TELR

Toll-Free Phone Book USA

A Directory of Toll-Free Telephone Numbers for Businesses and Organizations Nationwide

2016
20th Edition

Containing Toll-Free Numbers, Telephone Numbers, and Mailing Addresses for Leading U.S. Businesses, Organizations, Agencies, and Institutions, Including Companies, Associations, Educational Institutions, Media, Political Organizations, Societies, Travel Providers, and U.S. Government Agencies. Arranged Alphabetically by Name of Organization and in a Classified Section by Type of Business.

R **Rich's** Business Directories Inc.

Rich's Business Directories Inc.

Pearline Jaikumar, *Editor*
Karthikeyan Ponnambalam, *Research Manager*

★ ★ ★

Keith Jones,
Managing Editor

Copyright © 2016 Rich's Business Directories Inc.

In collaboration with Omnigraphics Inc.

ISBN 978-0-7808-1433-2

ISSN 1092-0085

Printed in the United States of America

Rich's Business Directories Inc., in collaboration with Omnigraphics Inc.
155 W. Congress, Ste. 200 Detroit, MI 48226
Phone Orders: 800-234-1340 • Fax Orders: 800-875-1340
Mail Orders: P.O. Box 8002 • Aston, PA 19014-8002
www.omnigraphics.com

Table of Contents

How To Use This Directory

Toll-Free Phone Book USA provides toll-free numbers, along with other key contact information, for some of the largest and most important corporations, organizations, and institutions in the United States. This 20th edition contains **more than 40,200** individual listings, presented alphabetically by company or organization name as well as in a classified subject arrangement according to business or organization type. The directory is intended as a convenient resource for toll-free calling nationwide, with supplemental contact data provided as an aid to follow-up correspondence or additional research.

What's Included in Toll-Free Phone Book USA?

Toll-free phone numbers, addresses, and local telephone numbers are provided for major businesses and industries located throughout the United States, as well as for organizations that serve as important information resources for businesses. Included also are listings for top Canadian companies and organizations.

Types of businesses listed in *Toll-Free Phone Book USA* include:
- manufacturing, retail, and wholesale companies;
- construction, mining, transportation, and utilities industries;
- agricultural interests;
- media and communications;
- and a full range of service industries.

Examples of other types of organizations listed include:
- associations;
- colleges and universities;
- libraries;
- research centers; and
- US Government agencies and offices.

How Do I Find What I'm Looking For?

Toll-Free Phone Book USA is organized in two main sections: an **Alphabetical Section,** in which listings are presented alphabetically according to company or organization name; and a **Classified Section**, where listings are organized under subject headings and subheadings according to business or organization type. All of the 40,000 plus entries are listed in each section.

- **Alphabetizing in *Toll-Free Phone Book USA***

Alphabetizing throughout *Toll-Free Phone Book USA* is on a word-by-word, rather than letter-by-letter, basis. No distinction is made between upper and lower case letters, and articles, conjunctions, and most prepositions are ignored for sorting purposes. Names that begin with symbols or numerals rather than letters file first. Symbols that may accompany numerals (e.g., a pound sign [#] or dollar sign [$]) are ignored for alphabetical sorting.

The following example illustrates these alphabetizing rules:

> 1 on 1 Computing
> $1 Sunglasses Ltd
> 3M Co
> All Weather Vacuuming
> C & S Inc
> Calido Hotels
> Cambridge Fire Insurance
> Damon Corp
> DAS Co
> Data Generation Inc
> La Quinta Motor Inns
> Laacke Co

- **Index to Classified Headings**

All of the subject headings under which listings are organized in the Classified Section of *Toll-Free Phone*

Book USA are identified in the Index to Classified Headings located at the back of the directory. Page numbers given for each index citation refer to the page on which a particular subject category begins, rather than to a specific company or organization name. "See" and "See also" references are included to help guide users to appropriate subject categories.

Content of Individual Listings

Each listing in *Toll-Free Phone Book USA* provides the official name of the company, organization, or institution; street or other mailing address; city, state, and zip code; tollfree telephone number; and local telephone number (with area code). For publicly traded companies, stock exchange information is provided as well.

Classification Codes

In addition to these items of contact information, each listing in *Toll-Free Phone Book USA* contains a **classification code.** Classification codes are numbers that appear to the left of subject headings in the Classified Section and in a "Class" column to the right of listings in the Alphabetical Section, thus providing a common element that links the two sections. Users can determine a company's business activity by matching a number in a "Class" column to the corresponding subject heading number in the Classified Section.

Some listings in the Classified Section may be organized under a second level of subheadings within the broader category named in a heading. In situations where there are two levels of headings, two levels of classification codes are given as well. For instance, if a heading numbered as 200 is followed by a series of subheadings, the first subheading would be numbered 200-1, the second would be 200-2, and so on. Headings that have been created only to provide a reference to another heading category—i.e., "See" and "See also" references—are **not** numbered.

• Company Names

As a general rule, complete official names are given for companies and organizations listed in *Toll-Free Phone Book USA*. In the case of listings for companies that are clearly named after individuals, information usually is presented both by the person's first name and by the last name. For example, LL Bean Inc would also be listed as Bean LL Inc.

Companies that are well-known by an acronym or initialism — for example, IBM — usually are listed both by acronym and by full name (i.e., "IBM" and "International Business Machines Corp").

• Addresses

Most of the addresses provided in this directory are street addresses, unless mail cannot be accepted at a particular location, in which case a post office box or other mailing address is provided. All listings include the city, state, and zip code as well.

• Toll-Free Numbers

All ten digits, including the area code (800, 855, 866, 877, or 888), are given for each listing's toll-free number. If the toll-free number is intended for a specific use (e.g., customer service, human resources, or technical support) rather than for general calling, an asterisk is printed to the right of the toll-free number and an explanatory note (e.g., *Cust Svc) is printed on the line below the name/address data.

• Telephone Numbers

Local telephone numbers given in *Toll-Free Phone Book USA* are usually for the main switchboard of a company or organization, and area codes are included with all phone numbers listed.

• Stock Exchange Information

Trading symbols and corresponding stock exchanges for publicly traded companies are provided below the company's name and address.

Comments Welcome

Comments from readers concerning this publication, including suggestions for additions and improvements, are welcome. Please send to:

Editor — *Toll-Free Phone Book USA*
Rich's Business Directories Inc.
155 W. Congress, Ste. 200,
Detroit MI 48226
editorial@omnigraphics.com

Area Codes in Numerical Order

Code	Location	Code	Location	Code	Location	Code	Location	Code	Location
201	New Jersey	331	Illinois	518	New York	707	California	850	Florida
202	District of Columbia	334	Alabama	519	Ontario	708	Illinois	855	Toll-free; all states
203	Connecticut	336	North Carolina	520	Arizona	709	Newfoundland	856	New Jersey
204	Manitoba	337	Louisiana	530	California	712	Iowa	857	Massachusetts
205	Alabama	339	Massachusetts	534	Wisconsin	713	Texas	858	California
206	Washington	340	US Virgin Islands	540	Virginia	714	California	859	Kentucky
207	Maine	345	Cayman Islands	541	Oregon	715	Wisconsin	860	Connecticut
208	Idaho	347	New York	551	New Jersey	716	New York	862	New Jersey
209	California	351	Massachusetts	559	California	717	Pennsylvania	863	Florida
210	Texas	352	Florida	561	Florida	718	New York	864	South Carolina
212	New York	360	Washington	562	California	719	Colorado	865	Tennessee
213	California	361	Texas	563	Iowa	720	Colorado	866	Toll-free; all states
214	Texas	385	Utah	567	Ohio	724	Pennsylvania	867	NorthWest Territories
215	Pennsylvania	386	Florida	570	Pennsylvania	727	Florida	868	Trinidad and Tobago
216	Ohio	401	Rhode Island	571	Virginia	731	Tennessee	869	Saint Kitts and Nevis
217	Illinois	402	Nebraska	573	Missouri	732	New Jersey	870	Arkansas
218	Minnesota	403	Alberta	574	Indiana	734	Michigan	876	Jamaica
219	Indiana	404	Georgia	575	New Mexico	740	Ohio	877	Toll-free; all states
224	Illinois	405	Oklahoma	580	Oklahoma	747	California	878	Pennsylvania
225	Louisiana	406	Montana	581	Quebec	754	Florida	880	Toll Calls: From Canada & The Caribbean
226	Ontario	407	Florida	585	New York	757	Virginia		
228	Mississippi	408	California	586	Michigan	758	Saint Lucia	881	Toll Calls: From Canada & The Caribbean
229	Georgia	409	Texas	587	Alberta	760	California		
231	Michigan	410	Maryland	601	Mississippi	762	Georgia	888	Toll-free; all states
234	Ohio	412	Pennsylvania	602	Arizona	763	Minnesota	901	Tennessee
239	Florida	413	Massachusetts	603	New Hampshire	765	Indiana	902	Nova Scotia
240	Maryland	414	Wisconsin	604	British Columbia	767	Dominica	903	Texas
242	Bahamas	415	California	605	South Dakota	769	Mississippi	904	Florida
246	Barbados	416	Ontario	606	Kentucky	770	Georgia	905	Ontario
248	Michigan	417	Missouri	607	New York	772	Florida	906	Michigan
250	British Columbia	418	Quebec	608	Wisconsin	773	Illinois	907	Alaska
251	Alabama	419	Ohio	609	New Jersey	774	Massachusetts	908	New Jersey
252	North Carolina	423	Tennessee	610	Pennsylvania	775	Nevada	909	California
253	Washington	424	California	612	Minnesota	778	British Columbia	910	North Carolina
254	Texas	425	Washington	613	Ontario	779	Illinois	912	Georgia
256	Alabama	430	Texas	614	Ohio	780	Alberta	913	Kansas
260	Indiana	432	Texas	615	Tennessee	781	Massachusetts	914	New York
262	Wisconsin	434	Virginia	616	Michigan	784	Saint Vincent & the Grenadines	915	Texas
264	Anguilla	435	Utah	617	Massachusetts			916	California
267	Pennsylvania	438	Quebec	618	Illinois	785	Kansas	917	New York
268	Antigua and Barbuda	440	Ohio	619	California	786	Florida	918	Oklahoma
269	Michigan	441	Bermuda	620	Kansas	787	Puerto Rico	919	North Carolina
270	Kentucky	442	California	623	Arizona	800	Toll-free; all states	920	Wisconsin
276	Virginia	443	Maryland	626	California	801	Utah	925	California
281	Texas	450	Quebec	630	Illinois	802	Vermont	928	Arizona
284	British Virgin Islands	458	Oregon	631	New York	803	South Carolina	931	Tennessee
289	Ontario	469	Texas	636	Missouri	804	Virginia	936	Texas
301	Maryland	470	Georgia	641	Iowa	805	California	937	Ohio
302	Delaware	473	Grenada	646	New York	806	Texas	939	Puerto Rico
303	Colorado	475	Connecticut	647	Ontario	807	Ontario	940	Texas
304	West Virginia	478	Georgia	649	Turks and Caicos	808	Hawaii	941	Florida
305	Florida	479	Arkansas	650	California	809	Dominican Republic	947	Michigan
306	Saskatchewan	480	Arizona	651	Minnesota	810	Michigan	949	California
307	Wyoming	484	Pennsylvania	657	California	812	Indiana	951	California
308	Nebraska	501	Arkansas	660	Missouri	813	Florida	952	Minnesota
309	Illinois	502	Kentucky	661	California	814	Pennsylvania	954	Florida
310	California	503	Oregon	662	Mississippi	815	Illinois	956	Texas
312	Illinois	504	Louisiana	664	Montserrat	816	Missouri	959	Connecticut
313	Michigan	505	New Mexico	671	Guam	817	Texas	970	Colorado
314	Missouri	506	New Brunswick	678	Georgia	818	California	971	Oregon
315	New York	507	Minnesota	681	West Virginia	819	Quebec	972	Texas
316	Kansas	508	Massachusetts	682	Texas	828	North Carolina	973	New Jersey
317	Indiana	509	Washington	684	American Samoa	829	Dominican Republic	978	Massachusetts
318	Louisiana	510	California	689	Florida	830	Texas	979	Texas
319	Iowa	512	Texas	701	North Dakota	831	California	980	North Carolina
320	Minnesota	513	Ohio	702	Nevada	832	Texas	985	Louisiana
321	Florida	514	Quebec	703	Virginia	843	South Carolina	989	Michigan
323	California	515	Iowa	704	North Carolina	845	New York		
325	Texas	516	New York	705	Ontario	847	Illinois		
330	Ohio	517	Michigan	706	Georgia	848	New Jersey		

Area Codes in State Order

Alabama
205 Birmingham & Tuscaloosa
251 Southwest
256 North & East Central
334 South

Alaska
907 All locations

American Samoa
684 All locations

Arizona
480 East of Phoenix including Tempe & Scottsdale
520 Southeast
602 Phoenix
623 West of Phoenix including Glendale
928 Most of State except South Central & Southeast areas

Arkansas
479 West Central & Northwest
501 Little Rock & surrounding areas
870 East & South

California
209 Central
213 Los Angeles
310 Long Beach/West
323 Los Angeles
408 West Central
415 San Francisco
424 Long Beach/West
442 Southeast except San Diego Area
510 Oakland
530 North
559 Central
562 Long Beach
619 San Diego & surrounding area (except North)
626 Pasadena/East
650 South of San Francisco
657 Northern Orange County
661 Bakersfield & Northern La County
707 Northwest
714 Northern Orange County
747 Burbank & Glendale Area
760 Southeast except San Diego Area
805 South
818 Burbank & Glendale Area
831 West Central
858 San Diego/North
909 San Bernardino & surrounding area
916 Sacramento & surrounding area
925 East of Oakland
949 Southern Orange County
951 Riverside & surrounding area (except North)

Canada
204 All locations in Manitoba
226 Southern Ontario
250 Outside Vancouver Area including Vancouver Island
289 North of Toronto
306 All locations in Saskatchewan
403 Southern Alberta
416 Toronto
418 Eastern Quebec
438 Montreal Metro Area
450 Outside Montreal Metro Area
506 All locations in New Brunswick
514 Montreal Metro Area

519 Southern Ontario
581 Eastern Quebec
587 All locations in Alberta
604 Vancouver Area
613 Northeast of Toronto
647 Toronto
705 Eastern Ontario
709 All locations in Newfoundland
778 Vancouver Area
780 Central & Northern Alberta
807 Western Ontario
819 Western Quebec
867 All locations in Yukon & Northwest Territories
902 All locations in Nova Scotia & Prince Edward Island
905 North of Toronto

Caribbean, Bahamas & Bermuda
242 Bahamas
246 Barbados
264 Anguilla
268 Antigua & Barbuda
284 British Virgin Islands
340 US Virgin Islands
345 Cayman Islands
441 Bermuda
473 Grenada
649 Turks & Caicos
664 Montserrat
758 Saint Lucia
767 Dominica
784 Saint Vincent & Grenadines
787 Puerto Rico
809 Dominican Republic
829 Dominican Republic
868 Trinidad & Tobago
869 Saint Kitts & Nevis
876 Jamaica
939 Puerto Rico

Colorado
303 Denver
719 South & East
720 Denver
970 West & North

Connecticut
203 Southwest
475 Southwest
860 Except Southwest
959 Except Southwest

Delaware
302 All locations

District of Columbia
202 All locations

Florida
239 Southwest (Lee, Collier & part of Monroe Counties)
305 Southeast
321 Central & East Central
352 Gainesville, Ocala & surrounding areas
386 Northeast except Jacksonville, St. Augustine & surrounding areas
407 Central
561 Palm Beach County
689 Central & East Central
727 Saint Petersburg/Clearwater
754 Fort Lauderdale & surrounding area
772 Martin, St. Lucie, Indian River & part of Brevard Counties
786 Southeast
813 Tampa
850 Northwest

863 South Central
904 Jacksonville, St. Augustine & surrounding areas
941 Southwest (Sarasota, Charlotte & Manatee Counties)
954 Fort Lauderdale & surrounding area

Georgia
229 Southwest
404 Atlanta
470 Atlanta & surrounding area
478 Central
678 Atlanta Area
706 North except Atlanta Area
762 North except Atlanta Area
770 Atlanta suburbs
912 Southeast

Guam
671 All locations

Hawaii
808 All locations

Idaho
208 All locations

Illinois
217 Central
224 Suburban Chicago
309 West
312 Chicago
331 Northeast
618 South
630 Northeast
708 Northeast
773 Chicago (outside central commercial area)
779 North
815 North
847 Suburban Chicago

Indiana
219 North West
260 Northeast
317 Indianapolis Metro Area
574 North Central
765 Central except Indianapolis Metro Area
812 South

Iowa
319 East Central
515 Central including Des Moines & Ames
563 East
641 South central & East Central
712 West

Kansas
316 Wichita & surrounding area
620 South except Wichita & surrounding area
785 North except Kansas City
913 Kansas City

Kentucky
270 West & Central
502 North including Louisville
606 East
859 North Central

Louisiana
225 East Central
318 North & West
337 West Central & Southwest
504 New Orleans Area
985 Southeast except New Orleans Area

Maine
207 All locations

Maryland
240 West
301 West
410 East
443 East

Massachusetts
339 Outside Metro Boston
351 North
413 West
508 Southeast
617 Boston Metro Area
774 Southeast
781 Outside Metro Boston
857 Boston Metro Area
978 North

Michigan
231 Northwest
248 East (Oakland County)
269 Southwest
313 Detroit & inner suburbs
517 South Central
586 East (Macomb County)
616 West/Southwest
734 West of Detroit
810 East (except Oakland & Macomb Counties)
906 North
947 East (Oakland County)
989 Central

Minnesota
218 North
320 Central except Minneapolis/ Saint Paul Metro Area
507 South
612 Minneapolis
651 Saint Paul & East Central
763 Suburbs North & Northwest of Minneapolis
952 Suburbs South & Southwest of Minneapolis

Mississippi
228 Gulfport/Biloxi & surrounding area
601 South except Gulfport/ Biloxi & surrounding area
662 North
769 South except Gulfport/ Biloxi & surrounding area

Missouri
314 Saint Louis
417 Southwest
573 East except Saint Louis Metro Area
636 East (outside Saint Louis)
660 North except Kansas City & Saint Joseph
816 Kansas City & Saint Joseph

Montana
406 All locations

Nebraska
308 West
402 East

Nevada
702 Las Vegas Area
775 All locations except Las Vegas

New Hampshire
603 All locations

New Jersey
201 Northeast
551 Northeast
609 Southeast
732 East Central
848 East Central
856 Southwest
862 Northwest
908 West Central
973 Northwest

Area Codes in State Order (continued)

New Mexico
505	Northwest
575	Entire State except Northwest

New York
212	New York City
315	North Central
347	New York City
516	Nassau County
518	Northeast
585	West-Central
607	South Central
631	Suffolk County
646	New York City
716	West
718	New York City
845	North & West of Westchester County
914	Westchester County
917	New York City

North Carolina
252	East
336	Greensboro & Winston-Salem areas
704	Southwest
828	West
910	South Central
919	North Central
980	Southwest

North Dakota
701	All locations

Ohio
216	Cleveland Metro Area
234	Northeast except Cleveland
330	Northeast except Cleveland
419	Northwest
440	North Central except Cleveland Metro Area
513	Southwest
567	Northwest
614	Columbus Area
740	East & Central except Columbus Area
937	Southwest except Cincinnati Area

Oklahoma
405	Central
580	South & West
918	Northeast

Oregon
458	Outside Portland Area
503	Portland Area
541	Outside Portland Area
971	Portland Area

Pennsylvania
215	Philadelphia
267	Philadelphia
412	Pittsburgh Metro Area
484	Southeast
570	Northeast
610	Southeast
717	Southeast
724	Outside Pittsburgh Metro Area
814	West
878	Pittsburgh & surrounding area

Rhode Island
401	All locations

South Carolina
803	Central
843	East
864	Northwest

South Dakota
605	All locations

Tennessee
423	Northeast & Southeast
615	North Central
731	West except Shelby, Fayette & Tipton Counties
865	Knoxville & surrounding area
901	Southwest (Shelby, Fayette & Tipton Counties)
931	Nashville & North Central

Texas
210	San Antonio Metro Area
214	Dallas
254	North Central
281	Houston
325	Central
361	Corpus Christi & surrounding Area
409	East of Houston Area
430	Northeast
432	West Central
469	Dallas
512	Austin & surrounding area
682	Fort Worth Metro Area & Arlington
713	Houston
806	Northwest
817	Fort Worth Metro Area & Arlington
830	South Central
832	Houston
903	Northeast
915	West (including El Paso)
936	North of Houston Area
940	North
956	South
972	Dallas
979	West of Houston Area

Toll Calls: From Canada & The Caribbean
880	
881	

Toll-Free; All States
800	
855	
866	
877	
888	

Utah
385	Salt Lake City, Ogden & Provo Metro areas
435	All locations except Salt Lake City/Ogden/Provo Metro areas
801	Salt Lake City, Ogden & Provo Metro areas

Vermont
802	All locations

Virginia
276	Southwest
434	South & Central
540	North
571	Northeast
703	Northeast
757	Norfolk & surrounding area
804	East

Washington
206	Seattle Area
253	Tacoma Area
360	West except Seattle, Tacoma & Everett areas
425	East of Seattle between Everett & Kent
509	East

West Virginia
304	All locations
681	All locations

Wisconsin
262	Southeast except Milwaukee
414	Milwaukee
534	North
608	Southwest
715	North
920	Southeast except Milwaukee & surrounding area (South)

Wyoming
307	All locations

Toll-Free
Phone Book USA

Alphabetical Section

Listings here are presented in alphabetical order by company or organization name. Alphabetizing is on a word-by-word rather than letter-by-letter basis. For a detailed explanation of the scope and arrangement of listings in this directory, please refer to "How To Use This Directory" at the beginning of this book. An explanation of individual page elements is also provided under the "Sample Entry" on the back inside cover of the book.

SYMBOLS & NUMERALS

				Toll-Free	Phone	Class
1 Biotechnology						
PO Box 758 .... Oneco	FL	34264		800-951-4246	941-355-8451	412
100 Fountain Spa at the Pillar & Post Inn						
48 John St						
PO Box 48 .... Niagara-on-the-Lake	ON	L0S1J0		888-669-5566	905-468-2123	698
1&1 Internet Inc						
701 Lee Rd Ste 300 ...... Chesterbrook	PA	19087		877-461-2631		681
1-800 Attorney Lawyer Holdings LLC						
2525 McKinnon Ave Ste 625 ..... Dallas	TX	75201		800-288-6763		628-6
OTC: ATTY						
1-800-Flowers.com Inc						
One Old Country Rd Ste 500 .... Carle Place	NY	11514		800-356-9377	516-237-6000	292
NASDAQ: FLWS						
1-800-Got-Junk						
301 - 887 Great Northern Way						
3rd Fl .... Vancouver	BC	V5T4T5		800-468-5865		309
1-800-Water Damage						
1167 Mercer St .... Seattle	WA	98109		800-928-3732	206-381-3041	150
1167 Mercer St .... Seattle	WA	98109		800-928-3732	206-381-3041	309
180s Inc						
700 S Caroline St .... Baltimore	MD	21231		877-725-4386	410-534-6320	153-8
1886 Crescent Hotel & Spa						
75 Prospect Ave ...... Eureka Springs	AR	72632		877-342-9766	479-253-9766	376
1888 Mills LLC						
1520 Kensington Rd Ste 115 ..... Oak Brook	IL	60523		800-346-3660		735
1928 Jewelry Co						
3000 W Empire Ave .... Burbank	CA	91504		800-227-1928	818-841-1928	405
1932 & 1980 Lake Placid Winter Olympic Museum						
Olympic Ctr 2634 Main St .... Lake Placid	NY	12946		800-462-6236	518-523-1655	515
1MAGE Software Inc						
384 Inverness Pkwy Ste 206 ..... Englewood	CO	80112		800-844-1468		179-1
1secureaudit LLC						
1600 Tysons Blvd Fl 8 .... Mc Lean	VA	22102		800-321-0706	703-245-3020	195
1st Choice Facilities Services Corp						
1941 Whitfield Park Loop ..... Sarasota	FL	34243		866-241-0070		187
1st Colonial Bancorp Inc						
1040 Haddon Ave ...... Collingswood	NJ	08108		800-500-1044	856-858-1100	69
OTC: FCOB						
1st Community Bank						
2911 N Westwood Blvd ...... Poplar Bluff	MO	63901		888-785-1772	573-778-0101	69
1st Discount Brokerage Inc						
8927 Hypoluxo Rd Ste A-5 ..... Lake Worth	FL	33467		888-642-2811	561-515-3200	681
1st Source Bank						
100 N Michigan St ...... South Bend	IN	46601		800-513-2360	574-235-2254	69
1stWEST Financial Corp						
32186 Castle Court Ste 220 ..... Evergreen	CO	80439		866-670-3443		461
2 Places At 1 Time Inc						
270 Peachtree St 20th Fl ..... Atlanta	GA	30303		877-275-2237		458
21st Century Christian Inc						
PO Box 40526 .... Nashville	TN	37204		800-251-2477	615-383-3842	94
220 Marketing						
3405 Kenyon St Ste 501 ..... San Diego	CA	92110		877-220-6584		196
24 Asset Management Corp						
2020 Camino del Rio N Ste 900 .... San Diego	CA	92108		855-414-2424		390
29 Prime Inc						
9701 Jeronimo Rd .... Irvine	CA	92618		888-513-7746		5
360 Solutions LLC						
2114 Austin Ave .... Waco	TX	76701		877-755-7888	254-755-7000	195
390th Memorial Museum						
6000 E Valencia Rd .... Tucson	AZ	85706		800-639-4992	520-574-0287	513
3D Exhibits Inc						
2900 Lively Blvd ...... Elk Grove Village	IL	60007		800-471-9617	847-250-9000	232
3D Systems Inc						
333 Three D Systems Cir ..... Rock Hill	SC	29730		800-793-3669	803-326-3900	179-8
3Dlabs Inc Ltd						
1901 McCarthy Blvd .... Milpitas	CA	95035		800-464-3348	408-530-4700	617
3DShopping.com						
28th Fl US Bank Tower ..... Los Angeles	CA	90071		800-442-5299		5
3M Canada Co						
300 Tartan Dr .... London	ON	N5V4M9		888-364-3577		722
3M Co						
3M Ctr Bldg 225-3S-06 ..... Saint Paul	MN	55144		800-364-3577	651-733-1110	186
NYSE: MMM						
3M Digital Signage						
600 Ericksen Ave NE						
Ste 200 .... Bainbridge Island	WA	98110		888-460-8866	206-855-2000	607
3M Electronic Handling & Protection Div						
6801 River Pl Blvd .... Austin	TX	78726		800-328-1368		253
3M ESPE Dental Products Div						
3M Ctr Bldg 0275-02-SE-03 ..... Saint Paul	MN	55144		800-634-2249	651-575-5144	228
3M Interconnect Solutions Div						
6801 River Pl Blvd .... Austin	TX	78726		800-225-5373	512-984-1800	253
3M Telecommunications Div						
6801 River Pl Blvd .... Austin	TX	78726		800-426-8688		248

				Toll-Free	Phone	Class
3M Touch Systems						
501 Griffin Brook Dr .... Methuen	MA	01844		866-407-6666	978-659-9000	174-2
3M Unitek						
2724 Peck Rd .... Monrovia	CA	91016		800-634-5300		228
3rd Federal Bank						
3 Penns Trail .... Newtown	PA	18940		800-822-3321	215-579-4600	69
4checks.com						
8245 N Union Blvd ...... Colorado Springs	CO	80920		866-923-0451		140
4D Inc						
3031 Tisch Way Ste 900 ..... San Jose	CA	95128		800-785-3303	408-557-4600	179-1
4Front Engineered Solutions Inc						
1612 Hutton Dr Ste 140 ..... Carrollton	TX	75006		877-778-3625	972-466-0707	465
4Life Research						
9850 South 300 West .... Sandy	UT	84070		888-454-3374*	801-256-3102	363
*Sales						
4over Inc						
5900 San Fernando Rd .... Glendale	CA	91202		877-782-2737		619
4-Star Trailers Inc						
10000 NW Tenth St ...... Oklahoma City	OK	73127		800-848-3095	405-324-7827	769
4th Source Inc						
2400 Veterans Blvd Ste 480 ..... Kenner	LA	70062		855-875-4700		178
5 Alarm Fire & Safety Equipment LLC						
350 Austin Cir .... Delafield	WI	53018		800-615-6789	262-646-5911	684
5.11 Inc						
4300 Spyres Way .... Modesto	CA	95356		866-451-1726	209-527-4511	155-5
600 WREC						
2650 Thousand Oaks Blvd						
Ste 4100 .... Memphis	TN	38118		800-474-9732	901-259-1300	636-66
63 Ranch						
PO Box 979 .... Livingston	MT	59047		888-395-5151		239
66 Federal Credit Union						
PO Box 1358 .... Bartlesville	OK	74005		800-897-6991	918-336-7662	219
7 D Ranch						
7D Ranch PO Box 100 .... Cody	WY	82414		888-587-9885	307-587-9885	239
70 Park Avenue Hotel						
70 Pk Ave at 38th St ..... New York	NY	10016		877-707-2752	212-973-2400	376
7-Eleven Inc						
1722 Routh Ste 100 .... Dallas	TX	75221		800-255-0711	972-828-7011	205
7-sigma Inc						
2843 26th Ave S ...... Minneapolis	MN	55406		888-722-8396	612-722-5358	601
7Summits LLC						
1110 Old World Third St						
Ste 500 .... Milwaukee	WI	53203		866-705-6372		196
82 Queen						
82 Queen St .... Charleston	SC	29401		800-849-0082	843-723-7591	662
84 Lumber Co						
1019 Rt 519 .... Eighty Four	PA	15330		800-664-1984	724-228-8820	192-3
89.1 WBOI						
3204 Clairmont Ct .... Fort Wayne	IN	46808		800-471-9264*	260-452-1189	636-44
*General						
8x8 Inc						
810 W Maude Ave .... Sunnyvale	CA	94085		888-898-8733	408-727-1885	687
NASDAQ: EGHT						
911 Restoration Enterprises Inc						
7721 Densmore Ave .... Van Nuys	CA	91406		888-243-6653		658
92.5 WESC-FM						
101 N Main St PO Box 100 ..... Greenville	SC	29601		800-248-0863	864-242-4660	636-49
930 AM The Answer						
9601 McAllister Fwy						
Ste 1200 .... San Antonio	TX	78216		866-308-8867	210-344-8481	636-95
98.5 KFOX						
201 Third St Ste 1200 ..... San Francisco	CA	94103		877-410-5369		636-98
99 Cents Only Stores						
4000 Union Pacific Ave ..... Commerce	CA	90023		888-582-5999	323-980-8145	779
@Comm Corp						
150 Dow St .... Manchester	NH	03101		800-641-5400	650-375-8188	179-7

A

				Toll-Free	Phone	Class
A & A Express Inc						
PO Box 707 .... Brandon	SD	57005		800-658-3549	605-582-2402	770
A & K Railroad Materials Inc						
1505 S Redwood Rd ...... Salt Lake City	UT	84104		800-453-8812*	801-974-5484	760
*Sales						
A & M Tool & Die Company Inc						
64 Mill St .... Southbridge	MA	01550		800-848-4628	508-764-3241	747
A & S Services Group LLC						
310 N Zarfoss Dr .... York	PA	17404		800-227-6782	717-759-3017	310
A & Z Hayward Co						
655 Waterman Ave ...... East Providence	RI	02914		800-556-7462	401-438-0550	405
A & Z Pharmaceutical Inc						
180 Oser Ave .... Hauppauge	NY	11788		800-810-9819	631-952-3802	231
A 1 Auto Recyclers						
7804 S Hwy 79 .... Rapid City	SD	57701		800-456-0715	605-348-8442	53
A Better Chance Inc						
253 W 35th St 6th Fl ..... New York	NY	10001		800-562-7865	646-346-1310	47-11

Alphabetical Section

	Toll-Free	Phone	Class
A Betterway Rent-a-car Inc 1110 Northchase Pkwy SE . . . . . . Marietta GA 30067	800-527-0700	770-240-3305	125
A C e International Company Inc 85 Independence Dr . . . . . . Taunton MA 02780	800-223-4685	508-884-9600	195
A C Nelson Rv World 11818 L St . . . . . . Omaha NE 68137	888-655-2332	402-333-1122	56
A Contemporary Theatre (ACT) 700 Union St Kreielsheimer Pl . . . . . . Seattle WA 98101	888-584-4849	206-292-7660	565
A Daigger & Company Inc 620 Lakeview Pkwy . . . . . . Vernon Hills IL 60061	800-621-7193	847-816-5060	596
A Duchini Inc 2550 McKinley Ave . . . . . . Erie PA 16514	800-937-7317	814-456-7027	184
A Duie Pyle Inc 650 Westtown Rd . . . . . . West Chester PA 19382	800-523-5020	610-696-5800	444
A Finkl & Sons Co 2011 N Southport Ave . . . . . . Chicago IL 60614	800-343-2562	773-975-2510	714
A H Belo Corp 508 Young St PO Box 224866 . . . . . . Dallas TX 75202 *NYSE: AHC*	800-230-1074	214-977-8200	573
A Homecrest Outdoor Living LLC 1250 Homecrest Ave . . . . . . Wadena MN 56482	888-346-4852	218-631-1000	318-4
A Matter of Fax 105 Harrison Ave . . . . . . Harrison NJ 07029	800-433-3329	973-482-3700	180
A Plus Benefits Inc 395 West 600 North . . . . . . Lindon UT 84042	800-748-5102	801-443-1090	387
A Plus International Inc 5138 Eucalyptus Ave . . . . . . Chino CA 91710	800-762-1123	909-591-5168	470
A Rifkin Co 1400 Sans Souci Pkwy . . . . . . Wilkes-Barre PA 18706 *Cust Svc	800-458-7300*	570-825-9551	66
A Schulman Inc 3550 W Market St . . . . . . Akron OH 44333 *NASDAQ: SHLM*	800-547-3746	330-666-3751	598-2
A Stucki Co 2600 Neville Rd . . . . . . Pittsburgh PA 15225	888-266-6630	412-771-7300	641
A Web That Works 2733 Concession Rd 7 . . . . . . Bowmanville ON L1C3K6	800-579-9253	905-263-2666	4
A Yankee Line 370 W First St . . . . . . Boston MA 02127	800-942-8890	617-268-8890	106
A'Gaci LLC 12460 Network Blvd Ste 106 . . . . . . San Antonio TX 78249	866-265-3036	210-377-3393	155-6
A+ School Apparel 401 Knoss Ave . . . . . . Star City AR 71667	800-227-3215		153-18
A. M. Ortega Construction Inc 10125 Ch Rd . . . . . . Lakeside CA 92040	800-909-1988	619-390-1988	190-4
A.g. Ferrari Foods 14234 Catalina St . . . . . . San Leandro CA 94577	877-878-2783	510-346-2100	342
A.R.M. Solutions Inc PO Box 2929 . . . . . . Camarillo CA 93011	888-772-6468		158
A/G (Assemblies of God) 1445 N Boonville Ave . . . . . . Springfield MO 65802	800-641-4310	417-862-2781	47-20
A10 Networks Inc Three W Plumeria Dr . . . . . . San Jose CA 95134	888-210-6363	408-325-8668	684
A123 Systems Inc 200 W St . . . . . . Waltham MA 02451	800-224-7654	617-778-5700	73
A2LA (American Assn for Laboratory Accreditation) 5301 Buckeystown Pike Ste 350 . . . . . . Frederick MD 21704	888-627-8318	301-644-3248	48-19
A2Z Science & Nature Store 57 King St . . . . . . NorthHampton MA 01060	877-261-6171	413-586-1611	751
AA Importing Co Inc 7700 Hall St . . . . . . Saint Louis MO 63147 *Cust Svc	800-325-0602*	314-383-8800	358
AA Wheel & Truck Supply Inc 717 E 16th Ave . . . . . . Kansas City MO 64116	800-486-4335	816-221-9556	60
AAA (American Academy of Audiology) 11730 Plz America Dr Ste 300 . . . . . . Reston VA 20190	800-222-2336	703-790-8466	48-8
AAA (American Angus Assn) 3201 Frederick Ave . . . . . . Saint Joseph MO 64506	800-821-5478	816-383-5100	47-2
AAA (American Arbitration Assn Inc) 1633 Broadway 10th Fl . . . . . . New York NY 10019	800-778-7879	212-716-5800	40
AAA (American Ambulance Assn) 8201 Greensboro Dr Ste 300 . . . . . . McLean VA 22102	800-523-4447	703-610-9018	48-21
AAA Allied Group Inc 15 W Central Pkwy . . . . . . Cincinnati OH 45202	800-543-2345	513-762-3100	52
AAA Carolinas 6600 AAA Dr . . . . . . Charlotte NC 28212	800-477-4222	704-569-3600	52
AAA Chicago Motor Club 975 Meridian Lake Dr . . . . . . Aurora IL 60504	866-968-7222		52
AAA Colorado 4100 E Arkansas Ave . . . . . . Denver CO 80222	866-625-3601	303-753-8800	52
AAA Cooper Transportation 1751 Kinsey Rd . . . . . . Dothan AL 36303	800-633-7571	334-793-2284	770
AAA East Penn 1020 W Hamilton St . . . . . . Allentown PA 18101	800-222-4357		52
AAA Financial Corp 4613 N University Dr . . . . . . Coral Springs FL 33065	800-881-2530	954-344-2530	502
Aaa Flag & Banner Manufacturing Co 8955 National Blvd . . . . . . Los Angeles CA 90034	800-266-4222		287
AAA Hawaii 1130 N Nimitz Hwy Ste A-170 . . . . . . Honolulu HI 96817	800-736-2886	808-593-2221	52
AAA Massillon Auto Club 1972 Wales Rd NE . . . . . . Massillon OH 44646	800-222-4357	330-833-1084	52
AAA Michigan 1 Auto Club Dr . . . . . . Dearborn MI 48126	800-222-6424	313-336-1920	52
AAA Minnesota/Iowa 600 W Travelers Trl . . . . . . Burnsville MN 55337	800-222-1333	952-707-4500	52
AAA Missouri 12901 N Forty Dr . . . . . . Saint Louis MO 63141	800-222-4357	314-523-7350	52
AAA MountainWest 2100 11th Ave . . . . . . Helena MT 59601	800-332-6119	406-447-8100	52
Aaa Moving & Storage Inc 747 E Ship Creek Ave . . . . . . Anchorage AK 99501	866-641-4446	907-276-3506	770
AAA Nebraska 910 N 96th St . . . . . . Omaha NE 68114	800-222-6327	402-390-1000	52
AAA North Penn 1035 N Washington Ave . . . . . . Scranton PA 18509	800-222-4357	570-348-2511	52
AAA Northern New England 68 Marginal Way . . . . . . Portland ME 04104	800-222-4357	207-780-6800	52
AAA Northway 112 Railroad St . . . . . . Schenectady NY 12305	866-222-7283	518-374-4696	52
AAA Northwest Ohio 7150 W Central Ave . . . . . . Toledo OH 43617	800-428-0060	419-843-1200	52
AAA Ohio Auto Club 90 E Wilson Bridge Rd . . . . . . Worthington OH 43085	888-222-6446	614-431-7901	52
AAA Oklahoma 2121 E 15th St . . . . . . Tulsa OK 74104	800-222-2582	918-748-1000	52
AAA Southern New England 110 Royal Little Dr . . . . . . Providence RI 02904	800-222-7448	401-868-2000	52
AAA Southern Pennsylvania 2840 Eastern Blvd . . . . . . York PA 17402	800-222-1469	717-600-8700	52
AAA Washington-Inland 1745 114th Ave SE . . . . . . Bellevue WA 98004	800-222-4357	425-646-2058	52
AAA Western & Central New York 100 International Dr . . . . . . Williamsville NY 14221	800-836-2582	716-633-9860	52
AAA Wisconsin 8401 Excelsior Dr . . . . . . Madison WI 53717	800-236-1300	608-836-6555	52
AAAAI (American Academy of Allergy Asthma & Immunology) 555 E Wells St Ste 1100 . . . . . . Milwaukee WI 53202	800-654-2452	414-272-6071	48-8
AAAASF (American Assn for Accreditation of Ambulatory Surgery Facilities Inc) 5101 Washington St Ste 2F PO Box 9500 . . . . . . Gurnee IL 60031	888-545-5222	847-775-1985	47-1
AAACCVB (Annapolis & Anne Arundel County Conference & Visitors Bureau) 26 W St . . . . . . Annapolis MD 21401	888-302-2852	410-280-0445	207
AAAE (American Assn of Airport Executives) 601 Madison St Ste 400 . . . . . . Alexandria VA 22314	800-609-7374	703-824-0500	48-21
AAAOM (American Assn of Acupuncture & Oriental Medicine) PO Box 162340 . . . . . . Sacramento CA 95816	866-455-7999	916-443-4770	47-17
AAAS (American Assn for the Advancement of Science) 1200 New York Ave NW . . . . . . Washington DC 20005	800-669-6820	202-326-6400	48-19
AAB (American Assn of Bioanalysts) 906 Olive St Ste 1200 . . . . . . Saint Louis MO 63101	800-457-3332	314-241-1445	48-8
AABBA (Anchorage Alaska Bed & Breakfast Assn) PO Box 242623 . . . . . . Anchorage AK 99524	888-584-5147	907-272-5909	373
AABBN (Alexandria & Arlington Bed & Breakfast Networks) 4938 Hampden Ln Ste 164 . . . . . . Bethesda MD 20814	888-549-3415	703-549-3415	373
AABC (American Amateur Baseball Congress) 100 W Broadway . . . . . . Farmington NM 87401	800-853-2414	505-327-3120	47-22
AABP (American Assn of Bovine Practitioners) 3320 Skyway Dr Ste 802 PO Box 3610 . . . . . . Auburn AL 36831	800-269-2227	334-821-0442	47-2
AACAP (American Academy of Child & Adolescent Psychiatry) 3615 Wisconsin Ave NW . . . . . . Washington DC 20016	800-333-7636	202-966-7300	48-15
AACC (Asset Acceptance Capital Corp) 28405 Van Dyke Ave . . . . . . Warren MI 48093 *NASDAQ: AACC*	800-545-9931	586-939-9600	158
AACC (American Assn for Clinical Chemistry Inc) 1850 K St NW Ste 625 . . . . . . Washington DC 20006 *Cust Svc	800-892-1400*	202-857-0717	48-19
AACD (American Academy of Cosmetic Dentistry) 402 W Wilson St . . . . . . Madison WI 53703	800-543-9220	608-222-8583	48-8
AACE (American Assn of Clinical Endocrinologists) 245 Riverside Ave Ste 2000 . . . . . . Jacksonville FL 32202	800-435-7352	904-353-7878	48-8
AACE (Association for the Advancement of Computing in Education) PO Box 1545 . . . . . . Chesapeake VA 23327	800-352-5397	757-366-5606	48-5
AACE International - Assn for the Advancement of Cost Engineering 209 Prairie Ave Ste 100 . . . . . . Morgantown WV 26501	800-858-2678	304-296-8444	48-1
AACN (American Assn of Critical-Care Nurses) 101 Columbia . . . . . . Aliso Viejo CA 92656	800-809-2273	949-362-2000	48-8
AACOM (American Assn of Colleges of Osteopathic Medicine) 5550 Friendship Blvd Ste 310 . . . . . . Chevy Chase MD 20815	800-356-7836	301-968-4100	48-8
AACPM (American Assn of Colleges of Podiatric Medicine) 15850 Crabbs Branch Way Ste 320 . . . . . . Rockville MD 20855	800-922-9266	301-948-9760	48-8
AACR (American Assn for Cancer Research) 615 Chestnut St 17th Fl . . . . . . Philadelphia PA 19106	866-423-3965	215-440-9300	48-8
AACRAO (American Assn of Collegiate Registrars & Admissions Officers) 1 Dupont Cir NW Ste 520 . . . . . . Washington DC 20036	800-222-4922	202-293-9161	48-5
AAD (American Academy of Dermatology) 930 E Woodfield Rd . . . . . . Schaumburg IL 60173	800-868-2472	847-330-0230	48-8
AADEP (American Academy of Disability Evaluating Physicians) 223 W Jackson Blvd Ste 1104 . . . . . . Chicago IL 60606	800-456-6095	312-663-1171	48-8
AADMM (American Assn of Daily Money Managers) 174 Crestview Dr . . . . . . Bellefonte PA 16823	877-326-5991		48-2
AADP (American Assn of Drugless Practitioners) 2200 Market St Ste 803 . . . . . . Galveston TX 77550	888-764-2237	409-621-2600	47-17
AAE (American Assn of Endodontists) 211 E Chicago Ave Ste 1100 . . . . . . Chicago IL 60611	800-872-3636	312-266-7255	48-8
AAEP (American Assn of Equine Practitioners) 4075 Iron Works Pkwy . . . . . . Lexington KY 40511	800-443-0177	859-233-0147	47-3
AAES (American Assn of Engineering Societies) 1620 'I' St NW Ste 210 . . . . . . Washington DC 20006 *Orders	888-400-2237*	202-296-2237	48-19
AAF (American Adv Federation) 1101 Vermont Ave NW Ste 500 . . . . . . Washington DC 20005	800-999-2231	202-898-0089	48-18
AAF International Corp 10300 Ormsby Pk Pl Ste 600 . . . . . . Louisville KY 40223	888-223-2003	502-637-0011	18
AAFA (American Apparel & Footwear Assn) 1601 N Kent St Ste 1200 . . . . . . Arlington VA 22209	800-520-2262	703-524-1864	48-4
AAFA (Asthma & Allergy Foundation of America) 8201 Corporate Dr Ste 1000 . . . . . . Landover MD 20785	800-727-8462	202-466-7643	47-17
AAFCS (American Assn of Family & Consumer Sciences) 400 N Columbus St Ste 202 . . . . . . Alexandria VA 22314	800-424-8080	703-706-4600	48-5
AAFD (American Assn of Franchisees & Dealers) PO Box 10158 . . . . . . Palm Desert CA 92255	800-733-9858	619-209-3775	48-18
AAFP (American Academy of Family Physicians) 11400 Tomahawk Creek Pkwy . . . . . . Leawood KS 66211	800-274-2237	913-906-6000	48-8
AAG (Association of American Geographers) 1710 16th St NW . . . . . . Washington DC 20009	800-696-7353	202-234-1450	48-19
AAGL (American Assn of Gynecological Laparoscopists) 6757 Katella Ave . . . . . . Cypress CA 90630	800-554-2245	714-503-6200	48-8
AAHA (American Animal Hospital Assn) 12575 W Bayaud Ave . . . . . . Lakewood CO 80228	800-252-2242	303-986-2800	47-3
AAH-PERD (American Alliance for Health Physical Education Recreation & Dance) 1900 Association Dr . . . . . . Reston VA 20191	800-213-7193	703-476-3400	47-22
AAI (American Assn of Immunologists) 9650 Rockville Pike . . . . . . Bethesda MD 20814	888-503-1050	301-634-7178	48-8
AAI (American Athletic Inc) 200 American Ave . . . . . . Jefferson IA 50129	800-247-3978	515-386-3125	343
AAIA (Automotive Aftermarket Industry Assn) 7101 Wisconsin Ave . . . . . . Bethesda MD 20814	800-936-8906	301-654-6664	48-21
AAIDD (American Assn on Intellectual & Developmental Disabilities) 444 N Capitol St NW Ste 846 . . . . . . Washington DC 20001	800-424-3688	202-387-1968	47-17
AAII (American Assn of Individual Investors) 625 N Michigan Ave Ste 1900 . . . . . . Chicago IL 60611	800-428-2244	312-280-0170	48-2
aaiPharma Inc 1726 N 23rd St . . . . . . Wilmington NC 28405	800-575-4224		576

	Toll-Free	Phone	Class

AAIS (American Assn of Insurance Services)
1745 S Naperville Rd .... Wheaton IL 60189 | **800-564-2247** | 630-681-8347 | 48-9

AAJ (American Assn for Justice)
777 Sixth St NW Ste 200 .... Washington DC 20001 | **800-424-2725** | 202-965-3500 | 48-10

AALDEF (Asian American Legal Defense & Education Fund)
99 Hudson St 12th Fl .... New York NY 10013 | **800-966-5946** | 212-966-5932 | 47-8

Aalfs Mfg Co
1005 Fourth St .... Sioux City IA 51101 | **888-412-2537** | 712-252-1877 | 153-10

AALU (Association for Advanced Life Underwriting)
11921 Freedom Dr Ste 1100 .... Reston VA 20190 | **888-275-0092** | 703-641-9400 | 48-9

AAM (American Assn of Museums)
1575 Eye St NW Ste 400 .... Washington DC 20005 | **866-226-2150** | 202-289-1818 | 47-4

AAMA (American Amusement Machine Assn)
450 E Higgins Rd
Ste 201 .... Elk Grove Village IL 60007 | **866-372-5190** | 847-290-9088 | 47-23

AAMA (American Assn of Medical Assistants)
20 N Wacker Dr Ste 1575 .... Chicago IL 60606 | **800-228-2262** | 312-899-1500 | 48-8

AAMC (Association of American Medical Colleges)
2450 N St NW .... Washington DC 20037 | **800-273-8255** | 202-828-0400 | 48-5

A-American Self Storage Management Co Inc
11560 Tennessee Ave .... Los Angeles CA 90064 | **888-333-6479** | 310-914-4022 | 791-3

AAMGA (American Assn of Managing General Agents)
150 S Warner Rd Ste 156 .... King of Prussia PA 19406 | **800-467-8725** | 610-225-1999 | 48-9

AAMI (Association for the Advancement of Medical Instrumentation)
4301 N Fairfax Dr Ste 301 .... Arlington VA 22203 | **800-332-2264** | 703-525-4890 | 48-8

AAMRO (American Assn of Medical Review Officers)
PO Box 12873 .... Research Triangle Park NC 27709 | **800-489-1839** | 919-489-5407 | 48-8

AAN (Association of Alternative Newsweeklies)
115615th St NW .... Washington DC 20005 | **866-415-0704** | 202-289-8484 | 48-14

AAN (American Academy of Neurology)
1080 Montreal Ave .... Saint Paul MN 55116 | **800-879-1960** | 651-695-1940 | 48-8

AANA (Arthroscopy Assn of North America)
6300 N River Rd Ste 104 .... Rosemont IL 60018 | **877-924-0305** | 847-292-2262 | 48-8

AANAPAC (American Assn of Nurse Anesthetists PAC)
222 S Prospect Ave .... Park Ridge IL 60068 | **855-526-2262** | 847-692-2051 | 608

AANEM (American Assn of Neuromuscular & Electrodiagnostic Medicine)
2621 Superior Dr NW .... Rochester MN 55901 | **844-347-3277** | 507-288-0100 | 48-8

AANN (American Assn of Neuroscience Nurses)
4700 W Lk Ave .... Glenview IL 60025 | **888-557-2266** | 847-375-4733 | 48-8

AANP (American Assn of Naturopathic Physicians)
4435 Wisconsin Ave NW
Ste 403 .... Washington DC 20016 | **866-538-2267** | 202-237-8150 | 47-17

AANS (American Assn of Neurological Surgeons)
5550 Meadowbrook Dr .... Rolling Meadows IL 60008 | **888-566-2267** | 847-378-0500 | 48-8

AAO (American Academy of Optometry)
6110 Executive Blvd Ste 506 .... Rockville MD 20852 | **800-368-6263** | 301-984-1441 | 48-8

AAO (American Assn of Orthodontists)
401 N Lindbergh Blvd .... Saint Louis MO 63141 | **800-522-1899** | 314-993-1700 | 48-8

AAO-HNS (American Academy of Otolaryngology-Head & Neck Surgery)
1650 Diagonal Rd .... Alexandria VA 22314 | **877-722-6467** | 703-836-4444 | 48-8

AAOMS (American Assn of Oral & Maxillofacial Surgeons)
9700 W Bryn Mawr Ave .... Rosemont IL 60018 | **800-822-6637** | 847-678-6200 | 48-8

AAOP (American Academy of Orthotists & Prosthetists)
526 King St Ste 201 .... Alexandria VA 22314 | **800-669-6024** | 703-836-0788 | 48-8

AAOS (American Academy of Orthopaedic Surgeons)
6300 N River Rd .... Rosemont IL 60018 | **800-346-2267** | 847-823-7186 | 48-8

AAP (American Academy of Pediatrics)
141 NW Pt Blvd .... Elk Grove Village IL 60007 | **800-433-9016** | 847-434-4000 | 48-8

AAP (American Academy of Periodontology)
737 N Michigan Ave Ste 800 .... Chicago IL 60611 | **800-282-4867** | 312-787-5518 | 48-8

AAP (Association of American Publishers Inc)
71 Fifth Ave .... New York NY 10003 | **866-271-4968** | 212-255-0200 | 48-16

AAPAR (American Assn for Physical Activity & Recreation)
1900 Assn Dr .... Reston VA 20191 | **800-213-7193** | 703-476-3400 | 47-23

AAPB (Association for Applied Psychophysiology & Biofeedback)
10200 W 44th Ave Ste 304 .... Wheat Ridge CO 80033 | **800-477-8892** | 303-422-8436 | 48-8

AAPCC (American Assn of Poison Control Centers)
3201 New Mexico Ave
Suite 310 .... Washington DC 20016 | **800-222-1222** | | 48-8

AAPD (American Academy of Pediatric Dentistry)
211 E Chicago Ave Ste 1700 .... Chicago IL 60611 | **800-974-3084** | 312-337-2169 | 48-8

AAPG (American Assn of Petroleum Geologists)
1444 S Boulder Ave PO Box 979 .... Tulsa OK 74119 | **800-364-2274** | 918-584-2555 | 47-12

AAPG Explorer Magazine
1444 S Boulder Ave .... Tulsa OK 74119 | **800-364-2274** | 918-584-2555 | 452-21

AAPL (American Academy of Psychiatry & the Law)
One Regency Dr PO Box 30 .... Bloomfield CT 06002 | **800-331-1389** | 860-242-5450 | 48-15

AAPM (American Academy of Pain Management)
13947 Mono Way Ste A .... Sonora CA 95370 | **888-519-9901** | 209-533-9744 | 48-8

AAPS (American Assn of Pharmaceutical Scientists)
2107 Wilson Blvd Ste 700 .... Arlington VA 22201 | **877-998-2277** | 703-243-2800 | 48-19

AAR (American Academy of Religion)
825 Houston Mill Rd NE Ste 300 .... Atlanta GA 30329 | **800-282-6632** | 404-727-3049 | 47-20

AAR (Alliance for Aging Research)
750 17th St NW Ste 1100 .... Washington DC 20006 | **866-840-6283** | 202-293-2856 | 47-17

AAR Aircraft Component Services
747 Zeckendorf Blvd .... Garden City NY 11530 | **800-422-2213** | 516-222-9000 | 24

AAR Aircraft Turbine Ctr
1100 N Wood Dale Rd 1 AAR Pl ...... Wood Dale IL 60191 | **800-422-2213*** | 630-227-2000 | 760
*General

AAR Composites
14201 Myerlake Cir .... Clearwater FL 33760 | **800-422-2213** | 727-539-8585 | 22

AAR Corp
1100 N Wood Dale Rd 1 AAR Pl ...... Wood Dale IL 60191 | **800-422-2213** | 630-227-2000 | 21
NYSE: AIR

AAR Distribution
1100 N Wood Dale Rd 1 AAR Pl ...... Wood Dale IL 60191 | **800-422-2213** | 630-227-2000 | 760

AAR Landing Gear Services
9371 NW 100th St .... Miami FL 33178 | **800-422-2213** | 305-887-4027 | 24

AARDA (American Autoimmune Related Disease Assn)
22100 Gratiot Ave .... Eastpointe MI 48021 | **800-598-4668** | 586-776-3900 | 47-17

Aaron & Company Inc
PO Box 8310 .... Piscataway NJ 08855 | **800-734-4822** | 732-752-8200 | 605

AaronEquipment Company Inc
735 E Green St PO Box 80 .... Bensenville IL 60106 | **800-492-2766** | 630-350-2200 | 382

AARP
601 E St NW .... Washington DC 20049 | **888-687-2277** | 202-434-2277 | 47-6

AARP Grandparent Information Ctr
601 E St NW .... Washington DC 20049 | **888-687-2277** | 202-434-3525 | 47-6

AARP Health Care Options
PO Box 1017 .... Montgomeryville PA 18936 | **800-523-5800** | | 388-3

AARP Motoring Plan
601 E Street N.W. .... Washington DC 20049 | **800-555-1121** | | 52

AARP Public Policy Institute
601 E St NW .... Washington DC 20049 | **888-687-2277** | 202-434-2277 | 625

AARP the Magazine
601 E St NW .... Washington DC 20049 | **888-687-2277** | 202-434-3525 | 452-10

AASA (American Assn of School Administrators)
801 N Quincy St Ste 700 .... Arlington VA 22203 | **800-771-1162** | 703-528-0700 | 48-5

AASCU (American Assn of State Colleges & Universities)
1307 New York Ave NW
Fifth Fl .... Washington DC 20005 | **800-558-3417** | 202-293-7070 | 48-5

AASHTO (American Assn of State Highway & Transportation Officials)
444 N Capitol St NW Ste 249 ...... Washington DC 20001 | **800-880-4117** | 202-624-5800 | 48-7

AASL (American Assn of School Librarians)
50 E Huron St .... Chicago IL 60611 | **800-545-2433** | 312-280-4386 | 48-11

AATB (American Assn of Tissue Banks)
1320 Old Chain Bridge Rd Ste 450 ...... McLean VA 22101 | **800-635-2282** | 703-827-9582 | 48-8

AATBS (Association for Advanced Training in the Behavioral Sciences)
5126 Ralston St .... Ventura CA 93003 | **800-472-1931** | 805-676-3030 | 48-5

AATG (American Assn of Teachers of German)
112 Haddontowne Ct Ste 104 .... Cherry Hill NJ 08034 | **800-835-6770** | 856-795-5553 | 48-5

AATH (Association for Applied & Therapeutic Humor)
65 Enterprise .... Aliso Viejo CA 92656 | **888-747-2284** | 815-708-6587 | 47-17

AATS (American Assn for Thoracic Surgery)
900 Cummings Ctr Ste 221-U .... Beverly MA 01915 | **800-424-5249** | 978-927-8330 | 48-8

AATSP (American Assn of Teachers of Spanish & Portuguese)
900 Ladd Rd .... Walled Lake MI 48390 | **877-832-2457** | 248-960-2180 | 48-5

AAU (Amateur Athletic Union of the US)
1910 Hotel Plaza Blvd .... Lake Buena Vista FL 32830 | **800-228-4872** | 407-934-7200 | 47-22

AAUP (American Assn of University Professors)
1133 Nineteenth St Ste 200 .... Washington DC 20036 | **800-424-2973** | 202-737-5900 | 48-5

AAUW (American Assn of University Women)
1111 16th St NW .... Washington DC 20036 | **800-326-2289** | 202-785-7700 | 48-5

AAUW Outlook Magazine
1111 16th St NW .... Washington DC 20036 | **800-326-2289** | 202-785-7700 | 452-10

Aavid Thermalloy LLC
70 Commercial St Ste 200 .... Concord NH 03301 | **855-322-2843** | 603-224-9988 | 253

AAVSO (American Assn of Variable Star Observers)
49 Bay State Rd .... Cambridge MA 02138 | **888-802-7827** | 617-354-0484 | 48-19

AB (AllianceBernstein Holding LP)
1345 Ave of the Americas .... New York NY 10105 | **800-221-5672*** | 212-486-5800 | 398
NYSE: AB ▪ *Cust Svc

AB Watley Direct Inc
50 Broad St Ste 1614 .... New York NY 10004 | **877-993-4886** | 646-753-9301 | 681

A&B Wiper Supply Inc
5601 Paschall Ave .... Philadelphia PA 19143 | **800-333-7247** | 215-482-6100 | 501

AB Young Cos Inc
15305 Stony Creek Way .... Noblesville IN 46060 | **800-886-7001** | 317-565-5000 | 605

ABA (American Bicycle Assn)
1645 W Sunrise Blvd .... Gilbert AZ 85233 | **866-650-4867** | 480-961-1903 | 47-22

ABA (American Bankers Assn)
1120 Connecticut Ave NW .... Washington DC 20036 | **800-226-5377*** | 202-663-5000 | 48-2
*Cust Svc

ABA (American Baptist Assn)
4605 N State Line Ave .... Texarkana TX 75503 | **800-264-2482** | 903-792-2783 | 47-20

ABA (American Bar Assn)
321 N Clark St .... Chicago IL 60610 | **800-285-2221** | 312-988-5000 | 48-10

ABA (American Booksellers Assn)
200 White Plains Rd Ste 600 .... Tarrytown NY 10591 | **800-637-0037** | 914-591-2665 | 48-18

ABA (American Businesspersons Assn)
350 Fairway Dr Ste 200 .... Deerfield Beach FL 33441 | **800-221-2168** | 954-571-1877 | 48-12

ABA Commission on Domestic Violence
321 N Clark St Ninth Fl. .... Chicago IL 60654 | **800-799-7233** | 312-988-5000 | 48-10

ABA Marketing Network
1120 Connecticut Ave NW .... Washington DC 20036 | **800-226-5377** | 202-663-5000 | 48-2

Abacus Technology Corp
5454 Wisconsin Ave Ste 1100 ...... Chevy Chase MD 20815 | **800-225-2135** | 301-907-8500 | 181

Abalon Precision Mfg Corp
1040 Home St .... Bronx NY 10459 | **800-888-2225** | 718-589-5682 | 688

Abalonetti Seafood Trattoria
57 Fisherman's Wharf Ste 1 .... Monterey CA 93940 | **877-643-4972** | 831-373-1851 | 662

ABAPAC (American Bankers Assn PAC)
1120 Connecticut Ave NW .... Washington DC 20036 | **800-226-5377** | | 608

ABA-PGT Inc
10 Gear Dr PO Box 8270 .... Manchester CT 06040 | **877-840-2172** | 860-649-4591 | 747

Abatement Technologies
605 Satellite Blvd Ste 300 .... Suwanee GA 30024 | **800-634-9091** | 678-889-4200 | 36

Abatix Corp
2400 Skyline Dr Ste 400 .... Mesquite TX 75149 | **800-426-3983** | 214-381-0322 | 382

Abaxis Inc
3240 Whipple Rd .... Union City CA 94587 | **800-822-2947** | 510-675-6500 | 416
NASDAQ: ABAX

ABB Inc 501 Merritt 7 .... Norwalk CT 06851 | **800-626-4999*** | 203-750-2200 | 383
*Prod Info

ABB SSAC
8242 Loop Rd .... Baldwinsville NY 13027 | **800-377-7722*** | 315-638-1300 | 204
*Tech Supp

Abba Technologies Inc
1501 San Pedro Dr NE .... Albuquerque NM 87110 | **888-222-2832** | 505-889-3337 | 195

Abbco Inc
2401 American Ln .... Elkgrove Vlg IL 60007 | **866-986-6546** | 630-595-7115 | 450

Abbey Delray
2000 Lowson Blvd .... Delray Beach FL 33445 | **888-791-9363** | 561-454-2000 | 663

Abbey Resort & Fontana Spa
269 Fontana Blvd .... Fontana WI 53125 | **800-709-1323** | 262-275-9000 | 660

Abbot & Abbot Box Corp
37-11 Tenth St .... Long Island City NY 11101 | **888-525-7186** | | 201

Abbott Ambulance Inc
2500 Abbott Pl .... Saint Louis MO 63143 | **888-974-7035** | 314-768-1000 | 30

Abbott Interfast Corp
190 Abbott Dr .... Wheeling IL 60090 | **800-877-0789** | 847-459-6200 | 614

Abbott Laboratories Abbott Diagnostics Div
100 Abbott Pk Rd .... Abbott Park IL 60064 | **800-387-8378** | 847-937-6100 | 231

Abbott Laboratories Animal Health Div
1401 Sheridan Rd .... North Chicago IL 60064 | **888-299-7416** | 847-937-6100 | 575

Abbott Laboratories Pharmaceutical Products Div
100 Research Dr
Bioresearch Ctr. .... Worcester MA 01605 | **866-427-8477** | 847-937-6100 | 576

Abbott Laboratories Ross Products Div
625 Cleveland Ave .... Columbus OH 43215 | **800-227-5767*** | 614-624-7485 | 295-10
*PR

Abbott Vascular
26531 Ynez Rd .... Temecula CA 92591 | **800-227-9902** | | 110

Abbozzo Gallery
401 Richmond Stt W Ste 128 .... Toronto ON M5V3A8 | **866-844-4481** | 416-260-2220 | 41

Abbyland Foods Inc
502 E Linden St PO Box 69 .... Abbotsford WI 54405 | **800-732-5483** | 715-223-6386 | 468

Listing	Toll-Free	Phone	Class
ABC (America's Blood Centers) 725 15th St NW Ste 700 — Washington DC 20005	888-872-5663	202-393-5725	48-8
ABC (Associated Builders & Contractors Inc) 4250 Fairfax Dr — Arlington VA 22203	866-262-0540	703-812-2000	48-3
ABC (Audit Bureau of Circulations) 48 W Seegers Road — Arlington Heights IL 60005	800-759-6397	224-366-6939	48-18
ABC Appliance Inc 1 Silverdome Industrial Pk — Pontiac MI 48343	800-981-3866	248-335-4222	34
ABC Compounding Company Inc & Acme Wholesale 6970 Jonesboro Rd — Morrow GA 30260	800-795-9222	770-968-9222	149
ABC Fine Wines & Spirits 8989 S Orange Ave — Orlando FL 32824	800-854-7283	407-851-0000	439
ABC Global Services 6400 Shafer Ct Ste 310 — Rosemont IL 60018	800-722-5179		761
ABC Home Medical Supply Inc 15 E Uwchlan Ave Ste 430 — Exton PA 19341	866-897-8588		470
ABC Industrie PO Box 77 — Warsaw IN 46581	800-426-0921	574-267-5166	367
ABC Metals Inc 500 W Clinton St — Logansport IN 46947	800-238-8470		487
A-B-C Packaging Machine Corp 811 Live Oak St — Tarpon Springs FL 34689	800-237-5975	727-937-5144	540
ABC Seamless 3001 Fiechtner Dr — Fargo ND 58103	800-732-6577	701-293-5952	192-4
ABC Supply Company Inc One ABC Pkwy — Beloit WI 53511	888-492-1047	608-362-7777	192-4
ABC-CLIO Inc 130 Cremona Dr — Goleta CA 93117	800-368-6868	805-968-1911	628-2
Abco Cleaning Products 6800 NW 36th Ave — Miami FL 33147	888-694-2226	305-694-2226	501
Abco Distribution Inc 6282 Proprietors Rd — Worthington OH 43085	800-821-9435		620
Abco Inc 1621 Wall St — Dallas TX 75215	800-969-2226	214-565-1191	85
Abco Laboratories Inc 2450 S Watney Way — Fairfield CA 94533	800-678-2226	707-432-2200	295-37
Abco Office Furniture 4121 Rushton St — Florence AL 35630	800-336-0070	256-767-4100	318-1
ABCT (Association for Behavioral & Cognitive Therapies) 305 Seventh Ave 16th Fl — New York NY 10001	800-685-2228	212-647-1890	48-15
Abe's of Maine Cameras & Electronics Five Fernwood Ave — Edison NJ 08837	800-992-2237	732-225-1777	118
Abel Automatics Inc 165 Aviador St — Camarillo CA 93010	866-511-7444	805-484-8789	701
Abel Reel, The 165 Aviador St — Camarillo CA 93010	866-511-7444	805-484-8789	746
Abelconn LLC 9210 Science Ctr Dr — New Hope MN 55428	800-526-2828	763-533-3533	617
Abell Corp 2500 Sterlington Rd — Monroe LA 71203	800-325-7204		280
Abell-Howe Crane Inc 10321 Werch Dr Ste 100 — Woodridge IL 60517	800-366-0068		465
Aberdeen & Rockfish Railroad Co 101 E Main St — Aberdeen NC 28315	800-849-8985	910-944-2341	639
Aberdeen American News 124 S Second St — Aberdeen SD 57402	800-925-4100	605-225-4100	525-2
Aberdeen Area Chamber of Commerce 516 S Main St — Aberdeen SD 57401	800-874-9038	605-225-2860	137
Aberdeen Convention & Visitors Bureau 10 Railroad Ave SW PO Box 78 — Aberdeen SD 57401	800-645-3851	605-225-2414	207
Aberdeen LLC 9130 Norwalk Blvd — Santa Fe Springs CA 90670	800-500-9526	562-699-6998	174-1
ABF Freight Systems Inc 3801 Old Greenwood Rd — Fort Smith AR 72903	800-610-5544	479-785-8913	770
ABHES (Accrediting Bureau of Health Education Schools) 7777 Leesburg Pike Ste 314 N — Falls Church VA 22043	800-228-9290	703-917-9503	47-1
ABI (Advanced Biotechnologies Inc) 9108 Guilford Rd — Columbia MD 21046	800-426-0764	410-792-9779	231
ABI (Atkinson-Baker Inc) 500 N Brand Blvd 3rd Fl — Glendale CA 91203	800-288-3376	818-551-7300	440
Abilene Christian University Brown Library (ACU) 760 Library Ct — Abilene TX 79699	800-460-6228	325-674-2000	431-6
Abilene Convention & Visitors Bureau 1101 N First St — Abilene TX 79601	800-727-7704	325-676-2556	207
Abilene Machine Inc PO Box 129 — Abilene KS 67410	800-255-0337	785-655-9455	274
Abilene Reporter-News 101 Cypress St — Abilene TX 79601	800-588-6397	325-673-4271	525-2
ABIM (American Board of Internal Medicine) 510 Walnut St Ste 1700 — Philadelphia PA 19106	800-441-2246	215-446-3500	47-1
Abingdon Convention & Visitors Bureau 335 Cummings St — Abingdon VA 24210	800-435-3440	276-676-2282	207
ABIOMED Inc 22 Cherry Hill Dr — Danvers MA 01923 *NASDAQ: ABMD*	800-422-8666	978-777-5410	250
Abipa Canada Inc 2000, Blvd Dagenais ouest — Laval QC H7L5W2	877-963-6888	450-963-6888	21
Abita Brewing Co 21084 Hwy 36 — Covington LA 70433	800-737-2311	985-893-3143	101
Abitec Corp Inc PO Box 569 — Columbus OH 43215 *Sales	800-555-1255*	614-429-6464	295-29
ABL (American Beverage Licensees) 5101 River Rd Ste 108 — Bethesda MD 20816	800-656-3241	301-656-1494	48-6
Able 2 Products Company Inc PO Box 543 — Cassville MO 65625	800-641-4098	417-847-4791	434
Able Services 868 Folsom St — San Francisco CA 94107	800-461-9577	415-546-6534	256
Able Steel Equipment Co Inc 50-02 23rd St — Long Island City NY 11101	800-428-8722	718-361-9240	286
ABMA (American Boiler Manufacturers Assn) 8221 Old Courthouse Rd Ste 207 — Vienna VA 22182	800-227-1966	703-356-7172	48-13
ABMC (American Bio Medica Corp) 122 Smith Rd — Kinderhook NY 12106 *OTC: ABMC ■ *General*	800-227-1243*	518-758-8158	84
ABMP (Associated Bodywork & Massage Professionals) 25188 Genesee Trl Rd Ste 200 — Golden CO 80401	800-458-2267	303-674-8478	47-17
Abraham Baldwin Agricultural College 2802 Moore Hwy ABAC 3 — Tifton GA 31793	800-733-3653	229-391-5001	160
Abraham Lincoln Presidential Library & Museum 112 N Sixth St — Springfield IL 62701	800-610-2094	217-557-6250	431-2
Abrams Construction Inc Seven Kent St Ste 2 — Brookline MA 02445	800-935-9350	617-566-9090	187
Abresist Corp PO Box 38 — Urbana IN 46990	800-348-0717	260-774-3327	184
Abric (North America) Inc 220 Barren Springs Dr Ste 1 — Houston TX 77090	888-922-7429	281-569-7100	325
Abrisa Technologies 200 S Hallock Dr — Santa Paula CA 93060	877-622-7472		330
ABRY Partners LLC 111 Huntington Ave 29th Fl — Boston MA 02199	800-777-3674	617-859-2959	402
ABS Global Inc 1525 River Rd PO Box 459 — DeForest WI 53532 *Cust Svc	800-356-5331*	608-846-3721	11-2
Absocold Corp PO Box 1545 — Richmond IN 47375	800-843-3714	765-935-7501	603
Absolut Aire Inc 5496 N Riverview Dr — Kalamazoo MI 49004	800-804-4000	269-382-1875	14
Absopure Water Co 8835 General Dr — Plymouth MI 48170	800-422-7678	313-898-1200	793
Absorbent Ink 5812 Trade Ctr Dr Ste 100 — Austin TX 78744	866-618-3471		7
ABT Internet Inc 175 E Shore Rd — Great Neck NY 11023	800-367-3414	516-829-5484	395
ABTA (American Brain Tumor Assn) 2720 River Rd — Des Plaines IL 60018	800-886-2282	847-827-9910	47-17
ABWA (American Business Women's Assn) 11050 Roe Ave Ste 200 — Overland Park KS 66211	800-228-0007		48-12
ABX Air Inc 145 Hunter Dr — Wilmington OH 45177	800-736-3973	937-382-5591	12
Abx Engineering 880 Hinckley Rd — Burlingame CA 94010	800-366-4588	650-552-2322	256
AC & T Company Inc 11535 Hopewell Rd — Hagerstown MD 21740	800-458-3835	301-582-2700	315
AC Central Reservations Inc 201 Tilton Rd London Sq Mall Ste 17B — Northfield NJ 08225	888-227-6667	609-383-8880	373
Ac Coin & Slot 201 W Decatur Ave — Pleasantville NJ 08232	800-284-7568	609-641-7811	321
AC Corp 301 Creek Ridge Rd — Greensboro NC 27406	800-422-7378	336-273-4472	190-10
AC Doctor LLC 2151 W Hillsboro Blvd Ste 400 — Deerfield Beach FL 33442	866-264-1479		779
AC Miller Concrete Products Inc 31 E Bridge St PO Box 199 — Spring City PA 19475	800-229-2922	610-948-4600	184
AC Nutrition 158 N Main St — Winters TX 79567	800-588-3333	325-754-4546	442
ACA (American Council on Alcoholism) 1000 E Indian School Rd — Phoenix AZ 85014	800-527-5344		47-17
ACA (Auto Club of America Corp) 9411 N Georgia St — Oklahoma City OK 73120	800-411-2007	405-751-4430	52
ACA (American Camp Assn) 5000 State Rd 67 N — Martinsville IN 46151	800-428-2267	765-342-8456	47-23
ACA (American Chiropractic Assn) 1701 Clarendon Blvd Second Fl — Arlington VA 22209	800-986-4636	703-276-8800	48-8
ACA (American Correctional Assn) 206 N Washington St Ste 200 — Alexandria VA 22314	800-222-5646	703-224-0000	48-7
ACA (American Counseling Assn) 5999 Stevenson Ave — Alexandria VA 22304	800-347-6647	703-823-9800	48-15
ACA (American AgCredit) PO Box 1120 — Santa Rosa CA 95402	800-800-4865	707-545-1200	216
ACA International - Assn of Credit & Collection Professionals 4040 W 70th St PO Box 390106 — Minneapolis MN 55439	800-844-5654	952-926-6547	48-2
ACAAI (American College of Allergy Asthma & Immunology) 85 W Algonquin Rd Ste 550 — Arlington Heights IL 60005	800-466-3649	847-427-1200	48-8
Acacia Life Insurance Co 7315 Wisconsin Ave — Bethesda MD 20814	800-444-1889	301-280-1000	388-2
Acacia National Life 7315 Wisconsin Ave — Bethesda MD 20814	800-444-1889	800-368-2745	388-2
Academe Magazine 1133 19th St NW Ste 200 — Washington DC 20036	800-424-2973	202-737-5900	452-8
Academic Apparel 20644 Superior St — Chatsworth CA 91311	800-626-5000	818-886-8697	153-13
Academy Bus LLC 111 Paterson Ave — Hoboken NJ 07030	800-442-7272	201-420-7000	750
Academy for Guided Imagery Inc 10780 Santa Monica Blvd Ste 290 — Los Angeles CA 90025	800-726-2070		756
Academy Hotel Colorado Springs, The 8110 N Academy Blvd — Colorado Springs CO 80920	800-766-8524	719-598-5770	376
Academy of Art University 79 New Montgomery St — San Francisco CA 94105	800-544-2787	415-274-2200	166
Academy of Court Reporting Clawson 1055 W Maple Rd — Clawson MI 48017	888-314-7780		788
Academy of Court Reporting Cleveland 2044 Euclid Ave — Cleveland OH 44115	888-314-7780		788
Academy of Court Reporting Columbus 150 E Gay St — Columbus OH 43215	866-865-8067	614-221-7770	788
Academy of General Dentistry (AGD) 211 E Chicago Ave Ste 900 — Chicago IL 60611	888-243-3368	312-440-4300	48-8
Academy of Managed Care Pharmacy (AMCP) 100 N Pitt St Ste 400 — Alexandria VA 22314	800-827-2627	703-683-8416	48-8
Academy of Management (AOM) 235 Elm Rd PO Box 3020 — Briarcliff Manor NY 10510	800-633-4931	914-923-2607	48-12
Academy of Model Aeronautics (AMA) 5161 E Memorial Dr — Muncie IN 47302	800-435-9262	765-287-1256	47-18
Academy of Osseointegration 85 W Algonquin Rd Ste 550 — Arlington Heights IL 60005	800-656-7736	847-439-1919	48-8
Academy of Pharmacy Practice & Management American Pharmacists Assn 1100 15th St NW Ste 400 — Washington DC 20005	800-237-2742	202-628-4410	48-8
Academy of Students of Pharmacy American Pharmacists Assn 1100 15th St NW Ste 400 — Washington DC 20005	800-237-2742	202-628-4410	48-8
Academy Sports & Outdoors 1800 N Mason Rd — Katy TX 77449	888-922-2336	281-646-5200	702
Acadia Divinity College 38 Highland Ave — Wolfville NS B4P2R6	866-875-8975	902-585-2210	167-3
Acadia Inn 98 Eden St — Bar Harbor ME 04609	800-638-3636	207-288-3500	376

Name / Address	City	State	ZIP	Toll-Free	Phone	Class
Acadia Realty Trust						
1311 Mamaroneck Ave						
Ste 260	White Plains	NY	10605	**800-937-5449**	914-288-8100	646
NYSE: AKR						
Acadia University						
15 University Ave	Wolfville	NS	B4P2R6	**877-585-1121**	902-542-2201	773
Acadian Ambulance Service Inc						
300 Hopkins St	Lafayette	LA	70501	**800-259-3333**		30
Acadian Asset Management Inc						
260 Franklin St	Boston	MA	02110	**800-946-0166**	617-850-3500	398
Acadiana Symphony Orchestra						
412 Travis St	Lafayette	LA	70503	**800-259-8852**	337-232-4277	566-3
ACAOM (Accreditation Commission for Acupuncture & Oriental Medicine)						
7501 Greenway Ctr Dr Ste 760	Greenbelt	MD	20770	**800-735-2968**	301-313-0855	47-1
ACA-PAC (American Chiropractic Assn PAC)						
1701 Clarendon Blvd	Arlington	VA	22209	**800-986-4636**	703-276-8800	608
Acapulco Hotel & Resort						
2505 S						
Atlantic Ave	Daytona Beach Shores	FL	32118	**855-922-3224**	386-761-2210	376
ACAT (Accreditation Council for Accountancy & Taxation)						
1010 N Fairfax St	Alexandria	VA	22314	**888-289-7763**	703-549-2228	47-1
ACB (American Council of the Blind)						
1155 15th St NW Ste 1004	Washington	DC	20005	**800-424-8666**	202-467-5081	47-17
ACB (America's Community Bankers)						
1120 Connecticut Ave NW	Washington	DC	20036	**800-226-5377**		48-2
ACBL (American Contract Bridge League)						
6575 Windchase Blvd	Horn Lake	MS	38637	**800-264-2743***	662-253-3100	47-18
*Sales						
ACC (Alpena Community College)						
665 Johnson St	Alpena	MI	49707	**888-468-6222**	989-356-9021	160
ACC (American College of Cardiology)						
2400 N St NW	Washington	DC	20037	**800-253-4636***	202-375-6000	48-8
*Cust Svc						
ACC (Association of Corporate Counsel)						
1025 Connecticut Ave NW						
Ste 200	Washington	DC	20036	**877-647-3411**	202-293-4103	48-10
ACC (Austin Community College)						
5930 Middle Fiskville Rd	Austin	TX	78752	**877-442-3522**	512-223-7000	160
ACCE (American Chamber of Commerce Executives)						
4875 Eisenhower Ave Ste 250	Alexandria	VA	22304	**800-394-2223**	703-998-0072	48-12
Accel Networks LLC						
4905 34th StS #227	St. Petersburg	FL	33711	**877-406-8585**		224
Accelerated Genetics						
E 10890 Penny Ln	Baraboo	WI	53913	**800-451-9275**	608-356-8357	11-2
Accelrys Inc						
10188 Telesis Ct Ste 100	San Diego	CA	92121	**888-249-2284**	858-799-5000	179-5
NASDAQ: ACCL						
Accent Health						
60 E 42nd St Ste 1543	New York	NY	10165	**800-235-4930**		729
Accent Inns Vancouver Airport						
10551 St Edwards Dr	Richmond	BC	V6X3L8	**800-663-0298**	604-273-3311	376
Accent Inns Vancouver-Burnaby						
3777 Henning Dr	Burnaby	BC	V5C6N5	**800-663-0298**	604-473-5000	376
Accent' Windows Inc						
14175 E 42nd Ave	Denver	CO	80239	**888-284-3948**	303-420-2002	494
Access America						
673 Emory Vly Rd	Oak Ridge	TN	37830	**800-860-2140**	865-482-2140	726
Access Business Group						
7575 Fulton St E	Ada	MI	49355	**800-253-6500***	616-787-6000	444
*Cust Svc						
Access Energy Co-op						
1800 W Washington St	Mount Pleasant	IA	52641	**866-242-4232**	319-385-1577	245
Access Innovations Inc						
4725 Indian School Rd NE						
Ste 100	Albuquerque	NM	87110	**800-926-8328**	505-265-3591	178
Access Intelligence LLC						
Four Choke Cherry Rd						
Second Fl	Rockville	MD	20850	**800-777-5006**	301-354-2000	628-9
Access Magazine						
444 N Michigan Ave Ste 3400	Chicago	IL	60611	**800-243-2342**	312-440-8900	452-16
Access National Corp						
1800 Robert Fulton Dr Ste 310	Reston	VA	20191	**800-931-0370**	703-871-2100	357-2
NASDAQ: ANCX						
Access Point Inc						
1100 Crescent Green	Cary	NC	27518	**877-419-4274**	919-851-4838	726
Access Securities Inc						
30 Buxton Farm Rd	Stamford	CT	06905	**800-331-6171**	203-322-3377	681
Access Specialties International LLC						
15230 Carrousel Way	Rosemount	MN	55068	**800-332-1013**	651-453-1283	175
Access To Media						
432 Front St	Chicopee	MA	01013	**866-612-0034**		7
Access US						
712 N Second St Ste 300	Saint Louis	MO	63102	**800-638-6373**	314-655-7700	395
Accident Fund Co						
232 S Capitol Ave PO Box 40790	Lansing	MI	48901	**888-276-0327***	517-342-4200	388-4
*Mktg						
ACCO Engineered Systems						
6265 San Fernando Rd	Glendale	CA	91201	**800-998-2226***	818-243-1727	190-10
*Cust Svc						
Accord Creditor Services LLC						
PO Box 10005	Newnan	GA	30271	**800-373-0760**		390
Accord Industries						
4001 Forsyth Rd	Winter Park	FL	32792	**800-876-6989***	407-671-6989	184
*General						
Accounting Principals						
10151 Deerwood Park Blvd						
Ste 400	Jacksonville	FL	32256	**800-981-3849**		712
AccountingWEB Inc						
PO Box 2252	Westerville	OH	43086	**866-688-1678**		523
Accounts Receivable Funding Corp (ARFC)						
PO Box 35750	Houston	TX	77235	**800-992-1717**		272
Accoutrements						
10915 47th Ave W	Mukilteo	WA	98275	**800-886-2221**	425-349-3838	327
ACCP (American College of Chest Physicians)						
3300 Dundee Rd	Northbrook	IL	60062	**800-343-2227**	847-498-1400	48-8
Accram Inc						
2901 W Clarendon Ave	Phoenix	AZ	85017	**800-786-0288**		176
Accreditation Commission for Acupuncture & Oriental Medicine (ACAOM)						
7501 Greenway Ctr Dr Ste 760	Greenbelt	MD	20770	**800-735-2968**	301-313-0855	47-1
Accreditation Council for Accountancy & Taxation (ACAT)						
1010 N Fairfax St	Alexandria	VA	22314	**888-289-7763**	703-549-2228	47-1
Accrediting Bureau of Health Education Schools (ABHES)						
7777 Leesburg Pike						
Ste 314 N	Falls Church	VA	22043	**800-228-9290**	703-917-9503	47-1
Accrediting Council for Independent Colleges & Schools (ACICS)						
750 First St NE Ste 980	Washington	DC	20002	**800-258-3826**	202-336-6780	47-1
Accredo Health Group Inc						
1640 Century Ctr Pkwy	Memphis	TN	38134	**877-222-7336**	901-385-3688	580
ACCT (Association of Community College Trustees)						
1233 20th St NW Ste 605	Washington	DC	20036	**866-895-2228**	202-775-4667	48-5
Accu Therm Inc						
PO Box 249	Monroe City	MO	63456	**888-925-4332**	573-735-1060	383
Accucaps Industries Ltd						
2125 Ambassador Dr	Windsor	ON	N9C3R5	**800-665-7210**	519-969-5404	576
AccuCode Inc						
6886 S Yosemite St Ste 100	Centennial	CO	80112	**866-705-9879**	303-639-6111	178
Accufax PO Box 35563	Tulsa	OK	74153	**800-256-8898**		626
Accugenix Inc						
223 Lake Dr	Newark	DE	19702	**800-886-9654**	302-292-8888	415
Accuplan Benefits Services						
515 East 4500 South						
Ste G200	Salt Lake City	UT	84107	**800-454-2649**	801-266-9900	48-2
Accuracy in Media Inc (AIM)						
4455 Connecticut Ave NW						
Ste 330	Washington	DC	20008	**800-787-4567**	202-364-4401	48-14
Accurate Air Engineering Inc						
16207 Carmennita Rd	Cerritos	CA	90703	**800-438-5577**	562-484-6370	382
Accurate Alloys Inc						
5455 Irwindale Ave	Irwindale	CA	91706	**800-842-2222**	626-338-4012	487
Accurate Bushing Company Inc						
443 N Ave	Garwood	NJ	07027	**800-932-0076***	908-789-1121	74
*Sales						
Accurate Chemical & Scientific Corp						
300 Shames Dr	Westbury	NY	11590	**800-645-6264**	516-333-2221	231
Accurate Dial & Nameplate Inc						
329 Mira Loma Ave	Glendale	CA	91204	**800-400-4455**	323-245-9181	410
Accurate Mailings Inc						
215 O'Neill Ave	Belmont	CA	94002	**800-732-3290**	650-508-8885	5
Accurate Perforating Co						
3636 S Kedzie Ave	Chicago	IL	60632	**800-621-0273**	773-254-3232	483
Accurate Surgical & Scientific Instruments Corp						
300 Shames Dr	Westbury	NY	11590	**800-645-3569**	516-333-2570	471
Accuray Inc						
1310 Chesapeake Terr	Sunnyvale	CA	94089	**888-522-3740**	408-716-4600	471
NASDAQ: ARAY						
Accuride Corp						
7140 Office Cir	Evansville	IN	47715	**800-823-8332***	812-962-5000	59
NYSE: ACW ■ *Cust Svc						
Accuristix						
2844 Bristol Cir	Oakville	ON	L6H6G4	**866-356-6830**	905-829-9927	357-2
Accu-Sort Systems Inc						
511 School House Rd	Telford	PA	18969	**800-227-2633**	215-723-0981	174-7
Accu-Systems Inc						
1810 West 5000 South	Salt Lake City	UT	84118	**800-369-5746**		279
Accutest Laboratories						
2235 Rt 130 Bldg B	Dayton	NJ	08810	**800-329-0204**	732-329-0200	732
Accu-time Systems Inc						
420 Somers Rd	Ellington	CT	06029	**800-355-4648**	860-870-5000	55
Accutron Inc						
1733 Parkside Ln	Phoenix	AZ	85027	**800-531-2221**	623-780-2020	228
Accuvant Inc						
1125 17th St Ste 1700	Denver	CO	80202	**800-574-0896**	303-298-0600	684
AccuWeather Inc						
385 Science Pk Rd	State College	PA	16803	**800-566-6606***	814-235-8650	523
*Sales						
ACD Systems International Inc						
129-1335 Bear Mtn Pkwy	Victoria	BC	V9B6T9	**800-579-5309**	250-419-6700	179-8
ACDA (American Choral Directors Assn)						
545 Couch Dr	Oklahoma City	OK	73102	**800-624-0166**	405-232-8161	47-4
ACDI/VOCA						
50 F St NW Ste 1075	Washington	DC	20001	**800-929-8622**	202-638-4661	47-5
ACE (American Council on Exercise)						
4851 Paramount Dr	San Diego	CA	92123	**800-825-3636**	858-576-6500	47-17
ACE (Altamont Commuter Express)						
949 E Ch St	Stockton	CA	95202	**800-411-7245**		463
ACE (Association of Conservation Engineers)						
Missouri Dept of Conservation						
PO Box 180	Jefferson City	MO	65102	**866-633-8110**	573-522-4115	48-7
ACE Cash Express						
1231 Greenway Dr Ste 600	Irving	TX	75038	**800-817-5106**	972-550-5000	139
ACE Conference Ctr						
800 Ridge Pk	Lafayette Hill	PA	19444	**800-523-3000**	610-825-8000	374
Ace Doran Hauling & Rigging Co Inc						
1601 Blue Rock St	Cincinnati	OH	45223	**800-829-0929**	513-681-7900	770
Ace Forms of Kansas Inc						
2900 N Rotary Terr	Pittsburg	KS	66762	**800-223-9287**		109
Ace Glass Inc						
1430 NW Blvd PO Box 688	Vineland	NJ	08360	**800-223-4524**	856-692-3333	331
Ace ImageWear						
4120 Truman Rd	Kansas City	MO	64127	**800-366-0564**	816-231-5737	438
Ace Mart - Downtown San Antonio						
1220 S St Mary's	San Antonio	TX	78210	**888-898-8079**	210-224-0082	113
Ace Medical Inc						
94-910 Moloalo St	Waipahu	HI	96797	**866-678-3601**	808-678-3600	470
Ace Parking Management Inc						
645 Ash St	San Diego	CA	92101	**800-925-7275***	619-233-6624	555
*General						
Ace Relocation Systems Inc						
5608 Eastgate Dr	San Diego	CA	92121	**800-453-0964**	858-677-5500	770
ACE Rent A Car						
5773 W Washington St	Indianapolis	IN	46241	**800-242-7368**	317-248-5686	125
Ace Tool Co						
7337 Bryan Dairy Rd	Largo	FL	33777	**800-777-5910**	727-544-4331	60
Ace Wire & Cable Co Inc						
7201 51st Ave	Woodside	NY	11377	**800-225-2354**	718-458-9200	800
Ace World Wide Moving						
1900 E College Ave	Cudahy	WI	53110	**800-558-3980**	414-764-1000	512
ACEC (Allamakee-Clayton Electric Co-op)						
229 Hwy 51 PO Box 715	Postville	IA	52162	**888-788-1551**	563-864-7611	245
Aceco 4419 Federal Way	Boise	ID	83716	**800-359-7012**	208-343-7712	347
ACEI (Association for Childhood Education International)						
1101 16th St NW Ste 300	Washington	DC	20036	**800-423-3563**	202-372-9986	48-5
ACEP (American College of Emergency Physicians)						
1125 Executive Cir PO Box 619911	Dallas	TX	75261	**800-798-1822**	972-550-0911	48-8
Acer America Corp						
333 W San Carlos St Ste 1500	San Jose	CA	95110	**800-253-2687**	408-533-7700	174-1
Ace-Tex Enterprises						
7601 Central St	Detroit	MI	48210	**800-444-3800**	313-834-4000	438

Listing	Toll-Free	Phone	Class
ACF (Association of Consulting Foresters of America)			
312 Montgomery St Ste 208 . . . Alexandria VA 22314	**888-540-8733**	703-548-0990	47-2
ACF (American Culinary Federation Inc)			
180 Ctr Pl Way . . . Saint Augustine FL 32095	**800-624-9458**	904-824-4468	48-6
ACF Components & Fasteners Inc			
31012 Huntwood Ave . . . Hayward CA 94544	**800-227-2901***	510-487-2100	246
*Cust Svc			
ACFA (Alameda County Fair Assn)			
4501 Pleasanton Ave . . . Pleasanton CA 94566	**800-874-9253**	925-426-7600	633
ACFAS (American College of Foot & Ankle Surgeons)			
8725 W Higgins Rd Ste 555 . . . Chicago IL 60631	**800-421-2237**	773-693-9300	48-8
ACFC (American Coalition for Fathers & Children)			
1718 M St NW Ste 1187 . . . Washington DC 20036	**800-978-3237**		47-6
ACFC (Atlantic Coast Bank)			
505 Haines Ave . . . Waycross GA 31501	**800-342-2824**	912-283-4711	357-2
NASDAQ: ACFC			
ACFE (Association of Certified Fraud Examiners)			
716 W Ave . . . Austin TX 78701	**800-245-3321**	512-478-9000	48-1
ACFEI (American College of Forensic Examiners International)			
2750 E Sunshine St . . . Springfield MO 65804	**800-423-9737**	417-881-3818	48-8
ACG (American Cotton Growers Textile Div)			
PO Box 2827 PO Box 430 . . . Lubbock TX 79408	**800-333-8011**	806-763-8011	734-1
ACG (Association for Corporate Growth)			
71 S Wacker Dr Ste 2760 . . . Chicago IL 60606	**877-358-2220**	312-957-4260	48-12
ACH Food Cos Inc			
7171 Goodlet Farms Pkwy . . . Cordova TN 38016	**800-691-1106**	901-381-3000	295-30
ACHE (Association for Continuing Higher Education)			
1700 Asp Ave . . . Norman OK 73072	**800-807-2243**		48-5
Achieva Inc			
197 Funder Dr PO Box 729 . . . Mocksville NC 27028	**800-788-7213**	336-751-7104	318-3
Achilles Guard Inc			
4201 Spring Vly Rd Ste 1400 . . . Dallas TX 75244	**866-525-8680**		181
ACI (Arkansas Correctional Industries)			
2403 E Harding St . . . Pine Bluff AR 71601	**877-635-7213**	870-850-8431	622
ACI (Axis Communications Inc)			
100 Apollo Dr . . . Chelmsford MA 01824	**800-444-2947**	978-614-2000	177
ACI (AREBA Casriel Inc)			
500 W 57th St . . . New York NY 10019	**800-724-4444**	212-293-3000	717
ACI Worldwide			
4965 Preston Pk Blvd Ste 800 . . . Plano TX 75093	**877-238-3095**	972-599-5600	179-1
Acic Fine Chemicals Inc			
81 St Claire Blvd . . . Brantford ON N3S7X6	**800-265-6727**	519-751-3668	474
ACICS (Accrediting Council for Independent Colleges & Schools)			
750 First St NE Ste 980 . . . Washington DC 20002	**800-258-3826**	202-336-6780	47-1
Acier Picard Inc			
3000 Rue De L' Etchemin . . . Levis QC G6W7X6	**888-834-0646**	418-834-8300	487
ACIL (American Council of Independent Laboratories)			
1875 I St NW Ste 500 . . . Washington DC 20006	**800-368-1131**	202-887-5872	48-19
ACIPCO (American Cast Iron Pipe Co)			
1501 31st Ave N . . . Birmingham AL 35207	**800-442-2347**	205-325-7701	306
Ackermann Public Relations & Marketing			
1111 Northshore Dr Ste N-400 . . . Knoxville TN 37919	**877-325-9453***	865-584-0550	627
*General			
ACL (Atlantic Container Line)			
50 Cardinal Dr . . . Westfield NJ 07090	**800-225-1235**	908-518-5300	312
ACLU (American Civil Liberties Union)			
125 Broad St 18th Fl . . . New York NY 10004	**877-867-1025**	212-549-2500	47-8
ACM (Association for Computing Machinery)			
Two Penn Plz Ste 701 . . . New York NY 10121	**800-342-6626**	212-626-0500	47-9
ACMA Computers Inc			
1565 Reliance Way . . . Fremont CA 94539	**800-800-6328***	510-651-8886	174-1
*Sales			
ACMC (Affiliated Community Medical Centers)			
101 Willmar Ave SW . . . Willmar MN 56201	**888-225-6580**	320-231-5000	371-3
ACME (Association for Couples in Marriage Enrichment)			
PO Box 21374 . . . Winston-Salem NC 27120	**800-634-8325**	336-724-1526	47-6
Acme Brick Co			
3024 Acme Brick Plaza . . . Fort Worth TX 76109	**866-430-2263**	817-332-4101	148
Acme Cryogenics Inc			
2801 Mitchell Ave . . . Allentown PA 18103	**800-422-2790**	610-966-4488	449
Acme Distribution Centers Inc			
18101 E Colfax Ave . . . Aurora CO 80011	**800-444-3614**	303-340-2100	791-1
Acme Dynamics Inc			
3608 Sydney Rd PO Box 1780 . . . Plant City FL 33566	**800-622-9355**	813-752-3137	632
Acme Electric			
N85 W12545 Westbrook			
Crossing . . . Menomonee Falls WI 53051	**800-334-5214**	910-738-1121	383
Acme Food Sales Inc			
5940 1st Ave S . . . Seattle WA 98108	**800-777-2263**	206-762-5150	296-8
Acme Industrial Co			
441 Maple Ave . . . Carpentersville IL 60110	**800-323-5582**	847-428-3911	488
Acme Markets Inc			
75 Valley Stream Pkwy . . . Malvern PA 19355	**877-932-7948**	610-889-4000	342
Acme Metal Cap Inc Co			
33-53 62nd St . . . Woodside NY 11377	**800-338-3581**	718-335-3000	483
Acme Paper & Supply Company Inc			
8229 Sandy Ct PO Box 422 . . . Savage MD 20763	**800-462-5812**	410-792-2333	541
Acme Pizza & Bakery Equipment Inc			
7039 E Slauson Blvd . . . Commerce CA 90040	**800-428-2263**	323-722-7900	297
Acme Spirally Wound Paper Products Inc			
4810 W 139th St PO Box 35320 . . . Cleveland OH 44135	**800-274-2797**	216-267-2950	124
Acme Truck Line Inc			
121 Pailet Dr . . . Harvey LA 70058	**800-825-6246**	504-368-2510	770
Acme United Corp			
60 Round Hill Rd . . . Fairfield CT 06824	**800-835-2263**	203-254-6060	471
NYSE: ACU			
ACOFP (American College of Osteopathic Family Physicians)			
330 E Algonquin Rd			
Ste 1 . . . Arlington Heights IL 60005	**800-323-0794**	847-952-5100	48-8
ACOM Solutions Inc			
2850 E 29th St . . . Long Beach CA 90806	**800-347-3638**	562-424-7899	179-1
Acor Orthopaedic Inc			
18530 S Miles Pkwy . . . Cleveland OH 44128	**800-237-2267**	216-662-4500	300
ACORD (Association for Co-op Operations Research & Development)			
One Blue Hill Plz			
PO Box 1529 . . . Pearl River NY 10965	**800-444-3341**	845-620-1700	48-9
Acorn Deck House Co			
852 Main St . . . Acton MA 01720	**800-727-3325**	978-263-6800	105
Acorn Engineering Co			
15125 Proctor Ave			
PO Box 3527 . . . City of Industry CA 91744	**800-488-8999**	626-336-4561	602
Acorn Manufacturing Company Inc			
457 School St . . . Mansfield MA 02048	**800-835-0121**		347

Listing	Toll-Free	Phone	Class
Acorn Wire & Iron Works Inc			
2035 S Racine Ave . . . Chicago IL 60608	**800-552-2676**	773-585-0600	279
Acosta Sales & Marketing Co			
665 W N Ave Ste 300 . . . Lombard IL 60148	**888-281-9810***	630-620-7600	196
*General			
Acousti Engineering Co of Florida Inc			
4656 34th St SW . . . Orlando FL 32811	**800-434-3467**	407-425-3467	190-9
Acoustic Neuroma Assn (ANA)			
600 Peachtree Pkwy Ste 108 . . . Cumming GA 30041	**877-200-8211**	770-205-8211	47-17
Acoustical Material Services Inc			
1620 S Maple Ave . . . Montebello CA 90640	**888-531-1416**	323-721-9011	192-2
ACP (American College of Physicians)			
190 N Independence Mall W . . . Philadelphia PA 19106	**800-523-1546**	215-351-2400	48-8
ACPA (American Chronic Pain Assn)			
PO Box 850 . . . Rocklin CA 95677	**800-533-3231**	916-632-0922	47-17
ACPE (American College of Physician Executives)			
400 N Ashley Dr Ste 4001 . . . Tampa FL 33602	**800-562-8088**	813-287-2000	48-8
ACPHS (Albany College of Pharmacy)			
106 New Scotland Ave . . . Albany NY 12208	**888-203-8010***	518-694-7221	166
*General			
Acqua Hotel			
555 Redwood Hwy . . . Mill Valley CA 94941	**888-662-9555**	415-380-0400	376
Acqualina			
17875 Collins Ave . . . Sunny Isles Beach FL 33160	**877-312-9742**	305-918-8000	376
ACR (Applied Computer Research Inc)			
PO Box 41730 . . . Phoenix AZ 85080	**800-234-2227**		628-11
ACR (American College of Radiology)			
1892 Preston White Dr . . . Reston VA 20191	**800-227-5463**	703-648-8900	48-8
ACR (Association for Conflict Resolution)			
12100 Sunset Hills Rd Ste 130 . . . Reston VA 20190	**800-880-7303**	703-234-4141	48-10
ACR Electronics Inc			
5757 Anglers Ave . . . Fort Lauderdale FL 33312	**800-432-0227**	954-981-3333	669
ACRL (Association of College & Research Libraries)			
50 E Huron St . . . Chicago IL 60611	**800-545-2433**	312-280-2519	48-11
Acro Labels Inc			
2530 Wyandotte Rd . . . Willow Grove PA 19090	**800-355-2235**	215-657-5366	410
Acro Media Inc			
2303 Leckie Rd Ste 103 . . . Kelowna BC V1X6Y5	**877-763-8844**	250-763-8884	796
Acromag Inc			
30765 S Wixom Rd . . . Wixom MI 48393	**877-295-7092**	248-624-1541	617
Acroprint Time Recorder Co			
5640 Departure Dr . . . Raleigh NC 27616	**800-334-7190**	919-872-5800	527
ACRP (Association of Clinical Research Professionals)			
500 Montgomery St Ste 800 . . . Alexandria VA 22314	**888-508-5731**	703-254-8100	48-8
ACRT Inc 1333 Home Ave . . . Akron OH 44310	**800-622-2562**	330-945-7500	194
Acry Fab Inc			
584 Progress Way . . . Sun Prairie WI 53590	**800-747-2279**	608-837-0045	601
Acrylic Design Assoc			
6050 Nathan Ln N . . . Plymouth MN 55442	**800-445-2167**	763-559-8395	233
Acryline USA Inc			
2015 Becancour . . . Lyster QC G0S1V0	**800-567-0920**		347
ACS (American Cancer Society)			
250 William St NW Ste 6001 . . . Atlanta GA 30303	**800-227-2345**	404-320-3333	47-17
ACS (American Chemical Society)			
1155 16th St NW . . . Washington DC 20036	**800-227-5558**	202-872-4600	48-19
ACS (American College of Surgeons)			
633 N St Clair St . . . Chicago IL 60611	**800-621-4111**	312-202-5000	48-8
ACS Group			
1100 E Woodfield Rd Ste 588 . . . Schaumburg IL 60173	**800-783-7835**	847-273-7700	14
ACS Industries Inc			
191 Social St . . . Woonsocket RI 02895	**866-783-4838**	401-769-4700	679
ACSA (Association of Collegiate Schools of Architecture)			
1735 New York Ave NW 3rd Fl . . . Washington DC 20006	**877-426-6323**	202-785-2324	48-5
ACSH (American Council on Science & Health)			
1995 Broadway Second Fl . . . New York NY 10023	**866-905-2694**	212-362-7044	48-19
ACSI (Association of Christian Schools International)			
731 Chapel Hills Dr . . . Colorado Springs CO 80920	**800-367-0798***	719-528-6906	48-5
*Cust Svc			
ACT (A Contemporary Theatre)			
700 Union St Kreielsheimer Pl . . . Seattle WA 98101	**888-584-4849**	206-292-7660	565
ACT Conferencing			
1526 Cole Blvd Bldg 3 Ste 300 . . . Lakewood CO 80401	**800-433-2900**	303-233-3500	726
ACTE (Association for Career & Technical Education)			
1410 King St . . . Alexandria VA 22314	**800-826-9972**	703-683-3111	48-5
ACTE (Association of Corporate Travel Executives)			
515 King St Ste 440 . . . Alexandria VA 22314	**800-375-2283**	703-683-5322	47-23
Actel Corp			
2061 Stierlin Ct . . . Mountain View CA 94043	**800-262-1060**	650-318-4200	687
ACTFL (American Council on the Teaching of Foreign Languages)			
1001 N Fairfax St Ste 200 . . . Alexandria VA 22314	**844-685-4373**	703-894-2900	48-5
Action Against Hunger			
247 W 37th St 10th Fl . . . New York NY 10018	**877-777-1420**	212-967-7800	47-5
Action Bolt & Tool Co (WURTH)			
2051 E Blue Heron Blvd . . . Riviera Beach FL 33404	**800-423-0700**		348
Action Capital Corp			
230 Peachtree St Ste 910 . . . Atlanta GA 30343	**800-525-7767**	404-524-3181	272
Action Co			
1425 N Tennessee St . . . McKinney TX 75069	**800-937-3700***	972-542-8700	428
*Sales			
Action Reporter Media			
N6637 Rolling Meadows Dr			
PO Box 1955 . . . Fond du Lac WI 54936	**800-261-5325**	920-922-4600	525-2
Action Sports Systems Inc			
617 Carbon City Rd			
PO Box 1442 . . . Morganton NC 28655	**800-631-1091**	828-584-8000	153-18
Action Stainless & Alloys Inc			
1505 Halsey Way . . . Carrollton TX 75007	**800-749-2523**	972-466-1500	487
Action Technologies Inc			
10970 International Blvd			
Second Fl . . . Oakland CA 94603	**800-967-5356**	510-638-8300	179-1
ActionCOACH			
5781 S Ft Apache Rd . . . Las Vegas NV 89148	**888-483-2828**	702-795-3188	755
ActionTec Electronics Inc			
760 N Mary Ave . . . Sunnyvale CA 94085	**888-436-0657***	408-752-7700	174-3
*Tech Supp			
Active Aero Group			
2068 E St . . . Belleville MI 48111	**800-872-5387***	734-547-7200	13
*Cust Svc			
Active Captive Management			
16485 Laguna Canyon Rd Ste 200 . . . Irvine CA 92618	**800-921-0155**	949-727-0155	2
Active Day/Senior Care Inc			
400 Redland Ct Ste 114 . . . Owings Mills MD 21117	**866-724-9599**		446
Active Network			
10182 Telesis Ct Ste 100 . . . San Diego CA 92121	**888-543-7223**	858-964-3800	7

Alphabetical Section

	Toll-Free	Phone	Class
Active Organics Inc			
1097 Yates St ....Lewisville TX 75057	800-541-1478	972-221-7500	296-8
Active Parenting Publishers			
1955 Vaughn Rd Ste 108 ....Kennesaw GA 30144	800-825-0060	770-429-0565	506
Active Power Inc			
2128 W Breaker Ln ....Austin TX 78758	800-625-1731	512-836-6464	757
NASDAQ: ACPW			
Activeforevercom			
10799 N 90th St ....Scottsdale AZ 85260	800-377-8033	480-459-3202	320
activePDF Inc			
27405 Puerta Real Ste 100 ....Mission Viejo CA 92691	866-468-6733	949-582-9002	179-12
Acton Institute for the Study of Religion & Liberty			
161 Ottawa Ave NW Ste 301 ....Grand Rapids MI 49503	800-345-2286	616-454-3080	625
Actors Theatre of Louisville			
316 W Main St ....Louisville KY 40202	800-428-5849	502-584-1205	738
Actsoft Inc			
8910 N Dale Mabry Hwy ....Tampa FL 33614	888-732-6638	813-936-2331	178
Actuarial Systems Corp			
15840 Monte St Ste 108.............Sylmar CA 91342	800-950-2082		387
Actuate Corp			
2207 Bridgepointe Pkwy			
Ste 500 ....San Mateo CA 94404	800-914-2259*	650-645-3000	179-1
NASDAQ: OTEX ▨ *Sales*			
ACU (Abilene Christian University Brown Library)			
760 Library Ct ....Abilene TX 79699	800-460-6228	325-674-2000	431-6
Acura 101 West			
24650 Calabasas Rd ....Calabasas CA 91302	800-472-3173	818-222-5555	56
Acushnet Co			
333 Bridge St ....Fairhaven MA 02719	800-225-8500	508-979-2000	701
AcuSport Corp			
1 Hunter Pl ....Bellefontaine OH 43311	800-543-3150	937-593-7010	701
Acxiom Corp			
601 E Third St ....Little Rock AR 72201	888-337-7699	501-342-7799	5
NASDAQ: ACXM			
Ad Art Co			
3260 E 26th St ....Los Angeles CA 90058	800-266-7522	323-981-8941	692
ADA (American Diabetes Assn)			
1701 N Beauregard St ....Alexandria VA 22311	800-232-3472	703-549-1500	47-17
ADA (American Dietetic Assn)			
120 S Riverside Plz Ste 2000 ....Chicago IL 60606	800-877-1600	312-899-0040	48-8
ADA (Americans for Democratic Action)			
1625 K St NW Ste 210 ....Washington DC 20006	855-712-8441	202-785-5980	47-7
ADA Technologies Inc			
8100 Shaffer Pkwy Ste 130.............Littleton CO 80127	800-232-0296	303-792-5615	659
ADAA (American Dental Assistants Assn)			
35 E Wacker Dr Ste 1730 ....Chicago IL 60601	877-874-3785	312-541-1550	48-8
ADA-ES Inc			
8100 Southpark Way Ste B..........Littleton CO 80120	888-822-8617	303-734-1727	143
NASDAQ: ADES			
Adair Printing Technologies			
7850 Second St ....Dexter MI 48130	800-637-5025	734-426-2822	618
Adamatic Equipment Corp			
607 Industrial Way W ....Eatontown NJ 07724	800-526-2807	732-544-8400	297
Adams & Brooks Inc			
1915 S Hoover St			
PO Box 7303..................Los Angeles CA 90007	800-999-9808*	213-749-3226	295-8
*Orders			
Adams Construction Co			
523 Rutherford Ave NE ....Roanoke VA 24016	800-237-6060	540-982-2366	189-4
Adams County Travel & Visitors Bureau			
509 E Main St ....West Union OH 45693	877-232-6764	937-544-5639	137
Adams Electric Co-op			
700 Eastwood St PO Box 247 ....Camp Point IL 62320	800-232-4797	217-593-7701	245
Adams Electric Co-op Inc			
1338 Biglerville Rd			
PO Box 1055...............Gettysburg PA 17325	888-232-6732	717-334-2171	245
Adams Elevator Equipment Co			
6310 W Howard St ....Niles IL 60714	800-929-9247	847-581-2900	669
Adams Express Co			
Seven St Paul St Ste 1140 ....Baltimore MD 21202	800-638-2479	410-752-5900	402
NYSE: ADX			
Adams Golf			
2801 E Plano Pkwy ....Plano TX 75074	800-709-6142	972-673-9000	701
Adams Keegan Inc			
6055 Primacy Pkwy Ste 300..........Memphis TN 38119	800-621-1308	901-683-5353	623
Adams Oceanfront Resort			
Four Read St ....Dewey Beach DE 19971	800-448-8080	302-227-3030	376
Adams Products Co			
5701 McCrimmon Pkwy			
PO Box 189..................Morrisville NC 27560	800-672-3131	919-467-2218	184
Adams Remco Inc			
PO Box 3968 ....South Bend IN 46619	800-627-2113	574-288-2113	111
Adams Rite Manufacturing Co			
260 W Santa Fe St ....Pomona CA 91767	800-872-3267	909-632-2300	347
Adams Rural Electric Co-op Inc			
4800 SR 125 ....West Union OH 45693	800-283-1846	937-544-2305	245
Adams State College			
208 Edgemont Blvd ....Alamosa CO 81102	800-824-6494	719-587-7712	166
Adams USA Inc			
610 S Jefferson Ave ....Cookeville TN 38501	800-251-6857		701
Adams-Burch Inc			
1901 Stanford Ct ....Landover MD 20785	800-347-8093*	301-276-2000	299
*Cust Svc			
Adams-Columbia Electric Co-op			
401 E Lake St ....Friendship WI 53934	800-831-8629	608-339-3346	245
Adamson Global Technology Corp			
13101 N Eron Church Rd ....Chester VA 23836	800-525-7703		90
Adaptive Micro Systems Inc			
7840 N 86th St ....Milwaukee WI 53224	800-558-4187	414-357-2020	179-7
ADB (American Drill Bushings Co)			
5740 Hunt Rd ....Valdosta GA 31606	800-423-4425	229-253-8928	488
AdCare Hospital of Worcester			
107 Lincoln St ....Worcester MA 01605	800-252-6465	508-799-9000	717
Adco Inc			
1909 W Oakridge ....Albany GA 31707	800-821-7556		149
Adconion Media Group Ltd			
950 Tower Ln ....Santa Monica CA 94404	800-542-2811	650-802-8871	507
ADDCO LLC			
240 Arlington Ave E ....Saint Paul MN 55117	800-616-4408	651-488-8600	691
Adden Furniture Inc			
710 Chelmsford St ....Lowell MA 01851	800-625-3876	978-454-7848	318-3
Addison Biological Laboratory Inc			
507 N Cleveland Ave ....Fayette MO 65248	800-331-2530	660-248-2215	575
Addison Insurance Co			
118 Second Ave SE			
PO Box 73909..................Cedar Rapids IA 52401	800-332-7977	319-399-5700	388-4
Adducent Technology Inc			
230 Parque Margarita ....Rohnert Park CA 94928	800-648-0656	707-478-8136	522
Addus HealthCare Inc			
2401 S Plum Grove Rd ....Palatine IL 60067	888-233-8746	847-303-5300	350
NASDAQ: ADUS			
ADEA (American Dental Education Assn)			
1400 K St NW Ste 1100 ....Washington DC 20005	800-353-2237	202-289-7201	48-5
A-dec Inc			
2601 Crestview Dr ....Newberg OR 97132	800-547-1883*	503-538-7478	228
*Cust Svc			
Adecco Inc			
175 Broad Hollow Rd ....Melville NY 11747	800-978-3729*	631-844-7650	712
*General			
Adell Plastics Inc			
4530 Annapolis Rd ....Baltimore MD 21227	800-638-5218	410-789-7780	734-2
Adelman Travel Group			
6980 N Port Washington Rd ....Milwaukee WI 53217	800-248-5562*	414-352-7600	761
*Cust Svc			
Adelphi University			
PO Box 701 ....Garden City NY 11530	800-233-5744	516-877-3050	166
Manhattan Ctr			
75 Varick St Second Fl.............New York NY 10013	800-233-5744	212-965-8340	166
Adelphia Steel Equipment Co			
7372 State Rd ....Philadelphia PA 19136	800-865-8211	215-333-6300	318-1
Adept Technology Inc			
5960 Inglewood Dr ....Pleasanton CA 94588	800-292-3378	925-245-3400	383
NASDAQ: ADEP			
Aderans Hair Goods Inc			
Simplicity Hair Extensions			
5130 N State Rd			
Seven ft Ninth Fl.............Lauderdale FL 33319	877-413-5225*		345
*Sales			
ADESA Inc			
13085 Hamilton Crossing Blvd ....Carmel IN 46032	800-923-3725	317-815-1100	50
Adexa Inc			
5933 W Century Blvd 12th Fl........Los Angeles CA 90045	888-300-7692	310-642-2100	179-1
ADG Promotional Products			
2300 Main St ....Hugo MN 55038	800-852-5208		9
ADHA (American Dental Hygienists' Assn)			
444 N Michigan Ave Ste 3400 ....Chicago IL 60611	800-243-2342	312-440-8900	48-8
Adhesive Applications Inc			
41 O'Neill St ....EastHampton MA 01027	800-356-3572*	413-527-7120	722
*General			
Adhesive Packaging Specialties Inc			
PO Box 31 ....Peabody MA 01960	800-222-1117	978-531-3300	541
Adhesives Research Inc			
400 Seaks Run Rd PO Box 100..........Glen Rock PA 17327	800-445-6240	717-235-7979	3
Adi American Distributors Inc			
Two Emery Ave Ste 1 ....Randolph NJ 07869	800-877-0510	973-328-1181	246
Adirondack Council			
103 Hand Ave Ste 3			
PO Box 2...............Elizabethtown NY 12932	877-873-2240	518-873-2240	47-13
Adirondack Direct			
3040 48th Ave ....Long Island City NY 11101	800-221-2444	718-204-4500	319
Adirondack Mountain Club			
814 Goggins Rd ....Lake George NY 12845	800-395-8080*	518-668-4447	47-23
*Orders			
Adirondack Regional Chambers of Commerce			
136 Glen St Ste 3 ....Glens Falls NY 12801	888-516-7247	518-798-1761	137
Adirondack Trailways			
499 Hurley Ave ....Hurley NY 12443	800-858-8555	845-339-4230	107
ADL (Anti-Defamation League)			
605 Third Ave ....New York NY 10158	866-386-3235	212-885-7700	47-8
Adleta Co			
1645 Diplomat Dr Ste 200 ....Carrollton TX 75006	800-423-5382	972-620-5600	358
ADM (Archer Daniels Midland Co)			
4666 E Faries Pkwy ....Decatur IL 62526	800-637-5843	217-424-5200	186
NYSE: ADM			
ADM (ADM Milling Co)			
8000 W 110th St ....Overland Park KS 66210	800-422-1688	913-491-9400	295-23
ADM Alliance Nutrition Inc			
1000 N 30th St ....Quincy IL 62301	800-292-3333	217-222-7100	442
ADM Cocoa Div			
12500 W Carmen Ave ....Milwaukee WI 53225	800-637-5843	217-424-5200	295-8
ADM Corn Processing Div			
4666 E Faries Pkwy ....Decatur IL 62526	800-637-5843	217-424-5200	295-23
ADM Corp			
100 Lincoln Blvd ....Middlesex NJ 08846	800-327-0718	732-469-0900	263
ADM Milling Co (ADM)			
8000 W 110th St ....Overland Park KS 66210	800-422-1688	913-491-9400	295-23
ADM Natural Health & Nutrition			
Archer Daniels Midland Co			
4666 Faries Pkwy ....Decatur IL 62526	800-637-5843	217-451-7231	787
Adm Productions Inc			
40 Seaview Blvd ....Port Washington NY 11050	800-236-3425	516-484-6900	507
ADM Specialty Food Ingredients Div			
4666 E Faries Pkwy ....Decatur IL 62526	800-637-5843	217-424-5200	295-17
Admar Supply Co Inc			
1950 Brighton Henriett ....Rochester NY 14623	800-836-2367	585-272-9390	355
Administrative-Maximum US Penitentiary			
Florence PO Box 8500 ....Florence CO 81226	877-623-8426	719-784-9464	
Admiral Craft Equipment Corp			
940 S Oyster Bay Rd ....Hicksville NY 11801	800-223-7750	516-433-3535	483
Admiral Fell Inn			
888 S Broadway			
Historic Fell's Pt ....Baltimore MD 21231	866-583-4162	410-522-7377	376
Admiral Inc			
10 Taylor Ave ....Annapolis MD 21401	800-864-4429	410-267-8381	423
Admiral on Baltimore			
2 Baltimore Ave ....Rehoboth Beach DE 19971	888-882-4188	302-227-1300	376
Admiral Packaging Inc			
10 Admiral St ....Providence RI 02908	800-556-6454	401-274-7000	541
Admiralty Room			
666 Wisconsin Ave ....Madison WI 53703	800-922-5512	608-256-9071	662
AdMobilize LLC			
1680 Michigan Ave Ste 736 ....Miami FL 33139	855-236-6245		384
ADMS (American Donkey & Mule Society)			
1346 Morningside Ave ....Lewisville TX 75057	877-752-4068	972-219-0781	47-3
Ado Corp			
851 Simuel Rd ....Spartanburg SC 29301	800-845-0918*		735
*Cust Svc			

	Toll-Free	Phone	Class
Adobe Systems Inc			
345 Pk Ave ....San Jose CA 95110	800-833-6687	408-536-6000	179-8
NASDAQ: ADBE			
Adobe Ventures LP			
345 Pk Ave ....San Jose CA 95110	877-722-7088	408-536-6000	780
Adolphus, The			
1321 Commerce St ....Dallas TX 75202	800-221-9083	214-742-8200	376
Adoption ARC Inc			
4701 Pine St Ste J-7...Philadelphia PA 19143	800-884-4004	215-748-1441	47-6
Adoptive Families Magazine			
108 West 39th St Ste 805.....New York NY 10018	800-372-3300	646-366-0830	452-10
Adorama Camera Inc			
42 W 18th St ....New York NY 10011	800-223-2500	212-741-0052	118
ADP (Association of Directory Publishers)			
116 Cass St ....Traverse City MI 49684	800-267-9002	231-486-2182	48-16
ADP (Automatic Data Processing Inc)			
One ADP Blvd ....Roseland NJ 07068	800-225-5237	973-994-5000	225
NASDAQ: ADP			
ADP TotalSource Co			
10200 Sunset Dr ....Miami FL 33173	800-447-3237	305-630-1000	623
ADRA (Adventist Development & Relief Agency International)			
12501 Old Columbia Pk ....Silver Spring MD 20904	800-424-2372	301-680-6380	47-5
Adrian College			
110 S Madison St ....Adrian MI 49221	800-877-2246*	517-265-5161	166
*Admissions			
Adrienne Arsht Ctr for the Performing Arts of Miami-Dade County Inc			
1300 Biscayne Blvd ....Miami FL 33132	877-949-6722	786-468-2000	565
Adroit Medical Systems Inc			
1146 CaRding Machine Rd ....Loudon TN 37774	800-267-6077		472
ADS Environmental Services			
4940 Research Dr ....Huntsville AL 35805	800-633-7246	256-430-3366	202
ADS Tactical Inc			
Lynnwood Plz 621 Lynnhaven Pkwy			
Ste 400 ....Virginia Beach VA 23452	800-948-9433	757-481-7758	444
ADS/Transicoil			
Nine Iron Bridge Dr ....Collegeville PA 19426	800-323-7115	484-902-1100	511
ADSA (American Dairy Science Assn)			
1111 N Dunlap Ave ....Savoy IL 61874	888-670-2250	217-356-5146	47-2
ADT Security Services Inc			
14200 E Exposition Ave ....Aurora CO 80012	800-238-2455		683
Ad-tech Medical Instrument Inc			
1901 William St ....Racine WI 53404	800-776-1555	262-634-1555	471
ADTRAN Inc			
901 Explorer Blvd ....Huntsville AL 35806	800-923-8726	256-963-8000	725
NASDAQ: ADTN			
ADTRAV Travel Management			
4555 S Lake Pkwy ....Birmingham AL 35244	800-476-2952	205-444-4800	761
Advance America Cash Advance Centers Inc			
135 N Church St ....Spartanburg SC 29306	800-538-1579	864-342-5600	139
NYSE: AEA			
Advance Auto Parts Inc			
5008 Airport Rd ....Roanoke VA 24012	877-238-2623	540-561-8452	53
NYSE: AAP			
Advance Bag & Packaging Technologies			
5720 Williams Lk Rd ....Waterford MI 48329	800-475-2247	248-674-3126	593
Advance Carbon Products Inc			
2036 National Ave ....Hayward CA 94545	800-283-1249	510-293-5930	126
Advance Corp Braille-Tac Div			
8200 97th St S ....Cottage Grove MN 55016	800-328-9451	651-771-9297	692
Advance Energy Technologies Inc			
One Solar Dr ....Clifton Park NY 12065	800-724-0198	518-371-2140	655
Advance Engineering Co			
7505 Baron Dr ....Canton MI 48187	800-497-6388	313-537-3500	484
Advance Food Company Inc			
9987 Carver Rd Ste 500 ....Cincinnati OH 45242	800-969-2747		298
Advance Insurance Company of Kansas			
1133 SW Topeka Blvd ....Topeka KS 66629	800-530-5989	785-273-9804	388-2
Advance Lifts Inc			
701 Kirk Rd ....Saint Charles IL 60174	800-843-3625	630-584-9881	465
Advance Reservations Inn Arizona			
PO Box 950 ....Tempe AZ 85280	800-456-0682	480-990-0682	373
Advance Tabco			
200 Heartland Blvd ....Edgewood NY 11717	800-645-3166	631-242-4800	299
Advanced Bionics LLC			
28515 Westinghouse Pl ....Valencia CA 91355	877-829-0026	661-362-1400	253
Advanced Biotechnologies Inc (ABI)			
9108 Guilford Rd ....Columbia MD 21046	800-426-0764	410-792-9779	231
Advanced Cell Diagnostics Inc			
3960 Point Eden Way ....Hayward CA 94545	877-576-3636	510-576-8800	659
Advanced Circuits Inc			
21101 E 32nd Pkwy ....Aurora CO 80011	800-979-4722	303-576-6610	617
Advanced Digital Data Inc			
Six Laurel Dr ....Flanders NJ 07836	800-922-0972	973-584-4026	178
Advanced Drainage Systems Inc			
4640 Trueman Blvd ....Hilliard OH 43026	800-821-6710		589
Advanced Energy Industries Inc			
1625 Sharp Pt Dr ....Fort Collins CO 80525	800-446-9167	970-221-4670	686
NASDAQ: AEIS			
Advanced Hydraulics Inc			
13568 Vintage Pl ....Chino CA 91710	888-581-8079	909-590-7644	451
Advanced Image Direct			
1415 S Acacia Ave ....Fullerton CA 92831	800-540-3848	714-502-3900	454
Advanced Industrial Services Inc			
3250 Susquehanna Trial ....York PA 17406	800-544-5080	717-764-9811	187
Advanced Information Systems Group Inc			
11315 Corporate Blvd Ste 210 ....Orlando FL 32817	800-593-8359	407-581-2929	181
Advanced Lighting Technologies Inc			
32000 Aurora Rd ....Solon OH 44139	888-440-2358	440-519-0500	433
Advanced Looseleaf Technologies Inc			
1424 Somerset Ave ....Dighton MA 02715	800-339-6354	508-669-6354	85
Advanced Machine & Engineering Co			
2500 Latham St ....Rockford IL 61103	800-225-4263	815-962-6076	488
Advanced Micro Devices Inc (AMD)			
One AMD PI PO Box 3453 ....Sunnyvale CA 94088	800-538-8450	408-749-4000	687
NYSE: AMD			
Advanced MP Technology			
1010 Calle Sombra ....San Clemente CA 92673	800-492-3113	949-492-3113	246
Advanced Photographic Solutions			
1525 Hardeman Ln ....Cleveland TN 37312	800-241-9234	423-479-5481	581
Advanced Probing Systems Inc			
2300 Central Ave ....Boulder CO 80301	800-631-0005	303-939-9384	587
Advanced Sterilization Products (ASP)			
33 Technology Dr ....Irvine CA 92618	888-783-7723		472
Advanced Technology Co			
2858 E Walnut St ....Pasadena CA 91107	800-447-2442	626-449-2696	22
Advancement LLC			
32200 Solon Rd ....Solon OH 44139	866-364-3370	440-248-8550	195
Advanstar Veterinary Healthcare Communications			
8033 Flint St ....Lenexa KS 66214	800-255-6864	913-871-3800	628-9
Advantage Engineering Inc			
525 E S- 18 Rd ....Greenwood IN 46142	800-669-1282	317-887-0729	14
Advantage Funding Corp			
1000 Parkwood Cir SE ....Atlanta GA 30339	800-241-2274	770-955-2274	272
Advantage Limousine Services Inc			
8310 Castleford St Ste 200...........Houston TX 77040	888-983-9991	713-983-9991	437
Advantage Metals Recycling LLC			
3005 Manchester Trfy ....Kansas City MO 64129	866-527-4733	816-861-2700	677
Advantage Mktg Inc			
14 W Main St ....Ashland OH 44805	800-670-7479	419-281-4762	94
Advantage Payroll Services Inc			
126 Merrow Rd PO Box 1330...........Auburn ME 04211	800-876-0178*	207-784-0178	563
*Cust Svc			
Advantage Performance Group Inc			
700 Larkspur Landing Cir ....Larkspur CA 94939	800-494-6646	415-925-6832	195
Advantage Rent-A-Car			
1288 Old Bayshore Hwy			
Ste 116 ....Burlingame CA 94010	800-777-5500*	650-343-3052	125
*Cust Svc			
Advantage Resourcing			
220 Norwood Pk S ....Norwood MA 02062	800-343-4314	781-251-8000	712
Advantage Truck Accessories Inc			
5400 S State Rd PO Box 1747 ....Ann Arbor MI 48108	800-773-3110		60
Advantec MFS Inc			
6723 Sierra Ct Ste A...........Dublin CA 94568	800-334-7132	925-479-0625	18
Advantech International Inc			
PO Box 6739 ....Somerset NJ 08875	800-322-6150	732-805-1900	60
Advantix Solutions Group			
1202 Richardson Dr Ste 200.....Richardson TX 75080	866-238-2684		384
Advantor Systems Corp			
12612 Challenger Pkwy Ste 300.........Orlando FL 32809	800-238-2686	407-859-3350	683
Advent Capital Management LLC			
1065 Ave of the Americas			
31st Fl...............New York NY 10018	888-523-8368	212-482-1600	398
Advent Software Inc			
600 Townsend St Ste 500			
5th Fl ....San Francisco CA 94103	800-727-0605	415-543-7696	179-1
NASDAQ: ADVS			
Adventist Behavioral Health			
14901 Broschart Rd ....Rockville MD 20850	800-204-8600	301-251-4500	371-5
Adventist Community Services			
12501 Old Columbia Pk ....Silver Spring MD 20904	877-227-2702	301-680-6438	47-5
Adventist Development & Relief Agency International (ADRA)			
12501 Old Columbia Pk ....Silver Spring MD 20904	800-424-2372	301-680-6380	47-5
Adventist Health			
2100 Douglas Blvd ....Roseville CA 95661	877-336-3566	916-781-2000	350
Adventure 16 Inc			
4620 Alvarado Canyon Rd ....San Diego CA 92120	800-854-2672	619-283-2362	702
Adventure Alaska Tours Inc			
PO Box 64 ....Hope AK 99605	800-365-7057	907-782-3730	750
Adventure Aquarium			
1 Riverside Dr ....Camden NJ 08103	800-616-5297	856-365-3300	39
Adventure Connection			
PO Box 475 ....Coloma CA 95613	800-556-6060	530-626-7385	750
Adventure Cycling Assn			
150 E Pine St PO Box 8308 ....Missoula MT 59807	800-755-2453	406-721-1776	47-22
Adventure Life South America			
1655 S Third St W Ste 1...........Missoula MT 59801	800-344-6118	406-541-2677	750
Adventuredome			
2880 Las Vegas Blvd S ....Las Vegas NV 89109	866-456-8894	702-691-5861	32
Adventureland Inn			
305 34th Ave NW ....Altoona IA 50009	800-910-5382	515-265-7321	376
Adventureland Park			
305 34th Ave NW ....Altoona IA 50009	800-532-1286	515-266-2121	32
Adventures Out West			
1680 S 21st St ....Colorado Springs CO 80904	800-755-0935		750
Advertising Council Inc			
815 Second Ave Fl 9.............New York NY 10016	888-200-4005	212-922-1500	48-18
Advertising Specialties Institute			
4800 St Rd ....Trevose PA 19053	800-546-1350	215-942-8600	628-9
Advice Media LLC			
PO Box 982064 ....Park City UT 84098	800-260-9497		623
Advion BioSciences Inc			
19 Brown Rd ....Ithaca NY 14850	877-523-8466	607-266-0665	659
Advisor Today			
2901 Telestar Ct ....Falls Church VA 22042	800-247-4074		452-5
Advisors Excel LLC			
1300 SW Arrowhead Rd Ste 200.......Topeka KS 66604	866-363-9595		196
Advisory Board Co, The			
2445 M St NW ....Washington DC 20037	800-784-8669	202-266-5600	195
NASDAQ: ABCO			
Advocare International Lp			
2801 Summit Ave ....Plano TX 75074	800-542-4800	972-665-5800	363
Advocate Sherman Hospital			
1425 N Randall Rd ....Elgin IL 60123	800-397-9000	847-742-9800	371-3
Advocate, The			
7290 Blue Bonnet Blvd ....Baton Rouge LA 70810	800-960-6397	225-383-1111	525-2
Advocates for Highway & Auto Safety			
750 First St NE Ste 901 ....Washington DC 20002	877-366-0711	202-408-1711	47-10
Advocates for Self-Government			
1010 N Tennessee St			
Ste 215...............Cartersville GA 30120	800-932-1776	770-386-8372	47-7
Adwerx Inc			
307 W Main St ....Durham NC 27701	888-746-5678		5
Adzzup LLC			
8240 S Kyrene Rd Ste 101 ....Tempe AZ 85284	888-723-9987		5
AEA Advocate Magazine			
345 E Palm Ln ....Phoenix AZ 85004	800-352-5411	602-264-1774	452-8
Aearo Co			
5457 W 79th St ....Indianapolis IN 46268	877-327-4332	317-692-6666	569
AEB (American Egg Board)			
1460 Renaissance Dr Ste 301.....Park Ridge IL 60068	888-549-2140	847-296-7043	47-2
AEB (American Exchange Bank)			
510 W Main St PO Box 818 .....Henryetta OK 74437	888-652-3321	918-652-3321	69
AEC (Aluminum Extruders Council)			
1000 N Rand Rd Ste 214 ....Wauconda IL 60084	800-354-5892	847-526-2010	48-13
AEC (Applied Energy Company Inc)			
1205 Venture Ct Ste 100...........Carrollton TX 75006	800-580-1171	214-355-4200	631

Alphabetical Section

	Toll-Free	Phone	Class
AED (Associated Equipment Distributors)			
600 22nd St Ste 220 . . . . Oak Brook IL 60523	800-388-0650	630-574-0650	48-18
AEE (Association of Energy Engineers)			
4025 Pleasantdale Rd Ste 420 . . . . Atlanta GA 30340	877-407-0784	770-447-5083	47-12
Aegis Assisted Living			
17602 NE Union Hill Rd . . . . Redmond WA 98052	888-252-3447	425-861-9993	446
Aegis Communications Group Inc			
8201 Ridgepoint Dr . . . . Irving TX 75063	877-892-3447	972-830-1800	727
Aegis Security Inc			
PO Box 3153 . . . . Harrisburg PA 17105	800-233-2160	717-657-9671	388-4
Aehr Test Systems			
400 Kato Terr . . . . Fremont CA 94539	800-962-4284	510-623-9400	686
NASDAQ: AEHR			
AEI (American Enterprise Institute for Public Policy Research)			
1150 17th St NW Ste 1100 . . . . Washington DC 20036	800-862-5801	202-862-5800	625
AEI Speakers Bureau			
214 Lincoln St Ste 113 . . . . Allston MA 02134	800-447-7325	617-782-3111	699
AELE (Americans for Effective Law Enforcement)			
841 W Touhy Ave . . . . Park Ridge IL 60068	800-763-2802	847-685-0700	47-8
AELI (Agape English Language Institute)			
610 Pickens St PO Box 12504 . . . . Columbia SC 29201	877-476-2354	803-799-3452	420
AEM (Association of Equipment Manufacturers)			
6737 W Washington St Ste 2400 . . . . . . Milwaukee WI 53214	866-236-0442	414-272-0943	48-13
AEP Industries Inc			
125 Phillips Ave . . . . South Hackensack NJ 07606	800-999-2374	201-641-6600	593
NASDAQ: AEPI			
AEP River Operations			
16150 Main Cir Dr Ste 400 . . . . Chesterfield MO 63017	800-621-3362	636-530-2100	460
AEPhi (Alpha Epsilon Phi Sorority)			
11 Lake Ave Ext Ste 1-A . . . . Danbury CT 06811	888-668-4293	203-748-0029	47-16
Aer Lingus Airlines Gold Cir Club			
300 Jericho Quad Ste 130 . . . . Jericho NY 11753	800-474-7424		26
Aer Mfg Inc			
PO Box 979 . . . . Carrollton TX 75011	800-753-5237	972-417-2582	59
AERA (American Educational Research Assn)			
1430 K St NW Ste 1200 . . . . Washington DC 20005	800-893-7950	202-238-3200	48-5
AERA (Automotive Engine Rebuilders Assn)			
500 Coventry Ln Ste 180 . . . . Crystal Lake IL 60014	888-326-2372	847-541-6550	48-21
Aerco International Inc			
159 Paris Ave . . . . Northvale NJ 07647	800-526-0288	201-768-2400	354
Aermotor Pumps Inc			
293 Wright St . . . . Delavan WI 53115	800-230-1816		632
Aero Air LLC			
2050 NE 25th Ave . . . . Hillsboro OR 97124	800-448-2376	503-640-3711	13
Aero Industries Inc			
4243 W Bradbury Ave . . . . Indianapolis IN 46241	800-535-9545*	317-244-2433	723
Sales			
Aero Rubber Company Inc			
8100 W 185th St . . . . Tinley Park IL 60487	800-662-1009	708-430-4900	367
Aero Tec Labs Inc			
45 Spear Rd Industrial Pk . . . . Ramsey NJ 07446	800-526-5330	201-825-1400	667
Aerobics & Fitness Assn of America (AFAA)			
15250 Ventura Blvd Ste 200 . . . . . . Sherman Oaks CA 91403	877-968-7263	818-905-0040	47-22
Aerodyne Alloys LLC			
350 Pleasant Vly Rd . . . . South Windsor CT 06074	800-243-4344	860-289-6011	482
Aerofin Corp			
4621 Murray Pl PO Box 10819 . . . . Lynchburg VA 24506	800-237-6346	434-845-7081	90
Aeroflex			
400 New Century Pkwy . . . . . New Century KS 66031	800-843-1553	913-764-2452	248
Aeroflex Inc			
35 S Service Rd PO Box 6022 . . . . Plainview NY 11803	800-843-1553	516-694-6700	687
TSE: ARX			
Aeroflot Russian International Airlines			
10 Rockefeller Plaza Ste 1015 . . . . New York NY 10020	866-879-7647	212-944-2300	25
Aeroflow Inc			
3165 Sweeten Creek Rd . . . . Asheville NC 28803	888-345-1780		470
Aeroglide Corp			
100 Aeroglide Dr . . . . Cary NC 27511	800-722-7483	919-851-2000	383
Aeronet Worldwide			
42 Corporate Pk . . . . Irvine CA 92606	800-552-3869	949-474-3000	12
Aeroshade Inc			
433 Oakland Ave . . . . Waukesha WI 53186	800-331-7179	262-547-2101	86
Aerosoles Inc			
201 Meadow Rd . . . . Edison NJ 08817	800-798-9478	732-985-6900	300
Aerospace America Inc			
900 Harry Truman Pkwy			
PO Box 189 . . . . Bay City MI 48706	800-237-6414	989-684-2121	475
Aerospace America Magazine			
1801 Alexander Bell Dr Ste 500 . . . . Reston VA 20191	800-639-2422	703-264-7500	452-21
Aerospace Industries Assn of America (AIA)			
1000 Wilson Blvd Ste 1700 . . . . Arlington VA 22209	866-923-7797	703-358-1000	48-21
Aerospace Optics Inc			
3201 Sandy Ln . . . . Fort Worth TX 76112	888-848-4786	817-451-1141	802
Aerospace Products International (API)			
3778 Distriplex Dr N . . . . Memphis TN 38118	888-274-2497	901-365-3470	22
Aero-Space Southwest Inc			
21450 N Third Ave . . . . Phoenix AZ 85027	800-289-2779	623-582-2779	348
Aerotech Inc			
101 Zeta Dr . . . . Pittsburgh PA 15238	888-492-8950	412-967-6440	511
Aerotek Inc			
7301 Pkwy Dr . . . . Hanover MD 21076	800-237-6835	410-694-5100	712
AeroTurbine Inc			
2323 NW 82nd Ave . . . . Miami FL 33122	877-747-2370*	305-590-2600	23
Cust Svc			
AeroVironment Inc			
181 W Huntington Dr Ste 202 . . . . Monrovia CA 91016	888-833-2148	626-357-9983	20
NASDAQ: AVAV			
Aervoe Industries Inc			
PO Box 485 . . . . Gardnerville NV 89410	800-227-0196	775-783-3100	543
AES (American Epilepsy Society)			
342 N Main St . . . . West Hartford CT 06117	888-233-2334	860-586-7505	47-17
AES Electrophoresis Society			
1202 Ann St . . . . Madison WI 53713	800-242-4363	608-258-1565	48-19
AESC (Association of Energy Service Cos)			
14531 Fm 529 Ste 250 . . . . Houston TX 77095	800-692-0771	713-781-0758	47-12
Aesco Electronics Inc			
2230 Picton Pkwy . . . . Akron OH 44312	877-442-6987	330-245-2630	246
AESCULAP Inc			
3773 Corporate Pkwy . . . . Center Valley PA 18034	800-282-9000		471
AESP Inc			
16295 NW 13th Ave . . . . Miami FL 33169	800-446-2377	305-944-7710	253
AESU Travel Inc			
3922 Hickory Ave . . . . Baltimore MD 21211	800-638-7640	410-366-5494	761
AETEA Information Technology Inc			
1445 Research Blvd Ste 300 . . . . Rockville MD 20850	888-772-3832	301-721-4200	181
AETEK UV Systems			
1229 Lakeview Ct . . . . Romeoville IL 60446	800-333-2304	630-226-4200	433
AETN (Arkansas Educational Television Network)			
350 S Donaghey Ave . . . . Conway AR 72034	800-662-2386	501-682-2386	624
Aetna Felt Corp			
2401 W Emaus Ave . . . . Allentown PA 18103	800-526-4451	610-791-0900	734-6
Aetna Inc			
151 Farmington Ave . . . . Hartford CT 06156	800-872-3862	860-273-0123	388-3
NYSE: AET			
Aetna Plastics Corp			
1702 St Clair Ave . . . . Cleveland OH 44114	800-634-3074	216-781-4421	596
Aetna US Healthcare Inc			
980 Jolly Rd . . . . Blue Bell PA 19422	800-872-3862	215-775-4800	388-3
AFA (American Fence Assn)			
800 Roosevelt Rd Bldg C-312 . . . . . Glen Ellyn IL 60137	800-822-4342	630-942-6598	48-3
AFA (American Federation of Astrologers)			
6535 S Rural Rd . . . . Tempe AZ 85283	888-301-7630	480-838-1751	47-18
AFA (American Finance Assn)			
350 Main St . . . . Malden MA 02148	800-835-6770	781-388-8599	48-2
AFA (Air Force Assn)			
1501 Lee Hwy Fourth Fl . . . . Arlington VA 22209	800-727-3337	703-247-5800	47-19
AFAA (Aerobics & Fitness Assn of America)			
15250 Ventura Blvd Ste 200 . . . . . . Sherman Oaks CA 91403	877-968-7263	818-905-0040	47-22
AFAR (American Federation for Aging Research)			
55 W 39th St 16th Fl . . . . New York NY 10018	888-582-2327	212-703-9977	48-8
AFB (American Foundation for the Blind)			
2 Penn Plaza . . . . New York NY 10001	800-232-5463	212-502-7600	47-17
AFC (AMPAC Fine Chemicals)			
MS 1007 PO Box 1718 . . . . Rancho Cordova CA 95741	800-311-9668	916-357-6880	143
AFC (Automotive Finance Corp)			
13085 Hamilton Crossing Blvd . . . . Carmel IN 46032	888-335-6675	865-384-8250	216
AFC Cable Systems Inc			
272 Duchaine Blvd . . . . New Bedford MA 02745	800-757-6996	508-998-1131	800
AFC Industries Inc			
13-16 133rd Pl . . . . College Point NY 11356	800-663-3412	718-747-0237	195
AFCA (American Football Coaches Assn)			
100 Legends Ln . . . . Waco TX 76706	877-557-5338	254-754-9900	47-22
AFCEA (Armed Forces Communications & Electronics Assn)			
4400 Fair Lakes Ct . . . . Fairfax VA 22033	800-336-4583	703-631-6100	47-19
AFCI (Association of Film Commissioners International)			
109 E 17th St . . . . Cheyenne WY 82001	888-765-5777	307-637-4422	47-4
AFCO (Alex C Fergusson LLC)			
5000 Letterkenny Rd . . . . Chambersburg PA 17201	800-345-1329		143
AFCO Credit Corp			
14 Wall St . . . . New York NY 10005	800-288-6901	212-401-4400	216
Afco Industries Inc			
3400 Roy St . . . . Alexandria LA 71302	800-551-6576		477
AFCU (Andrews Federal Credit Union)			
5711 Allentown Rd . . . . Suitland MD 20746	800-487-5500	301-702-5500	219
Afexa Life Sciences			
9604 20th Ave . . . . Edmonton AB T6N1G1	888-280-0022	780-432-0022	787
Affiliated Car Rental			
105 Hwy 36 . . . . Eatontown NJ 07724	800-367-5159		125
Affiliated Chamber of Commerce of Greater Springfield			
1441 Main St . . . . Springfield MA 01103	888-283-3757	413-787-1555	137
Affiliated Community Medical Centers (ACMC)			
101 Willmar Ave SW . . . . Willmar MN 56201	888-225-6580	320-231-5000	371-3
Affiliated Foods Inc			
1401 W Farmers Ave . . . . Amarillo TX 79118	800-234-3661	806-372-3851	296-8
Affiliated Power Purchasers International LLC			
224 Phillip Morris Dr Ste 402 . . . . Salisbury MD 21804	800-520-6685		195
Affina Dumont			
150 E 34th St . . . . New York NY 10016	866-233-4642	212-481-7600	376
Affinia 50			
155 E 50th St . . . . New York NY 10022	866-246-2203	212-751-5710	376
Affinia Chicago			
155 E 50th St . . . . New York NY 10022	866-246-2203	212-751-5710	376
Affinia Gardens			
215 E 64th St . . . . New York NY 10065	866-233-4642	212-355-1230	376
Affinia Manhattan			
371 Seventh Ave . . . . New York NY 10001	866-246-2203	212-563-1800	376
Affinion Group Inc			
6 High Ridge Pk . . . . Stamford CT 06905	800-251-2148	203-956-1000	387
Affinitas Corp			
1015 N 98th St Ste 100 . . . . Omaha NE 68114	800-369-6495	402-505-5000	195
Affinity Federal Credit Union			
73 Mountain View Blvd			
PO Box 621 . . . . Basking Ridge NJ 07920	800-325-0808		219
Affinity Medical Ctr			
875 Eigth St NE . . . . Massillon OH 44646	800-999-6673	330-832-8761	371-3
Affirmative Insurance Holdings Inc			
150 Harvester Dr Ste 250 . . . . Burr Ridge IL 60527	800-877-0226	972-728-6300	357-4
OTC: AFFM			
Affordable Car Rental LC			
105 Hwy 36 . . . . Eatontown NJ 07724	800-367-5159	732-272-8736	125
Affordable Housing Update			
8204 Fenton St . . . . Silver Spring MD 20910	800-666-6380	301-588-6380	524-8
Affymetrix Inc			
3420 Central Expy . . . . Santa Clara CA 95051	888-362-2447	408-731-5000	250
NASDAQ: AFFX			
Afghanistan Embassy			
2341 Wyoming Ave NW . . . . Washington DC 20008	866-323-8609	202-483-6410	257
AFI (Armed Forces Insurance Exchange)			
PO Box G . . . . Fort Leavenworth KS 66027	800-255-0187	800-255-6792	388-4
Afinety Inc			
1956 Cotner Ave . . . . Los Angeles CA 90025	877-423-4638	310-996-2700	320
AFLAC (American Family Life Assurance Company of Columbus)			
1932 Wynnton Rd . . . . Columbus GA 31999	800-992-3522*	706-323-3431	388-2
Cust Svc			
AFLAC Inc			
1932 Wynnton Rd . . . . Columbus GA 31999	800-992-3522	706-323-3431	357-4
NYSE: AFL			
AFLAC PAC (American Family Life Assurance Co PAC)			
1932 Wynnton Rd Ste 300 . . . . Columbus GA 31999	800-992-3522*	706-323-3431	608
*NYSE: AFL ▪ *Cust Svc*			
AFL-CIO (American Federation of Labor & Congress of Industrial Organizations)			
815 16th St NW . . . . Washington DC 20006	877-850-4959	202-637-5000	411
AFM (American Federation of Musicians of the US & Canada)			
1501 Broadway Ste 600 . . . . New York NY 10036	800-762-3444	212-869-1330	411
AFMR (American Federation for Medical Research)			
900 Cummings Ctr Ste 221-U . . . . Beverly MA 01915	888-737-9477	978-927-8330	48-8

	Toll-Free	Phone	Class
AFOP (Association of Farmworker Opportunity Programs) 1726 M St NW Ste 602 Washington DC 20036	866-487-9243	202-828-6006	47-2
AFP (Association of Fundraising Professionals) 4300 Wilson Blvd Ste 300 Arlington VA 22203	800-666-3863	703-684-0410	48-12
AFP Transformers Inc 206 Talmedge Rd Edison NJ 08817	800-843-1215	732-248-0305	757
AF&PA (American Forest & Paper Assn) 1111 19th St NW Ste 800 Washington DC 20036	800-878-8878	202-463-2700	47-2
Africa Adventure Co, The 5353 N Federal Hwy Ste 300 Fort Lauderdale FL 33308	800-882-9453	954-491-8877	750
African American Historical Museum & Cultural Ctr of Iowa 55 12th Ave SE Cedar Rapids IA 52406	877-526-1863	319-862-2101	513
African Lion Safari & Game Farm RR 1 Cambridge ON N1R5S2	800-461-9453	519-623-2620	810
African Safari Wildlife Park 267 S Lightner Rd Port Clinton OH 43452	800-521-2660	419-732-3606	810
African Travel Inc 330 N Brand Blvd Glendale CA 91205	800-421-8907	818-507-7893	750
African Wildlife Foundation (AWF) 1400 16th St NW Ste 120 Washington DC 20036	888-494-5354	202-939-3333	47-3
AFRL (Air Force Research Laboratory) AFRL/PA 1864 Fourth St Bldg 15 Rm 225 Wright-Patterson AFB OH 45433	800-222-0336		659
Afro-American Newspapers Co 2519 N Charles St Baltimore MD 21218	800-237-6892	410-554-8200	628-8
AFS (American Folklore Society) Ohio State Univ Mershon Ctr 1501 Neil Ave Columbus OH 43201	866-311-1200	614-292-4715	47-14
AFS (American Foundry Society) 1695 N Penny Ln Schaumburg IL 60173	800-537-4237	847-824-0181	48-13
AFSA (American Foreign Service Assn) 2101 E St NW Washington DC 20037	800-704-2372	202-338-4045	48-7
AFSP (American Foundation for Suicide Prevention) 120 Wall St 22nd Fl New York NY 10005	888-333-2377	212-363-3500	47-17
AFT (American Farmland Trust) 1200 18th St Washington DC 20036	800-431-1499	202-331-7300	47-2
AFT (American Federation of Teachers) 555 New Jersey Ave NW Washington DC 20001	800-238-1133	202-879-4400	411
AFT Healthcare 555 New Jersey Ave NW Washington DC 20001	800-238-1133	202-879-4491	411
After Six 118 W 20th St New York NY 10011	800-444-8304	646-638-9600	153-11
Afton State Park 6959 Peller Ave S Hastings MN 55033	800-366-8917	651-436-5391	558
AG Partners Inc 512 S Eigth St PO Box 467 Lake City MN 55041	800-772-2990	651-345-3328	442
Ag Processing Inc 12700 W Dodge Rd PO Box 2047 Omaha NE 68103	800-247-1345	402-496-7809	295-29
Ag West Supply Inc 9055 Rickreall Rd Rickreall OR 97371	800-842-2224	503-363-2332	274
AGA (American Gastroenterological Assn) 4930 Del Ray Ave Bethesda MD 20814	800-228-9290	301-654-2055	48-8
AGA (American Galvanizers Assn) 6881 S Holly Cir Ste 108 Centennial CO 80112	800-468-7732	720-554-0900	48-13
AGA (Association of Government Accountants) 2208 Mt Vernon Ave Alexandria VA 22301	800-242-7211	703-684-6931	48-1
Aga Khan Foundation USA (AKF) 1825 K St NW Ste 901 Washington DC 20006	800-267-2532	202-293-2537	47-5
Agape English Language Institute (AELI) 610 Pickens St PO Box 12504 Columbia SC 29201	877-476-2354	803-799-3452	420
Agar Supply Company Inc 225 John Hancock Rd Taunton MA 02780	800-669-6040	508-821-2060	296-9
AGB (Association of Governing Boards of Universities & Colleges) 1133 20th St NW Ste 300 Washington DC 20036	800-356-6317	202-296-8400	48-5
AGBU (Armenian General Benevolent Union) 55 E 59th St 7th Fl New York NY 10022	800-368-4262	212-319-6383	47-14
AGC (Associated General Contractors of America) 2300 Wilson Blvd Ste 400 Arlington VA 22201	800-242-1766	703-548-3118	48-3
AGC Flat Galss North America Inc 11175 Cicero Dr Ste 400 Alpharetta GA 30022	800-251-0441	404-446-4200	328
AGCO (AGCO Corp) 4205 River Green Pkwy Duluth GA 30096 *NYSE: AGCO*	877-525-4384	770-813-9200	273
AGCO Corp (AGCO) 4205 River Green Pkwy Duluth GA 30096 *NYSE: AGCO*	877-525-4384	770-813-9200	273
AGD (Academy of General Dentistry) 211 E Chicago Ave Ste 900 Chicago IL 60611	888-243-3368	312-440-4300	48-8
Agency for Healthcare Research & Quality 540 Gaither Rd Rockville MD 20850	800-358-9295	301-427-1200	338-8
Agency for Toxic Substances & Disease Registry 4770 Buford Hwy NE Atlanta GA 30341	800-232-4636		338-8
Agency Revolution 698 NW Bend OR 97701	800-606-0477		5
Agency Software Inc 215 W Commerce Dr Hayden Lake ID 83835	800-342-7327	208-762-7188	387
Aget Manufacturing Co 1408 E Church St Adrian MI 49221	800-832-2438	517-263-5781	18
AGF Management Ltd 66 Wellington St W 31st Fl Toronto ON M5K1E9	800-268-8583	905-214-8203	398
Agfa Corp 611 River Dr Elmwood Park NJ 07407	888-274-8626	201-440-2500	584
AGFA HealthCare Corp 10 S Academy St Greenville SC 29601	877-777-2432	864-421-1600	179-10
Agfinity 260 Factory Rd Eaton CO 80615	800-433-4688	970-454-4000	276
AGI (American Geological Institute) 4220 King St Alexandria VA 22302	800-334-2564	703-379-2480	48-19
AGI (Alan Guttmacher Institute) 125 Maiden Ln Seventh Fl New York NY 10038	800-355-0244	212-248-1111	47-5
AgilQuest Corp 9407 Hull St Rd Richmond VA 23236	888-745-7455	804-745-0467	179-1
Aging News Alert 8204 Fenton St Silver Spring MD 20910	800-666-6380	301-588-6385	524-8
Agissar Corp 526 Benton St Stratford CT 06615	800-627-8256	203-375-8662	110
AGL Corp 2202 N Redmond Rd PO Box 189 Jacksonville AR 72076	800-643-9696	501-982-4433	422
AGM Container Controls Inc PO Box 40020 Tucson AZ 85717	800-995-5590	520-881-2130	347
AGM Industries Inc 16 Jonathan Dr Brockton MA 02301	800-225-9990	508-587-3900	798
AGMA (American Guild of Musical Artists) 1430 Broadway 14th Fl New York NY 10018	800-543-2462	212-265-3687	47-4
AGN International-North America 2851 S Parker Rd Ste 850 Aurora CO 80014	800-782-2272	303-743-7880	48-1
Agnes Scott College 141 E College Ave Decatur GA 30030	800-868-8602	404-471-6000	166
Agnico-Eagle Mines Ltd 145 King St E Ste 500 Toronto ON M5C2Y7 *NYSE: AEM*	888-822-6714	416-947-1212	497
AGPA (American Group Psychotherapy Assn) 25 E 21st St Sixth Fl New York NY 10010	877-668-2472	212-477-2677	48-15
Agralite Electric Co-op 320 Hwy 12 SE Benson MN 56215	800-950-8375	320-843-4150	245
Agrex Inc 10975 Grandview Dr St Ste 200 Overland Park KS 66210	800-334-6788	913-851-6300	10-3
Agri Beef Co 1555 Shoreline Dr Ste 320 Boise ID 83702	800-657-6305	208-338-2500	10-1
agriCAREERS Inc 613 Main St PO Box 140 Massena IA 50853	800-633-8387		260
Agricredit Acceptance LLC 8001 Birchwood Ct Ste C PO Box 2000 Johnston IA 50131	800-577-8504	515-314-9203	216
Agricultural Workers Mutual Auto Insurance Co PO Box 88 Fort Worth TX 76101	800-772-7424	817-831-9900	388-4
AgriGold Hybrids 5381 Akin Rd Saint Francisville IL 62460	800-262-7333	618-943-5776	685
Agri-King Inc 18246 Waller Rd Fulton IL 61252	800-435-9560	815-589-2525	442
AgriNorthwest 7404 W Hood Pl Ste B Kennewick WA 99336	888-632-5511	509-734-1195	10-4
Agri-Service 3204 Kimberly Rd E Twin Falls ID 83301	800-388-3599	208-734-7772	274
Agrium Inc 13131 Lk Fraser Dr SE Calgary AB T2J7E8 *NYSE: AGU*	877-247-4861	403-225-7000	280
AGS (American Gem Society) 8881 W Sahara Ave Las Vegas NV 89117	866-805-6500	702-255-6500	48-4
AGS (Augusta Regional Airport - Bush Field) 1501 Aviation Way Augusta GA 30906	866-289-9673	706-798-3236	27
AGSI 3343 Peachtree Rd NE Ste 510 Atlanta GA 30326	800-768-2474	404-816-7577	181
AGTA (American Gem Trade Assn) 3030 LBJ Fwy Ste 840 Dallas TX 75234	800-972-1162	214-742-4367	48-4
AGU (American Geophysical Union) 2000 Florida Ave NW Washington DC 20009	800-966-2481	202-462-6900	48-19
Agua Caliente Casino Resort Spa 32-250 Bob Hope Dr Rancho Mirage CA 92270	888-999-1995	760-321-2000	132
AGVA (American Guild of Variety Artists) 363 Seventh Ave 17th Fl New York NY 10001	800-331-0890	212-675-1003	47-4
AgVantage FS Inc 1600 Eigth St SW Waverly IA 50677	800-346-0058	319-483-4900	276
AH Harris & Son Inc 367 Alumni Rd Newington CT 06111	800-382-6555	860-665-9494	264-3
AHA (American Heart Assn) 7272 Greenville Ave Dallas TX 75231	800-242-8721	214-373-6300	47-17
AHA (American Historical Assn) 400 A St SE Washington DC 20003	888-444-6664	202-544-2422	48-5
AHA (American Hospital Assn) 155 N Wacker Dr Chicago IL 60606	800-424-4301	312-422-3000	48-8
AHA (American Humane Assn) 63 Inverness Dr E Englewood CO 80112	800-227-4645	303-792-9900	47-6
AHAM (Association of Home Appliance Manufacturers) 1111 19th St NW Ste 402 Washington DC 20036	888-258-3247	202-872-5955	48-4
AHAPAC (American Hospital Assn PAC) 325 Seventh St NW Washington DC 20004	800-424-4301	202-638-1100	608
AHAVA North America 330 7th Avenue New York NY 10001	800-366-7254		215
AHC Media LLC 3525 Piedmont Rd NE Bldg 6 Ste 400 Atlanta GA 30305 *Cust Svc	800-688-2421*	404-262-5476	628-9
AHCA (American Health Care Assn) 1201 L St NW Washington DC 20005	800-321-0343	202-842-4444	48-8
AHDI (Association for Healthcare Documentation Integrity) 4230 Kiernan Ave Ste 130 Modesto CA 95356	800-982-2182	209-527-9620	48-8
Ahead LLC 270 Samuel Barnet Blvd New Bedford MA 02745	800-282-2246	508-985-9898	153-8
AheadTek Inc 6410 Via Del Oro San Jose CA 95119	800-971-9191	408-226-9991	638
Ahearn & Soper Inc 100 Woodbine Downs Blvd Rexdale ON M9W5S6	800-263-4258	416-675-3999	175
AHEPA (American Hellenic Educational Progressive Assn) 1909 Q St NW Ste 500 Washington DC 20009	855-473-3512	202-232-6300	47-14
Ahern Rentals Inc 4241 Arville St Las Vegas NV 89103	800-589-6797	702-362-0623	264-3
AHI International Corp 6400 Shafer Ct Rosemont IL 60018	800-323-7373		750
AHI Supply Inc PO Box 884 Friendswood TX 77549	800-873-5794	281-331-0088	192-1
AHIA (Association of Healthcare Internal Auditors) 10200 W 44th Ave Ste 304 Wheat Ridge CO 80033	888-275-2442	303-327-7546	48-1
AHIMA (American Health Information Management Assn) 233 N Michigan Ave Ste 2100 Chicago IL 60601	800-335-5535	312-233-1100	48-8
AHIP (America's Health Insurance Plans) 601 Pennsylvania Ave NW Ste 500 Washington DC 20004 *Cust Svc	877-291-2247*	202-778-3200	48-9
AHLA (Alberta Hotel & Lodging Assn) 2707 Ellwood Dr Edmonton AB T6X0P7	888-436-6112	780-436-6112	47-23
AHNA (American Holistic Nurses' Assn) 323 N San Francisco St Ste 201 Flagstaff AZ 86001	800-278-2462	928-526-2196	47-17
Ahola Corp, The 6820 W Snowville Rd Brecksville OH 44141	800-727-2849	440-717-7620	2
AHRA (American Healthcare Radiology Administrators) 490-B Boston Post Rd Ste 200 Sudbury MA 01776	800-334-2472	978-443-7591	48-8
Ahrberg Milling Co 200 S Depot St PO Box 968 Cushing OK 74023	800-324-0267	918-225-0267	442
AHS (American Horticultural Society) 7931 E Blvd Dr Alexandria VA 22308	800-777-7931	703-768-5700	47-18
AHS (American Helicopter Society International) 217 N Washington St Alexandria VA 22314	855-247-4685	703-684-6777	48-21

				Toll-Free	Phone	Class
Al Friedman Company Inc						
44 W 18th St Fourth Fl	New York	NY	10011	**800-204-6352**	212-243-9000	44
AIA (AIA Corporation)						
800 Winneconne Ave	Neenah	WI	54956	**800-460-7836**	920-886-3700	9
AIA (Aerospace Industries Assn of America)						
1000 Wilson Blvd Ste 1700	Arlington	VA	22209	**866-923-7797**	703-358-1000	48-21
AIA (American Institute of Architects)						
1735 New York Ave NW	Washington	DC	20006	**800-242-3837***	202-626-7300	47-4
*Orders						
AIA (Archaeological Institute of America)						
656 Beacon St 4th Fl	Boston	MA	02215	**877-524-6300**	617-353-9361	47-11
AIA Corporation (AIA)						
800 Winneconne Ave	Neenah	WI	54956	**800-460-7836**	920-886-3700	9
AIAA (American Institute of Aeronautics & Astronautics Inc)						
1801 Alexander Bell Dr Ste 500	Reston	VA	20191	**800-639-2422**	703-264-7500	48-19
AIADA (American International Automobile Dealers Assn)						
500 Montgomery St Ste 800	Alexandria	VA	22314	**800-462-4232**	703-519-7800	48-18
AIAG (Automotive Industry Action Group)						
26200 Lahser Rd Ste 200	Southfield	MI	48033	**877-275-2424**	248-358-3570	48-21
AIB (Art Institute of Boston at Lesley)						
700 Beacon St Ste 202	Boston	MA	02215	**800-773-0494**	617-585-6600	162
AIB College of Business						
2500 Fleur Dr	Des Moines	IA	50321	**800-444-1921**	515-244-4221	788
AIBS (American Institute of Biological Sciences)						
1444 'I' St NW Ste 200	Washington	DC	20005	**800-992-2427**	202-628-1500	48-19
AIC (American Institute of Chemists)						
315 Chestnut St	Philadelphia	PA	19106	**800-829-0115**	215-873-8224	48-19
AICA (American-International Charolais Assn)						
11700 NW Plaza Cir	Kansas City	MO	64153	**800-270-7711**	816-464-5977	47-2
AIChE (American Institute of Chemical Engineers)						
120 Wall St Fl 23	New York	NY	10005	**800-242-4363***	203-702-7660	48-19
*Cust Svc						
AICPA (American Institute of Certified Public Accountants)						
1211 Ave of the Americas	New York	NY	10036	**888-777-7077**	212-596-6200	48-1
AICPCU/IIA (American Institute for CPCU & Insurance Institute of America)						
720 Providence Rd Ste 100	Malvern	PA	19355	**800-644-2101**	610-644-2100	48-9
AICR Newsletter						
1759 R St NW	Washington	DC	20009	**800-843-8114**	202-328-7744	524-8
Aidells Sausage Co						
1625 Alvarado St	San Leandro	CA	94577	**877-243-3557**	510-614-5450	295-26
AIDS Library						
1233 Locust St 2nd Fl	Philadelphia	PA	19107	**877-613-4533**	215-985-4851	431-4
AIDSinfo						
PO Box 6303	Rockville	MD	20849	**800-448-0440**	301-519-0459	338-8
AIFD (American Institute of Floral Designers)						
720 Light St	Baltimore	MD	21230	**877-865-5320**	410-752-3318	48-4
AIFP (American International Forest Products LLC)						
5560 SW 107th Ave	Beaverton	OR	97005	**800-366-1611**	503-641-1611	192-3
AIG SunAmerica Inc						
21650 Oxnard St	Woodland Hills	CA	91367	**800-445-7862**		357-4
AIGA (American Institute of Graphic Arts)						
164 Fifth Ave	New York	NY	10010	**800-548-1634**	212-807-1990	47-4
Aigner Index Inc						
23 Mac Arthur Ave	New Windsor	NY	12553	**800-242-3919**	845-562-4510	601
Aiken County						
828 Richland Ave W	Aiken	SC	29801	**866-876-7074**	803-642-2012	336
Aiken Electric Co-op Inc						
2790 Wagener Rd	Aiken	SC	29802	**877-264-5368***	803-649-6245	245
*Tech Supp						
Aiken Regional Medical Centers						
302 University Pkwy	Aiken	SC	29801	**800-245-3679**	803-641-5000	371-3
AIL (American Income Life Insurance Co)						
1200 Wooded Acres	Waco	TX	76710	**800-433-3405**	254-761-6400	388-2
AIM (Accuracy in Media Inc)						
4455 Connecticut Ave NW						
Ste 330	Washington	DC	20008	**800-787-4567**	202-364-4401	48-14
AIM Supply Co						
7337 Bryan Dairy Rd	Largo	FL	33777	**800-999-0125**	727-544-6211	382
Aimco						
10000 SE Pine St	Portland	OR	97216	**800-852-1368**		382
Aims Community College						
5401 W 20th St	Greeley	CO	80634	**800-301-5388**	970-330-8008	160
AIMS Inc						
235 Desiard St	Monroe	LA	71201	**800-729-2467**	318-323-2467	179-10
AIN Plastics Inc						
1750 E Heights Dr	Madison Heights	MI	48071	**877-246-7700***	248-356-4000	596
*Cust Svc						
AIPB (American Institute of Professional Bookkeepers)						
6001 Montrose Rd Ste 500	Rockville	MD	20852	**800-622-0121**		48-1
AIPC (Amphenol Interconnect Products Corp)						
20 Valley St	Endicott	NY	13760	**888-275-2472**	607-754-4444	253
AIPG (American Institute of Professional Geologists)						
1400 W 122nd Ave Ste 250	Westminster	CO	80234	**800-772-3773**	303-412-6205	48-19
Air & Waste Management Assn (A&WMA)						
420 Fort Duquesne Blvd						
1 Gateway Ctr 3rd Fl	Pittsburgh	PA	15222	**800-270-3444**	412-232-3444	47-12
Air Charter Team						
4151 N Mulberry Dr Ste 250	Kansas City	MO	64116	**800-205-6610**	816-283-3280	13
Air Comfort Corp						
2550 Braga Dr	Broadview	IL	60155	**800-466-3779**	708-345-1900	190-10
Air Conditioning Heating & Refrigeration News						
2401 W Big Beaver Rd Ste 700	Troy	MI	48084	**800-837-8337**	248-362-3700	452-21
Air Contact Transport Inc						
PO Box 570	Budd Lake	NJ	07828	**800-765-2769**		188
Air Cycle Corp						
2200 Ogden Ave Ste 100	Lisle	IL	60532	**800-909-9709**		294
Air Force Assn (AFA)						
1501 Lee Hwy Fourth Fl	Arlington	VA	22209	**800-727-3337**	703-247-5800	47-19
Air Force Federal Credit Union						
1560 Cable Ranch Rd Ste 200	San Antonio	TX	78245	**800-227-5328**	210-673-5610	219
Air Force Magazine						
1501 Lee Hwy	Arlington	VA	22209	**800-727-3337**	703-247-5800	452-12
Air Force Research Laboratory (AFRL)						
AFRL/PA						
1864 Fourth St Bldg 15 Rm 225	Wright-Patterson AFB	OH	45433	**800-222-0336**		659
Air Force Times Magazine						
6883 Commercial Dr	Springfield	VA	22159	**800-368-5718**	703-750-7400	452-12
Air India						
570 Lexington Ave 15th Fl	New York	NY	10022	**800-223-7776**		25
Air Jamaica 7th Heaven						
9200 S Dadeland Blvd	Miami	FL	33156	**800-523-5585**	305-670-3222	26
Air Line Pilots Assn						
535 Herndon Pkwy	Herndon	VA	20170	**877-331-1223**	703-689-2270	411

				Toll-Free	Phone	Class
Air Liquide America LP						
2700 Post Oak Blvd Ste 1800	Houston	TX	77056	**877-855-9533**		141
Air Logistics Inc						
4605 Industrial Dr	New Iberia	LA	70560	**800-365-6771**	337-365-6771	356
Air Monitor Corp						
1050 Hopper Ave	Santa Rosa	CA	95403	**800-247-3569**	707-544-2706	605
Air New Zealand Ltd						
1960 E Grand Ave Ste 300	El Segundo	CA	90245	**800-262-1234**	310-648-7104	25
Air Palm Springs						
145 S Gene Autry Trl						
Ste 14	Palm Springs	CA	92262	**800-760-7774**	760-322-1104	13
Air Products & Chemicals Inc						
7201 Hamilton Blvd	Allentown	PA	18195	**800-345-3148***	610-481-4911	141
NYSE: APD ■ *Prod Info						
Air Quality Engineering Inc						
7140 Northland Dr N	Brooklyn Park	MN	55428	**800-328-0787**	763-531-9823	18
Air Sunshine Inc						
PO Box 22237	Fort Lauderdale	FL	33335	**800-435-8900**	954-434-8900	25
Air Systems International Inc						
829 Juniper Crescent	Chesapeake	VA	23320	**800-866-8100**	757-424-3967	632
Air Tahiti Nui						
1990 E Grand Ave	El Segundo	CA	90245	**877-824-4846***	310-662-1860	25
*Cust Svc						
Air Technical Industries						
7501 Clover Ave	Mentor	OH	44060	**800-321-9680**	440-951-5191	465
Air Techniques Inc						
1295 Walt Whitman Rd	Melville	NY	11747	**888-247-8481**	516-433-7676	228
Air Traffic Control Assn (ATCA)						
1101 King St Ste 300	Alexandria	VA	22314	**866-953-2189**	703-299-2430	48-21
Air Van Moving Group						
2340 130th Ave NE Ste 201	Bellevue	WA	98005	**800-989-8905**	425-629-4101	512
Air Vent Inc						
4117 Pinnacle Pnt Dr Ste 400	Dallas	TX	75211	**800-247-8368**		688
Airbiquity Inc						
1011 Western Ave Ste 600	Seattle	WA	98104	**888-334-7741**	206-219-2700	638
Airbus Helicopters Inc						
2701 Forum Dr	Grand Prairie	TX	75052	**800-873-0001**	972-641-0000	20
Airbus North America Holdings						
198 Van Buren St Ste 300	Herndon	VA	20170	**888-340-2375**	703-834-3400	195
AirClic Inc						
900 Northbrook Dr Ste 100	Trevose	PA	19053	**800-419-8495**	215-504-0560	174-7
AIRCO Group						
1853 S Eisenhower Ct	Wichita	KS	67209	**800-835-2243**	316-945-0445	760
Aircom Mfg Inc						
6205 E 30th St	Indianapolis	IN	46219	**800-925-2426**	317-545-5383	688
Aircraft Owners & Pilots Assn (AOPA)						
421 Aviation Way	Frederick	MD	21701	**800-872-2672**	301-695-2000	48-21
Aircraft Technical Publishers						
101 S Hill Dr	Brisbane	CA	94005	**800-227-4610**	415-330-9500	628-11
Aire Serv Heating & Air Conditioning Inc						
5387 Texas 6 Fwy Ste 101	Woodway	TX	76712	**855-983-0630**	254-523-3600	190-10
Airefco Inc						
18755 SW Teton Ave PO Box 1349	Tualatin	OR	97062	**800-869-1349**	503-692-3210	15
Aire-Master of America Inc						
1821 N State Hwy Cc	Nixa	MO	65714	**800-525-0957**	417-725-2691	309
AirFlite Inc						
3250 AirFlite Way	Long Beach	CA	90807	**800-241-3548**	562-490-6200	13
Airfloat LLC						
2230 Brush College Rd	Decatur	IL	62526	**800-888-0018**	217-423-6001	208
Airflow Systems Inc						
11221 Pagemill Rd	Dallas	TX	75243	**800-818-6185**	214-503-8008	18
Airgas Inc						
259 N Radnor-Chester Rd Ste 100	Radnor	PA	19087	**800-255-2165**	610-687-5253	144
NYSE: ARG						
Airgas Specialty Products						
2530 Sever Rd Ste 300	Lawrenceville	GA	30043	**800-295-2225**		280
Airguard Industries Inc						
100 River Ridge Cir	Jeffersonville	IN	47130	**800-999-3458**	866-247-4827	18
AirLiance Materials LLC						
450 Medinah Rd	Roselle	IL	60172	**877-233-5800***	847-233-5800	760
*General						
Airlie Conference Ctr						
6809 Airlie Rd	Warrenton	VA	20187	**800-288-9573**	540-347-1300	374
Airmate Co Inc						
16280 County Rd D	Bryan	OH	43506	**800-544-3614**	419-636-3184	9
Airosol Company Inc						
1206 Illinois St	Neodesha	KS	66757	**800-633-9576**	620-325-2666	143
AirPair Inc						
875 Howard St	San Francisco	CA	94103	**800-487-0668**		384
Airparts Company Inc						
2310 NW 55th Ct	Fort Lauderdale	FL	33309	**800-392-4999**	954-739-3575	760
Airport Settle Inn						
2620 S Packerland Dr	Green Bay	WI	54313	**800-688-9052**	920-499-1900	376
AIR-serv Group LLC						
1370 Mendota						
Heights Rd	Mendota Heights	MN	55120	**800-247-8363**	651-454-0465	54
Airtek Inc PO Box 466	Irwin	PA	15642	**800-424-7835**	724-863-1350	173
Airtel Plaza Hotel						
7277 Valjean Ave	Van Nuys	CA	91406	**800-224-7835**	818-997-7676	376
Airtex Consumer Products a Div of Federal Foam Technologies						
150 Industrial Pk Blvd	Cokato	MN	55321	**800-851-8887**		734-6
Airtex Products						
407 W Main St	Fairfield	IL	62837	**800-880-3056**	618-842-2111	59
Airvoice Wireless LLC						
2425 Franklin Rd	Bloomfield Hills	MI	48302	**888-944-2355**		726
Air-Way Manufacturing Co						
586 N Main St	Olivet	MI	49076	**800-253-1036***	269-749-2161	778
*Cust Svc						
Airways Freight Corp						
3849 W Wedington Dr	Fayetteville	AR	72704	**800-643-3525**	479-442-6301	310
AIS (AmSouth Investment Services Inc)						
250 Riverchase Pkwy E 4th Fl	Birmingham	AL	35244	**866-512-3479**		398
AIS RealTime						
4440 Bowen Blvd SE	Grand Rapids	MI	49508	**877-314-1100**		196
AISES (American Indian Science & Engineering Society)						
2305 Renard SE Ste 200	Albuquerque	NM	87106	**800-759-5219**	505-765-1052	48-19
AIST (Association for Iron & Steel Technology)						
186 Thorn Hill Rd	Warrendale	PA	15086	**800-732-0999**	724-814-3000	48-13
AIT (Avante International Technology Inc)						
70 Washington Rd	Princeton Junction	NJ	08550	**800-735-5040**	609-799-9388	789
AITDomains.com						
421 Maiden Ln	Fayetteville	NC	28301	**877-549-2881**		393
Aitken Products Inc						
566 N Eagle St PO Box 151	Geneva	OH	44041	**800-569-9341**	440-466-5711	14

	Toll-Free	Phone	Class
AIUM (American Institute of Ultrasound in Medicine)			
14750 Sweitzer Ln Ste 100 ... Laurel MD 20707	800-638-5352	301-498-4100	48-8
AIUSA (Amnesty International USA)			
5 Penn Plaza 16th Fl ... New York NY 10001	866-273-4466	212-807-8400	47-5
AJ Desmond & Sons Funeral Directors			
2600 Crooks Rd ... Troy MI 48084	800-210-7135	248-362-2500	503
Ajax Paving Industries Inc			
PO Box 7058 ... Troy MI 48007	888-468-5489	248-244-3300	189-4
Ajax Rolled Ring & Machine Inc			
500 Wallace Way ... York SC 29745	800-727-6333	803-684-3133	478
Ajax Tocco Magnethermic Corp			
1745 Overland Ave NE ... Warren OH 44483	800-547-1527	330-372-8511	317
Ajilon Communications			
970 Peachtree Industrial Blvd Ste 200 ... Suwanee GA 30024	800-843-6910	678-482-5103	197
AJLI (Association of Junior Leagues International Inc)			
80 Maiden Ln Ste 305 ... New York NY 10038	800-955-3248	212-951-8300	47-15
AJS (American Judicature Society)			
2700 University Ave ... Des Moines IA 50311	800-626-4089	515-271-2281	48-10
AJWS (American Jewish World Service)			
45 W 36th St ... New York NY 10018	800-889-7146	212-792-2900	47-5
AK Steel Corp			
9227 Centre Pt Dr ... West Chester OH 45069	800-331-5050	513-425-5000	714
NYSE: AKS			
AK Tube LLC			
30400 E Broadway ... Walbridge OH 43465	800-955-8031	419-661-4150	485
Akal Security Inc			
Seven Infinity Loop ... Espanola NM 87532	888-325-2527	505-692-6600	683
Akamai Technologies Inc			
Eight Cambridge Ctr ... Cambridge MA 02142	877-425-2624	617-444-3000	179-7
NASDAQ: AKAM			
Akcros Chemicals America			
500 Jersey Ave ... New Brunswick NJ 08901	800-500-7890*	732-220-6882	598-2
*Cust Svc			
Akdo Intertrade Inc			
1435 State St ... Bridgeport CT 06605	800-811-2536	203-336-5199	715
AKF (American Kidney Fund)			
6110 Executive Blvd Ste 1010 ... Rockville MD 20852	800-638-8299		47-17
AKF (Aga Khan Foundation USA)			
1825 K St NW Ste 901 ... Washington DC 20006	800-267-2532	202-293-2537	47-5
Akorn Inc			
1925 W Field Ct ... Lake Forest IL 60045	800-932-5676	847-279-6100	231
NASDAQ: AKRX			
AKRF Inc			
440 Pk Ave S ... New York NY 10016	800-899-2573	212-696-0670	261
Akrochem Corp			
255 Fountain St ... Akron OH 44304	800-321-2260	330-535-2100	598-3
Akro-Mils Inc			
1293 S Main St ... Akron OH 44301	800-253-2467		200
Akron Auto Auction Inc			
2471 Ley Dr ... Akron OH 44319	800-773-0033	330-773-8245	50
Akron Gasket & Packing Enterprises Inc			
445 NE Ave ... Tallmadge OH 44278	800-888-2088	330-633-3742	325
Akron General Medical Ctr			
400 Wabash Ave ... Akron OH 44307	800-221-4601	330-344-6000	371-3
Akron Paint & Varnish Inc			
1390 Firestone Pkwy ... Akron OH 44301	800-772-3452	330-773-8911	543
Akron Porcelain & Plastics Co			
2739 Cory Ave PO Box 15157 ... Akron OH 44314	800-737-9664	330-745-2159	597
Akron/Summit County Convention & Visitors Bureau			
77 E Mill St ... Akron OH 44308	800-245-4254	330-374-8900	207
Akron-Canton Airport			
5400 Lauby Rd NW ... North Canton OH 44720	888-434-2359	330-499-4221	27
AKSM (American Kidney Stone Management Ltd)			
797 Thomas Ln ... Columbus OH 43214	800-637-5188	614-447-0281	350
AKT Enterprises			
6424 Forest City Rd ... Orlando FL 32810	877-306-3651		5
Akzo Nobel Chemicals Inc			
10 Finderne Ave ... Bridgewater NJ 08807	888-331-6212		143
AkzoNobel Surface Chemistry LLC			
525 W Van Buren St ... Chicago IL 60607	877-565-8432*	312-544-7000	141
*Cust Svc			
Al Betz & Assoc Inc			
125 Airport Dr Ste 30 ... Westminster MD 21157	877-402-3376	410-875-3376	440
Al Copeland Investments Inc			
1001 Harimaw Ct S ... Metairie LA 70001	800-401-0401	504-830-1000	661
Al Hirschfeld Theatre			
302 W 45th St ... New York NY 10036	800-432-7780	212-239-6262	736
Al Hoffer's Pest Protection Inc			
12329 NW 35 St ... Coral Springs FL 33065	866-549-7987		570
Al Neyer Inc			
302 W Third St Ste 800 ... Cincinnati OH 45202	877-271-6400	513-271-6400	644
ALA (Alliance for Lupus Research)			
28 W 44th St Ste 501 ... New York NY 10036	800-867-1743	212-218-2840	47-17
ALA (American Library Assn)			
50 E Huron St ... Chicago IL 60611	800-545-2433	312-944-6780	48-11
ALA (American Logistics Assn)			
1133 15th St NW Ste 640 ... Washington DC 20005	800-791-7146	202-466-2520	47-19
ALA (American Lung Assn)			
14 Wall St ... New York NY 10005	800-586-4872	212-315-8700	47-17
ALA (Legal Management: Journal of the Assn of Legal Administrators)			
75 Tri State International Ste 222 ... Lincolnshire IL 60069	800-801-3830	847-267-1252	452-15
ALA (Association of Legal Administrators)			
75 Tri-State International Ste 222 ... Lincolnshire IL 60069	877-675-5571	847-267-1252	48-10
ALA (American Lighting Assn)			
2050 Stemmons Fwy Ste 10046 ... Dallas TX 75207	800-605-4448	214-698-9898	48-4
Ala Moana Hotel			
410 Atkinson Dr ... Honolulu HI 96814	800-367-6025	808-955-4811	376
Alabama			
Administrative Office of Alabama Courts			
300 Dexter Ave ... Montgomery AL 36104	866-954-9411	334-954-5000	337-1
Conservation & Natural Resources Dept			
64 N Union St PO Box 301450 ... Montgomery AL 36130	800-262-3151	334-242-3486	337-1
Crime Victims Compensation Commission			
5845 Carmichael Rd ... Montgomery AL 36117	800-541-9388	334-290-4420	337-1
Emergency Management Agency			
5898 County Rd 41 PO Box 2160 ... Clanton AL 35046	800-843-0699	205-280-2200	337-1
Mental Health & Mental Retardation Dept			
100 N Union St PO Box 301410 ... Montgomery AL 36130	800-367-0955	334-242-3454	337-1
Public Health Dept			
201 Monroe St ... Montgomery AL 36104	800-252-1818	334-206-5300	337-1
Public Service Commission			
100 N Union St RSA Union PO Box 304260 ... Montgomery AL 36130	800-392-8050	334-242-5218	337-1
Rehabilitation Services Dept			
602 S Lawrence St ... Montgomery AL 36104	800-441-7607	334-293-7500	337-1
Securities Commission			
770 Washington Ave Ste 570 ... Montgomery AL 36130	800-222-1253	334-242-2984	337-1
State Parks Div			
64 N Union St ... Montgomery AL 36130	800-252-7275		337-1
Tourism Department			
401 Adams Ave PO Box 4927 ... Montgomery AL 36104	800-252-2262	334-242-4169	337-1
Alabama Agricultural & Mechanical University			
4900 Meridian St PO Box 1087 ... Huntsville AL 35810	800-553-0816	256-372-5000	166
Alabama Art Supply Inc			
1006 23rd St S ... Birmingham AL 35205	800-749-4741*	205-322-4741	44
*Cust Svc			
Alabama Assn of Realtors			
522 Washington Ave PO Box 4070 ... Montgomery AL 36104	800-446-3808	334-262-3808	647
Alabama Card Systems Inc			
500 Gene Reed Dr Ste 102 ... Birmingham AL 35215	800-985-7507	205-833-1116	751
Alabama Constitution Village			
109 Gates Ave ... Huntsville AL 35801	800-678-1819	256-564-8100	513
Alabama Correctional Industries			
1400 Lloyd St ... Montgomery AL 36107	800-224-7007	334-261-3600	622
Alabama Crown Distributing			
421 Industrial Ln ... Birmingham AL 35211	800-548-1869	205-941-1155	80-3
Alabama Educational Television Commission			
2112 11th Ave S Ste 400 ... Birmingham AL 35205	800-239-5233	205-328-8756	624
Alabama Eye Bank			
500 Robert Jemison Rd ... Birmingham AL 35209	800-423-7811		269
Alabama Farmers Co-op Inc			
PO Box 2227 ... Decatur AL 35601	888-255-2667	256-353-6843	280
Alabama Gas Corp (Alagasco)			
605 Richard Arrington Jr Blvd N. ... Birmingham AL 35203	800-292-4005	205-326-8100	775
Alabama Gulf Coast Convention & Visitors Bureau			
3150 Gulf Shores Pkwy PO Box 457. ... Gulf Shores AL 36547	800-745-7263	251-968-7511	207
Alabama Lawyer Magazine			
415 Dexter Ave ... Montgomery AL 36104	800-354-6154	334-269-1515	452-15
Alabama Medical Assn			
19 S Jackson St ... Montgomery AL 36104	800-239-6272		469
Alabama Metal Industries Corp (AMICO)			
3245 Fayette Ave ... Birmingham AL 35208	800-366-2642	205-787-2611	486
Alabama Motor Express Inc			
10720 E US Hwy 84 E ... Ashford AL 36312	800-633-7590		770
Alabama Outdoors Inc			
3054 Independence Dr ... Birmingham AL 35209	800-870-0011	205-870-1919	702
Alabama Pharmacy Assn			
1211 Carmichael Way ... Montgomery AL 36106	800-529-7533*	334-271-4222	578
*General			
Alabama Prepaid Affordable College Tuition (PACT) Program			
100 N Union St Ste 660 ... Montgomery AL 36130	800-252-7228	334-242-7514	716
Alabama Public Television (APT)			
2112 11th Ave S Ste 400 ... Birmingham AL 35205	800-239-5233	205-328-8756	624
Alabama Republican Party			
3505 Lorna Rd Ste 219. ... Birmingham AL 35216	800-274-8683	205-212-5900	609-2
Alabama School Journal			
422 Dexter Ave ... Montgomery AL 36104	800-392-5839	334-834-9790	452-8
Alabama Shakespeare Festival			
One Festival Dr ... Montgomery AL 36117	800-841-4273	334-271-5300	738
Alabama Southern Community College			
30755 Hwy 43 ... Thomasville AL 36784	866-901-1117	334-636-9642	160
Alabama Specialty Products Inc			
152 Metal Samples Rd PO Box 8 ... Munford AL 36268	888-388-1006	256-358-5200	317
Alabama State Bar			
415 Dexter Ave ... Montgomery AL 36104	800-392-5660	334-269-1515	71
Alabama State Legislature			
State House 11 S Union St ... Montgomery AL 36130	800-499-3051	334-242-7600	430
Alabama State Nurses Assn (ASNA)			
360 N Hull St ... Montgomery AL 36104	800-270-2762	334-262-8321	526
Alabama State University			
915 S Jackson St ... Montgomery AL 36104	800-253-5037*	334-229-4100	166
*Admissions			
Alabama Theatre			
4750 Hwy 17 S ... North Myrtle Beach SC 29582	800-342-2262	843-272-1111	565
Alacare Home Health & Hospice			
2400 John Hawkins Pkwy ... Birmingham AL 35244	800-852-4724	205-981-8000	360
Alachua County Library District			
401 E University Ave ... Gainesville FL 32601	866-341-2730	352-334-3900	431-3
Alachua County Visitors & Convention Bureau			
30 E University Ave ... Gainesville FL 32601	866-778-5002	352-374-5260	207
ALACO Ladder Co			
5167 G St ... Chino CA 91710	888-310-7040	909-591-7561	418
Aladdin Steel Inc			
PO Box 89 ... Gillespie IL 62033	800-637-4455	217-839-2121	487
Alagasco (Alabama Gas Corp)			
605 Richard Arrington Jr Blvd N. ... Birmingham AL 35203	800-292-4005	205-326-8100	775
Alaglass Swimming Pools			
165 Sweet Bay Rd ... Saint Matthews SC 29135	877-655-7179		372
Alaka'i Mechanical Corp			
2655 Waiwai Loop ... Honolulu HI 96819	800-600-1085	808-834-1085	190-10
Alamance Community College			
PO Box 8000 ... Graham NC 27253	877-667-7533	336-578-2002	160
Alamance-Burlington School District			
1712 Vaughn Rd ... Burlington NC 27217	888-764-7001	336-570-6060	676
Alamar Resort Inn			
311 16th St ... Virginia Beach VA 23451	800-346-5681	757-428-7582	660
Alameda County Fair Assn (ACFA)			
4501 Pleasanton Ave ... Pleasanton CA 94566	800-874-9253	925-426-7600	633
Alameda County Water District			
43885 S Grimmer Blvd ... Fremont CA 94537	866-275-3772	510-668-4200	775
Alameda Times-Star			
7677 Oakport St Ste 950 ... Oakland CA 94604	866-225-5277	510-208-6300	628-8
Alameda-Contra Costa Transit District			
1600 Franklin St 10th Fl. ... Oakland CA 94612	877-878-8883	510-891-4777	463
Alamo Group Inc			
1627 E Walnut ... Seguin TX 78155	800-788-6066*	830-379-1480	273
*NYSE: ALG *Cust Svc*			
Alamo Industrial Inc			
1502 East Walnut St ... Seguin TX 78155	800-356-6286		294

Alphabetical Section

Name / Address	City	State	Zip	Toll-Free	Phone	Class
Alamo Iron Works Inc						
943 AT&T Ctr Pkwy	San Antonio	TX	78219	**800-292-7817**	210-223-6161	382
Alamo Lumber Co						
10800 Sentinel Dr	San Antonio	TX	78217	**855-828-9792**	210-352-1300	192-3
Alamo Music Ctr						
425 N Main Ave	San Antonio	TX	78205	**800-822-5010**	210-224-1010	519
Alamo Tissue Service Ltd						
5844 Rocky Point Dr Ste 167	San Antonio	TX	78249	**800-226-9091**	210-738-2663	538
Alamo Travel Group Inc						
8930 Wurzbach Rd Ste 100	San Antonio	TX	78240	**800-692-5266**	210-593-0084	761
Alamodome						
100 Montana St	San Antonio	TX	78203	**800-884-3663**	210-207-3663	711
Alamogordo Chamber of Commerce						
1301 N White Sands Blvd	Alamogordo	NM	88310	**800-826-0294**	575-437-6120	137
Alan Gordon Enterprises Inc						
5625 Melrose Ave	Hollywood	CA	90038	**800-825-6684**	323-466-3561	584
Alan Guttmacher Institute (AGI)						
125 Maiden Ln Seventh Fl	New York	NY	10038	**800-355-0244**	212-248-1111	47-5
Alan Ritchey Inc						
740 S I-35 E Frontage Rd	Valley View	TX	76272	**800-877-0273**	940-726-3276	770
Al-Anon Family Group Inc						
1600 Corporate Landing Pkwy	Virginia Beach	VA	23454	**888-425-2666**	757-563-1600	47-21
Alaska						
Banking Securities & Corporations Div 333 Willoughby Ave Fl 9 PO Box 110807	Juneau	AK	99801	**888-925-2521**	907-465-2521	337-2
Enterprise Technology Services Div PO Box 110206	Juneau	AK	99811	**888-565-8680**		337-2
Housing Finance Corp 4300 Boniface Pkwy 99504 PO Box 101020	Anchorage	AK	99504	**800-478-2432**	907-338-6100	337-2
Military & Veterans Affairs Dept (DMVA) PO Box 5800	Fort Richardson	AK	99505	**888-248-3682**	907-428-6896	337-2
Postsecondary Education Commission 3030 Vintage Blvd PO Box 110510	Juneau	AK	99801	**800-441-2962**	907-465-2962	337-2
Vocational Rehabilitation Div 801 W Tenth St Ste 200	Juneau	AK	99801	**800-478-2815**	907-465-2814	337-2
Alaska Bar Assn						
550 W Seventh Ave Ste 1900 PO Box 100279	Anchorage	AK	99501	**800-478-4372**	907-272-7469	71
Alaska Bible College						
248 E Elmwood Ave	Palmer	AK	99645	**800-478-7884**	907-822-3201	159
Alaska Business Monthly						
501 W Northern Lights Blvd Ste 100	Anchorage	AK	99503	**800-770-4373**	907-276-4373	452-5
Alaska Commercial Co						
550 W 64th Ave Ste 200	Anchorage	AK	99518	**800-563-0002**	907-273-4600	342
Alaska Commission on Postsecondary Education						
PO Box 110510	Juneau	AK	99811	**800-441-2962**	907-465-2962	716
Alaska Communications Systems Group Inc						
600 Telephone Ave	Anchorage	AK	99503	**800-808-8083**	907-563-8000	726
NASDAQ: ALSK						
Alaska Industrial Hardware Inc						
2192 Viking Dr	Anchorage	AK	99501	**800-478-7201**	907-276-7201	361
Alaska Magazine						
301 Arctic Slope Ave Ste 300	Anchorage	AK	99518	**800-288-5892**	386-246-0444	452-22
Alaska Marine Highway System						
6858 Glacier Hwy PO Box 112505	Juneau	AK	99801	**800-642-0066**	907-465-3941	463
Alaska Marine Lines Inc						
5615 W Marginal Way SW	Seattle	WA	98106	**800-326-8346***	206-763-4244	311
*Cust Svc						
Alaska Native Heritage Ctr						
8800 Heritage Ctr Dr	Anchorage	AK	99504	**800-315-6608**	907-330-8000	513
Alaska Native Medical Ctr (ANMC)						
4315 Diplomacy Dr	Anchorage	AK	99508	**800-478-6661***	907-563-2662	371-3
*Admitting						
Alaska Pacific University						
4101 University Dr	Anchorage	AK	99508	**800-252-7528**	907-564-8248	166
Alaska Pharmacist's Assn						
203 W 15th Ave Ste 100	Anchorage	AK	99501	**800-228-9290**	907-563-8880	578
Alaska Power & Telephone Co						
193 Otto St PO Box 3222	Port Townsend	WA	98368	**800-982-0136***	360-385-1733	775
OTC: APTL ▪ *Cust Svc						
Alaska Salmon Bake In Alaskaland						
2300 Airport Way	Fairbanks	AK	99701	**800-354-7274**	907-452-7274	662
Alaska State Medical Assn						
4107 Laurel St	Anchorage	AK	99508	**800-951-8712**	907-562-0304	469
Alaska State Museum						
395 Whittier St	Juneau	AK	99801	**800-440-2919**	907-465-2901	513
Alaska Stock Images						
2505 Fairbanks St	Anchorage	AK	99503	**800-487-4285**	907-276-1343	586
Alaska Tour & Travel						
9170 Jewel Lk Rd Ste 202 PO Box 221011	Anchorage	AK	99502	**800-208-0200**	907-245-0200	761
Alaska Travel Adventures Inc						
9085 Glacier Hwy Ste 301	Juneau	AK	99801	**800-323-5757**	907-789-0052	761
Alaska USA Federal Credit Union						
4000 Credit Union Dr PO Box 196613	Anchorage	AK	99503	**800-525-9094**	907-563-4567	219
Alaskan Copper & Brass Co						
3223 Sixth Ave S	Seattle	WA	98134	**800-552-7661**	206-623-5800	487
Alba Wheels Up International Inc						
525 Washington Blvd	Jersey City	NJ	07310	**888-720-9917**	201-435-7050	310
Alban Tractor Co						
8531 Pulaski Hwy	Baltimore	MD	21237	**800-492-6994**	410-686-7777	355
Albany Area Chamber of Commerce						
225 W Broad Ave	Albany	GA	31701	**800-475-8700**	229-434-8700	137
Albany College of Pharmacy (ACPHS)						
106 New Scotland Ave	Albany	NY	12208	**888-203-8010***	518-694-7221	166
*General						
Albany County Convention & Visitors Bureau						
25 Quackenbush Sq	Albany	NY	12207	**800-258-3582**	518-434-1217	207
Albany Democrat-Herald						
600 Lyons St SW PO Box 130	Albany	OR	97321	**877-634-2867**	541-926-2211	525-2
Albany Herald Publishing Company Inc						
126 N Washington St	Albany	GA	31702	**800-234-3725**	229-888-9300	628-8
Albany Industries Inc						
504 N Glenfield Rd	New Albany	MS	38652	**877-534-9804**	662-534-9800	318-2
Albany International Corp						
1373 Broadway PO Box 1907	Albany	NY	12204	**888-797-6735**	518-445-2200	734-3
NYSE: AIN						
Albany International Research Co						
216 Airport Dr	Rochester	NH	03867	**888-797-6735**	603-330-5850	659
Albany Law School of Union University (ALS)						
80 New Scotland Ave	Albany	NY	12208	**800-448-3500**	518-445-2311	167-1
Albany Public Library (APL)						
161 Washington Ave	Albany	NY	12210	**800-733-2767**	518-427-4300	431-3
Albany Steel Inc						
566 Broadway	Albany	NY	12204	**800-342-9317**	518-436-4851	190-14
Albany Visitors Assn						
300 Second Ave SW	Albany	OR	97321	**800-526-2256**	541-928-0911	207
Albemarle Electric Membership Corp						
P.O. Box 69	Hertford	NC	27944	**800-215-9915**	252-426-5735	245
Alberic Colon Auto Sales Inc						
Ave John F Kennedy Carr Ste 2 KM 3.4	San Juan	PR	00920	**877-292-4610**		56
Albert at Bay Suite Hotel						
435 Albert St	Ottawa	ON	K1R7X4	**800-267-6644**	613-238-8858	376
Albert Einstein Healthcare Network						
5501 Old York Rd	Philadelphia	PA	19141	**800-346-7834**	215-456-7890	350
Albert Einstein Medical Ctr						
5501 Old York Rd	Philadelphia	PA	19141	**800-346-7834**		371-3
Albert Guarnieri Co						
1133 E Market St	Warren	OH	44483	**800-686-2639**	330-394-5636	296-8
Albert H Notini & Sons Inc						
225 Aiken St	Lowell	MA	01854	**800-366-8464**	978-459-7151	746
Albert Lea Seed House						
1414 W Main St	Albert Lea	MN	56007	**800-352-5247**	507-373-3161	685
Albert Lea Tribune, The						
808 W Front St PO Box 60	Albert Lea	MN	56007	**800-657-4996**	507-373-1411	628-8
Albert Screen Print Inc						
3704 Summit Rd	Norton	OH	44203	**800-759-2774**	330-753-7559	734-7
Albert's Organics Inc						
3268 E Vernon Ave	Vernon	CA	90058	**800-899-5944**		296-7
Alberta Bair Theater for the Performing Arts						
2722 Third Ave N Ste 200 PO Box 1556	Billings	MT	59103	**877-321-2074**	406-256-8915	565
Alberta Blue Cross						
10009 108th St NW	Edmonton	AB	T5J3C5	**800-661-6995**	780-498-8100	388-3
Alberta Chambers of Commerce						
10025 - 102A Ave Edmonton Ctr Ste 1808	Edmonton	AB	T5J2Z2	**800-272-8854**	780-425-4180	136
Alberta College of Art & Design						
1407 14th Ave NW	Calgary	AB	T2N4R3	**800-251-8290**	403-284-7600	773
Alberta Hotel & Lodging Assn (AHLA)						
2707 Ellwood Dr	Edmonton	AB	T6X0P7	**888-436-6112**	780-436-6112	47-23
Alberta-Pacific Forest Industries Inc						
PO Box 8000	Boyle	AB	T0A0M0	**800-661-5210**	780-525-8000	629
Albertus Magnus College						
700 Prospect St	New Haven	CT	06511	**800-578-9160***	203-773-8550	166
*Admissions						
Albertville Quality Foods Inc						
130 Quality Dr PO Box 756	Albertville	AL	35950	**800-353-2806**	256-840-9923	295-26
Albion College						
611 E Porter St	Albion	MI	49224	**800-858-6770**	517-629-1000	166
Albion Hotel						
1650 James Ave	Miami Beach	FL	33139	**877-782-3557***	305-913-1000	376
*General						
Albion Laboratories Inc						
101 N Main St	Clearfield	UT	84015	**800-453-2406**	801-773-4631	442
Albright College						
1621 N 13th St	Reading	PA	19604	**800-252-1856**	610-921-2381	166
Albuquerque Convention & Visitors Bureau						
20 First Plz Ste 601	Albuquerque	NM	87102	**800-733-9918**	505-842-9918	207
Albuquerque Journal						
7777 Jefferson St NE	Albuquerque	NM	87109	**800-990-5765**	505-823-7777	525-2
Albuquerque Public Schools (APS)						
6400 Uptown Blvd NE	Albuquerque	NM	87110	**866-563-9297**	505-880-3700	676
Alcan Cable						
3 Ravinia Dr Ste 1600	Atlanta	GA	30346	**800-347-0571**	770-394-9886	800
Alcoa Inc						
390 Park Ave PO Box 8001	New York	NY	10022	**800-523-9596**	412-553-4545	480
Alcoa Primary Metals						
900 S Gay St Riverview Twr Ste 1100	Knoxville	TN	37902	**800-852-0238**	865-594-4700	480
Alcoa Wheel Products International						
1600 Harvard Ave	Cleveland	OH	44105	**800-242-9898**	216-641-3600	478
Alcohol & Tobacco Tax & Trade Bureau						
1310 G St NW Ste 300	Washington	DC	20220	**877-882-3277**	202-453-2000	338-16
Alcoholic Beverage Control						
PO Box 27491	Richmond	VA	23261	**800-552-3200**	804-213-4565	524-7
Alcon Laboratories Inc						
6201 S Fwy	Fort Worth	TX	76134	**800-862-5266**	817-293-0450	269
Alcorn County Electric Power Assn						
1909 S Tate St	Corinth	MS	38834	**866-448-3046**	662-287-4402	245
Alcott Group						
71 Executive Blvd	Farmingdale	NY	11735	**888-425-2688**	631-420-0100	623
ALCTS (Association for Library Collections & Technical Services)						
50 E Huron St	Chicago	IL	60611	**800-545-2433**	312-280-5038	48-11
Aldelo LP						
4641 Spyres Way Ste 4	Modesto	CA	95356	**800-801-6036**	209-338-5488	253
Alderbrook Resort & Spa						
7101 E SR-106	Union	WA	98592	**800-622-9370**	360-898-2200	660
Alderfer Inc						
382 Main St PO Box 2	Harleysville	PA	19438	**800-341-1121***	215-256-8818	295-26
*Sales						
Alderson Reporting Co						
1155 Connecticut Ave NW Ste 200	Washington	DC	20036	**800-367-3376**	202-289-2260	440
Alderson-Broaddus College						
101 College Hill Rd CB 2003	Philippi	WV	26416	**800-263-1549***	304-457-1700	166
*Admissions						
ALDI Inc						
1200 N Kirk Rd	Batavia	IL	60510	**800-388-2534**	630-879-8100	342
Aldila Inc						
14145 Danielson St Ste B	Poway	CA	92064	**800-854-2786**	858-513-1801	701
OTC: ALDA						
Aldo Shoes						
2300 Emile Belanger	Montreal	QC	H4R3J4	**888-818-2536**	514-747-2536	300
ALDOT (Alabama)						
300 Dexter Ave	Montgomery	AL	36104	**866-954-9411**	334-954-5000	337-1
Alembic Inc						
3005 Wiljan Ct	Santa Rosa	CA	95407	**800-322-5893**	707-523-2611	520
Alemite LLC						
1057-521 Corporate Ctr Dr Ste 100	Fort Mill	SC	29715	**800-267-8022**	803-802-0001	383

Toll-Free Phone Class

ALerCHEK Inc
15 Oak St Ste 302 Springvale ME 04083 **877-282-9542** 207-490-2266 231

Alere Inc
51 Sawyer Rd Ste 200 Waltham MA 02453 **877-441-7440** 781-647-3900 231

Alere San Diego Inc
9975 Summers Ridge Rd San Diego CA 92121 **800-286-2111** 781-647-3900 231

Aleris International Inc
25825 Science Pk Dr Ste 400 Beachwood OH 44122 **866-266-2586** 216-910-3400 714

AlertOne Services Inc
1000 Commerce Park Dr
Ste 300 Williamsport PA 17701 **866-581-4540*** 568
*Cust Svc

Alerus Retirement Solutions
Two Pine Tree Dr Ste 400 Arden Hills MN 55112 **800-795-2697** 521

Alesco Data Group LLC
5276 Summerlin Commons Way Fort Myers FL 33907 **800-701-6531** 239-275-5006 4

Aleutians East Borough
3380 C St Ste 205 Anchorage AK 99503 **888-383-2699** 907-274-7555 336

Alex C Fergusson LLC (AFCO)
5000 Letterkenny Rd Chambersburg PA 17201 **800-345-1329** 143

Alex R Masson Inc
12819 198th St Linwood KS 66052 **800-879-2539*** 913-301-3281 366
*General

Alexander & Baldwin Inc
822 Bishop St Honolulu HI 96813 **800-454-0477** 808-525-6611 186
NYSE: ALEX

Alexander Communications Group Inc
712 Main St Ste 187-B Boonton NJ 07005 **800-232-4317** 973-265-2300 628-9

Alexander Mfg Co
12978 Tesson Ferry Rd Sappington MO 63128 **800-258-2743*** 314-842-3344 9
*General

Alexander Open Systems Inc
12851 Foster St Overland Park KS 66213 **800-473-1110** 913-307-2300 175

Alexandria & Arlington Bed & Breakfast Networks (AABBN)
4938 Hampden Ln Ste 164 Bethesda MD 20814 **888-549-3415** 703-549-3415 373

Alexandria Archaeology Museum
105 N Union St Ste 327 Alexandria VA 22314 **800-367-7623** 703-746-4399 513

Alexandria Black History Museum
902 Wythe St Alexandria VA 22314 **800-367-7623** 703-838-4356 513

Alexandria Convention & Visitors Assn
221 King St Alexandria VA 22314 **800-388-9119** 703-746-3301 207

Alexandria Daily Town Talk
PO Box 7558 Alexandria LA 71306 **800-523-8391** 318-487-6397 525-2

Alexandria Extrusion Co
401 County Rd 22 NW Alexandria MN 56308 **800-568-6601** 320-763-6537 482

Alexandria Lakes Area Chamber of Commerce
206 Broadway Alexandria MN 56308 **800-235-9441** 320-763-3161 137

Alexandria Moulding
20352 Powerdam Rd Alexandria ON K0C1A0 **866-377-2539** 613-525-2784 308

Alexandria National Cemetery
209 E Shamrock St Pineville LA 71360 **800-827-1000** 318-449-1793 135

Alexandria Real Estate Equities Inc
385 E Colorado Blvd Ste 299 Pasadena CA 91101 **800-776-9437** 626-578-0777 646
NYSE: ARE

Alexandria Veterans Affairs Medical Ctr
2495 Shreveport Hwy 71 N Pineville LA 71360 **800-375-8387** 318-473-0010 371-8

Alexandria/Pineville Area Convention & Visitors Bureau (APACVB)
707 Main St PO Box 1070 Alexandria LA 71301 **800-551-9546** 318-442-9546 207

Alexian Bros Medical Ctr
800 Biesterfield Rd Elk Grove Village IL 60007 **800-432-5005** 847-437-5500 371-3

Alexis Hotel
1007 First Ave Seattle WA 98104 **866-356-8894** 206-624-4844 376

Alexis Park Resort
375 E Harmon Ave Las Vegas NV 89169 **800-582-2228** 702-796-3300 660

ALF (American Liver Foundation)
39 Broadway New York NY 10006 **800-465-4837** 212-668-1000 47-17

Alfa Aesar Co
26 Parkridge Rd Second Fl Ward Hill MA 01835 **800-343-0660** 978-521-6300 143

Alfalfa Electric Co-op Inc
121 E Main St Cherokee OK 73728 **888-736-3837** 580-596-3333 245

Alforex Seeds
38001 County Rd 27 Woodland CA 95695 **877-560-5181** 530-666-3331 276

Alfred A. Loeb State Park
725 Summer St NE Ste C Salem OR 97301 **800-551-6949** 503-986-0707 558

Alfred Angelo Inc
1301 Virginia Dr Fort Washington PA 19034 **888-218-0044** 215-659-5300 153-20

Alfred Hitchcock Mystery Magazine
44 Wall St Ste 904 New York NY 10005 **800-220-7443** 212-686-7188 452-11

Alfred Nickles Bakery Inc
26 N Main St Navarre OH 44662 **800-635-1110** 330-879-5635 295-1

Alger Family of Funds
PO Box 8480 Boston MA 02266 **800-992-3863** 521

Alger Mfg Company Inc
724 S Bon View Ave Ontario CA 91761 **800-854-9833** 909-986-4591 614

Algoa Correctional Ctr
8501 No More Victims Rd Jefferson City MO 65102 **800-392-1111** 573-751-3911 213

Algoma Hardwoods Inc
1001 Perry St Algoma WI 54201 **800-678-8910** 920-487-5221 236

Algy Team Collection
440 NE First Ave Hallandale FL 33009 **800-458-2549** 954-457-8100 153-18

ALI (American Law Institute)
4025 Chestnut St Philadelphia PA 19104 **800-253-6397** 215-243-1600 48-10

Alice Lloyd College
100 Purpose Rd Pippa Passes KY 41844 **888-280-4252*** 606-368-6000 166
*Admissions

Alikar Gardens Resort, The
1123 Verde Dr Colorado Springs CO 80910 **800-456-1123** 719-475-2564 211

Aliments Asta Inc
511 Ave De
La Gare St Alexandre-De-Kamouraska QC G0L2G0 **800-463-1355** 418-495-2728 295-26

ALine Inc
2206 E Gladwick St Rancho Dominguez CA 90220 **877-707-8575** 732

Alion Science & Technology
1750 Tysons Blvd Ste 1300 McLean VA 22102 **877-439-9227** 703-918-4480 261

Alisal Guest Ranch & Resort
1054 Alisal Rd Solvang CA 93463 **800-425-4725** 805-688-6411 660

Alisal Union Elementary School District
1205 E Market St Salinas CA 93905 **800-782-7463** 831-753-5700 676

ALISE (Association for Library & Information Science Education)
65 E Wacker Pl Ste 1900 Chicago IL 60601 **800-522-0772** 312-795-0996 48-11

Alishaev Bros Inc
20 W 47th St Ste 203 New York NY 10036 **877-859-6020** 408

Alive Hospice Inc
1718 Patterson St Nashville TN 37203 **800-327-1085** 615-327-1085 368

Alken Inc
40 Hercules Dr Colchester VT 05446 **800-357-4777** 802-655-3159 683

Alkermes Inc
852 Winter St Waltham MA 02451 **800-848-4876** 781-609-6000 84
NASDAQ: ALKS

Alkinco PO Box 278 New York NY 10116 **800-424-7118** 212-719-3070 345

All Aboard Benefits
6162 E Mockingird Ln Ste 104 Dallas TX 75214 **800-462-2322** 214-821-6677 388-7

All Aboard Cruises Inc
11114 SW 127th Ct Miami FL 33186 **800-883-8657** 305-385-8657 761

All American Moving Group LLC
PO Box 271277 Memphis TN 38167 **800-467-2900** 901-353-3900 770

All American Ticket Service
2616 Philadelphia Pike Ste E Claymont DE 19703 **800-669-0571** 740

All Business Machines Inc
2555 Third St Ste 100 Sacramento CA 95818 **888-880-7801** 744

All Classical Portland
515 NE 15th Ave Portland OR 97232 **888-306-5277** 503-943-5828 636-86

All Cruise Travel
1723 Hamilton Ave San Jose CA 95125 **800-227-8473** 408-295-1200 761

All Foils Inc
16100 Imperial Pkwy Strongsville OH 44149 **800-521-0054** 440-572-3645 487

All Freight Systems Inc
PO Box 5279 Kansas City KS 66119 **800-377-7575** 913-281-1203 770

All Inc
185 Plato Blvd W Saint Paul MN 55107 **800-829-2127** 651-227-6331 37

All Line Inc
16851 E Parkview Ave
Unit 2 Fountain Hills AZ 85268 **800-843-5733** 480-306-6001 209

All Makes Office Equipment Co
2558 Farnam St Omaha NE 68131 **800-341-2413** 402-341-2413 320

All Metals Industries Inc
PO Box 807 Belmont NH 03220 **800-654-6043** 603-267-7023 487

All New Stamping Co
10801 Lower Azusa Rd El Monte CA 91731 **800-877-7775** 483

All Nippon Airways Company Ltd
2050 W 190th St Ste 100 Torrance CA 90504 **800-235-9262** 25

All Source Security Container Mfg Corp
40 Mills Rd Barrie ON L4N6H4 **866-526-4579** 705-726-6460 791-1

All Star Glass Co Inc
1845 Morena Blvd San Diego CA 92110 **800-225-4184** 619-275-3343 61-2

All States Inc
602 N 12th St Saint Charles IL 60174 **800-621-5837*** 773-728-0525 601
*Cust Svc

All Tile Inc
1201 Chase Ave Elk Grove Village IL 60007 **877-255-8453** 847-979-2500 192-1

All Tune & Lube Brakes & More Inc
8334 Veteran's Hwy Millersville MD 21108 **877-978-1758** 410-987-1011 61-5

All Tune & Lube International Inc
ATL International Inc
8334 Veterans Hwy Millersville MD 21108 **877-978-1758*** 410-987-1011 61-5
*Cust Svc

All Tune Transmissions
8334 Veteran's Hwy Millersville MD 21108 **877-978-1758** 410-987-1011 61-6

All Weather Inc
1165 National Dr Sacramento CA 95834 **800-824-5873** 916-928-1000 467

All West Coach Lines
7701 Wilbur Way Sacramento CA 95828 **800-843-2121** 916-423-4000 106

All West Select Sires
450 N Hill Blvd Burlington WA 98233 **800-426-2697** 441

Alladin Plastics Inc
140 Industrial Dr Surgoinsville TN 37873 **877-536-4693** 423-345-2351 597

Allamakee-Clayton Electric Co-op (ACEC)
229 Hwy 51 PO Box 715 Postville IA 52162 **888-788-1551** 563-864-7611 245

All-American Co-op
PO Box 125 Stewartville MN 55976 **888-354-4058** 507-533-4222 273

Allamon Tool Company Inc
18935 Freeport Dr Montgomery TX 77356 **877-449-5433** 532

Allan A Myers Inc
1805 Berks Rd PO Box 1340 Worcester PA 19490 **800-596-6118** 610-222-8800 189-4

Allant Group Inc, The
2056 Westings Ave Ste 500 Naperville IL 60563 **800-367-7311** 195

Allcare Medical Inc
125 Newtown Rd Ste 300 Plainview NY 11803 **800-244-4660** 360

All-Clad Metalcrafters LLC
424 Morganza Rd Canonsburg PA 15317 **800-255-2523*** 724-745-8300 481
*Cust Svc

Allegacy Federal Credit Union
1691 Westbrook Plaza Dr Winston-Salem NC 27103 **800-782-4670** 336-774-3400 219

Allegan County Tourist & Recreational Council
3255 122nd Ave Ste 103 Allegan MI 49010 **888-425-5342** 269-686-9088 207

Allegany College of Maryland
12401 Willowbrook Rd SE Cumberland MD 21502 **800-974-0203** 301-784-5000 160

Allegheny College
520 N Main St Meadville PA 16335 **800-521-5293** 814-332-4351 166

Allegheny Design Management Inc
1154 Parks Industrial Dr Vandergrift PA 15690 **800-927-2611** 724-845-7336 770

Allegheny Institute for Public Policy
305 Mt Lebanon Blvd Ste 208 Pittsburgh PA 15234 **800-242-2184** 412-440-0079 625

Allegheny Petroleum Products Co
999 Airbrake Ave Wilmerding PA 15148 **800-600-2900** 412-829-1990 573

Allegheny Power
800 Cabin Hill Dr Greensburg PA 15601 **800-255-3443*** 724-837-3000 775
*Cust Svc

Allegheny Technologies Inc
1000 Six PPG Pl Pittsburgh PA 15222 **800-258-3586*** 412-394-2800 714
NYSE: ATI ■ *Sales

Allegheny Valley Bank
5137 Butler St Pittsburgh PA 15201 **800-889-6440** 412-781-1464 357-2
OTC: AVLY

Allegheny Wesleyan College
2161 Woodsdale Rd Salem OH 44460 **800-292-3153** 330-337-6403 159

Allegiance Health
205 NE Ave Jackson MI 49201 **800-872-6480** 517-788-4800 371-3

Allegiance Security Group LLC
2900 Arendell St Ste 18 Morehead City NC 28557 **866-747-2748** 252-247-1138 684

Allegis Group Inc
7301 Pkwy Dr Hanover MD 21076 **800-927-8090** 410-579-3000 712

Allegra Network LLC
47585 Galleon Dr Plymouth MI 48170 **800-726-9050*** 248-596-8600 112
*General

Allegro Coffee Co
12799 Claude Ct Thornton CO 80241 **800-530-3995** 303-444-4844 295-7

	City	State	ZIP	Toll-Free	Phone	Class
Allegro Corp						
20048 NE San Rafael St	Portland	OR	97230	**800-288-2007**	503-491-8480	516
Allen & Co Inc						
1401 South Florida Avenue	Lakeland	FL	33803	**800-950-2526**	863-688-9000	681
Allen Bros Inc						
3737 S Halsted St	Chicago	IL	60609	**800-548-7777**	773-890-5100	468
Allen Co						
712 E Main St	Blanchester	OH	45107	**800-329-2491**	937-783-2491	9
Allen Communication Learning Services						
55 West 900 South						
Ste 100	Salt Lake City	UT	84101	**866-310-7800**	801-537-7800	179-3
Allen Company Inc						
525 Burbank St PO Box 445	Broomfield	CO	80020	**800-876-8600**	303-469-1857	189-4
Allen County Community College						
1801 N Cottonwood St	Iola	KS	66749	**800-444-0535**	620-365-5116	160
Allen County Public Library						
900 Library Plaza	Fort Wayne	IN	46802	**800-448-6160**	260-421-1200	431-3
Allen County War Memorial Coliseum						
4000 Parnell Ave	Fort Wayne	IN	46805	**800-745-3000**	260-482-9502	711
Allen Extruders Inc						
1305 Lincoln Ave	Holland	MI	49423	**800-833-1305**	616-394-3810	593
Allen Industries Inc						
6434 Burnt Poplar Rd	Greensboro	NC	27409	**800-967-2553**	336-668-2791	692
Allen Memorial Hospital						
1825 Logan Ave	Waterloo	IA	50703	**888-343-4165**	319-235-3941	371-3
Allen Millwork Inc						
6969 Fern Loop PO Box 6480	Shreveport	LA	71105	**800-551-8737**	318-629-5300	494
Allen Parish						
PO Box 1280	Oberlin	LA	70655	**888-639-4868**	337-639-4868	336
Allen Press Inc						
810 E Tenth St PO Box 1897	Lawrence	KS	66044	**800-627-0932**	785-843-1235	46
Allen Systems Group Inc (ASG)						
1333 Third Ave S	Naples	FL	34102	**800-932-5536**	239-435-2200	179-12
Allen University						
1530 Harden St	Columbia	SC	29204	**877-625-5368**	803-376-5700	166
Allen Ventures Inc						
517 State Farm Rd	Deerfield	WI	53531	**877-423-9800**	608-423-9800	652
Allenberry Resort						
1559 Boiling						
Springs Rd	Boiling Springs	PA	17007	**800-430-5468**	717-258-3211	660
Allen-Edmonds Shoe Corp						
201 E Seven Hills Rd	Port Washington	WI	53074	**800-235-2348***	262-235-6512	300
*Cust Svc						
Allentown Equipment						
1733 90th St	Sturtevant	WI	53177	**800-553-3414**		383
Allentown School District (ASD)						
31 S Penn St	Allentown	PA	18105	**877-262-1492**	484-765-4000	676
Allen-Vanguard Corp						
2400 St Laurent Blvd	Ottawa	ON	K1G5B4	**800-644-9078**	613-739-9646	569
Allergan						
2525 Dupont Dr PO Box 19534	Irvine	CA	92612	**800-347-4500**	714-246-4500	472
Allergan Inc						
2525 Dupont Dr	Irvine	CA	92612	**800-347-4500**	714-246-4500	576
NYSE: AGN						
Allermed Laboratories Inc						
7203 Convoy Ct	San Diego	CA	92111	**800-221-2748**		231
ALLETE Inc						
30 W Superior St	Duluth	MN	55802	**800-228-4966**	218-279-5000	357-5
NYSE: ALE						
Allevity HR & Payroll						
870 Manzanita Ct Ste A	Chico	CA	95926	**800-447-8233**	530-345-2486	623
Alliance Bank						
541 Lawrence Rd	Broomall	PA	19008	**800-472-3272**	610-353-2900	69
NASDAQ: ALLB						
Alliance Foods Inc						
605 W Chicago Rd	Coldwater	MI	49036	**800-388-4158**	517-278-2396	342
Alliance for Aging Research (AAR)						
750 17th St NW Ste 1100	Washington	DC	20006	**866-840-6283**	202-293-2856	47-17
Alliance for Children & Families Inc						
11700 W Lk Pk Dr	Milwaukee	WI	53224	**800-221-3726**	414-359-1040	47-6
Alliance For Employee Growth & Development Inc, The						
80 Cottontail Ln Ste 320	Somerset	NJ	08873	**800-323-3436**		194
Alliance for Excellent Education						
1201 Connecticut Ave Ste 901	Washington	DC	20036	**800-695-0285**	202-828-0828	47-11
Alliance for International Educational & Cultural Exchange						
1776 Massachusetts Ave NW						
Ste 620	Washington	DC	20036	**888-304-9023**	202-293-6141	47-11
Alliance for Lupus Research (ALA)						
28 W 44th St Ste 501	New York	NY	10036	**800-867-1743**	212-218-2840	47-17
Alliance for Retired Americans						
815 16th St NW Fourth Fl	Washington	DC	20006	**888-373-6497**	202-637-5399	47-6
Alliance for Telecommunications Industry Solutions (ATIS)						
1200 G St NW Ste 500	Washington	DC	20005	**800-649-1202**	202-628-6380	48-20
Alliance Grain Co						
1306 W Eigth St	Gibson City	IL	60936	**800-222-2451**	217-784-4284	275
Alliance Imaging Inc						
100 Bayview Cir Ste 400	Newport Beach	CA	92660	**800-544-3215**	949-242-5300	380
Alliance Limousine Inc						
14553 Delano St Unit 210	Van Nuys	CA	91411	**800-954-5466**		437
Alliance One International Inc						
8001 Aerial Ctr Pkwy						
PO Box 2009	Morrisville	NC	27560	**800-937-5449**	919-379-4300	746
NYSE: AOI						
Alliance Reservations Network						
21640 N 19th Ave Ste C102	Phoenix	AZ	85027	**800-419-1545***	602-444-9993	373
*Cust Svc						
Alliance Rubber Co						
210 Carpenter Dam Rd	Hot Springs	AR	71901	**800-626-5940**		667
Alliance to Save Energy (ASE)						
1850 M St NW Ste 600	Washington	DC	20036	**800-862-2086**	202-857-0666	47-12
Alliance Wood Group Engineering LP						
330 Barker Cypress Rd	Houston	TX	77094	**866-313-0052**	281-828-6000	192-2
Alliance Worldwide Investigative Group Inc						
Four Executive Park Dr	Clifton Park	NY	12065	**800-579-2911**	518-514-2944	387
Alliance, The						
810 Tate St	Corinth	MS	38834	**877-347-0545**	662-287-5269	137
AllianceBernstein Holding LP (AB)						
1345 Ave of the Americas	New York	NY	10105	**800-221-5672***	212-486-5800	398
NYSE: AB ■ *Cust Svc						
AllianceOne Inc						
4850 E St Rd Ste 300	Trevose	PA	19053	**866-405-7241**	215-354-5511	158
Alliant Energy Corp						
4902 N Biltmore Ln Ste 1000	Madison	WI	53718	**800-255-4268**		775
NYSE: LNT						
Alliant International University						
10455 Pomerado Rd	San Diego	CA	92131	**866-825-5426**	858-635-4772	166
Alliant Powder						
2299 Snake River Ave PO Box 6	Lewiston	ID	83501	**800-276-9337**	800-379-1732	268
Allianz Life Insurance Company of North America						
PO Box 1344	Minneapolis	MN	55416	**800-950-5872**		388-2
Allied Aerofoam Products LLC						
216 Kelsey Ln	Tampa	FL	33619	**800-338-9140**	813-626-0090	594
Allied Air Enterprises						
215 Metropolitan Dr	West Columbia	SC	29170	**800-448-5872**		15
Allied Automotive Group						
2302 ParkLake Dr						
Bldg 15 Ste 600	Atlanta	GA	30345	**800-476-2058**		770
Allied Bldg Products Corp						
15 E Union Ave	East Rutherford	NJ	07073	**800-541-2198**	201-507-8400	192-3
Allied Body Works Inc						
625 S 96th St	Seattle	WA	98108	**800-733-7450***	206-763-7811	509
*General						
Allied Construction Products LLC						
3900 Kelley Ave	Cleveland	OH	44114	**800-321-1046***	216-431-2600	191
*Cust Svc						
Allied Construction Services & Color Inc						
2122 Fleur Dr PO Box 937	Des Moines	IA	50304	**800-365-4855**	515-288-4855	190-9
Allied Container Systems Inc						
201 N Civic Dr Ste 180	Walnut Creek	CA	94596	**800-943-6510**		542
Allied Controls Inc						
150 E Aurora St	Waterbury	CT	06708	**800-788-0955**	203-757-4200	204
Allied Corrosion Industries Inc						
1550 Cobb Industrial Dr	Marietta	GA	30066	**800-241-0809**	770-425-1355	256
Allied Court Reporters Inc						
115 Phenix Ave	Cranston	RI	02920	**888-443-3767**	401-946-5500	440
Allied Electronics Inc						
7151 Jack Newell Blvd S	Fort Worth	TX	76118	**866-433-5722**	817-595-3500	246
Allied Employer Group						
4400 Buffalo Gap Rd Ste 4500	Abilene	TX	79606	**800-495-3836**	325-695-5822	623
Allied Erecting & Dismantling Company Inc						
2100 Poland Ave	Youngstown	OH	44502	**800-624-2867**	330-744-0808	190-16
Allied Fire & Security Inc						
425 W Second Ave	Spokane	WA	99201	**888-333-2632***	509-321-8778	683
*Acctg						
Allied Fire Protection LP						
PO Box 2842	Pearland	TX	77588	**800-604-2600**	281-485-6803	190-10
ALLIED Group Inc						
1100 Locust St	Des Moines	IA	50391	**800-532-1436**	515-508-4211	388-4
Allied Group Inc, The						
25 Amflex Dr	Cranston	RI	02921	**800-556-6310**	401-946-6100	175
Allied Health Group LLC						
145 Technology Pkwy NW	Norcross	GA	30092	**800-741-4674**		712
Allied Healthcare Products Inc						
1720 Sublette Ave	Saint Louis	MO	63110	**800-444-3954**	314-771-2400	472
NASDAQ: AHPI						
Allied Insurance						
1601 Exposition Blvd	Sacramento	CA	95815	**800-552-2437**	916-924-4000	388-4
Allied International						
13207 Bradley Ave	Sylmar	CA	91342	**800-533-8333***	818-364-2333	348
*General						
Allied International Credit Corp						
16635 Young St Unit 26	Newmarket	ON	L3X1V6	**877-451-2594**		158
Allied International NA Inc						
700 Oakmont Ln	Westmont	IL	60559	**800-444-6787**	630-570-3500	512
Allied Machine & Engineering Corp						
120 Deeds Dr	Dover	OH	44622	**800-321-5537**	330-343-4283	488
Allied Mechanical Services Inc						
5688 E MI Ave Ste A	Kalamazoo	MI	49048	**888-237-3017**	269-344-0191	190-10
Allied Motion Technologies Inc						
495 Commerce Dr Ste 3	Amherst	NY	14228	**888-392-5543**	716-242-8634	248
NASDAQ: AMOT						
Allied Moulded Products Inc						
222 N Union St	Bryan	OH	43506	**800-722-2679**	419-636-4217	803
Allied Oil & Supply Inc						
2209 S 24th St	Omaha	NE	68108	**800-333-3717**	402-344-4343	572
Allied Plastics Company Inc						
2001 Walnut St	Jacksonville	FL	32206	**800-999-0386***	904-359-0386	318-1
*Cust Svc						
Allied Services Rehabilitation Hospital						
475 Morgan Hwy	Scranton	PA	18508	**888-734-2272**	570-348-1300	371-6
Allied Sinterings Inc						
29 Briar Ridge Rd	Danbury	CT	06810	**877-875-0464**		487
Allied Steel Construction Co Inc						
2211 NW First Terr						
PO Box 1111	Oklahoma City	OK	73107	**800-522-4658**	405-232-7531	264-3
Allied Supply Company Inc						
1100 E Monument Ave	Dayton	OH	45402	**800-589-5690**	937-224-9833	656
Allied Systems Co						
21433 SW Oregon St	Sherwood	OR	97140	**800-285-7000**	503-625-2560	273
Allied Technology Inc						
1803 Research Blvd Ste 601	Rockville	MD	20850	**888-294-8560**	301-309-1234	181
Allied Telesyn International Corp						
19800 N Creek Pkwy Ste 100	Bothell	WA	98011	**800-424-4284**	425-481-3895	177
Allied Tool Products						
9334 N 107th St	Milwaukee	WI	53224	**800-558-5147**	414-355-8280	450
Allied Toyotalift						
1640 Island Home Ave	Knoxville	TN	37920	**866-538-0667**	865-573-0995	56
Allied Vaughn						
7600 Parklawn Ste 300	Minneapolis	MN	55435	**800-323-0281**	952-832-3100	649
AlliedBarton Security Services						
150 S Warner Rd	King of Prussia	PA	19406	**866-703-7666**	484-654-3800	684
Allied-Locke Industries						
1088 Corregidor Rd	Dixon	IL	61021	**800-435-7752**	815-288-1471	613
All-Inclusive Vacations Inc						
1595 Iris St	Lakewood	CO	80215	**866-980-6483**	303-980-6483	761
Allison Payment Systems LLC						
2200 Production Dr	Indianapolis	IN	46241	**800-755-2440**		109
Allmar Inc						
287 Riverton Ave	Winnipeg	MB	R2L0N2	**800-230-5516**	204-668-1000	236
AllMeds Inc						
151 Lafayette Dr Ste 401	Oak Ridge	TN	37830	**888-343-6337**	865-482-1999	38
Allomatic Products Co						
102 Jericho Tpke						
Ste 104 Floral Pk	Floral Park	NY	11001	**800-568-0330**	516-775-0330	60
Allor Manufacturing Inc						
12534 Emerson Dr	Brighton	MI	48116	**888-244-4028**	248-486-4500	208
AlloSource						
6278 S Troy Cir	Centennial	CO	80111	**888-873-8330**	720-873-0213	538

Alphabetical Section

	Toll-Free	Phone	Class
Allot Communications			
300 Tradecenter Ste 4680 .... Woburn MA 01801	**877-255-6826**	781-939-9300	179-10
Alloy Engineering & Casting Co			
1700 W Washington St .... Champaign IL 61821	**866-352-8001**	217-398-3200	306
Alloy Stainless Products Co			
611 Union Blvd .... Totowa NJ 07512	**800-631-8372**	973-256-1616	588
All-Pro Fasteners Inc			
1916 Peyco Dr N .... Arlington TX 76001	**800-361-6627**	817-467-5700	348
Allscripts Healthcare Solutions			
222 Merchandise Mart Plz			
Ste 2024 .... Chicago IL 60654	**800-654-0889**		179-10
NASDAQ: MDRX			
All-Search & Inspection Inc			
1108 E S Union Ave .... Midvale UT 84047	**800-227-3152**	801-984-8160	626
All-South Subcontractors Inc			
2678 Queenstown Rd .... Birmingham AL 35210	**800-873-8110**	205-836-8111	190-12
Allstar Fire Equipment Inc			
12328 Lower Azusa Rd .... Arcadia CA 91006	**800-425-5787**	626-652-0900	670
Allstar Magnetics LLC			
6205 NE 63rd St .... Vancouver WA 98661	**800-356-5977**	360-693-0213	246
All-Star Recruiting LLC			
4400 W Sample Rd Ste 250 .... Coconut Creek FL 33073	**800-928-0229**		260
Allstate Corp			
2775 Sanders Rd Allstate Plz .... Northbrook IL 60062	**800-255-7828**	847-402-5000	357-4
NYSE: ALL			
Allstate Floral & Craft Inc			
14038 Park Pl .... Cerritos CA 90703	**800-433-4056**	562-926-2302	293
Allstate Leasing Inc			
One Olympic Pl .... Towson MD 21204	**800-223-4885**	410-363-6500	289
Allstate Life Insurance Co			
3100 Sanders Rd			
Allstate W Plz .... Northbrook IL 60062	**800-366-1411***	847-402-5000	388-2
*Cust Svc			
Allsteel Inc			
2210 Second Ave .... Muscatine IA 52761	**888-255-7833***	563-272-4800	318-1
*Cust Svc			
Allstream Corp			
200 Wellington St W .... Toronto ON M5V3G2	**888-288-2273***	416-345-2000	726
*Cust Svc			
Allsup Inc			
300 Allsup Pl .... Belleville IL 62223	**800-854-1418**		195
Alltech Inc			
3031 Catnip Hill Pike .... Nicholasville KY 40356	**800-289-8324**	859-885-9613	575
All-Temp Refrigeration Services Inc			
271 Hwy 1085 .... Madisonville LA 70447	**888-626-1277**		603
ALL-TEST Pro LLC			
123 Spencer Plain Rd .... Old Saybrook CT 06475	**800-952-8776**	860-399-4222	202
Allvac Inc			
2020 Ashcraft Ave PO Box 5030 .... Monroe NC 28110	**800-841-5491**	704-289-4511	480
Allway Tools Inc			
1255 Seabury Ave .... Bronx NY 10462	**800-422-5592**	718-792-3636	748
All-Ways Adv Co			
1442 Broad St .... Bloomfield NJ 07003	**800-255-9291**	973-338-0700	4
Allwire Inc			
16395 Ave 24 1/2 PO Box 1000 .... Chowchilla CA 93610	**800-255-3828**	559-665-4893	800
ALM (American Lawyer Media Inc)			
120 Broadway Fifth Fl. .... New York NY 10271	**877-256-2472**	212-457-9400	628-9
Alma College			
614 W Superior St .... Alma MI 48801	**800-321-2562**	989-463-7139	166
Alma Products Co			
2000 Michigan Ave .... Alma MI 48801	**877-427-2624**	989-463-1151	59
Almatis Inc			
501 W Pk Rd .... Leetsdale PA 15056	**800-643-8771**	412-630-2800	141
Almo Corp			
2709 Commerce Way .... Philadelphia PA 19154	**800-345-2566**	215-698-4000	37
Almost Family Inc			
9510 Ormsby Stn Rd Ste 300 .... Louisville KY 40223	**800-828-9769**	502-891-1000	360
NASDAQ: AFAM			
Alnylam Pharmaceuticals Inc			
300 Third St 3rd Fl. .... Cambridge MA 02142	**866-330-0326**	617-551-8200	84
NASDAQ: ALNY			
ALOA (Associated Locksmiths of America)			
3500 Easy St .... Dallas TX 75247	**800-532-2562**	214-819-9733	48-3
Aloha Medicinals Inc			
2300 Arrowhead Dr .... Carson City NV 89706	**877-835-6091**	775-886-6300	231
Aloha Petroleum Ltd			
1132 Bishop St Ste 1700 .... Honolulu HI 96813	**800-621-4654**	808-522-9700	112
Alostar Bank			
3680 Grandview Pkwy Ste 200 .... Birmingham AL 35243	**877-738-6391**	205-298-6391	69
ALP Industries Inc			
1229 W Lincoln Hwy .... Coatesville PA 19320	**800-220-2571**	610-384-1300	669
Alpena Area Chamber of Commerce			
235 W Chisholm St .... Alpena MI 49707	**800-425-7362**	989-354-4181	137
Alpena Area Convention & Visitors Bureau			
235 W Chisholm St .... Alpena MI 49707	**800-425-7362**	989-354-4181	207
Alpena Community College (ACC)			
665 Johnson St .... Alpena MI 49707	**888-468-6222**	989-356-9021	160
Alpena County George N Fletcher Public Library			
211 N First Ave .... Alpena MI 49707	**877-737-4106**	989-356-6188	431-3
Alpena Oil Co Inc			
235 Water St .... Alpena MI 49707	**800-968-1098**	989-356-1098	323
Alpena Regional Medical Ctr			
1501 W Chisholm St .... Alpena MI 49707	**800-556-8842**	989-356-7000	371-3
Alpenhof Lodge			
3255 W Village Dr			
PO Box 288. .... Teton Village WY 83025	**800-732-3244**	307-733-3242	376
Alpha & Omega Financial Management Consultants Inc			
8580 La Mesa Blvd Ste 100 .... La Mesa CA 91942	**800-755-5060**		195
Alpha 1 Induction Service Ctr Inc			
1525 Old Alum Creek Dr .... Columbus OH 43209	**800-991-2599**	614-253-8900	317
Alpha Assoc Inc			
145 Lehigh Ave .... Lakewood NJ 08701	**800-631-5399**	732-634-5700	734-2
Alpha Card Services Inc			
475 Veit Rd .... Huntingdon Valley PA 19006	**866-253-2227**		251
Alpha Chi Omega			
5939 Castle Creek			
Pkwy N Dr. .... Indianapolis IN 46250	**800-328-0522**	317-579-5050	47-16
Alpha Chi Sigma			
2141 N Franklin Rd .... Indianapolis IN 46219	**800-252-4369**	317-357-5944	47-16
Alpha Epsilon Phi Sorority (AEPhi)			
11 Lake Ave Ext Ste 1-A .... Danbury CT 06811	**888-668-4293**	203-748-0029	47-16
Alpha Epsilon Pi Fraternity Inc			
8815 Wesleyan Rd .... Indianapolis IN 46268	**800-684-3608**	317-876-1913	47-16

	Toll-Free	Phone	Class
Alpha Gamma Rho			
10101 NW Ambassador Dr .... Kansas City MO 64153	**888-241-4546**	816-891-9200	47-16
Alpha Group, The			
3767 Alpha Way .... Bellingham WA 98226	**800-322-5742**	360-647-2360	253
Alpha Imaging Inc			
4455 Glenrock Rd .... Willoughby OH 44094	**800-331-7327**	440-953-3800	470
Alpha Industries Inc			
14200 Pk Meadow Dr Ste 110S .... Chantilly VA 20151	**866-631-0719***	703-378-1420	153-5
*General			
Alpha Natural Resources Inc			
1 Alpha Pl PO Box 16429 .... Bristol VA 24209	**866-322-5742**	276-619-4410	496
OTC: ANR			
Alpha Omega International Dental Fraternity			
50 W Edmonston Dr .... Rockville MD 20852	**877-368-6326**	301-738-6400	47-16
Alpha Omicron Pi International			
5390 Virginia Way .... Brentwood TN 37027	**855-230-1183**	615-370-0920	47-16
Alpha Packaging			
1555 Page Industrial Blvd .... Saint Louis MO 63132	**800-421-4772**	314-427-4300	97
Alpha Pro Tech Ltd			
60 Centurian Dr Ste 112 .... Markham ON L3R9R2	**800-749-1363**	905-479-0654	228
Alpha Sigma Phi National Fraternity			
710 Adams St .... Carmel IN 46032	**866-515-4747**	317-843-1911	47-16
Alpha Tau Omega Fraternity (ATO)			
One N Pennsylvania St			
12th Fl .... Indianapolis IN 46204	**800-798-9286**	317-684-1865	47-16
Alpha Technologies Services LLC			
3030 Gilchrist Rd .... Akron OH 44305	**800-356-9886**	330-745-1641	202
Alpha Wire Co			
711 Lidgerwood Ave .... Elizabeth NJ 07207	**800-522-5742**	908-925-8000	801
AlphaGary Corp			
170 Pioneer Dr .... Leominster MA 01453	**800-232-9741**	978-537-8071	598-2
AlphaGraphics Inc			
215 S State St Ste 320 .... Salt Lake City UT 84111	**800-955-6246**	801-595-7270	619
Alphanumeric Systems Inc			
3801 Wake Forest Rd .... Raleigh NC 27609	**800-638-6556**	919-781-7575	112
AlphaStaff Inc			
800 Corporate Dr			
Ste 600 .... Fort Lauderdale FL 33334	**888-335-9545**	954-267-1760	623
Alphin Bros Inc			
2302 US 301 S .... Dunn NC 28334	**800-672-4502**	910-892-8751	295-36
Alpine Access Inc			
1120 Lincoln St Ste 1400 .... Denver CO 80203	**866-279-0585***	303-279-0585	194
*General			
Alpine Adventure Trails Tours Inc			
7495 Lower Thomaston Rd .... Macon GA 31220	**888-478-4004**		750
Alpine Bank of Colorado			
2200 Grand Ave .... Glenwood Springs CO 81601	**888-425-7463**	970-945-2424	357-2
Alpine Electronics of America			
19145 Gramercy Pl .... Torrance CA 90501	**800-257-4631**	310-326-8000	51
Alpine Engineered Products Inc			
1100 Pk Central Blvd S			
PO Box 2225. .... Pompano Beach FL 33064	**800-786-6086***	954-781-3333	804
*General			
Alpine Fresh Inc			
9300 NW 58th St Ste 201 .... Miami FL 33178	**800-292-8777**	305-594-9117	296-7
Alpine Helen/White County Convention & Visitors Bureau			
726 Bruckenstrasse PO Box 730. .... Helen GA 30545	**800-858-8027**	706-878-2181	207
Alpine Innovations			
275 North 950 East .... Lehi UT 84043	**866-489-6788**	801-766-4994	195
Alpine Lumber Co			
1120 W 122nd Ave Ste 301 .... Denver CO 80234	**800-499-1634**	303-451-8001	192-3
Alpine Meadows Ski Resort			
2600 Alpine Meadows Rd .... Tahoe City CA 96145	**800-403-0206**		660
Alpine Meats			
9850 Lowr Sacramento Rd .... Stockton CA 95210	**800-399-6328**	209-477-2691	468
Alpine Power Systems Inc			
24355 Capitol .... Redford MI 48239	**877-769-3762**	313-531-6600	749
Alro Steel Corp			
3100 E High St .... Jackson MI 49204	**800-877-2576**	517-787-5500	487
ALS (Albany Law School of Union University)			
80 New Scotland Ave .... Albany NY 12208	**800-448-3500**	518-445-2311	167-1
ALS (American Littoral Society)			
18 Hartshorne Dr Ste 1 .... Highlands NJ 07732	**800-424-8802**	732-291-0055	47-13
ALSAC (American Lebanese Syrian Associated Charities)			
501 St Jude Pl .... Memphis TN 38105	**800-822-6344**	901-578-2000	47-5
Alsay Inc			
6615 Gant St .... Houston TX 77066	**800-833-5969**	281-444-6960	190-15
ALSC (Association for Library Service to Children)			
50 E Huron St .... Chicago IL 60611	**800-545-2433**	312-280-2163	48-11
Alsea Bay Historic Interpretive Ctr			
725 Summer St NE Ste C .... Salem OR 97301	**800-551-6949**		558
ALTA (American Land Title Assn)			
1828 L St NW Ste 705 .... Washington DC 20036	**800-787-2582**	202-296-3671	48-10
Alta California			
N8350 High Road .... Watertown WI 53094	**800-932-2855**	920-261-5065	11-2
Alta Dena Dairy			
17851 E Railrd .... City of Industry CA 91748	**800-535-1369***		295-27
*Orders			
Alta Lodge PO Box 8040 .... Alta UT 84092	**800-707-2582***	801-742-3500	660
*Cust Svc			
Alta Resources			
120 N Commercial St .... Neenah WI 54956	**877-464-2582**		727
Alta Via Consulting LLC			
127 ConKinnon Dr .... Lenoir City TN 37772	**877-258-2842**		178
ALTAFF (Association for Library Trustees, Advocates, Friends & Foundations)			
50 E Huron St .... Chicago IL 60611	**800-545-2433**		48-11
Altair Customer Intelligence			
341 Cool Springs Blvd Ste 450 .... Franklin TN 37067	**800-241-6631**	615-468-6938	195
Altair Engineering Inc			
1820 E Big Beaver Rd .... Troy MI 48083	**888-222-7822**	248-614-2400	195
Altamaha Electric Membership Corp			
611 W Liberty Ave PO Box 346. .... Lyons GA 30436	**800-822-4563**	912-526-8181	245
Altamed Health Services Corp			
500 Citadel Dr Ste 490 .... Los Angeles CA 90040	**877-462-2582**	323-725-8751	360
Altametrics Inc			
3191 Red Hill Ave Ste 100 .... Costa Mesa CA 92626	**800-676-1281**		175
Altamont Commuter Express (ACE)			
949 E Ch St .... Stockton CA 95202	**800-411-7245**		463
Altech LLC			
242 America Pl .... Jeffersonville IN 47130	**800-264-8256**	812-282-8256	480
Altech Services Inc			
1160 Parsippany Blvd Ste 202 .... Parsippany NJ 07054	**888-725-8324**		178
Alter Group			
5500 W Howard St .... Skokie IL 60077	**800-637-4842**	847-676-4300	644

Name / Address	Toll-Free	Phone	Class
Alter Trading Corp			
700 Office Pkwy .... Saint Louis MO 63141	**888-337-2727**	314-872-2400	677
Altera Corp			
101 Innovation Dr .... San Jose CA 95134	**800-767-3753***	408-544-7000	687
NASDAQ: ALTR ▣ *Cust Svc*			
Altera Payroll Inc			
2400 Northside Crossing .... Macon GA 31210	**877-474-6060**	478-477-6060	2
Althoff Industries Inc			
8001 S Rt 31 .... Crystal Lake IL 60014	**800-225-2443**	815-455-7000	190-10
AltiGen Communications Inc			
410 E Plumeria Dr .... San Jose CA 95134	**888-258-4436**	408-597-9000	725
OTC: ATGN			
Altimate Medical Inc			
262 W First St .... Morton MN 56270	**800-342-8968**	507-697-6393	471
Altium Inc			
3207 Grey Hawk Ct Ste 100 .... Carlsbad CA 92010	**800-544-4186***	760-231-0760	179-5
*Sales			
Altius Health Plans			
10421 S Jordan Gateway			
Ste 400 .... South Jordan UT 84095	**800-365-1334**	801-355-1234	388-3
Altman Lighting Inc			
57 Alexander St .... Yonkers NY 10701	**800-425-8626**	914-476-7987	435
Altman Specialty Plants Inc			
3742 Blue Bird Canyon Rd .... Vista CA 92084	**800-773-7667**	760-744-8191	366
Altman Weil Inc			
PO Box 625 .... Newtown Square PA 19073	**866-886-3600**	610-359-9900	195
Altmeyer Home Stores Inc			
6515 Rt 22 .... Delmont PA 15626	**800-394-6628**	724-468-3434	359
Alton National Cemetery			
600 Pearl St .... Alton IL 62003	**800-535-1117**	314-845-8320	135
Alton Regional Convention & Visitors Bureau (ARCVB)			
200 Piasa St .... Alton IL 62002	**800-258-6645**	618-465-6676	207
Altoona Mirror			
301 Cayuga Ave .... Altoona PA 16602	**800-222-1962**	814-946-7411	525-2
Altoona Regional Health System Altoona Hospital			
620 Howard Ave .... Altoona PA 16601	**877-855-8152**	814-889-2011	371-3
Altoona VA Medical Ctr			
2907 Pleasant Vly Blvd .... Altoona PA 16602	**877-626-2500**		371-8
Altoros Systems			
830 Stewart Dr Ste 119 .... Sunnyvale CA 94085	**855-258-6767**	650-395-7002	195
Alto-Shaam Inc			
W 164 N 9221 Water St			
PO Box 450 .... Menomonee Falls WI 53052	**800-329-8744**	262-251-3800	297
Altran Solutions USA			
2525 Rt 130 S .... Cranbury NJ 08512	**855-425-8726**	609-409-9790	732
Altrec.com Inc			
725 SW Umatilla Ave .... Redmond OR 97756	**800-369-3949**	541-316-2400	702
ALTRES Inc			
967 Kapiolani Blvd .... Honolulu HI 96814	**888-425-8737**	808-591-4940	712
Altru Hospital			
1200 S Columbia Rd .... Grand Forks ND 58201	**800-732-4277**	701-780-5000	371-3
Aluchem Inc			
One Landy Ln .... Cincinnati OH 45215	**800-336-8519**	513-733-8519	482
Alumaweld Boats Inc			
1601 Ave F .... White City OR 97503	**800-401-2628**	541-826-7171	89
Alumicor Ltd			
290 Humberline Dr .... Toronto ON M9W5S2	**877-258-6426**	416-745-4222	476
Aluminum & Stainless Inc			
PO Box 3484 .... Lafayette LA 70502	**800-252-9074**	337-837-4381	487
Aluminum Extruders Council (AEC)			
1000 N Rand Rd Ste 214 .... Wauconda IL 60084	**800-354-5892**	847-526-2010	48-13
Aluminum Ladder Co			
1430 W Darlington St .... Florence SC 29501	**800-752-2526**	843-662-2595	482
Aluminum Line Products Co			
24460 Sperry Cir .... Westlake OH 44145	**800-321-3154**	440-835-8880	688
Aluminum Precision Products Inc			
3333 W Warner St .... Santa Ana CA 92704	**800-411-8983**	714-546-8125	478
Alutiiq LLC			
3909 Arctic Blvd Ste 400 .... Anchorage AK 99503	**800-829-8547**	907-222-9500	357-3
Alva-Amco Pharmacal Cos Inc			
7711 Merrimac Ave .... Niles IL 60714	**800-792-2582**	847-663-0700	576
Alvah Bushnell Co			
519 E Chelten Ave .... Philadelphia PA 19144	**800-255-7434**	215-842-9520	553
Alvarado Mfg Company Inc			
12660 Colony St .... Chino CA 91710	**800-423-4143**	909-591-8431	486
Alvernia College			
540 Upland Ave .... Reading PA 19611	**888-258-3764**	610-796-8200	166
Alverno College			
PO Box 343922 .... Milwaukee WI 53234	**800-933-3401**	414-382-6100	166
Alvin & Company Inc			
1335 Blue Hills Ave .... Bloomfield CT 06002	**800-444-2584**	860-243-8991	42
Alvin C York Medical Ctr			
3400 Lebanon Pike .... Murfreesboro TN 37129	**800-228-4973**	615-867-6000	371-8
Alvin Hollis & Co			
One Hollis St .... South Weymouth MA 02190	**800-649-5090**	781-335-2100	315
Alvin-Manvel Area Chamber of Commerce			
105 W Willis St .... Alvin TX 77511	**888-755-6864**	281-331-3944	137
Alyeska Prince Hotel & Resort			
1000 Arlberg Ave PO Box 249 .... Girdwood AK 99587	**800-880-3880**	907-754-1111	660
Alzheimer's Assn			
225 N Michigan Ave Ste 1700 .... Chicago IL 60601	**800-272-3900**	312-335-8700	47-17
Alzheimer's Disease Education & Referral Ctr			
PO Box 8250 .... Silver Spring MD 20907	**800-438-4380**	301-495-1080	198
AM 570 LA Sports			
3400 W Olive Ave Ste 550 .... Burbank CA 91505	**866-987-2570**	818-559-2252	636
AM Best Co .... Ambest Rd .... Oldwick NJ 08858	**800-424-2378**	908-439-2200	628-10
AM Kinney			
150 E Fourth St Ste 6 .... Cincinnati OH 45202	**800-265-3682**	513-421-2265	261
A&M Supply Corp			
6701 90th Ave N .... Pinellas Park FL 33782	**800-877-8551**	727-541-6631	807
AMA (American Marketing Assn)			
311 S Wacker Dr Ste 5800 .... Chicago IL 60606	**800-262-1150**	312-542-9000	48-18
AMA (American Medical Assn)			
515 N State St .... Chicago IL 60610	**800-621-8335**	312-464-5000	48-8
AMA (Academy of Model Aeronautics)			
5161 E Memorial Dr .... Muncie IN 47302	**800-435-9262**	765-287-1256	47-18
AMACO (American Art Clay Co)			
6060 Guion Rd .... Indianapolis IN 46254	**800-374-1600**	317-244-6871	42
Amada America Inc			
7025 Firestone Blvd .... Buena Park CA 90621	**800-626-6612**	714-739-2111	451
Amadeus North America Inc			
3470 NW 82nd Ave Ste 1000 .... Miami FL 33122	**888-262-3387**	305-499-6000	333
Amador County Chamber of Commerce			
115 Main St PO Box 596 .... Jackson CA 95642	**800-822-9466***	209-223-0350	137
*General			
AMAG Technology Inc			
20701 Manhattan Pl .... Torrance CA 90501	**800-889-9138**	310-518-2380	683
Amalgamated Bank of New York			
275 Seventh Ave .... New York NY 10001	**800-662-0860**		69
Amalgamated Transit Union (ATU)			
5025 Wisconsin Ave NW			
Third Fl .... Washington DC 20016	**888-240-1196**	202-537-1645	411
Amana Appliances Inc			
2800 220th Trl .... Amana IA 52204	**800-843-0304***	319-622-5511	15
*Cust Svc			
Amana Colonies			
622 46th Ave .... Amana IA 52203	**800-579-2294**	319-622-7622	10-3
Amana Colonies Convention & Visitors Bureau			
622 46th Ave .... Amana IA 52203	**800-579-2294**	319-622-7622	207
Amangani Resort			
1535 NE Butte Rd .... Jackson WY 83001	**877-734-7333**	307-734-7333	660
Amano Cincinnati Inc			
140 Harrison Ave .... Roseland NJ 07068	**800-526-2559**	973-403-1900	110
Amarillo Convention & Visitor Council			
1000 S Polk St PO Box 9480 .... Amarillo TX 79105	**800-692-1338**	806-374-1497	207
Amarillo National Bank			
410 S Taylor St Plaza 1 .... Amarillo TX 79101	**800-253-1031**	806-378-8000	69
Amarillo Wind Machine Co			
20513 Ave 256 .... Exeter CA 93221	**800-311-4498**	559-592-4256	273
Amateur Athletic Union of the US (AAU)			
1910 Hotel Plaza Blvd .... Lake Buena Vista FL 32830	**800-228-4872**	407-934-7200	47-22
Amateur Softball Assn of America Inc (ASA)			
2801 NE 50th St .... Oklahoma City OK 73111	**800-654-8337**	405-424-5266	47-22
Amateur Trapshooting Assn (ATA)			
601 W National Rd .... Vandalia OH 45377	**800-671-8042**	937-898-4638	47-22
Amatex Corp			
1032 Stambridge St .... Norristown PA 19404	**800-441-9680**	610-277-6100	734-3
Amatom Electronic Hardware LLC			
Five Pasco Hill Rd .... Cromwell CT 06416	**800-243-6032**	860-828-0847	482
AmaWaterways			
26010 Mureau Rd .... Calabasas CA 91302	**800-626-0126**		750
Amax Engineering Corp			
1565 Reliance Way .... Fremont CA 94539	**800-889-2629***	510-651-8886	174-1
*Cust Svc			
Amax Nutrasource Inc			
14291 E Don Julian Rd .... City Of Industry CA 91746	**800-893-5306**	626-961-6600	342
Amazing Recycled Products Inc			
PO Box 312 .... Denver CO 80201	**800-241-2174**	303-699-7693	652
Amazon.com Inc			
1200 12th Ave S Ste 1200 .... Seattle WA 98144	**800-201-7575***	206-266-1000	95
NASDAQ: AMZN ▣ *Cust Svc*			
AMB Financial Corp			
8230 Hohman Ave .... Munster IN 46321	**800-436-5113**	219-836-5870	357-2
OTC: AMFC			
AMBAC Assurance Corp			
1 State St Plaza 15th Fl .... New York NY 10004	**800-221-1854**	212-658-7470	388-5
AMBAC Financial Group Inc			
One State St Plz 15th Fl .... New York NY 10004	**800-221-1854**	212-668-0340	357-4
OTC: ABKFQ			
AMBAC International Inc			
910 Spears Creek Ct .... Elgin SC 29045	**800-628-6894**	803-735-1400	59
Ambassador Hotel			
535 Tchoupitoulas St .... New Orleans LA 70130	**800-455-3417**	504-527-5271	376
Ambassadors Group Inc			
110 S Ferrall St .... Spokane WA 99202	**800-652-8683**	509-534-6200	750
NASDAQ: EPAX			
Amber Lotus Publishing			
PO Box 11329 .... Portland OR 97211	**800-326-2375**	503-284-6400	129
AMBEST Inc			
5115 Maryland Way .... Brentwood TN 37027	**800-910-7220**	615-371-5187	323
Ambion Inc			
2130 Woodward St .... Austin TX 78744	**866-952-3559**	512-651-0200	231
Amboy Bancorp			
3590 US Hwy 9 S .... Old Bridge NJ 08857	**800-942-6269**	732-591-8700	357-2
Amboy National Bank			
3590 US Hwy 9 S .... Old Bridge NJ 08857	**800-942-6269**	732-591-8700	69
Ambriola Company Inc			
Seven Patton Dr .... West Caldwell NJ 07006	**800-962-8224**		296-4
Ambrosia House Tropical Lodging			
622 Fleming St .... Key West FL 33040	**800-535-9838**	305-296-9838	376
AMBUCS (National AMBUCS Inc)			
4285 Regency Ct PO Box 5127 .... High Point NC 27265	**800-838-1845**	336-852-0052	47-5
AMC (Augusta Medical Ctr)			
78 Medical Ctr Dr			
PO Box 1000 .... Fishersville VA 22939	**800-932-0262**	540-932-4000	371-3
AMC (Appalachian Mountain Club)			
Five Joy St .... Boston MA 02108	**800-262-4455***	617-523-0655	47-13
*Orders			
AMC Entertainment Inc			
920 Main St .... Kansas City MO 64105	**877-341-6397**	816-221-4000	737
AMC Star Theatres			
25333 W 12-Mile Rd .... Southfield MI 48034	**888-262-4386**	248-368-1802	737
AMC Theatres			
920 Main St .... Kansas City MO 64105	**877-341-6397**	816-221-4000	737
AMCOL International Corp			
2870 Forbs Ave .... Hoffman Estates IL 60192	**800-962-8586***	847-851-1500	498-2
NYSE: ACO ▣ *General*			
Amcom Software Inc			
10400 Yellow Cir Dr .... Eden Prairie MN 55343	**800-852-8935**	952-230-5200	179-7
AMCON Distributing Co			
7405 Irvington Rd .... Omaha NE 68122	**888-201-5997**	402-331-3727	746
NYSE: DIT			
AMCP (Academy of Managed Care Pharmacy)			
100 N Pitt St Ste 400 .... Alexandria VA 22314	**800-827-2627**	703-683-8416	48-8
AMD (Advanced Micro Devices Inc)			
One AMD Pl PO Box 3453 .... Sunnyvale CA 94088	**800-538-8450**	408-749-4000	687
NYSE: AMD			
AMD Industries Inc			
4620 W 19th St .... Cicero IL 60804	**800-367-9999**	708-863-8900	233
AMDA (American Medical Directors Assn)			
11000 Broken Land Pkwy Ste 400 .... Columbia MD 21044	**800-876-2632**	410-740-9743	48-8
Amdocs Ltd			
1390 Timberlake			
Manor Pkwy .... Chesterfield MO 63017	**866-426-8003**	314-212-7000	179-10
NYSE: DOX			

Name / Address	City	State	ZIP	Toll-Free	Phone	Class
AME Inc						
2467 Coltharp Rd	Fort Mill	SC	29715	800-849-7766	803-548-7766	189-6
AME Label Corp						
25155 W Ave Stanford	Valencia	CA	91355	866-278-9268	661-257-2200	410
Amedisys Hospice						
1423 W Morris Blvd Ste C	Morristown	TN	37813	800-659-2633	423-587-9484	368
Amedisys Inc						
5959 S Sherwood Forest Blvd						
Ste 300	Baton Rouge	LA	70816	800-464-0020	225-292-2031	349
NASDAQ: AMED						
Amegy Bank of Texas						
4400 Post Oak Pkwy	Houston	TX	77027	800-287-0301	713-235-8800	69
Amelia Island Plantation						
39 Beach Lagoon Rd	Amelia Island	FL	32034	800-834-4900	904-261-6161	660
AmerCable Inc						
350 Bailey Rd	El Dorado	AR	71730	800-643-1516	870-862-4919	800
Amerco Real Estate Co						
2727 N Central Ave Ste 500	Phoenix	AZ	85004	800-528-0463*	602-263-6555	644
*General						
Ameren Corp						
1901 Chouteau Ave	Saint Louis	MO	63103	800-552-7583	314-621-3222	357-5
NYSE: AEE						
Ameresco Canada Inc						
90 Sheppard Ave E 7th Fl	North York	ON	M2N6X3	877-358-3853	416-512-7700	461
Ameresco Inc						
111 Speen St Ste 410	Framingham	MA	01701	866-263-7372	508-661-2200	193
Ameriana Bancorp						
2118 Bundy Ave PO Box H	New Castle	IN	47362	866-844-7584	765-529-2230	357-2
NASDAQ: ASBI						
America First Credit Union						
1344 West 4675 South	Ogden	UT	84405	800-999-3961	801-627-0900	219
America II Electronics Inc						
2600 118th Ave N	Saint Petersburg	FL	33716	800-767-2637	727-573-0900	246
America Outdoors						
5816 Kingston Pk	Knoxville	TN	37919	800-524-4814	865-558-3595	47-23
America's Best Franchising Inc						
America's Best Inns & Suites						
50 Glen Lake Pkwy NE Ste 350	Atlanta	GA	30328	800-237-8466	770-393-2662	376
America's Blood Centers (ABC)						
725 15th St NW Ste 700	Washington	DC	20005	888-872-5663	202-393-5725	48-8
America's Community Bankers (ACB)						
1120 Connecticut Ave NW	Washington	DC	20036	800-226-5377		48-2
America's Health Insurance Plans (AHIP)						
601 Pennsylvania Ave NW						
Ste 500	Washington	DC	20004	877-291-2247*	202-778-3200	48-9
*Cust Svc						
America's Second Harvest						
35 E Wacker Dr Ste 2000	Chicago	IL	60601	800-771-2303	312-263-2303	47-5
American Academy McAllister Institute of Funeral Service						
619 W 54th St 2nd Fl	New York	NY	10019	866-932-2264	212-757-1190	788
American Academy of Actuaries						
1100 17th St NW 7th Fl	Washington	DC	20036	888-888-1778	202-223-8196	48-9
American Academy of Allergy Asthma & Immunology (AAAAI)						
555 E Wells St Ste 1100	Milwaukee	WI	53202	800-654-2452	414-272-6071	48-8
American Academy of Art						
332 S Michigan Ave 3rd Fl	Chicago	IL	60604	888-461-0600	312-461-0600	162
American Academy of Arts & Sciences						
136 Irving St	Cambridge	MA	02138	800-666-2211	617-576-5000	47-4
American Academy of Audiology (AAA)						
11730 Plz America Dr Ste 300	Reston	VA	20190	800-222-2336	703-790-8466	48-8
American Academy of Child & Adolescent Psychiatry (AACAP)						
3615 Wisconsin Ave NW	Washington	DC	20016	800-333-7636	202-966-7300	48-15
American Academy of Cosmetic Dentistry (AACD)						
402 W Wilson St	Madison	WI	53703	800-543-9220	608-222-8583	48-8
American Academy of Dermatology (AAD)						
930 E Woodfield Rd	Schaumburg	IL	60173	800-868-2472	847-330-0230	48-8
American Academy of Disability Evaluating Physicians (AADEP)						
223 W Jackson Blvd Ste 1104	Chicago	IL	60606	800-456-6095	312-663-1171	48-8
American Academy of Dramatic Arts						
120 Madison Ave	New York	NY	10016	800-463-8990	212-686-9244	162
American Academy of Family Physicians (AAFP)						
11400 Tomahawk Creek Pkwy	Leawood	KS	66211	800-274-2237	913-906-6000	48-8
American Academy of Neurology (AAN)						
1080 Montreal Ave	Saint Paul	MN	55116	800-879-1960	651-695-1940	48-8
American Academy of Ophthalmology						
655 Beach St	San Francisco	CA	94109	866-561-8558	415-561-8500	48-8
American Academy of Ophthalmology PAC						
Governmental Affairs Div						
20 F St NW Ste 400	Washington	DC	20001	866-561-8558	202-737-6662	608
American Academy of Optometry (AAO)						
6110 Executive Blvd Ste 506	Rockville	MD	20852	800-368-6263	301-984-1441	48-8
American Academy of Orthopaedic Surgeons (AAOS)						
6300 N River Rd	Rosemont	IL	60018	800-346-2267	847-823-7186	48-8
American Academy of Orthotists & Prosthetists (AAOP)						
526 King St Ste 201	Alexandria	VA	22314	800-669-6024	703-836-0788	48-8
American Academy of Otolaryngology-Head & Neck Surgery (AAO-HNS)						
1650 Diagonal Rd	Alexandria	VA	22314	877-722-6467	703-836-4444	48-8
American Academy of Pain Management (AAPM)						
13947 Mono Way Ste A	Sonora	CA	95370	888-519-9901	209-533-9744	48-8
American Academy of Pediatric Dentistry (AAPD)						
211 E Chicago Ave Ste 1700	Chicago	IL	60611	800-974-3084	312-337-2169	48-8
American Academy of Pediatrics (AAP)						
141 NW Pt Blvd	Elk Grove Village	IL	60007	800-433-9016	847-434-4000	48-8
American Academy of Periodontology (AAP)						
737 N Michigan Ave Ste 800	Chicago	IL	60611	800-282-4867	312-787-5518	48-8
American Academy of Psychiatry & the Law (AAPL)						
One Regency Dr PO Box 30	Bloomfield	CT	06002	800-331-1389	860-242-5450	48-15
American Academy of Religion (AAR)						
825 Houston Mill Rd NE Ste 300	Atlanta	GA	30329	800-282-6632	404-727-3049	47-20
American Accounts & Advisors						
PO Box 250	Cottage Grove	MN	55016	866-714-0489	651-287-6100	158
American Achievement Corp						
7211 Cir S Rd	Austin	TX	78745	800-531-5055	512-444-0571	406
American Adv Federation (AAF)						
1101 Vermont Ave NW Ste 500	Washington	DC	20005	800-999-2231	202-898-0089	48-18
American Aerospace Controls Inc						
570 Smith St	Farmingdale	NY	11735	888-873-8559	631-694-5100	256
American AgCredit (ACA)						
PO Box 1120	Santa Rosa	CA	95402	800-800-4865	707-545-1200	216
American Agriculturist						
5227-B Baltimore Pike	Littlestown	PA	17340	800-441-1410	717-359-0150	452-1
American Air Charter Inc						
577 Bell Ave	Chesterfield	MO	63005	888-532-2710	636-532-2707	13
American Airlines CR Smith Museum						
4601 Hwy 360 at FAA Rd	Fort Worth	TX	76155	877-277-6484	817-967-1560	513
American Airlines Ctr						
2500 Victory Ave	Dallas	TX	75219	800-745-3000	214-222-3687	711
American Airlines Employees Federal Credit Union						
4151 Amon Carter Blvd						
PO Box 155489	Fort Worth	TX	76155	800-533-0035	817-952-4500	219
American Airlines Inc						
4333 Amon Carter Blvd	Fort Worth	TX	76155	800-433-7300	817-963-1234	25
American Alliance for Health Physical Education Recreation & Dance (AAH-PERD)						
1900 Assn Dr	Reston	VA	20191	800-213-7193	703-476-3400	47-22
American Amateur Baseball Congress (AABC)						
100 W Broadway	Farmington	NM	87401	800-853-2414	505-327-3120	47-22
American Ambulance Assn (AAA)						
8201 Greensboro Dr Ste 300	McLean	VA	22102	800-523-4447	703-610-9018	48-21
American Amicable Life Insurance Co						
PO Box 2549	Waco	TX	76702	800-736-7311	254-297-2777	388-2
American Amusement Machine Assn (AAMA)						
450 E Higgins Rd						
Ste 201	Elk Grove Village	IL	60007	866-372-5190	847-290-9088	47-23
American Angus Assn (AAA)						
3201 Frederick Ave	Saint Joseph	MO	64506	800-821-5478	816-383-5100	47-2
American Animal Hospital Assn (AAHA)						
12575 W Bayaud Ave	Lakewood	CO	80228	800-252-2242	303-986-2800	47-3
American Anti-Slavery Group, The						
198 Tremont St	Boston	MA	02116	800-884-0719	617-426-8161	47-5
American Apparel & Footwear Assn (AAFA)						
1601 N Kent St Ste 1200	Arlington	VA	22209	800-520-2262	703-524-1864	48-4
American Apparel & Footwear Assn PAC						
1601 N Kent St Ste 1200	Arlington	VA	22209	800-520-2262	703-524-1864	608
American Apparel LLC						
747 Warehouse St	Los Angeles	CA	90021	888-747-0070	213-488-0226	153-11
American Arbitration Assn Inc (AAA)						
1633 Broadway 10th Fl	New York	NY	10019	800-778-7879	212-716-5800	40
American Arium						
14811 Myford Rd	Tustin	CA	92780	877-508-3970	714-731-1661	687
American Art Clay Co (AMACO)						
6060 Guion Rd	Indianapolis	IN	46254	800-374-1600	317-244-6871	42
American Assn for Accreditation of Ambulatory Surgery Facilities Inc (AAAASF)						
5101 Washington St Ste 2F						
PO Box 9500	Gurnee	IL	60031	888-545-5222	847-775-1985	47-1
American Assn for Cancer Research (AACR)						
615 Chestnut St 17th Fl	Philadelphia	PA	19106	866-423-3965	215-440-9300	48-8
American Assn for Clinical Chemistry Inc (AACC)						
1850 K St NW Ste 625	Washington	DC	20006	800-892-1400*	202-857-0717	48-19
*Cust Svc						
American Assn for Justice (AAJ)						
777 Sixth St NW Ste 200	Washington	DC	20001	800-424-2725	202-965-3500	48-10
American Assn for Laboratory Accreditation (A2LA)						
5301 Buckeystown Pike Ste 350	Frederick	MD	21704	888-627-8318	301-644-3248	48-19
American Assn for Physical Activity & Recreation (AAPAR)						
1900 Assn Dr	Reston	VA	20191	800-213-7193	703-476-3400	47-23
American Assn for the Advancement of Science (AAAS)						
1200 New York Ave NW	Washington	DC	20005	800-669-6820	202-326-6400	48-19
American Assn for Thoracic Surgery (AATS)						
900 Cummings Ctr Ste 221-U	Beverly	MA	01915	800-424-5249	978-927-8330	48-8
American Assn of Acupuncture & Oriental Medicine (AAAOM)						
PO Box 162340	Sacramento	CA	95816	866-455-7999	916-443-4770	47-17
American Assn of Airport Executives (AAAE)						
601 Madison St Ste 400	Alexandria	VA	22314	800-609-7374	703-824-0500	48-21
American Assn of Bioanalysts (AAB)						
906 Olive St Ste 1200	Saint Louis	MO	63101	800-457-3332	314-241-1445	48-8
American Assn of Bovine Practitioners (AABP)						
3320 Skyway Dr Ste 802						
PO Box 3610	Auburn	AL	36831	800-269-2227	334-821-0442	47-2
American Assn of Clinical Endocrinologists (AACE)						
245 Riverside Ave Ste 2000	Jacksonville	FL	32202	800-435-7352	904-353-7878	48-8
American Assn of Colleges of Osteopathic Medicine (AACOM)						
5550 Friendship Blvd						
Ste 310	Chevy Chase	MD	20815	800-356-7836	301-968-4100	48-8
American Assn of Colleges of Podiatric Medicine (AACPM)						
15850 Crabbs Branch Way						
Ste 320	Rockville	MD	20855	800-922-9266	301-948-9760	48-8
American Assn of Collegiate Registrars & Admissions Officers (AACRAO)						
1 Dupont Cir NW Ste 520	Washington	DC	20036	800-222-4922	202-293-9161	48-5
American Assn of Critical-Care Nurses (AACN)						
101 Columbia	Aliso Viejo	CA	92656	800-809-2273	949-362-2000	48-8
American Assn of Daily Money Managers (AADMM)						
174 Crestview Dr	Bellefonte	PA	16823	877-326-5991		48-2
American Assn of Drugless Practitioners (AADP)						
2200 Market St Ste 803	Galveston	TX	77550	888-764-2237	409-621-2600	47-17
American Assn of Endodontists (AAE)						
211 E Chicago Ave Ste 1100	Chicago	IL	60611	800-872-3636	312-266-7255	48-8
American Assn of Engineering Societies (AAES)						
1620 'I' St NW Ste 210	Washington	DC	20006	888-400-2237*	202-296-2237	48-19
*Orders						
American Assn of Equine Practitioners (AAEP)						
4075 Iron Works Pkwy	Lexington	KY	40511	800-443-0177	859-233-0147	47-3
American Assn of Family & Consumer Sciences (AAFCS)						
400 N Columbus St Ste 202	Alexandria	VA	22314	800-424-8080	703-706-4600	48-5
American Assn of Franchisees & Dealers (AAFD)						
PO Box 10158	Palm Desert	CA	92255	800-733-9858	619-209-3775	48-18
American Assn of Gynecological Laparoscopists (AAGL)						
6757 Katella Ave	Cypress	CA	90630	800-554-2245	714-503-6200	48-8
American Assn of Immunologists (AAI)						
9650 Rockville Pike	Bethesda	MD	20814	888-503-1050	301-634-7178	48-8
American Assn of Individual Investors (AAII)						
625 N Michigan Ave Ste 1900	Chicago	IL	60611	800-428-2244	312-280-0170	48-2
American Assn of Insurance Services (AAIS)						
1745 S Naperville Rd	Wheaton	IL	60189	800-564-2247	630-681-8347	48-9
American Assn of Managing General Agents (AAMGA)						
150 S Warner Rd Ste 156	King of Prussia	PA	19406	800-467-8725	610-225-1999	48-9
American Assn of Medical Assistants (AAMA)						
20 N Wacker Dr Ste 1575	Chicago	IL	60606	800-228-2262	312-899-1500	48-8
American Assn of Medical Review Officers (AAMRO)						
PO Box 12873	Research Triangle Park	NC	27709	800-489-1839	919-489-5407	48-8
American Assn of Museums (AAM)						
1575 Eye St NW Ste 400	Washington	DC	20005	866-226-2150	202-289-1818	47-4
American Assn of Naturopathic Physicians (AANP)						
4435 Wisconsin Ave NW						
Ste 403	Washington	DC	20016	866-538-2267	202-237-8150	47-17
American Assn of Neurological Surgeons (AANS)						
5550 Meadowbrook Dr	Rolling Meadows	IL	60008	888-566-2267	847-378-0500	48-8

Listing	Toll-Free	Phone	Class
American Assn of Neuromuscular & Electrodiagnostic Medicine (AANEM)			
2621 Superior Dr NW .... Rochester MN 55901	844-347-3277	507-288-0100	48-8
American Assn of Neuroscience Nurses (AANN)			
4700 W Lk Ave .... Glenview IL 60025	888-557-2266	847-375-4733	48-8
American Assn of Nurse Anesthetists PAC (AANAPAC)			
222 S Prospect Ave .... Park Ridge IL 60068	855-526-2262	847-692-2051	608
American Assn of Oral & Maxillofacial Surgeons (AAOMS)			
9700 W Bryn Mawr Ave .... Rosemont IL 60018	800-822-6637	847-678-6200	48-8
American Assn of Orthodontists (AAO)			
401 N Lindbergh Blvd .... Saint Louis MO 63141	800-522-1899	314-993-1700	48-8
American Assn of Orthodontists PAC			
401 N Lindbergh Blvd .... Saint Louis MO 63141	800-424-2841	314-993-1700	608
American Assn of Petroleum Geologists (AAPG)			
1444 S Boulder Ave PO Box 979 .... Tulsa OK 74119	800-364-2274	918-584-2555	47-12
American Assn of Pharmaceutical Scientists (AAPS)			
2107 Wilson Blvd Ste 700 .... Arlington VA 22201	877-998-2277	703-243-2800	48-19
American Assn of Poison Control Centers (AAPCC)			
3201 New Mexico Ave			
Suite 310 .... Washington DC 20016	800-222-1222		48-8
American Assn of School Administrators (AASA)			
801 N Quincy St Ste 700 .... Arlington VA 22203	800-771-1162	703-528-0700	48-5
American Assn of School Librarians (AASL)			
50 E Huron St .... Chicago IL 60611	800-545-2433	312-280-4386	48-11
American Assn of State Colleges & Universities (AASCU)			
1307 New York Ave NW			
Fifth Fl .... Washington DC 20005	800-558-3417	202-293-7070	48-5
American Assn of State Highway & Transportation Officials (AASHTO)			
444 N Capitol St NW Ste 249 .... Washington DC 20001	800-880-4117	202-624-5800	48-7
American Assn of Teachers of German (AATG)			
112 Haddontowne Ct Ste 104 .... Cherry Hill NJ 08034	800-835-6770	856-795-5553	48-5
American Assn of Teachers of Spanish & Portuguese (AATSP)			
900 Ladd Rd .... Walled Lake MI 48390	877-832-2457	248-960-2180	48-5
American Assn of Tissue Banks (AATB)			
1320 Old Chain Bridge Rd Ste 450 .... McLean VA 22101	800-635-2282	703-827-9582	48-8
American Assn of University Professors (AAUP)			
1133 Nineteenth St Ste 200 .... Washington DC 20036	800-424-2973	202-737-5900	48-5
American Assn of University Women (AAUW)			
1111 16th St NW .... Washington DC 20036	800-326-2289	202-785-7700	48-5
American Assn of Variable Star Observers (AAVSO)			
49 Bay State Rd .... Cambridge MA 02138	888-802-7827	617-354-0484	48-19
American Assn on Intellectual & Developmental Disabilities (AAIDD)			
444 N Capitol St NW Ste 846 .... Washington DC 20001	800-424-3688	202-387-1968	47-17
American Association for Justice			
777 6th St NW Ste 200 .... Washington DC 20001	800-424-2727	202-965-3500	524-7
American Athletic Inc (AAI)			
200 American Ave .... Jefferson IA 50129	800-247-3978	515-386-3125	343
American Auction Co			
951 W Watkins .... Phoenix AZ 85007	800-801-8880	602-252-4842	50
American Augers Inc			
135 US Rt 42 .... West Salem OH 44287	800-324-4930	419-869-7107	56
American Autoimmune Related Disease Assn (AARDA)			
22100 Gratiot Ave .... Eastpointe MI 48021	800-598-4668	586-776-3900	47-17
American Automobile Association, Inc.			
435 E Broadway .... Louisville KY 40202	800-727-2552	502-582-3311	52
American Avionics			
7023 Perimeter Rd S .... Seattle WA 98108	800-518-5858*	206-763-8530	24
*Sales			
American Baler Co			
800 E Centre St .... Bellevue OH 44811	800-843-7512	419-483-5790	383
American Bank of Texas NA			
200 N Austin St .... Seguin TX 78155	800-567-1817	830-379-5236	69
American Banker Magazine			
one State St Plaza 27th Fl .... New York NY 10004	800-221-1809	212-803-8200	452-5
American Bankers Assn (ABA)			
1120 Connecticut Ave NW .... Washington DC 20036	800-226-5377*	202-663-5000	48-2
*Cust Svc			
American Bankers Assn PAC (ABAPAC)			
1120 Connecticut Ave NW .... Washington DC 20036	800-226-5377		608
American Baptist Assn (ABA)			
4605 N State Line Ave .... Texarkana TX 75503	800-264-2482	903-792-2783	47-20
American Baptist Churches USA			
PO Box 851 .... Valley Forge PA 19482	800-222-3872	610-768-2000	47-20
American Baptist News Service			
PO Box 851 .... Valley Forge PA 19482	800-222-3872	610-768-2000	523
American Baptist Seminary of the West			
2606 Dwight Way .... Berkeley CA 94704	800-799-7233	510-841-1905	167-3
American Bar Assn (ABA)			
321 N Clark St .... Chicago IL 60610	800-285-2221	312-988-5000	48-10
American Behavioral Benefits Managers			
2204 Lakeshore Dr Ste 135 .... Birmingham AL 35209	800-925-5327	205-871-7814	457
American Benefits Council			
1501 M St NW Ste 600 .... Washington DC 20005	877-829-5500	202-289-6700	48-2
American Beverage Licensees (ABL)			
5101 River Rd Ste 108 .... Bethesda MD 20816	800-656-3241	301-656-1494	48-6
American Bible Society			
1865 Broadway .... New York NY 10023	800-322-4253	212-408-1200	628-3
American Bicycle Assn (ABA)			
1645 W Sunrise Blvd .... Gilbert AZ 85233	866-650-4867	480-961-1903	47-22
American Bio Medica Corp (ABMC)			
122 Smith Rd .... Kinderhook NY 12106	800-227-1243*	518-758-8158	84
OTC: ABMC ■ *General			
American Biologics			
1180 Walnut Ave .... Chula Vista CA 91911	800-227-4473	619-429-8200	416
American Biophysics Corp			
140 Frenchtown Rd .... North Kingstown RI 02852	877-699-8727	800-953-5737	426
American Board of Internal Medicine (ABIM)			
510 Walnut St Ste 1700 .... Philadelphia PA 19106	800-441-2246	215-446-3500	47-1
American Boiler Manufacturers Assn (ABMA)			
8221 Old Courthouse Rd Ste 207 .... Vienna VA 22182	800-227-1966	703-356-7172	48-13
American Bolt & Screw Manufacturing Corp			
601 Kettering Dr .... Ontario CA 91761	800-325-0844	909-390-0522	347
American Booksellers Assn (ABA)			
200 White Plains Rd Ste 600 .... Tarrytown NY 10591	800-637-0037	914-591-2665	48-18
American Borate Corp			
5700 Cleveland St			
Ste 420 .... Virginia Beach VA 23462	800-486-1072	757-490-2242	498-1
American Botanical Council			
6200 Manor Rd PO Box 144345 .... Austin TX 78723	800-373-7105	512-926-4900	47-17
American Boychoir School			
19 Lambert Dr .... Princeton NJ 08540	888-269-2464	609-924-5858	615
American Brain Tumor Assn (ABTA)			
2720 River Rd .... Des Plaines IL 60018	800-886-2282	847-827-9910	47-17
American Brass Manufacturing Co			
5000 Superior Ave .... Cleveland OH 44103	800-431-6440	216-431-6565	602

Listing	Toll-Free	Phone	Class
American Buildings Co			
1150 State Docks Rd .... Eufaula AL 36027	888-307-4338	334-687-2032	104
American Bullion Inc			
12301 Wilshire Blvd Ste 650 .... Los Angeles CA 90025	800-326-9598	310-689-7720	780
American Business Systems Inc			
315 Littleton Rd .... Chelmsford MA 01824	800-356-4034		179-1
American Business Women's Assn (ABWA)			
11050 Roe Ave Ste 200 .... Overland Park KS 66211	800-228-0007		48-12
American Businesspersons Assn (ABA)			
350 Fairway Dr Ste 200 .... Deerfield Beach FL 33441	800-221-2168	954-571-1877	48-12
American Camp Assn (ACA)			
5000 State Rd 67 N .... Martinsville IN 46151	800-428-2267	765-342-8456	47-23
American Cancer Society (ACS)			
250 William St NW Ste 6001 .... Atlanta GA 30303	800-227-2345	404-320-3333	47-17
American Cancer Society Hope Lodge of Baltimore			
636 W Lexington St .... Baltimore MD 21201	888-227-6333	410-547-2522	369
American Cancer Society Hope Lodge of Charleston			
269 Calhoun St .... Charleston SC 29401	800-227-2345	843-958-0930	369
American Cancer Society Joe Lee Griffin Hope Lodge			
1104 Ireland Way .... Birmingham AL 35205	888-513-9933	205-558-7860	369
American Capital Group Inc			
8105 Irvine Ctr Dr Ste 250 .... Irvine CA 92618	877-814-6871	949-485-3005	780
American Carrier Equipment Trailer Sales LLC			
2285 E Date Ave .... Fresno CA 93706	800-344-2174	559-442-1500	769
American Cast Iron Pipe Co (ACIPCO)			
1501 31st Ave N .... Birmingham AL 35207	800-442-2347	205-325-7701	306
American Casting & Manufacturing Corp			
51 Commercial St .... Plainview NY 11803	800-342-0333	516-349-7010	325
American Century Investments Inc			
4500 Main St PO Box 419200 .... Kansas City MO 64111	800-345-2021	816-531-5575	398
American Century Proprietary Holdings Inc			
PO Box 419200 .... Kansas City MO 64141	800-345-2021	816-531-5575	521
American Chamber of Commerce Executives (ACCE)			
4875 Eisenhower Ave Ste 250 .... Alexandria VA 22304	800-394-2223	703-998-0072	48-12
American Chemical Society (ACS)			
1155 16th St NW .... Washington DC 20036	800-227-5558	202-872-4600	48-19
American Chiropractic Assn (ACA)			
1701 Clarendon Blvd Second Fl .... Arlington VA 22209	800-986-4636	703-276-8800	48-8
American Chiropractic Assn PAC (ACA-PAC)			
1701 Clarendon Blvd .... Arlington VA 22209	800-986-4636	703-276-8800	608
American Chiropractor, The			
8619 NW 68Th St .... Miami FL 33166	888-369-1396		523
American Choral Directors Assn (ACDA)			
545 Couch Dr .... Oklahoma City OK 73102	800-624-0166	405-232-8161	47-4
American Chronic Pain Assn (ACPA)			
PO Box 850 .... Rocklin CA 95677	800-533-3231	916-632-0922	47-17
American Cinematographer Magazine			
1782 N Orange Dr .... Los Angeles CA 90028	800-448-0145	323-969-4333	452-9
American Civil Liberties Union (ACLU)			
125 Broad St 18th Fl .... New York NY 10004	877-867-1025	212-549-2500	47-8
American Clay Enterprises LLC			
2418 Second St SW .... Albuquerque NM 87102	866-404-1634	505-243-5300	498-6
American Cleaning Solutions			
39-30 Review Ave .... Long Island City NY 11101	888-929-7587	718-392-8080	149
American Club, The			
419 Highland Dr .... Kohler WI 53044	800-344-2838	920-457-8000	660
American Coach Limousine			
1100 Jorie Blvd Ste 314 .... Oak Brook IL 60523	888-709-5466	630-629-0001	437
American Coalition for Fathers & Children (ACFC)			
1718 M St NW Ste 1187 .... Washington DC 20036	800-978-3237		47-6
American College			
270 S Bryn Mawr Ave .... Bryn Mawr PA 19010	888-263-7265	610-526-1000	788
American College of Allergy Asthma & Immunology (ACAAI)			
85 W Algonquin Rd			
Ste 550 .... Arlington Heights IL 60005	800-466-3649	847-427-1200	48-8
American College of Cardiology (ACC)			
2400 N St NW .... Washington DC 20037	800-253-4636*	202-375-6000	48-8
*Cust Svc			
American College of Chest Physicians (ACCP)			
3300 Dundee Rd .... Northbrook IL 60062	800-343-2227	847-498-1400	48-8
American College of Emergency Physicians (ACEP)			
1125 Executive Cir PO Box 619911 .... Dallas TX 75261	800-798-1822	972-550-0911	48-8
American College of Foot & Ankle Surgeons (ACFAS)			
8725 W Higgins Rd Ste 555 .... Chicago IL 60631	800-421-2237	773-693-9300	48-8
American College of Forensic Examiners International (ACFEI)			
2750 E Sunshine St .... Springfield MO 65804	800-423-9737	417-881-3818	48-8
American College of Osteopathic Family Physicians (ACOFP)			
330 E Algonquin Rd			
Ste 1 .... Arlington Heights IL 60005	800-323-0794	847-952-5100	48-8
American College of Physician Executives (ACPE)			
400 N Ashley Dr Ste 4001 .... Tampa FL 33602	800-562-8088	813-287-2000	48-8
American College of Physicians (ACP)			
190 N Independence Mall W .... Philadelphia PA 19106	800-523-1546	215-351-2400	48-8
American College of Radiology (ACR)			
1892 Preston White Dr .... Reston VA 20191	800-227-5463	703-648-8900	48-8
American College of Surgeons (ACS)			
633 N St Clair St .... Chicago IL 60611	800-621-4111	312-202-5000	48-8
American Commerce Insurance Co			
3590 Twin Creeks Dr .... Columbus OH 43204	800-848-2945	614-308-3366	388-4
American Commercial Barge Lines Inc			
1701 E Market St .... Jeffersonville IN 47130	800-457-6377	812-288-0100	313
American Commercial Lines Inc			
1701 E Market St .... Jeffersonville IN 47130	800-899-7195	812-288-0100	313
American Contract Bridge League (ACBL)			
6575 Windchase Blvd .... Horn Lake MS 38637	800-264-2743*	662-253-3100	47-18
*Sales			
American Coolair Corp			
3604 Mayflower St .... Jacksonville FL 32205	877-250-2822	904-389-3646	14
American Correctional Assn (ACA)			
206 N Washington St Ste 200 .... Alexandria VA 22314	800-222-5646	703-224-0000	48-7
American Cotton Growers Textile Div (ACG)			
PO Box 2827 PO Box 430 .... Lubbock TX 79408	800-333-8011	806-763-8011	734-1
American Council of Independent Laboratories (ACIL)			
1875 I St NW Ste 500 .... Washington DC 20006	800-368-1131	202-887-5872	48-19
American Council of the Blind (ACB)			
1155 15th St NW Ste 1004 .... Washington DC 20005	800-424-8666	202-467-5081	47-17
American Council on Alcoholism (ACA)			
1000 E Indian School Rd .... Phoenix AZ 85014	800-527-5344		47-17
American Council on Exercise (ACE)			
4851 Paramount Dr .... San Diego CA 92123	800-825-3636	858-576-6500	47-17
American Council on Science & Health (ACSH)			
1995 Broadway Second Fl .... New York NY 10023	866-905-2694	212-362-7044	48-19
American Council on the Teaching of Foreign Languages (ACTFL)			
1001 N Fairfax St Ste 200 .... Alexandria VA 22314	844-685-4373	703-894-2900	48-5

Alphabetical Section

Name / Address	Toll-Free	Phone	Class
American Counseling Assn (ACA) 5999 Stevenson Ave .... Alexandria VA 22304	800-347-6647	703-823-9800	48-15
American Craft Council 72 Spring St Sixth Fl .... New York NY 10012	800-836-3470	212-274-0630	47-4
American Crane & Equipment Corp 531 Old Swede Rd .... Douglassville PA 19518	877-877-6778	610-385-6061	465
American Cruise Lines 741 Boston Post Rd Ste 200 .... Guilford CT 06437	800-814-6880	203-453-6800	221
American Culinary Federation Chef & Child Foundation 180 Ctr Pl Way .... Saint Augustine FL 32095	800-624-9458	904-824-4468	47-6
American Culinary Federation Inc (ACF) 180 Ctr Pl Way .... Saint Augustine FL 32095	800-624-9458	904-824-4468	48-6
American Cutting Edge Inc 480 Congress Pk Dr .... Centerville OH 45459 *General	800-543-6860*	888-252-3372	488
American Dairy Science Assn (ADSA) 1111 N Dunlap Ave .... Savoy IL 61874	888-670-2250	217-356-5146	47-2
American Dehydrated Foods Inc 3801 E Sunshine .... Springfield MO 65809	800-456-3447	417-881-7755	612
American Dental Assistants Assn (ADAA) 35 E Wacker Dr Ste 1730 .... Chicago IL 60601	877-874-3785	312-541-1550	48-8
American Dental Assn 1111 14th St NW Ste 1100 .... Washington DC 20005	800-353-2237	202-898-2424	608
American Dental Education Assn (ADEA) 1400 K St NW Ste 1100 .... Washington DC 20005	800-353-2237	202-289-7201	48-5
American Dental Hygienists' Assn (ADHA) 444 N Michigan Ave Ste 3400 .... Chicago IL 60611	800-243-2342	312-440-8900	48-8
American Dental Partners Inc 401 Edgewater Pl Ste 430 .... Wakefield MA 01880 NASDAQ: ADPI	800-838-6563	781-213-6500	458
American Desk 1302 Industrial Blvd .... Temple TX 76504	800-433-3142		318-3
American Diabetes Assn (ADA) 1701 N Beauregard St .... Alexandria VA 22311	800-232-3472	703-549-1500	47-17
American Dietetic Assn (ADA) 120 S Riverside Plz Ste 2000 .... Chicago IL 60606	800-877-1600	312-899-0040	48-8
American Donkey & Mule Society (ADMS) 1346 Morningside Ave .... Lewisville TX 75057	877-752-4068	972-219-0781	47-3
American Douglas Metals Inc 783 Thorpe Rd .... Orlando FL 32824	800-428-0023	407-855-6590	487
American Drill Bushings Co (ADB) 5740 Hunt Rd .... Valdosta GA 31606	800-423-4425	229-253-8928	488
American Driving Records Inc 2860 Gold Tailings Ct PO Box 1970 .... Rancho Cordova CA 95670	800-766-6877	916-456-3200	626
American Eagle Federal Credit Union 417 Main St .... East Hartford CT 06118	800-842-0145	860-568-2020	219
American Eagle Outfitters Inc 77 Hot Metal St .... Pittsburgh PA 15203 NYSE: AEO ▪ *Cust Svc	888-232-4535*	412-432-3300	155-4
American Educational Products Inc 401 Hickory St PO Box 2121 .... Fort Collins CO 80522	800-289-9299	970-484-7445	243
American Educational Research Assn (AERA) 1430 K St NW Ste 1200 .... Washington DC 20005	800-893-7950	202-238-3200	48-5
American Educator Magazine 555 New Jersey Ave NW .... Washington DC 20001	800-238-1133	202-879-4400	452-8
American Egg Board (AEB) 1460 Renaissance Dr Ste 301 .... Park Ridge IL 60068	888-549-2140	847-296-7043	47-2
American Electric Power Company Inc One Riverside Plz .... Columbus OH 43215 NYSE: AEP ▪ *Cust Svc	800-277-2177*	614-716-1000	357-5
American Electronic Components 1101 Lafayette St .... Elkhart IN 46516	888-847-6552	574-295-6330	247
American Engineering Testing Inc 550 Cleveland Ave N .... Saint Paul MN 55114	800-972-6364	651-659-9001	261
American Enterprise Institute for Public Policy Research (AEI) 1150 17th St NW Ste 1100 .... Washington DC 20036	800-862-5801	202-862-5800	625
American Epilepsy Society (AES) 342 N Main St .... West Hartford CT 06117	888-233-2334	860-586-7505	47-17
American Equity Investment Life Holding Co 6000 Westown Pkwy Ste 440 PO Box 71216 .... West Des Moines IA 50266 NYSE: AEL	888-221-1234	515-221-0002	357-4
American Equity Investment Life Insurance Co 6000 Westown Pkwy .... West Des Moines IA 50266	888-221-1234	515-221-0002	388-2
American Excelsior Co 850 Ave H E PO Box 5067 .... Arlington TX 76005	800-777-7645		594
American Exchange Bank (AEB) 510 W Main St PO Box 818 .... Henryetta OK 74437	888-652-3321	918-652-3321	69
American Express Company Inc World Financial Ctr 200 Vesey St .... New York NY 10285 NYSE: AXP	800-528-4800	212-640-2000	217
American Exteriors LLC 1169 W Littleton Blvd .... Littleton CO 80120	800-794-6369	303-794-6369	235
American Family Association PO Drawer 2440 .... Tupelo MS 38803	800-326-4543	662-844-5036	635
American Family Care 2147 Riverchase Office Rd .... Birmingham AL 35244	800-258-7535	205-403-8902	349
American Family Life Assurance Co PAC (AFLAC PAC) 1932 Wynnton Rd Ste 300 .... Columbus GA 31999 NYSE: AFL ▪ *Cust Svc	800-992-3522*	706-323-3431	608
American Family Life Assurance Company of Columbus (AFLAC) 1932 Wynnton Rd .... Columbus GA 31999 *Cust Svc	800-992-3522*	706-323-3431	388-2
American Family Life Insurance Co 6000 American Pkwy .... Madison WI 53783	800-692-6326	608-249-2111	388-2
American Family Mutual Insurance Co 6000 American Pkwy .... Madison WI 53783 *Cust Svc	800-374-0008*	608-249-2111	388-2
American Fan Company Inc 2933 Symmes Rd .... Fairfield OH 45014	866-771-6266	513-874-2400	18
American Farmland Trust (AFT) 1200 18th St .... Washington DC 20036	800-431-1499	202-331-7300	47-2
American Federation for Aging Research (AFAR) 55 W 39th St 16th Fl .... New York NY 10018	888-582-2327	212-703-9977	48-8
American Federation for Medical Research (AFMR) 900 Cummings Ctr Ste 221-U .... Beverly MA 01915	888-737-9477	978-927-8330	48-8
American Federation of Astrologers (AFA) 6535 S Rural Rd .... Tempe AZ 85283	888-301-7630	480-838-1751	47-18
American Federation of Government Employees 80 F St NW .... Washington DC 20001	888-844-2343	202-737-8700	411
American Federation of Labor & Congress of Industrial Organizations (AFL-CIO) 815 16th St NW .... Washington DC 20006	877-850-4959	202-637-5000	411
American Federation of Musicians of the US & Canada (AFM) 1501 Broadway Ste 600 .... New York NY 10036	800-762-3444	212-869-1330	411
American Federation of Police & Concerned Citizens 6350 Horizon Dr .... Titusville FL 32780	800-435-7352	321-264-0911	48-7
American Federation of Teachers (AFT) 555 New Jersey Ave NW .... Washington DC 20001	800-238-1133	202-879-4400	411
American Fence Assn (AFA) 800 Roosevelt Rd Bldg C-312 .... Glen Ellyn IL 60137	800-822-4342	630-942-6598	48-3
American Fence Inc 2502 N 27th Ave .... Phoenix AZ 85009	888-691-4565	602-272-2333	192-2
American Fidelity Assurance Co 2000 N Classen Blvd .... Oklahoma City OK 73106	800-654-8489	405-523-2000	357-4
American Finance Assn (AFA) 350 Main St .... Malden MA 02148	800-835-6770	781-388-8599	48-2
American Fitness Magazine 15250 Ventura Blvd Ste 200 .... Sherman Oaks CA 91403	800-446-2322	818-905-0040	452-13
American Floor Products Company Inc 7977 Cessna Ave .... Gaithersburg MD 20879	800-342-0424		291
American Fluorescent Corp 2345 Ernie Krueger Cir .... Waukegan IL 60087	800-873-2326	847-249-5970	435
American Folklore Society (AFS) Ohio State Univ Mershon Ctr 1501 Neil Ave .... Columbus OH 43201	866-311-1200	614-292-4715	47-14
American Food & Vending Corp 124 Metropolitan Pk Dr .... Syracuse NY 13088	800-466-9261	315-457-9950	298
American Foods Group Inc 544 Acme St .... Green Bay WI 54302	800-345-0293	920-437-6330	468
American Football Coaches Assn (AFCA) 100 Legends Ln .... Waco TX 76706	877-557-5338	254-754-9900	47-22
American Foreign Service Assn (AFSA) 2101 E St NW .... Washington DC 20037	800-704-2372	202-338-4045	48-7
American Forest & Paper Assn (AF&PA) 1111 19th St NW Ste 800 .... Washington DC 20036	800-878-8878	202-463-2700	47-2
American Forests 734 15th St NW .... Washington DC 20005	800-368-5748	202-737-1944	47-13
American Foundation for Suicide Prevention (AFSP) 120 Wall St 22nd Fl .... New York NY 10005	888-333-2377	212-363-3500	47-17
American Foundation for the Blind (AFB) 2 Penn Plaza .... New York NY 10001	800-232-5463	212-502-7600	47-17
American Foundry Society (AFS) 1695 N Penny Ln .... Schaumburg IL 60173	800-537-4237	847-824-0181	48-13
American Furniture Warehouse Co 8501 Grant St .... Thornton CO 80229	888-615-9415	303-289-3300	320
American Galvanizers Assn (AGA) 6881 S Holly Cir Ste 108 .... Centennial CO 80112	800-468-7732	720-554-0900	48-13
American Gaming & Electronics 9500 W 55th St Ste A .... Countryside IL 60525	800-336-6630	708-290-2100	321
American Gastroenterological Assn (AGA) 4930 Del Ray Ave .... Bethesda MD 20814	800-228-9290	301-654-2055	48-8
American Gelbvieh Assn 10900 Dover St .... Westminster CO 80021	877-279-2195	303-465-2333	47-2
American Gem Society (AGS) 8881 W Sahara Ave .... Las Vegas NV 89117	866-805-6500	702-255-6500	48-4
American Gem Trade Assn (AGTA) 3030 LBJ Fwy Ste 840 .... Dallas TX 75234	800-972-1162	214-742-4367	48-4
American Geological Institute (AGI) 4220 King St .... Alexandria VA 22302	800-334-2564	703-379-2480	48-19
American Geophysical Union (AGU) 2000 Florida Ave NW .... Washington DC 20009	800-966-2481	202-462-6900	48-19
American Girl Inc 8400 Fairway Pl .... Middleton WI 53562 *Orders	800-845-0005*	608-836-4848	752
American Golf Corp 2951 28th St .... Santa Monica CA 90405	800-238-7267	310-664-4000	646
American Gramaphone LLC 9130 Mormon Bridge Rd .... Omaha NE 68152	800-348-3434	402-457-4341	648
American Granby Inc 7652 Morgan Rd .... Liverpool NY 13090	800-776-2266	315-451-1100	605
American Greetings Corp 1 American Rd .... Cleveland OH 44144 NYSE: AM ▪ *Sales	800-777-4891*	216-252-7300	129
American Greetings Corp Carlton Cards Div 1 American Rd .... Cleveland OH 44144	800-777-4891	216-252-7300	128
American Grinding & Machine Co 2000 N Mango Ave .... Chicago IL 60639	877-988-4343	773-889-4343	449
American Group Psychotherapy Assn (AGPA) 25 E 21st St Sixth Fl .... New York NY 10010	877-668-2472	212-477-2677	48-15
American Guild of Musical Artists (AGMA) 1430 Broadway 14th Fl .... New York NY 10018	800-543-2462	212-265-3687	47-4
American Guild of Variety Artists (AGVA) 363 Seventh Ave 17th Fl .... New York NY 10001	800-331-0890	212-675-1003	47-4
American Gypsum Co 3811 Turtle Creek Blvd Ste 1200 .... Dallas TX 75219	866-439-5800	214-530-5500	344
American Health Associates 671 Ohio Pk Ste K .... Cincinnati IN 45245	800-522-7556		412
American Health Care Assn (AHCA) 1201 L St NW .... Washington DC 20005	800-321-0343	202-842-4444	48-8
American Health Information Management Assn (AHIMA) 233 N Michigan Ave Ste 2100 .... Chicago IL 60601	800-335-5535	312-233-1100	48-8
American Healthcare Radiology Administrators (AHRA) 490-B Boston Post Rd Ste 200 .... Sudbury MA 01776	800-334-2472	978-443-7591	48-8
American Healthcare Services LLC 1000 John R Ste 250 .... Troy MI 48083	866-227-9998	248-588-9700	712
American Heart Assn (AHA) 7272 Greenville Ave .... Dallas TX 75231	800-242-8721	214-373-6300	47-17
American Helicopter Society International (AHS) 217 N Washington St .... Alexandria VA 22314	855-247-4685	703-684-6777	48-21
American Hellenic Educational Progressive Assn (AHEPA) 1909 Q St NW Ste 500 .... Washington DC 20009	855-473-3512	202-232-6300	47-14
American Heritage Bank 2 S Main PO Box 1408 .... Sapulpa OK 74067	866-669-2427	918-224-3210	69
American Historical Assn (AHA) 400 A St SE .... Washington DC 20003	888-444-6664	202-544-2422	48-5
American History Illustrated Magazine 19300 Promenade Dr .... Leesburg VA 20176	800-435-0715	310-922-2159	452-14
American Holistic Nurses' Assn (AHNA) 323 N San Francisco St Ste 201 .... Flagstaff AZ 86001	800-278-2462	928-526-2196	47-17
American Home Base 428 Childers St .... Pensacola FL 32534 *General	800-549-0595*	850-857-0860	727
American Home Furnishings 3535 Menaul Blvd NE .... Albuquerque NM 87107	800-854-6755	505-883-2211	320

	Toll-Free	Phone	Class
American Home Shield			
889 Ridge Lake Blvd PO Box 851 .... Memphis TN 38120	800-776-4663	901-537-8000	364
American HomePatient Inc			
5200 Maryland Way Ste 400 .... Brentwood TN 37027	800-890-7271	615-221-8884	360
American Homestar Corp			
2450 S Shore Blvd Ste 300 .... League City TX 77573	800-313-5570	281-334-9700	500
American Honda Motor Company Inc			
1919 Torrance Blvd .... Torrance CA 90501	800-999-1009	310-783-3170	58
American Horticultural Society (AHS)			
7931 E Blvd Dr .... Alexandria VA 22308	800-777-7931	703-768-5700	47-18
American Hose & Rubber Co			
3645 E 44th St .... Tucson AZ 85713	800-272-7537	520-514-1666	367
American Hospital Assn (AHA)			
155 N Wacker Dr .... Chicago IL 60606	800-424-4301	312-422-3000	48-8
American Hospital Assn PAC (AHAPAC)			
325 Seventh St NW .... Washington DC 20004	800-424-4301	202-638-1100	608
American Hotel Register Co			
100 S Milwaukee Ave .... Vernon Hills IL 60061	800-323-5686	847-743-3000	552
American Humane Assn (AHA)			
63 Inverness Dr E .... Englewood CO 80112	800-227-4645	303-792-9900	47-6
American Income Life Insurance Co (AIL)			
1200 Wooded Acres .... Waco TX 76710	800-433-3405	254-761-6400	388-2
American Indian College Fund			
8333 Greenwood Blvd .... Denver CO 80221	800-776-3863	303-426-8900	47-11
American Indian College of the Assemblies of God			
10020 N 15th Ave .... Phoenix AZ 85021	800-621-7440	602-944-3335	166
American Indian Science & Engineering Society (AISES)			
2305 Renard SE Ste 200 .... Albuquerque NM 87106	800-759-5219	505-765-1052	48-19
American Institute for Cancer Research			
1759 R St NW .... Washington DC 20009	800-843-8114	202-328-7744	659
American Institute for CPCU & Insurance Institute of America (AICPCU/IIA)			
720 Providence Rd Ste 100 .... Malvern PA 19355	800-644-2101	610-644-2100	48-9
American Institute of Aeronautics & Astronautics Inc (AIAA)			
1801 Alexander Bell Dr Ste 500 .... Reston VA 20191	800-639-2422	703-264-7500	48-19
American Institute of Architects (AIA)			
1735 New York Ave NW .... Washington DC 20006	800-242-3837*	202-626-7300	47-4
*Orders			
American Institute of Biological Sciences (AIBS)			
1444 'I' St NW Ste 200 .... Washington DC 20005	800-992-2427	202-628-1500	48-19
American Institute of Certified Public Accountants (AICPA)			
1211 Ave of the Americas .... New York NY 10036	888-777-7077	212-596-6200	48-1
American Institute of Chemical Engineers (AIChE)			
120 Wall St Fl 23 .... New York NY 10005	800-242-4363*	203-702-7660	48-19
*Cust Svc			
American Institute of Chemists (AIC)			
315 Chestnut St .... Philadelphia PA 19106	800-829-0115	215-873-8224	48-19
American Institute of Floral Designers (AIFD)			
720 Light St .... Baltimore MD 21230	877-865-5320	410-752-3318	48-4
American Institute of Graphic Arts (AIGA)			
164 Fifth Ave .... New York NY 10010	800-548-1634	212-807-1990	47-4
American Institute of Professional Bookkeepers (AIPB)			
6001 Montrose Rd Ste 500 .... Rockville MD 20852	800-622-0121		48-1
American Institute of Professional Geologists (AIPG)			
1400 W 122nd Ave Ste 250 .... Westminster CO 80234	800-772-3773	303-412-6205	48-19
American Institute of Ultrasound in Medicine (AIUM)			
14750 Sweitzer Ln Ste 100 .... Laurel MD 20707	800-638-5352	301-498-4100	48-8
American Institutes for Research			
1000 Thomas Jefferson St NW ...... Washington DC 20007	877-334-3499	202-403-5000	659
American InterContinental University			
Atlanta			
6600 Peachtree Dunwoody Rd			
500 Embassy Row NE .... Atlanta GA 30328	800-491-0182	404-965-6500	166
Dunwoody			
6600 Peachtree-Dunwoody Rd			
500 Embassy Row .... Atlanta GA 30328	855-377-1888	404-965-6500	166
American InterContinental University Los Angeles			
231 N Martingale Rd Sixth Fl .... Schaumburg IL 60173	877-701-3800		166
American Intercontinental University South Florida			
2250 N Commerce Pkwy .... Weston FL 33326	855-377-1888	954-446-6100	166
American International Automobile Dealers Assn (AIADA)			
500 Montgomery St Ste 800 .... Alexandria VA 22314	800-462-4232	703-519-7800	48-18
American International College			
1000 State St .... Springfield MA 01109	800-242-3142*	413-205-3201	166
*Admissions			
American International Forest Products LLC (AIFP)			
5560 SW 107th Ave .... Beaverton OR 97005	800-366-1611	503-641-1611	192-3
American International Inc			
1040 Avendia Acaso .... Camarillo CA 93012	800-336-6500	805-388-6800	253
American Iron Magazine			
1010 Summer St .... Stamford CT 06905	877-693-3572*	203-425-8777	452-3
*Cust Svc			
American Jazz Museum			
1616 E 18th St .... Kansas City MO 64108	800-745-3000	816-474-8463	513
American Jewish World Service (AJWS)			
45 W 36th St .... New York NY 10018	800-889-7146	212-792-2900	47-5
American Journal of Psychiatry			
1000 Wilson Blvd Ste 1825 .... Arlington VA 22209	800-368-5777	703-907-7300	452-16
American Journalism Review			
University of Maryland			
1117 Journalism Bldg			
1117 Journalism Bldg Rm 2116 ... College Park MD 20742	800-827-0771	301-405-8803	452-5
American Judicature Society (AJS)			
2700 University Ave .... Des Moines IA 50311	800-626-4089	515-271-2281	48-10
American Kidney Fund (AKF)			
6110 Executive Blvd Ste 1010 .... Rockville MD 20852	800-638-8299		47-17
American Kidney Stone Management Ltd (AKSM)			
797 Thomas Ln .... Columbus OH 43214	800-637-5188	614-447-0281	350
American Land Title Assn (ALTA)			
1828 L St NW Ste 705 .... Washington DC 20036	800-787-2582	202-296-3671	48-10
American Language Communication Ctr			
229 W 36th St .... New York NY 10018	800-364-5474	212-736-2373	420
American Laser Skincare			
24555 Hallwood Ct .... Farmington Hills MI 48335	877-252-2010	248-426-8250	797
American Law Institute (ALI)			
4025 Chestnut St .... Philadelphia PA 19104	800-253-6397	215-243-1600	48-10
American Lawyer Media Inc (ALM)			
120 Broadway Fifth Fl .... New York NY 10271	877-256-2472	212-457-9400	628-9
American Lebanese Syrian Associated Charities (ALSAC)			
501 St Jude Pl .... Memphis TN 38105	800-822-6344	901-578-2000	47-5
American Lecithin Company Inc			
115 Hurley Rd Unit 2B .... Oxford CT 06478	800-364-4416	203-262-7100	295-29
American Legend Co-op			
PO Box 58308 .... Seattle WA 98138	800-266-3314	425-251-3200	

	Toll-Free	Phone	Class
American Legion, The			
700 N Pennsylvania St .... Indianapolis IN 46204	800-433-3318*	317-630-1200	47-19
*Cust Svc			
American Libraries Magazine			
50 E Huron St .... Chicago IL 60611	800-545-2433		452-8
American Library Assn (ALA)			
50 E Huron St .... Chicago IL 60611	800-545-2433	312-944-6780	48-11
American Library Assn Committee on Accreditation			
50 E Huron St .... Chicago IL 60611	800-545-2433	312-944-6780	47-1
American Library Assn Library			
50 E Huron St .... Chicago IL 60611	800-545-2433	312-944-6780	431-4
American Lighting Assn (ALA)			
2050 Stemmons Fwy Ste 10046 .... Dallas TX 75207	800-605-4448	214-698-9898	48-4
American Littoral Society (ALS)			
18 Hartshorne Dr Ste 1 .... Highlands NJ 07732	800-424-8802	732-291-0055	47-13
American Liver Foundation (ALF)			
39 Broadway .... New York NY 10006	800-465-4837	212-668-1000	47-17
American Locker Group Inc			
815 S Main St .... Grapevine TX 76051	800-828-9118	817-329-1600	683
OTC: ALGI			
American Locker Security Systems Inc			
608 Allen St .... Jamestown NY 14701	800-828-9118*	716-664-9600	683
*Sales			
American Logistics Assn (ALA)			
1133 15th St NW Ste 640 .... Washington DC 20005	800-791-7146	202-466-2520	47-19
American Louver Co			
7700 N Austin Ave .... Skokie IL 60077	800-772-0355	847-470-3300	435
American Lung Assn (ALA)			
14 Wall St .... New York NY 10005	800-586-4872	212-315-8700	47-17
American Machine & Tool Company Inc			
400 Spring St .... Royersford PA 19468	888-268-7867	610-948-3800	632
American Marazzi Tile Inc			
359 Clay Rd .... Sunnyvale TX 75182	800-289-8453	972-232-3801	741
American Marketing Assn (AMA)			
311 S Wacker Dr Ste 5800 .... Chicago IL 60606	800-262-1150	312-542-9000	48-18
American Marking Systems Inc			
1015 Paulison Ave PO Box 1677 .... Clifton NJ 07011	800-782-6766	973-478-5600	462
American Massage Therapy Assn (AMTA)			
500 Davis St Ste 900 .... Evanston IL 60201	877-905-2700	847-864-0123	47-17
American Mathematical Society (AMS)			
201 Charles St .... Providence RI 02904	800-321-4267*	401-455-4000	48-19
*Cust Svc			
American Medical Assn (AMA)			
515 N State St .... Chicago IL 60610	800-621-8335	312-464-5000	48-8
American Medical Directors Assn (AMDA)			
11000 Broken Land Pkwy Ste 400 ...... Columbia MD 21044	800-876-2632	410-740-9743	48-8
American Medical ID			
949 Wakefield Ste 100 .... Houston TX 77018	800-363-5985		470
American Medical Rehabilitation Providers Assn (AMRPA)			
1710 N St NW .... Washington DC 20036	888-346-4624	202-223-1920	48-8
American Medical Response (AMR)			
6200 S Syracuse Way			
Ste 200 .... Greenwood Village CO 80111	877-244-4890	303-495-1200	30
American Medical Security (AMS)			
3100 AMS Blvd PO Box 19032 .... Green Bay WI 54307	800-232-5432	800-657-8205	357-4
American Medical Student Assn (AMSA)			
1902 Assn Dr .... Reston VA 20191	800-767-2266	703-620-6600	48-5
American Medical Systems Holdings Inc			
10700 Bren Rd W .... Minnetonka MN 55343	800-328-3881	952-930-6000	472
American Medical Technologies Inc			
5655 Bear Ln .... Corpus Christi TX 78405	800-359-1959	361-289-1145	228
OTC: ADLI			
American Medical Technologists (AMT)			
10700 W Higgins Rd Ste 150 .... Rosemont IL 60018	800-275-1268	847-823-5169	48-8
American Megatrends Inc (AMI)			
5555 Oakbrook Pkwy Bldg 200 .... Norcross GA 30093	800-828-9264	770-246-8600	177
American Mensa Ltd			
1229 Corporate Dr W .... Arlington TX 76006	800-666-3672	817-607-0060	47-15
American Mental Health Counselors Assn (AMHCA)			
801 N Fairfax St Ste 304 .... Alexandria VA 22314	800-326-2642	703-548-6002	48-15
American Metal & Plastics Inc			
450 32nd St SW .... Grand Rapids MI 49548	800-382-0067	616-452-6061	484
American Metal Bearing Co			
7191 Acacia Ave .... Garden Grove CA 92841	800-888-3048	714-892-5527	613
American Metalcraft Inc			
2074 George St .... Melrose Park IL 60160	800-333-9133	708-345-1177	483
American Meteorological Society (AMS)			
45 Beacon St .... Boston MA 02108	800-824-0405	617-227-2425	48-19
American Modern Home Insurance Co			
PO Box 5323 .... Cincinnati OH 45201	800-543-2644	513-943-7200	388-4
American Morgan Horse Assn (AMHA)			
4066 Shelburne Rd Ste 5 .... Shelburne VT 05482	888-436-3700	802-985-4944	47-3
American Motel Management			
2200 Northlake Pkwy Ste 277 .... Tucker GA 30084	800-580-8258	770-939-1801	646
American Motorcyclist Assn			
101 Constitution Ave NW			
Ste 800W .... Washington DC 20001	888-985-6090	202-742-4301	608
American Moving & Storage Assn (AMSA)			
1611 Duke St .... Alexandria VA 22314	888-849-2672	703-683-7410	48-21
American Moving & Storage Assn PAC			
1611 Duke St .... Alexandria VA 22314	888-849-2672	703-683-7410	608
American Muscle			
7 Lee Blvd .... Malvern PA 19355	888-332-7930	610-251-2397	779
American Museum of Fly Fishing			
4104 Main Rd .... Manchester VT 05254	800-333-1550	802-362-3300	515
American Musical Supply			
PO Box 152 .... Spicer MN 56288	800-458-4076	320-796-2088	519
American Musicological Society (AMS)			
6010 College Stn .... Brunswick ME 04011	888-421-1442	207-798-4243	47-4
American National Bank			
PO Box 2139 .... Omaha NE 68103	800-279-0007*	402-399-5000	69
*Cust Svc			
American National Property & Casualty Co			
1949 E Sunshine St .... Springfield MO 65899	800-333-2860	417-887-0220	388-4
American National Rubber Co			
Main & High St .... Ceredo WV 25507	800-624-3410*	304-453-1311	668
*Cust Svc			
American National Standards Institute (ANSI)			
25 W 43rd St 4th fl .... New York NY 10036	800-374-3818	212-642-4900	47-1
American Naturopathic Medical Assn (ANMA)			
150 S Hwy 160 Ste 8-528 .... Pahrump NV 89048	888-202-4440	702-897-7053	47-17
American Nephrology Nurses Assn (ANNA)			
200 E Holly Ave .... Sewell NJ 08080	888-600-2662	856-256-2320	48-8

Name / Address	Toll-Free	Phone	Class
American Nickeloid Co			
2900 Main St . . . Peru IL 61354	**800-645-5643**	815-223-0373	476
American Nuclear Insurers (ANI)			
95 Glastonbury Blvd Ste 300 . . . Glastonbury CT 06033	**866-301-1301**	860-682-1301	48-9
American Nuclear Society (ANS)			
555 N Kensington Ave . . . La Grange Park IL 60526	**800-323-3044**	708-352-6611	48-19
American Nurse Magazine			
8515 Georgia Ave Ste 400 . . . Silver Spring MD 20910	**800-274-4262**	301-628-5000	452-16
American Nurses Assn (ANA)			
8515 Georgia Ave Ste 400 . . . Silver Spring MD 20910	**800-274-4262**	301-628-5000	48-8
American Nurses Assn PAC (ANA PAC)			
8515 Georgia Ave Ste 400 . . . Silver Spring MD 20910	**800-274-4262**	301-628-5000	608
American Occupational Therapy Assn Inc (AOTA)			
4720 Montgomery Ln			
PO Box 31220 . . . Bethesda MD 20824	**800-877-1383**	301-652-2682	48-8
American Oil Chemists Society (AOCS)			
2710 S Boulder PO Box 17190 . . . Urbana IL 61802	**866-535-2730**	217-359-2344	47-12
American Orthodontics Corp			
1714 Cambridge Ave . . . Sheboygan WI 53081	**800-558-7687**	920-457-5051	228
American Orthopaedic Society for Sports Medicine (AOSSM)			
6300 N River Rd Ste 500 . . . Rosemont IL 60018	**877-321-3500**	847-292-4900	48-8
American Osteopathic Assn (AOA)			
142 E Ontario St . . . Chicago IL 60611	**800-621-1773**	312-202-8000	48-8
American Outdoor Products Inc			
6350 Gunpark Dr . . . Boulder CO 80301	**800-641-0500**	303-581-0518	295-37
American Packaging Corp			
777 Driving Pk Ave . . . Rochester NY 14613	**800-551-8801**	585-254-9500	541
American Packaging Corp Extrusion Div			
777 Driving Pk Ave . . . Rochester NY 14613	**800-551-8801**	585-254-9500	541
American Packing & Gasket Co (APG)			
6039 Armour Dr PO Box 213 . . . Houston TX 77020	**800-888-5223**	713-675-5271	325
American Pain Society (APS)			
4700 W Lake Ave . . . Glenview IL 60025	**877-752-4754**	847-375-4715	47-17
American Panel Corp			
5800 SE 78th St . . . Ocala FL 34472	**800-327-3015**	352-245-7055	655
American Paper & Twine Co			
7400 Cockrill Bend Blvd . . . Nashville TN 37209	**800-251-2437**	615-350-9000	552
American Paper Recycling Corp			
301 W Lake St . . . Northlake IL 60164	**800-762-6790***	708-344-6789	651
*Cust Svc			
American Park & Recreation Society (APRS)			
22377 Belmont Ridge Rd . . . Ashburn VA 20148	**800-765-3110**	703-858-0784	47-23
American Parkinson Disease Assn (APDA)			
135 Parkinson Ave . . . Staten Island NY 10305	**800-223-2732**	718-981-8001	47-17
American Parkinson's Disease Assn Newsletter			
135 Parkinson Ave . . . Staten Island NY 10305	**800-223-2732**	718-981-8001	524-8
American Permanent Ware Inc			
729 Third Ave . . . Dallas TX 75226	**800-527-2100**	214-421-7366	297
American Pet Products Manufacturers Assn (APPMA)			
255 Glenville Rd . . . Greenwich CT 06831	**800-452-1225**	203-532-0000	48-4
American Pharmacists Assn PAC			
2215 Constitution Ave NW . . . Washington DC 20037	**800-237-2742**	202-628-4410	608
American Photo Magazine			
1633 Broadway 43rd Fl . . . New York NY 10019	**800-274-4514**	212-767-6000	452-14
American Physical Society (APS)			
1 Physics Ellipse . . . College Park MD 20740	**888-221-9425**	301-209-3200	48-19
American Physical Therapy Assn (APTA)			
1111 N Fairfax St . . . Alexandria VA 22314	**800-999-2782**	703-684-2782	48-8
American Plastic Molding Corp			
965 S Elm St . . . Scottsburg IN 47170	**877-527-8427**	812-752-7000	597
American Plastic Toys Inc			
799 Ladd Rd . . . Walled Lake MI 48390	**800-521-7080**	248-624-4881	752
American Playground Corp			
505 E 31st St Ste X . . . Anderson IN 46016	**800-541-1602**	765-642-0288	343
American Pneumatic Tool Inc			
9949 Tabor Pl . . . Santa Fe Springs CA 90670	**800-532-7402**	562-204-1555	749
American Podiatric Medical Assn (APMA)			
9312 Old Georgetown Rd . . . Bethesda MD 20814	**800-275-2762**	301-581-9200	48-8
American Polarizers Inc			
141 S Seventh St . . . Reading PA 19602	**800-736-9031**	610-373-5177	537
American Polywater Corp			
11222 60th St N . . . Stillwater MN 55082	**800-328-9384**	651-430-2270	143
American Portwell Technology Inc			
44200 Christy St . . . Fremont CA 94538	**877-278-8899**	510-403-3399	175
American Power Conversion Corp (APC)			
132 Fairgrounds Rd . . . West Kingston RI 02892	**800-788-2208***	401-789-5735	253
*Cust Svc			
American Power Pull Corp			
550 W Linfoot St PO Box 109 . . . Wauseon OH 43567	**800-808-5922**	419-335-7050	465
American Press			
4900 Hwy 90 E . . . Lake Charles LA 70615	**800-442-2511***	337-494-4080	525-2
*News Rm			
American Pride Co-Op			
55 W Bromley Ln . . . Brighton CO 80601	**800-332-6478**	303-659-1230	276
American Printing House for the Blind			
1839 Frankfort Ave			
PO Box 6085 . . . Louisville KY 40206	**800-223-1839**	502-895-2405	628-10
American Product Distributors Inc (APD)			
8350 Arrowridge Blvd . . . Charlotte NC 28273	**800-849-5842**	704-522-9411	527
American Products LLC			
597 Evergreen Rd . . . Strafford MO 65757	**855-736-2135**	417-736-2135	483
American Psychiatric Assn (APA)			
1000 Wilson Blvd Ste 1825 . . . Arlington VA 22209	**888-357-7924**	703-907-7300	48-15
American Psychiatric Nurses Assn (APNA)			
1555 Wilson Blvd Ste 530 . . . Arlington VA 22209	**866-243-2443**	703-243-2443	48-8
American Psychiatric Publishing Inc			
1000 Wilson Blvd Ste 1825 . . . Arlington VA 22209	**800-368-5777**	703-907-7322	628-9
American Psychological Assn (APA)			
750 First St NE . . . Washington DC 20002	**800-374-2721**	202-336-5500	48-15
American Psychologist Magazine			
750 First St NE . . . Washington DC 20002	**800-374-2721**	202-336-5500	452-16
American Public Communications Council Inc (APCC)			
625 Slaters Ln Ste 104 . . . Alexandria VA 22314	**800-868-2722**	703-739-1322	48-20
American Public Gas Assn (APGA)			
201 Massachusetts Ave NE			
Ste C-4 . . . Washington DC 20002	**800-927-4204**	202-464-2742	47-12
American Public Life Insurance Co			
2305 Lakeland Dr PO Box 925 . . . Jackson MS 39205	**800-256-8606**	601-936-6600	388-5
American Public Power Assn (APPA)			
1875 Connecticut Ave			
Ste 1200 . . . Washington DC 20009	**800-515-2772**	202-467-2900	47-12
American Public University System (AMU)			
111 W Congress St . . . Charles Town WV 25414	**877-777-9081**	304-724-3700	167
American Public Works Assn (APWA)			
2345 Grand Blvd Ste 700 . . . Kansas City MO 64108	**800-848-2792**	816-472-6100	48-7
American Quarter Horse Assn (AQHA)			
1600 Quarter Horse Dr . . . Amarillo TX 79104	**800-291-7323**	806-376-4811	47-3
American Radio Relay League (ARRL)			
225 Main St . . . Newington CT 06111	**888-277-5289**	860-594-0200	48-14
American Radiolabeled Chemicals Inc (ARC)			
101 ARC Dr . . . Saint Louis MO 63146	**800-331-6661**	314-991-4545	143
American Railcar Industries Inc			
100 Clark St . . . Saint Charles MO 63301	**800-489-9888**	636-940-6000	641
NASDAQ: ARII			
American Realty Investors Inc			
1800 Vly View Ln Ste 300 . . . Dallas TX 75234	**800-400-6407**	469-522-4200	646
NYSE: ARL			
American Recycled Plastic Inc			
773 N. Union Grove Rd . . . Friendsville TN 37737	**866-674-1525**	865-738-3439	652
American Red Ball International			
9750 Third Ave NE Ste 200 . . . Seattle WA 98115	**800-669-6424**	206-526-1730	512
American Red Ball Transit Company Inc			
PO Box 1127 . . . Indianapolis IN 46206	**800-733-8139**		512
American Red Cross In Greater New York (Inc)			
520 W 49th St . . . New York NY 10019	**877-733-2767**		349
American Reeling Devices Inc			
15 Airpark Vista Blvd . . . Dayton NV 89403	**800-354-7335***		116
*Sales			
American Refugee Committee (ARC)			
430 Oak Grove St Ste 204 . . . Minneapolis MN 55403	**800-875-7060**	612-872-7060	47-5
American Registry of Diagnostic Medical Sonographers (ARDMS)			
51 Monroe St Plz E 1 . . . Rockville MD 20850	**800-541-9754**	301-738-8401	48-8
American Religious Town Hall Meeting Inc			
PO Box 180118 . . . Dallas TX 75218	**800-783-9828**	214-328-9828	446
American Renal Assoc Inc			
66 Cherry Hill Dr . . . Beverly MA 01915	**877-997-3625**	978-922-3080	350
American Rental Assn (ARA)			
1900 19th St . . . Moline IL 61265	**800-334-2177**	309-764-2475	48-4
American Republic Insurance Co			
601 Sixth Ave . . . Des Moines IA 50309	**800-247-2190***		388-2
*Cust Svc			
American Residential Services LLC			
9010 Maier Rd Ste 105 . . . Laurel MD 20723	**866-399-2885**	901-271-9700	190-10
American River Bankshares			
3100 Zinfandel Dr			
Ste 450 . . . Rancho Cordova CA 95670	**800-544-0545**		357-2
NASDAQ: AMRB			
American Rivers			
1101 14th St NW Ste 1400 . . . Washington DC 20005	**877-347-7550**	202-347-7550	47-13
American Road & Transportation Builders Assn (ARTBA)			
1219 28th St NW . . . Washington DC 20007	**800-636-2377**	202-289-4434	48-3
American Roentgen Ray Society (ARRS)			
44211 Slatestone Ct . . . Leesburg VA 20176	**800-438-2777**	703-729-3353	48-8
American Rose Society (ARS)			
8877 Jefferson Paige Rd . . . Shreveport LA 71119	**800-637-6534**	318-938-5402	47-18
American Royal Assn			
1701 American Royal Ct . . . Kansas City MO 64102	**800-767-8487**	816-221-9800	47-2
American Royal Museum & Visitors Ctr			
1701 American Royal Ct . . . Kansas City MO 64102	**866-844-2295***	816-221-9800	513
*General			
American Running Assn			
4405 E W Hwy Ste 405 . . . Bethesda MD 20814	**800-776-2732**	301-913-9517	47-22
American Saddlebred Museum			
4083 Iron Works Pkwy . . . Lexington KY 40511	**800-829-4438**	859-259-2746	513
American Safety Technologies Inc			
565 Eagle Rock Ave . . . Roseland NJ 07068	**800-631-7841**	973-403-2600	543
American Salon Magazine			
757 Third Ave 5th Fl . . . New York NY 10017	**866-871-0656**	212-895-8200	452-21
American Savings Bank FSB			
1001 Bishop St PO Box 2300 . . . Honolulu HI 96813	**800-272-2566**	808-539-7843	69
American School Counselor Assn (ASCA)			
1101 King St Ste 625 . . . Alexandria VA 22314	**800-306-4722**	703-683-2722	48-5
American Science & Engineering Inc			
829 Middlesex Tpke . . . Billerica MA 01821	**800-225-1608**	978-262-8700	683
NASDAQ: ASEI			
American Scientist Magazine			
3106 E NC Hwy 54			
PO Box 13975 . . . Research Triangle Park NC 27709	**800-243-6534**	919-549-4691	452-19
American Seating Co			
401 American Seating			
Ctr NW . . . Grand Rapids MI 49504	**800-748-0268***	616-732-6600	318-3
*Cust Svc			
American Security Products Inc			
11925 Pacific Ave . . . Fontana CA 92337	**800-421-6142**	951-685-9680	683
American Seed Trade Assn (ASTA)			
225 Reinekers Ln Ste 650 . . . Alexandria VA 22314	**888-890-7333**	703-837-8140	47-2
American Seminar Leaders Assn (ASLA)			
2405 E Washington Blvd . . . Pasadena CA 91104	**800-801-1886**	626-791-1211	48-12
American Services Inc			
1300 Rutherford Rd . . . Greenville SC 29609	**877-292-7450**	864-292-7450	684
American Shared Hospital Services			
Four Embarcadero Ctr			
Ste 3700 . . . San Francisco CA 94111	**800-735-0641**	415-788-5300	264-4
NYSE: AMS			
American Shore & Beach Preservation Assn (ASBPA)			
5460 Beaujolais Ln . . . Fort Myers FL 33919	**800-331-1600**	239-489-2616	47-13
American Sleep Apnea Assn (ASAA)			
6856 Eastern Ave NW #203 . . . Washington DC 20012	**888-292-6522**	202-293-3650	47-17
American Society for Aesthetic Plastic Surgery, The (ASAPS)			
11262 Monarch St . . . Garden Grove CA 92841	**800-364-2147**	562-799-2356	48-8
American Society for Clinical Pathology (ASCP)			
33 W Monroe St Ste 1600 . . . Chicago IL 60603	**800-621-4142***	312-541-4999	48-8
*Cust Svc			
American Society for Colposcopy & Cervical Pathology (ASCCP)			
152 W Washington St . . . Hagerstown MD 21740	**800-787-7227**	301-733-3640	48-8
American Society for Gastrointestinal Endoscopy (ASGE)			
1520 Kensington Rd Ste 202 . . . Oak Brook IL 60523	**866-353-2743**	630-573-0600	48-8
American Society for Horticultural Science (ASHS)			
1018 Duke St . . . Alexandria VA 22314	**800-331-1600**	703-836-4606	47-2
American Society for Laser Medicine & Surgery Inc (ASLMS)			
2100 Stewart Ave Ste 240 . . . Wausau WI 54401	**877-258-6028**	715-845-9283	48-8
American Society for Nondestructive Testing Inc (ASNT)			
1711 Arlingate Ln PO Box 28518 . . . Columbus OH 43228	**800-222-2768***	614-274-6003	48-19
*Orders			
American Society for Nutrition (ASNS)			
9650 Rockville Pike Ste L3503A . . . Bethesda MD 20814	**800-627-8723**	301-634-7050	48-6

	Toll-Free	Phone	Class
American Society for Parenteral & Enteral Nutrition (ASPEN)			
8630 Fenton St Ste 412 ... Silver Spring MD 20910	**800-727-4567**	301-587-6315	48-8
American Society for Photobiology (ASP)			
PO Box 1897 ... Lawrence KS 66044	**800-627-0326**	785-843-1234	48-19
American Society for Quality (ASQ)			
600 N Plankinton Ave ... Milwaukee WI 53203	**800-248-1946**	414-272-8575	48-13
American Society for Surgery of the Hand (ASSH)			
822 W. Washington Blvd ... Chicago IL 60607	**888-343-6337**	312-880-1900	48-8
American Society for Therapeutic Radiology & Oncology (ASTRO)			
8280 Willow Oaks Corporate Dr			
Ste 500 ... Fairfax VA 22031	**800-962-7876**	703-502-1550	48-8
American Society for Training & Development (ASTD)			
1640 King St Third Fl			
PO Box 1443 ... Alexandria VA 22313	**800-628-2783**	703-683-8100	48-5
American Society of Agricultural Consultants (ASAC)			
N78W14573 Appleton Ave ... Menomonee Falls WI 53051	**800-327-6789**	262-253-6902	47-2
American Society of Agronomy (ASA)			
5585 Guilford Rd ... Madison WI 53711	**866-359-9161**	608-273-8080	47-2
American Society of Anesthesiologists (ASA)			
520 N NW Hwy ... Park Ridge IL 60068	**800-331-1600**	847-825-5586	48-8
American Society of Appraisers (ASA)			
555 Herndon Pkwy Ste 125 ... Herndon VA 20170	**800-272-8258**	703-478-2228	48-17
American Society of Assn Executives (ASAE)			
1575 'I' St NW ... Washington DC 20005	**888-950-2723**	202-626-2723	48-12
American Society of Cataract & Refractive Surgery (ASCRS)			
4000 Legato Rd Ste 700 ... Fairfax VA 22033	**800-451-1339**	703-591-2220	48-8
American Society of Cinematographers (ASC)			
1782 N Orange Dr ... Hollywood CA 90028	**800-448-0145**	323-969-4333	47-4
American Society of Civil Engineers (ASCE)			
1801 Alexander Bell Dr ... Reston VA 20191	**800-548-2723**	703-295-6300	452-21
American Society of Clinical Hypnosis (ASCH)			
140 N Bloomingdale Rd ... Bloomingdale IL 60108	**866-986-8779**	630-980-4740	48-8
American Society of Clinical Oncology (ASCO)			
2318 Mill Rd Ste 800 ... Alexandria VA 22314	**888-282-2552**	571-483-1300	48-8
American Society of Consultant Pharmacists (ASCP)			
1321 Duke St ... Alexandria VA 22314	**800-355-2727**	703-739-1300	48-8
American Society of Dermatopathology, The			
111 Deer Lake Rd Ste 100 ... ÿDeerfield IL 60015	**800-445-8667**	847-400-5820	48-8
American Society of Health-System Pharmacists (ASHP)			
7272 Wisconsin Ave ... Bethesda MD 20814	**866-279-0681**	301-664-8700	48-8
American Society of Heating Refrigerating & Air-Conditioning Engineers Inc (ASHRAE)			
1791 Tullie Cir NE ... Atlanta GA 30329	**800-527-4723***	404-636-8400	48-3
*Cust Svc			
American Society of Home Inspectors (ASHI)			
932 Lee St Ste 101 ... Des Plaines IL 60016	**800-743-2744**	847-759-2820	48-3
American Society of Human Genetics (ASHG)			
9650 Rockville Pike ... Bethesda MD 20814	**866-486-4363**	301-634-7300	48-19
American Society of Landscape Architects (ASLA)			
636 'I' St NW ... Washington DC 20001	**888-999-2752**	202-898-2444	47-2
American Society of Limnology & Oceanography (ASLO)			
5400 Bosque Blvd Ste 680 ... Waco TX 76710	**800-929-2756**	254-399-9635	48-19
American Society of Military Comptrollers (ASMC)			
415 N Alfred St ... Alexandria VA 22314	**800-462-5637**	703-549-0360	47-19
American Society of Naval Engineers (ASNE)			
1452 Duke St ... Alexandria VA 22314	**800-995-3579**	703-836-6727	48-21
American Society of PeriAnesthesia Nurses (ASPAN)			
90 Frontage Rd ... Cherry Hill NJ 08034	**877-737-9696**	856-616-9600	48-8
American Society of Plastic Surgeons (ASPS)			
444 E Algonquin Rd ... Arlington Heights IL 60005	**888-475-2784**	847-228-9900	48-8
American Society of Professional Estimators (ASPE)			
2525 Perimeter Pl Dr Ste 103 ... Nashville TN 37214	**888-378-6283**	615-316-9200	48-3
American Society of Radiologic Technologists (ASRT)			
15000 Central Ave SE ... Albuquerque NM 87123	**800-444-2778**	505-298-4500	48-8
American Society of Regional Anesthesia & Pain Medicine (ASRA)			
239 Fourth Ave Ste 1714 ... Pittsburgh PA 15222	**855-795-2772**	412-471-2718	48-8
American Society of Travel Agents (ASTA)			
1101 King St Ste 200 ... Alexandria VA 22314	**800-275-2782**	703-739-2782	47-23
American Society of Travel Agents PAC			
1101 King St Ste 490 ... Alexandria VA 22314	**800-275-2782**	703-739-2782	608
American Society on Aging (ASA)			
71 Stevenson St Ste 1450 ... San Francisco CA 94105	**800-537-9728**	415-974-9600	47-6
American Sociological Assn (ASA)			
1307 New York Ave ... Washington DC 20005	**800-524-9400**	202-383-9005	48-5
American Software Inc			
470 E Paces Ferry Rd ... Atlanta GA 30305	**800-726-2946**	404-261-4381	179-1
NASDAQ: AMSWA			
American Solutions for Business			
31 E Minnesota Ave PO Box 218 ... Glenwood MN 56334	**800-862-3690**		527
American Southern Insurance Co			
3715 Northside Pkwy NW			
Bldg 400 Ste 800 ... Atlanta GA 30327	**800-241-1172**	404-266-9599	388-4
American Soybean Assn (ASA)			
12125 Woodcrest Executive Dr			
Ste 100 ... Saint Louis MO 63141	**800-688-7692**	314-576-1770	47-2
American Speaker			
PO Box 787 ... Williamsport PA 17703	**800-791-8699**	570-567-1982	524-2
American Specialty Health Plans			
10221 Wateridge Cir ... San Diego CA 92121	**800-848-3555**		388-3
American Spectator Magazine			
1611 N Kent St Ste 901 ... Arlington VA 22209	**800-524-3469**	703-807-2011	452-17
American Spectrum Realty Inc			
2401 Fountain View Ste 510 ... Houston TX 77057	**888-315-2776**	713-706-6200	646
NYSE: AQQ			
American Speech-Language-Hearing Assn (ASHA)			
2200 Research Blvd ... Rockville MD 20850	**800-498-2071**	301-296-5700	48-8
American Spoon Foods Inc			
1668 Clarion Ave ... Petoskey MI 49770	**800-222-5886**	231-347-9030	295-20
American Sports			
74 Albe Dr Ste 1 ... Newark DE 19702	**866-207-3179**	302-369-9480	701
American Staffing Assn (ASA)			
277 S Washington St Ste 200 ... Alexandria VA 22314	**800-456-4324**	703-253-2020	48-12
American Stair Corp Inc			
642 Forestwood Dr ... Romeoville IL 60446	**800-872-7824**		486
American Standard Cos Inc			
1 Centennial Ave ... Piscataway NJ 08855	**800-442-1902**		357-3
American Standard Cos Inc Bath & Kitchen Products Div			
One Centennial Ave			
PO Box 6820 ... Piscataway NJ 08855	**800-442-1902**		604
American Standard Insurance Company of Wisconsin			
6000 American Pkwy ... Madison WI 53783	**800-692-6326**	608-249-2111	388-2
American State Bank			
1401 Ave Q ... Lubbock TX 79401	**800-531-1401**	806-767-7000	357-2

	Toll-Free	Phone	Class
American States Water Co			
630 E Foothill Blvd ... San Dimas CA 91773	**800-999-4033**	909-394-3600	357-5
NYSE: AWR			
American Statistical Assn (ASA)			
732 N Washington St ... Alexandria VA 22314	**888-231-3473**	703-684-1221	48-19
American String Teachers Assn (ASTA)			
4155 Chain Bridge Rd ... Fairfax VA 22030	**800-821-7303**	703-279-2113	48-5
American Strip Steel Inc			
901 Coopertown Rd ... Delanco NJ 08075	**800-526-1216**		487
American Studies Assn (ASA)			
1120 19th St NW Ste 301 ... Washington DC 20036	**800-468-3571**	202-467-4783	48-5
American Subcontractors Assn Inc (ASA)			
1004 Duke St ... Alexandria VA 22314	**866-378-8866**	703-684-3450	48-3
American Systems Corp			
14151 Pk Meadow Dr Ste 500 ... Chantilly VA 20151	**800-733-2721**	703-968-6300	181
American Tank & Fabricating Co (AT&F)			
12314 Elmwood Ave ... Cleveland OH 44111	**800-544-5316**	216-252-1500	714
American Teacher Magazine			
555 New Jersey Ave NW ... Washington DC 20001	**800-238-1133**	202-879-4400	452-8
American Technology Network Corp			
1341 San Mateo Ave ... South San Francisco CA 94080	**800-910-2862**	650-875-0130	537
American Textile Co			
10 N Linden St ... Duquesne PA 15110	**800-289-2826***	412-948-1020	735
*Cust Svc			
American Theological Library Assn (ATLA)			
300 S Wacker Dr Ste 2100 ... Chicago IL 60606	**888-665-2852**	312-454-5100	47-20
American Therapeutic Recreation Assn (ATRA)			
629 N Main St ... Hattiesburg MS 39401	**800-433-5255**	601-450-2872	47-17
American Thermoplastic Co (ATC)			
106 Gamma Dr ... Pittsburgh PA 15238	**800-245-6600**		85
American Thoracic Society (ATS)			
61 Broadway 4th Fl ... New York NY 10006	**866-316-2673**	212-315-8600	48-8
American Tinnitus Assn (ATA)			
522 SW Fifth Ave Ste 825 ... Portland OR 97204	**800-634-8978**	503-248-9985	47-17
American Tire Depot			
1123 W Commonwealth Ave ... Fullerton CA 92833	**855-333-2823**	714-525-2306	745
American Tort Reform Assn (ATRA)			
1101 Connecticut Ave NW			
Ste 400 ... Washington DC 20036	**877-333-2227**	202-682-1163	48-10
American Tower Corp			
116 Huntington Ave 11th Fl ... Boston MA 02116	**877-282-7483**	617-375-7500	171
NYSE: AMT			
American Traffic Safety Services Assn (ATSSA)			
15 Riverside Pkwy			
Ste 100 ... Fredericksburg VA 22406	**800-272-8772**	540-368-1701	48-21
American Trails			
PO Box 491797 ... Redding CA 96049	**866-363-7226**	530-547-2060	47-23
American Trails West (ATW)			
92 Middle Neck Rd ... Great Neck NY 11021	**800-645-6260**	516-487-2800	750
American Translators Assn (ATA)			
225 Reinekers Ln Ste 590 ... Alexandria VA 22314	**800-253-2252**	703-683-6100	48-5
American Trucking Assn (ATA)			
950 N Glebe Rd Ste 210 ... Arlington VA 22203	**800-282-5463**	703-838-1700	48-21
American Type Culture Collection (ATCC)			
10801 University Blvd			
PO Box 1549 ... Manassas VA 20108	**800-638-6597***	703-365-2700	659
*Cust Svc			
American Ultraviolet Co			
40 Morristown Rd ... Bernardsville NJ 07924	**800-288-9288**	908-696-1130	798
American United Life Insurance Co			
One American Sq 510A			
PO Box 6010 ... Indianapolis IN 46282	**800-537-6442**	317-285-1877	388-2
American University			
4400 Massachusetts Ave NW ... Washington DC 20016	**800-829-1040**	202-885-1000	166
American University Washington College of Law			
4801 Massachusetts Ave NW ... Washington DC 20016	**800-995-6423**	202-274-4101	167-1
American Urban Radio Networks			
960 Penn Ave Fourth Fl ... Pittsburgh PA 15222	**800-456-4211**	412-456-4000	637
American Urological Assn (AUA)			
1000 Corporate Blvd ... Linthicum MD 21090	**866-746-4282**	410-689-3700	48-8
American Vending Sales Inc			
750 Morse Ave ... Elk Grove Village IL 60007	**800-441-0009**	847-439-9400	54
American Veterinary Medical Assn (AVMA)			
1931 N Meacham Rd Ste 100 ... Schaumburg IL 60173	**800-248-2862**	847-925-8070	48-8
American Veterinary Medical Assn Council on Education			
1931 N Meacham Rd Ste 100 ... Schaumburg IL 60173	**800-248-2862**	847-925-8070	47-1
American Veterinary Medical Assn PAC (AVMA)			
1910 Sunderland Pl NW ... Washington DC 20036	**800-321-1473**	202-789-0007	608
American Volkssport Assn (AVA)			
1001 Pat Booker Rd			
Ste 101 ... Universal City TX 78148	**855-999-5200**	210-659-2112	47-22
American Watchmakers-Clockmakers Institute (AWI)			
701 Enterprise Dr ... Harrison OH 45030	**866-367-2924**	513-367-9800	48-4
American Water Ski Hall of Fame & Museum			
1251 Holy Cow Rd ... Polk City FL 33868	**800-533-2972**	863-324-2472	515
American Water Works Assn (AWWA)			
6666 W Quincy Ave ... Denver CO 80235	**800-926-7337**	303-794-7711	47-12
American Water Works Co Inc			
1025 Laurel Oak Rd ... Voorhees NJ 08043	**888-282-6816**	856-346-8200	357-5
NYSE: AWK			
American Welding & Tank Co			
4718 Old Gettysburg Rd			
Ste 300 ... Mechanicsburg PA 17055	**800-345-2495**	717-763-5080	90
American Welding Society (AWS)			
550 NW 42nd Ave ... Miami FL 33126	**800-443-9353**	305-443-9353	48-3
American Whitewater (AW)			
PO Box 1540 ... Cullowhee NC 28723	**866-262-8429**	828-586-1930	47-23
American Wholesale Marketers Assn (AWMA)			
2750 Prosperity Ave Ste 530 ... Fairfax VA 22031	**800-482-2962**	703-208-3358	48-18
American Woman's Society of Certified Public Accountants (AWSCPA)			
136 S Keowee St ... Dayton OH 45402	**800-297-2721**	937-222-1872	48-1
American Youth Soccer Organization (AYSO)			
19750 S Vermont Ave Ste 200 ... Torrance CA 90502	**800-872-2976**		47-22
Americana Tickets NY			
1535 Broadway ... New York NY 10036	**800-833-3121**	212-581-6660	740
AmericanChurch Inc			
525 McClurg Rd PO Box 3120 ... Youngstown OH 44513	**800-446-3035**	330-758-4545	263
American-International Charolais Assn (AICA)			
11700 NW Plaza Cir ... Kansas City MO 64153	**800-270-7711**	816-464-5977	47-2
Americanna Co			
29 Aldrin Rd ... Plymouth MA 02360	**888-747-5550***	508-747-5550	9
*Cust Svc			
Americano Beach Resort			
1260 N Atlantic Ave ... Daytona Beach FL 32118	**800-874-1824**	386-255-7431	660

Name / Address	City	State	ZIP	Toll-Free	Phone	Class
Americans for Democratic Action (ADA) 1625 K St NW Ste 210	Washington	DC	20006	**855-712-8441**	202-785-5980	47-7
Americans for Effective Law Enforcement (AELE) 841 W Touhy Ave	Park Ridge	IL	60068	**800-763-2802**	847-685-0700	47-8
Americans for Peace Now (APN) 1101 14th St NW 6th Fl	Washington	DC	20005	**877-429-0678**	202-728-1893	47-7
Americans for the Arts 1000 Vermont Ave NW 6th Fl	Washington	DC	20005	**866-471-2787**	202-371-2830	47-4
Americans United for Separation of Church & State 518 C St NE	Washington	DC	20002	**800-875-3707**	202-466-3234	47-7
AmericanTours International LLC (ATI) 6053 W Century Blvd	Los Angeles	CA	90045	**800-800-8942**	310-641-9953	750
AmericanWest Bancorp 41 W Riverside Ave Ste 100	Spokane	WA	99201	**800-772-5479**	509-927-3028	357-2
AmeriCares Foundation 88 Hamilton Ave	Stamford	CT	06902	**800-486-4357**	203-658-9500	47-5
AmericasMart 240 Peachtree St NW Ste 2200	Atlanta	GA	30303	**800-285-6278**	404-220-3000	206
Americhem Inc 2000 Americhem Way	Cuyahoga Falls	OH	44221	**800-228-3476**	330-929-4213	141
AmericInn Inn-Pressive Club 250 Lake Dr E	Chanhassen	MN	55317	**800-634-3444**	952-294-5000	375
AmericInn International LLC 250 Lake Dr E *Resv	Chanhassen	MN	55317	**800-396-5007***	952-294-5000	376
Americo Financial Life & Annuity Insurance Co PO Box 410288	Kansas City	MO	64141	**800-231-0801**		388-2
Americo Life Inc 300 W 11th St *General	Kansas City	MO	64105	**800-231-0801***	816-391-2000	357-4
AmeriCom Inc PO Box 2146	Sandy	UT	84091	**800-820-6296**	801-571-2446	726
Americomm 804 Greenbrier Cir	Chesapeake	VA	23320	**800-527-6757**	757-622-2724	5
Ameridial Inc 4535 Strausser St NW	North Canton	OH	44720	**800-445-7128**		727
Ameridrives Couplings 1802 Pittsburgh Ave PO Box 4000	Erie	PA	16512	**800-352-0141**	814-480-5000	613
AmeriDrives International 1802 Pittsburgh Ave	Erie	PA	16502	**800-352-0141**	814-480-5000	613
AmeriFactors 215 Celebration Pl Ste 340	Celebration	FL	34747	**800-884-3863**	407-566-1150	272
Ameri-Fax Corp 6520 W 20th Ave Ste 2	Hialeah	FL	33016	**800-262-8214**		547
Ameriflight Inc 4700 Empire Ave Hngr 1	Burbank	CA	91505	**800-800-4538**	818-847-0000	12
AmeriGas Partners LP 460 N Gulph Rd *NYSE: APU*	King of Prussia	PA	19406	**800-427-4968**	610-337-7000	315
AMERIGROUP Corp 4425 Corporation Ln *NYSE: AGP*	Virginia Beach	VA	23462	**800-600-4441**	757-490-6900	388-3
AmeriHealth Mercy Health Plan 8040 Carlson Rd Ste 500	Harrisburg	PA	17112	**888-991-7200**	717-651-3540	349
Ameril-Co Carriers Inc 1702 E Overland PO Box 1649	Scottsbluff	NE	69361	**800-445-5400**	308-635-3157	770
Amerijet International Inc 2800 S Andrews Ave	Fort Lauderdale	FL	33316	**800-927-6059**	954-320-5300	12
Amerimade Technology Inc 449 Mtn Vista Pkwy	Livermore	CA	94551	**800-938-3824**	925-243-9090	601
Amerimax Bldg Products Inc 5208 Tennyson Pkwy	Plano	TX	75024	**800-448-4033**	469-366-3200	475
Amerimax Home Products Inc 450 Richardson Dr	Lancaster	PA	17603	**800-347-2586**	717-299-3711	475
Amerinet Inc Two City Pl Dr Ste 400	St. Louis	MO	63141	**877-711-5700**		246
Ameripack Inc 107 N Gold Dr	Robbinsville	NJ	08691	**800-456-7963**	609-259-7004	5
AmeriPride Services Inc 10801 Wayzata Blvd *Cust Svc	Minnetonka	MN	55305	**800-750-4628***	952-738-4200	438
Ameriprise Brokerage 70400 Ameriprise Financial Ctr	Minneapolis	MN	55474	**800-535-2001**		681
Ameriprise Financial Inc 834 Ameriprise Financial Ctr *NYSE: AMP*	Minneapolis	MN	55474	**866-673-3673**	612-671-3131	398
Ameriprise Financial Services Inc 70100 Ameriprise Financial Ctr	Minneapolis	MN	55474	**866-483-8434**		398
Ameris Bancorp 24 Second Ave SE *NASDAQ: ABCB*	Moultrie	GA	31768	**800-347-9680**	229-890-1111	357-2
Ameris Bank 24 Second Ave SE PO Box 3668	Moultrie	GA	31768	**866-616-6020**		187
AMERISAFE Inc 2301 Hwy 190 W *NASDAQ: AMSF*	DeRidder	LA	70634	**800-256-9052**	337-463-9052	388-4
Ameriserv Financial 216 Franklin St PO Box 520 *NASDAQ: ASRV*	Johnstown	PA	15907	**800-837-2265**	814-533-5300	69
AmerisourceBergen Corp 1300 Morris Dr Ste 100 PO Box 959 *NYSE: ABC*	Chesterbrook	PA	19087	**800-829-3132**	610-727-7000	238
AmeriSpan Unlimited 1334 Walnut St 6 Fl	Philadelphia	PA	19107	**800-879-6640**	215-751-1100	420
AmeriSpec Inc 889 Ridge Lk Blvd	Memphis	TN	38120	**800-426-2270**	901-820-8500	362
Ameristar Casino & Hotel 3200 N Ameristar Dr	Kansas City	MO	64161	**888-777-8700**	816-414-7000	376
Ameristar Casino Hotel Council Bluffs 2200 River Rd	Council Bluffs	IA	51501	**866-667-3386**	712-328-8888	132
Ameristar Casinos Inc 3773 Howard Hughes Pkwy Ste 490-S *NASDAQ: ASCA*	Las Vegas	NV	89169	**888-203-1112**	702-567-7000	131
Ameristar Fence Products Inc 1555 N Mingo Rd	Tulsa	OK	74116	**888-333-3422**	918-835-0898	486
Amerisure Insurance Co 26777 Halsted Rd Ste 200	Farmington Hills	MI	48331	**800-257-1900**	248-615-9000	388-4

Name / Address	City	State	ZIP	Toll-Free	Phone	Class
Ameritas Direct 5900 'O' St	Lincoln	NE	68510	**800-555-4655**		388-2
Ameritas Holding Co 5900 O St	Lincoln	NE	68510	**800-311-7871**	402-467-1122	357-4
Ameritas Life Insurance Corp 5900 'O' St	Lincoln	NE	68510	**800-745-1112**	402-467-1122	388-2
Ameritas Managed Dental Plan Inc 5900 'O' St	Lincoln	NE	68510	**800-404-8019**	402-467-1122	388-3
Ameritas Variable Life Insurance Co 5900 'O' St	Lincoln	NE	68510	**800-634-8353**	402-467-1122	388-2
Ameritel Inn Boise Towne Square 7965 W Emerald St	Boise	ID	83704	**800-600-6001**	208-378-7000	376
Ameritel Inn Pocatello 1440 Pocatello Bench Rd	Pocatello	ID	83201	**800-600-6001**	208-234-7500	376
Ameriwood Industries Inc 410 E S First St *General	Wright City	MO	63390	**800-489-3351***	636-745-3351	318-2
Amery Regional Medical Ctr 265 Griffin St E	Amery	WI	54001	**800-424-5273**	715-268-8000	350
Ames Community School District 415 Stanton Ave	Ames	IA	50014	**800-262-3867**	515-268-6600	676
Ames Taping Tools Inc 3350 Breckinridge Blvd Ste 100	Duluth	GA	30096	**800-408-2801**	800-303-1827	748
Ames True Temper Inc 465 Railroad Ave	Camp Hill	PA	17011	**800-393-1846**		748
AMETEK Automation & Process Technologies 1080 N Crooks	Clawson	MI	48017	**800-635-0289**	248-435-0700	202
Ametek HDR Power Systems Inc 3563 Interchange Rd	Columbus	OH	43204	**888-797-2685**	614-308-5500	253
AMETEK Inc 1100 Cassatt Rd PO Box 1764 *NYSE: AME*	Berwyn	PA	19312	**800-473-1286**	610-647-2121	357-3
AMETEK Inc Chemical Products Div 455 Corporate Blvd *Orders	Newark	DE	19702	**800-441-7777***	302-456-4400	734-3
AMETEK Inc Dixson Div 287 27 Rd	Grand Junction	CO	81503	**888-302-0639**	970-242-8863	490
AMETEK Inc Test & Calibration Instruments Div 8600 Somerset Dr	Largo	FL	33773	**800-733-5427**	727-538-6132	467
AMETEK National Controls Corp 1725 Western Dr	West Chicago	IL	60185	**800-323-2593**	630-231-5900	204
AMETEK Sensor Technology Drexelbrook Div 205 Keith Valley Rd *Cust Svc	Horsham	PA	19044	**800-553-9092***	215-674-1234	490
AMETEK Solidstate Controls 875 Dearborn Dr	Columbus	OH	43085	**800-635-7300**	614-846-7500	253
AMETEK US Gauge 820 Pennsylvania Blvd	Feasterville	PA	19053	**888-631-5454**	215-355-6900	467
AMF Bakery Systems 2115 W Laburnum Ave	Richmond	VA	23227	**800-225-3771**	804-355-7961	208
AMF Bowling Worldwide Inc 7313 Bell Creek Rd	Mechanicsville	VA	23111	**800-342-5263**		98
Amfed Cos LLC 576 Highland Colony Pkwy	Ridgeland	MS	39157	**800-264-8085**	601-853-4949	387
AMFM Inc 240 Capitol St Ste 500	Charleston	WV	25301	**800-348-1623**	304-344-1623	458
AMG Resources Corp 2 Robinson Plaza # 350	Pittsburgh	PA	15205	**800-633-3606**	412-777-7300	677
Amgen Canada Inc 6775 Financial Dr Ste 100	Mississauga	ON	L5N0A4	**800-665-4273**	905-285-3000	84
Amgen Inc One Amgen Ctr Dr	Thousand Oaks	CA	91320	**800-563-9798**	805-447-1000	84
AMHA (American Morgan Horse Assn) 4066 Shelburne Rd Ste 5	Shelburne	VT	05482	**888-436-3700**	802-985-4944	47-3
AMHCA (American Mental Health Counselors Assn) 801 N Fairfax St Ste 304	Alexandria	VA	22314	**800-326-2642**	703-548-6002	48-15
Amherst College 220 S Pleasant St	Amherst	MA	01002	**866-542-4438**	413-542-2000	166
AMI (American Megatrends Inc) 5555 Oakbrook Pkwy Bldg 200	Norcross	GA	30093	**800-828-9264**	770-246-8600	177
Ami Adini & Assoc Inc 4609 Russell Ave	Los Angeles	CA	90027	**888-400-4260**	323-913-4073	195
AMI Metals Inc 1738 General George Patton Dr	Brentwood	TN	37027	**800-727-1903**	615-377-0400	487
Amica Mutual Insurance Co 100 Amica Way	Lincoln	RI	02865	**800-652-6422**		388-4
Amicalola Electric Membership Corp 544 Hwy 515 S	Jasper	GA	30143	**800-282-7411**	706-253-5200	245
Amick Farms Inc 2079 Batesburg Hwy	Batesburg	SC	29006	**800-926-4257**	803-532-1400	10-7
AMICO (Alabama Metal Industries Corp) 3245 Fayette Ave	Birmingham	AL	35208	**800-366-2642**	205-787-2611	486
Amidon Graphics 1966 Benson Ave	Saint Paul	MN	55116	**800-328-6502**	651-690-2401	619
Amigos de las Americas 5618 Star Ln	Houston	TX	77057	**800-231-7796**	713-782-5290	47-5
Amigos Library Services 14400 Midway Rd	Dallas	TX	75244	**800-843-8482**	972-851-8000	384
Amino Transport Inc 223 NE Loop 820 Ste 101	Hurst	TX	76053	**800-304-3360**		195
Amivest Capital Management 703 Market St 18th Fl	San Francisco	CA	94103	**800-541-7774**		398
AML Partners LLC Four Grand Cove Way	Edgewater	NJ	07020	**866-790-5095**	201-484-8835	461
Ammeraal Beltech USA 7501 N St Louis Ave *Cust Svc	Skokie	IL	60076	**800-323-4170***	847-673-6720	367
AMN Healthcare Services Inc 12400 High Bluff Dr Ste 100 *NYSE: AHS*	San Diego	CA	92130	**866-871-8519**		712
Amneal Pharmaceuticals LLC 75 Adams Ave *NYSE: IPAH*	Hauppauge	NY	11788	**866-525-7270**	631-952-0214	576
Amnesty International USA (AIUSA) 5 Penn Plaza 16th Fl	New York	NY	10001	**866-273-4466**	212-807-8400	47-5
AMOA (Amusement & Music Operators Assn) 600 Spring Hill Ring Rd Ste 111	West Dundee	IL	60118	**800-937-2662**	847-428-7699	47-23
AMOA-National Dart Assn (NDA) 9100 PuRdue Rd Ste 200	Indianapolis	IN	46268	**800-808-9884**	317-387-1299	47-22
Amoco Federal Credit Union PO Box 889	Texas City	TX	77592	**800-231-6053**	409-948-8541	219

	Toll-Free	Phone	Class
Amon Carter Museum			
3501 Camp Bowie Blvd .... Fort Worth TX 76107	800-573-1933	817-738-1933	513
Amoroso's Baking Co			
845 S 55th St .... Philadelphia PA 19143	800-377-6557	215-471-4740	295-1
Amos Press Inc			
911 S Vandemark Rd .... Sidney OH 45365	866-468-1622	937-498-0850	628-9
AMPAC Fine Chemicals (AFC)			
MS 1007 PO Box 1718......... Rancho Cordova CA 95741	800-311-9668	916-357-6880	143
Ampac Packaging LLC			
12025 Tricon Rd .... Cincinnati OH 45246	800-543-7030	513-671-1777	65
Ampac Seed Co			
32727 Hwy 99 E .... Tangent OR 97389	800-547-3230	541-928-1651	685
Ampacet Corp			
660 White Plains Rd .... Tarrytown NY 10591	800-888-4267*	914-631-6600	141
*Cust Svc			
Ampco Metal Inc			
1117 E Algonquin Rd .... Arlington Heights IL 60005	800-844-6008	847-437-6000	480
Ampco Pumps Company Inc			
2045 W Mill Rd .... Glendale WI 53209	800-737-8671	414-643-1852	632
Ampersand Art Supply			
1235 S Loop 4 Ste 400.................. Buda TX 78610	800-822-1939	512-322-0278	42
Ampersand Capital Partners			
55 William St Ste 240................ Wellesley MA 02481	800-477-6834	781-239-0700	780
Ampex Corp			
500 Broadway .... Redwood City CA 94063	800-835-5095	650-367-2011	649
Amphastar Pharmaceuticals Inc			
11570 Sixth St .... Rancho Cucamonga CA 91730	800-423-4136	909-980-9484	576
Amphenol Aerospace			
40-60 Delaware Ave .... Sidney NY 13838	800-678-0141	607-563-5011	253
Amphenol Corp			
358 Hall Ave .... Wallingford CT 06492	877-267-4366	203-265-8900	802
NYSE: APH			
Amphenol Interconnect Products Corp (AIPC)			
20 Valley St .... Endicott NY 13760	888-275-2472	607-754-4444	253
Amphenol Optimize Manufacturing Co			
180 N Freeport Dr Bldg W-10........... Nogales AZ 85621	800-288-4746	520-397-7015	461
Amphenol RF			
Four Old Newtown Rd .... Danbury CT 06810	800-627-7100	203-743-9272	253
Amphenol Spectra-Strip			
720 Sherman Ave .... Hamden CT 06514	800-846-6400	203-281-3200	253
Amphenol-Tuchel Electronics			
6900 Haggerty Rd Ste 200 .... Canton MI 48187	800-380-8052	734-451-6400	253
AMPI 315 N Broadway .... New Ulm MN 56073	800-533-3580	507-354-8295	296-4
AmpliPhi Biosciences Corp			
4870 Sadler Rd Ste 300 .... Glen Allen VA 23060	877-795-3647	804-205-5069	84
OTC: APHB			
AmpliVox Sound Systems LLC			
3995 Commercial Ave .... Northbrook IL 60062	800-267-5486	847-498-9000	51
Ampronix Inc			
15 Whatney .... Irvine CA 92618	800-400-7972	949-273-8000	470
AMR (American Medical Response)			
6200 S Syracuse Way			
Ste 200 .... Greenwood Village CO 80111	877-244-4890	303-495-1200	30
AmRad Engineering Inc			
32 Hargrove Grade .... Palm Coast FL 32137	800-445-6033	386-445-6000	253
AmRent			
950 Threadneedle Ste 255 .... Houston TX 77079	800-324-4595	713-266-1870	626
AMREP Inc			
990 Industrial Pk Dr .... Marietta GA 30062	800-241-7766*	770-422-2071	143
*Cust Svc			
Amresco Inc			
6681 Cochran Rd .... Solon OH 44139	800-448-4442	440-349-1313	231
Amridge University			
1200 Taylor Rd .... Montgomery AL 36117	888-790-8080	334-387-3877	166
Amro Music Stores			
2918 Poplar Ave .... Memphis TN 38111	800-626-2676*	901-323-8888	519
*General			
AMRPA (American Medical Rehabilitation Providers Assn)			
1710 N St NW .... Washington DC 20036	888-346-4624	202-223-1920	48-8
AMS (American Musicological Society)			
6010 College Stn .... Brunswick ME 04011	888-421-1442	207-798-4243	47-4
AMS (American Mathematical Society)			
201 Charles St .... Providence RI 02904	800-321-4267*	401-455-4000	48-19
*Cust Svc			
AMS (American Meteorological Society)			
45 Beacon St .... Boston MA 02108	800-824-0405	617-227-2425	48-19
AMS (American Medical Security)			
3100 AMS Blvd PO Box 19032......... Green Bay WI 54307	800-232-5432	800-657-8205	357-4
AMS Health Sciences Inc			
4000 N Lindsay .... Oklahoma City OK 73105	800-426-4267	405-842-0131	295-11
Ams Mechanical Systems Inc			
140 E Tower Dr .... Burr Ridge IL 60527	800-794-5033	630-887-7700	261
AMS Servicing LLC			
3374 Walden Ave Ste 120............... Depew NY 14043	866-919-5608		502
AMSA (American Medical Student Assn)			
1902 Assn Dr .... Reston VA 20191	800-767-2266	703-620-6600	48-5
AMSA (American Moving & Storage Assn)			
1611 Duke St .... Alexandria VA 22314	888-849-2672	703-683-7410	48-21
AmSan			
3031 N Andrews Ave Exd .... Pompano Beach FL 33064	866-412-6726	954-972-1700	403
Amscan Inc			
80 Grasslands Rd .... Elmsford NY 10523	800-444-8887	914-345-2020	559
Amsco Steel Co			
PO Box 11037 .... Fort Worth TX 76110	800-772-2743	817-926-3355	487
Amsco Windows Inc			
1880 S 1045 W .... Salt Lake City UT 84104	800-748-4661	801-978-5000	234
Amsoil Inc			
925 Tower Ave .... Superior WI 54880	800-777-7094*	715-392-7101	534
*Sales			
AmSouth Investment Services Inc (AIS)			
250 Riverchase Pkwy E 4th Fl........ Birmingham AL 35244	866-512-3479		398
Amstan Logistics			
101 Knightsbridge Dr .... Hamilton OH 45011	800-322-5546	513-863-4627	770
Amsterdam Printing & Litho Corp			
166 Wallins Corners Rd .... Amsterdam NY 12010	800-833-6231*	518-842-6000	9
*Cust Svc			
Amster-Kirtz Co			
2830 Cleveland Ave NW .... Canton OH 44709	800-257-9338	330-535-6021	296-8
AmSurg Corp			
1A Burton Hills Blvd 5th Fl............ Nashville TN 37215	800-945-2301	615-665-1283	349
NASDAQ: AMSG			
AMSUS (Association of Military Surgeons of the United States)			
9320 Old Georgetown Rd .... Bethesda MD 20814	800-761-9320	301-897-8800	48-8
AMT (American Medical Technologists)			
10700 W Higgins Rd Ste 150......... Rosemont IL 60018	800-275-1268	847-823-5169	48-8
AMT (Association for Mfg Technology)			
7901 Westpark Dr .... McLean VA 22102	800-524-0475	703-893-2900	48-12
AMT Datasouth Corp			
803 Camarillo Springs Rd			
Ste D.............................. Camarillo CA 93012	800-215-9192	805-388-5799	174-6
AMTA (American Massage Therapy Assn)			
500 Davis St Ste 900 .... Evanston IL 60201	877-905-2700	847-864-0123	47-17
Amtelco			
4800 Curtin Dr .... McFarland WI 53558	800-356-9148	608-838-4194	725
Amtote International Inc			
11200 Pepper Rd .... Hunt Valley MD 21031	800-345-1566	410-771-8700	321
AmTrust Bank			
1801 E Ninth St .... Cleveland OH 44114	888-696-4444	216-736-3480	69
AMU (American Public University System)			
111 W Congress St .... Charles Town WV 25414	877-777-9081	304-724-3700	167
Amusement & Music Operators Assn (AMOA)			
600 Spring Hill Ring Rd			
Ste 111 .... West Dundee IL 60118	800-937-2662	847-428-7699	47-23
Amvac Chemical Corp			
4100 E Washington Blvd .... Los Angeles CA 90023	800-424-9300	323-264-3910	280
AMVETS			
4647 Forbes Blvd .... Lanham MD 20706	877-726-8387	301-459-9600	47-19
Amway Corp			
7575 Fulton St E .... Ada MI 49355	800-253-6500	616-787-4000	363
Amway Grand Plaza Hotel			
187 Monroe Ave NW .... Grand Rapids MI 49503	800-253-3590	616-774-2000	376
AMX Corp			
3000 Research Dr .... Richardson TX 75082	855-269-8585	469-624-8585	204
AN Deringer Inc			
64 N Main St .... Saint Albans VT 05478	800-448-8108	802-524-8110	444
ANA (Acoustic Neuroma Assn)			
600 Peachtree Pkwy Ste 108........... Cumming GA 30041	877-200-8211	770-205-8211	47-17
ANA (American Nurses Assn)			
8515 Georgia Ave Ste 400 .... Silver Spring MD 20910	800-274-4262	301-628-5000	48-8
ANA PAC (American Nurses Assn PAC)			
8515 Georgia Ave Ste 400 .... Silver Spring MD 20910	800-274-4262	301-628-5000	608
ANAC (Association of Nurses in AIDS Care)			
3538 Ridgewood Rd .... Akron OH 44333	800-260-6780	330-670-0101	48-8
Anacom General Corp			
1240 S Claudina St .... Anaheim CA 92805	800-955-9540	714-774-8484	389
Anadarko Petroleum Corp			
1201 Lk Robbins Dr .... Spring TX 77380	800-800-1101	832-636-1000	529
NYSE: APC			
Anaheim Automation			
910 E Orangefair Ln .... Anaheim CA 92801	800-345-9401*	714-992-6990	204
*Sales			
Anaheim Custom Extruders			
4640 E La Palma Ave .... Anaheim CA 92807	800-229-2760*	714-693-8508	593
*Cust Svc			
Anaheim Ducks			
2695 E Katella Ave .... Anaheim CA 92806	877-945-3946		707
Anaheim Extrusion Company Inc			
1330 N Kraemer Blvd PO Box 6380 ..... Anaheim CA 92806	800-660-3318	714-630-3111	480
Anaheim Marriott			
700 W Convention Way .... Anaheim CA 92802	800-845-5279	714-750-8000	662
Anaheim Mfg Co			
2680 Orbiter St PO Box 4146.............. Brea CA 92821	800-854-3229*	310-542-5259	35
*Cust Svc			
Anaheim Plaza Hotel & Suites			
1700 S Harbor Blvd .... Anaheim CA 92802	800-631-4144	714-772-5900	376
Anaheim/Orange County Visitor & Convention Bureau			
800 W Katella Ave PO Box 4270........ Anaheim CA 92802	855-405-5020	714-765-8888	207
Analog Devices Inc			
Three Technology Way .... Norwood MA 02062	800-262-5643	781-329-4700	687
NASDAQ: ADI			
Analysts Inc			
22750 Hawthorne Blvd Ste 220 .... Torrance CA 90505	800-336-3637		732
Analysts International Corp			
7700 France Ave S Ste 200.......... Minneapolis MN 55435	800-800-5044	952-838-3000	181
NASDAQ: ANLY			
Analytic Investors LLC			
555 W Fifth St 50th Fl.............. Los Angeles CA 90013	800-618-1872	213-688-3015	398
Analytical Graphics Inc			
220 Vly Creek Blvd .... Exton PA 19341	800-220-4785	610-981-8000	178
Anaqua Grill			
555 S Alamo St .... San Antonio TX 78205	800-845-5279	210-229-1000	662
Anaren Microwave Inc			
6635 Kirkville Rd .... East Syracuse NY 13057	800-544-2414	315-432-8909	253
NASDAQ: ANEN			
AnaSpec Inc			
34801 Campus Dr .... Fremont CA 94555	800-452-5530	510-791-9560	231
Ancestry 360 W 4800 N .... Provo UT 84604	800-262-3787	801-705-7000	394
Ancestry.com			
360 W 4800 N .... Provo UT 84604	800-262-3787*	801-705-7000	394
*Cust Svc			
Anchor BanCorp Wisconsin Inc			
25 W Main St .... Madison WI 53707	800-252-6246	608-252-8700	357-2
NYSE: ABCW			
Anchor Bank			
1055 Wayzata Blvd E .... Wayzata MN 55391	800-425-5150	952-473-4606	69
Anchor Bay School District			
5201 County Line Rd			
Ste 100.......................... Casco Township MI 48064	800-285-4460	586-725-2861	676
Anchor Brewing Co			
1705 Mariposa St .... San Francisco CA 94107	800-478-2227	415-863-8350	101
Anchor Computer Inc			
1900 New Hwy .... Farmingdale NY 11735	800-728-6262	631-293-6100	179-10
Anchor Fabrication Ltd			
1200 Lawson Rd .... Fort Worth TX 76131	800-635-0386	817-498-2521	475
Anchor Industries Inc			
1100 Burch Dr .... Evansville IN 47725	800-544-4445	812-867-2421	723
Anchor Paper Company Inc			
480 Broadway St .... Saint Paul MN 55101	800-652-9755	651-298-1311	546
Anchor QEA LLC			
720 Olive Way Ste 1900 .... Seattle WA 98101	800-887-8681	206-287-9130	195
Anchorage Alaska Bed & Breakfast Assn (AABBA)			
PO Box 242623 .... Anchorage AK 99524	888-584-5147	907-272-5909	373
Anchorage Convention & Visitors Bureau			
524 W Fourth Ave .... Anchorage AK 99501	800-445-8667	907-276-4118	207
Anchorage Daily News			
1001 Northway Dr .... Anchorage AK 99508	800-478-4200	907-257-4200	525-2

Company	Address	City	State	ZIP	Toll-Free	Phone	Class
AnchorBank	25 W Main St PO Box 7933	Madison	WI	53703	**800-252-6246**	608-252-8827	69
Anchor-Harvey Components LLC	600 W Lamm Rd	Freeport	IL	61032	**888-367-4464**	815-235-4400	478
Ancient Cedars Spa at the Wickaninnish Inn	500 Osprey Ln PO Box 250	Tofino	BC	V0R2Z0	**800-333-4604**	250-725-3113	698
Ancira Winton Chevrolet	6111 Bandera Rd *General	San Antonio	TX	78238	**800-299-5286***	210-390-6255	56
ANCO Insurance	1111 Briarcrest Dr PO Box 3889	Bryan	TX	77802	**800-749-1733**	979-776-2626	387
Anco Products Inc (API)	2500 S 17th St	Elkhart	IN	46517	**800-837-2626**	574-293-5574	386
Ancra International LLC	4880 W Rosecrans Ave	Hawthorne	CA	90250	**800-973-5092**	310-973-5000	669
Andaluz	125 Second St NW	Albuquerque	NM	87102	**877-987-9090**	505-242-9090	376
Andaz San Diego	600 F St	San Diego	CA	92101	**877-489-4489**	619-849-1234	376
Anderol Inc	215 Merry Ln PO Box 518	East Hanover	NJ	07936	**888-263-3765**	973-887-7410	534
Andersen Corp	100 Fourth Ave N	Bayport	MN	55003	**888-888-7020**	651-264-5150	236
Andersen Manufacturing Inc	3125 N Yellowstone Hwy	Idaho Falls	ID	83401	**800-635-6106**	208-523-6460	638
Anderson Area Chamber of Commerce	907 N Main St Ste 200	Anderson	SC	29621	**800-922-1150**	864-226-3454	137
Anderson Brass Co	1629 W Bobo Newsome Hwy	Hartsville	SC	29550	**800-476-9876**	843-332-4111	777
Anderson Chemical Co	325 S Davis	Litchfield	MN	55355	**800-366-2477**	320-693-2477	143
Anderson Coach & Travel	One Anderson Plz	Greenville	PA	16125	**800-345-3435**	724-588-8310	750
Anderson Copper & Brass Co	4325 Frontage Rd	Oak Forest	IL	60452	**800-323-5284**	708-535-9030	602
Anderson Electrical Products Inc	1615 Moores St PO Box 455	Leeds	AL	35094	**800-423-0730**	573-682-5521	347
Anderson Equipment Co	1000 Washington Pk	Bridgeville	PA	15017	**800-414-4554**	412-343-2300	355
Anderson Erickson Dairy Co	2420 E University Ave	Des Moines	IA	50317	**800-234-7257**	515-265-2521	295-27
Anderson Forest Products Inc	1267 Old Edmonton Rd PO Box 520	Tompkinsville	KY	42167	**800-489-6778**	270-487-6778	544
Anderson Independent-Mail	PO Box 2507	Anderson	SC	29622	**800-859-6397**	864-224-4321	525-2
Anderson Instrument Co	156 Auriesville Rd	Fultonville	NY	12072	**800-833-0081**	518-922-5315	202
Anderson International Corp	6200 Harvard Ave	Cleveland	OH	44105	**800-336-4730**	216-641-1112	297
Anderson Ranch Arts Ctr	5263 Owl Creek Rd PO Box 5598	Snowmass Village	CO	81615	**800-525-6363**	970-923-3181	49-1
Anderson Trucking Service Inc	725 Opportunity St PO Box 1377	Saint Cloud	MN	56301	**800-328-2316**	320-255-7400	770
Anderson University	1100 E Fifth St *Admissions	Anderson	IN	46012	**800-428-6414***	765-649-9071	166
Anderson Wood Products Co	1381 Beech St	Louisville	KY	40211	**800-825-5591**	502-778-5591	494
Anderson/Madison County Visitors & Convention Bureau	6335 S Scatterfield Rd	Anderson	IN	46013	**800-533-6569**	765-643-5633	207
Anderson-DuBose Co	5300 Tod Ave SW	Lordstown	OH	44481	**800-248-1080**	440-248-8800	299
Andersons Inc	480 W Dussel Dr *NASDAQ: ANDE*	Maumee	OH	43537	**800-537-3370**	419-893-5050	186
Andersons Inc Rail Group	480 W Dussel Dr PO Box 119 *General	Maumee	OH	43537	**800-537-3370***	419-893-5050	264-5
Andersons Inc Retail Group	480 W Dussel Dr PO Box 119	Maumee	OH	43537	**800-537-3370**	419-893-5050	779
Andex Industries Inc	1911 Fourth Ave N	Escanaba	MI	49829	**800-338-9882**		87
Andis Co	1800 County Rd H	Sturtevant	WI	53177	**800-558-9441**	262-884-2600	36
Andover College	265 Western Ave	South Portland	ME	04106	**800-639-3110**	207-774-6126	788
Andover Healthcare Inc	9 Fanaras Dr	Salisbury	MA	01952	**800-432-6686**	978-465-0044	471
Andover Newton Theological School	210 Herrick Rd	Newton Centre	MA	02459	**800-964-2687**	617-964-1100	167-3
Andreini & Co	220 W 20th Ave	San Mateo	CA	94403	**800-969-2522**	650-573-1111	387
Andrew College	501 College St	Cuthbert	GA	39840	**800-664-9250**		160
Andrew Technologies LLC	1421 Edinger Ave Ste D	Tustin	CA	92780	**888-959-7674**		470
Andrews Federal Credit Union (AFCU)	5711 Allentown Rd	Suitland	MD	20746	**800-487-5500**	301-702-5500	219
Andrews Hotel	624 Post St	San Francisco	CA	94109	**800-926-3739**	415-563-6877	376
Andrews McMeel Universal	1130 Walnut	Kansas City	MO	64106	**800-851-8923**	816-581-7500	523
Andrews Osborne Academy	38588 Mentor Ave	Willoughby	OH	44094	**800-753-4683**	440-942-3600	615
Andrews University	3976 Rose Dr	Berrien Springs	MI	49103	**800-253-2874**	269-471-7771	166
Andrews University James White Library	4190 Admin Dr	Berrien Springs	MI	49104	**800-253-2874**	269-471-3264	431-6
Andrews University Seventh-day Adventist Theological Seminary	4145 E Campus Cir Dr Andrews University	Berrien Springs	MI	49104	**800-253-2874**	269-471-3537	167-3
Andrews Van Lines Inc	310 S Seventh St *Cust Svc	Norfolk	NE	68701	**800-228-8146***	402-371-5440	512
Andrie Inc	561 E Western Ave	Muskegon	MI	49442	**800-722-2421**	231-728-2226	313
Androscoggin Home Health Services Inc	PO Box 819	Lewiston	ME	04243	**800-482-7412**	207-777-7740	360
Andrus Transportation Services LLC	3185 East Deseret Dr North PO Box 880	Saint George	UT	84790	**800-888-5838**	435-673-1566	357-2
Andy Frain Services Inc	761 Shoreline Dr	Aurora	IL	60504	**877-707-4771**	630-820-3820	684
Andy Williams Moon River Theatre	2500 Hwy 76	Branson	MO	65616	**800-666-6094**	417-334-1800	565
Anemostat	1220 Watsoncenter Rd PO Box 4938	Carson	CA	90745	**877-423-7426**	310-835-7500	234
ANG Federal Credit Union	PO Box 170204	Birmingham	AL	35217	**800-237-6211**	205-841-4525	219
Angel Fire Resort	PO Box 130	Angel Fire	NM	87710	**800-633-7463**	575-377-6401	660
Angel Stadium	2000 Gene Autry Way	Anaheim	CA	92806	**866-800-1275**	714-940-2000	711
Angela Hospice Home Care	14100 Newburgh Rd *General	Livonia	MI	48154	**866-464-7810***	734-464-7810	368
Angelo State University	2601 W Ave N ASU Stn 11014	San Angelo	TX	76909	**800-946-8627**	325-942-2041	166
Angelo State University Henderson Library	2025 S Johnson St	San Angelo	TX	76909	**800-946-8627**	325-942-2051	431-6
Angie's Cantina	11 E Buchanan St	Duluth	MN	55802	**800-706-7672**	218-727-6117	662
Angler's Inn	265 N Millward	Jackson	WY	83001	**800-867-4667**	307-733-3682	376
Angola Wire Products Inc	803 Wohlert St	Angola	IN	46703	**800-800-7225**	260-665-9447	286
Angstrom Graphics	2025 McKinley St	Hollywood	FL	33020	**800-634-1262**	954-920-7300	619
Angstrom Graphics Inc	4437 E 49th St	Cleveland	OH	44125	**800-634-1262**	216-271-5300	619
Angstrom Technologies Inc	7880 Foundation Dr *Cust Svc	Florence	KY	41042	**800-543-7358***	859-282-0020	143
Anguil Environmental Systems Inc	8855 N 55th St	Milwaukee	WI	53223	**800-488-0230**	414-365-6400	18
Anguilla Tourist Marketing Office	246 Central Ave	White Plains	NY	10606	**800-553-4939**	914-287-2400	765
Angus Barn	9401 Glenwood Ave	Raleigh	NC	27617	**800-277-2270**	919-781-2444	662
Anheuser-Busch Cos Inc	1200 Lynch St	Saint Louis	MO	63118	**800-379-2739**	314-577-3559	79-1
ANI (American Nuclear Insurers)	95 Glastonbury Blvd Ste 300	Glastonbury	CT	06033	**866-301-1301**	860-682-1301	48-9
Animal Supply Company LLC	32001 32nd Ave S Ste 420	Federal Way	WA	98001	**800-323-2963**	253-237-0400	296-8
Animas Corp	200 Lawrence Dr	West Chester	PA	19380	**877-937-7867**	610-644-8990	472
Animation Mentor	1400 65th St Ste 250	Emeryville	CA	94608	**877-326-4628**		754
Anixter Inc	2301 Patriot Blvd	Glenview	IL	60026	**800-264-9837**	224-521-8000	190-4
Anixter International Inc	2301 Patriot Blvd *NYSE: AXE*	Glenview	IL	60025	**800-492-1212**	224-521-8000	246
Anlin Industries	1665 Tollhouse Rd	Clovis	CA	93611	**800-287-7996**	559-322-1531	494
ANMA (American Naturopathic Medical Assn)	150 S Hwy 160 Ste 8-528	Pahrump	NV	89048	**888-202-4440**	702-897-7053	47-17
ANMC (Alaska Native Medical Ctr)	4315 Diplomacy Dr *Admitting	Anchorage	AK	99508	**800-478-6661***	907-563-2662	371-3
Ann Arbor Area Convention & Visitors Bureau	120 W Huron St	Ann Arbor	MI	48104	**800-888-9487**	734-995-7281	207
Ann Inc	Seven Times Sq *NYSE: ANN*	New York	NY	10036	**800-677-6788**	212-541-3300	155-6
Ann Sacks Tile & Stone Inc	8120 NE 33rd Dr	Portland	OR	97211	**800-278-8453**	503-281-7751	741
ANNA (American Nephrology Nurses Assn)	200 E Holly Ave	Sewell	NJ	08080	**888-600-2662**	856-256-2320	48-8
Anna Griffin Inc	99 Armour Dr	Atlanta	GA	30324	**888-817-8170**	404-817-8170	545-2
Anna Maria College	50 Sunset Ln	Paxton	MA	01612	**800-344-4586**		166
Anna's Linens Inc	3550 Hyland Ave	Costa Mesa	CA	92626	**866-266-2728**	714-850-0504	359
Annals of Internal Medicine Magazine	190 N Independence Mall W	Philadelphia	PA	19106	**800-523-1546**	215-351-2400	452-16
Annapolis & Anne Arundel County Conference & Visitors Bureau (AAACCVB)	26 W St	Annapolis	MD	21401	**888-302-2852**	410-280-0445	207
Annapolis Bancorp Inc	1000 Bestgate Rd *NASDAQ: ANNB*	Annapolis	MD	21401	**800-555-5455**	410-224-4483	357-2
Annenberg Media	1301 Pennsylvania Ave NW ste302	Washington	DC	20004	**800-532-7637**		624
Annex Brands Inc	7580 Metropolitan Dr Ste 200	San Diego	CA	92108	**877-722-5236**	619-563-4800	112
Annie E Casey Foundation	701 St Paul St	Baltimore	MD	21202	**800-222-1099**	410-547-6600	304
Annin & Co	105 Eisenhower Pkwy	Roseland	NJ	07068	**800-534-5611**	973-228-9400	287
Anniston Sportswear Corp	P.O. Box 189	Anniston	AL	36201	**866-814-9253**	256-236-1551	153-11
Anniston Star	4305 McClellan Blvd PO Box 189	Anniston	AL	36202	**866-814-9253**	256-236-1551	525-2
AnnTaylor Inc	Seven Times Sq	New York	NY	10036	**800-677-6788**	212-541-3300	155-6
Annual Reviews	4139 El Camino Way	Palo Alto	CA	94303	**800-523-8635**	650-493-4400	628-9
Ano-Coil Corp	60 E Main St	Rockville	CT	06066	**800-492-7286**	860-871-1200	771
Anoka Technical College	1355 W Hwy 10	Anoka	MN	55303	**800-627-3529**	763-433-1100	788
Anoka-Hennepin Independent School District 11	2727 N Ferry St	Anoka	MN	55303	**800-729-6164**	763-506-1000	676
ANR Pipeline Co	717 Texas St	Houston	TX	77002	**800-827-5267**	832-320-5230	324
Anritsu Co	490 Jarvis Dr	Morgan Hill	CA	95037	**800-267-4878**	408-778-2000	248
ANS (American Nuclear Society)	555 N Kensington Ave	La Grange Park	IL	60526	**800-323-3044**	708-352-6611	48-19
Ansar Group Inc, The	240 S Eigth St	Philadelphia	PA	19107	**888-883-7804**	215-922-6088	470

	Toll-Free	Phone	Class
Ansell Healthcare Inc			
111 S Wood Ave Ste 200 .... Iselin NJ 08830	800-365-2282	732-345-5400	569
ANSI (American National Standards Institute)			
25 W 43rd St 4th fl .... New York NY 10036	800-374-3818	212-642-4900	47-1
AnswerDash Inc			
4000 Mason Rd New Ventures Facility			
Fluke Hall .... Seattle WA 98195	800-311-5786		384
Answers Corp			
237 W 35th St Ste 1101 .... New York NY 10001	888-885-5008	646-502-4778	179-7
ANSYS Inc			
275 Technology Dr .... Canonsburg PA 15317	800-937-3321	724-746-3304	179-5
NASDAQ: ANSS			
Antea Group			
5910 Rice Creek Pkwy Ste 100 .... Saint Paul MN 55126	800-477-7411	651-639-9449	658
Antec Inc			
47900 Fremont Blvd .... Fremont CA 94538	800-222-6832	510-770-1200	253
Antelope Valley Press			
37404 Sierra Hwy .... Palmdale CA 93550	888-874-2527	661-273-2700	525-2
Anthem Blue Cross & Blue Shield			
2015 Staples Mill Rd .... Richmond VA 23230	800-451-1527	804-354-7000	388-3
Anthem Blue Cross & Blue Shield Maine			
Two Gannett Dr ....South Portland ME 04106	800-482-0966*	207-822-7000	388-3
*Cust Svc			
Anthem Blue Cross & Blue Shield of Connecticut			
370 Bassett Rd .... North Haven CT 06473	800-922-1742	800-922-4670	388-3
Anthem Blue Cross & Blue Shield of Nevada			
9133 W Russell Rd .... Las Vegas NV 89148	800-332-3842	702-228-2583	388-3
Anthem Blue Cross Blue Shield Colorado			
700 Broadway .... Denver CO 80273	800-654-9338	303-831-2131	388-3
Anthem Inc			
120 Monument Cir ....Indianapolis IN 46204	800-999-7222	317-488-6000	457
Anthem Insurance Cos Inc			
120 Monument Cir Ste 200 ....Indianapolis IN 46204	800-331-1476	317-488-6000	357-4
Anthem Life Insurance Co			
6740 N High St Ste 200 ....Worthington OH 43085	800-551-7265	614-436-0688	388-2
Anthony & Sylvan Pools Corp			
3739 Easton Rd Rt 611 .... Doylestown PA 18901	800-366-7958	215-489-5600	719
Anthony Forest Products Co			
309 N Washington Ave ....El Dorado AR 71730	800-221-2326	870-862-3414	674
Anthony International			
12391 Montera Ave .... Sylmar CA 91342	800-772-0900	818-365-9451	328
Anthony-Thomas Candy Co			
1777 Arlingate Ln .... Columbus OH 43228	877-226-3921	614-274-8405	295-8
Anthro Corp			
10450 SW Manhasset Dr .... Tualatin OR 97062	800-325-3841	503-691-2556	318-1
Antibodies Inc			
PO Box 1560 .... Davis CA 95617	800-824-8540		84
AntiCancer Inc			
7917 Ostrow St .... San Diego CA 92111	800-511-2555	858-654-2555	231
Anti-Defamation League (ADL)			
605 Third Ave .... New York NY 10158	866-386-3235	212-885-7700	47-8
Antigua & Barbuda			
Embassy			
3216 New Mexico Ave NW .... Washington DC 20016	866-978-7299	202-362-5122	257
Antigua & Barbuda Dept of Tourism & Trade			
305 E 47th St 6th fl .... New York NY 10017	888-268-4227	212-541-4117	765
Antigua Sportswear Inc			
16651 N 84 Ave .... Peoria AZ 85382	800-528-3133	623-523-6000	153-11
Antioch University			
2326 Sixth Ave .... Seattle WA 98121	888-268-4477	206-441-5352	166
Antiochian Orthodox Christian Archdiocese of North America			
358 Mountain Rd .... Englewood NJ 07631	888-421-1442	201-871-1355	47-20
Antique Car Museum/Grovewood Gallery			
111 Grovewood Rd .... Asheville NC 28804	877-622-7238	828-253-7651	513
Antique Collectors Club			
116 Pleasant St ....EastHampton MA 01027	800-254-4100	413-529-0861	628-2
Antique Mall			
1251 S Virginia St .... Reno NV 89502	888-316-6255	775-324-4141	455
Antique Trader			
700 E State St .... Iola WI 54990	800-258-0929	715-445-2214	452-14
Antique World			
11111 Main St .... Clarence NY 14031	800-321-2211	716-759-8483	455
Antitrust & Trade Regulation Daily			
1801 S Bell St .... Arlington VA 22202	800-372-1033		524-2
Antler Inn			
43 W Pearl St PO Box 575 ....Jackson WY 83001	800-483-8667	307-733-2535	376
Anton/Bauer Inc			
14 Progress Dr .... Shelton CT 06484	800-422-3473	203-929-1100	584
Antonelli Institute			
300 Montgomery Ave ....Erdenheim PA 19038	800-722-7871	215-836-2222	162
Anvil Cases			
15730 Salt Lake Ave .... City of Industry CA 91745	800-359-2684	626-968-4100	448
Anvil Corp			
1675 W Bakerview Rd .... Bellingham WA 98226	877-412-6845	360-671-1450	261
AnyDoc Software Inc			
28500 Clemens Road Ste 800 .... Westlake OH 44145	888-495-2638		179-7
AO Smith Corp			
11270 W Pk Pl Ste 170			
PO Box 245008 ....Milwaukee WI 53224	800-359-4065	414-359-4000	511
NYSE: AOS			
AO Smith Electrical Products Co			
531 N Fourth St .... Tipp City OH 45371	800-543-9450	937-667-2431	511
AO Smith Water Products Co			
500 Tennessee Waltz Pkwy .... Ashland City TN 37015	800-527-1953		35
AOA (American Osteopathic Assn)			
142 E Ontario St .... Chicago IL 60611	800-621-1773	312-202-8000	48-8
AOAC International			
481 N Frederick Ave			
Ste 500 .... Gaithersburg MD 20877	800-379-2622	301-924-7077	48-19
AOC (Association of Old Crows)			
1000 N Payne St Ste 300 .... Alexandria VA 22314	800-247-5626	703-549-1600	47-19
AOCA (Automotive Oil Change Assn)			
330 N. Wabash Ave Ste 2000 .... Chicago IL 60611	800-230-0702	312-321-5132	48-21
AOCS (American Oil Chemists Society)			
2710 S Boulder PO Box 17190..........Urbana IL 61802	866-535-2730	217-359-2344	47-12
AODME (Association of Osteopathic Directors & Medical Educators)			
142 E Ontario St ....Chicago IL 60611	800-621-1773	312-202-8211	48-8
AOM (Academy of Management)			
235 Elm Rd PO Box 3020 ....Briarcliff Manor NY 10510	800-633-4931	914-923-2607	48-12
Aon Corp			
200 E Randolph St .... Chicago IL 60601	877-384-4276	312-381-1000	357-4
Aon Risk Services Inc			
200 E Randolph St .... Chicago IL 60601	877-384-4276	312-381-1000	387
AOPA (Aircraft Owners & Pilots Assn)			
421 Aviation Way .... Frederick MD 21701	800-872-2672	301-695-2000	48-21
AOPA Pilot Magazine			
421 Aviation Way .... Frederick MD 21701	800-872-2672	301-695-2000	452-14
AORN Inc			
2170 S Parker Rd Ste 300............Denver CO 80231	800-755-2676	303-755-6300	48-8
AOSSM (American Orthopaedic Society for Sports Medicine)			
6300 N River Rd Ste 500 .... Rosemont IL 60018	877-321-3500	847-292-4900	48-8
AOTA (American Occupational Therapy Assn Inc)			
4720 Montgomery Ln			
PO Box 31220............... Bethesda MD 20824	800-877-1383	301-652-2682	48-8
AP Exhaust Technologies Inc			
300 Dixie Trial ....Goldsboro NC 27530	800-277-2787	919-580-2000	59
APA (American Psychiatric Assn)			
1000 Wilson Blvd Ste 1825 .... Arlington VA 22209	888-357-7924	703-907-7300	48-15
APA (American Psychological Assn)			
750 First St NE .... Washington DC 20002	800-374-2721	202-336-5500	48-15
APA Services			
4150 International Plz Tower I			
Ste 510 .... Fort Worth TX 76109	877-425-5023		724
Apache Corp			
2000 Post Oak Blvd Ste 100...........Houston TX 77056	800-272-2434	713-296-6000	529
NYSE: APA			
Apache Hose & Belting Co Inc			
4805 Bowling St SW			
PO Box 1719...........Cedar Rapids IA 52404	800-553-5455*	319-365-0471	367
*Sales			
Apache Stainless Equipment Corp			
200 W Industrial Dr			
PO Box 538............Beaver Dam WI 53916	800-444-0398	920-356-9900	383
APACVB (Alexandria/Pineville Area Convention & Visitors Bureau)			
707 Main St PO Box 1070 .... Alexandria LA 71301	800-551-9546	318-442-9546	207
Apalachicola Bay Chamber of Commerce			
122 Commerce St .... Apalachicola FL 32320	866-269-3022	850-653-9419	137
Aparaa Corp			
14900 Landmark Blvd Ste 630 .... Dallas TX 75254	888-441-2535		178
Apartment Investment & Management Co			
4582 S Ulster St Pkwy Ste 1100..........Denver CO 80237	888-789-8600*	303-691-4350	646
NYSE: AIV *General			
APC (American Power Conversion Corp)			
132 Fairgrounds Rd ....West Kingston RI 02892	800-788-2208*	401-789-5735	253
*Cust Svc			
APC Integrated Services Inc			
770 SPIRIT OF SAINT			
LOUIS Blvd ...............CHESTERFIELD MO 63005	888-294-7886		316
APCC (American Public Communications Council Inc)			
625 Slaters Ln Ste 104 .... Alexandria VA 22314	800-868-2722	703-739-1322	48-20
APCO Bulletin			
351 N Williamson Blvd ....Daytona Beach FL 32114	888-272-6911	386-322-2500	524-8
APCO Employees Credit Union			
750 17th St N ....Birmingham AL 35203	800-249-2726	205-257-3601	219
Apco Extruders Inc			
180 National Rd .... Edison NJ 08817	800-942-8725*	732-287-3000	541
*Orders			
APCO Graphics Inc			
388 Grant St SE .... Atlanta GA 30312	877-988-2726	404-688-9000	692
APCON Inc			
9255 SW Pioneer Ct ....Wilsonville OR 97070	800-624-6808	503-682-4050	175
APD (American Product Distributors Inc)			
8350 Arrowridge Blvd ....Charlotte NC 28273	800-849-5842	704-522-9411	527
APDA (American Parkinson Disease Assn)			
135 Parkinson Ave .... Staten Island NY 10305	800-223-2732	718-981-8001	47-17
Aperio Technologies Inc			
1360 Park Ctr Dr Ste 106 .... Vista CA 92081	866-478-4111		471
APEX Analytix Inc			
1501 Highwoods Blvd			
Ste 200-A .... Greensboro NC 27410	866-577-8183	336-272-4669	179-9
Apex Color			
200 N Lee St .... Jacksonville FL 32204	800-367-6790		109
Apex Digital Imaging Inc			
16057 Tampa Palms Blvd W .... Tampa FL 33647	866-973-3034	813-973-3034	692
Apex Geoscience Inc			
2120 Brandon Dr .... Tyler TX 75703	800-755-8461	903-581-8080	256
Apex Homes Inc			
7172 Rt 522 .... Middleburg PA 17842	800-326-9524	570-837-2333	187
Apex Industries Inc			
100 Millennium Blvd .... Moncton NB E1E2G8	800-268-3331	506-857-1620	475
Apex Mills Corp			
168 Doughty Blvd ....Inwood NY 11096	800-989-2739	516-239-4400	734-4
Apex Paper Box Co			
5601 Walworth Ave ....Cleveland OH 44102	800-438-2269*	216-416-9475	100
*Cust Svc			
Apex Piping Systems Inc			
302 Falco Dr .... Wilmington DE 19804	888-995-2739	302-995-6136	603
APEX Systems Inc			
4400 Cox Rd Ste 100 .... Glen Allen VA 23060	800-452-7391	804-254-2600	712
Apex Voice Communications Inc			
21031 Ventura Blvd			
Second Fl .... Woodland Hills CA 91364	800-727-3970	818-379-8400	179-7
APG (Automation Products Group Inc)			
1025 West 1700 North .... Logan UT 84321	888-525-7300	435-753-7300	202
APG (American Packing & Gasket Co)			
6039 Armour Dr PO Box 213...........Houston TX 77020	800-888-5223	713-675-5271	325
APGA (American Public Gas Assn)			
201 Massachusetts Ave NE			
Ste C-4 .... Washington DC 20002	800-927-4204	202-464-2742	47-12
ApHC (Appaloosa Horse Club)			
2720 W Pullman Rd ....Moscow ID 83843	888-304-7768	208-882-5578	47-3
APHL (Association of Public Health Laboratories)			
8515 Georgia Ave Ste 700 .... Silver Spring MD 20910	800-899-2278	240-485-2745	48-7
API (Anco Products Inc)			
2500 S 17th St ....Elkhart IN 46517	800-837-2626	574-293-5574	386
API (Aerospace Products International)			
3778 Distriplex Dr N ....Memphis TN 38118	888-274-2497	901-365-3470	22
APi Construction Co			
1100 Old Hwy 8 NW ....New Brighton MN 55112	800-223-4922	651-636-4320	190-9
APi Group Inc			
1100 Old Hwy 8 NW ....New Brighton MN 55112	800-223-4922		186
APi Group Inc Fabrication & Mfg Group			
1100 Old Hwy 8 NW ....New Brighton MN 55112	800-223-4922		475
APi Group Inc Fire Protection Group			
1100 Old Hwy 8 NW ....New Brighton MN 55112	800-223-4922		190-13
APi Group Inc Materials Distribution Group			
1100 Old Hwy 8 NW ....New Brighton MN 55112	800-223-4922		192-2

	Toll-Free	Phone	Class

APi Group Inc Specialty Construction Services Group
1100 Old Hwy 8 NW ....New Brighton MN 55112　800-223-4922　　190-1
API Heat Transfer Inc
2777 Walden Ave ....Buffalo NY 14225　877-274-4328　716-684-6700　90
APi Systems Group Inc
10575 Vista Park Rd ....Dallas TX 75238　877-828-1200*　214-291-1200　683
　*General
Apio Inc PO Box 727 ....Guadalupe CA 93434　800-454-1355*　805-343-2835　295-21
　*Sales
APL (Albany Public Library)
161 Washington Ave ....Albany NY 12210　800-733-2767　518-427-4300　431-3
APL Access & Security Inc
115 S William Dillard Dr ....Gilbert AZ 85233　866-873-2288　480-497-9471　684
APL Logistics Inc
16220 N Scottsdale Rd
Ste 300 ....Scottsdale AZ 85254　866-896-2005　　444
Aplus.net Internet Services
10350 Barnes Canyon Rd ....San Diego CA 92121　877-275-8763　858-410-6929　395
APM Hexseal Corp
44 Honeck St ....Englewood NJ 07631　800-498-9034　201-569-5700　325
APMA (American Podiatric Medical Assn)
9312 Old Georgetown Rd ....Bethesda MD 20814　800-275-2762　301-581-9200　48-8
Apmetrix Inc
5414 Oberlin Dr Ste 200 ....San Diego CA 92121　800-490-3184　　384
APN (Americans for Peace Now)
1101 14th St NW 6th Fl ....Washington DC 20005　877-429-0678　202-728-1893　47-7
APN Media LLC
PO Box 20113 ....New York NY 10023　800-470-7599　212-581-3380　628-9
APNA (American Psychiatric Nurses Assn)
1555 Wilson Blvd Ste 530 ....Arlington VA 22209　866-243-2443　703-243-2443　48-8
Apogee Enterprises Inc
4400 W 78th St Ste 520 ....Minneapolis MN 55435　877-752-3432　952-835-1874　328
　NASDAQ: APOG
Apollo Design Technology Inc
4130 Fourier Dr ....Fort Wayne IN 46818　800-288-4626　260-497-9191　713
Apollo Group Inc
4025 E Elwood St ....Phoenix AZ 85040　800-990-2765　　242
　NASDAQ: APOL
Apollo Oil LLC
1175 Early Dr ....Winchester KY 40391　800-473-5823　859-744-5444　315
Apollo Professional Svc
29 Stiles Rd Ste 302 ....Salem NH 03079　866-277-3343　　261
Apotex Corp
2400 N Commerce Pkwy Ste 400 ......Weston FL 33326　877-427-6839　　577
Apotex Inc
150 Signet Dr ....Toronto ON M9L1T9　800-268-4623　416-749-9300　576
Apothecary Products
11750 12th Ave S Burnsville ....Burnsville MN 55337　800-328-2742　　215
Apothecus Pharmaceutical Corp
220 Townsend Sq ....Oyster Bay NY 11771　800-227-2393　516-624-8200　576
APPA (American Public Power Assn)
1875 Connecticut Ave
Ste 1200 ....Washington DC 20009　800-515-2772　202-467-2900　47-12
Appalachian Mountain Club (AMC)
Five Joy St ....Boston MA 02108　800-262-4455*　617-523-0655　47-13
　*Orders
Appalachian Regional Healthcare Service (ARH)
2285 Executive Dr PO Box 8086 .....Lexington KY 40505　877-243-4782　859-226-2440　350
Appalachian School of Law
1169 Edgewater Dr ....Grundy VA 24614　800-895-7411　276-935-4349　167-1
Appalachian State University
Belk Library
218 College St PO Box 32026 ....Boone NC 28608　877-423-0086　828-262-2300　431-6
Appalachian Trail Conservancy (ATC)
799 Washington St
PO Box 807 ....Harpers Ferry WV 25425　888-287-8673*　304-535-6331　47-23
　*Sales
Appaloosa Horse Club (ApHC)
2720 W Pullman Rd ....Moscow ID 83843　888-304-7768　208-882-5578　47-3
Apparelmaster
123 Harrison Ave ....Harrison OH 45030　877-543-1678　513-202-1600　438
Appeal-Democrat
1530 Ellis Lk Dr PO Box 431 ....Marysville CA 95901　800-831-2345　530-741-2345　525-2
Apple & Eve Inc
2 Seaview Blvd ....Port Washington NY 11050　800-969-8018　516-621-1122　295-20
Apple Bank for Savings
122 E 42nd St Ninth Fl ....New York NY 10168　800-824-0710　914-902-2775　69
Apple Inc
One Infinite Loop ....Cupertino CA 95014　800-275-2273*　408-996-1010　174-1
　*NASDAQ: AAPL ■ *Cust Svc
Apple Rehab 46 Maple St ....Kent CT 06757　800-353-5368*　860-927-5368　445
　*General
Apple Rubber Products Inc
310 Erie St ....Lancaster NY 14086　800-828-7745*　716-684-6560　325
　*Cust Svc
Apple Saddlery
1875 Innes Rd ....Ottawa ON K1B4C6　800-867-8225　613-744-4040　702
Apple Tree Inn
9508 N Div St ....Spokane WA 99218　800-323-5796　509-466-3020　376
Apple Vacations Inc
101 NW Pt Blvd ....Elk Grove Village IL 60007　800-517-2000　　761
Apple Valley Chamber of Commerce
14800 Galaxie Ave Ste 101 ....Apple Valley MN 55124　800-301-9435　952-432-8422　137
Applegate Insulation Manufacturing Inc
1000 Highview Dr ....Webberville MI 48892　800-627-7536　517-521-3545　386
AppleOne Employment Services Inc
327 W Broadway ....Glendale CA 91204　800-872-2677　310-750-3400　712
AppleSeeds Magazine
30 Grove St Ste C ....Peterborough NH 03458　800-821-0115　　452-6
Appleton Medical Ctr
1818 N Meade St ....Appleton WI 54911　800-236-4101　920-731-4101　371-3
Appleton Papers Inc
825 E Wisconsin Ave PO Box 359 ....Appleton WI 54912　888-593-9546　920-734-9841　545-1
Appleton Partners Inc
One Post Office Sq 6th Fl ....Boston MA 02109　800-338-0745　617-338-0700　398
Applewood Books Inc
1 River Rd ....Carlisle MA 01741　800-277-5312*　781-271-0055　628-2
　*General
Applewood Manor Inn
62 Cumberland Cir ....Asheville NC 28801　800-442-2197　828-254-2244　376
Appliance Recycling Centers of America Inc
7400 Excelsior Blvd ....Minneapolis MN 55426　800-452-8680　952-930-9000　651
　NASDAQ: ARCI

	Toll-Free	Phone	Class

Applicant Insight Ltd
5396 School Rd
PO Box 458. ....New Port Richey FL 34652　800-771-7703　　626
Applied Card Systems
50 Applied Card Way ....Glen Mills PA 19342　866-227-5627　　217
Applied Computer Research Inc (ACR)
PO Box 41730 ....Phoenix AZ 85080　800-234-2227　　628-11
Applied Dynamics International Inc
3800 Stone School Rd ....Ann Arbor MI 48108　888-465-4329　734-973-1300　179-2
Applied Energy Company Inc (AEC)
1205 Venture Ct Ste 100. ....Carrollton TX 75006　800-580-1171　214-355-4200　631
Applied Energy Solutions LLC
One Technology Pl ....Caledonia NY 14423　800-836-2132　585-538-4421　73
Applied Fiber Inc
PO Box 1339 ....Leesburg GA 31763　800-226-5394　229-759-8301　537
Applied Materials Inc
3050 Bowers Ave
PO Box 58039. ....Santa Clara CA 95054　877-356-9175　408-727-5555　686
　NASDAQ: AMAT
Applied Materials/Semitool
655 W Reserve Dr ....Kalispell MT 59901　877-356-9175　406-752-2107　686
Applied Mechanical Systems Inc
5598 Wolf Creek Pk ....Dayton OH 45426　888-854-3073　937-854-3073　603
Applied Membranes Inc
2325 Cousteau Ct ....Vista CA 92081　800-321-9321　760-727-3711　605
Applied Microstructures Inc
1020 Rincon Cir ....San Jose CA 95131　877-683-2678　408-907-2885　202
Applied Process Cooling Corp
555 Price Ave ....Redwood City CA 94063　877-231-6406　650-595-0665　655
Applied Research & Technology
215 Tremont St ....Rochester NY 14608　800-775-2427　585-436-2720　51
Applied Software Inc
3919 National Dr Ste 200 ....Burtonsville MD 20866　888-624-8439　　178
Applied Systems Inc
200 Applied Pkwy ....University Park IL 60466　800-999-5368*　708-534-5575　179-11
　*Sales
Applied Technology & Management Inc
5550 NW 111th Blvd ....Gainesville FL 32653　800-275-6488　　261
Appling County Board of Education
249 Blackshear Hwy ....Baxley GA 31513　866-632-9992　912-367-8600　676
APPMA (American Pet Products Manufacturers Assn)
255 Glenville Rd ....Greenwich CT 06831　800-452-1225　203-532-0000　48-4
Appraisal Institute
550 W Van Buren St Ste 1000 ....Chicago IL 60607　888-756-4624　312-335-4100　48-17
Appraisal Journal
200 W Madison Ste 1500 ....Chicago IL 60606　888-756-4624　　452-5
Appro International Inc
901 Fifth Ave Ste 1000 ....Seattle WA 98164　800-950-2729　206-701-2000　174-8
AppsHosting Inc
13772 Goldenwest St Ste 321 .....Westminster CA 92683　877-625-6610　　384
Apptis Inc
4800 Westfields Blvd ....Chantilly VA 20151　888-277-8478　703-579-0471　179-4
APPX Software Inc
11363 San Jose Blvd
Ste 301 ....Jacksonville FL 32223　800-879-2779　904-880-5560　179-1
APQC
123 N Post Oak Ln Ste 300. ....Houston TX 77024　800-776-9676　713-681-4020　48-12
APRA (Automotive Parts Remanufacturers Assn)
4215 Lafayette Ctr Dr Ste 3. ....Chantilly VA 20151　877-734-4827　703-968-2772　48-21
Apria Healthcare Group Inc
26220 Enterprise Ct ....Lake Forest CA 92630　800-277-4288　949-639-2000　360
Apricorn Inc
12191 Kirkham Rd ....Poway CA 92064　800-458-5448　858-513-2000　174-8
APRO (Association of Progressive Rental Organizations)
1504 Robin Hood Trl ....Austin TX 78703　800-204-2776　512-794-0095　48-18
APRS (American Park & Recreation Society)
22377 Belmont Ridge Rd ....Ashburn VA 20148　800-765-3110　703-858-0784　47-23
APS (American Pain Society)
4700 W Lake Ave ....Glenview IL 60025　877-752-4754　847-375-4715　47-17
APS (Albuquerque Public Schools)
6400 Uptown Blvd NE ....Albuquerque NM 87110　866-563-9297　505-880-3700　676
APS (American Physical Society)
1 Physics Ellipse ....College Park MD 20740　888-221-9425　301-209-3200　48-19
APS (Arizona Public Service Co)
400 N Fifth St PO Box 53999 ....Phoenix AZ 85004　800-253-9405　602-371-7171　775
APS Healthcare Inc
44 S Broadway Ste 1200. ....White Plains NY 10601　800-305-3720　　457
Apscreen Inc
PO Box 80639 ....Rancho Santa Margarita CA 92688　800-277-2733　949-646-4003　626
APSP (Association of Pool & Spa Professionals)
2111 Eisenhower Ave Ste 500 ....Alexandria VA 22314　800-323-3996　703-838-0083　48-4
APT (Alabama Public Television)
2112 11th Ave S Ste 400 ....Birmingham AL 35205　800-239-5233　205-328-8756　624
APTA (American Physical Therapy Assn)
1111 N Fairfax St ....Alexandria VA 22314　800-999-2782　703-684-2782　48-8
Aptech Computer Systems Inc
135 Delta Dr ....Pittsburgh PA 15238　800-245-0720　412-963-7440　179-11
Aptima Inc
12 Gill St Ste 1400 ....Woburn MA 01801　866-461-7298　781-935-3966　659
APTS (Association of Public Television Stations)
2100 Crystal Dr Ste 700 ....Arlington VA 22202　855-948-5853　202-654-4200　48-14
APV
1415 California Ave ....Brockville ON K6V7H7　800-263-3958　613-345-2280　297
APWA (American Public Works Assn)
2345 Grand Blvd Ste 700 ....Kansas City MO 64108　800-848-2792　816-472-6100　48-7
AQHA (American Quarter Horse Assn)
1600 Quarter Horse Dr ....Amarillo TX 79104　800-291-7323　806-376-4811　47-3
Aqua America Inc
762 W Lancaster Ave ....Bryn Mawr PA 19010　877-987-2782　　775
　NYSE: WTR
Aqua Bamboo
2425 Kuhio Ave ....Honolulu HI 96815　855-747-0754　808-922-7777　376
Aqua Bath Company Inc
921 Cherokee Ave ....Nashville TN 37207　800-232-2284　615-227-0017　603
Aqua Hospitality Corp
445 Seaside Ave ....Honolulu HI 96815　855-747-0755　808-923-2345　376
Aqua Waikiki Wave
2299 Kuhio Ave ....Honolulu HI 96815　855-747-0754　808-921-1262　376
Aqua-Aerobic Systems Inc
6306 N Alpine Rd ....Loves Park IL 61111　800-940-5008　815-654-2501　794
Aquae Sulis Spa at the JW Marriott Resort Las Vegas
221 N Rampart Blvd ....Las Vegas NV 89144　877-869-8777　702-869-7807　698
Aqua-Leisure Industries Inc
PO Box 239 ....Avon MA 02322　866-807-3998　　701

	Toll-Free	Phone	Class
Aqualung America Inc			
2340 Cousteau Ct .... Vista CA 92083	800-446-2671	760-597-5000	701
Aquarion Co			
835 Main St .... Bridgeport CT 06604	800-732-9678	203-336-7662	775
Aquarius Casino Resort			
1900 S Casino Dr .... Laughlin NV 89029	888-662-5825	702-298-5111	132
Aquatherm Industries Inc			
1940 Rutgers University Blvd .... Lakewood NJ 08701	800-535-6307		354
Aqueduct Medical Inc			
665 Third St Ste 20........ San Francisco CA 94107	877-365-4325		470
Aquent LLC			
711 Boylston St .... Boston MA 02116	855-767-6333	617-535-5000	712
Aquila Group of Funds			
380 Madison Ave Ste 2300........... New York NY 10017	800-437-1020	212-697-6666	521
Aquinas College			
4210 HaRding Rd .... Nashville TN 37205	800-649-9956*	615-297-7545	166
*Admissions			
Aquinas Institute of Theology			
23 S Spring Ave .... Saint Louis MO 63108	800-977-3869	314-256-8800	167-3
Aquion Water Treatment Products LLC Rainsoft Div			
2080 E Lunt Ave .... Elk Grove Village IL 60007	800-860-7638	847-437-9400	794
A-r Editions Inc			
8551 Research Way Ste 180.......... Middleton WI 53562	800-736-0070	608-836-9000	516
AR Thomson Group			
7930 130th St .... Surrey BC V3W0H7	800-410-9116	604-507-6050	325
AR Wilfley & Sons Inc			
7350 E Progress Pl Ste 200 ....Englewood CO 80111	800-525-9930	303-779-1777	632
ARA (American Rental Assn)			
1900 19th St .... Moline IL 61265	800-334-2177	309-764-2475	48-4
ARA (Awards & Recognition Assn)			
4700 W Lake Ave .... Glenview IL 60025	800-344-2148	847-375-4800	48-4
ARA (Automotive Recyclers Assn)			
3975 Fair Ridge Dr Ste 20N .... Fairfax VA 22033	888-385-1005	703-385-1001	48-21
Arabel Inc			
16301 NW 49th Ave .... Hialeah FL 33014	800-759-5959*	305-623-8302	192-2
*Sales			
Arabian Horse World Magazine			
1316 Tamson Dr Ste 101 .... Cambria CA 93428	800-955-9423	805-771-2300	452-14
Arachnid Inc			
6212 Material Ave ....Loves Park IL 61111	800-435-8319	815-654-0212	321
Arakansas Ethics Commission			
PO Box 1917 .... Little Rock AR 72203	800-422-7773	501-324-9600	265
ARAMARK Corp			
1101 Market St ....Philadelphia PA 19107	800-388-3300	937-660-4708	186
ARAMARK Food & Support Services			
1101 Market St ....Philadelphia PA 19107	800-388-3300	215-238-3000	298
Aramark Parks & Destinations			
27655 Hwy 26 & 287 .... Moran WY 83013	866-278-4245	307-543-2847	660
ARAMARK Uniform & Career Apparel LLC			
1101 Market St ....Philadelphia PA 19107	800-272-6275		271
Aramco Services Co			
9009 W Loop S ....Houston TX 77096	866-287-3592	713-432-4000	529
Aramsco Inc			
1480 Grandview Ave .... Paulsboro NJ 08086	800-767-6933	856-686-7700	144
Arandell Inc			
N 82 W 13118 Leon Rd .. Menomonee Falls WI 53051	800-558-8724	262-255-4400	619
Arapahoe Community College			
5900 S Santa Fe Dr .... Littleton CO 80160	888-800-9198	303-797-0100	160
ARB Inc			
26000 Commercentre Dr .... Lake Forest CA 92630	800-622-2699	949-598-9242	189-9
Arbella Mutual Insurance Co			
1100 Crown Colony Dr ....Quincy MA 02169	800-972-5348	617-328-2800	388-4
Arbill			
PO Box 820542 ....Philadelphia PA 19154	800-523-5367		670
Arbitration Forums Inc			
3350 Buschwood Pk Dr Ste 295.......... Tampa FL 33618	800-967-8889*	813-931-4004	40
*Cust Svc			
Arbitron Inc			
9705 Patuxent Woods Dr .... Columbia MD 21046	800-543-7300	410-312-8000	461
NYSE: ARB			
Arbor Acres			
1240 Arbor Rd .... Winston-Salem NC 27104	866-658-2724	336-724-7921	663
Arbor Centers for Eyecare			
2640 183rd St Ste 2 .... Homewood IL 60430	866-798-6633	708-798-6633	237
Arbor Hospice & Home Care			
2366 Oak Vly Dr .... Ann Arbor MI 48103	888-992-2273	734-662-5999	368
Arbor Realty Trust Inc			
333 Earle Ovington Blvd			
Ste 900.................... Uniondale NY 11553	800-272-6710		645
NYSE: ABR			
Arbors of Hop Brook			
403 W Ctr St .... Manchester CT 06040	866-689-0846	860-647-9343	663
ARC (Austin Ribbon & Computer Supplies Inc)			
9211 Waterford Centre Blvd			
Ste 202...................... Austin TX 78758	800-783-7459	512-452-0651	195
ARC (American Radiolabeled Chemicals Inc)			
101 ARC Dr .... Saint Louis MO 63146	800-331-6661	314-991-4545	143
ARC (American Refugee Committee)			
430 Oak Grove St Ste 204........Minneapolis MN 55403	800-875-7060	612-872-7060	47-5
ARC Industries Inc			
2879 Johnstown Rd .... Columbus OH 43219	800-734-7007		712
Arc of the US			
1010 Wayne Ave Ste 650 .... Silver Spring MD 20910	800-433-5255	301-565-3842	47-17
ARC Resources Ltd			
308 Fourth Ave SW Ste 1200 .... Calgary AB T2P0H7	888-272-4900	403-503-8600	666
TSE: ARX			
ARC the Hotel Ottawa			
140 Slater St .... Ottawa ON K1P5H6	800-699-2516	613-238-2888	376
Arcadia University			
450 S Easton Rd .... Glenside PA 19038	888-232-8373	215-572-2900	166
Arcet Equipment Company Inc			
1700 Chamberlayne Ave .... Richmond VA 23222	800-388-0302		202
Arch Chemicals Inc			
1200 Old Lower River Rd			
PO Box 800.............Charleston TN 37310	800-638-8174	423-780-2724	143
NYSE: ARJ			
Arch Crown Tags Inc			
460 Hillside Ave .... Hillside NJ 07205	800-526-8353	973-731-6300	410
Arch Insurance Group Inc			
One Liberty Plz 53rd Fl .... New York NY 10006	866-993-9978	212-651-6500	388-2
Archadeck			
2924 Emerywood Pkwy Ste 101 .... Richmond VA 23294	800-722-4668	804-353-6999	190-2
Archaeological Institute of America (AIA)			
656 Beacon St 4th Fl .... Boston MA 02215	877-524-6300	617-353-9361	47-11
Archaeology Magazine			
36-36 33rd St .... Long Island City NY 11106	877-275-9782	718-472-3050	452-19
Archbold Container Corp			
800 W Barre Rd PO Box 10......... Archbold OH 43502	800-446-2520	419-445-8865	233
Archdiocese of Portland in Oregon			
2838 E Burnside St .... Portland OR 97214	800-235-8722	503-234-5334	47-20
Archdiocese of Saint Paul & Minneapolis			
226 Summit Ave .... Saint Paul MN 55102	877-290-1605	651-291-4411	47-20
Archer Daniels Midland Co (ADM)			
4666 E Faries Pkwy .... Decatur IL 62526	800-637-5843	217-424-5200	186
NYSE: ADM			
Archer Rubber Co			
213 Central St ....Milford MA 01757	800-804-2074	508-473-1870	734-2
Architectural & Transportation Barriers Compliance Board			
1331 F St NW Ste 1000 .... Washington DC 20004	800-872-2253	202-272-0080	338-18
Architectural Bronze Aluminum Corp			
655 Deerfield Rd Ste 100 .... Deerfield IL 60015	800-339-6581		767
Architectural Digest			
Four Times Sq 18th Fl ....New York NY 10036	800-365-8032		452-2
Architectural Floor Systems Inc			
595 Supreme Dr .... Bensenville IL 60106	877-437-3567		130
Architectural Record Magazine			
2 Penn Plaza 9th Fl.................New York NY 10121	800-393-6343	212-904-2594	452-2
Architectural Woodwork Institute (AWI)			
46179 Westlake Dr Ste 120 .... Potomac Falls VA 20165	866-877-6933	571-323-3636	48-3
Architex International			
3333 Commercial Ave .... Northbrook IL 60062	800-621-0827	847-205-1333	358
Archway Marketing Services Inc			
19850 S Diamond Lake Rd ....Rogers MN 55374	866-779-9855	763-428-3300	458
ARCO Coffee Company			
2206 Winter St ....Superior WI 54880	800-283-2726	715-392-4771	295-7
Arco Electric Products Corp			
2325 E Michigan Rd .... Shelbyville IN 46176	800-428-4370	317-398-9713	511
Arcos Industries			
One Arcos Dr .... Mount Carmel PA 17851	800-233-8460	570-339-5200	798
Arctic Cat Inc			
601 Brooks Ave S ....Thief River Falls MN 56701	877-228-2687	218-681-8558	696
NASDAQ: ACAT			
Arctic Glacier Holdings Inc			
625 Henry Ave ....Winnipeg MB R3A0V1	888-573-9237	204-772-2473	571
Arctic Industries Inc			
9731 NW 114th Way .... Miami FL 33178	800-325-0123	305-883-5581	14
Arctic Slope Regional Corp			
1230 Agvik St PO Box 129 ....Barrow AK 99723	800-770-2772	907-852-8633	531
Arctic Star Refrigeration Mfg Company Inc			
3540 W Pioneer Pkwy .... Arlington TX 76013	800-229-6562	817-274-1396	655
Arctic Storm Management Group LLC			
2727 Alaskan Way Pier 69 .... Seattle WA 98121	800-929-0908	206-547-6557	285
ARCVB (Alton Regional Convention & Visitors Bureau)			
200 Piasa St .... Alton IL 62002	800-258-6645	618-465-6676	207
Arcweb Technologies LLC			
234 Market St Fifth Fl............Philadelphia PA 19106	800-846-7980		458
Ardenwood Historic Farm			
34600 Ardenwood Blvd ....Fremont CA 94555	888-327-2757	510-544-2797	513
ARDMS (American Registry of Diagnostic Medical Sonographers)			
51 Monroe St Plz E 1 .... Rockville MD 20850	800-541-9754	301-738-8401	48-8
Ards Trucking Company Inc			
1702 N Gov Williams Hwy .... Darlington SC 29540	800-845-7462	843-393-5101	770
ARE (Association for Research & Enlightenment)			
215 67th St .... Virginia Beach VA 23451	800-333-4499	757-428-3588	47-17
ARE (Association for Retail Environment)			
4651 Sheridan St Ste 470............ Hollywood FL 33021	800-421-3483	954-893-7300	48-3
Area 51 Esg Inc			
51 Post ....Irvine CA 92618	877-476-8751	949-387-0051	246
Area Agency On Aging			
9549 Koger Blvd			
Gadsden Bldg Ste 100 ....St Petersburg FL 33702	800-963-5337	727-570-9696	445
Area Agency On Aging 10b Inc			
1550 Corporate Woods Pkwy ....Uniontown OH 44685	800-421-7277	330-896-9172	445
Area Development Magazine			
400 Post Ave Ste 304 .... Westbury NY 11590	800-735-2732	516-338-0900	452-5
Area Development Partnership			
One Convention Ctr Plz .... Hattiesburg MS 39401	800-238-4288	601-296-7500	137
Area Temps Inc			
1228 Euclid Ave ....Cleveland OH 44115	866-995-5627	440-646-1333	712
AREBA Casriel Inc (ACI)			
500 W 57th St ....New York NY 10019	800-724-4444	212-293-3000	717
Arena Hotel			
817 The Alameda .... San Jose CA 95126	800-954-6835	408-294-6500	376
Arends & Sons Inc			
715 S Sangamon Ave .... Gibson City IL 60936	800-637-6052	217-784-4241	274
Arends Bros Inc			
1190 E 1200N Rd .... Melvin IL 60952	800-356-6811	217-388-7717	274
ARFC (Accounts Receivable Funding Corp)			
PO Box 35750 ....Houston TX 77235	800-992-1717		272
ARG Trucking Corp			
369 Bostwick Rd .... Phelps NY 14532	800-334-1314	315-789-8871	770
Argo International Corp			
160 Chubb Ave ....Lyndhurst NJ 07071	877-274-6468	201-561-7010	246
Argonaut Hotel			
495 Jefferson St .... San Francisco CA 94109	866-415-0704	415-563-0800	376
Argosy University			
1515 Central Pkwy ....Eagan MN 55121	888-844-2004	651-846-2882	166
Argosy University Hawaii			
400 ASB Tower 1001 Bishop St .... Honolulu HI 96813	888-323-2777	808-536-5555	788
Argosy's Alton Belle Casino			
One Piasa St .... Alton IL 62002	800-711-4263		132
Argus Interactive Agency Inc			
217 N Main St Ste 200 .... Santa Ana CA 92701	866-595-9597		523
Argus International Ltd			
108 Whispering Pines Dr			
Ste 110 .... Scotts Valley CA 95066	800-862-7487	831-461-4700	798
Argus Leader			
200 S Minnesota Ave ....Sioux Falls SD 57104	800-530-6397	605-331-2200	525-2
ARH (Appalachian Regional Healthcare Service)			
2285 Executive Dr PO Box 8086.......Lexington KY 40505	877-243-4782	859-226-2440	350
ARHP (Association of Reproductive Health Professionals)			
1901 L St NW Ste 300 .... Washington DC 20036	877-311-8972	202-466-3825	48-8
ARi Industries Inc			
381 Ari Ct .... Addison IL 60101	800-237-6725	630-953-9100	202
ARI Network Services Inc			
10850 W Pk Pl Ste 1200........... Milwaukee WI 53224	877-805-0803	414-973-4300	179-10
Aria			
200 N Columbus Dr ....Chicago IL 60601	888-495-1829	312-444-9494	662

	City	State	ZIP	Toll-Free	Phone	Class
Aria Communications Corp						
717 W Saint Germain St	St. Cloud	MN	56301	**800-955-9924**		727
Aria Spa & Club at the Vail Cascade Resort						
1300 Westhaven Dr	Vail	CO	81657	**888-824-5772**	970-479-5942	698
Ariba Inc						
807 11th Ave	Sunnyvale	CA	94089	**866-772-7422**	650-390-1000	38
NASDAQ: ARBA						
ARINC Inc						
2551 Riva Rd	Annapolis	MD	21401	**866-321-6060**	410-266-4000	672
Ariosa Diagnostics Inc						
5945 Optical Ct	San Jose	CA	95138	**855-927-4672**		415
Aris Horticulture Inc						
115 Third St SE	Barberton	OH	44203	**800-232-9557**		366
Aristocrat Technologies						
7230 Amigo St	Las Vegas	NV	89119	**800-748-4156**	702-270-1000	321
Aristotle Capital Management LLC						
11100 Santa Monica Blvd Ste 1700	Los Angeles	CA	90025	**877-478-4722**	310-478-4005	398
Aristotle Inc						
205 Pennsylvania Ave SE	Washington	DC	20003	**800-296-2747***	202-543-8345	179-11
*Sales						
Arizona						
Attorney General						
1275 W Washington St	Phoenix	AZ	85007	**888-377-6108**	602-542-5025	337-3
Children Youth & Families Div						
1789 W Jefferson St	Phoenix	AZ	85007	**866-229-5553**	602-542-0419	337-3
Historic Preservation Office						
1300 W Washington St	Phoenix	AZ	85007	**800-285-3703**	602-542-4174	337-3
Legislature						
Capitol Complex 1700 W Washington St.	Phoenix	AZ	85007	**800-352-8404**	602-926-3559	337-3
Motor Vehicle Div						
PO Box 2100	Phoenix	AZ	85001	**800-251-5866**	602-255-0072	337-3
Rehabilitation Services Admin						
1789 W Jefferson St 2nd Fl NW	Phoenix	AZ	85007	**800-563-1221**	602-542-3332	337-3
Tourism Office						
1110 W Washington St Ste 155	Phoenix	AZ	85007	**888-520-3434**	602-364-3700	337-3
Treasurer						
1700 W Washington St 1st Fl.	Phoenix	AZ	85007	**877-365-8310**	602-542-7800	337-3
Weights & Measures Dept						
4425 W Olive Ave Ste 134	Glendale	AZ	85302	**800-277-6675**	602-771-4920	337-3
Arizona Art Supply						
4025 N 16th St	Phoenix	AZ	85016	**877-264-9514**	602-264-9514	44
Arizona Assn of Realtors						
255 E Osborne Rd Ste 200	Phoenix	AZ	85012	**800-426-7274**	602-248-7787	647
Arizona Attorney Magazine						
4201 N 24th St Ste 200	Phoenix	AZ	85016	**866-482-9227**	602-252-4804	452-15
Arizona Biltmore Resort & Spa						
2400 E Missouri	Phoenix	AZ	85016	**800-950-0086**	602-955-6600	660
Arizona Cardinals						
8701 S Hardy Dr	Tempe	AZ	85284	**800-999-1402**	602-379-0101	706-3
Arizona Chamber of Commerce & Industry						
3200 N Central Ave Ste 1125	Phoenix	AZ	85012	**800-498-6973**	602-248-9172	138
Arizona Charlie's Boulder Casino & Hotel						
4575 Boulder Hwy	Las Vegas	NV	89121	**888-236-9066**	702-951-5800	376
Arizona Charlie's Decatur Casino & Hotel						
740 S Decatur Blvd	Las Vegas	NV	89107	**888-236-8645**	702-258-5200	132
Arizona Community Foundation						
2201 E Camelback Rd Ste 405B	Phoenix	AZ	85016	**800-222-8221**	602-381-1400	302
Arizona Culinary Institute						
10585 N 114th St Ste 401	Scottsdale	AZ	85259	**866-294-2433**	480-603-1066	161
Arizona Daily Star						
4850 S Pk Ave	Tucson	AZ	85714	**800-695-4492**	520-573-4343	525-2
Arizona Dental Assn						
3193 N Drinkwater Blvd	Scottsdale	AZ	85251	**800-866-2732**	480-344-5777	227
Arizona Federal Credit Union						
PO Box 60070	Phoenix	AZ	85082	**800-523-4603**	602-683-1000	219
Arizona Golf Resort & Conference Ctr						
425 S Power Rd	Mesa	AZ	85206	**800-528-8282**	480-832-3202	660
Arizona Grand Resort						
8000 S Arizona Grand Pkwy	Phoenix	AZ	85044	**866-267-1321**	602-438-9000	660
Arizona Highways Magazine						
2039 W Lewis Ave	Phoenix	AZ	85009	**800-543-5432**		452-22
Arizona Historical Society Museum						
1300 N College Ave	Tempe	AZ	85281	**800-249-7737**	480-929-0292	513
Arizona Inn						
2200 E Elm St	Tucson	AZ	85719	**800-933-1093**	520-325-1541	376
Arizona Leather Company Inc						
4235 Schaefer Ave	Chino	CA	91710	**888-669-5328**	909-993-5101	320
Arizona Limousines Inc						
8900 N Central Ave Ste 101	Phoenix	AZ	85020	**800-678-0033**	602-267-7097	437
Arizona Medical Assn, The (ArMA)						
810 W Bethany Home Rd	Phoenix	AZ	85013	**800-482-3480**	602-246-8901	469
Arizona Mills						
5000 Arizona Mills Cir	Tempe	AZ	85282	**877-746-6642**	480-491-7300	455
Arizona Partsmaster Inc						
7125 W Sherman St PO Box 23169	Phoenix	AZ	85043	**888-924-7278**	602-233-3580	605
Arizona Precision Sheet Metal						
2140 W Pinnacle Peak Rd	Phoenix	AZ	85027	**800-443-7039**	623-516-3700	688
Arizona Public Service Co (APS)						
400 N Fifth St PO Box 53999	Phoenix	AZ	85004	**800-253-9405**	602-371-7171	775
Arizona Publishing Cos						
PO Box 1950	Phoenix	AZ	85001	**800-331-9303**	602-444-8000	628-8
Arizona Republic						
200 E Van Buren St	Phoenix	AZ	85004	**800-331-9303**	602-444-8000	525-2
Arizona State Capitol Museum						
1700 W Washington St	Phoenix	AZ	85007	**800-228-4710**	602-542-4675	513
Arizona State Hospital						
2500 E Van Buren St	Phoenix	AZ	85008	**877-588-5163**	602-244-1331	371-5
Arizona State Prison Complex-Eyman						
4374 E Butte Ave PO Box 3500	Florence	AZ	85132	**866-333-2039**	520-868-0201	213
Arizona State University						
Sandra Day O'Connor College of Law						
PO Box 877906	Tempe	AZ	85287	**855-278-5080**	480-965-6181	167-1
West PO Box 37100	Phoenix	AZ	85069	**855-278-5080**	602-543-5500	166
Arizona State University Art Museum						
10th St & Mill Ave Nelson Fine Arts Ctr Arizona State University	Tempe	AZ	85287	**855-278-5080**	480-965-2787	513
Arizona Western College						
2020 S Ave 8 E	Yuma	AZ	85366	**888-293-0392**	928-317-6000	160
Arizona Wholesale Supply Co						
2020 E University Dr	Phoenix	AZ	85034	**866-977-6849**	602-258-7901	605
Ark Agency						
310 Washburne Ave	Paynesville	MN	56362	**800-328-8894**	320-243-7250	388-1
ARK Diagnostics Inc						
48089 Fremont Blvd	Fremont	CA	94538	**877-869-2320**	510-270-6270	360
Ark TeleServices						
Two E Merrick Rd	Valley Stream	NY	11580	**800-898-5367**		390
Ark Valley Electric Co-op Assn						
10 E Tenth St	South Hutchinson	KS	67504	**888-297-9212**	620-662-6661	245
Arkadin Inc						
Five Concourse Pkwy Ste 1600	Atlanta	GA	30328	**866-551-1432**		384
Arkansas						
Attorney General						
323 Ctr St Ste 200	Little Rock	AR	72201	**800-482-8982***	501-682-2007	337-4
*Consumer Info						
Child Support Enforcement Office						
1509 W Seventh St	Little Rock	AR	72201	**800-264-2445**	501-682-8398	337-4
Crime Victims Reparations Board						
323 Ctr St Ste 200	Little Rock	AR	72201	**800-448-3014**	501-682-1020	337-4
Game & Fish Commission						
2 Natural Resource Dr	Little Rock	AR	72205	**800-364-4263**	501-223-6300	337-4
Highway & Transportation Dept						
10324 I- 30	Little Rock	AR	72209	**800-245-1672**	501-569-2000	337-4
Insurance Dept						
1200 W Third St	Little Rock	AR	72201	**800-282-9134**	501-371-2600	337-4
Parks & Tourism Dept						
1 Capitol Mall	Little Rock	AR	72201	**800-628-8725**	501-682-7777	337-4
Rehabilitation Services						
525 W Capitol Ave	Little Rock	AR	72201	**800-330-0632**	501-296-1600	337-4
Securities Dept						
201 E Markham St Rm 300	Little Rock	AR	72201	**800-981-4429**	501-324-9260	337-4
Vital Records Div						
4815 W Markham St Slot 44	Little Rock	AR	72205	**800-637-9314**	501-661-2000	337-4
Worker's Compensation Commission						
PO Box 950	Little Rock	AR	72203	**800-622-4472**	501-682-3930	337-4
Arkansas Alligator Farm & Petting Zoo						
847 Whittington Ave	Hot Springs	AR	71901	**800-750-7891**	501-623-6172	810
Arkansas Arts Ctr						
501 E Ninth St	Little Rock	AR	72202	**800-264-2787**	501-372-4000	513
Arkansas Blue Cross Blue Shield						
PO Box 2181	Little Rock	AR	72203	**800-238-8379**	501-378-2000	388-3
Arkansas Business LP						
122 E Second St	Little Rock	AR	72201	**888-322-6397**	501-372-1443	452-5
Arkansas Capital Corp Group						
200 S Commerce St Ste 400	Little Rock	AR	72201	**800-216-7237**	501-374-9247	216
Arkansas Correctional Industries (ACI)						
2403 E Harding St	Pine Bluff	AR	71601	**877-635-7213**	870-850-8431	622
Arkansas Democrat-Gazette						
121 E Capital St	Little Rock	AR	72203	**800-482-1121***	501-378-3400	525-2
*Cust Svc						
Arkansas Dept of Corrections Maximum Security Unit						
2501 State Farm Rd	Tucker	AR	72168	**866-801-3435**	501-842-3800	213
Arkansas Dept of Corrections Tucker Unit						
2400 State Farm Rd PO Box 240	Tucker	AR	72168	**800-682-7377**	501-842-2519	213
Arkansas Distributing Company LLC						
800 E Barton Ave	West Memphis	AR	72301	**877-735-3506**	870-735-3506	80-1
Arkansas Educational Television Network (AETN)						
350 S Donaghey Ave	Conway	AR	72034	**800-662-2386**	501-682-2386	624
Arkansas Educator Magazine						
1500 W Fourth St	Little Rock	AR	72201	**800-632-0624**	501-375-4611	452-8
Arkansas Financial Aid Office						
114 Silas Hunt Hall	Fayetteville	AR	72701	**800-547-8839**	479-575-3806	716
Arkansas Hospice						
14 Parkstone Cir	North Little Rock	AR	72116	**877-257-3400**	501-748-3333	368
Arkansas Juvenile Access & Treatment Ctr						
425 W Capitol Ste 1620	Little Rock	AR	72201	**877-727-3468**	501-324-8900	409
Arkansas Lawyer Magazine						
2224 Cottondale Ln	Little Rock	AR	72202	**800-609-5668**	501-375-4606	452-15
Arkansas Museum of Natural Resources						
3853 Smackover Hwy	Smackover	AR	71762	**888-287-2757**	870-725-2877	558
Arkansas Museum of Science & History						
Museum of Discovery						
500 President Clinton Ave Ste 150	Little Rock	AR	72201	**800-880-6475**	501-396-7050	513
Arkansas Realtors Assn						
11224 Executive Ctr Dr	Little Rock	AR	72211	**888-333-2206**	501-225-2020	647
Arkansas State Chamber of Commerce						
1200 W Capitol Ave PO Box 3645	Little Rock	AR	72203	**800-482-1127**	501-372-2222	138
Arkansas State Library						
900 W Capitol Ste 100	Little Rock	AR	72201	**866-801-3435**	501-682-2053	431-5
Arkansas State University						
PO Box 1630	State University	AR	72467	**800-382-3030**	870-972-3024	166
Arkansas State University Museum						
PO Box 490	State University	AR	72467	**800-342-2923**	870-972-2074	513
Arkansas State University Newport						
7648 Victory Blvd	Newport	AR	72112	**800-976-1676**	870-512-7800	160
Arkansas Trailer Manufacturing Co						
3200 S Elm St	Little Rock	AR	72204	**800-666-5417**	501-666-5417	769
Arkansas Valley Electric Co-op Corp						
1811 W Commercial St PO Box 47	Ozark	AR	72949	**800-468-2176**	479-667-2176	245
Arkansas Valley Regional Medical Ctr (AVRMC)						
1100 Carson Ave	La Junta	CO	81050	**877-696-6775**	719-384-5412	371-3
Arkwin Industries Inc						
686 Main St	Westbury	NY	11590	**800-284-2551**	516-333-2640	778
Arkwright Inc						
538 Main St	Fiskeville	RI	02823	**800-556-6866***	401-821-1000	545-1
*Cust Svc						
Arlington Central School District						
144 Todd Hill Rd	LaGrangeville	NY	12540	**800-225-2527**	845-486-4460	676
Arlington Coal & Lumber Company Inc						
41 Pk Ave	Arlington	MA	02476	**800-649-8101**	781-643-8100	361
Arlington Computer Products Inc						
851 Commerce Ct	Buffalo Grove	IL	60089	**800-548-5105***	847-541-6333	181
*Orders						
Arlington Convention & Visitors Bureau						
1905 E Randol Mill Rd	Arlington	TX	76011	**800-433-5374**	817-265-7721	207
Arlington Industries Inc						
1616 Lakeside Dr	Waukegan	IL	60085	**800-323-4147**	847-689-2754	527
Arlington Public Library						
101 E Abram St	Arlington	TX	76010	**888-227-7669**	817-459-6900	431-3
Arlington Resort Hotel & Spa						
239 Central Ave	Hot Springs	AR	71901	**800-643-1502**	501-623-7771	660
Arlington School District						
315 N French Ave	Arlington	WA	98223	**888-535-0747**	360-618-6200	676
Arlo G. Lott Trucking Inc						
257 S 100 E	Jerome	ID	83338	**800-443-5688**	208-324-5053	770

				Toll-Free	Phone	Class
Arlon Graphics						
2811 S Harbor Blvd	Santa Ana	CA	92704	**800-232-7161**	714-540-2811	3
ARM (Associated Risk Managers)						
2 Pierce Pl	Itasca	IL	60143	**800-735-5441**	630-285-4324	48-9
ArMA (Arizona Medical Assn, The)						
810 W Bethany Home Rd	Phoenix	AZ	85013	**800-482-3480**	602-246-8901	469
ARMA (Asphalt Roofing Manufacturers Assn)						
529 14th St NW Ste 750	Washington	DC	20045	**800-247-6637**	202-207-0917	48-3
ARMA International						
11880 College Blvd						
Ste 450	Overland Park	KS	66210	**800-422-2762**	913-341-3808	48-12
Armada Group Inc, The						
325 Soquel Ave Ste A	Santa Cruz	CA	95062	**800-408-2120**		341
Armada Rubber Mfg Co						
24586 Armada Ridge Rd PO Box 579	Armada	MI	48005	**800-842-8311**	586-784-9135	668
Armand Manufacturing Inc						
2399 Silver Wolf Dr	Henderson	NV	89011	**800-669-9811**	702-565-7500	65
Armani Exchange						
568 Broadway	New York	NY	10012	**800-717-2929**	212-431-6000	277
Armanino Foods of Distinction Inc						
30588 San Antonio St	Hayward	CA	94544	**800-255-5855**	510-441-9300	295-36
OTC: AMNF						
Armatron International Inc						
15 Highland Ave	Malden	MA	02148	**800-343-3280**	781-321-2300	426
Armature Dns 2000 Inc						
11001 Jean Meunier	Montreal	QC	H1G4S7	**800-363-7996**	514-324-1141	779
Armed Forces Communications & Electronics Assn (AFCEA)						
4400 Fair Lakes Ct	Fairfax	VA	22033	**800-336-4583**	703-631-6100	47-19
Armed Forces Insurance Exchange (AFI)						
PO Box G	Fort Leavenworth	KS	66027	**800-255-0187**	800-255-6792	388-4
Armed Forces Retirement Home - Gulfport						
1800 Beach Dr	Gulfport	MS	39507	**800-422-9988**		663
Armed Forces Retirement Home - Washington						
3700 N Capitol St NW	Washington	DC	20011	**800-422-9988***		445
*Admissions						
Armed Services Mutual Benefit Assn (ASMBA)						
PO Box 160384	Nashville	TN	37216	**800-251-8434**	615-851-0800	47-19
Armellini Express Lines Inc						
3446 SW Armellini Ave	Palm City	FL	34990	**800-327-7887**	772-287-0575	770
Armenian General Benevolent Union (AGBU)						
55 E 59th St 7th Fl	New York	NY	10022	**800-368-4262**	212-319-6383	47-14
Armistead Mechanical Inc						
168 Hopper Ave	Waldwick	NJ	07463	**800-587-5267**	201-447-6740	190-10
Armor Group Inc, The						
4600 N Mason-Montgomery Rd	Mason	OH	45040	**800-255-0393**		317
Armor Protective Packaging						
951 Jones St	Howell	MI	48843	**800-365-1117**	517-546-1117	550
Arms Acres						
75 Seminary Hill Rd	Carmel	NY	10512	**800-989-2676**	845-225-3400	717
Armstrong Atlantic State University						
11935 Abercorn St	Savannah	GA	31419	**800-633-2349**		166
Armstrong County Tourist Bureau						
125 Market St Ste 2	Kittanning	PA	16201	**888-265-9954**	724-543-4003	207
Armstrong International Inc						
2081 SE Ocean Blvd 4th Fl	Stuart	FL	34996	**866-738-5125**	772-286-7175	777
Armstrong Lumber Co Inc						
2709 Auburn Way N	Auburn	WA	98002	**800-868-9066**	253-833-6666	804
Armstrong Medical Industries Inc						
575 Knightsbridge Pkwy	Lincolnshire	IL	60069	**800-323-4220***	847-913-0101	472
*Cust Svc						
Armstrong Mfg Co						
2700 SE Tacoma St	Portland	OR	97202	**800-426-6226**	503-228-8381	489
Armstrong School District						
410 Main St	Ford City	PA	16226	**888-573-5733**	724-763-5200	676
Armstrong World Industries Inc						
2500 Columbia Ave	Lancaster	PA	17603	**800-233-3823***	717-397-0611	291
NYSE: AWI ■ *Cust Svc						
Army & Navy Academy						
2605 Carlsbad Blvd PO Box 3000	Carlsbad	CA	92018	**888-762-2338**	760-729-2385	615
Army Distaff Foundation						
6200 Oregon Ave NW	Washington	DC	20015	**800-541-4255**	202-541-0149	47-19
ARMY Magazine						
2425 Wilson Blvd	Arlington	VA	22201	**800-336-4570**	703-841-4300	452-12
Army National Guard						
Army National Guard Readiness Ctr						
111 S George Mason Dr	Arlington	VA	22204	**800-404-8273**	703-607-2584	338-4
Army Residence Community						
7400 Crestway	San Antonio	TX	78239	**800-725-0083**	210-646-5316	663
ARN (Association of Rehabilitation Nurses)						
4700 W Lk Ave	Glenview	IL	60025	**800-229-7530**	847-375-4710	48-8
Arnaud's						
813 Bienville St	New Orleans	LA	70112	**866-230-8895**	504-523-5433	662
Arnoff Moving & Storage Inc						
1282 Dutchess Tpke	Poughkeepsie	NY	12603	**800-633-6683**	845-471-1504	512
Arnold & Porter LLP						
555 12th St NW	Washington	DC	20004	**877-470-8792**	202-942-5000	425
Arnold Lumber Co						
251 Fairgrounds Rd	West Kingston	RI	02892	**800-339-0116**	401-783-2266	192-3
Arnold Machinery Co						
2975 West 2100 South	Salt Lake City	UT	84119	**800-821-0548***	801-972-4000	355
*Cust Svc						
Arnold Palmer Hospital for Children & Women						
92 W Miller St	Orlando	FL	32806	**800-648-3818**	407-649-9111	371-1
Arnold Transportation Services Inc						
9523 Florida Mining Blvd	Jacksonville	FL	32257	**800-846-4321**	972-986-3154	770
Aroostook Home Health Services						
658 Main St Ste 2	Caribou	ME	04736	**877-688-9977**	207-492-8290	360
AroundWire.Com LLC						
18107 Sherman Way Ste 206	Reseda	CA	91335	**888-382-3793**		384
ARPAC Group						
9511 W River St	Schiller Park	IL	60176	**800-496-7210**	847-678-9034	540
ArQule Inc						
19 Presidential Way	Woburn	MA	01801	**800-373-7827**	781-994-0300	84
NASDAQ: ARQL						
Array BioPharma Inc						
3200 Walnut St	Boulder	CO	80301	**877-633-2436**	303-381-6600	84
NASDAQ: ARRY						
Array Marketing						
45 Progress Ave	Toronto	ON	M1P2Y6	**800-295-4120**	416-299-4865	233
Arris						
60 Decibel Rd	State College	PA	16801	**800-233-2267**	814-238-2461	638
Arris Group Inc						
3871 Lakefield Dr	Suwanee	GA	30024	**866-362-7747**	678-473-2000	638
NASDAQ: ARRS						

				Toll-Free	Phone	Class
ARRL (American Radio Relay League)						
225 Main St	Newington	CT	06111	**888-277-5289**	860-594-0200	48-14
Arrow Electric Company Inc						
317 Wabasso Ave	Louisville	KY	40209	**888-999-5591**	502-367-0141	190-4
Arrow Engine Co						
2301 E Independence St	Tulsa	OK	74110	**800-331-3662**	918-583-5711	262
Arrow Fastener Co Inc						
271 Mayhill St	Saddle Brook	NJ	07663	**800-776-2228**	201-843-6900	748
Arrow Financial Corp						
250 Glen St	Glens Falls	NY	12801	**800-937-5449**	518-745-1000	357-2
NASDAQ: AROW						
Arrow Florist & Park Avenue Greenhouses Inc						
757 Pk Ave	Cranston	RI	02910	**800-556-7097**	401-785-1900	292
Arrow Freight Management Inc						
PO Box 371974	El Paso	TX	79937	**888-598-9891**	915-778-3999	310
Arrow Lock Co						
100 Arrow Dr	New Haven	CT	06511	**800-839-3157**		347
Arrow Stage Lines						
720 E Norfolk Ave	Norfolk	NE	68701	**800-672-8302**	402-371-3850	106
Arrow Tank & Engineering Co						
650 N Emerson St	Cambridge	MN	55008	**888-892-7769**	763-689-3360	90
Arrow Truck Sales Inc						
3200 Manchester Trfy	Kansas City	MO	64129	**800-311-7144**	816-923-5000	56
Arrow Tru-Line Inc						
2211 S Defiance St	Archbold	OH	43502	**877-285-7253**	419-446-2785	483
Arrow Uniform Rental Inc						
6400 Monroe Blvd	Taylor	MI	48180	**888-332-7769**	313-299-5000	438
Arrow Value Recovery						
9101 Burnet Rd Ste 203	Austin	TX	78758	**800-393-7627**		651
Arrowhead Electric Co-op Inc						
5401 W Hwy 61 PO Box 39	Lutsen	MN	55612	**800-864-3744**	218-663-7239	245
Arrowhead Library System						
210 Dodge St	Janesville	WI	53548	**855-352-9003**	608-758-6690	431-3
Arrowhead Regional Medical Ctr						
400 N Pepper Ave	Colton	CA	92324	**855-422-8029**	909-580-1000	371-3
Arrow-Magnolia International						
2646 Rodney Ln	Dallas	TX	75229	**800-527-2101**	972-247-7111	149
Arrowpoint Capital						
Whitehall Corporate Ctr Ste 3						
3600 Arco Corporate Dr	Charlotte	NC	28273	**866-236-7750**	704-522-2000	388-4
Arrowwood Resort & Conference Ctr						
2100 Arrowwood Ln NW	Alexandria	MN	56308	**866-386-5263***	320-762-1124	660
*Resv						
ARRS (American Roentgen Ray Society)						
44211 Slatestone Ct	Leesburg	VA	20176	**800-438-2777**	703-729-3353	48-8
ARS (American Rose Society)						
8877 Jefferson Paige Rd	Shreveport	LA	71119	**800-637-6534**	318-938-5402	47-18
Art Academy of Cincinnati						
1212 Jackson St	Cincinnati	OH	45202	**800-323-5692**	513-562-6262	162
Art in America Magazine						
575 Broadway	New York	NY	10012	**800-925-8059***	212-941-2800	452-2
*Cust Svc						
Art Institute of Atlanta						
6600 Peachtree Dunwoody Rd NE						
100 Embassy Row	Atlanta	GA	30328	**800-275-4242**	770-394-8300	162
Art Institute of Boston at Lesley (AIB)						
700 Beacon St Ste 202	Boston	MA	02215	**800-773-0494**	617-585-6600	162
Inland Empire						
674 E Brier Dr	San Bernardino	CA	92408	**800-353-0812**	909-915-2100	162
Los Angeles						
2900 31st St	Santa Monica	CA	90405	**888-646-4610**	310-752-4700	162
Art Institute of California						
San Diego						
7650 Mission Valley Rd	San Diego	CA	92108	**888-624-0300**	858-598-1200	162
San Francisco						
1170 Market St	San Francisco	CA	94102	**888-493-3261**	415-865-0198	162
Art Institute of Charlotte						
2110 Water Ridge Pkwy						
3 LakePointe Plz	Charlotte	NC	28217	**800-872-4417**	704-357-8020	162
Art Institute of Colorado						
1200 Lincoln St	Denver	CO	80203	**800-275-2420**	303-837-0825	162
Art Institute of Dallas						
8080 Pk Ln Ste 100	Dallas	TX	75231	**800-275-4243**	214-692-8080	162
Art Institute of Fort Lauderdale						
1799 SE 17th St	Fort Lauderdale	FL	33316	**800-275-7603**	954-463-3000	162
Art Institute of Houston						
1900 Yorktown St	Houston	TX	77056	**800-275-4244**	713-623-2040	162
Art Institute of Indianapolis						
3500 Depauw Blvd	Indianapolis	IN	46268	**866-441-9031**	317-613-4800	162
Art Institute of Las Vegas						
2350 Corporate Cir	Henderson	NV	89074	**800-833-2678**	702-369-9944	162
Art Institute of Ohio						
Cincinnati						
8845 Covernor's Hill Dr						
Ste 100	Cincinnati	OH	45249	**866-613-5184**	513-833-2400	162
Art Institute of Philadelphia						
1622 Chestnut St	Philadelphia	PA	19103	**800-275-2474**	215-567-7080	162
Art Institute of Pittsburgh						
420 Blvd of the Allies	Pittsburgh	PA	15219	**800-275-2470**	412-263-6600	162
Art Institute of Portland						
1122 NW Davis St	Portland	OR	97209	**888-228-6528**	503-228-6528	162
Art Institute of Seattle						
2323 Elliott Ave	Seattle	WA	98121	**800-275-2471**	206-448-0900	162
Art Institute of Tampa						
4401 N Himes Ave Ste 150	Tampa	FL	33614	**866-703-3277**	813-873-2112	162
Art Institute of Washington						
1820 N Ft Myer Dr	Arlington	VA	22209	**877-303-3771**	703-358-9550	162
Art Institutes International Minnesota						
15 S Ninth St	Minneapolis	MN	55402	**800-777-3643**	612-332-3361	162
Art Iron Inc						
860 Curtis St	Toledo	OH	43609	**800-472-1113**	419-241-1261	487
Art Morrison Enterprises Inc						
5301 Eighth St E	Fife	WA	98424	**888-640-0516**	253-922-7188	56
ART Studio Clay Co						
9320 Michigan Ave	Sturtevant	WI	53177	**800-323-0212**	262-884-4278	42
Art Supply Warehouse						
6672 Westminster Blvd	Westminster	CA	92683	**800-854-6467**	714-891-3626	44
ARTBA (American Road & Transportation Builders Assn)						
1219 28th St NW	Washington	DC	20007	**800-636-2377**	202-289-4434	48-3
Artco-Bell Corp						
1302 Industrial Blvd	Temple	TX	76504	**877-778-1811**	254-778-1811	318-3
Artcraft Company Inc, The						
200 John L						
Dietsch Blvd	North Attleboro	MA	02763	**800-659-4042**	508-695-4042	426

Name / Address	City	State	ZIP	Toll-Free	Phone	Class
Art-Craft Optical Company Inc 57 Goodway Dr S	Rochester	NY	14623	**800-828-8288**	585-546-6640	535
Artech Information Systems LLC 240 Cedar Knolls Rd Ste 100	Cedar Knolls	NJ	07927	**800-950-9496**	973-998-2500	712
Artel Video Systems Corp 5B Lyberty Way	Westford	MA	01886	**800-225-0228**	978-263-5775	638
Artesian Resources Corp 664 Churchmans Rd *NASDAQ: ARTNA*	Newark	DE	19702	**800-332-5114**	302-453-6900	357-5
Artforum International Magazine 350 Seventh Ave 19th Fl	New York	NY	10001	**800-966-2783**	212-475-4000	452-2
Arthrex Inc 1370 Creekside Blvd	Naples	FL	34108	**800-934-4404**	239-643-5553	472
Arthritis Foundation 1330 W Peachtree St Ste 100	Atlanta	GA	30309	**800-283-7800**	404-872-7100	47-17
Arthroscopy Assn of North America (AANA) 6300 N River Rd Ste 104	Rosemont	IL	60018	**877-924-0305**	847-292-2262	48-8
Arthur Blank & Co Inc 225 Rivermoor St	Boston	MA	02132	**800-776-7333**	617-325-9600	9
Arthur G James Cancer Hospital & Richard J Solove Research Institute *Bone Marrow Transplant Program* 300 W Tenth Ave Ste 519	Columbus	OH	43210	**800-293-5066**		759
Arthur J Gallagher & Co 2 Pierce Pl *NYSE: AJG*	Itasca	IL	60143	**888-285-5106**	630-773-3800	387
Arthur J. Glatfelter Agency Inc PO Box 2726	York	PA	17405	**800-233-1957**	717-741-0911	387
Arthur Rutenberg Homes Inc 13922 58th St N	Clearwater	FL	33760	**800-274-6637**	727-536-5900	188
Arthur State Bank 100 E Main St PO Box 769	Union	SC	29379	**877-226-5246**	864-427-1213	69
Arthur Vining Davis Foundations 225 Water St	Jacksonville	FL	32202	**800-222-3448**	904-359-0670	304
Artifex Technology Consulting Inc 614 George Washington Hwy	Lincoln	RI	02865	**888-278-4339**	401-723-6644	195
Artillery Park Heritage Site Two D'Auteuil St PO Box 10 Stn B	Quebec	QC	G1K7A1	**888-773-8888**	418-648-7016	49-2
Artisan Funds PO Box 8412 *Cust Svc	Boston	MA	02266	**800-344-1770***		521
Artisan's Bank 2961 Centerville Rd	Wilmington	DE	19808	**800-282-8255**	302-658-6881	69
Artisans Inc W4146 Second St PO Box 278	Glen Flora	WI	54526	**800-311-8756**	715-322-5285	130
Artist Brand Canvas 2448 Loma Ave *Orders	South El Monte	CA	91733	**888-579-2704***	626-579-2740	42
Artist's Magazine, The 4700 E Galbraith Rd	Cincinnati	OH	45236	**800-422-2550**	513-531-2222	452-2
Artistic Carton Co 1975 Big Timber Rd	Elgin	IL	60123	**800-735-7225**	847-741-0247	99
Artistic Checks Inc PO Box 40003 PO Box 1000	Colorado Springs	CO	80935	**800-243-2577**		140
Artistic Maintenance Inc 23676 Birtcher Dr *General	Lake Forest	CA	92630	**800-698-9834***	949-581-9817	419
ARTnews Magazine 48 W 38th St Ninth Fl	New York	NY	10018	**800-284-4625**	212-398-1690	452-2
Artpark 450 S Fourth St	Lewiston	NY	14092	**877-325-5787**	716-754-9000	565
Art-Phyl Creations 16250 NW 48th Ave	Hialeah	FL	33014	**800-327-8318**	305-624-2333	233
Arts & Business Council of Americans for the Arts 1 E 53rd St 2nd Fl	New York	NY	10022	**866-471-2787**	212-223-2787	47-4
Arts Ctr of Coastal Carolina 14 Shelter Cove Ln	Hilton Head Island	SC	29928	**888-860-2787**	843-686-3945	565
Arts-Way Mfg Co Inc 5556 Hwy 9 PO Box 288 *NASDAQ: ARTW*	Armstrong	IA	50514	**800-535-4517**	712-864-3131	273
Aruba Networks Inc 1344 Crossman Ave *NASDAQ: ARUN*	Sunnyvale	CA	94089	**800-943-4526**	408-227-4500	178
Aruba Tourism Authority 1750 Powder Springs St Ste 190	Marietta	GA	30064	**800-862-7822**	404-892-7822	765
Arvato Digital Services LLC 29011 Commerce Ctr Dr	Valencia	CA	91355	**800-223-1478**		390
Arvco Container Corp 845 Gibson St	Kalamazoo	MI	49001	**800-968-9127**	269-381-0900	99
Arvinyl Metal Laminates Corp 233 N Sherman Ave	Corona	CA	92882	**800-278-4695**		480
Arzel Zoning Technology Inc 4801 Commerce Pkwy	Cleveland	OH	44128	**800-611-8312**	216-831-6068	202
ASA (Autism Society of America) 7910 Woodmont Ave Ste 300	Bethesda	MD	20814	**800-328-8476**	301-657-0881	47-17
ASA (American Studies Assn) 1120 19th St NW Ste 301	Washington	DC	20036	**800-468-3571**	202-467-4783	48-5
ASA (Amateur Softball Assn of America Inc) 2801 NE 50th St	Oklahoma City	OK	73111	**800-654-8337**	405-424-5266	47-22
ASA (American Society of Agronomy) 5585 Guilford Rd	Madison	WI	53711	**866-359-9161**	608-273-8080	47-2
ASA (American Society of Anesthesiologists) 520 N NW Hwy	Park Ridge	IL	60068	**800-331-1600**	847-825-5586	48-8
ASA (American Society of Appraisers) 555 Herndon Pkwy Ste 125	Herndon	VA	20170	**800-272-8258**	703-478-2228	48-17
ASA (American Society on Aging) 71 Stevenson St Ste 1450	San Francisco	CA	94105	**800-537-9728**	415-974-9600	47-6
ASA (American Sociological Assn) 1307 New York Ave	Washington	DC	20005	**800-524-9400**	202-383-9005	48-5
ASA (American Soybean Assn) 12125 Woodcrest Executive Dr Ste 100	Saint Louis	MO	63141	**800-688-7692**	314-576-1770	47-2
ASA (American Statistical Assn) 732 N Washington St	Alexandria	VA	22314	**888-231-3473**	703-684-1221	48-19
ASA (American Subcontractors Assn Inc) 1004 Duke St	Alexandria	VA	22314	**866-378-8866**	703-684-3450	48-3
ASA (Automotive Service Assn) 1901 Airport Fwy *Cust Svc	Bedford	TX	76021	**800-272-7467***		48-21
ASA (American Staffing Assn) 277 S Washington St Ste 200	Alexandria	VA	22314	**800-456-4324**	703-253-2020	48-12
ASA Computers Inc 645 National Ave	Mountain View	CA	94043	**800-732-5727**	650-230-8000	177
ASA Tire Systems Inc 651 S Stratford Dr	Meridian	ID	83642	**800-241-8472**	208-855-0781	175
ASAA (American Sleep Apnea Assn) 6856 Eastern Ave NW #203	Washington	DC	20012	**888-292-6522**	202-293-3650	47-17
ASAC (American Society of Agricultural Consultants) N78W14573 Appleton Ave	Menomonee Falls	WI	53051	**800-327-6789**	262-253-6902	47-2
ASAE (American Society of Assn Executives) 1575 'I' St NW	Washington	DC	20005	**888-950-2723**	202-626-2723	48-12
Asahi Kasei Plastics North America Inc 900 E Van Riper Rd *Cust Svc	Fowlerville	MI	48836	**800-993-5382***	517-223-2000	598-2
Asante Technologies Inc 673 S Milpitas Blvd Ste 100 *OTC: ASNL*	Milpitas	CA	95035	**800-303-9121**	408-435-8388	177
ASAPS (American Society for Aesthetic Plastic Surgery, The) 11262 Monarch St	Garden Grove	CA	92841	**800-364-2147**	562-799-2356	48-8
ASBO (Association of School Business Officials International) 11401 N Shore Dr	Reston	VA	20190	**866-682-2729**		48-5
ASBPA (American Shore & Beach Preservation Assn) 5460 Beaujolais Ln	Fort Myers	FL	33919	**800-331-1600**	239-489-2616	47-13
Asbury College One Macklem Dr *Admissions	Wilmore	KY	40390	**800-888-1818***	859-858-3511	166
Asbury Methodist Village 201 Russell Ave	Gaithersburg	MD	20877	**800-327-2879**	301-216-4100	663
Asbury Park Press 3601 Hwy 66 PO Box 1550	Neptune	NJ	07754	**800-883-7737**	732-922-6000	525-2
Asbury Theological Seminary 204 N Lexington Ave	Wilmore	KY	40390	**800-227-2879**	859-858-3581	167-3
ASC (American Society of Cinematographers) 1782 N Orange Dr	Hollywood	CA	90028	**800-448-0145**	323-969-4333	47-4
ASC Profiles Inc 2110 Enterprise Blvd *Cust Svc	West Sacramento	CA	95691	**800-360-2477***	916-372-0933	688
ASCA (American School Counselor Assn) 1101 King St Ste 625	Alexandria	VA	22314	**800-306-4722**	703-683-2722	48-5
ASCCP (American Society for Colposcopy & Cervical Pathology) 152 W Washington St	Hagerstown	MD	21740	**800-787-7227**	301-733-3640	48-8
ASCD (Association for Supervision & Curriculum Development) 1703 N Beauregard St	Alexandria	VA	22311	**800-933-2723**	703-578-9600	48-5
ASCE (American Society of Civil Engineers) 1801 Alexander Bell Dr	Reston	VA	20191	**800-548-2723**	703-295-6300	452-21
Ascend Federal Credit Union 520 Airpark Dr PO Box 1210	Tullahoma	TN	37388	**800-342-3086**	931-455-5441	219
Ascend Therapeutics Inc 607 Herndon Pkwy Ste 110	Herndon	VA	20170	**888-412-5751**	703-471-4744	231
Ascendant Advisors LLC Four Oaks Pl 1330 Post Oak Blvd Ste 1550	Houston	TX	77056	**800-552-6010**		521
Ascentium Capital LLC 23970 Hwy 59 N	Kingwood	TX	77339	**866-722-8500**		502
ASCH (American Society of Clinical Hypnosis) 140 N Bloomingdale Rd	Bloomingdale	IL	60108	**866-986-8779**	630-980-4740	48-8
Aschinger Electric Co 877 Horan Dr PO Box 26322	Fenton	MO	63026	**800-280-4061**	636-343-1211	190-4
ASCLA (Association of Specialized & Co-op Library Agencies) 50 E Huron St	Chicago	IL	60611	**800-545-2433**	312-280-4395	48-11
ASCO (Association of Schools & Colleges of Optometry) 6110 Executive Blvd Ste 420	Rockville	MD	20852	**888- 26-8377**	301-231-5944	48-8
ASCO (American Society of Clinical Oncology) 2318 Mill Rd Ste 800	Alexandria	VA	22314	**888-282-2552**	571-483-1300	48-8
ASCP (American Society of Consultant Pharmacists) 1321 Duke St	Alexandria	VA	22314	**800-355-2727**	703-739-1300	48-8
ASCP (American Society for Clinical Pathology) 33 W Monroe St Ste 1600 *Cust Svc	Chicago	IL	60603	**800-621-4142***	312-541-4999	48-8
ASCRS (American Society of Cataract & Refractive Surgery) 4000 Legato Rd Ste 700	Fairfax	VA	22033	**800-451-1339**	703-591-2220	48-8
ASD (Allentown School District) 31 S Penn St	Allentown	PA	18105	**877-262-1492**	484-765-4000	676
ASD 6255 Sunset Blvd 19th Fl	Los Angeles	CA	90028	**888-441-7575**	323-817-2200	185
ASD Data Services LLC PO Box 1184	Manchester	TN	37349	**877-742-7297**		628-6
ASE (Alliance to Save Energy) 1850 M St NW Ste 600	Washington	DC	20036	**800-862-2086**	202-857-0666	47-12
Asel Art Supply 2701 Cedar Springs	Dallas	TX	75201	**888-273-5278**	214-871-2425	44
AseraCare Hospice of Austin 14205 Burnet Rd	Austin	TX	78728	**800-332-3982**	512-218-9890	368
AseraCare Hospice of Milwaukee 7160 Dallas Pkwy Ste 400	Plano	TX	75024	**800-598-5132**	262-785-1356	368
ASF (Atlantic Salmon Federation) PO Box 5200	Saint Andrews	NB	E5B3S8	**800-565-5666**	506-529-1033	47-3
ASG (Allen Systems Group Inc) 1333 Third Ave S	Naples	FL	34102	**800-932-5536**	239-435-2200	179-12
ASG Renaissance 22226 Garrison St	Dearborn	MI	48124	**800-238-0890**	313-565-4700	261
ASGE (American Society for Gastrointestinal Endoscopy) 1520 Kensington Rd Ste 202	Oak Brook	IL	60523	**866-353-2743**	630-573-0600	48-8
Ash Grove Cement Co 8900 Indian Creek Pkwy *OTC: ASHG*	Overland Park	KS	66210	**800-545-1882**	913-451-8900	134
ASHA (American Speech-Language-Hearing Assn) 2200 Research Blvd	Rockville	MD	20850	**800-498-2071**	301-296-5700	48-8
Ashaway Line & Twine Manufacturing Co 24 Laurel St	Ashaway	RI	02804	**800-556-7260**	401-377-2221	209
Ashbrook Ctr 401 College Ave Ashland University	Ashland	OH	44805	**877-289-5411**	419-289-5411	625
Ashe County Chamber of Commerce 1 N Jefferson Ave Ste C	West Jefferson	NC	28694	**888-343-2743**	336-846-9550	336
Asher's Chocolates 80 Wambold Rd	Souderton	PA	18964	**800-223-4420**	215-721-3000	295-8
Asheville Area Chamber of Commerce 36 Montford Ave	Asheville	NC	28802	**888-314-1041**	828-258-6101	137
Asheville Area Convention & Visitors Bureau 36 Montford Ave	Asheville	NC	28801	**800-257-5583**	828-258-6101	207
Asheville Chevrolet Inc 205 Smokey Pk Hwy	Asheville	NC	28806	**866-921-1073**	828-665-4444	56
Asheville Citizen Times 14 O'Henry Ave	Asheville	NC	28801	**800-800-4204**	828-252-5622	525-2
Asheville Civic Ctr 87 Haywood St	Asheville	NC	28801	**888-464-4218**	828-259-5743	206

Toll-Free · Phone · Class

Asheville Regional Airport
61 Terminal Dr Ste 1 ... Fletcher NC 28732 **866-719-3910** 828-684-2226 27
Ashford University
400 N Bluff Blvd ... Clinton IA 52732 **800-242-4153** 563-242-4023 166
ASHG (American Society of Human Genetics)
9650 Rockville Pike ... Bethesda MD 20814 **866-486-4363** 301-634-7300 48-19
ASHI (American Society of Home Inspectors)
932 Lee St Ste 101 ... Des Plaines IL 60016 **800-743-2744** 847-759-2820 48-3
Ashland Alliance Chamber of Commerce
1733 Winchester Ave ... Ashland KY 41101 **800-233-3826** 606-324-5111 137
Ashland Community & Technical College
1400 College Dr ... Ashland KY 41101 **800-928-4256** 606-326-2000 160
Ashland Inc
50 E River Ctr Blvd
PO Box 391 ... Covington KY 41012 **877-546-2782** 859-815-3333 186
NYSE: ASH
Ashland Independent School District
PO Box 3000 ... Ashland KY 41105 **800-752-6200** 606-327-2706 676
Ashland Springs Hotel
212 E Main St ... Ashland OR 97520 **888-795-4545** 541-488-1700 376
Ashland University
401 College Ave ... Ashland OH 44805 **800-882-1548** 419-289-4142 166
Ashland University Library
509 College Ave ... Ashland OH 44805 **866-434-5222** 419-289-5400 431-6
Ashland-The Henry Clay Estate
120 Sycamore Rd ... Lexington KY 40502 **800-735-5251** 859-266-8581 49-2
Ashlar Inc
9600 Great Hills Trl
Ste 150W-1625 ... Austin TX 78759 **800-877-2745** 512-250-2186 179-5
Ashley Furniture Industries Inc
One Ashley Way ... Arcadia WI 54612 **800-477-2222** 608-323-6225 318-2
Ashley-Chicot Electric Co-op Inc
307 E Jefferson St ... Hamburg AR 71646 **800-281-5212** 870-853-5212 245
Ashmore Inn & Suites
4019 S Loop 289 ... Lubbock TX 79423 **800-785-0061** 806-785-0060 376
ASHP (American Society of Health-System Pharmacists)
7272 Wisconsin Ave ... Bethesda MD 20814 **866-279-0681** 301-664-8700 48-8
ASHRAE (American Society of Heating Refrigerating & Air-Conditioning Engineers Inc)
1791 Tullie Cir NE ... Atlanta GA 30329 **800-527-4723*** 404-636-8400 48-3
*Cust Svc
ASHS (American Society for Horticultural Science)
1018 Duke St ... Alexandria VA 22314 **800-331-1600** 703-836-4606 47-2
Ashta Chemicals Inc
3509 Middle Rd ... Ashtabula OH 44004 **800-492-5082*** 440-997-5221 141
*Cust Svc
Ashtead Technology Inc
19407 Pk Row Ste 170 ... Houston TX 77084 **800-242-3910** 281-398-9533 194
Ashton Hotel
610 Main St ... Fort Worth TX 76102 **866-327-4866** 817-332-0100 376
ASI Corp
48289 Fremont Blvd ... Fremont CA 94538 **800-200-0274** 510-226-8000 175
ASI DataMyte Inc
2800 Campus Dr Ste 60 ... Plymouth MN 55441 **800-207-5631** 763-553-1040 179-10
Asi System Integration Inc
48 W 37th St ... New York NY 10018 **866-308-3920** 112
Asi Technologies Inc
5848 N 95th Ct ... Milwaukee WI 53225 **800-558-7068** 414-464-6200 234
Asian American Legal Defense & Education Fund (AALDEF)
99 Hudson St 12th Fl ... New York NY 10013 **800-966-5946** 212-966-5932 47-8
Asics America Corp
29 Parker Ste 100 ... Irvine CA 92618 **800-333-8404** 949-453-8888 300
ASK Services Inc
42180 Ford Rd Ste 101 ... Canton MI 48187 **888-416-1313** 734-983-9040 397
ASKO Appliances Inc
PO Box 44848 ... Madison WI 53744 **800-898-1879** 35
ASKO Inc
501 W Seventh Ave ... Homestead PA 15120 **800-321-1310** 412-461-4110 488
ASLA (American Seminar Leaders Assn)
2405 E Washington Blvd ... Pasadena CA 91104 **800-801-1886** 626-791-1211 48-12
ASLA (American Society of Landscape Architects)
636 'I' St NW ... Washington DC 20001 **888-999-2752** 202-898-2444 47-2
ASLMS (American Society for Laser Medicine & Surgery Inc)
2100 Stewart Ave Ste 240 ... Wausau WI 54401 **877-258-6028** 715-845-9283 48-8
ASLO (American Society of Limnology & Oceanography)
5400 Bosque Blvd Ste 680 ... Waco TX 76710 **800-929-2756** 254-399-9635 48-19
ASM Industries Inc Pacer Pumps Div
41 Industrial Cir ... Lancaster PA 17601 **800-233-3861*** 717-656-2161 632
*Cust Svc
ASM International
9639 Kinsman Rd ... Materials Park OH 44073 **800-336-5152** 440-338-5151 48-13
ASMBA (Armed Services Mutual Benefit Assn)
PO Box 160384 ... Nashville TN 37216 **800-251-8434** 615-851-0800 47-19
ASMC (American Society of Military Comptrollers)
415 N Alfred St ... Alexandria VA 22314 **800-462-5637** 703-549-0360 47-19
ASML US Inc
8555 S River Pkwy ... Tempe AZ 85284 **800-227-6462** 480-383-4422 686
ASNA (Alabama State Nurses Assn)
360 N Hull St ... Montgomery AL 36104 **800-270-2762** 334-262-8321 526
ASNE (American Society of Naval Engineers)
1452 Duke St ... Alexandria VA 22314 **800-995-3579** 703-836-6727 48-21
ASNS (American Society for Nutrition)
9650 Rockville Pike Ste L3503A ... Bethesda MD 20814 **800-627-8723** 301-634-7050 48-6
ASNT (American Society for Nondestructive Testing Inc)
1711 Arlingate Ln PO Box 28518 ... Columbus OH 43228 **800-222-2768*** 614-274-6003 48-19
*Orders
Asnuntuck Community College
170 Elm St ... Enfield CT 06082 **800-501-3967** 860-253-3000 160
Asolo Repertory Theatre
5555 N Tamiami Tr ... Sarasota FL 34243 **800-361-8388** 941-351-9010 738
ASP (American Society for Photobiology)
PO Box 1897 ... Lawrence KS 66044 **800-627-0326** 785-843-1234 48-19
ASP (Advanced Sterilization Products)
33 Technology Dr ... Irvine CA 92618 **888-783-7723** 472
ASP Inc
460 Brant St Ste 212 ... Burlington ON L7R4B6 **877-552-5535** 905-333-4242 684
ASPAN (American Society of PeriAnesthesia Nurses)
90 Frontage Rd ... Cherry Hill NJ 08034 **877-737-9696** 856-616-9600 48-8
ASPCA Animal Poison Control Ctr
424 E 92nd St ... New York NY 10128 **888-426-4435** 212-876-7700 47-3
ASPE (American Society of Professional Estimators)
2525 Perimeter Pl Dr Ste 103 ... Nashville TN 37214 **888-378-6283** 615-316-9200 48-3
ASPE Inc
114 Edinburgh S Dr Ste 200 ... Cary NC 27511 **877-800-5221** 754

ASPEN (American Society for Parenteral & Enteral Nutrition)
8630 Fenton St Ste 412 ... Silver Spring MD 20910 **800-727-4567** 301-587-6315 48-8
Aspen Chamber Resort Assn
425 Rio Grande Pl ... Aspen CO 81611 **800-670-0792** 970-925-1940 137
Aspen Marketing Services
1240 N Ave ... West Chicago IL 60185 **800-848-0212** 630-293-9600 4
Aspen Meadows Resort
845 Meadows Rd ... Aspen CO 81611 **800-452-4240** 970-925-4240 660
Aspen Medical Products
6481 Oak Cyn ... Irvine CA 92618 **800-295-2776** 949-681-0200 471
Aspen Santa Fe Ballet
0245 Sage Way ... Aspen CO 81611 **866-449-0464** 970-925-7175 566-1
Aspen Skiing Co 117 ABC ... Aspen CO 81611 **855-754-2863** 970-925-1220 660
Aspen Surgical
6945 Southbelt Dr SE ... Caledonia MI 49316 **888-364-7004** 616-698-7100 472
Aspen Technology Inc
200 Wheeler Rd ... Burlington MA 01803 **888-996-7100** 781-221-6400 179-5
NASDAQ: AZPN
Asphalt Roofing Manufacturers Assn (ARMA)
529 14th St NW Ste 750 ... Washington DC 20045 **800-247-6637** 202-207-0917 48-3
Aspirus Wausau Hospital
333 Pine Ridge Blvd ... Wausau WI 54401 **800-283-2881** 715-847-2121 371-3
Asplundh Tree Expert Co
708 Blair Mill Rd ... Willow Grove PA 19090 **800-248-8733** 215-784-4200 766
ASPR (Association of Staff Physician Recruiters)
1000 Westgate Dr Ste 252 ... Saint Paul MN 55114 **800-830-2777** 48-8
ASPS (American Society of Plastic Surgeons)
444 E Algonquin Rd ... Arlington Heights IL 60005 **888-475-2784** 847-228-9900 48-8
Aspyra Inc
4360 Pk Terr Dr
Ste 100 ... Westlake Village CA 91361 **800-437-9000** 818-449-8671 179-10
OTC: APYI
ASQ (American Society for Quality)
600 N Plankinton Ave ... Milwaukee WI 53203 **800-248-1946** 414-272-8575 48-13
ASRA (American Society of Regional Anesthesia & Pain Medicine)
239 Fourth Ave Ste 1714 ... Pittsburgh PA 15222 **855-795-2772** 412-471-2718 48-8
ASRT (American Society of Radiologic Technologists)
15000 Central Ave SE ... Albuquerque NM 87123 **800-444-2778** 505-298-4500 48-8
ASSA ABLOY
110 Sargent Dr ... New Haven CT 06511 **800-377-3948** 234
ASSA Inc
110 Sargent Dr ... New Haven CT 06511 **800-235-7482** 203-624-5225 347
Assateague State Park
7307 Stephen Decatur Hwy ... Berlin MD 21811 **888-432-2267** 410-641-2120 558
Assay Technology Inc
1382 Stealth St ... Livermore CA 94551 **800-833-1258** 925-461-8880 630
Assemblies of God (A/G)
1445 N Boonville Ave ... Springfield MO 65802 **800-641-4310** 417-862-2781 47-20
Assemblies of God Theological Seminary
1435 N Glenstone Ave ... Springfield MO 65802 **800-467-2487** 417-268-1000 167-3
Assembly of Turkish American Assn (ATAA)
1526 18th St NW ... Washington DC 20036 **800-627-7692** 202-483-9090 47-14
Assent Consulting Inc
10054 Pasadena Ave ... Cupertino CA 95014 **800-747-0940** 408-366-8820 623
Assessment Technology Inc
6700 E Speedway Blvd ... Tucson AZ 85710 **800-367-4762** 520-323-9033 225
Asset Acceptance Capital Corp (AACC)
28405 Van Dyke Ave ... Warren MI 48093 **800-545-9931** 586-939-9600 158
NASDAQ: AACC
Asset Based Lending Consultant
1641 NW 71st Ter ... Hollywood FL 33024 **800-861-5711** 954-962-0099 195
Asset Marketing Systems Insurance Services LLC
15050 Ave of Science ... San Diego CA 92128 **888-303-8755** 364
AssetMark Inc
1655 Grant St 10th Fl ... Concord CA 94520 **800-664-5345** 398
ASSH (American Society for Surgery of the Hand)
822 W. Washington Blvd ... Chicago IL 60607 **888-343-6337** 312-880-1900 48-8
Assiniboine Park Zoo
55 Pavilion Crescent ... Winnipeg MB R3P2N6 **877-927-6006** 204-927-8080 810
Assist Cornerstone Technologies Inc
150 West Civic Ctr Dr Ste 601 ... Sandy UT 84070 **800-732-0136** 178
Assist-2-Sell Inc
1610 Meadow Wood Ln ... Reno NV 89502 **800-528-7816** 775-688-6060 643
Associated Bag Co
400 W Boden St ... Milwaukee WI 53207 **800-926-6100** 65
Associated Banc-Corp
1200 Hansen Rd ... Green Bay WI 54304 **800-236-2722*** 920-491-7000 357-2
NYSE: ASB ■ *PR
Associated Bank
2870 Holmgren Way ... Green Bay WI 54304 **800-728-3501** 262-879-0133 69
Associated Bank Green Bay NA
200 N Adams St ... Green Bay WI 54301 **800-728-3501** 920-433-3200 69
Associated Bank Illinois NA
612 N Main St ... Rockford IL 61103 **800-236-8866** 815-987-3500 69
Associated Bank Milwaukee
401 E Kilbourn Ave ... Milwaukee WI 53202 **800-236-8866** 414-271-1786 69
Associated Bank North
303 S First Ave ... Wausau WI 54401 **800-236-8866** 715-848-4793 69
Associated Behavioral Health Care Inc
4700 42nd Ave SW Ste 480 ... Seattle WA 98116 **800-858-6702** 206-935-1282 457
Associated Bodywork & Massage Professionals (ABMP)
25188 Genesee Trl Rd Ste 200 ... Golden CO 80401 **800-458-2267** 303-674-8478 47-17
Associated Builders & Contractors Inc (ABC)
4250 Fairfax Dr ... Arlington VA 22203 **866-262-0540** 703-812-2000 48-3
Associated Distributors LLC
401 Woodlake Dr ... Chesapeake VA 23320 **800-308-2600** 757-424-6300 80-1
Associated Equipment Corp
5043 Farlan Ave ... Saint Louis MO 63115 **800-949-1472** 314-385-5178 248
Associated Equipment Distributors (AED)
600 22nd St Ste 220 ... Oak Brook IL 60523 **800-388-0650** 630-574-0650 48-18
Associated Estates Realty Corp
One AEC Pkwy ... Richmond Heights OH 44143 **800-440-2372** 216-261-5000 646
NYSE: AEC
Associated Fabrics Corp
15-01 Pollitt Dr Unit 7 ... Fair Lawn NJ 07410 **800-232-4077** 587
Associated Floors
32 Morris Ave ... Springfield NJ 07081 **800-800-4320** 190-2
Associated Food Stores Inc
1850 West 2100 South ... Salt Lake City UT 84119 **888-574-7100*** 801-973-4400 296-8
*Cust Svc
Associated General Contractors of America (AGC)
2300 Wilson Blvd Ste 400 ... Arlington VA 22201 **800-242-1766** 703-548-3118 48-3
Associated General Contractors PAC
2300 Wilson Blvd Ste 400 ... Arlington VA 22201 **800-242-1767** 703-548-3118 608

	Toll-Free	Phone	Class
Associated Global Systems Inc			
3333 New Hyde Pk Rd . . . New Hyde Park NY 11042	**800-645-8300***	516-627-8910	444
*Cust Svc			
Associated Grocers Inc			
8600 Anselmo Ln . . . Baton Rouge LA 70810	**800-637-2021**	225-444-1000	296-8
Associated Grocers of New England Inc			
11 Co-op Way . . . Pembroke NH 03275	**800-242-2248**	603-223-6710	296-8
Associated Grocers of the South			
3600 Vanderbilt Rd . . . Birmingham AL 35217	**800-695-6051**	205-841-6781	296-8
Associated Hygienic Products LLC			
3400 River Green Ct Ste 600 . . . Duluth GA 30096	**800-757-0927***	770-497-9800	551
*General			
Associated Industries Of Massachusetts Mutual Insurance Com			
PO Box 4070 . . . Burlington MA 01803	**866-270-3354**	781-221-1600	388-4
Associated Locksmiths of America (ALOA)			
3500 Easy St . . . Dallas TX 75247	**800-532-2562**	214-819-9733	48-3
Associated Materials Inc			
3773 State Rd . . . Cuyahoga Falls OH 44223	**800-257-4335**	330-929-1811	688
Associated Materials Inc Alside Div			
PO Box 2010 . . . Akron OH 44309	**800-922-6009***		235
*Cust Svc			
Associated Mennonite Biblical Seminary			
3003 Benham Ave . . . Elkhart IN 46517	**800-964-2627**	574-295-3726	167-3
Associated Petroleum Carriers Inc			
PO Box 2808 . . . Spartanburg SC 29304	**800-573-9301***	864-573-9301	770
*Cust Svc			
Associated Press			
1100 13th St NW Ste 700 . . . Washington DC 20005	**800-824-5498**	202-641-9000	637
Associated Risk Managers (ARM)			
2 Pierce Pl . . . Itasca IL 60143	**800-735-5441**	630-285-4324	48-9
Associated Steel Corp			
18200 Miles Rd . . . Cleveland OH 44128	**800-321-9300**		348
Associated Wholesalers Inc			
PO Box 67 . . . Robesonia PA 19551	**800-927-7771**	610-693-3161	296-8
Association for Advanced Life Underwriting (AALU)			
11921 Freedom Dr Ste 1100 . . . Reston VA 20190	**888-275-0092**	703-641-9400	48-9
Association for Advanced Training in the Behavioral Sciences (AATBS)			
5126 Ralston St . . . Ventura CA 93003	**800-472-1931**	805-676-3030	48-5
Association for Applied & Therapeutic Humor (AATH)			
65 Enterprise . . . Aliso Viejo CA 92656	**888-747-2284**	815-708-6587	47-17
Association for Applied Psychophysiology & Biofeedback (AAPB)			
10200 W 44th Ave Ste 304 . . . Wheat Ridge CO 80033	**800-477-8892**	303-422-8436	48-8
Association for Assessment & Accreditation of Laboratory Animal Care International			
5283 Corporate Dr Ste 203 . . . Frederick MD 21703	**800-926-0066**	301-696-9626	47-1
Association for Behavioral & Cognitive Therapies (ABCT)			
305 Seventh Ave 16th Fl . . . New York NY 10001	**800-685-2228**	212-647-1890	48-15
Association for Career & Technical Education (ACTE)			
1410 King St . . . Alexandria VA 22314	**800-826-9972**	703-683-3111	48-5
Association for Childhood Education International (ACEI)			
1101 16th St NW Ste 300 . . . Washington DC 20036	**800-423-3563**	202-372-9986	48-5
Association for Computing Machinery (ACM)			
Two Penn Plz Ste 701 . . . New York NY 10121	**800-342-6626**	212-626-0500	47-9
Association for Conflict Resolution (ACR)			
12100 Sunset Hills Rd Ste 130 . . . Reston VA 20190	**800-880-7303**	703-234-4141	48-10
Association for Continuing Higher Education (ACHE)			
1700 Asp Ave . . . Norman OK 73072	**800-807-2243**		48-5
Association for Co-op Operations Research & Development (ACORD)			
One Blue Hill Plz			
PO Box 1529 . . . Pearl River NY 10965	**800-444-3341**	845-620-1700	48-9
Association for Corporate Growth (ACG)			
71 S Wacker Dr Ste 2760 . . . Chicago IL 60606	**877-358-2220**	312-957-4260	48-12
Association for Couples in Marriage Enrichment (ACME)			
PO Box 21374 . . . Winston-Salem NC 27120	**800-634-8325**	336-724-1526	47-6
Association for Healthcare Documentation Integrity (AHDI)			
4230 Kiernan Ave Ste 130 . . . Modesto CA 95356	**800-982-2182**	209-527-9620	48-8
Association for Iron & Steel Technology (AIST)			
186 Thorn Hill Rd . . . Warrendale PA 15086	**800-732-0999**	724-814-3000	48-13
Association for Library & Information Science Education (ALISE)			
65 E Wacker Pl Ste 1900 . . . Chicago IL 60601	**800-522-0772**	312-795-0996	48-11
Association for Library Collections & Technical Services (ALCTS)			
50 E Huron St . . . Chicago IL 60611	**800-545-2433**	312-280-5038	48-11
Association for Library Service to Children (ALSC)			
50 E Huron St . . . Chicago IL 60611	**800-545-2433**	312-280-2163	48-11
Association for Library Trustees, Advocates, Friends & Foundations (ALTAFF)			
50 E Huron St . . . Chicago IL 60611	**800-545-2433**		48-11
Association for Linen Management			
2161 Lexington Rd Ste 2 . . . Richmond KY 40475	**800-669-0863**	859-624-0177	48-4
Association for Mfg Technology (AMT)			
7901 Westpark Dr . . . McLean VA 22102	**800-524-0475**	703-893-2900	48-12
Association for Research & Enlightenment (ARE)			
215 67th St . . . Virginia Beach VA 23451	**800-333-4499**	757-428-3588	47-17
Association for Research & Enlightenment Library			
215 67th St . . . Virginia Beach VA 23451	**800-333-4499**	757-428-3588	431-4
Association for Retail Environment (ARE)			
4651 Sheridan St Ste 470 . . . Hollywood FL 33021	**800-421-3483**	954-893-7300	48-3
Association for Supervision & Curriculum Development (ASCD)			
1703 N Beauregard St . . . Alexandria VA 22311	**800-933-2723**	703-578-9600	48-5
Association for the Advancement of Computing in Education (AACE)			
PO Box 1545 . . . Chesapeake VA 23327	**800-352-5397**	757-366-5606	48-5
Association for the Advancement of Medical Instrumentation (AAMI)			
4301 N Fairfax Dr Ste 301 . . . Arlington VA 22203	**800-332-2264**	703-525-4890	48-8
Association for Vascular Access (AVA)			
5526 West 13400 South Ste 229 . . . Herriman UT 84096	**888-576-2826**	801-792-9079	48-8
Association for Women in Science Inc (AWIS)			
1321 Duke St Ste 210 . . . Alexandria VA 22314	**800-303-0129**	703-894-4490	48-19
Association Managers Inc			
12427 Hedges Run Dr Ste 104 . . . Lake Ridge VA 22192	**800-403-3374**	703-426-8100	46
Association of Alternative Newsweeklies (AAN)			
115615th St NW . . . Washington DC 20005	**866-415-0704**	202-289-8484	48-14
Association of American Chambers of Commerce in Latin America			
1615 H St NW 3rd Fl . . . Washington DC 20062	**800-638-6582**	202-463-5485	
Association of American Geographers (AAG)			
1710 16th St NW . . . Washington DC 20009	**800-696-7353**	202-234-1450	48-19
Association of American Medical Colleges (AAMC)			
2450 N St NW . . . Washington DC 20037	**800-273-8255**	202-828-0400	48-5
Association of American Publishers Inc (AAP)			
71 Fifth Ave . . . New York NY 10003	**866-271-4968**	212-255-0200	48-16
Association of Certified Fraud Examiners (ACFE)			
716 W Ave . . . Austin TX 78701	**800-245-3321**	512-478-9000	48-1
Association of Christian Schools International (ACSI)			
731 Chapel Hills Dr . . . Colorado Springs CO 80920	**800-367-0798***	719-528-6906	48-5
*Cust Svc			
Association of Clinical Research Professionals (ACRP)			
500 Montgomery St Ste 800 . . . Alexandria VA 22314	**888-508-5731**	703-254-8100	48-8
Association of College & Research Libraries (ACRL)			
50 E Huron St . . . Chicago IL 60611	**800-545-2433**	312-280-2519	48-11
Association of Collegiate Schools of Architecture (ACSA)			
1735 New York Ave NW 3rd Fl . . . Washington DC 20006	**877-426-6323**	202-785-2324	48-5
Association of Community College Trustees (ACCT)			
1233 20th St NW Ste 605 . . . Washington DC 20036	**866-895-2228**	202-775-4667	48-5
Association of Conservation Engineers (ACE)			
Missouri Dept of Conservation			
PO Box 180 . . . Jefferson City MO 65102	**866-633-8110**	573-522-4115	48-7
Association of Consulting Foresters of America (ACF)			
312 Montgomery St Ste 208 . . . Alexandria VA 22314	**888-540-8733**	703-548-0990	47-2
Association of Corporate Counsel (ACC)			
1025 Connecticut Ave NW			
Ste 200 . . . Washington DC 20036	**877-647-3411**	202-293-4103	48-10
Association of Corporate Travel Executives (ACTE)			
515 King St Ste 440 . . . Alexandria VA 22314	**800-375-2283**	703-683-5322	47-23
Association of Directory Publishers (ADP)			
116 Cass St . . . Traverse City MI 49684	**800-267-9002**	231-486-2182	48-16
Association of Energy Engineers (AEE)			
4025 Pleasantdale Rd Ste 420 . . . Atlanta GA 30340	**877-407-0784**	770-447-5083	47-12
Association of Energy Service Cos (AESC)			
14531 Fm 529 Ste 250 . . . Houston TX 77095	**800-692-0771**	713-781-0758	47-12
Association of Equipment Manufacturers (AEM)			
6737 W Washington St Ste 2400 . . . Milwaukee WI 53214	**866-236-0442**	414-272-0943	48-13
Association of Farmworker Opportunity Programs (AFOP)			
1726 M St NW Ste 602 . . . Washington DC 20036	**866-487-9243**	202-828-6006	47-2
Association of Film Commissioners International (AFCI)			
109 E 17th St . . . Cheyenne WY 82001	**888-765-5777**	307-637-4422	47-4
Association of Fundraising Professionals (AFP)			
4300 Wilson Blvd Ste 300 . . . Arlington VA 22203	**800-666-3863**	703-684-0410	48-12
Association of Governing Boards of Universities & Colleges (AGB)			
1133 20th St NW Ste 300 . . . Washington DC 20036	**800-356-6317**	202-296-8400	48-5
Association of Government Accountants (AGA)			
2208 Mt Vernon Ave . . . Alexandria VA 22301	**800-242-7211**	703-684-6931	48-1
Association of Healthcare Internal Auditors (AHIA)			
10200 W 44th Ave Ste 304 . . . Wheat Ridge CO 80033	**888-275-2442**	303-327-7546	48-1
Association of Home Appliance Manufacturers (AHAM)			
1111 19th St NW Ste 402 . . . Washington DC 20036	**888-258-3247**	202-872-5955	48-4
Association of Junior Leagues International Inc (AJLI)			
80 Maiden Ln Ste 305 . . . New York NY 10038	**800-955-3248**	212-951-8300	47-15
Association of Legal Administrators (ALA)			
75 Tri-State International			
Ste 222 . . . Lincolnshire IL 60069	**877-675-5571**	847-267-1252	48-10
Association of Military Surgeons of the United States (AMSUS)			
9320 Old Georgetown Rd . . . Bethesda MD 20814	**800-761-9320**	301-897-8800	48-8
Association of Nurses in AIDS Care (ANAC)			
3538 Ridgewood Rd . . . Akron OH 44333	**800-260-6780**	330-670-0101	48-8
Association of Old Crows (AOC)			
1000 N Payne St Ste 300 . . . Alexandria VA 22314	**800-247-5626**	703-549-1600	47-19
Association of Osteopathic Directors & Medical Educators (AODME)			
142 E Ontario St . . . Chicago IL 60611	**800-621-1773**	312-202-8211	48-8
Association of Performing Arts Presenters			
1211 Connecticut Ave NW			
Ste 200 . . . Washington DC 20036	**888-820-2787**	202-833-2787	47-4
Association of Pool & Spa Professionals (APSP)			
2111 Eisenhower Ave Ste 500 . . . Alexandria VA 22314	**800-323-3996**	703-838-0083	48-4
Association of Professional Flight Attendants			
1004 W Euless Blvd . . . Euless TX 76040	**800-395-2732**	817-540-0108	411
Association of Progressive Rental Organizations (APRO)			
1504 Robin Hood Trl . . . Austin TX 78703	**800-204-2776**	512-794-0095	48-18
Association of Public Health Laboratories (APHL)			
8515 Georgia Ave Ste 700 . . . Silver Spring MD 20910	**800-899-2278**	240-485-2745	48-7
Association of Public Television Stations (APTS)			
2100 Crystal Dr Ste 700 . . . Arlington VA 22202	**855-948-5853**	202-654-4200	48-14
Association of Public-Safety Communications Officials International Inc			
351 N Williamson Blvd . . . Daytona Beach FL 32114	**888-272-6911**	386-322-2500	48-7
Association of Rehabilitation Nurses (ARN)			
4700 W Lk Ave . . . Glenview IL 60025	**800-229-7530**	847-375-4710	48-8
Association of Reproductive Health Professionals (ARHP)			
1901 L St NW Ste 300 . . . Washington DC 20036	**877-311-8972**	202-466-3825	48-8
Association of School Business Officials International (ASBO)			
11401 N Shore Dr . . . Reston VA 20190	**866-682-2729**		48-5
Association of Schools & Colleges of Optometry (ASCO)			
6110 Executive Blvd Ste 420 . . . Rockville MD 20852	**888- 26-8377**	301-231-5944	48-8
Association of Social Work Boards (ASWB)			
400 S Ridge Pkwy Ste B . . . Culpeper VA 22701	**800-225-6880**	540-829-6880	48-7
Association of Specialized & Co-op Library Agencies (ASCLA)			
50 E Huron St . . . Chicago IL 60611	**800-545-2433**	312-280-4395	48-11
Association of Staff Physician Recruiters (ASPR)			
1000 Westgate Dr Ste 252 . . . Saint Paul MN 55114	**800-830-2777**		48-8
Association of State Wetland Managers			
32 Tandberg Trail Suite 2A . . . Windham ME 04062	**800-451-6027**	207-892-3399	48-7
Association of Surgical Technologists (AST)			
Six W Dry Creek Cir Ste 200 . . . Littleton CO 80120	**800-637-7433**	303-694-9130	48-8
Association of Test Publishers			
601 Pennsylvania Ave NW			
Ste 900 . . . Washington DC 20004	**866-240-7909**		48-5
Association of the US Army (AUSA)			
2425 Wilson Blvd . . . Arlington VA 22201	**800-336-4570**	703-841-4300	47-19
Association of Universities for Research in Astronomy (AURA)			
1200 New York Ave NW Ste 350 . . . Washington DC 20005	**888-624-8373**	202-483-2101	48-5
Association of University Centers on Disabilities (AUCD)			
1100 Wayne Avenue			
Suite 1000 . . . Silver Spring MD 20910	**888-572-2249**	301-588-8252	48-5
Association of University Programs in Health Administration (AUPHA)			
2000 N 14th St Ste 780 . . . Arlington VA 22201	**877-275-6462**	703-894-0941	48-8
Association of Washington Business			
PO Box 658 . . . Olympia WA 98507	**800-521-9325**	360-943-1600	138
Association of Water Technologies (AWT)			
15245 Shady Grove Rd Ste 130 . . . Rockville MD 20850	**800-858-6683**	301-740-1421	47-2
Association of Women's Health Obstetric & Neonatal Nurses (AWHONN)			
2000 L St NW Ste 740 . . . Washington DC 20036	**800-673-8499**	202-261-2400	48-8
Association of Zoos & Aquariums (AZA)			
8403 Colesville Rd			
Ste 710 . . . Silver Spring MD 20910	**800-821-4557**	301-562-0777	47-3
Assumption College			
500 Salisbury St . . . Worcester MA 01609	**888-882-7786**	508-767-7000	166
AssuranceAmerica Corp			
5500 I- N Pkwy Ste 600 . . . Atlanta GA 30328	**800-450-7857**	770-952-0200	388-4
Assurant Employee Benefits			
2323 Grand Blvd . . . Kansas City MO 64108	**800-733-7879**	816-474-2345	388-2
Assurant Group			
11222 Quail Roost Dr . . . Miami FL 33157	**800-852-2244**	305-253-2244	357-4

	Toll-Free	Phone	Class
Assurity Life Insurance Co			
1526 K St ....Lincoln NE 68508	800-869-0355	402-476-6500	387
AST (Association of Surgical Technologists)			
Six W Dry Creek Cir Ste 200..........Littleton CO 80120	800-637-7433	303-694-9130	48-8
AST Bearings			
115 Main Rd ....Montville NJ 07045	800-526-1250	973-335-2230	74
AST Products Inc			
Nine Linnell Cir ....Billerica MA 01821	877-667-4500	978-667-4500	476
AST Sports Science Inc			
120 Capitol Dr ....Golden CO 80401	800-627-2788	303-278-1420	787
ASTA (American Seed Trade Assn)			
225 Reinekers Ln Ste 650..........Alexandria VA 22314	888-890-7333	703-837-8140	47-2
ASTA (American String Teachers Assn)			
4155 Chain Bridge Rd ....Fairfax VA 22030	800-821-7303	703-279-2113	48-5
ASTA (American Society of Travel Agents)			
1101 King St Ste 200 ....Alexandria VA 22314	800-275-2782	703-739-2782	47-23
Asta Funding Inc			
210 Sylvan Ave ....Englewood Cliffs NJ 07632	866-389-7627	201-567-5648	272
NASDAQ: ASFI			
ASTD (American Society for Training & Development)			
1640 King St Third Fl			
PO Box 1443. ....Alexandria VA 22313	800-628-2783	703-683-8100	48-5
Astea International Inc			
240 Gibraltar Rd Ste 300 ....Horsham PA 19044	800-878-4657	215-682-2500	179-1
NASDAQ: ATEA			
Astellas Pharma US Inc			
One Astellas Way ....Northbrook IL 60062	800-695-4321		84
AstenJohnson			
4399 Corporate Rd ....Charleston SC 29405	800-529-7990	843-747-7800	734-3
Astex Pharmaceuticals			
4140 Dublin Blvd Ste 200..........Dublin CA 94568	877-534-2590	925-560-0100	84
Asthma & Allergy Foundation of America (AAFA)			
8201 Corporate Dr Ste 1000..........Landover MD 20785	800-727-8462	202-466-7643	47-17
Asticou Inn			
15 Peabody Dr ....Northeast Harbor ME 04662	800-258-3373	207-276-3344	376
ASTM International			
100 Barr Harbor Dr			
PO Box C700 ....West Conshohocken PA 19428	800-814-1017	610-832-9500	48-19
Aston Hotel & Resorts Sunvalley			
333 S Main St ....Ketchum ID 83340	877-997-6667	208-622-6400	660
Aston Hotels & Resorts			
2155 Kalakaua Ave Ste 500 ....Honolulu HI 96815	800-775-4228	808-931-1400	376
Astor Crowne Plaza			
739 Canal St ....New Orleans LA 70130	877-408-9661	504-962-0500	376
Astor Hotel, The			
924 E Juneau Ave ....Milwaukee WI 53202	800-558-0200	414-271-4220	376
Astoria Ford			
710 W Marine Dr ....Astoria OR 97103	888-760-9303	503-325-6411	56
Astoria-Pacific Inc			
15130 SE 82nd Dr ....Clackamas OR 97015	800-536-3111	503-657-3010	292
Astorino			
227 Fort Pitt Blvd ....Pittsburgh PA 15222	800-518-0464	412-765-1700	261
AstraZeneca Canada Inc			
1004 Middlegate Rd ....Mississauga ON L4Y1M4	800-565-5877	905-277-7111	576
AstraZeneca Pharmaceuticals LP			
1800 Concord Pk PO Box 15437 .....Wilmington DE 19850	800-236-9933		576
Astrex Inc			
205 Express St ....Plainview NY 11803	800-633-6360	516-433-1700	246
ASTRO (American Society for Therapeutic Radiology & Oncology)			
8280 Willow Oaks Corporate Dr			
Ste 500 ....Fairfax VA 22031	800-962-7876	703-502-1550	48-8
Astro Chemicals Inc			
126 Memorial Dr ....Springfield MA 01104	800-223-0776	413-781-7240	144
Astro Industries Inc			
4403 Dayton-Xenia Rd ....Dayton OH 45432	800-543-5810	937-429-5900	800
Astro Pak Corp			
270 E Baker St Ste 100..........Costa Mesa CA 92626	866-492-7876		732
Astrodyne Corp			
375 Forbes Blvd ....Mansfield MA 02048	800-823-8082	508-964-6300	256
Astro-Med Inc			
600 E Greenwich Ave ....West Warwick RI 02893	800-343-4039	401-828-4000	174-6
NASDAQ: ALOT			
Asure Softwar			
110 Wild Basin Rd ....Austin TX 78746	888-323-8835	512-437-2700	179-7
NASDAQ: ASUR			
ASW Global LLC			
3375 Gilchrist Rd ....Mogadore OH 44260	888-826-5087	330-733-6291	791-1
ASWB (Association of Social Work Boards)			
400 S Ridge Pkwy Ste B ....Culpeper VA 22701	800-225-6880	540-829-6880	48-7
AT & T Inc			
175 E Houston St			
PO Box 2933..........San Antonio TX 78299	800-351-7221	210-821-4105	726
NYSE: AT&T			
AT Clayton & Co Inc			
300 Atlantic St ....Stamford CT 06901	800-282-5298	203-658-1200	546
At Health Inc			
7829 Center Blvd SE ....Snoqualmie WA 98065	888-284-3258	425-292-0329	353
At Last Naturals Inc			
401 Columbus Ave ....Valhalla NY 10595	800-527-8123		215
ATA (American Tinnitus Assn)			
522 SW Fifth Ave Ste 825..........Portland OR 97204	800-634-8978	503-248-9985	47-17
ATA (Amateur Trapshooting Assn)			
601 W National Rd ....Vandalia OH 45377	800-671-8042	937-898-4638	47-22
ATA (American Trucking Assn)			
950 N Glebe Rd Ste 210 ....Arlington VA 22203	800-282-5463	703-838-1700	48-21
ATA (American Translators Assn)			
225 Reinekers Ln Ste 590..........Alexandria VA 22314	800-253-2252	703-683-6100	48-5
ATAA (Assembly of Turkish American Assn)			
1526 18th St NW ....Washington DC 20036	800-627-7692	202-483-9090	47-14
Ataco Steel Products Corp			
PO Box 270 ....Cedarburg WI 53012	800-536-4822	262-377-3000	483
ATAP Inc PO Box 98 ....Eastaboga AL 36260	800-362-2827	256-362-2221	465
ATAS International Inc			
6612 Snowdrift Rd ....Allentown PA 18106	800-468-1441	610-395-8445	486
Atascadero Chamber of Commerce			
6904 El Camino Real ....Atascadero CA 93422	877-204-9830	805-466-2044	137
Atascadero State Hospital			
10333 S Camino Real ....Atascadero CA 93422	844-210-6207	805-468-2000	371-5
ATC (American Thermoplastic Co)			
106 Gamma Dr ....Pittsburgh PA 15238	800-245-6600		85
ATC (Appalachian Trail Conservancy)			
799 Washington St			
PO Box 807. ....Harpers Ferry WV 25425	888-287-8673*	304-535-6331	47-23
*Sales			
ATC Assoc Inc			
104 E 25th St 10th Fl ....New York NY 10010	800-476-5886	212-353-8280	193
ATCA (Air Traffic Control Assn)			
1101 King St Ste 300 ....Alexandria VA 22314	866-953-2189	703-299-2430	48-21
ATCC (American Type Culture Collection)			
10801 University Blvd			
PO Box 1549. ....Manassas VA 20108	800-638-6597*	703-365-2700	659
*Cust Svc			
Atchison County			
405 S Main St PO Box 243 ....Rock Port MO 64482	800-989-4115	660-744-6562	336
Atchison-Holt Electric Co-op			
18585 Industrial Rd			
PO Box 160. ....Rock Port MO 64482	888-744-5366	660-744-5344	245
ATCO Ltd			
700 909 11th Ave SW ....Calgary AB T2R1N6	800-242-3447	403-292-7500	775
TSE: ACO/X			
Atco Rubber Products Inc			
7101 Atco Dr ....Fort Worth TX 76118	800-877-3828	817-595-2894	367
ATD-American Co			
135 Greenwood Ave ....Wyncote PA 19095	866-283-9327	215-576-1380	319
Ateeco Inc			
600 E Ctr St PO Box 606 ....Shenandoah PA 17976	800-233-3170	570-462-2745	295-36
ATEL Capital Group			
600 California St			
Sixth Fl ....San Francisco CA 94108	800-543-2835	415-989-8800	216
Aten Technology Inc			
23 Hubble ....Irvine CA 92618	888-999-2836	949-428-1111	174-2
AT&F (American Tank & Fabricating Co)			
12314 Elmwood Ave ....Cleveland OH 44111	800-544-5316	216-252-1500	714
Athabasca University			
One University Dr ....Athabasca AB T9S3A3	800-788-9041	780-675-6111	773
Athana Inc			
1624 W 240 St ....Harbor City CA 90710	800-421-1591	310-539-7280	649
Athea Laboratories Inc			
1900 W Cornell St ....Milwaukee WI 53209	800-743-6417		143
Athena Controls Inc			
5145 Campus Dr ....Plymouth Meeting PA 19462	800-782-6776	610-828-2490	202
Athena Diagnostics Inc			
377 Plantation St 2nd Fl ....Worcester MA 01605	800-394-4493	508-756-2886	231
Athena Engineering Inc			
456 E Foothill Blvd ....San Dimas CA 91773	877-777-4778	909-599-0947	190-4
athenahealth Inc			
311 Arsenal St ....Watertown MA 02472	800-981-5084	617-402-1000	179-1
NASDAQ: ATHN			
Atheneum Suite Hotel & Conference Ctr			
1000 Brush Ave ....Detroit MI 48226	800-772-2323	313-962-2323	376
Athens Area Chamber of Commerce			
449 E State St Ste 1 ....Athens OH 45701	877-360-3608	740-594-2251	137
Athens Banner-Herald			
One Press Pl ....Athens GA 30601	800-533-4252	706-549-0123	525-2
Athens Convention & Visitors Bureau			
300 N Thomas St ....Athens GA 30601	800-653-0603	706-357-4430	207
Athens County Convention & Visitors Bureau			
667 E State St ....Athens OH 45701	800-878-9767	740-592-1819	207
Athens Pastries & Frozen Foods Inc			
13600 Snow Rd ....Brookpark OH 44142	800-837-5683	216-676-8500	295-2
Athens Services			
14048 Valley Blvd ....La Puente CA 91746	888-336-6100	626-336-3636	792
Athens State Bank			
6530 N State Rt 29 ....Springfield IL 62707	800-367-7576	217-487-7766	69
Atherotech Inc			
201 London Pkwy ....Birmingham AL 35211	800-719-9807		415
Athletic Supply Co			
16101 NE 87th St ....Redmond WA 98052	800-732-9259	425-882-1456	702
ATI (AmericanTours International LLC)			
6053 W Century Blvd ....Los Angeles CA 90045	800-800-8942	310-641-9953	750
ATI Allegheny Ludlum Corp			
100 River Rd ....Brackenridge PA 15014	800-258-3586*	724-224-1000	714
*Sales			
ATI Metal Working Products			
1 Teledyne Pl ....La Vergne TN 37086	888-926-4211	615-641-4200	488
ATIS (Alliance for Telecommunications Industry Solutions)			
1200 G St NW Ste 500 ....Washington DC 20005	800-649-1202	202-628-6380	48-20
Atkins & Pearce Inc			
1 Braid Way ....Covington KY 41017	800-837-7477	859-356-2001	209
Atkins Nutritionals Inc			
1050 17th St Ste 1000 ....Denver CO 80265	800-628-5467	303-633-2840	787
Atkinson Candy Co			
1608 W Frank Ave ....Lufkin TX 75904	800-231-1203	936-639-2333	295-8
Atkinson County School System			
98 Roberts Ave E ....Pearson GA 31642	800-639-0850	912-422-7373	676
Atkinson-Baker Inc (ABI)			
500 N Brand Blvd 3rd Fl ....Glendale CA 91203	800-288-3376	818-551-7300	440
ATLA (American Theological Library Assn)			
300 S Wacker Dr Ste 2100 ....Chicago IL 60606	888-665-2852	312-454-5100	47-20
Atlanta Attachment Co Inc			
362 Industrial Pk Dr ....Lawrenceville GA 30045	877-206-5116	770-963-7369	35
Atlanta Braves			
PO Box 4064 ....Atlanta GA 30302	800-326-4000	404-522-7630	704
Atlanta Bread Co			
1200 Wilson Way Ste 100 ....Smyrna GA 30082	800-398-3728	770-432-0933	67
Atlanta Christian College			
2605 Ben Hill Rd ....East Point GA 30344	855-377-6468	404-761-8861	166
Atlanta Convention & Visitors Bureau			
233 Peachtree St NE Ste 1400 ....Atlanta GA 30303	800-285-2682	404-521-6600	207
Atlanta Cutlery Corp			
2147 Gees Mill Rd ....Conyers GA 30013	800-883-0300	770-922-3700	222
Atlanta Fixture & Sales Co			
3185 NE Expy ....Atlanta GA 30341	800-282-1977	770-455-8844	299
Atlanta Hardwood Corp			
5596 Riverview Rd SE ....Mableton GA 30126	800-476-5393	404-792-2290	361
Atlanta Motor Speedway			
PO Box 500 ....Hampton GA 30228	877-926-7849	770-946-4211	508
Atlanta Postal Credit Union			
501 Pulliam St SW Ste 350 ....Atlanta GA 30312	800-849-8431	404-768-4126	219
Atlanta's DeKalb Convention & Visitors Bureau			
1957 Lakeside Pkwy Ste 510 ....Tucker GA 30084	800-999-6055	770-492-5000	207
Atlanta's Gwinnett Convention & Visitors Bureau (GCVB)			
6500 Sugarloaf Pkwy Ste 200 ....Duluth GA 30097	888-494-6638	770-623-3600	207
Atlantic Bay Mortgage Group			
596 Lynnhaven Pkwy			
Ste 102 ....Virginia Beach VA 23452	866-877-3143	757-213-1660	214

Alphabetical Section

	Toll-Free	Phone	Class
Atlantic British Ltd			
Halfmoon Light Industrial Pk 6			
Enterprise Ave .... Clifton Park NY 12065	800-533-2210	518-664-6169	56
Atlantic Bulk Carrier Corp			
PO Box 112 ....Providence Forge VA 23140	800-966-0030	804-966-5459	444
Atlantic City Convention & Visitors Authority			
2314 Pacific Ave .... Atlantic City NJ 08401	888-228-4748	609-348-7100	207
Atlantic City Free Public Library			
1 N Tennessee Ave .... Atlantic City NJ 08401	800-621-3362	609-345-2269	431-3
Atlantic Coast Bank (ACFC)			
505 Haines Ave ....Waycross GA 31501	800-342-2824	912-283-4711	357-2
NASDAQ: ACFC			
Atlantic Concrete Products Inc			
8900 Old Rt 13 .... Tullytown PA 19007	888-318-9473	215-945-5600	184
Atlantic Construction Fabrics Inc			
2831 CaRdwell Rd .... Richmond VA 23234	800-448-3636	804-271-2363	191
Atlantic Container Line (ACL)			
50 Cardinal Dr .... Westfield NJ 07090	800-225-1235	908-518-5300	312
Atlantic Council of the United States			
1101 15th St NW 11th Fl .... Washington DC 20005	800-311-9410	202-463-7226	625
Atlantic Credit & Finance Inc			
2727 Franklin Rd ....Roanoke VA 24014	800-888-9419	540-772-7800	158
Atlantic Eyrie Lodge			
Six Norman Rd .... Bar Harbor ME 04609	800-422-2883		376
Atlantic Gasket Corp			
3908 Frankford Ave ....Philadelphia PA 19124	800-229-8881	215-533-6400	325
Atlantic India Rubber Co			
1437 Kentucky Rt 1428 .... Hagerhill KY 41222	800-476-6638		668
Atlantic Information Services Inc			
1100 17th St NW Ste 300 .... Washington DC 20036	800-521-4323	202-775-9008	628-9
Atlantic Lift Truck Inc			
2945 Whittington Ave ....Baltimore MD 21230	800-638-4566	410-644-7777	382
Atlantic Monthly Magazine			
600 New Hampshire Ave NW .... Washington DC 20037	800-234-2411*	202-266-6000	452-11
*Cust Svc			
Atlantic Oakes			
119 Eden St .... Bar Harbor ME 04609	800-356-3585	207-288-5801	660
Atlantic Packaging Co			
806 N 23rd St .... Wilmington NC 28405	800-722-5841	910-343-0624	546
Atlantic Paper & Twine Co Inc			
85 York Ave .... Pawtucket RI 02904	800-613-0950	401-725-0950	552
Atlantic Premium Shutters			
29797 Beck Rd ....Wixom MI 48393	866-288-2726	248-668-6408	690
Atlantic Publishing Co			
315 E Washington St .... Starke FL 32091	800-814-1132		628-2
Atlantic Relocation Systems Inc			
1314 Chattahoochee Ave NW .... Atlanta GA 30318	800-241-1140*	404-351-5311	512
*Cust Svc			
Atlantic Salmon Federation (ASF)			
PO Box 5200 .... Saint Andrews NB E5B3S8	800-565-5666	506-529-1033	47-3
Atlantic Sands Hotel			
101 N Boardwalk ....Rehoboth Beach DE 19971	800-422-0600	302-227-2511	376
Atlantic Scale Co Inc			
136 Washington Ave .... Nutley NJ 07110	888-627-5836	973-661-7090	358
Atlantic Spas & Billiards			
8721 Glenwood Ave .... Raleigh NC 27617	800-849-8827	919-783-7447	372
Atlantic Spring			
PO Box 650 .... Flemington NJ 08822	877-231-6474	908-788-5800	710
Atlantic States Cast Iron Pipe Co			
183 Sitgreaves St ....Phillipsburg NJ 08865	800-634-4746	908-454-1161	306
Atlantic Track & Turnout Co			
270 N Broad St ....Bloomfield NJ 07003	800-631-1274	973-748-5885	760
Atlantic Trust			
100 E Pratt St 23rd Fl ....Baltimore MD 21202	866-644-4144	410-539-4660	398
Atlantic Union College			
338 Main St ....South Lancaster MA 01561	800-282-2030	978-368-2000	166
Atlantica Hotel & Marina Oak Island			
36 Treasure Dr PO Box 6 .... Western Shore NS B0J3M0	800-565-5075	902-627-2600	660
Atlantis Casino Resort			
3800 S Virginia St .... Reno NV 89502	800-723-6500	775-825-4700	660
Atlantis Seafood Steakhouse			
3800 S Virginia St			
Atlantis Casino Resort................. Reno NV 89502	800-723-6500		662
Atlantix Global Systems			
One Sun Ct .... Norcross GA 30092	877-552-8526	770-248-7700	175
Atlas Air Worldwide Holdings Inc			
2000 Westchester Ave .... Purchase NY 10577	866-434-1617	914-701-8000	12
NASDAQ: AAWW			
Atlas Bolt & Screw Co			
1628 Troy Rd .... Ashland OH 44805	800-321-6977	419-289-6171	278
Atlas Carpet Mills Inc			
2200 Saybrook Ave .... City of Commerce CA 90040	800-272-8527	323-724-9000	130
Atlas Construction Supply Inc			
4640 Brinnell St .... San Diego CA 92111	877-588-2100	858-277-2100	192-1
Atlas Container Corp			
8140 Telegraph Rd .... Severn MD 21144	800-394-4894	410-551-6300	99
Atlas Copco North America LLC			
7 Campus Dr Ste 200 ....Parsippany NJ 07054	877-342-8527	973-397-3432	357-3
Atlas Copco Tools & Assembly Systems			
2998 Dutton Rd .... Auburn Hills MI 48326	800-859-3746	248-373-3000	749
Atlas Distributing Corp			
44 Southbridge St ....Auburn MA 01501	800-649-6221	508-791-6221	80-1
Atlas Food Systems & Services Inc			
205 Woods Lk Rd .... Greenville SC 29607	800-476-1123	864-232-1885	298
Atlas Match LLC			
1801 S Airport Cir .... Euless TX 76040	800-628-2426	817-267-1500	9
Atlas Metal Industries			
1135 NW 159th Dr ....Miami FL 33169	800-762-7565*	305-625-2451	297
*Cust Svc			
Atlas Minerals & Chemicals Inc			
1227 Valley Rd ....Mertztown PA 19539	800-523-8269*	610-682-7171	3
*Cust Svc			
Atlas Model Railroad Company Inc			
378 Florence Ave .... Hillside NJ 07205	800-872-2521*	908-687-0880	752
*Orders			
Atlas Oil Co			
24501 Ecorse Rd ....Taylor MI 48180	800-878-2000	313-292-5500	572
Atlas Pacific Engineering Co			
1 Atlas Ave ....Pueblo CO 81001	800-588-5438	719-948-3040	297
Atlas Paper Mills LLC			
3301 NW 107th St ....Miami FL 33167	800-562-2860	305-636-5740	551
Atlas Pipeline Partners LP			
110 W 7th Ste 2300 ....Tulsa OK 74119	877-950-7473	918-574-3500	324

	Toll-Free	Phone	Class
Atlas Railroad Construction LLC			
1370 Washington Pike			
Ste 202 ....Bridgeville PA 15017	800-829-4059	412-677-2020	189-8
Atlas Roofing Corp			
2322 Valley Rd .... Meridian MS 39307	800-478-0258*	601-483-7111	45
*Cust Svc			
Atlas Roofing Falcon Foam Div			
8240 Byron Ctr Rd SW .... Byron Center MI 49315	800-917-9138		593
Atlas Sound			
1601 Jack McKay Blvd ....Ennis TX 75119	800-876-3333	972-875-8413	51
Atlas Steel Products Co			
7990 Bavaria Rd .... Twinsburg OH 44087	800-444-1682	330-425-1600	487
Atlas Tube			
1855 E 122nd St .... Chicago IL 60633	800-733-5683	773-646-4500	485
Atlas Van Lines Inc			
1212 St George Rd .... Evansville IN 47711	800-638-9797	812-424-2222	512
Atlas Water Systems Inc			
301 Second Ave .... Waltham MA 02451	888-877-0561	781-373-4700	794
Atlas World Group Inc			
1212 St George Rd .... Evansville IN 47711	800-252-8885	812-424-2222	357-3
Atmos Energy Corp			
5430 LBJ Fwy Ste 1800 .... Dallas TX 75240	888-954-4321	972-934-9227	357-5
NYSE: ATO			
ATO (Alpha Tau Omega Fraternity)			
One N Pennsylvania St			
12th Fl ....Indianapolis IN 46204	800-798-9286	317-684-1865	47-16
Atomic USA			
2030 Lincoln Ave .... Ogden UT 84401	800-258-5020		701
Atos Origin			
2500 Westchester Ave Ste 300 .... Purchase NY 10577	866-875-8902	914-881-3000	179-1
ATRA (Automatic Transmission Rebuilders Assn)			
2400 Latigo Ave ....Oxnard CA 93030	866-464-2872	805-604-2000	48-21
ATRA (American Therapeutic Recreation Assn)			
629 N Main St .... Hattiesburg MS 39401	800-433-5255	601-450-2872	47-17
ATRA (American Tort Reform Assn)			
1101 Connecticut Ave NW			
Ste 400 .... Washington DC 20036	877-333-2227	202-682-1163	48-10
Atrex Inc			
175 Industrial Loop S ....Orange Park FL 32073	800-874-4505	904-264-9086	638
AtriCure Inc			
6217 Centre Pk Dr .... West Chester OH 45069	888-347-6403	513-755-4100	84
NASDAQ: ATRC			
Atrion Networking Corp			
30 Service Ave ....Warwick RI 02886	800-890-4526	401-736-6400	197
Atris Inc			
1151 S Trooper Rd Ste E .... Norristown PA 19403	800-724-3384		725
Atrium Hotel			
18700 MacArthur Blvd ....Irvine CA 92612	800-854-3012	949-833-2770	376
Atrium Medical Corp			
5 Wentworth Dr .... Hudson NH 03051	800-528-7486	603-880-1433	471
Atrium Medical Ctr			
One Medical Ctr Dr .... Middletown OH 45005	800-338-4057	513-424-2111	371-3
ATS (American Thoracic Society)			
61 Broadway 4th Fl .... New York NY 10006	866-316-2673	212-315-8600	48-8
Ats All Tire Supply Co			
6600 Long Point Rd Ste 101..........Houston TX 77055	888-339-6665		53
ATS Systems Inc			
30222 Esperanza ....Rancho Santa Margarita CA 92688	800-321-1833	949-888-1744	688
Ats Systems Oregon Inc			
2121 NE Jack London St .... Corvallis OR 97330	800-564-6253	541-758-3329	383
ATS Tours			
300 Continental Blvd Ste 350........ El Segundo CA 90245	888-410-5770		750
Atsco ReMfg Inc			
4525 N 43rd Ave .... Phoenix AZ 85031	800-470-2387	623-842-4047	60
ATSSA (American Traffic Safety Services Assn)			
15 Riverside Pkwy			
Ste 100 ....Fredericksburg VA 22406	800-272-8772	540-368-1701	48-21
AT&T Ctr			
One AT&T Ctr Pkwy ....San Antonio TX 78219	800-745-3000*	210-444-5000	711
*Resv			
AttachmateWRQ			
1500 Dexter Ave N .... Seattle WA 98109	800-872-2829*	206-217-7500	179-1
*Sales			
AtticSalt Greetings Inc			
PO Box 5773 ....Topeka KS 66605	888-345-6005		129
Attorney's Title Insurance Fund Inc			
6545 Corporate Ctr Blvd .... Orlando FL 32822	800-336-3863	407-240-3863	388-6
Attraction Inc			
672 Rue du Parc ....Lac-Drolet QC G0Y1C0	800-567-6095	819-549-2477	153-3
Attunity Inc			
70 BlanchaRd Rd ....Burlington MA 01803	866-288-8648	781-730-4070	179-1
Attwood Corp			
1016 N Monroe St .... Lowell MI 49331	844-808-5704	616-897-9241	347
ATU (Amalgamated Transit Union)			
5025 Wisconsin Ave NW			
Third Fl ....Washington DC 20016	888-240-1196	202-537-1645	411
ATW (American Trails West)			
92 Middle Neck Rd ....Great Neck NY 11021	800-645-6260	516-487-2800	750
Atwood Mobile Products			
1120 N Main St ....Elkhart IN 46514	800-546-8759	574-264-2131	59
Au Bon Pain			
19 Fid Kennedy Ave ....Boston MA 02210	800-825-5227	617-423-2100	67
Au Naturel Wellness & Medical Spa at the Brookstreet Hotel			
525 Legget Dr ....Ottawa ON K2K2W2	888-826-2220	613-271-1800	698
AUA (American Urological Assn)			
1000 Corporate Blvd .... Linthicum MD 21090	866-746-4282	410-689-3700	48-8
Auberge du Soleil			
180 Rutherford Hill Rd ....Rutherford CA 94573	800-348-5406	707-963-1211	376
Auberge du Vieux-Port			
97 Rue de la Commune E ....Montreal QC H2Y1J1	888-660-7678	514-876-0081	376
Auberge et spa Le Nordik Inc			
16 ch Nordik ....Old Chelsea QC J9B2P7	866-575-3700	819-827-1111	351
Auberge Saint-Antoine			
Eight rue Saint-Antoine ....Quebec QC G1K4C9	888-692-2211	418-692-2211	376
Auburn Area Chamber of Commerce			
601 Lincoln Way ....Auburn CA 95603	800-310-2355	530-885-5616	137
Auburn City School District			
PO Box 3270 ....Auburn AL 36831	866-277-9644	334-887-2100	676
Auburn Corp			
10490 164th Pl ....Orland Park IL 60467	800-393-1826		192-3
Auburn Leather Co			
125 N Caldwell St ....Auburn KY 42206	800-635-0617	270-542-4116	428
Auburn Manufacturing Co			
29 Stack St ....Middletown CT 06457	800-427-5387	860-346-6677	325

	City	State	ZIP	Toll-Free	Phone	Class
Auburn Publishers Inc						
25 Dill St	Auburn	NY	13021	**800-878-5311**	315-253-5311	628-8
Auburn Regional Medical Ctr						
202 N Div St Plaza 1	Auburn	WA	98001	**866-268-7223**	253-833-7711	371-3
Auburn University						
202 Mary Martin Hall	Auburn University	AL	36849	**866-389-6770***	334-844-6425	166
*Admissions						
Montgomery						
7440 E Dr	Montgomery	AL	36117	**800-227-2649**	334-244-3000	166
Auburn-Opelika Tourism Bureau						
714 E Glenn Ave	Auburn	AL	36830	**866-880-8747**	334-887-8747	207
AUCD (Association of University Centers on Disabilities)						
1100 Wayne Avenue						
Suite 1000	Silver Spring	MD	20910	**888-572-2249**	301-588-8252	48-5
Audi of America						
3800 Hamlin Rd	Auburn Hills	MI	48326	**888-237-2834**		58
Audible Inc						
One Washington Pk	Newark	NJ	07102	**888-283-5051**	973-820-0400	392
Audio Advisor						
3427 Kraft Ave SE	Grand Rapids	MI	49512	**800-942-0220**	616-254-8870	195
Audio Command Systems						
694 Main St	Westbury	NY	11590	**800-382-2939**	516-997-5800	51
Audio Direct						
2004 E Irvington Rd Ste 264	Tucson	AZ	85714	**888-628-3467***		34
*Cust Svc						
Audio Engineering Society						
60 E 42nd St Rm 2520	New York	NY	10165	**800-541-7299**	212-661-8528	48-19
Audio-Digest Foundation						
1577 E Chevy Chase Dr	Glendale	CA	91206	**800-423-2308**	818-240-7500	756
AudioQuest Inc						
2621 White Rd	Irvine	CA	92614	**800-747-2770**	949-585-0111	253
Audiosears Corp						
Two S St	Stamford	NY	12167	**800-533-7863**	607-652-7305	51
Audio-technica Us Inc						
1221 Commerce Dr	Stow	OH	44224	**800-667-3745**	330-686-2600	246
Audiovox Corp						
180 Marcus Blvd	Hauppauge	NY	11788	**800-645-4994**	631-231-7750	51
NASDAQ: VOXX						
Audit & Adjustment Company Inc						
20700 44th Ave W Ste 100	Lynnwood	WA	98036	**800-526-1074**	425-776-9797	528
Audit Bureau of Circulations (ABC)						
48 W Seegers Road	Arlington Heights	IL	60005	**800-759-6397**	224-366-6939	48-18
Audubon Aquarium of the Americas						
6500 Magazine St	New Orleans	LA	70118	**800-774-7394**	504-581-4629	39
Audubon Magazine						
225 Varick St Seventh Fl	New York	NY	10014	**800-274-4201***	212-979-3000	452-19
*Cust Svc						
Audubon Naturalist Society						
8940 Jones Mill Rd	Chevy Chase	MD	20815	**888-744-4723**	301-652-9188	47-13
Audubon Zoo						
6500 Magazine St	New Orleans	LA	70118	**800-774-7394**	504-581-4629	810
Auer Steel & Heating Supply Co						
2935 W Silver Spring Dr	Milwaukee	WI	53209	**800-242-0406**	414-463-1234	14
Auglaize & Mercer Counties Convention & Visitors Bureau						
900 Edgewater Dr	Saint Marys	OH	45885	**800-860-4726**	419-394-1294	207
Augsburg College						
2211 Riverside Ave	Minneapolis	MN	55454	**800-788-5678**	612-330-1000	166
Augsburg Fortress Publishers						
100 S Fifth St Ste 600	Minneapolis	MN	55402	**800-426-0115**	612-330-3300	628-3
August Wilson						
245 W 52nd St	New York	NY	10019	**800-432-7250**	212-239-6200	736
August Winter & Sons Inc						
2323 N Roemer Rd	Appleton	WI	54911	**800-236-8882**	920-739-8881	190-13
Augusta Chronicle						
725 Broad St	Augusta	GA	30901	**866-249-8223**	706-724-0851	525-2
Augusta Medical Ctr (AMC)						
78 Medical Ctr Dr						
PO Box 1000	Fishersville	VA	22939	**800-932-0262**	540-932-4000	371-3
Augusta Metropolitan Convention & Visitors Bureau						
1450 Greene St Ste 110	Augusta	GA	30901	**800-726-0243**	706-823-6600	207
Augusta Regional Airport - Bush Field (AGS)						
1501 Aviation Way	Augusta	GA	30906	**866-289-9673**	706-798-3236	27
Augusta State Airport						
75 Airport Rd	Augusta	ME	04330	**800-654-3131**	207-626-2306	27
Augusta State University						
2500 Walton Way	Augusta	GA	30904	**800-341-4373**	706-737-1632	166
Augustana College						
639 38th St	Rock Island	IL	61201	**800-798-8100**	309-794-7000	166
Augustine Casino						
84-001 Ave 54	Coachella	CA	92236	**888-752-9294**	760-391-9500	132
AUPHA (Association of University Programs in Health Administration)						
2000 N 14th St Ste 780	Arlington	VA	22201	**877-275-6462**	703-894-0941	48-8
AURA (Association of Universities for Research in Astronomy)						
1200 New York Ave NW Ste 350	Washington	DC	20005	**888-624-8373**	202-483-2101	48-5
Aura Systems Inc						
1310 E Grand Ave	El Segundo	CA	90245	**800-909-2872**	310-643-5300	511
OTC: AUSI						
Auragan LLC						
PO Box 1501	New Canaan	CT	06840	**866-644-2872**		726
Aureole						
135 W 42nd St	New York	NY	10036	**800-889-7188**	212-319-1660	662
Aurico Reports Inc						
116 W Eastman St	Arlington Heights	IL	60004	**866-255-1852**		397
Aurora Area Convention & Visitors Bureau						
43 W Galena Blvd	Aurora	IL	60506	**800-477-4369**	630-897-5581	207
Aurora Chamber of Commerce						
14305 E Alameda Ave Ste 300	Aurora	CO	80012	**877-770-4438**	303-344-1500	137
Aurora Contractors Inc						
100 Raynor Ave	Ronkonkoma	NY	11779	**866-423-2197**	631-981-3785	603
Aurora Co-op Elevator Co						
605 12th St PO Box 209	Aurora	NE	68818	**800-642-6795**	402-694-2106	275
Aurora Corp of America						
3500 Challenger St	Torrance	CA	90503	**800-327-8508**	310-793-5650	527
Aurora Las Encinas Hospital						
2900 E Del Mar Blvd	Pasadena	CA	91107	**800-792-2345**	626-795-9901	371-5
Aurora National Life Assurance Co						
PO Box 4490	Hartford	CT	06147	**800-265-2652**		388-2
Aurora Sentinel						
14305 E Alameda Ave Ste 200	Aurora	CO	80012	**855-269-4484**	303-750-7555	525-4
Aurora Sinai Medical Ctr						
945 N 12th St	Milwaukee	WI	53201	**888-863-5502**	414-219-2000	371-3
Aurora Textile Finishing Co						
911 N Lake St PO Box 70	Aurora	IL	60507	**800-864-0303**	630-892-7651	734-7

	City	State	ZIP	Toll-Free	Phone	Class
Aurora University						
347 S Gladstone Ave	Aurora	IL	60506	**800-742-5281**	630-844-5533	166
Aurora VNA Zilber Family Hospice						
1155 N Honey Creek Pkwy	Wauwatosa	WI	53213	**888-206-6955**	414-615-5900	368
Aurum Ceramic Dental Laboratories Ltd						
115 17 Ave SW	Calgary	AB	T2S0A1	**800-665-8815**	403-228-5120	415
AUSA (Association of the US Army)						
2425 Wilson Blvd	Arlington	VA	22201	**800-336-4570**	703-841-4300	47-19
Auspex Pharmaceuticals Inc						
3366 N Torrey Pines Ct Ste 225	La Jolla	CA	92037	**800-487-7671**	858-558-2400	238
Austad's Golf						
2801 E 10th St	Sioux Falls	SD	57103	**800-444-1234***	316-838-5557	702
*Cust Svc						
Austin American-Statesman						
305 S Congress Ave	Austin	TX	78704	**800-445-9898**	512-445-3500	525-2
Austin Chronicle						
PO Box 49066	Austin	TX	78765	**866-271-4900**	512-454-5766	525-5
Austin College						
900 N Grand Ave	Sherman	TX	75090	**866-776-0056**	903-813-3000	166
Austin Community College (ACC)						
5930 Middle Fiskville Rd	Austin	TX	78752	**877-442-3522**	512-223-7000	160
Eastview						
3401 Webberville Rd	Austin	TX	78702	**888-626-1697**	512-223-5100	160
Northridge						
11928 Stonehollow Dr	Austin	TX	78758	**877-990-0462**	512-223-4000	160
Pinnacle						
7748 Hwy 290 W	Austin	TX	78736	**888-626-1697**	512-223-8001	160
Rio Grande						
1212 Rio Grande St	Austin	TX	78701	**877-990-0462**	512-223-3000	160
Riverside						
1020 Grove Blvd	Austin	TX	78741	**877-990-0462**	512-223-6000	160
Austin Convention & Visitors Bureau						
301 Congress Ave Ste 200	Austin	TX	78701	**800-926-2282**	512-474-5171	207
Austin Film Festival						
1801 Salina St Ste 210	Austin	TX	78702	**800-310-3378**	512-478-4795	282
Austin Graduate School of Theology						
7640 Guadalupe St	Austin	TX	78752	**866-287-4723**	512-476-2772	166
Austin Hotel & Spa						
305 Malvern Ave	Hot Springs	AR	71901	**877-623-6697**	501-623-6600	376
Austin Industrial Inc						
2801 E 13th S PO Box 87888	La Porte	TX	77571	**866-308-2592**	713-641-3400	189-9
Austin Peay State University						
601 College St	Clarksville	TN	37044	**800-844-2778***	931-221-7661	166
*Admissions						
Austin Powder Co						
25800 Science Pk Dr Ste 300	Cleveland	OH	44122	**800-321-0752**	216-464-2400	268
Austin Pump & Supply Co						
PO Box 17037	Austin	TX	78760	**800-252-9692**	512-442-2348	382
Austin Ribbon & Computer Supplies Inc (ARC)						
9211 Waterford Centre Blvd						
Ste 202	Austin	TX	78758	**800-783-7459**	512-452-0651	195
Austin State Hospital						
4110 Guadalupe St	Austin	TX	78751	**866-407-3773**	512-452-0381	371-5
Austin Symphony Orchestra						
1101 Red River St	Austin	TX	78701	**888-462-3787**	512-476-6064	566-3
Austin Travel						
6801 Jericho Tpke Ste 100	Syosset	NY	11791	**800-645-7466**	516-465-1000	761
AustinMohawk & Company Inc						
2175 Beechgrove Pl	Utica	NY	13501	**800-765-3110**	315-793-3000	90
Australia						
Consulate General						
1000 Bishop St PH	Honolulu	HI	96813	**866-343-3086**	808-529-8100	257
Embassy						
2005 Massachusetts Ave NW	Washington	DC	20036	**800-345-6541**	202-558-2216	257
Austria						
Consulate General						
11859 Wilshire Blvd Ste 501	Los Angeles	CA	90025	**800-255-2414**	310-444-9310	257
Embassy						
3524 International Ct NW	Washington	DC	20008	**800-255-2414**	202-895-6700	257
Austro Mold Inc						
3 Rutter St	Rochester	NY	14606	**800-637-7774**	585-458-1410	747
Authentix Inc						
4355 Excel Pkwy Ste 100	Addison	TX	75001	**866-434-1402**	469-737-4400	683
Author House						
1663 Liberty Dr Ste 200	Bloomington	IN	47403	**888-728-8467**	812-339-6000	628-2
Authorize.Net Corp						
PO Box 8999	San Francisco	CA	94128	**877-447-3938**	801-492-6450	179-7
Autism Society of America (ASA)						
7910 Woodmont Ave Ste 300	Bethesda	MD	20814	**800-328-8476**	301-657-0881	47-17
Auto Club Ltd						
PO Box 162526	Austin	TX	78716	**866-247-3728**		52
Auto Club of America Corp (ACA)						
9411 N Georgia St	Oklahoma City	OK	73120	**800-411-2007**	405-751-4430	52
Auto Club Speedway						
9300 Cherry Ave	Fontana	CA	92335	**800-944-7223**	909-429-5000	508
Auto Crane Co						
PO Box 580697	Tulsa	OK	74158	**888-848-5445**	918-836-0463	509
Auto Europe						
39 Commercial St	Portland	ME	04101	**800-223-5555**	207-842-2000	125
Auto FX Software						
141 Village St Ste 2	Birmingham	AL	35242	**800-839-2008**	205-980-0056	179-8
Auto Meter Products Inc						
413 W Elm St	Sycamore	IL	60178	**866-248-6356**	815-895-8141	490
Auto Truck Inc						
1420 Brewster Creek Blvd	Bartlett	IL	60103	**877-284-4440**	630-860-5600	509
Autobell Car Wash Inc						
1521 E Third St	Charlotte	NC	28204	**800-582-8096**	704-527-9274	61-1
Autobytel Inc						
18872 MacArthur Blvd	Irvine	CA	92612	**888-422-8999**	949-225-4500	57
NASDAQ: ABTL						
Autocam Corp						
4070 E Paris Ave	Kentwood	MI	49512	**800-747-6978**	616-698-0707	59
Autocrat Coffee Inc						
10 Blackstone Vly Pl	Lincoln	RI	02865	**800-288-6272**	401-333-3300	295-7
Autodesk Inc						
111 McInnis Pkwy	San Rafael	CA	94903	**800-964-6432***	415-507-5000	179-5
NASDAQ: ADSK ■ *Tech Supp						
Autofusion Corp						
6215 Ferris Sq Ste 200	San Diego	CA	92121	**800-410-7354**	858-270-9444	57
Auto-Graphics Inc						
430 N Vineyard Ave	Ontario	CA	91764	**800-776-6939**	909-595-7004	771
Autoland						
170 Rt 22 E	Springfield	NJ	07081	**877-813-7239***	973-467-2900	56
*Sales						

Alphabetical Section

Business / Address	Toll-Free	Phone	Class
Autolog Corp 401 Commerce Rd ... Linden NJ 07036	800-526-6078		770
Automark Marking Systems 13475 Lakefront Dr ... Earth City MO 63045	888-777-2303	314-739-0430	462
Automated Bldg Components Inc 2359 Grant Rd ... North Baltimore OH 45872	800-837-2152	419-257-2152	804
Automated Medical Systems Inc 2310 N Patterson St Bldg H ... Valdosta GA 31602	800-256-3240		180
Automated Packaging Systems Inc 10175 Phillip Pkwy ... Streetsboro OH 44241 *Sales	800-527-0733*	330-528-2000	540
Automated Quality Technologies Inc 563 Shoreview Park Rd ... St Paul MN 55126	800-250-9297	651-484-6544	688
Automatic Data Processing Inc (ADP) One ADP Blvd ... Roseland NJ 07068 *NASDAQ: ADP*	800-225-5237	973-994-5000	225
Automatic Equipment Manufacturing Co One Mill Rd Industrial Pk ... Pender NE 68047	800-228-9289	402-385-3051	273
Automatic Fire Sprinkler Inc 7272 Mars Dr ... Huntington Beach CA 92647	800-436-2066	714-841-2066	603
Automatic Funds Transfer Services 151 S Landers St Ste C ... Seattle WA 98134	800-275-2033	206-254-0975	68
Automatic Products International Ltd 165 Bridgepoint Dr ... Saint Paul MN 55075	800-523-8363		54
Automatic Systems Inc 9230 E 47th St ... Kansas City MO 64133	800-366-3488	816-356-0660	208
Automatic Transmission Rebuilders Assn (ATRA) 2400 Latigo Ave ... Oxnard CA 93030	866-464-2872	805-604-2000	48-21
Automation Products Group Inc (APG) 1025 West 1700 North ... Logan UT 84321	888-525-7300	435-753-7300	202
Automation Service 13871 Parks Steed Dr ... Earth City MO 63045	800-325-4808	314-785-6600	202
Automobile Club of Southern California 2601 S Figueroa St ... Los Angeles CA 90007	800-400-4222	213-741-3686	52
Automobile Consumer Services Inc 6249 Stewart Rd ... Cincinnati OH 45227	800-223-4882	513-527-7700	57
Automobile Protection Corp 6010 Atlantic Blvd ... Norcross GA 30071 *Cust Svc	800-230-2434*		387
Automobile Racing Club of America 8117 Lewis Ave ... Temperance MI 48182	800-385-2503	734-847-6726	56
Automotive Aftermarket Industry Assn (AAIA) 7101 Wisconsin Ave ... Bethesda MD 20814	800-936-8906	301-654-6664	48-21
Automotive Distribution Network 3085 Fountainside Dr Ste 210 ... Germantown TN 38138	800-727-8112	901-682-9090	48-18
Automotive Distributors Company Inc 2981 Morse Rd ... Columbus OH 43231	800-421-5556		60
Automotive Engine Rebuilders Assn (AERA) 500 Coventry Ln Ste 180 ... Crystal Lake IL 60014	888-326-2372	847-541-6550	48-21
Automotive Executive Magazine 8400 Westpark Dr ... McLean VA 22102	800-672-3888	703-821-7150	452-21
Automotive Finance Corp (AFC) 13085 Hamilton Crossing Blvd ... Carmel IN 46032	888-335-6675	865-384-8250	216
Automotive Industry Action Group (AIAG) 26200 Lahser Rd Ste 200 ... Southfield MI 48033	877-275-2424	248-358-3570	48-21
Automotive Information Ctr 18872 MacArthur Blvd ... Irvine CA 92612	888-422-8999		57
Automotive News Magazine 1155 Gratiot Ave ... Detroit MI 48207	877-812-1584	313-446-0450	452-21
Automotive Oil Change Assn (AOCA) 330 N. Wabash Ave Ste 2000 ... Chicago IL 60611	800-230-0702	312-321-5132	48-21
Automotive Parts Headquarters 2959 Clearwater Rd ... Saint Cloud MN 56301	800-247-0339	320-252-5411	60
Automotive Parts Remanufacturers Assn (APRA) 4215 Lafayette Ctr Dr Ste 3 ... Chantilly VA 20151	877-734-4827	703-968-2772	48-21
Automotive Racing Products Inc 1863 Eastman Ave ... Ventura CA 93003	800-826-3045	805-339-2200	347
Automotive Recyclers Assn (ARA) 3975 Fair Ridge Dr Ste 20N ... Fairfax VA 22033	888-385-1005	703-385-1001	48-21
Automotive Service Assn (ASA) 1901 Airport Fwy ... Bedford TX 76021 *Cust Svc	800-272-7467*		48-21
Automotive Service Inc 910 Mtn Home Rd PO Box 2157 ... Sinking Spring PA 19608	800-383-3421	610-678-3421	315
Auto-Owners Insurance Co 6101 Anacapri Blvd ... Lansing MI 48917	800-346-0346	517-323-1200	388-4
Auto-Owners Life Insurance Co 6101 Anacapri Blvd ... Lansing MI 48917	800-288-8740	517-323-1200	388-2
Autoquip Corp 1058 W Industrial Rd ... Guthrie OK 73044	888-811-9876	405-282-5200	465
AutoRevo LTD 7920 Belt Line Rd Ste 450 ... Dallas TX 75254	888-311-7386	972-715-8600	56
AutoStar 114 Ave of the Americas Ste 39 ... New York NY 10036	800-288-6782	212-930-9400	645
Autostar Solutions Inc 1300 Summit Ave Ste 800 ... Fort Worth TX 76102	800-682-2215		175
Autotrol Corp 365 E Prairie St PO Box 557 ... Crystal Lake IL 60039	800-228-6207	815-459-3080	511
Autotruck Controls Corp 1490 Henry Brennan Dr ... El Paso TX 79936	800-213-3083	915-857-5200	247
Autotruck Federal Credit Union 3611 Newburg Rd PO Box 18880 ... Louisville KY 40218	800-459-2328	502-459-8981	219
AutoVision Wireless Inc 360 Deerhide Crescent ... Toronto ON M9M2Y6	866-514-8030	416-747-4444	225
AutoWeek Magazine 1155 Gratiot Ave ... Detroit MI 48207 *Circ	888-288-6954*	313-446-6000	452-3
AutoZone Inc 123 S Front St ... Memphis TN 38103 *NYSE: AZO*	800-288-6966	901-495-6500	53
Autry Greer & Sons Inc 2850 W Main St ... Mobile AL 36612	800-999-7750	251-457-8655	342
AV Homes Inc 8601 N Scottsdale Rd Ste 225 ... Scottsdale AR 85283 *NASDAQ: AVHI*	866-392-4286	480-214-7400	644
AVA (Association for Vascular Access) 5526 West 13400 South Ste 229 ... Herriman UT 84096	888-576-2826	801-792-9079	48-8
AVA (American Volkssport Assn) 1001 Pat Booker Rd Ste 101 ... Universal City TX 78148	855-999-5200	210-659-2112	47-22
AVAD Canada Ltd 205 Courtneypark Dr W ... Mississauga ON L5W0A5	866-523-2823		175
Avalon Beverly Hills 9400 W Olympic Blvd ... Beverly Hills CA 90212	800-670-6183	310-277-5221	376
Avalon Corporate Furnished Apartments 1553 Empire Blvd ... Webster NY 14580	800-934-9763	585-671-4421	376
Avalon Hotel 16 W Tenth St ... Erie PA 16501	888-295-4949	814-459-2220	376
Avancen MOD Corp 1156 Bowman Rd Ste 200 ... Mount Pleasant SC 29464	800-607-1230		250
Avant Ministries 10000 N Oak Trafficway ... Kansas City MO 64155	800-468-1892	816-734-8500	47-20
Avante International Technology Inc (AIT) 70 Washington Rd ... Princeton Junction NJ 08550	800-735-5040	609-799-9388	789
Avanti Destinations Inc 1629 SW Salmon St ... Portland OR 97205	800-422-5053	503-295-1100	761
Avanti Foods 109 Depot St ... Walnut IL 61376	800-243-3739	815-379-2155	295-36
Avanti Polar Lipids Inc 700 Industrial Pk Dr ... Alabaster AL 35007	800-227-0651	205-663-2494	474
Avanti Press Inc 155 W Congress St Ste 200 ... Detroit MI 48226	800-228-2684	313-961-0022	129
Avantus 15 W Strong St Ste 20A ... Pensacola FL 32501	800-600-2510	850-470-9336	179-10
Avatier Corp 2603 Camino Ramon Ste 110 ... San Ramon CA 94583	800-609-8610	925-217-5170	179-12
Avaya Government Solutions Inc 12730 Fair Lakes Cir ... Fairfax VA 22033	800-492-6769	703-653-8000	179-10
Avaya Inc 211 Mt Airy Rd ... Basking Ridge NJ 07920	800-237-3239	908-953-6000	177
Avcorp Industries Inc 10025 River Way ... Delta BC V4G1M7	866-781-3111	604-582-6677	22
Ave Intervision LLC 1840 W State St ... Alliance OH 44601	800-448-9126		676
Ave Maria University 5050 Ave Maria Blvd ... Naples FL 34119	877-283-8648	239-280-2500	166
Aveda Corp 4000 Pheasant Ridge Dr ... Blaine MN 55449	800-644-4831	763-951-4000	215
Avedis Zildjian Co 22 Longwater Dr ... Norwell MA 02061	800-229-8672	781-871-2200	520
Avemco Insurance Co 411 Aviation Way ... Frederick MD 21701	800-874-9125	301-694-5700	388-4
Aventura Hospital 20900 Biscayne Blvd ... Aventura FL 33180	800-523-5772	305-682-7000	371-3
Avenue Inn & Spa 33 Wilmington Ave ... Rehoboth Beach DE 19971	800-433-5870		376
Avenue Plaza Resort 2111 St Charles Ave ... New Orleans LA 70130	800-614-8685	504-566-1212	376
Avenue Stores Inc 365 W Passaic St ... Rochelle Park NJ 07662	888-843-2836	201-845-0880	155-6
Avera Queen of Peace Hospital 525 N Foster St ... Mitchell SD 57301	888-531-1685	605-995-2000	371-3
Avera Saint Luke's Hospital 305 S State St ... Aberdeen SD 57401	800-658-3535	605-622-5000	371-3
Avere Systems Inc 5000 Mcknight Rd Ste 404 ... Pittsburgh PA 15237	888-882-8373	412-894-2570	174-8
Averitt Express Inc 1415 Neal St ... Cookeville TN 38501	800-283-7488		770
Avery Dennison 950 German St ... Lenoir NC 28645	800-444-4947	828-758-2338	734-5
Avery Dennison Corp 207 Goode Ave ... Glendale CA 91203 *NYSE: AVY ■ *Cust Svc	888-567-4387*	626-304-2000	722
Avery Dennison Fastener Div 224 Industrial Rd ... Fitchburg MA 01420	800-225-5913		601
Avery Dennison Specialty Tapes Div 250 Chester St Bldg 5 ... Painesville OH 44077	866-462-8379	626-304-2000	722
Avery Dennison Worldwide Graphics Div 250 Chester St Bldg 5 ... Painesville OH 44077	800-443-9380	440-358-3700	545-1
Avery Dennison Worldwide Office Products Div 207 Goode Ave ... Glendale CA 91203	800-462-8379	626-304-2000	527
Avery Weigh-Tronix Inc 1000 Armstrong Dr ... Fairmont MN 56031	800-458-7062	507-238-4461	675
Aves Audio Visual Systems Inc PO Box 500 ... Sugar Land TX 77487	800-365-2837	281-295-1300	37
AVG Automation 4140 Utica St ... Bettendorf IA 52722	877-774-3279		253
Avi Systems Inc 9675 W 76th St Ste 200 ... Eden Prairie MN 55344	800-488-4954	952-949-3700	638
Aviagen Group 5015 Bradford Dr ... Huntsville AL 35805	800-826-9685	256-890-3800	10-7
Aviation Institute of Maintenance Houston 7651 Airport Blvd ... Houston TX 77061	888-349-5387	713-644-7777	788
Aviation Week & Space Technology Magazine 1200 G St NW Ste 922 ... Washington DC 20005	800-525-5003		452-19
AviationWeek 1200 G St NW Ste 900 ... Washington DC 20005	800-525-5003		524-13
Avid Payment Solutions 950 S Old Woodward Ste 220 ... Birmingham MI 48009	888-855-8644		255
Avid Technology Inc 65-75 Network Dri ... Burlington MA 01803 *NASDAQ: AVID*	800-949-2843	978-640-6789	179-8
Avila University 11901 Wornall Rd ... Kansas City MO 64145	800-862-3678	816-501-2400	166
Avionic Instruments Inc 1414 Randolph Ave ... Avenel NJ 07001	800-468-3571	732-388-3500	253
Avis Rent A Car System Inc 6 Sylvan Way ... Parsippany NJ 07054	800-331-1212	973-496-3500	125
Avisen Securities Inc 3620 American River Dr Ste 145 ... Sacramento CA 95864	800-230-7704	916-480-2747	681
Avista Corp 1411 E Mission St ... Spokane WA 99202 *NYSE: AVA*	800-936-6629	509-489-0500	775
Avista Utilities 1411 E Mission St ... Spokane WA 99252	800-227-9187		775
Avistar Communications Corp 1875 S Grant St 10th Fl ... San Mateo CA 94402 *OTC: AVSR*	800-803-0153	650-525-3300	179-7
Avitus Group P.O. Box 81590 ... Billings MT 59108	800-454-2446		724
AVMA (American Veterinary Medical Assn PAC) 1910 Sunderland Pl NW ... Washington DC 20036	800-321-1473	202-789-0007	608
AVMA (American Veterinary Medical Assn) 1931 N Meacham Rd Ste 100 ... Schaumburg IL 60173	800-248-2862	847-925-8070	48-8

Alphabetical Section

		Toll-Free	Phone	Class
AvMed				
4300 NW 89th Blvd ....Gainesville FL 32606		800-346-0231	352-372-8400	388-3
Avnet Electronics Marketing Inc				
2211 S 47th St ....Phoenix AZ 85034		888-822-8638	480-643-2000	253
Avnet Inc				
2211 S 47th St ....Phoenix AZ 85034		888-822-8638	480-643-2000	246
NYSE: AVT				
Avnet Technology Solutions				
8700 S Price Rd ....Tempe AZ 85284		800-409-1483	480-794-6500	175
Avocent Corp				
4991 Corporate Dr ....Huntsville AL 35805		866-286-2368	256-430-4000	174-3
Avon Old Farms School				
500 Old Farms Rd ....Avon CT 06001		800-464-2866	860-404-4100	615
Avon Products Inc				
1345 Ave of the Americas ....New York NY 10017		800-367-2866*	212-282-7000	215
NYSE: AVP ■ *Cust Svc				
Avox Systems Inc				
225 Erie St ....Lancaster NY 14086		866-278-3237	716-683-5100	22
Avoyelles Journal				
105 N Main St ....Marksville LA 71351		800-565-4321	318-253-5413	525-4
AVRMC (Arkansas Valley Regional Medical Ctr)				
1100 Carson Ave ....La Junta CO 81050		877-696-6775	719-384-5412	371-3
AVS Inc 60 Fitchburg Rd ....Ayer MA 01432		800-772-0710	978-772-0710	317
AVS Science & Technology Society				
120 Wall St 32nd Fl ....New York NY 10005		800-547-1406	212-248-0200	48-19
Avstar Aviation Ltd				
12 N Haven Ln ....East Northport NY 11731		800-575-2359	631-499-0048	13
AVT Inc				
341 Bonnie Cir Ste 102 ....Corona CA 92880		877-424-3663		181
Avtec Inc				
Six Industrial Pk ....Cahokia IL 62206		800-552-8832	618-337-7800	434
AW (American Whitewater)				
PO Box 1540 ....Cullowhee NC 28723		866-262-8429	828-586-1930	47-23
Awards & Recognition Assn (ARA)				
4700 W Lake Ave ....Glenview IL 60025		800-344-2148	847-375-4800	48-4
AWC Commercial Window Coverings Inc				
825 Williamson Ave ....Fullerton CA 92832		800-252-2280	714-879-3880	190-1
AWF (African Wildlife Foundation)				
1400 16th St NW Ste 120 ....Washington DC 20036		888-494-5354	202-939-3333	47-3
AWHONN (Association of Women's Health Obstetric & Neonatal Nurses)				
2000 L St NW Ste 740 ....Washington DC 20036		800-673-8499	202-261-2400	48-8
AWI (American Watchmakers-Clockmakers Institute)				
701 Enterprise Dr ....Harrison OH 45030		866-367-2924	513-367-9800	48-4
AWI (Architectural Woodwork Institute)				
46179 Westlake Dr Ste 120 ......Potomac Falls VA 20165		866-877-6933	571-323-3636	48-3
AWIS (Association for Women in Science Inc)				
1321 Duke St Ste 210...........Alexandria VA 22314		800-303-0129	703-894-4490	48-19
A&WMA (Air & Waste Management Assn)				
420 Fort Duquesne Blvd				
1 Gateway Ctr 3rd Fl ....Pittsburgh PA 15222		800-270-3444	412-232-3444	47-12
AWMA (American Wholesale Marketers Assn)				
2750 Prosperity Ave Ste 530 ....Fairfax VA 22031		800-482-2962	703-208-3358	48-18
Awrey Bakeries Inc				
12301 Farmington Rd ....Livonia MI 48150		800-950-2253	734-522-1100	67
AWS (American Welding Society)				
550 NW 42nd Ave ....Miami FL 33126		800-443-9353	305-443-9353	48-3
AWSCPA (American Woman's Society of Certified Public Accountants)				
136 S Keowee St ....Dayton OH 45402		800-297-2721	937-222-1872	48-1
AWT (Association of Water Technologies)				
15245 Shady Grove Rd Ste 130 ....Rockville MD 20850		800-858-6683	301-740-1421	47-2
AWWA (American Water Works Assn)				
6666 W Quincy Ave ....Denver CO 80235		800-926-7337	303-794-7711	47-12
Axcera Corp				
103 Freedom Dr ....Lawrence PA 15055		800-215-2614	724-873-8100	638
Axcet HR Solutions				
Axet				
8325 Lenexa Dr Ste 410...........Lenexa KS 66214		800-801-7557	913-383-2999	623
Axcient Inc				
1161 San Antonio Rd ....Mountain View CA 94043		800-715-2339		178
Axeda Systems Inc				
25 Forbes Blvd ....Foxboro MA 02035		800-613-7535	508-337-9200	179-7
Axial Inc				
45 E 20th St 12th Fl ....New York NY 10003		800-860-4519		682
Axiom Memory Solutions LLC				
19651 Descartes ....Foothill Ranch CA 92610		888-658-3326	949-581-1450	175
Axiom Resource Management Inc				
5203 Leesburg Pk Ste 300 ....Falls Church VA 22041		800-566-9305	703-208-3000	195
Axis Communications Inc (ACI)				
100 Apollo Dr ....Chelmsford MA 01824		800-444-2947	978-614-2000	177
Axis Dance Co				
1428 Alice St Ste 200...............Oakland CA 94612		800-838-3006	510-625-0110	566-1
Axsun Technologies Inc				
One Fortune Dr ....Billerica MA 01821		866-462-9786	978-262-0049	687
AXYS Technologies Inc				
2045 Mills Rd ....Sidney BC V8L5X2		877-792-7878	250-655-5850	601
AY McDonald Manufacturing Co				
4800 Chavenelle Rd PO Box 508 ....Dubuque IA 52002		800-292-2737*	563-583-7311	588
*Cust Svc				
Aycock LLC				
8261 Derry St ....Hummelstown PA 17036		800-772-5066	717-566-5066	190-1
Aydin Displays Inc				
One Riga Ln ....Birdsboro PA 19508		866-367-2934	610-404-7400	174-4
Ayres Hotel Anaheim				
2550 E Katella Ave ....Anaheim CA 92806		800-595-5692	714-634-2106	376
AYSO (American Youth Soccer Organization)				
19750 S Vermont Ave Ste 200 ....Torrance CA 90502		800-872-2976		47-22
AZ Countertops Inc				
1445 S Hudson Ave ....Ontario CA 91762		800-266-3524	909-983-5386	715
AZA (Association of Zoos & Aquariums)				
8403 Colesville Rd				
Ste 710 ....Silver Spring MD 20910		800-821-4557	301-562-0777	47-3
Azar Nut Co				
1800 NW Dr ....El Paso TX 79912		800-351-8178	915-877-4079	295-28
Azon USA Inc				
643 W Crosstown Pkwy ....Kalamazoo MI 49008		800-788-5942	269-385-5942	383
Azonix Corp				
900 Middlesex Tpke Bldg 6 ....Billerica MA 01821		800-967-5558	978-670-6300	202
Aztec International Inc				
3010 Henson Rd ....Knoxville TN 37921		800-369-5357	865-588-5357	149
Aztec Supply				
954 N Batavia St ....Orange CA 92867		800-836-3210	714-771-6580	596
AzTx Cattle Co				
PO Box 390 ....Hereford TX 79045		800-999-5065	806-364-8871	10-1

		Toll-Free	Phone	Class
Azul Systems Inc				
1600 Plymouth St ....Mountain View CA 94043		800-258-4199	650-230-6500	174-1
Azusa Pacific University				
901 E Alosta Ave PO Box 7000............Azusa CA 91702		800-825-5278	626-969-3434	166

B

		Toll-Free	Phone	Class
B & B Agency of Boston				
47 Commercial Wharf Ste 3 ....Boston MA 02110		800-248-9262		373
B & B Electronics Manufacturing Co				
PO Box 1040 ....Ottawa IL 61350		800-346-3119	815-433-5100	687
B & B Media Group				
109 S Main St ....Corsicana TX 75110		800-927-0517	903-872-0517	627
B & B Trade Distribution Centre				
675 York St ....London ON N5W2S6		800-265-0382	519-679-1770	603
B & C Transportation Inc				
427 Continental Dr ....Maryville TN 37804		877-812-2287	865-983-4653	106
B & F System Inc				
3920 S Walton Walker ....Dallas TX 75236		877-586-2926	214-333-2111	358
B & G Mfg Company Inc				
3067 Unionville Pk ....Hatfield PA 19440		800-366-3067	215-822-1925	278
B & H Manufacturing Co				
3461 Roeding Rd ....Ceres CA 95307		888-643-0444	209-556-6160	540
B & H Manufacturing Inc				
141 County Rd 34 E ....Jackson MN 56143		800-240-3288	507-847-2802	273
B & H Photo-Video-Pro Audio Corp				
420 Ninth Ave ....New York NY 10001		800-947-9954	212-444-6600	118
B & O Railroad Museum				
901 W Pratt St ....Baltimore MD 21223		800-228-3748	410-752-2490	513
B & W Press Inc				
401 E Main St ....Georgetown MA 01833		877-246-3467	978-352-6100	263
B Berger Co				
1380 Highland Rd ....Macedonia OH 44056		800-288-8400*	330-425-3838	587
*Cust Svc				
B Braun Medical Inc				
824 12th Ave ....Bethlehem PA 18018		800-523-9676	610-691-5400	471
B Carroll Reece Museum				
PO Box 70660 ....Johnson City TN 37614		855-590-3878	423-439-4392	513
B E Meyers & Co Inc				
9461 Willows Rd NE ....Redmond WA 98052		800-327-5648	425-881-6648	537
B Frank Joy LLC				
5355 Kilmer Pl ....Hyattsville MD 20781		800-992-3569	301-779-9400	189-10
B Green Innovations Inc				
750 Hwy 34 ....Matawan NJ 07747		877-996-9333	732-441-7700	181
B H G Inc PO Box 309 ....Garrison ND 58540		800-658-3485	701-463-2201	619
B M Ross & Assoc Ltd				
62 N St ....Goderich ON N7A2T4		888-524-2641	519-524-2641	256
B'nai B'rith International				
2020 K St NW Seventh Fl ....Washington DC 20006		888-388-4224	202-857-6600	47-20
B'Nai B'Rith Magazine				
2020 K St NW Seventh Fl ....Washington DC 20006		888-388-4224	202-857-6600	452-18
B. E. Smith Inc				
9777 Ridge Dr ....Lenexa KS 66219		800-467-9117		194
B2 Gold Corp				
595 Burrard St Ste 3100				
PO Box 49143..............Vancouver BC V7X1J1		800-316-8855	604-681-8371	497
BA (British Airways PLC)				
75-20 Astoria Blvd ....Flushing NY 11370		800-403-0882	347-418-4000	25
BAB Inc				
500 Lk Cook Rd Ste 475..............Deerfield IL 60015		800-251-6101		661
OTC: BABB				
Babcock & Wilcox Inc				
20 S Van Buren Ave ....Barberton OH 44203		800-222-2625	330-753-4511	90
Babcock Lumber Company Inc				
2220 Palmer St PO Box 8348.......Pittsburgh PA 15218		800-553-4441	412-351-3515	192-3
Babcock Power Inc				
One Corporate Place				
55 Ferncroft Road Ste 210 ....Danvers MA 01923		800-523-0480	978-646-3300	90
Babcock State Park				
486 Babcock Rd ....Clifftop WV 25831		800-225-5982	304-438-3004	558
Babcock-Davis				
9300 73rd Ave N ....Brooklyn Park MN 55428		888-412-3726	763-488-9247	234
Babe Ruth League Inc				
1770 Brunswick Pk PO Box 5000..........Trenton NJ 08638		800-880-3142	609-695-1434	47-22
Babe Winkelman Productions				
PO Box 407 ....Brainerd MN 56401		800-333-0471		731
Babson College				
231 Forest St ....Babson Park MA 02457		800-488-3696*	781-235-1200	166
*Admissions				
Baby Jogger Co				
8575 Magellan Pkwy Ste 1000 ....Richmond VA 23227		800-241-1848		63
Baby Trend Inc				
1567 S Campus Ave ....Ontario CA 91761		800-328-7363*		63
*Cust Svc				
Baby's Dream Furniture Inc				
411 Industrial Blvd				
PO Box 579...............Buena Vista GA 31803		800-835-2742	229-649-4404	318-2
Babybug Magazine				
30 Grove St Ste C...........Peterborough NH 03458		800-821-0115		452-6
BabyCenter LLC				
163 Freelon St ....San Francisco CA 94107		866-241-2229	415-537-0900	353
BAC (International Union of Bricklayers & Allied Craftworkers)				
1776 eye St NW ....Washington DC 20006		888-880-8222	202-783-3788	411
Bacara Resort & Spa				
8301 Hollister Ave ....Santa Barbara CA 93117		855-968-0100	805-968-0100	660
Bacardi USA Inc				
2701 S Le Jeune Rd Ste 400........Coral Gables FL 33134		800-222-2734	305-573-8511	79-1
Baccala Concrete Corp				
100 Armento St ....Johnston RI 02919		866-705-2382	401-231-8300	183
Bacharach Inc				
621 Hunt Vly Cir ....New Kensington PA 15068		800-736-4666	724-334-5000	202
Bachem Bioscience Inc				
3132 Kashiwa St ....Torrance CA 90505		800-634-3183	310-539-4171	474
Bachem-Peninsula Laboratories Inc				
305 Old County Rd ....San Carlos CA 94070		800-922-1516	650-801-6090	231
Bachman's Inc				
6010 Lyndale Ave S ....Minneapolis MN 55419		888-222-4626	612-861-7311	292

Alphabetical Section

	Toll-Free	Phone	Class
Bachmann Industries Inc			
1400 E Erie Ave ....Philadelphia PA 19124	800-356-3910*	215-533-1600	752
*Cust Svc			
Back Country Horsemen of America (BCHA)			
PO Box 1367 ....Graham WA 98338	888-893-5161	360-832-2461	47-23
Backcountry.com			
2607 South 3200 West			
Ste A.............West Valley City UT 84119	800-409-4502*		454
*Orders			
Background Bureau Inc			
2019 Alexandria Pike ...Highland Heights KY 41076	800-854-3990	859-781-3400	626
Background Information Services Inc			
1800 30th St Ste 204 ....Boulder CO 80301	800-433-6010	303-442-3960	626
Backroads			
801 Cedar St ....Berkeley CA 94710	800-462-2848	510-527-1555	750
Bacon Veneer Co			
6951 High Grove Blvd ......Burr Ridge IL 60527	800-443-7995	630-323-1414	606
Bacone College			
2299 Old Bacone Rd .....Muskogee OK 74403	888-682-5514*	918-683-4581	166
*Admissions			
Bacon-Universal Company Inc			
918 Ahua St ....Honolulu HI 96819	800-352-3508	808-839-7202	355
BACVA (Baltimore Area Convention & Visitors Assn)			
100 Light St 12th Fl ....Baltimore MD 21202	877-225-8466	410-659-7300	207
Badge A Minit Ltd			
345 N Lewis Ave ....Oglesby IL 61348	800-223-4103	815-883-8822	451
Badger Air Brush Co			
9128 Belmont Ave ....Franklin Park IL 60131	800-247-2787	847-678-3104	42
Badger Bus			
5501 Femrite Dr ....Madison WI 53718	800-442-8259	608-255-1511	106
Badger Coaches Inc			
5501 Femrite Dr ....Madison WI 53718	800-442-8259	608-255-1511	750
Badger Express LLC			
181 Quality Ct ....Fall River WI 53932	800-972-0084	920-484-5808	193
Badger Liquor Company Inc			
850 S Morris St ....Fond du Lac WI 54936	800-242-9708	920-923-8160	80-3
Badger Meter Inc			
4545 W Brown Deer Rd ....Milwaukee WI 53223	800-876-3837	414-355-0400	490
NYSE: BMI			
Badger Mining Corp			
409 S Church St PO Box 328 .....Berlin WI 54923	800-932-7263	920-361-2388	497
Badger Mutual Insurance Co			
1635 W National Ave ......Milwaukee WI 53204	800-837-7833	414-383-1234	387
Badger Sportswear Inc			
111 Badger Ln ....Statesville NC 28625	888-871-0990	704-871-0990	153-3
Badger State Industries (BSI)			
3099 E Washington Ave			
PO Box 8990.................Madison WI 53708	800-862-1086	608-240-5200	622
Badger West Wine & Spirits LLC			
5400 Old Town Hall Rd			
PO Box 869.................Eau Claire WI 54701	800-472-6674	715-836-8600	80-3
Badorf Shoe Co Inc			
1958 Auction Road PO Box 367 ...Manheim PA 17545	800-325-1545	717-653-0155	300
Baer Supply Co			
909 Forest Edge Dr ......Vernon Hills IL 60061	800-944-2237	847-913-2237	348
BAF Industries Inc			
1451 Edinger Ave ....Tustin CA 92780	800-437-9893	714-258-8055	149
Bag Makers Inc			
6606 S Union Rd ....Union IL 60180	800-458-9031		65
BagcraftPapercon			
3900 W 43rd St ....Chicago IL 60632	800-621-8468	773-254-8000	547
Bagdad Roller Mills Inc			
5740 Elmburg Rd PO Box 7 ....Bagdad KY 40003	800-928-3333	502-747-8968	442
Baggett Transportation Co			
2 S 32nd St ....Birmingham AL 35233	800-633-8982	888-224-4388	770
Baghouse & Industrial Sheet Metal Services Inc			
1731 Pomona Rd ....Corona CA 92880	888-224-4687	951-272-6610	18
Bahama Breeze			
8849 International Dr ....Orlando FL 32819	877-500-9715	407-248-2499	662
Bahama House			
2001 S Atlantic			
Ave ....Daytona Beach Shores FL 32118	888-687-1894		376
Bahamas			
Embassy			
2220 Massachusetts Ave NW .....Washington DC 20008	800-883-7421	202-319-2660	257
Bahamas Tourism Office			
1200 S Pine Island Rd			
Ste 750................Plantation FL 33324	800-327-7678	954-236-9292	765
Bahia Mar Beach Resort & Yachting Ctr			
801 Seabreeze Blvd ......Fort Lauderdale FL 33316	888-802-2442	954-764-2233	660
Bahia Resort Hotel			
998 W Mission Bay Dr ....San Diego CA 92109	800-576-4229	858-488-0551	660
Bahl & Gaynor Inc			
212 E Third St Ste 200 ....Cincinnati OH 45202	800-341-1810	513-287-6100	398
BAI (Bank Administration Institute)			
115 S LaSalle St Ste 3300 ....Chicago IL 60603	800-224-9889*	312-683-2464	48-2
*Cust Svc			
Baier Marine Company Inc			
2920 Airway Ave ....Costa Mesa CA 92626	800-455-3917		347
Bailey Farms LLC			
549 Karem Dr ....Marshall WI 53559	800-655-1705	608-655-3439	571
Bailey Lauerman & Assoc Inc			
1248 O St Ste 900 ....Lincoln NE 68508	800-869-0411	402-475-2800	4
Bailey Matthews Shell Museum			
3075 Sanibel-Captiva Rd			
PO Box 1580.................Sanibel FL 33957	888-679-6450	239-395-2233	513
Bailey's Express Inc			
61 Industrial Pk Rd ......Middletown CT 06457	800-523-3758	860-632-0388	770
Baille Lumber Co			
4002 Legion Dr PO Box 6......Hamburg NY 14075	800-950-2850	716-649-2850	192-3
Baillio's Inc			
5301 Menaul Blvd NE ....Albuquerque NM 87110	800-540-7511	505-883-7511	38
Baird Patrick & Company Inc			
305 Plz Ten ....Jersey City NJ 07311	800-221-7747	201-680-7300	681
Baisch & Skinner Inc			
2721 Lasalle St ....Saint Louis MO 63104	800-523-0013	314-664-1212	292
Baja Duty Free (BDF)			
4590 Border Village Rd .....San Ysidro CA 92173	877-438-8937	619-428-6671	241
Baja Expeditions Inc			
3096 Palm St ....San Diego CA 92104	800-843-6967	858-581-3311	220
Baja Fresh			
320 Commerce Ste 100 ....Irvine CA 92602	877-225-2373	949-270-8900	662
Bake'n Joy Foods Inc			
351 Willow St ....North Andover MA 01845	800-666-4937	978-683-1414	295-16
Baker & Taylor Inc			
2550 W Tyvola Rd Ste 300 ......Charlotte NC 28217	800-775-1800		94
Baker Book House Company Inc			
6030 E Fulton St ....Ada MI 49301	800-877-2665*	616-676-9185	628-3
*Orders			
Baker Book House Company Inc Revell Div			
6030 E Fulton St ....Ada MI 49301	800-877-2665*	616-676-9185	628-3
*Orders			
Auburn Hills			
1500 University Dr ....Auburn Hills MI 48326	888-429-0410	248-340-0600	166
Cadillac			
9600 E 13th St ....Cadillac MI 49601	888-313-3463	231-876-3100	166
Clinton Township			
34950 Little Mack Ave ....Clinton Township MI 48035	888-272-2842	586-791-6610	166
Flint 1050 W Bristol Rd ....Flint MI 48507	800-964-4299	810-767-7600	166
Baker College			
Jackson			
2800 Springport Rd ....Jackson MI 49202	888-343-3683	517-788-7800	166
Owosso			
1020 S Washington St ....Owosso MI 48867	800-879-3797	989-729-3350	166
Port Huron			
3403 Lapeer Rd ....Port Huron MI 48060	888-262-2442	810-985-7000	166
Baker Company Inc			
161 Gatehouse Rd PO Box E.......Sanford ME 04073	800-992-2537	207-324-8773	417
Baker Concrete Construction Inc			
900 N Garver Rd ....Monroe OH 45050	800-359-3935	513-539-4000	190-3
Baker County Visitors & Convention Bureau			
490 Campbell St ....Baker City OR 97814	800-523-1235	541-523-3356	207
Baker Cummins			
4400 Biscayne Blvd ....Miami FL 33173	800-226-8629		231
Baker Distributing Co			
PO Box 2954 Ste 100 ....Jacksonville FL 32203	800-217-4698		605
Baker Group			
4224 Hubbell Ave ....Des Moines IA 50317	855-262-4000	515-262-4000	190-10
Baker Hughes Inc (BHI)			
2929 Allen Pkwy Ste 1200 ....Houston TX 77019	800-229-7447	713-439-8600	532
NYSE: BHI			
Baker Hughes Inc Baker Petrolite Div			
12645 W Airport Blvd ......Sugar Land TX 77478	800-231-3606	281-276-5400	143
Baker Products			
55480 Hwy 21 N PO Box 128 ....Ellington MO 63638	800-548-6914	573-663-7711	808
Baker Rock Resources			
21880 SW Farmington Rd ....Beaverton OR 97007	800-340-7625	503-642-2531	45
Baker Roofing Co			
517 Mercury St ....Raleigh NC 27603	800-849-4096	919-828-2975	190-12
Baker Triangle			
415 Highway 80 East			
PO Box 850227................Mesquite TX 75150	800-458-3480	972-289-5534	190-9
Bal Seal Engineering Company Inc			
19650 Pauling ....Foothill Ranch CA 92610	800-366-1006	949-460-2100	325
Balance Rock Inn			
21 Albert Meadow ....Bar Harbor ME 04609	800-753-0494	207-288-2610	376
Balboa Park Inn			
3402 Pk Blvd ....San Diego CA 92103	800-938-8181	619-298-0823	376
Balboa Travel Management Inc			
5414 Oberlin Dr Ste 300 ....San Diego CA 92121	800-359-8773	858-678-3300	761
Balchem Corp			
52 Sunrise Pk Rd PO Box 600 .....New Hampton NY 10958	877-407-8289	845-326-5613	474
NASDAQ: BCPC			
Baldwin & Lyons Inc			
111 Congressional Blvd Ste 500 ......Carmel IN 46032	800-644-5501	317-636-9800	388-4
NASDAQ: BWINB			
Baldwin County Electric Membership Corp			
19600 Hwy 59 ....Summerdale AL 36580	800-837-3374	251-989-6247	245
Baldwin Filters			
4400 Hwy 30 ....Kearney NE 68847	800-822-5394		59
Baldwin Hardware Corp			
841 E Wyomissing Blvd ....Reading PA 19611	800-566-1986	610-777-7811	347
Baldwin Richardson Foods Company Inc			
20201 S La Grange Rd Ste 200........Frankfort IL 60423	866-644-2732*	815-464-9994	295-25
*Cust Svc			
Baldwin Technology Co Inc			
2 Trap Falls Rd Ste 402..........Shelton CT 06484	800-728-5839	203-402-1000	621
NYSE: BLD			
Baldwin-Wallace College			
275 Eastland Rd ....Berea OH 44017	877-292-7759	440-826-2222	166
Balfour 7211 Cir S Rd ....Austin TX 78745	800-225-3687		406
Balihoo Inc			
404 S Eighth St Ste 300 ....Boise ID 83702	866-446-9914		180
Ball Bounce & Sport Inc/Hedstrom Plastics			
One Hedstrom Dr ....Ashland OH 44805	800-765-9665	419-289-9310	752
Ball Homes LLC			
3609 Walden Dr ....Lexington KY 40517	888-268-1101	859-268-1191	188
Ball Horticultural Co			
622 Town Rd ....West Chicago IL 60185	800-879-2255	630-231-3600	293
Ball State University			
2000 W University Ave ....Muncie IN 47306	800-382-8540	765-289-1241	166
Ballantyne Resort Hotel			
10000 Ballantyne			
Commons Pkwy ....Charlotte NC 28277	866-248-4824	704-248-4000	660
Ballantyne Strong Inc			
13710 FNB Pkwy ....Omaha NE 68154	800-424-1215*		584
NYSE: BTN *General			
Ballard's Farm Sausage Inc			
2131 Right Fork Wilson Creek Rd			
PO Box 699...................Wayne WV 25570	800-346-7675*	304-272-5147	295-26
*General			
Ballet Magnificat			
5406 I-55 N ....Jackson MS 39211	866-617-3257	601-977-1001	566-1
Balloons Everywhere Inc			
16474 Greeno Rd ....Fairhope AL 36532	800-239-2000		559
Bally's Atlantic City			
1900 Pacific Ave ....Atlantic City NJ 08401	800-772-7777	609-340-2000	660
Bally's Casino Tunica			
1450 Bally's Blvd ....Robinsonville MS 38664	866-422-5597		132
Bally's Las Vegas			
3645 Las Vegas Blvd S ......Las Vegas NV 89109	800-522-4700*	702-967-4111	132
*Resv			
Ballymore Co			
501 Gunnard Carlson Dr ....Coatesville PA 19365	800-762-8327	610-593-5062	418
Balmoral Inn			
120 Balmoral Ave ....Biloxi MS 39531	800-393-9131	228-388-6776	376
Baltimore Area Convention & Visitors Assn (BACVA)			
100 Light St 12th Fl ....Baltimore MD 21202	877-225-8466	410-659-7300	207

Name / Address	City ST ZIP	Toll-Free	Phone	Class
Baltimore Behavioral Health (BBH) 1101 W Pratt St	Baltimore MD 21223	800-789-2647	410-962-7180	717
Baltimore City Community College 2901 Liberty Heights Ave	Baltimore MD 21215	888-203-1261	410-462-8000	160
Baltimore County Public Library 320 York Rd	Towson MD 21204	800-705-3493	410-887-6100	431-3
Baltimore County Revenue Authority 115 Towsontown Blvd E	Baltimore MD 21286	888-246-5384	410-887-3127	555
Baltimore Gas & Electric Co 110 W Fayette St P.O. Box 1475	Baltimore MD 21201	800-685-0123	410-470-7433	775
Baltimore International College 17 Commerce St	Baltimore MD 21202	800-624-9926	410-752-4710	161
Baltimore Life Cos 10075 Red Run Blvd	Owings Mills MD 21117	800-628-5433	410-581-6600	388-2
Baltimore Magazine 1000 Lancaster St Ste 400 *Cust Svc	Baltimore MD 21202	800-935-0838*	410-752-4200	452-22
Baltimore Museum of Art 10 Art Museum Dr	Baltimore MD 21218	800-735-2964	443-573-1700	513
Baltimore National Cemetery 5501 Frederick Ave	Baltimore MD 21228	800-535-1117	410-644-9696	135
Baltimore Rigging Company Inc, The 8149 Norris Ln PO Box 18401	Dundalk MD 21222	800-626-2150	443-696-4001	190-1
Baltimore Sun 501 N Calvert St	Baltimore MD 21278	800-829-8000	410-332-6000	525-2
Baltimore Symphony Orchestra 1212 Cathedral St	Baltimore MD 21201	877-276-1444	410-783-8100	566-3
Baltimore Times 2513 N Charles St	Baltimore MD 21218	800-944-7403	410-366-3900	525-4
Baltimore Washington Medical Ctr 301 Hospital Dr	Glen Burnie MD 21061	800-994-6610	410-787-4000	371-3
Baltimore/Washington International Thurgood Marshall Airport (BWI) PO Box 8766	Baltimore MD 21240	800-435-9294	410-859-7111	27
Balzer Pacific Equipment Co 2136 SE Eigth Ave	Portland OR 97214	800-442-0966	503-232-5141	355
Bamberger Polymers Inc Two Jericho Plz Ste 109	Jericho NY 11753	800-888-8959	516-622-3600	596
BAMC (Brooke Army Medical Ctr) 3551 Roger Brooke Dr	Fort Sam Houston TX 78234	800-443-2262	210-916-4141	371-4
BAMC (Bay Area Medical Ctr) 3100 Shore Dr	Marinette WI 54143	888-788-2070	715-735-4200	371-3
Banacol Marketing Corp 355 Alhambra Cir Ste 1510	Coral Gables FL 33134	877-324-7619	305-441-9036	296-7
Banana Bay Resort 4590 Overseas Hwy	Marathon FL 33050	866-689-4217		660
Bancorp Bank 409 Silverside Rd Ste 105 NASDAQ: TBBK ▪ *Cust Svc	Wilmington DE 19809	800-545-0289*	302-385-5000	69
BancorpSouth Inc 2910 W Jackson St NYSE: BXS	Tupelo MS 38801	888-797-7711	662-680-2000	357-2
Bancroft Bag Inc 425 Bancroft Blvd	West Monroe LA 71292	800-551-4950	318-387-2550	64
Bandera County Convention & Visitors Bureau 126 State Hwy 16 S PO Box 171	Bandera TX 78003	800-364-3833	830-796-3045	207
Bandera Electric Co-op Inc 3172 State Hwy 16 N	Bandera TX 78003	866-226-3372		245
Bandimere Speedway 3051 S Rooney Rd	Morrison CO 80465	800-664-8946	303-697-6001	508
Bandit Industries Inc 6750 W Millbrook Rd	Remus MI 49340	800-952-0178	989-561-2270	191
Band-It-IDEX Inc 4799 Dahlia St	Denver CO 80216	800-525-0758	303-320-4555	347
Bane Machinery Inc PO Box 541355	Dallas TX 75354	800-594-2263	214-352-2468	355
Banff Adventures Unlimited 211 Bear St Bison Courtyard	Banff AB T1L1A8	800-644-8888	403-762-4554	750
Banff Centre, The 107 Tunnel Mtn Dr PO Box 1020	Banff AB T1L1H5	800-884-7574	403-762-6100	374
Banff National Park PO Box 900	Banff AB T1L1K2	877-737-3783	403-762-1550	556
Banfield the Pet Hospital 8000 NE Tillamook St	Portland OR 97213	866-894-7927		782
Bang Printing Inc 3323 Oak St	Brainerd MN 56401	800-328-0450	218-829-2877	618
Bangor Daily News 491 Main St PO Box 1329	Bangor ME 04402	800-432-7964	207-990-8000	525-2
Bangor Hydro Electric Co PO Box 932	Bangor ME 04402	800-499-6600	207-945-5621	775
Bangor International Airport 287 Godfrey Blvd	Bangor ME 04401	866-359-2264	207-992-4600	27
Bangor Public Library 145 Harlow St	Bangor ME 04401	800-442-4293	207-947-8336	431-3
Bangor Savings Bank Three State St	Bangor ME 04401	877-226-4671	207-942-5211	69
Bangor Symphony Orchestra PO Box 1441 *General	Bangor ME 04402	800-639-3221*	207-942-5555	566-3
Bangor Theological Seminary 159 State St	Portland ME 04101	800-287-6781	207-942-6781	167-3
Bank Administration Institute (BAI) 115 S LaSalle St Ste 3300 *Cust Svc	Chicago IL 60603	800-224-9889*	312-683-2464	48-2
Bank Financial 6415 W 95th St	Chicago Ridge IL 60415	800-894-6900		69
Bank Independent 710 S Montgomery Ave	Sheffield AL 35660	877-865-5050	256-386-5000	357-2
Bank Leumi USA 579 Fifth Ave	New York NY 10017	800-892-5430	917-542-2343	69
Bank Mutual Corp 4949 W Brown Deer Rd NASDAQ: BKMU	Milwaukee WI 53223	844-256-8684	414-354-1500	357-2
Bank of America Card Services One Commercial Pl Second Fl	Norfolk VA 23510	800-732-9194	757-441-4770	217
Bank of Commerce Holdings 1901 Churn Creek Rd NASDAQ: BOCH	Redding CA 96002	800-421-2575	530-224-3333	357-2
Bank of Georgia, The 100 Westpark Dr	Peachtree City GA 30269	866-645-1139	770-631-9488	69
Bank of Hawaii Corp 130 Merchant St 20th Fl NYSE: BOH	Honolulu HI 96813	888-643-3888		357-2
Bank of Highland Park Financial Corp 1835 First St PO Box 546	Highland Park IL 60035	877-651-7800	847-432-7800	676
Bank of Louisiana 300 St Charles Ave	New Orleans LA 70130	866-392-9952	504-592-0600	69
Bank of Marin 504 Tamalpais Dr NASDAQ: BMRC	Corte Madera CA 94925	800-654-5111	415-927-2265	69
Bank of McKenney 20718 First St OTC: BOMK	McKenney VA 23872	800-528-2273	804-478-4434	69
Bank of Nevada 2700 W Sahara Ave	Las Vegas NV 89102	877-750-0010	702-248-4200	69
Bank of North Dakota 1200 Memorial Hwy	Bismarck ND 58504	800-472-2166	701-328-5600	69
Bank of Nova Scotia 1 Liberty Plaza 26th Fl TSE: BNS	New York NY 10006	800-472-6842	212-225-5011	69
Bank of Oklahoma NA PO Box 2300	Tulsa OK 74192	800-234-6181	918-588-6010	69
Bank of South Carolina Corp 256 Meeting St NASDAQ: BKSC	Charleston SC 29401	800-523-4175	843-724-1500	357-2
Bank of Stanly PO Box 338	Albemarle NC 28002	800-438-6864	704-983-6181	69
Bank of Stockton PO Box 1110	Stockton CA 95201	800-941-1494	209-929-1600	69
Bank of Sunset & Trust Co 863 Napoleon Ave	Sunset LA 70584	800-264-5578	337-662-5222	69
Bank of the Carolinas 135 Boxwood Village Dr OTC: BCAR	Mocksville NC 27028	877-751-5755	336-751-5755	69
Bank of the Orient 233 Sansome St	San Francisco CA 94104	877-275-3342	415-338-0843	187
Bank of the Ozarks 4328 Old Spanish Trail	Houston TX 77021	800-274-4482	713-747-9000	69
Bank of the Ozarks Inc 12615 Chenal Pkwy PO Box 8811 NASDAQ: OZRK	Little Rock AR 72211	800-628-3552	501-978-2265	357-2
Bank of the Sierra PO Box 1930 *Cust Svc	Porterville CA 93258	888-454-2265*	559-782-4900	69
Bank Of Utica 222 Genesee St OTC: BKUT	Utica NY 13502	800-442-1028	315-797-2700	69
Bank of Virginia 11730 Hull St Rd NASDAQ: BOVA	Midlothian VA 23112	800-500-1044	804-744-7576	69
BankAtlantic 200 W Second St	Winston-Salem NC 27101	800-226-5228	888-628-3926	69
Bankers Fidelity Life Insurance Co 4370 Peachtree Rd NASDAQ: AAME	Atlanta GA 30319	800-241-1439	404-266-5500	388-2
Bankers Life & Casualty Co 111 E Wacker Dr Ste 2100	Chicago IL 60601	800-231-9150	312-396-6000	388-2
Bankers' Bank 7700 Mineral Point Rd	Madison WI 53717	800-388-5550	608-833-5550	69
Bank-Fund Staff Federal Credit Union PO Box 27755	Washington DC 20038	800-923-7328	202-458-4300	219
Banking Daily 1801 S Bell St	Arlington VA 22202	800-372-1033		524-1
Banking Strategies Magazine 115 S LaSalle St Ste 3300	Chicago IL 60603	888-224-0037	312-553-4600	452-5
Banko Beverage Co 5001 Crackersport Rd *General	Allentown PA 18104	800-322-9295*	610-434-0147	80-1
Bankruptcy Court Decisions 360 Hiatt Dr	Palm Beach Gardens FL 33418	800-621-5463	561-622-6520	524-1
Bankruptcy Law Letter 610 Opperman Dr	Eagan MN 55123	800-937-8529	651-687-7000	524-7
Bankruptcy Management Solutions Inc Eight Corporate Park Ste 230	Irvine CA 92606	800-634-7734		458
Bankshot Sports Organization 842 B Rockville Pike	Rockville MD 20852	800-933-0140	301-309-0260	701
Bankwest Corporation 2050 N California Blvd	Walnut Creek CA 94597	888-389-8668	925-933-7810	69
Bankwest Inc 420 S Pierre St PO Box 998	Pierre SD 57501	800-253-0362	605-224-7391	69
Bannack State Park 4200 Bannack Rd	Dillon MT 59725	855-922-6768	406-834-3413	558
Banneker-Douglas Museum 84 Franklin St	Annapolis MD 21401	877-634-6361	410-216-6180	513
Banner Bank 10 S First Ave PO Box 907	Walla Walla WA 99362	800-272-9933	509-527-3636	69
Banner Behavioral Health Hospital 7575 E Earll Dr	Scottsdale AZ 85251	800-254-4357	480-941-7500	371-5
Banner Del E Webb Memorial Hospital 14502 W Meeker Blvd	Sun City West AZ 85375	800-254-4357	623-214-4000	371-3
Banner Engineering Corp 9714 Tenth Ave N	Minneapolis MN 55441	888-373-6767	763-544-3164	253
Banner Life Insurance Co 1701 Research Blvd	Rockville MD 20850	800-638-8428	301-279-4800	388-2
Banner Pharmacaps Inc 4100 Mendenhall Oaks Pkwy *Cust Svc	High Point NC 27265	866-529-2922*	336-812-3442	576
Banner Supply Co 7195 NW 30th St	Miami FL 33122	888-511-4004	305-593-2946	192-3
Banner-Gazette 490 E State Rd 60 PO Box 38	Pekin IN 47165	800-889-3390	812-967-3176	525-4
Bannister & Assoc Inc 34 N High St	New Albany OH 43054	800-995-3579	614-895-1355	46
Bannister Family House 406 Dickinson St	San Diego CA 92103	800-926-8273	619-543-7977	369
Bannister's Wharf 1 Bannister's Wharf	Newport RI 02840	800-395-1343	401-846-4500	49-5
Banterra Corp 1404 US Rt 45 S	Eldorado IL 62930	877-541-2265	618-273-9346	69
Banyan Air Service 5360 NW 20th Terr	Fort Lauderdale FL 33309	800-200-2031	954-491-3170	62
Banyan Resort 323 Whitehead St	Key West FL 33040	866-371-9222	305-296-7786	660
Banyan Water Inc 11002-B Metric Blvd	Austin TX 78758	800-276-1507		458

	Toll-Free	Phone	Class
Baptist Bible College			
538 VenaRd Rd ....Clarks Summit PA 18411	**800-451-7664***	570-586-2400	159
*General			
Baptist College of Florida			
5400 College Dr ....Graceville FL 32440	**800-328-2660**	850-263-3261	166
Baptist Health			
1 Trillium Way ....Corbin KY 40701	**800-395-4435**	606-528-1212	371-3
Baptist Health Louisville			
4000 Kresge Way ....Louisville KY 40207	**800-489-3002**	502-897-8100	371-3
Baptist Health Paducah (WBH)			
2501 Kentucky Ave ....Paducah KY 42003	**877-271-4176**	270-575-2100	371-3
Baptist Health South Florida Inc			
6855 Red Rd Ste 600 ....Coral Gables FL 33143	**800-622-2838**	786-662-7000	350
Baptist Hospital of Miami			
8900 SW 88th St ....Miami FL 33176	**800-994-6610**	786-596-1960	371-3
Baptist Medical Ctr			
800 Prudential Dr ....Jacksonville FL 32207	**800-874-8567**	904-202-2000	371-3
Baptist Memorial Health Care Corp			
350 N Humphreys Blvd ....Memphis TN 38120	**800-422-7847**	901-227-5920	350
Baptist Memorial Hospital Golden Triangle			
2520 Fifth St N ....Columbus MS 39703	**800-422-7847**	662-244-1000	371-3
Baptist Missionary Assn Theological Seminary			
1530 E Pine St ....Jacksonville TX 75766	**800-259-5673**	903-586-2501	167-3
Baptist Theological Seminary at Richmond			
8040 Villa Park Dr Ste 250 ....Richmond VA 23227	**888-345-2877**	804-355-8135	167-3
Baptist Trinity Home Care & Hospice			
6019 Walnut Grove Rd ....Memphis TN 38120	**800-422-7847**	901-226-5000	368
Baptist University of the Americas			
8019 S Pan Am Expy ....San Antonio TX 78224	**800-721-1396**	210-924-4338	159
Baptist World Alliance			
405 N Washington St ....Falls Church VA 22046	**866-291-7809**	703-790-8980	47-20
Bar Harbor Bankshares			
82 Main St PO Box 400 ......Bar Harbor ME 04609	**888-853-7100**	207-288-3314	357-2
NYSE: BHB			
Bar Harbor Chamber of Commerce			
Two Cottage St ....Bar Harbor ME 04609	**888-540-9990**	207-288-5103	137
Bar Harbor Hotel-Bluenose Inn			
90 Eden St ....Bar Harbor ME 04609	**800-445-4077**	207-288-3348	376
Bar Harbor Inn Oceanfront Resort			
Newport Dr PO Box 7 ....Bar Harbor ME 04609	**800-248-3351**	207-288-3351	660
Bar Lazy J Guest Ranch			
447 County Rd 3 PO Box N ......Parshall CO 80468	**800-396-6279**	970-725-3437	239
Bar None Auction Inc			
4751 Power Inn Rd ....Sacramento CA 95826	**866-372-1700**		188
Bar Productscom Inc			
1990 Lake Ave SE ....Largo FL 33771	**800-256-6396**	727-584-2093	320
Barbara Ann Karmanos Cancer Institute			
4100 John R St ....Detroit MI 48201	**800-527-6266**		659
Barbara B Mann Performing Arts Hall			
13350 FSW Pkwy ....Fort Myers FL 33919	**800-440-7469**	239-489-3033	565
Barbershop Harmony Society			
110 Seventh Ave N ....Nashville TN 37203	**800-876-7464**	615-823-3993	47-18
Barbey Electronics Corp			
210 Corporate Dr PO Box 2 ......Reading PA 19605	**800-822-2251**	610-916-7955	246
Barbour Welting Company Div Barbour Corp			
1001 N Montello St ....Brockton MA 02301	**800-955-9649**	508-583-8200	300
BARC Electric Co-op			
84 High St PO Box 264............Millboro VA 24460	**800-846-2272**		245
Barclay College			
607 N Kingman St ....Haviland KS 67059	**800-862-0226**	620-862-5252	159
Barclay International Group			
6800 Jericho Tpke ....Syosset NY 11791	**800-845-6636**	516-364-0064	373
Barclays Capital Inc			
200 Pk Ave ....New York NY 10166	**888-227-2275**	212-412-4000	681
Barco Electronic Systems Pvt Ltd			
11101 Trade Ctr Dr ....Rancho Cordova CA 95670	**888-414-7226**	916-859-2500	174-4
BARCO Industries Inc			
1020 MacArthur Rd ....Reading PA 19605	**800-234-8665***		748
*Cust Svc			
Barco Uniforms Inc			
350 W Rosecrans Ave ....Gardena CA 90248	**800-421-1874**	310-323-7315	153-18
Barcoding Inc			
2220 Boston St ....Baltimore MD 21231	**888-412-7226**	410-385-8532	180
Bard Access Systems Inc			
605 North 5600 West ....Salt Lake City UT 84116	**800-443-5505**	801-522-5000	471
Bard College			
PO Box 5000 ....Annandale-on-Hudson NY 12504	**800-872-7423**	845-758-7472	166
Bard Inc Peripheral Vascular			
1625 W Third St ....Tempe AZ 85281	**800-321-4254**	480-894-9515	471
Bard Mfg Co Inc			
1914 Randolph Dr ....Bryan OH 43506	**877-347-6456**	419-636-1194	15
Barden & Robeson Corp			
103 Kelly Ave ....Middleport NY 14105	**800-724-0141**	716-735-3732	105
Barden Corp			
200 Pk Ave ....Danbury CT 06810	**800-243-1060**	203-744-2211	613
Bardes Plastics Inc			
5225 W Clinton Ave ....Milwaukee WI 53223	**800-558-5161***		595
*Cust Svc			
Barefoot Landing			
4898 Hwy 17 S ....North Myrtle Beach SC 29582	**800-217-1511**	843-272-8349	49-5
Barefoot Resort & Golf			
4980 Barefoot Resort			
Bridge Rd ....North Myrtle Beach SC 29582	**866-638-4818**	843-390-3200	660
Barfield Inc			
4101 NW 29th St ....Miami FL 33142	**800-321-1039**	305-894-5300	24
Bargain Supply Co			
844 E Jefferson St ....Louisville KY 40206	**800-322-5226**	502-562-5000	348
Barger Packaging Inc			
2901 Oakland Ave ....Elkhart IN 46517	**888-525-2845**		594
Bargreen Ellingson Inc			
2925 70th Ave E ....Fife WA 98424	**866-722-2665**	253-722-2600	299
Barix Clinics			
135 S Prospect St ....Ypsilanti MI 48198	**800-282-0066**	734-547-4700	797
Barker Steel Co Inc			
55 Sumner St ....Milford MA 01757	**866-977-3227**	508-473-8484	475
Barksdale Inc			
3211 Fruitland Ave ....Los Angeles CA 90058	**800-835-1060**	323-589-6181	202
Barlovento LLC			
431 Technology Dr ....Dothan AL 36303	**877-498-6039**	334-983-9979	187
Barlow			
1305 Grand Dd SE ....Faucett MO 64448	**800-688-1202**	816-238-3373	770
Barn Furniture Mart Inc			
6206 N Sepulveda Blvd ....Van Nuys CA 91411	**888-302-2276**	818-780-4070	320
Barnes & Thornburg			
11 S Meridian St ....Indianapolis IN 46204	**800-236-1352**	317-236-1313	425
Barnes Distribution			
1301 E Ninth St Ste 700 ....Cleveland OH 44114	**800-726-9626**	216-416-7200	382
Barnes Farming Corp			
7840 Old Bailey Hwy .....Spring Hope NC 27882	**800-367-2799**		10-10
Barnes Group Inc			
123 Main St ....Bristol CT 06011	**800-877-8803**	860-583-7070	709
NYSE: B			
Barnes International Inc			
814 Chestnut St PO Box 1203 ....Rockford IL 61105	**800-435-4877**	815-964-8661	450
Barnes Lodge			
4520 Clayton Ave ....Saint Louis MO 63110	**800-551-3492**	314-652-4319	369
Barnes Transportation Services Inc			
2309 Whitley Rd ....Wilson NC 27895	**800-898-5897**		357-2
barnesandnoble.com Inc			
76 Ninth Ave Fl 9 ....New York NY 10011	**800-843-2665**	212-414-6000	95
Barnet Associates LLC			
Two Round Lk Rd ....Ridgefield CT 06877	**888-827-7070**		316
Barnet-Dulaney Eye Ctr			
4800 N 22nd St ....Phoenix AZ 85016	**866-742-6581**	602-955-1000	786
Barnett & Ramel Optical Co			
7154 N 16th St ....Omaha NE 68112	**800-228-9732**		536
Barnett Implement Co Inc			
4220 Old Hwy 99 S ....Snohomish WA 98273	**800-453-9274**	425-334-4048	274
Barnett Inc			
801 W Bay St ....Jacksonville FL 32204	**888-803-4467**	904-384-6530	605
Barney Trucking Inc			
235 State Rt 24 ....Salina UT 84654	**800-524-7930**		676
Barnhardt Mfg Co			
1100 Hawthorne Ln ....Charlotte NC 28205	**800-277-0377**		228
Barnhart Crane & Rigging Co			
1701 Dunn Ave ....Memphis TN 38106	**800-727-0149**	901-775-3000	191
Barnhill Bolt Company Inc			
2500 Princeton Dr Ne ....Albuquerque NM 87107	**800-472-3900**	505-884-1808	347
Barnsley Gardens			
597 Barnsley Gardens Rd ....Adairsville GA 30103	**877-773-2447**	770-773-7480	660
Barnstead Inn			
349 Bonnet St ....Manchester Center VT 05255	**800-331-1619**	802-362-1619	376
Baron Funds			
767 Fifth Ave 49th Fl ....New York NY 10153	**800-992-2766**	212-583-2000	521
Baron Mfg Company LLC			
1200 Capitol Dr ....Addison IL 60101	**800-368-8585**	630-628-9110	347
Barona Resort & Casino			
1932 Wildcat Canyon Rd ....Lakeside CA 92040	**888-722-7662**	619-443-2300	132
Baronne Plaza Hotel			
201 Baronne St ....New Orleans LA 70112	**888-756-0083**	504-522-0083	376
Barr Engineering Co			
4700 W 77th St ....Minneapolis MN 55435	**800-632-2277**	952-832-2600	261
Barracks, The			
43 Pinkney St ....Annapolis MD 21401	**800-603-4020**	410-267-7619	49-2
Barrett Business Services Inc			
8100 NE Pkwy Dr Ste 200...........Vancouver WA 98662	**800-494-5669**	360-828-0700	623
NASDAQ: BBSI			
Barrick Gold Corp			
TD Canada Trust Tower 161 Bay St			
PO Box 212.....................Toronto ON M5J2S1	**800-720-7415**	416-861-9911	497
NYSE: ABX			
Barrie House Coffee Company Inc			
Four Warehouse In ....Elmsford NY 10523	**800-876-2233**		296-2
Barriere Construction Co LLC			
1 Galleria Blvd Ste 1650 ....Metairie LA 70001	**866-645-3060**	504-581-7283	189-4
Barrington Hotel & Suites			
263 Shepherd of the Hills Expy ....Branson MO 65616	**800-760-8866**	417-334-8866	376
Barron Electric Co-op			
1434 State Hwy 25 N ....Barron WI 54812	**800-322-1008**	715-537-3171	245
Barron Motor Inc			
1850 McCloud Pl NE			
PO Box 1327...................Cedar Rapids IA 52402	**800-332-7953**		60
Barron's Educational Series Inc			
250 Wireless Blvd ....Hauppauge NY 11788	**800-645-3476**	631-434-3311	628-2
Barry Bunker Chevrolet Inc			
1307 N Wabash Ave ....Marion IN 46952	**866-603-8625***	765-664-1275	56
*Sales			
Barry Callebaut USA LLC			
400 Industrial Pk Rd ....Saint Albans VT 05478	**800-556-8845**	802-524-9711	295-8
Barry Electric Co-op			
4015 Main St PO Box 307 ....Cassville MO 65625	**866-847-2333**	417-847-2131	245
Barry University			
Barry Memorial Library			
11300 NE Second Ave ....Miami Shores FL 33161	**800-756-6000**	305-899-3000	431-6
Orlando			
1650 Sandlake Rd Ste 390 ....Orlando FL 32809	**800-756-6000**	407-438-4150	166
Tallahassee			
325 John Knox Rd Bldg A ....Tallahassee FL 32303	**800-756-6000**	850-385-2279	166
Barry-owen Co Inc			
5625 Smithway St ....Los Angeles CA 90040	**800-682-6682**	323-724-4800	292
Barry-Wehmiller Cos Inc			
8020 Forsyth Blvd ....Saint Louis MO 63105	**800-862-8020**	314-862-8000	540
Barry-Wehmiller Cos Inc Accraply Div			
3580 Holly Ln N ....Plymouth MN 55447	**800-328-3997**	763-557-1313	540
Bar-S Foods Co			
PO Box 29049 ....Phoenix AZ 85038	**800-699-4115**		295-26
Barstow College			
2700 Barstow Rd ....Barstow CA 92311	**877-823-2378**	760-252-2411	160
Bar-T-5 Covered Wagon Cook Out & Wild West Show			
812 Cache Creek Dr ....Jackson WY 83001	**800-772-5386**	307-733-5386	662
Bartech Group			
17199 N Laurel Pk Dr Ste 224 ....Livonia MI 48152	**800-828-4410**	734-953-5050	712
Bartell Machinery Systems LLC			
6321 Elmer Hill Rd ....Rome NY 13440	**800-537-8473**	315-336-7600	489
Bartender Magazine			
PO Box 158 ....Liberty Corner NJ 07938	**800-463-7465***	908-766-6006	452-21
*Sales			
Barth Electric Company Inc			
1934 N Illinois St ....Indianapolis IN 46202	**800-666-6226**	317-924-6226	190-4
Barthco International Inc			
5101 S Broad St ....Philadelphia PA 19112	**877-401-6400***	215-238-8600	310
*General			
Bartholomew County Rural Electric Membership Corp			
1697 W. Deaver Rd ....Columbus IN 47201	**800-927-5672**	812-372-2546	245
Bartizan Corp			
217 Riverdale Ave ....Yonkers NY 10705	**800-899-2278**	914-965-7977	527

	Toll-Free	Phone	Class
Bartlett & Co			
600 Vine St Ste 2100 . . . . Cincinnati OH 45202	**800-800-4612**	513-621-4612	398
Bartlett & West Engineers Inc			
1200 SW Executive Dr . . . . Topeka KS 66615	**888-200-6464**	785-272-2252	261
Barton College			
PO Box 5000 . . . . Wilson NC 27893	**800-345-4973**	252-399-6300	166
Barton Cotton Inc			
3030 Waterview Ave . . . . Baltimore MD 21230	**800-638-4652**	800-348-1102	316
Barton County Community College			
245 NE 30th Rd . . . . Great Bend KS 67530	**800-722-6842**	620-792-2701	160
Barton County Electric Co-op			
91 W Hwy 160 PO Box 459 . . . . Lamar MO 64759	**800-286-5636**	417-682-5636	245
Barton Solvents Inc			
1920 NE Broadway Ave . . . . Des Moines IA 50313	**800-728-6488**	515-265-7998	144
Baruch College			
55 Lexington Ave at 24th St . . . . . . New York NY 10010	**800-273-8255**	646-312-1000	166
Basalite Concrete Products LLC			
605 Industrial Way . . . . Dixon CA 95620	**800-776-6690**	707-678-1901	184
Basco Shower Enclosures			
7201 Snider Rd . . . . Mason OH 45040	**800-543-1938**	513-573-1900	328
Bascom Palmer Eye Institute			
900 NW 17th St . . . . Miami FL 33136	**800-329-7000**	305-326-6000	371-7
Baseball Express Inc			
5750 NW Pkwy Ste 100 . . . . San Antonio TX 78249	**800-937-4824**	210-348-7000	702
Baseball Hall of Fame			
910 S 3rd St . . . . Minneapolis MN 55415	**888-375-9707**	612-375-9707	515
BASF Canada			
100 Milverton Dr Fifth Fl . . . . Mississauga ON L5R4H1	**866-485-2273***	289-360-1300	141
*Cust Svc			
BASF Corp			
100 Campus Dr . . . . Florham Park NJ 07932	**800-526-1072**	973-245-6000	141
BASF Corp/Bldg Systems			
889 Valley Pk Dr . . . . Shakopee MN 55379	**800-433-9517***	952-496-6000	3
*Cust Svc			
Bashas Inc			
22402 S Bashas Rd . . . . Chandler AZ 85248	**800-755-7292**	480-895-9350	342
Basic American Foods			
2185 N California Blvd			
Ste 215 . . . . Walnut Creek CA 94596	**800-227-4050**	925-472-4000	295-18
Basic Carbide Corp			
900 Main St . . . . Lowber PA 15660	**800-426-4291**	724-446-1630	1
Basic Commodities Inc			
863 S Orlando Ave . . . . Winter Park FL 32789	**800-338-7006**	407-629-2000	170
Basic Components Inc			
1201 S Second Ave . . . . Mansfield TX 76063	**800-452-1780**	817-473-7224	192-2
Basic Metals Inc			
W180 Nn11819 River Ln . . . . Germantown WI 53022	**800-989-1996**	262-255-9034	487
Basin Disposal Inc			
2021 N Commercial Ave . . . . Pasco WA 99301	**800-642-6447**	509-547-2476	792
Basin Harbor Club			
4800 Basin Harbor Rd . . . . Vergennes VT 05491	**800-622-4000**	802-475-2311	660
Basin Tire & Auto Inc			
2700 E Main St . . . . Farmington NM 87402	**800-832-9832**	505-326-2231	61-5
Basis International Ltd			
5901 Jefferson St NE . . . . Albuquerque NM 87109	**800-423-1394***	505-345-5232	179-12
*Orders			
Baskin Auto Truck & Tractor Inc			
1844 Hwy 51 S . . . . Covington TN 38019	**877-476-2626**	901-476-2626	56
Baskin-Robbins Inc			
130 Royall St . . . . Canton MA 02021	**800-859-5339**	781-737-3000	378
Bass Performance Hall			
4th & Calhoun Sts . . . . Fort Worth TX 76102	**877-212-4280**	817-212-4200	565
Bass Player Magazine			
28 E 28th St 12th Fl . . . . New York NY 10016	**866-246-3595***	212-378-0400	452-9
*Cust Svc			
Bassett Furniture Industries Inc			
3525 Fairystone Pk Hwy			
PO Box 626. Bassett VA 24055	**877-525-7070**	714-222-1010	318-2
NASDAQ: BSET			
Bassett Healthcare Network			
1 Atwell Rd . . . . Cooperstown NY 13326	**800-227-7388**	607-547-3456	371-3
Bassett Printing Corp			
3321 Fairystone Park Hwy . . . . Bassett VA 24055	**800-336-5102**		619
Bassmaster Magazine			
3500 Blue Lake Dr Suite 330 . . . . . Birmingham FL 35243	**877-227-7872**		452-20
Bastian Material Handling LLC (BMH)			
10585 N Meridian St			
Third Fl . . . . Indianapolis IN 46290	**800-772-0464**	317-575-9992	54
Bastian Trucking Inc			
440 South Main . . . . Aurora UT 84620	**800-452-5126**	435-529-7453	770
Bat Conservation International (BCI)			
500 N Capital of Texas Hwy . . . . Austin TX 78746	**800-538-2287**	512-327-9721	47-3
Batavia VA Medical Ctr			
222 Richmond Ave . . . . Batavia NY 14020	**800-273-8255**	585-297-1000	371-8
BatchMaster Software Inc			
24461 Ridge Rt Dr Ste 210 . . . . Laguna Hills CA 92653	**800-359-0920**	949-583-1646	179-10
Bates College			
2 Andrews Rd Ln Hall . . . . Lewiston ME 04240	**888-522-8371**	207-786-6255	166
Bates Container			
6433 Davis Blvd . . . . North Richland Hills TX 76182	**800-792-8736**	817-498-3200	99
Batesville Casket Co			
1 Batesville Blvd . . . . Batesville IN 47006	**800-622-8373***	812-934-7500	133
*Cust Svc			
Bath & Body Works			
Seven Limited Pkwy E . . . . Reynoldsburg OH 43068	**800-395-1001**		215
Bath Veterans Affairs Medical Ctr			
76 Veterans Ave . . . . Bath NY 14810	**877-845-3247**	607-664-4000	371-8
Bathcrest Inc			
5195 W 4700 S . . . . Salt Lake City UT 84118	**800-826-6790**	801-957-1400	190-11
Bath-Tec Inc			
PO Box 1118 . . . . Ennis TX 75120	**800-526-3301**	972-646-5279	372
Baton Rouge Community College (BRCC)			
201 Community College Dr . . . . . Baton Rouge LA 70806	**866-217-9823**	225-216-8000	160
Baton Rouge Convention & Visitors Bureau			
359 Third St . . . . Baton Rouge LA 70801	**800-527-6843**	225-383-1825	207
Baton Rouge Metropolitan Airport			
9430 Jackie Cochran Dr			
Ste 300 . . . . Baton Rouge LA 70807	**877-359-2538**	225-355-0333	27
Battelle Memorial Institute Inc			
505 King Ave . . . . Columbus OH 43201	**800-201-2011**	614-424-6424	659
Battered Women's Justice Project			
1801 Nicollet Ave S Ste 102 . . . . . . Minneapolis MN 55403	**800-903-0111**	612-824-8768	48-10
Battle Creek Enquirer			
155 W Van Buren St . . . . Battle Creek MI 49017	**800-333-4139**	269-964-7161	525-2

	Toll-Free	Phone	Class
Battle Creek/Calhoun County Convention & Visitors Bureau			
77 E Michigan Ave Ste 100. . . . . Battle Creek MI 49017	**800-397-2240**	269-962-2240	207
Battle Ground Lake State Park			
18002 NE 249th St . . . . Battle Ground WA 98604	**888-226-7688**	360-687-4621	558
Battlefield Farms Inc			
23190 Clarks Mtn Rd . . . . Rapidan VA 22733	**800-722-0744**		366
Bauder College			
384 N Yards Blvd NW Ste 190 . . . . Atlanta GA 30313	**800-935-1857**	404-237-7573	788
Baudville Inc			
5380 52nd St SE . . . . Grand Rapids MI 49512	**800-728-0888***	616-698-0889	179-1
*Orders			
Baue Funeral Homes			
620 Jefferson St . . . . Saint Charles MO 63301	**888-724-0073**		503
Bauer Built Inc			
PO Box 248 . . . . Durand WI 54736	**800-268-5114**	715-672-4295	745
Bauer Premium Fly Reels			
585 Clover Ln Ste 1 . . . . Ashland OR 97520	**888-484-4165**	541-488-8246	701
Bauer-Pileco Inc			
100 N FM 3083 E . . . . Conroe TX 77303	**800-474-5326**	713-691-3000	383
Baum Textile Mills Inc			
812 Jersey Ave . . . . Jersey City NJ 07310	**866-842-7631**	201-659-0444	587
Baumfolder Corp			
1660 Campbell Rd . . . . Sidney OH 45365	**800-543-6107**	937-492-1281	549
Baumgarten's			
144 Ottley Dr . . . . Atlanta GA 30324	**800-247-5547**	404-874-7675	527
Bausch & Lomb Inc			
1400 N Goodman St . . . . Rochester NY 14609	**800-553-5340**	585-338-6000	535
Bausch & Lomb Inc Vision Care Div			
1400 Goodman St N . . . . Rochester NY 14609	**800-828-9030**	585-338-6000	535
Bausch & Lomb Pharmaceuticals Inc			
8500 Hidden River Pkwy . . . . Tampa FL 33637	**800-323-0000***	800-553-5340	576
*Cust Svc			
Baxter Assistance Services Inc			
2800 E Broadway Ste C-416. . . . . Pearland TX 77581	**866-443-0005**		457
Baxter Corp			
7125 Mississauga Rd . . . . Mississauga ON L5N0C2	**866-234-2345**	905-369-6000	231
BaxterBoo			
7025 S Fulton St Ste 150 . . . . Centennial CO 80112	**888-887-0063**		681
Bay Area Medical Ctr (BAMC)			
3100 Shore Dr . . . . Marinette WI 54143	**888-788-2070**	715-735-4200	371-3
Bay Bank			
2328 W Joppa Rd . . . . Lutherville MD 21093	**800-222-6566**	410-494-2580	357-2
NASDAQ: BYBK			
Bay City Flower Company Inc			
2265 Cabrillo Hwy S . . . . Half Moon Bay CA 94019	**800-399-5858***	650-726-5535	366
*Sales			
Bay City Times			
311 Fifth St . . . . Bay City MI 48708	**800-727-7661**	989-895-8551	525-2
Bay City Tribune			
2901 16th St . . . . Bay City TX 77414	**877-322-8228**	979-245-5555	525-2
Bay Club Hotel & Marina			
2131 Shelter Island Dr . . . . San Diego CA 92106	**800-672-0800**	619-224-8888	376
Bay de Noc Community College			
2001 N Lincoln Rd . . . . Escanaba MI 49829	**800-221-2001**	906-786-5802	160
Bay Hill Golf Club & Lodge			
9000 Bay Hill Blvd . . . . Orlando FL 32819	**888-422-9445**	407-876-2429	660
Bay Houston Towing Co			
2243 Milford St . . . . Houston TX 77253	**800-324-3755**	713-529-3755	460
Bay Mechanical Inc			
2696 Reliance Dr Ste 200. . . . . . . Virginia Beach VA 23452	**888-229-6324**	757-468-6700	190-10
Bay Medical Ctr			
615 N Bonita Ave . . . . Panama City FL 32401	**800-222-1222**	850-769-1511	371-3
Bay Mills Community College			
12214 W Lakeshore Dr . . . . Brimley MI 49715	**800-844-2622**	906-248-3354	163
Bay Park Hotel			
1425 Munras Ave . . . . Monterey CA 93940	**800-338-3564***	831-649-1020	376
*Resv			
Bay Path College			
588 Longmeadow St . . . . Longmeadow MA 01106	**800-782-7284**		166
Bay Regional Medical Ctr (BRMC)			
1900 Columbus Ave . . . . Bay City MI 48708	**800-656-3950**	989-894-3000	371-3
Bay Shore Systems Inc			
14206 N Ohio St . . . . Rathdrum ID 83858	**888-569-3745**	208-687-3311	191
Bay State College			
122 Commonwealth Ave . . . . Boston MA 02116	**800-815-3276**	617-217-9000	788
Bay State Milling Co			
100 Congress St . . . . Quincy MA 02169	**800-553-5687**		295-23
Bay Swiss Mfg Company Inc			
Five Airpark Vista Blvd . . . . Dayton NV 89403	**800-247-3207**	775-246-7100	614
Bay Technical Assoc Inc			
5239 Ave A . . . . Long Beach Industrial Park MS 39560	**800-523-2702**	228-563-7334	175
Bay Valley Hotel & Resort			
2470 Old Bridge Rd . . . . Bay City MI 48706	**888-241-4653**	989-686-3500	660
Bay Watch Resort & Conference Ctr			
2701 S Ocean Blvd . . . . North Myrtle Beach SC 29582	**866-270-2172**	843-272-4600	660
Bayco Products Inc			
640 Sanden Blvd . . . . Wylie TX 75098	**800-233-2155**	469-326-9400	433
Bayer Corp			
100 Bayer Rd . . . . Pittsburgh PA 15205	**800-422-9374**	412-777-2000	576
Bayer Inc			
77 Belfield Rd . . . . Toronto ON M9W1G6	**800-622-2937**	416-248-0771	576
Bayer MaterialScience LLC			
100 Bayer Rd . . . . Pittsburgh PA 15205	**800-662-2927**	412-777-2000	598-2
Bayfield Electric Co-op Inc			
7400 Iron River Dam Rd . . . . Iron River WI 54847	**800-278-0166**	715-372-4287	245
Bayfront Inn			
138 Avenida Menendez . . . . . . Saint Augustine FL 32084	**800-558-3455**	904-824-1681	376
Bayhead Products Corp			
173 Crosby Rd . . . . Dover NH 03820	**800-229-4323**	603-742-3000	465
Bayhealth Medical Ctr			
21 W Clarke Ave . . . . Milford DE 19963	**877-453-7107**	302-430-5738	371-3
Baylake Bank			
217 N Fourth Ave . . . . Sturgeon Bay WI 54235	**800-267-3610**	920-743-5551	69
Baylis Medical Company Inc			
5959 Trans-Canada Hwy . . . . Montreal QC H4T1A1	**800-850-9801**	514-488-9801	472
Baylor Plaza Hotel			
3600 Gaston Ave . . . . Dallas TX 75246	**800-422-9567**		369
Baylor Regional Medical Ctr at Grapevine			
1650 W College St . . . . Grapevine TX 76051	**800-422-9567**	817-481-1588	371-3
Baylor Trucking Inc			
9269 E State Rd 48 . . . . Milan IN 47031	**800-322-9567**	812-623-2020	770
Baylor University			
1311 S Fifth St 1 Bear Pl 98013 . . . . . . Waco TX 76798	**800-229-5678**	254-710-3718	166

Alphabetical Section

	Toll-Free	Phone	Class
Baylor University School of Law 1114 S University Parks Dr 1 Bear Pl 97288 .... Waco TX 76798	800-229-5678	254-710-1911	167-1
Baymont Inn 4025 McDonald Dr .... Dubuque IA 52003	800-337-0550	563-582-3752	376
Bayou Segnette State Park 7777 Westbank Expy .... Westwego LA 70094	888-677-2296	504-736-7140	558
BayPort Credit Union Inc 3711 Huntington Ave .... Newport News VA 23607	800-928-8801	757-928-8850	219
Bayshore Medical Ctr 4000 Spencer Hwy .... Pasadena TX 77504	866-503-7546	713-359-2000	371-3
Bayshore Town Center 5800 N Bayshore Dr Ste A256 .... Glendale WI 53217	800-235-4636	414-963-8780	455
Bayshore Transportation System Inc 901 Dawson Dr .... Newark DE 19713	800-523-3319	302-366-0220	770
Bayside Resort Hotel 225 Massachusetts 28 .... West Yarmouth MA 02673	800-243-1114	508-775-5669	660
Baystate Visiting Nurse Assn & Hospice 50 Maple St .... Springfield MA 01103	800-249-8298	413-794-6411	368
Bayview Limousine Service 15701 Nelson Pl S .... Seattle WA 98188	800-606-7880	206-824-6200	437
Bayview Press 30 Knox St PO Box 153 .... Thomaston ME 04861	800-903-2346	207-354-9919	129
Baywood Homes 1140 Sheppard Ave W Ste 13 .... Toronto ON M3K2A2	888-751-2223	416-633-7333	187
Bazz Houston Co 12700 Western Ave .... Garden Grove CA 92841	800-385-9608	714-898-2666	483
BB & T Corp 200 W Second St .... Winston-Salem NC 27101 NYSE: BBT	800-226-5228	336-733-2500	357-2
B&B Image Group 1712 Marshall St NE .... Minneapolis MN 55413	888-788-9461	612-788-9461	341
BBCN Bank 3731 Wilshire Blvd Ste 1000 .... Los Angeles CA 90010 NASDAQ: NARA	888-811-6272	213-639-1700	357-2
BBH (Baltimore Behavioral Health) 1101 W Pratt St .... Baltimore MD 21223	800-789-2647	410-962-7180	717
BCAA (British Columbia Automobile Assn) 4567 Canada Way .... Burnaby BC V5G4T1	800-222-4357	604-268-5000	52
BCC (Brevard Community College) 1519 Clearlake Rd .... Cocoa FL 32922	888-747-2802	321-632-1111	160
BCC Research LLC 49 Walnut Pk Bldg 2 .... Wellesley MA 02481	866-285-7215	781-489-7301	628-9
BCCR (Brown College of Court Reporting & Medical Transcription) 1900 Emery St NW Ste 200 .... Atlanta GA 30318	800-849-0703	404-876-1227	788
BCCVB (Bucks County Conference & Visitors Bureau) 3207 St Rd .... Bensalem PA 19020	800-836-2825	215-639-0300	207
BCHA (Back Country Horsemen of America) PO Box 1367 .... Graham WA 98338	888-893-5161	360-832-2461	47-23
BCI (Bat Conservation International) 500 N Capital of Texas Hwy .... Austin TX 78746	800-538-2287	512-327-9721	47-3
BCI Burke Company Inc 660 Van Dyne Rd .... Fond du Lac WI 54937	800-356-2070	920-921-9220	343
B&CMA (Biscuit & Cracker Manufacturers Assn) 6325 Woodside Ct Ste 125 .... Columbia MD 21046	877-701-8111	443-545-1645	48-6
BCN (Bliss Clearing Niagara) 1004 E State St .... Hastings MI 49058	800-642-5477	269-948-3300	451
BCSCVB (Bryan/College Station Convention & Visitors Bureau) 715 University Dr E .... College Station TX 77840	800-777-8292	979-260-9898	207
BCVB (Bloomington Convention & Visitors Bureau) 7900 International Dr Ste 990 .... Bloomington MN 55425	800-346-4289	952-858-8500	207
BCWSA (Bucks County Water & Sewer Authority) 1275 Almshouse Rd .... Warrington PA 18976	800-222-2068	215-343-2538	794
BD Biosciences 2350 Qume Dr .... San Jose CA 95131	800-223-8226	408-432-9475	416
BD Biosciences PharMingen 10975 Torreyana Rd .... San Diego CA 92121	800-848-6227	858-812-8800	84
BD Diagnostics Seven Loveton Cir .... Sparks MD 21152	800-666-6433	410-316-4000	231
BD Medical 9450 S State St .... Sandy UT 84070	888-237-2762	801-565-2300	471
BD Week 9737 Washingtonian Blvd Ste 100 .... Gaithersburg MD 20878	866-777-8567	646-223-6771	524-7
BDA (Bensinger DuPont & Assoc) 134 N LaSalle St Ste 2200 .... Chicago IL 60602	800-227-8620	312-726-8620	457
BDA (Bensussen Deutsch & Assoc Inc) 15525 Woodinville-Redmond Rd NE .... Woodinville WA 98072	800-451-4764	425-492-6111	461
BDB Payroll Inc 768 Bedford Ave .... Brooklyn NY 11205	800-729-7687	718-522-2000	724
BDF (Baja Duty Free) 4590 Border Village Rd .... San Ysidro CA 92173	877-438-8937	619-428-6671	241
B-D-R Transport Inc 7994 US Rt 5 .... Westminster VT 05158	800-421-0126	802-463-0606	770
BE Implement Co 1645 FM 403 PO Box 752 .... Brownfield TX 79316	800-725-5435	806-637-3594	274
BEA (Broadcast Education Assn) 1771 N St NW .... Washington DC 20036	888-326-1415	202-429-3935	48-5
Beach Camera 203 Rt 22 E .... Green Brook NJ 08812	800-572-3224	732-968-6400	118
Beach Colony Resort 5308 N Ocean Blvd .... Myrtle Beach SC 29577 *General	800-222-2141*	843-449-4010	660
Beach Haven Inn 4740 Mission Blvd .... San Diego CA 92109	800-831-6323	858-272-3812	376
Beach Manufacturing Co PO Box 129 .... Donnelsville OH 45319	800-543-5942	937-882-6372	59
Beach Realty & Construction 4826 N Croatan Hwy .... Kitty Hawk NC 27949	800-635-1559	252-261-3815	643
Beachcomber Resort Hotel & Villas 1200 S Ocean Blvd .... Pompano Beach FL 33062	800-231-2423	954-941-7830	660
Beacher's Lodge 6970 A1A S .... Saint Augustine FL 32080	800-527-8849	904-471-8849	376
Beacon Assoc Inc 900-A S Main St Ste 102 .... Bel Air MD 21014	877-846-5046	410-638-7279	195
Beacon Container Corp 700 W First St .... Birdsboro PA 19508	800-422-8383	610-582-2222	99
Beacon Credit Union PO Box 627 .... Wabash IN 46992	800-762-3136	260-563-7443	219
Beacon Hotel 720 Ocean Dr .... Miami Beach FL 33139	877-674-8200	305-674-8200	376
Beacon Hotel & Corporate Quarters 1615 Rhode Island Ave NW .... Washington DC 20036	800-823-1700	202-296-2100	376
Beacon House 1301 N Third St .... Marquette MI 49855	800-562-9753	906-225-7100	369
Beacon Industries Inc 12300 Old Tesson Rd .... Saint Louis MO 63128	800-454-7159	314-487-7600	21
Beacon Power Corp 65 Middlesex Rd .... Tyngsboro MA 01879	888-938-9112	978-694-9121	253
Beacon Products LLC 2041 58th Ave Cir E .... Bradenton FL 34203	800-345-4928		359
Beacon Rock State Park 34841 State Rd 14 .... Skamania WA 98648	888-226-7688	509-427-8265	558
Beacon Roofing Supply Inc One Lakeland Pk Dr .... Peabody MA 01960 NASDAQ: BECN	877-645-7663	978-535-7668	192-4
Bead & Button Magazine 21027 Crossroads Cir .... Waukesha WI 53186 *Cust Svc	800-533-6644*	262-796-8776	452-14
Bead Industries Inc 11 Cascade Blvd .... Milford CT 06460	800-297-4851	203-301-0270	482
Beadles Lumber Company Inc 900 Sixth St NE PO Box 3457 .... Moultrie GA 31776	800-763-2400	229-985-6996	674
BeadStyle Magazine 21027 Crossroads Cir .... Waukesha WI 53186 *Cust Svc	800-533-6644*	262-796-8776	452-14
Beal College 99 Farm Rd .... Bangor ME 04401	800-660-7351	207-947-4591	788
Beall Corp 9200 N Ramsey Blvd .... Portland OR 97203	855-219-5686		769
Beam Industries 1700 W Second St .... Webster City IA 50595	800-369-2326	515-832-4620	776
Beam Mack Sales & Service Inc 2674 W Henrietta Rd .... Rochester NY 14623	877-650-8789	585-424-4860	770
Beamers Hells Canyon Tours & Excursions PO Box 1243 .... Lewiston ID 83501	800-522-6966	509-758-4800	750
Beanstalk Data 656 michael wylie dr .... Charlotte NC 28217	800-892-3997		225
Bear Creek Lake State Park 22 Bear Creek Lk Rd .... Cumberland VA 23040	800-933-7275	804-492-4410	558
Bearcom Inc 4009 Distribution Dr Ste 200 .... Garland TX 75041 *Sales	800-527-1670*		246
Bearings Distributors Inc 8000 Hub Pkwy .... Cleveland OH 44125	888-435-7234	216-642-9100	382
Bearing Inspection Inc 4500 Mount Pleasant NW .... North Canton OH 44720 *Cust Svc	800-416-8881*	234-262-3000	74
Bearing Service Co of Pennsylvania 630 Alpha Dr RIDC Park .... Pittsburgh PA 15238	800-783-2327	412-963-7710	74
Bearskin Airlines 1475 W Walsh St .... Thunder Bay ON P7E4X6	800-465-2327	807-577-1141	25
Beartooth Electric Co-op Inc 1306 N Broadway St PO Box 1110 .... Red Lodge MT 59068	800-472-9821	406-446-2310	245
Beartown State Park HC 64 PO Box 189 .... Hillsboro WV 24946 *General	800-225-5982*	304-653-4254	558
Beason & Nalley Inc 101 Monroe St Ne .... Huntsville AL 35801	800-416-1946	256-533-1720	2
Beatty Group International 9800 Beaverton Hillsdale Ste 105 .... Beaverton OR 97005	800-285-6215	503-644-3340	381
Beau Rivage Resort & Casino 875 Beach Blvd .... Biloxi MS 39530	888-750-7111	228-386-7111	660
Beauchamp Distributing Co 1911 S Santa Fe Ave .... Compton CA 90221	800-734-5102	310-639-5320	80-1
Beaufort Memorial Hospital 955 Ribaut Rd .... Beaufort SC 29902	877-532-6472	843-522-5200	371-3
Beaufort National Cemetery 1601 Boundary St .... Beaufort SC 29902	800-273-8255	843-524-3925	135
Beaufurn LLC 5269 US Hwy 158 .... Advance NC 27006	888-766-7706		320
Beaulieu of America Inc 1502 Coronet Dr PO Box 1248 .... Dalton GA 30722	800-227-7211		130
Beaulieu Vineyard 1960 St Helena Hwy .... Rutherford CA 94573	800-373-5896	707-967-5233	79-3
Beaumont Civic Ctr Complex 701 Main St .... Beaumont TX 77701	800-782-3081	409-838-3435	206
Beaumont Convention & Visitors Bureau 505 Willow St .... Beaumont TX 77701	800-392-4401	409-880-3749	207
Beauregard Electric Co-op Inc 1010 E First St .... DeRidder LA 70634	800-367-0275	337-463-6221	245
Beauregard Parish Library 205 S Washington Ave .... DeRidder LA 70634	800-524-6239	337-463-6217	431-3
BeautiControl Inc 2121 Midway Rd PO Box 815189 .... Carrollton TX 75006	800-232-8841	972-458-0601	215
Beauti-Vue Products Inc 8555 194th Ave Bristol Industrial Pk .... Bristol WI 53104	800-558-9431	262-857-2306	86
Beauty Brands Inc 4600 Madison St Ste 400 .... Kansas City MO 64112	877-640-2248	816-531-2266	76
Beaver Creek Lodge 26 Avon Dale Ln .... Beaver Creek CO 81620	800-525-7280	970-845-9800	376
Beaver Creek Nature Area 20641 SD Hwy 1806 25495 485th Ave. .... Fort Pierre SD 57532	800-710-2267	605-223-7660	558
Beaver Express Service LLC 4310 Oklahoma Ave PO Box 1147 .... Woodward OK 73802	800-593-2328	580-256-6460	770
Beaver Run Resort & Conference Ctr 620 Village Rd .... Breckenridge CO 80424	800-525-2253	970-453-6000	660
Beaver Street Fisheries Inc 1741 W Beaver St .... Jacksonville FL 32209	800-874-6426	904-354-8533	295-13
Beaverton Foods Inc 7100 NW Century Blvd .... Hillsboro OR 97124	800-223-8076	503-646-8138	295-19
Beavertooth Oak Inc 401 S Fir St .... Medford OR 97501	800-306-1942	541-779-1942	192-3
bebe stores inc 400 Valley Dr .... Brisbane CA 94005 NASDAQ: BEBE	877-232-3777	415-715-3900	153-20
Becharas Bros Coffee Co Inc 14501 Hamilton Ave .... Highland Park MI 48203	800-944-9675	313-869-4700	296-2
Bechik Products Inc 1020 Discovery Rd Ste 150 .... Eagan MN 55121	800-328-6569	651-698-0364	466

Name	Address	City	State	ZIP	Toll-Free	Phone	Class
Becker Capital Management Inc	1211 S W Fifth Ave Ste 2185	Portland	OR	97204	**800-551-3998**	503-223-1720	398
Becker College	61 Sever St	Worcester	MA	01609	**877-523-2537**	508-791-9241	166
Becker Electric Supply Inc	1341 E Fourth St	Dayton	OH	45402	**800-762-9515**	937-226-1341	246
Becker''s ASC Review	77 Wacker	Chicago	IL	60611	**800-417-2035**	312-750-6016	195
Becket Fund for Religious Liberty	1350 Connecticut Ave NW Ste 605	Washington	DC	20036	**800-743-7734**	202-955-0095	47-8
Beckett Air Inc	37850 Beckett Pkwy	North Ridgeville	OH	44039	**800-831-7839**	440-327-9999	18
Beckett Corp	3250 Skyway Cir N	Irving	TX	75038	**888-232-5388**	972-871-8000	632
Beckley-Raleigh County Chamber of Commerce	245 N Kanawha St	Beckley	WV	25801	**877-987-3847**	304-252-7328	137
Beckman Coulter Genomics	36 Cherry Hill Dr	Danvers	MA	01923	**800-361-7780**	978-867-2600	231
Beckmanxmo	376 Morrison Rd	Columbus	OH	43213	**800-864-2232**	614-864-2232	619
Becton Dickinson & Co	One Becton Dr *NYSE: BDX* *Cust Svc	Franklin Lakes	NJ	07417	**888-237-2762***	201-847-6800	472
Becton Dickinson Consumer Healthcare	One Becton Dr	Franklin Lakes	NJ	07417	**888-237-2762**	201-847-6800	472
Becton Dickinson Pharmaceutical Systems	1 Becton Dr MC407	Franklin Lakes	NJ	07417	**800-638-8663**	201-847-6800	471
Bed & Breakfast Atlanta	790 N Ave Ste 202	Atlanta	GA	30306	**800-967-3224**	404-875-0525	373
Bed & Breakfast Cape Cod	PO Box 2250	Mashpee	MA	02649	**800-556-3815**	508-255-3824	373
Bed & Breakfast of Hawaii	PO Box 449	Kapaa	HI	96746	**800-733-1632**	808-822-7771	373
Bed Bath & Beyond Inc	650 Liberty Ave *NASDAQ: BBBY*	Union	NJ	07083	**800-462-3966**	908-688-0888	359
BedandBreakfast.com	700 Brazos St Ste B-700 *Sales	Austin	TX	78701	**800-462-2632***	512-322-2700	763
Beden-Baugh Products Inc	105 Lisbon Rd	Laurens	SC	29360	**866-598-5794**	864-682-3136	200
Bedford County Chamber of Commerce	137 E Pitt St	Bedford	PA	15522	**800-732-0999**	814-623-2233	137
Bedford County Visitors Bureau	131 S Juliana St	Bedford	PA	15522	**800-765-3331**	814-623-1771	207
Bedford Industries Inc	1659 Rowe Ave *Cust Svc	Worthington	MN	56187	**800-533-5314***	507-376-4136	541
Bedford Laboratories Inc	300 Northfield Rd	Bedford	OH	44146	**800-562-4797**	440-232-3320	474
Bedford Machine & Tool Inc	2103 John Williams Blvd	Bedford	IN	47421	**800-264-1948**	812-275-1948	486
Bedford Materials Co Inc	7676 Allegheny Rd	Manns Choice	PA	15550	**800-773-4276**		803
Bedford Public Schools	1623 W Sterns Rd	Temperance	MI	48182	**866-261-9184**	734-850-6000	676
Bedford Road Pharmacy Inc	11306 Bedford Rd Ne	Cumberland	MD	21502	**800-788-6693**	301-777-1771	238
Bedford Rural Electric Co-op Inc	8846 Lincoln Hwy	Bedford	PA	15522	**800-808-2732**	814-623-5101	245
Bedford Technology LLC	2424 Armour Rd PO Box 609	Worthington	MN	56187	**800-721-9037**	507-372-5558	652
Beech-Nut Nutrition Corp	One Nutritious Pl	Amsterdam	NY	12010	**800-233-2468**		295-36
Beechwood Hotel	363 Plantation St	Worcester	MA	01605	**800-344-2589**	508-754-5789	376
Beef Magazine	7900 International Dr Ste 300 *Cust Svc	Minneapolis	MN	55425	**800-722-5334***	952-851-9329	452-1
Beef O'Bradys Inc	5660 W Cypress St Ste A	Tampa	FL	33607	**800-728-8878**	813-226-2333	661
Beehive Botanicals Inc	16297 W Nursery Rd	Hayward	WI	54843	**800-233-4483**	715-634-4274	787
Beelman Truck Co	One Racehorse Dr *Sales	East Saint Louis	IL	62205	**800-541-5918***	618-646-5300	770
Beemac Trucking	2747 Litionville Rd	Ambridge	PA	15003	**800-282-8781**	724-266-8781	676
Beemer Precision Inc	230 New York Dr PO Box 3080	Fort Washington	PA	19034	**800-836-2340**	215-646-8440	613
BeenVerified Inc	307 Fifth Ave 16th Fl	New York	NY	10016	**888-579-5910**		316
Beepi	5050 El Camino Real Ste 116	Los Altos	CA	94022	**888-542-3374**		384
Beer Institute	122 C St NW Ste 350	Washington	DC	20001	**800-379-2739**	202-737-2337	48-6
BEGINNINGS for Parents of Children Who Are Deaf or Hard of Hearing Inc	302 Jefferson St Ste 110	Raleigh	NC	27605	**800-541-4327**	919-715-4092	47-17
Behavioral Science Technology Inc	417 Bryant Cir	Ojai	CA	93023	**800-548-5781**	805-646-0166	195
Behlen Manufacturing Co	4025 E 23rd St	Columbus	NE	68601	**800-553-5520**	402-564-3111	104
Behr Process Corp	3400 W Segerstrom Ave	Santa Ana	CA	92704	**800-854-0133**	714-545-7101	543
BEI Technologies Inc Industrial Encoder Div	7230 Hollister Ave *Sales	Goleta	CA	93117	**800-350-2727***	805-968-0782	253
Beitler-Mckee Optical Co	160 S 22nd St	Pittsburgh	PA	15203	**800-989-4700**	412-481-4700	535
Bekins Van Lines LLC	8010 Castleton Rd	Indianapolis	IN	46250	**800-456-8092**		512
Bel Fuse Inc	206 Van Vorst St *NASDAQ: BELFA*	Jersey City	NJ	07302	**800-235-3873**	201-432-0463	720
Belair Produce Company Inc	7226 Pkwy Dr	Hanover	MD	21076	**888-782-8008**	410-782-8000	296-7
Belaire Products Inc	763 S Broadway St	Akron	OH	44311	**800-886-3224**	330-253-3116	9
Bel-Art Products Inc	Six Industrial Rd	Pequannock	NJ	07440	**800-423-5278**	973-694-0500	417
Belarus Tractor International Inc	7842 N Faulkner Rd	Milwaukee	WI	53224	**800-356-2336**		274
Belcam Inc Delagar Div	27 Montgomery St	Rouses Point	NY	12979	**800-328-3006**	518-297-3366	215
Belcan Corp	10200 Anderson Way	Cincinnati	OH	45242	**800-423-5226**	513-891-0972	261
Belco Mfg Company Inc	2303 Taylors Vly Rd	Belton	TX	76513	**800-251-8265**	254-933-9000	200
Belco Packaging Systems Inc	910 S Mountain Ave	Monrovia	CA	91016	**800-833-1833**	626-357-9566	540
Belden Inc Americas Div	2200 US Hwy 27 S PO Box 1980	Richmond	IN	47375	**800-235-3362**	765-983-5200	801
Belding Tank Technologies Inc	200 N Gooding St PO Box 160	Belding	MI	48809	**800-253-4252**	616-794-1130	603
Beldon Enterprises Inc	PO Box 13380	San Antonio	TX	78213	**800-688-7663**	210-341-3100	190-12
Belfast Area Chamber of Commerce	14 Main St	Belfast	ME	04915	**877-338-9015**	207-338-5900	137
Belhaven College	1500 Peachtree St PO Box 153	Jackson	MS	39202	**800-960-5940**	601-968-5940	166
Believe In Tomorrow National Children's Foundation	6601 Frederick Rd	Baltimore	MD	21228	**800-933-5470**	410-744-1032	47-6
Bell Aliant Regional Communications	7 S Maritime Centre 1505 Barrington St *TSE: BA*	Halifax	NS	B3J3K5	**800-555-1212**	800-267-1110	726
Bell Canada	1050 Beaver Hall Hill Bureau 3700	Montreal	QC	H2Z1S4	**800-667-0123**		726
Bell County	101 E Central Ave PO Box 480	Belton	TX	76513	**800-460-2355**	254-933-5160	336
Bell Electrical Contractors Inc	128 Millwell Dr	Maryland Heights	MO	63043	**800-717-2355**	314-739-7744	190-4
Bell Equipment Inc	511 Fourth St	Nezperce	ID	83543	**800-343-2355**	208-937-2402	274
Bell Harbor International Conference Ctr	2211 Alaskan Way Pier 66	Seattle	WA	98121	**888-772-4422**	206-441-6666	206
Bell Helicopter Textron Inc	600 E Hurst Blvd (State Hwy 10)	Hurst	TX	76053	**888-874-5884**	817-280-2011	20
Bell Industries Inc Recreational Products Group	580 Yankee Doodle Rd	Eagan	MN	55121	**800-866-5017**	651-450-9020	60
Bell Lumber & Pole Co	778 First St NW PO Box 120786	New Brighton	MN	55112	**877-633-4334**	651-633-4334	805
Bell Sports Corp	6225 N St Hwy 161 Ste 300	Irving	TX	75038	**866-525-2357**	469-417-6600	569
Bell Supply Inc	7221 Rt 130	Pennsauken	NJ	08110	**888-834-2371**	856-663-3900	681
Bell Techlogix	5777 Decatur Blvd	Indianapolis	IN	46241	**866-782-2355**	317-333-7777	181
Bell Tower Hotel	300 S Thayer St	Ann Arbor	MI	48104	**800-562-3559**	734-769-3010	376
Bell Tower Inn	1235 Second St SW	Rochester	MN	55902	**800-448-7583**	507-289-2233	376
Bellacino's Corp	10096 Shaver Rd	Portage	MI	49024	**877-379-0700**	269-329-0782	661
Bellagio Conservatory & Botanical Gardens	3600 S Las Vegas Blvd	Las Vegas	NV	89109	**888-987-6667**	702-693-7111	96
Bellagio Hotel & Casino	3600 Las Vegas Blvd S	Las Vegas	NV	89109	**888-987-7111**	702-693-7111	660
Bellarmine University	2001 Newburg Rd	Louisville	KY	40205	**800-274-4723**	502-272-8000	166
Bellasera Hotel	221 Ninth St S	Naples	FL	34102	**855-990-0301**	239-649-7333	376
Bellco First Federal Credit Union	7600 E OrchaRd Rd Ste 400N	Greenwood Village	CO	80111	**800-235-5261**	303-689-7800	219
Bellco Glass Inc	340 Edrudo Rd	Vineland	NJ	08360	**800-257-7043**	856-691-1075	331
Belle Bonfils Memorial Blood Ctr	717 Yosemite St	Denver	CO	80230	**800-365-0006**	303-341-4000	88
Belle Meade Plantation	5025 Harding Pk	Nashville	TN	37205	**800-270-3991**	615-356-0501	513
Belle of Baton Rouge Casino	103 France St	Baton Rouge	LA	70802	**800-676-4847**		132
Belle Tire Inc	1000 Enterprise Dr	Allen Park	MI	48101	**888-462-3553**	313-271-9400	61-5
Bellefonte Area School District	318 N Allegheny St	Bellefonte	PA	16823	**866-632-9992**	814-355-4814	676
Belleville & District Chamber of Commerce	Five Moira St E	Belleville	ON	K8N5B3	**888-852-9992**	613-962-4597	136
Belleville General Hospital	265 Dundas St E	Belleville	ON	K8N5A9	**800-483-2811**	613-969-7400	371-2
Belleville News-Democrat	120 S Illinois St	Belleville	IL	62220	**800-293-0795**	618-234-1000	525-2
Belleville Wire Cloth Inc	18 Rutgers Ave	Cedar Grove	NJ	07009	**800-631-0490**	973-239-0074	679
Bellevue Arts Museum	510 Bellevue Way NE	Bellevue	WA	98004	**800-367-2648**	425-519-0770	513
Bellevue Club Hotel	11200 SE Sixth St	Bellevue	WA	98004	**800-579-1110**	425-454-4424	376
Bellevue Leader	604 Fort Crook Rd N	Bellevue	NE	68005	**800-284-6397**	402-733-7300	525-4
Bellevue University	1000 Galvin Rd S	Bellevue	NE	68005	**800-756-7920**	402-293-2000	166
Bellin College of Nursing	3201 Eaton Rd	Green Bay	WI	54311	**800-236-8707**	920-433-6699	166
Bellingham Marine Industries Inc	1001 C St	Bellingham	WA	98225	**800-733-5679**	360-676-2800	189-5
Bellingrath Gardens & Home	12401 Bellingrath Garden Rd	Theodore	AL	36582	**800-247-8420**	251-973-2217	96
Bellisio Foods Inc	1201 Harman Pl Ste 302	Minneapolis	MN	55403	**800-368-7337**	612-371-8222	295-36
Bellmoor, The	Six Christian St	Rehoboth Beach	DE	19971	**800-425-2355**	302-227-5800	376
Bellomy Research Inc	175 Sunnynoll Ct	Winston Salem	NC	27106	**800-443-7344**		196
Bellus Health Inc	275 Armand Frappier Blvd *TSE: BLU*	Laval	QC	H7V4A7	**877-680-4500**	450-680-4500	84
Belmont Abbey College	100 Belmont-Mt Holly Rd	Belmont	NC	28012	**888-222-0110**	704-461-6748	166
Belmont University	1900 Belmont Blvd	Nashville	TN	37212	**800-563-6765**	615-460-6000	166

Name / Address	City	State	ZIP	Toll-Free	Phone	Class
Beloit College						
700 College St	Beloit	WI	53511	**800-331-4943***	608-363-2500	166
*Admissions						
Beloit Convention & Visitors Bureau						
500 Public Ave	Beloit	WI	53511	**800-423-5648**	608-365-4838	207
Beloit Daily News						
149 State St	Beloit	WI	53511	**800-356-3411**	608-365-8811	525-2
Beloit Health System						
1969 W Hart Rd	Beloit	WI	53511	**800-637-2641**	608-363-5724	371-3
Beloit Regional Hospice						
655 Third St Ste 200	Beloit	WI	53511	**877-363-7421**	608-363-7421	368
Bel-Rea Institute of Animal Technology						
1681 S Dayton St	Denver	CO	80247	**800-950-8001**	303-751-8700	788
Belshaw Bros Inc						
1750 22nd Ave S	Seattle	WA	98144	**800-578-2547**	206-322-5474	297
Belson Outdoors Inc						
111 N River Rd	North Aurora	IL	60542	**800-323-5664**	630-897-8489	318-4
Belstra Milling Company Inc						
424 15th St PO Box 460	Demotte	IN	46310	**800-276-2789**		442
Belt Railway Co of Chicago						
6900 S Central Ave	Bedford Park	IL	60638	**877-772-5772**	708-496-4000	642
Belterra Casino Resort						
777 Belterra Dr	Florence	IN	47020	**888-235-8377**	812-427-7777	660
Belting Industries Company Inc						
20 Boright Ave	Kenilworth	NJ	07033	**800-843-2358**	908-272-8591	367
Belton Industries Inc						
1205 Hanby Rd PO Box 127	Belton	SC	29627	**800-845-8753**	864-338-5711	734-3
Beltone Electronics Corp						
2601 Patriot Blvd	Glenview	IL	60026	**800-235-8663**	847-832-3300	472
Beltrami Electric Co-op Inc						
4111 Technology Dr NW	Bemidji	MN	56601	**800-955-6083**	218-444-2540	245
Beltservice Corp						
4143 Rider Trl N	Earth City	MO	63045	**800-727-2358**	314-344-8500	208
Belvac Production Machinery Inc						
237 Graves Mill Rd	Lynchburg	VA	24502	**800-423-5822**	434-239-0358	489
Belvedere Hotel						
319 W 48th St	New York	NY	10036	**800-492-8122**	212-245-7000	376
Belvedere USA Corp						
1 Belvedere Blvd	Belvidere	IL	61008	**800-435-5491**	815-544-3131	75
Belwith International Ltd						
3100 Broadway Ave	Grandville	MI	49418	**800-235-9484**		347
Bema Incorporated						
744 N Oaklawn Ave	Elmhurst	IL	60126	**800-833-6657**	630-279-7800	65
Bement School						
94 Main St	Deerfield	MA	01342	**877-405-3949**	413-774-7061	615
Bemidji Area Chamber of Commerce						
300 Bemidji Ave	Bemidji	MN	56601	**800-458-2223**	218-444-3541	137
Bemidji State University						
1500 Birchmont Dr NE	Bemidji	MN	56601	**800-475-2001***	218-755-2001	166
*Admissions						
Bemis Co Inc Bemis Clysar Div						
2451 Badger Ave	Oshkosh	WI	54903	**888-425-9727**	920-303-7800	541
Bemis Company Inc Paper Packaging Div						
2445 Deer Pk Blvd	Omaha	NE	68105	**800-541-4303**		64
Bemis Manufacturing Co						
300 Mill St	Sheboygan Falls	WI	53085	**800-558-7651**	920-467-4621	318-4
Ben Arnold Beverage Company LP						
101 Beverage Blvd	Ridgeway	SC	29130	**888-262-9787***	803-337-3500	80-3
*Acctg						
Ben Bridge Jeweler Inc						
PO Box 1908	Seattle	WA	98111	**888-917-9171***	206-239-6811	407
*Cust Svc						
Ben Lippen School						
7401 Monticello Rd	Columbia	SC	29203	**800-777-2227**	803-786-7200	615
Ben Lomond Suites LLC						
2510 Washington Blvd	Ogden	UT	84401	**877-627-1900**	801-627-1900	376
Ben Moss Jewellers						
300-201 Portage Ave	Winnipeg	MB	R3B3K6	**888-236-6677**		407
Ben Tire Distributors Ltd						
203 E Madison St PO Box 158	Toledo	IL	62468	**800-252-8961**		745
Ben Venue Laboratories Inc						
300 Northfield Rd	Bedford	OH	44146	**800-989-3320***	440-232-3320	474
*General						
Bench & Bar of Minnesota Magazine						
600 Nicollet Mall Ste 380	Minneapolis	MN	55402	**800-366-4812**	612-333-1183	452-15
Benchmark Group						
4053 Maple Rd	Amherst	NY	14226	**800-876-0160**	716-833-4986	645
BenchmarkQA Inc						
7301 Ohms Ln Ste 590	Edina	MN	55439	**877-425-2581**	952-392-2400	179-12
Benco Electric Co-op						
20946 549 Ave PO Box 8	Mankato	MN	56002	**888-792-3626**	507-387-7963	245
Bend Chamber of Commerce						
777 NW Wall St Ste 200	Bend	OR	97701	**800-905-2363**	541-382-3221	137
Bender Group						
345 Parr Cir	Reno	NV	89512	**800-621-9402**	775-788-8800	444
Bendix Commercial Vehicle Systems LLC						
901 Cleveland St	Elyria	OH	44035	**800-247-2725**	440-329-9000	60
Benedict College						
1600 Harden St	Columbia	SC	29204	**800-868-6598**	803-253-5000	166
Benedictine College						
1020 N Second St	Atchison	KS	66002	**800-467-5340**	913-367-5340	166
Benedictine Health System						
503 E Third St Ste 400	Duluth	MN	55805	**800-833-7208**	218-786-2370	350
Benedictine University						
5700 College Rd	Lisle	IL	60532	**888-829-6363**	630-829-6300	166
Benefact Consulting Group						
6285 Northam Dr Ste 112	Mississauga	ON	L4V1X5	**855-829-2225**		458
Beneficial Financial Group						
55 N 300 W	Salt Lake City	UT	84145	**800-233-7979**	801-933-1100	388-2
Beneficial Mutual Savings Bank						
530 Walnut St	Philadelphia	PA	19106	**800-784-8490**	215-864-6000	69
Benefis Healthcare						
East Campus						
1101 26th St S	Great Falls	MT	59405	**800-648-6632**	406-455-5000	371-3
Benefit & Risk Management Services Inc						
10860 Gold Ctr Dr						
Ste 300	Rancho Cordova	CA	95670	**888-326-2555**	916-858-2950	387
BeneFit Cosmetics						
225 Bush St	San Francisco	CA	94104	**800-781-2336***	415-781-8153	215
*Cust Svc						
BenefitHelp Solutions Inc						
10505 SE 17th Ave	Milwaukie	OR	97222	**888-398-8057**	503-219-3679	528
BenefitMall						
3450 Lakeside Dr Ste 400	Miramar	FL	33027	**877-729-6299**	954-874-4800	2
BenefitMall Inc						
4851 LBJ Fwy Ste 1100	Dallas	TX	75244	**888-338-6293**	469-791-3300	179-10
Benefitvision Inc						
4522 RFD	Long Grove	IL	60047	**800-810-2200**		197
Benemax Inc						
Seven W Mill St	Medfield	MA	02052	**800-528-1530**		195
Benesyst Inc						
800 Washington Ave N 8th Fl	Minneapolis	MN	55401	**866-786-3366**	800-422-4661	256
Benjamin Franklin Institute of Technology						
41 Berkeley St	Boston	MA	02116	**877-400-2348**	617-423-4630	788
Benjamin Franklin Plumbing						
50 Central Ave Ste 920	Sarasota	FL	34236	**800-471-0809**	941-366-9692	309
Benjamin Moore & Co						
101 Paragon Dr	Montvale	NJ	07645	**800-344-0400**	201-573-9600	543
Benjamin N Cardozo School of Law Yeshiva University						
55 Fifth Ave Brookdale Ctr	New York	NY	10003	**800-232-5463**	212-790-0200	167-1
Benjamin, The						
125 E 50th St	New York	NY	10022	**866-233-4642**	212-715-2500	376
Benner-Nawman Inc						
3450 Sabin Brown Rd	Wickenburg	AZ	85390	**800-992-3833**	928-684-2813	286
Bennett Auto Supply Inc						
3141 SW Tenth St	Pompano Beach	FL	33069	**800-766-5913**	954-335-8700	53
Bennett College						
900 E Washington St	Greensboro	NC	27401	**800-413-5323***	336-370-8624	166
*Admissions						
Bennett Pump Co						
1218 Pontaluna Rd	Spring Lake	MI	49456	**800-235-7618**	231-798-1310	630
Bennington Area Chamber of Commerce						
100 Veterans Memorial Dr	Bennington	VT	05201	**800-229-0252**	802-447-3311	137
Bennington Battlefield State Historic Site						
c/o Grafton Lakes State Pk						
PO Box 163	Grafton	NY	12082	**800-456-2267**	518-686-7109	558
Bennington College						
One College Dr	Bennington	VT	05201	**800-833-6845**	802-442-5401	166
Bennington County						
100 Veterans Memorial Dr	Bennington	VT	05201	**800-229-0252**	802-447-3311	336
Benny Hinn Ministries						
PO Box 162000	Irving	TX	75016	**800-433-1900**	817-722-2000	47-20
Benny Whitehead Inc						
3265 S Eufaula Ave	Eufaula	AL	36027	**800-633-7617**	334-687-8055	357-2
BenQ America Corp						
15375 Barranca Ste A205	Irvine	CA	92618	**866-600-2367**	949-255-9500	174-7
Bensinger DuPont & Assoc (BDA)						
134 N LaSalle St Ste 2200	Chicago	IL	60602	**800-227-8620**	312-726-8620	457
Benson Industries LLC						
1650 NW Naito Pkwy Ste 250	Portland	OR	97209	**800-999-5113**	503-226-7611	190-6
Benson's Gourmet Seasonings						
PO Box 638	Azusa	CA	91702	**800-325-5619**	626-969-4443	295-37
Benson, The						
309 SW Broadway	Portland	OR	97205	**800-663-1144**	503-228-2000	376
Bensussen Deutsch & Assoc Inc (BDA)						
15525 Woodinville-Redmond						
Rd NE	Woodinville	WA	98072	**800-451-4764**	425-492-6111	461
Bentley College						
175 Forest St	Waltham	MA	02452	**800-642-7131***	781-891-2244	166
*Admissions						
Bentley Historical Library						
1150 Beal Ave	Ann Arbor	MI	48109	**866-233-6661**	734-764-3482	431-4
Bentley Prince Street						
14641 E Don Julian Rd	City of Industry	CA	91746	**800-423-4709**		130
Bentley Systems Inc						
685 Stockton Dr	Exton	PA	19341	**800-236-8539**	610-458-5000	179-5
Benton Express Inc						
1045 S River Industrial						
Blvd SE	Atlanta	GA	30315	**888-423-6866**	404-267-2200	770
Benton Rural Electric Assn (BREA)						
402 Seventh St PO Box 1150	Prosser	WA	99350	**800-221-6987**	509-786-2913	245
Bentsen-Rio Grande Valley State Park						
2800 S Bensen Palm Dr	Mission	TX	78572	**800-792-1112**	956-585-1107	558
Bentz Whaley Flessner						
7251 Ohms Ln	Minneapolis	MN	55439	**800-921-0111**	952-921-0111	316
Benz Communications LLC						
209 Mississippi St	San Francisco	CA	94107	**888-550-5251**		194
Benzel's Pretzel Bakery Inc						
5200 Sixth Ave	Altoona	PA	16602	**800-344-4438**	814-942-5062	295-9
Berchtold Equipment Co Inc						
330 E 19th St	Bakersfield	CA	93305	**800-691-7817**	661-323-7817	274
Berea College						
101 Chestnut St	Berea	KY	40403	**800-326-5948**	859-985-3500	166
Berea College Weatherford Planetarium						
101 Chestnut St	Berea	KY	40404	**800-326-5948**	859-985-3000	591
Berendsen Fluid Power						
401 S Boston Ave Ste 1200	Tulsa	OK	74103	**800-360-2327**	918-592-3781	382
Beretta USA Corp						
17601 Beretta Dr	Accokeek	MD	20607	**800-237-3882**	301-283-2191	284
Berg Equipment Co						
2700 W Veterans Pkwy	Marshfield	WI	54449	**800-494-1738**	715-384-2151	273
Bergad Inc						
747 Eljer Way	Ford City	PA	16226	**888-476-8664**	724-763-2883	466
Bergamot Inc						
820 E Wisconsin St	Delavan	WI	53115	**800-922-6733***	262-728-5572	9
*Cust Svc						
Bergdorf Goodman Inc						
754 Fifth Ave	New York	NY	10019	**800-558-1855***	212-753-7300	155-4
*Cust Svc						
Bergelectric Corp						
5650 W Centinela Ave	Los Angeles	CA	90045	**800-734-2374**	310-337-1377	190-4
Bergen Community College						
400 Paramus Rd	Paramus	NJ	07652	**877-612-5381**	201-447-7200	160
Berger Bldg Products Inc						
805 Pennsylvania Blvd	Feasterville	PA	19053	**800-523-8852***	215-355-1200	688
*Cust Svc						
Berger Transfer & Storage Inc						
2950 Long Lk Rd	Saint Paul	MN	55113	**877-268-2101**		512
Bergey's Inc						
462 Harleysville Pike	Souderton	PA	18964	**800-237-4397**	215-723-6071	61-5
Bergmann Assoc Inc						
28 E Main St						
200 1st Federal Plaza	Rochester	NY	14614	**800-724-1168**	585-232-5135	261
Bergquist Co						
18930 W 78th St	Chanhassen	MN	55317	**800-347-4572**	952-835-2322	253
Bergstrom of Kaukauna						
2929 Lawe St	Kaukauna	WI	54130	**866-939-0130**		56

Name / Address	City	State	Zip	Toll-Free	Phone	Class
Bering Air						
1470 Sepalla Dr PO Box 1650	Nome	AK	99762	**800-478-5422**	907-443-5464	25
Berkeley Chamber of Commerce						
1834 University Ave	Berkeley	CA	94703	**800-847-4823**	510-549-7000	137
Garrett Mountain						
44 Rifle Camp Rd	Woodland Park	NJ	07424	**800-446-5400**	973-278-5400	788
Berkeley College						
Paramus						
64 E Midland Ave	Paramus	NJ	07652	**800-446-5400**	201-967-9667	788
Woodbridge						
430 Rahway Ave	Woodbridge	NJ	07095	**800-446-5400**	732-750-1800	788
Berkeley College New York City						
Three E 43rd St	New York	NY	10017	**800-446-5400**	212-986-4343	788
Berkeley College White Plains						
99 Church St	White Plains	NY	10601	**800-446-5400**	914-694-1122	788
Berkeley Communications Corp						
1321 67th St	Emeryville	CA	94608	**877-237-5266**	510-644-1599	195
Berkeley County Chamber of Commerce						
PO Box 968	Moncks Corner	SC	29461	**800-882-0337**	843-761-8238	137
Berkeley Hotel, The						
1200 E Cary St	Richmond	VA	23219	**888-780-4422**	804-780-1300	376
Berkeley Sensor & Actuator Ctr (BSAC)						
University of California						
497 Cory Hall MC Ste 1774	Berkeley	CA	94720	**800-549-1002**	510-643-6690	659
Berklee College of Music						
1140 Boylston St	Boston	MA	02215	**800-421-0084**	617-747-2221	166
Berklee Performance Ctr						
136 Massachusetts Ave	Boston	MA	02115	**877-237-5533**	617-747-2261	565
Berkley Risk Administrators Company LLC						
222 S Ninth St Ste 1300	Minneapolis	MN	55402	**800-449-7707**	612-766-3000	387
Berkowitz Dick Pollack & Brant LLP						
200 S Biscayne Blvd Sixth Fl	Miami	FL	33131	**800-999-1272**	305-379-7000	2
Berks Packing Company Inc						
307-323 Bingaman St PO Box 5919	Reading	PA	19610	**800-882-3757**	610-376-7291	295-26
Berks VNA						
1170 Berkshire Blvd	Wyomissing	PA	19610	**855-843-8627**		368
Berkshire Bank						
PO Box 1308	Pittsfield	MA	01202	**800-773-5601**	413-443-5601	69
Berkshire Eagle						
75 S Church St PO Box 1171	Pittsfield	MA	01202	**800-234-7404**	413-447-7311	525-2
Berkshire Gas Company Inc						
115 Cheshire Rd	Pittsfield	MA	01201	**800-292-5012**	413-442-1511	775
Berkshire Hathaway Group (BHG)						
3024 Harney St	Omaha	NE	68131	**800-223-2064**	402-536-3100	388-4
Berkshire Hathaway Homestates Cos (BHHC)						
PO Box 2048	Omaha	NE	68103	**888-495-8949**		388-4
Berkshire Hathaway Inc						
3555 Farnam St Ste 1440	Omaha	NE	68131	**800-223-2064**	402-346-1400	186
NYSE: BRK/A						
Berkshire Hills Bancorp Inc						
24 N St	Pittsfield	MA	01201	**800-773-5601**	413-443-5601	357-2
NYSE: BHLB						
Berkshire School						
245 N Undermountain Rd	Sheffield	MA	01257	**866-738-5500**	413-229-8511	615
Berlex Laboratories Inc						
Six W Belt	Wayne	NJ	07470	**888-842-2937**	973-694-4100	231
Berlin Metals LLC						
3200 Sheffield Ave	Hammond	IN	46327	**800-754-8867**	219-933-0111	487
Bermuda Dept of Tourism						
675 Third Ave 20th Fl	New York	NY	10017	**800-223-6106**	212-818-9800	765
Bermuda Village						
142 Bermuda Village Dr	Advance	NC	27006	**800-843-5433***		663
*Mktg						
Bernard Food Industries Inc						
1125 Hartrey Ave	Evanston	IL	60204	**800-323-3663**	847-869-5222	295-18
Bernard Hodes Group						
220 E 42 St	New York	NY	10017	**888-438-9911**	212-999-9000	4
Bernard L Madoff Investment Securities Co						
885 Third Ave 18th Fl	New York	NY	10022	**800-334-1343**	212-230-2424	681
Bernards Inn						
27 Mine Brook Rd	Bernardsville	NJ	07924	**888-766-0002**	908-766-0002	376
Bernardus Lodge						
415 Carmel Valley Rd	Carmel Valley	CA	93924	**800-223-2533**	831-658-3400	376
Bernatello's						
PO Box 729	Maple Lake	MN	55358	**800-622-6935**	952-831-6622	295-21
Berne Apparel Co						
2210 Summit St	New Haven	IN	46774	**800-843-7657**	260-469-3136	153-18
Berner Foods Inc						
2034 E Factory Rd	Dakota	IL	61018	**800-819-8199**	815-563-4222	295-5
Berney-Karp Inc						
3350 E 26th St	Los Angeles	CA	90058	**800-237-6395**	323-260-7122	332
Berns Co						
1250 W 17th St	Long Beach	CA	90813	**800-421-3773**	562-437-0471	465
Berry Aviation Inc						
1807 Airport Dr	San Marcos	TX	78666	**800-229-2379**	512-353-2379	13
Berry College						
2277 Martha Berry Hwy						
PO Box 490159	Mount Berry	GA	30149	**800-237-7942**	706-232-5374	166
Berry Dunn Mcneil & Parker						
100 Middle St 4th Fl	Portland	ME	04101	**800-908-4490**	207-775-2387	2
Berry Plastics Corp						
101 Oakley St	Evansville	IN	47710	**877-662-3779**	812-424-2904	200
Berryman & Henigar						
11590 W Bernardo Ct Ste 100	San Diego	CA	92127	**800-272-9829**	858-451-6100	261
Berryman Products Inc						
3800 E Randol Mill Rd	Arlington	TX	76011	**800-433-1704**	817-640-2376	144
Berthel Fisher & Co						
701 Tama St Bldg B PO Box 609	Marion	IA	52302	**800-356-5234**	319-447-5700	681
Bertram Yacht Inc						
3663 NW 21st St	Miami	FL	33142	**800-256-4646**	305-633-8011	89
Berwick Offray LLC						
2015 W Front St	Berwick	PA	18603	**800-327-0350***	570-752-5934	734-6
*General						
Berwyn Development Corp						
3322 S Oak Pk Ave 2nd Fl	Berwyn	IL	60402	**877-247-7792**	708-788-8100	137
Besco Electric Supply Co						
711 S 14th St	Leesburg	FL	34748	**800-541-6618**		359
Besl Transfer Co						
5700 Este Ave	Cincinnati	OH	45232	**800-456-2375**	513-242-3456	770
Besly Cutting Tools Inc						
16200 Woodmint Ln	South Beloit	IL	61080	**800-435-2965**	815-389-2231	488
Bessemer Area Chamber of Commerce						
321 N 18th St	Bessemer	AL	35020	**888-423-7736**	205-425-3253	137
Bessemer Trust Co						
630 Fifth Ave 6th Fl	New York	NY	10111	**800-255-7688**	212-708-9100	398
Besser Co						
801 Johnson St	Alpena	MI	49707	**800-530-9980**	989-354-4111	383
Best Access Systems						
6161 E 75th St	Indianapolis	IN	46250	**855-365-2407**	317-849-2250	347
Best Bath Systems						
723 Garber St	Caldwell	ID	83605	**866-333-8657**	208-342-6823	372
Best Buy Company Inc						
7601 Penn Ave S	Minneapolis	MN	55423	**888-237-8289**	612-291-1000	34
NYSE: BBY						
Best Chevrolet Inc						
128 Derby St	Hingham	MA	02043	**866-208-7873**		56
Best Label Co						
2900 Faber St	Union City	CA	94587	**800-637-5333**	510-489-5400	410
Best Maid Products Inc						
PO Box 1809	Fort Worth	TX	76101	**800-447-3581**	817-335-5494	295-19
Best Material Handling Inc						
4754 N Chestnut St	Colorado Springs	CO	80907	**800-933-5270**	719-599-9191	320
Best Plumbing Specialties						
3039 Ventrie Ct	Myersville	MD	21773	**800-448-6710**		605
Best Provision Company Inc						
144 Avon Ave	Newark	NJ	07108	**800-631-4466**	973-242-5000	295-26
Best Registration Services Inc						
1418 S Third St	Louisville	KY	40208	**800-977-3475**	502-637-4528	393
Best Sand Corp						
11830 Ravenna Rd PO Box 87	Chardon	OH	44024	**800-237-4986**	440-285-3132	498-4
Best Sweet Inc						
288 Mazeppa Rd	Mooresville	NC	28115	**888-211-5530**	704-664-4300	295-8
Best Telecom Inc						
262 E End Ave	Beaver	PA	15009	**888-365-2273**		384
Best Travel Inc						
8600 W Bryn Mawr Ave	Chicago	IL	60631	**800-840-4822**	773-380-0150	761
Best Vascular						
4350 International Blvd Ste E	Norcross	GA	30093	**800-668-6783**	770-717-0904	471
Best Western Carson Station Hotel & Casino						
900 S Carson St	Carson City	NV	89701	**800-501-2929**	775-883-0900	132
Best Western Chincoteague Island						
7105 Maddox Blvd	Chincoteague Island	VA	23336	**800-553-6117**	757-336-6557	376
Best Western Grandma's Feather Bed						
9300 Glacier Hwy	Juneau	AK	99801	**888-781-5005**	907-789-5005	662
Best Western Inn of the Ozarks						
207 W Van Buren	Eureka Springs	AR	72632	**800-552-3785**	479-253-9768	660
Best Western International Inc						
6201 N 24th Pkwy	Phoenix	AZ	85016	**800-528-1234**	602-957-4200	376
Best Western Laguna Brisas Spa Hotel						
1600 S Coast Hwy	Laguna Beach	CA	92651	**888-296-6834**	949-497-7272	376
Best Western Victorian Inn						
487 Foam St	Monterey	CA	93940	**800-232-4141**	831-373-8000	376
Bestar Inc						
4220 Villeneuve St	Lac-Megantic	QC	G6B2C3	**888-823-7827**	819-583-1017	318-1
Bestforms Inc						
1135 Avenida Acaso	Camarillo	CA	93012	**800-350-0618**	805-383-6993	109
Bestolife Corp						
2777 Stemmons Fwy Ste 1800	Dallas	TX	75207	**855-243-9164**	214-583-0271	3
Best-Rite Mfg						
2885 Lorraine Ave PO Box D	Temple	TX	76501	**800-749-2258**		286
Bestway Inc						
12400 Coit Rd Ste 950	Dallas	TX	75251	**800-316-4567**	214-630-6655	264-2
Bestway Tours & Safaris						
8678 Greenall Ave	Burnaby	BC	V5J3M6	**800-663-0844**	604-264-7378	750
Beta Gamma Sigma Inc (BGS)						
125 Weldon Pkwy	Maryland Heights	MO	63043	**800-337-4677**	314-432-5650	47-16
Beta LaserMike Inc						
8001 Technology Blvd	Dayton	OH	45424	**800-886-9935**	937-233-9935	467
Beta Screen Corp						
707 Commercial Ave	Carlstadt	NJ	07072	**800-272-7336**	201-939-2400	584
Beta Theta Pi						
5134 Bonham Rd PO Box 6277	Oxford	OH	45056	**800-800-2382**	513-523-7591	47-16
Bete Fog Nozzle Inc						
50 Greenfield St	Greenfield	MA	01301	**800-235-0049**	413-772-0846	347
Beth Israel Deaconess Medical Ctr (BIDMC)						
330 Brookline Ave	Boston	MA	02215	**800-667-5356**	617-667-7000	371-3
Beth Israel Deaconess Medical Ctr Hematologic Malignancies/Bone Marrow Transplantation Program						
330 Brookline Ave	Boston	MA	02215	**800-439-0183**	617-667-9920	759
Bethany Bible College						
26 Western St	Sussex	NB	E4E1E6	**888-432-4444**	506-432-4400	773
Bethany College						
One Main St	Bethany	WV	26032	**800-922-7611**	304-829-7000	166
Bethany House Publishers						
11400 Hampshire Ave S	Bloomington	MN	55438	**800-328-6109**	616-676-9185	628-3
Bethany Lutheran College						
700 Luther Dr	Mankato	MN	56001	**800-944-3066**	507-344-7000	166
Bethany Theological Seminary						
615 National Rd W	Richmond	IN	47374	**800-287-8822**	765-983-1800	167-3
Bethel College						
1001 W McKinley Ave	Mishawaka	IN	46545	**800-422-4101***	574-807-7000	166
*Admissions						
Beth-El College of Nursing & Health Sciences						
1420 Austin						
Bluffs Pkwy	Colorado Springs	CO	80918	**800-990-8227**	719-255-8227	166
Bethel Inn & Country Club						
21 Broad St PO Box 49	Bethel	ME	04217	**800-654-0125**	207-824-2175	660
Bethel Seminary						
3949 Bethel Dr	Saint Paul	MN	55112	**800-255-8706**	651-638-6400	167-3
Bethel University						
3900 Bethel Dr	Saint Paul	MN	55112	**800-255-8706**	651-638-6400	166
Bethesda Hospital						
2951 Maple Ave	Zanesville	OH	43701	**800-322-4762**	740-454-4000	371-3
Bethlehem Area Public Library						
11 W Church St	Bethlehem	PA	18018	**800-732-0999**	610-867-3761	431-3
Bethpage Federal Credit Union						
899 S Oyster Bay Rd	Bethpage	NY	11714	**800-628-7070**		219
Bethpage State Park						
Bethpage Pkwy	Farmingdale	NY	11735	**800-456-2267**	516-249-0701	558
Bethune-Cookman College						
640 Dr Mary McLeod						
Bethune Blvd	Daytona Beach	FL	32114	**800-448-0228***	386-481-2900	166
*Admissions						
Betson Enterprises Inc						
303 Patterson Plank Rd	Carlstadt	NJ	07072	**800-524-2343**	201-438-1300	54
Betsy Hotel						
1440 Ocean Dr	Miami Beach	FL	33139	**866-792-3879**	305-531-6100	376

	Toll-Free	Phone	Class
Bettcher Industries Inc			
PO Box 336 . . . . Vermilion OH 44089	**800-321-8763**	440-965-4422	297
Bettendorf-stanford			
1370 W Main St . . . . Salem IL 62881	**800-548-2253**	618-548-3555	358
Better Business Bureau Heartland			
11811 P St . . . . Omaha NE 68137	**800-649-6814**	402-391-7612	78
Better Business Bureau Inc			
1000 Broadway Ste 625 . . . . Oakland CA 94607	**866-411-2221**	510-844-2000	78
Better Business Bureau of Ark-La-Tex			
401 Edwards St Ste 135 . . . . Shreveport LA 71101	**800-372-4222**	318-222-7575	78
Better Business Bureau of Canton Region/West Virginia			
1434 Cleveland Ave NW . . . . Canton OH 44703	**800-362-0494**	330-454-9401	78
Better Business Bureau of Central & Eastern Kentucky			
1460 Newtown Pk . . . . Lexington KY 40511	**800-866-6668**	859-259-1008	78
Better Business Bureau of Central East Texas			
3600 Old BullaRd Rd Bldg 1 . . . . Tyler TX 75701	**800-443-0131**	903-581-5704	78
Better Business Bureau of Central East Texas Longview Branch			
102 Commander Ste 7 . . . . Longview TX 75605	**800-443-0131**	903-758-3222	78
Better Business Bureau of Central Illinois			
112 Harrison St . . . . Peoria IL 61602	**800-763-4222**	309-688-3741	78
Better Business Bureau of Central Indiana			
151 N Delaware St . . . . Indianapolis IN 46204	**866-463-9222**	317-488-2222	78
Better Business Bureau of Central Louisiana & Ark-La-Tex			
5220-C Rue Verdun . . . . Alexandria LA 71303	**800-372-4222***	318-473-4494	78
*General			
Better Business Bureau of Central Northeast Northwest & Southwest Arizona			
4428 N 12th St . . . . Phoenix AZ 85014	**877-291-6222**	602-264-1721	78
Better Business Bureau of Central Ohio			
1169 Dublin Rd . . . . Columbus OH 43215	**800-759-2400**	614-486-6336	78
Better Business Bureau of Eastern Massachusetts Maine Rhode Island & Vermont			
290 Donald Lynch Blvd			
Ste 102 . . . . Marlborough MA 01752	**800-422-2811**	508-652-4800	78
Better Business Bureau of Greater Kansas City			
8080 Ward Pkwy Ste 401 . . . . Kansas City MO 64114	**877-606-0695**	816-421-7800	78
Better Business Bureau of Hawaii			
1132 Bishop St Ste 615 . . . . Honolulu HI 96813	**877-222-6551**	808-536-6956	78
Better Business Bureau of Kansas Inc			
345 N Riverview St Ste 720 . . . . Wichita KS 67203	**800-856-2417**	316-263-3146	78
Better Business Bureau of Louisville Southern Indiana & Western Kentucky			
844 S Fourth St . . . . Louisville KY 40203	**800-388-2222**	502-583-6546	78
Better Business Bureau of Maine			
290 Donald Lynch Blvd			
Ste 102 . . . . Marlborough MA 01752	**800-422-2811**	508-652-4800	78
Better Business Bureau of New Jersey			
1700 Whitehorse-Hamilton Sq Rd			
Ste D-5 . . . . Trenton NJ 08690	**888-494-4009**	609-588-0808	78
Better Business Bureau of Northeast Florida & The Southeast Atlantic			
4417 Beach Blvd Ste 202 . . . . Jacksonville FL 32207	**800-713-6661**	904-721-2288	78
Better Business Bureau of Northeast Louisiana			
1900 N 18th St Ste 411 . . . . Monroe LA 71201	**800-960-7756**	318-387-4600	78
Better Business Bureau of Northeast Ohio			
2800 Euclid Ave Fourth Fl . . . . Cleveland OH 44115	**800-233-0361**	216-241-7678	78
Better Business Bureau of Northern Colorado & East Central Wyoming			
8020 S County Rd 5 Ste 100 . . . . . . Fort Collins CO 80528	**800-564-0371**	970-484-1348	78
Better Business Bureau of Northwest North Carolina			
500 W Fifth St Ste 202 . . . . Winston-Salem NC 27101	**800-777-8348**	336-725-8348	78
Better Business Bureau of Northwest Ohio & Southeast Michigan			
7668 King's Pt Rd . . . . Toledo OH 43617	**800-743-4222**	419-531-3116	78
Better Business Bureau of Rockford			
330 North Wabash Ave Ste 3120 . . . . . Chicago IL 60611	**800-955-5100**	312-832-0500	78
Better Business Bureau of Southeast Florida & the Caribbean			
4411 Beacon Cir Ste 4 . . . . West Palm Beach FL 33407	**866-966-7226**	561-842-1918	78
Better Business Bureau of Southeast Tennessee & Northwest Georgia			
508 N Market St . . . . Chattanooga TN 37405	**800-548-4456**	423-266-6144	78
Better Business Bureau of Southeast Texas			
550 Fannin St Ste 100 . . . . Beaumont TX 77701	**800-685-7650**	409-835-5348	78
Better Business Bureau of Southwest Georgia			
PO Box 2587 . . . . Columbus GA 31902	**800-768-4222**	706-324-0712	78
Better Business Bureau of Southwest Idaho & Eastern Oregon			
1200 N Curtis Rd PO Box 9817 . . . . Boise ID 83706	**800-218-1001**	208-342-4649	78
Better Business Bureau of Southwest Louisiana Inc			
2309 E Prien Lk Rd . . . . Lake Charles LA 70601	**800-542-7085**	337-478-6253	78
Better Business Bureau of the Akron Inc			
222 W Market St . . . . Akron OH 44303	**800-825-8887**	330-253-4590	78
Better Business Bureau of the Bakersfield Area			
1601 H St Ste 101 . . . . Bakersfield CA 93301	**800-675-8118**	661-322-2074	78
Better Business Bureau of the Denver-Boulder Metro Area			
1020 Cherokee St . . . . Denver CO 80204	**800-356-6333**	303-758-2100	78
Better Business Bureau of the Mid-South			
3693 Tyndale Dr . . . . Memphis TN 38125	**800-222-8754**	901-759-1300	78
Better Business Bureau of Utah			
5673 S Redwood Rd Ste 22 . . . . . . Salt Lake City UT 84123	**800-456-3907**	801-892-6009	78
Better Business Bureau of Vancouver Island			
220-1175 Cook St Ste 220 . . . . Victoria BC V8V4A1	**877-826-4222**	250-386-6348	77
Better Business Bureau of West Florida			
2655 McCormick Dr . . . . Clearwater FL 33759	**800-525-1447**	727-535-5522	78
Better Business Bureau of West Georgia & East Alabama			
PO Box 2587 . . . . Columbus GA 31902	**800-768-4222**	706-324-0712	78
Better Business Bureau of Western Massachusetts			
35 Ctr St Ste 203 . . . . Chicopee MA 01013	**866-566-9222**		78
Better Business Bureau Online			
Council of Better Business Bureaus, The			
4200 Wilson Blvd Ste 800 . . . . Arlington VA 22203	**800-459-8875**	703-276-0100	78
Better Business Bureau Serving Central California			
4201 W Shaw Ave Ste 107 . . . . Fresno CA 93722	**800-675-8118**	559-222-8111	78
Better Business Bureau Serving Mainland British Columbia			
788 Beatty St Ste 404 . . . . Vancouver BC V6B2M1	**888-803-1222**	604-682-2711	77
Better Business Bureau Serving Western Ontario			
200 Queens Ave Ste 308			
PO Box 2153 . . . . London ON N6A3M8	**877-283-9222**	519-673-3222	77
Better Business Bureau Serving Winnipeg & Manitoba			
1030B Empress St . . . . Winnipeg MB R3G3H4	**800-385-3074**	204-989-9010	77
Better Homes & Gardens Test Garden			
1716 Locust St . . . . Des Moines IA 50309	**800-374-4244**	515-284-3994	96
Better Homes & Gardens WOOD Magazine			
1716 Locust St . . . . Des Moines IA 50309	**800-374-9663**		452-14
Better Investing			
PO Box 220 . . . . Royal Oak MI 48068	**877-275-6242**	248-583-6242	48-2
Better Investing Magazine			
PO Box 220 . . . . Royal Oak MI 48068	**877-275-6242**	248-583-6242	452-11
Better Made Snack Foods Inc			
10148 Gratiot Ave . . . . Detroit MI 48213	**800-332-2394**	313-925-4774	295-35
Better Management Corp (BMC)			
41738 Esterly Dr . . . . Columbiana OH 44408	**877-293-4300**	330-482-7070	651

	Toll-Free	Phone	Class
Better Packages Inc			
255 Canal St PO Box 711 . . . . Shelton CT 06484	**800-237-9151**	203-926-3722	110
Better Vision Institute, The (BVI)			
Vision Council, The			
225 Reinekers Ln Ste 700 . . . . Alexandria VA 22314	**800-372-3937**	703-548-4560	47-17
Bettinger Farms Inc			
11602 Frankfort Rd . . . . Swanton OH 43558	**855-629-7661**	419-829-2771	366
Betty Dain Creations Inc			
9701 NW 112 Ave Ste 10 . . . . Miami FL 33178	**800-327-5256***	305-769-3451	75
*General			
Betty Ford Ctr			
39000 Bob Hope Dr . . . . Rancho Mirage CA 92270	**800-854-9211**	760-773-4100	717
Beulah Heights Bible College			
892 Berne St SE PO Box 18145 . . . . Atlanta GA 30316	**888-777-2422**	404-627-2681	159
Beutler Air Conditioning Service			
855 National Dr Ste 109 . . . . Sacramento CA 95834	**866-559-0108**		190-10
Bevco Precision Manufacturing Co			
21320 Doral Rd . . . . Waukesha WI 53186	**800-864-2991**	262-798-9200	318-1
Beverage Distributors Co			
14200 E Moncrieff Pl . . . . Aurora CO 80011	**800-772-2096***	303-371-3421	80-3
*General			
Beverage Marketing Corp			
850 Third Ave 18th Fl . . . . New York NY 10022	**800-275-4630**	212-688-7640	196
Beverage-Air Corp			
3779 Champion Blvd . . . . Winston-Salem NC 27105	**800-845-9800**	336-245-6400	655
Beverly Hills Chamber of Commerce			
239 S Beverly Dr . . . . Beverly Hills CA 90212	**800-345-2210**	310-248-1000	137
Beverly Hills Conference & Visitors Bureau			
239 S Beverly Dr . . . . Beverly Hills CA 90212	**800-345-2210**	310-248-1000	207
Beverly Hills Hotel			
9641 Sunset Blvd . . . . Beverly Hills CA 90210	**800-283-8885**	310-276-2251	376
Beverly Hills Transfer & Storage Co			
15500 S Main St . . . . Gardena CA 90248	**800-999-7114**		512
Beverly Hills Unified School District			
255 S Lasky Dr . . . . Beverly Hills CA 90212	**800-334-5847**	310-551-5100	676
Beverly Hilton			
9876 Wilshire Blvd . . . . Beverly Hills CA 90210	**800-605-8896**	310-274-7777	376
Beverly Wilshire - A Four Seasons Hotel			
9500 Wilshire Blvd . . . . Beverly Hills CA 90212	**800-545-4000**	310-275-5200	376
Bevill State Community College			
Jasper			
1411 Indiana Ave . . . . Jasper AL 35501	**800-648-3271**	205-387-0511	160
Bexley City School District			
348 S Cassingham Rd . . . . Columbus OH 43209	**800-282-1780**	614-231-7611	676
Beyond			
1060 First Ave Ste 100 . . . . King of Prussia PA 19406	**800-227-7469**	610-878-2800	260
Beyond Components			
5 Carl Thompson Rd . . . . Westford MA 01886	**800-971-4242**		246
Beyond Digital Imaging			
36 Apple Creek Blvd . . . . Markham ON L3R4Y4	**888-689-1888**	905-415-1888	692
Beyond Pesticides			
701 E St SE Ste 200 . . . . Washington DC 20003	**866-260-6653**	202-543-5450	47-13
Beyond the Arc Inc			
2600 Tenth St Ste 616 . . . . Berkeley CA 94710	**877-676-3743**		458
BFC Forms Service Inc			
1051 N Kirk Rd . . . . Batavia IL 60510	**800-774-6840**	630-879-9240	619
BFGoodrich Tires Inc			
One Pkwy S . . . . Greenville SC 29602	**877-788-8899**		745
BFMA (Business Forms Management Assn)			
3800 Old Cheney Rd Ste 101-285 . . . . Lincoln NE 68516	**888-367-3078**	402-216-0479	48-12
B-G Mechanical Service Inc			
12 Second Ave . . . . Chicopee MA 01020	**800-992-7386**	413-888-1500	190-10
BG Products Inc			
740 S Wichita St . . . . Wichita KS 67213	**800-961-6228**	316-265-2686	534
BGA (Lincoln Botanical Garden & Arboretum)			
University of Nebraska			
1309 N 17th St . . . . Lincoln NE 68588	**800-742-8800**	402-472-2679	96
BGD Cos Inc			
5323 Lakeland Ave N . . . . Minneapolis MN 55429	**800-699-3537**	612-338-6804	318-1
BGF Industries Inc			
3802 Robert Porcher Way . . . . Greensboro NC 27410	**800-476-4845**		734-3
BGK Finishing Systems			
4131 Pheasant Ridge Dr NE . . . . . Minneapolis MN 55449	**800-663-5498**	763-784-0466	465
BGR Inc			
6392 Gano Rd . . . . West Chester OH 45069	**800-628-9195**	513-755-7100	552
BGS (Beta Gamma Sigma Inc)			
125 Weldon Pkwy . . . . Maryland Heights MO 63043	**800-337-4677**	314-432-5650	47-16
BGSU (Bowling Green State University Jerome Library)			
1001 E Wooster St . . . . Bowling Green OH 43403	**866-246-6732**	419-372-2051	431-6
B-H Transfer Co			
750 Sparta Rd PO Box 151 . . . . Sandersville GA 31082	**888-786-3664**	478-552-5119	444
BHG (Berkshire Hathaway Group)			
3024 Harney St . . . . Omaha NE 68131	**800-223-2064**	402-536-3100	388-4
BHHC (Berkshire Hathaway Homestates Cos)			
PO Box 2048 . . . . Omaha NE 68103	**888-495-8949**		388-4
BHI (Baker Hughes Inc)			
2929 Allen Pkwy Ste 1200 . . . . Houston TX 77019	**800-229-7447**	713-439-8600	532
NYSE: BHI			
BHK Securities LLC			
2200 Lakeshore Dr Ste 250 . . . . . . Birmingham AL 35209	**888-529-2610**	205-322-2025	681
BHN Corp			
435 Madison Ave . . . . Memphis TN 38103	**800-238-9046**	901-521-9500	190-9
BI Inc			
6400 Lookout Rd . . . . Boulder CO 80301	**800-241-2911**	303-218-1000	683
BIA (Bureau of Indian Affairs Regional Offices)			
3601 C St Ste 1100 . . . . Anchorage AK 99503	**800-645-8397**	907-271-1536	338-11
BIA (Brick Industry Assn)			
1850 Centennial Pk Dr Ste 301 . . . . Reston VA 20191	**866-644-1293**	703-620-0010	48-18
BIA Financial Network Inc			
15120 Enterprise Ct . . . . Chantilly VA 20151	**800-331-5086**	703-818-2425	195
Biamp Systems Inc			
9300 SW Gemini Dr . . . . Beaverton OR 97008	**800-826-1457**		51
Bianchi Motors Inc			
8430 Peach St PO Box 3086 . . . . Erie PA 16509	**866-979-8132**		509
Bibbero Systems Inc			
1300 N McDowell Blvd . . . . Petaluma CA 94954	**800-242-2376**	707-778-3131	619
Bibby Financial Services			
1901 South Congress ave			
Ste 150 . . . . Boynton Beach, FL 33426	**877-882-4229**		272
Bible Broadcasting Network Inc			
11530 Carmel Commons Blvd			
PO Box 7300 . . . . Charlotte NC 28226	**800-888-7077**	704-523-5555	634
Bible League			
PO Box 28000 . . . . Chicago IL 60628	**866-825-4636**	817-595-1664	47-20

	Toll-Free	Phone	Class
Biblical Archaeology Review 4710 41st St NW .... Washington DC 20016	800-221-4644	202-364-3300	452-18
Biblical Theological Seminary 200 N Main St .... Hatfield PA 19440	800-235-4021	215-368-5000	167-3
Bickel's Snack Foods 1120 Zinns Quarry Rd ....York PA 17404	800-233-1933	717-843-0738	295-35
Bickford's Family Restaurants Inc 37 Oak St Ext .... Brockton MA 02301	800-969-5653		661
Bicon LLC 501 Arborway ....Boston MA 02130	800-882-4266	617-524-4443	228
Bicycling Magazine 400 S Tenth St ....Emmaus PA 18098	800-666-2806		452-14
Biddeford Blankets 300 Terr Dr ....Mundelein IL 60060	800-789-6441		735
Biddle Precision Components Inc 701 S Main St .... Sheridan IN 46069	800-428-4387	317-758-4451	614
BIDMC (Beth Israel Deaconess Medical Ctr) 330 Brookline Ave .... Boston MA 02215	800-667-5356	617-667-7000	371-3
Bid-Well Corp PO Box 97 ....Canton SD 57013	800-843-9824		191
Bienville House Hotel 320 Decatur St .... New Orleans LA 70130	800-535-7836	504-529-2345	376
Bierlein Cos Inc 2000 Bay City Rd ....Midland MI 48642	800-336-6626	989-496-0066	190-16
Bierschbach Equipment & Supply Co PO Box 1444 ....Sioux Falls SD 57101	800-843-3707	605-332-4466	192-1
Biery Cheese Co 6544 Paris Ave ....Louisville OH 44641	800-243-3731	330-875-3381	295-5
Biesanz Stone Co Inc 4600 Goodview Rd .... Winona MN 55987	800-247-8322	507-454-4336	715
Big 5 Sporting Goods Corp 2525 E El Segundo Blvd .... El Segundo CA 90245 *NASDAQ: BGFV*	800-898-2994	310-536-0611	702
Big Apple Bagels 500 Lk Cook Rd Ste 475.......... Deerfield IL 60015	800-251-6101	847-948-7520	67
Big Apple Circus One Metrotech Ctr Third Fl.......... Brooklyn NY 11201	800-922-3772	212-268-2500	147
Big Bend Electric Co-op 1373 N Hwy 261 PO Box 348.......... Ritzville WA 99169	866-844-2363	509-659-1700	245
Big Bend Telephone Company Inc 808 N Fifth St ....Alpine TX 79830	800-520-0092	432-364-1000	115
Big C Lumber Inc 50860 Princess Way PO Box 176........ Granger IN 46530	888-297-0010	574-277-4550	192-3
Big Country Electric Co-op 1010 W S First St PO Box 518 ....Roby TX 79543	888-662-2232	325-776-2244	245
Big Dogs 519 Lincoln County Pkwy ....Lincolnton NC 28092	800-244-3647		153-3
Big Fitness 190 Frenchtown Rd .... North Kingstown RI 02852	800-383-2008	401-885-5200	351
Big Five Tours & Expeditions 1551 SE Palm Ct ....Stuart FL 34994	800-244-3483	772-287-7995	750
Big Flat Electric Co-op Inc 333 S Seventh St ....Malta MT 59538	800-242-2040	406-654-2040	245
Big Foot Beach State Park 1452 Wells St .... Lake Geneva WI 53147	888-936-7463	262-248-2528	558
Big G Cereals PO Box 9452 PO Box 9452.......... Minneapolis MN 55440	800-248-7310		295-4
Big G Express Inc PO Box 1650 ....Shelbyville TN 37162	800-955-9140	800-684-9140	770
Big Horn Rural Electric Co-op 208 S Fifth St PO Box 270 ....Basin WY 82410	800-564-2419	307-568-2419	245
Big Kaiser Precision Tooling Inc 641 Fargo Ave ....Elk Grove Village IL 60007	888-866-5776	847-228-7660	488
Big Lots Inc (BLI) 300 Phillipi Rd .... Columbus OH 43228 *NYSE: BIG*	877-998-1697	614-278-6800	779
Big River Industries Inc 900 Ashwood Pkwy Ste 500 ....Atlanta GA 30338	800-342-5483	770-640-3008	495
Big River Zinc Corp 2401 Mississippi Ave ....Sauget IL 62201	800-274-4002	618-274-5000	480
Big Rock Sports LLC 173 Hankison Dr ....Newport NC 28570	800-334-2661	252-808-3500	701
Big Sandy Community & Technical College One Bert T Combs Dr ....Prestonsburg KY 41653	888-641-4132	606-886-3863	160
Big Sandy Rural Electric Co-op Corp 504 11th St ....Paintsville KY 41240	888-789-7322	606-789-4095	245
Big Sky Resort One Lone Mtn Trl PO Box 160001 .... Big Sky MT 59716	800-548-4486	406-995-5000	660
Big Sky Technologies 9325 Sky Pk Ct Ste 120 ....San Diego CA 92123	800-736-2751	858-715-5000	179-7
Big Spring Convention & Visitor Bureau 215 W Third St PO Box 3359 ....Big Spring TX 79720	866-222-7100	432-264-6032	207
Big Spring Independent School District 708 E 11th Pl ....Big Spring TX 79720	866-632-9992	432-264-3600	676
Big Stone Lake State Park 35889 Meadowbrook State Pk Rd ....Ortonville MN 56278	888-646-6367	320-839-3663	558
Big Texan Steak Ranch 7701 I-40 E ....Amarillo TX 79118 *Cust Svc	800-657-7177*	806-372-6000	662
Big Y Foods Inc 2145 Roosevelt Ave ....Springfield MA 01102 *Cust Svc	800-828-2688*	413-784-0600	342
Bigbend Hospice 1723 Mahan Ctr Blvd ....Tallahassee FL 32308	800-772-5862	850-878-5310	368
Bigelow Tea 201 Black Rock Tpke ....Fairfield CT 06825	888-244-3569		295-40
Bigge Crane & Rigging Company Inc 10700 Bigge St PO Box 1657........ San Leandro CA 94577	888-337-2444	510-638-8100	190-1
Biggers Chevrolet 1385 E Chicago St ....Elgin IL 60120	866-431-1555	847-742-9000	56
BII (Burgess Industries Inc) 7500 Boone Ave N Ste 111.... Brooklyn Park MN 55428	800-233-2589	763-553-7800	621
Bil-Jax Inc 125 Taylor Pkwy ....Archbold OH 43502	800-537-0540	419-445-8915	486
Bilkays Express Co 2400 Bedle Place ....Linden NJ 07036	800-526-4006	908-289-2400	770
Bill & Melinda Gates Foundation PO Box 23350 ....Seattle WA 98102	800-728-3843	206-709-3100	304
Bill Barrett Corp 1099 18th St Ste 2300 ....Denver CO 80202 *NYSE: BBG*	800-826-6762	303-293-9100	531
Bill Collins 4220 BaRdstown Rd ....Louisville KY 40218	888-327-9095	502-459-9550	56
Bill Miller Bar-B-Q Inc 430 S Santa Rosa St PO Box 839925.................. San Antonio TX 78207	800-339-3111	210-225-4461	661
Bill Snethkamp Lansing Dodge Inc 6131 S Pennsylvania Ave ....Lansing MI 48911	800-863-6343	517-394-1200	56
Billings Area Chamber of Commerce 815 S 27th St .... Billings MT 59101	855-328-9116	406-245-4111	137
Billings C'mon Inn Hotel 2020 Overland Ave .... Billings MT 59102	800-655-1170	406-655-1100	376
Billings Clinic 2800 Tenth Ave N .... Billings MT 59101	800-332-7156	406-657-4000	371-3
Billings Convention & Visitors Bureau 815 S 27th St PO Box 31177 .... Billings MT 59107	800-735-2635	406-245-4111	207
Billings Gazette 401 N 28th St .... Billings MT 59101	800-543-2505	406-657-1200	525-2
Billings Hotel & Convention Ctr 1223 Mullowney Ln .... Billings MT 59101	800-537-7286	406-248-7151	376
Billows Electric Supply Co 9100 State Rd ....Philadelphia PA 19136	877-519-7302	215-332-9700	246
Billy Graham Evangelistic Assn One Billy Graham Pkwy PO Box 1270.................. Charlotte NC 28201	877-247-2426	704-401-2432	47-20
BI-LO LLC PO Box 99 ....Mauldin SC 29662	800-862-9293		342
BILS (Braille Institute of America Library Services) 741 N Vermont Ave ....Los Angeles CA 90029	800-808-2555	323-660-3880	431-3
Biltmore Greensboro Hotel 111 W Washington St .... Greensboro NC 27401 *General	800-332-0303*	336-272-3474	376
Biltmore Hotel & Conference Ctr of the Americas 1200 Anastasia Ave .... Coral Gables FL 33134 *Cust Svc	800-727-1926*	305-445-1926	660
Biltmore Hotel & Suites 2151 Laurelwood Rd .... Santa Clara CA 95054	800-255-9925	408-988-8411	376
Biltmore Hotel Oklahoma 401 S Meridian Ave ....Oklahoma City OK 73108	800-522-6620	405-947-7681	376
Biltmore Suites 205 W Madison St ....Baltimore MD 21201	800-868-5064	410-728-6550	376
Bilt-Rite Conveyors 735 Industrial Loop Rd .... New London WI 54961	800-558-3616	920-982-6600	208
Biltrite Corp 51 Sawyer Rd ....Waltham MA 02454	800-877-8775	781-647-1700	667
Bimbo Bakeries USA PO Box 976 ....Horsham PA 19044	800-984-0989		295-1
Bimeda-MTC Animal Health Inc 420 Beaverdale Rd ....Cambridge ON N3C2W4	888-524-6332	519-654-8000	575
Bindagraphics Inc 2701 Wilmarco Ave ....Baltimore MD 21223	800-326-0300	410-362-7200	91
Binghamton Knitting Co Inc 11 Alice St ....Binghamton NY 13904	877-746-3368	607-722-6941	153-15
Binghamton University 4400 Vestal Pkwy E ....Binghamton NY 13902	800-782-0289	607-777-2000	166
Binkley & Hurst LP 133 Rothsville Stn Rd ....Lititz PA 17543	800-414-4705	717-626-4705	426
Binkley & Ober Inc 2742 Lancaster Rd ....Manheim PA 17545	800-682-5625	717-569-0441	184
Binswanger Glass 965 Ridge Lk Blvd Ste 305 ....Memphis TN 38120	800-365-9922		328
Bio Medic Data Systems Inc One Silas Rd ....Seaford DE 19973	800-526-2637	302-628-4100	82
Bio Medical Innovations 814 Airport Way ....Sandpoint ID 83864	800-201-3958		250
Bio/Data Corp PO Box 347 ....Horsham PA 19044	800-257-3282	215-441-4000	416
Bioanalytical Systems Inc 2701 Kent Ave .... West Lafayette IN 47906 *NASDAQ: BASI*	800-845-4246	765-463-4527	416
Bio-Botanica Inc 75 Commerce Dr ....Hauppauge NY 11788	800-645-5720	631-231-5522	474
BioCardia Inc 125 Shoreway Rd Ste B ....San Carlos CA 94070	800-624-1179	650-226-0120	471
Biocell Laboratories Inc 2001 University Dr .... Rancho Dominguez CA 90220	800-222-8382	310-537-3300	231
Biodex Medical Systems Inc 20 Ramsay Rd ....Shirley NY 11967	800-224-6339	631-924-9000	471
Bioethics Legal Review 1617 JFK Blvd Ste 1750 ....Philadelphia PA 19103	877-256-2472	215-557-2300	524-7
Biofit Engineered Products 15500 Biofit Way ....Bowling Green OH 43402	800-597-0246	419-823-1089	318-1
Biogen Idec Inc 133 Boston Post Rd ....Weston MA 02493 *NASDAQ: BIIB*	877-750-8536	781-464-2000	84
BioGenex Laboratories Inc 4600 Norris Canyon Rd ....San Ramon CA 94583	800-421-4149	925-275-0550	231
Biohelix Corp 500 Cummings Ste 5550 ....Beverly MA 01915	866-800-5458	978-927-5056	231
BioHorizons Inc 2300 Riverchase Ctr ....Birmingham AL 35244	888-246-8338	205-967-7880	472
Bioject Medical Technologies Inc 20245 SW 95 Ave ....Tualatin OR 97062 *OTC: BJCT*	800-683-7221	503-692-8001	471
Biola University 13800 Biola Ave ....La Mirada CA 90639 *Admissions	800-652-4652*	562-903-6000	166
Bio-Lab Inc 1725 N Brown Rd PO Box 30000..................Lawrenceville GA 30043	800-859-7946	678-502-4000	141
BioLase Technology Inc Four Cromwell ....Irvine CA 92618	800-699-9462	888-424-6527	421
BioLegend Inc 11080 Roselle St ....San Diego CA 92121	877-246-5343	858-455-9588	659
bioLytical Laboratories Inc 1108 - 13351 Commerce Pkwy ..... Richmond BC V6V2X7	866-674-6784	604-204-6784	659
Biomarine Inc 456 Creamery Way ....Exton PA 19341	800-378-2287	610-524-8800	569
Biomerica Inc 1533 Monrovia Ave ....Newport Beach CA 92663 *OTC: BMRA* ▩ *Cust Svc	800-854-3002*	949-645-2111	231
BioMerieux Inc 595 Anglum Rd ....Hazelwood MO 63042	800-634-7656	314-731-8500	471
Biomerix Corp 47757 Fremont Blvd ....Fremont CA 94538	888-308-3620	510-933-3450	659
Biomet Inc 56 E Bell Dr PO Box 587.................. Warsaw IN 46582	800-348-9500	574-267-6639	472

				Toll-Free	Phone	Class
Biomet Microfixation Inc						
1520 Tradeport Dr	Jacksonville	FL	32218	**800-874-7711**	904-741-4400	471
BioMotiv LLC						
3605 Warrensville Ctr Rd	Cleveland	OH	44122	**800-477-6307**	216-455-3200	238
Bionetics Corp, The						
101 Production Dr Ste 100	Yorktown	VA	23693	**800-868-0330**	757-873-0900	261
Bioniche Life Sciences Inc.						
231 Dundas St E	Belleville	ON	K8N1E2	**800-265-5464**	613-966-8058	575
TSE: BNC						
Bionostics Inc						
Seven Jackson Rd	Devens	MA	01434	**800-776-3856***	978-772-7070	231
*General						
BIOPAC Systems Inc						
42 Aero Camino	Goleta	CA	93117	**877-524-6722**	805-685-0066	732
Bioquant Image Analysis Corp						
5611 Ohio Ave	Nashville	TN	37209	**800-221-0549**	615-350-7866	507
Bio-Rad Laboratories						
1000 Alfred Nobel Dr	Hercules	CA	94547	**800-424-6723**	510-724-7000	231
NYSE: BIO						
Bio-Recovery Corp						
1863 Pond Rd Ste 4	Ronkonkoma	NY	11779	**800-556-0621**	631-676-2600	83
Bio-Reference Laboratories Inc						
481 Edward H Ross Dr	Elmwood Park	NJ	07407	**800-229-5227**	201-421-2001	413
NASDAQ: BRLI						
BioReliance Corp						
14920 Broschart Rd	Rockville	MD	20850	**800-553-5372**	301-738-1000	84
Bio-Research Products Inc						
323 W Cherry St	North Liberty	IA	52317	**800-326-3511**	319-626-6707	732
Bio-Scene Recovery						
13191 Meadow St NE	Alliance	OH	44601	**877-380-5500**	330-823-5500	83
BioScience						
1444 'I' St NW Ste 200	Washington	DC	20005	**800-992-2427**	202-628-1500	452-19
BioScrip						
10050 Crosstown Cir						
Ste 300	Eden Prairie	MN	55344	**800-444-5951**		579
NASDAQ: BIOS						
Biosense Webster Inc						
3333 S Diamond Canyon Rd	Diamond Bar	CA	91765	**800-729-9010**	909-839-8500	471
Bio-Serv						
3 Foster Lane Suite 201	Flemington	NJ	08822	**800-996-9908**	908-284-2155	575
BioSource International Inc						
542 Flynn Rd	Camarillo	CA	93012	**800-242-0607**	805-987-0086	231
BioSpace Inc						
90 New Montgomery St						
Ste 414	San Francisco	CA	94105	**888-246-7722**	877-277-7585	394
BiosPacific Inc						
5980 Horton St Ste 225	Emeryville	CA	94608	**800-344-6686**	510-652-6155	231
BioTechniques						
52 Vanderbilt Ave 7th Fl	New York	NY	10017	**800-606-6246**	212-520-2777	452-19
Biotechnology Industry Organization						
1201 Maryland Ave SW Ste 900	Washington	DC	20024	**866-356-5155**	202-962-9200	48-19
Biotechnology Software						
140 Huguenot St Third Fl	New Rochelle	NY	10801	**800-654-3237**	914-740-2100	524-3
BioTek Instruments Inc						
100 Tigan St PO Box 998	Winooski	VT	05404	**888-451-5171**	802-655-4740	416
Bio-Tissue						
7000 SW 97th Ave Ste 211	Miami	FL	33173	**888-296-8858**	305-412-4430	538
Biovet Inc						
4375 Ave Beaudry	Saint-Hyacinthe	QC	J2S8W2	**888-824-6838**	450-771-7291	575
Biovet USA Inc						
9025 Penn Ave S Ste 100	Minneapolis	MN	55431	**877-824-6838**	952-884-3113	575
BioZyme Inc						
6010 Stockyards Expy	Saint Joseph	MO	64504	**800-821-3070**	816-238-3326	442
Birch Communications Inc						
2300 Main St 6th Fl	Kansas City	MO	64108	**866-424-5100**	816-300-3000	726
Birchcraft Studios Inc						
10 Railroad St	Abington	MA	02351	**800-333-0405**	781-878-5152	129
Birchwood Laboratories Inc						
7900 Fuller Rd	Eden Prairie	MN	55344	**800-328-6156**	952-937-7900	143
Bird Electronic Corp						
30303 Aurora Rd	Solon	OH	44139	**866-695-4569**	440-248-1200	248
Bird Precision						
One Spruce St PO Box 540569	Waltham	MA	02454	**800-454-7369***	781-894-0160	613
*Cust Svc						
Bird Studies Canada						
115 Front St PO Box 160	Port Rowan	ON	N0E1M0	**888-448-2473**	519-586-3531	47-3
Bird Talk Magazine						
Three Burroughs	Irvine	CA	92618	**800-695-6088***	949-855-8822	452-14
*Resv						
Bird Technologies Group Inc						
30303 Aurora Rd	Solon	OH	44139	**866-695-4569**	440-248-1200	248
Birdair Inc						
65 Lawrence Bell Dr	Amherst	NY	14221	**800-622-2246**	716-633-9500	190-12
Birds & Blooms Magazine						
5400 S 60th St	Greendale	WI	53129	**888-860-8040**	414-423-0100	452-14
BirdWatching Magazine						
25 Braintree Hill Office Pk						
Ste 404	Braintree	MA	02184	**877-252-8141**		452-14
Birmingham Civil Rights Institute						
520 16th St N	Birmingham	AL	35203	**866-328-9696**	205-328-9696	513
Birmingham International Forest Products LLC						
300 Riverhills Business Pk	Birmingham	AL	35242	**800-767-2437**	205-972-1500	192-3
Birmingham News						
2201 Fourth Ave N	Birmingham	AL	35203	**800-283-4001**	205-325-4444	525-2
Birmingham Race Course						
1000 John Rogers Dr	Birmingham	AL	35210	**800-998-8238**	205-838-7500	132
Birmingham Rail & Locomotive Company Inc						
PO Box 530157	Birmingham	AL	35253	**800-241-2260**	205-424-7245	760
Birmingham Times						
115 Third Ave W	Birmingham	AL	35204	**866-456-4995**	205-251-5158	525-4
Birmingham Vending Co						
540 Second Ave N	Birmingham	AL	35204	**800-288-7635**	205-324-7526	54
Birmingham-Southern College						
900 Arkadelphia Rd	Birmingham	AL	35254	**800-523-5793**	205-226-4600	166
Birner Dental Management Services Inc						
1777 S Harrison St Ste 1400	Denver	CO	80210	**877-898-1083**	303-691-0680	458
Birnie Bus Service Inc						
248 Otis St	Rome	NY	13441	**800-734-3950**	315-336-3950	108
Biscayne Rod Manufacturing Inc						
425 E Ninth St	Hialeah	FL	33010	**866-969-0808**	305-884-0808	701
Bisco Industries Inc						
1500 N Lakeview Ave	Anaheim	CA	92807	**800-323-1232**		246
Biscom Inc						
321 Billerica Rd	Chelmsford	MA	01824	**800-477-2472**	978-250-1800	174-3
Biscuit & Cracker Manufacturers Assn (B&CMA)						
6325 Woodside Ct Ste 125	Columbia	MD	21046	**877-701-8111**	443-545-1645	48-6
Bishop Distributing Co						
5200 36th St SE	Grand Rapids	MI	49512	**800-748-0363***		358
*Cust Svc						
Bishop International Airport						
G-3425 W Bristol Rd	Flint	MI	48507	**800-433-7300**	810-235-6560	27
Bishop's University						
2600 College St	Sherbrooke	QC	J1M0C8	**800-567-2792**	819-822-9600	773
Bishop-Wisecarver Corp						
2104 Martin Way	Pittsburg	CA	94565	**888-580-8272**	925-439-8272	613
Bismarck Expressway Suites						
180 E Bismarck Expy	Bismarck	ND	58504	**888-774-5566**	701-222-3311	376
Bismarck State College						
1500 Edwards Ave	Bismarck	ND	58501	**800-445-5073**	701-224-5400	160
Bismarck Tribune						
707 E Front Ave	Bismarck	ND	58504	**866-476-5348**	701-223-2500	525-2
Bismarck-Mandan Convention & Visitors Bureau						
1600 Burnt Boat Dr	Bismarck	ND	58503	**800-767-3555**	701-222-4308	207
Bison Gear & Engineering Corp						
3850 Ohio Ave	Saint Charles	IL	60174	**800-282-4766**	630-377-4327	700
Bison Inc 603 L St	Lincoln	NE	68508	**800-247-7668**	402-474-3353	701
Bisque Imports						
406 E Catawba St	Belmont	NC	28012	**888-568-5991**	704-829-9290	358
Bituminous Insurance Cos						
320 18th St	Rock Island	IL	61201	**800-475-4477**		388-4
Bix Beiderbecke Memorial Society						
PO Box 3688 Ste 201	Davenport	IA	52808	**888-249-5487**	563-324-7170	47-4
Bix Produce Co						
1415 L'Orient St	Saint Paul	MN	55117	**800-642-9514**	651-487-8000	296-7
Bixby International Corp						
1 Preble Rd	Newburyport	MA	01950	**800-466-4102**	978-462-4100	593
BizLand Inc						
70 BlanchaRd Rd	Burlington	MA	01803	**800-249-5263**		38
Bizlink Technology Inc						
3400 Gateway Blvd	Fremont	CA	94538	**800-326-4193**	510-252-0786	802
BKR International						
19 Fulton St Ste 401	New York	NY	10038	**800-257-4685**	212-964-2115	48-1
BL Cos						
355 Research Pkwy	Meriden	CT	06450	**800-301-3077**	203-630-1406	261
BL Downey Company LLC						
2125 Gardner Rd	Broadview	IL	60155	**800-323-1206**	708-345-8000	476
Blach Distributing Co						
131 W Main St	Elko	NV	89801	**800-310-5099**	775-738-7111	80-1
Blachford Corp						
401 Ctr Rd	Frankfort	IL	60423	**800-435-5942**	905-823-3200	534
Blachly-Lane Inc						
PO Box 70	Junction City	OR	97448	**800-446-8418**	541-688-8711	245
Black Bear Casino Resort						
1785 Hwy 210 PO Box 777	Carlton	MN	55718	**888-771-0777**	218-878-2327	132
Black Box Corp						
1000 Pk Dr	Lawrence	PA	15055	**877-877-2269**	724-746-5500	177
NASDAQ: BBOX						
Black Butte Ranch						
12930 Hawks BeaRd Rd						
PO Box 8000	Black Butte Ranch	OR	97759	**866-901-2961**	541-595-1252	660
Black Cultural Centre for Nova Scotia						
10 Cherry Brook Rd	Cherry Brook	NS	B2Z1A8	**800-465-0767**	902-434-6223	513
Black Enterprise Magazine						
130 Fifth Ave	New York	NY	10011	**800-727-7777***	212-242-8000	452-5
*Cust Svc						
Black Forest Decor LLC						
PO Box 297	Jenks	OK	74037	**800-605-0915**		779
Black Hat Inc						
1932 First Ave Ste 204	Seattle	WA	98101	**866-203-8081**	206-443-5489	683
Black Hawk College						
East						
1501 State Hwy 78	Kewanee	IL	61443	**800-233-5671**	309-852-5671	160
Quad Cities						
6600 34th Ave	Moline	IL	61265	**800-334-1311**	309-796-5000	160
Black Hills Bentonite LLC						
PO Box 9	Mills	WY	82644	**800-788-9443***	307-265-3740	498-2
*Orders						
Black Hills Caverns						
2600 Cavern Rd	Rapid City	SD	57702	**800-837-9358**	605-343-0542	49-4
Black Hills Corp						
625 Ninth St	Rapid City	SD	57701	**866-264-8003**	605-721-1700	357-5
NYSE: BKH						
Black Hills Electric Co-op						
25191 Co-op Way PO Box 792	Custer	SD	57730	**800-742-0085**	605-673-4461	245
Black Hills State University						
1200 University St Unit 9502	Spearfish	SD	57799	**800-255-2478**	605-642-6343	166
Black Mountain Ranch						
4000 Conger Mesa Rd	McCoy	CO	80463	**800-967-2401**	970-653-4226	239
Black Mountain-Swannanoa Chamber of Commerce						
201 E State St	Black Mountain	NC	28711	**800-669-2301**	828-669-2300	137
Black Photo Corp						
200 Consilium Pl Ste 1600	Toronto	ON	M1H3J3	**800-668-3826**	416-279-0007	118
Black Radio Network						
166 Madison Ave	New York	NY	10016	**800-226-8276**	212-686-6850	635
Black River Electric Co-op						
2600 Hwy 67 PO Box 31	Fredericktown	MO	63645	**800-392-4711**	573-783-3381	245
Black River State Forest						
101 S Webster St PO Box 7921	Madison	WI	53707	**888-936-7463**	608-266-2621	558
Black River Technical College						
1410 Hwy 304 E	Pocahontas	AR	72455	**866-890-6933**	870-248-4000	160
Blackbaud Inc						
2000 Daniel Island Dr	Charleston	SC	29492	**800-468-8996**	843-216-6200	179-1
NASDAQ: BLKB						
BlackBerry						
295 Phillip St	Waterloo	ON	N2L3W8	**877-255-2377**	519-888-7465	224
Blackboard Inc						
1899 L St NW Fifth Fl	Washington	DC	20036	**800-424-9299**	202-463-4860	179-3
Blackbourn						
200 Fourth Ave N	Edgerton	MN	56128	**800-842-7550**		85
Blackburn College						
700 College Ave	Carlinville	IL	62626	**800-233-3550**	217-854-3231	166
Blackburn's Physicians Pharmacy Inc						
301 Corbet St	Tarentum	PA	15084	**800-472-2440**	724-224-9100	471
Blackfoot Inn						
5940 Blackfoot Trl SE	Calgary	AB	T2H2B5	**800-661-1151**	403-252-2253	376
Blackhawk Bank						
PO Box 719	Beloit	WI	53511	**888-769-2600**	608-364-4534	68

	Toll-Free	Phone	Class
Blackhawk Technical College			
6004 S County Rd G ....Janesville WI 53546	800-498-1282	608-758-6900	788
Blackman Kallick			
10 S Riverside Plaza ....Chicago IL 60606	866-939-3921	312-207-1040	2
Blackmer			
1809 Century Ave ....Grand Rapids MI 49503	888-363-7886	616-241-1611	632
Blackmore Company Inc			
10800 Blackmore Ave ....Belleville MI 48111	800-874-8660	734-483-8661	601
BlackRock Inc			
601 Union St 56th Fl ....Seattle WA 98101	800-441-7450	206-613-6700	780
NYSE: BLK			
Blackstone Valley Chamber of Commerce			
110 Church St ....Whitinsville MA 01588	800-841-0919	508-234-9090	137
Blackwell, The			
2110 Tuttle Pk Pl ....Columbus OH 43210	866-247-4003	614-247-4000	376
Blade			
541 N Superior St ....Toledo OH 43660	800-245-3317	419-724-6000	525-2
Blade Energy Partners Ltd			
2600 Network Blvd Ste 550 ....Frisco TX 75034	800-849-1545	972-712-8407	193
Blade-Tech Industries Inc			
5530 184th St East ....Puyallup WA 98375	877-331-5793	253-655-8059	702
Bladon Springs State Park			
3921 Bladon Rd ....Bladon Springs AL 36919	800-252-7275	251-754-9207	558
Blaine County			
420 Ohio St ....Chinook MT 59523	800-666-6124	406-442-9830	336
Blaine Tech Services Inc			
1680 Rogers Ave ....San Jose CA 95112	800-545-7558	408-573-0555	195
Blaine's Art Supply			
1025 Photo Ave ....Anchorage AK 99503	866-561-4278	907-561-5344	44
Blair Cedar & Novelty Works Inc			
680 W US Hwy 54 ....Camdenton MO 65020	800-325-3943	573-346-2235	327
Blair Concrete Services			
1410-B Diggs Dr ....Raleigh NC 27603	800-815-7395	919-833-9088	190-3
Blair Packaging Inc			
1515 Independence St ....Cape Girardeau MO 63703	800-624-3150	573-334-2146	85
Blaise Alexander Chevrolet Inc			
933 Broad St ....Montoursville PA 17754	877-575-4256	570-368-8677	56
Blakely New York			
136 W 55th St ....New York NY 10019	800-735-0710	212-245-1800	376
Blakeslee Arpaia Chapman Inc			
200 N Branford Rd ....Branford CT 06405	800-922-6203	203-488-2500	184
Blanchard Compact Equipment			
1410 Ashville Hwy ....Spartanburg SC 29303	888-799-3606	864-582-1245	274
Blanco America Inc			
110 Mount Holly By-Pass ....Lumberton NJ 08048	800-451-5782		359
Blank Quilting Corp			
Blank Quilting			
49 West 37th St 14th fl. ....New York NY 10018	800-294-9495		587
Blanks Printing & Imaging Inc			
2343 N Beckley Ave ....Dallas TX 75208	800-325-7651	214-741-3905	771
Blanks/USA Inc			
7700 68th Ave N #7 ....Minneapolis MN 55428	800-328-7311		553
Blanton & Assoc Inc			
5 Lakeway Centre Ct Ste 200 ....Austin TX 78734	888-863-5881	512-264-1095	195
Blantyre			
16 Blantyre Rd PO Box 995 ....Lenox MA 01240	844-881-0104	413-637-3556	376
Blast Inc			
220 Chatham Business Dr			
PO Box 818. ....Pittsboro NC 27312	800-242-5278	919-533-0143	179-7
Blauch Bros Inc			
911 Chicago Ave ....Harrisonburg VA 22802	888-881-3939	540-434-2589	603
Blauer Mfg Co Inc			
20 Aberdeen St ....Boston MA 02215	800-225-6715	617-536-6606	153-18
Blazer Industries Inc			
PO Box 489 ....Aumsville OR 97325	877-211-3437	503-749-1900	105
Bledsoe Telephone Co-op Corp (BTC)			
338 Cumberland Ave PO Box 609 ....Pikeville TN 37367	888-382-1222	423-447-2121	726
Blendex Company Inc			
11208 Electron Dr ....Louisville KY 40299	800-626-6325	502-267-1003	295-23
Blenko Glass Co			
PO Box 67 ....Milton WV 25541	877-425-3656	304-743-9081	332
BLET (Brotherhood of Locomotive Engineers & Trainmen)			
1370 Ontario St			
Mezzanine Level ....Cleveland OH 44113	877-772-5772	216-241-2630	411
Bleyhl Farm Service Inc			
940 E Wine Country Rd ......Grandview WA 98930	800-862-6806*	509-882-2248	276
*Cust Svc			
BLI (Bulk Lift International Inc)			
1013 Tamarac Dr ....Carpentersville IL 60110	800-879-2247	847-428-6059	66
BLI (Big Lots Inc)			
300 Phillipi Rd ....Columbus OH 43228	877-998-1697	614-278-6800	779
NYSE: BIG			
Blish-Mize Co			
223 S Fifth St ....Atchison KS 66002	800-995-0525	913-367-1250	348
Bliss Clearing Niagara (BCN)			
1004 E State St ....Hastings MI 49058	800-642-5477	269-948-3300	451
Bliss Communications Inc			
PO Box 5001 ....Janesville WI 53547	800-362-6712	608-754-3311	634
Blissfield Manufacturing Co			
626 Depot St ....Blissfield MI 49228	800-626-1772*	517-486-2121	14
*Cust Svc			
Blistex Inc			
1800 Swift Dr ....Oak Brook IL 60523	800-837-1800*		576
*Cust Svc			
Bloch Industries			
140 Commerce Dr ....Rochester NY 14623	800-992-5624	585-334-9600	114
Blodgett Supply Co Inc			
100 Ave D PO Box 759 ....Williston VT 05495	888-888-3424	802-864-9831	37
Blommer Chocolate Co			
600 W Kinzie St ....Chicago IL 60654	800-621-1606	312-226-7700	295-8
Blonder Tongue Laboratories Inc			
1 Jake Brown Rd ....Old Bridge NJ 08857	877-407-8033	732-679-4000	638
NYSE: BDR			
Blood Assurance Inc			
705 E Fourth St ....Chattanooga TN 37403	800-962-0628	423-756-0966	88
Blood Bank of Delmarva			
100 Hygeia Dr ....Newark DE 19713	800-548-4009	302-737-8405	88
Blood Bank of Hawaii			
2043 Dillingham Blvd ....Honolulu HI 96819	800-372-9966	808-845-9966	88
Blood Bank of the Redwoods			
2324 Bethards Dr ....Santa Rosa CA 95405	888-393-4483	707-545-1222	88
Blood Centers of the Pacific			
250 Bush St ....San Francisco CA 94104	888-393-4483	415-567-6400	88
Blood Ctr of New Jersey			
45 S Grove St ....East Orange NJ 07018	866-228-1500	973-676-4700	88
Blood Ctr, The			
2609 Canal St ....New Orleans LA 70112	800-862-5663	504-524-1322	88
Blood Donor Ctr at Presbyterian/St Luke's Medical Ctr			
1719 E 19th Ave ....Denver CO 80218	800-231-2222	303-839-6000	759
Blood Systems Laboratories			
2424 W Erie Dr ....Tempe AZ 85282	800-288-2199	602-343-7000	414
BloodCenter of Wisconsin			
638 N 18th St ....Milwaukee WI 53233	877-232-4376	414-933-5000	88
Blood-Horse Magazine			
PO Box 911088 ....Lexington KY 40591	800-866-2361	859-278-2361	452-14
BloodSource			
1608 Q St ....Sacramento CA 95811	800-995-4420	916-456-1500	88
Bloom Engineering Co Inc			
5460 Curry Rd ....Pittsburgh PA 15236	800-451-5491	412-653-3500	317
Bloomfield College			
467 Franklin St ....Bloomfield NJ 07003	800-848-4555	973-748-9000	166
Bloomfield Township Public Library			
1099 Lone Pine Rd ....Bloomfield Hills MI 48302	800-318-2596	248-642-5800	431-3
Bloomingdale's			
1000 Third Ave ....New York NY 10022	800-950-0047	212-705-2000	229
Bloomington Convention & Visitors Bureau (BCVB)			
7900 International Dr			
Ste 990 ....Bloomington MN 55425	800-346-4289	952-858-8500	207
Bloomington/Monroe County Convention & Visitors Bureau			
2855 N Walnut St ....Bloomington IN 47404	800-800-0037	812-334-8900	207
Bloomington-Normal Area Convention & Visitors Bureau			
3201 CIRA Dr Ste 201 ....Bloomington IL 61704	800-433-8226	309-665-0033	207
BloomNation LLC			
8889 W Olympic Blvd ....Beverly Hills CA 90211	877-702-5666		292
BloomNet Inc			
One Old Country Rd Ste 500........Carle Place NY 11514	866-256-6663		384
Bloomsburg Carpet Industries Inc			
4999 Columbia Blvd ....Bloomsburg PA 17815	800-233-8773	570-784-9188	130
Bloomsburg University			
400 E Second St ....Bloomsburg PA 17815	888-651-6117	570-389-3900	166
Blossman Gas Inc			
809 Washington Ave ....Ocean Springs MS 39564	800-256-7762	888-256-7762	315
Blossom Music Ctr Tickets			
1145 W Steels			
Corners Rd ....Cuyahoga Falls OH 44223	800-745-3000	330-920-8040	565
Blount Inc Oregon Cutting Systems Div			
4909 SE International Way ....Portland OR 97222	800-223-5168	503-653-8881	749
Blount Seafood Corp			
630 Currant Rd ....Fall River MA 02720	800-274-2526*	774-888-1300	295-14
*Hotline			
Blount Small Ship Adventures			
461 Water St ....Warren RI 02885	800-556-7450	401-247-0955	220
Blower Application Company Inc			
N 114 W 19125 Clinton Dr ....Germantown WI 53022	800-959-0880	262-255-5580	383
Blowfish Direct LLC			
11130 Holder St ....Cypress CA 90630	877-725-6934		681
Blowing Rock Chamber of Commerce			
7738 Vly Blvd ....Blowing Rock NC 28605	800-295-7851	828-295-7851	137
BLR (Business & Legal Reports Inc)			
141 Mill Rock Rd E ....Old Saybrook CT 06475	800-727-5257	860-510-0100	628-9
Blue & Co			
12800 N Meridian St Ste 400 ....Carmel IN 46032	800-717-2583	317-848-8920	2
Blue Box Group Inc			
119 Pine St Ste 200 ....Seattle WA 98101	800-613-4305		384
Blue Care Network of Michigan			
20500 Civic Ctr Dr ....Southfield MI 48076	800-662-6667	248-799-6400	388-3
Blue Cat Design			
Mastwoods Rd ....Welcome ON L1A3V5	888-258-3228	905-753-1017	7
Blue Chip Casino Inc			
777 Blue Chip Dr ....Michigan City IN 46360	888-879-7711	219-879-7711	132
Blue Chip Venture Co			
312 Walnut St Ste 1120 ....Cincinnati OH 45202	800-775-1812	513-723-2300	780
Blue Coat Systems Inc			
420 N Mary Ave ....Sunnyvale CA 94085	866-302-2628	408-220-2200	177
NASDAQ: BCSI			
Blue Cross & Blue Shield Assn			
225 N Michigan Ave ....Chicago IL 60601	800-810-2583	312-297-6000	48-9
Blue Cross & Blue Shield of Alabama			
450 Riverchase Pkwy E ....Birmingham AL 35244	800-292-8868	205-988-2200	388-3
Blue Cross & Blue Shield of Kansas City			
2301 Main St ....Kansas City MO 64108	800-892-6048	816-395-2222	388-3
Blue Cross & Blue Shield of Mississippi			
PO Box 1043 ....Jackson MS 39215	800-222-8046	601-932-3704	388-3
Blue Cross & Blue Shield of Montana			
560 N Pk Ave PO Box 4309 ....Helena MT 59604	800-447-7828	406-437-5000	388-3
Blue Cross & Blue Shield of Nebraska			
1919 Aksarben Dr PO Box 3248.........Omaha NE 68180	800-422-2763	402-982-7000	388-3
Blue Cross & Blue Shield of New Mexico			
PO Box 27630 ....Albuquerque NM 87125	800-835-8699	505-291-3500	388-3
Blue Cross & Blue Shield of North Carolina			
1965 Ivory Creek Blvd ....Durham NC 27702	800-446-8053*	919-489-7431	388-3
*Cust Svc			
Blue Cross & Blue Shield of Oklahoma			
1215 S Boulder Ave ....Tulsa OK 74119	800-942-5837*	918-560-3500	388-3
*Cust Svc			
Blue Cross & Blue Shield of Rhode Island			
500 Exchange St ....Providence RI 02903	800-637-3718	401-459-1000	388-3
Blue Cross & Blue Shield of Texas Inc			
1001 E Lookout Dr ....Richardson TX 75082	800-521-2227	972-766-6900	388-3
Blue Cross & Blue Shield of Vermont			
445 Industrial Ln ....Montpelier VT 05602	800-247-2583*	802-223-6131	388-3
*Cust Svc			
Blue Cross Blue Shield of Arizona			
2444 W Las Palmaritas Dr ....Phoenix AZ 85021	800-232-2345	602-864-4400	388-3
Blue Cross Blue Shield of Delaware			
PO Box 1991 ....Wilmington DE 19899	800-572-4400	800-876-7639	388-3
Blue Cross Blue Shield of Georgia			
3350 Peachtree Rd NE ....Atlanta GA 30326	800-441-2273*	404-842-8000	388-3
*Cust Svc			
Blue Cross Blue Shield of Kansas			
1133 SW Topeka Blvd ....Topeka KS 66629	800-432-0216	785-291-7000	388-3
Blue Cross Blue Shield of Louisiana			
5525 Reitz Ave ....Baton Rouge LA 70898	800-599-2583	225-295-3307	388-3
Blue Cross Blue Shield of Massachusetts			
401 Pk Dr ....Boston MA 02215	888-247-2583	617-246-5000	388-3
Blue Cross Blue Shield of North Dakota			
4510 13th Ave S ....Fargo ND 58121	800-342-4718	701-282-1100	388-3

				Toll-Free	Phone	Class
Blue Cross Blue Shield of Wyoming						
4000 House Ave	Cheyenne	WY	82001	**800-851-9145**	307-634-1393	388-3
Blue Cross of California						
Two Gannett Dr	South Portland	ME	04106	**800-999-3643**	800-482-0966	388-3
Blue Cross of Idaho						
3000 E Pine Ave	Meridian	ID	83642	**800-274-4018**	208-345-4550	388-3
Blue Cross of Northeastern Pennsylvania						
19 N Main St	Wilkes-Barre	PA	18711	**800-577-3742***		388-3
*Cust Svc						
Blue Generation Div of M Rubin & Sons Inc						
34-01 38th Ave	Long Island City	NY	11101	**888-336-4687**	718-361-2800	153-18
Blue Grass Energy Co-op Corp						
1201 Lexington Rd	Nicholasville	KY	40356	**888-546-4243**	859-885-4191	245
Blue Grass Regional Library						
104 E Sixth St	Columbia	TN	38401	**888-345-5575**	931-388-9282	431-3
Blue Grass Regional Mental Health-Mental Retardation Board Inc						
1351 Newtown Pike Bldg 1	Lexington	KY	40511	**800-928-8000**	859-253-1686	47-6
Blue Grass Stockyard						
375 Lisle Industrial Ave						
PO Box 1023	Lexington	KY	40588	**800-621-3972**	859-255-7701	441
Blue Grass Tours Inc						
817 Enterprise Dr	Lexington	KY	40510	**800-755-6956**	859-233-2152	750
Blue Heaven						
729 Thomas St	Key West	FL	33040	**800-986-0958**	305-296-8666	662
Blue Horizon Hotel						
1225 Robson St	Vancouver	BC	V6E1C3	**800-663-1333**	604-688-1411	376
Blue Lakes Charters & Tours						
12154 N Saginaw Rd	Clio	MI	48420	**800-282-4287**	810-686-4287	106
Blue Lance Inc						
410 Pierce St Ste 950	Houston	TX	77002	**800-856-2583**	713-255-4800	179-12
Blue Licks Battlefield State Resort Park						
Hwy 68	Mount Olivet	KY	41064	**800-443-7008**		558
Blue Line Foodservice Distribution						
24120 Haggerty Rd	Farmington Hills	MI	48335	**800-892-8272***		298
*General						
Blue Moon Hotel						
944 Collins Ave	Miami Beach	FL	33139	**800-553-7739**	305-673-2262	376
Blue Mounds State Park						
1410 161st St	Luverne	MN	56156	**888-646-6367**	507-283-1307	558
Blue Mountain Arts Inc						
PO Box 4549	Boulder	CO	80306	**800-545-8573***	303-449-0536	129
*Sales						
Blue Mountain College						
PO Box 160	Blue Mountain	MS	38610	**800-235-0136**	662-685-4771	166
Blue Mountain Wallcoverings Inc						
15 Akron Rd	Etobicoke	ON	M8W1T3	**866-563-9872**	416-251-1678	790
Blue Nile Inc						
705 Fifth Ave S Ste 900	Seattle	WA	98104	**800-242-2728**	206-336-6700	407
NASDAQ: NILE						
Blue North Fisheries Inc						
2930 Westlake Ave N Ste 300	Seattle	WA	98109	**877-878-3263**	206-352-9252	285
Blue Parrot Inn						
916 Elizabeth St	Key West	FL	33040	**800-231-2473**	305-296-0033	376
Blue Pillar Inc						
9025 N River Rd Ste 150	Indianapolis	IN	46240	**888-234-3212**		193
Blue Ribbon Home Warranty Inc						
95 S Wadsworth Blvd	Lakewood	CO	80226	**800-571-0475**	303-986-3900	364
Blue Ribbon Tag & Label Corp						
4035 N 29th Ave	Hollywood	FL	33020	**800-433-4974**	954-922-9292	410
Blue Ridge Bank & Trust Co						
4240 Blue Ridge Blvd						
Ste 100	Kansas City	MO	64133	**800-569-4287**	816-358-5000	69
Blue Ridge Community College						
1 College Ln PO Box 80	Weyers Cave	VA	24486	**888-750-2722**	540-234-9261	160
Blue Ridge Electric Membership Corp						
1216 Blowing Rock Blvd	Lenoir	NC	28645	**800-451-5474**	828-758-2383	245
Blue Ridge Public Television						
1215 McNeil Dr	Roanoke	VA	24015	**888-332-7788**	540-344-0991	624
Blue Ridge X-Ray Company Inc						
120 Vista Blvd	Arden	NC	28704	**800-727-7290**		470
Blue Seal Feeds Inc						
2905 US Hwy 61 N	Muscatine	IA	52761	**866-647-1212***		442
*Cust Svc						
Blue Sky Swimwear						
729 E International						
Speedway Blvd	Daytona Beach	FL	32118	**800-799-6445***	386-255-2590	153-16
*Orders						
Blue Water Area Chamber of Commerce						
512 McMorran Blvd	Port Huron	MI	48060	**800-361-0526**	810-985-7101	137
Blue Water Resort						
291 S Shore Dr	South Yarmouth	MA	02664	**800-367-9393**	508-398-2288	660
Blue Water Sailing Magazine						
747 Aquidneck Ave Ste 201						
Ste 201	Middletown	RI	02842	**888-800-7245**	401-847-7612	452-4
BlueCross BlueShield of Western New York						
257 W Genesee St	Buffalo	NY	14240	**800-888-0757**	716-887-6900	388-3
Bluefield College						
3000 College Dr	Bluefield	VA	24605	**800-872-0175**	276-326-3682	166
Bluefield Regional Medical Ctr (BRMC)						
500 Cherry St	Bluefield	WV	24701	**800-994-6610**	304-327-1100	371-3
Bluefield State College						
219 Rock St	Bluefield	WV	24701	**800-654-7798**	304-327-4000	166
Bluefly Inc						
42 W 39th St Ninth Fl	New York	NY	10018	**877-258-3359***	212-944-8000	155-6
NASDAQ: BFLY ■ *Cust Svc						
Blue-Grace Logistics LLC						
2846 S Falkenburg Rd	Riverview	FL	33578	**800-697-4477**	813-641-0357	310
Bluegrass Cellular Inc						
2902 Ring Rd PO Box 5012	Elizabethtown	KY	42702	**800-928-2355**	270-769-0339	726
Bluegrass Community & Technical College						
Cooper Campus						
470 Cooper Dr	Lexington	KY	40506	**866-774-4872**	859-246-6200	160
Bluegreen Corp						
4960 Conference Way N						
Ste 100	Boca Raton	FL	33431	**800-456-2582**	561-912-8000	743
NYSE: BXG						
Blueharbor Bank						
106 Corporate Park Dr	Mooresville	NC	28117	**877-322-8228**	704-662-7700	69
Bluelock LLC						
6325 Morenci Trl	Indianapolis	IN	46268	**888-402-2583**		181
Bluemetal Architects Inc						
44 Pleasant St	Watertown	MA	02472	**866-252-0111**		197
Bluenose Inn & Suites						
636 Bedford Hwy	Halifax	NS	B3M2L8	**800-553-5339**	902-443-3171	376
BlueSpire Strategic Marketing						
7650 Edinborough Way						
Ste 500	Minneapolis	MN	55435	**800-727-6397**		5
Bluestem Electric Co-op Inc						
614 E Hwy 24 PO Box 5	Wamego	KS	66547	**800-558-1580**	785-456-2212	245
BlueTie Inc						
2480 Browncroft Blvd Ste 2b	Rochester	NY	14625	**800-258-3843**	585-586-2000	225
Bluewater Adventures Ltd						
252 E First St Ste 3	North Vancouver	BC	V7L1B3	**888-877-1770**	604-980-3800	220
Bluewater Bay Resort						
2000 Bluewater Blvd	Niceville	FL	32578	**800-874-2128**	850-897-3613	660
Bluewater Resort						
2001 S Ocean Blvd	Myrtle Beach	SC	29577	**800-845-6994**	843-626-8345	660
Bluewater Thermal Solutions						
201 Brookfield Pwy Ste 102	Greenville	SC	29607	**877-990-0050**	864-990-0050	479
Bluffton Flying Service Co						
1080 Navajo Dr	Bluffton	OH	45817	**800-468-6359**	419-358-7045	13
Bluffton Motor Works LLC						
410 E Spring St	Bluffton	IN	46714	**800-579-8527**	260-827-2200	511
Bluffton Today						
52 Persimmon St	Bluffton	SC	29910	**855-665-8549**	843-815-0800	525-4
Bluffton University						
1 University Dr	Bluffton	OH	45817	**800-488-3257**	419-358-3000	166
Blum Inc						
7733 Old Plank Rd	Stanley	NC	28164	**800-438-6788**	704-827-1345	347
Blum Shapiro						
29 S Main St						
PO Box 272000	West Hartford	CT	06107	**866-356-2586**	860-561-4000	2
Blumenthal Lansing Co						
30 Two Bridges Rd Ste 110	Fairfield	NJ	07004	**800-448-9749**	201-935-6220	587
Blytheco LLC						
23161 Mill Creek Dr	Laguna Hills	CA	92653	**800-425-9843**	949-583-9500	181
BMA (Business Marketing Assn)						
708 Third Ave 33rd Fl	New York	NY	10017	**800-664-4262**	212-697-5950	48-18
BMC (Better Management Corp)						
41738 Esterly Dr	Columbiana	OH	44408	**877-293-4300**	330-482-7070	651
BMC Software Inc						
2101 City W Blvd	Houston	TX	77042	**800-841-2031**	713-918-8800	179-1
NASDAQ: BMC						
BMG Aviation Inc						
984 S Kirby Rd	Bloomington	IN	47403	**888-457-3787**	812-825-7979	62
BMG Metals Inc						
950 Masonic Ln	Richmond	VA	23231	**800-552-1510**	804-226-1024	487
BMH (Bastian Material Handling LLC)						
10585 N Meridian St						
Third Fl	Indianapolis	IN	46290	**800-772-0464**	317-575-9992	54
BMH Books						
1104 Kings Hwy PO Box 544	Winona Lake	IN	46590	**800-348-2756**		628-8
BMI (Brotherhood Mutual Insurance Co)						
6400 Brotherhood Way						
PO Box 2589	Fort Wayne	IN	46825	**800-333-3735***		388-4
*Cust Svc						
BMI Educational Services						
PO Box 800	Dayton	NJ	08810	**800-222-8100**	732-329-6991	94
BMI Imaging Systems						
1115 E Arques Ave	Sunnyvale	CA	94085	**800-359-3456**	408-736-7444	491
Bmo Bankcorp Inc						
111 W Monroe St	Chicago	IL	60603	**888-340-2265**		357-2
BMO Financial Corp						
1 First Canadian Place 11th Fl	Toronto	ON	M5X1A1	**800-553-0332**	416-359-4440	216
BMO Harris Bank						
111 W Monroe St	Chicago	IL	60603	**888-340-2265**	847-238-2265	69
BMS (Broadcast Microwave Services Inc)						
12367 Crosthwaite Cir	Poway	CA	92064	**800-669-9667**	858-391-3050	224
BMW of North America LLC						
300 Chestnut Ridge Rd	Woodcliff Lake	NJ	07677	**800-831-1117**	201-307-4000	58
BNC National Bank						
322 E Main Ave PO Box 4050	Bismarck	ND	58501	**800-262-2265**	701-250-3000	69
BNN (Business News Network)						
299 Queen St W	Toronto	ON	M5V2Z5	**855-326-6266**	416-384-6600	729
BNSF (Burlington Northern & Santa Fe Railway)						
2650 Lou Menk Dr	Fort Worth	TX	76131	**800-795-2673**		639
BNSF (Burlington Northern Santa Fe Corp)						
500 New Jersey Ave NW						
Ste 550	Washington	DC	20001	**800-964-9386**	202-347-8662	608
BNZ Materials Inc						
6901 S Pierce St Ste 260	Littleton	CO	80128	**800-999-0890**	303-978-1199	653
Boar's Head Inn						
200 Ednam Dr	Charlottesville	VA	22903	**800-476-1988**	434-296-2181	660
Boarder to Boarder Trucking Inc						
PO Box 328	Edinburg	TX	78541	**800-678-8789**	956-316-4444	676
Boardman Park						
375 BoaRdman-Poland Rd	Boardman	OH	44512	**888-795-2707**	330-726-8107	49
Boardroom Communications Inc						
Bank Of America Plaza 1776 N Pine Island Rd						
Ste 320	Fort Lauderdale	FL	33322	**877-773-4761**	954-370-8999	627
Boardroom Inc						
281 Tresser Blvd 8th Fl	Stamford	CT	06901	**800-274-5611**		628-9
Boardwalk Pipeline Partners LP						
3800 Frederica St	Owensboro	KY	42301	**866-913-2122**	270-686-3620	324
NYSE: BWP						
Boardwalk Plaza Hotel						
Two Olive Ave	Rehoboth Beach	DE	19971	**800-332-3224**	302-227-7169	376
Boart Longyear Co						
2640 W 1700 S	Salt Lake City	UT	84104	**800-453-8740**	801-972-6430	191
Boat Owners Assn of the US						
880 S Pickett St	Alexandria	VA	22304	**800-395-2628**	703-823-9550	47-22
Bob Allen Ford						
9239 Metcalf Ave	Overland Park	KS	66212	**888-573-6364**	913-381-3000	56
Bob Barker Company Inc						
PO Box 429	Fuquay Varina	NC	27526	**800-334-9880**	919-552-3431	587
Bob Bullock Texas State History Museum						
1800 N Congress Ave	Austin	TX	78701	**866-369-7108**	512-936-8746	513
Bob Davidson Ford Lincoln						
1845 E Joppa Rd	Baltimore	MD	21234	**888-643-0263**	410-661-6400	56
Bob Evans Farms Inc						
3776 S High St	Columbus	OH	43207	**800-939-2338**		661
NASDAQ: BOBE						
Bob Jones University						
1700 Wade Hampton Blvd	Greenville	SC	29614	**800-252-6363***	864-242-5100	166
*Admissions						
Bob Stall Chevrolet						
7601 Alvarado Rd	La Mesa	CA	91942	**800-295-2695**	619-460-1311	56

Name / Address	Toll-Free	Phone	Class
Bob Straub State Park US 101 ... Pacific City OR 97135	800-551-6949		558
Bob Ward & Sons Inc 3015 Paxson St ... Missoula MT 59801	800-800-5083	406-728-3220	702
Bob's Red Mill Natural Foods Inc 13521 SE Pheasant Ct ... Milwaukie OR 97222	800-553-2258	503-654-3215	295-4
Bob's Sporting Goods 1111 Hudson St ... Longview WA 98632	800-292-5551	360-425-3870	229
Bob's Stores Inc 160 Corporate Ct ... Meriden CT 06450	866-333-2627	203-235-5775	155-2
Bobby Jones Retail Corp 2093 Old Route 15 PO Box 214 ... New Columbia PA 17856 *Cust Svc	855-437-5537*	855-785-1930	153-3
Bobco Metals Co 2000 S Alameda St ... Los Angeles CA 90058	877-952-6226		487
Bobit Business Media 3520 Challenger St ... Torrance CA 90503	888-239-2455	310-533-2400	628-9
Boca Raton Museum of Art 501 Plaza Real Mizner Pk ... Boca Raton FL 33432	888-472-4732	561-392-2500	513
Boca Raton Resort & Club 501 E Camino Real ... Boca Raton FL 33432	888-543-1224	561-447-3000	660
Boca Resorts 501 E Camino Real ... Boca Raton FL 33432	888-543-1277	561-447-3000	357-3
Bocada Inc 5555 Lakeview Dr ... Kirkland WA 98033	866-262-2321	425-818-4400	384
Bodega Bay Lodge 103 Coast Hwy 1 ... Bodega Bay CA 94923 *Resv	888-875-2250*	707-875-3525	376
Bodine Co 236 S Mt Pleasant Rd ... Collierville TN 38027	800-223-5728	901-853-7211	757
Bodine Electric Co 201 Northfield Rd ... Northfield IL 60093	800-726-3463	773-478-3515	511
Body & Soul 42 Pleasant St ... Watertown MA 02472	800-755-1178	617-449-5506	452-18
Body-Borneman Insurance PO Box 584 ... Boyertown PA 19512	800-326-5290	610-367-1100	387
Body-Solid Inc 1900 Des Plaines Ave ... Forest Park IL 60130	800-833-1227	708-427-3500	267
BoeFly LLC 50 W 72nd St Ste C6 ... New York NY 10023	800-277-3158		384
Boehringer Ingelheim Ltd 5180 S Service Rd ... Burlington ON L7L5H4	800-263-9107	905-639-0333	576
Boehringer Ingelheim Pharmaceuticals Inc 900 Ridgebury Rd ... Ridgefield CT 06877	800-243-0127	203-798-9988	576
Boehringer Ingelheim Vetmedica Inc 2621 N Belt Hwy ... Saint Joseph MO 64506	800-821-7467	816-233-2571	575
Boekel Scientific 855 Pennsylvania Blvd ... Feasterville PA 19053	800-336-6929	215-396-8200	417
Boelter Cos Inc N22W23685 Ridgeview Pkwy W ... West Waukesha WI 53188	800-263-5837	262-523-6200	299
Boesen the Florist 3422 Beaver Ave ... Des Moines IA 50310	800-274-4761	515-274-4761	292
Bogdahn Group, The 4901 Vineland Rd Ste 600 ... Orlando FL 32811	866-240-7932		398
Bogen Communications International Inc 50 Spring St ... Ramsey NJ 07446 OTC: BOGN	800-999-2809	201-934-8500	51
Boh Bros Construction Co LLC 730 S Tonti St ... New Orleans LA 70119	800-284-3377	504-821-2400	189-4
Bohannan Huston Inc 7500 Jefferson St NE Courtyard 1 ... Albuquerque NM 87109	800-877-5332	505-823-1000	179-5
Boheme, The 325 S Orange Ave ... Orlando FL 32801	866-663-0024	407-313-9000	662
Bohemian Hotel Celebration 700 Bloom St ... Celebration FL 34747	888-249-4007	407-566-6000	376
Bohler-Uddeholm North America 2505 Millenium Dr ... Elgin IL 60124	800-638-2520	630-883-3100	487
Bohrens Moving & Storage Inc Three Applegate Dr ... Robbinsville NJ 08691	800-326-4736	609-208-1470	512
Boies Schiller & Flexner LLP 5301 Wisconsin Ave NW ... Washington DC 20015	877-224-0464	202-237-2727	425
Boiling Springs Savings Bank (BSSB) 25 Orient Way ... Rutherford NJ 07070	888-388-7459	201-939-5000	69
Boingo Wireless Inc 10960 Wilshire Blvd Ste 800 ... Los Angeles CA 90024	800-880-4117	310-586-5180	178
Boise Bible College 8695 W Marigold St ... Boise ID 83714	800-893-7755	208-376-7731	159
Boise Cascade Bldg Materials Distribution Div 1111 W Jefferson Ste 300 PO Box 50 ... Boise ID 83728	800-367-4611	208-384-7700	192-3
Boise Convention & Visitors Bureau 1199 Main St ... Boise ID 83702	800-635-5240	208-344-7777	207
Boise State University 1910 University Dr ... Boise ID 83725	800-824-7017	208-426-1156	166
Boise-Winnemucca Stage Lines Inc 1105 S La Pt St ... Boise ID 83706	800-448-5692	208-336-3300	106
Boisfeuillet Jones Atlanta Civic Ctr 395 Piedmont Ave ... Atlanta GA 30308	877-430-7596	404-523-6275	565
Bojangles' Restaurants Inc 9432 Southern Pine Blvd ... Charlotte NC 28273	800-366-9921	704-335-1804	661
Boker's Inc 3104 Snelling Ave ... Minneapolis MN 55406	800-927-4377	612-729-9365	614
Bolger LLC 3301 Como Ave SE ... Minneapolis MN 55414	866-264-3287	651-645-6311	619
Bolivar County Library 104 S Leflore Ave ... Cleveland MS 38732	888-268-8076	662-843-2774	431-3
Bolle Inc 9200 Cody St ... Overland Park KS 66214	800-222-6553	913-752-3400	535
Bollinger Insurance 101 JFK Pkwy ... Short Hills NJ 07078	800-526-1379	973-467-0444	387
Bollman Hat Co 110 E Main St PO Box 517 ... Adamstown PA 19501	800-959-4287	717-484-4361	153-8
BOLT Solutions Inc 90 Park Ave Ste 1700 ... New York NY 10016	888-608-4646	212-608-4646	618
Bolthouse Farms 7200 E Brundage Ln ... Bakersfield CA 93307	800-467-4683		10-10
Bolton & Hay Inc 2701 Delaware Ave ... Des Moines IA 50317	800-362-1861	515-265-2554	299
Bolttech Mannings 501 Mosside Blvd ... North Versailles PA 15137	888-846-8827	724-872-4873	382

Name / Address	Toll-Free	Phone	Class
BOMA (Building Owners & Managers Assn International) 1101 15th St NW Ste 800 ... Washington DC 20005	800-426-6292	202-408-2662	48-17
Bomag Americas Inc 2000 Kentville Rd ... Kewanee IL 61443	800-782-6624	309-853-3571	191
Bombardier Aerospace 400 Cote-Vertu Rd W ... Dorval QC H4S1Y9 *General	866-855-5001*	514-855-5000	20
Bombardier Capital Group 261 Mountain View Dr 4th Fl ... Colchester VT 05446	800-949-5568	802-764-5232	216
Bombet Cashio & Assoc 11220 N Harrells Ferry Rd ... Baton Rouge LA 70816	800-256-5333	225-275-0796	397
Bommarito Automotive Group 15736 Manchester Rd ... Ellisville MO 63011	800-367-2289	636-391-7200	56
Bommer Industries Inc PO Box 187 ... Landrum SC 29356	800-334-1654	864-457-3301	347
Bon Homme Yankton Electric Assn 134 S Lidice St ... Tabor SD 57063	800-925-2929	605-463-2507	245
Bon Secour Fisheries Inc 17449 County Rd 49 S ... Bon Secour AL 36511	800-633-6854	251-949-7411	296-5
Bon Secours Memorial Regional Medical Ctr 8260 Atlee Rd ... Mechanicsville VA 23116	888-455-3766	804-764-6000	371-3
Bon Secours Saint Mary's Hospital 5801 Bremo Rd ... Richmond VA 23226	877-342-1500	804-285-2011	371-3
Bon Voyage Travel 1640 E River Rd Ste 115 ... Tucson AZ 85718	800-439-7963	520-797-1110	761
Bonadio Group, The 171 Sully's Trail Ste 201 ... Pittsford NY 14534	877-917-3077	585-381-1000	2
Bonair Daydreams PO Box 1522 ... Wrightsville Beach NC 28480	888-226-6247	910-617-3887	129
Bonaire Government Tourist Office 80 Broad St Ste 3202 32nd Fl. ... New York NY 10004	800-328-2288	212-956-5912	765
Bonanza Beverage Co 6333 Ensworth St ... Las Vegas NV 89119 *Cust Svc	800-677-4166*	702-361-4166	80-1
Bonanza Creek Country Guest Ranch 523 Bonanza Creek Rd ... Martinsdale MT 59053	800-476-6045	406-572-3366	239
Bonanza Trade & Supply 6853 Lankershim Blvd ... North Hollywood CA 91605	888-965-6577	818-765-6577	195
Bonaventure Tours 8 Boudreau Ln ... Haute-Aboujagane NB E4P5N1	800-561-1213	506-532-3674	750
Bond Auto Parts 45 Summer St ... Barre VT 05641	800-639-1982	802-476-3108	53
Bond Place Hotel 65 Dundas St E ... Toronto ON M5B2G8	800-268-9390	416-362-6061	376
Bond Pro LLC 1501 E Second Ave ... Tampa FL 33605	888-789-4985		388-5
Bondcote Corp PO Box 729 ... Pulaski VA 24301	800-368-2160	540-980-2640	734-2
Bonded Concrete Inc 303 Rt 155 ... Watervliet NY 12189	800-252-8589	518-273-5800	183
Bondhus Corp 1400 E Broadway St PO Box 660 ... Monticello MN 55362 *Cust Svc	800-328-8310*	763-295-2162	748
Bone Bank Allografts 4808 Research Dr ... San Antonio TX 78240 *Sales	800-397-0088*	210-696-7616	538
Bonfit America Inc 8460 Higuera St ... Culver City CA 90232	800-526-6348	310-204-7880	561
Bonhams & Butterfields 220 San Bruno Ave ... San Francisco CA 94103	800-223-2854	415-861-7500	50
Bonita Pioneer Packaging Products Inc 7333 SW Bonita Rd ... Portland OR 97224	800-677-7725		64
Bonita Springs Area Chamber of Commerce 25071 Chamber of Commerce Dr ... Bonita Springs FL 34135	800-226-2943	239-992-2943	137
Bonland Industries Inc 50 Newark-Pompton Tpke ... Wayne NJ 07470	800-232-6600	973-694-3211	190-12
Bonneville Billing & Collection Inc 1186 East 4600 South Ste 100 ... Ogden UT 84403	888-621-7880	801-621-7880	158
Bonnie Castle Resort 31 Holland St ... Alexandria Bay NY 13607	800-955-4511	315-482-4511	660
Bonnie Lure State Recreation Area 11321 SW Terwilliger Blvd ... Portland OR 97219	800-551-6949		558
Bon-Ton Stores Inc 2801 E Market St ... York PA 17402 NASDAQ: BONT	800-945-4438	717-757-7660	229
Book House Inc, The 208 W Chicago St ... Jonesville MI 49250	800-248-1146		95
Book Marketing Update P O Box 2887 ... Taos NM 87571	888-468-7386	575-751-3398	524-10
Book Passage 51 Tamal Vista Blvd ... Corte Madera CA 94925	800-999-7909	415-927-0960	95
Book Soup 8818 Sunset Blvd ... West Hollywood CA 90069	888-527-8238	310-659-3110	95
Bookazine Company Inc 75 Hook Rd ... Bayonne NJ 07002	800-221-8112	201-339-7777	94
Booklist Magazine 50 E Huron St ... Chicago IL 60611	800-545-2433		452-11
BookPal LLC 18101 Von Karman Ave Ste 1240 ... Irvine CA 92612	866-522-6657		95
BookPeople 603 N Lamar ... Austin TX 78703	800-853-9757	512-472-5050	95
Books on the Square 471 Angell St ... Providence RI 02906	888-669-9660	401-331-9097	95
Books-A-Million Inc 402 Industrial Ln ... Birmingham AL 35211 NASDAQ: BAMM	800-201-3550	205-942-3737	95
BookSense.com 200 White Plains Rd ... Tarrytown NY 10591	800-637-0037	914-631-2415	95
Booksource Inc 1230 Macklind Ave ... Saint Louis MO 63110	800-444-0435	314-647-0600	94
Boomer Consulting 610 Humboldt St ... Manhattan KS 66502	800-739-9998	785-537-2358	195
Boomers & Beyond Inc 1998 Ruffin Mill Rd ... Colonial Heights VA 23834	800-958-8324	804-524-9888	196
Boomtown Casino & Hotel Reno 2100 Garson Rd ... Verdi NV 89439 *Resv	800-648-3790*	775-345-6000	132
Boomtown Casino Biloxi 676 Bayview Ave ... Biloxi MS 39530	800-627-0777	228-435-7000	132
Boomtown Casino New Orleans 4132 Peters Rd ... Harvey LA 70058	800-366-7711	504-366-7711	132
Boomtown Inc 2100 Garson Rd ... Verdi NV 89439	800-648-3790	775-345-6000	131

Name / Address	City	State	Zip	Toll-Free	Phone	Class
Boone County National Bank 720 E Broadway PO Box 678	Columbia	MO	65201	**800-842-2262**	573-874-8535	69
Boone County Rural Electric Membership Corp 1207 Indianapolis Ave	Lebanon	IN	46052	**800-897-7362**	765-482-2390	245
Boone Electric Co-op 1413 Rangeline St	Columbia	MO	65201	**800-225-8143**	573-449-4181	245
Boone Tavern Hotel of Berea College 100 S Main St	Berea	KY	40403	**800-366-9358**	859-985-3700	376
Boonville Correctional Ctr 1216 E Morgan St	Boonville	MO	65233	**800-392-8486**	660-882-6521	213
Boos Dental Laboratory 1000 Boone Ave N Ste 660	Golden Valley	MN	55427	**800-333-2667**	763-544-1446	412
Boostability Inc 2600 West Executive Pkwy Ste 200	Lehi	UT	84043	**800-261-1537**		5
Booth Michigan 169 Monroe Ave Ste 100	Grand Rapids	MI	49503	**800-886-5529**	800-878-1400	628-8
Booth Theatre 222 W 45th St	New York	NY	10036	**800-432-7780**	212-239-6200	736
Booz Allen Hamilton Inc 8283 Greensboro Dr	McLean	VA	22102	**866-390-3908**	703-902-5000	195
BOP (Brookfield Properties Corp) 181 Bay St Ste 330 *NYSE: BPO*	Toronto	ON	M5J2T3	**800-387-0825**	416-369-2300	646
Boral Bricks Inc 9143 Bob Williams Pkwy	Covington	GA	30014	**800-526-7255**	678-625-4051	148
Border States Electric Supply 105 25th St N	Fargo	ND	58102	**800-800-0199**	701-293-5834	246
Borderland Tours 2550 W Calle Padilla	Tucson	AZ	85745	**800-525-7753**	520-882-7650	750
Boreal Genomics Inc 5150 El Camino Real	Los Altos	CA	94022	**800-681-5644**	604-822-8268	231
Borgata Hotel Casino & Spa 1 Borgata Way	Atlantic City	NJ	08401	**877-786-9900**	609-317-1000	376
Borla Performance Industries Inc 500 Borla Dr	Johnson City	TN	37604	**877-462-6752**	423-979-4000	59
Born Free USA United with Animal Protection Institute 1122 S St	Sacramento	CA	95814	**800-348-7387**	916-447-3085	47-3
Born Into It Inc 185 New Boston St	Woburn	MA	01801	**800-560-2840**	781-491-0707	155-6
Borough of Manhattan Community College 199 Chambers St Rm S-300	New York	NY	10007	**877-222-8387**	212-220-1265	160
Borroughs Corp 3002 N Burdick St	Kalamazoo	MI	49004	**800-748-0227**	269-342-0161	286
Borsheim's Inc 120 Regency Pkwy	Omaha	NE	68114	**800-642-4438**	402-391-0400	407
Bosch Rexroth PO Box 394	Wooster	OH	44691	**800-739-7684**	330-263-3300	778
Bosch Rexroth Corp 5150 Prairie Stone Pkwy	Hoffman Estates	IL	60192	**800-860-1055**	847-645-3600	511
Bosch Rexroth Corp Piston Pump Div 8 Southchase Ct	Fountain Inn	SC	29644	**877-266-7811**	864-967-2777	631
Bosch Security Systems 130 Perinton Pkwy	Fairport	NY	14450	**800-289-0096**	585-223-4060	683
Bose Corp The Mountain *Sales	Framingham	MA	01701	**800-379-2073***	508-766-1099	51
Boss Chair Inc 5353 Jillson St	Commerce	CA	90040	**800-593-1888**	323-262-1919	320
Bosshardt Realty Services LLC 5542 NW 43rd St	Gainesville	FL	32653	**800-284-6110**	352-371-6100	643
Bossier Chamber of Commerce 710 Benton Rd	Bossier City	LA	71111	**888-414-2695**	318-746-0252	137
Bossier Civic Ctr 620 Benton Rd	Bossier City	LA	71111	**800-522-4842**	318-741-8900	206
Bostik Inc 11320 Watertown Plank Rd	Wauwatosa	WI	53226	**800-726-7845**	414-774-2250	3
Boston Academy of English 38 Chauncy St Eighth Fl	Boston	MA	02111	**800-704-9313**		420
Boston Academy of English inc 38 Chauncy St 8th Fl	Boston	MA	02111	**800-704-9313**		420
Boston Advisors Inc One Liberty Sq 10th Fl	Boston	MA	02109	**800-523-5903**	617-348-3100	398
Boston Architectural College 320 Newbury St	Boston	MA	02115	**877-585-0100**	617-262-5000	788
Boston Beer Co One Design Ctr Pl Ste 850 *NYSE: SAM*	Boston	MA	02210	**888-661-2337**	617-368-5000	101
Boston College 140 Commonwealth Ave	Chestnut Hill	MA	02467	**800-360-2522**	617-552-3100	166
Boston College Law School 885 Centre St	Newton	MA	02459	**800-321-2211**	617-552-8550	167-1
Boston Duck Tours Ltd Four Copley Pl Ste 310	Boston	MA	02116	**800-226-7442**	617-450-0065	750
Boston Financial Data Services 2000 Crown Colony Dr	Quincy	MA	02169	**888-772-2337**	617-483-5000	398
Boston Group 400 Riverside Ave	Medford	MA	02155	**800-225-1633**		286
Boston Harbor Hotel 70 Rowes Wharf	Boston	MA	02110	**800-752-7077**	617-439-7000	376
Boston Harbor Islands National Recreation Area 408 Atlantic Ave Ste 228	Boston	MA	02110	**877-874-2478**	617-223-8666	557
Boston Language Institute Inc 648 Beacon St Kenmore Sq	Boston	MA	02215	**877-998-3500**	617-262-3500	758
Boston Market Corp 14103 Denver W Pkwy *General	Golden	CO	80401	**800-877-2870***	303-278-9500	661
Boston Mutual Life Insurance Co 120 Royall St	Canton	MA	02021	**800-669-2668**	781-463-6068	388-2
Boston Park Plaza Hotel & Towers 50 Pk Plz	Boston	MA	02116	**800-225-2008**	617-426-2000	376
Boston Pizza Restaurants LP 1501 LBJ Fwy Ste 450	Dallas	TX	75234	**866-277-8721**	972-484-9022	661
Boston Pops 301 Massachusetts Ave Symphony Hall	Boston	MA	02115	**888-266-1200**	617-266-1492	566-3
Boston Private Financial Holdings Inc 10 Post Office Sq *NASDAQ: BPFH*	Boston	MA	02109	**855-738-8916**	617-912-1900	357-2
Boston Sand & Gravel Company Inc 100 N Washington St PO Box 9187 *OTC: BSND*	Boston	MA	02114	**800-624-2724**	617-227-9000	183
Boston Scientific Corp One Boston Scientific Pl *NYSE: BSX*	Natick	MA	01760	**888-272-1001**	508-650-8000	471
Boston Symphony Hall 301 Massachusetts Ave	Boston	MA	02115	**888-266-1200**	617-266-1492	565
Boston Symphony Orchestra 301 Massachusetts Ave Symphony Hall	Boston	MA	02115	**888-266-1200**	617-266-1492	566-3
Boston University School of Law 765 Commonwealth Ave	Boston	MA	02215	**800-321-2211**	617-353-3100	167-1
Boston Warehouse Trading Corp 59 Davis Ave	Norwood	MA	02062	**888-923-2982**	781-769-8550	358
Boston Whaler Inc 100 Whaler Way	Edgewater	FL	32141	**877-294-5645**		89
Boston's Best Chimney Sweep 76 Bacon St *Cust Svc	Waltham	MA	02451	**800-660-6708***	781-893-6611	150
Bostwick-Braun Co PO Box 912	Toledo	OH	43697	**800-777-9640**	419-259-3600	348
Botanical Gardens at Asheville 151 WT Weaver Blvd	Asheville	NC	28804	**888-823-4622**	828-252-5190	96
Botanical Laboratories Inc 1441 W Smith Rd	Ferndale	WA	98248	**800-232-4005**	360-384-5656	576
Bott Radio Network 10550 Barkley St Ste 100	Overland Park	KS	66212	**800-875-1903**	913-642-7770	634
Bottom Line/Personal 281 Tresser Blvd Eighth Fl *Cust Svc	Stamford	CT	06901	**800-678-5835***	800-274-5611	524-6
Bottomline Technologies 325 Corporate Dr *NASDAQ: EPAY*	Portsmouth	NH	03801	**800-243-2528**	603-436-0700	179-1
Boulder Arts & Crafts 1421 Pearl St Mall	Boulder	CO	80302	**866-656-2667**	303-443-3683	455
Boulder Book Store 1107 Pearl St	Boulder	CO	80302	**800-244-4651**	303-447-2074	95
Boulder Convention & Visitors Bureau 2440 Pearl St	Boulder	CO	80302	**800-444-0447**	303-442-2911	207
Boulder Daily Camera 1048 Pearl St	Boulder	CO	80302	**800-783-1202**	303-442-1202	525-2
Boulder Mountain Lodge 91 Four Mile Canyon Rd	Boulder	CO	80302	**800-458-0882**	303-444-0882	376
Boulder Station Hotel & Casino 4111 Boulder Hwy	Las Vegas	NV	89121	**800-683-7777**	702-432-7777	132
Boulder Valley Credit Union Inc 5505 Arapahoe Ave	Boulder	CO	80303	**800-783-8850**	303-442-8850	219
Boulders Resort & Golden Door Spa 34631 N Tom Darlington Dr PO Box 2090	Carefree	AZ	85377	**888-579-2631**	480-488-9009	660
Bound to Stay Bound Books Inc (BTSB) 1880 W Morton Ave	Jacksonville	IL	62650	**800-637-6586**	217-245-5191	91
Bourbon & Boots Inc 419 Main St	North Little Rock	AR	72114	**855-623-3562**		681
Bourbon Orleans - A Wyndham Historic Hotel 717 Orleans St	New Orleans	LA	70116	**866-513-9744**	504-523-2222	376
Bourns Inc 1200 Columbia Ave	Riverside	CA	92507	**877-426-8767**	951-781-5690	617
Boutique Spa at the Ritz-Carlton Georgetown 3100 S St NW	Washington	DC	20007	**800-241-3333**	202-912-4175	698
Bovie Medical Corp 734 Walt Whitman Rd Ste 207 *NYSE: BVX*	Melville	NY	11747	**800-888-4999**	631-421-5452	250
Bowden Oil Company Inc PO Box 145	Sylacauga	AL	35150	**800-280-0393**	256-245-5611	315
Bowdoin College 5000 College Stn	Brunswick	ME	04011	**800-829-1040**	207-725-3000	166
BOWE Bell + Howell 760 S Wolf Rd	Wheeling	IL	60090	**800-220-3030**	847-675-7600	174-7
Bowhunting World Magazine 6121 Baker Rd Ste 101	Minnetonka	MN	55345	**800-766-0039**	952-405-2280	452-20
Bowie Industries Inc 1004 E Wise St	Bowie	TX	76230	**800-433-0934**	940-872-1106	273
Bowie State University 14000 Jericho Pk Rd	Bowie	MD	20715	**877-772-6943**	301-860-4000	166
Bowie-Cass Electric Co-op Inc 117 N St	Douglassville	TX	75560	**800-794-2919**	903-846-2311	245
Bowles Mattress Co Inc 1220 Watt St	Jeffersonville	IN	47130	**800-223-7509**	812-288-8614	466
Bowling Green Area Chamber of Commerce 710 College St	Bowling Green	KY	42101	**866-330-2422**	270-781-3200	137
Bowling Green State University 1001 E Wooster St	Bowling Green	OH	43403	**866-246-6732**	419-372-2531	166
Bowling Green State University Jerome Library (BGSU) 1001 E Wooster St	Bowling Green	OH	43403	**866-246-6732**	419-372-2051	431-6
Bowling Green Technical College 1845 Loop Dr	Bowling Green	KY	42101	**866-590-9238**	270-901-1000	788
Bowling Proprietors' Assn of America (BPAA) 621 Six Flags Dr PO Box 5802	Arlington	TX	76011	**800-343-1329**	817-649-5105	47-23
Bowman Hollis Manufacturing Inc 2925 Old Steele Creek Rd	Charlotte	NC	28208	**888-269-2358**	704-374-1500	733
Boyajian Inc 144 Will Dr *General	Canton	MA	02021	**800-965-0665***	781-828-9966	295-41
Boyce Thompson Arboretum 37615 US Hwy 60	Superior	AZ	85273	**877-763-5315**	520-689-2723	96
Boyce Thompson Arboretum State Park 37615 US Hwy 60	Superior	AZ	85273	**800-858-7378**	520-689-2811	558
Boyd Bros Transportation Inc 3275 Alabama 30	Clayton	AL	36016	**800-700-2693**	334-775-1400	770
Boyd Coffee Co 19730 NE Sandy Blvd *Cust Svc	Portland	OR	97230	**800-545-4077***	503-666-4545	295-7
Boyd Gaming Corp 3883 Howard Hughes Pkwy 9th Fl *NYSE: BYD*	Las Vegas	NV	89169	**800-522-4700**	702-792-7200	131
Boyden Caverns 74101 E Kings Canyon Rd	Kings Canyon National Park	CA	93633	**866-762-2837**	209-736-2708	49-4
Boyden World Corp 50 Broadway	Hawthorne	NY	10532	**877-226-9336**	914-747-0093	266
Boyds Collection Ltd 300 Frederick St	Hanover	PA	17331	**800-436-3726**	717-633-9898	327
Boyett Petroleum 601 McHenry Ave	Modesto	CA	95350	**800-545-9212**	209-577-6000	572

Name / Address	City	State	ZIP	Toll-Free	Phone	Class
Boyne Country Sports						
1200 Bay View Rd	Petoskey	MI	49770	**800-462-6963**	231-439-4906	702
Boyne Highlands Resort						
600 Highlands Dr	Harbor Springs	MI	49740	**800-462-6963**	231-526-3000	660
Boyne Mountain Resort						
11521 Huffman Lake Rd						
PO Box 91252	Boyne Falls	MI	49713	**800-462-6963**	231-549-6060	660
Boynton Beach Mall						
801 N Congress Ave	Boynton Beach	FL	33426	**877-746-6642**	561-736-7902	455
Boys & Girls Clubs of America						
1230 W Peachtree St NW	Atlanta	GA	30309	**800-995-3579**	404-487-5700	47-15
Boys Town						
14100 Crawford St	Boys Town	NE	68010	**800-448-3000**	402-498-1300	47-6
Bozzuto Group						
7850 Walker Dr Ste 400	Greenbelt	MD	20770	**866-698-7513***	301-220-0100	188
*General						
BP Canada Energy Co						
240 Fourth Ave SW	Calgary	AB	T2P2H8	**877-833-1359**	403-233-1359	529
BP Lubricants USA Inc						
1500 Valley Rd	Wayne	NJ	07470	**800-333-3991**	973-633-2200	534
BP MotorClub						
PO Box 4441	Carol Stream	IL	60197	**800-334-3300**		52
BP PLC						
28100 Torch Pkwy	Warrenville	IL	60555	**877-638-5672**	630-420-5111	573
NYSE: BP						
BPAA (Bowling Proprietors' Assn of America)						
621 Six Flags Dr PO Box 5802	Arlington	TX	76011	**800-343-1329**	817-649-5105	47-23
BPM Inc						
200 W Front St	Peshtigo	WI	54157	**800-826-0494**	715-582-4551	550
BPMLLP (Burr Pilger & Mayer LLP)						
600 California St						
Ste 1300	San Francisco	CA	94108	**866-312-4390**	415-421-5757	2
BPRR (Buffalo & Pittsburgh Railroad Inc)						
1200-C Scottsville Rd Ste 200	Rochester	NY	14624	**800-603-3385**	585-463-3307	639
BR 111 Exotic Hardwood Flooring						
1 NE 40th St	Miami	FL	33137	**800-525-2711**		3
BR Funsten & Co						
5200 Watt Ct Ste B	Fairfield	CA	94534	**888-261-2871**	209-825-5375	358
BR Kreider & Son Inc						
63 Kreider Ln	Manheim	PA	17545	**800-689-7651**	717-898-7651	190-5
Brackett Inc						
451 Forbes Field Bldg 451 J Ste	Topeka	KS	66619	**800-255-3506**	785-862-2205	621
Bradbury Company Inc						
1200 E Cole	Moundridge	KS	67107	**800-397-6394**	620-345-6394	451
Braden Mfg LLC						
5199 N Mingo Rd	Tulsa	OK	74117	**800-272-3360**		475
Braden Sutphin Ink Co						
3650 E 93rd St	Cleveland	OH	44105	**800-289-6872**	216-271-2300	385
Bradford Health Services						
2101 Magnolia Ave S Ste 518	Birmingham	AL	35205	**800-217-2849**	205-251-7753	717
Bradford School						
2469 Stelzer Rd	Columbus	OH	43219	**800-678-7981**	614-416-6200	788
Bradford White Corp						
725 Talamore Dr	Ambler	PA	19002	**800-523-2931**	215-641-9400	35
Bradley Academy for the Visual Arts						
1409 Williams Rd	York	PA	17402	**800-864-7725**	717-755-2300	162
Bradley Caldwell Inc						
200 Kiwanis Blvd	Hazleton	PA	18202	**800-257-9100***	570-455-7511	276
*Cust Svc						
Bradley Corp						
W 142 N 9101						
Fountain Blvd	Menomonee Falls	WI	53051	**800-272-3539**	262-251-6000	602
Bradley Inn						
3063 Bristol Rd	New Harbor	ME	04554	**800-942-5560**	207-677-2105	376
Bradley University						
1501 W Bradley Ave	Peoria	IL	61625	**800-447-6460***	309-676-7611	166
*Admissions						
Bradley University Cullom-Davis Library						
1501 W Bradley Ave	Peoria	IL	61625	**800-858-6843**	309-677-2850	431-6
Bradmark Technologies Inc						
4265 San Felipe St Ste 700	Houston	TX	77027	**800-621-2808**	713-621-2808	179-1
Brady Campaign to Prevent Gun Violence						
1225 'I' St NW Ste 1100	Washington	DC	20005	**800-732-0999**	202-898-0792	47-7
Brady Coated Products						
6555 W Good Hope Rd	Milwaukee	WI	53223	**800-662-1191**	414-358-6600	722
Brady Corp						
6555 W Good Hope Rd	Milwaukee	WI	53223	**800-541-1686***	414-358-6600	410
NYSE: BRC ■ *Cust Svc						
Brady Enterprises Inc						
167 Moore Rd	East Weymouth	MA	02189	**800-225-5126**	781-337-5000	295-15
Brady Identification Solutions						
6555 W Good Hope Rd	Milwaukee	WI	53223	**800-537-8791***	414-358-6600	179-1
*Cust Svc						
Brady Industries Inc						
7055 Lindell Rd	Las Vegas	NV	89118	**800-293-4698**	702-876-3990	403
Brady Marketing Co						
1331N California Blvd						
Ste 320	Walnut Creek	CA	94596	**800-326-6080**	925-676-1300	37
Braemar Inc						
1285 Corporate Ctr Dr	Eagan	MN	55121	**800-328-2719**	651-286-8620	471
Braille Institute of America Inc						
741 N Vermont Ave	Los Angeles	CA	90029	**800-272-4553**	323-663-1111	47-11
Braille Institute of America Library Services (BILS)						
741 N Vermont Ave	Los Angeles	CA	90029	**800-808-2555**	323-660-3880	431-3
Brain Injury Assn of America						
1608 Spring Hill Rd Ste 110	Vienna	VA	22182	**800-444-6443**	703-761-0750	47-17
Brainerd Compressor Rebuilders Inc						
3034 Sandbrook St	Memphis	TN	38116	**800-228-4138**		14
Brainerd Industries Inc						
680 Precision Ct	Miamisburg	OH	45342	**800-790-0430**	937-228-0488	478
Brainerd International Raceway						
5523 Birchdale Rd	Brainerd	MN	56401	**866-444-4455**	218-824-7223	508
Brainerd Lakes Area Chamber of Commerce						
124 N Sixth St PO Box 356	Brainerd	MN	56401	**800-450-2838**	218-829-2838	137
Brainerd Mfg Company Inc						
140 Business Pk Dr	Winston-Salem	NC	27107	**800-652-7277**	336-769-4077	347
BrainLAB Inc						
Three Westbrook Corp Ctr						
Ste 400	Westchester	IL	60154	**800-784-7700**	708-409-1343	379
Brainworks Software Inc						
100 S Main St	Sayville	NY	11782	**800-755-1111**	631-563-5000	179-1
Brake Supply Company Inc						
5501 Foundation Blvd	Evansville	IN	47725	**800-457-5788**	812-467-1000	382
Brakebush Bros Inc						
N4993 Sixth Dr	Westfield	WI	53964	**800-933-2121**	608-296-2121	612
Brakeley Briscoe Inc						
322 W Bellevue Ave Ste 204	San Mateo	CA	94402	**800-416-3086**	650-344-8883	316
Brakewell Steel Fabricator Inc						
55 Leone Ln	Chester	NY	10918	**888-914-9131**	845-469-9131	477
Brakke Consulting Inc						
2735 Villa Creek Ste 140	Dallas	TX	75234	**877-399-6354**	972-243-4033	195
Brame Specialty Company Inc						
PO Box 27	Durham	NC	27702	**800-533-2041**	919-683-1331	552
Branch Banking & Trust Company of South Carolina						
301 College St	Greenville	SC	29601	**800-226-5228**		69
Brand Energy & Infrastructure Services Inc						
1325 Cobb International Dr						
Ste A-1	Kennesaw	GA	30152	**855-746-4477**	678-285-1400	486
Branded Emblem Co Inc						
7920 Foster St	Overland Park	KS	66204	**800-448-2267**	913-648-0573	258
Brandeis University						
415 S St	Waltham	MA	02454	**800-622-0622**	781-736-3500	166
BrandEquity International						
2330 Washington St	Newton	MA	02462	**800-969-3150**		341
Brandes Investment Partners LP						
11988 El Camino Real Ste 500	San Diego	CA	92130	**800-237-7119**	858-755-0239	398
Brandmovers Inc						
590 Means St Ste 250	Atlanta	GA	30318	**888-463-4933**		623
Brandom Cabinets Co						
404 Hawkins St	Hillsboro	TX	76645	**800-366-8001***	512-805-0280	114
*Cust Svc						
BrandsMart USA Corp						
3200 SW 42nd St	Fort Lauderdale	FL	33312	**800-432-8579**		34
Brandtjen & Kluge Inc						
539 Blanding						
Woods Rd	Saint Croix Falls	WI	54024	**800-826-7320**	715-483-3265	621
Brandywine Capital Associates						
113 East Evans St	West Chester	PA	19380	**888-344-2920**	610-344-2910	398
Brandywine Conference & Visitors Bureau						
1501 N Providence Rd	Media	PA	19063	**800-343-3983**	610-565-3679	207
Brandywine Global Investment Management LLC						
2929 Arch St Eighth Fl	Philadelphia	PA	19104	**800-348-2499**	215-609-3500	398
Brandywine Investment Group Homalite Div						
11 Brookside Dr	Wilmington	DE	19804	**800-346-7802**	302-652-3686	593
Brandywine Realty Trust						
555 E Lancaster Ave Ste 100	Radnor	PA	19087	**866-426-5400**	610-325-5600	646
NYSE: BDN						
Brannan Paving Coltd						
111 Elk Dr PO Box 3403	Victoria	TX	77903	**800-626-7064**	361-573-3130	187
Brannen Banks Of Florida Inc						
PO Box 1929	Inverness	FL	34451	**866-546-8273**	352-726-1221	357-2
Branson's Best Reservations						
2875 Green Mtn Dr	Branson	MO	65616	**800-335-2555**	417-339-2204	373
Branson/Lakes Area Chamber of Commerce						
PO Box 1897	Branson	MO	65615	**800-214-3661**	417-334-4084	137
Branson/Lakes Area Lodging Assn						
PO Box 430	Branson	MO	65615	**877-781-1218**	417-332-1400	373
Bran-Zan Holdings Inc						
1548 Barclay Blvd	Buffalo Grove	IL	60089	**866-266-9670**		298
Brasfield & Gorrie LLC						
3021 Seventh Ave S	Birmingham	AL	35233	**800-239-8017**	205-328-4000	187
Brasher Motor Company of Weimar Inc						
1700 I- 10	Weimar	TX	78962	**800-783-1746**	979-725-8515	56
Brasseler USA						
One Brasseler Blvd	Savannah	GA	31419	**800-841-4522**		228
Brasstown Valley Resort						
6321 US Hwy 76	Young Harris	GA	30582	**800-201-3205**	706-379-9900	660
Braswell Food Co						
226 N Zetterower Ave	Statesboro	GA	30458	**800-673-9388**	912-764-6191	295-20
Brattleboro Area Chamber of Commerce						
180 Main St	Brattleboro	VT	05301	**877-254-4565**	802-254-4565	137
Brattleboro Memorial Hospital Inc						
17 Belmont Ave Ste 1	Brattleboro	VT	05301	**866-972-5266**	802-257-0341	371-3
Brauer Material Handling Systems Inc						
226 Molly Walton Dr	Hendersonville	TN	37075	**800-645-6083**	615-859-2930	382
Braun Intertec Corp						
11001 Hampshire Ave S	Bloomington	MN	55438	**800-279-6100**	952-995-2000	261
Brava LLC						
14221 SW 142nd St Ste 725	Miami	FL	33186	**800-422-5350**	305-856-4242	471
BRAVO | BRIO Restaurant Group						
777 Goodale Blvd Ste 100	Columbus	OH	43212	**888-452-7286**	614-326-7944	661
Bravo Sports Corp						
12801 Carmenita Rd	Santa Fe Springs	CA	90670	**800-234-9737***	562-484-5100	701
*Cust Svc						
Bray Real Estate						
637 N Ave	Grand Junction	CO	81501	**888-760-4251**	970-242-8450	643
Brazil						
Consulate General						
1233 W Loop S Ste 1150	Houston	TX	77027	**800-326-2289**	713-961-3063	257
Consulate General						
8484 Wilshire Blvd						
Ste 711	Beverly Hills	CA	90211	**877-782-5477**	323-651-2664	257
Brazilian Court, The						
301 Australian Ave	Palm Beach	FL	33480	**800-552-0335**	561-655-7740	376
Brazilian Travel Service (BTS)						
16 W 46th St Second Fl	New York	NY	10036	**800-342-5746**	212-764-6161	16
Brazos Urethane Inc						
1031 Sixth St N	Texas City	TX	77590	**866-527-2967**	409-965-0011	190-12
Brazosport College						
500 College Dr	Lake Jackson	TX	77566	**877-717-7873**	979-230-3000	160
Brazosport Facts						
720 S Main St	Clute	TX	77531	**800-864-8340**	979-265-7411	525-2
BRB Contractors Inc						
3805 NW 25th St	Topeka	KS	66618	**800-833-6747**	785-232-1245	189-10
BRB Publications Inc						
PO Box 27869	Tempe	AZ	85285	**800-929-3811**	480-829-7475	628-2
BRCC (Baton Rouge Community College)						
201 Community College Dr	Baton Rouge	LA	70806	**866-217-9823**	225-216-8000	160
BREA (Benton Rural Electric Assn)						
402 Seventh St PO Box 1150	Prosser	WA	99350	**800-221-6987**	509-786-2913	245
Bread for the World						
50 F St NW Ste 500	Washington	DC	20001	**800-822-7323***	202-639-9400	47-5
*Cust Svc						
Breakaway Tours						
3300 Bloor St Ste 1800	Toronto	ON	M8X2X2	**800-465-4257**	416-915-9880	750
Breakers at Waikiki, The						
250 Beach Walk	Honolulu	HI	96815	**800-426-0494**	808-923-3181	376

	City	State	ZIP	Toll-Free	Phone	Class
Breakers Hotel & Suites						
105 Second St	Rehoboth Beach	DE	19971	**800-441-8009**	302-227-6688	376
Breakers Resort						
3002 N Ocean Blvd	Myrtle Beach	SC	29577	**800-952-4507**	843-448-8082	660
Breakers Resort Inn						
16th & Oceanfront	Virginia Beach	VA	23451	**800-237-7532**	757-428-1821	660
Breakers, The						
One S County Rd	Palm Beach	FL	33480	**888-273-2537**	561-655-6611	660
Breakwater Inn						
1711 Glacier Ave	Juneau	AK	99801	**888-586-6303**	907-586-6303	376
BREC (Butler Rural Electric Co-op Inc)						
3888 Still-Beckett Rd	Oxford	OH	45056	**800-255-2732**	513-867-4400	245
Breckinridge County School District						
86 Airport Rd	Hardinsburg	KY	40143	**800-325-1713**	270-756-2186	676
Breeden Homes Inc						
366 E 40th Ave	Eugene	OR	97405	**800-870-1367***	541-686-9431	188
*Sales						
Breezy Point Resort						
9252 Breezy Pt Dr	Breezy Point	MN	56472	**800-432-3777**	218-562-7811	660
Breg Inc						
2611 Commerce Way Ste C	Vista	CA	92081	**800-897-2734**	760-599-3000	47-2
Breitburn Energy Partners LP						
515 S Flower St Ste 4800	Los Angeles	CA	90071	**800-732-0330**	213-225-5900	531
NASDAQ: BBEP						
Bremen Castings Inc						
500 N Baltimore St	Bremen	IN	46506	**800-837-2411**		306
Bremer Financial Corp						
2100 Bremer Tower						
445 Minnesota St	Saint Paul	MN	55101	**800-908-2265**	651-227-7621	68
Bremner Biscuit Co						
4600 Joliet St	Denver	CO	80239	**866-972-6879**	303-371-8180	295-9
Brenau University						
500 Washington St	Gainesville	GA	30501	**800-252-5119**	770-534-6299	166
Brendan Vacations						
21625 Prairie St	Chatsworth	CA	91311	**800-421-8446**	800-687-1002	750
Brenden Theatres						
531 Davis St	Vacaville	CA	95688	**877-638-3456**	707-469-0190	737
Brendle Sprinkler Co Inc						
3635 S Montgomery St	Tacoma	WA	98409	**800-392-8021**	334-270-8571	190-13
Brenham Wholesale Grocery Co						
602 W First St	Brenham	TX	77833	**800-392-4869**	979-836-7925	296-8
Brenham/Washington County Convention & Visitor Bureau						
314 S Austin St	Brenham	TX	77833	**888-273-6426**	979-836-3695	207
Brenner Tank LLC						
450 Arlington Ave	Fond du Lac	WI	54935	**800-558-9750**	920-922-5020	769
Brenntag Canada Inc						
35 Vulcan St	Rexdale	ON	M9W1L3	**866-516-9707**	416-243-9615	144
Brenntag Great Lakes LLC						
PO Box 444	Butler	WI	53007	**800-558-8501**	262-252-3550	144
Brenntag Mid-South Inc						
1405 Hwy 136 W	Henderson	KY	42419	**800-950-1727**	270-830-1200	144
Brenntag Pacific						
4545 Ardine St	South Gate	CA	90280	**800-732-0562**	323-832-5000	144
Brenntag Southeast Inc						
2000 E Pedigree St	Durham	NC	27703	**800-849-7000**	919-596-0681	144
Brenntag Southwest Inc						
610 Fisher Rd	Longview	TX	75604	**800-945-4528**	903-759-7151	144
Brent House Hotel						
1512 Jefferson Hwy	New Orleans	LA	70121	**800-535-3986**	504-842-4140	376
Brent's Place						
11980 E 16th Ave	Aurora	CO	80010	**800-895-1999**	303-831-4545	369
Brenton LLC						
4750 County Rd 13 NE	Alexandria	MN	56308	**800-535-2730**	320-852-7705	540
Brentwood A Behavioral Health Co						
1006 Highland Ave	Shreveport	LA	71101	**877-678-7500**	318-678-7500	371-5
Brescia University						
717 Frederica St	Owensboro	KY	42301	**877-273-7242***	270-685-3131	166
*Admissions						
Bresser's Cross Index Directory Co						
684 W Baltimore St	Detroit	MI	48202	**800-995-0570**	313-874-0570	628-6
Bretford Manufacturing Inc						
11000 Seymour Ave	Franklin Park	IL	60131	**800-521-9614**	847-678-2545	318-3
Brethren Press						
1451 Dundee Ave	Elgin	IL	60120	**800-441-3712**		628-3
Bretthauer Oil Co						
453 SW Washington St	Hillsboro	OR	97123	**800-359-3113**	503-648-2531	572
Brevard College						
One Brevard College Dr	Brevard	NC	28712	**800-527-9090***	828-883-8292	166
*Admissions						
Brevard Community College (BCC)						
Cocoa 1519 Clearlake Rd	Cocoa	FL	32922	**888-747-2802**	321-632-1111	160
Melbourne						
3865 N Wickham Rd	Melbourne	FL	32935	**888-747-2802**	321-632-1111	160
Palm Bay						
250 Community College Pkwy	Palm Bay	FL	32909	**888-747-2802**	321-632-1111	160
Titusville						
1311 N US 1	Titusville	FL	32796	**888-747-2802**	321-632-1111	160
Brevard County Tourism Development						
430 Brevard Ave Ste 150	Cocoa Village	FL	32922	**877-572-3224**	321-433-4470	207
Brevard Zoo						
8225 N Wickham Rd	Melbourne	FL	32940	**800-435-7352**	321-254-9453	810
Brevard-Transylvania Chamber of Commerce						
175 E Main St	Brevard	NC	28712	**800-648-4523**	828-883-3700	137
Brewer Co						
1354 US Hwy 50	Milford	OH	45150	**800-394-0017**	513-576-6300	45
Brewer-Cantelmo Company Inc						
55 W 39th St Ste 205	New York	NY	10018	**800-246-1233**	212-244-4600	448
Brewmatic Co						
20333 S Normandie Ave						
PO Box 2959	Torrance	CA	90509	**800-421-6860**	310-787-5444	297
Brewster Academy						
80 Academy Dr	Wolfeboro	NH	03894	**800-842-9961**	603-569-7200	615
Brewster Rocky Mountain Adventures						
PO Box 370	Banff	AB	T1L1A5	**800-691-5085**	403-762-5454	750
Brewster Travel Canada						
100 Gopher St PO Box 1140	Banff	AB	T1L1J3	**866-606-6700**	403-762-6700	750
Brewton-Parker College						
201 David-Eliza Fountain Cir Hwy 280						
PO Box 197	Mount Vernon	GA	30445	**800-342-1087**	912-583-2241	166
BRG (Business Resource Group)						
10440 N Central Expy Ste 1150	Dallas	TX	75231	**888-391-9166**	214-777-5100	195
Briar Cliff University						
3303 Rebecca St	Sioux City	IA	51104	**800-662-3303**	712-279-5321	166
Briarhurst Manor						
404 Manitou Ave	Manitou Springs	CO	80829	**877-685-1448**	719-685-1864	662
Briarwood College						
2279 Mt Vernon Rd	Southington	CT	06489	**800-952-2444**	860-628-4751	166
BRIC Engineered Systems Ltd						
1101 Wentworth St W Ste D1	Oshawa	ON	L1J8P7	**800-937-5135**	905-436-8867	256
Brice's Crossroads National Battlefield Site						
2680 Natchez Trace Pkwy	Tupelo	MS	38804	**800-305-7417**	662-680-4025	557
Brick Bodies Fitness Services Inc						
201 Old Padonia Rd	Cockeysville	MD	21030	**866-952-7425**	410-252-8058	351
Brick Industry Assn (BIA)						
1850 Centennial Pk Dr Ste 301	Reston	VA	20191	**866-644-1293**	703-620-0010	48-18
Brick Township Chamber of Commerce						
270 Chambers Bridge Rd	Brick	NJ	08723	**877-539-2020**	732-477-4949	137
Brickell Financial Services Motor Club Inc						
7300 Corporate Ctr Dr Ste 601	Miami	FL	33126	**800-262-7262**	305-392-4300	52
BrickKicker Inc						
849 N Ellsworth St	Naperville	IL	60563	**800-821-1820**	630-420-9900	362
Bricmont Inc						
500 Technology Dr						
Southpointe Industrial Pk	Canonsburg	PA	15317	**888-274-2462**	724-746-2300	261
Bridal Guide Magazine						
330 Seventh Ave 10th Fl	New York	NY	10001	**800-472-7744**	212-838-7733	452-11
Bridal Veil Falls State Scenic Viewpoint						
E Bridal Veil Rd PO Box 100	Bridal Veil	OR	97010	**800-551-6949**		558
Bridge Capital Holdings						
55 Almaden Blvd Ste 200	San Jose	CA	95113	**866-273-4265***	408-423-8500	357-2
NASDAQ: BBNK ■ *General						
Bridge Home Health & Hospice						
15100 Birchaven Ln	Findlay	OH	45840	**800-982-3306**	419-423-5351	368
Bridge Metrics LLC						
830 S Greenville Ave	Allen	TX	75002	**877-801-7158**		461
Bridgeline Digital						
80 BlanchaRd Rd	Burlington	MA	01803	**800-603-9936**	781-376-5555	181
Bridgepoint Education Inc						
13500 Evening Creek Dr N						
Ste 600	San Diego	CA	92128	**866-475-0317**	858-668-2586	242
NYSE: BPI						
BridgePort Brewing Co						
1318 NW Northrup St	Portland	OR	97209	**888-834-7546**	503-241-7179	101
Bridgeport News						
1000 Bridgeport Ave	Shelton	CT	06484	**855-247-8573***	203-926-2080	525-4
*Advestisement						
Bridger Valley Extreme Access						
40014 Business Loop 1-80						
PO Box 399	Mountain View	WY	82939	**800-276-3481**	307-786-2800	245
Bridgestone Americas Holding Inc						
535 Marriott Dr	Nashville	TN	37214	**877-201-2373***	615-937-1000	744
*Cust Svc						
Bridgestone Golf Inc						
15320 Industrial Pk Blvd NE	Covington	GA	30014	**800-358-6319**	770-787-7400	701
BridgeSTOR LLC						
18060 Old Coach Dr	Poway	CA	92064	**800-280-8204**	858-375-7076	174-8
Bridgewater College						
402 E College St	Bridgewater	VA	22812	**800-759-8328**	540-828-5375	166
Bridgewater Hotel						
723 First Ave	Fairbanks	AK	99701	**800-528-4916**		376
Bridgford Foods Corp						
1308 N Patt St	Anaheim	CA	92801	**800-854-3255**	714-526-5533	295-26
NASDAQ: BRID						
Bridon Cordage LLC						
909 E 16th St	Albert Lea	MN	56007	**800-533-6002**	507-377-1601	209
Briefing.com Inc						
401 N Michigan Ste 2910	Chicago	IL	60611	**800-752-3013***	312-670-4463	401
*General						
Brierley & Partners						
5465 Legacy Dr Ste 300	Plano	TX	75024	**800-899-8700**	214-760-8700	5
Briggs & Stratton Corp						
12301 W Wirth St	Milwaukee	WI	53222	**800-444-7774**	414-259-5333	262
NYSE: BGG						
Briggs Equipment						
10540 N Stemmons Fwy Ste 1525	Dallas	TX	75220	**800-606-1833**	214-630-0808	382
Briggs Industrial Equipment						
10550 N Stemmons Fwy	Dallas	TX	75220	**800-516-9206**	214-630-0808	382
Briggs Plumbing Products						
300 Eagle Rd	Goose Creek	SC	29445	**800-888-4458**		604
Brigham & Women's Hospital						
75 Francis St	Boston	MA	02115	**800-722-5520**	617-732-5500	371-7
Bright Chair Co						
51 Railroad Ave PO Box 269	Middletown	NY	10940	**888-524-5997**	845-343-2196	318-1
Bright Co-op Inc						
803 W Seale St	Nacogdoches	TX	75964	**800-562-0730**	936-564-8378	753
Bright Horizons Family Solutions LLC						
200 Talcott Ave S	Watertown	MA	02472	**800-324-4386**	617-673-8000	146
Bright Image Corp						
2830 S18th Ave	Broadview	IL	60155	**888-449-5656**		204
BrightMove Inc						
320 High Tide Dr # 201	Saint Augustine	FL	32080	**877-482-8840**		197
Brighton Hospital						
12851 E Grand River Ave	Brighton	MI	48116	**800-523-8198***	810-227-1211	717
*Cust Svc						
Brill Securities Inc						
152 W 57th St 16th Fl	New York	NY	10019	**800-933-0800**	212-957-5700	681
Brillacademic Publishers Inc						
2 liberty Sq 11th Fl	Boston	MA	02109	**800-337-9255**	617-263-2323	628-2
Brillio						
100 Town Sq Pl Ste 308	Jersey City	NJ	07310	**800-317-0575**		458
Brillion Iron Works Inc						
200 Pk Ave PO Box 127	Brillion	WI	54110	**855-320-0373**	920-756-2121	273
Bri-Mar Mfg LLC						
1080 S Main St	Chambersburg	PA	17201	**800-732-5845**	717-263-6116	769
Brine Inc						
32125 Hollingsworth Ave	Warren	MI	48092	**800-968-7845**		701
Brinjac Engineering Inc						
114 N Second St Ste 1	Harrisburg	PA	17101	**877-274-6526**	717-233-4502	261
Brink's Inc						
555 Dividend Dr Ste 100	Coppell	TX	75019	**800-274-6575**	469-549-6000	684
Brinker International Inc						
6820 LBJ Fwy	Dallas	TX	75240	**800-983-4637**	972-980-9917	661
NYSE: EAT						
Brinkmann Corp						
4215 McEwen Rd	Dallas	TX	75244	**800-527-0717**	972-770-8500	435
Brinly-Hardy Co						
3230 Industrial Pkwy	Jeffersonville	IN	47130	**800-626-5329**	812-218-7200	426

	Toll-Free	Phone	Class
Brisk Waterproofing Company Inc			
720 Grand Ave .... Ridgefield NJ 07657	800-325-2801	201-945-0210	190-7
BriskHeat Corp			
1055 Gibbard Ave .... Columbus OH 43201	800-848-7673	614-294-3376	317
Bristol Herald-Courier			
320 Bob Morrison Blvd .... Bristol VA 24201	888-228-2098	276-669-2181	525-2
Bristol Hotel			
1055 First Ave .... San Diego CA 92101	800-662-4477	619-232-6141	376
Bristol Memorial Works Inc			
797 King St .... Bristol CT 06010	888-987-7821	860-583-1654	715
Bristol Motor Speedway			
151 Speedway Blvd .... Bristol TN 37620	866-415-4158	423-989-6933	508
Bristol Products Corp			
700 Shelby St .... Bristol TN 37620	800-336-8775*	423-968-4140	153-1
*Orders			
Bristol Public Library			
5 High St .... Bristol CT 06010	877-603-7323	860-584-7787	431-3
Bristol, The			
200 Boylston St .... Boston MA 02116	800-819-5053	617-338-4400	662
Bristol-Myers Squibb Canada Inc			
2344 Alfred-Nobel Blvd Ste 300 .... Montreal QC H4S0A4	800-267-0005*	514-333-3200	576
*Cust Svc			
Bristow Alaska Inc			
1915 Donald Ave .... Fairbanks AK 99701	800-686-4080	907-452-1197	356
Brita Products Co			
1221 Broadway PO Box 24305 .... Oakland CA 94612	800-242-7482	510-271-7000	794
Britax Child Safety Inc			
13501 S Ridge Dr .... Charlotte NC 28273	888-427-4829	704-409-1700	63
Brite-Line LLC			
10660 E 51st Ave .... Denver CO 80239	888-201-6448		722
British Airways Executive Club			
PO Box 300743 .... Jamaica NY 11430	800-452-1201		26
British Airways PLC (BA)			
75-20 Astoria Blvd .... Flushing NY 11370	800-403-0882	347-418-4000	25
British Columbia Automobile Assn (BCAA)			
4567 Canada Way .... Burnaby BC V5G4T1	800-222-4357	604-268-5000	52
British Columbia's Women's Hospital & Health Centre			
4500 Oak St .... Vancouver BC V6H3N1	888-300-3088	604-875-2424	371-2
British Heritage Magazine			
19300 Promenade Dr .... Leesburg VA 20176	800-358-6327		452-14
British Standards Institution, The			
12110 Sunset Hills Rd Ste 200 .... Reston VA 20190	800-862-4977	703-437-9000	452-5
Brittany Pointe Estates			
1001 S Valley Forge Rd .... Lansdale PA 19446	800-504-2287	215-855-4109	663
Britton Lumber Company Inc			
Seven Ely Rd PO Box 389 .... Fairlee VT 05045	800-343-5300	802-333-4388	192-3
Brivo Systems LLC			
4350 E W Hwy Ste 201 .... Bethesda MD 20814	866-692-7486*	301-664-5242	683
*Tech Supp			
BRK Brands Inc			
3901 Liberty St Rd .... Aurora IL 60504	800-323-9005	630-851-7330	283
3901 Liberty St Rd .... Aurora IL 60504	800-323-9005	630-851-7330	739
BRMC (Bay Regional Medical Ctr)			
1900 Columbus Ave .... Bay City MI 48708	800-656-3950	989-894-3000	371-3
BRMC (Bluefield Regional Medical Ctr)			
500 Cherry St .... Bluefield WV 24701	800-994-6610	304-327-1100	371-3
Broad River Electric Co-op Inc			
811 Hamrick St .... Gaffney SC 29342	866-687-2667	864-489-5737	245
Broadband Dynamics LLC			
8757 E Via De Commercio .... Scottsdale AZ 85258	888-801-1034		384
Broadcast Education Assn (BEA)			
1771 N St NW .... Washington DC 20036	888-326-1415	202-429-3935	48-5
Broadcast Microwave Services Inc (BMS)			
12367 Crosthwaite Cir .... Poway CA 92064	800-669-9667	858-391-3050	224
Broadcom Corp			
5300 California Ave .... Irvine CA 92617	877-577-2726	949-926-5000	687
NASDAQ: BRCM			
Broadfield Distributing Inc			
67A Glen Cove Ave .... Glen Cove NY 11542	800-634-5178	516-676-2378	246
Broadhurst Theatre			
235 W 44th St .... New York NY 10036	800-447-7400	212-239-6200	736
Broadlawns Medical Ctr			
1801 Hickman Rd .... Des Moines IA 50314	866-904-5755	515-282-2200	371-3
Broadman & Holman Publishers			
127 Ninth Ave N MSN 114 .... Nashville TN 37234	800-448-8032		628-3
Broadmoor, The			
One Lake Ave .... Colorado Springs CO 80906	866-837-9520	719-577-5775	660
Broadview Networks Holdings Inc			
800 Westchester Ave Ste N-501 .... Rye Brook NY 10573	800-260-8766	914-922-7000	726
Broadway Ctr for the Performing Arts			
901 Broadway .... Tacoma WA 98402	800-291-7593	253-591-5890	565
Broadway Financial Corp			
4800 Wilshire Blvd .... Los Angeles CA 90010	800-227-0845	323-634-1700	357-2
NASDAQ: BYFC			
Broadway League, The			
729 Seventh Ave 5th Fl .... New York NY 10019	866-442-9878	212-764-1122	47-4
Broadway Mechanical			
873 81st Ave .... Oakland CA 94621	800-862-4930	510-746-4000	603
Broadway.com			
729 Seventh Ave .... New York NY 10019	800-762-3929	212-541-8457	740
Broan-NuTone LLC			
926 W State St PO Box 140 .... Hartford WI 53027	800-558-1711*	262-673-4340	36
*Cust Svc			
Brocade Communications Systems Inc			
130 Holger Way .... San Jose CA 95134	800-752-8061	408-333-8000	177
NASDAQ: BRCD			
Brock & Company Inc			
257 Great Vly Pkwy .... Malvern PA 19355	866-468-2783	610-647-5656	661
Brock Grain Systems			
611 N Higbee St P.O. Box 2000 .... Milford IN 46542	800-541-7900	574-658-4191	273
Brock Services LLC			
1675 Spindletop Rd .... Beaumont TX 77705	800-600-9675	409-833-7571	190-8
Brock Solutions Inc			
86 Ardelt Ave .... Kitchener ON N2C2C9	877-702-7625	519-571-1522	261
Brockway-Smith Co (BWAY)			
146 Dascomb Rd .... Andover MA 01810	800-225-7912	978-475-7100	494
Broco Inc			
10868 Bell Ct .... Rancho Cucamonga CA 91730	800-845-7259	909-483-3222	480
Brodart Co			
500 Arch St .... Williamsport PA 17701	800-233-8467	570-326-2461	179-10
Brodart Company Automation Div			
500 Arch St .... Williamsport PA 17701	800-233-8467	570-326-2461	628-10
Brodart Company Book Services Div			
500 Arch St .... Williamsport PA 17701	800-474-9816	570-326-2461	94
Brody School of Medicine at East Carolina University			
600 Moye Blvd .... Greenville NC 27834	800-722-3281	252-744-1020	167-2
Broedell Plumbing Supply Inc			
1601 Commerce Ln .... Jupiter FL 33458	888-328-2383	561-747-8000	605
Broich Enterprises Inc			
6440 City W Pkwy .... Eden Prairie MN 55344	800-853-3508	952-941-2270	656
Brokers Worldwide			
701C Ashland Ave .... Folcroft PA 19032	800-624-5287	610-461-3661	454
Brolite Products Inc			
1900 S Pk Ave .... Streamwood IL 60107	888-276-5483	630-830-0340	295-42
Bronco Billy's Casino			
233 E Bennett Ave			
PO Box 590 .... Cripple Creek CO 80813	877-989-2142	719-689-2142	132
Bronco Wine Co			
6342 Bystrum Rd .... Ceres CA 95307	855-874-2394	209-538-3131	79-3
Bronner Bros Inc			
2141 Powers Ferry Rd .... Marietta GA 30067	800-241-6151	770-988-0015	215
Bronson Methodist Hospital			
601 John St .... Kalamazoo MI 49007	800-276-6766	269-341-7654	371-3
Bronx Community College			
2155 University Ave .... Bronx NY 10453	866-888-8777	718-289-5100	160
Bronx Council on the Arts			
1738 Hone Ave .... Bronx NY 10461	866-564-5226	718-931-9500	455
Bronx Library Ctr			
310 E Kings Bridge Rd .... Bronx NY 10458	800-342-3688	718-579-4244	431-3
Bronx Psychiatric Ctr			
1500 Waters Pl .... Bronx NY 10461	800-597-8481	718-931-0600	371-5
Bronx Zoo			
2300 Southern Blvd .... Bronx NY 10460	800-433-4149	718-220-5100	810
BronxCare Family Wellness Center			
1276 Fulton Ave .... Bronx NY 10456	877-451-9361	718-590-1800	371-3
Bronze Craft Corp			
37 Will St .... Nashua NH 03060	800-488-7747	603-883-7747	347
Brook Furniture Rental Inc			
100 N Field Dr Ste 220 .... Lake Forest IL 60045	877-285-7368	847-810-4000	264-2
Brook Mays Music Co			
8605 John Carpenter Fwy .... Dallas TX 75247	800-637-8966*	214-631-0928	519
*Cust Svc			
Brookdale Community College			
765 Newman Springs Rd .... Lincroft NJ 07738	866-767-9512	732-842-1900	160
Brookdale Senior Living Inc			
111 Westwood Pl Ste 400 .... Brentwood TN 37027	866-785-9025	615-221-2250	663
Brooke Army Medical Ctr (BAMC)			
3551 Roger Brooke Dr .... Fort Sam Houston TX 78234	800-443-2262	210-916-4141	371-4
Brooke Distributors Inc			
16250 NW 52nd Ave .... Hialeah FL 33014	800-275-8792	305-624-9752	37
Brookfield Engineering Lab Inc			
11 Commerce Blvd .... Middleboro MA 02346	800-628-8139	508-946-6200	202
Brookfield Properties Corp (BOP)			
181 Bay St Ste 330 .... Toronto ON M5J2T3	800-387-0825	416-369-2300	646
NYSE: BPO			
Brookfield Public Library			
1900 N Calhoun Rd .... Brookfield WI 53005	866-868-3947	262-782-4140	431-3
Brookfield Suites Hotel & Convention Ctr			
1200 S Moorland Rd .... Brookfield WI 53005	800-444-6404	262-782-2900	376
Brookgreen Gardens			
1931 Brookgreen Dr .... Murrells Inlet SC 29576	800-849-1931	843-235-6000	96
Brookhaven-Lincoln County Chamber of Commerce			
230 S Whitworth Ave .... Brookhaven MS 39601	800-613-4667	601-833-1411	137
Brookings Institution			
1775 Massachusetts Ave NW .... Washington DC 20036	800-275-1447	202-797-6000	625
Brookline Bank			
PO Box 470469 .... Brookline MA 02445	877-668-2265*	617-730-3520	357-2
NASDAQ: BRKL ■ *Cust Svc			
Brooks Automation Inc			
15 Elizabeth Dr .... Chelmsford MA 01824	800-698-6149	978-262-2400	686
NASDAQ: BRKS			
Brooks Automation Inc Polycold Systems			
3800 Lakeville Hwy .... Petaluma CA 94954	800-698-6149	707-769-7000	14
Brooks Equipment Company Inc			
10926 David Taylor Dr Ste 300 .... Charlotte NC 28269	800-826-3473		670
Brooks Lake Lodge & Guest Ranch			
458 Brooks Lk Rd .... Dubois WY 82513	866-213-4022		239
Brooks Resources Corp			
409 NW Franklin Ave .... Bend OR 97701	877-475-9779	541-382-1662	644
Brooks Sports Inc			
19910 N Creek Pkwy Ste 200 .... Bothell WA 98011	800-227-6657		300
Brooks Tropicals Inc			
18400 SW 256th St			
PO Box 900160 .... Homestead FL 33090	800-327-4833	305-247-3544	314-4
Brooks Utility Products Group			
23847 Industrial			
Park Dr .... Farmington Hills MI 48335	888-687-3008	248-477-0250	630
Brookshire Bros Ltd			
1201 Ellen Trout Dr .... Lufkin TX 75904	855-467-7837	936-634-8155	342
Brookshire Suites			
120 E Lombard St .... Baltimore MD 21202	855-345-5033	410-625-1300	376
Brookside Gardens			
1800 Glenallan Ave .... Wheaton MD 20902	800-366-2012	301-962-1400	96
Brookside Resort			
463 E Pkwy .... Gatlinburg TN 37738	800-251-9597	865-436-5611	660
Brookstone Inc			
1 Innovation Way .... Merrimack NH 03054	800-846-3000*	603-880-9500	326
*Cust Svc			
Brookstown Inn			
200 Brookstown Ave .... Winston-Salem NC 27101	800-845-4262	336-725-1120	376
Brookstreet Hotel			
525 Legget Dr .... Ottawa ON K2K2W2	888-826-2220	613-271-1800	376
Brooksville Regional Hospital			
17240 Cortez Blvd .... Brooksville FL 34601	844-455-8708	352-796-5111	371-3
Brookwood Cos Inc			
25 W 45th St 11th Fl .... New York NY 10036	800-426-5468	212-551-0100	587
Broome Community College			
901 Front St .... Binghamton NY 13905	800-836-0689	607-778-5000	160
Bro-Tex Inc			
800 Hampden Ave .... Saint Paul MN 55114	800-328-2282	651-645-5721	501
Brother International Corp			
100 Somerset			
Corporate Blvd .... Bridgewater NJ 08807	877-552-6255*	908-704-1700	110
*Cust Svc			
Brotherhood Mutual Insurance Co (BMI)			
6400 Brotherhood Way			
PO Box 2589 .... Fort Wayne IN 46825	800-333-3735*		388-4
*Cust Svc			

Name / Address	City	State	ZIP	Toll-Free	Phone	Class
Brotherhood of Locomotive Engineers & Trainmen (BLET)						
1370 Ontario St						
Mezzanine Level	Cleveland	OH	44113	**877-772-5772**	216-241-2630	411
Brothers Inc						
1000 Sussex Blvd	Broomall	PA	19008	**866-276-7462**	610-328-0670	190-4
Broughton Foods Co						
1701 Green St	Marietta	OH	45750	**800-283-2479**	740-373-4121	295-27
Broussard Bros Inc						
25817 Louisiana Hwy 333	Abbeville	LA	70510	**800-299-5303**	337-893-5303	264-3
Broward Community College						
Downtown Ctr						
111 E Las Olas Blvd	Fort Lauderdale	FL	33301	**888-654-6482**	954-201-7350	160
North						
1000 Coconut Creek Blvd	Coconut Creek	FL	33066	**888-654-6482**	954-201-2240	160
Broward County Historical Commission						
151 SW Second St	Fort Lauderdale	FL	33301	**866-682-2258**	954-765-4670	513
Broward Ctr for the Performing Arts						
201 SW Fifth Ave	Fort Lauderdale	FL	33312	**877-311-7469**	954-462-0222	565
Broward Fire Equipment & Service Inc						
101 SW Sixth St	Fort Lauderdale	FL	33301	**800-866-3473**	954-467-6625	670
Brower Mechanical Inc						
4060 Alvis Ct	Rocklin	CA	95677	**800-360-9276**	916-624-0808	603
Brown & Bigelow Inc						
345 Plato Blvd E	Saint Paul	MN	55107	**800-628-1755***	651-293-7000	9
*Cust Svc						
Brown & Brown Insurance						
PO Box 1718	Tacoma	WA	98401	**800-562-8171**	253-396-5500	388-4
Brown & Haley						
PO Box 1596	Tacoma	WA	98401	**800-426-8400**	253-620-3085	295-8
Brown & Saenger						
711 W Russell St						
PO Box 84040	Sioux Falls	SD	57118	**800-952-3509**	605-336-1960	319
Brown Capital Management Inc						
1201 N Calvert St	Baltimore	MD	21202	**800-809-3863**	410-837-3234	398
Brown Coach Inc						
50 Venner Rd	Amsterdam	NY	12010	**800-424-4700**	518-843-4700	106
Brown College						
1345 Mendota						
Heights Rd	Mendota Heights	MN	55120	**888-574-3777**	651-905-3400	788
Brown College of Court Reporting & Medical Transcription (BCCR)						
1900 Emery St NW Ste 200	Atlanta	GA	30318	**800-849-0703**	404-876-1227	788
Brown County Convention & Visitors Bureau						
10 N Van Buren St PO Box 840	Nashville	IN	47448	**800-753-3255**	812-988-7303	207
Brown County Inn						
51 State Rd 46	Nashville	IN	47448	**800-772-5249**	812-988-2291	376
Brown County Rural Electric Assn						
24386 State Hwy 4 PO Box 529	Sleepy Eye	MN	56085	**800-658-2368**	507-794-3331	245
Brown Hotel, The						
335 W Broadway St	Louisville	KY	40202	**888-387-0498**	502-583-1234	376
Brown Jordan Co						
9860 Gidley St	El Monte	CA	91731	**800-743-4252**		318-4
Brown Machine LLC						
330 N Ross St	Beaverton	MI	48612	**877-702-4142**	989-435-7741	144
Fort Wayne						
3000 E Coliseum Blvd	Fort Wayne	IN	46805	**866-433-2289***	260-484-4400	788
*General						
Merrillville						
1000 E 80th Pl Ste 101N	Merrillville	IN	46410	**800-258-3321**	219-769-3321	788
Brown Mackie College						
Michigan City						
1001 E US Hwy 20	Michigan City	IN	46360	**800-519-2416**	219-877-3100	788
South Bend						
3454 Douglas Rd	South Bend	IN	46635	**800-743-2447**	574-237-0774	788
Brown Mackie College Atlanta						
4370 Peachtree Rd NE	Atlanta	GA	30319	**877-479-8419**	404-799-4500	788
Brown Mackie College Bettendorf						
2119 E Kimberly Rd	Bettendorf	IA	52722	**888-420-1652**	563-344-1500	788
Brown Mackie College Findlay						
1700 Fostoria Ave Ste 100	Findlay	OH	45840	**800-842-3687**	419-423-2211	788
Brown Mackie College Hopkinsville						
4001 Ft Campbell Blvd	Hopkinsville	KY	42240	**800-359-4753**	270-886-1302	788
Brown Mackie College Lenexa						
9705 Lenexa Dr	Lenexa	KS	66215	**800-635-9101**	913-768-1900	788
Brown Mackie College Louisville						
3605 Fern Vly Rd	Louisville	KY	40219	**800-999-7387**	502-968-7191	788
Brown Mackie College Miami						
3700 Lakeside Dr	Miramar	FL	33132	**866-505-0335**	305-341-6600	788
Brown Mackie College Northern Kentucky						
309 Buttermilk Pk	Fort Mitchell	KY	41017	**800-888-1445**	859-341-5627	788
Brown Mackie College Salina						
2106 S Ninth St	Salina	KS	67401	**800-365-0433**	785-825-5422	788
Brown Mfg Corp						
6001 E Hwy 27	Ozark	AL	36360	**800-633-8909**		273
Brown Palace Hotel						
321 17th St	Denver	CO	80202	**800-321-2599**	303-297-3111	376
Brown Stove Works Inc						
1422 Carolina Ave	Cleveland	TN	37320	**800-251-7485***	423-476-6544	35
*All						
Brown University Rockefeller Library						
10 Prospect St	Providence	RI	02912	**877-668-4493**	401-863-2162	431-6
Brown Wood Preserving Company Inc						
6201 Camp Ground Rd	Louisville	KY	40216	**800-537-1765**	502-448-2337	805
Brown Wood Products Co						
7040 N Lawndale Ave	Lincolnwood	IL	60712	**800-328-5858**		807
Brown's Wharf Inn						
121 Atlantic Ave	Boothbay Harbor	ME	04538	**800-334-8110**	207-633-5440	376
Browne & Co						
100 Esna Pk Dr	Markham	ON	L3R1E3	**866-306-3672**	905-475-6104	299
Browne-Halco Inc						
2840 Morris Ave	Union	NJ	07083	**888-289-1005**	973-232-1065	299
Brownell World Travel						
216 Summit Blvd Ste 220	Birmingham	AL	35243	**800-999-3960**	205-802-6222	761
Brown-Forman Corp						
850 Dixie Hwy PO Box 1080	Louisville	KY	40210	**800-831-9146**	502-585-1100	186
NYSE: BFB						
Brownstone Real Estate Co						
1840 Fishburn Rd	Hershey	PA	17033	**877-533-6222**	717-533-6222	643
Brownstown Electric Supply Company Inc						
690 E State Rd 250 PO Box L	Brownstown	IN	47220	**800-742-8492**	812-358-4555	775
Brown-Strauss Steel						
2495 Uravan St	Aurora	CO	80011	**800-677-2778***	303-371-2200	487
*Sales						
Brownsville Convention & Visitors Bureau						
650 Ruben M Torres Sr Blvd	Brownsville	TX	78521	**800-626-2639**	956-546-3721	207
Brownsville Herald, The						
1135 E Van Buren St	Brownsville	TX	78520	**800-488-4301**	956-542-4301	525-2
Browntrout Publishers Inc						
201 Continental Blvd	El Segundo	CA	90245	**800-777-7812**	310-607-9010	628-2
Broyhill Co						
One N Market Sq	Dakota City	NE	68731	**800-228-1003**	402-987-3412	273
Broyhill Furniture Industries Inc						
3483 Hickory Blvd	Hudson	NC	28638	**800-327-6944***	828-396-2361	318-2
*Cust Svc						
BRP Manufacturing Co						
637 N Jackson St	Lima	OH	45801	**800-858-0482**	419-228-4441	667
BRT Laboratories Inc						
400 W Franklin St	Baltimore	MD	21201	**800-765-5170**	410-225-9595	414
BRT Realty Trust						
60 Cutter Mill Rd Ste 303	Great Neck	NY	11021	**800-450-5816**	516-466-3100	502
NYSE: BRT						
Bruce & Merrilees Electric Co						
930 Cass St	New Castle	PA	16101	**800-652-5560**	724-652-5566	190-4
Bruce Foods Corp						
PO Drawer 1030	New Iberia	LA	70561	**800-299-9082**	337-365-8101	295-20
Bruce Fox Inc						
1909 McDonald Ln	New Albany	IN	47150	**877-336-9601**	812-945-3511	767
Bruel & Kjaer Instruments Inc						
2815 Colonnades Ct Ste A	Norcross	GA	30071	**800-332-2040**	770-209-6907	248
Brueton Industries Inc						
146 Hanse Ave	Freeport	NY	11520	**800-221-6783***	516-379-3400	318-2
*Cust Svc						
Brulin & Company Inc						
2920 Dr AJ Brown Ave	Indianapolis	IN	46205	**800-776-7149**	317-923-3211	143
Brundage Management Co Inc						
254 Spencer Ln	San Antonio	TX	78201	**800-531-7652**	210-735-9393	791-1
Brunswick & The Golden Isles of Georgia Visitors Bureau						
Four Glynn Ave	Brunswick	GA	31520	**800-933-2627**	912-265-0620	207
Brunswick Community College						
50 College Rd	Bolivia	NC	28422	**800-754-1050**	910-755-7300	160
Brunswick County Board of Education						
35 Referendum Dr	Bolivia	NC	28422	**800-662-7030**	910-253-2900	676
Brunswick County Chamber of Commerce						
4948 Main St	Shallotte	NC	28459	**800-426-6644**	910-754-6644	137
Brunswick Electric Membership Corp						
795 Ocean Hwy PO Box 226	Shallotte	NC	28459	**800-842-5871**	910-754-4391	245
Brunswick-Glynn County Regional Library						
208 Gloucester St	Brunswick	GA	31520	**800-222-6748**	912-267-1212	431-3
Bruss Co						
3548 N Kostner Ave	Chicago	IL	60641	**800-621-3882**	773-282-2900	296-9
Bry-Air Inc						
10793 SR 37 W	Sunbury	OH	43074	**877-427-9247**	740-965-2974	14
Bryan College						
721 Bryan Dr PO Box 7000	Dayton	TN	37321	**800-277-9522**	423-775-2041	166
Bryan LGH Medical Ctr East						
1600 S 48th St	Lincoln	NE	68506	**800-742-7844**	402-481-7333	371-3
Bryan Systems						
14020 US 20A Hwy	Montpelier	OH	43543	**800-745-2796**		770
Bryan/College Station Convention & Visitors Bureau (BCSCVB)						
715 University Dr E	College Station	TX	77840	**800-777-8292**	979-260-9898	207
Bryan-College Station Chamber of Commerce						
4001 E 29th St Ste 175	Bryan	TX	77802	**800-777-8292**	979-260-5200	137
Bryant & Stratton College						
Cleveland						
3121 Euclid Ave	Cleveland	OH	44115	**866-948-0571**	216-771-1700	788
Bryant & Stratton College Milwaukee						
310 W Wisconsin Ave Ste 500-E	Milwaukee	WI	53203	**866-948-0571**	414-276-5200	788
Bryant & Stratton College Richmond						
8141 Hull St Rd	Richmond	VA	23235	**866-948-0571**	804-745-2444	788
Bryant University						
1150 Douglas Pk	Smithfield	RI	02917	**800-622-7001***	401-232-6000	166
*Admissions						
Bryce Corp						
4505 Old Lamar Ave PO Box 18338	Memphis	TN	38118	**800-238-7277**	901-369-4400	541
BryCoat Inc						
207 Vollmer Ave	Oldsmar	FL	34677	**800-989-8788**	727-490-1000	543
BryLin Hospitals						
1263 Delaware Ave	Buffalo	NY	14209	**800-727-9546**	716-886-8200	371-5
Bryn Mawr Bank Corp						
801 Lancaster Ave	Bryn Mawr	PA	19010	**855-381-2631**	610-525-1700	357-2
NASDAQ: BMTC						
Bryn Mawr College						
101 N Merion Ave	Bryn Mawr	PA	19010	**800-262-2586***	610-526-5000	166
*Admissions						
Bryn Mawr Rehab Hospital						
414 Paoli Pike	Malvern	PA	19355	**888-876-8764**	484-596-5400	371-6
BSAC (Berkeley Sensor & Actuator Ctr)						
497 Cory Hall MC Ste 1774	Berkeley	CA	94720	**800-549-1002**	510-643-6690	659
BSC America Inc						
803 Bel Air Rd	Bel Air	MD	21014	**800-764-7400**		458
BSCAI (Building Service Contractors Assn International)						
401 N Michigan Ave Ste 2200	Chicago	IL	60611	**800-368-3414**	312-321-5167	48-13
BSI (Badger State Industries)						
3099 E Washington Ave						
PO Box 8990	Madison	WI	53708	**800-862-1086**	608-240-5200	622
BSI (Burner Systems International Inc)						
3600 Cummings Rd	Chattanooga	TN	37419	**800-251-6318**	423-822-3600	354
BSI (Building Service Inc)						
W222 N630 Cheaney Rd	Waukesha	WI	53186	**866-353-3600**	262-955-6400	390
BSM Wireless Inc						
75 International Blvd Ste 100	Toronto	ON	M9W6L9	**866-768-4771**	416-675-1201	683
BSN Medical Inc						
5825 Carnegie Blvd	Charlotte	NC	28209	**800-552-1157**	704-554-9933	472
BSQUARE Corp						
110 110th Ave NE Ste 200	Bellevue	WA	98004	**888-820-4500**	425-519-5900	179-2
NASDAQ: BSQR						
BSSB (Boiling Springs Savings Bank)						
25 Orient Way	Rutherford	NJ	07070	**888-388-7459**	201-939-5000	69
BT Americas Inc						
2160 E Grand Ave	El Segundo	CA	90245	**888-767-2988**	408-330-2700	391
BT Conferencing Inc						
150 Newport Ave. Ext,						
Ste 300	North Quincy	MA	02171	**866-770-8777**		357-3
BT Mancini Co Inc						
876 S Milpitas Blvd	Milpitas	CA	95035	**800-787-6381**	408-942-7900	190-12
BT Mancini Co Inc Brookman Div						
876 S Milpitas Blvd	Milpitas	CA	95035	**800-787-6381**	408-942-7900	187
BTA (Business Technology Assn)						
12411 Wornall Rd Ste 200	Kansas City	MO	64145	**800-325-7219**	816-941-3100	48-18

Alphabetical Section

Name / Address	Toll-Free	Phone	Class
BTC (Bledsoe Telephone Co-op Corp) 338 Cumberland Ave PO Box 609 . . . Pikeville TN 37367	888-382-1222	423-447-2121	726
Btd Mfg Inc 1111 13th Ave SE . . . Detroit Lakes MN 56501	866-562-3986		483
BTS (IEEE Broadcast Technology Society) 445 Hoes Ln . . . Piscataway NJ 08854	800-678-4333	732-562-5407	48-19
BTS (Brazilian Travel Service) 16 W 46th St Second Fl . . . New York NY 10036	800-342-5746	212-764-6161	16
BTS Asset Management Inc 420 Bedford St Ste 340 . . . Lexington MA 02420	800-343-3040		398
BTS USA Inc 300 Stamford Pl Ste 425 . . . Stamford CT 06902	800-445-7089	203-316-2740	195
BTSB (Bound to Stay Bound Books Inc) 1880 W Morton Ave . . . Jacksonville IL 62650	800-637-6586	217-245-5191	91
BTU International Inc 23 Esquire Rd . . . North Billerica MA 01862 *NASDAQ: BTUI*	800-998-0666	978-667-4111	686
Bubba Gump Shrimp Co LLC 2501 Seawall Blvd . . . Galveston TX 77550	800-552-6379	409-766-4952	661
Buca di Beppo 1204 Harmon Pl . . . Minneapolis MN 55403	866-328-2822	612-288-0138	661
Buca Inc 1204 Harmon Pl . . . Minneapolis MN 55403	866-328-2822	612-288-0138	661
Buchanan Automotive Group 50 Central Ave Ste 900 . . . Sarasota FL 34236	888-292-4883	941-364-9500	56
Buchanan Hauling & Rigging 4625 Industrial Rd . . . Fort Wayne IN 46825	888-544-4285	260-471-1877	770
Buchanan Ingersoll & Rooney PC 301 Grant St 1 Oxford Ctr 20th Fl . . . Pittsburgh PA 15219	800-444-6738	412-562-8800	425
Bucher & Christian Consulting Inc 10 W Market St Ste 1300 . . . Indianapolis IN 46204	866-363-1132	317-423-8980	195
Buck & Knobby Equipment Co 6220 Sterns Rd . . . Ottawa Lake MI 49267	855-213-2825	734-856-2811	264-3
Buck Chuck Co 2155 Traversefield Dr . . . Traverse City MI 49686	800-228-2825		488
Buck Distributing Company Inc 15827 Commerce Ct . . . Upper Marlboro MD 20774 *Cust Svc	800-750-2825*	301-952-0400	80-1
Buck Knives Inc 660 S Lochsa St . . . Post Falls ID 83854	800-326-2825	208-262-0500	222
Buck's Pizza Franchising Corp Inc PO Box 405 . . . Du Bois PA 15801	800-310-8848		661
Buck's Pocket State Park 393 County Rd 174 . . . Grove Oak AL 35975	800-760-4089	256-659-2000	558
Buckeye Business Products Inc 3830 Kelley Ave . . . Cleveland OH 44114	800-837-4323		620
Buckeye Container Inc 3350 Long Rd . . . Wooster OH 44691	800-968-6894	330-264-6336	99
Buckeye International Inc 2700 Wagner Pl . . . Maryland Heights MO 63043	800-321-2583	314-291-1900	149
Buckeye Nutrition 330 E Schultz Ave PO Box 505 . . . Dalton OH 44618	800-417-6460		442
Buckeye Pacific LLC 4386 SW Macadam Ave Ste 200 . . . Portland OR 97207	800-767-9191	503-274-2284	192-3
Buckeye Power Sales Company Inc 6850 Commerce Ct Dr PO Box 489 . . . Blacklick OH 43004	800-523-3587	614-861-6000	613
Buckeye Rural Electric Co-op PO Box 200 . . . Rio Grande OH 45674	800-231-2732	740-379-2025	245
Buckeye ShapeForm 555 Marion Rd . . . Columbus OH 43207	800-728-0776	614-445-8433	254
Buckhorn Inc 55 W Techne Ctr Dr . . . Milford OH 45150	800-543-4454	513-831-4402	200
Buckhorn Lake State Resort Park 4441 Kentucky Hwy 1833 . . . Buckhorn KY 41721	800-325-0058		558
Buckle Inc 2407 W 24th St . . . Kearney NE 68845 *NYSE: BKE*	800-626-1255	308-236-8491	155-4
Buckles-Smith 801 Savaker Ave . . . San Jose CA 95126	800-833-7362	408-280-7777	246
Buckley Industries Inc 1850 E 53rd St N . . . Wichita KS 67219	800-835-2779	316-744-7587	596
Buckley Powder Co 42 Inverness Dr E . . . Englewood CO 80112	800-333-2266	303-790-7007	268
Bucklin Tractor & Implement Co 115 W Railroad PO Box 127 . . . Bucklin KS 67834	800-334-4823	620-826-3271	273
Buckman Laboratories Inc 1256 N McLean Blvd . . . Memphis TN 38108	800-282-5626	901-278-0330	143
Buckner International 600 N Pearl St Ste 2000 20th Fl . . . Dallas TX 75201	800-442-4800	214-758-8000	47-6
Bucks County Conference & Visitors Bureau (BCCVB) 3207 St Rd . . . Bensalem PA 19020	800-836-2825	215-639-0300	207
Bucks County Water & Sewer Authority (BCWSA) 1275 Almshouse Rd . . . Warrington PA 18976	800-222-2068	215-343-2538	794
Buddy Moore Trucking Inc PO Box 10047 . . . Birmingham AL 35202	866-704-1598	205-949-2260	770
Buddy Rogers Music Inc 6891 Simpson Ave . . . Cincinnati OH 45239	800-536-2263	513-729-1950	519
Buddy's Home Furnishings 6608 E Adamo Dr . . . Tampa FL 33619	866-779-5085		264-2
Budget Blinds Inc 1927 N Glassell St . . . Orange CA 92865	800-800-9250	714-637-2100	86
Budget Finance Co 1849 Sawtelle Blvd . . . Los Angeles CA 90025	800-225-6267	310-696-4050	214
Budget Host International 2307 Roosevelt Dr . . . Arlington TX 76016	800-283-4678	817-861-6088	376
Budget Rent A Car System Inc Six Sylvan Way . . . Parsippany NJ 07054	800-527-0700	800-283-4382	125
Budget Suites of America 2770 N Hwy 360 . . . Grand Prairie TX 75050	866-877-2000	972-647-2500	376
Budgetext Corp 1936 N Shiloh Dr . . . Fayetteville AR 72704	800-621-4272	479-684-3300	431
Budreck Truck Lines Inc 8040 S Roberts Rd . . . Bridgeview IL 60455	800-621-0013	708-496-0522	187
Buehler Ltd 41 Waukegan Rd . . . Lake Bluff IL 60044 *Sales	800-283-4537*	847-295-6500	416
Buehler Moving & Storage 3899 Jackson St . . . Denver CO 80205	800-234-6683	303-388-4000	512
Buehner Block Co 2800 SW Temple . . . Salt Lake City UT 84115	800-999-2565	801-467-5456	184
Buena Park Convention & Visitors Office 6601 Beach Blvd . . . Buena Park CA 90621	800-541-3953		207
Buena Vista Palace Hotel & Spa 1900 N Buena Vista Dr . . . Lake Buena Vista FL 32830	866-397-6516		660
Buena Vista Regional Medical Ctr PO Box 309 . . . Storm Lake IA 50588	877-401-8030	712-732-4030	371-3
Buena Vista Suites 8203 World Ctr Dr . . . Orlando FL 32821 *Resv	800-537-7737*	407-239-8588	376
Buena Vista University 610 W Fourth St . . . Storm Lake IA 50588	800-383-9600	712-749-2253	166
Buettner Bros Lumber Co 700 Seventh Ave SW . . . Cullman AL 35055	800-500-0669	256-734-4221	804
Buffalo & Pittsburgh Railroad Inc (BPRR) 1200-C Scottsville Rd Ste 200 . . . Rochester NY 14624	800-603-3385	585-463-3307	639
Buffalo Bill's Resort & Casino 31900 Las Vegas Blvd S . . . Primm NV 89019	888-386-7867	702-386-7867	132
Buffalo Bills Ralph Wilson Stadium 1 Bills Dr . . . Orchard Park NY 14127	877-228-4257	716-648-1800	706-3
Buffalo Crushed Stone Co Inc 2544 Clinton St . . . Buffalo NY 14224	800-543-3860	716-826-7310	495
Buffalo Games Inc 220 James E Casey Dr . . . Buffalo NY 14206	855-895-4290		752
Buffalo General Hospital 100 High St . . . Buffalo NY 14203	800-506-6480	716-859-5600	371-3
Buffalo Hotel Supply Company Inc 375 Commerce Dr . . . Amherst NY 14228	800-333-1678	716-691-8080	299
Buffalo Industries Inc 99 S Spokane St . . . Seattle WA 98134	800-683-0052	206-682-9900	734-8
Buffalo Museum of Science 1020 Humboldt Pkwy . . . Buffalo NY 14211	866-291-6660	716-896-5200	513
Buffalo News One News Plz PO Box 100 . . . Buffalo NY 14240	800-777-8640	716-849-4444	525-2
Buffalo Niagara Convention & Visitors Bureau 617 Main St Ste 200 . . . Buffalo NY 14203	800-283-3256	716-852-2356	207
Buffalo Niagara Convention Ctr 153 Franklin St Convention Ctr Plz . . . Buffalo NY 14202	800-995-7570	716-855-5555	206
Buffalo Niagara Partnership 665 Main St Ste 200 . . . Buffalo NY 14203	800-241-0474	716-852-7100	137
Buffalo Psychiatric Ctr 400 Forest Ave . . . Buffalo NY 14213	800-597-8481	716-885-2261	371-5
Buffalo Rock Co 111 Oxmoor Rd . . . Birmingham AL 35209	800-822-9799	205-942-3435	80-2
Buffalo Sabres HSBC Arena 1 Seymour H Knox III Plz . . . Buffalo NY 14203	888-467-2273	716-855-4100	707
Buffalo Spree Magazine 100 Corporate Pkwy Ste 220 . . . Buffalo NY 14226	855-697-7733	716-783-9119	452-22
Buffalo Supply Inc 1650A Coal Creek Dr . . . Lafayette CO 80026	800-366-1812		238
Buffalo Wire Works Co 1165 Clinton St . . . Buffalo NY 14206	800-828-7028	716-826-4666	679
Buffalo's Franchise Concepts Inc 9606 Santa Monica Blvd Ste 105 . . . Beverly Hills CA 90210	800-459-4647	310-402-0606	661
Buglisi Dance Theatre 229 W 42nd St Ste 502 . . . New York NY 10036	800-754-0797	212-719-3301	566-1
BUG-O Systems Inc 161 Hillpointe Dr . . . Canonsburg PA 15317	800-245-3186	412-331-1776	798
Buhler Inc 13105 12th Ave N . . . Plymouth MN 55441	800-722-7483	763-847-9900	202
Buhler Versatile Inc 1260 Clarence Ave . . . Winnipeg MB R3T1T2	888-524-1003	204-661-8711	273
Build-A-Bear Workshop Inc 1954 Innerbelt Business Ctr Dr . . . Saint Louis MO 63114 *NYSE: BBW*	888-560-2327	314-423-8000	751
Builder Magazine 1 Thomas Cir NW Ste 600 . . . Washington DC 20005	800-325-6180	202-452-0800	452-21
Builders General Supply Co 15 Sycamore Ave . . . Little Silver NJ 07739	800-570-7227		192-3
Builders Hardware & Supply Company Inc 1516 15th Ave W PO Box C-79005 . . . Seattle WA 98119	800-828-1437	206-281-3700	348
Builders Redi-Mix Inc 30701 W 10 Mile Rd Ste 500 PO Box 2900 . . . Farmington Hills MI 48333	888-988-4400		183
Building & Construction Trades Dept AFL-CIO 815 16th St NW Ste 600 . . . Washington DC 20006	800-772-1213	202-347-1461	48-3
Building 19 Inc 319 Lincoln St . . . Hingham MA 02043	800-225-5061	781-749-6900	779
Building Design & Construction Magazine 3030 W Salt Creek Ln Ste 201 . . . Arlington Heights IL 60005	888-811-3288	847-391-1000	452-21
Building Owners & Managers Assn International (BOMA) 1101 15th St NW Ste 800 . . . Washington DC 20005	800-426-6292	202-408-2662	48-17
Building Performance Institute Inc 107 Hermes Rd Ste 110 . . . Malta NY 12020	877-274-1274	518-899-2727	195
Building Products Corp 950 Freeburg Ave . . . Belleville IL 62220	800-233-1996	618-233-4427	183
Building Products Plus 12317 Almeda Rd . . . Houston TX 77045	800-460-8627		805
Building Service Contractors Assn International (BSCAI) 401 N Michigan Ave Ste 2200 . . . Chicago IL 60611	800-368-3414	312-321-5167	48-13
Building Service Inc (BSI) W222 N630 Cheaney Rd . . . Waukesha WI 53186	866-353-3600	262-955-6400	390
Bulgaria Embassy 1621 22nd St NW . . . Washington DC 20008	800-961-6836	202-387-0174	257
Bulk Lift International Inc (BLI) 1013 Tamarac Dr . . . Carpentersville IL 60110	800-879-2247	847-428-6059	66
Bulk Transit Corp 7177 Industrial Pkwy . . . Plain City OH 43064	800-345-2855	614-873-4632	770
Bulkmatic Transport Co 2001 N Cline Ave . . . Griffith IN 46319	800-535-8505		770
Bulk-pack Inc 1025 N Ninth St . . . Monroe LA 71201	800-498-4215	318-387-3260	99
Bull Moose Tube Co 1819 Clarkson Rd Ste 100 . . . Chesterfield MO 63017	800-325-4467	636-537-2600	485
Bull Wealth Management Group Inc 4100 Yonge St Ste 612 . . . Toronto ON M2P2B5	866-623-2053	416-223-2053	681
Bullard Abrasives Inc Six Carol Dr . . . Lincoln RI 02865	800-227-4469	401-333-3000	1
Bullard Co 1898 Safety Way . . . Cynthiana KY 41031	800-227-0423	859-234-6611	569

	Toll-Free	Phone	Class
Bulldog Hiway Express			
3390 Buffalo Ave ....Charleston SC 29418	**800-331-9515**	843-744-1651	444
Bulldog Solutions LLC			
7600 N Capital of Texas Hwy Bldg C			
Ste 250 ....Austin TX 78731	**877-402-9199**		5
Bullen Cos			
1640 Delmar Dr PO Box 37 ....Folcroft PA 19032	**800-444-8900**	610-534-8900	149
Bullen Midwest			
900 E 103rd St ....Chicago IL 60628	**800-621-8553**	773-785-2300	143
Bulletin, The			
1777 SW Chandler Ave ....Bend OR 97702	**800-503-3933**	541-382-1811	525-2
Bullfrog Films Inc			
372 Dautrich Rd ....Reading PA 19606	**800-543-3764**	610-779-8226	507
Bullhead Area Chamber of Commerce			
1251 Hwy 95 ....Bullhead City AZ 86429	**800-987-7457**	928-754-4121	137
Bulloch & Bulloch Inc			
309 Cash Memorial Blvd ....Forest Park GA 30297	**800-339-8177**	404-762-5063	25
Bullock Creek Public Schools			
1420 S Badour Rd ....Midland MI 48640	**877-706-2508**	989-631-9022	676
Bullseye Glass Co			
3722 SE 21st Ave ....Portland OR 97202	**888-220-3002**	503-232-8887	328
Bulova Corp			
1 Bulova Ave ....Woodside NY 11377	**800-228-5682**	718-204-3300	151
Bumble Bee Seafoods Inc			
9655 Granite Ridge Dr Ste 100...San Diego CA 92123	**800-800-8572**	858-715-4000	295-13
Bunker Hill Community College			
Charlestown			
250 New Rutherford Ave ....Boston MA 02129	**877-218-8829**	617-228-2000	160
Bunn-O-Matic Corp			
1400 Stevenson Dr ....Springfield IL 62703	**800-637-8606**	217-529-6601	36
Bunting Bearings Corp			
1001 Holland Pk Blvd ....Holland OH 43528	**888-286-8464**	419-866-7000	307
Bunting Magnetics Co			
500 S Spencer Ave ....Newton KS 67114	**800-835-2526**	316-284-2020	480
Burch Fabrics Group			
4200 Brockton Dr SE ....Grand Rapids MI 49512	**800-841-8111**	616-698-2800	587
Burchell Nursery Inc, The			
12000 Hwy 120 ....Oakdale CA 95361	**800-828-8733**	209-845-8733	292
Burchfield Group Inc, The			
1295 Northland Dr Ste 350........St Paul MN 55120	**800-778-1359**	651-389-5640	195
Burco Molding Inc			
15015 Herriman Blvd ....Noblesville IN 46060	**888-883-6656**	317-773-5699	601
Burd & Fletcher			
3000 W Geospace Dr ....Independence MO 64056	**800-821-2776**	816-257-0291	100
Bureau of Consular Affairs			
2201 C St NW SA-29 ....Washington DC 20520	**888-407-4747**	202-501-4444	338-14
Office of Children's Issues			
SA-17 9th Fl ....Washington DC 20522	**888-407-4747**	202-501-4444	338-14
Passport Services			
1111 19th St NW Ste 500........Washington DC 20524	**888-874-7793**	877-487-2778	338-14
Bureau of Engraving & Printing			
14th & C Sts SW ....Washington DC 20228	**877-874-4114**		338-16
Bureau of Indian Affairs Regional Offices (BIA)			
Alaska Region			
3601 C St Ste 1100 ....Anchorage AK 99503	**800-645-8397**	907-271-1536	338-11
Bureau of Land Management			
National Wild Horse & Burro Program			
1849 C Street NW Rm. 5665 ......Washington DC 20240	**866-468-7826**	202-208-3801	338-11
Bureau of National Affairs Inc			
1801 S Bell St ....Arlington VA 22202	**800-372-1033**	703-341-3000	628-2
Bureau of National Affairs Inc BNA Books Div			
1801 S Bell St ....Arlington VA 22202	**800-372-1033***	703-341-3500	628-2
*Sales			
Bureau of the Public Debt			
TreasuryDirect			
PO Box 7015 ....Parkersburg WV 26106	**800-722-2678**	304-480-7711	338-16
Burger King Corp			
5505 Blue Lagoon Dr ....Miami FL 33126	**855-673-3725**	305-378-3000	661
Burger's Ozark Country Cured Hams Inc			
32819 hwy 87 ....California MO 65018	**800-203-4424**	573-796-3134	295-26
Burgerville USA			
109 W 17th St ....Vancouver WA 98660	**888-827-8369**	360-694-1521	661
Burgess & Niple Inc			
5085 Reed Rd ....Columbus OH 43220	**800-282-1761**	614-459-2050	261
Burgess Industries Inc (BII)			
7500 Boone Ave N Ste 111...Brooklyn Park MN 55428	**800-233-2589**	763-553-7800	621
Burgess Pigment Company Inc			
525 Beck Blvd PO Box 349........Sandersville GA 31082	**800-841-8999**	478-552-2544	495
Burgett Floral Inc			
868 Fuller NE ....Grand Rapids MI 49503	**800-404-2999**	616-456-1999	366
Burkart-Phelan Inc			
2 Shaker Rd Ste D-107 ....Shirley MA 01464	**800-236-4343**	978-425-4500	520
Burke & Herbert Bank & Trust Co			
100 S Fairfax St ....Alexandria VA 22314	**877-440-0800**	703-751-7701	69
Burke Inc			
1800 Merriam Ln ....Kansas City KS 66106	**800-255-4147***		472
*Sales			
Burke International Tours Inc			
PO Box 890 ....Newton NC 28658	**800-476-3900**	828-465-3900	750
Burke Rehabilitation Hospital			
785 Mamaroneck Ave ....White Plains NY 10605	**888-992-8753**	914-597-2500	371-6
Burkhalter Travel Agency			
6501 Mineral Pt Rd ....Madison WI 53705	**800-556-9286**	608-833-5200	761
Burkhart Dental Supply Co			
2502 S 78th St ....Tacoma WA 98409	**800-562-8176***	253-474-7761	470
*Cust Svc			
Burkholder Paving			
621 Martindale Rd ....Ephrata PA 17522	**866-839-3426**	717-354-1340	45
Burkina Faso Embassy			
2005 Massachusetts Ave NW ....Washington DC 20008	**800-345-6541**	202-332-5577	257
Burklund Distributors Inc			
2500 N Main St Ste 3..........East Peoria IL 61611	**800-322-2876**	309-694-1900	296-3
Burks Tractor Co Inc			
3140 Kimberly Rd ....Twin Falls ID 83301	**800-247-7419**	208-733-5543	274
Burlington Coat Factory			
1830 Rt 130 N ....Burlington NJ 08016	**855-355-2875**	609-387-7800	359
Burlington College			
351 N Ave ....Burlington VT 05401	**800-862-9616**		166
Burlington Drug Co Inc			
91 Catamount Dr ....Milton VT 05468	**800-338-8703**	802-893-5105	231
Burlington Free Press			
100 Bank St ....Burlington VT 05401	**800-427-3124**	802-863-3441	525-2
Burlington Hawk Eye Co			
800 S Main St PO Box 10..........Burlington IA 52601	**800-397-1708**	319-754-8461	628-8

	Toll-Free	Phone	Class
Burlington Mall			
75 Middlesex Tpke ....Burlington MA 01803	**877-746-6642**	781-272-8667	455
Burlington Northern & Santa Fe Railway (BNSF)			
2650 Lou Menk Dr ....Fort Worth TX 76131	**800-795-2673**		639
Burlington Northern Santa Fe Corp (BNSF)			
500 New Jersey Ave NW			
Ste 550 ....Washington DC 20001	**800-964-9386**	202-347-8662	608
Burlington/Alamance County Convention & Visitors Bureau			
610 S Lexington Ave			
PO Box 519...................Burlington NC 27216	**800-637-3804**	336-570-1444	207
Burlington/West Burlington Area Chamber of Commerce			
610 N Fourth St Ste 200.............Burlington IA 52601	**800-827-4837**	319-752-6365	137
Burmax Co			
28 Barretts Ave ....Holtsville NY 11742	**800-645-5118**		75
Burndy LLC			
47 E Industrial Park Dr ....Manchester NH 03109	**800-346-4175**		802
Burner Systems International Inc (BSI)			
3600 Cummings Rd ....Chattanooga TN 37419	**800-251-6318**	423-822-3600	354
Burnett Dairy Co-op			
11631 SR- 70 ....Grantsburg WI 54840	**800-854-2716**	715-689-2468	295-5
Burns Engineering Inc			
10201 Bren Rd E ....Minnetonka MN 55343	**800-328-3871**	952-935-4400	256
Burns Motor Freight Inc			
500 Seneca Trl N ....Marlinton WV 24954	**800-598-5674**	304-799-6106	770
Burr Pilger & Mayer LLP (BPMLLP)			
600 California St			
Ste 1300 ....San Francisco CA 94108	**866-312-4390**	415-421-5757	2
Burr Truck & Trailer Sales Inc			
2901 Vestal Rd ....Vestal NY 13850	**866-230-2383**	607-729-2211	56
Burrell Imaging			
1311 Merrillville Rd ....Crown Point IN 46307	**800-348-8732**	219-663-3210	581
BurrellesLuce			
30 B Vreeland Rd			
PO Box 674...................Florham Park NJ 07932	**800-631-1160**	973-992-6600	384
Burris Company Inc			
331 E Eigth St ....Greeley CO 80631	**888-228-7747**	970-356-1670	537
Burris Logistics			
501 SE Fifth St PO Box 219 ....Milford DE 19963	**800-805-8135**	302-839-5157	791-2
Burrows Paper Corp			
501 W Main St ....Little Falls NY 13365	**800-272-7122**	315-823-2300	550
Burrows Paper Corp Packaging Group			
2000 Commerce Ctr Dr ....Franklin OH 45005	**800-732-1933**	937-746-1933	541
Burrtec Waste Industries Inc			
9890 Cherry Ave ....Fontana CA 92335	**888-287-7832**	909-429-4200	792
Bursma Electronic Distributing Inc			
2851 Buchanan Ave SW ....Grand Rapids MI 49548	**800-777-2604**	616-831-0080	37
Burst Communication Inc			
8200 S Akron St Ste 108 ....Centennial CO 80112	**800-891-8593**	303-649-9600	246
Burt County Public Power District			
613 N 13th St PO Box 209 ....Tekamah NE 68061	**888-835-1620**	402-374-2631	245
Burton & Mayer Inc			
W140 N9000 Lilly Rd ....Menomonee Falls WI 53051	**800-236-1770**	262-781-0770	619
Bus Andrews Truck Equipment Inc			
2828 N E Ave ....Springfield MO 65803	**800-273-0733**	417-869-1541	56
Busch Gardens Williamsburg			
1 Busch Gardens Blvd ....Williamsburg VA 23185	**800-343-7946**		32
Buse Timber & Sales Inc			
3812 28th Pl NE ....Everett WA 98201	**800-305-2577**	425-258-2577	674
Bush Industries Inc			
1 Mason Dr ....Jamestown NY 14701	**800-950-4782**	716-665-2000	318-2
Bushnell Corp			
9200 Cody St ....Overland Park KS 66214	**800-423-3537**	913-752-3400	537
Bushnell Ctr for the Performing Arts			
166 Capitol Ave ....Hartford CT 06106	**888-824-2874**	860-987-6000	565
Bushwacker Inc			
6710 N Catlin Ave ....Portland OR 97203	**800-234-8920**	503-283-4335	59
Business & Legal Reports Inc (BLR)			
141 Mill Rock Rd E ....Old Saybrook CT 06475	**800-727-5257**	860-510-0100	628-9
Business Council of Alabama			
Two N Jackson St PO Box 76 ....Montgomery AL 36101	**800-665-9647**	334-834-6000	138
Business Council of New York State Inc			
152 Washington Ave ....Albany NY 12210	**800-358-1202**	518-465-7511	138
Business Facilities Magazine			
44 Apple St Ste 3 ....Tinton Falls NJ 07724	**800-524-0337**	732-842-7433	452-5
Business Forms Management Assn (BFMA)			
3800 Old Cheney Rd Ste 101-285 ....Lincoln NE 68516	**888-367-3078**	402-216-0479	48-12
Business Furniture Corp			
6102 Victory Way ....Indianapolis IN 46278	**800-774-5544**	317-216-1600	319
Business Inn			
180 MacLaren St ....Ottawa ON K2P0L3	**800-363-1777**	613-232-1121	376
Business Insurance Magazine			
711 Third Ave ....New York NY 10017	**877-812-1587**	212-210-0100	452-5
Business Intelligence Advisor			
37 Broadway Ste 1 ....Arlington MA 02474	**800-964-5118**	781-648-8700	524-3
Business Journal, The			
25 E Boardman St ....Youngstown OH 44501	**800-837-6397**	330-744-5023	452-5
Business Marketing Assn (BMA)			
708 Third Ave 33rd Fl ....New York NY 10017	**800-664-4262**	212-697-5950	48-18
Business News Network (BNN)			
299 Queen St W ....Toronto ON M5V2Z5	**855-326-6266**	416-384-6600	729
Business News Publishing Co			
2401 W Big Beaver Rd Ste 700..........Troy MI 48084	**800-837-7370**	248-362-3700	628-9
Business Professionals of America			
5454 Cleveland Ave ....Columbus OH 43231	**800-334-2007**	614-895-7277	48-5
Business Resource Group (BRG)			
10440 N Central Expy Ste 1150 ......Dallas TX 75231	**888-391-9166**	214-777-5100	195
Business Stationery LLC			
4944 Commerce Pkwy ....Cleveland OH 44128	**800-234-9954**	216-514-1277	527
Business Technology Assn (BTA)			
12411 Wornall Rd Ste 200 ....Kansas City MO 64145	**800-325-7219**	816-941-3100	48-18
Buskirk Lumber Co			
319 Oak St ....Freeport MI 49325	**800-860-9663**	616-765-5103	674
Busler Enterprises Inc			
2601 N St Joseph Ave ....Evansville IN 47720	**800-457-3232**	812-424-7511	323
BUSPAC			
700 13th St NW Ste 575 ....Washington DC 20005	**800-283-2877**	202-842-1645	608
Busse/SJI Corp			
124 N Columbus St ....Randolph WI 53956	**800-882-4995**		465
Busy Beaver Bldg Centers			
2940 Library Rd ....Pittsburgh PA 15234	**800-732-0999**	412-882-6633	361
Busy Body Home Fitness			
9990 Empire St ....San Diego CA 92126	**800-466-3348**		702
Butchart Gardens, The			
800 Benvenuto Ave ....Brentwood Bay BC V8M1J8	**866-652-4422**	250-652-4422	96

	Toll-Free	Phone	Class
Butcher Distributors Inc			
101 Boyce Rd ....Broussard LA 70518	800-960-0008	337-837-2088	605
Butler Animal Health Supply LLC			
400 Metro Pl N ....Dublin OH 43017	888-691-2724*	614-761-9095	470
*PR			
Butler Area School District			
110 Campus Ln ....Butler PA 16001	888-800-5583	724-287-8720	676
Butler Automatic Inc			
41 Leona Dr ....Middleboro MA 02346	800-544-0070*	508-923-0544	540
*Cust Svc			
Butler County			
205 W Central Ave ....El Dorado KS 67042	800-822-6104	316-322-4300	336
Butler County Community College			
107 College Dr ....Butler PA 16002	888-826-2829	724-287-8711	160
Butler County Rural Electric Co-op			
521 N Main PO Box 98 ....Allison IA 50602	888-267-2726	319-267-2726	245
Butler County Rural Public Power District			
1331 N Fourth St ....David City NE 68632	800-230-0569	402-367-3081	245
Butler Home Products LLC			
237 Cedar Hill St ....Marlborough MA 01752	888-318-8521	508-597-8000	501
Butler National Corp			
19920 W 161st St ....Olathe KS 66062	800-690-6903	913-780-9595	522
OTC: BUKS			
Butler Rural Electric Co-op Assn Inc			
216 S Vine St PO Box 1242 ....El Dorado KS 67042	800-464-0060	316-321-9600	245
Butler Rural Electric Co-op Inc (BREC)			
3888 Still-Beckett Rd ....Oxford OH 45056	800-255-2732	513-867-4400	245
Butler Supply Inc			
965 Horan Dr ....Fenton MO 63026	800-850-9949	636-349-9000	246
Butler Technologies Inc			
231 W Wayne St ....Butler PA 16001	800-494-6656	724-283-6656	175
Butler Transport Inc			
347 N James St ....Kansas City KS 66118	800-345-8158	913-321-0047	770
Butler University			
4600 Sunset Ave ....Indianapolis IN 46208	800-368-6852	317-940-8100	166
Butler University Irwin Library			
4600 Sunset Ave ....Indianapolis IN 46208	888-940-8100	317-940-9227	431-6
Butler-Dearden Paper Service Inc			
PO Box 1069 ....Boylston MA 01505	800-634-7070	508-869-9000	552
Butte College			
3536 Butte Campus Dr ....Oroville CA 95965	800-933-8322*	530-895-2511	160
*Hum Res			
Butte Electric Co-op			
PO Box 137 ....Newell SD 57760	800-928-8839	605-456-2494	245
Butterfly House - Faust Park, The			
15193 Olive Blvd ....Chesterfield MO 63017	800-642-8842	636-530-0076	49-4
Butte-Silver Bow Chamber of Commerce			
1000 George St ....Butte MT 59701	800-735-6814	406-723-3177	137
Butts Foods Inc			
432 N Royal St PO Box 2466 ....Jackson TN 38301	800-962-8570	731-423-3456	296-10
Buurma Farms Inc			
3909 Kok Rd ....Willard OH 44890	888-428-8762	419-935-6411	10-10
Buxton Co			
245 Cadwell Dr PO Box 1650 ....Springfield MA 01104	800-426-3638	413-734-5900	427
BUYandHOLD.com Securities Corp			
c/o Freedom Investments, Inc			
375 Raritan Ctr Pkwy Ste D ....Edison NJ 08837	800-646-8212		681
Buyatab Online Inc			
204 - 576 Seymour St ....Vancouver BC V6B3K1	888-267-0447		224
Buyers Laboratory Inc			
20 Railroad Ave ....Hackensack NJ 07601	800-578-5902	201-488-0404	628-9
BVI (Better Vision Institute, The)			
225 Reinekers Ln Ste 700 ....Alexandria VA 22314	800-372-3937	703-548-4560	47-17
BW Container Systems			
1305 Lakeview Dr ....Romeoville IL 60446	800-527-0494	630-759-6800	208
BWAY (Brockway-Smith Co)			
146 Dascomb Rd ....Andover MA 01810	800-225-7912	978-475-7100	494
BWAY Corp			
8607 Roberts Dr Ste 250 ....Atlanta GA 30350	800-527-2267	770-645-4800	123
BWI (Baltimore/Washington International Thurgood Marshall Airport)			
PO Box 8766 ....Baltimore MD 21240	800-435-9294	410-859-7111	27
bx.com Inc			
1 W Exchange St ....Providence RI 02903	877-447-2355	401-274-8991	796
Byard F Brogan Inc			
PO Box 0369 ....Glenside PA 19038	800-232-7642	215-885-3550	406
Bybee Stone Company Inc			
6293 N Matthews Dr ....Ellettsville IN 47429	800-457-4530	812-876-2215	715
Byer California			
66 Potrero Ave ....San Francisco CA 94103	844-628-4498	415-626-7844	153-4
Byerly Ford			
4041 Dixie Hwy ....Louisville KY 40216	888-436-0819	502-448-1661	56
Byline Bank			
3639 N Broadway St ....Chicago IL 60613	866-957-7700	773-244-7000	69
Byram Healthcare Centers Inc			
120 Bloomingdale Rd ....White Plains NY 10605	800-354-4054	914-286-2000	470
Byram Laboratories Inc			
One Columbia Rd ....Branchburg NJ 08876	800-766-1212		246
Byrd Cookie Company Inc			
6700 Waters Ave ....Savannah GA 31406	800-291-2973	912-355-1716	342
Bytespeed LLC			
3131 24th Ave S ....Moorhead MN 56560	877-553-0777	218-227-0445	174-1

C

	Toll-Free	Phone	Class
C & A Industries Inc			
13609 California St ....Omaha NE 68154	800-574-9829	402-891-0009	712
C & D Technologies Inc			
1400 Union Meeting Rd			
PO Box 3053 ....Blue Bell PA 19422	800-543-8630	215-619-2700	73
C & F Financial Corp			
802 Main St PO Box 391 ....West Point VA 23181	800-583-3863	804-843-4584	357-2
NASDAQ: CFFI			
C & H Chemical Inc			
13505 Industrial Park Blvd ....Plymouth MN 55441	800-966-2909	763-582-1140	149
C & H Distributors LLC			
770 S 70th St ....Milwaukee WI 53214	800-558-9966*	414-443-1700	382
*Sales			

	Toll-Free	Phone	Class
C & H International			
4751 Wilshire Blvd Ste 201 ....Los Angeles CA 90010	800-833-8888	323-933-2288	16
C & H Sugar Co Inc			
850 Loring Ave ....Crockett CA 94525	800-773-1803		295-38
C & L Supply Co			
PO Box 578 ....Vinita OK 74301	800-256-6411	918-256-6411	37
C & M Conveyor			
4598 SR 37 ....Mitchell IN 47446	800-551-3195	812-849-5647	208
C & R Mechanical			
12825 Pennridge Dr ....Bridgeton MO 63044	800-524-3828	314-739-1800	190-10
C & R Research Services Inc			
500 N Michigan Ave Ste 1200 ....Chicago IL 60611	800-543-9393	312-828-9200	461
C & S Companies (CSCOS)			
499 Col Eileen Collins Blvd ....Syracuse NY 13212	877-277-6583	315-455-2000	261
C Cowles & Co Inc			
83 Water St ....New Haven CT 06511	800-624-4483	203-865-3117	484
C Cretors & Co			
3243 N California Ave ....Chicago IL 60618	800-228-1885	773-588-1690	297
C H Garmong & Son Inc			
3050 Poplar St ....Terre Haute IN 47803	800-894-2962	812-234-3714	603
C Paul Phelps Correctional Ctr			
14925 Hwy 27 N PO Box 1056 ....Dequincy LA 70633	888-524-3578	337-786-7963	213
C Spire			
1018 Highland Colony Pkwy			
Ste 300 ....Ridgeland MS 39157	855-277-4735		384
C'mon Inn Grand Forks			
3051 32nd Ave S ....Grand Forks ND 58201	800-255-2323	701-775-3320	376
C. L. Smith Co			
1311 S 39th St ....Saint Louis MO 63110	800-264-1202	314-771-1202	601
C.a. Murren & Sons Co Inc			
2275 Loganville Hwy ....Grayson GA 30017	800-523-2200	770-682-2940	187
C2F Inc			
6600 SW 111th Ave ....Beaverton OR 97008	800-544-8825	503-643-9050	94
CA (Cocaine Anonymous World Services Inc)			
3740 Overland Ave Ste C ....Los Angeles CA 90034	800-347-8998	310-559-5833	47-21
CA Inc One CA Plz ....Islandia NY 11749	800-225-5224	631-342-6000	179-1
NASDAQ: CA			
Ca Lindman Inc			
10401 Guilford Rd ....Jessup MD 20794	877-737-8675	301-470-4700	187
CAA (Canadian Automobile Assn)			
2151 Thurston Dr Ste 200 ....Ottawa ON K1G6C9	800-267-8713	613-820-1890	47-23
CAA (Council on Aviation Accreditation)			
3410 Skyway Dr ....Auburn AL 36830	800-767-4767	334-844-2431	47-1
CAA Central Ontario			
60 Commerce Vly Dr E ....Thornhill ON L3T7P9	800-268-3750	905-771-3000	52
CAA Manitoba			
870 Empress St ....Winnipeg MB R3C2Z3	800-222-4357	204-262-6166	52
CAA Maritimes Ltd			
378 Westmorland Rd ....Saint John NB E2J2G4	800-471-1611	506-634-1400	52
CAA North & East Ontario			
PO Box 8350 ....Ottawa ON K1G3T2	800-267-8713	613-820-1890	52
CAA Quebec			
444 Bouvier St ....Quebec QC G2J1E3	800-222-4357	418-624-8222	52
CAA Stoney Creek			
163 Centennial Pkwy N ....Hamilton ON L8E1H8	800-992-8143	905-664-8000	52
CAAHEP (Commission on Accreditation of Allied Health Education Programs)			
1361 Pk St ....Clearwater FL 33756	800-228-2262	727-210-2350	47-1
Cabarrus County Convention & Visitors Bureau			
3003 Dale Earnhardt Blvd ....Kannapolis NC 28083	800-848-3740	704-782-4340	207
Cabela's Inc			
One Cabela Dr ....Sidney NE 69160	800-237-8888	308-254-5505	702
NYSE: CAB			
Cabela's Outdoor Adventures Inc			
610 Glover Rd Ste A ....Sidney NE 69162	800-346-8747		702
Cabell-Huntington Convention & Visitors Bureau			
PO Box 347 ....Huntington WV 25708	800-635-6329	304-525-7333	207
CabelTel International Corp			
1603 Lyndon B Johnson Fwy ....Dallas TX 75234	888-407-8400	972-407-8400	446
Caber Sure Fit Inc			
35 Valleywood Dr Ste 1 ....Markham ON L3R5L9	800-520-3152	905-479-5803	358
Cabinet Tronix LLC			
290 Trousdale Dr Ste A ....Chula Vista CA 91910	866-876-6199		806
Cabinetry By Karman Inc			
6000 Stratler St ....Salt Lake City UT 84107	800-255-3581	801-281-6400	114
CABLCF (Creditors Adjustment Bureau-LC Financial)			
14226 Ventura Blvd ....Sherman Oaks CA 91423	800-800-4523	818-990-4800	158
Cable Connection, The			
52 Heppner Dr ....Carson City NV 89706	800-851-2961	775-885-1443	115
Cable Markers Company Inc			
13805-C Alton Pkwy ....Irvine CA 92618	800-746-7655		462
Cable One Inc			
210 E Earll Drive ....Phoenix AZ 85012	877-692-2253	602-364-6000	115
Cable Public Affairs Ch (CPAC)			
PO Box 81099 ....Ottawa ON K1P1B1	877-287-2722		729
CableAmerica Corp			
350 E 10th Dr ....Mesa AZ 85210	866-871-4492		115
Cable-Dahmer Chevrolet Inc			
1834 S Noland Rd ....Independence MO 64055	888-738-5260	816-521-7508	56
Cables to Go Inc			
3599 Dayton Pk Dr ....Dayton OH 45414	800-826-7904	937-224-8646	801
Cabot Corp			
2 Seaport Ln Ste 1300 ....Boston MA 02210	800-322-1236	617-345-0100	143
NYSE: CBT			
Cabot Creamery			
One Home Farm Way ....Montpelier VT 05602	888-792-2268	802-229-9361	295-5
Cabot Heritage Corp			
176 N St PO Box 2049 ....Salem MA 01970	800-654-1514	978-745-5532	628-9
Cabot Market Letter			
176 N St PO Box 2049 ....Salem MA 01970	800-387-8588*	978-745-5532	524-9
*Orders			
Cabot Microelectronics Corp			
870 N Commons Dr ....Aurora IL 60504	800-811-2756	630-375-6631	143
NASDAQ: CCMP			
Cabot Oil & Gas Corp			
840 Gessner Rd Ste 1200 ....Houston TX 77024	800-434-3985	281-848-2799	775
NYSE: COG			
Cabot Specialty Fluids Inc			
Waterway Plaza Two 10001 Woodlock Forest Dr			
Ste 275 ....The Woodlands TX 77380	800-322-1236	281-298-9955	143
Cabrillo College			
6500 Soquel Dr ....Aptos CA 95003	800-218-0013	831-479-6100	160
Cabrillo National Monument			
1800 Cabrillo Memorial Dr ....San Diego CA 92106	800-236-7916	619-557-5450	557

				Toll-Free	Phone	Class
Cabrini College						
610 King of Prussia Rd	Radnor	PA	19087	**800-848-1003**	610-902-8552	166
CAC (Coating & Adhesive Corp)						
1901 Popular St PO Box 1080	Leland	NC	28451	**800-410-2999**	910-371-3184	543
Cache County School District						
2063 N 1200 E	North Logan	UT	84341	**888-837-6437**	435-752-3925	676
Cache Valley Electric Inc						
875 N 1000 W	Logan	UT	84321	**888-558-0600**	435-752-6405	190-4
CACI International Inc						
1100 N Glebe Rd	Arlington	VA	22201	**866-606-3471**	703-841-7800	181
NYSE: CACI						
Cacique Inc						
14923 Procter Ave	La Puente	CA	91746	**800-521-6987**	626-961-3399	295-5
Cactus Feeders Inc						
2209 W Seventh Ave	Amarillo	TX	79106	**877-698-7355**	806-373-2333	10-1
Cactus Flower Florists						
10822 N Scottsdale Rd	Scottsdale	AZ	85254	**800-922-2887**	480-483-9200	292
CACU (Community America Credit Union)						
9777 Ridge Dr	Lenexa	KS	66219	**800-892-7957**	913-905-7000	219
CAD/CAM Consulting Services Inc (CCCS)						
996 Lawrence Dr Ste 101	Newbury Park	CA	91320	**888-375-7676**	805-375-7676	175
Cadbury Retirement Community						
2150 Rt 38	Cherry Hill	NJ	08002	**800-422-3287**	856-667-4550	663
CADCA (CPA Auto Dealer Consultants Assn)						
624 Grassmere Pk Dr Ste 15	Nashville	TN	37211	**800-231-2524**	615-373-9880	48-1
Caddo Electric Co-op						
PO Box 70	Binger	OK	73009	**800-522-6543**	405-656-2322	245
CADE (Commission on Accreditation for Dietetics Education)						
120 S Riverside Plz Ste 2000	Chicago	IL	60606	**800-877-1600**	312-899-0040	47-1
Cade & Assoc Adv Inc						
1645 Metropolitan Blvd	Tallahassee	FL	32308	**800-715-2233**	850-385-0300	4
Cadeau Express Inc						
3494 E Sunset Rd	Las Vegas	NV	89120	**800-240-0301**	702-433-1333	238
Cadec Corp						
645 Harvey Rd	Manchester	NH	03103	**800-252-2332**	603-668-1010	175
Cadence Capital Management						
265 Franklin St 4th Fl	Boston	MA	02110	**800-298-2194**	617-624-3500	398
Cadence Design Systems Inc						
2655 Seely Ave	San Jose	CA	95134	**800-746-6223***	408-943-1234	179-5
NASDAQ: CDNS ■ *Cust Svc						
Cadet Mfg Company Inc						
2500 W Fourth Plain Blvd	Vancouver	WA	98660	**800-442-2338**	360-693-2505	36
Cadillac Area Visitors Bureau						
201 N Mitchell St	Cadillac	MI	49601	**800-225-2537**	231-775-0657	207
Cadillac Coffee Co						
194 E Maple Rd	Troy	MI	48083	**800-438-6900**	248-545-2266	295-7
Cadre Computer Resources Co						
201 East Fifth Street						
Suite 1800	Cincinnati	OH	45202	**866-762-6700**	513-762-7350	181
Cadwell Laboratories Inc						
909 N Kellogg St	Kennewick	WA	99336	**800-245-3001**	509-735-6481	471
CAE (Center of the American Experiment)						
12 S Sixth St						
1024 Plymouth Bldg	Minneapolis	MN	55402	**800-657-3717**	612-338-3605	625
CAE Inc						
8585 Cote de Liesse	Saint Laurent	QC	H4T1G6	**866-999-6223**	514-341-6780	694
NYSE: CAE						
CAEP (Canadian Assn of Emergency Physicians)						
1785 Alta Vista Dr Ste 104	Ottawa	ON	K1G3Y6	**800-463-1158**	613-523-3343	48-8
Caesar's Palace						
3570 Las Vegas Blvd S						
Caesar's Palace	Las Vegas	NV	89109	**800-634-6001**	702-731-7110	662
Caesars Atlantic City Hotel Casino						
2100 Pacific Ave	Atlantic City	NJ	08401	**800-522-4700**	609-348-4411	660
Caesars Head State Park						
8155 Geer Hwy	Cleveland	SC	29635	**866-345-7275**	864-836-6115	558
Caesars License Company LLC						
377 Riverside Dr E	Windsor	ON	N9A7H7	**800-991-7777**	519-258-7878	132
Cafe Fina						
47 Fisherman's Wharf Ste 1	Monterey	CA	93940	**800-843-3462**	831-372-5200	662
Cafe, The						
3434 Peachtree Rd NE						
Ritz-Carlton Buckhead	Atlanta	GA	30326	**800-241-3333**	404-237-2700	662
CAGW (Citizens Against Government Waste)						
1301 Pennsylvania Ave NW						
Ste 1075	Washington	DC	20004	**800-232-6479**	202-467-5300	47-7
Cagwin & Dorward Inc						
1565 S Novato Blvd Ste B	Novato	CA	94947	**800-891-7710**	415-892-7710	419
CAI (Community Assns Institute)						
6402 Arlington Blvd						
Ste 500	Falls Church	VA	22042	**888-224-4321**	703-970-9220	47-7
CAI (Chrysler Aviation Inc)						
7120 Hayvenhurst Ave Ste 309	Van Nuys	CA	91406	**800-995-0825**	818-989-7900	13
CAI (Computer Aid Inc)						
1390 Ridgeview Dr	Allentown	PA	18104	**877-432-7228**	610-530-5000	178
Cain's Foods Inc						
114 E Main St	Ayer	MA	01432	**800-225-0601**	978-772-0300	295-19
Cajun Constructors Inc						
15635 Airline Hwy	Baton Rouge	LA	70817	**877-401-5911**	225-753-5857	189-7
Cal Farley's Boys Ranch						
600 W 11th St PO Box 1890	Amarillo	TX	79174	**800-687-3722**	806-372-2341	47-6
Cal Spas Inc						
1462 E Ninth St	Pomona	CA	91766	**800-225-7727**	909-623-8781	372
Calabro Cheese Corp						
580 Coe Ave PO Box 120186	East Haven	CT	06512	**800-969-1311**	203-469-1311	295-5
CALAMCO (California Ammonia Co)						
1776 W March Ln Ste 420	Stockton	CA	95207	**800-624-4200**	209-982-1000	280
Calamos Asset Management Inc						
2020 Calamos Ct	Naperville	IL	60563	**800-582-6959**	630-245-7200	398
NASDAQ: CLMS						
Cal-a-Vie Spa						
29402 Spa Havens Way	Vista	CA	92084	**866-772-4283**	760-945-2055	697
Calavo Growers Inc						
1141-A Cummings Rd	Santa Paula	CA	93060	**800-654-8758**	805-525-1245	314-4
NASDAQ: CVGW						
Calbag Metals Co						
2495 NW Nicolai St	Portland	OR	97210	**800-398-3441**	503-226-3441	677
Cal-Coast Dairy Systems Inc						
424 S Tegner Rd	Turlock	CA	95380	**800-732-6826***	209-634-9026	273
*Cust Svc						
Calculated Industries Inc						
4840 Hytech Dr	Carson City	NV	89706	**800-854-8075**	775-885-4900	117
Calder Casino & Race Course						
21001 NW 27th Ave	Miami	FL	33056	**800-522-4700**	305-625-1311	633
Caldwell Chamber of Commerce						
704 Blaine St	Caldwell	ID	83605	**877-375-7382**	208-459-7493	137
Caldwell College						
Nine Ryerson Ave	Caldwell	NJ	07006	**888-864-9516***	973-618-3500	166
*Admissions						
Caldwell Securities Ltd						
150 King St W Ste 1710	Toronto	ON	M5H1J9	**800-387-0859**	416-862-7755	681
CALEA (Commission on Accreditation for Law Enforcement Agencies)						
13575 Heathcote Blvd						
Ste 320	Gainesville	VA	20155	**877-789-6904**	703-352-4225	48-7
Caledon State Park						
11617 Caledon Rd	King George	VA	22485	**800-933-7275**	540-663-3861	558
Caledonia Haulers LLC						
420 W Lincoln St PO Box 31	Caledonia	MN	55921	**800-325-4728**	507-725-9000	463
Calex Express Inc						
58 Pittston Ave	Pittston	PA	18640	**800-292-2539**	570-603-0180	770
CALEX Manufacturing Co						
2401 Stanwell Dr	Concord	CA	94520	**800-542-3355**	925-687-4411	511
Calgary Herald						
215-16th St SE						
PO Box 2400 Stn M	Calgary	AB	T2E7P5	**800-372-9219**	403-235-7100	525-1
Calgary International Airport						
2000 Airport Rd NE	Calgary	AB	T2E6W5	**877-254-7427**	403-735-1200	27
Calgary Sun						
2615 12th St NE	Calgary	AB	T2E7W9	**877-624-1463**	403-410-1010	525-1
Calgary Zoo Botanical Garden & Prehistoric Park						
1300 Zoo Rd NE	Calgary	AB	T2E7V6	**800-588-9993**	403-232-9300	810
Calgon Carbon Corp						
500 Calgon Carbon Dr	Pittsburgh	PA	15205	**800-422-7266***	412-787-6700	141
NYSE: CCC ■ *Cust Svc						
Huntsville						
102B Wynn Dr	Huntsville	AL	35805	**800-626-3628**	256-890-4701	160
Calhoun Community College						
Redstone Arsenal						
6250 Hwy 31 N	Tanner	AL	35671	**800-626-3628**	256-306-2500	160
Calhoun County Electric Co-op Assn						
1015 Tonawanda St						
PO Box 312	Rockwell City	IA	50579	**800-821-4879**	712-297-7112	245
Calhoun Falls State Recreation Area						
46 Maintenance Shop Rd	Calhoun Falls	SC	29628	**866-345-7275**	864-447-8267	558
Calian Technology Ltd						
340 Legget Dr Ste 101	Ottawa	ON	K2K1Y6	**877-225-4264**	613-599-8600	712
TSE: CTY						
Calibre Systems Inc						
6354 Walker Ln						
Ste 300 Metro Pk	Alexandria	VA	22310	**888-225-4273**	703-797-8500	181
Califone International Inc						
1145 Arroyo St Ste A	San Fernando	CA	91340	**800-722-0500**	818-407-2400	253
Arts Council						
1300 'I' St Ste 930	Sacramento	CA	95814	**800-201-6201**	916-322-6555	337-5
Child Support Services Dept						
PO Box 419064	Sacramento	CA	95741	**866-901-3212**	916-464-5000	337-5
California						
Corporations Dept						
1515 K St Ste 200	Sacramento	CA	95814	**866-275-2677**	916-445-7205	337-5
Corrections Dept						
PO Box 942883	Sacramento	CA	94283	**877-256-6877**		337-5
Fish & Game Dept						
1416 Ninth St 12th Fl	Sacramento	CA	95814	**888-334-2258**	916-445-0411	337-5
Health Care Services Dept						
PO Box 997413 MS 8502	Sacramento	CA	95899	**800-735-2929**		337-5
Housing Finance Agency						
500 Capitol Mall Ste 1400	Sacramento	CA	95814	**877-922-5432**	916-322-3991	337-5
Parks & Recreation Dept						
PO Box 942896	Sacramento	CA	94296	**800-777-0369**	916-653-6995	337-5
Public Utilities Commission						
505 Van Ness Ave	San Francisco	CA	94102	**800-848-5580**	415-703-2782	337-5
Teacher Credentialing Commission						
1900 Capitol Ave	Sacramento	CA	95814	**888-921-2682**	916-445-7254	337-5
Veterans Affairs Dept						
1227 'O' St	Sacramento	CA	95814	**800-221-8998**	916-653-2158	337-5
Victim Compensation Program						
PO Box 3036	Sacramento	CA	95812	**800-777-9229**		337-5
California Ammonia Co (CALAMCO)						
1776 W March Ln Ste 420	Stockton	CA	95207	**800-624-4200**	209-982-1000	280
California Analytical Instruments Inc						
1312 W Grove Ave	Orange	CA	92865	**800-959-0949**	714-974-5560	416
California Bank & Trust						
11622 El Camino Real Ste 200	San Diego	CA	92130	**800-400-6080**	858-793-7400	69
California Baptist University						
8432 Magnolia Ave	Riverside	CA	92504	**877-228-8866**	951-689-5771	166
California Cartage Company Inc						
2931 Redondo Ave	Long Beach	CA	90806	**888-537-1432**		770
California Casualty Insurance Group						
1900 Alameda De Las Pulgas	San Mateo	CA	94403	**866-680-5143**	650-574-4000	388-4
California Closet Co						
610A DuBois St	San Rafael	CA	94901	**888-336-9707***	415-256-8500	190-11
*General						
California College of the Arts						
Oakland 5212 Broadway	Oakland	CA	94618	**800-447-1278**	510-594-3600	162
San Francisco						
1111 Eigth St	San Francisco	CA	94107	**800-447-1278**	415-703-9500	162
California Cryobank Inc						
11915 La Grange Ave	Los Angeles	CA	90025	**866-927-9622**	310-443-5244	538
California Ctr for the Arts						
340 N Escondido Blvd	Escondido	CA	92025	**800-988-4253**	760-839-4138	565
California Dental Assn						
1201 K St	Sacramento	CA	95853	**800-736-7071**	916-443-0505	227
California Design College						
3440 Wilshire Blvd 10th Fl	Los Angeles	CA	90010	**877-468-6232**	213-251-3636	162
California Fair Political Practices Commission						
428 J St Ste 620	Sacramento	CA	95814	**866-275-3772**	916-322-5660	265
California Flexrake Corp						
9620 Gidley St	Temple City	CA	91780	**800-266-4200**	626-443-4026	426
California Gasket & Rubber Corp						
533 W Collins Ave	Orange	CA	92867	**800-635-7084**	310-323-4250	325
California Grill						
11999 Harbor Blvd						
Hyatt Regency Orange County	Garden Grove	CA	92840	**800-233-1234**	714-740-6047	662
California Hotel & Casino						
12 E Ogden Ave	Las Vegas	NV	89101	**800-634-6505**	702-385-1222	132
California Institute of Technology						
1200 E California Blvd	Pasadena	CA	91125	**800-568-8324**	626-395-6811	166

	Toll-Free	Phone	Class
California Institute of the Arts			
24700 McBean Pkwy .... Valencia CA 91355	800-545-2787	661-255-1050	162
California ISO			
151 Blue Ravine Rd PO Box 639014...... Folsom CA 95630	800-220-4907	916-351-4400	775
California Kitchen Cabinet Door Corp			
400 Cochrane Cir .... Morgan Hill CA 95037	888-225-3667	408-782-5700	114
California Lutheran University			
60 W Olsen Rd .... Thousand Oaks CA 91360	877-258-3678	805-493-3135	166
California Lutheran University Pearson Library			
60 W Olsen Rd .... Thousand Oaks CA 91360	877-258-3678	805-493-3250	431-6
California Maritime Academy			
200 Maritime Academy Dr .... Vallejo CA 94590	800-561-1945	707-654-1330	166
California Market Ctr			
110 E Ninth St .... Los Angeles CA 90079	800-225-6278	213-630-3600	206
California Neon Products Inc			
4530 Mission Gorge Pl .... San Diego CA 92120	800-822-6366	619-283-2191	692
California Office Furniture			
1724 Tenth St .... Sacramento CA 95811	877-442-6959	916-442-6959	319
California Pacific Medical Ctr Research Institute			
475 Brannan St Ste 220 .... San Francisco CA 94107	855-354-2778	415-600-1600	659
California Panel & Veneer Co			
14055 Artesia Blvd .... Cerritos CA 90703	800-451-1745	562-926-5834	606
California Parlor Car Tours			
500 Sutter St Ste 401 .... San Francisco CA 94102	800-227-4250	415-474-7500	750
California Pharmacists Assn (CPhA)			
4030 Lennane Dr .... Sacramento CA 95834	866-365-7472	916-779-1400	578
California Pizza Kitchen Inc			
18601 Airport Way Ste 135... Santa Ana CA 92707	800-919-3227	949-252-6125	661
NASDAQ: CPKI			
California Polytechnic State University			
1 Grand Ave .... San Luis Obispo CA 93407	800-424-6723	805-756-1111	166
California Portland Cement Co			
2025 E Financial Way Ste 200 .... Glendora CA 91741	800-272-1891*	626-852-6200	134
*Cust Svc			
California Products Corp			
150 Dascomb Rd .... Andover MA 01810	800-225-1141	978-623-9980	543
California Real Estate Magazine			
525 S Virgil Ave ....Los Angeles CA 90020	888-811-5281	213-739-8200	452-5
California Saw & Knife Works			
721 Brannan St .... San Francisco CA 94103	888-729-6533	415-861-0644	673
California Southern Baptist Convention			
678 E Shaw Ave .... Fresno CA 93710	888-462-7729	559-229-9533	47-20
California State Archives			
1020 'O' St .... Sacramento CA 95814	800-633-5155	916-653-7715	513
California State Automobile Assn			
150 Van Ness Ave .... San Francisco CA 94102	800-922-8228*		52
*Cust Svc			
California State Library			
900 N St .... Sacramento CA 95814	800-952-5666	916-654-0261	431-5
California State Railroad Museum			
125 "I" St 111 'I' St .... Sacramento CA 95814	866-240-4655	916-323-9280	558
California State University			
401 Golden Shore .... Long Beach CA 90802	800-325-4000	562-951-4000	774
Chico CSU Chico .... Chico CA 95929	800-542-4426*	530-898-6321	166
*Admissions			
Dominguez Hills			
1000 E Victoria St .... Carson CA 90747	888-545-6512	310-243-3300	166
East Bay			
25800 Carlos Bee Blvd ....Hayward CA 94542	877-829-5500	510-885-3000	166
Fresno			
5241 N Maple Ave .... Fresno CA 93740	800-700-2320	559-278-4240	166
Fullerton			
800 N State College Blvd .... Fullerton CA 92834	888-433-9406	714-278-2011	166
Long Beach			
1250 Bellflower Blvd .... Long Beach CA 90840	800-663-1144	562-985-4111	166
Northridge			
18111 Nordhoff St ....Northridge CA 91330	800-399-4529	818-677-1200	166
San Bernardino			
5500 University Pkwy .... San Bernardino CA 92407	866-275-3772	909-537-5188	166
San Marcos			
333 S Twin Oaks Valley Rd .... San Marcos CA 92096	888-225-5427	760-750-4000	166
Stanislaus			
1 University Cir ....Turlock CA 95382	800-235-9292	209-667-3152	166
California Steel & Tube			
16049 Stephens St .... City of Industry CA 91745	800-338-8823	626-968-5511	485
California Student Aid Commission			
PO Box 419027 .... Rancho Cordova CA 95741	888-224-7268	916-526-8999	716
California Theatre of Performing Arts			
562 W Fourth St .... San Bernardino CA 92401	800-745-3000	909-885-5152	565
California University of Pennsylvania			
250 University Ave ....California PA 15419	888-412-0479	724-938-4000	166
California Water Service Group			
1720 N First St .... San Jose CA 95112	800-750-8200	408-367-8200	775
NYSE: CWT			
California Western School of Law			
225 Cedar St .... San Diego CA 92101	800-255-4252	619-525-1401	167-1
Caliper Life Sciences Inc			
68 Elm St .... Hopkinton MA 01748	800-762-4000	508-435-9500	416
Calise & Sons Bakery Inc			
Two Quality Dr .... Lincoln RI 02865	800-225-4737	401-334-3444	295-1
Calista Corp			
301 Calista Ct Ste A .... Anchorage AK 99518	800-277-5516	907-279-5516	646
Calistoga Beverage Co			
865 Silverado Trl .... Calistoga CA 94515	800-365-4446		793
Calistoga Ranch			
580 Lommel Rd .... Calistoga CA 94515	800-942-4220	707-254-2800	660
Calistoga Spa Hot Springs			
1006 Washington St .... Calistoga CA 94515	866-822-5772	707-942-6269	697
Calix Society, The			
3881 Highland Ave Ste 201 .... St Paul MN 55110	800-398-0524	651-773-3117	47-21
Call One Inc			
400 Imperial Blvd			
PO Box 9002............ Cape Canaveral FL 32920	800-749-3160	321-783-2400	725
Callahan Chemical Co			
200 Industrial Ave .... Ridgefield Park NJ 07660	800-526-7000	201-440-9000	144
Callan & Woodworth Moving & Storage			
900 Hwy 212 .... Michigan City IN 46360	800-584-0551	269-447-1578	512
Callan Assoc Inc			
101 California St			
Ste 3500 .... San Francisco CA 94111	800-227-3288	415-974-5060	398
Callaway Electric Co-op			
1313 Co-op Dr PO Box 250 .... Fulton MO 65251	888-642-4840	573-642-3326	245
Callaway Gardens			
17800 Hwy 27 ....Pine Mountain GA 31822	800-225-5292	706-663-2281	660

	Toll-Free	Phone	Class
Callaway Golf Co			
2180 Rutherford Rd .... Carlsbad CA 92008	800-588-9836	760-931-1771	701
NYSE: ELY			
Callbright Corp			
6700 Hollister ....Houston TX 77040	877-462-2552		387
CallDirek			
2200 S Dixie Hwy Ste 401 .... Miami FL 33133	866-673-4735		384
Callenor Company Inc			
N 60 W 15725 Kohler Ln ...... Menomonee Falls WI 53051	800-813-7429	262-252-3343	124
Caller-Times			
820 N Lower Broadway ......Corpus Christi TX 78401	800-827-2011	361-884-2011	525-2
Calling Solutions By Phone Power Inc			
2200 McCullough Ave ....San Antonio TX 78212	800-683-5500*	210-822-7400	727
*Cust Svc			
Callisto Integration			
635 Fourth Line Ste 16............Oakville ON L6L5B3	800-387-0467	905-339-0059	195
Callon Petroleum Co			
200 N Canal St .... Natchez MS 39120	800-451-1294	601-442-1601	533
NYSE: CPE			
Callware Technologies Inc			
9100 S 500 W .... Sandy UT 84070	800-888-4226	801-988-6800	179-7
CalMet Services Inc			
7202 Peterson Ln ....Paramount CA 90723	800-990-6387	562-259-1239	792
Calnet Inc			
12359 Sunrise Vly Dr Ste 270 ......Reston VA 20191	877-322-5638*	703-547-6800	195
*General			
Calolympic Glove & Safety Company Inc			
1720 Delilah St ....Corona CA 92879	800-421-6630	951-340-2229	670
Calphalon Corp			
PO Box 583 .... Toledo OH 43697	800-809-7267		481
Calpico Inc			
1387 San Mateo Ave .... South San Francisco CA 94080	800-998-9115	650-588-2241	325
Calpine Corp			
717 Texas Ave Ste 1000 ....Houston TX 77002	800-367-5690	713-830-2000	775
NYSE: CPN			
CalPortland Co			
5975 E Marginal Way S			
PO Box 1730............ Seattle WA 98134	800-750-0123	206-764-3000	183
Cal-Royal Products Inc			
6605 Flotilla St ....City Of Commerce CA 90040	800-876-9258	323-888-6601	347
Calsak Corp			
1411 West 190th St Suite 400 ....Gardena CA 90248	888-663-6005	310-719-9500	596
CalSurance			
681 S Parker St Ste 300 ....Orange CA 92868	800-762-7800	714-939-0800	387
Calton & Assoc Inc			
14497 N Dale Mabry Hwy .... Tampa FL 33618	800-942-0262	813-264-0440	681
Calumet College of Saint Joseph			
2400 New York Ave .... Whiting IN 46394	877-700-9100	219-473-4215	166
Calumet Diversified Meats Inc			
10000 80th Ave ....Pleasant Prairie WI 53158	800-752-7427	262-947-7200	296-9
Calumet Lubricants Co			
2780 Waterfront Pkwy Dr E			
Ste 200............Indianapolis IN 46214	800-437-3188	317-328-5660	573
Calumet Specialty Products Partners LP			
2780 Waterfront Pkwy E Dr			
Ste 200............Indianapolis IN 46214	800-437-3188	317-328-5660	573
NASDAQ: CLMT			
Cal-Van Tools			
4300 Waterleaf Ct .... Greensboro NC 27410	800-537-1077		748
Calvary Bible College & Theological Seminary			
15800 Calvary Rd .... Kansas City MO 64147	800-326-3960	816-322-3960	159
Calvert Investments Inc			
4550 Montgomery Ave Ste 1000N ... Bethesda MD 20814	800-368-2748	301-951-4800	521
Calvert Labs			
1225 Crescent Green Ste 115...............Cary NC 27518	800-300-8114	919-459-8653	415
Calvert Marine Museum			
14200 Solomons Island Rd			
PO Box 97............ Solomons MD 20688	800-735-2258	410-326-2042	513
Calverton National Cemetery			
210 Princeton Blvd ....Calverton NY 11933	800-829-1040	631-727-5410	135
Calvin College			
3201 Burton St SE ....Grand Rapids MI 49546	800-688-0122	616-526-6000	166
Calvin College Hekman Library			
3201 Burton St SE ....Grand Rapids MI 49546	800-688-0122	616-526-6000	431-6
Calvin Theological Seminary			
3233 Burton St SE ....Grand Rapids MI 49546	800-388-6034	616-957-6036	167-3
Calzone Case Co			
225 Black Rock Ave ....Bridgeport CT 06605	800-243-5152*	203-367-5766	448
*Cust Svc			
CAM Commerce Solutions Inc			
17075 Newhope St Ste A .... Fountain Valley CA 92708	800-726-3282	714-241-9241	179-10
Camanchaca Inc			
7200 NW 19th St Ste 410 .... Miami FL 33126	800-335-7553	305-406-9560	295-14
Camas-Washougal Chamber of Commerce			
422 NE Fourth Ave .... Camas WA 98607	800-468-5865	360-834-2472	137
Cambelt International Corp			
2820 West 1100 South ......Salt Lake City UT 84104	855-226-2358	801-972-5511	208
Camber Corp			
635 Discovery Dr NW .... Huntsville AL 35806	800-998-7988	256-922-0200	181
Cambex Corp			
337 Tpke Rd .... Southborough MA 01772	800-325-5565	508-281-0209	177
OTC: CBEX			
Cambiar Investors Inc			
2401 E Second Ave Ste 500 .... Denver CO 80206	888-673-9950		398
Cambrex Corp			
1 Meadowlands Plaza			
15th Fl .... East Rutherford NJ 07073	866-286-9133	201-804-3000	474
NYSE: CBM			
Cambria Capital LLC			
488 E Winchester St			
Ste 200............Salt Lake City UT 84107	877-226-0477		398
Cambria-Rowe Business College (CRBC)			
221 Central Ave .... Johnstown PA 15902	800-639-2273	814-536-5168	788
Cambridge Chamber of Commerce			
750 Hespeler Rd .... Cambridge ON N3H5L8	800-749-7560*	519-622-2221	136
*General			
Cambridge College Inc			
1000 Mass Ave Ste 31 ....Cambridge MA 02138	800-829-4723	617-868-1000	788
Cambridge Engineering Inc			
PO Box 1010 .... Chesterfield MO 63006	800-899-1989	636-532-2233	317
Cambridge Heart Inc			
46 Jonspin Rd .... Wilmington MA 01887	888-226-9283	978-654-7600	471
Cambridge Inc			
105 Goodwill Rd PO Box 399........ Cambridge MD 21613	800-638-9560	410-228-3000	208

	City	State	ZIP	Toll-Free	Phone	Class
Cambridge Isotope Laboratories Inc						
50 Frontage Rd	Andover	MA	01810	**800-322-1174**	978-749-8000	143
Cambridge Medical Ctr (CMC)						
701 S Dellwood St	Cambridge	MN	55008	**800-252-4133**	763-689-7700	371-3
Cambridge Packing Co Inc						
41-43 Foodmart Rd	Boston	MA	02118	**800-722-6726**	617-269-6700	296-9
Cambridge Public Library						
244 S Birch St	Cambridge	MN	55008	**877-721-4862**	763-689-7390	431-3
Cambridge Savings Bank						
1374 Massachusetts Ave	Cambridge	MA	02138	**800-540-6322**	617-441-4155	69
Cambridge Silversmith Ltd						
116 Lehigh Dr	Fairfield	NJ	07004	**800-890-3366**	973-227-4400	358
Cambridge Street Metal Corp (CSM)						
82 Stevens St	East Taunton	MA	02718	**800-254-7580**	508-822-2278	487
Cambridge Suites Hotel Halifax						
1583 Brunswick St	Halifax	NS	B3J3P5	**800-565-1263**	902-420-0555	376
Cambridge Suites Hotel Toronto						
15 Richmond St E	Toronto	ON	M5C1N2	**800-463-1990**	416-368-1990	376
Cambridge Technology Inc						
25 Hartwell Ave	Lexington	MA	02421	**800-342-3757**	781-541-1600	467
Cambridgeport Air Systems						
Eight Fanaras Dr	Salisbury	MA	01952	**877-648-2872**	978-465-8481	603
CambridgeSoft Corp						
100 CambridgePark Dr	Cambridge	MA	02140	**800-315-7300**	617-588-9100	179-5
CambridgeWorld						
34 Franklin Ave	Brooklyn	NY	11205	**800-221-2253**	718-858-5002	118
Cambro Manufacturers Co						
5801 Skylab Rd	Huntington Beach	CA	92647	**800-833-3003**	714-848-1555	299
Cambrooke Foods Inc						
Four Copeland Dr	Ayer	MA	01432	**866-456-9776**	508-782-2300	296-8
Camco Chemical Co						
8145 Holton Dr	Florence	KY	41042	**800-354-1001***	859-727-3200	149
*Cust Svc						
Camden County Chamber of Commerce						
2603 Osborne Rd Ste R	Saint Marys	GA	31558	**888-837-4002**	912-729-5840	137
Camden County College						
200 College Dr	Blackwood	NJ	08012	**888-228-2466**	856-227-7200	160
Camden County Library						
203 Laurel Rd	Voorhees	NJ	08043	**877-222-3737**	856-772-1636	431-3
Camden National Corp						
Two Elm St	Camden	ME	04843	**800-860-8821**	207-236-8821	357-2
NYSE: CAC						
Camden Property Trust						
11 Greenway Plz Ste 2400	Houston	TX	77046	**800-922-6336**	713-354-2500	646
NYSE: CPT						
Camden Publications						
331 E Bell St	Camden	MI	49232	**800-222-6336**	517-368-0365	525-4
Camden-Clark Memorial Hospital (CCMH)						
800 Garfield Ave	Parkersburg	WV	26101	**800-541-3160**	304-424-2111	371-3
Camel Grinding Wheels						
7525 N Oak Pk Ave	Niles	IL	60714	**800-447-4248**	847-647-5994	1
Camel Rock Casino						
17486A Hwy 84/285	Santa Fe	NM	87506	**800-483-1040**	505-983-2667	132
Camelback Inn JW Marriott Resort Golf Club & Spa						
5402 E Lincoln Dr	Scottsdale	AZ	85253	**800-242-2635**	480-948-1700	660
CAMELBACK MOUNTAIN						
301 Resort Dr	Tannersville	PA	18372	**888-337-6966**	570-629-1661	31
Camelot Carpet Mills Inc						
17111 Red Hill Ave	Irvine	CA	92614	**800-854-8331**	949-474-4000	130
Camelot Community Care Inc						
4910 D Creekside Dr	Clearwater	FL	33760	**866-343-8606**	727-593-0003	47-6
Camera Corner Inc						
PO Box 1899	Burlington	NC	27216	**800-868-2462**	336-228-0251	118
Cameron Balloons US						
PO Box 3672	Ann Arbor	MI	48106	**866-423-6178**	734-426-5525	28
Cameron Compression Systems						
16250 Port NW Dr	Houston	TX	77041	**800-323-9160**	713-354-1900	173
Cameron Thomson Group Ltd						
390 Bay St Ste 1706	Toronto	ON	M5H2Y2	**800-395-9943**	416-350-5009	398
Cameron Turbocompressor						
3101 Broadway	Buffalo	NY	14225	**877-805-7911**	716-896-6600	173
Cameron University						
2800 W Gore Blvd	Lawton	OK	73505	**888-454-7600***	580-581-2289	166
*Admissions						
Camesa Inc						
1615 Spur 529	Rosenberg	TX	77471	**800-866-0001**	281-342-4494	253
Camin Cargo Control Inc						
230 Marion Ave	Linden	NJ	07036	**800-756-8798**	908-862-1899	732
Camino Real Foods Inc						
2638 E Vernon Ave	Vernon	CA	90058	**800-421-6201**	323-585-6599	295-36
Camp Butler National Cemetery						
5063 Camp Butler Rd	Springfield	IL	62707	**877-907-8585**	217-492-4070	135
Camp Creek State Forest						
2390 Camp Creek Rd	Camp Creek	WV	25820	**800-225-5982**	304-425-9481	558
Camp Nelson National Cemetery						
6980 Danville Rd	Nicholasville	KY	40356	**800-827-1000**	859-885-5727	135
Camp Olympia						
723 Olympia Dr	Trinity	TX	75862	**800-735-6190**	936-594-2541	296-8
Campaign Legal Ctr						
Media Policy Program Campaign						
Legal Ctr	Washington	DC	20036	**877-855-5007**	202-736-2200	47-7
Campbell Alliance Group Inc						
8045 Arco Corporate Dr Ste 500	Raleigh	NC	27617	**888-297-2001**	919-844-7100	190-4
Campbell County Board of Education						
101 Orchard Ln	Alexandria	KY	41001	**800-942-3767**	859-635-2173	676
Campbell County Chamber of Commerce						
314 S Gillette Ave	Gillette	WY	82716	**877-682-3481**	307-682-3673	137
Campbell County Public Library						
2101 S 4-J Rd	Gillette	WY	82718	**888-250-1879**	307-682-3223	431-3
Campbell Manufacturing Inc						
127 E Spring St	Bechtelsville	PA	19505	**800-523-0224**	610-367-2107	588
Campbell Oil Company Inc						
611 Erie St S	Massillon	OH	44646	**800-589-8555**	330-833-8555	572
Campbell Soup Co						
One Campbell Pl	Camden	NJ	08103	**800-257-8443**	856-342-4800	295-36
NYSE: CPB						
Campbell University						
450 Leslie Campbell Ave						
PO Box 546	Buies Creek	NC	27506	**800-334-4111**	910-893-1290	166
Campbell University Norman Adrian Wiggins School of Law						
113 Main St	Buies Creek	NC	27506	**800-334-4111**	919-865-5991	167-1
Campbell Wrapper Corp						
1415 Fortune Ave	De Pere	WI	54115	**800-727-4210**	920-983-7100	540

	City	State	ZIP	Toll-Free	Phone	Class
Campbell's Resort						
104 W Woodin Ave PO Box 278	Chelan	WA	98816	**800-553-8225**	509-682-2561	660
Campbellsville University						
One University Dr	Campbellsville	KY	42718	**800-264-6014***	270-789-5000	166
*Admissions						
Camperoo Inc						
2900 Weslayan St Ste 545	Houston	TX	77027	**888-538-8809**		384
Campion College at the University of Regina						
3737 Wascana Pkwy	Regina	SK	S4S0A2	**800-667-7282**	306-586-4242	773
Campus Crusade for Christ International						
100 Lk Hart Dr	Orlando	FL	32832	**888-278-7233**	407-826-2500	47-20
Campus Federal Credit Union						
PO Box 98036	Baton Rouge	LA	70898	**888-769-8841**	225-769-8841	219
Campus Inn & Suites						
390 E Broadway	Eugene	OR	97401	**800-888-6313**	541-343-3376	376
Campus Special LLC, The						
3575 Koger Blvd Ste 300	Duluth	GA	30096	**800-365-8520**		196
Campus Televideo Inc						
100 First Stamford Pl	Stamford	CT	06902	**866-615-8674**	203-983-5400	115
Campus USA Credit Union						
PO Box 147029	Gainesville	FL	32614	**800-367-6440**	352-335-9090	219
Cam-Wal Electric Co-op Inc						
404 W Scranton St PO Box 135	Selby	SD	57472	**800-269-7676**		245
Can Lines Engineering						
9839 Downey Norwalk Rd						
PO Box 7039	Downey	CA	90241	**800-233-4597**	562-861-2996	208
Can Manufacturers Institute (CMI)						
1730 Rhode Island Ave NW						
Ste 1000	Washington	DC	20036	**800-363-2726**	202-232-4677	48-13
Canaan Valley Resort & Conference Ctr						
230 Main Lodge Rd	Davis	WV	26260	**800-622-4121**	304-866-4121	660
Canaan Valley Resort State Park						
230 Main Lodge Rd	Davis	WV	26260	**800-622-4121**	304-866-4121	558
CANAC Inc						
6505 Trans-Canada Hwy						
Ste 405	St Laurent	QC	H4T1S3	**800-588-4387**	514-734-4700	641
Canad Inns - Club Regent Casino Hotel						
1415 Regent Ave W	Winnipeg	MB	R2C3B2	**888-332-2623**	204-667-5560	376
Canad Inns Fort Garry						
1824 Pembina Hwy	Winnipeg	MB	R3T2G2	**888-332-2623**	204-261-7450	376
Canad Inns Garden City						
2100 McPhillips St	Winnipeg	MB	R2V3T9	**888-332-2623**	204-633-0024	376
Canad Inns Polo Park						
1405 St Matthews Ave	Winnipeg	MB	R3G0K5	**888-332-2623**	204-775-8791	376
Canada						
885 Second Ave 14th Fl	New York	NY	10017	**800-267-8376**	212-848-1100	
Consulate General						
500 N Akard St Ste 2900	Dallas	TX	75201	**800-267-8376**	214-922-9806	257
Consulate General						
1251 Ave of the Americas						
Concourse Level	New York	NY	10020	**800-267-8376**	212-596-1628	257
Embassy						
501 Pennsylvania Ave NW	Washington	DC	20001	**800-567-6868**	202-682-1740	257
Canada Agriculture Museum						
Prince of Wales Dr						
PO Box 9724 Stn T	Ottawa	ON	K1G5A3	**866-442-4416**	613-991-3044	513
Canada Flowers						
4073 Longhurst Ave	Niagara Falls	ON	L2E6G5	**888-705-9999**	905-354-2713	292
Canada Forgings Inc						
130 Hagar St	Welland	ON	L3B5P8	**800-263-0440**	905-735-1220	534
Canada Life Assurance Co, The						
330 University Ave	Toronto	ON	M5G1R8	**888-252-1847**	416-597-1456	388-4
Canada Science & Technology Museum						
1867 St Laurent Blvd PO Box 9724	Ottawa	ON	K1G5A3	**866-442-4416**	613-991-3044	513
Canada's Research-Based Pharmaceutical Cos (Rx&D)						
55 Metcalfe St Ste 1220	Ottawa	ON	K1P6L5	**800-363-0203**	613-236-0455	48-8
Canadian Academy of Sport Medicine (CASM)						
180 Elgin St Ste 1400	Ottawa	ON	K2P2K3	**877-585-2394**	613-748-5851	48-8
Canadian Assn of Emergency Physicians (CAEP)						
1785 Alta Vista Dr Ste 104	Ottawa	ON	K1G3Y6	**800-463-1158**	613-523-3343	48-8
Canadian Assn of Occupational Therapists (CAOT)						
1125 Colonel By Dr	Ottawa	ON	K1S5R1	**800-434-2268**	613-523-2268	47-1
Canadian Assn of Speech-Language Pathologists & Audiologists (CASLPA)						
One Nicholas St Ste 1000	Ottawa	ON	K1N7B7	**800-259-8519**	613-567-9968	47-1
Canadian Automobile Assn (CAA)						
2151 Thurston Dr Ste 200	Ottawa	ON	K1G6C9	**800-267-8713**	613-820-1890	47-23
Canadian Bearings Ltd						
1600 Drew Rd	Mississauga	ON	L5S1S5	**800-229-2327**	905-670-6700	382
Canadian College of Naturopathic Medicine						
1255 Sheppard Ave E	Toronto	ON	M2K1E2	**866-241-2266**	416-498-1255	773
Canadian Federation of Humane Societies (CFHS)						
30 Concourse Gate Ste 102	Ottawa	ON	K2E7V7	**888-678-2347**	613-224-8072	47-3
Canadian Fishing Co						
Foot of Gore Ave	Vancouver	BC	V6A2Y7	**877-506-1294**	604-681-0211	285
Canadian Golf Hall of Fame & Museum						
Glen Abbey Golf Course						
1333 Dorval Dr Ste 1	Oakville	ON	L6M4X7	**800-263-0009**	905-849-9700	515
Canadian Gypsum Company Inc						
350 Burnhamthorpe Rd W						
Fifth Fl	Mississauga	ON	L5B3J1	**800-565-6607**	905-803-5600	344
Canadian Imperial Bank of Commerce (CIBC)						
199 Bay St Commerce Ct W	Toronto	ON	M5L1A2	**800-465-2422**		69
NYSE: CM						
Canadian Industrial Distributors Inc						
175 Sun Pac Blvd Ste 2A	Brampton	ON	L6S5Z6	**877-280-0243**	905-595-0411	94
Canadian Information Processing Society (CIPS)						
5090 Explorer Dr Ste 801	Mississauga	ON	L4W4T9	**877-275-2477**	905-602-1370	47-1
Canadian Kennel Club (CKC)						
200 Ronson Dr Ste 400	Etobicoke	ON	M9W5Z9	**800-250-8040**	416-675-5511	47-3
Canadian Livestock Insurance						
480 University Ave Ste 412	Toronto	ON	M5G1V2	**800-727-1502**	416-510-8191	388-1
Canadian Living Magazine						
25 Sheppard Ave W Ste 100	Toronto	ON	M2N6S7	**800-387-6332**	416-733-7600	452-11
Canadian Medical Assn (CMA)						
1867 Alta Vista Dr	Ottawa	ON	K1G5W8	**800-663-7336**	613-731-9331	48-8
Canadian Medical Laboratories Ltd						
6560 Kennedy Rd	Mississauga	ON	L5T2X4	**800-263-0801**		415
Canadian Museum of Civilization						
100 Laurier St	Gatineau	QC	K1A0M8	**800-555-5621**	819-776-7000	513
Canadian Museum of Contemporary Photography						
380 Sussex Dr PO Box 427 Stn A	Ottawa	ON	K1N9N4	**800-319-2787**	613-990-1985	513
Canadian Museum of Nature						
240 McLeod St	Ottawa	ON	K2P2R1	**800-263-4433**	613-566-4700	513

Name / Address	City	State	ZIP	Toll-Free	Phone	Class
Canadian Musician Magazine						
4056 Dorchester Rd	Niagara Falls	ON	L2E6M9	**877-746-4692**	905-374-8878	452-9
Canadian National Railway Co						
935 Rue de la Gauchetiere O	Montreal	QC	H3B2M9	**888-668-4626**	888-888-5909	639
TSE: CNR						
Canadian Natural Resources Ltd (CNRL)						
855 Second St SW Ste 2500	Calgary	AB	T2P4J8	**888-878-3700**	403-517-6700	529
NYSE: CNQ						
Canadian Newspaper Assn						
890 Yonge St Ste 200	Toronto	ON	M4W3P4	**877-305-2262**	416-923-3567	48-16
Canadian Pacific Railway Co						
401 9 Ave SW Ste 500	Calgary	AB	T2P4Z4	**888-333-6370**	403-319-7000	639
Canadian Parks & Wilderness Society (CPAWS)						
250 City Ctr Ave Ste 506	Ottawa	ON	K1R6K7	**800-333-9453**	613-569-7226	47-13
Canadian Peregrine Foundation						
1450 O'Connor Dr Bldg B Ste 214	Toronto	ON	M4B2T8	**888-709-3944**	416-481-1233	47-3
Canadian Southern Baptist Seminary						
200 Seminary View	Cochrane	AB	T4C2G1	**877-922-2727**	403-932-6622	167-3
Canadian Tire Corp Ltd						
2180 Yonge St PO Box 770 Stn K	Toronto	ON	M4P2V8	**800-387-8803**	416-480-3000	186
TSE: CTC						
Canadian Valley Electric Co-op						
11277 S 356 PO Box 751	Seminole	OK	74868	**877-382-3680**	405-382-3680	245
Canadian Western Bank						
10303 Jasper Ave Ste 3000	Edmonton	AB	T5J3X6	**866-317-0356**	780-423-8888	69
TSE: CWB						
Canadian Wildlife Federation (CWF)						
350 Michael Cowpland Dr	Kanata	ON	K2M2W1	**800-563-9453**	613-599-9594	47-13
Canal Insurance Co						
400 E Stone Ave PO Box 7	Greenville	SC	29601	**800-452-6911**		388-4
Canal Park Lodge						
250 Canal Pk Dr	Duluth	MN	55802	**800-777-8560**	218-279-6000	376
Canal Park Stadium						
300 S Main St	Akron	OH	44308	**855-977-8225**	330-253-5151	711
Canal Wood LLC						
2430 Main St	Conway	SC	29526	**866-587-1460**	843-488-9663	443
Canaletto						
3355 Las Vegas Blvd S	Las Vegas	NV	89109	**866-659-9643**	702-414-1000	662
Canam Group Inc						
11505 First Ave						
Bureau 500	Saint-Georges	QC	G5Y7H5	**877-499-6049**	418-228-8031	714
TSE: CAM						
Can-am Plumbing Inc						
151 Wyoming St	Pleasanton	CA	94566	**800-786-9797**	925-846-1833	603
Canandaigua Inn on the Lake						
770 S Main St	Canandaigua	NY	14424	**800-228-2801**	585-394-7800	376
Canandaigua Wine Company Inc						
235 N Bloomfield Rd	Canandaigua	NY	14424	**888-659-7900**	585-396-7600	79-3
Canary Hotel						
31 W Carrillo	Santa Barbara	CA	93101	**866-999-5401**	805-884-0300	376
Canberra Corp						
3610 Holland Sylvania Rd	Toledo	OH	43615	**800-832-8992**	419-841-6616	149
Canberra Industries Inc						
800 Research Pkwy	Meriden	CT	06450	**800-243-3955***	203-238-2351	467
*Sales						
Canby School District						
1130 S Ivy St	Canby	OR	97013	**800-475-7785**	503-266-7861	676
Cancap Pharmaceutical Ltd						
13111 Vanier Pl Ste 180	Richmond	BC	V6V2J1	**877-998-2378**	604-278-2188	231
Cancer Care Inc						
275 Seventh Ave 22nd Fl	New York	NY	10001	**800-813-4673**	212-712-8400	47-17
Cancer Genetics Inc						
Meadows Office Complex 201 Rt 17 N						
Second Fl	Rutherford	NJ	07070	**888-334-4988**	201-528-9200	231
Cancer Letter						
PO Box 9905	Washington	DC	20016	**800-513-7042**	202-362-1809	524-8
Cancer Letter Business & Regulatory Report						
PO Box 9905	Washington	DC	20016	**800-513-7042**	202-362-1809	524-8
Candela Corp						
530 Boston Post Rd	Wayland	MA	01778	**800-733-8550**	508-358-7400	421
NASDAQ: CLZR						
Candid Color Systems Inc						
1300 Metropolitan Ave	Oklahoma City	OK	73108	**800-336-4550**	405-947-8747	581
Candlelighters Childhood Cancer Foundation						
10920 Connecticut Ave Suuite A						
PO Box 498	Kensington	MD	20895	**800-366-2223**	301-962-3520	47-17
Candy Bouquet International Inc						
510 Mclean St	Little Rock	AR	72202	**877-226-3901**	501-375-9990	122
Cane Creek Cycling Components						
355 Cane Creek Rd	Fletcher	NC	28732	**800-234-2725**	828-684-3551	81
Cane Creek State Park						
50 State Pk Rd	Star City	AR	71667	**888-287-2757**	870-628-4714	558
Caney Fork Electric Co-op Inc						
920 Smithville Hwy						
PO Box 272	McMinnville	TN	37110	**888-505-3030**	931-473-3116	245
Caney Valley Electric Co-op Assn Inc, The						
401 Lawrence St PO Box 308	Cedar Vale	KS	67024	**800-310-8911**	620-758-2262	245
Canfield & Tack Inc						
925 Exchange St	Rochester	NY	14608	**800-836-0861***	585-235-7710	619
*General						
Canfield Connector Div						
8510 Foxwood Ct	Youngstown	OH	44514	**800-554-5071**		202
Cangene bioPharma Inc						
1111 S Paca St	Baltimore	MD	21230	**800-441-4225**	410-843-5000	231
Cangene Corp						
155 Innovation Dr	Winnipeg	MB	R3T5Y3	**800-768-2304**	204-275-4200	84
TSE: CNJ						
Cangro Industries Long Island Transmission Co						
495 Smith St	Farmingdale	NY	11735	**800-422-9210**	631-454-9000	613
Canine Companions for Independence Inc (CCI)						
2965 Dutton Ave PO Box 446	Santa Rosa	CA	95402	**800-572-2275**	707-577-1700	47-17
Canisius College						
2001 Main St	Buffalo	NY	14208	**800-843-1517**	716-888-2200	166
Cankdeska Cikana Community College						
PO Box 269	Fort Totten	ND	58335	**888-783-1463**	701-766-4415	163
Cannery Casino & Hotel, The						
Cannery Casino Resorts LLC						
2121 E Craig Rd	North Las Vegas	NV	89030	**866-999-4899**	702-507-5700	376
Cannon Air Force Base						
110 E Sextant Ave Ste 1150	Cannon AFB	NM	88103	**877-283-3858**	575-784-4131	492-1
Cannon Design						
2170 Whitehaven Rd	Grand Island	NY	14072	**800-340-9511**	716-773-6800	261
Cannon Muskegon Corp						
2875 Lincoln St PO Box 506	Muskegon	MI	49441	**800-253-0371**	231-755-1681	480
Canoga Perkins Corp						
20600 Prairie St	Chatsworth	CA	91311	**800-360-6642***	818-718-6300	174-3
*Tech Supp						
Canon Business Solutions-Central						
425 N Martingale Rd Ste 100	Schaumburg	IL	60173	**800-706-3303**	847-706-3400	111
Canon Business Solutions-Southeast Inc						
300 Commerce Sq Blvd	Burlington	NJ	08016	**844-443-4636**	609-387-8700	111
Canon Business Solutions-West						
One Canon Park	Melville	CA	11747	**844-443-4636**		111
Canon City Chamber of Commerce						
403 Royal Gorge Blvd	Canon City	CO	81212	**800-876-7922**	719-275-2331	137
Canoochee Electric Membership Corp						
342 E Brazell St	Reidsville	GA	30453	**800-342-0134**		245
Canplas Industries Ltd						
500 Veterans Dr	Barrie	ON	L4M4V3	**800-461-1771**	705-726-3361	598-2
Canson Inc						
21 Industrial Dr	South Hadley	MA	01075	**800-628-9283**	413-538-9250	42
Canteen Service Co						
712 Industrial Dr	Owensboro	KY	42301	**800-467-2471**	270-683-2471	298
Canteen Vending Services						
Compass Group						
2400 Yorkmont Rd	Charlotte	NC	28217	**800-357-0012**	704-328-4000	298
Canter & Assoc LLC						
12975 Coral Tree Pl	Los Angeles	CA	90066	**800-669-9011***	310-578-4700	756
*Cust Svc						
Canterbury International						
5632 W Washington Blvd	Los Angeles	CA	90016	**800-935-7111**	323-936-7111	151
Canterbury Park Holding Corp						
1100 Canterbury Rd	Shakopee	MN	55379	**800-340-6361**	952-445-7223	633
NASDAQ: CPHC						
Canton Public Library						
1200 S Canton Ctr Rd	Canton	MI	48188	**888-988-6300**	734-397-0999	431-3
Canton Regional Chamber of Commerce						
222 Market Ave N	Canton	OH	44702	**800-533-4302**	330-456-7253	137
Canton/Stark County Convention & Visitors Bureau						
222 Market Ave N	Canton	OH	44702	**800-552-6051**	330-454-1439	207
Canvas Products Co						
274 S Waterman St	Detroit	MI	48209	**877-293-1669**		723
Canyon Chamber of Commerce						
1518 Fifth Ave	Canyon	TX	79015	**800-999-9481**	806-655-7815	137
Canyon Creek Cabinet Co						
16726 Tye St SE	Monroe	WA	98272	**800-228-1830**	360-348-4973	114
Canyon Ranch Lenox						
165 Kemble St	Lenox	MA	01240	**800-742-9000***	413-637-4100	660
*Resv						
Canyon Ranch SpaClub at the Venetian						
3355 Las Vegas Blvd S						
Ste 1159	Las Vegas	NV	89109	**877-220-2688**	702-414-3606	698
Canyon Ranch Tucson						
8600 E Rockcliff Rd	Tucson	AZ	85750	**800-742-9000**	520-749-9000	660
Canyons Resort, The						
4000 The Canyons Resort Dr	Park City	UT	84098	**888-226-9667**	435-649-5400	660
CAO Group Inc						
4628 Skyhawk Dr	West Jordan	UT	84084	**877-877-9778**	801-256-9282	416
CAOT (Canadian Assn of Occupational Therapists)						
1125 Colonel By Dr	Ottawa	ON	K1S5R1	**800-434-2268**	613-523-2268	47-1
CAP (College of American Pathologists)						
325 Waukegan Rd	Northfield	IL	60093	**800-323-4040**	847-832-7000	48-8
CAP (Children Awaiting Parents Inc)						
595 Blossom Rd Ste 306	Rochester	NY	14610	**888-835-8802**	585-232-5110	47-6
Cape Air						
660 Barnstable Rd	Hyannis	MA	02601	**866-227-3247**	508-771-6944	25
Cape Breton University						
1250 Grand Lk Rd	Sydney	NS	B1P6L2	**888-959-9995**	902-539-5300	773
Cape Cod Canal Regional Chamber of Commerce						
70 Main St	Buzzards Bay	MA	02532	**888-332-2732**	508-759-6000	137
Cape Cod Chamber of Commerce						
Five Shoot Flying Hill Rd	Centerville	MA	02632	**888-332-2732**	508-362-3225	137
Cape Cod Coast Guard Air Station						
2300 Wilson Blvd Ste 500	Arlington	VA	20598	**877-669-8724**	202-372-4620	156
Cape Cod Community College						
2240 Iyanough Rd	West Barnstable	MA	02668	**877-846-3672**	508-362-2131	160
Cape Cod Five Cents Savings Bank						
19 W Rd PO Box 20	Orleans	MA	02653	**800-678-1855**	508-240-0555	69
Cape Cod Life Magazine						
13 Steeple St Ste 204						
PO Box 1439	Mashpee	MA	02649	**800-698-1717**	508-419-7381	452-22
Cape Cod Lumber Co Inc						
225 Groveland St	Abington	MA	02351	**800-368-3117**	781-878-0715	361
Cape Cod Potato Chip Co						
100 Breed's Hill Rd	Hyannis	MA	02601	**888-881-2447**	508-775-3358	295-35
Cape Cod Regional Transit Authority (CCRTA)						
215 Iyannough Rd PO Box 1988	Hyannis	MA	02601	**800-352-7155**	508-775-8504	463
Cape Cod Times						
319 Main St	Hyannis	MA	02601	**800-451-7887**	508-775-1200	525-2
Cape Codder Resort & Spa						
1225 Iyanough Rd						
Rt 132 Bearse's Way	Hyannis	MA	02601	**888-297-2200**	508-771-3000	660
Cape Fear Coast Convention & Visitors Bureau						
505 Nutt St Unit A	Wilmington	NC	28401	**877-406-2356**	910-341-4030	207
Cape Fear Community College						
411 N Front St	Wilmington	NC	28401	**877-498-8868**	910-362-7000	160
Cape Girardeau Convention & Visitors Bureau						
400 Broadway Ste 100	Cape Girardeau	MO	63701	**800-777-0068**	573-335-1631	207
Cape Hatteras Electric Co-op						
47109 Light Plant Rd PO Box 9	Buxton	NC	27920	**800-454-5616**	252-995-5616	245
Cape Verde						
Embassy						
3415 Massachusetts Ave NW	Washington	DC	20007	**800-343-2347**	202-965-6820	257
Capel Inc 831 N Main St	Troy	NC	27371	**800-334-3711**	800-382-6574	130
Capella Education Co						
225 S Sixth St Ninth Fl	Minneapolis	MN	55402	**888-227-3552***	612-339-8650	242
NASDAQ: CPLA ■ *Cust Svc						
Capezio/Ballet Makers Inc						
One Campus Rd	Totowa	NJ	07512	**800-533-1887***	973-595-9000	300
*Acctg						
CapFinancial Partners LLC						
4208 Six Forks Rd Ste 1700	Raleigh	NC	27609	**800-216-0645**	919-870-6822	398
Capistrano Scion						
33395 Camino						
Capistrano	San Juan Capistrano	CA	92675	**888-493-0040**	949-493-4100	56
Capital Agricultural Property Services Inc						
801 Warrenville Rd Ste 150	Lisle	IL	60532	**800-243-2060**	630-434-9150	314-3

Name / Address	City	State	ZIP	Toll-Free	Phone	Class
Capital Analysts Inc 218 Glenside Ave	Wyncote	PA	19095	**800-242-1421**		387
Capital Automotive Real Estate Services Inc 8270 Greensboro Dr Ste 950	McLean	VA	22102	**877-422-7288**	703-288-3075	645
Capital City Bank 2111 N Monroe St PO Box 900	Tallahassee	FL	32302	**888-671-0400**	850-402-7500	69
Capital City Bank Group Inc PO Box 900 *NASDAQ: CCBG*	Tallahassee	FL	32302	**888-671-0400**	850-402-7500	357-2
Capital Community College 950 Main St	Hartford	CT	06103	**800-894-6126**	860-906-5000	160
Capital Culinary Institute of Keiser College *Melbourne* 900 S Babcock St	Melbourne	FL	32901	**877-636-3618**	321-409-4800	161
Capital District Physicians' Health Plan 500 Patroon Creek Blvd	Albany	NY	12206	**888-258-0477**	518-641-3000	388-3
Capital Farm Credit Aca 7000 Woodway Dr PO Box 20097	Waco	TX	76702	**877-944-5500**	254-776-7506	68
Capital Ford Inc 4900 Capital Blvd	Raleigh	NC	27616	**877-659-2496**	919-790-4600	56
Capital Gazette Communications LLC 2000 Capital Dr	Annapolis	MD	21401	**888-607-8365**	410-268-5000	628-8
Capital Grille 900 Boylston St	Boston	MA	02115	**866-518-9113**		662
Capital Group Cos Inc 333 S Hope St	Los Angeles	CA	90071	**800-421-8511**	213-615-0514	398
Capital Growth Management LP 1 International Pl	Boston	MA	02110	**800-345-4048**	617-737-3225	398
Capital Health Plan PO Box 15349	Tallahassee	FL	32317	**800-390-1434**	850-383-3333	388-3
Capital Hill Hotel & Suites 88 Albert St	Ottawa	ON	K1P5E9	**800-463-7705**	613-235-1413	376
Capital Hotel 111 W Markham St	Little Rock	AR	72201	**877-637-0037**	501-374-7474	376
Capital Journal 333 W Dakota Ave	Pierre	SD	57501	**800-537-0025**	605-224-7301	525-2
Capital Manor 1955 Dallas Hwy NW	Salem	OR	97304	**800-637-0327**	503-362-4101	663
Capital Medical Ctr 3900 Capital Mall Dr SW	Olympia	WA	98502	**888-677-9757**	360-754-5858	371-3
Capital Newspapers 1901 Fish Hatchery Rd	Madison	WI	53713	**888-798-4468**	920-887-0321	628-8
Capital One Auto Finance Inc PO Box 60511	City of Industry	CA	91716	**800-946-0332**		69
Capital One Financial Corp 1680 Capital One Dr *NYSE: COF*	McLean	VA	22102	**800-655-2265**	800-926-1000	217
Capital Public Radio Inc 7055 Folsom Blvd	Sacramento	CA	95826	**877-480-5900**	916-278-8900	636-92
Capital Region International Airport 4100 Capital City Blvd	Lansing	MI	48906	**866-841-4900**	517-321-6121	27
Capital Regional Medical Ctr (CRMC) 2626 Capital Medical Blvd	Tallahassee	FL	32308	**800-994-6610**	850-325-5000	371-3
Capital Research & Management Co (CRMC) 333 S Hope St	Los Angeles	CA	90071	**800-421-4225**	213-486-9200	398
Capital Research Ctr 1513 16th St NW	Washington	DC	20036	**800-459-3950**	202-483-6900	625
Capital Resource Partners 31 State St 6th Fl	Boston	MA	02109	**800-623-2880**	617-478-9600	780
Capital Southwest Corp 12900 Preston Rd Ste 700 *NASDAQ: CSWC*	Dallas	TX	75230	**877-870-5176**	972-233-8242	780
Capital Times 1901 Fish Hatchery Rd	Madison	WI	53713	**800-362-8333**	608-252-6400	525-2
Capital University College & Main St	Columbus	OH	43209	**866-544-6175**	614-236-6101	166
Capital University Law School 303 E Broad St	Columbus	OH	43215	**800-362-2779**	614-236-6500	167-1
Capitol Aggregates Ltd 12625 Wetmore Rd Ste 301	San Antonio	TX	78247	**800-292-5315**	210-871-6100	45
Capitol Broadcasting Co Inc 2619 Western Blvd	Raleigh	NC	27606	**800-234-4857**	919-890-6000	728
Capitol Chevrolet Montgomery 711 Eastern Blvd *Sales	Montgomery	AL	36117	**800-410-1137***	334-272-8700	56
Capitol City Bancshares Inc 562 Lee St	Atlanta	GA	30310	**866-758-6395**	404-752-6067	357-2
Capitol City Produce 16550 Commercial Ave	Baton Rouge	LA	70816	**800-349-1583**	225-272-8153	295-21
Capitol City Speakers Bureau 1620 S Fifth St	Springfield	IL	62703	**800-397-3183**	217-544-8552	699
Capitol Detective Agency 2922 N 18th Pl	Phoenix	AZ	85016	**800-346-0347**	602-265-3462	397
Capitol Distributing Inc 3500 E Commercial Ct	Meridian	ID	83642	**800-769-5659**	208-888-5112	342
Capitol Federal Financial 700 Kansas Ave *NASDAQ: CFFN*	Topeka	KS	66603	**888-822-7333**	785-235-1341	357-2
Capitol FSB 700 S Kansas Ave	Topeka	KS	66603	**800-432-2926**	785-235-1341	69
Capitol Indemnity Corp 1600 Aspen Commons	Middleton	WI	53562	**800-475-4450**	608-829-4200	388-4
Capitol Insurance Cos 1600 Aspen Commons PO Box 5900	Middleton	WI	53562	**800-475-4450**	608-829-4200	388-4
Capitol Mitsubishi 750 Capitol Expy Automall	San Jose	CA	95136	**888-479-0842**	408-264-9999	56
Capitol Plaza Hotel 415 W McCarty St	Jefferson City	MO	65101	**800-338-8088**	573-635-1234	662
Capitol Plaza Hotel & Conference Ctr 100 State St	Montpelier	VT	05602	**800-274-5252**	802-223-5252	376
Capitol Plaza Hotel Jefferson City 415 W McCarty St	Jefferson City	MO	65101	**800-338-8088**	573-635-1234	376
Capitol Plywood Inc 160 Commerce Cir	Sacramento	CA	95815	**800-326-1505**	916-922-8861	606
Capitol Services Inc 800 Brazos St Ste 400	Austin	TX	78701	**800-345-4647**		626
Capitol Steps Productions Inc 210 N Washington St	Alexandria	VA	22314	**800-733-7837**	703-683-8330	624
Capitol Technology University 11301 Springfield Rd	Laurel	MD	20708	**800-950-1992**	301-369-2800	166
Capitol Transamerica Corp 1600 Aspen Commons	Middleton	WI	53562	**800-475-4450**	608-829-4200	357-4
Caplugs LLC 2150 Elmwood Ave *Cust Svc	Buffalo	NY	14207	**888-227-5847***	716-876-9855	152
CAPP/USA 201 Marple Ave	Clifton Heights	PA	19018	**800-356-8000**	610-394-1100	203
Capricorn Coffees Inc 353 Tenth St	San Francisco	CA	94103	**800-541-0758**	415-621-8500	296-2
Capsmith Inc 2240 Old Lk Mary Rd	Sanford	FL	32771	**800-228-3889**	407-328-7660	155-6
Capstead Mortgage Corp 8401 N Central Expy Ste 800 *NYSE: CMO*	Dallas	TX	75225	**800-358-2323**	214-874-2323	645
Capstone Therapeutics Corp 1275 W Washington St Ste 101 *OTC: CAPS*	Tempe	AZ	85281	**800-937-5520**	602-286-5520	472
Capstone Turbine Corp 21211 Nordhoff St *NASDAQ: CPST*	Chatsworth	CA	91311	**866-422-7786**	818-734-5300	262
Capt Hirams Resort 1606 Indian River Dr	Sebastian	FL	32958	**888-447-2671**	772-589-4345	376
Captain D's LLC 624 Grassmere Park Dr Ste 30	Nashville	TN	37211	**800-314-4819**	615-391-5461	661
Captain Daniel Stone Inn 10 Water St	Brunswick	ME	04011	**877-573-2374**	207-373-1824	376
Captain Merry Guesthouse & Fine Dining 399 Sinsinawa Ave	East Dubuque	IL	61025	**866-351-9586**	815-747-3644	662
CAPTE (Commission on Accreditation in Physical Therapy Education) 1111 N Fairfax St	Alexandria	VA	22314	**800-999-2782**	703-706-3245	47-1
Captive Fastener Corp 19 Thornton Rd	Oakland	NJ	07436	**800-526-4430**	201-337-6800	278
Captive-aire Systems Inc 4641 Paragon Pk Rd	Raleigh	NC	27616	**800-334-9256**	919-882-2410	688
Car City Motor Company Inc 3100 S US Hwy 169	Saint Joseph	MO	64503	**800-525-7008**	816-233-9149	56
Car Clinic Productions 5675 N Davis Hwy	Pensacola	FL	32503	**888-227-2546**	850-478-3139	637
Car Craft Magazine 6420 Wilshire Blvd	Los Angeles	CA	90048	**800-230-3030**	323-782-2000	452-3
Car Toys Inc 20 W Galer St	Seattle	WA	98119	**800-997-3644**	206-443-0980	51
Cara Operations Ltd 199 Four Valley Dr	Vaughan	ON	L4K0B8	**800-860-4082**	905-760-2244	298
Carahsoft Technology Corp 12369 Sunrise Vly Dr Ste D2	Reston	VA	20191	**888-662-2724**	703-871-8500	225
Caraustar Industries Inc 5000 Austell-Powder Springs Rd Ste 300	Austell	GA	30106	**800-223-1373**	770-948-3100	547
Caravan Facilities Management LLC 1400 Weiss St	Saginaw	MI	48602	**855-211-7450**		193
Caravan Products Company Inc 100 Adams Dr	Totowa	NJ	07512	**800-526-5261**	973-256-8886	295-16
Caravelle Resort Hotel & Villas 6900 N Ocean Blvd	Myrtle Beach	SC	29572	**800-507-9145**	843-918-8000	660
Carbo Ceramics Inc 575 N. Dairy Ashford Rd. Ste 300 *NYSE: CRR*	Houston	TX	77079	**800-551-3247**	281-921-6400	530
Carboline Co 350 Hanley Industrial Ct	Saint Louis	MO	63144	**800-848-4645**	314-644-1000	543
Carbon County PO Box 1017	Rawlins	WY	82301	**800-228-3547**		336
Carbon Power & Light Inc 100 E Willow Ave PO Box 579	Saratoga	WY	82331	**800-359-0249**	307-326-5206	245
Carbro Corp 15724 Condon Ave PO Box 278	Lawndale	CA	90260	**888-738-4400**	310-643-8400	488
Carcinoid Cancer Foundation Inc 333 Mamaroneck Ave Ste 492	White Plains	NY	10605	**888-722-3132**	212-722-3132	47-17
CARCO Group Inc 5000 Corporate Ct	Holtsville	NY	11742	**800-645-4556**	631-862-9300	626
Carco International Inc 2721 Midland Blvd	Fort Smith	AR	72904	**800-824-3215**	479-441-3270	274
Carco National Lease Inc 2905 N 32nd St	Fort Smith	AR	72904	**800-643-2596**	479-441-3200	768
Card Pak Inc 29601 Solon Rd	Solon	OH	44139	**800-824-3342**	440-542-3100	87
Cardiac Science Corp 3303 Monte Villa Pkwy *Cust Svc	Bothell	WA	98021	**800-426-0337***	425-402-2000	250
CardiacAssist Inc 240 Alpha Dr	Pittsburgh	PA	15238	**800-373-1607**	412-963-7770	471
Cardica Inc 900 Saginaw Dr *NASDAQ: CRDC*	Redwood City	CA	94063	**888-544-7194**	650-364-9975	471
Cardinal Aluminum Co 6910 Preston Hwy *Cust Svc	Louisville	KY	40219	**800-398-7833***	502-969-9302	480
Cardinal Detecto Scale Manufacturing Co 203 E Daugherty St	Webb City	MO	64870	**800-441-4237**	417-673-4631	675
Cardinal Financial Corp 8270 Greensboro Dr Ste 500 *NASDAQ: CFNL*	McLean	VA	22102	**800-473-3247**	703-584-3400	357-2
Cardinal Gates 79 Amlajack Way	Newnan	GA	30265	**800-318-3380**	770-252-4200	63
Cardinal Health Nuclear Pharmacy Services 7000 Cardinal Pl	Dublin	OH	43017	**800-326-6457**	614-757-5000	238
Cardinal Hill Healthcare System 2050 Versailles Rd	Lexington	KY	40504	**877-794-7328**	859-254-5701	371-6
Cardinal Industries Inc 21-01 51st Ave	Long Island City	NY	11101	**800-524-8697**	718-784-3000	752
Cardinal Meat Specialists Ltd 155 Hedgedale Rd	Brampton	ON	L6T5P3	**800-363-1439**	905-459-4436	296-9
Cardinal Office Products Inc 576 E Main St	Frankfort	KY	40601	**800-589-5886**	502-875-3300	527
Cardinal Stritch University 6801 N Yates Rd	Milwaukee	WI	53217	**800-347-8822**	414-410-4000	166
Cardinal Transport Inc 7180 E Reed Rd	Coal City	IL	60416	**800-435-9302**	815-634-4443	770
Cardiome Pharma Corp 6190 Agronomy Rd 6th Fl. *NASDAQ: CRME*	Vancouver	BC	V6T1Z3	**800-330-9928**	604-677-6905	84
Cardiovascular Systems Inc 651 Campus Dr	St Paul	MN	55112	**877-274-0360**	651-259-1600	471
CardLogix 16 Hughes Ste 100	Irvine	CA	92618	**866-392-8326**	949-380-1312	695

	Toll-Free	Phone	Class
Cardlytics Inc			
675 Ponce de Leon Ave NE Ste 6000 . . . . Atlanta GA 30308	888-798-5802		5
Cardolite Corp			
500 Doremus Ave . . . . Newark NJ 07105	800-322-7365		142
Cardone Industries Inc			
5501 Whitaker Ave . . . . Philadelphia PA 19124	800-777-4780*	215-912-3000	59
*Cust Svc			
CardScan Inc			
25 First St Ste 107 . . . . Cambridge MA 02141	800-942-6739	617-492-4200	174-7
CardSmart Retail Corp			
11 Executive Ave . . . . Edison NJ 08817	888-782-7050		309
CARE (Coalition for Auto Repair Equality)			
105 Oronoco St Ste 115 . . . . Alexandria VA 22314	800-229-5380	703-519-7555	48-21
Care Partners			
68 Sweeten Creek Rd . . . . Asheville NC 28803	800-627-1533	828-252-2255	360
CARE USA			
151 Ellis St NE . . . . Atlanta GA 30303	800-521-2273	404-681-2552	47-5
CareCentric Inc			
20 Church Street 12th Fl. . . . . Hartford CT 06103	866-467-8263	800-808-1902	179-10
Career Education Corp (CEC)			
2895 Greenspoint Pkwy Ste 600 . . . . Hoffman Estates IL 60196	877-559-9222	847-781-3600	242
NASDAQ: CECO			
CareerStaff Unlimited Inc			
6363 N State Hwy 161 Ste 525 . . . . Irving TX 75038	888-993-4599		712
Carefree of Colorado			
2145 W Sixth Ave . . . . Broomfield CO 80020	800-621-2617	303-469-3324	723
Carefree Resort & Conference Ctr			
37220 Mule Train Rd . . . . Carefree AZ 85377	888-692-4343		698
Carefree Vacations Inc			
9710 Scranton Rd Ste 300 . . . . San Diego CA 92121	800-266-3476	858-459-4074	761
CareFusion Corp			
3750 Torrey View Ct . . . . San Diego CA 92130	888-876-4287	858-617-2000	471
NYSE: CFN			
Carelink Health Plans			
500 Virginia St E Ste 400 . . . . Charleston WV 25301	800-348-2922	304-348-2900	388-3
Caremark Rx Inc			
PO Box 832407 . . . . Richardson TX 75083	877-460-7766		579
Carenet Healthcare Services			
11845 Interstate 10 W Ste 400 . . . . San Antonio TX 78230	800-809-7000		390
CarePartners Mountain Area Hospice			
PO Box 5779 . . . . Asheville NC 28813	800-627-1533	828-255-0231	368
CareSource			
230 N Main St . . . . Dayton OH 45402	800-488-0134	937-224-3300	349
Caresource Health Plan			
740 SE Seventh St . . . . Grants Pass OR 97526	888-460-0185	541-471-4106	360
Care-Tech Laboratories Inc			
3224 S KingsHwy Blvd . . . . Saint Louis MO 63139	800-325-9681	314-772-4610	576
Carey Digital			
1718 Central Pkwy . . . . Cincinnati OH 45214	800-767-6071	513-241-5210	771
Carey Executive Limousine			
245 University Ave . . . . Atlanta GA 30315	800-241-3943	404-223-2000	437
Carey International Inc			
4530 Wisconsin Ave NW 5th Fl . . . . Washington DC 20016	800-336-4646	202-895-1200	437
CARF (Commission on Accreditation of Rehabilitation Facilities International)			
6951 E Southpoint Rd . . . . Tucson AZ 85756	888-281-6531	520-325-1044	47-1
Carfax Inc			
10304 Eaton Pl Ste 500 . . . . Fairfax VA 10304	800-274-2277	703-934-2664	57
CARF-CCAC (Continuing Care Accreditation Commission)			
1730 Rhode Island Ave NW Ste 209 . . . . Washington DC 20036	866-888-1122	202-587-5001	47-1
Car-Freshner Corp			
21205 Little Tree Dr PO Box 719. . . . . Watertown NY 13601	800-545-5454	315-788-6250	149
Cargill Assoc Inc			
4701 Altamesa Blvd . . . . Fort Worth TX 76133	800-433-2233	817-292-9374	316
Cargill Energy			
PO Box 9300 . . . . Minneapolis MN 55440	800-227-4455	952-742-7575	572
Cargill Foundation			
15407 McGinty Rd W Ste 46 . . . . Wayzata MN 55391	800-227-4455	877-765-8867	303
Cargill Inc			
15407 McGinty Rd W . . . . Wayzata MN 55391	800-227-4455	952-742-7575	275
Cargill Salt Inc			
PO Box 5621 . . . . Minneapolis MN 55440	888-385-7258		671
Carhartt Inc			
5750 Mercury Dr . . . . Dearborn MI 48126	800-833-3118	313-271-8460	153-18
Caribbean Gardens			
1590 Goodlette-Frank Rd . . . . Naples FL 34102	888-520-3756	239-262-5409	810
Caribbean Products Ltd			
3624 Falls Rd . . . . Baltimore MD 21211	888-689-5068	410-235-7700	295-26
Caribbean Resort & Villas			
3000 N Ocean Blvd . . . . Myrtle Beach SC 29577	800-552-8509		660
Caribbean Travel & Life Magazine			
460 N Orlando Ave Ste 200 . . . . Winter Park FL 32789	800-289-9399*	407-628-4802	452-22
*Sales			
Caribe Royale Orlando All-Suites Hotel & Convention Ctr			
8101 World Ctr Dr . . . . Orlando FL 32821	800-823-8300*	407-238-8000	376
*Resv			
Caribou Coffee Company Inc			
3900 Lakebreeze Ave N . . . . . Minneapolis MN 55429	888-227-4268*	763-592-2200	157
NASDAQ: CBOU ■ *Cust Svc			
Caribou County			
159 S Main . . . . Soda Springs ID 83276	800-972-7660	208-547-4324	336
Caribou Highlands Lodge			
371 Ski Hill Rd PO Box 99 . . . . Lutsen MN 55612	800-642-6036	218-663-7241	660
Carilion New River Valley Medical Ctr			
2900 Lamb Cir . . . . Christiansburg VA 24073	800-432-7874	540-731-2000	371-3
Carithers Wallace Courtenay Co			
4343 NE Expy . . . . Atlanta GA 30340	800-292-8220	770-493-8200	319
Carl Buddig & Co			
950 175th St . . . . Homewood IL 60430	888-633-5684	708-798-0900	295-26
Carl Fischer Inc			
65 Bleecker St 28th Fl. . . . . . . New York NY 10012	800-762-2328	212-777-0900	628-7
Carl R Bieber Tourways Inc			
320 Fair St PO Box 180 . . . . Kutztown PA 19530	800-243-2374	610-683-7333	106
Carl Sandburg College			
2400 Tom L Wilson Blvd . . . . Galesburg IL 61401	877-236-1862	309-344-2518	160
Carl Sandburg Home National Historic Site			
81 Carl Sadburg Ln . . . . Flat Rock NC 28731	877-642-4743	828-693-4178	557
Carl Vinson Veterans Affairs Medical Ctr			
1826 Veterans Blvd . . . . Dublin GA 31021	800-595-5229	478-272-1210	371-8
Carl Zeiss Industrial Metrology			
6250 Sycamore Ln N . . . . . . Maple Grove MN 55369	800-752-6181	763-744-2400	488
Carle Hospice			
611 W Park St . . . . Urbana IL 61801	800-239-3620	217-383-3311	368
Carleton College			
100 S College St . . . . Northfield MN 55057	800-995-2275*	507-646-4000	166
*Admissions			
Carleton University			
1125 Colonel By Dr . . . . Ottawa ON K1S5B6	888-354-4414	613-520-7400	773
Carley State Park			
19041 Hwy 74 . . . . Altura MN 55910	888-646-6367	507-932-3007	558
Carling Technologies Inc			
60 Johnson Ave . . . . Plainville CT 06062	800-243-8556	860-793-9281	802
Carlisle Cos Inc			
13925 Ballantyne Corporate Pl Ste 400 . . . . Charlotte NC 28277	800-248-5995	704-501-1100	59
NYSE: CSL			
Carlisle FoodService Products Inc			
4711 E Hefner Rd . . . . Oklahoma City OK 73131	800-654-8210	405-475-5600	299
Carlisle Industrial Brake			
1031 E Hillside Dr . . . . Bloomington IN 47401	800-873-6361	812-336-3811	59
Carlisle Sanitary Maintenance Products			
402 S Black River St . . . . Sparta WI 54656	800-654-8210	608-269-2151	102
Carlisle SynTec			
1285 Ritner Hwy PO Box 7000 . . . . Carlisle PA 17013	800-479-6832	717-245-7000	192-4
Carlisle Tire & Wheel Mfg			
23 Windham Blvd . . . . Aiken SC 29805	800-827-1001*	803-643-2919	744
*Sales			
Carlow University			
3333 Fifth Ave . . . . Pittsburgh PA 15213	800-333-2275	412-578-6000	166
Carlsbad Chamber of Commerce			
302 S Canal St PO Box 910 . . . . Carlsbad NM 88220	866-822-9226	575-887-6516	137
Carlsbad Convention & Visitors Bureau			
400 Carlsbad Village Dr . . . . Carlsbad CA 92008	800-227-5722	760-434-6093	207
Carlsbad State Beach			
c/o San Diego Coast District Office 4477 Pacific Hwy . . . . San Diego CA 92110	800-777-0369	760-438-3143	558
Carlson			
Radisson Hotels & Resorts 701 Carlson Pkwy . . . . Minnetonka MN 55305	800-333-3333	763-212-5000	376
Carlson Hotels Worldwide			
Country Inns & Suites by Carlson 11340 Blondo St Ste 100 . . . . Omaha NE 68164	800-600-7275		376
Carlson Restaurants			
4201 Marsh Ln . . . . Carrollton TX 75007	800-374-3297	972-662-5400	661
Carlson Tool & Manufacturing Corp			
W57 N14386 Doerr Way PO Box 85. . . . . Cedarburg WI 53012	800-532-2252	262-377-2020	747
Carlson Wagonlit Travel Inc			
701 Carlson Pkwy . . . . Minnetonka MN 55305	800-213-7295		762
Carlstar Group LLC, The			
725 Cool Springs Blvd Ste 500 . . . . Franklin TN 37067	866-773-2926	615-503-0220	367
Carlton Bates Co			
3600 W 69th St . . . . Little Rock AR 72209	800-482-9313	501-562-9100	246
Carlton Foods Corp			
880 Texas 46 . . . . New Braunfels TX 78130	800-628-9849	830-625-7583	295-26
Carlton Group Inc			
120 Landmark Dr . . . . Greensboro NC 27409	800-722-7824	336-668-7677	358
Carlton on Madison Ave			
88 Madison Ave . . . . New York NY 10016	800-601-8500*	212-532-4100	376
*Resv			
Carlyle Hotel, The			
1731 New Hampshire Ave NW . . . . . . Washington DC 20009	877-301-0019	202-234-3200	376
Carlyle Johnson Machine Co (CJM)			
291 Boston Tpke . . . . Bolton CT 06043	888-629-4867	860-643-1531	613
CarMax Inc			
12800 Tuckahoe Creek Pkwy . . . . Richmond VA 23238	888-722-7629	804-747-0422	56
NYSE: KMX			
Carmel Clay Public Library			
55 Fourth Ave SE . . . . Carmel IN 46032	800-908-4490	317-844-3361	431-3
Carmel River Inn			
26600 Oliver Rd . . . . Carmel CA 93923	800-882-8142	831-624-1575	376
Carmel Valley Manor			
8545 Carmel Vly Rd . . . . Carmel CA 93923	800-544-5546	831-624-1281	663
Carmel Valley Ranch Resort			
One Old Ranch Rd . . . . Carmel CA 93923	866-405-5037	831-625-9500	660
Carmeuse North America			
11 Stanwix St 11th Fl . . . . Pittsburgh PA 15222	866-243-0965	412-995-5500	436
Carnegie Body Co			
9500 Brookpark Rd . . . . Cleveland OH 44129	800-362-1989	216-749-5000	509
Carnegie Corp of New York			
437 Madison Ave 26th Fl . . . . New York NY 10022	800-336-7323	212-371-3200	304
Carnegie Endowment for International Peace			
1779 Massachusetts Ave NW . . . . . Washington DC 20036	877-866-3070	202-483-7600	625
Carnegie Hall			
881 Seventh Ave . . . . New York NY 10019	800-728-3843	212-247-7800	565
Carnegie Hotel			
1216 W State of Franklin Rd . . . . Johnson City TN 37604	866-757-8277	423-979-6400	376
Carnegie Learning Inc			
437 Grant St . . . . Pittsburgh PA 15219	888-851-7094	412-690-6284	178
Carnegie Mellon University			
5000 Forbes Ave . . . . Pittsburgh PA 15213	844-625-4600	412-268-2000	166
Carnegie Regional Library			
49 W Seventh St . . . . Grafton ND 58237	800-568-5964	701-352-2754	431-3
Carneros Inn, The			
4048 Sonoma Hwy . . . . Napa CA 94559	888-400-9000	707-299-4900	698
Carnival Corp			
3655 NW 87th Ave . . . . Miami FL 33178	800-438-6744	305-599-2600	357-3
NYSE: CCL			
Carnival Cruise Lines			
3655 NW 87th Ave . . . . Miami FL 33178	800-764-7419	305-599-2600	220
Carnow Conibear & Assoc Ltd			
600 W Van Buren Ste 500. . . . . Chicago IL 60607	800-860-4486	312-782-4486	194
Caro Foods Inc			
2324 Bayou Blue Rd . . . . Houma LA 70364	800-395-2276	985-872-1483	296-7
Carol Stream Public Library			
616 Hiawatha Dr . . . . Carol Stream IL 60188	800-829-1040	630-653-0755	431-3
Carol Woods Retirement Community			
750 Weaver Dairy Rd . . . . Chapel Hill NC 27514	800-518-9333	919-968-4511	663
Carole Fabrics Inc			
PO Box 1436 . . . . Augusta GA 30903	800-241-0920	706-863-4742	735

Alphabetical Section

Listing	Toll-Free	Phone	Class
Carole Joy Creations Inc 1087 Federal Rd Unit 8 ... Brookfield CT 06804 *Sales	800-223-6945*	203-740-4490	129
Carolina Ballet Inc 3401-131 Atlantic Ave ... Raleigh NC 27604	800-841-2787	919-719-0800	566-1
Carolina Bank Holdings Inc 101 N Spring St ... Greensboro NC 27401 NASDAQ: CLBH	800-472-3272	336-288-1898	357-2
Carolina Biological Supply Co 2700 York Rd ... Burlington NC 27215	800-334-5551	336-584-0381	243
Carolina Business Furniture LLC 535 Archdale Blvd ... Archdale NC 27263	800-763-0212	336-431-9400	318-1
Carolina Carports Inc 187 Cardinal Ridge Trl ... Dobson NC 27017	800-670-4262		482
Carolina Casualty Insurance Co 4600 Touchton Rd E Bldg 100 Ste 400 ... Jacksonville FL 32246	800-874-8053	904-363-0900	388-4
Carolina Container Co 909 Prospect St ... High Point NC 27260	800-627-0825	336-883-7146	99
Carolina Farms Real Estate 547 S Main St ... King NC 27021	800-559-2113	336-983-5263	643
Carolina Filters Inc 109 E Newberry Ave PO Box 716 ... Sumter SC 29151	800-849-5646	803-773-6842	794
Carolina Glove Co 116 Mclin Creek Rd PO Box 999 ... Conover NC 28613	800-335-1918	828-464-1132	153-7
Carolina Hurricanes RBC Ctr 1400 EdwaRds Mill Rd ... Raleigh NC 27607	800-521-7521	919-467-7825	707
Carolina Inn 211 Pittsboro St ... Chapel Hill NC 27516	800-962-8519	919-933-2001	376
Carolina International Trucks Inc 1619 Bluff Rd ... Columbia SC 29201	800-868-4923	803-799-4923	56
Carolina Material Handling Services Inc PO Box 6 ... Columbia SC 29202	800-922-6709	803-695-0149	382
Carolina Meadows 100 Carolina Meadows ... Chapel Hill NC 27517	800-458-6756	919-942-4014	663
Carolina Mfg 7025 Augusta Rd ... Greenville SC 29605	800-845-2744	864-299-0600	153-12
Carolina Mountain Water Co 150 Central Ave ... Hot Springs AR 71902	800-828-0836		793
Carolina Opry 8901 Hwy 17 N Ste A ... Myrtle Beach SC 29572	800-843-6779		565
Carolina Packers Inc 2999 S Bright Leaf Blvd PO Box 1109 ... Smithfield NC 27577	800-682-7675	919-934-2181	468
Carolina Panthers Bank of America Stadium 800 S Mint St ... Charlotte NC 28202	888-297-8673	704-358-7000	706-3
Carolina Rim & Wheel Co 1308 Upper Asbury Ave ... Charlotte NC 28206	800-247-4337	704-334-7276	60
Carolina Skiff Inc 3231 Fulford Rd ... Waycross GA 31503	800-422-7282	912-287-0547	89
Carolina Trust Bank 901 E Main St ... Lincolnton NC 28092 NASDAQ: CART	877-983-5537	704-735-1104	69
Carolinas Auto Supply House Inc 2135 Tipton Dr ... Charlotte NC 28206	800-438-4070	704-334-4646	60
Carolinas Medical Center-NorthEast 920 Church St N ... Concord NC 28025	800-575-1275	704-403-1275	371-3
Carolinas Medical Center-University 8800 N Tryon St ... Charlotte NC 28262	800-821-1535	704-863-6000	371-3
Carolinas Medical Ctr Mercy 2001 Vail Ave ... Charlotte NC 28207	800-821-1535		371-3
Caroline County Public Library 100 Market St ... Denton MD 21629	800-832-3277	410-479-1343	431-3
Carollo Engineers 2700 Ygnacio Vly Rd Ste 300 ... Walnut Creek CA 94598	800-523-5826	925-932-1710	261
Caron Compactor Co 1204 Ullrey Ave ... Escalon CA 95320	800-542-2766	209-838-2062	191
Caroplast Inc PO Box 668405 ... Charlotte NC 28266	800-327-5797	704-394-4191	605
Carousel Beachfront Hotel & Suites 11700 Coastal Hwy ... Ocean City MD 21842	800-641-0011	410-524-1000	376
Carousel Industries of North America Inc 659 S County Trl ... Exeter RI 02822	800-401-0760		224
Carousel Inn & Suites 1530 S Harbor Blvd ... Anaheim CA 92802	800-854-6767	714-758-0444	376
Carpedia International Ltd 75 Navy St ... Oakville ON L6J2Z1	877-445-8288		458
Carpenter Co 5016 Monument Ave ... Richmond VA 23230	800-288-3830	804-359-0800	594
Carpenter Contractors of America Inc 3900 Ave D NW ... Winter Haven FL 33880	800-959-8806	863-294-6449	190-2
Carpenter Powder Products 600 Mayer St ... Bridgeville PA 15017	866-790-9092	412-257-5102	588
Carpenter Specialty Alloys Operations 101 W Bern St ... Reading PA 19601	800-654-6543	610-208-2000	714
Carpenter Technology Corp PO Box 14662 ... Reading PA 19612 NYSE: CRS	800-654-6543	610-208-2000	714
Carquest Corp 2635 E Millbrook Rd ... Raleigh NC 27604	800-876-1291	919-573-3000	60
Carr Business Systems Inc 130 Spagnoli Rd ... Melville NY 11747	800-244-1880	631-249-9880	111
Carr Corp 1547 11th St ... Santa Monica CA 90401	800-952-2398	310-587-1113	584
Carriage House Cos Inc, The 196 Newton St ... Fredonia NY 14063	800-828-8915	716-673-1000	295-20
Carriage Services Inc 3040 Post Oak Blvd Ste 300 ... Houston TX 77056 NYSE: CSV	866-332-8400	713-332-8400	503
Carrico Implement Company Inc 3160 US 24 Hwy ... Beloit KS 67420	877-542-4099	785-738-5744	274
Carrier Clinic 252 County Rd 601 ... Belle Mead NJ 08502	800-933-3579	908-281-1000	371-5
Carrier Corp 1 Carrier Pl ... Farmington CT 06034	800-227-7437	860-674-3000	14
Carrier Vibrating Equipment Inc 3400 Fern Vly Rd ... Louisville KY 40213	800-547-7278	502-969-3171	208
Carrillo Business Technologies Inc 750 The City Dr S Ste 225 ... Orange CA 92868	888-241-7585		180
Carrington Convention & Visitors Bureau 871 Main St PO Box 439 ... Carrington ND 58421	800-641-9668	701-652-2524	207
Carroll & Co 425 N Canon Dr ... Beverly Hills CA 90210	800-238-9400	310-273-9060	155-3
Carroll Co 2900 W Kingsley Rd ... Garland TX 75041	800-527-5722	972-278-1304	149
Carroll College 1601 N Benton Ave ... Helena MT 59625	800-992-3648	406-447-4300	166
Carroll Cos Inc 1640 Old Hwy 421 S ... Boone NC 28607	800-884-2521	828-264-2521	428
Carroll County 8215 Black Oak Road ... Mount Carroll IL 61053	800-485-0145	815-244-2035	336
Carroll County Chamber of Commerce & Economic Development 61 N Lisbon St PO Box 277 ... Carrollton OH 44615	800-956-4684	330-627-4811	137
Carroll County District Library 70 Second St NE ... Carrollton OH 44615	800-827-1000	330-627-2613	431-3
Carroll Electric Co-op Corp 920 Hwy 62 Spur ... Berryville AR 72616	800-432-9720	870-423-2161	245
Carroll Electric Co-op Inc 350 Canton Rd NW ... Carrollton OH 44615	800-232-7697	330-627-2116	245
Carroll Hospice 292 Stoner Ave ... Westminster MD 21157	844-211-5403	410-871-8000	368
Carroll Independent Fuel Co 2700 Loch Raven Rd ... Baltimore MD 21218	800-834-8590	410-235-1070	315
Carroll Lutheran Village 300 St Luke Cir ... Westminster MD 21158	877-848-0095	410-848-0090	663
Carroll Publishing Co 4701 Sangamore Rd Ste S-155 ... Bethesda MD 20816	800-336-4240	301-263-9800	628-2
Carroll Seating Company Inc 10 Lincoln St ... Kansas City KS 66103	800-972-3779	816-471-2929	319
Carroll University 100 NE Ave ... Waukesha WI 53186	800-227-7655	262-547-1211	166
Carroll Valley Golf Resort 78 Country Club Trail ... Carroll Valley PA 17320	855-784-0330	717-642-8282	660
Carrollton Public Library 4220 N Josey Ln ... Carrollton TX 75010	888-727-2978	972-466-4800	431-3
Carrom 218 E Dowland St ... Ludington MI 49431	800-223-6047	231-845-1263	318-2
Carron Net Company Inc 1623 17th St PO Box 177 ... Two Rivers WI 54241	800-558-7768	920-793-2217	209
Cars.com 175 W Jackson Blvd Ste 800 ... Chicago IL 60604	888-246-6298	312-601-5000	57
CarsDirect.com Inc 909 N Sepulveda Blvd 11th Fl ... El Segundo CA 90245 *Cust Svc	888-227-7347*		57
Carson City Nugget 507 N Carson St ... Carson City NV 89701	800-426-5239	775-882-1626	132
Carson Helicopters 952 Blooming Glen Rd ... Perkasie PA 18944	800-523-2335	215-249-3535	356
Carson Hot Springs 1500 Hot Springs Rd ... Carson City NV 89706	888-917-3711	775-885-8844	49-4
Carson Oil Company Inc 3125 NW 35th Ave PO Box 10948 ... Portland OR 97296	800-998-7767	503-224-8500	572
Carson Valley Chamber of Commerce & Visitors Authority 1477 Hwy 395 N Ste A ... Gardnerville NV 89410	800-727-7677	775-782-8144	137
Carson-Dellosa Publishing Company Inc 7027 Albert Pick Rd ... Greensboro NC 27409	800-321-0943	336-632-0084	243
Carsonite Composites LLC 19845 US Hwy 76 ... Newberry SC 29108	800-648-7916	803-321-1185	669
Carson-Newman College 1646 Russell Ave ... Jefferson City TN 37760	800-678-9061	865-471-2000	166
CARSTAR Quality Collision Service 8400 W 110th St Ste 200 ... Overland Park KS 66210 *Cust Svc	800-227-7827*	913-451-1294	61-4
Carswell Distributing Co 3750 N Liberty St ... Winston Salem NC 27105	800-929-1948	336-767-7700	426
Cartec International Inc 106 Powder Mill Rd ... Canton CT 06019	800-821-4434	860-693-9395	598-2
Carter & Holmes N1510 Geneva Ave ... Lake Geneva WI 53147	800-621-4646	262-215-5494	153-12
Carter BloodCare 2205 Hwy 121 ... Bedford TX 76021	800-366-2834	817-412-5000	88
Carter Bros LLC 100 Hartsfield Ctr Pkwy Ste 140 ... Atlanta GA 30354	888-818-0152		683
Carter County 101 1St Ave SW ... Ardmore OK 73401	800-231-8668	580-223-8162	336
Carter Ctr One Copenhill Ave 453 Freedom Pkwy ... Atlanta GA 30307	800-550-3560	404-420-5100	625
Carter Healthcare 3105 S Meridian Ave ... Oklahoma City OK 73119	888-951-1112	405-947-7700	360
Carter Lumber Co Inc 601 Tallmadge Rd ... Kent OH 44240	877-586-2374	330-673-6100	361
Carteret County Chamber of Commerce 801 Arendell St Ste 1 ... Morehead City NC 28557	800-622-6278	252-726-6350	137
Carteret-Craven Electric Co-op (CCEC) 1300 Hwy 24 W PO Box 1490 ... Newport NC 28570	800-682-2217	252-247-3107	245
Carthage College 2001 Alford Pk Dr ... Kenosha WI 53140 *Admissions	800-351-4058*	262-551-8500	166
Carthage Mills 4243 Hunt Rd ... Cincinnati OH 45242 *Sales	800-543-4430*	513-794-1600	734-3
Cartier Place Suite Hotel 180 Cooper St ... Ottawa ON K2P2L5	800-236-8399	613-236-5000	376
Carton Service Inc First Quality Dr PO Box 702 ... Shelby OH 44875 *General	800-533-7744*	419-342-5010	100
Cartwright Cos, The 11901 Cartwright Ave ... Grandview MO 64030	800-821-2334		512
CartwrightDownes Inc 950 Lee St Ste 110 ... Des Plaines IL 60016	800-323-2049	847-685-2700	195
Carus Corp 315 Fifth St ... Peru IL 61354	800-435-6856	815-223-1500	141
Caruso Inc 3465 Hauck Rd ... Cincinnati OH 45241	800-759-7659	513-860-9200	10-10
Carvel Express 200 Glenridge Pt Pkwy Ste 200 ... Atlanta GA 30342	800-322-4848		378
Carvin Corp 12340 World Trade Dr ... San Diego CA 92128	800-854-2235	858-487-1600	520
Car-X Assoc Corp 1375 E Woodfield Rd Ste 500 ... Schaumburg IL 60173	800-359-2359	847-273-8920	309
Cary Oil Company Inc 110 Mackenan Dr PO Box 5189 ... Cary NC 27511	800-227-9645	919-462-1100	574
Carylon Corp 2500 W Arthington St ... Chicago IL 60612	800-621-4342	312-666-7700	658

Name / Address	City	State	ZIP	Toll-Free	Phone	Class
CAS (Center for Auto Safety)						
1825 Connecticut Ave NW						
Ste 330	Washington	DC	20009	**800-424-9393**	202-328-7700	48-21
CAS (Chemical Abstracts Service)						
2540 Olentangy River Rd	Columbus	OH	43202	**800-848-6538**	614-447-3600	384
CAS Inc						
PO Box 11190	Huntsville	AL	35814	**800-729-8686**	256-971-6126	261
CAS Medical Systems Inc						
44 E Industrial Rd	Branford	CT	06405	**800-227-4414**	203-488-6056	471
NASDAQ: CASM						
CASA (National Court Appointed Special Advocate Assn)						
100 W Harrison St N Twr Ste 500	Seattle	WA	98119	**800-628-3233**	206-270-0072	47-6
Casa Colina Ctr for Rehabilitation						
255 E Bonita Ave	Pomona	CA	91769	**800-926-5462**	909-596-7733	445
Casa Esperanza						
1005 Yale NE	Albuquerque	NM	87106	**866-654-1338**	505-277-9880	369
Casa Grande Ruins National Monument						
1100 W Ruins Dr	Coolidge	AZ	85128	**877-642-4743**	520-723-3172	557
Casa Grande Valley Newspaper Inc						
PO Box 15002	Casa Grande	AZ	85130	**800-352-3796**	520-836-7461	628-8
Casa Herrerra Inc						
2655 N Pine St	Pomona	CA	91767	**800-624-3916**	909-392-3930	297
Casa Madrona Hotel						
801 Bridgeway	Sausalito	CA	94965	**800-288-0502***	415-332-0502	376
*General						
Casa Marina Resort & Beach Club						
1500 Reynolds St	Key West	FL	33040	**888-303-5717**		660
Casa Monica Hotel						
95 Cordova St	Saint Augustine	FL	32084	**800-648-1888***	904-827-1888	376
*Help Line						
Casa Munras Hotel						
700 Munras Ave	Monterey	CA	93940	**800-222-2446**	831-375-2411	376
Casa Palmero						
1518 Cypress Dr	Pebble Beach	CA	93953	**800-654-9300**	831-622-6650	660
Casa Via Mar Inn & Tennis Club						
377 W Ch Islands Blvd	Port Hueneme	CA	93041	**800-992-5522**	805-984-6222	376
Casa Ybel Resort						
2255 W Gulf Dr	Sanibel Island	FL	33957	**800-276-4753**	239-472-3145	660
Casablanca Fan Co						
761 Corporate Ctr Dr	Pomona	CA	91768	**888-227-2178**	909-689-1477	36
Casablanca Hotel						
147 W 43rd St	New York	NY	10036	**888-922-7225**	212-869-1212	376
Casablanca Resort						
950 W Mesquite Blvd	Mesquite	NV	89027	**800-459-7529**	702-346-7529	660
Cascade Bancorp						
1100 NW Wall St	Bend	OR	97701	**877-617-3400***	541-385-6205	357-2
NASDAQ: CACB ■ *Cust Svc						
Cascade Corp						
2201 NE 201st Ave	Fairview	OR	97024	**800-227-2233**	503-669-6300	465
NYSE: CASC						
Cascade Designs Inc						
4000 First Ave S	Seattle	WA	98134	**800-531-9531***	206-505-9500	701
*Cust Svc						
Cascade Federal Credit Union						
18020 80th Ave S	Kent	WA	98032	**800-562-2853**	425-251-8888	216
Cascade Financial Management Inc						
950 17th St Ste 950	Denver	CO	80202	**800-353-0008**		195
Cascade General Inc						
5555 N Ch Ave	Portland	OR	97217	**855-844-6799**	503-247-1777	689
Cascade Lodge						
3719 W Hwy 61	Lutsen	MN	55612	**800-322-9543**	218-387-1112	660
Cascade Machinery & Electric Inc						
4600 E Marginal Way S						
PO Box 3575	Seattle	WA	98134	**800-289-0500**	206-762-0500	382
Cascade Microtech Inc						
2430 NW 206th Ave	Beaverton	OR	97006	**800-854-8400**	503-601-1000	248
NASDAQ: CSCD						
Cascade Natural Gas Corp (CNGC)						
8113 W Grandridge Blvd	Kennewick	WA	99336	**888-522-1130**	206-624-3900	775
Cascade Receivables Management LLC						
101 Second St Ste 100	Petaluma	CA	94952	**888-417-1531**		390
Cascade Regional Blood Services						
220 S 'I' St	Tacoma	WA	98405	**877-242-5663**	253-383-2553	88
Cascade Steel Rolling Mills Inc (CSRM)						
3200 N Hwy 99 W PO Box 687	McMinnville	OR	97128	**800-283-2776**	503-472-4181	714
Cascade Wholesale Hardware Inc						
5650 NW	Hillsboro	OR	97124	**800-877-9987***	503-614-2600	348
*General						
Cascade Wood Products Inc						
PO Box 2429	White City	OR	97503	**800-423-3311**	541-826-2911	494
Cascades Inc						
404 Marie-Victorin Blvd	Kingsey Falls	QC	J0A1B0	**800-361-4070**	819-363-5100	554
TSE: CAS						
Cascades Inn						
3226 Shepherd of the						
Hills Expy	Branson	MO	65616	**800-588-8424**	417-335-8424	376
Cascio Interstate Music						
13819 W National Ave	New Berlin	WI	53151	**800-462-2263**	262-789-7600	519
CASE (Council of Administrators of Special Education)						
Osigian Office Centre 101 Katelyn Cir						
Ste E	Warner Robins	GA	31088	**800-585-1753**	478-333-6892	48-5
CASE (Council for Advancement & Support of Education)						
1307 New York Ave NW						
Ste 1000	Washington	DC	20005	**800-554-8536***	202-328-5900	48-5
*Orders						
Case Design Corp						
333 School Ln	Telford	PA	18969	**800-847-4176**	215-703-0130	200
Case Logic Inc						
6303 Dry Creek Pkwy	Longmont	CO	80503	**800-925-8111**	303-652-1000	527
Case Management Society of America (CMSA)						
6301 Ranch Dr	Little Rock	AR	72223	**800-216-2672**	501-225-2229	48-8
Case Paper Company Inc						
500 Mamaroneck Ave Second Fl	Harrison	NY	10528	**800-222-2922**	914-899-3500	547
Case Western Reserve University						
2061 Cornell Rd	Cleveland	OH	44106	**800-967-8898**	216-368-2000	166
Case Western Reserve University School of Law						
11075 E Blvd	Cleveland	OH	44106	**800-756-0036**	216-368-3600	167-1
Casella Waste Systems Inc						
25 Greens Hill Ln	Rutland	VT	05701	**800-227-3552**	802-775-0325	792
NASDAQ: CWST						
Casey Research LLC						
PO Box 1427	Stowe	VT	05672	**888-512-2739**	602-445-2736	398
Casey State Bank						
305-307 N Central Ave	Casey	IL	62420	**866-666-2754**	217-932-2136	69

Name / Address	City	State	ZIP	Toll-Free	Phone	Class
Casgrain & Company Ltd						
1200 Mcgill College Ave						
21st Fl	Montreal	QC	H3B4G7	**800-361-8738**	514-871-8080	398
Cash Plus Inc						
3002 Dow Ave Ste 120	Tustin	CA	92780	**888-707-2274**	714-731-2274	139
Cashtown Inn Restaurant						
1325 Old Rt 30	Cashtown	PA	17310	**800-367-1797**	717-334-9722	662
Cash-Wa Distributing Co						
401 W Fourth St	Kearney	NE	68845	**800-652-0010**	308-237-3151	296-8
CASI (Computer Analytical Systems Inc)						
1418 S Third St	Louisville	KY	40208	**800-977-3475**	502-635-2019	181
Casiano Communications Inc						
1700 Fernandez Juncos Ave						
PO Box 12130	San Juan	PR	00909	**844-723-2351**	787-728-3000	628-8
Casino Arizona at Salt River						
524 N 92nd St	Scottsdale	AZ	85256	**866-877-9897***	480-850-7777	132
*General						
Casino Aztar						
421 NW Riverside Dr	Evansville	IN	47708	**800-342-5386**	812-433-4000	132
Casino New Brunswick LP						
21 Casino Dr	Moncton	NB	E1G0R7	**877-859-7775**	506-859-7770	132
Casino Niagara						
5705 Falls Ave	Niagara Falls	ON	L2E6T3	**888-325-5788**	905-374-3598	132
Casino Nova Scotia						
1983 Upper Water St	Halifax	NS	B3J3Y5	**888-642-6376**	902-425-7777	132
Casino Queen						
200 S Front St	East Saint Louis	IL	62201	**800-777-0777**	618-874-5000	132
Casino Royale Hotel						
3411 Las Vegas Blvd S	Las Vegas	NV	89109	**800-854-7666**	702-737-3500	376
Casio Inc						
570 Mt Pleasant Ave	Dover	NJ	07801	**800-634-1895***	973-361-5400	584
*Cust Svc						
Cask 'n' Cleaver						
8689 Ninth St	Rancho Cucamonga	CA	91730	**800-995-4452**	909-981-5771	661
CASLPA (Canadian Assn of Speech-Language Pathologists & Audiologists)						
One Nicholas St Ste 1000	Ottawa	ON	K1N7B7	**800-259-8519**	613-567-9968	47-1
CASM (Canadian Academy of Sport Medicine)						
180 Elgin St Ste 1400	Ottawa	ON	K2P2K3	**877-585-2394**	613-748-5851	48-8
Casper Area Chamber of Commerce						
500 N Ctr St	Casper	WY	82601	**866-234-5311**	307-234-5311	137
Casper Area Convention & Visitors Bureau						
992 N Poplar St	Casper	WY	82601	**800-852-1889**	307-234-5362	207
Casper College						
125 College Dr	Casper	WY	82601	**800-442-2963**	307-268-2110	160
Casper Events Ctr						
1 Events Dr	Casper	WY	82601	**800-442-2256**	307-235-8441	206
Cass Cable Tv Inc						
100 Redbud Rd	Virginia	IL	62691	**800-252-1799**	217-452-7725	115
Cass County Electric Co-op Inc						
4100 32nd Ave SW	Fargo	ND	58104	**800-248-3292**	701-356-4400	245
Cass Tours						
2621 Green River Rd Ste 105-222	Corona	CA	92882	**800-593-6510**	951-371-3511	761
Casselman River Bridge State Park						
580 Taylor Ave						
Tawes State Ofc Bldg	Annapolis	MD	21401	**877-620-8367**		558
Casswood Insurance Agency Ltd						
Five Executive Pk Dr	Clifton Park	NY	12065	**800-972-2242**	518-373-8700	387
Castalloy Inc						
1701 Industrial Ln PO Box 827	Waukesha	WI	53189	**800-211-0900**	262-547-0070	306
Castine Moving & Storage						
1235 Chestnut St	Athol	MA	01331	**800-225-8068**	978-249-9105	512
Castle Brands Inc						
122 E 42nd St Ste 4700	New York	NY	10168	**800-882-8140**	646-356-0200	80-3
NYSE: ROX						
Castle Hill Inn & Resort						
590 Ocean Dr	Newport	RI	02840	**888-466-1355**	401-849-3800	660
Castle in the Sand Hotel						
3701 Atlantic Ave	Ocean City	MD	21842	**800-552-7263**	410-289-6846	376
Castle Inn & Suites						
1734 S Harbor Blvd	Anaheim	CA	92802	**800-227-8530**	714-774-8111	376
Castle on the Hudson						
400 Benedict Ave	Tarrytown	NY	10591	**800-616-4487**	914-631-1980	376
Castle Worldwide Inc						
900 Perimeter Pk Rd Ste G	Morrisville	NC	27560	**800-655-4845**	919-572-6880	244
Castleton State College						
86 Seminary St	Castleton	VT	05735	**800-639-8521**	802-468-5611	166
Casto Travel Inc						
2560 N First St Ste 150	San Jose	CA	95131	**800-832-3445**	408-984-7000	761
Castrol Industrial North America Inc						
150 W Warrenville Rd	Naperville	IL	60563	**877-641-1600**		534
Cat Fancy Magazine						
Three Burroughs	Irvine	CA	92618	**800-546-7730***	949-855-8822	452-14
*Cust Svc						
Catalina Express						
Berth 95	San Pedro	CA	90731	**800-481-3470**	310-519-7971	463
Catalina Graphic Films Inc						
27001 Agoura Rd Ste 100	Calabasas Hills	CA	91301	**800-333-3136**	818-880-8060	593
Catalina Marketing Corp						
200 Carillon Pkwy	Saint Petersburg	FL	33716	**888-322-3814**	727-579-5000	5
Catalog.com Inc						
14000 Quail Springs Pkwy						
Ste 3600	Oklahoma City	OK	73134	**888-932-4376**	405-753-9300	795
Catalyst Awareness Inc						
355 Elmira Rd N Ste 127	Guelph	ON	N1K1S5	**866-749-3697**		260
Catapult Systems Inc						
1221 S MoPac Expwy Ste 350	Austin	TX	78746	**800-528-6248**	512-328-8181	181
Catawba College						
2300 W Innes St	Salisbury	NC	28144	**800-228-2922**	704-637-4111	166
Catawba Hospital						
5525 Catawba Hospital Dr	Catawba	VA	24070	**800-451-5544**	540-375-4200	371-5
Catawba Valley Community College						
2550 US Hwy 70 SE	Hickory	NC	28602	**800-433-3243**	828-327-7000	160
Cathay General Bancorp Inc						
777 N Broadway	Los Angeles	CA	90012	**800-922-8429**	213-625-4700	357-2
NASDAQ: CATY						
Cathay Pacific Cargo						
6040 Avion Dr Ste 338	Los Angeles	CA	90045	**800-628-6960**	310-417-0052	12
Cathedral Caverns State Park						
637 Cave Rd	Woodville	AL	35776	**800-252-7275**	256-728-8193	558
Cathedral Church of Saint Peter & Saint Paul						
3101 Wisconsin Ave NW	Washington	DC	20016	**800-622-6304**	202-537-6200	513
Cathedral of Our Lady of the Angels						
555 W Temple St	Los Angeles	CA	90012	**800-838-1356**	213-680-5200	49

Name / Address	City	State	Zip	Toll-Free	Phone	Class
Cathedral Press Inc						
600 NE Sixth St	Long Prairie	MN	56347	**800-874-8332***	320-732-6143	628-10
*Cust Svc						
Cathedral State Park						
Rt 1 12 Cathedral Way	Aurora	WV	26705	**800-225-5982**	304-735-3771	558
Catholic Church Extension Society of the USA						
150 S Wacker Dr 20th Fl	Chicago	IL	60606	**800-842-7804**		47-20
Catholic Digest						
PO Box 6015	New London	CT	06320	**800-678-2836**	860-437-3012	452-18
Catholic Diocese of Peoria, The						
607 NE Madison Ave	Peoria	IL	61603	**800-340-5630**	309-682-5823	49
Catholic Healthcare Partners						
615 Elsinore Pl	Cincinnati	OH	45202	**800-367-9212**	513-639-2800	350
Catholic Medical Ctr (CMC)						
100 McGregor St	Manchester	NH	03102	**800-437-9666**	603-668-3545	371-3
Catholic Medical Mission Board (CMMB)						
10 W 17th St	New York	NY	10011	**800-678-5659**	212-242-7757	47-5
Catholic Mutual Group						
10843 Old Mill Rd	Omaha	NE	68154	**800-228-6108**	402-551-8765	388-5
Catholic Press Assn (CPA)						
205 W Monroe St Ste 470	Chicago	IL	60606	**800-777-7432**	312-380-6789	48-14
Catholic Relief Services (CRS)						
228 W Lexington St	Baltimore	MD	21201	**800-235-2772**	410-625-2220	47-5
Catholic Supply of st Louis Inc						
6759 Chippewa St	Saint Louis	MO	63109	**800-325-9026**	314-644-0643	47-20
Catholic University of America Press						
620 Michigan Ave NE						
240 Leahy Hall	Washington	DC	20064	**800-537-5487**	202-319-5052	628-4
CatholicMatch LLC						
211 E Grandview Ave	Zelienople	PA	16063	**888-605-3977**		384
Cato Corp, The						
8100 Denmark Rd	Charlotte	NC	28273	**800-526-9169**	704-554-8510	155-6
Catskill Area Hospice & Palliative Care Inc						
One Birchwood Dr	Oneonta	NY	13820	**800-306-3870**	607-432-6773	368
Catskill Regional Medical Ctr						
68 Harris-Bushville Rd						
PO Box 800	Harris	NY	12742	**888-846-5945**	845-794-3300	371-3
Cattaneo Bros Inc						
769 Caudill St	San Luis Obispo	CA	93401	**800-243-8537**	805-543-7188	295-26
CattleLog						
10305 102nd Terrace	Sebastian	FL	32958	**866-239-2665**		461
Causeway Lumber Co						
3318 SW Second Ave	Fort Lauderdale	FL	33315	**800-375-5050**	954-763-1224	192-3
Cauthorne Paper Co						
12124 S Washington Hwy	Ashland	VA	23005	**800-552-3011**	804-798-6999	550
Cavalier Homes Inc						
32 Wilson Blvd Ste 100	Addison	AL	35540	**800-743-2284**		500
Cavalier Hotel						
4201 Atlantic Ave	Virginia Beach	VA	23451	**800-446-8199**	757-425-8555	660
Cavalier Telephone LLC						
2134 W Laburnum Ave	Richmond	VA	23227	**800-683-3944**	800-442-2410	726
Cavanagh Law Firm, The						
1850 N Central Ave	Phoenix	AZ	85004	**888-824-3476**	602-322-4000	425
Cavco Industries Inc						
1001 N Central Ave Eighth Fl	Phoenix	AZ	85004	**800-790-9111**	602-256-6263	500
NASDAQ: CVCO						
Cayenta Canada Corp						
4200 N Fraser Way Ste 201	Burnaby	BC	V5J5K7	**866-229-3682**	604-570-4300	38
Cayman Airways Cargo Services						
6103 NW 72nd Ave	Miami	FL	33166	**800-252-2746**	305-526-3190	12
Cayman Airways Ltd						
91 Owen Roberts Dr	Grand Cayman	KY	10092	**800-422-9626**	345-949-8200	25
Cayman Islands Dept of Tourism						
350 Fifth Ave	New York	NY	10118	**800-235-5888**	212-889-9009	765
Cayuga Community College						
197 Franklin St	Auburn	NY	13021	**866-598-8883**	315-255-1743	160
Cazenovia College						
Eight Sullivan St	Cazenovia	NY	13035	**800-654-3210**	315-655-7208	166
CB Fleet Co Inc						
4615 Murray Pl	Lynchburg	VA	24502	**866-255-6960**	434-528-4000	576
CB Ragland Co						
2720 Eugenia Ave	Nashville	TN	37211	**866-770-5263**	615-254-2841	296-8
CBAN (Community Banking Advisory Network)						
624 Grassmere Pk Dr Ste 15	Nashville	TN	37211	**800-231-2524**	615-373-9880	48-2
CBB (Citizens Business Bank)						
701 N Haven Ave	Ontario	CA	91764	**888-222-5432***	909-980-4030	69
*Cust Svc						
CBI Laboratories						
4201 Diplomacy Rd	Fort Worth	TX	76155	**800-822-7546**	972-241-7546	215
CBI Services Inc						
24 Read's Way	New Castle	DE	19720	**800-642-8675**	302-325-8400	190-14
CBIZ Benefits & Insurance Services of Maryland Inc						
44 Baltimore St	Cumberland	MD	21502	**800-615-8418***	301-777-1500	387
*Cust Svc						
CBIZ Tofias PC						
500 Boylston St	Boston	MA	02116	**888-761-8835**	617-761-0600	2
CBM (Christian Blind Mission)						
450 E Pk Ave	Greenville	SC	29601	**800-937-2264**	864-239-0065	47-5
CBMC (Connecting Businessmen to Christ)						
5746 Marlin Rd						
Ste 602 Osborne Ctr	Chattanooga	TN	37411	**800-566-2262**	423-698-4444	47-20
CBMR (Crested Butte Mountain Resort)						
12 Snowmass Rd						
PO Box 5700	Crested Butte	CO	81224	**800-810-7669**	970-349-2222	660
CBN (Christian Broadcasting Network)						
977 Centerville Tpke						
CBN Ctr	Virginia Beach	VA	23463	**800-759-0700**	757-226-7000	729
CBOE (Chicago Board Options Exchange)						
400 S La Salle St	Chicago	IL	60605	**800-678-4667**	312-786-5600	682
CBRL Group Inc						
PO Box 787	Lebanon	TN	37088	**800-333-9566**		357-3
CBV-FM 106.3 (CBC)						
PO Box 500 Stn A	Toronto	ON	M5W1E6	**866-306-4636**		636
Cc Pollen Co						
3627 E Indian School Rd Ste 209	Phoenix	AZ	85018	**800-875-0096**	602-957-0096	787
CCA (Coastal Conservation Assn)						
6919 Portwest Dr Ste 100	Houston	TX	77024	**800-201-3474**	713-626-4234	47-13
CCA Global Partners						
4301 Earth City Expy	Earth City	MO	63045	**800-466-6984**	314-506-0000	358
CCA Industries Inc						
200 Murray Hill Pkwy	East Rutherford	NJ	07073	**800-524-2720***	201-935-3232	215
NYSE: CAW ■ *Cust Svc						
CCC (Copyright Clearance Ctr Inc)						
222 Rosewood Dr	Danvers	MA	01923	**855-239-3415**	978-750-8400	48-16
CCC (Consolidated Container Co)						
3101 Towercreek Pkwy Ste 300	Atlanta	GA	30339	**888-831-2184***	678-742-4600	541
*Sales						
CCC (Clovis Community College)						
417 Schepps Blvd	Clovis	NM	88101	**800-769-1409**	575-769-2811	160
CCC Information Services Inc						
222 Merchandise Mart Plz	Chicago	IL	60654	**800-621-8070**		225
CCCC (Conference on College Composition & Communication)						
1111 W Kenyon Rd	Urbana	IL	61801	**877-369-6283**	217-328-3870	48-5
CCCS (CAD/CAM Consulting Services Inc)						
996 Lawrence Dr Ste 101	Newbury Park	CA	91320	**888-375-7676**	805-375-7676	175
CCCVB (Clermont County Convention & Visitors Bureau)						
410 E Main St PO Box 100	Batavia	OH	45103	**800-796-4282**	513-732-3600	207
CCDNCVB (Crescent City-Del Norte County Chamber of Commerce)						
1001 Front St	Crescent City	CA	95531	**800-343-8300**	707-464-3174	207
CCEC (Carteret-Craven Electric Co-op)						
1300 Hwy 24 W PO Box 1490	Newport	NC	28570	**800-682-2217**	252-247-3107	245
CCFA (Crohn's & Colitis Foundation of America)						
386 Pk Ave S 17th Fl	New York	NY	10016	**800-932-2423**	212-685-3440	47-17
CCH (Covenant Children's Hospital)						
4015 22nd Pl	Lubbock	TX	79410	**800-378-4189**	806-725-0000	371-1
CCH Small Firm Services						
225 Chastain Meadows Ct NW						
Ste 200	Kennesaw	GA	30144	**866-345-4171***		179-10
*Sales						
CCH Washington Service Bureau Inc						
1015 15th St NW 10th Fl	Washington	DC	20005	**800-955-5219**	202-312-6600	626
CCI (Canine Companions for Independence Inc)						
2965 Dutton Ave PO Box 446	Santa Rosa	CA	95402	**800-572-2275**	707-577-1700	47-17
CCI (Charlestown Retirement Community)						
715 Maiden Choice Ln	Catonsville	MD	21228	**800-917-8649**	410-242-2880	663
CCI (Computer Consultants Inc)						
43252 Woodward Ave						
Ste 240	Bloomfield Hills	MI	48302	**800-693-1066**	248-858-7701	225
CCI Thermal Technologies Inc						
5918 Roper Rd	Edmonton	AB	T6B3E1	**800-661-8529***	780-466-3178	317
*Cust Svc						
CCIM Institute						
430 N Michigan Ave Ste 800	Chicago	IL	60611	**800-621-7027**	312-321-4460	48-17
CCL Label Inc						
161 Worcester Rd Ste 502	Framingham	MA	01701	**877-240-9772**	508-872-4511	410
CCM (Comprehensive Care Management Corp)						
1250 Waters Pl Tower 1 Ste 602	Bronx	NY	10461	**877-226-8500**		445
CCMcD (Clark-Cutler-McDermott Co)						
5 Fisher St	Franklin	MA	02038	**800-922-3019**	508-528-1200	734-6
CCMG (Clark Capital Management Group Inc)						
1650 Market St						
1 Liberty Pl 53rd Fl	Philadelphia	PA	19103	**800-766-2264**	215-569-2224	398
CCMH (Camden-Clark Memorial Hospital)						
800 Garfield Ave	Parkersburg	WV	26101	**800-541-3160**	304-424-2111	371-3
CCON (Columbia College of Nursing)						
4425 N Port Washington Rd	Glendale	WI	53212	**800-221-5573**	414-326-2330	166
CCPS (Center for Chemical Process Safety)						
120 Wall St	New York	NY	10005	**800-242-4363**	646-495-1371	48-19
CCRKBA (Citizens Committee for the Right to Keep & Bear Arms)						
12500 NE Tenth Pl	Bellevue	WA	98005	**800-426-4302**	425-454-4911	47-7
CCRTA (Cape Cod Regional Transit Authority)						
215 Iyannough Rd PO Box 1988	Hyannis	MA	02601	**800-352-7155**	508-775-8504	463
CCS (Credit Control Services Inc)						
2 Wells Ave Ste 1	Newton	MA	02459	**800-526-0532**	617-965-2000	158
CCS (Custom Computer Specialists Inc)						
70 Suffolk Ct	Hauppauge	NY	11788	**800-598-8989**	631-864-6699	181
CCS Medical Inc						
1505 LBJ Fwy Ste 600	Farmers Branch	TX	75234	**800-726-9811**	800-260-8193	470
CCSAA (Cross Country Ski Areas Assn)						
259 Bolton Rd	Winchester	NH	03470	**877-779-2754**	603-239-4341	47-22
CCSD (Charleston County School District)						
75 Calhoun St	Charleston	SC	29401	**800-255-7688**	843-937-6300	676
CCSD (Clark County School District)						
5100 W Sahara Ave	Las Vegas	NV	89146	**866-799-8997**	702-799-5000	676
CCT (Chesapeake Conventions & Tourism Bureau)						
860 Greenbrier Cir Ste 101	Chesapeake	VA	23320	**888-889-5551**	757-502-4898	207
CCUSD (Culver City Unified School District)						
4034 Irving Pl	Culver City	CA	90232	**855-446-2673**	310-842-4220	676
CD Ford & Sons Inc						
PO Box 300	Geneseo	IL	61254	**800-383-4661**	309-944-4661	366
CD Publications						
8204 Fenton St	Silver Spring	MD	20910	**800-666-6380**	301-588-6380	524-2
C&D Technologies						
11 Cabot Blvd	Mansfield	MA	02048	**800-233-2765**	508-339-3000	253
CD Universe						
101 N Plains Industrial Rd	Wallingford	CT	06492	**800-231-7937**	203-294-1648	518
CD Warehouse						
900 N Broadway	Oklahoma City	OK	73102	**800-641-9394**	919-577-6000	518
CDA (Chemically Dependent Anonymous)						
PO Box 423	Severna Park	MD	21146	**888-232-4673**		47-21
CDC Small Business Finance Corp						
2448 Historic Decatur Rd						
Ste 200	San Diego	CA	92106	**800-611-5170**	619-291-3594	216
CDC Trade Beam Inc						
Two Waters Pk Dr Ste 100	San Mateo	CA	94403	**888-311-1415**	650-653-4800	179-1
CDF (Children's Defense Fund)						
25 E St NW	Washington	DC	20001	**800-233-1200**	202-628-8787	47-6
CDGRA (Colorado Dude & Guest Ranch Assn)						
PO Box D	Shawnee	CO	80475	**866-942-3472**		47-23
CDI (Consolidated Devices Inc)						
19220 San Jose Ave	City of Industry	CA	91748	**800-525-6319**	626-965-0668	748
CDI Corporation						
1717 Arch St 35th Fl	Philadelphia	PA	19103	**866-472-2203**	215-569-2200	261
CDI Credit Inc						
6160 Peachtree Dunwoody Rd NE						
Ste B-210	Atlanta	GA	30328	**800-633-3961**	770-350-5070	626
CdLS (Cornelia de Lange Syndrome Foundation Inc)						
302 W Main St Ste 100	Avon	CT	06001	**800-753-2357**	860-676-8166	47-17
CDMA (Chain Drug Marketing Assn)						
43157 W Nine-Mile Rd PO Box 995	Novi	MI	48376	**800-935-2362**	248-449-9300	48-18
Cdo Technologies Inc						
5200 Sprngfeld St Ste 320	Dayton	OH	45431	**866-307-6616**	937-258-0022	444
CDS Analytical Inc						
465 Limestone Rd PO Box 277	Oxford	PA	19363	**800-541-6593**	610-932-3636	416
CDS Logistics Management Inc						
1225 Bengies Rd Ste A	Baltimore	MD	21220	**866-649-9559**	410-314-8000	310
CDS-John Blue Co						
290 Pinehurst Dr	Huntsville	AL	35806	**800-253-2583**	256-721-9090	632

	Toll-Free	Phone	Class
Cdspi 155 Lesmill Rd . . . . Toronto ON M3B2T8	800-561-9401	416-296-9401	388-3
CDT (Center for Democracy & Technology) 1634 'I' St NW 11th Fl. . . . . Washington DC 20006	800-869-4499	202-637-9800	47-7
CDW Corp 200 N Milwaukee Ave . . . . Vernon Hills IL 60061	800-800-4239	847-465-6000	180
CE Conover & Company Inc 4106 Blanche Rd . . . . Bensalem PA 19020	800-266-6837	215-639-6666	325
CE Niehoff & Co 2021 Lee St . . . . Evanston IL 60202 *Tech Supp	800-643-4633*	847-866-6030	247
CE Resource Inc 1482 Stone Point Dr Ste 100 . . . . Roseville CA 95661	800-707-5644		458
CE Rogers Co 1895 Frontage Rd . . . . Mora MN 55051	800-279-8081	320-679-2172	297
CE Thurston & Sons Inc 3335 Croft St . . . . Norfolk VA 23513	800-444-7713	757-855-7700	190-9
CEA (Cultural Experiences Abroad) 2999 N 44th St Ste 200 . . . . Phoenix AZ 85018	800-266-4441	480-557-7900	750
CEC (Career Education Corp) 2895 Greenspoint Pkwy Ste 600 . . . . Hoffman Estates IL 60196 *NASDAQ: CECO*	877-559-9222	847-781-3600	242
Cec Controls Co Inc 14555 Barber Ave . . . . Warren MI 48088	877-924-0303	586-779-0222	202
CEC Entertainment Inc 4441 W Airport Fwy PO Box 152077 . . . . . . Irving TX 75062 *NYSE: CEC*	888-778-7193	972-258-8507	661
CECO (Compressor Engineering Corp) 5440 Alder Dr . . . . Houston TX 77081	800-879-2326	713-664-7333	173
Ceco Concrete Construction LLC 9135 Barton . . . . Overland Park KS 66214	800-285-1131	913-362-1855	190-3
CED (Committee for Economic Development) 2000 L St NW Ste 700 . . . . Washington DC 20036	800-676-7353	202-296-5860	625
Cedar Breaks National Monument 2390 W Hwy 56 Ste 11 . . . . Cedar City UT 84720	877-642-4743	435-586-9451	557
Cedar City-Brian Head Tourism & Convention Bureau 581 N Main St Ste A. . . . . Cedar City UT 84721	800-354-4849	435-586-5124	207
Cedar Crest College 100 College Dr . . . . Allentown PA 18104 *Admissions	800-360-1222*	610-437-4471	166
Cedar Crest Specialties Inc 7269 Hwy 60 PO Box 260. . . . . Cedarburg WI 53012 *Hotline	800-877-8341*	262-377-7252	295-25
Cedar Fair Parks 14523 Carowinds Blvd . . . . Charlotte NC 28273	800-888-4386	704-588-2600	32
Cedar Grove Composting Inc 7343 E Marginal Way S . . . . Seattle WA 98108	888-832-3008	206-832-3000	187
Cedar Rapids Area Convention & Visitors Bureau 119 First Ave SE PO Box 5339. . . . . Cedar Rapids IA 52401	800-735-5557	319-398-5009	207
Cedar Rapids Truck Ctr Inc 9201 Sixth St SW . . . . Cedar Rapids IA 52404	866-602-1597	319-848-6230	770
Cedar Springs Behavioral Health System 2135 Southgate Rd . . . . Colorado Springs CO 80906	800-888-1088	719-633-4114	371-5
Cedar Springs Post 36 E Maple PO Box 370 . . . . Cedar Springs MI 49319	888-937-4514	616-696-3655	525-4
Cedar Valley Hospice 2101 Kimball Ave Ste 401 . . . . Waterloo IA 50702	800-617-1972	319-272-2002	368
Cedara Software Corp 6303 Airport Rd Ste 500. . . . . Mississauga ON L4V1R8	800-724-5970	905-364-8000	179-10
Cedarlane Laboratories Inc 4410 Paletta St . . . . Burlington ON L7L5R2	800-268-5058	905-878-8891	231
Cedars of Lebanon State Park 328 Cedar Forest Rd . . . . Lebanon TN 37087	800-342-3145	615-443-2769	558
Cedars-Sinai Medical Ctr (CSMC) 8700 Beverly Blvd . . . . Los Angeles CA 90048	800-233-2771	310-423-3277	371-3
Cedars-Sinai Medical Ctr Blood & Marrow Transplant Program 8700 Beverly Blvd AC1060. . . . . Los Angeles CA 90048	800-265-4186	310-423-1160	759
Cedarville University 251 N Main St . . . . Cedarville OH 45314	800-233-2784	937-766-7700	166
Cedarville University Centennial Library 251 N Main St . . . . Cedarville OH 45314	800-233-2784	937-766-7700	431-6
CEDIA (Custom Electronic Design & Installation Assn) 7150 Winton Dr Ste 300. . . . . Indianapolis IN 46268	800-669-5329	317-328-4336	48-19
Ceeva Inc 643 First Ave Ste 300 . . . . Pittsburgh PA 15219	866-233-8248	412-690-2300	195
CEF Industries Inc 320 S Church St . . . . Addison IL 60101	800-888-6419	630-628-2299	22
CEI (Culbertson Enterprises Inc) 600A Snyder Ave . . . . West Chester PA 19382	800-382-2685	610-436-6400	190-7
CEI Enterprises Inc 245 WoodwaRd Rd SE . . . . Albuquerque NM 87102	800-545-4034		14
Ceiva Logic Inc 214 E Magnolia Blvd . . . . Burbank CA 91502 *Tech Supp	877-693-7263*	818-562-1495	584
Cejka Search Inc Four Cityplace Dr Ste 300. . . . . Saint Louis MO 63141	800-678-7858	314-726-1603	712
Celadon Trucking Services Inc 9503 E 33rd St . . . . Indianapolis IN 46235	800-235-2366	317-972-7000	770
Celesco Transducer Products Inc 20630 Plummer St . . . . Chatsworth CA 91311	800-423-5483	818-701-2750	202
Celestial Seasonings Inc 4600 Sleepytime Dr . . . . Boulder CO 80301	800-351-8175	303-530-5300	295-40
Celestica Inc 844 Don Mills Rd . . . . Toronto ON M3C1V7 *NYSE: CLS*	888-899-9998	416-448-5800	253
Celgene Corp 86 Morris Ave . . . . Summit NJ 07901 *NASDAQ: CELG*	888-771-0141	908-673-9000	84
Cell Response Formulation LLC 4115 S Pub Pl . . . . Jackson WY 83002	888-364-7839	307-734-7839	296-9
Cell Signaling Technology Inc Three Trask Ln . . . . Danvers MA 01923	877-678-8324	978-867-2300	415
Cell Therapeutics Inc (CTI) 501 Elliott Ave W Ste 400 . . . . Seattle WA 98119 *NASDAQ: CTIC*	800-215-2355	206-282-7100	84
Cell-con Inc 305 Commerce Dr Ste 300 . . . . Exton PA 19341	800-771-7139	610-280-7630	73
Cellmark Forensics 13988 Diplomat Dr Ste 100 . . . . Dallas TX 75234	800-752-2774	214-271-8400	414
Cello Professional Products 1354 Old Post Rd . . . . Havre de Grace MD 21078	800-638-4850	410-939-1234	149
Cellofoam North America Inc 1917 Rockdale Industrial Blvd . . . . Conyers GA 30012	800-241-3634	770-929-3688	594
Cello-Pack Corp 55 Innsbruck Dr . . . . Cheektowaga NY 14227	800-778-3111	716-668-3111	541
Cellotape Inc 47623 Fremont Blvd . . . . Fremont CA 94538	800-231-0608	510-651-5551	410
Cell-Tel Government Systems Inc 8226-B Phillips Hwy Ste 290 . . . . Jacksonville FL 32256	800-737-7545	904-363-1111	246
CEL-SCI Corp 8229 Boone Blvd Ste 802 . . . . Vienna VA 22182 *NYSE: CVM*	800-422-6237	703-506-9460	84
Celsion Corp 10220-L Old Columbia Rd . . . . Columbia MD 21046 *NASDAQ: CLSN*	888-504-7965	410-290-5390	471
Celsis International 600 W Chicago Ave Ste 625 . . . . Chicago IL 60654	800-222-8260	312-476-1282	732
Celtic Healthcare 150 Scharberry Ln . . . . Mars PA 16046	800-355-8894		368
CEM Corp 3100 Smith Farm Rd . . . . Matthews NC 28104	800-726-3331	704-821-7015	416
CEMCO 263 N Covina Ln . . . . City Of Industry CA 91744	800-775-2362		104
Cemen Tech Inc 1700 N 14th St . . . . Indianola IA 50125	800-247-2464	515-961-7407	191
Cement Industries Inc 2925 Hanson St PO Box 823 . . . . Fort Myers FL 33902	800-332-1440	239-332-1440	184
Cement Products & Supply Co Inc 516 W Main St . . . . Lakeland FL 33815	800-248-2385	863-686-5141	184
Cemex USA 840 Gessner Ste 1400 . . . . Houston TX 77024 *NYSE: CX*	888-292-0070	713-650-6200	134
Cemline Corp PO Box 55 . . . . Cheswick PA 15024	800-245-6268	724-274-5430	35
Cemstone Products Co 2025 Centre Pt Blvd Ste 300 . . . . Mendota Heights MN 55120	800-236-7866	651-688-9292	183
Cenergistic Inc 5950 Sherry Ln Ste 900 . . . . Dallas TX 75225	888-782-7937	214-346-5950	195
Cengage Learning PO Box 6904 . . . . Florence KY 41022	800-354-9706		628-2
Centegra Memorial Medical Ctr 3701 Doty Rd . . . . Woodstock IL 60098	877-236-8347	815-338-2500	371-3
Centenary College 400 Jefferson St . . . . Hackettstown NJ 07840 *Admissions	800-236-8679*	908-852-1400	166
Centenary College of Louisiana 2911 Centenary Blvd . . . . Shreveport LA 71104 *Admissions	800-234-4448*	318-869-5131	166
Centenary State Historic Site 3522 College St . . . . Jackson LA 70748	888-677-2364	225-634-7925	558
Centene Corp 7700 Forsyth Blvd . . . . Saint Louis MO 63105 *NYSE: CNC* ■ *General	800-293-0056*	314-725-4477	388-3
Centennial Hall Convention Ctr 101 Egan Dr . . . . Juneau AK 99801	800-478-4176	907-586-5283	206
Centennial Hotel 96 Pleasant St . . . . Concord NH 03301	800-360-4839	603-227-9000	376
Centennial Travelers 311 S College Ave . . . . Fort Collins CO 80524	800-223-0675	970-484-4988	750
Center Court Historic Inn & Cottages 1075 Duval St C-19 . . . . Key West FL 33040	800-797-8787	305-296-9292	376
Center Enterprises Inc 30 Shield St . . . . West Hartford CT 06110 *Orders	800-542-2214*	860-953-4423	243
Center for Animals & Public Policy Tufts Univ School of Veterinary Medicine 200 Westboro Rd . . . . North Grafton MA 01536	888-748-8387	508-839-7920	625
Center for Assn Growth 1926 Waukegan Rd Ste 1 . . . . Glenview IL 60025	800-492-6462	847-657-6700	46
Center for Assn Resources Inc 1901 N Roselle Rd Ste 920. . . . . Schaumburg IL 60195	888-705-1434		46
Center for Auto Safety (CAS) 1825 Connecticut Ave NW Ste 330 . . . . Washington DC 20009	800-424-9393	202-328-7700	48-21
Center for Automation Research University of Maryland AV Williams Bldg 115 Rm 4413 . . . College Park MD 20742	800-868-0094	301-405-4526	659
Center for Chemical Process Safety (CCPS) 120 Wall St . . . . New York NY 10005	800-242-4363	646-495-1371	48-19
Center for Creative Photography 1030 N Olive Rd . . . . Tucson AZ 85721	888-472-4732	520-621-7968	513
Center for Democracy & Technology (CDT) 1634 'I' St NW 11th Fl. . . . . Washington DC 20006	800-869-4499	202-637-9800	47-7
Center for Diagnostic Imaging 5775 Wayzata Blvd Ste 400 . . . . Saint Louis Park MN 55416	877-885-8797	952-541-1840	380
Center for Genetic Testing at Saint Francis 6465 S Yale Ave . . . . Tulsa OK 74136	877-789-6001	918-502-1720	414
Center for Grain & Animal Health Research 1515 College Ave . . . . Manhattan KS 66502	800-627-0388		659
Center for Hospice Care Inc 111 Sunnybrook Ct . . . . South Bend IN 46637	800-413-9083	574-243-3100	368
Center for Individual Rights (CIR) 1233 20th St NW Ste 300 . . . . Washington DC 20036	877-426-2665	202-833-8400	47-8
Center for Lasik Ophthalmology Consultants, The 5800 Colonial Dr Ste 103 . . . . Margate FL 33063	800-448-8770	954-969-0090	786
Center for Law & Social Policy (CLASP) 1015 15th St NW Ste 400 . . . . Washington DC 20005	800-821-4367	202-906-8000	625
Center for Nutrition Policy & Promotion (CNPP) 3101 Pk Ctr Dr 10th Fl . . . . Alexandria VA 22302	888-779-7264	703-305-7600	338-1
Center for Organ Recovery & Education (CORE) 204 Sigma Dr RIDC Pk . . . . Pittsburgh PA 15238	800-366-6777	412-963-3550	269
Center for Policy Research Syracuse University 426 Eggers Hall . . . . Syracuse NY 13244	800-325-3535	315-443-3114	625
Center for Practical Bioethics 1111 Main St Ste 500. . . . . Kansas City MO 64105	800-344-3829	816-221-1100	47-17
Center for Puppetry Arts 1404 Spring St NW . . . . Atlanta GA 30309	800-642-3629	404-873-3089	49-1
Center for Research in Mathematics & Science Education San Diego State University 6475 Alvarado Rd Ste 206 . . . . San Diego CA 92120	800-573-8804	619-594-5090	659
Center for Space Plasma & Aeronomic Research University of Alabama Huntsville . . . . Huntsville AL 35899	800-824-2255	256-961-7403	659

Name / Address	City	State	ZIP	Toll-Free	Phone	Class
Center for the Arts						
103 Ctr for the Arts	Buffalo	NY	14260	**800-745-3000**	716-645-2787	565
Center for Western Studies						
2101 S Summit Ave						
Augustana College	Sioux Falls	SD	57197	**800-727-2844**	605-274-4007	513
Center of the American Experiment (CAE)						
12 S Sixth St						
1024 Plymouth Bldg	Minneapolis	MN	55402	**800-657-3717**	612-338-3605	625
Center on Education & Training for Employment						
Ohio State University						
1900 Kenny Rd	Columbus	OH	43210	**800-848-4815**	614-292-6869	659
Center on Human Development & Disability						
University of Washington 1701 NE Columbia Rd						
PO Box 357920	Seattle	WA	98195	**800-636-1089**	206-543-2832	659
Centerplate						
2187 Atlantic St	Stamford	CT	06902	**800-698-6992**	203-975-5900	298
CenterPoint Energy Inc						
1111 Louisiana St	Houston	TX	77002	**800-495-9880***	713-207-1111	357-5
NYSE: CNP ■ *Cust Svc						
National Center for Chronic Disease Prevention & Health Promotion (NCCDPHP)						
4770 Buford Hwy NE	Atlanta	GA	30341	**800-232-4636**		338-8
National Center for Emerging & Zoonotic Infectious Diseases						
1600 Clifton Rd	Atlanta	GA	30333	**800-232-4636**	404-639-3311	338-8
National Center for Environmental Health						
4770 Buford Hwy Bldg 101	Atlanta	GA	30341	**800-232-4636**	404-639-3311	338-8
National Center for Health Marketing						
1600 Clifton Rd NE	Atlanta	GA	30333	**800-311-3435**	404-498-1515	338-8
National Center for HIV/AIDS Viral Hepatitis STD & TB Prevention						
1600 Clifton Rd	Atlanta	GA	30333	**800-232-4636**		338-8
National Center for Immunization & Respiratory Diseases						
1600 Clifton Rd NE MS E-05	Atlanta	GA	30333	**800-232-4636**		338-8
National Center for Injury Prevention & Control (NCIPC)						
4770 Buford Hwy NE	Atlanta	GA	30341	**800-232-4636**		338-8
National Center for Public Health Informatics						
1600 Clifton Rd NE MS E-78	Atlanta	GA	30333	**800-232-4636**		338-8
National Center on Birth Defects & Developmental Disabilities						
1600 Clifton Rd	Atlanta	GA	30329	**800-232-4636**	770-498-3800	338-8
National Institute for Occupational Safety & Health						
200 Independence Ave SW	Washington	DC	20201	**800-356-4674**	404-639-3286	338-8
Centers for Disease Control & Prevention						
Travelers Health						
1600 Clifton Rd NE	Atlanta	GA	30333	**800-232-4636**		338-8
Centers for Medicare & Medicaid Services (CMS)						
7500 Security Blvd	Baltimore	MD	21244	**800-633-4227**		338-8
Medicare Hotline						
7500 Security Blvd	Baltimore	MD	21244	**800-633-4227**		338-8
Centimark Corp						
12 Grandview Cir	Canonsburg	PA	15317	**800-558-4100**		190-12
Centon Electronics Inc						
15 Argonaut	Aliso Viejo	CA	92656	**800-836-1986**	949-855-9111	617
Centra Health Inc						
1920 Atherholt Rd	Lynchburg	VA	24501	**877-635-4651**	434-947-3000	350
Central Alabama Community College						
1675 Cherokee Rd	Alexander City	AL	35010	**800-643-2657**	256-234-6346	160
Central Alabama Electric Co-op						
1802 Hwy 31 N	Prattville	AL	36067	**800-545-5735**	334-365-6762	245
Central Arizona College						
8470 N Overfield Rd	Coolidge	AZ	85228	**800-237-9814**	520-494-5444	160
Central Baptist Theological Seminary						
6601 Monticello Rd	Shawnee	KS	66226	**800-677-2287**	913-667-5700	167-3
Central Boston Elder Services Inc						
2315 Washington St	Boston	MA	02119	**800-922-2275**	617-277-7416	445
Central Brass Mfg Company Inc						
2950 E 55th St	Cleveland	OH	44127	**800-321-8630**	216-883-0220	602
Central Builders Supply Company Inc						
125 Bridge Ave PO Box 152	Sunbury	PA	17801	**800-326-9361**	570-286-6461	183
Central Carolina Hospital						
1135 Carthage St	Sanford	NC	27330	**800-292-2262**	919-774-2100	371-3
Central Christian College						
PO Box 1403	McPherson	KS	67460	**800-835-0078**	620-241-0723	166
Central Christian College of the Bible						
911 E Urbandale Dr	Moberly	MO	65270	**888-263-3900**	660-263-3900	159
Central College						
812 University St	Pella	IA	50219	**877-462-3687**	641-628-5285	166
Central Concrete Supply Company Inc						
755 Stockton Ave	San Jose	CA	95126	**866-404-1000**	408-293-6272	183
Central Connecticut Co-op Farmers Assn						
10 Apel Pl PO Box 8500	Manchester	CT	06042	**800-640-4523**	860-649-4523	275
Central Crude Inc						
4187 Hwy 3059 PO Box 1863	Lake Charles	LA	70602	**800-245-8408**	337-436-1000	574
Central Distributors Inc						
15 Foss Rd	Lewiston	ME	04240	**800-427-5757***	207-784-4026	80-1
*Cust Svc						
Central DuPage Hospital						
25 N Winfield Rd	Winfield	IL	60190	**800-223-9776**	630-933-1600	371-3
Central Electric Membership Corp						
128 Wilson Rd	Sanford	NC	27331	**800-446-7752**	919-774-4900	245
Central Federal Corp						
2923 Smith Rd	Fairlawn	OH	44333	**866-668-4606**	330-666-7979	357-2
NASDAQ: CFBK						
Central Florida Electric Co-op Inc						
1124 N Young Blvd	Chiefland	FL	32644	**800-227-1302**	352-493-2511	245
Central Florida Investments Inc						
5601 Windhover Dr	Orlando	FL	32819	**800-218-4363**	407-351-3351	743
Central Florida Visitors & Convention Bureau						
101 Adventure Ct	Davenport	FL	33837	**800-828-7655**	863-420-2586	207
Central Florida Zoological Park						
3755 NW Hwy 17-92 & I-4						
PO Box 470309	Lake Monroe	FL	32747	**800-435-7352**	407-323-4450	810
Central Flying Service Inc						
1501 Bond St	Little Rock	AR	72202	**800-888-5387**	501-375-3245	62
Central Freight Lines Inc						
PO Box 2638	Waco	TX	76702	**800-782-5036**		770
Central Georgia Electric Membership Corp						
923 S Mulberry St	Jackson	GA	30233	**800-222-4877**	770-775-7857	245
Central Georgia Technical College						
3300 Macon Tech Dr	Macon	GA	31206	**866-430-0135**	478-757-3400	788
Central Hudson Gas & Electric Corp						
284 S Ave	Poughkeepsie	NY	12601	**800-527-2714**	845-452-2700	775
Central Illinois Community Blood Ctr						
1134 S Seventh St	Springfield	IL	62703	**800-448-3253***	217-753-1530	88
*Help Line						
Central Industries Inc						
11438 Cronridge Dr Ste W	Owings Mills	MD	21117	**800-304-8484**		532
Central Ink Corp						
1100 Harvester Rd	West Chicago	IL	60185	**800-345-2541**	630-231-6500	385
Central Insurance Cos						
800 S Washington St	Van Wert	OH	45891	**800-736-7000**	419-238-1010	388-4
Central Iowa Co-op						
2829 Westown Pkwy						
Ste 350	West Des Moines	IA	50266	**800-513-3938**	515-225-1334	275
Central Jersey Blood Ctr						
494 Sycamore Ave	Shrewsbury	NJ	07702	**888-712-5663**	732-842-5750	88
Central Kentucky Blood Ctr						
3121 Beaumont Centre Cir	Lexington	KY	40513	**800-775-2522**	859-276-2534	88
Brainerd						
501 W College Dr	Brainerd	MN	56401	**800-933-0346**	218-855-8199	160
Central Lakes College						
Staples						
1830 Airport Rd	Staples	MN	56479	**800-247-6836**	218-894-5100	160
Central Louisiana State Hospital						
242 W Shamrock St	Pineville	LA	71360	**866-666-8335**	318-484-6200	371-5
Central Maine Community College						
1250 Turner St	Auburn	ME	04210	**800-891-2002***	207-755-5100	788
*Admissions						
Central Maine Power Co						
83 Edison Dr	Augusta	ME	04336	**800-565-0121**	207-623-3521	775
Central Maintenance & Welding Inc (CMW)						
2620 E Keysville Rd	Lithia	FL	33547	**877-704-7411**	813-737-1402	190-14
Central Methodist University						
411 Central Methodist Sq	Fayette	MO	65248	**877-268-1854**	660-248-3391	166
Central Michigan University						
102 Warriner Hall	Mount Pleasant	MI	48859	**888-292-5366***	989-774-4000	166
*Admissions						
Central Mine Equipment Company Inc						
4215 Rider Trl N	Earth City	MO	63045	**800-325-8827**	314-291-7700	191
Central Minnesota Fabricating Inc						
2725 W Gorton Ave	Willmar	MN	56201	**800-839-8857**	320-235-4181	475
Central Nebraska Packing Inc						
2800 E Eigth St	North Platte	NE	69103	**800-445-2881***	308-532-1250	468
*Cust Svc						
Central New York Business Journal, The						
269 W Jefferson St	Syracuse	NY	13202	**800-836-3539**	315-579-3919	452-5
Central Pacific Bank						
PO Box 3590	Honolulu	HI	96811	**800-342-8422***	808-544-0500	69
NYSE: CPF ■ *Cust Svc						
Central Pacific Financial Corp						
PO Box 3590	Honolulu	HI	96811	**800-342-8422**	808-544-0500	357-2
NYSE: CPF						
Central Paper Products Co Inc						
350 Gay St						
Brown Ave Industrial Pk	Manchester	NH	03103	**800-339-4065**	603-624-4065	552
Central Pennsylvania Blood Bank						
8167 Adams Dr	Hummelstown	PA	17036	**800-771-0059**	717-566-6161	88
Central Pennsylvania College						
600 Valley Rd PO Box 309	Summerdale	PA	17093	**800-759-2727**	717-732-0702	788
Central Petroleum Transport Inc (CPT)						
6115 Mitchell St	Sioux City	IA	51111	**800-798-6357**	712-258-6357	770
Central Piedmont Community College						
1201 Elizabeth Ave	Charlotte	NC	28204	**877-530-8815**	704-330-2722	160
Central Pipe Supply Inc						
101 Ware Rd PO Box 5470	Pearl	MS	39288	**800-844-7700**	601-939-3322	588
Central Puget Sound Regional Transit Authority						
401 S Jackson St	Seattle	WA	98104	**800-201-4900**	206-398-5000	463
Central Refrigerated Service Inc						
5175 W 2100 S	West Valley City	UT	84120	**800-777-0069**	801-924-7000	770
Central Rural Electric Co-op						
3304 S Boomer Rd PO Box 1809	Stillwater	OK	74076	**800-375-2884**	405-372-2884	245
Central Securities Corp						
630 Fifth Ave Ste 820	New York	NY	10111	**866-593-2507**	212-698-2020	402
NYSE: CET						
Central Service Assn						
93 S Coley Rd	Tupelo	MS	38801	**877-842-5962**	662-842-5962	225
Central Signaling						
2033 Hamilton Rd	Columbus	GA	31904	**800-554-1104**	706-322-3756	683
Central Specialties Ltd						
220 Exchange Dr	Crystal Lake	IL	60014	**800-873-4370**	815-459-6000	63
Central State University						
1400 Brush Row Rd						
PO Box 1004	Wilberforce	OH	45384	**800-388-2781**	937-376-6011	166
Central States Business Forms Inc						
2500 Industrial Pkwy	Dewey	OK	74029	**800-331-0920**		109
Central States Coach Repairs						
3426 Gilbert Rd	Grand Prairie	TX	75050	**800-533-1939**	972-399-1059	106
Central States Health & Life Company of Omaha						
1212 N 96th St	Omaha	NE	68114	**800-826-6587**	402-397-1111	388-2
Central Street Health Ctr						
26 Central St	Somerville	MA	02143	**800-909-2677**	617-591-6033	717
Central Texas College						
PO Box 1800	Killeen	TX	76540	**800-792-3348**	254-526-7161	160
Central Texas Electric Co-op Inc (CTEC)						
386 Friendship Ln						
PO Box 553	Fredericksburg	TX	78624	**800-900-2832***	830-997-2126	245
*General						
Central Texas Medical Ctr (CTMC)						
1301 Wonder World Dr	San Marcos	TX	78666	**800-927-9004**	512-353-8979	371-3
Central Texas Veterans Health Care System						
1901 Veterans Memorial Dr	Temple	TX	76504	**800-423-2111**	254-778-4811	371-8
Central Transportation Systems Inc						
4105 Rio Bravo Ste 100	El Paso	TX	79902	**800-283-3106**		444
Central Valley Bank						
537 W Second Ave	Toppenish	WA	98948	**800-422-1566***	509-865-2511	69
*General						
Central Valley Community Bancorp						
7100 N Financial Dr Ste 101	Fresno	CA	93720	**866-294-9588**	559-298-1775	357-2
NASDAQ: CVCY						
Central Valley Co-op						
900 30th Pl NW	Owatonna	MN	55060	**800-270-2339**	507-451-1230	276
Central Vermont Chamber of Commerce						
33 Stewart Rd	Berlin	VT	05602	**877-887-3678**	802-229-5711	137
Central Vermont Public Service Corp						
77 Grove St	Rutland	VT	05701	**800-649-2877**		775
Central Virginia Electric Co-op						
800 Co-op Way PO Box 247	Lovingston	VA	22949	**800-367-2832**	434-263-8336	245
Central Washington Hospital						
1201 S Miller St	Wenatchee	WA	98801	**800-365-6428**	509-662-1511	371-5

Name / Address	City	State	ZIP	Toll-Free	Phone	Class
Central Washington University						
400 E University Way	Ellensburg	WA	98926	**866-298-4968***	509-963-1111	166
*Admissions						
Central Woodwork Inc						
870 Keough Rd	Collierville	TN	38017	**800-788-3775**	901-363-4141	494
Central Wyoming College						
2660 Peck Ave	Riverton	WY	82501	**800-735-8418**	307-855-2000	160
Centralia-Chehalis Chamber of Commerce						
500 NW Chamber of						
Commerce Way	Chehalis	WA	98532	**800-525-3323**	360-748-8885	137
CentralVac International						
23455 Hellman Ave PO Box 259	Dollar Bay	MI	49922	**800-666-3133**		776
Centrav Inc						
511 E Travelers Trl	Burnsville	MN	55337	**800-874-2033**	952-886-7650	16
Centre College						
600 W Walnut St	Danville	KY	40422	**800-423-6236**	859-238-5350	166
Centre County Convention & Visitors Bureau						
800 E Pk Ave	State College	PA	16803	**800-358-5466**	814-231-1400	207
Centre Daily Times						
3400 E College Ave	State College	PA	16801	**800-327-5500**	814-238-5000	525-2
Centre for Well-Being at the Phoenician						
6000 E Camelback Rd	Scottsdale	AZ	85251	**800-843-2392**		698
Centre Hospitalier Le Gardeur						
911 Montee des Pionniers	Terrebonne	QC	J6V2H2	**888-654-7525**	450-654-7525	371-2
Centre Hospitalier Pierre Boucher						
1333 Boul Jacques-Cartier E	Longueuil	QC	J4M2A5	**866-277-3553**	450-468-8111	371-2
Centre in the Square						
101 Queen St N	Kitchener	ON	N2H6P7	**800-265-8977**	519-578-1570	565
Centrex Clinical Laboratories Inc						
28 Campion Rd	New Hartford	NY	13413	**800-753-8653**	315-797-0791	415
CENTRIA						
1005 Beaver Grade Rd	Moon Township	PA	15108	**800-759-7474**	412-299-8000	475
Centrix Inc						
770 River Rd	Shelton	CT	06484	**800-235-5862**	203-929-5582	228
Centron Data Services Inc						
1175 Devin Dr	Norton Shores	MI	49441	**800-732-8787***		5
*Cust Svc						
Centrus Energy Corp						
6903 Rockledge Dr Ste 400	Bethesda	MD	20817	**800-273-7754**	301-564-3200	141
NYSE: USU						
Centurion Industries Inc						
1107 N Taylor Rd	Garrett	IN	46738	**888-832-4466**	260-357-6665	191
Centurion Medical Products						
100 Centurion Way	Williamston	MI	48895	**800-248-4058**	517-546-5400	472
CENTURY 21 Sweyer & Assoc						
1630 Military Cutoff Rd	Wilmington	NC	28403	**800-848-0021**	910-256-0021	643
Century Bancorp Inc						
400 Mystic Ave	Medford	MA	02155	**866-823-6887**	781-393-4160	357-2
NASDAQ: CNBKA						
Century Casinos Inc						
2860 S Cir Dr Ste 350	Colorado Springs	CO	80906	**888-966-2257**	719-527-8300	131
NASDAQ: CNTY						
Century City Chamber of Commerce						
2029 Century Pk E						
Concourse Level	Los Angeles	CA	90067	**800-462-7899**	310-553-2222	137
Century College						
3300 Century Ave N	White Bear Lake	MN	55115	**800-228-1978**	651-779-3300	160
Century Fasteners Corp						
50-20 Ireland St	Elmhurst	NY	11373	**800-221-0769**	718-446-5000	246
Century Furniture LLC						
401 11th St NW	Hickory	NC	28601	**800-852-5552**	828-328-1851	318-2
Century Graphics & Metals Inc						
550 S N Lake Blvd						
Ste 1000	Altamonte Springs	FL	32701	**800-327-5664**		692
Century Group Inc, The						
1106 W Napoleon St PO Box 228	Sulphur	LA	70664	**800-527-5232**	337-527-5266	184
Century Health Solutions Inc						
2951 SW Woodside Dr	Topeka	KS	66614	**800-227-0089**	785-233-1816	195
Century Hotel South Beach						
140 Ocean Dr	Miami Beach	FL	33139	**877-659-8855**	305-674-8855	376
Century Insurance Group						
465 Cleveland Ave	Westerville	OH	43082	**877-855-8462**	614-895-2000	388-5
Century Interactive LLC						
8750 N Central Expy Ste 720	Dallas	TX	75231	**877-921-7992**	214-446-7867	726
Century Marketing Solutions LLC						
3000 Cameron St	Monroe	LA	71201	**800-256-6000**		619
Century Martial Art Supply Inc						
1000 Century Blvd	Oklahoma City	OK	73110	**800-626-2787***	405-732-2226	702
*Sales						
Century National Bank						
14 S Fifth St	Zanesville	OH	43701	**800-548-3557***	740-454-2521	69
*Cust Svc						
Century Plaza Hotel & Spa						
1015 Burrard St	Vancouver	BC	V6Z1Y5	**800-663-1818**	604-687-0575	376
Century Ready-Mix Corp						
3250 Armand St PO Box 4420	Monroe	LA	71211	**800-732-3969**	318-322-4444	183
Century Roof Tile						
23135 Saklan Rd	Hayward	CA	94545	**888-233-7548**	510-780-9489	192-1
Century Sports Inc						
1995 Rutgers University Blvd	Lakewood	NJ	08701	**800-526-7548***	732-905-4422	701
*Sales						
Century Spring Corp						
222 E 16th St	Los Angeles	CA	90015	**800-237-5225**	213-749-1466	710
Century Steel Erectors Co						
210 Washington Ave						
PO Box 490	Dravosburg	PA	15034	**888-601-8801**	412-469-8800	190-14
Century Suites Hotel						
300 SR-446	Bloomington	IN	47401	**800-766-5446**	812-336-7777	376
Century Tile Supply Co						
747 E Roosevelt Rd	Lombard	IL	60148	**888-845-3968**	630-495-2300	290
Century Tool & Mfg						
90 McMillen Rd	Antioch	IL	60002	**800-635-3831**		701
Century-National Insurance Co						
12200 Sylvan St						
PO Box 3999	North Hollywood	CA	91606	**800-894-8384***	818-760-0880	388-4
*Cust Svc						
CenturyTel Inc						
100 Centurylink Dr PO Box 4065	Monroe	LA	71211	**877-290-5458**	318-388-9000	357-3
NYSE: CTL						
CEOExpress Co						
1 Broadway 14th Fl	Cambridge	MA	02142	**888-686-1181**	617-482-1200	394
Cepheid						
904 E Caribbean Dr	Sunnyvale	CA	94089	**888-838-3222**	408-541-4191	416
NASDAQ: CPHD						

Name / Address	City	State	ZIP	Toll-Free	Phone	Class
Cepia LLC						
121 Hunter Ave Ste 103	Saint Louis	MO	63124	**800-225-9319**	314-725-4900	752
Cequent Towing Products						
47774 Anchor Ct W	Plymouth	MI	48170	**800-521-0510**		753
Cequent Trailer Products						
1050 Indianhead Dr	Mosinee	WI	54455	**800-604-9466**	715-693-1700	753
Ceradyne Inc						
3169 Redhill Ave	Costa Mesa	CA	92626	**877-992-7749**	714-549-0421	249
NYSE: MMM						
Ceragon Networks Inc						
10 Forest Ave	Paramus	NJ	07652	**877-342-3247***	201-845-6955	725
NASDAQ: CRNT ■ *Tech Supp						
Ceramics Monthly						
600 N Cleveland Ave Ste 210	Westerville	OH	43082	**800-342-3594**	614-794-5867	452-14
Ceramo Company Inc						
681 Kasten Dr	Jackson	MO	63755	**800-325-8303**	573-243-3138	332
CERC (Columbia Environmental Research Ctr)						
4200 New Haven Rd	Columbia	MO	65201	**888-283-7626**	573-875-5399	659
Ceres Solutions LLP						
2112 Indianapolis Rd						
PO Box 432	Crawfordsville	IN	47933	**800-878-0952***	765-362-6700	275
*General						
Cerex Advanced Fabrics Inc						
610 Chemstrand Rd	Cantonment	FL	32533	**800-572-3739**	850-968-0100	734-6
Cermetek Microelectronics Inc						
374 Turquoise St	Milpitas	CA	95035	**800-882-6271**	408-752-5000	174-3
Cernan Earth & Space Ctr						
2000 N Fifth Ave						
Triton College	River Grove	IL	60171	**800-972-7000**	708-456-0300	591
Cerner Corp						
2800 Rockcreek Pkwy	North Kansas City	MO	64117	**888-827-7220**	816-221-1024	179-11
NASDAQ: CERN						
Ceros Financial Services Inc						
1445 Research Blvd Ste 530	Rockville	MD	20850	**866-842-3356**		681
Cerritos Civic Ctr						
18025 Bloomfield Ave	Cerritos	CA	90703	**866-402-7433**	562-916-1350	431-3
Cerritos Ctr for the Performing Arts						
12700 Ctr Ct Dr	Cerritos	CA	90703	**800-300-4345**	562-916-8501	565
Cerro Coso Community College						
Bishop 4090 W Line St	Bishop	CA	93514	**888-537-6932**	760-872-1565	160
Indian Wells Valley						
3000 College Heights Blvd	Ridgecrest	CA	93555	**888-537-6932**	760-384-6100	160
Kern River Valley						
5520 Lk Isabella Blvd	Lake Isabella	CA	93240	**888-537-6932**	760-379-5501	160
Mammoth						
101 College Pkwy						
PO Box 1865	Mammoth Lakes	CA	93546	**888-537-6932**	760-934-2875	160
Cerro Flow Products Inc						
PO Box 66800	Saint Louis	MO	63166	**888-237-7611**	618-337-6000	485
Cerro Wire & Cable Company Inc						
1099 Thompson Rd SE	Hartselle	AL	35640	**800-523-3869**	256-773-2522	800
Cersosimo Lumber Co Inc						
1103 Vernon St	Brattleboro	VT	05301	**800-326-5647**	802-254-4508	674
CertainTeed Corp						
750 E Swedesford Rd	Valley Forge	PA	19482	**800-782-8777***	610-341-7000	386
*Prod Info						
CertainTeed Corp Pipe & Plastics Div						
750 E Swedesford Rd						
PO Box 860	Valley Forge	PA	19482	**800-274-8530**	610-341-7000	589
CertainTeed Gypsum						
2424 Lakeshore Rd W	Mississauga	ON	L5J1K4	**800-233-8990**	905-823-9881	344
CertaPro Painters Ltd						
150 Green Tree Rd Ste 1003	Oaks	PA	19456	**800-689-7271**		190-8
Certicom Corp						
4701 Tahoe Blvd Bldg A	Mississauga	ON	L4W0B5	**800-561-6100**	905-507-4220	179-12
Certified Financial Planner Board of Standards Inc						
1425 K St NW Ste 500	Washington	DC	20005	**800-487-1497**	202-379-2200	48-2
Certified General Accountants Assn of British Columbia						
300-1867 W Broadway	Vancouver	BC	V6J5L4	**800-565-1211**	604-732-1211	2
Certified Horsemanship Assn (CHA)						
1795 Alysheba Way Ste 7102	Lexington	KY	40509	**800-399-0138**	859-259-3399	47-3
Certified Power Inc						
970 Campus Dr	Mundelein	IL	60060	**888-905-7411**	847-573-3800	613
Certified Restoration DryCleaning Network LLC						
2060 Coolidge Hwy	Berkley	MI	48072	**800-963-2736**		309
Certipay						
199 Ave B NW Ste 270	Winter Haven	FL	33881	**800-422-3782**	863-299-2400	2
Certis USA LLC						
9145 Guilford Rd Ste 175	Columbia	MD	21046	**800-250-5024**		280
Cerus Corp						
2550 Stanwell Dr	Concord	CA	94520	**800-401-1957**	925-288-6000	84
NASDAQ: CERS						
CES (IEEE Consumer Electronics Society)						
445 Hoes Ln	Piscataway	NJ	08854	**800-678-4333**	732-981-0060	48-19
Cetac Technologies Inc						
14306 Industrial Rd	Omaha	NE	68144	**800-369-2822**	402-733-2829	416
CETCO (Colloid Environmental Technologies Co)						
2870 Forbs Ave	Hoffman Estates	IL	60192	**800-527-9948**	847-851-1899	3
Cetera Financial Group Inc						
200 N Sepulveda Blvd						
Ste 1200	El Segundo	CA	90245	**866-489-3100**		681
Cev Multimedia Ltd						
1020 SE Loop 289	Lubbock	TX	79404	**877-610-5017**	806-745-8820	507
CEVA Inc						
1943 Landings Dr	San Jose	CA	94043	**800-894-0972**	650-417-7900	687
CF Martin & Company Inc						
510 Sycamore St PO Box 329	Nazareth	PA	18064	**888-433-9177**	610-759-2837	520
CFA (Consumer Federation of America)						
1620 I St NW Ste 200	Washington	DC	20006	**877-382-4357**	202-387-6121	47-10
CFA Institute						
915 E High St						
PO Box 3668	Charlottesville	VA	22903	**800-247-8132**	434-951-5499	48-2
CFC Farm & Home Ctr						
15172 Brandy Rd PO Box 2002	Culpeper	VA	22701	**800-284-2667**	540-825-2200	280
CFC International Inc						
500 State St	Chicago Heights	IL	60411	**800-393-4505**	708-891-3456	3
CFCA (Christian Foundation for Children & Aging)						
One Elmwood Ave	Kansas City	KS	66103	**800-875-6564**	913-384-6500	47-6
CFG (Creative Financial Group)						
16 Campus Blvd	Newtown Square	PA	19073	**800-893-4824**	610-325-6100	398
CFG Community Bank						
1422 Clarkview Rd	Baltimore	MD	21209	**866-619-1417**	410-823-0500	69
CFHS (Canadian Federation of Humane Societies)						
30 Concourse Gate Ste 102	Ottawa	ON	K2E7V7	**888-678-2347**	613-224-8072	47-3

	City	State	ZIP	Toll-Free	Phone	Class
CFMA (Construction Financial Management Assn)						
100 Village Blvd Ste 200A	Princeton	NJ	08540	**877-462-7827**	609-452-8000	48-1
CFO Magazine						
253 Summer St	Boston	MA	02210	**800-772-1119**	617-345-9700	452-5
CFS Bancorp Inc						
707 Ridge Rd	Munster	IN	46321	**866-622-1370**	219-513-5123	357-2
NASDAQ: CITZ						
CFS the School at Church Farm						
PO Box 2000	Paoli	PA	19301	**800-439-4745**	610-363-7500	615
CG Schmidt Inc						
11777 W Lake Pk Dr	Milwaukee	WI	53224	**800-248-1254**	414-577-1177	187
CGH (Coral Gables Hospital Inc)						
3100 Douglas Rd	Coral Gables	FL	33134	**866-728-3677**	305-445-8461	371-3
CGH Medical Ctr (CGHMC)						
100 E LeFevre Rd	Sterling	IL	61081	**800-625-4790**	815-625-0400	371-3
CGHMC (CGH Medical Ctr)						
100 E LeFevre Rd	Sterling	IL	61081	**800-625-4790**	815-625-0400	371-3
CGI Communications Inc						
130 E Main St Ste 800	Rochester	NY	14604	**800-398-3029**	585-427-0020	507
CGI Group Inc						
1130 Sherbrooke St W						
Seventh Fl	Montreal	QC	H3A2M8	**800-828-8377**	514-841-3200	181
TSE: GIB/A						
CGM Funds						
38 Newbury St Ste 8	Boston	MA	02116	**800-345-4048**	617-859-7714	521
CGM Inc 1445 Ford Rd	Bensalem	PA	19020	**800-523-6570**	215-638-4400	134
Cgn & Assoc Inc						
415 SW Washington St	Peoria	IL	61602	**888-746-4246**	309-495-2100	195
CGNAD (Compass Group North American Div)						
2400 Yorkmont Rd	Charlotte	NC	28217	**800-357-0012**	704-328-4000	298
CGR Products Inc						
4655 US Hwy 29 N	Greensboro	NC	27405	**877-313-6785**	336-621-4568	325
CH (Clarion Hospital)						
One Hospital Dr	Clarion	PA	16214	**800-522-0505**	814-226-9500	371-3
CH Ellis Co Inc						
2432 SE Ave	Indianapolis	IN	46201	**800-466-3351***	317-636-3351	448
*Sales						
CH Energy Group Inc						
284 S Ave	Poughkeepsie	NY	12601	**800-527-2714**	845-452-2000	357-5
NYSE: CHG						
CH Hanson Co						
2000 N Aurora Rd	Naperville	IL	60563	**800-827-3398**	630-848-2000	462
CH Robinson Worldwide Inc						
14701 Charlson Rd	Eden Prairie	MN	55347	**855-229-6128***	952-683-3950	444
NASDAQ: CHRW ■ *Cust Svc						
CHA (Certified Horsemanship Assn)						
1795 Alysheba Way Ste 7102	Lexington	KY	40509	**800-399-0138**	859-259-3399	47-3
CHA (Craft & Hobby Assn)						
319 E 54th St	Elmwood Park	NJ	07407	**800-822-0494**	201-835-1200	47-18
CHA (Clough Harbour & Assoc)						
Three Winners Cir PO Box 5269	Albany	NY	12205	**800-836-0817**	518-453-4500	261
CHA (Community Hospital Anderson)						
1515 N Madison Ave	Anderson	IN	46011	**800-777-7775**	765-298-4242	371-3
ChaCha Search Inc						
14550 Clay Terr Blvd Ste 130	Carmel	IN	46032	**800-224-2242**	317-660-6680	195
Chaco Culture National Historical Park						
PO Box 220	Nageezi	NM	87037	**877-642-4743**	505-786-7014	557
Chad Therapeutics Inc						
2975 Horseshoe Dr S Ste 600	Naples	FL	34104	**800-423-8870**	239-687-1285	471
OTC: CHADQ						
CHADD (Children & Adults with Attention-Deficit/Hyperactivity Disorder)						
8181 Professional Pl Ste 150	Landover	MD	20785	**800-233-4050**	301-306-7070	47-17
Chadderton Trucking Inc						
40 Stewart Way	Sharon	PA	16146	**800-327-6868**	724-981-5050	770
Chadron State College						
1000 Main St	Chadron	NE	69337	**800-242-3766**	308-432-6263	166
Chadwick's of Boston						
500 Bic Dr Bldg 4	Milford	CT	06461	**877-330-3393**		454
Chadwick-BaRoss Inc						
160 Warren Ave	Westbrook	ME	04092	**800-804-0775**	207-854-8411	355
Chain Drug Marketing Assn (CDMA)						
43157 W Nine-Mile Rd PO Box 995	Novi	MI	48376	**800-935-2362**	248-449-9300	48-18
Chain Store Guide						
10117 Princess Palm Ave Ste 375	Tampa	FL	33610	**800-927-9292**		628-6
Chalk & Vermilion Fine Arts Inc						
55 Old Post Rd Ste 2	Greenwich	CT	06830	**800-877-2250**	203-869-9500	628-10
Challenge Printing Co, The						
Two Bridewell Pl	Clifton	NJ	07014	**800-654-1234**	973-471-4700	619
Challenge Publications Inc						
9509 Vassar Ave Ste A	Chatsworth	CA	91311	**800-562-9182**	818-700-6868	628-9
Challenger Ctr for Space Science Education						
422 First St SE Third Fl	Washington	DC	20003	**800-969-5747***	202-827-1580	47-11
*General						
Challenger Learning Ctr (CLC)						
316 Washington Ave						
Wheeling Jesuit University	Wheeling	WV	26003	**800-624-6992**	304-243-2279	513
Chalmers & Kubeck Inc						
150 Commerce Dr	Aston	PA	19014	**800-242-5637**	610-494-4300	449
Chamber Music America (CMA)						
305 Seventh Ave 5th Fl	New York	NY	10001	**888-221-9836**	212-242-2022	47-4
Chamber of Business & Industry of Centre County						
200 Innovation Blvd						
Ste 150	State College	PA	16803	**877-234-5050**	814-234-1829	137
Chamber of Commerce Mountain View						
580 Castro St	Mountain View	CA	94041	**800-229-7728**	650-968-8378	137
Chamber of Commerce of Harrison County						
111 W Walnut St	Corydon	IN	47112	**800-666-0255**	812-738-0120	137
Chamber of Commerce serving Middletown Monroe & Trenton						
1500 Central Ave	Middletown	OH	45044	**800-837-3200**	513-422-4551	137
Chamber of Schenectady County						
306 State St	Schenectady	NY	12305	**800-962-8007**	518-372-5656	137
Chamber Orchestra of Philadelphia						
1520 Locust St Ste 500	Philadelphia	PA	19102	**800-732-0999**	215-545-5451	566-3
Chamber South						
6410 SW 80th St	South Miami	FL	33143	**800-206-3715**	305-661-1621	137
Chamberlain College of Nursing						
11830 Westline Industrial						
Ste 106	Saint Louis	MO	63146	**888-556-8226**	314-991-6200	166
Chamberlain Group						
845 Larch Ave	Elmhurst	IL	60126	**800-528-9131**	630-279-3600	347
Chamberlain West Hollywood						
1000 Westmount Dr	West Hollywood	CA	90069	**800-201-9652**	310-657-7400	376
Chambers of Commerce / Tourism						
106 E Jefferson St	Tallahassee	FL	32301	**800-628-2866**	850-606-2305	207
Chaminade						
One Chaminade Ln	Santa Cruz	CA	95065	**800-283-6569**	831-475-5600	374
Chaminade College Preparatory School						
425 S Lindbergh Blvd	Saint Louis	MO	63131	**877-378-6847**	314-993-4400	615
Chaminade University						
3140 Waialae Ave	Honolulu	HI	96816	**800-735-3733**	808-735-4711	166
Chamizal National Memorial						
800 S San Marcial St	El Paso	TX	79905	**877-642-4743**	915-532-7273	557
Champaign County Chamber of Commerce						
113 Miami St	Urbana	OH	43078	**877-873-5764**	937-653-5764	137
Champaign County Convention & Visitors Bureau						
108 S Neil St	Champaign	IL	61820	**800-369-6151**	217-351-4133	207
Champion Athletic Wear						
1000 E Hanes Mill Rd	Winston-Salem	NC	27105	**800-315-0563**		153-17
Champion Bus Inc						
331 Graham Rd	Imlay City	MI	48444	**800-776-4943**	810-724-6474	509
Champion Chemical Co						
8319 S Greenleaf Ave	Whittier	CA	90602	**800-424-9300**		149
Champion Co						
400 Harrison St	Springfield	OH	45505	**800-328-0115***	937-324-5681	199
*Sales						
Champion College Services Inc						
4600 S Mill Ave Ste 180	Tempe	AZ	85282	**800-761-7376**	480-947-7375	195
Champion Inc						
180 Traders Mine Rd						
PO Box 490	Iron Mountain	MI	49801	**800-568-8881***	906-779-2300	183
*Sales						
Champion Industries Inc						
PO Box 2968 PO Box 2968	Huntington	WV	25728	**800-624-3431**	304-528-2791	619
OTC: CHMP						
Champion Mfg Industries Inc						
6021 N Galena Rd	Peoria	IL	61614	**800-452-7473**	309-685-1031	588
Champion Power Equipment Inc						
10006 Santa Fe						
Springs Rd	Santa Fe Springs	CA	90670	**877-338-0999**	562-236-9422	60
Champion Shuffleboard Ltd						
7216 Burns St	Richland Hills	TX	76118	**800-826-7856**	817-284-3499	701
Champion Solutions Group						
791 Pk of Commerce Blvd						
Ste 200	Boca Raton	FL	33487	**800-771-7000**	561-997-2900	175
Champion Window Mfg Inc						
12121 Champion Way	Cincinnati	OH	45241	**877-424-2674**	513-346-4600	235
Champion-Arrowhead LLC						
5147 Alhambra Ave	Los Angeles	CA	90032	**800-332-4267**	323-221-9137	602
Champlain Cable Corp						
175 Hercules Dr	Colchester	VT	05446	**800-451-5162**		801
Champlain College						
163 S Willard St	Burlington	VT	05401	**800-570-5858**	802-860-2700	166
Champps Entertainment Inc						
19111 Dallas Pkwy Ste 370	Dallas	TX	75287	**800-229-2118***	972-581-1171	661
*General						
Champs Sports						
311 Manatee Ave W	Bradenton	FL	34205	**800-991-6813**		702
Chancellor Hotel on Union Square						
433 Powell St	San Francisco	CA	94102	**800-428-4748**	415-362-2004	376
Chandler Chamber of Commerce						
25 S Arizona Pl Ste 201	Chandler	AZ	85225	**800-963-4571**	480-963-4571	137
Chandler Hall Hospice						
99 Barclay St	Newtown	PA	18940	**888-603-1973**	215-860-4000	368
Chandler Inn						
26 Chandler St	Boston	MA	02116	**800-842-3450**	617-482-3450	376
Chandler Regional Hospital						
475 S Dobson Rd	Chandler	AZ	85224	**877-728-5414**	480-728-3000	371-3
Chandlers Plywood Products Inc						
3716 Waverly Rd	Huntington	WV	25704	**800-414-1311**	304-429-1311	114
Chanel Inc						
15 E 57th St	New York	NY	10022	**800-550-0005**	212-355-5050	567
Chaney Enterprises						
12480 Mattawoman Dr PO Box 548	Waldorf	MD	20604	**888-244-0411**	301-932-5000	184
Channel Solutions LLC						
3145 E Chandler Blvd Ste 110	Phoenix	AZ	85048	**866-501-9690**		197
Channellock Inc						
1306 S Main St	Meadville	PA	16335	**800-724-3018***		748
*Cust Svc						
Channelnet						
Three Harbor Dr Ste 206	Sausalito	CA	94965	**800-667-6858**	415-332-4704	178
Channing Bete Co						
One Community Pl	South Deerfield	MA	01373	**800-477-4776**	413-665-7611	628-10
Chanticleer Inn						
1458 E Dollar Lk Rd	Eagle River	WI	54521	**800-752-9193**	715-479-4486	660
CHAP (Community Health Accreditation Program Inc)						
1275 K St NW Ste 800	Washington	DC	20005	**800-656-9656**	202-862-3413	47-1
Chaparral Energy Inc						
701 Cedar Lake Blvd	Oklahoma City	OK	73114	**866-478-8770**	405-478-8770	531
Chaparral Suites Resort & Conference Ctr						
5001 N Scottsdale Rd	Scottsdale	AZ	85250	**866-534-1797**	480-949-1414	660
Chapel Hill/Orange County Visitors Bureau						
501 W Franklin St	Chapel Hill	NC	27516	**888-968-2060**		207
Chapel Steel Co						
590 N Bethlehem Pk						
PO Box 1000	Lower Gwynedd	PA	19002	**800-570-7674**	215-793-0899	449
Chapman University						
One University Dr	Orange	CA	92866	**888-282-7759**	714-997-6815	166
Chapman/Leonard Studio Equipment Inc						
12950 Raymer St	North Hollywood	CA	91605	**888-883-6559**	818-764-6726	713
Chapters Health System						
12973 Telecom Pkwy						
Ste 100	Temple Terrace	FL	33637	**866-204-8611**	813-871-8111	368
Char-Broil						
1442 Belfast Ave	Columbus	GA	31902	**866-239-6777***	706-571-7000	35
*Cust Svc						
Charisma Magazine						
600 Rinehart Rd	Lake Mary	FL	32746	**800-749-6500**	407-333-0600	452-18
Chariton Valley Electric Co-op						
2090 Hwy 5 PO Box 486	Albia	IA	52531	**800-475-1702**	641-932-7126	245
CharityUSA.com LLC						
600 University St						
Ste 1000 One Union Square	Seattle	WA	98101	**888-811-5271**	206-268-5400	384
Charles & Colvard Ltd						
170 Southport Dr	Morrisville	NC	27560	**877-202-5467**		408
NASDAQ: CTHR						
Charles A. Lindbergh State Park						
1615 Lindbergh Dr S						
PO Box 364	Little Falls	MN	56345	**888-646-6367**	320-616-2525	558

Company / Address	City	State	ZIP	Toll-Free	Phone	Class
Charles C Thomas Publisher						
2600 S First St						
PO Box 19265	Springfield	IL	62704	800-258-8980*	217-789-8980	628-2
*Sales						
Charles C. Parks Co						
500 Belvedere Dr	Gallatin	TN	37066	800-873-2406	615-452-2406	296-11
Charles County Chamber of Commerce						
101 Centennial St Ste A	La Plata	MD	20646	800-992-3194	301-932-6500	137
Charles Craft Inc						
21381 Charles Craft Ln						
Laurinburg-Maxton Airport	Laurinburg	NC	28352	800-277-1009	910-844-3521	734-9
Charles E Egeler Correctional Facility						
3855 Cooper St	Jackson	MI	49201	855-444-3911	517-780-5600	213
Charles Gabus Ford Inc						
4545 Merle Hay Rd	Des Moines	IA	50310	800-934-2287*	515-270-0707	56
*Sales						
Charles GG Schmidt & Company Inc						
301 W Grand Ave	Montvale	NJ	07645	800-724-6438	201-391-5300	748
Charles Hotel Harvard Square						
One Bennett St	Cambridge	MA	02138	800-882-1818	617-864-1200	376
Charles Industries Ltd						
5600 Apollo Dr	Rolling Meadows	IL	60008	800-458-4747	847-806-6300	725
Charles Jones LLC						
PO Box 8488	Trenton	NJ	08650	800-792-8888		626
Charles Leonard Inc						
145 Kennedy Dr	Hauppauge	NY	11788	800-999-7202	631-273-6700	347
Charles Machine Works Inc						
PO Box 66	Perry	OK	73077	800-654-6481*	580-336-4402	191
*Cust Svc						
Charles Mix Electric Assn Inc						
440 Lake St	Lake Andes	SD	57356	800-208-8587	605-487-7321	245
Charles River Analytics Inc						
625 Mt Auburn St Ste 3	Cambridge	MA	02138	877-547-4600	617-491-3474	178
Charles River Laboratories Inc						
251 Ballardvale St	Wilmington	MA	01887	800-522-7287	781-222-6000	659
NYSE: CRL						
Charles Ross & Son Co						
710 Old Willets Path	Hauppauge	NY	11788	800-243-7677	631-234-0500	383
Charles Ryan Assoc Inc						
601 Morris St Ste 301	Charleston	WV	25301	877-342-0161		627
Charles Schwab & Co Inc						
211 Main St	San Francisco	CA	94105	800-648-5300*	415-667-1009	681
*Cust Svc						
Charles Towne Landing State Historic Site						
1500 Old Towne Rd	Charleston	SC	29407	866-345-7275	843-852-4200	558
Charleston Area Convention & Visitors Bureau						
423 King St	Charleston	SC	29403	800-868-8118	843-853-8000	207
Charleston Auto Parts Inc						
3108 Losee Rd	North Las Vegas	NV	89030	800-879-7901		60
Charleston County School District (CCSD)						
75 Calhoun St	Charleston	SC	29401	800-255-7688	843-937-6300	676
Charleston Gazette						
1001 Virginia St E	Charleston	WV	25301	800-982-6397	304-348-5140	525-2
Charleston Place						
205 Meeting St	Charleston	SC	29401	800-611-5545	843-722-4900	376
Charleston Regional Chamber of Commerce						
1116 Smith St	Charleston	WV	25301	800-792-4326	304-340-4253	137
Charleston Southern University						
9200 University Blvd	Charleston	SC	29423	800-947-7474	843-863-7050	166
Charlestown Retirement Community (CCI)						
715 Maiden Choice Ln	Catonsville	MD	21228	800-917-8649	410-242-2880	663
Charley's Grilled Subs						
2500 Farmers Dr Ste 140	Columbus	OH	43235	800-437-8325	614-923-4700	661
Charlie Palmer Steak						
101 Constitution Ave NW	Washington	DC	20001	877-632-7800	202-547-8100	662
Charlotte Anodizing Products Inc						
591 E Packard Hwy	Charlotte	MI	48813	800-818-6945	517-543-1911	476
Charlotte Convention & Visitors Bureau						
500 S College St Ste 300	Charlotte	NC	28202	800-722-1994	704-334-2282	207
Charlotte Institute of Rehabilitation						
1100 Blythe Blvd	Charlotte	NC	28203	800-634-2256	704-355-4300	371-6
Charlotte Motor Speedway						
5555 Concord Pkwy S	Concord	NC	28027	800-455-3267	704-455-3200	633
Charlotte Nature Museum						
1658 Sterling Rd	Charlotte	NC	28209	800-935-0553	704-372-6261	513
Charlotte Observer, The						
600 S Tryon St	Charlotte	NC	28202	800-332-0686	704-358-5000	525-2
Charlotte Pipe & Foundry Co						
2109 Randolph Rd	Charlotte	NC	28207	800-438-6091	704-372-5030	485
Charlotte Russe Inc						
5910 Pacific Center Blvd	San Diego	CA	92121	888-211-7271		155-6
Charlotte-Mecklenburg Schools						
701 E ML King Jr Blvd	Charlotte	NC	28202	800-244-6224	980-343-3000	676
Charm Sciences Inc						
659 Andover St	Lawrence	MA	01843	800-343-2170	978-687-9200	474
Charmer Sunbelt Group, The						
60 E 42nd St Ste 1915	New York	NY	10165	800-772-2096	212-699-7000	80-3
Chart House Restaurants						
1510 W Loop S	Houston	TX	77027	800-552-6379	713-850-1010	661
Charter at Beaver Creek						
120 Offerson Rd PO Box 5310	Avon	CO	81620	800-525-6660	970-949-6660	376
Charter Communications Inc						
12405 Powerscourt Dr						
Ste 100	Saint Louis	MO	63131	888-438-2427	314-965-0555	115
NASDAQ: CHTR						
Charter Dura-Bar						
2100 W Lake Shore Dr	Woodstock	IL	60098	800-227-6455	815-338-3900	306
Charter Films Inc						
1901 Winter St PO Box 277	Superior	WI	54880	877-411-3456	715-395-8258	541
Charter Flight Inc						
1928 S Blvd	Charlotte	NC	28208	800-521-3148	704-359-9124	13
Charter Wire						
3700 W Milwaukee Rd	Milwaukee	WI	53208	800-436-9074	414-390-3000	800
CharterBank						
1233 OG Skinner Dr	West Point	GA	31833	800-763-4444	706-645-1391	69
Chartis Group LLC						
220 W Kinzie St Fifth Fl	Chicago	IL	60654	877-667-4700		458
Chartist Newsletter						
PO Box 758	Seal Beach	CA	90740	800-942-4278	562-596-2385	524-9
Chartpak Inc 1 River Rd	Leeds	MA	01053	800-628-1910	413-584-5446	42
Chartway Federal Credit Union						
160 Newtown Rd	Virginia Beach	VA	23462	800-678-8765	757-552-1000	219
Chase & Sons Inc						
295 University Ave	Westwood	MA	02090	800-323-4182	781-332-0700	803
Chase Bank						
One Chase Manhattan Plz	New York	NY	10081	800-935-9935		69
Chase Brass & Copper Co						
14212 County Rd M 50						
PO Box 152	Montpelier	OH	43543	800-537-4291	419-485-3193	480
Chase Hotel at Palm Springs						
200 W Arenas Rd	Palm Springs	CA	92262	877-532-4273	760-320-8866	376
Chase Industries Inc						
10021 Commerce Park Dr	Cincinnati	OH	45246	800-543-4455	513-860-5565	475
Chase Park Plaza						
212 N KingsHwy Blvd	Saint Louis	MO	63108	877-587-2427*	314-633-3000	376
*Resv						
Chase Paymentech Solutions LLC						
14221 Dallas Pkwy	Dallas	TX	75254	800-708-3740*		255
*Cust Svc						
Chase Plastic Services Inc						
6467 Waldon Ctr Dr	Clarkston	MI	48346	800-232-4273	248-620-2120	681
Chateau Elan Resort & Conference Ctr						
100 Rue Charlemagne	Braselton	GA	30517	800-233-9463	678-425-0900	374
Chateau Elan Spa at the Chateau Elan Atlanta						
100 Rue Charlemagne	Braselton	GA	30517	800-233-9463	678-425-0900	698
Chateau Elan Winery						
100 Tour de France	Braselton	GA	30517	800-233-9463	678-425-0900	49-6
Chateau Grille						
415 N State Hwy 265	Branson	MO	65616	888-333-5253	417-334-1161	662
Chateau Louis Hotel & Conference Centre						
11727 Kingsway	Edmonton	AB	T5G3A1	800-661-9843	780-452-7770	376
Chateau Morrisette Winery						
287 Winery Rd SW	Floyd	VA	24091	866-695-2001	540-593-2865	49-6
Chateau on the Lake						
415 N State Hwy 265	Branson	MO	65616	888-333-5253	417-334-1161	376
Chateau Ste Michelle Winery						
14111 NE 145th St	Woodinville	WA	98072	800-267-6793	425-415-3300	49-6
Chateau Vaudreuil Suites Hotel						
21700 Rt Transcanada						
Hwy.	Vaudreuil-Dorion	QC	J7V8P3	800-363-7896	450-455-0955	376
Chateau Versailles						
1659 Sherbrooke St W	Montreal	QC	H3H1E3	888-933-8111	514-933-3611	376
Chatham Bars Inn						
297 Shore Rd	Chatham	MA	02633	800-527-4884	508-945-0096	660
Chatham Steel Corp						
501 W Boundary St	Savannah	GA	31401	800-800-1337	912-233-5751	487
Chatham University						
1 Woodland Rd	Pittsburgh	PA	15232	800-837-1290	412-365-1100	166
chatr wireless						
333 Bloor St E Eighth Fl	Toronto	ON	M4W1G9	800-485-9745		224
Chatsworth Data Corp						
9735 Lurline Ave	Chatsworth	CA	91311	877-380-6855	818-350-5072	248
Chatsworth Products Inc						
31425 Agoura Rd	Westlake Village	CA	91361	800-834-4969	818-735-6100	177
Chatsworth-Murray County Chamber of Commerce						
PO Box 516	Chatsworth	GA	30705	800-969-9490	706-695-2834	137
Chattahoochee River National Recreation Area						
1978 Island Ford Pkwy	Atlanta	GA	30350	877-874-2478	678-538-1200	557
Chattanooga Area Chamber of Commerce						
811 Broad St	Chattanooga	TN	37402	877-756-7684	423-756-2121	137
Chattanooga Area Convention & Visitors Bureau						
215 Broad St	Chattanooga	TN	37402	800-322-3344	423-756-8687	207
Chattanooga Convention Ctr						
1150 Carter St PO Box 6008	Chattanooga	TN	37402	800-962-5213	423-756-0001	206
Chattanooga Group						
4717 Adams Rd	Hixson	TN	37343	800-592-7329	423-870-2281	472
Chattanooga National Cemetery						
1200 Bailey Ave	Chattanooga	TN	37404	877-907-8585	423-855-6590	135
Chattanooga State Technical Community College						
4501 Amnicola Hwy	Chattanooga	TN	37406	866-547-3733	423-697-4400	160
Chattanoogan, The						
1201 Broad St	Chattanooga	TN	37402	877-756-1684	423-756-3400	374
Chautauqua County Visitors Bureau						
Chautauqua Main Gate Rt 394						
PO Box 1441	Chautauqua	NY	14722	800-242-4569	716-357-4569	207
CHCBC (Community Health Ctr of Branch County)						
274 E Chicago St	Coldwater	MI	49036	800-994-6610	517-279-5400	371-3
Cheaha Resort State Park						
19644 Hwy 281	Delta	AL	36258	800-610-5801	256-488-5111	558
Check Point Software Technologies Ltd						
800 Bridge Pkwy	Redwood City	CA	94065	800-429-4391	650-628-2000	179-12
NASDAQ: CHKP						
Check Printers Inc						
1530 Antioch Pike	Antioch	TN	37013	800-766-1217		140
Checkered Flag Motor Car Corp						
5225 Virginia						
Beach Blvd	Virginia Beach	VA	23462	866-414-7820	757-687-3486	56
Checkers Drive-In Restaurants Inc						
4300 W Cypress St Ste 600	Tampa	FL	33607	800-800-8072	813-283-7000	661
CheckPoint HR						
2035 Lincoln Hwy Ste 1080	Edison	NJ	08817	800-385-0331	732-287-8270	563
Checkpoint Systems Inc						
101 Wolf Dr	Thorofare	NJ	08086	800-257-5540	856-848-1800	683
NYSE: CKP						
Checks In The Mail Inc						
2435 Goodwin Ln	New Braunfels	TX	78135	800-733-4443	830-609-5500	140
Checks Unlimited						
8245 N Union Blvd						
PO Box 35630	Colorado Springs	CO	80920	800-634-2563		140
Cheeca Lodge & Spa						
81801 Overseas Hwy						
Mile Marker 82	Islamorada	FL	33036	800-327-2888	305-664-4651	698
Cheekwood Museum of Art & Botanical Garden						
1200 Forrest Pk Dr	Nashville	TN	37205	877-356-8150	615-356-8000	96
Chef's Catalog						
5070 Centennial Blvd	Colorado Springs	CO	80919	800-541-6390*		359
*Cust Svc						
Chelsea Bldg Products						
565 Cedar Way	Oakmont	PA	15139	800-424-3573		235
Chelsea Lumber Co						
One Old Barn Cir	Chelsea	MI	48118	800-875-9126	734-475-9126	192-3
Chelsea Milling Co						
201 W N St PO Box 460	Chelsea	MI	48118	800-727-2460	734-475-1361	295-23
Chelsea Savoy Hotel						
204 W 23rd St	New York	NY	10011	866-929-9353	212-929-9353	376
Chem Processing Inc						
3910 Linden Oaks Dr	Rockford	IL	61109	800-262-2119	815-874-8118	476

Alphabetical Section

	Toll-Free	Phone	Class
Chem USA Corp			
38507 Cherry St ....Newark CA 94560	800-866-2436	510-608-8818	174-1
Chemart Co			
15 New England Way ....Lincoln RI 02865	800-521-5001	401-333-9200	476
Chematics Inc			
PO Box 293 ....North Webster IN 46555	800-348-5174	574-834-2406	231
Chembio Diagnostics Inc			
3661 Horseblock Rd ....Medford NY 11763	844-243-6246	631-924-1135	576
NASDAQ: CEMI			
Chemed Corp			
255 E Fifth St Ste 2600........Cincinnati OH 45202	800-982-7650*	513-762-6900	186
NYSE: CHE ■ *General			
Chemetal			
39 O'Neil St ....EastHampton MA 01027	800-807-7341	413-529-0718	294
Chemetron Fire Systems			
16 W 361 S Frontage Rd			
Ste 125..............Burr Ridge IL 60527	800-878-5631*	708-748-1503	283
Ste 125..............Burr Ridge IL 60527	800-878-5631*	708-748-1503	739
*Cust Svc			
Chemical Abstracts Service (CAS)			
2540 Olentangy River Rd ....Columbus OH 43202	800-848-6538	614-447-3600	384
Chemical Financial Corp			
333 E Main St ....Midland MI 48640	800-867-9757	989-839-5350	357-2
NASDAQ: CHFC			
Chemical Processing Magazine			
555 W Pierce Rd Ste 301 ....Itasca IL 60143	800-343-4048	630-467-1300	452-21
Chemical Products Corp			
102 Old Mill Rd ....Cartersville GA 30120	877-210-9814*	770-382-2144	141
*Cust Svc			
Chemical Regulation Reporter			
1801 S Bell St ....Arlington VA 22202	800-372-1033		524-5
Chemical Safety Corp			
5901 Christie Ave Ste 502 ....Emeryville CA 94608	888-594-1100	510-594-1000	38
Chemical Specialties Manufacturing Corp			
901 N Newkirk St ....Baltimore MD 21205	800-638-7370*	410-675-4800	149
*Sales			
Chemical Waste Management Inc			
1001 Fannin St Ste 4000 ....Houston TX 77002	800-633-7871	713-512-6200	658
Chemical Week Magazine			
140 East 45th Street			
2 Grand Central Tower,40th Fl..........New York NY 10017	866-501-7540*	212-884-9528	452-21
*Cust Svc			
Chemically Dependent Anonymous (CDA)			
PO Box 423 ....Severna Park MD 21146	888-232-4673		47-21
Chemin-A-Haut State Park			
14656 State Pk Rd ....Bastrop LA 71220	888-677-2436	318-283-0812	558
Chemineer Inc			
5870 Poe Ave ....Dayton OH 45414	800-643-0641	937-454-3200	383
Chemprene Inc			
483 Fishkill Ave PO Box 471 ....Beacon NY 12508	800-431-9981	845-831-2800	367
Chemsolv Inc			
1140 Industry Ave SE ....Roanoke VA 24013	800-523-3099	540-427-4000	144
Chemstar Products Co			
3915 Hiawatha Ave ....Minneapolis MN 55406	800-328-5037	612-722-0079	142
Chem-Tainer Industries Inc			
361 Neptune Ave ....West Babylon NY 11704	800-275-2436	631-661-8300	200
Chemtex International Inc			
1979 Eastwood Rd ....Wilmington NC 28403	877-243-6839	910-509-4400	261
Chem-Trend LP			
1445 McPherson Pk Dr ....Howell MI 48843	800-727-7730	517-546-4520	534
Chemtrol Div NIBCO Inc			
1516 Middlebury St ....Elkhart IN 46516	800-234-0227	574-295-3000	589
Chemtronics Inc			
8125 Cobb Centre Dr ....Kennesaw GA 30152	800-645-5244	770-424-4888	143
Chemung County Chamber of Commerce			
400 E Church St ....Elmira NY 14901	800-627-5892*	607-734-5137	137
*General			
Chemung Supply Corp			
PO Box 527 ....Elmira NY 14903	800-733-5508	607-733-5506	192-2
Cheney Lime & Cement			
478 Graystone Rd PO Box 160 ....Allgood AL 35013	800-752-8282	205-625-3031	436
Cheniere Energy Inc			
700 Milam St Ste 800..............Houston TX 77002	877-375-5002	713-375-5000	324
NYSE: LNG			
Chenille Kraft Co			
65 Ambrogio Dr PO Box 269 ....Gurnee IL 60031	800-621-1261		243
CHEP USA			
8517 S Pk Cir ....Orlando FL 32819	866-855-2437*	407-370-2437	639
*Cust Svc			
Cher-Make Sausage Co			
2915 Calumet Ave ....Manitowoc WI 54220	800-242-7679	920-683-5980	295-26
Cherokee Brick & Tile Co Inc			
3250 Waterville Rd ....Macon GA 31206	800-277-2745	478-781-6800	148
Cherokee Casino & Resort			
777 W Cherokee St ....Catoosa OK 74015	800-760-6700		660
Cherokee County			
165 E Sixth St Ste 203 PO Box 259 ....Rusk TX 75785	800-541-2524	903-683-6540	336
Cherokee Electric Co-op			
1550 Clarence Chestnut Bypass			
PO Box O ....Centre AL 35960	800-952-2667	256-927-5524	245
Cherokee Heritage Ctr & National Museum			
21192 S Keeler Dr ....Park Hill OK 74451	888-999-6007	918-456-6007	513
Cherokee Park Ranch			
436 Cherokee Hills Dr ....Livermore CO 80536	800-628-0949	970-493-6522	239
Cherokee Tribal Travel & Promotions			
498 Tsali Blvd PO Box 460 ....Cherokee NC 28719	877-440-9990	828-359-6492	207
Cherry Corp			
11200 88th Ave ....Pleasant Prairie WI 53158	800-510-1689	262-942-6500	802
Cherry Creek Dodge			
2727 S Havana St ....Denver CO 80014	888-891-7522*	303-751-1104	56
*Sales			
Cherry Creek State Park			
4201 S Parker Rd ....Aurora CO 80014	866-265-6447	303-699-3860	558
Cherry Demolition			
6131 Selinsky Rd ....Houston TX 77048	800-444-1123	713-987-0000	190-16
Cherry Hill Photo Enterprises Inc			
4 East Stow Rd ....Marlton NJ 08053	800-969-2440		583
Cherry Hill Regional Chamber of Commerce			
1060 Kings Hwy N Ste 200..........Cherry Hill NJ 08034	800-669-6801	856-667-1600	137
Cherry's Industrial Equipment			
600 Morse Ave ....Elk Grove Village IL 60007	800-350-0011		355
Cherrydale Farms Fundraising			
707 N Vly Forge Rd ....Lansdale PA 19446	877-619-4822		295-8
Cherryland Electric Co-op			
5930 US 31 S PO Box 298 ....Grawn MI 49637	800-442-8616	231-486-9200	245
Cherryroad Technologies Inc			
301 Gibraltar Dr Ste 2C ....Morris Plains NJ 07950	877-402-7804	973-402-7802	178
Cheryl & Co			
646 McCorkle Blvd ....Westerville OH 43082	800-443-8124		67
Chesapeake Bay Magazine			
1819 Bay Ridge Ave Ste 180..........Annapolis MD 21403	800-283-2883	410-263-2662	452-22
Chesapeake Conventions & Tourism Bureau (CCT)			
860 Greenbrier Cir Ste 101..........Chesapeake VA 23320	888-889-5551	757-502-4898	207
Chesapeake Lodging Trust (CLT)			
1997 Annapolis Exchange Pkwy			
Ste 410 ....Annapolis MD 21401	800-698-2820		645
NYSE: CHSP			
Chesapeake Regional Medical Ctr			
736 Battlefield Blvd N ....Chesapeake VA 23320	800-582-8350	757-312-8121	371-3
Chess Life Magazine			
PO Box 3967 ....Crossville TN 38557	800-903-8723*	931-787-1234	452-14
*Sales			
Chester County			
313 W Market St Ste 6202			
PO Box 2748. ....West Chester PA 19380	800-692-1100	610-344-6100	336
Chester Fritz Auditorium			
3475 University Ave			
PO Box 9028. ....Grand Forks ND 58202	800-375-4068	701-777-3076	565
Chester Inc			
555 Eastport Ctr Dr ....Valparaiso IN 46383	800-778-1131	219-465-7555	295-35
Chester Mental Health Ctr			
1315 Lehman Dr ....Chester IL 62233	800-843-6154	618-826-4571	371-5
Chester Water Authority			
PO Box 467 ....Chester PA 19016	800-793-2323	610-876-8185	793
Chester's International LLC			
3500 Colonnade Pkwy Ste 325..........Birmingham AL 35243	800-554-4537	205-949-4690	309
Chesterfield Chamber of Commerce			
101 Chesterfield			
Business Pkwy ....Chesterfield MO 63005	888-242-4262	636-532-3399	137
Chesterfield Hotel			
363 Cocoanut Row ....Palm Beach FL 33480	800-243-7871	561-659-5800	376
Chester-Jensen Company Inc			
PO Box 908 ....Chester PA 19016	800-685-3750	610-876-6276	297
Chestnut Hill College			
9601 Germantown Ave ....Philadelphia PA 19118	800-248-0052	215-248-7001	166
Chestnut Hill Hotel			
8229 Germantown Ave ....Philadelphia PA 19118	800-628-9744	215-242-5905	376
Chestnut Mountain Resort			
8700 Chestnut Dr ....Galena IL 61036	800-397-1320		375
Chestnut Ridge Foam Inc			
PO Box 781 ....Latrobe PA 15650	800-234-2734*	724-537-9000	594
*Cust Svc			
Chevron Canada Ltd			
1200 - 1050 W Pender St ....Vancouver BC V6E3T4	800-663-1650	604-668-5300	573
Chevron Corp			
6001 Bollinger Canyon Rd ....San Ramon CA 94583	800-243-8766*	925-842-1000	529
NYSE: CVX ■ *Cust Svc			
Chevron Energy Solutions			
345 California St 18th Fl..........San Francisco CA 94104	800-368-8357	415-733-4500	261
Chevron Phillips Chemical Company LP			
10001 Six Pines Dr ....The Woodlands TX 77380	800-231-1212	832-813-4100	142
Chevron Phillips Chemical Company Performance Pipe Div			
5085 W Pk Blvd Ste 500..............Plano TX 75093	800-527-0662	972-599-6600	589
Chevron Texaco Credit Card Ctr			
PO Box P ....Concord CA 94524	800-243-8766		217
Chewacla State Park			
124 Shell Toomer Pkwy ....Auburn AL 36830	800-252-7275	334-887-5621	558
Cheyenne Area Convention & Visitors Bureau			
121 W 15th St Ste 202 ....Cheyenne WY 82001	800-426-5009	307-778-3133	207
Cheyenne Civic Ctr			
510 W 20th St ....Cheyenne WY 82001	877-691-2787	307-637-6364	565
Cheyenne Depot Museum			
121 W 15th St Ste 300 ....Cheyenne WY 82001	800-544-2151	307-632-3905	513
Cheyenne Mountain Conference Resort			
3225 Broadmoor Vly Rd ....Colorado Springs CO 80906	800-428-8886	719-538-4000	374
Cheyenne Newspaper Inc			
702 W Lincolnway ....Cheyenne WY 82001	800-561-6268	307-634-3361	628-8
Cheyney University of Pennsylvania			
1837 University Cir PO Box 200..........Cheyney PA 19319	800-243-9639	610-399-2275	166
CHF Industries Inc			
One Pk Ave Ninth Fl ....New York NY 10016	800-243-7090*	212-951-7800	735
*Cust Svc			
Chi Phi Fraternity			
1160 Satellite Blvd ....Suwanee GA 30024	800-849-1824	404-231-1824	47-16
CHI St. Joseph's Health			
2500 Fairway St ....Dickinson ND 58601	800-446-6215*	701-456-4000	371-3
*General			
Chicago Board Options Exchange (CBOE)			
400 S La Salle St ....Chicago IL 60605	800-678-4667	312-786-5600	682
Chicago Boiler Co			
1300 NW Ave ....Gurnee IL 60031	800-522-7343*	847-662-4000	90
*Cust Svc			
Chicago Boiler Co CB Mills Div			
1300 NW Ave ....Gurnee IL 60031	800-522-7343	847-662-4000	90
Chicago Botanic Garden			
1000 Lake Cook Rd ....Glencoe IL 60022	877-829-5500	847-835-5440	96
Chicago Bridge & Iron Co			
6001 Rogerdale Rd ....Houston TX 77072	866-235-5687*	713-485-1000	190-14
NYSE: CBI ■ *General			
Chicago Cutting Die Co			
3555 Woodhead Dr ....Northbrook IL 60062	800-747-3437	847-509-5800	747
Chicago Display Marketing Corp			
2021 W St ....River Grove IL 60171	800-681-4340	708-842-0001	233
Chicago Dowel Company Inc			
4700 W Grand Ave ....Chicago IL 60639	800-333-6935	773-622-2000	807
Chicago Extruded Metals Co (CXM)			
1601 S 54th Ave ....Cicero IL 60804	800-323-8102*		480
*Cust Svc			
Chicago Faucets A Geberit Co			
2100 S Clearwater Dr ....Des Plaines IL 60018	800-323-5060	847-803-5000	602
Chicago Fire			
7000 S Harlem Ave ....Bridgeview IL 60455	888-657-3473	708-594-7200	708
Chicago Gasket Co			
1285 W N Ave ....Chicago IL 60622	800-833-5666	773-486-3060	325
Chicago Heights Steel Acquisition Corp			
211 E Main St ....Chicago Heights IL 60411	800-424-4487	708-756-5648	714

Name / Address	City	State	ZIP	Toll-Free	Phone	Class
Chicago International Film Festival Cinema Chicago 30 E Adams St Ste 800	Chicago	IL	60603	**800-982-2787**	312-683-0121	282
Chicago Lakeshore Hospital 4840 N Marine Dr *Cust Svc	Chicago	IL	60640	**800-888-0560***	773-878-9700	371-5
Chicago Lumber Company of Omaha, The 1324 Pierce St PO Box 3487	Omaha	NE	68103	**800-642-8210**	402-342-0840	192-3
Chicago Magazine 435 N Michigan Ave Ste 1100	Chicago	IL	60611	**800-999-0879**	312-222-8999	452-22
Chicago Meat Authority Inc (CMA) 1120 W 47th Pl	Chicago	IL	60609	**800-383-3811**	773-254-3811	295-26
Chicago Metallic Corp 4849 S Austin Ave	Chicago	IL	60638	**800-323-7164**	708-563-4600	486
Chicago Midway Airport 5700 S Cicero Ave	Chicago	IL	60638	**800-832-6352**	773-838-0600	27
Chicago Office of Tourism & Culture 78 E Washington St 4th Fl	Chicago	IL	60602	**866-966-5335**	312-744-2400	207
Chicago Pneumatic Tool Co 1800 Overview Dr	Rock Hill	SC	29730	**800-624-4735**	803-817-7000	749
Chicago Reader 11 E Illinois St	Chicago	IL	60611	**888-473-5362**	312-828-0350	525-5
Chicago Southland Convention & Visitors Bureau 2304 173rd St	Lansing	IL	60438	**888-895-8233**	708-895-8200	207
Chicago Southshore & South Bend Railroad 505 N Carroll Ave	Michigan City	IN	46360	**800-356-2079**	219-874-9000	639
Chicago Symphony Orchestra 220 S Michigan Ave	Chicago	IL	60604	**800-223-7114**	312-294-3000	566-3
Chicago Title & Trust Co 171 N Clark St	Chicago	IL	60601	**800-621-1919**	312-223-2000	388-6
Chicago Tribune 435 N Michigan Ave	Chicago	IL	60611	**800-874-2863**	312-222-3232	525-2
Chicago Tube & Iron Co One Chicago Tube Dr *Cust Svc	Romeoville	IL	60446	**800-972-0217***	815-834-2500	487
Chicago-Wilcox Mfg Co 16928 State St PO Box 126	South Holland	IL	60473	**800-323-5282**		325
Chick Master Incubator Co 945 Lafayette Rd PO Box 704	Medina	OH	44258	**800-727-8726**	330-722-5591	273
Chickasaw Electric Co-op 17970 US Hwy 64 E PO Box 459	Somerville	TN	38068	**866-465-3591**	901-465-3591	245
Chickasaw Nation, The 520 Arlington St PO Box 1548	Ada	OK	74821	**866-466-1481**	580-436-2603	47-11
Chickasaw State Park 26955 US Hwy 43	Gallion	AL	36742	**800-760-4089**	334-295-8230	558
Chick-fil-A Inc 5200 Buffington Rd	Atlanta	GA	30349	**800-232-2677**	404-765-8000	661
Chico Chamber of Commerce 441 Main St	Chico	CA	95928	**800-852-8570**	530-891-5556	137
Chico Enterprise Record 400 E Pk Ave PO Box 9	Chico	CA	95927	**800-827-1421**	530-891-1234	525-2
Chico News & Review 353 E Second St	Chico	CA	95928	**866-703-3873**	530-894-2300	525-5
Chico's FAS Inc 11215 Metro Pkwy *NYSE: CHS*	Fort Myers	FL	33966	**800-690-6903**	888-855-4986	155-6
Chicopee Provision Co Inc 19 Sitarz St	Chicopee	MA	01013	**800-924-6328**	413-594-4765	295-26
Chicot State Park 3469 Chicot Pk Rd	Ville Platte	LA	70586	**888-677-2442**	337-363-2403	558
Chief Automotive Systems Inc 1924 E Fourth St	Grand Island	NE	68802	**800-445-9262**	308-384-9747	383
Child Development Assoc Inc 678 Third Ave Ste 201	Chula Vista	CA	91910	**888-755-2445**	619-427-4411	146
Child Evangelism Fellowship Inc 17482 Hwy M	Warrenton	MO	63383	**800-748-7710**	636-456-4321	47-20
Child Find Canada 212-2211 McPhillips St	Winnipeg	MB	R2V3M5	**800-387-7962**	204-339-5584	47-6
Child Lures Prevention 5166 Shelburne Rd	Shelburne	VT	05482	**800-552-2197**	802-985-8458	47-6
Child Welfare Information Gateway 1250 Maryland Ave SW 8th Fl	Washington	DC	20024	**800-394-3366**	703-385-7565	338-8
Childcare Network Inc 1501 13th St Ste D	Columbus	GA	31901	**866-521-5437**	706-562-8600	146
Childhaven 316 Broadway	Seattle	WA	98122	**877-300-9164**	206-624-6477	350
Childhelp USA 4350 E Camelback Rd Bldg F250	Phoenix	AZ	85018	**800-422-4453**	480-922-8212	47-6
Children & Adults with Attention-Deficit/Hyperactivity Disorder (CHADD) 8181 Professional Pl Ste 150	Landover	MD	20785	**800-233-4050**	301-306-7070	47-17
Children & Youth Funding Report 8204 Fenton St	Silver Spring	MD	20910	**800-666-6380**	301-588-6380	524-8
Children Awaiting Parents Inc (CAP) 595 Blossom Rd Ste 306	Rochester	NY	14610	**888-835-8802**	585-232-5110	47-6
Children Inc 4205 Dover Rd	Richmond	VA	23221	**800-538-5381**	804-359-4562	47-6
Children International 2000 E Red Bridge Rd	Kansas City	MO	64131	**800-888-3089**	816-942-2000	47-5
Children of Lesbians & Gays Everywhere (COLAGE) 1550 Bryant St Ste 830	San Francisco	CA	94103	**855-426-5243**	415-861-5437	47-21
Children of the Night 14530 Sylvan St	Van Nuys	CA	91411	**800-551-1300**	818-908-4474	47-6
Children's Bureau of Southern California 1910 Magnolia Ave	Los Angeles	CA	90004	**800-730-3933**	213-342-0100	349
Children's Defense Fund (CDF) 25 E St NW	Washington	DC	20001	**800-233-1200**	202-628-8787	47-6
Children's Healthcare of Atlanta at Egleston 1405 Clifton Rd NE	Atlanta	GA	30322	**888-785-7778**	404-785-6000	371-1
Children's Healthcare of Atlanta at Scottish Rite 1001 Johnson Ferry Rd NE	Atlanta	GA	30342	**888-785-7778**	404-785-5252	371-1
Children's Hope House 7922 W Jefferson Blvd	Fort Wayne	IN	46804	**800-706-9941**	260-459-8550	369
Children's Hospital 200 Henry Clay Ave	New Orleans	LA	70118	**800-299-9511**	504-899-9511	371-1
Children's Hospital & Research Ctr at Oakland Blood & Marrow Transplantation Program 747 52nd St	Oakland	CA	94609	**888-433-9042**	510-428-3000	759
Children's Hospital Central California 9300 Valley Children's Pl	Madera	CA	93638	**800-548-5435**	559-353-3000	371-1
Children's Hospital Medical Ctr of Akron one Perkins Sq	Akron	OH	44308	**800-262-0333**	330-543-1000	371-1
Children's Hospital of Eastern Ontario 401 Smyth Rd	Ottawa	ON	K1H8L1	**866-797-0007**	613-737-7600	371-2
Children's Hospital of New York-Presbyterian *Pediatric Blood & Marrow Transplantation Program* 3959 Broadway 11 Central	New York	NY	10032	**866-463-2778**	212-305-5593	759
Children's Hospital of Orange County Blood & Donor Services 505 S Main St	Orange	CA	92868	**800-228-5234**	714-532-8339	759
Children's Hospital of Wisconsin Bone Marrow Transplant Clinic (CHW) 9000 W Wisconsin Ave PO Box 1997	Milwaukee	WI	53226	**877-266-8989**	414-266-2000	759
Children's Hospitals & Clinics Minneapolis 2525 Chicago Ave	Minneapolis	MN	55404	**866-225-3251**	612-813-6000	371-1
Children's House at Johns Hopkins 1915 McElderry St	Baltimore	MD	21205	**800-933-5470**	410-614-2560	369
Children's Institute of Pittsburgh 1405 Shady Ave	Pittsburgh	PA	15217	**877-433-1109**	412-420-2400	371-1
Children's Medical Ctr one Children's Plaza	Dayton	OH	45404	**800-228-4055**	937-641-3000	371-1
Children's Medical Ctr of Dallas Ctr for Cancer & Blood Disorders (CMC) 1935 Medical District Dr	Dallas	TX	75235	**800-222-1222**	214-456-7000	759
Children's Mercy Hospital & Clinics 2401 Gillham Rd	Kansas City	MO	64108	**866-512-2168**	816-234-3000	371-1
Children's Museum of Oak Ridge 461 W Outer Dr	Oak Ridge	TN	37830	**877-524-1223**	865-482-1074	514
Children's Museum of Richmond 2626 W Broad St	Richmond	VA	23220	**866-737-5965**	804-474-7000	514
Children's National Medical Ctr (CNMC) 111 Michigan Ave NW	Washington	DC	20010	**800-884-5433**	202-476-5000	371-1
Children's Organ Transplant Assn (COTA) 2501 W Cota Dr	Bloomington	IN	47403	**800-366-2682**	812-336-8872	47-17
Children's Place Retail Stores Inc 500 Plz Dr *NASDAQ: PLCE*	Secaucus	NJ	07094	**877-752-2387**	201-558-2400	155-1
Children's Research Institute Children's National Medical Ctr 111 Michigan Ave NW Research Fl 5	Washington	DC	20010	**888-884-2327**		659
Children's Tumor Foundation 95 Pine St 16th Fl	New York	NY	10005	**800-323-7938**	212-344-6633	47-17
Children's Wish Foundation International 8615 Roswell Rd	Atlanta	GA	30350	**800-323-9474**	770-393-9474	47-17
Childrens Plus Inc 1387 Dutch American Way	Beecher	IL	60401	**800-230-1279**		95
Chillicothe Correctional Ctr 3151 Litton Rd	Chillicothe	MO	64601	**800-392-8486**	660-646-4032	213
Chillicothe Gazette 50 W Main St	Chillicothe	OH	45601	**877-424-0215**	740-773-2111	525-2
Chiltern Inn 11 Cromwell Harbor Rd	Bar Harbor	ME	04609	**800-709-0114**	207-288-3371	376
Chime Master Systems PO Box 936	Lancaster	OH	43130	**800-344-7464**		520
Chimney Rock Park 431 Main St	Chimney Rock	NC	28720	**800-277-9611**	828-625-9611	96
Chimney Rock Public Power District 805 W Eigth St PO Box 608	Bayard	NE	69334	**877-773-6300**	308-586-1824	245
Chimo Hotel 1199 Joseph Cyr St	Ottawa	ON	K1J7T4	**800-387-9779**	613-744-1060	376
China Airlines Cargo Sales & Service 11201 Aviation Blvd	Los Angeles	CA	90045	**800-778-4838**	310-646-4293	12
China Ocean Shipping Co Americas Inc (COSCO) 100 Lighting Way	Secaucus	NJ	07094	**800-242-7354**	201-422-0500	220
Chinatrust Bank USA 801 S Figueroa St Ste 2300	Los Angeles	CA	90017	**888-839-9000**	310-791-2828	69
Chinese Chamber of Commerce of Los Angeles 977 N Broadway Ground Fl Ste E	Los Angeles	CA	90012	**800-400-7115**	213-617-0396	
Chinese Laundry Shoes 3485 S La Cienega Blvd	Los Angeles	CA	90016	**888-935-8825**	310-838-2103	300
Chino Valley Ranchers 5611 Peck Rd	Arcadia	CA	91006	**800-354-4503**		296-10
Chinois on Main 2709 Main St	Santa Monica	CA	90405	**888-646-3387**	310-392-9025	662
Chippewa Falls Area Chamber of Commerce 10 S Bridge St	Chippewa Falls	WI	54729	**888-723-0024**	715-723-0331	137
Chippewa Trails 510 E S Ave	Chippewa Falls	WI	54729	**866-777-1399**	715-726-2457	106
Chippewa Valley Electric Co-op 317 S Eigth St	Cornell	WI	54732	**800-300-6800**	715-239-6800	245
Chippewa Valley Technical College 620 W Clairemont Ave	Eau Claire	WI	54701	**800-547-2882**	715-833-6200	788
Chipton-ross Inc 343 Main St	El Segundo	CA	90245	**800-927-9318**	310-414-7800	623
Chiropractic Health Plan of California PO Box 190	Clayton	CA	94517	**800-995-2442**	310-210-5400	388-3
Chisago County 313 N Main St	Center City	MN	55012	**888-234-1246**	651-257-1300	336
Chisesi Bros Meat Packing Co 5221 Jefferson Hwy	New Orleans	LA	70123	**800-966-3550**	504-822-3550	468
Chisholm Fleming & Assoc 317 Renfrew Dr Ste 301	Markham	ON	L3R9S8	**888-241-4149**	905-474-1458	256
CHN (Coalition on Human Needs) 1120 Connecticut Ave NW	Washington	DC	20036	**800-822-7323**	202-223-2532	47-5
Chocolates a la Carte Inc 28455 Livingston Ave *Cust Svc	Valencia	CA	91355	**800-818-2462***		295-8
Choctaw Electric Co-op Inc 1033 N 4250 Rd	Hugo	OK	74743	**800-780-6486**	580-326-6486	245
Choctawhatchee Electric Co-op Inc 1350 W Baldwin Ave	DeFuniak Springs	FL	32435	**800-342-0990**	850-892-2111	245
Choi Bros Inc 3401 W Div St	Chicago	IL	60651	**800-524-2464**	773-489-2800	153-1
Choice Books LLC 2387 Grace Chapel Rd	Harrisonburg	VA	22801	**800-224-5006**	540-434-1827	94
Choice Hotels International Inc 10750 Columbia Pk *NYSE: CHH*	Silver Spring	MD	20901	**800-424-6423**	301-592-5000	376
Choice Hotels International, Inc. 997 New Loudon Rd	Latham	NY	12110	**800-424-6423**	518-785-0931	376
Cholestech Corp 9975 Summers Ridge Rd	San Diego	CA	92121	**800-733-0404**	510-732-7200	231
CHOMP (Community Hospital of the Monterey Peninsula) 23625 Holman Hwy	Monterey	CA	93940	**888-452-4667**	831-624-5311	371-3
Chopra Ctr at La Costa Resort & Spa 2013 Costa del Mar Rd	Carlsbad	CA	92009	**888-424-6772**	760-494-1600	664
Choptank Electric Co-op Inc 24820 Meeting House Rd PO Box 430	Denton	MD	21629	**877-892-0001**		245

Alphabetical Section

	Toll-Free	Phone	Class
Choristers Guild			
2834 W Kingsley Rd .... Garland TX 75041	800-246-7478	972-271-1521	47-4
Chowan University			
1 University Pl .... Murfreesboro NC 27855	888-424-6926*	252-398-6439	166
*Admissions			
CHQR-AM 770 (N/T)			
200 Barclay Parade SW Ste 170 .... Calgary AB T2P4R5	800-563-7770	403-716-6500	636-20
Chris-Craft Boats			
8161 15th St E .... Sarasota FL 34243	800-845-5255	941-351-4900	89
Christ Hospital			
2139 Auburn Ave .... Cincinnati OH 45219	800-527-8919	513-585-2000	371-3
Christ in Youth Inc			
PO Box B .... Joplin MO 64801	800-693-9653	417-781-2273	47-20
Christ School			
500 Christ School Rd .... Arden NC 28704	800-422-3212	828-684-6232	615
Christchurch School			
49 Seahorse Ln .... Christchurch VA 23031	800-296-2306	804-758-2306	615
Christel DeHaan Fine Arts Ctr			
1400 E Hanna Ave			
University of Indianapolis .... Indianapolis IN 46227	800-232-8634	317-788-3566	565
Christendom College			
134 Christendom Dr ...... Front Royal VA 22630	800-877-5456	540-636-2900	166
Christenson Transportation Inc			
2001 W Old Rt 66 .... Strafford MO 65757	800-880-6711	417-866-5993	770
Christian & Missionary Alliance			
8595 Explorer Dr .... Colorado Springs CO 80920	800-700-2651	719-599-5999	47-20
Christian & Timbers			
25825 Science Pk Dr .... Cleveland OH 44122	800-299-9630	216-464-8710	266
Christian Appalachian Project			
6550 S KY Rt 321 PO Box 459 ...... Hagerhill KY 41222	800-755-5322		47-5
Christian Blind Mission (CBM)			
450 E Pk Ave .... Greenville SC 29601	800-937-2264	864-239-0065	47-5
Christian Broadcasting Network (CBN)			
977 Centerville Tpke			
CBN Ctr .... Virginia Beach VA 23463	800-759-0700	757-226-7000	729
Christian Bros University			
650 E Pkwy S .... Memphis TN 38104	800-288-7576*	901-321-3000	166
*Admissions			
Christian Coalition of America			
PO Box 37030 .... Washington DC 20013	888-999-6778	202-479-6900	47-7
Christian County Public Schools			
200 Glass Ave PO Box 609 .... Hopkinsville KY 42240	800-274-7374	270-887-7000	676
Christian Dior			
712 Fifth Ave 37th Fl .... New York NY 10019	800-929-3467	212-582-0500	277
Christian Foundation for Children & Aging (CFCA)			
One Elmwood Ave .... Kansas City KS 66103	800-875-6564	913-384-6500	47-6
Christian Homes Inc			
200 N Postville Dr .... Lincoln IL 62656	800-535-8717	217-732-9651	360
Christian Leadership Alliance (CLA)			
635 Camino De Los Mares			
Ste 216 .... San Clemente CA 92673	800-263-6317	949-487-0900	48-12
Christian Medical & Dental Assn (CMDA)			
2604 Hwy 421 PO Box 7500 .... Bristol TN 37620	888-231-2637	423-844-1000	48-8
Christian Reformed Church in North America (CRC)			
2850 Kalamazoo Ave SE .... Grand Rapids MI 49560	800-272-5125	616-241-1691	47-20
Christian Reformed World Relief Committee (CRWRC)			
2850 Kalamazoo Ave SE .... Grand Rapids MI 49560	800-552-7972	616-241-1691	47-5
Christian Schools International (CSI)			
3350 E Paris Ave SE ...... Grand Rapids MI 49512	800-635-8288	616-957-1070	48-5
Christian Science Monitor			
210 Massachusetts Ave .... Boston MA 02115	800-453-3432	617-450-2000	525-3
Christian Science Publishing Society			
210 Massachusetts Ave P02-15 .... Boston MA 02115	800-456-2220	617-450-2000	628-8
Christian Television Network Inc (CTN)			
6922 142nd Ave N .... Largo FL 33771	800-716-7729	727-535-5622	728
Christian Theological Seminary			
1000 W 42nd St .... Indianapolis IN 46208	800-585-0108	317-924-1331	167-3
Christianity Today			
465 Gundersen Dr .... Carol Stream IL 60188	800-222-1840*	630-260-6200	452-11
*Cust Svc			
Christianity Today Magazine			
465 Gundersen Dr .... Carol Stream IL 60188	800-999-1704	630-260-6200	452-18
Christianson Systems Inc			
20421 15th St SE PO Box 138 .... Blomkest MN 56216	800-328-8896	320-995-6141	208
Christie Cookie Co			
1205 Third Ave N .... Nashville TN 37208	800-458-2447	615-242-3817	295-9
Christine Alexander Inc			
34210 Ninth Ave S Ste 101 .... Federal Way WA 98003	800-554-2539*	253-874-5570	153-20
*General			
Christopher Enterprises			
155 West 2050 North .... Spanish Fork UT 84660	800-453-1406		352
Christopher Newport University			
One University Pl .... Newport News VA 23606	800-333-4268*	757-594-7015	166
*Admissions			
Christopher Ranch			
305 Bloomfield Ave .... Gilroy CA 95020	800-779-1156	408-847-1100	10-10
Christopher Reeve Foundation			
636 Morris Tpke Ste 3A .... Short Hills NJ 07078	800-225-0292	973-379-2690	47-17
Christophers, The			
Five Hanover Sq 11th Fl .... New York NY 10004	888-298-4050	212-759-4050	47-20
CHRISTUS Hospital - St Elizabeth			
2830 Calder St .... Beaumont TX 77702	866-683-3627	409-892-7171	371-3
CHRISTUS Saint Mary Hospital			
3600 Gates Blvd Ste 3 ...... Port Arthur TX 77642	866-683-3627	409-985-7431	371-3
CHRISTUS Schumpert Health System			
1 St Mary Pl .... Shreveport LA 71101	844-444-8440	318-681-4500	350
CHRISTUS Spohn Health System			
1702 Santa Fe St ...... Corpus Christi TX 78404	800-247-6574	361-881-3000	350
CHRISTUS Spohn Hospice			
6200 Saratoga Blvd			
Bldg B Ste 104 .... Corpus Christi TX 78414	844-444-8440	361-994-3400	368
ChromaGen Vision LLC			
326 W Cedar St Ste 1 ...... Kennett Square PA 19348	855-473-2323		537
Chromaline Corp			
4832 Grand Ave .... Duluth MN 55807	800-328-4261	218-628-2217	620
Chromaprobe Inc			
378 Fee Fee Rd ...... Maryland Heights MO 63043	888-964-1400	314-738-0001	231
Chronicle Books			
680 Second St .... San Francisco CA 94107	800-722-6657	415-537-4200	628-2
Chronicle Herald, The			
PO Box 610 .... Halifax NS B3J2T2	800-563-1187	902-426-2811	525-1
Chronicle Independent			
909 W Dekalb St .... Camden SC 29020	800-698-3514*	803-432-6157	525-4
*General			

	Toll-Free	Phone	Class
Chronicle of Higher Education, The			
1255 23rd St NW Ste 700 .... Washington DC 20037	800-728-2803	202-466-1000	452-8
Chronicle-Telegram			
225 E Ave .... Elyria OH 44035	800-848-6397	440-329-7000	525-2
Chronicle-Tribune			
610 S Adams St .... Marion IN 46953	800-955-7888	765-664-5111	525-2
Chrysalis Inn & Spa			
804 Tenth St .... Bellingham WA 98225	888-808-0005	360-756-1005	376
Chrysler Aviation Inc (CAI)			
7120 Hayvenhurst Ave Ste 309 .... Van Nuys CA 91406	800-995-0825	818-989-7900	13
Chrysler Group LLC			
1000 Chrysler Dr .... Auburn Hills MI 48326	800-423-6343*		58
*Cust Svc			
CHS Inc			
3520 E River Rd PO Box 6878 .... Rochester MN 55903	888-254-0632	507-289-4086	574
CHSI (Comprehensive Health Services Inc)			
10701 Parkridge Blvd Ste 200 .... Reston VA 20191	800-638-8083	703-760-0700	388-3
CHU Sainte-Justine			
3175 Ch de la Cote-Sainte-			
Catherine .... Montreal QC H3T1C5	888-235-3667	514-345-4931	371-2
Chubb & Son			
15 Mountain View Rd .... Warren NJ 07059	800-252-4670	908-903-2000	388-4
Chubb Corp			
15 Mountain View Rd .... Warren NJ 07059	800-252-4670	908-903-2000	357-4
NYSE: CB			
Chubb Specialty Insurance			
82 Hopmeadow St .... Simsbury CT 06070	800-252-4670	860-408-2000	388-5
Chugach Electric Assn Inc			
5601 Electron Dr .... Anchorage AK 99518	800-478-7494	907-563-7494	245
Chugach State Park			
18620 Seward Highway .... Anchorage AK 99516	800-478-6196	907-345-5014	558
Chukchansi Gold Resort & Casino			
711 Lucky Ln .... Coarsegold CA 93614	866-794-6946		375
Chula Vista Resort			
2501 River Rd .... Wisconsin Dells WI 53965	800-388-4782	608-254-8366	660
Chungs Gourmet Foods			
3907 Dennis St .... Houston TX 77004	800-824-8640	713-741-2118	295-36
Church & Chapel Metal Arts Inc			
2616 W Grand Ave .... Chicago IL 60612	800-992-1234		503
Church & Stagg Office Supply Company Inc			
3421 Sixth Ave .... Birmingham AL 35222	800-239-5336	205-251-2951	528
Church Mutual Insurance Co			
3000 Schuster Ln .... Merrill WI 54452	800-554-2642	715-536-5577	388-4
Church of God in Christ Inc			
930 Mason St .... Memphis TN 38126	877-746-8578	901-947-9300	47-20
Church of God Ministries			
1201 E Fifth St .... Anderson IN 46012	800-848-2464	765-642-0256	47-20
Church of God World Missions (COGWM)			
2490 Keith St PO Box 8016 .... Cleveland TN 37320	800-345-7492	423-478-7190	47-20
Church of the Brethren			
1451 Dundee Ave .... Elgin IL 60120	800-323-8039	847-742-5100	47-20
Church Women United (CWU)			
475 Riverside Dr Ste 243 .... New York NY 10115	800-298-5551	212-870-2347	47-20
Church World Service			
28606 Phillips St PO Box 968 .... Elkhart IN 46515	800-297-1516	574-264-3102	47-5
Church World Service Emergency Response Program			
475 Riverside Dr Ste 700 .... New York NY 10115	888-297-2767	212-870-3151	47-5
Churchill Cabinet Co			
4616 W 19th St .... Cicero IL 60804	800-379-9776*	708-780-0070	286
*Sales			
Churchill Corporate Services			
56 Utter Ave .... Hawthorne NJ 07506	800-941-7458	973-636-9400	211
Churchill County School District			
545 E Richards St .... Fallon NV 89406	800-232-6382	775-423-5184	676
Churchill Downs Inc			
700 Central Ave .... Louisville KY 40208	800-994-9909	502-636-4400	633
NASDAQ: CHDN			
Churchill Hotel			
1914 Connecticut Ave NW .... Washington DC 20009	800-424-2464	202-797-2000	376
Churchill Nature Tours			
PO Box 429 .... Erickson MB R0J0P0	877-636-2968	204-636-2968	750
Churchwell Co			
814 S Edgewood Ave .... Jacksonville FL 32205	877-537-6166	904-356-5721	9
CHW (Children's Hospital of Wisconsin Bone Marrow Transplant Clinic)			
9000 W Wisconsin Ave			
PO Box 1997 .... Milwaukee WI 53226	877-266-8989	414-266-2000	759
Chyron Corp 5 Hub Dr .... Melville NY 11747	800-642-1687	631-845-2000	179-8
NASDAQ: CHYR			
CI (Conservation International)			
2011 Crystal Dr Ste 500 .... Arlington VA 22202	800-406-2306	703-341-2400	47-13
CIBA Vision Corp			
11460 Johns Creek Pkwy .... Duluth GA 30097	800-875-3001		535
CIBC (Canadian Imperial Bank of Commerce)			
199 Bay St Commerce Ct W .... Toronto ON M5L1A2	800-465-2422		69
NYSE: CM			
CIBC Wood Gundy Capital			
425 Lexington Ave .... New York NY 10017	800-999-6726	212-856-4000	780
CIBER Inc			
6363 S Fiddler's Green Cir			
Ste 1400 .... Greenwood Village CO 80111	800-242-3799	303-220-0100	181
NYSE: CBR			
CIBO (Council of Industrial Boiler Owners)			
6035 Burke Ctr Pkwy Ste 360 .... Burke VA 22015	800-542-6096	703-250-9042	48-13
CICA-TV Ch 19 (Ind)			
2180 Yonge St Stn Q PO Box 200 .... Toronto ON M4T2T1	800-613-0513	416-484-2600	730-78
Cicero Inc			
8000 Regency Pkwy Ste 542 .... Cary NC 27518	866-538-3588	919-380-5000	179-1
CiDRA Corp			
50 Barnes Pk N .... Wallingford CT 06492	877-243-7277	203-265-0035	725
CIEE (Council on International Educational Exchange)			
300 Fore St Second Fl .... Portland ME 04101	888-268-6245*	207-553-4000	48-5
*Cust Svc			
CIENA Corp			
1201 Winterson Rd .... Linthicum MD 21090	800-921-1144	410-694-5700	725
NASDAQ: CIEN			
Cigar.com Inc			
1911 Spillman Dr .... Bethlehem PA 18015	800-357-9800		746
CIGNA			
900 Cottage Grove Rd .... Hartford CT 06002	800-997-1654	860-226-6000	388-2
CIGNA Behavioral Health Inc			
11095 Viking Dr Ste 350 .... Eden Prairie MN 55344	800-753-0540	703-907-7730	457
CIGNA Foundation			
900 Cottage Grove Rd .... Bloomfield CT 06002	866-438-2446		303
NYSE: CI			

Name / Address	City	State	ZIP	Toll-Free	Phone	Class
CIGNA Healthcare 900 Cottage Grove Rd	Hartford	CT	06152	**800-997-1654**	860-226-6000	388-3
CIGNA Healthcare of North Carolina Inc 701 Corporate Ctr Dr	Raleigh	NC	27607	**800-997-1654**	919-854-7000	388-3
Cimarron Electric Co-op PO Box 299	Kingfisher	OK	73750	**800-375-4121**	405-375-4121	245
Cimmaron Field Services Inc 303 W Wall St Bank of America Tower Ste 600	Midland	TX	79701	**877-944-2705**		529
Cinch Connectors Inc 1700 Findley Rd	Lombard	IL	60148	**800-323-9612**	630-705-6000	802
Cincinnati Art Museum 953 Eden Pk Dr	Cincinnati	OH	45202	**877-472-4226**	513-721-2787	513
Cincinnati Ballet 1555 Central Pkwy	Cincinnati	OH	45214	**800-745-3000**	513-621-5219	566-1
Cincinnati Bell Inc 221 E Fourth St *NYSE: CBB*	Cincinnati	OH	45202	**800-387-3638**	513-397-9900	726
Cincinnati Bengals One Paul Brown Stadium	Cincinnati	OH	45202	**866-621-8383**	513-621-3550	706-3
Cincinnati Children's Hospital Medical Ctr 3333 Burnet Ave	Cincinnati	OH	45229	**800-344-2462**	513-636-4200	371-1
Cincinnati Children's Hospital Research Foundation 3333 Burnet Ave	Cincinnati	OH	45229	**800-344-2462**	513-636-4200	659
Cincinnati Christian University 2700 Glenway Ave	Cincinnati	OH	45204	**800-949-4228**	513-244-8100	159
Cincinnati College of Mortuary Science 645 W N Bend Rd	Cincinnati	OH	45224	**888-377-8433**	513-761-2020	788
Cincinnati Enquirer 312 Elm St	Cincinnati	OH	45202	**800-876-4500**	513-721-2700	525-2
Cincinnati Floor Company Inc 5162 Broerman Ave	Cincinnati	OH	45217	**800-886-4501**	513-641-4500	190-2
Cincinnati History Museum 1301 Western Ave Cincinnati Museum Ctr	Cincinnati	OH	45203	**800-733-2077**	513-287-7000	513
Cincinnati Playhouse in the Park 962 Mt Adams Cir PO Box 6537	Cincinnati	OH	45202	**800-582-3208**	513-345-2242	565
Cincinnati Preserving Company Inc 3015 E Kemper Rd *Cust Svc	Cincinnati	OH	45241	**800-222-9966***	513-771-2000	295-20
Cincinnati Reds 100 Joe Nuxhall Way	Cincinnati	OH	45202	**877-647-7337**	513-381-7337	704
Cincinnati State Technical & Community College 3520 Central Pkwy	Cincinnati	OH	45223	**877-569-0115**	513-569-1500	160
Cincinnati Test Systems Inc 5555 Dry Fork Rd	Cleves	OH	45002	**800-850-3189**	513-367-6699	202
Cincinnati Zoo & Botanical Garden 3400 Vine St	Cincinnati	OH	45220	**800-944-4776**	513-281-4700	810
Cincinnatian Hotel 601 Vine St	Cincinnati	OH	45202	**800-942-9000**	513-381-3000	376
Cincom Systems Inc 55 Merchant St	Cincinnati	OH	45246	**800-224-6266**	513-612-2300	179-1
Cindus Corp 515 Stn Ave	Cincinnati	OH	45215	**800-543-4691**		547
Cine Magnetics Inc 100 Business Pk Dr Ste 1	Armonk	NY	10504	**800-431-1102**	914-273-7500	649
Cinemark USA Inc 3900 Dallas Pkwy Ste 500	Plano	TX	75093	**800-246-3627**	972-665-1000	737
Cineplex Entertainment LP 1303 Yonge St	Toronto	ON	M4T2Y9	**800-333-0061**	416-323-6600	737
Cinergy Children's Museum 1301 Western Ave Cincinnati Museum Ctr	Cincinnati	OH	45203	**800-733-2077**	513-287-7000	514
Cinmar LLC 5566 W Chester Rd	West Chester	OH	45069	**888-263-9850**		454
Cintas Corp PO Box 625737 *NASDAQ: CTAS*	Cincinnati	OH	45262	**800-786-4367**	513-459-1200	438
Cintrex Audio Visual 656 Axminister Dr	Fenton	MO	63026	**800-325-9541**	636-343-0178	507
Cipher Systems LLC 2661 Riva Rd Ste 1000	Annapolis	MD	21401	**888-899-1523**	410-412-3326	195
CIPS (Canadian Information Processing Society) 5090 Explorer Dr Ste 801	Mississauga	ON	L4W4T9	**877-275-2477**	905-602-1370	47-1
CIR (Center for Individual Rights) 1233 20th St NW Ste 300	Washington	DC	20036	**877-426-2665**	202-833-8400	47-8
CIR Law Offices LLP 8665 Gibbs Dr Ste 150	San Diego	CA	92123	**800-496-8909**		40
Circa Inc 415 Madison Ave 19th Fl	New York	NY	10017	**877-876-5493**	212-486-6013	408
Circa39 Hotel 3900 Collins Ave *Resv	Miami Beach	FL	33140	**877-824-7223***	305-538-4900	376
Circadian Technologies Inc Two Main St Ste 310	Stoneham	MA	02180	**800-284-5001**	781-439-6300	195
Circle in the Square Theatre 1633 Broadway	New York	NY	10019	**800-432-7250**	212-239-6200	736
Circle J Trailers 312 W Simplot Blvd	Caldwell	ID	83605	**800-247-2535**	208-459-0842	769
Circle Media Inc 5817 Old Leeds Rd	Irondale	AL	35210	**800-356-9916**		525-3
Circle Seal Controls Inc 2301 Wardlow Cir	Corona	CA	92880	**800-991-2726**	951-270-6200	777
Circle Z Ranch PO Box 194	Patagonia	AZ	85624	**888-854-2525**		239
Circleville City School District 388 Clark Dr	Circleville	OH	43113	**800-418-6423**	740-474-4340	676
Circuit Playhouse, The 51 S Cooper St	Memphis	TN	38104	**888-648-8154**	901-725-0776	565
Circus Circus Hotel & Casino Reno 500 N Sierra St	Reno	NV	89503	**800-648-5010**	775-329-0711	132
Circus Circus Hotel Casino & Theme Park Las Vegas 2880 Las Vegas Blvd S *Resv	Las Vegas	NV	89109	**800-634-3450***	702-734-0410	132
Circus World Museum 550 Water St	Baraboo	WI	53913	**866-693-1500**	608-356-8341	513
Cirque Corp 2463 South 3850 West Ste A	Salt Lake City	UT	84120	**800-454-3375**	801-467-1100	174-2
Cirque du Soleil Inc 8400 Second Ave	Montreal	QC	H1Z4M6	**800-678-2119**	514-722-2324	147
Cirrascale Corp 12140 Community Rd	Poway	CA	92064	**888-942-3800**	858-874-3800	174-8
Cirrus Logic Inc 2901 Via Fortuna *NASDAQ: CRUS*	Austin	TX	78746	**800-888-5016**	512-851-4000	687
Cisco Systems Foundation 170 W Tasman Dr	San Jose	CA	95134	**800-553-6387**	408-527-3040	303
Cisco Systems Inc 170 W Tasman Dr *NASDAQ: CSCO*	San Jose	CA	95134	**800-553-6387**	408-526-4000	177
Cisco-Eagle 2120 Valley View Ln	Dallas	TX	75234	**888-877-3861**	972-406-9330	382
Cision Inc 12051 Indian Creek Ct *NASDAQ: VOCS*	Beltsville	MD	20705	**866-639-5087**	301-459-2590	38
Citadel Federal Credit Union 520 Eagleview Blvd	Exton	PA	19341	**800-666-0191**	610-380-6000	219
Citadel, The 171 Moultrie St	Charleston	SC	29409	**800-868-1842**	843-953-5230	166
CITGO Petroleum Corp 1293 Eldridge Pkwy	Houston	TX	77077	**800-424-9300**	832-486-4700	573
Citi Trends Inc 104 Coleman Blvd *NASDAQ: CTRN*	Savannah	GA	31408	**800-605-8174**	912-236-1561	155-2
Citibank (Delaware) 4500 New Linden Hill Rd	Wilmington	DE	19808	**800-374-9700**	302-323-3600	69
Citibank NA 399 Pk Ave	New York	NY	10022	**800-627-3999**		69
Citibank (South Dakota) NA 701 E 60th St N	Sioux Falls	SD	57104	**800-627-3999**	605-370-6261	69
Cities of Gold Casino 10-B Cities of Gold Rd	Santa Fe	NM	87506	**800-455-3313**	505-455-3313	132
CitiMortgage Inc 1000 Technology Dr *Cust Svc	O'Fallon	MO	63368	**800-283-7918***		502
CitiusTech Inc Two Research Way Second Fl	Princeton	NJ	08540	**877-248-4871**		225
Citizen Auto Stage Co 67 E Baffert Dr	Nogales	AZ	85621	**800-276-1528**	520-281-0400	106
Citizen Systems America Corp 363 Van Ness Way Ste 404	Torrance	CA	90501	**800-421-6516**	310-781-1460	174-6
Citizen Tribune 1609 W First N St PO Box 625	Morristown	TN	37815	**800-624-0281**	423-581-5630	525-2
Citizen Watch Co of America Inc 1000 W 190th St	Torrance	CA	90502	**800-321-1023**		151
Citizens Against Government Waste (CAGW) 1301 Pennsylvania Ave NW Ste 1075	Washington	DC	20004	**800-232-6479**	202-467-5300	47-7
Citizens Bank of Clovis 420 Wheeler	Texico	NM	88135	**844-657-3553**	575-482-3381	69
Citizens Bank of Massachusetts 28 State St	Boston	MA	02109	**800-610-7300**		69
Citizens Bank of Mukwonago 301 N Rochester St PO Box 223	Mukwonago	WI	53149	**877-546-5868**	262-363-6500	69
Citizens Bank of Rhode Island One Citizens Plz *Cust Svc	Providence	RI	02903	**800-922-9999***	401-456-7000	69
Citizens Business Bank (CBB) 701 N Haven Ave *Cust Svc	Ontario	CA	91764	**888-222-5432***	909-980-4030	69
Citizens Committee for the Right to Keep & Bear Arms (CCRKBA) 12500 NE Tenth Pl	Bellevue	WA	98005	**800-426-4302**	425-454-4911	47-7
Citizens Equity First Credit Union 5401 W Dirksen Pkwy *Cust Svc	Peoria	IL	61607	**800-633-7077***	309-633-7000	219
Citizens Federal Savings & Loan Assn 110 N Main St PO Box 9	Bellefontaine	OH	43311	**800-436-5177**	937-593-0015	68
Citizens Financial Corp 12910 Shelbyville Rd Ste 300 *OTC: CFIN*	Louisville	KY	40243	**800-843-7752**	502-244-2420	357-4
Citizens Financial Group Inc One Citizens Dr	Riverside	RI	02915	**800-922-9999**	401-456-7000	357-2
Citizens Financial Services 707 Ridge Rd	Munster	IN	46321	**866-622-1370**	219-836-5500	69
Citizens for Tax Justice (CTJ) 1616 P St NW Ste 200-B	Washington	DC	20036	**888-626-2622**	202-299-1066	47-7
Citizens Gas & Coke Utility 2020 N Meridian St	Indianapolis	IN	46202	**800-427-4217**	317-924-3311	775
Citizens Inc 400 E Anderson Ln *NYSE: CIA* ■ *General	Austin	TX	78752	**877-785-9659***	512-837-7100	357-4
Citizens Insurance Company of America 400 E Anderson Ln	Austin	TX	78752	**800-880-5044**	512-837-7100	388-2
Citizens Security Life Insurance Co 12910 Shelbyville Rd Ste 300	Louisville	KY	40243	**800-843-7752**	502-244-2420	388-2
Citizens South Banking Corp 519 S New Hope Rd PO Box 2249 *NASDAQ: CSBC*	Gastonia	NC	28054	**877-311-2265**	704-868-5200	357-2
Citizens State Bank 1300 W Hildebrand Ave PO Box 5970	San Antonio	TX	78201	**800-870-2472**	210-785-2300	69
Citizens Telephone Co-op PO Box 137	Floyd	VA	24091	**800-941-0426**	540-745-2111	726
Citizens Trust Bank 1700 3rd Ave N	Birmingham	AL	35203	**888-214-3099**	205-328-2041	69
Citizens' Electric Co 1775 Industrial Blvd PO Box 551	Lewisburg	PA	17837	**877-487-9384**	570-524-2231	245
Citrix Systems Inc 851 W Cypress Creek Rd *NASDAQ: CTXS*	Fort Lauderdale	FL	33309	**800-393-1888**	954-267-3000	179-12
Citterio USA Corp 2008 SR 940	Freeland	PA	18224	**800-435-8888**	570-636-3171	295-26
City Auto Glass Inc 116 S Concord Exchange	South Saint Paul	MN	55075	**888-552-4272**	651-552-1000	61-2
City Carton Company Inc Three E Benton St	Iowa City	IA	52240	**800-369-6112**	319-351-2848	677
City College of New York 138th St & Convent Ave *Admissions	New York	NY	10031	**800-286-9937***	212-650-6448	166
City College of San Francisco 50 Phelan Ave	San Francisco	CA	94112	**800-433-3243**	415-239-3000	160
City Colleges of Chicago 226 W Jackson	Chicago	IL	60606	**866-908-7582**	312-553-2500	160

Name / Address	City	State	ZIP	Toll-Free	Phone	Class
City Escape Holidays						
13470 Washington Blvd Ste 101	Marina del Rey	CA	90292	**800-222-0022**		761
City Furniture Inc						
6701 N Hiatus Rd	Tamarac	FL	33321	**866-930-4233**	954-597-2200	320
City Hospital						
2500 Hospital Dr	Martinsburg	WV	25401	**888-988-1362**	304-264-1000	371-3
City National Bank						
400 N Roxbury Dr	Beverly Hills	CA	90210	**800-773-7100***	310-888-6000	69
*Cust Svc						
City National Bank of Florida						
450 E Las Olas Blvd Ste 160	Fort Lauderdale	FL	33301	**800-762-2489**	954-467-6667	69
City National Bank of New Jersey (CNB)						
900 Broad St	Newark	NJ	07102	**877-350-3524**	973-624-0865	69
City National Bank of West Virginia						
3601 McCorckle Ave	Charleston	WV	25304	**888-816-8064**	304-926-3324	69
City of Carlsbad Library						
1250 Carlsbad Village Dr	Carlsbad	CA	92008	**866-230-2273**	760-434-2870	431-3
City of Chula Vista						
276 Fourth Ave	Chula Vista	CA	91910	**877-478-5478**	619-691-5047	51
City of Clarksville						
199 10th St	Clarksville	TN	37040	**800-342-1003**	931-645-7464	256
City of Hope National Medical Ctr						
1500 E Duarte Rd	Duarte	CA	91010	**800-826-4673***	626-256-4673	371-3
*Admissions						
City of Hope National Medical Ctr Hematology & Hematopoietic Cell Transplantation Div						
1500 E Duarte Rd	Duarte	CA	91010	**800-535-7119**	626-256-4673	759
City of Palm Springs						
300 S Sunrise Way	Palm Springs	CA	92262	**800-611-1911**	760-322-7323	431-3
City of Pendleton						
500 SW Dorion Ave	Pendleton	OR	97801	**800-238-5355**	541-966-0201	206
City of Thomasville Tourism Authority						
144 E Jackson St	Thomasville	GA	31792	**800-533-4587**	229-226-3424	207
City Pipe & Supply Corp						
PO Box 2112	Odessa	TX	79760	**844-307-4044**	432-332-1541	487
City Public Service Board						
PO Box 1771	San Antonio	TX	78296	**800-870-1006**	210-353-2222	775
City Securities Corp						
30 S Meridian St Ste 600	Indianapolis	IN	46204	**800-800-2489**	317-634-4400	681
City Tours Mainey						
P.O. Box 167	Nobleboro	ME	04555	**800-537-5378**	207-563-2288	750
City University						
11900 NE First St	Bellevue	WA	98005	**800-426-5596***	425-637-1010	166
*Admissions						
City University of New York (CUNY)						
535 E 80th St	New York	NY	10075	**877-769-7441**	212-794-5555	774
Civacon						
4304 N Mattox Rd	Kansas City	MO	64150	**888-526-5657***	816-741-6600	778
*Sales						
CIVCO Medical Instruments						
102 First St	Kalona	IA	52247	**800-445-6741**	319-656-4447	379
Civil & Environmental Consultants Inc						
333 Baldwin Rd	Pittsburgh	PA	15205	**800-365-2324**	412-429-2324	261
Civil Engineering Magazine						
1801 Alexander Bell Dr	Reston	VA	20191	**800-548-2723**	703-295-6300	452-21
Civil Service Employees Insurance Co						
2121 N California Blvd Ste 555	Walnut Creek	CA	94596	**800-282-6848**		388-4
Civil War Preservation Trust (CWPT)						
1331 H St NW Ste 1001	Washington	DC	20005	**888-606-1400**	202-367-1861	47-13
Civista Bank						
100 E Water St	Sandusky	OH	44870	**888-645-4121**	419-625-4121	68
Civitan International						
PO Box 130744	Birmingham	AL	35213	**800-248-4826**	205-591-8910	47-15
CJ Duffey Paper Co						
528 Washington Ave N	Minneapolis	MN	55401	**800-752-8190**	612-338-8701	546
CJ Vitner & Co						
4202 W 45th St	Chicago	IL	60632	**800-523-7900***	773-523-7900	295-35
*General						
CJK						
3962 Virginia Ave	Cincinnati	OH	45227	**800-598-7808**	513-271-6035	618
CJM (Carlyle Johnson Machine Co)						
291 Boston Tpke	Bolton	CT	06043	**888-629-4867**	860-643-1531	613
CJT Koolcarb Inc						
494 Mission St	Carol Stream	IL	60188	**800-323-2299**	630-690-5933	488
CJW Medical Ctr						
7101 Jahnke Rd	Richmond	VA	23225	**800-468-6620**	804-320-3911	371-3
CK Worldwide Inc						
3501 C St NE	Auburn	WA	98002	**800-426-0877**	253-854-5820	798
CKC (Canadian Kennel Club)						
200 Ronson Dr Ste 400	Etobicoke	ON	M9W5Z9	**800-250-8040**	416-675-5511	47-3
CKHS (Crozer-Keystone Health System)						
190 W Sproul Rd	Springfield	PA	19064	**800-254-3258**	610-328-8700	350
CKLW-AM 800 (N/T)						
1640 Ouellette Ave	Windsor	ON	N8X1L1	**800-263-2559**	519-258-8888	636
CKVR-TV Ch 3 (Ind)						
299 Queen St W	Toronto	ON	M5V2Z5	**866-690-6179**	416-384-5000	730
CKY-FM 102.3 (AC)						
4-166 Osborne St	Winnipeg	MB	R3L1Y8	**877-413-7970**	204-788-3400	
CLA (Christian Leadership Alliance)						
635 Camino De Los Mares Ste 216	San Clemente	CA	92673	**800-263-6317**	949-487-0900	48-12
CLA (Coin Laundry Assn)						
1s660 Midwest Rd Ste 205	Oakbrook Terrace	IL	60181	**800-570-5629**	630-953-7920	48-4
Claflin University						
400 Magnolia St	Orangeburg	SC	29115	**800-922-1276**	803-535-5000	166
Claiborne County Chamber of Commerce						
1732 Main St PO Box 649	Tazewell	TN	37879	**800-332-8164**	423-626-4149	137
Claims Verification Inc						
6700 N Andrews Ave Ste 200	Ft. Lauderdale	FL	33309	**888-284-2000**		397
Claimsnet.com Inc						
14860 Montfort Dr Ste 250	Dallas	TX	75254	**800-356-1511**	972-458-1701	225
Claire Manufacturing Co						
1005 S Westgate Ave	Addison	IL	60101	**800-252-4731***	630-543-7600	143
*Sales						
Claire's Accessories						
2400 W Central Rd	Hoffman Estates	IL	60192	**800-252-4737**	847-765-1100	155-6
Claitor's Law Books & Publishing						
PO Box 261333	Baton Rouge	LA	70826	**800-274-1403**	225-344-0476	618
Clamp Swing Pricing Company Inc						
8386 Capwell Dr	Oakland	CA	94621	**800-227-7615**	510-567-1600	410
Clamshell Structures Inc						
1101 Maulhardt Ave	Oxnard	CA	93030	**800-360-8853**	805-988-1340	723
Clarcor Inc						
840 Crescent Ctr Dr Ste 600	Franklin	TN	37067	**800-252-7267**	615-771-3100	18
NYSE: CLC						
Claremont Resort & Spa						
41 Tunnel Rd	Berkeley	CA	94705	**800-551-7266**	510-843-3000	660
Claremont Sales Corp						
35 Winsome Dr PO Box 430	Durham	CT	06422	**800-222-4448**	860-349-4499	386
Claremont School of Theology						
1325 N College Ave	Claremont	CA	91711	**800-733-5181**	909-447-2500	167-3
Clarendon College						
1122 College Dr PO Box 968	Clarendon	TX	79226	**800-687-9737**	806-874-3571	160
Clarendon County Chamber of Commerce						
19 N Brooks St	Manning	SC	29102	**800-731-5253**	803-435-4405	137
Claricent Inc						
22 Preserve way	Sturbridge	MA	01566	**888-325-6496**		178
Claridge Products & Equipment Inc						
601 Hwy 62 65	Harrison	AR	72601	**800-434-4610**	870-743-2200	243
Clarion Corp of America						
6200 Gateway Dr	Cypress	CA	90630	**800-347-8667**	310-327-9100	51
Clarion Hospital (CH)						
One Hospital Dr	Clarion	PA	16214	**800-522-0505**	814-226-9500	371-3
Clarion Hotel & Conference Ctr Antietam Creek						
901 Dual Hwy	Hagerstown	MD	21740	**888-528-6738**	301-733-5100	374
Clarion University of Pennsylvania						
840 Wood St	Clarion	PA	16214	**800-672-7171**	814-393-2306	166
Venango						
1801 W First St	Oil City	PA	16301	**800-672-7171**	814-676-6591	166
Clarion-Ledger, The						
201 S Congress St	Jackson	MS	39201	**877-850-5343**	601-961-7000	525-2
Clark Atlanta University						
223 James P Brawley Dr SW	Atlanta	GA	30314	**800-688-3228***	404-880-8000	166
*Admissions						
Clark Capital Management Group Inc (CCMG)						
1650 Market St 1 Liberty Pl 53rd Fl	Philadelphia	PA	19103	**800-766-2264**	215-569-2224	398
Clark Construction Group LLC						
7500 Old Georgetown Rd	Bethesda	MD	20814	**800-655-1330**	301-272-8100	187
Clark Consulting						
2100 Ross Ave	Dallas	TX	75201	**800-999-3125**	214-871-8717	194
Clark Cos NA						
156 Oak St	Newton Upper Falls	MA	02464	**800-211-5461***	617-964-1222	300
*Cust Svc						
Clark County REMC						
7810 State Rd 60 PO Box 411	Sellersburg	IN	47172	**800-462-6988**	812-246-3316	245
Clark County School District (CCSD)						
5100 W Sahara Ave	Las Vegas	NV	89146	**866-799-8997**	702-799-5000	676
Clark Electric Co-op						
124 N Main St PO Box 190	Greenwood	WI	54437	**800-272-6188**	715-267-6188	245
Clark Energy Co-op Inc						
2640 Ironworks Rd	Winchester	KY	40391	**800-992-3269**	859-744-4251	245
Clark Foam Products Corp						
655 Remington Blvd	Bolingbrook	IL	60440	**888-284-2290**	630-226-5900	594
Clark Material Handling Co						
700 Enterprise Dr	Lexington	KY	40510	**866-252-5275**	859-422-6400	465
Clark Nuber PS						
10900 NE Fourth St Ste 1700	Bellevue	WA	98004	**800-504-8747***	425-454-4919	2
*General						
Clark Pest Control Inc						
555 N Guild Ave	Lodi	CA	95240	**877-918-9988**		193
Clark Tire & Auto Supply Co Inc						
220 S Ctr St	Hickory	NC	28602	**800-968-3092**	828-322-2303	61-5
Clark Transfer Inc						
800A Paxton St	Harrisburg	PA	17104	**800-488-7585**	717-238-0801	187
Clark University						
950 Main St	Worcester	MA	01610	**800-462-5275**	508-793-7711	166
Clark, Gagliardi & Miller PC						
99 Court St	White Plains	NY	10601	**800-734-5694**		425
Clark-Cutler-McDermott Co (CCMcD)						
5 Fisher St	Franklin	MA	02038	**800-922-3019**	508-528-1200	734-6
Clarke College						
1550 Clarke Dr	Dubuque	IA	52001	**888-825-2753**	563-588-6300	166
Clark-Floyd Counties Convention & Tourism Bureau						
315 Southern Indiana Ave	Jeffersonville	IN	47130	**800-552-3842**	812-282-6654	207
Clark-Lindsey Village						
101 W Windsor Rd	Urbana	IL	61802	**800-998-2581**	217-344-2144	663
Clark-Reliance Corp						
16633 Foltz Pkwy	Strongsville	OH	44149	**800-238-4027**	440-572-1500	490
Clarksburg Exponent Telegram						
324 Hewes Ave	Clarksburg	WV	26301	**800-982-6034**	304-626-1400	525-2
Clarksdale Municipal School District						
101 McGuire St PO Box 1088	Clarksdale	MS	38614	**877-820-7831**	662-627-8500	187
Clarksdale-Coahoma County Chamber of Commerce & Industrial Foundation						
1540 DeSoto Ave	Clarksdale	MS	38614	**800-626-3764**	662-627-7337	137
Clarkson College						
101 S 42nd St	Omaha	NE	68131	**800-647-5500**	402-552-3100	166
Clarkson University						
10 Clarkson Ave	Potsdam	NY	13699	**800-527-6577***	315-268-6480	166
*Admissions						
Clarkston Consulting						
1007 Slater Rd Ste 400	Durham	NC	27703	**800-652-4274**	919-484-4400	181
Clarksville Area Chamber of Commerce						
25 Jefferson St Ste 300	Clarksville	TN	37040	**800-530-2487**	931-647-2331	137
Clarksville Montgomery County Public Library						
350 Pageant Ln	Clarksville	TN	37040	**877-239-6635**	931-648-8826	431-3
Clarksville/Montgomery County Tourist Commission						
25 Jefferson St Ste 300	Clarksville	TN	37040	**800-530-2487**	931-647-2331	207
Clary Corp						
150 E Huntington Dr	Monrovia	CA	91016	**800-551-6111**	626-359-4486	253
CLASP (Center for Law & Social Policy)						
1015 15th St NW Ste 400	Washington	DC	20005	**800-821-4367**	202-906-8000	625
Class Act Federal Credit Union						
3620 Fern Vly Rd	Louisville	KY	40219	**800-292-2960**	502-964-7575	219
Class Action Litigation Report						
1801 S Bell St	Arlington	VA	22202	**800-372-1033**		524-7
Classic Brass Inc						
2051 Stoneman Cir	Lakewood	NY	14750	**800-869-3173**	716-763-1400	347
Classic Custom Vacations						
5893 Rue Ferrari	San Jose	CA	95138	**800-635-1333**		761
Classic Medallics Inc						
520 S Fulton Ave	Mount Vernon	NY	10550	**800-221-1348**	914-530-6259	767

	Toll-Free	Phone	Class
Classic Party Rentals			
11766 Wilshire Blvd Ste 350 ....Los Angeles CA 90025	800-678-3854	310-535-3660	264-2
Classic Sleep Products Inc			
8214 Wellmoor Ct ....Jessup MD 20794	877-707-7533	410-904-0006	466
Classic Student Tours			
75 Rhoads Ctr Dr ....Dayton OH 45458	800-860-0246	937-439-0032	750
Classic Trains Magazine			
21027 Crossroads Cir PO Box 1612 ....Waukesha WI 53186	800-533-6644	262-796-8776	452-14
Classic Transportation Group			
1600 Locust Ave ....Bohemia NY 11716	800-291-8090	631-567-5100	437
Clatsop Community College			
1653 Jerome Ave ....Astoria OR 97103	855-252-8767	503-325-0910	160
Claverack Rural Electric Co-op Inc			
32750 W US 6 ....Wysox PA 18854	800-326-9799	570-265-2167	245
Clawson Tank Co			
4545 Clawson Tank Dr ....Clarkston MI 48346	800-272-1367	248-625-8700	90
Claxton Poultry Farms			
8816 Hwy 301 PO Box 428 ....Claxton GA 30417	888-739-3181	912-739-3181	612
Clay County Chamber of Commerce			
1734 Kingsley Ave ....Orange Park FL 32073	800-435-7352	904-264-2651	137
Clay County Electric Co-op Corp			
300 N Missouri Ave ....Corning AR 72422	800-521-2450	870-857-3521	245
Clay Electric Co-op Inc			
7450 State Rd 100 ....Keystone Heights FL 32656	800-224-4917	352-473-8000	245
Clay Lacy Aviation			
7435 Valjean Ave ....Van Nuys CA 91406	800-423-2904	818-989-2900	13
Clay Today			
3513 US Hwy 17 ....Fleming Island FL 32003	888-434-9844	904-264-3200	525-4
Claybar Constracting Inc			
424 Macnab St ....Dundas ON L9H2L3	866-801-9305	905-627-8000	603
Claymore C Sieck Wholesale Florist			
311 E Chase St ....Baltimore MD 21202	800-624-7134	410-685-4660	293
Clayton Block Co			
PO Box 3015 ....Lakewood NJ 08701	800-662-3044		184
Clayton Corp			
866 Horan Dr ....Fenton MO 63026	800-729-8220*	636-349-5333	594
*Cust Svc			
Clayton Cos, The			
PO Box 3015 ....Lakewood NJ 08701	800-662-3044		184
Clayton County Chamber of Commerce			
2270 Mt Zion Rd ....Jonesboro GA 30236	877-790-1831	678-610-4021	137
Clayton Holdings LLC			
100 BeaRd Sawmill Rd Ste 200 ....Shelton CT 06484	877-291-5301	203-926-5600	357-3
Clayton Industries			
17477 Hurley St ....City of Industry CA 91744	800-423-4585	626-435-1200	467
Clayton Metals Inc			
546 Clayton Ct ....Wood Dale IL 60191	800-323-7628		487
Clay-Union Electric Corp			
1410 E Cherry St PO Box 317 ....Vermillion SD 57069	800-696-2832	605-624-2673	245
CLC (Challenger Learning Ctr)			
316 Washington Ave			
Wheeling Jesuit University ....Wheeling WV 26003	800-624-6992	304-243-2279	513
Clean Air Report			
1919 S Eads St Ste 201 ....Arlington VA 22202	800-424-9068	703-416-8516	524-5
Clean Air Technology Inc			
41105 Capital Dr ....Canton MI 48187	800-459-6320	734-459-6320	444
Clean Diesel Technologies Inc			
4567 Telephone Rd Ste 206 ....Ventura CA 93003	800-661-9963	805-639-9458	383
NASDAQ: CDTI			
Clean Earth of North Jersey Inc			
115 Jacobus Ave ....South Kearny NJ 07032	877-445-3478	973-344-4004	651
Clean Harbors Inc			
42 Longwater Dr PO Box 9149 ....Norwell MA 02061	800-282-0058	781-792-5000	658
NYSE: CLH			
Clean Ones Corp			
PO Box 40008 ....Portland OR 97204	800-367-4587	503-224-5211	256
Clean Power LLC			
124 N 121st St ....Milwaukee WI 53226	888-566-1717	414-302-3000	150
Clean Venture/Cycle Chem Inc			
201 S First St ....Elizabeth NJ 07206	800-347-7672	908-355-5800	658
Clean Water Action			
4455 Connecticut Ave NW ....Washington DC 20008	800-234-7284	202-895-0420	47-13
Cleaning Authority			
7230 Lee DeForest Dr Ste 200 ....Columbia MD 21046	888-658-0659	410-740-1900	309
CleanNet USA			
9861 Brokenland Pkwy Ste 208 ....Columbia MD 21046	800-735-8838	410-720-6444	150
Cleanroom Systems			
7000 Performance Dr ....North Syracuse NY 13212	800-825-3268	315-452-7400	18
Cleanwise Inc			
1100 E Woodfield Rd Ste 200 ....Schaumburg IL 60173	877-255-5230		390
Clear Brook Manor			
1100 E Northampton St ....Laurel Run PA 18706	800-582-6241		717
Clear Edge Technical Fabrics			
7160 Northland Cir N ....Minneapolis MN 55428	800-328-3036	763-535-3220	734-3
Clear Lake Area Chamber of Commerce			
1201 NASA Pkwy ....Houston TX 77058	800-877-8339	281-488-7676	137
Clear Lake Convention & Visitors Bureau			
205 Main Ave PO Box 188 ....Clear Lake IA 50428	800-285-5338	641-357-2159	207
Clear View Bag Co			
5 Burdick Dr ....Albany NY 12205	800-458-7153	518-458-7153	65
Clearfield Bank & Trust Co			
11 N Second St PO Box 171 ....Clearfield PA 16830	888-765-7551	814-765-7551	69
Clearfield Hospital			
809 Tpke Ave PO Box 992 ....Clearfield PA 16830	800-281-8000	814-765-5341	371-3
ClearOne Communications Inc			
5225 Wiley Post Way ....Salt Lake City UT 84116	800-945-7730	801-975-7200	725
ClearSail Communications LLC			
3950 Braxton ....Houston TX 77063	888-905-0888	713-230-2800	395
Clearwater Christian College			
3400 Gulf to Bay Blvd ....Clearwater FL 33759	800-348-4463*	727-726-1153	166
*Admissions			
Clearwater Power Co			
4230 Hatwai Rd PO Box 997 ....Lewiston ID 83501	888-743-1501	208-743-1501	245
Clearwater Public Library			
100 N Osceola Ave ....Clearwater FL 33755	800-342-8060	727-562-4970	431-3
Clearwater Regional Chamber of Commerce			
401 Cleveland St ....Clearwater FL 33755	877-447-7356	727-461-0011	137
Clearwater-Polk Electric Co-op			
315 Main Ave N ....Bagley MN 56621	888-694-3833	218-694-6241	245
Cleary Millwork Company Inc			
235 Dividend Rd ....Rocky Hill CT 06067	800-486-7600	860-721-0520	192-3
Cleary University			
3601 Plymouth Rd ....Ann Arbor MI 48105	800-686-1883	734-332-4477	788

	Toll-Free	Phone	Class
Livingston			
3750 Cleary Dr ....Howell MI 48843	800-686-1883	517-548-3670	788
Cleburne Chamber of Commerce			
1511 W Henderson St ....Cleburne TX 76033	888-253-2876	817-645-2455	137
Cleco Corp			
2030 Donahue Ferry Rd ....Pineville LA 71361	800-622-6537*	318-484-7400	775
*Cust Svc			
Cleft Palate Foundation (CPF)			
1504 E Franklin St Ste 102 ....Chapel Hill NC 27514	800-242-5338	919-933-9044	47-17
Cleftstone Manor			
92 Eden St ....Bar Harbor ME 04609	888-288-4951	207-288-8086	376
Clement Communications Inc			
Three Creek Pkwy PO Box 2208 ....Boothwyn PA 19061	800-253-6368	610-459-4200	628-10
Clement Industries Inc			
PO Box 914 ....Minden LA 71058	800-562-5948*	318-377-2776	769
*Cust Svc			
Clement Pappas & Company Inc			
One Colons Dr Ste 200 ....Carneyspoint NJ 08069	800-257-7019	856-455-1000	295-20
Clements National Co			
6650 S Narragansett Ave ....Chicago IL 60638	800-966-0016	708-594-5890	18
Clemson University			
105 Sikes Hall ....Clemson SC 29634	800-640-2657	864-656-3311	166
Clermont County Convention & Visitors Bureau (CCCVB)			
410 E Main St PO Box 100 ....Batavia OH 45103	800-796-4282	513-732-3600	207
Clermont State Historic Site			
1 Clermont Ave ....Germantown NY 12526	800-456-2267	518-537-4240	558
Cleveland Bros Equipment Company Inc			
5300 Paxton St ....Harrisburg PA 17111	866-551-4602	717-564-2121	355
Cleveland Cavaliers			
Quicken Loans Arena 1 Ctr Ct ....Cleveland OH 44115	800-332-2287	216-420-2000	705-1
Cleveland Clinic			
9500 Euclid Ave ....Cleveland OH 44195	800-223-2273	216-444-2200	371-3
Cleveland Clinic Bone Marrow Transplantation Program			
9500 Euclid Ave ....Cleveland OH 44195	800-223-2273	216-444-0261	759
Cleveland Clinic Hospital			
2950 Cleveland Clinic Blvd ....Weston FL 33331	866-293-7866	954-689-5000	371-3
Cleveland Corp			
42810 N Green Bay Rd ....Zion IL 60099	800-281-3464	847-872-7200	677
Cleveland Electric Company Inc			
1281 Fulton Industrial Blvd NW ....Atlanta GA 30336	800-282-7150	404-696-4550	190-4
Cleveland Gear Co			
3249 E 80th St ....Cleveland OH 44104	800-423-3169	216-641-9000	700
Cleveland Golf Co			
5601 Skylab Rd ....Huntington Beach CA 92647	800-999-6263*		701
*Cust Svc			
Cleveland Group Inc			
1281 Fulton Industrial Blvd ....Atlanta GA 30336	800-282-7150	404-696-4550	190-4
Cleveland HeartLab Inc			
6701 Carnegie Ave Ste 500 ....Cleveland OH 44103	866-358-9828		412
Cleveland Indians Team Shops			
2401 Ontario St ....Cleveland OH 44115	800-388-7423	216-420-4444	711
Cleveland Institute of Art			
11141 E Blvd ....Cleveland OH 44106	800-223-4700		162
Cleveland Institute of Electronics			
1776 E 17th St ....Cleveland OH 44114	800-243-6446	216-781-9400	788
Cleveland Magazine			
1422 Euclid Ave Ste 730 ....Cleveland OH 44115	800-210-7293	216-771-2833	452-22
Cleveland Motion Controls Inc			
7550 Hub Pkwy ....Cleveland OH 44125	800-321-8072	216-524-8800	204
Cleveland Museum of Art			
11150 E Blvd ....Cleveland OH 44106	800-469-4449*	216-421-7340	513
*Sales			
Cleveland Museum of Natural History			
One Wade Oval Dr			
University Cir ....Cleveland OH 44106	800-317-9155	216-231-4600	513
Cleveland Orchestra, The			
11001 Euclid Ave			
Severance Hall ....Cleveland OH 44106	800-686-1141	216-231-1111	566-3
Cleveland Plant & Flower Co			
12920 Corporate Dr ....Cleveland OH 44130	800-688-8012	216-898-3500	293
Cleveland Plumbing Supply Company Inc			
143 E Washington St ....Chagrin Falls OH 44022	800-331-1078	440-247-2555	605
Cleveland Punch & Die Co			
666 Pratt St PO Box 769 ....Ravenna OH 44266	888-451-4342		747
Cleveland Range Co			
1333 E 179th St ....Cleveland OH 44110	800-338-2204	216-481-4900	297
Cleveland State University			
2121 Euclid Ave ....Cleveland OH 44115	888-278-6446	216-687-2000	166
Cleveland State University Cleveland-Marshall College of Law			
1801 Euclid Ave LB 138 ....Cleveland OH 44115	866-687-2304	216-687-2344	167-1
Cleveland Wire Cloth & Manufacturing Co			
3573 E 78th St ....Cleveland OH 44105	800-321-3234	216-341-1832	679
Cleveland/Bradley Chamber of Commerce			
225 Keith St ....Cleveland TN 37311	800-533-9930	423-472-6587	137
Clever Devices Ltd			
300 Crossways Pk Dr ....Woodbury NY 11797	800-872-6129	516-433-6100	181
CLIA (Cruise Lines International Assn)			
910 SE 17th St Ste 400 ....Fort Lauderdale FL 33316	877-486-9222	754-224-2200	47-23
Click Magazine			
30 Grove St Ste C ....Peterborough NH 03458	800-821-0115		452-6
ClickSafety.com Inc			
2185 N California Blvd			
Ste 425 ....Walnut Creek CA 94596	800-971-1080		755
ClickSoftware Inc			
35 Corporate Dr Ste 400 ....Burlington MA 01803	888-438-3308	781-272-5903	179-7
NASDAQ: CKSW			
Clients First Business Solutions LLC			
670 N Beers St Bldg 4 ....Holmdel NJ 07733	866-677-6290		178
Cliff House at Pikes Peak			
306 Canyon Ave ....Manitou Springs CO 80829	888-212-7000		376
Cliff Spa at Snowbird			
Hwy 210 PO Box 929000 ....Snowbird UT 84092	800-453-3000	801-933-2225	698
Cliff Viessman Inc			
215 First Ave PO Box 175 ....Gary SD 57237	800-328-2408	605-272-5241	463
Cliff Weil Inc			
8043 Industrial Pk Rd ....Mechanicsville VA 23116	800-446-9345	804-746-1321	536
Clifton Savings Bancorp Inc			
1433 Van Houten Ave 3rd Fl ....Clifton NJ 07015	888-562-6727	973-473-2200	357-2
NASDAQ: CSBK			
Clifton Springs Hospital & Clinic			
2 Coulter Rd ....Clifton Springs NY 14432	888-786-4347	315-462-9561	371-3
Clifton T Perkins Hospital Ctr			
8450 Dorsey Run Rd ....Jessup MD 20794	877-463-3464	410-724-3000	371-5

Alphabetical Section

Name / Address	City	ST	ZIP	Toll-Free	Phone	Class
CliftonLarsonAllen - CLA 301 SW Adams St Ste 1000	Peoria	IL	61602	800-354-5849	309-671-4500	2
Climate Registry, The 523 W Sixth St Ste 445	Los Angeles	CA	90014	866-523-0764		193
ClimateMaster Inc 7300 SW 44th St	Oklahoma City	OK	73179	800-299-9747	405-745-6000	14
Climax Manufacturing Co 7840 SR 26	Lowville	NY	13367	800-225-4629	315-376-8000	550
Climax Packaging Inc 4515 Easton Rd	Saint Joseph	MO	64503	800-225-4629	816-233-3181	100
Climbing Magazine 2291 Arapahoe Ave	Boulder	CO	80302	800-829-5895		452-20
Clinch-Tite Corp 5264 Lake St PO Box 456 *General	Sandy Lake	PA	16145	800-241-0900*	724-376-7315	544
Cline Falls State Scenic Viewpoint 62976 OB Riley Rd	Bend	OR	97701	800-551-6949		558
C-Line Products Inc 1100 E Business Ctr Dr	Mount Prospect	IL	60056	800-323-6084	847-827-6661	527
Cline Tool & Service Co PO Box 866	Newton	IA	50208	866-561-3022	641-792-7081	488
Clinical Testing & Research Inc 20 Wilsey Sq	Ridgewood	NJ	07450	888-837-5267		414
CliniComp International 9655 Towne Ctr Dr	San Diego	CA	92121	800-350-8202	858-546-8202	179-10
Clinique Laboratories Inc 767 Fifth Ave 37th Fl	New York	NY	10153	800-419-4041	212-572-3983	215
Clinton Community College 1000 Lincoln Blvd	Clinton	IA	52732	877-495-3320	563-244-7001	160
Clinton County Economic Partnership 212 N Jay St	Lock Haven	PA	17745	888-388-6991	570-748-5782	137
Clinton County Electric Co-op Inc 475 N Main St PO Box 40	Breese	IL	62230	800-526-7282	618-526-7282	245
Clinton Inn Hotel 145 Dean Dr	Tenafly	NJ	07670	800-275-4411	201-871-3200	376
Clinton Junior College 1029 Crawford Rd	Rock Hill	SC	29730	877-837-9645	803-327-7402	160
Clinton Memorial Hospital (CMH) 610 W Main St PO Box 600	Wilmington	OH	45177	800-803-9648	937-382-6611	371-3
Clio Area School District 430 N Mill St	Clio	MI	48420	866-984-3962	810-591-0500	676
Clippard Instrument Lab 7390 Colerain Ave	Cincinnati	OH	45239	877-245-6247	513-521-4261	223
Clipper Exxpress Inc 9014 Heritage Pkwy Ste 300	Woodridge	IL	60517	800-678-2547	630-739-0700	444
Clipper Fund 2949 E Elvira Rd Ste 101	Tucson	AZ	85756	800-432-2504		521
Clipper Navigation Inc 2701 Alaskan Way Pier 69	Seattle	WA	98121	800-888-2535	206-443-2560	761
CLLA (Commercial Law League of America) 70 E Lake St Ste 630	Chicago	IL	60601	800-978-2552	312-781-2000	48-10
Clock Mobility 6700 Clay Ave	Grand Rapids	MI	49548	800-732-5625	616-698-9400	61-7
Clocktower Inn Hotel 181 E Santa Clara St	Ventura	CA	93001	800-727-1027	805-652-0141	376
Clofine Dairy Products Inc 1407 New Rd	Linwood	NJ	08221	800-441-1001	609-653-1000	296-4
Cloisters Museum Fort Tryon Pk	New York	NY	10040	800-662-3397	212-923-3700	513
Clopay Bldg Products Inc 8585 Duke Blvd	Mason	OH	45040	800-225-6729		234
Clopay Plastic Products Co 8585 Duke Blvd	Mason	OH	45040	800-282-2260	513-770-4800	593
Cloquet Area Chamber of Commerce 225 Sunnyside Dr	Cloquet	MN	55720	800-554-4350	218-879-1551	137
Clorox Co 1221 Broadway *NYSE: CLX ▓ *Cust Svc	Oakland	CA	94612	800-424-9300*	510-271-7000	186
Clos du Bois 19410 Geyserville Ave *Sales	Geyserville	CA	95441	800-222-3189*	707-857-1651	79-3
Close Up Foundation 1330 Braddock Pl Ste 400	Alexandria	VA	22314	800-256-7387	703-706-3300	47-7
Closet Factory 12800 S Broadway	Los Angeles	CA	90061	800-838-7995	310-516-7000	190-11
Cloud County Community College 2221 Campus Dr	Concordia	KS	66901	800-729-5101	785-243-1435	160
Cloud Peak Energy Inc (RTEA) 505 S Gillette Ave PO Box 3009	Gillette	WY	82717	866-470-4300	307-687-6000	496
CloudSway LLC 711 Pacific Ave	Tacoma	WA	98402	855-212-5683		384
Clough Harbour & Assoc (CHA) Three Winners Cir PO Box 5269	Albany	NY	12205	800-836-0817	518-453-4500	261
Clougherty Packing Co 3049 E Vernon Ave *Sales	Los Angeles	CA	90058	800-846-7635*		468
Clover Farms Dairy PO Box 14627	Reading	PA	19612	800-323-0123	610-921-9111	295-27
Cloverdale Equipment Co 13133 Cloverdale St	Oak Park	MI	48237	888-388-9182	248-399-6600	264-3
Cloverdale Foods Co 3015 34th St NW	Mandan	ND	58554	800-669-9511		295-26
Cloverland Green Spring Dairy Inc 2701 Loch Raven Rd *Orders	Baltimore	MD	21218	800-492-0094*	410-235-4477	295-27
Clover-Stornetta Farms Inc PO Box 750369	Petaluma	CA	94975	800-237-3315	707-769-3235	296-4
Clovis Community College (CCC) 417 Schepps Blvd	Clovis	NM	88101	800-769-1409	575-769-2811	160
Clovis Unified School District 1450 Herndon Ave	Clovis	CA	93611	800-498-9055	559-327-9000	676
Clovis/Curry County Chamber of Commerce 105 E Third St	Clovis	NM	88101	800-261-7656	575-763-3435	137
Clow Valve Co 902 S Second St	Oskaloosa	IA	52577	800-829-2569	641-673-8611	777
Clowns of America International (COAI) PO Box 1171	Englewood	FL	34295	877-816-6941	941-474-4351	47-4
CLT (Chesapeake Lodging Trust) 1997 Annapolis Exchange Pkwy Ste 410 *NYSE: CHSP	Annapolis	MD	21401	800-698-2820		645
Club Cal Neva Hotel Casino, The 38 E Second St PO Box 2071	Reno	NV	89501	877-777-7303	775-323-1046	660
Club Deportivo Chivas USA Home Depot Ctr 18400 Avalon Blvd Ste 500 *Sales	Carson	CA	90746	877-244-8271*	310-630-4550	708
Club Europa 802 W Oregon St	Urbana	IL	61801	800-331-1882	217-344-5863	750
Club Intrawest 375 Water St Ste 326	Vancouver	BC	V6B5C6	800-649-9243		743
Club Managers Assn of America (CMAA) 1733 King St	Alexandria	VA	22314	800-777-3529	703-739-9500	48-12
Club Med Sandpiper 4500 SE Pine Vly St	Port Saint Lucie	FL	34952	888-932-2582	772-398-5100	660
ClubCorp Inc 3030 Lyndon B Johnson Fwy Ste 600	Dallas	TX	75234	800-433-5079	972-243-6191	646
Clubfurniture.com 11535 Carmel Commons Blvd Ste 202	Charlotte	NC	28226	888-378-8383		779
ClubHouse Hotel & Suites Sioux Falls 2320 S Louise Ave	Sioux Falls	SD	57106	866-534-8700	605-361-8700	376
ClubLink Corp 15675 Dufferin St	King City	ON	L7B1K5	800-661-1818	905-841-3730	646
Clyde Peeling's Reptiland 18628 US Rt 15	Allenwood	PA	17810	800-737-8452		810
CLYDE UNION Pumps 4600 W Dickman Rd	Battle Creek	MI	49037	800-877-7867	269-966-4600	632
Clyde's Transfer Inc 8015 Industrial Pk Rd	Mechanicsville	VA	23116	800-342-8758	804-746-1135	676
CM Almy Inc One Ruth Rd	Pittsfield	ME	04967	800-225-2569	207-487-3232	153-13
CM Paula Co 6049 Hi-Tek Ct	Mason	OH	45040	800-543-4464		326
CM Ranch 167 Fish Hatchery Rd PO Box 217	Dubois	WY	82513	800-455-0721	307-455-2331	239
CM Services Inc 800 Roosevelt Rd Bldg C Ste 312	Glen Ellyn	IL	60137	800-613-6672	630-858-7337	46
CM Trailers Inc 200 County Rd PO Box 680	Madill	OK	73446	888-268-7577	580-795-5536	769
CMA (Chicago Meat Authority Inc) 1120 W 47th Pl	Chicago	IL	60609	800-383-3811	773-254-3811	295-26
CMA (Chamber Music America) 305 Seventh Ave 5th Fl	New York	NY	10001	888-221-9836	212-242-2022	47-4
CMA (Canadian Medical Assn) 1867 Alta Vista Dr	Ottawa	ON	K1G5W8	800-663-7336	613-731-9331	48-8
CMA (Country Music Assn Inc) 1 Music Cir S	Nashville	TN	37203	800-788-3045	615-244-2840	47-4
CMA (Crystal Meth Anonymous General Service Organization) 4470 W Sunset Blvd Ste 107 PO Box 555	Los Angeles	CA	90027	877-262-6691		47-21
CMA Consulting Services Inc 700 Troy Schenectady Rd	Latham	NY	12110	800-276-6101	518-783-9003	178
CMA Dishmachines 12700 Knott St	Garden Grove	CA	92841	800-854-6417	714-898-8781	383
CMAA (Crane Manufacturers Assn of America) 8720 Red Oak Blvd Ste 201	Charlotte	NC	28217	800-345-1815	704-676-1190	48-13
CMAA (Club Managers Assn of America) 1733 King St	Alexandria	VA	22314	800-777-3529	703-739-9500	48-12
CMC (Catholic Medical Ctr) 100 McGregor St	Manchester	NH	03102	800-437-9666	603-668-3545	371-3
CMC (Communications Manufacturing Co) 2234 Colby Ave *Orders	Los Angeles	CA	90064	800-462-5532*	310-828-3200	248
CMC (Community Medical Ctr) 99 Hwy 37 W	Toms River	NJ	08755	888-724-7123	732-557-8000	371-3
CMC (Children's Medical Ctr of Dallas Ctr for Cancer & Blood Disorders) 1935 Medical District Dr	Dallas	TX	75235	800-222-1222	214-456-7000	759
CMC (Cambridge Medical Ctr) 701 S Dellwood St	Cambridge	MN	55008	800-252-4133	763-689-7700	371-3
CMC Alamo Steel Co 2784 Old Dallas Rd	Waco	TX	76705	800-500-0333	254-799-2471	475
CMC Capitol City Steel 14501 S IH 35	Buda	TX	78610	888-682-7337	512-282-8820	475
CMC Construction Services 9103 E Almeda Rd	Houston	TX	77054	877-297-9111	713-799-1150	382
CMC Rebar Georgia 251 Hosea Rd	Lawrenceville	GA	30045	888-682-7337	770-963-6251	475
CMD Products 1410 Flightline Dr Ste D	Lincoln	CA	95648	800-210-9949	916-434-0228	426
CMDA (Christian Medical & Dental Assn) 2604 Hwy 421 PO Box 7500	Bristol	TN	37620	888-231-2637	423-844-1000	48-8
CME Group Inc 20 S Wacker Dr *NASDAQ: CME	Chicago	IL	60606	866-716-7274	312-930-1000	682
CMG (Computer Measurement Group) 151 Fries Mill Rd Ste 104	Turnersville	NJ	08012	800-436-7264	856-401-1700	47-9
CMH (Clinton Memorial Hospital) 610 W Main St PO Box 600	Wilmington	OH	45177	800-803-9648	937-382-6611	371-3
CMI (Can Manufacturers Institute) 1730 Rhode Island Ave NW Ste 1000	Washington	DC	20036	800-363-2726	202-232-4677	48-13
CMI EFCO Inc 435 W Wilson St	Salem	OH	44460	877-225-2674	330-332-4661	317
CMI Inc 316 E Ninth St	Owensboro	KY	42303	866-835-0690	270-685-6545	522
CMMB (Catholic Medical Mission Board) 10 W 17th St	New York	NY	10011	800-678-5659	212-242-7757	47-5
CMS (College Music Society) 312 E Pine St	Missoula	MT	59802	800-729-0235	406-721-9616	48-5
CMS (Centers for Medicare & Medicaid Services) 7500 Security Blvd	Baltimore	MD	21244	800-633-4227		338-8
Cms Communications Inc 722 Goddard Ave	Chesterfield	MO	63005	800-755-9169		246
CMS Electric Co-op Inc 509 E Carthage St	Meade	KS	67864	800-794-2353	620-873-2184	245
CMS Energy Corp One Energy Plz *NYSE: CMS	Jackson	MI	49201	800-477-5050	517-788-0550	357-5
CMS Mid-Atlantic Inc 295 Totowa Rd	Totowa	NJ	07512	800-267-1981		390
CMS Peripherals Inc 12 Mauchly Unit E	Irvine	CA	92618	800-327-5773	714-424-5520	174-8
CMSA (Case Management Society of America) 6301 Ranch Dr	Little Rock	AR	72223	800-216-2672	501-225-2229	48-8

Name / Address	City	State	ZIP	Toll-Free	Phone	Class
CMW (Central Maintenance & Welding Inc)						
2620 E Keysville Rd	Lithia	FL	33547	**877-704-7411**	813-737-1402	190-14
CNA Corp						
4825 Mark Ctr Dr	Alexandria	VA	22311	**800-344-0007**	703-824-2000	659
CNA Financial Corp						
333 S Wabash Ave	Chicago	IL	60604	**800-262-4357**	312-822-5000	357-4
NYSE: CNA						
CNA Surety Corp						
333 S Wabash Ave	Chicago	IL	60604	**877-672-6115**	312-822-5000	388-5
NYSE: L						
CNB (City National Bank of New Jersey)						
900 Broad St	Newark	NJ	07102	**877-350-3524**	973-624-0865	69
CNB Financial Corp						
One S Second St PO Box 42	Clearfield	PA	16830	**800-492-3221**	814-765-9621	357-2
NASDAQ: CCNE						
CNBS Inc						
7200 W 132nd St Ste 240	Overland Park	KS	66213	**800-222-0978**		681
CNGC (Cascade Natural Gas Corp)						
8113 W Grandridge Blvd	Kennewick	WA	99336	**888-522-1130**	206-624-3900	775
Cnlbank						
450 S Orange Ave Ste 400	Orlando	FL	32801	**800-910-2187**	407-244-3100	69
CNMC (Children's National Medical Ctr)						
111 Michigan Ave NW	Washington	DC	20010	**800-884-5433**	202-476-5000	371-1
CNPP (Center for Nutrition Policy & Promotion)						
3101 Pk Ctr Dr 10th Fl	Alexandria	VA	22302	**888-779-7264**	703-305-7600	338-1
CNRL (Canadian Natural Resources Ltd)						
855 Second St SW Ste 2500	Calgary	AB	T2P4J8	**888-878-3700**	403-517-6700	529
NYSE: CNQ						
COA (Council on Accreditation)						
45 Broadway 29th Fl	New York	NY	10006	**866-262-8088**	212-797-3000	47-1
Coach & Equipment Manufacturing Corp						
130 Horizon Pk Dr PO Box 36	Penn Yan	NY	14527	**800-724-8464**		509
Coach House Inc						
3480 Technology Dr	Nokomis	FL	34275	**800-235-0984**	941-485-0984	119
Coach Inc						
516 W 34th St	New York	NY	10001	**800-444-3611**	212-594-1850	427
NYSE: COH						
Coach Tours Ltd						
475 Federal Rd	Brookfield	CT	06804	**800-822-6224**	203-740-1118	750
Coachman Inn						
32959 SR-Hwy 20	Oak Harbor	WA	98277	**800-635-0043**	360-675-0727	376
Co-Advantage Resources						
111 W Jefferson St Ste 100	Orlando	FL	32801	**800-868-1016**	407-422-8448	623
COAI (Clowns of America International)						
PO Box 1171	Englewood	FL	34295	**877-816-6941**	941-474-4351	47-4
Coal Outlook						
1200 G St NW Ste 1100	Washington	DC	20005	**800-752-8878**	212-904-3070	524-5
Coalition Against Insurance Fraud						
1012 14th St NW Ste 200	Washington	DC	20005	**800-835-6422**	202-393-7330	48-9
Coalition for Auto Repair Equality (CARE)						
105 Oronoco St Ste 115	Alexandria	VA	22314	**800-229-5380**	703-519-7555	48-21
Coalition on Human Needs (CHN)						
1120 Connecticut Ave NW	Washington	DC	20036	**800-822-7323**	202-223-2532	47-5
Co-Alliance LLP						
5250 E US Hwy 36 Bldg 1000	Avon	IN	46123	**800-525-0272**	317-745-4491	275
Co-Anon Family Groups						
PO Box 12722	Tucson	AZ	85732	**800-898-9985**	520-513-5028	47-21
Coast Capital Savings						
645 Tyee Rd Ste 400	Victoria	BC	V9A6X5	**888-517-7000**	250-483-7000	69
Coast Central Credit Union Inc						
2650 Harrison Ave	Eureka	CA	95501	**800-974-9727**	707-445-8801	219
Coast Dental Services Inc						
4010 W Boy Scout Blvd Ste 1100	Tampa	FL	33607	**800-327-6453**	813-288-1999	458
Coast Distribution System						
350 Woodview Ave	Morgan Hill	CA	95037	**800-495-5858**	408-782-6686	60
NYSE: CRV						
Coast Edmonton House Suite Hotel						
1090 W Georgia S Ste 900	Vancouver	BC	V6E3V7	**800-716-6199**	604-682-7982	376
Coast Electric Power Assn						
18020 Hwy Ste 603	Kiln	MS	39556	**800-624-3348***	228-363-7000	245
*Cust Svc						
Coast to Coast Corporate Housing						
10773 Los Alamitos Blvd	Los Alamitos	CA	90720	**800-451-9466**	562-795-0250	211
Coast to Coast Moving & Storage Co						
136 41st St	Brooklyn	NY	11232	**800-872-6683**	718-443-5800	512
Coast2Coast Diagnostics Inc						
600 N Tustin Ave Ste 110	Santa Ana	CA	92705	**800-730-9263**		412
Coastal Agrobusiness Inc						
3702 Evans St PO Box 856	Greenville	NC	27835	**800-758-1828**	252-756-1126	280
Coastal Bend Blood Ctr						
209 N Padre Island Dr	Corpus Christi	TX	78406	**800-299-4943**	361-855-4943	88
Coastal Bend College						
Beeville						
3800 Charco Rd	Beeville	TX	78102	**866-722-2838**	361-358-2838	160
Coastal Carolina University						
PO Box 261954	Conway	SC	29528	**800-277-7000**	843-349-2170	166
Coastal Cement Corp						
36 Drydock Ave	Boston	MA	02210	**800-828-8352**	617-350-0183	134
Coastal Conservation Assn (CCA)						
6919 Portwest Dr Ste 100	Houston	TX	77024	**800-201-3474**	713-626-4234	47-13
Coastal Electric Co-op						
1265 S Coastal Hwy PO Box 109	Midway	GA	31320	**800-421-2343**	912-884-3311	245
Coastal Electric Co-op Inc						
2269 Jefferies Hwy	Walterboro	SC	29488	**866-708-0913**	843-538-5700	245
Coastal Federal Credit Union						
1000 St Albans Dr	Raleigh	NC	27609	**800-868-4262**	919-420-8000	219
Coastal Helicopters Inc						
8995 Yandukin Dr	Juneau	AK	99801	**800-789-5610**	907-789-5600	356
Coastal Hospice & Palliative Care						
2604 Old Ocean City Rd						
PO Box 1733	Salisbury	MD	21804	**800-780-7886**	410-742-8732	368
Coastal Inn Concorde						
379 Windmill Rd	Dartmouth	NS	B3A1J6	**800-565-1565**	902-465-7777	376
Coastal Inns Inc						
111 Warwick St Box 280	Digby	NS	B0V1A0	**800-665-7829**	800-401-1155	376
Coastal Journal						
97 Commercial St Ste 3	Bath	ME	04530	**800-649-6241**	207-443-6241	525-4
Coastal Mechanical Services LLC						
394 E Dr	Melbourne	FL	32904	**866-584-9528**	321-725-3061	190-10
Coastal Pacific Food Distributors Inc (CPFD)						
1015 Performance Dr	Stockton	CA	95206	**800-500-2611**	209-983-2454	296-8
Coastal Palms Hotel						
120th St Coastal Hwy	Ocean City	MD	21842	**800-641-0011**		376
Coastal Training Technologies Corp						
500 Studio Dr	Virginia Beach	VA	23452	**866-333-6888**	757-498-9014	506
Coastal Transport Co Inc						
1603 Ackerman Rd	San Antonio	TX	78219	**800-523-8612**	210-661-4287	770
Coastal Transportation Inc						
4025 13th Ave W	Seattle	WA	98119	**800-544-2580**	206-282-9979	311
Coastline Community College						
11460 Warner Ave	Fountain Valley	CA	92708	**866-422-2645**	714-546-7600	160
Coating & Adhesive Corp (CAC)						
1901 Popular St PO Box 1080	Leland	NC	28451	**800-410-2999**	910-371-3184	543
Coats North America						
3430 Toringdon Way Ste 301	Charlotte	NC	28277	**800-631-0965**	704-329-5800	734-9
Coaxial Dynamics						
6800 Lake Abrams Dr	Middleburg Heights	OH	44130	**800-262-9425**	440-243-1100	638
COBA/Select Sires Inc						
1224 Alton Darby Creek Rd	Columbus	OH	43228	**800-837-2621**	614-878-5333	11-2
Cobalt Boats LLC						
1715 N Eigth St	Neodesha	KS	66757	**800-468-5764**	620-325-2653	89
Cobalt Group Inc						
2200 First Ave S Ste 400	Seattle	WA	98134	**800-909-8244**		179-10
Cobb Chamber of Commerce						
240 I- N Pkwy	Atlanta	GA	30339	**800-228-2545**	770-980-2000	137
Cobb Mechanical Contractors						
2906 W Morrison	Colorado Springs	CO	80904	**800-808-2622***	719-471-8958	190-10
*General						
Cobb Travel & Tourism						
One Galleria Pkwy	Atlanta	GA	30339	**800-451-3480**	678-303-2622	207
Cobblestone Magazine						
30 Grove St Ste C	Peterborough	NH	03458	**800-821-0115**	603-924-7209	452-6
Cobblestone Publishing Co						
30 Grove St Ste C	Peterborough	NH	03458	**800-821-0115**	603-924-7209	628-9
Cobb-Vantress Inc						
PO Box 1030	Siloam Springs	AR	72761	**800-748-9719**	479-524-3166	11-2
Cobra Mfg Co Inc						
7909 E 148th St S	Bixby	OK	74008	**800-352-6272**	918-366-7484	701
Coburn Supply Company Inc						
390 Pk St Ste 100	Beaumont	TX	77701	**800-832-8492**	409-838-6363	605
Coca-Cola Bottling Co Consolidated						
4100 Coca-Cola Plaza	Charlotte	NC	28211	**800-777-2653**	704-557-4000	80-2
NASDAQ: COKE						
Coca-Cola Co						
One Coca-Cola Plz PO Box 1734	Atlanta	GA	30313	**800-438-2653**	404-676-2121	79-2
NYSE: KO						
Coca-Cola Foundation Inc						
PO Box 1734	Atlanta	GA	30301	**800-438-2653**	800-306-2653	303
Coca-Cola Nonpartisan Committee for Good Government						
PO Box 1734	Atlanta	GA	30301	**800-438-2653**		608
Cocaine Anonymous World Services Inc (CA)						
3740 Overland Ave Ste C	Los Angeles	CA	90034	**800-347-8998**	310-559-5833	47-21
Cocca's Inn & Suites						
Corner of Wolf Rd & Central Ave	Albany	NY	12205	**888-426-2227**	518-459-2240	376
Cochise College						
4190 W Hwy 80	Douglas	AZ	85607	**800-966-7943**	520-364-7943	160
Sierra Vista						
901 N Colombo Ave	Sierra Vista	AZ	85635	**800-966-7943**	520-515-0500	160
Cochran Firm LLC						
111 E Main St	Dothan	AL	36301	**800-843-3476**	334-793-1555	425
Cochrane Technologies Inc						
PO Box 81276	Lafayette	LA	70598	**800-346-3745**	337-837-3334	718
Cocoa Beach Area Chamber of Commerce						
400 Fortenberry Rd	Merritt Island	FL	32952	**888-874-2674**	321-459-2200	137
Coconino Community College						
Lonetree						
2800 S Lone Tree Rd	Flagstaff	AZ	86001	**800-350-7122**	928-527-1222	160
Coconino County						
219 E Cherry Ave	Flagstaff	AZ	86001	**800-559-9289**	928-774-5011	336
Coconut Malorie Resort						
200 59th St	Ocean City	MD	21842	**855-826-6361**	443-513-0175	660
Codale Electric Supply Inc						
5225 West 2400 South						
PO Box 702070	Salt Lake City	UT	84120	**800-300-6634**	801-975-7300	246
Code Hennessy & Simmons Inc						
10 S Wacker Dr Ste 3175	Chicago	IL	60606	**888-603-5847**	312-876-1840	780
Codington-Clark Electric Co-op						
3520 Ninth Ave SW PO Box 880	Watertown	SD	57201	**800-463-8938**	605-886-5848	245
Codman & Shurtleff Inc						
325 Paramount Dr	Raynham	MA	02767	**800-225-0460**	800-382-4682	472
Coe College						
1220 First Ave NE	Cedar Rapids	IA	52402	**877-225-5263**	319-399-8500	166
Coe College Permanent Collection of Art						
1220 First Ave NE	Cedar Rapids	IA	52402	**800-273-8255**	319-399-8500	513
COECO Office Systems Co						
2521 N Church St						
PO Box 2088	Rocky Mount	NC	27804	**800-682-6844**	252-977-1121	319
Coeur d'Alene Area Chamber of Commerce						
105 N First St Ste 100	Coeur d'Alene	ID	83814	**877-782-9232**	208-664-3194	137
Coeur d'Alene Resort						
115 S Second St	Coeur d'Alene	ID	83814	**800-688-5253**	208-765-4000	660
Coface Services North America Inc						
50 Millstone Rd	East Windsor	NJ	08520	**877-626-3223**	609-469-0400	218
Coffee Bean International						
9120 NE Alderwood Rd	Portland	OR	97220	**800-877-0474**	503-227-4490	296-2
Coffee Beanery Ltd, The						
3429 Pierson Pl	Flushing	MI	48433	**800-441-2255**		157
Coffee Holding Company Inc						
3475 Victory Blvd	Staten Island	NY	10314	**800-458-2233**	718-832-0800	295-7
NASDAQ: JVA						
Coffee Masters Inc						
7606 Industrial Ct	Spring Grove	IL	60081	**800-334-6485**	815-675-0088	296-2
Coffee People Inc						
33 Coffee Ln	Waterbury	VT	05676	**888-879-4627**		157
Coffeyville Community College						
400 W 11th St	Coffeyville	KS	67337	**877-517-2836**	620-251-7700	160
Coffeyville Regional Medical Ctr						
1400 W Fourth St	Coffeyville	KS	67337	**800-540-2762**	620-251-1200	371-3
Coffin Turbo Pump Inc						
326 S Dean St	Englewood	NJ	07631	**800-568-9798**	201-568-2826	632
Coffman Truck Sales						
1149 W Lake S PO Box 151	Aurora	IL	60507	**800-255-7641**	630-892-7093	56
Cogeco Cable Inc						
5 Pl Ville-Marie Ste 915	Montreal	QC	H3B2G2	**800-855-0511**	514-874-2600	115
Cogent Communications Group Inc						
1015 31st St NW	Washington	DC	20007	**877-875-4432**	202-295-4200	391
NASDAQ: CCOI						

Name / Address	City	State	ZIP	Toll-Free	Phone	Class
Cognizant Technology Solutions Corp						
500 Frank W Burr Blvd	Teaneck	NJ	07666	**888-937-3277**	201-801-0233	181
NASDAQ: CTSH						
Cogswell Polytechnical College						
1175 Bordeaux Dr	Sunnyvale	CA	94089	**800-264-7955**	408-541-0100	166
COGWM (Church of God World Missions)						
2490 Keith St PO Box 8016	Cleveland	TN	37320	**800-345-7492**	423-478-7190	47-20
Cohasset Harbor Inn						
124 Elm St	Cohasset	MA	02025	**800-252-5287**	781-383-6650	376
Cohen & Grigsby Pc						
625 Liberty Ave	Pittsburgh	PA	15222	**800-235-8619**	412-297-4900	425
Cohen & Steers Inc						
280 Pk Ave 10th Fl	New York	NY	10017	**800-330-7348**	212-832-3232	398
NYSE: CNS						
Cohen Bros Inc						
1723 Woodlawn Ave	Middletown	OH	45044	**800-878-3697**	513-422-3696	677
Coherent Inc						
5100 Patrick Henry Dr	Santa Clara	CA	95054	**800-527-3786***	408-764-4000	422
NASDAQ: COHR ▩ *Sales						
Cohu Inc						
12367 Crosthwaite Cir	Poway	CA	92064	**800-685-5050**	858-848-8100	248
NASDAQ: COHU						
Coilcraft Inc						
1102 Silver Lk Rd	Cary	IL	60013	**800-322-2645**	847-639-2361	253
Coilhose Pneumatics Inc						
19 Kimberly Rd	East Brunswick	NJ	08816	**800-424-9300**	732-390-8480	367
Coin Acceptors Inc						
300 Hunter Ave	Saint Louis	MO	63124	**800-325-2646**	314-725-0100	54
Coin Laundry Assn (CLA)						
1s660 Midwest Rd						
Ste 205	Oakbrook Terrace	IL	60181	**800-570-5629**	630-953-7920	48-4
Coin World Magazine						
911 S Vandemark Rd	Sidney	OH	45365	**866-519-7298**	937-498-0800	452-14
Coinmach Service Corp						
303 Sunnyside Blvd Ste 70	Plainview	NY	11803	**877-264-6622**	516-349-8555	423
Coinstar Inc						
1800 114th Ave SE	Bellevue	WA	98004	**800-928-2274**	425-943-8000	54
Coker College						
300 E College Ave	Hartsville	SC	29550	**800-950-1908**	843-383-8000	166
Coker Consulting						
2400 Lakeview Pkwy Ste 400	Alpharetta	GA	30009	**800-345-5829**		458
COLA						
9881 Broken Land Pkwy Ste 200	Columbia	MD	21046	**800-981-9883**	410-381-6581	48-8
Colad Group						
801 Exchange St	Buffalo	NY	14210	**800-950-1755**	716-961-1776	548
COLAGE (Children of Lesbians & Gays Everywhere)						
1550 Bryant St Ste 830	San Francisco	CA	94103	**855-426-5243**	415-861-5437	47-21
Colbert County Tourism & Convention Bureau						
719 Hwy 72 W PO Box 740425	Tuscumbia	AL	35674	**800-344-0783**	256-383-0783	207
Colby Attorneys Service Company Inc						
111 Washington Ave Ste 703	Albany	NY	12210	**800-832-1220**		626
Colby College						
4800 Mayflower Hill	Waterville	ME	04901	**800-723-3032***	207-859-4800	166
*Admissions						
Colby Community College						
1255 S Range Ave	Colby	KS	67701	**888-634-9350**	785-462-3984	160
Colby Convention & Visitors Bureau						
350 S Range Ste 10	Colby	KS	67701	**800-611-8835**	785-460-7643	207
Colby Hill Inn						
33 The Oaks PO Box 779	Henniker	NH	03242	**800-531-0330**	603-428-3281	376
Colby-Sawyer College						
541 Main St	New London	NH	03257	**800-272-1015***	603-526-3700	166
*Admissions						
Colchester Regional Hospital						
207 Willow St	Truro	NS	B2N5A1	**800-460-2110**	902-893-4321	371-2
Colcord Hotel						
15 N Robinson Ave	Oklahoma City	OK	73102	**866-781-3800**	405-601-4300	376
Cold Spring Granite Inc						
17482 Granite W Rd	Cold Spring	MN	56320	**800-328-5040**	320-685-3621	715
Cold Stone Creamery Inc						
9311 E Via De Ventura	Scottsdale	AZ	85258	**866-452-4252***	480-362-4800	378
*Cust Svc						
Coldspring						
17482 Granite W Rd	Cold Spring	MN	56320	**800-328-5040**		715
Coldwell Banker Gundaker						
2458 Old Dorsett Rd						
Ste 300	Maryland Heights	MO	63043	**800-325-1978**	314-298-5000	643
Coldwell Banker Residential Brokerage						
600 Grant St Ste 925	Denver	CO	80203	**800-552-6787***	303-409-1500	643
*All						
Coldwell Banker Residential Real Estate						
5951 Cattleridge Ave	Sarasota	FL	34232	**888-937-6426**	941-378-8211	643
Cole Hersee Co						
20 Old Colony Ave	Boston	MA	02127	**800-365-2653**	617-268-2100	802
Cole Information Services						
3401 NW 39th St	Lincoln	NE	68524	**800-800-3271**	402-555-5678	628-6
Cole Papers Inc						
1300 N 38th St	Fargo	ND	58102	**800-800-8090**	701-282-5311	546
Cole Warren & Long Inc						
Two Penn Ctr Ste 312	Philadelphia	PA	19102	**800-394-8517**	215-563-0701	266
Cole-Haan						
8701 Keystone Crossing	Indianapolis	IN	46240	**800-695-8945**	317-810-0160	300
Coleman American Cos Inc						
PO Box 960	Midland City	AL	36350	**877-693-7060**	334-983-6500	444
Coleman American Moving Services Inc						
PO Box 960	Midland City	AL	36350	**877-693-7060**	866-929-1482	770
Coleman Co						
1100 Stearns Dr	Sauk Rapids	MN	56379	**800-328-3208**	320-252-1642	701
Coleman Company Inc						
3600 N Hydraulic	Wichita	KS	67219	**800-835-3278***	316-832-2653	701
*Cust Svc						
Coleman County Electric Co-op Inc						
3300 N Hwy 84 PO Box 860	Coleman	TX	76834	**800-560-2128**	325-625-2128	245
Coleman Dairy Inc						
6901 I-30	Little Rock	AR	72209	**800-365-1551**	501-748-1700	295-27
Coleman E Adler & Sons Inc						
722 Canal St Third Fl	New Orleans	LA	70130	**800-925-7912**	504-523-5292	407
Cole-Parmer Instrument Co						
625 E Bunker Ct	Vernon Hills	IL	60061	**800-323-4340**	847-549-7600	417
Coles-Moultrie Electric Co-op						
104 DeWitt Ave E PO Box 709	Mattoon	IL	61938	**888-661-2632**	217-235-0341	245
Colgate Rochester Crozer Divinity School						
1100 S Goodman St	Rochester	NY	14620	**888-937-3732**	585-271-1320	167-3
Colgate University Case Library						
13 Oak Dr	Hamilton	NY	13346	**888-827-4434**	315-228-7300	431-6
CollabNet Inc						
8000 Marina Blvd Ste 600	Brisbane	CA	94005	**888-532-6823**	650-228-2500	178
Collaborative Consulting LLC						
70 BlanchaRd Rd Ste 500	Burlington	MA	01803	**877-376-9900**	781-565-2600	194
Collage Dance Theatre						
2934 1/2 Beverly Glen Cir	Los Angeles	CA	90077	**866-300-4287**	818-784-8669	566-1
Collective Technologies LLC						
9433 Bee Caves Rd	Austin	TX	78733	**800-994-1640**	512-263-5500	225
Collectors Universe Inc						
PO Box 6280	Newport Beach	CA	92658	**800-325-1121**	949-567-1234	50
NASDAQ: CLCT						
College & University Professional Assn for Hum Res (CUPA-HR)						
1811 Commons Pt Dr	Knoxville	TN	37932	**877-287-2474**	865-637-7673	48-5
College Board						
45 Columbus Ave	New York	NY	10023	**800-927-4302**	212-713-8000	244
College Health Services LLC						
144 Turnpike Rd Ste 240	Southboro	MA	01772	**866-636-8336**		178
College Hospital						
10802 College Pl	Cerritos	CA	90703	**800-352-3301**	562-924-9581	371-5
College Hospital Costa Mesa						
301 Victoria St	Costa Mesa	CA	92627	**800-773-8001**	949-642-2734	371-5
College Merici						
755 Ch St-Louis	Quebec City	QC	G1S1C1	**800-208-1463**	418-683-1591	160
College Music Society (CMS)						
312 E Pine St	Missoula	MT	59802	**800-729-0235**	406-721-9616	48-5
College of American Pathologists (CAP)						
325 Waukegan Rd	Northfield	IL	60093	**800-323-4040**	847-832-7000	48-8
College of American Pathologists PAC						
1350 I St NW Ste 590	Washington	DC	20005	**800-392-9994**	202-354-7100	608
College of Charleston						
66 George St	Charleston	SC	29424	**800-355-9983**	843-805-5507	166
College of Court Reporting Inc						
111 W Tenth St Ste 111	Hobart	IN	46342	**866-294-3974**	219-942-1459	788
College of Eastern Utah						
451 E 400 N	Price	UT	84501	**800-336-2381**	435-797-1000	160
San Juan						
639 West 100 South	Blanding	UT	84511	**800-395-2969**	435-678-2201	160
College of Idaho						
2112 Cleveland Blvd	Caldwell	ID	83605	**800-224-3246***	208-459-5011	166
*Admissions						
College of Menominee Nation						
PO Box 1179	Keshena	WI	54135	**800-567-2344**	715-799-5600	163
College of Mount Saint Joseph						
5701 Delhi Rd	Cincinnati	OH	45233	**800-654-9314**	513-244-4200	166
College of Mount Saint Vincent						
6301 Riverdale Ave	Riverdale	NY	10471	**877-392-6844**	718-405-3304	166
College of New Jersey						
2000 Pennington Rd PO Box 7718	Ewing	NJ	08628	**800-644-3562**	609-771-1855	166
College of New Rochelle						
29 Castle Pl	New Rochelle	NY	10805	**800-933-5923**	914-654-5000	166
College of Notre Dame of Maryland						
4701 N Charles St	Baltimore	MD	21210	**800-753-3757***	410-435-0100	166
*Admissions						
College of Saint Catherine						
2004 Randolph Ave	Saint Paul	MN	55105	**800-945-4599**	651-690-6000	166
Minneapolis						
601 25th Ave S	Minneapolis	MN	55454	**800-945-4599**	651-690-7700	166
College of Saint Elizabeth						
2 Convent Rd	Morristown	NJ	07960	**800-210-7900***	973-290-4700	166
*Admissions						
College of Saint Joseph in Vermont						
71 Clement Rd	Rutland	VT	05701	**877-270-9998***	802-773-5900	166
*Admissions						
College of Saint Mary						
7000 Mercy Rd	Omaha	NE	68106	**800-926-5534**	402-399-2400	166
College of Saint Rose						
432 Western Ave	Albany	NY	12203	**800-637-8556**	518-454-5150	166
College of Saint Scholastica						
1200 Kenwood Ave	Duluth	MN	55811	**800-447-5444**	218-723-6046	166
College of Santa Fe						
1600 St Michaels Dr	Santa Fe	NM	87505	**800-862-7759**	505-473-6011	166
College of Southern Maryland						
Leonardtown						
22950 Hollywood Rd	Leonardtown	MD	20650	**800-933-9177**	240-725-5300	160
Prince Frederick						
115 J W Williams Rd	Prince Frederick	MD	20678	**800-933-9177**	443-550-6000	160
College of Staten Island						
2800 Victory Blvd	Staten Island	NY	10314	**888-442-4551**	718-982-2000	166
College of the Atlantic						
105 Eden St	Bar Harbor	ME	04609	**800-528-0025***	207-288-5015	166
*Admissions						
College of the Holy Cross						
1 College St	Worcester	MA	01610	**800-442-2421**	508-793-2011	166
College of the Holy Cross Dinand Library						
1 College St	Worcester	MA	01610	**877-433-1843**	508-793-2642	431-6
College of the Ozarks						
1 Industrial Dr PO Box 17	Point Lookout	MO	65726	**800-222-0525***	417-334-6411	166
*Admissions						
College of the Redwoods						
7351 Tompkins Hill Rd	Eureka	CA	95501	**800-641-0400**	707-476-4100	160
Del Norte						
883 W Washington Blvd	Crescent City	CA	95531	**800-641-0400**	707-465-2300	160
Mendocino Coast						
440 Alger St	Fort Bragg	CA	95437	**800-641-0400**	707-962-2600	160
College of the Siskiyous						
800 College Ave	Weed	CA	96094	**888-397-4339**	530-938-4461	160
College of the Southwest						
6610 N Lovington Hwy	Hobbs	NM	88240	**800-530-4400**	575-392-6561	166
College of Westchester (CW)						
325 Central Ave	White Plains	NY	10606	**800-660-7093**		788
College of William & Mary Swem Library						
PO Box 8794	Williamsburg	VA	23187	**800-462-3683**	757-221-3072	431-6
College of Wooster						
1189 Beall Ave	Wooster	OH	44691	**800-877-9905**	330-263-2000	166
College Outlook & Career Opportunities Magazine						
20 E Gregory Blvd	Kansas City	MO	64114	**800-274-8867**	816-361-0616	452-11
College Parents of America (CPA)						
2200 Wilson Blvd Ste 102-396	Arlington	VA	22201	**888-761-6702**		47-11
College Savings Bank						
Five Vaughn Dr Ste 100	Princeton	NJ	08540	**800-888-2723**		69
College Station Ford						
1351 Earl Rudder Fwy S	College Station	TX	77845	**888-508-0241**	979-694-2022	56

Name / Address	City	State	Zip	Toll-Free	Phone	Class
Collin County						
200 S McDonald St Ste 120	McKinney	TX	75069	**800-336-5996**		336
Collin Street Bakery Inc						
401 W Seventh Ave	Corsicana	TX	75151	**800-504-1896***	903-872-8111	67
*Sales						
Collins Bus Corp						
PO Box 2946	Hutchinson	KS	67504	**800-533-1850**	620-662-9000	58
Collins Cos						
1618 SW First Ave Ste 500	Portland	OR	97201	**800-329-1219**		674
Collins Electric Co Inc						
53 Second Ave	Chicopee	MA	01020	**877-553-2810**	413-592-9221	190-4
Collins Manufacturing Co						
2000 Bowser Rd	Cookeville	TN	38506	**800-292-6450**	931-528-5151	75
Colloid Environmental Technologies Co (CETCO)						
2870 Forbs Ave	Hoffman Estates	IL	60192	**800-527-9948**	847-851-1899	3
Colmac Coil Manufacturing Inc						
370 N Lincoln St PO Box 571	Colville	WA	99114	**800-845-6778**	509-684-2595	14
Colmac Industries Inc						
PO Box 72	Colville	WA	99114	**800-926-5622**	509-684-4505	424
Colmery-O'Neil Veterans Affairs Medical Ctr						
2200 SW Gage Blvd	Topeka	KS	66622	**800-574-8387**	785-350-3111	371-8
Coloma Frozen Foods Inc						
4145 Coloma Rd	Coloma	MI	49038	**800-642-2723**	269-849-0500	295-21
Colonial Bag Co						
One Ocean Pond Ave PO Box 929	Lake Park	GA	31636	**800-392-4875**	229-559-8484	64
Colonial Bag Corp						
205 E Fullerton Ave	Carol Stream	IL	60188	**800-445-7496**	630-690-3999	65
Colonial Bronze Co						
511 Winsted Rd	Torrington	CT	06790	**800-355-7903***	860-489-9233	347
*All						
Colonial Downs						
10515 Colonial Downs Pkwy	New Kent	VA	23124	**888-482-8722**	804-966-7223	633
Colonial Engineering Inc						
6400 Corporate Ave	Portage	MI	49002	**800-374-0234**	269-323-2495	588
Colonial Farm Credit Aca						
7104 Mechanicsville Tpke						
PO Box 727	Mechanicsville	VA	23111	**800-777-8908**	804-746-4581	216
Colonial Freight Systems Inc						
10924 McBride Ln	Knoxville	TN	37932	**800-826-1402**	865-966-9711	770
Colonial House Inn						
277 Main St Rt 6A	Yarmouth Port	MA	02675	**800-999-3416**	508-362-4348	662
Colonial Life & Accident Insurance Co						
1200 Colonial Life Blvd	Columbia	SC	29210	**800-325-4368**	803-213-7250	388-2
Colonial National Historical Park						
PO Box 210	Yorktown	VA	23690	**866-945-7920**	757-898-3400	557
Colonial Parking Inc						
1050 Thomas Jefferson St NW						
Ste 100	Washington	DC	20007	**877-777-4778**	202-295-8100	555
Colonial Penn Life Insurance Co						
399 Market St	Philadelphia	PA	19181	**800-523-9100**	215-928-8000	388-2
Colonial Pipeline Co						
1185 Sanctuary Pkwy Ste 100	Alpharetta	GA	30009	**800-275-3004**	678-762-2200	590
Colonial Truck Co						
1833 Commerce Rd	Richmond	VA	23224	**800-234-8782**	804-232-3492	770
Colonial Williamsburg Foundation						
PO Box 1776	Williamsburg	VA	23187	**800-447-8679**	757-229-1000	304
Colonial Williamsburg Reservation Ctr						
PO Box 1776	Williamsburg	VA	23187	**800-447-8679**	757-229-1000	373
ColonialWebb Contractors Co						
2820 Ackley Ave	Richmond	VA	23228	**877-208-3894**	804-916-1400	190-10
Colonna's Shipyard Inc						
400 E Indian River Rd	Norfolk	VA	23523	**800-265-6627**	757-545-2414	689
Colonnade Hotel						
120 Huntington Ave	Boston	MA	02116	**800-962-3030**	617-424-7000	376
Colony Capital Management						
3050 Peachtree Rd NW Suite 200	Atlanta	GA	30305	**877-365-5050**	404-365-5050	398
Colony Hotel						
140 Ocean Ave	Kennebunkport	ME	04046	**800-552-2363**	207-967-3331	660
Colony Inc						
2500 Galvin Dr	Elgin	IL	60123	**800-735-1300**	847-426-5300	233
Colony South Hotel						
7401 Surratts Rd	Clinton	MD	20735	**800-537-1147**	301-856-4500	376
Color Communication Inc						
4000 W Fillmore St	Chicago	IL	60624	**800-458-5743**		771
Color Imaging Inc						
4350 Peachtree Industrial Blvd						
Ste 100	Norcross	GA	30071	**800-783-1090**	770-840-1090	620
Color Me Beautiful						
7000 Infantry Ridge Rd Ste 200	Manassas	VA	20109	**800-265-6763**		363
Color Me Mine Enterprises Inc						
3722 San Fernando Rd	Glendale	CA	91204	**888-265-6764**	818-291-5900	309
Color Resolutions International						
575 Quality Blvd	Fairfield	OH	45014	**800-346-8570**	513-552-7200	385
Color Spot Nurseries Inc						
2575 Olive Hill Rd	Fallbrook	CA	92028	**800-554-4065**	760-695-1480	366
Color Wheel Paint Mfg Co Inc						
2814 Silver Star Rd	Orlando	FL	32808	**855-862-6639**	407-293-6810	543
Colorado						
Aging & Adult Services Div						
1575 Sherman St Ground Fl	Denver	CO	80203	**800-773-1366**	303-866-2636	337-6
Housing & Finance Authority						
1981 Blake St	Denver	CO	80202	**800-877-2432**	303-297-2432	337-6
Natural Resources Dept						
1313 Sherman St Rm 718	Denver	CO	80203	**800-536-5308**	303-866-3311	337-6
Parks & Outdoor Recreation Div						
1313 Sherman St Rm 618	Denver	CO	80203	**800-678-2267***	303-866-3437	337-6
*Campground Resv						
Public Health & Environment Dept (CDPHE)						
4300 Cherry Creek Dr S	Denver	CO	80246	**800-886-7689**	303-692-2000	337-6
Public Utilities Commission						
1560 Broadway Ste 250	Denver	CO	80203	**800-888-0170**	303-894-2000	337-6
Regulatory Agencies Dept						
1560 Broadway Ste 1550	Denver	CO	80202	**800-886-7675**	303-894-7855	337-6
State Court Administrator						
1301 Pennsylvania St Ste 300	Denver	CO	80203	**800-888-0001**	303-837-3668	337-6
Supreme Court						
1560 Broadway Ste 1800	Denver	CO	80202	**877-888-1370**	303-866-6400	337-6
Victims Programs Office						
700 Kipling St Ste 1000	Lakewood	CO	80215	**888-282-1080**	303-239-5719	337-6
Vocational Rehabilitation Div						
1575 Sherman St 4th Fl	Denver	CO	80203	**866-870-4595**	303-866-4150	337-6
Workers Compensation Div						
633 17th St Ste 400	Denver	CO	80202	**888-390-7936**	303-318-8700	337-6
Colorado Assn of Realtors						
309 Inverness Way S	Englewood	CO	80112	**800-944-6550**	303-790-7099	647
Colorado Belle Hotel & Casino						
2100 S Casino Dr	Laughlin	NV	89029	**877-460-0777***	702-298-4000	132
*Resv						
Colorado Business Bank						
821 17th St	Denver	CO	80202	**800-574-4714**	303-293-2265	357-2
Colorado Charter Lines						
4960 Locust St	Commerce City	CO	80022	**800-821-7491**	303-287-0239	106
Colorado Christian University						
8787 W Alameda Ave	Lakewood	CO	80226	**800-443-2484**	303-963-3200	166
Loveland						
3553 Clydesdale Pkwy Ste 300	Loveland	CO	80538	**800-443-2484**	970-669-8700	166
Colorado College						
14 E Cache La						
Poudre St	Colorado Springs	CO	80903	**800-542-7214**	719-389-6344	166
Colorado CollegeInvest						
1560 Broadway Ste 1700	Denver	CO	80202	**800-448-2424**	303-376-8800	716
Colorado Correctional Industries						
2862 S Cir Dr	Colorado Springs	CO	80906	**800-685-7891***	719-226-4206	212
*Cust Svc						
Colorado Dental Assn						
3690 S Yosemite St Ste 400	Denver	CO	80237	**866-777-4771**	303-740-6900	227
Colorado Dude & Guest Ranch Assn (CDGRA)						
PO Box D	Shawnee	CO	80475	**866-942-3472**		47-23
Colorado Farm Bureau Mutual Insurance Co						
PO Box 5647	Denver	CO	80217	**800-315-5998**	303-749-7500	388-4
Colorado Fsb						
8400 E Prentice Ave						
Ste 545	Greenwood Village	CO	80111	**877-484-2372**	303-793-3555	69
Colorado Labor & Employment Dept						
633 17th St Ste 201	Denver	CO	80203	**800-390-7936**	303-318-8000	259
Colorado Lawyer Magazine						
1900 Grant St Ninth Fl	Denver	CO	80203	**800-332-6736**	303-860-1115	452-15
Colorado Lottery						
212 W Third St Ste 210	Pueblo	CO	81003	**800-999-2959**	719-546-2400	447
Colorado Medical Society						
7351 Lowry Blvd	Denver	CO	80230	**800-654-5653**	720-859-1001	469
Alpine						
1330 Bob Adams Dr	Steamboat Springs	CO	80487	**800-621-8559**	970-870-4444	160
Aspen 0255 Sage Way	Aspen	CO	81611	**800-621-8559**	970-925-7740	160
Colorado Mountain College						
Roaring Fork-Spring Valley						
3000 County Rd 114	Glenwood Springs	CO	81601	**800-621-8559**	970-945-7481	160
Colorado National Monument						
1750 Rim Rock Dr	Fruita	CO	81521	**866-945-7920**	970-858-3617	557
Colorado Northwestern Community College						
500 Kennedy Dr	Rangely	CO	81648	**800-562-1105**	970-675-3335	160
Craig 50 College Dr	Craig	CO	81625	**800-562-1105**		160
Colorado Passport Agency						
Colorado Agency						
3151 S Vaughn Way Ste 600	Aurora	CO	80014	**888-874-7793**	877-487-2778	338-14
Colorado Petroleum Products Co						
4080 Globeville Rd	Denver	CO	80216	**800-580-4080**	303-294-0302	534
Colorado Prime Foods						
500 Bi-County Blvd Ste 400	Farmingdale	NY	11735	**800-365-2404**	631-694-1111	363
Colorado Railroad Museum						
17155 W 44th Ave	Golden	CO	80403	**800-365-6263**	303-279-4591	513
Colorado School Journal						
1500 Grant St	Denver	CO	80203	**800-336-7678**	800-332-5939	452-8
Colorado School of Mines						
1600 Maple St	Golden	CO	80401	**800-446-9488**	303-273-3000	166
Colorado Serum Co						
4950 York St PO Box 16428	Denver	CO	80216	**800-525-2065***	303-295-7527	84
*Orders						
Colorado Springs City Auditorium						
221 E Kiowa St	Colorado Springs	CO	80903	**800-888-4748**	719-385-5969	206
Colorado Springs Convention & Visitors Bureau						
515 S Cascade Ave	Colorado Springs	CO	80903	**800-888-4748**	719-635-7506	207
Colorado Springs School District #11						
1115 N El Paso St	Colorado Springs	CO	80903	**800-273-8255**	719-520-2000	676
Colorado Springs Utilities						
111 S Cascade Ave						
PO Box 1103	Colorado Springs	CO	80903	**800-238-5434**	719-448-4800	775
Colorado State University						
Pueblo						
2200 Bonforte Blvd	Pueblo	CO	81001	**877-307-5678**	719-549-2100	166
Colorado Symphony Orchestra						
1000 14th St Unit 15	Denver	CO	80202	**877-292-7979**	303-623-7876	566-3
Colorado Technical University						
4435 N Chestnut St	Colorado Springs	CO	80907	**855-230-0555**	719-598-0200	166
Colorado Technical University Denver						
1865 W 121st Ave						
Bldg C Ste 100	Westminster	CO	80234	**877-250-9372**	303-362-2900	788
Colorado Time Systems						
1551 E 11th St	Loveland	CO	80537	**800-279-0111**	970-667-1000	692
Colorado Trails Ranch						
12161 County Rd 240	Durango	CO	81301	**800-323-3833**	970-247-5055	239
Colorado Trust						
1600 Sherman St	Denver	CO	80203	**888-847-9140**	303-837-1200	302
Colorado Valley Transit Inc						
108 Cardinal Ln PO Box 940	Columbus	TX	78934	**800-548-1068**	979-732-6281	107
Colorado Veterinary Medical Assn						
191 Yuma St	Denver	CO	80223	**800-228-5429**	303-318-0447	783
Coloradoan, The						
1300 Riverside Ave	Fort Collins	CO	80524	**877-424-0063**	970-493-6397	525-2
ColorDynamics						
200 E Bethany Dr	Allen	TX	75002	**800-445-0017**	972-390-6500	619
Color-Fi Inc						
320 Neeley St	Sumter	SC	29150	**800-843-6382**	803-436-4200	598-1
Color-Glo International						
7111 Ohms Ln	Minneapolis	MN	55439	**800-333-8523**	952-835-1338	61-1
Colors By Design						
7723 Densmore Ave	Van Nuys	CA	91406	**800-832-8436**		129
Colors on Parade						
125 Daytona St PO Box 50940	Conway	SC	29526	**866-756-4207***	843-347-8818	61-4
*Cust Svc						
Colquitt Regional Medical Ctr (CRMC)						
3131 S Main St PO Box 40	Moultrie	GA	31768	**888-262-2762**	229-985-3420	371-3
Colt's Plastics Co						
969 N Main St PO Box 429	Dayville	CT	06241	**800-222-2658**	860-774-2301	97
Coltene/Whaledent Inc						
235 Ascot Pkwy	Cuyahoga Falls	OH	44223	**800-221-3046**	330-916-8800	228

Listing	Toll-Free	Phone	Class
Columbia Air Services 175 Tower Ave Groton-New London Airport, Groton CT 06340	800-787-5001	860-449-1400	62
Columbia Bank 1301 A St Ste 800, Tacoma WA 98402 *NASDAQ: COLB*	800-305-1905	253-305-1900	357-2
Columbia Bank, The 7168 Columbia Gateway Dr, Columbia MD 21046	888-822-2265		69
Columbia Cascade Co 1300 SW Sixth Ave Ste 310, Portland OR 97201	800-547-1940	503-223-1157	343
Columbia College 600 S Michigan Ave 3rd Fl, Chicago IL 60605	866-705-0200	312-663-1600	166
Columbia College Hollywood 18618 Oxnard St, Tarzana CA 91356	800-785-0585	818-345-8414	166
Columbia College Jefferson City 3314 Emerald Ln, Jefferson City MO 65109	800-231-2391	573-634-3250	166
Columbia College Lake of the Ozarks 900 College Blvd, Osage Beach MO 65065	800-231-2391	573-348-6463	166
Columbia College of Nursing (CCON) 4425 N Port Washington Rd, Glendale WI 53212	800-221-5573	414-326-2330	166
Columbia College Orlando 2600 Technology Dr Ste 100, Orlando FL 32804	800-231-2391	407-293-9911	166
Columbia Convention & Visitors Bureau 300 S Providence Rd, Columbia MO 65203	800-652-0987	573-875-1231	207
Columbia Crest Winery Hwy 221 Columbia Crest Dr PO Box 231, Paterson WA 99345	888-309-9463	509-875-4227	79-3
Columbia Daily Tribune 101 N Fourth St, Columbia MO 65201	800-333-6799	573-815-1700	525-2
Columbia Data Products Inc 925 Sunshine Ln Ste 1080, Altamonte Springs FL 32714 *Sales	800-613-6288*	407-869-6700	179-12
Columbia Distributing Co 6840 N Cutter Cir, Portland OR 97217	888-417-5001	503-289-9600	80-1
Columbia Elevator Products Company Inc 380 Horace St, Bridgeport NY 06610	888-858-1558		190-1
Columbia Environmental Research Ctr (CERC) 4200 New Haven Rd, Columbia MO 65201	888-283-7626	573-875-5399	659
Columbia Forest Products Inc 7900 Triad Ctr Dr Ste 200, Greensboro NC 27409	800-637-1609	336-291-5905	606
Columbia Forest Products Inc Columbia Plywood Div 7900 Triad Ctr Dr Ste 200, Greensboro NC 27409	800-637-1609		606
Columbia Gas of Ohio Inc 200 Civic Ctr Dr, Columbus OH 43215	800-807-9781	614-460-6000	775
Columbia Gas of Virginia Inc 8063 Cedon Rd, Woodford VA 22580 *Cust Svc	800-543-8911*		775
Columbia Gear Corp 530 County Rd 50, Avon MN 56310	800-323-9838	320-356-7301	700
Columbia Gorge Hotel 4000 Westcliff Dr, Hood River OR 97031	800-345-1921	541-386-5566	376
Columbia Industries Inc PO Box 746, Hopkinsville KY 42240	800-531-5920	270-881-1300	701
Columbia International University 7435 Monticello Rd, Columbia SC 29203	800-777-2227	803-754-4100	159
Columbia Magazine 1 Columbus Plaza, New Haven CT 06510	800-380-9995	203-752-4000	452-10
Columbia Management Investment Advisers LLC 1 Financial Ctr, Boston MA 02111	800-426-3750		398
Columbia Memorial Hospital 71 Prospect Ave, Hudson NY 12534	866-539-1370	518-828-7601	371-3
Columbia Metropolitan Airport 3000 Aviation Way W PO Box 280037, Columbia SC 29170	888-562-5002	803-822-5010	27
Columbia Metropolitan Convention & Visitors Bureau 1101 Lincoln St PO Box 15, Columbia SC 29202	800-264-4884	803-545-0000	207
Columbia Mfg Corp 14400 S San Pedro St, Gardena CA 90248	800-729-3667	310-327-9300	234
Columbia ParCar Corp 1115 Commercial Ave, Reedsburg WI 53959	800-222-4653	608-524-8888	509
Columbia Pipe & Supply Co 1120 W Pershing Rd, Chicago IL 60609	888-429-4635	773-927-6600	487
Columbia Rural Electric Assn Inc 115 E Main St, Dayton WA 99328	800-642-1231	509-382-2578	245
Columbia Savings Bank 19-01 Rt 208, Fair Lawn NJ 07410 *Cust Svc	800-747-4428*	800-522-4167	69
Columbia Sportswear Co 14375 NW Science Pk Dr, Portland OR 97229 *NASDAQ: COLM*	800-622-6953	503-985-4000	153-1
Columbia State Bank PO Box 2156, Tacoma WA 98401	800-305-1905	253-305-1900	69
Columbia Steel Casting Co Inc 10425 N Bloss Ave, Portland OR 97203	800-547-9471	503-286-0685	306
Columbia TriStar Motion Picture Group 10202 W Washington Blvd, Culver City CA 90232	855-327-7669	310-244-4000	507
Columbia Ultimate Business Systems Inc 4400 NE 77th Ave Ste 100, Vancouver WA 98662	800-488-4420	360-256-7358	175
Columbia University Press 61 W 62nd St 3rd Fl, New York NY 10023	800-944-8648	212-459-0600	628-4
Columbia Winery 14030 NE 145th St PO Box 1248, Woodinville WA 98072	800-488-2347	425-488-2776	49-6
Columbia-Greene Community College 4400 Rt 23, Hudson NY 12534	888-668-4293	518-828-4181	160
Columbia-Montour Visitors Bureau 121 Papermill Rd, Bloomsburg PA 17815	800-847-4810	570-784-8279	207
Columbian 701 W Eigth St PO Box 180, Vancouver WA 98660	800-743-3391	360-694-3391	525-2
Columbian Chemicals Co 1800 W Oak Commons Ct, Marietta GA 30062	800-235-4003	770-792-9400	143
Columbian Park Zoo 1915 Scott St, Lafayette IN 47904	800-438-9926	765-807-1540	810
Columbian Tectank 2101 S 21st St PO Box 996, Parsons KS 67357	800-555-8265	620-421-0200	90
Columbus Area Visitors Ctr 506 Fifth St, Columbus IN 47201	800-468-6564	812-378-2622	207
Columbus Bank & Trust Co 1148 Broadway, Columbus GA 31901	800-334-9007	706-649-4900	69
Columbus Business First 303 W Nationwide Blvd, Columbus OH 43215	800-486-3289	614-461-4040	452-5
Columbus Chamber of Commerce 150 S Front St Ste 200, Columbus OH 43215	888-382-1574	614-221-1321	137
Columbus Civic Ctr 400 Fourth St, Columbus GA 31901	800-745-3000	706-653-4482	711
Columbus College of Art & Design 60 Cleveland Ave, Columbus OH 43215	877-997-2223	614-224-9101	162
Columbus Convention & Visitors Bureau 318 7th St N, Columbus MS 39701	800-327-2686	662-329-1191	207
Columbus Dispatch 34 S Third St, Columbus OH 43215	800-942-2745	614-461-5000	525-2
Columbus Electric Co-op Inc 900 N Gold St PO Box 631, Deming NM 88031	800-950-2667	505-546-8838	245
Columbus Industries Inc 2938 SR-752, Ashville OH 43103	800-766-2552	740-983-2552	18
Columbus Ledger-Enquirer 17 W 12th St, Columbus GA 31901	800-282-7859	706-324-5526	525-2
Columbus Life Insurance Co 400 E Fourth St PO Box 5737, Cincinnati OH 45201	800-677-9595	800-677-9696	388-2
Columbus Marble Works Corp 2415 Hwy 45 N PO Box 791, Columbus MS 39703 *Cust Svc	800-647-1055*	662-328-1477	715
Columbus McKinnon Corp 140 John James Audubon Pkwy, Amherst NY 14228 *NASDAQ: CMCO*	800-888-0985	716-689-5400	465
Columbus Regional Hospital 2400 E 17th St, Columbus IN 47201	800-841-4938	812-379-4441	371-3
Columbus State Community College 550 E Spring St, Columbus OH 43215	800-621-6407	614-287-2400	160
Columbus State University 4225 University Ave, Columbus GA 31907	866-264-2035	706-507-8800	166
Columbus Symphony Orchestra 55 E State St, Columbus OH 43215	800-745-3000	614-228-9600	566-3
Columbus Zoo & Aquarium 4850 W Powell Rd, Powell OH 43065	800-945-3543	614-645-3400	810
Columns, The 3811 St Charles Ave, New Orleans LA 70115	800-445-9308	504-899-9308	376
Comag Marketing Group LLC 155 Village Blvd 3rd Fl, Princeton NJ 08540	866-790-9353	609-524-1800	94
Comal County 199 Main Plaza, New Braunfels TX 78130	877-724-9475	830-221-1100	336
Comanche Electric Co-op Assn 201 W Wrights Ave, Comanche TX 76442	800-915-2533	325-356-2533	245
Comanche Nation College 1608 SW Ninth St, Lawton OK 73501	877-591-0203	580-591-0203	160
Comar LLC 141 N Fifth St, Saddle Brook NJ 07663	800-962-6627	201-909-3400	97
Comarco Inc 25541 Commerce Ctr Dr, Lake Forest CA 92630 *OTC: CMRO*	800-792-0250	949-599-7400	725
Comarco Wireless Technologies Inc 25541 Commerce Ctr Dr, Lake Forest CA 92630 *Cust Svc	800-792-0250*	949-599-7400	725
COMARK Communications 104 Feeding Hills Rd, Southwick MA 01077	800-288-8364	413-998-1100	638
Comark Corp 93 W St, Medfield MA 02052	800-280-8522	508-359-8161	174-1
Comark Direct 507 S Main St, Ft. Worth TX 76104	888-742-0405		5
Combe Inc 1101 Westchester Ave, White Plains NY 10604	800-431-2610	914-694-5454	215
CombiMatrix Corp 300 Goddard Ste 100, Irvine CA 92618 *NASDAQ: CBMX*	800-710-0624	949-753-0624	84
Combined Transport Inc 5656 Crater Lake Ave, Central Point OR 97502	800-547-2870	541-734-7418	770
Comcar Industries Inc 502 E Bridgers Ave, Auburndale FL 33823 *Cust Svc	800-524-1101*	863-967-1101	770
Comcast Corp 1701 JFK Blvd, Philadelphia PA 19103 *NASDAQ: CMCSA*	800-266-2278	215-665-1700	357-3
Comco Inc 2151 N Lincoln St, Burbank CA 91504	800-796-6626	818-841-5500	1
Comdata Corp 5301 Maryland Way, Brentwood TN 37027	800-266-3282	615-370-7000	68
Comdel Inc 11 Kondelin Rd, Gloucester MA 01930	800-468-3144	978-282-0620	253
Comer Packing 1000 Poplar St PO Box 33, Aberdeen MS 39730	800-748-8916	662-369-9325	468
Comerica Bank 411 W Lafayette, Detroit MI 48226	800-643-4418	313-222-3344	69
Comerica Bank-California 333 W Santa Clara St, San Jose CA 95113	800-522-2265	408-556-5300	69
Comerica Bank-Texas 1717 Main St, Dallas TX 75201	800-925-2160		69
Comerica Inc 1717 Main St Comerica Bank Tower, Dallas TX 75201 *NYSE: CMA*	800-266-3742		69
Cometic Gasket Inc 8090 Auburn Rd, Concord OH 44077	800-752-9850	440-354-0777	325
Com-Fab Inc 4657 Price HilliaRds Rd, Plain City OH 43064	866-522-1794	740-857-1107	753
ComForcare Senior Services Inc 2520 Telegraph Rd Ste 100, Bloomfield Hills MI 48302	800-886-4044	248-745-9700	309
Comfort Inn & Suites Milwaukee 916 E State St, Milwaukee WI 53202	800-424-6423	414-276-8800	376
Comfort Systems USA Inc 675 Bering Ste 400, Houston TX 77057 *NYSE: FIX*	800-723-8431	713-830-9600	190-10
Comfortex Inc 1680 Wilkie Dr PO Box 850, Winona MN 55987	800-445-4007	507-454-6579	466
Comfortex Window Fashions Inc 21 Elm St, Maplewood NY 12189 *Cust Svc	800-843-4151*	518-273-3333	86
Command Alkon Inc 1800 International Pk Dr Ste 400, Birmingham AL 35243	800-624-1872	205-879-3282	179-10
Command Ctr Inc 3901 N Schreiber Wy, Coeur D Alene ID 83815 *OTC: CCNI*	866-464-5844	208-773-7450	712
Command Plastic Corp 124 W Ave, Tallmadge OH 44278	800-321-8001	330-434-3497	541
Command Security Corp 388 Westchester Ave Ste 1J/H, Port Chester NY 10573	877-331-8056	914-937-2969	684

				Toll-Free	Phone	Class
Commander Hotel						
1401 Atlantic Ave	Ocean City	MD	21842	**888-289-6166**	410-289-6166	376
Commemorative Brands Inc						
7211 Cir S Rd	Austin	TX	78745	**800-225-3687**		628-2
Commentary Magazine						
561 7th Ave 16th Fl	New York	NY	10018	**800-829-6270**	212-891-1400	452-10
Commerce Bank & Trust Co						
386 Main St	Worcester	MA	01608	**800-698-2265**	508-797-6842	69
Commerce Corp						
7603 Energy Pkwy	Baltimore	MD	21226	**800-883-0234**	410-255-3500	426
Commerce Insurance Co						
211 Main St	Webster	MA	01570	**800-221-1605**	508-943-9000	388-4
Commercial & Architectural Products Inc						
PO Box 250	Dover	OH	44622	**800-377-1221**	330-343-6621	494
Commercial Appeal						
495 Union Ave	Memphis	TN	38103	**800-444-6397**	901-529-2345	525-2
Commercial Bank						
301 N State St PO Box 638	Alma	MI	48801	**800-547-8531**	989-463-2185	69
OTC: CEFC						
Commercial Distributing Co Inc						
46 S Broad St	Westfield	MA	01085	**800-332-8999***	413-562-9691	80-1
*Cust Svc						
Commercial Driver Training						
600 Patton Ave	West Babylon	NY	11704	**800-649-7447**	631-249-1330	788
Commercial Law League of America (CLLA)						
70 E Lake St Ste 630	Chicago	IL	60601	**800-978-2552**	312-781-2000	48-10
Commercial Lending Litigation News						
360 Hiatt Dr	Palm Beach Gardens	FL	33418	**800-621-5463**	561-622-6520	524-1
Commercial Lighting Industries						
81161 Indio Blvd	Indio	CA	92201	**800-755-0155**	760-343-2704	435
Commercial Mailing Accessories Inc						
28220 Playmor Beach Rd	Rocky Mount	MO	65072	**800-325-7303**		4
Commercial National Financial Corp						
900 Ligonier St	Latrobe	PA	15650	**800-803-2265**	724-539-3501	357-2
OTC: CNAF						
Commercial Programming Systems Inc						
4400 Coldwater Canyon Ave	Studio City	CA	91604	**888-277-4562**	323-851-2681	178
Commercial Properties Realty Trust						
402 N Fourth St	Baton Rouge	LA	70802	**800-648-9064**	225-924-7206	645
Commercial Siding & Maintenance Co, The						
8059 Crile Rd	Painesville	OH	44077	**800-229-4276**	440-352-7800	190-12
Commercial-News						
17 W N St	Danville	IL	61832	**877-732-8258**	217-446-1000	525-2
Commission Junction Inc						
530 E Montecito St	Santa Barbara	CA	93103	**800-761-1072**	805-730-8000	7
Commission on Accreditation for Dietetics Education (CADE)						
120 S Riverside Plz Ste 2000	Chicago	IL	60606	**800-877-1600**	312-899-0040	47-1
Commission on Accreditation for Law Enforcement Agencies (CALEA)						
13575 Heathcote Blvd						
Ste 320	Gainesville	VA	20155	**877-789-6904**	703-352-4225	48-7
Commission on Accreditation in Physical Therapy Education (CAPTE)						
1111 N Fairfax St	Alexandria	VA	22314	**800-999-2782**	703-706-3245	47-1
Commission on Accreditation of Allied Health Education Programs (CAAHEP)						
1361 Pk St	Clearwater	FL	33756	**800-228-2262**	727-210-2350	47-1
Commission on Accreditation of Rehabilitation Facilities International (CARF)						
6951 E Southpoint Rd	Tucson	AZ	85756	**888-281-6531**	520-325-1044	47-1
Commission on Collegiate Nursing Education						
1 Dupont Cir NW Ste 530	Washington	DC	20036	**800-441-1414**	202-887-6791	47-1
Commission on Dental Accreditation of Canada						
1815 Alta Vista Dr	Ottawa	ON	K1G3Y6	**866-521-2322**	613-523-7114	47-1
Committee for Economic Development (CED)						
2000 L St NW Ste 700	Washington	DC	20036	**800-676-7353**	202-296-5860	625
Commodity Components International Inc						
100 Summit St	Peabody	MA	01960	**800-424-7364**	978-538-0020	246
Commodity Futures Trading Commission						
3 Lafayette Ctr						
1155 21 St NW	Washington	DC	20581	**866-366-2382**	202-418-5000	338-18
Commodity Information Systems Inc						
3030 NW Expy Ste 725	Oklahoma City	OK	73112	**800-231-0477**	405-604-8726	628-9
Commodity Research Bureau						
330 S Wells St Ste 612	Chicago	IL	60606	**800-621-5271**	312-554-8456	524-9
Commonwealth Altadis Inc						
5900 N Andrews Ave						
Ste 1000	Fort Lauderdale	FL	33309	**800-446-5797***	954-772-9000	746
*Orders						
Commonwealth Biotechnologies Inc						
601 Biotech Dr	Richmond	VA	23235	**800-735-9224**	804-648-3820	414
Commonwealth Canvas Inc						
Five Perkins Way	Newburyport	MA	01950	**877-922-6827**	978-499-3900	723
Commonwealth Club of California						
595 Market St Second Fl	San Francisco	CA	94105	**800-933-7548**	415-597-6700	624
Commonwealth Credit Union						
PO Box 978	Frankfort	KY	40602	**800-228-6420**	502-564-4775	219
Commonwealth Financial Network						
29 Sawyer Rd	Waltham	MA	02453	**800-237-0081**	781-736-0700	398
Commonwealth Laminating & Coating Inc						
345 Beaver Creek Dr	Martinsville	VA	24112	**888-321-5111***	276-632-4991	690
*General						
Commonwealth Land Title Insurance Co						
601 Riverside Ave	Jacksonville	FL	32204	**888-866-3684**		388-6
Commonwealth Park Suites Hotel						
901 Bank St	Richmond	VA	23219	**888-343-7301**	804-343-7300	376
Commonwealth Telephone Co						
1 Newbury Street Suite 103	Peabody	MA	01960	**800-439-7170**	978-536-9500	726
CommScope Inc						
1100 Commscope Pl SE PO Box 339	Hickory	NC	28603	**800-982-1708**	828-324-2200	801
Communication Data Services						
1901 Bell Ave	Des Moines	IA	50315	**866-897-7987**	515-246-6837	225
Communication Technologies Inc						
14151 Newbrook Dr Ste 400	Chantilly	VA	20151	**888-266-8358**	703-961-9080	725
Communications & Power Industries Inc EIMAC Div (CPI)						
607 Hansen Way	Palo Alto	CA	94304	**800-414-8823**		253
Communications & Power Industries LLC						
607 Hansen Way	Palo Alto	CA	94303	**800-231-4818**	650-846-2900	253
Communications Daily						
2115 Ward Ct NW	Washington	DC	20037	**800-771-9202**	202-872-9200	524-11
Communications Manufacturing Co (CMC)						
2234 Colby Ave	Los Angeles	CA	90064	**800-462-5532***	310-828-3200	248
*Orders						
Communications News						
PO Box 866	Osprey	FL	34229	**800-827-9715**	941-539-7579	452-5
Communications Supply Corp (CSC)						
200 E Lies Rd	Carol Stream	IL	60188	**800-468-2121**	630-221-6400	246
Communications Supply Service Assn (CSSA)						
5700 Murray St	Little Rock	AR	72209	**800-252-2772**	501-562-7666	48-20
Communications Test Design Inc						
1339 Enterprise Dr	West Chester	PA	19380	**800-223-3910**	610-436-5203	725
CommuniGate Systems Inc						
655 Redwood Hwy Ste 275	Mill Valley	CA	94941	**800-262-4722**	415-383-7164	179-12
Communispond Inc						
12 Barns Ln	East Hampton	NY	11937	**800-529-5925**	631-907-8010	195
Community America Credit Union (CACU)						
9777 Ridge Dr	Lenexa	KS	66219	**800-892-7957**	913-905-7000	219
Community Asphalt Corp						
9675 NW 117 Ave Ste 108	Miami	FL	33178	**800-741-0806***	305-884-9444	45
*General						
Community Assns Institute (CAI)						
6402 Arlington Blvd						
Ste 500	Falls Church	VA	22042	**888-224-4321**	703-970-9220	47-7
Community Bank						
790 E Colorado Blvd	Pasadena	CA	91101	**800-788-9999**		68
Community Bank of Florida						
28801 SW 157th Ave	Homestead	FL	33033	**866-820-1533**	305-245-2211	69
Community Bank of Raymore						
PO Box 200	Raymore	MO	64083	**800-322-6772**	816-322-2100	69
Community Bank Shares of Indiana Inc						
101 W Spring St	New Albany	IN	47150	**866-944-2004**	812-944-2224	357-2
NASDAQ: YCB						
Community Bank System Inc						
5790 Widewaters Pkwy	Syracuse	NY	13214	**800-847-2911**	315-445-2282	357-2
NYSE: CBU						
Community Banking Advisory Network (CBAN)						
624 Grassmere Pk Dr Ste 15	Nashville	TN	37211	**800-231-2524**	615-373-9880	48-2
Community Blood Bank of Northwest Pennsylvania						
2646 Peach St	Erie	PA	16508	**877-842-0631**	814-456-4206	88
Community Blood Ctr						
349 S Main St	Dayton	OH	45402	**800-388-4483**	937-461-3450	88
Blue Springs Ctr						
4040 Main St	Kansas City	MO	64111	**888-647-4040**	816-753-4040	88
Community Blood Ctr Inc						
4406 W Spencer St	Appleton	WI	54914	**800-280-4102**	920-738-3131	88
Community Blood Ctr of the Ozarks						
220 W Plainview Rd	Springfield	MO	65810	**800-280-5337**	417-227-5000	88
Community Blood Services of Illinois						
1408 W University Ave	Urbana	IL	61801	**800-217-4483**	217-367-2202	88
Community Care						
218 W Sixth St	Tulsa	OK	74119	**800-278-7563**	918-594-5200	388-3
Community Coffee Co						
PO Box 2311	Baton Rouge	LA	70821	**800-688-0990**	800-884-5282	295-7
Community College of Aurora						
16000 E Centretech Pkwy	Aurora	CO	80011	**844-493-8255**	303-360-4700	160
Community College of Baltimore County						
Essex						
7201 Rossville Blvd	Baltimore	MD	21237	**877-557-2575**	410-682-6000	160
Owings Mills						
110 Painters Mill Rd	Owings Mills	MD	21117	**877-557-2575**	410-363-4111	160
Community College of Beaver County						
One Campus Dr	Monaca	PA	15061	**800-335-0222**	724-775-8561	160
Community College of Southern Nevada Planetarium & Observatory						
3200 E Cheyenne Ave	North Las Vegas	NV	89030	**800-630-7563**	702-651-4759	591
Community College of Vermont						
Bennington						
324 Main St	Bennington	VT	05201	**800-431-0025**	802-447-2361	160
Brattleboro						
70 Landmark Hill Ste 101	Brattleboro	VT	05301	**800-431-0025**	802-254-6370	160
Middlebury						
10 Merchants Row Ste 223	Middlebury	VT	05753	**800-431-0025**	802-388-3032	160
Montpelier						
PO Box 489	Montpelier	VT	05602	**800-228-6686**	802-828-4060	160
Morrisville						
197 Harrell St Ste 2	Morrisville	VT	05661	**800-431-0025**	802-888-4258	160
Newport						
100 Main St Ste 150	Newport	VT	05855	**800-431-0025**	802-334-3387	160
Rutland 60 W St	Rutland	VT	05701	**800-228-6686**	802-786-6996	160
Upper Valley						
145 Billings						
Farm Rd	White River Junction	VT	05001	**800-431-0025**	802-295-8822	160
Community Development Digest						
8204 Fenton St	Silver Spring	MD	20910	**800-666-6380**	301-588-6380	524-7
Community Development Partnership						
410 Poplar Ave						
256 W Beacon	Philadelphia	MS	39350	**877-752-2643**	601-656-1000	137
Community Electric Co-op						
52 W Windsor Blvd	Windsor	VA	23487	**855-700-2667**	757-242-6181	245
Community Food Bank of New Jersey Inc						
31 Evans Terminal	Hillside	NJ	07205	**866-527-1087**	908-355-3663	47-5
Community Foundation for Greater New Haven						
70 Audubon St	New Haven	CT	06510	**877-829-5500**	203-777-2386	302
Community Health Accreditation Program Inc (CHAP)						
1275 K St NW Ste 800	Washington	DC	20005	**800-656-9656**	202-862-3413	47-1
Community Health Charities						
200 N Glebe Rd Ste 801	Arlington	VA	22203	**800-654-0845**	703-528-1007	47-5
Community Health Ctr of Branch County (CHCBC)						
274 E Chicago St	Coldwater	MI	49036	**800-994-6610**	517-279-5400	371-3
Community Health Funding Week						
8204 Fenton St	Silver Spring	MD	20910	**800-666-6380**	301-588-6380	524-7
Community Health Systems Inc						
4000 Meridian Blvd	Franklin	TN	37067	**888-373-9600**	615-465-7000	350
NYSE: CYH						
Community Hospice						
1480 Carter Ave	Ashland	KY	41101	**800-926-6184**	606-329-1890	368
Community Hospice Inc						
4368 Spyres Way	Modesto	CA	95356	**866-645-4567**	209-578-6300	368
Community Hospice of Texas						
6100 Western Pl Ste 500	Fort Worth	TX	76107	**800-226-0373**	817-870-2795	368
Community Hospital Anderson (CHA)						
1515 N Madison Ave	Anderson	IN	46011	**800-777-7775**	765-298-4242	371-3
Community Hospital of Long Beach						
1720 Termino Ave	Long Beach	CA	90804	**800-994-6610**	562-498-1000	371-3
Community Hospital of the Monterey Peninsula (CHOMP)						
23625 Holman Hwy	Monterey	CA	93940	**888-452-4667**	831-624-5311	371-3
Community Investors Bancorp Inc						
119 S Sandusky Ave	Bucyrus	OH	44820	**800-222-4955**	419-562-7055	357-2
OTC: CIBN						
Community Medical Ctr (CMC)						
99 Hwy 37 W	Toms River	NJ	08755	**888-724-7123**	732-557-8000	371-3

	Toll-Free	Phone	Class
Community Newspaper Co Inc 72 Cherry Hill Dr .... Beverly MA 01915	800-281-6498	978-739-1300	628-8
Community of Christ 1001 W Walnut St .... Independence MO 64050	800-825-2806	816-833-1000	47-20
Community Oriented Policing Services (COPS) 1100 Vermont Ave NW 10th Fl ...... Washington DC 20530	800-421-6770	202-616-2888	338-12
Community Pharmacies LP 16 Commerce Dr Ste 1 .... Augusta ME 04332	800-730-4840		237
Community Professional Loudspeakers 333 E Fifth St .... Chester PA 19013	800-523-4934	610-876-3400	51
Community Resource Federal Credit Union 20 Wade Rd .... Latham NY 12110	888-783-2211	518-783-2211	219
Community Services Group (CSG) 320 Highland Dr PO Box 597 .... Mountville PA 17554	877-907-7970	717-285-7121	350
Community Shores Bank Corp 1030 W Norton Ave .... Muskegon MI 49441 OTC: CSHB	888-853-6633	231-780-1800	357-2
Community State Bank 208 N Ctr .... Shelbina MO 63468 *General	877-588-4121*	573-588-4101	357-2
Community Suffolk Inc 304 Second St .... Everett MA 02149	800-225-4470	617-389-5200	296-7
Community Surgical Supply Inc 1390 Rt 37 W .... Toms River NJ 08755	800-349-2990	732-349-2990	472
Community Tissue Services 3573 Bristol Pike Ste 201 .... Bensalem PA 19020	800-684-7783	215-245-4506	538
Community Title & Escrow Ltd 2600 State St Bldg D .... Alton IL 62002	800-854-4049	618-466-7755	388-6
Community Transportation Assn of America (CTAA) 1341 G St NW 10th Fl. .... Washington DC 20005	800-891-0590	202-628-1480	48-21
Community Trust Bancorp Inc 346 N Mayo Trl .... Pikeville KY 41501 NASDAQ: CTBI	800-422-1090	606-432-1414	357-2
Community Trust Bank NA 346 N Mayo Trl PO Box 2947 .... Pikeville KY 41501	800-422-1090	606-432-1414	69
Community VNA 10 Emory St .... Attleboro MA 02703	800-220-0110	508-222-0118	368
Comm-Works Holdings LLC 1405 Xenium Ln N Ste 120 .... Minneapolis MN 55441	800-853-8090	763-258-5800	252
ComNet Marketing Group Inc 1214 Stowe Ave .... Medford OR 97501	877-581-2565		196
Co-Mo Electric Co-op Inc 29868 Hwy 5 PO Box 220 .... Tipton MO 65081	800-781-0157	660-433-5521	245
Comox Valley Chamber of Commerce 2040 Cliffe Ave .... Courtenay BC V9N2L3	888-357-4471	250-334-3234	136
Compaction Technologies Inc 1171 Northland Dr Ste 121 .... Mendota Heights MN 55120	877-860-6900		193
Compak Asset Management 1801 Dove St .... Newport Beach CA 92660	800-388-9700		398
Companion Life Insurance Co 7909 Parklane Rd Ste 200 .... Columbia SC 29223	800-753-0404	803-735-1251	388-2
Companion Pets Inc (CPI) 2001 N Black Canyon Hwy .... Phoenix AZ 85009	800-646-3611	602-255-0166	571
Companion Professional Services LLC 1301 Gervais St Ste 1700 .... Columbia SC 29201	800-780-1170	803-765-1310	178
Companions & Homemakers Inc 613 New Britain Ave .... Farmington CT 06032	800-348-4663	860-677-4948	797
Compass Bancshares Inc 15 S 20th St .... Birmingham AL 35233	800-266-7277	205-297-3584	357-2
Compass Cove Ocean Resort 2311 S Ocean Blvd .... Myrtle Beach SC 29577	800-331-0934	843-448-8373	660
Compass Group North American Div (CGNAD) 2400 Yorkmont Rd .... Charlotte NC 28217	800-357-0012	704-328-4000	298
Compass Minerals International 9900 W 109th St Ste 100 .... Overland Park KS 66210 NYSE: CMP ■ *Cust Svc	866-755-1743*	913-344-9200	671
Compassion & Choices PO Box 101810 .... Denver CO 80250	800-247-7421	303-639-1202	47-17
Compassion International 12290 Voyager Pkwy .... Colorado Springs CO 80921	800-336-7676	719-487-7000	47-5
Compassionate Care Hospice 3331 St Rd Ste 410. .... Bensalem PA 19020	800-584-8165	215-245-3525	368
Compassionate Care Hospice of Delaware 702 Wilmington Ave .... Wilmington DE 19805 *General	800-219-0092*	302-993-9090	368
Compassionate Friends PO Box 3696 .... Oak Brook IL 60522	877-969-0010	630-990-0010	47-21
CompassLearning Inc 203 Colorado St .... Austin TX 78701	800-232-9556	512-478-9600	179-3
CompBenefits Corp 100 Mansell Ct E Ste 400 .... Roswell GA 30076	800-633-1262	770-552-7101	388-3
Compensation Resources Inc 310 Rt 17 N .... Upper Saddle River NJ 07458	877-934-0505	201-934-0505	195
Competition Cams Inc 3406 Democrat Rd .... Memphis TN 38118	800-999-0853	901-795-2400	59
Competitor Magazine 9477 Waples St Ste 150 .... San Diego CA 92121	800-311-1255		452-20
Compex Inc 7918 Jones Branch Dr .... Mclean VA 22102	800-279-8891	703-642-5910	177
Compex Legal Services Inc 325 S Maple Ave .... Torrance CA 90503 *Cust Svc	800-426-6739*		440
CompHealth Inc 6440 S Millrock Dr Ste 175 Ste 175 .... Salt Lake City UT 84121	800-453-3030	801-930-3000	712
Complemar Partners 500 Lee Rd Ste 200 .... Rochester NY 14606	800-388-7254	585-647-5800	548
Complete Payroll Processing Inc 7488 SR- 39 Po Box 190 .... Perry NY 14530	888-237-5800	585-237-5800	2
CompleteCampaigns.com Inc 3635 Ruffin Rd Third Fl .... San Diego CA 92123	888-217-9600		384
Complex Steel & Wire Corp 36254 Annapolis Rd .... Wayne MI 48184	800-521-0666	734-326-1600	306
Compmanagement Inc PO Box 884 .... Dublin OH 43017	800-825-6755	614-376-5300	458
Component Enterprises Co Inc 235 E Penn St PO Box 189 .... Norristown PA 19401	877-232-7253		802
Component Hardware Group Inc 1890 Swarthmore Ave .... Lakewood NJ 08701	800-526-3694	732-363-4700	347
ComponentOne LLC 201 S Highland Ave Third Fl 3rd Fl .... Pittsburgh PA 15206	800-858-2739	412-681-4343	179-12
Comporium Communications 332 E Main St .... Rock Hill SC 29730	866-922-5922	888-403-2667	726
Composite Panel Assn 19465 Deerfield Ave Ste 306 .... Leesburg VA 20176	866-426-6767	703-724-1128	48-3
Composition Materials Company Inc 249 Pepes Farm Rd .... Milford CT 06460	800-262-7763	203-874-6500	1
Comprehensive Care Management Corp (CCM) 1250 Waters Pl Tower 1 Ste 602 .... Bronx NY 10461	877-226-8500		445
Comprehensive EAP 5 Militia Dr .... Lexington MA 02421	800-344-1011		457
Comprehensive Health Services Inc (CHSI) 10701 Parkridge Blvd Ste 200 .... Reston VA 20191	800-638-8083	703-760-0700	388-3
Comprehensive Pharmacy Services Inc (CPS) 6409 N Quail Hollow Rd .... Memphis TN 38120	800-968-6962	901-748-0470	195
Comprehensive Tissue Ctr 11402 University Ave Rm 7415 .... Edmonton AB T6G2J3	866-407-1970	780-407-7510	538
Comprehensive Traffic Systems Inc 4860 Robb St Ste 205. .... Wheat Ridge CO 80033	888-353-9002	303-432-3777	175
Compressed Air Systems Inc 9303 Stannum St .... Tampa FL 33619	800-626-8177	813-626-8177	173
Compressor Engineering Corp (CECO) 5440 Alder Dr .... Houston TX 77081	800-879-2326	713-664-7333	173
Compressor Products International 4410 Greenbriar Dr .... Stafford TX 77477	800-675-6646	281-207-4600	127
ComPsych Corp 455 N City Front Plaza Dr NBC Tower 13th Fl .... Chicago IL 60611	800-851-1714	312-595-4000	457
Comptroller of the Currency 250 E St SW .... Washington DC 20219 *Cust Svc	800-613-6743*	202-874-5000	338-16
CompuCom Systems Inc 7171 Forest Ln .... Dallas TX 75230 *Cust Svc	800-597-0555*	972-856-3600	177
Compulink Inc 1205 Gandy Blvd N .... Saint Petersburg FL 33702	800-231-6685	727-579-1500	801
CompuMed Inc 5777 W Century Blvd Ste 360. .... Los Angeles CA 90045	800-421-3395	310-258-5000	416
Compunetix Inc 2420 Mosside Blvd .... Monroeville PA 15146	800-879-4266	412-373-8110	725
Compunnel Software Group Inc 103 Morgan Ln Suite 102 .... Plainsboro NJ 08536	800-696-8128		712
Compusearch Software Systems Inc 21251 Ridgetop Cir .... Dulles VA 20166	855-817-2720	703-481-3699	178
Computer Aid Inc (CAI) 1390 Ridgeview Dr .... Allentown PA 18104	877-432-7228	610-530-5000	178
Computer Aided Technology Inc 165 N Arlington Heights Rd Ste 101 .... Buffalo Grove IL 60089	888-308-2284		175
Computer Analytical Systems Inc (CASI) 1418 S Third St .... Louisville KY 40208	800-977-3475	502-635-2019	181
Computer Connection of Central New York Inc 11206 Cosby Manor Rd .... Utica NY 13502	800-566-4786	315-724-2209	175
Computer Consultants Inc (CCI) 43252 Woodward Ave Ste 240 .... Bloomfield Hills MI 48302	800-693-1066	248-858-7701	225
Computer Credit Inc 640 W Fourth St .... Winston-Salem NC 27101	800-942-2995	336-761-1524	158
Computer Dynamics Inc 3030 Whitehall Pk Dr .... Charlotte NC 28273	866-599-6512		175
Computer Economics Report, The 2082 Business Ctr Dr Ste 240 .... Irvine CA 92612	800-326-8100	949-831-8700	524-3
Computer Explorers 12715 Telge Rd .... Cypress TX 77429	800-531-5053		146
Computer Guidance Corp 15035 N 75th St .... Scottsdale AZ 85260	888-361-4551	480-444-7000	178
Computer Magazine 10662 Los Vaqueros Cir .... Los Alamitos CA 90720 *Orders	800-272-6657*	714-821-8380	452-7
Computer Measurement Group (CMG) 151 Fries Mill Rd Ste 104 .... Turnersville NJ 08012	800-436-7264	856-401-1700	47-9
Computer Programs & Systems Inc (CPSI) 6600 Wall St .... Mobile AL 36695 NASDAQ: CPSI	800-711-2774	251-639-8100	38
Computer Sciences Corp 2100 E Grand Ave .... El Segundo CA 90245 NYSE: CSC	866-310-0950	310-615-0311	181
Computer Services Inc 3901 Technology Dr .... Paducah KY 42001 OTC: CSVI	800-545-4274	270-442-7361	225
Computer Task Group Inc (CTG) 800 Delaware Ave .... Buffalo NY 14209 OTC: CTG	800-992-5350	716-882-8000	181
Computer Technology Law Report 1801 S Bell St .... Arlington VA 22202	800-372-1033		524-7
Computer Troubleshooters USA 755 Commerce Dr Ste 605 .... Decatur GA 30030	877-704-1702	404-477-1302	309
ComputerJobs.com Inc 1995 N Pk Pl SE .... Atlanta GA 30339	800-850-0045	770-850-0045	260
ComputerPlus Sales & Service Inc Five Northway Ct .... Greer SC 29651	800-849-4426		176
Computers in Libraries Magazine 143 Old Marlton Pk .... Medford NJ 08055	800-300-9868	609-654-6266	452-7
Computers Unlimited 2407 Montana Ave .... Billings MT 59101	800-763-0308	406-255-9500	179-10
Computershare Plans Software Two Enterprise Dr .... Shelton CT 06484	888-340-4267	203-944-7300	179-1
Computerwise Inc 302 N Winchester Ln .... Olathe KS 66062	800-255-3739	913-829-0600	174-7
Computerworld Magazine One Speen St .... Framingham MA 01701	800-343-6474	508-879-0700	452-7
Computrition Inc 19808 Nordhoff Pl .... Chatsworth CA 91311	800-222-4488		178
Compuware Corp One Campus Martius St .... Detroit MI 48226 NASDAQ: CPWR	800-292-7432	313-227-7300	179-1
Compuware Corp Professional Services Div 7760 France Ave S Ste 430. .... Bloomington MN 55435	800-288-8974	612-851-2200	712
comScore Inc 11950 Democracy Dr # 600 .... Reston VA 20190	866-276-6972	703-438-2000	461
Comstar Enterprises Inc PO Box 6698 .... Springdale AR 72766	800-533-2343	479-361-2111	47-11
ComStar Networks LLC 1820 NE Jensen Beach Blvd Ste 564 .... Jensen Beach FL 34957	800-516-1595		196

Name / Address	City	State	ZIP	Toll-Free	Phone	Class
Comstock Resources Inc						
5300 Town & Country Blvd Ste 500	Frisco	TX	75034	**800-877-1322**	972-668-8800	529
NYSE: CRK						
Comstor Inc						
14850 Conference Ctr Dr Ste 200	Chantilly	VA	20151	**800-955-9590**	703-345-5100	175
Comstor Productivity Ctr Inc						
2219 N Dickey Rd	Spokane	WA	99212	**800-776-2451**	509-534-5080	491
ComTech21						
One Barnes Park S	Wallingford	CT	06492	**877-312-5564**		384
Comtel Corp						
39810 Grand River Ave Ste 180	Novi	MI	48375	**800-335-2505**	248-888-4730	246
Comtrol Corp						
6655 Wedgewood Rd Ste 120	Maple Grove	MN	55311	**800-926-6876**	763-494-4100	177
Con Cast Pipe LP						
299 Brock Rd S RR#3	Guelph	ON	N1H6H9	**800-668-7473**		184
Con Forms						
777 Maritime Dr	Port Washington	WI	53074	**800-223-3676**	262-284-7800	184
ConAgra Foods Inc						
One ConAgra Dr	Omaha	NE	68102	**877-266-2472**	402-240-4000	357-3
NYSE: CAG						
ConAgra Foods Retail Products Co Deli Foods Group						
215 W Field Rd	Naperville	IL	60563	**877-266-2472**	630-857-1000	468
Conair Corp						
One Cummings Pt Rd	Stamford	CT	06902	**800-326-6247**	203-351-9000	36
OTC: CNGA						
Conant Auto Retail Group						
18900 Studebaker Rd	Cerritos	CA	90703	**888-318-5001**		56
Conax Buffalo Technologies LLC						
2300 Walden Ave	Buffalo	NY	14225	**800-223-2389**	716-684-4500	202
Concentra Inc						
5080 Spectrum Dr Ste 1200 W	Addison	TX	75001	**866-944-6046**		458
Concentrix Corp						
3750 Monroe Ave	Pittsford	NY	14534	**800-747-0583**	585-218-5300	112
Concept Boats Corp						
2410 NW 147th St	Opa Locka	FL	33054	**888-635-8712**	305-635-8712	89
Concepts In Data Management Inc						
205 Oxford St E	London	ON	N6A5G6	**800-668-8768**		180
Concepts NREC						
217 Billings Farm Rd	White River Junction	VT	05001	**888-299-8057**	802-296-2321	261
Concern America						
2015 N Broadway	Santa Ana	CA	92706	**800-266-2376**	714-953-8575	47-5
Concerned United Birthparents Inc (CUB)						
PO Box 503475	San Diego	CA	92150	**800-822-2777**		47-21
Concerns of Police Survivors Inc (COPS)						
846 Old S 5 PO Box 3199	Camdenton	MO	65020	**800-784-2677**	573-346-4911	47-21
Conch House Heritage Inn						
625 Truman Ave	Key West	FL	33040	**800-207-5806**	305-293-0020	376
Conch House Marina Resort						
57 Comares Ave	Saint Augustine	FL	32080	**800-940-6256**	904-829-8646	376
Conch House Restaurant						
57 Comares Ave Conch House Marina Resort	Saint Augustine	FL	32080	**800-940-6256**	904-829-8646	662
Concord Coalition						
1011 Arlington Blvd Ste 300	Arlington	VA	22209	**888-333-4248**	703-894-6222	47-7
Concord Confections Ltd						
345 Courtland Ave	Concord	ON	L4K5A6	**800-267-0037**	905-660-8989	295-6
Concord Group Insurance Cos						
Four Bouton St	Concord	NH	03301	**800-852-3380**		388-4
Concord Litho Group						
92 Old Tpke Rd	Concord	NH	03301	**800-258-3662**	603-225-3328	619
Concord Mills						
8111 Concord Mills Blvd	Concord	NC	28027	**877-789-2327**	704-979-3000	455
Concord University						
PO Box 1000	Athens	WV	24712	**800-344-6679**	304-384-3115	166
Concorde Career Colleges						
5800 Foxridge Dr Ste 500	Mission	KS	66202	**800-693-7010**	913-831-9977	788
Concorde Career Colleges Inc						
San Bernardino						
201 E Airport Dr	San Bernardino	CA	92408	**800-852-8434**	909-884-8891	788
Concorde Career Colleges inc Miramar						
10933 Marks Way	Miramar	FL	33025	**800-693-7010**	954-731-8880	788
Concordia College						
901 Eigth St S	Moorhead	MN	56562	**800-699-9897**	218-299-4000	166
Concordia College New York						
171 White Plains Rd	Bronxville	NY	10708	**800-937-2655***	914-337-9300	166
*Admissions						
Concordia Electric Co-op Inc						
1865 Hwy 84 W PO Box 98	Jonesville	LA	71343	**800-617-6282**	318-339-7969	245
Concordia Hospital						
1095 Concordia Ave	Winnipeg	MB	R2K3S8	**888-315-9257**	204-667-1560	371-2
Concordia Publishing House Inc						
3558 S Jefferson Ave	Saint Louis	MO	63118	**800-325-3040***	314-268-1000	628-3
*Cust Svc						
Concordia Seminary						
801 Seminary Pl	Saint Louis	MO	63105	**800-822-9545**	314-505-7000	167-3
Concordia Theological Seminary						
6600 N Clinton St	Fort Wayne	IN	46825	**800-481-2155**	260-452-2100	167-3
Concordia University Ann Arbor						
4090 Geddes Rd	Ann Arbor	MI	48105	**888-282-2338**	734-995-7322	166
Concordia University Austin						
3400 IH-35 N	Austin	TX	78705	**800-865-4282**	512-486-2000	166
Concordia University Chicago						
7400 Augusta St	River Forest	IL	60305	**888-258-6773**	708-771-8300	166
Concordia University College of Alberta						
7128 Ada Blvd NW	Edmonton	AB	T5B4E4	**866-479-5200**	780-479-9220	773
Concordia University Irvine						
1530 Concordia W	Irvine	CA	92612	**800-229-1200**	949-854-8002	166
Concordia University Nebraska						
800 N Columbia Ave	Seward	NE	68434	**800-535-5494**	402-643-3651	166
Concordia University Portland						
2811 NE Holman St	Portland	OR	97211	**800-321-9371**	503-288-9371	166
Concordia University Wisconsin						
12800 N Lake Shore Dr	Mequon	WI	53097	**888-628-9472***	262-243-5700	166
*Admissions						
Concurrent						
4375 River Green Pkwy Ste 100	Duluth	GA	30096	**877-978-7363**	678-258-4000	179-8
NASDAQ: CCUR						
Conde Group Inc						
4141 Jutland Dr Ste 130	San Diego	CA	92117	**800-838-0819**		197
Conde Nast Publications Inc						
Four Times Sq	New York	NY	10036	**800-897-8666**	212-286-2860	628-9
Condo Control Central						
First Canadian Pl 100 King St W Ste 5700	Toronto	ON	M5X1C7	**888-762-6636**		224
Condon Oil Co						
126 E Jackson St	Ripon	WI	54971	**800-452-1212**	920-748-3186	572
Condor Earth Technologies Inc						
PO Box 3905	Sonora	CA	95370	**800-800-0490**	209-532-0361	195
Conductix 10102 F St	Omaha	NE	68127	**800-521-4888**	402-339-9300	116
Conduit Pipe Products Co						
1501 W Main St	West Jefferson	OH	43162	**800-848-6125**	614-879-9114	803
Condusiv Technologies						
7590 N Glenoaks Blvd	Burbank	CA	91504	**800-829-6468***	818-771-1600	179-12
*Sales						
Cone Denim LLC						
804 Green Valley Rd Ste 300	Greensboro	NC	27408	**800-763-0123**	336-379-6220	734-1
Cone Drive Operations Inc - A Textron Co						
240 E 12th St	Traverse City	MI	49685	**888-994-2663***	231-946-8410	700
*Sales						
Conergy Inc						
2460 W 26th Ave Ste 280C	Denver	CO	80211	**888-396-6611**		775
Conestoga Valley School District						
2110 Horseshoe Rd	Lancaster	PA	17601	**800-732-0025**	717-397-2421	676
Conestoga Wood Specialties Inc						
245 Reading Rd	East Earl	PA	17519	**800-964-3667**		114
Conexant Systems Inc						
1901 Main St Ste 300	Irvine	CA	92614	**888-855-4562**	949-483-4600	687
Confer Plastics Inc (CPI)						
97 Witmer Rd	North Tonawanda	NY	14120	**800-635-3213**	716-693-2056	597
Conference & Travel						
5655 Coventry Ln	Fort Wayne	IN	46804	**800-346-9807**	260-434-6600	185
Conference & Visitors Bureau of Montgomery County MD Inc						
111 Rockville Pk Ste 800	Rockville	MD	20850	**877-789-6904**	240-777-2060	207
Conference Ctr at NorthPointe						
100 Green Meadows Dr S	Lewis Center	OH	43035	**866-233-9393**	614-880-4300	374
Conference of State Bank Supervisors (CSBS)						
1129 20th St NW Fifth Fl	Washington	DC	20036	**800-886-2727**	202-296-2840	48-7
Conference on College Composition & Communication (CCCC)						
1111 W Kenyon Rd	Urbana	IL	61801	**877-369-6283**	217-328-3870	48-5
Confident Care Corp						
Three University Plz Dr	Hackensack	NJ	07601	**866-839-2273**	201-498-9400	360
Confluence Watersports Co						
575 Mauldin Rd Ste 200	Greenville	SC	29607	**800-595-2925**		701
Conforma Laboratories Inc						
4705 Colley Ave	Norfolk	VA	23508	**800-426-1700**	757-321-0200	535
Congoleum Corp						
3500 Quakerridge Rd PO Box 3127	Mercerville	NJ	08619	**800-274-3266**	609-584-3000	291
Congress Daily						
600 New Hampshire Ave The Watergate	Washington	DC	20037	**800-424-2921**	202-266-7000	524-7
Congress Plaza Hotel & Convention Ctr						
520 S Michigan Ave	Chicago	IL	60605	**800-635-1666**	312-427-3800	376
Congress Watch						
215 Pennsylvania Ave SE	Washington	DC	20003	**800-289-3787**	202-546-4996	47-7
Congressional Quarterly Budget Tracker						
77 K St NE	Washington	DC	20002	**800-432-2250**	202-650-6500	524-7
Congressional Quarterly HealthBeat						
77 K St NE	Washington	DC	20002	**800-432-2250**	202-650-6500	524-7
Congressional Quarterly House Action Reports						
77 K St NE	Washington	DC	20002	**800-432-2250**	202-650-6500	524-7
Conifer Park						
79 Glenridge Rd	Schenectady	NY	12302	**800-989-6446**	518-399-6446	717
CONIX Systems Inc						
7252 Main St	Manchester Center	VT	05255	**800-332-1899**		178
Conklin Company Inc						
551 Valley Pk Dr	Shakopee	MN	55379	**800-888-8838**	952-445-6010	363
Conley Transport Ii Inc						
2104 Eastline Rd	Searcy	AR	72143	**800-338-8700**	501-268-4672	444
Conlin Travel Inc						
3270 Washtenaw Ave	Ann Arbor	MI	48104	**800-426-6546**	734-677-0900	761
Conmed Corp						
525 French Rd	Utica	NY	13502	**800-448-6506**	315-797-8375	471
NASDAQ: CNMD						
ConMed Endoscopic Technologie						
525 French Rd	Utica	NY	13502	**800-225-1332**	315-797-8375	471
CONMED Linvatec						
11311 Concept Blvd	Largo	FL	33773	**800-448-6506***	727-392-6464	471
*Cust Svc						
Conn's Inc						
3295 College St	Beaumont	TX	77701	**800-511-5750***	409-832-1696	34
NASDAQ: CONN ■ *Cust Svc						
Conneaut Savings Bank						
305 Main St PO Box 740	Conneaut	OH	44030	**888-453-2311**	440-599-8121	69
Connect America LLC						
2193 W Chester Pk	Broomall	PA	19008	**800-654-6100**		470
Connect PR						
One Market St 36th Fl	San Francisco	CA	94105	**800-455-8855**	415-222-9691	627
ConnectiCare Inc						
175 Scott Swamp Rd	Farmington	CT	06032	**800-251-7722***	860-674-5700	388-3
*Cust Svc						
Connecticut						
Banking Dept						
260 Constitution Plaza	Hartford	CT	06103	**800-831-7225**	860-240-8299	337-7
Chief Medical Examiner						
11 Shuttle Rd	Farmington	CT	06032	**800-842-1508**	860-679-3980	337-7
Consumer Protection Dept						
165 Capitol Ave	Hartford	CT	06106	**800-842-2649**	860-713-6100	337-7
Emergency Management and Homeland Security Div						
25 Sigourney St 6th Fl	Hartford	CT	06106	**800-397-8876**	860-256-0800	337-7
Higher Education Dept						
61 Woodland St	Hartford	CT	06105	**800-842-0229**	860-947-1800	337-7
Public Utility Control Dept						
10 Franklin Sq	New Britain	CT	06051	**800-382-4586**	860-827-2935	337-7
Rehabilitation Services Bureau						
25 Sigourney St 11th Fl	Hartford	CT	06106	**800-537-2549**	860-424-4844	337-7
State Parks Div						
79 Elm St	Hartford	CT	06106	**866-287-2757**	860-424-3000	337-7
Veterans Affairs Dept						
287 W St	Rocky Hill	CT	06067	**800-447-0961**	860-721-5891	337-7
Victim Services Office						
225 Spring St 4th Fl	Wethersfield	CT	06109	**800-822-8428**		337-7
Workers' Compensation Commission						
21 Oak St 4th Fl	Hartford	CT	06106	**800-223-9675**	860-493-1500	337-7

Name / Address	City	State	ZIP	Toll-Free	Phone	Class
Connecticut Assn of Realtors						
111 Founders Plz Ste 1101	East Hartford	CT	06108	**800-335-4862**	860-290-6601	647
Connecticut College						
270 Mohegan Ave	New London	CT	06320	**800-892-3363**	860-439-2000	166
Connecticut Innovations Inc						
865 Brook St Third Fl	Rocky Hill	CT	06067	**800-733-4763**	860-563-5851	780
Connecticut Laminating Company Inc						
162 James St	New Haven	CT	06513	**800-753-9119**	203-787-2184	592
Connecticut Light & Power Co						
107 Selden St	Berlin	CT	06037	**800-286-2000***	860-665-5000	775
*Cust Svc						
Connecticut Magazine						
35 Nutmeg Dr	Trumbull	CT	06611	**800-645-4328**	203-380-6600	452-22
Connecticut Medicine Magazine						
160 St Ronan St	New Haven	CT	06511	**800-842-8440**	203-865-0587	452-16
Connecticut Post						
410 State St	Bridgeport	CT	06604	**800-293-0795***	203-333-0161	525-2
*Edit						
Connecticut Public Broadcasting Inc (CPBI)						
1049 Asylum Ave	Hartford	CT	06105	**800-683-2112**	860-278-5310	624
Connecticut Real Estate & Professional Trades Div						
Dept of Consumer Protection						
165 Capitol Ave	Hartford	CT	06106	**800-842-2649**	860-713-6100	337-7
Connecticut State Library						
231 Capitol Ave	Hartford	CT	06106	**866-886-4478**	860-757-6510	431-5
Connecticut State Medical Society						
160 St Ronan St	New Haven	CT	06511	**800-406-1527**	203-865-0587	469
Connecticut Sun						
1 Mohegan Sun Blvd	Uncasville	CT	06382	**877-329-9622**	860-862-4000	705-2
Connecticut Valley Arms (CVA)						
1685 Boggs Rd Ste 300	Duluth	GA	30096	**800-320-8767**	770-449-4687	284
Connecticut Valley Railroad State Park						
1 Railroad Ave PO Box 452	Essex	CT	06426	**866-526-2014**	860-767-0103	558
Connecticut Water Service Inc						
93 W Main St	Clinton	CT	06413	**800-286-5700**	860-669-8636	357-5
NASDAQ: CTWS						
Connecticut Weights & Measures Div						
Dept of Consumer Protection						
165 Capitol Ave	Hartford	CT	06106	**800-842-2649**	860-713-6100	337-7
Connecting Businessmen to Christ (CBMC)						
5746 Marlin Rd						
Ste 602 Osborne Ctr	Chattanooga	TN	37411	**800-566-2262**	423-698-4444	47-20
Connecting Generations						
100 W Tenth St Ste 1115	Wilmington	DE	19801	**877-202-9050**	302-656-2122	47-6
Connection, The						
11351 Rupp Dr	Burnsville	MN	55337	**800-883-5777***	952-948-5488	727
*Sales						
Connectria Corp						
10845 Olive Blvd Ste 300	Saint Louis	MO	63141	**800-781-7820**	314-587-7000	38
ConnectWise Inc						
4110 George Rd Ste 200	Tampa	FL	33634	**800-671-6898**	813-463-4700	180
Connell Bros Co Ltd						
345 California St 27th Fl	San Francisco	CA	94104	**800-210-9839**	415-772-4000	144
Connell Realty & Development Co						
200 Connell Dr	Berkeley Heights	NJ	07922	**800-233-3240**	908-673-3700	644
Connell's Map Lee Flowers & Gifts						
2408 E Main St	Bexley	OH	43209	**800-790-8980**	614-237-8653	292
Conner Prairie Living History Museum						
13400 Allisonville Rd	Fishers	IN	46038	**800-966-1836**	317-776-6000	513
Connexus Energy Co-op						
14601 Ramsey Blvd	Ramsey	MN	55303	**877-382-4357**	763-323-2650	245
Connors State College						
1000 College Rd	Warner	OK	74469	**888-594-5171**	918-463-2931	160
Conolog Corp						
Five Columbia Rd	Somerville	NJ	08876	**800-526-3984**	908-722-8081	638
OTC: CNLG						
Conoptics International Sales Corp						
19 Eagle Rd	Danbury	CT	06810	**800-748-3349**	203-743-3349	537
Conrac Inc						
5124 Commerce Dr	Baldwin Park	CA	91706	**800-451-5288**	626-480-0095	174-4
Conrad Forest Products						
68765 Wildwood Dr	North Bend	OR	97459	**800-356-7146**		805
Conrad Miami						
1395 Brickell Ave	Miami	FL	33131	**800-002-6672**	305-503-6500	376
Conrad-American Inc						
PO Box 2000	Houghton	IA	52631	**800-553-1791***		273
*General						
Conroe Regional Medical Ctr						
504 Medical Ctr Blvd	Conroe	TX	77304	**888-633-2687**	936-539-1111	371-3
Conseco Annuity Assurance Co						
11825 N Pennsylvania St	Carmel	IN	46032	**866-595-2255**		388-2
Conseco Health Insurance Co						
11825 N Pennsylvania St	Carmel	IN	46032	**866-595-2255**		388-2
Conseco Inc						
11825 N Pennsylvania St	Carmel	IN	46032	**866-595-2255**	317-817-3012	357-4
NYSE: CNO						
Conseco Senior Health Insurance Co						
11825 N Pennsylvania St						
PO Box 1980	Carmel	IN	46032	**866-595-2255**		388-2
Conservation Fund						
1655 N Fort Myer Dr Ste 1300	Arlington	VA	22209	**800-672-5839**	703-525-6300	47-13
Conservation International (CI)						
2011 Crystal Dr Ste 500	Arlington	VA	22202	**800-406-2306**	703-341-2400	47-13
CONSOL Energy Inc						
1000 Consol Energy Dr	Canonsburg	PA	15317	**800-544-8024**	724-485-4000	357-3
NYSE: CNX						
Consolidated Beverages Inc						
12 St Mark St	Auburn	MA	01501	**800-922-8128**	508-832-5311	80-1
Consolidated Casting Corp						
1501 S I-45	Hutchins	TX	75141	**800-649-5289**	972-225-7305	305
Consolidated Catfish Cos LLC						
299 S St PO Box 271	Isola	MS	38754	**800-228-3474**	662-962-3101	295-14
Consolidated Container Co (CCC)						
3101 Towercreek Pkwy Ste 300	Atlanta	GA	30339	**888-831-2184***	678-742-4600	541
*Sales						
Consolidated Devices Inc (CDI)						
19220 San Jose Ave	City of Industry	CA	91748	**800-525-6319**	626-965-0668	748
Consolidated Disposal Services Inc						
12949 Telegraph Rd	Santa Fe Springs	CA	90670	**800-299-4898**		792
Consolidated Edison Inc						
Four Irving Pl	New York	NY	10003	**800-752-6633**	212-460-4600	357-5
NYSE: ED						
Consolidated Electric Co-op						
3940 E Liberty St	Mexico	MO	65265	**800-621-0091**	573-581-3630	245

Name / Address	City	State	ZIP	Toll-Free	Phone	Class
Consolidated Electronic Wire & Cable Co						
11044 King St	Franklin Park	IL	60131	**800-621-4278**	847-455-8830	801
Consolidated Energy Co						
910 Main St PO Box 317	Jesup	IA	50648	**800-338-3021**	319-827-1211	572
Consolidated Fibers						
8100 S Blvd	Charlotte	NC	28273	**800-243-8621**		598-1
Consolidated Graphics Group Inc						
1614 E 40th St	Cleveland	OH	44103	**888-884-9191***	216-881-9191	619
*General						
Consolidated Metco Inc						
13940 N Rivergate Blvd	Portland	OR	97203	**800-547-9473***		59
*Sales						
Consolidated Pipe & Supply Inc						
1205 Hilltop Pkwy	Birmingham	AL	35204	**800-467-7261***	205-323-7261	487
*Sales						
Consolidated Publishing Co						
PO Box 189	Anniston	AL	36202	**866-814-9253**	256-236-1551	628-8
Consolidated Rail Corp						
1717 Arch St Ste 3210	Philadelphia	PA	19103	**800-272-0911**	215-209-2000	639
Consolidated Shoe Company Inc						
22290 Timberlake Rd	Lynchburg	VA	24502	**800-368-7463**	434-239-0391	300
Consolidated Steel Services Inc						
632 Glendale Vly Blvd	Fallentimber	PA	16639	**800-237-8783**	814-944-5890	487
Consolidated Storage Cos						
225 Main St	Tatamy	PA	18085	**800-323-0801***	610-253-2775	286
*Cust Svc						
Consolidated Supply Co						
7337 SW Kable Ln	Tigard	OR	97224	**800-929-5810**	503-620-7050	605
Consolidated Systems Inc						
650 Rosewood Dr	Columbia	SC	29202	**800-654-1912**		688
Consortium for School Networking (CoSN)						
1025 Vermont Ave NW Ste 1010	Washington	DC	20005	**866-267-8747**	202-861-2676	47-9
Constantine's Wood Ctr						
1040 E Oakland Pk Blvd	Fort Lauderdale	FL	33334	**800-443-9667**	954-561-1716	606
Constellation Brands Inc						
207 High Pt Dr Bldg 100	Victor	NY	14564	**888-724-2169**		80-3
NYSE: STZ						
Constellation Technology Corp						
7887 Bryan Dairy Rd Ste 100	Largo	FL	33777	**800-335-7355**	727-547-0600	218
Constitutional Rights Foundation						
601 S Kingsley Dr	Los Angeles	CA	90005	**800-488-4273**	213-487-5590	47-7
Construction Claims Monthly						
2222 Sedwick Dr	Durham	NC	27713	**800-223-8720**		524-13
Construction Financial Management Assn (CFMA)						
100 Village Blvd Ste 200A	Princeton	NJ	08540	**877-462-7827**	609-452-8000	48-1
Construction Labor Report						
1801 S Bell St	Arlington	VA	22202	**800-372-1033**		524-13
Construction Products Inc						
1631 Ashport Rd	Jackson	TN	38305	**800-238-8226**	731-668-7305	184
Construction Software Technologies Inc						
4500 W Lake Forest Drive						
Ste 502	Cincinnati	OH	45242	**800-364-2059**	513-645-8004	179-10
Construction Specialties Inc						
Three Werner Way	Lebanon	NJ	08833	**800-972-7214**	908-236-0800	486
Construction Systems Software Inc						
494 Covered Bridge	Schertz	TX	78154	**800-531-1035**	210-979-6494	179-10
Construction Testing & Engineering Inc						
1441 Montiel Road Ste 115	Escondido	CA	92026	**800-576-2271**	760-746-4955	732
Construx Software						
11820 Northup Way Ste E-200	Bellevue	WA	98005	**866-296-6300**	425-636-0100	178
Consultnet LLC						
10813 S River Front Pkwy						
Ste 150	South Jordan	UT	84095	**888-215-9675**	801-208-3700	712
Consumer Bankruptcy News						
360 Hiatt Dr	Palm Beach Gardens	FL	33418	**800-621-5463**	561-622-6520	524-1
Consumer Federation of America (CFA)						
1620 I St NW Ste 200	Washington	DC	20006	**877-382-4357**	202-387-6121	47-10
Consumer Financial Services Law Report						
360 Hiatt Dr	Palm Beach Gardens	FL	33418	**800-621-5463**	561-622-6520	524-7
Consumer Product Safety Commission (CPSC)						
4340 E W Hwy Ste 502	Bethesda	MD	20814	**800-638-2772**	301-504-7923	338-18
Consumer Reports Magazine						
101 Truman Ave	Yonkers	NY	10703	**800-333-0663***	914-378-2000	452-11
*Orders						
Consumer Reports On Health						
101 Truman Ave	Yonkers	NY	10703	**800-234-1645**	914-378-2000	524-8
Consumers Energy						
2074 242nd St	Marshalltown	IA	50158	**800-696-6552**	641-752-1593	245
Consumers Energy Co						
One Energy Plz	Jackson	MI	49201	**800-477-5050***	517-788-0550	775
*Cust Svc						
Consumers Pipe & Supply Co						
5832 E 61st St	Los Angeles	CA	90040	**800-338-7473**	323-685-6870	487
Consumers Power Inc (CPI)						
6990 W Hills Rd PO Box 1180	Philomath	OR	97370	**800-872-9036**	541-929-3124	245
Consumers Union of US Inc						
101 Truman Ave	Yonkers	NY	10703	**800-927-4357**	914-378-2000	628-9
Consumers' Research Council of America (CRCA)						
2020 Pennsylvania Ave NW						
Ste 300-A	Washington	DC	20006	**800-675-5376**	202-835-9698	47-10
Contact Industries Inc						
9200 SE Sunnybrook Blvd						
Ste 200	Clackamas	OR	97015	**800-547-1038**	503-228-7361	494
Contact Lens Manufacturers Assn						
PO Box 29398	Lincoln	NE	68529	**800-344-9060**	402-465-4122	48-4
Container Research Corp (CRC)						
1 Hollow Hill Rd	Glen Riddle	PA	19037	**844-220-9574**	610-459-2160	199
Container Store, The						
500 Freeport Pkwy	Coppell	TX	75019	**800-733-3532**	972-538-6000	359
ContainerWorld Forwarding Services Inc						
16133 Blundell Rd	Richmond	BC	V6W0A3	**877-838-8880**	604-276-1300	310
Contech Construction Products Inc						
9025 Centre Pt Dr Ste 400	West Chester	OH	45069	**800-338-1122**	513-645-7000	688
Con-Tech Lighting						
2783 Shermer Rd	Northbrook	IL	60062	**800-728-0312**	847-559-5500	435
Contemporary Arts Ctr						
900 Camp St	New Orleans	LA	70130	**800-568-6968**	504-528-3805	565
Contemporary Tours						
1400 Old Country Rd Ste 100	Westbury	NY	11590	**800-627-8873**	516-484-5032	750
Conterra Ultra Broadband LLC						
2101 Rexford Rd Ste 200E	Charlotte	NC	28211	**800-634-1374**	704-936-1800	643
Contiki Holidays						
801 E Katella Ave 3rd Fl	Anaheim	CA	92805	**800-944-5708**	714-935-0808	750

				Toll-Free	Phone	Class
Continental Airlines Inc						
900 Grand Plz Dr	Houston	TX	77067	**800-621-7467**	713-952-1630	26
Continental Assurance Co						
333 S Wabash Ave	Chicago	IL	60604	**800-251-2148**	312-822-5000	388-2
Continental Battery Corp						
4919 Woodall St	Dallas	TX	75247	**800-442-0081**	214-631-5701	73
Continental Binder & Specialty Corp						
407 W Compton Blvd	Gardena	CA	90248	**800-872-2897**	310-324-8227	85
Continental Cast Stone Manufacturing Inc						
22001 W 83rd St	Shawnee	KS	66227	**800-989-7866**		715
Continental Casualty Co						
333 S Wabash Ave	Chicago	IL	60685	**800-303-9744**	312-822-5000	388-4
Continental Cement Company LLC						
14755 N Outer 40 Ste 514	Chesterfield	MO	63017	**800-625-1144**	636-532-7440	134
Continental Coin Corp						
5627 Sepulveda Blvd	Van Nuys	CA	91411	**800-552-6467**	818-781-4232	408
Continental Concession Supplies Inc						
575 Jericho Turnpike Ste 300	Jericho	NY	11753	**800-516-0090**	516-739-8777	296-3
Continental Electric Motors Inc						
23 Sebago St	Clifton	NJ	07013	**800-335-6718**		511
Continental Electronics Corp						
4212 S Buckner Blvd	Dallas	TX	75227	**800-733-5011**	214-381-7161	638
Continental Fire Sprinkler Co						
4518 S 133rd St	Omaha	NE	68137	**800-543-5170**	402-330-5170	603
Continental Graphics Corp						
4060 N Lakewood Blvd						
Bldg 801 5th Fl	Long Beach	CA	90808	**800-862-5691**	714-503-4200	225
Continental Linen Services						
4200 Manchester Rd	Kalamazoo	MI	49001	**800-878-4357**		438
Continental Loose Leaf Inc						
1122 16th Ave	Minneapolis	MN	55414	**888-719-5013**	612-378-4800	85
Continental Manufacturing Co						
305 Rock Industrial Pk Dr	Bridgeton	MO	63044	**800-325-1051**	314-656-4301	501
Continental Maritime of San Diego Inc						
1995 Bay Front St	San Diego	CA	92113	**877-631-0020**	619-234-8851	689
Continental Motors Inc						
2039 Broad St	Mobile	AL	36615	**800-718-3411**	251-438-3411	21
Continental Resources Inc						
175 Middlesex Tpke	Bedford	MA	01730	**800-937-4688**	781-275-0850	177
Continental Safety Equipment						
2935 Waters Rd Ste 140	Eagan	MN	55121	**800-844-7003**	651-454-7233	670
Continental Service Group Inc						
200 Cross Keys Office Pk	Fairport	NY	14450	**800-724-7500**	585-421-1000	158
Continental Studwelding Ltd						
35 Devon Rd	Brampton	ON	L6T5B6	**800-848-9442**	905-792-3650	476
Continental Tire North America Inc						
1800 Continental Blvd	Charlotte	NC	28273	**877-235-0102**	704-583-3900	744
Continental Traffic Service Inc (CTSI)						
5100 Poplar Ave 15th Fl	Memphis	TN	38137	**888-836-5135**	901-766-1500	310
Continental Western Group						
11201 Douglas Ave	Urbandale	IA	50322	**800-235-2942**	515-473-3000	388-4
Contingent Workforce Solutions Inc						
2430 Meadowpine Blvd						
Ste 101	Mississauga	ON	L5N6S2	**866-837-8630**		2
Continucare Corp						
7200 Corporate Ctr Dr Ste 600	Miami	FL	33126	**866-312-7154**	305-500-2000	360
Continuing Care Accreditation Commission (CARF-CCAC)						
1730 Rhode Island Ave NW						
Ste 209	Washington	DC	20036	**866-888-1122**	202-587-5001	47-1
Continuum						
3150 Central Expy	Santa Clara	CA	95051	**888-532-1064**	408-727-3240	422
Contour Saws Inc						
1217 E Thacker St	Des Plaines	IL	60016	**800-458-9034**	847-824-1146	673
Contours Express Inc						
156 Imperial Way	Nicholasville	KY	40356	**855-589-9662**		351
Contra Costa County Library						
75 Santa Barbara Rd	Pleasant Hill	CA	94523	**800-984-4636**	925-646-6423	431-3
Contra Costa Federal Credit Union						
PO Box 509	Martinez	CA	94553	**888-387-8632**	925-228-7550	219
Contra Costa Health Services						
2500 Alhambra Ave	Martinez	CA	94553	**877-661-6230**	925-370-5000	371-3
Contract Design Magazine						
770 Broadway	New York	NY	10004	**800-697-8859**		452-5
Contract Land Staff LLC						
2245 Texas Dr Ste 200	Sugar Land	TX	77479	**800-874-4519**	281-240-3370	195
Contractors Register Inc						
800 E Main St						
PO Box 500	Jefferson Valley	NY	10535	**800-431-2584**		628-6
Contractors Steel Co						
36555 Amrhein Rd	Livonia	MI	48150	**800-521-3946**	734-464-4000	487
Contrex Inc						
8900 Zachary Ln N	Maple Grove	MN	55369	**800-342-4411**	763-424-7800	204
Control Flow Inc						
9201 Fairbanks N Houston Rd	Houston	TX	77064	**800-231-9922**	281-890-8300	778
Controlled Access Inc						
1515 W 130th St	Hinckley	OH	44233	**800-942-0829**	330-273-6185	630
Controlled Contamination Services LLC						
4182 Sorrento Valley Blvd	San Diego	CA	92121	**888-263-9886**	858-457-7598	256
Controlled Power Co						
1955 Stephenson Hwy Ste G	Troy	MI	48083	**800-521-4792**	248-528-3700	757
Controller Magazine						
120 W Harvest Dr	Lincoln	NE	68521	**800-247-4890**	402-479-2143	452-21
Convention & Visitors Bureau of Marion County						
1000 Cole St Ste A	Fairmont	WV	26554	**800-834-7365**	304-368-1123	207
Convention & Visitors Bureau-Village of Pinehurst Southern Pines Aberdeen Area						
10677 Hwy 15-501	Southern Pines	NC	28387	**800-346-5362**	910-692-3330	207
Convergent Laser Technologies						
1660 S Loop Rd	Alameda	CA	94502	**800-848-8200**	510-832-2130	421
ConvergeOne LLC						
175B Rennell Dr	Southport	CT	06890	**888-321-6227**		384
Convergys Corp						
201 E Fourth St	Cincinnati	OH	45202	**888-284-9900**	513-723-7000	727
NYSE: CVG						
Converse College						
580 E Main St	Spartanburg	SC	29302	**800-766-1125***	864-596-9000	166
*Admissions						
Conveyco Technologies Inc						
PO Box 1000	Bristol	CT	06011	**800-229-8215**	860-589-8215	382
Conveyor Components Co						
130 Seltzer Rd	Croswell	MI	48422	**800-233-3233***	810-679-4211	208
*Cust Svc						
Conway Area Chamber of Commerce						
203 Main St	Conway	SC	29526	**888-272-8700**	843-248-2273	137
Conway Cemetery State Park						
c/o Arkansas State Parks						
1 Capitol Mall	Little Rock	AR	72201	**888-287-2757**		558
Con-way Freight						
2211 Old Earhart Rd	Ann Arbor	MI	48105	**800-755-2728**	734-994-6600	770
Conway Import Co Inc						
11051 W Addison St	Franklin Park	IL	60131	**800-323-8801**	847-455-5600	295-19
Con-way Inc						
2855 Campus Dr Ste 300	San Mateo	CA	94403	**800-755-2728**	650-378-5200	770
NYSE: CNW						
Cook Aviation Inc						
970 S Kirby Rd	Bloomington	IN	47403	**800-880-3499**	812-825-2392	62
Cook Biotech Inc						
1425 Innovation Pl	West Lafayette	IN	47906	**888-299-4224**	765-497-3355	84
Cook Communications Ministries						
4050 Lee Vance View	Colorado Springs	CO	80918	**800-708-5550**	719-536-0100	628-9
Cook Hotel & Conference Ctr						
3848 W Lakeshore Dr	Baton Rouge	LA	70808	**866-610-2665**	225-383-2665	374
Cook Inc						
PO Box 4195	Bloomington	IN	47402	**800-457-4500**	812-339-2235	471
Cook Medical Inc						
1186 Montgomery Ln	Vandergrift	PA	15690	**800-245-4715***	724-845-8621	471
*General						
Cook Moving Systems Inc						
1845 Dale Rd	Buffalo	NY	14225	**800-828-7144**		512
Cook Urological Inc						
1100 W Morgan St PO Box 227	Spencer	IN	47460	**800-457-4500**	812-829-4891	471
Cook's Ham Inc						
200 S Second St	Lincoln	NE	68508	**800-332-8400**	402-475-6700	295-26
Cook's Illustrated Magazine						
PO Box 470739	Brookline	MA	02447	**800-526-8442***	617-232-1000	452-11
*Circ						
Cookbook Publishers Inc						
9825 Widmer Rd	Lenexa	KS	66215	**800-227-7282**	913-492-5900	618
Cooke County Electric Co-op						
11799 W US Hwy 82 PO Box 530	Muenster	TX	76252	**800-962-0296**	940-759-2211	245
Cooke Trucking Co Inc						
1759 S Andy Griffith Pkwy	Mount Airy	NC	27030	**800-888-9502**	336-786-5181	770
Cookeville Area-Putnam County Chamber of Commerce						
One W First St	Cookeville	TN	38501	**800-264-5541**	931-526-2211	137
Cookies By Design Inc						
1865 Summit Ave Ste 605	Plano	TX	75074	**800-945-2665**	972-398-9536	309
Cooking & Hospitality Institute of Chicago						
361 W Chestnut St	Chicago	IL	60610	**877-828-7772***	312-944-0882	161
*Admissions						
Cooking Light Magazine						
2100 Lakeshore Dr	Birmingham	AL	35209	**800-366-4712**	205-445-6000	452-13
Cooking.com						
2850 Ocean Pk Blvd Ste 310	Santa Monica	CA	90405	**800-663-8810**	310-450-3270	359
Cookson Co						
2417 S 50th Ave	Phoenix	AZ	85043	**800-294-4358**	602-272-4244	234
Cookson Hills Electric Co-op Inc						
1002 E Main St	Stigler	OK	74462	**800-328-2368**	918-967-4614	245
CookTek LLC						
156 N Jefferson St Ste 300	Chicago	IL	60661	**888-266-5835**	312-563-9600	35
Cool Amphibious Manufacturers International LLC						
714 Okeetee Rd	Ridgeland	SC	29936	**888-926-6553**	843-717-2444	119
Cool Gear International LLC						
10 Cordage Park Cir	Plymouth	MA	02360	**855-393-2665**	508-830-3440	358
Coolant Control Inc						
5353 Spring Grove Ave	Cincinnati	OH	45217	**800-535-3885**	513-471-8770	144
Cooley Godward Kronish LLP						
3000 El Camino Real	Palo Alto	CA	94306	**888-654-2411**	650-843-5000	425
Cooley Group						
50 Esten Ave	Pawtucket	RI	02860	**800-992-0072***	401-724-9000	734-2
*Cust Svc						
Cooley Motors Corp						
401 N Greenbush Rd	Rensselaer	NY	12144	**866-308-0724**	518-283-2902	56
Co-op America						
1612 K St NW Ste 600	Washington	DC	20006	**800-584-7336**	202-872-5307	47-13
Co-op Communciations Inc						
210 Clay Ave	Lyndhurst	NJ	07071	**800-833-2700**		726
Co-op Elevator Co						
7211 E Michigan Ave	Pigeon	MI	48755	**800-968-0601**	989-453-4500	275
Co-op Feed Dealers Inc						
380 Broome Corporate Pkwy						
PO Box 670	Conklin	NY	13748	**800-333-0895***	607-651-9078	276
*Cust Svc						
Co-op Finance Assn Inc, The						
10100 N Ambassador Dr Ste 315						
PO Box 901532	Kansas City	MO	64153	**877-835-5232**	816-214-4200	216
CO-OP Financial Services Inc						
9692 Haven Ave	Rancho Cucamonga	CA	91730	**800-782-9042**		390
Cooper Atkins Corp						
33 Reeds Gap Rd	Middlefield	CT	06455	**800-835-5011***	860-349-3473	202
*Sales						
Cooper B-Line Inc						
509 W Monroe St	Highland	IL	62249	**800-851-7415**	618-654-2184	803
Cooper Bussmann Inc						
114 Old State Rd	Ellisville	MO	63021	**855-287-7626**	636-394-2877	802
Cooper Cos Inc						
6140 Stoneridge Mall Rd						
Ste 590	Pleasanton	CA	94588	**888-822-2660**	925-460-3600	535
NYSE: COO						
Cooper Crouse-Hinds						
1201 Wolf St	Syracuse	NY	13208	**866-764-5454**	315-477-5531	802
Cooper Farms						
22348 County Rd 140 PO Box 547	Oakwood	OH	45873	**800-423-2765**	419-594-3325	10-7
Cooper Hotel & Conference Ctr						
12230 Preston Rd	Dallas	TX	75230	**800-444-5187**	972-386-0306	376
Cooper Industries						
600 Travis St Ste 5400	Houston	TX	77002	**866-853-4293**	713-209-8400	802
NYSE: ETN						
Cooper Tire & Rubber Co						
701 Lima Ave	Findlay	OH	45840	**800-854-6288**	419-423-1321	744
NYSE: CTB						
Cooper Union for the Advancement of Science & Art						
30 Cooper Sq	New York	NY	10003	**800-872-2777**	212-353-4100	166
Cooper University Hospital						
Three Cooper Plz	Camden	NJ	08103	**800-826-6737**	856-342-2000	371-3
Cooper Wellness Program						
12230 Preston Rd	Dallas	TX	75230	**800-444-5192**	972-386-4777	697

	Toll-Free	Phone	Class
Cooper Wiring Devices Inc			
203 Cooper Cir ....Peachtree City GA 30269	866-853-4293*	770-631-2100	802
*Cust Svc			
Coopers Rock State Forest			
61 County Line Dr ....Bruceton Mills WV 26525	800-225-5982	304-594-1561	558
CooperSurgical Inc			
95 Corporate Dr ....Trumbull CT 06611	800-645-3760	203-929-6321	471
CooperVision Inc			
370 Woodcliff Dr Ste 200 ....Fairport NY 14450	800-538-7850	585-385-6810	535
Coordinating Research Council Inc (CRC)			
3650 Mansell Rd Ste 140 ....Alpharetta GA 30022	800-445-8667	678-795-0506	48-19
Coors Credit Union			
816 Washington Ave ....Golden CO 80401	800-770-6414	303-279-6414	219
CoorsTek Inc			
600 Ninth St ....Golden CO 80401	800-821-6110	303-278-4000	249
Coos Bay-North Bend Visitor & Convention Bureau			
50 Central Ave ....Coos Bay OR 97420	800-824-8486	541-269-0215	207
Coosa Pines Federal Credit Union			
17591 Plant Rd ....Childersburg AL 35044	800-237-9789	256-378-5559	219
Coosa Valley Electric Co-op			
69220 Alabama Hwy 77			
PO Box 837.................Talladega AL 35160	800-273-7210	256-362-4180	245
COPE Inc			
1120 G St NW Ste 550 ....Washington DC 20005	800-247-3054	202-628-5100	457
Cope Plastics Inc			
4441 Industrial Dr ....Godfrey IL 62002	800-851-5510	618-466-0221	596
Copesan Services Inc			
W175 N5711			
Technology Dr...............Menomonee Falls WI 53051	800-267-3726		570
Copia International Ltd			
1220 Iroquois Dr Ste 180 ....Naperville IL 60563	800-689-8898*	630-778-8898	174-3
*Sales			
Copiah-Lincoln Community College			
PO Box 649 ....Wesson MS 39191	866-296-6522	601-643-8488	160
Natchez 11 Co-Lin Cir ....Natchez MS 39120	866-296-6522	601-442-9111	160
Copic Insurance Co			
7351 Lowry Blvd ....Denver CO 80230	800-421-1834	720-858-6000	388-5
Copiers Northwest Inc			
601 Dexter Ave N ....Seattle WA 98109	866-692-0700	206-282-1200	111
Copley Place			
100 Huntington Ave Ste 100.............Boston MA 02116	877-746-6642	617-262-6600	455
Copley Square Hotel			
47 Huntington Ave ....Boston MA 02116	800-225-7062	617-536-9000	376
Copper Development Assn Inc			
260 Madison Ave 16th Fl ....New York NY 10016	800-232-3282	212-251-7200	48-13
Copper Hills Youth Ctr			
5899 Rivendell Dr ....West Jordan UT 84081	800-776-7116		371-1
Copper Mountain Resort			
209 Ten Mile Cir			
PO Box 3001.................Copper Mountain CO 80443	888-219-2441	970-968-2882	660
Copper Valley Electric Assn Inc (CVEA)			
Mile 187 Glenn Hwy PO Box 45.......Glennallen AK 99588	866-835-2832	907-822-3211	245
Copperas Cove Independent School District			
703 W Ave D ....Copperas Cove TX 76522	866-632-9992	254-547-1227	676
CopperWynd Resort & Club			
13225 N Eagle Ridge Dr ....Fountain Hills AZ 85268	877-707-7760	480-333-1900	660
CopperWynd Resort and Club			
13225 N Eagle Ridge Dr ....Fountain Hills AZ 85268	877-707-7760	480-333-1831	698
Coppin State University			
2500 W N Ave ....Baltimore MD 21216	800-635-3674*	410-951-3600	166
*Admissions			
COPS (Community Oriented Policing Services)			
1100 Vermont Ave NW 10th Fl.......Washington DC 20530	800-421-6770	202-616-2888	338-12
COPS (Concerns of Police Survivors Inc)			
846 Old S 5 PO Box 3199.............Camdenton MO 65020	800-784-2677	573-346-4911	47-21
Copyright Clearance Ctr Inc (CCC)			
222 Rosewood Dr ....Danvers MA 01923	855-239-3415	978-750-8400	48-16
Coquille Myrtle Grove State Natural Site			
PO Box 569 ....Bandon OR 97411	800-551-6949		558
Coral Beach Resort & Suites			
1105 S Ocean Blvd ....Myrtle Beach SC 29577	800-843-2684	800-556-1754	660
Coral Chemical Co			
1915 Industrial Ave ....Zion IL 60099	800-228-4646	847-246-6666	143
Coral Gables Hospital Inc (CGH)			
3100 Douglas Rd ....Coral Gables FL 33134	866-728-3677	305-445-8461	371-3
Coral Springs Auto Mall			
9400 W Atlantic Blvd ....Coral Springs FL 33071	800-353-8660	954-796-4525	56
Coram Healthcare Corp			
555 17th St Ste 1500 ....Denver CO 80202	800-267-2642		360
Corban College			
5000 Deer Pk Dr SE ....Salem OR 97317	800-845-3005	503-581-8600	166
Corbett Lighting Inc			
14508 Nelson Ave ....City of Industry CA 91744	800-533-8769	626-336-4511	435
Corbin			
2360 Technology Pkwy ....Hollister CA 95023	800-538-7035	831-634-1100	510
Corbin Russwin Inc			
225 Episcopal Rd ....Berlin CT 06037	800-438-1951	860-225-7411	347
Corbis Corp			
710 Second Ave Ste 200.............Seattle WA 98104	800-260-0444	206-373-6000	586
Corby Industries Inc			
1501 E Pennsylvania St ....Allentown PA 18109	800-652-6729*	610-433-1412	683
*Sales			
Corcoran Group Inc, The			
660 Madison Ave ....New York NY 10021	800-544-4055	212-355-3550	643
Cord Sets Inc			
1015 Fifth St N ....Minneapolis MN 55411	800-752-0580	612-337-9700	802
Cordis Corp			
14201 NW 60th Ave ....Miami Lakes FL 33014	800-327-7714	800-447-7585	471
CORE (Center for Organ Recovery & Education)			
204 Sigma Dr RIDC Pk...........Pittsburgh PA 15238	800-366-6777	412-963-3550	269
Core Vision IT Solutions			
600 Dakota Ste D ....Crystal Lake IL 60012	855-788-5835		197
Corel Corp			
1600 Carling Ave ....Ottawa ON K1Z8R7	800-772-6735*	613-728-8200	179-8
*Orders			
CoreLogic SafeRent			
7300 Westmore Rd Ste 3 ....Rockville MD 20850	866-873-3651		626
Core-Mark International			
395 Oyster Pt Blvd			
Ste 415.................South San Francisco CA 94080	800-622-1713	650-589-9445	746
CoreNet Global Inc			
260 Peachtree St NW Ste 1500.........Atlanta GA 30303	800-726-8111	404-589-3200	48-17
CoreSource Inc			
400 Field Dr ....Lake Forest IL 60045	800-832-3332	847-604-9200	579
CoreTech			
660 American Ave ....King of Prussia PA 19406	800-220-3337		195
Corey Delta Inc			
4931 Park Rd PO Box 637 ....Benicia CA 94510	800-727-2260	707-747-7500	189-5
Corey Steel Co			
2800 S 61st Ct ....Cicero IL 60804	800-323-2750	708-735-8000	714
Coriell Institute for Medical Research			
403 Haddon Ave ....Camden NJ 08103	800-752-3805	856-966-7377	659
Corinth Area Convention & Visitors Bureau			
215 N Fillmore St ....Corinth MS 38834	800-748-9048	662-287-8300	207
Corinth National Cemetery			
1551 Horton St ....Corinth MS 38834	800-273-8255	901-386-8311	135
Corinthian Colleges Inc			
6 Hutton Centre Dr Ste 400.........Santa Ana CA 92707	888-370-7589	916-431-6959	242
NASDAQ: COCO			
Corinthian Partners LLC			
10 E 53rd St 28th Fl ....New York NY 10022	800-899-8950	212-287-1500	681
Corizon			
105 Westpark Dr Ste 200 ....Brentwood TN 37027	800-729-0069		458
Corken Inc			
3805 NW 36th St ....Oklahoma City OK 73112	800-631-4929	405-946-5576	632
Corn Belt Energy Corp			
One Energy Way ....Bloomington IL 61705	800-879-0339	309-662-5330	245
Corn Palace			
604 N Main St ....Mitchell SD 57301	800-289-7469	605-996-5031	49-2
Corn Refiners Assn Inc (CRA)			
1701 Pennsylvania Ave ....Washington DC 20006	800-284-5779	202-331-1634	47-2
Corn Stock Theatre			
1700 Pk Rd ....Peoria IL 61604	800-220-1185	309-676-2196	566-4
Cornelia Day Resort			
663 Fifth Ave Eighth Fl ....New York NY 10022	866-663-1700	212-871-3050	697
Cornelia de Lange Syndrome Foundation Inc (CdLS)			
302 W Main St Ste 100.................Avon CT 06001	800-753-2357	860-676-8166	47-17
Cornelius Seed Corn Co			
14760 317th Ave ....Bellevue IA 52031	800-218-1862	563-672-3463	295-20
Cornell College			
600 First St SW ....Mount Vernon IA 52314	800-747-1112*	319-895-4215	166
*Admissions			
Cornell Iron Works Inc			
24 Elmwood Rd ....Mountain Top PA 18707	800-233-8366	570-474-6773	234
Cornell Plantations			
1 Plantations Rd ....Ithaca NY 14850	800-269-8368	607-255-2400	96
Cornell University Press			
750 Cascadilla St PO Box 6525 ....Ithaca NY 14850	800-666-2211*	607-277-2338	628-4
*Sales			
Corner Bakery Cafe			
12700 Pk Central Dr Ste 1300 ....Dallas TX 75251	800-309-4642*	972-619-4100	67
*General			
Cornerstone Equity Investors LLC			
281 Tresser Blvd 12th Fl.............Stamford CT 06901	800-438-7465	212-753-0901	780
Cornerstone Group			
2100 Hollywood Blvd ....Hollywood FL 33020	800-809-4099	305-443-8288	644
Cornerstone Medical Arts Ctr Hospital			
159-05 Union Tpke ....Fresh Meadows NY 11366	800-233-9999	718-906-6700	717
Cornerstone Systems Inc			
3250 Players Club Pkwy ....Memphis TN 38125	855-288-7720	901-842-0660	195
Cornerstone University			
1001 E Beltline Ave NE ....Grand Rapids MI 49525	800-787-9778*	616-222-1426	166
*Admissions			
Cornhusker Casualty Co			
PO Box 2048 ....Omaha NE 68103	888-495-8949		388-4
Cornhusker Hotel, The			
333 S 13th St ....Lincoln NE 68508	866-706-7706	402-474-7474	376
Cornhusker State Industries			
800 Pioneers Blvd ....Lincoln NE 68502	800-348-7537	402-471-4597	622
Corning Area Chamber of Commerce			
One W Market St Ste 302 ....Corning NY 14830	866-463-6264	607-936-4686	137
Corning Cable Systems			
800 17th St NW ....Hickory NC 28603	800-743-2671	828-901-5000	801
Corning Gilbert Inc			
5310 W Camelback Rd ....Glendale AZ 85301	800-528-0199*	623-245-1050	253
*Cust Svc			
Corning Hospital			
176 Denison Pkwy E ....Corning NY 14830	877-750-2042	607-937-7200	371-3
Corning Inc Life Sciences Div			
836 N St Bldg 300 Ste 3401 ....Tewksbury MA 01876	800-492-1110	978-442-2200	416
Corning Museum of Glass			
One Museum Way ....Corning NY 14830	800-732-6845*	607-937-5371	513
*Cust Svc			
Cornish College of the Arts			
710 E Roy St ....Seattle WA 98121	800-726-2787	206-323-1400	162
Cornucopia Tool & Plastics Inc			
448 Sherwood Rd PO Box 1915.......Paso Robles CA 93447	800-235-4144	805-369-0030	253
Cornwell Quality Tools			
667 Seville Rd ....Wadsworth OH 44281	800-321-8356	330-336-3506	748
Corona Brushes Inc			
5065 Savarese Cir ....Tampa FL 33634	800-458-3483	813-885-2525	102
Corona Clipper Inc			
22440 Tomasco Canyon Rd ....Corona CA 92883	800-234-2547	951-737-6515	426
Coronet Lighting			
PO Box 2065 ....Gardena CA 90248	800-421-2748	310-327-6700	435
Corotec Corp			
145 Hyde Rd ....Farmington CT 06032	800-423-0348	860-678-0038	383
Corp for National & Community Service			
AmeriCorps USA			
1201 New York Ave NW ....Washington DC 20525	800-833-3722	202-606-5000	338-18
Learn & Serve America			
1201 New York Ave NW ....Washington DC 20525	800-833-3722	202-606-5000	338-18
Senior Corps			
1201 New York Ave NW ....Washington DC 20525	800-833-3722	202-606-5000	338-18
Corpak Medsystems Inc			
1001 Asbury Dr ....Buffalo Grove IL 60089	800-323-6305	847-403-3400	471
CorpCare Assoc Inc			
7000 Peachtree Dunwoody Rd			
Bldg 4 Ste 300 ....Atlanta GA 30328	800-728-9444		457
Corporate Accountability International			
10 Milk St Ste 610 ....Boston MA 02108	800-688-8797	617-695-2525	47-8
Corporate Air LLC			
15 Allegheny			
County Airport ....West Mifflin PA 15122	888-429-5377	412-469-6800	62
Corporate Care Works			
8649 Baypine Rd Ste 101 ....Jacksonville FL 32256	800-327-9757	904-296-9436	457
Corporate Compliance & Regulatory			
1617 JFK Blvd Ste 1750 ....Philadelphia PA 19103	877-256-2472	215-557-2300	524-7

Company / Address	City	State	Zip	Toll-Free	Phone	Class
Corporate Disk Co 4610 Crime Pkwy	McHenry	IL	60050	**800-634-3475**	815-331-6000	240
Corporate Executive Board Co 1919 N Lynn St *NYSE: CEB*	Arlington	VA	22209	**866-913-2632**	571-303-3000	195
Corporate Fitness Works Inc 1200 16th St N	St Petersburg	FL	33705	**855-417-9697**	301-417-9697	351
Corporate Helicopters of San Diego 3753 John J Montgomery Dr Ste 2	San Diego	CA	92123	**800-345-6737**	858-505-5650	356
Corporate It Solutions Inc 661 Pleasant St	Norwood	MA	02062	**888-521-2487**		197
Corporate Telephone Services 184 W Second St	Boston	MA	02127	**800-274-1211**	617-625-1200	246
Corporate Travel Management Group 450 E 22nd St	Lombard	IL	60148	**866-545-6789**	630-691-8000	761
Corporate Writer & Editor 111 E Wacker Dr Ste 500	Chicago	IL	60601	**800-878-5331**	312-960-4140	524-2
Corporation for Public Broadcasting (CPB) 401 Ninth St NW	Washington	DC	20004	**800-272-2190**	202-879-9600	304
Corporation Service Co 2711 Centerville Rd Ste 400	Wilmington	DE	19808	**866-403-5272**	302-636-5400	112
Corps Network, The 1100 G St NW Ste 1000	Washington	DC	20005	**800-245-5627**	202-737-6272	47-6
Corptax LLC 1751 Lk Cook Rd Ste 100	Deerfield	IL	60015	**800-966-1639**		178
Corpus Christi Convention & Visitors Bureau 101 N Shoreline Blvd Ste 430	Corpus Christi	TX	78401	**800-678-6232**	361-881-1888	207
Corpus Christi Gasket & Fastener Inc PO Box 4074	Corpus Christi	TX	78469	**800-460-6366**	361-884-6366	325
Corpus Christi Symphony Orchestra 555 N Carancahua St Tower II Ste 410 Ste 410	Corpus Christi	TX	78401	**877-286-6683**	361-883-6683	566-3
Corradino Group 200 s Fifth st	Louisville	KY	40202	**800-880-8241**	502-587-7221	256
Correct Craft Inc 14700 Aerospace Pkwy	Orlando	FL	32809	**800-346-2092**	407-855-4141	89
Correctional Enterprises of Connecticut 24 Wolcott Hill Rd	Wethersfield	CT	06109	**800-842-1146**	860-263-6839	622
Corrections Corp of America 10 Burton Hills Blvd *NYSE: CXW*	Nashville	TN	37215	**800-624-2931**	615-263-3000	212
Correlated Products Inc 5616 Progress Rd	Indianapolis	IN	46242	**800-428-3266**	317-243-3248	149
Corrigan Moving Systems 23923 Research Dr	Farmington Hills	MI	48335	**800-267-7442**		512
Corrpro Canada Inc 10848 - 214 St	Edmonton	AB	T5S2A7	**800-661-8390**	780-447-4565	256
Corrpro Cos Inc 1055 W Smith Rd	Medina	OH	44256	**800-443-3516**	330-723-5082	261
Corsair Memory Inc 46221 Landing Pkwy	Fremont	CA	94538	**888-222-4346**	510-657-8747	174-5
Corsicana Area Chamber of Commerce 120 N 12th St	Corsicana	TX	75110	**866-222-7100**	903-874-4731	137
Corsicana Bedding Inc PO Box 1050	Corsicana	TX	75151	**800-323-4349**	903-872-2591	466
Cortec Corp 4119 White Bear Pkwy	Saint Paul	MN	55110	**800-426-7832**	651-429-1100	143
Cortelco Inc 1703 Sawyer Rd	Corinth	MS	38834	**800-288-3132**	662-287-5281	246
Corunna Public School District 124 N Shiawassee St	Corunna	MI	48817	**866-632-9992**	989-743-6338	676
Corvallis Tourism 420 NW Second St	Corvallis	OR	97330	**800-334-8118**	541-757-1544	207
CorVel Corp 2010 Main St Ste 600 *NASDAQ: CRVL*	Irvine	CA	92614	**888-726-7835**	949-851-1473	458
Corvirtus LLC 1011 N Weber St	Colorado Springs	CO	80903	**800-322-5329**		458
Corwin Press Inc 2455 Teller Rd *Orders	Thousand Oaks	CA	91320	**800-233-9936***	805-499-9734	628-2
Cosanti Originals Inc 6433 Doubletree Ranch Rd	Paradise Valley	AZ	85253	**800-752-3187**	480-948-6145	49-2
COSCO (China Ocean Shipping Co Americas Inc) 100 Lighting Way	Secaucus	NJ	07094	**800-242-7354**	201-422-0500	220
Cosco Fire Protection Inc 1075 W Lambert Rd Bldg D	Brea	CA	92821	**800-485-3795**	714-989-1800	190-13
Cosco Industries Inc 7220 W Wilson Ave	Harwood Heights	IL	60706	**800-296-8970**	708-867-5800	462
CoServ Electric 7701 S Stemmons Fwy	Corinth	TX	76210	**800-274-4014**	940-321-7800	245
COSI Columbus 333 W Broad St	Columbus	OH	43215	**888-819-2674**	614-228-2674	513
Cosi Inc 1751 Lk Cook Rd Ste 600 *NASDAQ: COSI*	Deerfield	IL	60015	**800-822-2076**	847-597-8800	661
Cosmopolitan Hotel Toronto Eight Colborne St	Toronto	ON	M5E1E1	**800-958-3488**	416-350-2000	376
Cosmopolitan International 7341 W 80th St PO Box 4588	Shawnee Mission	KS	66204	**800-648-4331**	913-648-4330	47-15
Cosmopolitan Magazine 300 W 57th St	New York	NY	10019	**800-888-2676**	212-649-2000	452-11
Cosmopolitan Translation Bureau Inc 53 W Jackson Blvd Ste 1260	Chicago	IL	60604	**866-370-1439**	312-726-2610	758
Cosmos Communications Inc 11-05 44th Dr	Long Island City	NY	11101	**800-223-5751**	718-482-1800	619
CoSN (Consortium for School Networking) 1025 Vermont Ave NW Ste 1010	Washington	DC	20005	**866-267-8747**	202-861-2676	47-9
Cossatot River State Park-Natural Area 1980 Hwy 278 W	Wickes	AR	71973	**877-665-6343**	870-385-2201	558
Cost Plus Inc 200 Fourth St *NASDAQ: CPWM*	Oakland	CA	94607	**877-967-5362**	510-893-7300	359
Costa Cruise Lines 200 S Pk Rd Ste 200	Hollywood	FL	33021	**800-462-6782**	954-266-5600	220
Costa Del Mar 2361 Mason Ave Ste 100	Daytona Beach	FL	32117	**800-447-3700**	386-274-4000	535
Costa Fruit & Produce 18 Bunker Hill Industrial Pk PO Box 290754	Boston	MA	02129	**800-322-1374**	617-241-8007	296-7
Costa Nursery Farms Inc 21800 SW 162nd Ave	Miami	FL	33170	**800-327-7074**		366
Costanoa Coastal Lodge & Camp 2001 Rossi Rd	Pescadero	CA	94060	**877-262-7848**	650-879-1100	660
CoStar Group Inc Two Bethesda Metro Ctr 10th Fl *NASDAQ: CSGP*	Bethesda	MD	20814	**800-613-1303**	301-215-8300	179-10
Costco Wholesale Corp 999 Lake Dr *NASDAQ: COST* ■ *Cust Svc	Issaquah	WA	98027	**800-774-2678***	425-313-8100	799
Costume Gallery 4451 Rt 130	Burlington	NJ	08016	**800-222-8125**	609-386-6501	153-6
Costume Specialists Inc 211 N Fifth St	Columbus	OH	43215	**800-596-9357**	614-464-2115	153-6
COTA (Children's Organ Transplant Assn) 2501 W Cota Dr	Bloomington	IN	47403	**800-366-2682**	812-336-8872	47-17
Cothern Computer Systems Inc 1640 Lelia Dr Ste 200	Jackson	MS	39216	**800-844-1155**	601-969-1155	179-7
Cott Corp 6525 Viscount Rd *NYSE: COT*	Mississauga	ON	L4V1H6	**888-378-4361**	905-672-1900	79-2
Cotterman Co 130 Seltzer Rd	Croswell	MI	48422	**800-552-3337**	810-679-4400	418
Cottey College 1000 W Austin Blvd	Nevada	MO	64772	**888-526-8839**	417-667-8181	160
Cotton & Co 633 SE Fifth St	Stuart	FL	34994	**800-266-9076**	772-287-6612	4
Cotton Belt Inc 401 E Sater St	Pinetops	NC	27864	**800-849-4192**	252-827-4192	466
Cotton Electric Co-op Inc 226 N Broadway	Walters	OK	73572	**800-522-3520**	580-875-3351	245
Cotton Inc 6399 Weston Pkwy	Cary	NC	27513	**800-334-5868**	919-678-2220	47-2
Cotton's Week 7193 Goodlett Farms Pkwy	Cordova	TN	38016	**888-232-1738**	901-274-9030	524-13
Cottrell Inc 2125 Candler Rd *Sales	Gainesville	GA	30507	**800-827-0132***	770-532-7251	769
Cottrell Paper Company Inc 1135 Rock City Rd PO Box 35	Rock City Falls	NY	12863	**800-948-3559**	518-885-1702	803
Couch & Philippi Inc 10680 Fern Ave PO Box A *Orders	Stanton	CA	90680	**800-854-3360***	714-527-2261	692
Coulter Cadillac Inc 1188 E Camelback Rd	Phoenix	AZ	85014	**800-843-4237**	602-264-1188	56
Coulter Lake Guest Ranch 80 County Rd 273	Rifle	CO	81650	**800-858-3046**	970-625-1473	239
Council Bluffs Area Chamber of Commerce 149 W Bdwy	Council Bluffs	IA	51503	**800-228-6878**	712-325-1000	137
Council for Advancement & Support of Education (CASE) 1307 New York Ave NW Ste 1000 *Orders	Washington	DC	20005	**800-554-8536***	202-328-5900	48-5
Council For Economic Opportunities In Greater Cleveland 1228 Euclid Ave Ste 700	Cleveland	OH	44115	**888-262-3226**	216-696-9077	47-11
Council for Opportunity in Education 1025 Vermont Ave NW Ste 900	Washington	DC	20005	**800-633-7313**	202-347-7430	47-11
Council for Professional Recognition 2460 16th St NW	Washington	DC	20009	**800-424-4310**	202-265-9090	48-5
Council for Responsible Genetics (CRG) 5 Upland Rd Ste 3	Cambridge	MA	02140	**888-591-3911**	617-868-0870	48-19
Council of Administrators of Special Education (CASE) Osigian Office Centre 101 Katelyn Cir Ste E	Warner Robins	GA	31088	**800-585-1753**	478-333-6892	48-5
Council of Better Business Bureaus Inc *Dispute Resolution Services & Mediation Training* 4200 Wilson Blvd Ste 800	Arlington	VA	22203	**800-537-4600**	703-276-0100	40
Council of Industrial Boiler Owners (CIBO) 6035 Burke Ctr Pkwy Ste 360	Burke	VA	22015	**800-542-6096**	703-250-9042	48-13
Council of Insurance Agents & Brokers 701 Pennsylvania Ave NW Ste 750	Washington	DC	20004	**877-267-9855**	202-783-4400	48-9
Council of Real Estate Brokerage Managers (CRB) 430 N Michigan Ave Ste 300	Chicago	IL	60611	**800-621-8738**		48-17
Council of Residential Specialists 430 N Michigan Ave Ste 300	Chicago	IL	60611	**800-462-8841**	312-321-4400	48-17
Council of State & Territorial Epidemiologists (CSTE) 2872 Woodcock Blvd Ste 303	Atlanta	GA	30341	**866-577-9956**	770-458-3811	48-7
Council of State Governments (CSG) 2760 Research Pk Dr *Sales	Lexington	KY	40511	**800-800-1910***	859-244-8000	48-7
Council of the Great City Schools 1301 Pennsylvania Ave NW Ste 702	Washington	DC	20004	**888-280-7903**	202-393-2427	48-5
Council on Academic Accreditation in Audiology & Speech-Language Pathology 2200 Research Blvd	Rockville	MD	20850	**800-498-2071**	301-296-5700	47-1
Council on Accreditation (COA) 45 Broadway 29th Fl	New York	NY	10006	**866-262-8088**	212-797-3000	47-1
Council on Accreditation of Nurse Anesthesia Educational Programs 222 S Prospect Ave	Park Ridge	IL	60068	**855-526-2262**	847-692-7050	47-1
Council on Aviation Accreditation (CAA) *Aviation Accreditation Board International* 3410 Skyway Dr	Auburn	AL	36830	**800-767-4767**	334-844-2431	47-1
Council on Aviation Accreditation (CAA) *Aviation Accreditation Board International* 5750 Main St NE *Sales	Fridley	MN	55432	**800-328-2403***	763-571-2400	808
Council on Chiropractic Education Commission on Accreditation 8049 N 85th Way	Scottsdale	AZ	85258	**888-443-3506**	480-443-8877	47-1
Council on Foundations 2121 Crystal Dr Ste 700	Arlington	VA	22202	**800-673-9036**	703-879-0600	47-5
Council on International Educational Exchange (CIEE) 300 Fore St Second Fl *Cust Svc	Portland	ME	04101	**888-268-6245***	207-553-4000	48-5
Council on Occupational Education 7840 Roswell Rd Bldg 300 Ste 325	Atlanta	GA	30350	**800-917-2081**	770-396-3898	47-1
Counsel Corp 1211 Ave of the Americas Ste 2902 *NYSE: CXS*	New York	NY	10036	**866-296-3743**	212-696-0100	402
Count Me In LLC 1530 E Dundee Ste 150	Palatine	IL	60074	**866-514-5888**		82

	Toll-Free	Phone	Class
Counter Pro Inc			
210 Lincoln St . . . . Manchester NH 03103	800-899-2444	603-647-2444	192-3
Country Bank for Savings			
75 Main St . . . . Ware MA 01082	800-322-8233	413-967-6221	69
Country Curtains			
PO Box 955 . . . . Stockbridge MA 01262	800-937-1237	413-243-1474	155-5
Country Home Products Inc			
75 Meigs Road . . . . Vergennes VT 05491	800-376-9637	802-877-1200	454
Country Inn at the Mall			
936 Stillwater Ave . . . . Bangor ME 04401	800-244-3961*	207-941-0200	376
*Resv			
Country Inn Lake Resort			
1332 Airport Rd . . . . Hot Springs AR 71913	800-822-7402	501-767-3535	376
COUNTRY Insurance & Financial Services			
1705 Towanda Ave . . . . Bloomington IL 61701	888-211-2555	866-268-6879	388-2
Country Lane Flower Shop			
729 S Michigan Ave . . . . Howell MI 48843	800-764-7673	517-546-1111	292
Country Living Magazine			
300 W 57th St . . . . New York NY 10019	800-888-0128	212-649-3204	452-11
Country Magazine			
1610 North 2nd St Ste 102 . . . . Milwaukee WI 53212	888-861-1265	414-423-0100	452-11
Country Mark Co-op			
1200 Refinery Rd . . . . Mount Vernon IN 47620	800-832-5490		590
Country Music Assn Inc (CMA)			
1 Music Cir S . . . . Nashville TN 37203	800-788-3045	615-244-2840	47-4
Country Music Hall of Fame & Museum			
222 Fifth Ave S . . . . Nashville TN 37203	800-852-6437	615-416-2001	513
Country Mutual Insurance Co			
1701 Towanda Ave . . . . Bloomington IL 61701	888-211-2555*	309-821-3000	388-4
*Cust Svc			
Country Pride Co-op (CPC)			
648 W Second St PO Box 529 . . . . Winner SD 57580	888-325-7743	605-842-2711	10-4
Country Today			
701 S Farwell St . . . . Eau Claire WI 54701	800-236-4004	715-833-9270	525-4
Country Woman Magazine			
5400 S 60th St . . . . Greendale WI 53129	800-828-4548	414-423-0100	452-14
Country's Barbecue			
2016 12th Ave . . . . Columbus GA 31901	800-285-4267*	706-327-7702	662
*General			
Countryside Co-op			
514 E Main St . . . . Durand WI 54736	800-236-7585	715-672-8947	276
CountryTyme Inc			
3451 Cincinnati-Zanesville			
Rd SW . . . . Lancaster OH 43130	800-213-8365	740-475-6001	644
County College of Morris			
214 Ctr Grove Rd . . . . Randolph NJ 07869	888-726-3260	973-328-5000	160
County of Greene			
93 E High St . . . . Waynesburg PA 15370	888-852-5399	724-852-5210	336
Coup de Pouce Magazine			
1100 boul Rene-Levesque O			
24e Etage . . . . Montreal QC H3B4X9	800-528-3836	514-392-9000	452-11
Courier Printing			
One Courier Pl . . . . Smyrna TN 37167	800-467-0444	615-355-4000	619
Courier-Journal			
525 W Broadway PO Box 740031 . . . . . . Louisville KY 40201	800-765-4011	502-582-4011	525-2
Courier-Post			
301 Cuthbert Blvd . . . . Cherry Hill NJ 08002	800-677-6289	856-663-6000	525-2
Courier-Tribune			
500 Sunset Ave . . . . Asheboro NC 27203	800-488-0444	336-625-2101	525-2
Court Reporting Institute of Dallas			
1341 W Mockingbird Ln Ste 200-E . . . . . . Dallas TX 75247	866-382-1284	214-350-9722	788
Court Reporting Institute of Houston			
13101 NW Fwy Ste 100 . . . . Houston TX 77040	866-996-8300	713-996-8300	788
Courtesy Assoc			
2025 M St NW Ste 800 . . . . Washington DC 20036	800-647-4689		185
Courtesy Chevrolet			
1233 E Camelback Rd . . . . Phoenix AZ 85014	877-295-4648	602-235-0255	56
Courtroom Sciences Inc			
4950 N O'Connor Rd			
Corporate Plaza 1 1st Fl . . . . Irving TX 75062	800-514-5879	972-717-1773	440
Courtyard Cafe			
18 St Thomas St . . . . Toronto ON M5S3E7	877-999-2767*	416-921-2921	662
*Cust Svc			
Courtyard Fort Lauderdale Beach			
440 Seabreeze Blvd . . . . Fort Lauderdale FL 33316	888-236-2427	954-524-8733	376
Coushatta Casino Resort			
777 Coushatta Dr PO Box 1510 . . . . Kinder LA 70648	800-584-7263		132
Cousins Submarines Inc			
N83 W13400 Leon Rd . . . . . . Menomonee Falls WI 53051	800-238-9736	262-253-7700	661
Covance Inc			
210 Carnegie Ctr . . . . Princeton NJ 08540	888-268-2623	609-419-2240	84
NYSE: CVD			
Covansys Corp			
32605 W 12 Mile Rd			
Ste 250 . . . . Farmington Hills MI 48334	866-310-0950	248-488-2088	181
Cove Haven Pocono Palace			
5222 Milford Rd . . . . East Stroudsburg PA 18302	877-822-3333	800-432-9932	660
Cove Inn			
900 Broad Ave S . . . . Naples FL 34102	800-255-4365	239-262-7161	376
Cove Lake State Park			
110 Cove Lake Ln . . . . Caryville TN 37714	800-342-3145	423-566-9701	558
Covenant Children's Hospital (CCH)			
4015 22nd Pl . . . . Lubbock TX 79410	800-378-4189	806-725-0000	371-1
Covenant College			
14049 Scenic Hwy . . . . Lookout Mountain GA 30750	888-451-2683	706-820-1560	166
Covenant Hospice			
5041 N 12th Ave . . . . Pensacola FL 32504	800-541-3072	850-433-2155	368
Covenant House			
Five Penn Plz Third Fl . . . . New York NY 10001	800-999-9999	212-727-4000	47-6
Covenant Transport Inc			
400 Birmingham Hwy . . . . Chattanooga TN 37419	800-334-9686	423-821-1212	770
NASDAQ: CVTI			
Covenant Village of Golden Valley			
5800 St Croix Ave . . . . Minneapolis MN 55422	877-224-5051	763-546-6125	663
Covenant Village of Turlock			
2125 N Olive Ave . . . . Turlock CA 95382	800-485-7844	209-216-5610	663
Coventry First LLC			
7111 Vly Green Rd . . . . Fort Washington PA 19034	877-836-8300		784
Coventry Health Care Inc			
6705 Rockledge Dr Ste 900 . . . . Bethesda MD 20817	866-667-3062	301-581-0600	388-3
NYSE: CVH			
Coventry Health Care of Delaware Inc			
750 Prides Crossing Ste 200 . . . . Newark DE 19713	800-833-7423		388-3
Coventry Health Care of Georgia Inc			
1100 Cir 75 Pkwy Ste 1400 . . . . Atlanta GA 30339	800-470-2004	678-202-2100	388-3
Coventry Health Care of Iowa Inc			
4320 114th St . . . . Urbandale IA 50322	800-470-6352	515-225-1234	388-3
Coventry Health Care of Kansas Inc			
8320 Ward Pkwy . . . . Kansas City MO 64114	800-969-3343		388-3
Coventry Health Care of Louisiana Inc			
1720 S Sykes Dr . . . . Bismarck ND 58504	800-341-6613*		388-3
*Sales			
Coventry Health Care of Nebraska Inc			
15950 W Dodge Rd Ste 100 . . . . Omaha NE 68164	855-449-2889	402-498-9030	388-3
Coventry Lumber Inc			
2030 Nooseneck Hill Rd . . . . Coventry RI 02816	800-390-0919	401-821-2800	192-3
Covera Solutions Inc			
1021 Watervliet-Shaker Rd			
PO Box 13539 . . . . Albany NY 12205	866-526-8372		255
Coverall Cleaning Concepts			
5201 Congress Ave Ste 275 . . . . Boca Raton FL 33487	800-537-3371	866-296-8944	150
Coverbind Corp			
3200 Corporate Dr . . . . Wilmington NC 28405	800-366-6060	910-799-4116	601
Coverstar LLC			
1795 West 200 North . . . . Lindon UT 84042	800-617-7283	801-373-4777	701
Covington Electric Co-op Inc			
18836 US Hwy 84 . . . . Andalusia AL 36421	800-239-4121	334-222-4121	245
Covington International Travel			
4401 Dominion Blvd . . . . Glen Allen VA 23060	800-922-9238	804-747-7077	761
Covisint			
1 Campus Martius Suite 700 . . . . Detroit MI 48226	800-229-4125		179-4
Cowboy Village Resort			
120 S Flat Creek Dr PO Box 38 . . . . Jackson WY 83001	800-962-4988	307-733-3121	376
Coweta-Fayette Electric Membership Corp			
807 Collinsworth Rd . . . . Palmetto GA 30268	877-746-4362	770-502-0226	245
Cowley County Community College & Area Vocational-Technical School			
PO Box 1147 . . . . Arkansas City KS 67005	800-593-2222	620-442-0430	160
Cowtown Boots			
11401 Gateway Blvd W . . . . El Paso TX 79936	800-580-2698	915-593-2709	300
Cox Arboretum MetroPark			
6733 Springboro Pike . . . . Dayton OH 45449	877-359-3291	937-434-9005	96
Cox Communications Inc			
1400 Lake Hearn Dr . . . . Atlanta GA 30319	866-961-0027	404-843-5000	115
Cox Industries Inc			
860 Cannon Bridge Rd			
PO Box 1124 . . . . Orangeburg SC 29116	800-476-4401	803-534-7467	805
Cox Interior Inc			
1751 Old Columbia Rd . . . . Campbellsville KY 42718	800-733-1751		494
Cox Manufacturing Co			
5500 N Loop 1604 E . . . . San Antonio TX 78247	800-900-7981	210-657-7731	614
Cox Media Group Tampa			
11300 Fourth St N			
Ste 300 . . . . Saint Petersburg FL 33716	888-723-9388	727-579-2000	636-111
Cox Transportation Services Inc			
10448 Dow Gil Rd . . . . Ashland VA 23005	800-288-8118	804-798-1477	770
Coyle Reproductions Inc			
14949 Firestone Blvd . . . . La Mirada CA 90638	866-269-5373	714-690-8200	619
Coyne Textile Services Inc			
140 Cortland Ave . . . . Syracuse NY 13202	800-672-6963	315-475-1626	438
Coyote Lake Feedyard Inc			
1287 FM 1731 . . . . Muleshoe TX 79347	800-299-3321	806-946-3321	10-1
Coyote Logistics LLC			
191 E Deerpath Rd . . . . Lake Forest IL 60045	877-626-9683	847-295-2424	444
Cozen O'Connor			
1900 Market St . . . . Philadelphia PA 19103	800-523-2900	215-665-2000	425
C-P Flexible Packaging			
15 Grumbacher Rd . . . . York PA 17406	800-815-0667	717-764-1193	547
CP Franchising LLC			
3300 University Dr . . . . Coral Springs FL 33065	800-683-0206	954-344-8060	762
CPA (College Parents of America)			
2200 Wilson Blvd Ste 102-396 . . . . Arlington VA 22201	888-761-6702		47-11
CPA (Catholic Press Assn)			
205 W Monroe St Ste 470 . . . . Chicago IL 60606	800-777-7432	312-380-6789	48-14
CPA Auto Dealer Consultants Assn (CADCA)			
624 Grassmere Pk Dr Ste 15 . . . . Nashville TN 37211	800-231-2524	615-373-9880	48-1
CPA2Biz Inc			
100 Broadway Sixth Fl . . . . New York NY 10005	888-777-7077	646-233-5000	726
CPAC (Cable Public Affairs Ch)			
PO Box 81099 . . . . Ottawa ON K1P1B1	877-287-2722		729
CPAmerica International			
11801 Research Dr . . . . Alachua FL 32615	800-992-2324	386-418-4001	48-1
CPAWS (Canadian Parks & Wilderness Society)			
250 City Ctr Ave Ste 506 . . . . Ottawa ON K1R6K7	800-333-9453	613-569-7226	47-13
CPB (Corporation for Public Broadcasting)			
401 Ninth St NW . . . . Washington DC 20004	800-272-2190	202-879-9600	304
CPB (First NBC)			
29092 Kretel Rd . . . . Lacombe LA 70445	800-423-7503	985-819-1200	69
CPBI (Connecticut Public Broadcasting Inc)			
1049 Asylum Ave . . . . Hartford CT 06105	800-683-2112	860-278-5310	624
CPC (Country Pride Co-op)			
648 W Second St PO Box 529 . . . . Winner SD 57580	888-325-7743	605-842-2711	10-4
CPC Aeroscience Inc			
2700 SW 14th St . . . . Pompano Beach FL 33069	800-327-1835*		143
*Cust Svc			
CPC Logistics Inc			
14528 S Outer 40 Rd			
Ste 210 . . . . Chesterfield MO 63017	800-274-3746	314-542-2266	712
CPCU Society			
720 Providence Rd . . . . Malvern PA 19355	800-932-2728		48-9
CPF (Cleft Palate Foundation)			
1504 E Franklin St Ste 102 . . . . Chapel Hill NC 27514	800-242-5338	919-933-9044	47-17
CPFD (Coastal Pacific Food Distributors Inc)			
1015 Performance Dr . . . . Stockton CA 95206	800-500-2611	209-983-2454	296-8
CPH Engineers			
500 W Fulton St PO Box 2808 . . . . Sanford FL 32771	866-609-0688		261
CPhA (California Pharmacists Assn)			
4030 Lennane Dr . . . . Sacramento CA 95834	866-365-7472	916-779-1400	578
CPI (Companion Pets Inc)			
2001 N Black Canyon Hwy . . . . Phoenix AZ 85009	800-646-3611	602-255-0166	571
CPI (Consumers Power Inc)			
6990 W Hills Rd PO Box 1180 . . . . Philomath OR 97370	800-872-9036	541-929-3124	245
CPI (Confer Plastics Inc)			
97 Witmer Rd . . . . North Tonawanda NY 14120	800-635-3213	716-693-2056	597
CPI (Communications & Power Industries Inc EIMAC Div)			
607 Hansen Way . . . . Palo Alto CA 94304	800-414-8823		253

	Toll-Free	Phone	Class
CPI Corp			
1706 Washington Ave .... Saint Louis MO 63103	800-422-9410	314-231-1575	583
OTC: CPIC			
CPM Wolverine Proctor LLC			
251 Gibraltar Rd .... Horsham PA 19044	800-428-0846	215-443-5200	297
CPR Institute for Dispute Resolution			
575 Lexington Ave 21st Fl .... New York NY 10022	866-723-1781	212-949-6490	40
CPS (Comprehensive Pharmacy Services Inc)			
6409 N Quail Hollow Rd .... Memphis TN 38120	800-968-6962	901-748-0470	195
CPSC (Consumer Product Safety Commission)			
4340 E W Hwy Ste 502 .... Bethesda MD 20814	800-638-2772	301-504-7923	338-18
CPSI (Computer Programs & Systems Inc)			
6600 Wall St .... Mobile AL 36695	800-711-2774	251-639-8100	38
NASDAQ: CPSI			
CPT (Central Petroleum Transport Inc)			
6115 Mitchell St .... Sioux City IA 51111	800-798-6357	712-258-6357	770
CR Bard Inc Medical Div			
8195 Industrial Blvd .... Covington GA 30014	800-526-4455	770-784-6100	471
CR Bard Inc Urological Div			
8195 Industrial Blvd .... Covington GA 30014	800-526-4455	770-784-6100	471
CR Daniels Inc			
3451 Ellicott Ctr Dr .... Ellicott City MD 21043	800-933-2638	410-461-2100	723
CR England & Sons Inc			
4701 West 2100 South .... Salt Lake City UT 84120	800-453-8826	801-972-2712	770
CR Laurence Company Inc			
2503 E Vernon Ave			
PO Box 58923 .... Los Angeles CA 90058	800-421-6144	323-588-1281	192-2
CRA (Corn Refiners Assn Inc)			
1701 Pennsylvania Ave .... Washington DC 20006	800-284-5779	202-331-1634	47-2
Crabtree & Evelyn Ltd			
102 Peake Brook Rd .... Woodstock CT 06281	800-272-2873	860-928-2761	215
Cracker Barrel Old Country Store Inc			
PO Box 787 .... Lebanon TN 37088	800-333-9566	615-444-5533	661
NASDAQ: CBRL			
Crafco Inc			
420 N Roosevelt Ave .... Chandler AZ 85226	800-528-8242	602-276-0406	45
Craft & Hobby Assn (CHA)			
319 E 54th St .... Elmwood Park NJ 07407	800-822-0494	201-835-1200	47-18
Craft Inc			
1929 County St			
PO Box 3049. .... South Attleboro MA 02703	800-827-2388	508-761-7917	347
Craftmade International Inc			
650 S Royal Ln .... Coppell TX 75019	800-486-4892	972-393-3800	36
OTC: CRFT			
Crafts 'n Things Magazine			
PO Box 926 .... Sidney OH 45365	866-222-3621		452-14
Crafts Technology			
91 Joey Dr .... Elk Grove Village IL 60007	800-323-6802	847-758-3100	450
Cragun's Conference & Golf Resort			
11000 Cragun's Dr .... Brainerd MN 56401	800-272-4867		660
Craig Hospital			
3425 S Clarkson St .... Englewood CO 80113	800-247-0257	303-789-8000	371-6
Craig Transportation Co			
26699 Eckel Rd .... Perrysburg OH 43551	800-521-9119	419-872-3333	770
Craighead Electric Co-op Corp			
4314 Stadium Blvd PO Box 7503 ...... Jonesboro AR 72403	800-794-5012	870-932-8301	245
Crain Communications Inc			
1155 Gratiot Ave .... Detroit MI 48207	888-288-6954	313-446-6000	628-9
Crain's Chicago Business Magazine			
150 N Michigan Ave 16th Fl ...... Chicago IL 60601	877-812-1590	312-649-5200	452-5
Crain's Cleveland Business Magazine			
700 W St Clair Ave Ste 310 .... Cleveland OH 44113	888-909-9111	216-522-1383	452-5
Crain's Detroit Business Magazine			
1155 Gratiot Ave .... Detroit MI 48207	888-909-9111	313-446-6000	452-5
Crain's New York Business Magazine			
685 Third Ave 3rd Fl. .... New York NY 10017	888-909-9111	212-210-0100	452-5
Cramer Inc			
1222 Quebec St .... North Kansas City MO 64116	800-366-6700		318-1
Cramer Products Inc			
153 W Warren St .... Gardner KS 66030	800-345-2231	913-856-7511	472
Crandall University			
333 Gorge Rd .... Moncton NB E1G3H9	888-968-6228	506-858-8970	773
Crane & Co Inc 30 S St .... Dalton MA 01226	800-268-2281*		545-2
*Cust Svc			
Crane Company Dynalco Controls Div			
3690 NW 53rd St .... Fort Lauderdale FL 33309	800-368-6666	954-739-4300	202
Crane Company Stockham Div			
2129 Third Ave SE .... Cullman AL 35055	800-786-2542	256-775-3800	777
Crane Composites Inc			
23525 W Eames St .... Channahon IL 60410	800-435-0080	815-467-8600	599
Crane Manufacturers Assn of America (CMAA)			
8720 Red Oak Blvd Ste 201 ...... Charlotte NC 28217	800-345-1815	704-676-1190	48-13
Crane Nuclear Inc			
2825 Cobb International Blvd .... Kennesaw GA 30152	800-795-8013	770-424-6343	467
Crane Worldwide Logistics LLC			
1500 Rankin Rd .... Houston TX 77073	888-870-2726	281-443-2777	444
Cranel Inc			
8999 Gemini Pkwy .... Columbus OH 43240	800-288-3475*	614-431-8000	175
*General			
Craneveyor Corp			
1524 Potrero Ave .... South El Monte CA 91733	888-501-0050		465
Cranmore Mountain Resort			
One Skimobile Rd			
PO Box 1640. .... North Conway NH 03860	800-786-6754	603-356-5543	660
Cranston Machinery Company Inc			
2251 SE Oak Grove Blvd .... Oak Grove OR 97267	800-547-1012	503-654-7751	549
Cranston Print Works Co			
1381 Cranston St .... Cranston RI 02920	800-876-2756	401-943-4800	734-7
Cranwell Resort Spa & Golf Club			
55 Lee Rd .... Lenox MA 01240	800-272-6935	413-637-1364	660
CRAssoc Inc			
8580 Cinderbed Rd Ste 2400 .... Newington VA 22122	877-272-8960	703-550-8145	458
Craters & Freighters			
331 Corporate Cir Ste J .... Golden CO 80401	800-736-3335		309
Craven County Convention & Visitors Bureau			
203 S Front St .... New Bern NC 28560	800-437-5767	252-637-9400	207
Crawdaddy's			
6414 W Greenfield Ave .... Milwaukee WI 53214	800-727-9477	414-778-2228	662
Crawford Electric Co-op Inc			
10301 N Service Rd PO Box 10 ...... Bourbon MO 65441	800-677-2667	573-732-4415	245
Crawford Industries LLC			
1414 Crawford Dr .... Crawfordsville IN 47933	800-428-0840		541
Crazy Shirts Inc			
99-969 Iwaena St .... Aiea HI 96701	800-771-2720	808-487-9919	153-3
Crazy Woman Creek Bancorp Inc			
PO Box 1020 .... Buffalo WY 82834	877-684-2766	307-684-5591	357-2
CRB (Council of Real Estate Brokerage Managers)			
430 N Michigan Ave Ste 300 ...... Chicago IL 60611	800-621-8738		48-17
CRBC (Cambria-Rowe Business College)			
221 Central Ave .... Johnstown PA 15902	800-639-2273	814-536-5168	788
CRC (Christian Reformed Church in North America)			
2850 Kalamazoo Ave SE .... Grand Rapids MI 49560	800-272-5125	616-241-1691	47-20
CRC (Container Research Corp)			
1 Hollow Hill Rd .... Glen Riddle PA 19037	844-220-9574	610-459-2160	199
CRC (Coordinating Research Council Inc)			
3650 Mansell Rd Ste 140 .... Alpharetta GA 30022	800-445-8667	678-795-0506	48-19
CRC Evans Pipeline International Inc			
10700 E Independence St .... Tulsa OK 74116	800-664-9224	918-438-2100	191
CRC Industries Inc			
885 Louis Dr .... Warminster PA 18974	800-556-5074*	215-674-4300	534
*Cust Svc			
CRC Press LLC			
6000 Broken Sound Pkwy NW			
Ste 300 .... Boca Raton FL 33487	800-272-7737*	561-994-0555	628-9
*Cust Svc			
CRCA (Consumers' Research Council of America)			
2020 Pennsylvania Ave NW			
Ste 300-A .... Washington DC 20006	800-675-5376	202-835-9698	47-10
Creamland Dairies Inc			
10 Indian School Rd NW .... Albuquerque NM 87105	800-334-3865	505-247-0721	295-25
Cream-O-Land Dairy Inc			
529 Cedar Ln PO Box 146 .... Florence NJ 08518	800-220-6455	609-499-3601	296-4
Creating Keepsakes Magazine			
14850 Pony Express Rd .... Bluffdale UT 84065	888-247-5282	801-816-8300	452-14
Creative Alliance Inc			
437 W Jefferson St .... Louisville KY 40202	800-525-0294	502-584-8787	4
Creative Colors International Inc			
19015 S Jodi Rd Ste E .... Mokena IL 60448	800-933-2656	708-478-1437	309
Creative Communications For The Parish Inc			
1564 Fencorp Dr .... Fenton MO 63026	800-325-9414	636-305-9777	628-2
Creative Environments			
8920 S Hardy Dr .... Tempe AZ 85284	855-777-9305	480-458-4100	419
Creative Financial Group (CFG)			
16 Campus Blvd .... Newtown Square PA 19073	800-893-4824	610-325-6100	398
Creative Foam Corp			
300 N Alloy Dr .... Fenton MI 48430	800-529-4149	810-629-4149	594
Creative Hobbies Inc			
900 Creek Rd Ste A .... Bellmawr NJ 08031	800-843-5456	856-933-2540	43
Creative Impact Group Inc			
801 Skokie Blvd Ste 108 .... Northbrook IL 60062	800-445-2171	847-945-7401	185
Creative Kid Stuff			
3939 E 46th St .... Minneapolis MN 55406	800-353-0710	612-929-2431	751
Creative Kids Magazine			
PO Box 8813 .... Waco TX 76714	800-998-2208	254-756-3337	452-6
Creative Labs Inc			
1901 McCarthy Blvd .... Milpitas CA 95035	800-998-1000*	408-428-6600	617
*Cust Svc			
Creative Loafing Atlanta			
384 Northyards Blvd Ste 600 .... Atlanta GA 30313	888-242-0208	404-688-5623	525-5
Creative Outdoor Advertising			
2402 Stouffville Rd .... Gormley ON L0H1G0	800-661-6088		7
Creative Pultrusions Inc			
214 Industrial Ln .... Alum Bank PA 15521	888-274-7855	814-839-4186	192-3
Creative Teaching Press Inc			
6262 Katella Ave .... Cypress CA 92649	800-444-4287	714-895-5047	243
Creative Training Techniques International Inc			
14530 Martin Dr .... Eden Prairie MN 55344	800-383-9210	952-829-1954	755
Creativity for Kids			
9450 Allen Dr .... Cleveland OH 44125	800-311-8684	216-643-4660	752
Creators Syndicate Inc			
5777 W Century Blvd Ste 700 .... Los Angeles CA 90045	877-563-4645	310-337-7003	523
Credant Technologies Inc			
15303 Dallas Pkwy Ste 1420 .... Addison TX 75001	800-929-8331	972-458-5400	178
Credit Acceptance Corp			
25505 W 12 Mile Rd .... Southfield MI 48034	800-634-1506	248-353-2700	214
Credit Card Systems Inc			
180 Shepard Ave .... Wheeling IL 60090	800-747-1269	847-459-8320	695
Credit Control Services Inc (CCS)			
2 Wells Ave Ste 1 .... Newton MA 02459	800-526-0532	617-965-2000	158
Credit Management LP			
4200 International Pkwy .... Carrollton TX 75007	800-377-7713		158
Credit Research Foundation (CRF)			
8840 Columbia 100 Pkwy .... Columbia MD 21045	866-265-3298	410-740-5499	48-2
Credit Suisse			
11 Madison Ave .... New York NY 10010	800-222-8977	212-325-2000	681
Credit Union Directors Newsletter			
5710 Mineral Pt Rd .... Madison WI 53705	800-356-9655	608-231-4000	524-1
Credit Union Executive Newsletter			
5710 Mineral Pt Rd .... Madison WI 53705	800-356-9655*	608-231-4000	524-1
*Circ			
Credit Union Executives Society (CUES)			
5510 Research Pk Dr .... Madison WI 53711	800-252-2664	608-271-2664	48-2
Credit Union of Denver			
9305 W Alameda Ave .... Lakewood CO 80226	800-951-9014	303-234-1700	69
Credit Union of Southern California			
PO Box 200 .... Whittier CA 90608	866-287-6225	562-698-8326	219
Credit Union of Texas			
PO Box 517028 .... Dallas TX 75251	800-314-3828	972-263-9497	219
Credit Valley Hospital			
2200 Eglinton Ave W .... Mississauga ON L5M2N1	877-292-4284	905-813-2200	371-2
Creditors Adjustment Bureau-LC Financial (CABLCF)			
14226 Ventura Blvd .... Sherman Oaks CA 91423	800-800-4523	818-990-4800	158
Cree Inc			
4600 Silicon Dr .... Durham NC 27703	800-533-2583	919-313-5300	687
NASDAQ: CREE			
Creedmoor Psychiatric Ctr			
79-25 Winchester Blvd .... Queens Village NY 11427	800-597-8481	718-464-7500	371-5
Creform Corp PO Box 830 .... Greer SC 29652	800-839-8823	864-989-1700	714
Creighton University			
2500 California Plz .... Omaha NE 68178	800-282-5835	402-280-2700	166
Creighton University School of Medicine			
2500 California Plz .... Omaha NE 68178	800-325-4405	402-280-2799	167-2
Crescent Cardboard Company LLC			
100 W Willow Rd .... Wheeling IL 60090	800-323-1055		553
Crescent City-Del Norte County Chamber of Commerce (CCDNCVB)			
1001 Front St .... Crescent City CA 95531	800-343-8300	707-464-3174	207
Crescent Ford Truck Sales			
6121 Jefferson Hwy .... Harahan LA 70123	800-575-8785	504-818-1818	56

				Toll-Free	Phone	Class
Crescent Manufacturing Co 1310 Majestic Dr	Fremont	OH	43420	**800-537-1330**	419-332-6484	222
Crescent-News 624 W Second St PO Box 249	Defiance	OH	43512	**800-589-5441**	419-784-5441	525-2
Cresco Lines Inc 15220 S Halsted St	Harvey	IL	60426	**800-323-4476**	708-339-1186	770
Cres-Cor 5925 Heisley Rd	Mentor	OH	44060	**877-273-7267**	440-350-1100	286
Crest Electronics Inc 3706 Alliance Dr	Greensboro	NC	27407	**888-502-7378**	336-855-6422	51
Crest Healthcare Supply 195 Third St	Dassel	MN	55325	**800-328-8908**	320-275-3382	389
Crest Hotel & Suites 1670 James Ave	Miami Beach	FL	33139	**800-531-3880**	305-531-0321	376
Crest Ultrasonics Corp 10 Grumman Ave	Trenton	NJ	08628	**800-992-7378**	609-883-4000	772
Crested Butte Mountain Resort (CBMR) 12 Snowmass Rd PO Box 5700	Crested Butte	CO	81224	**800-810-7669**	970-349-2222	660
Crestmark Bank 5480 Corporate Dr Ste 350	Troy	MI	48098	**888-999-8050**		272
Crestwood Manor 50 Lacey Rd *General	Whiting	NJ	08759	**877-467-1652***	732-849-4900	663
Crete Carrier Corp 400 NW 56th St PO Box 81228 *Cust Svc	Lincoln	NE	68528	**800-998-4095***	402-475-9521	770
Creutzfeldt-Jakob Disease Foundation Inc 341 W 38th St Ste 501	New York	NY	10018	**800-659-1991**	212-719-5900	47-17
Crew Outfitters Inc 1001 Virginia Ave	Atlanta	GA	30354	**888-345-5353**		154
CRF (Credit Research Foundation) 8840 Columbia 100 Pkwy	Columbia	MD	21045	**866-265-3298**	410-740-5499	48-2
CRG (Council for Responsible Genetics) 5 Upland Rd Ste 3	Cambridge	MA	02140	**888-591-3911**	617-868-0870	48-19
Cricket Media Inc 30 Grove St Ste C	Peterborough	NH	03458	**800-821-0115**		452-6
Criminal Law Reporter 1801 S Bell St	Arlington	VA	22202	**800-372-1033**		524-7
Crissey Field State Recreation Site 1655 Hwy 101 N	Brookings	OR	97415	**800-551-6949**	541-469-2021	558
CRISTA Ministries 19303 Fremont Ave N *Cust Svc	Seattle	WA	98133	**800-346-9140***	206-546-7200	47-5
Cristek Interconnects Inc 5395 E Hunter Ave	Anaheim	CA	92807	**888-265-9162**	714-696-5200	802
Criswell College 4010 Gaston Ave	Dallas	TX	75246	**800-899-0012**	214-821-5433	166
Criterion Thread Company Inc 21744 98th Ave *General	Queens Village	NY	11429	**800-695-0080***	718-464-4200	587
Critical Path Inc 2655 Campus Dr Ste 250	San Mateo	CA	94403	**800-353-8437**	650-480-7300	38
Criticare Systems Inc N7W22025 Johnson Dr	Waukesha	WI	53186	**800-458-4615**	262-798-8282	471
Criticom Inc 4211 Forbes Blvd	Lanham	MD	20706	**800-449-3384**	301-306-0600	726
Critter Control Inc 9435 E Cherry Bend Rd	Traverse City	MI	49684	**800-451-6544**	231-947-2400	309
CRM Dynamics Inc 245 Glenforest Rd	Toronto	ON	M4N2A5	**866-740-2424**		197
CRM Learning 2218 Faraday Ave Ste 110	Carlsbad	CA	92008	**800-421-0833**	760-431-9800	506
CRMC (Capital Research & Management Co) 333 S Hope St	Los Angeles	CA	90071	**800-421-4225**	213-486-9200	398
CRMC (Capital Regional Medical Ctr) 2626 Capital Medical Blvd	Tallahassee	FL	32308	**800-994-6610**	850-325-5000	371-3
CRMC (Colquitt Regional Medical Ctr) 3131 S Main St PO Box 40	Moultrie	GA	31768	**888-262-2762**	229-985-3420	371-3
CRN Digital Talk Radio 10487 Sunland Blvd	Sunland	CA	91040	**800-336-2225**	818-352-7152	729
Croatian National Tourist Office 350 Fifth Ave Ste 4003	New York	NY	10118	**800-829-4416**	212-279-8672	765
Crocker & Winsor Seafoods Inc PO Box 51905	Boston	MA	02205	**800-225-1597**	617-269-3100	295-14
Crockett Hotel 320 Bonham St	San Antonio	TX	78205	**800-292-1050**	210-225-6500	376
Crocs Inc 6328 Monarch Pk Pl *NASDAQ: CROX*	Niwot	CO	80503	**866-306-3179**	303-848-7000	300
Croda Inc 300 Columbus Cir Ste A	Edison	NJ	08837	**888-842-7632**	732-417-0800	143
Croft LLC 107 Oliver Emmerich Dr	McComb	MS	39648	**800-437-8421**	601-684-6121	480
Crohn's & Colitis Foundation of America (CCFA) 386 Pk Ave S 17th Fl	New York	NY	10016	**800-932-2423**	212-685-3440	47-17
Cromers Inc 1700 Huger St	Columbia	SC	29201	**800-322-7688**		295-36
Cronos Containers Inc 1 Front St Ste 925	San Francisco	CA	94111	**866-275-3711**	415-677-8990	264-5
CropKing Inc 134 W Dr	Lodi	OH	44254	**800-321-5656**	330-302-4203	276
CropLife America 1156 15th St NW Ste 400	Washington	DC	20005	**800-266-9432**	202-296-1585	47-2
CROPP Co-op One Organic Way	LaFarge	WI	54639	**888-444-6455**		10-10
Crosby & Overton Inc 1610 W 17th St	Long Beach	CA	90813	**800-827-6729**	562-432-5445	658
Crosby Group, The 2801 Dawson Rd	Tulsa	OK	74110	**800-772-1500**	918-834-4611	465
Crosman Corp 7629 Rt 5 & 20	Bloomfield	NY	14469	**800-724-7486**	585-657-6161	284
Cross Automation Inc 2001 Oak Pkwy PO Box 1026 *General	Belmont	NC	28012	**800-272-7537***	704-523-2222	246
Cross Bros Inc 5255 Sheila St	Los Angeles	CA	90040	**866-939-1057**	323-266-2000	477
Cross Co 4400 Piedmont Pkwy	Greensboro	NC	27410	**800-858-1737**	336-856-6000	382
Cross Country Healthcare Inc 6551 Pk of Commerce Blvd *NASDAQ: CCRN*	Boca Raton	FL	33487	**800-347-2264**	561-998-2232	712
Cross Country Home Services 1625 NW 136th Ave Ste 200 *Cust Svc	Fort Lauderdale	FL	33323	**800-778-8000***	954-845-2468	364
Cross Country Ski Areas Assn (CCSAA) 259 Bolton Rd	Winchester	NH	03470	**877-779-2754**	603-239-4341	47-22
Cross Creek Resort 3815 Pennsylvania 8	Titusville	PA	16354	**800-461-3173**	814-827-9611	376
Cross Financial Corp 74 Gilman Rd PO Box 1388	Bangor	ME	04401	**800-999-7345**	207-947-7345	387
Cross Keys Village 2990 Carlisle Pk PO Box 128 *Mktg	New Oxford	PA	17350	**888-624-8242***	717-624-5350	663
Cross Oil Refining & Marketing Inc 484 E Sixth St	Smackover	AR	71762	**800-725-3066**	870-881-8700	573
Crosscom National LLC 900 Deerfield Pkwy	Buffalo Grove	IL	60089	**888-471-6050**	847-520-9200	225
Crosscountry Courier Inc PO Box 4030	Bismarck	ND	58502	**800-521-0287**	701-222-8498	539
Crosset Company Inc 10295 Toebben Dr	Independence	KY	41051	**800-347-4902**	859-283-5830	296-7
Crossett Inc PO Box 946 *General	Warren	PA	16365	**800-876-2778***		770
Crossman Post Production LLC 35 Lone Hollow	Sandy	UT	84092	**888-553-1958**	801-553-1958	505
Crossmark Inc 5100 Legacy Dr	Plano	TX	75024	**877-699-6275**	469-814-1000	196
Crossmatch 720 Bay Rd Ste 100	Redwood City	CA	94063	**866-463-7792**	650-474-4000	82
Crossroads Bible College 601 N Shortridge Rd	Indianapolis	IN	46219	**800-822-3119**	317-352-8736	159
Crossroads College 920 Mayowood Rd SW	Rochester	MN	55902	**800-456-7651**	507-288-4563	159
Crossroads Systems Inc 8300 N MoPac Expy *NASDAQ: CRDS*	Austin	TX	78759	**800-643-7148**	512-349-0300	177
Crossville Cumberland County Chamber of Commerce 34 S Main St	Crossville	TN	38555	**877-465-3861**	931-484-8444	137
Crossville Porcelain Stone/USA PO Box 1168	Crossville	TN	38557	**800-221-9093**	931-484-2110	741
Croswell Bus Lines Inc 975 W Main St	Williamsburg	OH	45176	**800-782-8747**	513-724-2206	106
Crow Executive Air Inc 28331 Lemoyne Rd Toledo Metcalf Airport	Millbury	OH	43447	**800-972-2769**	419-838-6921	62
Crow Wing Co-op Power & Light Co Hwy 371 N PO Box 507	Brainerd	MN	56401	**800-648-9401**	218-829-2827	245
Crow Wing County 326 Laurel St	Brainerd	MN	56401	**888-829-6680**	218-824-1067	336
Crow Wing State Park 3124 State Pk Rd	Brainerd	MN	56401	**888-646-6367**	218-825-3075	558
Crowder College 601 Laclede Ave	Neosho	MO	64850	**866-238-7788**	417-451-3223	160
Crowder Construction Company Inc PO Box 30007	Charlotte	NC	28230	**800-849-2966**	704-372-3541	189-4
CrowdSource Solutions Inc 33 Bronze Pointe	Swansea	IL	62226	**855-276-9376**		623
Crowell Weedon & Co One Wilshire Blvd 26th Fl	Los Angeles	CA	90017	**800-227-0319**	213-620-1850	681
Crowley Maritime Corp 9487 Regency Square Blvd Ste 2130	Jacksonville	FL	32225	**800-276-9539**	904-727-2200	311
Crowley's Ridge College 100 College Dr	Paragould	AR	72450	**800-264-1096**	870-236-6901	160
Crown Battery Manufacturing Co 1445 Majestic Dr	Fremont	OH	43420	**800-487-2879**	419-334-7181	73
Crown Castle International Corp 1220 Augusta Dr Ste 500 *NYSE: CCI*	Houston	TX	77057	**877-486-9377**	713-570-3000	171
Crown Castle USA Inc 2000 Corporate Dr	Canonsburg	PA	15317	**877-486-9377**	724-746-3600	171
Crown College 8700 College View Dr	Saint Bonifacius	MN	55375	**800-682-7696**	952-446-4100	159
Crown Crafts Inc 916 S Burnside *NASDAQ: CRWS*	Gonzales	LA	70737	**800-433-9560**	225-647-9100	735
Crown Crafts Infant Products Inc 711 W Walnut St	Compton	CA	90220	**800-421-0526**	310-763-8100	63
Crown Financial Ministries 601 Broad St SE	Gainesville	GA	30501	**800-722-1976**	770-534-1000	398
Crown Holdings Inc One Crown Way *NYSE: CCK*	Philadelphia	PA	19154	**800-523-3644**	215-698-5100	123
Crown Management Services Inc 1501 N Guillemard St	Pensacola	FL	32501	**800-844-5280**	850-438-7578	423
Crown Media Holdings Inc 12700 Ventura Blvd Ste 200 *NASDAQ: CRWN*	Studio City	CA	91604	**800-479-7328**	818-755-2400	729
Crown Micro Inc 48351 Fremont Blvd	Fremont	CA	94538	**800-963-7070**	510-490-8187	175
Crown Motors Ltd 196 Regent Blvd	Holland	MI	49423	**800-466-7000**	616-396-5268	56
Crown Packaging Corp 17854 Chesterfld Airport Rd	Chesterfield	MO	63005	**800-883-9400**	636-681-8000	541
Crown Point State Historic Site 21 Grandview Dr	Crown Point	NY	12928	**800-456-2267**	518-597-4666	558
Crown Products Company Inc 6390 Phillips Hwy	Jacksonville	FL	32216	**800-683-7144**	904-737-7144	688
Crown Reef Resort 2913 S Ocean Blvd	Myrtle Beach	SC	29577	**877-435-9125**	843-626-8077	376
Crown Roll Leaf Inc 91 Illinois Ave	Paterson	NJ	07503	**800-631-3831**	973-742-4000	294
Crown Travel & Cruises 240 Newton Rd Ste 106	Raleigh	NC	27615	**800-869-7447**	919-870-1986	761
Crowne Plaza Syracuse 701 E Genesee St	Syracuse	NY	13210	**888-227-6963**	315-479-7000	376
CrownTonka Inc 15600 37th Ave N Ste 100	Plymouth	MN	55446	**800-523-7337**	763-541-1410	655
Crozer-Keystone Health System (CKHS) 190 W Sproul Rd	Springfield	PA	19064	**800-254-3258**	610-328-8700	350
CRS (Catholic Relief Services) 228 W Lexington St	Baltimore	MD	21201	**800-235-2772**	410-625-2220	47-5

Name / Address	City	State	ZIP	Toll-Free	Phone	Class
CRS Inc						
4851 White Bear Pkwy	Saint Paul	MN	55110	**800-333-4949**	651-294-2700	111
CRS Jet Spares Inc						
6701 NW 12th Ave	Fort Lauderdale	FL	33309	**800-338-5387**	954-972-2807	22
CRS Onesource						
2803 Tamarack Rd PO Box 1984	Owensboro	KY	42302	**800-264-0710**	270-684-1469	296-11
CRST International Inc						
3930 16th Ave SW PO Box 68	Cedar Rapids	IA	52406	**800-736-2778**		770
CRU Acquisitions Group LLC						
1000 SE Tech Ctr Dr Ste 160	Vancouver	WA	98683	**800-260-9800**	360-816-1800	174-8
Crucial Technology						
3475 E Commercial Ct	Meridian	ID	83642	**800-336-8915**	208-363-5790	617
Crucible Materials Corp						
575 State Fair Blvd	Syracuse	NY	13209	**800-365-1180**	315-487-4111	714
Cruise America						
11 W Hampton Ave	Mesa	AZ	85210	**800-671-8042**	480-464-7300	119
Cruise Brokers						
2803 W Busch Blvd Ste 100	Tampa	FL	33618	**800-409-1919**	813-288-9597	761
Cruise Concepts						
1329 Eniswood Pkwy	Palm Harbor	FL	34683	**800-752-7963**	727-784-7245	761
Cruise Connection LLC						
7932 N Oak Ste 210	Kansas City	MO	64118	**800-572-0004**	816-420-8688	761
Cruise Connections Inc						
3411 Healy Dr Ste D	Winston-Salem	NC	27103	**800-248-7447**		761
Cruise Industry News						
441 Lexington Ave Ste 809	New York	NY	10017	**800-333-7300**	212-986-1025	524-13
Cruise Lines International Assn (CLIA)						
910 SE 17th St Ste 400	Fort Lauderdale	FL	33316	**877-486-9222**	754-224-2200	47-23
Cruise People Inc						
10191 W Sample Rd Ste 215	Coral Springs	FL	33065	**800-642-2469**	954-753-0069	761
Cruise People Ltd						
1252 Lawrence Ave E Ste 210	Don Mills	ON	M3A1C3	**800-268-6523**	416-444-2410	761
Cruise Shop, The						
700 Pasquinelli Dr Ste C	Westmont	IL	60559	**800-622-6456**	630-325-7447	761
Cruise Vacation Ctr						
2042 Central Pk Ave	Yonkers	NY	10710	**800-803-7245**		761
Cruise Web Inc						
8100 Corporate Dr Ste 300	Landover	MD	20785	**800-377-9383**	240-487-0155	761
Cruise West						
3826 18th Ave W Suite 401	Seattle	WA	98119	**888-862-8881**	206-283-9322	220
CruiseOne Inc						
1201 W Cypress Creek Rd Ste 100	Fort Lauderdale	FL	33309	**800-278-4731**		762
Cruises Cruises						
6604 Antoine Dr	Houston	TX	77091	**800-245-9806**	713-681-9866	761
Cruises Inc						
1201 W Cypress Creek Rd Ste 100	Fort Lauderdale	FL	33309	**888-282-1249***		761
*Cust Svc						
Cruises.com						
100 Fordham Rd Bldg C	Wilmington	MA	01887	**800-288-6006**		763
Crum & Forster Insurance Inc						
305 Madison Ave PO Box 1973	Morristown	NJ	07962	**800-690-5520**	973-490-6600	388-4
Crum Electric Supply Co						
1165 W English Ave	Casper	WY	82601	**800-726-2239**	307-266-1278	246
Crunch Fitness International						
220 W 19th St	New York	NY	10011	**888-227-8624**	212-370-0998	351
Crusader Paper Company Inc						
350 Holt Rd	North Andover	MA	01845	**800-421-0007**		547
Crutchfield Corp						
One Crutchfield Pk	Charlottesville	VA	22911	**800-955-3000***	434-817-1000	454
*Sales						
CRWRC (Christian Reformed World Relief Committee)						
2850 Kalamazoo Ave SE	Grand Rapids	MI	49560	**800-552-7972**	616-241-1691	47-5
Cryobiology Inc						
4830D Knightsbridge Blvd	Columbus	OH	43214	**800-359-4375**	614-451-4375	538
Cryogenic Laboratories Inc						
1944 Lexington Ave N	Roseville	MN	55113	**800-466-2796**	651-489-8000	538
Cryolife Inc						
1655 Roberts Blvd NW	Kennesaw	GA	30144	**800-438-8285**	770-419-3355	84
NYSE: CRY						
Cryovac Food Packaging & Food Solutions						
100 Rogers Bridge Rd	Duncan	SC	29334	**800-391-5645**		541
Crystal Beach Suites & Health Club						
6985 Collins Ave	Miami Beach	FL	33141	**888-643-4630**	305-865-9555	376
Crystal Cabinet Works Inc						
1100 Crystal Dr	Princeton	MN	55371	**800-347-5045**		114
Crystal Group Inc						
850 Kacena Rd	Hiawatha	IA	52233	**877-279-7863**	319-378-1636	177
Crystal Inn						
185 S State St Ste 202	Salt Lake City	UT	84111	**800-662-2525***	801-320-7200	376
*General						
Crystal Inn Salt Lake City Downtown						
230 W 500 S	Salt Lake City	UT	84101	**800-662-2525**	801-328-4466	376
Crystal Lake Chamber of Commerce						
427 W Virginia St	Crystal Lake	IL	60014	**800-946-2248**	815-459-1300	137
Crystal Lake Manufacturing Inc						
2225 Alabama 14 PO Box 159	Autaugaville	AL	36003	**800-633-8720**	334-365-3342	102
Crystal Meth Anonymous General Service Organization (CMA)						
4470 W Sunset Blvd Ste 107 PO Box 555	Los Angeles	CA	90027	**877-262-6691**		47-21
Crystal Mountain Resort						
12500 Crystal Mtn Dr	Thompsonville	MI	49683	**800-968-7686**	231-378-2000	660
Crystal River Preserve State Park						
3266 N Sailboat Ave	Crystal River	FL	34428	**800-326-3521**	352-563-0450	558
Crystal Rock Holdings Inc						
1050 Buckingham St	Watertown	CT	06795	**800-525-0070**	860-945-0661	79-2
NYSE: AMEX						
Crystal Valley Coop						
721 W Humphrey PO 210	Lake Crystal	MN	56055	**800-622-2910**	507-726-6455	276
Crystallex International Corp						
Eight King St E Ste 1201	Toronto	ON	M5C1B5	**800-738-1577**	416-203-2448	497
Crystal-Like Plastics						
2547 N Ontario St	Burbank	CA	91504	**800-554-6091**	323-849-1735	601
Crysteel Mfg Inc						
52182 Ember Rd	Lake Crystal	MN	56055	**800-533-0494***	507-726-2728	465
*Orders						
Crysteel Truck Equipment Inc						
55248 Ember Rd	Lake Crystal	MN	56055	**800-722-0588***	507-726-6041	770
*General						
Crystek Crystals Corp						
12730 Commonwealth Dr	Fort Myers	FL	33913	**800-237-3061**	239-561-3311	253
Crystex Composites LLC						
125 Clifton Blvd	Clifton	NJ	07011	**800-638-8235**	973-779-8866	495

Name / Address	City	State	ZIP	Toll-Free	Phone	Class
CS Mott Children's Hospital						
1500 E Medical Ctr Dr	Ann Arbor	MI	48109	**800-211-8181**	734-936-4000	371-1
CSA Inc						
280 I- N Cir SE Ste 250	Atlanta	GA	30339	**800-844-6584**	770-955-3518	179-5
CSBS (Conference of State Bank Supervisors)						
1129 20th St NW Fifth Fl	Washington	DC	20036	**800-886-2727**	202-296-2840	48-7
CSC (Communications Supply Corp)						
200 E Lies Rd	Carol Stream	IL	60188	**800-468-2121**	630-221-6400	246
CSC (Curtis Steel Company LLC)						
6504 Hurst St PO Box 7469	Houston	TX	77008	**800-749-4621**	713-861-4621	480
CSCOS (C & S Companies)						
499 Col Eileen Collins Blvd	Syracuse	NY	13212	**877-277-6583**	315-455-2000	261
CSE Corp						
600 Seco Rd	Monroeville	PA	15146	**800-245-2224**	412-856-9200	669
CSG (Council of State Governments)						
2760 Research Pk Dr	Lexington	KY	40511	**800-800-1910***	859-244-8000	48-7
*Sales						
CSG (Community Services Group)						
320 Highland Dr PO Box 597	Mountville	PA	17554	**877-907-7970**	717-285-7121	350
CSI (Christian Schools International)						
3350 E Paris Ave SE	Grand Rapids	MI	49512	**800-635-8288**	616-957-1070	48-5
CSI Aviation Services Inc						
3700 Rio Grand Blvd NW	Albuquerque	NM	87107	**800-765-9464**	505-761-9000	13
CSI Compressor Systems Inc						
3809 S FM 1788 PO Box 60760	Midland	TX	79711	**800-676-0654**	432-563-1170	173
Csi Industries Inc						
6910 W Ridge Rd	Fairview	PA	16415	**800-937-9033**	814-474-9353	199
CSI International Inc						
8120 State Rt 138	Williamsport	OH	43164	**800-795-4914**	740-420-5400	179-12
CSM (Cambridge Street Metal Corp)						
82 Stevens St	East Taunton	MA	02718	**800-254-7580**	508-822-2278	487
CSM Metal Fabricating & Engineering Inc						
1800 S San Pedro St	Los Angeles	CA	90015	**800-272-4806**	213-748-7321	477
CSMC (Cedars-Sinai Medical Ctr)						
8700 Beverly Blvd	Los Angeles	CA	90048	**800-233-2771**	310-423-3277	371-3
CSP Inc						
43 Manning Rd	Billerica	MA	01821	**800-325-3110**	978-663-7598	174-1
NASDAQ: CSPI						
CSRM (Cascade Steel Rolling Mills Inc)						
3200 N Hwy 99 W PO Box 687	McMinnville	OR	97128	**800-283-2776**	503-472-4181	714
CSRS (D+H CollateralGuard RC)						
4126 Norland Ave Ste 200	Burnaby	BC	V5G3S8	**866-873-9780**	604-637-4000	626
CSS Laboratories Inc						
1641 McGaw Ave	Irvine	CA	92614	**800-852-2680**	949-852-8161	174-1
CSSA (Communications Supply Service Assn)						
5700 Murray St	Little Rock	AR	72209	**800-252-2772**	501-562-7666	48-20
CSS-Dynamac Corp						
10301 Democracy Ln Ste 300	Fairfax	VA	22030	**800-888-4612**	703-691-4612	261
CST Technologies Inc						
55 Northern Blvd Ste 200	Great Neck	NY	11021	**800-448-4407**	516-482-9001	231
CST/Berger Corp						
255 W Fleming St	Watseka	IL	60970	**800-435-1859**	815-432-5237	537
CSTE (Council of State & Territorial Epidemiologists)						
2872 Woodcock Blvd Ste 303	Atlanta	GA	30341	**866-577-9956**	770-458-3811	48-7
CSTM (Mexico Tourism Board)						
225 N Michigan Ave Ste 1800	Chicago	IL	60601	**800-446-3942***		765
*General						
CT Consultants Inc						
8150 Sterling Ct	Mentor	OH	44060	**800-925-0988**	440-951-9000	261
Ct Gasket & Polymer Company Inc						
12308 Cutten Rd	Houston	TX	77066	**800-299-1685**		325
CT Lien Solutions						
2727 Allen Pkwy Ste 1000	Houston	TX	77019	**800-833-5778**		626
CTAA (Community Transportation Assn of America)						
1341 G St NW 10th Fl	Washington	DC	20005	**800-891-0590**	202-628-1480	48-21
CTB Inc						
611 N Higbee St PO Box 2000	Milford	IN	46542	**800-261-8651**	574-658-4191	273
CTEC (Central Texas Electric Co-op Inc)						
386 Friendship Ln PO Box 553	Fredericksburg	TX	78624	**800-900-2832***	830-997-2126	245
*General						
CTG (Computer Task Group Inc)						
800 Delaware Ave	Buffalo	NY	14209	**800-992-5350**	716-882-8000	181
OTC: CTG						
CTI (Cell Therapeutics Inc)						
501 Elliott Ave W Ste 400	Seattle	WA	98119	**800-215-2355**	206-282-7100	84
NASDAQ: CTIC						
CTI Inc						
11105 Norrth Casa Grande Hwy	Rillito	AZ	85654	**800-362-4952**	520-624-2348	770
CTJ (Citizens for Tax Justice)						
1616 P St NW Ste 200-B	Washington	DC	20036	**888-626-2622**	202-299-1066	47-7
CTL Distribution Inc						
4201 Bonnie Mine Rd	Mulberry	FL	33860	**800-237-9088**	863-428-2373	770
Ctl Engineering Inc						
PO Box 44548	Columbus	OH	43204	**866-366-3832**	614-276-8123	261
CTLGroup						
5400 Old OrchaRd Rd	Skokie	IL	60077	**800-522-2285**	847-965-7500	732
CTMC (Central Texas Medical Ctr)						
1301 Wonder World Dr	San Marcos	TX	78666	**800-927-9004**	512-353-8979	371-3
CTN (Christian Television Network Inc)						
6922 142nd Ave N	Largo	FL	33771	**800-716-7729**	727-535-5622	728
CTS Corp 905 W Blvd N	Elkhart	IN	46514	**800-757-6686**	574-293-7511	253
NYSE: CTS						
CTSI (Continental Traffic Service Inc)						
5100 Poplar Ave 15th Fl	Memphis	TN	38137	**888-836-5135**	901-766-1500	310
CTV-TV Ch 5 (CTV)						
345 Graham Ave Ste 400	Winnipeg	MB	R3C5S6	**800-461-1542**	204-788-3300	730-82
CU Conferences						
8711 Watson Rd Ste 200	St. Louis	MO	63119	**888-465-6010**		384
CUB (Concerned United Birthparents Inc)						
PO Box 503475	San Diego	CA	92150	**800-822-2777**		47-21
Cuba						
315 Lexington Ave	New York	NY	10016	**800-553-3210***	212-689-7215	
*General						
Cubic Corp						
9333 Balboa Ave PO Box 85587	San Diego	CA	92186	**800-937-5449**	858-277-6780	694
NYSE: CUB						
Cubic Defense Systems						
9333 Balboa Ave	San Diego	CA	92123	**800-937-5449**	858-277-6780	694
Cubic Transportation Systems Inc						
5650 Kearny Mesa Rd	San Diego	CA	92111	**800-937-5449**	858-268-3100	467
Cubist Pharmaceuticals Inc						
65 Hayden Ave	Lexington	MA	02421	**877-282-4786**	781-860-8660	84
NASDAQ: CBST						

	Toll-Free	Phone	Class
Cubix Corp 2800 Lockheed Way ...... Carson City NV 89706 *Sales	800-829-0550*	775-888-1000	177
Cudahy Patrick Inc One Sweet Apple-Wood Ln .... Cudahy WI 53110	800-486-6900	414-744-2000	468
CUE Inc 11 Leonberg Rd .... Cranberry Township PA 16066	800-283-4621	724-772-5225	593
CUES (Credit Union Executives Society) 5510 Research Pk Dr ...... Madison WI 53711	800-252-2664	608-271-2664	48-2
Cuesta College PO Box 8106 ...... San Luis Obispo CA 93403	800-675-2526	805-546-3100	160
Cuisinart 1 Cummings Pt Rd ...... Stamford CT 06902	800-726-0190	203-975-4609	36
Cuisine Magazine 2200 Grand Ave ...... Des Moines IA 50312	800-311-3995		452-11
Cuisine Solutions Inc 4106 Wheeler Ave Ste 450 .... Alexandria VA 22304 OTC: CUSI	888-285-4679	703-270-2900	295-36
Cuivre River Electric Co-op 1112 E Cherry St ...... Troy MO 63379	800-392-3709	636-528-8261	245
Culbertson Enterprises Inc (CEI) 600A Snyder Ave .... West Chester PA 19382	800-382-2685	610-436-6400	190-7
Culinary Depot Inc Two Melnick Dr ...... Monsey NY 10952	888-845-8200		403
Culinary Institute Alain & Marie LeNotre 7070 Allensby ...... Houston TX 77022	888-536-6873	713-692-0077	161
Culinary Institute of America 1946 Campus Dr ...... Hyde Park NY 12538 *Admissions	800-285-4627*	845-452-9430	161
Culinary Institute of Charleston 7000 Rivers Ave ...... Charleston SC 29406	877-349-7184	843-574-6111	161
Cullen/Frost Bankers Inc 100 W Houston St ...... San Antonio TX 78205 NYSE: CFR	800-562-6732	210-220-4011	357-2
Culligan International Co 9399 W Higgins Rd Ste 1100 .... Rosemont IL 60018	800-285-5442	847-430-2800	794
Cullman Area Chamber of Commerce 301 Second Ave SW ...... Cullman AL 35055	800-313-5114	256-734-0454	137
Cullman County Public Library System 200 Clark St NE ...... Cullman AL 35055	800-752-7389	256-734-1068	431-3
Cullman Electric Co-op 1749 Eva Rd NE PO Box 1168 .... Cullman AL 35055	800-242-1806	256-737-3201	245
Culpeper Baptist Retirement Community 12425 Village Loop ...... Culpeper VA 22701	800-894-2411	540-825-2411	663
Culpeper National Cemetery 305 US Ave ...... Culpeper VA 22701	800-827-1000	540-825-0027	135
Cultural Ctr for Language Studies 3191 Coral Way Ste 114 .... Miami FL 33145	800-704-8181	305-529-2257	420
Cultural Experiences Abroad (CEA) 2999 N 44th St Ste 200 .... Phoenix AZ 85018	800-266-4441	480-557-7900	750
Culver Academies 1300 Academy Rd ...... Culver IN 46511	800-528-5837	574-842-7000	615
Culver City Unified School District (CCUSD) 4034 Irving Pl ...... Culver City CA 90232	855-446-2673	310-842-4220	676
Culver Duck Farms Inc PO Box 910 ...... Middlebury IN 46540	800-825-9225	574-825-9537	10-7
Cumberland Chrysler Ctr 1550 Interstate Dr ...... Cookeville TN 38501	888-277-4902		56
Cumberland County College 3322 College Dr ...... Vineland NJ 08360	800-433-3243	856-691-8600	160
Cumberland County Public Library 300 Maiden Ln ...... Fayetteville NC 28301	866-488-7386	910-483-1580	431-3
Cumberland Falls State Resort Park 7351 Hwy 90 ...... Corbin KY 40701	800-325-0063		558
Cumberland Gap National Historical Park 91 Bartlett Pk Rd PO Box 1848 ...... Middlesboro KY 40965	888-831-7526	606-248-2817	557
Cumberland Insurance Group 633 Shiloh Pike ...... Bridgeton NJ 08302	800-232-6992		388-4
Cumberland Island National Seashore 101 Wheeler St PO Box 806 .... Saint Marys GA 31558	877-860-6787	912-882-4336	557
Cumberland Mutual Fire Insurance Co 633 Shiloh Pk ...... Bridgeton NJ 08302	800-232-6992		388-4
Cumberland Times-News 19 Baltimore St ...... Cumberland MD 21502	800-742-8149	301-722-4600	525-2
Cumberland University One Cumberland Sq ...... Lebanon TN 37087	800-467-0562	615-444-2562	166
Cumberland Valley Co-op Assn 908 Mt Rock Rd ...... Shippensburg PA 17257	800-488-2197	717-532-2197	442
Cumberland Valley Electric Inc 6219 N US Hwy 25 E ...... Gray KY 40734	800-513-2677		245
Cumbre Inc 3333 Concours Ste 5100 ...... Ontario CA 91764	800-998-7986	909-484-2456	387
Cuming Corp 225 Bodwell St ...... Avon MA 02322	800-432-6464	508-580-2660	530
Cuming County Public Power District 500 S Main St ...... West Point NE 68788	877-572-2463	402-372-2463	245
Cummings Signs Inc 15 Century Blvd Ste 200 ...... Nashville TN 37214	800-489-7446		692
Cummins Construction Company Inc 1420 W Chestnut Ave ...... Enid OK 73702	800-375-6001	580-233-6000	189-4
Cummins Filtration 2931 Elm Hill Pike ...... Nashville TN 37214	800-777-7064	615-367-0040	59
Cummins Inc 500 Jackson St PO Box 3005 .... Columbus IN 47201 NYSE: CMI	800-343-7357	812-377-5000	262
Cummins Southern Plains Inc PO Box 90027 ...... Arlington TX 76004	800-516-4354	817-640-6801	382
Cummins-Allison Corp 852 Feehanville Dr .... Mount Prospect IL 60056	800-786-5528	847-299-9550	110
CUNA Mutual Group 5910 Mineral Pt Dr ...... Madison WI 53705	800-937-2644	608-238-5851	357-4
Cunard Line Ltd 24303 Town Ctr Dr Ste 200 .... Valencia CA 91355	800-728-6273	661-753-1000	220
Cunningham Brick Co Inc 701 N Main St ...... Lexington NC 27292	800-672-6181	336-248-8541	148
Cunningham Manufacturing Co 318 S Webster St ...... Seattle WA 98108	800-767-0038	206-767-3713	223
Cunningham Memorial Library 510 N 6 1/2 St ...... Terre Haute IN 47809	800-851-4279	812-237-2580	431-6
CUNO Inc 400 Research Pkwy ...... Meriden CT 06450	800-243-6894	203-237-5541	383
CUNY (City University of New York) 535 E 80th St ...... New York NY 10075	877-769-7441	212-794-5555	774
CUPA-HR (College & University Professional Assn for Hum Res) 1811 Commons Pt Dr ...... Knoxville TN 37932	877-287-2474	865-637-7673	48-5
CuraScript Inc 6272 Lee Vista Blvd ...... Orlando FL 32822	888-773-7376		579
Curatel LLC 1605 W Olympic Blvd Ste 800 .... Los Angeles CA 90015	866-287-2366		384
Curecanti National Recreation Area 102 Elk Creek ...... Gunnison CO 81230	866-713-9688	970-641-2337	557
CureSearch for Children's Cancer 4600 East-West Hwy Ste 600 .... Bethesda MD 20814	800-458-6223	301-718-0047	659
Currency Museum of the Bank of Canada 245 Sparks St ...... Ottawa ON K1A0G9 *Hotline	800-303-1282*	613-782-8914	513
Current Analysis Inc 21335 Signal Hill Plz Ste 200 .... Sterling VA 20164	877-787-8947	703-404-9200	179-1
Current Inc 30 Tyler St PO Box 120183 .... East Haven CT 06512	877-436-6542	203-469-1337	592
Current USA Inc 1005 E Woodmen Rd .... Colorado Springs CO 80920 *Cust Svc	800-848-2848*		454
Curriculum Assoc Inc 153 Rangeway Rd .... North Billerica MA 01862	800-225-0248		628-2
Curry College 1071 Blue Hill Ave ...... Milton MA 02186	800-669-0686	617-333-2210	166
Curtain Call Costumes 333 E Seventh Ave ...... York PA 17404	888-808-0801	717-852-6910	153-6
Curtis 1000 Inc 1725 Breckinridge Pkwy Ste 500 .... Duluth GA 30096	877-287-8715	678-380-9095	263
Curtis Dyna-Fog Ltd 17335 US Hwy 31 N ...... Westfield IN 46074	800-544-8990	317-896-2561	173
Curtis Industries Inc 2400 S 43rd St PO Box 343925 .... Milwaukee WI 53219	800-657-0853	414-649-4200	802
Curtis Industries LLC 111 Higgins St ...... Worcester MA 01606	800-343-7676		509
Curtis Institute of Music 1726 Locust St ...... Philadelphia PA 19103	800-640-4155	215-893-5252	166
Curtis Instruments Inc 200 Kisco Ave ...... Mount Kisco NY 10549	800-777-3433	914-666-2971	248
Curtis M Phillips Ctr for the Performing Arts 315 Hull Rd PO Box 112750 .... Gainesville FL 32611	800-905-2787	352-392-1900	565
Curtis Packing Co 2416 Randolph Ave PO Box 1470 ...... Greensboro NC 27406	800-852-7890	336-275-7684	468
Curtis Restaurant Supply & Equipment Co 6577 E 40th St ...... Tulsa OK 74145	800-766-2878	918-622-7390	299
Curtis Screw Company Inc 50 Thielman Dr ...... Buffalo NY 14206	800-914-6276	716-898-7800	614
Curtis Steel Company LLC (CSC) 6504 Hurst St PO Box 7469 .... Houston TX 77008	800-749-4621	713-861-4621	480
Curtis, The 1405 Curtis St ...... Denver CO 80202	800-525-6651	303-571-0300	376
Curtiss-Wright Corp 10 Waterview Blvd 2nd Fl .... Parsippany NJ 07054 NYSE: CW	855-449-0995	973-541-3700	22
Curtis-Toledo Inc 1905 Kienlen Ave ...... Saint Louis MO 63133	800-925-5431	314-383-1300	173
Curwood Inc 2200 Badger Ave PO Box 2968 .... Oshkosh WI 54903	800-544-4672	920-303-7300	541
Cusack Wholesale Meat Inc 301 SW 12th St .... Oklahoma City OK 73109	800-241-6328	405-232-2114	296-9
Cushing-Malloy Inc 1350 N Main St ...... Ann Arbor MI 48104	888-295-7244	734-663-8554	618
Custer Public Power District 625 E SE St PO Box 10 .... Broken Bow NE 68822	888-749-2453	308-872-2451	245
Custom Accents 1940 Lunt Ave .... Elk Grove Village IL 60007	888-553-6789	847-640-4725	601
Custom Aluminum Products Inc 414 Div St ...... South Elgin IL 60177	800-745-6333	847-717-5000	480
Custom Bldg Products 13001 Seal Beach Blvd .... Seal Beach CA 90740	800-272-8786	562-598-8808	3
Custom Business Forms Inc 210 Edge Pl ...... Minneapolis MN 55418 *General	800-234-1221*	612-789-0002	109
Custom Cable Industries Inc 3221 Cherry Palm Dr ...... Tampa FL 33619	800-552-2232	813-623-2232	190-4
Custom Chrome Inc 155 E Main Ave Ste 150 .... Morgan Hill CA 95037	800-729-3332	408-778-0500	60
Custom Computer Specialists Inc (CCS) 70 Suffolk St ...... Hauppauge NY 11788	800-598-8989	631-864-6699	181
Custom Coolers LLC 5609 Azle Ave ...... Fort Worth TX 76114	800-627-0488	817-626-3737	655
Custom Culinary 2505 S Finley Rd ...... Lombard IL 60148 *Cust Svc	800-621-8827*	630-928-4898	295-18
Custom Drapery Blinds & Shutters 3402 E T C Jester ...... Houston TX 77018	800-929-9211	713-225-9211	735
Custom Electronic Design & Installation Assn (CEDIA) 7150 Winton Dr Ste 300 .... Indianapolis IN 46268	800-669-5329	317-328-4336	48-19
Custom Fiberglass Mfg Corp Snugtop 1711 Harbor Ave PO Box 121 .... Long Beach CA 90813	800-768-4867	562-432-5454	119
Custom Global Logistics LLC 317 W Lk St ...... Northlake IL 60164	800-446-8336		313
Custom Hotel 8639 Lincoln Blvd .... Los Angeles CA 90045	877-287-8601	310-645-0400	376
Custom Medical Stock Photo Inc 3660 W Irving Pk Rd ...... Chicago IL 60618	800-373-2677	773-267-3100	586
Custom Mold Engineering Inc 9780 S Franklin Dr ...... Franklin WI 53132	800-448-2005	414-421-5444	747
Custom Pack Inc 662 Exton Cmns ...... Exton PA 19341	800-722-7005	610-321-2525	594
Custom Paper Tubes Inc 15900 Industrial Pkwy ...... Cleveland OH 44135	800-343-8823	216-362-2964	124
Custom Products of Litchfield Inc 1715 S Sibley Ave ...... Litchfield MN 55355	800-222-5463	320-693-3221	273
Custom Toll Free 914 164Th St SE #1670 .... Mill Creek WA 98012	800-222-2222		384
Custom Truck Accessories Inc 13408 Hwy 65 Ne .... Ham Lake MN 55304	800-333-1282	763-757-5326	53
Customer Communicator, The (TCC) 712 Main St Ste 187B .... Boonton NJ 07005	800-232-4317	973-265-2300	524-2
Customer Service Delivery Platform Corp 15615 Alton Pkwy Ste 310 .... Irvine CA 92618	888-741-2737		178

Name / Address	Toll-Free	Phone	Class
Cut Flower Wholesale Inc 2122 Faulkner Rd NE ... Atlanta GA 30324	888-997-8367	404-320-1619	293
Cutco Corp 1116 E State St ... Olean NY 14760	800-828-0448	716-372-3111	222
Cutera Inc 3240 Bayshore Blvd ... Brisbane CA 94005 *NASDAQ: CUTR*	888-428-8372	415-657-5500	471
Cuthbert Greenhouses Inc 4900 Hendron Rd ... Groveport OH 43125	800-321-1939	614-836-3866	366
Cut-Heal Animal Care Products Inc 923 S Cedar Hill Rd ... Cedar Hill TX 75104	800-288-4325	972-293-9700	575
Cutler Majestic Theatre at Emerson College 219 Tremont St ... Boston MA 02116	888-627-7115	617-824-8000	565
Cutlery & More LLC 135 Prairie Lk Rd ... East Dundee IL 60118	800-650-9866		359
Cutter & Buck Inc 701 N 34th St Ste 400 ... Seattle WA 98103	800-713-7810	888-338-9944	153-1
Cutter Aviation 2802 E Old Tower Rd ... Phoenix AZ 85034	800-234-5382	602-273-1237	24
Cutter Consortium 37 Broadway Ste 1 ... Arlington MA 02474	800-964-5118	781-648-8700	524-3
Cutter Information Corp 37 Broadway Ste 1 ... Arlington MA 02474	800-964-5118	781-648-8700	628-9
Cutter IT Journal 37 Broadway Ste 1 ... Arlington MA 02474	800-964-5118	781-648-8700	524-3
Eastern 4250 Richmond Rd ... Highland Hills OH 44122	800-954-8742	216-987-2024	160
Cuyahoga Community College *Metropolitan* 2900 Community College Ave ... Cleveland OH 44115	800-954-8742	216-987-4200	160
Western 11000 Pleasant Valley Rd ... Parma OH 44130	800-954-8742	216-987-2800	160
Cuyahoga County Public Library 2111 Snow Rd ... Parma OH 44134	800-749-5560	216-398-1800	431-3
Cuyahoga Falls News-Press 1050 W Main St PO Box 5199 ... Kent OH 44240	800-560-9657	330-541-9421	525-4
Cuyahoga Hills Juvenile Correctional Facility 4321 Green Rd ... Highland Hills OH 44128	800-872-3132	216-464-8200	409
Cuyahoga Molded Plastics Corp 1265 Babbitt Rd ... Cleveland OH 44132	800-805-9549	216-261-2744	597
Cuyahoga Valley National Park 15610 Vaughn Rd ... Brecksville OH 44141	800-445-9667	216-524-1497	557
Cuyamaca College 900 Rancho San Diego Pkwy ... El Cajon CA 92019	800-234-1597	619-660-4000	160
Cuyamaca Rancho State Park 13652 Hwy 79 ... Julian CA 92036	800-444-7275	760-765-0755	558
CVA (Connecticut Valley Arms) 1685 Boggs Rd Ste 300 ... Duluth GA 30096	800-320-8767	770-449-4687	284
CVB Financial Corp 701 N Haven Ave PO Box 51000 ... Ontario CA 91764 *NASDAQ: CVBF*	888-222-5432	909-980-4030	357-2
CVEA (Copper Valley Electric Assn Inc) Mile 187 Glenn Hwy PO Box 45 ... Glennallen AK 99588	866-835-2832	907-822-3211	245
CVS Corp One CVS Dr ... Woonsocket RI 02895 *Cust Svc	888-607-4287*	401-765-1500	237
CW (College of Westchester) 325 Central Ave ... White Plains NY 10606	800-660-7093		788
CWCVB (Wausau Central Wisconsin Convention & Visitors Bureau) 10204 Pk Plz Ste B ... Rothschild WI 54474	888-948-4748	715-355-8788	207
CWF (Canadian Wildlife Federation) 350 Michael Cowpland Dr ... Kanata ON K2M2W1	800-563-9453	613-599-9594	47-13
CWI Gifts & Crafts 77 Cypress St SW ... Reynoldsburg OH 43068	800-666-5858	740-964-6210	43
CWPS Inc 14120 A Sullyfield Cir ... Chantilly VA 20151	877-297-7472		181
CWPT (Civil War Preservation Trust) 1331 H St NW Ste 1001 ... Washington DC 20005	888-606-1400	202-367-1861	47-13
CWU (Church Women United) 475 Riverside Dr Ste 243 ... New York NY 10115	800-298-5551	212-870-2347	47-20
CXM (Chicago Extruded Metals Co) 1601 S 54th Ave ... Cicero IL 60804 *Cust Svc	800-323-8102*		480
CXR Larus Corp 894 Faulstich Ct ... San Jose CA 95112	800-999-9946	408-573-2700	248
CXtec 5404 S Bay Rd PO Box 4799 ... Syracuse NY 13212 *Orders	800-767-3282*	315-476-3000	801
Cyanotech Corp 73-4460 Queen Kaahumanu Hwy Ste 102 ... Kailua-Kona HI 96740 *NASDAQ: CYAN ■ *Sales	800-453-1187*	808-326-1353	474
Cyber Power Systems Inc 4241 12th Ave E Ste 400 ... Shakopee MN 55379	877-297-6937	952-403-9500	253
Cyber-Ark Software Inc 60 Wells Ave Ste 20A ... Newton MA 02459	888-808-9005	617-965-1544	178
Cyberdata Corp Three Justin Ct ... Monterey CA 93940	800-363-8010	831-373-2601	177
Cyberex 5900 Eastport Blvd ... Richmond VA 23231	800-238-5000	804-236-3300	253
Cyberonics Inc 100 Cyberonics Blvd The Cyberonics Bldg ... Houston TX 77058 *NASDAQ: CYBX*	800-332-1375	281-228-7262	472
CyberOptics Corp 5900 Golden Hills Dr ... Minneapolis MN 55416 *NASDAQ: CYBE ■ *Cust Svc	800-746-6315*	763-542-5000	248
Cyber-Rain Inc 6345 Balboa Blvd Ste 230 ... Encino CA 91316	877-888-1452		404
Cybex International Inc 10 Trotter Dr ... Medway MA 02053 *NASDAQ: CYBI*	888-462-9239	508-533-4300	267
Cycle Country Access Corp 205 N Depot St PO Box 107 ... Fox Lake WI 53933 *Sales	800-841-2222*		29
Cycle World Magazine 1499 Monrovia Ave ... Newport Beach CA 92663	800-456-3084	949-720-5300	452-3
Cyclonaire Corp PO Box 366 ... York NE 68467	800-445-0730	402-362-2000	208
Cyclone Drilling Inc PO Box 908 ... Gillette WY 82717	800-318-3724	307-682-4161	533
Cygnus Business Media Inc 1233 Janesville Ave ... Fort Atkinson WI 53538	800-547-7377	631-845-2700	628-9
Cyma Systems Inc 2330 W University Dr Ste 4 ... Tempe AZ 85281	800-292-2962		179-1
Cynosure Inc Five Carlisle Rd ... Westford MA 01886 *NASDAQ: CYNO*	800-886-2966	978-256-4200	421
Cynthia C. & William E. Perry Pavilion 9400 Turkey Lake Rd ... Orlando FL 32819	800-447-1435	321-842-8844	369
CypherWorX Inc 3349 Monroe Ave ... Rochester NY 14618	888-685-4440		384
Cypremort Point State Park 306 Beach Ln ... Cypremort Point LA 70538	888-867-4510	337-867-4510	558
Cypress Bayou Casino 832 Martin Luther King Rd ... Charenton LA 70523	800-284-4386		447
Cypress Care Inc 2736 Meadow Church Rd Ste 300 ... Duluth GA 30097	800-419-7191		364
Cypress Communications Inc 3565 Piedmont Rd NE ... Atlanta GA 30305	844-276-2386	404-869-2500	726
Cypress Hills National Cemetery 625 Jamaica Ave ... Brooklyn NY 11208	800-535-1117	631-454-4949	135
Cypress Semiconductor Corp 198 Champion Ct ... San Jose CA 95134 *NASDAQ: CY*	800-541-4736	408-943-2600	687
CYR Bus Lines 153 Gilman Falls Ave ... Old Town ME 04468	800-244-2335	207-827-2335	106
CYR Bus Tours 153 Gilman Falls Ave ... Old Town ME 04468	800-244-2335	207-827-2335	750
Cyril Bath Co 1610 Airport Rd ... Monroe NC 28110	800-801-1418	704-289-8531	451
Cystic Fibrosis Foundation 6931 Arlington Rd Ste 200 ... Bethesda MD 20814	800-344-4823	301-951-4422	47-17
Cytec Industries Inc Five Garret Mtn Plz ... West Paterson NJ 07424 *NYSE: CYT*	800-652-6013	973-357-3100	143
Cytokinetics Inc 280 E Grand Ave ... South San Francisco CA 94080 *NASDAQ: CYTK*	800-546-5141	650-624-3000	84
Cytolab Pathology Services 6825 216th St Sw ... Lynnwood WA 98036	800-845-6167	425-712-8020	412
CytoSport Inc 4795 Industrial Way ... Benicia CA 94510	888-313-1922	707-751-3942	787
Cyveillance Inc 11091 Sunset Hills Rd Ste 210 ... Reston VA 20190	888-243-0097	703-351-1000	38
Czech Airlines 1 Penn Plaza Ste 1416 ... New York NY 10001	855-359-2932		25
Czech Airlines OK Plus 147 W 35th St Ste 1505 ... New York NY 10001	855-359-2932		26

D

Name / Address	Toll-Free	Phone	Class
D & B 103 JFK Pkwy ... Short Hills NJ 07078 *NYSE: DNB*	800-234-3867	973-921-5500	628-2
D & D Commodities Ltd PO Box 359 ... Stephen MN 56757	800-543-3308		442
D & D Foods Inc 9425 N 48th St ... Omaha NE 68152	800-208-0364	402-571-4113	295-36
D & D Manufacturing Inc 500 Territorial Dr ... Bolingbrook IL 60440	888-300-6869		747
D & H Distributing Company Inc 2525 N Seventh St ... Harrisburg PA 17110	800-340-1001		175
D & R Sports Ctr Inc 8178 W Main St ... Kalamazoo MI 49009	800-992-1520	269-372-2277	702
D & T Trucking Inc 3686 140th St E PO Box 510 ... Rosemount MN 55068	800-624-8130	651-480-7961	676
D & W Inc 941 Oak St ... Elkhart IN 46514	800-255-0829	574-264-9674	328
D Hilton Assoc Inc 9450 Grogans Mill Rd ... Spring TX 77380	800-367-0433	281-292-5088	195
D L Evans Bank 397 N Overland PO Box 1188 ... Burley ID 83318	888-873-9777	208-678-9076	69
D M Bowman Inc 10226 Governor Ln Blvd Ste 4009 ... Williamsport MD 21795	800-326-3274	301-582-2784	770
D River State Recreation Site 1110 NW U.S. 101 198 NE 123rd St ... Lincoln City OR 97367	800-551-6949	541-994-7341	558
D'Angelo Sandwich Shops 600 Providence Hwy ... Dedham MA 02026	800-727-2446	781-461-1200	661
D'Arrigo Bros Company of California Inc PO Box 850 ... Salinas CA 93902 *Cust Svc	800-995-5939*	831-455-4500	10-10
D'vontz 7208 E 38th St ... Tulsa OK 74145	877-322-3600	918-622-3600	603
D'Youville College 320 Porter Ave ... Buffalo NY 14201	800-777-3921	716-829-7600	166
D+H CollateralGuard RC (CSRS) 4126 Norland Ave Ste 200 ... Burnaby BC V5G3S8	866-873-9780	604-637-4000	626
D. P. Curtis Trucking Inc 1450 South Hwy 118 ... Richfield UT 84701	800-257-9151		770
D3 Technologies Inc 4838 Ronson Ct ... San Diego CA 92111	866-487-2365	858-571-1685	261
DA (Debtors Anonymous) PO Box 920888 ... Needham MA 02492	800-421-2383	781-453-2743	47-21
Da Camera of Houston 1427 Branard St ... Houston TX 77006	800-233-2226	713-524-7601	566-3
DA Davidson & Company Inc Eight Third St N ... Great Falls MT 59401	800-332-5915	406-727-4200	681
D-A Lubricant Co 1340 W 29th St ... Indianapolis IN 46208	800-645-5823	317-923-5321	534
Dabney State Recreation Area 30701 Historic Columbia River Hwy PO Box 100 ... Troutdale OR 97060	800-551-6949	503-695-2261	558
DAC (Dougherty Arts Ctr, The) 1110 Barton Springs Rd ... Austin TX 78704	855-787-2227	512-974-4000	49-1
DAC International Inc 6702 McNeil Dr ... Austin TX 78729	800-527-2531	512-331-5323	760
DAC Vision 3630 W Miller Ste 350 ... Garland TX 75041	800-800-1550	972-677-2700	535

Name / Address	City	State	ZIP	Toll-Free	Phone	Class
DACC (Dona Ana Branch Community College)						
2800 N Sonoma Ranch Blvd						
PO Box 30001	Las Cruces	NM	88011	**800-903-7503**	575-528-7000	160
DACCO Transmission Parts						
741 Dacco Dr PO Box 2789	Cookeville	TN	38502	**866-645-1452***	931-528-7581	59
*Cust Svc						
Dacotah Paper Co						
3940 15th Ave NW	Fargo	ND	58102	**800-270-6352**	701-281-1734	552
Dadant & Sons Inc						
51 S Second St	Hamilton	IL	62341	**888-922-1293**	217-847-3324	121
Daemen College						
4380 Main St	Amherst	NY	14226	**800-462-7652**	716-839-8225	166
DAG Media Inc						
125-10 Queens Blvd Ste 14	Kew Gardens	NY	11415	**800-261-2799**	718-263-8454	628-6
Daggett Truck Line Inc						
32717 County Rd 10	Frazee	MN	56544	**800-262-9393**	218-334-3711	770
Dahle North America Inc						
49 Vose Farm Rd Ste 110	Peterborough	NH	03458	**800-243-8145**	603-924-0003	527
Dahlgren & Co Inc						
1220 Sunflower St	Crookston	MN	56716	**877-312-9198**	218-281-2985	295-28
Dahlmann Campus Inn						
615 E Huron St	Ann Arbor	MI	48104	**800-666-8693**	734-769-2200	376
Dahlsten Truck Line Inc						
101 W Edgar PO Box 95	Clay Center	NE	68933	**800-228-4313**	402-762-3511	770
DAI (Denali Advance Integration)						
17735 NE 65th St Ste 130	Redmond	WA	98052	**877-467-8008**	425-885-4000	181
Daikin America Inc						
20 Olympic Dr	Orangeburg	NY	10962	**800-365-9570***	845-365-9500	598-2
*Cust Svc						
Daily Advertiser, The						
1100 Bertrand Dr	Lafayette	LA	70506	**888-522-6278**	337-289-6300	525-2
Daily American Republic						
208 Poplar St PO Box 7	Poplar Bluff	MO	63901	**888-276-2242**	573-785-1414	525-2
Daily Breeze						
5215 Torrance Blvd	Torrance	CA	90503	**800-356-7057**	310-540-5511	525-2
Daily Commercial						
212 E Main St	Leesburg	FL	34748	**866-273-2273**	352-365-8200	525-2
Daily Courier						
409 SE Seventh St	Grants Pass	OR	97526	**800-228-0457**	541-474-3700	525-2
Daily Environment Report						
1801 S Bell St	Arlington	VA	22202	**800-372-1033**		524-5
Daily Express Inc						
1072 Harrisburg Pk	Carlisle	PA	17013	**800-735-3136**	717-243-5757	770
Daily Gazette						
2345 Maxon Rd Ext						
PO Box 1090	Schenectady	NY	12301	**800-262-2211**	518-374-4141	525-2
Daily Globe, The						
118 E McLeod Ave PO Box 548	Ironwood	MI	49938	**800-236-2887**	906-932-2211	628-8
Daily Herald						
1555 N Freedom Blvd	Provo	UT	84604	**800-880-8075**	801-373-5050	525-2
Daily Journal						
8 Dearborn Sq	Kankakee	IL	60901	**866-299-9256**	815-937-3300	525-2
NASDAQ: DJCO						
Daily Labor Report						
1801 S Bell St	Arlington	VA	22202	**800-372-1033**		524-7
Daily News						
724 Bell Fork Rd						
PO Box 196	Jacksonville	NC	28541	**800-659-2873**	910-353-1171	525-2
Daily News of Los Angeles						
21221 Oxnard St	Woodland Hills	CA	91367	**800-559-1950**	818-713-3000	525-2
Daily Nonpareil						
535 W Broadway Ste 300	Council Bluffs	IA	51503	**800-283-1882**	712-328-1811	525-2
Daily Press						
13891 Pk Ave PO Box 1389	Victorville	CA	92393	**844-287-3897**	760-241-7744	525-2
Daily Progress						
685 W Rio Rd	Charlottesville	VA	22902	**866-469-4866**	434-978-7200	628-8
Daily Racing Form						
100 Broadway Seventh Fl	New York	NY	10005	**800-306-3676***	212-366-7600	452-14
*Cust Svc						
Daily Record						
212 E Liberty St PO Box 918	Wooster	OH	44691	**800-686-2958**	330-264-1125	525-2
Daily Report for Executives						
1801 S Bell St	Arlington	VA	22202	**800-372-1033**		524-2
Daily Review						
22533 Foothill Blvd	Hayward	CA	94541	**800-595-9595**	510-783-6111	525-2
Daily Sentinel						
PO Box 668	Grand Junction	CO	81502	**800-332-5832**	970-242-5050	525-2
Daily Star						
102 Chestnut St PO Box 250	Oneonta	NY	13820	**800-721-1000**	607-432-1000	525-2
Daily Sun						
1100 Main St	The Villages	FL	32159	**800-726-6592**	352-753-1119	525-4
Daily Tax Report						
1801 S Bell St	Arlington	VA	22202	**800-372-1033**		524-2
Daily Telegram						
133 N Winter St	Adrian	MI	49221	**800-968-5111**	517-265-5111	525-2
Daily Times						
201 N Allen Ave	Farmington	NM	87401	**877-599-3331**	505-325-4545	525-2
Daily World						
315 S Michigan St	Aberdeen	WA	98520	**800-829-7880**	360-532-4000	525-2
DailyAccess Corp						
307 University Blvd N Bldg 3						
Ste 1500	Mobile	AL	36688	**877-859-5735**	251-665-1800	387
DaimlerChrysler Corp Jeep Div						
PO Box 21-8004	Auburn Hills	MI	48321	**800-992-1997***		58
*Cust Svc						
Dairiconcepts LP						
3253 E Chestnut Expy	Springfield	MO	65802	**877-596-4374**	417-829-3400	295-5
Dairy Council Digest						
10255 W Higgins Rd Ste 900	Rosemont	IL	60018	**800-426-8271***	847-803-2000	524-8
*Cust Svc						
Dairy Farmers of America Inc						
10220 N Ambassador Dr						
Northpointe Tower	Kansas City	MO	64153	**888-332-6455**	816-801-6455	295-5
Dairy Farmers of America PAC						
10220 N Ambassador Dr						
Northpointe Twr	Kansas City	MO	64153	**888-332-6455**	816-801-6455	608
Dairy Herd Management						
10901 W 84th Terr	Lenexa	KS	66214	**800-255-5113**	913-438-8700	452-1
Dairy Management Inc (DMI)						
10255 W Higgins Rd Ste 900	Rosemont	IL	60018	**800-853-2479**		47-2
Dairy One						
730 Warren Rd	Ithaca	NY	14850	**800-344-2697**	607-257-1272	11-2
Dairy Queen						
7505 Metro Blvd	Minneapolis	MN	55439	**800-883-4279**	952-830-0200	378
Dairyamerica Inc						
7815 N Palm Ave Ste 250	Fresno	CA	93711	**800-722-3110**	559-251-0992	48-18
Dairyland Greyhound Park						
5522 104th Ave	Kenosha	WI	53144	**800-233-3357**	262-657-8200	132
Dairyland Insurance Co						
1800 N Pt Dr	Stevens Point	WI	54481	**866-445-5364***	715-346-6000	388-4
*Sales						
Daisy IT Supplies Sales & Service						
8575 Red Oak Ave	Rancho Cucamonga	CA	91730	**800-266-5585**	909-989-5585	111
Daisy Outdoor Products						
400 W Stribling Dr	Rogers	AR	72756	**800-643-3458**	479-636-1200	701
Daisy Rock Guitars						
16320 Roscoe Blvd Ste 100	Van Nuys	CA	91410	**877-693-2479**		520
Daiwa Corp						
12851 Midway Pl	Cerritos	CA	90703	**800-736-4653**	562-802-9589	701
DakoCytomation						
6392 Via Real	Carpinteria	CA	93013	**800-400-3256***	805-566-6655	231
*Cust Svc						
Dakota Central Telecommunications Co-op						
630 Fifth St N	Carrington	ND	58421	**800-771-0974**	701-652-3184	726
Dakota County Technical College						
1300 E 145th St	Rosemount	MN	55068	**877-937-3282**	651-423-8301	788
Dakota Drug Inc						
28 Main St N	Minot	ND	58703	**800-437-2018**	701-852-2141	238
Dakota Electric Assn						
4300 220th St W	Farmington	MN	55024	**800-874-3409**	651-463-6144	245
Dakota Energy Co-op Inc						
PO Box 830	Huron	SD	57350	**800-353-8591**	605-352-8591	245
Dakota Gasification Co						
PO Box 5540	Bismarck	ND	58506	**800-759-0555**	701-221-4400	775
Dakota Granite Co						
48391 150th St PO Box 1351	Milbank	SD	57252	**800-843-3333**	605-432-5580	715
Dakota Growers Pasta Company Inc						
One Pasta Ave	Carrington	ND	58421	**800-543-5561**	701-652-2855	295-31
Dakota Homestead Title Insurance Co						
315 S Phillips Ave	Sioux Falls	SD	57104	**800-425-0388**	605-336-0388	388-6
Dakota Line Inc						
PO Box 476	Vermillion	SD	57069	**800-532-5682**	605-624-5228	770
Dakota Marble Inc						
902 W 19th St	Yankton	SD	57078	**800-697-7241**	605-665-7241	715
Dakota Mfg Company Inc						
1909 S Rowley St	Mitchell	SD	57301	**800-232-5682**	605-996-5571	769
Dakota Plains Co-op						
151 Ninth Ave NW	Valley City	ND	58072	**800-288-7922**	701-845-0812	323
Dakota Smith Signature Eyewear						
498 N Oak St	Inglewood	CA	90302	**800-765-3937**	310-330-2700	535
Dakota State University						
820 N Washington Ave	Madison	SD	57042	**888-378-9988**	605-256-5139	166
Dakota Supply Group (DSG)						
2601 Third Ave N	Fargo	ND	58102	**800-437-4702**	701-237-9440	246
Dakota Valley Electric Co-op						
7296 Hwy 281	Edgeley	ND	58433	**800-342-4671**	701-493-2281	245
Dakota Wesleyan University						
1200 W University Ave	Mitchell	SD	57301	**800-333-8506**	605-995-2600	166
Dakotacare						
2600 W 49th St PO Box 7406	Sioux Falls	SD	57117	**800-325-5598**	605-334-4000	388-3
Daktronics Inc						
201 Daktronics Dr	Brookings	SD	57006	**800-325-8766**	605-692-0200	174-4
NASDAQ: DAKT						
Dale Carnegie & Assoc Inc						
290 Motor Pkwy	Hauppauge	NY	11788	**800-231-5800**		755
Dale Laboratories						
2960 Simms St	Hollywood	FL	33020	**800-327-1776**	954-925-0103	581
Dale Medical Products Inc						
PO Box 1556	Plainville	MA	02762	**800-343-3980**		471
Da-Lite Screen Company Inc						
3100 N Detroit St	Warsaw	IN	46581	**800-622-3737**	574-267-8101	584
Dallas Baptist University						
3000 Mtn Creek Pkwy	Dallas	TX	75211	**800-460-1328**	214-333-7100	166
Dallas Christian College						
2700 Christian Pkwy	Dallas	TX	75234	**800-688-1029**	972-241-3371	159
Dallas Convention & Visitors Bureau						
325 N St Paul St Ste 700	Dallas	TX	75201	**800-232-5527**	214-571-1000	207
Dallas Convention Ctr						
650 S Griffin St	Dallas	TX	75202	**877-850-2100**	214-939-2750	206
Dallas County Hospital						
610 10th St	Perry	IA	50220	**800-877-7541**	515-465-3547	371-3
Dallas Independent School District						
3700 Ross Ave	Dallas	TX	75204	**866-796-3682**	972-925-3700	676
Dallas Institute of Funeral Service						
3909 S Buckner Blvd	Dallas	TX	75227	**800-235-5444**	214-388-5466	788
Dallas Johnson Greenhouse Inc						
2802 Twin City Dr	Council Bluffs	IA	51501	**800-445-4794**	712-366-0407	366
Dallas Market Ctr						
2100 Stemmons Fwy Ste 113	Dallas	TX	75207	**800-325-6587**	214-655-6100	206
Dallas Morning News						
508 Young St	Dallas	TX	75202	**800-431-0010**	214-977-8222	525-2
Dallas Opera						
8350 N Central Expy Ste 210	Dallas	TX	75206	**888-353-4537**	214-443-1000	566-2
Dallas Theological Seminary						
3909 Swiss Ave	Dallas	TX	75204	**800-992-0998**	800-387-9673	167-3
Dallas-Fort Worth International Airport (DFW)						
3200 E Airfield Dr PO Box 619428	Dallas	TX	75261	**800-252-7522**	972-973-8888	27
Dalmation Press						
113 Seaboard Ln Ste C-250	Franklin	TN	37067	**800-815-8696**		628-2
Dal-Tile International Inc						
7834 Hawn Fwy	Dallas	TX	75217	**800-933-8453**	214-398-1411	741
Dalton Enterprises Inc						
131 Willow St	Cheshire	CT	06410	**800-851-5606**	203-272-3221	45
Dalton Gear Co						
212 Colfax Ave N	Minneapolis	MN	55405	**800-328-7485**	612-374-2150	700
Dalton State College						
650 N College Dr	Dalton	GA	30720	**800-829-4436**	706-272-4436	166
Daly City Public Library						
40 Wembley Dr	Daly City	CA	94015	**888-227-7669**	650-991-8025	431-3
Daly Computers Inc						
22521 Gateway Ctr Dr	Clarksburg	MD	20871	**800-955-3259**	301-670-0381	177
Daly Seven Inc						
4829 Riverside Dr	Danville	VA	24541	**800-466-5337**	434-822-2161	376
Daman Products Co Inc						
1811 N Home St	Mishawaka	IN	46545	**800-959-7841**	574-259-7841	778
Damascus Bakery Inc						
56 Gold St	Brooklyn	NY	11201	**800-367-7482**		67

	City	State	ZIP	Toll-Free	Phone	Class
Damascus Steel Casting Co						
Blockhouse Rd Run Extn	New Brighton	PA	15066	**800-920-2210**	724-846-2770	487
Damon G Douglas Co						
245 Birchwood Ave	Cranford	NJ	07016	**800-724-1759**	908-272-0100	190-3
Damon Industries Inc						
12435 Rockhill Ave NE	Alliance	OH	44601	**800-362-9850**	330-821-5310	149
Dan Schantz Farm & Greenhouses LLC						
8025 Spinnerstown Rd	Zionsville	PA	18092	**800-451-3064**	610-967-2181	366
Dan Wolf Chevrolet of Naperville						
1515 W Ogden Ave	Naperville	IL	60540	**800-243-8872**	630-596-1189	56
Dan'l Webster Inn						
149 Main St	Sandwich	MA	02563	**800-444-3566**	508-888-3622	376
Dana Innovations						
212 Avenida Fabricante	San Clemente	CA	92672	**800-582-7777**	949-492-7777	51
Dana Transport Inc						
210 Essex Ave E	Avenel	NJ	07001	**800-733-3262**	732-750-9100	770
Dana-Farber Cancer Institute						
44 Binney St	Boston	MA	02115	**866-408-3324**	617-632-3000	371-7
Dana-Farber Cancer Institute Stem Cell/Bone Marrow Transplant Program						
44 Binney St Dana Bldg 1B Rm 30	Boston	MA	02115	**866-408-3324**	617-632-3591	759
Danaher Controls						
1675 Delany Rd	Gurnee	IL	60031	**800-873-8731**	847-662-2666	490
Danaher Corp						
2200 Pennsylvania Ave NW						
Ste 800	Washington	DC	20037	**800-833-9200**	202-828-0850	467
NYSE: DHR						
Danbury Hospital (DH)						
24 Hospital Ave	Danbury	CT	06810	**800-516-3658**	203-739-6398	371-3
Dance Magazine						
333 Seventh Ave 11th Fl	New York	NY	10001	**800-331-1750**	212-979-4800	452-9
Dance Theatre of Harlem Inc						
466 W 152nd St	New York	NY	10031	**800-538-2538**	212-690-2800	566-1
Dancker Sellew & Douglas						
291 Evans Way	Somerville	NJ	08876	**800-326-2537**	908-231-1600	319
Dane Media LLC						
385 Sylvan Ave Ste 24	Englewood Cliffs	NJ	07632	**888-233-2863**		196
Danfords Hotel & Marina						
25 E Broadway	Port Jefferson	NY	11777	**800-332-6367**		375
Dangerous Goods Advisory Council (DGAC)						
1100 H St NW Ste 740	Washington	DC	20005	**800-923-9123**	202-289-4550	48-21
Daniel & Henry Co						
1001 Highlands Plaza Dr W						
Ste 500	Saint Louis	MO	63110	**800-256-3462**	314-421-1525	387
Daniel & Yeager (D&Y)						
6767 Old Madison Pk Ste 690	Huntsville	AL	35806	**800-955-1919**		266
Daniel Boone Regional Library						
100 W Broadway	Columbia	MO	65203	**800-324-4806**	573-443-3161	431-3
Daniel F Young Inc						
1235 Westlakes Dr Ste 255	Berwyn	PA	19312	**866-407-0083**	610-725-4000	444
Daniel Measurement & Control Inc						
5650 Brittmoore Rd	Houston	TX	77041	**800-518-1623**	713-467-6000	202
Daniel Smith Artist Materials						
PO Box 84268	Seattle	WA	98124	**800-426-6740**	206-223-9599	454
Daniel Webster College						
20 University Dr	Nashua	NH	03063	**800-325-6876**	603-577-6000	166
Daniele Inc						
PO Box 106	Pascoag	RI	02859	**800-451-2535**	401-568-6228	295-26
DANK (German-American National Congress)						
4740 N Western Ave Ste 206	Chicago	IL	60625	**888-872-3265**	773-275-1100	47-14
Danly IEM						
6779 Engle Rd Ste A-F	Cleveland	OH	44130	**877-534-8986**		747
Danner Shoe Manufacturing Co						
17634 NE Airport	Portland	OR	97230	**800-345-0430***	503-251-1100	300
*Cust Svc						
Danny Herman Trucking Inc						
PO Box 55	Mountain City	TN	37683	**800-251-7500**	423-727-9061	444
Danos & Curole Marine Contractors Inc						
13083 Louisiana 308	Larose	LA	70373	**800-487-5971**	985-693-3313	532
Dantom Systems Inc						
29241 Beck Rd	Wixom	MI	48393	**866-536-2376**	248-567-7300	225
Danver						
One Grand St	Wallingford	CT	06492	**888-441-0537**	203-269-2300	318-1
Danville Area Community College						
2000 E Main St	Danville	IL	61832	**877-342-3042**	217-443-3222	160
Danville Community College						
1008 S Main St	Danville	VA	24541	**800-560-4291**	434-797-2222	160
Danville National Cemetery						
1900 E Main St	Danville	IL	61832	**800-827-1000**	217-554-4550	135
Danville Public Library						
319 N Vermilion St	Danville	IL	61832	**866-235-6096**	217-477-5220	431-3
Danville Regional Medical Ctr						
142 S Main St	Danville	VA	24541	**800-688-3762**	434-799-2100	371-3
DAP Products Inc						
2400 Boston St Ste 200	Baltimore	MD	21224	**800-543-3840***	410-675-2100	3
*Cust Svc						
Dapper Tire Company Inc						
4025 Lockridge St	San Diego	CA	92102	**800-266-7172**	619-266-1397	745
Daptiv						
1008 Western Ave Suite 700	Seattle	WA	98101	**888-621-8361**	206-341-9117	38
Darby Group Cos Inc						
300 Jericho Quad	Jericho	NY	11753	**888-683-5001**	516-683-1800	576
Dardanelle & Russellville Railroad Co						
4416 S Arkansas Ave	Russellville	AR	72802	**888-877-7267**	479-968-6455	639
Dare Products Inc						
860 Betterly Rd PO Box 157	Battle Creek	MI	49015	**800-922-3273**	269-965-2307	279
Darex						
210 E Hersey St PO Box 730	Ashland	OR	97520	**800-418-1439**	541-488-2224	450
Darice Inc						
13000 Darice Pkwy	Strongsville	OH	44149	**800-321-1494**	866-432-7433	43
Darien Lake Theme Park Resort						
9993 Allegheny Rd						
PO Box 91	Darien Center	NY	14040	**866-640-0652**	585-599-4641	32
Dark Horse Comics Inc						
10956 SE Main St	Milwaukie	OR	97222	**800-862-0052**	503-652-8815	628-5
Darke Rural Electric Co-op Inc						
1120 Fort Jefferson Rd	Greenville	OH	45331	**866-692-6330**	937-548-4114	245
Darling International Inc						
251 O'Connor Ridge Blvd Ste 300	Irving	TX	75038	**855-327-7761**	972-717-0300	295-12
NYSE: DAR						
Darlington Raceway						
1301 Harry Bird Hwy	Darlington	SC	29532	**866-459-7223**		508
Darlington School						
1014 Cave Spring Rd	Rome	GA	30161	**800-368-4437**	706-235-6051	615
Darlington Veneer Company Inc						
225 Fourth St	Darlington	SC	29532	**800-845-2388**	843-393-3861	606
Darlingtonia State Natural Site						
84505 Hwy 101 S	Florence	OR	97439	**800-551-6949**	541-997-3851	558
Darnall Army Medical Ctr						
36000 Darnall Loop	Fort Hood	TX	76544	**800-305-6421**	254-288-8000	371-4
Dar-Ran Furniture Industries						
2402 Shore St	High Point	NC	27263	**800-334-7891**	336-861-2400	318-1
Darrow School						
110 Darrow Rd	New Lebanon	NY	12125	**877-432-7769**	518-794-6000	615
Dart Appraisalcom						
2600 W Big Beaver Rd Ste 100	Troy	MI	48084	**888-327-8123**		643
Dart Container Corp						
500 Hogsback Rd	Mason	MI	48854	**800-248-5960**		594
Dar-tech Inc						
16485 Rockside Rd	Cleveland	OH	44137	**800-228-7347**	216-663-7600	144
Darton College						
2400 Gillionville Rd	Albany	GA	31707	**866-775-1214**	229-430-6742	160
Darue of California Inc						
14102 S Broadway	Los Angeles	CA	90061	**877-693-2783**	310-323-1350	153-20
Darvin Furniture						
15400 S La Grange Rd	Orland Park	IL	60462	**800-232-7846**	708-460-4100	320
Daryl Flood Inc						
450 Airline Dr Ste 100	Coppell	TX	75019	**888-454-9481**	972-471-1496	187
DAS Inc 724 Lawn Rd	Palmyra	PA	17078	**866-622-7979**	717-964-3642	37
Dasco Pro Inc						
340 Blackhawk Pk Ave	Rockford	IL	61104	**800-327-2690**	815-962-3727	748
Dash Multi-Corp Inc						
2500 Adie Rd	Maryland Heights	MO	63043	**888-889-9655**	314-432-3200	357-3
Dash Point State Park						
5700 SW Dash Pt Rd	Federal Way	WA	98023	**888-226-7688**	253-661-4955	558
Dash Tours						
1024 Winnipeg St	Regina	SK	S4R8P8	**800-265-0000**	306-352-2222	750
Dassault Falcon Jet Corp						
PO Box 2000	South Hackensack	NJ	07606	**800-527-2463**	201-440-6700	20
Data Access Corp						
14000 SW 119th Ave	Miami	FL	33186	**800-451-3539**	305-238-0012	179-2
Data Device Corp						
105 Wilbur Pl	Bohemia	NY	11716	**800-332-5757***	631-567-5600	253
*Cust Svc						
Data Exchange Corp						
3600 Via Pescador	Camarillo	CA	93012	**800-237-7911**	805-388-1711	176
Data I/O Corp						
6464 185th Ave NE Ste 101	Redmond	WA	98052	**800-426-1045**	425-881-6444	686
NASDAQ: DAIO						
Data Impressions						
17418 Studebaker Rd	Cerritos	CA	90703	**800-777-6488**	562-207-9050	175
Data Interchange Standards Assn (DISA)						
7600 Leesburg Pike Ste 430	Falls Church	VA	22043	**866-205-5001**	703-970-4480	47-9
Data Label Inc						
1000 Spruce St	Terre Haute	IN	47807	**800-457-0676**	812-232-0408	410
Data Management Inc						
537 New Britain Ave	Farmington	CT	06034	**800-243-1969***	860-677-8586	85
*Orders						
Data Papers Inc						
468 Industrial Pk Rd	Muncy	PA	17756	**800-233-3032**		109
Data Pro Acctg Software Inc						
111 Second Ave NE						
Ste 1200	Saint Petersburg	FL	33701	**800-237-6377**	727-803-1500	179-1
Data Sales Company Inc						
3450 W Burnsville Pkwy	Burnsville	MN	55337	**800-328-2730**	952-890-8838	175
Data Source Inc						
1400 Universal Ave	Kansas City	MO	64120	**877-846-9120**	816-483-3282	109
Data Storage Systems Ctr (DSSC)						
Carnegie Mellon University ECE Dept						
5000 Forbes Ave	Pittsburgh	PA	15213	**800-864-8287**	412-268-6600	659
Data Technology Inc						
14225 Dayton Cir Ste 4	Omaha	NE	68137	**888-334-9300***	402-891-0711	540
*General						
Data Translation Inc						
100 Locke Dr	Marlborough	MA	01752	**800-525-8528**	508-481-3700	617
OTC: DATX						
Data Transmission Network Corp						
9110 W Dodge Rd Ste 200	Omaha	NE	68114	**800-485-4000**	402-390-2328	384
DataBank						
12000 Baltimore Ave	Beltsville	MD	20705	**800-873-9426**	301-837-0197	225
DataCard Corp						
11111 Bren Rd W	Minnetonka	MN	55343	**800-328-8623**	952-933-1223	695
Datacolor						
5 Princess Rd	Lawrenceville	NJ	08648	**800-340-1007***	609-924-2189	416
*General						
DataDirect Networks						
9320 Lurline Ave	Chatsworth	CA	91311	**800-837-2298**	818-700-7600	174-8
Dataflux Corp						
940 NW Cary Pkwy Ste 201	Cary	NC	27513	**800-727-0025**	919-447-3000	178
Dataforth Corp						
3331 E Hemisphere Loop	Tucson	AZ	85706	**800-444-7644**	520-741-1404	174-3
Dataium LLC						
2525 Perimeter Pl Dr Ste 105	Nashville	TN	37214	**877-896-3282**		384
Dataline LLC						
7918 Jones Branch Dr Ste 650	McLean	VA	22102	**800-666-9858**	703-847-7412	261
Datalink Corp						
8170 Upland Cir	Chanhassen	MN	55317	**800-448-6314**	952-944-3462	174-8
NASDAQ: DTLK						
Datalogic Scanning						
959 Terry St	Eugene	OR	97402	**800-695-5700**	541-683-5700	174-7
Datalok Co						
5990 Malburg Way	Los Angeles	CA	90058	**800-232-8256**	323-582-6100	791-1
Datalux Corp						
155 Aviation Dr	Winchester	VA	22602	**800-328-2589**	540-662-1500	174-1
Datamann Inc						
1994 Hartford Ave	Wilder	VT	05088	**800-451-4263**	802-295-6600	179-11
Datamatics Management Services Inc						
330 New Brunswick Ave	Fords	NJ	08863	**800-673-0366**	732-738-9600	179-1
Datamax Corp						
4501 Pkwy Commerce Blvd	Orlando	FL	32808	**800-656-2062**	407-578-8007	174-6
Datamax Office Systems Inc						
6717 Waldemar Ave	Saint Louis	MO	63139	**800-325-9299**	314-633-1400	111
Dataminr Inc						
99 Madison Ave Third Fl	New York	NY	10016	**888-764-4959**		384
DataMotion Inc						
35 Airport Rd Ste 120	Morristown	NJ	07960	**800-672-7233**	973-455-1245	179-7
DataPipe						
10 Exchange Pl	Jersey City	NJ	07302	**877-773-3306**	201-792-4847	795

	City	State	Zip	Toll-Free	Phone	Class
Dataram Corp						
777 Alexander Rd Ste 100	Princeton	NJ	08540	**800-328-2726**	609-799-0071	617
NASDAQ: DRAM						
Datarealm Internet Services Inc						
PO Box 1616	Hudson	WI	54016	**877-227-3783**		795
Datatel Inc						
4375 Fair Lakes Ct	Fairfax	VA	22033	**800-223-7036**		179-10
Datatel Resources Corp						
1729 Pennsylvania Ave	Monaca	PA	15061	**800-245-2688**	724-775-5300	109
DataViz Inc						
612 Wheelers Farms Rd	Milford	CT	06460	**800-733-0030**	203-874-0085	179-12
Datawatch Corp						
271 Mill Rd	Chelmsford	MA	01824	**800-445-3311**	978-441-2200	179-12
NASDAQ: DWCH						
DATTCO Inc						
583 S St	New Britain	CT	06051	**800-229-4879**	860-229-4878	106
Datum Filing Systems Inc						
89 Church Rd	Emigsville	PA	17318	**800-828-8018**	717-764-6350	286
Dauphin County						
2 S Second St 3rd Fl	Harrisburg	PA	17101	**800-328-0058**	717-780-6636	336
Dauphin North America						
300 Myrtle Ave	Boonton	NJ	07005	**800-631-1186***	973-263-1100	318-1
*Cust Svc						
Dauphine Orleans Hotel						
415 Dauphine St	New Orleans	LA	70112	**800-521-7111**	504-586-1800	376
DAV (Disabled American Veterans)						
3725 Alexandria Pike	Cold Spring	KY	41076	**877-426-2838**	859-441-7300	47-19
DavCo Restaurants Inc						
1657 Crofton Blvd	Crofton	MD	21114	**800-523-1411***	410-721-3770	661
*General						
Davco Technology LLC						
1600 Woodland Dr PO Box 487	Saline	MI	48176	**800-328-2611**	734-429-5665	59
Dave & Buster's						
3000 Oakwood Blvd	Hollywood	FL	33020	**844-515-5157**	954-923-5505	662
Dave & Buster's Inc						
2481 Manana Dr	Dallas	TX	75220	**800-842-5369**	214-357-9588	650
Dave Thomas Foundation for Adoption						
716 Mt Airyshire Blvd Ste 100	Columbus	OH	43235	**800-275-3832**		304
Davenport & Co LLC						
901 E Cary St						
One James Center Ste 1100	Richmond	VA	23219	**800-846-6666**	804-780-2000	681
Davenport Hotel, The						
10 S Post St	Spokane	WA	99201	**800-899-1482**	509-455-8888	376
Davenport Insulation Inc						
7400 Gateway Ct	Manassas	VA	20109	**855-626-6459**	703-631-7744	190-9
Davenport Machine Inc						
167 Ames St	Rochester	NY	14611	**800-344-5748**	585-235-4545	450
Dearborn						
4801 Oakman Blvd	Dearborn	MI	48126	**800-585-1479**	313-581-4400	166
Flint						
4318 Miller Rd Ste A	Flint	MI	48507	**800-727-1443**	810-732-9977	166
Lansing						
220 E Kalamazoo St	Lansing	MI	48933	**800-686-1600**	517-484-2600	166
Davenport University						
Lettinga Campus						
6191 Kraft Ave SE	Grand Rapids	MI	49512	**866-925-3884**	616-698-7111	166
Saginaw 5300 Bay Rd	Saginaw	MI	48604	**800-968-8133**	989-799-7800	166
Warren						
27650 Dequindre Rd	Warren	MI	48092	**800-724-7708**	586-558-8700	166
Davey Tree Expert Co						
1500 N Mantua St	Kent	OH	44240	**800-445-8733**	330-673-9511	766
David A. Straz Jr Ctr for, The Performing Arts, The						
1010 N WC MacInnes Pl	Tampa	FL	33602	**800-955-1045**	813-222-1000	565
David Clark Company Inc						
360 Franklin St	Worcester	MA	01615	**800-298-6235***	508-751-5800	569
*Cust Svc						
David Evans & Assoc Inc (DEA)						
2100 SW River Pkwy	Portland	OR	97201	**800-721-1916**	503-223-6663	261
David Grant US Air Force Medical Ctr						
101 Bodin Cir	Travis AFB	CA	94535	**800-264-3462**	707-423-3735	371-4
David H Fell & Company Inc						
6009 Bandini Blvd	Commerce	CA	90040	**800-822-1996**	323-722-9992	404
David Michael & Co Inc						
10801 Decatur Rd	Philadelphia	PA	19154	**800-363-5286**	215-632-3100	295-15
David Weekley Homes Inc						
1111 N Post Oak Rd	Houston	TX	77055	**800-390-6774**	713-963-0500	644
David's Bridal Inc						
1001 Washington St	Conshohocken	PA	19428	**800-823-2403**	610-943-5000	155-6
Davidsmeyer Bus Service Inc						
2513 E Higgins Rd	Elk Grove Village	IL	60007	**800-323-0312**	847-437-3767	108
Davidson College						
PO Box 7156	Davidson	NC	28035	**800-768-0380**	704-894-2000	166
Davidson County Community College						
PO Box 1287	Lexington	NC	27293	**800-233-4050**	336-249-8186	160
Davidson Plyforms Inc						
5505 33rd St SE	Grand Rapids	MI	49512	**800-505-4732**	616-956-0033	807
Davidson Transfer & Storage Co						
1701 Florida Ave NW	Washington	DC	20009	**800-736-6825**	202-234-5600	512
Davies Consulting Inc						
6935 Wisconsin Ave Ste 600	Chevy Chase	MD	20815	**800-811-8336**	301-652-4535	195
Davies Molding LLC						
350 Kehoe Blvd	Carol Stream	IL	60188	**800-554-9208**	630-510-8188	614
Daviess County Metal Sales Inc						
9929 E US Hwy 50	Cannelburg	IN	47519	**800-279-4299**	812-486-4299	688
Daviess-Martin County REMC						
12628 E 75 N PO Box 430	Loogootee	IN	47553	**800-762-7362**	812-295-4200	245
Davis & Elkins College						
100 Campus Dr	Elkins	WV	26241	**800-624-3157**	304-637-1900	166
Davis College						
4747 Monroe St	Toledo	OH	43623	**800-477-7021**	419-473-2700	788
Davis Cos						
325 Donald J Lynch Blvd	Marlborough	MA	01752	**800-482-9494**	508-481-9500	712
Davis Elen Adv						
865 S Figueroa St Ste 1200	Los Angeles	CA	90017	**800-729-4322**	213-688-7236	4
Davis Express Inc						
PO Box 1276	Starke	FL	32091	**800-874-4270**		770
Davis Funds						
2949 E Elvira Rd Ste 101	Tucson	AR	85756	**800-279-0279**		521
Davis Hospital & Medical Ctr (DHMC)						
1600 W Antelope Dr	Layton	UT	84041	**877-898-6080**	801-807-1000	371-3
Davis Instrument Corp						
3465 Diablo Ave	Hayward	CA	94545	**800-678-3669**	510-732-9229	467

	City	State	Zip	Toll-Free	Phone	Class
Davis Paint Company Inc						
1311 Iron St						
PO Box 7589	North Kansas City	MO	64116	**800-821-2029**	816-471-4447	543
Davis Vision Inc						
711 Troy-Schenectady Rd	Latham	NY	12110	**800-999-5431**		388-3
Davisco International Inc						
719 N Main St	Le Sueur	MN	56058	**800-757-7611**	507-665-8811	295-10
Davis-Ulmer Sprinkler Company Inc						
One Commerce Dr	Amherst	NY	14228	**877-691-3200**	716-691-3200	383
DaVita Inc						
1551 Wewatta St	Denver	CO	80202	**800-310-4872**	303-405-2100	349
NYSE: DVA						
Davitt & Hanser Music Co						
3015 Kustom Dr	Hebron	KY	41048	**800-999-5558**	859-817-7100	520
Davol Inc						
100 Crossings Blvd	Warwick	RI	02886	**800-556-6756***		471
*Cust Svc						
Davy Crockett Birthplace State Park						
1245 Davy Crockett Pk Rd	Limestone	TN	37681	**800-342-3145**	423-257-2167	558
Daw Construction Group LLC						
12552 South 125 West	Draper	UT	84020	**800-748-4778**	801-553-9111	187
Dawahares Inc						
1845 Alexandria Dr	Lexington	KY	40504	**800-677-9108**	859-278-0422	155-2
Dawes Arboretum						
7770 Jacksontown Rd SE	Newark	OH	43056	**800-443-2937**	740-323-2355	96
Dawn Food Products Inc						
3333 Sargent Rd	Jackson	MI	49201	**800-292-1362***	517-789-4400	295-16
*Cust Svc						
Dawson Community College						
300 College Dr	Glendive	MT	59330	**800-821-8320**		160
Dawson County Board of Education, The						
517 Allen St	Dawsonville	GA	30534	**866-632-9992**	706-265-3246	676
Dawson Geophysical Co						
508 W Wall St Ste 800	Midland	TX	79701	**800-332-9766**	432-684-3000	531
NASDAQ: DWSN						
Dawson Public Power District						
75191 Rd 433	Lexington	NE	68850	**800-752-8305**	308-324-2386	245
Day & Zimmermann Group Inc						
1818 Market St	Philadelphia	PA	19130	**877-319-0270**	215-299-8000	718
Day Pitney LLP						
242 Trumbull St	Hartford	CT	06103	**800-882-8684**	860-275-0100	425
Day Publishing Co						
47 Eugene O'Neill Dr	New London	CT	06320	**800-542-3354**	860-442-2200	628-8
Daybreak Star Ctr						
3801 W Government Way						
PO Box 99100	Seattle	WA	98199	**800-321-4321**	206-285-4425	49-1
Day-Glo Color Corp						
4515 St Clair Ave	Cleveland	OH	44103	**800-424-9300**	216-391-7070	543
Daylight Donut Flour Company LLC						
11707 E 11th St	Tulsa	OK	74128	**800-331-2245**	918-438-0800	67
Daylight Transport						
1501 Hughes Way Ste 200	Long Beach	CA	90810	**800-468-9999**		770
Days Inns Worldwide Inc						
215 W 94th St Broadway	New York	NY	10025	**800-834-2972**	212-866-6400	376
DaySpa Magazine						
7628 Densmore Ave	Van Nuys	CA	91406	**800-442-5667**	818-782-7328	452-21
DaySpring Cards Inc						
21154 Hwy 16 E	Siloam Springs	AR	72761	**800-944-8000**	479-524-9301	129
Daystar Television Network						
3901 Hwy 121 PO Box 610546	Bedford	TX	76021	**800-329-0029**	817-571-1229	729
Dayton Area Chamber of Commerce						
1 Chamber Plaza Ste 200	Dayton	OH	45402	**800-621-9131**	937-226-1444	137
Dayton Art Institute						
456 Belmonte Pk N	Dayton	OH	45405	**800-272-8258**	937-223-5277	513
Dayton Ballet						
140 N Main St	Dayton	OH	45402	**800-745-3000**	937-449-5060	566-1
Dayton Contemporary Dance Co						
840 Germantown St	Dayton	OH	45402	**888-228-3630**	937-228-3232	566-1
Dayton Foundation						
40 N Main St Ste 500	Dayton	OH	45423	**877-222-0410**	937-222-0410	302
Dayton International Airport						
3600 Terminal Dr Ste 300	Vandalia	OH	45377	**800-433-7300**	937-454-8200	27
Dayton National Cemetery						
4100 W Third St	Dayton	OH	45428	**800-273-8255**	937-262-2115	135
Dayton Parts LLC						
3500 Industrial Rd						
PO Box 5795	Harrisburg	PA	17110	**800-225-2159***	717-255-8500	59
*Cust Svc						
Dayton Power & Light Co						
PO Box 1247	Dayton	OH	45401	**800-433-8500**	937-331-3900	775
Dayton Reliable Air Filter Inc						
2294 N Moraine Dr	Dayton	OH	45439	**800-699-0747***		17
*Orders						
Dayton Rogers Manufacturing Co						
8401 W 35 W Service Dr	Minneapolis	MN	55449	**800-677-8881**	763-784-7714	483
Dayton Superior Corp						
1125 Byers Rd	Miamisburg	OH	45342	**800-745-3700**	937-866-0711	347
Dayton T Brown Inc						
1175 Church St	Bohemia	NY	11716	**800-232-6300**	631-589-6300	732
Dayton Va Medical Ctr						
4100 W Third St	Dayton	OH	45428	**800-368-8262**	937-268-6511	371-8
Dayton/Montgomery County Convention & Visitors Bureau						
One Chamber Plz Ste A	Dayton	OH	45402	**800-221-8235**	937-226-8211	207
Daytona Beach Community College						
1200 W International						
Speedway Blvd	Daytona Beach	FL	32114	**800-352-2583**	386-506-3000	160
Daytona Beach Resort & Conference Ctr						
2700 N Atlantic Ave	Daytona Beach	FL	32118	**800-654-6216**	386-672-3770	376
Daytona Inn Beach Resort						
219 S Atlantic Ave	Daytona Beach	FL	32118	**800-874-1822***	386-252-3626	376
*General						
Dayton-Phoenix Group Inc						
1619 Kuntz Rd	Dayton	OH	45404	**800-657-0707**	937-496-3974	641
Dazian Inc						
18 Central Blvd	South Hackensack	NJ	07606	**877-232-9426**		734-2
Dazor Manufacturing Corp						
2079 Congressional	Saint Louis	MO	63146	**800-345-9103**	314-652-2400	435
DB Aviation Inc						
3550 N McAree Rd	Waukegan	IL	60087	**888-362-6738**	847-336-9220	62
DB Becker Company Inc						
46 Leigh St	Clinton	NJ	08809	**800-394-3991**	908-730-6010	144
D&B Sales & Marketing Solutions						
460 Totten Pond Rd	Waltham	MA	02451	**866-473-3932**	781-672-9200	179-1

	Toll-Free	Phone	Class
DBI Inc 912 E Michigan Ave ....Lansing MI 48912	800-968-1324	517-485-3200	528
DBK Concepts Inc 12905 SW 129 Ave ....Miami FL 33186	800-725-7226	305-596-7226	176
DBS Bank Ltd 725 N Figueroa St ....Los Angeles CA 90017	800-232-5901	213-627-0222	69
DBSA (Depression & Bipolar Support Alliance) 730 N Franklin St Ste 501.............Chicago IL 60610	800-826-3632	312-642-0049	47-17
DBU (Duluth Business University) 4724 Mike Colalillo Dr ....Duluth MN 55807	800-777-8406	218-722-4000	788
DC Group Inc 1977 W River Rd N ....Minneapolis MN 55411	800-838-7927		757
DC Humphrys Inc 5744 Woodland Ave ....Philadelphia PA 19143 *Sales	800-645-2059*	215-724-8181	723
DC Taylor Co 312 29th St NE ....Cedar Rapids IA 52402	800-876-6346	319-363-2073	190-12
DC Tuition Assistance Grant Program 810 First St NE ....Washington DC 20001	877-485-6751	202-727-2824	716
DCA (Diamond Council of America) 3212 W End Ave Ste 202 ....Nashville TN 37203	877-283-5669	615-385-5301	48-4
DCAT (Drug Chemical & Associated Technologies Assn) One Washington Blvd Ste 7 ......Robbinsville NJ 08691	800-640-3228	609-448-1000	48-19
DCCI (Dow Chemical Canada Inc) 450 First St SW Ste 2100 ....Calgary AB T2P5H1	800-447-4369	403-267-3500	142
DCH (Delnor-Community Hospital) 300 Randall Rd ....Geneva IL 60134	800-223-9776	630-208-3000	371-3
DCH Honda of Nanuet 10 Rt 304 ....Nanuet NY 10954	888-495-8660	845-623-1200	56
DCI (Drum Corps International) PO Box 3129 ....Indianapolis IN 46206 *Orders	800-495-7469*	317-275-1212	47-4
DCI Marketing Inc 2727 W Good Hope Rd ....Milwaukee WI 53209	800-778-4805	414-228-7000	196
DCL (Downey City Library) 11121 Brookshire Ave ....Downey CA 90241	877-846-3452	562-904-7360	431-3
DCM (Distribution Ctr Management) 712 Main St Ste 187B.............Boonton NJ 07005	800-232-4317	973-265-2300	524-2
DCOTA (Design Ctr of the Americas) 1855 Griffin Rd ....Dania Beach FL 33004	877-992-9204	954-920-7997	455
DCT (Diversified Chemical Technologies Inc) 15477 Woodrow Wilson St ....Detroit MI 48238	800-243-1424	313-867-5444	143
DD Bean & Sons Co 207 Peterborough St ....Jaffrey NH 03452	800-366-2824	603-532-8311	464
DD Jones Transfer & Warehouse Co Inc 2121 Old Greenbrier Rd ....Chesapeake VA 23320	800-335-4787	757-494-0225	791-1
D&D Sexton Inc PO Box 156 ....Carthage MO 64836	800-743-0265	417-358-8727	770
DD Williamson & Company Inc 100 S Spring St ....Louisville KY 40206	800-227-2635	502-895-2438	295-15
DDA (Directory Distributing Assoc) 1602 Pk 370 Ct ....Hazelwood MO 63042 *General	800-325-1964*	314-592-8600	94
De Marque inc 400 Boul Jean-Lesage Bureau 540 ......Quebec QC G1K8W1	888-458-9143	418-658-9143	175
De Ronde Tire Supply Inc 95 Rapin Pl ....Buffalo NY 14211	800-227-4647	716-897-6690	745
de Saisset Museum at Santa Clara University 500 El Camino Real ....Santa Clara CA 95053	866-554-6800	408-554-4528	513
De Soto National Memorial 8300 Desoto Memorial Hwy ....Bradenton FL 34209	888-831-7526	941-792-0458	557
De Wafelbakkers LLC 10000 Crystal Hill Rd. ....North Little Rock AR 72113	800-924-3391	501-791-3320	295-1
DEA (David Evans & Assoc Inc) 2100 SW River Pkwy ....Portland OR 97201	800-721-1916	503-223-6663	261
Deacon Industrial Supply Co Inc 165 Boro Line Rd ....King of Prussia PA 19406	800-726-9800	610-265-5322	382
Deaconess Hospital 311 Straight St ....Cincinnati OH 45219	800-398-5699	513-559-2100	371-3
Deaf Smith Electric Co-op Inc 1501 E First St ....Hereford TX 79045	800-687-8189	806-364-1166	245
Deal Interactive LLC Three Park Ave 39th Fl ....New York NY 10016	888-415-4888		384
Deal LLC, The 20 Broad St ....New York NY 10005 *Cust Svc	888-667-3325*	212-313-9325	628-9
Dealers Truck Equipment Co 2460 Midway St ....Shreveport LA 71108	800-259-7569	318-635-7567	509
DealersEdge PO Box 606 ....Barnegat Light NJ 08006	800-321-5312	609-879-4456	524-13
DealerTrack Holdings Inc 1111 Marcus Ave Ste M04 .....New Hyde Park NY 11042 NASDAQ: TRAK	877-357-8725	516-734-3600	179-10
DealNet Capital Corp 325 Milner Ave Ste 300 ....Toronto ON M1B5N1	855-912-3444		458
Dean Cluck Feedyard Inc 105 Dean Cluck Ave ....Gruver TX 79040	888-458-4787	806-733-5021	10-1
Dean College 99 Main St ....Franklin MA 02038	877-879-3326	508-541-1508	160
Dean Foods Co 2711 N Haskell Ave Ste 3400 ....Dallas TX 75204 NYSE: DF	800-395-7004	214-303-3400	295-27
Dean Health Insurance Inc 1277 Deming Way ....Madison WI 53717	800-279-1301	608-836-1400	388-3
Dean Transportation Inc 4812 Aurelius Rd ....Lansing MI 48910	800-282-3326	517-319-8300	108
Dean Word Company Ltd 1245 River Rd PO Box 310330. ....New Braunfels TX 78131	800-683-3926	830-625-2365	189-4
Dearborn Chamber of Commerce 22100 Michigan Ave ....Dearborn MI 48124	800-844-5440	313-584-6100	137
Dearborn County Chamber of Commerce 320 Walnut St ....Lawrenceburg IN 47025	800-322-8198	812-537-0814	137
Dearborn Federal Credit Union 400 Town Ctr Dr ....Dearborn MI 48126	888-336-2700	313-336-2700	219
Dearborn Inn the - A Marriott Hotel 20301 Oakwood Blvd ....Dearborn MI 48124	800-228-9290	313-271-2700	376
Dearborn Times-Herald 13730 Michigan Ave ....Dearborn MI 48126	866-468-7630	313-584-4000	525-4
Dearth Motors Inc 520 Eigth St ....Monroe WI 53566	877-495-5321	608-325-3181	56
Death Valley National Park PO Box 579 ....Death Valley CA 92328	866-713-9688	760-786-3200	557
Deauville Beach Resort 6701 Collins Ave ....Miami Beach FL 33141	800-327-6656	305-865-8511	660
DEB Inc 2815 Coliseum Centre Dr Ste 600 ....Charlotte NC 28217	800-248-7190	704-263-4240	215
Deb-El Food Products LLC 2 Papetti Plaza ....Elizabeth NJ 07206	800-421-0330	908-351-0330	296-8
DeBourgh Manufacturing Co 27505 Otero Ave PO Box 981 ....La Junta CO 81050	800-328-8829		286
DeBra-Kuempel 3976 Southern Ave ....Cincinnati OH 45227	800-395-5741	513-271-6500	190-10
DebtFolio Inc 384 Merrow Rd Ste G ....Tolland CT 06084	866-876-3654		384
Debtors Anonymous (DA) PO Box 920888 ....Needham MA 02492	800-421-2383	781-453-2743	47-21
DeCarolis Truck Rental Inc 333 Colfax St ....Rochester NY 14606	800-666-1169	585-254-1169	768
Decatur Area Convention & Visitors Bureau 202 E N St ....Decatur IL 62523	800-331-4479	217-423-7000	207
Decatur Co-op Assn 305 S York Ave PO Box 68 ....Oberlin KS 67749	800-886-2293	785-475-2234	47-2
Decatur County Rural Electric Membership Corp 1430 W Main St PO Box 46 ....Greensburg IN 47240	800-844-7362	812-663-3391	245
Decatur Daily 201 First Ave SE ....Decatur AL 35601	888-353-4612	256-353-4612	525-2
Decatur Memorial Hospital 2300 N Edward St ....Decatur IL 62526	866-364-3600	217-876-8121	371-3
Decatur/Morgan County Convention & Visitors Bureau (DMCCVB) 719 Sixth Ave SE PO Box 2349 ....Decatur AL 35602	800-232-5449	256-350-2028	207
Deccofelt Corp 555 S Vermont Ave ....Glendora CA 91740 *Cust Svc	800-543-3226*	626-963-8511	734-2
Dechert LLP 2929 Arch St Cira Ctr ....Philadelphia PA 19104	800-328-4880	215-994-4000	425
DecisionOne Corp 426 W Lancaster Ave ....Devon PA 19333	800-767-2876	610-296-6000	176
DecisionPoint Systems Inc 19655 Descartes ....Foothill Ranch CA 92610 OTC: DPSI	800-336-3670	949-465-0065	178
DecisionQuest 21535 Hawthorne Blvd Ste 310 ....Torrance CA 90503	877-833-2474	310-618-9600	440
Decker Steel & Supply Inc 4500 Train Ave ....Cleveland OH 44102	800-321-6100	216-281-7900	487
Decker Tape Products Inc Six Stewart Pl ....Fairfield NJ 07004	800-227-5252	973-227-5350	722
Decker Truck Line Inc 4000 Fifth Ave S ....Fort Dodge IA 50501	800-247-2537	515-576-4141	770
Deckers Outdoor Corp 495-A S Fairview Ave ....Goleta CA 93117 NYSE: DECK	877-337-8333	805-967-7611	300
Decko Products Inc 2105 Superior St ....Sandusky OH 44870 *General	800-537-4487*	419-626-5757	295-8
Declara Inc 977 Commercial St ....Palo Alto CA 94303	877-216-0604		384
Deco Products Co 506 Sanford St ....Decorah IA 52101	800-327-9751	563-382-4264	307
DecoArt Inc 49 Cotton Ave ....Stanford KY 40484	800-367-3047	606-365-3193	42
Decoma International Inc Magna Exteriors & Interiors 50 Casmir Ct ....Concord ON L4K4J5	888-348-2398	905-669-2888	484
Decor & You Inc 900 Main St S ....Southbury CT 06488	800-477-3326	203-264-3500	309
Decorating Den Systems Inc 8659 Commerce Dr ....Easton MD 21601	800-332-3367	410-822-9001	390
Decorative Crafts Inc 50 Chestnut St ....Greenwich CT 06830	800-431-4455	203-531-1500	358
Decore-ative Specialties Inc 2772 S Peck Rd ....Monrovia CA 91016	800-729-7277	626-254-9191	114
DeCoty Coffee Company Inc 1920 Austin St ....San Angelo TX 76903	800-588-8001		295-7
Dectron International Inc 4300 Poirier Blvd ....Montreal QC H4R2C5	888-332-8766	514-334-9609	357-3
Dedham Institution For Savings 55 Elm St PO Box 9107 ....Dedham MA 02026	888-289-0342	781-329-6700	69
Dedicated Computing N26 W23880 Commerce Cir ....Waukesha WI 53188	877-523-3301	262-951-7200	174-1
Dedicated Distribution Inc 640 Miami Ave ....Kansas City KS 66105	800-325-8367	913-371-2200	470
Dee Cramer Inc 4221 E Baldwin Rd ....Holly MI 48442	888-342-6995	810-579-5000	190-12
Dee Electronics Inc 2500 16th Ave SW ....Cedar Rapids IA 52404	800-747-3331	319-365-7551	246
Dee Paper Box Company Inc 100 Broomall St ....Chester PA 19013	800-359-0041	610-876-9285	100
Deen Meats PO Box 4155 PO Box 4155...........Fort Worth TX 76164	800-333-3953	817-335-2257	296-9
Deep East Texas Electric Co-op Inc 880 Texas Hwy 21 E PO Box 736..............San Augustine TX 75972	800-392-5986	936-275-2314	245
Deepwater Chemicals Inc 1210 Airpark Rd ....Woodward OK 73801	800-854-4064	580-256-0500	794
Deer Path Inn 255 E Illinois Rd ....Lake Forest IL 60045	800-788-9480	847-234-2280	376
Deer Valley Federal Credit Union 16215 N 28th Ave ....Phoenix AZ 85053	800-579-5051	602-375-7300	219
Deer Valley Resort Lodging PO Box 889 ....Park City UT 84060	800-558-3337	435-645-6626	660
Deerfield Communications Co 4241 Old US 27 S PO Box 851 ....Gaylord MI 49735	800-599-8856	989-732-8856	179-7
Deerfield Correctional Ctr 21360 Deerfield Dr ....Capron VA 23829	800-560-4292	434-658-4368	213
Deerfield Episcopal Retirement Community 1617 Hendersonville Rd ....Asheville NC 28803	800-284-1531	828-274-1531	663
Deerfield Spa 650 Resica Falls Rd ....East Stroudsburg PA 18302	800-852-4494	570-223-0160	697
Deerfoot Inn & Casino 1000 11500 35th St SE ....Calgary AB T2Z3W4	877-236-5225	403-236-7529	376
Deerhurst Resort 1235 Deerhurst Dr ....Huntsville ON P1H2E8 *Sales	800-461-6522*	705-789-6411	660
Deering Banjo Co 3733 Kenora Dr ....Spring Valley CA 91977	800-845-7791	619-464-8252	520

				Toll-Free	Phone	Class
DeFehr Furniture Ltd						
125 Furniture Pk	Winnipeg	MB	R2G1B9	**877-333-3471**	204-988-5630	318-2
Defender Industries Inc						
42 Great Neck Rd	Waterford	CT	06385	**800-628-8225**	860-701-3400	760
Defenders Magazine						
1130 17th St NW	Washington	DC	20036	**800-385-9712**	202-682-9400	452-19
Defenders of Wildlife						
1130 17th St NW	Washington	DC	20036	**800-385-9712**	202-682-9400	47-3
Defense Finance & Accounting Service						
8899 E 56th St	Indianapolis	IN	46249	**888-332-7411**		724
Defense Group Inc						
307 Annandale Rd Ste 110	Falls Church	VA	22042	**877-233-5789**	703-532-0802	261
Defense Hotline for Fraud Waste & Abuse						
The Pentagon	Washington	DC	20301	**800-424-9098**	703-604-8799	338-3
Defense Nuclear Facilities Safety Board						
625 Indiana Ave NW Ste 700	Washington	DC	20004	**800-788-4016**	202-694-7000	338-18
Defense Research Institute (DRI)						
55 W Monroe St Ste 20	Chicago	IL	60603	**866-525-6466**	312-795-1101	48-10
Defense Technical Information Ctr (DTIC)						
8725 John J Kingman Rd						
Ste 0944	Fort Belvoir	VA	22060	**800-225-3842**	703-767-9100	338-3
Defense Technology/Federal Laboratories						
1855 S Loop PO Box 248	Casper	WY	82601	**877-248-3835**	307-235-2136	284
Defense Threat Reduction Agency						
8725 John T Kingman Rd						
MS 6201	Fort Belvoir	VA	22060	**800-701-5096**	703-767-5870	338-3
Deffenbaugh Industries Inc						
2601 Midwest Dr	Kansas City	KS	66111	**800-631-3301**	913-631-3300	792
Defiance College						
701 N Clinton St	Defiance	OH	43512	**800-520-4632**	419-784-4010	166
Deflect-O Corp						
7035 E 86th St	Indianapolis	IN	46250	**800-428-4328**		527
Degesch America Inc						
PO Box 116	Weyers Cave	VA	24486	**800-330-2525**	540-234-9281	280
DeGraaf Nature Ctr						
600 Graafschap Rd	Holland	MI	49423	**888-535-5792**	616-355-1057	49-4
DeGrazia Gallery in the Sun						
6300 N Swan Rd	Tucson	AZ	85718	**800-545-2185**	520-299-9191	513
Degree Controls Inc						
18 Meadowbrook Dr	Milford	NH	03055	**877-334-7332**	603-672-8900	256
DEI Holdings Inc						
One Viper Way	Vista	CA	92081	**800-876-0800**	760-598-6200	51
OTC: DEIX						
Dejana Truck & Utility Equipment Company Inc						
490 Pulaski Rd	Kings Park	NY	11754	**877-335-2621**	631-544-9000	770
DeKalb Chamber of Commerce						
125 Clairemont Ave Ste 235	Tucker	GA	30084	**800-428-7337**	404-378-8000	137
DeKalb County Public Library						
215 Sycamore St	Decatur	GA	30030	**800-677-1116**	404-370-3070	431-3
DeKalb Public Library						
309 Oak St	DeKalb	IL	60115	**888-268-2824**	815-756-9568	431-3
Del Amo Fashion Ctr						
3525 Carson St	Torrance	CA	90503	**877-746-6642**	310-542-8525	455
Del Amo Hospital						
23700 Camino Del Sol	Torrance	CA	90505	**800-533-5266**	310-530-1151	371-5
Del Mar Avionics						
1601 Alton Pkwy Ste C	Irvine	CA	92606	**800-854-0481**	949-250-3200	522
Del Mar College						
East						
101 Baldwin Blvd	Corpus Christi	TX	78404	**800-652-3357**	361-698-1200	160
Del Mar Die Casting Co						
12901 S Western Ave	Gardena	CA	90249	**800-624-7468**	323-321-0600	307
Del Monte Foods Co						
1 Maritime Plaza	San Francisco	CA	94111	**800-543-3090***	415-247-3000	295-20
*Cust Svc						
Del Monte Fresh Produce Co						
241 Sevilla Ave	Coral Gables	FL	33134	**800-950-3683***	305-520-8400	296-7
*Cust Svc						
Del Monte Lodge Renaissance Rochester Hotel & Spa, The						
41 N Main St	Pittsford	NY	14534	**866-237-5979**	585-381-9900	376
Del Rey Beach State Recreation Site						
100 Peter Iredale Rd	Hammond	OR	97121	**800-551-6949**		558
Del Rio Chamber of Commerce (DRCoC)						
1915 Veterans Blvd	Del Rio	TX	78840	**800-889-8149***	830-775-3551	137
*General						
Del Taco Inc						
25521 Commercentre Dr						
Ste 200	Lake Forest	CA	92630	**800-852-7204***	949-462-9300	661
*Cust Svc						
DelaGet LLC						
6608 Flying Cloud Dr	Eden Prairie	MN	55344	**866-264-5050**		197
Delaine James Inc						
10508C Boyer Blvd Ste 400	Austin	TX	78758	**800-999-5333***	512-835-5333	86
*Claims						
Delair Group LLC						
8600 River Rd	Delair	NJ	08110	**800-235-0185**		719
DELAMAR Greenwich Harbor						
500 Steamboat Rd	Greenwich	CT	06830	**866-335-2627**	203-661-9800	376
DeLand Area Chamber of Commerce						
336 N Woodland Blvd	DeLand	FL	32720	**800-611-5207**	386-734-4331	137
Delaware						
Agriculture Dept						
2320 S DuPont Hwy	Dover	DE	19901	**800-282-8685**	302-739-4811	337-8
Child Support Enforcement Div (DCSE)						
84A Christiana Rd	New Castle	DE	19720	**800-464-4357**	302-577-7171	337-8
Emergency Management Agency						
165 Brick Store Landing Rd	Smyrna	DE	19977	**877-729-3362**	302-659-3362	337-8
Parks & Recreation Div						
89 Kings Hwy	Dover	DE	19901	**877-987-2757***	302-739-9200	337-8
*Campground Resv						
Tourism Office						
99 Kings Hwy	Dover	DE	19901	**866-284-7483**	302-739-4271	337-8
Weights & Measures Office						
2320 S DuPont Hwy	Dover	DE	19901	**800-282-8685**	302-739-4811	337-8
Delaware Art Museum						
2301 Kentmere Pkwy	Wilmington	DE	19806	**800-272-8258**	302-571-9590	513
Delaware Assn of Realtors						
134 E Water St	Dover	DE	19901	**800-305-4445**	302-734-4444	647
Delaware County Community College						
901 Media Line Rd	Media	PA	19063	**800-908-9946**	610-359-5000	160
Delaware County District Library						
84 E Winter St	Delaware	OH	43015	**866-862-7286**	740-362-3861	431-3
Delaware County Intermediate Unit						
200 Yale Ave	Morton	PA	19070	**800-441-3215**	610-938-9000	676
Delaware Div of Libraries						
497 S Red Haven Ln	Dover	DE	19901	**800-829-4059**	302-739-4748	431-5
Delaware Electric Co-op Inc						
PO Box 600	Greenwood	DE	19950	**800-282-8595**	302-349-3147	245
Delaware Hospice Inc						
3515 Silverside Rd	Wilmington	DE	19810	**800-838-9800**	302-478-5707	360
Delaware Mfg Industries Corp						
3776 Commerce Ct	Wheatfield	NY	14120	**800-248-3642**	716-743-4360	262
Delaware North Cos Gaming & Entertainment						
40 Fountain Plz	Buffalo	NY	14202	**800-828-7240**	716-858-5000	633
Delaware North Cos Inc						
40 Fountain Plz	Buffalo	NY	14202	**800-828-7240**	716-858-5000	186
Delaware North Cos Parks & Resorts						
40 Fountain Plz	Buffalo	NY	14202	**800-828-7240**	716-858-5000	271
Delaware Nurses Assn (DNA)						
4765 Ogletown-Stanton Rd Ste L10	Newark	DE	19713	**800-626-4081**	302-733-5880	526
Delaware Park Racetrack & Slots Casino						
777 Delaware Pk Blvd	Wilmington	DE	19804	**800-417-5687**	302-994-2521	633
Delaware Psychiatric Ctr						
1901 N Dupont Hwy Main Bldg	New Castle	DE	19720	**800-652-2929**	302-255-9399	371-5
Delaware State Bar Assn						
405 N King St	Wilmington	DE	19801	**855-872-5911**	302-658-5279	71
Delaware State Chamber of Commerce						
1201 N Orange St Ste 200						
PO Box 671	Wilmington	DE	19899	**800-292-9507**	302-655-7221	138
Delaware State News						
110 Galaxy Dr PO Box 737	Dover	DE	19903	**800-282-8586**	302-674-3600	525-2
Delaware State Park						
5202 US Rt 23 N	Delaware	OH	43015	**866-644-6727**	740-548-4631	558
Delaware State University						
1200 N DuPont Hwy	Dover	DE	19901	**800-845-2544***	302-857-6351	166
*Admissions						
Delaware Transit Corp						
119 Lower Beach St Ste 100	Wilmington	DE	19805	**800-652-3278**	302-576-6000	463
Delaware Valley College						
700 E Butler Ave	Doylestown	PA	18901	**800-233-5825**	215-489-2211	166
Delaware Valley Wholesale Florist Inc (DVWF)						
520 Mantua Blvd N	Sewell	NJ	08080	**800-676-1212**	856-468-7000	293
DeLeon's Bromeliads Co						
13745 SW 216th St	Miami	FL	33170	**800-448-8649**	305-238-6028	366
Delfield Co						
980 S Isabella Rd	Mount Pleasant	MI	48858	**800-733-8821**	989-773-7981	297
Deli Express						
16101 W 78th St	Eden Prairie	MN	55344	**800-328-8184**		295-36
Delicious Living Magazine						
1401 Pearl St Ste 200	Boulder	CO	80302	**866-458-4935**	303-939-8440	452-11
Delight Grecian Foods Inc						
1201 Tonne Rd	Elk Grove Village	IL	60007	**800-621-4387**	847-364-1010	295-1
Delkor Systems Inc						
8700 Rendova St NE	Circle Pines	MN	55014	**800-328-5558**	763-783-0855	540
Dell						
8270 Willow Oaks Corporate Dr						
Ste 300	Fairfax	VA	22031	**877-219-6982**	703-289-8000	195
Dell Inc						
One Dell Way	Round Rock	TX	78682	**800-879-3355**	512-338-4400	174-1
NASDAQ: DELL						
Dellenbach Motors						
3111 S College Ave	Fort Collins	CO	80525	**866-963-5689**		56
Delmarva Foundation For Medical Care Inc (DFMC)						
28464 Marlboro Ave	Easton	MD	21601	**800-999-3362**	410-822-0697	469
Delmarva Power						
PO Box 231	Wilmington	DE	19899	**800-898-8042***		775
*Cust Svc						
Delmont Laboratories Inc						
715 Harvard Ave PO Box 269	Swarthmore	PA	19081	**800-562-5541**	610-543-3365	575
Delnor-Community Hospital (DCH)						
300 Randall Rd	Geneva	IL	60134	**800-223-9776**	630-208-3000	371-3
DeLorme						
Two DeLorme Dr PO Box 298	Yarmouth	ME	04096	**800-452-5931***	207-846-7000	628-1
*Sales						
Delphos Herald Inc						
405 N Main St	Delphos	OH	45833	**800-589-6950**	419-695-0015	628-8
Delsey Luggage						
6735 Business Pkwy Ste A	Elkridge	MD	21075	**800-558-3344**	410-796-5655	448
DelStar Technologies Inc						
220 E St Elmo Rd	Austin	TX	78745	**800-521-6713**	512-447-7000	601
Delta Air Cargo						
PO Box 20559 Dept 670	Atlanta	GA	30320	**800-352-2737**		12
Delta Air Lines Inc						
1030 Delta Blvd	Atlanta	GA	30354	**800-221-1212**	404-715-2600	25
NYSE: DAL						
Delta Apparel Inc						
2750 Premier Pkwy Ste 100	Duluth	GA	30097	**800-285-4456**	678-775-6900	153-3
NYSE: DLA						
Delta Blood Bank						
65 N Commerce St	Stockton	CA	95201	**888-942-5663**	209-943-3830	88
Delta Carbona LP						
376 Hollywood Ave Ste 208	Fairfield	NJ	07004	**888-746-5599**	973-808-6260	149
Delta Centrifugal Corp						
PO Box 1043	Temple	TX	76503	**888-433-3100***	254-773-9055	306
*Sales						
Delta Chemical Corp						
2601 Cannery Ave	Baltimore	MD	21226	**800-282-5322**	410-354-0100	143
Delta Chi Fraternity Inc						
314 Church St	Iowa City	IA	52245	**888-827-9702**	319-337-4811	47-16
Delta College						
1961 Delta Rd	University Center	MI	48710	**888-636-4211**	989-686-9000	160
Delta Consolidated Industries Inc						
4800 Krueger Dr	Jonesboro	AR	72401	**800-643-0084**	870-935-3711	483
Delta Cooling Towers Inc						
PO Box 315	Rockaway	NJ	07866	**800-289-3358**	973-586-2201	467
Delta Corporate Services Inc						
129 Littleton Rd	Parsippany	NJ	07054	**800-335-8220**	973-334-6260	181
Delta County Area Chamber of Commerce						
230 Ludington St	Escanaba	MI	49829	**888-335-8264**	906-786-2192	137
Delta Democrat Times						
988 N Broadway St	Greenville	MS	38701	**800-273-8255**	662-335-1155	525-2
Delta Dental Insurance Company of Alaska						
PO Box 1809	Alpharetta	GA	30023	**800-521-2651**		388-3
Delta Dental of Arizona						
PO Box 43026	Phoenix	AZ	85080	**800-352-6132**		388-3
Delta Dental of Arkansas						
1513 Country Club Rd						
PO Box 15965	Sherwood	AR	72120	**800-462-5410**	501-835-3400	388-3

Name / Address	City	State	ZIP	Toll-Free	Phone	Class
Delta Dental of Colorado						
4582 S Ulster St Ste 800	Denver	CO	80237	**800-233-0860**	303-741-9300	388-3
Delta Dental of Georgia						
PO Box 1803	Alpharetta	GA	30023	**800-422-4234**		388-3
Delta Dental of Idaho						
555 E Parkcenter Blvd PO Box 2870	Boise	ID	83706	**800-356-7586**	208-489-3580	388-3
Delta Dental of Indiana						
PO Box 30416	Lansing	MI	48909	**800-524-0149**		388-3
Delta Dental of Iowa						
9000 Northpark Dr Ste 13	Johnston	IA	50131	**800-544-0718***	515-261-5500	388-3
*Cust Svc						
Delta Dental of Kansas						
1619 N Waterfront Pkwy						
PO Box 789769	Wichita	KS	67201	**800-234-3375**	316-264-4511	388-3
Delta Dental of Kentucky						
10100 Linn Stn Rd						
PO Box 242810	Louisville	KY	40223	**800-955-2030***		388-3
*Cust Svc						
Delta Dental of Louisiana						
PO Box 1803	Alpharetta	GA	30023	**800-422-4234**		388-3
Delta Dental of Maryland						
One Delta Dr	Mechanicsburg	PA	17055	**800-932-0783**	717-766-8500	388-3
Delta Dental of Massachusetts						
465 Medford St	Boston	MA	02129	**800-872-0500***	617-886-1000	388-3
*Cust Svc						
Delta Dental of Michigan						
PO Box 30416	Lansing	MI	48909	**800-524-0149**		388-3
Delta Dental of Minnesota						
PO Box 330	Minneapolis	MN	55440	**800-553-9536**	651-406-5900	388-3
Delta Dental of Mississippi						
PO Box 1803	Alpharetta	GA	30023	**800-422-4234**		388-3
Delta Dental of Missouri						
12399 Gravois Rd Ste 2	Saint Louis	MO	63127	**800-392-1167**	314-656-3000	388-3
Delta Dental of Montana						
PO Box 1803	Alpharetta	GA	30023	**800-422-4234**		388-3
Delta Dental of New Jersey						
1639 State Rt 10	Parsippany	NJ	07054	**800-624-2633**	973-285-4000	388-3
Delta Dental of New Jersey Inc						
PO Box 222	Parsippany	NJ	07054	**800-452-9310**		388-3
Delta Dental of New Mexico						
2500 Louisiana Blvd NE						
Ste 600	Albuquerque	NM	87110	**800-999-0963**	505-883-4777	388-3
Delta Dental of New York						
One Delta Dr	Mechanicsburg	PA	17055	**800-932-0783**	717-766-8500	388-3
Delta Dental of Ohio						
PO Box 30416	Lansing	MI	48909	**800-524-0149**		388-3
Delta Dental of Oklahoma						
16 NW 63rd St Ste 201	Oklahoma City	OK	73116	**800-522-0188**	405-607-2100	388-3
Delta Dental of Pennsylvania						
One Delta Dr	Mechanicsburg	PA	17055	**800-932-0783**		388-3
Delta Dental of Rhode Island						
10 Charles St	Providence	RI	02904	**800-598-6684**	401-752-6000	388-3
Delta Dental of South Dakota						
720 N Euclid Ave PO Box 1157	Pierre	SD	57501	**800-627-3961**	605-224-7345	388-3
Delta Dental of Tennessee						
240 Venture Cir	Nashville	TN	37228	**800-223-3104***	615-255-3175	388-3
*Cust Svc						
Delta Dental of Texas						
PO Box 1803	Alpharetta	GA	30023	**800-422-4234**		388-3
Delta Dental of Utah						
PO Box 1803	Alpharetta	GA	30023	**800-422-4234**		388-3
Delta Dental of Virginia						
4818 Starkey Rd	Roanoke	VA	24014	**800-367-3531**	540-989-8000	388-3
Delta Dental of West Virginia						
One Delta Dr	Mechanicsburg	PA	17055	**800-932-0783**	717-766-8500	388-3
Delta Dental of Wisconsin						
2801 Hoover Rd PO Box 828	Stevens Point	WI	54481	**800-236-3713**	715-344-6087	388-3
Delta Dental of Wyoming						
6234 Yellowstone Rd Ste 100	Cheyenne	WY	82009	**800-735-3379**	307-632-3313	388-3
Delta Dental Plan of North Carolina						
343 E Six Forks Rd Ste 180	Raleigh	NC	27609	**800-662-8856**	919-832-6015	388-3
Delta Design Inc						
12367 Crosthwaite Cir	Poway	CA	92064	**877-660-6853**	858-848-8000	248
Delta Downs Racetrack						
2717 Delta Downs Dr	Vinton	LA	70668	**800-589-7441**		633
Delta Education LLC						
80 NW Blvd	Nashua	NH	03063	**800-258-1302**	603-889-8899	243
Delta Employees Credit Union						
1025 Virginia Ave	Atlanta	GA	30354	**800-544-3328**	404-715-4725	219
Delta Enterprises						
114 W 26th St Eighth Fl	New York	NY	10001	**800-377-3777**	212-736-7000	63
Delta Implement Co Inc						
3180 U.S. 82	Greenville	MS	38703	**800-264-2741**	662-332-2683	274
Delta King Riverboat Hotel						
1000 Front St	Sacramento	CA	95814	**800-825-5464**	916-444-5464	376
Delta M Corp						
1003 Larsen Dr	Oak Ridge	TN	37830	**800-922-0083**		404
Delta Meadowvale						
6750 Mississauga Rd	Mississauga	ON	L5N2L3	**800-422-8238**	905-821-1981	660
Delta Natural Gas Co Inc						
3617 Lexington Rd	Winchester	KY	40391	**800-262-2012**	859-744-6171	775
NASDAQ: DGAS						
Delta Sherbrooke Hotel & Conference Centre						
2685 Rue King O	Sherbrooke	QC	J1L1C1	**800-268-1133**	819-822-1989	374
Delta Sigma Theta Sorority Inc						
1707 New Hampshire Ave NW	Washington	DC	20009	**866-615-6464**	202-986-2400	47-16
Delta Star Inc						
270 Industrial Rd	San Carlos	CA	94070	**800-892-8673**		757
Delta State University						
1003 W Sunflower Rd	Cleveland	MS	38733	**800-468-6378**	662-846-4020	166
Delta T Inc						
8323 Loch Lomond Dr	Pico Rivera	CA	90660	**800-928-5828**		605
Delta Tau Delta Fraternity						
10000 Allisonville Rd	Fishers	IN	46038	**800-335-8795**	317-284-0203	47-16
Delta Theta Phi						
225 Hillsborough St Ste 432	Raleigh	NC	27603	**800-783-2600**		47-16
Delta Victoria Ocean Pointe Resort & Spa						
45 Songhees Rd	Victoria	BC	V9A6T3	**800-667-4677**	250-360-2999	660
Delta Waterfowl Foundation						
PO Box 3128	Bismarck	ND	58502	**888-987-3695**	701-222-8857	47-3
Delta Whistler Village Suites						
4308 Main St	Whistler	BC	V0N1B4	**888-299-3987**	604-905-3987	660
Deltacom Inc						
7037 Old Madison Pike	Huntsville	AL	35806	**800-239-3000**		726
deltathree Inc						
75 Broad St	New York	NY	10004	**888-335-8230**	212-500-4850	726
PINK: DDDC						
DeltaTRAK Inc						
PO Box 398	Pleasanton	CA	94566	**800-962-6776**	925-249-2250	203
Deltec Homes Inc						
69 Bingham Rd	Asheville	NC	28806	**800-642-2508**	828-253-0483	187
Deltech Corp						
11911 Scenic Hwy	Baton Rouge	LA	70807	**800-424-9300**	225-775-0150	598-1
Deltek Inc						
13880 Dulles Corner Ln	Herndon	VA	20171	**800-456-2009**	703-734-8606	179-1
NASDAQ: PROJ						
Deltona Corp						
8014 SW 135th St Rd	Ocala	FL	34473	**800-935-6378**	352-347-2322	644
Deltrol Fluid Products						
3001 Grant Ave	Bellwood	IL	60104	**800-477-9772**	708-547-0500	778
Deltronic Corp						
3900 W Segerstrom Ave	Santa Ana	CA	92704	**800-451-6922**	714-545-5800	488
Deluxe Bldg Systems Inc						
499 W Third St	Berwick	PA	18603	**800-843-7372**	570-752-5914	105
Deluxe Business Forms						
3680 Victoria St N	Shoreview	MN	55126	**800-328-7205***	651-483-7111	140
*Cust Svc						
Deluxe Corp						
3680 N Victoria St	Shoreview	MN	55126	**800-328-7205**	651-483-7111	357-3
NYSE: DLX						
Delyse Inc						
505 Reactor Way	Reno	NV	89502	**800-441-6887**	775-857-1811	295-9
DEMA (Diving Equipment & Marketing Assn)						
3750 Convoy St Ste 310	San Diego	CA	92111	**800-862-3483**	858-616-6408	48-4
Demag Cranes & Components						
29201 Aurora Rd	Solon	OH	44139	**866-920-3000**	440-248-2400	191
Dematic						
507 Plymouth Ave NE	Grand Rapids	MI	49505	**877-725-7500***		465
*Cust Svc						
DEMCO (Dixie Electric Membership Corp)						
PO Box 15659	Baton Rouge	LA	70895	**800-262-0221**	225-261-1221	245
DEMCO (Dethmers Manufacturing Co)						
4010 320th St PO Box 189	Boyden	IA	51234	**800-543-3626**	712-725-2311	753
Demco Inc						
4810 Forest Run Rd	Madison	WI	53704	**800-356-1200***	608-241-1201	553
*Orders						
Democrat & Chronicle						
55 Exchange Blvd	Rochester	NY	14614	**800-790-9565**	585-232-7100	525-2
DeMolay International						
10200 NW Ambassador Dr	Kansas City	MO	64153	**800-336-6529***	816-891-8333	47-15
*Orders						
DeMontrond 888 I- 45 S	Conroe	TX	77304	**888-843-6583***	281-443-2500	56
*Sales						
DeMoulin Bros & Company Inc						
1025 S Fourth St	Greenville	IL	62246	**800-228-8134**	618-664-2000	153-18
Demsey Manufacturing Co						
78 New Wood Rd	Watertown	CT	06795	**800-533-6739**	860-274-6209	477
Demtec Inc						
50, Blvd Industriel	Princeville	QC	G6L4P2	**800-560-2043**	819-364-2043	105
Den Hartog Industries Inc						
4010 Hospers Dr S PO Box 425	Hospers	IA	51238	**800-342-3408**	712-752-8432	601
Denali Advance Integration (DAI)						
17735 NE 65th St Ste 130	Redmond	WA	98052	**877-467-8008**	425-885-4000	181
Denali Commission						
510 L St Ste 410	Anchorage	AK	99501	**888-480-4321**	907-271-1414	338-18
Denali State Park						
7278 E Bogard Rd	Wasilla	AK	99654	**800-478-6196**	907-745-3975	558
Denbury Resources Inc						
5320 Legacy Dr	Plano	TX	75024	**800-348-9030***	972-673-2000	529
NYSE: DNR ■ *General						
Dendreon Corp						
3005 First Ave	Seattle	WA	98121	**877-256-4545**	206-256-4545	84
OTC: DNDNQ						
Denier Electric Co Inc						
10891 SR- 128	Harrison	OH	45030	**800-676-3282**	513-738-2641	245
Denim Group Ltd						
1354 N Loop 1604 E Ste 110	San Antonio	TX	78232	**844-572-4400**		178
Denison University						
100 W College St	Granville	OH	43023	**800-336-4766**	740-587-6394	166
Denison University Doane Library						
400 W Loop PO Box L	Granville	OH	43023	**800-336-4766**	740-587-6235	431-6
Denmark						
Consulate General						
875 N Michigan Ave Ste 3950	Chicago	IL	60611	**800-345-6541**		257
Den-Mat Corp						
2727 Skyway Dr	Santa Maria	CA	93455	**800-433-6628**	805-922-8491	228
Dennis K Burke Inc						
284 Eastern Ave PO Box 6069	Chelsea	MA	02150	**800-289-2875**	617-884-7800	444
Dennis Paper Co						
910 Acorn Dr	Nashville	TN	37210	**800-441-5684**	615-883-9010	546
Dennis Supply Co						
PO Box 3376	Sioux City	IA	51102	**800-352-4618**	712-255-7637	656
Dennis Uniform Mfg Company Inc						
135 SE Hawthorne Blvd	Portland	OR	97214	**800-544-7123**	503-234-7431	153-18
Denny's Corp						
203 E Main St	Spartanburg	SC	29319	**800-733-6697***	864-597-8000	661
NASDAQ: DENN ■ *Cust Svc						
Denso International America Inc						
24777 Denso Dr	Southfield	MI	48033	**800-321-6021**	248-350-7500	59
Denso North America Inc						
9747 Whithorn Dr	Houston	TX	77095	**888-821-2300**	281-821-3355	144
Dent Clinic						
711 48th Ave SE	Calgary	AB	T2G2A7	**888-722-3368**	403-255-3111	61-4
Dent Wizard International						
4710 Earth City Expway	Bridgeton	MO	63044	**800-267-9369**	314-592-1800	61-4
Dental Economics Magazine						
1421 S Sheridan Rd	Tulsa	OK	74112	**800-331-4463**		452-16
Dental Lifeline Network						
1800 15th St Unit 100	Denver	CO	80202	**888-471-6334**	303-534-5360	47-17
Dental Technologies Inc (DTI)						
5601 Arnold Rd	Dublin	CA	94568	**800-229-0936**	925-829-3611	412
DEN-TAL-EZ Group Inc						
Two W Liberty Blvd Ste 160	Malvern	PA	19355	**866-383-4636**	610-725-8004	228
DEN-TAL-EZ Inc Equipment Div						
2500 Hwy 31 S	Bay Minette	AL	36507	**800-383-4636**	251-937-6781	228
Dentists Insurance Co						
1201 K St 17th Fl	Sacramento	CA	95814	**800-733-0634**		388-5

Alphabetical Section

	City	State	Zip	Toll-Free	Phone	Class
Denton Chamber of Commerce						
414 W Pkwy St	Denton	TX	76201	**800-747-2316**	940-382-9693	137
Denton Record-Chronicle						
314 E Hickory St	Denton	TX	76201	**800-275-1722**	940-387-3811	525-2
Dentsply Caulk						
38 W Clarke Ave	Milford	DE	19963	**800-532-2855**	302-422-4511	228
DENTSPLY International						
221 W Philadelphia St P.O. Box 872	York	PA	17405	**800-800-2888**	717-845-7511	228
Dentsply International Inc						
221 W Philadelphia St PO Box 872	York	PA	17405	**800-877-0020**	717-845-7511	228
NASDAQ: XRAY						
Dentsply International Inc Rinn Div						
1212 Abbott Dr	Elgin	IL	60123	**800-323-0970**	847-742-1115	228
Dentsply International Inc Tulsa Dental Div						
5100 E Skelly Dr Ste 300	Tulsa	OK	74135	**800-662-1202**	918-493-6598	228
Denver Academy of Court Reporting						
9051 Harlan St Ste 20	Westminster	CO	80031	**866-712-2425**	303-427-5292	788
Denver Ctr for the Performing Arts						
1101 13th St	Denver	CO	80204	**800-641-1222**	303-893-4000	565
Denver Fire Dept Federal Credit Union (DFDFCU)						
2201 Federal Blvd	Denver	CO	80211	**866-880-7770**	303-228-5300	219
Denver International Airport						
8500 Pena Blvd	Denver	CO	80249	**800-247-2336**	303-342-2000	27
Denver International Film Festival						
1510 York 3rd Fl	Denver	CO	80206	**800-228-5838**	303-595-3456	282
Denver Metro Convention & Visitors Bureau						
1555 California St Ste 300	Denver	CO	80202	**800-480-2010**	303-892-1112	207
Denver Newspaper Agency						
101 W Colfax Ave	Denver	CO	80202	**800-336-7678**	303-954-1010	628-8
Denver Performing Arts Complex						
1245 Champa St 1St Fl	Denver	CO	80204	**800-745-3000**	720-865-4220	565
Denver Post						
101 W Colfax Ave	Denver	CO	80202	**800-336-7678**	303-820-1010	525-2
Denver Public Schools						
900 Grant St	Denver	CO	80203	**866-726-0033**	720-423-3200	676
Denver Seminary						
6399 S Santa Fe Dr	Littleton	CO	80120	**800-922-3040**	303-761-2482	167-3
Denver Veterans Affairs Medical Ctr						
1055 Clermont St	Denver	CO	80220	**888-336-8262**	303-399-8020	371-8
Denver Wholesale Florists Co						
4800 Dahlia St	Denver	CO	80216	**800-829-8280**	303-399-0970	293
Department of Education						
400 Maryland Ave SW	Washington	DC	20202	**800-872-5327**	202-401-2000	338-6
Inspector General's Fraud & Abuse Hotline						
400 Maryland Ave SW	Washington	DC	20202	**800-647-8733**		338-6
Office of Elementary & Secondary Education						
400 Maryland Ave SW	Washington	DC	20202	**800-872-5327**		338-6
Office of Vocational & Adult Education						
400 Maryland Ave SW						
Room 4W116	Washington	DC	20202	**800-872-5327**		338-6
Department of Energy (DOE)						
1000 Independence Ave SW	Washington	DC	20585	**800-342-5363**	202-586-5450	338-7
Office of Civilian Radioactive Waste Management						
1000 Independence Ave SW	Washington	DC	20585	**888-363-7289**	202-586-4940	338-7
Office of Energy Efficiency & Renewable Energy						
1000 Independence Ave SW	Washington	DC	20585	**877-337-3463**	202-586-9171	338-7
Office of Nuclear Energy						
1000 Independence Ave SW	Washington	DC	20585	**800-342-5363**		338-7
Department of Health & Human Services (HHS)						
330 Independence Ave SW	Washington	DC	20201	**877-696-6775**	202-619-0150	338-8
Department of Housing & Urban Development (HUD)						
451 Seventh St SW	Washington	DC	20410	**800-569-4287**	202-708-0685	338-10
Public Affairs Office						
451 Seventh St SW	Washington	DC	20410	**800-333-4636**	202-708-0980	338-10
Department of Housing & Urban Development Regional Offices						
Boston						
10 Cswy St 3rd Fl	Boston	MA	02222	**800-225-5342**	617-994-8200	338-10
Mid-Atlantic Region						
100 Penn Sq E	Philadelphia	PA	19107	**800-225-5342**	215-656-0500	338-10
New York City Regional Office						
26 Federal Plaza Ste 3541	New York	NY	10278	**800-496-4294**	212-264-8000	338-10
Pacific/Hawaii Region						
600 Harrison St 3rd Fl	San Francisco	CA	94107	**800-347-3739**	415-489-6572	338-10
Rocky Mountain Region						
1670 Bdwy 25th Fl	Denver	CO	80202	**800-955-2232**	303-672-5440	338-10
Job Corps						
200 Constitution Ave NW						
Ste N4463	Washington	DC	20210	**800-733-5627**	202-693-3000	338-13
Office of Administrative Law Judges						
200 Constitution Ave NW						
Ste 400 N	Washington	DC	20210	**877-889-5627**	202-693-7300	338-13
Department of Labor						
Public Affairs Office						
200 Constitution Ave NW	Washington	DC	20210	**866-487-2365**	202-693-4650	338-13
Department of Veterans Affairs (VA)						
810 Vermont Ave NW	Washington	DC	20420	**800-827-1000***	202-461-7600	338-17
*Cust Svc						
Public & Intergovernmental Affairs Office						
810 Vermont Ave NW	Washington	DC	20420	**800-273-8255**		338-17
Departures Magazine						
1120 Ave of the Americas	New York	NY	10036	**800-333-7483**	212-642-1999	452-22
DePaul University College of Law						
25 E Jackson Blvd	Chicago	IL	60604	**800-445-8667**	312-362-8701	167-1
DePauw University						
101 E Seminary St	Greencastle	IN	46135	**800-447-2495**	765-658-4006	166
DePauw University West Library						
11 E Larabee St	Greencastle	IN	46135	**800-447-2495**	765-658-4420	431-6
DePelchin Children's Ctr						
4950 Memorial Dr	Houston	TX	77007	**888-730-2335**	713-730-2335	47-6
Dependable Component Supply Corp						
1003 E Newport Ctr Dr	Deerfield Beach	FL	33442	**800-336-7100**	954-283-5800	246
Dependable Highway Express Inc						
2440 S 48th Ave	Phoenix	AZ	85043	**800-472-2037**	602-278-4401	444
Depobook Reporting Services						
1600 G St Ste 101	Modesto	CA	95354	**800-830-8885**	209-544-6466	440
Depoe Bay Whale Center						
Oregon Parks and Recreation Department						
58 US-101 198 NE 123rd St	Depoe Bay	OR	97341	**800-551-6949**	541-765-3304	558
DepoNet						
2700 Centennial Tower 101 Marietta St						
101 Marietta St	Atlanta	GA	30303	**800-337-6638**	404-495-0777	440
Deposition Sciences Inc						
3300 Coffey Ln	Santa Rosa	CA	95403	**866-433-7724**	707-573-6700	476

	City	State	Zip	Toll-Free	Phone	Class
Depression & Bipolar Support Alliance (DBSA)						
730 N Franklin St Ste 501	Chicago	IL	60610	**800-826-3632**	312-642-0049	47-17
Derby Industries LLC						
4451 Robards Ln	Louisville	KY	40218	**800-569-4812**	502-451-7373	791-1
Derma Sciences Inc						
214 Carnegie Ctr Ste 100	Princeton	NJ	08540	**800-825-4325**	609-514-4744	470
Dermatology Assoc of Atlanta						
5555 Pchtrdnwyd Ste 190	Atlanta	GA	30324	**800-233-0706**	404-256-4457	371-7
Dero Bike Racks Inc						
504 Malcolm Ave SE Ste 100	Minneapolis	MN	55414	**888-337-6729**	612-359-0689	60
DeRoyal Industries Inc						
200 DeBusk Ln	Powell	TN	37849	**800-251-9864**	865-938-7828	472
DeRoyal Textiles						
141 E York St PO Box 400	Camden	SC	29020	**800-845-1062**	803-432-2403	734-1
Derr Flooring Company Inc						
525 Davisville Rd						
PO Box 912	Willow Grove	PA	19090	**800-523-3457**	215-657-6300	358
Derrick Publishing Co						
1510 W First St	Oil City	PA	16301	**800-352-1002**	814-676-7444	628-8
Derse Exhibits Inc						
3800 W Canal St	Milwaukee	WI	53208	**800-562-2300**	414-257-2000	232
Der-Tex Corp						
One Lehner Rd	Saco	ME	04072	**800-669-0364**		734-2
Des Moines Area Community College						
Ankeny						
2006 S Ankeny Blvd	Ankeny	IA	50021	**800-362-2127**	515-964-6200	160
Boone 1125 Hancock Dr	Boone	IA	50036	**800-362-2127**	515-432-7203	160
Carroll						
906 N Grant Rd	Carroll	IA	51401	**800-622-3334**	712-792-1755	160
Urban/Des Moines						
1100 Seventh St	Des Moines	IA	50314	**800-622-3334**	515-244-4226	160
Des Moines Independent School District						
901 Walnut St	Des Moines	IA	50309	**800-452-1111**	515-242-7911	676
Des Moines International Airport						
5800 Fleur Dr	Des Moines	IA	50321	**877-686-0029**	515-256-5050	27
Des Moines Register						
715 Locust St	Des Moines	IA	50309	**800-247-5346**	515-284-8000	525-2
Des Plaines Public Library						
1501 Ellinwood Ave	Des Plaines	IL	60016	**800-829-1040**	847-827-5551	431-3
DeSales University						
2755 Stn Ave	Center Valley	PA	18034	**877-433-7253**	610-282-1100	166
Descartes Systems Group Inc						
120 Randall Dr	Waterloo	ON	N2V1C6	**800-419-8495**	519-746-8110	179-12
TSE: DSG						
Deschutes Public Library						
507 NW Wall St	Bend	OR	97701	**855-268-3767**	541-312-1020	431-3
Deseret Book Co						
57 W S Temple	Salt Lake City	UT	84111	**800-453-4532**	801-534-1515	628-3
Deseret News						
30 E 100 S Suite 400						
PO Box 1257	Salt Lake City	UT	84110	**800-999-7511**	801-236-6000	525-2
Desert Canyon Golf Resort						
1201 Desert Canyon Blvd	Orondo	WA	98843	**800-258-4173**	509-784-1111	660
Desert Dog Marketing LLC						
4641 N 12th St Ste 200	Phoenix	AZ	85014	**800-506-0398**		225
Desert European Motorcars Ltd						
71387 Hwy 111	Rancho Mirage	CA	92270	**877-839-3035**	760-773-5000	56
Desert Hot Springs Spa Hotel						
10805 Palm Dr	Desert Hot Springs	CA	92240	**800-808-7727**	760-329-6000	660
Desert Regional Medical Ctr						
1150 N Indian Canyon Dr	Palm Springs	CA	92262	**800-491-4990**	760-323-6511	371-3
Desert Schools Federal Credit Union						
148 N 48th St	Phoenix	AZ	85034	**800-456-9171**	602-433-7000	219
Desert Springs Marriott Resort & Spa						
74855 Country Club Dr	Palm Desert	CA	92260	**888-538-9459**	760-341-2211	660
Desert Sun						
750 N Gene Autry Trl	Palm Springs	CA	92263	**800-233-3741**	760-322-8889	525-2
Desert Sun Publishing Co						
PO Box 2734	Palm Springs	CA	92263	**800-233-3741***	760-322-8889	628-8
*Advertising						
Design Ctr of the Americas (DCOTA)						
1855 Griffin Rd	Dania Beach	FL	33004	**877-992-9204**	954-920-7997	455
Design Design Inc						
19 La Grave SE	Grand Rapids	MI	49503	**800-334-3348**	616-774-2448	129
Design Homes Inc						
600 N Marquette Rd	Prairie du Chien	WI	53821	**800-627-9443**	608-326-6041	105
Design Management Institute (DMI)						
38 Chauncy St Ste 800	Boston	MA	02111	**800-200-5909**	617-338-6380	47-4
Design News						
225 Wyman St	Waltham	MA	02451	**800-869-6882**	763-746-2792	452-21
Design ProfessionalXL Group						
2959 Salinas Hwy	Monterey	CA	93940	**800-227-4284**	831-649-5522	398
Design Strategy Corp						
805 Third Ave 11th Fl	New York	NY	10016	**800-331-8726**	212-370-0000	181
Design Toscano Inc						
1400 Morse Ave	Elk Grove Village	IL	60007	**800-525-5141**	847-952-0100	454
Design Within Reach Inc						
711 Canal St 3rd fl 3rd Fl	Stamford	CT	06902	**800-944-2233**	203-614-0600	359
OTC: DWRI						
Design/Build Business Magazine						
3030 Salt Creek Ln						
Ste 200	Arlington Heights	IL	60005	**800-547-7377**	847-454-2714	452-2
Designatronics Inc						
2101 Jericho Tpke	New Hyde Park	NY	11040	**800-345-1144***	516-328-3300	700
*Orders						
Designer Decal Inc						
1120 E First Ave	Spokane	WA	99202	**800-622-6333**	509-535-0267	678
Designfax Magazine						
2506 Tamiami Trail North	Nokomis	FL	34275	**877-245-6247**	941-966-9521	452-21
Designs on Talent LLC						
1579 Monroe Dr F155	Atlanta	GA	30324	**888-360-3360**		458
Desire2Learn Inc						
151 Charles SW Ste 400	Kitchener	ON	N2G1H6	**888-772-0325**	519-772-0325	175
Desktop Consulting Services						
43311 Joy Rd	Canton	MI	48187	**888-600-2731**		176
DeskTop Labels						
7277 Boone Ave N	Minneapolis	MN	55428	**800-241-9730**		410
Desmond Albany Hotel, The						
660 Albany-Shaker Rd	Albany	NY	12211	**800-448-3500**	518-869-8100	662
Desoto Parish School District						
201 Crosby St	Mansfield	LA	71052	**888-741-0205**	318-872-2836	676
DeSoto Public Library						
211 E Pleasant Run Rd Ste C	DeSoto	TX	75115	**800-886-9008**	972-230-9656	431-3

Name / Address	City	State	ZIP	Toll-Free	Phone	Class
Desoto Sales Inc						
20945 Osborne St	Canoga Park	CA	91304	**800-826-9779**	818-998-0853	348
Despatch Industries Inc						
8860 207th St W	Lakeville	MN	55044	**800-726-0110**	952-469-5424	317
DesPeres Hospital						
2345 Dougherty Ferry Rd	Saint Louis	MO	63122	**888-457-5203**	314-966-9100	371-3
Dessert Innovations Inc						
25-B Enterprise Blvd	Atlanta	GA	30336	**800-359-7351**	404-691-5000	295-2
DE-STA-CO						
1025 Doris Rd	Auburn Hills	MI	48326	**888-337-8226**	248-836-6700	347
Destin Area Chamber of Commerce						
4484 Legendary Dr Ste A	Destin	FL	32541	**877-487-2671**	850-837-6241	137
Destination Hotels & Resorts Inc						
10333 E Dry Creek Rd Ste 450	Englewood	CO	80112	**855-893-1011**	303-799-3830	376
Destination Maternity Corp						
456 N Fifth St	Philadelphia	PA	19123	**800-466-6223**	215-873-2200	155-6
NASDAQ: DEST						
Destination Resources						
5435 Balboa Blvd Ste 106	Encino	CA	91316	**800-422-6524**	818-995-7915	185
Destination Services of Colorado Inc (DSC)						
PO Box 3660	Avon	CO	81620	**800-372-7686**	970-476-6565	185
Destiny Industries LLC						
250 R W Bryant Rd	Moultrie	GA	31788	**866-782-6600**		500
Destrehan Plantation						
13034 River Rd	Destrehan	LA	70047	**877-453-2095**	985-764-9315	49-2
Destron Fearing						
490 Villaume Ave	South Saint Paul	MN	55075	**800-328-0118**	651-552-6300	638
Detecto Scale Co						
203 E Daugherty St PO Box 151	Webb City	MO	64870	**800-641-2008**	417-673-4631	675
Detex Corp						
302 Detex Dr	New Braunfels	TX	78130	**800-729-3839**	830-629-2900	683
Dethmers Manufacturing Co (DEMCO)						
4010 320th St PO Box 189	Boyden	IA	51234	**800-543-3626**	712-725-2311	753
Detroit Edge Tool Co						
6570 E Nevada St	Detroit	MI	48234	**800-404-2038**	313-366-4120	488
Detroit Free Press						
615 W Lafayette Blvd	Detroit	MI	48226	**800-395-3300**	313-222-6400	525-2
Detroit Hoist Co						
6650 Sterling Dr N	Sterling Heights	MI	48312	**800-521-9126**	586-268-2600	465
Detroit Lakes Regional Chamber of Commerce						
700 Summit Ave	Detroit Lakes	MN	56501	**800-542-3992**	218-847-9202	137
Detroit Legal News Co						
1409 Allen Rd Ste B	Troy	MI	48083	**800-875-5275**	248-577-6100	628-8
Detroit Lions						
222 Republic Dr	Allen Park	MI	48101	**800-745-3000**	313-216-4000	706-3
Detroit Metropolitan Convention & Visitors Bureau						
211 W Fort St Ste 1000	Detroit	MI	48226	**877-424-5554**	313-202-1800	207
Detroit News						
615 W Lafayette Blvd	Detroit	MI	48226	**800-395-3300***	313-222-2300	525-2
*General						
Detroit Public Schools						
3031 W Grand Blvd	Detroit	MI	48202	**800-656-4673**	313-873-7927	676
Detroit Pump & Mfg Co						
450 Fair St Bldg D	Ferndale	MI	48220	**800-686-1662**	248-544-4242	382
Detroit Quality Brush Mfg						
32165 Schoolcraft Rd	Livonia	MI	48150	**800-722-3037**	734-525-5660	102
Detroit Radiant Product Co						
21400 Hoover Rd	Warren	MI	48089	**800-222-1100**	586-756-0950	317
Detroit Stoker Co						
1510 E First St	Monroe	MI	48161	**800-786-5374**	734-241-9500	317
Detroit Symphony Orchestra						
3711 Woodward Ave	Detroit	MI	48201	**800-434-6340**	313-576-5111	566-3
Detroit Tigers						
Comerica Pk 2100 Woodward Ave	Detroit	MI	48201	**866-800-1275**	313-962-4000	704
Devcon Inc						
30 Endicott St	Danvers	MA	01923	**800-626-7226**	855-489-7262	3
Developers Diversified Realty Corp						
3300 Enterprise Pkwy	Beachwood	OH	44122	**877-225-5337**	216-755-5500	646
NYSE: DDR						
Development Dimensions International						
1225 Washington Pike	Bridgeville	PA	15017	**800-933-4463***	412-257-0600	194
*Mktg						
Development Director's Letter						
8204 Fenton St	Silver Spring	MD	20910	**800-666-6380**	301-588-6380	524-7
Development Planning & Financing Group Inc						
27127 Calle Arroyo						
Ste 1910	San Juan Capistrano	CA	92675	**800-535-5795**	949-388-9269	643
Devereux						
1291 Stanley Rd NW PO Box 1688	Kennesaw	GA	30156	**800-342-3357**	678-303-5233	371-1
Devereux Cleo Wallace						
8405 Church Ranch Blvd	Westminster	CO	80021	**800-456-2536**	303-466-7391	371-1
deView Electronics USA Inc						
708 Vly Ridge Cir Ste 1	Lewisville	TX	75057	**877-433-8439**	214-222-3332	683
Devil's Den State Park						
11333 W Arkansas Hwy 74	West Fork	AR	72774	**888-742-8701**	479-761-3325	558
Devil's Head Resort & Convention Ctr						
S 6330 Bluff Rd	Merrimac	WI	53561	**800-472-6670**	608-493-2251	660
Devil's Lake State Recreation Area						
198 NE 123rd St	Newport	OR	97365	**800-551-6949**		558
Devil's Punchbowl State Natural Area						
198 NE 123rd St	Newport	OR	97365	**800-551-6949**		558
Devils Fork State Park						
161 Holcombe Cir	Salem	SC	29676	**866-345-7275**	864-944-2639	558
Devon Bank						
6445 N Western Ave	Chicago	IL	60645	**866-683-3866**		69
Devon Energy Corp						
20 N Broadway	Oklahoma City	OK	73102	**877-860-5820**	405-235-3611	529
NYSE: DVN						
Devon Self Storage Holdings LLC						
2000 Powell St Ste 1240	Emeryville	CA	94608	**800-326-3199**	510-450-1300	791-3
DeVry University						
Calgary						
2700 Third Ave SE	Calgary	AB	T2A7W4	**800-363-5558***	403-235-3450	788
*General						
Colorado Springs						
1175 Kelly						
Johnson Blvd	Colorado Springs	CO	80920	**877-784-1997***	719-632-3000	788
*Help Line						
DeVry University Addison						
1221 N Swift Rd	Addison	IL	60101	**800-346-5420**	630-953-1300	788
DeVry University Federal Way						
3600 S 344th Way	Federal Way	WA	98001	**877-923-3879**	253-943-2800	788
DeVry University Fremont						
6600 Dumbarton Cir	Fremont	CA	94555	**800-363-5558**	510-574-1200	788
DeVry University Houston						
11125 Equity Dr	Houston	TX	77041	**866-703-3879**	713-973-3100	788
DeVry University Irving						
4800 Regent Blvd	Irving	TX	75063	**800-633-3879**	972-929-6777	788
DeVry University Kansas City						
11224 Holmes Rd	Kansas City	MO	64131	**800-821-3766**	816-941-0430	788
DeVry University Long Beach						
3880 Kilroy Airport Way	Long Beach	CA	90806	**800-597-1333**	562-997-5300	788
DeVry University Long Island City						
3020 Thomson Ave	Long Island City	NY	11101	**888-713-3879**	718-472-2728	788
DeVry University North Brunswick						
630 US Hwy 1	North Brunswick	NJ	08902	**800-333-3879**		788
DeVry University Orlando						
4000 Millenia Blvd	Orlando	FL	32839	**888-857-5757**	407-345-2800	788
DeVry University Phoenix						
2149 W Dunlap Ave	Phoenix	AZ	85021	**800-528-0250***	602-870-9222	788
*Cust Svc						
DeVry University Pomona						
901 Corporate Ctr Dr	Pomona	CA	91768	**800-243-3660**	909-622-8866	788
Dew Distribution Services Inc						
2201 Touhy Ave	Elk Grove Village	IL	60007	**800-837-3391**		640
DeWAL Industries Inc						
15 Ray Trainor Dr	Narragansett	RI	02882	**800-366-8356**	401-789-9736	722
Dew-El Corp						
10841 Paw Paw Dr	Holland	MI	49424	**800-443-3935**	616-396-6554	363
Dewey Ford Inc						
3055 SE Delaware Ave	Ankeny	IA	50021	**888-378-8516**	515-289-4949	125
Dewied International Inc						
5010 IH- 10 E	San Antonio	TX	78219	**800-992-5600**	210-661-6161	295-26
Dewitt Products Co						
5860 Plumer Ave	Detroit	MI	48209	**800-962-8599***	313-554-0575	45
*Cust Svc						
DeWitt Wallace Decorative Arts Museum						
325 Francis St	Williamsburg	VA	23185	**800-447-8679**		513
DexCom Inc						
6340 Sequence Dr	San Diego	CA	92121	**888-738-3646**	858-200-0200	84
NASDAQ: DXCM						
Dexter Axle						
2900 Industrial Pkwy	Elkhart	IN	46516	**800-522-7291**	574-295-7888	59
Dexter-Russell Inc						
44 River St	Southbridge	MA	01550	**800-343-6042**	508-765-0201	222
DFC (Duke Diet & Fitness Ctr)						
501 Douglas St	Durham	NC	27705	**800-235-3853**	919-688-3079	697
DFDFCU (Denver Fire Dept Federal Credit Union)						
2201 Federal Blvd	Denver	CO	80211	**866-880-7770**	303-228-5300	219
DFMC (Delmarva Foundation For Medical Care Inc)						
28464 Marlboro Ave	Easton	MD	21601	**800-999-3362**	410-822-0697	469
DFS Group 500 Main St	Groton	MA	01471	**800-225-9528***		109
*General						
DFW (Dallas-Fort Worth International Airport)						
3200 E Airfield Dr PO Box 619428	Dallas	TX	75261	**800-252-7522**	972-973-8888	27
DGAC (Dangerous Goods Advisory Council)						
1100 H St NW Ste 740	Washington	DC	20005	**800-923-9123**	202-289-4550	48-21
DGA-PAC						
7920 W Sunset Blvd	Los Angeles	CA	90046	**800-421-4173**	310-289-2000	608
DGKR (DoubleTree Resort by Hilton Hotel Grand Key)						
3990 S Roosevelt Blvd	Key West	FL	33040	**888-844-0454**	305-293-1818	660
DGSE Cos Inc						
11311 Reeder Rd	Dallas	TX	75229	**800-527-5307**	972-484-3662	407
NYSE: DGSE						
DH (Danbury Hospital)						
24 Hospital Ave	Danbury	CT	06810	**800-516-3658**	203-739-6398	371-3
DH Blattner & Sons Inc						
392 County Rd 50	Avon	MN	56310	**800-877-2866**	320-356-7351	189-4
DHI Computing Service Inc						
1525 West 820 North PO Box 51427	Provo	UT	84601	**800-992-1344**	801-373-8518	179-11
DHI Mortgage Co Ltd						
10700 Pecan Park Blvd Suite 450	Austin	TX	78750	**800-315-8434**	512-502-0545	214
DHL Global Mail						
2700 S Commerce Pkwy Ste 400	Weston	FL	33331	**800-805-9306**	954-903-6300	539
DHMC (Davis Hospital & Medical Ctr)						
1600 W Antelope Dr	Layton	UT	84041	**877-898-6080**	801-807-1000	371-3
Diabetes Advisor Magazine						
1701 N Beauregard St	Alexandria	VA	22311	**800-342-2383**	800-806-7801	452-16
Diabetes Forecast Magazine						
1701 N Beauregard St	Alexandria	VA	22311	**800-676-4065**	703-549-1500	452-13
Diablo Mfg Company Inc						
900 Golden Gate Terr						
PO Box 1108	Grass Valley	CA	95945	**800-551-2233***	530-272-2241	406
*Cust Svc						
Diablo Valley College						
312 Golf Club Rd	Pleasant Hill	CA	94523	**800-227-1060**	925-685-1230	160
Dial800 LLC						
9911 Pico Blvd Ste 1200	Los Angeles	CA	90035	**800-342-5800**		224
Dialog						
2250 Perimeter Pk Dr						
Ste 300	Morrisville	NC	27560	**800-334-2564**	919-804-6400	384
Dialog, The						
1925 Delaware Ave	Wilmington	DE	19806	**877-225-7870**	302-573-3109	525-4
Dialogic Inc						
1504 Mccarthy Blvd	Milpitas	CA	95035	**800-755-4444**	408-750-9400	181
Diamond Brand Canvas Products						
145 Cane Creek Industrial Pk Rd						
Ste 1	Fletcher	NC	28732	**800-459-6262***	828-684-9848	723
*Sales						
Diamond Chain Co						
402 Kentucky Ave	Indianapolis	IN	46225	**800-872-4246***	317-638-6431	613
*Cust Svc						
Diamond Chemical Company Inc						
Union Ave & Dubois St	East Rutherford	NJ	07073	**800-654-7627**	201-935-4300	149
Diamond Coach Corp						
2300 W Fourth St PO Box 489	Oswego	KS	67356	**800-442-4645**	620-795-2191	509
Diamond Comic Distributors Inc						
1966 Greenspring Dr Ste 300	Timonium	MD	21093	**800-452-6642**	410-560-7100	628-5
Diamond Council of America (DCA)						
3212 W End Ave Ste 202	Nashville	TN	37203	**877-283-5669**	615-385-5301	48-4
Diamond Drugs Inc						
645 Kolter Dr	Indiana	PA	15701	**800-882-6337**	724-349-1111	231
Diamond Equipment Inc						
1060 E Diamond Ave	Evansville	IN	47711	**800-258-4428**	812-425-4428	355
Diamond Head Inn						
605 Diamond St	San Diego	CA	92109	**888-478-7829**	858-273-1900	376
Diamond Hill Nursing & Rehabilitation						
100 New Tpke Rd	Troy	NY	12182	**800-697-5374**	518-235-1410	445

Alphabetical Section

	Toll-Free	Phone	Class
Diamond Manufacturing Co			
243 W Eigth St ....Wyoming PA 18644	**800-233-9601**	570-693-0300	483
Diamond Offshore Drilling Inc			
15415 Katy Fwy ....Houston TX 77094	**800-848-1980**	281-492-5300	533
NYSE: DO			
Diamond Packaging Company Inc			
111 Commerce Dr PO Box 23620......Rochester NY 14692	**800-333-4079**	585-334-8030	100
Diamond Parking Inc			
605 First Ave Ste 6000 ....Seattle WA 98104	**800-340-7275**	206-284-3100	555
Diamond Perforated Metals Inc			
7300 W Sunnyview Ave ....Visalia CA 93291	**800-642-4334**	559-651-1889	483
Diamond Plastics Corp			
1212 Johnstown Rd			
PO Box 1608. ....Grand Island NE 68802	**800-782-7473**	308-384-4400	589
Diamond Power International Inc			
2600 E Main St ....Lancaster OH 43130	**800-848-5086**	740-687-6500	383
Diamond Saw Works Inc			
12290 Olean Rd ....Chaffee NY 14030	**800-828-1180**	716-496-7417	673
Diamond Services Corp			
503 S DeGravelle Rd ....Amelia LA 70340	**800-879-1162**	985-631-2187	532
Diamond Tool & Die Inc			
508 29th Ave ....Oakland CA 94601	**800-227-1084**	510-534-7050	747
Diamond Transportation System Inc			
5021 21st St ....Racine WI 53406	**800-927-5702**	262-554-5400	770
Diamond V Mills Inc			
PO Box 74570 ....Cedar Rapids IA 52407	**800-373-7234**	319-366-0745	442
DiamondJacks Casino Resort			
711 Diamond Jacks Blvd ....Bossier City LA 71111	**866-552-9629**	318-678-7777	132
DiamondRock Hospitality Co (DRHC)			
3 Bethesda Metro Ctr Ste 1500....Bethesda MD 20814	**888-246-5941**	240-744-1150	645
NYSE: DRH			
Dian Fossey Gorilla Fund International			
800 Cherokee Ave SE ....Atlanta GA 30315	**800-851-0203**	404-624-5881	47-3
Diana Wortham Theatre at Pack Place			
2 S Pack Sq ....Asheville NC 28801	**800-999-2160**	828-257-4530	565
Diane Von Furstenberg			
440 W 14th St ....New York NY 10014	**888-472-2383**	212-741-6607	277
DIANON Systems Inc			
One Forest Pkwy ....Shelton CT 06484	**800-328-2666**	203-926-7100	415
DiaSorin Inc			
1951 NW Ave ....Stillwater MN 55082	**855-677-0600**	651-439-9710	231
Diaz Wholesale & Mfg Co Inc			
5501 Fulton Industrial Blvd ....Atlanta GA 30336	**800-394-4639**	404-344-5421	296-11
DiAZiT Company Inc			
941 US 1 Hwy PO Box 276..........Youngsville NC 27596	**800-334-6641***	919-556-5188	692
*Cust Svc			
DiCarlo Distributors Inc			
1630 N Ocean Ave ....Holtsville NY 11742	**800-342-2756**	631-758-6000	296-8
Dice Inc			
4101 NW Urbandale Dr ....Urbandale IA 50322	**877-386-3323**	515-280-1144	260
Dick Blick Co			
PO Box 1267 ....Galesburg IL 61402	**800-447-8192***	309-343-6181	44
*Orders			
Dick Gores Rv World			
14590 Duval Pl W ....Jacksonville FL 32218	**800-635-7008**	904-741-5100	509
Dick Lavy Trucking Inc			
8848 State Rt 121 ....Bradford OH 45308	**800-345-5289**	937-448-2104	770
Dickens Books Ltd			
219 N Milwaukee St Third Fl ....Milwaukee WI 53202	**800-236-7323**		95
Dickenson County School District			
PO Box 1127 ....Clintwood VA 24228	**866-632-9992**	276-926-4643	676
Dickey Transport			
401 E Fourth St ....Packwood IA 52580	**800-247-1081**	319-695-3601	572
DICKEY-john Corp			
5200 Dickey-John Rd ....Auburn IL 62615	**800-637-2952**	217-438-3371	630
Dickinson Area Partnership			
600 S Stephenson Ave ....Iron Mountain MI 49801	**888-543-2139**	906-774-2002	137
Dickinson Brands Inc			
31 E High St ....East Hampton CT 06424	**888-860-2279**	860-267-2279	576
Dickinson College			
PO Box 1773 ....Carlisle PA 17013	**800-644-1773**	717-243-5121	166
Dickinson Convention & Visitors Bureau			
72 E Museum Dr ....Dickinson ND 58601	**800-279-7391**	701-483-4988	207
Dickinson Homes Inc			
404 N Stephenson Ave Hwy US-2			
PO Box 2245. ....Iron Mountain MI 49801	**800-438-4687**	906-774-2186	105
Dickinson State University			
291 Campus Dr ....Dickinson ND 58601	**800-279-4295**	701-483-2507	166
Dickman Directories Inc			
6145 Columbus Pk ....Lewis Center OH 43035	**877-836-4154**	740-548-6130	628-6
Dickson Co			
930 S Westwood Ave ....Addison IL 60101	**800-757-3747**	630-543-3747	202
Dickson County Chamber of Commerce			
119 Hwy 70 E ....Dickson TN 37055	**877-718-4967**	615-446-2349	137
Dickstein Shapiro LLP			
1825 Eye St NW ....Washington DC 20006	**800-733-2767**	202-420-2200	425
Didax Inc 395 Main St ....Rowley MA 01969	**800-458-0024**	978-948-2340	243
Diebold Inc			
5995 Mayfair Rd ....North Canton OH 44720	**800-999-3600**	330-490-4000	789
NYSE: DBD			
Diehl Automotive Group Inc			
258 Pittsburgh Rd ....Butler PA 16002	**866-543-4523**	724-282-8898	56
Dielectric Laboratories Inc			
2777 US Rt 20 ....Cazenovia NY 13035	**800-656-9499**	315-655-8710	253
Dielectrics Industries Inc			
300 Burnett Rd ....Chicopee MA 01020	**800-472-7286**	413-594-8111	593
Dieterich-Post Co			
616 Monterey Pass Rd ......Monterey Park CA 91754	**800-955-3729**	626-289-5021	111
Dietz & Watson Inc			
5701 Tacony St ....Philadelphia PA 19135	**800-333-1974**	215-831-9000	295-26
Diffenbaugh Inc			
6865 Airport Dr ....Riverside CA 92504	**800-394-5334**	951-351-6865	187
Dig Corp			
1210 Activity Dr ....Vista CA 92081	**800-322-9146**	760-727-0914	273
Digerati Technologies Inc			
3463 Magic Dr Ste 355.......San Antonio TX 78229	**855-202-5683**	210-614-7240	726
OTC: DTGI			
Digestive Care Inc			
1120 Win Dr ....Bethlehem PA 18017	**877-882-5950**	610-882-0349	231
Digi International Inc			
11001 Bren Rd E ....Minnetonka MN 55343	**877-912-3444**	952-912-3444	177
NASDAQ: DGII			
Digi-Key Corp			
701 Brooks Ave S ....Thief River Falls MN 56701	**800-344-4539**	218-681-6674	246

	Toll-Free	Phone	Class
DigiLink Inc			
840 S Pickett St ....Alexandria VA 22304	**877-806-3453**	703-340-1800	175
Digimarc Corp			
9405 SW Gemini Dr ....Beaverton OR 97008	**800-344-4627**	503-469-4800	179-12
NASDAQ: DMRC			
Digirad Corp			
13950 Stowe Dr ....Poway CA 92064	**800-947-6134**	858-726-1600	379
NASDAQ: DRAD			
Digiscribe International LLC			
150 Clearbrook Rd Ste 125..........Elmsford NY 10523	**800-686-7577**		226
Digital Design Inc			
67 Sand Pk Rd ....Cedar Grove NJ 07009	**800-967-7746**	973-857-0900	174-6
Digital Employees' Federal Credit Union			
220 Donald Lynch Blvd ....Marlborough MA 01752	**800-328-8797**	508-263-6700	219
Digital Excellence			
300 York Ave ....Saint Paul MN 55101	**800-608-8008**	651-772-5100	649
Digital Innovations			
3436 N Kennicott			
Ste 200 ....Arlington Heights IL 60004	**888-762-7858**	847-463-9000	51
Digital Monitoring Products Inc			
2500 N Partnership Blvd ....Springfield MO 65803	**800-641-4282**	417-831-9362	659
Digital Peripheral Solutions Inc			
8015 E Crystal Dr ....Anaheim CA 92807	**877-998-3440**		174-8
Digital Photographer Magazine			
12121 Wilshire Blvd 12th Fl........Los Angeles CA 90025	**800-537-4619**	310-820-1500	452-14
Digital Power Corp			
41324 Christy St ....Fremont CA 94538	**866-344-7697**	510-353-4023	253
Digital River Inc			
10380 Bren Rd W Ste 150 ....Minnetonka MN 55343	**800-598-7450**		38
NASDAQ: DRIV			
Digital Solutions Inc			
955 SE Olson Dr ....Waukee IA 50263	**888-464-8770***	515-987-6227	179-11
*Cust Svc			
Digital Storage Inc			
7611 Green Meadows Dr ......Lewis Center OH 43035	**800-232-3475**	740-548-7179	175
Digital Video Services			
4592 40th St SE ....Grand Rapids MI 49512	**800-747-8273**	616-975-9911	240
Digital Voice Corp			
1201 S Beltline Rd Ste 150..........Coppell TX 75019	**800-777-8329***	469-635-6500	725
*Cust Svc			
DigitalWork Inc			
2345 S Alma School Rd Suite 105 ....Mesa AZ 85210	**877-496-7571**		38
Digitec Inc			
2731 Van Dorn Rd ....Milford NE 68405	**888-761-3382**	402-761-3382	659
Dignity Memorial			
1929 Allen Pkwy ....Houston TX 77019	**800-894-2024**	713-522-5141	503
DignityUSA Inc			
PO Box 376 ....Medford MA 02155	**800-877-8797**	202-861-0017	47-21
DII (Doucette Industries Inc)			
20 Leigh Dr ....York PA 17406	**800-445-7511**	717-845-8746	14
Dilley Manufacturing Co			
215 E Third St ....Des Moines IA 50309	**800-247-5087**	515-288-7289	85
Dilmar Oil Company Inc			
1951 W Darlington St			
PO Box 5629. ....Florence SC 29501	**800-922-5823**		770
DiMare Fresh Inc			
1049 Ave H E ....Arlington TX 76011	**800-322-2184***	817-385-3000	296-7
*General			
Dimco Steel Inc			
3901 S Lamar St ....Dallas TX 75215	**877-428-8336**	214-428-8336	677
Dime Bank, The			
820 Church St PO Box 509. ....Honesdale PA 18431	**888-469-3463**	570-253-1902	69
Dime Community Bancshares Inc			
209 Havemeyer St ....Brooklyn NY 11211	**800-321-3463**	718-782-6200	357-2
NASDAQ: DCOM			
Dinah's Garden Hotel			
4261 El Camino Real ....Palo Alto CA 94306	**800-227-8220**	650-493-2844	376
Diners Club International			
111 W Monroe ....Chicago IL 60603	**800-234-6377**		217
Dings Co			
4740 W Electric Ave ....Milwaukee WI 53219	**800-494-1918**	414-672-7830	383
Dinkel's Bakery			
3329 N Lincoln Ave ....Chicago IL 60657	**800-822-8817***	773-281-7300	295-1
*Orders			
Dinklage Feedyards			
PO Box 274 ....Sidney NE 69162	**888-343-5940**	308-254-5940	10-1
Dino's Trucking Inc			
9615 Continental Indus Dr ....Saint Louis MO 63123	**800-771-7805**	314-631-3001	770
Diocese of Greensburg			
723 E Pittsburgh St ....Greensburg PA 15601	**866-409-6455**	724-837-0901	47-20
Diocese of St. Augustine Inc			
11625 Old St Augustine ....Jacksonville FL 32258	**800-775-4659**	904-262-3200	47-20
Dipert Travel & Transportation Ltd			
PO Box 580 ....Arlington TX 76004	**800-433-5335**		750
Diplomatic Language Services LLC			
1901 N Ft Myer Dr Sixth Fl..........Arlington VA 22209	**800-642-7974**	703-243-4855	420
Dircks Moving Services Inc			
4340 W Mohave St ....Phoenix AZ 85043	**800-523-5038**	602-267-9401	770
Direct Federal Credit Union			
PO Box 9123 ....Needham MA 02494	**800-449-7728**	781-455-6500	219
Direct Internet Access			
141 Desiard St PO Box 7263 ....Monroe LA 71201	**800-296-2249**		395
Direct Marketing Assn Inc (DMA)			
1120 Ave of the Americas ....New York NY 10036	**855-422-0749**	212-768-7277	48-18
Direct Relief International			
27 S La Patera Ln ....Goleta CA 93117	**800-676-1638**	805-964-4767	47-5
Direct Source Inc			
8176 Mallory Ct ....Chanhassen MN 55317	**800-934-8055**	952-934-8000	179-5
Direct Travel			
95 New Jersey 17 ....Paramus NJ 07652	**800-831-1366**	201-847-9000	761
DirectBuy Inc			
8450 Broadway ....Merrillville IN 46410	**800-320-3462**	219-736-1100	309
DirectMailcom			
201 Skipjack Rd ....Prince Frederick MD 20678	**866-284-5816**	301-855-1700	5
Directors Guild of America			
7920 W Sunset Blvd ....Los Angeles CA 90046	**800-421-4173**	310-289-2000	411
Directory Distributing Assoc (DDA)			
1602 Pk 370 Ct ....Hazelwood MO 63042	**800-325-1964***	314-592-8600	94
*General			
DIRECTV Inc			
2230 E Imperial Hwy ....El Segundo CA 90245	**800-531-5000***	310-535-5000	115
*Cust Svc			
Dirt Pros of Fort Lauderdale			
PO Box 16453 ....Plantation FL 33318	**877-750-7767**	954-318-2477	256

Name / Address	Toll-Free	Phone	Class
DIS Corp 1315 Cornwall Ave — Bellingham WA 98225 *Cust Svc	800-426-8870*	360-733-7610	179-10
DISA (Data Interchange Standards Assn) 7600 Leesburg Pike Ste 430 — Falls Church VA 22043	866-205-5001	703-970-4480	47-9
Disa Systems Inc 150 Transit Ave — Thomasville NC 27360	800-845-8508	336-889-9187	18
Disability Funding Week 8204 Fenton St — Silver Spring MD 20910	800-666-6380		524-8
Disability Law Compliance Report 610 Opperman Dr — Eagan MN 55123 *Cust Svc	800-328-4880*	651-687-7000	524-7
Disability Rights Ctr Inc 18 Low Ave — Concord NH 03301	800-834-1721	603-228-0432	47-17
Disabled & Alone/Life Services for the Handicapped 1440 Broadway 23rd Floor — New York NY 10018	800-995-0066	212-532-6740	47-17
Disabled American Veterans (DAV) 3725 Alexandria Pike — Cold Spring KY 41076	877-426-2838	859-441-7300	47-19
Disabled American Veterans Magazine 3725 Alexandria Pike PO Box 14301 — Cold Spring KY 41076	877-426-2838	859-441-7300	452-10
Disabled Sports USA (DS/USA) 451 Hungerford Dr Ste 100 — Rockville MD 20850	800-543-2754	301-217-0960	47-22
Disaster News Network (DNN) PO Box 1746 — Ellicott City MD 21041	888-384-3028	443-393-3330	523
Disc Makers 7905 N Rt 130 — Pennsauken NJ 08110	800-468-9353	856-663-9030	174-8
Disco Inc 1895 Brannan Rd — McDonough GA 30253	800-325-1051	770-474-7575	501
Discount Car & Truck Rentals Ltd 720 Arrow Rd — North York ON M9M2M1	866-742-5968		125
Discount Drug Mart Inc 211 Commerce Dr — Medina OH 44256	800-833-6278	330-725-2340	237
Discount Labels Inc 4115 Profit Ct — New Albany IN 47150	800-995-9500		410
Discount RampsCom LLC 760 S Indiana Ave — West Bend WI 53095	888-651-3431	262-338-3431	475
Discount School Supplies Two Lower Ragsdale Rd Ste 125 — Monterey CA 93940	800-919-5238		751
DiscountMugs.com 12610 NW 115th Ave — Medley FL 33178	800-569-1980		681
Discover Bank PO Box 30416 — Salt Lake City UT 84130	800-347-7000	302-323-7810	69
Discover Group Inc 2741 W 23rd St — Brooklyn NY 11224	866-456-6555	718-456-4500	528
Discover Klamath 205 Riverside Dr Ste B — Klamath Falls OR 97601	800-445-6728	541-882-1501	207
Discovery Communications Inc One Discovery Pl — Silver Spring MD 20910 NASDAQ: DISCA	877-324-5850	240-662-2000	729
Discovery Cove 6000 Discovery Cove Way Ste B. — Orlando FL 32821	877-434-7268	407-370-1280	810
Discovery Cruises Inc 1775 NW 70th Ave — Miami FL 33126	800-866-8687	305-597-0336	220
Discovery Ctr of Springfield 438 E St Louis St — Springfield MO 65806	888-636-4395	417-862-9910	514
Discovery Place 301 N Tryon St — Charlotte NC 28202	800-935-0553	704-372-6261	514
Discovery Research Group 6975 Union Pk Ctr Ste 150 — Midvale UT 84047	800-678-3748		225
Disguise 12120 Kear Pl — Poway CA 92064	877-875-2557	858-391-3600	153-6
DISH Network LLC 9601 S Meridian Blvd — Englewood CO 80112 NASDAQ: DISH	800-823-4929		115
Disney Consumer Products 500 S Buena Vista St — Burbank CA 91521 *PR	877-282-8322*	818-560-1000	628-8
Disney Vacation Club 1390 Celebration Blvd — Celebration FL 34747	800-500-3990	407-566-3100	743
Disney's Animal Kingdom Lodge 2901 Osceola Pkwy — Lake Buena Vista FL 32830	855-878-9582	407-938-3000	660
Disney's California Adventure 1313 S Disneyland Dr — Anaheim CA 92802	800-225-2024	714-781-7290	32
Disney's Grand Floridian Spa 4401 Floridian Wy — Lake Buena Vista FL 32830	800-169-0730	407-824-2332	698
Disney/Little Blue State Park Hwy 28 E — Disney OK 74340	800-622-6317	918-435-8066	558
Dispatch Printing Co 34 S Third St — Columbus OH 43215	800-282-0263	614-461-5000	628-8
Dispatch, The 116 E Market St — Blairsville PA 15717	844-743-2015	724-459-6100	525-2
Dispensing Dynamics International 1020 Bixby Dr — City of Industry CA 91745	800-888-3698	626-961-3691	603
Display Smart LLC 801 W 27th Terr — Lawrence KS 66046	888-843-1870	785-843-1869	233
Display Technologies LLC 1111 Marcus Ave Ste M68 — Lake Success NY 11042	800-424-4220		233
Disston Precision Inc 6795 State Rd — Philadelphia PA 19135 *Cust Svc	800-238-1007*	215-338-1200	673
Distillata Co 1608 E 24th St — Cleveland OH 44114 *Cust Svc	800-999-2906*	216-771-2900	793
Distinctive Designs International Inc 120 Sibley Dr — Russellville AL 35654	800-243-4787	256-332-7390	293
Distinguished Programs Group LLC, The 1180 Ave Of The Americas 16th Fl — New York NY 10036	888-355-4626	212-297-3100	387
Distribution Ctr Management (DCM) 712 Main St Ste 187B — Boonton NJ 07005	800-232-4317	973-265-2300	524-2
District of Columbia Convention & Tourism Corp 901 7th St NW 4th Fl — Washington DC 20001	800-422-8644	202-789-7000	337-9
District of Columbia Bar, The 1101 K St NW Ste 200 — Washington DC 20005	877-333-2227	202-737-4700	71
DistTech Inc 4366 Mt. Pleasant St NW — North Canton OH 44720	800-969-5419		770
DIT-MCO International Corp 5612 Brighton Terr — Kansas City MO 64130	800-821-3487	816-444-9700	248
Dittrick Museum of Medical History 11000 Euclid Ave — Cleveland OH 44106	800-368-4723	216-368-3648	513
Divers Academy International 1500 Liberty Pl — Erial NJ 08081	800-238-3483		788
Diverse Power Inc 1400 S Davis Rd — LaGrange GA 30241	800-845-8362	706-845-2000	245
Diversified Chemical Technologies Inc (DCT) 15477 Woodrow Wilson St — Detroit MI 48238	800-243-1424	313-867-5444	143
Diversified Electronics Co Inc PO Box 566 — Forest Park GA 30298	800-646-7278	404-361-4840	246
Diversified Funding Services Inc 255 N Main St Ste 873 — Jonesboro GA 30237	888-603-0055	770-603-0055	272
Diversified Hum Res Inc 3020 E Camelback Rd Ste 213 — Phoenix AZ 85016	888-870-5588	480-941-5588	623
Diversified Labeling Solutions 1285 Hamilton Pkwy — Itasca IL 60143	800-397-3013	630-625-1225	545-1
Diversified Lenders Inc 5607 S Ave Q — Lubbock TX 79412	800-288-3024		195
Diversified Maintenance Systems Inc 5110 Eisenhower Blvd Ste250 — Tampa FL 33634	800-351-1557	813-383-0238	150
Diversified Search Cos 2005 Market St 33rd Fl — Philadelphia PA 19103	800-423-3932	215-732-6666	266
DiversiTech Inc 6650 Sugarloaf Pkwy Ste 100 — Duluth GA 30097	800-995-2222	678-542-3600	14
Dividend Capital Trust 518 17th St Ste 1700 — Denver CO 80202	866-324-7348	303-228-2200	645
Divine Word College 102 Jacoby Dr SW — Epworth IA 52045	800-553-3321	563-876-3353	166
Diving Equipment & Marketing Assn (DEMA) 3750 Convoy St Ste 310 — San Diego CA 92111	800-862-3483	858-616-6408	48-4
DIX (Downtown Idea Exchange) 712 Main St Ste 187B — Boonton NJ 07005	800-232-4317	973-265-2300	524-2
Dixie Construction Products Inc 970 Huff Rd NW — Atlanta GA 30318	800-992-1180	404-351-1100	348
Dixie Electric Co-op 9100 Atlanta Hwy — Montgomery AL 36117	888-349-4332	334-288-1163	245
Dixie Electric Membership Corp (DEMCO) PO Box 15659 — Baton Rouge LA 70895	800-262-0221	225-261-1221	245
Dixie Electric Power Assn PO Box 88 — Laurel MS 39441	888-465-9209	601-425-2535	245
Dixie Group Inc 104 Nowlin Ln Ste 101 — Chattanooga TN 37421 NASDAQ: DXYN	800-289-4811	423-510-7000	130
Dixie Gun Works Inc 1412 W Reelfoot Ave PO Box 130 — Union City TN 38281 *Orders	800-238-6785*	731-885-0700	702
Dixie Industries 3510 N Orchard Knob Ave — Chattanooga TN 37406	800-933-4943	423-698-3323	347
Dixie Pipe Sales Inc 2407 Broiler PO Box 300650 — Houston TX 77054	800-733-3494	713-796-2021	485
Dixie State College of Utah 225 S 700 E — Saint George UT 84770	855-628-8140	435-652-7500	166
Dixie Store Fixtures & Sales Company Inc 2425 First Ave N — Birmingham AL 35203	800-323-4943	205-322-2442	286
Dixie-Escalante Rural Electric Assn 71 E Hwy 56 — Beryl UT 84714	800-874-0904	435-439-5311	245
Dixie-Narco Inc 3330 Dixie-Narco Blvd — Williston SC 29853	800-688-9090	803-266-5000	54
Dixon Ticonderoga Co 195 International Pkwy — Heathrow FL 32746	800-824-9430	407-829-9000	564
DJ & A PC 3203 S Russell St — Missoula MT 59801	800-398-3522	406-721-4320	256
DJ Jacobetti Home for Veterans 425 Fisher St — Marquette MI 49855	800-433-6760	906-226-3576	781
DJ Orthopedics Inc 1430 Decision St — Vista CA 92081	800-321-9549	760-727-1280	472
DKRW Advanced Fuels LLC 5444 Westheimer Ste 1560 — Houston TX 77056	855-876-4595		529
D&L Art Glass Supply 1440 W 52nd Ave — Denver CO 80221	800-525-0940	303-449-8737	43
DLH Holdings Corp 1776 Peachtree St NW Ste 300S — Atlanta GA 30309 NASDAQ: DLHC	866-352-5304	770-554-3545	712
D-Link Systems Inc 17595 Mt Herrmann St — Fountain Valley CA 92708	800-326-1688	714-885-6000	177
Dlt Solutions 13861 Sunrise Valley Dr Ste 400 — Herndon VA 20171	800-262-4358	703-709-7172	175
DLZ Corp 6121 Huntley Rd — Columbus OH 43229	800-336-5352	614-888-0040	261
DM Figley Company Inc 10 Kelly Ct — Menlo Park CA 94025	800-292-9919	650-329-8700	144
DM Transportation Management Services Inc PO Box 621 — Boyertown PA 19512	888-399-0162	610-367-0162	195
DMA (Direct Marketing Assn Inc) 1120 Ave of the Americas — New York NY 10036	855-422-0749	212-768-7277	48-18
DMCCVB (Decatur/Morgan County Convention & Visitors Bureau) 719 Sixth Ave SE PO Box 2349 — Decatur AL 35602	800-232-5449	256-350-2028	207
D-M-E Co 29111 Stephenson Hwy — Madison Heights MI 48071	800-626-6653	248-398-6000	597
DME-Direct Inc 28486 Westinghouse Pl Ste 120 — Valencia CA 91355	877-721-7701		195
DMI (Dairy Management Inc) 10255 W Higgins Rd Ste 900 — Rosemont IL 60018	800-853-2479		47-2
DMI (Design Management Institute) 38 Chauncy St Ste 800 — Boston MA 02111	800-200-5909	617-338-6380	47-4
DMI Furniture Inc 9780 Ormsby Stn Rd Ste 2000 — Louisville KY 40223	888-750-5834	502-426-4351	318-2
DMS Facility Services Inc 417 East Huntington Dr — Monrovia CA 91016	800-443-8677	626-305-8500	103
DMS Laboratories Inc Two Darts Mill Rd — Flemington NJ 08822	800-567-4367	908-782-3353	575
DMS Pharmaceutical Group Inc 810 Busse Hwy — Park Ridge IL 60068	877-788-1100	847-518-1100	231
DMX Music Inc 1703 W Fifth St Ste 600 — Austin TX 78703	800-345-5000	512-380-8500	517
DN Tanks 351 Cypress Ln — El Cajon CA 92020	800-227-8181	619-440-8181	184
DNA (Delaware Nurses Assn) 4765 Ogletown-Stanton Rd Ste L10 — Newark DE 19713	800-626-4081	302-733-5880	526
DNA Diagnostics Ctr 1 DDC Way — Fairfield OH 45014	800-362-2368	513-881-7800	414
DNA Paternity Lab of Utah 2749 E Parleys Way — Salt Lake City UT 84109	800-362-5559	801-466-3872	414
DNN (Disaster News Network) PO Box 1746 — Ellicott City MD 21041	888-384-3028	443-393-3330	523

Alphabetical Section

	Toll-Free	Phone	Class
Doane College			
1014 Boswell Ave ....Crete NE 68333	800-333-6263	402-826-2161	166
Grand Island			
3180 W US Hwy 34 ....Grand Island NE 68801	800-333-6263	308-398-0800	166
Lincoln 303 N 52nd St ....Lincoln NE 68504	888-803-6263	402-466-4774	166
DOAR Litigation Consulting			
170 Earle Ave ....Lynbrook NY 11563	800-875-8705	516-823-4000	440
Dober Chemical Group			
11230 Katherine Crossing			
Ste 100....................Woodridge IL 60517	800-323-4983	630-410-7300	143
Doble Engineering Co Inc			
85 Walnut St ....Watertown MA 02472	800-759-5219	617-926-4900	248
DocMan Technologies			
31300 Bainbridge Rd ....Cleveland OH 44122	888-636-2626		38
Doctor's Assoc Inc			
325 Bic Dr ....Milford CT 06461	800-888-4848	203-877-4281	661
Doctors Foster & Smith Inc			
2253 Air Pk Rd PO Box 100 ....Rhinelander WI 54501	800-826-7206	715-369-3305	571
Doctors Hospital at White Rock Lake			
9440 Poppy Dr ....Dallas TX 75218	866-893-8446	214-324-6100	371-3
Doctors Hospital of Laredo			
10700 McPherson Rd ....Laredo TX 78045	844-244-4874	956-523-2000	371-3
Doctors Medical Ctr			
1441 Florida Ave ....Modesto CA 95350	800-994-6610	209-578-1211	371-3
Doctors Vision Ctr			
413 Mill St PO Box 7396 ....Rocky Mount NC 27804	888-414-4442	252-442-0802	536
Doctors Without Borders USA Inc			
333 Seventh Ave Second Fl ....New York NY 10001	888-392-0392	212-679-6800	47-5
Doctors' Co, The			
185 Greenwood Rd ....Napa CA 94558	800-421-2368		388-5
Docufree Corp			
1175 Northmeadow Pkwy Ste 140 ....Roswell GA 30076	877-220-4350	770-643-2900	225
Document Access Systems			
9019 Forest Hill Ave Ste 9C ....Richmond VA 23235	866-544-9876		197
Document Security Systems Inc			
28 E Main St Ste 1525 ....Rochester NY 14614	877-407-8031	585-325-3610	179-10
NYSE: DSS			
Doc-U-Search Inc			
63 Pleasant St PO Box 777..........Concord NH 03301	800-332-3034		626
Dodd Camera			
2077 E 30th St ....Cleveland OH 44115	800-507-1676	216-361-6800	118
Dodge & Cox			
555 California St 40th Fl..........San Francisco CA 94104	800-254-8494	415-981-1710	398
Dodge & Cox Funds			
30 Dan Rd PO Box 8422..............Canton MA 02021	800-621-3979		521
Dodge City Community College			
2501 N 14th Ave ....Dodge City KS 67801	800-367-3222	620-225-1321	160
Dodger Industries			
2075 Stultz Rd PO Box 711 ....Martinsville VA 24112	800-247-7879*		153-1
*Cust Svc			
DOE (Department of Energy)			
1000 Independence Ave SW ....Washington DC 20585	800-342-5363	202-586-5450	338-7
Doe Run Co			
1801 Pk 270 Dr Ste 300 ....Saint Louis MO 63146	800-356-3786	314-453-7100	480
Doerfer Engineering Corp			
PO Box 816 ....Waverly IA 50677	877-483-4700		261
Dog Fancy Magazine			
Three Burroughs ....Irvine CA 92618	800-546-7730*	949-855-8822	452-14
*Cust Svc			
Dogwood Hills Golf Resort			
1252 State Hwy KK ....Osage Beach MO 65065	800-220-6571	573-348-1735	660
Doheny Eye Institute			
1450 San Pablo St ....Los Angeles CA 90033	800-872-2273	323-442-7100	371-7
Doherty Employment Group			
7625 Parklawn Ave ....Edina MN 55435	888-297-0495*	952-832-8383	623
*Sales			
Dohrn Transfer Co			
625 Third Ave ....Rock Island IL 61201	888-364-7621	309-794-0723	444
Doka USA Ltd			
214 Gates Rd ....Little Ferry NJ 07643	877-365-2872	201-329-7839	192-3
Dolce Atlanta-Peachtree			
201 Aberdeen Pkwy ....Peachtree City GA 30269	800-983-6523	770-487-2666	374
Dolce Hayes Mansion			
200 Edenvale Ave ....San Jose CA 95136	866-981-3300	408-226-3200	374
Dole Food Company Hawaii			
802 Mapunapuna St ....Honolulu HI 96819	800-697-9100	808-861-8015	296-7
Dole Food Company Inc			
One Dole Dr ....Westlake Village CA 91362	800-232-8888	818-879-6600	314-4
NYSE: DOLE			
Dole Refrigerating Co			
1420 Higgs Rd ....Lewisburg TN 37091	800-251-8990	931-359-6211	655
Dolese Bros Co			
20 NW 13th St ....Oklahoma City OK 73103	800-375-2311	405-235-2311	184
Dollar Bank FSB			
225 Forbes Ave ....Pittsburgh PA 15222	800-828-5527	412-261-2343	69
Dollar General Corp			
100 Mission Ridge ....Goodlettsville TN 37072	800-777-1410	615-855-4000	779
NYSE: DG			
Dollar Loan Ctr LLC			
6122 W Sahara Ave ....Las Vegas NV 89146	866-550-4352	702-693-5626	214
Dollar Rent A Car Inc			
5330 E 31st St ....Tulsa OK 74135	800-800-4000	918-669-3000	125
Dollar Thrifty Automotive Group Inc			
5330 E 31st St PO Box 35985 ....Tulsa OK 74135	800-334-1705	918-660-7700	125
Dollar Tree Stores Inc			
500 Volvo Pkwy ....Chesapeake VA 23320	877-530-8733		779
NASDAQ: DLTR			
Dollars for Scholars			
Scholarship America			
1 Scholarship Way ....Saint Peter MN 56082	800-248-8080	507-931-1682	716
Dolly's Pizza Franchising Inc			
1097 Union Lake Rd ....White Lake MI 48386	866-336-5597	248-360-6440	661
Dollywood			
2700 Dollywood			
Parks Blvd...............Pigeon Forge TN 37863	800-365-5996		32
Dolphin Carpet & Tile			
3550 NW 77th Ct ....Miami FL 33122	800-639-3566	305-591-4141	290
Dolphin Inn			
1705 Atlantic Ave ....Virginia Beach VA 23451	800-365-3467	757-491-1420	376
Domain Assoc			
1 Palmer Sq Ste 515..............Princeton NJ 08542	866-803-9204	609-683-5656	780
Domain Registration Services			
PO Box 447 ....Palmyra NJ 08065	888-339-9001		393

	Toll-Free	Phone	Class
Domaine Chandon Inc			
One California Dr ....Yountville CA 94599	888-242-6366		79-3
Domain-It!			
9891 Montgomery Rd ....Cincinnati OH 45242	866-269-2355*	513-351-4222	393
*General			
DomainPeople Inc			
550 Burrard St			
Ste 200 Bentall Twr 5 ....Vancouver BC V6C2B5	877-734-3667	604-639-1680	393
Domestic Linen Supply & Laundry Co Inc			
30555 NW Hwy ....Farmington Hills MI 48334	800-344-3555	248-737-2000	438
Domestic Securities Inc			
160 Summit Ave ....Montvale NJ 07645	877-690-2274	201-505-9855	681
Dometic Corp			
2320 Industrial Pkwy PO Box 490 ....Elkhart IN 46516	800-544-4881	574-294-2511	14
Domini Social Investments			
PO Box 9785 ....Providence RI 02940	800-582-6757		521
Dominican College			
470 Western Hwy ....Orangeburg NY 10962	866-432-4636	845-359-7800	166
Dominican School of Philosophy & Theology			
2301 Vine St ....Berkeley CA 94708	888-450-3778	510-849-2030	167-3
Dominican University			
7900 W Div St ....River Forest IL 60305	800-828-8475	708-366-2490	166
Dominican University of California			
50 Acacia Ave ....San Rafael CA 94901	888-323-6763*	415-457-4440	166
*Admissions			
Dominion Bldg Products			
6949 Fairbanks N Houston Rd ....Houston TX 77040	800-826-2617		234
Dominion East Ohio			
PO Box 26532 ....Richmond VA 23261	800-362-7557*		775
*Cust Svc			
Dominion Electric Supply Company Inc			
5053 Lee Hwy ....Arlington VA 22207	800-525-5006	703-536-4400	246
Dominion Hope			
701 E Cary St ....Richmond VA 23219	866-366-4357	888-366-8280	775
Dominion Lending Centres Inc			
2215 Coquitlam Ave ....Port Coquitlam BC V3B1J6	866-928-6810		502
Dominion North Carolina Power			
701 E Cary St ....Richmond VA 23219	888-667-3000	757-857-2112	775
Dominion Resources Inc			
120 Tredegar St ....Richmond VA 23219	800-552-4034	804-819-2000	357-5
NYSE: D			
Dominion Veterinary Laboratories Inc			
1199 Sanford St ....Winnipeg MB R3E3A1	800-465-7122	204-589-7361	575
Dominion Virginia Power			
120 Tredegar St ....Richmond VA 23219	800-688-4673		775
Domtar Corp			
395 de Maisonneuve W ....Montreal QC H3A1L6	877-848-4466	514-848-5555	674
NYSE: UFS			
Don CeSar Beach Resort - A Loews Hotel			
3400 Gulf Blvd ....Saint Pete Beach FL 33706	866-563-9792	727-360-1881	660
Don Garlits Museums			
13700 SW 16th Ave ....Ocala FL 34473	877-271-3278	352-245-8661	515
Don Hall's Guesthouse			
1313 W Washington Ctr Rd ....Fort Wayne IN 46825	800-348-1999*	260-489-2524	376
*General			
Don Hummer Trucking Corp			
1486 Hwy 6 NW PO Box 310 ....Oxford IA 52322	888-642-7249	319-828-2000	770
Don Hutson Organization			
516 Tennessee St Ste 219........Memphis TN 38103	800-647-9166	901-767-0000	755
Don Laughlin's Riverside Resort & Casino			
1650 Casino Dr ....Laughlin NV 89029	800-227-3849	702-298-2535	132
Don McGill Toyota Inc			
11800 Katy Fwy ....Houston TX 77079	877-259-6888	281-496-2000	56
Don Miguel Mexican Foods Inc			
One Hormel Pl ....Austin MN 55912	800-725-7212		295-36
Don Pepino Sales Co			
123 Railroad Ave ....Williamstown NJ 08094	888-281-6400	856-629-7429	295-20
Don Stevens Inc			
980 Discovery Rd ....Eagan MN 55121	800-444-2299	651-452-0872	656
Don Young Co			
8181 Ambassador Row ....Dallas TX 75247	800-367-0390	214-630-0934	475
Dona Ana Branch Community College (DACC)			
2800 N Sonoma Ranch Blvd			
PO Box 30001................Las Cruces NM 88011	800-903-7503	575-528-7000	160
Donan Engineering Co Inc			
11321 Plantside Dr ....Louisville KY 40299	800-482-5611		397
Donatello, The			
501 Post St ....San Francisco CA 94102	800-258-2366	415-441-7100	376
Donatos Pizza			
935 Taylor Stn Rd ....Columbus OH 43230	800-366-2867		661
Donegal Group Inc			
1195 River Rd ....Marietta PA 17547	800-877-0600	717-426-1931	357-4
NASDAQ: DGICA			
Donegal Mutual Insurance Co			
1195 River Rd PO Box 302...........Marietta PA 17547	800-877-0600	717-426-1931	388-4
Donelson-Hermitage Chamber of Commerce			
125 Donelson Pike			
PO Box 140200................Nashville TN 37214	800-688-9889	615-883-7896	137
Donlen Corp			
2315 Sanders Rd ....Northbrook IL 60062	800-323-1483	847-714-1400	289
Donna Karan International Inc			
550 Seventh Ave 15th Fl........New York NY 10018	888-737-5743*	212-789-1500	153-20
*General			
Donnelly College			
608 N 18th St ....Kansas City KS 66102	800-908-9946	913-621-6070	160
Donning Company Publishers			
184 Business Pk Dr			
Ste 206 ....Virginia Beach VA 23462	800-296-8572		628-2
Donor Alliance Inc			
720 S Colorado Blvd Ste 800-N ....Denver CO 80246	888-868-4747	303-329-4747	538
Donor Network of Arizona			
201 W Coolidge St ....Phoenix AZ 85013	800-447-9477	602-222-2200	269
Donovan Marine Inc			
6316 Humphreys St ....Harahan LA 70123	800-347-4464	504-488-5731	760
Donzi Marine			
1653 WhichaRds Beach Rd			
PO Box 457................Washington NC 27889	800-624-3304		89
Dooney & Bourke Inc			
1 Regent St ....East Norwalk CT 06855	800-347-5000*	203-853-7515	427
*Cust Svc			
Door Components Inc			
7980 Redwood Ave ....Fontana CA 92336	866-989-3667	909-770-5700	234
Door Engineering & Mfg LLC			
400 Cherry St ....Kasota MN 56050	800-959-1352	507-931-6910	347

Company / Address	City	State	Zip	Toll-Free	Phone	Class
Door Systems Inc PO Box 511	Framingham	MA	01704	**800-545-3667**	508-875-3508	192-3
Doral Arrowwood Conference Resort 975 Anderson Hill Rd	Rye Brook	NY	10573	**844-211-0512**	844-214-5500	374
Doral Desert Princess Palm Springs Resort 67967 Vista Chino	Cathedral City	CA	92234	**800-433-0431**	760-322-7000	660
Doral Financial Corp 1441 F D Roosevelt Ave *NYSE: DRL*	San Juan	PR	00920	**866-296-3743**	787-749-4949	357-2
Doral Golf Resort & Spa 4400 NW 87th Ave	Miami	FL	33178	**800-713-6725**	305-592-2000	660
Dordt College 498 Fourth Ave NE	Sioux Center	IA	51250	**800-343-6738**	712-722-6080	166
Dorel Juvenile Group USA 2525 State St	Columbus	IN	47201	**800-544-1108**	812-372-0141	63
Dorling Kindersley Publishing 375 Hudson St *Cust Svc	New York	NY	10014	**800-631-8571***	646-674-4047	628-2
DORMA Architectural Hardware DORMA Dr Drawer AC	Reamstown	PA	17567	**800-523-8483**	717-336-3881	483
DORMA Group North America Dorma Dr	Reamstown	PA	17567	**800-523-8483**	717-336-3881	347
Dorman Products Inc 3400 E Walnut St *NASDAQ: DORM*	Colmar	PA	18915	**800-523-2492**	215-997-1800	59
Dormont Manufacturing Co 6015 Enterprise Dr	Export	PA	15632	**800-367-6668**		367
Dornbracht Americas Inc 1700 Executive Dr S Ste 600	Duluth	GA	30096	**800-774-1181**		603
Dorney Park & Wildwater Kingdom 3830 Dorney Pk Rd	Allentown	PA	18104	**800-747-0561**	610-395-3724	32
Dornier MedTech America Inc 1155 Roberts Blvd	Kennesaw	GA	30144	**800-367-6437**	770-426-1315	379
Dorsett & Jackson Inc 3800 Noakes St	Los Angeles	CA	90023	**800-871-8365**	323-268-1815	144
Dorsett Industries Inc 1304 May St PO Box 805	Dalton	GA	30721	**800-241-4035**	706-278-1961	130
Dorsey & Whitney LLP 50 S Sixth St Ste 1500	Minneapolis	MN	55402	**800-759-4929**	612-340-2600	425
Doskocil Mfg Company Inc PO Box 1246	Arlington	TX	76004	**877-738-6283**		571
Dostal Alley Casino 1 Dostal Alley	Central City	CO	80427	**888-949-2757**	303-582-1610	132
Dot Foods Inc One Dot Way PO Box 192	Mount Sterling	IL	62353	**800-366-3687**	217-773-4411	296-6
Dot Hill Systems Corp 1351 S Sunset St *NASDAQ: HILL*	Longmont	CO	80501	**800-872-2783**	303-845-3200	177
Dothan Area Chamber of Commerce 102 Jamestown Blvd	Dothan	AL	36301	**800-221-1027**	334-792-5138	137
Dothan Area Convention & Visitors Bureau 3311 Ross Clark Cir PO Box 8765	Dothan	AL	36301	**888-449-0212**	334-794-6622	207
Dothan Chrysler-Dodge Inc 4074 Ross Clark Cir NW	Dothan	AL	36303	**877-674-9574**		56
Dothan Eagle PO Box 1968	Dothan	AL	36302	**800-811-1771**	334-792-3141	525-2
Dot-Line Transportation PO Box 8739	Fountain Valley	CA	92728	**800-423-3780**	323-780-9010	189-5
Dotronix Inc 160 First St SE	New Brighton	MN	55112	**800-720-7218**	651-633-1742	174-4
Dotster 8100 NE Pkwy Dr Ste 300 PO Box 821066	Vancouver	WA	98682	**800-401-5250**	360-449-5800	393
Dotster Inc PO Box 821066	Vancouver	WA	98682	**800-401-5250**	360-253-2210	393
Double Diamond Co 5495 Belt Line Rd Suite 200	Dallas	TX	75254	**800-324-7438**	214-706-9801	644
Double Eagle Hotel & Casino 442 E Bennett Ave	Cripple Creek	CO	80813	**800-711-7234**	719-689-5000	132
Double H Plastics Inc 50 W St Rd	Warminster	PA	18974	**800-523-3932**	215-674-4100	597
Doubletree Claremont 555 W Foothill Blvd	Claremont	CA	91711	**800-222-8733**	909-626-2411	376
Doubletree Hotel Downtown Wilmington Legal District 700 N King St	Wilmington	DE	19801	**800-222-8733**	302-655-0400	376
Doubletree North Shore Hotel 9599 Skokie Blvd	Skokie	IL	60077	**800-445-8667**	847-679-7000	376
Doubletree Paradise Valley Resort 5401 N Scottsdale Rd	Scottsdale	AZ	85250	**800-222-8733**	480-947-5400	660
DoubleTree Resort by Hilton Hotel Grand Key (DGKR) 3990 S Roosevelt Blvd	Key West	FL	33040	**888-844-0454**	305-293-1818	660
Doucette Industries Inc (DII) 20 Leigh Dr	York	PA	17406	**800-445-7511**	717-845-8746	14
Doug Mockett & Company Inc 1915 Abalone Ave	Torrance	CA	90501	**800-523-1269**	310-318-2491	347
Doug Varone & Dancers 37 W 32nd St	New York	NY	10001	**800-366-2100**	212-279-3344	566-1
Dougherty & Company LLC 90 S Seventh St Ste 4300	Minneapolis	MN	55402	**800-328-4000**	612-376-4000	681
Dougherty Arts Ctr, The (DAC) 1110 Barton Springs Rd	Austin	TX	78704	**855-787-2227**	512-974-4000	49-1
Douglas & Sturgess Inc 1023 Factory St	Richmond	CA	94801	**800-762-0744**	510-235-8411	44
Douglas Baldwin & Assoc PO Box 1249	La Canada	CA	91012	**800-392-3950**	818-952-4433	397
Douglas Battery Manufacturing Co 500 Battery Dr	Winston-Salem	NC	27107	**800-368-4527**		73
Douglas Bros 423 Riverside Industrial Pkwy	Portland	ME	04103	**800-341-0926**	207-797-6771	588
Douglas Cuddle Toys Company Inc 69 Krif Rd PO Box D	Keene	NH	03431	**800-992-9002**	603-352-3414	752
Douglas Industries Co 3441 S 11th Ave	Eldridge	IA	52748	**800-553-8907**	563-285-4162	701
Douglas Laboratories Inc 600 Boyce Rd	Pittsburgh	PA	15205	**800-245-4440**	412-494-0122	787
Douglas Press Inc 2810 Madison St	Bellwood	IL	60104	**800-323-0705**	708-547-8400	321
Douglas Stewart Co, The 2402 Advance Rd	Madison	WI	53718	**800-279-2795**	608-221-1155	527
Douglas/Quikut Co 118 E Douglas Rd	Walnut Ridge	AR	72476	**800-982-5233**		222
Douglas-Coffee County Chamber of Commerce 211 S Gaskin Ave	Douglas	GA	31533	**888-426-3334**	912-384-1873	137
Douglas-Guardian Services Corp 14800 St Mary's Ln	Houston	TX	77079	**800-255-0552**	281-531-0500	396
Douglass Truck Bodies Inc 231 21st St	Bakersfield	CA	93301	**800-635-7641**	661-327-0258	509
Douthat State Park 14239 Douthat State Pk Rd *General	Millboro	VA	24460	**800-933-7275***	540-862-8100	558
Douthitt Corp 245 Adair St	Detroit	MI	48207	**800-368-8448**	313-259-1565	584
Dover Chemical Corp 3676 Davis Rd NW *General	Dover	OH	44622	**800-321-8805***	330-343-7711	143
Dover Downs Hotel & Casino 1131 N DuPont Hwy *NYSE: DDE*	Dover	DE	19901	**800-711-5882**	302-674-4600	633
Dover International Speedway 1131 N DuPont Hwy PO Box 843	Dover	DE	19901	**800-441-7223**	302-883-6500	633
Dover Motorsports Inc 1131 N Dupont Hwy *NYSE: DVD*	Dover	DE	19901	**800-441-7223**	302-883-6500	633
Dover Post 1196 S Little Creek Rd	Dover	DE	19901	**800-942-1616**	302-678-3616	525-4
Dover Saddlery Inc 525 Great Rd PO Box 1100 *NASDAQ: DOVR*	Littleton	MA	01460	**800-406-8204**	978-952-8062	701
Dow AgroSciences LLC 9330 Zionsville Rd	Indianapolis	IN	46268	**800-258-1470**	317-337-3000	280
Dow Chemical Canada Inc (DCCI) 450 First St SW Ste 2100	Calgary	AB	T2P5H1	**800-447-4369**	403-267-3500	142
Dow Chemical Co 2030 Dow Ctr *NYSE: DOW* ■ *Cust Svc	Midland	MI	48674	**800-422-8193***	989-636-1463	142
Dow Chemical Company Foundation 2030 Dow Ctr	Midland	MI	48674	**800-331-6451**	989-636-1000	303
Dow Chemical Company, The 1881 W Oak Pkwy	Marietta	GA	30062	**800-331-6451**	770-428-2684	594
Dow Chemical Employees' Credit Union 600 E Lyon Rd	Midland	MI	48640	**800-835-7794**	989-835-7794	219
Dow Corning Corp PO Box 994 *Cust Svc	Midland	MI	48686	**800-248-2481***	989-496-4000	142
Dow Cover Co Inc 373 Lexington Ave	New Haven	CT	06513	**800-735-8877**	203-469-5394	346
Dow Electronics Inc 8603 E Adamo Dr	Tampa	FL	33619	**800-627-2900**	813-626-5195	246
Dow Liquid Separations PO Box 1206	Midland	MI	48642	**800-447-4369**	989-636-1000	794
Dow Theory Forecasts 7412 Calumet Ave	Hammond	IN	46324	**800-233-5922**		524-9
Dow-Key Microwave Corp 4822 McGrath St	Ventura	CA	93003	**800-266-3695**	805-650-0260	253
Dowling College 150 Idle Hour Blvd	Oakdale	NY	11769	**800-369-5464**	631-244-3000	166
Down Beat Magazine 102 N Haven Rd PO Box 906	Elmhurst	IL	60126	**800-554-7470**	651-251-9682	452-9
Down East 680 Commercial St	Rockport	ME	04856	**800-766-1670**	207-594-9544	452-22
Downers Grove Area Chamber of Commerce & Industry 2001 Butterfield Rd Ste 105	Downers Grove	IL	60515	**800-922-3565**	630-968-4050	137
Downey Chamber of Commerce 11131 Brookshire Ave	Downey	CA	90241	**877-345-4633**	562-923-2191	137
Downey City Library (DCL) 11121 Brookshire Ave	Downey	CA	90241	**877-846-3452**	562-904-7360	431-3
Downing Displays Inc 550 Techne Ctr Dr	Milford	OH	45150	**800-883-1800**	513-248-9800	232
Downs Crane & Hoist Company Inc 8827 Juniper St	Los Angeles	CA	90002	**800-748-5994**	323-589-6061	465
Downtown Athletic Store Inc 1180 Seminole Trail Ste 210	Charlottesville	VA	22901	**800-348-2649**	434-975-3696	702
Downtown Idea Exchange (DIX) 712 Main St Ste 187B	Boonton	NJ	07005	**800-232-4317**	973-265-2300	524-2
Downtown Promotion Reporter (DPR) 712 Main St Ste 187B	Boonton	NJ	07005	**800-232-4317**	973-265-2300	524-10
DoxTek Inc 264 W Center St	Orem	UT	84057	**877-705-7226**		225
Doyle Security Systems Inc 792 Calkins Rd	Rochester	NY	14623	**800-836-9538**	585-244-3400	683
Doyon Drilling Inc 11500 C St Ste 200	Anchorage	AK	99515	**800-478-9675**	907-563-5530	533
DP Technology Corp 1150 Avenida Acaso	Camarillo	CA	93012	**800-627-8479**	805-388-6000	179-5
D-Patrick Inc 200 N Green River Rd	Evansville	IN	47716	**800-831-6870**	812-473-6500	56
DPC DATA Inc 103 Eisenhower Pkwy Ste 300	Roseland	NJ	07068	**800-996-4747**	201-346-0701	175
DPE Systems Inc 425 Pontius Ave N Ste 430	Seattle	WA	98109	**800-541-6566**	206-223-3737	181
DPEC Capital Inc 135 Fifth Ave	New York	NY	10010	**844-574-3577**	301-590-6500	402
DPF Data Services Group Inc 1990 Swarthmore Ave	Lakewood	NJ	08701	**800-431-4416**	732-370-8840	225
DPL Inc 1065 Woodman Dr *NYSE: DPL*	Dayton	OH	45432	**800-433-8500**	800-736-3001	357-5
DPNM (New Mexico Democratic Party) 8214 Second St NW ste A	Albuquerque	NM	87114	**800-624-2457**	505-830-3650	609-1
DPR (Downtown Promotion Reporter) 712 Main St Ste 187B	Boonton	NJ	07005	**800-232-4317**	973-265-2300	524-10
DPSI Inc 1801 Stanley Rd Ste 301	Greensboro	NC	27407	**800-897-7233**	336-854-7700	179-11
DPT Laboratories Ltd 318 McCullough	San Antonio	TX	78215	**866-225-5378**	210-476-8150	576
Dr Delphinium Designs & Events 5806 W Lovers Ln & Tollway	Dallas	TX	75225	**800-783-8790**	214-522-9911	292
DR Horton Inc 301 Commerce St Ste 500 *NYSE: DHI*	Fort Worth	TX	76102	**800-846-7866**	817-390-8200	644
Dr Kern USA Inc 221 S Franklin Rd	Indianapolis	IN	46219	**800-908-9885**	317-472-0873	75
Dr Pepper Snapple Group Inc 5301 Legacy Dr *NYSE: DPS*	Plano	TX	75024	**800-686-7398**	972-673-7000	295-15

Name / Address	City	State	Zip	Toll-Free	Phone	Class
Dr Pepper/Seven-Up Inc 5301 Legacy Dr	Plano	TX	75024	**800-696-5891**	972-673-7000	79-2
DR Sperry & Co 623 Rathbone Ave	Aurora	IL	60506	**888-997-9297**	630-892-4361	451
Dr Vinyl & Assoc Ltd 1350 SE Hamblen Rd *General	Lees Summit	MO	64081	**800-531-6600***	816-525-6060	61-1
Dr. Denim Inc 1136 Market St	Philadelphia	PA	19107	**888-761-6520**	215-564-2767	155-3
Dr. Sinatra 95 Old Shoals Rd	Arden	NC	28704	**800-304-1708**		524-8
Draeger Medical Inc 3135 Quarry Rd	Telford	PA	18969	**800-437-2437**		250
Dragon Claw USA Inc 16033 Arrow Hwy	Irwindale	CA	91706	**800-238-5296**	626-480-0068	276
Dragon Products Co 960 Ocean Ave	Portland	ME	04103	**800-828-8352**	207-774-6355	134
Draka Comteq Americas 2512 Penny Rd	Claremont	NC	28610	**800-879-9862**	828-459-9821	801
Drake Ctr 151 W Galbraith Rd	Cincinnati	OH	45216	**800-948-0003**	513-418-2500	371-6
Drake Hotel, The 140 E Walton Pl	Chicago	IL	60611	**800-553-7253**	312-787-2200	376
Drake Petroleum Co Inc 221 Quinebaug Rd PO Box 866	North Grosvenordale	CT	06255	**800-243-6366**		572
Drake Software 235 E Palmer St	Franklin	NC	28734	**800-890-9500**		179-1
Drake University 2507 University Ave	Des Moines	IA	50311	**800-443-7253**	515-271-3181	166
Drake University School of Law 2507 University Ave	Des Moines	IA	50311	**800-443-7253**	515-271-2824	167-1
Drake-Scruggs Equipment Inc 2000 S Dirksen Pkwy	Springfield	IL	62703	**877-799-0398**	217-753-3871	465
Drama Book Shop Inc 250 E 40th St Frnt 2	New York	NY	10018	**800-322-0595**	212-944-0595	95
Dramm & Echter Inc 1150 Quail Gardens Dr	Encinitas	CA	92024	**800-854-7021**	760-436-0188	366
Dranetz-BMI 1000 New Durham Rd	Edison	NJ	08818	**800-372-6832**	732-287-3680	248
Draper Knitting Co 28 Draper Ln	Canton	MA	02021	**800-808-7707**	781-828-0029	734-4
Draper Shade & Screen Co 411 S Pearl St	Spiceland	IN	47385	**800-238-7999**	765-987-7999	584
Drapers & Damons Nine Pasteur Ste 200	Irvine	CA	92618	**800-843-1174**		155-6
Draughons Junior College 340 Plus Pk Blvd	Nashville	TN	37217	**877-849-7921**	615-361-7555	788
DRAXIMAGE Inc 16751 Transcanada Hwy	Kirkland	QC	H9H4J4	**888-633-5343**	514-630-7080	238
Drayton Group 2295 N Opdyke Rd Ste D	Auburn Hills	MI	48326	**888-655-4442**		103
DRCoC (Del Rio Chamber of Commerce) 1915 Veterans Blvd *General	Del Rio	TX	78840	**800-889-8149***	830-775-3551	137
Dreamland BBQ 1427 14th Ave S	Birmingham	AL	35205	**800-752-0544**	205-933-2133	662
Dreamline Mfg Inc 1514 S Second St PO Box 1250	Cabot	AR	72023	**800-888-3585**	501-843-3585	466
DreamMaker Bath & Kitchen by Worldwide 510 N Valley Mills Dr Ste 304	Waco	TX	76710	**800-583-2133**		190-11
Dreamworld Backdrops 6450 Lusk Blvd Ste E-106	San Diego	CA	92121	**800-737-9869**		713
Drees Co 211 Grandview Dr	Fort Mitchell	KY	41017	**866-265-2980**	859-578-4200	188
Dreher Island State Recreation Area 3677 State Pk Rd	Prosperity	SC	29127	**866-345-7275**	803-364-4152	558
Dremel Inc 4915 21st St	Racine	WI	53406	**800-437-3635**	262-554-1390	749
Dresser-Rand Co Reciprocating Products Div 100 Chemung St	Painted Post	NY	14870	**877-590-7858**	619-656-4740	173
Dreumex USA 3445 BoaRd Rd	York	PA	17406	**800-233-9382**	717-767-6881	149
Drew Shoe Corp 252 Quarry Rd	Lancaster	OH	43130	**800-837-3739**	740-653-4271	300
Drexel University 3141 Chestnut St *Admissions	Philadelphia	PA	19104	**866-358-1010***	215-895-2000	166
Drexel University Hagerty Library 33rd St & Market St	Philadelphia	PA	19104	**888-278-8825**	215-895-2767	431-6
Dreyfus Family of Funds PO Box 55299	Boston	MA	02205	**800-843-5466**		521
Dreyfus-Cortney & Lowery Bros Rigging 4400 N Galvez St	New Orleans	LA	70117	**800-228-7660**	504-944-3366	760
Dreyfuss Planetarium 49 Washington St	Newark	NJ	07102	**888-370-6765**	973-596-6529	591
DRHC (DiamondRock Hospitality Co) 3 Bethesda Metro Ctr Ste 1500 *NYSE: DRH*	Bethesda	MD	20814	**888-246-5941**	240-744-1150	645
DRI (Defense Research Institute) 55 W Monroe St Ste 20	Chicago	IL	60603	**866-525-6466**	312-795-1101	48-10
Dri Mark Products Inc 999 S Oyster Bay Rd Ste 312	Bethpage	NY	11714	**800-645-9118**	516-484-6200	564
Driehaus Capital Management Inc 25 E Erie St	Chicago	IL	60611	**800-688-8819**	312-587-3800	398
Driftwood Beach State Recreation Site 5580 S Coast Hwy	Newport	OR	97366	**800-551-6949**		558
Driftwood Hotel 435 Willoughby Ave	Juneau	AK	99801	**800-544-2239**	907-586-2280	376
Driftwood on the Oceanfront Oceanfront at 16th Ave N	Myrtle Beach	SC	29578	**855-741-7986**	843-448-1544	376
Driftwood Shores Resort 88416 First Ave	Florence	OR	97439	**800-422-5091**	541-997-8263	376
Drillers Service Inc 1792 Highland Ave NE PO Box 1407	Hickory	NC	28601	**800-334-2308**	828-322-1100	530
Dril-Quip Inc 13550 Hempstead Hwy *NYSE: DRQ*	Houston	TX	77040	**877-316-2631**	713-939-7711	530
Drink More Water Store 7595-A Rickenbacker Dr	Gaithersburg	MD	20879	**800-697-2070**		14
Dripping Springs State Park 16830 Dripping Springs Rd	Okmulgee	OK	74447	**800-622-6317**	918-756-5971	558
Driscoll Children's Hospital 3533 S Alameda St	Corpus Christi	TX	78411	**800-324-5683**	361-694-5000	371-1
Driscoll Strawberry Assoc Inc 345 Westridge Dr	Watsonville	CA	95077	**800-871-3333**		314-1
Driskill Hotel 604 Brazos St	Austin	TX	78701	**800-252-9367**	512-474-5911	376
DRISTEEM Corp 14949 Technology Dr	Eden Prairie	MN	55344	**800-328-4447**	952-949-2415	14
Drive Thru Technology Inc 1755 N Main St	Los Angeles	CA	90031	**800-933-8388**	323-576-1400	174-1
Drive Train Industries Inc 5555 Joliet St	Denver	CO	80239	**800-525-6177**	303-292-5176	60
DriverDO LLC 734 Massachusetts St	Lawrence	KS	66044	**844-366-6837**		224
Drivers License Guide Co 1492 Oddstad Dr	Redwood City	CA	94063	**800-227-8827**	650-369-4849	628-10
DriveTime Corp 4020 E Indian School Rd	Phoenix	AZ	85018	**888-418-1212**		56
Driving Records Facilities PO Box 1086	Glen Burnie	MD	21061	**800-772-5510**		626
DrivingSales LLC 8871 S Sandy Pkwy Ste 250	Sandy	UT	84070	**866-943-8371**		384
DRMP (Dyer Riddle Mills & Precourt Inc) 941 Lk Baldwin Ln	Orlando	FL	32814	**800-375-3767**	407-896-0594	261
Dropbox Inc 1805 N Second St	Ironton	OH	45638	**888-388-7768**		475
Drowsy Water Ranch PO Box 147	Granby	CO	80446	**800-845-2292**	970-725-3456	239
DRS C3 Systems LLC 400 Professional Dr	Gaithersburg	MD	20879	**800-694-5005**	301-921-8100	522
DRS Sustainment Systems Inc 7375 Industrial Rd	Florence	KY	41042	**800-694-5005**	859-372-8204	14
DRS Technologies Inc Five Sylvan Way	Parsippany	NJ	07054	**800-694-5005**	973-898-1500	522
DRS Training & Control Systems 645 Anchors St NW	Fort Walton Beach	FL	32548	**800-694-5005**	850-302-3000	522
Drug Chemical & Associated Technologies Assn (DCAT) One Washington Blvd Ste 7	Robbinsville	NJ	08691	**800-640-3228**	609-448-1000	48-19
Drug Package Inc 901 Drug Package Ln	O'Fallon	MO	63366	**800-325-6137**		619
Drug Topics Magazine 24950 Country Club Blvd Ste 200 *Cust Svc	North Olmsted	OH	44070	**877-922-2022***	440-891-2792	452-5
Drugstore.com Inc 411 108th Ave NE Ste 1400	Bellevue	WA	98004	**800-378-4786**		237
Drum Corps International (DCI) PO Box 3129 *Orders	Indianapolis	IN	46206	**800-495-7469***	317-275-1212	47-4
Drury Hotels Company LLC 721 Emerson Rd Ste 400	Saint Louis	MO	63141	**800-378-7946**	314-429-2255	376
Drury University 900 N Benton Ave	Springfield	MO	65802	**800-922-2274**	417-873-7879	166
Druva Software Inc 150 Mathilda Place, STE 450	Sunnyvale	CA	94086	**888-248-4976**		384
Drycleaning & Laundry Institute 14700 Sweitzer Ln	Laurel	MD	20707	**800-638-2627**	301-622-1900	48-4
Dryden District Chamber of Commerce 284 Government St Hwy 17	Dryden	ON	P8N2P3	**877-934-6922**	807-223-2622	136
Dryhead Schively Ranch 1062 Rd 15	Lovell	WY	82431	**800-628-9081**	307-548-6688	239
Drysdales Inc 3220 S Memorial Dr	Tulsa	OK	74145	**800-444-6481**	918-664-6481	327
Dryvit Systems Inc 1 Energy Way	West Warwick	RI	02893	**800-556-7752**	401-822-4100	386
DS Brown Co 300 E Cherry St	North Baltimore	OH	45872	**800-848-1730**	419-257-3561	192-2
DS Waters of America Inc 5660 New Northside Dr Ste 500 *Cust Svc	Atlanta	GA	30328	**800-201-6218***		793
DS/USA (Disabled Sports USA) 451 Hungerford Dr Ste 100	Rockville	MD	20850	**800-543-2754**	301-217-0960	47-22
DSC (Destination Services of Colorado Inc) PO Box 3660	Avon	CO	81620	**800-372-7686**	970-476-6565	185
DSC Logistics 1750 S Wolf Rd	Des Plaines	IL	60018	**800-372-1960**		444
DSG (Dakota Supply Group) 2601 Third Ave N	Fargo	ND	58102	**800-437-4702**	701-237-9440	246
DSG Tag Systems Inc 5455 152nd St Ste 214	Surrey	BC	V3S5A5	**877-589-8806**		384
DSLextreme.com 21540 Plummer St Ste A	Chatsworth	CA	91311	**866-243-8638**		395
DSM Chemicals North America Inc 1 Columbia Nitrogen Rd	Augusta	GA	30901	**800-526-0189**	706-849-6600	142
DSM Desotech Inc 1122 St Charles St	Elgin	IL	60120	**800-222-7189**	847-697-0400	143
DSM Engineering Plastics Inc 2267 W Mill Rd	Evansville	IN	47720	**800-333-4237**	812-435-7500	598-2
DSM Food Specialties Inc 45 Waterview Blvd	Parsippany	NJ	07054	**800-526-0189**	973-257-1063	295-42
DS&O Electric Cooperative Inc 129 W Main St PO Box 286	Solomon	KS	67480	**800-376-3533**	785-655-2011	245
DSSC (Data Storage Systems Ctr) 5000 Forbes Ave	Pittsburgh	PA	15213	**800-864-8287**	412-268-6600	659
DST Controls 651 Stone Rd	Benicia	CA	94510	**800-251-0773**	707-745-5117	204
DST Output 5220 Robert J Mathews Pkwy	El Dorado Hills	CA	95762	**800-441-7587**	916-939-4960	491
DSX Access Systems Inc 10731 Rockwall Rd	Dallas	TX	75238	**888-419-8353**	214-553-6140	684
DTE Energy Co One Energy Plz *NYSE: DTE*	Detroit	MI	48226	**800-477-4747**	313-235-4000	357-5
DTI (Dental Technologies Inc) 5601 Arnold Rd	Dublin	CA	94568	**800-229-0936**	925-829-3611	412
DTIC (Defense Technical Information Ctr) 8725 John J Kingman Rd Ste 0944	Fort Belvoir	VA	22060	**800-225-3842**	703-767-9100	338-3
Dtreds LLC 1329 Shepard Dr Ste 2	Sterling	VA	20164	**877-694-7766**		224
Dts Cos Inc 1640 Monad Rd	Billings	MT	59101	**877-896-3420**	406-245-4695	770

	Toll-Free	Phone	Class
Du Page Airport Authority			
2700 International Dr Ste 200 .... West Chicago IL 60185	800-208-5690	630-584-2211	27
Dualite Sales & Service Inc			
1 Dualite Ln .... Williamsburg OH 45176	800-543-7271	513-724-7100	692
Duane's			
3649 Mission Inn Ave .... Riverside CA 92501	800-843-7755	951-784-0300	662
Duarte Unified School District			
1620 Huntington Dr .... Duarte CA 91010	888-225-7377	626-599-5000	676
Dublin Convention & Visitors Bureau			
Nine S High St .... Dublin OH 43017	800-245-8387	614-792-7666	207
Dublin Villager			
7801 N Central Dr .... Lewis Center OH 43035	866-790-4502	740-888-6100	525-4
Dublin-Laurens County Chamber of Commerce			
1200 Bellvue .... Dublin GA 31021	800-829-4933	478-272-5546	137
DuBois Business College			
1 Beaver Dr .... Du Bois PA 15801	800-692-6213	814-371-6920	788
Dubois Chemicals			
3630 E Kemper Rd .... Cincinnati OH 45241	800-438-2647		149
Dubose National Energy Services Inc			
PO Box 499 .... Clinton NC 28329	800-590-2150	910-590-2151	487
Dubuque Area Chamber of Commerce			
300 Main St Ste 200 .... Dubuque IA 52001	800-798-4748	563-557-9200	137
Dubuque Symphony Orchestra			
2728 Asbury Rd Ste 900 .... Dubuque IA 52001	866-803-9280	563-557-1677	566-3
Duckback Products			
2644 Hegan Ln PO Box 980 .... Chico CA 95927	800-825-5382		543
Ducks Unlimited Inc			
One Waterfowl Way .... Memphis TN 38120	800-453-8257	901-758-3825	47-3
Ducks Unlimited Magazine			
One Waterfowl Way .... Memphis TN 38120	800-453-8257	901-758-3825	452-20
Ducommun Inc			
23301 Wilmington Ave .... Carson CA 90745 *NYSE: DCO*	800-667-6589	310-513-7280	204
Duct-O-Wire Co			
345 Adams Cir .... Corona CA 92882	800-752-6001	951-735-8220	204
Dude Rancher Lodge			
415 N 29th St .... Billings MT 59101	800-221-3302	406-259-5561	376
Dude Ranchers' Assn			
1122 12th St PO Box 2307 .... Cody WY 82414	866-399-2339	307-587-2339	47-23
Dudnyk			
5 Walnut Grove Dr Ste 280 .... Horsham PA 19044	800-767-3263	215-443-9406	4
Dueck Auto Group			
12100 Featherstone Way .... Richmond BC V6W1K9	877-993-8325	604-273-1311	56
Dueco			
N4 W22610 Bluemound Rd .... Waukesha WI 53186	800-558-4004	262-547-8500	382
Duffens Langley Optical Co			
8140 Marshall Dr .... Lenexa KS 66214	800-397-2020	913-492-5379	535
Duffield Assoc Inc			
5400 Limestone Rd .... Wilmington DE 19808	877-732-9633	302-239-6634	187
Duffy's Collectible Cars			
1195 Boyson Rd .... Hiawatha IA 52233	877-670-3937	319-364-7000	513
Duininck Inc			
408 Sixth St PO Box 208 .... Prinsburg MN 56281 *General	800-328-8949*		189-4
Duke Diet & Fitness Ctr (DFC)			
501 Douglas St .... Durham NC 27705	800-235-3853	919-688-3079	697
Duke Energy Corp			
5400 Westheimer C Mail Drop WP 890 ....Houston TX 77056	800-521-2232	713-627-5400	775
Duke Manufacturing Co			
2305 N Broadway .... Saint Louis MO 63102	800-735-3853	314-231-1130	297
Duke Towers- All Condominium Hotel			
807 W Trinity Ave .... Durham NC 27701	866-385-3869	919-687-4444	376
Duke University Divinity School			
407 Chapel Drive PO Box 90968 .... Durham NC 27708	800-367-3853	919-660-3400	167-3
Duke University Press			
905 W Main St Ste 18-B .... Durham NC 27701 *Cust Svc	888-651-0122*	919-687-3600	628-4
Duke University School of Law			
201 Science Dr PO Box 90362 .... Durham NC 27708	888-529-2586	919-613-7006	167-1
Duke University School of Medicine			
Office of Admissions DUMC 3710 ...... Durham NC 27710	888-275-3853	919-684-2985	167-2
Duke's 8th Avenue Hotel			
630 W Eigth Ave .... Anchorage AK 99501	800-478-4837	907-274-6213	376
Dulles Aviation Inc			
10501 Observation Rd Manassas Regl Airport .... Manassas VA 20110	888-835-9324	703-361-2171	62
Dultmeier Sales LLC			
13808 Industrial Rd .... Omaha NE 68137	888-677-5054	402-333-1444	426
Duluth Area Chamber of Commerce			
5 W First St Ste 101 .... Duluth MN 55802	800-385-8842	218-722-5501	137
Duluth Business University (DBU)			
4724 Mike Colalilo Dr .... Duluth MN 55807	800-777-8406	218-722-4000	788
Duluth Convention & Visitors Bureau			
21 W Superior St Ste 100 .... Duluth MN 55802	800-438-5884	218-722-4011	207
Duluth Entertainment Convention Ctr			
350 Harbor Dr .... Duluth MN 55802	800-628-8385	218-722-5573	206
Duluth International Airport			
4701 Grinden Dr .... Duluth MN 55811	855-787-2227	218-727-2968	27
Duluth News-Tribune			
424 W First St .... Duluth MN 55802 *Circ	800-456-8080*	218-723-5281	525-2
Dumbell Man Fitness Equipment, The			
655 Hawaii Ave .... Torrance CA 90503	800-432-6266	310-381-2900	351
DuMor Inc			
PO Box 142 .... Mifflintown PA 17059	800-598-4018	717-436-2106	318-4
Dumore Corp			
1030 Veterans St .... Mauston WI 53948	888-467-8288	608-847-6420	511
Dunbar Mechanical Inc			
2806 N Reynolds Rd .... Toledo OH 43615	800-719-2201	419-537-1900	190-10
Dunbarton Corp			
PO Box 8577 .... Dothan AL 36304	800-633-7553		234
Duncan & Son Lines Inc			
23860 W US Hwy 85 .... Buckeye AZ 85326	800-528-4283	623-386-4511	770
Duncan Aviation Inc			
3701 Aviation Rd .... Lincoln NE 68524	800-228-4277	402-475-2611	24
Duncan Enterprises			
5673 E Shields Ave .... Fresno CA 93727	800-438-6226	559-291-4444	42
Duncan Industrial Solutions			
3450 S MacArthur Blvd ...... Oklahoma City OK 73179	800-375-9470	405-688-2300	382
Duncan Solutions Inc			
633 W Wisconsin Ave Ste 1600 .... Milwaukee WI 53203	888-993-8622		490
Duncan Supply Company Inc			
910 N Illinois St .... Indianapolis IN 46204	800-382-5528	317-634-1335	605
Duncan Valley Electric Co-op Inc			
PO Box 440 .... Duncan AZ 85534	800-669-2503	928-359-2503	245
Duncan-Parnell Inc			
900 S McDowell St .... Charlotte NC 28204	800-849-7708	704-372-7766	112
Duncanville Public Library			
201 James Collins Blvd .... Duncanville TX 75116	866-332-4558	972-780-5050	431-3
Dunes Manor Hotel			
2800 Baltimore Ave .... Ocean City MD 21842	800-523-2888	410-289-1100	376
Dunhill Hotel			
237 N Tryon St .... Charlotte NC 28202	800-354-4141	704-332-4141	376
Dunkin' Donuts			
130 Royall St .... Canton MA 02021 *Cust Svc	800-859-5339*	781-737-3000	67
Dunkley International Inc			
1910 Lake St .... Kalamazoo MI 49001	800-666-1264	269-343-5583	297
Dunlap Industries Inc			
123 State St .... Dunlap TN 37327	800-251-7214	423-949-4021	587
Dunlap Oil Company Inc			
759 S Haskell Ave .... Willcox AZ 85643	800-854-1646	520-384-2248	323
Dunlop Tires			
PO Box 1109 .... Buffalo NY 14240	800-845-8378		744
Dunmore Corp			
145 Wharton Rd .... Bristol PA 19007	800-444-0242	215-781-8895	593
Dunn Energy Co-op			
PO Box 220 .... Menomonie WI 54751	800-924-0630	715-232-6240	245
Dunn Manufacturing Inc			
1400 Goldmine Rd .... Monroe NC 28110	800-868-7111	704-283-2147	9
Dunn School			
2555 Hwy 154 PO Box 98 .... Los Olivos CA 93441	800-287-9197	805-688-6471	615
Dunn-Edwards Corp			
4885 E 52nd Pl .... Los Angeles CA 90058	800-537-4098	323-771-3330	543
Dunwoody College of Technology			
818 Dunwoody Blvd .... Minneapolis MN 55403	800-292-4625	612-374-5800	788
Duo Fast Northeast			
22 Tolland St .... East Hartford CT 06108	888-399-5712	860-289-6861	347
Duo-Fast Corp			
2400 Galvin Dr .... Elgin IL 60123 *Cust Svc	888-386-3278*	847-783-5500	748
DuPage Convention & Visitors Bureau			
915 Harger Rd Ste 240 .... Oak Brook IL 60523	800-232-0502	630-575-8070	207
Dupli Graphics Corp			
One Dupli Park Dr .... Syracuse NY 13204	800-724-2477		619
Duplication Factory Inc			
4275 Norex Dr .... Chaska MN 55318	800-279-2009	952-227-8106	649
Dupli-Systems Inc			
8260 Dow Cir .... Strongsville OH 44136	800-321-1610	440-234-9415	109
DuPont Advanced Fibers Systems			
5401 Jefferson Davis Hwy .... Richmond VA 23234	800-441-7515	804-383-2000	598-1
DuPont Automotive			
950 Stephenson Hwy PO Box 7013 .... Troy MI 48007	800-533-1313	248-583-8000	543
DuPont Chemical Solutions			
1007 Market St .... Wilmington DE 19898	800-441-7515	302-774-1000	143
DuPont Crop Protection			
PO Box 80705 .... Wilmington DE 19880	888-638-7668	302-774-1000	280
DuPont Engineering Polymers			
Lancaster Pike Rt 141 Barley Mill Plz Bldg 22 .... Wilmington DE 19805	800-441-7515	302-999-4592	598-2
DuPont Packaging & Industrial Polymers			
Barley Mill Plaza 26-2122 PO Box 80026 .... Wilmington DE 19880	800-438-7225	703-305-7666	541
DuPont Performance Coatings			
1007 Market St .... Wilmington DE 19898	800-441-7515	302-774-1000	543
DuPont Qualicon			
Henry Clay Rd Bldg 400 Rt 141 PO Box 80357 .... Wilmington DE 19880	800-863-6842	302-695-5300	231
DuPont Surfaces			
4417 Lancaster Pk CRP 728/3105 .... Wilmington DE 19805	800-448-9835	302-774-1000	592
DuPont Theatre			
1007 N Market St .... Wilmington DE 19801	800-338-0881	302-656-4401	565
DuPont Titanium Technologies			
1007 Market St .... Wilmington DE 19898	800-441-7515	302-774-1000	141
Duquesne Light Co			
411 Seventh Ave .... Pittsburgh PA 15219 *Cust Svc	888-393-7000*	412-393-7000	775
Duquesne Light Holdings Inc			
411 Seventh Ave .... Pittsburgh PA 15219	888-393-7000	412-393-7000	357-5
Duquesne University			
600 Forbes Ave .... Pittsburgh PA 15282	800-456-0590	412-396-6000	166
Duquesne University Gumberg Library			
600 Forbes Ave .... Pittsburgh PA 15282	800-283-3853	412-396-6130	431-6
Duquesne University School of Law			
600 Forbes Ave .... Pittsburgh PA 15282	800-732-8353	412-396-6300	167-1
DuQuoin Tourism Commission			
20 N Chestnut St PO Box 1037 .... Du Quoin IL 62832	800-455-9570	618-542-8338	207
Dura Automotive Systems Inc			
1780 Pond Run .... Auburn Hills MI 48326	800-362-3872	248-299-7500	59
Dura Wax Co			
4101 W Albany St .... McHenry IL 60050	800-435-5705	815-385-5000	149
Durable Products Inc			
PO Box 826 .... Crossville TN 38557	800-373-3502	931-484-3502	667
Duracell			
14 Research Dr .... Bethel CT 06801	800-551-2355	203-791-3014	73
Duraclean International Inc			
220 W Campus Dr .... Arlington Heights IL 60004	800-862-5326	847-704-7100	150
DuraColor			
1840 Oakdale Ave .... Racine WI 53406	877-899-7900		619
Duracote Corp			
350 N Diamond St .... Ravenna OH 44266	800-321-2252	330-296-3487	734-2
Duralee Fabrics Ltd Inc			
1775 Fifth Ave .... Bay Shore NY 11706 *Cust Svc	800-275-3872*	631-273-8800	587
DuraLine Imaging Inc			
110 Commercial Blvd .... Flat Rock NC 28731	866-359-2506	828-692-1301	620
Duran Human Capital Partners Inc			
300 Orchard City Dr Ste 142 .... Campbell CA 95008	800-287-9682	408-540-0070	712
Durand Forms Inc			
6200 Equitable Rd .... Kansas City MO 64120	800-545-6342		688
Durango Area Chamber of Commerce			
111 S Camino del Rio .... Durango CO 81303	888-414-0835	970-247-0312	137
Durango Area Tourism Office			
111 S Camino del Rio .... Durango CO 81301	800-525-8855	970-247-3500	207

Company / Address	City	State	ZIP	Toll-Free	Phone	Class
Durango Arts Ctr 802 E Second Ave	Durango	CO	81301	**800-838-3006**	970-259-2606	49-1
Durango Herald 1275 Main Ave	Durango	CO	81301	**800-530-8318**	970-247-3504	525-2
Durango Mountain Resort One Skier Pl	Durango	CO	81301	**800-982-6103**	970-247-9000	660
Dura-Stress Inc 11325 County Rd 44 *General	Leesburg	FL	34788	**800-342-9239***	352-787-1422	184
DuraTech Industries International Inc PO Box 1940	Jamestown	ND	58401	**800-243-4601**	701-252-4601	273
Durham Academy Inc 3130 Pickett Rd	Durham	NC	27705	**888-904-9149**	919-489-9118	676
Durham Convention & Visitors Bureau 101 E Morgan St	Durham	NC	27701	**800-446-8604**	919-687-0288	207
Durham Cos Inc 6300 Transit Rd	Depew	NY	14043	**800-633-7724**	716-684-3333	712
Durham Manufacturing Co 201 Main St	Durham	CT	06422	**800-243-3774**	860-349-3427	286
Durkan Patterned Carpet Inc 405 Virgil Dr	Dalton	GA	30721	**800-981-2009**		130
Duro Dyne Corp 81 Spence St	Bay Shore	NY	11706	**800-899-3876**	631-249-9000	14
Durocher Auto Sales Inc 4651 Rt 9	Plattsburgh	NY	12901	**877-215-8954**		56
Durr Marketing Assoc Inc PO Box 17600	Pittsburgh	PA	15235	**800-937-3877**		144
Durrset Amigos Ltd 4669 Hwy 90 W	San Antonio	TX	78237	**800-580-3477**	210-798-5360	295-36
Dury's 701 Ewing Ave	Nashville	TN	37203	**800-824-2379**	615-255-3456	118
DUSA Pharmaceuticals Inc 25 Upton Dr *NASDAQ: DUSA*	Wilmington	MA	01887	**877-533-3872**	978-657-7500	84
Dutailier Group Inc 299 Rue Chaput	Sainte-Pie	QC	J0H1W0	**800-363-9817**	450-772-2403	318-2
Dutch Gold Honey Inc 2220 Dutch Gold Dr	Lancaster	PA	17601	**800-846-2753**	717-393-1716	295-24
Dutch Valley Bulk Food Distributors Inc 7615 Lancaster Ave	Myerstown	PA	17067	**800-733-4191**	717-933-4191	296-8
Dutch Wonderland Family Amusement Park 2249 Lincoln Hwy E	Lancaster	PA	17602	**866-386-2839**	717-291-1888	32
Dutchess Beer Distributors Inc 5 Laurel St *Cust Svc	Poughkeepsie	NY	12601	**800-427-6308***	845-452-0940	80-1
Dutchess County Regional Chamber of Commerce 1 Civic Ctr Plaza Ste 400	Poughkeepsie	NY	12601	**800-817-2918**	845-454-1700	137
Dutchmen Mfg Inc 2164 Caragana Ct PO Box 2164	Goshen	IN	46527	**866-425-4369**	574-537-0600	119
Dutt & Wagner of Virginia Inc 1142 W Main St	Abingdon	VA	24210	**800-688-2116**	276-628-2116	296-10
Dutton Family Theatre 3454 W 76 Country Blvd	Branson	MO	65616	**888-388-8661**	417-332-2772	513
Duvinage Corp 60 W Oak Ridge Dr	Hagerstown	MD	21740	**800-541-2645**	301-733-8255	486
DVD Empire 2140 Woodland Rd	Warrendale	PA	15086	**888-383-1880**		785
DVWF (Delaware Valley Wholesale Florist Inc) 520 Mantua Blvd N	Sewell	NJ	08080	**800-676-1212**	856-468-7000	293
Dwight D Eisenhower Presidential Library & Museum 200 SE Fourth St	Abilene	KS	67410	**877-746-4453**	785-263-6700	431-2
Dwight D Eisenhower V A Medical Ctr 4101 South 4th St	Leavenworth	KS	66048	**800-952-8387**	913-682-2000	371-8
Dwyer Products Corp 1226 Michael Dr Ste F	Wood Dale	IL	60191	**800-822-0092**	630-741-7900	35
DXP Enterprises Inc 7272 Pinemont Dr *NASDAQ: DXPE*	Houston	TX	77040	**800-830-3973**	713-996-4700	382
D&Y (Daniel & Yeager) 6767 Old Madison Pk Ste 690	Huntsville	AL	35806	**800-955-1919**		266
Dyad Constructors Inc 8505 Holt St	Houston	TX	77054	**800-803-9202**	713-799-9380	187
Dyatech LLC 805 S Wheatley St Ste 600	Ridgeland	MS	39157	**866-651-4222**	601-914-1004	387
Dycor Technologies Ltd 1851 94 St	Edmonton	AB	T6N1E6	**800-663-9267**	780-486-0091	659
Dyer Riddle Mills & Precourt Inc (DRMP) 941 Lk Baldwin Ln	Orlando	FL	32814	**800-375-3767**	407-896-0594	261
Dylan Hotel 52 E 41st St	New York	NY	10017	**866-553-9526**	212-338-0500	376
Dymax Corp 318 Industrial Ln Ste 2	Torrington	CT	06790	**877-396-2963**	860-482-1010	3
Dynabrade Inc 8989 Sheridan Dr *Cust Svc	Clarence	NY	14031	**800-828-7333***	716-631-0100	749
Dynacast Inc 14045 Ballantyne Corporate Pl	Charlotte	NC	28277	**866-662-2750**	704-927-2790	307
Dynadot LLC PO Box 345 *Cust Svc	San Mateo	CA	94401	**866-652-2039***	650-585-1961	393
Dynalectric Corp 4462 Corporate Ctr Dr	Los Alamitos	CA	90720	**866-890-7794**	714-828-7000	190-4
Dynaloy LLC 6445 Olivia Ln	Indianapolis	IN	46226	**800-669-5709**	317-788-5694	143
Dynamet Inc 195 Museum Rd	Washington	PA	15301	**800-237-9655**	724-228-1000	480
DynaMetric Inc 717 S Myrtle Ave	Monrovia	CA	91016	**800-525-6925**	626-358-2559	725
Dynamex Inc 5429 LBJ Fwy Ste 1000 *Cust Svc	Dallas	TX	75240	**888-478-1660***	214-560-9000	539
Dynamic Computer Corp 23400 Industrial Pk Ct	Farmington Hills	MI	48335	**866-257-2111**	248-473-2200	175
Dynamic Design Solutions Inc 3565 Centre Cir	Fort Mill	SC	29715	**866-337-2010**	803-548-3609	256
Dynamic Homes LLC 525 Roosevelt Ave	Detroit Lakes	MN	56501	**800-492-4833**	218-847-2611	105
Dynamic Instruments Inc 3860 Calle Fortunada	San Diego	CA	92123	**800-793-3358**	858-278-4900	51
Dynamic Network Factory Inc 21353 Cabot Blvd	Hayward	CA	94545	**800-947-4742**	510-265-1122	174-8
Dynamic Recovery Services Inc 4101 McEwen Rd Ste 150	Farmers Branch	TX	75244	**800-886-8088**	972-241-5611	158
Dynamics Edge Inc 2635 N First St Ste #148	San Jose	CA	95134	**800-453-5961**		197
Dynapar 1675 Delany Rd *General	Gurnee	IL	60031	**800-873-8731***		789
Dynaquip Controls 10 Harris Industrial Pk	Saint Clair	MO	63077	**800-545-3636**	636-629-3700	778
Dynarex Corporation 10 Glenshaw St	Orangeburg	NY	10962	**888-335-7500**	845-365-8200	472
Dynaric Inc 5740 Bayside Rd	Virginia Beach	VA	23455	**800-526-0827**		540
Dynasplint Systems Inc 770 Ritchie Hwy Ste W21	Severna Park	MD	21146	**800-638-6771**	410-544-9530	264-4
Dynastar 1413 Crt Dr	Park City	UT	84098	**888-243-6722**	435-252-3300	701
Dynasty Suites 1235 W Colton Ave *General	Redlands	CA	92374	**800-874-8958***	909-793-6648	376
Dynatem Inc 23263 Madero Ste C	Mission Viejo	CA	92691	**800-543-3830**	949-855-3235	617
Dynatronics Corp 7030 Pk Centre Dr *NASDAQ: DYNT*	Salt Lake City	UT	84121	**800-874-6251**	801-568-7000	250
Dynavax Technologies Corp 2929 Seventh St Ste 100 *NASDAQ: DVAX*	Berkeley	CA	94710	**877-848-5100**	510-848-5100	576
Dynegy Inc 601 Travis St Ste 1400 *NYSE: DYN*	Houston	TX	77002	**800-633-4704**	713-507-6400	357-5
Dynetics Engineering Corp 515 Bond St	Lincolnshire	IL	60069	**800-888-8110**	847-541-7300	110
Dynisco LLC 38 Forge Pkwy *General	Franklin	MA	02038	**800-396-4726***	508-541-9400	467
Dyno Nobel Inc 2795 E Cottonwood Pkwy Ste 500	Salt Lake City	UT	84121	**800-473-2675**	801-364-4800	268
Dyonyx LP 1235 N Loop W *General	Houston	TX	77008	**855-749-6758***	713-485-7000	181
Dystonia Medical Research Foundation One E Wacker Dr Ste 2810 *General	Chicago	IL	60601	**800-377-3978***	312-755-0198	47-17
Dywidag Systems International 320 Marmon Dr	Bolingbrook	IL	60440	**800-457-7633**	630-739-1100	190-3

E

Company / Address	City	State	ZIP	Toll-Free	Phone	Class
E & M Bindery Inc 11 Peekay Dr	Clifton	NJ	07014	**800-736-2463**	973-777-9300	618
E & O Mari Inc 256 Broadway	Newburgh	NY	12550	**800-750-3034**	845-562-4400	520
E Dillon & Co 2522 Swords Creek Rd PO Box 160	Swords Creek	VA	24649	**800-234-8970**	276-873-6816	184
E Fougera & Co 60 Baylis Rd	Melville	NY	11747	**800-645-9833**	631-454-6996	577
E Gluck Corp 60-15 Little Neck Pkwy	Little Neck	NY	11362	**800-840-2933**	718-784-0700	151
E Ink Holdings Inc 733 Concord Ave	Cambridge	MA	02138	**866-311-1999**	617-499-6000	225
E J Harrison & Sons PO Box 4009	Ventura	CA	93007	**800-418-7274**	805-647-1414	792
E S Robbins Corp 2802 Avalon Ave	Muscle Shoals	AL	35661	**866-934-6018**	256-248-2400	593
E Sam Jones Distributor Inc 4898 S Atlanta Rd	Smyrna	GA	30080	**800-624-9849**	404-351-3250	246
E Tour & Travel 3626 Quadrangle Blvd Ste 400 *Sales	Orlando	FL	32817	**800-339-5120***	407-515-2400	761
E*Trade Bank 671 N Glebe Rd	Arlington	VA	22203	**800-387-2331**	877-800-1208	69
E*Trade Financial Corp 1271 Ave of the Americas 14th Fl *NASDAQ: ETFC*	New York	NY	10020	**800-387-2331**		681
E*Trade Financial Corp Corporate Services 4500 Bohannon Dr	Menlo Park	CA	94025	**800-786-2575**	650-331-6000	179-1
E/g Electro-graph Inc 2365 Camino Vida Roble	Carlsbad	CA	92011	**800-782-6659**	760-438-9090	687
E/The Environmental Magazine 28 Knight St PO Box 5098	Norwalk	CT	06851	**800-321-6742**	203-854-5559	452-19
E2 Consulting Engineers Inc 450 E 17th Ave Ste 200	Denver	CO	80203	**888-772-9773**	303-232-9800	261
EAA (Experimental Aircraft Assn) 3000 Poberezny Rd	Oshkosh	WI	54902	**800-236-4800**	920-426-4800	47-18
EAA AirVenture Museum 3000 Poberezny Rd	Oshkosh	WI	54902	**888-322-3229**	920-426-4800	513
eAcceleration Corp 1050 NE Hostmark St Ste 100-B *Sales	Poulsbo	WA	98370	**800-803-4588***	360-779-6301	179-7
EADS Group 1126 Eigth Ave	Altoona	PA	16602	**800-626-0904**	814-944-5035	261
EADS North American Defense Test & Services Inc 4 Goodyear *Cust Svc	Irvine	CA	92618	**800-722-2528***	949-859-8999	248
Eagan Convention & Visitors Bureau 1501 Central Pkwy	Eagan	MN	55121	**866-324-2620**	651-675-5546	207
Eagan Insurance Agency Inc 2629 N Cswy Blvd	Metairie	LA	70002	**888-882-9600**	504-836-9600	387
Eagle Affiliates Inc 1000 S Second St	Plainfield	NJ	07063	**800-237-9255**	908-757-4464	600
Eagle Asset Management 880 Carillon Pkwy	Saint Petersburg	FL	33716	**800-237-3101**		398

Alphabetical Section

Listing	Toll-Free	Phone	Class
Eagle Aviation 2861 Aviation Way Columbia Metropolitan Airport .... West Columbia SC 29170	800-849-3245	803-822-5555	62
Eagle Bancorp Inc 7815 Woodmont Ave ... Bethesda MD 20814 NASDAQ: EGBN	800-364-8313	240-497-2044	357-2
Eagle Burgmann Industries LP 10035 Brookriver Dr ... Houston TX 77040 *General	800-303-7735*		325
Eagle Communications Inc 2703 Hall St Ste 15 Ste 15 ... Hays KS 67601	877-613-2453	785-625-5910	634
Eagle Comtronics Inc 7665 Henry Clay Blvd ... Liverpool NY 13088	800-448-7474	315-622-3402	638
Eagle Express Lines Inc 715 W 172nd St PO Box 348 ... South Holland IL 60473	888-868-2501	708-333-8400	770
Eagle Family Foods Inc One Strawberry Ln ... Orrville OH 44667	888-656-3245		295-27
Eagle Group Inc 100 Industrial Blvd ... Clayton DE 19938	800-441-8440	302-653-3000	299
Eagle Magazine 1623 Gateway Cir S ... Grove City OH 43123	800-236-5450	614-883-2200	452-10
Eagle Marketing Inc Perfume Originals Products Div 2412 Sequoia Pk ... Yukon OK 73099	800-233-7424		567
Eagle Mountain Casino 681 S Tule Resv Rd ... Porterville CA 93257	800-903-3353	559-788-6220	132
Eagle Mountain House 179 Carter Notch Rd PO Box 804 ... Jackson NH 03846	800-966-5779	603-383-9111	376
Eagle One Golf Products Inc 1340 N Jefferson St ... Anaheim CA 92807	800-448-4409	714-983-0050	701
Eagle Pack Pet Foods Inc 200 Ames Pond Dr ... Tewksbury MA 01876	800-255-5959	574-259-7834	571
Eagle Parts & Products Inc 1411 Marvin Griffin Rd ... Augusta GA 30906	888-972-9911	706-790-6687	60
Eagle Pass Chamber of Commerce 400 E Garrison St ... Eagle Pass TX 78852	888-355-3224	830-773-3224	137
Eagle Point National Cemetery 2763 Riley Rd ... Eagle Point OR 97524	800-535-1117	541-826-2511	135
Eagle Point Software Corp 4131 Westmark Dr ... Dubuque IA 52002	800-678-6565	563-556-8392	179-10
Eagle Professional Resources Inc 67 Yonge St Ste 200 ... Toronto ON M5E1J8	800-281-2339	416-861-0636	712
Eagle Publishing Co 75 S Church St ... Pittsfield MA 01201	800-245-0254	413-447-7311	628-8
Eagle Radio Inc 2300 Hall ... Hays KS 67601	877-613-2453	785-625-2578	634
Eagle Ridge Inn & Resort 444 Eagle Ridge Dr ... Galena IL 61036	800-892-2269	815-777-2444	660
Eagle Roller Mill Co 1101 Airport Rd ... Shelby NC 28150	800-223-9108	704-487-5061	442
Eagle Transport Corp 300 S Wesleyan Blvd Ste 202 ... Rocky Mount NC 27804	800-776-9937	252-937-2464	770
Eagle-Picher Minerals Inc 9785 Gateway Dr Ste 1000 PO Box 12130 ... Reno NV 89521 *Cust Svc	800-228-3865*	775-824-7600	495
Eagleville Hospital 100 Eagleville Rd ... Eagleville PA 19408 *General	800-255-2019*	610-539-6000	717
Eaglewood Resort & Spa 1401 Nordic Rd ... Itasca IL 60143	877-285-6150	630-773-1400	660
Eakes Office Plus 617 W Third St ... Grand Island NE 68801	800-652-9396	308-382-8026	528
EANGUS (Enlisted Assn of the National Guard of the US) 3133 Mt Vernon Ave ... Alexandria VA 22305	800-234-3264	703-519-3846	47-19
EAP Consultants Inc 3901 Roswell Rd Ste 340 ... Marietta GA 30062	800-869-0276	770-951-9970	457
EAP Systems 500 W Cummings Pk ... Woburn MA 01801	800-535-4841	781-935-8850	457
Earhart Petroleum Inc 1494 Lytle Rd ... Troy OH 45373	800-686-2928	937-335-2928	572
Earl Burns Miller Japanese Garden 1250 Bellflower Blvd ... Long Beach CA 90840	800-985-8880	562-985-8885	96
Earl G Graves Ltd 130 Fifth Ave 10th Fl ... New York NY 10011 *Cust Svc	800-727-7777*	212-242-8000	628-9
Earl Industries LLC 2 Harper Ave ... Portsmouth VA 23707	800-433-7300	757-215-2500	689
Earl L Henderson Trucking Inc 206 W Main St ... Salem IL 62881	800-447-8084	618-548-4667	770
Earl May Seed & Nursery 208 N Elm St ... Shenandoah IA 51603	877-800-5556	712-246-1020	322
Earl's Apparel Inc 908 S Fourth St PO Box 939 ... Crockett TX 75835	800-527-3148	936-544-5521	153-18
Earle M Jorgensen Co 10650 S Alameda St ... Lynwood CA 90262 *Sales	800-336-5365*	323-567-1122	485
Earlham College 801 National Rd W ... Richmond IN 47374	800-327-5426	765-983-1600	166
Earlham School of Religion 228 College Ave ... Richmond IN 47374	800-432-1377	765-983-1423	167-3
Early Bird, The 5312 Sebring Warner Rd ... Greenville OH 45331	866-627-4557	937-548-3330	525-4
Early Childhood Report 360 Hiatt Dr ... Palm Beach Gardens FL 33418	800-621-5463	561-622-6520	524-4
Earnest Machine Products Co 12502 Plz Dr ... Cleveland OH 44130	800-327-6378	216-362-1100	348
Earnest Partners LLC 1180 Peachtree St Ste 2300 ... Atlanta GA 30309	800-322-0068	404-815-8772	398
Earnhardt Auto Centers 7300 W Orchid Ln ... Chandler AZ 85226	888-378-7711	480-926-4000	56
Earth Share 7735 Old Georgetown Rd Ste 900 ... Bethesda MD 20814	800-875-3863	240-333-0300	47-13
Earth Systems Services Inc 895 Aerovista Pl Ste 102 ... San Luis Obispo CA 93401	866-781-0112	805-781-0112	193
Earthbound Farm 1721 San Juan Hwy ... San Juan Bautista CA 95045	800-690-3200	831-623-7880	10-10
EarthLink Inc 1375 Peachtree St NE ... Atlanta GA 30309 NASDAQ: ELNK	866-383-3080	404-815-0770	395
EarthRights International 1612 K St NW Ste 401 ... Washington DC 20006	888-224-9043	202-466-5188	47-13
Earthwatch Institute 114 Western Ave ... Boston MA 02134	800-776-0188	978-461-0081	47-13
EarthWay Products Inc 1009 Maple St ... Bristol IN 46507	800-294-0671	574-848-7491	426
East Balt Inc 1801 W 31st Pl ... Chicago IL 60608	800-621-8555	773-376-4444	67
East Bay Chamber of Commerce 16 Cutler St Ste 102 ... Warren RI 02885	877-797-9790	401-245-0750	137
East Bay Ford Truck Sales Inc 70 Hegenberger Loop ... Oakland CA 94621	888-219-8551	510-272-4400	56
East Bay Tire Co 2200 Huntington Dr Unit C ... Fairfield CA 94533	800-831-8473	707-437-4700	745
East Boston Savings Bank 10 Meridian St ... Boston MA 02128	800-657-3272	617-567-1500	69
East Brunswick Public Library 2 Jean Walling Civic Ctr ... East Brunswick NJ 08816	800-829-1040	732-390-6950	431-3
East Canyon Hotel & Spa 288 E Camino Monte Vista ... Palm Springs CA 92262	877-324-6835	760-320-1928	376
East Central College 1964 Prairie Dell Rd ... Union MO 63084	800-273-8255	636-583-5193	160
East Central Community College PO Box 129 ... Decatur MS 39327	877-462-3222	601-635-2111	160
East Central Energy PO Box 39 ... Braham MN 55006	800-254-7944		245
East Central Oklahoma Electric Co-op Inc 2001 S Wood Dr PO Box 1178 ... Okmulgee OK 74447	800-783-9317	918-756-0833	245
East Central University Linscheid Library 1100 E 14th St ... Ada OK 74820	800-772-1213	580-332-8000	431-6
East Coast Security Services Inc 68 Stiles Rd ... Salem NH 03079	800-639-2086	603-898-6823	684
East End Hospice 481 Westhampton-Riverhead Rd PO Box 1048 ... WestHampton Beach NY 11978	877-513-0099	631-288-8400	368
East Georgia College 131 College Cir ... Swainsboro GA 30401	800-715-4255	478-289-2000	160
East Georgia Regional Medical Ctr (EGRMC) 1499 Fair Rd ... Statesboro GA 30458	844-455-8708	912-486-1000	371-3
East Hampton Star Inc, The 153 Main St PO Box 5002 ... East Hampton NY 11937	800-968-7364	631-324-0002	628-8
East Jefferson General Hospital (EJGH) 4200 Houma Blvd ... Metairie LA 70006	866-280-7737	504-454-4000	371-3
East Lansing Public Library 950 Abbott Rd ... East Lansing MI 48823	866-861-2010	517-351-2420	431-3
East Lion Corp 318 Brea Canyon Rd ... City of Industry CA 91789	877-939-1818	626-912-1818	300
East Maine School District 63 (EMSD) 10150 Dee Rd ... Des Plaines IL 60016	866-752-6850	847-299-1900	676
East Mfg Corp 1871 State Rt 44 PO Box 277 ... Randolph OH 44265	888-405-3278	330-325-9921	769
East Moline Metal Products Co 1201 Seventh St ... East Moline IL 61244 *Sales	800-325-4151*	309-752-1350	483
East Ridge Retirement Village 19301 SW 87th Ave ... Miami FL 33157	800-856-8097		663
East Side Moving & Storage 4836 SE Powell Blvd ... Portland OR 97206	800-547-4600	503-777-4181	512
East Side Plating Inc 8400 SE 26th Pl ... Portland OR 97202	800-394-8554	503-654-3774	476
East St Tammany Chamber of Commerce 118 W Hall Ave ... Slidell LA 70460	800-870-3673	985-643-5678	137
East Stroudsburg University 200 Prospect St ... East Stroudsburg PA 18301 *Admissions	877-230-5547*	570-422-3542	166
East Stroudsburg University Kemp Library 200 Prospect St ... East Stroudsburg PA 18301	877-422-1378	570-422-3465	431-6
East Teak Trading Group Inc 1106 Drake Rd ... Donalds SC 29638	800-338-5636	864-379-2111	347
East Tennessee Public Communications Corp 1611 E Magnolia Ave ... Knoxville TN 37917	844-686-2378	865-595-0220	624
East Tennessee State University PO Box 70731 ... Johnson City TN 37614	800-462-3878	423-439-4213	166
East Texas Baptist University 1209 N Grove St ... Marshall TX 75670	800-804-3828	903-935-7963	166
East Valley Tribune 120 W First Ave ... Mesa AZ 85210	888-887-4286	480-898-6500	525-2
East Valley Water District 3654 E Highland Ave Ste 18 ... Highland CA 92346	866-275-3772	909-889-9501	794
East West Bancorp Inc 1881 W Main St ... Alhambra CA 91801 NASDAQ: EWBC	888-895-5650	626-308-2012	357-2
East West Label Co 1000 E Hector St ... Conshohocken PA 19428	800-441-7333	610-825-0410	410
East-Central Iowa Rural Electric Co-op 2400 Bing Miller Ln ... Urbana IA 52345	877-850-4343	319-443-4343	245
Eastco Multi Media Solutions Inc 3646 California Rd ... Orchard Park NY 14127	800-365-8273	716-662-0536	507
Easter Seals 230 W Monroe St Ste 1800 ... Chicago IL 60606	800-221-6827	312-726-6200	47-17
Eastern Arizona College 615 N Stadium Ave ... Thatcher AZ 85552	800-678-3808	928-428-8472	160
Eastern Baltimore Area Chamber of Commerce 102 W Pennsylvania Ave Ste 101 ... Towson MD 21204	888-224-9740	410-825-6200	137
Eastern Bank One Eastern Pl ... Lynn MA 01901	800-327-8376	781-599-2100	69
Eastern Bank Corp 265 Franklin St ... Boston MA 02110 *Cust Svc	800-327-8376*	617-897-1008	357-2
Eastern Business Forms Inc PO Box 10 ... Mauldin SC 29662	800-387-2648		109
Eastern Carolina Nissan 3315 Hwy 70 E ... New Bern NC 28564	888-944-7822	252-636-1000	56
Eastern Concrete Materials Inc 475 Market St ... Elmwood Park NJ 07407	800-822-7242	201-797-7979	183
Eastern Connecticut State University 83 Windham St ... Willimantic CT 06226 *Admissions	877-353-3278*	860-465-5000	166
Eastern Connecticut State University Smith Library 83 Windham St ... Willimantic CT 06226	800-578-1449	860-465-4506	431-6
Eastern Floral & Gift Shop 818 Butterworth St SW ... Grand Rapids MI 49504	800-494-2202	616-949-2200	292
Eastern Foods Inc 1000 Naturally Fresh Blvd ... Atlanta GA 30349	800-765-1950		295-19
Eastern Gateway Community College 4000 Sunset Blvd ... Steubenville OH 43952	800-682-6553	740-264-5591	788

Company / Address	City	State	ZIP	Toll-Free	Phone	Class
Eastern Idaho Technical College						
1600 S 25th E	Idaho Falls	ID	83404	**800-662-0261**	208-524-3000	788
Eastern Illini Electric Co-op						
330 W Ottawa PO Box 96	Paxton	IL	60957	**800-824-5102**	217-379-2131	245
Eastern Illinois University						
600 Lincoln Ave	Charleston	IL	61920	**800-252-5711***	217-581-2223	166
*Admissions						
Eastern Iowa Light & Power Co-op						
600 E Fifth St PO Box 3003	Wilton	IA	52778	**800-728-1242**	563-732-2211	245
Eastern Kentucky University						
521 Lancaster Ave	Richmond	KY	40475	**800-465-9191**	859-622-2106	166
Eastern Lancaster County School District						
669 E Main St PO Box 609	New Holland	PA	17557	**877-935-5655**	717-354-1500	676
Eastern Lift Truck Company Inc						
549 E Linwood Ave	Maple Shade	NJ	08052	**866-980-7175**	856-779-8880	382
Eastern Maine Community College						
354 Hogan Rd	Bangor	ME	04401	**800-286-9357**	207-974-4600	788
Eastern Maine Electric Co-op Inc						
21 Union St	Calais	ME	04619	**800-696-7444**	207-454-7555	245
Eastern Mennonite University						
1200 Pk Rd	Harrisonburg	VA	22802	**800-368-2665***	540-432-4118	166
*Admissions						
Eastern Metal/USA-SIGN						
1430 Sullivan St	Elmira	NY	14901	**800-872-7446***	607-734-2295	692
*Sales						
Eastern Michigan University						
1000 College Pl	Ypsilanti	MI	48197	**800-468-6368**	734-487-1849	166
Eastern Michigan University Halle Library						
955 W Cir Dr	Ypsilanti	MI	48197	**888-888-3465**	734-487-0020	431-6
Eastern Mountain Sports						
1 Vose Farm Rd	Peterborough	NH	03458	**888-463-6367**	603-924-7231	702
Eastern Nazarene College						
23 E Elm Ave	Quincy	MA	02170	**800-883-6288**	617-745-3000	166
Eastern New Mexico Medical Ctr						
405 W Country Club Rd	Roswell	NM	88201	**800-222-1222**	575-622-8170	371-3
Eastern New Mexico University						
1500 S Ave K Stn 7	Portales	NM	88130	**800-367-3668**	575-562-1011	166
Eastern New Mexico University Roswell						
52 University Blvd PO Box 6000	Roswell	NM	88202	**800-243-6687**		160
Eastern Oregon University						
One University Blvd	La Grande	OR	97850	**800-452-8639**	541-962-3393	166
Eastern Pennsylvania Supply Co						
700 Scott St	Wilkes-Barre	PA	18705	**800-432-8075**	570-823-1181	605
Eastern Shore Natural Gas Co						
1110 Forest Ave Ste 201	Dover	DE	19904	**877-650-1257**	302-734-6720	775
Eastern State Hospital (ESH)						
4601 Ironbound Rd	Williamsburg	VA	23188	**800-994-6610**	757-253-5161	371-5
Eastern University						
1300 Eagle Rd	Wayne	PA	19087	**800-452-0996***	610-341-5800	166
*Admissions						
Eastern Virginia Bankshares Inc						
330 Hospital Rd	Tappahannock	VA	22560	**866-296-3743***	804-443-8400	357-2
NASDAQ: EVBS ■ *General						
Eastern West Virginia Community & Technical College						
316 Eastern Dr	Moorefield	WV	26836	**877-982-2322**	304-434-8000	160
Eastern Wyoming College						
3200 W 'C' St	Torrington	WY	82240	**800-658-3195**	307-532-8200	160
Eastex Telephone Co-op Inc						
PO Box 150	Henderson	TX	75653	**800-232-7839**	903-854-1000	726
Eastfield College						
3737 Motley Dr	Mesquite	TX	75150	**800-260-8000**	972-860-7100	160
Eastland Shoe Mfg Corp						
4 Meeting House Rd	Freeport	ME	04032	**888-988-1998**	207-865-6314	300
Eastman Chemical Co						
200 S Wilcox Dr	Kingsport	TN	37660	**800-327-8626***	423-229-2000	142
NYSE: EMN ■ *Cust Svc						
Eastman Machine Co						
779 Washington St	Buffalo	NY	14203	**800-872-5571**	716-856-2200	733
Eastridge Workforce Solutions						
2375 Northside Dr Ste 360	San Diego	CA	92108	**877-862-2632**	877-337-5422	724
Eastside Union School District						
45006 30th St E	Lancaster	CA	93535	**877-263-7995**	661-952-1200	676
East-West University						
816 S Michigan Ave Ste 800	Chicago	IL	60605	**877-398-9376**	312-939-0111	166
Easy Ice LLC						
925 W Washington St Ste 100	Marquette	MI	49855	**866-327-9423**		779
easyDNS						
219 Dufferin St Ste 304A	Toronto	ON	M6K3J1	**888-677-4741**	416-535-8672	393
EasyLink Services Corp						
6025 The Corners Pwy Ste 100	Norcross	GA	30092	**800-209-6245**	678-823-4600	179-12
Eat'n Park Hospitality Group Inc						
285 E Waterfront Dr						
PO Box 3000	Homestead	PA	15120	**800-947-4033**	412-461-2000	661
EATELCORP Inc						
913 S Burnside Ave	Gonzales	LA	70737	**800-621-4211**	225-621-4300	726
Eaton Farm Confectioners Inc						
30 Burbank Rd	Sutton	MA	01590	**800-343-9300**	508-865-5235	295-8
Eaton Metal Products Co						
4803 York St	Denver	CO	80216	**800-208-2657**	303-296-4800	90
Eaton Office Supply Company Inc						
180 John Glenn Dr	Buffalo	NY	14228	**800-365-3237**	716-691-6100	527
Eaton Steel Corp						
10221 Capital Ave	Oak Park	MI	48237	**800-527-3851**	248-398-3434	487
Eaton Vance Mutual Funds						
Two International Pl	Boston	MA	02110	**800-225-6265**	617-482-8260	521
Eatons' Ranch						
270 Eatons' Ranch Rd	Wolf	WY	82844	**800-210-1049**	307-655-9285	239
EatStreet Inc						
131 W Wilson St Ste 400	Madison	WI	53715	**866-654-8777**		384
Eau Claire Press Co						
701 S Farwell St	Eau Claire	WI	54701	**800-236-8808**	715-833-9200	628-8
EB Bradley Co						
5080 S Alameda St	Los Angeles	CA	90058	**800-533-3030**	323-585-9201	348
EBAA (Eye Bank Assn of America)						
1015 18th St NW Ste 1010	Washington	DC	20036	**888-491-8833**	202-775-4999	48-8
Ebara Technologies Inc						
51 Main Ave	Sacramento	CA	95838	**800-535-5376**	916-920-5451	686
eBay Enterprise Inc						
935 First Ave	King of Prussia	PA	19406	**877-255-2857**	610-491-7000	7
NASDAQ: EBAY						
eBay Inc						
2065 Hamilton Ave	San Jose	CA	95125	**800-322-9266**	408-376-7400	50
NASDAQ: EBAY						
Ebbtide Corp						
2545 Jones Creek Rd	White Bluff	TN	37187	**866-467-4010**	615-797-3193	89
Eberhard Mfg Co						
PO Box 368012	Cleveland	OH	44149	**800-334-6706**	440-238-9720	347
Ebix Inc						
5 Concourse Pkwy Ste 3200	Atlanta	GA	30328	**800-755-2326**	678-281-2020	179-11
NASDAQ: EBIX						
Ebonite International Inc						
PO Box 746	Hopkinsville	KY	42241	**800-326-6483**	270-881-1200	701
EBSCO Creative Concepts						
3500 Blue Lake Dr Ste 150	Birmingham	AL	35243	**800-756-7023**	205-262-2696	9
EBSCO Industries Inc						
5724 Hwy 280	Birmingham	AL	35242	**800-527-5901**	205-991-6600	186
EBSCO Industries Inc Vulcan Information Packaging Div						
PO Box 29	Vincent	AL	35178	**800-633-4526**		85
EBSCO Information Services						
PO Box 1943	Birmingham	AL	35201	**800-758-5995**	205-991-6600	384
EBSCO Publishing Inc						
10 Estes St	Ipswich	MA	01938	**800-653-2726**	978-356-6500	628-10
EBSCO Subscription Services						
110 Olmsted St Ste 100	Birmingham	AL	35242	**800-653-2726**	205-995-1596	94
EBSCO TeleServices						
4150 Belden Village Ave NW						
Ste 401	Canton	OH	44718	**800-456-5105**	330-492-5105	727
E-Builder Inc						
1800 NW 69 Ave Ste 201	Plantation	FL	33313	**800-580-9322**	954-556-6701	38
eBX LLC						
65 Franklin St Ste 201	Boston	MA	02110	**800-958-4813**	617-350-1600	681
Eby Co 4300 H St	Philadelphia	PA	19124	**800-329-3430**	215-537-4700	253
Eby-Brown Co						
280 W Shuman Blvd Ste 280	Naperville	IL	60563	**800-553-8249**	630-778-2800	746
EC Co PO Box 10286	Portland	OR	97296	**800-462-3370**	800-659-3511	190-4
EC Ernst Inc						
132 Log Canoe Cir	Stevensville	MD	21666	**800-683-7770**	301-350-7770	190-4
ECA (Evangelical Church Alliance)						
205 W Broadway St PO Box 9	Bradley	IL	60915	**888-855-6060**	815-937-0720	47-20
ECCB (Erie 2-Chautauqua Cattaraugus Boces)						
8685 Erie Rd	Angola	NY	14006	**800-228-1184**	716-549-4454	676
Ecclesia College						
9653 Nations Dr	Springdale	AR	72762	**800-735-9926**	479-248-7236	159
ECCO 833 W Diamond St	Boise	ID	83705	**800-635-5900**	208-395-8000	691
Ecco Business Systems Inc						
60 W 38th St 4th Fl	New York	NY	10018	**800-558-6777**	212-921-4545	110
Ecessa Corp						
2800 Campus Dr Ste 140	Plymouth	MN	55441	**800-669-6242**	763-694-9949	725
ECFA (Evangelical Council for Financial Accountability)						
440 W Jubal Early Dr Ste 130	Winchester	VA	22601	**800-323-9473**	540-535-0103	47-5
ECG Management Consultants Inc						
1111 Third Ave Ste 2700	Seattle	WA	98101	**800-729-7635**	206-689-2200	195
Echelon Corp						
550 Meridian Ave	San Jose	CA	95126	**888-324-3566**	408-938-5200	177
NASDAQ: ELON						
Echo Design Group						
10 E 40th St 16th Fl	New York	NY	10016	**800-331-3246***	212-686-8771	153-12
*General						
Echo Global Logistics Inc						
600 W Chicago Ave Ste 725	Chicago	IL	60654	**800-354-7993**		195
Echo Inc						
400 Oakwood Rd	Lake Zurich	IL	60047	**800-673-1558**	847-540-8400	426
E-Church Depot						
75 Utley Dr Ste 101	Camp Hill	PA	17011	**800-233-4443**		628-3
ECI (Engine Components Inc)						
9503 Middlex	San Antonio	TX	78217	**800-324-2359**	210-820-8101	21
ECII (Engineered Controls International Inc)						
100 Rego Dr PO Box 247	Elon	NC	27244	**800-650-0061**	336-449-7707	777
eCivis Inc						
418 N Fair Oaks Ave Ste 301	Pasadena	CA	91103	**877-232-4847**		68
Eckel Mfg Company Inc						
8035 N County Rd W	Odessa	TX	79764	**800-654-4779**	432-362-4336	223
Eckerd College						
4200 54th Ave S	Saint Petersburg	FL	33711	**800-456-9009***	727-867-1166	166
*Admissions						
Eckhart & Company Inc						
4011 W 54th St	Indianapolis	IN	46254	**800-443-3791**	317-347-2665	85
Eclectic Products Inc						
1075 Arrowsmith St PO Box 2280	Eugene	OR	97402	**800-693-4667**	541-284-9621	3
Eclectik						
1332 W Lake St	Chicago	IL	60607	**866-308-1231**	312-676-2442	129
Eclipse Inc						
1665 Elmwood Rd	Rockford	IL	61103	**888-826-3473**	815-877-3031	317
Eclipse Marketing Services Inc						
490 Headquarters Plz						
N Tower 10th Fl	Morristown	NJ	07960	**800-837-4648**		196
ECMD Inc						
Two Grandview St	North Wilkesboro	NC	28659	**888-222-3961**	336-667-5976	681
Ecoa Industrial Products						
7700 Nw 74th Ave	Medley	FL	33166	**800-433-3833**		355
Ecodyne Ltd						
4475 Corporate Dr	Burlington	ON	L7L5T9	**888-326-3963**	905-332-1404	383
ECOF (Eye Centers of Florida)						
4101 Evans Ave	Fort Myers	FL	33901	**888-393-2455**	239-939-3456	786
Ecojustice Canada						
131 Water St Ste 214	Vancouver	BC	V6B4M3	**800-926-7744**	604-685-5618	47-13
eCollect LLC						
5000 Euclid Ave Ste 303	Cleveland	OH	44103	**888-569-6001**		390
e-Commerce Law & Strategy						
1617 JFK Blvd Ste 1750	Philadelphia	PA	19103	**877-256-2472**	215-557-2300	524-7
E-Commerce Times (ECT)						
16133 Ventura Blvd Ste 700	Encino	CA	91436	**877-328-5500**	818-461-9700	452-5
Econo Foods						
1600 Stephenson						
PO Box 1107	Iron Mountain	MI	49801	**877-295-4558**	906-774-1911	342
Econoco Corp						
300 Karin Ln	Hicksville	NY	11801	**800-645-7032**	516-935-7700	286
Econ-o-copy Inc						
4437 Trenton St Ste A	Metairie	LA	70006	**877-256-0310**	504-457-0032	528
Econolite Control Products Inc						
3360 E La Palma Av	Anaheim	CA	92806	**800-225-6480**	714-630-3700	691
Economical Insurance Group, The						
111 Westmount Rd S PO Box 2000	Waterloo	ON	N2J4S4	**800-265-2180**	519-570-8200	388-4
Economy Spring & Stamping Co						
29 DePaolo Dr PO Box 651	Southington	CT	06489	**800-237-5225**	860-621-7358	710
eContent Magazine						
143 Old Marlton Pike Ste 3	Medford	NJ	08055	**800-300-9868**	609-654-6266	452-7

				Toll-Free	Phone	Class
eCredit						
777 Yamato Rd Ste 500	Boca Raton	FL	33431	**800-276-2321**	561-226-9000	179-1
ECRI Institute						
5200 Butler Pike	Plymouth Meeting	PA	19462	**866-247-3004**	610-825-6000	47-17
ECRM Inc						
554 Clark Rd	Tewksbury	MA	01876	**800-537-3276**	978-851-0207	110
ECS (Electronic Cash Systems Inc)						
30352 Esperanza Ste 110	Rancho Santa Margarita	CA	92688	**888-327-2860**	949-888-8580	55
ECS (Education Commission of the States)						
700 Broadway Ste 810	Denver	CO	80203	**877-584-8642**	303-299-3600	48-5
ECT (E-Commerce Times)						
16133 Ventura Blvd Ste 700	Encino	CA	91436	**877-328-5500**	818-461-9700	452-5
Ectaco Inc						
31-21 31st St	Long Island City	NY	11106	**800-710-7920**	718-728-6110	174-1
ECU (Educators Credit Union)						
1400 N Newman Rd PO Box 81040	Racine	WI	53406	**800-236-5898**	262-260-9393	219
ECWA (Erie County Water Authority)						
295 Main St Rm 350	Buffalo	NY	14203	**855-748-1076**	716-849-8484	775
ED Etnyre & Co						
1333 S Daysville Rd	Oregon	IL	61061	**800-995-2116**	815-732-2116	191
Ed Fagan Inc						
769 Susquehanna Ave	Franklin Lakes	NJ	07417	**800-335-6827**	201-891-4003	487
Ed Necco & Assoc						
178 Private Dr	South Point	OH	45680	**866-996-3226**	513-771-9600	756
Ed Staub & Sons Petroleum Inc						
1301 Esplanade Ave	Klamath Falls	OR	97601	**800-435-3835**		315
EDC (Education Development Ctr Inc)						
55 Chapel St	Newton	MA	02458	**800-225-4276**	617-969-7100	47-11
Edco & Arrowhead Products Inc						
8700 Excelsior Blvd	Hopkins	MN	55343	**800-333-2580**	952-945-2680	688
Eddie Bauer LLC						
PO Box 7001	Groveport	OH	43125	**800-426-8020***		155-4
*Orders						
Eddington Thread Manufacturing Co						
PO Box 446	Bensalem	PA	19020	**800-220-8901**	215-639-8900	734-9
Eddy Packing Company Inc						
404 Airport Dr	Yoakum	TX	77995	**800-292-2361**	361-293-2361	468
Edelbrock Corp						
2700 California St	Torrance	CA	90503	**800-739-3737**	310-781-2222	59
Eden Foods Inc						
701 Tecumseh Rd	Clinton	MI	49236	**800-248-0320***	517-456-7424	295-36
*Cust Svc						
Eden House						
1015 Fleming St	Key West	FL	33040	**800-533-5397**		376
Eden Roc - A Renaissance Beach Resort & Spa						
4525 Collins Ave	Miami Beach	FL	33140	**855-433-3676**	305-531-0000	660
Eden Theological Seminary						
475 E Lockwood Ave	Saint Louis	MO	63119	**800-969-3627**	314-961-3627	167-3
Eder Flag Mfg Company Inc						
1000 W Rawson Ave	Oak Creek	WI	53154	**800-558-6044**	414-764-3522	287
Edgar Allan Poe Museum						
1914 E Main St	Richmond	VA	23223	**866-229-8580**	804-648-5523	513
Edgar Lomax Co						
6564 Loisdale Ct Ste 310	Springfield	VA	22150	**866-205-0524**	703-719-0026	398
EDGAR Online Inc						
11200 Rockville Pk Ste 310	Rockville	MD	20852	**800-732-0330**	301-287-0300	401
NASDAQ: EDGR						
Edge Electronics Inc						
75 Orville Dr	Bohemia	NY	11716	**800-647-3343**	631-471-3343	174-8
Edge Information Management Inc						
1682 W Hibiscus Blvd	Melbourne	FL	32901	**800-725-3343**	321-722-3343	626
Edge Products						
1080 S Depot Dr	Ogden	UT	84404	**888-360-3343**	801-476-3343	247
Edge Systems LLC						
3S721 W Ave Ste 200	Warrenville	IL	60555	**800-352-3343***	630-810-9669	178
*Tech Supp						
Edge Technologies Inc						
3702 Pender Dr Ste 250	Fairfax	VA	22030	**888-771-3343**	703-691-7900	179-1
Edgecombe Community College						
2009 W Wilson St	Tarboro	NC	27886	**877-823-2378**	252-823-5166	160
Edgecombe-Martin County Electric Membership Corp						
NC Hwy 33 E	Tarboro	NC	27886	**800-445-6486**	252-823-2171	245
Edgemont Pharmaceuticals LLC						
1250 Capital of Texas Hwy S Bldg 3 Ste 400	Austin	TX	78746	**888-594-4332**	512-550-8555	231
Edgen Corp						
18444 Highland Rd	Baton Rouge	LA	70809	**866-334-3648**	225-756-9868	382
Edgenet Inc						
3445 Peachtree Rd NE	Atlanta	GA	30326	**866-865-6602**	615-371-3848	178
Edgewater Beach Hotel						
1901 Gulf Shore Blvd N	Naples	FL	34102	**888-564-1308**		376
Edgewater Hotel						
2411 Alaskan Way Pier 67	Seattle	WA	98121	**800-624-0670**	206-728-7000	376
Edgewater Hotel & Casino						
2020 S Casino Dr	Laughlin	NV	89029	**800-677-4837***	702-298-2453	132
*Resv						
Edgewater Pointe Estates						
23315 Blue Water Cir	Boca Raton	FL	33433	**888-339-2287***	561-391-6305	663
*General						
Edgewater Resort						
200 Edgewater Cir	Hot Springs	AR	71913	**800-234-3687**	501-767-3311	376
Edgewater Resort & Waterpark						
2400 London Rd	Duluth	MN	55812	**800-777-7925**	218-728-3601	376
Edgewood College						
1000 Edgewood College Dr	Madison	WI	53711	**800-444-4861**	608-663-2294	166
Edible Arrangements LLC						
95 Barnes Rd	Wallingford	CT	06492	**877-363-7848***	304-894-8901	309
*Cust Svc						
Edinboro University of Pennsylvania						
200 E Normal St	Edinboro	PA	16444	**888-846-2676**	814-732-2761	166
Edinboro University of Pennsylvania Baron-Forness Library (EUB)						
200 Tartan Rd	Edinboro	PA	16444	**888-845-2890**	814-732-2273	431-6
Edinburg Chamber of Commerce						
602 W University Dr	Edinburg	TX	78540	**800-800-7214**	956-383-4974	137
Edinburg Regional Medical Ctr (ERMC)						
1102 W Trenton Rd	Edinburg	TX	78539	**800-465-5585**	956-388-6000	371-3
e-Discovery Law & Strategy						
1617 JFK Blvd Ste 1750	Philadelphia	PA	19103	**877-256-2472**	215-557-2300	524-7
Edison Biotechnology Institute						
Ohio University Konneker Research Laboratories The Ridges	Athens	OH	45701	**800-444-2420**	740-593-4713	659
Edison Chouest Offshore						
16201 E Main St	Galliano	LA	70354	**866-925-5161**	985-601-4444	460
Charlotte						
26300 Airport Rd	Punta Gorda	FL	33950	**800-749-2322**	941-637-5629	160
Collier County						
7007 Lely Cultural Pkwy	Naples	FL	34113	**800-749-2322**	239-732-3701	160
Edison College						
Lee County						
8099 College Pkwy SW	Fort Myers	FL	33919	**800-749-2322**	239-489-9054	160
Edison Community College						
1973 Edison Dr	Piqua	OH	45356	**800-922-3722**	937-778-8600	160
Edison Electric Institute (EEI)						
701 Pennsylvania Ave NW	Washington	DC	20004	**800-649-1202**	202-508-5000	47-12
Edison International						
2244 Walnut Grove Ave	Rosemead	CA	91770	**800-655-4555***	626-302-1212	357-5
NYSE: EIX ■ *Cust Svc						
Edison Properties LLC						
100 Washington St	Newark	NJ	07102	**888-727-5327**	973-643-0895	555
eDist 97 McKee Dr	Mahwah	NJ	07430	**800-800-6624**	201-512-1400	683
Edisto Beach State Park						
8377 State Cabin Rd	Edisto Island	SC	29438	**800-315-3087**	843-869-2756	558
Edisto Electric Co-op Inc						
896 Calhoun St	Bamberg	SC	29003	**800-433-3292**	803-245-5141	245
Edith J Carrier Arboretum & Botanical Gardens at James Madison University						
780 University Blvd MSC 3705	Harrisonburg	VA	22807	**888-568-2586**	540-568-3194	96
Editor & Publisher Magazine						
17782 Cowan Ste C	Irvine	CA	92614	**855-896-7433**	949-660-6150	452-5
Editorial Freelancers Assn (EFA)						
71 W 23rd St 4th Fl	New York	NY	10010	**866-929-5400**	212-929-5400	48-16
Edlund Company Inc						
159 Industrial Pkwy	Burlington	VT	05401	**800-772-2126**	802-862-9661	297
EDMC (Education Management Corp)						
210 Sixth Ave 33rd Fl	Pittsburgh	PA	15222	**800-275-2440**	412-562-0900	242
NASDAQ: EDMC						
Edmo Distributors Inc						
12830 E Mirabeau Pkwy	Spokane Valley	WA	99216	**800-235-3300**	509-535-8280	760
Edmonds Community College						
20000 68th Ave W	Lynnwood	WA	98036	**866-886-4854**	425-640-1500	160
Edmonds Harbor Inn & Suites						
130 W Dayton	Edmonds	WA	98020	**800-441-8033**	425-771-5021	376
Edmonton International Airport						
8340 Sparrow Crescent	Edmonton	AB	T9E8B7	**800-854-9517**	780-980-0986	27
Edmonton Journal						
10006 - 101 St	Edmonton	AB	T5J2S6	**800-232-9486**	780-429-5100	525-1
Edmonton Oilers						
11230 110th St	Edmonton	AB	T5G3H7	**866-414-4625**	780-414-4000	707
Edmonton Sun						
4990 92nd Ave Ste 250	Edmonton	AB	T6B3A1	**877-468-2401**	780-468-0100	525-1
Edmonton Symphony Orchestra						
9720 102nd Ave	Edmonton	AB	T5J4B2	**800-563-5081**	780-428-1108	566-3
Edmund Optics Inc						
101 E Gloucester Pk	Barrington	NJ	08007	**800-363-1992**	856-547-3488	537
Edmunds Gages						
45 Spring Ln	Farmington	CT	06032	**800-878-1622**	860-677-2813	488
EDN Magazine						
303 Second St	San Francisco	CA	94107	**800-446-6551***	415-947-6000	452-21
*Orders						
Edo Japan International Inc						
32 St SE Ste 4838	Calgary	AB	T2B2S6	**888-336-9888**	403-215-8800	661
Edon Farmers Co-op Assn Inc						
205 S Michigan PO Box 308	Edon	OH	43518	**800-878-4093**	419-272-2121	276
Edro Corp						
37 Commerce St	East Berlin	CT	06023	**800-628-6434***	860-828-0311	424
*Sales						
EDS (IEEE Electron Devices Society)						
IEEE Operations Ctr 445 Hoes Ln	Piscataway	NJ	08854	**800-678-4333**	732-981-0060	48-19
Edstrom Industries Inc						
819 Bakke Ave	Waterford	WI	53185	**800-558-5913**	262-534-5181	417
Education Commission of the States (ECS)						
700 Broadway Ste 810	Denver	CO	80203	**877-584-8642**	303-299-3600	48-5
Education Ctr Inc						
3515 W Market St Ste 200	Greensboro	NC	27403	**800-714-7991**	336-854-0309	243
Education Development Ctr Inc (EDC)						
55 Chapel St	Newton	MA	02458	**800-225-4276**	617-969-7100	47-11
Education Grants Alert						
360 Hiatt Dr	Palm Beach Gardens	FL	33418	**800-621-5463**	561-622-6520	524-4
Education Management Corp (EDMC)						
210 Sixth Ave 33rd Fl	Pittsburgh	PA	15222	**800-275-2440**	412-562-0900	242
NASDAQ: EDMC						
Education Management Solutions Inc						
436 Creamery Way Ste 300	Exton	PA	19341	**877-367-5050**	610-701-7002	179-7
Education Resource Information Ctr (ERIC)						
c/o CSC 655 15th St NW Ste 500	Washington	DC	20005	**800-538-3742**		198
Education Week Magazine						
6935 Arlington Rd	Bethesda	MD	20814	**800-346-1834**	301-280-3100	452-8
Educational Development Corp						
10302 E 55th Pl	Tulsa	OK	74146	**800-475-4522**	918-622-4522	94
NASDAQ: EDUC						
Educational Employees Credit Union						
PO Box 5242	Fresno	CA	93755	**800-538-3328**	559-437-7700	219
Educational Housing Services Inc						
55 Clark St	Brooklyn	NY	11201	**800-385-1689**	212-977-7622	48-5
Educational Insights Inc						
380 N Fairway Dr	Vernon Hills	IL	60061	**800-995-4436**		243
Educational Leadership Magazine						
1703 N Beauregard St	Alexandria	VA	22311	**800-933-2723**	703-578-9600	452-8
Educational Media Foundation						
5700 W Oaks Blvd	Rocklin	CA	95765	**800-525-5683***	916-251-1600	634
*General						
Educational Research Newsletter						
PO Box 2347	South Portland	ME	04116	**800-321-7471**	207-632-1954	524-4
Educational Technology Inc						
300 Bedford Ave Ste 202	Bellmore	NY	11710	**800-942-2136***	516-221-8440	51
*Cust Svc						
Educational Tours						
1123 Sterling Rd	Inverness	FL	34450	**800-343-9003**		750
Educational Travel Consultants (ETC)						
PO Box 1580	Hendersonville	NC	28793	**800-247-7969**	828-693-0412	750
Educators Credit Union (ECU)						
1400 N Newman Rd PO Box 81040	Racine	WI	53406	**800-236-5898**	262-260-9393	219
Educators Publishing Service Inc (EPS)						
625 Mt Auburn St Third Fl PO Box 9031	Cambridge	MA	02139	**800-225-5750**		628-2

				Toll-Free	Phone	Class
Educators Resource Inc						
2575 Schillingers Rd	Semmes	AL	36575	**800-868-2368***		243
*Cust Svc						
Edufii Inc						
2078 Parker St Ste 200	San Luis Obispo	CA	93401	**800-439-8505**		384
EdVenture Children's Museum						
211 Gervais St	Columbia	SC	29201	**800-915-4522**	803-779-3100	514
EdVest PO Box 55244	Boston	MA	02205	**888-338-3789**		716
Edward A Sherman Publishing Co						
101 Malbone Rd	Newport	RI	02840	**800-320-2378**	401-849-3300	628-8
Edward C Levy Co						
9300 Dix Ave	Dearborn	MI	48120	**877-938-0007**	313-843-7200	498-5
Edward Don & Co						
2500 S Harlem Ave	North Riverside	IL	60546	**800-777-4366***		299
*Cust Svc						
Edward J Darby & Son Inc						
2200 N Eigth St						
PO Box 50049	Philadelphia	PA	19133	**800-875-6374**	215-236-2203	679
Edwards Instrument Co						
530 S Hwy H	Elkhorn	WI	53121	**800-562-6838**	262-723-4221	520
Edwards Jet Ctr						
1691 Aviation Pl	Billings	MT	59105	**866-353-8245**	406-252-0508	62
Edwards Lifesciences Corp						
One Edwards Way	Irvine	CA	92614	**800-424-3278**	949-250-2500	576
NYSE: EW						
Edwards Manufacturing Co						
1107 Sykes St PO Box 166	Albert Lea	MN	56007	**800-373-8206**	507-373-8206	451
Edwards-Freeman Inc						
441 E Hector St	Conshohocken	PA	19428	**877-448-6887**		295-32
Edwin Gaynor Corp						
200 Charles St	Stratford	CT	06615	**800-342-9667**	203-378-5545	802
Edwin L Heim Co						
1918 Greenwood St	Harrisburg	PA	17104	**800-692-7316**	717-233-8711	190-4
Edwin Shaw Rehab						
1621 Flickinger Rd	Akron	OH	44312	**800-221-4601**	330-784-1271	371-6
EE Schenck Co						
6000 N Cutter Cir	Portland	OR	97217	**800-433-0722**	503-284-4124	587
EE Times Magazine						
600 Community Dr	Manhasset	NY	11030	**800-645-6278**	408-930-7372	452-21
EECO Switch						
880 Columbia St	Brea	CA	92821	**800-854-3808**	714-835-6000	802
EEI (Edison Electric Institute)						
701 Pennsylvania Ave NW	Washington	DC	20004	**800-649-1202**	202-508-5000	47-12
EEI (Environmental Enterprises Inc)						
10163 Cincinnati Dayton Rd	Cincinnati	OH	45241	**800-722-2818**	513-772-2818	658
EEOC (Equal Employment Opportunity Commission)						
1801 L St NW	Washington	DC	20507	**800-669-4000**	202-663-4191	338-18
EF Tours						
One Education St	Cambridge	MA	02141	**800-872-8439**	877-205-9909	750
EFA (Editorial Freelancers Assn)						
71 W 23rd St 4th Fl	New York	NY	10010	**866-929-5400**	212-929-5400	48-16
EFC (Evangelical Fellowship of Canada)						
600 Alden Rd Ste 300 Markham						
Industrial Pk	Markham	ON	L3R0E7	**866-302-3362**	905-479-5885	47-20
EFCO Corp						
1000 County Rd	Monett	MO	65708	**800-221-4169**	417-235-3193	234
Effanbee Doll Co						
459 Hurley Ave	Hurley	NY	12443	**888-362-3655**	845-339-8246	752
Effective Solar Products LLC						
601 Crescent Ave	Lockport	LA	70374	**888-824-0090**	985-532-0800	603
Efficas Inc						
7007 Winchester Cir Ste 120	Boulder	CO	80301	**866-446-0388**	303-381-2070	571
Effingham Convention & Visitors Bureau						
201 E Jefferson Ave	Effingham	IL	62401	**800-772-0750**	217-342-5305	207
Effingham County Chamber of Commerce						
520 W Third St PO Box 1078	Springfield	GA	31329	**800-241-3333**	912-754-3301	137
Effingham Equity Inc						
201 W Roadway Ave	Effingham	IL	62401	**800-223-1337**	217-342-4101	275
EFJohnson Technologies						
1440 Corporate Dr	Irving	TX	75038	**800-328-3911**	972-819-0700	638
EFP Corp						
223 Middleton Run Rd	Elkhart	IN	46516	**800-205-8537**	574-295-4690	597
EG Fisher Public Library						
1289 Ingleside Ave	Athens	TN	37303	**800-552-6843**	423-745-7782	431-3
eGain Communications Corp						
345 E Middlefield Rd	Mountain View	CA	94043	**888-603-4246**	650-230-7500	38
NASDAQ: EGAN						
Egan Bernard & Co						
1900 Old Dixie Hwy	Fort Pierce	FL	34946	**800-327-6676**		314-2
Egenera Inc						
80 Central St	Boxborough	MA	01719	**866-301-3117**	978-206-6300	177
Egg Harbor Yachts Inc						
801 Philadelphia Ave						
PO Box 702	Egg Harbor City	NJ	08215	**800-960-6764**	609-965-2300	89
Eglin Federal Credit Union						
838 Eglin Pkwy NE	Fort Walton Beach	FL	32547	**800-367-6159**	850-862-0111	219
Egon Zehnder International Inc						
1 N Wacker Dr Ste 2300	Chicago	IL	60606	**800-367-3989**	312-260-8800	266
EGRMC (East Georgia Regional Medical Ctr)						
1499 Fair Rd	Statesboro	GA	30458	**844-455-8708**	912-486-1000	371-3
EGS Electrical Group LLC						
9377 W Higgins Rd	Rosemont	IL	60018	**800-621-1506**	847-268-6000	803
EGS Electrical Group LLC EasyHeat Div						
9377 W Higgins Rd	Rosemont	IL	60018	**800-621-1506**	847-268-6000	14
eGumBall Inc						
8687 Research Dr Ste 200	Irvine	CA	92618	**800-890-8940**		196
EGW.com Inc						
4075 Papazian Way	Fremont	CA	94538	**800-546-4754***	510-668-0268	628-9
*Cust Svc						
Egyptian Electric Co-op Assn						
PO Box 38	Steeleville	IL	62288	**800-606-1505**	618-965-3434	245
Egyptian Stationers Inc						
129 W Main St	Belleville	IL	62220	**800-642-3949***	618-234-2323	528
*Cust Svc						
EH Wachs Co						
600 Knightsbridge Pkwy	Lincolnshire	IL	60069	**800-323-8185**	847-537-8800	450
Ehlers & Assoc Inc						
3060 Centre Pointe Dr	Roseville	MN	55113	**800-552-1171**	651-697-8500	195
Ehob Inc						
250 N Belmont Ave	Indianapolis	IN	46222	**800-899-5553**	317-972-4600	472
Ehrhardt Tool & Machine Co						
25 Central Industrial Dr	Granite City	IL	62040	**877-386-7856**	314-436-6900	747
EI Electronics LLC						
1800 Shames Dr	Westbury	NY	11590	**877-346-3837**	516-334-0870	36
EIA (Environmental Information Assn)						
6935 Wisconsin Ave Ste 306	Chevy Chase	MD	20815	**888-343-4342**	301-961-4999	47-13
Eide Industries Inc						
16215 Piuma Ave	Cerritos	CA	90703	**800-422-6827**	562-402-8335	723
Eielson Air Force Base						
354 Broadway St Unit 2B	Eielson AFB	AK	99702	**800-538-6647**	907-377-1110	492-1
Eikos Inc						
2 Master Dr	Franklin	MA	02038	**888-345-6712**	508-528-0300	659
Eisai Inc						
100 Tice Blvd	Woodcliff Lake	NJ	07677	**866-613-4724**	201-692-1100	576
Eizo Nanao Technologies Inc						
5710 Warland Dr	Cypress	CA	90630	**800-800-5202**	562-431-5011	174-4
EJ Bartells Co						
700 Powell Ave SW PO Box 4160	Renton	WA	98057	**800-468-9528**	425-228-4111	192-4
EJ Group Inc						
301 Spring St	East Jordan	MI	49727	**800-874-4100**	231-536-2261	306
EJ Thomas Performing Arts Hall						
198 Hill St University of Akron	Akron	OH	44325	**800-745-3000**	330-972-7570	565
EJGH (East Jefferson General Hospital)						
4200 Houma Blvd	Metairie	LA	70006	**866-280-7737**	504-454-4000	371-3
E&K Companies						
343 Carol Ln	Elmhurst	IL	60126	**800-365-5760**	630-530-9001	190-9
Ekahau Inc						
1851 Alexander Bell Dr Ste 300	Reston	VA	20191	**866-435-2428**		384
Ektron Inc						
542 Amherst St (Rt 101A)	Nashua	NH	03063	**866-435-8766**	603-594-0249	6
El Al Israel Airlines Ltd						
15 E 26th St Sixth Fl	New York	NY	10010	**800-223-6700**	212-852-0600	25
El Camino Store, The						
420 Athena Dr	Athens	GA	30601	**888-685-5987**	706-546-9217	56
El Centro Public Library						
539 State St	El Centro	CA	92243	**877-482-5656**	760-337-4565	431-3
El Conquistador Resort & Golden Door Spa						
1000 El Conquistador Ave	Fajardo	PR	00738	**888-543-1282***	787-863-1000	660
*Resv						
El Cortez Hotel & Casino						
600 E Fremont St	Las Vegas	NV	89101	**800-634-6703**	702-385-5200	132
El Dorado County Chamber of Commerce						
542 Main St	Placerville	CA	95667	**800-457-6279**	530-621-5885	137
El Dorado Furniture Corp						
4200 NW 167th St	Miami	FL	33054	**888-451-7800**	305-624-2400	320
El Dorado Nature Ctr						
7550 E Spring St	Long Beach	CA	90815	**800-662-8887**	562-570-1745	49-4
El Dorado Savings Bank						
4040 El Dorado Rd	Placerville	CA	95667	**800-874-9779**	530-622-1492	69
El Dorado Trading Group Inc						
760 San Antonio Rd	Palo Alto	CA	94303	**800-227-8292**		111
El Encanto Inc						
2001 Fourth St SW						
PO Box 293	Albuquerque	NM	87103	**800-888-7336**	505-243-2722	295-36
El Fenix Corp						
11075 Harry Hines Blvd	Dallas	TX	75229	**877-591-1918**	972-241-2171	661
EL Harvey & Sons Inc						
68 Hopkinton Rd	Westborough	MA	01581	**800-321-3002**	508-836-3000	792
El Mar Plastics Inc						
109 W 134th St	Los Angeles	CA	90061	**800-255-5210**	310-436-6444	596
El Nuevo Herald						
3511 NW 91st Ave	Doral	FL	33172	**800-437-2535**	305-376-3535	525-2
El Paso Community College						
Valle Verde						
919 Hunter Dr	El Paso	TX	79915	**800-531-8292**	915-831-2000	160
El Paso Convention & Performing Arts Ctr						
One Civic Ctr Plz	El Paso	TX	79901	**800-351-6024**	915-534-0600	206
El Paso Convention & Visitors Bureau						
One Civic Ctr Plz	El Paso	TX	79901	**800-351-6024**	915-534-0600	207
El Paso Electric Co						
100 N Stanton Stanton Tower	El Paso	TX	79901	**800-351-1621**	915-543-5711	775
NYSE: EE						
El Paso First Health Plans Inc						
1145 Westmoreland Dr	El Paso	TX	79925	**877-532-3778**	915-532-3778	47-17
El Pollo Loco						
3535 Harbor Blvd Ste 100	Costa Mesa	CA	92626	**877-375-4968**	714-599-5000	661
El Ran Furniture Ltd						
2751 Transcanada Hwy	Pointe-Claire	QC	H9R1B4	**800-361-6546**	514-630-5656	318-2
El Rey Inn						
1862 Cerillos Rd	Santa Fe	NM	87505	**800-521-1349**	505-982-1931	376
El Tovar Hotel						
1 Main Street	Grand Canyon	AZ	86023	**888-297-2757**	928-638-2631	376
Elaine P Nunez Community College						
3710 Paris Rd	Chalmette	LA	70043	**866-825-1954**	504-278-7497	160
Elam Construction Inc						
556 Struthers Ave	Grand Junction	CO	81501	**800-675-4598**	970-242-5370	189-4
Elan Financial Services						
225 W Sta Sq Dr Ste 620	Pittsburgh	PA	15219	**877-935-2637**		398
Elan Hotel						
8435 Beverly Blvd	Los Angeles	CA	90048	**866-203-2212**	323-658-6663	376
Elance Inc						
441 Logue Ave Ste 150	Mountain View	CA	94043	**877-435-2623**	650-316-7500	179-7
Elanco Animal Health						
2500 Innovation Way	Greenfield	IN	46140	**877-352-6261**	317-276-2000	575
Elant Inc						
46 Harriman Dr	Goshen	NY	10924	**800-501-3936**		387
Elantas PDG Inc						
5200 N Second St	Saint Louis	MO	63147	**800-325-7492**	314-621-5700	143
Elat Chayyim						
116 Johnson Rd	Falls Village	CT	06031	**800-398-2630**		664
Elavon						
Two Concourse Pkwy Ste 300	Atlanta	GA	30328	**800-725-1243**	678-731-5000	179-4
eLawMarketing						
25 Robert Pitt Dr Ste 209G	Monsey	NY	10952	**866-833-6245**		316
Elbeco Inc						
4418 Pottsville Pk	Reading	PA	19605	**800-468-4654**	610-921-0651	153-18
ELCA (Evangelical Lutheran Church in America)						
8765 W Higgins Rd	Chicago	IL	60631	**800-638-3522**	773-380-2700	47-20
Elco Corp						
1000 Belt Line St	Cleveland	OH	44109	**800-321-0467**	216-749-2605	534
ELCO Mutual Life & Annuity						
916 Sherwood Dr	Lake Bluff	IL	60044	**888-872-7954**	847-295-6000	388-2
Elder Wood Preserving Co Inc						
334 Elder Wood Rd	Mansura	LA	71350	**800-467-8018**	318-964-2196	805
Eldercare Locator						
1730 Rhode Island Ave NW						
Ste 1200	Washington	DC	20036	**800-677-1116**		198

	Toll-Free	Phone	Class
Elderhostel Inc			
11 Ave de Lafayette ....Boston MA 02111	800-454-5768		47-23
Elderly Instruments			
1100 N Washington Ave ....Lansing MI 48906	888-473-5810	517-372-7890	519
ElderWood Senior Care			
Seven Limestone Dr ....Williamsville NY 14221	888-826-9663	716-633-3900	446
Eldorado Canyon State Park			
9 Kneale Rd PO Box B ....Eldorado Springs CO 80025	866-265-6447	303-494-3943	558
Eldorado Gold Corp			
550 Burrard St Ste 1188 ....Vanouver BC V6C2B5	888-353-8166	604-687-4018	497
NYSE: ELD			
Eldorado Hotel			
309 W San Francisco St ....Santa Fe NM 87501	800-955-4455	505-988-4455	376
Eldorado Hotel Casino			
345 N Virginia St ....Reno NV 89501	800-879-8879*	775-786-5700	376
*Resv			
Eldorado National Inc			
9670 Galena St ....Riverside CA 92509	800-338-3211	909-591-9557	58
Eldorado Resort Casino Shreveport			
451 Clyde Fant Pkwy ....Shreveport LA 71101	877-602-0711	318-220-0711	132
Eldridge Hotel			
701 Massachusetts St ....Lawrence KS 66044	800-527-0909	785-749-5011	376
Eldridge Products Inc			
2700 Garden Rd Bldg A ....Monterey CA 93940	800-321-3569	831-648-7777	202
Eleanor Roosevelt National Historic Site			
4097 Albany Post Rd ....Hyde Park NY 12538	800-337-8474	845-229-9115	557
Eleanor Slater Hospital			
14 Harrington Rd ....Cranston RI 02920	800-438-8477	401-462-2339	371-7
Election Systems & Software Inc			
11208 John Galt Blvd ....Omaha NE 68137	877-377-8683*	402-593-0101	789
*General			
Elections USA Inc			
1927 E Saw Mill Rd ....Quakertown PA 18951	800-789-8683	215-538-0779	789
Electralloy Corp			
175 Main St ....Oil City PA 16301	800-458-7273	814-678-4100	714
Electrex Inc			
PO Box 948 ....Hutchinson KS 67504	800-319-3676		253
Electric City Trolley Station & Museum			
300 Cliff St ....Scranton PA 18503	800-732-0999	570-963-6590	513
Electric Heater Co			
45 Seymour St ....Stratford CT 06615	800-647-3165	203-378-2659	35
Electric Mail Company Inc			
3999 Henning Dr Ste 300 ....Burnaby BC V5C6P9	800-419-7463	604-482-1111	38
Electric Materials Co			
50 S Washington St ....North East PA 16428	800-356-2211	814-725-9621	307
Electric Regulator Corp			
6189 El Camino Real ....Carlsbad CA 92009	800-458-6566	760-438-7873	204
Electric Research & Mfg Co-op Inc			
PO Box 1228 ....Dyersburg TN 38025	800-238-5587	731-285-9121	757
Electric Supply & Equipment Co			
1812 E Wendover Ave ....Greensboro NC 27405	800-632-0268	336-272-4123	246
Electric Supply Inc			
4407 N Manhattan Ave ....Tampa FL 33614	800-678-1894	813-872-1894	246
Electric Utility Week			
Two Penn Plz 25th Fl ....New York NY 10121	800-752-8878	212-904-3070	524-5
Electrical Distributing Inc			
4600 NW St Helens Rd ....Portland OR 97210	800-877-4229	503-226-4044	37
Electri-Cord Mfg Co Inc			
312 E Main St ....Westfield PA 16950	888-278-8253	814-367-2265	802
Electri-Flex Co			
222 Central Ave ....Roselle IL 60172	800-323-6174	630-529-2920	803
Electro Brand Inc			
1127 S Mannheim Rd Ste 305 ....Westchester IL 60154	800-982-3954	708-338-4400	246
Electro Enterprises Inc			
3601 N I-35 Service Rd ....Oklahoma City OK 73111	800-324-6591	405-427-6591	56
Electro Rent Corp			
6060 Sepulveda Blvd ....Van Nuys CA 91411	800-688-1111*	818-787-2100	264-1
NASDAQ: ELRC ■ *Sales			
Electro Scientific Industries Inc			
13900 NW Science Pk Dr ....Portland OR 97229	800-331-4708*	503-641-4141	422
NASDAQ: ESIO ■ *Cust Svc			
Electro Standards Laboratories Inc			
36 Western Industrial Dr ....Cranston RI 02921	877-943-1164	401-943-1164	725
Electro Static Technology			
31 Winterbrook Rd ....Mechanic Falls ME 04256	866-738-1857	207-998-5140	630
Electro Steam Generator Corp			
50 Indel Ave PO Box 438 ....Rancocas NJ 08073	866-617-0764	609-288-9071	262
Electrocube Inc			
3366 Pomona Blvd ....Pomona CA 91768	800-515-1112	909-595-4037	253
Electro-Flex Heat Inc			
Five Northwood Rd ....Bloomfield CT 06002	800-585-4213	860-242-6287	354
Electrolux Appliances			
PO Box 212237 ....Augusta GA 30907	877-435-3287		35
Electrolux Home Care Products Inc			
PO Box 3900 ....Peoria IL 61612	800-282-2886*		776
*Cust Svc			
Electro-Matic Products Inc			
23409 Industrial Pk Ct. ....Farmington Hills MI 48335	888-879-1088	248-478-1182	246
Electro-Motive Diesel Inc			
9301 W 55th St ....La Grange IL 60525	800-255-5355	708-387-6000	641
Electron Energy Corp			
924 Links Ave ....Landisville PA 17538	800-824-2735	717-898-2294	453
Electronic Cash Systems Inc (ECS)			
30352 Esperanza Ste 110 ....Rancho Santa Margarita CA 92688	888-327-2860	949-888-8580	55
Electronic Commerce & Law Report			
1801 S Bell St ....Arlington VA 22202	800-372-1033		524-1
Electronic Component News			
100 Enterprise Dr Ste 600. ....Rockaway NJ 07866	877-650-5160	973-920-7000	452-21
Electronic Contracting Co			
PO Box 29195 ....Lincoln NE 68529	800-366-5320	402-466-8274	190-4
Electronic Environments Corp			
410 Forest St ....Marlborough MA 01752	800-342-5332	508-229-1400	175
Electronic Security Assn Inc (ESA)			
2300 Vly View Ln Ste 230. ....Irving TX 75062	888-447-1689	214-260-5970	48-3
Electronic Tele-Communications Inc			
1915 MacArthur Rd ....Waukesha WI 53188	888-746-4382	262-542-5600	725
OTC: ETCIA			
Electronic Theatre Controls Inc			
3031 Pleasantview Rd ....Middleton WI 53562	800-688-4116	608-831-4116	204
Electronic Warfare Assoc Inc (EWA Inc)			
13873 Pk Ctr Rd Ste 500 ....Herndon VA 20171	888-392-0002*	703-904-5700	181
*General			
Electronics for Imaging Inc			
303 Velocity Way ....Foster City CA 94404	888-334-8650	650-357-3500	177
NASDAQ: EFII			
Electronics Representatives Assn (ERA)			
300 W Adams St Ste 617 ....Chicago IL 60606	800-776-7377	312-527-3050	48-18
Electronics Technicians Assn International (ETA)			
Five Depot St ....Greencastle IN 46135	800-288-3824	765-653-8262	48-19
Electro-Sensors Inc			
6111 Blue Cir Dr ....Minnetonka MN 55343	800-328-6170	952-930-0100	490
NASDAQ: ELSE			
Electroswitch			
2010 Yonkers Rd ....Raleigh NC 27604	888-768-2797	919-833-0707	802
ElectroTech Inc			
7101 Madison Ave W ....Minneapolis MN 55427	800-544-4288	763-544-4288	246
Electrovaya Inc			
2645 Royal Windsor Dr ....Mississauga ON L5J1K9	800-388-2865	905-855-4610	174-1
TSE: EFL			
Elegant Voyages			
1802 Keesling Ct ....San Jose CA 95125	800-555-3534	408-239-0300	761
Elektrisola Inc			
126 High St ....Boscawen NH 03303	800-325-2022	603-796-2114	800
Elementis Specialties Inc			
469 Old Trenton Rd ....East Windsor NJ 08512	800-866-6800		141
Elenbaas Co			
411 W Front St ....Sumas WA 98295	800-808-6954	360-988-5811	442
Eleni's 75 Ninth Ave ....New York NY 10011	888-435-3647		67
Elevating Boats LLC			
201 Dean Ct ....Houma LA 70363	800-843-2895	985-868-9655	689
Elevator Equipment Corp			
4035 Goodwin Ave ....Los Angeles CA 90039	888-577-3326	323-245-0147	256
ELF Fastening Systems Inc			
29019 Solon Rd ....Solon OH 44139	800-248-2376	440-248-8655	278
Elgin Area Chamber of Commerce			
31 S Grove Ave ....Elgin IL 60120	800-621-3362	847-741-5660	137
Elgin Area Convention & Visitors Bureau			
77 S Riverside Dr Ste 1. ....Elgin IL 60120	800-217-5362	847-695-7540	207
Elgin Community College			
1700 Spartan Dr ....Elgin IL 60123	855-850-2525	847-697-1000	160
Elgin Molded Plastics			
909 Grace St ....Elgin IL 60120	800-548-5483	847-931-2455	597
ELI (Environmental Law Institute)			
2000 L St NW Ste 620 ....Washington DC 20036	800-433-5120	202-939-3800	48-10
Eli Lilly & Co			
Lilly Corporate Ctr ....Indianapolis IN 46285	800-545-5979*	317-276-2000	576
NYSE: LLY ■ *Prod Info			
Eli Lilly & Co Foundation			
Lilly Corporate Ctr ....Indianapolis IN 46285	800-545-5979	317-276-2000	303
Eli Lilly Canada Inc			
3650 Danforth Ave ....Toronto ON M1N2E8	888-545-5972	416-694-3221	576
Eli Lilly Federal Credit Union			
225 SE St Ste 300. ....Indianapolis IN 46202	800-621-2105	317-276-2105	70
Eli's Cheesecake Co			
6701 W Forest Preserve Dr ....Chicago IL 60634	800-999-8300	773-736-3417	295-2
Eliason Corp			
9229 Shaver Rd ....Portage MI 49024	800-828-3655*	269-327-7003	655
*Cust Svc			
Elim Park Baptist Home Inc			
140 Cook Hill Rd ....Cheshire CT 06410	800-994-1776	203-272-7550	445
Elim Park Place			
140 Cook Hill Rd ....Cheshire CT 06410	800-994-1776	203-272-3547	663
Eliot Hotel, The			
370 Commonwealth Ave ....Boston MA 02215	800-443-5468	617-267-1607	376
Elisa Act Biotechnologies			
109 Carpenter Dr ....Sterling VA 20165	800-553-5472		412
Elisabet Ney Museum			
304 E 44th St ....Austin TX 78751	800-680-7289	512-458-2255	513
Elite Business Services			
PO Box 9630 ....Rancho Santa Fe CA 92067	800-204-3548		755
Elite Coach			
1685 W Main St ....Ephrata PA 17522	800-722-6206	717-733-7710	106
Elite Limousine Service Inc			
1059 12th Ave Ste E ....Honolulu HI 96816	800-776-2098	808-735-2431	437
Elite Sportswear LP			
2136 N 13th St ....Reading PA 19604	800-345-4087*	610-921-1469	153-1
*Cust Svc			
Elixir Industries Inc			
24800 Chrisanta Dr Ste 210 ....Mission Viejo CA 92691	800-421-1942	949-860-5000	234
Elizabeth Arden Inc			
2400 NE 145th Ave 2nd Fl ....Miramar FL 33027	800-326-7337	954-364-6900	567
NASDAQ: RDEN			
Elizabeth Arden Red Door Spa at Mystic Marriott Hotel & Spa			
625 N Rd ....Groton CT 06340	866-449-7390	860-446-2500	698
Elizabeth City State University			
1704 Weeksville Rd ....Elizabeth City NC 27909	800-347-3278*	252-335-3400	166
*Admissions			
Elizabeth Glaser Pediatric AIDS Foundation			
1140 Connecticut Ave NW Ste 200 ....Washington DC 20036	888-499-4673	202-296-9165	47-17
Elizabeth Hospice			
150 W Crest St ....Escondido CA 92025	800-797-2050	760-737-2050	368
Elizabethtown Community & Technical College			
600 College St Rd ....Elizabethtown KY 42701	877-246-2322	270-769-2371	160
Elizabethtown Gas Co			
One Elizabethtown Plz ....Union NJ 07083	800-242-5830	908-289-5000	775
Eljer Inc			
1 Centennial Ave ....Piscataway NJ 08855	800-442-1902		604
Elk Grove Village Public Library			
1001 Wellington Ave ....Elk Grove Village IL 60007	800-252-8980	847-439-0447	431-3
ELK Lighting			
12 Willow Ln ....Nesquehoning PA 18240	800-613-3261		435
Elk Lighting Inc			
12 Willow Lane ....Nesquehoning PA 18240	866-283-1953		435
Elk Mountain Ranch			
PO Box 910 ....Buena Vista CO 81211	800-432-8812		239
ELK Products Inc			
3266 Us 70 W ....Connelly Springs NC 28612	800-797-9355	828-397-4200	683
Elk River Systems Inc			
777 E Main Ste 108 ....Bozeman MT 59715	888-771-0809	406-632-4763	175
Elkhart County Convention & Visitors Bureau			
219 Caravan Dr ....Elkhart IN 46514	800-250-4827	574-262-8161	207
Elkhart Products Corp			
1255 Oak St ....Elkhart IN 46514	800-284-4851	574-264-3181	588

				Toll-Free	Phone	Class
Elkhorn Rural Public Power District						
206 N Fourth St	Battle Creek	NE	68715	**800-675-2185**	402-675-2185	245
Elkins Constructors Inc						
701 W Adams St	Jacksonville	FL	32204	**800-772-1213**	904-353-6500	189-10
Elko Convention & Visitors Authority						
700 Moren Way	Elko	NV	89801	**800-248-3556**	775-738-4091	206
Elks Magazine						
425 W Diversey Pkwy	Chicago	IL	60614	**800-273-8255**	773-755-4700	452-10
Elle Magazine						
1633 Broadway 44th Fl	New York	NY	10019	**800-876-8775**	212-903-5000	452-11
Ellenton Premium Outlets						
5461 Factory Shops Blvd	Ellenton	FL	34222	**888-267-2121**	941-723-1150	455
Ellie Fashion Group Inc						
1447 Second St Third Fl	Santa Monica	CA	90401	**888-926-9615**		681
Elliot Hospital						
1 Elliot Way Ste 100	Manchester	NH	03103	**800-922-4999**	603-627-1669	371-3
Elliott & Frantz Inc						
450 E Church Rd	King Of Prussia	PA	19406	**800-220-3025**	610-279-5200	355
Elliott Aviation Inc						
6601 74th Ave PO Box 100	Milan	IL	61264	**800-447-6711**	309-799-3183	24
Elliott Bay Book Co						
101 S Main St	Seattle	WA	98104	**800-962-5311**	206-624-6600	95
Elliott Company of Indianapolis Inc						
9200 Zionsville Rd	Indianapolis	IN	46268	**800-545-1213***	317-291-1213	594
*Orders						
Elliott Davis Decosimo LLC						
2 Union Sq						
Tallan Bldg Ste 1100	Chattanooga	TN	37402	**800-782-8382**	423-756-7100	2
Elliott Davis LLC						
200 E Broad St PO Box 6286	Greenville	SC	29606	**800-503-4721**	864-242-3370	2
Elliott Electric Supply Co						
2526 N Stallings Dr						
PO Box 630610	Nacogdoches	TX	75963	**877-777-0242**	936-569-1184	246
Elliott Group						
901 N Fourth St	Jeannette	PA	15644	**800-635-2208**	724-527-2811	173
Elliott Wave International (EWI)						
PO Box 1618	Gainesville	GA	30503	**800-336-1618***	770-536-0309	628-9
*Cust Svc						
Elliott Wave Theorist						
200 Main St	Gainesville	GA	30501	**800-336-1618**	770-536-0309	524-9
Ellis Coffee Co						
2835 Bridge St	Philadelphia	PA	19137	**800-822-3984**	215-537-9500	296-11
Ellis Corp						
1400 W Bryn Mawr Ave	Itasca	IL	60143	**800-611-6806**	630-250-9222	424
Ellmaker State Wayside						
198 NE 123rd St	Newport	OR	97365	**800-551-6949**		558
Ellsworth Area Chamber of Commerce						
163 High St	Ellsworth	ME	04605	**855-635-6278**	207-667-5584	137
Ellsworth Community College						
1100 College Ave	Iowa Falls	IA	50126	**800-322-9235**	641-648-4611	160
Ellsworth Corp						
PO Box 1002	Germantown	WI	53022	**877-454-9224**	262-253-8600	144
Ellucian						
4375 Fair Lakes Ct	Fairfax	VA	22033	**800-223-7036**	610-647-5930	179-10
Ellwood City Forge						
800 Commercial Ave	Ellwood City	PA	16117	**800-843-0166**	724-752-0055	478
Elm Chevrolet Co Inc						
301 E Church St	Elmira	NY	14901	**877-265-6708**	607-734-4141	56
ELM Resources						
12950 Race Track Rd Ste 201	Tampa	FL	33626	**866-524-8198**		384
Elmar Worldwide Inc						
200 Gould Ave PO Box 245	Depew	NY	14043	**800-443-5468***	716-681-5650	540
*Cust Svc						
Elmer's Products Inc						
One Easton Oval	Columbus	OH	43219	**888-435-6377**		3
Elmet Technologies Inc						
1560 Lisbon St	Lewiston	ME	04240	**800-343-8008**	207-333-6100	480
Elmhurst College						
190 Prospect Ave	Elmhurst	IL	60126	**800-697-1871**	630-617-3400	166
Elmira College 1 Pk Pl	Elmira	NY	14901	**800-935-6472***	607-735-1724	166
*Admissions						
Elmira Psychiatric Ctr						
100 Washington St	Elmira	NY	14901	**800-597-8481**	607-737-4711	371-5
Elmira Savings Bank						
333 E Water St	Elmira	NY	14901	**888-372-9299**	607-734-3374	69
NASDAQ: ESBK						
ELMS College						
291 Springfield St	Chicopee	MA	01013	**800-255-3567***	413-592-3189	166
*Admissions						
Elo TouchSystems Inc						
301 Constitution Dr	Menlo Park	CA	94025	**800-557-1458**	650-361-4700	174-2
eLocal Listing LLC						
28765 Single Oak Dr Ste 250	Temecula	CA	92590	**800-285-0484**		5
Elon University						
314 E Haggard Ave	Elon	NC	27244	**800-334-8448**	336-278-2000	166
ELS Language Centers						
7 Roszel Rd	Princeton	NJ	08540	**800-468-8978**	609-759-5500	420
Elsevier Science Ltd						
360 Pk Ave S	New York	NY	10010	**888-437-4636**	212-989-5800	628-9
Elster American Meter Co						
2221 Industrial Rd	Nebraska City	NE	68410	**800-461-4076**	402-873-8200	490
Elvis Presley Enterprises Inc						
3734 Elvis Presley Blvd	Memphis	TN	38116	**800-238-2000**	901-332-3322	357-3
Elvis Presley's Heartbreak Hotel						
3677 Elvis Presley Blvd	Memphis	TN	38116	**877-777-0606**	901-332-1000	376
Elward Construction Co						
680 Harlan St	Lakewood	CO	80214	**800-933-5339**	303-239-6303	190-1
Elwood Corp High Performance Motors Group						
2701 N Green Bay Rd	Racine	WI	53404	**800-558-9489**	262-637-6591	511
Elyria Mfg Corp						
145 Northrup St PO Box 479	Elyria	OH	44035	**866-365-4171**	440-365-4171	614
Elzinga & Volkers						
86 E Sixth St	Holland	MI	49423	**800-632-7734***	616-392-2383	676
*General						
EMA (Envelope Manufacturers Assn)						
500 Montgomery St Ste 550	Alexandria	VA	22314	**800-354-5892**	703-739-2200	48-4
eMag Solutions LLC						
3495 Piedmont Rd						
11 Piedmont Ctr Ste 500	Atlanta	GA	30305	**800-364-9838**	404-995-6060	179-12
Email Co, The						
15 Kainona Ave	Toronto	ON	M3H3H4	**877-933-6245**		363
E-Markets Inc						
807 Mountain Ave Ste 200	Berthoud	CO	80513	**877-674-7419**		38

				Toll-Free	Phone	Class
Embassy Hotel & Suites						
25 Cartier St	Ottawa	ON	K2P1J2	**800-661-5495**	613-237-2111	376
Embassy West Hotel						
1400 Carling Ave	Ottawa	ON	K1Z7L8	**800-267-8696**	613-729-4331	376
EmblemHealth Co						
55 Water St	New York	NY	10041	**800-447-8255**	646-447-5000	388-3
EmbroidMe Inc						
2121 Vista Pkwy	West Palm Beach	FL	33411	**877-877-0234**	561-640-7367	309
Embryotech Laboratories Inc						
140 Hale St	Haverhill	MA	01830	**800-673-7500**	978-373-7300	732
Embry-Riddle Aeronautical University						
Daytona Beach						
600 S Clyde Morris Blvd	Daytona Beach	FL	32114	**800-862-2416**	386-226-6000	166
Embry-Riddle Aeronautical University Prescott						
3700 Willow Creek Rd	Prescott	AZ	86301	**800-888-3728**	928-777-3728	166
EMC (Grady Electric Membership Corp)						
1499 US Hwy 84 W PO Box 270	Cairo	GA	39828	**800-942-4362**	229-377-4182	245
EMC (IEEE Electromagnetic Compatibility Society)						
IEEE Operations Ctr						
445 Hoes Ln	Piscataway	NJ	08854	**800-678-4333**	732-981-0060	48-19
EMC (Equipment Manufacturing Corp)						
14930 Marquardt Ave	Santa Fe Springs	CA	90670	**888-833-9000**	562-623-9394	383
EMC Corp						
2831 Mission College Blvd	Santa Clara	CA	95054	**877-534-2867***	408-566-2000	179-12
*Tech Supp						
EMC Insurance Group Inc						
717 Mulberry St	Des Moines	IA	50309	**800-447-2295**	515-280-2511	357-4
NASDAQ: EMCI						
EMCO (Engineering Measurements Co)						
1150 Northpoint Blvd Ste C	Blythewood	SC	29016	**800-575-0394**		490
EMCOR Group Inc						
301 Merritt 7 Sixth Fl	Norwalk	CT	06851	**866-890-7794**	203-849-7800	190-4
NYSE: EME						
EMC-Paradigm Publishing Co						
875 Montreal Way	Saint Paul	MN	55102	**800-328-1452**	651-290-2800	628-2
EMD Serono Inc						
1 Technology Pl	Rockland	MA	02370	**800-283-8088**	781-982-9000	84
Emeco						
805 W Elm Ave PO Box 179	Hanover	PA	17331	**800-366-5951**	717-637-5951	318-1
eMedicine.com Inc						
8420 W Dodge Rd Ste 402	Omaha	NE	68114	**866-241-9601**	402-341-3222	353
Emerald City Graphics						
23328 66th Ave S	Kent	WA	98032	**877-631-5178***	253-520-2600	619
*General						
Emerald Downs						
2300 Emerald Downs Dr PO Box 617	Auburn	WA	98001	**888-931-8400**	253-288-7000	132
Emerald Kalama Chemical LLC						
1296 Third St NW	Kalama	WA	98625	**877-300-9545**	360-673-2550	295-15
Emerald Queen Casino (EQC)						
2024 E 29th St	Tacoma	WA	98404	**888-831-7655**	253-594-7777	132
Emerald Queen Hotel & Casino						
5700 Pacific Hwy E	Fife	WA	98424	**888-820-3555**	253-922-2000	376
Emerge Financial Wellness Inc						
530 Church St Ste 301	Nashville	TN	37219	**800-791-1725**		260
Emergency Nurses Assn (ENA)						
915 Lee St	Des Plaines	IL	60016	**800-900-9659**	847-460-4000	48-8
Emeritus Corp						
3131 Elliott Ave Ste 500	Seattle	WA	98121	**855-444-7658**	206-298-2909	446
NYSE: ESC						
Emerson Climate Technologies - Retail Solutions						
1065 Big Shanty Rd NW Ste 100	Kennesaw	GA	30144	**800-829-2724**	770-425-2724	203
Emerson College						
10 Boylston Pl	Boston	MA	02116	**888-627-7115**	617-824-8500	166
Emerson Network Power Connectivity Solutions						
1050 Dearborn Dr	Columbus	OH	43085	**800-275-3500**	614-888-0246	253
Emerson Process Management CSI						
835 Innovation Dr	Knoxville	TN	37932	**800-675-4726**	865-675-2110	467
Emerson Resort & Spa						
5340 Rt 28	Mount Tremper	NY	12457	**877-688-2828**	845-688-7900	376
Emerson-Swan Inc						
300 Pond St	Randolph	MA	02368	**800-346-9219**	781-986-2000	605
Emery Winslow Scale Co						
73 Cogwheel Ln	Seymour	CT	06483	**800-891-3952**	203-881-9333	675
Emily Morgan Hotel						
705 E Houston St	San Antonio	TX	78205	**800-824-6674**	210-225-5100	376
EMILY's List						
1800 M St NW Ste 375N	Washington	DC	20036	**800-683-6459**	202-326-1400	47-7
Eminence Speaker LLC						
838 Mulberry Pike PO Box 360	Eminence	KY	40019	**800-897-8373**	502-845-5622	51
Emkay Inc						
805 W Thorndale Ave	Itasca	IL	60143	**800-621-2001**	630-250-7400	289
EMKF (Ewing Marion Kauffman Foundation)						
4801 Rockhill Rd	Kansas City	MO	64110	**800-385-1607**	816-932-1000	304
EMM (Episcopal Migration Ministries)						
815 Second Ave	New York	NY	10017	**800-334-7626**	212-716-6258	47-5
Emmanuel College						
181 Spring St	Franklin Springs	GA	30639	**800-860-8800**	706-245-7226	166
Emmaus Bible College						
2570 Asbury Rd	Dubuque	IA	52001	**800-397-2425**	563-588-8000	159
Emme E2MS LLC						
PO Box 2251	Bristol	CT	06011	**800-396-0523**		404
Emory & Henry College						
PO Box 10	Emory	VA	24327	**800-848-5493***	276-944-4121	166
*Admissions						
Emory Conference Ctr Hotel						
1615 Clifton Rd	Atlanta	GA	30329	**800-933-6679**	404-712-6000	374
Emory University						
201 Dowman Dr	Atlanta	GA	30322	**800-727-6036***	404-727-6036	166
*Admissions						
Emory University Oxford College						
201 Dowman Dr PO Box 1418	Atlanta	GA	30322	**800-723-8328**	404-727-6069	160
Emoteq Corp						
10002 E 43rd St S	Tulsa	OK	74146	**800-221-7572***	918-627-1845	511
*Sales						
Empire Bank						
PO Box 3397	Springfield	MO	65808	**888-231-4637**	417-881-3100	69
Empire Bldg Materials Inc						
PO Box 220	Bozeman	MT	59771	**800-332-4577**	800-548-8201	192-2
Empire Cleaning Supply						
12821 S Figueroa St	Los Angeles	CA	90061	**888-868-7336**	310-527-0132	149
Empire Comfort Systems Inc						
918 Freeburg Ave	Belleville	IL	62222	**800-851-3153**	618-233-7420	354
Empire Diamond Corp						
350 Fifth Ave Ste 4000	New York	NY	10118	**800-728-3425**	212-564-4777	408

Company / Address	City	State	ZIP	Toll-Free	Phone	Class
Empire District Electric Co, The						
602 Joplin St PO Box 127	Joplin	MO	64802	**800-206-2300**	417-625-5100	775
NYSE: EDE						
Empire Electric Assn Inc						
801 N Broadway	Cortez	CO	81321	**800-709-3726**	970-565-4444	245
Empire Industries Inc						
180 Olcott St	Manchester	CT	06040	**800-243-4844**	860-647-1431	588
Empire Landmark Hotel & Conference Centre						
1400 Robson St	Vancouver	BC	V6G1B9	**800-830-6144**	604-687-0511	376
Empire Level Manufacturing Corp						
929 Empire Dr PO Box 800	Mukwonago	WI	53149	**800-558-0722**		748
Empire Livestock Marketing LLC						
5001 Brittonfield Pkwy	East Syracuse	NY	13057	**800-462-8802**	315-433-9129	441
Empire Office Inc						
105 Madison Ave Ste 15	New York	NY	10016	**877-533-6747**	212-607-5500	319
Empire Safety & Supply Inc						
10624 Industrial Ave	Roseville	CA	95678	**800-995-1341**	916-781-3003	670
Empire Southwest Co						
1725 S Country Club Dr	Mesa	AZ	85210	**800-367-4731**	480-633-4000	355
Empire State Bldg						
350 Fifth Ave Ste 100	New York	NY	10118	**877-692-8439**	212-736-3100	49-3
Empire State Plaza Art Collection						
Empire State Plz Curatorial & Services						
41st Fl Corning Twr	Albany	NY	12242	**877-659-4377**	518-474-3899	513
Empire Telephone Corp						
34 Main St PO Box 349	Prattsburgh	NY	14873	**800-338-3300**	607-522-3712	726
Empire Vision Centers						
2921 Erie Blvd E	Syracuse	NY	13224	**877-959-4160**	315-446-5120	536
Empire West Inc						
9270 Graton Rd PO Box 511	Graton	CA	95444	**800-521-4261**	707-823-1190	595
Empire Wire & Supply						
2119 Austin Ave	Rochester Hills	MI	48309	**800-826-1265**		433
EmplawyerNet						
2331 Westwood Blvd	Los Angeles	CA	90064	**800-270-2688**		260
Employee Benefit News						
1325 G St NW Ste 900	Washington	DC	20005	**800-221-1809**	202-504-1122	452-5
Employee Management Services						
435 Elm St	Cincinnati	OH	45202	**888-651-1536**	513-651-3244	623
Employer Flexible						
7850 N Sam Houston Parkway W						
Ste 100	Houston	TX	77064	**866-501-4942**		724
Employers Insurance Company of Nevada						
9790 Gateway Dr Ste 100	Reno	NV	89521	**888-682-6671**		387
Employers Resource Management Co						
1301 S Vista Ave Ste 200	Boise	ID	83705	**800-574-4668**	208-376-3000	563
Employment & Training Administration Regional Offices						
Region III - Atlanta						
Federal Ctr						
61 Forsyth St SW Rm 6M12	Atlanta	GA	20210	**877-872-5627**		338-13
Employment Discrimination Report						
1801 S Bell St	Arlington	VA	22202	**800-372-1033**		524-7
Employment Screening Services Inc						
627 E Sprague St Ste 100	Spokane	WA	99202	**800-473-7778**	509-624-3851	626
Employment Standards Administration						
200 Constitution Ave NW						
Rm S2321	Washington	DC	20210	**866-487-2365**	202-693-0200	338-13
EmploymentGuide.com						
150 Granby St	Norfolk	VA	23510	**877-876-4039**		260
Emporia Area Chamber of Commerce						
719 Commercial St	Emporia	KS	66801	**800-279-3730**	620-342-1600	137
Emporia State University						
1200 Commercial St CB 4023	Emporia	KS	66801	**877-468-6378**	620-341-1200	166
Empress Hotel						
7766 Fay Ave	La Jolla	CA	92037	**888-369-9900**	858-454-3001	376
Empress Software Inc						
11785 Beltsville Dr	Beltsville	MD	20705	**866-626-8888**	301-220-1919	179-2
Emprise Financial Corp						
257 N Broadway St PO Box 2970	Wichita	KS	67202	**800-201-7118***	316-383-4301	68
*Cust Svc						
EMS (IEEE Engineering Management Society)						
IEEE Operations Ctr						
445 Hoes Ln	Piscataway	NJ	08854	**800-678-4333**	732-981-0060	48-19
EMSD (East Maine School District 63)						
10150 Dee Rd	Des Plaines	IL	60016	**866-752-6850**	847-299-1900	676
Emtek Products Inc						
15250 Stafford St	City of Industry	CA	91744	**800-356-2741**	626-961-0413	347
Emteq Inc						
5349 S Emmer Dr	New Berlin	WI	53151	**888-679-6170**	262-679-6170	24
Emulation Technology Inc						
759 Flynn Rd	Camarillo	CA	93012	**800-232-7837**	805-383-8480	202
Emulex Corp						
3333 Susan St	Costa Mesa	CA	92626	**800-854-7112**	714-662-5600	177
NYSE: ELX						
ENA (Emergency Nurses Assn)						
915 Lee St	Des Plaines	IL	60016	**800-900-9659**	847-460-4000	48-8
Enbridge Energy Management LLC						
1100 Louisiana St Ste 3300	Houston	TX	77002	**866-337-4636**	713-821-2000	357-5
NYSE: EEQ						
Enbridge Energy Partners LP						
1100 Louisiana Ste 3300	Houston	TX	77002	**800-481-2804**	713-821-2000	590
NYSE: EEP						
EnCana Corp						
855 Second St SW Po Box 2850	Calgary	AB	T2P2S5	**888-568-6322**	403-645-2000	529
NYSE: ECA						
Enchantment Resort						
525 Boynton Canyon Rd	Sedona	AZ	86336	**800-826-4180**		660
Encinitas Chamber of Commerce						
527 Encinitas Blvd	Encinitas	CA	92024	**800-953-6041**	760-753-6041	137
Encision Inc						
6797 Winchester Cir	Boulder	CO	80301	**800-998-0986**	303-444-2600	471
OTC: ECIA						
Enclave Suites of Orlando						
6165 Carrier Dr	Orlando	FL	32819	**800-457-0077**	407-351-1155	376
Enclos Corp						
2770 Blue Water Rd	Eagan	MN	55121	**888-234-2966**	651-796-6100	190-6
Encoder Products Co						
464276 Hwy 95 S PO Box 249	Sagle	ID	83860	**800-366-5412**	208-263-8541	202
Encompass Group LLC						
615 Macon Rd	McDonough	GA	30253	**800-284-4540**	770-957-1211	153-18
Encon Safety Products Co						
6825 W Sam Houston Pkwy N						
PO Box 3826	Houston	TX	77041	**800-283-6266**	713-466-1449	669
Encore Bank						
3003 Tamiami Trail N Ste 100	Naples	FL	34103	**800-472-3272**	239-919-5888	69

Company / Address	City	State	ZIP	Toll-Free	Phone	Class
Encore Capital Group Inc						
8875 Aero Dr Ste 200	San Diego	CA	92123	**877-445-4581**	858-560-2600	158
NASDAQ: ECPG						
Encore Medical Corp						
9800 Metric Blvd	Austin	TX	78758	**800-456-8696**	512-832-9500	84
Encore Wire Corp						
1329 Millwood Rd	McKinney	TX	75069	**800-962-9473**	972-562-9473	800
NASDAQ: WIRE						
Encyclopaedia Britannica Inc						
331 N La Salle St	Chicago	IL	60654	**800-323-1229**	312-347-7159	628-2
Encyclopedia Britannica Inc						
331 N Las Salle St	Chicago	IL	60654	**800-323-1229***	312-347-7159	628-10
*Cust Svc						
Enderes Tool Co						
1103 Hershey St	Albert Lea	MN	56007	**800-874-7776**		748
Endevco Corp						
30700 Rancho						
Viejo Rd	San Juan Capistrano	CA	92675	**800-982-6732**	949-493-8181	467
Endicott College						
376 Hale St	Beverly	MA	01915	**800-325-1114***	978-232-2021	166
*Admissions						
Endo Pharmaceuticals Holdings Inc						
100 Endo Blvd	Chadds Ford	PA	19317	**800-462-3636***	610-558-9800	576
*Cust Svc						
Endocrine Society						
8401 Connecticut Ave						
Ste 900	Chevy Chase	MD	20815	**888-363-6274**	301-941-0200	48-8
Endologix Inc						
11 Studebaker	Irvine	CA	92618	**800-983-2284**	949-457-9546	471
NASDAQ: ELGX						
Endometriosis Assn						
8585 N 76th Pl	Milwaukee	WI	53223	**800-992-3636**	414-355-2200	47-17
Endot Industries Inc						
60 Green Pond Rd	Rockaway	NJ	07866	**800-443-6368**	973-625-8500	589
Endress+Hauser Inc						
2350 Endress Pl	Greenwood	IN	46143	**888-363-7377**	317-535-7138	202
Endries International Inc						
714 W Ryan St PO Box 69	Brillion	WI	54110	**800-852-5821**	920-756-5381	382
Endura Products Inc						
8817 W Market St	Colfax	NC	27235	**800-334-2006**	336-668-2472	236
Endurance Reinsurance Corp of America						
750 Third Ave Fl 2 & 10	New York	NY	10017	**888-221-3894**	212-471-2800	388-4
Endurance Specialty Holdings Ltd						
767 Third Ave 5th Fl	New York	NY	10017	**855-838-7792**	212-209-6500	387
NYSE: ENH						
Enercon Engineering Inc						
One Altorfer Ln	East Peoria	IL	61611	**800-218-8831**	309-694-1418	204
Enerfab Inc						
4955 Spring Grove Ave	Cincinnati	OH	45232	**800-772-5066**	513-641-0500	90
Enerflex Systems Ltd						
1331 Macleod Trail SE Ste 904	Calgary	AB	T2G0K3	**800-242-3178**	403-387-6377	383
TSE: EFX						
Ener-G Foods Inc						
5960 First Ave S PO Box 84487	Seattle	WA	98124	**800-331-5222**	206-767-3928	295-36
Energen Corp						
605 Richard Arrington						
Blvd N	Birmingham	AL	35203	**800-654-3206**	205-326-2700	357-5
NYSE: EGN						
Energy Alloys LLC						
350 Glenborough Ste 300	Houston	TX	77067	**866-448-9831**	832-601-5800	485
Energy Concepts Inc						
404 Washington Blvd	Mundelein	IL	60060	**800-621-1247**	847-837-8191	694
Energy Efficiency & Renewable Energy Information Ctr						
1000 Independence Ave SW	Washington	DC	20585	**877-337-3463**	202-586-4849	198
Energy Exchanger Co						
1844 N Garnett Rd	Tulsa	OK	74116	**800-760-6700**	918-437-3000	90
Energy Focus Inc						
32000 Aurora Rd	Solon	OH	44139	**800-327-7877**	440-715-1300	435
OTC: EFOI						
Energy Northwest						
76 N Power Plant Loop	Richland	WA	99354	**800-468-6883**	509-372-5000	245
Energy Recovery Inc						
1717 Doolittle Dr	San Leandro	CA	94577	**888-455-2263**	510-483-7370	794
NASDAQ: ERII						
Energy West Inc						
1 First Ave S	Great Falls	MT	59401	**800-570-5688**	406-791-7500	775
EnergyExplorium						
13339 Hagers Ferry Rd	Huntersville	NC	28078	**800-777-0003**	980-875-5600	513
EnergyUnited Electric Membership Corp						
PO Box 1831	Statesville	NC	28687	**800-522-3793**	704-873-5241	245
Enerpac						
P.O. Box 3241	Milwaukee	WI	53201	**800-433-2766***	262-293-1600	749
*Cust Svc						
Enerplus Resources Fund						
333 Seventh Ave SW Ste 3000	Calgary	AB	T2P2Z1	**800-319-6462**	403-298-2200	402
EnerSys						
2366 Bernville Rd	Reading	PA	19605	**800-538-3627**	610-208-1991	73
NYSE: ENS						
EnerVision Inc						
4170 Ashford Dunwoody Rd						
Ste 550	Atlanta	GA	30319	**888-999-8840**	678-510-2900	195
Enesco LLC						
225 Windsor Dr	Itasca	IL	60143	**800-436-3726**	630-875-5300	332
Enflo Corp						
315 Lake Ave	Bristol	CT	06010	**888-887-4093**	860-589-0014	593
Enforcer Products Inc						
PO Box 1060	Cartersville	GA	30120	**888-805-4357**		280
EngenderHealth						
440 Ninth Ave 13th Fl	New York	NY	10001	**800-564-2872**	212-561-8000	47-17
Engent Inc						
3140 Northwoods Pkwy Ste 300A	Norcross	GA	30071	**888-768-4357**	678-990-3320	686
Enghouse Systems Ltd						
80 Tiverton Ct Ste 800	Markham	ON	L3R0G4	**866-206-0240**	905-946-3200	179-10
TSE: ESL						
Engine Components Inc (ECI)						
9503 Middlex	San Antonio	TX	78217	**800-324-2359**	210-820-8101	21
Engine Power Source Inc						
348 Bryant Blvd	Rock Hill	SC	29732	**800-374-7522**	704-944-1999	511
Engineered Controls International Inc (ECII)						
100 Rego Dr PO Box 247	Elon	NC	27244	**800-650-0061**	336-449-7707	777
Engineered Plastics Inc						
211 Chase St	Gibsonville	NC	27249	**800-711-1740**	336-449-4121	595
Engineered Polymer Solutions Inc						
1400 N State St	Marengo	IL	60152	**800-654-4242**		598-2

	Toll-Free	Phone	Class
Engineered Polymers Corp (EPC)			
1020 Maple Ave E .... Mora MN 55051	800-388-2155	320-679-3232	601
Engineered Products Co (EPCO)			
601 Kelso St PO Box 108 ....Flint MI 48506	888-414-3726	810-767-2050	347
Engineered Products Inc			
500 Furman Hall Rd .... Greenville SC 29609	888-301-1421	864-234-4888	208
Engineered Protection Systems Inc			
750 Front Ave NW Ste 300 ....Grand Rapids MI 49504	800-966-9199	616-459-0281	190-4
Engineered Storage Products Co			
345 Harvestore Dr ....DeKalb IL 60115	800-880-3663	815-756-1551	90
Engineering Measurements Co (EMCO)			
1150 Northpoint Blvd Ste C .... Blythewood SC 29016	800-575-0394		490
Engineering News-Record (ENR)			
Two Penn Plz Ninth Fl. ....New York NY 10121	877-876-8208	212-904-3507	452-21
Engineers Canada			
180 Elgin St Ste 1100...........Ottawa ON K2P2K3	877-408-9273	613-232-2474	47-1
Enginetech Inc			
1205 W Crosby Rd .... Carrollton TX 75006	800-869-8711	972-245-0110	60
Engis Corp			
105 W Hintz Rd .... Wheeling IL 60090	800-993-6447	847-808-9400	383
England Logistics Inc			
1325 South 4700 West ....Salt Lake City UT 84104	800-848-7810	801-656-4500	195
Englander Northeast			
12 Esquire Rd .... North Billerica MA 01862	800-370-8700		466
Englefield Oil Co			
447 James Pkwy ....Heath OH 43056	800-837-4458*	740-928-8215	323
*Cust Svc			
Englewood Electrical Supply			
716 Belvedere Dr ....Kokomo IN 46901	800-417-7543	765-452-4087	246
Englewood Meridian			
3455 S Corona St ....Englewood CO 80113	855-444-7658	888-221-7317	663
Englewood Public Library			
1000 Englewood Pkwy			
Englewood Civic Ctr 1st Fl ....Englewood CO 80110	866-922-9006	303-762-2560	431-3
Englewood-Cape Haze Area Chamber of Commerce			
601 S Indiana Ave ....Englewood FL 34223	800-603-7198	941-474-5511	137
English Inn, The			
677 S Michigan Rd .... Eaton Rapids MI 48827	800-858-0598	517-663-2500	662
Englund Marine & Industrial Supply Company Inc			
95 Hamburg Ave PO Box 296 .... Astoria OR 97103	800-228-7051	503-325-4341	221
Engman-Taylor Company Inc (ETCO)			
W142 N9351			
Fountain Blvd .... Menomonee Falls WI 53051	800-236-1975	262-255-9300	382
Enid News & Eagle			
227 W Broadway PO Box 3451.............Enid OK 73701	800-299-6397	580-548-8186	525-2
Enidine Inc			
7 Centre Dr .... Orchard Park NY 14127	800-852-8508	716-662-1900	467
Enlisted Assn of the National Guard of the US (EANGUS)			
3133 Mt Vernon Ave ....Alexandria VA 22305	800-234-3264	703-519-3846	47-19
Enloe Medical Ctr			
1531 Esplanade ....Chico CA 95926	800-822-8102	530-332-7300	371-3
Ennis Inc PO Box D .... Wolfe City TX 75496	800-527-1008		410
Enoch Manufacturing Co			
14242 SE 82nd Dr PO Box 98 ..... Clackamas OR 97015	888-659-2660	503-659-2660	614
ENOCHS Examining Room Furniture			
PO Box 50559 .... Indianapolis IN 46250	800-428-2305*		318-3
*Cust Svc			
Enor Corp			
245 Livingston St ....Northvale NJ 07647	800-977-6427	201-750-1680	601
Enphase Energy Inc			
1420 N Mcdowell Blvd .... Petaluma CA 94954	877-797-4743	707-763-4784	687
Enpro Inc			
121 S LombaRd Rd ....Addison IL 60101	800-323-2416	630-629-3504	382
EnPro Industries Inc			
5605 Carnegie Blvd Ste 500.........Charlotte NC 28209	800-356-6955	704-731-1500	325
NYSE: NPO			
EnPro Industries Inc Fairbanks Morse Engine			
701 White Ave ....Beloit WI 53511	800-356-6955		262
ENR (Engineering News-Record)			
Two Penn Plz Ninth Fl. ....New York NY 10121	877-876-8208	212-904-3507	452-21
ENSCO Inc			
3110 Fairview Pk Dr			
Ste 300 .... Falls Church VA 22042	800-367-2682	703-321-9000	261
Ensearch Management Consultants			
905 E Cotati Ave ....Cotati CA 94931	888-667-5627		712
Ensemble Travel			
256 W 38th St 11th Fl. ....New York NY 10018	800-576-2378	212-545-7460	762
Enseo Inc			
1680 Prospect Dr Ste 100.........Richardson TX 75081	800-270-8747	972-234-2513	175
Ensinger Putnam Precision Molding			
11 Danco Rd ....Putnam CT 06260	800-752-7865	860-928-7911	597
Ent Federal Credit Union			
7250 Campus Dr .... Colorado Springs CO 80920	800-525-9623	719-574-1100	219
Entegee Inc			
70 BlanchaRd Rd Ste 102...........Burlington MA 01803	800-230-7232	781-221-5800	712
Entegris Inc			
129 Concord Rd Bldg 2 ....Billerica MA 01821	877-695-7654	978-436-6500	686
NASDAQ: ENTG			
Entercom Communications Corp			
401 City Ave Ste 809 .... Bala Cynwyd PA 19004	800-776-9437	610-660-5610	634
NYSE: ETM			
Enterey Inc			
9900 Irvine Ctr Dr Ste 100 ....Irvine CA 92618	800-691-2349		458
Entergy Arkansas Inc			
425 W Capitol Ave .... Little Rock AR 72201	800-368-3749		775
Entergy Corp			
639 Loyola Ave .... New Orleans LA 70113	800-368-3749	504-576-4000	357-5
NYSE: ETR			
Entergy Louisiana Inc			
639 Loyola Ave .... New Orleans LA 70113	800-368-3749*	504-576-6116	775
*Cust Svc			
Entergy New Orleans Inc			
639 Loyola Ave .... New Orleans LA 70113	800-368-3749*		775
*Cust Svc			
Entergy Texas Inc			
350 Pine St .... Beaumont TX 77701	800-368-3749	409-981-3245	775
Enterprise Bank of SC			
13497 Broxton Bridge Rd			
PO Box 8. ....Ehrhardt SC 29081	800-554-8969	803-267-3191	69
Enterprise Community Partners Inc			
10227 Wincopin Cir ....Columbia MD 21044	800-624-4298	410-964-1230	47-5
Enterprise Financial Services Corp			
150 N Meramec Ave ....Clayton MO 63105	800-396-8141	314-725-5500	357-2
NASDAQ: EFSG			
Enterprise Fredericton			
10 Knowledge Pk Dr Ste 110 .... Fredericton NB E3C2M7	866-534-9270	506-444-4686	136
Enterprise Rent-A-Car			
600 Corporate Pk Dr .... Saint Louis MO 63105	800-325-8007	314-512-5000	125
Enterprise Wireless Alliance (EWA)			
8484 Westpark Dr Ste 630 ....McLean VA 22102	800-482-8282	703-528-5115	48-20
Enterprise-Ozark Community College			
1975 Ave C ....Mobile AL 36615	877-701-0033	251-438-2816	788
Entertainment Properties Trust			
909 Walnut Ste 200 .... Kansas City MO 64106	888-377-7348	816-472-1700	646
NYSE: EPR			
Entertainment Weekly Magazine			
1675 Broadway 29th Fl. ....New York NY 10019	800-828-6882	212-522-5600	452-9
Enthone Inc			
350 Frontage Rd .... West Haven CT 06516	800-431-2200	203-934-8611	143
Entitle Direct Group Inc			
281 Tresser Blvd Sixth Fl .... Stamford CT 06901	877-936-8485	203-724-1150	388-6
Entomological Society of America			
10001 Derekwood Ln Ste 100.......... Lanham MD 20706	800-523-8635	301-731-4535	48-19
Entrepreneur Magazine			
2445 McCabe Way Ste 400 ....Irvine CA 92614	800-274-6229	949-261-2325	452-5
Entrepreneur Media Inc			
2445 McCabe Way Ste 400 ....Irvine CA 92614	877-652-5295	949-261-2325	628-9
Entropic Communications Inc			
6290 Sequence Dr .... San Diego CA 92121	888-510-1765	858-768-3600	252
NASDAQ: ENTR			
Entrust Inc			
5400 LBJ Fwy Ste 1340 .... Dallas TX 75240	888-690-2424*	972-728-0447	179-12
*Sales			
Entwistle Co Dietzco Div			
6 Bigelow St .... Hudson MA 01749	800-445-8909	508-481-4000	549
Envelope Manufacturers Assn (EMA)			
500 Montgomery St Ste 550......... Alexandria VA 22314	800-354-5892	703-739-2200	48-4
EnviroLogix Inc			
500 Riverside Industrial Pkwy ....Portland ME 04103	866-408-4597	207-797-0300	732
Environment of Care Leader			
9737 Washintonian Blvd			
Ste 100 .... Gaithersburg MD 20878	800-929-4824*	301-287-2700	524-8
*Cust Svc			
Environment Reporter			
1801 S Bell St .... Arlington VA 22202	800-372-1033		524-5
Environmental & Safety Designs Inc			
5724 Summer Trees Dr .... Memphis TN 38134	800-588-7962	901-372-7962	193
Environmental Compliance Bulletin			
1801 S Bell St .... Arlington VA 22202	800-372-1033		524-5
Environmental Data Resources Inc			
440 Wheelers Farms Rd ....Milford CT 06460	800-352-0050	203-783-0300	384
Environmental Defense			
257 Pk Ave S ....New York NY 10010	800-505-0703	212-505-2100	47-13
Environmental Earthscapes Inc			
5075 S Swan Rd ....Tucson AZ 85706	800-571-1575	520-571-1575	419
Environmental Enterprises Inc (EEI)			
10163 Cincinnati Dayton Rd ..... Cincinnati OH 45241	800-722-2818	513-772-2818	658
Environmental Health & Engineering Inc			
117 Fourth Ave ....Needham MA 02494	800-825-5343	781-247-4300	256
Environmental Industry Assn			
4301 Connecticut Ave NW			
Ste 300 .... Washington DC 20008	800-424-2869	202-244-4700	47-12
Environmental Information Assn (EIA)			
6935 Wisconsin Ave Ste 306 .... Chevy Chase MD 20815	888-343-4342	301-961-4999	47-13
Environmental Law Institute (ELI)			
2000 L St NW Ste 620 .... Washington DC 20036	800-433-5120	202-939-3800	48-10
Environmental Management Inc			
5200 NE Hwy 33 ....Guthrie OK 73044	800-510-8510	405-282-8510	659
Environmental Protection Agency (EPA)			
1200 Pennsylvania Ave NW .... Washington DC 20460	888-372-8255	202-564-4700	338-18
US National Response Team			
1200 Pennsylvania Ave NW .... Washington DC 20593	800-424-9346	202-267-2675	338-18
Region 1			
1 Congress St Ste 1100 ....Boston MA 02114	888-372-7341	617-918-1111	338-18
Region 3			
1650 Arch St ....Philadelphia PA 19103	800-438-2474	215-814-5000	338-18
Environmental Protection Agency Regional Offices			
Region 4			
Federal Ctr 61 Forsyth St SW.......... Atlanta GA 30303	800-241-1754	404-562-9900	338-18
Region 6			
1445 Ross Ave Ste 1200 ....Dallas TX 75202	800-887-6063	214-665-2200	338-18
Region 8			
1595 Wynkoop St ....Denver CO 80202	800-227-8917	303-312-6312	338-18
Region 9			
75 Hawthorne St .... San Francisco CA 94105	866-372-9378	415-947-8000	338-18
Region 10			
1200 Sixth Ave Ste 900 .... Seattle WA 98101	800-424-4372	206-553-1200	338-18
Environmental Systems Research Institute Inc			
380 New York St ....Redlands CA 92373	800-447-9778*	909-793-2853	179-10
*Sales			
Enviro-Tote Inc			
4 Cote Ln ....Bedford NH 03110	800-868-3224	603-647-7171	65
Envision Inc			
610 N Main St ....Wichita KS 67203	888-425-7072	316-440-1500	47-6
Envision Peripherals Inc (EPI)			
47490 Seabridge Dr ....Fremont CA 94538	888-838-6388*	510-770-9988	174-4
*Tech Supp			
Envoy Plan Services Inc			
901 Calle Amanecer Ste 200....... San Clemente CA 92673	800-248-8858	949-366-5070	528
Enwood Structures Inc			
5724 McCrimmon Pkwy			
PO Box 2002..............Morrisville NC 27560	800-777-8648	919-518-0464	804
Enzo Biochem Inc			
527 Madison Ave ....New York NY 10022	800-522-5052	212-583-0100	231
NYSE: ENZ			
Enzo Life Sciences Inc			
10 Executive Blvd ....Farmingdale NY 11735	800-942-0430	631-694-7070	231
Enzymatic Therapy			
825 Challenger Dr .... Green Bay WI 54311	800-783-2286	920-469-1313	787
EOG Resources Inc			
1111 Bagby Sky Lobby 2 ....Houston TX 77002	877-363-3647	713-651-7000	531
NYSE: EOG			
Eola Hills Wine Cellars			
501 S Pacific Hwy 99 W ....Rickreall OR 97371	800-291-6730	503-623-2405	49-6
EP Henry Corp			
201 Pk Ave ....Woodbury NJ 08096	800-444-3679	856-845-6200	184
EPA (Environmental Protection Agency)			
1200 Pennsylvania Ave NW .... Washington DC 20460	888-372-8255	202-564-4700	338-18

Name / Address	City	State	ZIP	Toll-Free	Phone	Class
E-pak Machinery Inc 1535 S State Rd 39	La Porte	IN	46350	**800-328-0466**	219-393-5541	540
EPC (Engineered Polymers Corp) 1020 Maple Ave E	Mora	MN	55051	**800-388-2155**	320-679-3232	601
EPCO (Engineered Products Co) 601 Kelso St PO Box 108	Flint	MI	48506	**888-414-3726**	810-767-2050	347
Epes Carriers Inc 3400 Edgefield Ct	Greensboro	NC	27409	**800-869-3737**	336-668-3358	770
Ephor Group LLC 24 E Greenway Plz Ste 440	Houston	TX	77046	**800-379-9330**		458
Ephraim McDowell Regional Medical Ctr 217 S Third St	Danville	KY	40422	**800-686-4121**	859-239-1000	371-3
EPI (Envision Peripherals Inc) 47490 Seabridge Dr *Tech Supp	Fremont	CA	94538	**888-838-6388***	510-770-9988	174-4
Epic Life Insurance Co 1765 W Broadway *Sales	Madison	WI	53713	**800-236-8809***	608-223-2100	388-2
Epic Metals Corp 11 Talbot Ave	Rankin	PA	15104	**877-696-3742**	412-351-3913	688
Epicomm (NAPL) 1 Meadowlands Plaza Ste 1511	East Rutherford	NJ	07073	**800-642-6275**	201-634-9600	48-16
EPIEN Medical Inc 4225 White Bear Pkwy Ste 600	St Paul	MN	55110	**888-884-4675**	651-653-3380	659
Epilepsy Foundation 8301 Professional Pl E	Landover	MD	20785	**800-332-1000**	301-459-3700	47-17
Episcopal Church USA 815 Second Ave	New York	NY	10017	**800-334-7626**	212-716-6000	47-20
Episcopal Divinity School 99 Brattle St	Cambridge	MA	02138	**866-333-8742**	617-868-3450	167-3
Episcopal High School 1200 N Quaker Ln	Alexandria	VA	22302	**877-933-4347**	703-933-4062	615
Episcopal Life Magazine 815 Second Ave Episcopal Church Ctr	New York	NY	10017	**800-334-7626**	212-716-6000	452-18
Episcopal Migration Ministries (EMM) 815 Second Ave	New York	NY	10017	**800-334-7626**	212-716-6258	47-5
Episcopal Relief & Development 815 Second Ave	New York	NY	10017	**800-334-7626**	855-312-4325	47-5
Episcopal Theological Seminary of the Southwest (SSW) 501 E 32nd PO Box 2247	Austin	TX	78705	**800-252-5400**	512-472-4133	167-3
Epitomics Inc 863 Mitten Rd Ste 103	Burlingame	CA	94010	**888-772-2226**	650-583-6688	659
ePlus Inc 13595 Dulles Technology Dr *NASDAQ: PLUS*	Herndon	VA	20171	**888-482-1122**	703-984-8400	38
EPM Communications Inc 19 W 21st St Ste 303	New York	NY	10010	**888-852-9467**	212-941-0099	628-9
Epoch Senior Living 51 Sawyer Rd Ste 500	Waltham	MA	02453	**877-376-2475**	781-891-0777	663
Eppinger Manufacturing Co 6340 Schaefer Rd	Dearborn	MI	48126	**888-771-8277**	313-582-3205	701
Epps Aviation Inc One Aviation Way DeKalb Peachtree Airport	Atlanta	GA	30341	**800-241-6807**	770-458-9851	62
EPRI Journal 3420 Hillview Ave	Palo Alto	CA	94304	**800-313-3774**	650-855-2121	452-21
Epro Tile Inc 10890 E CR 6	Bloomville	OH	44818	**866-818-3776**		741
ePromos Promotional Products Inc 120 Broadway Ste 1360	New York	NY	10271	**877-377-6667**	212-286-8008	94
EPS (Educators Publishing Service Inc) 625 Mt Auburn St Third Fl PO Box 9031	Cambridge	MA	02139	**800-225-5750**		628-2
EPS Corp 150 Paularino Ave Ste A120	Costa Mesa	CA	92626	**866-377-7834**		458
Epson America Inc 3840 Kilroy Airport Way	Long Beach	CA	90806	**800-463-7766**	562-981-3840	174-6
Epson Electronics America Inc 150 River Oaks Pkwy	San Jose	CA	95134	**800-228-3964**	408-922-0200	687
Epworth Villa 14901 N Pennsylvania Ave	Oklahoma City	OK	73134	**800-579-8776**	405-752-1200	663
EQC (Emerald Queen Casino) 2024 E 29th St	Tacoma	WA	98404	**888-831-7655**	253-594-7777	132
EQT Corp 625 Liberty Ave Ste 1700 *NYSE: EQT*	Pittsburgh	PA	15222	**800-242-1776**	412-553-5700	775
Equal Employment Opportunity Commission (EEOC) 1801 L St NW	Washington	DC	20507	**800-669-4000**	202-663-4191	338-18
Equal Employment Opportunity Commission Regional Offices						
Atlanta District 100 Alabama St SW Ste 4R30	Atlanta	GA	30303	**800-669-6820**		338-18
Birmingham District 1130 22nd St S Ste 2000	Birmingham	AL	35205	**800-669-4000**	205-212-2100	338-18
Charlotte District 129 W Trade St Ste 400	Charlotte	NC	28202	**800-669-4000**	704-344-6682	338-18
Dallas District 207 S Houston St 3rd Fl	Dallas	TX	75202	**800-669-4000**	214-253-2700	338-18
Houston District 1201 Louisiana St 6th Fl	Houston	TX	77002	**800-669-4000**		338-18
Los Angeles District 255 E Temple St 4th Fl	Los Angeles	CA	90012	**800-669-4000**		338-18
New York District 33 Whitehall St 5th Fl	New York	NY	10004	**866-408-8075**	212-336-3620	338-18
Saint Louis District 1222 Spruce St Rm 8.100	Saint Louis	MO	63103	**800-669-4000**	314-539-7800	338-18
San Francisco District 450 Golden Gate Ave 5 W PO Box 36025	San Francisco	CA	94102	**800-669-4000**		338-18
Equal Energy Ltd 500 Fourth Ave SW	Calgary	AB	T2P2V6	**877-263-0262**	403-263-0262	531
Equal Rights Advocates (ERA) 1170 Market St Ste 700	San Francisco	CA	94102	**800-839-4372**	415-621-0672	47-24
Equifax Credit Marketing Services 1550 Peachtree St NW *NYSE: EFX* ■ *Sales	Atlanta	GA	30309	**800-660-5125***	404-885-8000	218
Equifax Inc 1550 Peachtree St NW *NYSE: EFX* ■ *Sales	Atlanta	GA	30309	**888-202-4025***	404-885-8000	218
Equilibrium Inc 3 Harbor Dr	Sausalito	CA	94965	**855-378-4542**	415-332-4343	179-8
Equine Canada 2685 Queensview Dr	Ottawa	ON	K2B8K2	**866-282-8395**	613-248-3484	643
Equinox Fitness Holdings Inc 895 Broadway	New York	NY	10003	**866-332-6549**	212-677-0180	351
Equinox, The 3567 Main St Rt 7A	Manchester Village	VT	05254	**800-362-4747**	802-362-4700	660
Equipment Manufacturing Corp (EMC) 14930 Marquardt Ave	Santa Fe Springs	CA	90670	**888-833-9000**	562-623-9394	383
Equipment Technology LLC 341 NW 122nd St	Oklahoma City	OK	73114	**888-748-3841**		264-3
Equipoise Dental Laboratory Inc 85 Portland Ave	Bergenfield	NJ	07621	**800-999-4950**	201-385-4750	415
EQUIPTO 225 Main St	Tatamy	PA	18085	**800-323-0801**	610-253-2775	286
Equipto Electronics Corp 351 Woodlawn Ave	Aurora	IL	60506	**800-204-7225**	630-897-4691	254
Equis International 90 South 400 West Ste 620 *Sales	Salt Lake City	UT	84101	**800-882-3040***	801-265-9996	179-10
Equisport Agency Inc 2306 Eastways Rd PO Box 269	Bloomfield Hills	MI	48304	**800-432-1215**	248-644-1215	388-1
Equitable Gas Co PO Box 6766	Pittsburgh	PA	15212	**800-654-6335**		775
Equitable Life & Casualty Insurance Co Three Triad Ctr *Cust Svc	Salt Lake City	UT	84180	**877-358-4060***		388-2
Equity Co-op Livestock Sales Assn 401 Commerce Ave	Baraboo	WI	53913	**800-362-3989**	608-356-8311	441
Equity Funding 12505 Bel-Red Rd Ste 200	Bellevue	WA	98005	**866-332-3863**	425-283-1040	216
Equity Lifestyle Properties Inc Two N Riverside Plz Ste 800 *NYSE: ELS*	Chicago	IL	60606	**800-274-7314**	312-279-1400	646
Equus Computer Systems Inc 5801 Clearwater Dr	Minnetonka	MN	55343	**866-378-8727**	612-617-6200	174-1
Equus Magazine 656 Quince OrchaRd Rd Ste 600 *Cust Svc	Gaithersburg	MD	20878	**800-829-5910***	301-977-3900	452-14
EQUUS Total Return Inc 700 Louisiana St 48th Fl	Houston	TX	77002	**888-323-4533**		780
ER Wagner Mfg Company Inc 4611 N 32nd St	Milwaukee	WI	53209	**800-558-5596**	414-871-5080	347
ERA (Equal Rights Advocates) 1170 Market St Ste 700	San Francisco	CA	94102	**800-839-4372**	415-621-0672	47-24
ERA (Electronics Representatives Assn) 300 W Adams St Ste 617	Chicago	IL	60606	**800-776-7377**	312-527-3050	48-18
Era Helicopters LLC 600 Airport Service Rd PO Box 6550	Lake Charles	LA	70606	**800-256-2372**	337-478-6131	13
ERA Wilder Realty 120A Columbia Ave PO Box 610	Chapin	SC	29036	**866-593-7653**	803-345-6713	643
Erb Equipment Co Inc 200 Erb Industrial Dr	Fenton	MO	63026	**800-634-9661**	636-349-0200	355
ERDC (US Army Engineer Research & Development Ctr) 3909 Halls Ferry Rd	Vicksburg	MS	39180	**800-522-6937**	601-634-3188	659
Erect-A-Tube Inc 701 W Pk St PO Box 100	Harvard	IL	60033	**800-624-9219**	815-943-4091	104
eResearch Technology Inc 1818 Market St Ste 1000 *NASDAQ: ERT*	Philadelphia	PA	19103	**800-704-9698**	215-972-0420	179-10
Ergodyne Corp 1021 Bandana Blvd E Ste 220	Saint Paul	MN	55108	**800-225-8238**	651-642-9889	472
ErgoGenesis LLC One BodyBilt Pl	Navasota	TX	77868	**800-364-5299**	936-825-1700	318-3
Ergon Properties Inc PO Box 1639	Jackson	MS	39215	**800-824-2626**	601-933-3174	644
Ergon Refining 2611 Haining Rd	Vicksburg	MS	39183	**877-888-9758**	601-933-3000	573
Ergotron Inc 1181 Trapp Rd *Sales	Saint Paul	MN	55121	**800-888-8458***	651-681-7600	318-1
Erhard Bmw Of Bloomfield Hills 4065 W Maple Rd	Bloomfield Hills	MI	48301	**888-481-4058**	248-642-6565	56
ERIC (Education Resource Information Ctr) c/o CSC 655 15th St NW Ste 500	Washington	DC	20005	**800-538-3742**		198
Eric Electronics 2220 Lundy Ave *General	San Jose	CA	95131	**800-495-3742***	408-432-1111	246
Erickson Air-Crane Co 5550 SW Macadam Ave Ste 200	Portland	OR	97239	**800-424-2413**	503-505-5800	20
Erickson Oil Products Inc 1231 Industrial St	Hudson	WI	54016	**800-521-0104**	715-386-8241	323
Erickson Transport Corp 2255 N Packer Rd	Springfield	MO	65803	**800-641-4595**	417-862-6741	770
ERICO Products Inc 34600 Solon Rd	Solon	OH	44139	**800-813-3378**	440-248-0100	802
Ericsson 1 Telcordia Dr	Piscataway	NJ	08854	**800-521-2673**	732-699-2000	179-10
Erie 2-Chautauqua Cattaraugus Boces (ECCB) 8685 Erie Rd	Angola	NY	14006	**800-228-1184**	716-549-4454	676
Erie County Water Authority (ECWA) 295 Main St Rm 350	Buffalo	NY	14203	**855-748-1076**	716-849-8484	775
Erie Family Life Insurance Co 100 Erie Insurance Pl	Erie	PA	16530	**800-458-0811**	814-870-2000	388-2
Erie Foods International Inc 401 Seventh Ave PO Box 648	Erie	IL	61250	**800-447-1887**	309-659-2233	295-10
Erie Indemnity Co *Erie Insurance Group* 100 Erie Insurance Pl *NASDAQ: ERIE*	Erie	PA	16530	**800-458-0811**	814-870-2000	388-4
Erie Insurance Exchange 100 Erie Insurance Pl	Erie	PA	16530	**800-458-0811**	814-870-2000	388-4
Erie Insurance Property & Casualty Co 100 Erie Insurance Pl	Erie	PA	16530	**800-458-0811**	814-870-2000	388-4
Erie Press Systems 1253 W 12th St PO Box 4061	Erie	PA	16512	**800-222-3608**	814-455-3941	451
Erie Regional Chamber & Growth Partnership 208 E Bayfront Pkwy	Erie	PA	16507	**888-300-3743**	814-454-7191	137
Erie Times-News 205 W 12th St	Erie	PA	16534	**800-352-0043**	814-870-1600	525-2
Erie VA Medical Ctr 135 E 38th St	Erie	PA	16504	**800-274-8387**	814-868-8661	371-8
Erie Zoo 423 W 38th St	Erie	PA	16508	**877-371-5422**	814-864-4091	810

Alphabetical Section

	City	State	ZIP	Toll-Free	Phone	Class
Erlanger Medical Ctr						
975 E Third St	Chattanooga	TN	37403	**877-849-8338**	423-778-7000	371-3
ERMC (Edinburg Regional Medical Ctr)						
1102 W Trenton Rd	Edinburg	TX	78539	**800-465-5585**	956-388-6000	371-3
Ernest F Mariani Company Inc						
573 West 2890 South	Salt Lake City	UT	84115	**800-453-2927**		656
Ernest Maier Inc						
4700 Annapolis Rd	Bladensburg	MD	20710	**888-927-8303**	301-927-8300	184
Ernest Paper Products						
5777 Smithway St	Commerce	CA	90040	**800-233-7788**		552
Ernie Ball						
151 Suburban Rd	San Luis Obispo	CA	93401	**866-823-2255**	805-544-7726	520
Ernst & Young						
Ernst & Young Tower 222 Bay St						
PO Box 251	Toronto	ON	M5K1J7	**800-291-3380**	416-864-1234	2
Ernst Enterprises Inc						
3361 Successful Way	Dayton	OH	45414	**800-353-1555**	937-233-5555	183
Ernst Publishing Co LLC						
one Commerce Plaza 99 Washington Ave						
Ste 309	Albany	NY	12210	**800-345-3822**		628-9
ERS Industries Inc						
1005 Indian Church Rd	West Seneca	NY	14224	**800-993-6446**	716-675-2040	760
Erskine College						
Two Washington St	Due West	SC	29639	**800-241-8721***	864-379-2131	166
*Admissions						
Erskine Theological Seminary						
2 Washington St PO Box 338	Due West	SC	29639	**888-359-4358**	864-379-8885	167-3
Ervin Industries Inc						
3893 Research Pk Dr	Ann Arbor	MI	48108	**800-748-0055**	734-769-4600	1
Ervin Leasing Co						
3893 Research Pk Dr	Ann Arbor	MI	48108	**800-748-0015**		264-3
ES (IEEE Education Society)						
IEEE Operations Ctr						
445 Hoes Ln	Piscataway	NJ	08854	**800-678-4333**	732-981-0060	48-19
ES Originals Inc						
440 9th Ave 7th Fl	New York	NY	10001	**800-677-6577***	212-736-8124	300
*General						
ESA (Evangelicals for Social Action)						
PO Box 367	Wayne	PA	19087	**800-650-6600**	484-384-2990	47-7
ESA (Electronic Security Assn Inc)						
2300 Vly View Ln Ste 230	Irving	TX	75062	**888-447-1689**	214-260-5970	48-3
Esab Welding & Cutting Products Inc						
411 S Ebenezer Rd						
PO Box 100545	Florence	SC	29501	**800-372-2123**	843-669-4411	798
Escalade Inc						
817 Maxwell Ave	Evansville	IN	47711	**800-426-1421***	812-467-1200	701
NASDAQ: ESCA ■ *Cust Svc						
Escalera Inc						
708 S Industrial Dr						
PO Box 1359	Yuba City	CA	95993	**800-622-1359**	530-673-6318	465
Escalon Premier Brands						
1905 McHenry Ave	Escalon	CA	95320	**800-255-5750**	209-838-7341	295-20
Escambia River Electric Co-op Inc						
3425 Florida 4	Jay	FL	32565	**800-235-3848**	850-675-4521	245
Escanaba Public Library						
400 Ludington St	Escanaba	MI	49829	**800-992-9012**	906-786-4463	431-3
Escapees RV Club						
100 Rainbow Dr	Livingston	TX	77399	**800-231-9896**	936-327-8873	47-23
Esco Corp						
2141 NW 25th Ave	Portland	OR	97210	**800-523-3795**	503-228-2141	191
ESCO Technologies Inc						
9900A Clayton Rd	Saint Louis	MO	63124	**800-368-5948**	314-213-7200	357-3
NYSE: ESE						
eScreen Inc						
7500 W 110th St Ste 500	Overland Park	KS	66210	**800-881-0722**	913-327-5915	384
ESD (Etiwanda School District)						
6061 E Ave	Etiwanda	CA	91739	**800-300-1506**	909-899-2451	676
ESE Inc						
PO Box 1107	Marshfield	WI	54449	**800-236-4778**	715-387-4778	256
Eseeola Lodge, The						
175 Linville Ave PO Box 99	Linville	NC	28646	**800-742-6717**	828-733-4311	660
ESGR (National Committee for Employer Support of the Guard & Reserve)						
1555 Wilson Blvd Ste 319	Arlington	VA	22209	**800-336-4590**	703-696-1386	47-19
ESH (Eastern State Hospital)						
4601 Ironbound Rd	Williamsburg	VA	23188	**800-994-6610**	757-253-5161	371-5
eSignal						
3955 Pt Eden Way	Hayward	CA	94545	**800-815-8256**	510-266-6000	179-1
Eskaton Village						
3939 Walnut Ave	Carmichael	CA	95608	**800-300-3929**	916-974-2000	663
Esker Inc						
1212 Deming Way Ste 350	Madison	WI	53717	**800-368-5283**	608-828-6000	179-12
ESL Instruction & Consulting Inc						
42 Broad St NW	Atlanta	GA	30303	**877-579-2366**	404-577-2366	420
Esmark Steel Group						
2500 Euclid Ave	Chicago Heights	IL	60411	**800-323-0340**	708-756-0400	357-3
Esmeralda County						
PO Box 547	Goldfield	NV	89013	**800-884-4072**	775-485-6309	336
eSoft Inc						
295 Interlocken Blvd Ste 500	Broomfield	CO	80021	**888-903-7638**	303-444-1600	177
ESOP Assn						
1726 M St NW Ste 501	Washington	DC	20036	**866-366-3832**	202-293-2971	48-12
ESOP Assn PAC						
1726 M St NW Ste 501	Washington	DC	20036	**866-366-3832**	202-293-2971	608
ESPE Mfg Company Inc						
9220 Ivanhoe St	Schiller Park	IL	60176	**800-367-3773***	847-678-8950	347
*Cust Svc						
Esplanade Tours						
160 Commonwealth Ave Ste U-1A	Boston	MA	02116	**800-628-4893**	617-266-7465	750
Esplendor Resort at Rio Rico						
1069 Camino Caralampi	Rio Rico	AZ	85648	**800-288-4746**	520-281-1901	660
ESPN Deportes						
Two Alhambra Plz Ninth Fl	Coral Gables	FL	33134	**800-337-6783**	305-567-3797	729
Esprit Miami						
3043 NW 107th Ave	Miami	FL	33172	**800-327-2320**	305-591-2244	293
Esquire Magazine						
300 W 57th St 21st Fl	New York	NY	10019	**800-888-5400**	212-649-4020	452-11
Essco Inc						
1933 Highland Rd	Twinsburg	OH	44087	**800-321-2664**	216-524-4141	598-2
Essen Haus						
514 E Wilson St	Madison	WI	53703	**800-448-0158**	608-255-4674	662
Essence Communications Inc						
135 W 50th St 4th Fl	New York	NY	10020	**800-274-9398***		628-9
*Sales						
Essence Magazine						
135 W 50th St Fourth Fl	New York	NY	10020	**800-274-9398**		452-11
Essential Technologies Inc						
1107 Hazeltine Blvd Ste 477	Chaska	MN	55318	**800-818-1125**	952-368-9001	176
Essentra PLC 3123 Stn Rd	Erie	PA	16510	**800-847-0486**	814-899-9263	152
Essex Boat Works Inc						
Ferry St PO Box 37	Essex	CT	06426	**866-378-3748**	860-767-8276	689
Essex Grain Products						
Nine Lee Blvd	Frazer	PA	19355	**800-441-1017**	610-647-3800	296-11
Essex Meadows						
30 Bokum Rd	Essex	CT	06426	**800-767-7201**	860-767-7201	663
Essex Mfg Inc						
350 Fifth Ave Ste 501	New York	NY	10118	**800-648-6010**	212-239-0080	153-5
Essex National Securities Inc						
550 Gateway Dr Ste 210	Napa	CA	94558	**855-444-3674**	707-258-5000	681
Essex Savings Bank						
PO Box 950	Essex	CT	06426	**877-377-3922**	860-767-4414	69
Essick Air Products Inc						
5800 Murray St	Little Rock	AR	72209	**800-643-8341**	501-562-1094	90
Essmueller Co						
334 Ave A PO Box 1966	Laurel	MS	39440	**800-325-7175**	601-649-2400	208
ESSROC Materials Inc						
3251 Bath Pike	Nazareth	PA	18064	**800-437-7762**	610-837-6725	134
Estancia La Jolla Hotel & Spa						
9700 N Torrey Pines Rd	La Jolla	CA	92037	**866-437-8262**	858-550-1000	698
Esterline Interface Technologies						
600 W Wilbur Ave	Coeur d'Alene	ID	83815	**800-444-5923**	208-765-8000	174-2
Esterline Mason						
13955 Balboa Blvd	Sylmar	CA	91342	**800-232-7700**	818-361-3366	499
Estes-Cox Corp						
1295 H St	Penrose	CO	81240	**800-525-7561**	719-372-6565	752
Estes-Winn Memorial Automobile Museum						
111 Grovewood Rd	Asheville	NC	28804	**877-622-7238**	828-253-7651	513
Estex Mfg Co Inc						
402 E Broad St PO Box 368	Fairburn	GA	30213	**800-749-1224**		723
Esther Price Candies Inc						
1709 Wayne Ave	Dayton	OH	45410	**800-782-0326**	937-253-2121	295-8
Estrada Hinojosa & Company Inc						
1717 Main St LB47	Dallas	TX	75201	**800-676-5352**	214-658-1670	398
ET Horn Co						
16050 Canary Ave	La Mirada	CA	90638	**800-442-4676**	714-523-8050	144
ETA (Evangelical Training Assn)						
PO Box 327	Wheaton	IL	60187	**800-369-8291***	630-384-6920	47-20
*General						
ETA (Electronics Technicians Assn International)						
Five Depot St	Greencastle	IN	46135	**800-288-3824**	765-653-8262	48-19
Eta Sigma Gamma						
2000 University Ave	Muncie	IN	47306	**800-715-2559**	765-285-2258	47-16
ETC (Educational Travel Consultants)						
PO Box 1580	Hendersonville	NC	28793	**800-247-7969**	828-693-0412	750
ETCO (Engman-Taylor Company Inc)						
W142 N9351						
Fountain Blvd	Menomonee Falls	WI	53051	**800-236-1975**	262-255-9300	382
ETCO Inc						
25 Bellows St	Warwick	RI	02888	**800-689-3826**	401-467-2400	802
ETCO Inc Automotive Products Div						
3004 62nd Ave E	Bradenton	FL	34203	**800-689-3826**	941-756-8426	247
Eternabond						
75 E Div St	Mundelein	IL	60060	**888-336-2663**	847-837-9400	722
Eternity Healthcare Inc						
Ste 1 8755 Ash St	Vancouver	BC	V6P6T3	**855-324-1110**		471
Etex Telephone Co-op Inc						
1013 Hwy 155 N	Gilmer	TX	75644	**877-482-3839**	903-797-2711	726
Ethan Allen Hotel						
21 Lake Ave Ext	Danbury	CT	06811	**800-742-1776**	203-744-1776	376
Etheridge Printing Co						
4434 Mcewen Rd	Dallas	TX	75244	**800-834-2709**	214-827-8151	390
Etiwanda School District (ESD)						
6061 E Ave	Etiwanda	CA	91739	**800-300-1506**	909-899-2451	676
Etm Electromatic Inc						
35451 Dumbarton Ct	Newark	CA	94560	**800-883-4386**	510-797-1100	638
ETS (Praxis Series Online Educational Testing Service Teaching & Learning Div)						
PO Box 6051	Princeton	NJ	08541	**800-772-9476**	609-771-7395	244
Ettore Products Co						
2100 N Loop Rd	Alameda	CA	94502	**800-438-8673**	510-748-4130	501
EUB (Edinboro University of Pennsylvania Baron-Forness Library)						
200 Tartan Rd	Edinboro	PA	16444	**888-845-2890**	814-732-2273	431-6
Eubanks Engineering Co						
3022 Inland Empire Blvd	Ontario	CA	91764	**800-729-4208**	909-483-2456	800
Euclid Chemical Co						
19218 Redwood Rd	Cleveland	OH	44110	**800-321-7628**	216-531-9222	3
Eudora Welty Library, The						
300 N State St	Jackson	MS	39201	**800-968-5803**	601-968-5811	431-3
Eugene Burger Management Corp						
6600 Hunter Dr	Rohnert Park	CA	94928	**800-788-0233**	707-584-5123	646
Eugene Ernst Products Company Inc						
PO Box 925	Farmingdale	NJ	07727	**800-992-2843**	732-938-5641	490
Eugene O'Neill National Historic Site						
1000 Kuss Rd	Danville	CA	94526	**866-945-7920**	925-838-0249	557
Eugene Weekly						
1251 Lincoln St	Eugene	OR	97401	**866-233-2250**	541-484-0519	525-5
Euler Hermes ACI						
800 Red Brook Blvd						
Fourth Fl	Owings Mills	MD	21117	**877-883-3224**	410-753-0753	388-5
Eureka College						
300 E College Ave	Eureka	IL	61530	**888-438-7352***	309-467-6350	166
*Admissions						
Eureka Welding Alloys Inc						
2000 E Avis Dr	Madison Heights	MI	48071	**800-962-8560**	248-588-0001	798
Euro Lloyd Travel Inc						
1640 Hempstead Tpke	East Meadow	NY	11554	**800-334-2724**	516-228-4970	761
Euro Pacific Capital Inc						
88 Post Rd W Third Fl	Westport	CT	06880	**800-727-7922**	203-662-9700	69
Europa Restaurant						
1620 S Indian Trl	Palm Springs	CA	92264	**800-245-2314**	760-327-2314	662
Europe by Car						
40 Exchange Pl Ste 1720	New York	NY	10005	**800-223-1516**	212-581-3040	125
EuroPharma Inc						
955 Challenger Dr	Green Bay	WI	54311	**866-598-5487**	920-406-6500	342

Name / Address	City	State	ZIP	Toll-Free	Phone	Class
Euro-Suites Hotel University Centre 501 Chestnut Ridge Rd	Morgantown	WV	26505	**800-678-4837**		376
Eutectic Corp N 94 W 14355 Garwin Mace Dr	Menomonee Falls	WI	53051	**800-558-8524**	262-532-4677	798
ev3 Inc 3033 Campus Dr	Plymouth	MN	55441	**800-716-6700**	763-398-7000	471
EVA Airways 200 N Sepulveda Blvd Ste 1600	El Segundo	CA	90245	**800-695-1188**	310-362-6600	25
Evan B Donaldson Adoption Institute 120 E 38th St	New York	NY	10016	**800-837-2655**	212-925-4089	47-6
Evana Automation 5825 Old Boonville Hwy	Evansville	IN	47715	**800-468-6774**	812-479-8246	208
Evangel University 1111 N Glenstone Ave	Springfield	MO	65802	**800-382-6435**	417-865-2815	166
Evangelical Church Alliance (ECA) 205 W Broadway St PO Box 9	Bradley	IL	60915	**888-855-6060**	815-937-0720	47-20
Evangelical Council for Financial Accountability (ECFA) 440 W Jubal Early Dr Ste 130	Winchester	VA	22601	**800-323-9473**	540-535-0103	47-5
Evangelical Fellowship of Canada (EFC) 600 Alden Rd Ste 300 Markham Industrial Pk	Markham	ON	L3R0E7	**866-302-3362**	905-479-5885	47-20
Evangelical Lutheran Church in America (ELCA) 8765 W Higgins Rd	Chicago	IL	60631	**800-638-3522**	773-380-2700	47-20
Evangelical School of Theology 121 S College St	Myerstown	PA	17067	**800-532-5775**	717-866-5775	167-3
Evangelical Training Assn (ETA) PO Box 327 *General	Wheaton	IL	60187	**800-369-8291***	630-384-6920	47-20
Evangelicals for Social Action (ESA) PO Box 367	Wayne	PA	19087	**800-650-6600**	484-384-2990	47-7
Evan-Moor Educational Publishers Inc 18 Lower Ragsdale Dr	Monterey	CA	93940	**800-777-4362**	831-649-5901	243
Evans & Sutherland Computer Corp 770 Komas Dr *OTC: ESCC* ▪ *Sales	Salt Lake City	UT	84108	**800-327-5707***	801-588-1000	694
Evans Bancorp Inc One Grimsby Dr *NYSE: EVBN*	Hamburg	NY	14075	**866-310-0763**	716-926-2000	357-2
Evans Dedicated Systems Inc PO Box 9	Maywood	CA	90270	**800-427-6387**	323-725-2928	770
Evans Delivery Company Inc PO Box 268	Pottsville	PA	17901	**800-666-7885**	570-385-9048	310
Evans Distribution Systems 18765 Seaway Dr	Melvindale	MI	48122	**800-653-8267**	313-388-3200	791-1
Evans Enterprises Inc 1536 S Western Ave	Oklahoma City	OK	73109	**800-423-8267**	405-631-1344	246
Evans Food Group Ltd 4118 S Halsted St	Chicago	IL	60609	**866-254-7400**	773-254-7400	295-35
Evans Tire & Service Centers Inc 510 N Broadway	Escondido	CA	92025	**877-338-2678**		61-5
Evans-Hydro 18128 S Santa Fe Ave	Rancho Dominguez	CA	90221	**800-429-7867**	310-608-5801	632
Evans-Sherratt Co 13050 Northend Ave	Oak Park	MI	48237	**800-248-3826**	248-584-5500	470
Evanston Hospital 2650 Ridge Ave	Evanston	IL	60201	**888-364-6400**	847-570-2000	371-3
Evanston Public Library 1703 Orrington Ave	Evanston	IL	60201	**888-253-7003**	847-448-8600	431-3
Evansville Auditorium & Convention Ctr 715 Locust St	Evansville	IN	47708	**844-381-4751**	812-435-5770	206
Evansville Convention & Visitors Bureau 401 SE Riverside Dr	Evansville	IN	47713	**800-433-3025**	812-421-2200	207
Evansville Courier & Press 300 E Walnut St	Evansville	IN	47713	**800-288-3200**	812-424-7711	525-2
Evansville Teachers Federal Credit Union PO Box 5129	Evansville	IN	47716	**800-800-9271**	812-477-9271	219
Evco Plastics 100 W N St PO Box 497	DeForest	WI	53532	**800-507-6000**		597
Evenflo Company Inc 1801 Commerce Dr	Piqua	OH	45356	**800-233-5921**		63
Evening Observer 8-10 E Second St PO Box 391	Dunkirk	NY	14048	**800-836-0931**	716-366-3000	525-2
Evening Sun 135 Baltimore St PO Box 514	Hanover	PA	17331	**800-877-3786**	717-637-3736	525-2
Event Planning International Corp 10900 Granite St	Charlotte	NC	28273	**800-940-2164**	980-233-3777	185
Everbrite Inc 4949 S 110th St PO Box 20020	Greenfield	WI	53220	**800-558-3888**	414-529-3500	692
Evercoat 6600 Cornell Rd	Cincinnati	OH	45242	**800-729-7600**	513-489-7600	59
Everest College 1010 W Sunshine St	Springfield	MO	65807	**888-223-8556**	417-864-7220	788
Everest College Alhambra 2215 W Mission Rd	Alhambra	CA	91803	**888-223-8556**	626-979-4940	788
Everest College Anaheim 511 N Brookhurst Ste 300	Anaheim	CA	92801	**888-224-6684**	714-953-6500	788
Everest College Aurora 14280 E Jewell Ave Ste 100	Aurora	CO	80012	**888-223-8556**	303-745-6244	788
Everest College City of Industry 12801 Crossroads Pkwy S	City of Industry	CA	91746	**888-224-6684**	562-908-2500	788
Everest College San Bernardino 217 E Club Ctr Dr Ste A	San Bernardino	CA	92408	**888-224-6684**	909-777-3300	788
Everest College San Jose 1245 S Winchester Blvd Ste 102	San Jose	CA	95128	**888-223-8556**	408-246-4171	788
Everest College Thornton 9065 Grant St	Thornton	CO	80229	**888-223-8556**	303-457-2757	788
Everest Institute 21107 Lahser Rd *General	Southfield	MI	48033	**800-611-2101***	248-799-9933	788
Everest Institute Long Beach 2161 Technology Pl	Long Beach	CA	90810	**888-223-8556**	562-624-9530	788
Everest Re Group Ltd 477 Martinsville Rd PO Box 830	Liberty Corner	NJ	07938	**800-269-6660**	908-604-3000	357-4
Everest Reinsurance Co 477 Martinsville Rd	Liberty Corner	NJ	07938	**800-269-6660**	908-604-3000	388-5
Brandon 3924 Coconut Palm Dr *Cust Svc	Tampa	FL	33619	**877-439-0003***	813-621-0041	788
Jacksonville 8226 Phillips Hwy	Jacksonville	FL	32256	**800-611-2101**	904-731-4949	788
Lakeland 995 E Memorial Blvd Ste 110	Lakeland	FL	33801	**888-223-8556**	863-686-1444	788
Largo 1199 E Bay Dr	Largo	FL	33770	**888-223-8556**	727-725-2688	788
Everest University *North Orlando* 5421 Diplomat Cir	Orlando	FL	32810	**888-223-8556**	407-628-5870	788
Orange Park 805 Wells Rd	Orange Park	FL	32073	**888-223-8556**	904-264-9122	788
Pompano Beach 225 N Federal Hwy	Pompano Beach	FL	33062	**888-223-8556**	954-783-7339	788
South Orlando 9200 Southpark Ctr Loop	Orlando	FL	32819	**800-611-2101**	407-851-2525	788
Tampa 3319 W Hillsborough Ave	Tampa	FL	33614	**888-223-8556**	813-879-6000	788
Everett Community College 2000 Tower St	Everett	WA	98201	**866-575-9027**	425-388-9100	160
Everett J Prescott Inc 32 Prescott St	Gardiner	ME	04345	**800-357-2447**	207-582-1851	605
Everfast Inc 203 Gale Ln *Cust Svc	Kennett Square	PA	19348	**800-213-6366***	610-444-9700	270
eVerge Group Inc 4965 Preston Pk Blvd Ste 700	Plano	TX	75093	**888-548-1973**	972-608-1803	181
Everglades Boats 544 Air Pk Rd	Edgewater	FL	32132	**800-368-5647**	386-409-2202	89
Evergreen Enterprises Inc 5915 Midlothian Trnpk	Richmond	VA	23225	**877-558-1511**	804-231-1800	319
Evergreen FS Inc 402 N Hershey Rd	Bloomington	IL	61704	**877-963-2392**	309-663-2392	276
Evergreen Hospice Services 12822 124th Ln NE	Kirkland	WA	98034	**877-980-7500**	425-899-1070	368
Evergreen Lodge 250 S Frontage Rd W	Vail	CO	81657	**800-284-8245**	970-476-7810	376
Evergreen Marriott Conference Resort 4021 Lakeview Dr	Stone Mountain	GA	30083	**800-228-9290**	770-879-9900	374
Evergreen Resort 7880 Mackinaw Trail	Cadillac	MI	49601	**800-634-7302**		660
Evergreen State College 2700 Evergreen Pkwy	Olympia	WA	98505	**888-492-9480**	360-867-6000	166
Evergreen Woods 88 Notch Hill Rd *General	North Branford	CT	06471	**866-413-6378***	203-488-8000	663
Evergreens, The 309 Bridgeboro Rd	Moorestown	NJ	08057	**877-673-8234**	856-439-2000	663
EverHome Mortgage Co 301 W Bay St *Cust Svc	Jacksonville	FL	32202	**800-669-9721***		502
Everi Holdings Inc (GCA) 7250 S Tenaya Way Ste 100 *NYSE: EVRI*	Las Vegas	NV	89113	**800-833-7110**	702-855-3000	55
Everist Genomics Inc 709 W Ellsworth Rd	Ann Arbor	MI	48108	**855-383-7478**		732
Everlaw 2020 Milvia St Ste 220	Berkeley	CA	94704	**844-383-7529**		384
Everprint International Inc 18021 Cortney Ct	City of Industry	CA	91748	**800-984-5777**		176
Everpure LLC 1040 Muirfield Dr	Hanover Park	IL	60133	**800-323-7873**	630-307-3000	794
Eversource 1 Nstar Way NW200 *Cust Svc	Westwood	MA	02090	**800-592-2000***	781-441-8011	775
EverTrue LLC 330 Congress St Second Fl	Boston	MA	02210	**855-387-8783**		384
Everwise Corp 1178 Broadway Fourth Fl	New York	NY	10001	**888-734-0011**		384
EVH Mfg Company LLC 4895 Red Bluff Rd	Loris	SC	29569	**888-990-2555**	843-756-2555	273
EVINE Live Inc 6740 Shady Oak Rd	Eden Prairie	MN	55344	**800-676-5523**		729
Evogi Group Inc, The 20645 N Pima Rd Bldg N Ste 130	Scottsdale	AZ	85255	**888-277-5573**		197
Evolution Computing 7000 N 16th St Ste 120 514	Phoenix	AZ	85020	**800-874-4028**		179-5
EW Kaufmann Co 140 Wharton Rd	Bristol	PA	19007	**800-635-5358**	215-364-0240	144
EW Scripps Co 312 Walnut St Ste 2800 *NYSE: SSP*	Cincinnati	OH	45202	**800-888-3000**	513-977-3000	628-8
EW Wylie Corp 1520 Second Ave NW *Cust Svc	West Fargo	ND	58078	**800-437-4132***	701-282-5550	770
EWA (Enterprise Wireless Alliance) 8484 Westpark Dr Ste 630	McLean	VA	22102	**800-482-8282**	703-528-5115	48-20
EWA Inc (Electronic Warfare Assoc Inc) 13873 Pk Ctr Rd Ste 500 *General	Herndon	VA	20171	**888-392-0002***	703-904-5700	181
EWI (Executive Women International) 7414 S State St	Midvale	UT	84047	**877-439-4669**	801-355-2800	48-12
EWI (Elliott Wave International) PO Box 1618 *Cust Svc	Gainesville	GA	30503	**800-336-1618***	770-536-0309	628-9
Ewing Marion Kauffman Foundation (EMKF) 4801 Rockhill Rd	Kansas City	MO	64110	**800-385-1607**	816-932-1000	304
eWorkplace Solutions Inc 24461 Ridge Rt Dr Ste 210	Laguna Hills	CA	92653	**888-477-7989**	949-583-1646	179-8
Exactech Inc 2320 NW 66th Ct *NASDAQ: EXAC*	Gainesville	FL	32653	**800-392-2832**	352-377-1140	472
ExaDigm Inc 2871 Pullman St	Santa Ana	CA	92705	**800-933-0064**	949-486-0320	195
Exalpha Biologicals Inc Five Clock Tower Pl Ste 255	Maynard	MA	01754	**800-395-1137**		231
ExamWorks Inc 3280 Peachtree Rd Ste 2625	Atlanta	GA	30305	**877-628-4703**		412
Excalibur Extrusions Inc 110 E Crowther Ave	Placentia	CA	92870	**800-648-6804**	714-528-8834	589

Alphabetical Section

Company / Address	City	State	Zip	Toll-Free	Phone	Class
Excalibur Hotel & Casino						
3850 Las Vegas Blvd S						
PO Box 96776	Las Vegas	NV	89109	**877-750-5464**	702-597-7777	132
Excel Homes Inc						
10642 S Susquehanna Trail	Liverpool	PA	17045	**800-521-8599***	717-444-3395	188
*Sales						
Excel Telecommunications						
433 Las Colinas Blvd Ste 400	Irving	TX	75039	**877-668-0808**	972-910-1900	726
Excelda Manufacturing Co						
12785 Emerson Dr	Brighton	MI	48116	**877-486-3801**	248-486-3800	143
Ex-Cell Metal Products Inc						
11240 Melrose St	Franklin Park	IL	60131	**800-392-3557**	847-451-0451	286
Excelligence Learning Corp						
2 Lower Ragsdale Dr Ste 125	Monterey	CA	93940	**800-627-2829**	831-333-5572	243
Excellon Automation Inc						
20001 S Rancho Way	Rancho Dominguez	CA	90220	**800-392-3556**	310-668-7700	465
Excellus BlueCross BlueShield						
PO Box 22999	Rochester	NY	14692	**800-278-1247**	585-454-1700	388-3
Excellus BlueCross BlueShield of Central New York						
333 Butternut Dr	Syracuse	NY	13214	**800-633-6066**	315-671-6400	388-3
Excelsior College						
Seven Columbia Cir	Albany	NY	12203	**888-647-2388**	518-464-8500	166
Excelsior Grand						
2380 Hylan Blvd	Staten Island	NY	10306	**888-233-6743**	718-987-4800	298
Excelsior Marking Products						
888 W Waterloo Rd	Akron	OH	44314	**800-433-3615**	330-745-2300	462
Exchange State Bank						
3992 Chandler St PO Box 68	Carsonville	MI	48419	**888-488-9300**	810-657-9333	69
Exchange, The						
3911 S Walton Walker Blvd	Dallas	TX	75236	**800-527-2345**	214-312-2011	779
EXCO Resources Inc						
12377 Merit Dr Ste 1700	Dallas	TX	75251	**888-788-9449**	214-368-2084	531
NYSE: XCO						
Exec Air Montana Inc						
2430 Airport Rd	Helena	MT	59601	**800-513-2190**	406-442-2190	13
ExecSuite						
Third Ave SW Ste 702	Calgary	AB	T2P3B4	**800-667-4980**	403-294-5800	211
ExecUNet Inc						
295 Westport Ave	Norwalk	CT	06851	**800-637-3126**	203-750-1030	260
Executive Car Leasing Inc						
7807 Santa Monica Blvd	Los Angeles	CA	90046	**800-994-2277**	323-654-5000	289
Executive Enterprises Institute						
12 Skyline Dr	Hawthorne	NY	10532	**877-334-4273**	914-517-1122	755
Executive Hotel Vintage Court						
650 Bush St	San Francisco	CA	94108	**888-388-3932**	415-392-4666	376
Executive Inn						
978 Phillips Ln	Louisville	KY	40209	**888-205-8144**	502-367-6161	376
Executive Inn Group Corp						
Executive Hotels & Resorts						
1080 Howe St Eighth Fl	Vancouver	BC	V6Z2T1	**866-642-6888**	604-642-5250	376
Executive Jet						
4556 Airport Rd	Cincinnati	OH	45226	**877-356-5387**	513-979-6600	13
Executive Office Concepts Inc						
1705 S Anderson Ave	Compton	CA	90220	**800-421-5927**	310-537-1657	318-1
Executive Pacific Plaza Hotel						
400 Spring St	Seattle	WA	98104	**888-388-3932**	206-623-3900	376
Executive Speakers Bureau						
8567 Cordes Cir	Germantown	TN	38139	**800-754-9404**	901-754-9404	699
Executive Suite Hotel						
4360 SpenaRd Rd	Anchorage	AK	99517	**800-770-6366**	907-243-6366	376
Executive Women International (EWI)						
7414 S State St	Midvale	UT	84047	**877-439-4669**	801-355-2800	48-12
Exel						
570 Polaris Pkwy	Westerville	OH	43082	**800-272-1052**	614-865-8500	444
eXelate						
Seven W 22nd St Ninth Fl	New York	NY	10010	**877-896-3282**	646-380-4400	461
EXFO Inc 400 Godin Ave	Quebec	QC	G1M2K2	**800-663-3936**	418-683-0211	248
NASDAQ: EXFO						
Exide Technologies						
13000 Deerfield Pkwy Bldg 200	Milton	GA	30004	**800-782-7848**	678-566-9000	73
NASDAQ: XIDE						
Exopack LLC						
3070 Southport Rd						
PO Box 5687	Spartanburg	SC	29302	**877-447-3539**	864-596-7140	541
Exp Pharmaceutical Services Corp						
48021 Warm Springs Blvd	Fremont	CA	94539	**800-350-0397**	510-476-0909	792
Expanding Light						
14618 Tyler Foote Rd	Nevada City	CA	95959	**800-346-5350**	530-478-7518	664
Expanko Inc						
180 Gordon Dr Ste 113	Exton	PA	19341	**800-345-6202**		291
Expansion Management Magazine						
1300 E Ninth St	Cleveland	OH	44114	**866-505-7173**	216-696-7000	452-5
Expedient Communications						
810 Parish St	Pittsburgh	PA	15220	**877-570-7827**	412-316-7800	395
Expeditors International of Washington Inc						
1015 Third Ave 12th Fl	Seattle	WA	98104	**800-284-7474**	206-674-3400	444
NASDAQ: EXPD						
Experian Information Solutions Inc						
475 Anton Blvd	Costa Mesa	CA	92626	**888-397-3742***	714-830-7000	218
*Cust Svc						
Experience Works Inc						
2200 Clarendon Blvd Ste 1000	Arlington	VA	22203	**866-397-9757**	703-522-7272	47-6
Experimental Aircraft Assn (EAA)						
3000 Poberezny Rd	Oshkosh	WI	54902	**800-236-4800**	920-426-4800	47-18
Expert Choice Inc						
1501 Lee Hwy Ste 302	Arlington	VA	22209	**888-259-6400**	703-243-5595	179-12
Expert Evidence Report						
1801 S Bell St	Arlington	VA	22202	**800-372-1033**		524-7
Expert Global Solutions, Inc						
507 Prudential Rd	Horsham	PA	19044	**800-220-2274**	215-441-3000	158
Experts Inc, The						
2400 E Commercial Blvd						
Ste 614	Fort Lauderdale	FL	33308	**888-748-3526**	954-493-8040	178
Exploration Place						
300 N McLean Blvd	Wichita	KS	67203	**877-904-1444**	316-660-0600	514
Exploratorium, The						
3601 Lyon St	San Francisco	CA	94123	**800-232-9698**	415-561-0360	513
Explore Information Services LLC						
2900 Lone Oak Pkwy Ste 140						
PO Box 21636	St. Paul	MN	55121	**800-531-9125**		626
Explorica Inc						
145 Tremont St	Boston	MA	02111	**888-310-7120**		750
Expo Group, The						
5931 W Campus Cir Dr	Irving	TX	75063	**800-736-7775**	972-580-9000	185

Company / Address	City	State	Zip	Toll-Free	Phone	Class
Expo Square						
4145 E 21st St	Tulsa	OK	74114	**877-781-2660**	918-744-1113	206
Expon Exhibits						
909 Fee Dr	Sacramento	CA	95815	**800-783-9766**	916-924-1600	232
Exponent Inc						
149 Commonwealth Dr	Menlo Park	CA	94025	**888-656-3976**	650-326-9400	659
NASDAQ: EXPO						
Exponent Telegram						
324 Hewes Ave	Clarksburg	WV	26301	**800-982-6034**		525-2
Export-Import Bank of the US						
811 Vermont Ave NW	Washington	DC	20571	**800-565-3946**	202-565-3946	338-18
Express						
One Limited Pkwy	Columbus	OH	43230	**888-397-1980**		155-6
NYSE: EXPR						
Express Employment Professionals						
8516 NW Expy	Oklahoma City	OK	73162	**800-222-4057**	405-840-5000	712
Express Oil Change						
1880 S Pk Dr	Hoover	AL	35244	**888-945-1771**	205-945-1771	61-5
Express-News Corp						
PO Box 2171	San Antonio	TX	78297	**800-555-1551**	210-250-3000	628-8
Express-Times						
30 N Fourth St	Easton	PA	18042	**800-360-3601**	610-258-7171	525-2
Expressway Hotels						
4303 17th Ave S	Fargo	ND	58103	**877-239-4303**	701-239-4303	376
Extended Care Hospital Westminster						
206 Hospital Cir	Westminster	CA	92683	**800-236-9747**	714-891-2769	445
Extended Stay America						
11525 N Community House Rd						
Ste 100	Charlotte	NC	28277	**800-804-3724**	980-345-1600	376
Crossland Economy Studios						
11525 N Community House Rd						
Ste 100	Charlotte	NC	28277	**800-804-3724**	980-345-1600	376
Extended StayAmerica						
11525 N Community House Rd						
Ste 100	Charlotte	NC	28277	**800-804-3724**	980-345-1600	376
Extended Stay Hotels						
StudioPLUS Deluxe Studios						
530 Woods Lake Rd	Greenville	SC	29607	**800-804-3724**	864-288-4300	376
Extensis						
1800 SW First Ave Ste 500	Portland	OR	97201	**800-796-9798**	503-274-2020	178
Exterran						
16666 Northchase Dr	Houston	TX	77060	**800-975-9090***	281-836-7000	382
*Sales						
EXTOL International Inc						
529 Terry Reiley Way	Pottsville	PA	17901	**800-542-7284**	570-628-5500	179-7
Extreme Networks Inc						
3585 Monroe St	Santa Clara	CA	95051	**888-257-3000**	408-579-2800	177
NASDAQ: EXTR						
Extreme Pita						
2187 Dunwin Dr	Mississauga	ON	L5L1X2	**888-729-7482**	905-820-7887	309
Extreme Plastics Plus Inc						
148 Roush Cir	Fairmont	WV	26554	**866-408-2837**		529
Extreme Reach Inc						
75 2nd Ave Ste 720	Needham	MA	02494	**888-326-8733**	781-577-2016	504
NASDAQ: DGIT						
Extron Electronics						
1230 S Lewis St	Anaheim	CA	92805	**800-633-9876***	714-491-1500	51
*Tech Supp						
Extrude Hone Corp						
235 Industry Blvd	Irwin	PA	15642	**800-367-1109**	724-863-5900	450
Exxon Mobil Corp						
5959 Las Colinas Blvd	Irving	TX	75039	**800-252-1800**	972-444-1000	529
NYSE: XOM						
Eyde Co						
4660 S Hagadorn Ste 660	East Lansing	MI	48823	**800-422-3933**	517-351-2480	188
Eye Bank Assn of America (EBAA)						
1015 18th St NW Ste 1010	Washington	DC	20036	**888-491-8833**	202-775-4999	48-8
Eye Bank for Sight Restoration Inc						
120 Wall St 3rd Fl	New York	NY	10005	**866-287-3937**	212-742-9000	269
Eye Centers of Florida (ECOF)						
4101 Evans Ave	Fort Myers	FL	33901	**888-393-2455**	239-939-3456	786
Eye Communication Systems Inc						
455 E Industrial Dr	Hartland	WI	53029	**800-558-2153**	262-367-1360	491
Eye Glass World Inc						
296 Grayson Hwy	Lawrenceville	GA	30046	**800-637-3597**		536
Eye Lighting International NA						
9150 Hendricks Rd	Mentor	OH	44060	**888-665-2677***	440-350-7000	433
*Cust Svc						
Eyefinity Inc						
10875 International Dr						
Ste 200	Rancho Cordova	CA	95670	**877-448-0707**		178
Eye-Kraft Optical Inc						
8 McLeland Rd	Saint Cloud	MN	56303	**888-455-2022**		535
Eye-Mart Express Inc						
13800 Senlac Dr Ste 200	Dallas	TX	75234	**888-372-2763**	972-488-2002	536
EyeMed Vision Care						
4000 Luxottica Pl	Mason	OH	45040	**800-521-3605**	513-765-4321	388-3
Eyre Bus Service Inc						
13600 Triadelphia Rd PO Box 239	Glenelg	MD	21737	**800-321-3973**	410-442-1330	106
EZ Loader Boat Trailers Inc						
717 N Hamilton St	Spokane	WA	99202	**800-398-5623**	509-489-0181	753
E-Z Mart Stores						
602 W Falvey Ave PO Box 1426	Texarkana	TX	75501	**800-234-6502**	903-832-6502	205
EZ Trail Inc						
1050 E Columbia St PO Box 168	Arthur	IL	61911	**800-677-2802**	217-543-3471	273
ezCater Inc						
101 Arch St Ste 410	Boston	MA	02110	**800-488-1803**		384
EZCORP Inc						
1901 Capital Pkwy	Austin	TX	78746	**800-873-7296**	512-314-3400	562
NASDAQ: EZPW						
Eze Castle Integration Inc						
260 Franklin St 12th Fl	Boston	MA	02110	**800-752-1382**	617-217-3000	196
Ezenia! Inc						
14 Celina Ave Unit 17	Nashua	NH	03063	**800-966-2301**	781-505-2100	177
E-Z-GO						
1451 Marvin Griffin Rd	Augusta	GA	30906	**800-241-5855**		509
E-Z-GO Division of Textron Inc						
1451 Marvin Griffin Rd	Augusta	GA	30906	**800-241-5855**	706-798-4311	760

F

Company / Address	City	State	ZIP	Toll-Free	Phone	Class
F & H Ribbon Co Inc						
3010 S Pipeline Rd	Euless	TX	76040	**800-877-5775**		767
F & M Hat Co Inc						
103 Walnut St PO Box 40	Denver	PA	17517	**800-953-4287**	717-336-5505	153-8
F C Kerbeck & Sons						
100 Rt 73 N	Palmyra	NJ	08065	**855-846-1500***	856-829-8200	56
*General						
F Mcconnell & Sons Inc						
11102 Lincoln Hwy E	New Haven	IN	46774	**800-552-0835**	260-493-6607	296-8
F+W, A Content + eCommerce Company						
10151 Carver Rd Ste 200	Cincinnati	OH	45236	**800-289-0963***	513-531-2690	628-9
*Sales						
F-11 Photographic Supplies						
16 E Main St	Bozeman	MT	59715	**888-548-0203**	406-586-3281	118
F5 Networks Inc						
401 Elliott Ave W	Seattle	WA	98119	**888-882-4447**	206-272-5555	177
NASDAQ: FFIV						
FA Bartlett Tree Expert Co						
1290 E Main St	Stamford	CT	06902	**877-227-8538**	203-323-1131	766
FA Davis Co						
1915 Arch St	Philadelphia	PA	19103	**800-323-3555**	215-568-2270	628-2
FAA (Federal Aviation Administration)						
800 Independence Ave SW	Washington	DC	20591	**866-835-5322**		338-15
FAA Credit Union						
PO Box 26406	Oklahoma City	OK	73126	**800-448-1990**	405-682-1990	219
Faac Inc						
1229 Oak Valley Dr	Ann Arbor	MI	48108	**877-322-2387**	734-761-5836	694
FAAN (Food Allergy & Anaphylaxis Network)						
11781 Lee Jackson Hwy Ste 160	Fairfax	VA	22033	**800-929-4040**	703-691-3179	47-17
Fabcon Inc						
6111 Hwy 13 W	Savage	MN	55378	**800-727-4444**	952-890-4444	184
Fabian's Investment Resources						
300 New Jersey Ave NW						
Ste 500	Washington	DC	20001	**800-950-8765**	267-295-8713	524-9
Fabral Inc						
3449 Hempland Rd	Lancaster	PA	17601	**800-477-2741**	717-397-2741	475
Fabreeka International Inc						
1023 Tpke St	Stoughton	MA	02072	**800-322-7352***	781-341-3655	668
*Cust Svc						
Fabricated Components Inc						
PO Box 431	Stroudsburg	PA	18360	**800-233-8163**	570-421-4110	477
Fabrication JR Tardif Inc						
62 Blvd Cartier	Rivi Re-Du-Loup	QC	G5R6B2	**877-962-7273**	418-862-7273	273
Fabricators & Manufacturers Assn International (FMA)						
833 Featherstone Rd	Rockford	IL	61107	**888-394-4362**	815-399-8700	48-13
Fabricon Products						
1721 W Pleasant Ave	River Rouge	MI	48218	**800-676-9727**	313-841-8200	547
Fabricut Inc						
9303 E 46th St	Tulsa	OK	74145	**800-999-8200**	918-622-7700	358
Fabri-Form Co						
200 S Friendship Dr	New Concord	OH	43762	**800-837-2574**	740-826-5000	595
Fabri-Kal Corp						
600 Plastics Pl	Kalamazoo	MI	49001	**800-888-5054**	269-385-5050	595
Fabri-Quilt Inc						
901 E 14th Ave	North Kansas City	MO	64116	**800-279-0622**	816-421-2000	258
Fabritech Inc						
5740 Salmen St	New Orleans	LA	70123	**888-733-5009**	504-733-5009	734-8
FACC (Franklin Area Chamber of Commerce)						
1259 Liberty St	Franklin	PA	16323	**888-547-2377**	814-432-5823	137
Face Stockholm Ltd						
324 Joslen Blvd	Hudson	NY	12534	**888-334-3223**	518-828-6600	231
Facets Multimedia Inc						
1517 W Fullerton Ave	Chicago	IL	60614	**800-331-6197***	773-281-9075	504
*Cust Svc						
Facility Solutions Group (FSG)						
4401 Westgate Blvd Ste 310	Austin	TX	78745	**800-854-6465**	512-440-7985	246
Facing History & Ourselves						
16 HuRd Rd	Brookline	MA	02445	**800-856-9039**	617-232-1595	47-11
Faction Media LLP						
1730 Blake St Ste 200	Denver	CO	80202	**866-788-5306**		7
FactSet Research Systems Inc						
601 Merritt 7 Third Fl	Norwalk	CT	06851	**877-322-8738**	203-810-1000	401
NYSE: FDS						
FACVB (Fayetteville Area Convention & Visitors Bureau)						
245 Person St	Fayetteville	NC	28301	**800-255-8217**	910-483-5311	207
FAE (New York State Society of Certified Public Accountant)						
14 Wall St 19th Fl	New York	NY	10005	**800-537-3635***	212-719-8300	48-1
*General						
Faegre & Benson LLP						
90 S Seventh St						
2200 Wells Fargo Bldg	Minneapolis	MN	55402	**800-328-4393**	612-766-7000	425
FAF (Form-A-Feed Inc)						
740 Bowman St	Stewart	MN	55385	**800-422-3649**	320-562-2413	442
Fafco Inc						
435 Otterson Dr	Chico	CA	95928	**800-994-7652**	530-332-2100	90
FAHC (University of Vermont Medical Center, The)						
111 Colchester Ave	Burlington	VT	05401	**800-358-1144**	802-847-0000	371-3
Fahlgren Inc						
4030 Easton Station Ste 300	Columbus	OH	43219	**800-731-8927**	614-383-1500	4
FAIA (Pekin Insurance)						
2505 Ct St	Pekin	IL	61558	**800-322-0160**	309-346-1161	388-4
FAIR (Federation for American Immigration Reform)						
25 Massachusetts Ave NW						
Ste 330	Washington	DC	20009	**877-627-3247**	202-328-7004	47-7
Fair Grounds Race Course						
1751 Gentilly Blvd	New Orleans	LA	70119	**800-262-7983**	504-944-5515	633
Fair Haven Beach State Park						
14985 State Park Rd	Sterling	NY	13156	**800-456-2267***	315-947-5205	558
*General						
Fair Hills Resort						
24270 County Hwy 20	Detroit Lakes	MN	56501	**800-323-2849***	218-847-7638	660
*Resv						
Fair Isaac Corp						
2665 Long Lake Rd Bldg C	Roseville	MN	55113	**888-342-6336***	612-758-5200	225
NYSE: FICO ■ *Cust Svc						

Company / Address	City	State	ZIP	Toll-Free	Phone	Class
Fair Meadows at Tulsa						
4609 E 21st St	Tulsa	OK	74114	**877-781-2660**	918-743-7223	633
Fair Oaks Hospital						
5352 Linton Blvd	Delray Beach	FL	33484	**866-904-6871**	561-498-4440	371-5
Fair Winds Air Charter Inc						
2525 SE Witham Field Hngr 7	Stuart	FL	34996	**800-989-9665**	772-288-4130	13
Fairbanks Chamber of Commerce						
100 Cushman St Ste 102	Fairbanks	AK	99701	**800-770-8255**	907-452-1105	137
Fairbanks Convention & Visitors Bureau						
101 Dunkel St Ste 111	Fairbanks	AK	99701	**800-327-5774**	907-456-5774	207
Fairbanks Correctional Ctr						
1931 Eagan Ave	Fairbanks	AK	99701	**877-741-0741**	907-458-6700	213
Fairbanks Hospital						
8102 Clearvista Pkwy	Indianapolis	IN	46256	**800-225-4673**	317-849-8222	717
Fairbanks Princess Riverside Lodge						
4477 Pikes Landing Rd	Fairbanks	AK	99709	**800-426-0500**	907-455-4477	376
Fairbanks Scales Inc						
821 Locust St	Kansas City	MO	64106	**800-451-4107**	816-471-0231	675
Fairbanks Youth Facility						
1502 Wilbur St	Fairbanks	AK	99701	**800-478-2686**	907-451-2150	409
FairBridge Inns LLC						
421 W Riverside Ave Ste 407	Spokane	WA	99201	**877-866-8090**		375
Fairchild Auto-mated Parts Inc						
10 White St	Winsted	CT	06098	**800-927-2545**	860-379-2725	614
Fairchild Controls Corp						
540 Highland St	Frederick	MD	21701	**800-695-5378**	301-228-3400	22
Fairchild Imaging Inc						
1801 McCarthy Blvd	Milpitas	CA	95035	**800-325-6975**	408-433-2500	687
Fairchild Industrial Products Co						
3920 Westpoint Blvd	Winston-Salem	NC	27103	**800-334-8422**	336-659-3400	202
Fairchild Semiconductor Corp						
82 Running Hill Rd	South Portland	ME	04106	**800-341-0392**	207-775-8100	687
NASDAQ: FCS						
Fairfax County Convention & Visitors Bureau (FXVA)						
3702 Pender Dr Ste 420	Fairfax	VA	22030	**800-732-4732**	703-790-0643	207
Fairfax Hospital						
10200 NE 132nd St	Kirkland	WA	98034	**800-435-7221**	425-821-2000	371-5
Fairfax PET Imaging Ctr						
8503 Arlington Blvd						
Ste 120 Lowr Level	Fairfax	VA	22031	**800-358-8831**	703-698-4441	759
Fairfield Industries Inc						
1111 Gillingham Ln	Sugar Land	TX	77478	**800-231-9809**	281-275-7500	467
Fairfield Medical Ctr (FMC)						
401 N Ewing St	Lancaster	OH	43130	**800-548-2627**	740-687-8000	371-3
Fairfield Processing Corp						
88 Rose Hill Ave	Danbury	CT	06810	**800-980-8000**	203-744-2090	598-1
Fairfield University						
Fairfield University						
1073 N Benson Rd	Fairfield	CT	06824	**877-278-7396**	203-254-4010	565
Fairhaven						
7200 Third Ave	Sykesville	MD	21784	**877-696-6775**	410-795-8801	663
FairHope Hospice & Palliative Care Inc						
282 Sells Rd	Lancaster	OH	43130	**800-994-7077**	740-654-7077	368
Fairlane Town Ctr						
18900 Michigan Ave	Dearborn	MI	48126	**800-992-9500**		455
Fairleigh Dickinson University						
285 Madison Ave	Madison	NJ	07940	**800-338-8803**	973-443-8500	166
Metropolitan						
1000 River Rd	Teaneck	NJ	07666	**800-338-8803**	201-692-2000	166
FairMarket Life Settlements Corp						
435 Ford Rd Ste 120	St Louis Park	MN	55426	**866-326-3757**		387
Fairmont Banff Springs						
PO Box 960	Banff	AB	T1L1J4	**800-441-1414**	403-762-2211	660
Fairmont Chateau Lake Louise						
111 Lk Louise Dr	Lake Louise	AB	T0L1E0	**800-441-1414**	403-522-3511	660
Fairmont Chateau Whistler						
4599 Chateau Blvd	Whistler	BC	V0N1B4	**800-441-1414**	604-938-8000	660
Fairmont Convention & Visitors Bureau						
323 E Blue Earth Ave	Fairmont	MN	56031	**800-657-3280**	507-235-8585	207
Fairmont Hot Springs Resort						
1500 Fairmont Rd	Fairmont	MT	59711	**800-332-3272**	406-797-3241	660
Fairmont Hotels & Resorts Inc						
100 Wellington St W						
TD Ctr Ste 1600	Toronto	ON	M5K1B7	**800-441-3313***	416-874-2600	376
*General						
Fairmont Kea Lani Maui						
4100 Wailea Alanui Dr	Wailea-makena	HI	96753	**800-659-4100**	808-875-4100	660
Fairmont Le Chateau Montebello						
392 Notre Dame St	Montebello	QC	J0V1L0	**800-441-1414**	819-423-6341	660
Fairmont Orchid Hawaii						
One N Kaniku Dr	Kamuela	HI	96743	**800-845-9905**	808-885-2000	660
Fairmont San Francisco Hotel, The						
950 Mason St	San Francisco	CA	94108	**800-257-7544**	415-772-5000	375
Fairmont Scottsdale Princess						
7575 E Princess Dr	Scottsdale	AZ	85255	**800-257-7544**	480-585-4848	660
Fairmont Sonoma Mission Inn & Spa, The						
PO Box 1447	Sonoma	CA	95476	**866-540-4499**	707-938-9000	660
Fairmont State University						
1201 Locust Ave	Fairmont	WV	26554	**800-641-5678***	304-367-4892	166
*Admissions						
Fairmount Behavioral Health System						
561 Fairthorne Ave	Philadelphia	PA	19128	**800-235-0200**	215-487-4000	371-5
Fairmount Hotel, The						
401 S Alamo St	San Antonio	TX	78205	**877-229-8808**	210-224-8800	376
FairPoint Communications Inc						
521 E Morehead St Ste 250	Charlotte	NC	28202	**866-740-2764**	704-344-8150	726
NASDAQ: FRP						
Fair-Rite Products Corp						
One Commerical Row PO Box J	Wallkill	NY	12589	**888-324-7748**	845-895-2055	249
Fairview Health Services						
2450 Riverside Ave	Minneapolis	MN	55454	**800-824-1953**	612-672-6000	350
Fairview Hospice						
2450 26th Ave S	Minneapolis	MN	55406	**800-285-5647**	612-728-2455	368
Fairview Hospital						
18101 Lorain Ave	Cleveland	OH	44111	**800-801-2273**	216-476-7000	371-3
Fairview University Medical Ctr Mesabi						
750 E 34th St	Hibbing	MN	55746	**888-870-8626**	218-262-4881	371-3
Fairview-Riverside State Park						
119 Fairview Dr	Madisonville	LA	70447	**888-677-3247**	985-845-3318	558
Fairweather LLC						
9525 King St	Anchorage	AK	99515	**800-319-8802**	907-346-3247	532
Fairwinds Federal Credit Union						
3087 N Alafaya Trl	Orlando	FL	32826	**800-443-6887**	407-277-5045	219

Name / Address	City	State	ZIP	Toll-Free	Phone	Class
Faith Baptist Bible College 1900 NW Fourth St	Ankeny	IA	50023	**800-409-3305**	515-964-0601	159
Faith Popcorn's BrainReserve 885 Second Ave 16th Fl 1 Dad Hammarskjold Plz	New York	NY	10017	**800-873-6337**	212-772-7778	196
FaithTrust Institute 2400 N 45th St Ste 101	Seattle	WA	98103	**877-860-2255**	206-634-1903	47-17
Falcon Crest Aviation Supply Inc 8318 Braniff	Houston	TX	77061	**800-833-8229**	713-644-2290	256
Falcon Express Inc 2250 E Church St PO Box 4897	Philadelphia	PA	19124	**800-544-6566**	215-992-3140	770
Falcon Foundry Co 96 Sixth St	Lowellville	OH	44436	**800-253-8624**	330-536-6221	307
Falcon Safety Products Inc 25 Chubb Way	Somerville	NJ	08876	**800-332-5266**	908-707-4900	149
Fall River Area Chamber of Commerce & Industry 200 Pocasset St	Fall River	MA	02721	**800-647-2824**	508-676-8226	137
Fall River Public Library 104 N Main St	Fall River	MA	02720	**800-331-3764**	508-324-2700	431-3
Fall River Rural Electric Co-op Inc 1150 N 3400 E	Ashton	ID	83420	**800-632-5726**	208-652-7431	245
Fallbrook Ctr 6633 Fallbrook Ave	West Hills	CA	91307	**866-718-1649**	818-885-9700	455
Fallon 901 Marquette Ave Ste 2400	Minneapolis	MN	55402	**888-758-2345**	612-758-2345	4
Fallon Community Health Plan Inc 10 Chestnut St Ste 7	Worcester	MA	01608	**800-333-2535**	508-799-2100	388-3
Fallsview Casino Resort 6380 Fallsview Blvd	Niagara Falls	ON	L2G7X5	**888-325-5788**		660
Falmouth Chamber of Commerce 20 Academy Ln	Falmouth	MA	02540	**800-526-8532**	508-548-8500	137
Falmouth Inn 824 Main St	Falmouth	MA	02540	**800-255-4157**	508-540-2500	376
False Cape State Park 4001 Sandpiper Rd *General	Virginia Beach	VA	23456	**800-933-7275***	757-426-7128	558
Fam Funds 384 N Grand St PO Box 310	Cobleskill	NY	12043	**800-721-5391**	518-234-4393	316
FAME (Maine Finance Authority of Maine) 5 Community Dr PO Box 949	Augusta	ME	04332	**800-228-3734**	207-623-3263	716
Families Against Mandatory Minimums (FAMM) 1612 K St NW Ste 700	Washington	DC	20006	**800-435-7352**	202-822-6700	47-8
Families USA 1201 New York Ave NW Ste 1100	Washington	DC	20005	**888-392-5132**	202-628-3030	47-7
Family Brands International LLC 1001 Elm Hill Rd PO Box 429	Lenoir City	TN	37771	**800-356-4455**		295-26
Family Career & Community Leaders of America (FCCLA) 1910 Assn Dr	Reston	VA	20191	**800-234-4425**	703-476-4900	47-11
Family Caregiver Alliance (FCA) 180 Montgomery St Ste 900	San Francisco	CA	94104	**800-445-8106**	415-434-3388	47-17
Family Cir Magazine 375 Lexington Ave 9th Fl	New York	NY	10017	**800-627-4444**		452-11
Family Credit Counseling Service 111 N Wabash Ste 1408	Chicago	IL	60602	**800-994-3328**		40
Family Dollar Stores Inc PO Box 1017 *NYSE: FDO*	Charlotte	NC	28201	**866-377-6420**	704-847-6961	779
Family Handyman Magazine 2915 Commers Dr Ste 700	Eagan	MN	55121	**800-285-4961**		452-14
Family Home Hospice 2724 N Tenaya Way Ste 201	Las Vegas	NV	89128	**800-748-6773**	702-242-7000	368
Family Hospice & Palliative Care 50 Moffett St	Pittsburgh	PA	15243	**800-513-2148**	412-572-8800	368
Family Law Reporter 1801 S Bell St	Arlington	VA	22202	**800-372-1033**		524-7
Family Life Communications Inc PO Box 35300	Tucson	AZ	85740	**800-776-1070**		635
Family Motor Coach Assn (FMCA) 8291 Clough Pk	Cincinnati	OH	45244	**800-543-3622**	513-474-3622	47-23
Family Motor Coaching Magazine 8291 Clough Pk	Cincinnati	OH	45244	**800-543-3622**	513-474-3622	452-22
Family of the Americas Foundation PO Box 1170	Dunkirk	MD	20754	**800-443-3395**	301-627-3346	47-17
Family Practice Management 11400 Tomahawk Creek Pkwy	Leawood	KS	66211	**800-274-2237**	913-906-6000	452-16
Family Radio 290 Hegenberger Rd	Oakland	CA	94621	**800-543-1495**		634
Family Research Council (FRC) 801 G St NW	Washington	DC	20001	**800-225-4008**	202-393-2100	47-6
Family Stations Inc 290 Hegenberger Rd	Oakland	CA	94621	**800-543-1495**		636
Family Video 2500 Lehigh Ave	Glenview	IL	60026	**888-332-6843**	847-904-9000	785
FamilySearch 35 N W Temple St	Salt Lake City	UT	84150	**866-406-1830**		384
FAMM (Families Against Mandatory Minimums) 1612 K St NW Ste 700	Washington	DC	20006	**800-435-7352**	202-822-6700	47-8
Famous Dave's of America Inc 12701 Whitewater Dr Ste 200 *NASDAQ: DAVE*	Minnetonka	MN	55343	**800-929-4040**	952-294-1300	661
Famous Footwear 7010 Mineral Pt Rd *Cust Svc	Madison	WI	53717	**800-888-7198***	608-833-3340	300
Fannie Mae 3900 Wisconsin Ave NW *OTC: FNMA*	Washington	DC	20016	**800-732-6643**	202-752-7000	502
Fannin County Board of Education 2290 E First St	Blue Ridge	GA	30513	**800-308-2145**	706-632-3771	676
Fanning/Howey Assoc Inc 1200 Irmscher Blvd	Celina	OH	45822	**888-499-2292**	419-586-2292	261
Fantagraphics Books 7563 Lk City Way NE	Seattle	WA	98115	**800-657-1100**	206-524-1967	628-5
Fantastic Tours & Travel 6143 Jericho Tpke	Commack	NY	11725	**800-552-6262**	631-462-6262	750
Fan-Tastic Vent Corp 2083 S Almont Ave	Imlay City	MI	48444	**800-521-0298**	810-724-3818	36
Fantasy Diamond Corp 1550 W Carrol Ave	Chicago	IL	60607	**800-621-4445**	312-583-3200	407
Fantasy Springs Resort Casino 84-245 Indio Springs Pkwy *Cust Svc	Indio	CA	92203	**800-827-2946***	760-342-5000	132
Fantini Baking Company Inc 375 Washington St	Haverhill	MA	01832	**800-223-9037**	978-373-1273	295-1
Fantus Paper Products P.S. Greetings Inc 5730 N Tripp Ave *Sales	Chicago	IL	60646	**800-621-8823***	773-267-6069	129
FANUC America Corp 3900 W Hamlin Rd	Rochester Hills	MI	48309	**800-477-6268**	248-377-7000	383
Fanzz 2657 South 1030 West	Salt Lake City	UT	84119	**888-326-9946**	801-325-2700	702
FAO Schwarz 767 Fifth Ave 58th St	New York	NY	10153	**800-426-8697**	212-644-9400	751
Fapco Inc 216 Post Rd	Buchanan	MI	49107	**800-782-0167**	269-695-6889	542
FAPD (Federal APD Inc) 28100 Cabot Dr Ste 200	Novi	MI	48377	**877-992-7749**	248-374-9600	683
Far East Broadcasting Co Inc 15700 Imperial Hwy PO Box 1	La Mirada	CA	90638	**800-523-3480**		634
Fargo C'mon Inn Hotel 4338 20th Ave SW	Fargo	ND	58103	**800-334-1570**	701-277-9944	376
FARGODOME 1800 N University Dr	Fargo	ND	58102	**855-694-6367**	701-241-9100	711
Fargo-Moorhead Convention & Visitors Bureau 2001 44th St S	Fargo	ND	58103	**800-235-7654**	701-282-3653	207
Farm Boy Meats 2761 N Kentucky Ave	Evansville	IN	47711	**800-852-3976**	812-425-5231	468
Farm Bureau Bank 2165 Green Vista Dr Ste 204	Sparks	NV	89431	**800-492-3276**	775-673-4566	69
Farm Bureau Life Insurance Co 5400 University Ave	West Des Moines	IA	50266	**800-247-4170**	515-225-5400	388-2
Farm Credit Council 50 F St NW Ste 900	Washington	DC	20001	**866-632-9992**	202-626-8710	48-2
Farm Credit Leasing (FCL) 600 Hwy 169 S Ste 300	Minneapolis	MN	55426	**800-444-2929**	952-417-7800	216
Farm Credit Of Central Florida Aca 115 S Missouri Ave Ste 400	Lakeland	FL	33815	**800-533-2773**	863-682-4117	216
Farm Credit Of Northwest Florida Aca 5052 Hwy 90	Marianna	FL	32446	**800-527-0647**	850-526-4910	216
Farm Credit of The Virginias Aca 106 Sangers Ln	Staunton	VA	24401	**800-559-1016**	540-886-3435	214
Farm Family Casualty Insurance Co PO Box 656	Albany	NY	12201	**800-843-3276**	518-431-5000	388-4
Farm Family Life Insurance Co PO Box 656	Albany	NY	12201	**800-948-3276**	518-431-5000	388-2
Farm Implement & Supply Company Inc 1200 S Washington Hwy 183	Plainville	KS	67663	**888-589-6029**	785-434-4824	274
Farm Industry News 7900 International Dr Ste 300 *Cust Svc	Minneapolis	MN	55425	**800-722-5334***	952-851-9329	452-1
Farm Journal 30 S 15th Ste 900	Philadelphia	PA	19102	**800-331-9310**	215-557-8900	452-1
Farm Service Co-op 2308 Pine St	Harlan	IA	51537	**800-452-4372**	712-755-3185	276
Farm Show Magazine 20088 Kenwood Trial	Lakeville	MN	55044	**800-834-9665**		452-1
Farmer Boy Ag Systems Inc PO Box 435	Myerstown	PA	17067	**800-845-3374**		274
Farmer Bros Co 20333 S Normandie Ave *NASDAQ: FARM*	Torrance	CA	90502	**800-735-2878**	310-787-5200	295-7
Farmer State Bank of Sublette 303 S Pennsylvania Ave PO Box 20	Sublette	IL	61367	**866-269-1722**	815-849-5242	357-2
Farmer's Co-op Assn 110 S Keokuk Wash Rd	Keota	IA	52248	**877-843-4893**	641-636-3748	47-2
Farmers Alliance Mutual Insurance Co 1122 N Main PO Box 1401	McPherson	KS	67460	**800-362-1075**	620-241-2200	388-4
Farmers Bank, The 9 E Clinton St PO Box 129	Frankfort	IN	46041	**800-883-0131**	765-654-8731	69
Farmers Capital Bank Corp PO Box 309 *NASDAQ: FFKT*	Frankfort	KY	40602	**800-776-9437**	502-227-1668	357-2
Farmers Co-op 208 W Depot	Dorchester	NE	68343	**800-642-6439**	402-946-2211	275
Farmers Co-op Assn 105 Jackson St	Jackson	MN	56143	**800-864-3847**	507-847-4160	276
Farmers Co-op Union, The 225 S Broadway PO Box 159	Sterling	KS	67579	**800-238-1843**	620-278-2141	11-1
Farmers Educational & Co-op Union of America 20 F St NW Ste 300	Washington	DC	20001	**800-331-1212**	202-554-1600	47-2
Farmers Electric Co-op Inc 2000 E I-30	Greenville	TX	75402	**800-541-2662**	903-455-1715	245
Farmers Fire Insurance Co 2875 Eastern Blvd	York	PA	17402	**800-537-0928**	717-751-4435	387
Farmers Insurance Exchange 4680 Wilshire Blvd	Los Angeles	CA	90010	**855-808-6599**	323-932-3200	388-4
Farmers Insurance Group 4680 Wilshire Blvd	Los Angeles	CA	90010	**800-327-6377**	323-932-3200	357-4
Farmers Mutual Hail Insurance Company of Iowa 6785 Westown Pkwy	West Des Moines	IA	50266	**800-247-5248**	515-282-9104	388-4
Farmers Mutual Insurance Company of Nebraska 1220 Lincoln Mall	Lincoln	NE	68508	**800-742-7433**	402-434-8300	388-4
Farmers Rice Co-op PO Box 15223	Sacramento	CA	95851	**800-326-2799**	916-923-5100	295-23
Farmers Rural Electric Co-op Corp 504 S Broadway St	Glasgow	KY	42141	**800-253-2191**	270-651-2191	245
Farmers Supply Sales Inc 1409 E Ave	Kalona	IA	52247	**800-493-4917**	319-656-2291	274
Farmers Telecommunications Co-op (FTC) 144 McCurdy Ave N PO Box 217	Rainsville	AL	35986	**866-638-2144**	256-638-2144	726
Farmers Telephone Co-op Inc 1101 E Main St	Kingstree	SC	29556	**888-218-5050**	843-382-2333	726
Farmers West 5300 Foothill Rd	Carpinteria	CA	93013	**800-549-0085**	805-684-5531	366
farmers win coop (FFC) 110 N Jefferson	Fredericksburg	IA	50630	**800-562-8389**	563-237-5324	10-3
Farmers' Electric Co-op 201 W Business 36 PO Box 680	Chillicothe	MO	64601	**800-279-0496**	660-646-4281	245
Farmington Convention & Visitors Bureau 3041 E Main St	Farmington	NM	87402	**800-448-1240**	505-326-7602	207
Farmington Press 218 N Washington St PO Box 70	Farmington	MO	63640	**800-455-0206**	573-756-8927	525-4

Name / Address	City	State	ZIP	Toll-Free	Phone	Class
FarmTek						
1440 Field of Dreams Way	Dyersville	IA	52040	**800-327-6835**	563-875-2288	10-3
Farner-Bocken Co						
1751 US Hwy 30 E PO Box 368	Carroll	IA	51401	**800-274-8692**	712-792-3503	296-8
Farouk Systems Inc						
250 Pennbright Dr	Houston	TX	77090	**800-237-9175**	281-876-2000	215
Farr Regional Library						
1939 61st Ave	Greeley	CO	80634	**888-861-7323**	970-506-8550	431-3
Farrel Corp						
25 Main St	Ansonia	CT	06401	**800-800-7290**	203-736-5500	383
Farrell-Calhoun Inc						
221 E Carolina Ave	Memphis	TN	38126	**888-832-7735**	901-526-2211	543
Farrey's Wholesale Hardware Company Inc						
1850 NE 146th St	North Miami	FL	33181	**888-854-5483**	305-947-5451	358
Farris Evans Insurance Agency Inc						
1568 Union Ave	Memphis	TN	38104	**800-395-8207**	901-274-5424	387
Farrs Better Foods						
2575 South						
300 West	South Salt lake City	UT	84115	**877-553-2777**	801-484-8724	295-25
Farwest Corrosion Control Co						
1480 W Artesia Blvd	Gardena	CA	90248	**888-532-7937**	310-532-9524	261
FASB (Financial Acctg Standards Board)						
401 Merritt 7 PO Box 5116	Norwalk	CT	06856	**800-748-0659**	203-847-0700	48-1
FASCore LLC						
8515 E Orchard Rd	Greenwood Village	CO	80111	**800-232-0859**	800-537-2033	528
FASEB (Federation of American Societies for Experimental Biology)						
9650 Rockville Pk	Bethesda	MD	20814	**800-433-2732**	301-634-7000	48-19
Fashion Institute of Design & Merchandising						
Los Angeles						
919 S Grand Ave	Los Angeles	CA	90015	**800-624-1200***	213-624-1200	162
*Admissions						
Orange County						
17590 Gillette Ave	Irvine	CA	92614	**888-974-3436**	949-851-6200	162
San Diego						
350 Tenth Ave	San Diego	CA	92101	**800-243-3436**	619-235-2049	162
San Francisco						
55 Stockton St	San Francisco	CA	94108	**800-422-3436**	415-675-5200	162
Fashion Wallcoverings						
4005 Carnegie Ave	Cleveland	OH	44103	**800-362-9930***	216-432-1600	790
*Orders						
Fasig-Tipton Co Inc						
2400 Newtown Pike	Lexington	KY	40511	**877-945-2020**	859-255-1555	50
Fasken Martineau DuMoulin LLP						
333 Bay St Bay Adelaide Centre						
Ste 2400 PO Box 20	Toronto	ON	M5H2T6	**800-268-8424**	416-366-8381	40
Fast Company Magazine						
Seven World Trade Ctr	New York	NY	10007	**800-542-6029**	212-389-5300	452-5
Fast Heat Inc						
776 Oaklawn Ave	Elmhurst	IL	60126	**877-747-8575**	630-833-5400	317
Fastbolt Corp						
200 Louis St	South Hackensack	NJ	07606	**800-631-1980**	201-440-9100	347
Fastec Industrial						
2219 Eddie Williams Rd	Johnson City	TN	37601	**800-837-2505**		348
Fastenal Co						
2001 Theurer Blvd	Winona	MN	55987	**877-507-7555**	507-454-5374	348
NASDAQ: FAST						
Fastener Supply Co						
13410 S Ridge Dr PO Box 7369	Charlotte	NC	28241	**800-888-9519**	704-596-7634	681
Fast-Fix Jewelry & Watch Repairs						
451 Altamonte Ave	Altamonte Springs	FL	32701	**800-359-0407**	407-261-1595	309
Fastframe USA Inc						
1200 Lawrence Dr Ste 300	Newbury Park	CA	91320	**888-863-7263**	805-498-4463	44
Fastfurnishings.com						
340 S Lemon Ave Ste 6043	Walnut	CA	91789	**877-404-6072**	443-371-3278	320
FasTracKids International Ltd						
6900 E Belleview Ave						
Ste 100	Greenwood Village	CO	80111	**888-576-6888**	303-224-0200	309
FASTSIGNS International Inc						
2542 Highlander Way	Carrollton	TX	75006	**800-827-7446**	972-447-0777	692
FastWeb Inc						
444 N Michigan Ave Ste 3000	Chicago	IL	60611	**800-829-1040**	444-536-1212	716
FATA Hunter Inc						
1040 Iowa Ave Ste 100	Riverside	CA	92507	**800-248-6837**	951-328-0200	261
Fatburger North America Inc						
301 Arizona Ave Ste 200	Santa Monica	CA	90401	**800-315-3901**	310-319-1850	661
Father Hennepin State Park						
41294 Father Hennepin Pk Rd						
PO Box 397	Isle	MN	56342	**888-646-6367**	320-676-8763	558
FAU (Florida Atlantic University)						
777 Glades Rd	Boca Raton	FL	33431	**800-299-4328***	561-297-3000	166
*Admissions						
Faulk & Winkler LLC						
6811 Jefferson Hwy	Baton Rouge	LA	70806	**800-927-6811**	225-927-6811	195
Faulkner Information Services						
7905 Browning Rd	Pennsauken	NJ	08109	**800-843-0460**	856-662-2070	628-11
Faulkner State Community College						
Bay Minette						
1900 Hwy 31 S	Bay Minette	AL	36507	**800-381-3722**	251-580-2111	160
Fairhope						
440 Fairhope Ave	Fairhope	AL	36532	**800-231-3752**	251-990-0420	160
Gulf Shores						
3301 Gulf Shores Pkwy	Gulf Shores	AL	36542	**800-231-3752**	251-968-3101	160
Faulkner University						
5345 Atlanta Hwy	Montgomery	AL	36109	**800-879-9816**	334-272-5820	166
Faultless Caster						
3438 Briley Pk Blvd N	Nashville	TN	37207	**800-322-7359***		347
*Cust Svc						
Fauquier Bank, The (TFB)						
10 Courthouse Sq PO Box 561	Warrenton	VA	20186	**800-638-3798**	540-347-2700	69
Fauquier Bankshares Inc						
10 Courthouse Sq	Warrenton	VA	20186	**800-638-3798**	540-347-2700	357-2
NASDAQ: FBSS						
Fauquier Times-Democrat						
39 Culpeper St	Warrenton	VA	20186	**888-351-1660**	540-347-4222	525-4
Fauske & Assoc LLC						
16w070 83rd St	Burr Ridge	IL	60527	**877-328-7531**	630-323-8750	193
Faxaway						
417 Second Ave W	Seattle	WA	98119	**800-906-4329**	206-301-7000	726
FaxBack Inc						
7007 SW Cardinal Ln Ste 105	Portland	OR	97224	**800-329-2225**	503-597-5350	726
Fay School						
48 Main St	Southborough	MA	01772	**800-933-2925**	508-485-0100	615
Fay Spofford & Thorndike LLC						
5 Burlington Woods	Burlington	MA	01803	**800-835-8666**	781-221-1000	261
FAYBLOCK Materials Inc						
130 Builders Blvd	Fayetteville	NC	28302	**800-326-9198**	910-323-9198	192-1
Fayette Chamber of Commerce						
65 W Main St	Uniontown	PA	15401	**800-916-9365**	724-437-4571	137
Fayette County Board of Education						
210 Stonewall Ave	Fayetteville	GA	30214	**800-550-5131**	770-460-3535	676
Fayette County Chamber of Commerce						
200 Courthouse Sq	Fayetteville	GA	30214	**877-527-3712**	770-461-9983	137
Fayette County Library						
216 W Market St	Somerville	TN	38068	**866-465-3591**	901-465-5248	431-3
Fayette County Public Library						
531 Summit St	Oak Hill	WV	25901	**855-275-5737**	304-465-0121	431-3
Fayette Electric Co-op Inc						
357 N Washington St	La Grange	TX	78945	**800-874-8290**	979-968-3181	245
Fayetteville Area Convention & Visitors Bureau (FACVB)						
245 Person St	Fayetteville	NC	28301	**800-255-8217**	910-483-5311	207
Fayetteville Chamber of Commerce						
123 W Mountain St	Fayetteville	AR	72702	**866-893-5007**	479-521-1710	137
Fayetteville Observer						
458 Whitfield St	Fayetteville	NC	28306	**800-345-9895**	910-323-4848	525-2
Fayetteville Public Utilities						
408 W College St	Fayetteville	TN	37334	**800-379-2534**	931-433-1522	245
Fayetteville State University						
1200 Murchison Rd	Fayetteville	NC	28301	**800-222-2594***	910-672-1371	166
*Admissions						
Fayetteville Technical Community College						
2201 Hull Rd	Fayetteville	NC	28303	**877-245-5520**	910-678-8400	160
Fayetteville-Lincoln County Chamber of Commerce						
208 S Elk Ave	Fayetteville	TN	37334	**888-433-1238**	931-433-1234	137
FBFC (First Bank Financial Centre)						
155 W Wisconsin Ave						
PO Box 1004	Oconomowoc	WI	53066	**888-569-9909**	262-569-9900	69
FBG Service Corp						
407 S 27th Ave	Omaha	NE	68131	**800-777-8326**	402-346-4422	103
FBLA-PBL (Future Business Leaders of America-Phi Beta Lambda Inc)						
1912 Assn Dr	Reston	VA	20191	**800-325-2946**		47-11
FBS (Fullerton Bldg Systems Inc)						
34620 250th St PO Box 308	Worthington	MN	56187	**800-450-9782**	507-376-3128	804
FC Haab Company Inc						
2314 Market St	Philadelphia	PA	19103	**800-486-5663**	215-563-0800	315
FCA (Family Caregiver Alliance)						
180 Montgomery St Ste 900	San Francisco	CA	94104	**800-445-8106**	415-434-3388	47-17
FCA (Fellowship of Christian Athletes)						
8701 Leeds Rd	Kansas City	MO	64129	**800-289-0909**	816-921-0909	47-22
FCA (First Co-op Assn)						
960 Riverview Dr PO Box 60	Cherokee	IA	51012	**877-753-5400**	712-225-5400	442
FCC (First Community Corp)						
5455 Sunset Blvd	Lexington	SC	29072	**800-829-6372**	803-951-0555	357-2
NASDAQ: FCCO						
FCC (Federal Communications Commission)						
445 12th St SW	Washington	DC	20554	**888-225-5322**		338-18
FCC (Fremont Contract Carriers Inc)						
865 S Bud Blvd	Fremont	NE	68025	**800-228-9842**		444
FCC Services						
7951 E Maplewood Ave						
Ste 225	Greenwood Village	CO	80111	**888-275-3227**		458
FCCI Insurance Group						
6300 University Pkwy						
PO Box 58004	Sarasota	FL	34232	**800-226-3224**	941-907-3224	388-4
FCCLA (Family Career & Community Leaders of America)						
1910 Assn Dr	Reston	VA	20191	**800-234-4425**	703-476-4900	47-11
FCCU (First Community Credit Union)						
PO Box 1030	Chesterfield	MO	63006	**800-767-8880**	636-728-3333	219
FCFC (First Community Financial Corp)						
4000 N Central Ave Ste 100	Phoenix	AZ	85012	**877-777-4778**	602-265-7715	216
OTC: FMFP						
FCG (Florida City Gas)						
955 E 25th St	Hialeah	FL	33013	**800-993-7546**	305-691-8710	775
FCI Inc						
4661 Giles Rd	Cleveland	OH	44135	**800-321-1032**	216-251-5200	614
FCL (Farm Credit Leasing)						
600 Hwy 169 S Ste 300	Minneapolis	MN	55426	**800-444-2929**	952-417-7800	216
FCNL (Friends Committee on National Legislation)						
245 Second St NE	Washington	DC	20002	**800-630-1330**	202-547-6000	608
FCPL (Flagler County Public Library)						
2500 Palm Coast Pkwy NW	Palm Coast	FL	32137	**877-863-5244**	386-446-6763	431-3
FCx Performance						
3000 E 14th Ave	Columbus	OH	43219	**800-253-6223**	614-324-6050	382
FD Lawrence Electric Company Inc						
3450 Beekman St	Cincinnati	OH	45223	**800-582-4490***	513-542-1100	246
*Cust Svc						
FD Roosevelt State Park						
2970 GA Hwy 190	Pine Mountain	GA	31822	**800-864-7275**	706-663-4858	558
FDB (First DataBank Inc)						
701 Gateway Blvd						
Ste 600	South San Francisco	CA	94080	**800-633-3453***		179-10
*General						
FDLI (Food & Drug Law Institute)						
1155 15th St NW Ste 800	Washington	DC	20005	**800-956-6293**	202-371-1420	48-10
Feather Publishing Co Inc						
287 Lawrence St	Quincy	CA	95971	**866-849-8390**	530-283-0800	628-8
Feather River College						
570 Golden Eagle Ave	Quincy	CA	95971	**800-442-9799**	530-283-0202	160
Featherlite Trailers						
Hwy 63 & 9 PO Box 320	Cresco	IA	52136	**800-800-1230**	563-547-6000	769
Fechheimer Bros Company Inc						
4545 Malsbary Rd	Cincinnati	OH	45242	**800-543-1939**	513-793-5400	153-18
Federal APD Inc (FAPD)						
28100 Cabot Dr Ste 200	Novi	MI	48377	**877-992-7749**	248-374-9600	683
Federal Assistance Monitor						
8204 Fenton St	Silver Spring	MD	20910	**800-666-6380**	301-588-6380	524-7
Federal Aviation Administration (FAA)						
800 Independence Ave SW	Washington	DC	20591	**866-835-5322**		338-15
Aviation Research Div						
800 Independence Ave SW						
Rm 528A	Washington	DC	20591	**866-835-5322**	202-267-9251	659
Safety Hotline						
800 Independence Ave SW	Washington	DC	20591	**800-255-1111**		338-15
Federal Aviation Administration Northwest Mountain Region						
1601 Lind Ave SW	Renton	WA	98057	**800-220-5715**	425-227-2001	338-15
Federal Bldg Services Inc						
1641 Barclay Blvd	Buffalo Grove	IL	60089	**800-982-9234**	847-279-7360	150
Federal Block Corp						
247 Walsh Ave	New Windsor	NY	12553	**800-724-1999**	845-561-4108	184

	Toll-Free	Phone	Class
Federal Bureau of Prisons			
National Institute of Corrections			
320 First St NW .... Washington DC 20534	**800-995-6423**	202-307-3106	338-12
National Institute of Corrections Information Cent			
11900 E Cornell Ave Unit C .... Aurora CO 80014	**800-877-1461**		338-12
Federal Business Products Inc			
95 Main Ave .... Clifton NJ 07014	**800-927-5123**	973-667-9800	109
Federal Cartridge Co			
900 Ehlen Dr .... Anoka MN 55303	**800-379-1732**		284
Federal Communications Commission (FCC)			
445 12th St SW .... Washington DC 20554	**888-225-5322**		338-18
Federal Computer Week Magazine			
3141 Fairview Pk Dr			
Ste 777 .... Falls Church VA 22042	**877-534-2208**	703-876-5100	452-7
Federal Contracts Report			
1801 S Bell St .... Arlington VA 22202	**800-372-1033**		524-7
Federal Correctional Complex			
Coleman			
846 NE 54th Terr .... ÿColeman FL 33521	**877-623-8426**	352-689-5000	
Butner			
Old NC Hwy 75 PO Box 1000 .... Butner NC 27509	**877-623-8426**	919-575-4541	
Danbury Rt 37 .... Danbury CT 06811	**877-623-8426**	203-743-6471	
Englewood			
9595 W Quincy Ave .... Littleton CO 80123	**877-623-8426**	303-985-1566	
Fairton			
655 Fairton-Millville Rd			
PO Box 280 .... Fairton NJ 08320	**877-623-8426**	856-453-1177	
Federal Correctional Institution			
Forrest City			
1400 Dale Bumpers Rd			
PO Box 8000 .... Forrest City AR 72335	**877-623-8426**	870-630-6000	
Loretto PO Box 1000 .... Loretto PA 15940	**877-623-8426**	814-472-4140	
Manchester			
805 Fox Hollow Rd			
PO Box 4000 .... Manchester KY 40962	**877-623-8426**	606-598-1900	
McKean			
6975 Rt 59 PO Box 8000 .... Lewis Run PA 16738	**877-623-8426**	814-362-8900	
Yazoo City			
2225 Haley Barbour Pkwy			
PO Box 5050 .... Yazoo City MS 39194	**877-623-8426**	662-751-4800	
Federal Deposit Insurance Corp			
550 17th St NW .... Washington DC 20429	**877-275-3342**	202-898-7192	338-18
Federal Deposit Insurance Corp Regional Offices			
Atlanta Area Office			
10 Tenth St NW Ste 800 .... Atlanta GA 30309	**800-765-3342**	678-916-2200	338-18
Boston Area Office			
15 Braintree Hill Office Pk			
Ste 300 .... Braintree MA 02184	**866-728-9953**	781-794-5500	338-18
Chicago Area Office			
300 S Riverside Plaza Ste 1700 .... Chicago IL 60606	**800-944-5343**	312-382-6000	338-18
Dallas Area Office			
1601 Bryan St .... Dallas TX 75201	**800-568-9161**	214-754-0098	338-18
Kansas City Area Office			
2345 Grand Blvd Ste 1200 .... Kansas City MO 64108	**800-209-7459**	816-234-8000	338-18
Memphis Area Office			
5100 Poplar Ave Ste 1900 .... Memphis TN 38137	**800-210-6354**	901-685-1603	338-18
New York Area Office			
350 5th Ave Ste 1200 .... New York NY 11215	**800-334-9593**	917-320-2500	338-18
San Francisco Area Office			
25 Jessie St at Ecker Sq			
Ste 2300 .... San Francisco CA 94105	**800-756-3558**	415-546-0160	338-18
Federal Detention Ctr			
SeaTac PO Box 13901 .... Seattle WA 98198	**877-623-8426**	206-870-5700	
Federal EEO Advisor			
360 Hiatt Dr .... Palm Beach Gardens FL 33418	**800-341-7874**	561-622-6520	524-2
Federal Election Commission			
999 E St NW .... Washington DC 20463	**800-424-9530**	202-694-1100	265
Federal Emergency Management Agency			
FEMA for Kids			
500 C St SW Ste 714 .... Washington DC 20472	**800-621-3362**		338-9
National Flood Insurance Program			
500 C St SW .... Washington DC 20472	**888-379-9531**		338-9
Region 1 99 High St .... Boston MA 02110	**877-336-2734**	617-956-7551	338-9
Region 3			
1 Independence Mall			
615 Chestnut St 6th Fl .... Philadelphia PA 19106	**800-621-3362**	215-931-5500	338-9
Region 5			
536 S Clark St 6th Fl .... Chicago IL 60605	**877-336-2627**	312-408-5500	338-9
Region 6			
800 N Loop 288 .... Denton TX 76209	**800-426-5460**	940-898-5399	338-9
Federal Emergency Management Agency Regional Offices			
Region 9			
1111 Broadway Ste 1200 .... Oakland CA 94607	**877-336-2627**	510-627-7100	338-9
Region 10			
Federal Regional Ctr			
130 228th St SW .... Bothell WA 98021	**800-772-1252***	425-487-4600	338-9
*General			
Federal Energy Regulatory Commission			
888 First St NE .... Washington DC 20426	**866-208-3372**	202-502-8004	338-7
Federal Equipment Co			
5298 River Rd .... Cincinnati OH 45233	**877-435-4723**	513-621-5260	173
Federal Express Europe Inc			
3610 Hacks Cross Rd .... Memphis TN 38125	**800-463-3339**	901-369-3600	539
Federal Flange			
4014 Pinemont St .... Houston TX 77018	**800-231-0150**	713-681-0606	478
Federal Foam Technologies Inc			
600 Wisconsin Dr .... New Richmond WI 54017	**800-898-9559**	715-246-9500	594
Federal Highway Administration			
National Highway Institute			
4600 Fairfax Dr Ste 800 .... Arlington VA 22203	**877-558-6873**	703-235-0500	338-15
Federal Industries Div Standex Corp			
215 Federal Ave .... Belleville WI 53508	**800-356-4206**		655
Federal International Inc			
7935 Clayton Rd .... Saint Louis MO 63117	**800-972-7277**	314-721-3377	651
Federal Life Insurance Co Mutual			
3750 W Deerfield Rd Ste A .... Riverwoods IL 60015	**800-233-3750**	847-520-1900	388-2
Federal Management Systems Inc			
462 K St NW .... Washington DC 20001	**877-637-8277**	202-842-3003	2
Federal Motor Carrier Safety Administration (FMCSA)			
1200 New Jersey Ave SE .... Washington DC 20590	**800-832-5660**		338-15
Federal Prison Camp			
Duluth			
6902 Airport Rd PO Box 1400 .... Duluth MN 55814	**877-623-8426**	218-722-8634	
Montgomery			
Maxwell AFB .... Montgomery AL 36112	**877-623-8426**	334-293-2100	
Federal Prison Industries Inc			
320 First St NW .... Washington DC 20534	**800-827-3168**		622
Federal Protection Inc			
2500 N Airport			
Commerce Ave .... Springfield MO 65803	**800-299-5400**	417-869-9192	684
Federal Railroad Administration Regional Offices (FRA)			
Region 1			
55 Broadway Room 1077 .... Cambridge MA 02142	**800-724-5991**	617-494-2302	338-15
Region 2			
Baldwin Tower Ste 660			
1510 Chester Pike .... Crum Lynne PA 19022	**800-724-5992**	610-521-8200	338-15
Region 3			
61 Forsyth St SW Ste 16T20 .... Atlanta GA 30303	**800-724-5993**	404-562-3800	338-15
Region 4			
200 W Adams St .... Chicago IL 60606	**800-724-5040**	312-353-6203	338-15
Region 6			
901 Locust St Ste 464 .... Kansas City MO 64106	**800-724-5996**	816-329-3840	338-15
Region 8			
703 Broadway St Ste 650 .... Vancouver WA 98660	**800-724-5998**	360-696-7536	338-15
Federal Realty Investment Trust			
1626 E Jefferson St .... Rockville MD 20852	**800-658-8980**	301-998-8100	646
NYSE: FRT			
Federal Reserve Bank of Atlanta			
1000 Peachtree St NE .... Atlanta GA 30309	**888-500-7390**	404-498-8353	70
Birmingham Branch			
524 Liberty Pkwy .... Birmingham AL 35242	**800-257-7013**	205-968-6700	70
Federal Reserve Bank of Cleveland			
Cincinnati Branch			
150 E Fourth St .... Cincinnati OH 45202	**877-372-2457**	513-721-4787	70
Federal Reserve Bank of Dallas			
2200 N Pearl St PO Box 655906 .... Dallas TX 75201	**800-333-4460**	214-922-6000	70
San Antonio Branch			
402 Dwyer Ave .... San Antonio TX 78204	**800-333-4460**	210-978-1200	70
Federal Reserve Bank of Kansas City			
1 Memorial Dr PO Box 1200 .... Kansas City MO 64198	**800-333-1010**	816-881-2000	70
Denver Branch			
1 Memorial Dr .... Kansas City MO 64198	**888-851-1920**		70
Oklahoma City Branch			
226 Dean A McGee Ave .... Oklahoma City OK 73102	**800-333-1030**	405-270-8400	70
Omaha Branch			
2201 Farnam St .... Omaha NE 68102	**800-333-1040**	402-221-5500	70
Federal Reserve Bank of Minneapolis			
90 Hennepin Ave .... Minneapolis MN 55401	**800-553-9656**	612-204-5000	70
Federal Reserve Bank of Philadelphia			
10 Independence Mall .... Philadelphia PA 19106	**877-574-1776**	215-574-6000	70
Federal Reserve Bank of Saint Louis			
411 Locust St .... Saint Louis MO 63102	**800-333-0810**	314-444-8444	70
Little Rock Branch			
111 Ctr St			
Ste 1000 Stephens Bldg .... Little Rock AR 72201	**877-372-2457**	501-324-8300	70
Federal Reserve Bank of San Francisco (FRBSF)			
101 Market St .... San Francisco CA 94105	**800-227-4133**	415-974-2000	70
Portland Branch			
1500 SW First Ave Ste 100 .... Portland OR 97201	**800-227-4133**	503-276-3000	70
Salt Lake City Branch			
101 Market St .... San Francisco CA 94105	**800-227-4133**	415-974-2000	70
Federal Trade Commission (FTC)			
600 Pennsylvania Ave NW .... Washington DC 20580	**877-382-4357**	202-326-2222	338-18
National Do Not Call Registry			
600 Pennsylvania Ave NW .... Washington DC 20580	**888-382-1222**		338-18
East Central Region			
1111 Superior Ave Ste 200 .... Cleveland OH 44114	**877-382-4357**	216-263-3455	338-18
Midwest Region			
55 W Monroe St Ste 1825 .... Chicago IL 60603	**877-382-4357**	312-960-5634	338-18
Northwest Region			
915 Second Ave Rm 2896 .... Seattle WA 98174	**877-382-4357**		338-18
Federal Trade Commission Regional Offices			
Southeast Region			
60 Forsyth St SW .... Atlanta GA 30303	**877-282-4357**	404-656-1390	338-18
Southwest Region			
1999 Bryan St Ste 2150 .... Dallas TX 75201	**877-382-4357**		338-18
Western Region			
901 Market Street Ste 570 .... San Francisco CA 94103	**877-382-4357**		338-18
Federal White Cement Ltd			
PO Box 1609 .... Woodstock ON N4S0A8	**800-265-1806***	519-485-5410	134
*Sales			
Federal-Mogul Corp			
27300 W 11 Mile Rd .... Southfield MI 48034	**800-325-8886***	248-354-7700	59
NASDAQ: FDML ■ *Cust Svc			
Federated Co-ops Inc			
502 S Second St .... Princeton MN 55371	**800-638-8228**	763-389-2582	572
Federated Group Inc			
3025 W Salt Creek Ln .... Arlington Heights IL 60005	**800-234-0011**	847-577-1200	342
Federated Insurance Cos			
121 E Pk Sq PO Box 328 .... Owatonna MN 55060	**800-533-0472**	507-455-5200	357-4
Federated Investors			
1001 Liberty Ave			
Federated Investors Twr .... Pittsburgh PA 15222	**800-245-0242**	412-288-1900	398
NYSE: FII			
Federated Life Insurance Co			
121 E Pk Sq PO Box 328 .... Owatonna MN 55060	**800-533-0472**	507-455-5200	388-2
Federated Mutual Insurance Co			
121 E Pk Sq PO Box 328 .... Owatonna MN 55060	**800-533-0472**	507-455-5200	388-2
Federated Rural Electric Assn			
77100 US Hwy 71 PO Box 69 .... Jackson MN 56143	**800-321-3520**	507-847-3520	245
Federation Co-op			
108 N Water St .... Black River Falls WI 54615	**800-944-1784**	715-284-5354	276
Federation for American Immigration Reform (FAIR)			
25 Massachusetts Ave NW			
Ste 330 .... Washington DC 20009	**877-627-3247**	202-328-7004	47-7
Federation of American Societies for Experimental Biology (FASEB)			
9650 Rockville Pk .... Bethesda MD 20814	**800-433-2732**	301-634-7000	48-19
Federation of State Medical Boards of the US Inc (FSMB)			
400 Fuller Wiser Rd Ste 300 .... Euless TX 76039	**800-793-7939**	817-868-4000	48-8
FedEx 450 W First Ave .... Roselle NJ 07203	**800-463-3339**	908-245-4400	109
FedEx Corp			
3610 Hacks Cross Rd .... Memphis TN 38125	**800-463-3339**	901-369-3600	357-3
NYSE: FDX			
FedEx Custom Critical Inc			
1475 Boettler Rd .... Uniontown OH 44685	**800-463-3339***	234-310-4090	539
*Cust Svc			

	Toll-Free	Phone	Class
FedEx Supply Chain Services Inc			
5455 Darrow Rd .... Hudson OH 44236	800-463-3339	901-369-3600	444
Fedmet Resources Corp			
PO Box 278 .... Montreal QC H3Z2T2	800-609-5711	514-931-5711	654
Fednav Ltd			
1000 Rue de la GauchetiFre O			
Bureau 3500 .... Montreal QC H3B4W5	800-678-4842*	514-878-6500	312
*General			
Fedway Assoc Inc			
505 Westgate Dr .... Basking Ridge NJ 07920	800-447-4736	973-624-6444	80-3
FedWorld.gov			
National Technical Information Service			
5285 Port Royal Rd .... Alexandria VA 22312	800-553-6847	703-605-6000	198
FEE (Foundation for Economic Education)			
30 S Broadway .... Irvington-on-Hudson NY 10533	800-960-4333	914-591-7230	625
Feeco International Inc			
3913 Algoma Rd .... Green Bay WI 54311	800-373-9347	920-468-1000	208
Feed the Children (FTC)			
PO Box 36 .... Oklahoma City OK 73101	800-627-4556	405-942-0228	47-5
Feesers Inc			
5561 Grayson Rd .... Harrisburg PA 17111	800-326-2828	717-564-4636	296-8
Feheley Fine Arts			
65 George St .... Toronto ON M5A4L8	877-904-9114	416-323-1373	41
FEI Behavioral Health			
11700 W Lk Pk Dr .... Milwaukee WI 53224	800-782-1948	414-359-1055	457
FEI Co			
5350 NE Dawson Creek Dr .... Hillsboro OR 97124	866-693-3426*	503-640-7500	416
NASDAQ: FEIC ■ *Cust Svc			
Feingold Assn of the US			
37 Shell Rd Second Fl .... Rocky Point NY 11778	800-321-3287	631-369-9340	47-17
Felbro Inc			
3666 E Olympic Blvd .... Los Angeles CA 90023	800-733-5276	323-263-8686	233
Feldmeier Equipment Inc			
6800 Townline Rd .... Syracuse NY 13211	800-258-0118	315-454-8608	297
Felician College			
Rutherford			
223 Montross Ave .... Rutherford NJ 07070	888-442-4551	201-559-6000	166
Felix Neck Wildlife Sanctuary			
100 Felix Neck Dr .... Edgartown MA 02539	866-627-2267	508-627-4850	810
Felker Bros Corp			
22 N Chestnut Ave .... Marshfield WI 54449	800-826-2304	715-384-3121	485
Fellowes Inc			
1789 Norwood Ave .... Itasca IL 60143	800-945-4545	630-893-1600	110
Fellowship Hall Inc			
5140 Dunstan Rd .... Greensboro NC 27405	800-659-3381	336-621-3381	717
Fellowship of Christian Athletes (FCA)			
8701 Leeds Rd .... Kansas City MO 64129	800-289-0909	816-921-0909	47-22
Felly's Flowers Inc			
PO Box 6620 .... Madison WI 53716	800-993-7673		292
Felton Brush Inc			
Seven Burton Dr .... Londonderry NH 03053	800-258-9702	603-425-0200	102
Felts Field Aviation Inc			
5829 E Rutter Ave .... Spokane WA 99212	800-676-5538	509-535-9011	62
FEM Electric Assn Inc			
PO Box 468 .... Ipswich SD 57451	800-587-5880	605-426-6891	245
Region 1 99 High St .... Boston MA 02110	877-336-2734	617-956-7551	338-9
Female Health Co			
515 N State St Ste 2225 .... Chicago IL 60654	800-860-2442	312-595-9123	472
Femco Machine Co			
754 S Main St Ext .... Punxsutawney PA 15767	800-458-3445	814-938-9763	449
Feminist Press at the City University of New York			
365 Fifth Ave Ste 5406 .... New York NY 10016	800-283-3572	212-817-7922	628-2
Fender Musical Instruments Corp			
17600 N Perimeter Dr Ste 100 .... Scottsdale AZ 85255	800-488-1818*	480-596-9690	520
*Cust Svc			
Fenner Drives			
311 W Stiegel St .... Manheim PA 17545	800-243-3374*	717-665-2421	367
*Sales			
Fenton Art Glass Co			
700 Elizabeth St .... Williamstown WV 26187	800-933-6766*	304-375-6122	332
*Cust Svc			
Fenway Park			
Four Yawkey Way .... Boston MA 02215	877-733-7699	617-226-6000	711
Fenwick Inn			
13801 Coastal Hwy .... Ocean City MD 21842	800-492-1873	410-250-1100	376
Ferguson Enterprises Inc			
12500 Jefferson Ave .... Newport News VA 23602	877-616-2885	757-874-7795	605
Ferguson Perforating & Wire Co			
130 Ernest St .... Providence RI 02905	800-341-9800	401-941-8876	478
Ferguson Supply & Box Manufacturing Co			
10820 Quality Dr .... Charlotte NC 28278	800-821-1023	704-597-0310	99
Ferma Corp			
1265 Montecito Ave .... Mountain View CA 94043	877-337-6211	650-961-2742	190-16
Fernco Inc			
300 S Dayton St .... Davison MI 48423	800-521-1283	810-653-9626	589
Ferno-Washington Inc			
70 Weil Way .... Wilmington OH 45177	800-733-3766	937-382-1451	472
Fernwood Resort			
5785 Milford Rd .... East Stroudsburg PA 18302	888-337-6966		660
Feroleto Steel Company Inc			
300 Scofield Ave .... Bridgeport CT 06605	800-243-2839	203-366-3263	714
Ferrandino & Son Inc			
71 Carolyn Blvd .... Farmingdale NY 11735	866-571-4609	516-735-0097	603
Ferrara Cafe			
195 Grand St .... New York NY 10013	800-871-6068	212-226-6150	295-9
Ferrara Fire Apparatus Inc			
PO Box 249 .... Holden LA 70744	800-443-9006	225-567-7100	58
Ferrellgas Partners LP			
1 Liberty Plaza .... Liberty MO 64068	888-337-7355	816-792-1600	315
NYSE: FGP			
Ferring Pharmaceuticals Inc			
100 Interpace Pkwy Third Fl .... Parsippany NJ 07054	888-337-7464	973-796-1600	238
Ferris School			
959 Centre Rd .... Wilmington DE 19805	800-292-9582	302-993-3800	409
Ferris State University			
FLITE Library			
1010 Campus Dr .... Big Rapids MI 49307	800-433-7747	231-591-3602	431-6
Traverse City			
2200 Dendrinos Dr			
Ste 200H .... Traverse City MI 49684	866-857-1954	231-995-1734	166
Ferro Corp			
6060 Parkland Blvd .... Mayfield Heights IN 44124	800-321-3314	216-875-5600	543
Ferro Corp Plastics Colorants Div			
Three Railroad Ave .... Stryker OH 43557	800-521-9094	419-682-3311	543
Ferrum College			
215 Ferrum Mtn Rd .... Ferrum VA 24088	800-868-9797	540-365-2121	166
FESCO Agencies NA Inc			
1000 Second Ave Ste 1310 .... Seattle WA 98104	800-275-3372	206-583-0860	310
FESCO Ltd			
1000 Fesco Ave .... Alice TX 78332	800-375-3479	361-661-7000	532
Fesnak & Associates LLP			
1777 Sentry Pkwy W Ste 300 ...... Blue Bell PA 19422	800-274-3978	267-419-2200	724
Fess Parker's Doubletree Resort (FPDTR)			
633 E Cabrillo Blvd .... Santa Barbara CA 93103	800-879-2929	805-564-4333	660
Festiva Resorts			
One Vance Gap Rd .... Asheville NC 28805	866-933-7848*	828-254-3378	743
*Resv			
Festival Concert Hall			
North Dakota State University			
PO Box 5691 .... Fargo ND 58105	800-726-1724	701-231-7932	565
Festival Flea Market Mall			
2900 W Sample Rd ...... Pompano Beach FL 33073	800-353-2627	954-979-4555	455
Festival Plaza			
101 Crockett St Ste A .... Shreveport LA 71101	888-458-4748	318-673-5100	206
Festive Holidays Inc			
5501 New Jersey Ave .... Wildwood Crest NJ 08260	800-257-8920	609-522-6316	750
Fetch Logistics Inc			
25 Northpointe Pkwy Ste 200 .... Amherst NY 14228	800-964-4940	716-689-4556	310
Fey Industries Inc			
200 Fourth Ave N .... Edgerton MN 56128	800-533-5340	507-442-4311	85
FFB (First Financial Bancorp)			
255 E Fifth St Ste 700 .... Cincinnati OH 45202	877-322-9530	513-979-5837	357-2
NASDAQ: FFBC			
FFC (farmers win coop)			
110 N Jefferson .... Fredericksburg IA 50630	800-562-8389	563-237-5324	10-3
FFD Financial Corp			
321 N Wooster Ave .... Dover OH 44622	800-558-3424	330-364-7777	357-2
OTC: FFDF			
FFE Transportation Inc			
1145 Empire Central Pl .... Dallas TX 75247	800-569-9200	214-630-8090	770
FFF Enterprises Inc			
41093 County Ctr Dr .... Temecula CA 92591	800-843-7477	951-296-2500	5
FFP (Food for the Poor Inc)			
6401 Lyons Rd .... Coconut Creek FL 33073	800-427-9104	954-427-2222	47-5
FFW Corp			
1205 N Cass St .... Wabash IN 46992	800-377-4984	260-563-3185	357-2
OTC: FFWC			
FGI (FOIA Group Inc)			
1250 Connecticut Ave NW			
Ste 200 .... Washington DC 20036	888-461-7951		384
FGS (Freedom Graphic Systems Inc)			
1101 S Janesville St .... Milton WI 53563	800-334-3540		109
FGX International Inc			
500 George Washington Hwy .... Smithfield RI 02917	800-480-4846	401-231-3800	405
FH Bonn Co			
4300 Gateway Blvd .... Springfield OH 45502	800-323-0143	937-323-7024	734-3
FHA (HUD Office of Housing and Urban Development)			
451 Seventh St SW Ste 9100 .. Washington DC 20410	800-767-7468	202-708-1112	338-10
Fhm Insurance Co			
4601 Touchton Rd E			
Bldg 300 Ste 3150 .... Jacksonville FL 32246	800-393-0001	904-724-9890	388-4
FHN Memorial Hospital			
1045 W Stephenson St .... Freeport IL 61032	800-747-4131	815-599-6000	371-3
Fiber Instruments Sales Inc			
161 Clear Rd .... Oriskany NY 13424	800-500-0347*	315-736-2206	467
*Sales			
Fiber SenSys LLC			
2925 NW Aloclek Dr Ste 130 .... Hillsboro OR 97124	800-641-8150	503-692-4430	683
Fibercel Packaging LLC			
46 Brooklyn St PO Box 610 .... Portville NY 14770	800-545-8546*	716-933-8703	541
*Sales			
Fiberglass Specialties Inc			
PO Box 1340 .... Henderson TX 75653	800-527-1459	903-657-6522	601
Fibergrate Composite Structures Inc			
5151 Beltline Rd Ste 700 .... Dallas TX 75254	800-527-4043	972-250-1633	599
FiberMark North America, Inc.			
161 Wellington Rd .... Brattleboro VT 05302	800-784-8558*	802-257-0365	554
*Cust Svc			
Fiberoptics Technology Inc			
One Quassett Rd .... Pomfret CT 06258	800-433-5248*	860-928-0443	329
*Cust Svc			
Fiber-Tech Industries Inc			
2000 Kenskill			
Ave .... Washington Court House OH 43160	800-879-4377	740-335-9400	606
Fiberwave Corp			
140 58th St Bldg B Unit 6E.......... Brooklyn NY 11220	800-280-9011	718-802-9011	800
Fibre-Metal			
2000 Plainfield Pk PO Box 248........ Cranston RI 02921	800-430-4110		569
Fidelifacts			
42 Broadway Ste 1548 .... New York NY 10004	800-678-0007	212-425-1520	626
Fidelity Advisor Funds			
PO Box 770002 .... Cincinnati OH 45277	800-522-7297		521
Fidelity Bancshares Nc Inc			
PO Box 8 .... Fuquay Varina NC 27526	800-816-9608	919-552-2242	69
Fidelity Bank			
100 E English St .... Wichita KS 67201	800-658-1637		69
Fidelity Engineering Corp			
25 Loveton Cir PO Box 2500 .... Sparks MD 21152	800-787-6000	410-771-9400	14
Fidelity Exploration & Production Co			
1801 California St Ste 2500 .... Denver CO 80202	800-986-3133	303-893-3133	531
Fidelity Investment Funds			
PO Box 770001 .... Cincinnati OH 45277	800-343-3548		521
Fidelity Investments Charitable Gift Fund			
PO Box 770001 .... Cincinnati OH 45277	800-262-6039		402
Fidelity Investments Institutional Operations Company Inc			
PO Box 770002 .... Cincinnati OH 45277	877-208-0098		521
Fidelity Investments Institutional Services Company Inc			
82 Devonshire St .... Boston MA 02109	800-343-3548	617-563-9840	398
Fidelity National Title Group Inc			
601 Riverside Ave .... Jacksonville FL 32204	888-866-3684	904-854-8100	388-6
Fidelity National Title Insurance Co			
7025 N Scottsdale Rd .... Scottsdale AZ 85258	888-934-3354	480-344-6400	388-6
Fidelity National Title Insurance Company of Oregon			
900 SW Fifth Ave			
Mezzanine Level .... Portland OR 97204	888-934-3354	503-223-8338	388-6
Fiducial			
1370 Ave of the Americas			
31st Fl. .... New York NY 10019	866-343-8242	212-207-4700	724

Alphabetical Section

Company / Address	City	State	ZIP	Toll-Free	Phone	Class
Fiducial Franchising						
10100 Old Columbia Rd Third Fl	Columbia	MD	21046	**800-323-9000**	410-290-8296	724
Fiduciary Management Inc of Milwaukee						
100 E Wisconsin Ave Ste 2200	Milwaukee	WI	53202	**800-264-7684**	414-226-4545	398
Field Nation LLC						
310 Fourth Ave S Ste 8100	Minneapolis	MN	55415	**877-573-4353**		316
Field Paper Co						
3950 D St	Omaha	NE	68107	**800-969-3435**	402-733-3600	546
Fieldale Farms Corp						
555 Broiler Blvd	Baldwin	GA	30511	**800-241-5400**	706-778-5100	612
Fieldpoint Private Bank & Trust						
100 Field Pt Rd	Greenwich	CT	06830	**877-438-4338**	203-413-9300	681
Fields Company LLC						
2240 Taylor Way	Tacoma	WA	98421	**800-627-4098**		45
Fields Group Inc						
12335 Bridgewater Rd	Indianapolis	IN	46256	**800-600-2969**	317-578-4414	381
Fieldstone Homes						
Two Ada	Irvine	CA	92618	**800-665-0661**	949-790-5400	644
Fiesta Henderson						
777 W Lk Mead Pkwy	Henderson	NV	89015	**888-899-7770**	702-558-7000	376
Fiesta Rancho Casino Hotel						
2400 N Rancho Dr	Las Vegas	NV	89130	**800-731-7333***	702-631-7000	132
*Resv						
Fifield Land Co						
4307 Fifield Rd	Brawley	CA	92227	**800-536-6395**	760-344-6391	276
Fifteen Beacon Hotel						
15 Beacon St	Boston	MA	02108	**877-982-3226**	617-670-1500	376
Fifth Third Bank Central Ohio						
21 E State St	Columbus	OH	43215	**800-972-3030**		69
Figaro's Italian Pizza Inc						
1500 Liberty St SE Ste 160	Salem	OR	97302	**888-344-2767**	503-371-9318	661
Figueroa Hotel						
939 S Figueroa St	Los Angeles	CA	90015	**800-421-9092***	213-627-8971	376
*General						
Fiji Embassy						
2000 M St NW Ste 710	Washington	DC	20036	**800-932-3454**	202-337-8320	257
Fiji Water Company LLC						
11444 W Olympic Blvd Second Fl	Los Angeles	CA	90064	**888-426-3454**	310-312-2850	79-2
Fike Corp						
704 SW Tenth St	Blue Springs	MO	64015	**877-342-3453**	816-229-3405	283
704 SW Tenth St	Blue Springs	MO	64015	**877-342-3453**	816-229-3405	739
Fiksdal Hotel & Suites						
1215 Second St SW	Rochester	MN	55902	**800-366-3451**	507-288-2671	376
File Keepers LLC						
6277 E Slauson Ave	Los Angeles	CA	90040	**800-332-3463**	323-728-3133	458
FileMaker Inc						
5201 Patrick Henry Dr	Santa Clara	CA	95054	**800-325-2747***	408-987-7000	179-1
*Cust Svc						
Fillauer Inc						
PO Box 5189	Chattanooga	TN	37406	**800-251-6398**	423-624-0946	472
Fillip Metal Cabinet Co						
4500 W 47th St	Chicago	IL	60632	**800-535-0733**	773-733-7527	318-1
Fillmore Glen State Park						
1686 St Rt 38	Moravia	NY	13118	**800-456-2267**	315-497-0130	558
Film Comment Magazine						
165 W 65th St	New York	NY	10023	**888-313-6085**	212-875-5610	452-9
Filoli 86 Canada Rd	Woodside	CA	94062	**866-691-9080**	650-364-8300	96
Filterspun						
624 N Fairfield St	Amarillo	TX	79107	**800-323-5431**	806-383-3840	794
Filtertek Inc						
11411 Price Rd	Hebron	IL	60034	**800-248-2461**	815-648-1001	597
Filtration Group Inc						
912 E Washington St	Joliet	IL	60433	**800-739-4600**	815-726-4600	18
FinAid Page LLC						
PO Box 2056	Cranberry Township	PA	16066	**800-433-3243**	724-538-4500	716
Final Draft Inc						
26707 W Agoura Rd Ste 205	Calabasas	CA	91302	**800-231-4055**	818-995-8995	179-10
Finance & Commerce						
730 Second Ave S US Trust Bldg Ste 100	Minneapolis	MN	55402	**800-451-9998**	612-333-4244	452-5
Finance Ctr Federal Credit Union						
PO Box 26501	Indianapolis	IN	46226	**800-473-2328**	317-916-7700	219
Finance Factors Ltd						
1164 Bishop St	Honolulu	HI	96813	**800-648-7136**	808-548-4940	214
Financial Acctg Standards Board (FASB)						
401 Merritt 7 PO Box 5116	Norwalk	CT	06856	**800-748-0659**	203-847-0700	48-1
Financial Engines Inc						
1804 Embarcadero Rd	Palo Alto	CA	94303	**888-443-8577**	650-565-4900	179-10
NASDAQ: FNGN						
Financial Guaranty Insurance Co						
125 Pk Ave Sixth Fl	New York	NY	10017	**800-352-0001**	212-312-3000	388-5
Financial Institutions Inc						
220 Liberty St	Warsaw	NY	14569	**866-296-3743**	585-786-1100	357-2
NASDAQ: FISI						
Financial Managers Society (FMS)						
100 W Monroe St Ste 810	Chicago	IL	60603	**800-275-4367***	312-578-1300	48-2
*Cust Svc						
Financial Pacific Co						
3455 S 344th Way Ste 300	Federal Way	WA	98001	**800-447-7107**		216
Financial Partners Credit Union						
PO Box 7005	Downey	CA	90241	**800-950-7328**	562-923-0311	219
Financial Planning Assn (FPA)						
7535 E Hampden Ave Ste 400	Denver	CO	80231	**800-322-4237**	303-759-4900	48-2
Financial Publishing Co						
PO Box 570	South Bend	IN	46624	**800-433-0090***	574-243-6040	628-2
*Cust Svc						
Financial Service Corp						
2300 Windy Ridge Pkwy Ste 1100	Atlanta	GA	30339	**800-547-2382**	770-916-6500	681
Financial Times						
1330 Ave of the Americas	New York	NY	10019	**800-628-8088**	212-641-6500	525-2
FinancialCAD Corp						
13450 102nd Ave Ste 1750	Surrey	BC	V3T5X3	**800-304-0702**	604-957-1200	38
Fincantieri Marine Systems North America Inc						
800-C Principal Ct	Chesapeake	VA	23320	**877-436-7643**	757-548-6000	681
Finch Paper LLC						
One Glen St	Glens Falls	NY	12801	**800-833-9983**	518-793-2541	550
Finck Cigar Co						
414 Vera Cruz St	San Antonio	TX	78207	**800-221-0638***	210-226-4191	746
*Orders						
Find the Children						
2656 29th St Ste 203	Santa Monica	CA	90405	**888-477-6721**	310-314-3213	47-6
Findings Inc						
160 Water St	Keene	NH	03431	**800-225-2706**	603-352-3717	404
Findlay Automobile Club						
1550 Tiffin Ave	Findlay	OH	45840	**800-222-4357**	419-422-4961	52
Findlay Inn & Conference Ctr						
200 E Main Cross St	Findlay	OH	45840	**800-825-1455***	419-422-5682	376
*Cust Svc						
Fine Homebuilding Magazine						
63 S Main St PO Box 5506	Newtown	CT	06470	**800-283-7252**	203-426-8171	452-21
Fine Line Production						
2221 Regal Pkwy	Euless	TX	76040	**800-887-5625**	817-267-6750	478
Fine Organics Corp						
420 Kuller Rd PO Box 2277	Clifton	NJ	07015	**800-526-7480**	973-478-1000	149
Fine Woodworking Magazine						
63 S Main St PO Box 5506	Newtown	CT	06470	**800-283-7252**	203-426-8171	452-14
Finger Lakes Gaming & Race Track						
5857 Rt 96	Farmington	NY	14425	**877-846-7369**	585-924-3232	633
Finger Lakes Library System						
119 E Green St	Ithaca	NY	14850	**800-909-3557**	607-273-4074	431-3
Finger Lakes Times						
218 Genesse St PO Box 393	Geneva	NY	14456	**800-388-6652**	315-789-3333	628-8
Finger Lakes Visitors Connection						
25 Gorham St	Canandaigua	NY	14424	**877-386-4669**	585-394-3915	207
Fingerhut						
6509 Flying Cloud Dr	Eden Prairie	MN	55344	**800-208-2500**		454
Finish Line Ford Inc						
2211 W Pioneer Pkwy	Peoria	IL	61615	**888-841-4002**	309-693-2525	56
Finish Line Inc, The						
3308 N Mitthoeffer Rd	Indianapolis	IN	46235	**888-777-3949**	317-899-1022	300
NASDAQ: FINL						
FinishMaster Inc						
54 Monument Cir Eighth Fl	Indianapolis	IN	46204	**888-311-3678**	317-237-3678	543
Finken Plumbing Heating & Cooling						
628 19th Ave NE	Saint Joseph	MN	56374	**877-346-5367**	320-258-2005	603
Finks Jewelry Inc						
3545 Electric Rd	Roanoke	VA	24018	**800-699-7464**	540-342-2991	407
Finlandia University						
601 Quincy St	Hancock	MI	49930	**800-682-7604**	906-482-5300	166
Finley Hospital						
350 N Grandview Ave	Dubuque	IA	52001	**800-582-1891**	563-582-1881	371-3
Finn Corp						
9281 Le St Dr	Fairfield	OH	45014	**800-543-7166**	513-874-2818	273
Finn's Point National Cemetery						
454 Ft. Mott Rd	Pennsville	NJ	08070	**800-827-1000**	215-504-5610	135
Finney County Convention & Visitors Bureau						
1511 E Fulton Terr	Garden City	KS	67846	**866-267-4638**	620-275-1900	207
Finnleo Sauna						
575 Cokato St E	Cokato	MN	55321	**800-346-6536**		318-2
FINRA 1735 K St NW	Washington	DC	20006	**800-289-9999**	202-728-8000	48-2
Finzer Roller Co						
129 Rawls Rd	Des Plaines	IL	60018	**888-486-1900**	847-390-6200	668
Fire & Life Safety America						
3017 Vernon Rd Ste 100	Richmond	VA	23228	**800-252-5069**	804-222-1381	283
3017 Vernon Rd Ste 100	Richmond	VA	23228	**800-252-5069**	804-222-1381	739
Fire Fighter Sales & Service Co						
791 Commonwealth Dr	Warrendale	PA	15086	**888-412-3473**	724-720-6000	603
Firecom Inc						
39-27 59th St	Woodside	NY	11377	**888-347-3269**	718-899-6100	283
39-27 59th St	Woodside	NY	11377	**888-347-3269**	718-899-6100	739
Fire-End & Croker Corp						
Seven Westchester Plz	Elmsford	NY	10523	**800-759-3473**	914-592-3640	569
Firefighters Community Credit Union Inc						
2300 St Clair Ave NE	Cleveland	OH	44114	**800-621-4644**	216-621-4644	219
Firehouse Restaurant Group Inc						
3400 Kori Rd Ste 8	Jacksonville	FL	32257	**877-309-7332**	904-886-8300	309
FireKing Security Group						
101 Security Pkwy	New Albany	IN	47150	**800-457-2424**	812-948-8400	683
Firelands Electric Co-op Inc						
One Energy Pl PO Box 32	New London	OH	44851	**800-533-8658**	419-929-1571	245
Firelands Regional Medical Ctr						
1111 Hayes Ave	Sandusky	OH	44870	**800-342-1177**	419-557-7400	371-3
Fireman's Fund Insurance Co						
777 San Marin Dr	Novato	CA	94998	**866-386-3932**	800-558-1606	388-5
Fireside Hearth & Home						
7571 215th St W	Lakeville	MN	55044	**800-669-4328**		110
Fireside Inn & Suites						
25 Airport Rd	West Lebanon	NH	03784	**877-258-5900**	603-298-5900	376
FireSky Resort & Spa						
4925 N Scottsdale Rd	Scottsdale	AZ	85251	**800-528-7867**	480-945-7666	660
Firestone Fibers & Textiles Co						
100 Firestone Ln PO Box 1369	Kings Mountain	NC	28086	**800-441-1336**	704-734-2132	734-3
Firestone Industrial Products Co						
250 W 96th St	Indianapolis	IN	46260	**800-888-0650**	317-818-8600	59
Fireworks Fine Crafts Gallery						
3307 Utah Ave S	Seattle	WA	98134	**800-505-8882**	206-682-8707	513
Firm Consulting Group						
2107 W Cass St Ste B	Tampa	FL	33606	**877-636-9525**		458
FIRST						
200 Bedford St	Manchester	NH	03101	**800-871-8326**	603-666-3906	47-11
First Act Inc						
745 Boylston St	Boston	MA	02116	**888-551-1115**	617-226-7888	519
First Action Security Security Team Inc						
18702 Crestwood Dr	Hagerstown	MD	21742	**800-372-7447***	301-797-2124	683
*Cust Svc						
First Alarm Security & Patrol Inc						
1111 Estates Dr	Aptos	CA	95003	**800-684-1111**	831-476-1111	684
First Alert Inc						
3901 Liberty St Rd	Aurora	IL	60504	**800-323-9005**	630-851-7330	283
3901 Liberty St Rd	Aurora	IL	60504	**800-323-9005**	630-851-7330	739
First American Bank & Trust						
2785 Hwy 20 W PO Box 550	Vacherie	LA	70090	**800-738-2265**	225-265-2265	69
First American Corp						
One First American Way	Santa Ana	CA	92707	**800-854-3643**	714-250-3000	388-6
NYSE: FAF						
First American Funds						
PO Box 701	Milwaukee	WI	53201	**800-677-3863**		521
First American Home Buyers Protection Corp						
7833 Haskell Ave PO Box 10180	Van Nuys	CA	91410	**800-444-9030**	818-781-5050	364
First BanCorp						
PO Box 9146	San Juan	PR	00908	**866-695-2511**	787-725-2511	357-2
NYSE: FBP						
First Banctrust Corp						
101 S Central Ave	Paris	IL	61944	**800-228-6381**	217-465-6381	357-2
OTC: FIRT						

				Toll-Free	Phone	Class
First Bank Financial Centre (FBFC)						
155 W Wisconsin Ave						
PO Box 1004	Oconomowoc	WI	53066	**888-569-9909**	262-569-9900	69
First Banks Inc						
135 N Meramec Ave	Clayton	MO	63105	**800-760-2265**	314-854-4600	357-2
First Busey Corp						
100 W University Ave	Champaign	IL	61820	**800-672-8739**	217-365-4516	357-2
NASDAQ: BUSE						
First Business Financial Services Inc						
401 Charmany Dr	Madison	WI	53719	**888-455-2263**	608-238-8008	69
NASDAQ: FBIZ						
First Calgary Savings						
510 16th Ave NE	Calgary	AB	T2E1K4	**866-923-4778**		69
First Candle						
1314 Bedford Ave Ste 210	Baltimore	MD	21208	**800-221-7437**	410-653-8226	47-17
First Carolina Corporate Credit Union						
7900 Triad Ctr Dr Ste 410	Greensboro	NC	27409	**800-585-4317**		216
First Century Bank NA						
500 Federal St	Bluefield	WV	24701	**877-214-9426**	304-325-8181	69
First Chemical Corp						
1001 Industrial Rd	Pascagoula	MS	39581	**877-243-6178**	228-762-0870	142
First Choice Health Plan						
600 University St Ste 1400	Seattle	WA	98101	**800-467-5281**		388-3
First Church of Christ Scientist						
210 Massachusetts Ave P05-10	Boston	MA	02115	**800-288-7155**	617-450-2000	47-20
First Citizens Bancorp Inc						
PO Box 29	Columbia	SC	29202	**888-612-4444**		357-2
OTC: FCBN						
First Citizens Bank						
1801 Century Pk E Ste 800	Los Angeles	CA	90067	**888-323-4732**		357-2
First Citizens Bank & Trust Co Inc						
1230 Main St	Columbia	SC	29201	**888-612-4444**	803-733-2025	69
First Citizens National Bank Charitable Foundation						
PO Box 1708	Mason City	IA	50402	**800-423-1602**	641-423-1600	357-2
First Class Services Inc						
9355 US Hwy 60 E	Lewisport	KY	42351	**800-467-8684***	270-295-3746	770
*General						
First Commonwealth Financial Corp						
601 Philadelphia St	Indiana	PA	15701	**800-711-2265**	724-349-7220	357-2
NYSE: FCF						
First Community Corp (FCC)						
5455 Sunset Blvd	Lexington	SC	29072	**800-829-6372**	803-951-0555	357-2
NASDAQ: FCCO						
First Community Credit Union (FCCU)						
PO Box 1030	Chesterfield	MO	63006	**800-767-8880**	636-728-3333	219
First Community Financial Corp (FCFC)						
4000 N Central Ave Ste 100	Phoenix	AZ	85012	**877-777-4778**	602-265-7715	216
OTC: FMFP						
First Community Village						
1800 Riverside Dr	Columbus	OH	43212	**877-364-2570**	614-324-4455	663
First Co-op Assn (FCA)						
960 Riverview Dr PO Box 60	Cherokee	IA	51012	**877-753-5400**	712-225-5400	442
First Corporate Sedans Inc						
60 E 42nd St Ste 2424	New York	NY	10165	**800-473-8876**	212-972-2282	315
First DataBank Inc (FDB)						
701 Gateway Blvd						
Ste 600	South San Francisco	CA	94080	**800-633-3453***		179-10
*General						
First Defiance Financial Corp						
601 Clinton St	Defiance	OH	43512	**800-472-6292**	419-782-5015	357-2
NASDAQ: FDEF						
First Dental Health						
5771 Copley Dr Ste 101	San Diego	CA	92111	**800-334-7244**		412
First Draft						
316 N Michigan Ave Ste 400	Chicago	IL	60601	**800-878-5331**	800-493-4867	524-11
First Eastern Mortgage Corp						
100 Brickstone Sq	Andover	MA	01810	**800-777-2240**	978-749-3100	502
First Electric Co-op Corp						
1000 S JP Wright Loop Rd	Jacksonville	AR	72076	**800-489-7405**	501-982-4545	245
First Environment Inc						
91 Fulton St	Boonton	NJ	07005	**800-486-5869**	973-334-0003	193
First Equipment Co						
PO Box 2129	Addison	TX	75001	**888-780-8631**	972-380-2300	264-1
First Equity Mortgage Bankers						
9300 S Dadeland Blvd Ste 500	Miami	FL	33156	**800-973-3654**	305-666-3333	502
First Farmers & Merchants National Bank						
816 S Garden St PO Box 1148	Columbia	TN	38401	**800-882-8378**	931-388-3145	676
OTC: FIME						
First Federal Bancshares of Arkansas Inc						
1401 Hwy 62-65 N	Harrison	AR	72601	**866-242-3324**	870-741-7641	357-2
NASDAQ: FFBH						
First Federal Lakewood						
14806 Detroit Ave	Lakewood	OH	44107	**800-966-7300**	216-529-2700	69
First Federal of Northern Michigan						
100 S Second Ave	Alpena	MI	49707	**800-916-8800**	989-356-9041	70
NASDAQ: FFNM						
First Financial Bancorp (FFB)						
255 E Fifth St Ste 700	Cincinnati	OH	45202	**877-322-9530**	513-979-5837	357-2
NASDAQ: FFBC						
First Financial Bank						
300 High St	Hamilton	OH	45011	**877-322-9530***	513-867-4744	69
*Cust Svc						
First Financial Bankshares Inc						
PO Box 701	Abilene	TX	79604	**888-588-2623**	325-627-7155	357-2
NASDAQ: FFIN						
First Financial Corp						
One First Financial Plz	Terre Haute	IN	47807	**800-511-0045**	812-238-6000	357-2
NASDAQ: THFF						
First Foundation Bank						
18101 Von Karman Ave Ste 750	Irvine	CA	92612	**800-224-7931**	949-202-4100	69
First FSB						
633 La Salle St	Ottawa	IL	61350	**800-443-8780**	815-434-3500	70
First FSB of Frankfort						
216 W Main St PO Box 535	Frankfort	KY	40602	**888-818-3372**	502-223-1638	357-2
First Gold Hotel						
270 Main St	Deadwood	SD	57732	**800-274-1876**	605-578-9777	376
First Hartford Corp						
149 Colonial Rd	Manchester	CT	06042	**888-646-6555**	860-646-6555	644
OTC: FHRT						
First Hawaiian Bank						
999 Bishop St	Honolulu	HI	96813	**888-844-4444**	808-525-6340	69
First Health Group Corp						
Coventry						
3200 Highland Ave	Downers Grove	IL	60515	**800-247-2898**	630-737-7900	458

				Toll-Free	Phone	Class
First Horizon National Corp						
165 Madison	Memphis	TN	38103	**800-489-4040**	901-523-4444	357-2
NYSE: FHN						
First Independence Corp						
112 E Myrtle St PO Box 947	Independence	KS	67301	**800-455-0744**	620-331-1660	357-2
NYSE: FFSL						
First Insurance Company of Hawaii Ltd						
1100 Ward Ave PO Box 2866	Honolulu	HI	96803	**800-272-5202**	808-527-7777	388-4
First Insurance Funding Corp						
450 Skokie Blvd Ste 1000	Northbrook	IL	60062	**800-837-3707**		214
First Interstate Bancsystem Inc						
401 N 31st St	Billings	MT	59101	**888-752-3341**	406-255-5000	357-2
NASDAQ: FIBK						
First Interstate Bank						
401 N 31st St PO Box 30918	Billings	MT	59101	**888-752-3341**	406-255-5000	69
First Investors Corp						
110 Wall St	New York	NY	10005	**800-832-7783***		357-4
*General						
First Investors Life Insurance Co						
Raritan Plz 1 PO Box 7836	Edison	NJ	08818	**800-423-4026**		388-2
First Lease Inc						
1300 Virginia Dr						
Ste 450	Fort Washington	PA	19034	**866-493-4778**		264-4
First Mercantile Trust Co						
57 Germantown Ct Fourth Fl	Cordova	TN	38018	**800-753-3682**	901-753-9080	69
First Merchants Corp						
200 E Jackson St	Muncie	IN	47305	**800-205-3464**	765-747-1500	357-2
NASDAQ: FRME						
First Midwest Bancorp Inc						
One Pierce Pl Ste 1500	Itasca	IL	60143	**800-322-3623**	630-875-7200	357-2
NASDAQ: FMBI						
First Mutual Bancshares Inc						
400 108th Ave NE PO Box 1647	Bellevue	WA	98009	**800-735-7303**	425-455-7300	357-2
First National Bank						
4220 William Penn Hwy	Monroeville	PA	15146	**800-555-5455**		357-2
First National Bank Alaska						
101 W 36 Ave PO Box 100720	Anchorage	AK	99510	**800-856-4362**	907-777-4362	69
OTC: FBAK						
First National Bank Creston						
PO Box 445	Creston	IA	50801	**877-782-2195**	641-782-2195	69
First National Bank of Muscatine						
300 E Second St	Muscatine	IA	52761	**800-722-2678**	563-263-4221	69
First National Bank of Omaha						
1620 Dodge St	Omaha	NE	68197	**800-228-4411**	402-341-0500	69
First National Bank of Oneida, The						
18418 Alberta St PO Box 4699	Oneida	TN	37841	**866-546-8273**	423-569-8586	69
First National Bank of Santa Fe						
PO Box 609	Santa Fe	NM	87504	**888-912-2265**	505-992-2000	69
First National Bankers Bankshares Inc (FNBB)						
7813 Office Pk Blvd	Baton Rouge	LA	70809	**800-421-6182**	225-924-8015	69
First National Lincoln Corp						
223 Main St PO Box 940	Damariscotta	ME	04543	**800-564-3195**	207-563-3195	357-2
First National of Nebraska Inc						
PO BOX 2490	Omaha	NE	68197	**800-688-7070**	402-341-0500	357-2
Northern						
1301 Central Ave	Prince Albert	SK	S6V4W1	**800-267-6303**	306-765-3333	773
First Nations University of Canada						
Saskatoon						
226 20th St E	Saskatoon	SK	S7K0A6	**800-267-6303**	306-931-1800	773
First NBC (CPB)						
29092 Kretel Rd	Lacombe	LA	70445	**800-423-7503**	985-819-1200	69
First Niagara Ctr						
One Seymour Knox III Plz	Buffalo	NY	14203	**888-223-6000**	716-855-4100	711
First Niagara Financial Group						
726 Exchange St Ste 618	Buffalo	NY	14210	**800-421-0004**	716-625-7500	69
First Niagara RISK Management						
1215 Manor Dr	Mechanicsburg	PA	17055	**800-421-0004**	717-795-8666	195
First of Long Island Corp						
10 Glen Head Ave	Glen Head	NY	11545	**800-554-8969**	516-671-4900	357-2
NASDAQ: FLIC						
First Office						
1204 E Sixth St	Huntingburg	IN	47542	**800-983-4415**		318-1
First Pacific Advisors Inc						
11400 W Olympic Blvd						
Ste 1200	Los Angeles	CA	90064	**800-982-4372**	310-473-0225	398
First Palmetto Savings Bank Fsb						
PO Box 430	Camden	SC	29021	**800-922-7411**	803-432-2265	69
First Priority Health						
19 N Main St	Wilkes-Barre	PA	18711	**800-822-8753**		388-3
First Priority Inc						
1590 Todd Farm Dr	Elgin	IL	60123	**800-650-4899**	847-289-1600	576
First Quantum Minerals Ltd						
543 Granville St 8th Fl	Vancouver	BC	V6C1X8	**888-688-6577**	604-688-6577	497
TSE: FM						
First Regional Library						
370 W Commerce St	Hernando	MS	38632	**800-446-0892**	662-429-4439	431-3
First Republic Bank						
111 Pine St Third Fl	San Francisco	CA	94111	**800-392-1400**	415-392-1400	69
NYSE: FRC						
First Run Features						
630 Ninth Ave Ste 1213	New York	NY	10036	**800-229-8575**	212-243-0600	504
First Savings Bank						
2804 N Telshor Blvd	Las Cruces	NM	88011	**800-555-6895**	575-521-7931	69
First Shore Federal						
106-108 S Div St PO Box 4248	Salisbury	MD	21803	**800-634-6309**	410-546-1101	70
First South Bancorp Inc						
1311 Carolina Ave	Washington	NC	27889	**800-946-4178**	252-946-4178	357-2
NASDAQ: FSBK						
First South FarmCredit						
713 S Pear OrchaRd Rd Ste 300	Ridgeland	MS	39158	**800-955-1722**	601-977-8381	216
First Southern Bank						
301 S Ct St	Florence	AL	35630	**800-625-7131***	256-718-4200	357-2
*General						
First Southwest Co						
325 N St Paul St Ste 800	Dallas	TX	75201	**800-678-3792**	214-953-4000	681
First State Bank						
730 Harry Sauner Rd	Hillsboro	OH	45133	**800-987-2566***	937-393-9170	357-2
*General						
First State Bank & Trust Co						
1005 E 23rd St	Fremont	NE	68025	**888-674-4344**	402-721-2500	69
First State Bank of Kansas City						
650 Kansas Ave	Kansas City	KS	66105	**800-883-1242**	913-371-1242	69
First Supply LLC						
6800 Gisholt Dr	Madison	WI	53713	**800-236-9795**	608-222-7799	605

Company / Address	City	State	ZIP	Toll-Free	Phone	Class
First Tennessee Bank						
165 Madison Ave	Memphis	TN	38103	**800-382-5465**	901-523-4883	69
First Texas Bank						
501 E Third St PO Box 671	Lampasas	TX	76550	**866-220-1598**	512-556-3691	69
First Truck Centre Inc						
11313 170 St	Edmonton	AB	T5M3P5	**888-882-8530**	780-413-8800	56
First United Corp						
19 S Second St	Oakland	MD	21550	**888-692-2654**		357-2
NASDAQ: FUNC						
First UNUM Life Insurance Co						
2211 Congress St	Portland	ME	04122	**800-633-7491**	207-575-2211	388-2
First Western Bank & Trust						
PO Box 1090	Minot	ND	58702	**800-688-2584**	701-852-3711	69
FirstCare						
1901 W Loop 289 Ste #9	Lubbock	TX	79407	**800-884-4901**	806-784-4300	388-2
FirstCom Music						
1325 Capital Pkwy Ste 109	Carrollton	TX	75006	**800-858-8880***	972-446-8742	518
*Cust Svc						
FirstEnergy Corp						
76 S Main St	Akron	OH	44308	**800-633-4766**		357-5
NYSE: FE						
Firstexpress Inc						
1135 Freightliner Dr	Nashville	TN	37210	**800-848-9203**		770
FirstFed Bancorp Inc						
1630 Fourth Ave N PO Box 340	Bessemer	AL	35020	**800-436-5112**	205-428-8472	357-2
First-Knox National Bank						
One S Main St	Mount Vernon	OH	43050	**800-837-5266**	740-399-5500	69
Firstrust Savings Bank						
15 E Ridge Pike 4th Fl	Conshohocken	PA	19428	**800-220-2265**	610-941-9898	69
Firstwave Technologies Inc						
6263 N Scottsdale Rd Ste 180	Scottsdale	AZ	85250	**800-540-6061**	678-672-3112	179-11
Fisc Investment Services Corp						
1849 Clairmont Rd	Decatur	GA	30033	**800-241-3203**	404-321-1212	681
Fischer Environmental Service Inc						
1980 Surgi Dr	Mandeville	LA	70448	**800-391-2565**		570
Fischer Francis Trees & Watts Inc						
200 Pk Ave 11th Fl	New York	NY	10166	**888-367-3389**	212-681-3000	398
Fischer International Systems Corp						
5801 Pelican Bay Blvd Ste 300	Naples	FL	34108	**800-776-7258***	239-643-1500	179-1
*Tech Supp						
Fiserv Inc						
255 Fiserv Dr PO Box 979	Brookfield	WI	53008	**800-872-7882***	262-879-5000	68
NASDAQ: FISV ■ *Sales						
Fish & Richardson PC						
225 Franklin St 31st Fl	Boston	MA	02110	**800-818-5070**	617-542-5070	425
Fish Oven & Equipment Corp						
120 W Kent Ave	Wauconda	IL	60084	**877-526-8720**	847-526-8686	297
Fish Window Cleaning Services Inc						
200 Enchanted Pkwy	Manchester	MO	63021	**877-707-3474**	636-779-1500	309
Fisher & Arnold Inc						
9180 Crestwyn Hills Dr	Memphis	TN	38125	**888-583-9724**	901-748-1811	195
Fisher & Ludlow Tru-Weld Grating						
2000 Corporate Dr Ste 400	Wexford	PA	15090	**800-334-2047**	724-934-5320	486
Fisher & Paykel Appliances Inc						
5900 Skylab Rd	Huntington Beach	CA	92647	**888-936-7872**		35
Fisher & Paykel Healthcare Inc						
15365 Barranca Pkwy	Irvine	CA	92618	**800-446-3908**	949-453-4000	250
Fisher Bio Svc Inc						
14665 Rothgeb Dr	Rockville	MD	20850	**888-462-7246**	301-315-8460	580
Fisher Canvas Products Inc						
415 St Mary St	Burlington	NJ	08016	**800-892-6688**		723
Fisher College						
118 Beacon St	Boston	MA	02116	**866-266-6007**	617-236-8800	160
Fisher Container Corp						
1111 Busch Pkwy	Buffalo Grove	IL	60089	**800-837-2247**	847-541-0000	541
Fisher Investments						
13100 Skyline Blvd	Woodside	CA	94062	**800-550-1071**		398
Fisher Island Club & Resort						
One Fisher Island Dr	Miami	FL	33109	**800-537-3708***	305-535-6000	660
*Resv						
Fisher Manufacturing Co						
PO Box 60	Tulare	CA	93275	**800-421-6162**		602
Fisher Sand & Gravel Co						
3948 First ST SW	Underwood	ND	58576	**800-932-8740**	701-442-5600	498-4
Fisher Science Education						
4500 Turnberry Dr	Hanover Park	IL	60133	**800-955-1177**	800-766-7000	243
Fisher Textiles Inc						
139 Business Pk Dr	Indian Trail	NC	28079	**800-554-8886**	704-821-8870	734-6
Fisheries Museum of the Atlantic						
68 Bluenose Dr PO Box 1363	Lunenburg	NS	B0J2C0	**866-579-4909**	902-634-4794	513
Fisheries Supply Co						
1900 N Northlake Way	Seattle	WA	98103	**800-426-6930**	206-632-4462	760
Fisherman's Wharf Inn						
22 Commercial St	Boothbay Harbor	ME	04538	**800-628-6872**	207-633-5090	376
Fisher-Price Inc						
636 Girard Ave	East Aurora	NY	14052	**800-432-5437**	716-687-3000	752
Fisher-Titus Medical Ctr (FTMC)						
272 Benedict Ave	Norwalk	OH	44857	**800-589-3862**	419-668-8101	371-3
FishHound LLC						
15720 Ventura Blvd Ste 220	Encino	CA	91436	**800-469-0224**		384
FishNet Security						
2575 E Camelback Rd	Phoenix	AZ	85016	**888-732-9406**	602-343-2300	179-10
Fisk University						
1000 17th Ave N	Nashville	TN	37208	**888-702-0022**	615-329-8500	166
Fiskars Brands Inc						
2537 Daniels St	Madison	WI	53718	**866-348-5661**		222
Fiske Bros Refining Co						
129 Lockwood St	Newark	NJ	07105	**800-733-4755**	973-589-9150	534
Fit America MD						
4864 Arthur Kill Rd	Staten Island	NY	10309	**800-940-7546**	718-227-4980	797
Fitch Co						
2201 Russell St	Baltimore	MD	21230	**800-933-4824**	410-539-1953	403
Fitch Ratings Inc						
One State St Plz	New York	NY	10004	**800-753-4824**	212-908-0500	218
Fitger's Brewery Complex						
600 E Superior St	Duluth	MN	55802	**888-348-4377**	218-722-8826	662
Fitger's Brewery Museum						
600 E Superior St	Duluth	MN	55802	**888-348-4377**	218-722-8826	513
Fitness Depot						
1808 Lower Roswell Rd	Marietta	GA	30068	**800-974-6828**	770-971-6828	351
Fitness Rx for Men Magazine						
21 Bennetts Rd	Setauket	NY	11733	**800-653-1151**	631-751-9696	452-13
Fitness Zone						
3439 Colonnade Pkwy Se 800	Birmingham	AL	35243	**800-875-9145**		702
Fitzgerald Contractors Inc						
7103 St Vincent Ave	Shreveport	LA	71106	**800-259-3264**	318-869-3262	190-10
Fitzgeralds Casino & Hotel Tunica						
711 Lucky Ln	Robinsonville	MS	38664	**888-766-5825**	662-363-5825	132
Fitzpatrick Manhattan Hotel						
687 Lexington Ave	New York	NY	10022	**800-367-7701**	212-355-0100	376
Five Star Dodge						
3068 Riverside Dr	Macon	GA	31210	**877-748-9845**	478-474-3700	56
Five Star Electric of Houston Inc						
19424 Pk Row Ste 100	Houston	TX	77084	**888-492-7090**	281-492-7090	511
Five Star Food Service Inc						
6005 Century Oaks Dr						
Ste 100	Chattanooga	TN	37416	**800-327-0043**	423-643-2600	298
Five Star Quality Care Inc						
400 Centre St	Newton	MA	02458	**866-230-1286**	617-796-8387	446
NYSE: FVE						
Five Star Trucking Inc						
4380 Glenbrook Rd	Willoughby	OH	44094	**800-321-3658**	440-953-9300	770
FIX Flyer LLC						
225 Broadway Ste 1600	New York	NY	10007	**888-349-3593**		251
FJC Security Services Inc						
275 Jericho Tpke	Floral Park	NY	11001	**888-832-6352**	516-328-6000	684
Fkg Oil Co						
721 W Main	Belleville	IL	62220	**800-873-3546**	618-233-6754	205
FL Crane & Sons Inc						
508 S Spring St PO Box 428	Fulton	MS	38843	**800-748-9523**	662-862-2172	190-9
FL Emmert Co Inc						
2007 Dunlap St	Cincinnati	OH	45214	**800-441-3343**	513-721-5808	442
FL Smidth Inc						
2040 Ave C	Bethlehem	PA	18017	**800-523-9482**	610-264-6011	465
FLA (Forest Landowners Assn)						
900 Cir 75 Pkwy Ste 205	Atlanta	GA	30339	**800-325-2954**	404-325-2954	47-13
Flagler College						
74 King St	Saint Augustine	FL	32084	**800-304-4208***	904-829-6481	166
*Admissions						
Flagler County Public Library (FCPL)						
2500 Palm Coast Pkwy NW	Palm Coast	FL	32137	**877-863-5244**	386-446-6763	431-3
Flagship All Suites Resort						
60 N Maine Ave	Atlantic City	NJ	08401	**800-647-7890**	609-343-7447	376
Flagship Press Inc						
150 Flagship Dr	North Andover	MA	01845	**800-733-1520**	978-975-3100	619
Flagstaff Convention & Visitors Bureau						
323 W Aspen Ave	Flagstaff	AZ	86001	**800-217-2367**	928-779-7611	207
Flagstaff Pulliam Airport						
6200 S Pulliam Dr	Flagstaff	AZ	86001	**800-463-1389**	928-556-1234	27
Flagstaff Symphony Orchestra						
113 E Aspen Ave # A	Flagstaff	AZ	86001	**888-520-7214**	928-774-5107	566-3
Flagstar Bank FSB						
5151 Corporate Dr	Troy	MI	48098	**800-945-7700**	248-312-2000	69
FlagZone LLC						
105A Industrial Dr	Gilbertsville	PA	19525	**800-976-4201**		258
Flair Communications Agency Inc						
214 W Erie St	Chicago	IL	60654	**800-621-8317**	312-943-5959	9
Flambeau Inc						
15981 Valplast Rd	Middlefield	OH	44062	**800-457-5252**	440-632-1631	597
Flame Enterprises Inc						
21500 Gledhill St	Chatsworth	CA	91311	**800-854-2255**	818-700-2905	246
Flame Retardancy News						
49 Walnut Pk Bldg 2	Wellesley	MA	02481	**866-285-7215**	781-489-7301	524-12
Flamers Charbroiled Hamburgers						
1515 International Pkwy						
Ste 2013	Heathrow	FL	32746	**866-749-4889**	407-574-8363	661
Flamingo Gardens						
3750 S Flamingo Rd	Davie	FL	33330	**800-435-7352**	954-473-2955	96
Flamingo Resort Hotel & Conference Ctr						
2777 Fourth St	Santa Rosa	CA	95405	**800-848-8300**	707-545-8530	660
Flanders Corp						
531 Flanders Filters Rd	Washington	NC	27889	**800-637-2803**	252-946-8081	18
OTC: FLDR						
FLANDERS Inc						
8101 Baumgart Rd						
PO Box 23130	Evansville	IN	47724	**855-875-5888**	812-867-7421	511
Flash Technology Corp						
332 Nichol Mill Ln	Franklin	TN	37067	**888-313-5274**	615-503-2000	522
Flashes Publishers Inc						
595 Jenner Dr	Allegan	MI	49010	**800-968-4415**	269-673-2141	628-8
Flathead Convention & Visitors Bureau						
15 Depot Pk	Kalispell	MT	59901	**800-543-3105**	406-756-9091	207
Flathead Electric Co-op Inc						
2510 Hwy 2 E	Kalispell	MT	59901	**800-735-8489**	406-751-4483	245
Flathead Valley Community College						
777 Grandview Dr	Kalispell	MT	59901	**800-313-3822**	406-756-3822	160
Flatout Inc						
1422 Woodland Dr	Saline	MI	48176	**866-944-5445**	734-944-4262	295
Flavor Dynamics Inc						
640 Montrose Ave	South Plainfield	NJ	07080	**888-271-8424**	908-822-8855	296-8
Flax Art & Design						
1699 Market St	San Francisco	CA	94103	**844-352-9278**	415-552-2355	44
Fleet Engineers Inc						
1800 E Keating Ave	Muskegon	MI	49442	**800-333-7890***	231-777-2537	509
*Cust Svc						
Fleet Equipment Corp						
567 Commerce St	Franklin Lakes	NJ	07417	**800-631-0873**	201-337-3294	509
Fleet Landing Retirement Community						
1 Fleet Landing Blvd	Atlantic Beach	FL	32233	**877-591-6547***	904-246-9900	663
*General						
Fleet Owner Magazine						
11 Riverbend Dr S PO Box 4211	Stamford	CT	06907	**800-776-1246**	203-358-4205	452-5
Fleet Reserve Assn (FRA)						
125 NW St	Alexandria	VA	22314	**800-372-1924**	703-683-1400	47-19
FleetBoss Global Positioning Solutions Inc						
241 O'Brien Rd	Fern Park	FL	32730	**877-265-9559**	407-265-9559	725
Fleetwash Inc						
PO Box 1577	West Caldwell	NJ	07007	**800-847-3735**		61-1
Fleetwood Group Inc						
11832 James St	Holland	MI	49424	**800-257-6390**	616-396-1142	318-3
Fleetwood Homes of Idaho Inc						
2611 E Comstock Ave	Nampa	ID	83687	**800-334-8958**	208-466-2438	500
Fleetwood-Signode						
2222 Windsor Ct	Addison	IL	60101	**800-862-7997**	630-268-9999	552
Fleming Door Products Ltd						
101 Ashbridge Cir	Woodbridge	ON	L4L3R5	**800-263-7515**		234
Fleming Mason Energy Co-op						
1449 Elizaville Rd	Flemingsburg	KY	41041	**800-464-3144**	606-845-2661	245

Name / Address	City	State	ZIP	Toll-Free	Phone	Class
Flesh Co						
2118 59th St	Saint Louis	MO	63110	**800-869-3330**	314-781-4400	109
Fletch's Inc						
825 Charlevoix Ave PO Box 265	Petoskey	MI	49770	**877-238-0816**	231-347-9651	56
FletchAir Inc						
103 Turkey Run Ln	Comfort	TX	78013	**800-329-4647**	830-995-5900	22
Fletcher Granite Company Inc						
534 Groton Rd	Westford	MA	01886	**800-253-8168**	978-251-4031	498-6
Fletcher Jones Imports						
7300 W Sahara Ave	Las Vegas	NV	89117	**888-350-8850**	702-364-2700	56
Fletcher Music Centers Inc						
3966 Airway Cir	Clearwater	FL	33762	**800-258-1088**	727-571-1088	519
Fletcher'S Medical Supplies Inc						
6851 S Distribution Ave	Jacksonville	FL	32256	**855-541-7809**	904-387-4481	360
Fletcher-Terry Company Inc						
65 Spring Ln	Farmington	CT	06032	**800-843-3826***	860-677-7331	748
*Cust Svc						
Flex Checks Inc						
PO Box 141215	Grand Rapids	MI	49514	**866-791-7900**	616-791-7900	2
Flex Foam						
617 N 21st Ave	Phoenix	AZ	85009	**800-266-3626**	602-252-5819	130
Flex Hr						
10700 Medlock Bridge Rd						
Ste 206	Johns Creek	GA	30097	**877-735-3947**	770-814-4225	351
Flex Magazine						
21100 Erwin St	Woodland Hills	CA	91367	**877-527-8342**	412-235-0203	452-13
Flexaust Co						
1510 Armstrong Rd	Warsaw	IN	46580	**800-343-0428**	574-267-7909	367
Flexbar Machine Corp						
250 Gibbs Rd	Islandia	NY	11749	**800-879-7575**	631-582-8440	688
Flex-Cable Inc						
5822 N Henkel Rd	Howard City	MI	49329	**800-245-3539**	231-937-8000	803
Flexible Materials Inc						
1202 Port Rd	Jeffersonville	IN	47130	**800-244-6492**	812-280-7000	606
Flexible Steel Lacing Co						
2525 Wisconsin Ave	Downers Grove	IL	60515	**800-323-3444**	630-971-0150	208
Flexible-Montisa						
323 Acorn St	Plainwell	MI	49080	**800-875-6836***	269-924-0730	318-1
*Cust Svc						
Flexicon Corp						
2400 Emrick Blvd	Bethlehem	PA	18020	**888-353-9426**	610-814-2400	540
Flexicore of Texas						
PO Box 450049	Houston	TX	77245	**888-359-4267**	281-437-5700	184
FlexiInternational Software Inc						
Two Enterprise Dr	Shelton	CT	06484	**800-353-9492**	203-925-3040	179-1
OTC: FLXI						
Flexi-Van Leasing Inc						
251 Monroe Ave	Kenilworth	NJ	07033	**866-965-9288**	908-276-8000	264-5
Flexmag Industries Inc						
107 Industry Rd	Marietta	OH	45750	**800-543-4426**	740-374-8024	453
Flex-N-Gate Corp						
1306 E University Ave	Urbana	IL	61802	**800-398-1496**	217-278-2600	59
Flex-O-Lite Inc						
50 Crestwood Executive Ctr						
Ste 522	Saint Louis	MO	63126	**800-325-9525**		330
Flexospan Steel Buildings Inc						
253 Railroad St	Sandy Lake	PA	16145	**800-245-0396**	724-376-7221	105
Flex-Pay Business Services Inc						
723 Coliseum Dr Ste 200	Winston-Salem	NC	27106	**800-457-2143**	336-773-0128	195
Flexsys America LP						
260 Springside Dr	Akron	OH	44333	**800-455-5622**	330-666-4111	667
Flextron Industries Inc						
720 Mt Rd	Aston	PA	19014	**800-633-2181**	610-459-4600	541
Flex-Y-Plan Industries Inc						
6960 W Ridge Rd	Fairview	PA	16415	**800-458-0552***	814-474-1565	318-1
*Cust Svc						
Flight Dimensions International Inc						
4835 Cordell Ave Ste 150	Bethesda	MD	20814	**866-235-6870**	301-634-8201	21
Flight Systems Inc						
505 Fishing Creek Rd	Lewisberry	PA	17339	**800-403-3728**	717-932-9900	247
Flightstar Corp						
Seven Airport Rd Willard Airport	Savoy	IL	61874	**800-747-4777**	217-351-7700	13
Flinchbaugh Engineering Inc						
4387 Run Way	York	PA	17406	**866-967-5334**	717-755-1900	482
Flint & Walling Inc						
95 N Oak St	Kendallville	IN	46755	**800-345-9422***	260-347-1600	632
*Sales						
Flint Cultural Ctr Corp						
1310 E Kearsley St	Flint	MI	48503	**888-823-6837**	810-237-7333	49-1
Flint Energies						
103 Macon Rd	Reynolds	GA	31076	**800-342-3616**	478-847-3415	245
Flint Journal						
200 E First St	Flint	MI	48502	**800-875-6200***	810-766-6100	525-2
*Circ						
Flint River Mills Inc						
1100 Dothan Rd PO Box 280	Bainbridge	GA	39817	**800-841-8502***	229-246-2232	442
*Cust Svc						
Flintco LLC						
1624 W 21st St	Tulsa	OK	74107	**800-947-2828**	918-587-8451	187
FLIR Systems Inc						
27700-A SW Pkwy Ave	Wilsonville	OR	97070	**877-773-3547**	503-498-3547	522
NASDAQ: FLIR						
Floor Coverings International						
5250 Triangle Pwy Ste 100	Norcross	GA	30092	**800-955-4324***	770-874-7600	290
*Sales						
Flooring Sales Group						
1251 First Ave S	Seattle	WA	98134	**877-478-3577**	206-624-7800	290
Flora Mfg & Distributing Ltd						
7400 Fraser Park Dr	Burnaby	BC	V5J5B9	**888-436-6697**	604-436-6000	474
Florence Area Chamber of Commerce						
290 Hwy 101	Florence	OR	97439	**800-585-3737**	541-997-3128	137
Florence Convention & Visitors Bureau						
3290 W Radio Dr	Florence	SC	29501	**800-325-9005***	843-664-0330	207
*General						
Florence Eiseman company LLC						
1966 S Fourth St	Milwaukee	WI	53204	**800-558-9013**		153-4
Florence Events Ctr						
715 Quince St	Florence	OR	97439	**888-968-4086**	541-997-1994	206
Florence National Cemetery						
803 E National Cemetery Rd	Florence	SC	29506	**877-907-8585**	843-669-8783	135
Florence-Darlington Technical College						
2715 W Lucas St	Florence	SC	29502	**800-228-5745**	843-661-8324	788
Florentine Opera Co						
700 N Water St Ste 950	Milwaukee	WI	53202	**800-326-7372**	414-291-5700	566-2

Name / Address	City	State	ZIP	Toll-Free	Phone	Class
Florestone Products Company Inc						
2851 Falcon Dr	Madera	CA	93637	**800-446-8827**	559-661-4171	603
Florida						
Attorney General						
State Capitol PL-01	Tallahassee	FL	32399	**866-966-7226**	850-487-1963	337-10
Business & Professional Regulation Dept						
1940 N Monroe St	Tallahassee	FL	32399	**866-532-1440**	850-487-1395	337-10
Consumer Services Div						
2005 Apalachee Pkwy	Tallahassee	FL	32399	**800-435-7352**		337-10
Education Dept						
325 W Gaines St Ste 1514	Tallahassee	FL	32399	**800-445-6739**	850-245-0505	337-10
Financial Services Dept						
200 E Gaines St	Tallahassee	FL	32399	**800-342-2762**	850-413-3100	337-10
Insurance Regulation Office						
200 E Gaines St	Tallahassee	FL	32301	**800-342-2762**	850-413-3140	337-10
Recreation & Parks Div						
3900 Commonwealth Blvd						
MS 500	Tallahassee	FL	32399	**800-326-3521***	850-245-2157	337-10
*Campground Resv						
Secretary of State						
RA Gray Bldg						
500 S Bronough St	Tallahassee	FL	32399	**800-955-8771**	850-245-6500	337-10
Vocational Rehabilitation Services Div						
2002 Old St Augustine Rd						
Bldg A	Tallahassee	FL	32301	**800-451-4327**	850-245-3399	337-10
Florida A & M University						
Coleman Memorial Library						
1500 S Martin Luther						
King Blvd	Tallahassee	FL	32307	**800-540-6754**	850-599-3370	431-6
Florida Aquarium						
701 Channelside Dr	Tampa	FL	33602	**800-353-4741**	813-273-4000	39
Florida Atlantic University (FAU)						
777 Glades Rd	Boca Raton	FL	33431	**800-299-4328***	561-297-3000	166
*Admissions						
Davie 3200 College Ave	Davie	FL	33314	**800-764-2222**	954-236-1000	166
Fort Lauderdale						
111 E Las Olas Blvd	Fort Lauderdale	FL	33301	**800-764-2222**	954-236-1000	166
MacArthur						
5353 Parkside Dr	Jupiter	FL	33458	**888-328-2586**	561-799-8500	166
Florida Bar						
651 E Jefferson St	Tallahassee	FL	32399	**800-342-8060**	850-561-5600	71
Florida Bar Journal						
651 E Jefferson St	Tallahassee	FL	32399	**800-342-8060**	850-561-5600	452-15
Florida Bill Status						
111 W Madison St Rm 704	Tallahassee	FL	32399	**800-342-1827**	850-488-4371	430
Florida Chamber of Commerce						
136 S Bronough St						
PO Box 11309	Tallahassee	FL	32302	**877-521-1230**	850-521-1200	138
Florida Christian College						
1011 Bill Beck Blvd	Kissimmee	FL	34744	**888-468-6322**	407-847-8966	159
Florida City Gas (FCG)						
955 E 25th St	Hialeah	FL	33013	**800-993-7546**	305-691-8710	775
Florida Coastal School of Law						
8787 Bay Pine Rd	Jacksonville	FL	32256	**877-210-2591**	904-680-7700	167-1
Florida College						
119 N Glen Arven Ave	Temple Terrace	FL	33617	**800-326-7655**	813-988-5131	166
Florida Community College at Jacksonville						
Downtown						
101 State St W	Jacksonville	FL	32202	**877-633-5950**	904-633-8100	160
Florida Culinary Institute						
2410 Metro Centre Blvd	West Palm Beach	FL	33407	**800-254-0547**	561-842-8324	161
Florida Democratic Party						
214 S Bronough St	Tallahassee	FL	32301	**855-352-7233**	850-222-3411	609-1
Florida Dental Assn						
1111 E Tennessee St	Tallahassee	FL	32308	**800-877-9922**	850-681-3629	227
Florida Detroit Diesel-Allison Inc						
5040 University Blvd W	Jacksonville	FL	32216	**888-812-4440**	904-737-7330	382
Florida Family Insurance Services LLC						
27599 Riverview Ctr Blvd Ste 100						
PO Box 136001	Bonita Springs	FL	34136	**888-850-4663**	239-495-4700	388-4
Florida Farm Bureau Insurance Cos						
5700 SW 34th St	Gainesville	FL	32608	**866-275-7322**	352-378-1321	388-4
Florida Grand Opera						
8390 NW 25th St	Miami	FL	33122	**800-741-1010**	305-854-1643	566-2
Florida Heritage Museum						
167 San Marco Ave	Saint Augustine	FL	32084	**800-268-7252**	904-829-9729	513
Florida Holocaust Museum						
55 Fifth St S	Saint Petersburg	FL	33701	**800-388-4069**	727-820-0100	513
Florida Hospital Heartland Medical Ctr						
4200 Sun 'n Lake Blvd						
PO Box 9400	Sebring	FL	33871	**800-756-4447**	863-314-4466	371-3
Florida Institute of Technology						
150 W University Blvd	Melbourne	FL	32901	**800-888-4348**	321-674-8000	166
Florida International University						
11200 SW Eigth St	Miami	FL	33199	**800-677-6337**	305-348-2000	166
Florida Keys Community College						
5901 College Rd	Key West	FL	33040	**866-567-2665**	305-296-9081	160
Florida Keys Electric Co-op Assn						
91630 Overseas Hwy	Tavernier	FL	33070	**800-858-8845**	305-852-2431	245
Florida Memorial University						
15800 NW 42nd Ave	Miami Gardens	FL	33054	**800-822-1362**	305-626-3600	166
Florida National Cemetery						
6502 SW 102nd Ave	Bushnell	FL	33513	**877-907-8585**	352-793-7740	135
Florida Newsclips LLC						
PO Box 2190	Palm Harbor	FL	34682	**800-442-0332**		616
Florida Pneumatic Manufacturing Corp						
851 Jupiter Pk Ln	Jupiter	FL	33458	**800-327-9403**	561-744-9500	749
Florida Presbyterian Homes						
16 Lk Hunter Dr	Lakeland	FL	33803	**866-294-3352**	863-688-5521	663
Florida Public Utilities Co (FPUC)						
401 S Dixie Hwy	West Palm Beach	FL	33401	**800-427-7712**		775
Florida Solar Energy Ctr						
1679 Clearlake Rd	Cocoa	FL	32922	**877-777-4778**	321-638-1000	659
Florida Southern College						
111 Lk Hollingsworth Dr	Lakeland	FL	33801	**800-274-4131***	863-680-4131	166
*Admissions						
Florida Student Financial Assistance Office						
1940 N Monroe St Ste 70	Tallahassee	FL	32303	**888-827-2004**	850-410-5200	716
Florida Technical College						
12900 Challenger Pkwy Ste 130	Orlando	FL	32826	**888-678-2929***	407-447-7300	788
*General						
Florida Tile Industries Inc						
998 Governors Ln Ste 300	Lexington	KY	40513	**800-352-8453***	859-219-5200	741
*Cust Svc						

Name / Address	City	State	ZIP	Toll-Free	Phone	Class
Florida Times-Union One Riverside Ave	Jacksonville	FL	32202	800-472-6397	904-359-4111	525-2
Florim USA Inc 300 International Blvd	Clarksville	TN	37040	877-356-7461	931-645-5100	741
Florist Distributing Inc 2403 Bell Ave	Des Moines	IA	50321	800-373-3741	515-243-5228	293
Florsheim Inc 333 W Estabrook Blvd	Glendale	WI	53212	866-454-0449		300
Flow Dry Technology Inc 379 Albert Rd PO Box 190	Brookville	OH	45309	800-533-0077	937-833-2161	325
Flow International Corp 23500 64th Ave S *NASDAQ: FLOW*	Kent	WA	98032	800-446-3569	253-850-3500	450
Flower City Tissue Mills Inc 700 Driving Pk Ave	Rochester	NY	14613	800-595-2030	585-458-9200	541
Flower Patch Inc 4370 S 300 W *General	Murray	UT	84107	888-865-6858*	801-747-2824	292
Flower Pot Florists 2314 N Broadway St	Knoxville	TN	37917	800-824-7792	865-523-5121	292
FlowerClub PO Box 60910	Los Angeles	CA	90060	800-493-5610	310-966-8644	292
Flowers Auto Parts Co 935 Hwy 70 SE *Cust Svc	Hickory	NC	28602	800-538-6272*	828-322-5414	60
Flowers Hospital 4370 W Main St	Dothan	AL	36305	877-456-9617	334-793-5000	371-3
Flow-Eze Co 3209 Auburn St	Rockford	IL	61101	800-435-4873	815-965-1062	678
Flowserve Corp 5215 N O'Connor Blvd Ste 2300 *NYSE: FLS*	Irving	TX	75039	800-350-1082	972-443-6500	632
Floyd Blinsky Trucking Inc 210 Keys Rd	Yakima	WA	98901	800-537-9599	509-457-3484	676
Floyd Browne Group 3875 Embassy Parkway *General	Akron	OH	44333	800-325-7647*	330-375-0800	194
Floyd County 100 S Main St	Floydada	TX	79235	800-521-8565	806-983-2197	336
Floyd E Tut Fann State Veterans Home 2701 Meridian St	Huntsville	AL	35811	855-212-8028	256-851-2807	781
Floyd Medical Ctr 304 Turner McCall Blvd	Rome	GA	30165	866-874-2772	706-509-5000	371-3
Floyd Memorial Hospital 1850 State St	New Albany	IN	47150	800-423-1513	812-944-7701	371-3
Fluent Home Ltd 7319 104 St NW	Edmonton	AB	T6E4B9	855-238-4826		684
Fluid Components International 1755 La Costa Meadows Dr	San Marcos	CA	92078	800-863-8703	760-744-6950	202
Fluid Management Inc 1023 S Wheeling Rd	Wheeling	IL	60090	800-462-2466	847-537-0880	383
Fluid Metering Inc Five Aerial Way Ste 500	Syosset	NY	11791	800-223-3388	516-922-6050	631
Fluidmaster Inc 30800 Rancho Viejo Rd	San Juan Capistrano	CA	92675	800-631-2011	949-728-2000	602
Fluidware 12 York St Second Fl	Ottawa	ON	K1N5S6	866-218-5127		384
Fluke Biomedical 6920 Seaway Blvd	Everett	WA	98203	800-443-5853	425-446-6945	248
Fluke Corp 6920 Seaway Blvd	Everett	WA	98203	877-355-3225	425-446-6100	248
Fluke Networks Inc 6920 Seaway Blvd	Everett	WA	98203	800-283-5853	425-446-4519	248
Fluor Corp 6700 Las Colinas Blvd	Irving	TX	75039	800-405-6637	469-398-7000	195
Flushing Financial Corp 1979 Marcus Ave *NASDAQ: FFIC*	New Hyde Park	NY	11042	800-581-2889	718-961-5400	357-2
FlyData Inc 1043 N Shoreline Blvd Ste 200	Mountain View	CA	94043	855-427-9787		616
Flying E Ranch 2801 W Wickenburg Way	Wickenburg	AZ	85390	888-684-2650	928-684-2690	239
Flying Leatherneck Aviation Museum Anderson Ave MCAS Miramar	San Diego	CA	92145	877-359-8762	858-693-1723	513
Flying Magazine 460 N. Orlando Ave. Suite 200 *Cust Svc	Winter Park	FL	32789	800-678-0797*	407-628-4802	452-14
Flying W Ranch Inc 3330 Chuckwagon Rd	Colorado Springs	CO	80919	800-232-3599	719-598-4000	662
Flynn Canada Ltd 1390 Spruce St *General	Winnipeg	MB	R3E2V7	877-856-8566*	204-786-6951	190-12
F&M Bank PO Box 1130	Clarksville	TN	37041	800-645-4199	931-645-2400	69
FM Brown's Sons Inc 205 Woodrow Ave PO Box 2116	Sinking Spring	PA	19608	800-334-8816	610-678-4567	442
FM Global 270 Central Ave PO Box 7500	Johnston	RI	02919	800-343-7722	401-275-3000	388-4
F&M Mafco Inc PO Box 11013	Cincinnati	OH	45211	800-333-2151	513-367-2151	191
FM NEWS 101 KXL 1211 SW Fifth Ave	Portland	OR	97204	877-733-1011	503-517-6000	636-86
FMA (Fabricators & Manufacturers Assn International) 833 Featherstone Rd	Rockford	IL	61107	888-394-4362	815-399-8700	48-13
FMC (Fairfield Medical Ctr) 401 N Ewing St	Lancaster	OH	43130	800-548-2627	740-687-8000	371-3
FMC Corp 1735 Market St *NYSE: FMC*	Philadelphia	PA	19103	888-548-4486	215-299-6000	141
FMC Corp Industrial Chemicals Group 1735 Market St	Philadelphia	PA	19103	800-323-7107	215-299-6000	141
FMC Technologies Inc 1803 Gears Rd *NYSE: FTI*	Houston	TX	77067	800-356-4898	281-591-4000	530
FMCA (Family Motor Coach Assn) 8291 Clough Pk	Cincinnati	OH	45244	800-543-3622	513-474-3622	47-23
FMCI (Grassley Group, The) 409 Washington St Ste A	Cedar Falls	IA	50613	866-619-5580		46
FMCSA (Federal Motor Carrier Safety Administration) 1200 New Jersey Ave SE	Washington	DC	20590	800-832-5660		338-15
FMG Enterprises Inc 1125 Memorex Dr	Santa Clara	CA	95050	800-327-6177	408-982-0110	632
FMI (Food Marketing Institute) 2345 Crystal Dr Ste 800	Arlington	VA	22202	800-732-2639	202-220-0600	48-18
FMI Corp 5171 Glenwood Ave Ste 200 *General	Raleigh	NC	27612	800-669-1364*	919-787-8400	195
FMR Corp 82 Devonshire St	Boston	MA	02109	800-343-3548		398
FMS (Financial Managers Society) 100 W Monroe St Ste 810 *Cust Svc	Chicago	IL	60603	800-275-4367*	312-578-1300	48-2
FMS Inc 8150 Leesburg Pk Ste 600	Vienna	VA	22182	866-367-7801	703-356-4700	179-2
FNBB (First National Bankers Bankshares Inc) 7813 Office Pk Blvd	Baton Rouge	LA	70809	800-421-6182	225-924-8015	69
FNW Industrial Plastics Inc 12500 Jefferson Ave PO Box 2778	Newport News	VA	23602	800-721-2590	757-874-7795	595
FOA (Friends of Animals Inc) 777 Post Rd Ste 205	Darien	CT	06820	800-321-7387	203-656-1522	47-3
Foam Molders & Specialty Corp 20004 State Rd	Cerritos	CA	90703	800-378-8987		594
Focus Camera Inc 905 McDonald Ave	Brooklyn	NY	11218	800-221-0828	718-437-8810	118
Focus Direct LLC 9707 Broadway	San Antonio	TX	78217	800-555-1551	210-805-9185	5
Focus on the Family 8605 Explorer Dr *Sales	Colorado Springs	CO	80920	800-232-6459*	719-531-3400	47-6
Focus Receivables Management LLC 1130 Northchase Pkwy Ste 150	Marietta	GA	30067	877-362-8766	678-305-9606	158
Focus Services Inc 4102 South 1900 West Ste 7	Roy	UT	84067	888-362-8711		390
Focus Strategic Communications Inc 2474 Waterford St	Oakville	ON	L6L5E6	866-263-6287	905-825-8757	93
Foellinger-Freimann Botanical Conservatory 1100 S Calhoun St	Fort Wayne	IN	46802	866-220-8842	260-427-6440	96
Fogarty Creek State Recreation Area 5150 Oregon Coast Hwy 198 NE 123rd St	Depoe Bay	OR	97341	800-551-6949		558
FOIA Group Inc (FGI) 1250 Connecticut Ave NW Ste 200	Washington	DC	20036	888-461-7951		384
Folbot Inc 4209 Pace St	Charleston	SC	29405	800-533-5099	843-744-3483	701
Foldcraft Co 615 Centennial Dr	Kenyon	MN	55946	800-759-6653	507-789-5111	318-1
Foley & Lardner LLP 777 E Wisconsin Ave	Milwaukee	WI	53202	855-225-5341	414-271-2400	425
Foley House Inn 14 W Hull St Chippewa Sq	Savannah	GA	31401	800-647-3708	912-232-6622	376
Foley Inc 855 Centennial Ave	Piscataway	NJ	08854	888-417-6464	732-885-5555	61-7
Folger Adam Security Inc 4634 S Presa St	San Antonio	TX	78223	888-745-0530	210-533-1231	347
Folk Art Ctr PO Box 9545	Asheville	NC	28815	888-672-7717	828-298-7928	513
Follett Corp 3 Westbrook Corporate Center Ste 200	Westchester	IL	60154	800-365-5388		94
Follett Educational Services 1433 International Pkwy	Woodridge	IL	60517	800-621-4272	630-972-5600	94
Follett Higher Education Group Three Westbrook Corporate Ctr Ste 200	Westchester	IL	60154	800-323-4506		95
Follett Software Co 1391 Corporate Dr	McHenry	IL	60050	800-323-3397	815-344-8700	179-10
Folsom Lake Ford 12755 Folsom Blvd	Folsom	CA	95630	800-730-0457	916-353-2000	56
Fomo Products Inc 2775 Barber Rd	Norton	OH	44203	800-321-5585	330-753-4585	594
Fonar Corp 110 Marcus Dr *NASDAQ: FONR*	Melville	NY	11747	877-694-2929	631-694-2929	379
Fond du Lac Area Assn of Commerce 207 N Main St	Fond du Lac	WI	54935	800-279-8811	920-921-9500	137
Fond du Lac Band of Lake Superior Chippewa 1720 Big Lake Rd	Cloquet	MN	55720	888-888-6007	218-879-4593	131
Fond du Lac Convention & Visitors Bureau 171 S Pioneer Rd	Fond du Lac	WI	54935	800-937-9123	920-923-3010	207
Fond du Lac Tribal & Community College 2101 14th St	Cloquet	MN	55720	800-657-3712	218-879-0800	163
Fontaine Fifth Wheel 7574 Commerce Cir	Trussville	AL	35173	800-874-9780	205-661-4900	59
Fontaine Modification Co 9827 Mt Holly Rd	Charlotte	NC	28214	800-366-8246	704-391-1355	509
Fontaine Trailer Co 430 Letson Rd PO Box 619	Haleyville	AL	35565	800-821-6535	205-486-5251	769
Fontaine Truck Equipment Co 7574 Commerce Cir	Trussville	AL	35173	800-874-9780	205-661-4900	509
Fontainebleau Miami Beach 4441 Collins Ave	Miami Beach	FL	33140	800-548-8886	305-538-2000	660
Fontainebleau State Park 67825 US Hwy 190	Mandeville	LA	70448	888-677-3668	985-624-4443	558
Fontana Village Resort 300 Woods Rd PO Box 68	Fontana Dam	NC	28733	800-849-2258	828-498-2211	660
Center for Devices & Radiological Health (CDRH) 10903 New Hampshire Ave WO66-5429	Silver Spring	MD	20993	800-638-2041	301-796-7100	338-8
Center for Drug Evaluation & Research 10001 New Hampshire Ave Hillandale Bldg 4th Fl	Silver Spring	MD	20993	855-543-3784	301-796-3400	338-8
Center for Food Safety & Applied Nutrition 5100 Paint Branch Pkwy	College Park	MD	20740	888-723-3366		338-8
Food & Drug Administration *National Center for Toxicological Research* 3900 N Ctr Rd	Jefferson	AR	72079	800-638-3321	870-543-7000	338-8
Food & Drug Law Institute (FDLI) 1155 15th St NW Ste 800	Washington	DC	20005	800-956-6293	202-371-1420	48-10
Food & Nutrition Service *Food Stamp Program* 3101 Pk Ctr Dr	Alexandria	VA	22302	800-221-5689	703-305-2022	338-1

Name / Address	City	State	ZIP	Toll-Free	Phone	Class
Food & Wine Magazine 1120 Ave of the Americas	New York	NY	10036	**800-333-6569**	813-979-6625	452-11
Food Allergy & Anaphylaxis Network (FAAN) 11781 Lee Jackson Hwy Ste 160	Fairfax	VA	22033	**800-929-4040**	703-691-3179	47-17
Food Bank For New York City 39 Broadway 10th Fl	New York	NY	10006	**866-692-3663**	212-566-7855	298
Food City 1005 N Arizona Ave	Chandler	AZ	85224	**800-755-7292**	480-857-2198	342
Food for the Poor Inc (FFP) 6401 Lyons Rd	Coconut Creek	FL	33073	**800-427-9104**	954-427-2222	47-5
Food Ingredient News 49 Walnut Pk Bldg 2	Wellesley	MA	02481	**866-285-7215**	781-489-7301	524-12
Food Marketing Institute (FMI) 2345 Crystal Dr Ste 800	Arlington	VA	22202	**800-732-2639**	202-220-0600	48-18
Food Processing Magazine 555 W Pierce Rd Ste 301	Itasca	IL	60143	**800-755-5505**	630-467-1300	452-21
Food Processing Suppliers Assn (FPSA) 1451 Dolley Madison Blvd Ste 101	McLean	VA	22101	**800-772-9247**	703-761-2600	48-13
Food Services of America Inc 16100 N 71st St Ste 400	Scottsdale	AZ	85254	**800-528-9346**	480-927-4000	296-8
Food Warming Equipment Company Inc 7900 S Rt 31 *Sales	Crystal Lake	IL	60014	**800-222-4393***	815-459-7500	297
Foodscience Corp 20 New England Dr Ste 10	Essex Junction	VT	05452	**800-451-5190**	802-878-5508	787
Foot Locker Inc 112 W 34th St *NYSE: FL*	New York	NY	10120	**800-952-5210**	212-720-3700	300
Foot of the Mountain Motel 200 W Arapahoe Ave	Boulder	CO	80302	**866-773-5489**	303-442-5688	376
Foot Solutions Inc 2359 Windy Hill Rd Ste 400 *General	Marietta	GA	30067	**888-358-3668***	770-984-0844	309
Footaction Inc 112 W 34th St	New York	NY	10120	**800-863-8932**	715-261-9588	300
Foothill College 12345 El Monte Rd	Los Altos Hills	CA	94022	**800-234-1597**	650-949-7777	160
Foothills Inn 1625 N La Crosse St	Rapid City	SD	57701	**877-428-5666**	605-348-5640	376
Footstar Inc 933 MacArthur Blvd	Mahwah	NJ	07430	**800-322-2885**	201-934-2000	300
FOP (Fraternal Order of Police) 701 Marriott Dr	Nashville	TN	37214	**800-451-2711**	615-399-0900	47-15
For Eyes/Insight Optical 285 W 74th Pl	Hialeah	FL	33014	**877-688-9891**	305-557-9004	536
Forbes Hospice 4800 Friendship Ave	Pittsburgh	PA	15224	**800-381-8080**	412-578-5000	368
Forbes Inc 60 Fifth Ave	New York	NY	10011	**800-295-0893**	212-620-2200	628-9
Forbes Magazine 60 Fifth Ave	New York	NY	10011	**800-295-0893**	212-366-8900	452-5
Forbes Snyder Tristate Cash 54 Northampton St	Easthampton	MA	01027	**800-222-4064**	413-529-2950	253
Forbo Flooring Systems Eight Maplewood Dr Humboldt Industrial Pk *Cust Svc	Hazleton	PA	18202	**800-842-7839***		291
Force 3 Inc 2151 Priest Bridge Dr Ste 7	Crofton	MD	21114	**800-391-0204**	301-261-0204	181
Force Control Industries Inc 3660 Dixie Hwy	Fairfield	OH	45014	**800-829-3244**	513-868-0900	613
Force Flow Inc 2430 Stanwell Dr	Concord	CA	94520	**800-893-6723**		359
Force10 Networks Inc 1415 N McDowell Blvd	Petaluma	CA	94954	**866-600-5100**	707-665-4400	672
Ford Audio-Video Systems Inc 4800 W I- 40	Oklahoma City	OK	73128	**800-654-6744**	405-946-9966	51
Ford Equity Research Inc 11722 Sorrento Vly Rd Ste I	San Diego	CA	92121	**800-842-0207**	858-755-1327	398
Ford Fasteners Inc 110 S Newman St	Hackensack	NJ	07601	**800-272-3673**	201-487-3151	278
Ford Motor Co PO Box 6248 *NYSE: F*	Dearborn	MI	48126	**800-392-3673**	313-845-8540	58
Ford Motor Credit Co One American Rd PO Box 1732	Dearborn	MI	48121	**800-727-7000**	313-322-3000	214
Ford of Montebello Inc 2747 Via Campo	Montebello	CA	90640	**888-313-2305**	323-838-6920	56
Ford of Ocala Inc 2816 NW Pine Ave	Ocala	FL	34475	**888-255-1788**	352-732-4800	509
FordDirect 1740 Us Hwy 60 PO Box 700	Republic	MO	65738	**888-865-2576**		56
Fordham Auto Sales Inc 236 W Fordham Rd	Bronx	NY	10468	**800-407-1153**		56
Fordham Equipment Co 1204 Village Market Place Suite 262	Morrisville	NC	27560	**866-467-0708**	919-467-0708	318-3
College at Lincoln Ctr 113 W 60th St	New York	NY	10023	**800-367-3426**	212-636-6710	166
Fordham University *Westchester* 400 Westchester Ave	West Harrison	NY	10604	**800-606-6090**	914-332-8295	166
Forecast International 22 Commerce Rd	Newtown	CT	06470	**800-451-4975**	203-426-0800	628-10
Foreign Affairs 58 E 68th St *Cust Svc	New York	NY	10065	**800-829-5539***	212-434-9527	452-17
Foreign Candy Company Inc One Foreign Candy Dr	Hull	IA	51239	**800-831-8541**	712-439-1496	296-3
Foreign Policy Assn (FPA) 470 Pk Ave S	New York	NY	10016	**800-628-5754**	212-481-8100	47-7
Foremost Farms USA E10889A Penny Ln	Baraboo	WI	53913	**800-362-9196**	608-355-8700	295-10
Foremost Industries Inc 2375 Buchanan Trl W	Greencastle	PA	17225	**877-284-5334**	717-597-7166	105
Foremost Insurance Co 5600 Beech Tree Ln	Caledonia	MI	49316	**800-532-4221**		388-4
Foremostco Inc 8457 NW 66th St	Miami	FL	33166	**800-421-8986**	305-592-8986	685
Forensic Fluids Laboratories Inc 225 Parsons St	Kalamazoo	MI	49007	**866-492-2517**	269-492-7700	732
Forest at Duke 2701 Pickett Rd	Durham	NC	27705	**800-474-0258**	919-490-8000	663
Forest City Residential Management Inc 50 Public Sq Ste 1515	Cleveland	OH	44113	**800-750-0750**	216-416-3906	502
Forest City Trading Group LLC 10250 SW Greenburg Rd Ste 200 PO Box 4209	Portland	OR	97223	**800-767-3284**	503-246-8500	192-3
Forest Hills Journal 394 WaRds Corner Rd Ste 170	Loveland	OH	45140	**888-894-2113**	513-248-8600	525-4
Forest Lake Area School District 6100 210th St N	Forest Lake	MN	55025	**866-632-9992**	651-982-8100	676
Forest Landowners Assn (FLA) 900 Cir 75 Pkwy Ste 205	Atlanta	GA	30339	**800-325-2954**	404-325-2954	47-13
Forest Lawn Memorial-Parks & Mortuaries 1712 S Glendale Ave	Glendale	CA	91205	**800-204-3131**	323-254-3131	503
Forest Lawn Museum 1712 S Glendale Ave	Glendale	CA	91205	**800-204-3131**		513
Forest Pharmaceutical Inc 13600 Shoreline Dr	Earth City	MO	63045	**800-678-1605**	314-493-7000	576
Forest Service (USFS) 1400 Independence Ave SW	Washington	DC	20050	**800-832-1355**	202-205-8333	338-1
Forest Service Employees for Environmental Ethics (FSEEE) PO Box 11615	Eugene	OR	97440	**800-270-7504**	541-484-2692	48-7
Forest Service Regional Offices *Region 8 (Southern Region)* 1720 Peachtree St Ste 760S	Atlanta	GA	30309	**877-372-7248**	404-347-4177	338-1
Forestry Suppliers Inc 205 W Rankin St *Cust Svc	Jackson	MS	39201	**800-752-8460***	601-354-3565	454
Forestville/Mystery Cave State Park 21071 County 118	Preston	MN	55965	**888-646-6367**	507-352-5111	558
Forethought Financial Services Inc Forethought Ctr	Batesville	IN	47006	**877-454-4777**	713-212-4600	388-2
Foretravel Motorcoach Inc 1221 NW Stallings Dr	Nacogdoches	TX	75964	**800-955-6226**	936-564-8367	119
Forever 21 Inc 2001 S Alameda St *Cust Svc	Los Angeles	CA	90058	**800-966-1355***	213-741-5100	155-6
Forever Living Products International Inc 7501 E McCormick Pkwy	Scottsdale	AZ	85258	**888-440-2563**	480-998-8888	215
Forever Spring 2629 E Craig Rd Ste E	Las Vegas	NV	89030	**800-523-4334**	702-633-4283	238
Forex Newscom 55 Water St 50th Fl	New York	NY	10041	**888-503-6739**		384
Forged Products Inc (FPI) 6505 N Houston Rosslyn Rd	Houston	TX	77091	**800-876-3416**	713-462-3416	478
Forged Vessel Connections Inc 2525 DeSoto St *Cust Svc	Houston	TX	77091	**800-231-2701***	713-688-9705	478
Forkardt 2155 Traverse Field Dr	Traverse City	MI	49686	**800-544-3823**	231-995-8300	488
Forklifts of Minnesota Inc 2201 W 94th St	Bloomington	MN	55431	**800-752-4300**	952-887-5400	382
Forks of Cheat Winery 2811 Stewart Town Rd	Morgantown	WV	26508	**877-989-4637**	304-598-2019	49-6
Form-A-Feed Inc (FAF) 740 Bowman St	Stewart	MN	55385	**800-422-3649**	320-562-2413	442
Formall Inc 3908 Fountain Vly Dr	Knoxville	TN	37918	**800-643-3676**	865-922-7514	595
Formax Manufacturing Corp 168 Wealthy St SW	Grand Rapids	MI	49503	**800-242-2833**	616-456-5458	1
Former Governors' Mansion State Historic Site 612 E Blvd Ave	Bismarck	ND	58505	**866-243-5352**	701-328-2666	558
Formetco Inc 2963 Pleasant Hill Rd	Duluth	GA	30096	**800-367-6382**	770-476-7000	692
Formflex Inc PO Box 218	Bloomingdale	IN	47832	**800-255-7659**		85
Formica Corp 10155 Reading Rd	Cincinnati	OH	45241	**800-367-6422**	513-786-3400	592
Forms Manufacturers Inc 312 E Forest Ave	Girard	KS	66743	**800-835-0614**	620-724-8225	109
Formtek Metal Forming Inc 4899 Commerce Pkwy	Cleveland	OH	44128	**800-631-0520**	216-292-4460	665
Forney Corp 3405 Wiley Post Rd *Cust Svc	Carrollton	TX	75006	**800-356-7740***	972-458-6100	202
Forney Industries Inc 1830 LaPorte Ave	Fort Collins	CO	80521	**800-521-6038**		798
Forrest General Hospital 6051 US Hwy 49	Hattiesburg	MS	39402	**800-503-5980**	601-288-7000	371-3
Forrest Hills Mountain Resort & Conference Ctr 135 Forrest Hills Rd	Dahlonega	GA	30533	**800-654-6313**	706-864-6456	660
Forsbergs Inc 1210 Pennington Ave PO Box 510 *Cust Svc	Thief River Falls	MN	56701	**800-654-1927***	218-681-1927	273
Forsyth County Public Library 660 W Fifth St	Winston-Salem	NC	27101	**866-345-1884**	336-703-2665	431-3
Forsyth Technical Community College 2100 Silas Creek Pkwy	Winston-Salem	NC	27103	**800-870-3676**	336-723-0371	788
Fort Atkinson State Historical Park PO Box 240	Fort Calhoun	NE	68023	**800-742-7627**	402-468-5611	558
Fort Bliss National Cemetery PO Box 6342	El Paso	TX	79906	**800-273-8255**	915-564-0201	135
Fort Bragg Unified School District 312 S Lincoln St	Fort Bragg	CA	95437	**800-734-7793**	707-961-2850	676
Fort Caspar Museum 4001 Fort Caspar Rd	Casper	WY	82604	**800-877-7353**	307-235-8462	513
Fort Cobb Lake State Park 27022 Copperhead Rd	Fort Cobb	OK	73038	**800-622-6317**	405-643-2249	558
Fort Collins Area Chamber of Commerce 225 S Meldrum St	Fort Collins	CO	80521	**877-652-8607**	970-482-3746	137
Fort Collins Convention & Visitors Bureau 19 Old Town Sq Ste 137	Fort Collins	CO	80524	**800-274-3678**	970-232-3840	207
Fort Custer National Cemetery 15501 Dickman Rd	Augusta	MI	49012	**800-273-8255**	269-731-4164	135
Fort Edward Express Company Inc 1402 Rt 9	Fort Edward	NY	12828	**800-342-1233**	518-792-6571	770
Fort Erie Race Track 230 Catherine St PO Box 1130	Fort Erie	ON	L2A5N9	**800-295-3770**	905-871-3200	633
Fort Garry, The 222 Broadway	Winnipeg	MB	R3C0R3	**800-665-8088**	204-942-8251	376
Fort Hays State University 600 Pk St *Admissions	Hays	KS	67601	**800-628-3478***	785-628-4000	166

Alphabetical Section

Name / Address	City	State	ZIP	Toll-Free	Phone	Class
Fort Henry National Historic Site						
PO Box 213	Kingston	ON	K7L4V8	**800-437-2233***	613-542-7388	513
*Cust Svc						
Fort Jesup State Historic Site						
32 Geoghagan Rd	Many	LA	71449	**888-677-5378**	318-256-4117	558
Fort Knox Federal Credit Union						
PO Box 900	Radcliff	KY	40159	**800-756-3678**	502-942-0254	219
Fort Lauderdale Grande Hotel & Yacht Club						
1881 SE 17th St	Fort Lauderdale	FL	33316	**888-554-2131**	954-463-4000	660
Fort Lauderdale Hospital						
1601 E Las Olas Blvd	Fort Lauderdale	FL	33301	**800-585-7527**	954-463-4321	371-5
Fort Lauderdale/Hollywood International Airport						
100 Aviation Blvd	Fort Lauderdale	FL	33315	**866-682-2258**	954-359-1200	27
Fort Leonard Wood						
Bldg 744	Fort Leonard Wood	MO	65473	**800-350-7746**	573-596-0131	492-2
Fort Lewis College						
1000 Rim Dr	Durango	CO	81301	**877-352-2656**	970-247-7010	166
Fort MacArthur Museum						
3601 S Gaffey St	San Pedro	CA	90731	**800-232-5505**	310-548-2631	513
Fort Madison						
614 Ninth St	Fort Madison	IA	52627	**800-210-8687**	319-372-5471	207
Fort Marcy Hotel Suites						
321 Kearney Ave	Santa Fe	NM	87501	**888-667-2775**	505-988-2800	376
Fort McAllister State Historic Park						
3894 Ft McAllister Rd	Richmond Hill	GA	31324	**800-864-7275**	912-727-2339	558
Fort McDowell Casino						
10424 N Ft McDowell Rd	Fort Mcdowell	AZ	85264	**800-843-3678**	480-837-1424	132
Fort McHenry National Monument & Historic Shrine						
2400 E Fort Ave	Baltimore	MD	21230	**866-945-7920**	410-962-4290	513
Fort Meade						
4550 Parade Field Ln Rm 102	Fort Meade	MD	20755	**877-372-3337**	301-677-1361	492-2
Fort Meigs State Memorial						
29100 W River Rd	Perrysburg	OH	43551	**800-283-8916**	419-874-4121	49-2
Fort Morgan Area Chamber of Commerce						
300 Main St	Fort Morgan	CO	80701	**800-354-8660**	970-867-6702	137
Fort Myers Beach Chamber of Commerce						
17200 San Carlos Blvd	Fort Myers Beach	FL	33931	**866-998-9250**	239-454-7500	137
Fort Pillow State Historic Park						
3122 Pk Rd	Henning	TN	38041	**800-342-3145**	731-738-5581	558
Fort Polk						
2030 14th St	Fort Polk	LA	71459	**800-752-4658**	337-531-2911	492-2
Fort Richardson						
Richardson Dr Bldg 600	Fort Richardson	AK	99505	**800-984-1517**	907-384-0763	492-2
Fort Ridgely State Park						
72158 County Rd 30	Fairfax	MN	55332	**888-646-6367**	507-426-7840	558
Fort Riley						
405 Pershing Ct	Fort Riley	KS	66442	**800-273-8255**	785-239-2022	492-2
Fort Rock State Natural Area						
c/o LaPine Management Unit						
15800 State Recreation Rd	Lake County	OR	97739	**800-551-6949**		558
Fort Saint Jean Baptiste State Historic Site						
155 Jefferson St	Natchitoches	LA	71457	**888-677-7853**	318-357-3101	558
Fort Scott Community College						
2108 S Horton St	Fort Scott	KS	66701	**800-874-3722**	620-223-2700	160
Fort Smith Convention & Visitors Bureau						
2 N 'B'	Fort Smith	AR	72901	**800-637-1477**	479-783-8888	207
Fort Smith National Cemetery						
522 Garland Ave	Fort Smith	AR	72901	**800-535-1117**	479-783-5345	135
Fort Smith Public Library						
3201 Rogers Ave	Fort Smith	AR	72903	**866-660-0885**	479-783-0229	431-3
Fort Smith Regional Airport						
6700 McKennon Blvd Ste 200	Fort Smith	AR	72903	**800-992-7433**	479-452-7000	27
Fort Snelling State Park						
101 Snelling Lake Rd	Saint Paul	MN	55111	**888-646-6367**	612-725-2389	558
Fort Valley State University						
1005 State University Dr	Fort Valley	GA	31030	**877-462-3878**	478-825-6211	166
Fort Vancouver National Historic Site						
612 E Reserve St	Vancouver	WA	98661	**800-832-3599**	360-816-6230	557
Fort Ward Museum & Historic Site						
4301 W Braddock Rd	Alexandria	VA	22304	**800-468-8894**	703-838-4848	513
Fort Wayne Newspapers Inc						
600 W Main St	Fort Wayne	IN	46802	**800-444-3303**	260-461-8444	628-8
Fort Wayne/Allen County Convention & Visitors Bureau						
927 S Harrison St	Fort Wayne	IN	46802	**800-767-7752**	260-424-3700	207
Fort Worth City Credit Union						
PO Box 100099	Fort Worth	TX	76185	**888-732-3085**	817-732-2803	219
Fort Worth Community Credit Union						
1905 Forest Ridge Dr						
PO Box 210848	Bedford	TX	76021	**800-817-8234**	817-835-5000	219
Fort Worth Convention & Visitors Bureau						
111 W Fourth St Ste 200	Fort Worth	TX	76102	**800-433-5747**	817-336-8791	207
Fort Worth Convention Ctr						
1201 Houston St	Fort Worth	TX	76102	**866-630-2588**	817-392-6338	206
Fort Worth Museum of Science & History						
1600 Gendy St	Fort Worth	TX	76107	**888-255-9300**	817-255-9300	513
Fort Worth Opera						
1300 Gendy St	Fort Worth	TX	76107	**877-396-7372**	817-731-0833	566-2
Forth Inc						
5959 W Century Blvd Ste 700	Los Angeles	CA	90045	**800-553-6784**	310-999-6784	179-2
Fortifiber Building Systems Group						
300 Industrial Dr	Fernley	NV	89408	**800-773-4777**	775-333-6400	545-1
Fortitude Business Solutions LLC						
PO Box 2095	Daphne	AL	36526	**877-577-2644**		390
Fortrend Corp						
687 N Pastoria Ave	Sunnyvale	CA	94085	**888-937-3637**	408-734-9311	686
Fortress Integrated Technologies						
100 Delawanna Ave	Clifton	NJ	07014	**888-734-9320**	973-572-1070	795
Fortress Technology Inc						
51 Grand Marshall Dr	Toronto	ON	M1B5N6	**888-220-8737**	416-754-2898	683
Fortun Insurance Agency Inc						
365 Palermo Ave	Coral Gables	FL	33134	**877-643-2055**	305-445-3535	387
Fortune Brands Inc						
520 Lk Cook Rd	Deerfield	IL	60015	**800-225-2719**	847-484-4400	186
NYSE: FBHS						
Fortune Plastics Inc						
One Williams Ln	Old Saybrook	CT	06475	**800-243-0306**	860-388-3426	65
Forum Communications Co						
101 Fifth St N	Fargo	ND	58102	**800-747-7311**	701-451-5629	628-8
Forum Corp						
265 Franklin St 4th Fl	Boston	MA	02110	**800-367-8611**	617-523-7300	755
Forum Credit Union						
PO Box 50738	Indianapolis	IN	46250	**800-382-5414**	317-558-6000	219
Forum Publishing Co						
383 E Main St	Centerport	NY	11721	**800-635-7654**	631-754-5000	628-9

Name / Address	City	State	ZIP	Toll-Free	Phone	Class
Forum, The						
101 N Fifth St	Fargo	ND	58102	**800-747-7311**	701-235-7311	525-2
Forward Air Corp						
430 Airport Rd PO Box 1058	Greeneville	TN	37744	**800-726-6654**	423-636-7100	770
NASDAQ: FWRD						
Forward Corp						
219 N Front St	Standish	MI	48658	**800-664-4501**	989-846-4501	323
Forward Publishing						
125 Maiden Ln	New York	NY	10038	**800-266-0773**	212-889-8200	628-8
Forward Technology Inc						
260 Jenks Ave	Cokato	MN	55321	**800-307-6040***	320-286-2578	383
*Cust Svc						
Foseco Metallurgical Inc						
20200 Sheldon Rd	Cleveland	OH	44142	**800-321-3132**	440-826-4548	143
Foss Maritime Co						
660 W Ewing St	Seattle	WA	98119	**800-426-2885**	800-562-2711	460
Foss Mfg Co LLC						
11 Merrill Industrial Dr						
PO Box 5000	Hampton	NH	03842	**800-343-3277**	603-929-6000	734-6
Foss State Park						
10252 Hwy 44	Foss	OK	73647	**800-622-6317**	580-592-4433	558
Fosta-Tek Optics Inc						
320 Hamilton St	Leominster	MA	01453	**866-221-9157**	978-534-6511	537
Foster City Flowers & Gifts						
1160 Chess Dr Ste 1	Foster City	CA	94404	**800-970-7673**	650-573-6607	292
Foster Construction Products Inc						
1105 S Frontenac St	Aurora	IL	60504	**800-231-9541**		3
Foster Farms Inc						
1000 Davis St PO Box 457	Livingston	CA	95334	**800-255-7227**		10-7
Foster Grandparent Program c/o Senior Corps						
1201 New York Ave NW	Washington	DC	20525	**800-424-8867**	202-606-5000	198
Foster Pepper Pllc						
1111 Third Ave Ste 3400	Seattle	WA	98101	**800-995-5902**	206-447-4400	425
Foster Wheeler AG						
53 Frontage Rd PO Box 9000	Hampton	NJ	08827	**888-288-1464**	908-730-4000	261
NYSE: LSE						
Foster's Daily Democrat						
150 Venture Dr	Dover	NH	03820	**800-660-8310**	603-742-4455	525-2
Foundation Constructors Inc						
81 Big Break Rd PO Box 97	Oakley	CA	94561	**800-841-8740**	925-754-6633	190-5
Foundation Ctr						
79 Fifth Ave Second Fl	New York	NY	10003	**800-424-9836**	212-620-4230	47-11
Foundation Fighting Blindness						
11435 Cron Hill Dr	Owings Mills	MD	21117	**800-683-5555**	410-568-0150	47-17
Foundation for Economic Education (FEE)						
30 S Broadway	Irvington-on-Hudson	NY	10533	**800-960-4333**	914-591-7230	625
Foundation for the Carolinas						
217 S Tryon St	Charlotte	NC	28202	**800-973-7244**	704-973-4500	302
Foundation Technologies Inc						
1400 Progress						
Industrial Blvd	Lawrenceville	GA	30043	**800-773-2368**	678-407-4640	192-1
Founders Federal Credit Union						
607 N Main St	Lancaster	SC	29720	**888-918-7403***	803-289-5927	219
*Tech Supp						
Founders Inn						
5641 Indian River Rd	Virginia Beach	VA	23464	**800-926-4466**	757-424-5511	374
Fountain Valley Regional Hospital & Medical Ctr						
17100 Euclid St	Fountain Valley	CA	92708	**866-904-6871**	714-966-7200	371-3
Fountainhead College of Technology						
3203 Tazewell Pk	Knoxville	TN	37918	**888-218-7335**	865-688-9422	788
Fountainhead Group Inc						
23 Garden St	New York Mills	NY	13417	**800-311-9903**	315-736-0037	173
Four County Electric Membership Corp						
1822 NC Hwy 53 W PO Box 667	Burgaw	NC	28425	**888-368-7289**	910-259-2171	245
Four Oaks Bank & Trust Co						
PO Box 309	Four Oaks	NC	27524	**877-963-6257**	919-963-2177	69
Four Points by Sheraton Charlotte						
315 E Woodlawn Rd	Charlotte	NC	28217	**800-368-7764**	704-522-0852	376
Four Points by Sheraton French Quarter						
541 Bourbon St	New Orleans	LA	70130	**800-535-7891**	504-524-7611	376
Four Queens Hotel & Casino						
202 Fremont St	Las Vegas	NV	89101	**800-634-6045**	702-385-4011	376
Four Sails Resort Hotel						
3301 Atlantic Ave	Virginia Beach	VA	23451	**800-227-4213**	757-491-8100	376
Four Seasons Hospice & Palliative Care						
571 S Allen Rd	Flat Rock	NC	28731	**866-466-9734**	828-692-6178	368
Four Seasons Hotels & Resorts						
1165 Leslie St	Toronto	ON	M3C2K8	**800-332-3442**	416-449-1750	743
Four Seasons Hotels Inc						
1165 Leslie St	Toronto	ON	M3C2K8	**800-332-3442**	416-449-1750	376
Four Seasons Inc						
1801 Waters Ridge Dr	Lewisville	TX	75057	**800-433-7508**	972-316-8100	605
Four Seasons Resort & Club Dallas at Las Colinas						
4150 N MacArthur Blvd	Irving	TX	75038	**800-332-3442**	972-717-0700	660
Four Seasons Resort Hualalai						
100 Ka'upulehu Dr	Kailua Kona	HI	96740	**888-340-5662**	808-325-8000	660
Four Seasons Resort Jackson Hole						
7680 Granite Loop Rd						
PO Box 544	Teton Village	WY	83025	**800-914-5110**	307-732-5000	660
Four Seasons Resort Maui at Wailea						
3900 Wailea Alanui Dr	Wailea	HI	96753	**800-334-6284**	808-874-8000	660
Four Seasons Resort Palm Beach						
2800 S Ocean Blvd	Palm Beach	FL	33480	**800-432-2335**	561-582-2800	660
Four Seasons Resort Santa Barbara						
1260 Ch Dr	Santa Barbara	CA	93108	**800-819-5053**	805-969-2261	660
Four Seasons Resort Scottsdale at Troon North						
10600 E Crescent Moon Dr	Scottsdale	AZ	85262	**800-332-3442**	480-515-5700	660
Four Seasons Solar Products LLC						
5005 Veterans Memorial Hwy	Holbrook	NY	11741	**800-368-7732**	631-563-4000	104
Four Seasons Spa at the Four Seasons Hotel Las Vegas						
3960 Las Vegas Blvd S	Las Vegas	NV	89119	**800-332-3442**	702-632-5302	698
Four Seasons Spa at the Four Seasons Hotel Los Angeles at Beverly Hills						
300 S Doheny Dr	Los Angeles	CA	90048	**800-819-5053**	310-786-2229	698
Four Seasons Spa at the Four Seasons Resort Jackson Hole						
7680 Granite Loop Rd						
PO Box 544	Teton Village	WY	83025	**800-819-5053**	307-732-5120	698
Four Seasons Spa at the Four Seasons Resort Maui						
3900 Wailea Alanui Dr	Wailea	HI	96753	**800-334-6284**	808-874-2925	698
Four Seasons Spa at the Four Seasons Resort Santa Barbara						
1260 Ch Dr	Santa Barbara	CA	93108	**800-819-5053***	805-565-8250	698
*General						
Four Wheel Campers						
1460 Churchill Downs Ave	Woodland	CA	95776	**800-242-1442**	530-666-1442	119

	Toll-Free	Phone	Class
Four Winds Casino Resort			
11111 Wilson Rd .... New Buffalo MI 49117	**866-494-6371**		131
Four Winds Hospital			
800 Cross River Rd .... Katonah NY 10536	**800-528-6624**	914-763-8151	371-5
Foursome Inc			
3570 Vicksveurg Ln N Ste 100 .... Plymouth MN 55447	**888-368-7766**	763-473-4667	155-2
Fourwinds Resort & Marina			
9301 Fairfax Rd .... Bloomington IN 47401	**800-824-2628**	812-824-2628	660
Fowler State Bank			
300 E Fifth St PO Box 511 .... Fowler IN 47944	**800-439-3951**	765-884-1200	69
Fowler's Chocolate Co			
100 River Rock Dr Ste 102 .... Buffalo NY 14207	**800-824-2263**	716-877-9983	295-8
Fownes Bros & Company Inc			
16 E 34th St .... New York NY 10016	**800-345-6837***	212-683-0150	153-7
*All			
Fox Chase Cancer Ctr			
333 Cottman Ave .... Philadelphia PA 19111	**888-369-2427**	215-728-6900	371-7
Fox Chase Cancer Ctr Bone Marrow Transplant Program			
333 Cottman Ave .... Philadelphia PA 19111	**888-369-2427**		759
Fox Cities Chamber of Commerce & Industry			
125 N Superior St .... Appleton WI 54911	**800-456-0152**	920-734-7101	137
Fox Cities Convention & Visitors Bureau			
3433 W College Ave .... Appleton WI 54914	**800-236-6673**	920-734-3358	207
Fox Harb'r Resort & Spa			
1337 Fox Harbour Rd .... Wallace NS B0K1Y0	**866-257-1801**	902-257-1801	698
Fox Hills Resort & Convention Ctr			
250 W Church St .... Mishicot WI 54228	**800-950-7615**	920-755-2376	660
Fox Industries Inc			
3100 Falls Cliff Rd .... Baltimore MD 21211	**888-760-0369**	410-243-8856	3
Fox Pool Corp			
3490 BoaRd Rd .... York PA 17406	**800-723-1011**	717-764-8581	719
Fox River Mills Inc			
227 Poplar Stq PO Box 298 .... Osage IA 50461	**800-247-1815**	641-732-3798	153-9
Fox Service Co			
PO Box 19047 .... Austin TX 78760	**866-668-4749**	512-442-6782	190-10
Fox Theater			
2001 H St .... Bakersfield CA 93301	**888-825-5484**	661-324-1369	565
Fox Theatre			
660 Peachtree St NE .... Atlanta GA 30308	**855-285-8499**	404-881-2100	565
Fox Valley Technical College			
1825 N Bluemound Dr			
PO Box 2277 .... Appleton WI 54912	**800-735-3882**	920-735-5600	788
Fox's Pizza Den Inc			
4425 Willaim Penn Hwy .... Murrysville PA 15668	**800-899-3697**	724-733-7888	661
Foxcom Inc			
136 Main St Ste 300b .... Princeton NJ 08540	**866-663-7284**	609-514-1800	246
Foxcroft School			
22407 Foxhound Ln .... Middleburg VA 20117	**800-858-2364**	540-687-5555	615
Foxdale Village			
500 E Marylyn Ave .... State College PA 16801	**800-253-4951**	814-272-2117	663
Foxes Music Co			
416 S Washington St .... Falls Church VA 22046	**800-446-4414**	703-533-7393	519
Foxworth-Galbraith Lumber Co			
4965 Preston Pk Blvd Ste 400 .... Plano TX 75093	**800-688-8082**	972-665-2400	192-3
FP Mailing Solutions			
140 N Mitchell Ct .... Addison IL 60101	**800-341-6052**	630-827-5500	111
FPA (Foreign Policy Assn)			
470 Pk Ave S .... New York NY 10016	**800-628-5754**	212-481-8100	47-7
FPA (Financial Planning Assn)			
7535 E Hampden Ave Ste 400 .... Denver CO 80231	**800-322-4237**	303-759-4900	48-2
FPC Flexible Packaging Corp			
1891 Eglinton Ave E .... Toronto ON M1L2L7	**888-288-7386**	416-288-3060	541
FPDTR (Fess Parker's Doubletree Resort)			
633 E Cabrillo Blvd .... Santa Barbara CA 93103	**800-879-2929**	805-564-4333	660
FPI (Forged Products Inc)			
6505 N Houston Rosslyn Rd .... Houston TX 77091	**800-876-3416**	713-462-3416	478
FPL Group Inc			
NextEra Energy Inc			
700 Universe Blvd .... Juno Beach FL 33408	**800-979-3967**	561-694-4000	357-5
NYSE: NEE			
FPM LLC			
1501 S Lively Blvd .... Elk Grove Village IL 60007	**877-437-6432**	847-228-2525	479
FPMI Solutions Inc			
1033 N Fairfax St Ste 200 .... Alexandria VA 22314	**888-644-3764**		194
FPSA (Food Processing Suppliers Assn)			
1451 Dolley Madison Blvd Ste 101 .... McLean VA 22101	**800-772-9247**	703-761-2600	48-13
FPUC (Florida Public Utilities Co)			
401 S Dixie Hwy .... West Palm Beach FL 33401	**800-427-7712**		775
FRA (Federal Railroad Administration Regional Offices)			
55 Broadway Room 1077 .... Cambridge MA 02142	**800-724-5991**	617-494-2302	338-15
FRA (Fleet Reserve Assn)			
125 NW St .... Alexandria VA 22314	**800-372-1924**	703-683-1400	47-19
FRA Today			
125 NW St .... Alexandria VA 22314	**800-372-1924**	703-683-1400	452-12
Frac Tech Services LLC			
301 E 18th St .... Cisco TX 76437	**866-877-1008**	817-850-1008	143
Fraen Corp			
80 Newcrossing Rd .... Reading MA 01867	**800-370-0078**	781-205-5300	483
Framingham State College			
100 State St PO Box 9101 .... Framingham MA 01701	**866-361-8970**	508-620-1220	166
France			
Consulate General			
205 N Michigan Ave Ste 3700 .... Chicago IL 60601	**888-642-2787**	312-327-5200	257
Consulate General			
1395 Brickell Ave Ste 1050 .... Miami FL 33131	**877-624-8737**	305-403-4185	257
Consulate General			
777 Post Oak Blvd Ste 600 .... Houston TX 77056	**888-902-5322**	713-572-2799	257
Consulate General			
934 Fifth Ave .... New York NY 10021	**800-772-1213**	212-606-3600	257
Consulate General			
540 Bush St .... San Francisco CA 94108	**800-843-3779**	415-397-4330	257
Consulate General			
3475 Piedmont Rd NE Ste 1840 .... Atlanta GA 30305	**866-347-2523**	404-495-1660	257
Embassy			
4101 Reservoir Rd NW .... Washington DC 20007	**800-622-6232**	202-944-6000	257
Franchise Brands LLC			
325 Bic Dr .... Milford CT 06461	**800-797-2308**		458
Franchise Co, The (TFC)			
5399 Eglinton Ave W Ste 110 .... Etobicoke ON M9C5K9	**800-294-5591**	416-620-3960	458
Franchise Handbook			
5555 N Port Washington Rd			
Ste 305 .... Milwaukee WI 53217	**800-272-0246**	414-882-2878	452-11
Franchise Information Services Inc			
4300 Wilson Blvd Ste 480 .... Arlington VA 22203	**800-485-9570**	703-740-4700	384

	Toll-Free	Phone	Class
Franchising Business & Law Alert			
1617 JFK Blvd Ste 1750 .... Philadelphia PA 19103	**877-256-2472**	215-557-2300	524-7
Franchising World Magazine			
1501 K St NW Ste 350 .... Washington DC 20005	**800-543-1038**	202-628-8000	452-5
Franchoice Inc			
7500 Flying Cloud Dr .... Eden Prairie MN 55344	**877-396-4238**	952-345-8400	195
Francis Investment Counsel LLC			
21180 W Capitol Dr .... Pewaukee WI 53072	**866-232-6457**		784
Francis Marion Hotel, The			
387 King St .... Charleston SC 29403	**877-756-2121**	843-722-0600	376
Francis Marion University			
PO Box 100547 .... Florence SC 29501	**800-368-7551**	843-661-1231	166
Francis Marion University Rogers Library			
PO Box 100547 .... Florence SC 29502	**800-368-7551**		431-6
Francis Scott Key Family Resort			
12806 Ocean Gateway			
PO Box 468 .... Ocean City MD 21842	**800-213-0088**	410-213-0088	660
Franciscan Alliance, Inc			
St Francis Hospital 1600			
Albany St .... Beech Grove IN 46107	**800-361-0016**	317-528-5500	759
Franciscan Estates			
1178 Galleron Rd .... Saint Helena CA 94574	**800-529-9463**	707-967-3830	79-3
Franciscan Oaks			
19 Pocono Rd .... Denville NJ 07834	**800-237-3330**	973-586-6000	663
Franciscan School of Theology			
1712 Euclid Ave .... Berkeley CA 94709	**855-355-1550**	760-547-1800	167-3
Franciscan Sisters of Chicago Inc			
1055 175th St Ste 202 .... Homewood IL 60430	**800-524-6126**	708-647-6500	47-20
Franciscan St. Elizabeth Health			
1501 Hartford St .... Lafayette IN 47904	**800-371-6011**	765-423-6011	371-3
Francisco Grande Hotel & Golf Resort			
26000 Gila Bend Hwy .... Casa Grande AZ 85222	**800-237-4238***	520-836-6444	660
*General			
Frank B Fuhrer Wholesale Co			
3100 E Carson St .... Pittsburgh PA 15203	**800-837-2212**	412-488-8844	80-1
Frank C. Alegre Trucking Inc			
PO Box 1508 .... Lodi CA 95241	**800-769-2440**	209-334-2112	770
Frank Edmunds & Co			
6111 S Sayre .... Chicago IL 60638	**800-447-3516**	773-586-2772	807
Frank Edwards Co			
3626 Pkwy Blvd .... West Valley City UT 84120	**800-366-8851**	801-736-8000	60
Frank Jackson State Park			
100 Jerry Adams Dr .... Opp AL 36467	**800-760-4089**	334-493-6988	558
Frank Lill & Son Inc			
785 Old Dutch Road .... Victoriaville NY 14564	**800-756-0490**	585-265-0490	190-10
Frank Lloyd Wright's Martin House Complex			
125 Jewett Pkwy .... Buffalo NY 14214	**877-377-3858**	716-856-3858	49-2
Frank Mayer & Assoc Inc			
1975 Wisconsin Ave .... Grafton WI 53024	**855-294-2875**		233
Frank Paxton Lumber Co			
7455 Dawson Rd .... Cincinnati OH 45243	**800-325-9800**	513-984-8200	192-3
Frank Roberts & Sons Inc			
1130 Robertsville Rd .... Punxsutawney PA 15767	**800-262-8955**	814-938-5000	192-4
Frankel Lois (Rep D - FL)			
1037 Longworth Bldg .... Washington DC 20515	**866-264-0957**	202-225-9890	
Frankenmuth Convention & Visitors Bureau			
635 S Main St .... Frankenmuth MI 48734	**800-386-8696**	989-652-6106	207
Frankenmuth Insurance			
1 Mutual Ave .... Frankenmuth MI 48787	**800-234-4433**	989-652-6121	388-4
Frankfort Convention Ctr			
405 Mero St .... Frankfort KY 40601	**800-426-7866**	502-564-5335	206
Frankfort Regional Medical Ctr			
299 King's Daughters Dr .... Frankfort KY 40601	**888-696-4505**	502-875-5240	371-3
Frankfort/Franklin County Tourist & Convention Commission			
100 Capitol Ave .... Frankfort KY 40601	**800-960-7200**	502-875-8687	207
Franklin & Marshall College			
PO Box 3003 .... Lancaster PA 17604	**877-678-9111**	717-291-3951	166
Franklin & Marshall College Shadek-Fackenthal Library			
450 College Ave .... Lancaster PA 17604	**866-366-7655**	717-291-4223	431-6
Franklin Area Chamber of Commerce (FACC)			
1259 Liberty St .... Franklin PA 16323	**888-547-2377**	814-432-5823	137
Franklin College			
101 Branigin Blvd .... Franklin IN 46131	**800-852-0232**	317-738-8000	166
Franklin Community Health Network			
111 Franklin Health Commons .... Farmington ME 04938	**800-398-6031**	207-778-6031	371-3
Franklin County			
355 W Main St .... Malone NY 12953	**800-397-8686**	518-483-6770	336
Franklin County Chamber of Commerce			
44 Chamber Way PO Box 280 .... Winchester TN 37398	**866-462-5991**	931-967-6788	137
Franklin Covey Co			
2200 West PkwyBlvd .... Salt Lake City UT 84119	**800-827-1776**	801-817-1776	755
NYSE: FC			
Franklin Credit Management Corp			
101 Hudson St .... Jersey City NJ 07302	**800-255-5897**	201-604-1800	214
Franklin D Roosevelt Presidential Library & Museum			
4079 Albany Post Rd .... Hyde Park NY 12538	**800-337-8474**	845-486-7770	431-2
Franklin Electric Co Inc			
9255 Coverdale Rd .... Fort Wayne IN 46809	**800-962-3787**	260-824-2900	511
NASDAQ: FELE			
Franklin Electric Co-op Inc			
225 Franklin St NW .... Russellville AL 35653	**800-410-2732**	256-332-2730	245
Franklin Electronic Publishers Inc			
One Franklin Plz .... Burlington NJ 08016	**800-266-5626**	609-386-2500	174-1
Franklin Empire Inc			
8421 Darnley Rd .... Montreal QC H4T2B2	**800-361-5044**	514-341-9720	253
Franklin Fibre-Lamitex Corp			
903 E 13th St .... Wilmington DE 19802	**800-233-9739**	302-652-3621	592
Franklin Homes Inc			
10655 Hwy 43 .... Russellville AL 35653	**800-332-4511**		500
Franklin Institute Science Museum			
222 N 20th St .... Philadelphia PA 19103	**800-732-0999**	215-448-1200	513
Franklin International			
2020 Bruck St .... Columbus OH 43207	**800-877-4583**	614-443-0241	3
Franklin Local School District			
PO Box 428 .... Duncan Falls OH 43734	**800-846-4976**	740-674-5203	676
Franklin Mills			
1455 Franklin Mills Cir .... Philadelphia PA 19154	**877-746-6642***	215-632-1500	455
*General			
Franklin Mutual Insurance Co			
Five Broad St .... Branchville NJ 07826	**800-842-0551**	973-948-3120	388-4
Franklin Park Conservatory & Botanical Gardens			
1777 E Broad St .... Columbus OH 43203	**800-241-7275**	614-715-8000	96
Concord			
Five Chenell Dr .... Concord NH 03301	**800-437-0048**	603-228-1155	166

Listing	Toll-Free	Phone	Class
Franklin Pierce University			
Keene 17 Bradco St .... Keene NH 03431	**800-325-1090**	603-357-0079	166
Lebanon			
24 Airport Rd Ste 19 .... West Lebanon NH 03784	**800-325-1090**	603-298-5549	166
Manchester			
670 N Commercial St .... Manchester NH 03101	**800-437-0048***	603-626-4972	166
*Admissions			
Portsmouth			
73 Corporate Dr .... Portsmouth NH 03801	**800-325-1090**	603-433-2000	166
Rindge			
40 University Dr .... Rindge NH 03461	**800-437-0048***	603-899-4000	166
*Admissions			
Franklin Resources Inc			
One Franklin Pkwy			
Bdge 970 First Fl .... San Mateo CA 94403	**800-632-2301**	650-312-2000	398
NYSE: BEN			
Franklin Rural Electric Co-op			
1560 Hwy 65 PO Box 437 .... Hampton IA 50441	**800-750-3557**	641-456-2557	245
Franklin Sports Inc			
17 Campanelli Pkwy PO Box 508 .... Stoughton MA 02072	**800-225-8649**	781-344-1111	701
Franklin Square Hospital Ctr			
9000 Franklin Sq Dr .... Baltimore MD 21237	**855-633-8880**	443-777-7000	371-3
Franklin Street Properties Corp			
401 Edgewater Pl Ste 200 .... Wakefield MA 01880	**877-686-9496**	781-557-1300	645
NYSE: FSP			
Franklin Templeton Investments			
3344 Quality Dr .... Rancho Cordova CA 95670	**800-632-2350**	650-312-2000	681
Franklin University			
201 S Grant Ave .... Columbus OH 43215	**877-341-6300**	614-797-4700	166
Franks Supply Company Inc			
3311 Stanford Dr NE .... Albuquerque NM 87107	**800-432-5254**	505-884-0000	355
FRAN-PAC			
1501 K St Ste 350 .... Washington DC 20005	**800-543-1038**	202-628-8000	608
Fraternal Order of Alaska State Troopers Museum			
245 W Fifth Ave .... Anchorage AK 99501	**800-770-5050**	907-279-5050	513
Fraternal Order of Police (FOP)			
701 Marriott Dr .... Nashville TN 37214	**800-451-2711**	615-399-0900	47-15
Frazier Healthcare			
601 Union 2 Union Sq Ste 3200 .... Seattle WA 98101	**800-638-4817**	206-621-7200	780
Frazier Industrial Co			
91 Fairview Ave .... Long Valley NJ 07853	**800-859-1342**	908-876-3001	286
Frazier Rehabilitation Institute			
220 Abraham Flexner Way .... Louisville KY 40202	**800-333-2230**	502-582-7400	371-6
FRBSF (Federal Reserve Bank of San Francisco)			
101 Market St .... San Francisco CA 94105	**800-227-4133**	415-974-2000	70
FRC (Family Research Council)			
801 G St NW .... Washington DC 20001	**800-225-4008**	202-393-2100	47-6
FRCC (Front Range Community College)			
2190 Miller Dr .... Longmont CO 80501	**888-800-9198**	303-678-3722	160
Fred Loya Insurance			
1800 Lee Trevino Ste 201 .... El Paso TX 79936	**800-554-0595**	915-590-5692	387
Fred M Schildwachter & Sons Inc			
1400 Ferris Pl .... Bronx NY 10461	**800-642-3646**	718-828-2500	315
Fred Pryor Seminars			
9757 Metcalf Ave .... Overland Park KS 66212	**800-780-8476**		755
Fred Usinger Inc			
1030 N Old World Third St .... Milwaukee WI 53203	**800-558-9998**	414-276-9100	295-26
Fred Weber Inc			
2320 Creve Coeur			
Mill Rd .... Maryland Heights MO 63043	**866-739-8855**	314-344-0070	189-4
Fred's Inc			
4300 New Getwell Rd .... Memphis TN 38118	**800-374-7417**	901-365-8880	229
NASDAQ: FRED			
Freddie Mac			
8200 Jones Branch Dr .... McLean VA 22102	**800-424-5401**	703-903-2000	502
North Central Region			
333 W Wacker Dr Ste 2500 .... Chicago IL 60606	**800-373-3343**	312-407-7400	502
Northeast Region			
8200 Jones Branch Dr .... McLean VA 22102	**800-373-3343**	703-903-2000	502
Southeast/Southwest Region			
2300 Windy Ridge Pkwy Ste 200N .... Atlanta GA 30339	**800-373-3343**	770-857-8800	502
Freddie Mac Foundation			
8250 Jones Branch Dr .... McLean VA 22102	**800-424-5401**	703-918-5000	303
Frederick News Post			
200 E Patrick St .... Frederick MD 21701	**800-486-1177**	301-662-1177	525-2
Frederick Taylor University			
346 Rheem Blvd Ste 203 .... Moraga CA 94556	**800-988-4622**		
Frederick Wildman & Sons Ltd			
307 E 53rd St .... New York NY 10022	**800-733-9463***	212-355-0700	80-3
*General			
Frederick's of Hollywood Inc			
PO Box 2949 .... Phoenix AZ 85062	**800-323-9525**		155-6
Fredericksburg Chamber of Commerce			
302 E Austin St .... Fredericksburg TX 78624	**888-997-3600**	830-997-6523	207
Fredericksburg City Public Schools			
817 Princess Anne St .... Fredericksburg VA 22401	**800-846-4464**	540-372-1130	676
Fredericksburg Regional Chamber of Commerce			
2300 Fall Hill Ave			
Ste 240 .... Fredericksburg VA 22401	**888-338-0252**	540-373-9400	137
Frederik Meijer Gardens & Sculpture Park			
1000 E Beltline Ave NE .... Grand Rapids MI 49525	**877-975-3171**	616-957-1580	96
Free Flow Packaging International Inc			
1090 Mills Way .... Redwood City CA 94063	**800-866-9946**	650-261-5300	594
Free Lance Star			
616 Amelia St .... Fredericksburg VA 22401	**800-877-0500**	540-374-5000	525-2
Free Library of Philadelphia			
1901 Vine St .... Philadelphia PA 19103	**800-732-0999**	215-686-5322	431-3
Free Press			
418 S Second St .... Mankato MN 56001	**800-657-4662**	507-625-4451	525-2
Free Service Tire Co Inc			
PO Box 6187 .... Johnson City TN 37602	**855-646-1423**	423-979-2250	745
Free Will Baptist Bible College			
3606 W End Ave .... Nashville TN 37205	**800-763-9222**	615-844-5000	159
Freeborn-Mower Co-op Services			
2501 E Main St .... Albert Lea MN 56007	**800-734-6421**	507-373-6421	245
Freed-Hardeman University			
158 E Main St .... Henderson TN 38340	**800-348-3481**	731-989-6651	166
Freedman Seating Co			
4545 W Augusta Blvd .... Chicago IL 60651	**800-443-4540**	773-524-2440	680
Freedom Communications Inc			
17666 Fitch .... Irvine CA 92614	**866-262-7678**	949-253-2300	628-8
Freedom from Hunger			
1644 DaVinci Ct .... Davis CA 95618	**800-708-2555**	530-758-6200	47-5

Listing	Toll-Free	Phone	Class
Freedom Graphic Systems Inc (FGS)			
1101 S Janesville St .... Milton WI 53563	**800-334-3540**		109
Freedom Greeting Card Company Inc			
774 American Dr .... Bensalem PA 19020	**800-359-3301***	215-604-0300	129
*Sales			
Freedom Investments Inc			
375 Raritan Ctr Pkwy .... Edison NJ 08837	**800-944-4033**		681
Freedom Medical Inc			
219 Welsh Pool Rd .... Exton PA 19341	**800-784-8849**	610-903-0200	264-4
Freedom Village			
23442 El Toro Rd .... Lake Forest CA 92630	**800-584-8084**	949-472-4700	663
FreedomWorks			
601 Pennsylvania Ave NW			
Ste 700-N .... Washington DC 20004	**888-564-6273**	202-783-3870	47-7
Freelin-Wade Co			
1730 NE Miller St .... McMinnville OR 97128	**888-373-9233**	503-434-5561	367
Freeman Gas Inc			
1186 Asheville Hwy			
PO Box 4366 .... Spartanburg SC 29303	**800-277-5730**	864-582-5475	354
Freeman Jewelers Inc			
76 Merchants Row .... Rutland VT 05701	**800-451-4167**	802-773-2792	407
Freeman Manufacturing Co			
900 W Chicago Rd .... Sturgis MI 49091	**800-253-2091**	269-651-2371	472
Freeman Mfg & Supply Co			
1101 Moore Rd .... Avon OH 44011	**800-321-8511**	440-934-1902	560
Freeman, The			
30 S Broadway .... Irvington-on-Hudson NY 10533	**800-960-4333***	914-591-7230	452-17
*Sales			
Freeport Area Chamber of Commerce			
27 W Stephenson St .... Freeport IL 61032	**877-881-7339**	815-233-1350	137
Freescale Semiconductor Inc			
6501 William Cannon Dr W .... Austin TX 78735	**800-521-6274***	512-895-2000	687
*Tech Supp			
Freeservers.com			
1253 N Research Way Ste Q-2500 .... Orem UT 84097	**800-396-1999**		795
Freestone Inn at Wilson Ranch			
31 Early Winters Dr .... Mazama WA 98833	**800-639-3809**	509-996-3906	660
Freestyle Photo Biz			
5124 Sunset Blvd .... Hollywood CA 90027	**800-292-6137**		583
FreeWave Technologies Inc			
1880 S Flatiron Ct Ste F .... Boulder CO 80301	**866-923-6168***	303-444-3862	174-3
*Cust Svc			
Freight Logistics Inc			
PO Box 1712 .... Medford OR 97501	**800-866-7882**	541-734-5617	310
FreightCar America Inc			
17 Johns St .... Johnstown PA 15901	**800-458-2235**		641
NASDAQ: RAIL			
Freightliner of Hartford Inc			
222 Roberts St .... East Hartford CT 06108	**800-453-6967**	860-289-0201	56
Freightliner Specialty Vehicles Inc			
2300 S 13th St .... Clinton OK 73601	**800-358-7624**	580-323-4100	58
FreightPros			
3307 Northland Dr Ste 360 .... Austin TX 78731	**888-297-6968**		473
Freightquote.com Inc			
16025 W 113th St .... Lenexa KS 66219	**800-323-5441**	913-642-4700	311
Fremont Bank			
PO Box 5101 .... Fremont CA 94538	**800-359-2265**	510-792-2300	69
Fremont Contract Carriers Inc (FCC)			
865 S Bud Blvd .... Fremont NE 68025	**800-228-9842**		444
Fremont County			
450 N Second St .... Lander WY 82520	**800-967-2297**	307-332-2405	336
Fremont Hotel & Casino			
200 Fremont St .... Las Vegas NV 89101	**800-634-6460**	702-385-3232	132
Fremont Industries Inc			
4400 Vly Industrial Blvd N			
PO Box 67 .... Shakopee MN 55379	**800-436-1238**	952-445-4121	143
Fremont Main Library			
2400 Stevenson Blvd .... Fremont CA 94538	**800-434-0222**	510-745-1400	431-3
Fremont Public Schools			
220 W Pine St .... Fremont MI 49412	**800-822-9433**	231-924-2350	676
Fremont Unified School District			
PO Box 5008 .... Fremont CA 94537	**800-544-5248**	510-657-2350	676
Fremont/Sandusky County Convention & Visitors Bureau			
712 N St Ste 102 .... Fremont OH 43420	**800-255-8070**	419-332-4470	207
French Country Waterways Ltd			
PO Box 2195 .... Duxbury MA 02331	**800-222-1236**	781-934-2454	221
French Culinary Institute			
462 Broadway .... New York NY 10013	**888-324-2433**		161
French Lick Resort			
8670 W State Rd 56 .... French Lick IN 47432	**888-936-9360**	812-936-9300	660
French Paper Co			
100 French St .... Niles MI 49120	**800-253-5952**	269-683-1100	545-1
French Quarter Suites Hotel			
1119 N Rampart St .... New Orleans LA 70116	**800-457-2253**	504-524-7725	376
French-American Chamber of Commerce in New York			
1350 Broadway Ste 2101 .... New York NY 10018	**800-821-2241**	212-867-0123	
Frenchman Valley Farmers Co-op Exchange			
202 Broadway .... Imperial NE 69033	**800-538-2667**	308-882-3200	276
Fresenius Medical Care North America			
920 Winter St .... Waltham MA 02451	**800-662-1237**	781-699-9000	349
Fresh Air Fund			
633 Third Ave 14th Fl .... New York NY 10017	**800-367-0003**		239
Fresh Del Monte Produce Co			
241 Sevilla Ave			
PO Box 149222 .... Coral Gables FL 33134	**800-950-3683***	305-520-8400	357-3
NYSE: FDP ■ *Cust Svc			
Fresh Enterprises Inc			
5900-A Katella Ave Ste 101 .... Cypress CA 90630	**877-225-2373**	562-391-2400	661
Fresh Express Inc			
550 South Caldwell St			
Ste 1212 .... Charlotte NC 28202	**800-242-5472***		11-1
*Cust Svc			
Fresh Frozen Foods LLC			
1814 Washington St PO Box 215 .... Jefferson GA 30549	**800-277-9851**	706-367-9851	295-21
FreshDirect Inc			
23-30 Borden Ave .... Long Island City NY 11101	**866-511-1240**	718-928-1000	342
FreshGrade Inc			
301-1447 Ellis St .... Kelowna BC V1Y2A3	**877-957-7757**		224
Freshwater Farm Products LLC			
4554 State Hwy 12 E PO Box 850 .... Belzoni MS 39038	**800-748-9338**	662-247-4205	295-14
Freshwater Society			
2500 Shadywood Rd .... Excelsior MN 55331	**888-471-9773**	952-471-9773	47-13
Freskeeto Frozen Foods Inc			
8019 Rt 209 .... Ellenville NY 12428	**800-356-3663**	845-647-5111	295-18

Name / Address	Toll-Free	Phone	Class
Fresno & Clovis Convention & Visitors Bureau 1550 E Shaw Ave Ste 101 — Fresno CA 93710	800-788-0836	559-981-5500	207
Fresno Bee 1626 E St — Fresno CA 93786	800-877-3400	559-441-6111	525-2
Fresno City College 1101 E University Ave — Fresno CA 93741	866-245-3276	559-442-4600	160
Fresno Distributing Company Inc 2055 E McKinley Ave — Fresno CA 93703	800-655-2542	559-442-8800	605
Fresno District Fair 1121 S Chance Ave — Fresno CA 93702	866-275-3772	559-650-3247	633
Fresno Pacific University 1717 S Chestnut Ave PO Box 2005 — Fresno CA 93702	800-660-6089	559-453-2039	166
Fresno Valves & Castings Inc 7736 E Springfield Ave PO Box 40 — Selma CA 93662	800-333-1658	559-834-2511	778
Fresno Yosemite International Airport 5175 E Clinton Way — Fresno CA 93727	800-244-2359	559-621-4500	27
Freud America Inc 218 Feld Ave — High Point NC 27263	800-334-4107	336-434-3171	347
Freundlich Supply Co Inc 2200 Arthur Kill Rd — Staten Island NY 10309	800-221-0260	718-356-1500	760
Friary of Lakeview Ctr, The 4400 Hickory Shores Blvd — Gulf Breeze FL 32563	800-332-2271	850-932-9375	717
Frick Hospital 508 S Church St — Mount Pleasant PA 15666	877-771-1234	724-547-1500	371-3
Fridgedoor.com 65 School St — Quincy MA 02169	800-955-3741	617-770-7913	327
Frieda's Inc 4465 Corporate Ctr Dr — Los Alamitos CA 90720	800-241-1771	714-826-6100	296-7
Friedberg Smith & Co PC 855 Main St — Bridgeport CT 06604	800-772-1213	203-366-5876	2
Friedman Billings Ramsey Group Inc 1001 19th St N — Arlington VA 22209	800-846-5050	703-312-9500	681
Friedman Bros Decorative Arts 9015 NW 105th Way — Medley FL 33178	800-327-1065	305-887-3170	332
Friedman Electric 1321 Wyoming Ave — Exeter PA 18643	800-545-5517	570-654-3371	246
Friedman LLP 1700 Broadway — New York NY 10019	800-372-1033	212-842-7000	2
Friedrich 10001 Reunion Pl Ste 500 — San Antonio TX 78216	800-541-6645	210-546-0500	14
Friend Tire Co 11 Industrial Dr — Monett MO 65708	800-950-8473		745
Friend's Professional Stationery Inc 1535 Lewis Ave — Zion IL 60099	800-323-4394		528
Friendfinder Network Inc 6800 Broken Sound Pkwy Ste 200 — Boca Raton FL 33487 *TSE: FFN*	800-388-0760	561-912-7000	226
Friendly Cruises 3081 S Sycamore Village Dr — Superstition Mountain AZ 85118	888-842-1786	480-358-1496	761
Friendly Excursions Inc PO Box 69 — Sunland CA 91041	800-775-5018	818-353-7726	750
Friendly Ice Cream Corp 1855 Boston Rd — Wilbraham MA 01095	800-966-9970	413-731-4000	661
Friends Committee on National Legislation (FCNL) 245 Second St NE — Washington DC 20002	800-630-1330	202-547-6000	608
Friends Hospital 4641 Roosevelt Blvd — Philadelphia PA 19124	800-889-0548	215-831-4600	371-5
Friends of Animals Inc (FOA) 777 Post Rd Ste 205 — Darien CT 06820	800-321-7387	203-656-1522	47-3
Friends of the Earth 1717 Massachusetts Ave NW Ste 600 — Washington DC 20036	877-843-8687	202-783-7400	47-13
Friends of the Earth Magazine 1100 15th St NW — Washington DC 20005	877-843-8687	202-783-7400	452-19
Friends of the River 1418 20th St Ste 100 — Sacramento CA 95811	888-464-2477	916-442-3155	47-13
Friends Research Institute Inc 1040 Pk Ave Ste 103 — Baltimore MD 21201	800-822-3677	410-823-5116	659
Friends University 2100 University St — Wichita KS 67213	800-794-6945	316-295-5000	166
Friendship Manor 1209 21st Ave — Rock Island IL 61201	888-382-1222	309-786-9667	663
Friendship Village Kalamazoo 1400 N Drake Rd — Kalamazoo MI 49006	800-613-3984	269-381-0560	663
Friendship Village of Tempe 2645 E Southern Ave — Tempe AZ 85282	800-824-1112	480-831-5000	663
Friendsview Retirement Community 1301 E Fulton St — Newberg OR 97132	866-307-4371	503-538-3144	663
Friendswood Public Library 416 S Friendswood Dr — Friendswood TX 77546	800-696-3493	281-482-7135	431-3
Fringe Benefits Management Co 3101 Sessions Rd — Tallahassee FL 32303	800-872-0345	850-425-6200	387
Friona Feedyard 2370 FM 3140 — Friona TX 79035	800-658-6014	806-265-3574	10-1
Friona Industries LP 500 S Taylor St Ste 601 PO Box 15568 — Amarillo TX 79101	800-658-6014	806-374-1811	10-1
Frisch's Restaurants Inc 2800 Gilbert Ave — Cincinnati OH 45206 *NYSE: FRS*	800-873-3633	513-961-2660	661
Frit Industries Inc 1792 Jodie Parker Rd — Ozark AL 36360	800-633-7685	334-774-2515	280
Frito-Lay North America 7701 Legacy Dr — Plano TX 75024	800-352-4477	972-334-7000	295-35
Fritz Industries Inc 180 Gordon Dr Ste 113 — Exton PA 19341	800-345-6202		184
FRL Furniture 460 Grand Blvd — Westbury NY 11590	800-529-4375	516-333-4400	655
Froedtert Hospital Bone Marrow Transplant Program 9200 W Wisconsin Ave — Milwaukee WI 53226	800-272-3666	414-805-3666	759
Frog Street Press Inc 800 Industrial Blvd Ste 100 — Grapevine TX 76051	800-884-3764		243
Frog Switch & Mfg Co 600 E High St — Carlisle PA 17013	800-233-7194	717-243-2454	306
Fromm Electric Supply Corp 2101 Centre Ave PO Box 15147 — Reading PA 19605	800-360-4441	610-374-4441	246
Front Porch Communities & Services 303 N Glenoaks Blvd — Burbank CA 91502	800-233-3709		445
Front Range Community College (FRCC) *Boulder County* 2190 Miller Dr — Longmont CO 80501	888-800-9198	303-678-3722	160
Larimer 4616 S Shields St — Fort Collins CO 80526	888-800-9198	970-226-2500	160
Front Row USA Entertainment 900 N Federal Hwy Ste 200 — Hallandale FL 33009	800-277-8499	305-940-8499	740
Front Runner Consulting LLC 6850 O'Bannon Bluff — Loveland OH 45140	877-328-3360	513-697-6850	195
Frontenac Bank 3330 Rider Trl S — Earth City MO 63045	877-205-5777	314-298-8200	69
Frontenac Co 135 S La Salle St Ste 3800 — Chicago IL 60603	800-368-3681	312-368-0044	780
Frontenac State Park 29223 County 28 Blvd — Frontenac MN 55026	888-646-6367	651-345-3401	558
Frontera Foods Inc 449 N Clark St Ste 205 — Chicago IL 60654	800-509-4441	312-595-1624	342
Frontier Adjusters of America Inc 4745 N Seventh St Ste 320 — Phoenix AZ 85014	800-426-7228		387
Frontier Airlines Ctr 400 W Wisconsin Ave — Milwaukee WI 53203	800-745-3000	414-908-6000	206
Frontier Airlines Inc 7001 Tower Rd — Denver CO 80249	800-432-1359	720-374-4200	357-1
Frontier Communications 1522 N Walker St — Princeton WV 24740	877-378-9289	304-487-1502	137
Frontier Communications Corp Three High Ridge Pk — Stamford CT 06905 *NASDAQ: FTR*	800-877-4390	203-614-5600	726
Frontier Computer Corp 1275 Business Pk Dr — Traverse City MI 49686	866-226-6344	231-929-1386	181
Frontier Co-op 211 S Lincoln PO Box 37 — Brainard NE 68626	800-869-0379	402-545-2811	275
Frontier Electronic Systems Corp 4500 W Sixth Ave — Stillwater OK 74074	800-677-1769	405-624-1769	522
Frontier Logistics LP 1806 S 16th St — La Porte TX 77571	800-610-6808		310
Frontier Metal Stamping Inc 3764 Puritan Way — Erie CO 80516	888-316-1266	303-458-5129	478
Frontier Natural Products Co-op 3021 78th St PO Box 299 — Norway IA 52318	800-669-3275	319-227-7996	295-37
Frontier Power Co 770 S 2nd St PO Box 280 — Coshocton OH 43812	800-624-8050	740-622-6755	245
Frontier Supply Inc 981 Van Horn Rd — Fairbanks AK 99701	800-478-7867	907-374-3500	605
Frontier-Kemper Constructors Inc 1695 Allen Rd — Evansville IN 47710	877-554-8600	812-426-2741	189-10
Frontiers International Travel PO Box 959 — Wexford PA 15090	800-245-1950	724-935-1577	750
Frontline Communications PO Box 98 — Orangeburg NY 10962	888-376-6854		395
Frontline Group of Texas LLC 15021 Katy Fwy Ste 575 — Houston TX 77094	800-285-5512	281-453-6000	755
FrontRange Solutions USA Inc 5675 Gibraltar Dr — Pleasanton CA 94588	800-776-7889	925-398-1800	179-1
Frost & Sullivan 7550 IH 10 W Ste 400 — San Antonio TX 78229	877-463-7678	210-348-1000	524-12
Frost Brown Todd LLC 201 E Fifth St 2200 PNC Ctr — Cincinnati OH 45202	866-559-6446	513-651-6800	425
Frozen Head State Natural Area 964 Flat Fork Rd — Wartburg TN 37887	800-342-3145	423-346-3318	558
Fruit Co, The 2900 Van Horn Dr — Hood River OR 97031	800-387-3100	541-387-3100	292
Fruit of The Earth Inc 3101 High Rver Rd Ste 175 — Fort Worth TX 76155	800-527-7731	972-790-0808	215
Fruit of the Loom Inc One Fruit of the Loom Dr PO Box 90015 — Bowling Green KY 42102	888-378-4829	270-781-6400	153-3
Frullati Cafe & Bakery 9311 E Via de Ventura — Scottsdale AZ 85258	866-452-4252	480-362-4800	661
Frutarom Corp 9500 Railroad Ave — North Bergen NJ 07047	866-229-7198	201-861-9500	295-15
Fruth Pharmacy Inc 4016 Ohio River Rd — Point Pleasant WV 25550	800-438-5390	304-675-1612	237
Fry's Food Stores of Arizona Inc 500 S 99th Ave — Tolleson AZ 85353	866-221-4141		342
Fryeburg Academy 745 Main St — Fryeburg ME 04037	877-935-2013	207-935-2013	615
Frymaster LLC 8700 Line Ave — Shreveport LA 71106 *Cust Svc*	800-221-4583*	318-865-1711	297
Fry-Wagner Moving & Storage Co 3700 Rider Trl S — Earth City MO 63045	800-899-4035	314-291-4100	770
FS Tool Corp 71 Hobbs Gate — Markham ON L3R9T9	800-387-9723	905-475-1999	688
FSEEE (Forest Service Employees for Environmental Ethics) PO Box 11615 — Eugene OR 97440	800-270-7504	541-484-2692	48-7
FSG (Facility Solutions Group) 4401 Westgate Blvd Ste 310 — Austin TX 78745	800-854-6465	512-440-7985	246
FSG Lighting 4401 Westgate Blvd Ste 310 — Austin TX 78745	800-854-6465	512-440-7985	246
FSI Technologies Inc 668 E Western Ave — Lombard IL 60148	800-468-6009	630-932-9380	204
FSMB (Federation of State Medical Boards of the US Inc) 400 Fuller Wiser Rd Ste 300 — Euless TX 76039	800-793-7939	817-868-4000	48-8
FTC (Federal Trade Commission) 600 Pennsylvania Ave NW — Washington DC 20580	877-382-4357	202-326-2222	338-18
FTC (Farmers Telecommunications Co-op) 144 McCurdy Ave N PO Box 217 — Rainsville AL 35986	866-638-2144	256-638-2144	726
FTC (Feed the Children) PO Box 36 — Oklahoma City OK 73101	800-627-4556	405-942-0228	47-5
FTD Inc 3113 Woodcreek Dr — Downers Grove IL 60515 *Cust Svc*	800-736-3383*		292
FTG Inc 725 Marshall Phelps Rd — Windsor CT 06095	888-610-6020	860-610-6000	246
FTI Consulting 909 Commerce Rd Ste 1400 — Annapolis MD 21401 *NYSE: FCN*	800-334-5701	410-224-8770	440
FTJ FundChoice LLC 2300 Litton Ln Ste 102 — Hebron KY 41048	800-379-2513		384
FTMC (Fisher-Titus Medical Ctr) 272 Benedict Ave — Norwalk OH 44857	800-589-3862	419-668-8101	371-3
Fuchs Lubricants Co 17050 Lathrop Ave — Harvey IL 60426	800-323-7755	708-333-8900	534
Fuchs North America 9740 Reisterstown Rd — Owings Mills MD 21117	800-365-3229	410-363-1700	295-37
Fuego 330 E Palace Ave — Santa Fe NM 87501 *Sales*	855-811-0050*	505-986-0000	662

Company / Address	City	State	Zip	Toll-Free	Phone	Class
Fuel Education LLC 7506 Broadway Ext	Oklahoma City	OK	73116	**800-222-2811**		179-3
Fuel Tech Inc 27601 Bella Vista Pkwy *NASDAQ: FTEK* ■ *General	Warrenville	IL	60555	**800-666-9688***	630-845-4500	18
Fuji Health Science Inc Three Terri Ln Ste 12	Burlington	NJ	08016	**877-385-4777**	609-386-3030	296-8
FUJIFILM Graphic System USA Inc 45 Crosby Dr	Bedford	MA	01730	**800-755-3854**	781-271-4400	382
Fujitsu America Inc 1250 E Arques Ave	Sunnyvale	CA	94085	**800-538-8460**	408-746-6200	725
Fujitsu Computer Products of America Inc 1255 E Arques Ave	Sunnyvale	CA	94085	**800-626-4686**	408-746-7000	174-8
Fujitsu Computer Systems Corp 1250 E Arques Ave	Sunnyvale	CA	94085	**800-538-8460**	408-746-6000	177
Fujitsu Consulting 1250 E Arques Ave	Sunnyvale	CA	94085	**800-831-3183**		181
Fujitsu General America Inc 353 Rt 46 W	Fairfield	NJ	07004	**888-888-3424**	973-575-0380	603
Fujitsu Ten Corp of America 19600 S Vermont Ave	Torrance	CA	90502	**800-233-2216**	310-327-2151	51
Fulbright & Jaworski LLP 1301 McKinney St Ste 5100	Houston	TX	77010	**866-385-2744**	713-651-5151	425
Fulcrum Analytics Inc 70 W 40th St 10th Fl	New York	NY	10018	**888-245-9450**	212-651-7000	196
Fulflex Inc 32 Justin Holden Dr	Brattleboro	VT	05301	**800-283-2500**	802-257-5256	734-5
Fulghum Industries 317 S Main St	Wadley	GA	30477	**800-841-5980**	478-252-5223	674
Full Cir Bookstore 1900 NW Expy	Oklahoma City	OK	73118	**800-683-7323**	405-842-2900	95
Full House Resorts Inc 4670 S Fort Apache Rd Ste 190 *NASDAQ: FLL*	Las Vegas	NV	89147	**800-240-6709**	702-221-7800	131
Full Sail University 3300 University Blvd Ste 160	Winter Park	FL	32792	**800-226-7625**	407-679-6333	788
Fullen Dock & Warehouse Inc 382 Klinke Rd	Memphis	TN	38127	**800-467-7104**	901-358-9544	192-1
Fuller Brush Co, The P.O. Box 729 1 Fuller Way *Cust Svc	Great Bend	KS	67530	**800-522-0499***	620-792-1711	102
Fuller Theological Seminary 135 N Oakland Ave	Pasadena	CA	91182	**800-235-2222**	626-584-5200	167-3
Fullerton Bldg Systems Inc (FBS) 34620 250th St PO Box 308	Worthington	MN	56187	**800-450-9782**	507-376-3128	804
Fullerton Tool Company Inc 121 Perry St	Saginaw	MI	48602	**855-722-7243**	989-799-4550	488
Fulmer Co 122 Gayoso Ave	Memphis	TN	38103	**800-467-2400**	901-525-5711	510
Fulton Corp 303 Eigth Ave	Fulton	IL	61252	**800-252-0002**		347
Fulton County Rural Electric Membership Corp 1448 W State Rd 14 PO Box 230	Rochester	IN	46975	**800-286-2265**	574-223-3156	245
Fulton Industries Inc 135 E Linfoot St PO Box 377	Wauseon	OH	43567	**800-537-5012**	419-335-3015	435
Fulton Mansion 317 N Fulton Beach Rd	Rockport	TX	78382	**800-792-1112**	361-729-0386	49-2
Fulton Opera House Foundation 12 N Prince St PO Box 1865	Lancaster	PA	17603	**888-480-1265**	717-397-7425	565
Fun 101.3 FM 1996 Auction Rd	Manheim	PA	17545	**877-870-5678**	717-653-0800	636
Fundcraft Publishing Inc PO Box 340	Collierville	TN	38027	**800-964-5715**	901-853-7070	619
FundThrough Inc 260 Spadina Ave Ste 400	Toronto	ON	M5T2E4	**800-766-0460**		224
Funeral Consumers Alliance 33 Patchen Rd	South Burlington	VT	05403	**800-765-0107**	802-865-8300	47-10
Funeral Service Insider 3349 Hwy 138 Bldg D Ste D	Wall	NJ	07719	**800-500-4585**		524-13
Funnel Science Internet Marketing LLC 1802 N Carson St	Carson City	NV	89701	**877-301-0001**		5
Furman Sound LLC 1690 Corporate Cir	Petaluma	CA	94954	**877-486-4738**	707-763-1010	51
Furmanite America 101 Old Underwood Rd Unit E	La Porte	TX	77571	**800-444-5572**	281-842-5100	449
Furmano Foods Inc 770 Cannery Rd PO Box 500	Northumberland	PA	17857	**877-877-6032**	570-473-3516	295-20
Furnace Creek Inn & Ranch Resort Hwy 190 PO Box 187	Death Valley	CA	92328	**800-236-7916**	760-786-2345	660
Furniture Medic 3839 S Forest Hill Irene Rd	Memphis	TN	38125	**800-877-9933**		309
Furniture Outlets USA Inc 140 E Hinks Ln	Sioux Falls	SD	57104	**877-395-8998**	605-336-5000	290
FurnitureDealer.net Inc PO Box 22251	Eagan	MN	55122	**866-387-6357**		523
Furst-McNess Co 120 E Clark St	Freeport	IL	61032	**800-435-5100**	815-235-6151	442
Fusion Inc 4658 E 355th St	Willoughby	OH	44094	**800-626-9501**	440-946-3300	383
Fusion Optix Inc 19 Wheeling Ave	Woburn	MA	01801	**866-506-8300**	781-995-0805	601
Fusion Solutions Inc 16901 N Dallas Pkwy Ste 114	Dallas	TX	75001	**888-817-1951**	972-764-1708	195
Fusion Telecommunications International Inc 420 Lexington Ave Ste 1718 *OTC: FSNN*	New York	NY	10170	**888-301-1721**	212-201-2400	726
FusionStorm Two Bryant St Ste 150	San Francisco	CA	94105	**800-228-8324**	415-623-2626	178
Fuss & O'Neill Consulting Engineers Inc 146 Hartford Rd	Manchester	CT	06040	**800-286-2469**	860-646-2469	261
FUTEK Advanced Sensor Technology Inc 10 Thomas	Irvine	CA	92618	**800-233-8835**	949-465-0900	256
Future Business Leaders of America-Phi Beta Lambda Inc (FBLA-PBL) 1912 Assn Dr	Reston	VA	20191	**800-325-2946**		47-11
Future Electronics 237 Hymus Blvd *Cust Svc	Pointe-Claire	QC	H9R5C7	**800-675-1619***	514-694-7710	246
Future Foam Inc 1610 Ave N Council Bluffs	Council Bluffs	IA	51501	**800-733-8061**	712-323-9122	594
Futurebiotics LLC 70 Commerce Dr	Hauppauge	NY	11788	**800-645-1721**	631-273-6300	787
FutureMark Paper Co 13101 S Pulaski Rd	Alsip	IL	60803	**866-580-8325**	708-272-8700	550
FutureSoft Inc 1660 Townhurst Dr Ste E	Houston	TX	77043	**800-989-8908**	281-496-9400	179-7
Futurex Inc 864 Old Boerne Rd	Bulverde	TX	78163	**800-251-5112**	830-980-9782	177
Futurist Magazine 7910 Woodmont Ave Ste 450	Bethesda	MD	20814	**800-989-8274**	301-656-8274	452-11
FW Gartner Thermal Spraying Ltd 25 Southbelt Industrial Dr	Houston	TX	77047	**888-439-4872**	713-225-0010	476
FW Webb Co 160 Middlesex Tpke	Bedford	MA	01730	**800-343-7555**	781-272-6600	382
FXCM Inc 32 Old Slip *NYSE: FXCM*	New York	NY	10005	**888-503-6739**	212-897-7660	179-10
FXI 1400 N Providence Rd	Media	PA	19063	**800-355-3626**	610-744-2300	594
FXVA (Fairfax County Convention & Visitors Bureau) 3702 Pender Dr Ste 420	Fairfax	VA	22030	**800-732-4732**	703-790-0643	207
Fyda Freightliner Youngstown Inc 5260 76th Dr	Youngstown	OH	44515	**800-837-3932**	330-797-0224	61-5

G

Company / Address	City	State	Zip	Toll-Free	Phone	Class
G & D Transportation Inc 50 Commerce Dr	Morton	IL	61550	**800-451-6680**	309-266-1472	187
G & G Instrument Corp 466 Saw Mill River Rd	Ardsley	NY	10502	**800-882-2288**	914-693-6000	471
G & H Decoys Inc PO Box 1208 *Orders	Henryetta	OK	74437	**800-443-3269***	918-652-3314	701
G & H Wire Company Inc 2165 Earlywood Dr	Franklin	IN	46131	**800-526-1026**	317-346-6655	228
G & K Services Inc 5995 Opus Pkwy Ste 500	Minnetonka	MN	55343	**800-452-2737**	952-912-5500	438
G & T Industries Inc 1001 76th St SW	Byron Center	MI	49315	**800-968-6035**		594
G & W Laboratories Inc 111 Coolidge St	South Plainfield	NJ	07080	**800-922-1038**	908-753-2000	576
G G Schmitt & Sons Inc 2821 Old Tree Dr	Lancaster	PA	17603	**866-724-6488**	717-394-3701	347
G r Manufacturing Inc 4800 Commerce Dr	Trussville	AL	35173	**800-841-8001**	205-655-8001	296-8
G Robert Cotton Correctional Facility 3500 N Elm Rd	Jackson	MI	49201	**855-444-3911**	517-780-5000	213
G6 Hospitality LLC *Motel 6* 4001 International Pkwy	Carrollton	TX	75007	**800-466-8356**	972-360-9000	376
GA (Gamblers Anonymous) PO Box 17173	Los Angeles	CA	90017	**888-424-3577**	626-960-3500	47-21
GA Braun Inc 461 E Brighton Ave	Syracuse	NY	13212	**800-432-7286**	315-475-3123	424
G&A Partners 4801 Woodway Dr Ste 210W	Houston	TX	77056	**800-253-8562**	713-784-1181	712
GA Wintzer & Son Co 204 W Auglaize St	Wapakoneta	OH	45895	**800-331-1801**	419-739-4900	295-12
GableSigns Inc 7440 Ft Smallwood Rd	Baltimore	MD	21226	**800-854-0568**	410-255-6400	692
Gabriel Roeder Smith & Co 1 Towne Sq Ste 800	Southfield	MI	48076	**800-521-0498**	248-799-9000	194
Gachman Metals & Recycling Company Inc 2600 Shamrock Ave	Fort Worth	TX	76107	**800-749-0423**	817-334-0211	677
Gaco Western Inc 200 W Mercer St Ste 202	Seattle	WA	98119	**800-456-4226**	206-575-0450	594
Gadabout Vacations 1801 E Tahquitz Canyon Way Ste 100	Palm Springs	CA	92262	**800-952-5068**	760-325-5556	750
Gadsden & Etowah County Chamber One Commerce Sq	Gadsden	AL	35901	**800-659-2955**	256-543-3472	137
Gadsden County Chamber of Commerce 208 N Adams St	Quincy	FL	32351	**800-627-9231**	850-627-9231	137
Gadsden State Community College 1001 George Wallace Dr PO Box 227	Gadsden	AL	35902	**800-226-5563**	256-549-8200	160
Gadsden Times 401 Locust St	Gadsden	AL	35901	**800-762-2464**	256-549-2000	525-2
GAF Materials Corp 1361 Alps Rd	Wayne	NJ	07470	**800-365-7353**	973-628-3000	45
Gagemaker LP 712 Southmore Ave	Pasadena	TX	77502	**800-767-7633**	713-472-7360	630
Gaiam Inc 833 W S Boulder Rd Ste C *NASDAQ: GAIA*	Louisville	CO	80027	**877-989-6321**	303-222-3600	454
Gaines Motor Lines Inc 2349 13th Ave SW PO Box 1549	Hickory	NC	28603	**800-438-7311**	828-322-2000	187
Gainesville Area Chamber of Commerce 300 E University Ave Ste 100	Gainesville	FL	32601	**888-795-2707**	352-334-7100	137
Gainesville City Schools 508 Oak St	Gainesville	GA	30501	**800-533-0682**	770-536-5275	676
Gainesville Times 345 Green St NW	Gainesville	GA	30501	**800-395-5005**	770-532-1234	525-2
Gainey Ceramics Inc 1200 Arrow Hwy *Cust Svc	La Verne	CA	91750	**800-451-8155***	909-593-3533	332
GAI-Tronics Corp 400 E Wyomissing Ave	Mohnton	PA	19540	**800-492-1212**	610-777-1374	725
Galaxy Hotel Systems LLC 15621 Red Hill Ave Ste 100	Tustin	CA	92780	**800-434-9990**	714-258-5800	179-11
Galaxy Nutritional Foods Inc 66 Whitecap Dr	North Kingstown	RI	02852	**800-441-9419**	401-667-5000	295-5
Galco Industrial Electronics Inc 26010 Pinehurst Dr	Madison Heights	MI	48071	**888-783-4611**	248-542-9090	246
Galderma Laboratories Inc 14501 N Fwy	Fort Worth	TX	76177	**866-735-4137**	817-961-5000	576
Gale Cengage Learning 27500 Drake Rd *Cust Svc	Farmington Hills	MI	48331	**800-877-4253***	248-699-4253	628-2

	City	State	Zip	Toll-Free	Phone	Class
Gale Force Petroleum Inc						
Ste 5700 100 King St W	Toronto	ON	M5X1C7	**888-440-3411**		316
Galectin Therapeutics						
Seven Wells Ave Ste 34	Newton	MA	02459	**888-286-8010**	617-559-0033	84
Galena Gazette						
716 S Bench St	Galena	IL	61036	**800-373-6397**	815-777-0019	525-4
Galesburg Area Convention & Visitors Bureau						
2163 E Main St	Galesburg	IL	61401	**800-916-3330**	309-343-2485	207
Galesburg Printing & Publishing Co						
140 S Prairie St	Galesburg	IL	61401	**800-733-2767**	309-343-7181	628-8
Galison Publishing LLC						
28 W 44th St Ste 1411	New York	NY	10036	**800-670-7441**	212-354-8840	129
Gallade Chemical Inc						
1230 E St Gertrude Pl	Santa Ana	CA	92707	**888-830-9092**	714-546-9901	144
Gallagher Asphalt Corp						
18100 S Indiana Ave	Thornton	IL	60476	**800-536-7160**	708-877-7160	189-4
Gallagher Corp						
3908 Morrison Dr	Gurnee	IL	60031	**800-524-8597**	847-249-3440	598-2
Gallant Greetings Corp						
4300 United Pkwy	Schiller Park	IL	60176	**800-621-4279**	847-671-6500	129
Gallaudet University						
800 Florida Ave NE	Washington	DC	20002	**800-995-0550**	202-651-5000	166
Gallaudet University Library						
800 Florida Ave NE	Washington	DC	20002	**800-995-0550**	202-651-5217	431-6
Gallaudet University Press						
800 Florida Ave NE	Washington	DC	20002	**800-621-2736**	202-651-5488	628-4
Gallegos Corp PO Box 821	Vail	CO	81658	**800-425-5346**	970-926-3737	190-7
Galleon Resort & Marina						
617 Front St	Key West	FL	33040	**800-544-3030**	305-296-7711	660
Gallery 78 Inc						
796 Queen St	Fredericton	NB	E3B1C6	**888-883-8322**	506-454-5192	41
Gallery of History Inc						
3601 W Sahara Ave						
Ste Promenade	Las Vegas	NV	89102	**800-425-5379**	702-364-1000	50
Galliard Capital Management Inc						
800 La Salle Ave Ste 1100	Minneapolis	MN	55402	**800-717-1617**	612-667-3220	399
Galliker Dairy Company Inc						
143 Donald Ln	Johnstown	PA	15907	**800-477-6455**	814-266-8702	295-27
Gallina LLP						
2870 Gold Tailings Crt						
2nd Fl	Rancho Cordova	CA	95670	**877-638-1188**	916-638-1188	2
Galls Inc						
2680 Palumbo Dr	Lexington	KY	40509	**800-477-7766**	859-266-7227	569
Gallup Organization						
901 F St NW	Washington	DC	20004	**877-242-5587**	202-715-3030	461
Galpin Motors Inc						
15505 Roscoe Blvd	North Hills	CA	91343	**800-256-7137**	818-787-3800	56
Galt House Hotel						
140 N Fourth St	Louisville	KY	40202	**800-843-4258**	502-589-5200	376
Galvan Industries Inc						
7320 Millbrook Rd	Harrisburg	NC	28075	**888-256-6929***	704-455-5102	476
*General						
Galveston College						
4015 Ave Q	Galveston	TX	77550	**866-483-4242**	409-763-6551	160
Galveston County Daily News						
8522 Teichman Rd PO Box 628	Galveston	TX	77553	**800-561-3611**	409-683-5200	525-2
Galveston Independent School District (GISD)						
3904 Ave PO Box 660	Galveston	TX	77550	**877-262-1492**	409-766-5100	676
Galvin Flying Services						
7149 Perimeter Rd	Seattle	WA	98108	**800-341-4102**	206-763-9706	62
GAMA (General Aviation Manufacturers Assn)						
1400 K St NW Ste 801	Washington	DC	20005	**800-728-9607**	202-393-1500	48-21
GAMA International						
2901 Telestar Ct	Falls Church	VA	22042	**800-345-2687***		48-9
*Cust Svc						
Gamajet Cleaning Systems Inc						
604 Jeffers Cir	Exton	PA	19341	**877-426-2538***	610-408-9940	383
*Sales						
Gamblers Anonymous (GA)						
PO Box 17173	Los Angeles	CA	90017	**888-424-3577**	626-960-3500	47-21
Gambrill State Park						
8602 Gambrill Pk Rd	Frederick	MD	21702	**800-830-3974**	301-271-7574	558
Gambrinus Co, The						
14800 San Pedro Ave						
Third Fl	San Antonio	TX	78232	**800-596-6486**	210-490-9128	80-1
Gambro BCT						
10811 W Collins Ave	Lakewood	CO	80215	**877-339-4228**	303-231-4357	416
Gambro Renal Products						
14143 Denver W Pkwy	Lakewood	CO	80401	**800-525-2623**	303-232-6800	250
GAMCO Investors Inc						
One Corporate Ctr	Rye	NY	10580	**800-422-3554**	914-921-5100	521
NYSE: GBL						
GamePlan Financial Marketing LLC						
300 ParkBrooke Pl Ste 200	Woodstock	GA	30189	**800-886-4757***	678-238-0601	399
*Cust Svc						
GameStop Corp						
625 Westport Pkwy	Grapevine	TX	76051	**800-883-8895**	817-424-2000	180
NYSE: GME						
Gamewell FCI						
12 Clintonville Rd	Northford	CT	06472	**800-606-1983**	203-484-7161	283
12 Clintonville Rd	Northford	CT	06472	**800-606-1983**	203-484-7161	739
Gaming Partners International Corp						
1700 Industrial Rd	Las Vegas	NV	89102	**800-728-5766**	702-384-2425	321
NASDAQ: GPIC						
Gamla Enterprises North America Inc						
875 Ave of The Americas						
Ste 205	New York	NY	10001	**800-442-6526**	212-947-3790	37
Gamma Beta Phi Society						
78 Mitchell Rd Ste A	Oak Ridge	TN	37830	**800-628-9920**	865-483-6212	47-16
Gamma Sports						
200 Waterfront Dr	Pittsburgh	PA	15222	**800-333-0337**	412-323-0335	701
Gammex Inc						
7600 Discovery Dr	Middleton	WI	53562	**800-426-6391**	608-828-7000	630
GANA (Glass Assn of North America)						
800 SW Jackson St Ste 1500	Topeka	KS	66612	**877-275-2421**	785-271-0208	48-13
Gandy Co						
528 Gandrud Rd	Owatonna	MN	55060	**800-443-2476**	507-451-5430	273
Gandy Dancer						
401 Depot St	Ann Arbor	MI	48104	**800-552-6379**	734-769-0592	662
Gandy's Dairies Inc						
201 University Blvd	Lubbock	TX	79415	**877-382-4357**	806-765-8833	295-25
Gannett Fleming Inc						
207 Senate Ave	Camp Hill	PA	17011	**800-233-1055**	717-763-7211	261
Gannett Offset						
7950 Jones Branch Dr	McLean	VA	22107	**800-255-1457**	703-750-8673	619
Gannett Welsh & Kotler LLC						
222 Berkeley St 15th Fl	Boston	MA	02116	**800-225-4236**	617-236-8900	398
Gannon University						
109 University Sq	Erie	PA	16541	**800-426-6668***	814-871-7000	166
*Admissions						
Gans Ink & Supply Company Inc						
1441 Boyd St	Los Angeles	CA	90033	**800-421-6167**	323-264-2200	385
Gant Travel Management						
304 W Kirkwood Ave Ste 1	Bloomington	IN	47404	**800-742-4198***		761
*Cust Svc						
Gap Inc						
Two Folsom St	San Francisco	CA	94105	**800-333-7899**	650-952-4400	155-4
NYSE: GPS						
Garaga Inc						
8500 25th Ave	St Georges	QC	G6A1K5	**800-464-2724**	418-227-2828	475
GARBC (General Assn of Regular Baptist Churches)						
1300 N Meacham Rd	Schaumburg	IL	60173	**888-588-1600**	847-585-0816	47-20
Garco Bldg Systems						
2714 S Garfield Rd	Airway Heights	WA	99001	**800-941-2291**	509-244-5611	104
Garda World Security Corp						
1390 Barre St	Montreal	QC	H3C1N4	**800-859-1599**	514-281-2811	684
TSE: GW						
Gardco Lighting						
1611 Clovis Barker Rd	San Marcos	TX	78666	**800-227-0758**	512-753-1000	435
Garden City Community College						
801 N Campus Dr	Garden City	KS	67846	**800-658-1696**	620-276-7611	160
Garden City Feed Yard						
1805 W Annie Scheer Rd	Garden City	KS	67846	**800-272-4191**	620-275-4191	10-1
Garden City Group LLC						
105 Maxess Rd	Melville	NY	11747	**888-404-8013**	631-470-5000	425
Garden City Hotel						
45 Seventh St	Garden City	NY	11530	**877-549-0400**	516-747-3000	376
Garden Court Hotel						
520 Cowper St	Palo Alto	CA	94301	**800-824-9028**	650-322-9000	376
Garden Fresh Restaurant Corp						
15822 Bernardo Ctr Dr Ste A	San Diego	CA	92127	**800-874-1600**	858-675-1600	661
Garden Grove Chamber of Commerce						
12866 Main St Ste 102	Garden Grove	CA	92840	**800-959-5560**	714-638-7950	137
Garden of Life Inc						
5500 Village Blvd						
Ste 102	West Palm Beach	FL	33407	**866-465-0051**		787
Garden Place Hotel						
6461 Transit Rd	Depew	NY	14043	**877-456-4097**	716-683-7990	376
Garden Spa at MacArthur Place						
29 E MacArthur St	Sonoma	CA	95476	**800-722-1866**	707-933-3193	698
Garden State Community Bank (GSCB)						
36 Ferry St	Newark	NJ	07105	**877-786-6560**	973-589-8616	69
NYSE: NYB						
Garden State Engine & Equipment Co						
3509 US Hwy 22	Somerville	NJ	08876	**800-479-3857**	908-534-5444	355
Garden State Growers						
99 Locust Grove Rd	Pittstown	NJ	08867	**800-288-8484**	908-730-8888	366
Gardena Valley News						
15005 S Vermont Ave	Gardena	CA	90247	**800-329-6351**	310-329-6351	525-4
Gardener's Supply Co						
128 Intervale Rd	Burlington	VT	05401	**800-863-1700**	802-660-3500	322
Gardens Alive Inc						
5100 Schenley Pl	Lawrenceburg	IN	47025	**800-222-1222**	513-354-1482	454
Gardens Hotel						
526 Angela St	Key West	FL	33040	**800-526-2664**	305-294-2661	376
Gardens of the American Rose Ctr						
8877 Jefferson-Paige Rd	Shreveport	LA	71119	**800-637-6534**	318-938-5402	96
Gardenside Ltd						
808 Anthony St Ste 140	Berkeley	CA	94710	**888-999-8325**	415-455-4500	318-4
Gardner Denver Compressor Div						
1800 Gardner Expwy	Quincy	IL	62305	**800-682-9868**	217-222-5400	173
Gardner Denver Inc						
1800 Gardner Expy	Quincy	IL	62305	**800-682-9868**	217-222-5400	173
NYSE: GDI						
Gardner Denver Nash						
1800 Gardner Expy	Quincy	IL	62305	**800-637-5729**	217-222-5400	173
Gardner Denver Water Jetting Systems Inc						
12300 N Houston Rosslyn	Houston	TX	77086	**800-682-9868***	281-448-5800	173
*General						
Gardner Glass Products Inc						
301 Elkin Hwy						
PO Box 1570	North Wilkesboro	NC	28659	**800-334-7267**		332
Gardner Inc						
3641 Interchange Rd	Columbus	OH	43204	**800-848-8946**	614-456-4000	274
Gardner Mattress Corp						
254 Canal St	Salem	MA	01970	**800-564-2736**	978-744-1810	320
Gardner Publications Inc						
6915 Valley Ave	Cincinnati	OH	45244	**800-950-8020**	513-527-8800	628-9
Gardner Village						
1100 West 7800 South	West Jordan	UT	84088	**800-662-4335**	801-566-8903	455
Gardner-Gibson						
PO Box 5449	Tampa	FL	33675	**800-237-1155**	813-248-2101	45
Gardners Candies Inc						
2600 Adams Ave PO Box E	Tyrone	PA	16686	**800-242-2639**	814-684-3925	122
Gardner-Webb University						
PO Box 817	Boiling Springs	NC	28017	**800-253-6472**	704-406-4498	166
Gare Inc						
165 Rosemont St	Haverhill	MA	01832	**888-289-4273**	978-373-9131	42
Gared Sports Inc						
707 N Second St Ste 220	Saint Louis	MO	63102	**800-325-2682**	314-421-0044	701
Garfield County						
375 North 700 West	Panguitch	UT	84759	**800-636-8826**	435-676-2678	336
Garfield Suites Hotel						
Two Garfield Pl	Cincinnati	OH	45202	**800-367-2155**	513-421-3355	376
Garkane Energy Co-op Inc						
120 West 300 South PO Box 465	Loa	UT	84747	**800-747-5403**	435-836-2795	245
Garland C Norris Co						
1101 Terry Rd PO Box 28	Apex	NC	27502	**800-331-8920**	919-387-1059	552
Garland Commercial Industries						
185 S St	Freeland	PA	18224	**800-424-2411**	570-636-1000	297
Garland Company Inc						
3800 E 91st St	Cleveland	OH	44105	**800-321-9336**	216-641-7500	45
Garland Independent School District (GISD)						
501 S Jupiter PO Box 469026	Garland	TX	75046	**800-252-5555**	972-494-8201	676
Garland Resort						
4700 N Red Oak Rd	Lewiston	MI	49756	**877-442-7526**	989-786-2211	660

Alphabetical Section

Company	Address	City	State	ZIP	Toll-Free	Phone	Class
Garland Sales Inc	PO Box 1870	Dalton	GA	30720	**800-524-0361**	706-278-7880	130
Garland, The	4222 Vineland Ave	North Hollywood	CA	91602	**800-238-3759**	818-980-8000	376
Garlich Printing Co	525 Rudder Rd	Fenton	MO	63026	**800-276-2622**	636-349-8000	618
Garmin Ltd	1200 E 151st St	Olathe	KS	66062	**888-442-7646**	913-397-8200	522
NASDAQ: GRMN							
Garner Industries Inc	7201 N 98th St PO Box 29709	Lincoln	NE	68507	**800-228-0275**	402-434-9100	601
Garnet Hill Inc	231 Main St	Franconia	NH	03580	**800-870-3513**	603-823-5545	734-1
Garr Tool Co	7800 N Alger Rd	Alma	MI	48801	**800-248-9003**	989-463-6171	488
Garrett College	687 Mosser Rd	McHenry	MD	21541	**866-554-2773**	301-387-3000	160
Garrett County Chamber of Commerce	15 Visitors Ctr Dr	McHenry	MD	21541	**888-387-5237**	301-387-4386	137
Garrett Metal Detectors	1881 W State St	Garland	TX	75042	**800-234-6151**	972-494-6151	467
Garrett's Desert Inn	311 Old Santa Fe Trl	Santa Fe	NM	87501	**800-888-2145**	505-982-1851	376
Garry Packing Inc	11272 E Central Ave PO Box 249	Del Rey	CA	93616	**800-248-2126**	559-888-2126	295-18
Garsite LLC	539 S Tenth St	Kansas City	KS	66105	**888-427-7483**	913-342-5600	21
Gartner Inc	56 Top Gallant Rd	Stamford	CT	06902	**800-863-8863**	203-964-0096	461
NYSE: IT							
Garton Tractor Inc	2400 N Golden State Blvd	Turlock	CA	95382	**877-872-2767**	209-632-3931	274
Garvan Woodland Gardens	550 Arkridge Rd PO Box 22240	Hot Springs	AR	71903	**800-366-4664**	501-262-9300	96
Garver Engineers	4701 Northshore Dr	North Little Rock	AR	72118	**800-264-3633**	501-376-3633	261
Garvey Corp	208 S Rt 73	Blue Anchor	NJ	08037	**800-257-8581**	609-561-2450	208
Gary Plastic Packaging Corp	1340 Viele Ave	Bronx	NY	10474	**800-221-8150**	718-893-2200	593
Gary Soren Smith Ctr for the Fine & Performing Arts *Ohlone College*	43600 Mission Blvd	Fremont	CA	94539	**800-309-2131**	510-659-6031	565
GAS (Glass Art Society)	6512 23rd Ave NW Ste 329	Seattle	WA	98121	**800-636-2377**	206-382-1305	47-4
Gas Co, The	515 Kamake'e St	Honolulu	HI	96814	**866-499-3941**	808-535-5933	775
Gas Daily	1200 G St NW Ste 1000	Washington	DC	20005	**800-752-8878**	202-383-2000	524-5
Gas Technology Energy Concepts LLC	401 William L Gaiter Pkwy Ste 4	Buffalo	NY	14215	**800-451-8294**		173
GasAmerica Services Inc	2700 W Main St	Greenfield	IN	46140	**800-643-1948**	317-468-2515	323
Gasboy International Inc	7300 W Friendly Ave	Greensboro	NC	27420	**800-444-5579***	336-547-5000	630
*Sales							
Gascosage Electric Co-op	803 S Hwy 28 PO Box G	Dixon	MO	65459	**866-568-8243**	573-759-7146	245
Gas-Fired Products Inc	305 Doggett St	Charlotte	NC	28203	**800-830-3983**	704-372-3485	317
Gaska-Tape Inc	1810 W Lusher Ave	Elkhart	IN	46517	**800-423-1571**	574-294-5431	722
Gasket Manufacturing Co	18001 Main St	Gardena	CA	90248	**800-442-7538**	310-217-5600	325
Gaskets Inc	301 W Hwy 16	Rio	WI	53960	**800-558-1833**	920-992-3137	325
Gaslamp Plaza Suites	520 E St	San Diego	CA	92101	**800-874-8770**	619-232-9500	376
Gaspard Inc	200 N Janacek Rd	Brookfield	WI	53045	**800-784-6868**	262-784-6800	153-13
Gassco	7515 Lindsay Rd	Bakersfield	CA	93313	**800-390-7837**	661-832-7406	572
Gast Mfg Inc	2300 M-139 Hwy PO Box 97	Benton Harbor	MI	49023	**800-665-1196**	269-926-6171	173
Gaston Chamber of Commerce	601 W Franklin Blvd	Gastonia	NC	28052	**800-933-3909**	704-864-2621	137
Gaston College	201 Hwy 321-S	Dallas	NC	28034	**800-634-7854**	704-922-6200	160
Gaston County Public Library	1555 E Garrison Blvd	Gastonia	NC	28054	**888-241-3115**	704-868-2164	431-3
Gaston County Travel & Tourism	620 N Main St	Belmont	NC	28012	**800-849-9994**	704-825-4044	207
Gaston Gazette	1893 Remount Rd	Gastonia	NC	28054	**800-527-5226**	704-869-1700	525-2
Gastonian, The	220 E Gaston St	Savannah	GA	31401	**800-322-6603**	912-232-2869	376
Gate Petroleum Co	9540 San Jose Blvd PO Box 23627	Jacksonville	FL	32241	**866-571-1982**	904-737-7220	323
GateHouse Media Inc	350 Willowbrook Office Pk	Fairport	NY	14450	**866-487-9243**	585-598-0030	628-8
NYSE: GHSE							
Gatekeeper Systems Inc	8 Studebaker	Irvine	CA	92618	**888-808-9433**	949-453-1940	200
Gates Albert Inc	3434 Union St	North Chili	NY	14514	**800-937-9311**	585-594-9401	614
Gates Bar-B-Q	4621 Paseo Blvd	Kansas City	MO	64110	**800-662-7427**	816-923-0900	661
Gates Corp	1551 Wewatta St	Denver	CO	80202	**800-709-6001**	303-744-1911	367
Gates County	200 Ct St	Gatesville	NC	27938	**800-272-9829**	252-357-2411	336
Gates Family Foundation	1390 Lawrence Street	Denver	CO	80204	**866-590-4377**	303-722-1881	304
Gates of the Arctic National Park & Preserve	4175 Geist Rd	Fairbanks	AK	99709	**866-869-6887**	907-457-5752	557
Gateway Community & Technical College (GCTC)	1025 Amsterdam Rd	Covington	KY	41011	**855-346-4282**	859-441-4500	788
GateWay Community College	108 N 40th St	Phoenix	AZ	85034	**888-994-4433**	602-286-8000	160
Gateway Ctr	One Gateway Dr	Collinsville	IL	62234	**800-289-2388**	618-345-8998	206
Gateway Foundation Inc	1080 E Pk St	Carbondale	IL	62901	**877-505-4673**		717
Gateway Inc	7565 Irvine Ctr Dr	Irvine	CA	92618	**800-846-2000**	949-471-7040	174-1
Gateway Industrial Power Inc	921 Fournie Ln	Collinsville	IL	62234	**888-865-8675**	618-345-0123	56
Gateway Limousines	1550 Gilbreth Rd	Burlingame	CA	94010	**800-486-7077**	650-697-5548	437
Gateway Mortgage Group LLC	6910 E 14th St	Tulsa	OK	74112	**877-406-8109**	918-712-9000	214
Gateway News	1050 West Main St	Kent	OH	44240	**800-560-9657**	330-541-9400	525-4
Gateway Newstands	240 Chrislea Rd	Woodbridge	ON	L4L8V1	**800-942-5351**	905-851-9652	523
Gateway Regional Medical Ctr (GRMC)	2100 Madison Ave	Granite City	IL	62040	**800-422-6237***	618-798-3000	371-3
*General							
Gateway Shoe Co	910 Kehro Mill Rd Ste 112	Ballwin	MO	63011	**800-539-6063**	636-256-7050	300
Gateway Supply Company Inc	1312 Hamrick St	Columbia	SC	29202	**800-922-5312**	803-771-7160	605
Gateway Technical College	3520 30th Ave	Kenosha	WI	53144	**800-247-7122**	262-564-2200	788
Gateways Inn	51 Walker St	Lenox	MA	01240	**888-492-9466**	413-637-2532	376
Gator Park	24050 SW Eigth St	Miami	FL	33187	**800-559-2205**	305-559-2255	810
Gatorade Sports Science Institute	617 W Main St	Barrington	IL	60010	**800-616-4774**		659
Gatorland	14501 S Orange Blossom Trl	Orlando	FL	32837	**800-393-5297**	407-855-5496	810
Gavel International Corp	300 Tri State International Ste 320	Lincolnshire	IL	60069	**800-544-2835**	847-945-8150	185
Gavis Pharmaceuticals LLC	400 Campus Dr	Somerset	NJ	08873	**866-403-7592**	908-603-6080	238
Gay Men's Health Crisis (GMHC)	119 W 24th St	New York	NY	10011	**800-243-7692**	212-367-1000	47-17
Gayla Industries Inc	PO Box 920800	Houston	TX	77292	**800-231-7508**	905-857-5207	752
Gaylor Electric	5750 Castle Creek Pkwy N Dr Ste 400	Indianapolis	IN	46250	**800-878-0577**	317-843-0577	190-4
Gaylord Bros	7282 William Barry Blvd	Syracuse	NY	13212	**800-345-5330**	315-457-5070	318-3
Gaylord Hospital	Gaylord Farms Rd PO Box 400	Wallingford	CT	06492	**866-429-5673**	203-284-2800	371-6
Gaylord Industries Inc	10900 SW Avery St	Tualatin	OR	97062	**800-547-9696**	503-691-2010	18
Gaylord Manufacturing Co	1088 Montclaire Dr	Ceres	CA	95307	**800-375-0091**	209-538-3313	803
Gaylord Opryland Hotel & Convention Ctr	2800 Opryland Dr	Nashville	TN	37214	**888-236-2427**	615-889-1000	376
Gaymar Industries Inc	10 Centre Dr	Orchard Park	NY	14127	**800-828-7341**	716-662-2551	471
Gaytan Foods	15430 Proctor Ave	City Of Industry	CA	91745	**800-242-9826**	626-330-4553	295-26
Gazette Newspapers Inc	9030 Comprint Ct	Gaithersburg	MD	20877	**888-670-7100**	301-948-3120	628-8
Gazette Publishing Inc	1114 Broadway	Wheaton	MN	56296	**800-567-8303**	320-563-8146	619
Gazette, The	501 Second Ave SE	Cedar Rapids	IA	52401	**800-397-8333**	319-398-8333	525-2
GBCVB (Greater Boston Convention & Visitors Bureau)	Two Copley Pl Ste 105	Boston	MA	02116	**888-733-2678**	617-536-4100	207
GBH Communications Inc	1309 S Myrtle Ave	Monrovia	CA	91016	**800-222-5424**		246
GBPD (Guardian Building Products)	979 Batesville Rd	Greer	SC	29651	**800-569-4262**	864-297-6101	192-3
GBS Corp	7233 Freedom Ave NW	North Canton	OH	44720	**800-552-2427**	330-494-5330	527
GBS Filing Solutions	224 Morges Rd	Malvern	OH	44644	**800-873-4427**	330-494-5330	553
GBTA (Global Business Travel Assn, The)	123 N Pitt St	Alexandria	VA	22314	**888-574-6447**	703-684-0836	47-23
GC America Inc	3737 W 127th St	Alsip	IL	60803	**800-323-7063***	708-597-0900	228
*Cust Svc							
GC Services LP	6330 Gulfton St	Houston	TX	77081	**800-756-6524**	713-777-4441	158
GCA (Greeting Card Assn)	1133 Westchester Ave Ste N136	White Plains	NY	10604	**866-799-5384**	914-421-3331	48-16
GCA (Everi Holdings Inc)	7250 S Tenaya Way Ste 100	Las Vegas	NV	89113	**800-833-7110**	702-855-3000	55
NYSE: EVRI							
GCA Services Group	1350 Euclid Ave Ste 1500	Cleveland	OH	44115	**800-422-8760**		150
GCC Printers USA	209 Burlington Rd	Bedford	MA	01730	**800-422-7777***	781-275-1115	174-6
*Sales							
GCEC (Grayson-Collin Electric Co-op)	PO Box 548	Van Alstyne	TX	75495	**800-967-5235**	903-482-7100	245
GCF (General Credit Forms Inc)	3595 Rider Trl S	Earth City	MO	63045	**888-423-6397**	314-216-8600	109
GCS (Georgia Cancer Specialists Pc)	1872 Montreal Rd	Tucker	GA	30084	**800-491-5991**	770-496-9443	371-7
GCS Service Inc	370 Wabasha St N	St. Paul	MN	55102	**800-822-2303**		390
GCSAA (Golf Course Superintendents Assn of America)	1421 Research Pk Dr	Lawrence	KS	66049	**800-472-7878**	785-841-2240	47-2
GCTC (Gateway Community & Technical College)	1025 Amsterdam Rd	Covington	KY	41011	**855-346-4282**	859-441-4500	788
GCube Insurance Services Inc	3101 Wcoast Hwy Ste 100	Newport Beach	CA	92663	**877-903-4777**	949-515-9981	387
GCVB (Atlanta's Gwinnett Convention & Visitors Bureau)	6500 Sugarloaf Pkwy Ste 200	Duluth	GA	30097	**888-494-6638**	770-623-3600	207
GDI Infotech Inc	3775 Varsity Dr	Ann Arbor	MI	48108	**800-608-7682**	734-477-6900	178
GE Analytical Instruments Inc	6060 Spine Rd	Boulder	CO	80301	**800-255-6964**	303-444-2009	683
GE Betz	4636 Somerton Rd	Trevose	PA	19053	**866-439-2837***	215-355-3300	143
*Cust Svc							
GE Capital Fleet Services	Three Capital Dr	Eden Prairie	MN	55344	**800-469-0044**		289

	City	State	ZIP	Toll-Free	Phone	Class
GE Capital Solutions Franchise Finance						
8377 E Hartford Dr Ste 200	Scottsdale	AZ	85255	**866-438-4333**		645
GE Digital Energy						
650 Markland St	Markham	ON	L6C0M1	**877-605-6777**	905-294-6222	204
GE Energy						
4200 Wildwood Pkwy	Atlanta	GA	30339	**800-368-1316**	203-373-2211	262
GE Fanuc Embedded Systems Inc						
7401 Snaproll NE	Albuquerque	NM	87109	**888-790-1820**	505-875-0600	617
GE Healthcare Information Technologies						
8200 W Tower Ave	Milwaukee	WI	53223	**800-558-5102**	414-355-5000	250
GE Infrastructure Sensing						
1100 Technology Pk Dr	Billerica	MA	01821	**800-833-9438**	978-437-1000	202
GE Johnson Construction Co						
25 N Cascade Ave						
Ste 400	Colorado Springs	CO	80903	**800-640-9501**	719-473-5321	187
GE Lighting Systems Inc						
3010 Spartanburg Hwy	East Flat Rock	NC	28726	**888-694-3533**	828-693-2000	435
GE Rail Car Services						
161 N Clark St 7th Fl	Chicago	IL	60601	**800-626-2000**	312-853-5000	264-5
GE Richards Graphic Supplies Company Inc						
928 Links Ave	Landisville	PA	17538	**800-233-0410**	717-898-3151	681
GE Transportation Rail						
2901 E Lake Rd	Erie	PA	16531	**800-626-2000***	814-875-2234	641
*Prod Info						
GE Vendor Financial Services						
10 Riverview Dr	Danbury	CT	06810	**800-626-2000**	203-373-2039	216
GE Water & Process Technologies						
4636 Somerton Rd	Trevose	PA	19053	**866-439-2837**	215-355-3300	794
GEA PHE Systems North America Inc						
100 Gea Dr	York	PA	17402	**800-774-0474**	717-268-6200	475
Gear for Sports Inc						
9700 Commerce Pkwy	Lenexa	KS	66219	**800-255-1065**	913-693-3200	153-1
Gearench Inc						
4450 S Hwy 6 PO Box 192	Clifton	TX	76634	**800-221-1848**	254-675-8651	530
Gearhart By the Sea						
1157 N Marion Ave	Gearhart	OR	97138	**800-547-0115**	503-738-8331	660
Geary Pacific Corp						
1908 N Enterprise St	Orange	CA	92865	**800-444-3279**	714-279-2950	681
GEARYS Beverly Hills						
351 N Beverly Dr	Beverly Hills	CA	90210	**800-793-6670**	310-273-4741	359
Geauga County Transit						
12555 Merritt Rd	Chardon	OH	44024	**888-287-7190***	440-279-2150	107
*Cust Svc						
Gebco Insurance Assoc						
8600 LaSalle Rd Ste 338	Towson	MD	21286	**800-464-3226**	410-668-3100	387
GEFCO (GEFCO Inc)						
2215 S Van Buren	Enid	OK	73703	**800-759-7441**	580-234-4141	530
GEFCO Inc (GEFCO)						
2215 S Van Buren	Enid	OK	73703	**800-759-7441**	580-234-4141	530
Gefran ISI Inc						
Eight Lowell Ave	Winchester	MA	01890	**888-888-4474**	781-729-5249	202
Gehl's Guernsey Farms Inc						
N116 W15970 Main St	Germantown	WI	53022	**800-521-2873**	262-251-8572	295-10
Gehr Industries						
7400 E Slauson Ave	Los Angeles	CA	90040	**800-688-6606**	323-728-5558	800
GEI Consultants Inc						
400 Unicorn Pk Dr	Woburn	MA	01801	**888-434-9679**	781-721-4000	261
Geiger International Inc						
6095 Fulton Industrial Blvd SW	Atlanta	GA	30336	**800-456-6452**	404-344-1100	318-1
Geisinger Health Plan						
100 N Academy Ave	Danville	PA	17822	**800-447-4000**	570-271-8760	388-3
Geisinger Health System						
100 N Academy Ave	Danville	PA	17822	**800-275-6401**	570-271-6211	350
Gelmart Industries Inc						
136 Madison Ave 4th Fl	New York	NY	10016	**800-746-0014***	212-743-6900	153-17
*General						
Gel-Pak LLC						
31398 Huntwood Ave	Hayward	CA	94544	**888-621-4147**	510-576-2220	687
Gem Dandy Inc						
200 W Academy St	Madison	NC	27025	**800-334-5101**	336-548-9624	153-2
GEM Edwards Inc						
5640 Hudson Industrial Pkwy						
PO Box 429	Hudson	OH	44236	**800-733-7976**		471
GEM Group						
Nine International Way	Lawrence	MA	01843	**800-800-3200**	978-691-2000	66
GEM Inc						
6842 Commodore Dr	Walbridge	OH	43465	**866-720-2700***	419-666-6554	190-10
*General						
Gem State Paper & Supply Co						
1801 Highland Ave E	Twin Falls	ID	83303	**800-727-2737**	208-733-6081	552
Gemex Systems Inc						
6040 W Executive Dr Ste A	Mequon	WI	53092	**866-694-3639**	262-242-1111	408
Gemini Coatings Inc						
421 SE 27th St	El Reno	OK	73036	**800-262-5710**	405-262-5710	543
Gemini Inc						
103 Mensing Way	Cannon Falls	MN	55009	**800-538-8377**	507-263-3957	692
Gemini Valve						
Two Otter Ct	Raymond	NH	03077	**800-370-0936**	603-895-4761	777
Gemological Institute of America (GIA)						
5345 Armada Dr	Carlsbad	CA	92008	**800-421-7250**	760-603-4000	48-4
Gems Sensors Inc						
One Cowles Rd	Plainville	CT	06062	**800-378-1600**	860-747-3000	202
Gemstone Systems Inc						
1260 NW Waterhouse Ave						
Ste 200	Beaverton	OR	97006	**800-243-4772**	503-533-3000	179-1
Gemtex Abrasives						
60 Belfield Rd	Toronto	ON	M9W1G1	**800-387-5100**	416-245-5605	1
Gemtor Inc						
One Johnson Ave	Matawan	NJ	07747	**800-405-9048**	732-583-6200	669
Genaera Corp						
5110 Campus Dr	Plymouth Meeting	PA	19462	**800-299-9156**	610-941-4020	84
GenBio						
15222 Ave of Science Ste A	San Diego	CA	92128	**800-288-4368***	858-592-9300	231
*Tech Supp						
Gencor Industries Inc						
5201 N Orange Blossom Trail	Orlando	FL	32810	**888-887-1266***	407-290-6000	191
NASDAQ: GENC ■ *General						
Genealogy.com						
360 West 4800 North	Provo	UT	84604	**800-262-3787**	801-705-7000	394
Genemed Biotechnologies Inc						
458 Carlton Ct S San						
Francisco	San Fransisco	CA	94080	**877-436-3633**	650-952-0110	659
Generac Power Systems Inc						
PO Box 8	Waukesha	WI	53187	**888-436-3722**	262-544-4811	511
General Air Service & Supply Company Inc						
1105 Zuni St	Denver	CO	80204	**877-782-8434**	303-892-7003	144
General Aluminum Company of Texas LLP						
1001 W Crosby Rd	Carrollton	TX	75006	**800-727-0835**	972-242-5271	234
General Assn of Regular Baptist Churches (GARBC)						
1300 N Meacham Rd	Schaumburg	IL	60173	**888-588-1600**	847-585-0816	47-20
General Atomics						
3550 General Atomics Ct						
PO Box 85608	San Diego	CA	92121	**800-669-6820**	858-455-3000	659
General Aviation Manufacturers Assn (GAMA)						
1400 K St NW Ste 801	Washington	DC	20005	**800-728-9607**	202-393-1500	48-21
General Aviation Services LLC						
1155 E Ensell Rd	Lake Zurich	IL	60047	**800-586-5336**	847-726-5000	760
General Bearing Corp						
44 High St	West Nyack	NY	10994	**800-431-1766***	845-358-6000	74
*Sales						
General Body Manufacturing Co						
7110 Jensen Dr	Houston	TX	77093	**800-395-8585**	713-692-5177	509
General Butler State Resort Park						
1608 US Hwy 227	Carrollton	KY	41008	**866-462-8853**	502-732-4384	660
General Cable Corp						
Four Tesseneer Dr	Highland Heights	KY	41076	**800-572-8000**	859-572-8000	801
NYSE: BGC						
General Carbide Corp						
1151 Garden St	Greensburg	PA	15601	**800-245-2465**	724-836-3000	747
General Chemical Group Inc						
90 E Halsey Rd	Parsippany	NJ	07054	**800-244-6224**	973-515-0900	141
General Communication Inc						
2550 Denali St Ste 1000	Anchorage	AK	99503	**800-770-7886**	907-265-5600	726
NASDAQ: GNCMA						
General Credit Forms Inc (GCF)						
3595 Rider Trl S	Earth City	MO	63045	**888-423-6397**	314-216-8600	109
General Crook House Museum						
5730 N 30th St Bldg 11B	Omaha	NE	68111	**800-393-6198**	402-455-9990	49-2
General Data Co Inc						
4354 Ferguson Dr	Cincinnati	OH	45245	**800-733-5252**	513-752-7978	175
General Devices Company Inc						
1410 S Post Rd	Indianapolis	IN	46239	**800-821-3520**	317-897-7000	202
General Die Casters Inc						
2150 Highland Rd	Twinsburg	OH	44087	**800-332-2278**	330-657-2300	307
General Digital Corp						
Eight Nutmeg Rd S	South Windsor	CT	06074	**800-952-2535**	860-282-2900	174-4
General Dynamics C4 Systems						
400 John Quincy Adams Rd						
Bldg 80	Taunton	MA	02780	**877-449-0600**		179-10
General Dynamics Information Technology						
3211 Jermantown Rd	Fairfax	VA	22030	**800-242-0230**	703-246-0200	181
General Dynamics SATCOM Technologies						
1500 Prodelin Dr	Newton	NC	28658	**888-874-7646**	828-464-4141	638
General Econopak Inc						
1725 N Sixth St	Philadelphia	PA	19122	**888-871-8568**	215-763-8200	569
General Equipment & Supplies Inc						
4300 Main Ave	Fargo	ND	58103	**800-437-2924**	701-282-2662	355
General Equipment Co						
620 Alexander Dr SW PO Box 334	Owatonna	MN	55060	**800-533-0524***	507-451-5510	383
*Cust Svc						
General Fasteners Co						
37584 Amrhein Rd Ste 150	Livonia	MI	48150	**800-945-2658**	734-452-2400	348
General Federation of Women's Clubs (GFWC)						
1734 N St NW	Washington	DC	20036	**800-443-4392**	202-347-3168	47-24
General Filters Inc						
43800 Grand River Ave	Novi	MI	48375	**866-476-5101**		18
General Formulations Inc						
309 S Union St	Sparta	MI	49345	**800-253-3664**	616-887-7387	593
General Grand Chapter Order of the Eastern Star						
1618 New Hampshire Ave NW	Washington	DC	20009	**800-648-1182**	202-667-4737	47-15
General Growth Properties Inc						
110 N Wacker Dr	Chicago	IL	60606	**888-395-8037**	312-960-5000	646
NYSE: GGP						
General Healthcare Resources Inc						
2250 Hickory Rd						
Ste 240	Plymouth Meeting	PA	19462	**800-879-4471**	610-834-1122	360
General Insulation Company Inc						
278 Mystic Ave Ste 209	Medford	MA	02155	**800-442-6662**	781-391-2070	192-4
General Loose Leaf Bindery Co						
3811 Hawthorn Ct	Waukegan	IL	60087	**800-621-0493**	847-244-9700	85
General Machine Products Company Inc						
3111 Old Lincoln Hwy	Trevose	PA	19053	**800-345-6009***	215-357-5500	748
*Tech Supp						
General Magnaplate Corp						
1331 Us Rt 1	Linden	NJ	07036	**800-441-6173**	908-862-6200	482
General Mills Foundation						
PO Box 9452	Minneapolis	MN	55440	**800-248-7310**		303
General Mills Inc						
One General Mills Blvd	Minneapolis	MN	55426	**800-248-7310**		298
NYSE: GIS						
General Monitors Inc						
26776 Simpatica Cir	Lake Forest	CA	92630	**866-686-0741**	949-581-4464	283
26776 Simpatica Cir	Lake Forest	CA	92630	**866-686-0741**	949-581-4464	739
General Morgan Inn						
111 N Main St	Greeneville	TN	37743	**800-223-2679**	423-787-1000	376
General Motors Acceptance Corp (GMAC)						
200 Renaissance Ctr	Detroit	MI	48265	**800-200-4622**	877-320-2559	214
General Motors Corp Buick Motor Div						
300 Renaissance Ctr						
PO Box 33136	Detroit	MI	48265	**800-521-7300***		58
*Cust Svc						
General Motors Foundation Inc						
PO Box 33170	Detroit	MI	48232	**800-222-1020**		303
General Music Corp						
1164 Tower Ln	Bensenville	IL	60106	**800-323-0280**	630-766-8230	520
General Pet Supply Inc						
7711 N 81st St	Milwaukee	WI	53223	**800-433-9786**	414-365-3400	94
General Plastic Extrusions Inc						
1238 Kasson Dr	Prescott	WI	54021	**800-532-3888**	715-262-3806	541
General Plastics Mfg Co						
4910 S Burlington Way	Tacoma	WA	98409	**800-806-6051**	253-473-5000	594
General Plug & Mfg Co Inc						
455 Main St	Grafton	OH	44044	**800-289-7584**	440-926-2411	588
General Produce Co						
1330 N 'B' St	Sacramento	CA	95814	**800-366-4991**	916-441-6431	296-7
General Revenue Corp						
4660 Duke Dr Ste 300	Mason	OH	45040	**800-234-6258**		158

Name / Address	City	State	ZIP	Toll-Free	Phone	Class
General Services Administration						
FCIC National Contact Ctr						
PO Box 100	Pueblo	CO	81009	**888-878-3256**		338-18
Region 1 - New England						
10 Cswy St Rm 1010						
Thomas P O'Neill Federal Bldg.	Boston	MA	02222	**866-734-1727**	617-565-5860	338-18
Region 3 - Mid-Atlantic						
Strawbridge Bldg						
20 N 8th St	Philadelphia	PA	19107	**800-333-4636**	215-446-5100	338-18
Region 4 - Southeast Sunbelt						
1800 F St NW Ste 600	Washington	DC	20405	**800-333-4636**		338-18
General Services Administration Regional Offices						
Region 8 - Rocky Mountain						
Denver Federal Ctr Bldg 41	Denver	CO	80225	**888-999-4777**	303-236-7329	338-18
General Shale Products LLC						
3015 Bristol Hwy	Johnson City	TN	37601	**800-414-4661**	423-282-4661	148
General Star National Insurance Co						
695 E Main St Financial Ctr	Stamford	CT	06901	**800-431-9994**	203-328-5000	388-4
General Steamship Agencies Inc						
575 Redwood Hwy Ste 200	Mill Valley	CA	94941	**855-859-3123**	415-389-5200	460
General Steel Inc						
PO Box 1503	Macon	GA	31202	**800-476-2794**	478-746-2794	487
General Theological Seminary						
440 W 21st St	New York	NY	10011	**888-487-5649**	212-243-5150	167-3
General Tool & Supply Co Inc						
2705 NW Nicolai St	Portland	OR	97210	**800-526-9328**	503-226-3411	382
General Tool Co						
101 Landy Ln	Cincinnati	OH	45215	**800-314-9817**	513-733-5500	747
General Tools Mfg Company LLC						
80 White St	New York	NY	10013	**800-697-8665**	212-431-6100	748
General Tours						
53 Summer St	Keene	NH	03431	**800-221-2216**		750
General Truck Parts & Equipment Co						
3835 W 42nd St	Chicago	IL	60632	**800-621-3914**	773-247-6900	60
General Vision Services LLC						
520 Eigth Ave 9th Fl	New York	NY	10018	**855-653-0586**	212-729-5300	536
General Wax & Candle Co						
6863 Beck Ave						
PO Box 9398	North Hollywood	CA	91605	**800-929-7867**	818-765-5800	121
General Wire Spring Co						
1101 Thompson Ave	McKees Rocks	PA	15136	**800-245-6200**	412-771-6300	709
Generations United (GU)						
1333 H St NW Ste 500-W	Washington	DC	20005	**800-677-1116**	202-289-3979	47-6
Generex Biotechnology Corp						
555 Richmond St W Ste 202	Toronto	ON	M5J2G2	**800-391-6755**	416-364-2551	84
OTC: GNBT						
Generic Pharmaceutical Assn (GPhA)						
2300 Clarendon Blvd Ste 400	Arlington	VA	22201	**800-859-8003**	703-647-2480	48-19
Genesee Community College						
1 College Rd	Batavia	NY	14020	**866-225-5422**	585-343-0068	160
Genesee County Chamber of Commerce						
210 E Main St	Batavia	NY	14020	**800-622-2686**	585-343-7440	137
Genesee County Parks & Recreation						
5045 Stanley Rd	Flint	MI	48506	**800-648-7275**	810-736-7100	49-4
Genesee District Library						
G-4195 W Pasadena Ave	Flint	MI	48504	**866-732-1120**	810-732-0110	431-3
Genesee Grande Hotel						
1060 E Genesee St	Syracuse	NY	13210	**800-365-4663**	315-476-4212	376
Genesee Regional Chamber of Commerce						
519 S Saginaw St Ste 200	Flint	MI	48502	**888-823-6837**	810-600-1404	137
Genesee Valley Ctr						
3341 S Linden Rd	Flint	MI	48507	**866-236-1128**	810-732-4000	455
Genesis Capital LLC						
3414 Peachtree Rd Ne Ste 700	Atlanta	GA	30326	**800-998-8479**	404-816-7540	69
Genesis Corp						
950 Third Ave Fl 26	New York	NY	10022	**800-261-1776**	212-688-5522	181
Genesis Energy LP						
919 Milam Ste 2100	Houston	TX	77002	**800-284-3365**	713-860-2500	590
NYSE: GEL						
Genesis HealthCare Corp						
101 E State St	Kennett Square	PA	19348	**800-944-7776**	610-444-6350	446
Genesis Medical Ctr Illini Campus						
801 Illini Dr	Silvis	IL	61282	**800-250-6020**	309-792-9363	371-3
Genesis Publisher Services						
3310 Eagle Pk Dr NE						
Ste 200	Grand Rapids	MI	49525	**800-828-1022**	616-831-2800	628-6
Genesisfour Corp						
7747 Ten Acre Rd	Andrews	SC	29510	**800-937-4364**	843-461-4117	178
Genesys Telecommunications Laboratories Inc						
2001 Junipero Serra Blvd	Daly City	CA	94014	**888-436-3797**	650-466-1100	725
Genetec Inc						
2280 Alfred-Nobel Blvd Ste 400	Montreal	QC	H4S2A4	**866-684-8006**	514-332-4000	225
Genetic Engineering News						
140 Huguenot St 3rd Fl	New Rochelle	NY	10801	**800-799-9436**	914-740-2100	524-12
Genetic Profiles Corp						
10675 Treena St Ste 103	San Diego	CA	92131	**800-551-7763**		414
Genetica DNA Laboratories Inc						
8740 Montgomery Rd	Cincinnati	OH	45236	**800-433-6848**	513-985-9777	414
Genetics Society of America (GSA)						
9650 Rockville Pk	Bethesda	MD	20814	**866-486-4363**	301-634-7300	48-19
Geneva Capital LLC						
522 Broadway St Ste 4	Alexandria	MN	56308	**800-408-9352**		195
Geneva College						
3200 College Ave	Beaver Falls	PA	15010	**800-847-8255**	724-847-6500	166
Geneva on the Lake						
1001 Lochland Rd	Geneva	NY	14456	**800-343-6382**	315-789-7190	376
Geneva Rock Products Inc						
302 W 5400 S Ste 200	Murray	UT	84107	**855-614-6497**	801-281-7900	183
Geneva Scientific Inc						
11 N Batavia Ave	Batavia	IL	60510	**800-338-2697**		382
Genex Co-op Inc/CRI						
117 E Green Bay St	Shawano	WI	54166	**888-333-1783**	715-526-2141	11-2
Genex Services Inc						
440 E Swedesford Rd Ste 1000	Wayne	PA	19087	**888-464-3639**	610-964-5100	195
Genie Co						
One Door Dr PO Box 67	Mount Hope	OH	44660	**800-354-3643**		347
Genie Industries Inc						
18340 NE 76th St	Redmond	WA	98052	**800-536-1800**	425-881-1800	465
Genieco Inc						
200 N Laflin St	Chicago	IL	60607	**800-223-8217**	312-421-2383	143
Genmark Automation Inc						
1201 Cadillac Ct	Milpitas	CA	95035	**866-467-6268**	408-678-8500	383
Genoa Business Forms Inc						
445 Pk Ave	Sycamore	IL	60178	**800-383-2801**		109
Genomic Health Inc						
101 Galveston Dr	Redwood City	CA	94063	**866-662-6897**	650-556-9300	84
NASDAQ: GHDX						
Genova Diagnostics						
63 Zillicoa St	Asheville	NC	28801	**800-522-4762**	828-253-0621	415
Genova Products Inc						
7034 E Court St	Davison	MI	48423	**800-521-7488**	810-744-4500	601
Genpak Carthage						
505 E Cotton St	Carthage	TX	75633	**800-626-6695**	903-693-7151	299
Genpak Corp						
68 Warren St	Glens Falls	NY	12801	**800-626-6695**	518-798-9511	541
GenPore						
1136 Morgantown Rd PO Box 380	Reading	PA	19607	**800-654-4391**	610-374-5171	601
Gen-Probe Inc						
10210 Genetic Ctr Dr	San Diego	CA	92121	**800-523-5001**	858-410-8000	231
GenQuest DNA Analysis Laboratory						
133 Coney Island Dr	Sparks	NV	89431	**877-362-5227**	775-358-0652	414
Gensco Inc						
4402 20th St E	Tacoma	WA	98424	**877-620-8203**	253-620-8203	605
Gentek Bldg Products Inc						
11 Craigwood Rd	Avenel	NJ	07001	**800-548-4542**	732-381-0900	688
Gentex Optics Inc						
324 Main St	Simpson	PA	18407	**800-736-0554**	570-282-3550	535
Genzyme Corp						
500 Kendall St	Cambridge	MA	02142	**800-745-4447**	617-252-7500	84
Genzyme Genetics						
3400 Computer Dr	Westborough	MA	01581	**800-255-7357**	508-898-9001	414
GEO Drilling Fluids Inc						
1431 Union Ave	Bakersfield	CA	93305	**800-438-7436**	661-325-5919	533
Geo Products LLC						
8615 Golden Spike Ln	Houston	TX	77086	**800-434-4743**	281-820-5493	806
Geocel Corp						
PO Box 398	Elkhart	IN	46515	**800-348-7615**	574-264-0645	3
Geocomp Corp						
1145 Massachusetts Ave	Boxborough	MA	01719	**800-822-2669***	978-635-0012	179-5
*Cust Svc						
GeoEngineers Inc						
8410 154th Ave NE	Redmond	WA	98052	**888-624-8373**	425-861-6000	261
Geographics						
108 Main St Third Fl.	Norwalk	CT	06851	**800-436-4919**		545-2
Geo-instruments Inc						
24 Celestial Dr Ste B.	Narragansett	RI	02882	**800-477-2506**		458
Geological Museum						
1000 E University Ave	Laramie	WY	82071	**800-842-2776**	307-766-2646	513
Geological Society of America, The (GSA)						
3300 Penrose Pl PO Box 9140	Boulder	CO	80301	**800-472-1988**	303-357-1000	48-19
GeoLogics Corp						
5285 Shawnee Rd Ste 300	Alexandria	VA	22312	**800-684-3455**	703-750-4000	181
Geomet Technologies LLC						
20251 Century Blvd	Germantown	MD	20874	**877-407-8033**	301-428-9898	194
Geophysical Research Letter						
2000 Florida Ave NW	Washington	DC	20009	**800-966-2481**	202-462-6900	524-12
GeoResources Inc						
110 Cypress Stn Dr Ste 220	Williston	ND	58802	**855-538-0599**	281-537-9920	529
NASDAQ: GEOI						
George E DeLallo Co Inc						
6390 Rt 30	Jeannette	PA	15644	**877-335-2556**	724-523-6577	296-8
George Fox Evangelical Seminary						
12753 SW 68th Ave	Portland	OR	97223	**800-493-4937**	503-554-6150	167-3
George Fox University						
414 N Meridian St	Newberg	OR	97132	**800-765-4369**	503-538-8383	166
George H. Crosby Manitou State Park						
c/o Tettegouche State Pk						
5702 Hwy 61	Silver Bay	MN	55614	**888-646-6367**	218-226-6365	558
George J Foster Co Inc						
150 Venture Dr	Dover	NH	03820	**800-462-2265**	603-742-4455	628-8
George K Baum & Co						
4801 Main St Ste 500						
Ste 500	Kansas City	MO	64112	**800-821-7195**	816-474-1100	681
George Koch Sons LLC						
10 S 11th Ave	Evansville	IN	47712	**888-873-5624**	812-465-9600	383
George Mason Mortgage Corp						
4100 Monu Crnr Dr Ste 100	Fairfax	VA	22030	**800-867-6859**	703-273-2600	502
George Mason University						
4400 University Dr	Fairfax	VA	22030	**888-627-6612**	703-993-1000	166
George Patton Assoc Inc						
55 Broadcommon Rd	Bristol	RI	02809	**800-572-2194**	401-247-0333	692
George R Brown Convention Ctr						
1001 Avenida de Las Americas	Houston	TX	77010	**800-427-4697**	713-853-8000	206
George R Peters Assoc Inc						
PO Box 850	Troy	MI	48099	**800-929-5972**	248-524-2211	246
George Risk Industries Inc						
802 S Elm St	Kimball	NE	69145	**800-523-1227***	308-235-4645	683
OTC: RSKIA ■ *Sales						
George S Coyne Chemical Co						
3015 State Rd	Croydon	PA	19021	**800-523-1230**	215-785-3000	144
George School						
1690 Newtown-Langhorne Rd	Newtown	PA	18940	**888-804-1300**	215-579-6547	615
George STREET Photo & Video LLC						
230 W Huron St Ste 3W	Chicago	IL	60654	**866-831-4103**		583
George Uhe Company Inc						
219 River Dr	Garfield	NJ	07026	**800-850-4075**	201-843-4000	474
George Washington Masonic National Memorial						
101 Callahan Dr	Alexandria	VA	22301	**800-435-7352**	703-683-2007	49-3
George Washington University						
Mount Vernon College						
2100 Foxhall Rd NW	Washington	DC	20007	**800-447-3765**	202-994-1000	166
George Washington University Hospital						
900 23rd St NW	Washington	DC	20037	**888-449-3627**	202-715-4000	371-3
George Washington University Inn						
824 New Hampshire Ave NW	Washington	DC	20037	**800-426-4455**	202-337-6620	376
George Washington University School of Medicine & Health Sciences						
2300 'I' St NW Ross Hall 716	Washington	DC	20037	**866-846-1107**	202-994-3506	167-2
George Weston Ltd						
22 St Clair Ave E	Toronto	ON	M4T2S7	**800-564-6253**	416-922-2500	357-3
TSE: WN						
Georgeson Securities Corp						
480 Washington Blvd 27th Fl	Jersey City	NJ	07310	**800-428-0717**		681
Georgetown College						
400 E College St	Georgetown	KY	40324	**800-788-9985***	502-863-8000	166
*Admissions						
Georgetown Convention & Visitors Bureau						
1101 N College St	Georgetown	TX	78626	**800-436-8696**	512-930-3545	207

	Toll-Free	Phone	Class
Georgetown County Chamber of Commerce			
531 Front St ....Georgetown SC 29440	800-777-7705	843-546-8436	137
Georgetown Inn			
1310 Wisconsin Ave ....Washington DC 20007	866-971-6618	202-333-8900	376
Georgetown Railroad Co			
5300 S IH-35 PO Box 529 ....Georgetown TX 78626	888-456-6777	512-863-2538	639
Georgetown Times			
615 Front St ....Georgetown SC 29440	800-772-1213	843-546-4148	525-4
Georgetown University Hotel & Conference Ctr			
3800 Reservoir Rd NW ....Washington DC 20057	800-228-9290	202-687-3200	374
Georgia			
Arts Council			
260 14th St NW Ste 401..........Atlanta GA 30318	800-222-6006	404-685-2400	337-11
Corrections Dept			
300 Patrol Rd Forsyth ....Atlanta GA 31029	888-343-5627	404-656-4661	337-11
Emergency Management Agency (GEMA)			
935 E Confederate Ave SE			
PO Box 18055 ....Atlanta GA 30316	800-879-4362	404-635-7000	337-11
Environmental Protection Div			
2 Martin Luther King Jr Dr			
Ste 1152 E Tower ....Atlanta GA 30334	888-373-5947	404-657-5947	337-11
Governor's Office of Consumer Protection			
2 ML King Jr Dr Ste 356..........Atlanta GA 30334	800-869-1123		337-11
Securities & Business Regulation Div			
2 Martin Luther King Jr Dr			
W Tower Ste 802 ....Atlanta GA 30334	844-753-7825	478-207-2440	337-11
State Government Information			
7 Martin Luther King JrDr			
Ste 643......................Atlanta GA 30303	800-436-7442	678-436-7442	337-11
Tourism Div			
75 Fifth St NW Ste 1200..........Atlanta GA 30308	800-255-0056*	404-962-4000	337-11
*Resv			
Georgia Assn of Realtors			
3200 Presidential Dr ....Atlanta GA 30340	866-280-0576	770-451-1831	647
Georgia Bar Journal			
104 Marietta St NW Ste 100..........Atlanta GA 30303	866-773-2782	404-527-8700	452-15
Georgia Boot Inc			
39 E Canal St ....Nelsonville OH 45764	877-795-2410	740-753-1951	300
Georgia Cancer Specialists Pc (GCS)			
1872 Montreal Rd ....Tucker GA 30084	800-491-5991	770-496-9443	371-7
Georgia Chamber of Commerce			
233 Peachtree St NE Ste 2000 ....Atlanta GA 30303	800-241-2286	404-223-2264	138
Georgia College & State University			
Macon 433 Cherry St ....Macon GA 31206	800-342-0471	478-752-4278	166
Georgia Correctional Industries			
2984 Clifton Springs Rd ....Decatur GA 30034	800-282-7130	404-244-5100	622
Georgia Crown Distributing Co			
100 Georgia Crown Dr ....McDonough GA 30253	800-342-2350	770-302-3000	80-3
Georgia Dental Assn			
7000 Peachtree Dnwdy Rd NE			
Ste 200 Bldg 17 ....Atlanta GA 30328	800-432-4357	404-636-7553	227
Georgia Dome			
1 Georgia Dome Dr NW ....Atlanta GA 30313	888-333-4406	404-223-9200	711
Georgia Farm Bureau News			
1620 Bass Rd ....Macon GA 31210	800-342-1192	478-474-8411	452-1
Cartersville			
5441 Hwy 20 NE ....Cartersville GA 30121	800-332-2406	678-872-8000	160
Georgia Highlands College			
Floyd 3175 Cedartown Hwy ....Rome GA 30161	800-332-2406	706-802-5000	160
Georgia Institute of Technology Library			
225 N Ave NW ....Atlanta GA 30332	888-225-7804	404-894-4500	431-6
Georgia International Convention Ctr			
2000 Convention Ctr			
Concourse ....College Park GA 30337	888-331-4422	770-997-3566	206
Georgia Military College			
201 E Green St ....Milledgeville GA 31061	800-342-0413	478-387-4900	160
Georgia Nurses Assn (GNA)			
3032 Briarcliff Rd NE ....Atlanta GA 30329	800-324-0462	404-325-5536	526
Georgia Ports Authority			
PO Box 2406 ....Savannah GA 31402	800-342-8012	912-964-3811	611
Georgia Power Co			
241 Ralph McGill Blvd NE ....Atlanta GA 30308	866-506-5333*	404-506-5000	775
*Cust Svc			
Georgia Printco			
90 S Oak St ....Lakeland GA 31635	866-572-0146		619
Georgia Public Broadcasting (GPB)			
260 14th St NW ....Atlanta GA 30318	800-222-6006		624
Georgia Regional Hospital at Savannah			
1915 Eisenhower Dr ....Savannah GA 31406	800-436-7442	912-356-2011	371-5
Georgia Southwestern State University			
800 Gsw State University Dr ....Americus GA 31709	800-338-0082*	229-928-1273	166
*Admissions			
Georgia Student Finance Commission			
2082 E Exchange Pl Ste 200..........Tucker GA 30084	800-505-4732	770-724-9000	716
Georgia Transparency & Campaign Finance Commission			
200 Piedmont Ave SE Ste 1402 ....Atlanta GA 30334	866-589-7327	404-463-1980	265
Georgia Veterinary Medical Assn			
233 Peachtree St NE Ste 2205 ....Atlanta GA 30303	800-853-1625	678-309-9800	783
Georgia's Own Credit Union			
1155 Peachtree St NE Ste 400			
PO Box 105205..................Atlanta GA 30309	800-533-2062	404-874-1166	219
Georgian Court Hotel			
773 Beatty St ....Vancouver BC V6B2M4	800-663-1155	604-682-5555	376
Georgian Court University			
900 Lakewood Ave ....Lakewood NJ 08701	800-458-8422		166
Georgian Hotel			
1415 Ocean Ave ....Santa Monica CA 90401	800-538-8147	310-395-9945	376
Georgian Plantation Shutter Co			
455 Wilbanks Dr ....Ball Ground GA 30107	888-684-0382	678-454-1100	358
Georgian Resort			
384 Canada St ....Lake George NY 12845	800-525-3436	518-668-5401	376
Georgian Terrace Hotel			
659 Peachtree St NE ....Atlanta GA 30308	800-651-2316	404-897-1991	376
Georgie's Ceramic & Clay Company Inc			
756 NE Lombard St ....Portland OR 97211	800-999-2529	503-283-1353	42
GEOSPAN Corp			
10900 73rd Ave N Ste 136..........Minneapolis MN 55369	800-436-7726	763-493-9320	225
GeoSyntec Consultants Inc			
5901 Broken Sound Pkwy NW			
Ste 300 ....Boca Raton FL 33487	866-676-1101	561-995-0900	261
Geotech Environmental Equipment Inc			
2650 E 40th Ave ....Denver CO 80205	800-833-7958	303-320-4764	202
Geotek Engineering & Testing Services Inc			
909 E 50th St N ....Sioux Falls SD 57104	800-354-5512	605-335-5512	256
GeoTrust Inc			
350 Ellis St Bldg J ....Mountain View CA 94043	866-511-4141	650-426-5010	179-7
Gerald H Phipps			
5995 Greenwood Florida Plaza Blvd			
Ste 100..............Greenwood Village CO 80111	866-487-2365	303-571-5377	187
Gerald R Ford Conservation Ctr			
1326 S 32nd St ....Omaha NE 68105	800-634-6932	402-595-1180	49-1
Gerald R Ford International Airport			
5500 44th St SE ....Grand Rapids MI 49512	866-289-9673	616-233-6000	27
Gerald R Ford Museum			
303 Pearl St NW ....Grand Rapids MI 49504	800-888-9487	616-254-0400	513
Gerard Daniel Worldwide			
34 Barnhart Dr ....Hanover PA 17331	800-232-3332	717-637-5901	679
Gerber Auto Collision & Glass Centers Inc			
8250 Skokie Blvd ....Skokie IL 60077	877-743-7237	847-679-0510	61-4
Gerber Childrenswear Inc			
7005 Pelham Rd Ste D ....Greenville SC 29602	800-642-4452	864-987-5200	153-4
Gerber Collision & Glass			
44700 Enterprise Dr ....Clinton Township MI 48038	877-743-7237*	586-954-3850	61-4
*General			
Gerber Life Insurance Co			
1311 Mamaroneck Ave ....White Plains NY 10605	800-704-2180	914-272-4000	388-2
Gerber Plumbing Fixtures LLC			
2500 International Pkwy ....Woodridge IL 60517	888-648-6466		604
Gerber Products Co			
445 State St ....Fremont MI 49413	800-284-9488		295-36
Gerber Technology Inc			
24 Industrial Pk Rd W ....Tolland CT 06084	800-826-3243	860-871-8082	733
Gerber Tours Inc			
1400 Old Country Rd Ste 100..........Westbury NY 11590	800-645-9145	516-826-5000	750
Gerdau AmeriSteel Corp			
4221 W Boy Scout Blvd Ste 600..........Tampa FL 33607	800-876-7833*	813-286-8383	714
*Sales			
Gerloff Company Inc			
14955 Bulverde Rd ....San Antonio TX 78247	800-486-3621	210-490-2777	187
German American Bancorp			
711 Main St ....Jasper IN 47546	800-482-1314	812-482-1314	357-2
NASDAQ: GABC			
German-American National Congress (DANK)			
4740 N Western Ave Ste 206 ....Chicago IL 60625	888-872-3265	773-275-1100	47-14
Germania Farm Mutual Insurance Assn			
507 Hwy 290 E ....Brenham TX 77833	800-392-2202	979-836-5224	388-4
Germany			
Consulate General			
285 Peachtree Ctr Ave NE			
Ste 901..................Atlanta GA 30303	866-687-8561	404-659-4760	257
Germiphene Corp			
1379 Colborne St E			
PO Box 1748..................Brantford ON N3T5M1	800-265-9931	519-759-7100	576
Gerontological Society of America, The			
1220 L St NW Ste 901 ....Washington DC 20005	800-677-1116	202-842-1275	48-8
Gerry Cosby & Company Inc			
11 Pennsylvania Plz ....New York NY 10001	877-563-6464	212-563-6464	702
Gershwin Hotel			
7 E 27th St ....New York NY 10016	855-468-3501	212-545-8000	376
Gerson Co			
1450 S Lone Elm Rd ....Olathe KS 66061	800-444-8172	913-262-7400	408
Gertrude Hawk Chocolates Inc			
9 Keystone Pk ....Dunmore PA 18512	866-932-4295	800-822-2032	295-8
GES (Grangeville Environmental Services)			
585 McAllister St ....Hanover PA 17331	866-437-5151	717-637-6152	83
GES Exposition Services			
7000 Lindell Rd ....Las Vegas NV 89118	800-443-9767	702-515-5500	185
Gesa Credit Union			
51 Gage Blvd PO Box 500 ....Richland WA 99352	888-946-4372	509-946-1611	219
GET Engineering Corp			
9350 Bond Ave ....El Cajon CA 92021	877-494-1820	619-443-8295	204
Getconnect			
14114 Dallas Pkwy Ste 430 ....Dallas TX 75254	888-200-1831		363
Getty Realty Corp			
125 Jericho Tpke Ste 103 ....Jericho NY 11753	866-399-4335	516-478-5400	323
NYSE: GTY			
Gettysburg College			
300 N Washington St ....Gettysburg PA 17325	800-431-0803	717-337-6000	166
Gettysburg Convention & Visitors Bureau			
571 W Middle St PO Box 4117........Gettysburg PA 17325	800-337-5015	717-334-6274	207
Gettysburg Heritage Center			
297 Steinwehr Ave ....Gettysburg PA 17325	800-887-7775*	717-334-6245	513
*General			
Gettysburg-Adams County Area Chamber of Commerce			
18 Carlisle St Ste 203............Gettysburg PA 17325	800-699-1176	717-334-8151	137
Getzen Company Inc			
530 S Cty Hwy H PO Box 440............Elkhorn WI 53121	800-366-5584	262-723-4221	520
GF Health Products Inc			
2935 NE Pkwy ....Atlanta GA 30360	800-347-5678	770-447-1609	472
GF Machining Solutions			
560 Bond St ....Lincolnshire IL 60069	800-282-1336	847-913-5300	450
GFC Leasing Co			
2675 Research Pk Dr ....Madison WI 53711	800-333-5905	800-677-7877	264-2
GfG Instrumentation Inc			
1194 Oak Vly Dr Ste 20 ....Ann Arbor MI 48108	800-959-0329	734-769-0573	202
GFI Genfare			
751 Pratt Blvd ....Elk Grove Village IL 60007	877-247-3797	847-593-8855	467
GFI Group Inc			
55 Water St ....New York NY 10041	888-750-5884	212-968-4100	170
NYSE: GFIG			
GFWC (General Federation of Women's Clubs)			
1734 N St NW ....Washington DC 20036	800-443-4392	202-347-3168	47-24
GGB North America			
700 Mid Atlantic Pkwy			
PO Box 189..................Thorofare NJ 08086	888-840-2349	856-848-3200	613
GGS Technical Publications Services			
3265 Farmtrail Rd ....York PA 17406	800-927-4474	717-764-2222	771
Ghafari Assoc Inc			
17101 Michigan Ave ....Dearborn MI 48126	800-289-7822	313-441-3000	261
Gheens Science Hall & Rauch Planetarium			
Rauch Planetarium			
University of Louisville ....Louisville KY 40292	800-996-7566	502-852-6664	591
Ghent Manufacturing Inc			
2999 Henkle Dr ....Lebanon OH 45036	800-543-0550	513-932-3445	243
GHG Corp			
960 Clear Lk City Blvd ....Webster TX 77598	866-380-4146	281-488-8806	179-10
Ghirardelli Chocolate Co			
1111 139th Ave ....San Leandro CA 94578	800-877-9338		295-8

Company / Address	City	State	ZIP	Toll-Free	Phone	Class
GHS (Greenville Hospital System)						
701 Grove Rd	Greenville	SC	29605	**877-447-4636**	864-455-8976	350
GHS Corp						
2813 Wilber Ave	Battle Creek	MI	49037	**800-388-4447**		520
GHS Interactive Security Inc						
2081 Arena Blvd Ste 260	Sacramento	CA	95834	**855-208-2447**		684
GHX (Global Health Care Exchange LLC)						
1315 W Century Dr	Louisville	CO	80027	**800-968-7449**	720-887-7000	225
GIA (Gemological Institute of America)						
5345 Armada Dr	Carlsbad	CA	92008	**800-421-7250**	760-603-4000	48-4
Giant Eagle Inc						
101 Kappa Dr	Pittsburgh	PA	15238	**800-553-2324***	412-963-6200	342
*Cust Svc						
Giant Food Inc						
8301 Professional Pl Ste 115	Landover	MD	20785	**888-469-4426**		342
Giant Food Stores Inc						
1149 Harrisburg Pike	Carlisle	PA	17013	**888-814-4268**	717-249-4000	342
Giant Springs State Park						
4600 Giant Springs Rd	Great Falls	MT	59405	**855-922-6768**	406-454-5840	558
Giantbank.com						
6300 NE First Ave	Fort Lauderdale	FL	33334	**877-446-4200**	954-958-0001	69
Gibbs & Assoc						
323 Science Dr	Moorpark	CA	93021	**800-654-9399***	805-523-0004	179-5
*Cust Svc						
Gibbs Wire & Steel Company Inc						
Metals Dr PO Box 520	Southington	CT	06489	**800-800-4422**	860-621-0121	487
Gibraltar Industries Inc						
3556 Lakeshore Rd	Buffalo	NY	14219	**800-247-8368**	716-826-6500	714
NASDAQ: ROCK						
Gibson & Barnes						
1900 Weld Blvd Ste 140	El Cajon	CA	92020	**800-748-6693***	619-440-6977	153-18
*Sales						
Gibson Arnold & Assoc						
5433 Westheimer Rd Ste 1016	Houston	TX	77056	**800-879-2007**	713-572-3000	712
Gibson Dunn & Crutcher LLP						
333 S Grand Ave Ste 4600	Los Angeles	CA	90071	**888-203-1112**	213-229-7000	425
Gibson Guitar Corp						
309 Plus Pk Blvd	Nashville	TN	37217	**800-444-2766**	615-871-4500	520
Gibson Laboratories Inc						
1040 Manchester St	Lexington	KY	40508	**800-477-4763**	859-254-9500	231
Gibson Piano Ventures Inc						
309 Plus Pk Blvd	Nashville	TN	37217	**800-444-2766**	615-871-4500	520
Gideon Putnam Resort & Spa						
24 Gideon Putnam Rd	Saratoga Springs	NY	12866	**800-452-7275**	518-584-3000	376
Giffin Koerth Inc						
40 University Ave Ste 800	Toronto	ON	M5J1T1	**800-564-5313**	416-368-1700	256
Gift of Hope Organ & Tissue Donor Network						
425 Spring Lake Dr	Itasca	IL	60143	**877-577-3747**	630-758-2600	538
Gift of Life Bone Marrow Foundation						
800 Yamato Rd Ste 101	Boca Raton	FL	33431	**800-962-7769**	561-982-2900	47-17
Gift of Life Donor Program						
401 N Third St	Philadelphia	PA	19123	**800-543-6391**	215-557-8090	538
Gift of Life Transplant House						
705 Second St SW	Rochester	MN	55902	**800-479-7824**	507-288-7470	369
Gift Wrap Co						
338 Industrial Blvd	Midway	GA	31320	**800-443-4429***		541
*General						
GiftCertificates.com						
11510 Blondo St	Omaha	NE	68164	**800-773-7368**		326
Giftware News						
20 W Kinzie St 12th Fl	Chicago	IL	60654	**800-229-1967**	312-849-2220	452-21
Giga-Tronics Inc						
4650 Norris Canyon Rd	San Ramon	CA	94583	**800-726-4442**	925-328-4650	248
NASDAQ: GIGA						
GigMasters.com Inc						
33 S Main St	Norwalk	CT	06854	**866-342-9794**		384
Gil Tours Travel Inc						
1511 Walnut St Ste 200	Philadelphia	PA	19102	**800-223-3855**	215-568-6655	761
Gila County						
1400 E Ash St	Globe	AZ	85501	**800-304-4452**	928-425-3231	336
Gilbane Bldg Co						
Seven Jackson Walkway	Providence	RI	02903	**800-445-2263**	401-456-5800	189-7
Gilbane Bldg Co New England Regional Office						
7 Jackson Walkway	Providence	RI	02903	**800-445-2263**	401-456-5800	187
Gilbane Bldg Company Mid-Atlantic Regional Office						
7901 Sandy Spring Rd Ste 500	Laurel	MD	20707	**800-445-2263**	301-317-6100	187
Gilbane Bldg Company Southwest Regional Office						
1331 Lamar St Ste 1170	Houston	TX	77010	**800-445-2263**	713-209-1873	187
Gilbane Inc						
Seven Jackson Walkway	Providence	RI	02903	**800-445-2263**	401-456-5890	644
Gilbert Displays Inc						
110 Spagnoli Rd	Melville	NY	11747	**855-577-1100**	631-577-1100	232
Gilbreth Packaging Systems						
3001 State Rd	Croydon	PA	19021	**800-630-2413**		410
Gilchrist Hospice Care						
11311 McCormick Rd	Hunt Valley	MD	21031	**800-735-2258**	443-849-8200	368
Gilcrease Museum						
1400 N Gilcrease Museum Rd	Tulsa	OK	74127	**888-655-2278**	918-596-2700	513
Gilead Sciences Inc						
333 Lakeside Dr	Foster City	CA	94404	**800-445-3235**	650-574-3000	84
NASDAQ: GILD						
Giles & Ransome Inc Ransome Engine Power Div						
2975 Galloway Rd	Bensalem	PA	19020	**877-726-7663**	215-639-4300	274
Giles Engineering Assoc Inc						
N8 W22350 Johnson Rd Ste A1	Waukesha	WI	53186	**800-782-0610**	262-544-0118	256
Giles Industries Inc						
405 S Broad St	New Tazewell	TN	37825	**800-844-4537**	423-626-7243	500
Gilford Securities Inc						
777 Third Ave	New York	NY	10017	**800-445-3673**	212-888-6400	681
Gill Athletics Inc						
2808 Gemini Ct	Champaign	IL	61822	**800-637-3090***	217-367-8438	701
*Cust Svc						
Gillespie County Fairgrounds						
530 Fair Dr PO Box 526	Fredericksburg	TX	78624	**800-280-9531**	830-997-2359	633
Gillespie Museum of Minerals						
421 N Woodland Blvd Unit 8403	DeLand	FL	32723	**800-688-0101**	386-822-7330	513
Gillette Children's Specialty Healthcare						
200 E University Ave	Saint Paul	MN	55101	**800-719-4040**	651-291-2848	371-1
Gillig Corp						
25800 Clawiter Rd	Hayward	CA	94545	**800-735-1500**	510-785-1500	509
Gilligan & Ferneman LLC						
1754 Business Ctr Ln	Kissimmee	FL	34758	**800-720-4152**		316
Gillman Cos						
10595 W Sam Houston Pkwy S	Houston	TX	77099	**888-532-8956**	713-776-7000	56
Gillmore Security Systems Inc						
26165 Broadway Ave	Cleveland	OH	44146	**800-899-8995**	440-232-1000	684
Gilman & Pastor LLP						
63 Atlantic Ave Third Fl	Boston	MA	02110	**877-428-7374**	617-742-9700	193
Gilman USA						
1230 Cheyenne Ave PO Box 5	Grafton	WI	53024	**800-445-6267**	262-377-2434	488
Gilmore Entertainment Group						
8901-A Business 17 N	Myrtle Beach	SC	29572	**800-843-6779**	843-913-4000	182
Gilmour Academy						
34001 Cedar Rd	Gates Mills	OH	44040	**800-533-5140**	440-442-1104	615
Gilmour Mfg Group						
492 Drum Ave Somerset	Somerset	PA	15501	**800-458-0107***	814-443-4802	426
*Cust Svc						
Gilroy Chevrolet Cadillac Inc						
6720 Bear Cat Ct	Gilroy	CA	95020	**800-201-7241**	408-842-9301	56
Gilsbar Inc						
PO Box 998	Covington	LA	70434	**800-445-7227**	985-892-3520	457
Gilton Solid Waste Management						
755 S Yosemite Ave	Oakdale	CA	95361	**800-894-8980**	209-527-3781	792
Gina B Designs Inc						
12700 Industrial Pk Blvd						
Ste 40	Plymouth	MN	55441	**800-228-4856**	763-559-7595	129
Ginger Cove						
4000 River Crescent Dr	Annapolis	MD	21401	**800-299-2683**	410-266-7300	663
Gino Morena Enterprises LLC						
111 Starlite St	South San Francisco	CA	94080	**800-227-6905**		76
Ginsberg's Foods Inc						
29 Ginsberg Ln PO Box 17	Hudson	NY	12534	**800-999-6006**	518-828-4004	352
Giorgio Foods Inc						
PO Box 96	Temple	PA	19560	**800-220-2139**	610-926-2139	295-20
Giovanni's Restaurant & Convention Ctr						
610 N Bell School Rd	Rockford	IL	61107	**800-383-7829**	815-398-6411	662
Girl Scouts of the USA						
420 Fifth Ave	New York	NY	10018	**800-223-0624**	212-852-8000	47-15
Girls Inc						
120 Wall St Third Fl	New York	NY	10005	**800-374-4475**	212-509-2000	47-24
Girls' Life Acqusition Co						
4529 Hartford Rd	Baltimore	MD	21214	**888-999-3222**	410-426-9600	452-6
Giroux Glass Inc						
850 W Washington Blvd	Los Angeles	CA	90015	**800-684-5277**	213-747-7406	190-6
GISD (Garland Independent School District)						
501 S Jupiter PO Box 469026	Garland	TX	75046	**800-252-5555**	972-494-8201	676
GISD (Galveston Independent School District)						
3904 Ave PO Box 660	Galveston	TX	77550	**877-262-1492**	409-766-5100	676
Giselle's Travel Inc						
1300 Ethan Way Ste 100	Sacramento	CA	95825	**800-782-5545**	916-922-5500	761
Gitman & Co						
2309 Chestnut St	Ashland	PA	17921	**800-526-3929**	570-875-3100	153-11
Gitman Bros Shirt Company Inc						
641 Lexington Ave 19th Fl	New York	NY	10019	**800-526-3929***	212-581-6968	153-11
*General						
GIW Industries Inc						
5000 Wrightsboro Rd	Grovetown	GA	30813	**888-832-4449**	706-863-1011	632
GK Industries Ltd						
50 Precidio Ct	Brampton	ON	L6S6E3	**800-463-8889**	905-799-1972	60
GKG (Global Knowledge Group Inc)						
302 N Bryan Ave	Bryan	TX	77803	**866-776-7584**		795
G-L Veneer Co Inc						
2224 E Slauson Ave	Huntington Park	CA	90255	**800-588-5003**	323-582-5203	606
Glacial Energy						
2701 N Dallas Pkwy Ste 120	Plano	TX	75093	**877-569-2841**		193
Glacial Lakes State Park						
25022 County Rd 41	Starbuck	MN	56381	**888-646-6367**	320-239-2860	558
Glacial Ridge Hospital Foundation Inc						
10 Fourth Ave SE	Glenwood	MN	56334	**866-667-4747**	320-634-4521	371-3
Glacial Waters Spa at Grand View Lodge						
23521 Nokomis Ave	Nisswa	MN	56468	**866-801-2951**	218-963-2234	698
Glacier Bancorp Inc						
PO Box 27	Kalispell	MT	59903	**800-735-4371**	406-756-4200	357-2
NASDAQ: GBCI						
Glacier Bay Catamarans						
1090 W Saint James St	Tarboro	NC	27886	**855-662-4855**		89
Glacier Bay Country Inn						
35 Tong Rd	Gustavus	AK	99826	**800-628-0912**		376
Glacier Clear Enterprises Inc						
3291 Thomas St	Innisfil	ON	L9S3W3	**800-668-5118***	705-436-6363	793
*Cust Svc						
Glacier Electric Co-op Inc						
410 E Main St	Cut Bank	MT	59427	**800-347-6795**	406-873-5566	245
Glacier National Park						
PO Box 350	Revelstoke	BC	V0E2S0	**866-787-6221**	250-837-7500	556
Glacier Water Services Inc						
1385 Pk Ctr Dr	Vista	CA	92081	**800-452-2437**	760-560-1111	54
OTC: GWSV						
Glade Springs Resort						
255 Resort Dr	Daniels	WV	25832	**866-562-8054**		660
Gladstone Dodge						
5610 N Oak Trafficway	Gladstone	MO	64118	**866-695-2043**		56
Gladstone School District 115						
17789 Webster Rd	Gladstone	OR	97027	**800-328-0272**	503-655-2777	676
Gladys Porter Zoo						
500 Ringgold St	Brownsville	TX	78520	**800-424-8802**	956-546-7187	810
Glamos Wire Products Company Inc						
5561 N 152nd St	Hugo	MN	55038	**800-328-5062**	651-429-5386	72
Glance Networks Inc						
1167 Massachusetts Ave	Arlington	MA	02476	**877-452-6236**	781-646-8505	225
Glasforms Inc						
1226 Lincoln Ave	San Jose	CA	95125	**888-297-3800**	408-297-9300	593
Glasgow Inc						
104 Willow Grove Ave	Glenside	PA	19038	**877-222-5514**	215-884-8800	189-4
Glasgow-Barren County Chamber of Commerce						
118 E Public Sq	Glasgow	KY	42141	**800-264-3161**	270-651-3161	137
Glass Art Society (GAS)						
6512 23rd Ave NW Ste 329	Seattle	WA	98121	**800-636-2377**	206-382-1305	47-4
Glass Assn of North America (GANA)						
800 SW Jackson St Ste 1500	Topeka	KS	66612	**877-275-2421**	785-271-0208	48-13
Glass House Inn						
3202 W 26th St	Erie	PA	16506	**800-956-7222**	814-833-7751	376
Glass Molders Pottery Plastics & Allied Workers International Union						
608 E Baltimore Pike	Media	PA	19063	**855-670-4787**	610-565-5051	411
GlassCraft Door Co						
2002 Brittmoore Rd	Houston	TX	77043	**800-766-2196**	713-690-8282	234
Glassmere Fuel Service Inc						
1967 Saxonburg Blvd	Tarentum	PA	15084	**800-235-9054**	724-265-4646	315

Company / Address	City	State	ZIP	Toll-Free	Phone	Class
Glasteel-stabilit America Inc 285 Industrial Dr	Moscow	TN	38057	**800-238-5546**	901-877-3010	601
Glastender Inc 5400 N Michigan Rd	Saginaw	MI	48604	**800-748-0423**	989-752-4275	383
Glastic Corp 4321 Glenridge Rd	Cleveland	OH	44121	**800-360-1319**	216-486-0100	599
Glastonbury Southern Gage 46 Industrial Pk Rd	Erin	TN	37061	**800-251-4243**	931-289-4243	488
Glastron Boats 710 Co Rd 75	St Joseph	MN	56374	**855-272-2709**	320-433-2141	89
Glaucoma Research Foundation 251 Post St Ste 600	San Francisco	CA	94108	**800-826-6693**	415-986-3162	47-17
Glaval Bus 914 County Rd 1	Elkhart	IN	46514	**800-445-2825**	574-262-2212	58
GlaxoSmithKline Inc 7333 Mississauga Rd N	Mississauga	ON	L5N6L4	**800-387-7374**	905-819-3000	576
Glazer's Wholesale Drug Company Inc 14911 Quorum Dr Ste 400	Dallas	TX	75254	**800-275-2854**	972-392-8200	80-3
Glazier Foods Co 11303 Antoine Dr *General	Houston	TX	77066	**800-989-6411***	832-375-6300	296-8
Glaz-Tech Industries Inc 2207 E Elvira Rd	Tucson	AZ	85756	**800-755-8062**	520-629-0268	328
GLC (God's Learning Ch) PO Box 61000	Midland	TX	79711	**800-707-0420**	432-563-0420	729
Gleason Corp 1000 University Ave	Rochester	NY	14607	**800-727-6333**	585-473-1000	450
Gleason M & M Precision Systems Corp 300 Progress Rd	Dayton	OH	45449	**800-727-6333**	937-859-8273	248
Gleason Reel Corp 600 S Clark St	Mayville	WI	53050	**888-504-5151**	920-387-4120	116
Glen Cove Mansion Hotel & Conference Ctr 200 Dosoris Ln	Glen Cove	NY	11542	**877-782-9426**	516-671-6400	374
Glen Ellyn Chamber of Commerce 800 Roosevelt Rd Bldg D Ste 108	Glen Ellyn	IL	60137	**800-622-9000**	630-469-0907	137
Glen Grove Suites 2837 Yonge St	Toronto	ON	M4N2J6	**800-565-3024**	416-489-8441	376
Glen Meadows 11630 Glen Arm Rd	Glen Arm	MD	21057	**800-630-4689**		663
Glen Oaks Community College 62249 Shimmel Rd	Centreville	MI	49032	**888-994-7818**	269-467-9945	160
Glen Raven Inc 232 Glen Raven Rd	Glen Raven	NC	27217	**800-675-0032**	336-227-6211	734-1
Glen Research Corp 22825 Davis Dr	Sterling	VA	20164	**800-327-4536**	703-437-6191	659
Glenair Inc 1211 Air Way	Glendale	CA	91201	**888-465-4094**	818-247-6000	802
Glenbeigh Health Source 2863 SR 45	Rock Creek	OH	44084	**800-234-1001**	440-563-3400	717
Glencoe/McGraw-Hill 8787 Orion Pl	Columbus	OH	43240	**800-848-1567**		628-2
Glencrest Farm 1576 Moores Mill Rd PO Box 4468	Midway	KY	40347	**800-903-0136**	859-233-7032	365
Glendale Infiniti 812 S Brand Blvd	Glendale	CA	91204	**800-449-9375**	818-543-5000	56
Glendinning Marine Products 740 Century Cir	Conway	SC	29526	**800-500-2380**	843-399-6146	204
Glendora Chamber of Commerce 131 E Foothill Blvd	Glendora	CA	91741	**866-987-1611**	626-963-4128	137
Glendora Public Library & Cultural Ctr 140 S Glendora Ave	Glendora	CA	91741	**866-275-3772**	626-852-4891	431-3
Glendorn 1000 Glendorn Dr	Bradford	PA	16701	**800-843-8568**	814-362-6511	376
Gleneden Beach State Recreation Site 198 NE 123rd St	Newport	OR	97365	**800-551-6949**		558
Glenerin Inn, The 1695 The Collegeway	Mississauga	ON	L5L3S7	**877-991-9971**	905-828-6103	376
Glenmede Funds 1650 Market St Ste 1200	Philadelphia	PA	19103	**800-966-3200**	215-419-6000	521
Glenmede Trust Co 1650 Market St Ste 1200	Philadelphia	PA	19103	**800-966-3200**	215-419-6000	398
Glenmore Inn 2720 Glenmore Trl SE	Calgary	AB	T2C2E6	**800-661-3163**	403-279-8611	376
Glenn O Hawbaker Inc 1952 Waddle Rd Ste 203	State College	PA	16803	**800-221-1355**	814-237-1444	45
GlenOaks Hospital 701 Winthrop Ave	Glendale Heights	IL	60139	**866-751-7127**	630-545-8000	371-3
Glenro Inc 39 McBride Ave	Paterson	NJ	07501	**888-453-6761**	973-279-5900	317
Glenrock International Inc 985 E Linden Ave	Linden	NJ	07036	**800-453-6762**	908-862-3433	715
Glens Falls Hospital 100 Pk St	Glens Falls	NY	12801	**800-994-6610**	518-926-1000	371-3
Glensheen Mansion 3300 London Rd	Duluth	MN	55804	**888-454-4536**	218-726-8910	49-2
Glentek Inc 208 Standard St	El Segundo	CA	90245	**877-470-6742**	310-322-3026	511
Glenville State College 200 High St *Admissions	Glenville	WV	26351	**800-924-2010***	304-462-7361	166
Glenwood LLC 111 Cedar Ln	Englewood	NJ	07631	**800-542-0772**	201-569-0050	577
Glenwood State Bank 5 E Minnesota Ave PO Box 197	Glenwood	MN	56334	**800-207-7333**	320-634-5111	69
Glessner House Museum 1800 S Prairie Ave	Chicago	IL	60616	**800-657-0687**	312-326-1480	513
Glidden House 1901 Ford Dr	Cleveland	OH	44106	**866-812-4537**	216-231-8900	376
Glidewell Laboratories Inc 4141 MacArthur Blvd	Newport Beach	CA	92660	**800-854-7256**		732
Glimmerglass Festival 7300 State Hwy 80 PO Box 191	Cooperstown	NY	13326	**866-568-2388**	607-547-0700	566-2
Glimmerglass Networks Inc 26142 Eden Landing Rd	Hayward	CA	94545	**877-723-1900**	510-723-1900	179-10
Glines & Rhodes Inc 189 E St PO Box 2285	Attleboro	MA	02703	**800-343-1196**	508-226-2000	480
Glit/Microtron 809 Broad St PO Box 709	Wrens	GA	30833	**800-325-1051**	314-739-8585	1
GLM Industries LP 1508 - Eighth St	Nisku	AB	T9E7S6	**800-661-9828**	780-955-2233	475
Global Air Response 5919 Approach Rd	Sarasota	FL	34238	**800-631-6565**		30
Global Business Travel Assn, The (GBTA) 123 N Pitt St	Alexandria	VA	22314	**888-574-6447**	703-684-0836	47-23
Global Computer Supplies Inc 11 Harbor Pk Dr	Port Washington	NY	11050	**800-446-9662**		175
Global Consultants Inc 25 Airport Rd	Morristown	NJ	07960	**877-264-6424**	973-889-5200	181
Global Educational Tours 7216 Madison Ave Ste U	Indianapolis	IN	46227	**888-508-6877**	317-787-2787	750
Global Electronic Music Marketplace PO Box 2186	La Jolla	CA	92038	**800-207-4366**	858-456-0894	518
Global Equipment Marketing Inc PO Box 810483	Boca Raton	FL	33481	**866-750-8662**	561-750-8662	355
Global Exchange 2017 Mission St Ste 303	San Francisco	CA	94110	**800-497-1994**	415-255-7296	47-7
Global Filtration Inc 9207 Emmott St	Houston	TX	77040	**888-717-0888**	713-856-9800	56
Global Ground Support LLC 540 Old Hwy 56	Olathe	KS	66061	**888-780-0303**	913-780-0300	22
Global Health Care Exchange LLC (GHX) 1315 W Century Dr	Louisville	CO	80027	**800-968-7449**	720-887-7000	225
Global Help Desk Services Inc 2080 Silas Deane Hwy	Rocky Hill	CT	06067	**800-770-1075**		181
Global Imaging Systems Inc 3820 Northdale Blvd Ste 200A	Tampa	FL	33624	**888-628-7834**	813-960-5508	111
Global Industries Inc 17 W Stow Rd	Marlton	NJ	08053	**800-220-1900**	856-596-3390	318-1
Global Industries Ltd 8000 Global Dr	Sulphur	LA	70665	**800-525-3483**	337-583-5000	532
Global Knowledge Group Inc (GKG) 302 N Bryan Ave	Bryan	TX	77803	**866-776-7584**		795
Global Knowledge Training LLC 9000 Regency Pkwy Ste 500	Cary	NC	27518	**800-268-7737**	919-461-8600	754
Global Market Perspective PO Box 1618	Gainesville	GA	30503	**800-336-1618**	770-536-0309	524-9
Global Medical Imaging LLC 222 Rampart St	Charlotte	NC	28203	**800-958-9986**		470
Global Medical LLC 8332 Bristol Ct Ste 108	Jessup	MD	20794	**800-528-1001**		470
Global Neuro-Diagnostics LP 2670 Firewheel Dr Ste B	Flower Mound	TX	75028	**866-848-2522**		415
Global Offset & Countertrade Assn (GOCA) 818 Connecticut Ave NW 12th Fl	Washington	DC	20006	**800-343-6074**	202-887-9011	48-18
Global Pacific Financial Services Ltd 10430 144 St	Surrey	BC	V3T4V5	**800-561-1177**		316
Global Partners LP 800 S St Ste 200 *NYSE: GLP*	Waltham	MA	02454	**800-685-7222**	781-894-8800	572
Global Payments Inc 10 Glenlake Pkwy N Twr *NYSE: GPN*	Atlanta	GA	30328	**800-560-2960**	770-829-8000	255
Global Power Report Two Penn Plz 25th Fl	New York	NY	10121	**800-752-8878**		524-5
Global R&D Consulting Group 555 N Point Ctr E	Alpharetta	GA	30022	**866-770-5577**		390
Global Shop Solutions Inc 975 Evergreen Cir *Sales	The Woodlands	TX	77380	**800-364-5958***	281-681-1959	179-1
Global Software Inc 3201 Beechleaf Ct Ste 170	Raleigh	NC	27604	**800-326-3444**	919-872-7800	179-1
Global Solar Energy Inc 8500 S Rita Rd	Tucson	AZ	85747	**866-999-8422**	520-546-6313	687
Global Technology Resources Inc 990 S Broadway Ste 400	Denver	CO	80209	**877-603-1984**	303-455-8800	181
Global Travel 900 W Jefferson St	Boise	ID	83702	**800-584-8888**	208-387-1000	761
Global Travel International 2600 Lk Lucien Dr Ste 201	Maitland	FL	32751	**800-715-4440**	407-660-7800	762
Global Turnkey Systems Inc 2001 US 46	Parsippany	NJ	07054	**800-221-1746**	973-331-1010	179-10
Global TV 121 Bloor St E	Toronto	ON	M4W3M5	**877-345-9195**	416-967-1174	730
Global University 1211 S Glenstone Ave	Springfield	MO	65804	**800-443-1083**	417-862-9533	756
GlobalDie 1130 Minot Ave PO Box 1120	Auburn	ME	04211	**888-271-4735**	207-514-7252	747
Globalspec Inc 350 Jordan Rd	Troy	NY	12180	**800-261-2052**	518-880-0200	181
Globalstar LP 3200 Zanker Rd Bldg 260	San Jose	CA	95134	**877-728-7466**	408-933-4000	672
Globe Consultants Inc 3112 Porter St Ste D	Soquel	CA	95073	**800-208-0663**		194
Globe Electronic Hardware Inc 34-24 56th St	Woodside	NY	11377	**800-221-1505**	718-457-0303	204
Globe Food Equipment Co 2153 Dryden Rd	Dayton	OH	45439	**800-347-5423**	937-299-5493	297
Globe Mfg Co 37 Loudon Rd PO Box 128	Pittsfield	NH	03263	**800-232-8323**	603-435-8323	569
Globe Motors Inc 2275 Stanley Ave	Dayton	OH	45404	**800-433-5700**	937-228-3171	56
Globecomm Systems Inc 45 Oser Ave *NASDAQ: GCOM*	Hauppauge	NY	11788	**866-499-0223**	631-231-9800	638
Globe-Gazette 300 N Washington St PO Box 271	Mason City	IA	50402	**800-421-0546**	641-421-0500	525-2
Globex Corp 3620 Stutz Dr	Canfield	OH	44406	**800-533-8610**	330-533-0030	256
Globus 5301 S Federal Cir	Littleton	CO	80123	**866-755-8581**	303-703-7000	750
Glo-Quartz Electric Heater Company Inc 7084 Maple St *Sales	Mentor	OH	44060	**800-321-3574***	440-255-9701	317
Glorietta Bay Inn 1630 Glorietta Blvd	Coronado	CA	92118	**800-283-9383**	619-435-3101	376
Glorybee Foods Inc 120 N Seneca Rd	Eugene	OR	97402	**800-456-7923**	541-689-0913	295-24
Glover Sales Group LLC 221 Cockeysville Rd	Cockeysville	MD	21030	**800-966-9016**	410-771-8000	319
Gloves Inc 1950 Collins Boulevard	Austell	MA	30106	**800-476-4568**	770-944-9186	153-7
Glovia International Inc 2250 E Imperial Hwy Ste 200	El Segundo	CA	90245	**888-245-6842**	310-563-7000	179-1

Name	Address	City	State	ZIP	Toll-Free	Phone	Class
GLS (Government Liaison Services Inc)	200 N Glebe Rd Ste 321	Arlington	VA	22203	**800-642-6564**	703-524-8200	626
GM Nameplate Inc	2040 15th Ave W	Seattle	WA	98119	**800-366-7668**	206-284-2200	476
GMAC (General Motors Acceptance Corp)	200 Renaissance Ctr	Detroit	MI	48265	**800-200-4622**	877-320-2559	214
GMAC (Graduate Management Admission Council)	11921 Freedom Dr Ste 300	Reston	VA	20190	**866-505-6559**	703-668-9600	47-11
GMAC Insurance Holdings Inc	PO Box 3199	Winston-Salem	NC	27102	**888-293-5108**		357-4
GMHC (Gay Men's Health Crisis)	119 W 24th St	New York	NY	10011	**800-243-7692**	212-367-1000	47-17
GMI Building Services Inc	8001 Vickers St	San Diego	CA	92111	**866-803-4464**		256
GMI Composites Inc	1355 W Sherman Blvd	Muskegon	MI	49441	**800-330-4045**	231-755-1611	599
GMP Metal Products Inc	3883 Delor St	Saint Louis	MO	63116	**800-325-9808**	314-481-0300	273
GMX Resources Inc	9400 Bdwy Extension Hwy *NYSE: GMXRQ*	Oklahoma City	OK	73114	**877-600-0711**	405-600-0711	529
GN ReSound North America	8001 E Bloomington Fwy	Bloomington	MN	55420	**888-735-4327**		250
GN US Inc	77 NE Blvd	Nashua	NH	03062	**800-327-2230**	603-598-1100	725
GNA (Georgia Nurses Assn)	3032 Briarcliff Rd NE	Atlanta	GA	30329	**800-324-0462**	404-325-5536	526
GNC Inc	300 Sixth Ave 14th Fl *NYSE: GNC*	Pittsburgh	PA	15222	**877-462-4700**		352
GNFCC (Greater North Fulton Chamber of Commerce)	11605 Haynes Bridge Rd Ste 100	Alpharetta	GA	30009	**866-840-5770**	770-993-8806	137
Gnuco LLC	20 N Wacker Dr Ste 1870	Chicago	IL	60606	**800-800-8805**	312-669-9600	178
GO Carlson Inc	350 Marshallton Thorndale Rd	Downingtown	PA	19335	**800-338-5622**	610-384-2800	714
Go Edit Inc	5614 Cahuenga Blvd	North Hollywood	CA	91601	**800-833-9200**	818-284-6260	505
Go Next	8000 W 78th St Ste 345	Minneapolis	MN	55439	**800-842-9023**	952-918-8950	750
Go...With Jo! Tours & Travel Inc	910 Dixieland Rd	Harlingen	TX	78552	**800-999-1446**	956-423-1446	750
Goal Sporting Goods Inc	37 Industrial Pk Rd PO Box 236	Essex	CT	06426	**800-334-4625**		701
Goals & Poles	7575 Jefferson Hwy	Baton Rouge	LA	70806	**800-275-0317**	225-923-0622	701
Goalsetter Systems Inc	1041 Cordova Ave	Lynnville	IA	50153	**800-362-4625**		701
Gobin's Inc	615 N Santa Fe Ave	Pueblo	CO	81003	**800-425-2324**	719-544-2324	528
GOCA (Global Offset & Countertrade Assn)	818 Connecticut Ave NW 12th Fl	Washington	DC	20006	**800-343-6074**	202-887-9011	48-18
God's Bible School & College	1810 Young St	Cincinnati	OH	45202	**800-486-4637**	513-721-7944	159
God's Learning Ch (GLC)	PO Box 61000	Midland	TX	79711	**800-707-0420**	432-563-0420	729
Goddard College	123 Pitkin Rd	Plainfield	VT	05667	**800-468-4888**	802-454-8311	166
Goddard Institute for Space Studies	2880 Broadway	New York	NY	10025	**888-661-1620**	212-678-5510	659
Goddard Systems Inc	1016 W Ninth Ave	King of Prussia	PA	19406	**800-463-3273**	610-265-8510	309
Godfrey Trucking Inc	6173 West 2100 South	West Valley City	UT	84128	**800-444-7669**	801-972-0660	770
Goebel Fixture Co	528 Dale St	Hutchinson	MN	55350	**800-727-4646**	320-587-2112	286
Goethe Institut Atlanta/German Cultural Ctr	1197 Peachtree St NE	Atlanta	GA	30361	**888-446-3843**	404-892-2388	513
Goetze's Candy Company Inc	3900 E Monument St *Orders	Baltimore	MD	21205	**800-295-8058***	410-342-2010	295-8
GOG (Gynecologic Oncology Group)	1600 JFK Blvd Ste 1020	Philadelphia	PA	19103	**800-225-3053**	215-854-0770	48-8
Gogebic Community College	E 4946 Jackson Rd	Ironwood	MI	49938	**800-682-5910**	906-932-4231	160
GOGO WorldWide Vacations	69 Spring St	Ramsey	NJ	07446	**800-254-3477**		761
GOJO Industries Inc	One GOJO Plz Ste 500	Akron	OH	44311	**800-321-9647**	330-255-6000	215
Gold Canyon Golf Resort	6100 S Kings Ranch Rd	Gold Canyon	AZ	85118	**800-624-6445**	480-982-9090	660
Gold Coast Freightways Inc	12250 NW 28th Ave	Miami	FL	33167	**877-465-3585**	305-687-3560	310
Gold Coast Hotel & Casino	4000 W Flamingo Rd	Las Vegas	NV	89103	**800-331-5334**	702-367-7111	132
Gold Coast Ingredients Inc	2429 Yates Ave	Commerce	CA	90040	**800-352-8673**	323-724-8935	296-8
Gold Dust West Carson City	2171 E William St	Carson City	NV	89701	**877-519-5567**	775-885-9000	132
Gold Eagle Co	4400 S Kildare Ave	Chicago	IL	60632	**800-367-3245**		143
Gold Medal	PO Box 9452	Minneapolis	MN	55440	**800-248-7310**		295-23
Gold Medal Bakery Inc	1397 Bay St	Fall River	MA	02724	**800-642-7568**	508-674-5766	67
Gold Newsletter	PO Box 84900	Phoenix	AZ	85071	**800-877-8847**		524-9
Gold Ranch Casino & RV Resort	350 Gold Ranch Rd PO Box 160	Verdi	NV	89439	**877-914-6789**	775-345-6789	132
Gold Reserve Inc	926 W Sprague Ave Ste 200 *TSE: GRZ*	Spokane	WA	99201	**800-625-9550**	509-623-1500	497
Gold Room	127 N Franklin St	Juneau	AK	99801	**800-544-0970**	907-586-2660	662
Gold Standard Enterprises Inc	5100 W Dempster St	Skokie	IL	60077	**888-942-9463**	847-674-4200	439
Gold Star Chili	650 Lunken Pk Dr	Cincinnati	OH	45226	**800-643-0465**	513-231-4541	661
Gold Star FS Inc	101 NE St PO Box 79	Cambridge	IL	61238	**800-443-8497**	309-937-3369	276
Gold Strike Casino Resort	1010 Casino Ctr Dr *Resv	Tunica Resorts	MS	38664	**888-245-7829***	662-357-1111	132
Gold Strike Hotel & Gambling Hall	One Main St PO Box 19278	Jean	NV	89019	**800-634-1359**	702-477-5000	132
Goldbelt Hotel Juneau	51 Egan Dr	Juneau	AK	99801	**888-478-6909**	907-586-6900	376
Goldcorp Inc	666 Burrard St Ste 3400 *NYSE: G*	Vancouver	BC	V6C2X8	**800-567-6223**	604-696-3000	497
Goldcrest Wallcoverings	PO Box 245	Slingerlands	NY	12159	**800-535-9513**	518-478-7214	790
Gold-eagle Co-op	515 N Locust St PO Box 280	Goldfield	IA	50542	**800-825-3331**		10-3
Golden Artists Colors Inc	188 Bell Rd	New Berlin	NY	13411	**800-959-6543**	607-847-6154	42
Golden Door	PO Box 463077	Escondido	CA	92046	**866-420-6414**	760-744-5777	697
Golden Eagle Insurance Corp	525 B St	San Diego	CA	92101	**888-398-8924**	619-744-6000	388-4
Golden Eagle Resort	511 Mountain Rd PO Box 1090	Stowe	VT	05672	**800-626-1010**	802-253-4811	376
Golden Equipment Co	721 Candelaria NE	Albuquerque	NM	87107	**800-880-8580**	505-345-7811	355
Golden Flake Snack Foods Inc	One Golden Flake Dr	Birmingham	AL	35205	**800-239-2447**	205-323-6161	295-35
Golden Foods/Golden Brands LLC	2520 Seventh St Rd	Louisville	KY	40208	**800-622-3055**	502-636-3712	295-30
Golden Gate Baptist Theological Seminary	201 Seminary Dr	Mill Valley	CA	94941	**888-442-8701**	415-380-1300	167-3
Golden Gate Bridge	Golden Gate Bridge Toll Plz Presidio Stn PO Box 9000	San Francisco	CA	94129	**877-229-8655**	415-921-5858	49-3
Golden Gate Canyon State Park	92 Crawford Gulch Rd	Golden	CO	80403	**866-265-6447**	303-582-3707	558
Golden Gate University	*San Francisco* 536 Mission St	San Francisco	CA	94105	**800-448-4968**	415-442-7000	788
Golden Gate University School of Law	536 Mission St	San Francisco	CA	94105	**800-448-4968**	415-442-6600	167-1
Golden Grain Energy LLC	1822 43rd St SW	Mason City	IA	50401	**888-443-2676**	641-423-8525	10-4
Golden Hotel, The	800 11th St	Golden	CO	80401	**800-233-7214**	303-279-0100	376
Golden Neo-Life Diamite International	3500 Gateway Blvd	Fremont	CA	94538	**800-432-5842**		363
Golden Nugget Hotel	129 E Fremont St	Las Vegas	NV	89101	**800-634-3454**	702-385-7111	660
Golden Nugget Hotels & Casinos	151 Beach Blvd	Biloxi	MS	39530	**800-777-7568**	228-435-5400	132
Golden Nugget Laughlin	2300 S Casino Dr	Laughlin	NV	89029	**800-950-7700**	702-298-7111	132
Golden Oaks Village	5801 N Oakwood Rd	Enid	OK	73703	**800-259-0914**	580-249-2600	663
Golden Rule Insurance Co	7440 Woodlands *Cust Svc	Indianapolis	IN	46278	**800-444-8990***		388-3
Golden Spike Equipment Co	1352 W Main St PO Box 70	Tremonton	UT	84337	**800-821-4474**	435-257-5346	274
Golden Sports Tours	301 W Parker Rd Ste 206	Plano	TX	75023	**800-966-8258**		761
Golden Star Inc	4770 N Belleview Ave Ste 209	Kansas City	MO	64116	**800-821-2792**	816-842-0233	501
Golden Star Resources Ltd	10901 W Toller Dr Ste 300 *NYSE: GSS*	Littleton	CO	80127	**800-553-8436**	303-830-9000	497
Golden State Cellular	17400 High School Rd	Jamestown	CA	95327	**800-453-8255**	209-984-8700	726
Golden State Medical Supply Inc	5187 Camino Ruiz	Camarillo	CA	93012	**800-284-8633**	805-477-9866	231
Golden State Warriors	1011 Broadway	Oakland	CA	94607	**866-648-4668**	510-986-2200	705-1
Golden Valley Bank Community Foundation	190 Cohasset Rd Ste 170	Chico	CA	95926	**800-808-2070**	530-894-1000	69
Golden Valley Electrical Assn Inc	758 Illinois St	Fairbanks	AK	99701	**800-770-4832**	907-452-1151	245
Golden Valley Memorial Hospital	1600 N Second St	Clinton	MO	64735	**888-225-6903**	660-885-5511	371-3
Golden West Casino	1001 S Union Ave	Bakersfield	CA	93307	**800-267-3983**	661-324-6936	132
Golden West Telecommunications	415 Crown St PO Box 411	Wall	SD	57790	**866-279-2161**	605-279-2161	726
Goldener Hirsch Inn	7570 Royal St E *Cust Svc	Park City	UT	84060	**800-252-3373***	435-649-7770	376
GoldenRAM Computer Products	13 Whatney	Irvine	CA	92618	**800-222-8861**	949-460-9000	617
Golden-Tech International Inc	2461 152nd Ave NE	Redmond	WA	98052	**800-311-8090**	425-869-1461	296-5
Goldey Beacom College	4701 Limestone Rd	Wilmington	DE	19808	**800-833-4877**	302-998-8814	166
Goldline International Inc	1601 Cloverfield Blvd 100 S Tower	Santa Monica	CA	90404	**877-376-2646**	310-587-1423	486
Goldman Sachs	200 W St *NYSE: GS*	New York	NY	10282	**800-526-7384**	212-902-1000	521
Goldman Sachs Asset Management (GSAM)	200 W St	New York	NY	10282	**800-526-7384**	212-902-1000	398
Goldshield Elite	1501 Northpoint Pkwy	West Palm Beach	FL	33407	**866-218-8142**	561-615-4701	363
Goldsmith & Eggleton Inc	300 First St	Wadsworth	OH	44281	**800-321-0954**	330-336-6616	598-2
Goleta Valley Chamber of Commerce	271 N Fairview Ave Ste 104	Goleta	CA	93117	**800-646-5382**	805-967-2500	137
Golf Course Superintendents Assn of America (GCSAA)	1421 Research Pk Dr	Lawrence	KS	66049	**800-472-7878**	785-841-2240	47-2
Golf Etc of America Inc	2201 Commercial Ln	Granbury	TX	76048	**800-806-8633**	817-579-5263	702
Golf Mill Shopping Ctr	239 Golf Mill Ctr	Niles	IL	60714	**866-853-9491**	847-699-1070	455
Golf Shack Inc	1631 N Bell School Rd	Rockford	IL	61107	**888-446-5390**	815-397-3709	702

Name / Address	City	State	Zip	Toll-Free	Phone	Class
Golf Tips Magazine						
12121 Wilshire Blvd						
Ste 1200	Los Angeles	CA	90025	**877-505-9447**	310-820-1500	452-20
Golflogix Inc						
15685 N Greenway-Hayden Loop						
Ste 100A	Scottsdale	AZ	85260	**877-977-0162**		146
Golfsmith International Inc						
11000 N IH-35	Austin	TX	78753	**800-396-0099***	512-821-4050	702
*Sales						
GolfWorks, The						
4820 Jacksontown Rd PO Box 3008	Newark	OH	43055	**800-848-8358**	740-328-4193	701
Goliad Independent School District						
PO Box 830	Goliad	TX	77963	**800-750-9911**	361-645-3259	676
Golub Corp						
461 Nott St	Schenectady	NY	12308	**800-666-7667**		342
gomembers Inc						
1155 Perimeter Center West						
Bldg 700	Atlanta	GA	30338	**888-288-4634**	855-411-2783	179-10
Gonnella Baking Co						
1001 W Chicago Ave	Chicago	IL	60642	**800-262-3442**	312-733-2020	67
Gonzaga University						
502 E Boone Ave	Spokane	WA	99258	**800-986-9585**	509-323-6572	166
Gonzaga University Foley Library						
502 E Boone Ave	Spokane	WA	99258	**800-498-5941**	509-323-5931	431-6
Gonzaga University School of Law						
721 N Cincinnati St PO Box 3528	Spokane	WA	99220	**800-793-1710***	509-313-3700	167-1
*Admissions						
Good Eats Inc						
12200 Stemmons Fwy Ste 100	Dallas	TX	75234	**800-275-1337**	972-241-5500	661
Good Hotel						
Good Hotel						
112 Seventh St	San Francisco	CA	94103	**800-444-5819**	415-621-7001	376
Good Printers Inc						
213 Dry River Rd	Bridgewater	VA	22812	**800-296-3731**	540-828-4663	175
Good Sam Club						
PO Box 6888	Englewood	CO	80155	**800-234-3450**		47-23
Good Samaritan Hospice						
2408 Electric Rd	Roanoke	VA	24018	**888-466-7809**	540-776-0198	368
Good Samaritan Hospital						
10 E 31st St	Kearney	NE	68847	**800-277-4306**	308-865-7100	371-3
Good Samaritan Regional Medical Ctr						
3600 NW Samaritan Dr	Corvallis	OR	97330	**888-872-0760**	541-768-5111	371-3
Good Shepherd Hospice						
4350 Will Rogers Pkwy						
Ste 400	Oklahoma City	OK	73108	**800-687-9808**	405-943-0903	368
Good Time Tours						
455 Corday St	Pensacola	FL	32503	**800-446-0886**	850-476-0046	750
Good Times Travel Inc						
17132 Magnolia St	Fountain Valley	CA	92708	**888-488-2287**	714-848-1255	750
Good Zoo & Benedum Planetarium						
Rt 88 N Oglebay Pk	Wheeling	WV	26003	**800-624-6988**	304-243-4030	810
Goodall Manufacturing Co						
7558 Washington Ave S	Eden Prairie	MN	55344	**800-328-7730**	952-941-6666	247
Goodell Devries Leech & Dann LLP						
One S St 20th Fl	Baltimore	MD	21202	**888-229-4354**	410-783-4000	425
Goodheart-Willcox Publisher						
18604 W Creek Dr	Tinley Park	IL	60477	**800-323-0440**	708-687-5000	628-2
Goodhue County Co-op Electric Assn						
1410 Northstar Dr	Zumbrota	MN	55992	**800-927-6864**	507-732-5117	245
Goodin Co						
2700 N Second St	Minneapolis	MN	55411	**800-328-8433**	612-588-7811	605
Goodman Correctional Institution						
4556 Broad River Rd	Columbia	SC	29210	**866-230-7761**	803-896-8565	213
Goodman Factors						
3010 LBJ Fwy Ste 140	Dallas	TX	75234	**877-446-6362**	972-241-3297	272
Good-Nite Inn Fremont						
4135 Cushing Pkwy	Fremont	CA	94538	**800-648-3466**	510-656-9307	376
Goodrich Corp						
2730 W Tyvola Rd						
4 Coliseum Ctr	Charlotte	NC	28217	**800-735-7899**	704-423-7000	522
NYSE: GR						
Goodrich Corp Aircraft Interior Products Div						
3420 S Seventh St	Phoenix	AZ	85040	**877-808-7575**	602-243-2200	22
Goodspeed Musicals						
PO Box A	East Haddam	CT	06423	**800-262-8721**	860-873-8664	738
Goodwill Industries International Inc						
15810 Indianola Dr	Rockville	MD	20855	**800-741-0197**	301-530-6500	47-5
Goodwill Industries of Akron Ohio Inc, The						
570 E Waterloo Rd	Akron	OH	44319	**800-989-8428**	330-724-6995	194
Goodwill Industries of Central Texas						
1015 Norwood Pk Blvd	Austin	TX	78753	**800-735-2989**	512-637-7100	47-15
Goodwin Biotechnology Inc						
1850 NW 69th Ave	Plantation	FL	33313	**800-814-8600**	954-327-9656	231
Goodyear Tire & Rubber Co						
200 Innovation Way	Akron	OH	44316	**800-321-2136***	330-796-2121	744
NASDAQ: GT ■ *Cust Svc						
Goold Health Systems Inc						
PO Box 1090	Augusta	ME	04332	**800-832-9672**	207-622-7153	225
Goose Creek State Park						
2190 Camp Leach Rd	Washington	NC	27889	**877-722-6762**	252-923-2191	558
Gooseberry Falls State Park						
3206 Hwy 61	Two Harbors	MN	55616	**888-646-6367**	218-834-3855	558
Gooseneck Trailer Mfg Co						
4400 E Hwy 21 PO Box 832	Bryan	TX	77808	**800-688-5490***	979-778-0034	753
*Cust Svc						
Gopher Sign Co						
1310 Randolph Ave	Saint Paul	MN	55105	**800-383-3156**	651-698-5095	692
Gordman 12100 W Ctr Rd	Omaha	NE	68144	**800-456-7463**	402-691-4000	229
Gordon Bros Group LLC						
101 Huntington Ave 10th Fl	Boston	MA	02199	**888-424-1903**		50
Gordon Brush Mfg Company Inc						
6247 Randolph St	Commerce	CA	90040	**800-950-7950**	323-724-7777	102
Gordon College						
255 Grapevine Rd	Wenham	MA	01984	**800-343-1379**	978-927-2300	166
Gordon County Chamber of Commerce						
300 S Wall St	Calhoun	GA	30701	**800-887-3811**	706-625-3200	137
Gordon Paper Company Inc						
PO Box 1806	Norfolk	VA	23501	**800-457-7366**	757-464-3581	545-2
Gordon Trucking Inc						
151 Stewart Rd SW	Pacific	WA	98047	**800-426-8486**	253-863-7777	770
Gordon-Conwell Theological Seminary						
130 Essex St	South Hamilton	MA	01982	**800-428-7329**	978-468-7111	167-3
Goria Enterprises						
PO Box 14489	Greensboro	NC	27415	**800-446-7421**		184
Gorton's Inc						
128 Rogers St	Gloucester	MA	01930	**800-222-6846**	978-283-3000	295-14
Goshen Chamber of Commerce						
232 S Main St	Goshen	IN	46526	**800-307-4204**	574-533-2102	137
Goshen College						
1700 S Main St	Goshen	IN	46526	**800-348-7422**	574-535-7000	166
Goshen News						
114 S Main St PO Box 569	Goshen	IN	46527	**800-487-2151**	574-533-2151	525-2
Gosiger Inc						
108 McDonough St	Dayton	OH	45402	**877-288-1538**	937-228-5174	382
GoSolo Technologies Inc						
5410 Mariner St Ste 175	Tampa	FL	33609	**866-246-7656**		610
Gospel Light Publications						
1957 Eastman Ave	Ventura	CA	93003	**800-446-7735**	805-644-9721	628-3
Gospel Publishing House						
1445 N Boonville Ave	Springfield	MO	65802	**800-641-4310***	417-862-2781	618
*Orders						
Goss Inc						
1511 William Flynn Hwy	Glenshaw	PA	15116	**800-367-4677**	412-486-6100	798
Gossen /Corp						
2030 W Bender Rd	Milwaukee	WI	53209	**800-558-8984**	414-228-9800	192-2
Gossner Foods Inc						
1051 N 1000 W	Logan	UT	84321	**800-944-0454**	435-713-6100	295-5
Gotham Distributing Corp						
60 Portland Rd	Conshohocken	PA	19428	**800-446-8426**	610-649-7650	516
Gotham Sales Co						
302 Main St	Millburn	NJ	07041	**800-292-7726**	973-912-8412	37
Goucher College						
1021 Dulaney Vly Rd	Towson	MD	21204	**800-468-2437**	410-337-6000	166
Gougler Industries Inc						
711 Lake St	Kent	OH	44240	**800-527-2282**	330-673-5826	383
Gould & Goodrich Leather Inc						
709 E McNeil St	Lillington	NC	27546	**800-277-0732**	910-893-2071	428
Gould Paper Corp						
11 Madison Ave 14th Fl	New York	NY	10010	**800-275-4685**	212-301-0000	546
Goulds Pumps Inc Goulds Water Technologies Group						
240 Fall St	Seneca Falls	NY	13148	**800-327-7700**	315-568-2811	777
Gouverneur Hotel Montreal (Place-Dupuis)						
1000 Sherbrooke St W Ste 2300	Montreal	QC	H3A3R3	**888-910-1111**		376
Govconnection Inc						
7503 Standish Pl	Rockville	MD	20855	**800-998-0009**		180
Gove Group Real Estate LLC						
70 Portsmouth Ave	Stratham	NH	03885	**866-778-6400**	603-778-6400	643
Governing Magazine						
1100 Connecticut Ave NW						
Ste 1300	Washington	DC	20036	**800-940-6039**	202-862-8802	452-12
Government Employee Relations Report						
1801 S Bell St	Arlington	VA	22202	**800-372-1033**		524-2
Government Island State Recreation Area						
725 Summer St NE Ste C	Salem	OR	97301	**800-551-6949**		558
Government Liaison Services Inc (GLS)						
200 N Glebe Rd Ste 321	Arlington	VA	22203	**800-642-6564**	703-524-8200	626
Government Research Service						
1516 SW Boswell Ave	Topeka	KS	66604	**800-346-6898**	785-232-7720	628-2
Governor Calvert House						
58 State Cir	Annapolis	MD	21401	**800-847-8882**	410-263-2641	376
Governor Daniel Dunklin's Grave State Historic Site						
PO Box 176 2901 Hwy 61	Jefferson City	MO	65102	**800-334-6946**		558
Governor Hotel						
621 S Capitol Way	Olympia	WA	98501	**800-716-6199**	360-352-7700	376
Governor Patterson Memorial State Recreation Site						
5580 S Coast Hwy						
5580 S Coast Hwy	Newport	OR	97394	**800-551-6949**		558
Governor's Inn						
210 Richards Blvd	Sacramento	CA	95814	**800-999-6689**	916-448-7224	376
Governors State University						
1 University Pkwy	University Park	IL	6048	**800-478-8478**	708-534-5000	166
Gowan Company LLC						
PO Box 5569	Yuma	AZ	85366	**800-883-1844**	928-783-8844	276
Gowans-Knight Co Inc						
49 Knight St	Watertown	CT	06795	**800-352-4871**	860-274-8801	509
Goyette Mechanical Co						
3842 Gorey Ave	Flint	MI	48501	**877-469-3883**	810-743-6883	190-10
GP Strategies Corp						
11000 Broken Land Parkway						
Suite 200	Columbia	MD	21044	**888-843-4784**	443-367-9600	181
Gpa Specialty Printable Sbstrt						
8740 W 50th St	McCook	IL	60525	**800-395-9000**	773-650-2020	546
GPB (Georgia Public Broadcasting)						
260 14th St NW	Atlanta	GA	30318	**800-222-6006**		624
GPB Education						
260 14th St NW	Atlanta	GA	30318	**888-501-8960**	404-685-2550	624
GPCCVB (Greenville-Pitt County Convention & Visitors Bureau)						
303 SW Greenville Blvd						
PO Box 8027	Greenville	NC	27835	**800-537-5564**	252-329-4200	207
GPhA (Generic Pharmaceutical Assn)						
2300 Clarendon Blvd Ste 400	Arlington	VA	22201	**800-859-8003**	703-647-2480	48-19
GPK Products Inc						
1601 43rd St NW	Fargo	ND	58102	**800-437-4670**	701-277-3225	601
GPM Industries Inc						
110 Gateway Dr	Macon	GA	31210	**888-476-7867**	478-471-7867	632
GPO (US Government Printing Office Bookstore)						
732 N Capitol St NW	Washington	DC	20401	**866-512-1800**	202-512-1800	340
GPRMC (Great Plains Regional Medical Ctr)						
601 W Leota St PO Box 1167	North Platte	NE	69101	**800-662-0011**	308-696-8000	371-3
GPSB (Grant Parish School Board)						
512 Main St PO Box 208	Colfax	LA	71417	**877-277-3812**	318-627-3274	187
GRAA (Greater Rockford Auto Auction Inc)						
5937 Sandy Hollow Rd	Rockford	IL	61109	**800-830-4722**	815-874-7800	50
Graber Olive House Inc						
315 E Fourth St	Ontario	CA	91764	**800-996-5483**		334
Grabill Cabinet Company Inc						
13844 Sawmill Dr	Grabill	IN	46741	**877-472-2782**		114
Grace A Dow Memorial Library						
1710 W St Andrews Rd	Midland	MI	48640	**888-400-5530**	989-837-3430	431-3
Grace Bible College						
1011 Aldon St SW						
PO Box 910	Grand Rapids	MI	49509	**800-968-1887**	616-538-2330	159
Grace College						
200 Seminary Dr	Winona Lake	IN	46590	**800-544-7223**	574-372-5100	166
Grace Communion International						
PO Box 5005	Glendora	CA	91740	**800-423-4444**	626-650-2300	628-9
Grace Darex Packaging Technologies						
62 Whittemore Ave	Cambridge	MA	02140	**866-333-3726**	617-498-4987	3

	Toll-Free	Phone	Class
Grace Davison			
7500 Grace Dr ....Columbia MD 21044	**800-638-6014**	410-531-4000	143
Grace Financial Group LLC			
83 Jobs Ln ....Southampton NY 11968	**866-817-6047**	631-287-4633	681
Grace Theological Seminary			
200 Seminary Dr ....Winona Lake IN 46590	**800-544-7223**	574-372-5100	167-3
Grace University			
1311 S Ninth St ....Omaha NE 68108	**800-383-1422**	402-449-2800	159
Graceland (Elvis Presley Mansion)			
3734 Elvis Presley Blvd ....Memphis TN 38116	**800-238-2000**	901-332-3322	513
Graceland Fruit Inc			
1123 Main St ....Frankfort MI 49635	**800-352-7181**	231-352-7181	295-18
Graceland University			
1 University Pl ....Lamoni IA 50140	**800-859-1215**	641-784-5000	166
Graceland University Independence			
1401 W Truman Rd ....Independence MO 64050	**800-833-0524**	816-833-0524	166
Gracious Home			
1220 Third Ave ....New York NY 10021	**800-338-7809**	212-517-6300	359
Graco Inc			
88 11th Ave NE PO Box 1441........Minneapolis MN 55413	**800-328-0211***	612-623-6000	632
NYSE: GGG ■ *Cust Svc			
Grade Finders Inc			
PO Box 944 ....Exton PA 19341	**800-777-8074**	610-524-7070	628-2
Graduate Management Admission Council (GMAC)			
11921 Freedom Dr Ste 300.........Reston VA 20190	**866-505-6559**	703-668-9600	47-11
Graduate Theological Union			
2400 Ridge Rd ....Berkeley CA 94709	**800-826-4488**	510-649-2400	167-3
Grady Electric Membership Corp (EMC)			
1499 US Hwy 84 W PO Box 270..........Cairo GA 39828	**800-942-4362**	229-377-4182	245
Grady Management Inc			
8630 Fenton St Ste 625 ....Silver Spring MD 20910	**800-544-7239**	301-587-3330	646
Grady Memorial Hospital			
2220 Iowa Ave ....Chickasha OK 73018	**800-299-9665**	405-224-2300	371-3
Graebel Van Lines Inc			
16346 Airport Cir ....Aurora CO 80011	**800-568-0031**	303-214-6683	512
Graeter's Inc			
2145 Reading Rd ....Cincinnati OH 45202	**800-721-3323**	513-721-3323	295-25
Graff Truck Centers Inc			
1401 S Saginaw St ....Flint MI 48503	**888-870-4203**	810-239-8300	56
Grafton National Cemetery			
431 Walnut St ....Grafton WV 26354	**800-535-1117**	304-265-2044	135
Grafton on Sunset			
8462 W Sunset Blvd ....West Hollywood CA 90069	**800-821-3660**	323-654-4600	376
Graham Architectural Products Corp			
1551 Mt Rose Ave ....York PA 17403	**800-755-6274**	717-849-8100	234
Graham Cadillac			
1515 W Fourth St ....Mansfield OH 44906	**866-472-4261**		509
Graham Co, The			
One Penn Sq W 25th Fl ....Philadelphia PA 19102	**888-472-4262**	215-567-6300	387
Graham Corp			
20 Florence Ave ....Batavia NY 14020	**800-828-8150***	585-343-2216	383
NYSE: GHM ■ *Orders			
Graham County			
34 Wall St Suite 407..............Asheville NC 28801	**866-962-6246**	828-255-0182	336
Graham County Chamber of Commerce			
1111 Thatcher Blvd ....Safford AZ 85546	**888-837-1841**	928-428-2511	137
Graham County Electric Inc			
9 W Center St ....Pima AZ 85543	**800-577-9266**	928-485-2451	245
Graham Medical Products			
2273 Larsen Rd ....Green Bay WI 54303	**800-558-6765***	920-494-8701	569
*Cust Svc			
Graham, The			
1075 Thomas Jefferson St NW ......Washington DC 20007	**855-341-1292**	202-337-0900	376
Grain Belt Supply Company Inc			
PO Box 615 ....Salina KS 67402	**800-447-0522**	785-827-4491	475
Grain Dealers Mutual Insurance Co			
6201 Corporate Dr ....Indianapolis IN 46278	**800-428-7081**	317-388-4500	388-4
Grambling State University			
403 Main St ....Grambling LA 71245	**800-569-4714**	318-247-3811	166
Gramercy Park Hotel			
2 Lexington Ave ....New York NY 10010	**866-784-1300**	212-920-3300	376
Grammer Industries Inc			
18375 E 345 S ....Grammer IN 47236	**800-333-7410**	812-579-5655	770
Grammy Magazine			
3030 Olympic Blvd ....Santa Monica CA 90404	**800-423-2017**	310-392-3777	452-9
Grand 1894 Opera House			
2020 Postoffice St ....Galveston TX 77550	**800-821-1894**	409-765-1894	565
Grand Aerie Fraternal Order of Eagles			
1623 Gateway Cir S ....Grove City OH 43123	**877-829-5500**	614-883-2200	47-15
Grand Aire Express Inc			
11777 W Airport Service Rd ....Swanton OH 43558	**800-704-7263**		62
Grand America Hotel			
555 S Main St ....Salt Lake City UT 84111	**800-621-4505**	801-258-6000	376
Grand Blanc Cement Products			
10709 Ctr Rd ....Grand Blanc MI 48439	**800-875-7500**	810-694-7500	184
Grand Canyon University			
3300 W Camelback Rd ....Phoenix AZ 85017	**800-800-9776**	602-639-7500	166
Grand Casino Hinckley			
777 Lady Luck Dr ....Hinckley MN 55037	**800-472-6321**		132
Grand Casino Mille Lacs			
777 Grand Ave PO Box 343 ....Onamia MN 56359	**800-626-5825**		132
Grand Country Inn			
Grand Country Sq 1945 W Hwy 76.......Branson MO 65616	**888-505-4096**	417-335-3535	376
Grand Del Mar			
5300 Grand Del Mar Ct ....San Diego CA 92130	**855-314-2030**	858-314-2000	376
Grand Electric Co-op Inc			
801 Coleman Ave PO Box 39 ....Bison SD 57620	**800-592-1803**	605-244-5211	245
Grand European Tours			
6000 Meadows Rd Ste 520.........Lake Oswego OR 97035	**877-622-9109**	503-718-2262	750
Grand Forks Chamber of Commerce			
202 N Third St ....Grand Forks ND 58203	**855-233-6362**	701-772-7271	137
Grand Gateway Hotel			
1721 N LaCrosse St ....Rapid City SD 57701	**866-742-1300**	605-342-8853	376
Grand Geneva Resort & Spa			
7036 Grand Geneva Way ....Lake Geneva WI 53147	**800-558-3417**	262-248-8811	660
Grand Harbor Resort & Waterpark			
350 Bell St ....Dubuque IA 52001	**866-690-4006**	563-690-4000	660
Grand Hotel & Suites Toronto			
225 Jarvis St ....Toronto ON M5B2C1	**877-324-7263**	416-863-9000	376
Grand Hotel Marriott Resort Golf Club & Spa			
One Grand Blvd PO Box 639..........Point Clear AL 36564	**800-544-9933**	251-928-9201	698
Grand Hotel Minneapolis, The			
615 Second Ave S ....Minneapolis MN 55402	**866-843-4726**	612-288-8888	376

	Toll-Free	Phone	Class
Grand Hyatt Kauai Resort & Spa			
1571 Poipu Rd ....Koloa HI 96756	**800-233-1234**	808-742-1234	660
Grand Island Independent			
422 W First St ....Grand Island NE 68801	**800-658-3160**	308-382-1000	525-2
Grand Island Veterans' Home			
2300 W Capital Ave ....Grand Island NE 68803	**800-358-8802**	308-385-6252	781
Grand Isle State Park			
Admiral Craik Dr ....Grand Isle LA 70358	**888-787-2559**	985-787-2559	558
Grand Junction Area Chamber of Commerce			
360 Grand Ave ....Grand Junction CO 81501	**800-352-5286**	970-242-3214	137
Grand Junction Visitors & Convention Bureau			
740 Horizon Dr ....Grand Junction CO 81506	**800-962-2547**	970-244-1480	207
Grand Lake Gardens			
401 Santa Clara Ave ....Oakland CA 94610	**800-416-6091**		663
Grand Lodge Crested Butte			
12 Snowmass Rd ....Crested Butte CO 81224	**877-547-5143**	970-349-2222	660
Grand Oaks Hotel			
2315 Green Mountain Dr ....Branson MO 65616	**800-553-6423**		376
Grand Pacific Palisades Resort & Hotel			
5805 Armada Dr ....Carlsbad CA 92008	**800-725-4723**	760-827-3200	660
Grand Palms Hotel & Golf Resort			
110 Grand Palms Dr ....Pembroke Pines FL 33027	**800-327-9246**	954-431-8800	660
Grand Portage Lodge & Casino			
PO Box 233 ....Grand Portage MN 55605	**800-543-1384**	218-475-2401	660
Grand Portage State Park			
9393 E Hwy 61 ....Grand Portage MN 55605	**888-646-6367**	218-475-2360	558
Grand Rapids Area Chamber of Commerce			
One NW Third St ....Grand Rapids MN 55744	**800-472-6366**	218-326-6619	137
Grand Rapids Art Museum			
101 Monroe Ctr ....Grand Rapids MI 49503	**800-272-8258**	616-831-1000	513
Grand Rapids Civic Theatre			
30 N Div Ave ....Grand Rapids MI 49503	**866-455-4728**	616-222-6650	565
Grand Rapids Label Co			
2351 Oak Industrial Dr NE ......Grand Rapids MI 49505	**800-552-5215**	616-459-8134	410
Grand Rapids/Kent County Convention & Visitors Bureau			
171 Monroe Ave NW Ste 700 ......Grand Rapids MI 49503	**800-678-9859**	616-459-8287	207
Grand Sierra Resort & Casino			
2500 E Second St ....Reno NV 89595	**800-501-2651**	775-789-2000	660
Grand Strand Regional Medical Ctr			
809 82nd Pkwy ....Myrtle Beach SC 29572	**800-342-2383**	843-692-1000	371-3
Grand Summit Hotel			
570 Springfield Ave ....Summit NJ 07901	**800-346-0773**	908-273-3000	376
Grand Targhee Resort			
3300 E Ski Hill Rd ....Alta WY 83414	**800-827-4433**	307-353-2300	660
Grand Teton Lodge Co			
5 Miles N Hwy 89 PO Box 250 ....Moran WY 83013	**800-628-9988***	307-543-2811	660
*Resv			
Grand Traverse Resort & Spa			
100 Grand Traverse Blvd PO Box 404.......Acme MI 49610	**800-236-1577**	231-534-6000	660
Grand Valley Rural Power Lines Inc			
845 22 Rd PO Box 190 ....Grand Junction CO 81505	**877-760-7435**	970-242-0040	245
Grand Valley State University			
1 Campus Dr ....Allendale MI 49401	**800-748-0246**	616-331-5000	166
Grand Valley State University Zumberge Library			
One Campus Dr ....Allendale MI 49401	**800-879-0581**	616-331-3252	431-6
Grand View College			
1200 Grandview Ave ....Des Moines IA 50316	**800-444-6083**	515-263-2800	166
Grand View Lodge			
23521 Nokomis Ave ....Nisswa MN 56468	**866-801-2951**	218-963-2234	660
Grand View Media Group Inc (GVMG)			
200 Croft St Ste 1 ....Birmingham AL 35242	**888-431-2877**	205-408-3700	628-9
Grand Wailea Resort & Spa			
3850 Wailea Alanui Dr ....Wailea HI 96753	**800-888-6100**	808-875-1234	660
Grand, The			
818 N Market St ....Wilmington DE 19801	**800-374-7263**	302-658-7897	565
Grande Cheese Co			
301 E Main St ....Lomira WI 53048	**800-772-3210**		295-5
Grande Colonial			
910 Prospect St ....La Jolla CA 92037	**888-828-5498**		376
Grande Prairie Public Library			
3479 W 183rd St ....Hazel Crest IL 60429	**800-321-9511**	708-798-5563	431-3
Grandite Inc			
PO Box 47133 ....Quebec QC G1S4X1	**866-808-3932**	581-318-2018	179-1
Grandma's Saloon & Grill			
522 Lake Ave S ....Duluth MN 55802	**800-706-7672**	218-727-4192	662
Grandmother's Buttons Museum			
9814 Royal St ....Saint Francisville LA 70775	**800-580-6941**	225-635-4107	513
Grandover Resort & Conference Ctr			
1000 Club Rd ....Greensboro NC 27407	**800-472-6301**	336-294-1800	374
Grandview Products Co			
1601 Superior Dr ....Parsons KS 67357	**800-247-9105**	620-421-6950	114
Grandwell Industries Inc			
121 Quantum St ....Holly Springs NC 27540	**800-338-6554***	919-557-1221	692
*Cust Svc			
Grange Insurance			
671 S High St ....Columbus OH 43206	**800-422-0550**		388-2
Grangetto's Farm & Garden Supply Co			
1105 W Mission Ave ....Escondido CA 92025	**800-536-4671**	760-745-4671	276
Grangeville Environmental Services (GES)			
GES Property Pros LLC			
585 McAllister St ....Hanover PA 17331	**866-437-5151**	717-637-6152	83
Granite City Electric Supply Co			
19 Quincy Ave ....Quincy MA 02169	**800-850-9400**	617-472-6500	359
Granite City Journal			
Two Executive Dr ....Collinsville IL 62234	**800-766-3278**	618-877-7700	525-4
Granite Falls Energy LLC			
15045 Hwy 23 SE ....Granite Falls MN 56241	**877-485-8595**	320-564-3100	296-8
Granite Falls School District			
307 N Alder Ave ....Granite Falls WA 98252	**888-651-8931**	360-691-7717	676
Granite Farms Estates			
1343 W Baltimore Pike ....Media PA 19063	**888-499-2287**	610-358-3440	663
Granite Group Wholesalers LLC			
6 Storrs St ....Concord NH 03301	**800-258-3690**	603-224-1901	605
Granite Knitwear Inc			
805 S Salberry Ave			
Hwy 52S ....Granite Quarry NC 28072	**800-476-9944***	704-279-5526	153-11
*Cust Svc			
Granite State College			
Eight Old Suncook Rd ....Concord NH 03301	**888-228-3000**	603-228-3000	166
Granite State Manufacturing Co			
124 Joliette St ....Manchester NH 03102	**800-464-7646**		449
Granite Telecommunications LLC			
100 Newport Ave Ext ....Quincy MA 02171	**866-847-1500**	617-933-5500	726

	Toll-Free	Phone	Class
Graniterock Co			
350 Technology Dr			
PO Box 50001 .... Watsonville CA 95077	**888-762-5100**	831-768-2000	192-1
Grant Assembly Technologies			
90 Silliman Ave .... Bridgeport CT 06605	**800-227-2150**	203-366-4557	451
Grant County			
301 W Main St .... John Day OR 97845	**800-769-5664**	541-575-0547	336
Grant Parish School Board (GPSB)			
512 Main St PO Box 208 .... Colfax LA 71417	**877-277-3812**	318-627-3274	187
Grant Piston Rings			
1360 Jefferson St .... Anaheim CA 92807	**800-854-3540**	714-996-0050	127
Grant Plaza Hotel			
465 Grant Ave .... San Francisco CA 94108	**800-472-6899**	415-434-3883	376
Grants Pass Chamber of Commerce			
1995 NW Vine St PO Box 970 .... Grants Pass OR 97526	**800-547-5927**	541-476-7717	137
Grants Pass Visitors & Convention Bureau			
1995 NW Vine St .... Grants Pass OR 97526	**800-547-5927**	541-476-5510	207
Grants State Bank			
824 W Santa Fe Ave PO Box 1088 .... Grants NM 87020	**877-285-6611**	505-285-6611	69
Grants.gov			
Dept of Health & Human Services			
200 Independence Ave SW			
HHH Bldg .... Washington DC 20201	**800-518-4726**		198
Grants/Cibola County Chamber of Commerce			
100 N Iron Ave .... Grants NM 87020	**866-270-5110**	505-287-4802	137
Granville Island Hotel			
1253 Johnston St .... Vancouver BC V6H3R9	**800-663-1840***	604-683-7373	376
*Resv			
Grapevine Canyon Ranch Inc			
PO Box 302 .... Pearce AZ 85625	**800-245-9202**	520-826-3185	239
Grapevine Chamber of Commerce			
200 Vine St .... Grapevine TX 76051	**866-322-8667**	817-481-1522	137
Grapevine Convention Ctr, The			
1209 S Main St .... Grapevine TX 76051	**866-782-7897**	817-410-3459	206
Graphel Corp			
6115 Centre Pk Dr			
PO Box 369. .... West Chester OH 45071	**800-255-1104**	513-779-6166	495
Graphic Controls LLC			
400 Exchange St .... Buffalo NY 14204	**800-669-1535**		620
Graphic Converting LLC			
877 N Larch Ave .... Elmhurst IL 60126	**800-447-1935**	630-758-4100	547
Graphic Packaging International			
1500 Riveredge Parkway NW .... Atlanta GA 30328	**888-548-8395**	770-240-7200	100
NYSE: GPK			
Graphic Products Inc			
PO Box 4030 .... Beaverton OR 97076	**888-326-9244**	503-644-5572	175
Graphic Reproduction			
1381 Franquette Ave Bldg B1 .... Concord CA 94520	**800-498-9939**	925-674-0900	341
Graphic Specialties Inc			
3110 Washington Ave N .... Minneapolis MN 55411	**800-486-4605**	612-522-5287	692
Graphique De France			
Nine State St .... Woburn MA 01801	**800-444-1464***	781-935-3405	129
*Sales			
Graphite Sales Inc			
16710 W Pk Cir Dr .... Chagrin Falls OH 44023	**800-321-4147**	440-543-8221	495
Graphnet Inc			
40 Fultron St 28th Fl. .... New York NY 10038	**800-327-1800**	212-994-1100	726
Grass America Inc			
1202 Hwy 66 S .... Kernersville NC 27284	**800-334-3512**		347
Grassland Dairy Products Company Inc			
N 8790 Fairgrounds Ave			
PO Box 160. .... Greenwood WI 54437	**800-428-8837**	715-267-6182	295-3
Grassland Equipment & Irrigation Corp			
892-898 Troy Schenectady Rd .... Latham NY 12110	**800-564-5587**	518-785-5841	426
Grassley Group, The (FMCI)			
409 Washington St Ste A .... Cedar Falls IA 50613	**866-619-5580**		46
Grassroots Motorsports Magazine			
915 Ridgewood Ave .... Holly Hill FL 32117	**800-520-8292**	386-239-0523	452-3
Gratz College			
7605 Old York Rd .... Melrose Park PA 19027	**800-475-4635**	215-635-7300	166
Gratz Park Inn			
120 W Second St .... Lexington KY 40507	**800-752-4166**	859-231-1777	662
Graver Technologies LLC			
200 Lake Dr .... Newark DE 19702	**800-249-1990**	302-731-1700	794
Graver Water Systems			
675 Central Ave Ste 3 .... New Providence NJ 07974	**877-472-8379**	908-516-1400	794
Graves Lumber Co			
1315 S Cleveland-Massillon Rd .... Copley OH 44321	**877-500-5515**	330-666-1115	494
Graves Piano & Organ Company Inc			
5798 Karl Rd .... Columbus OH 43229	**800-686-4322**	614-847-4322	519
Gravograph-New Hermes Inc			
2200 Northmont Pkwy .... Duluth GA 30096	**800-843-7637**	770-623-0331	621
Gray & Sons Inc			
430 W Padonia Rd .... Timonium MD 21093	**800-254-0752**	410-771-4311	189-4
Gray Construction			
10 Quality St .... Lexington KY 40507	**800-814-8468**	859-281-5000	187
Gray Glass Co			
217-44 98th Ave .... Queens Village NY 11429	**800-523-3320**	718-217-2943	328
Gray Transportation Inc			
2459 GT Dr .... Waterloo IA 50703	**800-234-3930**	319-234-3930	676
Graybar Electric Co Inc			
34 N Meramec Ave .... Saint Louis MO 63105	**800-472-9227**	314-573-9200	246
Grayling Industries			
1008 Branch Dr .... Alpharetta GA 30004	**800-635-1551**	770-751-9095	541
Graymills Corp			
3705 N Lincoln Ave .... Chicago IL 60613	**877-465-7867**	773-477-4100	632
Grays Harbor Chamber of Commerce			
506 Duffy St .... Aberdeen WA 98520	**800-321-1924**	360-532-1924	137
Grays Harbor College			
1620 Edward P Smith Dr .... Aberdeen WA 98520	**800-562-4830**	360-532-9020	160
Grays Harbor Raceway			
32 Elma McCleary Rd PO Box 768 .... Elma WA 98541	**800-667-7711**	360-482-4374	633
Grays Harbor Tourism			
PO Box 1229 .... Elma WA 98541	**800-621-9625**	360-482-2651	207
Grayson Rural Electric Co-op Corp			
109 Bagby Pk .... Grayson KY 41143	**800-562-3532**	606-474-5136	245
Grayson-Collin Electric Co-op (GCEC)			
PO Box 548 .... Van Alstyne TX 75495	**800-967-5235**	903-482-7100	245
GrayWolf Sensing Solutions LLC			
Six Research Dr .... Shelton CT 06484	**800-218-7997**	203-402-0477	416
GRE America Inc			
425 Harbor Blvd .... Belmont CA 94002	**800-233-5973**	650-591-1400	174-3
Grease Monkey International			
7450 E Progress Pl .... Greenwood Village CO 80111	**800-822-7706**	303-308-1660	61-5

	Toll-Free	Phone	Class
Great American Bancorp Inc			
1311 S Neil St .... Champaign IL 61820	**800-962-4284**	217-356-2265	357-2
OTC: GTPS			
Great American Cookie Company Inc			
1346 Oakbrook Dr Ste 170 .... Norcross GA 30093	**877-639-2361**		67
Great American Home Store			
5295 Pepper Chase Dr .... Southaven MS 38671	**877-303-1964**	662-996-1000	320
Great American Products Inc			
1661 S Seguin Ave .... New Braunfels TX 78130	**800-341-4436**	830-620-4400	693
Great American Supplemental Benefits			
PO Box 26580 .... Austin TX 78755	**866-459-4272**		388-3
Great Arrow Graphics			
2495 Main St Ste 457. .... Buffalo NY 14214	**800-835-0490**	716-836-0408	129
Great Basin College			
1500 College Pkwy .... Elko NV 89801	**888-590-6726**	775-738-8493	166
Great Books Foundation			
35 E Wacker Dr Ste 400 .... Chicago IL 60601	**800-222-5870**	312-332-5870	47-11
Great Clips Inc			
7700 France Ave S Ste 425. .... Minneapolis MN 55435	**800-999-5959**	952-893-9088	76
Great Day Improvements LLC			
700 E Highland Rd .... Macedonia OH 44056	**800-230-8301**	330-468-0700	236
Great Divide Lodge			
550 Village Rd PO Box 8059 ...... Breckenridge CO 80424	**888-400-9590**	970-547-5550	376
Great Events & TEAMS Inc			
2170 S Parker Rd Ste 290. .... Denver CO 80231	**866-706-7814**	303-394-2022	185
Great Falls Area Chamber of Commerce			
100 First Ave N .... Great Falls MT 59401	**800-735-8535**	406-761-4434	137
Great Falls Marketing LLC			
121 Mill St .... Auburn ME 04210	**800-221-8895**		196
Great Falls Tribune			
205 River Dr S .... Great Falls MT 59405	**800-438-6600**	406-791-1444	525-2
Great Harvest Bread Co			
28 S Montana St .... Dillon MT 59725	**800-442-0424**	406-683-6842	67
Great Lakes Aviation Ltd			
1022 Airport Pkwy .... Cheyenne WY 82001	**800-554-5111**	307-432-7000	25
OTC: GLUX			
Great Lakes Christian College			
6211 W Willow Hwy .... Lansing MI 48917	**800-937-4522***	517-321-0242	159
*Admissions			
Great Lakes Crossing Outlets			
4000 Baldwin Rd .... Auburn Hills MI 48326	**877-746-7452**	248-454-5000	49-5
Great Lakes Cruise Co			
3270 Washtenaw Ave .... Ann Arbor MI 48104	**888-891-0203**		220
Great Lakes Energy Co-op			
1323 Boyne Ave .... Boyne City MI 49712	**888-485-2537**		245
Great Lakes Filters			
301 Arch Ave .... Hillsdale MI 49242	**800-521-8565**		18
Great Lakes Mall			
7850 Mentor Ave .... Mentor OH 44060	**877-746-6642**	440-255-6900	455
Great Lakes Orthodontic Laboratories Div			
200 Cooper Ave .... Tonawanda NY 14150	**800-828-7626**		228
Great Lakes Packaging Corp			
W 190 N 11393 Carnegie Dr .... Germantown WI 53022	**800-261-4572**	262-255-2100	99
Great Lakes Towing Co			
4500 Div Ave .... Cleveland OH 44102	**800-321-3663**	216-621-4854	460
Great Neck Saw Manufacturing Inc			
165 E Second St .... Mineola NY 11501	**800-457-0600***	516-746-5352	673
*Cust Svc			
Great Northern Corp			
395 Stroebe Rd .... Appleton WI 54914	**800-236-3671**	920-739-3671	99
Great Northern Insurance Co			
15 Mtn View Rd .... Warren NJ 07059	**800-252-4670***	908-903-2000	388-4
*Cust Svc			
Great Northern Iron Ore Properties			
332 Minnesota St Rm W1290. .... Saint Paul MN 55101	**800-468-9716**	651-224-2385	666
NYSE: GNI			
Great Pacific Fixed Income Securities Inc			
151 Kalmus Dr Ste H-8. .... Costa Mesa CA 92626	**800-284-4804**	714-619-3000	681
Great Plains Coca-Cola Bottling Company Inc			
600 N May Ave .... Oklahoma City OK 73107	**800-753-2653**	405-280-2000	79-2
Great Plains Health Alliance Inc			
625 Third St .... Phillipsburg KS 67661	**800-432-2779**	785-543-2111	350
Great Plains Industries Inc			
5252 E 36th St N .... Wichita KS 67220	**800-835-0113***	316-686-7361	632
*Sales			
Great Plains Nature Ctr			
6232 E 29th St N .... Wichita KS 67220	**800-222-1222**	316-683-5499	49-4
Great Plains Regional Medical Ctr (GPRMC)			
601 W Leota St PO Box 1167 .... North Platte NE 69101	**800-662-0011**	308-696-8000	371-3
Great Plains State Park			
22487 E 1566 Rd .... Mountain Park OK 73559	**800-622-6317**	580-569-2032	558
Great Planes Model Distributors			
PO Box 9021 .... Champaign IL 61826	**800-637-7660**	217-398-3630	752
Great River Bluffs State Park			
43605 Kipp Dr .... Winona MN 55987	**888-646-6367**	507-643-6849	558
Great River Energy			
12300 Elm Creek Blvd .... Maple Grove MN 55369	**888-521-0130**	763-445-5000	245
Great Salt Lake Book Festival			
Utah Humanities Council			
202 W 300 N. .... Salt Lake City UT 84103	**877-786-7598**	801-359-9670	281
Great Seats Inc			
7338 Baltimore Ave			
Ste 108A. .... College Park MD 20740	**800-664-5056**	301-985-6250	740
Great Source Education Group			
181 Ballardvale St .... Wilmington MA 01887	**800-289-4490**		243
Great Southern Wood Preserving Inc			
1100 US Hwy 431 N .... Abbeville AL 36310	**800-633-7539**	334-585-2291	805
Great Steak & Potato Co			
9311 E Via de Ventura .... Scottsdale AZ 85258	**866-452-4252**	480-362-4800	661
Great West Casualty Co			
1100 W 29th St			
PO Box 277. .... South Sioux City NE 68776	**800-228-8602**	402-494-2084	388-4
Great Western Bank			
6015 NW Radial Hwy .... Omaha NE 68104	**800-952-2043**	402-952-6000	69
Great Western Mfg Co Inc			
2017 S Fourth St PO Box 149. ...... Leavenworth KS 66048	**800-682-3121**	913-682-2291	297
Great Wolf Lodge Williamsburg			
549 E Rochambeau Dr .... Williamsburg VA 23188	**800-551-9653**	757-229-9700	660
Greater Atlanta Christian			
1575 Indian Trl Lilburn Rd .... Norcross GA 30093	**800-450-1327**	770-243-2000	47-20
Greater Atlantic City Chamber			
12 S Virginia Ave .... Atlantic City NJ 08401	**800-123-4567**	609-345-4524	137
Greater Austin Chamber of Commerce			
535 E 5th St .... Austin TX 78701	**888-409-5380**	512-478-9383	137

Name / Address	City	State	ZIP	Toll-Free	Phone	Class
Greater Bakersfield Convention & Visitors Bureau						
515 Truxtun Ave	Bakersfield	CA	93301	**866-425-7353**	661-852-7282	207
Greater Bangor Convention & Visitors Bureau						
40 Harlow St	Bangor	ME	04401	**800-916-6673**	207-947-5205	207
Greater Beloit Chamber of Commerce						
500 Public Ave	Beloit	WI	53511	**866-981-5969**	608-365-8835	137
Greater Bethesda-Chevy Chase Chamber of Commerce						
7910 Woodmont Ave Ste 1204	Bethesda	MD	20814	**800-333-6778**	301-652-4900	137
Greater Big Rapids Convention & Visitors Bureau						
246 N State St	Big Rapids	MI	49307	**800-999-9069**	231-796-7640	207
Greater Birmingham Convention & Visitors Bureau						
2200 Ninth Ave N	Birmingham	AL	35203	**800-458-8085**	205-458-8000	207
Greater Boca Raton Chamber of Commerce						
1800 N Dixie Hwy	Boca Raton	FL	33432	**800-435-7352**	561-395-4433	137
Greater Boston Convention & Visitors Bureau (GBCVB)						
Two Copley Pl Ste 105	Boston	MA	02116	**888-733-2678**	617-536-4100	207
Greater Bridgeport Conference & Vistors Ctr						
164 W Main St	Bridgeport	WV	26330	**800-368-4324**	304-842-7272	207
Greater Bristol Chamber of Commerce						
200 Main St	Bristol	CT	06010	**855-344-1874**	860-584-4718	137
Greater Cedar Creek Lake Area Chamber of Commerce						
604 S Third St Ste E	Mabank	TX	75147	**800-331-6844**	903-887-3152	137
Greater Cedar Valley Chamber of Commerce						
10 W 4th St Ste 310	Waterloo	IA	50703	**800-288-1047**	319-232-1156	137
Greater Cincinnati Convention & Visitors Bureau						
525 Vine St Ste 1500	Cincinnati	OH	45202	**800-543-2613**	513-621-2142	207
Greater Cleveland Partnership						
50 Public Sq Ste 200	Cleveland	OH	44113	**888-304-4769**	216-621-3300	137
Greater Columbus Chamber of Commerce						
1200 Sixth Ave PO Box 1200	Columbus	GA	31902	**800-360-8552**	706-327-1566	137
Greater Columbus Convention & Visitors Bureau						
277 W Nationwide Blvd Ste 125	Columbus	OH	43215	**866-397-2657**	614-221-6623	207
Greater Columbus Convention Ctr						
400 N High St	Columbus	OH	43215	**800-626-0241**	614-827-2500	206
Greater Concord Chamber of Commerce						
2280 Diamond Blvd Ste 200	Concord	CA	94520	**800-427-8686**	925-685-1181	137
Greater Crofton Chamber of Commerce						
PO Box 4146	Crofton	MD	21114	**866-852-4237**	410-721-9131	137
Greater Des Moines Convention & Visitors Bureau						
400 Locust St Ste 265	Des Moines	IA	50309	**800-451-2625**	515-286-4960	207
Greater Des Moines Partnership						
700 Locust St Ste 100	Des Moines	IA	50309	**800-376-9059**	515-286-4950	137
Greater Enid Chamber of Commerce						
PO Box 907	Enid	OK	73702	**877-233-4232**	580-237-2494	137
Greater Eureka Chamber of Commerce, The						
2112 Broadway	Eureka	CA	95501	**866-267-4255**	707-442-3738	137
Greater Fort Lauderdale Chamber of Commerce						
512 NE Third Ave	Fort Lauderdale	FL	33301	**800-683-8338**	954-462-6000	137
Greater Fort Lauderdale Convention & Visitors Bureau						
100 E Broward Blvd						
Ste 200	Fort Lauderdale	FL	33301	**800-227-8669**	954-765-4466	207
Greater Fort Myers Chamber of Commerce						
2310 Edwards Dr	Fort Myers	FL	33901	**800-366-3622**	239-332-3624	137
Greater Fort Wayne Chamber of Commerce						
826 Ewing St	Fort Wayne	IN	46802	**888-259-9175**	260-424-1435	137
Greater Grand Forks Convention & Visitors Bureau						
4251 Gateway Dr	Grand Forks	ND	58203	**800-866-4566**	701-746-0444	207
Greater Greenbrier Chamber of Commerce						
200 W Washington St Ste C	Lewisburg	WV	24901	**800-833-2068**	304-645-2818	137
Greater Greenville Chamber of Commerce						
24 Cleveland St	Greenville	SC	29601	**866-485-5262**	864-242-1050	137
Greater Greenville Convention & Visitors Bureau						
148 River St Ste 222	Greenville	SC	29601	**800-351-7180**	864-421-0000	207
Greater Greenwood Chamber of Commerce						
65 Airport Pkwy	Greenwood	IN	46143	**800-462-7585**	317-888-4856	137
Greater Hartsville Chamber of Commerce						
PO Box 578	Hartsville	SC	29551	**866-747-0060**	843-332-6401	137
Greater Homestead/Florida City Chamber of Commerce						
455 N Flagler Ave	Homestead	FL	33030	**888-247-5012**	305-247-2332	137
Greater Houston Convention & Visitors Bureau						
901 Bagby St Ste 100	Houston	TX	77002	**800-446-8786**	713-437-5200	207
Greater Hutchinson Convention & Visitors Bureau						
117 N Walnut St PO Box 519	Hutchinson	KS	67504	**800-691-4262**	620-662-3391	207
Greater Issaquah Chamber of Commerce						
155 NW Gilman Blvd	Issaquah	WA	98027	**800-668-3030**	425-392-7024	137
Greater Jackson Chamber of Commerce						
141 S Jackson St	Jackson	MI	49201	**800-366-3699**	517-782-8221	137
Greater Jackson County Chamber of Commerce						
PO Box 973	Scottsboro	AL	35768	**800-259-5508**	256-259-5500	137
Greater Johnstown/Cambria County Chamber of Commerce						
245 Market St Ste 100	Johnstown	PA	15901	**800-790-4522**	814-536-5107	137
Greater Johnstown/Cambria County Convention & Visitors Bureau						
416 Main St Ste 100	Johnstown	PA	15901	**800-237-8590**	814-536-7993	207
Greater Kansas City Chamber of Commerce						
911 Main St Ste 2600	Kansas City	MO	64105	**800-767-7700**	816-221-2424	137
Greater Killeen Chamber of Commerce						
One Santa Fe Plz	Killeen	TX	76540	**866-790-4769**	254-526-9551	137
Greater Lansing Convention & Visitors Bureau						
500 E Michigan Ave Ste 180	Lansing	MI	48912	**888-252-6746**	517-487-0077	207
Greater Lawrence County Area Chamber of Commerce						
216 Collins Ave	South Point	OH	45680	**800-408-1334**	740-377-4550	137
Greater Lawrence Township Chamber of Commerce						
9120 Otis Ave Ste 100	Indianapolis	IN	46216	**800-473-2328**	317-541-9876	137
Greater Lehigh Valley Chamber of Commerce						
840 Hamilton St Ste 205	Allentown	PA	18101	**800-845-7941**	610-841-5800	137
Greater Limestone County Chamber of Commerce						
101 S Beaty St	Athens	AL	35611	**866-953-6565**	256-232-2600	137
Greater Lowell Chamber of Commerce						
131 Merrimack St	Lowell	MA	01852	**800-338-0221**	978-459-8154	137
Greater Madison Convention & Visitors Bureau						
615 E Washington Ave	Madison	WI	53703	**800-373-6376**	608-255-2537	207
Greater Mankato Growth						
1961 Premier Dr	Mankato	MN	56001	**800-697-0652**	507-385-6640	207
Greater Marathon Chamber of Commerce						
12222 Overseas Hwy	Marathon	FL	33050	**800-262-7284**	305-743-5417	137
Greater Marion Area Chamber of Commerce						
2305 W Main St	Marion	IL	62959	**800-699-1760**	618-997-6311	137
Greater Marshall Chamber of Commerce						
213 W Austin St	Marshall	TX	75670	**800-953-7868**	903-935-7868	137
Greater Menomonie Area Chamber of Commerce						
342 E Main St	Menomonie	WI	54751	**800-283-1862**	715-235-9087	137
Greater Merced Chamber of Commerce						
1640 N St Ste 120	Merced	CA	95340	**800-877-2345**	209-384-7092	137
Greater Meriden Chamber of Commerce						
3 Colony St Ste 301	Meriden	CT	06451	**877-283-8158**	203-235-7901	137
Greater Merrimack Valley Convention & Visitors Bureau						
40 French St Second Fl	Lowell	MA	01852	**800-443-3332**	978-459-6150	207
Greater Miami Chamber of Commerce						
1601 Biscayne Blvd	Miami	FL	33132	**888-660-5955**	305-350-7700	137
Greater Miami Convention & Visitors Bureau						
701 Brickell Ave Ste 2700	Miami	FL	33131	**800-933-8448**	305-539-3000	207
Greater Milwaukee Convention & Visitors Bureau						
648 N Plankinton Ave Ste 425	Milwaukee	WI	53203	**800-554-1448**	414-273-7222	207
Greater Monmouth Chamber of Commerce						
57 Schanck Rd Ste C-3	Freehold	NJ	07728	**800-700-6400**	732-462-3030	137
Greater Monticello Chamber of Commerce						
116 N Main St	Monticello	IN	47960	**800-541-7906**	574-583-7220	137
Greater Morgantown Convention & Visitors Bureau						
68 Donley St	Morgantown	WV	26501	**800-458-7373**	304-292-5081	207
Greater Mount Airy Chamber of Commerce						
200 N Main St	Mount Airy	NC	27030	**800-948-0949**	336-786-6116	137
Greater Naples Marco Island Everglades Convention & Visitors Bureau						
2800 Horseshoe Dr	Naples	FL	34104	**800-688-3600**	239-252-2384	207
Greater New Braunfels Chamber of Commerce Inc, The						
390 S Seguin Ave						
PO Box 311417	New Braunfels	TX	78130	**800-572-2626**	830-625-2385	207
Greater New Orleans Hotel & Lodging Assn						
2020 St Charles Ave 5th Fl	New Orleans	LA	70130	**866-366-1121**	504-525-2264	373
Greater Newport Chamber of Commerce						
555 SW Coast Hwy	Newport	OR	97365	**800-262-7844**	541-265-8801	137
Greater North Fulton Chamber of Commerce (GNFCC)						
11605 Haynes Bridge Rd						
Ste 100	Alpharetta	GA	30009	**866-840-5770**	770-993-8806	137
Greater Northampton Chamber of Commerce						
99 Pleasant St	NortHampton	MA	01060	**800-392-6090**	413-584-1900	137
Greater O'Hare Assn of Industry & Commerce						
PO Box 1516	Elk Grove Village	IL	60009	**877-355-4768**	630-773-2944	137
Greater Ocean City Chamber of Commerce						
12320 Ocean Gateway	Ocean City	MD	21842	**888-626-3386**	410-213-0144	137
Greater Omaha Convention & Visitors Bureau						
1001 Farnam St Ste 200	Omaha	NE	68102	**866-937-6624**	402-444-4660	207
Greater Omaha Packing Company Inc						
3001 L St	Omaha	NE	68107	**800-747-5400**	402-731-1700	468
Greater Parkersburg Convention & Visitors Bureau						
350 Seventh St	Parkersburg	WV	26101	**800-752-4982**	304-428-1130	207
Greater Paterson Chamber of Commerce						
100 Hamilton Plaza Ste 1201	Paterson	NJ	07505	**800-220-2892**	973-881-7300	137
Greater Peterborough Chamber of Commerce						
175 George St N	Peterborough	ON	K9J3G6	**877-640-4037**	705-748-9771	136
Greater Phoenix Convention & Visitors Bureau						
400 E Van Buren St Ste 600	Phoenix	AZ	85004	**877-225-5749**	602-254-6500	207
Greater Pittsburgh Convention & Visitors Bureau						
120 Fifth Ave						
Fifth Ave Pl, 1st Level	Pittsburgh	PA	15222	**800-359-0758**	412-281-7711	207
Greater Plant City Chamber of Commerce						
106 N Evers St	Plant City	FL	33563	**800-760-2315**	813-754-3707	137
Greater Pueblo Chamber of Commerce						
302 N Santa Fe Ave	Pueblo	CO	81003	**800-233-3446**	719-542-1704	137
Greater Raleigh Chamber of Commerce						
PO Box 2978	Raleigh	NC	27602	**866-291-0854**	919-664-7000	137
Greater Raleigh Convention & Visitors Bureau						
421 Fayetteville St Mall						
Ste 1505	Raleigh	NC	27602	**800-849-8499**	919-834-5900	207
Greater Reading Chamber of Commerce & Industry						
201 Penn St	Reading	PA	19601	**877-438-4338**	610-376-6766	137
Greater Renton Chamber of Commerce						
625 S Fourth St	Renton	WA	98057	**877-467-3686**	425-226-4560	137
Greater Reston Chamber of Commerce						
1763 Fountain Dr	Reston	VA	20190	**844-430-7073**	703-707-9045	137
Greater Rockford Airport						
60 Airport Dr	Rockford	IL	61109	**800-517-2000**	815-969-4000	27
Greater Rockford Auto Auction Inc (GRAA)						
5937 Sandy Hollow Rd	Rockford	IL	61109	**800-830-4722**	815-874-7800	50
Greater Rome Chamber of Commerce						
One Riverside Pkwy	Rome	GA	30161	**800-234-3154**	706-291-7663	137
Greater Rome Convention & Visitors Bureau						
402 Civics Ctr Dr	Rome	GA	30161	**800-444-1834**	706-295-5576	207
Greater Saint Charles Convention & Visitors Bureau						
230 S Main St	Saint Charles	MO	63301	**800-366-2427**	636-946-7776	207
Greater San Antonio Chamber of Commerce						
602 E Commerce St	San Antonio	TX	78205	**888-828-8680**	210-229-2100	137
Greater Seattle Chamber of Commerce						
1301 Fifth Ave Ste 1500	Seattle	WA	98101	**866-978-2997**	206-389-7200	137
Greater Shawnee Area Chamber of Commerce						
131 N Bell Ave	Shawnee	OK	74801	**800-762-7695**	405-273-6092	137
Greater Shreveport Chamber of Commerce						
400 Edwards St	Shreveport	LA	71101	**800-448-5432**	318-677-2500	137
Greater Sierra Vista Area Chamber of Commerce						
21 E Wilcox Dr	Sierra Vista	AZ	85635	**800-288-3861**	520-458-6940	137
Greater Spokane Inc						
801 W Riverside Ave Ste 100	Spokane	WA	99201	**800-776-5263**	509-624-1393	137
Greater Springfield Convention & Visitors Bureau						
1441 Main St	Springfield	MA	01103	**800-723-1548**	413-787-1548	207
Greater Starkville Development Partnership						
200 E Main St	Starkville	MS	39759	**800-649-8687**	662-323-3322	137
Greater Sumter Chamber of Commerce						
32 E Calhoun St	Sumter	SC	29150	**888-868-0737**	803-775-1231	137
Greater Susquehanna Valley Chamber of Commerce						
2859 N Susquehanna Trl						
PO Box 10	Shamokin Dam	PA	17876	**800-410-2880**	570-743-4100	137
Greater Tacoma Convention & Trade Ctr						
1500 Broadway	Tacoma	WA	98402	**800-745-3000**	253-830-6601	206
Greater Talent Network Inc						
437 Fifth Ave Seventh Fl	New York	NY	10016	**800-326-4211**	212-645-4200	699
Greater Tallahassee Chamber of Commerce						
115 N Calhoun St	Tallahassee	FL	32301	**866-566-6106**	850-224-8116	137
Greater Tampa Chamber of Commerce						
201 N Franklin St Ste 201	Tampa	FL	33602	**877-693-5236**	813-228-7777	137
Greater Toledo Convention & Visitors Bureau						
401 Jefferson Ave	Toledo	OH	43604	**800-243-4667**	419-321-6404	207
Greater Vineland Chamber of Commerce						
2115 S Delsea Dr	Vineland	NJ	08360	**800-922-1766**	856-691-7400	137
Greater Watertown-North Country Chamber of Commerce						
1241 Coffeen St	Watertown	NY	13601	**800-642-4272**	315-788-4400	137
Greater Wilkes-Barre Chamber of Business & Industry						
2 Public Sq PO Box 5340	Wilkes-Barre	PA	18710	**800-701-8449**	570-823-2101	137

Name / Address	City	State	ZIP	Toll-Free	Phone	Class
Greater Wilmington Chamber of Commerce						
1 Estell Lee Pl	Wilmington	NC	28401	**800-829-4477**	910-762-2611	137
Greater Wilmington Convention & Visitors Bureau						
100 W Tenth St Ste 20	Wilmington	DE	19801	**800-489-6664**		207
Greater Woodfield Convention & Visitors Bureau						
1375 E Woodfield Rd Ste 120	Schaumburg	IL	60173	**800-847-4849**	847-490-1010	207
Greater Yellowstone Coalition (GYC)						
13 S Willson Ave Ste 2	Bozeman	MT	59715	**800-775-1834**	406-586-1593	47-13
Great-West Life & Annuity Insurance Co						
8515 E OrchaRd Rd	Greenwood Village	CO	80111	**800-537-2033**	303-737-3000	388-2
Great-West Life Assurance Co						
100 Osborne St	Winnipeg	MB	R3C3A5	**800-990-6654**	204-946-1190	388-2
Greek Catholic Union of the USA						
5400 Tuscarawas Rd	Beaver	PA	15009	**800-722-4428**	724-495-3400	388-2
Greeley & Hansen						
100 S Wacker Dr Ste 1400	Chicago	IL	60606	**800-837-9779**	312-558-9000	261
Greeley Convention & Visitors Bureau						
902 Seventh Ave	Greeley	CO	80631	**800-449-3866**	970-352-3567	207
Greeley County						
510 Broadway PO Box 656	Tribune	KS	67879	**888-204-1781**	620-376-2548	336
Greeley-Weld Chamber of Commerce						
902 Seventh Ave	Greeley	CO	80631	**800-449-3866**	970-352-3566	137
Green Bay Botanical Garden						
2600 Larsen Rd	Green Bay	WI	54303	**877-355-4224**	920-490-9457	96
Green Bay Drop Forge						
1341 State St	Green Bay	WI	54304	**800-824-4896**	920-432-6401	478
Green Bay Packaging Inc						
1700 Webster Ct	Green Bay	WI	54302	**800-236-8400**	920-433-5111	541
Green Bay Packaging Inc Mill Div						
1700 N Webster Ct Box 19017	Green Bay	WI	54307	**800-445-4269**	920-433-5111	554
Green Bay Packers Hall of Fame						
1265 Lombardi Ave	Green Bay	WI	54304	**888-442-7225**	920-569-7512	515
Green Bay Press-Gazette						
PO Box 23430	Green Bay	WI	54305	**800-289-8221**	920-431-8400	525-2
Green County						
1016 16th Ave	Monroe	WI	53566	**800-947-3529**	608-328-9430	336
Green Field Paper Co						
7196 Clairemont Mesa Blvd	San Diego	CA	92111	**888-402-9979**	858-565-2585	550
Green Foods Corp						
2220 Camino Del Sol	Oxnard	CA	93030	**800-777-4430**	805-983-7470	295-25
Green Hills Antique Mall						
4108 Hillsboro Pk	Nashville	TN	37215	**888-316-6255**	615-383-9851	455
Green Hills Software Inc						
30 W Sola St	Santa Barbara	CA	93101	**800-765-4733**	805-965-6044	179-2
Green Mountain at Fox Run						
262 Fox Ln PO Box 358	Ludlow	VT	05149	**800-448-8106**	802-228-8885	697
Green Mountain College						
One Brennan Cir	Poultney	VT	05764	**800-776-6675***	802-287-8000	166
*Admissions						
Green Mountain Inn						
18 Main St PO Box 60	Stowe	VT	05672	**800-253-7302**	802-253-7301	376
Green Mountain Power Corp						
163 Acorn Ln	Colchester	VT	05446	**888-835-4672**	802-864-5731	775
Green Oaks Hospital						
7808 Clodus Fields Dr	Dallas	TX	75251	**800-866-6554**	972-991-9504	371-5
Green Plains Renewable Energy Inc						
450 Regency Pkwy Ste 400	Omaha	NE	68114	**877-886-2288**	402-884-8700	141
NASDAQ: GPRE						
Green Room at the Hotel duPont						
11th & Market St	Wilmington	DE	19801	**800-441-9019**	302-594-3100	662
Green Tortoise Adventure Travel & Hostels						
494 Broadway	San Francisco	CA	94133	**800-867-8647**	415-834-1000	750
Green Tree Packing Co						
65 Central Ave	Passaic	NJ	07055	**800-562-6934**	973-473-1305	295-26
Green Tree Servicing LLC						
345 St Peter St	Saint Paul	MN	55102	**800-643-0202**	800-423-9527	214
Green Valley Floral Co						
24999 Potter Rd	Salinas	CA	93908	**800-228-1255**	831-424-7691	366
Green Valley Ranch Resort Casino & Spa						
2300 Paseo Verde Pkwy	Henderson	NV	89052	**866-782-9487***	702-617-7777	376
*Resv						
Green Valley Spa & Resort						
1871 W Canyon View Dr	Saint George	UT	84770	**800-237-1068**		697
Greenbelt Electric Co-op Inc						
PO Box 948	Wellington	TX	79095	**800-527-3082**	806-447-2536	245
Greenbriar Inn, The						
8735 N Foothills Hwy	Boulder	CO	80302	**800-253-1474**	303-440-7979	662
Greenbrier Co						
One Centerpointe Dr Ste 200	Lake Oswego	OR	97035	**800-343-7188**	503-684-7000	641
NYSE: GBX						
Greenbrier County						
200 W Washington St	Lewisburg	WV	24901	**800-833-2068**	304-647-6602	336
Greenbrier County Convention & Visitors Bureau						
540 N Jefferson St Ste N	Lewisburg	WV	24901	**800-833-2068**	304-645-1000	207
Greenbrier Farms Inc						
225 Sign Pine Rd	Chesapeake	VA	23322	**800-829-2141**	757-421-2141	322
Greenbrier, The						
300 W Main St	White Sulphur Springs	WV	24986	**800-453-4858**	304-536-1110	660
Greene County Bancorp Inc						
302 Main St	Catskill	NY	12414	**888-439-4272**	518-943-2600	357-2
NASDAQ: GCBC						
Greene County Convention & Visitors Bureau						
1221 Meadowbridge Dr	Beavercreek	OH	45434	**800-733-9109**	937-429-9100	207
Greenerd Press & Machine Company Inc						
41 Crown St	Nashua	NH	03060	**800-877-9110**	603-889-4101	451
Greeneville Light & Power System						
PO Box 1690	Greeneville	TN	37744	**866-466-1438**	423-636-6200	245
Greenfield Village						
20900 Oakwood Blvd	Dearborn	MI	48124	**800-835-5237**	313-271-1620	513
Greenheart Farms Inc						
902 Zenon Way PO Box 1510	Arroyo Grande	CA	93420	**800-549-5531**	805-481-2234	10-10
Greenhorn Creek Guest Ranch						
2116 Greenhorn Ranch Rd	Quincy	CA	95971	**800-334-6939**	530-283-0930	239
Greenhorn Creek Resort						
711 McCauley Ranch Rd	Angels Camp	CA	95222	**888-736-5900**	209-729-8111	660
Greenleaf Ctr						
2209 Pineview Dr	Valdosta	GA	31602	**800-247-2747**	229-671-6700	717
Greenleaf Nursery Co						
28406 Hwy 82	Park Hill	OK	74451	**800-331-2982**	918-457-5172	366
Greenlee Textron						
1390 Aspen Way	Vista	CA	92081	**800-642-2155**	760-598-8900	253
Greenlee Textron Inc						
4455 Boeing Dr	Rockford	IL	61109	**800-435-0786**		749

Name / Address	City	State	ZIP	Toll-Free	Phone	Class
Greenline Equipment						
14750 S Pony Express Rd	Bluffdale	UT	84065	**888-201-5500**	801-966-4231	274
GreenLine Paper Company Inc						
631 S Pine St	York	PA	17403	**800-641-1117**	717-845-8697	546
Greenpages Inc						
33 Badgers Island W	Kittery	ME	03904	**888-687-4876**	207-439-7310	181
Greenpath Inc						
38505 Country Club Dr	Farmington Hills	MI	48331	**800-550-1961**	248-553-5400	797
Greenpeace Canada						
33 Cecil St	Toronto	ON	M5T1N1	**800-320-7183**	416-597-8408	47-13
Greenpeace USA						
702 H St NW Ste 300	Washington	DC	20001	**800-326-0959**	202-462-1177	47-13
Greensboro Area Convention & Visitors Bureau						
2200 Pinecroft Rd Ste 200	Greensboro	NC	27407	**800-344-2282**	336-274-2282	207
Greensboro College						
815 W Market St	Greensboro	NC	27401	**800-346-8226**	336-272-7102	166
GreenSky Trade Credit LLC						
1797 Northeast Expy Ste 100	Atlanta	GA	30329	**866-936-0602**		224
Greenstone Farm Credit Services Aca						
3515 West Road	East Lansing	MI	48823	**800-444-3276**	800-968-0061	216
Greenville Area Chamber of Commerce						
1 Depot Sq	Greenville	AL	36037	**800-959-0717**	334-382-3251	137
Greenville City Hall						
206 S Main St	Greenville	SC	29601	**800-829-4477**	864-232-2273	335
Greenville College						
315 E College Ave	Greenville	IL	62246	**800-345-4440**	618-664-7100	166
Greenville County Library						
25 Heritage Green Pl	Greenville	SC	29601	**866-275-7273**	864-242-5000	431-3
Greenville First Bank						
100 Verdae Blvd Ste 100	Greenville	SC	29072	**877-679-9646**	864-679-9000	69
Greenville Hospital System (GHS)						
701 Grove Rd	Greenville	SC	29605	**877-447-4636**	864-455-8976	350
Greenville News						
305 S Main St	Greenville	SC	29601	**800-800-5116**	864-298-4100	525-2
Greenville Technical College						
Barton						
506 S Pleasantburg Dr	Greenville	SC	29607	**800-723-0673***	864-250-8111	160
*All						
Greer						
2522 Locust Hill Rd	Taylors	SC	29687	**800-723-0673**		160
Greenville Zoo						
150 Cleveland Pk Dr	Greenville	SC	29601	**800-877-8339**	864-467-4300	810
Greenville-Muhlenberg Chamber of Commerce						
100 E Main Cross PO Box 313	Greenville	KY	42345	**866-227-4812**	270-338-5422	137
Greenville-Pitt County Convention & Visitors Bureau (GPCCVB)						
303 SW Greenville Blvd						
PO Box 8027	Greenville	NC	27835	**800-537-5564**	252-329-4200	207
Greenville-Spartanburg Airport (GSP)						
2000 GSP Dr Ste 1	Greer	SC	29651	**800-331-1212**	864-877-7426	27
Greenwald Industries						
212 Middlesex Ave	Chester	CT	06412	**800-221-0982**	860-526-0800	490
Greenwich Assoc LLC						
6 High Ridge Pk	Stamford	CT	06905	**800-704-1027**	203-629-1200	195
Greenwich Hospital						
5 Perryridge Rd	Greenwich	CT	06830	**800-657-8355**	203-863-3000	371-3
Greenwood Convention & Visitors Bureau						
111 E Market St	Greenwood	MS	38930	**800-748-9064**	662-453-9197	207
Greenwood Mop & Broom Inc						
312 Palmer St	Greenwood	SC	29646	**800-635-6849**	864-227-8411	102
Greenwood Park Mall						
1251 US Hwy 31 N	Greenwood	IN	46142	**877-746-6642**	317-881-6758	455
Greenwood Plantation						
6838 Highland Rd	Saint Francisville	LA	70775	**800-259-4475**	225-655-4475	49-2
Greenwood Racing Inc						
3001 St Rd	Bensalem	PA	19020	**888-238-2946**	215-639-9000	357-2
Greenwood School						
14 Greenwood Ln	Putney	VT	05346	**800-380-9218**	802-387-4545	615
Greenwood School District 50						
1855 Calhoun Rd PO Box 248	Greenwood	SC	29648	**888-260-9430**	864-941-5400	676
Greenwood-Heinemann						
361 Hanover St	Portsmouth	NH	03801	**800-541-2086**	603-431-7894	628-2
Greer Garson Theatre Ctr						
1600 St Michael's Dr						
College of Santa Fe	Santa Fe	NM	87505	**800-456-2673**	505-473-6011	565
Greer Laboratories Inc						
639 Nuway Cir NE PO Box 800	Lenoir	NC	28645	**800-378-3906***	828-754-5327	474
*Cust Svc						
Greer Steel Co 624 Blvd	Dover	OH	44622	**800-388-2868***	330-343-8811	714
*Sales						
Greeters of Hawaii Ltd						
300 Rodgers Blvd Ste 266	Honolulu	HI	96819	**800-366-8559**	808-836-0161	292
Greeting Card Assn (GCA)						
1133 Westchester Ave						
Ste N136	White Plains	NY	10604	**866-799-5384**	914-421-3331	48-16
Gregg Appliances Inc						
4151 E 96th St	Indianapolis	IN	46240	**800-284-7344**	317-848-8710	34
NYSE: HGG						
Gregg Investigations Inc						
222 S Hamilton St Ste 17	Madison	WI	53703	**800-866-1976**		397
Gregory Poole Equipment Co						
4807 Beryl Rd PO Box 469	Raleigh	NC	27606	**800-451-7278**	919-828-0641	383
Greif Inc						
425 Winter Rd	Delaware	OH	43015	**877-781-9797**	740-549-6000	199
NYSE: GEF						
Gretz Beer Co						
710 E Main St	Norristown	PA	19401	**800-310-5099***	610-275-0285	80-1
*General						
Grey Bonnet Inn						
831 Rt 100 N	Killington	VT	05751	**800-342-2086**	802-775-2537	376
Grey House Publishing						
4919 Rt 22 PO Box 56	Amenia	NY	12501	**800-562-2139**	518-789-8700	628-2
Greyfield Inn						
Four N Second St						
Ste 300	Fernandina Beach	FL	32034	**866-401-8581**	904-261-6408	376
Greyhound Canada Transportation Corp						
1111 International Blvd						
Ste 700	Burlington	ON	L7L6W1	**800-661-8747**		106
Greyhound Hall of Fame						
407 S Buckeye Ave	Abilene	KS	67410	**800-932-7881**	785-263-3000	515
Greylock Federal Credit Union						
150 W St	Pittsfield	MA	01201	**800-207-5555**	413-236-4000	219
Greyston Bakery Inc						
104 Alexander St	Yonkers	NY	10701	**800-289-2253**	914-375-1510	295-1

	Toll-Free	Phone	Class
Greystone of Lincoln Inc			
7 Wellington Rd .... Lincoln RI 02865	**800-446-1761**	401-333-0444	614
GRFI Ltd			
400 E Randolph St Ste 700 .... Chicago IL 60601	**888-856-5161**		461
Gridstore Inc			
1975 W El Camino Real Ste 306 .... Mountain View CA 94040	**855-786-7065**	650-316-5515	174-8
Griffin Gate Marriott Resort			
1800 Newtown Pk .... Lexington KY 40511	**800-228-9290**	859-231-5100	660
Griffin Memorial Hospital			
900 E Main St .... Norman OK 73071 *General	**800-955-3468***	405-321-4880	371-5
Griffin Thermal Products			
100 Hurricane Creek Rd .... Piedmont SC 29673	**800-722-3723**	864-845-5000	59
Griffith Laboratories Worldwide Inc			
1 Griffith Ctr .... Alsip IL 60803 *Cust Svc	**800-346-9494***	708-371-0900	295-37
Griffith Rubber Mills			
2625 NW Industrial St .... Portland OR 97210	**800-321-9677**	503-226-6971	668
Grifols USA LLC			
2410 Lillyvale Ave .... Los Angeles CA 90032	**888-474-3657**		84
Grill 225			
225 E Bay St .... Charleston SC 29401	**877-440-2250**	843-266-4222	662
Grill at Hacienda del Sol			
5501 N Hacienda del Sol Rd .... Tucson AZ 85718	**800-728-6514**	520-529-3500	662
Grimmway Farms Inc			
PO Box 81498 .... Bakersfield CA 93380	**800-301-3101**		10-10
Grindmaster Crathco Systems Inc			
4003 Collins Ln .... Louisville KY 40245	**800-695-4500**	502-425-4776	297
Grinnell College			
1115 8th Ave .... Grinnell IA 50112	**800-247-0113**	641-269-3600	166
Grinnell College Burling Library			
6th Ave High St .... Grinnell IA 50112	**800-247-0113**	641-269-3371	431-6
Grinnell Mutual Reinsurance Co			
4215 Hwy 146 PO Box 790 .... Grinnell IA 50112	**800-362-2041**	641-269-8000	388-4
Griswold Corp			
One River St PO Box 638 .... Moosup CT 06354	**800-472-8788**	860-564-3321	667
Griswold Machine & Engineering Inc			
8530 M 60 .... Union City MI 49094	**800-248-2054**	517-741-4300	470
Griswold Special Care Inc			
717 Bethlehem Pike Ste 300 .... Erdenheim PA 19038	**855-303-9470**	215-402-0200	309
Grizzly & Wolf Discovery Ctr			
201 S Canyon St .... West Yellowstone MT 59758	**800-257-2570**	406-646-7001	810
GRMC (Gateway Regional Medical Ctr)			
2100 Madison Ave .... Granite City IL 62040 *General	**800-422-6237***	618-798-3000	371-3
Grob Inc			
1731 Tenth Ave .... Grafton WI 53024	**800-225-6481**	262-377-1400	450
Grobet File Company of America Inc			
750 Washington Ave .... Carlstadt NJ 07072	**800-847-4188**	201-939-6700	748
Grocers Supply International Inc			
3131 E Holcombe Blvd PO Box 14200 .... Houston TX 77021	**800-352-8003**	713-747-5000	296-8
Grocery Supply Co			
130 Hillcrest Dr .... Sulphur Springs TX 75482	**800-231-1938**	903-885-7621	296-8
Groendyke Transport Inc			
2510 Rock Island Blvd .... Enid OK 73701	**800-843-2103**	580-234-4663	770
Grogans Health Care Supply Inc			
1016 S Broadway St .... Lexington KY 40504	**800-365-1020**	859-254-6661	470
Grohe America Inc			
241 Covington Dr .... Bloomingdale IL 60108	**800-444-7643**	630-582-7711	602
Groovfold Inc			
1050 W State St .... Newcomerstown OH 43832	**800-367-1133**	740-498-8363	308
Grosh Scenic Rentals			
4114 Sunset Blvd .... Los Angeles CA 90029	**877-363-7998**		713
Gros-Ite Industries			
1790 New Britain Ave .... Farmington CT 06032	**877-777-4778**	860-677-2603	21
Gross Electric Inc			
2807 N Reynolds Rd .... Toledo OH 43615	**800-824-7268**	419-537-1818	246
Grossenburg Implement Inc			
31341 US Hwy 18 .... Winner SD 57580	**800-658-3440**	605-842-2040	274
Grossman Iron & Steel			
Five N Market St .... Saint Louis MO 63102	**800-969-9423**	314-231-9423	677
Grote & Weigel Inc			
76 Granby St .... Bloomfield CT 06002	**800-943-6376**	860-242-8528	295-26
Grote Industries Inc			
2600 Lanier Dr .... Madison IN 47250	**800-628-0809**	812-273-2121	59
Groth Corp			
13650 N Promenade Blvd .... Stafford TX 77477	**800-354-7684**	281-295-6800	777
Grounds For Play Inc			
1401 E Dallas St .... Mansfield TX 76063	**800-552-7529**	817-453-5703	343
Group 1 Automotive Inc			
800 Gessner Ste 500 .... Houston TX 77024 NYSE: GPI	**888-707-4094**	713-647-5700	56
Group Dekko Services LLC			
2505 Dekko Dr .... Garrett IN 46738	**800-829-3101**	260-357-3621	802
Group Health Co-op			
320 Westlake Ave N Ste 100 .... Seattle WA 98109	**888-901-4636**	206-448-5600	388-3
Group Management Services Inc			
3296 Columbia Rd Ste 101 .... Richfield OH 44286	**888-823-2084**	330-659-0100	458
Group O Inc			
4905 77th Ave .... Milan IL 61264 *Cust Svc	**800-752-0730***	309-736-8300	112
Groupe Lacasse LLC			
99 St-Pierre St .... Sainte-Pie QC J0H1W0	**888-522-2773**	450-772-2495	318-1
Grove Park Inn Resort & Spa			
290 Macon Ave .... Asheville NC 28804	**800-438-5800**	828-252-2711	660
Grove, The			
189 The Grove Dr .... Los Angeles CA 90036	**888-315-8883**	323-900-8080	455
Grover Corp			
2759 S 28th St .... Milwaukee WI 53234	**800-776-3602**	414-384-9472	127
GroveWare Technologies Ltd			
Ste 411 90 Eglinton Ave E .... Toronto ON M4P2Y3	**877-701-9378**		316
Grower Direct Fresh Cut Flowers			
9613 41 Ave Ste 201 .... Edmonton AB T6E5X7	**877-277-4787**	780-436-7774	292
Growth Assn of Southwestern Illinois			
5800 Godfrey Rd Alden Hall .... Godfrey IL 62035	**855-852-9460**	618-467-2280	137
Growth Coach, The			
10700 Montgomery Rd Ste 300 .... Cincinnati OH 45242	**888-292-7992**		309
Growth Products Ltd			
80 Lafayette Ave .... White Plains NY 10603	**800-648-7626**	914-428-1316	276
GRSS (IEEE Geoscience & Remote Sensing Society)			
IEEE Operations Ctr 445 Hoes Ln .... Piscataway NJ 08854	**800-678-4333**	732-562-5550	48-19
Grubbs Infiniti Ltd			
1661 Airport Fwy .... Euless TX 76040	**800-685-1111**	817-318-1200	56
Gruber Systems Inc			
25636 Ave Stanford .... Valencia CA 91355	**800-257-4070**	661-257-4060	597
Gruet Winery			
8400 Pan American Fwy NE .... Albuquerque NM 87113	**888-857-9463**	505-821-0055	49-6
Gruma Corp			
1159 Cottonwood L Ste 200 .... Irving TX 75038	**800-627-3221**	972-232-5000	11-1
Grunau Company Inc			
1100 W Anderson Ct .... Oak Creek WI 53154	**800-365-1920**	414-216-6900	190-10
Grundfos Pumps Corp			
17100 W 118th Terr .... Olathe KS 66061	**800-345-4555**	913-227-3400	632
Grundy County Chamber of Commerce & Industry			
909 Liberty St .... Morris IL 60450	**800-825-1785**	815-942-0113	137
Grundy County Rural Electric Co-op			
102 E 'G' Ave .... Grundy Center IA 50638	**800-390-7605**	319-824-5251	245
Grundy Electric Co-op Inc			
4100 Oklahoma Ave .... Trenton MO 64683	**800-279-2249**	660-359-3941	245
GRW Engineers Inc			
801 Corporate Dr .... Lexington KY 40503	**800-432-9537**	859-223-3999	261
GS Blodgett Corp			
44 Lakeside Ave .... Burlington VT 05401	**800-331-5842**	802-658-6600	297
Gs Foods Inc			
5925 S Alcoa Ave .... Vernon CA 90058	**800-273-6637**	323-581-6161	342
G-S Supplies			
408 St Paul St .... Rochester NY 14605	**800-295-3050**	585-295-0250	537
GSA (Geological Society of America, The)			
3300 Penrose Pl PO Box 9140 .... Boulder CO 80301	**800-472-1988**	303-357-1000	48-19
GSA (Genetics Society of America)			
9650 Rockville Pk .... Bethesda MD 20814	**866-486-4363**	301-634-7300	48-19
GSAM (Goldman Sachs Asset Management)			
200 W St .... New York NY 10282	**800-526-7384**	212-902-1000	398
GSB (Guilford Savings Bank)			
PO Box 369 .... Guilford CT 06437	**866-878-1480**	203-453-2015	69
GSCB (Garden State Community Bank)			
36 Ferry St .... Newark NJ 07105 NYSE: NYB	**877-786-6560**	973-589-8616	69
GSE Lining Technology Inc			
19103 Gundle Rd .... Houston TX 77073	**800-435-2008**	281-443-8564	593
GSE Systems Inc			
1332 Londontown Blvd Ste 200 .... Sykesville MD 21784 NYSE: GVP ■ *Cust Svc	**800-638-7912***	410-970-7800	179-1
GSI Group Inc			
125 Middlesex Tpke .... Bedford MA 01730 NASDAQ: GSIG	**800-342-3757**	781-266-5700	422
GSP (Greenville-Spartanburg Airport)			
2000 GSP Dr Ste 1 .... Greer SC 29651	**800-331-1212**	864-877-7426	27
Gst Information Technology Solutions			
13043 166th St .... Cerritos CA 90703	**800-833-0128**	562-345-8700	178
GT Water Products Inc			
5239 N Commerce Ave .... Moorpark CA 93021	**800-862-5647**	805-529-2900	600
GTE Federal Credit Union			
PO Box 172599 .... Tampa FL 33672	**888-871-2690**	813-871-2690	219
GTSI Corp			
2553 Dulles View Dr Ste 100 .... Herndon VA 20171 NASDAQ: GTSI	**800-999-4874**	703-502-2000	175
GTT Communications Inc			
7900 Tysons One Pl Ste 1450 .... McLean VA 22102 NYSE: GTT	**866-250-3887**	703-442-5500	726
GTT Global			
4100 Spring Valley Rd Ste 202 .... Dallas TX 75244	**888-288-7182**	972-239-5069	16
GU (Generations United)			
1333 H St NW Ste 500-W .... Washington DC 20005	**800-677-1116**	202-289-3979	47-6
Guadalupe Credit Union			
3601 Mimbres Ln .... Santa Fe NM 87507	**800-540-5382**	505-982-8942	219
Guadalupe Valley Electric Co-op Inc			
825 E Sarah Dewitt Dr .... Gonzales TX 78629	**800-223-4832**	830-857-1200	245
Guadalupe Valley Telephone Co-op (GVTC)			
36101 FM 3159 .... New Braunfels TX 78132	**800-367-4882**	830-885-4411	726
Guarantee Electrical Co			
3405 Bent Ave .... Saint Louis MO 63116 *General	**800-854-4326***	314-772-5400	190-4
Guarantee Trust Life Insurance Co			
1275 Milwaukee Ave .... Glenview IL 60025	**800-338-7452**	847-699-0600	388-2
Guaranteed Rate Inc			
3940 N Ravenswood .... Chicago IL 60613	**866-934-7283**	773-290-0505	214
Guaranty Bancshares Inc			
100 W Arkansas St PO Box 1158 .... Mount Pleasant TX 75455	**888-572-9881**	903-572-9881	357-2
Guaranty Bank			
4000 W Brown Deer Rd .... Brown Deer WI 53209	**800-235-4636**	414-362-4000	69
Guaranty Bank & Trust Co			
PO Box 1807 .... Cedar Rapids IA 52406	**888-777-4590**	319-286-6200	69
Guard Systems Inc			
1190 Monterey Pass Rd .... Monterey Park CA 91754	**800-606-6711**	323-881-6711	684
Guardair Corp			
54 Second Ave .... Chicopee MA 01020	**800-482-7324**	413-594-4400	173
Guardian Alarm			
20800 Southfield Rd .... Southfield MI 48075	**800-782-9688**	248-423-1000	683
Guardian Building Products (GBPD)			
979 Batesville Rd .... Greer SC 29651	**800-569-4262**	864-297-6101	192-3
Guardian Electric Mfg Company Inc			
1425 Lake Ave .... Woodstock IL 60098	**800-762-0369**	815-334-3600	204
Guardian Industries Corp			
2300 Harmon Rd .... Auburn Hills MI 48326	**800-822-5599**	248-340-1800	328
Guardian Life Insurance Company of America			
Seven Hanover Sq .... New York NY 10004	**888-600-4667**	212-598-8000	388-2
Guardian Packaging Inc			
3615 Security St .... Garland TX 75042	**800-259-1502**	214-349-1500	594
Guardian Protection Services Inc			
174 Thorn Hill Rd .... Warrendale PA 15086 *Cust Svc	**877-314-7092***	855-779-2001	684
Guard-Line Inc			
215 S Louise St PO Box 1030 .... Atlanta TX 75551	**800-527-8822**	903-796-4111	153-7
guardNOW Inc			
16209 Victory Blvd Ste 302 .... Van Nuys CA 91406	**877-482-7366**		684
Guardsmark Inc			
10 Rockefeller Plz 12th Fl .... New York NY 10020	**800-238-5878**	212-765-8226	684
Guenther House			
205 E Guenther St .... San Antonio TX 78204	**800-235-8186**	210-227-1061	49-2
Guerbet LLC			
1185 W Second St .... Bloomington IN 47403	**877-729-6679**	812-333-0059	231
Guest Informant Magazine			
725 Broad St .... Augusta GA 30901	**800-622-6358**	706-724-0851	452-22

				Toll-Free	Phone	Class
Guest Services Inc						
3055 Prosperity Ave	Fairfax	VA	22031	**800-345-7534**	703-849-9300	298
Guest Supply Inc						
4301 US Hwy 1						
PO Box 902	Monmouth Junction	NJ	08852	**800-446-7819***	609-514-9696	215
*Cust Svc						
GuestHouse International LLC						
100 Bluegrass Commons Blvd						
Ste 110	Hendersonville	TN	37075	**800-214-8378**		376
Guggenheim Hermitage Museum						
3355 Las Vegas Blvd S						
Venetian Resort Hotel & Casino	Las Vegas	NV	89109	**800-329-6109**	212-423-3575	513
Guhring Inc						
1445 Commerce Ave	Brookfield	WI	53045	**800-776-6170**	262-784-6730	488
Guidance Software Inc						
215 N Marengo Ave 2nd Fl	Pasadena	CA	91101	**866-229-9199**	626-229-9191	179-10
Guida-Seibert Dairy Co						
433 Pk St	New Britain	CT	06051	**800-832-8929**	860-224-2404	295-27
Guide Dog Foundation for the Blind Inc						
371 E Jericho Tkpe	Smithtown	NY	11787	**800-548-4337**		47-17
Guide Dogs for the Blind						
350 Los Ranchitos Rd	San Rafael	CA	94903	**800-295-4050**	415-499-4000	47-17
Guide Dogs of America						
13445 Glenoaks Blvd	Sylmar	CA	91342	**800-459-4843**	818-362-5834	47-17
Guidecraft USA						
55508 Hwy 19 W PO Box U	Winthrop	MN	55396	**800-524-3555**	507-647-5030	752
Guided Tours of Trois-Rivieres						
1457 Rue Notre Dame	Trois-Rivieres	QC	G9A4X4	**800-313-1123**	819-375-1122	765
GuideOne Insurance Co						
1111 Ashworth Rd	West Des Moines	IA	50265	**877-448-4331**	515-267-5000	388-4
GuideOne Mutual Insurance Co						
1111 Ashworth Rd	West Des Moines	IA	50265	**877-448-4331**	515-267-5000	388-4
GuideOne Specialty Mutual Insurance Co						
1111 Ashworth Rd	West Des Moines	IA	50265	**877-448-4331**	515-267-5000	388-4
Guild Mortgage Co						
5898 Copley Dr						
Fourth & Fifth Fl	San Diego	CA	92111	**800-365-4441**		502
Guilford College						
5800 W Friendly Ave	Greensboro	NC	27410	**800-992-7759***	336-316-2000	166
*Admissions						
Guilford County Schools						
617 W Market St	Greensboro	NC	27401	**866-286-7337**	336-370-8100	676
Guilford Savings Bank (GSB)						
PO Box 369	Guilford	CT	06437	**866-878-1480**	203-453-2015	69
Guinness World Records Museum						
4943 Clifton Hill	Niagara Falls	ON	L2G3N5	**866-656-0310**	905-357-4330	513
Guitar Player Magazine						
28 E 28th St 12th Fl	New York	NY	10016	**800-289-9839***	212-378-0400	452-9
*Cust Svc						
Guittard Chocolate Co						
10 GuittaRd Rd	Burlingame	CA	94010	**800-468-2462**	650-697-4427	295-8
Gulf Business Forms Inc						
2460 S IH-35 PO Box 1073	San Marcos	TX	78667	**800-433-4853**	512-353-8313	109
Gulf Coast Bank						
4310 Johnston St	Lafayette	LA	70503	**800-722-5363**	337-989-1133	69
Gulf Coast Bank & Trust Co						
200 St Charles Ave	New Orleans	LA	70130	**800-223-2060**	504-561-6100	676
Gulf Coast Collection Bureau Inc						
5630 Marquesas Cir	Sarasota	FL	34233	**877-827-4820**	941-927-6999	158
Gulf Coast Community College						
5230 W Hwy 98	Panama City	FL	32401	**800-311-3685**	850-769-1551	160
Gulf Coast Electric Co-op Inc						
722 Florida 22	Wewahitchka	FL	32465	**800-333-9392**	850-639-2216	245
Gulf Coast Machine & Supply Company Inc						
6817 Industrial Rd	Beaumont	TX	77705	**800-231-3032**	409-842-1311	714
Gulf Coast Medical Ctr						
13681 Doctors Way	Fort Myers	FL	33912	**800-809-9906**	239-343-1000	371-3
Gulf Coast Regional Blood Ctr						
1400 La Concha Ln	Houston	TX	77054	**888-482-5663**	713-790-1200	88
Gulf Coast Treatment Ctr						
1015 Mar-Walt Dr	Fort Walton Beach	FL	32547	**800-537-5433**	850-863-4160	371-1
Gulf Hills Hotel						
13701 Paso Rd	Ocean Springs	MS	39564	**866-875-4211**	228-875-4211	660
Gulf of Maine Research Institute, The						
350 Commercial St	Portland	ME	04101	**866-447-2111**	207-772-2321	461
Gulf Offshore Logistics LLC						
120 White Rose Dr	Raceland	LA	70394	**866-532-1060**		532
Gulf Oil LP						
100 Crossing Blvd	Framingham	MA	01702	**800-256-4853**	508-270-8300	572
Gulf Publishing Company Inc						
Two Greenway Plz Ste 1020	Houston	TX	77046	**800-231-6275**	713-529-4301	628-9
Gulf Stream Coach Inc						
503 S Oakland Ave PO Box 1005	Nappanee	IN	46550	**800-289-8787**	574-773-7761	119
Gulf Winds International Inc						
411 Brisbane St	Houston	TX	77061	**866-238-4909**	713-747-4909	791-1
Gulfside Hospice Inc						
6224 Lafayette St	New Port Richey	FL	34652	**800-561-4883**	727-845-5707	368
Gulfstream Park						
901 S Federal Hwy	Hallandale	FL	33009	**866-840-8069**	954-454-7000	132
Gumbiner Savett Inc						
1723 Cloverfield Blvd	Santa Monica	CA	90404	**800-989-9798**	310-828-9798	2
Gump's						
135 Post St	San Francisco	CA	94108	**800-766-7628**	415-982-1616	359
Gun Parts Corp						
226 Williams Ln	Kingston	NY	12401	**866-686-7424**	845-679-4867	284
Gund Inc 1 Runyons Ln	Edison	NJ	08817	**800-448-4863***	732-248-1500	752
*Cust Svc						
Gundaker Property Management						
2458 Old Dorsett Rd						
Ste 100	Maryland Heights	MO	63043	**800-325-1978**	314-298-5200	646
Gundersen Lutheran at Home HomeCare & Hospice						
914 Green Bay St	La Crosse	WI	54601	**800-362-9567***	608-775-8400	368
*General						
Gundersen Lutheran Medical Ctr						
1836 S Ave	La Crosse	WI	54601	**800-362-9567**	608-782-7300	371-3
Gunite Corp						
302 Peoples Ave	Rockford	IL	61104	**800-677-3786**	815-964-3301	59
Gunite Supply & Equipment Company - West						
1726 S Magnolia Ave	Monrovia	CA	91016	**888-393-8635**	626-358-0143	325
Gunlocke Company LLC						
One Gunlocke Dr	Wayland	NY	14572	**800-828-6300***	585-728-5111	318-1
*Cust Svc						

				Toll-Free	Phone	Class
Gunnebo-Johnson Corp						
1240 N Harvard Ave	Tulsa	OK	74115	**800-331-5460***	918-832-8933	465
*Sales						
Gunnison County Electric Assn Inc						
37250 W Hwy 50 PO Box 180	Gunnison	CO	81230	**800-726-3523**	970-641-3520	245
Gunster Yoakley & Stewart Pa						
777 S Flagler Dr						
Ste 500 E	West Palm Beach	FL	33401	**800-749-1980**	561-655-1980	425
Gupton-Jones College of Funeral Service						
5141 Snapfinger Woods Dr	Decatur	GA	30035	**800-848-5352**	770-593-2257	788
Gurwitch Products LLC						
8 Greenway Plz	Stafford	TX	77046	**888-637-2437**	281-275-7000	215
Gustave A Larson Co						
PO Box 910	Pewaukee	WI	53072	**800-829-9609**	262-542-0200	656
Gustavus Adolphus College						
800 W College Ave	Saint Peter	MN	56082	**800-487-8288**	507-933-8000	166
Guthrie Healthcare System						
1 Guthrie Sq	Sayre	PA	18840	**888-448-8474**	570-887-4401	350
Guthrie Theater						
818 S Second St	Minneapolis	MN	55415	**877-447-8243***	612-377-2224	565
*Resv						
Guthy-Renker Television Network						
3340 Ocean Pk Blvd	Santa Monica	CA	90405	**800-778-1011**	310-581-6250	731
Gutsy Women Travel LLC						
801 E Katella Ave	Anaheim	CA	92806	**866-464-8879**		750
Guttenplans Frozen Dough						
100 Hwy 36	Middletown	NJ	07748	**888-422-4357***	732-495-9480	295-2
*General						
Guy M Turner Inc						
4514 S Holden Rd PO Box 7776	Greensboro	NC	27406	**800-432-4859**	336-294-4660	770
Guy Shavender Trucking Inc						
PO Box 206	Pantego	NC	27860	**800-682-2447**	252-943-3379	676
GVMG (Grand View Media Group Inc)						
200 Croft St Ste 1	Birmingham	AL	35242	**888-431-2877**	205-408-3700	628-9
GVTC (Guadalupe Valley Telephone Co-op)						
36101 FM 3159	New Braunfels	TX	78132	**800-367-4882**	830-885-4411	726
Gwin's Travel Planners Inc						
212 N Kirkwood Rd	Saint Louis	MO	63122	**800-433-9211**	314-822-1957	761
Gwynedd-Mercy College						
1325 Sunneytown Pk						
PO Box 901	Gwynedd Valley	PA	19437	**800-342-5462***	215-646-7300	166
*Admissions						
GXS Inc						
9711 Washingtonian Blvd	Gaithersburg	MD	20878	**800-560-4347**	301-340-4000	179-4
GYC (Greater Yellowstone Coalition)						
13 S Willson Ave Ste 2	Bozeman	MT	59715	**800-775-1834**	406-586-1593	47-13
Gym Source						
40 E 52nd St	New York	NY	10022	**800-496-3499**	212-688-4222	702
Gymboree Corp						
500 Howard St	San Francisco	CA	94105	**877-449-6932**	415-278-7000	155-1
NASDAQ: GYMB						
Gymboree Corp Play & Music Program						
500 Howard St	San Francisco	CA	94105	**877-449-6932***	415-278-7000	146
*Cust Svc						
Gynecologic Oncology Group (GOG)						
1600 JFK Blvd Ste 1020	Philadelphia	PA	19103	**800-225-3053**	215-854-0770	48-8
Gypsum Express Ltd						
8280 Sixty Rd PO Box 268	Baldwinsville	NY	13027	**800-621-7901**	315-638-2201	444
Gyration Inc						
3601-B Calle Tecate	Camarillo	CA	93012	**888-340-0033**		174-2

H

				Toll-Free	Phone	Class
H & E Equipment Services Inc						
11100 Mead Rd	Baton Rouge	LA	70809	**866-467-3682**	225-298-5200	264-3
NASDAQ: HEES						
H & H Color Lab Inc						
8906 E 67th St PO Box 219080	Raytown	MO	64133	**800-821-1305**	816-358-6677	581
H & H Industrial Corp						
7612 Rt 130	Pennsauken	NJ	08110	**800-982-0341**	856-663-4444	688
H & H Publishing Company Inc						
1231 Kapp Dr	Clearwater	FL	33765	**800-366-4079**	727-442-7760	244
H & H Swiss Screw Machine Products Company Inc						
1478 Chestnut Ave	Hillside	NJ	07205	**800-826-9985**		614
H & L Tooth Company Inc						
10055 E 56 St N	Tulsa	OK	74117	**800-458-6684**	918-272-0951	478
H & M International Transportation Inc						
485B Rt 1 S	Iselin	NJ	08830	**800-446-4685**	732-510-4640	770
H & R 1871						
60 Industrial Rowe	Gardner	MA	01440	**866-776-9292**		284
H & R Block Tax Services Inc						
4400 Main St	Kansas City	MO	64111	**800-472-5625**		724
H & S Bakery Inc						
601 S Caroline St	Baltimore	MD	21231	**800-959-7655**	410-276-7254	295-1
H & W Computer Systems Inc						
PO Box 46019	Boise	ID	83711	**800-338-6692**	208-377-0336	178
H & W Trucking Company Inc						
1772 N Andy Griffith Pkwy						
PO Box 1545	Mount Airy	NC	27030	**800-334-9181**	336-789-2188	770
H B Fuller Construction Products Inc						
1105 S Frontenac Rd	Aurora	IL	60504	**800-832-9002**		3
H Company Computer Products Inc						
16812 Hale Ave	Irvine	CA	92606	**800-726-2477**	949-833-3222	174-8
H E Whitlock Inc						
4808 Dillon Dr	Pueblo	CO	81008	**866-933-0709**		444
H Freeman & Son Inc						
411 N Cranberry Rd	Westminster	MD	21157	**800-876-7700**	410-857-5774	153-11
H G Makelim Co						
219 Shaw Rd	South San Francisco	CA	94080	**800-471-0590**	650-873-4757	382
H Kramer & Co						
1345 W 21st St	Chicago	IL	60608	**800-621-2305**	312-226-6600	480
H Lee Moffitt Cancer Ctr & Research Institute						
University of S Florida						
12902 Magnolia Dr	Tampa	FL	33612	**800-456-3434**	888-663-3488	371-7
H Lee Moffitt Cancer Ctr & Research Institute Blood & Marrow Transplantation Program						
12902 Magnolia Dr	Tampa	FL	33612	**888-663-3488**		759

Company / Address	City	State	ZIP	Toll-Free	Phone	Class
H Muehlstein & Company Inc 10 Westport Rd	Wilton	CT	06897	**800-257-3746**	203-855-6000	596
H O Wolding Inc PO Box 217	Amherst	WI	54406	**800-950-0054**	715-824-5513	770
H Pearce Real Estate Co 393 State St	North Haven	CT	06473	**800-373-3411**	203-281-3400	643
H Stern Jewelers Inc 645 Fifth Ave	New York	NY	10022	**800-747-8376**	212-688-0300	407
H Wilson Co 2245 Delany Rd	Waukegan	IL	60087	**800-245-7224**		318-1
H. B. Van Duzer Forest State Scenic Corridor 198 NE 123rd St	Newport	OR	97365	**800-551-6949**		558
H. F. Campbell & Son PO Box 260	Millerstown	PA	17062	**800-233-7112**	717-589-3194	770
H. T. Berry Co Inc PO Box B	Canton	MA	02021	**800-736-2206**	781-828-6000	552
H2O Plus Inc 845 W Madison St *Cust Svc	Chicago	IL	60607	**800-242-2284***	312-850-9283	215
HA Guden Company Inc 99 Raynor Ave	Ronkonkoma	NY	11779	**800-344-6437**	631-737-2900	347
HA Logistics Inc 5175 Johnson Dr	Pleasanton	CA	94588	**800-449-5778**	925-251-9300	310
Haas & Wilkerson Inc 4300 Shawnee Mission Pkwy	Fairway	KS	66205	**800-821-7703**	913-432-4400	387
Haas Automation Inc 2800 Sturgis Rd	Oxnard	CA	93030	**800-331-6746**	805-278-1800	449
Haas Cabinet Company Inc 625 W Utica St	Sellersburg	IN	47172	**800-457-6458**	812-246-4431	114
Habana Inn 2200 NW 40th St	Oklahoma City	OK	73112	**800-988-2221**	405-525-0730	376
Habasit ABT Inc 150 Industrial Pk Rd	Middletown	CT	06457	**800-522-2358**	860-632-2211	367
Habasit America 805 Satellite Blvd	Suwanee	GA	30024	**800-458-6431**		601
Habasit Belting Inc 1400 Clinton St	Buffalo	NY	14206	**800-325-1585**	716-824-8484	367
Habbersett Scrapple Inc 103 S Railroad Ave	Bridgeville	DE	19933	**800-338-4727**		295-26
Habco Beverage Systems Inc 501 Gordon Baker Rd	Toronto	ON	M2H2S6	**800-448-0244**	416-491-6008	791-1
Habersham County Chamber of Commerce 668 Clarkesville St	Cornelia	GA	30531	**800-835-2559**	706-778-4654	137
Habersham Electric Membership Corp 6135 Georgia 115	Clarkesville	GA	30523	**800-640-6812**	706-754-2114	245
Habersham Funding LLC 415 E Paces Ferry Rd NE Terr Level	Atlanta	GA	30305	**888-874-2402**	404-233-8275	784
Habitat for Humanity International Inc 121 Habitat St	Americus	GA	31709	**800-422-4828**	229-924-6935	47-5
Habitat Suites 500 E Highland Mall Blvd	Austin	TX	78752	**800-535-4663**	512-467-6000	376
Habitec Security Inc 2926 S Republic Blvd	Toledo	OH	43615	**888-422-4832**	419-537-6768	684
HAC (Housing Assistance Council) 1025 Vermont Ave NW Ste 606	Washington	DC	20005	**866-234-2689**	202-842-8600	47-5
Hach Co PO Box 389	Loveland	CO	80539	**800-227-4224**	970-669-3050	416
Hachette Book Group 237 Pk Ave	New York	NY	10017	**800-759-0190**		628-2
Hacienda del Sol Guest Ranch Resort 5501 N Hacienda Del Sol Rd	Tucson	AZ	85718	**800-728-6514**	520-299-1501	660
Hacienda Mexican Restaurants 1501 N Ironwood Dr	South Bend	IN	46635	**800-541-3227**		661
Hacienda The at Hotel Santa Fe 1501 Paseo del Peralta	Santa Fe	NM	87501	**855-825-9876**	505-955-7805	376
Hackbarth Delivery Service Inc 3504 Brookdale Dr N	Mobile	AL	36618	**800-277-3322**	251-478-1401	313
Hacker Johnson & Smith PA 500 N Wshore Blvd Ste 1000	Tampa	FL	33609	**800-366-7126**	813-286-2424	2
Hackney & Sons Inc 911 W 5th St PO Box 880	Washington	NC	27889	**800-763-0700**	252-946-6521	509
HACU (Hispanic Assn of Colleges & Universities) 8415 Datapoint Dr Ste 400	San Antonio	TX	78229	**800-780-4228**	210-692-3805	48-5
Hader/Seitz Inc 15600 W Lincoln Ave PO Box 510260	New Berlin	WI	53151	**877-388-2101**		223
Hadley House Co 4816 Nicollet Ave S	Minneapolis	MN	55419	**800-423-5390**		628-10
Hadronics Inc 4570 Steel Pl	Cincinnati	OH	45209	**800-829-0826**	513-321-9350	476
Haeger Industries Inc Seven Maiden Ln *Cust Svc	Dundee	IL	60118	**800-288-2529***	847-426-3441	332
Haemonetics Corp 400 Wood Rd *NYSE: HAE*	Braintree	MA	02184	**800-225-5242**	781-848-7100	471
Hafele America Company Inc 3901 Cheyenne Dr *Cust Svc	Archdale	NC	27263	**800-423-3531***	336-889-2322	486
Hagemeyer North America Inc 1460 Tobias Gadson Blvd	Charleston	SC	29407	**877-462-7070**	843-745-2400	382
Hager Co 139 Victor St	Saint Louis	MO	63104	**800-325-9995**	314-772-4400	347
Hagerstown/Washington County Convention & Visitors Bureau 16 Public Sq	Hagerstown	MD	21740	**888-257-2600**	301-791-3246	207
Hagerty Insurance Agency LLC 141 River's Edge Dr Ste 200 PO Box 1303	Traverse City	MI	49684	**877-922-9701**	231-947-6868	388-4
Haggar Clothing Co 11511 Luna Rd 2 Colinas Crossing	Dallas	TX	75234	**877-841-2219**	214-352-8481	153-11
Haggard & Stocking Assoc 5318 Victory Dr	Indianapolis	IN	46203	**800-622-4824**	317-788-4661	382
Haggerty Enterprises Inc 370 Kimberly Dr	Carol Stream	IL	60188	**800-336-5282**	630-315-3300	332
Hagie Manufacturing Co PO Box 273	Clarion	IA	50525	**800-247-4885**	515-532-2861	273
Hahn & Bowersock Corp 151 Kalmus Dr Ste L1	Costa Mesa	CA	92626	**800-660-3187**		440
Hahn Systems Co Inc 6312 SE Ave	Indianapolis	IN	46203	**800-201-4246**	317-243-3796	382
HAI (Helicopter Assn International) 1635 Prince St	Alexandria	VA	22314	**800-435-4976**	703-683-4646	48-21
HAI (Hohman Assoc Inc) 6951 W Little York	Houston	TX	77040	**800-324-0978**	713-896-0978	47-2

Company / Address	City	State	ZIP	Toll-Free	Phone	Class
Haida Corp PO Box 89	Hydaburg	AK	99922	**800-478-3721**	907-285-3721	742
Haights Cross Communications 136 Madison Ave 8th Fl	New York	NY	10016	**800-338-6519**	212-209-0500	628-2
Hain Celestial Group Inc 4600 Sleepytime Dr Ste 250 *NASDAQ: HAIN*	Boulder	CO	80301	**800-434-4246**		296-11
Hainen Ford Inc 800 Hwy 5 S	Tipton	MO	65081	**888-526-6979**		56
Haines & Company Inc 8050 Freedom Ave	North Canton	OH	44720	**800-843-8452**		628-6
Haines City Citrus Growers Assn (HCCGA) Eight Railroad Ave PO Box 337 *Sales	Haines City	FL	33844	**800-327-6676***	863-422-1174	11-1
Hajoca Corp 127 Coulter Ave	Ardmore	PA	19003	**888-328-2383**	610-649-1430	605
Hajoca Corp Keenan Supply Div 1341 Philadelphia St	Pomona	CA	91766	**800-332-0366**	909-613-1363	605
Hal Hays Construction Inc 4181 Latham St	Riverside	CA	92501	**888-425-4297**	951-788-0703	301
Hal Leonard Corp 960 E Mark St	Winona	MN	55987	**800-321-3408**	507-454-2920	628-7
Haldeman-Homme Inc 430 Industrial Blvd NE	Minneapolis	MN	55413	**800-795-0696**	612-331-4880	319
Hale Centre Theater 3333 S Decker Lake Dr	West Valley City	UT	84119	**877-829-5500**	801-984-9000	565
Hale Farm & Village 2686 Oakhill Rd PO Box 296	Bath	OH	44210	**800-589-9703**	330-666-3711	513
Hale Products Inc 700 Spring Mill Ave	Conshohocken	PA	19428	**800-220-4253**	610-825-6300	632
Hale Trailer Brake & Wheel Inc Rt 73 & Cooper Rd	Voorhees	NJ	08043	**800-232-6535**	856-768-1330	125
Halekulani Hotel 2199 Kalia Rd	Honolulu	HI	96815	**800-367-2343**	808-923-2311	376
Halex Co 23901 Aurora Rd	Bedford Heights	OH	44146	**800-749-3261**	440-439-1616	307
Halex Corp 750 S Reservoir St	Pomona	CA	91766	**800-576-1636**	909-622-3537	347
Haley Bros Inc 6291 Orangethorpe Ave	Buena Park	CA	90620	**800-854-5951**	714-670-2112	236
Half Moon Bay Lodge & Conference Ctr 2400 S Cabrillo Hwy	Half Moon Bay	CA	94019	**800-710-0778**	650-726-9000	376
Half Moon Bay State Beach c/o San Mateo Coast Sector Office 95 Kelly Ave	Half Moon Bay	CA	94019	**800-444-7275**	650-726-8819	558
Halifax County Public Schools 1030 Mary Bethune St PO Box 1849	Halifax	VA	24558	**800-253-2687**	434-476-2171	676
Halifax Marriott Harborfront Hotel 1919 Upper Water St	Halifax	NS	B3J3J5	**800-450-4442**	902-421-1700	376
Halifax Stanfield International Airport (HIAA) 1 Bell Blvd	Enfield	NS	B2T1K2	**800-565-5359**	902-873-4422	27
Hall County Schools 711 Green St NW Ste 100	Gainesville	GA	30501	**800-505-4732**	770-534-1080	676
Hall Electric Supply Company Inc 263 Main St	Stoneham	MA	02180	**800-444-3726**	781-438-3800	37
Hall Signs Inc 4495 W Vernal Pk	Bloomington	IN	47404	**800-284-7446**		692
Hallamore Motor Transportation Inc 795 Plymouth St	Holbrook	MA	02343	**800-242-1300**	781-767-2000	770
Hallcrest Inc 1820 Pickwick Ln *General	Glenview	IL	60026	**800-527-1419***	847-998-8580	203
Halliburton House Inn 5184 Morris St	Halifax	NS	B3J1B3	**888-512-3344**	902-420-0658	376
Hallie Ford Museum of Art 700 State St	Salem	OR	97301	**844-232-7228**	503-370-6855	513
Hallmark Cards Inc 2501 McGee St	Kansas City	MO	64108	**800-425-5627**	816-274-5111	129
Hallmark Ch 12700 Ventura Blvd Ste 200	Studio City	CA	91604	**888-390-7474**	818-755-2400	729
Hallmark Inns & Resorts 15455 Hallmark Dr Ste 200	Lake Oswego	OR	97035	**888-448-4449**		376
Hallmark International PO Box 419034	Kansas City	MO	64141	**800-425-5627**	816-274-5111	129
Hallmark Nameplate Inc 1717 E Lincoln Ave	Mount Dora	FL	32757	**800-874-9063**	352-383-8142	692
Halocarbon Products Corp PO Box 661	River Edge	NJ	07661	**800-338-5803**	201-262-8899	576
Halogen Software 495 March Rd	Kanata	ON	K2K3G1	**866-566-7778**	613-270-1011	179-1
Halsted Corp 78 Halladay St	Jersey City	NJ	07304	**800-843-5184**	201-433-3323	66
Halt Medical Inc 131 Sand Creek Rd Ste B	Brentwood	CA	94513	**877-412-3828**	925-634-7943	360
Halyard Health 20202 Windrow Dr	Lake Forest	CA	92630	**800-448-3569**	949-206-2700	472
Hamburg Sud North America Inc 465 S St	Morristown	NJ	07960	**888-228-8241**	973-775-5300	312
Hamilton Beach/Proctor-Silex Inc 4421 Waterfront Dr *Cust Svc	Glen Allen	VA	23060	**800-851-8900***	804-273-9777	36
Hamilton Chevrolet 5800 E 14 Mile Rd	Warren	MI	48092	**888-466-7827**	586-264-1400	56
Hamilton City Employees Federal Credit Union 309 Ct St	Hamilton	OH	45011	**800-264-5578**	513-868-5881	219
Hamilton Co 4970 Energy Way	Reno	NV	89502	**800-648-5950**	775-858-3000	416
Hamilton College 198 College Hill Rd *Admissions	Clinton	NY	13323	**800-843-2655***	315-859-4421	166
Hamilton County Convention & Visitors Bureau Inc 37 E Main St	Carmel	IN	46032	**800-776-8687**	317-848-3181	207
Hamilton County Educational Service Ctr (HCESC) 11083 Hamilton Ave	Cincinnati	OH	45231	**800-964-8211**	513-674-4200	676
Hamilton County Electric Co-op Assn 420 N Rice St PO Box 753	Hamilton	TX	76531	**800-595-3401**	254-386-3123	245
Hamilton Ctr Inc PO Box 4323	Terre Haute	IN	47804	**800-742-0787**	812-231-8323	371-5
Hamilton Group 100 Elwood Davis Rd	North Syracuse	NY	13212	**800-351-3066**	315-413-0086	272
Hamilton Park Hotel & Conference Ctr 175 Pk Ave	Florham Park	NJ	07932	**800-321-6000**	973-377-2424	374

Company / Address	City	State	ZIP	Toll-Free	Phone	Class
Hamilton Port Authority 605 James St N 6th Fl	Hamilton	ON	L8L1K1	**800-263-2131**	905-525-4330	611
Hamilton Sorter Co Inc 3158 Production Dr	Fairfield	OH	45014	**800-503-9966**	513-870-4400	286
Hamilton Telephone Co 1001 12th St	Aurora	NE	68818	**800-821-1831**	402-694-5101	115
Hamler State Bank 210 Randolph St PO Box 358	Hamler	OH	43524	**888-508-3955**	419-274-3955	69
Hamlin Beach State Park One Camp Rd	Hamlin	NY	14464	**800-456-2267**	585-964-2462	558
Hamline University 1536 Hewitt Ave	Saint Paul	MN	55104	**800-753-9753**	651-523-2207	166
Hamline University Bush Memorial Library 1536 Hewitt Ave	Saint Paul	MN	55104	**800-753-9753**	651-523-2375	431-6
Hamline University School of Law 1536 Hewitt Ave	Saint Paul	MN	55104	**800-388-3688**	651-523-2800	167-1
Hammacher Schlemmer & Co 9307 N Milwaukee Ave	Niles	IL	60714	**800-321-1484**		359
Hammel Green & Abrahamson Inc 701 Washington Ave N	Minneapolis	MN	55401	**888-442-8255**	612-758-4000	261
Hammelmann Corp 600 Progress Rd	Dayton	OH	45449	**800-783-4935**	937-859-8777	632
Hammer Nutrition Ltd 4952 Whitefish Stage Rd *Cust Svc	Whitefish	MT	59937	**800-336-1977***	406-862-1877	787
Hammerman Bros Inc 50 W 57th St 12th Fl	New York	NY	10019	**800-223-6436**	212-956-2800	406
Hammersmith Mfg & Sales Inc 401 Central Ave	Horton	KS	66439	**800-375-8245**	785-486-2121	90
Hammock Beach Resort 200 Ocean Crest Dr	Palm Coast	FL	32137	**866-841-0287**	386-246-5500	660
Hammond Communications Group Inc 173 Trade St	Lexington	KY	40511	**888-424-1878**	859-254-1878	506
Hammond Electronics Inc 1230 W Central Blvd *Sales	Orlando	FL	32805	**800-929-3672***	407-849-6060	246
Hammond Suzuki USA Inc 743 Annoreno Dr	Addison	IL	60101	**888-765-2900**	630-543-0277	520
Hammons Products Co 105 Hammons Dr PO Box 140	Stockton	MO	65785	**888-429-6887**		10-9
Hamon Research-Cottrell Inc 58 E Main St	Somerville	NJ	08876	**800-722-7580**	908-685-4000	383
Hampden-Sydney College PO Box 667 *Admissions	Hampden Sydney	VA	23943	**800-755-0733***	434-223-6120	166
Hampson Archeological Museum State Park PO Box 156	Wilson	AR	72395	**888-742-8701**	870-655-8622	558
Hampton Affiliates 9600 SW Barnes Rd Ste 200	Portland	OR	97225	**888-310-1464**	503-297-7691	674
Hampton Behavioral Health Center 650 Rancocas Rd	Westampton	NJ	08060	**800-603-6767**		717
Hampton Conventions & Visitors Bureau 1919 Commerce Dr Ste 290	Hampton	VA	23666	**800-487-8778**	757-722-1222	207
Hampton Inn Philadelphia Ctr City-Convention Ctr 1301 Race St	Philadelphia	PA	19107	**800-426-7866**	215-665-9100	206
Hampton Plantation State Historic Site 1950 Rutledge Rd	McClellanville	SC	29458	**800-315-3087**	843-546-9361	558
Hampton Products International Corp 50 Icon	Foothill Ranch	CA	92610	**800-562-5625**	949-472-4256	347
Hampton University 100 E Queen St	Hampton	VA	23668	**800-624-3341**	757-727-5000	166
Hamptons Magazine 67 Hampton Rd Ste 201	SouthHampton	NY	11968	**866-891-3144**	631-283-7125	452-22
Hamrick Inc 742 Peachoid Rd	Gaffney	SC	29341	**800-487-5411**	864-489-6095	153-3
Hamrick Mills Inc 515 W Buford St PO Box 48	Gaffney	SC	29341	**800-600-4305**	864-489-4731	734-1
Hana Hou Magazine (Hawaiian Airlines) 1144 Tenth Ave Ste 401	Honolulu	HI	96816	**888-733-3336**	808-733-3333	452-22
Hanalei Bay Resort & Suites 5380 Honoiki Rd	Princeville	HI	96722	**877-344-0688**	808-826-6522	660
Hanauma Bay Nature Preserve 100 Hanauma Bay Rd	Honolulu	HI	96825	**800-690-6200**	808-396-4229	49-4
Hanchett Entry Systems Inc (HES) 22630 N 17th Ave	Phoenix	AZ	85027	**800-626-7590**	623-582-4626	683
Hanchett Manufacturing Inc 906 N State St	Big Rapids	MI	49307	**800-454-7463**	231-796-7678	450
Hancock Concrete Products Inc 17 Atlantic Ave	Hancock	MN	56244	**800-321-1558**	320-392-5207	184
Hancock County 12630 Broad St	Sparta	GA	31087	**800-255-0135**	706-444-5746	336
Hancock County Co-op Oil Assn 245 State St	Garner	IA	50438	**800-924-2667**	641-923-2635	342
Hancock Holding Co 2510 14th St	Gulfport	MS	39501	**800-522-6542**	228-822-4371	357-2
Hancock-Wood Electric Co-op Inc (HWEC) 1399 Business Pk Dr S PO Box 190	North Baltimore	OH	45872	**800-445-4840**	419-257-3241	245
Hancor Inc PO Box 1047	Findlay	OH	45839	**888-892-2694**	419-422-6521	589
Handgards Inc 901 Hawkins Blvd	El Paso	TX	79915	**800-351-8161**		569
Handlery Hotel & Resort 950 Hotel Cir N	San Diego	CA	92108	**800-676-6567**	619-298-0511	660
Handlery Union Square Hotel 351 Geary St	San Francisco	CA	94102	**800-995-4874**	415-781-7800	376
Handley Industries Inc 2101 Brooklyn Rd	Jackson	MI	49203	**800-870-5088**	517-787-8821	200
Hands of Hope Hospice 137 N Belt Hwy	Saint Joseph	MO	64506	**800-443-1143**	816-271-7190	368
Handy Hardware Wholesale Inc 8300 Tewantin Dr	Houston	TX	77061	**800-364-3835**	713-644-1495	348
Handy Store Fixtures Inc 337 Sherman Ave	Newark	NJ	07114	**800-631-4280**	973-242-1600	286
Handyman Connection Inc 11115 Kenwood Rd	Cincinnati	OH	45242	**800-884-2639**	513-771-3003	190-11
Handyman Matters Inc 12567 W Cedar Dr Ste 250	Lakewood	CO	80228	**866-349-6946**	303-984-0177	309
HandyTrac Systems LLC 510 Staghorn Ct	Alpharetta	GA	30004	**800-665-9994**	678-990-2305	683
Hanes Cos Inc 500 N McLin Creek Rd	Conover	NC	28613	**877-252-3052**	828-464-4673	587
Hanger Orthopedic Group Inc 10910 Domain Dr Ste 300	Austin	TX	78758	**877-442-6437**	512-777-3800	349
Hanger Prosthetics & Orthopedics Inc 10910 Domain Dr Ste 300	Austin	TX	78758	**877-442-6437**		472
Hangsterfer's Laboratories Inc 175 Ogden Rd	Mantua	NJ	08051	**800-433-5823**	856-468-0216	534
Hankook Tire America Corp 1450 Valley Rd	Wayne	NJ	07470	**800-426-8252**	973-633-9000	744
Hanley Wood Market Intelligence 555 Anton Blvd Ste 950	Costa Mesa	CA	92626	**800-938-8839**	714-540-8500	194
Hanley-Wood LLC 1 Thomas Cir NW Ste 600	Washington	DC	20005	**800-227-8839**	202-452-0800	628-9
Hanmi Bank 3660 Wilshire Blvd Ste PH-A	Los Angeles	CA	90010	**877-808-4266**	213-382-2200	357-2
Hanna Andersson Corp 1010 NW Flanders St *Cust Svc	Portland	OR	97209	**800-222-0544***		454
Hanna Steel Corp 3812 Commerce Ave PO Box 558	Fairfield	AL	35064	**800-633-8252**	205-780-1111	485
Hannay Reels Inc 553 SR 143	Westerlo	NY	12193	**877-467-3357**	518-797-3791	116
Hannibal Carbide Tool Inc 5000 Paris Gravel Rd	Hannibal	MO	63401	**800-451-9436**	573-221-2775	488
Hannibal Convention & Visitors Bureau 505 N Third St	Hannibal	MO	63401	**866-263-4825**	573-221-2477	207
Hannibal Industries Inc 3851 S Santa Fe Ave	Los Angeles	CA	90058	**888-246-7074**	323-588-4261	485
Hannibal-LaGrange College 2800 Palmyra Rd *Admissions	Hannibal	MO	63401	**800-454-1119***	573-221-3675	166
Hannon Hydraulics LLC 625 N Loop 12	Irving	TX	75061	**800-333-4266**	972-438-2870	223
Hannon Security Services Inc 9036 Grand Ave S	Minneapolis	MN	55420	**800-328-3877**	952-881-5865	684
Hanover College 484 Ball Dr	Hanover	IN	47243	**800-213-2178**	812-866-7000	166
Hanover Foods Corp 1550 York St PO Box 334 *OTC: HNFSA*	Hanover	PA	17331	**800-888-4646**	717-632-6000	295-36
Hanover Hospital 300 Highland Ave	Hanover	PA	17331	**800-673-2426**	717-637-3711	371-3
Hanover Inn Two E Wheelock St	Hanover	NH	03755	**800-443-7024**	603-643-4300	376
Hanover Insurance Co 440 Lincoln St	Worcester	MA	01653	**800-853-0456**	508-855-1000	388-4
Hanover Insurance Group Inc 440 Lincoln St *NYSE: THG*	Worcester	MA	01653	**800-628-0250**	508-855-1000	357-4
Hans Johnsen Co 8901 Chancellor Row *Sales	Dallas	TX	75247	**800-879-1515***	214-879-1550	348
Hanscom Inc 331 Market St	Warren	RI	02885	**877-725-6788**	401-247-1999	601
Hansen Beverage Co One Monster Way	Corona	CA	92879	**800-426-7367**		296-8
Hansen Manufacturing Corp 5100 W 12th St	Sioux Falls	SD	57107	**800-328-1785**	605-332-3200	208
Hansen Technologies Corp 6827 High Grove Blvd	Burr Ridge	IL	60527	**800-426-7368**	630-325-1565	203
Hansgrohe Inc 1490 Bluegrass Lakes Pkwy	Alpharetta	GA	30004	**800-334-0455**	770-360-9880	602
Hanson Logistics 2900 S State St Ste 4 E	Saint Joseph	MI	49085	**888-772-1197**	269-982-1390	444
Hapag-Lloyd America Inc 401 E Jackson St	Tampa	FL	33602	**800-282-8977**	813-276-4600	312
Hapco Inc 26252 Hillman Hwy	Abingdon	VA	24210	**800-368-7171**	276-628-7171	486
Hapman 6002 E N Ave	Kalamazoo	MI	49048	**800-427-6260**	269-343-1675	208
Hapuna Beach Prince Hotel 62-100 Kauna'oa Dr	Kamuela	HI	96743	**800-882-6060**	808-880-1111	660
Harbec Plastics Inc 369 SR- 104	Ontario	NY	14519	**888-521-4416**	585-265-0010	601
Harben Inc 2010 Ronald Regan Blvd	Cumming	GA	30041	**800-327-5387**	770-889-9535	632
Harbin Hot Springs 18424 Harbin Springs Rd PO Box 782	Middletown	CA	95461	**800-622-2477**	707-987-2477	664
Harbison-Fischer 901 N Crowley Rd	Crowley	TX	76036	**800-364-7867**	817-297-2211	530
Harbor Court Hotel 550 Light St	Baltimore	MD	21202	**800-766-3782**	410-234-0550	376
Harbor Hospital Ctr 3001 S Hanover St	Baltimore	MD	21225	**800-280-9006**	410-350-3200	371-3
Harbor Industries Inc 14130 172nd Ave	Grand Haven	MI	49417	**800-968-6993**	616-842-5330	233
Harbor Light Hospice 800 Roosevelt Rd Bldg C Ste 206	Glen Ellyn	IL	60137	**800-419-0542**	630-942-0100	368
Harbor Sales 1000 Harbor Ct	Sudlersville	MD	21668	**800-345-1712**		606
Harbor View Hotel 131 N Water St Martha's Vineyard PO Box 7	Edgartown	MA	02539	**800-225-6005**	508-627-7000	376
Harborlite 130 Castilian Dr	Santa Barbara	CA	93117	**800-893-4445**	805-562-0200	498-3
HarborOne Credit Union 770 Oak St PO Box 720	Brockton	MA	02301	**800-244-7592**	508-895-1000	219
Harborplace & the Gallery 201 E Pratt St	Baltimore	MD	21202	**800-722-8614**	410-332-4191	49-5
Harborside Event Ctr 1375 Monroe St	Fort Myers	FL	33901	**800-294-9516**	239-321-8110	206
Harborside Hotel & Marina 55 W St	Bar Harbor	ME	04609	**800-328-5033**	207-288-5033	376
Harborside Inn One Christie's Landing	Newport	RI	02840	**800-427-9444**	401-846-6600	376
HARBORSIDE SUITES AT LITTLE HARBOR 611 Destiny Dr	Ruskin	FL	33570	**800-327-2773**		660
Harbour Industries Inc 4744 Shelburne Rd PO Box 188	Shelburne	VT	05482	**800-659-4733**	802-985-3311	801
Harbour's Edge 401 E Linton Blvd	Delray Beach	FL	33483	**888-417-9281**	561-272-7979	663
Harbourtowne Golf Resort & Conference Ctr 9784 Martingham Dr	Saint Michaels	MD	21663	**800-446-9066**	410-745-9066	660
Harco National Insurance Co PO Box 68309	Schaumburg	IL	60168	**800-448-4642**		388-4

	Toll-Free	Phone	Class
Harcourt Equipment			
313 Hwy 169 & 175 E ....Harcourt IA 50544	800-445-5646	515-354-5332	274
Harcourt Outlines Inc			
7765 S 175 W PO Box 128............. Milroy IN 46156	800-428-6584		54
Harcourt Pencil Co			
7765 S 175 W .... Milroy IN 46156	800-428-6584	765-629-2244	564
Harcros Chemicals Inc			
5200 Speaker Rd ....Kansas City KS 66106	800-504-8071	913-321-3131	144
Harcum College			
750 Montgomery Ave ....Bryn Mawr PA 19010	800-650-0035	610-525-4100	160
Hard Mfg Company Inc			
230 Grider St ....Buffalo NY 14215	800-873-4273		318-3
Hard Rock Cafe			
111 W Crocket St ....San Antonio TX 78205	888-519-6683	210-224-7625	662
Hard Rock Cafe International Inc			
6100 Old Pk Ln ....Orlando FL 32835	888-686-7625	407-445-7625	661
Hard Rock Hotel & Casino			
4455 Paradise Rd .... Las Vegas NV 89169	800-693-7625	702-693-5000	660
Hard Rock Hotel & Casino Biloxi			
777 Beach Blvd ....Biloxi MS 39530	877-877-6256	228-374-7625	132
Hard Rock Hotel at Universal Orlando Resort			
5800 Universal Blvd ....Orlando FL 32819	888-430-4999	407-503-2000	660
Hard Rock Hotel San Diego			
207 Fifth Ave ....San Diego CA 92101	866-751-7625	619-702-3000	376
Harder Mechanical Contractors Inc			
2148 NE M L King Blvd ....Portland OR 97212	800-392-3729	503-281-1112	190-10
HARDI Hydronic Heating & Cooling Council			
3455 Mill Run Dr Ste 820.............Hilliard OH 43026	888-253-2128	614-345-4328	48-18
Hardi Inc			
1500 W 76th St ....Davenport IA 52806	866-770-7063	563-386-1730	273
Hardin County Chamber of Commerce (HCCBA)			
225 S Detroit St ....Kenton OH 43326	888-642-7346	419-673-4131	137
Harding University			
900 E Ctr Ave ....Searcy AR 72149	800-477-4407	501-279-4000	166
Harding University Graduate School of Religion			
915 E Market Ave ....Searcy AR 72143	800-477-4407	501-279-4407	167-3
Hardinge Inc			
1 Hardinge Dr ....Elmira NY 14902	800-843-8801	607-734-2281	450
NASDAQ: HDNG			
Hardin-Simmons University			
2200 Hickory St ....Abilene TX 79698	877-464-7889	325-670-1206	166
Hardware Distribution Warehouses Inc (HDW)			
6900 Woolworth Rd ....Shreveport LA 71129	800-256-8527*	318-686-8527	348
*Cust Svc			
Hardware Suppliers of America Inc (HSI)			
1400 E Fire Tower Rd ....Greenville NC 27858	800-334-5625		348
Hardwick Clothes Inc			
3800 Old Tasso Rd ....Cleveland TN 37312	800-251-6392		153-11
Hardwoods of Michigan Inc			
430 Div St ....Clinton MI 49236	800-327-2812	517-456-7431	674
Hardy Bros Inc			
6406 Siloam Rd ....Siloam NC 27047	800-525-5354	336-374-5050	187
Hardy Corp			
350 Industrial Dr ....Birmingham AL 35211	800-289-4822	205-252-7191	190-10
Hardy County			
204 Washington St Rm 111 ....Moorefield WV 26836	800-222-1222	304-530-0250	336
Harford County Chamber of Commerce			
108 S Bond St ....Bel Air MD 21014	800-682-8536	410-838-2020	137
Harford County Public Library			
1221-A Brass Mill Rd ....Belcamp MD 21017	800-944-7403	410-575-6761	431-3
Hargrave Military Academy (HMA)			
200 Military Dr ....Chatham VA 24531	800-432-2480	434-432-2481	615
Hargray Communications			
856 William Hilton Pkwy			
PO Box 5986.........Hilton Head Island SC 29938	800-726-1266	843-341-1501	726
Harkcon			
1390 Chain Bridge Rd 570 ....Mclean VA 22101	800-499-6456		458
Harkins Builders Inc			
2201 Warwick Way ....Marriottsville MD 21104	800-227-2345	410-750-2600	187
Harlan ARH Hospital			
81 Ballpark Rd ....Harlan KY 40831	800-274-9375	606-573-8100	371-3
Harlan Bioproducts for Science Inc (HBPS)			
298 S Carroll Rd ....Indianapolis IN 46229	800-793-7287		231
Harlan County			
311 Main St ....Alma NE 68920	800-762-5498		336
Harlan Materials Handling Corp			
27 Stanley Rd ....Kansas City KS 66115	800-255-4262	913-342-5650	465
Harlem Globetrotters International Inc			
400 E Van Buren St Ste 300 ....Phoenix AZ 85004	800-641-4667	602-258-0000	182
Harlequin Enterprises Ltd			
225 Duncan Mill Rd ....Don Mills ON M3B3K9	888-343-9777	416-445-5860	628-2
Harlequin Enterprises Ltd Distribution Ctr			
3010 Walden Ave ....Depew NY 14043	888-432-4879	716-684-1800	94
Harlequin-Silhouette Books			
233 Broadway Ste 1001 ....New York NY 10279	800-873-8635	212-553-4200	628-2
Harley-Davidson Financial Services Inc			
PO Box 21489 ....Carson City NV 89721	888-691-4337		214
Harleysville Group Inc			
355 Maple Ave ....Harleysville PA 19438	800-523-6344	215-256-5000	357-4
NASDAQ: HGIC			
Harleysville Insurance Co of New Jersey			
112 W Park Dr ....Mount Laurel NJ 08054	800-322-5521	856-642-9779	388-4
Harleysville Life Insurance Co			
355 Maple Ave ....Harleysville PA 19438	800-222-1981*		388-2
*General			
Harleysville Mutual Insurance Co			
355 Maple Ave ....Harleysville PA 19438	800-523-6344	215-256-5000	388-2
Harleysville Pennland Insurance Co			
355 Maple Ave ....Harleysville PA 19438	800-523-6344	215-256-5000	388-4
Harleysville Preferred Insurance Co			
355 Maple Ave ....Harleysville PA 19438	800-523-6344	215-256-5000	388-4
Harleysville Savings Financial Corp			
271 Main St ....Harleysville PA 19438	888-256-8828	215-256-8828	357-2
NASDAQ: HARL			
Harleysville Worcester Insurance Co			
120 Front St Ste 400..............Worcester MA 01608	800-225-7387	508-754-6666	388-4
Harlo Corp			
PO Box 129 ....Grandville MI 49468	800-391-4151	616-538-0550	465
Harman International Industries Inc			
400 Atlantic St 15th Fl ....Stamford CT 06901	800-473-0602	203-328-3500	51
NYSE: HAR			
Harmon Electric Assn Inc (HEA)			
114 N First St PO Box 393 ....Hollis OK 73550	800-643-7769	580-688-3342	245

	Toll-Free	Phone	Class
Harmon Stores Inc			
650 Liberty Ave ....Union NJ 07083	866-427-6661		237
Harmonic Drive LLC			
247 Lynnfield St ....Peabody MA 01960	800-921-3332	978-532-1800	60
Harmonic Inc			
4300 N First St ....San Jose CA 95134	800-322-2885	408-542-2500	638
NASDAQ: HLIT			
Harms Charters			
532 S Vly View Rd ....Sioux Falls SD 57106	800-678-6543	605-336-3339	106
Harnack Co			
6016 Nordic Dr ....Cedar Falls IA 50613	800-772-2022*	319-277-0660	426
*Cust Svc			
Harness Racing Museum & Hall of Fame			
240 Main St ....Goshen NY 10924	877-800-8782	845-294-6330	515
Harnett County Board of Education			
1008 11th Street PO Box 1029.....Lillington NC 27546	800-942-3767	910-893-8151	676
Harney Rock & Paving Co			
457 S Date Ave ....Burns OR 97720	888-298-2681	541-573-7855	498-5
Harold G Butzer Inc			
730 Wicker Ln ....Jefferson City MO 65109	800-769-1065	573-636-4115	190-10
Harold Levinson Assoc (HLA)			
21 Banfi Plz ....Farmingdale NY 11735	800-325-2512	631-962-2400	296-3
Harper Brush Works Inc			
400 N Second St ....Fairfield IA 52556	800-223-7894	641-472-5186	102
Harper County			
201 N Jennings Ave ....Anthony KS 67003	877-537-2110	620-842-5555	336
Harper Industries Inc			
616 Northview St ....Paducah KY 42001	866-487-9243	270-442-2753	189-4
Harper Trucks Inc			
PO Box 12330 ....Wichita KS 67277	800-835-4099	316-942-1381	465
Harper's Bazaar Magazine			
300 W 57th St ....New York NY 10019	800-285-4274*	212-903-5000	452-11
*General			
Harper's Magazine			
666 Broadway 11th Fl............New York NY 10012	800-444-4653	212-420-5720	452-11
HarperCollins Publishers Inc			
10 E 53rd St ....New York NY 10022	800-242-7737	212-207-7000	628-2
Harps Food Stores Inc			
918 S Gutensohn Rd ....Springdale AR 72762	877-772-8193	479-751-7601	342
Harrah's Ak-Chin Casino Resort			
15406 Maricopa Rd ....Maricopa AZ 85139	800-427-7247*	480-802-5000	660
*General			
Harrah's Cherokee Casino & Hotel			
777 Casino Dr ....Cherokee NC 28719	877-811-0777*	828-497-7777	132
*General			
Harrah's Council Bluffs			
1 Harrahs Blvd ....Council Bluffs IA 51501	800-342-7724	712-329-6000	132
Harrah's Joliet			
151 N Joliet St ....Joliet IL 60432	800-522-4700	815-740-7800	132
Harrah's Las Vegas			
3475 Las Vegas Blvd S .... Las Vegas NV 89109	800-214-9110		131
Harrah's Laughlin			
2900 S Casino Dr ....Laughlin NV 89029	800-427-7247	702-298-4600	132
Harrah's New Orleans			
8 Canal St ....New Orleans LA 70130	800-427-7247	504-533-6000	132
Harrah's Reno			
219 N Ctr St ....Reno NV 89501	866-736-6427	775-788-3044	376
Harrah's Resort Atlantic City			
777 Harrah's Blvd ....Atlantic City NJ 08401	800-342-7724	609-441-5000	132
Harrah's Rincon Casino & Resort			
777 Harrah's Rincon Way ......Valley Center CA 92082	800-522-4700	760-751-3100	660
Harrah's Tunica			
1021 Casino Ctr Dr ....Robinsonville MS 38664	800-946-4946	800-303-7463	132
Harraseeket Inn			
162 Main St ....Freeport ME 04032	800-342-6423	207-865-9377	376
Harri Plumbing & Heating Inc			
809 W 12th St ....Juneau AK 99801	800-478-3190	907-586-3190	605
Harriman State Park			
3489 Green Canyon Rd ....Island Park ID 83429	866-634-3246	208-558-7368	558
Harrington College of Design			
200 W Madison St ....Chicago IL 60606	866-590-4423		166
Harrington Hoists Inc			
401 W End Ave ....Manheim PA 17545	800-233-3010	717-665-2000	383
Harrington Industrial Plastics LLC			
14480 Yorba Ave ....Chino CA 91710	800-213-4528	909-597-8641	382
Harrington Memorial Hospital (HMH)			
100 S St ....Southbridge MA 01550	800-416-6072	508-765-9771	371-3
Harrington Raceway			
15 W Rider Rd ....Harrington DE 19952	888-887-5687	302-398-7223	633
Harris Assoc LP			
111 South Wacker Dr Ste 4600........Chicago IL 60606	800-731-0700	312-646-3600	398
Harris Connect LLC			
1511 Rt 22 Ste C-25..............Brewster NY 10509	800-516-4915		628-2
Harris Corp			
1025 W NASA Blvd ....Melbourne FL 32919	800-442-7747	321-727-9100	638
NYSE: HRS			
Harris Corp RF Communications Div			
1680 University Ave ....Rochester NY 14610	866-264-8040	585-244-5830	638
Harris County			
112 S College St PO Box 426.........Hamilton GA 31811	888-478-0010	706-628-0010	336
Harris Farms Inc			
27366 W Oakland Ave ....Coalinga CA 93210	800-311-6211	559-884-2859	10-10
Harris Group Inc			
300 Elliott Ave W ....Seattle WA 98119	800-488-7410	206-494-9400	261
Harris Industries Inc			
5181 Argosy Ave ....Huntington Beach CA 92649	800-222-6866	714-898-8048	722
Harris Interactive Inc			
60 Corporate Woods ....Rochester NY 14623	800-866-7655	585-272-8400	461
NASDAQ: HPOL			
Harris Miniature Golf			
141 W Burk Ave ....Wildwood NJ 08260	888-294-6530	609-522-4200	189-3
Harris Moran Seed Co			
PO Box 4938 ....Modesto CA 95352	800-808-7333	800-320-4672	685
Harris myCFO Inc			
2200 Geng Rd Ste 100 ....Palo Alto CA 94303	866-966-1130	650-210-5000	401
Harris Products Group			
4501 Quality Pl ....Mason OH 45040	800-733-4043	513-754-2000	798
Harris Ranch Beef Co			
16277 S McCall Ave PO Box 220 ......Selma CA 93662	800-742-1955		468
Harris Soup Co, The			
17711 NE Riverside Pkwy ....Portland OR 97230	800-307-7687	503-257-7687	296-8
Harris Teeter Inc			
701 Crestdale Rd PO Box 10100 ......Matthews NC 28105	800-432-6111*	704-844-3100	342
*Cust Svc			

	Toll-Free	Phone	Class
Harrisburg Area Community College			
Gettysburg			
731 Old Harrisburg Rd ....Gettysburg PA 17325	**800-222-4222**	717-337-3855	160
Lebanon			
735 Cumberland St ....Lebanon PA 17042	**800-222-4222**	717-270-4222	160
Harrisburg Dairies Inc			
2001 Herr St ....Harrisburg PA 17105	**800-692-7429**	717-233-8701	295-27
Harrisburg Hospital			
111 S Front St ....Harrisburg PA 17101	**888-782-5678**	717-782-3131	371-3
Harrisburg International Airport			
One Terminal Dr Ste 300......Middletown PA 17057	**888-235-9442**	717-948-3900	27
Harrisburg Regional Chamber			
3211 N Front St Ste 201 ....Harrisburg PA 17110	**877-883-8339**	717-232-4099	137
HarrisData			
13555 Bishops Ct Ste 300 ....Brookfield WI 53005	**800-225-0585**	262-784-9099	179-1
Harrison Hot Springs Resort & Spa			
100 Esplanade Ave ......Harrison Hot Springs BC V0M1K0	**800-663-2266**	604-796-2244	660
Harrison Paint Co			
1329 Harrison Ave SW ....Canton OH 44706	**800-321-0680**	330-455-5125	543
Harrison Steel Castings Co Inc			
900 S Mound St ....Attica IN 47918	**888-782-7937**	765-762-2481	306
Harrisonville Telephone Co			
213 S Main St PO Box 149..........Waterloo IL 62298	**888-482-8353**	618-939-6112	726
Harrogate			
400 Locust St ....Lakewood NJ 08701	**888-551-5531**	732-905-7070	663
Harry & David Holdings Inc			
2500 S Pacific Hwy ....Medford OR 97501	**877-322-1200***		334
Cust Svc			
Harry Cooper Supply Company Inc			
605 N Sherman Pkwy ....Springfield MO 65802	**800-426-6737**	417-865-8392	605
Harry Davis & Co			
1725 Blvd of Allies ....Pittsburgh PA 15219	**800-775-2289**	412-765-1170	50
Harry G Barr Co			
6500 S Zero St ....Fort Smith AR 72903	**800-829-2277**	479-646-7891	235
Harry Hynes Memorial Hospice			
313 S Market St ....Wichita KS 67202	**800-767-4965**	316-265-9441	368
Harry Klitzner Co, The			
530 Wellington Ave Ste 11 ....Cranston RI 02910	**800-621-0161**		406
Harry London Candies Inc			
5353 Lauby Rd ....North Canton OH 44720	**800-333-3629***	330-494-0833	295-8
Cust Svc			
Harry Ritchie's Jewelers Inc			
956 Willamette St ....Eugene OR 97401	**800-935-2850***	541-686-1787	407
Cust Svc			
Harry S Truman College			
1145 W Wilson Ave ....Chicago IL 60640	**877-863-6339**	773-878-1700	160
Harry S Truman Memorial Veterans Hospital			
800 Hospital Dr ....Columbia MO 65201	**877-222-8387**	573-814-6000	371-8
Harry S Truman National Historic Site			
223 N Main St ....Independence MO 64050	**877-642-4743**	816-254-2720	557
Harry S Truman Presidential Library & Museum			
500 W Hwy 24 ....Independence MO 64050	**800-833-1225**	816-268-8200	431-2
Harry S Truman's Little White House Museum			
111 Front St Truman Annex ....Key West FL 33040	**800-435-7352**	305-294-9911	513
Harry Winston Inc			
718 Fifth Ave ....New York NY 10019	**800-988-4110**	212-399-1000	406
Harsco Corp			
350 Poplar Church Rd ....Camp Hill PA 17011	**866-470-3900**	717-763-7064	186
NYSE: HSC			
Harsco Industrial Air-X-Changers			
5215 Arkansas Rd PO Box 1804........Catoosa OK 74015	**800-404-3904**	918-619-8000	90
Hart & Price Corp			
PO Box 36368 ....Dallas TX 75235	**800-777-9129**	214-521-9129	656
Hart Corp			
900 Jaymor Rd ....SouthHampton PA 18966	**800-368-4278**	215-322-5100	643
Hart Electric Membership Corp			
1071 Elberton Hwy ....Hartwell GA 30643	**800-241-4109**	706-376-4714	245
Hart InterCivic			
15500 Wells Port Dr PO Box 80649.......Austin TX 78708	**800-223-4278**	512-252-6400	789
Hart Publications Inc			
1616 S Voss Rd Ste 1000..........Houston TX 77057	**800-874-2544**	713-260-6400	628-9
Hart Schaffner Marx (HSM)			
1680 E Touhy Ave ....Des Plaines IL 60018	**800-327-4466**		153-11
Hart Scientific Inc			
799 E Utah Vly Dr ....American Fork UT 84003	**800-438-4278**	801-763-1600	202
Harte Nissan Inc			
165 W Service Rd ....Hartford CT 06120	**866-687-8971**	860-549-2800	56
Harte-Hanks Inc			
9601 McAllister Fwy Ste 610 ....San Antonio TX 78216	**800-456-9748**	210-829-9000	5
NYSE: HHS			
Harte-Hanks Market Intelligence			
9980 Huennekens St ....San Diego CA 92121	**800-854-8409**		196
Harte-Hanks Response Management			
2800 Wells Branch Pkwy ....Austin TX 78728	**800-456-9748**	512-434-1100	727
Hartford Computer Group Inc			
10440 Little Patuxent Pkwy			
3rd Fl ....Columbia MD 21044	**800-370-5849**	410-740-3020	181
Hartford Courant			
285 Broad St ....Hartford CT 06115	**800-524-4242**	860-241-6200	525-2
Hartford Electric Supply Co (HESCO)			
30 Inwood Rd Ste 1 ....Rocky Hill CT 06067	**800-969-5444**	860-236-6363	246
Hartford Hospital			
80 Seymour St ....Hartford CT 06102	**800-545-7664**	860-545-5000	371-3
Hartford Life & Accident Insurance Co			
One Hartford Plz ....Hartford CT 06155	**800-833-5575**	860-547-5000	388-2
Hartford Mutual Funds			
30 Dan Rd Ste 55022 ....Canton MA 02021	**888-843-7824**		521
Hartford Seminary			
77 Sherman St ....Hartford CT 06105	**877-860-2255**	860-509-9500	166
Hartford Steam Boiler Inspection & Insurance Co, The (HSB)			
One State St PO Box 5024 ....Hartford CT 06102	**800-472-1866**		388-4
Hartford's Omni Auto Plan			
PO Box 105440 ....Atlanta GA 30348	**800-243-5860**	770-952-4500	388-4
Hartgrove Hospital			
5730 W Roosevelt Rd ....Chicago IL 60644	**800-478-4783**	773-722-3113	371-5
Hartnell College			
156 Homestead Ave ....Salinas CA 93901	**888-678-2871**	831-755-6700	160
Hartness House Inn			
30 Orchard St ....Springfield VT 05156	**800-732-4789**	802-885-2115	376
Hartness International Inc			
1200 Garlington Rd			
PO Box 26509...............Greenville SC 29616	**800-845-8791**	864-297-1200	540
Harton Regional Medical Ctr			
1801 N Jackson St ....Tullahoma TN 37388	**800-999-6673***	931-393-3000	371-3
*General			
Harts Nursery of Jefferson Inc			
4049 Jefferson-Scio Rd ....Jefferson OR 97352	**800-356-9335**	541-327-3366	366
Hartsfield-Jackson Atlanta International Airport			
6000 N Terminal Pkwy Ste 4000.........Atlanta GA 30320	**800-897-1910**	404-530-6600	27
Hartson-kennedy Cabinet Top Company Inc			
522 W 22nd St PO Box 3095..........Marion IN 46953	**800-388-8144**	765-668-8144	592
Hartung Agalite Glass Co			
17830 W Valley Hwy ....Seattle WA 98188	**800-552-2227**	425-656-2626	328
Hartung Bros Inc			
708 Heartland Trl Ste 2000 ....Madison WI 53717	**800-362-2522**	608-829-6000	10-10
Hartung Glass Industries			
10450 SW Ridder Rd ....Wilsonville OR 97070	**800-552-2227**	503-682-3846	328
Hartwick College			
One Hartwick Dr ....Oneonta NY 13820	**888-427-8942**	607-431-4150	166
Harty Press Inc, The			
PO Box 324 ....New Haven CT 06513	**800-654-0562**	203-562-5112	619
Hartz Mountain Corp, The			
400 Plz Dr ....Secaucus NJ 07094	**800-275-1414**		571
Hartzell Engine Technologies LLC			
2900 Selma Hwy ....Montgomery AL 36108	**877-359-5355**	334-386-5400	21
Hartzell Fan Inc			
910 S Downing St ....Piqua OH 45356	**800-336-3267**	937-773-7411	18
Harvard Bioscience Inc			
84 October Hill Rd ....Holliston MA 01746	**800-272-2775**	508-893-8999	416
NASDAQ: HBIO			
Harvard Business Review			
60 Harvard Way ....Boston MA 02163	**800-274-3214**	617-783-7500	452-5
Harvard Business School Publishing			
60 Harvard Way ....Boston MA 02163	**800-795-5200**		628-4
Harvard Educational Review			
Eight Story St First Fl ....Cambridge MA 02138	**877-930-4473**	617-495-3432	452-8
Harvard Medical School			
25 Shattuck St ....Boston MA 02115	**866-606-0573**	617-432-1550	167-2
Harvard Pilgrim Health Care Inc			
93 Worcester St ....Wellesley MA 02481	**888-888-4742**	617-509-1000	388-3
Harvard Square Hotel			
110 Mt Auburn St Harvard Sq......Cambridge MA 02138	**800-458-5886**	617-864-5200	376
Harvard University Press			
79 Garden St ....Cambridge MA 02138	**800-405-1619**	617-495-2600	628-4
Harvard Women's Health Watch			
PO Box 9308 ....Big Sandy TX 75755	**877-649-9457**		524-8
Harvest Energy Trust			
330 Fifth Ave SW Ste 2100.............Calgary AB T2P0L4	**866-666-1178**	403-265-1178	666
Harvest Inn			
1 Main St ....Saint Helena CA 94574	**800-950-8466**	707-963-9463	376
Harvest Land Co-op			
711 Front St PO Box 278 ....Morgan MN 56266	**800-245-5819**	507-249-3196	442
Harvest Partners			
280 Pk Ave 25th Fl ....New York NY 10017	**866-771-1000**	212-599-6300	780
Harvey Industries Inc			
1400 Main St ....Waltham MA 02451	**800-598-5400**		192-4
Harvey Mudd College			
301 Platt Blvd Kingston Hall.........Claremont CA 91711	**877-827-5462**	909-621-8011	166
Harvey Software Inc			
7050 Winkler Rd Ste 104 ....Fort Myers FL 33919	**800-231-0296**		178
Harvey Watt & Co			
475 N Central Ave ....Atlanta GA 30354	**800-241-6103**	404-767-7501	388-2
Harvey's			
424 S Gloster St ....Tupelo MS 38801	**888-222-9550**	662-842-6763	662
Harveys Lake Tahoe			
Hwy 50 at Stateline Ave			
PO Box 128...............Lake Tahoe NV 89449	**800-522-4700**	775-588-6611	132
Hasbro Inc			
1027 Newport Ave ....Pawtucket RI 02861	**800-242-7276**	401-431-8697	752
NASDAQ: HAS			
Hasbro Inc Playskool Div			
1027 Newport Ave ....Pawtucket RI 02861	**800-242-7276**	401-431-8697	752
HASCO America Inc			
270 Rutledge Rd Unit B ....Fletcher NC 28732	**800-387-9609**	828-650-2600	688
Haskel International Inc			
100 E Graham Pl ....Burbank CA 91502	**800-743-2720**	818-843-4000	632
Haskell Co			
111 Riverside Ave ....Jacksonville FL 32202	**800-622-4326**	904-791-4500	189-7
Hassayampa Inn			
122 E Gurley St ....Prescott AZ 86301	**800-322-1927***		376
Cust Svc			
Hassett Air Express			
877 S Rt 83 ....Elmhurst IL 60126	**800-323-9422**	630-530-6524	310
Hastings & Sons Publishing			
38 Exchange St ....Lynn MA 01901	**877-226-4267**	781-593-7700	628-8
Hastings Area Chamber of Commerce & Tourism Bureau			
111 E Third St ....Hastings MN 55033	**888-612-6122**	651-437-6775	137
Hastings Bus Co			
425 31st St E ....Hastings MN 55033	**800-210-6362**	651-437-1888	108
Hastings College			
710 N Turner Ave ....Hastings NE 68901	**800-532-7642**	402-463-2402	166
Hastings Entertainment Inc			
3601 Plains Blvd ....Amarillo TX 79102	**877-427-8464***		95
*NASDAQ: HAST ■ *Cust Svc*			
Hastings Equity Grain Bin Mfg Co			
1900 Summit Ave ....Hastings NE 68901	**888-883-2189**	402-462-2189	273
Hastings House Country House Hotel			
160 Upper Ganges Rd ....Salt Spring Island BC V8K2S2	**800-661-9255**	250-537-2362	376
Hastings HVAC Inc			
3606 Yost Ave PO Box 669 ....Hastings NE 68902	**800-228-4243***	402-463-9821	14
Cust Svc			
Hastings Manufacturing Co			
325 N Hanover St ....Hastings MI 49058	**800-776-1088**	269-945-2491	127
Hastings Public Library			
517 W Fourth St ....Hastings NE 68901	**800-318-2596**	402-461-2346	431-3
Hastings Veterans Home			
1200 E 18th St ....Hastings MN 55033	**877-838-3803**	651-438-8500	781
Hat World Corp			
7555 Woodland Dr ....Indianapolis IN 46278	**888-564-4287**		155-5
Hatboro-Horsham School District			
229 Meetinghouse Rd ....Horsham PA 19044	**866-771-3170**	215-672-5660	676
Hatch & Kirk Inc			
5111 Leary Ave NW ....Seattle WA 98107	**800-426-2818**	206-783-2766	262
Hatfield Quality Meats Inc			
2700 Clemens Rd ....Hatfield PA 19440	**800-743-1191**	215-368-2500	468

Alphabetical Section

	Toll-Free	Phone	Class
Hatteras Hammocks Inc			
305 Industrial Blvd .... Greenville NC 27834	800-643-3522	252-758-0641	318-4
Hattiesburg American			
825 N Main St .... Hattiesburg MS 39401	800-844-2637	601-582-4321	525-2
Hattiesburg-Laurel Regional Airport			
1002 Terminal Dr .... Moselle MS 39459	800-433-7300	601-649-2444	27
Hatton Brown Publishers Inc			
PO Box 2268 .... Montgomery AL 36102	800-669-5613	334-834-1170	628-9
Hauck & Assoc Inc			
1255 23rd St NW Ste 200.......... Washington DC 20037	800-767-7777	202-452-8100	46
Hauppauge Computer Works Inc			
91 Cabot Ct .... Hauppauge NY 11788	800-443-6284	631-434-1600	617
Hauppauge Digital Inc			
91 Cabot Ct .... Hauppauge NY 11788	800-443-6284	631-434-1600	617
OTC: HAUP			
Hause Machines			
809 S Pleasant St .... Montpelier OH 43543	800-932-8665	419-485-3158	450
Hausmann Industries Inc			
130 Union St .... Northvale NJ 07647	888-428-7626	201-767-0255	318-1
Havenwood-Heritage Heights Havenwood Campus			
33 Christian Ave .... Concord NH 03301	800-457-6833	603-224-5363	663
Havenwoods State Forest			
6141 N Hopkins St .... Milwaukee WI 53209	888-936-7463	414-527-0232	558
Havenwyck Hospital			
1525 University Dr .... Auburn Hills MI 48326	800-401-2727	248-373-9200	371-5
Haverford Trust Co			
Three Radnor Corp Ctr Ste 450.......... Radnor PA 19087	888-995-1979	610-995-8700	402
Haverhill Gazette			
181 Merrimack St .... Haverhill MA 01831	888-411-3245	978-374-0321	525-2
Haverty Furniture Cos Inc			
780 Johnson Ferry Rd NE Ste 800 .... Atlanta GA 30342	888-428-3789	404-443-2900	320
NYSE: HVT			
Haviland Enterprises Inc			
421 Ann St NW ....Grand Rapids MI 49504	800-456-1134	616-361-6691	144
Hawaii			
Child Support Enforcement Agency			
601 Kamokila Blvd Ste 251 .... Kapolei HI 96707	888-317-9081		337-12
Taxation Dept			
830 Punchbowl St Rm 221.......... Honolulu HI 96813	800-222-3229	808-587-4242	337-12
Vocational Rehabilitation Div			
1901 Bachelot St .... Honolulu HI 96817	800-316-8005	808-586-9744	337-12
Hawaii Assn of Realtors			
1136 12th Ave Ste 220 .... Honolulu HI 96816	866-693-6767	808-733-7060	647
Hawaii Bar Journal			
1100 Alakea St Ste 1000............. Honolulu HI 96813	888-586-1056	808-537-1868	452-15
Hawaii Coffee Company Inc			
1555 Kalani St .... Honolulu HI 96817	800-338-8353	808-847-3600	157
Hawaii Community Foundation			
65-1279 Kawaihae Rd Ste 203 .... Kamuela HI 96743	888-731-3863	808-537-6333	302
Hawaii Convention Ctr			
1801 Kalakaua Ave .... Honolulu HI 96815	800-295-6603	808-943-3500	206
Hawaii Dental Assn			
1345 S Beretania St Ste 301....... Honolulu HI 96814	800-359-6725	808-593-7956	227
Hawaii Dental Service			
700 Bishop St Ste 700 .... Honolulu HI 96813	800-232-2533	808-521-1431	388-3
Hawaii Dept of Education Honolulu District Office			
4967 Kilauea Ave .... Honolulu HI 96816	800-437-8641	808-733-4950	676
Hawaii Island Chamber of Commerce			
117 Keawe St .... Hilo HI 96720	877-482-4411	808-935-7178	137
Hawaii Medical Assn			
1360 S Beretania St Ste 200......... Honolulu HI 96814	888-536-2792	808-536-7702	469
Hawaii Medical Service Assn			
818 Keeaumoku St .... Honolulu HI 96822	800-776-4672	808-948-6111	388-3
Hawaii National Bank			
45 N King St .... Honolulu HI 96817	800-528-2273	808-528-7711	68
Hawaii Nurses Assn (HNA)			
949 Kapiolani Blvd Ste 107 .... Honolulu HI 96814	800-617-2677	808-531-1628	526
Meader Library			
1060 Bishop St .... Honolulu HI 96813	866-225-5478	808-544-0210	431-6
Hawaii Pacific University			
Windward Hawaii Loa			
1164 Bishop St .... Honolulu HI 96813	866-225-5478*	808-544-0200	166
*Admissions			
Hawaii Planing Mill Ltd (HPM)			
16-166 Melekahiwa St ....Keaau HI 96749	877-841-7633	808-966-5693	192-3
Hawaii Postsecondary Education Commission			
2444 Dole St			
Bachman Hall Rm 209 .... Honolulu HI 96822	877-531-2333	808-956-8213	716
Hawaii Preparatory Academy			
65-1692 Kohala Mountain Rd ....Kamuela HI 96743	800-644-4481	808-881-4007	615
Hawaii Prince Hotel Waikiki, The			
100 Holomoana St .... Honolulu HI 96815	888-977-4623		660
Hawaii Public Television			
2350 Dole St .... Honolulu HI 96822	800-238-4847	808-973-1000	624
Hawaii Visitors & Convention Bureau			
2270 Kalakaua Ave Ste 801 .... Honolulu HI 96815	800-464-2924		207
Hawaii's Best Bed & Breakfasts			
571 Pauku St .... Kailua HI 96734	800-262-9912	808-263-3100	373
Hawaiian Airlines HawaiianMiles			
PO Box 30008 .... Honolulu HI 96820	877-426-4537		26
Hawaiian Airlines Inc			
3375 Koapaka St Ste G350........... Honolulu HI 96819	800-367-5320	808-835-3700	25
Hawaiian Inn			
2301 S Atlantic			
Ave ....Daytona Beach Shores FL 32118	800-922-3023	386-255-5411	376
Hawaiian Isles Kona Coffee Co			
2839 Mokumoa St .... Honolulu HI 96819	800-657-7716*	808-839-3255	295-7
*Orders			
Hawaiian Tug & Barge			
1331 N Nimitz Hwy PO Box 3288 .... Honolulu HI 96817	800-572-2743	808-543-9311	460
Hawk Eye, The			
800 S Main St PO Box 10.......... Burlington IA 52601	800-397-1708	319-754-8461	525-2
Hawk Inn & Mountain Resort			
75 Billings Rd ....Plymouth VT 05056	800-685-4295	802-672-3811	660
Hawk's Cay Resort & Marina			
61 Hawk's Cay Blvd .... Duck Key FL 33050	888-395-5539	305-743-7000	660
Hawker Powersource Inc			
9404 Ooltewah Industrial Dr			
PO Box 808.................. Ooltewah TN 37363	800-238-8658	423-238-5700	73
Hawkeye Community College			
1501 E Orange Rd .... Waterloo IA 50704	800-670-4769	319-296-2320	160
Hawkeye REC			
24049 Iowa 9 .... Cresco IA 52136	800-658-2243	563-547-3801	245

	Toll-Free	Phone	Class
Hawkeye Stages Inc			
703 Dudley St ....Decorah IA 52101	877-464-2954	563-382-3639	106
Hawkins Inc			
3100 E Hennepin Ave ....Minneapolis MN 55413	800-328-5460	612-331-6910	141
NASDAQ: HWKN			
Hawkins Traffic Safety Supply			
1255 E Shore Hwy .... Berkeley CA 94710	800-772-3995	800-236-0112	669
Hawley Mountain Guest Ranch			
PO Box 4 .... McLeod MT 59052	877-496-7848	406-932-5791	239
Haworth Inc			
One Haworth Ctr .... Holland MI 49423	800-344-2600	616-393-3000	318-1
Haws Corp			
1455 Kleppe Ln .... Sparks NV 89431	888-640-4297	775-359-4712	655
Hawthorn Bancshares Inc			
300 SW Longview Blvd ....Lee's Summit MO 64081	800-761-8362	816-347-8100	357-2
NASDAQ: HWBK			
Hawthorn Ctr			
18471 Haggerty Rd .... Northville MI 48167	855-444-3911	248-349-3000	371-1
Hawthorn PNC Family Wealth			
1600 Market St .... Philadelphia PA 19103	888-947-3762		398
Hawthorne Chamber of Commerce			
12629 Crenshaw Blvd .... Hawthorne CA 90250	800-977-4770	310-676-1163	137
Hawthorne Hotel			
18 Washington Sq W .... Salem MA 01970	800-729-7829	978-744-4080	376
Hawthorne Inn & Conference Ctr			
420 High St .... Winston-Salem NC 27101	877-777-3099	336-777-3000	376
Hawthorne Machinery Co			
16945 Camino San Bernardo .... San Diego CA 92127	800-437-4228	858-674-7000	264-3
Hay Group Inc			
1650 Arch St Ste 2300 .... Philadelphia PA 19107	800-716-4429	215-861-2000	195
Hay House Inc			
PO Box 5100 .... Carlsbad CA 92018	800-654-5126	760-431-7695	628-3
Hayden Automotive			
1801 Waters Ridge Dr ....Lewisville TX 75057	888-505-4567		59
Hayden Twist Drill & Tool Company Inc			
22822 Globe St ....Warren MI 48089	800-521-1780	586-754-7700	488
Hayes & Stolz Industrial Manufacturing Co			
3521 Hemphill St			
PO Box 11217.................. Fort Worth TX 76110	800-725-7272	817-926-3391	297
Hayes Handpiece Franchises Inc			
5375 Avenida Encinas Ste C........... Carlsbad CA 92008	800-228-0521	760-602-0521	309
Hayes School Publishing Co Inc			
321 Pennwood Ave .... Pittsburgh PA 15221	800-926-0704	412-371-2373	243
Hayes Specialties Corp			
1761 E Genesee .... Saginaw MI 48601	800-248-3603	989-755-6541	327
Haynes International Inc			
1020 W Pk Ave PO Box 9013........... Kokomo IN 46904	800-354-0806	765-456-6000	480
NASDAQ: HAYN			
Hays Convention & Visitors Bureau			
2700 Vine St PO Box 490 .... Hays KS 67601	800-569-4505	785-628-8202	207
Hays Fluid Controls			
114 Eason Rd .... Dallas NC 28034	800-354-4297	704-922-9565	778
Hays Medical Ctr (HMC)			
2220 Canterbury Dr .... Hays KS 67601	800-248-0073	785-650-2759	371-3
Hayward Baker Inc			
1130 Annapolis Rd Ste 202 ....Odenton MD 21113	800-456-6548	410-551-8200	190-5
Haywood Community College			
185 Freedlander Dr ....Clyde NC 28721	866-468-6422	828-627-2821	160
Haywood County Chamber of Commerce			
28 Walnut Street .... Waynesville NC 28786	877-456-3073	828-456-3021	137
Haywood Electric Membership Corp			
376 Grindstone Rd .... Waynesville NC 28785	800-951-6088	828-452-2281	245
Hazard Community & Technical College			
One Community College Dr .... Hazard KY 41701	800-246-7521	606-436-5721	160
Hazard Campus			
101 Vo Tech Dr .... Hazard KY 41701	800-246-7521	606-435-6101	160
Lees Campus			
601 Jefferson Ave .... Jackson KY 41339	800-246-7521	606-666-7521	160
Hazel Park Raceway			
1650 E 10 Mile Rd .... Hazel Park MI 48030	800-794-8001	248-398-1000	633
Hazelden Chicago			
867 N Dearborn St ....Chicago IL 60610	800-257-7810	312-943-3534	717
Hazelden Ctr for Youth & Families (HCYF)			
11505 36th Ave N ....Plymouth MN 55441	800-257-7810	763-509-3800	717
Hazelden Foundation			
15251 Pleasant Vly Rd ....Center City MN 55012	800-257-7810	651-213-4200	717
Hazelden New York			
322 Eigth Ave 12th Fl .... New York NY 10001	800-257-7800	212-420-9520	717
Hazelden Springbrook			
1901 Esther St ....Newberg OR 97132	866-866-4662	503-554-4300	717
Hazelnut Growers of Oregon			
401 N 26th Ave ....Cornelius OR 97113	800-273-4676	503-648-4176	11-1
Hazen & Sawyer PC			
498 Seventh Ave 11th Fl .... New York NY 10018	800-858-9876	212-777-8400	261
Hazen Transport Inc			
27050 Wick Rd ....Taylor MI 48180	800-251-2120	313-292-2120	770
Hazle Park Packing Co			
260 Washington Ave			
Hazle Pk ....Hazletownship PA 18202	800-238-4331	570-455-7571	295-26
Hazleton Standard Speaker			
21 N Wyoming St ....Hazleton PA 18201	800-843-6680*	570-455-3636	525-2
*Cust Svc			
HB Communications Inc			
60 Dodge Ave ....North Haven CT 06473	800-243-4414	203-234-9246	37
HB Duvall Inc			
901 E Patrick St PO Box 70 .... Frederick MD 21701	800-325-2252	301-662-1125	274
HB Fuller Co			
1200 Willow Lk Blvd			
PO Box 64683................. Saint Paul MN 55164	888-423-8553	651-236-5900	3
NYSE: FUL			
HB Rentals LC			
5813 Hwy 90 E .... Broussard LA 70518	800-262-6790	337-839-1641	264-3
HBD Inc			
3901 Riverdale Rd .... Greensboro NC 27406	800-403-2247	336-275-4800	66
HBD/Thermoid Inc			
1301 W Sandusky Ave .... Bellefontaine OH 43311	800-543-8070	937-593-5010	367
HB&G Inc PO Box 589 .... Troy AL 36081	800-264-4424	334-566-5000	494
HBI (Hickory Brands Inc)			
429 27th St NW .... Hickory NC 28601	800-438-5777		734-5
HBP (Huttig Bldg Products Inc)			
555 Maryville University Dr			
Ste 400 .... Saint Louis MO 63141	800-325-4466	314-216-2600	494
OTC: HBPI			

Name / Address	City	State	ZIP	Toll-Free	Phone	Class
HBPL (Huntington Beach Public Library)						
7111 Talbert Ave	Huntington Beach	CA	92648	**800-565-0148**	714-842-4481	431-3
HBPS (Harlan Bioproducts for Science Inc)						
298 S Carroll Rd	Indianapolis	IN	46229	**800-793-7287**		231
HCA Midwest Health System						
903 E 104th St Ste 500	Kansas City	MO	64131	**800-386-9355**	816-508-4000	350
HCAA (National CPA Health Care Advisors Assn)						
624 Grassmere Pk Ste 15	Nashville	TN	37211	**800-231-2524**	615-373-9880	48-1
HCC Inc						
1501 First Ave	Mendota	IL	61342	**800-548-6633**	815-539-9371	273
HCC Life Insurance Co						
225 Townpark Dr Ste 145	Kennesaw	GA	30144	**800-447-0460**	770-973-9851	388-2
HCCBA (Hardin County Chamber of Commerce)						
225 S Detroit St	Kenton	OH	43326	**888-642-7346**	419-673-4131	137
HCCGA (Haines City Citrus Growers Assn)						
Eight Railroad Ave						
PO Box 337	Haines City	FL	33844	**800-327-6676***	863-422-1174	11-1
*Sales						
HCEA (Healthcare Convention & Exhibitors Assn)						
1100 Johnson Ferry Rd Ste 300	Atlanta	GA	30342	**800-236-1592**	404-252-3663	48-18
HCESC (Hamilton County Educational Service Ctr)						
11083 Hamilton Ave	Cincinnati	OH	45231	**800-964-8211**	513-674-4200	676
HCI (Health Communications Inc)						
3201 SW 15th St	Deerfield Beach	FL	33442	**800-441-5569***	954-360-0909	628-2
*Cust Svc						
HCI (Hospice of Central Iowa)						
401 Railroad Pl	West Des Moines	IA	50265	**800-806-9934**	515-333-5810	368
Hcpro Inc						
75 Sylvan St Ste A-10	Danvers	MA	01923	**800-650-6787**		196
HCREC (Humboldt County Rural Electric Co-op)						
1210 13th St N	Humboldt	IA	50548	**800-452-1111**	515-332-1616	245
HCSG (Healthcare Services Group Inc)						
3220 Tillman Dr Ste 300	Bensalem	PA	19020	**800-486-3289**	215-639-4274	438
HCYF (Hazelden Ctr for Youth & Families)						
11505 36th Ave N	Plymouth	MN	55441	**800-257-7810**	763-509-3800	717
H-D Electric Co-op Inc						
423 Third Ave S	Clear Lake	SD	57226	**800-781-7474**	605-874-2171	245
HD Hudson Manufacturing Co						
500 N Michigan Ave Ste 2300	Chicago	IL	60611	**800-977-7293**	312-644-2830	273
HD Supply Waterworks Ltd						
PO Box 1419	Thomasville	GA	31799	**800-492-6909**	800-950-7659	382
HD Vest Financial Services						
6333 N State Hwy 161 Fourth Fl	Irving	TX	75038	**866-218-8206**	972-870-6000	398
HDR Engineering Inc						
8404 Indian Hills Dr	Omaha	NE	68114	**800-366-4411**	402-399-1000	261
HDSA (Huntington's Disease Society of America)						
505 Eigth Ave Ste 902	New York	NY	10018	**800-345-4372**	212-242-1968	47-17
HDW (Hardware Distribution Warehouses Inc)						
6900 Woolworth Rd	Shreveport	LA	71129	**800-256-8527***	318-686-8527	348
*Cust Svc						
HE Neumann Inc						
100 Middle Creek Rd	Triadelphia	WV	26059	**800-627-5312**	304-232-3040	190-10
HE Williams Inc						
831 W Fairview Ave	Carthage	MO	64836	**866-358-4065**	417-358-4065	435
HEA (Harmon Electric Assn Inc)						
114 N First St PO Box 393	Hollis	OK	73550	**800-643-7769**	580-688-3342	245
HEAD USA Inc						
One Selleck St	Norwalk	CT	06855	**800-874-3235**	203-855-8666	701
HEAD/Penn Racquet Sports						
306 S 45th Ave	Phoenix	AZ	85043	**800-289-7366**		701
Headley-Whitney Museum						
4435 Old Frankfort Pike	Lexington	KY	40510	**800-310-5085**	859-255-6653	513
Headquarter Toyota						
5895 NW 167th St	Miami	FL	33015	**800-549-0947**	305-364-9800	56
Headstart Hair For Men Inc						
3395 Cypress Gardens Rd	Winter Haven	FL	33884	**800-645-6525**	863-324-5559	345
Healing the Children (HTC)						
2624 W Beacon Ave	Spokane	WA	99208	**888-233-9527**	509-327-4281	47-5
Health & Safety Institute Inc						
1450 Westec Dr	Eugene	OR	97402	**800-447-3177**		754
Health After 50						
500 Fifth Ave Ste 1900	New York	NY	10110	**800-829-0422**		524-8
Health Alliance Plan						
2850 W Grand Blvd	Detroit	MI	48202	**800-422-4641**	313-872-8100	388-3
Health Care Daily Report						
1801 S Bell St	Arlington	VA	22202	**800-372-1033**		524-8
Health Care Fraud Report						
1801 S Bell St	Arlington	VA	22202	**800-372-1033**		524-7
Health Care Policy Report						
1801 S Bell St	Arlington	VA	22202	**800-372-1033**		524-8
Health Care Property Investors Inc						
1920 Main St Ste 1200	Irvine	CA	92614	**888-604-1990**	949-407-0700	646
Health Care Software Inc						
PO Box 2430	Farmingdale	NJ	07727	**800-524-1038**		178
Health Communications Inc (HCI)						
3201 SW 15th St	Deerfield Beach	FL	33442	**800-441-5569***	954-360-0909	628-2
*Cust Svc						
Health Facilities Management Magazine						
155 N Wacker Dr Ste 400	Chicago	IL	60606	**800-621-6902**	312-893-6800	452-5
Health Forum						
155 North Wacker Drive						
Suite 400	Chicago	IL	60606	**800-621-6902**	312-422-2165	628-11
Health Industry Business Communications Council (HIBCC)						
2525 E Arizona Biltmore Cir						
Ste 127	Phoenix	AZ	85016	**800-755-5505**	602-381-1091	48-8
Health Industry Distributors Assn (HIDA)						
310 Montgomery St	Alexandria	VA	22314	**800-549-4432**	703-549-4432	48-18
Health Law Reporter						
1801 S Bell St	Arlington	VA	22202	**800-372-1033**		524-7
Health Law Week						
590 Dutch Vly Rd NE	Atlanta	GA	30324	**800-926-7926**	404-881-1141	524-8
Health Management Systems Inc						
401 Pk Ave S	New York	NY	10016	**877-467-0184**	212-857-5000	225
Health Net Inc						
21650 Oxnard St	Woodland Hills	CA	91367	**800-848-4747**	818-676-6000	388-3
NYSE: HNT						
Health Net Of Arizona Inc						
1230 W Washington St	Tempe	AZ	85281	**800-291-6911**	602-794-1400	350
Health Network Laboratory						
2024 Lehigh St	Allentown	PA	18103	**877-402-4221**	610-402-8170	415
Health Physics Society						
1313 Dolley Madison Blvd Ste 402	McLean	VA	22101	**888-624-8373**	703-790-1745	47-17
Health Resources & Services Administration (HRSA)						
5600 Fishers Ln	Rockville	MD	20857	**888-275-4772**	301-443-2216	338-8
Health Smart Rx						
1301 E Ninth St	Cleveland	OH	44114	**800-681-6912**		579
Health Tradition Health Plan						
1808 E Main St	Onalaska	WI	54650	**800-545-8499**	608-781-9692	388-3
HealthAmerica Pennsylvania Inc						
3721 Tecport Dr PO Box 67103	Harrisburg	PA	17111	**800-788-6445**		388-3
HealthAxis Inc						
7301 N State Hwy 161 Ste 300	Irving	TX	75039	**888-974-2947**	972-443-5000	458
Healthcare Automation Inc						
41 Sharpe Dr	Cranston	RI	02920	**800-738-8850**	401-572-3040	178
Healthcare Convention & Exhibitors Assn (HCEA)						
1100 Johnson Ferry Rd Ste 300	Atlanta	GA	30342	**800-236-1592**	404-252-3663	48-18
Healthcare Disparities Report						
8204 Fenton St	Silver Spring	MD	20910	**800-666-6380**	301-588-6385	524-8
Healthcare Financial Management Assn (HFMA)						
Two Westbrook Corporate Ctr						
Ste 700	Westchester	IL	60154	**800-252-4362**	708-531-9600	48-8
Healthcare Management Systems Inc (HMS)						
3102 W End Ave Ste 400	Nashville	TN	37203	**800-383-3317**	615-383-7300	384
Healthcare Services Group Inc (HCSG)						
3220 Tillman Dr Ste 300	Bensalem	PA	19020	**800-486-3289**	215-639-4274	438
HealthCare USA						
10 S Broadway Ste 1200	Saint Louis	MO	63102	**800-213-7792**	314-241-5300	388-3
HealthCareSource Inc						
100 Sylvan Rd Ste 100	Woburn	MA	01801	**800-869-5200**		260
HealthDrive Corp						
888 Worcester St	Wellesley	MA	02482	**888-964-6681**		349
Healthforce Partners Inc						
18323 Bothell Everett Hwy	Bothell	WA	98012	**877-437-2497**	425-806-5700	195
HealthLeaders-InterStudy						
One Vantage Way Ste B-300	Nashville	TN	37228	**800-643-7600**	615-385-4131	628-6
HealthMEDX						
5100 N Towne Ctr Dr	Ozark	MO	65721	**877-875-1200**	417-582-1816	38
HealthPartners Inc						
PO Box 1309	Minneapolis	MN	55440	**800-883-2177**	952-883-5000	388-3
Healthplex Inc						
333 Earl Ovington Blvd	Uniondale	NY	11553	**800-468-0608***	516-542-2200	388-3
*Cust Svc						
HealthPlus of Michigan						
2050 S Linden Rd	Flint	MI	48532	**800-332-9161**	810-230-2000	388-3
Healthpoint						
3909 Hulen St	Fort Worth	TX	76107	**800-441-8227***	817-900-4000	577
*Cust Svc						
HealthSCOPE Benefits Inc						
27 Corporate Hill Dr	Little Rock	AR	72205	**877-240-0135**	501-225-1551	387
HealthSource Saginaw						
3340 Hospital Rd	Saginaw	MI	48603	**800-662-6848**	989-790-7700	717
HealthSouth Chattanooga Rehabilitation Hospital						
3660 Grandview Pkwy Ste 200	Birmingham	AL	35243	**800-765-4772**	205-967-7116	371-6
HealthSouth Corp						
3660 Grandview Pkwy Ste 200	Birmingham	AL	35243	**800-765-4772**	205-967-7116	349
NYSE: HLS						
HealthSouth Harmarville Rehabilitation Hospital						
320 Guys Run Rd	Pittsburgh	PA	15238	**800-765-4772**	412-828-1300	371-6
HealthSouth Hospital of Pittsburgh						
320 Guys Run Rd	Pittsburgh	PA	15238	**800-765-4772**	412-828-1300	371-6
HealthSouth MountainView Regional Rehabilitation Hospital						
1160 Van Voorhis Rd	Morgantown	WV	26505	**800-388-2451**	304-598-1100	371-6
HealthSouth Nittany Valley Rehabilitation Hospital						
550 W College Ave	Pleasant Gap	PA	16823	**800-842-6026**	814-359-3421	371-6
HealthSouth Plano Rehabilitation Hospital						
2800 W 15th St	Plano	TX	75075	**800-765-4772**	972-612-9000	371-6
HealthSouth Rehabilitation Hospital of Altoona						
2005 Vly View Blvd	Altoona	PA	16602	**800-873-4220**	814-944-3535	371-6
HealthSouth Rehabilitation Hospital of Austin						
1215 Red River	Austin	TX	78701	**800-765-4772**	512-474-5700	371-6
HealthSouth Rehabilitation Hospital of Erie						
143 E Second St	Erie	PA	16507	**800-765-4772**	814-878-1230	371-6
HealthSouth Rehabilitation Hospital of Kingsport						
113 Cassel Dr	Kingsport	TN	37660	**800-454-7422**	423-246-7240	371-6
HealthStream Inc						
209 Tenth Ave S Ste 450	Nashville	TN	37203	**800-933-9293**	615-301-3100	755
NASDAQ: HSTM						
Healthtrax Fitness & Wellness						
2345 Main St	Glastonbury	CT	06033	**800-998-0880**	860-652-7066	351
HealthTronics Inc						
9825 Spectrum Dr Bldg 3	Austin	TX	78717	**888-252-6575**	512-328-2892	250
Healthways Inc						
701 Cool Springs Blvd Ste 300	Franklin	TN	37067	**800-327-3822**		349
NASDAQ: HWAY						
Healthy Directions LLC						
7811 Montrose Rd	Potomac	MD	20854	**866-599-9491**		628-9
Healthy Pet						
6960 Salashan Pkwy	Ferndale	WA	98248	**800-242-2287**	360-734-7415	571
Healy Group Inc, The						
53800 Generations Dr	South Bend	IN	46635	**800-667-4613**	574-271-6000	387
Hearing Loss Assn of America						
7910 Woodmont Ave Ste 1200	Bethesda	MD	20814	**800-221-6827**	301-657-2248	47-17
Hearn Kirkwood						
7251 Standard Dr	Hanover	MD	21076	**800-777-9489***	410-712-6000	296-7
*General						
Hearn Paper Co						
556 N Meridian Rd	Youngstown	OH	44509	**800-225-2989**	330-792-6533	546
Hearst Foundation, The						
300 W 57th St 26th Fl	New York	NY	10019	**800-841-7048**	212-649-3750	304
Hearst San Simeon State Historical Monument						
750 Hearst Castle Rd	San Simeon	CA	93452	**800-444-4445**	805-927-2020	558
Heart & Soul Magazine						
15480 Annapolis Rd Ste 202-225	Bowie	MD	20715	**800-834-8813**		452-13
Heart of Lancaster Regional Medical Ctr						
1500 Highland Dr	Lititz	PA	17543	**800-999-6673**	717-625-5000	371-3
Heart Six Ranch						
16985 Buffalo Vly Rd PO Box 70	Moran	WY	83013	**888-543-2477**		239
Heartland Blood Centers						
1200 N Highland Ave	Aurora	IL	60506	**800-786-4483**	630-892-7055	88
Heartland Co-op						
2829 Westown Pkwy						
Ste 350	West Des Moines	IA	50266	**800-513-3938**	515-225-1334	275
Heartland Equipment Inc						
2100 N Falls Blvd	Wynne	AR	72396	**800-530-7617**		273
Heartland Express Inc						
901 N Kansas Ave	North Liberty	IA	52317	**800-654-1175**		770
NASDAQ: HTLD						

Name	Address	City	State	ZIP	Toll-Free	Phone	Class
Heartland Financial USA Inc	1398 Central Ave *NASDAQ: HTLF*	Dubuque	IA	52001	**888-739-2100**	563-589-2100	357-2
Heartland Funds	789 N Water St Ste 500	Milwaukee	WI	53202	**800-432-7856**	414-347-7777	521
Heartland Health Care Ctr Bloomfield Hills	2975 N Adams Rd	Bloomfield Hills	MI	48304	**800-622-6757**	248-645-2900	445
Heartland Hospice Services	333 N Summit St	Toledo	OH	43604	**800-366-1232**	419-252-5500	368
Heartland Inns	87-2nd St *Resv	Coralville	IA	52241	**800-334-3277***	319-351-8132	376
Heartland Label Printers Inc	1700 Stephen St *General	Little Chute	WI	54140	**800-236-7914***		246
Heartland Lions Eye Bank	10100 N Ambassador Dr Ste 200	Kansas City	MO	64153	**800-756-4824**	816-454-5454	269
Heartland Meat Company Inc	3461 Main St	Chula Vista	CA	91911	**888-407-3668**	619-407-3668	296-9
Heartland Paper Co	808 W Cherokee St *Cust Svc	Sioux Falls	SD	57104	**800-843-7922***	605-336-1190	552
Heartland Park Topeka	7530 SW Topeka Blvd	Topeka	KS	66619	**800-437-2237**	785-862-4781	508
Heartland Payment Systems Inc	90 Nassau St Second Fl *NYSE: HPY*	Princeton	NJ	08542	**888-798-3131**	609-683-3831	251
Heartland Power Co-op	216 Jackson St PO Box 65	Thompson	IA	50478	**888-584-9732**	641-584-2251	245
Heartland Rural Electric Co-op	110 Enterprise St	Girard	KS	66743	**888-835-9585**	620-724-8251	245
Heartland Spa	1237 E 1600 N Rd	Gilman	IL	60938	**800-545-4853**		697
Heartline Fitness Products Inc	8041 Cessna Ave Ste 200	Gaithersburg	MD	20879	**800-262-3348**	301-921-0661	267
Heat & Control Inc	21121 Cabot Blvd	Hayward	CA	94545	**800-227-5980**	510-259-0500	297
Heat Seal LLC	4580 E 71st St	Cleveland	OH	44125	**800-342-6329**	216-341-2022	540
Heatcraft Refrigeration Products	2175 W Pk Pl Blvd	Stone Mountain	GA	30087	**800-321-1881**	770-465-5600	655
Heath Consultants Inc	9030 Monroe Rd	Houston	TX	77061	**800-432-8487**	713-844-1300	193
HeatMax Inc	513 Hill Rd PO Box 1191	Dalton	GA	30721	**800-432-8629**	706-226-1800	569
Heatrex Inc	PO Box 515	Meadville	PA	16335	**800-394-6589**	814-724-1800	317
Heaven's Best Carpet & Upholstery Cleaning	PO Box 607	Rexburg	ID	83440	**800-359-2095**	208-359-1106	150
Heavy Machines Inc	3926 E Rains Rd	Memphis	TN	38118	**888-366-9028**	901-260-2200	355
Hebeler Corp	2000 Military Rd	Tonawanda	NY	14150	**800-486-4709**	716-873-9300	613
Hebrew Immigrant Aid Society (HIAS)	333 Seventh Ave 16th Fl	New York	NY	10001	**800-442-7714**	212-967-4100	47-5
Hebrew Union College Los Angeles	3077 University Ave	Los Angeles	CA	90007	**800-899-0925**	213-749-3424	166
Hebron Academy	Rt 119 PO Box 309	Hebron	ME	04238	**888-432-7664**	207-966-2100	615
Heceta Head Lighthouse State Scenic Viewpoint	93111 Hwy 101 N	Florence	OR	97439	**800-551-6949**		558
Hedahls Inc	100 East Broadway	Bismarck	ND	58502	**800-433-2457**	701-223-8393	60
Hedwin Corp	1600 Roland Heights Ave	Baltimore	MD	21211	**800-638-1012**	410-467-8209	200
Heely-Brown Company Inc	1280 Chattahoochee Ave	Atlanta	GA	30318	**800-241-4628**	404-352-0022	45
Heeren Bros Inc	1060 Hall St SW	Grand Rapids	MI	49503	**800-733-5466**	616-452-8641	296-7
Heery International Inc	999 Peachtree St NE	Atlanta	GA	30309	**866-840-3940**	404-881-9880	261
Heffel Gallery Ltd	2247 Granville St	Vancouver	BC	V6H3G1	**800-528-9608**	604-732-6505	41
HEI Inc	1495 Steiger Lk Ln	Victoria	MN	55386	**866-720-2397**	952-443-2500	687
Heidel House Resort	643 Illinois Ave	Green Lake	WI	54941	**800-444-2812**	920-294-3344	660
Heidelberg University	310 E Market St	Tiffin	OH	44883	**800-434-3352**	419-448-2000	166
Heidelberg USA Inc	1000 Gutenberg Dr *Cust Svc	Kennesaw	GA	30144	**888-472-9655***	770-419-6500	621
Heidler Roofing Services Inc	2120 Alpha Dr	York	PA	17408	**866-792-3549**	717-792-3549	190-12
Heifer International	One World Ave	Little Rock	AR	72202	**800-422-0474**	501-907-2600	47-5
Heil Environmental Ltd	2030 Hamilton Pl Blvd Ste 200	Chattanooga	TN	37421	**866-367-4345**	423-899-9100	509
Heilind Electronics Inc	58 Jonspin Rd	Wilmington	MA	01887	**800-400-7041**	978-657-4870	246
Heiners Bakery Inc	1300 Adams Ave	Huntington	WV	25704	**800-776-8411**	304-523-8411	295-1
Heinrich Envelope Corp	925 Zane Ave N	Minneapolis	MN	55422	**800-346-7957**	763-544-3571	263
Heintz & Weber Co Inc	150 Reading Ave	Buffalo	NY	14220	**800-438-6878**	716-852-7171	295-41
Heinz Hall for the Performing Arts	600 Penn Ave	Pittsburgh	PA	15222	**800-743-8560**	412-392-4900	565
Heitman LLC	191 N Wacker Dr Ste 2500	Chicago	IL	60606	**800-225-5435**	312-855-5700	646
Helac Corp	225 Battersby Ave	Enumclaw	WA	98022	**800-327-2589**	360-825-1601	223
Helen B Hoffman Plantation Library	501 N Fig Tree Ln	Plantation	FL	33317	**800-774-5866**	954-797-2140	431-3
Helen DeVos Children's Hospital	100 Michigan St NE	Grand Rapids	MI	49503	**800-222-1222**	616-391-9000	371-1
Helen DeVos Children's Hospital Pediatric Hematology/Oncology Program	100 Michigan NE	Grand Rapids	MI	49503	**866-989-7999**	616-391-9000	759
Helen Hayes Theatre	240 W 44th St	New York	NY	10036	**800-447-7400**	212-239-6200	736
Helen Keller International	352 Pk Ave S Ste 1200	New York	NY	10010	**877-535-5374**	212-532-0544	47-5
Helena Area Chamber of Commerce	225 Cruse Ave	Helena	MT	59601	**800-743-5362**	406-442-4120	137
Helena Laboratories Inc	1530 Lindbergh Dr	Beaumont	TX	77704	**800-231-5663**	409-842-3714	231
Helical Products Co Inc	901 W McCoy Ln	Santa Maria	CA	93455	**877-353-9873**	805-928-3851	613
Helicopter Assn International (HAI)	1635 Prince St	Alexandria	VA	22314	**800-435-4976**	703-683-4646	48-21
Helicopter Support Inc (HSI)	124 Quarry Rd	Trumbull	CT	06611	**800-795-6051**	203-416-4000	760
Heliene Inc	520 Allen'S Side Rd	Sault Ste Marie	ON	P6A6K4	**855-363-2797**	705-575-6556	253
Heli-Mart Inc	3184 Airway Ave Ste E	Costa Mesa	CA	92626	**800-826-6899**	714-755-2999	760
Helix Energy Solutions Inc	400 N Sam Houston Pkwy E Ste 400 *NYSE: HLX*	Houston	TX	77060	**888-345-2347**	281-618-0400	532
Helix Medical LLC	1110 Mark Ave	Carpinteria	CA	93013	**800-266-4421**	805-684-3304	472
Hello Direct Inc	77 NE Blvd	Nashua	NH	03062	**800-435-5634**		454
HelloWorld	One ePrize Dr	Pleasant Ridge	MI	48069	**877-837-7493**		7
Helly Hansen US Inc	4104 C St NE Ste 200	Auburn	WA	98002	**800-435-5901**		153-5
Helmel Engineering Products Inc	6520 Lockport Rd	Niagara Falls	NY	14305	**800-237-8266**	716-297-8644	175
Helmerich & Payne Inc	1437 S Boulder Ave *NYSE: HP*	Tulsa	OK	74119	**800-205-4913**	918-742-5531	533
Helmsley Sandcastle Hotel	1540 Ben Franklin Dr	Sarasota	FL	34236	**800-225-2181**	941-388-2181	376
Help At Home Inc	One N State St Ste 800	Chicago	IL	60602	**800-404-3191**	312-762-0900	360
Helpjuice Inc	211 E Seventh St Ste 620	Austin	TX	78701	**888-230-3420**		384
Helton Industries Ltd	30840 Peardonville Rd	Abbotsford	BC	V2T6K2	**877-300-7412**	604-854-3660	347
Helvoet Pharma Inc	9012 Pennsauken Hwy	Pennsauken	NJ	08110	**800-874-3586**	856-663-2202	472
Helwig Carbon Products Inc	8900 W Tower Ave	Milwaukee	WI	53224	**800-365-3113**	414-354-2411	126
Helzberg Diamonds	1825 Swift Ave	North Kansas City	MO	64116	**800-669-7780**	816-842-7780	407
Hemacare Corp	15350 Sherman Way Ste 350	Van Nuys	CA	91406	**877-310-0717**	818-226-1968	88
Hemagen Diagnostics Inc	9033 Red Branch Rd *OTC: HMGN*	Columbia	MD	21045	**800-436-2436**	443-367-5500	231
Hemmings Motor News	222 Main St	Bennington	VT	05201	**800-227-4373**	802-442-3101	452-3
Henderson Auctions	13340 Florida Blvd PO Box 336	Livingston	LA	70754	**800-334-7443**	225-686-2252	50
Henderson Community College	2660 S Green St	Henderson	KY	42420	**800-696-9958**	270-827-1867	160
Henderson Convention Ctr	200 S Water St	Henderson	NV	89015	**877-775-5252**	702-267-2171	206
Henderson County Public Library	301 N Washington St	Hendersonville	NC	28739	**866-866-2362**	828-697-4725	431-3
Henderson County Tourist Commission	101 N Water St Ste B	Henderson	KY	42420	**800-648-3128**	270-826-3128	207
Henderson County Travel & Tourism	201 S Main St	Hendersonville	NC	28792	**800-828-4244**	828-693-9708	207
Henderson Glass Inc	715 S Blvd E	Rochester Hills	MI	48307	**800-694-0672**	855-543-8663	330
Henderson Global Investors	One Financial Plz Fl 19	Hartford	CT	06103	**888-832-6774**	860-723-8600	398
Henderson Hills Baptist Church	1200 E I 35 Frontage Rd	Edmond	OK	73034	**877-901-4639**	405-341-4639	47-20
Henderson Manufacturing Inc	1085 S Third St	Manchester	IA	52057	**800-359-4970**	563-927-2828	273
Henderson State University	1100 Henderson St	Arkadelphia	AR	71999	**800-228-7333**	870-230-5000	166
Henderson Wheel & Warehouse Supply	1825 South 300 West	Salt Lake City	UT	84115	**800-748-5111**	801-486-2073	60
Hendrick Buick GMC Cadillac	1151 W 104th St	Kansas City	MO	64114	**888-255-9362**	816-942-7100	56
Hendrick Hospice Care	1682 Hickory St	Abilene	TX	79601	**800-622-8516**	325-677-8516	368
Hendrick Manufacturing Co	One Seventh Ave *Cust Svc	Carbondale	PA	18407	**800-225-7373***		483
Hendrick Motorsports Museum	4400 Papa Joe Hendrick Blvd	Charlotte	NC	28262	**877-467-4890**		515
Hendricks County Flyer	8109 Kingston St Ste 500	Avon	IN	46123	**800-359-3747**	317-272-5800	525-4
Hendricks Power Co-op	86 N County Rd 500 E	Avon	IN	46123	**800-876-5473**	317-745-5473	245
Hendrickson International	800 S Frontage Rd	Woodridge	IL	60517	**855-743-3733**	630-910-2800	59
Hendrix College	1600 Washington Ave	Conway	AR	72032	**800-277-9017**	501-329-6811	166
Henkel Corp	One Henkel Way *Cust Svc	Rocky Hill	CT	06067	**800-243-4874***	860-571-5100	3
Henkels & McCoy Inc	985 Jolly Rd	Blue Bell	PA	19422	**800-523-2568**	215-283-7600	189-10
Henley Park Hotel	926 Massachusetts Ave NW	Washington	DC	20001	**800-222-8474**	202-638-5200	376
Henlopen Hotel	511 N Boardwalk	Rehoboth Beach	DE	19971	**800-441-8450**	302-227-2551	376
Hennepin Technical College	9000 Brooklyn Blvd	Brooklyn Park	MN	55445	**800-345-4655**	952-995-1300	788
Hennessy Industries Inc	1601 JP Hennesey Dr	La Vergne	TN	37086	**800-688-6359**	615-641-7533	59
Hennis Care Centre	1720 Cross St	Dover	OH	44622	**800-241-1044**	330-364-8849	445
Henny Penny Corp	1219 US 35 W PO Box 60	Eaton	OH	45320	**800-417-8417**	937-456-8400	297
Henri Bendel Inc	712 Fifth Ave	New York	NY	10019	**866-875-7975**	212-247-1100	155-6

Name / Address	Toll-Free	Phone	Class
Henricus Historical Park Henricus Pk Rd ... Chester VA 23836	800-514-3849	804-748-1613	513
Henry B Gonzalez Convention Ctr 200 E Market St ... San Antonio TX 78205	877-504-8895	210-207-8500	206
Henry Brick Co Inc 3409 Water Ave ... Selma AL 36703	800-218-3906	334-875-2600	148
Henry Co 909 N Sepulveda Blvd Ste 650 ... El Segundo CA 90245	800-598-7663	310-955-9200	45
Henry County Public Library System 1001 Florence McGarity Blvd ... McDonough GA 30252	877-527-3712	770-954-2806	431-3
Henry Equestrian Insurance Brokers 28 Victoria St ... Aurora ON L4G1P9	800-565-4321	905-727-1144	388-1
Henry Ford Community College 5101 Evergreen Rd ... Dearborn MI 48128	800-585-4322	313-845-9600	160
Henry Ford Health System One Ford Pl ... Detroit MI 48202	800-436-7936		350
Henry Ford Hospital 2799 W Grand Blvd ... Detroit MI 48202	800-999-4340	313-916-2600	371-3
Henry Ford Museum 20900 Oakwood Blvd ... Dearborn MI 48124	800-733-0345	313-271-1620	513
Henry Ford OptimEyes 655 W 13-Mile Rd ... Madison Heights MI 48071	800-393-2273	248-588-9300	536
Henry Glass & Co 49 W 37th St ... New York NY 10018	800-294-9495	917-229-1080	734-1
Henry Margu Inc 540 Commerce Dr ... Yeadon PA 19050	800-345-8284	610-622-0515	345
Henry Pratt Co 401 S Highland Ave ... Aurora IL 60506	877-436-7977	630-844-4000	778
Henry Products Inc 302 S 23rd Ave ... Phoenix AZ 85009	800-525-5533	602-253-3191	192-1
Henry Schein Inc 135 Duryea Rd ... Melville NY 11747 NASDAQ: HSIC	800-582-2702	631-843-5500	470
Henry Technologies 701 S Main St ... Chatham IL 62629	800-964-3679	217-483-2406	14
Henry Troemner LLC 201 Wolf Dr ... Thorofare NJ 08086	800-352-7705	856-686-1600	471
Hensel Phelps Construction Co 420 Sixth Ave PO Box 0 ... Greeley CO 80632	800-826-6309	970-352-6565	187
Hensley Industries Inc 2108 Joe Field Rd PO Box 29779 ... Dallas TX 75229	888-406-6262	972-241-2321	191
Hentzen Coatings Inc 6937 W Mill Rd ... Milwaukee WI 53218	800-236-6589	414-353-4200	543
Hepaco Inc 2711 Burch Dr PO Box 26308 ... Charlotte NC 28269	800-888-7689	704-598-9782	684
Hepatitis Foundation International (HFI) 504 Blick Dr ... Silver Spring MD 20904	800-891-0707	301-622-4200	47-17
Her Interactive Inc 1150 114th Ave SE Ste 200 ... Bellevue WA 98004 *Orders	800-461-8787*	425-460-8787	179-6
Heraeus 300 Heraeus Way ... South Bend IN 46614 *General	800-431-1785*		228
Herald & Review 601 E Williams St ... Decatur IL 62523	800-437-2533	217-429-5151	525-2
Herald Bulletin 1133 Jackson St ... Anderson IN 46016	800-750-5049	765-622-1212	525-2
Herald Democrat 603 S Sam Rayburn Fwy ... Sherman TX 75090	800-827-7183	903-893-8181	525-2
Herald Journal 75 W 300 N ... Logan UT 84321	800-275-0423	435-752-2121	525-2
Herald Publishing Co PO Box 153 ... Houston TX 77001	888-421-1866	713-630-0391	628-8
Herald Times Reporter 902 Franklin St ... Manitowoc WI 54221	800-783-7323	920-684-4433	525-2
Herald-Dispatch 946 Fifth Ave ... Huntington WV 25701	800-444-2446	304-526-4000	525-2
Herald-Mail Co, The 100 Summit Ave PO Box 439 ... Hagerstown MD 21741	800-626-6397	301-733-5131	628-8
Herald-Palladium 3450 Hollywood Rd PO Box 128 ... Saint Joseph MI 49085	800-356-4262	269-429-2400	525-2
Herald-Standard Eight E Church St Ste 18 ... Uniontown PA 15401	800-342-8254	724-439-7500	525-2
Herald-Star 401 Herald Sq ... Steubenville OH 43952	800-526-7987	740-283-4711	628-8
Herald-Sun, The 2828 Pickett Rd ... Durham NC 27705	877-627-6724	919-419-6500	525-2
Herb Chambers I 95 Inc 107 Andover St ... Danvers MA 01923	877-907-1965		56
Herb Easley Motors Inc 1125 Central Fwy ... Wichita Falls TX 76306	866-232-8859	940-723-6631	56
Herb Gordon Nissan 3131 Automobile Blvd ... Silver Spring MD 20904	855-414-4810	866-399-7502	56
Herb Research Foundation (HRF) 4140 15th St ... Boulder CO 80304	800-748-2617	303-449-2265	47-17
Herbalist, The 2106 NE 65th St ... Seattle WA 98115	800-694-3727	206-523-2600	787
Herbert H & Grace A Dow Foundation 1018 W Main St ... Midland MI 48640	800-362-4874	989-631-3699	304
Herbert H. Landy Insurance Agency Inc 75 Second Ave Ste 410 ... Needham MA 02494	800-336-5422		387
Herbert S Hiller Corp 401 Commerce Pt ... New Orleans LA 70123	800-833-5211	504-736-0008	669
Hercules Chemical Company Inc 111 S St ... Passaic NJ 07055	800-221-9330	973-778-5000	3
Hercules Engine Components Co 2770 S Erie St ... Massillon OH 44646	800-345-0662	330-830-2498	262
Hercules Industries Inc 1310 W Evans Ave ... Denver CO 80223	800-356-5350	303-937-1000	605
Hercules Manufacturing Co 800 Bob Posey St ... Henderson KY 42420	800-633-3031	270-826-9501	509
Hercules Offshore Inc 9 Greenway Plaza Ste 2200 ... Houston TX 77046 NASDAQ: HERO	888-647-1715	713-350-5100	533
Hercules Tire & Rubber Co 16380 E US Rt 224 - 200 ... Findlay OH 45840	800-677-9535	419-425-6400	744
Herc-U-Lift Inc 5655 Hwy 12 W PO Box 69 ... Maple Plain MN 55359	800-362-3500	763-479-2501	382
Herculite Products Inc 105 E Sinking Springs Ln ... Emigsville PA 17318 *Cust Svc	800-772-0036*	717-764-1192	734-2
Heritage Bags 1648 Diplomat Dr ... Carrollton TX 75006	800-527-2247		65
Heritage Bank 201 Fifth Ave SW ... Olympia WA 98501	800-455-6126	360-943-1500	357-2
Heritage Bible College 1747 Bud Hawkins Rd PO Box 1628 ... Dunn NC 28334	800-297-6351	910-892-3178	166
Heritage Canada Foundation Five Blackburn Ave ... Ottawa ON K1N8A2	866-964-1066	613-237-1066	47-13
Heritage Christian University 3625 Helton Dr PO Box HCU ... Florence AL 35630	800-367-3565	256-766-6610	159
Heritage Club 2020 S Monroe St ... Denver CO 80210	888-221-7317	303-756-0025	663
Heritage Co, The 2402 Wildwood Ave Ste 500 ... North Little Rock AR 72120	800-643-8822	501-835-5000	5
Heritage College & Seminary 175 Holiday Inn Dr ... Cambridge ON N3C3T2	800-465-1961	519-651-2869	773
Heritage Commerce Corp 150 Almaden Blvd ... San Jose CA 95113 NASDAQ: HTBK	800-468-9716	408-947-6900	357-2
Heritage Corridor Convention & Visitors Bureau 339 W Jefferson St ... Joliet IL 60435	800-926-2262	815-727-2323	207
Heritage Ctr 1201 W Buena Vista Rd ... Evansville IN 47710	800-704-0700	812-429-0700	445
Heritage Financial Corp 201 Fifth Ave SW ... Olympia WA 98501 NASDAQ: HFWA	800-962-4284	360-943-1500	357-2
Heritage Foods LLC 4002 Westminster Ave ... Santa Ana CA 92703 *Orders	800-321-5960*	714-775-5000	295-27
Heritage Foundation 214 Massachusetts Ave NE ... Washington DC 20002	800-546-2843	202-546-4400	625
Heritage Group Inc 1101 12th St ... Aurora NE 68818	888-463-6611	402-694-3136	69
Heritage Hills Golf Resort & Conference Ctr 2700 Mt Rose Ave ... York PA 17402	877-782-9752	717-755-0123	660
Heritage Hospice 120 Enterprise Dr PO Box 1213 ... Danville KY 40423	800-203-6633	859-236-2425	368
Heritage Hotel 522 Heritage Rd ... Southbury CT 06488	800-932-3466	203-264-8200	374
Heritage Inn, The 34521 Postal Ln ... Lewes DE 19958	800-669-9399		376
Heritage Mint Ltd PO Box 13750 ... Scottsdale AZ 85267	888-860-6245	480-860-1300	721
Heritage of the Americas Museum 12110 Cuyamaca College Dr W ... El Cajon CA 92019	800-234-1597	619-670-5194	513
Heritage Place Inc 2829 S MacArthur ... Oklahoma City OK 73128	888-343-9831	405-682-4551	50
Heritage Plastics Inc 1002 Hunt St ... Picayune MS 39466	800-245-4623	601-798-8663	598-2
Heritage Square Museum 3800 Homer St ... Los Angeles CA 90031	800-375-1771	323-225-2700	513
Heritage Summit HealthCare of Florida Inc PO Box 2928 ... Lakeland FL 33806	800-282-7644	863-665-6629	388-3
Heritage University 3240 Ft Rd ... Toppenish WA 98948	888-272-6190	509-865-8500	166
Heritage-Crystal Clean Inc 2175 Pt Blvd Ste 375 ... Elgin IL 60123	877-938-7948	847-836-5670	149
Herkimer County Chamber of Commerce 28 W Main St ... Mohawk NY 13407	877-984-4636	315-866-7820	137
Herkimer County Community College 100 Reservoir Rd ... Herkimer NY 13350	844-464-4375	315-866-0300	160
Herley-CTI Inc 9 Whippany Rd ... Whippany NJ 07981	866-606-5867	973-884-2580	253
Herman Davis State Park Corner of Ark 18 Baltimore St ... Manila AR 72201	888-287-2757		558
Herman Goldner Co Inc 7777 Brewster Ave ... Philadelphia PA 19153	800-355-5997	215-365-5400	190-10
Herman H Sticht Company Inc 45 Main St Ste 701 ... Brooklyn NY 11201	800-221-3203	718-852-7602	467
Herman Miller for Health Care 855 E Main Ave PO Box 302 ... Zeeland MI 49464	888-443-4357	616-654-3000	318-3
Herman Miller Inc 855 E Main Ave ... Zeeland MI 49464 NASDAQ: MLHR	888-443-4357	616-654-3000	318-1
Herman's Inc 2820 Blackhawk Rd ... Rock Island IL 61201	800-447-1295	309-788-9568	154
Hermann Oak Leather Co 4050 N First St ... Saint Louis MO 63147	800-325-7950	314-421-1173	429
Hermitage Hotel 231 Sixth Ave N ... Nashville TN 37219	888-888-9414	615-244-3121	376
hermo Fisher Scientific Inc 8365 Valley Pike PO Box 307 ... Middletown VA 22645	800-528-0494	800-556-2323	231
Hermosa Inn 5532 N Palo Cristi Rd ... Paradise Valley AZ 85253	800-241-1210	602-955-8614	376
Heroix Corp 165 Bay State Dr ... Braintree MA 02184	800-229-6500	781-848-1701	179-12
Herold's Salads Inc 17512 Miles Ave ... Cleveland OH 44128	800-427-2523	216-991-7500	295-33
Heron Point of Chestertown 501 E Campus Ave ... Chestertown MD 21620	800-327-9138	410-778-7300	663
Herr Foods Inc 20 Herr Dr PO Box 300 ... Nottingham PA 19362	800-344-3777	610-932-9330	295-35
Herr Tavern & Public House 900 Chambersburg Rd ... Gettysburg PA 17325	800-362-9849	717-334-4332	662
Herrman Lumber Co 1917 S State Hwy N ... Springfield MO 65802	888-238-9778	417-862-3737	361
Herrschners Inc 2800 Hoover Rd ... Stevens Point WI 54481	800-713-1239	715-341-8686	258
HERS (Hysterectomy Educational Resources & Services Foundation) 422 Bryn Mawr Ave ... Bala Cynwyd PA 19004	888-750-4377	610-667-7757	47-17
Hersam Acorn Newspapers 16 Bailey Ave ... Ridgefield CT 06877	800-372-2790	203-438-6544	628-8
Herschel-Adams Inc 1301 N 14th St ... Indianola IA 50125	800-247-2167		273
Hershey Co 100 Crystal A Dr ... Hershey PA 17033 NYSE: HSY *Cust Svc	800-468-1714*		295-8
Hershey Creamery Co 301 S Cameron St ... Harrisburg PA 17101	888-240-1905	717-238-8134	295-25
Hershey Entertainment & Resorts Co 27 W Chocolate Ave ... Hershey PA 17033	800-437-7439		660
Hershey Harrisburg Region Visitors Bureau 17 S Second St ... Harrisburg PA 17101	877-727-8573	717-231-7788	207
Hershey Lodge 325 University Dr ... Hershey PA 17033	800-437-7439	717-533-3311	376

Name / Address	City	State	ZIP	Toll-Free	Phone	Class
Hersheypark 100 Hershey Pk Dr	Hershey	PA	17033	**800-437-7439**	717-534-3900	32
Herson's Inc 15525 Frederick Rd	Rockville	MD	20855	**888-203-8318**		56
Hertz Equipment Rental Corp 225 Brae Blvd	Park Ridge	NJ	07656	**800-654-3131**	201-307-2000	264-3
Hertz Global Holdings Inc 225 Brae Blvd	Park Ridge	NJ	07656	**800-654-3131**	201-307-2000	125
NYSE: HTZ						
Herweck's Art & Drafting Supplies 300 Broadway St	San Antonio	TX	78205	**800-725-1349**	210-227-1349	44
Herzing College *Atlanta* 3393 Peachtree Rd Ste 1003	Atlanta	GA	30326	**800-573-4533**	404-816-4533	788
Herzing College Birmingham 280 W Valley Ave	Birmingham	AL	35209	**800-425-9432**	205-916-2800	788
Herzing College Madison 5218 E Terr Dr	Madison	WI	53718	**800-582-1227**	608-249-6611	788
Herzog Contracting Corp 600 S Riverside Rd	Saint Joseph	MO	64507	**800-541-7846**	816-233-9001	189-4
HES (Hanchett Entry Systems Inc) 22630 N 17th Ave	Phoenix	AZ	85027	**800-626-7590**	623-582-4626	683
HESCO (Hartford Electric Supply Co) 30 Inwood Rd Ste 1	Rocky Hill	CT	06067	**800-969-5444**	860-236-6363	246
Heska Corp 3760 Rocky Mtn Ave	Loveland	CO	80538	**800-464-3752**	970-493-7272	575
NASDAQ: HSKA						
Hesperia Chamber of Commerce 16816 Main St Ste D	Hesperia	CA	92345	**855-574-7337**	760-244-2135	137
HESS Construction + Engineering Services Inc 804 W Diamond Ave Ste 300	Gaithersburg	MD	20878	**800-544-6056**	301-670-9000	256
Hess Sweitzer Inc 2805 S 160th St	New Berlin	WI	53151	**800-491-4377**	262-641-9100	190-8
Hesse Inc 6700 St John Ave	Kansas City	MO	64123	**800-821-5562**	816-483-7808	769
Hesselgrave International PO Box 30768	Bellingham	WA	98228	**800-457-5522**	360-734-3570	750
Hesser College 3 Sundial Ave	Manchester	NH	03103	**888-971-2190**	603-668-6660	166
Hesston College 325 S College Dr PO Box 3000	Hesston	KS	67062	**800-995-2757**	620-327-4221	160
Heucotech Ltd 99 Newbold Rd	Fairless Hills	PA	19030	**800-483-2224**		142
Hewlett-Packard (Canada) Ltd (HP) 5150 Spectrum Way	Mississauga	ON	L4W5G1	**888-447-4636**	905-206-4725	174-1
Hewlett-Packard Co 3000 Hanover St	Palo Alto	CA	94304	**800-752-0900***	650-857-1501	174-1
NYSE: HPQ ■ *Sales						
Hexacon Electric Co 161 W Clay Ave	Roselle Park	NJ	07204	**888-765-3371**	908-245-6200	748
Hexagon Metrology Inc 250 Circuit Dr	North Kingstown	RI	02852	**855-443-9638**	401-886-2000	467
Hexaware Technologies Inc 1095 Cranbury Rd	Jamesburg	NJ	08831	**866-746-2133**	609-409-6950	181
Hexcel Corp 281 Tresser Blvd 16th Fl	Stamford	CT	06901	**800-444-3923**	800-688-7734	598-1
NYSE: HXL						
Heyburn State Park 57 Chatcolet Rd	Plummer	ID	83851	**866-634-3246**	208-686-1308	558
Heyco Products 1800 Industrial Way N	Toms River	NJ	08755	**800-526-4182**	732-286-1800	483
Heyman HospiceCare 420 E Second Ave	Rome	GA	30161	**800-324-1078**	706-509-3200	368
Heymann Performing Arts Ctr 1373 S College Rd	Lafayette	LA	70503	**800-745-3000**	337-291-5540	565
HF Financial Corp 225 S Main Ave	Sioux Falls	SD	57104	**800-244-2149**	605-333-7556	357-2
NASDAQ: HFFC						
HF Group Inc 203 W Artesia Blvd	Compton	CA	90220	**800-421-5000**	310-605-0755	491
HFA (Hospice Foundation of America) 1710 Rhode Island Ave NW Ste 400	Washington	DC	20036	**800-854-3402**	202-457-5811	48-8
HFES (Human Factors & Ergonomics Society) 1124 Montana Ave Ste B PO Box 1369	Santa Monica	CA	90406	**800-233-1234**	310-394-1811	47-17
HFI (Hepatitis Foundation International) 504 Blick Dr	Silver Spring	MD	20904	**800-891-0707**	301-622-4200	47-17
HFIA (Home Furnishings Independents Assn) 2050 Stemmons World Fwy Ste 292	Dallas	TX	75207	**800-422-3778**	214-741-7632	48-4
HFMA (Healthcare Financial Management Assn) Two Westbrook Corporate Ctr Ste 700	Westchester	IL	60154	**800-252-4362**	708-531-9600	48-8
HFTP (Hospitality Financial & Technology Professionals) 11709 Boulder Ln Ste 110	Austin	TX	78726	**800-646-4387**	512-249-5333	48-1
Hfw Industries Inc 196 Philadelphia St PO Box 8	Buffalo	NY	14207	**800-937-9311**	716-875-3380	383
HGI Skydyne 100 River Rd	Port Jervis	NY	12771	**800-428-2273**		200
HH Angus & Assoc Ltd 1127 Leslie St	Toronto	ON	M3C2J6	**866-955-8201**	416-443-8200	256
HH Arnold Co Inc 529 Liberty St	Rockland	MA	02370	**866-868-9603**	781-878-0346	733
HH Brown Shoe Company Inc 124 W Putnam Ave	Greenwich	CT	06830	**888-444-2769**	203-661-2424	300
HHP (Horizon House Publications Inc) 685 Canton St	Norwood	MA	02062	**800-225-9977**	781-769-9750	628-9
HHS (Department of Health & Human Services) 330 Independence Ave SW	Washington	DC	20201	**877-696-6775**	202-619-0150	338-8
HI TecMetal Group Inc 1101 E 55th St	Cleveland	OH	44103	**877-484-2867**	216-881-8100	479
HIAA (Halifax Stanfield International Airport) 1 Bell Blvd	Enfield	NS	B2T1K2	**800-565-5359**	902-873-4422	27
HIAS (Hebrew Immigrant Aid Society) 333 Seventh Ave 16th Fl	New York	NY	10001	**800-442-7714**	212-967-4100	47-5
HI-AYH (Hostelling International USA - American Youth Hostels) 8401 Colesville Rd Ste 600	Silver Spring	MD	20910	**800-725-2331**	301-495-1240	47-23
Hibbing Community College 1515 E 25th St	Hibbing	MN	55746	**800-224-4422**	218-262-6700	160
Hibbs Hallmark & Co 501 Shelley Dr	Tyler	TX	75701	**800-765-6767**		387
HIBCC (Health Industry Business Communications Council) 2525 E Arizona Biltmore Cir Ste 127	Phoenix	AZ	85016	**800-755-5505**	602-381-1091	48-8
Hibco Plastics Inc 1820 Us 601 Hwy	Yadkinville	NC	27055	**800-849-8683**	336-463-2391	594
Hickey Freeman 1155 N Clinton Ave	Rochester	NY	14621	**844-755-7344***	585-467-7021	153-11
*Cust Svc						
Hickman-Fulton Counties Rural Electric Co-op Corp 1702 Moscow Ave PO Box 190	Hickman	KY	42050	**800-633-1391**	270-236-2521	245
Hickok Inc 10514 Dupont Ave	Cleveland	OH	44108	**800-342-5080**	216-541-8060	248
OTC: HICKA						
Hickory Brands Inc (HBI) 429 27th St NW	Hickory	NC	28601	**800-438-5777**		734-5
Hickory Daily Record 1100 Pk Pl	Hickory	NC	28602	**800-849-8586**	828-322-4510	525-2
Hickory Farms Inc 811 Madison Ave	Toledo	OH	43604	**800-753-8558**		334
Hickory Knob State Resort Park 1591 Resort Dr	McCormick	SC	29835	**800-491-1764**	864-391-2450	558
Hickory Metro Convention & Visitors Bureau 1960 13th Ave Dr SE	Hickory	NC	28602	**800-509-2444**	828-322-1335	207
Hickory Motor Speedway 3130 Hwy 70 SE	Newton	NC	28658	**800-843-8725**	828-464-3655	508
Hickory Point Bank & Trust FSB PO Box 2548	Decatur	IL	62525	**800-872-0081***	217-875-3131	69
*Cust Svc						
Hickory Printing Group Inc 725 Reese Dr SW	Conover	NC	28613	**800-442-5679**	828-465-3431	619
Hickory Ridge Marriott Conference Hotel 10400 Fernwood Rd	Bethesda	IL	20817	**800-334-0344**	301-380-3000	374
Hickory Springs Mfg Co 235 Second Ave NW	Hickory	NC	28601	**800-438-5341**		710
Hickory Tech Corp 221 E Hickory St PO Box 3248	Mankato	MN	56002	**866-442-5679**	507-387-1151	357-3
NASDAQ: ENVE						
HID Global Corp 611 Center Ridge Dr	Austin	TX	78753	**800-237-7769**	512-776-9000	179-12
HIDA (Health Industry Distributors Assn) 310 Montgomery St	Alexandria	VA	22314	**800-549-4432**	703-549-4432	48-18
Hidalgo County PO Box 58	Edinburg	TX	78540	**888-318-2811**	956-318-2100	336
Hidden Valley Resort & Conference Ctr 1 Craighead Dr PO Box 4420	Hidden Valley	PA	15502	**800-452-2223**	814-443-8000	374
Hideout at Flitner Ranch Resort PO Box 206	Shell	WY	82441	**800-354-8637**	307-765-2080	239
Hie Electronics Inc 321 N Central Expy Ste 260	Mckinney	TX	75070	**888-782-7937**	972-542-2327	174-8
Higdon Florist 201 E 32nd St	Joplin	MO	64804	**800-641-4726**	417-624-7171	292
High Concrete Structures Inc 125 Denver Rd	Denver	PA	17517	**800-773-2278**	717-336-9300	184
High Country Bancorp Inc 7360 W Hwy 50 PO Box 309	Salida	CO	81201	**800-201-0557**	719-539-2516	357-2
OTC: HCBC						
High Country Transportation Inc PO Box 700	Cortez	CO	81321	**800-635-7687**		770
High Desert Museum 59800 S Hwy 97	Bend	OR	97702	**866-632-9992**	541-382-4754	513
High End Systems Inc 2105 Gracy Farms Ln	Austin	TX	78758	**800-890-8989**	512-836-2242	435
High Hampton Inn & Country Club 1525 Hwy 107 S	Cashiers	NC	28717	**800-334-2551**	828-743-2450	660
High Peaks Resort 2384 Saranac Ave	Lake Placid	NY	12946	**800-755-5598**	518-523-4411	660
High Performance Computing Collaboratory PO Box 9627	Mississippi State	MS	39762	**800-521-4041**	662-325-8278	659
High Plains Livestock Exchange LLC 28601 US Hwy 34	Brush	CO	80723	**866-842-5115**	970-842-5115	441
High Plains Power Inc 1775 E Monroe PO Box 713	Riverton	WY	82501	**800-445-0613**	307-856-9426	245
High Plains Publishers Inc 1500 W Wyatt Earp Blvd	Dodge City	KS	67801	**800-452-7171**	620-227-7171	628-8
High Point Chamber of Commerce 1634 N Main St	High Point	NC	27262	**877-852-9462**	336-882-5000	137
High Point Convention & Visitors Bureau 300 S Main St	High Point	NC	27260	**800-720-5255**	336-884-5255	207
High Point Furniture Industries Inc 1104 Bedford St PO Box 2063	High Point	NC	27261	**800-447-3462**	336-431-7101	318-1
High Point Public Library (HPPL) 901 N Main St	High Point	NC	27262	**877-772-8346**	336-883-3660	431-3
High Point Regional Health System (HPRHS) 601 N Elm St PO Box HP-5	High Point	NC	27262	**877-878-7644**	336-878-6000	371-3
High Point University 833 Montlieu Ave	High Point	NC	27262	**800-345-6993**	336-841-9216	166
High Power Technical Services Inc (HPTS) 2230 Ampere Dr	Louisville	KY	40299	**866-398-3474**		115
High Speed Productions Inc 1303 Underwood Ave	San Francisco	CA	94124	**888-520-9099**	415-822-3083	507
High Vacuum Apparatus LLC (HVA) 12880 Moya Blvd	Reno	NV	89506	**800-551-4422**	775-359-4442	777
High West Energy Inc (HWE) 6270 County Rd 212	Pine Bluffs	WY	82082	**888-834-1657**	307-245-3261	245
Higher Ed Growth LLC 5400 S Lakeshore Dr Ste 101	Tempe	AZ	85283	**866-433-8532**		444
HighJump Software 5600 W 83rd St Ste 600	Minneapolis	MN	55437	**800-328-3271**	952-947-4088	179-1
Highland Computer Forms Inc 1025 W Main St	Hillsboro	OH	45133	**800-669-5213**	937-393-4215	109
Highlands Regional Medical Ctr 5000 KY Rt 321	Prestonsburg	KY	41653	**800-533-4762**	606-886-8511	371-3
Highlands Today 315 US Hwy 27 N	Sebring	FL	33870	**800-645-3423***	863-386-5800	525-2
*General						
Highlights for Children Inc 1800 Watermark Dr	Columbus	OH	43216	**800-255-9517***	614-486-0631	628-9
*Cust Svc						
Highline Electric Assn 1300 S Interocean Ave	Holyoke	CO	80734	**800-816-2236**	970-854-2236	245
Highmark Inc 120 Fifth Ave Pl	Pittsburgh	PA	15222	**800-992-0246**	412-544-7000	388-3

	City	State	ZIP	Toll-Free	Phone	Class
Highway Machine Company Inc (HMC)						
3010 S Old US Hwy 41	Princeton	IN	47670	**866-990-9462**	812-385-3639	449
Highway To Health Inc						
One Radnor Corporate Ctr Ste 100	Radnor	PA	19087	**888-243-2358**		388-7
Highwoods Properties Inc						
3100 Smoketree Ct Ste 600	Raleigh	NC	27604	**866-449-6637**	919-872-4924	646
NYSE: HIW						
Hiland Dairy Co						
PO Box 2270	Springfield	MO	65801	**800-641-4022**	417-862-9311	295-27
Hilbert College						
5200 S Pk Ave	Hamburg	NY	14075	**800-649-8003**	716-649-7900	166
Hilco Electric Co-op Inc						
115 E Main PO Box 127	Itasca	TX	76055	**800-338-6425**	254-687-2331	245
Hilford Moving & Storage						
1595 Arundell Ave	Ventura	CA	93003	**800-739-6683**	805-642-0221	512
Hilgard House Hotel & Suites						
927 Hilgard Ave	Los Angeles	CA	90024	**800-826-3934**	310-208-3945	376
Hilgraeve Inc						
115 E Elm Ave	Monroe	MI	48162	**800-826-2760***	734-243-0576	179-7
*Sales						
Hill & Griffith Co						
1085 Summer St	Cincinnati	OH	45204	**800-543-0425**	513-921-1075	495
Hill Barth & King LLC						
7680 Market St	Youngstown	OH	44512	**800-733-8613**	330-758-8613	2
Hill Bros Chemical Co						
1675 N Main St	Orange	CA	92867	**800-994-8801**	714-998-8800	144
Hill County Electric Co-op Inc						
PO Box 2330	Havre	MT	59501	**877-394-7804**		245
Hill Crest Behavioral Health Services						
6869 Fifth Ave S	Birmingham	AL	35212	**800-292-8553**	205-833-9000	371-5
Hill Engineering Inc						
373 Randy Rd	Carol Stream	IL	60188	**800-631-0520**	630-834-4430	747
Hill Mfg Company Inc						
1500 Jonesboro Rd SE	Atlanta	GA	30315	**800-445-5123**	404-522-8364	149
Hill PHOENIX Inc						
1003 Sigman Rd	Conyers	GA	30013	**800-518-6630**	770-285-3264	655
Hill Physicians Medical Group Inc						
2409 Camino Ramon PO Box 5080	San Ramon	CA	94583	**800-445-5747**	925-820-8300	458
Hill School						
717 E High St	Pottstown	PA	19464	**877-651-2800**	610-326-1000	615
Hill Top Collections Inc						
38 W 32nd St Ste 1510	New York	NY	10001	**800-361-6871**	212-564-2322	158
Hill Wood Products Inc						
9483 Ashawa Rd	Cook	MN	55723	**800-788-9689**	218-666-5933	544
Hill's Pet Nutrition Inc						
400 SW Eigth St	Topeka	KS	66603	**800-569-7913***	785-354-8523	571
*General						
Hillcrest Foods						
2695 E 40th St	Cleveland	OH	44115	**800-952-4344**	216-361-4625	296-4
Hillerich & Bradsby Company Inc						
800 W Main St	Louisville	KY	40202	**800-282-2287**	502-585-5226	701
Hilliard This Week						
7801 N Central Dr	Lewis Center	OH	43035	**888-837-4342**	740-888-6100	525-4
Hillman Group Inc						
10590 Hamilton Ave	Cincinnati	OH	45231	**800-800-4900**	513-851-4900	348
Hill-Rom Services Inc						
1069 SR 46 E	Batesville	IN	47006	**800-267-2337**	812-934-7777	318-3
Hills Bank & Trust Co						
131 Main St PO Box 70	Hills	IA	52235	**800-445-5725**	319-679-2291	69
Hills Health Ranch						
4871 Caribou Hwy 97						
PO Box 26	108 Mile Ranch	BC	V0K2Z0	**800-668-2233**	250-791-5225	697
Hills Materials Co						
3975 Sturgis Rd PO Box 2320	Rapid City	SD	57709	**800-325-7056**	605-394-3300	498-4
Hillsboro Equipment Inc						
E18898 Hwy 33	Hillsboro	WI	54634	**800-521-5133**	608-489-2275	274
Hillsboro Public Library						
2850 NE Brookwood Pkwy	Hillsboro	OR	97124	**855-870-0049**	503-615-6500	431-3
Hillsborough County Public Schools						
901 E Kennedy Blvd	Tampa	FL	33602	**800-962-2873**	813-272-4000	676
Hillsborough Township Board of Education						
379 S Branch Rd	Hillsborough	NJ	08844	**800-272-1325**	908-431-6600	676
Hillsdale College						
33 E College St	Hillsdale	MI	49242	**888-886-1174**	517-437-7341	166
Hillsdale Free Will Baptist College						
PO Box 7208	Moore	OK	73153	**800-460-6328**	405-912-9000	166
Hillshire Brands						
PO Box 3901	Peoria	IL	61612	**800-323-7117**		215
Hillside Candy Co						
35 Hillside Ave	Hillside	NJ	07205	**800-524-1304**	973-926-2300	295-8
Hillside School						
404 Robin Hill Rd	Marlborough	MA	01752	**800-344-8328**	508-485-2824	615
Hillstone Restaurant Group						
147 S Beverly Dr	Beverly Hills	CA	90212	**800-230-9787**	310-385-7343	661
Hilltop Inn of Vermont						
3472 Airport Rd	Montpelier	VT	05602	**877-609-0003**	802-229-5766	376
Hillyard Chemical Company Inc						
302 N Fourth St	Saint Joseph	MO	64501	**800-365-1555**	816-233-1321	149
Hilman Inc						
12 Timber Ln	Marlboro	NJ	07746	**888-276-5548***	732-462-6277	465
*Cust Svc						
Hilmar Cheese Company Inc						
PO Box 910	Hilmar	CA	95324	**888-300-4465**	209-667-6076	295-5
Hilo Hattie						
700 N Nimitz Hwy	Honolulu	HI	96817	**800-233-8912**		155-5
Hilti Inc						
5400 S 122nd E Ave	Tulsa	OK	74146	**800-879-8000***	918-252-6000	749
*Cust Svc						
Hilton Galveston Island Resort						
5400 Seawall Blvd	Galveston	TX	77551	**800-475-3386**	409-744-5000	660
Hilton Grand Vacations Company LLC						
6355 Metro W Blvd Ste 180	Orlando	FL	32835	**800-230-7068**	407-722-3100	743
Hilton Hawaiian Village						
2005 Kalia Rd	Honolulu	HI	96815	**800-445-8667**	808-949-4321	660
Hilton Head Health Institute						
14 Valencia Rd	Hilton Head Island	SC	29928	**800-292-2440**	843-785-7292	697
Hilton Head Island Visitors & Convention Bureau						
1 Chamber Dr						
PO Box 5647	Hilton Head Island	SC	29938	**800-523-3373**	843-785-3673	207
Hilton Head Island-Bluffton Chamber of Commerce						
One Chamber Dr	Hilton Head Island	SC	29928	**800-523-3373**	843-785-3673	137
Hilton Head Library						
11 Beach City Rd	Hilton Head Island	SC	29926	**800-860-1444**	843-255-6500	431-3
Hilton Head Regional Medical Ctr						
25 Hospital Ctr						
Blvd	Hilton Head Island	SC	29926	**888-689-8207**	843-681-6122	371-3
Hilton Myrtle Beach Resort						
10000 Beach Club Dr	Myrtle Beach	SC	29572	**800-445-8667**	843-449-5000	660
Hilton San Diego Resort						
1775 E Mission Bay Dr	San Diego	CA	92109	**800-445-8667**	619-276-4010	660
Hilton Sandestin Beach Golf Resort & Spa						
4000 Sandestin Blvd S	Destin	FL	32550	**800-559-1805**	850-267-9500	660
Hilton Scranton & Conference Ctr						
100 Adams Ave	Scranton	PA	18503	**800-445-8667**	570-343-3000	374
Hilton Sedona Resort & Spa						
90 Ridge Trl Dr	Sedona	AZ	86351	**877-273-3762***	928-284-4040	660
*General						
Hilton Short Hills						
41 JFK Pkwy	Short Hills	NJ	07078	**800-445-8667**	973-379-0100	698
Hilton Suites Toronto/Markham Conference Centre & Spa						
8500 Warden Ave	Markham	ON	L6G1A5	**800-445-8667**	905-470-8500	698
Hilton University of Florida Conference Ctr						
1714 SW 34th St	Gainesville	FL	32607	**800-774-1500**	352-371-3600	374
Hilton Waikoloa Village						
425 Waikoloa Beach Dr	Waikoloa	HI	96738	**866-931-1679**	808-886-1234	660
Hilton Whistler Resort & Spa						
4050 Whistler Way	Whistler	BC	V0N1B4	**800-515-4050**	604-932-1982	660
Hilton Worldwide						
7930 Jones Branch Dr	McLean	VA	22102	**800-445-8667**	703-883-1000	376
Hinckley Co, The						
One Little Harbor Landing	Portsmouth	RI	02871	**866-446-2553**	401-683-7005	89
Hinda Incentives Inc						
2440 W 34th St	Chicago	IL	60608	**800-621-4112**	773-890-5900	755
Hindley Mfg Company Inc						
Nine Havens St	Cumberland	RI	02864	**800-323-9031**	401-722-2550	347
Hinds Community College						
501 E Main St PO Box 1100	Raymond	MS	39154	**800-446-3722**	601-857-5261	160
Hinds Hospice						
1616 W Shaw Ste C-1	Fresno	CA	93711	**800-400-4677**	559-248-8591	368
Hines Interest LP						
2800 Post Oak Blvd	Houston	TX	77056	**800-891-7017**	713-621-8000	644
Hines Nut Co Inc						
990 S St Paul St	Dallas	TX	75201	**800-561-6374**	214-939-0253	295-28
Hingham Institution for Savings						
55 Main St	Hingham	MA	02043	**877-447-2265**	781-749-2200	69
NASDAQ: HIFS						
Hingham Mutual Fire Insurance Co						
230 Beal St	Hingham	MA	02043	**800-341-8200**	781-749-0841	388-4
Hiniker Co						
58766 240th St	Mankato	MN	56002	**800-433-5620**	507-625-6621	273
Hinkley Lighting						
12600 Berea Rd	Cleveland	OH	44111	**800-446-5539**	216-671-3300	435
Hippocrates Health Institute Life-Change Ctr						
1443 Palmdale Ct	West Palm Beach	FL	33411	**800-842-2125**	561-471-8876	697
Hiram College PO Box 67	Hiram	OH	44234	**800-362-5280***	330-569-5169	166
*Admissions						
Hiregenics						
47742 Van Dyke Ave	Shelby Township	MI	48317	**866-315-5489**		563
Hireko Trading Company Inc						
16185 Stephens St	City of Industry	CA	91745	**800-367-8912**		701
HiRel Systems						
11100 Wayzata Blvd Ste 501	Minnetonka	MN	55305	**888-604-5888**	952-544-1344	253
HireRight Inc						
5151 California Ave	Irvine	CA	92617	**800-400-2761**	949-428-5800	626
Hirschbach Motor Lines Inc						
18355 US Hwy 20	East Dubuque	IL	61025	**800-554-2969**	402-494-5000	770
Hirsh Industries Inc						
3636 Westown Pkwy						
Ste 100	West Des Moines	IA	50266	**800-383-7414**	515-299-3200	318-1
Hirzel Canning Company & Farms						
411 Lemoyne Rd	Northwood	OH	43619	**800-837-1631**	419-693-0531	295-20
Hi-Shear Technology Corp (HSTC)						
24225 Garnier St	Torrance	CA	90505	**800-733-0321***	310-784-2100	499
*Mktg						
Hispanic Assn of Colleges & Universities (HACU)						
8415 Datapoint Dr Ste 400	San Antonio	TX	78229	**800-780-4228**	210-692-3805	48-5
Historic Annapolis Foundation Museum						
77 Main St	Annapolis	MD	21401	**800-603-4020**	410-268-5576	513
Historic Bullock Hotel						
633 Main St	Deadwood	SD	57732	**800-336-1876**		376
Historic French Market Inn						
509 Decatur St	New Orleans	LA	70130	**800-366-2743**	504-561-5621	376
Historic Inns of Annapolis						
58 State Cir	Annapolis	MD	21401	**800-847-8882**	410-263-2641	376
Historic Jonesborough Visitors Ctr & Museum						
117 Boone St	Jonesborough	TN	37659	**866-401-4223**	423-753-1010	513
Historic New England						
141 Cambridge St	Boston	MA	02114	**800-722-2256**	617-227-3956	47-13
Historic Old Town Fort Collins						
19 Old Town Sq Ste 230	Fort Collins	CO	80524	**866-203-5939**	970-484-6500	455
Historic Rock Ford Plantation						
881 Rockford Rd	Lancaster	PA	17602	**800-732-0999**	717-392-7223	49-2
Historic Roswell Convention & Visitors Bureau						
617 Atlanta St	Roswell	GA	30075	**800-776-7935**	770-640-3253	207
Historic Tours of America Inc						
201 Front St Ste 224	Key West	FL	33040	**800-844-7601***	305-296-3609	750
*General						
Historic Trinity Lutheran Church						
1345 Gratiot Ave	Detroit	MI	48207	**800-268-3058**	313-567-3100	49
Historical Research Ctr Inc						
2107 Corporate Dr	Boynton Beach	FL	33426	**800-985-9956**	561-732-5263	326
History Ch						
A&E Television Networks LLC						
235 E 45th St 8th Fl	New York	NY	10017	**866-582-5613**	212-210-1400	729
Hit Promotional Products Inc						
7150 Bryan Dairy Rd	Largo	FL	33777	**800-237-6305**	727-541-5561	9
Hitachi America Ltd						
50 Prospect Ave	Tarrytown	NY	10591	**800-448-2244**	914-332-5800	186
Hitachi America Ltd Computer Div						
2000 Sierra Pt Pkwy	Brisbane	CA	94005	**800-448-2244**		174-8
Hitachi Canada Ltd						
5450 Explore Dr Suite 501	Mississauga	ON	L4W5N1	**866-797-4332**	905-629-9300	253
Hitachi Chemical Diagnostics						
630 Clyde Ct	Mountain View	CA	94043	**800-233-6278**	650-961-5501	231
Hitachi Data Systems Corp						
750 Central Expy	Santa Clara	CA	95050	**877-437-3849**	408-970-1000	174-8

Name	Address	City	St	Zip	Toll-Free	Phone	Class
Hitachi Kokusai Electric America Ltd	150 Crossways Pk Dr	Woodbury	NY	11797	**888-687-6877**	516-921-7200	638
Hitachi Medical Systems America Inc	1959 Summit Commerce Pk	Twinsburg	OH	44087	**800-800-3106**	330-425-1313	379
Hitachi Metals America Ltd	2 Manhattanville Rd Ste 301	Purchase	NY	10577	**800-777-5757**	914-694-9200	306
Hitch Enterprises Inc	309 Northridge Cir PO Box 1308	Guymon	OK	73942	**800-951-2533**	580-338-8575	357-3
HITCO Carbon Composites Inc	1600 W 135th St	Gardena	CA	90249	**800-421-5444**	310-527-0700	499
Hite Co	3101 Beale Ave	Altoona	PA	16601	**800-252-3598**	814-944-6121	246
HITEC Group Ltd	1743 Quincy Ave Unit 155	Naperville	IL	60540	**800-288-8303**		246
Hi-Tech Pharmacal Co Inc	369 Bayview Ave	Amityville	NY	11701	**888-628-0581**	631-789-8228	576
	NASDAQ: HITK						
Hitt Marking Devices Inc	3231 W MacArthur Blvd	Santa Ana	CA	92704	**800-969-6699**	714-979-1405	462
Hiwassee College	225 Hiwassee College Dr	Madisonville	TN	37354	**800-356-2187**	423-442-2001	160
Hix Corp	1201 E 27th Terr	Pittsburg	KS	66762	**800-835-0606**	620-231-8568	733
HJ Heinz Co	One PPG Pl Ste 3100	Pittsburgh	PA	15230	**800-255-5750**	412-456-5700	295-20
HK Systems Inc	2855 S James Dr	New Berlin	WI	53151	**800-424-7365**	262-860-7000	179-1
Hkm Direct Market Communications Inc	5501 Cass Ave	Cleveland	OH	44102	**800-860-4456***	216-651-9500	5
	*General						
HL Dalis Inc	35-35 24th St	Long Island City	NY	11106	**800-453-2547**	718-361-1100	246
HLA (Harold Levinson Assoc)	21 Banfi Plz	Farmingdale	NY	11735	**800-325-2512**	631-962-2400	296-3
HLC Hotels Inc	7080 Abercorn St PO Box 13069	Savannah	GA	31416	**800-344-4378**	912-352-4493	376
HLI (Human Life International)	Four Family Life Ln	Front Royal	VA	22630	**800-549-5433***	540-635-7884	47-6
	*Orders						
Hli Properties Inc	PO Box 1052	Fort Dodge	IA	50501	**800-247-2000**	515-955-1600	628-9
HM Royal Inc	689 Pennington Ave	Trenton	NJ	08618	**800-257-9452**	609-396-9176	144
HM Stauffer & Sons Inc	33 Glenola Dr PO Box 567	Leola	PA	17540	**800-662-2226**	717-656-2811	804
HMA (Hargrave Military Academy)	200 Military Dr	Chatham	VA	24531	**800-432-2480**	434-432-2481	615
HMC (Highway Machine Company Inc)	3010 S Old US Hwy 41	Princeton	IN	47670	**866-990-9462**	812-385-3639	449
HMC (Hays Medical Ctr)	2220 Canterbury Dr	Hays	KS	67601	**800-248-0073**	785-650-2759	371-3
HMC Archtiect	3546 Councours St	Ontario	CA	91764	**800-350-9979**	909-989-9979	261
HMH (Harrington Memorial Hospital)	100 S St	Southbridge	MA	01550	**800-416-6072**	508-765-9771	371-3
HMN Financial Inc	1016 Civic Ctr Dr NW	Rochester	MN	55901	**888-257-2000**	507-535-1309	357-2
	NASDAQ: HMNF						
HMS (Healthcare Management Systems Inc)	3102 W End Ave Ste 400	Nashville	TN	37203	**800-383-3317**	615-383-7300	384
HNA (Hawaii Nurses Assn)	949 Kapiolani Blvd Ste 107	Honolulu	HI	96814	**800-617-2677**	808-531-1628	526
HNA (Hockey North America)	45570 Shepard Dr	Sterling	VA	20164	**800-446-2539**	703-430-8100	47-22
HO Bostrom Company Inc	818 Progress Ave	Waukesha	WI	53186	**800-332-5415**	262-542-0222	680
HO Trerice Co	12950 W Eight-Mile Rd	Oak Park	MI	48237	**888-873-7423**	248-399-8000	202
Hoard's Dairyman Magazine	28 Milwaukee Ave W PO Box 801	Fort Atkinson	WI	53538	**800-245-8222**	920-563-5551	452-1
Hoban & Assoc Dba Coast Real Estate Services	2829 Rucker Ave	Everett	WA	98201	**800-339-3634**	425-339-3638	643
Hobart & William Smith Colleges	300 Pulteney St	Geneva	NY	14456	**800-852-2256***	315-781-3000	166
	*Admissions						
Hobart Corp	701 S Ridge Ave	Troy	OH	45374	**800-333-7447***	937-332-3000	297
	*Cust Svc						
Hobas Pipe USA LP	1413 E Richey Rd	Houston	TX	77073	**800-856-7473**	281-821-2200	589
Hobbs Bonded Fibers Inc	200 Commerce Dr	Waco	TX	76710	**800-433-3357**	254-741-0040	734-6
Hobbs Chamber of Commerce	400 N Marland Blvd	Hobbs	NM	88240	**800-658-6291**	575-397-3202	137
Hobe Sound Bible College	PO Box 1065	Hobe Sound	FL	33475	**800-881-5534**	772-546-5534	159
Hobie Cat Co	4925 Oceanside Blvd	Oceanside	CA	92056	**800-462-4349**	760-758-9100	89
Hobson & Motzer Inc	30 Air Line Dr PO Box 427	Durham	CT	06422	**800-476-5111**	860-349-1756	483
Hobsons CollegeView	50 E Business Way Ste 300	Cincinnati	OH	45241	**800-927-8439**		628-9
Ho-Chunk Casino	S 3214 County Rd BD	Baraboo	WI	53913	**800-746-2486**		132
Hockessin Library	1023 Valley Rd	Hockessin	DE	19707	**888-352-7722**	302-239-5160	431-3
Hockey News Magazine	25 Sheppard Ave Ste 100	Toronto	ON	M2N6S7	**888-361-9768**		452-20
Hockey North America (HNA)	45570 Shepard Dr	Sterling	VA	20164	**800-446-2539**	703-430-8100	47-22
Hocking College	3301 Hocking Pkwy	Nelsonville	OH	45764	**877-462-5464**	740-753-3591	788
Hodell-natco Industries Inc	7825 Hub Pkwy	Cleveland	OH	44125	**800-321-4862**	216-447-0165	348
Hodge Products Inc	1410 Hill St	El Cajon	CA	92020	**800-778-2217**		294
Hodges Trucking Co LLC	4050 W I-40	Oklahoma City	OK	73108	**888-829-1370**	405-947-7764	770
Hodges University	2655 Northbrooke Dr	Naples	FL	34119	**800-466-8017**	239-513-1122	166
	Fort Myers 4501 Colonial Blvd	Fort Myers	FL	33966	**800-466-0019**	239-482-0019	166

Name	Address	City	St	Zip	Toll-Free	Phone	Class
Hodgson Mill Inc	1100 Stevens Ave	Effingham	IL	62401	**800-347-0105**	217-347-0105	295-23
Hoegemeyer Hybrids Inc	1755 Hoegemeyer Rd	Hooper	NE	68031	**800-245-4631**	402-654-3399	10-4
Hoerbiger Corp of America Inc	3350 Gateway Dr	Pompano Beach	FL	33069	**800-327-8961**	954-974-5700	777
Hoffman California Fabrics Inc	25792 Obrero Dr	Mission Viejo	CA	92691	**800-547-0100**		587
Hoffman Memorial State Wayside	PO Box 569	Bandon	OR	97411	**800-551-6949**		558
Hoffman Products	9600 Vly View Rd	Macedonia	OH	44056	**800-645-2014**	216-525-4320	802
Hoffmann Hospice of the Valley	8501 Brimhall Rd Bldg 100	Bakersfield	CA	93312	**888-833-3900**	661-410-1010	368
Hoffmann-LaRoche Inc	340 Kingsland St	Nutley	NJ	07110	**800-526-6367**	973-235-5000	576
Hoffmaster	2920 N Main St	Oshkosh	WI	54901	**800-327-9774**	920-235-9330	551
Hofstra University	1000 Fulton Ave	Hempstead	NY	11549	**800-463-7872**	516-463-6600	166
Hofstra University School of Law	121 Hofstra University	Hempstead	NY	11549	**800-463-7872**	516-463-5916	167-1
Hog Slat	200 N Meridian Line Rd	Camden	IN	46917	**800-949-4647**	574-967-3776	442
Hog Slat Inc	PO Box 300	Newton Grove	NC	28366	**800-949-4647**	910-594-0219	10-5
Hoggan Health Industries Inc	8020 South 1300 West	West Jordan	UT	84088	**800-678-7888**	801-572-6500	267
Hogue Cellars	2800 Lee Rd	Prosser	WA	99350	**800-565-9779**		79-3
Hohman Assoc Inc (HAI)	6951 W Little York	Houston	TX	77040	**800-324-0978**	713-896-0978	47-2
Hohmann & Barnard Inc	30 Rasons Ct	Hauppauge	NY	11788	**800-645-0616**	631-234-0600	278
Hohner Inc	1000 Technology Pk Dr	Glen Allen	VA	23059	**800-446-6010**	804-515-1900	520
Hoigaards Inc	5425 Excelsior Blvd	Minneapolis	MN	55416	**800-266-8157**	952-929-1351	702
Hoist Fitness Systems Inc	9990 Empire St Ste 130	San Diego	CA	92126	**800-548-5438**	858-578-7676	267
Hoke County	227 N Main St	Raeford	NC	28376	**888-302-9793**	910-875-8751	336
Holderness School	Chapel Ln PO Box 1879	Plymouth	NH	03264	**877-262-1492**	603-536-1747	615
Ho-Lee-Chow	2204 Danforth Ave	Toronto	ON	M4C1K3	**800-465-3324**	416-996-3333	661
Holiday Acres Resort	4060 S Shore Dr PO Box 460	Rhinelander	WI	54501	**800-261-1500**	715-369-1500	660
Holiday Builders Inc	2293 W Eau Gallie Blvd	Melbourne	FL	32935	**866-431-2533**	321-610-5172	644
Holiday Cos	4567 American Blvd W PO Box 1224	Bloomington	MN	55437	**800-745-7411**	952-830-8700	186
Holiday Express Corp	721 S 28th St	Estherville	IA	51334	**800-831-5078**	712-362-5812	676
Holiday Hair	7201 Metro Blvd	Minneapolis	MN	55439	**800-345-7811**		76
Holiday Inn	301 Government St	Mobile	AL	36602	**888-465-4329**	251-694-0100	376
Holiday Inn Express & Suites	5001 Brougham Dr	Drayton Valley	AB	T7A0A1	**877-444-3110**	780-515-9888	373
Holiday Inn Express & Suites Oceanfront	3301 S Atlantic Ave	Daytona Beach Shores	FL	32118	**800-633-8464**	386-767-1711	660
Holiday Inn Express DFW North	4550 W John Carpenter Fwy	Irving	TX	75063	**800-465-4329**		376
Holiday Inn Oceanfront at Surfside Beach	1601 N Ocean Blvd	Surfside Beach	SC	29575	**866-661-5139***	843-238-5601	660
	*Resv						
Holiday Inn Resort Daytona Beach Oceanfront	1615 S Atlantic Ave	Daytona Beach	FL	32118	**800-874-0975**	386-255-0921	376
Holiday Inn Resort Lake Buena Vista	13351 SR 535	Orlando	FL	32821	**866-808-8833***	407-239-4500	660
	*Sales						
Holiday Inn SunSpree Resort Wrightsville Beach	1706 N Lumina Ave	Wrightsville Beach	NC	28480	**888-211-9874**	910-256-2231	660
Holiday Isle Beach Resort & Marina	84001 Overseas Hwy	Islamorada	FL	33036	**800-327-7070**	305-664-2321	660
Holiday Retirement Corp	5885 Meadows Rd Ste 500	Lake Oswego	OR	97035	**800-322-0999**	503-370-7070	646
Holiday River Expeditions	544 East 3900 South	Salt Lake City	UT	84107	**800-624-6323**	801-266-2087	750
Holiday Stationstores	4567 American Blvd W	Bloomington	MN	55437	**800-745-7411**	952-830-8700	205
Holiday Trails Resorts (Western) Inc	53730 Bridal Falls Rd	Rosedale	BC	V0X1X1	**800-663-2265**	604-794-7876	120
Holiday Tree Farms Inc	800 NW Cornell Ave	Corvallis	OR	97330	**800-289-3684**	541-753-3236	742
Holiday Valley Resort	Rt 219 PO Box 370	Ellicottville	NY	14731	**800-323-0020**	716-699-2345	660
Holiday World & Splashin' Safari	452 E Christmas Blvd	Santa Claus	IN	47579	**877-463-2645**	812-937-4401	32
Holland America Line	300 Elliott Ave W	Seattle	WA	98119	**800-426-0327**	206-281-3535	220
Holland Area Chamber of Commerce	272 E Eigth St	Holland	MI	49423	**800-421-3512**	616-392-2389	137
Holland Area Convention & Visitors Bureau	76 E Eigth St	Holland	MI	49423	**800-506-1299**	616-394-0000	207
Holland Capital Management LP	303 W Madison St Ste 700	Chicago	IL	60606	**800-295-9779**	312-553-4830	398
Holland Co	1000 Holland Dr	Crete	IL	60417	**800-899-7754**	708-672-2300	641
Holland Mfg Co Inc	15 Main St PO Box 404	Succasunna	NJ	07876	**800-345-0492**	973-584-8141	722
Holland NASCAR Motorsports Complex	11586 Holland Glenwood Rd	Holland	NY	14080	**866-655-0257**	716-537-2272	508
Holland Sentinel	54 W Eigth St	Holland	MI	49423	**800-784-6776**	616-392-2311	525-2
Hollander Home Fashions Corp	6501 Congress Avenue Suite 300	Boca Raton	FL	33487	**800-233-7666**	561-997-6900	735
Hollandia Dairy Inc	622 E Mission Rd	San Marcos	CA	92069	**888-883-2479**	760-744-3222	10-2

	Toll-Free	Phone	Class
Hollar & Greene Produce Co Inc 230 Cabbage Rd PO Box 3500 Boone NC 28607	800-222-1077	828-264-2177	296-7
Holley Performance Products Inc 1801 Russellville Rd Bowling Green KY 42101 *Sales	800-638-0032*	270-782-2900	127
Holliday Lake State Park 2759 State Pk Rd Appomattox VA 24522	800-933-7275	434-248-6308	558
Hollingsworth Inc 1775 SW 30th St Ontario OR 97914	800-541-1612	541-889-7254	274
Hollins University PO BOX 9707 Roanoke VA 24020 *Admissions	800-456-9595*	540-362-6401	166
Hollister Inc 2000 Hollister Dr Libertyville IL 60048	800-323-4060	847-680-1000	472
Holloway Sportswear Inc 2633 Campbell Rd Sidney OH 45365	800-331-5156		153-5
Holly Energy Partners LP 100 Crescent Ct Ste 1600 Dallas TX 75201	800-642-1687	214-871-3555	357-5
Holly Hill Hospital 3019 Falstaff Rd Raleigh NC 27610	800-447-1800	919-250-7000	371-5
Holly Poultry Inc 2221 Berlin St Baltimore MD 21230	800-342-9464	410-727-6210	342
Hollyhock PO Box 127 Mansons Landing BC V0P1K0	800-933-6339	250-935-6576	664
Hollywood Bowl 2301 N Highland Ave Hollywood CA 90068	800-653-8000	323-850-2000	565
Hollywood Casino at Charles Town Races 750 Hollywood Dr Charles Town WV 25414	800-795-7001	304-725-7001	633
Hollywood Casino Baton Rouge 1717 River Rd N Baton Rouge LA 70802	800-447-6843	877-770-7867	132
Hollywood Casino Bay Saint Louis 711 Hollywood Blvd Bay Saint Louis MS 39520	866-758-2591		132
Hollywood Casino Joliet 777 Hollywood Blvd Joliet IL 60436	800-426-2537		132
Hollywood Reporter 5055 Wilshire Blvd Ste 600 Los Angeles CA 90036	866-525-2150	323-525-2000	452-9
Hollywood Ribbon Industries Inc 9000 Rochester Ave Rancho Cucamonga CA 91730	800-457-7652	323-266-0670	327
Hollywood Roosevelt Hotel 7000 Hollywood Blvd Los Angeles CA 90028	800-950-7667	323-466-7000	376
Hollywood Wax Museum 6767 Hollywood Blvd Hollywood CA 90028	800-214-3661	323-462-5991	513
Hol-Mac Corp 2730-A Hwy 15 PO Box 349 Bay Springs MS 39422	800-844-3019	601-764-4121	223
Holman Cadillac Co 1200 Rt 73 S Mount Laurel NJ 08054	866-865-6973	856-778-1000	56
Holman Group 9451 Corbin Ave Northridge CA 91324	800-321-2843	818-704-1444	457
Holman Transportation Services Inc 1010 Holman Ct Caldwell ID 83605	800-375-2416	208-454-0779	770
Holmberg Farms Inc 13430 Hobson Simmons Rd Lithia FL 33547	800-282-3562		293
Holmes Community College PO Box 399 Goodman MS 39079	800-465-6374	662-472-2312	160
Holmes Murphy & Assoc Inc 3001 Westown Pkwy West Des Moines IA 50266	800-247-7756	515-223-6800	387
Holmes Regional Medical Ctr 1350 Hickory St Melbourne FL 32901	800-716-7737	321-434-7000	371-3
Holmes-Wayne Electric Co-op Inc 6060 Ohio 83 Millersburg OH 44654	866-674-1055	330-674-1055	245
Holocaust Memorial Ctr 28123 OrchaRd Lake Rd Farmington Hills MI 48334	800-875-5275	248-553-2400	513
Hologic Inc 35 Crosby Dr Bedford MA 01730 *NASDAQ: HOLX*	800-523-5001	781-999-7300	379
Holophane 214 Oakwood Ave PO Box 3004 Newark OH 43058	866-465-6742	740-345-9631	435
Holstein Assn USA Inc One Holstein Pl Brattleboro VT 05302 *Orders	800-952-5200*	802-254-4551	47-2
Holsum Bakery Inc 2322 W Lincoln St Phoenix AZ 85009	888-246-5786	602-252-2351	67
Holt & Bugbee Co 1600 Shawsheen St Tewksbury MA 01876	800-325-6010	978-851-7201	192-3
HOLT Texas Ltd 3302 S WW White Rd San Antonio TX 78222	800-275-4658	210-648-1111	274
Holten Meat Inc 1682 Sauget Business Blvd Sauget IL 62206	800-851-4684	618-337-8400	296-9
Holts Cigar Co 1522 Walnut St Philadelphia PA 19102	800-523-1641	215-732-8500	746
Holtzbrinck Publishers 175 Fifth Ave New York NY 10010	800-221-7945	646-307-5151	628-2
Holum & Sons Company Inc 740 Burr Oak Dr Westmont IL 60559	800-447-4479	630-654-8222	85
Holy Cross Energy PO Box 2150 Glenwood Springs CO 81602	877-833-2555	970-945-5491	245
Holy Cross Family Ministries 518 Washington St North Easton MA 02356	800-299-7729	508-238-4095	47-20
Holy Cross Hospital 1500 Forest Glen Rd Silver Spring MD 20910	800-358-9001	301-754-7000	371-3
Holy Family Memorial Medical Ctr 2300 Western Ave PO Box 1450 Manitowoc WI 54220	800-994-3662	920-320-2011	371-3
Holy Family University 9801 Frankford Ave Philadelphia PA 19114	800-422-0010	215-637-7700	166
Holy Names University 3500 Mountain Blvd Oakland CA 94619	800-430-1321	510-436-1000	166
Holy Redeemer Hospital & Medical Ctr 1648 Huntingdon Pk Meadowbrook PA 19046	800-818-4747	215-947-3000	371-3
Holy Rosary Healthcare 2600 Wilson St Miles City MT 59301	800-843-3820	406-233-2600	371-3
Holyoke Community College 303 Homestead Ave Holyoke MA 01040	877-442-6222	413-538-7000	160
Holyoke Rehabilitation Ctr 260 Easthampton Rd Holyoke MA 01040	800-811-3535	413-538-9733	445
Holz Rubber Company Inc 1129 S Sacramento St Lodi CA 95240	800-285-1600	209-368-7171	668
Homasote Co 932 Lower Ferry Rd PO Box 7240 West Trenton NJ 08628 *OTC: HMTC*	800-257-9491	609-883-3300	806
Home & Away Magazine 10703 J St Ste 100 Omaha NE 68127	800-710-2267	402-592-5000	452-22
Home & Garden Showplace 8600 W Bryn Mawr Chicago IL 60631	877-502-4641	773-695-5000	322
Home Automated Living Inc 14401 Sweitzer Ln Sixth Fl Laurel MD 20707	800-935-5313	301-498-6000	175
Home Bound Healthcare Inc 1615 Vollmer Rd Flossmoor IL 60422	800-444-7028	708-798-0800	360
Home Capital Group Inc 145 King St W Ste 2300 Toronto ON M5H1J8 *TSE: HCG*	800-990-7881	416-360-4663	357-3
Home Care Industries Inc 1 Lisbon St Clifton NJ 07013	888-382-1222	973-365-1600	65
Home Care Industries Inc ALFCO Div One Lisbon St Clifton NJ 07013 *Cust Svc	800-325-1908*	973-365-1600	18
Home City Financial Corp 2454 N Limestone St PO Box 1288 Springfield OH 45503 *OTC: HCFL*	866-421-2331	937-390-0470	357-2
Home Depot Inc 2455 Paces Ferry Rd NW Atlanta GA 30339 *NYSE: HD* ■ *Cust Svc	800-553-3199*	770-433-8211	361
Home Depot Supply 3100 Cumberland Blvd Ste 1480 Atlanta GA 30339	855-615-8372	770-852-9000	348
Home Dynamix LLC One Carol Pl Moonachie NJ 07074	800-726-9290	201-807-0111	130
Home Entertainment Distribution Inc 120 Shawmut Rd Canton MA 02021	800-343-9619	781-821-0087	37
Home Essentials & Beyond Inc 200 Theodore Conrad Dr Jersey City NJ 07305	800-417-6218	732-590-3600	358
Home Federal Bank 1602 Cumberland Ave Middlesboro KY 40965 *OTC: HFBA*	800-354-0182	606-248-1095	357-2
Home Furnishings Independents Assn (HFIA) 2050 Stemmons World Fwy Ste 292 Dallas TX 75207	800-422-3778	214-741-7632	48-4
Home Health & Hospice Care Seven Executive Park Dr Merrimack NH 03054	800-887-5973	603-882-2941	368
Home Health Line 11300 Rockville Pk Ste 1100 Rockville MD 20852	800-929-4824	301-287-2700	524-8
Home Hospice Care of Rhode Island 1085 N Main St Providence RI 02904	800-338-6555	401-415-4200	368
Home Instead Inc 13330 California St Ste 200 Omaha NE 68154	888-484-5759	402-498-4466	360
Home IV Care & Nutritional Service PO Box 700 Stuarts Draft VA 24477	800-552-6576		360
Home Market Foods Inc 140 Morgan Dr Norwood MA 02062	800-367-8325	781-948-1500	295-36
Home Media Retailing 201 E Sandpointe Ave Ste 500 Santa Ana CA 92707	800-371-6897	714-759-4661	452-21
Home News Enterprises 333 Second St Columbus IN 47201	800-876-7811		628-8
Home News Tribune 92 E Main St Ste 202 Somerville NJ 08876	800-627-4663	732-246-5500	525-2
Home Paramount Pest Control Cos Inc PO Box 850 Forest Hill MD 21050	888-888-4663	410-510-0700	570
Home Products International Inc 4501 W 47th St Chicago IL 60632	800-327-3534	773-890-1010	600
Home Ranch PO Box 822 Clark CO 80428	800-688-2982	970-879-1780	239
Home Run Inn Inc 1300 Internationale Pkwy Woodridge IL 60517	800-636-9696	630-783-9696	661
Home Savings & Loan Company of Youngstown 275 W Federal St Youngstown OH 44503	888-822-4751	330-742-0500	69
Home Security of America Inc 310 N Midvale Blvd Madison WI 53705	800-367-1448		364
HomeAdvisor 14023 Denver W Pkwy Ste 200 Golden CO 80401	800-474-1596	303-963-7200	394
HomeCare & Hospice 1225 W State St Olean NY 14760	800-339-7011	716-372-5735	368
HomeCare of East Alabama Medical Ctr 665 Opelika Rd Auburn AL 36830	866-542-4768	334-826-3131	368
HomeCrest Cabinetry 1002 Eisenhower Dr N Goshen IN 46526	800-960-3660	574-535-9300	114
HomeGain.com Inc 6001 Shellmound St Ste 550 Emeryville CA 94608	888-542-0800	510-655-0800	643
Homeland Security Funding Week 8204 Fenton St Silver Spring MD 20910	800-666-6380	301-588-6380	524-7
Homeplace Ranch RR 1 Site 2 Priddis AB T0L1W0	877-931-3245	403-969-4444	239
Homer Electric Assn Inc 3977 Lake St Homer AK 99603	800-478-8551	907-235-8551	245
Homer Laughlin China Co 672 Fiesta Dr Newell WV 26050	800-452-4462	304-387-1300	721
Homer Optical Company Inc 2401 Linden Ln Silver Spring MD 20910	800-627-2710	301-585-9060	535
Homereach Hospice 800 McConnell Dr Columbus OH 43214	800-837-2455	614-566-5377	368
Homes & Land Magazine Affiliates LLC 1830 E Pk Ave Tallahassee FL 32301	800-277-7800	850-575-0189	628-9
Homes by Keystone Inc 13338 Midvale Rd PO Box 69 Waynesboro PA 17268	800-890-7926		105
Homes.com Inc 150 Granby St Norfolk VA 23510	866-675-1058		384
HomeServices of America Inc 333 S Seventh St 27th Fl Minneapolis MN 55402	888-485-0018		643
Homestead Mills 221 N River St PO Box 1115 Cook MN 55723	800-652-5233	218-666-5233	295-4
Homestead Resort 700 N Homestead Dr Midway UT 84049	888-327-7220		660
Homestead Technologies Inc 180 Jefferson Dr Menlo Park CA 94025	800-797-2958	650-944-3100	795
HomeSteps 500 Plano Pkwy Carrollton TX 75010	800-972-7555		502
HomeStreet Bank 601 Union St 2 Union Sq Ste 2000 Seattle WA 98101	800-654-1075	206-623-3050	69
HomeTeam Inspection Service Inc 575 Chamber Dr Milford OH 45150	800-598-5297		362
Hometown America LLC 150 N Wacker Dr Ste 2800 Chicago IL 60606	888-735-4310	312-604-7500	500
Hometown Bank 245 N Peters Ave Fond du Lac WI 54935	877-261-2220	920-907-2220	69
HomeVestors of America Inc 6500 Greenville Ave Ste 400 Dallas TX 75206	800-442-8937	972-761-0046	309
Homewood FSB 3228-30 Eastern Ave Baltimore MD 21224	800-554-8969	410-327-5220	69

Name / Address	City	State	ZIP	*Toll-Free*	*Phone*	*Class*
HomeWorks Tri-County Electric Co-op 7973 E Grand River Ave PO Box 350	Portland	MI	48875	**800-848-9333**	517-647-7554	245
HON Co 200 Oak St	Muscatine	IA	52761	**800-553-8230**	563-272-7100	318-1
Honat Bancorp Inc 733 Main St PO Box 350 *OTC: HONT*	Honesdale	PA	18431	**800-462-9515**	570-253-3355	357-2
Honda Ctr 2695 E Katella Ave	Anaheim	CA	92806	**877-945-3946**	714-704-2400	711
Honda of Santa Monica 1726 Santa Monica Blvd	Santa Monica	CA	90404	**800-269-2031**	310-264-4900	56
Honda World 10645 Studebaker Rd	Downey	CA	90241	**888-458-9404**	562-929-7000	56
Hondros College 4140 Executive Pkwy	Westerville	OH	43081	**888-466-3767**		166
Honduras *Embassy* 3007 Tilden St NW	Washington	DC	20008	**800-375-5283**	202-966-7702	257
Honey Acres 1557 Hwy 67 N	Ashippun	WI	53003	**800-558-7745**		295-24
Honey Creek State Park 901 State Pk Rd	Grove	OK	74344	**800-622-6317**	918-786-9447	558
Honey Dew Assoc Inc Two Taunton St	Plainville	MA	02762	**800-946-6393**	508-699-3900	67
Honeys Place Inc 640 Glenoaks Blvd	San Fernando	CA	91340	**800-910-3246**	818-256-1101	231
Honeytree Inc 8570 M 50	Onsted	MI	49265	**800-968-1889**	517-467-2482	295-24
Honeyville Grain Inc 11600 Dayton Dr	Rancho Cucamonga	CA	91730	**888-810-3212**	909-980-9500	295-4
Honeyville Metal Inc 4200 S 900 W	Topeka	IN	46571	**800-593-8377**	260-593-2266	18
Honeywell 101 Columbia Rd	Morristown	NJ	07960	**800-822-7673**	973-455-2000	143
Honeywell Aerospace 3520 Westmoor St	South Bend	IN	46628	**800-707-4555**	574-231-2000	22
Honeywell Fire Solutions One Fire-Lite Pl	Northford	CT	06472	**800-627-3473**	203-484-7161	283
One Fire-Lite Pl	Northford	CT	06472	**800-627-3473**	203-484-7161	739
Honeywell Fluorine Products 101 Columbia Rd	Morristown	NJ	07962	**800-951-1527**	973-455-2000	143
Honeywell International Inc 101 Columbia Rd PO Box M6/LM *NYSE: HON*	Morristown	NJ	07962	**877-841-2840**	480-353-3020	725
Honeywell Safety Products 2000 Plainfield Pike *Cust Svc	Cranston	RI	02921	**800-430-4110***	401-943-4400	569
Honeywell Security Group Two Corporate Ctr Dr Ste 100	Melville	NY	11747	**800-467-5875**	516-577-2000	683
Honeywell Sensing & Control 11 W Spring St *Cust Svc	Freeport	IL	61032	**800-537-6945***	815-235-5500	204
Honeywell Specialty Materials 101 Columbia Rd	Morristown	NJ	07962	**800-222-0094**	973-455-2145	598-1
Honeywood Winery 1350 Hines St SE	Salem	OR	97302	**800-726-4101**	503-362-4111	49-6
Hong Kong Tourism Board 5670 Wilshire Blvd Ste 1230	Los Angeles	CA	90036	**800-282-4582**	323-938-4582	765
Honkamp Krueger & Company PC 2345 JFK Rd PO Box 699	Dubuque	IA	52004	**888-556-0123**	563-556-0123	2
Honolulu Academy of Arts 900 S Beretania St	Honolulu	HI	96814	**866-385-3849**	808-532-8700	513
Honolulu Advertiser 500 Ala Moana Blvd	Honolulu	HI	96813	**877-233-1133**	808-529-4747	525-2
Honolulu Magazine 1000 Bishop St Ste 405	Honolulu	HI	96813	**800-788-4230**	808-534-7546	452-22
Honolulu Publishing Co Ltd 707 Richards St Ste PH3	Honolulu	HI	96813	**800-272-5245**	808-524-7400	628-9
Hoober Inc 3452 Old Philadelphia Pk PO Box 518	Intercourse	PA	17534	**800-732-0017**	717-768-8231	274
Hood College 401 Rosemont Ave	Frederick	MD	21701	**800-922-1599**	301-696-3400	166
Hood County Public Library 222 N Travis St	Granbury	TX	76048	**800-452-9292**	817-573-3569	431-3
Hood Packaging Corp 25 Woodgreen Pl	Madison	MS	39110	**800-321-8115**	601-853-7260	64
Hooker Furniture Corp 440 E Commonwealth Blvd *NASDAQ: HOFT* ■ *Cust Svc	Martinsville	VA	24112	**800-422-1511***	276-632-0459	318-2
Hooper Corp 2030 Pennsylvania Ave	Madison	WI	53704	**800-242-8511**	608-249-0451	190-10
Hoosier Co 5421 W 86th St PO Box 681064	Indianapolis	IN	46268	**800-521-4184**	317-872-8125	286
Hoosier Park Racing & Casino 4500 Dan Patch Cir	Anderson	IN	46013	**800-526-7223**	765-642-7223	633
Hooters Casino Hotel 115 E Tropicana Ave	Las Vegas	NV	89109	**866-584-6687**	702-739-9000	132
Hoover & Strong Inc 10700 Trade Rd *Cust Svc	North Chesterfield	VA	23236	**800-759-9997***		480
Hoover Construction Co Inc PO Box 1007	Virginia	MN	55792	**800-741-0970**	218-741-3280	189-4
Hoover Toyota 2686 Hwy 150	Hoover	AL	35244	**866-980-8082**	205-978-2600	56
Hoover's Inc 5800 Airport Blvd	Austin	TX	78752	**800-486-8666**	512-374-4500	628-6
Hop-A-Jet Inc 5525 NW 15th Ave Ste 150	Fort Lauderdale	FL	33309	**800-556-6633**	954-771-5779	13
Hope College 69 E Tenth St PO Box 9000 *Admissions	Holland	MI	49422	**800-968-7850***	616-395-7850	166
Hope College Van Wylen Library 53 Graves Pl	Holland	MI	49423	**800-968-7850**	616-395-7790	431-6
Hope Global Engineered Textile Solutions 50 Martin St *General	Cumberland	RI	02864	**800-854-7139***	401-333-8990	734-5
Hope Hospice 611 N Walnut Ave	New Braunfels	TX	78130	**800-499-7501**	830-625-7500	368
Hope International University 2500 E Nutwood Ave	Fullerton	CA	92831	**866-722-4673**	714-879-3901	166
Hope Network 3075 Orchard Vista Dr SE	Grand Rapids	MI	49546	**800-695-7273**	616-301-8000	445
Hope Pharmaceuticals Inc 16416 N 92nd St Ste 125	Scottsdale	AZ	85260	**800-755-9595**		576
Hopkins & Carley A Law Corp PO Box 1469	San Jose	CA	95109	**800-829-3676**	408-286-9800	425
Hopkins Ctr for the Arts 6041 Wilson Hall	Hanover	NH	03755	**800-451-4067**	603-646-2422	565
Hopkins Manufacturing Corp 428 Peyton St	Emporia	KS	66801	**800-524-1458**	620-342-7320	59
Hopkins-Carter Company Inc 3300 NW 21st St	Miami	FL	33142	**800-595-9656**	305-635-7377	460
Hopkinsville Community College 720 N Dr	Hopkinsville	KY	42240	**866-534-2224**	270-886-3921	160
Hopkinsville-Christian County Chamber of Commerce 2800 Port Campbell Blvd	Hopkinsville	KY	42240	**800-842-9959**	270-885-9096	137
Horace Mann Educators Corp One Horace Mann Plz *NYSE: HMN*	Springfield	IL	62715	**800-999-1030**	217-789-2500	357-4
Horace Mann Life Insurance Co 1 Horace Mann Plaza	Springfield	IL	62715	**800-999-1030**	217-789-2500	388-2
Horiba Instruments Inc 17671 Armstrong Ave	Irvine	CA	92614	**800-446-7422**	949-250-4811	416
Horizon Air Freight Inc 152-15 Rockaway Blvd	Jamaica	NY	11434	**800-221-6028**	718-528-3800	444
Horizon Convention Ctr 401 S High St	Muncie	IN	47305	**888-288-8860**	765-288-8860	206
Horizon Freight System Inc 6600 Bessemer Ave	Cleveland	OH	44127	**800-480-6829**	216-341-7410	463
Horizon Home Care & Hospice 11400 W Lake Park Dr	Milwaukee	WI	53224	**800-468-4660**	414-365-8300	368
Horizon Hospice 833 W Chicago Ave	Chicago	IL	60642	**866-733-6028**	312-733-8900	368
Horizon House Publications Inc (HHP) 685 Canton St	Norwood	MA	02062	**800-225-9977**	781-769-9750	628-9
Horizon Lines Inc 4064 Colony Rd Ste 200 *Cust Svc	Charlotte	NC	28211	**877-678-7447***	704-973-7000	311
Horizon Paper Co Inc 1010 Washington Blvd	Stamford	CT	06901	**866-358-0855**	203-358-0855	545-1
Horizon Termite & Pest Control Corp 45 Cross Ave	Midland Park	NJ	07432	**888-612-2847**	201-447-2530	570
Horizons Window Fashions Inc 1705 Waukegan Rd	Waukegan	IL	60085	**800-858-2352**		358
Hormel Foods Corp 1 Hormel Pl *NYSE: HRL*	Austin	MN	55912	**800-523-4635**	507-437-5611	295-26
Hornady Manufacturing Co 3625 W Old Potash Hwy	Grand Island	NE	68803	**800-338-3220**	308-382-1390	284
Hornbeck Offshore Services Inc 103 Northpark Blvd Ste 300 *NYSE: HOS*	Covington	LA	70433	**800-642-9816**	985-727-2000	460
Horner Millwork Corp 1255 Grand Army Hwy	Somerset	MA	02726	**800-543-5403**	508-679-6479	494
Hornerxpress Inc 5755 Powerline Rd	Fort Lauderdale	FL	33309	**800-432-6966**	954-772-6966	719
Hornor Townsend & Kent Inc (HTK) 600 Dresher Rd Ste C1C	Horsham	PA	19044	**800-289-9999**		399
Hornung's Golf Products Inc 815 Morris St	Fond du Lac	WI	54935	**800-323-3569**	920-922-2640	327
Horry Telephone Co-op Inc (HTC) 3480 Hwy 701 N PO Box 1820	Conway	SC	29528	**800-824-6779**	843-365-2151	726
Horry-Georgetown Technical College *Grand Strand Campus* 743 Hemlock Ave	Myrtle Beach	SC	29577	**855-544-4482**	843-477-0808	788
Horse Illustrated Magazine 3 Burroughs	Irvine	CA	92618	**888-588-4677**	949-855-8822	452-14
Horse Prairie Ranch 3300 Bachelor Mountain Rd	Dillon	MT	59725	**888-726-2454**	406-681-3166	239
Horsehead Corp 4955 Steubenville Pk Ste 405	Pittsburgh	PA	15205	**800-648-8897**	724-774-1020	141
HorseLoverZ com 254 N Cedar St	Hazleton	PA	18201	**877-804-7810**	570-579-0054	155-5
Horseshoe Bend Regional Library 207 NW St	Dadeville	AL	36853	**855-336-0333**	256-825-9232	431-3
Horseshoe Casino 777 Casino Ctr Dr	Hammond	IN	46320	**800-522-4700**	219-473-7000	132
Horseshoe Southern Indiana Hotel & Casino 711 Horseshoe Blvd	Bossier City	LA	71111	**800-895-0711**		132
Horsham Clinic 722 E Butler Pk	Ambler	PA	19002	**800-237-4447**	215-643-7800	371-5
Horspool & Romine Manufacturing Inc 5850 Marshall St	Oakland	CA	94608	**800-446-2263**		614
Horst Group Inc 320 Granite Run Dr PO Box 3330	Lancaster	PA	17604	**800-732-0330**	717-581-9800	187
Hortica Insurance One Horticultural Ln PO Box 428	Edwardsville	IL	62025	**800-851-7740**	618-656-4240	388-4
Horton Grand Hotel 311 Island Ave	San Diego	CA	92101	**800-542-1886**	619-544-1886	376
Horton Group, The 10320 Orland Pkwy	Orland Park	IL	60467	**800-383-8283**	708-845-3000	387
Horton Homes Inc 101 Industrial Blvd	Eatonton	GA	31024	**800-657-4000**	706-485-8506	500
Horton Inc 2565 Walnut St	Saint Paul	MN	55113	**800-621-1320**	651-361-6400	613
Horwith Trucks Inc PO Box 7	NorthHampton	PA	18067	**800-220-8807**	610-261-2220	56
Hosokawa Polymer Systems 63 Fuller Way	Berlin	CT	06037	**800-233-6112**	860-828-0541	383
Hosparus Inc 624 E Market St	New Albany	IN	47150	**800-895-5633**	812-945-4596	368
Hospice & Palliative Care of Cape Cod Inc 765 Attucks Ln	Hyannis	MA	02601	**800-642-2423**	508-957-0200	368
Hospice & Palliative Care of Northern Colorado 2726 W 11th St Rd	Greeley	CO	80634	**800-564-5563**	970-352-8487	368
Hospice & Palliative Care of Western Colorado 2754 Compass Dr Ste 377	Grand Junction	CO	81506	**866-310-8900**	970-241-2212	368
Hospice & Palliative CareCenter 101 Hospice Ln	Winston-Salem	NC	27103	**888-876-3663**	336-768-3972	368
Hospice Alliance 10220 Prairie Ridge Blvd	Pleasant Prairie	WI	53158	**800-830-8344**	262-652-4400	368

Alphabetical Section

	Toll-Free	Phone	Class
Hospice at Home			
4025 Health Pk Ln . . . . Saint Joseph MI 49085	800-717-3811	269-429-7100	368
Hospice at the Texas Medical Ctr			
1905 Holcombe Blvd . . . . Houston TX 77030	800-630-7894	713-467-7423	368
Hospice Atlanta-Visiting Nurse Health System			
1244 Pk Vista Dr . . . . Atlanta GA 30319	866-374-4776	404-869-3000	368
Hospice Austin			
4107 Spicewood Springs Rd			
Ste 100 . . . . Austin TX 78759	800-445-3261	512-342-4700	368
Hospice Brazos Valley			
502 W 26th St . . . . Bryan TX 77803	800-824-2326	979-821-2266	368
Hospice by the Sea			
1531 W Palmetto Pk Rd . . . . Boca Raton FL 33486	800-633-2577	561-395-5031	368
Hospice Care			
100 Sylvan Rd . . . . Woburn MA 01801	866-279-7103	781-569-2888	368
Hospice Care Inc			
4277 Middle Settlement Rd . . . . New Hartford NY 13413	800-317-5661	315-735-6484	368
Hospice Care Network			
99 Sunnyside Blvd . . . . Woodbury NY 11797	800-405-6731	516-832-7100	368
Hospice Care Team			
1708 N Amburn Rd Ste C . . . . Texas City TX 77591	800-545-8738	409-938-0070	368
Hospice Caring Project of Santa Cruz County			
940 Disc Dr . . . . Scotts Valley CA 95066	877-688-6144	831-430-3000	368
Hospice Community Care			
PO Box 993 . . . . Rock Hill SC 29731	800-895-2273	803-329-1500	368
Hospice Education Institute			
Three Unity Sq PO Box 98 . . . . Machiasport ME 04655	800-331-1620	207-255-8800	47-17
Hospice Family Care			
550 E Main St . . . . Batavia NY 14020	800-719-7129	585-343-7596	368
Hospice Foundation of America (HFA)			
1710 Rhode Island Ave NW			
Ste 400 . . . . Washington DC 20036	800-854-3402	202-457-5811	48-8
Hospice Home Care			
2200 S Bowman . . . . Little Rock AR 72211	800-479-1219	501-296-9043	368
Hospice Ministries			
450 Towne Ctr Blvd . . . . Ridgeland MS 39157	800-273-7724	601-898-1053	368
Hospice of Acadiana			
2600 Johnston St Ste 200 . . . . Lafayette LA 70503	800-738-2226	337-232-1234	368
Hospice of Alamance Caswell			
914 Chapel Hill Rd . . . . Burlington NC 27215	800-588-8879	336-532-0100	368
Hospice of Arizona			
19820 N Seventh Ave Ste 130 . . . . Phoenix AZ 85027	888-330-8560	602-678-1313	368
Hospice of Baton Rouge			
9063 Siegen Ln . . . . Baton Rouge LA 70810	888-447-0433	225-767-4673	368
Hospice of Central Iowa (HCI)			
401 Railroad Pl . . . . West Des Moines IA 50265	800-806-9934	515-333-5810	368
Hospice of Central Ohio			
2269 Cherry Vly Rd . . . . Newark OH 43055	800-804-2505	740-344-0311	368
Hospice of Central Pennsylvania			
1320 Linglestown Rd . . . . Harrisburg PA 17110	866-779-7374	717-732-1000	368
Hospice of Chattanooga			
4411 Oakwood Dr . . . . Chattanooga TN 37416	800-267-6828	423-892-4289	368
Hospice of Cincinnati			
4360 Cooper Rd . . . . Cincinnati OH 45242	800-691-7255	513-891-7700	368
Hospice of Dayton			
324 Wilmington Ave . . . . Dayton OH 45420	800-653-4490	937-256-4490	368
Hospice of East Texas			
4111 University Blvd . . . . Tyler TX 75701	800-777-9860	903-266-3400	368
Hospice of Henry Ford Health System			
655 W 13 Mile Rd 1st Fl . . . . Madison Heights MI 48071	800-436-7936	248-585-5270	368
Hospice of Holland Inc			
270 Hoover Blvd . . . . Holland MI 49423	800-255-3522	616-396-2972	368
Hospice of Huntington			
1101 Sixth Ave . . . . Huntington WV 25701	800-788-5480	304-529-4217	368
Hospice of Lake & Sumter Inc			
2445 Ln Pk Rd . . . . Tavares FL 32778	888-728-6234	352-343-1341	368
Hospice of Lake Cumberland			
100 Pkwy Dr . . . . Somerset KY 42503	800-937-9596	606-679-4389	368
Hospice of Lancaster County			
685 Good Dr PO Box 4125 . . . . Lancaster PA 17604	888-236-9563	717-295-3900	368
Hospice of Lansing			
4052 Legacy Pkwy Ste 200 . . . . Lansing MI 48911	877-882-4500	517-882-4500	368
Hospice of Lincolnland			
1000 Health Ctr Dr . . . . Mattoon IL 61938	800-454-4055		368
Hospice of Marion County			
3231 SW 34th Ave . . . . Ocala FL 34474	888-482-5018	352-873-7400	368
Hospice of Marshall County			
408 Martling Rd . . . . Albertville AL 35951	888-334-9336	256-891-7724	368
Hospice of Medina County			
5075 Windfall Rd . . . . Medina OH 44256	800-700-4771	330-722-4771	368
Hospice of Miami County			
550 Summit Ave Ste 101 . . . . Troy OH 45373	800-372-0009	937-335-5191	368
Hospice of Michigan			
400 Mack Ave . . . . Detroit MI 48201	888-247-5701	313-578-5000	368
Hospice of New Jersey			
400 Broadacres Dr 1St Fl . . . . Bloomfield NJ 07003	800-501-0451	973-893-0818	368
Hospice of North Central Ohio			
1050 Dauch Dr . . . . Ashland OH 44805	800-952-2207	419-281-7107	368
Hospice of North Iowa			
232 Second St SE . . . . Mason City IA 50401	800-297-4719	641-428-6208	368
Hospice of Northeast Florida			
4266 Sunbeam Rd . . . . Jacksonville FL 32257	866-253-6681	904-268-5200	368
Hospice of Northwest Ohio			
30000 E River Rd . . . . Perrysburg OH 43551	866-661-4001	419-661-4001	368
Hospice of Orange & Sullivan Counties			
800 Stony Brook Ct . . . . Newburgh NY 12550	800-924-0157	845-561-6111	368
Hospice of Palm Beach County			
5300 E Ave . . . . West Palm Beach FL 33407	800-287-4722	561-848-5200	368
Hospice of Reno County			
1600 N Lorraine . . . . Hutchinson KS 67502	800-267-6891	620-665-2473	368
Hospice of Rutherford County			
374 Hudlow Rd PO Box 336 . . . . Forest City NC 28043	800-218-2273	828-245-0095	368
Hospice of Saint Francis Inc			
1250 Grumman Pl Ste B . . . . Titusville FL 32780	866-269-4240	321-269-4240	368
Hospice of San Angelo			
36 E Twohig St PO Box 471 . . . . San Angelo TX 76903	800-499-6524	325-658-6524	368
Hospice of Siouxland			
4300 Hamilton Blvd . . . . Sioux City IA 51104	800-383-4545	712-233-4100	368
Hospice of South Texas			
605 E Locust Ave . . . . Victoria TX 77901	800-874-6908	361-572-4300	368
Hospice of Southeastern Connecticut Inc			
227 Dunham St . . . . Norwich CT 06360	877-654-4035	860-848-5699	368
Hospice of Southern Illinois			
305 S Illinois St . . . . Belleville IL 62220	800-233-1708	618-235-1703	368
Hospice of Southern Kentucky			
5872 Scottsville Rd . . . . Bowling Green KY 42104	800-344-9479	270-782-3402	368
Hospice of Southwest Georgia			
114 A Mimosa Dr . . . . Thomasville GA 31792	800-290-6567	229-584-5500	368
Hospice of Spokane			
121 S Arthur St . . . . Spokane WA 99202	888-459-0438	509-456-0438	368
Hospice of Stanly County			
960 N First St . . . . Albemarle NC 28001	800-230-4236	704-983-4216	368
Hospice of the Bluegrass			
2312 Alexandria Dr . . . . Lexington KY 40504	800-876-6005	859-276-5344	368
Hospice of the Calumet Area			
600 Superior Ave . . . . Munster IN 46321	855-225-5344	219-922-2732	368
Hospice of the Chesapeake			
445 Defense Hwy . . . . Annapolis MD 21401	877-462-1101*	410-987-2003	368
*General			
Hospice of the Cleveland Clinic			
6801 Brecksville Rd Ste 10. . . . . . . Independence OH 44131	800-263-0403	216-444-9819	368
Hospice of the Comforter			
480 W Central Pkwy . . . . Altamonte Springs FL 32714	877-696-6775	407-682-0808	368
Hospice of the North Shore			
75 Sylvan St Ste B102 . . . . Danvers MA 01923	888-283-1722	978-774-7566	368
Hospice of the Panhandle			
330 Hospice Ln . . . . Kearneysville WV 25430	800-345-6538	304-264-0406	368
Hospice of the Piedmont			
675 Peter Jefferson Pkwy			
Ste 300 . . . . Charlottesville VA 22911	800-975-5501	434-817-6900	368
Hospice of the Rapidan			
1200 Sunset Ln Ste 230 . . . . Culpeper VA 22701	800-676-2012	540-825-4840	368
Hospice of the Red River Valley			
1701 38th St S Ste 101. . . . . Fargo ND 58103	800-237-4629	701-356-1500	368
Hospice of the Treasure Coast			
5090 Dunn Rd . . . . Fort Pierce FL 34981	800-299-4677	772-462-8900	368
Hospice of the Upstate			
1835 Rogers Rd . . . . Anderson SC 29621	800-261-8636	864-224-3358	368
Hospice of the Valley			
240 Johnston St SE . . . . Decatur AL 35601	877-260-3657	256-350-5585	368
Hospice of Visiting Nurse Service			
3358 Ridgewood Rd . . . . Akron OH 44333	800-335-1455	330-665-1455	368
Hospice of Wake County Inc			
250 Hospice Cir 4th Fl . . . . Raleigh NC 27607	888-900-3959	919-828-0890	368
Hospice of West Alabama			
3851 Loop Rd . . . . Tuscaloosa AL 35404	877-362-7522	205-523-0101	368
Hospice Savannah Inc			
PO Box 13190 . . . . Savannah GA 31416	888-355-4911	912-355-2289	368
HospiceCare			
5395 E Cheryl Pkwy . . . . Madison WI 53711	800-553-4289	608-276-4660	368
HospiceCare of Southeast Florida Inc			
309 SE 18th St Ste 200. . . . . . Fort Lauderdale FL 33316	866-231-5695	954-467-7423	368
Hospira Inc			
275 N Field Dr . . . . Lake Forest IL 60045	877-946-7747	224-212-2000	472
NYSE: HSP			
Hospital Billing & Collection Service Ltd			
118 Lukens Dr . . . . New Castle DE 19720	877-254-9580	302-552-8000	158
Hospital Forms & Systems Corp			
8900 Ambassador Row . . . . Dallas TX 75247	800-527-5081	214-634-8900	109
Hospital Litigation Reporter			
590 Dutch Vly Rd NE . . . . Atlanta GA 30324	800-926-7926	404-881-1141	524-7
Hospital of Saint Raphael			
1450 Chapel St . . . . New Haven CT 06511	888-700-6543	203-789-3000	371-3
Hospitality Financial & Technology Professionals (HFTP)			
11709 Boulder Ln Ste 110 . . . . Austin TX 78726	800-646-4387	512-249-5333	48-1
Master Hosts Inns & Resorts			
1726 Montreal Cir . . . . Tucker GA 30084	800-247-4677		376
Passport Inn			
1726 Montreal Cir . . . . Tucker GA 30084	800-251-1962		376
Red Carpet Inn			
1726 Montreal Cir . . . . Tucker GA 30084	800-247-4677		376
Hospitality International Inc			
Scottish Inns			
1726 Montreal Cir . . . . Tucker GA 30084	800-251-1962		376
Hospitality International INNcentive Card Program			
1726 Montreal Cir . . . . Tucker GA 30084	800-247-4677		375
Hospitality Law			
360 Hiatt Dr . . . . Palm Beach Gardens FL 33418	800-621-5463	561-622-6520	524-7
Hospitality Suites Resort			
409 N Scottsdale Rd . . . . Scottsdale AZ 85257	800-445-5115	480-949-5115	376
Hospitals & Health Networks Magazine			
155 N Wacker Ste 400 . . . . Chicago IL 60606	800-621-6902	312-893-6800	452-5
Hoss's Steak & Sea House			
170 Patchway Rd . . . . Duncansville PA 16635	800-992-4677	814-695-7600	661
Host Department LLC			
45277 Fremont Blvd Ste 11 . . . . Fremont CA 94538	866-887-4678		384
Host Depot Inc			
2455 Paces Ferry Rd NW . . . . Atlanta GA 30339	888-340-3527	770-433-8211	795
Hostcentric Inc			
70 BlanchaRd Rd 3rd Fl . . . . Burlington MA 01803	866-897-5418*	602-716-5396	795
*Tech Supp			
Hostedware Corp			
16 Technology Dr Ste 116 . . . . Irvine CA 92618	800-211-6967	949-585-1500	795
Hostelling International USA - American Youth Hostels (HI-AYH)			
8401 Colesville Rd			
Ste 600 . . . . Silver Spring MD 20910	800-725-2331	301-495-1240	47-23
Hostos Community College			
500 Grand Concourse . . . . Bronx NY 10451	888-993-7650	718-518-4444	160
Hostway Corp			
100 N Riverside Plaza 8th Fl. . . . . Chicago IL 60606	866-467-8929	312-238-0125	795
Hot Dog on a Stick			
5942 Priestly Dr . . . . Carlsbad CA 92008	877-639-2361	760-930-0456	661
Hot Rod Magazine			
6420 Wilshire Blvd . . . . Los Angeles CA 90048	800-800-4681*	323-782-2000	452-3
*Orders			
Hot Rod Network			
774 S Placentia Ave . . . . Placentia CA 92870	800-926-8207		452-3
Hot Rooms			
875 N. Michigan Ave Ste 3100 . . . . Chicago IL 60611	800-468-3500	773-468-7666	373
Hot Shot Delivery Inc			
747 N Shepherd Dr Ste 100			
PO Box 701189. . . . . Houston TX 77007	866-261-3184	713-869-5525	539
Hot Springs Convention & Visitors Bureau			
134 Convention Blvd . . . . Hot Springs AR 71901	800-543-2284	501-321-2277	207
Hot Springs Convention Ctr (HSCVB)			
134 Convention Blvd			
PO Box 6000. . . . . Hot Springs AR 71902	800-625-7576	501-321-2277	206

	Toll-Free	Phone	Class
Hot Springs Lodge & Pool			
415 E Sixth St			
PO Box 308. . . . . .Glenwood Springs CO 81602	**800-537-7946**	970-945-6571	660
Hot Springs Memorial Field			
525 Airport Rd . . . . .Hot Springs AR 71913	**800-992-7433**	501-321-6750	27
Hot Stuff Pizza			
2930 W Maple St . . . . .Sioux Falls SD 57107	**800-336-1320**	605-336-6961	67
Hotel & Restaurant Supply Inc			
5020 Arundel Rd PO Box 6. . . . . Meridian MS 39302	**800-782-6651**	601-482-7127	299
Hotel & Suites Normandin			
4700 Pierre-Bertrand Blvd . . . . Quebec QC G2J1A4	**800-463-6721**	418-622-1611	376
Hotel 1000			
1000 First Ave . . . . .Seattle WA 98104	**877-315-1088**	206-957-1000	376
Hotel 140			
140 Clarendon St . . . . .Boston MA 02116	**800-714-0140**	617-585-5600	376
Hotel 43 981 Grove St . . . . .Boise ID 83702	**800-243-4622**	208-342-4622	376
Hotel 71			
71 St Pierre St . . . . .Quebec City QC G1K4A4	**888-692-1171**	418-692-1171	376
Hotel Abri			
127 Ellis St . . . . San Francisco CA 94102	**866-778-6169**	415-392-8800	376
Hotel Adagio			
550 Geary St . . . . San Francisco CA 94102	**800-738-7477**	415-775-5000	376
Hotel Alex Johnson			
523 Sixth St . . . . .Rapid City SD 57701	**800-888-2539**	605-342-1210	376
Hotel Allegro Chicago			
171 W Randolph St . . . . .Chicago IL 60601	**800-643-1500**	312-236-0123	376
Hotel Ambassadeur			
3401 Blvd Ste-Anne . . . . .Qu,bec QC G1E3L4	**800-363-4619**	418-666-2828	376
Hotel Ambassador			
1324 S Main St . . . . .Tulsa OK 74119	**888-408-8282***	918-587-8200	376
*General			
Hotel Andra			
2000 Fourth Ave . . . . .Seattle WA 98121	**877-448-8600**	206-448-8600	376
Hotel Andrew Jackson			
919 Royal St . . . . .New Orleans LA 70116	**844-561-5881**	504-561-5881	376
Hotel Astor			
956 Washington Ave . . . . Miami Beach FL 33139	**800-270-4981**	305-531-8081	376
Hotel at Auburn University & Dixon Conference Ctr, The			
241 S College St . . . . Auburn AL 36830	**800-228-2876**	334-821-8200	374
Hotel at Old Town Wichita			
830 E First St . . . . Wichita KS 67202	**877-265-3869**	316-267-4800	376
Hotel Avante			
860 E El Camino Real . . . . .Mountain View CA 94040	**800-538-1600**	650-940-1000	376
Hotel Beacon			
2130 Broadway . . . . .New York NY 10023	**800-572-4969**	212-787-1100	376
Hotel Bedford			
118 E 40th St . . . . .New York NY 10016	**800-221-6881**	212-697-4800	376
Hotel Bel-Air			
701 Stone Canyon Rd . . . . .Los Angeles CA 90077	**800-648-4097**	310-472-1211	376
Hotel Bethlehem			
437 Main St . . . . .Bethlehem PA 18018	**800-607-2384**	610-625-5000	376
Hotel Bijou			
111 Mason St . . . . San Francisco CA 94102	**877-568-2733**	415-771-1200	376
Hotel Boulderado			
2115 13th St . . . . .Boulder CO 80302	**800-433-4344**	303-442-4344	376
Hotel Burnham			
One W Washington St . . . . .Chicago IL 60602	**866-690-1986**	312-782-1111	376
Hotel Captain Cook			
939 W Fifth Ave . . . . .Anchorage AK 99501	**800-843-1950**	907-276-6000	376
Hotel Casa del Mar			
1910 Ocean Way . . . . .Santa Monica CA 90405	**800-898-6999**	310-581-5533	376
Hotel Chateau Bellevue			
16 Rue de la Porte . . . . .Quebec QC G1R4M9	**877-849-1877**	418-692-2573	376
Hotel Chateau Laurier			
1220 Pl George-V Ouest . . . . .Quebec QC G1R5B8	**877-522-8108**	418-522-8108	376
Hotel Cheribourg			
2603 Ch du Parc . . . . .Orford QC J1X8C8	**877-845-5344**	819-843-3308	660
Hotel Classique			
2815 Laurier Blvd . . . . .Quebec QC G1V4H3	**800-463-1885**	418-658-2793	376
Hotel Colorado			
526 Pine St . . . . .Glenwood Springs CO 81601	**800-544-3998**	970-945-6511	376
Hotel Commonwealth			
500 Commonwealth Ave . . . . .Boston MA 02215	**866-784-4000**	617-933-5000	376
Hotel Congress			
311 E Congress St . . . . .Tucson AZ 85701	**800-722-8848**	520-622-8848	376
Hotel Contessa			
306 W Market St . . . . .San Antonio TX 78205	**866-435-0900**	210-229-9222	376
Hotel de Anza			
233 W Santa Clara St . . . . .San Jose CA 95113	**800-843-3700**	408-286-1000	376
Hotel Deca			
4507 Brooklyn Ave NE . . . . .Seattle WA 98105	**800-899-0251**	206-634-2000	376
Hotel Del Coronado			
1500 Orange Ave . . . . .Coronado CA 92118	**800-468-3533**	619-435-6611	660
Hotel Del Sol			
3100 Webster St . . . . San Francisco CA 94123	**877-433-5765**	415-921-5520	376
Hotel Deluxe			
729 SW 15th Ave . . . . .Portland OR 97205	**866-895-2094**	503-219-2094	376
Hotel Derek			
2525 W Loop S . . . . .Houston TX 77027	**866-292-4100**	713-961-3000	376
Hotel Drisco			
2901 Pacific Ave . . . . San Francisco CA 94115	**800-738-7477**	415-346-2880	376
Hotel du Lac			
121 Rue Cuttle . . . . .Mont-Tremblant QC J8E1B9	**800-567-8341**	819-425-2731	660
Hotel du Pont			
11th & Market Sts . . . . .Wilmington DE 19801	**800-441-9019**	302-594-3100	376
Hotel Durant			
2600 Durant Ave . . . . .Berkeley CA 94704	**855-687-7262**	510-845-8981	376
Hotel Edison			
228 W 47th St . . . . .New York NY 10036	**800-637-7070**	212-840-5000	376
Hotel Fort Des Moines			
1000 Walnut St . . . . .Des Moines IA 50309	**800-532-1466**	515-243-1161	376
Hotel Galvez - A Wyndham Historic Hotel			
2024 Seawall Blvd . . . . .Galveston TX 77550	**800-996-3426**	409-765-7721	376
Hotel George			
15 E St NW . . . . .Washington DC 20001	**800-546-7866***	202-347-4200	376
*General			
Hotel Grand Pacific			
463 Belleville St . . . . .Victoria BC V8V1X3	**800-663-7550**	250-386-0450	376
Hotel Grand Victorian			
2325 W Hwy 76 . . . . .Branson MO 65616	**800-324-8751**	417-336-2935	376
Hotel Granduca			
1080 Uptown Pk Blvd . . . . .Houston TX 77056	**888-472-6382**	713-418-1000	376
Hotel Griffon			
155 Steuart St . . . . San Francisco CA 94105	**800-321-2201**	415-495-2100	376
Hotel Hershey, The			
100 Hotel Rd . . . . .Hershey PA 17033	**800-437-7439**	717-533-2171	660
Hotel Jerome			
330 E Main St .Aspen CO 81611	**855-331-7213**	970-429-5028	376
Hotel La Jolla			
7955 La Jolla Shores Dr . . . . .La Jolla CA 92037	**800-941-1149**	858-459-0261	376
Hotel La Rose			
308 Wilson St . . . . .Santa Rosa CA 95401	**800-527-6738**	707-579-3200	376
Hotel Lawrence			
302 S Houston St . . . . .Dallas TX 75202	**877-396-0334**	214-761-9090	376
Hotel Le Bleu			
370 Fourth Ave . . . . .Brooklyn NY 11215	**866-427-6073**	718-625-1500	376
Hotel Le Cantlie Suites			
1110 Sherbrooke St W . . . . .Montreal QC H3A1G9	**800-567-1110**	514-842-2000	376
Hotel Le Capitole			
972 St Jean St . . . . .Quebec QC G1R1R5	**800-363-4040**	418-694-4040	376
Hotel Le Clos Saint-Louis			
69 St Louis St . . . . .Quebec QC G1R3Z2	**800-461-1311**	418-694-1311	376
Hotel Le Germain			
2050 Mansfield St . . . . .Montreal QC H3A1Y9	**877-333-2050**	514-849-2050	376
Hotel Le Germain Toronto			
30 Mercer St . . . . .Toronto ON M5V1H3	**866-345-9501**	416-345-9500	376
Hotel Le Marais			
717 Conti St . . . . .New Orleans LA 70130	**800-935-8740**	504-525-2300	376
Hotel le Priori			
15 du Sault-au-Matelot St . . . . .Quebec QC G1K3Y7	**800-351-3992**	418-692-3992	376
Hotel Le Soleil			
567 Hornby St . . . . .Vancouver BC V6C2E8	**877-632-3030**	604-632-3000	376
Hotel Le St-James			
355 St Jacques St . . . . .Montreal QC H2Y1N9	**866-841-3111**	514-841-3111	376
Hotel Lombardy			
2019 Pennsylvania Ave NW . . . . Washington DC 20006	**800-424-5486**	202-828-2600	376
Hotel Lord-Berri			
1199 Berri St . . . . .Montreal QC H2L4C6	**888-363-0363**	514-845-9236	376
Hotel Lucia			
400 SW Broadway . . . . .Portland OR 97205	**877-225-1717**	503-225-1717	376
Hotel Lumen			
6101 Hillcrest Ave . . . . .Dallas TX 75205	**800-908-1140**	214-219-2400	376
Hotel Lusso			
808 West Sprague Avenue . . . . . . .Spokane WA 99201	**800-899-1482***	509-747-9750	376
*General			
Hotel Madera			
1310 New Hampshire Ave NW . . . . .Washington DC 20036	**800-546-7866**	202-296-7600	376
Hotel Manoir Victoria			
44 Cote du Palais . . . . .Quebec QC G1R4H8	**800-463-6283**	418-692-1030	376
Hotel Maritime Plaza			
1155 Guy St . . . . .Montreal QC H3H2K5	**877-768-4326**	514-932-1411	376
Hotel Mark Twain			
345 Taylor St . . . . San Francisco CA 94102	**877-854-4106**	415-673-2332	376
Hotel Marlowe Cambridge			
25 Edwind H Land Blvd . . . . .Cambridge MA 02141	**800-825-7140**	617-868-8000	376
Hotel Max			
620 Stewart St . . . . .Seattle WA 98101	**866-833-6299**	206-728-6299	376
Hotel Mead			
451 E Grand Ave . . . . .Wisconsin Rapids WI 54494	**800-843-6323**	715-423-1500	376
Hotel Mela			
120 W 44th St . . . . .New York NY 10036	**877-452-6352**	212-710-7000	376
Hotel Metro			
411 E Mason St . . . . .Milwaukee WI 53202	**877-638-7620**	414-272-1937	376
Hotel Monaco Chicago			
225 N Wabash Ave . . . . .Chicago IL 60601	**800-397-7661**	312-960-8500	376
Hotel Monaco Denver			
1717 Champa St . . . . .Denver CO 80202	**800-990-1303**	303-296-1717	376
Hotel Monaco Portland			
506 SW Washington at			
Fifth Ave . . . . .Portland OR 97204	**866-861-9514**	503-222-0001	376
Hotel Monaco Salt Lake City			
15 West 200 South . . . . .Salt Lake City UT 84101	**800-805-1801***	801-595-0000	376
*Resv			
Hotel Monaco San Francisco			
501 Geary St . . . . San Francisco CA 94102	**866-622-5284**	415-292-0100	376
Hotel Monaco Seattle			
1101 Fourth Ave . . . . .Seattle WA 98101	**800-715-6513**	206-621-1770	376
Hotel Monte Vista			
100 N San Francisco St . . . . .Flagstaff AZ 86001	**800-545-3068**	928-779-6971	376
Hotel Monteleone			
214 Royal St . . . . .New Orleans LA 70130	**800-535-9595**	504-523-3341	376
Hotel Murano			
1320 Broadway Plz . . . . .Tacoma WA 98402	**888-862-3255**	253-238-8000	376
Hotel Nikko San Francisco			
222 Mason St . . . . San Francisco CA 94102	**866-636-4556**	415-394-1111	376
Hotel Northampton			
36 King St . . . . .NortHampton MA 01060	**800-547-3529**	413-584-3100	376
Hotel Oceana			
Santa Barbara			
202 W Cabrillo Blvd . . . . .Santa Barbara CA 93101	**800-965-9776**	805-965-4577	376
Hotel Omni Mont-Royal			
1050 Sherbrooke St W . . . . .Montreal QC H3A2R6	**800-843-6664**	514-284-1110	376
Hotel Orrington			
1710 Orrington Ave . . . . .Evanston IL 60201	**888-677-4648**	847-866-8700	376
Hotel Pacific			
300 Pacific St . . . . .Monterey CA 93940	**800-554-5542**	831-373-5700	376
Hotel Palomar San Francisco			
12 Fourth St . . . . San Francisco CA 94103	**866-373-4941**	415-348-1111	376
Hotel Park City (HPC)			
2001 Pk Ave . . . . .Park City UT 84060	**866-933-0347**	435-200-2000	376
Hotel Phillips			
106 W 12th St . . . . .Kansas City MO 64105	**800-433-1426**	816-221-7000	376
Hotel Plaza Athenee			
37 E 64th St . . . . .New York NY 10065	**800-447-8800**	212-734-9100	376
Hotel Plaza Quebec			
3031 Laurier Blvd . . . . .Sainte-Foy QC G1V2M2	**800-567-5276**	418-658-2727	376
Hotel Plaza Real			
125 Washington Ave . . . . .Santa Fe NM 87501	**855-752-9273**	505-988-4900	376
Hotel Preston			
733 Briley Pkwy . . . . .Nashville TN 37217	**800-407-4324**	615-361-5900	376
Hotel Provincial			
1024 Rue Chartres . . . . .New Orleans LA 70116	**800-535-7922**	504-581-4995	376
Hotel Rex			
562 Sutter St . . . . San Francisco CA 94102	**800-433-4434***	415-433-4434	376
*Resv			
Hotel Roanoke & Conference Ctr			
110 Shenandoah Ave . . . . .Roanoke VA 24016	**800-222-8733**	540-985-5900	374

Name / Address	City	State	ZIP	Toll-Free	Phone	Class
Hotel Rodney						
142 Second St	Lewes	DE	19958	800-824-8754	302-645-6466	376
Hotel Roger Williams						
131 Madison Ave	New York	NY	10016	888-448-7788*	212-448-7000	376
*Resv						
Hotel Rouge						
1315 16th St NW	Washington	DC	20036	800-738-1202	202-232-8000	376
Hotel Royal Plaza						
1905 Hotel Plaza Blvd	Lake Buena Vista	FL	32830	888-662-4683	407-828-2828	376
Hotel Ruby Foo's						
7655 Decarie Blvd	Montreal	QC	H4P2H2	800-361-5419	514-731-7701	376
Hotel Saint Francis						
210 Don Gaspar Ave	Santa Fe	NM	87501	800-529-5700	505-983-5700	376
Hotel Saint Marie						
827 Toulouse St	New Orleans	LA	70112	800-366-2743	504-561-8951	376
Hotel Saint Pierre						
911 Burgundy St	New Orleans	LA	70116	800-225-4040*	504-524-4401	376
*Resv						
Hotel San Carlos						
202 N Central Ave	Phoenix	AZ	85004	866-253-4121	602-253-4121	376
Hotel Santa Barbara						
533 State St	Santa Barbara	CA	93101	888-259-7700	805-957-9300	376
Hotel Santa Fe						
1501 Paseo de Peralta	Santa Fe	NM	87501	855-825-9876	505-982-1200	376
Hotel Sax Chicago						
333 N Dearborn St	Chicago	IL	60610	855-880-1240	312-245-0333	376
Hotel Sepia						
3135 Ch St-Louis	Sainte-Foy	QC	G1W1R9	888-301-6837	418-653-4941	376
Hotel Shelley						
844 Collins Ave	Miami Beach	FL	33139	877-762-3477	305-531-3341	376
Hotel Solamar						
435 Sixth Ave	San Diego	CA	92101	877-230-0300	619-819-9500	376
Hotel Strasburg, The						
213 S Holliday St	Strasburg	VA	22657	800-348-8327	540-465-9191	376
Hotel Teatro						
1100 14th St	Denver	CO	80202	888-727-1200	303-228-1100	376
Hotel The Queen Mary						
1126 Queens Hwy	Long Beach	CA	90802	877-342-0738	562-435-3511	376
Hotel Triton						
342 Grant Ave	San Francisco	CA	94108	800-800-1299	415-394-0500	376
Hotel Universel						
2300 Ch St-Foy	Qu,bec	QC	G1V1S5	800-463-4495	418-653-5250	376
Hotel Utica						
102 Lafayette St	Utica	NY	13502	877-906-1912	315-724-7829	376
Hotel Valencia Santana Row						
355 Santana Row	San Jose	CA	95128	866-842-0100	408-551-0010	376
Hotel Valley Ho						
6850 E Main St	Scottsdale	AZ	85251	866-882-4484	844-993-9601	376
Hotel Victoria						
56 Yonge St	Toronto	ON	M5E1G5	800-363-8228	416-363-1666	376
Hotel Viking						
One Bellevue Ave	Newport	RI	02840	800-556-7126	401-847-3300	376
Hotel Vintage Park						
1100 Fifth Ave	Seattle	WA	98101	800-853-3914	206-624-8000	376
Hotel Vitale						
8 Mission St	San Francisco	CA	94105	888-890-8688	415-278-3700	376
Hotel Wales						
1295 Madison Ave	New York	NY	10128	866-925-3746	212-876-6000	376
Hotel XIXe Siecle						
Lhotel						
262 St Jacques St W	Vieux Montreal	QC	H2Y1N1	877-553-0019	514-985-0019	376
Hotel ZaZa Dallas						
2332 Leonard St	Dallas	TX	75201	800-597-8399	214-468-8399	376
Hotel ZaZa Houston						
5701 Main St	Houston	TX	77005	888-880-3244*	713-526-1991	376
*Resv						
Hotelrooms.com Inc						
108-18 Queens Blvd	Forest Hills	NY	11375	800-486-7000	718-730-6000	394
Hot-Line Freight System Inc						
PO Box 205	West Salem	WI	54669	800-468-4686	608-486-1600	770
Hotpadscom						
PO Box 53104	Washington	DC	20009	888-876-1992	202-232-1581	643
Hotwire Communications LLC						
One Belmont Ave Ste 1100	Bala Cynwyd	PA	19004	800-409-4733		224
Hotwire.com						
655 Montgomery St Ste 600	San Francisco	CA	94111	866-468-9473*	415-343-8400	763
*Cust Svc						
Houchen Bindery LTD						
340 First St	Utica	NE	68456	800-869-0420	402-534-2261	618
Houff Transfer Inc						
46 Houff Rd	Weyers Cave	VA	24486	800-476-4683	540-234-9233	770
Hougen Manufacturing Inc						
3001 Hougen Dr	Swartz Creek	MI	48473	800-426-7818*	810-635-7111	488
*Orders						
Houghton Chemical Corp						
52 Cambridge St	Allston	MA	02134	800-777-2466	617-254-1010	143
Houghton College						
One Willard Ave PO Box 128	Houghton	NY	14744	800-777-2556	585-567-9200	166
Houghton International Inc						
945 Madison Ave PO Box 930	Valley Forge	PA	19482	888-459-9844	610-666-4000	3
Houghton Mifflin Harcourt						
222 Berkeley St	Boston	MA	02116	877-866-2586	617-351-5000	628-2
Houma Area Convention & Visitors Bureau						
114 Tourist Dr	Gray	LA	70359	800-688-2732	985-868-2732	207
Houmas House Plantation & Gardens						
40136 Hwy 942	Darrow	LA	70725	800-979-3370	225-473-7841	49-2
Housatonic Community College						
900 Lafayette Blvd	Bridgeport	CT	06604	866-733-2463	203-332-5000	160
House Foods America Corp						
7351 Orangewood Ave	Garden Grove	CA	92841	877-333-7077	714-901-4350	295-20
House of Blues Entertainment Inc						
7060 Hollywood Blvd	Hollywood	CA	90028	877-632-7600	323-769-4600	182
House of Broel's Historic Mansion & Dollhouse Museum						
2220 St Charles Ave	New Orleans	LA	70130	800-827-4325	504-522-2220	513
House of Flavors Inc						
110 N William St	Ludington	MI	49431	800-930-7740	231-845-7369	377
House of Raeford Farms Inc						
520 E Central Ave	Raeford	NC	28376	800-888-7539	910-875-5161	612
House-Autry Mills Inc						
7000 US Hwy 301 S	Four Oaks	NC	27524	800-849-0802		295-23
House-Hasson Hardware Inc						
3125 Water Plant Rd	Knoxville	TN	37914	800-333-0520	865-525-0471	348
HouseMaster						
850 Bear Tavern RD Ste 303	Ewing	NJ	08628	800-526-3939	732-469-6565	362
Housing Assistance Council (HAC)						
1025 Vermont Ave NW Ste 606	Washington	DC	20005	866-234-2689	202-842-8600	47-5
Housing Authority Risk Retention Group Inc						
PO Box 189	Cheshire	CT	06410	800-873-0242	203-272-8220	387
Housley Communications Inc						
3550 S Bryant Blvd	San Angelo	TX	76903	800-880-9905	325-944-9905	187
Houston Arboretum & Nature Ctr						
4501 Woodway Dr	Houston	TX	77024	866-510-7219	713-681-8433	49-4
Houston Astros						
Minute Maid Pk 501 Crawford St	Houston	TX	77002	800-771-2303	713-259-8000	704
Houston Ballet						
601 Preston St	Houston	TX	77002	800-828-2787	713-523-6300	566-1
Houston Baptist University						
7502 Fondren Rd	Houston	TX	77074	800-969-3210*	281-649-3000	166
*Admissions						
Houston Chronicle						
801 Texas Ave	Houston	TX	77002	800-735-3800	713-362-7171	525-2
Houston Food Bank, The						
535 Portwall St	Houston	TX	77029	866-384-4277	713-223-3700	323
Houston Grand Opera						
510 Preston St Ste 500	Houston	TX	77002	800-626-7372	713-546-0200	566-2
Houston Harris Div Patrol Inc						
6420 Richmond Ave	Houston	TX	77057	877-975-9922	713-975-9922	684
Houston Independent School District						
228 McCarty St	Houston	TX	77029	800-446-2821	713-556-6000	676
Houston LifeStyle Magazine						
10707 Corporate Dr Ste 170	Stafford	TX	77477	866-505-4456	281-240-2445	452-22
Houston Mfg Specialty Company Inc						
9909 Wallisville Rd	Houston	TX	77013	800-231-6030	713-675-7400	325
Houston Numismatic Exchange Inc						
2486 Times Blvd	Houston	TX	77005	800-231-3650	713-528-2135	454
Houston Press						
1621 Milam St Ste 100	Houston	TX	77002	877-926-8300	713-280-2400	525-5
Houston Public Library						
500 McKinney St	Houston	TX	77002	800-318-2596	832-393-1313	431-3
Houston Rockets						
1510 Polk St	Houston	TX	77002	866-648-4668	713-758-7200	705-1
Houston Service Industries Inc						
7901 Hansen Rd	Houston	TX	77061	800-725-2291	713-947-1623	18
Houston Wire & Cable Co (HWC)						
10201 N Loop E	Houston	TX	77029	800-468-9473	713-609-2100	246
Houstonian Hotel Club & Spa						
111 N Post Oak Ln	Houston	TX	77024	800-231-2759*	713-680-2626	660
*Resv						
Hoveround Corp						
2151 Whitfield Industrial Way	Sarasota	FL	34243	800-542-7236	941-739-6200	472
HOW Design Magazine						
4700 E Galbraith Rd	Cincinnati	OH	45236	800-333-1115*	513-531-2690	452-2
*Cust Svc						
Howard Bros Florists						
8700 S Pennsylvania Ave	Oklahoma City	OK	73159	800-648-0524	405-632-4747	292
Howard College						
1001 Birdwell Ln	Big Spring	TX	79720	877-898-3833	432-264-5000	160
Howard Community College						
10901 Little Patuxent Pkwy	Columbia	MD	21044	888-442-4551	410-772-4800	160
Howard County Central Library						
10375 Little Patuxent Pkwy	Columbia	MD	21044	800-848-1555	410-313-7800	431-3
Howard County General Hospital						
5755 Cedar Ln	Columbia	MD	21044	866-323-4615	410-740-7890	371-3
Howard County Tourism Council						
8267 Main St Side Entrance	Ellicott City	MD	21043	800-243-3425	410-313-1900	207
Howard Electric Co-op						
205 Hwy 5 & 240 N PO Box 391	Fayette	MO	65248	877-352-0122	660-248-3311	245
Howard F Baer Inc						
1301 Foster Ave	Nashville	TN	37210	800-447-7430	615-255-7351	770
Howard Greeley Rural Power						
422 Howard Ave PO Box 105	Saint Paul	NE	68873	800-280-4962	308-754-4457	245
Howard Leight Industries						
7828 Waterville Rd	San Diego	CA	92154	800-430-5490		472
Howard Lumber Co						
475 Columbia Industrial Blvd PO Box 1039	Evans	GA	30809	800-868-3227	706-868-8400	192-3
Howard Payne University						
1000 Fisk Ave	Brownwood	TX	76801	800-950-8465	325-646-2502	166
Howard Precision Metals Inc						
PO Box 240127	Milwaukee	WI	53224	800-444-0311	414-355-9611	487
Howard R Green Co						
8710 Earhart Ln SW	Cedar Rapids	IA	52404	800-728-7805	319-841-4000	261
Howard Systems International						
2777 Summer St	Stamford	CT	06905	800-326-4860		181
Howard Uniform Co						
1915 Annapolis Rd	Baltimore	MD	21230	800-628-8299	410-727-3086	153-18
Howard University						
2400 Sixth St NW	Washington	DC	20059	800-822-6363	202-806-6100	166
Howard University School of Divinity						
1400 Shepherd St NE	Washington	DC	20017	800-822-6363	202-806-0500	167-3
Howard University School of Law						
2900 Van Ness St NW	Washington	DC	20008	800-829-9019	202-806-8000	167-1
Howco Metals Management						
9611 Telge Rd	Houston	TX	77095	800-392-7720	281-649-8800	306
Howe Military School						
PO Box 240	Howe	IN	46746	888-462-4693	260-562-2131	615
Howell Tractor & Equipment LLC						
480 Blaine St	Gary	IN	46406	800-852-8816		779
Howell's Craftand Imports						
6030 NE 112th Ave	Portland	OR	97220	800-547-0368		43
Howell's Motor Freight Inc						
PO Box 12308	Roanoke	VA	24024	800-444-0585	540-966-3200	770
Howell-Oregon Electric Co-op Inc						
6327 N US Hwy 63 PO Box 649	West Plains	MO	65775	855-385-9903	417-256-2131	245
Howred Corp						
7887 San Felipe St Ste 122	Houston	TX	77063	800-535-5053	713-781-3980	192-4
Hoxworth Blood Ctr University of Cincinnati Medical Ctr						
3130 Highland Ave ML0055	Cincinnati	OH	45267	800-265-1515	513-558-1200	88
HP (Hewlett-Packard (Canada) Ltd)						
5150 Spectrum Way	Mississauga	ON	L4W5G1	888-447-4636	905-206-4725	174-1
HP Pavilion at San Jose						
525 W Santa Clara St	San Jose	CA	95113	800-745-3000	408-287-7070	711
H-P Products Inc						
512 W Gorgas St	Louisville	OH	44641	800-822-8356	330-875-5556	588
HPC (Hotel Park City)						
2001 Pk Ave	Park City	UT	84060	866-933-0347	435-200-2000	376

Company / Address	City	State	ZIP	Toll-Free	Phone	Class
HPC Foods Ltd						
288 Libby St	Honolulu	HI	96819	**877-370-0919**	808-848-2431	295-21
HPD, LLC						
23563 W Main St	Plainfield	IL	60544	**866-362-0993**	815-609-2000	261
HPH Corp						
1529 SE 47th Terr	Cape Coral	FL	33904	**800-654-9884**	239-540-0085	345
HPL Stampings Inc						
425 Enterprise Pkwy	Lake Zurich	IL	60047	**800-927-0397**	847-540-1400	483
HPM (Hawaii Planing Mill Ltd)						
16-166 Melekahiwa St	Keaau	HI	96749	**877-841-7633**	808-966-5693	192-3
HPPL (High Point Public Library)						
901 N Main St	High Point	NC	27262	**877-772-8346**	336-883-3660	431-3
HPRHS (High Point Regional Health System)						
601 N Elm St PO Box HP-5	High Point	NC	27262	**877-878-7644**	336-878-6000	371-3
HPTS (High Power Technical Services Inc)						
2230 Ampere Dr	Louisville	KY	40299	**866-398-3474**		115
HRC (National Herpes Resource Ctr)						
PO Box 13827	Research Triangle Park	NC	27709	**877-478-5868**	919-361-8400	47-17
HRCPAC (Human Rights Campaign PAC)						
1640 Rhode Island Ave NW	Washington	DC	20036	**800-777-4723**	202-628-4160	608
HRF (Herb Research Foundation)						
4140 15th St	Boulder	CO	80304	**800-748-2617**	303-449-2265	47-17
HRI Inc						
1750 W College Ave	State College	PA	16801	**877-474-9999**		189-4
HRMagazine						
1800 Duke St	Alexandria	VA	22314	**800-283-7476**	703-548-3440	452-5
HRP Associates Inc						
197 Scott Swamp Rd	Farmington	CT	06032	**800-246-9021**		261
HRSA (Health Resources & Services Administration)						
5600 Fishers Ln	Rockville	MD	20857	**888-275-4772**	301-443-2216	338-8
HSB (Hartford Steam Boiler Inspection & Insurance Co, The)						
One State St PO Box 5024	Hartford	CT	06102	**800-472-1866**		388-4
HSB Group Inc						
1 State St	Hartford	CT	06103	**800-472-1866**	860-722-1866	388-4
HSBC Bank USA						
2929 Walden Ave	Depew	NY	14043	**800-338-4626**		502
HSBC North America Holdings Inc						
2700 Sanders Rd	Prospect Heights	IL	60070	**800-975-4722**	847-564-5000	357-2
HSC Pediatric Ctr						
1731 Bunker Hill Rd NE	Washington	DC	20017	**800-226-4444**	202-832-4400	371-1
HSCVB (Hot Springs Convention Ctr)						
134 Convention Blvd						
PO Box 6000	Hot Springs	AR	71902	**800-625-7576**	501-321-2277	206
HSI (Helicopter Support Inc)						
124 Quarry Rd	Trumbull	CT	06611	**800-795-6051**	203-416-4000	760
HSI (Hardware Suppliers of America Inc)						
1400 E Fire Tower Rd	Greenville	NC	27858	**800-334-5625**		348
HSM (Hart Schaffner Marx)						
1680 E Touhy Ave	Des Plaines	IL	60018	**800-327-4466**		153-11
HSQ Technology						
26227 Research Rd	Hayward	CA	94545	**800-486-6684**	510-259-1334	202
HSTC (Hi-Shear Technology Corp)						
24225 Garnier St	Torrance	CA	90505	**800-733-0321***	310-784-2100	499
*Mktg						
HT Hackney Co						
502 S Gay St PO Box 238	Knoxville	TN	37901	**800-406-1291**	865-546-1291	186
HTC (Healing the Children)						
2624 W Beacon Ave	Spokane	WA	99208	**888-233-9527**	509-327-4281	47-5
HTC (Horry Telephone Co-op Inc)						
3480 Hwy 701 N PO Box 1820	Conway	SC	29528	**800-824-6779**	843-365-2151	726
HTK (Hornor Townsend & Kent Inc)						
600 Dresher Rd Ste C1C	Horsham	PA	19044	**800-289-9999**		399
HTT Inc.						
1828 Oakland Ave	Sheboygan	WI	53081	**866-270-4710**	920-457-2311	483
Hub City Inc						
2914 Industrial Ave	Aberdeen	SD	57401	**800-482-2489**	605-225-0360	700
Hub Folding Box Co Inc						
774 Norfolk St	Mansfield	MA	02048	**800-334-1113**	508-339-0005	100
Hub Group Inc						
3050 Highland Pkwy						
Ste 100	Downers Grove	IL	60515	**800-377-5833**	630-271-3600	444
NASDAQ: HUBG						
Hub International Ltd						
1065 Ave of the Americas	New York	NY	10018	**800-456-5293**	212-338-2000	387
Hub Pattern Corp						
2113 Salem Ave	Roanoke	VA	24016	**800-482-3505**	540-342-3505	560
Hubbard & Drake General Mechanical Contractors Inc						
PO Box 1867	Decatur	AL	35602	**800-353-9245**	256-353-9244	190-10
Hubbard Construction Co						
1936 Lee Rd 3rd Fl	Winter Park	FL	32789	**800-476-1228**	407-645-5500	189-4
Hubbard Feeds Inc						
424 N Riverfront Dr PO Box 8500	Mankato	MN	56001	**800-869-7219**	507-388-9400	442
Hubbard House, The						
29 W Miller St	Orlando	FL	32806	**800-648-3818**	407-649-6886	369
Hubbard Publishing Co						
127 E Chillicothe Ave						
PO Box 40	Bellefontaine	OH	43311	**866-632-9992**	937-592-3060	628-8
Hubbard-Hall Inc						
563 S Leonard St	Waterbury	CT	06708	**800-331-6871**	203-756-5521	144
Hubbell Lighting Inc						
701 Millennium Blvd	Greenville	SC	29607	**800-465-7051**	864-678-1000	435
Hubbell Power Systems Inc						
210 N Allen St	Centralia	MO	65240	**800-346-3062**	573-682-5521	253
Hubbell Premise Wiring Inc						
23 Clara Dr	Mystic	CT	06355	**800-626-0005**		802
Hubbell RACO						
3902 W Sample St	South Bend	IN	46619	**800-722-6437**	574-234-7151	803
Hubbell Wiring Device-Kellems						
40 Waterview Dr	Shelton	CT	06484	**800-288-6000***	203-882-4800	802
*Cust Svc						
Huckstep & Assoc LLC						
3734 S Ave Ste E	Springfield	MO	65807	**800-269-6466**	417-889-8991	2
HUD (Department of Housing & Urban Development)						
451 Seventh St SW	Washington	DC	20410	**800-569-4287**	202-708-0685	338-10
HUD Office of Fair Housing & Equal Opportunity						
Housing Discrimination Hotline						
451 Seventh St SW	Washington	DC	20410	**800-333-4636**	202-708-1112	338-10
HUD Office of Housing and Urban Development (FHA)						
451 Seventh St SW Ste 9100	Washington	DC	20410	**800-767-7468**	202-708-1112	338-10
HUD Office of Public & Indian Housing						
451 Seventh St SW Rm 4100	Washington	DC	20410	**800-955-2232**	202-708-0950	338-10
Real Estate Assessment Ctr						
550 12th St SW Ste 100	Washington	DC	20410	**888-245-4860**	202-708-1112	338-10

Company / Address	City	State	ZIP	Toll-Free	Phone	Class
Hudson City Savings Bank						
W 80 Century Rd	Paramus	NJ	07652	**800-222-0194**	201-967-1900	69
Hudson Health Plan Inc						
303 S Broadway Ste 321	Tarrytown	NY	10591	**800-339-4557**	914-631-1611	388-2
Hudson Institute						
1015 15th St NW Ste 600	Washington	DC	20005	**888-554-1325**	202-974-2400	625
Hudson Lock Inc						
81 Apsley St	Hudson	MA	01749	**800-434-8960**		347
Hudson River Islands State Park						
Schodack Island						
State Pk	Schodack Landing	NY	12156	**800-456-2267**	518-732-0187	558
Hudson Seating & Mobility						
151 Rockwell Rd	Newington	CT	06111	**800-321-4442**	860-666-7500	319
Hudson Valley Community College						
80 Vandenburgh Ave	Troy	NY	12180	**877-325-4822**	518-629-4822	160
Hudson Valley Federal Credit Union						
159 Barnegat Rd	Poughkeepsie	NY	12601	**800-468-3011**	845-463-3011	219
Hudson Valley Magazine						
2678 S Rd 2nd Fl	Poughkeepsie	NY	12601	**855-658-1850***	845-463-0542	452-22
*General						
Hudson Valve Company Inc						
5301 Office Pk Dr Ste 330	Bakersfield	CA	93309	**800-748-6218**	661-869-1126	777
Hudson's on the Bend						
3509 Ranch Rd 620 N	Austin	TX	78734	**800-996-7655**	512-266-1369	662
Hudspeth County						
109 Brown St	Sierra Blanca	TX	79851	**888-368-4689**	915-369-2331	336
Hueco Tanks State Historic Site						
6900 Hueco Tanks Rd Ste 1	El Paso	TX	79938	**800-792-1112**	915-857-1135	558
Hueneme Elementary School Dist						
205 N Ventura Rd	Port Hueneme	CA	93041	**866-431-2478**	805-488-3588	676
Hufcor Inc						
2101 Kennedy Rd	Janesville	WI	53545	**800-356-6968**	608-756-1241	286
Huffman Corp						
1050 Huffman Way	Clover	SC	29710	**888-483-3626**	803-222-4561	450
Huffy Bicycle Co						
6551 Centerville						
Business Pkwy	Centerville	OH	45459	**800-872-2453**	937-865-2800	81
Hu-Friedy Mfg Company Inc						
3232 N Rockwell St	Chicago	IL	60618	**800-483-7433**	773-975-6100	228
Hughes Bros Inc						
210 N 13th St PO Box 159	Seward	NE	68434	**800-869-0359**	402-643-2991	803
Hughes Corp Weschler Instruments Div						
16900 Foltz Pkwy	Cleveland	OH	44149	**800-557-0064**	440-238-2550	248
Hughes Federal Credit Union Inc						
PO Box 11900	Tucson	AZ	85734	**866-760-3156**	520-794-8341	219
Hughes Network Systems LLC						
11717 Exploration Ln	Germantown	MD	20876	**888-748-6288**	301-428-5500	725
Hughes Supply Company of Thomasville Inc						
175 Kanoy Rd PO Box 1003	Thomasville	NC	27360	**800-747-8141**	336-475-8146	449
HughesNet						
11717 Exploration Ln	Germantown	MD	20876	**866-347-3292**	301-428-5500	395
Hughston Orthopedic Hospital						
100 Frist Ct	Columbus	GA	31908	**866-272-9452**	706-494-2100	371-7
Huhtamaki Inc North America						
9201 Packaging Dr	DeSoto	KS	66018	**800-255-4243**	913-583-3025	541
Huitt-Zollars Inc						
1717 McKinney Ave Ste 1400	Dallas	TX	75202	**866-667-6572**	214-871-3311	261
Hull Lift Truck Inc						
28747 Old US 33 W	Elkhart	IN	46516	**888-284-0364**	574-293-8651	382
Hultgren Implements Inc						
5698 State Hwy 175	Ida Grove	IA	51445	**800-827-1650**	712-364-3105	274
Human Arc Corp						
1457 East 40th St	Cleveland	OH	44103	**800-828-6453**	216-431-5200	387
Human Capital						
2055 Crooks Rd						
Lowr Level	Rochester Hills	MI	48309	**888-736-9071**		623
Human Factors & Ergonomics Society (HFES)						
1124 Montana Ave Ste B						
PO Box 1369	Santa Monica	CA	90406	**800-233-1234**	310-394-1811	47-17
Human Factors International Inc						
410 W Lowe Ave	Fairfield	IA	52556	**800-242-4480**	641-472-4480	178
Human Growth Foundation						
997 Glen Cove Ave Ste 5	Glen Head	NY	11545	**800-451-6434**	516-671-4041	47-17
Human Kinetics						
1607 N Market St	Champaign	IL	61820	**800-747-4457**	217-351-5076	628-2
Human Life International (HLI)						
Four Family Life Ln	Front Royal	VA	22630	**800-549-5433***	540-635-7884	47-6
*Orders						
Human Management Services Inc						
835 Springdale Dr	Exton	PA	19341	**800-343-2186**	610-363-6175	457
Human Resource Development Press Inc						
22 Amherst Rd	Amherst	MA	01002	**800-822-2801**	413-253-3488	195
Human Resource Executive Magazine						
747 Dresher Rd Ste 500	Horsham	PA	19044	**888-365-2763**	215-784-0910	452-5
Human Resources Report						
1801 S Bell St	Arlington	VA	22202	**800-372-1033**		524-2
Human Rights Campaign						
1640 Rhode Island Ave NW	Washington	DC	20036	**800-777-4723**	202-628-4160	47-8
Human Rights Campaign PAC (HRCPAC)						
1640 Rhode Island Ave NW	Washington	DC	20036	**800-777-4723**	202-628-4160	608
Human Touch						
3030 Walnut Ave	Long Beach	CA	90807	**800-742-5493**	562-426-8700	318-2
Humana Foundation Inc						
500 W Main St Ste 208	Louisville	KY	40202	**888-431-4748**	502-580-4140	303
Humana Inc						
500 W Main St	Louisville	KY	40202	**800-486-2620**	502-580-1000	388-3
NYSE: HUM						
Humana Military Healthcare Services						
500 W Main St	Louisville	KY	40201	**800-444-5445***	502-580-3200	388-3
*General						
Humboldt County Convention & Visitors Bureau						
1034 Second St	Eureka	CA	95501	**800-346-3482**	707-443-5097	207
Humboldt County Rural Electric Co-op (HCREC)						
1210 13th St N	Humboldt	IA	50548	**800-452-1111**	515-332-1616	245
Humboldt State University						
One Harpst St	Arcata	CA	95521	**866-850-9556**	707-826-3011	166
Humco Holding Group Inc						
7400 Alumax Dr	Texarkana	TX	75501	**800-662-3435**	903-334-6200	576
Hummert International Inc						
4500 Earth City Expy	Earth City	MO	63045	**800-325-3055**	314-506-4500	276
Humphrey Products Co						
5070 E N Ave PO Box 2008	Kalamazoo	MI	49048	**800-477-8707**	269-381-5500	777
Humphrey's Half Moon Inn & Suites						
2303 Shelter Island Dr	San Diego	CA	92106	**800-542-7400**	619-224-3411	376

Name / Address	City	State	ZIP	Toll-Free	Phone	Class
Humphreys College 6650 Inglewood Ave	Stockton	CA	95207	800-433-3243	209-478-0800	166
Humphreys Restaurant 2241 Shelter Island Dr	San Diego	CA	92106	800-377-1177	619-224-3411	662
Hunger Project, The Five Union Sq W	New York	NY	10003	800-228-6691	212-251-9100	47-5
Hunt & Sons Inc 5750 S Watt Ave	Sacramento	CA	95829	800-734-2999	916-383-4868	323
Hunt Consolidated Inc 1900 N Akard St Ste 1500	Dallas	TX	75201	800-424-9300	214-978-8000	357-3
Hunt Forest Products 401 E Reynolds Dr PO Box 1263	Ruston	LA	71273	800-390-8589	318-255-2245	674
Hunt Guillot & Assoc LLC 603 Reynolds Dr	Ruston	LA	71270	866-255-6825	318-255-6825	256
Hunt Insurance Agency Inc 12000 S Harlem Ave	Palos Heights	IL	60463	800-772-6484	708-361-5300	387
Hunt Midwest Enterprises Inc 8300 NE Underground Dr	Kansas City	MO	64161	800-551-6877	816-455-2500	646
Hunt Midwest Mining Inc 8300 NE Underground Dr	Kansas City	MO	64161	800-551-6877	816-455-2500	498-5
Hunt Midwest Residential Development 8300 NE Underground Dr	Kansas City	MO	64161	800-551-6877	816-455-2500	644
Hunt Pan Am Aviation Inc 505 Amelia Earhart Dr	Brownsville	TX	78521	800-888-7524	956-542-9111	62
Hunt Regional Healthcare 4215 Joe Ramsey Blvd	Greenville	TX	75401	800-984-9223	903-408-5000	371-3
Hunter Barth Adv Inc 2043 Wcliff Dr Ste 303	Newport Beach	CA	92660	877-524-2732	949-631-9900	4
Hunter Business Group LLC 4650 N Port Washington Rd	Milwaukee	WI	53212	800-423-4010	414-203-8060	196
Hunter Company Inc 3300 W 71st Ave	Westminster	CO	80030	800-676-4868	303-427-4626	701
Hunter Contracting Co 701 N Cooper Rd	Gilbert	AZ	85233	877-992-0521	480-892-0521	189-4
Hunter Display 14 Hewlett Ave	East Patchogue	NY	11772	800-767-2110	631-475-5900	233
Hunter Douglas Inc 1 Hunter Douglas Dr	Cumberland	MD	21502	800-365-3399	301-722-7700	86
Hunter Engineering Co 11250 Hunter Dr	Bridgeton	MO	63044	800-448-6848	314-731-3020	61-5
Hunter Fan Co 7130 Goodlett Farms Pkwy Ste 400	Memphis	TN	38016	888-830-1326	901-743-1360	36
Hunter Heavy Equipment Inc 2829 Texas Ave	Texas City	TX	77590	800-562-7368	409-945-2382	191
Hunter Public Relations 41 Madison Ave 5th Fl	New York	NY	10010	866-395-7710	212-679-6600	627
Hunter Woodworks Inc 21038 S Wilmington Ave PO Box 4937	Carson	CA	90749	800-966-4751	323-775-2544	544
Hunter's Specialties Inc 6000 Huntington Ct NE	Cedar Rapids	IA	52402	800-530-7149	319-395-0321	701
Hunterdon County Democrat 8 Minneakoning Rd	Flemington	NJ	08822	888-782-7533	908-782-4747	525-4
Hunting Island State Park 2555 Sea Island Pkwy	Hunting Island	SC	29920	800-315-3087	843-838-2011	558
Huntingdon College 1500 E Fairview Ave *Admissions	Montgomery	AL	36106	800-763-0313*	334-833-4497	166
Huntingdon County Visitors Bureau 6993 Seven Pt Rd Ste 2	Hesston	PA	16647	888-729-7869	814-658-0060	207
Huntington Bancshares Inc 7 Easton Oval *NASDAQ: HBAN*	Columbus	OH	43219	800-480-2265		357-2
Huntington Beach Marketing & Visitors Bureau 301 Main St Ste 208	Huntington Beach	CA	92648	800-729-6232	714-969-3492	207
Huntington Beach Public Library (HBPL) 7111 Talbert Ave	Huntington Beach	CA	92648	800-565-0148	714-842-4481	431-3
Huntington Beach State Park 16148 Ocean Hwy	Murrells Inlet	SC	29576	800-491-1764	843-237-4440	558
Huntington County Visitors & Convention Bureau 407 N Jefferson St	Huntington	IN	46750	800-848-4282	260-359-8687	207
Huntington Junior College 900 Fifth Ave	Huntington	WV	25701	800-344-4522	304-697-7550	788
Huntington Learning Centers Inc 496 Kinderkamack Rd	Oradell	NJ	07649	800-653-8400	201-261-8400	146
Huntington Mortgage Co 7575 Huntington Pk Dr	Columbus	OH	43235	800-323-4695	614-480-6505	502
Huntington National Bank 41 S High St Huntington Ctr	Columbus	OH	43287	800-480-2265	614-480-8300	69
Huntington Park Rubber Stamp 2761 E Slauson Ave PO Box 519	Huntington Park	CA	90255	800-882-0029	323-582-6461	462
Huntington State Park PO Box 1343	Huntington	UT	84528	800-322-3770	435-687-2491	558
Huntington Township Chamber of Commerce 164 Main St	Huntington	NY	11743	888-962-9932	631-423-6100	137
Huntington University 2303 College Ave *Admissions	Huntington	IN	46750	800-642-6493*	260-356-6000	166
Huntington Veterans Affairs Medical Ctr 1540 Spring Valley Dr	Huntington	WV	25704	800-827-8244	304-429-6741	371-8
Huntington's Disease Society of America (HDSA) 505 Eigth Ave Ste 902	New York	NY	10018	800-345-4372	212-242-1968	47-17
Huntleigh Securities Corp 7800 Forsyth Blvd Fifth Fl	Saint Louis	MO	63105	800-727-5405	314-236-2400	681
Hunton & Williams LLP 951 E Byrd St Riverfront Plaza E Tower	Richmond	VA	23219	800-669-6820	804-788-8200	425
Huntsman Corp 500 Huntsman Way *NYSE: HUN*	Salt Lake City	UT	84108	888-490-8484	801-584-5700	598-2
Huntsville Board of Education 200 White St	Huntsville	AL	35801	877-517-0020	256-428-6800	676
Huntsville Botanical Garden 4747 Bob Wallace Ave	Huntsville	AL	35805	800-300-4916	256-830-4447	96
Huntsville Museum of Art 300 Church St SW	Huntsville	AL	35801	800-786-9095	256-535-4350	513
Huntsville Times 2317 S Memorial Pkwy	Huntsville	AL	35801	800-239-5271	256-532-4000	525-2
Huntsville/Madison County Convention & Visitor's Bureau 500 Church St Ste 1	Huntsville	AL	35801	800-843-0468	256-551-2230	207
Huntsville-Walker County Chamber of Commerce 1327 11th St	Huntsville	TX	77340	800-289-0389	936-295-8113	137
Huntwood Industries 23800 E Apple Way	Liberty Lake	WA	99019	800-873-7350	509-924-5858	114
Huot Manufacturing Co 550 Wheeler St N	Saint Paul	MN	55104	800-832-3838	651-646-1869	318-1
Hurco Cos Inc One Technology Way *NASDAQ: HURC* ■ *Sales	Indianapolis	IN	46268	800-634-2416*	317-293-5309	450
Hurley Medical Ctr One Hurley Plz	Flint	MI	48503	800-336-8999	810-262-9000	371-3
Huron Automatic Screw Co PO Box 610068	Port Huron	MI	48061	800-500-4000	810-364-6636	614
Huron Chamber & Visitors Bureau 1725 Dakota Ave S	Huron	SD	57350	800-487-6673	605-352-0000	207
Huron Machine Products Inc 228 SW 21st Terr	Fort Lauderdale	FL	33312	800-327-8186		488
Huron Valley Correctional Facility 3201 Bemis Rd	Ypsilanti	MI	48197	855-444-3911	734-572-9900	213
Hurricane Convention & Visitors Bureau 3255 Teays Vly Rd PO Box 1086	Hurricane	WV	25526	877-487-7982	304-562-5896	207
Hurst Boiler & Welding Company Inc PO Box 530	Coolidge	GA	31738	877-994-8778	229-346-3545	90
Hurst Chemical Co 2360 Eastman Ave Ste 108 *Cust Svc	Oxnard	CA	93030	800-723-2004*		620
Hurst Farm Supply Inc 105 Ave D	Abernathy	TX	79311	800-535-8903	806-298-2541	274
Hurst Group 257 E Short St	Lexington	KY	40507	800-926-4423	859-255-4422	528
Hurst Place 209 Limeridge Rd E	Hamilton	ON	L9A2S6	888-521-8300	289-426-5302	457
Hurst Public Library 901 Precinct Line Rd	Hurst	TX	76053	800-344-8377	817-788-7300	431-3
Hurtigruten 405 Pk Ave	New York	NY	10022	866-552-0371	212-319-1300	220
Huse Publishing Co 525 Norfolk Ave PO Box 977	Norfolk	NE	68701	877-371-1020	402-371-1020	628-8
Hush Puppies Co 9341 Courtland Dr NE	Rockford	MI	49351	866-699-7365	616-866-5500	300
Husky Energy Inc 707 Eigth Ave SW PO Box 6525 *TSE: HSE*	Calgary	AB	T2P3G7	877-262-2111	403-298-6111	529
Husqvarna Construction Products 17400 W 119th St	Olathe	KS	66061	800-288-5040		488
Hussey Copper Ltd 100 Washington St	Leetsdale	PA	15056	800-733-8866	724-251-4200	480
Hussey Seating Co 38 Dyer St Ext	North Berwick	ME	03906	800-341-0401	207-676-2271	318-3
Hussmann Corp 12999 St Charles Rock Rd	Bridgeton	MO	63044	800-592-2060	314-291-2000	655
Husson College One College Cir	Bangor	ME	04401	800-448-7766	207-941-7000	166
Huston-Tillotson University 900 Chicon St	Austin	TX	78702	877-487-8702	512-505-3000	166
Hutchens Construction Co 1007 Main St	Cassville	MO	65625	888-728-3482	417-847-2489	189-4
Hutchens Industries Inc 215 N Patterson Ave	Springfield	MO	65802	800-654-8824	417-862-5012	59
Hutchings Court Reporters LLC 6055 E Washington Blvd Eighth Fl *Cust Svc	Los Angeles	CA	90040	800-697-3210*	323-888-6300	440
Hutchinson Aerospace & Industry Inc 82 S St	Hopkinton	MA	01748	800-227-7962	508-417-7000	667
Hutchinson Community College & Area Vocational School 1300 N Plum St	Hutchinson	KS	67501	800-289-3501	620-665-3500	160
Hutchinson Co-Op PO Box 158	Hutchinson	MN	55350	800-795-1299	320-587-4647	276
Hutchinson News 300 W Second St	Hutchinson	KS	67504	800-766-3311	620-694-5700	525-2
Hutchinson Zoo 6 Emerson Loop E Carey Pk	Hutchinson	KS	67501	800-362-3247	620-694-2693	810
Hutchinson/Mayrath/TerraTrack Industries 514 W Crawford PO Box 629	Clay Center	KS	67432	800-523-6993	785-632-2161	273
Hutchinson/Reno County Chamber of Commerce 117 N Walnut St	Hutchinson	KS	67501	800-691-4262	620-662-3391	137
Hutchison Inc 7460 Hwy 85 PO Box 1158	Adams City	CO	80022	800-525-0121	303-287-2826	192-3
Huthwaite Inc 901 N Glebe Rd Ste 200	Arlington	VA	22203	800-851-3842	703-467-3800	194
Huttig Bldg Products Inc (HBP) 555 Maryville University Dr Ste 400 *OTC: HBPI*	Saint Louis	MO	63141	800-325-4466	314-216-2600	494
HVA (High Vacuum Apparatus LLC) 12880 Moya Blvd	Reno	NV	89506	800-551-4422	775-359-4442	777
HVB AE Power Systems Inc 7250 Mcginnis Ferry Rd	Suwanee	GA	30024	866-362-0798	770-495-1755	720
HVH Transportation Inc 181 E 56th Ave Ste 200	Denver	CO	80216	800-525-4844	303-292-3656	770
HW Wilson Co 10 Estes St	Ipswich	MA	01938	800-653-2726	978-356-6500	628-2
HWC (Houston Wire & Cable Co) 10201 N Loop E	Houston	TX	77029	800-468-9473	713-609-2100	246
HWE (High West Energy Inc) 6270 County Rd 212	Pine Bluffs	WY	82082	888-834-1657	307-245-3261	245
HWEC (Hancock-Wood Electric Co-op Inc) 1399 Business Pk Dr S PO Box 190	North Baltimore	OH	45872	800-445-4840	419-257-3241	245
HWH Corp 2096 Moscow Rd	Moscow	IA	52760	800-321-3494	563-724-3396	59
Hyannis Holiday Motel 131 Ocean St	Hyannis	MA	02601	800-423-1551	508-775-1639	376
Hyannis Travel Inn 18 N St	Hyannis	MA	02601	800-352-7190	508-775-8200	376
Hyatt Carmel Highlands 120 Highlands Dr	Carmel	CA	93923	800-633-7313	831-620-1234	376
Hyatt Gold Passport Program 9805 Q St PO Box 27089	Omaha	NE	68127	800-233-1234		375
Grand Hyatt Hotels 71 S Wacker Dr *Resv	Chicago	IL	60606	800-233-1234*	312-750-1234	376
Hyatt Place Hotels 71 S Wacker Dr	Chicago	IL	60606	888-492-8847	312-750-1234	376

Toll-Free | Phone | Class

Hyatt Regency Hotels
71 S Wacker Dr .... Chicago IL 60606 **800-233-1234*** 312-750-1234 376
*Resv
Hyatt Hotels Corp
Park Hyatt Hotels
71 S Wacker Dr .... Chicago IL 60606 **800-233-1234*** 312-750-1234 376
*Resv
Hyatt Regency Huntington Beach Resort & Spa
21500 Pacific
Coast Hwy.................. Huntington Beach CA 92648 **800-633-7313** 714-698-1234 662
Hyatt Regency Lake Tahoe Resort & Casino
111 Country Club Dr .... Incline Village NV 89451 **800-233-1234** 775-832-1234 132
Hyatt Regency Maui Resort & Spa
200 Nohea Kai Dr .... Lahaina HI 96761 **800-633-7313** 808-661-1234 660
Hyatt Regency Scottsdale Resort at Gainey Ranch
7500 E Doubletree Ranch Rd .... Scottsdale AZ 85258 **800-233-1234** 480-483-5558 698
Hyatt Vacation Ownership Inc
140 Fountain Pkwy N
Ste 570..................... Saint Petersburg FL 33716 **800-926-4447** 727-803-9400 743
Hycor Biomedical Inc
7272 Chapman Ave .... Garden Grove CA 92841 **800-382-2527*** 231
*Cust Svc
Hyde Tools Co
54 Eastford Rd .... Southbridge MA 01550 **800-872-4933** 508-764-4344 748
Hydraforce Inc
500 Barclay Blvd .... Lincolnshire IL 60069 **877-237-9101** 847-793-2300 778
Hydrel
12881 Bradley Ave .... Sylmar CA 91342 **866-533-9901** 435
Hydrite Chemical Co
300 N Patrick Blvd .... Brookfield WI 53045 **800-543-4560** 262-792-1450 144
Hydro Aluminum North America
999 Corporate Blvd Ste 100 .... Linthicum MD 21090 **888-935-5752** 485
Hydro Carbide
4439 State Rte 982 .... Latrobe PA 15650 **800-245-2476** 724-539-9701 747
Hydro One Inc
483 Bay St 15th Fl .... Toronto ON M5G2P5 **888-664-9376** 416-345-5000 775
Hydro Systems Inc
29132 Ave Paine .... Valencia CA 91355 **800-747-9990** 661-775-0686 372
HydroCAD Software Solutions LLC
PO Box 477 .... Chocorua NH 03817 **800-927-7246** 603-323-8666 179-8
HYDRO-FIT Inc
160 Madison St .... Eugene OR 97402 **800-346-7295*** 541-484-4361 267
*Cust Svc
Hydromat Inc
11600 Adie Rd .... Saint Louis MO 63043 **800-552-3288** 314-432-4644 450
Hydromatic Pump Co
740 E Ninth St .... Ashland OH 44805 **888-957-8677** 632
Hydroseal Valve Co Inc
1500 SE 89th St................ Oklahoma City OK 73149 **800-398-2493** 405-631-1533 777
Hydrotex Inc
12920 Senlac D Ste 190......... Farmers Branch TX 75234 **800-527-9439** 534
Hydro-Thermal Corp
400 Pilot Ct .... Waukesha WI 53188 **800-952-0121** 262-548-8900 383
Hygenic Corp
1245 Home Ave .... Akron OH 44310 **800-321-2135** 330-633-8460 228
hygiena LLC
941 Avenida Acaso .... Camarillo CA 93012 **877-494-4364** 805-388-8007 416
Hygolet Inc
349 SE Second Ave .... Deerfield Beach FL 33441 **800-494-6538** 954-481-8601 601
Hygrade Metal Moulding Manufacturing Corp
1990 Highland Ave .... Bethlehem PA 18020 **800-645-9475** 610-866-2441 234
Hygrade Precision Technologies Inc
329 Cooke St .... Plainville CT 06062 **800-457-1666** 860-747-5773 747
HyGreen Inc
3630 SW 47th Ave Ste 100........... Gainesville FL 32608 **877-574-9473** 732
Hy-Ko Products Co
60 Meadow Ln .... Northfield OH 44067 **800-292-0550** 330-467-7446 692
Hyland Screw Machine Products
1900 Kuntz Rd .... Dayton OH 45404 **866-863-7282** 614
Hyland Software Inc
28500 Clemens Rd .... Westlake OH 44145 **888-495-2638** 440-788-5000 179-7
Hylant Group
811 Madison Ave .... Toledo OH 43624 **800-249-5268** 419-255-1020 387
Hynes Industries
3760 Oakwood .... Youngstown OH 44515 **800-321-9257** 487
Hyperion Capital Management Inc
200 Vessey St
3 World Financial Ctr .... New York NY 10281 **800-497-3746** 212-549-8400 398
Hypertension Diagnostics Inc
2915 Waters Rd Ste 108................ Eagan MN 55121 **888-785-7392** 651-687-9999 471
Hypertherm Inc
21 Great Hollow Rd PO Box 5010........ Hanover NH 03755 **800-643-0030** 603-643-3441 450
Hypro
375 Fifth Ave NW .... New Brighton MN 55112 **800-424-9776*** 651-766-6300 632
*Cust Svc
Hyson Products
10367 Brecksville Rd .... Brecksville OH 44141 **800-876-4976** 440-526-5900 778
Hysterectomy Educational Resources & Services Foundation (HERS)
422 Bryn Mawr Ave .... Bala Cynwyd PA 19004 **888-750-4377** 610-667-7757 47-17
Hy-Tape International Inc
PO Box 540 .... Patterson NY 12563 **800-248-0101** 472
Hyundai Motor America
10550 Talbert Ave .... Fountain Valley CA 92708 **800-633-5151*** 714-965-3000 58
*Cust Svc

I

Toll-Free | Phone | Class

I & I Sling Inc
PO Box 2423 .... Aston PA 19014 **800-874-3539** 610-485-8500 209
I Am Athlete LLC
PO Box 667 .... Santa Monica CA 90406 **877-462-7979** 384
I B M Southeast Employees Federal Credit Union
PO Box 5090 .... Boca Raton FL 33431 **888-567-8688** 561-982-4700 219
I D Booth Inc
PO Box 579 .... Elmira NY 14902 **888-432-6684** 607-733-9121 605

Toll-Free | Phone | Class

I Rice & Company Inc
11500 Roosevelt Blvd
Bldg D.......................... Philadelphia PA 19116 **800-232-6022** 215-673-7423 295-15
I Spiewak & Sons Inc
463 Seventh Ave .... New York NY 10018 **800-223-6850** 212-695-1620 153-18
I Wireless
4135 NW Urbandale Dr .... Urbandale IA 50322 **888-550-4497*** 515-258-7000 725
*Cust Svc
i Wireless Ctr
1201 River Dr .... Moline IL 61265 **800-745-3000** 309-764-2001 711
I.B.I.S. Inc
30 Technology Pkwy S Ste 400......... Norcross GA 30092 **888-477-7989** 770-368-4000 686
I.T. Blueprint Solutions Consulting Inc
170-422 Richards St .... Vancouver BC V6B2Z4 **866-261-8981** 197
IAABO (International Assn of Approved Basketball Officials)
PO Box 355 .... Carlisle PA 17013 **800-526-1379** 717-713-8129 47-22
IAAO (International Assn of Assessing Officers)
314 W Tenth St .... Kansas City MO 64105 **800-616-4226** 816-701-8100 48-7
IABC (International Assn of Business Communicators)
601 Montgomery St
Ste 1900...................... San Francisco CA 94111 **800-766-4222** 415-544-4700 48-12
IAC Industries
895 Beacon St .... Brea CA 92821 **800-989-1422** 714-990-8997 318-1
IACP (International Assn of Culinary Professionals)
1221 Ave of the Americas
42nd fl .... New York NY 10020 **800-928-4227** 866-358-2524 48-6
IACP (International Academy of Compounding Pharmacists)
4638 Riverstone Blvd .... Missouri City TX 77459 **800-927-4227** 281-933-8400 48-8
IACP (International Assn of Chiefs of Police)
515 N Washington St .... Alexandria VA 22314 **800-843-4227** 703-836-6767 48-7
IAEI (International Assn of Electrical Inspectors)
901 Waterfall Way Ste 602 .... Richardson TX 75080 **800-786-4234** 972-235-1455 48-3
IAFC (International Assn of Fire Chiefs)
4025 Fair Ridge Dr Ste 300 .... Fairfax VA 22033 **866-385-9110** 703-273-0911 48-7
IAFE (International Assn of Fairs & Expositions, The)
3043 E Cairo .... Springfield MO 65802 **800-516-0313** 417-862-5771 47-23
IAFP (International Assn for Food Protection)
6200 Aurora Ave Ste 200W.......... Des Moines IA 50322 **800-369-6337*** 515-276-3344 48-6
*General
IAHB (Institute for the Advancement of Human Behavior)
PO BOX 5527 .... Santa Rosa CA 95402 **800-258-8411** 650-851-8411 48-8
IAIA (Institute of American Indian Arts)
83 Avan Nu Po Rd .... Santa Fe NM 87508 **800-804-6422** 505-424-2300 163
IAMFC (International Assn of Marriage & Family Counselors)
5999 Stevenson Ave .... Alexandria VA 22304 **800-347-6647** 48-15
IAMGOLD Corp
401 Bay St Ste 3200 PO Box 153........ Toronto ON M5H2Y4 **888-464-9999** 416-360-4710 497
TSE: IMG
IAMS Co 3700 Ohio 65 .... Leipsic OH 45856 **800-675-3849*** 419-943-4267 571
*Cust Svc
IANA (Intermodal Assn of North America)
11785 Beltsville Dr Ste 1100 .... Calverton MD 20705 **877-438-8442** 301-982-3400 48-21
IAP Worldwide Services Inc
7315 N Atlantic Ave .... Cape Canaveral FL 32920 **877-296-8010** 321-784-7100 271
IAPA (International Airline Passengers Assn)
PO Box 700188 .... Dallas TX 75370 **800-821-4272** 972-404-9980 47-23
IAPES (International Assn of Workforce Professionals)
1801 Louisville Rd .... Frankfort KY 40601 **888-898-9960** 502-223-4459 48-12
IAPMO (International Assn of Plumbing & Mechanical Officials)
4755 E Philadelphia St .... Ontario CA 91761 **877-427-6601** 909-472-4100 48-7
IARW (International Assn of Refrigerated Warehouses)
1500 King St Ste 201 .... Alexandria VA 22314 **800-488-2900** 703-373-4300 48-21
IASIS Healthcare Corp
117 Seaboard Ln Bldg E............... Franklin TN 37067 **877-898-6080** 615-844-2747 350
IASP (International Assn for the Study of Pain)
111 Queen Anne Ave N Ste 501 .... Seattle WA 98109 **866-574-2654** 206-283-0311 47-17
IATAN (International Airlines Travel Agent Network)
800 Pl Victoria P.O. Box 113........... Montreal QC H4Z1A1 **877-734-2826** 514-868-8800 48-21
IATSE (International Alliance of Theatrical Stage Employees Moving Picture Technicians)
1430 Broadway 20th Fl............... New York NY 10018 **800-456-3863** 212-730-1770 411
IATSE PAC
1430 Broadway 20th Fl............... New York NY 10018 **844-422-9273** 212-730-1770 608
IAVM (International Assn of Venue Managers Inc)
635 Fritz Dr Ste 100 .... Coppell TX 75019 **800-935-4226** 972-906-7441 48-12
IBA (Institute of Business Appraisers)
1111 BrickyaRd Rd
Ste 200........................ Salt Lake City UT 84106 **800-299-4130** 48-17
Ibaset
27442 Portola Pkwy .... Foothill Ranch CA 92610 **877-422-7381** 949-598-5200 181
IBC Advanced Alloys Corp
570 Granville St Ste 1200............ Vancouver BC V6C3P1 **800-373-3251** 604-685-6263 497
IBERIABANK Corp
200 W Congress St .... Lafayette LA 70501 **800-968-0801** 357-2
NASDAQ: IBKC
Iberville Parish Chamber of Commerce
23675 Church St .... Plaquemine LA 70764 **800-266-2692** 225-687-3560 137
IBHS (Institute for Business & Home Safety)
4775 E Fowler Ave .... Tampa FL 33617 **866-657-4247** 813-286-3400 48-9
IBISWorld Inc
11755 Wilshire blvd 11th fl .... Los Angeles CA 90025 **800-330-3772** 384
IBM (International Business Machines Corp)
One New OrchaRd Rd .... Armonk NY 10504 **800-426-4968** 914-499-1900 174-1
NYSE: IBM
IBM Palisades Conference Ctr
334 Rt 9 W .... Palisades NY 10964 **800-426-0889** 845-732-6000 374
IBS (International Biometric Society)
1444 'I' St NW Ste 700 .... Washington DC 20005 **800-262-1171** 202-712-9049 48-19
IBS (International Bible Society)
1820 Jet Stream Dr .... Colorado Springs CO 80921 **800-524-1588*** 719-488-9200 47-20
*Cust Svc
IBS Direct
431 Yerkes Rd .... King of Prussia PA 19406 **800-220-1255** 610-265-8210 109
IBS Electronics Inc
3506 W Lk Ctr Dr Ste D .... Santa Ana CA 92704 **800-527-2888** 714-751-6633 246
IBT Enterprises LLC
1770 Indian Trail Rd Ste 300 .... Norcross GA 30093 **877-242-8428** 770-381-2023 195
IBT Inc
9400 W 55th St .... Merriam KS 66203 **800-332-2114** 913-677-3151 382
IBU (Inlandboatmen's Union of the Pacific)
1711 W Nickerson St Ste D .... Seattle WA 98119 **800-562-6000** 206-284-6001 411
IBWA (International Bottled Water Assn)
1700 Diagonal Rd Ste 650 .... Alexandria VA 22314 **800-928-3711** 703-683-5213 48-6
IC Bus LLC
4201 Winfield Rd .... Warrenville IL 60555 **800-892-7761** 630-753-5000 509

				Toll-Free	Phone	Class
ICA (International Chiropractors Assn PAC)						
6400 Arlington Blvd						
Ste 800	Falls Church	VA	22042	**800-423-4690**	703-528-5000	608
ICA (International Chiropractors Assn)						
6400 Arlington Blvd						
Ste 800	Falls Church	VA	22042	**800-423-4690**	703-528-5000	48-8
ICA (Independent Charities of America)						
1100 Larkspur Landing Cir						
Ste 340	Larkspur	CA	94939	**800-477-0733**	415-925-2600	47-5
ICAC (Institute of Clean Air Cos)						
1730 M St NW Ste 206	Washington	DC	20036	**888-383-5726**	202-457-0911	47-12
iCAD Inc						
Four Townsend W Ste 17	Nashua	NH	03063	**866-280-2239**	603-882-5200	379
NASDAQ: ICAD						
Icahn Enterprises LP						
767 Fifth Ave 47th Fl	New York	NY	10153	**800-255-2737**	212-702-4300	357-3
NASDAQ: IEP						
Icare Industries Inc						
4399 35th St N	Saint Petersburg	FL	33714	**877-422-7352**	727-526-0501	535
IcareLabs						
4399 35th St N	Saint Petersburg	FL	33714	**877-422-7352**		535
ICBA (Independent Community Bankers of America)						
1615 L St NW Ste 900	Washington	DC	20036	**800-422-8439**	202-659-8111	48-2
ICC (International Code Council)						
500 New Jersey Ave NW 6th Fl	Washington	DC	20001	**888-422-7233**	202-370-1800	48-3
ICC Chemical Corp						
460 Pk Ave	New York	NY	10022	**800-422-1720**	212-521-1700	144
ICC Industries Inc						
460 Pk Ave	New York	NY	10022	**800-422-1720**	212-521-1700	142
ICCFA (International Cemetery Cremation & Funeral Assn)						
107 Carpenter Dr Ste 100	Sterling	VA	20164	**800-645-7700**	703-391-8400	48-4
ICCP (Institute for Certification of Computing Professionals)						
2400 E Devon Ave Ste 281	Des Plaines	IL	60018	**800-843-8227**	847-299-4227	47-9
ICD (International College of Dentists)						
51 Monroe St Ste 1400	Rockville	MD	20850	**800-533-6825**	301-251-8861	48-8
ICD (Industrial Controls Distributors Inc)						
1776 Bloomsbury Ave	Ocean	NJ	07712	**800-281-4788***	732-918-9000	382
*Sales						
ICE (US Immigration & Customs Enforcement)						
425 'I' St NW	Washington	DC	20536	**866-347-2423**	202-514-1900	338-9
Ice Cream Specialties						
8419 Hanley Industrial Ct	Saint Louis	MO	63144	**800-662-7550**	314-962-2550	295-25
Icelandair North America						
1900 Crown Colony Dr	Quincy	MA	02169	**800-223-5500**		26
Icemakers Inc						
3711 Fifth Ct N	Birmingham	AL	35222	**800-467-2181***	205-591-2791	377
*General						
Ice-O-Matic						
11100 E 45th Ave	Denver	CO	80239	**800-423-3367**	303-371-3737	655
Iceptstechnology Group Inc						
1301 Fulling Mill Rd	Middletown	PA	17057	**888-477-7989**	717-704-1000	175
ICF (International Contract Furnishings Inc)						
19 Ohio Ave	Norwich	CT	06360	**800-237-1625**	860-886-1700	320
ICFG (International Church of the Foursquare Gospel)						
1910 W Sunset Blvd						
PO Box 26902	Los Angeles	CA	90026	**888-635-4234**	213-989-4234	47-20
ICFL (Idaho Commission for Libraries)						
325 W State St	Boise	ID	83702	**800-458-3271**	208-334-2150	431-5
ICG/Holliston						
905 Holliston Mills Rd						
PO Box 478	Church Hill	TN	37642	**800-251-0451**	423-357-6141	734-2
ICIA (International Communications Industries Assn)						
11242 Waples Mill Rd Ste 200	Fairfax	VA	22030	**800-659-7469**	703-273-7200	48-20
iCIMS Inc						
90 Matawan Rd Pkwy 120 Fifth Fl	Matawan	NJ	07747	**800-889-4422**	732-847-1941	179-1
ICLA (International Collegiate Licensing Assn)						
24651 Detroit Rd	Westlake	OH	44145	**877-887-2261**	440-892-4000	47-22
ICM Asset Management Inc						
601 W Main Ave	Spokane	WA	99201	**800-488-4075**	509-455-3588	398
Icm Controls Corp						
7313 William Barry Blvd	North Syracuse	NY	13212	**800-365-5525**	315-233-5266	204
ICMA (International City/County Management Assn)						
777 N Capitol St NE Ste 500	Washington	DC	20002	**800-745-8780**	202-289-4262	48-7
ICMARC						
777 N Capitol St NE Ste 600	Washington	DC	20002	**800-669-7471***	202-962-4600	521
*General						
ICOI (International Congress of Oral Implantologists)						
248 Lorraine Ave						
Third Fl	Upper Montclair	NJ	07043	**800-442-0525**	973-783-6300	48-8
iCollector Technologies Inc						
1750 Coast Meridian Rd						
Ste 114	Port Coquitlam	BC	V3C6R8	**866-313-0123**	604-941-2221	50
ICOM America Inc						
2380 116th Ave NE	Bellevue	WA	98004	**800-872-4266**	425-454-8155	638
ICON Health & Fitness Inc						
1500 South 1000 West	Logan	UT	84321	**800-999-3756**	435-750-5000	267
Icon Identity Solutions						
1418 Elmhurst Rd	Elk Grove Village	IL	60007	**888-724-0380**		692
Iconixx Software						
3420 Executive Ctr Dr Ste 250	Austin	TX	78731	**877-426-6499**		181
Iconma LLC						
850 Stephenson Hwy Ste 612	Troy	MI	48083	**888-451-2519**		623
ICP (International Comfort Products Corp)						
650 Heil Quaker Ave	Lewisburg	TN	37091	**800-458-6650**	931-359-3511	15
ICPI (Interlocking Concrete Pavement Institute)						
1444 'I' St NW Ste 700	Washington	DC	20005	**800-241-3652**	202-712-9036	48-3
ICPM (Institute of Certified Professional Managers)						
James Madison University						
MSC 5504	Harrisonburg	VA	22807	**800-460-8013**	540-568-3247	48-12
ICS (Information & Computing Services Inc)						
1650 Prudential Dr Ste 300	Jacksonville	FL	32207	**800-676-4427**	904-399-8500	179-1
ICS Blount Inc						
4909 SE International Way	Portland	OR	97222	**800-321-1240**		673
ICTC (Inter-Community Telephone Co)						
PO Box 8	Nome	ND	58062	**800-350-9137**	701-924-8815	726
ICU Medical Inc						
951 Calle Amanecer	San Clemente	CA	92673	**800-824-7890**	949-366-2183	472
NASDAQ: ICUI						
ICW Group						
11455 El Camino Real	San Diego	CA	92130	**800-877-1111**	858-350-2400	388-4
ICWM (Institute of Caster & Wheel Manufacturers)						
8720 Red Oak Blvd Ste 201	Charlotte	NC	28217	**877-522-5431**	704-676-1190	48-13

				Toll-Free	Phone	Class
ID Systems Inc						
123 Tice Blvd Ste 101	Woodcliff Lake	NJ	07677	**866-410-0152**	201-996-9000	638
NASDAQ: IDSY						
IDA (In Defense of Animals)						
3010 Kerner Blvd	San Rafael	CA	94901	**800-705-0425**	415-448-0048	47-3
IDA (International Dyslexia Assn, The)						
40 York Rd Fourth Fl	Towson	MD	21204	**800-222-3123**	410-296-0232	47-17
Aging Commission (ICOA)						
341 W Washington Fl 3						
PO Box 83720	Boise	ID	83702	**800-926-2588**	208-334-3833	337-13
Idaho						
Arts Commission						
2410 Old Penitentiary Rd	Boise	ID	83712	**800-278-3863**	208-334-2119	337-13
Board of Medicine						
1755 N Westgate Dr Ste 140						
PO Box 83720	Boise	ID	83704	**800-333-0073**	208-327-7000	337-13
Crime Victims Compensation Program						
PO Box 83720	Boise	ID	83720	**800-950-2110**	208-334-6000	337-13
Department of Commerce						
700 W State St PO Box 83720	Boise	ID	83720	**800-842-5858**	208-334-2470	337-13
Homeland Security Bureau						
4040 W Guard St Bldg 600	Boise	ID	83705	**800-344-0984**	208-422-3040	337-13
Housing & Finance Assn						
565 W Myrtle Ave	Boise	ID	83702	**800-526-7145**	208-331-4882	337-13
Parks & Recreation Dept						
5657 Warm Springs Ave	Boise	ID	83716	**855-514-2429**		337-13
Public Utilities Commission						
PO Box 83720	Boise	ID	83720	**800-432-0369**	208-334-0300	337-13
Real Estate Commission						
575 E Parkcenter Blvd Ste 180	Boise	ID	83706	**866-447-5411**	208-334-3285	337-13
Tax Commission						
800 E Pk Blvd	Boise	ID	83712	**800-972-7660**	208-334-7660	337-13
Tourism Development Div						
700 W State St PO Box 83720	Boise	ID	83720	**800-847-4843***	208-334-2470	337-13
*General						
Idaho Assn of Realtors						
10116 W Overland Rd	Boise	ID	83702	**800-621-7553**	208-342-3585	647
Idaho Botanical Garden						
2355 N Penitentiary Rd	Boise	ID	83712	**877-527-8233**	208-343-8649	96
Idaho Commission for Libraries (ICFL)						
325 W State St	Boise	ID	83702	**800-458-3271**	208-334-2150	431-5
Idaho County Light & Power Co-op						
1065 Hwy 13 PO Box 300	Grangeville	ID	83530	**877-212-0424**	208-983-1610	245
Idaho Democratic Party						
943 W Overland Rd	Meridian	ID	83642	**800-626-0471**	208-336-1815	609-1
Idaho Falls School District 91 Education Foundation Inc						
690 John Adams Pkwy	Idaho Falls	ID	83401	**888-993-7120**	208-525-7500	676
Idaho Lions Eye Bank						
1090 N Cole Rd	Boise	ID	83704	**800-546-6889**	208-338-5466	269
Idaho Lottery						
1199 Shoreline Ln Ste 100	Boise	ID	83702	**800-432-5688**	208-334-2600	447
Idaho National Laboratory (INL)						
2525 Fremont Ave						
PO Box 1625	Idaho Falls	ID	83415	**866-495-7440**		659
Idaho Nurses Assn (INA)						
1850 E Southern Ave Ste 1	Tempe	AZ	85224	**888-721-8904**	404-760-2803	526
Idaho Pacific Lumber Co (IdaPac)						
7255 Franklin Rd	Boise	ID	83709	**800-231-2310**	208-375-8052	192-3
Idaho Power Co						
1221 W Idaho St	Boise	ID	83702	**800-488-6151**	208-388-2200	775
Idaho Public Television (IPTV)						
1455 N Orchard St	Boise	ID	83706	**800-543-6868**	208-373-7220	624
Idaho State Bar						
525 W Jefferson St	Boise	ID	83702	**800-221-3295**	208-334-4500	71
Idaho State Journal						
305 S Arthur Ave	Pocatello	ID	83204	**800-669-9777**	208-232-4161	525-2
Idaho State Veterans Home-Lewiston						
821 21st Ave	Lewiston	ID	83501	**877-222-8387**	208-799-3422	781
Idaho State Veterans Home-Pocatello						
1957 Alvin Ricken Dr	Pocatello	ID	83201	**877-222-8387**	208-236-6340	781
Idaho Statesman						
PO Box 40	Boise	ID	83707	**800-635-8934**	208-377-6400	525-2
Idaho-Pacific Corp						
4723 E 100 N PO Box 478	Ririe	ID	83443	**800-238-5503***	208-538-6971	295-18
*Sales						
IdaPac (Idaho Pacific Lumber Co)						
7255 Franklin Rd	Boise	ID	83709	**800-231-2310**	208-375-8052	192-3
IDC (International Data Corp)						
Five Speen St	Framingham	MA	01701	**800-343-4952**	508-872-8200	461
IDDBA (International Dairy-Deli-Bakery Assn)						
636 Science Dr	Madison	WI	53705	**877-399-4925**	608-238-7908	48-6
IDEA Inc						
10455 Pacific Ctr Ct	San Diego	CA	92121	**800-999-4332**	858-535-8979	47-22
Ideal Adv & Printing						
116 N Winnebago St	Rockford	IL	61101	**800-208-0294**	815-965-1713	4
Ideal Chemical & Supply Co						
4025 Air Pk St	Memphis	TN	38118	**800-232-6776**	901-363-7720	144
Ideal Clamp						
8100 Tridon Dr	Smyrna	TN	37167	**800-251-3220**	615-459-5800	347
Ideal Industries Inc						
1000 Pk Ave	Sycamore	IL	60178	**800-435-0705**	815-895-5181	803
Ideal Shield LLC						
2525 Clark St	Detroit	MI	48209	**866-825-8659**	313-842-7290	294
Ideal Tape Co						
1400 Middlesex St	Lowell	MA	01851	**800-284-3325**		472
Idealease Inc						
430 N Rand Rd	North Barrington	IL	60010	**800-435-3273**	847-304-6000	768
Idealliance						
7200 France Ave S Ste 223	Edina	MN	55435	**800-255-8141**	952-896-1908	48-16
Idealstor LLC						
1100 Lakeway Dr Ste100	Lakeway	TX	78734	**888-864-3257**	512-279-4321	174-8
IDEC Corp						
1175 Elko Dr	Sunnyvale	CA	94089	**800-262-4332**	408-747-0550	204
Idenix Pharmaceuticals Inc						
One Merck Dr						
P.O. Box 100	Whitehouse Station	NJ	08889	**800-770-4674**	908-423-1000	84
NYSE: MRK						
Ident-A-Kid Services of America						
1780 102nd Ave N						
Ste 100	Saint Petersburg	FL	33716	**800-890-1000**	727-577-4646	309
Identatronics Inc						
165 N Lively Blvd	Elk Grove Village	IL	60007	**800-323-5403***	847-437-2654	584
*Cust Svc						

				Toll-Free	Phone	Class
IDenticard Systems Inc						
40 Citation Ln	Lititz	PA	17543	**800-233-0298**	717-569-5797	683
Identity Genetics Inc						
47927 213th St	Aurora	SD	57002	**800-861-1054**		414
IDEO 100 Forest Ave	Palo Alto	CA	94301	**866-369-9888**	650-289-3400	261
IDEXX Laboratories Inc						
One IDEXX Dr	Westbrook	ME	04092	**800-548-6733**	207-556-0300	231
NASDAQ: IDXX						
IDF (Immune Deficiency Foundation)						
40 W Chesapeake Ave Ste 308	Towson	MD	21204	**800-296-4433**	410-321-6647	47-17
IDFW (Institute for a Drug-Free Workplace)						
10701 Parkridge Blvd Ste 300	Reston	VA	20191	**877-696-6775**	703-391-7222	48-12
IDG (International Data Group Inc)						
1 Exeter Plaza 15th Fl	Boston	MA	02116	**800-343-4952***	617-534-1200	628-9
*Orders						
IDI (Interconnect Devices Inc)						
5101 Richland Ave	Kansas City	KS	66106	**866-433-5722**	913-342-5544	253
IDI Distributors Inc						
8303 Audubon Rd	Chanhassen	MN	55317	**888-843-1318**	952-279-6400	681
iDirect Technologies Inc						
13865 Sunrise Valley Dr Ste 100	Herndon	VA	20171	**888-362-5475**	703-648-8118	725
IDP (Insurance Data Processing Inc)						
8101 Washington Ln	Wyncote	PA	19095	**800-523-6745**	215-885-2150	179-11
IDSA (Infectious Diseases Society of America)						
1300 Wilson Blvd Ste 300	Arlington	VA	22209	**888-844-4372**	703-299-0200	48-8
IEAP (Interface EAP Inc)						
10370 Richmond Ave Ste 1100						
PO Box 421879	Houston	TX	77042	**800-324-4327**	713-781-3364	457
IEEE Broadcast Technology Society (BTS)						
445 Hoes Ln	Piscataway	NJ	08854	**800-678-4333**	732-562-5407	48-19
IEEE Computer Graphics & Applications Magazine						
10662 Los Vaqueros Cir						
PO Box 3014	Los Alamitos	CA	90720	**800-272-6657**	714-821-8380	452-7
IEEE Computer Society						
2001 L St NW Ste 700	Washington	DC	20036	**800-272-6657**	202-371-0101	48-19
IEEE Computer Society Press						
10662 Los Vaqueros Cir						
PO Box 3014	Los Alamitos	CA	90720	**800-272-6657**	714-821-8380	628-9
IEEE Consumer Electronics Society (CES)						
445 Hoes Ln	Piscataway	NJ	08854	**800-678-4333**	732-981-0060	48-19
IEEE Education Society (ES)						
IEEE Operations Ctr						
445 Hoes Ln	Piscataway	NJ	08854	**800-678-4333**	732-981-0060	48-19
IEEE Electromagnetic Compatibility Society (EMC)						
IEEE Operations Ctr						
445 Hoes Ln	Piscataway	NJ	08854	**800-678-4333**	732-981-0060	48-19
IEEE Electron Devices Society (EDS)						
IEEE Operations Ctr						
445 Hoes Ln	Piscataway	NJ	08854	**800-678-4333**	732-981-0060	48-19
IEEE Engineering Management Society (EMS)						
IEEE Operations Ctr						
445 Hoes Ln	Piscataway	NJ	08854	**800-678-4333**	732-981-0060	48-19
IEEE Geoscience & Remote Sensing Society (GRSS)						
IEEE Operations Ctr						
445 Hoes Ln	Piscataway	NJ	08854	**800-678-4333**	732-562-5550	48-19
IEEE Industrial Electronics Society (IES)						
IEEE Operations Ctr						
445 Hoes Ln	Piscataway	NJ	08854	**800-678-4333**	732-981-0060	48-19
IEEE Instrumentation & Measurement Society (IM)						
445 Hoes Ln	Piscataway	NJ	08854	**800-327-6677**	732-562-3844	48-19
IEEE Magnetics Society						
445 Hoes Ln PO Box 459	Piscataway	NJ	08855	**800-678-4333**	908-981-0060	48-19
IEEE Micro Magazine						
10662 Los Vaqueros Cir						
PO Box 3014	Los Alamitos	CA	90720	**800-272-6657**	714-821-8380	452-7
IEEE Microwave Theory & Techniques Society (MTT-S)						
IEEE Operations Ctr						
445 Hoes Ln	Piscataway	NJ	08555	**800-678-4333**	732-562-5400	48-19
IEEE Nuclear & Plasma Sciences Society (NPSS)						
445 Hoes Ln	Piscataway	NJ	08854	**800-678-4333**	732-981-0060	48-19
IEEE Power Engineering Society (PES)						
IEEE Operations Ctr						
445 Hoes Ln	Piscataway	NJ	08854	**800-678-4333**	732-562-3883	48-19
IEEE Product Safety Engineering Society						
IEEE Operations Ctr						
445 Hoes Ln	Piscataway	NJ	08854	**800-678-4333**	732-981-0060	48-19
IEEE Reliability Society (RS)						
IEEE Operations Ctr						
445 Hoes Ln	Piscataway	NJ	08854	**800-678-4333**	732-981-0060	48-19
IEEE Signal Processing Society						
IEEE Operations Ctr						
445 Hoes Ln	Piscataway	NJ	08854	**800-678-4333**	732-981-0060	48-19
IEEE Society on Social Implications of Technology (SSIT)						
IEEE Operations Ctr						
445 Hoes Ln	Piscataway	NJ	08854	**800-678-4333**	732-981-0060	48-19
IEEE Solid State Circuits Society (SSCS)						
445 Hoes Ln	Piscataway	NJ	08854	**800-678-4333**	732-981-3400	48-19
IEEE Ultrasonics Ferroelectrics & Frequency Control Society						
IEEE Operations Ctr						
445 Hoes Ln	Piscataway	NJ	08854	**800-678-4333**	732-981-0060	48-19
IEHA (International Executive Housekeepers Assn)						
1001 Eastwind Dr Ste 301	Westerville	OH	43081	**800-200-6342**	614-895-7166	48-4
iEntertainment Network Inc						
124 Quade Dr P.O. Box 3897	Cary	NC	27519	**800-395-8425**	919-238-4090	179-6
OTC: IENT						
IES (IEEE Industrial Electronics Society)						
IEEE Operations Ctr						
445 Hoes Ln	Piscataway	NJ	08854	**800-678-4333**	732-981-0060	48-19
IEWC (Industrial Electric Wire & Cable Inc)						
5001 S Towne Dr	New Berlin	WI	53151	**800-344-2323**	262-782-2323	246
IFA (International Franchise Assn)						
1501 K St NW Ste 350	Washington	DC	20005	**800-543-1038**	202-628-8000	48-18
IFAI (Industrial Fabrics Assn International)						
1801 County Rd 'B' W	Roseville	MN	55113	**800-225-4324**	651-222-2508	48-13
IFAW (International Fund for Animal Welfare)						
290 Summer St	Yarmouth Port	MA	02675	**800-932-4329**	508-744-2000	47-3
IFCA International						
3520 Fairlane Ave SW	Grandville	MI	49418	**800-347-1840**	616-531-1840	47-20
Ifco Systems						
6829 Flintlock Rd	Houston	TX	77040	**800-771-1148**	713-332-6200	544
IFEBP (International Foundation of Employee Benefit Plans)						
18700 W Bluemound Rd	Brookfield	WI	53045	**888-334-3327**	262-786-6700	260
IFH (Institution Food House Inc)						
543 12th St Dr NW	Hickory	NC	28601	**800-800-0434**		298
IFIC (International Fidelity Insurance Co)						
One Newark Ctr 20th Fl	Newark	NJ	07102	**800-333-4167**	973-624-7200	388-5
IFIC (International Food Information Council Foundation)						
1100 Connecticut Ave NW						
Ste 430	Washington	DC	20036	**888-723-3366**	202-296-6540	48-6
IFS North America Inc						
300 Pk Blvd Ste 555	Chicago	IL	60143	**888-437-4968**		179-1
IFT (Institute of Food Technologists)						
525 W Van Buren St Ste 1000	Chicago	IL	60607	**800-438-3663**	312-782-8424	48-6
IG Inc 720 S Sara Rd	Mustang	OK	73137	**800-654-8433**	405-376-9393	325
IGA Inc						
8725 W Higgins Rd Ste 350	Chicago	IL	60631	**800-321-5442**	773-693-4520	342
IGI (Information Gatekeepers Inc)						
1340 Soldiers Field Rd Ste 2	Brighton	MA	02135	**800-323-1088**	617-782-5033	628-11
IGI (Insight Global Inc)						
4170 Ashford Dunwoody Rd						
Ste 580	Atlanta	GA	30319	**888-336-7463**	404-257-7900	194
Igloo Products Corp						
777 Igloo Rd	Katy	TX	77494	**800-364-5566**	713-584-6800	600
IGLTA (International Gay & Lesbian Travel Assn)						
1201 NE 26th St Ste 103	Fort Lauderdale	FL	33305	**866-845-4472**	954-630-1637	47-23
IGM Financial Inc						
447 Portage Ave 1 Canada Ctr	Winnipeg	MB	R3C3B6	**888-746-6344**		398
NYSE: IGM						
Ignition Systems & Controls LP						
6300 W Hwy 80	Midland	TX	79706	**800-777-5559**	432-697-6472	247
iGo Inc						
17800 N Perimeter Dr Ste 200	Scottsdale	AZ	85255	**888-205-0093**	480-596-0061	177
NASDAQ: IGOI						
I-Go Van & Storage						
9820 S 142nd St	Omaha	NE	68138	**800-228-9276**	402-891-1222	512
IGS (Institute of General Semantics)						
72-11 Austin St	Forest Hills	NY	11375	**800-346-1359**	212-729-7973	47-11
IGS (Industrial Gasket & Shim Company Inc)						
200 Country Club Rd	Meadow Lands	PA	15347	**800-229-1447**	724-222-5800	325
IGSHPA (International Ground Source Heat Pump Assn)						
Oklahoma State University						
374 Cordell S	Stillwater	OK	74078	**800-626-4747**	405-744-5175	48-13
IGT (International Game Technology)						
9295 Prototype Dr	Reno	NV	89521	**800-522-4700**	775-448-7777	321
NYSE: IGT						
Ih Services Inc						
PO Box 5033	Greenville	SC	29606	**800-340-9088**	864-297-3748	150
IHA (International Housewares Assn)						
6400 Shafer Ct Ste 650	Rosemont	IL	60018	**888-689-2838**	847-292-4200	48-4
IHC (International Homes of Cedar Inc)						
PO Box 886	Woodinville	WA	98072	**800-767-7674**	360-668-8511	105
iHealth Lab Inc						
719 N Shoreline Blvd	Mountain View	CA	94043	**855-816-7705**		732
iHeartMedia, Inc						
200 E Basse Rd	San Antonio	TX	78209	**888-283-6901**	210-822-2828	186
IHFRA (International Home Furnishings Representatives Assn)						
209 S Main St PO Box 670	High Point	NC	27261	**800-667-9506**	336-889-3920	48-18
IHI (Institute for Healthcare Improvement)						
20 University Rd Seventh Fl	Cambridge	MA	02138	**866-787-0831**	617-301-4800	48-8
IHLIC (Investors Heritage Life Insurance Co)						
200 Capital Ave PO Box 717	Frankfort	KY	40602	**800-422-2011**	502-223-2361	388-2
IHMM (Institute of Hazardous Materials Management)						
11900 Parklawn Dr Ste 450	Rockville	MD	20852	**800-437-0137**	301-984-8969	47-12
IHOP Corp						
450 N Brand Blvd	Glendale	CA	91203	**800-901-5248**	818-240-6055	661
IHRIM (International Assn for Human Resource Information Management Inc)						
PO Box 1086	Burlington	MA	01803	**800-804-3983**		48-12
IHRSA (International Health Racquet & Sportsclub Assn)						
70 Fargo St	Boston	MA	02210	**800-228-4772**	617-951-0055	47-22
IHS (International Hearing Society)						
16880 Middlebelt Rd Ste 4	Livonia	MI	48154	**800-521-5247**	734-522-7200	47-17
IHS Energy Group						
15 Inverness Way E	Englewood	CO	80112	**800-447-2273**	303-736-3000	179-10
IHS Inc						
321 Inverness Dr S	Englewood	CO	80112	**800-525-7052**	303-790-0600	179-11
NYSE: IHS						
IIABA (Independent Insurance Agents & Brokers of America Inc)						
127 S Peyton St	Alexandria	VA	22314	**800-221-7917**	703-683-4422	48-9
IID (Imperial Irrigation District)						
PO Box 937	Imperial	CA	92251	**800-303-7756**	760-482-9600	204
IIDA (International Interior Design Assn)						
222 Merchandise Mart Plz						
Ste 567	Chicago	IL	60654	**888-799-4432**	312-467-1950	47-4
IIE (Institute of Industrial Engineers)						
3577 PkwyLn Ste 200	Norcross	GA	30092	**800-494-0460***	770-449-0460	48-13
*Cust Svc						
IIG (Industrial Insulation Group LLC)						
2100 Line St	Brunswick	GA	31520	**800-334-7997**		386
III (Insurance Information Institute Inc)						
110 William St	New York	NY	10038	**877-263-7995**	212-346-5500	48-9
IIMC (International Institute of Municipal Clerks)						
8331 Utica Ave Ste 200	Rancho Cucamonga	CA	91730	**800-251-1639**	909-944-4162	48-7
IIS Group LLC						
1015 Virginia Dr						
Ste 1 W	Fort Washington	PA	19034	**855-443-5777**		176
IJO (Independent Jewelers Organization)						
136 Old Post Rd	Southport	CT	06890	**800-624-9252**		48-4
Ika-Works Inc						
2635 Northchase Pkwy SE	Wilmington	NC	28405	**800-733-3037**	910-452-7059	417
IKEA						
420 Alan Wood Rd	Conshohocken	PA	19428	**800-434-4532**	610-834-0180	320
Ikegami Electronics USA Inc						
37 Brook Ave	Maywood	NJ	07607	**800-368-9171**	201-368-9171	638
Il Fornaio America Corp						
770 Tamalpais Dr Ste 400	Corte Madera	CA	94925	**888-454-6246**	415-945-0500	661
ILC Dover Inc						
One Moonwalker Rd	Frederica	DE	19946	**800-631-9567**	302-335-3911	569
ILC Resources						
3301 106th Cir	Urbandale	IA	50322	**800-247-2133**	515-243-8106	498-3
iLeads.com LLC						
567 San Nicolas Dr						
Ste 180	Newport Beach	CA	92660	**877-245-3237**		224
Ilene Industries Inc						
301 Stanley Blvd	Shelbyville	TN	37160	**800-251-1602**	931-684-8731	325
Ilex Construction & Woodworking						
131 N Washington St Ste 400	Easton	MD	21601	**866-551-4539**	410-820-4393	676
Iliff School of Theology						
2201 S University Blvd	Denver	CO	80210	**800-678-3360**	303-744-1287	167-3

	Toll-Free	Phone	Class
Ilikai Hotel & Suites			
1777 Ala Moana Blvd .... Honolulu HI 96815	866-536-7973	808-949-3811	376
iLinc Communications Inc			
2999 N 44th St Ste 650 .... Phoenix AZ 85018	800-767-9054	602-952-1200	177
Child Support Enforcement Div			
509 S Sixth St .... Springfield IL 62701	800-447-4278		337-14
Illinois			
Crime Victims Services Div			
100 W Randolf Rd 13th Fl .... Chicago IL 60601	800-228-3368	312-814-2581	337-14
Human Services Dept			
100 S Grand Ave E 3rd Fl .... Springfield IL 62762	800-843-6154	217-557-1601	337-14
Mental Health Div			
100 W Randolf St Ste 3-400 .... Chicago IL 60601	800-252-2923	312-814-2811	337-14
Revenue Dept			
101 W Jefferson St .... Springfield IL 62702	800-732-8866	217-782-3336	337-14
Secretary of State			
213 State Capitol .... Springfield IL 62756	800-252-8980	217-782-2201	337-14
Tourism Bureau			
100 W Randolph St Ste 3-400 .... Chicago IL 60601	800-226-6632	312-814-4732	337-14
Veterans Affairs Dept			
James R. Thompson Ctr 100 W Randolph Ste 5-570 .... Chicago IL 60601	800-437-9824	312-814-5391	337-14
Workers' Compensation Commission			
100 W Randolph St 8th Fl .... Chicago IL 60601	866-352-3033	312-814-6611	337-14
Illinois Auto Electric Co			
700 Enterprise St .... Aurora IL 60504	800-683-8484	630-862-3300	382
Illinois Capacitor Inc			
3757 W Touhy Ave .... Lincolnwood IL 60712	800-263-9275	847-675-1760	253
Illinois College			
1101 W College Ave .... Jacksonville IL 62650	866-464-5265*	217-245-3030	166
*Admissions			
Illinois Fair Plan Association			
130 East Randolph Ste 1050. .... Chicago IL 60601	800-972-4480	312-861-0385	681
Illinois Glove Co			
3701 Commercial Ave .... Northbrook IL 60062	800-342-5458	847-291-1700	153-7
Chicago			
350 N Orleans St Ste 136-L .... Chicago IL 60654	800-351-3450	312-280-3500	162
Illinois Institute of Art			
Schaumburg			
1000 N Plz Dr .... Schaumburg IL 60173	800-314-3450	847-619-3450	162
Illinois Institute of Technology			
10 W 33rd St .... Chicago IL 60616	800-448-2329	312-567-3025	166
Illinois International Port District			
3600 E 95th St .... Chicago IL 60617	800-843-7678	773-646-4400	611
Illinois Lottery			
101 W Jefferson St .... Springfield IL 62702	800-252-1775	217-524-6435	447
Illinois Mutual Life Insurance Co			
300 SW Adams St .... Peoria IL 61634	800-380-6688	309-674-8255	388-2
Illinois State Bar Assn			
424 S Second St .... Springfield IL 62701	800-252-8908	217-525-1760	71
Illinois State Dental Society			
1010 S Second St .... Springfield IL 62704	888-286-2447	217-525-1406	227
Illinois State Medical Inter-Insurance Exchange (ISMIE)			
20 N Michigan Ave Ste 700 .... Chicago IL 60602	800-782-4767	312-782-2749	388-5
Illinois State Medical Society			
20 N Michigan Ave Ste 700 .... Chicago IL 60602	800-782-4767	312-782-1654	469
Illinois State Military Museum			
1301 N MacArthur Blvd Ste 30 .... Springfield IL 62702	800-732-8868	217-761-3910	513
Illinois State University			
North and School Streets Hovey Hall 201 .... Normal IL 61790	800-366-2478*	309-438-2111	166
*Admissions			
Illinois Student Assistance Commission			
1755 Lake Cook Rd .... Deerfield IL 60015	800-899-4722	847-948-8500	716
Illinois Symphony Orchestera			
524 E Capitol Ave .... Springfield IL 62701	800-401-7222	217-522-2838	566-3
Illinois Tool Works Inc TACC Div			
56 Air Stn Industrial Pk .... Rockland MA 02370	888-751-0409*		3
*Hotline			
Illinois Veterans Home-Anna			
792 N Main St .... Anna IL 62906	888-261-3336	618-833-6302	781
Illinois Wesleyan University			
1312 Pk St .... Bloomington IL 61701	800-332-2498*	309-556-3031	166
*Admissions			
Illinois Wholesale Cash Register Inc			
2790 Pinnacle Dr .... Elgin IL 60124	800-544-5493	847-310-4200	111
Illumina Inc			
9885 Towne Centre Dr .... San Diego CA 92121	800-809-4566	858-202-4500	416
NASDAQ: ILMN			
ILS (International Launch Services)			
1875 Explorer St Ste 700 .... Reston VA 20190	800-852-4980	571-633-7400	499
ILSCO			
4730 Madison Rd .... Cincinnati OH 45227	800-776-9775*	513-533-6200	802
*Sales			
ILX Lightwave Corp			
31950 E Frontage Rd .... Bozeman MT 59715	800-459-9459	406-586-1244	248
IM (IEEE Instrumentation & Measurement Society)			
445 Hoes Ln .... Piscataway NJ 08854	800-327-6677	732-562-3844	48-19
IMA (Institute of Management Accountants Inc)			
10 Paragon Dr Ste 1 .... Montvale NJ 07645	800-638-4427	201-573-9000	48-1
Image Labs International			
PO Box 1545 .... Belgrade MT 59714	800-785-5995	406-585-7225	179-8
Image One Corp			
13201 Capital Ave .... Oak Park MI 48237	800-799-5377	248-414-9955	620
Image Works			
PO Box 443 .... Woodstock NY 12498	800-475-8801	845-679-8500	586
ImageWare Systems Inc			
10815 Rancho BernaRdo Rd Ste 310 .... San Diego CA 92127	800-842-4199	858-673-8600	179-10
ImageWorks			
250 Clearbrook Rd .... Elmsford NY 10523	800-592-6666	914-592-6100	379
Imagination Publishing			
600 W Fulton St Ste 600. .... Chicago IL 60661	800-482-0776	312-887-1000	628-10
Imaging Business Machines LLC			
2750 Crestwood Blvd .... Birmingham AL 35210	800-627-2269	205-439-7100	110
Imaging Diagnostic Systems Inc			
6531 NW 18th Ct .... Plantation FL 33313	800-992-9008	954-581-9800	379
OTC: IMDS			
Imaging Healthcare Specialists Medical Group Inc			
6256 Greenwich Dr Ste 150 .... San Diego CA 92122	866-558-4320		412
iMakeNews Inc			
200 Fifth Ave .... Waltham MA 02451	866-964-6397	781-890-4700	181

	Toll-Free	Phone	Class
I-many Inc			
1735 Market St 37th Fl. .... Philadelphia PA 19103	877-774-2451	215-344-1900	179-1
Imation Corp			
One Imation Pl .... Oakdale MN 55128	888-466-3456	651-704-4000	649
NYSE: IMN			
IMBA (International Mountain Bicycling Assn)			
207 Canyon Blvd Ste 301 PO Box 7578. .... Boulder CO 80306	888-442-4622	303-545-9011	47-23
IMC (InterAmerican Motor Corp)			
8901 Canoga Ave .... Canoga Park CA 91304	800-874-8925	818-678-1200	60
IMC (International Medical Corps)			
1919 Santa Monica Blvd Ste 400 .... Santa Monica CA 90404	800-481-4462	310-826-7800	47-5
IMC Networks Corp			
19772 Pauling .... Foothill Ranch CA 92610	800-624-1070	949-465-3000	177
IMC USA (Institute of Management Consultants USA Inc)			
2025 M St NW Ste 800. .... Washington DC 20036	800-221-2557	202-367-1134	48-12
IMCA (Investment Management Consultants Assn)			
5619 DTC Pkwy Ste 500. ...... Greenwood Village CO 80111	800-250-9083	303-770-3377	48-2
IMCOR-Interstate Mechanical Corp			
1841 E Washington St .... Phoenix AZ 85034	800-628-0211	602-257-1319	190-10
IMCU (Indiana Members Credit Union)			
7110 W Tenth St .... Indianapolis IN 46214	800-556-9268	317-248-8556	219
IME (Institute of Makers of Explosives)			
1120 19th St NW Ste 310. .... Washington DC 20036	800-461-8841	202-429-9280	48-13
Imecom Group			
Eight Governor Wentworth Hwy .... Wolfeboro NH 03894	800-329-9099	603-569-0600	179-7
Imedex Inc			
4325 Alexander Dr .... Alpharetta GA 30022	800-243-6969	770-751-7332	788
iMemories			
9181 E Bell Rd .... Scottsdale AZ 85260	800-845-7986		581
Imerys USA Inc			
100 Mansell Ct E Ste 300. .... Roswell GA 30076	800-374-3224	770-645-3300	498-2
IMETCO (Innovative Metals Company Inc)			
4648 S Old Peachtree Rd .... Norcross GA 30084	800-646-3826	770-908-1030	45
iMethods LLC			
10748 Deerwood Park Blvd Ste 150 .... Jacksonville FL 32256	888-306-2261		197
IMG (International Motor Coach Group Inc)			
8695 College Blvd Ste 260. .... Overland Park KS 66210	888-447-3466	913-906-0111	48-21
Imh Financial Corp			
4900 N Scottsdale Rd Ste 5000 .... Scottsdale AZ 85251	800-510-6445	480-840-8400	216
IMI (International Masonry Institute)			
42 E St .... Annapolis MD 21401	800-803-0295	410-280-1305	48-3
IMI Cornelius Inc			
101 Broadway St W .... Osseo MN 55369	800-238-3600	763-488-8200	655
IMI Data Search Inc			
275 E Hillcrest Dr Ste 102 .... Thousand Oaks CA 91360	800-860-7779	805-495-1149	626
IMLA (International Municipal Lawyers Assn)			
7910 Woodmont Ave Ste 1440. ...... Bethesda MD 20814	800-942-7732	202-466-5424	48-10
Immaculata University			
1145 King Rd .... Immaculata PA 19345	877-428-6329	610-647-4400	166
Immediatek Inc(NDA)			
Ste 200 3301 Airport Fwy .... Bedford TX 76021	888-661-6565		224
Immersion Corp			
30 Rio Robles .... San Jose CA 95134	877-223-6273	408-467-1900	174-2
NASDAQ: IMMR			
Immtech Pharmaceuticals			
One N End Ave .... New York NY 10282	877-898-8038	212-791-2911	576
ImmucorGamma Inc			
3130 Gateway Dr PO Box 5625. .... Norcross GA 30091	800-829-2553*	770-441-2051	231
NASDAQ: BLUD ■ *Cust Svc*			
Immune Deficiency Foundation (IDF)			
40 W Chesapeake Ave Ste 308 .... Towson MD 21204	800-296-4433	410-321-6647	47-17
Immuno Concepts NA Ltd			
9825 Goethe Rd Ste 350. .... Sacramento CA 95827	800-251-5115	916-363-2649	732
ImmunoDiagnostics Inc			
One Presidential Way Ste 104. .... Woburn MA 01801	800-573-1700	781-938-6300	231
Immunomedics Inc			
300 American Rd .... Morris Plains NJ 07950	800-327-7211	973-605-8200	84
NASDAQ: IMMU			
Immuno-Mycologics Inc (IMMY)			
2700 Technology Pl .... Norman OK 73071	800-654-3639		231
Immunovision Inc			
1820 Ford Ave .... Springdale AR 72764	800-541-0960	479-751-7005	231
IMMVAC Inc			
6080 Bass Ln .... Columbia MO 65201	800-944-7563	573-443-5363	575
IMMY (Immuno-Mycologics Inc)			
2700 Technology Pl .... Norman OK 73071	800-654-3639		231
Imo Pump			
1710 Airport Rd .... Monroe NC 28110	800-405-0148	704-289-6511	632
iMomentous			
20 Gibraltar Rd Ste 109 .... Horsham PA 19044	888-985-7755		197
Impac Mortgage Holdings Inc			
19500 Jamboree Rd .... Irvine CA 92612	800-597-4101	949-475-3600	645
NYSE: IMH			
Impact Drug & Alcohol Treatment Ctr			
1680 N Fair Oaks Ave PO Box 93607. .... Pasadena CA 91103	866-734-4200	626-798-0884	717
Impact Guns			
2710 South 1900 West .... Ogden UT 84401	888-505-3086	801-393-2474	674
Impact Label Corp			
3434 S Burdick St .... Kalamazoo MI 49001	800-820-0362	269-381-4280	410
Impact Products LLC			
2840 Centennial Rd .... Toledo OH 43617	800-333-1541*	419-841-2891	149
*Cust Svc			
Impact Seven Inc			
147 Le Almena Dr .... Almena WI 54805	800-685-9353	715-357-3334	399
Impax Laboratories Inc			
3735 Castor Ave .... Philadelphia PA 19124	877-994-6729	215-613-2400	577
NASDAQ: IPXL			
Imperial Bedding Co			
720 11th St PO Box 5347. .... Huntington WV 25703	800-529-3321	304-529-3321	466
Imperial Finance & Trading			
701 Pk of Commerce Blvd Ste 301 .... Boca Raton FL 33487	888-364-6775		214
Imperial Graphics Inc			
3100 Walkent Dr NW .... Grand Rapids MI 49544	800-777-2591		109
Imperial Industries Inc			
505 Industrial Pk Ave .... Rothschild WI 54474	800-558-2945	715-359-0200	104
Imperial Irrigation District (IID)			
PO Box 937 .... Imperial CA 92251	800-303-7756	760-482-9600	204

Name / Address	City	State	ZIP	Toll-Free	Phone	Class
Imperial of Waikiki						
205 Lewers St	Honolulu	HI	96815	**800-347-2582**	808-923-1827	376
Imperial Oil Resources Ltd						
237 Fourth Ave SW						
PO Box 2480 Stn M	Calgary	AB	T2P3M9	**800-567-3776**		573
Imperial PFS (UPAC)						
8245 Nieman Rd	Lenexa	KS	66214	**800-877-7848**	913-894-6150	216
Imperial Pools Inc						
33 Wade Rd	Latham	NY	12110	**800-444-9977**	518-786-1200	719
Imperial Theatre						
249 W 45th St	New York	NY	10036	**800-447-7400**	212-239-6200	736
Imperial Trading Co Inc						
701 Edwards Ave PO Box 23508	Elmwood	LA	70123	**800-775-4504***	504-733-1400	296-8
*Cust Svc						
Imperial Woodworks Inc						
7201 Mars Dr PO Box 7835	Waco	TX	76714	**800-234-6624**		318-3
Impinj Inc						
701 N 34th St Ste 300	Seattle	WA	98103	**866-467-4650**	206-517-5300	687
Implant Sciences Corp						
500 Research Dr	Wilmington	MA	01887	**877-732-7333**	978-752-1700	471
OTC: IMSC						
Impo International Inc						
PO Box 639	Santa Maria	CA	93456	**800-367-4676**	805-922-7753	300
Imprimis Group Inc						
4835 Lyndon B Johnson Fwy	Dallas	TX	75244	**888-772-9682**	972-419-1700	341
Improved Construction Methods						
1040 N Redmond Rd	Jacksonville	AR	72076	**877-494-5793**		355
IMS Inc						
340 Progress Dr	Manchester	CT	06040	**800-264-9837***	860-649-4415	246
*General						
IMSA (International Municipal Signal Assn)						
165 E Union St PO Box 539	Newark	NY	14513	**800-723-4672**	315-331-2182	48-7
IMT (Iowa Mold Tooling Co Inc)						
500 W US Hwy 18	Garner	IA	50438	**800-247-5958**	641-923-3711	465
IMT Group, The						
PO Box 1336	Des Moines	IA	50266	**800-274-3531**		388-4
In Defense of Animals (IDA)						
3010 Kerner Blvd	San Rafael	CA	94901	**800-705-0425**	415-448-0048	47-3
In The Swim Inc						
320 Industrial Dr	West Chicago	IL	60185	**800-288-7946**	630-876-0040	702
INA (Idaho Nurses Assn)						
1850 E Southern Ave Ste 1	Tempe	AZ	85224	**888-721-8904**	404-760-2803	526
Inc Magazine						
7 World Trade Ctr	New York	NY	10007	**800-234-0999**	212-389-5377	452-5
Inca Engineers Inc						
400 112th Ave NE Ste 400	Bellevue	WA	98004	**800-825-4622**	425-635-1000	195
Incentive Publications Inc						
2400 Crestmoor Dr	Nashville	TN	37215	**800-967-5325***	615-385-2934	243
*Mktg						
Incline Village/Crystal Bay Visitors Bureau						
969 Tahoe Blvd	Incline Village	NV	89451	**800-468-2463**	775-832-1606	207
InComm Conferencing Inc						
208 Harristown Rd Ste 101	Glen Rock	NJ	07452	**877-804-2062**		384
Incontact Inc						
7730 S Union Pk Ave						
Ste 500	Salt Lake City	UT	84047	**800-363-6177**	801-320-3200	179-11
NASDAQ: SAAS						
Indaco Metal						
Three American Way	Shawnee	OK	74804	**877-300-7334**		105
Indeck Power Equipment Co						
1111 Willis Ave	Wheeling	IL	60090	**800-446-3325**	847-541-8300	382
Indelco Plastics Corp						
6530 Cambridge St	Minneapolis	MN	55426	**800-486-6456**	952-925-5075	598-2
Indel-Davis Inc						
4401 S Jackson Ave	Tulsa	OK	74107	**800-331-6300**	918-587-2151	532
Indemnity Company of California						
17780 Fitch Ste 200	Irvine	CA	92614	**800-782-1546**	949-263-3300	388-5
Independence Blue Cross						
1901 Market St	Philadelphia	PA	19103	**800-275-2583**		388-3
Independence Community College						
1057 W College Ave						
PO Box 708	Independence	KS	67301	**800-842-6063**	620-331-4100	160
Independence Ctr						
2035 Independence Ctr Dr	Independence	MO	64057	**877-746-6642**	816-795-8600	455
Independence Excavating Inc						
5720 Schaaf Rd	Independence	OH	44131	**800-524-3478**	216-524-1700	190-5
Independent Bank Corp						
230 W Main St PO Box 491	Ionia	MI	48846	**888-300-3193**	616-527-2400	357-2
NASDAQ: IBCP						
Independent Charities of America (ICA)						
1100 Larkspur Landing Cir						
Ste 340	Larkspur	CA	94939	**800-477-0733**	415-925-2600	47-5
Independent Chemical Corp						
79-51 Cooper Ave	Glendale	NY	11385	**800-892-2578**	718-894-0700	144
Independent Community Bankers of America (ICBA)						
1615 L St NW Ste 900	Washington	DC	20036	**800-422-8439**	202-659-8111	48-2
Independent Community Bankers of America PAC						
1615 L St Ste 900	Washington	DC	20036	**800-422-8439**	202-659-8111	608
Independent Electric Supply Inc						
1370 Bayport Ave	San Carlos	CA	94070	**855-437-4968**	650-594-9440	246
Independent Health						
511 Farber Lakes Dr	Buffalo	NY	14221	**800-247-1466**	716-631-3001	388-3
Independent Ink Inc						
13700 Gramercy Pl	Gardena	CA	90249	**800-446-5538**	310-523-4657	385
Independent Institute						
100 Swan Way	Oakland	CA	94621	**800-927-8733**	510-632-1366	625
Independent Insurance Agents & Brokers of America Inc (IIABA)						
127 S Peyton St	Alexandria	VA	22314	**800-221-7917**	703-683-4422	48-9
Independent Jewelers Organization (IJO)						
136 Old Post Rd	Southport	CT	06890	**800-624-9252**		48-4
Independent Order of Foresters (IOF)						
789 Don Mills Rd	Toronto	ON	M3C1T9	**800-828-1540**	416-429-3000	47-5
Independent Order of Odd Fellows						
422 N Trade St	Winston-Salem	NC	27101	**800-235-8358**	336-725-5955	47-15
Independent Petroleum Assn of America (IPAA)						
1201 15th St NW Ste 300	Washington	DC	20005	**800-433-2851**	202-857-4722	47-12
Independent Protection Company Inc						
1607 S Main St	Goshen	IN	46526	**800-860-8388**	574-533-4116	802
Independent Publishers Group						
814 N Franklin St	Chicago	IL	60610	**800-888-4741***	312-337-0747	94
*Orders						
Independent Publishing Co						
1000 Williamston Rd	Anderson	SC	29621	**800-859-6397**	864-224-4321	628-8
Independent Record						
317 Cruse Ave	Helena	MT	59601	**800-523-2272**	406-447-4000	525-2
Independent Sector						
1602 L St NW Ste 900	Washington	DC	20036	**888-737-9477**	202-467-6100	47-5
Independent Television Service (ITVS)						
651 Brannan St Ste 410	San Francisco	CA	94107	**800-621-6196**	415-356-8383	731
Independent, The						
2250 First St	Livermore	CA	94550	**877-952-3588**	925-447-8700	525-4
Indera Mills Co						
350 W Maple St PO Box 309	Yadkinville	NC	27055	**800-334-8605**	336-679-4440	153-17
Index Fresh Inc						
18184 Slover Ave	Bloomington	CA	92316	**800-352-6931**	909-877-0999	11-1
India						
Consulate General						
540 Arguello Blvd	San Francisco	CA	94118	**866-978-0055**	415-668-0662	257
India Tourist Office						
1270 Ave of the Americas						
Ste 303	New York	NY	10020	**800-425-1414***	212-586-4901	765
*General						
Indian Arts & Crafts Board						
Dept of the Interior 1849 C St NW						
MS 2528-MIB	Washington	DC	20240	**888-278-3253**	202-208-3773	338-18
Indian Bible College						
2918 N Aris Ave	Flagstaff	AZ	86004	**866-503-7789**	928-774-3890	166
Indian Capital Technology Ctr						
2403 N 41st St E	Muskogee	OK	74403	**800-757-0877**	918-687-6383	788
Indian Creek Fabricators						
1350 Commerce Pk Dr	Tipp City	OH	45371	**877-769-5880**	937-667-5818	747
Indian Electric Co-op Inc						
2506 E Hwy 64	Cleveland	OK	74020	**800-482-2750**	918-358-2514	245
Indian Harvest Specialtifoods Inc						
1012 Paul Bunyan Dr SE	Bemidji	MN	56601	**800-346-7032***		295-23
*Orders						
Indian Head Industries Inc						
8530 Cliff Cameron Dr	Charlotte	NC	28269	**800-527-1534**	704-547-7411	59
Indian Head Industries Inc MGM Brakes Div						
8530 Cliff Cameron Dr	Charlotte	NC	28269	**800-527-1534**	704-547-7411	59
Indian Hills Community College						
525 Grandview Ave	Ottumwa	IA	52501	**800-726-2585**	641-683-5111	160
Indian Lakes Resort						
250 W Schick Rd	Bloomingdale	IL	60108	**800-334-3417**	630-529-0200	660
Indian Point Resort						
71 Dogwood Pk Trl	Branson	MO	65616	**800-888-1891**	417-338-2250	660
Indian Pueblo Cultural Ctr						
2401 12th St NW	Albuquerque	NM	87104	**866-855-7902**	505-843-7270	513
Indian River County Chamber of Commerce						
1216 21st St	Vero Beach	FL	32960	**888-703-8130**	772-567-3491	137
Indian River Estates						
2250 Indian Creek Blvd W	Vero Beach	FL	32966	**800-544-0277***	772-562-7400	663
*Mktg						
Indian River Lifesaving Station Museum						
25039 Costal Hwy	Rehoboth Beach	DE	19971	**877-987-2757**	302-227-6991	513
Indian River State College (IRSC)						
3209 Virginia Ave	Fort Pierce	FL	34981	**866-792-4772**	772-462-4772	160
Indian River Transport Co						
2580 Executive Rd	Winter Haven	FL	33884	**800-877-2430**	863-324-2430	770
Indian Springs Resort & Spa						
1712 Lincoln Ave	Calistoga	CA	94515	**800-877-3623**	707-942-4913	660
Indian Springs School						
190 Woodward Dr	Pelham	AL	35124	**888-843-9477***	205-988-3350	615
*General						
Indian Summer Carpet Mills Inc						
601 Callahan Rd PO Box 3577	Dalton	GA	30719	**800-824-4010**	706-277-6277	130
Indian Temple Mound Museum						
107 Miracle Strip						
Pkwy SW	Fort Walton Beach	FL	32548	**866-847-1301**	850-833-9500	513
Indian Trails Inc						
109 E Comstock St	Owosso	MI	48867	**800-292-3831**	989-725-5105	106
Indian Valley Industries Inc						
PO Box 810	Johnson City	NY	13790	**800-659-5111**	607-729-5111	66
Indian Wells Resort Hotel						
76-661 Hwy 111	Indian Wells	CA	92210	**800-248-3220**	760-345-6466	660
Child Support Bureau						
402 W Washington St	Indianapolis	IN	46204	**800-840-8757**	317-232-2350	337-15
Consumer Protection Div						
402 W Washington St 5th Fl	Indianapolis	IN	46204	**800-382-5516**	317-232-6330	337-15
Disability Aging & Rehabilitative Services Div						
402 W Washington St						
Rm W451	Indianapolis	IN	46204	**800-545-7763**	317-232-1147	337-15
Indiana						
Environmental Management Dept						
100 N Senate Ave Rm 1301	Indianapolis	IN	46204	**800-451-6027**	317-232-8611	337-15
General Assembly						
State House						
200 W Washington St	Indianapolis	IN	46204	**800-382-9842**	317-232-9600	337-15
Insurance Dept						
311 W Washington St						
Ste 300	Indianapolis	IN	46204	**800-622-4461***	317-232-2385	337-15
*Cust Svc						
State Government Information						
402 W Washington St						
Rm W160A	Indianapolis	IN	46204	**800-457-8283**	317-233-0800	337-15
State Parks & Reservoirs Div						
402 W Washington St						
Rm W298	Indianapolis	IN	46204	**800-622-4931**	317-232-4124	337-15
Tourism Development Office						
1 N Capitol Ave Ste 100	Indianapolis	IN	46204	**800-457-8283**	317-232-8860	337-15
Victims Services Div						
101 West Washington Street						
Suite 1170	East Tower Indianapolis	IN	46204	**800-353-1484**	317-232-1233	337-15
Indiana Assn of Realtors						
7301 N Shadeland Ave Ste A	Indianapolis	IN	46250	**800-284-0084**	317-842-0890	647
Indiana Beach						
5224 E Indiana Beach Rd	Monticello	IN	47960	**800-583-4306**	574-583-4141	32
Indiana County						
350 N Fourth St	Indiana	PA	15701	**888-559-6355**	724-465-3805	336
Indiana County Tourist Bureau						
2334 Oakland Ave Ste 68	Indiana	PA	15701	**877-746-3426**	724-463-7505	207
Indiana Credit Union League						
5975 Castle Creek Parkway N						
Ste 300	Indianapolis	IN	46250	**800-285-5300**	317-594-5300	219
Indiana Democratic Party						
115 W Washington St						
Ste 1165	Indianapolis	IN	46204	**800-223-3387**	317-231-7100	609-1

				Toll-Free	Phone	Class
Indiana Dental Assn						
401 W Michigan St	Indianapolis	IN	46202	**800-562-5646**	317-634-2610	227
INDIANA DONOR NETWORK						
3760 Guion Rd	Indianapolis	IN	46222	**888-275-4676**	317-685-0389	538
Indiana Dunes the Casual Coast						
1215 N State Rd 49	Porter	IN	46304	**800-283-8687**	219-926-2255	207
Indiana Farm Bureau Insurance Co						
225 SE St PO Box 1250	Indianapolis	IN	46206	**800-723-3276**	317-692-7200	388-2
Indiana Farmers Mutual Insurance Co						
10 W 106th St	Indianapolis	IN	46290	**800-666-6460**	317-846-4211	388-4
Indiana Fever						
Conseco Fieldhouse						
125 S Pennsylvania St	Indianapolis	IN	46204	**877-275-9007**	317-917-2500	705-2
Indiana Furniture						
1224 Mill St	Jasper	IN	47546	**800-422-5727**	812-482-5727	318-1
Indiana Lottery						
201 S Capitol Ave Ste 1100	Indianapolis	IN	46225	**800-955-6886**	317-264-4800	337-15
Indiana Members Credit Union (IMCU)						
7110 W Tenth St	Indianapolis	IN	46214	**800-556-9268**	317-248-8556	219
Indiana Pharmacists Alliance						
729 N Pennsylvania St	Indianapolis	IN	46204	**800-516-0313**	317-634-4968	578
Indiana Port Commission						
150 W Market St Ste 100	Indianapolis	IN	46204	**800-232-7678**	317-232-9200	611
Indiana Republican Party						
47 S Meridian St Ste 200	Indianapolis	IN	46204	**800-466-1087**	317-635-7561	609-2
Indiana Ribbon Inc						
106 N Second St	Wolcott	IN	47995	**800-531-3100**	219-279-2112	541
Indiana State Medical Assn						
322 Canal Walk	Indianapolis	IN	46202	**800-257-4762**	317-261-2060	469
Indiana State University						
200 N Seventh St	Terre Haute	IN	47809	**800-468-6478**		166
Indiana Students Assistance Commission						
150 W Market St Ste 500	Indianapolis	IN	46204	**888-528-4719**	317-232-2350	716
Indiana Tech						
1600 E Washington Blvd	Fort Wayne	IN	46803	**800-937-2448**	260-422-5561	166
Indiana University						
East						
2325 Chester Blvd	Richmond	IN	47374	**800-959-3278**	765-973-8208	166
Kokomo						
2300 S Washington St PO Box 9003	Kokomo	IN	46904	**888-875-4485**	765-455-9217	166
Northwest 3400 Broadway	Gary	IN	46408	**888-968-7486**	219-980-6500	166
South Bend						
1700 Mishawaka Ave						
PO Box 7111	South Bend	IN	46634	**877-462-4872**	574-520-4870	166
Indiana University Cancer Ctr Bone Marrow & Stem Cell Transplant Team						
550 N University Blvd	Indianapolis	IN	46202	**888-600-4822**	317-948-6997	759
Indiana University Hospital						
550 N University Blvd	Indianapolis	IN	46202	**800-248-1199**	317-274-5000	371-3
Indiana University of Pennsylvania						
1011 S Dr Sutton Hall Ste 117	Indiana	PA	15705	**800-442-6830**	724-357-2230	166
Indiana University of Pennsylvania Stapleton Library						
431 S 11th St	Indiana	PA	15705	**888-342-2383**	724-357-2340	431-6
Indiana University Press						
601 N Morton St	Bloomington	IN	47404	**800-842-6796**	812-855-8817	628-4
Indiana University-Purdue University						
Fort Wayne						
2101 E Coliseum Blvd	Fort Wayne	IN	46805	**800-324-4739**	260-481-6100	166
Indiana University-Purdue University Indianapolis						
Library						
755 W Michigan St	Indianapolis	IN	46202	**888-422-0499**	317-274-0462	431-6
Indiana Veterinary Medical Assn						
201 S Capitol Ave Ste 405	Indianapolis	IN	46225	**800-270-0747**	317-974-0888	783
Indiana Wesleyan University						
4201 S Washington St	Marion	IN	46953	**800-332-6901**	765-677-2138	166
Indiana Workforce Development Dept						
10 N Senate Ave	Indianapolis	IN	46204	**800-891-6499**	317-232-7670	259
Indianapolis Business Journal						
41 E Washington St Ste 200	Indianapolis	IN	46204	**800-428-7081**	317-634-6200	452-5
Indianapolis Colts						
7001 W 56th St	Indianapolis	IN	46254	**800-805-2658**	317-297-2658	706-3
Indianapolis Convention & Visitors Assn						
200 S Capitol Ave Ste 300	Indianapolis	IN	46225	**800-862-6912**	317-262-3000	207
Indianapolis Fruit Company Inc						
4501 Massachusetts Ave	Indianapolis	IN	46218	**800-377-2425**	317-546-2425	296-7
Indianapolis Monthly Magazine						
40 Monument Cir Ste 100	Indianapolis	IN	46204	**888-403-9005***	317-237-9288	452-22
*Circ						
Indianapolis Star						
307 N Pennsylvania St	Indianapolis	IN	46204	**800-669-7827**	317-444-4000	525-2
Indianapolis Symphony Orchestra						
45 Monument Cir	Indianapolis	IN	46204	**800-366-8457**	317-262-1100	566-3
Indianhead Federated Library System						
1538 Truax Blvd	Eau Claire	WI	54703	**800-321-5427**	715-839-5082	431-3
Indianhead Mountain Resort						
500 Indianhead Rd	Wakefield	MI	49968	**800-346-3426**		660
Indigo Books & Music Inc						
468 King St W Ste 500	Toronto	ON	M5V1L8	**800-832-7569***	416-364-4499	95
NYSE: IDG ■ *Cust Svc						
Indigo Inn						
One Maiden Ln	Charleston	SC	29401	**800-845-7639**	843-577-5900	376
Indio Chamber of Commerce						
82921 Indio Blvd	Indio	CA	92201	**800-464-7928**	760-347-0676	137
Individual Software Inc						
4255 HopyaRd Rd Ste 2	Pleasanton	CA	94588	**800-822-3522**	925-734-6767	179-3
Indoff Inc						
11816 Lackland Rd	Saint Louis	MO	63146	**800-486-7867**	314-997-1122	382
Indoor Purification Systems Inc						
Surround Air Div						
334 N Marshall Way Ste C	Layton	UT	84041	**888-812-1516**	801-547-1162	17
Inductoheat Inc						
32251 N Avis Dr	Madison Heights	MI	48071	**800-624-6297**	248-585-9393	317
Inductotherm Group						
10 Indel Ave PO Box 157	Rancocas	NJ	08073	**800-257-9527**	609-267-9000	317
Indus International Inc						
340 S Oak St PO Box 890	West Salem	WI	54669	**800-843-9377**	608-786-0300	491
Indusco Group						
1200 W Hamburg St	Baltimore	MD	21230	**800-727-0665**	410-727-0665	465
Industrial Alliance Insurance & Financial Services						
1080 Grande Allee W						
PO Box 1907 Stn Therminus	Quebec City	QC	G1K7M3	**800-463-6236**	418-684-5000	388-2
Industrial Battery & Charger Inc						
5831 Orr Rd	Charlotte	NC	28213	**800-833-8412**	704-597-7330	73
Industrial Brush Company Inc						
105 Clinton Rd	Fairfield	NJ	07004	**800-241-9860**	973-575-0455	102

				Toll-Free	Phone	Class
Industrial Chemicals Inc						
2042 Montreat Dr	Vestavia	AL	35216	**800-476-2042***	205-823-7330	144
*Cust Svc						
Industrial Container Services						
7152 First Ave S	Seattle	WA	98108	**800-273-3786**	206-763-2345	199
Industrial Contractors Inc						
701 Ch Dr	Bismarck	ND	58501	**800-467-3089**	701-258-9908	190-10
Industrial Controls Distributors Inc (ICD)						
1776 Bloomsbury Ave	Ocean	NJ	07712	**800-281-4788***	732-918-9000	382
*Sales						
Industrial Custom Products Inc						
2801 37th Ave NE	Minneapolis	MN	55421	**800-654-0886**	612-781-2255	325
Industrial Data Systems Inc						
3822 E La Palma Ave	Anaheim	CA	92807	**800-854-3311**	714-921-9212	675
Industrial Diesel Inc						
8705 Harmon Rd	Fort Worth	TX	76177	**800-323-3659**	817-232-1071	382
Industrial Door Company Inc						
360 Coon Rapids Blvd	Minneapolis	MN	55433	**888-798-0199**	763-786-4730	236
Industrial Dynamics Company Ltd						
3100 Fujita St	Torrance	CA	90505	**888-434-5832**	310-325-5633	467
Industrial Electric Wire & Cable Inc (IEWC)						
5001 S Towne Dr	New Berlin	WI	53151	**800-344-2323**	262-782-2323	246
Industrial Fabrics Assn International (IFAI)						
1801 County Rd 'B' W	Roseville	MN	55113	**800-225-4324**	651-222-2508	48-13
Industrial Gasket & Shim Company Inc (IGS)						
200 Country Club Rd	Meadow Lands	PA	15347	**800-229-1447**	724-222-5800	325
Industrial Insulation Group LLC (IIG)						
2100 Line St	Brunswick	GA	31520	**800-334-7997**		386
Industrial Louvers Inc						
511 Seventh St S	Delano	MN	55328	**800-328-3421**	763-972-2981	688
Industrial Paper Tube Inc						
1335 E Bay Ave	Bronx	NY	10474	**800-345-0960**		124
Industrial Piping Inc						
800 Culp Rd	Pineville	NC	28134	**800-951-0988**	704-588-1100	190-10
Industrial Power & Lighting Corp						
701 Seneca St Ste 500	Buffalo	NY	14210	**800-639-3702**	716-854-1811	190-4
Industrial Scientific Corp						
7848 Steubenville Pk	Oakdale	PA	15071	**800-338-3287**	412-788-4353	202
Industrial Steel Treating Inc						
613 Carroll St	Jackson	MI	49202	**800-253-9534**		479
Industrial Supply Solutions Inc						
520 Elizabeth St	Charleston	WV	25311	**800-346-5341**	304-346-5341	382
Industrial Tectonics Inc						
7222 Huron River Dr	Dexter	MI	48130	**800-482-2255**	734-426-4681	480
Industrial Timber & Lumber Corp (ITL)						
23925 Commerce Pk Rd	Beachwood	OH	44122	**800-829-9663**	216-831-3140	674
Industrial Tool Inc						
9210 52nd Ave N	New Hope	MN	55428	**800-776-4455***	763-533-7244	449
*Sales						
Industrial Tools Inc (ITI)						
1111 S Rose Ave	Oxnard	CA	93033	**800-266-5561**	805-483-1111	488
Industrial Towel & Uniform Inc						
2700 S 160th St	New Berlin	WI	53151	**800-767-2487**	262-782-1950	438
Industrial Tube & Steel Corp						
4658 Crystal Pkwy	Kent	OH	44240	**800-662-9567**	330-474-5530	681
Industrial Welders & Machinists Inc						
610 Opperman Dr	Eagan	MN	55123	**800-455-4565**		798
Industries for the Blind						
445 S Curtis Rd	West Allis	WI	53214	**800-642-8778**	414-778-3040	102
Industronics Service Co						
489 Sullivan Ave						
PO Box 649	South Windsor	CT	06074	**800-878-1551**	860-289-1551	317
Industry Specific Solutions LLC						
24901 Northwestern Hwy						
Ste 502	Southfield	MI	48075	**877-356-3450**		260
Industry-Railway Suppliers Inc						
811 Golf Ln	Bensenville	IL	60106	**800-728-0029**	630-766-5708	760
Indy Honda						
8455 US 31 S	Indianapolis	IN	46227	**888-752-4589**	317-887-0800	56
Inertia Dynamics Inc						
31 Industrial Pk Rd	New Hartford	CT	06057	**800-800-6445**	860-482-4444	204
INetU Inc						
744 Roble Rd Ste 70	Allentown	PA	18109	**888-664-6388**	610-266-7441	795
Infantino LLC						
4920 Carroll Canyon Rd						
Ste 200	San Diego	CA	92121	**800-840-4916**		63
Infectious Diseases Society of America (IDSA)						
1300 Wilson Blvd Ste 300	Arlington	VA	22209	**888-844-4372**	703-299-0200	48-8
Infinera Corp						
140 Caspian Ct	Sunnyvale	CA	94089	**877-742-3427**	408-572-5200	725
NASDAQ: INFN						
Infinite Graphics Inc						
4611 E Lake St	Minneapolis	MN	55406	**800-679-0676**	612-721-6283	179-5
OTC: INFG						
Info Tech Inc						
5700 SW 34th St Ste 1235	Gainesville	FL	32608	**888-352-2439**	352-381-4400	179-10
InfoCision Management Corp						
325 Springside Dr	Akron	OH	44333	**800-210-6269**	330-668-1400	727
InFocus Corp						
13190 SW 68th Pkwy Ste 200	Portland	OR	97223	**877-388-8385**	503-207-4700	584
INFOCUS Marketing Inc						
4245 Sigler Rd	Warrenton	VA	20187	**800-708-5478**		458
infoGroup Inc						
1020 E First St	Papillion	NE	68046	**866-414-7848**	402-836-5290	5
Infogrow Corp						
2140 Front St	Cuyahoga Falls	OH	44221	**800-897-9807**		197
InfoNow Corp						
1875 Lawrence St Ste 1200	Denver	CO	80202	**855-524-3282**	303-293-0212	179-7
Infor Global Solutions						
13560 Morris Rd Ste 4100	Alpharetta	GA	30004	**866-244-5479**	678-319-8000	179-10
Informatica Corp						
100 Cardinal Way	Redwood City	CA	94063	**800-653-3871**	650-385-5000	179-1
NASDAQ: INFA						
Information & Computing Services Inc (ICS)						
1650 Prudential Dr Ste 300	Jacksonville	FL	32207	**800-676-4427**	904-399-8500	179-1
Information Analysis Inc						
11240 Waples Mill Rd Ste 201	Fairfax	VA	22030	**800-829-7614**	703-383-3000	181
Information Builders Inc						
Two Penn Plz	New York	NY	10121	**800-969-4636**	212-736-4433	179-7
Information Gatekeepers Inc (IGI)						
1340 Soldiers Field Rd Ste 2	Brighton	MA	02135	**800-323-1088**	617-782-5033	628-11
Information Management Systems Inc						
114 W Main St Ste 211						
PO Box 2924	New Britain	CT	06050	**888-403-8347**	860-229-1119	626

	Toll-Free	Phone	Class
Information Network Assoc Inc 5235 N Front St .... Harrisburg PA 17110	800-443-0824	717-599-5505	684
Information Resources Inc 150 N Clinton St .... Chicago IL 60661	866-262-5973	312-726-1221	461
Information Systems Audit & Control Assn (ISACA) 3701 Algonquin Rd Ste 1010 ..... Rolling Meadows IL 60008	888-491-8833	847-253-1545	47-9
Information Television Network 6650 Pk of Commerce Blvd .... Boca Raton FL 33487	800-463-6488	561-997-5433	731
Information Today Inc 143 Old Marlton Pike ..... Medford NJ 08055	800-300-9868	609-654-6266	628-9
Information Today Magazine 143 Old Marlton Pk ..... Medford NJ 08055	800-300-9868	609-654-6266	452-7
InformationWeek Magazine 600 Community Dr .... Manhasset NY 11030	800-441-8826	516-562-5000	452-7
INFORMS (Institute for Operations Research & the Management Sciences) 7240 Pkwy Dr Ste 300 ..... Hanover MD 21076	800-446-3676	443-757-3500	48-19
Infosight Corp PO Box 5000 .... Chillicothe OH 45601	800-401-0716	740-642-3600	462
Infosource Inc 1300 City View Ctr .... Oviedo FL 32765	800-393-4636	407-796-5200	178
InfoTech Enterprises America Inc 330 Roberts St Ste 102 ..... East Hartford CT 06108	866-746-2133	860-528-5430	256
Infotel Distributors 6450 Poe Ave Ste 200 .... Dayton OH 45414	888-528-4504		175
Infotrieve Inc 20 Westport Rd PO Box 7102 ..... Wilton CT 06897 *Cust Svc	800-422-4633*	203-423-2130	384
infoUSA Inc 5711 S 86th Cir .... Omaha NE 68127	800-321-0869	800-835-5856	384
InfoVista Corp 12950 Worldgate Dr Ste 250 .... Herndon VA 20170	866-921-9219	703-435-2435	179-1
InfoWorld Magazine 501 Second St Ste 120 .... San Francisco CA 94107	800-227-8365	415-243-4344	452-7
InfoWorld Media Group Inc 501 Second St Ste 120 .... San Francisco CA 94107	800-227-8365	415-243-0500	628-9
Infrastructure Networks Inc 1718 Fry Rd Ste 116 .... Houston TX 77084	855-333-4638	281-740-3226	384
Infusion Nurses Society (INS) 315 Norwood Pk S .... Norwood MA 02062	800-694-0298	781-440-9408	48-8
InfySource Ltd 8345 NW 66th St .... Miami FL 33166	800-275-7503		616
ING Funds 7337 E Doubletree Ranch Rd .... Scottsdale AZ 85258	800-992-0180		521
Ingenix Inc 12125 Technology Dr .... Eden Prairie MN 55344	888-445-8745	952-833-7100	458
Ingenuity Ieq 3600 Centennial Dr .... Midland MI 48642	800-669-9726	989-496-2233	603
Ingle International 460 Richmond St W Ste 100 .... Toronto ON M5V1Y1	800-360-3234	416-730-8488	388-7
Ingles Markets Inc 2913 US Hwy 70 W .... Black Mountain NC 28711 NASDAQ: IMKTA	800-635-5066	828-669-2941	342
Ingleside Inn 200 W Ramon Rd .... Palm Springs CA 92264	800-772-6655	760-325-0046	376
Ingot Metal Company Ltd 111 Fenmar Dr .... Weston ON M9L1M3	800-567-7774	416-749-1372	476
Ingram Book Group 1 Ingram Blvd .... La Vergne TN 37086	800-937-8000	615-793-5000	94
Ingram Entertainment Inc 2 Ingram Blvd .... La Vergne TN 37089	800-621-1333	615-287-4000	504
Ingram Micro Inc 1600 E St Andrew Pl .... Santa Ana CA 92705 NYSE: IM ■ *Sales	800-456-8000*	714-566-1000	175
Ingram Park Mall 6301 NW Loop 410 .... San Antonio TX 78238	877-746-6642	210-684-9570	455
Injured Workers Insurance Fund 8722 Loch Raven Blvd .... Towson MD 21286	800-264-4943	410-494-2000	388-4
Ink Technology Corp 18320 Lanken Ave .... Cleveland OH 44119	800-633-2826	216-486-6720	620
INL (Idaho National Laboratory) 2525 Fremont Ave PO Box 1625 .... Idaho Falls ID 83415	866-495-7440		659
Inland Empire Magazine 3769 Tibbetts St Ste A .... Riverside CA 92506 *General	800-424-4232*	951-682-3026	452-22
Inland Empire Paper Co 3320 N Argonne .... Millwood WA 99212	866-437-7711	509-924-1911	550
Inland Group Inc 2901 Butterfield Rd .... Oak Brook IL 60523	800-826-8228	630-218-8000	646
Inland Mortgage Corp 2901 Butterfield Rd .... Oak Brook IL 60523	800-826-8228	630-218-8000	502
Inland Northwest Blood Ctr 210 W Cataldo Ave .... Spokane WA 99201	800-423-0151	509-624-0151	88
Inland Plywood Co 375 N Cass Ave .... Pontiac MI 48342	800-521-4355	248-334-4706	606
Inland Power & Light Company Inc 10110 W Hallett Rd .... Spokane WA 99224	800-747-7151	509-747-7151	245
Inland Real Estate Corp 2901 Butterfield Rd .... Oak Brook IL 60523 NYSE: IRC	888-331-4732	630-218-8000	645
Inland Real Estate Development Corp 2901 Butterfield Rd .... Oak Brook IL 60523	866-954-5692	630-218-8000	644
Inland Real Estate Sales Inc 2901 Butterfield Rd .... Oak Brook IL 60523	800-828-8999	630-218-8000	643
Inland Refractories Co 38600 Chester Rd PO Box 239 .... Avon OH 44011	800-321-0767	440-934-6600	654
Inland Seafood Corp 1651 Montreal Cir .... Tucker GA 30084	800-883-3474	404-350-5850	296-5
Inlandboatmen's Union of the Pacific (IBU) 1711 W Nickerson St Ste D .... Seattle WA 98119	800-562-6000	206-284-6001	411
Inlet Tower Suites 1200 L St .... Anchorage AK 99501	800-544-0786	907-276-0110	376
Inline Plastics Corp 42 Canal St .... Shelton CT 06484	800-826-5567	203-924-2015	595
Inmagic Inc 600 Unicorn Pk Dr .... Woburn MA 01801	800-229-8398	781-938-4444	179-10
Inman News 1100 Marina Village Pkwy Ste 102 .... Alameda CA 94501	800-775-4662	510-658-9252	523
Inmedius Inc 2247 Babcock Blvd Ste 200 .... Pittsburgh PA 15237	800-697-7110		178
Inn & Spa at Loretto 211 Old Santa Fe Trl .... Santa Fe NM 87501	800-727-5531	505-988-5531	376

	Toll-Free	Phone	Class
Inn at Aspen 38750 Hwy 82 .... Aspen CO 81611	800-222-7736		374
Inn at Bay Harbor, The 3600 Village Harbor Dr .... Bay Harbor MI 49770	800-462-6963	231-439-4000	660
Inn at Camachee Harbor 201 Yacht Club Dr .... Saint Augustine FL 32084	800-688-5379	904-825-0003	376
Inn at Ellis Square 201 W Bay St .... Savannah GA 31401	877-542-7666		375
Inn at Gig Harbor 3211 56th St NW .... Gig Harbor WA 98335	800-795-9980	253-858-1111	376
Inn at Harbour Town Seven Lighthouse Ln .... Hilton Head Island SC 29928 *Resv	800-732-7463*	843-363-8100	376
Inn at Henderson's Wharf 1000 Fell St .... Baltimore MD 21231	888-995-9560	410-522-7777	376
Inn at Langley 400 First St PO Box 835 .... Langley WA 98260	800-843-3779	360-221-3033	376
Inn at Mayo Clinic 4420 Mary Brigh Dr .... Jacksonville FL 32224	888-255-4458	904-992-9992	376
Inn at Montchanin Village 528 Montchanin Rd .... Montchanin DE 19710	800-269-2473	302-888-2133	376
Inn at Morro Bay 60 State Pk Rd .... Morro Bay CA 93442	800-321-9566	805-772-5651	376
Inn at Mystic 3 Williams Ave PO Box 526 .... Mystic CT 06355	800-237-2415	860-536-9604	376
Inn at Otter Crest 301 Otter Crest Loop .... Otter Rock OR 97369	800-452-2101	541-765-2111	376
Inn at Pelican Bay 800 Vanderbilt Beach Rd .... Naples FL 34108	800-597-8770	239-597-8777	376
Inn at Perry Cabin 308 Watkins Ln .... Saint Michaels MD 21663	800-722-2949	410-745-2200	376
Inn at Rancho Santa Fe 5951 Linea Del Cielo PO Box 869 .... Rancho Santa Fe CA 92067	800-843-4661	858-756-1131	660
Inn at Reading, The 1040 N Pk Rd .... Wyomissing PA 19610	800-383-9713	610-372-7811	376
Inn at Saint John 939 Congress St .... Portland ME 04102	800-636-9127	207-773-6481	376
Inn at Spanish Bay, The 2700 17-Mile Dr .... Pebble Beach CA 93953	800-654-9300	831-647-7500	660
Inn at Spanish Head 4009 SW Hwy 101 .... Lincoln City OR 97367	800-452-8127	541-996-2161	376
Inn at Stratton Mountain 5 Village Lodge Rd .... Stratton Mountain VT 05155	800-787-2886	802-297-2500	660
Inn at the Market 86 Pine St .... Seattle WA 98101	800-446-4484	206-443-3600	376
Inn At The Quay 900 Quayside Dr .... New Westminster BC V3M6G1	800-663-2001	604-520-1776	376
Inn at Union Square 440 Post St .... San Francisco CA 94102	800-288-4346	415-397-3510	376
Inn at Virginia Mason 1006 Spring St .... Seattle WA 98104	800-283-6453	206-583-6453	369
Inn at Virginia Tech & Skelton Conference Ctr 901 Prices Fork Rd MS 0104 .... Blacksburg VA 24061	877-200-3360	540-231-8000	374
Inn at, The Tides, The 800 Coast Hwy 1 PO Box 640 .... Bodega Bay CA 94923	800-541-7788	707-875-2751	376
Inn by the Lake 3300 Lk Tahoe Blvd .... South Lake Tahoe CA 96150	800-877-1466	530-542-0330	376
Inn by the Sea 40 Bowery Beach Rd .... Cape Elizabeth ME 04107	800-888-4287	207-799-3134	660
Inn of Chicago Magnificent Mile 162 E Ohio St .... Chicago IL 60611 *Resv	800-424-6423*	312-787-3100	376
Inn of Long Beach 185 Atlantic Ave .... Long Beach CA 90802	800-230-7500	562-435-3791	376
Inn of the Anasazi 113 Washington Ave .... Santa Fe NM 87501	888-767-3966	505-988-3030	376
Inn of the Governors 101 W Alameda St .... Santa Fe NM 87501	800-234-4534	505-982-4333	376
Inn of the Hills River Resort 1001 Junction Hwy .... Kerrville TX 78028	800-292-5690	830-895-5000	660
Inn of the Mountain Gods 287 Carrizo Canyon Rd .... Mescalero NM 88340	800-545-9011		660
Inn of the Six Mountains 2617 Killington Rd .... Killington VT 05751	800-228-4676	802-422-4302	376
Inn on Biltmore Estate 1 Antler Hill Rd .... Asheville NC 28803	800-411-3812	828-225-1333	376
Inn on Fifth 699 Fifth Ave S .... Naples FL 34102	888-403-8778	239-403-8777	376
Inn on Gitche Gumee 8517 Congdon Blvd .... Duluth MN 55804	800-317-4979	218-525-4979	376
Inn on Lake Superior 350 Canal Pk Dr .... Duluth MN 55802	888-668-4352	218-726-1111	376
Inn on the Alameda 303 E Alameda St .... Santa Fe NM 87501	888-984-2121	505-984-2121	376
Inn on the Paseo 630 Paseo de Peralta .... Santa Fe NM 87501	855-984-8200	505-984-8200	376
Inner Traditions International one Pk Row .... Rochester VT 05767	800-246-8648	802-767-3174	628-2
Innis Maggiore Group Inc 4715 Whipple Ave NW .... Canton OH 44718	800-460-4111	330-492-5500	4
Innisbrook Resort & Golf Club 36750 US Hwy 19 N .... Palm Harbor FL 34684	800-492-6899	727-942-2000	660
Innodata-Isogen Inc Three University Plz Dr .... Hackensack NJ 07601 NASDAQ: INOD	877-454-8400	201-371-8000	179-12
InnoMedia Inc 128 Baytech Dr .... San Jose CA 95134	888-251-6250	408-432-5400	725
Innotrac Corp 6465 E Johns Crossing .... Johns Creek GA 30097 NASDAQ: INOC	800-322-2885	678-584-4000	196
In-N-Out Burger Inc 4199 Campus Dr Ninth Fl .... Irvine CA 92612 *Cust Svc	800-786-1000*	949-509-6200	661
Innovasystems International LLC 2385 Northside Dr Ste 300 .... San Diego CA 92108	866-566-7778	619-955-5800	178
Innovate E-Commerce Inc 160 N Craig St .... Pittsburgh PA 15213	888-771-9606		623
Innovative Enterprises Inc 25 Town & Country Dr .... Washington MO 63090	800-280-0300	636-390-0300	541
Innovative Fluid Handling Systems 3300 E Rock Falls Rd .... Rock Falls IL 61071	800-435-7003	815-626-1018	199
Innovative Hearth Products 2701 S Harbor Blvd .... Santa Ana CA 92704	866-328-4537		358

	Toll-Free	Phone	Class
Innovative Industrial Solutions Inc			
2830 Skyline Dr .... Russellville AR 72802	888-684-8249	479-968-4266	684
Innovative Information Solutions Inc			
61 I- Ln .... Waterbury CT 06705	800-343-8121	203-756-4243	180
Innovative Metals Company Inc (IMETCO)			
4648 S Old Peachtree Rd .... Norcross GA 30084	800-646-3826	770-908-1030	45
Innovative Solutions & Support Inc			
720 Pennsylvania Dr .... Exton PA 19341	866-359-7876	610-646-9800	522
NASDAQ: ISSC			
Innovative Stamping Corp			
2068 E Gladwick St .... Compton CA 90220	800-400-0047	310-537-6996	483
Innovative Systems Group Inc			
799 Roosevelt Rd .... Glen Ellyn IL 60137	800-739-2400	630-858-8500	178
Innovative Systems Inc			
790 Holiday Dr Bldg 11 .... Pittsburgh PA 15220	800-622-6390	412-937-9300	179-1
Innovative Technologies Corp (ITC)			
1020 Woodman Dr Ste 100 .... Dayton OH 45432	800-745-8050	937-252-2145	179-10
Innovative Telecom Solutions Inc			
Nine Vela Way .... Edgewater NJ 07020	800-510-3000		384
Innovize Inc			
500 Oak Grove Pkwy .... Saint Paul MN 55127	877-605-6580		595
Inns at Mill Falls			
312 Daniel Webster Hwy .... Meredith NH 03253	800-622-6455		376
InnSuites Hospitality Trust			
1625 E Northern Ave Ste 105 .... Phoenix AZ 85020	800-842-4242	602-944-1500	645
NYSE: IHT			
InnSuites Hospitality Trust InnSuites Hotels & Suites			
475 N Granada Ave Ste 102 .... Tucson AZ 85701	800-842-4242	520-622-0923	376
InnSuites Hotel Tempe/Phoenix Airport			
1651 W Baseline Rd .... Tempe AZ 85283	800-841-4242	480-897-7900	376
InnSuites Hotel Tucson City Ctr			
475 N Granada Ave .... Tucson AZ 85701	888-784-8324	520-622-3000	376
Inolex Chemical Co			
2101 S Swanson St .... Philadelphia PA 19148	800-521-9891*	215-271-0800	142
*Cust Svc			
Inova Diagnostics Inc			
9900 Old Grove Rd .... San Diego CA 92131	800-545-9495	858-586-9900	231
Inova Health System			
8110 Gatehouse Rd .... Falls Church VA 22042	855-694-6682		350
Inova Payroll Inc			
176 Thompson Ln Ste 204 .... Nashville TN 37211	888-244-6106	615-921-0600	724
Inova Solutions Inc			
110 Avon St .... Charlottesville VA 22902	800-637-1077	434-817-8000	179-1
In-O-Vate Technologies Inc			
810 Saturn St Ste 21.............. Jupiter FL 33477	888-443-7937	561-743-8696	192-1
Inovex Industries Inc			
45681 Oakbrook Ct Ste 102 .... Sterling VA 20166	888-374-3366	703-421-9778	3
Inovio Pharmaceuticals Inc			
1787 Sentry PkwyW Bldg 18 .... Blue Bell PA 19422	877-446-6846	267-440-4200	250
NASDAQ: INOVIO			
Inovise Medical Inc			
8770 SW Nimbus Ave Ste D .... Beaverton OR 97008	877-466-8473	503-431-3800	471
InPath Devices			
3610 Dodge St Ste 200.............. Omaha NE 68131	800-988-1914	402-345-9200	174-7
Input 1 LLC			
6200 Canoga Ave Ste 400 .... Woodland Hills CA 91367	888-882-2554	818-713-2303	179-10
Inquipco			
2730 N Nellis Blvd .... Las Vegas NV 89115	800-598-3465	702-644-1700	191
INS (Infusion Nurses Society)			
315 Norwood Pk S .... Norwood MA 02062	800-694-0298	781-440-9408	48-8
Inscape Publishing Inc			
6465 Wayzata Blvd Ste 800 .... Minneapolis MN 55426	877-735-8383	763-765-2222	179-3
Insco Dico Group			
17780 Fitch Ste 200 .... Irvine CA 92614	800-782-1546	949-263-3300	388-5
Insco Distributing Inc			
12501 Network Blvd .... San Antonio TX 78249	855-282-4295	210-690-8400	656
Inside Energy			
Two Penn Plz 25th Fl .... New York NY 10121	800-752-8878		524-5
Inside FERC			
Two Penn Plz 25th Fl .... New York NY 10121	800-752-8878		524-5
Inside FERC's Gas Market Report			
Two Penn Plz 25th Fl .... New York NY 10121	800-752-8878	212-904-3070	524-5
Inside NRC			
Two Penn Plz 25th Fl .... New York NY 10121	800-752-8878		524-5
Inside Washington Publishers			
1919 S Eads St Ste 201 .... Arlington VA 22202	800-424-9068	703-416-8500	628-9
InsideFlyer Magazine			
1930 Frequent			
Flyer Pt.............. Colorado Springs CO 80915	800-767-8896	719-597-8889	452-22
Insight			
444 Scott Dr .... Bloomingdale IL 60108	800-467-4448		194
Insight Enterprises Inc			
6820 S Harl Ave .... Tempe AZ 85283	800-467-4448	480-333-3000	180
NASDAQ: NSIT			
Insight Global Inc (IGI)			
4170 Ashford Dunwoody Rd			
Ste 580.................... Atlanta GA 30319	888-336-7463	404-257-7900	194
Insight Imaging			
26250 Enterprise Ct Ste 100......... Lake Forest CA 92630	800-344-9555	949-282-6000	380
Insight Information			
214 King St W Ste 300 .... Toronto ON M5H3S6	888-777-1707	416-777-2020	755
Insight Media			
2162 Broadway .... New York NY 10024	800-233-9910	212-721-6316	504
Insight Technology Inc			
Nine Akira Way .... Londonderry NH 03053	866-509-2040	603-626-4800	21
Insignia Systems Inc			
8799 Brooklyn Blvd .... Minneapolis MN 55445	800-874-4648	763-392-6200	692
NASDAQ: ISIG			
In-Sink-Erator			
4700 21st St .... Racine WI 53406	800-558-5712	262-554-5432	35
Insituform Technologies Inc			
17988 Edison Ave .... Chesterfield MO 63005	800-234-2992*	636-530-8000	189-10
*Cust Svc			
Insl-X Products Corp			
101 Paragon Dr .... Montvale NJ 07645	800-225-5554*		543
*Cust Svc			
Inspirage Inc			
40 Lk Bellevue Dr Ste 100 .... Bellevue WA 98005	855-517-4250		623
Inspiration Software Inc			
5125 SW Macadam Ave Ste 145....... Beaverton OR 97239	800-877-4292	503-297-3004	179-1
Inspired eLearning Inc			
613 NW Loop 410 Ste 530 ...... San Antonio TX 78216	800-631-2078	210-579-0224	225
Instant Imprints			
5897 Oberlin Dr Ste 200............ San Diego CA 92121	800-542-3437	858-642-4848	309
Instantiations Inc			
Officers Row Ste 1325B .... Vancouver WA 98661	855-476-2558	503-649-3836	179-2
Instantwhip Foods Inc			
2200 Cardigan Ave .... Columbus OH 43215	800-544-9447*	614-488-2536	295-10
*Cust Svc			
Insteel Industries Inc			
1373 Boggs Dr .... Mount Airy NC 27030	800-334-9504	336-786-2141	800
NASDAQ: IIIN			
Institute for a Drug-Free Workplace (IDFW)			
10701 Parkridge Blvd Ste 300 .... Reston VA 20191	877-696-6775	703-391-7222	48-12
Institute for Astronomy			
University of Hawaii			
2680 Woodlawn Dr. .... Honolulu HI 96822	800-351-1330	808-956-8312	659
Institute for Business & Home Safety (IBHS)			
4775 E Fowler Ave .... Tampa FL 33617	866-657-4247	813-286-3400	48-9
Institute for Certification of Computing Professionals (ICCP)			
2400 E Devon Ave Ste 281 .... Des Plaines IL 60018	800-843-8227	847-299-4227	47-9
Institute for Corporate Productivity Inc			
411 First Ave S Ste 403 .... Seattle WA 98104	866-375-4427	206-624-6565	461
Institute for Healthcare Improvement (IHI)			
20 University Rd Seventh Fl .... Cambridge MA 02138	866-787-0831	617-301-4800	48-8
Institute for Humane Studies			
3301 N Fairfax Dr Ste 440 .... Arlington VA 22201	800-697-8799	703-993-4880	625
Institute for Justice			
901 N Glebe Rd Ste 900 .... Arlington VA 22203	888-322-6397	703-682-9320	625
Institute for Operations Research & the Management Sciences (INFORMS)			
7240 Pkwy Dr Ste 300 .... Hanover MD 21076	800-446-3676	443-757-3500	48-19
Institute for Policy Studies (IPS)			
1112 16th St NW Ste 600.......... Washington DC 20036	877-564-6833	202-234-9382	625
Institute for Research on Poverty			
University of Wisconsin Madison 1180 Observatory Dr			
3412 William H Sewell Social Sciences Bldg			
WI 53706	866-301-1753	608-262-6358	659
Madison			
Institute for Supply Management (ISM)			
2055 Centennial Cir .... Tempe AZ 85284	800-888-6276*	480-752-6276	48-12
*Cust Svc			
Institute for Systems Research			
University of Maryland			
2173 AV Williams Bldg.......... College Park MD 20742	866-675-8967	301-405-6615	659
Institute for the Advancement of Human Behavior (IAHB)			
PO BOX 5527 .... Santa Rosa CA 95402	800-258-8411	650-851-8411	48-8
Institute of American Indian Arts (IAIA)			
83 Avan Nu Po Rd .... Santa Fe NM 87508	800-804-6422	505-424-2300	163
Institute of Business Appraisers (IBA)			
1111 BrickyaRd Rd			
Ste 200.................. Salt Lake City UT 84106	800-299-4130		48-17
Institute of Caster & Wheel Manufacturers (ICWM)			
8720 Red Oak Blvd Ste 201 .... Charlotte NC 28217	877-522-5431	704-676-1190	48-13
Institute of Certified Professional Managers (ICPM)			
James Madison University			
MSC 5504 .... Harrisonburg VA 22807	800-460-8013	540-568-3247	48-12
Institute of Clean Air Cos (ICAC)			
1730 M St NW Ste 206.......... Washington DC 20036	888-383-5726	202-457-0911	47-12
Institute of Culinary Education			
50 W 23rd St .... New York NY 10010	800-522-4610	212-847-0700	161
Institute of Food Technologists (IFT)			
525 W Van Buren St Ste 1000 .... Chicago IL 60607	800-438-3663	312-782-8424	48-6
Institute of General Semantics (IGS)			
72-11 Austin St............ Forest Hills NY 11375	800-346-1359	212-729-7973	47-11
Institute of Gerontology			
University of Michigan			
300 N Ingalls St .... Ann Arbor MI 48109	877-865-2167	734-936-2107	659
Institute of Government & Public Affairs			
Univ of Illinois			
1007 W Nevada St .... Urbana IL 61801	866-794-3340	217-333-3340	625
Institute of Hazardous Materials Management (IHMM)			
11900 Parklawn Dr Ste 450 .... Rockville MD 20852	800-437-0137	301-984-8969	47-12
Institute of Industrial Engineers (IIE)			
3577 PkwyLn Ste 200.............. Norcross GA 30092	800-494-0460*	770-449-0460	48-13
*Cust Svc			
Institute of Makers of Explosives (IME)			
1120 19th St NW Ste 310.......... Washington DC 20036	800-461-8841	202-429-9280	48-13
Institute of Management Accountants Inc (IMA)			
10 Paragon Dr Ste 1 .... Montvale NJ 07645	800-638-4427	201-573-9000	48-1
Institute of Management Consultants USA Inc (IMC USA)			
2025 M St NW Ste 800.......... Washington DC 20036	800-221-2557	202-367-1134	48-12
Institute of Materials Science			
University of Connecticut			
97 N Eagleville Rd. .... Storrs CT 06269	800-528-7411	860-486-4623	659
Institute of Navigation Inc (ION)			
8551 Rixlew Ln Ste 360 .... Manassas VA 20109	800-696-7353	703-366-2723	48-21
Institute of Packaging Professionals (IoPP)			
1833 Centre Point Cir			
Ste 123.................. Naperville IL 60563	800-432-4085	630-544-5050	48-13
Institute of Paper Science & Technology (IPST)			
500 Tenth St NW .... Atlanta GA 30332	800-558-6611	404-894-5700	48-13
Institute of Real Estate Management (IREM)			
430 N Michigan Ave .... Chicago IL 60611	800-837-0706	312-329-6000	48-17
Institute of Scrap Recycling Industries Magazine			
1615 L St NW Ste 6000 .... Washington DC 20036	800-767-7236	202-662-8500	452-21
Institute of Texan Cultures			
801 E Durango Blvd .... San Antonio TX 78205	800-447-3372	210-458-2300	513
Institute of World Politics			
1521 16th St NW .... Washington DC 20036	888-566-9497	202-462-2101	625
Institution Food House Inc (IFH)			
543 12th St Dr NW .... Hickory NC 28601	800-800-0434		298
Institutional Investor Newsletters			
225 Pk Ave S 8th Fl .... New York NY 10003	800-437-9997	212-224-3300	628-9
Institutional Wholesale Co			
535 Dry Vly Rd .... Cookeville TN 38506	800-239-9588	931-537-4000	298
Instron Corp Wilson Instruments Div			
825 University Ave .... Norwood MA 02062	800-695-4273	781-828-2500	467
Instrument Sales & Service Inc			
16427 NE Airport Way .... Portland OR 97230	800-333-7976	503-239-0754	60
Instrumentation Laboratory Inc			
180 Hartwell Rd .... Bedford MA 01730	800-955-9525*	781-861-0710	416
*Sales			
Insulet Corp			
Nine Oak Park Dr .... Bedford MA 01730	800-591-3455	781-457-5000	471
Insulfab Plastics Inc			
834 Hayne St .... Spartanburg SC 29301	800-845-7599	864-582-7506	592
Insultab Inc			
45 Industrial Pkwy .... Woburn MA 01801	800-468-4822*	781-935-0800	592
*Cust Svc			

Name / Address	City	State	Zip	Toll-Free	Phone	Class
Insurance Auto Auctions Inc						
Two Westbrook Corporate Ctr						
Ste 500	Westchester	IL	60154	**800-872-1501**	708-492-7000	50
Insurance Company of the West						
11455 El Camino Real	San Diego	CA	92130	**800-877-1111**	858-350-2400	388-4
Insurance Consultants International						
19760 Knights Crossing Ste 1C	Monument	CO	80132	**800-576-2674**	719-573-9080	388-7
Insurance Coverage Law Bulletin, The						
1617 JFK Blvd Ste 1750	Philadelphia	PA	19103	**877-256-2472**	215-557-2300	524-7
Insurance Data Processing Inc (IDP)						
8101 Washington Ln	Wyncote	PA	19095	**800-523-6745**	215-885-2150	179-11
Insurance Information Institute Inc (III)						
110 William St	New York	NY	10038	**877-263-7995**	212-346-5500	48-9
Insurance Institute for Highway Safety						
1005 N Glebe Rd Ste 800	Arlington	VA	22201	**888-327-4236**	703-247-1500	48-9
Insurance Marketing Agencies Inc						
306 Main St	Worcester	MA	01608	**800-891-1226**	508-753-7233	388-2
Insurance Research Council (IRC)						
720 Providence Rd	Malvern	PA	19355	**800-644-2101**	610-644-2212	48-9
Insurance Services Office Inc (ISO)						
545 Washington Blvd	Jersey City	NJ	07310	**800-888-4476**	201-469-2000	387
InsurBanc						
10 Executive Dr	Farmington	CT	06032	**866-467-2262**	860-677-9701	69
InsWeb Inc						
11290 Pyrites Way Ste 200	Gold River	CA	95670	**866-697-9085**	916-853-3300	113
INTA (International Trademark Assn)						
655 Third Ave 10th Fl	New York	NY	10017	**800-995-3579**	212-768-9887	48-12
Intacct Corp						
125 S Market St Ste 600	San Jose	CA	95113	**877-437-7765**	408-878-0900	38
Intact Insurance						
700 University Ave Mn 3						
Ste 1500	Toronto	ON	M5G0A1	**877-341-1464**	416-341-1464	388-4
Intaglio LLC						
5809 Cross Roads Commerce Pkwy						
Ste 200	Grand Rapids	MI	49519	**800-632-9153**	616-243-3300	506
Intec Video Systems Inc						
23301 Vista Grande Dr	Laguna Hills	CA	92653	**800-468-3254**	949-859-3800	684
Intedge Mfg						
1875 Chumley Rd	Woodruff	SC	29388	**866-969-9605**	864-969-9601	299
Integra LifeSciences Holdings Corp						
311 Enterprise Dr	Plainsboro	NJ	08536	**800-654-2873**	609-275-0500	84
NASDAQ: IART						
Integra Telecom Inc						
1201 NE Lloyd Blvd Ste 500	Portland	OR	97232	**866-468-3472***	503-453-8000	726
*General						
IntegraColor						
3210 Innovative Way	Mesquite	TX	75149	**800-933-9511**	972-289-0705	619
Integrated Biometrics Inc						
121 Broadcast Dr	Spartanburg	SC	29303	**888-840-8034**	864-990-3711	683
Integrated BioPharma Inc						
225 Long Ave	Hillside	NJ	07205	**888-319-6962**	973-926-0816	787
OTC: INBP						
Integrated Design Tools Inc						
1202 E Pk Ave	Tallahassee	FL	32301	**800-462-4307**	850-222-5939	584
Integrated Device Technology Inc						
6024 Silver Creek Vly Rd	San Jose	CA	95138	**800-345-7015**	408-284-8200	687
NASDAQ: IDTI						
Integrated Flow Solutions LLC						
6461 Reynolds Rd	Tyler	TX	75708	**800-859-7867**	903-595-6511	632
Integrated Magnetics Inc						
11248 Playa Ct	Culver City	CA	90230	**800-421-6692**	310-391-7213	253
Integrated Regional Laboratories Inc						
5361 NW 33rd Ave	Ft. Lauderdale	FL	33309	**800-522-0232**		412
Integrated Silicon Solution Inc (ISSI)						
1940 Zanker Rd	San Jose	CA	95112	**800-379-4774**	408-969-6600	687
NASDAQ: ISSI						
Integrated Support Command Miami Beach						
100 MacArthur Cswy	Miami Beach	FL	33139	**866-772-8724**	305-535-4300	156
Integrated Systems Analysts Inc						
2001 N Beauregard St Ste 600	Alexandria	VA	22311	**800-929-1024**	703-824-0700	181
Integration Technologies Group Inc						
2745 Hartland Rd Ste 200	Falls Church	VA	22043	**800-835-7823**	703-698-8282	176
Integretel Inc						
5883 Rue Ferrari	San Jose	CA	95138	**888-302-2750**	408-362-4000	727
INTEGRIS Baptist Regional Health Ctr						
200 Second Ave SW	Miami	OK	74355	**888-951-2277**	918-542-6611	371-3
INTEGRIS Bass Baptist Health Ctr						
600 S Monroe	Enid	OK	73701	**888-951-2277**	580-233-2300	371-3
INTEGRIS Southwest Medical Ctr						
4401 S Western St	Oklahoma City	OK	73109	**888-949-3816**	405-636-7000	371-3
Integrity Music						
4050 Lee Vance View	Colorado Springs	CO	80918	**888-888-4726**	719-536-0100	648
Integrity Staffing Solutions Inc						
750 Shipyard Dr Ste 300	Wilmington	DE	19801	**888-458-8367**	302-661-8776	712
Integrys Energy Group Inc						
130 E Randolph Dr	Chicago	IL	60601	**800-699-1269**	312-228-5400	357-5
Intek Plastic Inc						
1000 Spiral Blvd	Hastings	MN	55033	**888-468-3531**		325
Intel Corp						
2200 Mission College Blvd	Santa Clara	CA	95052	**800-628-8686***	408-765-8080	687
NASDAQ: INTC ■ *Cust Svc						
Intel Museum						
2200 Mission College Blvd	Santa Clara	CA	95052	**800-628-8686**	408-765-0503	513
Intellect Resources Inc						
3824 N Elm St Ste 102	Greensboro	NC	27455	**877-554-8911**		260
Intelletrace Inc						
448 Ignacio Blvd	Novato	CA	94945	**800-618-5877**		384
Intelligencer Journal						
Eight W King St PO Box 1328	Lancaster	PA	17603	**800-809-4666**	717-291-8622	525-2
Intelligencer Printing Co						
330 Eden Rd	Lancaster	PA	17601	**800-233-0107**		619
Intelligent Computer Solutions Inc						
9350 Eton Ave	Chatsworth	CA	91311	**888-994-4678**	818-998-5805	175
Intelligent Decisions Inc						
21445 Beaumeade Cir	Ashburn	VA	20147	**800-929-8331**	703-554-1600	181
Intelligent Instrumentation Inc						
419 NE 10th Ave	Portland	OR	97232	**800-685-9911**	503-928-3188	202
Intelligent Mechatronic Systems Inc						
435 King St N	Waterloo	ON	N2J2Z5	**866-818-6637**	519-745-8887	659
Intelligent Transportation Society of America (ITS)						
1100 17th St NW Ste 1200	Washington	DC	20036	**800-374-8472**	202-484-4847	48-21
Intelligrated Products						
475 E High St PO Box 899	London	OH	43140	**866-936-7300**	513-701-7300	208
IntelliNet Technologies Inc						
1990 W New Haven Ave Ste 303	Melbourne	FL	32904	**888-726-0686**	321-726-0686	179-7
IntelliSoft Group LLC						
61 Spit Brook Rd	Nashua	NH	03060	**888-634-4464**		181
Interactive Business Systems Inc						
2625 Butterfield Rd	Oak Brook	IL	60523	**800-555-5427**	630-571-9100	181
Interactive Data Corp						
32 Crosby Dr	Bedford	MA	01730	**800-228-9715**	781-687-8500	628-10
Interactive Intelligence Inc						
7601 Interactive Way	Indianapolis	IN	46278	**800-267-1364**	317-872-3000	179-7
NASDAQ: ININ						
Interactive Services Group Inc						
600 Delran Pkwy Ste C	Delran	NJ	08075	**800-566-3310**		176
Inter-American Development Bank						
1300 New York Ave NW	Washington	DC	20577	**877-782-7432**	202-623-1000	
InterAmerican Motor Corp (IMC)						
8901 Canoga Ave	Canoga Park	CA	91304	**800-874-8925**	818-678-1200	60
Interbond Corp of America						
3200 SW 42nd St	Fort Lauderdale	FL	33312	**800-432-8579**		34
InterCall						
8420 W Bryn Mawr Ste 1100	Chicago	IL	60631	**800-374-2441**	773-399-1600	726
Interchem Corp						
120 Rt 17 N	Paramus	NJ	07652	**800-261-7332**	201-261-7333	474
Intercollegiate Studies Institute (ISI)						
3901 Centerville Rd	Wilmington	DE	19807	**800-526-7022**	302-652-4600	47-11
Inter-Community Telephone Co (ICTC)						
PO Box 8	Nome	ND	58062	**800-350-9137**	701-924-8815	726
Intercomp Co						
3839 County Rd 116	Medina	MN	55340	**800-328-3336**	763-476-2531	675
Interconnect Devices Inc (IDI)						
5101 Richland Ave	Kansas City	KS	66106	**866-433-5722**	913-342-5544	253
InterContinental Hotel Cleveland						
9801 Carnegie Ave	Cleveland	OH	44106	**877-707-8999**	216-707-4100	374
Holiday Inn Express						
3 Ravinia Dr Ste 100	Atlanta	GA	30346	**800-725-8232**	770-604-2000	376
Holiday Inn Hotels & Resorts						
3 Ravinia Dr Ste 100	Atlanta	GA	30346	**800-725-8232**	770-604-2000	376
InterContinental Hotels Group						
Hotel Indigo						
3 Ravinia Dr Ste 100	Atlanta	GA	30346	**800-334-5194**	770-604-2000	376
Staybridge Suites						
Three Ravinia Dr Ste 100	Atlanta	GA	30346	**800-465-4329**	770-604-2000	376
Intercontinental San Francisco						
888 Howard St	San Francisco	CA	94103	**888-811-4273**		375
Inter-County Bakers Inc						
1095 Long Island Ave Ste 1	Deer Park	NY	11729	**800-696-1350**	631-957-1350	69
Inter-County Energy Co-op						
1009 Hustonville Rd	Danville	KY	40422	**888-266-7322**	859-236-4561	245
Intercultural Communications College						
810 Richards St Ste 200	Honolulu	HI	96813	**800-545-2078**	808-946-2445	420
Interdenominational Theological Ctr						
700 Martin Luther King Jr Dr	Atlanta	GA	30314	**800-908-9946**	404-527-7700	168
Interdom LLC						
11800 S 75th Ave Ste 2N	Palos Heights	IL	60463	**800-935-0851**		310
Interface Inc						
7401 E Butherus Dr	Scottsdale	AZ	85260	**800-947-5598**	480-948-5555	467
Interface Security Systems LLC						
6340 International Pkwy Ste 100	Plano	TX	75093	**866-593-3480**	972-996-2800	683
Interface Solutions Inc						
216 Wohlsen Way	Lancaster	PA	17603	**800-942-7538**	717-207-6000	325
Interfaith Alliance						
1212 New York Ave NW						
Ste 1250	Washington	DC	20005	**800-510-0969**	202-238-3300	47-7
Intergraph Corp						
19 Interpro Rd	Madison	AL	35758	**800-345-4856**	256-730-2000	179-5
Interim HealthCare Inc						
1601 Sawgrass Corporate Pkwy	Sunrise	FL	33323	**800-338-7786**	954-858-6000	712
Interior Design Services Inc						
209 Powell Pl	Brentwood	TN	37027	**800-433-7446**	615-376-1200	320
Interlaken Inn						
74 Interlaken Rd Rt 12	Lakeville	CT	06039	**800-222-2909**	860-435-9878	660
Interlectric Corp						
1401 Lexington Ave	Warren	PA	16365	**800-722-2184**	814-723-6061	433
Interleukin Genetics Inc						
135 Beaver St 3rd Fl	Waltham	MA	02452	**800-826-6762***	781-398-0700	231
OTC: ILIU ■ *Cust Svc						
Interlocking Concrete Pavement Institute (ICPI)						
1444 'I' St NW Ste 700	Washington	DC	20005	**800-241-3652**	202-712-9036	48-3
Interlog USA Inc						
2818A Anthony Ln S	Minneapolis	MN	55418	**800-603-6030**	612-789-3456	312
Intermark Group Inc						
101 25th St N	Birmingham	AL	35243	**800-624-9239**	205-803-0000	4
Intermec Inc						
6001 36th Ave W	Everett	WA	98203	**800-755-5505**	425-348-2600	186
NYSE: IN						
Intermec Technologies Corp						
6001 36th Ave W	Everett	WA	98203	**800-934-3163***	425-348-2600	224
*Sales						
InterMetro Industries Corp						
651 N Washington St	Wilkes-Barre	PA	18705	**800-992-1776***	570-825-2741	72
*Cust Svc						
Intermodal Assn of North America (IANA)						
11785 Beltsville Dr Ste 1100	Calverton	MD	20705	**877-438-8442**	301-982-3400	48-21
Intermolecular Inc						
3011 N First St	San Jose	CA	95134	**877-251-1860**	408-582-5700	687
Intermountain Air LLC						
301 N 2370 W	Salt Lake City	UT	84116	**800-433-9617**	801-322-1645	760
Intermountain Gas Co Inc						
555 S Cole Rd	Boise	ID	83709	**800-548-3679***	208-377-6840	775
*Cust Svc						
Intermountain HealthCare						
36 S State St	Salt Lake City	UT	84111	**800-843-7820***	801-442-2000	350
*Hum Res						
Intermountain Healthcare Logan Regional Hospital						
500 E 1400 N	Logan	UT	84341	**800-442-4845**	435-716-1000	371-3
Intermountain Rural Electric Assn						
5496 Hwy 85	Sedalia	CO	80135	**800-332-9540**	303-688-3100	245
InterMune Inc						
3280 Bayshore Blvd	Brisbane	CA	94005	**877-862-2292**	415-466-2200	576
NASDAQ: ITMN						
Internal Medicine News						
5635 Fishers Ln Ste 6000	Rockville	MD	20852	**877-524-9336**	240-221-2400	452-16
Internal Revenue Service (IRS)						
1111 Constitution Ave NW	Washington	DC	20224	**800-829-1040**	202-622-9511	338-16

				Toll-Free	Phone	Class
Taxpayer Advocate Service						
77 K St NE Ste 1500	Washington	DC	20002	**877-777-4778**	202-803-9000	338-16
Internap Network Services Corp						
250 Williams St Ste E-100	Atlanta	GA	30303	**877-843-7627**	404-302-9700	38
NASDAQ: INAP						
International Academy of Compounding Pharmacists (IACP)						
4638 Riverstone Blvd	Missouri City	TX	77459	**800-927-4227**	281-933-8400	48-8
Chicago						
One N State St Ste 500	Chicago	IL	60602	**888-318-6111**	312-386-7681	162
Las Vegas						
2495 Village View Dr	Henderson	NV	89074	**866-400-4238**	702-990-0150	162
International Academy of Design & Technology						
Tampa						
5104 Eisenhower Blvd	Tampa	FL	33634	**866-302-4238***	813-881-0007	162
*General						
Toronto						
1835 Yonge St Second Fl	Toronto	ON	M4S1X8	**866-838-6542***		773
*General						
International Aid Inc						
17011 W Hickory St	Spring Lake	MI	49456	**800-968-7490**	616-846-7490	47-5
International Airline Passengers Assn (IAPA)						
PO Box 700188	Dallas	TX	75370	**800-821-4272**	972-404-9980	47-23
International Airlines Travel Agent Network (IATAN)						
800 Pl Victoria P.O. Box 113	Montreal	QC	H4Z1A1	**877-734-2826**	514-868-8800	48-21
International Alliance for Women (TIAW)						
1101 Pennsylvania Ave						
NW Fl 6	Washington	DC	20004	**888-712-5200**		47-24
International Alliance of Theatrical Stage Employees Moving Picture Technicians (IATSE)						
1430 Broadway 20th Fl	New York	NY	10018	**800-456-3863**	212-730-1770	411
International Assn for Food Protection (IAFP)						
6200 Aurora Ave Ste 200W	Des Moines	IA	50322	**800-369-6337***	515-276-3344	48-6
*General						
International Assn for Human Resource Information Management Inc (IHRIM)						
PO Box 1086	Burlington	MA	01803	**800-804-3983**		48-12
International Assn for the Study of Pain (IASP)						
111 Queen Anne Ave N Ste 501	Seattle	WA	98109	**866-574-2654**	206-283-0311	47-17
International Assn of Approved Basketball Officials (IAABO)						
PO Box 355	Carlisle	PA	17013	**800-526-1379**	717-713-8129	47-22
International Assn of Assessing Officers (IAAO)						
314 W Tenth St	Kansas City	MO	64105	**800-616-4226**	816-701-8100	48-7
International Assn of Bridge Structural Ornamental & Reinforcing Iron Workers						
1750 New York Ave NW Ste 400	Washington	DC	20006	**800-368-0105**	202-383-4800	411
International Assn of Business Communicators (IABC)						
601 Montgomery St						
Ste 1900	San Francisco	CA	94111	**800-766-4222**	415-544-4700	48-12
International Assn of Chiefs of Police (IACP)						
515 N Washington St	Alexandria	VA	22314	**800-843-4227**	703-836-6767	48-7
International Assn of Culinary Professionals (IACP)						
1221 Ave of the Americas						
42nd fl	New York	NY	10020	**800-928-4227**	866-358-2524	48-6
International Assn of Electrical Inspectors (IAEI)						
901 Waterfall Way Ste 602	Richardson	TX	75080	**800-786-4234**	972-235-1455	48-3
International Assn of Fairs & Expositions, The (IAFE)						
3043 E Cairo	Springfield	MO	65802	**800-516-0313**	417-862-5771	47-23
International Assn of Fire Chiefs (IAFC)						
4025 Fair Ridge Dr Ste 300	Fairfax	VA	22033	**866-385-9110**	703-273-0911	48-7
International Assn of Marriage & Family Counselors (IAMFC)						
5999 Stevenson Ave	Alexandria	VA	22304	**800-347-6647**		48-15
International Assn of Plumbing & Mechanical Officials (IAPMO)						
4755 E Philadelphia St	Ontario	CA	91761	**877-427-6601**	909-472-4100	48-7
International Assn of Refrigerated Warehouses (IARW)						
1500 King St Ste 201	Alexandria	VA	22314	**800-488-2900**	703-373-4300	48-21
International Assn of Venue Managers Inc (IAVM)						
635 Fritz Dr Ste 100	Coppell	TX	75019	**800-935-4226**	972-906-7441	48-12
International Assn of Workforce Professionals (IAPES)						
1801 Louisville Rd	Frankfort	KY	40601	**888-898-9960**	502-223-4459	48-12
International Bible Society (IBS)						
Biblica						
1820 Jet Stream Dr	Colorado Springs	CO	80921	**800-524-1588***	719-488-9200	47-20
*Cust Svc						
International Biometric Society (IBS)						
1444 'I' St NW Ste 700	Washington	DC	20005	**800-262-1171**	202-712-9049	48-19
International Bottled Water Assn (IBWA)						
1700 Diagonal Rd Ste 650	Alexandria	VA	22314	**800-928-3711**	703-683-5213	48-6
International Boundary & Water Commission - US & Mexico						
4171 N Mesa Ste C-100	El Paso	TX	79902	**800-262-8857**	915-832-4101	338-14
International Business & Finance Daily						
1801 S Bell St	Arlington	VA	22202	**800-372-1033**		524-1
International Business College						
5699 Coventry Ln	Fort Wayne	IN	46804	**800-589-6363**	260-459-4500	788
International Business Machines Corp (IBM)						
One New OrchaRd Rd	Armonk	NY	10504	**800-426-4968**	914-499-1900	174-1
NYSE: IBM						
International Carwash Assn						
230 East Ohio Street	Chicago	IL	60611	**888-422-8422**		48-21
International Cemetery Cremation & Funeral Assn (ICCFA)						
107 Carpenter Dr Ste 100	Sterling	VA	20164	**800-645-7700**	703-391-8400	48-4
International Ceramic Engineering						
235 Brooks St	Worcester	MA	01606	**800-779-3321**	508-853-4700	249
International Chauffeured Service Worldwide						
53 E 34th St Fourth Fl	New York	NY	10016	**800-266-5254**	212-213-0302	437
International Chemical Co						
2628 N Mascher St	Philadelphia	PA	19133	**888-225-5422**	215-739-2313	143
International Chimney Corp						
55 S Long St	Williamsville	NY	14221	**800-828-1446**		190-7
International Chiropractors Assn (ICA)						
6400 Arlington Blvd						
Ste 800	Falls Church	VA	22042	**800-423-4690**	703-528-5000	48-8
International Chiropractors Assn PAC (ICA)						
6400 Arlington Blvd						
Ste 800	Falls Church	VA	22042	**800-423-4690**	703-528-5000	608
International Church of the Foursquare Gospel (ICFG)						
1910 W Sunset Blvd						
PO Box 26902	Los Angeles	CA	90026	**888-635-4234**	213-989-4234	47-20
International City/County Management Assn (ICMA)						
777 N Capitol St NE Ste 500	Washington	DC	20002	**800-745-8780**	202-289-4262	48-7
International Civil Rights Ctr & Museum						
134 S Elm St	Greensboro	NC	27401	**800-748-7116**	336-274-9199	513
International Coatings Co						
13929 166th St	Cerritos	CA	90703	**800-423-4103**	562-926-1010	385
International Code Council (ICC)						
500 New Jersey Ave NW 6th Fl	Washington	DC	20001	**888-422-7233**	202-370-1800	48-3
International Coffee & Tea Inc						
1945 S La Cienega Blvd	Los Angeles	CA	90034	**877-653-1963**	310-237-2326	157
International Cold Storage Company Inc						
215 E 13th St	Andover	KS	67002	**800-835-0001**	316-733-1385	655
International College of Dentists (ICD)						
51 Monroe St Ste 1400	Rockville	MD	20850	**800-533-6825**	301-251-8861	48-8
International Collegiate Licensing Assn (ICLA)						
24651 Detroit Rd	Westlake	OH	44145	**877-887-2261**	440-892-4000	47-22
International Comfort Products Corp (ICP)						
650 Heil Quaker Ave	Lewisburg	TN	37091	**800-458-6650**	931-359-3511	15
International Communications Industries Assn (ICIA)						
11242 Waples Mill Rd Ste 200	Fairfax	VA	22030	**800-659-7469**	703-273-7200	48-20
International Conference of Funeral Service Examining Boards Inc						
1885 Shelby Ln	Fayetteville	AR	72704	**800-709-0180**	479-442-7076	48-7
International Congress of Oral Implantologists (ICOI)						
248 Lorraine Ave						
Third Fl	Upper Montclair	NJ	07043	**800-442-0525**	973-783-6300	48-8
International Contract Furnishings Inc (ICF)						
19 Ohio Ave	Norwich	CT	06360	**800-237-1625**	860-886-1700	320
International Converter Inc						
17153 Industrial Hwy	Caldwell	OH	43724	**800-848-6623**	740-732-5665	547
International Cornea Project						
9246 Lightwave Ave Ste 120	San Diego	CA	92123	**800-393-2265**	858-694-0400	269
International Ctr for Language Studies Inc						
1133 15th St NW Ste 600	Washington	DC	20005	**800-626-2427**	202-639-8800	420
International Dairy Queen Corp						
7505 Metro Blvd	Minneapolis	MN	55439	**866-793-7582**	952-830-0200	661
International Dairy-Deli-Bakery Assn (IDDBA)						
636 Science Dr	Madison	WI	53705	**877-399-4925**	608-238-7908	48-6
International Data Corp (IDC)						
Five Speen St	Framingham	MA	01701	**800-343-4952**	508-872-8200	461
International Data Group Inc (IDG)						
1 Exeter Plaza 15th Fl	Boston	MA	02116	**800-343-4952***	617-534-1200	628-9
*Orders						
International Dyslexia Assn, The (IDA)						
40 York Rd Fourth Fl	Towson	MD	21204	**800-222-3123**	410-296-0232	47-17
International Electronics Inc						
427 Tpke St	Canton	MA	02021	**800-343-9502**	781-821-5566	683
International Engraved Graphics Assn						
305 Plus Pk Blvd	Nashville	TN	37217	**800-821-3138**		48-4
International Executive Housekeepers Assn (IEHA)						
1001 Eastwind Dr Ste 301	Westerville	OH	43081	**800-200-6342**	614-895-7166	48-4
International Exposition Ctr						
1-X Ctr Dr	Cleveland	OH	44135	**855-436-8683**	216-676-6000	206
International Extrusions Inc						
5800 Venoy Rd	Garden City	MI	48135	**800-242-8876**	734-427-8700	477
International Federation of Accountants						
545 Fifth Ave 14th Fl	New York	NY	10017	**888-272-2001**	212-286-9344	48-1
International Fiber Corp						
50 Bridge St	North Tonawanda	NY	14120	**888-698-1936**	716-693-4040	598-1
International Fidelity Insurance Co (IFIC)						
One Newark Ctr 20th Fl	Newark	NJ	07102	**800-333-4167**	973-624-7200	388-5
International Food Information Council Foundation (IFIC)						
1100 Connecticut Ave NW						
Ste 430	Washington	DC	20036	**888-723-3366**	202-296-6540	48-6
International Foundation of Employee Benefit Plans (IFEBP)						
18700 W Bluemound Rd	Brookfield	WI	53045	**888-334-3327**	262-786-6700	260
International Franchise Assn (IFA)						
1501 K St NW Ste 350	Washington	DC	20005	**800-543-1038**	202-628-8000	48-18
International Fraternity of Phi Gamma Delta						
1201 Red Mile Rd PO Box 4599	Lexington	KY	40544	**888-668-4293**	859-255-1848	47-16
International Fund for Animal Welfare (IFAW)						
290 Summer St	Yarmouth Port	MA	02675	**800-932-4329**	508-744-2000	47-3
International Game Technology (IGT)						
9295 Prototype Dr	Reno	NV	89521	**800-522-4700**	775-448-7777	321
NYSE: IGT						
International Gay & Lesbian Travel Assn (IGLTA)						
1201 NE 26th St Ste 103	Fort Lauderdale	FL	33305	**866-845-4472**	954-630-1637	47-23
International Ground Source Heat Pump Assn (IGSHPA)						
Oklahoma State University						
374 Cordell S	Stillwater	OK	74078	**800-626-4747**	405-744-5175	48-13
International Group Inc						
85 Old Eagle School Rd	Wayne	PA	19087	**800-852-6537**	610-687-9030	573
International Health Racquet & Sportsclub Assn (IHRSA)						
70 Fargo St	Boston	MA	02210	**800-228-4772**	617-951-0055	47-22
International Hearing Society (IHS)						
16880 Middlebelt Rd Ste 4	Livonia	MI	48154	**800-521-5247**	734-522-7200	47-17
International Home Furnishings Representatives Assn (IHFRA)						
209 S Main St PO Box 670	High Point	NC	27261	**800-667-9506**	336-889-3920	48-18
International Homes of Cedar Inc (IHC)						
PO Box 886	Woodinville	WA	98072	**800-767-7674**	360-668-8511	105
International Hotel						
20 Second Ave SW	Rochester	MN	55902	**800-940-6811**		376
International House Hotel						
221 Camp St	New Orleans	LA	70130	**800-633-5770**	504-553-9550	376
International Housewares Assn (IHA)						
6400 Shafer Ct Ste 650	Rosemont	IL	60018	**888-689-2838**	847-292-4200	48-4
International Imaging Materials Inc						
310 Commerce Dr	Amherst	NY	14228	**888-464-4625**	716-691-6333	527
International Immunology Corp						
25549 Adams Ave	Murrieta	CA	92562	**800-843-2853**	951-677-5629	231
International Institute of Ammonia Refrigeration						
1001 N Fairfax St Ste 503	Alexandria	VA	22314	**800-937-8461**	703-312-4200	48-3
International Institute of Municipal Clerks (IIMC)						
8331 Utica Ave Ste 200	Rancho Cucamonga	CA	91730	**800-251-1639**	909-944-4162	48-7
International Interior Design Assn (IIDA)						
222 Merchandise Mart Plz						
Ste 567	Chicago	IL	60654	**888-799-4432**	312-467-1950	47-4
International Investigators Inc						
3216 N Pennsylvania St	Indianapolis	IN	46205	**800-403-8111**	317-925-1496	397
International Isotopes Inc						
4137 Commerce Cir	Idaho Falls	ID	83401	**800-699-3108**	208-524-5300	231
OTC: INIS						
International Jet Aviation Services						
8511 Aviator Ln	Centennial	CO	80112	**800-858-5891**	303-790-0414	13
International Label & Printing Company Inc						
2550 United Ln	Elk Grove Village	IL	60007	**800-244-1442**		410
International Launch Services (ILS)						
1875 Explorer St Ste 700	Reston	VA	20190	**800-852-4980**	571-633-7400	499
International Longshore & Warehouse Union						
1188 Franklin St 4th Fl	San Francisco	CA	94109	**866-266-0013**	415-775-0533	411
International Manufacturing Group Inc						
879 F St Ste 120	West Sacramento	CA	95605	**800-775-6412**		470
International Masonry Institute (IMI)						
42 E St	Annapolis	MD	21401	**800-803-0295**	410-280-1305	48-3

Alphabetical Section

	Toll-Free	Phone	Class
International Medical Corps (IMC) 1919 Santa Monica Blvd Ste 400 .... Santa Monica CA 90404	800-481-4462	310-826-7800	47-5
International Medical Device Regulatory Monitor 300 N Washington St Ste 200 .... Falls Church VA 22046	888-838-5578	703-538-7600	524-8
International Meeting Managers Inc 4550 Post Oak Pl Ste 342 .... Houston TX 77027	800-423-7175	713-965-0566	185
International Metal Hose Co 520 Goodrich Rd .... Bellevue OH 44811	800-458-6855	419-483-7690	485
International Microcomputer Software Inc 25 Leveroni Ct .... Novato CA 94949	800-833-8082	415-483-8000	179-8
International Montessori Council & The Montessori Foundation 2400 Miguel Bay Dr PO Box 130 .... Terra Ceia Island FL 34250	800-655-5843	941-729-9565	47-11
International Motor Coach Group Inc (IMG) 8695 College Blvd Ste 260 .... Overland Park KS 66210	888-447-3466	913-906-0111	48-21
International Mountain Bicycling Assn (IMBA) 207 Canyon Blvd Ste 301 PO Box 7578 .... Boulder CO 80306	888-442-4622	303-545-9011	47-23
International Municipal Lawyers Assn (IMLA) 7910 Woodmont Ave Ste 1440 .... Bethesda MD 20814	800-942-7732	202-466-5424	48-10
International Municipal Signal Assn (IMSA) 165 E Union St PO Box 539 .... Newark NY 14513	800-723-4672	315-331-2182	48-7
International Museum of the Horse 4089 Iron Works Pkwy .... Lexington KY 40511	800-678-8813	859-259-4232	513
International Order of the Golden Rule (OGR) 3520 Executive Ctr Dr Ste 300 .... Austin TX 78731	800-637-8030	512-334-5504	48-4
International Organization of Masters Mates & Pilots 700 Maritime Blvd .... Linthicum Heights MD 21090	877-667-5522	410-850-8700	411
International Orthodox Christian Charities (IOCC) 110 W Rd Ste 360 .... Towson MD 21204	877-803-4622	410-243-9820	47-5
International Paper Co 6400 Poplar Ave .... Memphis TN 38197 *NYSE: IP ■ *Prod Info*	800-223-1268*	901-419-9000	550
International Patterns Inc 50 Inez Dr .... Bay Shore NY 11706	800-471-6368	631-952-2000	692
International Planned Parenthood Federation - Western Hemisphere Region (IPPF/WHR) 120 Wall St 9th Fl .... New York NY 10005	866-477-3947	212-248-6400	47-5
International Plant Nutrition Institute (IPNI) 3500 PkwyLn Ste 550 .... Norcross GA 30092	800-521-3044	770-447-0335	47-2
International Playthings Inc 75D Lackawanna Ave .... Parsippany NJ 07054	800-631-1272	973-316-2500	752
International Poly Bag Inc 990 Pk Ctr Dr Ste F .... Vista CA 92081	800-976-5922	760-598-2468	65
International Port of Dutch Harbor PO Box 610 .... Unalaska AK 99685	800-526-6731	907-581-1251	611
International Public Management Assn for Hum Res (IPMA-HR) 1617 Duke St .... Alexandria VA 22314	800-381-8378	703-549-7100	48-12
International Reading Assn (IRA) 800 Barksdale Rd PO Box 6021 .... Newark DE 19714	800-336-7323	302-731-1600	48-5
International Reprographic Assn (IRgA) 401 N Michigan Ave Ste 2200 .... Chicago IL 60611	800-833-4742	312-245-1026	48-16
International Rescue Committee (IRC) 122 E 42nd St 12th Fl .... New York NY 10168	800-435-7352	212-551-3000	47-5
International Revolving Door Co 2138 N Sixth Ave .... Evansville IN 47710	800-745-4726	812-425-3311	234
International Safe Transit Assn (ISTA) 1400 Abbott Rd Ste 160 .... East Lansing MI 48823	888-299-2208	517-333-3437	48-21
International Sanitary Supply Assn (ISSA) 3300 Dundee Rd .... Northbrook IL 60062	800-225-4772	847-982-0800	48-18
International Shipholding Corp 11 N Water St 18290 .... Mobile AL 36602 *NYSE: ISH*	800-826-3513	251-243-9100	312
International Sight Restoration Inc 3808 Gunn Hwy Ste B .... Tampa FL 33618	877-477-3210	813-264-6003	269
International Sign Assn (ISA) 1001 N Fairfax St Ste 301 .... Alexandria VA 22314	866-949-7446	703-836-4012	48-4
International Society for Animal Rights (ISAR) PO Box F .... Clarks Summit PA 18411	888-589-6397	570-586-2200	47-3
International Society for Heart & Lung Transplantation (ISHLT) 14673 Midway Rd Ste 200 .... Addison TX 75001	888-722-2220	972-490-9495	48-8
International Society for Magnetic Resonance in Medicine (ISMRM) 2030 Addison St Ste 700 .... Berkeley CA 94704	877-837-4400	510-841-1899	48-8
International Society for Performance Improvement (ISPI) 1400 Spring St Ste 260 .... Silver Spring MD 20910	800-825-7550	301-587-8570	48-12
International Society for Pharmacoeconomics & Outcomes Research (ISPOR) 3100 Princeton Pk Bldg 3 Ste E .... Lawrenceville NJ 08648	800-992-0643	609-219-0773	48-8
International Society for Pharmacoepidemiology (ISPE) 5272 River Rd Ste 630 .... Bethesda MD 20816	888-887-7955	301-718-6500	48-8
International Society for Technology in Education (ISTE) 1710 Rhode Island Ave NW Ste 900 .... Washington DC 20036 *General	800-336-5191*	202-861-7777	48-5
International Society of Arboriculture (ISA) PO Box 3129 .... Champaign IL 61826	888-472-8733	217-355-9411	47-2
International Society of Certified Electronics Technicians (ISCET) 3608 Pershing Ave .... Fort Worth TX 76107	800-946-0201	817-921-9101	48-19
International Society of Certified Employee Benefit Specialists (ISCEBS) 18700 W Bluemond Rd PO Box 209 .... Brookfield WI 53008	888-334-3327	262-786-8771	48-12
International Society of Fire Service Instructors (ISFSI) 14001C St Germain Dr .... Centreville VA 20121	800-435-0005		48-7
International Society of Refractive Surgery (ISRS) 655 Beach St PO Box 7424 .... San Francisco CA 94109	866-561-8558	415-561-8581	48-8
International Society of Tropical Foresters (ISTF) 5400 Grosvenor Ln .... Bethesda MD 20814	866-897-8720	301-530-4514	47-13
International SOS Assistance Inc 3600 Horizon Blvd Ste 300 .... Trevose PA 19053	888-413-9071	215-244-1500	388-7
International Specialty Products Inc (ISP) 1361 Alps Rd .... Wayne NJ 07470	800-622-4423	973-628-4000	142
International Tax Monitor 1801 S Bell St .... Arlington VA 22202	800-372-1033		524-1
International Technidyne Corp Eight Olsen Ave .... Edison NJ 08820	800-631-5945	732-548-5700	472
International Tennis Hall of Fame & Museum 194 Bellevue Ave .... Newport RI 02840	800-745-3000	401-849-3990	515
International Trade Reporter 1801 S Bell St .... Arlington VA 22202	800-372-1033		524-2
International Trademark Assn (INTA) 655 Third Ave 10th Fl .... New York NY 10017	800-995-3579	212-768-9887	48-12
International Transplant Nurses Society (ITNS) 1739 E Carson St PO Box 351 .... Pittsburgh PA 15203	800-776-8636	412-343-4867	48-8
International Travel Systems Inc 64 Madison Ave 2nd Fl .... Wood-Ridge NJ 07075	800-258-0135	201-727-0470	16
International Union of Bricklayers & Allied Craftworkers (BAC) 1776 eye St NW .... Washington DC 20006	888-880-8222	202-783-3788	411
International Union of Painters & Allied Trades (IUPAT) 7234 Pkwy Dr .... Hanover MD 21076	800-554-2479	410-564-5900	411
International Union of Police Assn 1549 Ringling Blvd Ste 600 .... Sarasota FL 34236	800-247-4872	941-487-2560	411
International Union Security Police & Fire Professionals of America (SPFPA) 25510 Kelly Rd .... Roseville MI 48066	800-228-7492	586-772-7250	411
International Violin Co Ltd 1421 Clarkview Rd .... Baltimore MD 21209	800-542-3538	410-832-2525	519
International Visual Corp (IVC) 11839 Rodolphe Forget .... Montreal QC H1E7J8	866-643-0570	514-643-0570	286
International Window Corp 5625 E Firestone Blvd .... South Gate CA 90280	800-477-4032	562-928-6411	234
International Women's Air & Space Museum 1501 N Marginal Rd Burke Lakefront Airport .... Cleveland OH 44114	877-287-4752	216-623-1111	513
International Wood Products Assn (IWPA) 4214 King St .... Alexandria VA 22302	855-435-0005	703-820-6696	48-3
Internet America Inc 12853 Capricorn St .... Stafford TX 77477	800-232-4335		395
Internet Business Network 303 Ross Dr .... Mill Valley CA 94941	866-497-6747	415-377-2255	628-9
Internet Law & Strategy 1617 JFK Blvd Ste 1750 .... Philadelphia PA 19103	877-256-2472	215-557-2300	524-7
Internet Public Library University of Michigan School of Information 304 W Hall .... Ann Arbor MI 48109	800-545-2433	734-763-2285	394
InternetSafety.com Inc 3979 S Main St Ste 230 .... Acworth GA 30101	877-944-8080		179-7
Inter-Pacific Corp 2257 Colby Ave .... Los Angeles CA 90064	877-605-8414	310-473-7591	300
Interphase Corp 2901 N Dallas Pkwy Ste 200 .... Plano TX 75093 *NASDAQ: INPH*	800-327-8638	214-654-5000	177
Interplastic Corp 1225 Wolters Blvd .... Saint Paul MN 55110	800-736-5497	651-481-6860	598-2
Interpoint Corp PO Box 97005 .... Redmond WA 98073	800-822-8782	425-882-3100	253
Interpreters Unlimited Inc 11199 Sorrento Vly Rd Ste 203 .... San Diego CA 92121	800-726-9891		758
Interprint LLC 7111 Hayvenhurst Ave .... Van Nuys CA 91406	800-926-9873	818-989-3600	619
InterraTech Corp PO Box 4 .... Mount Ephraim NJ 08059	888-589-4889	856-854-5100	179-1
Interroll Corp 3000 Corporate Dr .... Wilmington NC 28405 *Sales	800-830-9680*	910-799-1100	208
Intersections Inc 3901 Stonecroft Blvd PO Box 222455 .... Chantilly VA 20151 *NASDAQ: INTX*	800-695-7536	703-488-6100	217
Interserve USA 7000 Ludlow St .... Upper Darby PA 19082	800-809-4440	610-352-0581	47-20
Intersil Corp 1001 Murphy Ranch Rd .... Milpitas CA 95035 *NASDAQ: ISIL*	888-468-3774	408-432-8888	687
Interstate Aviation 62 Johnson Ave .... Plainville CT 06062	800-573-5519	860-747-5519	62
Interstate Batteries 12770 Merit Dr Ste 400 .... Dallas TX 75251	800-541-8419	972-991-1444	60
Interstate Chemical Co Inc 2797 Freedland Rd .... Hermitage PA 16148	800-422-2436	724-981-3771	141
Interstate Connecting Components Inc 120 Mt Holly By Pass .... Lumberton NJ 08048	888-899-1990		246
Interstate Distributor Co 11707 21st Ave S .... Tacoma WA 98444	800-426-8560		770
Interstate Electrical Supply Inc 2300 Second Ave .... Columbus GA 31901	800-903-4409	706-324-1000	246
Interstate Electronics Corp 602 E Vermont Ave PO Box 3117 .... Anaheim CA 92803	800-854-6979	714-758-0500	522
Interstate Oil & Gas Compact Commission (IOGCC) 900 NE 23rd St PO Box 53127 .... Oklahoma City OK 73152	800-822-4015	405-525-3556	47-12
Interstate Transport Inc 324 First Ave N .... St Petersburg FL 33701	866-281-1281	727-822-9999	641
Interstates Construction Services Inc 1520 N Main Ave .... Sioux Center IA 51250	800-827-1662	712-722-1662	190-4
Interstyle Ceramics & Glass Ltd 3625 Brighton Ave .... Burnaby BC V5A3H5	800-667-1566	604-421-7229	741
Intertek Group PLC 801 Travis St Ste 1500 .... Houston TX 77002	800-967-5352	713-407-3500	261
Intertrade Industries Ltd 15632 Commerce Ln .... Huntington Beach CA 92649	800-944-9277	714-894-5566	594
InterTrust Technologies Corp 920 Stewart Dr Ste 100 .... Sunnyvale CA 94085	800-393-2272	408-616-1600	179-12
Interval International Inc 6262 Sunset Dr PO Box 431920 .... Miami FL 33143	800-828-8200	305-666-1861	743
InterVarsity Christian Fellowship/USA 6400 Schroeder Rd .... Madison WI 53711	866-734-4823	608-274-9001	47-20
Intervest Bancshares Corp 1 Rockefeller Plaza Ste 400 .... New York NY 10020 *NASDAQ: IBCA*	877-226-5462	212-218-8383	357-2
Interview Magazine 575 Broadway Fifth Fl .... New York NY 10012	800-925-9574	212-941-2900	452-11
InterWest Insurance Services Inc 3636 American River Dr 2nd Fl .... Sacramento CA 95864	800-444-4134	916-679-2960	387
InterWest Partners 2710 Sand Hill Rd 2nd Fl .... Menlo Park CA 94025	866-803-9204	650-854-8585	780
Intex Recreation Corp 1665 Hughes Way PO Box 1440 .... Long Beach CA 90801 *Cust Svc	800-234-6839*	310-847-6981	701
Intland GmbH 968 Inverness Way .... Sunnyvale CA 94087	866-468-5210		390
Intradiem 3650 Mansell Rd Ste 500 .... Alpharetta GA 30022	888-566-9457	678-356-3500	179-10
Intrado Inc 1601 Dry Creek Dr .... Longmont CO 80503	877-262-3775	720-494-5800	726
IntraLinks Inc 150 E 42nd St Ste 8 .... New York NY 10017	888-546-5383	212-543-7700	38

Name / Address				Toll-Free	Phone	Class
Intratek Computer Inc						
5431 Industrial Dr	Huntington Beach	CA	92649	800-892-8282		176
Intrepid Potash Inc						
700 17th St Ste 1700	Denver	CO	80202	800-451-2888	303-296-3006	280
NYSE: IPI						
Intrepid Sea-Air-Space Museum						
W 46th St & 12th Ave Pier 86	New York	NY	10036	877-957-7447	212-245-0072	513
Intrinsix Corp						
100 Campus Dr	Marlborough	MA	01752	800-783-0330	508-658-7600	261
Intrusion Inc						
1101 E Arapaho Rd	Richardson	TX	75081	888-637-7770	972-234-6400	179-12
Intsel Steel Distributors LP						
11310 W Little York	Houston	TX	77041	800-762-3316	713-937-9500	714
Intuit Inc						
2632 Marine Way	Mountain View	CA	94043	800-446-8848*	650-944-6000	179-9
*NASDAQ: INTU ■ *Cust Svc*						
Intuitive Surgical Inc						
1266 Kifer Rd Bldg 101	Sunnyvale	CA	94086	888-868-4647	408-523-2100	471
NASDAQ: ISRG						
Inuit Gallery of Vancouver Ltd						
206 Cambie St Gastown	Vancouver	BC	V6B2M9	888-615-8399	604-688-7323	41
Invacare Corp						
One Invacare Way	Elyria	OH	44036	800-333-6900	440-329-6000	472
NYSE: IVC						
Invent Now, Inc						
3701 Highland Park NW	North Canton	OH	44720	800-968-4332		513
Inventory Sales Co						
9777 Reavis Rd	St Louis	MO	63123	866-417-3801	314-776-6200	347
Inver Hills Community College						
2500 80th St E	Inver Grove Heights	MN	55076	866-576-0689	651-450-8500	160
Inverness Hotel & Golf Club						
200 Inverness Dr W	Englewood	CO	80112	800-346-4891	303-799-5800	660
Inverrary Resort						
3501 Inverrary Blvd	Fort Lauderdale	FL	33319	800-241-0363	954-485-0500	660
Invesco						
11 Greenway Plaza Ste 100	Houston	TX	77046	800-959-4246	713-626-1919	521
INVESCO Private Capital Inc						
1166 Ave of the Americas						
26th Fl	New York	NY	10036	800-959-4246	212-278-9000	780
Investment Management Consultants Assn (IMCA)						
5619 DTC Pkwy Ste 500	Greenwood Village	CO	80111	800-250-9083	303-770-3377	48-2
Investor's Business Daily						
12655 Beatrice St	Los Angeles	CA	90066	800-831-2525	310-448-6000	525-2
InvestorPlace.com						
2420A Gehman Ln						
2420A Gehman Ln	Lancaster	PA	17602	800-219-8592		401
Investors Heritage Life Insurance Co (IHLIC)						
200 Capital Ave PO Box 717	Frankfort	KY	40602	800-422-2011	502-223-2361	388-2
Investors Real Estate Trust						
1400 31st Ave Se 60	Minot	ND	58701	888-478-4738	701-837-4738	645
NYSE: IRET						
Investors Savings Bank						
101 Wood Ave S	Iselin	NJ	08830	855-422-6548	973-924-5100	69
NASDAQ: ISBC						
Investors Title Co						
121 N Columbia St	Chapel Hill	NC	27514	800-326-4842	919-968-2200	357-4
NASDAQ: ITIC						
Investrade Discount Securities						
950 N Milwaukee Ave Ste 102	Glenview	IL	60025	800-498-7120*	847-375-6080	681
*Cust Svc						
Invincible Office Furniture Co						
842 S 26th St PO Box 1117	Manitowoc	WI	54220	877-682-4601	920-682-4601	318-1
INVISTA						
4123 E 37th St N	Wichita	KS	67220	877-446-8478	316-828-1000	598-1
InVite Health Inc						
One Garden State Plz	Paramus	NJ	07652	800-349-0929	201-587-2222	342
Inviting Home.com						
4700 SW 51st St Unit 219	Davie	FL	33314	866-751-6606	781-444-8001	320
InVitro International						
17751 Sky Pk Cir Ste G	Irvine	CA	92614	800-246-8487	949-851-8356	231
Invivoscribe Technologies Inc						
6330 Nancy Ridge Dr Ste 106	San Diego	CA	92121	866-623-8105	858-224-6600	231
Invoke Solutions Inc						
375 Totten Pond Rd	Waltham	MA	02451	866-687-4367	781-810-2700	461
IOA Re Inc						
190 W Germantown Pk						
Ste 200	East Norriton	PA	19401	800-462-2300	610-940-9000	388-3
IOCC (International Orthodox Christian Charities)						
110 W Rd Ste 360	Towson	MD	21204	877-803-4622	410-243-9820	47-5
IOF (Independent Order of Foresters)						
789 Don Mills Rd	Toronto	ON	M3C1T9	800-828-1540	416-429-3000	47-5
IOGCC (Interstate Oil & Gas Compact Commission)						
900 NE 23rd St						
PO Box 53127	Oklahoma City	OK	73152	800-822-4015	405-525-3556	47-12
Iolani School						
563 Kamoku St	Honolulu	HI	96826	888-879-8970	808-949-5355	
Ioline Corp						
14140 NE 200th St	Woodinville	WA	98072	800-598-0029	425-398-8282	733
ION (Institute of Navigation Inc)						
8551 Rixlew Ln Ste 360	Manassas	VA	20109	800-696-7353	703-366-2723	48-21
Ion Media Networks						
601 Clearwater Pk Rd	West Palm Beach	FL	33401	800-987-9936	561-659-4122	729
Ion Networks Inc						
120 Corporate Blvd						
Ste A	South Plainfield	NJ	07080	800-722-8986	908-546-3900	179-7
Iona College						
715 N Ave	New Rochelle	NY	10801	800-264-6350	914-633-2502	166
IoPP (Institute of Packaging Professionals)						
1833 Centre Point Cir						
Ste 123	Naperville	IL	60563	800-432-4085	630-544-5050	48-13
Iowa						
Adult Children & Family Services Div						
1305 E Walnut St	Des Moines	IA	50319	800-735-2942	515-281-3094	337-16
Child Support Recovery Unit						
PO Box 9125	Des Moines	IA	50306	888-229-9223		337-16
Consumer Protection Div						
1305 E Walnut St 2nd Fl	Des Moines	IA	50319	888-777-4590	515-281-5926	337-16
Elder Affairs Dept						
510 E 12th Street Ste 2	Des Moines	IA	50309	800-532-3213	515-242-3333	337-16
Motor Vehicle Div						
100 Euclid Ave PO Box 9204	Des Moines	IA	50306	800-532-1121	515-244-9124	337-16
Revenue & Finance Dept						
1305 E Walnut	Des Moines	IA	50319	800-367-3388	515-281-3204	337-16
Utilities Board						
1375 E Ct Ave Rm 69	Des Moines	IA	50319	877-565-4450	515-725-7300	337-16
Iowa 80 Group Inc						
515 Sterling Dr PO Box 639	Walcott	IA	52773	800-336-9889	563-284-6965	323
Iowa Assn of Business & Industry						
400 E Ct Ave Ste 100	Des Moines	IA	50309	800-383-4224	515-280-8000	138
Iowa Assn of Realtors						
1370 NW 114th St Ste 100	Clive	IA	50325	800-532-1515	515-453-1064	647
Iowa Central Community College						
2031 Quail Ave	Fort Dodge	IA	50501	800-362-2793	515-576-7201	160
Iowa City Area Chamber of Commerce						
325 E Washington St Ste 100	Iowa City	IA	52240	800-283-6592	319-337-9637	137
Iowa City Public Library						
123 S Linn St	Iowa City	IA	52240	866-862-6877	319-356-5200	431-3
Iowa City/Coralville Area Convention & Visitors Bureau						
900 First Ave Hayden						
Fry Way	Coralville	IA	52241	800-283-6592	319-337-6592	207
Iowa College Student Aid Commission						
603 E 12th St Fl 5th	Des Moines	IA	50319	800-383-4222	515-725-3400	716
Iowa Dental Assn						
8797 NW 54th Ave Ste 100	Johnston	IA	50131	800-828-2181	515-331-2298	227
Iowa Farm Bureau Spokesman Magazine						
5400 University Ave	West Des Moines	IA	50266	866-598-3693	515-225-5413	452-1
Iowa Interstate Railroad						
5900 Sixth St SW	Cedar Rapids	IA	52404	800-321-3884	319-298-5400	639
Iowa Lakes Community College						
300 S 18th St	Estherville	IA	51334	800-242-5106	712-362-2604	160
Iowa Lakes Electric Co-op						
702 S First St	Estherville	IA	51334	800-225-4532	712-362-7870	245
Iowa Medical Society						
1001 Grand Ave	West Des Moines	IA	50265	800-747-3070	515-223-1401	469
Iowa Medicine Magazine						
1001 Grand Ave	West Des Moines	IA	50265	800-747-3070	515-223-1401	452-16
Iowa Mold Tooling Co Inc (IMT)						
500 W US Hwy 18	Garner	IA	50438	800-247-5958	641-923-3711	465
Iowa Pharmacy Assn						
8515 Douglas Ave Ste 16	Des Moines	IA	50322	866-512-1800	515-270-0713	578
Iowa Prison Industries (IPI)						
1445 E Grand Ave	Des Moines	IA	50316	800-670-4537	515-242-5770	622
Iowa Public Television						
6450 Corporate Dr	Johnston	IA	50131	800-532-1290	515-242-3100	730
Iowa Realty Company Inc						
3501 Westown Pkwy	West Des Moines	IA	50266	800-247-2430	515-453-6222	643
Iowa State University						
100 Alumni Hall	Ames	IA	50011	800-262-3810*	515-294-4111	166
*Admissions						
Iowa Veterans Home						
1301 Summit St Bldg 3465	Marshalltown	IA	50131	800-838-4692	515-252-4698	781
Iowa Veterinary Medical Assn						
1605 N Ankeny Blvd Ste 110	Ankeny	IA	50023	800-369-9564	515-965-9237	783
Iowa Veterinary Supply Co (IVESCO)						
124 Country Club Rd	Iowa Falls	IA	50126	800-457-0118	641-648-2529	470
Iowa Wesleyan College						
601 N Main St	Mount Pleasant	IA	52641	800-582-2383		166
Iowa Western Community College						
Clarinda						
923 E Washington St	Clarinda	IA	51632	800-521-2073	712-542-5117	160
Iowa Workforce Development						
1000 E Grand Ave	Des Moines	IA	50319	800-562-4692	515-281-5387	259
IP Casino Resort & Spa						
850 Bayview Ave	Biloxi	MS	39530	888-946-2847*	228-436-3000	132
*Resv						
IPAA (Independent Petroleum Assn of America)						
1201 15th St NW Ste 300	Washington	DC	20005	800-433-2851	202-857-4722	47-12
iPass Inc						
3800 Bridge Pkwy	Redwood Shores	CA	94065	877-236-3807	650-232-4100	391
NASDAQ: IPAS						
ipDataTel LLC						
13110 SW Fwy	Sugar Land	TX	77478	866-896-1818	713-452-2700	253
IPG Photonics Corp						
50 Old Webster Rd	Oxford	MA	01540	877-980-1550	508-373-1100	422
NASDAQ: IPGP						
IPI (Iowa Prison Industries)						
1445 E Grand Ave	Des Moines	IA	50316	800-670-4537	515-242-5770	622
IPMA-HR (International Public Management Assn for Hum Res)						
1617 Duke St	Alexandria	VA	22314	800-381-8378	703-549-7100	48-12
IPNI (International Plant Nutrition Institute)						
3500 PkwyLn Ste 550	Norcross	GA	30092	800-521-3044	770-447-0335	47-2
IPPF/WHR (International Planned Parenthood Federation - Western Hemisphere Region)						
120 Wall St 9th Fl	New York	NY	10005	866-477-3947	212-248-6400	47-5
IPS (Institute for Policy Studies)						
1112 16th St NW Ste 600	Washington	DC	20036	877-564-6833	202-234-9382	625
IPS Corp						
455 W Victoria St	Compton	CA	90220	800-888-8312	310-898-3300	3
Ipsen Inc						
PO Box 6266	Rockford	IL	61125	800-727-7625	815-332-4941	317
IPST (Institute of Paper Science & Technology)						
500 Tenth St NW	Atlanta	GA	30332	800-558-6611	404-894-5700	48-13
Ipswich Shellfish Co Inc						
8 Hayward St	Ipswich	MA	01938	800-477-9424	978-356-6800	296-5
Ipswitch Inc						
83 Hartwell Ave	Lexington	MA	02421	800-793-4825	781-676-5700	179-12
IPTV (Idaho Public Television)						
1455 N Orchard St	Boise	ID	83706	800-543-6868	208-373-7220	624
IRA (International Reading Assn)						
800 Barksdale Rd PO Box 6021	Newark	DE	19714	800-336-7323	302-731-1600	48-5
Ira Green Inc						
177 Georgia Ave	Providence	RI	02905	800-663-7487*	401-467-4770	406
*General						
IRC (International Rescue Committee)						
122 E 42nd St 12th Fl	New York	NY	10168	800-435-7352	212-551-3000	47-5
IRC (Insurance Research Council)						
720 Providence Rd	Malvern	PA	19355	800-644-2101	610-644-2212	48-9
Iredale Mineral Cosmetics Ltd						
28 Church St	Great Barrington	MA	01230	877-869-9420	413-528-1078	238
Ireland						
Embassy						
2234 Massachusetts Ave NW	Washington	DC	20008	866-560-1050	202-462-3939	257
IREM (Institute of Real Estate Management)						
430 N Michigan Ave	Chicago	IL	60611	800-837-0706	312-329-6000	48-17
Irex Contracting Group						
120 N Lime St	Lancaster	PA	17608	800-487-7255		190-9
IRgA (International Reprographic Assn)						
401 N Michigan Ave Ste 2200	Chicago	IL	60611	800-833-4742	312-245-1026	48-16

	Toll-Free	Phone	Class
Iridex Corp			
1212 Terra Bella Ave ....Mountain View CA 94043	**800-388-4747***	650-940-4700	421
NASDAQ: IRIX ■ *Cust Svc			
Iridium Satellite LLC			
6701 Democracy Blvd ....Bethesda MD 20817	**866-947-4348**	301-571-6200	726
IRIS International Inc			
9172 Eton Ave ....Chatsworth CA 91311	**877-920-4747**	818-709-1244	379
NASDAQ: IRIS			
Iris USA Inc			
11111 80th Ave ....Pleasant Prairie WI 53158	**800-320-4747**	262-612-1000	600
Irish Tourist Board			
345 Pk Ave 17th Fl ....New York NY 10154	**800-223-6470**	212-418-0800	765
Iron & Metals Inc			
5555 Franklin St ....Denver CO 80216	**800-776-7910**	303-292-5555	677
Iron City Distributing Co			
2670 Commercial Ave ...Mingo Junction OH 43938	**800-759-2671***	740-598-4171	80-1
*Cust Svc			
Iron City Uniform Rental			
6640 Frankstown Ave ....Pittsburgh PA 15206	**800-532-2010**	412-661-2001	438
Iron Mountain			
745 Atlantic Ave ....Boston MA 02111	**800-899-4766**	617-535-4766	791-1
NYSE: IRM			
Iron Range Tourism Bureau			
403 N First St ....Virginia MN 55792	**800-777-8497**	218-749-8161	207
Iron Tribe Franchise LLC			
300 27th St S ....Birmingham AL 35233	**855-226-8699**	205-226-8669	351
Ironman Magazine			
1701 Ives Ave ....Oxnard CA 93033	**800-447-0008**	805-385-3500	452-13
IronMaster LLC			
14562 167th Ave SE Ste E ....Monroe WA 98272	**800-533-3339**	360-217-7780	267
Ironplanet Inc			
3825 Hopyard Rd Ste 250...........Pleasanton CA 94588	**888-433-5426***	925-225-8600	50
*Cust Svc			
Ironrock Capital Inc			
1201 Millerton St SE ....Canton OH 44707	**800-325-3945**	330-484-4887	741
Ironworkers Political Action League			
1750 New York Ave NW Ste 400......Washington DC 20006	**800-368-0105**	202-383-4800	608
Iroquois Gas Transmission System LP			
1 Corporate Dr Ste 600............Shelton CT 06484	**800-888-3982**	203-925-7200	324
Iroquois New York			
49 W 44th St ....New York City NY 10036	**800-332-7220**	212-840-3080	376
Iroquois Products of Chicago			
2220 W 56th St ....Chicago IL 60636	**800-453-3355**		200
Irresistibles			
Seven Hawkes St ....Marblehead MA 01945	**800-555-9865**	781-631-1248	155-6
IRS (Internal Revenue Service)			
1111 Constitution Ave NW ......Washington DC 20224	**800-829-1040**	202-622-9511	338-16
IRS Practice Adviser			
1801 S Bell St ....Arlington VA 22202	**800-372-1033**		524-7
IRSC (Indian River State College)			
3209 Virginia Ave ....Fort Pierce FL 34981	**866-792-4772**	772-462-4772	160
Irvine Access Floors Inc			
9425 Washington Blvd ....Laurel MD 20723	**888-458-6339**	301-617-9333	486
Irvine Chamber of Commerce			
2485 McCabe Way Ste 150 ....Irvine CA 92614	**800-321-2211***	949-660-9112	137
*General			
Irvine Scientific			
2511 Daimler St ....Santa Ana CA 92705	**800-577-6097**	949-261-7800	84
Irvine Technology Corp			
201 E Sandpointe Ave Ste 300 ......Santa Ana CA 92707	**866-322-4482**		195
Irving Convention & Visitors Bureau			
222 W Las Colinas Blvd Ste 1550 .....Irving TX 75039	**800-247-8464**	972-252-7476	207
Irving Mall			
3880 Irving Mall ....Irving TX 75062	**877-746-6642**	972-255-0571	455
Irvington General Hospital			
95 Old Short Hills Rd ....West Orange NJ 07052	**888-724-7123**		371-3
Irwin Electric Membership Corp			
915 W Fourth St ....Ocilla GA 31774	**800-237-3745**	229-468-7415	245
Irwin Naturals			
5310 Beethoven St ....Los Angeles CA 90066	**800-297-3273**	310-306-3636	787
Irwin Seating Company Inc			
3251 Fruit Ridge NW ....Grand Rapids MI 49544	**866-464-7946**	616-574-7400	318-3
ISA (International Sign Assn)			
1001 N Fairfax St Ste 301.........Alexandria VA 22314	**866-949-7446**	703-836-4012	48-4
ISA (International Society of Arboriculture)			
PO Box 3129 ....Champaign IL 61826	**888-472-8733**	217-355-9411	47-2
Isaak Bond Investments Inc			
3900 S Wadsworth Blvd Ste 590 ......Lakewood CO 80202	**800-279-4426**	303-623-7500	681
Isabel Bloom LLC			
736 Federal St Ste 2100 ....Davenport IA 52803	**800-273-5436**		184
ISACA (Information Systems Audit & Control Assn)			
3701 Algonquin Rd			
Ste 1010....................Rolling Meadows IL 60008	**888-491-8833**	847-253-1545	47-9
Isagenix International LLC			
2225 S Price Rd ....Chandler AZ 85286	**877-877-8111**	480-889-5747	295-11
ISAR (International Society for Animal Rights)			
PO Box F ....Clarks Summit PA 18411	**888-589-6397**	570-586-2200	47-3
ISCEBS (International Society of Certified Employee Benefit Specialists)			
18700 W Bluemond Rd			
PO Box 209..................Brookfield WI 53008	**888-334-3327**	262-786-8771	48-12
ISCET (International Society of Certified Electronics Technicians)			
3608 Pershing Ave ....Fort Worth TX 76107	**800-946-0201**	817-921-9101	48-19
ISCO Inc			
4700 Superior St PO Box 82531.........Lincoln NE 68501	**800-228-4250**	402-464-0231	416
Isco Industries			
926 Baxter Ave PO Box 4545 ....Louisville KY 40204	**800-345-4726**	502-583-6591	589
ISCO International LLC			
1450 Arthur Ave Ste A .....Elk Grove Village IL 60007	**888-948-4726**	224-222-1666	725
ISFSI (International Society of Fire Service Instructors)			
14001C St Germain Dr ....Centreville VA 20121	**800-435-0005**		48-7
ISG Novasoft (ISGN)			
600 A N John Rodes Blvd ....Melbourne FL 32934	**800-939-8258**		179-1
ISGN (ISG Novasoft)			
600 A N John Rodes Blvd ....Melbourne FL 32934	**800-939-8258**		179-1
ISHLT (International Society for Heart & Lung Transplantation)			
14673 Midway Rd Ste 200 ....Addison TX 75001	**888-722-2220**	972-490-9495	48-8
ISI (Intercollegiate Studies Institute)			
3901 Centerville Rd ....Wilmington DE 19807	**800-526-7022**	302-652-4600	47-11
ISI Commercial Refrigeration LP			
9136 Viscount Row ....Dallas TX 75247	**800-777-5070**	214-631-7980	656
Isis Pharmaceuticals Inc			
2855 Gazelle Ct ....Carlsbad CA 92008	**800-679-4747**	760-931-9200	84
NASDAQ: ISIS			

	Toll-Free	Phone	Class
iSky			
1700 Pennsylvania Ave NW			
Ste 560 ....Washington DC 20006	**855-475-4759**		727
Islamorada Chamber of Commerce			
PO Box 915 ....Islamorada FL 33036	**800-322-5397**	305-664-4503	137
Islamorada Fish Co			
81532 Overseas Hwy			
PO Box 283. ....Islamorada FL 33036	**800-258-2559**		662
Island Express Helicopter Service			
1175 Queens Hwy S ....Long Beach CA 90802	**800-228-2566***	310-510-2525	356
*Cust Svc			
Island Federal Credit Union			
120 Motor Pkwy ....Hauppauge NY 11788	**800-475-5263**	631-851-1100	219
Island Hotel, The			
690 Newport Ctr Dr ....Newport Beach CA 92660	**866-554-4620**	949-759-0808	376
Island Lincoln-Mercury Inc			
1850 E Merritt			
Island Cswy ....Merritt Island FL 32952	**800-392-3673**	321-452-9220	56
Island Oasis			
141 Norfolk St PO Box 769...........Walpole MA 02081	**800-777-4752**	508-660-1176	298
Island Pacific Inc			
17310 Red Hill Ave Ste 320 ....Irvine CA 92614	**800-994-3847**		179-10
Island Packet			
10 Buck Island Rd ....Bluffton SC 29910	**877-706-8100**	843-706-8100	525-2
Island Press			
2000 M St NW Suite 650 ....Washington DC 20036	**800-621-2736**	202-232-7933	628-2
Island Runner Boats			
PO Box 530098 ....Lake Park FL 33403	**800-749-4322**	954-829-3252	89
Island View Casino Resort			
3300 W Beach Blvd PO Box 1600........Gulfport MS 39502	**888-777-9696***	228-314-2100	132
*General			
Island Windjammers Inc			
165 Shaw Dr ....Acworth GA 30102	**877-772-4549**		31
Islands in the Sun Cruises & Tours Inc			
121 Bayview ....Grasonville MD 21638	**800-278-7786**	410-827-3812	761
Islands Magazine			
460 N Orlando Ave Ste 200 ....Winter Park FL 32789	**800-250-1523**	515-237-3697	452-22
Isle of Capri Casino			
401 Main St ....Black Hawk CO 80422	**800-843-4753***	303-998-7777	132
*resv			
Isle of Capri Casino Hotel Lake Charles			
100 W Lake Ave ....Westlake LA 70669	**800-843-4753**		132
ISM (Institute for Supply Management)			
2055 Centennial Cir ....Tempe AZ 85284	**800-888-6276***	480-752-6276	48-12
*Cust Svc			
ISMIE (Illinois State Medical Inter-Insurance Exchange)			
20 N Michigan Ave Ste 700 ....Chicago IL 60602	**800-782-4767**	312-782-2749	388-5
ISMRM (International Society for Magnetic Resonance in Medicine)			
2030 Addison St Ste 700 ....Berkeley CA 94704	**877-837-4400**	510-841-1899	48-8
ISO (Insurance Services Office Inc)			
545 Washington Blvd ....Jersey City NJ 07310	**800-888-4476**	201-469-2000	387
Isolatek International Inc			
41 Furnace St ....Stanhope NJ 07874	**800-631-9600**	973-347-1200	386
Isolite Systems			
111 Castilian Dr ....Santa Barbara CA 93117	**800-560-6066**	805-560-9888	228
IsoRay Medical Inc			
350 Hills St Ste 106 ....Richland WA 99354	**877-447-6729**	509-375-1202	357-3
Iso-Tex Diagnostics Inc			
PO Box 909 ....Friendswood TX 77549	**800-477-4839**		231
ISP (International Specialty Products Inc)			
1361 Alps Rd ....Wayne NJ 07470	**800-622-4423**	973-628-4000	142
ISPE (International Society for Pharmacoepidemiology)			
5272 River Rd Ste 630 ....Bethesda MD 20816	**888-887-7955**	301-718-6500	48-8
ISPI (International Society for Performance Improvement)			
1400 Spring St Ste 260 ....Silver Spring MD 20910	**800-825-7550**	301-587-8570	48-12
ISPOR (International Society for Pharmacoeconomics & Outcomes Research)			
3100 Princeton Pk			
Bldg 3 Ste E ....Lawrenceville NJ 08648	**800-992-0643**	609-219-0773	48-8
Israel Government Tourist Office			
800 Second Ave 16th Fl ....New York NY 10017	**877-248-8687**	212-499-5660	765
Isram World of Travel Inc			
233 Pk Ave S 10th Fl ....New York NY 10003	**800-223-7460**	212-661-1193	750
ISRS (International Society of Refractive Surgery)			
655 Beach St PO Box 7424........San Francisco CA 94109	**866-561-8558**	415-561-8581	48-8
ISSA (International Sanitary Supply Assn)			
3300 Dundee Rd ....Northbrook IL 60062	**800-225-4772**	847-982-0800	48-18
ISSI (Integrated Silicon Solution Inc)			
1940 Zanker Rd ....San Jose CA 95112	**800-379-4774**	408-969-6600	687
NASDAQ: ISSI			
Isspro Inc			
2515 NE Riverside Way ....Portland OR 97211	**888-447-7776**	503-528-3400	490
ISTA (International Safe Transit Assn)			
1400 Abbott Rd Ste 160 ....East Lansing MI 48823	**888-299-2208**	517-333-3437	48-21
ISTA Advocate Magazine			
150 W Market St Ste 900 ....Indianapolis IN 46204	**800-382-4037**	317-263-3400	452-8
iStar Financial Inc			
1114 Ave of the Americas			
39th Fl ....New York NY 10036	**888-603-5847**	212-930-9400	216
NYSE: STAR			
ISTE (International Society for Technology in Education)			
1710 Rhode Island Ave NW			
Ste 900 ....Washington DC 20036	**800-336-5191***	202-861-7777	48-5
*General			
ISTF (International Society of Tropical Foresters)			
5400 Grosvenor Ln ....Bethesda MD 20814	**866-897-8720**	301-530-4514	47-13
ITAGroup			
4600 Westown Pkwy ....West Des Moines IA 50266	**800-257-1985**		381
Italgrani USA Inc			
7900 Van Buren St ....Saint Louis MO 63111	**800-274-1274**	314-638-1447	275
Italy			
Consulate General			
600 Atlantic Ave 17th Fl ....Boston MA 02210	**888-225-5427**	617-722-9201	257
Consulate General			
150 S Independence Mall W			
Public Ledger Bldg Ste 1026 ....Philadelphia PA 19106	**800-531-0840**	215-592-7329	257
Consulate General			
1300 Post Oak Blvd Ste 660 ....Houston TX 77056	**800-637-9314**	713-850-7520	257
Consulate General			
12400 Wilshire Blvd Ste 300 ...Los Angeles CA 90025	**800-313-7133**	310-820-0622	257
Embassy			
3000 Whitehaven St NW ......Washington DC 20008	**800-222-1222**	202-612-4400	257
Italy-America Chamber of Commerce Southeast Inc			
2 S Biscayne Blvd Ste 1880 ....Miami FL 33131	**800-428-3003**	305-577-9868	

	Toll-Free	Phone	Class
Itasca Community College			
1851 E Us Hwy 169 ...Grand Rapids MN 55744	800-996-6422	218-327-4460	160
Itawamba Community College			
Fulton 602 W Hill St ...Fulton MS 38843	800-433-3243	662-862-8000	160
ITC (Innovative Technologies Corp)			
1020 Woodman Dr Ste 100 ...Dayton OH 45432	800-745-8050	937-252-2145	179-10
ITC Learning Corp			
1616 Anderson Rd Ste 109 ...McLean VA 22102	800-638-3757		755
Iten Industries			
4602 Benefit Ave ...Ashtabula OH 44004	800-227-4836*	440-997-6134	592
*Orders			
ITG Inc			
One Liberty Plz 165 Broadway ...New York NY 10006	800-215-4484	212-588-4000	681
Ithaca College			
953 Danby Rd ...Ithaca NY 14850	800-429-4274*	607-274-3124	166
*Admissions			
Ithaca/Tompkins County Convention & Visitors Bureau			
904 E Shore Dr ...Ithaca NY 14850	800-284-8422	607-272-1313	207
ITI (Industrial Tools Inc)			
1111 S Rose Ave ...Oxnard CA 93033	800-266-5561	805-483-1111	488
ITL (Industrial Timber & Lumber Corp)			
23925 Commerce Pk Rd ...Beachwood OH 44122	800-829-9663	216-831-3140	674
ITNS (International Transplant Nurses Society)			
1739 E Carson St PO Box 351 ...Pittsburgh PA 15203	800-776-8636	412-343-4867	48-8
iTOK Inc			
3400 North Ashton Blvd Ste 260 ...Lehi UT 84043	866-515-4865		390
ITR Group Inc			
2520 Lexington Ave S Ste 500 ...Saint Paul MN 55120	866-290-3423		194
Itron Inc			
2111 N Molter Rd ...Liberty Lake WA 99019	800-635-5461	509-924-9900	248
NASDAQ: ITRI			
ITS (Intelligent Transportation Society of America)			
1100 17th St NW Ste 1200 ...Washington DC 20036	800-374-8472	202-484-4847	48-21
ITT Aerospace Controls			
28150 Industry Dr ...Valencia CA 91355	866-294-8691	661-295-4000	778
ITT Educational Services Inc			
13000 N Meridian St ...Carmel IN 46032	800-388-3368	317-706-9200	242
NYSE: ESI			
ITT Goulds Pumps Industries/Goulds Industrial Pumps Group			
240 Fall St ...Seneca Falls NY 13148	800-327-7700	315-568-2811	777
ITT Industries Inc			
1133 Westchester Ave ...White Plains NY 10604	800-254-2823	914-641-2000	253
NYSE: ITT			
ITT Industries Inc Engineered Valves Div			
33 Centerville Rd ...Lancaster PA 17603	800-366-1111	717-509-2200	777
ITT Night Vision & Imaging			
7635 Plantation Rd ...Roanoke VA 24019	800-448-8678	540-563-0371	537
ITT Standard			
175 Standard Pkwy ...Cheektowaga NY 14227	800-447-7700	800-281-4111	90
ITT Technical Institute			
Lathrop			
16916 S Harlan Rd ...Lathrop CA 95330	800-346-1786	209-858-0077	788
Oxnard			
2051 Solar Dr Ste 150 ...Oxnard CA 93036	800-530-1582	805-988-0143	788
Rancho Cordova			
10863 Gold Ctr Dr ...Rancho Cordova CA 95670	800-488-8466	916-851-3900	788
San Bernardino			
670 Carnegie Dr ...San Bernardino CA 92408	800-888-3801	909-806-4600	788
San Dimas			
650 W Cienega Ave ...San Dimas CA 91773	800-414-6522	909-971-2300	788
Sylmar			
12669 Encinitas Ave ...Sylmar CA 91342	800-363-2086	818-364-5151	788
ITT Technical Institute Albany			
13 Airline Dr ...Albany NY 12205	800-489-1191	518-452-9300	788
ITT Technical Institute Albuquerque			
5100 Masthead St NE ...Albuquerque NM 87109	800-636-1114	505-828-1114	788
ITT Technical Institute Arlington			
551 Ryan Plz Dr ...Arlington TX 76011	888-288-4950	817-794-5100	788
ITT Technical Institute Arnold			
1930 Meyer Drury Dr ...Arnold MO 63010	888-488-1082	636-464-6600	788
ITT Technical Institute Austin			
6330 Hwy 290 E Ste 150 ...Austin TX 78723	800-431-0677	512-467-6800	788
ITT Technical Institute Birmingham			
6270 Pk S Dr ...Bessemer AL 35022	800-488-7033	205-497-5700	788
ITT Technical Institute Boise			
12302 W Explorer Dr ...Boise ID 83713	800-666-4888	208-322-8844	788
ITT Technical Institute Canton			
1905 S Haggerty Rd ...Canton MI 48188	800-247-4477	734-397-7800	788
ITT Technical Institute Cordova			
7260 Goodlett Farms Pkwy ...Cordova TN 38016	866-444-5141	901-381-0200	788
ITT Technical Institute Dayton			
3325 S- Eight Rd ...Dayton OH 45414	800-568-3241	937-264-7700	788
ITT Technical Institute Earth City			
3640 Corporate Trl Dr ...Earth City MO 63045	800-235-5488	314-298-7800	788
ITT Technical Institute Fort Lauderdale			
3401 S University Dr ...Fort Lauderdale FL 33328	800-488-7797	954-476-9300	788
ITT Technical Institute Fort Wayne			
2810 Dupont Commerce Ct ...Fort Wayne IN 46825	800-866-4488	260-497-6200	788
ITT Technical Institute Getzville			
2295 Millersport Hwy ...Getzville NY 14068	800-469-7593	716-689-2200	788
ITT Technical Institute Grand Rapids			
1980 Metro Ct SW ...Wyoming MI 49519	800-632-4676	616-406-1200	788
ITT Technical Institute Greenville			
Six Independence Pointe			
Independence Corporate Pk ...Greenville SC 29615	800-932-4488	864-288-0777	788
ITT Technical Institute Harrisburg			
449 Eisenhower Blvd Ste 100 ...Harrisburg PA 17111	800-847-4756	717-565-1700	788
ITT Technical Institute Henderson			
168 Gibson Rd ...Henderson NV 89014	800-488-8459	702-558-5404	788
ITT Technical Institute High Point			
4050 Piedmont Pkwy ...High Point NC 27265	877-536-5231	336-819-5900	788
ITT Technical Institute Houston			
15651 N Fwy ...Houston TX 77090	800-879-6486	281-873-0512	788
ITT Technical Institute Indianapolis			
9511 Angola Ct ...Indianapolis IN 46268	800-937-4488	317-875-8640	788
ITT Technical Institute Jacksonville			
7011 AC Skinner Pkwy			
Ste 140 ...Jacksonville FL 32256	800-318-1264	904-573-9100	788
ITT Technical Institute Kansas City			
9150 E 41st Terr ...Kansas City MO 64133	877-488-1442	816-276-1400	788
ITT Technical Institute Kennesaw			
2065 Baker Rd NW ...Kennesaw GA 30144	800-564-9771	770-426-2300	788
ITT Technical Institute Liverpool			
235 Greenfield Pkwy ...Liverpool NY 13088	877-488-0011	315-461-8000	788
ITT Technical Institute Louisville			
9500 Ormsby Stn Rd Ste 100 ...Louisville KY 40223	888-790-7427	502-327-7424	788
ITT Technical Institute Murray			
920 Levoy Dr ...Murray UT 84123	800-365-2136	801-263-3313	788
ITT Technical Institute Nashville			
2845 Elm Hill Pk ...Nashville TN 37214	800-331-8386	615-889-8700	788
ITT Technical Institute Newburgh			
10999 Stahl Rd ...Newburgh IN 47630	800-832-4488	812-858-1600	788
ITT Technical Institute Norfolk			
5425 Robin Hood Rd Ste 100 ...Norfolk VA 23513	888-253-8324	757-466-1260	788
ITT Technical Institute Norwood			
4750 Wesley Ave ...Norwood OH 45212	800-314-8324	513-531-8300	788
ITT Technical Institute Omaha			
1120 N 103rd Plz Ste 200 ...Omaha NE 68114	800-677-9260	402-331-2900	788
ITT Technical Institute Owings Mills			
11301 Red Run Blvd ...Owings Mills MD 21117	877-411-6782	443-394-7115	788
ITT Technical Institute Portland			
9500 NE Cascades Pkwy ...Portland OR 97220	800-234-5488	503-255-6500	788
ITT Technical Institute Richardson			
2101 Waterview Pkwy ...Richardson TX 75080	888-488-5761	972-690-9100	788
ITT Technical Institute Richmond			
300 Gateway Centre Pkwy ...Richmond VA 23235	888-330-4888	804-330-4992	788
ITT Technical Institute San Antonio			
5700 NW Pkwy ...San Antonio TX 78249	800-880-0570	210-694-4612	788
ITT Technical Institute Seattle			
12720 Gateway Dr Ste 100 ...Seattle WA 98168	800-422-2029	206-244-3300	788
ITT Technical Institute Springfield			
7300 Boston Blvd ...Springfield VA 22153	866-817-8324	703-440-9535	788
ITT Technical Institute Strongsville			
14955 Sprague Rd ...Strongsville OH 44136	800-331-1488	440-234-9091	788
ITT Technical Institute Tampa			
4809 Memorial Hwy ...Tampa FL 33634	800-825-2831	813-885-2244	788
ITT Technical Institute Tempe			
5005 S Wendler Dr ...Tempe AZ 85282	800-879-4881	602-437-7500	788
ITT Technical Institute Troy			
1522 E Big Beaver Rd ...Troy MI 48083	800-832-6817	248-524-1800	788
ITT Technical Institute Tucson			
1455 W River Rd ...Tucson AZ 85704	800-870-9730	520-408-7488	788
ITT Technical Institute Warrensville Heights			
4700 Richmond Rd ...Warrensville Heights OH 44128	800-741-3494	216-896-6500	788
ITT Technical Institute Wilmington			
200 Ballardvale St Ste 200 ...Wilmington MA 01887	800-430-5097	978-658-2636	788
ITT Technical Institute Youngstown			
1030 N Meridian Rd ...Youngstown OH 44509	800-832-5001	330-270-1600	788
ITVS (Independent Television Service)			
651 Brannan St Ste 410 ...San Francisco CA 94107	800-621-6196	415-356-8383	731
ITW Brands			
955 National Pkwy Ste 95500 ...Schaumburg IL 60173	877-489-2726	847-944-2260	278
ITW Buildex			
1349 W Bryn Mawr ...Itasca IL 60143	800-284-5339	630-595-3500	278
ITW Dymon			
805 E Old 56 Hwy ...Olathe KS 66061	800-443-9536	913-829-6296	149
ITW Insulation Systems			
1370 E 40th St Ste 1 Bldg 7 ...Houston TX 77022	800-231-1024		386
ITW Ransburg			
320 Phillips Ave ...Toledo OH 43612	800-233-3366*	419-470-2000	173
*Cust Svc			
ITW Rocol North America			
3650 W Lake Ave ...Glenview IL 60026	800-452-5823	847-657-5278	534
ITW Switches			
2550 Mill Brook Dr ...Buffalo Grove IL 60089	800-544-3354	847-876-9400	720
ITW Vortec			
10125 Carver Rd ...Cincinnati OH 45242	800-441-7475	513-891-7485	14
ITW-GaleWrap			
1320 Leslie Dr ...Douglasville GA 30134	866-425-3727		594
iUniverse			
1663 Liberty Dr ...Bloomington IN 47403	800-288-4677		628-2
IUPAT (International Union of Painters & Allied Trades)			
7234 Pkwy Dr ...Hanover MD 21076	800-554-2479	410-564-5900	411
IV Most Consulting Inc			
25 Meadow Ln ...Chappaqua NY 10514	800-448-6678		178
iv3 Solutions Corp			
50 Minthorn Blvd Ste 301 ...Markham ON L3T7X8	877-995-2651		362
IVC (International Visual Corp)			
11839 Rodolphe Forget ...Montreal QC H1E7J8	866-643-0570	514-643-0570	286
IVCi LLC			
601 Old Willets Path ...Hauppauge NY 11788	800-224-7083	631-273-5800	726
Ivenuecom			
9925 Painter Ave Ste A ...Whittier CA 90605	800-683-8314		178
Ivers-Lee Inc			
31 Hansen S ...Brampton ON L6W3H7	800-265-1009	905-451-5535	84
IVESCO (Iowa Veterinary Supply Co)			
124 Country Club Rd ...Iowa Falls IA 50126	800-457-0118	641-648-2529	470
Ivey Spencer Leadership Centre			
551 Windermere Rd ...London ON N5X2T1	888-678-6926	519-679-4546	374
Ivinson Memorial Hospital			
255 N 30th St ...Laramie WY 82072	877-858-0990	307-742-2141	371-3
IVY Biomedical Systems Inc			
11 Business Pk Dr ...Branford CT 06405	800-247-4614	203-481-4183	250
Ivy Funds			
6300 Lamar Ave ...Overland Park KS 66202	888-923-3355	913-236-2000	521
Ivy Tech Columbus College			
Columbus			
4475 Central Ave ...Columbus IN 47203	800-922-4838	812-372-9925	788
Bloomington			
200 Daniels Way ...Bloomington IN 47404	866-447-0700	812-330-6137	788
Ivy Tech Community College			
Central Indiana			
50 W Fall Creek Pkwy N Dr ...Indianapolis IN 46208	888-489-5463	317-921-4800	788
Kokomo			
1815 E Morgan St ...Kokomo IN 46901	800-459-0561	765-459-0561	788
Muncie 4301 S Cowan Rd ...Muncie IN 47302	800-589-8324	765-289-2291	788
North Central			
220 Dean Johnson Blvd ...South Bend IN 46601	888-489-3478	574-289-7001	788
Richmond			
2357 Chester Blvd ...Richmond IN 47374	800-659-4562	765-966-2656	788
Southeast			
590 Ivy Tech Dr ...Madison IN 47250	800-403-2190	812-265-2580	788
Southern Indiana			
8204 Old Indiana 311 ...Sellersburg IN 47172	800-321-9021	812-246-3301	788
iWay Software			
Two Penn Plz ...New York NY 10121	800-736-6130	212-736-4433	195
IWLA (Izaak Walton League of America)			
707 Conservation Ln ...Gaithersburg MD 20878	800-453-5463	301-548-0150	47-13

Alphabetical Section

	Toll-Free	Phone	Class
IWPA (International Wood Products Assn)			
4214 King St . . . . Alexandria VA 22302	**855-435-0005**	703-820-6696	48-3
Ixia			
26601 W Agoura Rd . . . . Calabasas CA 91302	**877-367-4942**	818-871-1800	248
NASDAQ: XXIA			
Izaak Walton League of America (IWLA)			
707 Conservation Ln . . . . Gaithersburg MD 20878	**800-453-5463**	301-548-0150	47-13

J

	Toll-Free	Phone	Class
J & A Freight Systems Inc			
4704 Irving Park Rd Ste 8 . . . . Chicago IL 60641	**877-668-3378**		310
J & A Printing Inc			
PO Box 457 . . . . Hiawatha IA 52233	**800-793-1781**	319-393-1781	619
J & H Oil Co			
2696 Chicago Dr SW . . . . Wyoming MI 49519	**800-442-9110**	616-534-2181	323
J & J Industries Inc			
818 J & J Dr PO Box 1287 . . . . Dalton GA 30721	**800-241-4586**	706-529-2100	130
J & J Snack Foods Corp			
6000 Central Hwy . . . . Pennsauken NJ 08109	**800-486-9533**	856-665-9533	295-25
NASDAQ: JJSF			
J & M Industries Inc			
300 Ponchatoula Pkwy . . . . Ponchatoula LA 70454	**800-989-1002**	985-386-6000	66
J A T of Fort Wayne Inc			
5031 Industrial Rd . . . . Fort Wayne IN 46825	**800-522-3306**	260-482-8447	770
J Alexander's Corp			
3401 W End Ave Ste 260 . . . . Nashville TN 37203	**888-528-1991**	615-269-1900	661
NASDAQ: JAX			
J C Steele & Sons Inc			
710 S Mulberry St . . . . Statesville NC 28677	**800-278-3353**	704-872-3681	449
J Crew Group Inc			
770 Broadway . . . . New York NY 10003	**800-562-0258**	212-209-2500	454
J D Rush C Inc			
5900 E Lerdo Hwy . . . . Shafter CA 93263	**800-537-6284**	661-392-1900	485
J D'Addario & Company Inc			
595 Smith St . . . . Farmingdale NY 11735	**800-323-2746**	631-439-3300	520
J Edgar Eubanks & Assoc			
One Windsor Cove Ste 305 . . . . Columbia SC 29223	**800-445-8629**	803-252-5646	46
J Fletcher Creamer & Son Inc			
101 E Broadway . . . . Hackensack NJ 07601	**800-835-9801**	201-488-9800	190-5
J Freirich Foods Inc			
815 W Kerr St PO Box 1529 . . . . Salisbury NC 28144	**800-554-4788**	704-636-2621	468
J L Business Interiors Inc			
515 Schoenhaar Dr PO Box 303 . . . . West Bend WI 53090	**866-338-5524**	262-338-2221	319
J O Galloup Co			
135 Manufacturers Dr . . . . Holland MI 49424	**888-755-3110**	269-965-4005	192-2
J P Noonan Transportation Inc			
415 W St . . . . West Bridgewater MA 02379	**800-922-8026**	508-583-2880	770
J Polep Distribution Services Inc			
705 Meadow St . . . . Chicopee MA 01013	**800-447-6537**	413-592-4141	746
J R C Transportation Inc			
47 Maple Ave PO Box 366 . . . . Thomaston CT 06787	**800-346-3250***	860-283-0207	770
*General			
J Robert Scott Inc			
500 N Oak St . . . . Inglewood CA 90302	**877-207-5130**	310-680-4300	318-4
J s Logistics			
4550 Gustine Ave . . . . Saint Louis MO 63116	**800-814-2634**	314-832-6008	313
J Smith Lanier & Co			
300 W Tenth St . . . . West Point GA 31833	**800-226-4522**	706-645-2211	387
J Sosnick & Sons Inc			
258 Littlefield			
Ave . . . . South San Francisco CA 94080	**800-443-6737**	650-952-2226	296-11
J T M Technologies Inc			
204 Industrial Ct . . . . Wylie TX 75098	**877-586-8324**	972-429-6575	614
J. C. Macelroy Company Inc			
PO Box 850 . . . . Piscataway NJ 08855	**800-622-3576**	732-572-7100	475
J. Ennis Fabrics Ltd			
12122 - 68 St . . . . Edmonton AB T5B1R1	**800-663-6647**		403
J. H. Bennett & Company Inc			
PO Box 8028 . . . . Novi MI 48376	**800-837-5426***	248-596-5100	382
*General			
J.M. Bozeman Enterprises Inc			
166 Seltzer Ln . . . . Malvern AR 72104	**800-472-1836***	501-844-4060	676
*General			
J2 Global Communications Inc			
6922 Hollywood Blvd			
Eighth Fl . . . . Los Angeles CA 90028	**888-718-2000***	323-860-9200	726
*Sales			
JA (Jewelers of America)			
52 Vanderbilt Ave 19th Fl . . . . New York NY 10017	**800-223-0673**	646-658-0246	48-4
JA Billipp Co			
6925 Portwest Dr Ste 130 . . . . Houston TX 77024	**800-216-9013**	713-426-5000	644
Jabil Circuit Inc			
10560 ML King St N . . . . . . Saint Petersburg FL 33716	**877-217-6328**	727-577-9749	617
NYSE: JBL			
Jabo Supply Corp			
5164 County Rd 64/66 . . . . Huntington WV 25705	**800-334-5226**	304-736-8333	382
JACAN (Junior Achievement of Canada)			
1 Eva Rd Ste 218 . . . . Toronto ON M9C4Z5	**800-265-0699**	416-622-4602	47-11
Jace Holdings Ltd			
6649 Butler Crescent . . . . Saanichton BC V8M1Z7	**800-667-8280**	250-483-1715	296-8
Jack B Kelley Inc			
801 S Fillmore St Ste 505 . . . . Amarillo TX 79101	**800-225-5525**	806-353-3553	770
Jack B Parson Cos			
2350 South 1900 West . . . . Ogden UT 84401	**888-672-7766**	801-731-1111	189-4
Jack Becker Distributors Inc			
6800 Suemac Pl . . . . Jacksonville FL 32254	**800-488-8411**		574
Jack Conway			
137 Washington St . . . . Norwell MA 02061	**800-283-1030**	781-871-0080	643
Jack Cooper Transport Co Inc			
1100 Walnut St Ste 2400 . . . . Kansas City MO 64106	**866-449-6388**	816-983-4000	770
Jack Henry & Assoc Inc			
663 W Hwy 60 PO Box 807 . . . . Monett MO 65708	**800-299-4222**	417-235-6652	179-11
NASDAQ: JKHY			
Jack in the Box Inc			
9330 Balboa Ave . . . . San Diego CA 92123	**800-955-5225**	858-571-2121	661
NASDAQ: JACK			

	Toll-Free	Phone	Class
Jack London Inn			
444 Embarcadero W . . . . Oakland CA 94607	**800-549-8780**	510-444-2032	376
Jack Richeson & Company Inc			
557 Marcella Dr . . . . Kimberly WI 54136	**800-233-2404**	920-738-0744	42
Jack Williams Tire Co Inc			
PO Box 3655 . . . . Scranton PA 18505	**800-833-5051**		61-5
Jack's Family Restaurants Inc			
2831 19th St S . . . . Homewood AL 35209	**800-422-3893**	205-879-9321	661
Jacknob Corp			
290 Oser Ave PO Box 18032 . . . . Hauppauge NY 11788	**800-424-7495**	631-546-6560	347
Jackpot Junction Casino Hotel			
39375 County Hwy 24 PO Box 420 . . . . Morton MN 56270	**800-946-2274**	507-697-8000	132
Jackson & Perkins			
Two Floral Ave . . . . Hodges SC 29653	**800-292-4769***		454
*Cust Svc			
Jackson Area Chamber of Commerce			
197 Auditorium St . . . . Jackson TN 38301	**866-262-8867**	731-423-2200	137
Jackson Citizen Patriot			
100 E Michigan Ave Ste 100 . . . . Jackson MI 49201	**877-213-3754**		525-2
Jackson Community College			
2111 Emmons Rd . . . . Jackson MI 49201	**888-522-7344**	517-787-0800	160
Hillsdale			
3120 W Carleton Rd PO Box 712 . . . . . . Hillsdale MI 49242	**888-522-7344**	517-437-3343	160
Jackson County Area Chamber of Commerce			
270 Athens St PO Box 629 . . . . Jefferson GA 30549	**800-243-6921**	706-387-0300	137
Jackson County Chamber of Commerce			
773 W Main St . . . . Sylva NC 28779	**800-962-1911**	828-586-2155	137
Jackson County Convention & Visitors Bureau			
141 S Jackson St . . . . Jackson MI 49201	**800-245-5282**	517-764-4440	207
Jackson County Memorial Hospital			
1200 E Pecan St . . . . Altus OK 73521	**800-595-0455**	580-379-5000	371-3
Jackson County Public Library (JCPL)			
303 W Second St . . . . Seymour IN 47274	**877-275-7673**	812-522-3412	431-3
Jackson County Rural Electric Membership Corp			
274 E Base Rd . . . . Brownstown IN 47220	**800-288-4458**	812-358-4458	245
Jackson County School District 6			
300 Ash St . . . . Central Point OR 97502	**800-978-3040**	541-494-6200	676
Jackson County School System			
1660 Winder Hwy . . . . Jefferson GA 30549	**800-760-3727**	706-367-5151	676
Jackson Electric Co-op			
N6868 County Rd F			
PO Box 546 . . . . Black River Falls WI 54615	**800-370-4607**	715-284-5385	245
Jackson Electric Membership Corp			
850 Commerce Rd . . . . Jefferson GA 30549	**800-462-3691**	706-367-5281	245
Jackson Energy Co-op			
115 Jackson Energy Ln . . . . McKee KY 40447	**800-262-7480**	606-364-1000	245
Jackson Hewitt Inc			
Three Sylvan Way Ste 301 . . . . Parsippany NJ 07054	**800-234-1040**		724
OTC: JHTXQ			
Jackson Hole Central Reservations (JHCR)			
140 E Broadway Ste 24			
PO Box 2618 . . . . Jackson WY 83001	**888-838-6606**	307-733-4005	373
Jackson Hole Lodge			
420 W Broadway PO Box 1805 . . . . Jackson WY 83001	**800-604-9404**	307-733-2992	376
Jackson Hole Mountain Resort			
3395 Cody Ln PO Box 290 . . . . Teton Village WY 83025	**800-450-0477**	307-733-2292	660
Jackson HoleResort Lodging			
3200 W McCollister Dr			
PO Box 510 . . . . Teton Village WY 83025	**800-443-8613**	307-733-3990	660
Jackson ImmunoResearch Laboratories Inc			
872 W Baltimore Pk PO Box 9 . . . . . West Grove PA 19390	**800-367-5296**	610-869-4024	231
Jackson International Airport			
100 International Dr Ste 300 . . . . Jackson MS 39208	**800-227-7368**	601-939-5631	27
Jackson Lake Lodge			
PO Box 250 . . . . Moran WY 83013	**800-628-9988**	307-543-2811	660
Jackson Marking Products Co			
9105 N Rainbow Ln . . . . Mount Vernon IL 62864	**800-782-6722**	618-242-1334	462
Jackson Mattress Company Inc			
3154 Camden Rd . . . . Fayetteville NC 28306	**800-763-7378**	910-425-0131	466
Jackson National Life Insurance Co			
One Corporate Way . . . . Lansing MI 48951	**800-644-4565**	517-381-5500	388-2
Jackson Oil & Solvents Inc			
1970 Kentucky Ave . . . . Indianapolis IN 46221	**800-221-4603**	317-636-4421	534
Jackson Purchase Energy Corp			
2900 Irvin Cobb Dr . . . . Paducah KY 42002	**800-633-4044**	270-442-7321	245
Jackson Purchase Medical Ctr			
1099 Medical Ctr Cir . . . . Mayfield KY 42066	**800-994-6610**	270-251-4100	371-3
Jackson State University			
1400 John R Lynch St . . . . Jackson MS 39217	**800-848-6817**	601-979-2121	166
Jackson Sun			
245 W LaFayette St . . . . Jackson TN 38301	**800-372-3922**	731-427-3333	525-2
Jackson Tube Service Inc			
8210 Industry Pk Dr . . . . Piqua OH 45356	**800-543-8910**	937-773-8550	485
Jacksonville Bancorp Inc			
100 N Laura St . . . . Jacksonville FL 32202	**888-699-5292**	904-421-3040	357-2
NASDAQ: JAXB			
Jacksonville Chamber of Commerce			
200 Dupree Dr . . . . Jacksonville AR 72076	**888-857-3019**	501-982-1511	137
Jacksonville Convention & Visitors Bureau			
310 E State St . . . . Jacksonville IL 62650	**800-593-5678**	217-243-5678	207
Jacksonville Independent School District			
PO Box 631 . . . . Jacksonville TX 75766	**866-914-5202**	903-586-6511	676
Jacksonville Magazine			
1261 King St . . . . Jacksonville FL 32204	**800-962-0214**	904-389-3622	452-22
Jacksonville Municipal Stadium			
1 EverBank Field Dr . . . . Jacksonville FL 32202	**877-452-4784**	904-633-6000	711
Jacksonville State University			
700 Pelham Rd N . . . . Jacksonville AL 36265	**800-231-5291**	256-782-5781	166
Jacksonville Symphony Orchestra (JSO)			
300 W Water St Ste 200 . . . . Jacksonville FL 32202	**877-662-6731**	904-354-5479	566-3
Jacksonville University			
2800 University Blvd N . . . . Jacksonville FL 32211	**800-225-2027**	904-256-8000	166
Jacksonville/Onslow Chamber of Commerce			
1099 Gum Branch Rd . . . . Jacksonville NC 28541	**800-877-8339**	910-347-3141	137
Jacmel Jewelry Inc			
3030 47th Ave . . . . Long Island City NY 11101	**800-945-4300**		406
Jaco Electronics Inc			
415 Oser Ave . . . . Hauppauge NY 11788	**877-373-5226**		246
OTC: JACO			
Jacob Ash Company Inc			
301 Munson Ave . . . . McKees Rocks PA 15136	**800-245-6111**	412-331-6660	154
Jacob Holtz Co			
10 Industrial Hwy MS-6			
Airport Business Complex B . . . . Lester PA 19029	**800-445-4337**	215-423-2800	347

	Toll-Free	Phone	Class
Jacob Leinenkugel Brewing Co			
124 E Elm St ... Chippewa Falls WI 54729	**888-534-6437***	715-723-5558	101
*General			
Jacob Stern & Sons Inc			
1464 E Valley Rd ... Santa Barbara CA 93108	**800-223-7054***	805-565-1411	295-12
*Cust Svc			
Jacobs Theatre			
242 W 45th St ... New York NY 10036	**800-447-7400**	212-239-6200	736
Jacobsen			
11108 Quality Dr ... Charlotte NC 28273	**866-522-6273**	704-504-6600	426
Jacobsen Homes			
600 Packard Ct ... Safety Harbor FL 34695	**800-843-1559**	727-726-1138	500
Jacquelyn Wigs			
15 W 37th St Fourth Fl ... New York NY 10018	**800-272-2424**	212-302-2266	345
Jade Engineered Plastic Inc			
121 Broadcommon Rd ... Bristol RI 02809	**800-557-9155**	401-253-4440	325
JAE Electronics Inc			
142 Technology Dr Ste 100 ... Irvine CA 92618	**800-523-7278**	949-753-2600	253
Jaeckle Wholesale Inc			
4101 Owl Creek Dr ... Madison WI 53718	**800-236-7225**	608-838-5400	192-1
Jafra Cosmetics International			
2451 Townsgate Rd ... Westlake Village CA 91361	**800-551-2345**	805-449-3000	215
Jagemann Stamping Co			
5757 W Custer St PO Box 217 ... Manitowoc WI 54221	**888-337-7853**	920-682-4633	483
Jaipur Rugs Inc			
2775 Pacific Dr ... Norcross GA 30071	**888-676-7330**	404-351-2360	130
JAK Enterprises Inc			
8309 N Knoxville Ave ... Peoria IL 61615	**800-752-3295**	309-692-8222	536
Jake's Famous Crawfish			
401 SW 12th Ave SW Stark ... Portland OR 97205	**800-552-6379**	503-226-1419	662
Jake's Grill			
611 SW Tenth Ave ... Portland OR 97205	**800-552-6379**	503-220-1850	662
JAKKS Pacific Inc			
21749 Baker Pkwy ... Walnut CA 91789	**877-875-2557**	909-594-7771	752
NASDAQ: JAKK			
JAMA (Journal of the American Medical Assn)			
PO Box 10946 ... Chicago IL 60654	**800-262-2350**	312-670-7827	452-16
Jamaica Tourist Board			
5201 Blue Lagoon Dr Ste 670 ... Miami FL 33126	**800-233-4582**	305-665-0557	765
Jamak Fabrication Inc			
1401 N Bowie Dr ... Weatherford TX 76086	**800-543-4747**	817-594-8771	668
James A Rhodes State College			
4240 Campus Dr ... Lima OH 45804	**866-498-4968**	419-995-8320	788
James A Scott & Son Inc			
PO Box 10489 ... Lynchburg VA 24506	**800-365-0101**	434-832-2100	388-4
James Austin Co			
115 Downieville Rd PO Box 827 ... Mars PA 16046	**800-245-1942**	724-625-1535	149
James Avery Craftsman Inc			
145 Avery Rd N ... Kerrville TX 78029	**800-283-1770**	830-895-1122	406
James Candy Co			
1519 Boardwalk ... Atlantic City NJ 08401	**800-441-1404***	609-344-1519	295-8
*Orders			
James Chicago, The			
55 E Ontario ... Chicago IL 60611	**888-526-3778**	312-337-1000	376
James Gettys Hotel			
27 Chambersburg St ... Gettysburg PA 17325	**888-900-5275**	717-337-1334	376
James Graham Brown Cancer Ctr			
529 S Jackson St ... Louisville KY 40202	**866-530-5516**	502-562-4369	759
James H Drew Corp			
8701 Zionsville Rd ... Indianapolis IN 46268	**800-772-7342**	317-876-3739	189-4
James H Quillen Veterans Affairs Medical Ctr			
Corner of Lamont & Veterans Way			
PO Box 4000 ... Mountain Home TN 37684	**877-573-3529**	423-926-1171	371-8
James Hardie Bldg Products			
26300 La Alameda Ave			
Ste 400 ... Mission Viejo CA 92691	**888-542-7343**	949-348-1800	192-4
James J Hill House			
240 Summit Ave ... Saint Paul MN 55102	**888-727-8386**	651-297-2555	49-2
James L Allen Ctr			
2169 Campus Dr ... Evanston IL 60208	**877-755-2227**	847-467-7000	374
James L. Taylor Manufacturing Co			
108 Parker Ave ... Poughkeepsie NY 12601	**800-952-1320**	845-452-3780	808
James Machine Works LLC			
1521 Adams St ... Monroe LA 71201	**800-259-6104**	318-322-6104	190-1
James Skinner Baking Co			
4657 G St ... Omaha NE 68117	**800-358-7428**	402-734-1672	295-2
James Wood Motors Inc			
2111 Us Hwy 287 S ... Decatur TX 76234	**888-833-7230**	940-627-2177	56
Jameson Inns			
Jameson Inns			
115 Ann Denard Dr ... Washington GA 30673	**800-526-3766**	706-678-7925	376
Jameson Real Estate LLC			
425 W N Ave ... Chicago IL 60610	**888-751-4663**	312-751-0300	643
Jamestown College			
6000 College Ln ... Jamestown ND 58405	**800-336-2554**	701-252-3467	166
Jamestown Community College			
525 Faulkner St PO Box 20 ... Jamestown NY 14702	**800-388-8557**	716-338-1000	160
Cattaraugus County			
260 N Union St PO Box 5901 ... Olean NY 14760	**800-388-9776**	716-376-7500	160
Jamestown Promotions & Tourism Ctr			
404 Louis L'Amour Ln ... Jamestown ND 58401	**800-222-4766**	701-251-9145	207
Jamesway Incubator Co Inc			
30 High Ridge Ct ... Cambridge ON N1R7L3	**800-438-8077**	519-624-4646	273
Jamison Bedding Inc			
PO Box 681948 ... Franklin TN 37068	**800-255-1883***	615-794-1883	466
*Cust Svc			
Jamison Door Co			
55 JV Jamison Dr PO Box 70 ... Hagerstown MD 21740	**800-532-3667**	301-733-3100	234
JAMS/Endispute			
500 N State College Blvd 14th Fl ... Orange CA 92868	**800-352-5267**	714-939-1300	40
Jan Cos			
35 Sockanosset Cross Rd ... Cranston RI 02920	**888-693-6844**	401-946-4000	661
Jan Marini Skin Research Inc			
6951 Via Del Oro ... San Jose CA 95119	**800-347-2223**	408-362-0130	215
Jan's Mountain Outfitters			
1600 Pk Ave PO Box 280 ... Park City UT 84060	**800-745-1020**	435-649-4949	702
Janazzo Services Corp			
140 Norton St Rt 10 PO Box 469 ... Milldale CT 06467	**800-297-3931**	860-621-7381	190-10
Jane Addams Hull-House Museum			
800 S Halsted St ... Chicago IL 60607	**800-625-2013**	312-413-5353	49-2
Jane Goodall Institute for Wildlife Research Education & Conservation (JGI)			
4245 N Fairfax Dr Ste 600 ... Arlington VA 22203	**800-592-5263**	703-682-9220	47-3
Jane Rose Reporting			
80 Fifth Ave ... New York NY 10011	**800-825-3341**	212-727-7773	440
Jane's Information Group			
110 N Royal St Ste 200 ... Alexandria VA 22314	**800-824-0768**	703-683-3700	628-2
Janell Inc			
6130 Cornell Rd ... Cincinnati OH 45242	**888-489-9111**	513-489-9111	355
Janes Island State Park			
26280 Alfred Lawson Dr ... Crisfield MD 21817	**877-620-8367**	410-968-1565	558
Janesville Gazette			
One S Parker Dr PO Box 5001 ... Janesville WI 53547	**800-362-6712**	608-754-3311	525-2
Janesville Sand & Gravel Co (JSG)			
1110 Harding St ... Janesville WI 53547	**800-955-7702**	608-754-7701	498-4
Janesway Electronic Corp			
404 N Terr Ave ... Mount Vernon NY 10552	**800-431-1348**	914-699-6710	246
Janet Mcafee Inc			
9889 Clayton Rd ... Saint Louis MO 63124	**888-991-4800**	314-997-4800	643
Jani-King International Inc			
16885 Dallas Pkwy ... Addison TX 75001	**800-526-4546**	972-991-0900	150
Janlynn Corp			
2070 Westover Rd ... Chicopee MA 01022	**800-445-5565**	413-206-0002	587
Janney Montgomery Scott LLC			
1801 Market St ... Philadelphia PA 19103	**800-526-6397**	215-665-6000	681
Jan-Pro International Inc (JPI)			
2520 Northwinds Pkwy Ste 375 ... Alpharetta GA 30009	**866-355-1064**	678-336-1780	150
Janson Industries			
1200 Garfield Ave SW ... Canton OH 44706	**800-548-8982**	330-455-7029	713
Janssen Healthcare Learning Ctr			
PO Box 200 ... Titusville NJ 08560	**800-526-7736**		576
Janssen Pharmaceutica Inc			
1125 Trenton-Harbourton Rd ... Titusville NJ 08560	**800-526-7736**	609-730-2000	576
Janssen-Ortho Inc			
19 Green Belt Dr ... Toronto ON M3C1L9	**800-387-8781**	416-449-9444	576
Jantek Industries			
230 Rt 70 ... Medford NJ 08055	**888-782-7937**	609-654-1030	234
Janus Hotels & Resorts Inc			
2300 Corporate Blvd NW			
Ste 232 ... Boca Raton FL 33431	**800-327-2110**	561-997-2325	376
Japan Travel Bureau USA Inc			
156 W 56th St Third Fl ... New York NY 10019	**800-235-3523**	212-698-4900	761
Japanese American National Museum			
369 E First St ... Los Angeles CA 90012	**800-461-5266**	213-625-0414	513
Jarden Consumer Solutions			
2381 Executive Ctr Dr ... Boca Raton FL 33431	**800-777-5452**	561-912-4100	36
Jarden Home Brands			
14611 W Commerce Rd ... Daleville IN 47334	**800-240-3340***	765-557-3000	807
*Cust Svc			
Jared Coffin House			
29 Broad St ... Nantucket MA 02554	**800-248-2405***	508-228-2400	376
*Cust Svc			
Jaro Transportation Services Inc			
975 Post Rd PO Box 1890 ... Warren OH 44483	**800-451-3447**	330-393-5659	770
Jarrow Formulas Inc			
1824 S Robertson Blvd ... Los Angeles CA 90035	**800-726-0886**	310-204-6936	787
Jarvis Caster Co			
881 Lower Brownsville Rd ... Jackson TN 38301	**800-995-9876**		347
JAS (Jo-Ann Stores Inc)			
5555 Darrow Rd ... Hudson OH 44236	**888-739-4120**	330-656-2600	270
Jas. D. Collier & Co			
606 S Mendenhall Rd Ste 200 ... Memphis TN 38117	**800-511-1548***		387
*General			
Jasco Products Inc			
10 E Memorial Rd ... Oklahoma City OK 73114	**800-654-8483**	405-752-0710	246
Jasco Tools Inc			
1390 Mt Read Blvd			
PO Box 60497 ... Rochester NY 14606	**800-724-5497**	585-254-7000	488
Jason International Inc			
8328 MacArthur Dr ... North Little Rock AR 72118	**800-255-5766**	501-771-4477	372
Jasper County Rural Electric Membership Corp			
280 E 400 S ... Rensselaer IN 47978	**888-866-7362**	219-866-4601	245
Jasper Desk Co			
415 E Sixth St ... Jasper IN 47546	**800-365-7994***	812-482-4132	318-1
*Cust Svc			
JASPER Engines & Transmissions			
815 Wernsing Rd PO Box 650 ... Jasper IN 47547	**800-827-7455**	812-482-1041	59
Jasper Rubber Products Inc			
1010 First Ave ... Jasper IN 47546	**800-457-7457**	812-482-3242	668
Jasper Seating Company Inc			
Jasper Group			
225 Clay St ... Jasper IN 47546	**800-622-5661**	812-482-3204	318-1
Jasper Wyman & Son			
PO Box 100 ... Milbridge ME 04658	**800-341-1758***		314-1
*Sales			
Jatheon Technologies Inc			
British Colonial Bldg 8 Wellington St E			
Mezzanine Level ... Toronto ON M5E1C5	**888-528-4366**	416-840-0418	398
JatoTech Ventures			
6300 Bridgepoint Pkwy			
Bldg 1 Ste 500 ... Austin TX 78730	**800-626-4686**	512-795-5860	780
Javelin Capital Markets LLC			
443 Park Ave S 10th Fl ... New York NY 10016	**877-528-9244**	212-779-2300	681
Jay County Rural Electric Membership Corp			
484 S 200 W PO Box 904 ... Portland IN 47371	**800-835-7362**	260-726-7121	245
Jay Peak Resort			
830 Jay Peak Rd ... Jay VT 05859	**800-451-4449**	802-988-2611	660
Jayco Inc			
903 S Main St ... Middlebury IN 46540	**800-283-8267***	574-825-5861	119
*Cust Svc			
Jayhawk Bowling Supply Inc			
355 N Iowa St PO Box 685 ... Lawrence KS 66044	**800-255-6436**	785-842-3237	701
Jaynes Corp			
2906 Broadway NE ... Albuquerque NM 87107	**800-393-6343**	505-345-8591	187
Jaypro Sports Inc			
976 Hartford Tpke ... Waterford CT 06385	**800-243-0533***	860-447-3001	343
*Cust Svc			
Jazz Pharmaceuticals Inc			
3180 Porter Dr ... Palo Alto CA 94304	**866-997-3688**	650-496-3777	576
Jazzercise Inc			
2460 Impala Dr ... Carlsbad CA 92010	**800-348-4748***	760-476-1750	797
*Cust Svc			
Jazziz Magazine			
2650 N Military Trail			
Ste 140 ... Boca Raton FL 33431	**888-852-9987**	561-893-6868	452-9
JazzTimes Magazine			
85 Quincy Ave Ste 2 ... Quincy MA 02169	**800-437-5828**	617-706-9110	452-9

Company	Toll-Free	Phone	Class
JB Hunt Transport Services Inc 615 JB Hunt Corporate Dr ...... Lowell AR 72745 *NASDAQ: JBHT*	800-643-3622	479-820-0000	444
JB Martin Co 645 Fifth Ave Ste 400 ...... New York NY 10022	800-223-0525	212-421-2020	734-1
J&B Medical Supply Co Inc 50496 W Pontiac Trail ...... Wixom MI 48393	800-980-0047	248-896-6210	238
JB Sandlin Cos 5137 Davis Blvd ...... Fort Worth TX 76180	800-821-4663	817-281-3509	188
Jb Wholesale Roofing & Bldg Supplies Inc 21524 Nordhoff St PO Box 5289 ...... Chatsworth CA 91311 *General	800-464-2461*	818-998-0440	192-3
JBFCS (Jewish Board of Family & Children Services) 120 W 57th St ...... New York NY 10019	888-523-2769	212-582-9100	47-6
JBL Professional 8500 Balboa Blvd ...... Northridge CA 91329	800-852-5776	818-894-8850	51
JBMH (Joseph Brant Memorial Hospital) 1230 N Shore Blvd ...... Burlington ON L7S1W7	800-810-0000	905-632-3730	371-2
JBS United Inc 4310 State Rd 38 W ...... Sheridan IN 46069	800-382-9909	317-758-4495	442
JC Newman Cigar Co 2701 16th St ...... Tampa FL 33605 *Orders	800-477-1884*	813-248-2124	746
JC Penney Optical Co 821 N Central Expressway ...... Plano TX 75024	866-435-7111	972-516-1393	536
JC Raulston Arboretum North Carolina State University PO Box 7522 ...... Raleigh NC 27695	888-842-2442	919-513-7457	96
JC Whitney 761 Progress Pkwy ...... La Salle IL 61301	866-529-5530		454
JCI (Junior Chamber International) 15645 Olive Blvd ...... Chesterfield MO 63017	800-905-5499	636-449-3100	47-7
JCPL (Jackson County Public Library) 303 W Second St ...... Seymour IN 47274	877-275-7673	812-522-3412	431-3
JD Calato Mfg Company Inc 4501 Hyde Pk Blvd ...... Niagara Falls NY 14305 *Cust Svc	800-358-4590*	716-285-3546	520
JD Equipment Inc 1660 US 42 NE ...... London OH 43140	800-659-5646	614-879-6620	274
JD Ford & Company LLC 650 S Cherry St Ste 1200 ...... Denver CO 80246	888-999-9495	303-333-3673	681
JD Gould Co Inc 4707 Massachusetts Ave ...... Indianapolis IN 46218	800-634-6853		778
JD Heiskell & Co 116 W Cedar St ...... Tulare CA 93274	800-366-1886	559-685-6100	442
JD McCarty Ctr for Children with Developmental Disabilities 2002 E Robinson St ...... Norman OK 73071	800-777-1272	405-307-2800	371-1
JD Power & Assoc 2625 Townsgate Rd Ste 100 ...... Westlake Village CA 91361	800-274-5372	805-418-8000	461
JDG (Justice Design Group) 500 S Grand Ave Ste 110 ...... Los Angeles CA 90071	800-533-4799	213-437-0102	435
JDH Pacific Inc 15301 S Blackburn Ave ...... Norwalk CA 90650	800-818-9335	562-926-8088	487
JDR Microdevices Inc 229 Polaris Ave Ste 17 ...... Mountain View CA 94043	800-538-5000	650-625-1400	454
JDRF (Juvenile Diabetes Research Foundation International) 120 Wall St ...... New York NY 10005	800-533-2873	212-785-9500	47-17
JE Herndon Company Inc 1020 J E Herndon Access Rd ...... Kings Mountain NC 28086	800-277-0500	704-739-4711	734-8
JE Sawyer & Company Inc 64 Glen St ...... Glens Falls NY 12801	800-724-3983		605
Jean Coutu Group (PJC) Inc 530 Rue Beriault ...... Longueuil QC J4G1S8 *TSE: PJC.A	877-695-6175	450-646-9760	237
Jean Paree Weegs Inc 4041 South 700 East Ste 2 ...... Salt Lake City UT 84107 *Orders	800-422-9447*		345
Jeff Davis Bancshares Inc 507 N Main St PO Box 730 ...... Jennings LA 70546 *OTC: JDVB	866-889-8176	337-824-3424	69
Jefferds Corp 652 Winfield Rd PO Box 757 ...... Saint Albans WV 25177	888-848-6216	304-755-8111	382
Jefferies Socks 2203 Tucker St ...... Burlington NC 27215	800-334-6831	336-226-7315	153-9
Jeffers Inc 310 W Saunders Rd PO Box 100 ...... Dothan AL 36301	800-533-3377	334-793-6257	571
Jefferson Barracks County Park 345 N Dr ...... Saint Louis MO 63125	800-735-2966	314-544-5714	49-4
Jefferson Barracks National Cemetery 2900 Sheridan Rd ...... Saint Louis MO 63125	800-827-1000	314-845-8320	135
Jefferson Ceramic Tile Company Inc 405 S Main St ...... Jefferson WI 53549	888-739-8399	920-674-5725	741
Jefferson City Area Chamber of Commerce 213 Adams St ...... Jefferson City MO 65101	866-223-6535	573-634-3616	137
Jefferson City Convention & Visitors Bureau 100 E High St PO Box 2227 ...... Jefferson City MO 65101	800-769-4183	573-632-2820	207
Jefferson City National Cemetery 1024 E McCarty St ...... Jefferson City MO 65101	877-907-8585	314-845-8320	135
Jefferson City News Tribune 210 Monroe St ...... Jefferson City MO 65101	888-892-6333	573-636-3131	525-2
Jefferson College of Health Sciences 101 Elm Ave SE ...... Roanoke VA 24031	888-985-8483	540-985-8483	788
Jefferson Community & Technical College 109 E Broadway ...... Louisville KY 40202	855-246-5282	502-584-0181	160
Jefferson Community College 1220 Coffeen St ...... Watertown NY 13601	888-435-6522	315-786-2200	160
Jefferson Convention & Visitors Bureau 1221 Elmwood Pk Blvd Ste 411 ...... New Orleans LA 70123	877-572-7474	504-731-7083	207
Jefferson County PO Box 890 ...... Dandridge TN 37725	877-237-3847	865-397-9642	336
Jefferson County Chamber of Commerce 532 Patriot Dr ...... Dandridge TN 37725	877-237-3847	865-397-9642	137
Jefferson County Convention & Visitors Bureau 37 Washington Ct ...... Harpers Ferry WV 25425	866-435-5698	304-535-2627	207
Jefferson County Journal 1405 N Truman Blvd ...... Festus MO 63028	800-365-0820	636-937-9811	525-4
Jefferson Ctr 541 Luck Ave Ste 221 ...... Roanoke VA 24016	866-345-2550	540-343-2624	565
Jefferson Davis Electric Co-op 906 N Lk Arthur Ave PO Drawer 1229 ...... Jennings LA 70546	800-256-5332	337-824-4330	245
Jefferson Energy Co-op 3077 Hwy 17 PO Box 457 ...... North Wrens GA 30833	888-634-7336	706-547-2167	245
Jefferson Hotel 101 W Franklin St ...... Richmond VA 23220	800-424-8014	804-788-8000	376
Jefferson Lines 2100 E 26th St ...... Minneapolis MN 55404 *Cust Svc	800-767-5333*	612-359-3400	107
Jefferson Medical College of Thomas Jefferson University 1015 Walnut St ...... Philadelphia PA 19107	800-533-3669	215-955-6983	167-2
Jefferson National Expansion Memorial 11 N Fourth St ...... Saint Louis MO 63102	855-733-4522	314-655-1700	557
Jefferson Partners LP 2100 E 26th St ...... Minneapolis MN 55404 *Cust Svc	800-767-5333*	612-359-3400	107
Jefferson State Community College 2601 Carson Rd ...... Birmingham AL 35215	800-239-5900	205-853-1200	160
Jefferson-Madison Regional Library 201 E Market St ...... Charlottesville VA 22902	866-979-1555	434-979-7151	431-3
Jeffrey Byrne & Associates 4042 Central St ...... Kansas City MO 64111	800-222-9233		40
Jeffrey Hale - St Brigid's Hospital 1250 ch Sainte-Foy ...... Quebec QC G1S2M6	888-984-5333	418-684-5333	371-2
Jeffrey Matthews Financial Group LLC, The 30B Vreeland Rd Ste 210 ...... Florham Park NJ 07932	888-467-3636	973-805-6222	398
JEGS Performance Auto Parts 101 Jeg'S Pl ...... Delaware OH 43015	800-345-4545	614-294-5050	60
Jekyll Island Club Hotel 371 Riverview Dr ...... Jekyll Island GA 31527	800-535-9547	912-635-2600	660
Jekyll Island Convention Ctr 1 N Beachview Dr ...... Jekyll Island GA 31527	877-453-5955	912-635-5203	206
Jel Sert Co Rt 59 & Conde St ...... West Chicago IL 60185	800-323-2592	630-876-4838	295-15
Jeld-Wen Inc PO Box 1329 ...... Klamath Falls OR 97601	800-535-3936		494
Jelliff Corp 354 Pequot Ave ...... Southport CT 06890	800-243-0052	203-259-1615	679
Jelly Belly Candy Co 1 Jelly Belly Ln ...... Fairfield CA 94533	800-323-9380	707-428-2800	295-8
Jemez Mountains Electric Co-op PO Box 128 ...... Espanola NM 87532	888-755-2105	505-753-2105	245
Jencast PO Box 1509 ...... Coffeyville KS 67337	800-331-2662	620-251-5700	306
Jenkins Electric Inc 5933 Brookshire Blvd ...... Charlotte NC 28216	800-438-3003		253
Jenkins Mfg Company Inc 1608 Frank Akers Rd ...... Anniston AL 36207	800-633-2323	256-831-7000	236
Jennie Stuart Medical Ctr 320 W 18th St PO Box 2400 ...... Hopkinsville KY 42241	800-887-5762	270-887-0100	371-3
Jennie-O Turkey Store 2505 Willmar Ave SW ...... Willmar MN 56201	800-621-3505		612
Jennings County Schools 34 W Main St ...... North Vernon IN 47265	866-346-3724	812-346-4483	676
Jenny Craig International Inc 5770 Fleet St ...... Carlsbad CA 92008	800-443-2331	760-696-4000	797
Jenny Wiley State Resort Park 75 Theatre Ct ...... Prestonsburg KY 41653	800-325-0142		558
Jensen Distribution Services PO Box 3708 ...... Spokane WA 99220 *General	800-234-1321*		348
Jensen Precast 625 Bergin Way ...... Sparks NV 89431	800-648-1134	775-359-6200	184
Jenzabar Inc 101 Huntington Ave Ste 2200 ...... Boston MA 02199	800-593-0028	617-492-9099	179-10
Jeppesen Sanderson Inc 55 Inverness Dr E ...... Englewood CO 80112	800-621-5377	303-799-9090	628-2
Jergens Inc 15700 S Waterloo Rd ...... Cleveland OH 44110	800-537-4367	877-486-1454	488
Jerith Mfg Company Inc 14400 McNulty Rd ...... Philadelphia PA 19154	800-344-2242	215-676-4068	486
Jerome Cheese Co 547 W Nez Perce ...... Jerome ID 83338	800-757-7611	208-324-8806	295-5
Jerome's Furniture Warehouse 16960 Mesamint St ...... San Diego CA 92127	866-633-4094		320
Jerry L Pettis Memorial Veterans Affairs Medical Ctr 11201 Benton St ...... Loma Linda CA 92357	800-827-1000	909-825-7084	371-8
Jerry Lipps Inc 3888 Nash Rd PO Box F ...... Cape Girardeau MO 63702	800-325-3331	573-335-8204	770
Jerry Pate Turf & Irrigation Inc 301 Schubert Dr ...... Pensacola FL 32504	800-700-7004	850-479-4653	274
Jerry's Marine Service 100 SW 16th St ...... Fort Lauderdale FL 33315	800-432-2231	954-525-0311	760
Jerry's Sport Ctr Inc 100 Capital Rd ...... Jenkins Township PA 18640	800-234-2612		701
Jerry's Systems Inc 15942 Shady Grove Rd ...... Gaithersburg MD 20877	800-990-9176		661
Jersey Cape Realty Inc 739 Washington St ...... Cape May NJ 08204	800-643-0043	609-884-5800	643
Jersey Shore State Bank 300 Market St PO Box 967 ...... Williamsport PA 17701	888-412-5772	570-322-1111	69
Jersey Shore Steel Co 70 Maryland Ave PO Box 5055 ...... Jersey Shore PA 17740	800-833-0277	570-753-3000	714
Jersey Shore University Medical Ctr 1945 Rt 33 ...... Neptune NJ 07753	800-560-9990	732-775-5500	371-3
Jesco-Wipco Industries Inc 950 Anderson Rd PO Box 388 ...... Litchfield MI 49252	800-455-0019	517-542-2903	286
Jesuit School of Theology at Berkeley 1735 LeRoy Ave ...... Berkeley CA 94709	800-824-0122	510-549-5000	167-3
Jet Aviation 112 Charles A Lindbergh Dr ...... Teterboro NJ 07608	800-538-0832	201-288-8400	24
Jet Aviation Business Jets Inc 112 Charles A Lindbergh Dr ...... Teterboro NJ 07608	800-736-8538	201-462-4100	13
JET Equipment & Tools Ltd 49 Schooner St ...... Coquitlam BC V3K0B3	800-472-7685	604-523-8665	688
Jet Industries Inc 1935 Silverton Rd NE PO Box 7362 ...... Salem OR 97303	800-659-0620	503-363-2334	603
Jet Resource Inc 455 Wilmer Ave Lunken Airport Hngr 27 ...... Cincinnati OH 45226	800-404-5387	513-871-1554	13
Jet Star Inc 10825 Andrade Dr ...... Zionsville IN 46077	800-969-4222	317-873-4222	770

Company / Address	City	State	ZIP	Toll-Free	Phone	Class
JetBlue Airways						
29 Queens Blvd Ste 118	Forest Hills	NY	11375	**800-538-2583**	718-286-7900	25
NASDAQ: JBLU						
JetBlue Airways Corp						
118-29 Queens Blvd	Forest Hills	NY	11375	**800-538-2583**	718-286-7900	357-1
NASDAQ: JBLU						
Jet-Lube Inc						
4849 Homestead Rd Ste 232	Houston	TX	77226	**800-538-5823**	713-670-5700	534
Jetscape Inc						
10 S New River Dr E Ste 200	Fort Lauderdale	FL	33301	**800-355-5387**	954-763-4737	23
Jetstream of Houston LLP						
4930 Cranswick	Houston	TX	77041	**800-231-8192**	713-462-7000	778
Jeunesse Global LLC						
650 Douglas Ave	Altamonte Springs	FL	32714	**800-400-2676**	407-215-7414	75
Jewel Case Corp						
110 Dupont Dr	Providence	RI	02907	**800-441-4447**	401-943-1400	200
Jewel-Craft Inc						
4122 Olympic Blvd	Erlanger	KY	41018	**800-525-5482**	859-282-2400	408
Jewelers of America (JA)						
52 Vanderbilt Ave 19th Fl	New York	NY	10017	**800-223-0673**	646-658-0246	48-4
Jewelers Shipping Assn (JSA)						
125 Carlsbad St	Cranston	RI	02920	**800-688-4572**	401-943-6020	48-21
Jewell Instruments LLC						
850 Perimeter Rd	Manchester	NH	03103	**800-227-5955**	603-669-6400	522
JewelryWeb.com Inc						
98 Cuttermill Rd Ste 464	Great Neck	NY	11021	**800-955-9245**	516-482-3982	407
Jewett-Cameron Trading Company Ltd						
32275 NW Hillcrest PO Box 1010	North Plains	OR	97133	**800-547-5877**	503-647-0110	192-3
NASDAQ: JCTCF						
Jewish Board of Family & Children Services (JBFCS)						
120 W 57th St	New York	NY	10019	**888-523-2769**	212-582-9100	47-6
Jewish Home Lifecare						
120 W 106th St	New York	NY	10025	**800-544-0304**	212-870-5000	445
Jewish Hospital & St Mary's HealthCare						
2020 Newburg Rd	Louisville	KY	40205	**800-451-3637**	502-451-3330	371-5
Jewish Museum of Maryland						
15 Lloyd St	Baltimore	MD	21202	**800-235-4045***	410-732-6400	513
*All						
Jewish National Fund (JNF)						
42 E 69th St	New York	NY	10021	**800-542-8733**	212-879-9300	47-20
Jewish Publication Society						
2100 Arch St Second Fl	Philadelphia	PA	19103	**800-234-3151**	215-832-0600	628-3
Jewish Reconstructionist Federation (JRF)						
101 Greenwood Ave	Jenkintown	PA	19046	**877-226-7573**	215-885-5601	47-20
Jewish United Fund/Jewish Federation of Metropolitan Chicago (JUF)						
30 S Wells St	Chicago	IL	60606	**855-275-5237**	312-346-6700	47-20
Jews for Jesus						
60 Haight St	San Francisco	CA	94102	**800-366-5521**	415-864-2600	47-20
JF Ahern Co						
855 Morris St	Fond du Lac	WI	54935	**800-532-0155**	920-921-9020	190-10
JF Drake State Technical College						
3421 Meridian St N	Huntsville	AL	35811	**888-413-7253**	256-539-8161	788
JF Shea Construction Inc						
655 Brea Canyon Rd	Walnut	CA	91789	**888-779-7333**	909-594-9500	189-4
JF White Contracting Co						
10 Burr St	Framingham	MA	01701	**866-539-4400**	508-879-4700	189-4
JFC International Inc						
7101 E Slauson Ave	Los Angeles	CA	90040	**800-633-1004**	323-721-6100	296-11
JFKL (John F Kennedy Library)						
190 W 49th St	Hialeah	FL	33012	**877-738-5622**	305-821-2700	431-3
JFP (Joyner Fine Properties)						
2727 Enterprise Pkwy PO Box 31355	Richmond	VA	23294	**800-446-3858**	804-270-9440	643
JG Tax Group						
1430 S Federal Hwy	Deerfield Beach	FL	33441	**866-477-5291**		724
JGI (Jane Goodall Institute for Wildlife Research Education & Conservation)						
4245 N Fairfax Dr Ste 600	Arlington	VA	22203	**800-592-5263**	703-682-9220	47-3
JH Baxter & Co						
PO Box 5902	San Mateo	CA	94402	**800-556-1098**	650-349-0201	805
JH Cohn LLP						
Four Becker Farm Rd	Roseland	NJ	07068	**877-704-3500**	973-228-3500	2
JH Fletcher & Co Inc						
402 High St	Huntington	WV	25705	**800-327-6203**	304-525-7811	191
JH Industries Inc						
1981 E Aurora Rd	Twinsburg	OH	44087	**800-321-4968**	330-963-4105	475
JH Larson Co						
10200 51st Ave N	Plymouth	MN	55442	**800-292-7970**	763-545-1717	246
JH Routh Packing Company Inc						
4413 W Bogart Rd	Sandusky	OH	44870	**800-446-6759**	419-626-2251	468
JH Walker Trucking Company Inc						
152 N Hollywood Rd	Houma	LA	70364	**800-535-5992**	985-868-8330	770
JH Williams Oil Company Inc						
1237 E Twiggs St	Tampa	FL	33602	**800-683-0536**	813-228-7776	572
JHB International Inc						
1955 S Quince St	Denver	CO	80231	**800-525-9007**	303-751-8100	587
JHCR (Jackson Hole Central Reservations)						
140 E Broadway Ste 24 PO Box 2618	Jackson	WY	83001	**888-838-6606**	307-733-4005	373
JHL Industries						
10012 Nevada Ave	Chatsworth	CA	91311	**800-255-6636**	818-882-2233	722
Jiffy Lube						
PO Box 4427	Houston	TX	77210	**800-344-6933**		61-5
Jim Bishop Cabinets Inc						
5640 Bell Rd	Montgomery	AL	36116	**800-410-2444**		114
Jim Palmer Trucking Inc						
9730 Derby Dr	Missoula	MT	59801	**888-698-3422**	406-721-5151	770
Jim Walter Homes LLC						
3000 Riverchase Galleria Ste 1700	Birmingham	AL	35244	**800-643-0202**	205-745-2615	188
Jimbo's Jumbos Inc						
185 Peanut Dr PO Box 465	Edenton	NC	27932	**800-334-4771***		295-32
*General						
Jimmie Davis State Park						
1209 State Pk Rd	Chatham	LA	71226	**888-677-2263**	318-249-2595	558
Jimmy John's Franchise Inc						
2212 Fox Dr	Champaign	IL	61820	**800-546-6904**	217-356-9900	661
Jimmy Swaggart Ministries (JSM)						
8919 World Ministry Blvd PO Box 262550	Baton Rouge	LA	70810	**800-288-8350***	225-768-8300	47-20
*Orders						
Jive Communications Inc						
1275 West 1600 North Ste 100	Orem	UT	84057	**866-768-5429**		180

Company / Address	City	State	ZIP	Toll-Free	Phone	Class
JJ Haines & Company Inc						
6950 Aviation Blvd	Glen Burnie	MD	21061	**800-922-9248**		358
JJ Keller & Assoc Inc						
3003 Breezewood Ln PO Box 368	Neenah	WI	54957	**800-558-5011**	920-722-2848	628-11
JJB Hilliard WL Lyons Inc						
500 W Jefferson St	Louisville	KY	40202	**800-444-1854**	502-588-8400	681
JL Clark Mfg Co						
923 23rd Ave	Rockford	IL	61104	**877-482-5275**	815-962-8861	123
JL Industries Inc						
4450 W 78th St Cir	Bloomington	MN	55435	**800-554-6077**	952-835-6850	286
JLM Couture Inc						
525 Seventh Ave Ste 1703	New York	NY	10018	**800-924-6475**	212-221-8203	153-20
JM Huber Corp						
499 Thornall St 8th Fl	Edison	NJ	08837	**877-418-0038**	732-549-8600	529
JM Manufacturing Company Inc						
5200 West Century Blvd	Los Angeles	CA	90045	**800-621-4404**		589
JM Smucker Co						
One Strawberry Ln	Orrville	OH	44667	**888-550-9555**	330-682-3000	295-20
NYSE: SJM						
JM Swank Co						
395 Herky St	North Liberty	IA	52317	**800-593-6333**	319-626-3683	296-8
JM Test Systems Inc						
7323 Tom Dr	Baton Rouge	LA	70806	**800-353-3411**	225-925-2029	732
JM Turner Engineering Inc						
1325 College Ave	Santa Rosa	CA	95404	**800-514-4220**	707-528-4503	256
JMA Railroad Supply Co						
381 S Main Pl	Carol Stream	IL	60188	**800-874-0643**	630-653-9224	760
J-Mar Enterprises Inc						
PO Box 4143	Bismarck	ND	58502	**800-446-8283**	701-222-4518	770
JMC Communities						
2201 Fourth St N Ste 200	Saint Petersburg	FL	33704	**800-741-4106**	727-823-0022	644
JMFA (M Floyd John & Assoc Inc)						
125 N Burnett Dr	Baytown	TX	77520	**800-809-2307**		195
JMG Security Systems Inc						
17150 Newhope St Ste 109	Fountain Valley	CA	92708	**800-900-4564**	714-545-8882	684
JMMC (John Muir Medical Ctr)						
1601 Ygnacio Valley Rd	Walnut Creek	CA	94598	**844-398-5376**	925-939-3000	371-3
JMT (Johnson Mirmiran & Thompson)						
72 Loveton Cir	Sparks	MD	21152	**800-472-2310**	410-329-3100	261
JNF (Jewish National Fund)						
42 E 69th St	New York	NY	10021	**800-542-8733**	212-879-9300	47-20
JNJ Express Inc						
3935 Old Getwell Rd PO Box 30983	Memphis	TN	38130	**888-383-7157**	901-362-3444	770
Joan & Sanford Weill Medical College of Cornell University						
445 E 69th St	New York	NY	10021	**800-422-0711**	212-746-5454	167-2
Joan C Edwards School of Medicine at Marshall University						
1600 Medical Ctr Dr	Huntington	WV	25701	**877-691-1600**	304-691-1700	167-2
Jo-Ann Fabrics & Crafts						
5555 Darrow Rd	Hudson	OH	44236	**888-739-4120**	330-656-2600	270
Jo-Ann Stores Inc (JAS)						
5555 Darrow Rd	Hudson	OH	44236	**888-739-4120**	330-656-2600	270
JobMonkey Inc						
PO Box 3956	Seattle	WA	98124	**800-230-1095**		260
Jobpostings.ca						
100-25 Imperial St	Toronto	ON	M5P1B9	**877-900-5627**		260
Jobscope Corp						
355 Woodruff Rd	Greenville	SC	29607	**800-443-5794**	864-458-3100	179-11
JOC (Johnson Oil Co)						
1113 E Sara DeWitt Dr	Gonzales	TX	78629	**800-284-2432**	830-672-9574	572
JOC Group Inc						
2 Penn Plaza E 975 Raymond Blvd	Newark	NJ	07105	**800-223-0243***	973-776-7824	628-9
*Cust Svc						
Jo-Carroll Energy						
793 US Hwy 20 W	Elizabeth	IL	61028	**800-858-5522**	815-858-2207	245
Jockey International Inc						
2300 60th St PO Box 1417	Kenosha	WI	53140	**800-562-5391**		153-17
Jockeys' Guild Inc						
103 Wind Haven Dr Ste 200	Nicholasville	KY	40356	**866-465-6257**	859-305-0606	47-22
Joe Christensen Inc						
1540 Adams St	Lincoln	NE	68521	**800-228-5030**	402-476-7535	618
Joe Van Horn Chevrolet Inc						
PO Box 238	Plymouth	WI	53073	**800-236-1415**	920-893-6361	56
Joe Wheeler Electric Membership Corp						
PO Box 460	Trinity	AL	35673	**800-239-6518**	256-552-2300	245
Joe Wheeler Resort Lodge & Convention Ctr						
4401 McLean Dr	Rogersville	AL	35652	**800-544-5639**	256-247-5461	660
Joe's Jeans Inc						
2340 S Eastern Ave	Commerce	CA	90040	**877-528-5637**	323-837-3700	155-4
NASDAQ: JOEZ						
Joerns Healthcare						
5001 Joerns Dr	Stevens Point	WI	54481	**800-826-0270**	715-341-3600	318-3
Joey's Only Seafood Franchising Corp						
514-42nd Ave SE	Calgary	AB	T2G1Y6	**800-661-2123**	403-243-4584	661
JOFCO PO Box 71	Jasper	IN	47547	**800-235-6326**	812-482-5154	318-1
Joffrey's Coffee & Tea Co						
3803 Corporex Pk Dr	Tampa	FL	33619	**800-458-5282**	813-250-0404	296-11
Johanna Foods Inc						
20 Johanna Farm Rd PO Box 272	Flemington	NJ	08822	**800-727-6700**	908-788-2200	295-20
Johannes Flowers Inc						
4990 Foothill Rd	Carpinteria	CA	93013	**800-365-9476**	805-684-5686	366
Johanson Mfg Corp						
301 Rockaway Valley Rd	Boonton	NJ	07005	**800-477-1272**	973-334-2676	253
John A Van Den Bosch Co						
4511 Holland Ave	Holland	MI	49424	**800-968-6477**		442
John Amico Haircare Products						
4731 W 136th St	Crestwood	IL	60445	**800-676-5264**	708-824-4000	215
John Anson Ford Theatres						
2580 Cahuenga Blvd E	Hollywood	CA	90068	**800-466-3876**	323-461-3673	565
John Ascuaga's Nugget Hotel Casino						
1100 Nugget Ave	Sparks	NV	89431	**800-648-1177**	775-356-3300	660
John B Hynes Veterans Memorial Convention Ctr						
900 Boylston St	Boston	MA	02115	**800-392-6089**	617-954-2000	206
John B Sanfilippo & Son Inc						
1703 N Randall Rd	Elgin	IL	60123	**800-874-8734**	847-289-1800	295-28
NASDAQ: JBSS						
John Bean Co						
309 Exchange Ave	Conway	AR	72032	**800-225-5786**	501-450-1500	59
John Boos & Co						
3601 S Banker St PO Box 609	Effingham	IL	62401	**888-431-2667**	217-347-7701	286

	Toll-Free	Phone	Class
John Boyd Thacher State Park			
1 Hailes Cave Rd .... Voorheesville NY 12186	800-456-2267	518-872-1237	558
John Brown University			
2000 W University St .... Siloam Springs AR 72761	877-528-4636*	479-524-9500	166
*Admissions			
John Burroughs Memorial State Historic Site			
c/o Mine Kill State Pk			
PO Box 923 Rt 30 .... North Blenheim NY 12131	800-456-2267	518-827-6111	558
John C. Heath, Attorney at Law PLLC			
360 N Cutler Dr .... Salt Lake City UT 84054	800-756-9681		425
John Carroll University			
20700 N Pk Blvd .... Cleveland OH 44118	888-335-6800	216-397-1886	166
John Crane Inc			
6400 W Oakton St .... Morton Grove IL 60053	800-732-5464	847-967-2400	325
John D Archbold Memorial Hospital			
915 Gordon Ave .... Thomasville GA 31792	800-341-1009	229-228-2000	371-3
John Daugherty Realtors			
520 Post Oak Blvd Sixth Fl .... Houston TX 77027	800-231-2821	713-626-3930	643
John Day Co			
6263 Abbott Dr .... Omaha NE 68110	800-767-2273	402-455-8000	274
John Deere Credit Co			
6400 NW 86th St .... Johnston IA 50131	800-275-5322	515-267-3000	216
John Deere Planetarium			
820 38th St			
Augustana College .... Rock Island IL 61201	800-798-8100	309-794-7327	591
John Deere Power Systems			
3801 W Ridgeway Ave			
PO Box 5100. .... Waterloo IA 50704	800-533-6446		262
John E Conner Museum			
905 W Santa Gertrudis Ave			
700 University Blvd. .... Kingsville TX 78363	800-726-8192	361-593-2810	513
John E Jones Oil Co Inc			
1016 S Cedar PO Box 546 .... Stockton KS 67669	800-323-9821	785-425-6746	187
John E Koerner & Company Inc			
4820 Jefferson Hwy .... New Orleans LA 70121	800-333-1913		296-11
John F Buchan Homes			
2821 Northup Way Ste 100. .... Bellevue WA 98004	866-528-2426	425-827-2266	644
John F Kennedy Ctr for the Performing Arts			
2700 F St NW .... Washington DC 20566	800-444-1324	202-416-8000	565
John F Kennedy Library (JFKL)			
190 W 49th St .... Hialeah FL 33012	877-738-5622	305-821-2700	431-3
John F Kennedy Presidential Library & Museum			
Columbia Pt .... Boston MA 02125	866-535-1960	617-514-1600	431-2
John F Kennedy University			
100 Ellinwood Way .... Pleasant Hill CA 94523	800-696-5358	925-969-3300	166
John F. Kennedy			
Space Ctr .... Kennedy Space Center FL 32899	866-737-5235	321-867-5000	659
John Fabick Tractor Co			
1 Fabick Dr .... Fenton MO 63026	800-845-9188*	636-343-5900	355
*Cust Svc			
John Hancock Funds			
101 Huntington Ave 10th Fl .... Boston MA 02199	800-338-8080	617-375-1500	521
John Hancock New York			
100 Summit Lake Dr 2nd Fl .... Valhalla NY 10595	800-732-5543	877-391-3748	388-2
John Henry Co			
5800 W Grand River Ave .... Lansing MI 48906	800-748-0517	517-323-9000	618
John J Pershing Veterans Affairs Medical Ctr			
1500 N Westwood Blvd .... Poplar Bluff MO 63901	888-557-8262	573-686-4151	371-8
John Jay Homestead State Historic Site			
PO Box 832 .... Katonah NY 10536	800-456-2267	914-232-5651	558
John Johnson Co			
274 S Waterman St .... Detroit MI 48209	800-991-1394	313-496-0600	723
John Knox Village			
400 NW Murray Rd .... Lee's Summit MO 64081	800-892-5669	816-251-8000	663
John M Frey Co Inc			
2735 62nd St Ct .... Bettendorf IA 52722	800-397-3739	563-332-9200	605
John M. Campbell & Co			
1215 Crossroads Blvd .... Norman OK 73072	800-821-5933	405-321-1383	261
John Marshall Law School			
315 S Plymouth Ct .... Chicago IL 60604	800-285-2221	312-427-2737	167-1
John Morrell & Co			
805 E Kemper Rd .... Cincinnati OH 45246	800-722-1127	513-346-3540	468
John Muir Medical Ctr (JMMC)			
1601 Ygnacio Valley Rd .... Walnut Creek CA 94598	844-398-5376	925-939-3000	371-3
John Paul Jones State Historic Site			
c/o Bureau of Parks & Lands .... Bangor ME 04401	800-452-1942	207-941-4014	558
John Paul Mitchell Systems			
1888 Century Park E			
ste 1600 .... Los Angeles CA 90067	800-793-8790*		215
*Cust Svc			
John R Hess & Company Inc			
400 Stn St PO Box 3615. .... Cranston RI 02910	800-828-4377	401-785-9300	144
John R White Company Inc			
PO Box 10043 .... Birmingham AL 35202	800-245-1183	205-595-8381	144
John Reyer Shoe Store			
40 S Water Ave .... Sharon PA 16146	800-245-1550*		300
*Cust Svc			
John Roberts Co			
9687 E River Rd .... Coon Rapids MN 55433	800-551-1534	763-755-5500	619
John S Knight Ctr			
77 E Mill St .... Akron OH 44308	800-245-4254	330-374-8900	206
John T Cyr & Sons Inc			
153 Gilman Falls Ave .... Old Town ME 04468	800-244-2335	207-827-2335	108
John Volpi & Company Inc			
5263 Northrup Ave .... St Louis MO 63110	800-288-3439	314-772-8550	295-10
John W Danforth Co			
300 Colvin Woods Pkwy .... Tonawanda NY 14150	800-888-6119	716-832-1940	190-10
John Watson Chevrolet			
3535 Wall Ave .... Ogden UT 84401	866-647-9930	801-394-2611	56
John Wieland Homes & Neighborhoods			
4125 Atlanta Rd SE .... Smyrna GA 30080	800-376-4663	770-996-2400	644
John Wiley & Sons Inc			
111 River St .... Hoboken NJ 07030	800-225-5945*	201-748-6000	628-2
NYSE: JW/A ■ *Sales			
John Wolf Florist			
6228 Waters Ave .... Savannah GA 31406	800-944-6435	912-352-9843	292
John Zink Company LLC			
11920 E Apache St .... Tulsa OK 74116	800-421-9242	918-234-1800	354
John's Pass Village & Boardwalk			
150 John's Pass			
Boardwalk Pl .... Madeira Beach FL 33708	800-755-0677	727-398-6577	49-5
John-Kenyon Eye Ctr			
1305 Wall St Ste 200 .... Jeffersonville IN 47130	800-342-5393		786
Johnny Rockets			
1100 S Hayes St .... Arlington VA 22202	888-856-4669	703-415-3510	662
Johnny's Fine Foods Inc			
319 E 25th St .... Tacoma WA 98421	855-654-9590*	253-383-4597	295-37
*General			
Johnny's Selected Seeds			
955 Benton Ave .... Winslow ME 04901	877-564-6697	207-861-3900	685
Johns Eastern Co Inc			
PO Box 110259 Lakewood Branch ...... Sarasota FL 34211	800-452-4682*	941-907-3100	387
*General			
Johns Hopkins University Press			
2715 N Charles St .... Baltimore MD 21218	800-537-5487*	410-516-6900	628-4
*Orders			
Johns Manville Corp			
717 17th St PO Box 5108 .... Denver CO 80217	800-654-3103*	303-978-2000	386
*Prod Info			
Johnson & Johnson			
One Johnson &			
Johnson Plz .... New Brunswick NJ 08933	800-565-0122	732-524-0400	186
NYSE: JNJ			
Johnson & Johnson Consumer Products Co			
199 Grandview Rd .... Skillman NJ 08558	866-565-2229	908-874-1000	215
Johnson & Johnson Inc			
7101 Notre-Dame E .... Montreal QC H1N2G4	800-361-8990	514-251-5100	215
Johnson & Johnson Vision Care Inc			
7500 Centurion Pkwy .... Jacksonville FL 32256	800-843-2020	800-874-5278	535
Johnson & Wales University			
Providence			
Eight Abbott Pk Pl .... Providence RI 02903	800-342-5598	401-598-1000	166
Johnson & Wales University Charlotte			
801 W Trade St .... Charlotte NC 28202	866-598-2427	980-598-1100	166
Johnson & Wales University Denver			
7150 E Montview Blvd .... Denver CO 80220	877-598-3368	303-256-9300	166
Johnson & Wales University North Miami			
1701 NE 127th St .... North Miami FL 33181	866-598-3567	305-892-7551	166
Johnson Bros Bakery Supply			
10731 N Interstate 35 .... San Antonio TX 78233	877-446-2767	800-590-2575	296-8
Johnson Bros Wholesale Liquor Co			
1999 ShepaRd Rd .... Saint Paul MN 55116	800-723-2424	651-649-5800	80-3
Johnson C Smith University			
100 Beatties Ford Rd .... Charlotte NC 28216	800-782-7303*	704-378-1000	166
*Admissions			
Johnson City/Jonesborough/Washington County Chamber of Commerce			
603 E Market St .... Johnson City TN 37601	800-852-3392	423-461-8000	137
Johnson College			
3427 N Main Ave .... Scranton PA 18508	800-293-9675	570-342-6404	788
Johnson Controls Fire & Security Solutions			
4100 Gardian St Ste 200. .... Simi Valley CA 93063	800-229-4076	805-522-5555	683
Johnson Controls Systems			
9410 Bunsen Pkwy Ste 100-B ...... Louisville KY 40220	800-765-7773	502-671-7300	203
Johnson County Community College			
12345 College Blvd .... Overland Park KS 66210	866-896-5893	913-469-8500	160
Johnson County Library			
PO Box 2933 .... Shawnee Mission KS 66201	800-386-8501	913-826-4600	431-3
Johnson County Rural Electric Membership Corp			
750 International Dr .... Franklin IN 46131	800-382-5544	317-736-6174	245
Johnson Electric Coil Co			
821 Watson St .... Antigo WI 54409	800-826-9741	715-627-4367	757
Johnson Engineering Inc			
2122 Johnson St .... Fort Myers FL 33901	866-367-4400	239-334-0046	256
Johnson Gas Appliance Co			
520 E Ave NW .... Cedar Rapids IA 52405	800-553-5422	319-365-5267	317
Johnson Industries			
5944 Peachtree Corners E .... Norcross GA 30071	800-922-8111*	770-441-1128	60
*Orders			
Johnson Matthey Inc Pharmaceutical Materials Div			
2003 Nolte Dr .... Paulsboro NJ 08066	800-444-8544	856-384-7001	474
Johnson Matthey Medical Products			
1401 King Rd .... West Chester PA 19380	800-442-1405	610-648-8000	471
Johnson Matthey Pharma Services			
25 Patton Rd .... Devens MA 01434	800-444-8544	978-784-5000	474
Johnson Mirmiran & Thompson (JMT)			
72 Loveton Cir .... Sparks MD 21152	800-472-2310	410-329-3100	261
Johnson Motors Inc			
1891 Blinker Pkwy .... Du Bois PA 15801	800-537-1768	814-371-4444	56
Johnson Oil Co (JOC)			
1113 E Sara DeWitt Dr .... Gonzales TX 78629	800-284-2432	830-672-9574	572
Johnson Outdoors Inc			
555 Main St .... Racine WI 53403	800-468-9716	262-631-6600	701
NASDAQ: JOUT			
Johnson Refrigerated Truck Bodies			
215 E Allen St .... Rice Lake WI 54868	800-922-8360*	715-234-7071	509
*Sales			
Johnson Scale Company Inc			
36 Stiles Ln .... Pine Brook NJ 07058	800-572-2531		675
Johnson State College			
337 College Hill .... Johnson VT 05656	800-635-2356	802-635-2356	166
Johnson Storage & Moving Co			
221 Broadway .... Denver CO 80202	800-289-6683	303-778-6683	512
Johnson Supply Inc			
10151 Stella Link Rd .... Houston TX 77025	800-833-5455	713-830-2499	605
Johnson University			
7900 Johnson Dr .... Knoxville TN 37998	800-827-2122	865-573-4517	159
Johnson Youth Ctr			
3252 Hospital Dr .... Juneau AK 99801	800-780-9972	907-586-9433	409
Johnson's Garden Centers			
2707 W 13th St .... Wichita KS 67203	888-542-8463	316-942-1443	322
Johnsonite Inc			
16910 Munn Rd .... Chagrin Falls OH 44023	800-899-8916	440-543-8916	130
Johnsonville Sausage LLC			
PO Box 906 .... Sheboygan Falls WI 53085	888-556-2728		295-26
Johnston & Murphy Inc			
1415 Murfreesboro Rd .... Nashville TN 37217	800-424-2854	615-367-7168	300
Johnston Boiler Co			
300 Pine St .... Ferrysburg MI 49409	800-748-0295*	616-842-5050	354
*General			
Johnston County Convention & Visitors Bureau			
235 E Market St .... Smithfield NC 27577	800-441-7829	919-989-8687	207
Johnston Paper Co			
2 Eagle St .... Auburn NY 13021	800-800-7123	315-253-8435	552
Johnston the Florist Inc			
14179 Lincoln Way .... North Huntington PA 15642	800-356-9371	412-751-2821	292
Joliet Area Community Hospice			
250 Water Stone Cir .... Joliet IL 60431	800-360-1817	815-740-4104	368

Name / Address	City	State	ZIP	Toll-Free	Phone	Class
Joliet Equipment Corp One Doris Ave	Joliet	IL	60433	**800-435-9350**	815-727-6606	511
Joliet Junior College *North* 1215 Houbolt Rd	Joliet	IL	60431	**800-899-4722**	815-729-9020	160
Joliet Region Chamber of Commerce & Industry 63 N Chicago St	Joliet	IL	60432	**877-499-9669**	815-727-5371	137
Jolly Hotel Madison Towers 22 E 38th St *Resv	New York	NY	10016	**888-726-0528***	212-802-0600	376
Jolly Roger Inn 640 W Katella Ave	Anaheim	CA	92802	**888-296-5986**	714-782-7500	376
Jolt Consulting Group 112 Spring St Ste 301	Saratoga Springs	NY	12866	**877-249-6262**		458
Jomax LLC 14100 N 83rd Ave Ste 235	Peoria	AZ	85381	**888-866-0721**		390
Jon Renau Collection 2510 Island View Way	Vista	CA	92081	**800-462-9447**	760-598-0067	345
Jonas Fitness Inc 16969 n texas ave	Webster	TX	77598	**800-324-9800**		351
Jones Apparel Group Inc Jones New York Collection Div 1411 Broadway	New York	NY	10018	**800-999-1877**	212-355-4449	153-20
Jones College 5353 Arlington Expy	Jacksonville	FL	32211	**800-331-0176**	904-743-1122	166
Jones County Chamber of Commerce PO Box 527 *General	Laurel	MS	39441	**800-392-9629***	601-649-3031	137
Jones Dairy Farm 800 Jones Ave	Fort Atkinson	WI	53538	**800-635-6637**	920-563-2431	295-26
Jones Eye Clinic 4405 Hamilton Blvd PO Box 3246	Sioux City	IA	51104	**800-334-2015**	712-239-3937	786
Jones Hamilton Co 30354 Tracy Rd	Walbridge	OH	43465	**888-858-4425**	419-666-9838	141
Jones International Ltd 9697 E Mineral Ave	Centennial	CO	80112	**800-525-7002**		635
Jones International University Ltd 9697 E Mineral Ave	Centennial	CO	80112	**800-811-5663**	303-784-8904	788
Jones Knowledge Group Inc 9697 E Mineral Ave	Centennial	CO	80112	**800-350-6914**	303-792-3111	755
Jones Library Inc 43 Amity St	Amherst	MA	01002	**800-439-2370**	413-256-4090	431-3
Jones Metal Products Co 200 N Ctr St	West Lafayette	OH	43845	**888-868-6535**	740-545-6381	747
Jones Metal Products Inc 3201 Third Ave	Mankato	MN	56001	**800-967-1750**	507-625-4436	688
Jones Motor Company Inc 900 W Bridge St PO Box 137	Spring City	PA	19475	**800-825-6637**	610-948-7900	770
Jones Soda Co 234 Ninth Ave N *OTC: JSDA*	Seattle	WA	98109	**800-690-6903**	206-624-3357	79-2
Jonesboro Sun 518 Carson St	Jonesboro	AR	72401	**800-237-5341**	870-935-5525	525-2
Jones-Onslow Electric Membership Corp 259 Western Blvd	Jacksonville	NC	28546	**800-682-1515**	910-353-1940	245
Joplin Globe 117 E Fourth St	Joplin	MO	64801	**800-444-8514**	417-623-3480	525-2
Jordache Enterprises 1400 Broadway	New York	NY	10018	**888-295-3267**	212-944-1330	153-10
Jordan Hospital 275 Sandwich St	Plymouth	MA	02360	**800-256-7326**	508-746-2000	371-3
Jordan Lake State Recreation Area 280 State Pk Rd	Apex	NC	27523	**877-722-6762**	919-362-0586	558
Jordan Tourism Board (JTB) 1307 Dolley Madison Blvd Ste 2A	McLean	VA	22101	**877-733-5673**	703-243-7404	765
Jordano's Inc 550 S Patterson Ave	Santa Barbara	CA	93111	**800-325-2278**	805-964-0611	296-8
Jorgensen Conveyors Inc 10303 N Baehr Rd	Mequon	WI	53092	**800-325-7705**	262-242-3089	208
Jorgensen Forge Corp 8531 E Marginal Way S	Tukwila	WA	98108	**800-231-5382**	206-762-1100	478
Jorgensen Laboratories Inc 1450 Van Buren Ave	Loveland	CO	80538	**800-525-5614**	970-669-2500	470
Jos A Bank Clothiers 500 Hanover Pk	Hampstead	MD	21074	**800-999-7472***	410-239-2700	153-11
Josam Co 525 W US Hwy 20	Michigan City	IN	46360	**800-365-6726**	219-872-5531	602
Joseph Blank Inc 62 W 47th St Ste 808	New York	NY	10036	**800-223-7666**	212-575-9050	408
Joseph Brant Memorial Hospital (JBMH) 1230 N Shore Blvd	Burlington	ON	L7S1W7	**800-810-0000**	905-632-3730	371-2
Joseph Meyerhoff Symphony Hall 1212 Cathedral St	Baltimore	MD	21201	**877-276-1444**	410-783-8100	565
Josephine County Fairgrounds 1451 Fairgrounds Rd PO Box 672	Grants Pass	OR	97527	**800-773-1162**	541-476-3215	633
Joslyn Clark Corp 2100 W Broad St	Elizabethtown	NC	28337	**800-476-6952**		204
Joslyn Sunbank Co LLC 1740 Commerce Way	Paso Robles	CA	93446	**800-523-0727**	805-238-2840	803
Jostens Inc 3601 Minnesota Ave Ste 400	Minneapolis	MN	55435	**800-235-4774**	952-830-3300	406
Jottan Inc PO Box 166	Florence	NJ	08518	**800-364-4234**	609-447-6200	190-12
Joule Inc 1245 US Rt 1 S	Edison	NJ	08837	**800-341-0341**	732-548-5444	712
Journal & Courier 217 N Sixth St *News Rm	Lafayette	IN	47901	**800-407-5813***	765-423-5511	525-2
Journal Gazette 600 W Main St	Fort Wayne	IN	46802	**888-966-4532**	260-461-8773	525-2
Journal Graphics Inc 2840 NW 35th Ave Ste B	Portland	OR	97210	**888-609-6051**	503-790-9100	628-8
Journal Inquirer 306 Progress Dr PO Box 510	Manchester	CT	06045	**800-237-3606**	860-646-0500	525-2
Journal Le Droit 47 Clarence St	Ottawa	ON	K1N9K1	**800-267-6961**	613-562-0555	525-1
Journal of Accountancy 220 Leigh Farm Rd	Durham	NC	27707	**888-777-7077**		452-5
Journal of Employee Communication Management 316 N Michigan Ave Ste 400	Chicago	IL	60601	**800-878-5331**	312-960-4100	524-2
Journal of Financial Planning Assn 7535 E Hampden Ave Ste 600	Denver	CO	80231	**800-322-4237**	303-759-4900	452-5
Journal of Housing & Community Development 630 'I' St NW	Washington	DC	20001	**877-866-2476**	202-289-3500	452-5
Journal of Petroleum Technology 222 Palisades Creek Dr	Richardson	TX	75080	**800-456-6863**	972-952-9393	452-21
Journal of Practical Nursing (JPN) 1940 Duke St Ste 200	Alexandria	VA	22314	**800-655-4845**	703-933-1003	452-16
Journal of Property Management 430 N Michigan Ave	Chicago	IL	60611	**800-837-0706**		452-5
Journal of Protective Coatings & Linings 2100 Wharton St Ste 310	Pittsburgh	PA	15203	**800-837-8303**	412-431-8300	452-21
Journal of the American Medical Assn (JAMA) PO Box 10946	Chicago	IL	60654	**800-262-2350**	312-670-7827	452-16
Journal of the American Pharmacists Assn 2215 Constitution Ave NW	Washington	DC	20037	**800-237-2742**	202-628-4410	452-16
Journal of the Kansas Bar Assn 1200 SW Harrison St	Topeka	KS	66612	**800-928-3111**	785-234-5696	452-15
Journal of the Louisiana State Medical Society 6767 Perkins Rd Ste 100	Baton Rouge	LA	70808	**800-375-9508**	225-763-8500	452-16
Journal of the Medical Assn of Georgia 1849 The Exchange Ste 200	Atlanta	GA	30339	**800-282-0224**	678-303-9290	452-16
Journal of the Philosophy of Sport 1607 N Market St	Champaign	IL	61820	**800-747-4457**	217-351-5076	452-20
Journal Publishing Co 1242 S Green St	Tupelo	MS	38804	**800-264-6397**	662-842-2611	628-8
Journal, The 207 W King St	Martinsburg	WV	25402	**800-448-1895**	304-263-8931	525-2
Journal-Patriot PO Box 70	North Wilkesboro	NC	28659	**877-322-8228**	336-838-4117	525-4
Journal-Standard 27 S State Ave	Freeport	IL	61032	**800-325-6397**	815-232-1171	525-2
Journey Education Marketing Inc 13755 Hutton Dr Ste 500	Dallas	TX	75234	**800-874-9001**	972-481-2000	175
Journey Museum 222 New York St	Rapid City	SD	57701	**877-343-8220**	605-394-6923	513
Journyx Inc 7600 Burnet Rd Ste. 300	Austin	TX	78757	**800-755-9878**	512-834-8888	38
Joy Cone Co 3435 Lamor Rd	Hermitage	PA	16148	**800-242-2663**	724-962-5747	295-9
Joy Dog Food PO Box 305	Pinckneyville	IL	62274	**800-245-4125**		571
Joyce Florist 2729 S Hampton Rd	Dallas	TX	75224	**800-527-1520**	214-942-1776	292
Joyce Koons Buick Gmc 10660 Automotive Dr	Manassas	VA	20109	**866-224-9293**	703-368-9100	509
Joyce Motors Corp 3166 SR- 10	Denville	NJ	07834	**844-332-5955**	973-361-3000	56
Joyce Windows 1125 Berea Industrial Pkwy	Berea	OH	44017	**800-824-7988**	440-239-9100	234
Joyner Fine Properties (JFP) 2727 Enterprise Pkwy PO Box 31355	Richmond	VA	23294	**800-446-3858**	804-270-9440	643
JP Everhart & Co 1840 N Greenville Ave Ste 178	Richardson	TX	75081	**888-622-8575**		388-5
JP Maguire Assoc Inc 266 Brookside Rd	Waterbury	CT	06708	**877-576-2484**	203-755-2297	83
JPI (Jan-Pro International Inc) 2520 Northwinds Pkwy Ste 375	Alpharetta	GA	30009	**866-355-1064**	678-336-1780	150
JPMorgan Fleming Asset Management PO Box 8528	Boston	MA	02266	**800-480-4111**		398
JPN (Journal of Practical Nursing) 1940 Duke St Ste 200	Alexandria	VA	22314	**800-655-4845**	703-933-1003	452-16
JR Filanc Construction Company Inc 740 N Andreasen Dr	Escondido	CA	92029	**877-225-5428**	760-941-7130	189-10
JR O'Dwyer Co 271 Madison Ave Sixth Fl	New York	NY	10016	**866-395-7710**	212-679-2471	628-9
JR Simplot Co 999 W Main St Ste 1300	Boise	ID	83702	**800-832-8893**	208-336-2110	295-21
JR Watkins Inc 150 Liberty St PO Box 5570	Winona	MN	55987	**800-243-9423**	507-457-3300	363
JR's Place for Ribs 131st St & Coastal	Ocean City	MD	21842	**800-879-7742**	410-250-3100	662
JRF (Jewish Reconstructionist Federation) 101 Greenwood Ave	Jenkintown	PA	19046	**877-226-7573**	215-885-5601	47-20
JRM Industries Inc One Mattimore St	Passaic	NJ	07055	**800-533-2697**	973-779-9340	734-5
JSA (Junior State of America) 400 S El Camino Real Ste 300	San Mateo	CA	94402	**800-334-5353**	650-347-1600	47-11
JSA (Jewelers Shipping Assn) 125 Carlsbad St	Cranston	RI	02920	**800-688-4572**	401-943-6020	48-21
JSB Industries Inc 130 Crescent Ave	Chelsea	MA	02150	**800-554-2887**	617-846-1565	342
JSG (Janesville Sand & Gravel Co) 1110 Harding St	Janesville	WI	53547	**800-955-7702**	608-754-7701	498-4
JSJ Corp Dake Div 724 Robbins Rd	Grand Haven	MI	49417	**800-846-3253**	616-842-7110	348
JSM (Jimmy Swaggart Ministries) 8919 World Ministry Blvd PO Box 262550 *Orders	Baton Rouge	LA	70810	**800-288-8350***	225-768-8300	47-20
JSO (Jacksonville Symphony Orchestra) 300 W Water St Ste 200	Jacksonville	FL	32202	**877-662-6731**	904-354-5479	566-3
JTB (Jordan Tourism Board) 1307 Dolley Madison Blvd Ste 2A	McLean	VA	22101	**877-733-5673**	703-243-7404	765
JTech Communications Inc 6413 Congress Ave Ste 150	Boca Raton	FL	33487	**800-321-6221**		725
JTEKT Corporation 29570 Clemens Rd *Cust Svc	Westlake	OH	44145	**800-263-5163***	440-835-1000	74
Juanita K Hammons Hall for the Performing Arts 901 S National Ave	Springfield	MO	65897	**888-476-7849**	417-836-6776	565
Juanita's Foods Inc P.O. Box 847 PO Box 847	Wilmington	CA	90748	**800-303-2965**		295-36
Jubitz Corp 33 NE Middlefield Rd	Portland	OR	97211	**800-523-0600**	503-283-1111	323
Judaica Press Inc 123 Ditmas Ave	Brooklyn	NY	11218	**800-972-6201**	718-972-6200	628-2
Judd Wire Inc 124 Tpke Rd *Cust Svc	Turners Falls	MA	01376	**800-545-5833***	413-863-4357	801
Judge Group Inc 300 Conshohocken State Rd Ste 300	West Conshohocken	PA	19428	**888-228-7162**	610-667-7700	712
Judicate West 1851 E First St Ste 1450	Santa Ana	CA	92705	**800-488-8805**	714-834-1340	40

	Toll-Free	Phone	Class
Judicial Watch Inc			
425 Third St SW Ste 800 . . . . Washington DC 20024	**888-593-8442**	202-646-5172	47-7
Judson College			
302 Bibb St . . . . Marion AL 36756	**800-447-9472***	334-683-5110	166
*Admissions			
Judson Park			
23600 Marine View Dr S . . . . . . Des Moines WA 98198	**800-401-4113**	206-824-4000	663
Judson University			
1151 N State St . . . . Elgin IL 60123	**800-879-5376***	847-628-2500	166
*Admissions			
JUF (Jewish United Fund/Jewish Federation of Metropolitan Chicago)			
30 S Wells St . . . . Chicago IL 60606	**855-275-5237**	312-346-6700	47-20
Jugs Sports			
11885 SW Herman Rd . . . . Tualatin OR 97062	**800-547-6843**		701
Julian Charter School Inc			
1704 Cape Horn . . . . Julian CA 92036	**866-853-0003**	760-765-3847	676
Julian Tours			
1721 Crestwood Dr Ste 110 . . . . . . Alexandria VA 22302	**800-541-7936**	703-379-2300	750
Julius Koch USA Inc			
387 Church St . . . . New Bedford MA 02745	**800-522-3652***	508-995-9565	734-5
*Sales			
July Business Services			
215 Mary Ave Ste 302 . . . . Waco TX 76701	**888-333-5859**		40
Jump River Electric Co-op			
PO Box 99 . . . . Ladysmith WI 54848	**866-273-5111**	715-532-5524	245
Juneau Chamber of Commerce			
9301 Glacier Hwy Suite 110 . . . . Juneau AK 99801	**888-581-2201**	907-463-3488	137
Juneau Convention & Visitors Bureau			
101 Egan Dr . . . . Juneau AK 99801	**888-581-2201**	907-586-1737	207
Juneau International Airport			
1873 Shell Simmons Dr Ste 200 . . . . . . Juneau AK 99801	**800-478-4176**	907-789-7821	27
Juneau Public Libraries			
292 Marine Way . . . . Juneau AK 99801	**800-478-4176**	907-586-5324	431-3
Jungle Adventures			
26205 E Colonial Dr . . . . Christmas FL 32709	**877-424-2867**	407-568-2885	810
Juniata College			
1700 Moore St . . . . Huntingdon PA 16652	**877-586-4282**	814-641-3000	166
Juniata Valley Area Chamber of Commerce			
1 W Market St . . . . Lewistown PA 17044	**866-377-1234**	717-248-6713	137
Junior Achievement of Canada (JACAN)			
1 Eva Rd Ste 218 . . . . Toronto ON M9C4Z5	**800-265-0699**	416-622-4602	47-11
Junior Chamber International (JCI)			
15645 Olive Blvd . . . . Chesterfield MO 63017	**800-905-5499**	636-449-3100	47-7
Junior State of America (JSA)			
400 S El Camino Real Ste 300 . . . . . . San Mateo CA 94402	**800-334-5353**	650-347-1600	47-11
Juniper Networks Inc			
1194 N Mathilda Ave . . . . Sunnyvale CA 94089	**888-586-4737**	408-745-2000	177
NYSE: JNPR			
Juniper Pharmaceuticals Inc			
354 Eisenhower Pkwy			
Plaza 1 2nd Fl. . . . . Livingston NJ 07039	**866-566-5636**	973-994-3999	576
NASDAQ: CBRX			
Jupiter Aluminum Corp			
4825 Scott St . . . . Schiller Park IL 60176	**800-392-7265**	847-928-5930	651
Jupiter Beach Resort			
Five N A1A . . . . Jupiter FL 33477	**877-389-0571**	561-746-2511	660
Jurlique Spa			
4925 N Scottsdale Rd . . . . Scottsdale AZ 85251	**800-528-7867**	480-424-6072	698
Jury Research Institute			
2617 Danville Blvd PO Box 100 . . . . Alamo CA 94507	**800-233-5879**	925-932-5663	440
Just Born Inc			
1300 Stefko Blvd . . . . Bethlehem PA 18017	**800-445-5787**	610-867-7568	295-8
Justice Design Group (JDG)			
500 S Grand Ave Ste 110 . . . . . . Los Angeles CA 90071	**800-533-4799**	213-437-0102	435
Justin Boot Co Inc			
610 W Daggett St . . . . Fort Worth TX 76104	**866-240-8853***	817-332-7797	300
*Cust Svc			
Justin P. Wilson Cumberland Trail State Park			
220 Pk Rd . . . . Caryville TN 38555	**800-342-3145**	423-566-2229	558
Justiss Oil Company Inc			
1120 E Oak St . . . . Jena LA 71342	**800-256-2501**	318-992-4111	533
Justrite Manufacturing Co			
2454 E Dempster St Ste 300. . . . . . Des Plaines IL 60016	**800-798-9250**	847-298-9250	199
Juvenile Diabetes Research Foundation International (JDRF)			
120 Wall St . . . . New York NY 10005	**800-533-2873**	212-785-9500	47-17
JVC Professional Products Co			
1700 Valley Rd . . . . Wayne NJ 07470	**800-252-5722**	973-317-5000	51
JW Aluminum			
435 Old Mt Holly Rd . . . . Mount Holly SC 29445	**877-586-5314***		480
*Sales			
JW Jung Seed Co			
335 S High St . . . . Randolph WI 53956	**800-297-3123**		685
JW Marriott Desert Ridge Resort & Spa			
5350 E Marriott Dr . . . . Phoenix AZ 85054	**800-845-5279**	480-293-5000	660
JW Marriott Orlando Grande Lakes Resort			
4040 Central Florida Pkwy . . . . Orlando FL 32837	**800-576-5750**	407-206-2300	660
JW Marriott Resort Las Vegas			
221 N Rampart Blvd . . . . Las Vegas NV 89144	**877-869-8777**	702-869-7777	660
JW Pepper & Son Inc			
2480 Industrial Blvd . . . . Paoli PA 19301	**800-345-6296**	610-648-0500	519
JW Peters Inc			
500 W Market St . . . . Burlington WI 53105	**866-265-7888**	262-806-9009	184
JW Speaker Corp			
N 120 W 19434 Freistadt Rd			
PO Box 1011. . . . . Germantown WI 53022	**800-558-7288**	262-251-6660	434
JW Starr Pass Resort & Spa			
3800 W Starr Pass Blvd . . . . Tucson AZ 85745	**800-845-5279**	520-792-3500	698
JWCI (Providence Health & Services)			
2200 Santa Monica Blvd . . . . . . Santa Monica CA 90404	**800-262-6259**	310-582-7450	659
JWF Industries			
84 Iron St PO Box 1286 . . . . Johnstown PA 15907	**800-225-9359**	814-539-6922	798

K

	Toll-Free	Phone	Class
K & B Machine Works Inc			
212 Redmond Rd PO Box 10265 . . . . Houma LA 70363	**800-256-1526**	985-868-6730	383
K Line America Inc			
8730 Stony Pt Pkwy Ste 400. . . . . . . Richmond VA 23235	**800-609-3221**	804-560-3600	312

	Toll-Free	Phone	Class
K12 Inc			
2300 Corporate Pk Dr . . . . Herndon VA 20171	**866-512-2273**	703-483-7000	676
NYSE: LRN			
K2 Industrial Services			
5233 Hohman Ave . . . . Hammond IN 46320	**866-524-6387**	219-933-5300	190-8
K2 Sports			
4201 Sixth Ave S . . . . Seattle WA 98108	**800-426-1617**	206-805-4800	701
KA (Kraus-Anderson Co)			
523 S Eigth St . . . . Minneapolis MN 55404	**888-547-3983**	612-305-2934	186
KA Steel Chemicals Inc			
15185 Main St PO Box 729 . . . . Lemont IL 60439	**800-677-8335**	630-257-3900	144
Kaba Ilco Corp			
400 Jeffreys Rd . . . . Rocky Mount NC 27804	**800-334-1381**	252-446-3321	347
KA-BAR Knives Inc			
200 Homer St . . . . Olean NY 14760	**800-282-0130**	716-372-5952	222
KABB-TV Ch 29 (Fox)			
4335 NW Loop 410 . . . . San Antonio TX 78229	**800-987-6038**	210-366-1129	730-67
KABC-AM 790 (N/T)			
3321 S La Cienega Blvd			
PO Box 790. . . . . Los Angeles CA 90016	**800-222-5222**	310-840-4900	636-62
KABX-FM 97.5 (Oldies)			
1020 W Main St . . . . Merced CA 95340	**800-350-3777**	209-723-2191	636
KABZ-FM 103.7 (N/T)			
2400 Cottondale Ln . . . . Little Rock AR 72202	**800-477-1037**	501-661-1037	636-61
KACV-FM 90 (Alt)			
PO Box 447 . . . . Amarillo TX 79178	**800-766-0176**		636-5
Kadlec Regional Medical Ctr			
888 Swift Blvd . . . . Richland WA 99352	**800-780-6067**	509-946-4611	371-3
KAFT-TV Ch 13 (PBS)			
350 S Donaghey Ave . . . . Conway AR 72034	**800-662-2386**	501-682-2386	730
KAG (Kenan Advantage Group Inc)			
4366 Mt Pleasant St NW . . . . North Canton OH 44720	**800-969-5419**	330-491-0474	770
KAG West			
4076 Seaport Blvd . . . . West Sacramento CA 95691	**800-547-1587**	916-371-8241	770
Kagome Creative Foods LLC			
710 N Pearl St . . . . Osceola AR 72370	**800-643-0006**	870-563-2601	295-30
Kahala Corp			
9311 E Via de Ventura . . . . Scottsdale AZ 85258	**866-452-4252**	480-362-4800	661
Kahala Mandarin Oriental Hotel Hawaii Resort			
5000 Kahala Ave . . . . Honolulu HI 96816	**800-367-2525**	808-739-8888	376
Kahiki Foods Inc			
1100 Morrison Rd . . . . Columbus OH 43230	**855-524-4540**	614-322-3180	295-36
Kahn Litwin Renza & Company Ltd			
951 N Main St . . . . Providence RI 02904	**888-557-8557**	401-274-2001	2
Kahului Airport			
1 Kahului Airport Rd . . . . Kahului HI 96732	**800-321-3712**	808-872-3830	27
KAI (Kingsway America Inc)			
150 NW Pt Blvd . . . . Elk Grove Village IL 60007	**800-232-0631**	847-700-9100	357-4
Kai 20 Jay St Ste 530. . . . . Brooklyn NY 11201	**888-832-7832**	718-250-4000	662
Kailua Chamber of Commerce			
600 Kailua Rd Ste 107 . . . . Kailua HI 96734	**888-261-7997**	808-261-2727	137
Kaiser Aluminum Corp			
27422 Portola Pkwy			
Ste 200 . . . . Foothill Ranch CA 92610	**800-873-2011***	949-614-1740	480
*Sales			
Kaiser Foundation Health Plan Inc			
One Kaiser Plz 27th Fl . . . . Oakland CA 94612	**800-464-4000**	510-271-5800	388-3
Kaiser Permanente			
280 W MacArthur Blvd . . . . Oakland CA 94611	**800-464-4000**	510-752-1000	388-3
Kaiser Permanente Foundation Hospital			
9400 E Rosecrans Ave . . . . Bellflower CA 90706	**866-279-8954**	562-461-3000	371-3
Kaiser Permanente Harbor City Medical Ctr			
25825 S Vermont Ave . . . . Harbor City CA 90710	**800-464-4000**	310-325-5111	371-3
Kaiser Permanente Hawaii			
711 Kapiolani Blvd . . . . Honolulu HI 96813	**800-966-5955**	808-432-0000	388-3
Kaiser Permanente Hospital			
441 N Lakeview Ave . . . . Anaheim CA 92807	**800-464-4000**	714-279-4000	371-3
Kaiser Permanente Medical Center-South Sacramento			
6600 Bruceville Rd . . . . Sacramento CA 95823	**800-464-4000**	916-688-2000	371-3
Kaiser Permanente Medical Ctr			
710 Lawrence Expy . . . . Santa Clara CA 95051	**800-464-4000**	408-851-1717	371-3
Kaiser Permanente Northwest			
500 NE Multnomah St Ste 100 . . . . Portland OR 97232	**800-813-2000**	503-813-2000	388-3
Kaiser Permanente Parma Medical Ctr			
12301 Snow Rd . . . . Cleveland OH 44130	**800-524-7372**	216-362-2000	371-3
Kaiser Permanente Riverside Medical Ctr			
10800 Magnolia Ave . . . . Riverside CA 92505	**800-464-4000***	951-353-2000	371-3
*Cust Svc			
Kaiser Permanente Walnut Creek Medical Ctr			
1425 S Main St . . . . Walnut Creek CA 94596	**800-464-4000**	925-295-4000	371-3
KaiserAir Inc			
8735 Earhart Rd PO Box 2626 . . . . Oakland CA 94621	**800-538-2625**	510-569-9622	13
KAJA-FM 97.3 (Ctry)			
6222 NW IH-10 . . . . San Antonio TX 78201	**800-707-5150**	210-736-9700	636-95
Kalamazoo College			
1200 Academy St . . . . Kalamazoo MI 49006	**800-253-3602***	269-337-7166	166
*Admissions			
Kalamazoo County Convention & Visitors Bureau			
141 E Michigan Ave Ste 100. . . . . . . Kalamazoo MI 49007	**800-888-0509**	269-488-9000	207
Kalamazoo Gazette			
401 S Burdick St . . . . Kalamazoo MI 49007	**800-466-6397**	269-345-3511	525-2
Kalamazoo Technical Furniture			
6450 Vly Industrial Dr . . . . Kalamazoo MI 49009	**800-832-5227**		417
Kalani Oceanside Retreat			
12-6860 Kapoho Kalapana Rd . . . . Pahoa HI 96778	**800-800-6886**	808-965-7828	664
Kaleo Software Inc			
841 Apollo St Ste 330. . . . . El Segundo CA 90245	**888-937-8945**		384
Kalibrate Technologies PLC			
25B Hanover Rd . . . . Florham Park NJ 07932	**800-727-6774***	973-549-1850	179-11
*Cust Svc			
Kalido			
1 Wall St Ste 3 . . . . Burlington MA 01803	**866-466-3849**	781-202-3200	179-1
Kalispell Regional Medical Ctr			
310 Sunnyview Ln . . . . Kalispell MT 59901	**800-228-1574**	406-752-5111	371-3
Kalitta Charters LLC			
843 Willow Run Airport . . . . Ypsilanti MI 48198	**800-525-4882**	734-544-3400	21
Kalitta Flying Service			
818 Willow Run Airport . . . . Ypsilanti MI 48198	**800-521-1590**	734-484-0088	12
Kallista Inc			
1227 N Eigth St Ste 2 . . . . Sheboygan WI 53081	**888-452-5547***	920-457-4441	372
Kalman Floor Company Inc			
1202 Bergen Pkwy Ste 110. . . . . Evergreen CO 80439	**800-525-7840**	303-674-2290	190-2

	Toll-Free	Phone	Class
Kalsec Inc 3713 W Main St … Kalamazoo MI 49006	800-323-9320	269-349-9711	295-15
Kalwall Corp 1111 Candia Rd … Manchester NH 03109	800-258-9777	603-627-3861	601
Kam Wah Chung State Heritage Site (KWC) 725 Summer St NE Ste C … Salem OR 97301	800-551-6949	503-986-0707	558
Kam's 4500 Montrose Blvd … Houston TX 77006	800-510-3663	713-529-5057	662
Kama Corp 600 Dietrich Ave … Hazleton PA 18201	888-252-6212	412-553-4545	593
Kamatics Corp 1330 Blue Hills Ave … Bloomfield CT 06002	866-540-5760	860-243-9704	613
KaMMCO (Kansas Medical Mutual Insurance Co) 623 SW Tenth Ave Ste 200 … Topeka KS 66612	800-232-2259	785-232-2224	388-5
Kampgrounds of America Inc (KOA) PO Box 30558 … Billings MT 59114	888-562-0000		120
Kanawha Hospice Care 1606 Kanawha Blvd W … Charleston WV 25387	800-560-8523	304-768-8523	368
Kanawha Scales & Systems Inc Rock Branch Industrial Pk 303 Jacobson Dr … Poca WV 25159	800-955-8321	304-755-8321	358
Kane County 78 S 100 E … Kanab UT 84741	800-733-5263	435-644-5033	336
Kane Graphical Corp 2255 W Logan Blvd … Chicago IL 60647	800-992-2921	773-384-1200	341
Kane Manufacturing Corp 515 N Fraley St … Kane PA 16735	800-952-6399	814-837-6464	234
Kane Reid Securities Group Inc 13024 Ballantyne Corporate Pl Ste 500 … Charlotte NC 28277	877-495-5464		681
Kane Transport Inc 40925 403rd Ave PO Box 126 … Sauk Centre MN 56378	800-892-8557	320-352-2762	758
Kanebridge Corp 153 Bauer Dr … Oakland NJ 07436	888-222-9221	201-337-2300	347
Kanguru Solutions 1360 Main St … Millis MA 02054 *Sales	888-526-4878*	508-376-4245	174-8
Kankakee Community College 100 College Dr … Kankakee IL 60901	800-526-0844	815-802-8100	160
Kansas Consumer Protection Div 534 S Kansas Ave Ste 1210 … Topeka KS 66603	800-452-6727	785-296-5059	337-17
Healing Arts Board 800 SW Jackson Lower Level Ste A … Topeka KS 66612	888-886-7205	785-296-7413	337-17
Insurance Dept 420 SW Ninth St … Topeka KS 66612	800-432-2484	785-296-3071	337-17
Travel & Tourism Development Div 1020 S Kansas Ave Ste 200 … Topeka KS 66612	800-252-6727	785-296-2009	337-17
Treasurer 900 SW Jackson St Ste 201 … Topeka KS 66612	800-432-0386	785-296-3171	337-17
Workers' Compensation Div 401 SW Topeka Blvd Ste 2 … Topeka KS 66603	800-332-0353	785-296-4000	337-17
Kansas Assn of Realtors 3644 SW Burlingame Rd … Topeka KS 66611	800-366-0069	785-267-3610	647
Kansas Bar Assn 1200 SW Harrison St … Topeka KS 66612	800-928-3111	785-234-5696	71
Kansas Children's Service League (KCSL) 3545 SW 5th … Topeka KS 66606	877-530-5275	785-274-3100	47-6
Kansas City Art Institute 4415 Warwick Blvd … Kansas City MO 64111	800-522-5224	816-474-5224	162
Kansas City Aviation Ctr Inc 15325 S Pflumm Rd … Olathe KS 66062	800-720-5222	913-782-0530	62
Kansas City Chiefs Arrowhead Stadium 1 Arrowhead Dr … Kansas City MO 64129	800-332-6048	816-920-9300	706-3
Kansas City Convention & Entertainment Centers 301 W 13th St … Kansas City MO 64105	800-821-7060	816-513-5000	206
Kansas City Convention & Visitors Assn 1100 Main St Ste 2200 … Kansas City MO 64105	800-767-7700	816-221-5242	207
Kansas City Electrical Supply Co (KCES) 10900 MidAmerica Ave … Lenexa KS 66219	866-271-6456	913-563-7002	246
Kansas City Kansas Convention & Visitors Bureau Inc 901 N Eigth St PO Box 171517 … Kansas City KS 66117	800-264-1563	913-321-5800	207
Kansas City Life Insurance Co 3520 Broadway … Kansas City MO 64111 NASDAQ: KCLI	800-821-6164	816-753-7000	357-4
Kansas City Music Hall 301 W 13th St … Kansas City MO 64105	800-821-7060	816-513-5000	565
Kansas City Peterbilt Inc 8915 Woodend Rd … Kansas City KS 66111	800-489-1122	913-441-2888	61-5
Kansas City Power & Light Co 1200 Main … Kansas City MO 64141	888-471-5275	816-556-2200	775
Kansas City Royals Kauffman Stadium 1 Royal Way … Kansas City MO 64129 *Sales	800-676-9257*	816-921-8000	704
Kansas City Southern Railway Co 427 W 12th St … Kansas City MO 64105	800-468-6527	816-983-1303	639
Kansas City Star 1729 Grand Ave … Kansas City MO 64108	877-962-7827		525-2
Kansas City Symphony 1020 Central St Ste 300 … Kansas City MO 64105	877-829-5590	816-471-1100	566-3
Kansas Cosmosphere & Space Ctr 1100 N Plum St … Hutchinson KS 67501	800-397-0330	620-662-2305	514
Kansas Democratic Party 700 SW Jackson St Ste 706 … Topeka KS 66603	888-573-3547	785-234-0425	609-1
Kansas Expocentre One Expocentre Dr … Topeka KS 66612	800-745-3000	785-235-1986	206
Kansas Gas Service 7421 W 129th St … Overland Park KS 66213	888-482-4950		775
Kansas Living Magazine 2627 KFB Plz … Manhattan KS 66503	800-406-3053	785-587-6000	452-1
Kansas Lottery 128 N Kansas Ave … Topeka KS 66603	800-544-9467	785-296-5700	447
Kansas Medical Mutual Insurance Co (KaMMCO) 623 SW Tenth Ave Ste 200 … Topeka KS 66612	800-232-2259	785-232-2224	388-5
Kansas Medical Society 623 SW Tenth Ave … Topeka KS 66612	800-332-0156	785-235-2383	469
Kansas Museum of History 6425 SW Sixth St … Topeka KS 66615	888-537-1222	785-272-8681	513
Kansas Pharmacists Assn 1020 SW Fairlawn Rd … Topeka KS 66604	888-792-6273	785-228-2327	578
Kansas State University 119 Anderson Hall … Manhattan KS 66506 *Admissions	800-432-8270*	785-532-6250	166
Kansas Veterinary Medical Assn 816 SW Tyler St Ste 200 … Topeka KS 66612	888-545-5862	785-233-4141	783
Kansas Wesleyan University 100 E Claflin Ave … Salina KS 67401	800-874-1154	785-827-5541	166
Kanto Corp 13424 N Woodrush Way … Portland OR 97203	866-609-5571	503-283-0405	141
KANU-FM 91.5 (NPR) 1120 W 11th St Kansas Public Radio … Lawrence KS 66044	888-577-5268	785-864-4530	636
Kanzaki Specialty Papers 1 Monarch Pl Ste 800 … Springfield MA 01144	888-526-9254		547
Kao Brands Co 2535 Spring Grove Ave … Cincinnati OH 45214	800-742-8798	513-421-1400	215
Kao Specialties Americas LLC 243 Woodbine St PO Box 2316 … High Point NC 27261	800-727-2214	336-884-2214	143
Kapalua Villas, The 2000 Village Rd … Lahaina HI 96761	800-545-0018	808-665-5400	660
Kaplan & Zubrin Inc 146 Kaighns Ave … Camden NJ 08103	800-248-1736	856-964-1083	295-19
Kaplan Career Institute Franklin Mills 177 Franklin Mills Blvd … Philadelphia PA 19154	800-935-1857	215-612-6600	788
Kaplan Early Learning Co 1310 Lewisville-Clemmons Rd … Lewisville NC 27023	800-334-2014	336-766-7374	243
Kaplan Inc 6301 Kaplan University Ave … Fort Lauderdale FL 33309 *Cust Svc	800-258-2432*	954-515-3993	244
Kaplan Telephone Company Inc (KTC) 220 N Cushing Ave … Kaplan LA 70548	866-643-7171	337-643-7171	726
Kaplan University 6301 Kaplan University Ave … Fort Lauderdale FL 33309	866-522-7747	954-515-4015	788
Kaplan University Omaha 5425 N 103rd St … Omaha NE 68134	800-987-7734	402-572-8500	788
Kappa Alpha Order 115 Liberty Hall Rd … Lexington VA 24450	888-922-6335	540-463-1865	47-16
Kappa Alpha Theta Fraternity 8740 Founders Rd … Indianapolis IN 46268	800-526-1870	317-876-1870	47-16
Kappa Delta Pi 3707 Woodview Trace … Indianapolis IN 46268	800-284-3167	317-871-4900	47-16
Kappa Delta Sorority 3205 Players Ln … Memphis TN 38125	800-536-1897	901-748-1897	47-16
Kappa Kappa Gamma PO Box 38 … Columbus OH 43216	866-554-1870	614-228-6515	47-16
Kappler Inc 115 Grimes Dr PO Box 490 … Guntersville AL 35976	800-600-4019	256-505-4005	569
Kar's Nuts 1200 E 14 Mile Rd … Madison Heights MI 48071	800-527-6887	248-588-1903	295-28
Karas & Karas Glass Company Inc 455 Dorchester Ave … Boston MA 02127	800-888-1235	617-268-8800	190-6
Karbone Inc 130 W 42nd St 9th Fl … New York NY 10036	800-728-2056	646-291-2900	193
Kardex Systems Inc 114 Westview Ave PO Box 171 … Marietta OH 45750	800-639-5805	740-374-9300	286
Karen Ann Quinlan Hospice 99 Sparta Ave … Newton NJ 07860	800-882-1117	973-383-0115	368
KARE-TV Ch 11 (NBC) 8811 State Hwy 55 … Golden Valley MN 55427	888-966-4532	763-546-1111	730
Karges Furniture Company Inc 1501 W Maryland St … Evansville IN 47710	800-252-7437	812-425-2291	286
Karl Ehmer Inc 48 S Ocean Ave … Patchogue NY 11772	800-487-5275	631-289-3448	295-26
Karl Storz Endoscopy-america Inc 600 Corporate Pt Fl 5 … Culver City CA 90230	800-321-1304	310-338-8100	470
Karl's Transport Inc PO Box 333 … Antigo WI 54409	800-922-8707	715-623-2033	463
Karmanos Cancer Institute Bone Marrow/Stem Cell Transplant Program 4100 John R Rm 1308-A … Detroit MI 48201	800-527-6266		759
Karnak Corp, The 330 Central Ave … Clark NJ 07066	800-526-4236	732-388-0300	45
Karnes Electric Co-op Inc 1007 N Hwy 123 … Karnes City TX 78118	888-807-3952	830-780-3952	245
Karthauser & Sons Inc W 147 N 11100 Fond du Lac Ave … Germantown WI 53022	800-338-8620	262-255-7815	293
Kasa Industrial Controls Inc 418 E Ave B … Salina KS 67401	800-755-5272	785-825-7181	720
Kaseya Corp 400 Totten Pond Rd Ste 200 … Waltham MA 02451	877-926-0001		197
Kaslen Textiles 6099 Triangle Dr … Commerce CA 90040	800-777-5789	323-588-7700	735
Kason Industries Inc 57 Amlajack Blvd … Newnan GA 30265	800-935-3550	770-304-3000	347
Kaspar Wire Works Inc PO Box 667 … Shiner TX 77984	800-337-0610	361-594-3327	72
Katalyst Surgical LLC 754 Goddard Ave … Chesterfield MO 63005	888-452-8259		681
Kate Spade 135 5th Ave Set 7 … New York NY 10010	866-999-5283	212-358-0420	346
Katharine Beecher Candies 1250 Slate Hill Rd … Camp Hill PA 17011	800-233-7082	717-761-5440	295-8
Katharine Ordway Preserve 4245 N Fairfax Dr Ste 100 … Arlington VA 22203	800-628-6860	203-226-4991	49-4
Katherine Shaw Bethea Hospital 403 E First St … Dixon IL 61021	800-582-9731	815-288-5531	371-3
Katmai Coastal Bear Tours PO Box 1503 … Homer AK 99603	800-532-8338	907-235-8337	750
Katten Muchin Rosenman LLP 525 W Monroe St Ste 1300 … Chicago IL 60661	800-449-8114	312-902-5200	425
Katz Group 10104 103rd Ave Ste 1702 Bell Tower … Edmonton AB T5J0H8	866-323-9695	780-990-0505	237
Kauai Community College 3-1901 Kaumualii Hwy … Lihue HI 96766	800-776-4816	808-245-8311	160
Kauffman Stadium One Royal Way … Kansas City MO 64129	800-676-9257	816-921-8000	711
Kaufman Mfg Co 547 S 29th St PO Box 1056 … Manitowoc WI 54221	800-420-6641	920-684-6641	450
Kaufman Rossin & Co PA 2699 S Bayshore Dr … Miami FL 33133	866-357-9634	305-858-5600	2

	Toll-Free	Phone	Class
Kaw Valley Electric Co-op Inc			
1100 SW Auburn Rd ....Topeka KS 66615	**800-794-2011**	785-478-3444	245
Kawada Hotel			
200 S Hill St ....Los Angeles CA 90012	**800-752-9232**	213-621-4455	376
Kaweah Delta Hospital			
400 W Mineral King Ave ....Visalia CA 93291	**800-717-5670**	559-624-2000	371-3
Kay Automotive Graphics			
57 Kay Industrial Dr ....Lake Orion MI 48359	**800-443-0190**	248-377-4999	678
Kay Chemical Co			
8300 Capital Dr ....Greensboro NC 27409	**877-315-1115**	336-668-7290	149
Kay Dee Designs Inc			
177 Skunk Hill Rd ....Hope Valley RI 02832	**800-537-3433**	401-539-2405	735
Kay Dee Feed Company Inc			
1919 Grand Ave ....Sioux City IA 51106	**800-831-4815***	712-277-2011	442
*Cust Svc			
Kay El Bar Guest Ranch			
PO Box 2480 ....Wickenburg AZ 85358	**800-684-7583**	928-684-7593	239
Kay Electric Co-op (KEC)			
300 W Doolin Ave ....Blackwell OK 74631	**800-535-1079**	580-363-1260	245
Kay Green Design Inc			
859 Outer Rd ....Orlando FL 32814	**800-226-5186**	407-246-7155	390
Kay Jewelers			
375 Ghent Rd ....Akron OH 44333	**800-681-8796**	330-668-5000	407
Kay Park Recreation Corp			
1301 Pine St ....Janesville IA 50647	**800-553-2476***		318-4
*Cust Svc			
Kay Toledo Tag Inc			
PO Box 5038 ....Toledo OH 43612	**800-822-8247**	419-729-5479	619
Kayem Foods Inc			
75 Arlington St ....Chelsea MA 02150	**800-426-6100**	617-889-1600	295-26
Kaye-Smith			
4101 Oakesdale Ave SW ....Renton WA 98057	**800-822-9987**	425-228-8600	109
Kayline Processing Inc			
31 Coates St ....Trenton NJ 08611	**800-367-5546***	609-695-1449	593
*Sales			
Kayne Anderson Capital Advisors LP			
1800 Ave of the Stars			
Third Fl ....Los Angeles CA 90067	**800-638-1496**		398
Kaytee Products Inc			
521 Clay St ....Chilton WI 53014	**800-669-9580**	920-849-2321	571
KAZ Inc			
250 Tpke Rd ....Southborough MA 01772	**800-477-0457**		36
Kazan, McClain, Abrams, Fernandez, Lyons & Farrise PLC			
Jack London Market 55 Harrison St			
Ste 400 ....Oakland CA 94607	**877-995-6372**		461
KB Electronics Inc			
12095 NW 39th St ....Coral Springs FL 33065	**800-221-6570**	954-346-4900	204
KB Home			
10990 Wilshire Blvd			
Seventh Fl. ....Los Angeles CA 90024	**800-304-0657**	310-231-4000	644
NYSE: KBH			
KBAC-FM 98.1 (AAA)			
2502 Camino Entrada Ste C ....Santa Fe NM 87507	**888-321-5123**	505-988-5222	636-99
KBAY-FM 94.5 (AC)			
190 Pk Ctr Plz Ste 200 ....San Jose CA 95113	**800-948-5229**	408-287-5775	636-98
KBBY-FM 95.1 (AC)			
1376 Walter St ....Ventura CA 93003	**888-288-9242**	805-642-8595	636
KBFB-FM 97.9 (Urban)			
13331 Preston Rd Ste 1180 ....Dallas TX 75240	**888-362-8683**	972-331-5400	636-34
KBH Corp, The			
395 Anderson Blvd ....Clarksdale MS 38614	**800-843-5241**	662-624-5471	273
KBHC (Kristin Brooks Hope Ctr)			
1250 24th St NW ....Washington DC 20037	**800-784-2433**	202-536-3200	47-17
KBHE-FM 89.3 (NPR)			
555 N Dakota St PO Box 5000 ....Vermillion SD 57069	**800-456-0766**	605-677-5861	636
KBHE-TV Ch 9 (PBS)			
555 N Dakota St PO Box 5000 ....Vermillion SD 57069	**800-333-0789**		730
KBIA-FM 91.3 (NPR)			
409 Jesse Hall ....Columbia MO 65211	**800-292-9136**	573-882-3431	636
KBIG-FM 104.3 (AC)			
3400 W Olive Ave Ste 550 ....Burbank CA 91505	**866-544-6936**	818-559-2252	636
KBKS-FM 106.1 (CHR)			
645 Elliott Ave W Ste 400 ....Seattle WA 98119	**888-343-1061**	206-494-2000	636-101
KBME-TV Ch 3 (PBS)			
207 N Fifth St ....Fargo ND 58102	**800-359-6900**	701-241-6900	730-27
KBOS-FM 94.9 (CHR)			
83 E Shaw Ave Ste 150 ....Fresno CA 93710	**877-565-9467**	559-230-4300	636-45
KBR Inc			
601 Jefferson St ....Houston TX 77002	**866-313-3046**	713-753-2000	261
KBR Rural Public Power District			
374 N Pine St PO Box 187 ....Ainsworth NE 69210	**800-672-0009**	402-387-1120	245
KBRG-FM 100.3 (Span AC)			
750 Battery St Ste 200 ....San Francisco CA 94111	**888-808-1003**	415-989-5765	636
KBTC-TV Ch 28 (PBS)			
2320 S 19th St ....Tacoma WA 98405	**888-596-5282**	253-680-7700	730-69
KBXX-FM 97.9 (Urban)			
24 Greenway Plaza Ste 900. ....Houston TX 77046	**888-407-4747**	713-623-2108	636-52
KBYU-TV Ch 11 (PBS)			
2000 Ironton Blvd			
Brigham Young University ....Provo UT 84606	**800-298-5298**	801-422-8450	730
KBYZ-FM 96.5 (CR)			
4303 Memorial Hwy ....Mandan ND 58554	**888-663-9650**	701-663-9600	636
KC Electric Assn			
422 Third Ave ....Hugo CO 80821	**800-700-3123**	719-743-2431	245
KCCK-FM 88.3 (Jazz)			
6301 Kirkwood Blvd SW ....Cedar Rapids IA 52404	**800-373-5225**	319-398-5446	636-22
KCES (Kansas City Electrical Supply Co)			
10900 MidAmerica Ave ....Lenexa KS 66219	**866-271-6456**	913-563-7002	246
KCFR-FM 90.1 (NPR)			
7409 S Alton Ct ....Centennial CO 80112	**800-722-4449**	303-871-9191	636
KCI (Kinetic Concepts Inc)			
PO Box 659508 ....San Antonio TX 78265	**800-275-4524***		472
*Cust Svc			
KCI Technologies Inc			
936 Ridgebrook Rd ....Sparks MD 21152	**800-572-7496**	410-316-7800	261
KCLR-FM 99.3 (Ctry)			
3215 Lemone Industrial Blvd			
Ste 200 ....Columbia MO 65201	**800-455-5257**	573-875-1099	636
KCMQ-FM 96.7 (CR)			
3215 Lemone Industrial Blvd			
Ste 200 ....Columbia MO 65201	**800-455-1967**	573-875-1099	636
KCRG-TV Ch 9 (ABC)			
501 Second Ave SE ....Cedar Rapids IA 52401	**800-332-5443**	319-398-8422	730-12
KCRW-FM 89.9 (NPR)			
1900 Pico Blvd ....Santa Monica CA 90405	**877-527-9227**	310-450-5183	636
KCSD-FM 90.9 (NPR)			
555 N Dakota St PO Box 5000 ....Vermillion SD 57069	**800-456-0766**	605-677-5861	636
KCSL (Kansas Children's Service League)			
3545 SW 5th ....Topeka KS 66606	**877-530-5275**	785-274-3100	47-6
KCTS-TV Ch 9 (PBS)			
401 Mercer St ....Seattle WA 98109	**800-443-9991**	206-728-6463	730-69
KCUR-FM 89.3 (NPR)			
4825 Troost Ave Ste 202. ....Kansas City MO 64110	**855-778-5437**	816-235-1551	636-58
KCVB (Kingsport Convention & Visitors Bureau)			
400 Clinchfield St Ste 100 ....Kingsport TN 37660	**800-743-5282**	423-392-8820	207
KCWY-TV Ch 13 (NBC)			
141 Progress Cir PO Box 1450. ....Mills WY 82644	**800-955-5739**	307-577-0013	730
KDAQ-FM 89.9 (NPR)			
One University Pl			
PO Box 5250. ....Shreveport LA 71115	**800-552-8502**	318-797-5150	636-102
KDC Technologies			
27201 Tourney Rd Ste 201 ....Valencia CA 91355	**877-532-1112**		197
K-Dee Supply Inc			
621 E Lake St ....Lake Mills WI 53551	**800-268-3681**	920-648-8202	769
KDF Electronic & Vacuum Services Inc			
10 Volvo Dr ....Rockleigh NJ 07647	**877-533-3343**	201-784-5005	686
KDIndustries			
1525 E Lake Rd ....Erie PA 16511	**800-840-9577**	814-453-6761	655
KDLT-TV Ch 46 (NBC)			
3600 S Westport Ave ....Sioux Falls SD 57106	**800-727-5358**	605-361-5555	730-71
KDON-FM 102.5 (CHR)			
903 N Main St ....Salinas CA 93906	**888-558-5366**	831-755-8181	636
KDOT-FM 104.5 (Rock)			
2900 Sutro St ....Reno NV 89512	**800-227-1885**	775-329-9261	636-88
KDR (National Fraternity of Kappa Delta Rho)			
331 S Main St ....Greensburg PA 15601	**800-536-5371**	724-838-7100	47-16
KDRK-FM 93.7 (Ctry)			
1601 E 57th Ave ....Spokane WA 99223	**877-871-6772**	509-448-1000	636-104
KDSU-FM 91.9 (NPR)			
207 Fifth St N ....Fargo ND 58102	**800-359-6900**	701-241-6900	636-42
KDVR-TV Ch 31 (Fox)			
100 E Speer Blvd ....Denver CO 80203	**888-397-3742**	303-595-3131	730-20
KDWN-AM 720 (N/T)			
1455 E Tropicana Ave Ste 800 ....Las Vegas NV 89119	**866-297-5303**	702-730-0300	636-59
Kea Lani Spa at the Fairmont Kea Lani Maui			
4100 Wailea Alanui Dr ....Maui HI 96753	**800-659-4100**	808-875-2229	698
KEA News			
401 Capital Ave ....Frankfort KY 40601	**800-231-4532**	502-875-2889	452-8
Kean University			
1000 Morris Ave Kean Hall ....Union NJ 07083	**800-882-1037**	908-737-7100	166
Keane Care Inc			
8383 158th Ave NE Ste 100 ....Redmond WA 98052	**800-426-2675**		179-11
KEAN-FM 105.1 (Ctry)			
3911 S First St ....Abilene TX 79605	**800-588-5326**	325-676-5326	636-1
Kearney Area Chamber of Commerce			
1007 Second Ave PO Box 607 ....Kearney NE 68848	**800-227-8340**	308-237-3101	137
Kearny FSB			
120 Passaic Ave ....Fairfield NJ 07004	**800-273-3406**	973-244-4500	69
KEC (Kay Electric Co-op)			
300 W Doolin Ave ....Blackwell OK 74631	**800-535-1079**	580-363-1260	245
KEC (Kiamichi Electric Co-op Inc)			
966 SW Hwy 2 PO Box 340 ....Wilburton OK 74578	**800-888-2731**	918-465-2338	245
Keds Corp			
1400 Industries Rd ....Richmond IN 47374	**800-680-0966**		300
KEDT-FM 90.3 (NPR)			
4455 S Padre Island Dr			
Ste 38 ....Corpus Christi TX 78411	**800-307-5338**	361-855-2213	636-33
KEDT-TV Ch 16 (PBS)			
4455 S Padre Island Dr			
Ste 38 ....Corpus Christi TX 78411	**800-307-5338**	361-855-2213	730-17
Keefe Real Estate			
1155 E Geneva St ....Delavan WI 53115	**800-690-2292**	262-728-8757	643
Keeler Motor Car Co			
1111 Troy Schenectady Rd ....Latham NY 12110	**800-474-4197**	518-785-4197	56
Keeley Investment Corp			
401 S La Salle St Ste 1201 ....Chicago IL 60605	**800-533-5344**	312-786-5000	170
Keenan & Assoc			
2355 Crenshaw Blvd Ste 200			
PO Box 4328. ....Torrance CA 90501	**800-654-8102**	310-212-3344	387
Keene Publishing Corp			
PO Box 546 ....Keene NH 03431	**800-765-9994**	603-352-1234	628-8
Keene State College			
229 Main St ....Keene NH 03435	**800-572-1909**	603-352-1909	166
Keene State College Mason Library			
229 Main St ....Keene NH 03435	**800-572-1909**	603-358-2711	431-6
Keeney Manufacturing Co			
1170 Main St ....Newington CT 06111	**800-243-0526***	860-666-3342	602
*Cust Svc			
Keepers International Inc			
9420 Eton Ave ....Chatsworth CA 91311	**800-797-6257**		153-9
Keesler Federal Credit Union			
PO Box 7001 ....Biloxi MS 39534	**888-533-7537**	228-385-5500	219
KEGA-FM 101.5 (Ctry)			
50 West Broadway Ste 200 ....Salt Lake City UT 84101	**866-551-1015**	801-524-2600	636-94
Kegel's Produce Inc			
2851 Old Tree Dr ....Lancaster PA 17603	**800-535-3435**	717-392-6612	296-7
Kehoe Component Sales Inc			
34 Foley Dr ....Sodus NY 14551	**800-228-7223**		246
Keilson-Dayton Co			
107 Commerce Pk Dr ....Dayton OH 45404	**800-759-3174**	937-236-1070	746
Keim T S Inc			
1249 N Ninth St PO Box 226 ....Sabetha KS 66534	**800-255-2450**		770
Keiro Services			
325 S Boyle Ave ....Los Angeles CA 90033	**855-872-6060**	323-980-7555	458
Keiser Homes			
56 Mechanic Falls Rd PO Box 9000 ....Oxford ME 04270	**888-333-1748**		105
Keiser University			
Fort Lauderdale			
1500 W Commercial Blvd ..... Fort Lauderdale FL 33309	**800-749-4456**	954-776-4456	788
Sarasota			
6151 Lk Osprey Dr ....Sarasota FL 34240	**866-534-7372**	941-907-3900	788
Keith Titus Corp			
PO Box 920 ....Weedsport NY 13166	**800-233-2126**	315-834-6681	770
Keithley Instruments Inc			
28775 Aurora Rd ....Cleveland OH 44139	**800-552-1115**	440-248-0400	248
Keithly-Williams Seeds Inc			
420 Palm Ave PO Box 177 ....Holtville CA 92250	**800-533-3465**	760-356-5533	685

	Toll-Free	Phone	Class
Keller & Heckman LLP			
1001 G St NW Ste 500w . . . . Washington DC 20001	888-364-1200	202-434-4100	425
Keller Army Community Hospital			
900 Washington Rd . . . . West Point NY 10996	800-552-2907	845-938-7992	371-4
Keller Laboratories Inc			
160 Larkin Williams			
Industrial Ct . . . . Fenton MO 63026	800-325-3056	636-600-4200	415
Keller Supply Company Inc			
3209 17th Ave W . . . . Seattle WA 98119	800-285-3302	206-285-3300	605
Kellermeyer Co			
475 W Woodland Cir . . . . Bowling Green OH 43402	800-445-7415	419-255-3022	403
Kelley Blue Book Company Inc			
195 Technology Dr . . . . Irvine CA 92623	800-258-3266	949-770-7704	57
Kelley Manufacturing Co			
80 Vernon Dr PO Box 1467 . . . . Tifton GA 31793	800-444-5449	229-382-9393	273
Kellogg Co			
One Kellogg Sq PO Box 3599 . . . . Battle Creek MI 49016	800-962-1413*	269-961-2000	295-4
NYSE: K ■ *Cust Svc*			
Kellogg Hotel & Conference Ctr			
219 S Harrison Rd			
Michigan State University Campus . . . East Lansing MI 48824	800-875-5090	517-432-4000	376
Kellogg Marine Supply Inc			
Five Enterprise Dr . . . . Old Lyme CT 06371	800-243-9303	860-434-6002	760
Kelly Aerospace Turbine Rotables Inc			
3414 W 29th St S . . . . Wichita KS 67217	866-359-5287	316-943-6100	21
Kelly Home Care Services Inc			
999 W Big Beaver Rd . . . . Troy MI 48084	800-755-8636	248-362-4444	360
Kelly Paper Co			
288 Brea Canyon Rd . . . . Walnut CA 91789	800-675-3559		546
Kelly Pipe Company LLC			
11680 Bloomfield Ave . . . . Santa Fe Springs CA 90670	800-305-3559	562-868-0456	588
Kelly Ryan Equipment Co			
900 Kelly Ryan Dr . . . . Blair NE 68008	800-640-6967	402-426-2151	273
Kelly Systems Inc			
422 N Western Ave . . . . Chicago IL 60612	800-258-8237	312-733-3224	465
Kelly's Janitorial Service Inc			
228 Hazel Ave . . . . Ewing NJ 08638	800-227-0366	609-771-0365	256
Kelly's Pipe & Supply Co Inc			
2124 Industrial Rd . . . . Las Vegas NV 89102	888-382-4957		605
Kelly-Moore Paint Company Inc			
987 Commercial St . . . . San Carlos CA 94070	800-874-4436	650-592-8337	543
KELO-TV Ch 11 (CBS)			
501 S Phillips Ave . . . . Sioux Falls SD 57104	800-888-5356	605-336-1100	730-71
Kelowna General Hospital (KGH)			
2268 Pandosy St . . . . Kelowna BC V1Y1T2	888-877-4442	250-862-4000	371-2
Kelser Corp			
111 Roberts St Ste D . . . . East Hartford CT 06108	800-647-5316	860-528-9819	225
Kelsey Museum of Archaeology			
434 S State St			
University of Michigan . . . . Ann Arbor MI 48109	800-562-3559	734-763-3559	513
Kelty 6235 Lookout Rd . . . . Boulder CO 80301	800-423-2320	800-535-3589	63
Kelyniam Global Inc			
97 River Rd . . . . Canton CT 06019	800-280-8192		250
KEM Electric Co-op Inc			
107 S Broadway . . . . Linton ND 58552	800-472-2673	701-254-4666	245
KEMC-FM 91.7 (NPR)			
1500 University Dr . . . . Billings MT 59101	800-441-2941	406-657-2941	636-13
Kemco Systems Inc			
11500 47th St N . . . . Clearwater FL 33762	800-633-7055	727-573-2323	424
Kemin Industries Inc			
2100 Maury St . . . . Des Moines IA 50317	800-777-8307	515-559-5100	442
Kemper Arena & American Royal Centers			
1701 American Royal Ct . . . . Kansas City MO 64102	800-634-3942	816-221-5242	711
KemPharm Inc			
2656 Crosspark Rd Ste 100 . . . . Coralville IA 52241	877-695-3638	319-665-2575	659
Kemps LLC			
1270 Energy Ln . . . . Saint Paul MN 55108	800-322-9566	651-379-6500	295-27
Kemron Environmental Services Inc			
8521 Leesburg Pike Ste 175 . . . . Vienna VA 22182	888-429-3516	703-893-4106	193
Kemtah Group Inc			
7601 Jefferson St NE			
Ste 120 . . . . Albuquerque NM 87109	877-753-6824	505-346-4900	181
Kemwel Inc			
39 Commercial St . . . . Portland ME 04112	800-678-0678	207-842-2285	125
Ken Fowler Motors			
1265 Airport Pk Blvd . . . . Ukiah CA 95482	800-287-0107	707-468-0101	56
Ken Garff Automotive Group			
405 S Main St . . . . Salt Lake City UT 84111	888-630-6838	801-257-3400	56
Ken Jones Tire Inc			
73 Chandler St . . . . Worcester MA 01609	800-225-9513	508-755-5255	745
Ken's Flower Shop			
140 W S Boundary St . . . . Perrysburg OH 43551	800-253-0100	419-874-1333	292
Ken's Foods Inc			
1 D'Angelo Dr . . . . Marlborough MA 01752	800-633-5800*	508-229-1100	295-19
General			
Kenall Mfg			
1020 Lakeside Dr . . . . Gurnee IL 60031	800-453-6255	847-360-8200	435
Kenan Advantage Group Inc (KAG)			
4366 Mt Pleasant St NW . . . . . . North Canton OH 44720	800-969-5419	330-491-0474	770
Kenan Transport Co			
100 Europa Ctr Ste 320 . . . . Chapel Hill NC 27517	866-821-3444	919-967-8221	770
Kenco Group Inc			
2001 Riverside Dr . . . . Chattanooga TN 37406	800-758-3289		444
Kenda USA			
7095 Americana Pkwy . . . . Reynoldsburg OH 43068	866-536-3287	614-866-9803	745
Kendal at Ithaca			
2230 N Triphammer Rd . . . . Ithaca NY 14850	800-253-6325	607-266-5300	663
Kendal at Longwood & Crosslands			
PO Box 100 . . . . Kennett Square PA 19348	800-216-1920	610-388-1441	663
Kendal at Oberlin			
600 Kendal Dr . . . . Oberlin OH 44074	800-548-9469*		663
Mktg			
Kendall & Davis Company Inc			
3668 S Geyer Rd Ste 100 . . . . St. Louis MO 63127	866-675-3755		260
Kendall College			
900 N North Branch St . . . . Chicago IL 60622	866-667-3344	312-752-2000	161
Kendall College of Art & Design of Ferris State University			
17 Fountain St NW . . . . Grand Rapids MI 49503	800-676-2787	616-451-2787	166
Kendall Electric Inc			
131 Grand Trunk Ave . . . . Battle Creek MI 49037	800-632-5422	269-963-5585	246
Kendall Packaging Corp			
10200 N Port Washington Rd . . . . Mequon WI 53092	800-237-0951	262-404-1200	593
Kendall/Hunt Publishing Co			
4050 Westmark Dr PO Box 1840 . . . . Dubuque IA 52002	800-228-0810*	563-589-1000	628-2
Cust Svc			
Kendall-Jackson Wine Estates Ltd			
425 Aviation Blvd . . . . Santa Rosa CA 95403	800-769-3649	707-544-4000	79-3
Kendle International Inc			
441 Vine St 1200 Carew Twr . . . . Cincinnati OH 45202	800-733-1572	513-381-5550	659
Kendra Scott Design Inc			
1400 S Congress Ave Ste A-170 . . . . Austin TX 78704	866-677-7023	512-499-8400	408
Kenergy Corp			
6402 Old Corydon Rd . . . . Henderson KY 42419	800-844-4832	270-826-3991	245
Kenilworth Aquatic Gardens			
1550 Anacostia Ave NE . . . . Washington DC 20019	877-642-4743	202-426-6905	96
Kenlake State Resort Park			
542 Kenlake Rd . . . . Hardin KY 42048	800-325-0143	270-474-2211	558
Kenlee Precision Corp			
1701 Inverness Ave . . . . Baltimore MD 21230	800-969-5278	410-525-3800	614
Ken-Mac Metals Inc			
17901 Englewood Dr . . . . Cleveland OH 44130	800-831-9503	440-234-7500	487
Kenmore Air Harbor Inc			
6321 NE 175th St . . . . Kenmore WA 98028	866-435-9524	425-486-1257	25
Kenmore Camera Inc			
18031 67th Ave NE PO Box 82467 . . . . . . Kenmore WA 98028	888-485-7447	425-485-7447	118
Kenmore-Town of Tonawanda Chamber of Commerce			
3411 Delaware Ave . . . . Kenmore NY 14217	888-710-6626	716-874-1202	137
Kennametal Inc			
1600 Technology Way PO Box 231 . . . . . . Latrobe PA 15650	800-446-7738*	724-539-5000	488
NYSE: KMT ■ *Cust Svc*			
Kennebec Savings Bank			
150 State St PO Box 50 . . . . Augusta ME 04332	888-303-7788	207-622-5801	69
Kennebec Telephone Company Inc			
220 S Main St . . . . Kennebec SD 57544	888-868-3390	605-869-2220	726
Kennebec Valley Community College			
92 Western Ave . . . . Fairfield ME 04937	800-528-5882	207-453-5000	160
Kennedy Ctr Opera House Orchestra			
John F Kennedy Ctr for the Performing Arts			
2700 F St NW . . . . Washington DC 20566	800-444-1324		566-3
Kennedy Health System-Cherry Hill			
2201 Chapel Ave W . . . . Cherry Hill NJ 08002	866-224-0264	856-488-6500	371-3
Kennedy Krieger Institute			
707 N Broadway . . . . Baltimore MD 21205	800-873-3377	443-923-9200	371-1
Kennedy Manufacturing Co			
1260 Industrial Dr . . . . Van Wert OH 45891	800-413-8665	419-238-2442	483
Kennedy Office Supply			
4211-A Atlantic Ave . . . . Raleigh NC 27604	800-733-9401	919-878-5400	528
Kennedy Valve			
1021 E Water St . . . . Elmira NY 14902	800-782-5831	607-734-2211	777
Kennedy Wholesale Inc			
16014 Adelante St . . . . Irwindale CA 91706	877-292-2639	818-241-9977	296-3
Kennedy-Wilson Inc			
9701 Wilshire Blvd			
Ste 700 . . . . Beverly Hills CA 90212	800-522-6664	310-887-6400	50
Kennesaw State University			
1000 Chastain Rd . . . . Kennesaw GA 30144	800-542-2233	770-423-6000	166
Kenneth Cole Productions Inc			
603 W 50th St . . . . New York NY 10019	800-536-2653	212-265-1500	300
NYSE: KCP			
Kenney Mfg Co			
1000 Jefferson Blvd . . . . Warwick RI 02886	800-753-6639*	401-739-2200	86
Cust Svc			
Kennicott Bros			
452 N Ashland Ave . . . . Chicago IL 60622	866-346-2826	312-492-8200	293
Kennywood Entertainment Corp			
4800 Kennywood Blvd . . . . West Mifflin PA 15122	800-213-5861	412-461-8127	31
Kenosha Area Convention & Visitors Bureau			
812 56th St . . . . Kenosha WI 53140	800-654-7309	262-654-7307	207
Kenosha Medical Ctr			
6308 Eigth Ave . . . . Kenosha WI 53143	800-994-6610	262-656-2011	371-3
Kenosha News			
5800 Seventh Ave . . . . Kenosha WI 53140	800-292-2700	262-657-1000	525-2
Kenosha Public Museum			
5500 First Ave . . . . Kenosha WI 53140	888-258-9966	262-653-4140	513
Kensey Nash Corp			
735 Pennsylvania Dr . . . . Exton PA 19341	800-322-2885*	484-713-2100	471
NASDAQ: KNSY ■ *General*			
Kensington Computer Products Group			
333 Twin Dolphin Dr			
Sixth Fl . . . . Redwood Shores CA 94065	800-535-4242	650-572-2700	174-2
Kensington Court Ann Arbor			
610 Hilton Blvd . . . . Ann Arbor MI 48108	800-344-7829*	734-761-7800	376
Orders			
Kensington Park Hotel			
450 Post St . . . . San Francisco CA 94102	800-553-1900	415-202-8700	376
Kensington Publishing Corp			
119 W 40th St . . . . New York NY 10018	800-221-2647	212-407-1500	628-2
Kensington Riverside Inn			
1126 Memorial Dr NW . . . . Calgary AB T2N3E3	877-313-3733	403-228-4442	376
Kent Chamber of Commerce			
524 W Meeker St Ste 1 . . . . Kent WA 98032	800-321-2808	253-854-1770	137
Kent Corp			
4446 Pinson Valley Pkwy . . . . Birmingham AL 35215	800-252-5368	205-853-3420	286
Kent County & Greater Dover Delaware Convention & Visitors Bureau			
435 N DuPont Hwy . . . . Dover DE 19901	800-233-5368	302-734-1736	207
Kent District Library			
814 W River Ctr Dr NE . . . . . . Comstock Park MI 49321	877-243-2466	616-784-2007	431-3
Kent Elastomer Products Inc			
1500 St Claire Ave . . . . Kent OH 44240	800-331-4762*	330-673-1011	667
Cust Svc			
Kent General Hospital			
640 S State St . . . . Dover DE 19901	888-761-8300	302-674-4700	371-3
Kent Quality Foods Inc			
703 Leonard St NW . . . . Grand Rapids MI 49504	800-748-0141		295-26
Kent School PO Box 2006 . . . . Kent CT 06757	800-538-5368	860-927-6111	615
Kent Security Services Inc			
14600 Biscayne Blvd . . . . . North Miami Beach FL 33181	800-273-5368	305-919-9400	684
Kent State University			
800 E. Summit St PO Box 5190 . . . . Kent OH 44242	800-988-5368	330-672-2121	166
Ashtabula			
3300 Lake Rd W . . . . Ashtabula OH 44004	800-988-5368	440-964-3322	160
Stark			
6000 Frank Ave NW . . . . North Canton OH 44720	800-988-5368	330-499-9600	166
Trumbull Campus			
4314 Mahoning Ave NW . . . . Warren OH 44483	800-988-5368	330-847-0571	166

	Toll-Free	Phone	Class
Tuscarawas			
330 University Dr NE ....New Philadelphia OH 44663	800-988-5368	330-339-3391	166
Kent State University Museum			
PO Box 5190 ....Kent OH 44242	800-988-5368	330-672-3450	513
Kent, The			
1131 Collins Ave ....Miami Beach FL 33139	866-826-5368	305-604-5068	376
Kentec Inc			
3250 Centerville Hwy ....Snellville GA 30039	800-241-0148	770-985-1907	348
Kentec Medical Inc			
17871 Fitch ....Irvine CA 92614	800-825-5996	949-863-0810	470
Ken-Tron Manufacturing Inc			
PO Box 21250 ....Owensboro KY 42304	800-872-9336	270-684-0431	483
Arts Council			
500 Mero St			
21st Fl Capital Plaza Tower ....Frankfort KY 40601	888-833-2787	502-564-3757	337-18
Child Support Div			
730 Schenkel Ln ....Frankfort KY 40601	800-248-1163	502-564-2285	337-18
Consumer Protection Div			
1024 Capital Ctr Dr Ste 200 ....Frankfort KY 40601	888-432-9257	502-696-5389	337-18
Crime Victims Compensation Board			
130 Brighton Pk Blvd ....Frankfort KY 40601	800-469-2120	502-573-2290	337-18
Education Professional Standards Board			
100 Airport Dr 3rd Fl ....Frankfort KY 40601	888-598-7667	502-564-4606	337-18
Financial Institutions Dept			
1025 Capital Ctr Dr Ste 200 ....Frankfort KY 40601	800-223-2579	502-573-3390	337-18
Fish & Wildlife Resources Dept			
1 Game Farm Rd ....Frankfort KY 40601	800-858-1549	502-564-3400	337-18
General Assembly			
700 Capitol Ave			
State Capitol Bldg............Frankfort KY 40601	800-372-7181	502-564-8100	337-18
Historical Society			
100 W Broadway ....Frankfort KY 40601	877-444-7867	502-564-1792	337-18
Housing Corp			
1231 Louisville Rd ....Frankfort KY 40601	800-633-8896	502-564-7630	337-18
Insurance Dept			
215 W Main St ....Frankfort KY 40602	800-595-6053	502-564-3630	337-18
Kentucky			
Public Service Commission			
PO Box 615 ....Frankfort KY 40602	800-772-4636	502-564-3940	337-18
Real Estate Commission (KREC)			
10200 Linn Stn Rd Ste 201 ....Louisville KY 40223	888-373-3300*	502-429-7250	337-18
*General			
State Government Information			
229 W Main St Ste 400 ....Frankfort KY 40601	877-855-3573	502-875-3733	337-18
Travel and Tourism Dept			
500 Mero St Ste 2200 ....Frankfort KY 40601	800-225-8747	502-564-4930	337-18
Veterans Affairs Dept (KDVA)			
1111B Louisville Rd ....Frankfort KY 40601	800-572-6245	502-564-9203	337-18
Vocational Rehabilitation Dept			
275 E Main St MS 2E-K ....Frankfort KY 40601	800-372-7172	502-564-4440	337-18
Workers Claims Dept (DWC)			
657 Chamberlin Ave ....Frankfort KY 40601	800-554-8601	502-564-5550	337-18
Kentucky Assn of Realtors			
161 Prosperous Pl ....Lexington KY 40509	800-264-2185	859-263-7377	647
Kentucky Bank			
PO Box 157 ....Paris KY 40362	877-322-8228	859-987-1795	69
Kentucky Chamber of Commerce			
464 Chenault Rd ....Frankfort KY 40601	800-533-0127	502-695-4700	138
Kentucky Christian University			
100 Academic Pkwy ....Grayson KY 41143	800-522-3181*	606-474-3000	166
*Admissions			
Kentucky Correctional Industries			
1041 Leestown Rd ....Frankfort KY 40601	800-828-9524	502-573-1040	622
Kentucky Correctional Institution for Women			
3000 Ash Ave ....Pewee Valley KY 40056	877-687-6818	502-241-8454	213
Kentucky Dept for Libraries & Archives			
300 Coffee Tree Rd ....Frankfort KY 40602	800-372-2968	502-564-8300	431-5
Kentucky Derby Museum			
704 Central Ave ....Louisville KY 40208	800-273-3729	502-637-1111	513
Kentucky Educational Television (KET)			
600 Cooper Dr ....Lexington KY 40502	800-432-0951	859-258-7000	624
Kentucky Electric Steel LLC			
2704 S Big Run Rd W ....Ashland KY 41102	800-333-3012	606-929-1200	714
Kentucky Higher Education Assistance Authority (KHEAA)			
100 Airport Rd ....Frankfort KY 40602	800-928-8926		716
Kentucky Horse Park			
4089 Iron Works Pkwy ....Lexington KY 40511	800-678-8813	859-233-4303	810
Kentucky International Convention Ctr			
221 S Fourth St ....Louisville KY 40202	800-701-5831	502-595-4381	206
Kentucky Lottery Corp			
1011 W Main St ....Louisville KY 40202	800-937-8946	502-560-1500	447
Kentucky Mountain Bible College			
855 Hwy 541 PO Box 10 ....Vancleve KY 41385	800-879-5622	606-693-5000	159
Kentucky Opera Assn			
323 W Broadway Ste 601 ....Louisville KY 40202	800-690-9236	502-584-4500	566-2
Kentucky Organ Donor Affiliates (KODA)			
106 E Broadway ....Louisville KY 40202	800-525-3456	502-581-9511	538
Kentucky Pharmacists Assn			
1228 US 127 S ....Frankfort KY 40601	800-922-1557	502-227-2303	578
Kentucky Post			
1720 Gilbert Ave ....Cincinnati OH 45202	877-667-4265	513-721-9900	525-2
Kentucky Press Assn			
101 Consumer Ln ....Frankfort KY 40601	800-264-5721*	502-223-8821	616
*Cust Svc			
Kentucky Speedway			
1 Speedway Blvd ....Sparta KY 41086	888-652-7223*	859-567-3400	508
*Resv			
Kentucky State University			
400 E Main St ....Frankfort KY 40601	800-325-1716*	502-597-6000	166
*Admissions			
Kentucky Trailer			
7201 Logistics Dr ....Louisville KY 40258	888-598-7245	502-637-2551	769
Kentucky Trailer Technologies			
1240 N Pontiac Trial ....Walled Lake MI 48390	866-638-6080	248-960-9700	769
Kentucky Veterinary Medical Assn			
108 Consumer Ln ....Frankfort KY 40601	800-552-5862	502-226-5862	783
Kentucky Wesleyan College			
3000 Frederica St ....Owensboro KY 42301	800-999-0592*	270-852-3120	166
*Admissions			
Kentwood Office Furniture Inc			
3063 Breton Rd SE ....Grand Rapids MI 49512	877-698-6250	616-957-2320	319
Kenwood USA Corp			
2201 E Dominguez St ....Long Beach CA 90810	800-536-9663	310-639-9000	638

	Toll-Free	Phone	Class
Kenworth Northwest Inc			
20220 International Blvd S			
PO Box 98967 ....SeaTac WA 98198	800-562-0060	206-433-5911	56
Kenworth of Indianapolis Inc			
2929 S Holt Rd ....Indianapolis IN 46241	800-827-8421	317-247-8421	56
Kenworth Sales Co			
2125 Constitution			
Blvd ....West Valley City UT 84119	800-222-7831*	801-487-4161	770
*General			
Kenya			
866 UN Plaza Rm 304............New York NY 10017	866-445-3692	212-421-4740	
Kenya Embassy			
2249 R St NW ....Washington DC 20008	888-502-2642	202-387-6101	257
Kenya Tourism Board			
6442 City W Pkwy			
6442 City W Pkwy............Minneapolis MN 55344	800-223-6486	310-649-7718	765
Kenyon College			
103 College Dr ....Gambier OH 43022	800-848-2468	740-427-5000	166
Kenyon Plastering Inc			
4001 W Indian School Rd ....Phoenix AZ 85019	800-949-4319	602-233-1191	543
KEO Cutters Inc			
25040 Easy St ....Warren MI 48089	888-390-2050	586-771-2050	488
Keokuk National Cemetery			
1701 J St ....Keokuk IA 52632	800-273-8255	309-782-2094	135
Kepco Inc			
131-38 Sanford Ave ....Flushing NY 11355	800-526-2324	718-461-7000	253
Kepner-Tregoe Inc			
PO Box 704 ....Princeton NJ 08542	800-537-6378	609-921-2806	195
Ker & Downey Inc			
6703 Hwy Blvd ....Katy TX 77494	800-423-4236	281-371-2500	750
KERA-FM 90.1 (NPR)			
3000 Harry Hines Blvd ....Dallas TX 75201	800-456-5372	214-871-1390	636-34
Kerasotes ShowPlace Theatres LLC			
224 N Des Plaines Ave ....Chicago IL 60661	877-293-2000	312-756-3360	737
Kerite Co 49 Day St ....Seymour CT 06483	800-777-7483	203-888-2591	800
Kerkau Manufacturing Co			
1321 S Valley Ctr Dr ....Bay City MI 48706	800-248-5060	989-686-0350	478
Kern County Board of Trade			
2101 Oak St ....Bakersfield CA 93301	800-787-9920*	661-868-5376	137
*General			
Kern Health Systems			
9700 Stockdale Hwy ....Bakersfield CA 93311	888-466-2219	661-664-5000	231
Kern River Gas Transmission Co			
2755 E Cottonwood Pkwy			
Ste 300 ....Salt Lake City UT 84121	800-420-7500	801-937-6000	324
Kern Schools Federal Credit Union			
PO Box 9506 ....Bakersfield CA 93389	800-221-3311	661-833-7900	219
Kerr Lakeside Inc			
26841 Tungsten Rd ....Euclid OH 44132	800-487-5377	216-261-2100	614
Kerr Pump & Supply			
12880 Cloverdale St ....Oak Park MI 48237	800-482-8259	248-543-3880	632
Kerrville Bus Co			
One S Main St ....Del Rio TX 78840	800-474-3352	830-775-7515	106
Kerrville Convention & Visitors Bureau			
2108 Sidney Baker St ....Kerrville TX 78028	800-221-7958	830-792-3535	207
Kerrville National Cemetery			
3600 Memorial Blvd ....Kerrville TX 78028	800-273-8255	210-820-3891	135
Kerrville State Hospital			
721 Thompson Dr ....Kerrville TX 78028	888-963-7111	830-896-2211	371-5
Kerry's Nursery Inc			
21840 SW 258th St ....Homestead FL 33031	800-331-9127		366
Kershaw County Chamber of Commerce			
607 S Broad St ....Camden SC 29020	800-968-4037	803-432-2525	137
Keryx Biopharmaceuticals Inc			
750 Lexington Ave 20th Fl ....New York NY 10022	800-903-0247	212-531-5965	576
NASDAQ: KERX			
Kerzner International Ltd			
1000 S Pine Island Rd			
Ste 800 ....Plantation FL 33324	800-321-3000	954-809-2000	131
KESQ-TV Ch 3 (ABC)			
42650 Melanie Pl ....Palm Desert CA 92211	888-776-8538	760-568-6830	730
Kessler International			
45 Rockefeller Plz Ste 2000 ....New York NY 10111	800-932-2221	212-286-9100	397
Kessler's Inc			
1201 Hummel Ave ....Lemoyne PA 17043	800-382-1328	717-763-7162	295-26
Kester Inc			
800 W Thorndale Ave ....Itasca IL 60143	800-253-7837	630-616-4000	143
Keswick Hall			
701 Club Dr ....Keswick VA 22947	888-778-2565	434-979-3440	376
KET (Kentucky Educational Television)			
600 Cooper Dr ....Lexington KY 40502	800-432-0951	859-258-7000	624
Ketchikan Visitors Bureau			
131 Front St ....Ketchikan AK 99901	800-770-3300	907-225-6166	207
KETC-TV Ch 9 (PBS)			
3655 Olive St ....Saint Louis MO 63108	855-482-5382	314-512-9000	730-65
KETG-TV Ch 9 (PBS)			
350 S Donaghey Ave ....Conway AR 72034	800-662-2386	501-682-2386	730
KETS-TV Ch 2 (PBS)			
350 S Donaghey Ave ....Conway AR 72034	800-662-2386	501-682-2386	730
Kett Engineering Corp			
15500 Erwin St Ste 1029 ....Van Nuys CA 91411	877-372-6799	818-908-5388	732
Kettering University			
1700 University Ave ....Flint MI 48504	800-955-4464	810-762-9500	166
KETV-TV Ch 7 (ABC)			
2665 Douglas St ....Omaha NE 68131	800-279-5388	402-345-7777	730-51
Keuka College			
141 Central Ave ....Keuka Park NY 14478	800-335-3852*	315-279-5254	166
*Admissions			
Keurig Green Mountain Inc			
33 Coffee Ln ....Waterbury VT 05676	888-879-4627*		295-7
NASDAQ: GMCR ■ *Cust Svc			
Keurig Inc			
55 Walkers Brook Dr ....Reading MA 01867	866-901-2739		101
Kewaunee Scientific Corp			
2700 W Front St PO Box 1842 ....Statesville NC 28687	800-824-6626	704-873-7202	417
NASDAQ: KEQU			
Keweenaw Financial Corp			
235 Quincy St ....Hancock MI 49930	866-482-0404	906-482-0404	357-2
Keweenaw Peninsula Chamber of Commerce			
902 College Ave PO Box 336 ....Houghton MI 49931	800-796-0004	906-482-5240	137
KEX-AM 1190 (N/T)			
13333 SW 68th Parkway Suite 310 ....Tigard OR 97223	888-457-4838	503-323-6400	636-86
Key Air LLC			
Three Juliano Dr Ste 201 ....Oxford CT 06478	888-539-2471	203-264-0605	13

	Toll-Free	Phone	Class
Key Bank			
65 Dutch Hill Rd ....Orangeburg NY 10962	**800-539-2968***		69
*Cust Svc			
Key Club International			
3636 Woodview Trace ....Indianapolis IN 46268	**800-549-2647**	317-875-8755	47-15
Key Container Corp			
21 Campbell St ....Pawtucket RI 02861	**800-343-8811**	401-723-2000	99
Key Curriculum Press			
1150 65th St ....Emeryville CA 94608	**800-338-3987**	510-595-7000	628-2
Key Equipment Finance			
1000 S McCaslin Blvd ....Superior CO 80027	**888-301-6238**		216
Key Fire Hose Corp (KFH)			
PO Box 7107 ....Dothan AL 36302	**800-447-5666**	334-671-5532	367
Key Industries Inc			
400 Marble Rd ....Fort Scott KS 66701	**800-835-0365**	620-223-2000	153-18
Key Information Systems Inc			
21700 Oxnard St Ste 250 ......Woodland Hills CA 91367	**877-442-3249**	818-992-8950	179-11
Key Largo Chamber of Commerce			
106000 Overseas Hwy ....Key Largo FL 33037	**866-820-1533**	305-451-1414	137
Key Largo Marriott Bay Resort			
103800 Overseas Hwy ....Key Largo FL 33037	**888-731-9056***	305-453-0000	660
*Resv			
Key Lime Inn			
725 Truman Ave ....Key West FL 33040	**800-549-4430**	305-294-5229	376
Key Magazine			
PO Box 111266 ....Memphis TN 38111	**866-446-3674**	901-458-3912	452-22
Key Speakers Bureau Inc			
3500 E Coast Hwy Ste 6 ......Corona del Mar CA 92625	**800-675-1175**	949-675-7856	699
Key Technology Inc			
150 Avery St ....Walla Walla WA 99362	**877-341-5668**	509-529-2161	297
NASDAQ: KTEC			
Key West Aloe			
13095 N Telecom Pkwy ....Tampa FL 33637	**800-445-2563**	305-293-1885	215
Key West Aquarium			
One Whitehead St ....Key West FL 33040	**888-544-5927**	305-296-2051	39
Key West Key			
726 Passover Ln ....Key West FL 33040	**800-881-7321**		373
Key West Visitors Ctr			
510 Greene St 1st Fl ....Key West FL 33040	**800-533-5397***	305-294-2587	207
*General			
Key: This Week in Chicago Magazine			
226 E Ontario St Ste 300 ....Chicago IL 60611	**877-866-0966**	312-943-0838	452-22
Keyboard Magazine			
28 E 28th St 12th Fl ....New York NY 10016	**800-483-2433***	212-378-0400	452-9
*Cust Svc			
KeyCorp			
127 Public Sq ....Cleveland OH 44114	**800-539-9055**	216-689-8481	357-2
NYSE: KEY			
KEYE-TV Ch 42 (CBS)			
10700 Metric Blvd ....Austin TX 78758	**800-621-3362**	512-835-0042	730-5
Keynote Systems Inc			
777 Mariners Island Blvd ....San Mateo CA 94404	**888-539-7978**	650-403-2400	179-7
NASDAQ: KEYN			
KeyPoint Credit Union			
2805 Bowers Ave ....Santa Clara CA 95051	**888-255-3637**	408-731-4100	219
Keyston Bros			
2801 Academy Way Ste A..........Sacramento CA 95815	**800-453-1112**	916-646-1834	587
Keystone Aniline Corp			
2501 W Fulton St ....Chicago IL 60612	**800-522-4393**	312-666-2015	141
Keystone Automotive Operations Inc			
44 Tunkhannock Ave ....Exeter PA 18643	**800-521-9999**	570-655-4514	60
Keystone Aviation Services Inc			
288 Christian St ....Oxford CT 06478	**866-436-2177**	203-264-6525	62
Keystone College			
One College Green ....La Plume PA 18440	**800-824-2764**	570-945-5141	166
Keystone Consolidated Industries Inc			
7000 SW Adams St ....Peoria IL 61641	**800-447-6444***		800
*Sales			
Keystone Ctr			
2001 Providence Ave ....Chester PA 19013	**800-558-9600**	610-876-9000	717
Keystone Dental Inc			
144 Middlesex Tpke ....Burlington MA 01803	**866-902-9272**	781-328-3490	228
Keystone Electronics Corp			
31-07 20th Rd ....Astoria NY 11105	**800-221-5510**	718-956-8900	347
Keystone Equities Group, The			
1003 B Egypt Rd ....Oaks PA 19456	**800-715-9905**	610-415-6300	195
Keystone Fruit Marketing Inc			
11 N Carlisle St Ste 102			
PO Box 189. ....Greencastle PA 17225	**800-779-1156**	717-597-2112	195
Keystone Industries			
480 S Democrat Rd ....Gibbstown NJ 08027	**800-333-3131**	856-663-4700	470
Keystone Learning Systems LLC			
6030 Daybreak Cir			
Ste A150 116 ....Clarksville MD 21029	**800-949-5590**	410-800-4000	506
Keystone Pretzels			
124 W Airport Rd ....Lititz PA 17543	**888-572-4500**		295-9
Keystone Resort			
21996 Hwy 6 PO Box 38. ....Keystone CO 80435	**877-625-1556**	970-496-2316	660
Keystone Retaining Wall Systems Inc			
4444 W 78th St ....Minneapolis MN 55435	**800-642-3887**	952-897-1040	715
Keystone RV Co			
2642 Hackberry Dr PO Box 2000 ....Goshen IN 46527	**866-425-4369**	574-535-2100	119
Keystone State Park			
1926 S Hwy 151 ....Sand Springs OK 74063	**800-654-8240**	918-865-4991	558
Keystone Steel & Wire Co			
7000 S Adams St ....Peoria IL 61641	**800-447-6444**		714
KEYW Corp			
7740 Milestone Pkwy Ste 400 ....Hanover MD 21076	**800-340-1001**	443-733-1600	178
KF Industries Inc			
1500 SE 89th St ....Oklahoma City OK 73149	**800-654-4842**	405-631-1533	777
KFAN-AM 1130 (Sports)			
1600 Utica Ave S Ste 400 ....Minneapolis MN 55416	**800-320-5326**	952-417-3000	636-69
KFBB-TV			
3200 Old Havre Hwy			
PO Box 1139. ....Black Eagle MT 59414	**800-854-7720**	406-453-4377	730
KFC Corp			
1441 Gardiner Ln ....Louisville KY 40213	**800-225-5532**	818-780-6990	661
KFH (Key Fire Hose Corp)			
PO Box 7107 ....Dothan AL 36302	**800-447-5666**	334-671-5532	367
KFJM-FM 90.7 (AAA)			
207 N Fifth St ....Fargo ND 58102	**800-366-6888**	701-241-6900	636
KFMB-AM 760 (N/T)			
7677 Engineer Rd ....San Diego CA 92111	**800-760-5362**	858-292-7600	636-96
KFME-TV Ch 13 (PBS)			
207 N Fifth St ....Fargo ND 58102	**800-359-6900**	701-241-6900	730-27
KForce Government Soultions			
2750 Prosperity Ave Ste 300 ....Fairfax VA 22031	**800-200-7465**	703-245-7350	181
Kforce Inc			
1001 E Palm Ave ....Tampa FL 33605	**888-663-3626**	813-552-5000	712
NASDAQ: KFRC			
KFRG-FM 95.1 (Ctry)			
900 E Washington St Ste 315 ....Colton CA 92324	**888-431-3764**	909-825-9525	636
KFRX-FM 106.3 (CHR)			
3800 Cornhusker Hwy ....Lincoln NE 68504	**800-523-9101**	402-466-1234	
Kfs Inc			
1840 West Airfield Dr ....Dallas TX 75261	**800-364-4115**	817-488-4115	24
KFTV-TV Ch 21 (Uni)			
601 W Univision Plaza ....Fresno CA 93650	**866-783-2645**	212-455-5200	730-30
KFTX-FM 97.5 (Ctry)			
1520 S Port Ave ....Corpus Christi TX 78405	**866-975-5389**	361-883-5987	636-33
KFXA-TV Ch 28 (Fox)			
600 Old Marion Rd NE ....Cedar Rapids IA 52402	**800-222-5426**		730-12
KGAN-TV Ch 2 (CBS)			
600 Old Marion Rd NE ....Cedar Rapids IA 52402	**800-642-6140**	319-395-9060	730-12
KGBX-FM 105.9 (AC)			
1856 S Glenstone Ave ....Springfield MO 65804	**800-445-1059**	417-890-5555	636-106
KGFE-TV Ch 2 (PBS)			
207 N Fifth St ....Fargo ND 58102	**800-359-6900**	701-241-6900	730-27
KGGI-FM 99.1 (CHR)			
2030 Iowa Ave Ste A..............Riverside CA 92507	**866-991-5444**	951-684-1991	636-89
KGGN-AM 890 (Rel)			
1734 E 63rd St Ste 600. ....Kansas City MO 64110	**800-924-3177**	816-333-0092	636-58
KGH (Kelowna General Hospital)			
2268 Pandosy St ....Kelowna BC V1Y1T2	**888-877-4442**	250-862-4000	371-2
KGNC-AM 710 (N/T)			
3505 Olsen Blvd Ste 117 ....Amarillo TX 79109	**800-285-0710**	806-355-9801	636-5
KGNC-FM 97.9 (Ctry)			
3505 Olsen Blvd Ste 117 ....Amarillo TX 79109	**877-765-9790**	806-355-9801	636-5
KGNU-FM 88.5 (Var)			
4700 Walnut St ....Boulder CO 80301	**800-737-3030**	303-449-4885	636
KGNZ-FM 88.1 (Rel)			
542 Butternut St ....Abilene TX 79602	**800-588-8801**	325-673-3045	636-1
KGO-AM 810 (N/T)			
55 Hawthorne St ....San Francisco CA 94105	**855-847-7247**	415-995-5721	636-97
KGON-FM 92.3 (CR)			
0700 SW Bancroft St ....Portland OR 97239	**800-222-9236**	503-223-1441	636-86
KGOU-FM 106.3 (NPR)			
860 Van Vleet Oval Rm 300 ....Norman OK 73019	**866-533-2470**	405-325-3388	636
KGS Steel Inc			
3725 Pine Ln ....Bessemer AL 35022	**800-533-3846**	205-425-0800	487
KGW-TV Ch 8 (NBC)			
1501 SW Jefferson St ....Portland OR 97201	**800-669-9777**	503-226-5000	730-58
KGY-FM 96.9 (Ctry)			
1700 Marine Dr NE ....Olympia WA 98501	**855-549-1240**	360-943-1240	636
KHBS-TV Ch 40 (ABC)			
2415 N Albert Pike ....Fort Smith AR 72904	**855-253-7122***	479-783-4040	730-28
*General			
KHCC-FM 90.1 (NPR)			
815 N Walnut St Ste 300 ....Hutchinson KS 67501	**800-723-4657**	620-662-6646	636
KHEAA (Kentucky Higher Education Assistance Authority)			
100 Airport Rd ....Frankfort KY 40602	**800-928-8926**		716
KHHO-AM 850 (Sports)			
645 Elliott Ave W Ste 400 ....Seattle WA 98119	**800-829-0950**	206-494-2000	636-101
KHIP-FM 104.3 (CR)			
60 Garden Ct Ste 300 ....Monterey CA 93940	**877-762-5104**	831-658-5200	636-72
KHJZ-FM 93.9 (CHR)			
650 Iwilei Rd Ste 400 ....Honolulu HI 96817	**800-745-3000**	808-550-9200	
Khong Guan Corp			
30068 Eigenbrodt Way ....Union City CA 94587	**877-889-8968**	510-487-7800	196
KHON-TV Ch 2 (Fox)			
88 Piikoi St ....Honolulu HI 96814	**877-926-8300**	808-591-4278	730-33
Khoury Inc			
1129 Webster Ave PO Box 1746. ....Waco TX 76703	**800-725-6765**	254-754-5481	318-1
KHS & S Contractors Inc			
5422 Bay Ctr Dr Ste 200. ....Tampa FL 33609	**866-991-7277**	813-628-9330	190-9
KHTK-AM 1140 (Sports)			
5244 Madison Ave ....Sacramento CA 95841	**800-920-1140**	916-338-9200	636-92
KHTO-FM 96.7			
125 Corporate Terr ....Hot Springs AR 71913	**866-425-9600**	501-525-9700	636-51
KHVH-AM 830 (N/T)			
650 Iwilei Rd Ste 400 ....Honolulu HI 96817	**888-565-8383**	808-550-9200	
KI 1330 Bellevue St			
...................Green Bay WI 54302	**800-424-2432**	920-468-8100	318-1
Kiamichi Electric Co-op Inc (KEC)			
966 SW Hwy 2 PO Box 340 ....Wilburton OK 74578	**800-888-2731**	918-465-2338	245
Kiawah Island Golf Resort			
One Sanctuary Beach Dr ......Kiawah Island SC 29455	**800-654-2924***	843-768-2121	660
*Resv			
Kibble Equipment			
1150 S Victory Dr ....Mankato MN 56001	**800-624-8983**	507-387-8201	355
Kibow Biotech Inc			
4781 W Chester Pike Newtown			
Business Ctr ....Newtown Square PA 19073	**888-271-2560**	610-353-5130	231
Kice Industries Inc			
5500 N Mill Heights Dr ....Wichita KS 67219	**877-289-5423**	316-744-7151	208
Kichler Lighting			
7711 E Pleasant Vly Rd			
PO Box 318010. ....Cleveland OH 44131	**866-558-5706**		435
Kickhaefer Mfg Co (KMC)			
1221 S Pk St PO Box 348. ....Port Washington WI 53074	**800-822-6080**	262-377-5030	483
KidCo Inc			
1013 Technology Way ....Libertyville IL 60048	**800-553-5529**	847-549-8600	63
Kidde-Fenwal Inc			
400 Main St ....Ashland MA 01721	**800-872-6527***	508-881-2000	203
*Hum Res			
Kidron Auction Inc			
4885 Kidron Rd ....Kidron OH 44636	**800-589-9749**	330-857-2641	441
Kidron Inc			
13442 Emerson Rd ....Kidron OH 44636	**800-321-5421**	330-857-3011	509
Kids II			
555 N Pt Ctr E Ste 600 ....Alpharetta GA 30022	**877-325-7056**	770-751-0442	63
KidsPeace Orchard Hills Campus			
5300 Kids Peace Dr ....Orefield PA 18069	**800-257-3223**		371-1
Kiefer Specialty Flooring Inc			
2910 Falling Waters Blvd ....Lindenhurst IL 60046	**800-322-5448**	847-245-8450	358
Kieffer & Company Inc			
3322 Washington Ave ....Sheboygan WI 53081	**800-458-4394**		692

	Toll-Free	Phone	Class
KIII-TV Ch 3 (ABC)			
5002 S Padre Island Dr ....Corpus Christi TX 78411	**800-882-9539**	361-986-8300	730-17
KIK Custom Products			
2730 Middlebury St ....Elkhart IN 46516	**800-479-6603**	574-295-0000	143
KIK Pool Additives Inc			
5160 E Airport Dr ....Ontario CA 91761	**800-745-4536**	909-390-9912	143
Kilian Community College			
300 E Sixth St ....Sioux Falls SD 57103	**800-888-1147**	605-221-3100	160
Killen Group Inc			
1189 Lancaster Ave ....Berwyn PA 19312	**877-454-5536**	610-296-7222	398
Killington Grand Resort Hotel & Conference Ctr			
4763 Killington Rd ....Killington VT 05751	**800-621-6867**	802-422-5001	376
Killington Resort & Pico Mountain			
228 E Mountain Rd ....Killington VT 05751	**800-621-6867**	802-422-6200	660
Killion Industries Inc			
1380 Poinsettia Ave ....Vista CA 92081	**800-421-5352**	760-727-5102	286
KILO-FM 94.3 (Rock)			
1805 E Cheyenne Rd ....Colorado Springs CO 80905	**800-727-5456***	719-634-4896	636-29
*General			
Kilwins Quality Confections Inc (KQC)			
1050 Bay View Rd ....Petoskey MI 49770	**888-454-5946**		122
Kim Hotstart Manufacturing Co			
5723 E Alki Ave ....Spokane WA 99212	**800-224-5550**	509-536-8660	15
Kimball Electronics			
13700 Reptron Blvd ....Tampa FL 33626	**800-903-8328**	813-854-2000	617
Kimball Electronics Group			
1038 E 15th St ....Jasper IN 47549	**800-482-1616**	812-634-4200	617
Kimball Genetics Inc			
8490 Upland Dr Ste 100.........Englewood CO 80112	**800-444-9111**		412
Kimball Hospitality			
1180 E 16th St ....Jasper IN 47549	**800-634-9510**	276-666-8933	318-3
Kimball International Inc			
1600 Royal St ....Jasper IN 47549	**800-482-1616**	812-482-1600	186
NASDAQ: KBAL			
Kimball Midwest			
4800 Robert Rd ....Columbus OH 43228	**800-233-1294**	614-219-6100	382
Kimball Office Furniture Co			
1600 Royal St ....Jasper IN 47549	**800-482-1818**		318-1
Kimball Terrace Inn			
10 Huntington Rd ....Northeast Harbor ME 04662	**800-454-6225**	207-276-3383	376
Kimberly Hotel			
145 E 50th St ....New York NY 10022	**800-683-0400**	212-755-0400	376
Kimberly-Clark Corp			
351 Phelps Dr ....Irving TX 75038	**888-525-8388**	972-281-1200	551
NYSE: KMB			
Kimberly-Clark/Ballard Medical Products			
1400 Holcomb Bridge Rd ....Roswell GA 30076	**800-524-3577**		471
Kimco Realty Corp			
3333 New Hyde Pk Rd ....New Hyde Park NY 11042	**800-645-6292**	516-869-9000	646
NYSE: KIM			
Kimco Staffing Services Inc			
17872 Cowan Ave ....Irvine CA 92614	**800-649-5627**	949-752-6996	712
Kimoto Tech Inc			
PO Box 1783 ....Cedartown GA 30125	**888-546-6861**	770-748-2643	593
Kimpton Hotel & Restaurant Group			
422 SW Broadway ....Portland OR 97205	**800-263-2305**	503-228-1212	376
Kimpton Hotel & Restaurant Group LLC			
222 Kearny St Ste 200 ......San Francisco CA 94108	**800-546-7866**	415-397-5572	376
Kimpton Hotel & Restaurant Group, LLC			
10050 S DeAnza Blvd ....Cupertino CA 95014	**800-499-1408**	408-253-8900	376
Kimray Inc			
52 NW 42nd St ....Oklahoma City OK 73118	**866-586-7233**	405-525-6601	778
KIMT-TV Ch 3 (CBS)			
112 N Pennsylvania Ave ....Mason City IA 50401	**800-323-4883**	641-423-2540	730
Kimwood Corp			
77684 Oregon 99 ....Cottage Grove OR 97424	**800-942-4401**	541-942-4401	808
Kinaxis			
700 Silver Seven Rd ....Ottawa ON K2V1C3	**877-546-2947***	613-592-5780	179-10
*General			
Kincaid Coach Lines Inc			
9207 Woodend Rd ....Kansas City KS 66111	**800-998-1901**	913-441-6200	750
Kincardine Cable TV Ltd			
223 Bruce Ave ....Kincardine ON N2Z2P2	**800-265-3064**	519-396-8880	115
Kinco International			
4286 NE 185th Dr ....Portland OR 97230	**800-547-8410***		153-7
*General			
Kinder Morgan			
1001 Louisiana St Ste 1000 ....Houston TX 77002	**800-247-4122**	713-369-9000	324
NYSE: KMI			
Kinder Morgan Bulk Terminals Inc			
7116 Hwy 22 ....Sorrento LA 70778	**800-232-1627**	225-675-5387	460
Kinder Morgan Energy Partners LP			
500 Dallas St Ste 1000............Houston TX 77002	**866-208-3372**	713-369-9000	324
NYSE: KMI			
Kinder Morgan Inc			
500 Dallas St Ste 1000.............Houston TX 77002	**800-525-3752**	713-369-9000	775
NYSE: KMI			
Kinder Morgan Inc KN Energy Retail Div			
370 Van Gordon St ....Lakewood CO 80228	**800-232-1627**	303-989-1740	775
Kinder Morgan Management LLC			
500 Dallas St			
1 Allen Ctr Ste 1000 ....Houston TX 77002	**800-781-4152**	713-369-9000	324
NYSE: KMI			
Kinder Morgan Texas Pipeline LLC			
500 Dallas St Ste 1000.............Houston TX 77002	**800-324-2900**	713-369-9000	324
KinderCare Learning Centers Inc			
650 NE Holladay St Ste 1400			
PO Box 6760.....................Portland OR 97232	**800-633-1488**		146
Kinderdance International Inc			
1333 Gateway Dr Ste 1033 ....Melbourne FL 32901	**800-554-2334**	321-984-4448	309
Kindred Healthcare Inc			
680 S Fourth Ave ....Louisville KY 40202	**800-545-0749**	502-596-7300	350
NYSE: KND			
Kindred Hospital Atlanta			
705 Juniper St ....Atlanta GA 30308	**800-255-0135**	404-873-2871	371-7
Kindred Hospital Greensboro			
2401 Southside Blvd ....Greensboro NC 27406	**877-836-2671**	336-271-2800	445
Kindred Hospital Kansas City			
8701 Troost Ave ....Kansas City MO 64131	**800-545-0749**	816-995-2000	371-7
Kindred Hospital Philadelphia			
6129 Palmetto St ....Philadelphia PA 19111	**800-654-5988**	215-722-8555	445
Kindred Hospital Pittsburgh			
7777 Steubenville Pk ....Oakdale PA 15071	**800-654-5988**	412-494-5500	445

	Toll-Free	Phone	Class
Kinecta Federal Credit Union			
1440 Rosecrans Ave			
PO Box 10003..............Manhattan Beach CA 90266	**800-854-9846**	310-643-5400	219
Kinesis Corp			
22030 20th Ave SE Ste 102 ....Bothell WA 98021	**800-454-6374**	425-402-8100	174-2
Kinetic Concepts Inc (KCI)			
PO Box 659508 ....San Antonio TX 78265	**800-275-4524***		472
*Cust Svc			
Kinetico Inc			
10845 Kinsman Rd ....Newbury OH 44065	**800-944-9283**		794
Kinetics Mechanical Service Inc			
6691 Brisa St ....Livermore CA 94550	**866-567-7378**	925-245-6200	603
King & Prince Beach & Golf Resort			
201 Arnold Rd ....Saint Simons Island GA 31522	**800-342-0212**	912-638-3631	660
King & Prince Seafood Corp			
One King & Prince Blvd ....Brunswick GA 31520	**800-841-0205**	912-265-5155	295-14
KING 5 Television			
333 Dexter Ave N ....Seattle WA 98109	**800-456-3975**	206-448-5555	730-69
King Architectural Metals Inc			
PO Box 271169 ....Dallas TX 75227	**800-542-2379**		486
King Bio Pharmaceuticals Inc			
Three Westside Dr ....Asheville NC 28806	**800-543-3245**	828-255-0201	576
King College			
1350 King College Rd ....Bristol TN 37620	**800-362-0014***	423-652-4861	166
*Admissions			
King County			
401 5th Ave Ste 800 ....Seattle WA 98104	**800-325-6165**	206-296-1586	336
King Electrical Manufacturing Co			
9131 Tenth Ave S ....Seattle WA 98108	**800-603-5464**	206-762-0400	36
King Engineering Assoc Inc			
4921 Memorial Hwy Ste 300 ....Tampa FL 33634	**800-723-1403**	813-880-8881	261
King Engineering Corp			
3201 S State St ....Ann Arbor MI 48106	**800-242-8871***	734-662-5691	18
*Cust Svc			
King Estate Winery			
80854 Territorial Rd ....Eugene OR 97405	**800-884-4441**	541-942-9874	49-6
King Features Syndicate Inc			
300 W 57th St 15th Fl............New York NY 10019	**800-708-7311**	212-969-7550	523
King Industries Inc			
One Science Rd ....Norwalk CT 06852	**800-431-7900**	203-866-5551	143
King Kamehameha's Kona Beach Hotel			
75-5660 Palani Rd ....Kailua-Kona HI 96740	**800-367-2111**	808-329-2911	376
King Koil Licensing Company Inc			
7501 S Quincy St Ste 130........Willowbrook IL 60527	**800-525-8331**		466
King Nut Co			
31900 Solon Rd ....Solon OH 44139	**800-860-5464**	440-248-8484	295-28
King of Prussia Mall			
160 N Gulph Rd ....King of Prussia PA 19406	**877-746-6642**	610-265-5727	455
King Pacific Lodge			
255 W First St ....North Vancouver BC V7M3G8	**855-825-9378**	604-987-5452	376
King Plastic Corp			
1100 N Toledo Blade Blvd ....North Port FL 34288	**800-780-5502**	941-493-5502	601
King Precision Glass Inc			
177 S Indian Hill Blvd ....Claremont CA 91711	**866-554-2773**	909-626-3526	330
King Relocation Services			
13535 Larwin Cir ....Santa Fe Springs CA 90670	**800-854-3679**		512
King's College			
133 N River St ....Wilkes-Barre PA 18711	**800-955-5777**	570-208-5858	166
King's Material Inc			
650 12th Ave SW ....Cedar Rapids IA 52404	**800-332-5298**	319-363-0233	184
King's University College			
9125 50th St ....Edmonton AB T6B2H3	**800-661-8582**	780-465-3500	773
Kingbridge Centre, The			
12750 Jane St ....King City ON L7B1A3	**800-827-7221**	905-833-3086	374
Kingdom of Callaway Chamber of Commerce			
409 Ct St ....Fulton MO 65251	**800-257-3554**	573-642-3055	137
Kingman Regional Medical Ctr (KRMC)			
3269 Stockton Hill Rd ....Kingman AZ 86409	**877-757-2101**	928-757-2101	371-3
Kings Landing Historical Settlement			
5804 Rt 102 ....Prince William NB E6K0A5	**888-666-5547***	506-363-4999	513
*General			
Kingsbury Inc			
10385 Drummond Rd ....Philadelphia PA 19154	**866-581-5464***	215-824-4000	613
*Sales			
Kingsdown Inc			
126 W Holt St ....Mebane NC 27302	**800-354-5464***	919-563-3531	466
*Cust Svc			
Kingsgate Marriott Conference Ctr at the University of Cincinnati			
151 Goodman St ....Cincinnati OH 45219	**800-228-9290**	513-487-3800	374
Kingsley Plantation			
11676 Palmetto Ave ....Jacksonville FL 32226	**877-874-2478**	904-251-3537	513
Kingsmill Resort & Spa			
1010 Kingsmill Rd ....Williamsburg VA 23185	**800-832-5665**	757-253-1703	660
Kingsport Convention & Visitors Bureau (KCVB)			
400 Clinchfield St Ste 100 ....Kingsport TN 37660	**800-743-5282**	423-392-8820	207
Kingsport Times-News			
701 Lynn Garden Dr ....Kingsport TN 37660	**800-251-0328**	423-246-8121	525-2
Kingston National Bank			
Two N Main St PO Box 613 ....Kingston OH 45644	**866-642-2191**	740-642-2191	69
Kingston Oil Supply Corp			
2926 Rt 32 N ....Saugerties NY 12477	**800-755-6726**	845-247-2200	315
Kingston Technology Co			
17600 Newhope St ....Fountain Valley CA 92708	**800-835-6575**	714-435-2600	288
Kingsway America Inc (KAI)			
150 NW Pt Blvd ....Elk Grove Village IL 60007	**800-232-0631**	847-700-9100	357-4
Kingsway Charities			
1119 Commonwealth Ave ....Bristol VA 24201	**800-321-9234**	276-466-3014	47-20
Kingswood Senior Living Community			
10000 Wornall Rd ....Kansas City MO 64114	**888-942-2715***	816-942-0994	663
*Sales			
Kingwood College			
20000 Kingwood Dr ....Kingwood TX 77339	**800-883-7939**	281-312-1600	160
KINK-FM 101.9 (AAA)			
1211 SW Fifth Ave ....Portland OR 97204	**877-567-5465**	503-517-6000	636-86
Kinney Brick Co			
100 Prosperity Rd			
PO Box 1804................Albuquerque NM 87103	**800-464-4605**	505-877-4550	148
Kino International Corp			
333 W 39th St Rm 503 ....New York NY 10018	**800-562-3330**	212-629-6880	504
Kinray Inc			
152-35 Tenth Ave ....Whitestone NY 11357	**800-854-6729**	718-767-1234	238
Kinross Gold Corp			
25 York St 17th Fl................Toronto ON M5J2V5	**866-561-3636**	416-365-5123	497
NYSE: KGC			

Name / Address	City	State	ZIP	Toll-Free	Phone	Class
Kinsley & Sons Inc 24 S Church St Ste A *General	Union	MO	63084	800-468-4428*		406
Kinston Convention & Visitors Bureau 301 N Queen St	Kinston	NC	28501	800-869-0032	252-523-2500	207
Kintetsu World Express USA Inc One Jericho Plz Ste 100	Jericho	NY	11753	800-275-4045	516-933-7100	444
KINT-FM 93.9 (Span) 5426 N Mesa St	El Paso	TX	79912	866-560-5673	915-581-1126	636-37
Kinyo Company Inc 14235 Lomitas Ave	La Puente	CA	91746	800-735-4696	626-333-3711	174-5
Kinzie Hotel 20 W Kinzie St	Chicago	IL	60654	877-262-5341	312-395-9000	376
KIOA-FM 93.3 (Oldies) 1416 Locust St	Des Moines	IA	50309	877-984-8786	515-280-1350	
KIOI-FM 101.3 (AC) 340 Townsend St Fourth Fl	San Francisco	CA	94107	800-800-1013	415-975-5555	636-97
Kiosk Information Systems Inc (KIS) 346 S Arthur Ave *General	Louisville	CO	80027	800-509-5471*	303-466-5471	607
Kipin Industries Inc 4194 Green Garden Rd	Aliquippa	PA	15001	800-782-8050	724-495-6200	190-16
Kiplinger Agriculture Letter 1729 H St NW	Washington	DC	20006	800-544-0155	202-887-6400	524-13
Kiplinger California Letter 1729 H St NW	Washington	DC	20006	800-544-0155	202-887-6400	524-6
Kiplinger Tax Letter 1729 H St NW	Washington	DC	20006	800-544-0155	202-887-6400	524-7
Kiplinger Washington Editors Inc 1729 H St NW	Washington	DC	20006	800-544-0155	202-887-6400	628-9
Kipp Foundation 135 Main St Ste 1700	San Francisco	CA	94105	866-345-5477	415-399-1556	195
Kirby Agri Inc 500 Running Pump Rd PO Box 6277	Lancaster	PA	17607	800-745-7524	717-299-2541	280
Kirby Bldg Systems Inc 124 Kirby Dr	Portland	TN	37148	800-348-7799	615-325-4165	104
Kirby Co 1920 W 114th St	Cleveland	OH	44102	800-437-7170	216-228-2400	776
Kirk Rudy Inc 125 Lorraine Pkwy	Woodstock	GA	30188	800-897-1910	770-427-4203	540
Kirkegaard & Perry Laboratories Inc 910 Clopper Rd	Gaithersburg	MD	20878	800-638-3167	301-948-7755	231
Kirkland & Ellis LLP 200 E Randolph Dr	Chicago	IL	60601	800-647-7600	312-861-2000	425
Kirkland's Inc 431 Smith Ln *NASDAQ: KIRK*	Jackson	TN	38301	877-541-4855		359
Kirkpatrick & Lockhart Preston Gates Ellis LLP 210 Sixth Ave	Pittsburgh	PA	15222	800-452-8260	412-355-6500	425
Kirkpatrick Concrete Co 2000-A Southbridge Pkwy Ste 610	Birmingham	AL	35209	800-489-0205	205-423-2600	183
Kirkridge Retreat & Study Ctr 2495 Fox Gap Rd	Bangor	PA	18013	800-231-2222	610-588-1793	664
Kirkwood Community College 6301 Kirkwood Blvd SW	Cedar Rapids	IA	52404	800-332-2055	319-398-5411	160
Kirkwood Industries Inc 1239 Rockside Rd	Cleveland	OH	44134	800-262-2266	216-267-6200	511
Kirkwood Library 6000 Kirkwood Hwy	Wilmington	DE	19808	888-352-7722	302-995-7663	431-3
Kirtland Air Force Base 2000 Wyoming Blvd SE Ste A-1	Kirtland AFB	NM	87117	877-246-1453	505-846-5991	492-1
Kirtland Community College 10775 N St Helen Rd	Roscommon	MI	48653	866-632-9992	989-275-5000	160
KIS (Kiosk Information Systems Inc) 346 S Arthur Ave *General	Louisville	CO	80027	800-509-5471*	303-466-5471	607
Kish Bancorp Inc 4255 E Main St PO Box 917 *OTC: KISB*	Belleville	PA	17004	888-554-4748	717-935-2191	69
Kishwaukee College 21193 Malta Rd	Malta	IL	60150	888-656-7329	815-825-2086	160
Kishwaukee Community Hospital 1 Kish Hospital Dr	DeKalb	IL	60115	800-397-1521	815-756-1521	371-3
Kiski School 1888 Brett Ln	Saltsburg	PA	15681	877-547-5448	724-639-3586	615
KISS-FM 99.5 (Rock) 8122 Datapoint Dr Ste 600	San Antonio	TX	78229	866-333-6747	210-615-5400	636-95
Kissimmee Utility Authority Inc (KUA) 1701 W Carroll St	Kissimmee	FL	34741	877-582-7700	407-933-7777	775
Kistler Instrument Corp 75 John Glenn Dr	Amherst	NY	14228	888-547-8537	716-691-5100	467
Kistler-Morse Corp 150 Venture Blvd	Spartanburg	SC	29306	800-426-9010	864-574-2763	202
Kistner Concrete Products Inc 8713 Read Rd	East Pembroke	NY	14056	800-809-2801	585-762-8216	184
KISU-TV Ch 10 (PBS) Idaho State University CB 8111 921 S Eighth Ave	Pocatello	ID	83209	800-543-6868	208-282-2857	730-56
KIT HomeBuilders West LLC 1124 Garber St	Caldwell	ID	83605	800-859-0347	208-454-5000	105
Kitano New York 66 Pk Ave E 38th St	New York	NY	10016	800-548-2666	212-885-7000	376
Kitchen Academy 6370 W Sunset Blvd	Hollywood	CA	90028	866-548-2223		161
Kitchen Collection Inc 71 E Water St *General	Chillicothe	OH	45601	888-548-2651*	740-773-9150	359
Kitchen Tune-Up Inc 813 Cir Dr	Aberdeen	SD	57401	800-333-6385	605-225-4049	190-11
KITCO Fiber Optics Inc 5269 Cleveland St	Virginia Beach	VA	23462	866-643-5220	757-518-8100	603
Kite Realty Group Trust 30 S Meridian St Ste 1100 *NYSE: KRG*	Indianapolis	IN	46204	888-577-5600	317-577-5600	645
Kitsap Regional Library 1301 Sylvan Way	Bremerton	WA	98310	877-883-9900	360-405-9100	431-3
Kitsap Sun PO Box 259	Bremerton	WA	98337	888-377-3711	360-377-3711	525-2
KITS-FM 105.3 (Alt) 865 Battery St	San Francisco	CA	94111	800-696-1053		636-97
Kitt Peak National Observatory 950 N Cherry Ave	Tucson	AZ	85719	888-809-4012	520-318-8600	591
Kittery Trading Post 301 US 1	Kittery	ME	03904	888-587-6246	603-334-1157	155-2
Kittredge Equipment Co Inc 100 Bowles Rd	Agawam	MA	01001	800-423-7082	413-304-4100	299
Kitty Askins Hospice Ctr 107 Handley Pk Ct	Goldsboro	NC	27534	800-692-4442	919-735-5887	368
Kivort Steel 380 Hudson River Rd	Waterford	NY	12188	800-462-2616	518-590-7233	487
Kiwanis International Foundation 3636 Woodview Trace	Indianapolis	IN	46268	800-549-2647	317-875-8755	304
Kiwanis Magazine 3636 Woodview Trace	Indianapolis	IN	46268	800-549-2647	317-875-8755	452-10
Kiwash Electric Co-op Inc 120 W First St	Cordell	OK	73632	888-832-3362	580-832-3361	245
KIXI-AM 880 (Nost) 3650 131st Ave SE Ste 550	Bellevue	WA	98006	866-880-5494	425-562-8964	636
KJAQ-FM 96.5 (Var) 1000 Dexter Ave N Ste 100	Seattle	WA	98109	866-416-5225	206-805-1100	636-101
KJLA-TV Ch 57 (Ind) 2323 Corinth Ave	Los Angeles	CA	90064	800-588-5788	310-943-5288	730-40
KJR-AM 950 (Sports) 351 Elliott Ave W Ste 300	Seattle	WA	98119	800-829-0950	206-494-2000	636-101
KJUD-TV Ch 8 (ABC) 2700 E Tudor Rd	Anchorage	AK	99507	877-304-1313	907-561-1313	730-35
KKBB-FM 99.3 (Oldies) 3651 Pegasus Dr Ste 107	Bakersfield	CA	93308	866-758-4696	661-393-1900	636-9
KKBD-FM 95.9 (CR) 311 Lexington Ave	Fort Smith	AR	72901	866-503-1398	479-782-8888	
KKPT-FM 94.1 (CR) 2400 Cottondale Ln	Little Rock	AR	72202	800-844-0094	501-664-9410	636-61
KKRZ-FM 100.3 (CHR) 13333 SW 68th Pkwy Ste 310	Tigard	OR	97223	888-483-0100	503-460-0100	636-86
KKSF-FM 103.7 (NAC) 340 Townsend St Fourth Fl	San Francisco	CA	94107	866-900-1037	415-975-5555	636-97
KL Industries Inc 1790 Sun Dolphin Dr	Muskegon	MI	49444	800-733-2727	231-733-2725	701
Klafter's Inc 216 N Beaver St	New Castle	PA	16101	800-922-1233		746
Klamath County 305 Main St	Klamath Falls	OR	97601	800-377-6094	541-883-5134	336
KLAQ-FM 95.5 (Rock) 4180 N Mesa St	El Paso	TX	79902	877-566-8477	915-880-4955	636-37
KLAT-AM 1010 (Span N/T) 5100 SW Fwy	Houston	TX	77056	800-646-6779	713-407-1415	636-52
KLA-Tencor Corp One Technology Dr *NASDAQ: KLAC*	Milpitas	CA	95035	800-600-2829	408-875-3000	248
Klaussner Home Furnishings 405 Lewallen Rd	Asheboro	NC	27205	888-732-5948	336-625-6174	318-2
KLAZ-FM 105.9 (CHR) 208 Buena Vista Rd	Hot Springs	AR	71913	800-621-3362	501-525-4600	636-51
Kleet Lumber Company Inc 777 Pk Ave	Huntington	NY	11743	800-696-5533	631-427-7060	192-3
Klein & Company Corporate Housing Services Inc 914 Washington Ave	Golden	CO	80401	800-208-9826	303-796-2100	211
Klein Steel Service 105 Vanguarden Pkwy *Cust Svc	Rochester	NY	14606	800-477-6789*	585-328-4000	487
Klein Tools Inc 450 Bond St *Cust Svc	Lincolnshire	IL	60069	800-553-4676*		748
Kleiner Perkins Caufield & Byers (KPCB) 2750 Sand Hill Rd	Menlo Park	CA	94025	877-312-5521	650-233-2750	780
Kleinschmidt Inc 450 Lake Cook Rd	Deerfield	IL	60015	800-824-2330	847-945-1000	38
Klement Sausage Co Inc 207 E Lincoln Ave	Milwaukee	WI	53207	800-553-6368	414-744-2330	295-26
KLFC-FM 88.1 (Rel) 205 W Atlantic St	Branson	MO	65616	877-410-8592	417-334-5532	636-17
Kline & Company Inc 150 Clove Rd Seventh Fl	Little Falls	NJ	07424	800-290-5214	973-435-6262	195
Klingberg Family Centers Inc 370 Linwood St	New Britain	CT	06052	877-696-6775	860-224-9113	47-15
Klingelhofer Corp 165 Mill Ln	Mountainside	NJ	07092	800-879-5546	908-232-7200	450
Klipsch LLC 137 Hempstead 278	Hope	AR	71801	888-250-8561		51
KLJ Computer Solutions Inc 115 Joseph Zatzman Dr	Dartmouth	NS	B3B1N3	888-455-5669		180
KLLM Inc 135 Riverview Dr	Richland	MS	39218	800-925-5556	800-925-1000	770
KLN Steel Products Co Two Winnco Dr	San Antonio	TX	78218	800-624-9101	210-227-4747	318-3
KLNV-FM 106.5 (Span) 600 W Broadway Ste 2150	San Diego	CA	92101	800-879-4278	619-235-0600	636-96
KLO-AM 1430 (N/T) 257 East 200 South Ste 400	Salt Lake City	UT	84111	866-627-1430	801-364-9836	636-94
Klochko Equipment Rental Company Inc 2782 Corbin Ave	Melvindale	MI	48122	800-783-7368	313-386-7220	264-3
Kloehn Inc 10000 Banburry Cross Dr	Las Vegas	NV	89144	800-358-4342	702-243-7727	472
Kloppenberg & Co 2627 W Oxford Ave	Englewood	CO	80110	800-346-3246	303-761-1615	655
Klosterman Baking Company Inc 4760 Paddock Rd	Cincinnati	OH	45229	877-301-1004	513-242-1004	295-1
KLPB-TV Ch 24 (PBS) 7733 Perkins Rd	Baton Rouge	LA	70810	800-272-8161	225-767-5660	730-8
KLRN-TV Ch 9 (PBS) 501 Broadway St	San Antonio	TX	78215	800-627-8193	210-270-9000	730-67
KLSE-FM 91.7 (Clas) 206 S Broadway Ste 735	Rochester	MN	55904	800-652-9700	507-282-0910	636-91
Kluane National Park & Reserve of Canada PO Box 5495	Haines Junction	YT	Y0B1L0	877-852-3100	867-634-7250	556
Kluber Lubrication North America LP 32 Industrial Dr	Londonderry	NH	03053	800-447-2238	603-647-4104	534
KLUV-FM 98.7 (Oldies) 4131 N Central Expy Ste 1000	Dallas	TX	75204	855-987-5588	214-525-7000	636-34
KM Fabrics Inc 2 Waco St	Greenville	SC	29611	800-873-7326	864-295-2550	734-1
K&M Tire Inc 965 Spencerville Rd PO Box 279	Delphos	OH	45833	877-879-5407	419-695-1061	744

Alphabetical Section

	Toll-Free	Phone	Class
K-Mac Enterprises Inc PO Box 6538 ... Fort Smith AR 72906	800-947-9277	479-646-2053	661
KMAJ-AM 1440 (N/T) 825 S Kansas Ave Ste 100 ... Topeka KS 66612	877-297-1077	785-272-2122	636-113
KMAJ-FM 107.7 (AC) 825 S Kansas Ave Ste 100 ... Topeka KS 66612	877-297-1077	785-272-2122	636-113
KMAX-TV Ch 31 (CBS) 2713 Kovr Dr ... West Sacramento CA 95605	800-374-8813	916-374-1313	730
KMC (Kickhaefer Mfg Co) 1221 S Pk St PO Box 348 ... Port Washington WI 53074	800-822-6080	262-377-5030	483
KMC Controls Inc 19476 Industrial Dr ... New Paris IN 46553	877-444-5622	574-831-5250	203
KMI Diagnostics Inc 8201 Central Ave NE Ste P ... Minneapolis MN 55432	888-564-3424	763-231-3313	231
KMIZ-TV Ch 17 (ABC) 501 Business Loop 70 E ... Columbia MO 65201	800-345-4109	573-449-0917	730
KMJ-AM 580 (N/T) 1071 W Shaw Ave ... Fresno CA 93711	800-776-5858	559-490-5800	636-45
KMJ-FM 105.9 1071 W Shaw Ave ... Fresno CA 93711	800-491-1899	559-490-5800	636-45
KMLO-FM 100.7 (Ctry) 214 W Pleasant Dr ... Pierre SD 57501	800-658-5439	605-224-8686	636-84
KMOS-TV Ch 6 (PBS) University of Central Missouri ... Warrensburg MO 64093	800-753-3436		730
KMPH-TV Ch 26 (Fox) 5111 E McKinley Ave ... Fresno CA 93727	800-101-2045	559-453-8850	730-30
KMRQ-FM 96.7 (Rock) 2121 Lancey Dr ... Modesto CA 95355	800-505-3967	209-866-6677	636-71
KMS Ventures Inc 1301 W 25th St Ste 300 ... Austin TX 78705	844-282-7433	512-474-6312	262
Kmtelecom 18 Second Ave NW ... Kasson MN 55944	888-232-3796	507-634-2511	115
KMTV Action 3 News 10714 Mockingbird Dr ... Omaha NE 68127	800-800-6619	402-592-3333	730-51
KMVQ-FM 99.7 (AC) 865 Battery St ... San Francisco CA 94111	888-456-9970	415-765-4112	636-97
KMW Ltd PO Box 327 ... Sterling KS 67579	800-445-7388	620-278-3641	273
KMXB-FM 94.1 (AC) 7255 S Tenaya Way Ste 100 ... Las Vegas NV 89113	866-438-0220	702-257-9400	636-59
KMYS-TV Ch 35 (MNT) 4335 NW Loop 410 ... San Antonio TX 78229	800-987-6038	210-366-1129	730-67
Knaack Manufacturing Co 420 E Terra Cotta Ave ... Crystal Lake IL 60014	800-456-7865	815-459-6020	483
Knape & Vogt Manufacturing Co 2700 Oak Industrial Dr NE ... Grand Rapids MI 49505	800-253-1561	616-459-3311	347
Knapheide Mfg Co 1848 Westphalia Strasse PO Box 7140 ... Quincy IL 62305	855-264-4300	217-222-7131	509
Knappen Milling Co 110 S Water St ... Augusta MI 49012	800-562-7736	269-731-4141	295-23
Knauf Insulation One Knauf Dr ... Shelbyville IN 46176	800-825-4434	317-398-4434	386
KNAU-FM 88.7 (NPR) Bldg 83 ,515 E Pine Knoll Dr PO Box 5764 ... Flagstaff AZ 86011	800-523-5628	928-523-5628	636-43
KNBA-FM 90.3 (NPR) 3600 San Geronimo Dr Ste 480 ... Anchorage AK 99508	888-278-5622	907-793-3500	636-6
KNDR-FM 104.7 (Rel) 1400 NE Third St ... Mandan ND 58554	800-767-5095	701-663-2345	636
Knf Neuberger Inc 2 Black Forest Rd ... Trenton NJ 08691	800-323-4340	609-890-8600	417
Knight Capital Group Inc 545 Washington Blvd ... Jersey City NJ 07310 *NYSE: KCG*	800-544-7508	201-222-9400	681
Knight Electronics Inc 10557 Metric Dr ... Dallas TX 75243	800-323-2439	214-340-0265	195
Knight Hawk Coal LLC 500 Cutler-Trico Rd ... Percy IL 62272	855-611-2625	618-426-3662	496
Knight James E & Associates Pc 14825 Saint Marys Ln ... Houston TX 77079	800-896-4500	281-493-5080	724
Knight Publishing Co 600 S Tryon St ... Charlotte NC 28202	800-332-0686	704-358-5000	628-8
Knight Rifles 213 Dennis st Athens ... Athens TN 37303	866-518-4181		284
Knight Transportation Inc 5601 W Buckeye Rd ... Phoenix AZ 85043 *NYSE: KNX*	800-489-2000	602-269-2000	770
Knights of Columbus One Columbus Plz ... New Haven CT 06510 *Cust Svc	800-380-9995*	203-752-4000	47-15
KNIS-FM 91.3 (Rel) PO Box 21888 ... Carson City NV 89721	800-541-5647	775-883-5647	636-88
Knit Rite Inc 120 Osage Ave ... Kansas City KS 66105	800-821-3094	913-281-4600	471
Knitney Lines Inc PO Box 350 ... Scranton PA 18501 *General	800-266-7883*	570-457-5060	310
KNME-TV Ch 5 (PBS) 1130 University Blvd NE University of New Mexico ... Albuquerque NM 87102	800-328-5663	505-277-2121	730-2
KNML-AM 610 (Sports) 500 Fourth St NW Fifth Fl ... Albuquerque NM 87102	888-922-0610	505-767-6700	636-4
Knob Hill Inn 960 N Main St PO Box 1327 ... Ketchum ID 83340	800-526-8010	208-726-8010	376
Knockout Pest Control Inc 1009 Front St ... Uniondale NY 11553	800-244-7378	516-489-7817	570
Knoebels Amusement Resort 391 Knoebels Blvd ... Elysburg PA 17824	800-487-4386	570-672-2572	32
Knoll Inc 1235 Water St ... East Greenville PA 18041 *NYSE: KNL ■ *Cust Svc*	800-343-5665*	215-679-7991	318-1
Knollwood 6200 Oregon Ave NW ... Washington DC 20015	800-541-4255	202-541-0400	663
Knopp Inc 1307 66th St ... Emeryville CA 94608	800-227-1848	510-653-1661	248
Knorr Beeswax Products Inc 14906 Via De La Valle ... Del Mar CA 92014	800-807-2337	760-431-2007	121
Knot Inc, The 462 Broadway 6th Fl ... New York NY 10013	800-390-9784	212-219-8555	172
Knott's Berry Farm 8039 Beach Blvd ... Buena Park CA 90620	800-742-6427	714-220-5220	32
Knott's Berry Farm Resort 7675 Crescent Ave ... Buena Park CA 90620	866-752-2444	714-995-1111	660
Know Before You Go Reservations 8000 International Dr ... Orlando FL 32819	800-749-1993	407-352-9813	373
KNOW-FM 91.1 (NPR) 480 Cedar St ... Saint Paul MN 55101	800-228-7123	651-290-1500	636
Knowledge Information Solutions Inc 2877 Guardian Ln Ste 201 ... Virginia Beach VA 23452	877-547-7248	757-463-0033	180
Knowledge Works Inc 5750 Old Orchard Rd Ste 250 ... Skokie IL 60077	866-825-3400	847-853-6117	461
Knowles - Mcniff 12862 Garden Grove Blvd Ste C ... Garden Grove CA 92843	800-820-5254		178
KnowX LLC 730 Peachtree St ... Atlanta GA 30308	877-317-5000	404-541-0220	626
Knox College 2 E S St ... Galesburg IL 61401 *Admissions	800-678-5669*	309-341-7000	166
Knox County Convention & Visitors Bureau 107 S Main St ... Mount Vernon OH 43050	800-837-5282	740-392-6102	207
Knox Nursery Inc 940 Avalon Rd ... Winter Garden FL 34787	800-441-5669		366
Knoxville Civic Auditorium/Coliseum 500 Howard Baker Jr Ave ... Knoxville TN 37915	877-995-9961	865-215-8900	565
Knoxville News-Sentinel 2332 News Sentinel Dr ... Knoxville TN 37921	800-237-5821	865-521-8181	525-2
Knoxville Tourism & Sports Corp 301 S Gay St ... Knoxville TN 37902	800-727-8045	865-523-7263	207
KNPR-FM 89.5 (NPR) 1289 S Torrey Pines Dr ... Las Vegas NV 89146	888-258-9895	702-258-9895	636-59
KNRK-FM 94.7 (Alt) 0700 SW Bancroft St ... Portland OR 97239	800-777-0947	503-733-5470	636-86
KNWC-AM 96.5 (Rel) 6300 S Tallgrass Ave ... Sioux Falls SD 57108	800-569-5692	605-339-1270	636-103
KNWI-FM 107.1 (Rel) 3737 Woodland Ave Ste 300 ... West Des Moines IA 50266	800-701-3123	515-327-1071	636
KNXV-TV Ch 15 (ABC) 515 N 44th St ... Phoenix AZ 85008	800-222-4357	602-273-1500	730-54
KO Prime 90 Tremont St ... Boston MA 02108	866-906-9090	617-772-0202	662
KOA (Kampgrounds of America Inc) PO Box 30558 ... Billings MT 59114	888-562-0000		120
KOAT-TV Ch 7 (ABC) 3801 Carlisle Blvd NE ... Albuquerque NM 87107	877-871-0165	505-884-7777	730-2
Kobelco Stewart Bolling Inc (KSBI) 1600 Terex Rd ... Hudson OH 44236	800-464-0064	330-655-3111	383
Koberg Beach State Recreation Site 725 Summer St NE Ste C ... Salem OR 97301	800-551-6949	503-986-0707	558
Kobrin Builders Supply Inc 1924 W Princeton St ... Orlando FL 32804	800-273-5511	407-843-1000	192-1
Kobussen Buses Ltd W914 County Rd CE ... Kaukauna WI 54130	800-447-0116	920-766-0606	108
Koch Air LLC 1900 W Lloyd Expy PO Box 1167 ... Evansville IN 47712	877-456-2422	812-962-5200	605
Koch Bros 325 Grand Ave ... Des Moines IA 50309	800-944-5624	515-283-2451	528
Koch Filter Corp 625 W Hill St ... Louisville KY 40208	800-757-5624	502-634-4796	18
Koch Foods Inc 1300 Higgins Rd Ste 100 ... Park Ridge IL 60068	800-837-2778	847-384-5940	612
Koch Membrane Systems Inc 850 Main St ... Wilmington MA 01887	888-677-5624	978-694-7000	383
Koch Mineral Services LLC 4111 E 37th St N ... Wichita KS 67220	800-750-5834	316-828-5500	170
Koch Specialty Plant Services 12221 E Sam Houston Pkwy N ... Houston TX 77044	800-765-9177	713-427-7700	532
Koch Supply & Trading LP 4111 E 37th St N ... Wichita KS 67220	800-245-2243	713-544-4123	388-4
KODA (Kentucky Organ Donor Affiliates) 106 E Broadway ... Louisville KY 40202	800-525-3456	502-581-9511	538
Kodiak Port & Harbor 403 Marine Way ... Kodiak AK 99615	800-563-4254	907-486-8080	611
KODS-FM 103.7 (Oldies) 961 Matley Ln Ste 120 ... Reno NV 89502	855-354-9111	775-829-1964	636-88
Koehler-Bright Star Inc 380 Stewart Rd ... Hanover Township PA 18706 *Cust Svc	800-788-1696*	570-825-1900	435
Koeze Co PO Box 9470 ... Grand Rapids MI 49509	800-555-9688		295-8
Koger/Air Corp PO Box 2098 ... Martinsville VA 24113	800-368-2096	276-638-8821	149
Kohl & Frisch Ltd 7622 Keele St ... Concord ON L4K2R5	800-265-2520		231
Kohl's Corp N 56 W 17000 Ridgewood Dr ... Menomonee Falls WI 53051 *NYSE: KSS*	855-564-5705	262-703-7000	229
Kohl's House at Children's Memorial Hospital 225 E Chicago Ave ... Chicago IL 60611	800-543-7362	312-227-4000	369
Kohler Canada Company Hytec Plumbing Products Div 4150 Spallumcheen Dr ... Armstrong BC V0E1B6	800-871-8311	250-546-3067	603
Kohler Co Inc 444 Highland Dr ... Kohler WI 53044	800-456-4537	920-457-4441	186
Kohler Engines 444 Highland Dr ... Kohler WI 53044	800-544-2444	920-457-4441	262
Kohler Plumbing North America 444 Highland Dr ... Kohler WI 53044	800-456-4537	920-457-4441	602
Kohler Waters Spa 501 Highlands Dr ... Kohler WI 53044	866-928-3777	920-457-7777	698
KOI Warehouse Inc 2701 Spring Grove Ave ... Cincinnati OH 45225	800-354-0408	513-357-2400	53
Koike Aronson Inc 635 W Main St PO Box 307 ... Arcade NY 14009	800-252-5232	585-492-2400	450
Koinonia Partners 1324 Georgia Hwy 49 S ... Americus GA 31719	877-738-1741	229-924-0391	295-28
Kois Bros Equipment Company Inc 5200 Colorado Blvd ... Commerce City CO 80022	800-672-6010	303-298-7370	383
Kokomo Opalescent Glass Co 1310 S Market St ... Kokomo IN 46902	877-475-6329	765-457-8136	328
Kokomo Tribune (KT) 300 N Union St PO Box 9014 ... Kokomo IN 46901	800-382-0696	765-459-3121	525-2
Kokomo-Howard County Public Library 220 N Union St ... Kokomo IN 46901	800-257-4762	765-457-3242	431-3

	Toll-Free	Phone	Class
Kokosing Construction Company Inc 17531 Waterford Rd PO Box 226 .... Fredericktown OH 43019	800-800-6315	740-694-6315	189-4
Kokusai Semiconductor Equipment Corp 2460 N First St Ste 290 .... San Jose CA 95131	800-800-5321	408-456-2750	686
Kolcraft Enterprises Inc 10832 NC Hwy 211 E .... Aberdeen NC 28315 *Cust Svc	800-453-7673*	910-944-9345	466
Kolene Corp 12890 Westwood Ave .... Detroit MI 48223	800-521-4182	313-273-9220	143
Kolkhorst Petroleum Co 1685 E Washington PO Box 410 .... Navasota TX 77868	800-548-6671	936-825-6868	315
Kollmann Monumental Works Inc 1915 W Div St .... Saint Cloud MN 56301	800-659-8010	320-251-8010	715
Kollmorgen Corp Electro-Optical Div 50 Prince St .... NorthHampton MA 01060	877-282-1168	413-586-2330	537
Kollsman Inc 220 Daniel Webster Hwy .... Merrimack NH 03054	800-772-9603	603-889-2500	522
KOLN-TV Ch 10 (CBS) 840 N 40th .... Lincoln NE 68503	800-475-1011	402-467-4321	730-38
Kolosso Toyota 3000 W Wisconsin Ave .... Appleton WI 54914	888-565-6776	920-738-3666	56
Kolpak 2915 Tennessee Ave N .... Parsons TN 38363	800-826-7036	731-847-5328	655
Kolpin Powersports 205 N Depot St PO Box 107 .... Fox Lake WI 53933	877-956-5746	920-928-3118	701
Komet Of America Inc 2050 Mitchell Blvd .... Schaumburg IL 60193	800-865-6638	847-923-8400	614
Komline-Sanderson Engineering Corp 12 Holland Ave .... Peapack NJ 07977	800-225-5457	908-234-1000	383
KOMO-AM 1000 (N/T) 140 Fourth Ave N Ste 340 .... Seattle WA 98109	888-477-5666	206-404-4000	636-101
KomTeK Technologies 40 Rockdale St .... Worcester MA 01606	800-669-4500	508-853-4500	478
KOMU-TV Ch 8 (NBC) 5550 Hwy 63 S .... Columbia MO 65201	800-286-3932	573-884-6397	730
Kona Grill Inc 7150 E Camelback Rd Ste 220 .... Scottsdale AZ 85251 *NASDAQ: KONA*	866-328-5662	480-922-8100	661
Kona International Airport 73-200 Kupipi St .... Kailua-Kona HI 96740	800-321-3712	808-327-9520	27
Kona Kai Resort 1551 Shelter Island Dr .... San Diego CA 92106	800-566-2524	619-221-8000	376
Konami Gaming Inc 585 Trade Ctr Dr .... Las Vegas NV 89119	866-544-7568	702-616-1400	321
Konecranes America 7300 Chippewa Blvd .... Houston TX 77086	800-231-0241	281-445-2225	465
Koneta Inc 1400 Lunar Dr .... Wapakoneta OH 45895	800-331-0775	419-739-4200	667
Konica Minolta Sensing Americas Inc 101 Williams Dr .... Ramsey NJ 07446	888-473-2656	201-825-4000	467
Konop Cos 1725 Industrial Dr .... Green Bay WI 54302	800-770-0477	920-468-8517	295-34
Konsyl Pharmaceuticals Inc 8050 Industrial Pk Rd .... Easton MD 21601	800-356-6795	410-822-5192	576
Kontron Mobile Computing Inc 7631 Anagram Dr .... Eden Prairie MN 55344	888-343-5396	952-974-7000	174-1
KOOL-FM 94.5 (Oldies) 840 N Central Ave .... Phoenix AZ 85004	800-222-4357	602-260-9494	636-83
Koons Ford of Annapolis Inc 2540 Riva Rd .... Annapolis MD 21401	888-313-5524	410-224-2100	56
Koontz-Wagner Electric Company Inc 3801 Voorde Dr .... South Bend IN 46628	800-345-2051	574-232-2051	190-4
Kootenai Electric Co-op Inc 2451 W Dakota Ave .... Hayden ID 83835	800-240-0459	208-765-1200	245
Kop-Coat Inc 436 Seventh Ave 1850 Koppers Bldg .... Pittsburgh PA 15219	800-221-4466	412-227-2426	543
KOPN-FM 89.5 (Var) 915 E Broadway .... Columbia MO 65201	800-895-5676	573-874-1139	636
Koppers Inc 436 Seventh Ave .... Pittsburgh PA 15219 *NYSE: KOP*	800-321-9876	412-227-2001	805
KOR Water Inc 95 Enterprise Ste 310 .... Aliso Viejo CA 92656	877-708-7567	714-708-7567	123
Koral Industries Inc 1504 S Kaufman St .... Ennis TX 75119	800-627-2441	972-875-6555	372
Korber Hats Inc 394 Kilburn St .... Fall River MA 02724 *Cust Svc	800-428-9911*	508-672-7033	153-8
Korea National Tourism Organization Two Executive Dr Ste 750 .... Fort Lee NJ 07024	800-868-7567	201-585-0909	765
Korea Republic of *Consulate General* 2033 Sixth Ave Ste 1125 .... Seattle WA 98121	800-375-5283	206-441-1011	257
Korean Air 6101 W Imperial Hwy .... Los Angeles CA 90045	800-438-5000	310-417-5200	25
Korean Air Skypass 1813 Wilshire Blvd Ste 300 .... Los Angeles CA 90057	800-438-5000	213-484-1900	26
Kor-it Inc 2442 Rice Ave .... West Sacramento CA 95691	888-727-4560		191
Korn/Ferry International 1900 Ave of the Stars Ste 2600 .... Los Angeles CA 90067 *NYSE: KFY*	877-345-3610	310-552-1834	266
Kornylak Corp 400 Heaton St .... Hamilton OH 45011	800-837-5676	513-863-1277	465
Kosciusko County Convention & Visitors Bureau (KOSCVB) 111 Capital Dr .... Warsaw IN 46582	800-800-6090	574-269-6090	207
KOSCVB (Kosciusko County Convention & Visitors Bureau) 111 Capital Dr .... Warsaw IN 46582	800-800-6090	574-269-6090	207
Koss Corp 4129 N Port Washington Ave .... Milwaukee WI 53212 *NASDAQ: KOSS*	800-872-5677	414-964-5000	51
KOTA-TV Ch 3 (ABC) 518 St Joseph St .... Rapid City SD 57701	866-558-4554	605-342-2000	
KOTV-TV Ch 6 (CBS) PO Box 6 .... Tulsa OK 74101	888-434-8248	918-732-6000	
Kovack Securities Inc 6451 N Federal Hwy # 1201 .... Fort Lauderdale FL 33308	800-711-4078	954-782-4771	681
Kovasys Inc 3575 St Laurent Blvd Ste 511 .... Montreal QC H2X2T7	888-568-2747		260
KOZK-TV Ch 21 (PBS) 901 S National Ave .... Springfield MO 65897	866-684-5695	417-836-3500	730-74
KPBS-FM 89.5 (NPR) San Diego State University 5200 Campanile Dr .... San Diego CA 92182	888-399-5727	619-265-6438	636-96
KPBS-TV Ch 15 (PBS) 5200 Campanile Dr .... San Diego CA 92182	888-399-5727	619-594-1515	730-68
KPCB (Kleiner Perkins Caufield & Byers) 2750 Sand Hill Rd .... Menlo Park CA 94025	877-312-5521	650-233-2750	780
KPDQ-FM 93.9 (Rel) 6400 SE Lake Rd Ste 350 .... Portland OR 97222	800-845-2162	503-786-0600	636-86
KPDX-TV Ch 49 (MNT) 14975 NW Greenbrier Pkwy .... Beaverton OR 97006	866-906-1249	503-906-1249	730
KPLO-FM 94.5 (Ctry) 214 W Pleasant Dr .... Pierre SD 57501 *General	800-658-5439*	605-224-8686	636-84
KPLO-TV Ch 6 (CBS) 501 S Phillips Ave .... Sioux Falls SD 57104	800-888-5356	605-336-1100	730
KPLU-FM 88.5 (NPR) 12180 Pk Ave S .... Tacoma WA 98447	800-677-5758	253-535-7758	636
KPLZ-FM 101.5 (AC) 140 Fourth Ave N Ste 340 .... Seattle WA 98109	888-821-1015	206-404-4000	636-101
KPRF-FM 98.7 (CHR) 6214 W 34th St .... Amarillo TX 79109	866-930-5225	806-355-9777	636-5
KPRS-FM 103.3 (Urban) 11131 Colorado Ave .... Kansas City MO 64137	800-273-8255	816-763-2040	636-58
KPRX-FM 89.1 (NPR) 3437 W Shaw Ave Ste 101 .... Fresno CA 93711	800-275-0764	559-275-0764	636-45
KPTS-TV Ch 8 (PBS) 320 W 21 St .... Wichita KS 67203	800-794-8498	316-838-3090	730-81
KPTV-TV Ch 12 (Fox) 14975 NW Greenbrier Pkwy .... Beaverton OR 97006	866-906-1249	503-906-1249	730
KPVI-TV Ch 6 (NBC) 902 E Sherman St .... Pocatello ID 83201	800-829-3676	208-232-6666	730-56
KPVU-FM 91.3 (NPR) Prairie View A & M University MS 1415 .... Prairie View TX 77446	877-241-1752	936-261-3750	636
KPXE-TV Ch 50 (I) 4220 Shawnee Mission Pkwy Ste 110 B .... Fairway KS 66205	800-646-7296	913-722-0798	730
KPXO-TV Ch 66 (I) 875 Waimanu St Ste 630 .... Honolulu HI 96813	800-987-9936	808-591-1275	730-33
KQC (Kilwins Quality Confections Inc) 1050 Bay View Rd .... Petoskey MI 49770	888-454-5946		122
KQED-FM 88.5 (NPR) 2601 Mariposa St .... San Francisco CA 94110	800-723-3566	415-864-2000	636-97
KQED-TV Ch 9 (PBS) 2601 Mariposa St .... San Francisco CA 94110	866-573-3123	415-864-2000	
KQOD-FM 100.1 (Oldies) 2121 Lancey Dr .... Modesto CA 95355	877-967-6342	209-551-1306	636-71
KQQL-FM 107.9 (Oldies) 1600 Utica Ave S Ste 400 .... Minneapolis MN 55416	800-745-3000	952-417-3000	636-69
KQV-AM 1410 (N/T) 650 Smithfield St Ste 620 Ctr City Towers .... Pittsburgh PA 15222	800-289-2642	412-562-5900	636-85
Kraft Chemical Co 1975 N Hawthorne Ave .... Melrose Park IL 60160	800-345-5200	708-345-5200	144
Kraft Fluid Systems Inc 14300 Foltz Pkwy .... Strongsville OH 44149	800-257-1155	440-238-5545	632
Kraft Power Corp 199 Wildwood Ave .... Woburn MA 01801	800-969-6121	781-938-9100	511
Kraftmaid Cabinetry Inc 15535 S State Ave PO Box 1055 .... Middlefield OH 44062	888-562-7744		114
Kraftware Corp 270 Cox St .... Roselle NJ 07203 *Cust Svc	800-221-1728*		600
Kramer Laboratories Inc 8778 SW Eigth St .... Miami FL 33174	800-824-4894	305-223-1287	576
Kramig Insulation 323 S Wayne Ave .... Cincinnati OH 45215	888-579-0079	513-761-4010	190-9
Krannert Ctr for the Performing Arts 500 S Goodwin Ave .... Urbana IL 61801	800-527-2849	217-333-6700	565
Kraton Performance Polymers Inc 15710 John F Kennedy Blvd Ste 300 .... Houston TX 77032 *NYSE: KRA*	800-457-2866	281-504-4950	598-2
Kratos Defense & Security Solutions Inc 4820 Eastgate Mall Ste 200 .... San Diego CA 92121	877-548-7911	858-332-3700	261
Kraus-Anderson Capital Inc 523 S Eigth St Ste 523 .... Minneapolis MN 55404	888-547-3983	612-305-2934	216
Kraus-Anderson Co (KA) 523 S Eigth St .... Minneapolis MN 55404	888-547-3983	612-305-2934	186
Kraus-Anderson Insurance 420 Gateway Blvd .... Burnsville MN 55337	800-207-9261	952-707-8200	387
KRBE-FM 104.1 (CHR) 9801 Westheimer Rd Ste 700 .... Houston TX 77042	888-955-2993	713-266-1000	636-52
KRCC-FM 91.5 (NPR) 912 N Weber St .... Colorado Springs CO 80903	800-748-2727	719-473-4801	636-29
KRCD-FM 103.9 (Span) 655 N Central Ave Ste 2500 .... Glendale CA 91203	888-382-1222	818-500-4500	636
Kreamer Feed Inc PO Box 38 .... Kreamer PA 17833	800-767-4537	570-374-8148	276
Kreher Steel Company LLC 1550 N 25th Ave .... Melrose Park IL 60160	800-323-0745		487
Krehling Industries Inc 1399 Hagy Way .... Harrisburg PA 17110	800-839-1654	717-232-7936	183
Kreider Farms 1461 Lancaster Rd .... Manheim PA 17545	888-665-4415	717-665-4415	10-2
Kreisler Mfg Corp 180 Van Riper Ave .... Elmwood Park NJ 07407	888-750-5834	201-791-0700	21
KREM-TV Ch 2 (CBS) 4103 S Regal St .... Spokane WA 99223	888-404-3922	509-448-2000	730-72
Kress Employment Screening 320 Westcott St Ste 108 .... Houston TX 77007	888-636-3693	713-880-3693	626
Krieger Specialty Products Co 4880 Gregg Rd .... Pico Rivera CA 90660	866-203-5060	562-695-0645	234
Krillion Inc 607A W Dana St .... Irvine CA 92618	877-784-0805	949-784-0800	178
Kripalu Ctr for Yoga & Health 57 Interlaken Rd .... Stockbridge MA 01262	800-741-7353	413-448-3400	697
Krispy Kreme Doughnuts Corp 370 Knollwood St Ste 500 .... Winston-Salem NC 27103 *NYSE: KKD*	800-457-4779	336-725-2981	67

Name	Address	City	State	ZIP	Toll-Free	Phone	Class
Kristin Brooks Hope Ctr (KBHC)	1250 24th St NW	Washington	DC	20037	**800-784-2433**	202-536-3200	47-17
KRKS-FM 94.7 (Rel)	3131 S Vaughn Way Ste 601	Aurora	CO	80014	**888-346-4700**	303-750-5687	636
KRLD-AM 1080 (N/T)	4131 N Central Expy Ste 100	Dallas	TX	75204	**800-289-1080**	214-525-7000	636-34
KRMA-TV Ch 6 (PBS)	1089 Bannock St	Denver	CO	80204	**800-274-6666**	303-892-6666	730-20
KRMC (Kingman Regional Medical Ctr)	3269 Stockton Hill Rd	Kingman	AZ	86409	**877-757-2101**	928-757-2101	371-3
KRMG-AM 740 (N/T)	7136 S Yale Ave Ste 500	Tulsa	OK	74136	**855-297-9696**	918-493-7400	636-115
KRNO-FM 106.9 (AC)	961 Matley Ln Ste 120	Reno	NV	89502	**888-505-1261**	775-829-1964	636-88
Kroger Co	1014 Vine St	Cincinnati	OH	45202	**800-576-4377**	513-762-4000	342 *NYSE: KR*
Krohn Industries Inc	PO Box 98	Carlstadt	NJ	07072	**800-526-6299**	201-933-9696	404
Kroll Background America Inc	100 Centerview Dr Ste 300	Nashville	TN	37214	**800-697-7189**	615-320-9800	626
Kroll Factual Data Inc	5200 Hahns Peak Dr	Loveland	CO	80538	**800-929-3400**	970-663-5700	218
Kroll Ontrack Inc	9023 Columbine Rd	Eden Prairie	MN	55347	**800-872-2599**	952-937-5161	179-12
KROM-FM 92.9 (Span)	1777 NE Loop 410 Ste 400	San Antonio	TX	78217	**888-382-1222**	210-821-6548	636-95
Krones Inc	9600 S 58th St PO Box 321801	Franklin	WI	53132	**800-752-3787**	414-409-4000	540
Kronos Inc	297 Billerica Rd	Chelmsford	MA	01824	**888-293-5549**	978-250-9800	179-11
Kronos Micronutrients	213 W Moxee Ave PO Box 1167	Moxee	WA	98936	**800-541-4086**	509-248-4911	280
Kronos Products Inc	One Kronos Dr	Glendale Heights	IL	60139	**800-621-0099**		295-26
Kronos Worldwide Inc	14950 Heathrow Forest Prkwy Ste 230	Houston	TX	77060	**800-866-5600**	281-423-3300	143 *NYSE: KRO*
KROQ-FM 106.7 (Alt)	5901 Venice Blvd	Los Angeles	CA	90034	**800-520-1067**	323-930-1067	636-62
KROX-AM 1260 (Var)	208 S Main St	Crookston	MN	56716	**800-222-2537**	218-281-1140	636
Kroy LLC	3830 Kelley Ave	Cleveland	OH	44114	**888-888-5769***	216-426-5600	174-6 *Cust Svc
KRQE-TV Ch 13 (CBS)	13 Broadcast Plz SW	Albuquerque	NM	87104	**800-283-4227**	505-243-2285	730-2
KRRO-FM 103.7 (Rock)	500 S Phillips Ave	Sioux Falls	SD	57104	**877-263-7995**	605-331-5350	636-103
KRSD-FM 88.1 (Clas)	480 Cedar St	Saint Paul	MN	55101	**800-228-7123**	651-290-1500	636-103
KRTH-FM 101.1 (Oldies)	5670 Wilshire Blvd Ste 200	Los Angeles	CA	90036	**800-232-5784**	323-936-5784	636-62
Kruepke Trucking Inc	2881 Hwy P	Jackson	WI	53037	**800-798-5000***	262-677-3155	770 *Cust Svc
Kruger Street Toy & Train Museum	144 Kruger St	Wheeling	WV	26003	**877-242-8133**	304-242-8133	513
Kruse Adhesive Tape Inc	1610 E McFadden Ave	Santa Ana	CA	92705	**800-992-7702**	714-640-2130	722
KRVK-FM 107.9 (Rock)	150 N Nichols Ave	Casper	WY	82601	**800-442-2256**	307-266-5252	636-21
Kryptonite Kollectibles	1441 Plainfield Ave	Janesville	WI	53545	**877-646-1728**		779
KSA Engineers Inc	140 E Tyler St Ste 600 Ste 600	Longview	TX	75601	**877-572-3647**	903-236-7700	261
KSAN-FM 107.7 (Alt)	750 Battery St 3rd Fl	San Francisco	CA	94105	**888-303-2663**	415-995-6800	636-97
KSAZ-TV Ch 10 (Fox)	511 W Adams St	Phoenix	AZ	85003	**888-369-4762**	602-257-1234	730-54
KSBI (Kobelco Stewart Bolling Inc)	1600 Terex Rd	Hudson	OH	44236	**800-464-0064**	330-655-3111	383
Ksbj	1722 Treble Dr	Humble	TX	77338	**877-644-5725**	281-446-5725	115
Ksby-Tv	1772 Calle Joaquin	San Luis Obispo	CA	93405	**800-583-4135**	805-541-6666	115
KSCF-FM 103.7 (N/T)	8033 Linda Vista Rd	San Diego	CA	92111	**888-388-1037**	858-571-7600	636-96
KSGN-FM 89.7 (Rel)	2048 Orange Tree Ln Ste 200	Redlands	CA	92374	**888-897-5746**	909-583-2150	636-89
KSHB-TV Ch 41 (NBC)	4720 Oak St	Kansas City	MO	64112	**800-222-1222**	816-753-4141	
KSKN-TV Ch 22 (CW)	4103 S Regal St	Spokane	WA	99223	**888-404-3922**	509-448-2000	730-72
KSKS-FM 93.7 (Ctry)	1071 W Shaw Ave	Fresno	CA	93711	**800-767-5477**	559-490-5800	636-45
KSLR-AM 630 (Rel)	9601 McAllister Fwy Ste 1200	San Antonio	TX	78216	**888-346-4700**	210-344-8481	636-95
KSL-TV Ch 5 (NBC)	PO Box 1160	Salt Lake City	UT	84110	**800-862-9098**	801-575-5555	730-66
KSME-FM 96.1 (CHR)	4270 Byrd Dr	Loveland	CO	80538	**877-498-9600**	970-461-2560	636
KSMQ-TV Ch 15 (PBS)	2000 Eigth Ave NW	Austin	MN	55912	**800-658-2539**	507-433-0678	730
KSMS-FM 90.5 (NPR)	Missouri State University 901 S National Ave	Springfield	MO	65804	**800-767-5768**	417-836-5878	636-106
KSMU-FM 91.1 (NPR)	Missouri State University 901 S National Ave	Springfield	MO	65897	**800-767-5768**	417-836-5878	636-106
KSNT-TV Ch 27 (NBC)	6835 NW Hwy 24	Topeka	KS	66618	**800-222-8477**	785-582-4000	730-77
KSNW-TV	833 N Main St	Wichita	KS	67203	**800-325-0778**	316-265-3333	730-81
KSOF-FM 98.9 (AC)	83 E Shaw Ave Ste 150	Fresno	CA	93710	**800-423-5870**	559-230-4300	636-45
KSON-FM 97.3 (Ctry)	1615 Murray Canyon Rd Ste 710	San Diego	CA	92108	**800-988-4253**	619-291-9797	636-96
KSPR-TV Ch 33 (ABC)	1359 St Louis St	Springfield	MO	65802	**888-435-1464**	417-831-1333	730-74
KSPS Public TV	3911 S Regal St	Spokane	WA	99223	**800-735-2377**	509-443-7800	730-72
KSPX-TV Ch 29 (I)	3352 Mather Field Rd	Rancho Cordova	CA	95670	**800-987-9936**	916-368-2929	730
KSTP-AM 1500 (N/T)	3415 University Ave	Saint Paul	MN	55114	**877-615-1500**	651-646-8255	636-69
KSTW-TV Ch 11 (CW)	1000 Dexter Ave N Ste 205	Seattle	WA	98109	**866-313-5789**	206-441-1111	730
KSTX-FM 89.1 (NPR)	8401 Datapoint Dr Ste 800	San Antonio	TX	78229	**800-622-8977**	210-614-8977	636-95
KSWF-FM 100.5 (Ctry)	1856 S Glenstone Ave	Springfield	MO	65804	**844-289-7234**	417-890-5555	636-106
K-Swiss Inc	31248 Oak Crest Dr	Westlake Village	CA	91361	**800-938-8000**	818-706-5100	300 *NASDAQ: KSWS*
KSWV-AM 810 (Span)	102 Taos St	Santa Fe	NM	87505	**800-873-3372**	505-989-7441	636-99
K-Systems Inc	2104 Aspen Dr	Mechanicsburg	PA	17055	**800-221-0204**	717-795-7711	179-1
KT (Kokomo Tribune)	300 N Union St PO Box 9014	Kokomo	IN	46901	**800-382-0696**	765-459-3121	525-2
KTAL-TV Ch 6 (NBC)	3150 N Market St	Shreveport	LA	71107	**800-259-4929**	318-629-6000	730-70
Kta-Tator Inc	115 Technology Dr	Pittsburgh	PA	15275	**800-582-4243**	412-788-1300	261
KTBN-TV Ch 40 (TBN)	2442 Michelle Dr	Tustin	CA	92780	**888-731-1000**	714-832-2950	730
KTBS-TV Ch 3 (ABC)	312 E Kings Hwy	Shreveport	LA	71104	**866-543-3296**	318-861-5800	730-70
KTBY-TV Ch 4 (Fox)	2700 E Tudor Rd	Anchorage	AK	99507	**877-304-1313**	907-561-1313	730-3
KTC (Kaplan Telephone Company Inc)	220 N Cushing Ave	Kaplan	LA	70548	**866-643-7171**	337-643-7171	726
KTHT-FM	1990 Post Oak Blvd Ste 2300	Houston	TX	77056	**877-745-6591**	713-963-1200	636-52
KTHV-TV Ch 11 (CBS)	720 S Izard St	Little Rock	AR	72201	**800-621-3362**	501-376-1111	730-39
KTKZ-AM 1380 (N/T)	1425 River Pk Dr Ste 520	Sacramento	CA	95815	**888-923-1380**	916-924-0710	636-92
KTNV-TV Ch 13 (ABC)	3355 S Valley View Blvd	Las Vegas	NV	89102	**800-877-1620**	702-876-1313	730-37
KTOM-FM 92.7 (Ctry)	903 N Main St	Salinas	CA	93906	**800-660-5866***	831-755-8181	636 *General
KTOZ-FM 95.5 (AC)	1856 S Glenstone Ave	Springfield	MO	65804	**800-757-9550**	417-890-5555	636-106
KTRC-AM 1260 (N/T)	2502 Camino Entrada Ste C	Santa Fe	NM	87507	**888-321-5123**	505-471-1067	636-99
KTRS-AM 550 (N/T)	638 Westport Plaza	Saint Louis	MO	63146	**888-550-5877**	314-453-5500	636-93
KTRS-FM 104.7 (CHR)	150 N Nichols Ave	Casper	WY	82601	**800-442-2256**	307-266-5252	636-21
KTSA-AM 550 (N/T)	4050 Eisenhauer Rd	San Antonio	TX	78218	**800-299-5872**	210-654-5100	636-95
KTSD-FM 91.1 (NPR)	555 N Dakota St PO Box 5000	Vermillion	SD	57069	**800-456-0766**	605-677-5861	636
KTSD-TV Ch 10 (PBS)	555 N Dakota St PO Box 5000	Vermillion	SD	57069	**800-333-0789**		730
KTSF-TV Ch 26 (Ind)	100 Valley Dr	Brisbane	CA	94005	**800-772-1213**	415-468-2626	730
KTTC-TV Ch 10 (NBC)	6301 Bandel Rd NW	Rochester	MN	55901	**800-288-1656**	507-288-4444	730-63
KTTS-FM 94.7 (Ctry)	2330 W Grand St	Springfield	MO	65802	**855-574-2533**	417-865-6614	636-106
KTTW-TV Ch 7 (Fox)	2817 W 11th St	Sioux Falls	SD	57104	**800-369-4762**	605-338-0017	730-71
K-Tube Technologies	13400 Kirkham Way	Poway	CA	92064	**800-394-0058**	858-513-9229	472
KTVB-TV Ch 7 (NBC)	5407 Fairview	Boise	ID	83706	**800-537-8939**	208-375-7277	730-10
KTVF-TV Ch 11 (NBC)	3650 Braddock St	Fairbanks	AK	99701	**855-255-5975**	907-458-1800	730-26
KTVQ-TV Ch 2 (CBS)	3203 Third Ave N	Billings	MT	59101	**800-908-4490**	406-252-5611	
KTWB-FM 101.9 (Ctry)	500 S Phillips Ave	Sioux Falls	SD	57104	**877-263-7995**	605-331-5350	636-103
KTWU-TV Ch 11 (PBS)	1700 College	Topeka	KS	66621	**800-866-5898**	785-670-1111	730-77
KTXR-FM 101.3 (AC)	3000 E Chestnut Expy	Springfield	MO	65806	**855-586-8852***	417-862-3751	636-106 *General
KTXY-FM 106.9 (AC)	3215 Lemone Industrial Blvd Ste 200	Columbia	MO	65201	**800-500-9107**	573-875-1099	636
KUA (Kissimmee Utility Authority Inc)	1701 W Carroll St	Kissimmee	FL	34741	**877-582-7700**	407-933-7777	775
KUAC FM/TV	PO Box 755620	Fairbanks	AK	99775	**800-727-6543**	907-474-7491	624
KUAC-FM 89.9 (NPR)	312 Tanana Dr Ste 202 PO Box 755620	Fairbanks	AK	99775	**800-727-6543**	907-474-7491	636-41
KUAC-TV Ch 9 (PBS)	University of Alaska PO Box 755620	Fairbanks	AK	99775	**800-727-6543**	907-474-7491	730-26
KUAD-FM 99.1 (Ctry)	600 Main St	Windsor	CO	80550	**800-500-2599**		636
KUAF 91.3 Public Radio	9 S School Ave	Fayetteville	AR	72701	**800-522-5823**	479-575-2556	636
KUBE-FM 93.3 (AC)	351 Elliott Ave W Ste 300	Seattle	WA	98119	**877-933-9393**	206-494-2000	636-101
Kubin-Nicholson Corp	8440 N 87th St	Milwaukee	WI	53224	**800-858-9557**	414-586-4300	8
Kubota Tractor Corp	3401 Del Amo Blvd	Torrance	CA	90503	**888-458-2682**	310-370-3370	273
Kubotek USA	Two Mt Royal Ave Ste 500	Marlborough	MA	01752	**800-372-3872**	508-229-2020	179-5
KUED-TV Ch 7 (PBS)	101 Wasatch Dr Rm 215	Salt Lake City	UT	84112	**800-477-5833**	801-581-7777	730-66
Kuehne & Nagel Inc	10 Exchange Pl	Jersey City	NJ	07302	**866-914-0444**	201-413-5500	444
KUER-FM 90.1 (NPR)	101 S Wasatch Dr	Salt Lake City	UT	84112	**800-491-1148**	801-581-6625	636-94
KUFM-FM 89.1 (NPR)	32 Campus Dr University of Montana	Missoula	MT	59812	**800-325-1565**	406-243-4931	636
Kugler Co	209 W Third St PO Box 1748	McCook	NE	69001	**800-445-9116**	308-345-2280	276

Name	Address	City	State	ZIP	Toll-Free	Phone	Class
KUGN-AM 590 (N/T)	1200 Executive Pkwy Ste 440	Eugene	OR	97401	**800-590-5846**	541-284-8500	636-39
KUHF-FM 88.7 (Clas)	4343 Elgin St 3rd Fl	Houston	TX	77204	**877-252-0436**	713-743-0887	636-52
Kuhlman Corp	1845 Indian Woods Cir	Maumee	OH	43537	**800-669-3309**	419-897-6000	183
Kuhlman Inc	N 56 W 16865 Ridgewood Dr	Menomonee Falls	WI	53051	**800-781-9229**	262-252-9400	190-10
Kuhn Flowers Inc	3802 Beach Blvd	Jacksonville	FL	32207	**800-458-5846**	904-398-8601	292
Kula Hospital	100 Keokea Pl	Kula	HI	96790	**800-845-6733**	808-878-1221	445
Kultur International Films Ltd	PO Box 755	Forked River	NJ	08731	**888-329-2580**		506
Kumho Tire USA Inc	10299 Sixth St	Rancho Cucamonga	CA	91730	**800-445-8646**	909-428-3999	745
Kumon North America Inc	300 Frank W Burr Blvd Glenpointe Ctr E Ste 6	Teaneck	NJ	07666	**800-222-6284**	201-928-0444	146
KUNM-FM 89.9 (NPR)	1University of New Mexico MSC 06 3520	Albuquerque	NM	87131	**877-277-4806**	505-277-4806	636-4
Kuno Creative Group LLC	36901 American Wy Ste 2A	Avon	OH	44011	**800-303-0806**		4
Kuntzman Trucking Inc	13515 Oyster Rd	Alliance	OH	44601	**800-362-9779**	330-821-9160	770
KUOW-FM 94.9 (NPR)	4518 University Way NE Ste 310	Seattle	WA	98105	**800-289-5869**	206-543-2710	636-101
KUPX-TV Ch 16 (I)	466C Lawndale Dr	Salt Lake City	UT	84115	**888-467-2988**	801-474-0016	730-66
Kuraray America Inc	2625 Bay Area Blvd Ste 600	Houston	TX	77058	**800-423-9762**		734-1
Kuriyama of America Inc	360 E State Pkwy	Schaumburg	IL	60173	**800-800-0320**	847-755-0360	192-2
Kurt Manufacturing Co	5280 Main St NE	Minneapolis	MN	55421	**800-458-7855**	763-572-1500	449
Kurt S Adler Inc	Seven W 34th St	New York	NY	10001	**866-919-9757**	212-924-0900	327
Kurt Weiss Greenhouses Inc	95 Main St	Center Moriches	NY	11934	**800-344-7805**	631-878-2500	366
Kurtz Bros Company Inc	400 Reed St PO Box 392	Clearfield	PA	16830	**800-252-3811**	814-765-6561	85
Kurtzon Lighting Inc	1420 S Talman Ave	Chicago	IL	60608	**800-837-8937**	773-277-2121	435
Kurz Electric Solutions Inc	1325 McMahon Dr	Neenah	WI	54956	**800-776-3629**	920-886-8200	700
Kurz-Kasch Inc	511 Byers Rd	Miamisburg	OH	45342	**888-587-9527**	937-299-0990	597
KUSC-FM 91.5 (Clas)	1149 S Hill St Ste H100 PO Box 7913	Los Angeles	CA	90015	**877-587-2227**	213-225-7400	636-62
KUSD-TV Ch 2 (PBS)	555 N Dakota St PO Box 5000	Vermillion	SD	57069	**800-333-0789**		730
KUSM-TV Ch 9 (PBS)	Visual Communications Bldg Rm 183	Bozeman	MT	59717	**800-426-8243**	406-994-3437	730
KUSP-FM 88.9 (NPR)	203 Eigth Ave	Santa Cruz	CA	95062	**800-655-5877**	831-476-2800	636
Kussmaul Electronics Company Inc	170 Cherry Ave	West Sayville	NY	11796	**800-346-0857**	631-567-0314	256
Kustom Fl LLC	265 Hunt Park Cv	Longwood	FL	32750	**866-679-0699**		187
KUTV-TV Ch 2 (CBS)	299 S Main St Ste 150	Salt Lake City	UT	84111	**866-438-0220**	801-839-1234	730-66
Kutztown University	15200 Kutztown Rd	Kutztown	PA	19530	**877-628-1915**	610-683-4000	166
Kuukpik Corp	PO Box 89187	Nuiqsut	AK	99789	**866-480-6220**	907-480-6220	342
KUVO-FM 89.3 (Jazz)	2900 Welton St Ste 200	Denver	CO	80205	**800-574-5886**	303-480-9272	636-35
Kuwait Airways Oasis Club	400 Kelby St	Fort Lee	NJ	07024	**800-458-9248**	201-582-9222	26
Kuwait Embassy	2940 Tilden St NW	Washington	DC	20008	**800-688-9889**	202-966-0702	257
KUWS-FM 91.3 (NPR)	1805 Catlin Ave	Superior	WI	54880	**800-300-8530**	715-394-8530	636
Kuyper College	3333 E Beltline Ave NE	Grand Rapids	MI	49525	**800-511-3749**	616-222-3000	159
KVAL Inc	825 Petaluma Blvd S	Petaluma	CA	94952	**800-553-5825**	707-762-7367	808
K-VA-T Food Stores Inc	PO Box 1158	Abingdon	VA	24212	**800-826-8451**	276-623-5100	342
KVCR-FM 91.9 (NPR)	701 S Mt Vernon Ave	San Bernardino	CA	92410	**800-533-5827**	909-384-4444	636-89
KVIA-TV Ch 7 (ABC)	4140 Rio Bravo St	El Paso	TX	79902	**800-433-7300**	915-496-7777	730-23
KVIE-TV Ch 6 (PBS)	2030 W El Camino Ave	Sacramento	CA	95833	**800-347-5843**	916-929-5843	730-64
KVIL-FM 103.7 (AC)	4131 N Central Expy Ste 1000	Dallas	TX	75204	**877-787-1037**	214-525-7000	636-34
KVKI-FM 96.5 (AC)	6341 W Port Ave	Shreveport	LA	71129	**800-487-1840**	318-688-1130	636-102
KVLC-FM 101.1 (Oldies)	101 Perkins Dr	Las Cruces	NM	88005	**877-527-1011**	575-527-1111	636
KVLY-TV Ch 11 (NBC)	1350 21st Ave S	Fargo	ND	58103	**800-450-5844**	701-237-5211	730-27
KVOR-AM 740 (N/T)	6805 Corporate Dr Ste 130	Colorado Springs	CO	80919	**800-232-6459**	719-593-2700	636-29
KVPR-FM 89.3 (NPR)	3437 W Shaw Ave Ste 101	Fresno	CA	93711	**800-275-0764**	559-275-0764	636-45
KWC (Kam Wah Chung State Heritage Site)	725 Summer St NE Ste C	Salem	OR	97301	**800-551-6949**	503-986-0707	558
KWCG Inc	12255 Pkwy Centre Dr	San Diego	CA	92064	**877-464-5924**		260
KWCH-TV Ch 12 (CBS)	2815 E 37th St N	Wichita	KS	67219	**877-257-6921**	316-838-1212	730-81
KWEB-AM 1270 (Sports)	1530 Greenview Dr SW Ste 200	Rochester	MN	55902	**888-519-6683**	507-288-3888	636-91
KWHE-TV Ch 14 (Ind)	1188 Bishop St Ste 502	Honolulu	HI	96813	**800-218-1414**	808-538-1414	730-33
Kwik Goal Ltd	140 Pacific Dr	Quakertown	PA	18951	**800-531-4252**	215-536-2200	701
Kwik Lok Corp	2712 S 16th Ave PO Box 9548	Yakima	WA	98909	**800-688-5945**	509-248-4770	297
Kwik-Wall Co	1010 E Edwards St	Springfield	IL	62703	**800-280-5945**	217-522-5553	286
KWJ Engineering Inc	8430 Central Ave Ste C	Newark	CA	94560	**800-472-6626**	510-794-4296	683
KWJJ-FM 99.5 (Ctry)	0700 SW Bancroft St	Portland	OR	97239	**866-239-9653**	503-733-9653	636-86
KWPX-TV Ch 33 (I)	8112-C 304th Ave SE PO Box 426	Preston	WA	98050	**888-467-2988**	425-222-6010	730
KWS Mfg Company Ltd	3041 Conveyor Dr	Burleson	TX	76028	**800-543-6558**	817-295-2247	208
KWTV-TV Ch 9 (CBS)	7401 N Kelley Ave	Oklahoma City	OK	73111	**888-550-5988**	405-843-6641	730-50
KWWL-TV Ch 7 (NBC)	500 E Fourth St	Waterloo	IA	50703	**800-947-7746**	319-291-1200	730
KWYE-FM 101.1 (CHR)	1071 W Shaw Ave	Fresno	CA	93711	**800-345-9101**	559-490-5800	636-45
KWYR-FM 93.7 (AC)	PO Box 491	Winner	SD	57580	**800-388-5997**	605-842-3333	636
KWYY-FM 95.5 (Ctry)	150 N Nichols Ave	Casper	WY	82601	**800-339-4673**	307-266-5252	636-21
KXFG-FM 92.9 (Ctry)	900 E Washington Ste 315	Colton	CA	92324	**888-431-3764**	909-825-9525	636
KXJB-TV Ch 4 (CBS)	1350 21st Ave S	Fargo	ND	58103	**877-571-0774**	701-237-5211	730-27
KXJM-FM 107.5 (AC)	13333 SW 68th Pkwy Ste 310	Portland	OR	97223	**800-567-1075**	503-248-1075	636-86
KXLT-TV Ch 47 (Fox)	6301 Bandel Rd NW	Rochester	MN	55901	**800-452-4368**	507-252-4747	730-63
KXMR-AM 710 (Sports)	3500 E Rosser Ave PO Box 2156	Bismarck	ND	58501	**866-522-5710**	701-255-1234	636-15
KXPR-FM 88.9 (Clas)	7055 Folsom Blvd	Sacramento	CA	95826	**877-480-5900**	916-278-8900	636-92
KXTX-TV Ch 39 (Tele)	4805 Amon Carter Blvd	Fort Worth	TX	76155	**877-266-8365**		730-18
KYCC-FM 90.1 (Rel)	9019 W Ln	Stockton	CA	95210	**800-654-5254**	209-477-3690	636-108
KYE Systems Corp	1301 NW 84th Ave Ste 127	Doral	FL	33126	**800-488-3111**	305-468-9250	174-2
KYLD-FM 94.9 (Urban)	340 Townsend St Ste 5101	San Francisco	CA	94107	**888-333-9490**	415-975-5555	636-97
KYMG-FM 98.9 (AC)	800 E Dimond Blvd Ste 3-370	Anchorage	AK	99515	**877-868-8857**	907-522-1515	636-6
Kyocera America Inc	8611 Balboa Ave	San Diego	CA	92123	**888-955-0800**	858-576-2600	687
Kyocera Industrial Ceramics Corp	5713 E Fourth Plain Rd	Vancouver	WA	98661	**800-826-0527**	360-696-8950	249
Kyocera International Inc	8611 Balboa Ave	San Diego	CA	92123	**877-248-4237**	858-576-2600	357-3
Kyocera Solar Inc	7812 E Acoma Dr Ste 2	Scottsdale	AZ	85260	**800-544-6466**	480-948-8003	687
Kyocera Tycom Corp	3565 Cadillac	Costa Mesa	CA	92626	**800-823-7284**	714-428-3600	450
Kysela Pere Et Fils Ltd	331 Victory Rd	Winchester	VA	22602	**877-492-7917**	540-722-9228	79-3
Kysor Panel Systems	4201 N Beach St	Fort Worth	TX	76137	**800-633-3426**	817-281-5121	655
KYTV-TV Ch 3 (NBC)	PO Box 3500	Springfield	MO	65808	**888-435-1464**	417-268-3000	730-74
KYUR-TV Ch 13 (ABC)	2700 E Tudor Rd	Anchorage	AK	99507	**877-304-1313**	907-561-1313	730-3
KYXY-FM 96.5 (AC)	8033 Linda Vista Rd	San Diego	CA	92111	**888-560-9650**	858-571-7600	636-96
KYYY-FM 92.9 (AC)	3500 E Rosser Ave	Bismarck	ND	58501	**866-929-9393**	701-255-1234	636-15
KZBB-FM 97.9 (CHR)	311 Lexington Ave	Fort Smith	AR	72901	**866-503-1398**	479-782-8888	
KZCH-FM 96.3 (CHR)	9323 E 37th St N	Wichita	KS	67226	**800-800-1013**	316-494-6600	
KZHT-FM 97.1 (CHR)	2801 S Decker Lake Dr	Salt Lake City	UT	84119	**800-888-8499**	801-908-1300	636-94
KZOK-FM 102.5 (CR)	1000 Dexter Ave N	Seattle	WA	98109	**800-252-1025**	206-421-1025	636-101
KZSN-FM 102.1 (Ctry)	9323 E 37th St N	Wichita	KS	67226	**800-505-0098**	316-494-6600	
KZZP-FM 104.7 (CHR)	4686 E Van Buren St Ste 300	Phoenix	AZ	85008	**877-541-1966**	602-374-6000	636-83
KZZU-FM 92.9 (CHR)	500 W Boone Ave	Spokane	WA	99201	**866-845-0929**	509-324-4200	636-104

L

Name	Address	City	State	ZIP	Toll-Free	Phone	Class
L & H Packing Co	PO Box 831368	San Antonio	TX	78283	**800-999-3241**	210-532-3241	468
L & L Nursery Supply Co Inc	2552 Shenandoah Way	San Bernardino	CA	92407	**800-624-2517**	909-591-0461	293
L & M Radiator Inc	1414 E 37th St	Hibbing	MN	55746	**800-346-3500**	218-263-8993	60
L & N Federal Credit Union	9265 Smyrna Pkwy	Louisville	KY	40229	**800-443-2479**	502-368-5858	219
L & S Truck Ctr of Appleton Inc	330 N Bluemound Dr PO Box 1255	Appleton	WI	54914	**888-617-3140**	920-749-1700	56
L B L Group	4281 Katella Ave Ste 221	Los Alamitos	CA	90720	**800-451-8037**	714-236-8270	681
L B Plastics Inc	PO Box 907	Mooresville	NC	28115	**800-752-7739**	704-663-1543	603
L Bornstein & Co Inc	321 Washington St	Somerville	MA	02143	**800-842-1111**	617-776-3555	358
L C Industries	1 Signature Dr	Hazlehurst	MS	39083	**877-524-4722**	601-894-1771	501
L E Coppersmith Inc	525 S Douglas St	El Segundo	CA	90245	**888-827-4388**	310-607-8000	310
L M Scofield Co	6533 Bandini Blvd	Los Angeles	CA	90040	**800-800-9900**	323-720-8810	184
L Suzio Concrete Company Inc	975 Westfield Rd	Meriden	CT	06450	**888-789-4626**	203-237-8421	183

	Toll-Free	Phone	Class
L Thorn Co Inc			
6000 Grant Line Rd			
PO Box 198. . . . . New Albany IN 47150	800-662-4594	812-246-4461	192-1
L' Appartement Hotel			
455 Sherbrooke W . . . . Montreal QC H3A1B7	800-363-3010	514-284-3634	376
L'Academie de Cuisine Inc			
16006 Industrial Dr . . . . Gaithersburg MD 20877	800-664-2433	301-670-8670	161
L'Acadie-Nouvelle			
476 Boul St-Pierre Ouest			
PO Box 5536. . . . . Caraquet NB E1W1B7	800-561-2255	506-727-4444	525-1
L'Auberge de Sedona			
301 L'Auberge Ln . . . . Sedona AZ 86336	855-905-5745	928-282-1661	662
L'Auberge Del Mar			
1540 Camino del Mar PO Box 2880 . . . . . . Del Mar CA 92014	800-245-9757	858-259-1515	660
L'Ermitage Beverly Hills Hotel			
9291 Burton Way . . . . Beverly Hills CA 90210	877-235-7582	310-278-3344	376
L'Hotel du Vieux-Quebec			
1190 St Jean St . . . . Quebec QC G1R1S6	800-361-7787	418-692-1850	376
L'Hotel Quebec			
3115 des Hotels Ave . . . . Sainte-Foy QC G1W3Z6	800-567-5276	418-658-5120	376
L'Oreal USA			
575 Fifth Ave . . . . New York NY 10017	800-322-2036	212-818-1500	215
L-3 Avionics Systems			
5353 52nd St SE . . . . Grand Rapids MI 49512	800-253-9525	616-949-6600	522
L-3 Communications Corp			
600 Third Ave 34-35 Fl. . . . . New York NY 10016	800-351-8483	212-697-1111	725
NYSE: LLL			
L-3 Communications Corp Aviation Recorders Div			
6000 Fruitville Rd . . . . Sarasota FL 34232	877-726-2228	941-371-0811	522
L-3 Communications Corp Communication Systems East Div			
1 Federal St . . . . Camden NJ 08103	800-339-6197	856-338-3000	522
L-3 Communications Corp Randtron Antenna Systems Div			
130 Constitution Dr . . . . Menlo Park CA 94025	866-900-7270*	650-326-9500	522
*Sales			
L-3 Communications ESSCO			
90 Nemco Way . . . . Ayer MA 01432	877-282-1168	978-568-5100	638
L-3 Communications Flight International Aviation LLC			
One Lear Dr . . . . Newport News VA 23602	800-358-4685	757-886-5500	24
L-3 Communications Integrated Systems			
10001 Jack Finney Blvd . . . . Greenville TX 75402	877-282-1168	903-455-3450	22
L-3 Communications Telemetry West Div			
9020 Balboa Ave . . . . San Diego CA 92123	800-351-8483	858-694-7500	638
La Beau Bros Inc			
295 N Harrison Ave PO Box 246. . . . . . . Kankakee IL 60901	800-747-9519	815-933-5519	56
La Bella Strings			
256 Broadway . . . . Newburgh NY 12550	800-750-3034	845-562-4400	520
La Belle Dodge Chrysler Jeep Inc			
501 S Main St . . . . Labelle FL 33935	800-226-1193	863-675-2701	56
La Capitol Federal Credit Union			
PO Box 3398 . . . . Baton Rouge LA 70821	800-522-2748	225-342-5055	219
LA Care Health Plan			
555 W Fifth St 29th Fl. . . . . Los Angeles CA 90013	888-839-9909	213-694-1250	388-3
La Costa Resort & Spa			
2100 Costa del Mar Rd . . . . Carlsbad CA 92009	800-854-5000	760-438-9111	660
La Crosse Area Convention & Visitors Bureau			
410 Veterans Memorial Dr . . . . La Crosse WI 54601	800-658-9424	608-782-2366	207
La Crosse Tribune			
401 N Third St . . . . La Crosse WI 54601	800-262-0420	608-782-9710	525-2
LA Darling Co			
1401 Hwy 49B . . . . Paragould AR 72450	800-643-3499	870-239-9564	286
La Follette Utilities Board			
302 N Tennessee Ave			
PO Box 1411. . . . . La Follette TN 37766	800-352-1340	423-562-3316	245
La Fonda			
100 E San Francisco St . . . . Santa Fe NM 87501	800-523-5002	505-982-5511	376
La Grande-Union County Chamber of Commerce			
102 Elm St . . . . La Grande OR 97850	800-848-9969	541-963-8588	137
La Habra Products Inc			
4125 E La Palma Ave Ste 250. . . . . . . Anaheim CA 92807	866-516-0061	714-778-2266	495
La Hacienda Treatment Ctr			
145 La Hacienda Way . . . . Hunt TX 78024	800-749-6160	830-238-4222	717
La Jolla Beach & Tennis Club			
2000 Spindrift Dr . . . . La Jolla CA 92037	888-828-0948	858-454-7126	660
La Jolla Nursing & Rehabilitation Ctr			
2552 Torrey Pines Rd . . . . La Jolla CA 92037	800-861-0086	858-453-5810	445
La Leche League International Inc (LLLI)			
957 N Plum Grove Rd . . . . Schaumburg IL 60173	800-525-3243	847-519-7730	47-17
La Marche Mfg Co			
106 Bradrock Dr . . . . Des Plaines IL 60018	888-232-9562	847-299-1188	253
La Mesa Rv Ctr Inc			
7430 Copley Pk Pl . . . . San Diego CA 92111	888-509-4199*	858-874-8000	56
*Sales			
La Pensione Hotel			
606 W Date St . . . . San Diego CA 92101	800-232-4683	619-236-8000	376
La Petite Bretonne Inc			
1210 Boul Mich Le-Bohec . . . . Blainville QC J7C5S4	800-361-3381	450-435-3381	296-8
La Plata Electric Assn Inc			
45 Stewart St . . . . Durango CO 81303	888-839-5732	970-247-5786	245
La Playa Beach & Golf Resort			
9891 Gulf Shore Dr . . . . Naples FL 34108	800-237-6883	239-597-3123	660
La Porte Hospital (LPH)			
1007 Lincolnway PO Box 250. . . . . . . La Porte IN 46350	800-235-6204	219-326-1234	371-3
La Posada de Santa Fe Resort & Spa			
330 E Palace Ave . . . . Santa Fe NM 87501	866-280-3810	505-986-0000	660
La Posada Hotel & Suites			
1000 Zaragoza St . . . . Laredo TX 78040	800-444-2099*	956-722-1701	376
*Resv			
La Quinta Inn & Suites Secaucus Meadowlands			
350 Lighting Way . . . . Secaucus NJ 07094	800-753-3757*	201-863-8700	376
*General			
La Quinta Resort & Club			
49-499 Eisenhower Dr . . . . La Quinta CA 92253	800-598-3828	760-564-4111	660
La Reina Inc			
316 N Ford Blvd . . . . Los Angeles CA 90022	800-367-7522	323-268-2791	295-36
La Roche College			
9000 Babcock Blvd . . . . Pittsburgh PA 15237	800-838-4572*	412-367-9300	166
*Admissions			
La Rosa Del Monte Express Inc			
1133-35 Tiffany St . . . . Bronx NY 10459	800-452-7672	718-991-3300	770
La Salle University			
1900 W Olney Ave . . . . Philadelphia PA 19141	800-328-1910	215-951-1500	166
La Salsa Fresh Mexican Grill			
320 Commerce Ste 100 . . . . Irvine CA 92602	866-452-7257	949-270-8900	661

	Toll-Free	Phone	Class
La Sierra University			
4500 Riverwalk Pkwy . . . . Riverside CA 92515	800-874-5587	951-785-2000	166
La Veta/Cuchara Chamber of Commerce			
132 W Ryus Ave . . . . La Veta CO 81055	866-277-5550	719-742-3676	137
La Vida Llena			
10501 Lagrima de Oro NE . . . . Albuquerque NM 87111	800-922-1344	505-293-4001	663
Lab Products Inc			
742 Sussex Ave PO Box 639 . . . . Seaford DE 19973	800-526-0469	302-628-4300	72
Labatt Breweries of Canada			
207 Queen's Quay W Ste 299 . . . . . . Toronto ON M5J1A7	800-268-2337*	416-361-5050	101
*Cust Svc			
Labcon North America Inc			
3700 Lkeville Hwy . . . . Petaluma CA 94954	800-227-1466	707-766-2100	416
Labconco Corp			
8811 Prospect Ave . . . . Kansas City MO 64132	800-821-5525*	816-333-8811	417
*Cust Svc			
Label Works			
2025 Lookout Dr . . . . North Mankato MN 56002	800-522-3558		619
Labelmaster Co			
5724 N Pulaski Rd . . . . Chicago IL 60646	800-621-5808	773-478-0900	410
Labeltape Inc			
5100 Beltway Dr SE . . . . Caledonia MI 49316	800-928-4537	616-698-1830	410
Labette Bank			
Fourth & Huston PO Box 497. . . . . . . Altamont KS 67330	800-711-5311	620-784-5311	69
Labette Community College			
200 S 14th St . . . . Parsons KS 67357	888-522-3883	620-421-6700	160
LabOne Inc			
10101 Renner Blvd . . . . Lenexa KS 66219	800-646-7788	913-888-1770	415
Labor Finders International Inc			
11426 N Jog Rd . . . . Palm Beach Gardens FL 33418	800-864-7749	561-627-6507	712
Labor Law Center Inc			
12534 Vly view st . . . . Garden Grove CA 92845	800-745-9970		
Laboratory Corp of America Holdings			
358 S Main St . . . . Burlington NC 27215	800-334-5161	336-584-5171	415
NYSE: LH			
Laboratory Institute of Merchandising			
12 E 53rd St . . . . New York NY 10022	800-677-1323	212-752-1530	166
Laborchex Co, The			
2506 Lakeland Dr Ste 200 . . . . Jackson MS 39232	800-880-0366	601-664-6760	626
Labrada Nutrition			
403 Century Plz Dr Ste 440 . . . . Houston TX 77073	800-832-9948		787
Labrie Environmental Group			
175 du Pont . . . . Saint-Nicolas QC G7A2T3	800-463-6638	418-831-8250	509
LABS Inc			
6933 S Revere Pkwy . . . . Centennial CO 80112	866-393-2244	720-528-4750	414
Lac Courte Oreilles Ojibwa Community College			
13466 W Trepania Rd . . . . Hayward WI 54843	888-526-6221	715-634-4790	163
Lace For Less Inc			
1500 Main Ave Ste 3 . . . . Clifton NJ 07011	800-533-5223	973-478-2955	734-4
Lack's Valley Stores Ltd			
1300 San Patricia St . . . . Pharr TX 78577	800-870-6999	956-702-3361	320
Lackawanna College			
501 Vine St . . . . Scranton PA 18509	877-346-3552	570-961-7810	160
Lackawanna County Convention & Visitors Bureau			
99 Glenmaura National Blvd . . . . Scranton PA 18507	800-229-3526	570-496-1701	207
Laclede Electric Co-op			
1400 E Rt 66 . . . . Lebanon MO 65536	800-299-3164	417-532-3164	245
Laclede Gas Co			
720 Olive St . . . . Saint Louis MO 63101	800-887-4173	314-342-0500	775
Laclede Group Inc			
720 Olive St Rm 1517. . . . . Saint Louis MO 63101	800-884-4225	314-342-0500	357-5
NYSE: LG			
La-Co/Markal Co			
1201 Pratt Blvd . . . . Elk Grove Village IL 60007	800-621-4025	847-956-7600	462
LaCrosse Footwear Inc			
17634 NE Airport . . . . Portland OR 97230	800-323-2668*		300
Lacrosse Hall of Fame & Museum			
113 W University Pkwy . . . . Baltimore MD 21210	866-877-7550	410-235-6882	513
Ladenburg Thalmann Financial Services Inc			
4400 Biscayne Blvd 12th Fl . . . . Miami FL 33137	800-523-8425	212-409-2000	681
NYSE: LTS			
Ladies Auxiliary VFW Magazine			
406 W 34th St . . . . Kansas City MO 64111	800-843-1950	816-561-8655	452-10
Lady Bird Johnson Wildflower Ctr			
4801 LaCrosse Ave . . . . Austin TX 78739	877-945-3357	512-292-4200	96
Lady Foot Locker (LFL)			
112 W 34th St . . . . New York NY 10120	800-991-6686		300
Lady Grace Stores Inc			
Five Commonwealth Ave Ste 1 . . . . Woburn MA 01801	800-922-0504	781-569-0727	155-6
Lady of America Franchise Corp			
159 Weston RD Ste 1650 . . . . Weston FL 33326	800-833-5239	954-217-8660	351
Laetitia Vineyards & Winery Inc			
453 Laetitia Vineyard Dr . . . . Arroyo Grande CA 93420	888-809-8463	805-481-1772	79-3
Lafayette Convention & Visitors Commission			
1400 NW Evangeline Thwy . . . . Lafayette LA 70501	800-346-1958	337-232-3737	207
Lafayette Federal Credit Union (Inc)			
3535 University Blvd W . . . . Kensington MD 20895	800-888-6560	301-929-7990	219
Lafayette Hotel			
600 St Charles Ave . . . . New Orleans LA 70130	800-366-2743	504-524-4441	376
Lafayette Life Insurance Co			
400 Broadway . . . . Cincinnati OH 45202	800-443-8793		388-2
Lafayette Museum			
1122 Lafayette St . . . . Lafayette LA 70501	800-346-1958	337-234-2208	513
Lafayette Park Hotel			
3287 Mt Diablo Blvd . . . . Lafayette CA 94549	877-283-8787	925-283-3700	376
Lafayette Steel Erector Inc			
313 Westgate Rd . . . . Lafayette LA 70506	877-234-9435	337-234-9435	190-14
Lafayette Venetian Blind Inc			
3000 Klondike Rd.			
P.O. Box 2838 . . . . West Lafayette IN 47996	800-342-5523		86
Lafayette Wood-Works Inc			
3004 Cameron St . . . . Lafayette LA 70506	800-960-3311	337-233-5250	494
LaFayette-Walker County Library			
305 S Duke St . . . . La Fayette GA 30728	877-842-9733	706-638-2992	431-3
Lafayette-West Lafayette Convention & Visitors Bureau			
301 Frontage Rd . . . . Lafayette IN 47905	800-872-6648	765-447-9999	207
Laflamme Doors & Windows Corp			
39 Industrielle . . . . St. Apollinaire QC G0S2E0	800-463-1922		494
Lafontaine Honda			
2245 S Telegraph Rd . . . . Dearborn MI 48124	866-567-5088		56
LaForce Inc			
1060 W Mason St . . . . Green Bay WI 54303	800-236-8858	920-497-7100	234
Lafourche Parish			
402 Green St PO Box 5548. . . . . Thibodaux LA 70302	800-834-8832	985-446-8427	336

Name	Address	City	State	ZIP	Toll-Free	Phone	Class
LaFrance Equipment Corp	516 Erie St	Elmira	NY	14904	**800-873-8808**	607-733-5511	670
Lago Mar Resort & Club	1700 S Ocean Ln	Fort Lauderdale	FL	33316	**855-209-5677**	954-678-3915	660
Lagoon & Pioneer Village	375 N Lagoon Dr	Farmington	UT	84025	**800-748-5246**	801-451-8000	32
LaGrange College	601 Broad St *Admissions	LaGrange	GA	30240	**800-593-2885***	706-880-8005	166
LaGrange County Chamber of Commerce	901 S Detroit St Ste A	LaGrange	IN	46761	**877-735-0340**	260-463-2443	137
LaGrange County Rural Electric Membership Corp	1995 E US Hwy 20	LaGrange	IN	46761	**877-463-7165**	260-463-7165	245
Laguna Beach Visitors & Conference Bureau	381 Forest Ave	Laguna Beach	CA	92651	**800-877-1115**	949-497-9229	207
Laguna Cliffs Marriott Resort	25135 Pk Lantern	Dana Point	CA	92629	**800-545-7483**	949-661-5000	660
Laguna College of Art & Design	2222 Laguna Canyon Rd	Laguna Beach	CA	92651	**800-255-0762**	949-376-6000	166
Lahey Clinic Foundation Inc	41 Mall Rd	Burlington	MA	01805	**800-524-3955**	781-744-8000	371-3
Laird & Co	One LaiRd Rd	Scobeyville	NJ	07724	**877-438-5247**	732-542-0312	79-1
Laird Norton Tyee	801 Second Ave Ste 1600	Seattle	WA	98104	**800-426-5105**	206-464-5100	398
Laird Plastics Inc	6800 Broken Sound Pkwy Ste 150	Boca Raton	FL	33487	**800-243-9696**	561-443-9100	596
Laitner Brush Co	1561 Laitner Dr *Cust Svc	Traverse City	MI	49686	**800-423-6805***	231-929-3300	102
Laitram LLC	200 Laitram Ln	Harahan	LA	70123	**800-535-7631**	504-733-6000	522
Lake Agassiz Regional Library (LARL)	118 Fifth St S PO Box 900	Moorhead	MN	56560	**800-247-0449**	218-233-3757	431-3
Lake Air	7709 Winpark Dr	Minneapolis	MN	55427	**888-785-2422**	763-546-0994	484
Lake Area Technical Institute	230 11th St NE PO Box 730	Watertown	SD	57201	**800-657-4344**	605-882-5284	160
Lake Arrowhead Resort & Spa	27984 Hwy 189	Lake Arrowhead	CA	92352	**800-800-6792**	909-336-1511	660
Lake Austin Spa Resort	1705 S Quinlan Pk Rd	Austin	TX	78732	**800-847-5637**	512-372-7380	698
Lake Barkley State Resort Park	3500 State Pk Rd	Cadiz	KY	42211	**800-325-1708**		558
Lake Barkley Tourist Commission	82 Days Inn Dr	Kuttawa	KY	42055	**800-355-3885**	270-388-5300	207
Lake Bistineau State Park	103 State Pk Rd	Doyline	LA	71023	**888-677-2478**	318-745-3503	558
Lake Breeze Motel Resort	9000 Congdon Blvd	Duluth	MN	55804	**800-738-5884**	218-525-6808	660
Lake Bruin State Park	201 State Pk Rd	Saint Joseph	LA	71366	**888-677-2784**	318-766-3530	558
Lake Carmi State Park	460 Marsh Farm Rd *Resv	Enosburg Falls	VT	05450	**888-409-7579***	802-933-8383	558
Lake Cascade State Park	970 Dam Rd	Cascade	ID	83611	**866-634-3246**	208-382-6544	558
Lake Champlain Regional Chamber of Commerce	60 Main St Ste 100	Burlington	VT	05401	**877-686-5253**	802-863-3489	137
Lake Charles American Press Inc	PO Box 2893	Lake Charles	LA	70602	**800-737-2283**	337-433-3000	628-8
Lake Charles Civic Ctr	900 Lakeshore Dr	Lake Charles	LA	70601	**888-620-1749**	337-491-1256	565
Lake Claiborne State Park	225 State Pk Rd	Homer	LA	71040	**888-677-2524**	318-927-2976	558
Lake Country Power	2810 Elida Dr	Grand Rapids	MN	55744	**800-421-9959**		245
Lake County	895 Michigan Ave PO Box 130	Baldwin	MI	49304	**800-245-3240**	231-745-4331	336
Lake County Convention & Visitors Bureau	5465 W Grand Ave Ste 100	Gurnee	IL	60031	**800-525-3669**	847-662-2700	207
Lake D'Arbonne State Park	3628 Evergreen Rd	Farmerville	LA	71241	**888-677-5200**	318-368-2086	558
Lake Erie College	391 W Washington St	Painesville	OH	44077	**800-533-4996**	440-375-7050	166
Lake Erie Shores & Islands Welcome Ctr	770 SE Catawba Rd	Port Clinton	OH	43452	**800-441-1271**	419-734-4386	207
Lake Forest College	555 N Sheridan Rd	Lake Forest	IL	60045	**800-828-4751**	847-234-3100	166
Lake Havasu Area Chamber of Commerce	314 London Bridge Rd	Lake Havasu City	AZ	86403	**800-307-3610**	928-855-4115	137
Lake Immunogenics Inc	348 Berg Rd	Ontario	NY	14519	**800-648-9990**		575
Lake Kegonsa State Park	2405 Door Creek Rd *General	Stoughton	WI	53589	**888-947-2757***	608-873-9695	558
Lake Lanier Islands Resort	7000 Holiday Rd	Buford	GA	30518	**800-840-5253**	770-945-8787	660
Lake Lawn Resort	2400 E Geneva St	Delavan	WI	53115	**800-338-5253**	262-728-7950	660
Lake Louise Inn	210 Village Rd PO Box 209	Lake Louise	AB	T0L1E0	**800-661-9237**	403-522-3791	376
Lake Lure Inn & Spa, The	2771 Memorial Hwy	Lake Lure	NC	28746	**888-434-4970**	828-625-2526	376
Lake Lurleen State Park	13226 Lake Lurleen Rd	Coker	AL	35452	**800-760-4089**	205-339-1558	558
Bertrand Crossing	1905 Foundation Dr	Niles	MI	49120	**800-252-1562**	269-695-1391	160
Lake Michigan College *South Haven*	125 Veterans Blvd	South Haven	MI	49090	**800-252-1562**	269-639-8442	160
Lake Monitors Inc	8809 Industrial Dr	Franksville	WI	53126	**800-850-6110**	262-884-9800	202
Lake Morey Resort	One Clubhouse Rd	Fairlee	VT	05045	**800-423-1211**	802-333-4311	660
Lake Murray Resort Park	3323 Lodge Rd	Ardmore	OK	73401	**800-622-6317**	580-223-6600	660
Lake Murray State Park	120 N Robinson Ave Sixth Fl	Oklahoma City	OK	73152	**800-652-6552**		558
Lake Norman Chamber of Commerce	19900 W Catawba Ave Ste 101	Cornelius	NC	28031	**800-305-2508**	704-892-1922	137
Lake of the Ozarks Convention & Visitors Bureau	5815 Hwy 54 PO Box 1498	Osage Beach	MO	65065	**800-386-5253**	573-348-1599	207
Lake of the Torches Resort Casino	510 Old Abe Rd	Lac du Flambeau	WI	54538	**800-258-6724**	715-588-7070	132
Lake Owyhee State Park	725 Summer St NE Ste C	Salem	OR	97301	**800-551-6949**	503-986-0707	558
Lake Placid Convention & Visitors Bureau	49 Parkside Dr	Lake Placid	NY	12946	**800-447-5224**	518-523-2445	207
Lake Placid Lodge	144 Lodge Way	Lake Placid	NY	12946	**877-523-2700**	518-523-2700	376
Lake Placid/Essex County Visitors Bureau	49 Parkside Dr	Lake Placid	NY	12946	**800-447-5224**	518-523-2445	137
Lake Pointe Medical Ctr (LPMC)	6800 Scenic Dr	Rowlett	TX	75088	**866-525-5762**	972-412-2273	371-3
Lake Powell Resorts & Marinas	100 Lakeshore Dr	Page	AZ	86040	**800-622-6317**	888-896-3829	660
Lake Quinault Lodge	345 S Shore Rd	Quinault	WA	98575	**800-562-6672**	360-288-2900	660
Lake Region Co-op Electrical Assn	1401 S Broadway PO Box 643	Pelican Rapids	MN	56572	**800-552-7658**	218-863-1171	245
Lake Region Electric Assn Inc	1212 Main St	Webster	SD	57274	**800-657-5869**	605-345-3379	245
Lake Region Electric Co-op Inc	516 S Lake Region Rd	Hulbert	OK	74441	**800-364-5732**	918-772-2526	245
Lake Region Hospital	712 S Cascade St	Fergus Falls	MN	56537	**800-439-6424**	218-736-8000	371-3
Lake Region State College	1801 College Dr N	Devils Lake	ND	58301	**800-443-1313**	701-662-1514	160
Lake Seminole Square	8333 Seminole Blvd	Seminole	FL	33772	**866-785-9025**	727-391-0500	663
Lake Shore Cryotronics	575 McCorkle Blvd	Westerville	OH	43082	**877-969-0010**	614-891-2243	202
Lake Shore Industries Inc (LSI)	1817 Poplar St PO BOX 3427	Erie	PA	16508	**800-458-0463**		692
Lake Shore Railway Museum	31 Wall St Lake Shore Historical Society	North East	PA	16428	**800-945-0340**	814-725-1911	513
Lake Sunapee Bank	9 Main St PO Box 29	Newport	NH	03773	**800-281-5772**	603-863-5772	357-2
Lake Superior College	2101 Trinity Rd	Duluth	MN	55811	**800-432-2884**	218-733-7600	160
Lake Superior Ind Sch Dist 381	1640 2 Hwy	Two Harbors	MN	55616	**888-878-0136**	218-834-8201	676
Lake Superior State University	650 W Easterday Ave *Admissions	Sault Sainte Marie	MI	49783	**888-800-5778***	906-632-6841	166
Lake Tahoe Visitors Authority	3066 Lk Tahoe Blvd	South Lake Tahoe	CA	96150	**800-288-2463**	530-544-5050	207
Lake Wapello State Park	15248 Campground Rd	Drakesville	IA	52552	**866-495-4868**	641-722-3371	558
Lake Wissota State Park	18127 County Hwy O	Chippewa Falls	WI	54729	**800-847-9367**	715-382-4574	558
Lake Wister State Park	25567 US Hwy 270	Wister	OK	74966	**800-622-6317**	918-655-7212	558
Lakeland Bancorp Inc	250 Oak Ridge Rd *NASDAQ: LBAI*	Oak Ridge	NJ	07438	**866-224-1379**	973-697-2000	357-2
Lakeland College	PO Box 359	Sheboygan	WI	53082	**800-569-2166**	920-565-2111	166
Lakeland Community College	7700 Clocktower Dr	Kirtland	OH	44094	**800-589-8520**	440-525-7000	160
Lakeland Financial Corp	202 E Ctr St *NASDAQ: LKFN*	Warsaw	IN	46580	**800-827-4522**	574-267-6144	357-2
Lakeland Industries Inc	701-7 Koehler Ave *NASDAQ: LAKE*	Ronkonkoma	NY	11779	**800-645-9291**	631-981-9700	569
Lakeland Medical Center-Niles	31 N St Joseph Ave	Niles	MI	49120	**800-968-0115**	269-683-5510	371-3
Lakeland Plastics Inc (LP)	1550 McCormick Blvd	Mundelein	IL	60060	**800-454-4006**	847-680-1550	592
Lakeland Village Beach & Mountain Resort	3535 Lake Tahoe Blvd	South Lake Tahoe	CA	96150	**888-484-7094**	530-544-1685	660
Lakepoint Resort State Park	104 Lakepoint Dr	Eufaula	AL	36027	**800-544-5253**	334-687-8011	558
Lakeport Regional Chamber of Commerce	875 Lakeport Blvd PO Box 295	Lakeport	CA	95453	**866-525-3767**	707-263-5092	137
Lakeridge Health Oshawa	One Hospital Ct	Oshawa	ON	L1G2B9	**866-338-1778**	905-576-8711	371-2
Lakes Entertainment Inc	130 Cheshire Ln Ste 101	Minnetonka	MN	55305	**800-946-9464**	952-449-9092	131
Lakes Region Community College (LRCC)	379 Belmont Rd	Laconia	NH	03246	**800-357-2992**	603-524-3207	160
Lakeshirts Inc	750 Randolph Rd	Detroit Lakes	MN	56501	**800-627-2780**	218-847-2171	60
Lakeshore Chamber of Commerce	5246 Hohman Ave Ste 100	Hammond	IN	46320	**855-464-6368**	219-931-1000	137
Lakeshore Learning Materials	2695 E Dominguez St	Carson	CA	90895	**800-778-4456**		527
Lakeshore Staffing Inc	1 N Franklin St	Chicago	IL	60606	**877-685-2432**	312-251-7575	712
Lakeshore Technical College	1290 N Ave	Cleveland	WI	53015	**888-468-6582**	920-693-1000	788
Lakeside Bank	55 W Wacker Dr	Chicago	IL	60601	**866-892-1572**	312-435-5100	69
Lakeside Behavioral Health System	2911 Brunswick Rd	Memphis	TN	38133	**800-232-5253**	901-377-4700	371-5
Lakeside Foods Inc	808 Hamilton St	Manitowoc	WI	54220	**800-466-3834**	920-684-3356	295-20
Lakeside Inn	100 N Alexander St	Mount Dora	FL	32757	**800-556-5016**	352-383-4101	376
Lakeside International LLC	11000 W Silver Spring Rd	Milwaukee	WI	53225	**800-236-0444**	414-353-4800	56
Lakeside Manufacturing Inc	4900 W Electric Ave	West Milwaukee	WI	53219	**800-558-8565**	414-902-6400	318-1
Lakeside Toyota	3701 N Cswy Blvd *Sales	Metairie	LA	70002	**877-512-8274***	504-833-3311	56
Lakeview Golf Resort & Spa	One Lakeview Dr	Morgantown	WV	26508	**800-624-8300**	304-594-1111	660
Lakeview on the Lake	8696 E Lake Rd	Erie	PA	16511	**888-558-8439**	814-899-6948	376

	Toll-Free	Phone	Class
Lakeville Area Chamber of Commerce & Convention & Visitors Bureau			
19950 Dodd Blvd Ste 101 . . . . Lakeville MN 55044	888-525-3845	952-469-2020	137
Lakeville Journal Co LLC			
33 Bissell St PO Box 1688 . . . . Lakeville CT 06039	800-553-2234	860-435-9873	628-8
Lakewold Gardens			
12317 Gravelly Lk Dr SW . . . . Lakewood WA 98499	888-858-4106	253-584-4106	96
Lakewood Hospital			
14519 Detroit Ave . . . . Lakewood OH 44107	866-588-2264	216-521-4200	371-3
Lakewood Manor			
1900 Lauderdale Dr . . . . Richmond VA 23238	866-521-9100	804-740-2900	663
Lakewood Shores Resort			
7751 Cedar Lake Rd . . . . Oscoda MI 48750	800-882-2493	989-739-2073	660
Lakin Tire West Inc			
15305 Spring Ave . . . . Santa Fe Springs CA 90670	800-488-2752	562-802-2752	745
LallyPak Inc			
1209 Central Ave . . . . Hillside NJ 07205	800-523-8484	908-351-4141	541
Lam Research Corp			
4650 Cushing Pkwy . . . . Fremont CA 94538	800-526-7678	510-572-0200	686
NASDAQ: LRCX			
Lamar Adv Co			
5321 Corporate Blvd . . . . Baton Rouge LA 70808	800-235-2627	225-926-1000	8
NASDAQ: LAMR			
Lamar Community College			
2401 S Main St . . . . Lamar CO 81052	800-968-6920	719-336-2248	160
Lamar County Chamber of Commerce			
1125 Bonham St . . . . Paris TX 75460	800-727-4789	903-784-2501	137
Lamar County Electric Co-op Assn			
1485 N Main St . . . . Paris TX 75460	800-252-8080	903-784-4303	245
Lamar State College			
Port Arthur			
PO Box 310 . . . . Port Arthur TX 77641	800-477-5872	409-983-4921	160
Lamart Corp			
16 Richmond St . . . . Clifton NJ 07015	800-526-2799	973-772-6262	592
Lamartek Inc			
175 NW Washington St . . . . Lake City FL 32055	800-495-1046*	386-752-1087	701
*Orders			
Lamaze International			
2025 M St NW Ste 800 . . . . Washington DC 20036	800-368-4404	202-367-1128	48-8
Lamb County Electric Co-op Inc			
2415 S Phelps Ave . . . . Littlefield TX 79339	800-365-9000	806-385-5191	245
Lambda Chi Alpha International Fraternity			
8741 Founders Rd . . . . Indianapolis IN 46268	800-209-6837	317-872-8000	47-16
Lambda Legal Defense & Education Fund			
120 Wall St Ste 1500 . . . . New York NY 10005	866-542-8336	212-809-8585	47-8
Lambeau Telecom			
1807 N Ctr St . . . . Beaver Dam WI 53916	800-444-4014*	920-887-3148	726
*Cust Svc			
Lambert Saint Louis International Airport			
10701 Lambert International Blvd			
PO Box 10212 . . . . Saint Louis MO 63145	855-787-2227	314-426-8000	27
Lambuth University			
705 Lambuth Blvd . . . . Jackson TN 38301	800-526-2305	731-427-4725	166
Lamers Bus Lines Inc			
2407 S Pt Rd . . . . Green Bay WI 54313	800-236-1240	920-496-3600	106
Lamesa Independent School District			
PO Box 261 . . . . Lamesa TX 79331	888-286-6700	806-872-5461	676
Lamey-Wellehan Inc			
940 Turner St . . . . Auburn ME 04210	800-370-6900	207-784-6595	300
Laminate Technologies Inc			
161 Maule Rd . . . . Tiffin OH 44883	800-231-2523		804
Laminated Wood Systems Inc (LWS)			
1327 285th Rd PO Box 386 . . . . Seward NE 68434	800-949-3526	402-643-4708	804
Laminations			
3010 E Venture Dr . . . . Appleton WI 54911	800-925-2626	920-831-0596	541
Laminators Inc			
3255 Penn St . . . . Hatfield PA 19440	877-663-4277	215-723-8107	804
Lammes Candies Since 1885 Inc			
PO Box 1885 . . . . Austin TX 78767	800-252-1885	512-310-2223	295-8
Lamons Gasket Co			
7300 Airport Blvd . . . . Houston TX 77061	800-231-6906	713-222-0284	325
Lamont Engineers			
548 Main St . . . . Cobleskill NY 12043	800-882-9721	518-234-4028	195
Lamont Ltd			
1530 Bluff Rd . . . . Burlington IA 52601	800-553-5621	319-753-5131	318-2
Lamothe House Hotel			
621 Esplanade Ave . . . . New Orleans LA 70116	800-535-7815		376
LaMotte Co			
802 Washington Ave . . . . Chestertown MD 21620	800-344-3100	410-778-3100	416
Lamplight Farms Inc			
W140 N4900 Lilly Rd . . . . Menomonee Falls WI 53051	888-473-1088*	262-781-9590	435
*Cust Svc			
Lamson & Goodnow Mfg Co			
45 Conway St . . . . Shelburne Falls MA 01370	800-872-6564	413-625-0201	222
Lamvin Inc			
4675 N Ave . . . . Oceanside CA 92056	800-446-6329	760-806-6400	601
Lancaster Bible College			
901 Eden Rd PO Box 83403 . . . . Lancaster PA 17608	800-544-7335	717-569-7071	159
Lancaster City School District			
345 E Mulberry St . . . . Lancaster OH 43130	888-647-4729	740-687-7300	676
Lancaster Colony Commercial Products Inc			
3902 Indianola Ave . . . . Columbus OH 43214	800-292-7260	614-263-2850	299
Lancaster Distributing Co			
1310 Union St . . . . Spartanburg SC 29302	800-845-8287*	864-583-3011	543
*General			
Lancaster Eagle-Gazette			
138 W Chestnut St . . . . Lancaster OH 43130	877-513-7355	740-654-1321	525-2
Lancaster Host Resort			
2300 Lincoln Hwy E . . . . Lancaster PA 17602	800-233-0121*	717-299-5500	660
*Resv			
Lancaster Hotel			
701 Texas St . . . . Houston TX 77002	800-231-0336	713-228-9500	376
Lancaster Knives Inc			
165 Ct St . . . . Lancaster NY 14086	800-869-9666	716-683-5050	488
Lancaster New Era			
Eight W King St PO Box 1328 . . . . Lancaster PA 17603	800-809-4666	717-291-8733	525-2
Lancaster Newspapers Inc			
Eight W King St PO Box 1328 . . . . Lancaster PA 17603	800-809-4666	717-291-8811	628-8
Lancaster Regional Medical Ctr			
250 College Ave . . . . Lancaster PA 17603	800-999-6673	717-291-8211	371-3
Lancaster Theological Seminary			
555 W James St . . . . Lancaster PA 17603	800-393-0654	717-393-0654	167-3
Lancaster Toyota Inc			
5270 Manheim Pk . . . . East Petersburg PA 17520	888-424-1295		56

	Toll-Free	Phone	Class
Lance Camper Mfg Corp			
43120 Venture St . . . . Lancaster CA 93535	800-423-7996	661-949-3322	119
Lancer Corp			
6655 Lancer Blvd . . . . San Antonio TX 78219	800-729-1500	210-310-7000	655
Lancer Label			
301 S 74th St . . . . Omaha NE 68114	800-228-7074*		410
*Cust Svc			
Lancer Orthodontics Inc			
1493 Poinsettia Bldg 143 . . . . Vista CA 92081	800-854-2896*	760-744-5585	228
*NYSE: LANZ ■ *Cust Svc			
Land & Legal Solutions Inc			
300 S Hamilton Ave . . . . Greensburg PA 15601	800-245-7900	724-853-8992	179-10
Land Coast Insulation Inc			
4017 Second St . . . . New Iberia LA 70560	800-333-9424	337-367-7741	190-9
Land Line Magazine			
One NW Oodia Dr . . . . Grain Valley MO 64029	800-444-5791	816-229-5791	452-21
Land O'Frost Inc			
16850 Chicago Ave . . . . Lansing IL 60438	800-323-3308	708-474-7100	468
Land O'Lakes Inc			
4001 Lexington Ave N . . . . Arden Hills MN 55126	800-328-9680	651-481-2222	295-3
Land O'Lakes Inc Dairyman's Div			
400 S 'M' St . . . . Tulare CA 93274	800-328-4155	559-687-8287	295-27
Land O'Lakes Inc Western Feed Div			
4001 Lexington Ave N . . . . Arden Hills MN 55126	800-328-9680		442
Land Rover North America Inc			
555 MacArthur Blvd . . . . Mahwah NJ 07430	800-637-6837		58
Land Span Inc			
1120 Griffin Rd . . . . Lakeland FL 33805	800-248-4847	863-686-6872	770
Landacorp Inc			
500 Orient St Ste 110 . . . . Chico CA 95928	866-828-8263	530-891-0853	179-10
Landair Corp			
1110 Myers St . . . . Greeneville TN 37743	888-526-3247		770
Landau Uniforms Inc			
8410 W Sandidge Rd . . . . Olive Branch MS 38654	800-387-0641*	662-895-7200	153-18
*General			
Landauer Inc			
Two Science Rd . . . . Glenwood IL 60425	800-323-8830	708-755-7000	569
NYSE: LDR			
Landec Ag LLC			
201 N Michigan St . . . . Oxford IN 47971	800-241-7252	765-385-1000	280
Lander University			
320 Stanley Ave . . . . Greenwood SC 29649	800-922-1117*	864-388-8307	166
*Admissions			
Landers Ford Inc			
2082 W Poplar Ave . . . . Collierville TN 38017	888-281-5266		56
Landice Inc			
111 Canfield Ave . . . . Randolph NJ 07869	800-526-3423	973-927-9010	471
Landis Gyr Inc			
2800 Duncan Rd . . . . Lafayette IN 47904	888-390-5733	765-742-1001	248
Landiscor			
7310 N 16th St Ste 275 . . . . Phoenix AZ 85020	866-221-8578	602-248-8989	718
Landmark Aviation			
3501 Aviation Ave . . . . Sioux Falls SD 57104	800-888-1646*	605-336-7791	62
*General			
Landmark Community Newspapers Inc			
601 Taylorsville Rd . . . . Shelbyville KY 40065	800-939-9322	502-633-4334	628-8
Landmark Credit Union			
5445 S Westridge Dr			
PO Box 510910 . . . . New Berlin WI 53151	800-801-1449	262-796-4500	219
Landmark Inn			
230 N Front St . . . . Marquette MI 49855	888-752-6362*	906-228-2580	376
*General			
Landmark International Trucks Inc			
4550 Rutledge Pk . . . . Knoxville TN 37914	800-968-9999	865-637-4881	770
Landmark Lincoln-Mercury Inc			
5000 S Broadway . . . . Englewood CO 80113	866-971-7207	303-761-1560	56
Landmark Plastic Corp			
1331 Kelly Ave . . . . Akron OH 44306	800-242-1183	330-785-2200	601
Landmark Resort			
7643 Hillside Rd . . . . Egg Harbor WI 54209	800-273-7877	920-868-3205	660
Landmark Structures LP			
1665 Harmon Rd . . . . Fort Worth TX 76177	800-888-6816	817-439-8888	189-10
Landmark Theaters			
2222 S Barrington Ave . . . . Los Angeles CA 90064	888-724-6362*	310-473-6701	737
*Cust Svc			
Landmark Tours			
1304 University Ave NE			
Ste 201 . . . . Minneapolis MN 55413	888-231-8735	651-490-5408	750
Landoll Corp			
1900 N St . . . . Marysville KS 66508	800-446-5175*	785-562-5381	465
*Cust Svc			
Landor Assoc Ltd			
1001 Front St . . . . San Francisco CA 94111	888-252-6367	415-365-1700	196
Landry's Restaurants Inc			
1510 W Loop S . . . . Houston TX 77027	800-552-6379	713-850-1010	661
Landry's Seafood House			
6801 Gateway Blvd W . . . . El Paso TX 79925	800-394-3839	915-779-2900	662
Lands' End Inc			
One Lands' End Ln . . . . Dodgeville WI 53595	800-963-4816*		454
*Orders			
Landsberg Orora			
1640 S Greenwood Ave . . . . Montebello CA 90640	888-526-3723*	323-832-2000	552
*Cust Svc			
Landscape Concepts Management			
31745 Alleghany Rd . . . . Grayslake IL 60030	866-655-3800	847-223-3800	419
Landscape Structures Inc			
601 Seventh St S . . . . Delano MN 55328	800-328-0035	763-972-3391	343
Landshire Inc			
12 Tucker Dr . . . . Caseyville IL 62232	800-468-3354	618-293-6525	295-34
Landstar Express America Inc			
13410 Sutton Pk Dr S . . . . Jacksonville FL 32224	800-872-9400	904-398-9400	770
Landstar Gemini Inc			
13410 Sutton Pk Dr S . . . . Jacksonville FL 32224	800-872-9400	262-250-7582	770
Landstar Inway Inc			
1000 Simpson Rd . . . . Rockford IL 61102	800-435-7352	815-972-5000	770
Landstar Logistics Inc			
13410 Sutton Pk Dr S . . . . Jacksonville FL 32224	800-872-9400	904-398-9400	444
Landstar Ranger Inc			
13410 Sutton Pk Dr S . . . . Jacksonville FL 32224	800-872-9400	904-398-9400	770
Landstar System Inc			
13410 Sutton Pk Dr S . . . . Jacksonville FL 32224	800-872-9400	904-398-9400	770
NASDAQ: LSTR			
Lane Aviation Corp			
4389 International Gateway . . . . Columbus OH 43219	800-848-6263	614-237-3747	62

	City	State	ZIP	Toll-Free	Phone	Class
Lane Bryant Inc						
3344 Morse Crossing	Columbus	OH	43215	**866-886-4731***	954-970-2205	155-6
*Cust Svc						
Lane College						
545 Ln Ave	Jackson	TN	38301	**800-960-7533***	731-426-7500	166
*Admissions						
Lane Community College						
4000 E 30th Ave	Eugene	OR	97405	**800-321-2211**	541-463-3000	160
Florence 3149 Oak St	Florence	OR	97439	**800-222-3290**	541-997-8444	160
Lane Press Inc						
87 Meadowland Dr PO Box 130	Burlington	VT	05402	**800-733-3740**	802-863-5555	619
Lane's End Farm						
1500 Midway Rd PO Box 626	Versailles	KY	40383	**800-456-3412**	859-873-7300	365
Lane-Scott Electric Co-op Inc						
410 S High	Dighton	KS	67839	**800-407-2217**	620-397-5327	245
Langdon Hall Country House Hotel & Spa						
One Langdon Dr	Cambridge	ON	N3H4R8	**800-268-1898**	519-740-2100	376
Langer Inc						
2905 Veterans' Memorial Hwy	Ronkonkoma	NY	11779	**800-645-5520**		472
Langham Boston, The						
250 Franklin St	Boston	MA	02110	**800-791-7781**	617-451-1900	376
Langley Federal Credit Union						
1055 W Mercury Blvd	Hampton	VA	23666	**800-826-7490**	757-827-7200	219
Langley Porter Psychiatric Institute						
401 Parnassus Ave	San Francisco	CA	94143	**800-723-7140**	415-476-7000	371-5
Langlois Co						
10810 San Sevaine Way	Mira Loma	CA	91752	**800-962-5993**	951-360-3900	295-16
Langstons Co						
2034 NW Seventh St	Oklahoma City	OK	73106	**800-658-2831**	405-235-9536	229
Language Exchange International						
500 NE Spanish River Blvd						
Ste 19	Boca Raton	FL	33431	**800-223-5836**	561-368-3913	420
Language Line Services						
One Lower Ragsdale Dr Bldg 2	Monterey	CA	93940	**800-752-6096**		758
Language Services Associates Inc						
455 Business Ctr Dr - Ste 100	Horsham	PA	19044	**800-305-9673**		758
Lankenau Medical Ctr						
100 E Lancaster Ave	Wynnewood	PA	19096	**866-225-5654**	484-476-2000	371-3
LANL (Los Alamos National Laboratory)						
PO Box 1663	Los Alamos	NM	87545	**877-723-4101**	505-667-7000	659
Lanly Co, The						
26201 Tungsten Rd	Cleveland	OH	44132	**800-327-8064**	216-731-1115	317
Lanman Oil Co Inc						
PO Box 108	Charleston	IL	61920	**800-677-2819**		572
Lannett Company Inc (LCI)						
13200 Townsend Rd	Philadelphia	PA	19154	**800-325-9994**	215-333-9000	474
NYSE: LCI						
Lansco Colors						
1 Blue Hill Plaza 11th Fl						
PO Box 1685	Pearl River	NY	10965	**800-526-2783**	845-507-5942	543
Lansdowne Resort						
44050 Woodridge Pkwy	Leesburg	VA	20176	**877-509-8400**	703-729-4036	698
Lansing Bldg Products						
8501 Sanford Dr	Richmond	VA	23228	**800-768-5762**	804-266-8771	192-4
Lansing Community College						
419 N Washington Sq	Lansing	MI	48933	**800-644-4522**	517-483-1957	160
Lansing State Journal						
120 E Lenawee St	Lansing	MI	48919	**800-234-1719**	517-377-1111	525-2
Lansmont Corp						
Ryan Ranch Research Pk 17						
Mandeville Ct	Monterey	CA	93940	**800-526-7666**	831-655-6600	341
Lantal Textiles Inc						
1300 Langenthal Dr						
PO Box 965	Rural Hall	NC	27045	**800-334-3309**	336-969-9551	734-1
Lantana Communications Corp						
1700 Tech Centre Pkwy Ste 100	Arlington	TX	76014	**800-345-4211**		44
Lantech Inc						
11000 Bluegrass Pkwy	Louisville	KY	40299	**800-866-0322**	502-815-9109	540
Lantern Lodge Motor Inn						
411 N College St	Myerstown	PA	17067	**800-262-5564**	717-866-6536	376
Lantronix Inc						
167 Technology Dr	Irvine	CA	92618	**800-526-8766***	949-453-3990	725
NASDAQ: LTRX ■ *Orders						
Lanxess Corp						
111 RIDC Pk W Dr	Pittsburgh	PA	15275	**800-526-9377**	412-809-1000	598-3
Lanz Cabinet Shop Inc						
3025 W Seventh Pl	Eugene	OR	97402	**800-788-6332**	541-485-4050	358
Lapeer District Library						
201 Village W Dr S	Lapeer	MI	48446	**866-746-7252**	810-664-9521	431-3
Lapeer Regional Hospital						
1375 N Main St	Lapeer	MI	48446	**888-327-0671**	810-667-5500	371-3
Lapham-Hickey Steel Corp						
5500 W 73rd St	Chicago	IL	60638	**800-323-8443**	708-496-6111	487
LaPine State Park						
15800 State Recreation Rd	La Pine	OR	97739	**800-551-6949**		558
LapLink Software Inc						
600 108th Ave NE Ste 610	Bellevue	WA	98004	**800-343-8080**	425-952-6000	179-12
Lapmaster International LLC						
501 W Algonquin Rd	Mount Prospect	IL	60056	**877-352-8637**	224-659-7101	486
LaPorte County Convention & Visitors Bureau						
4073 S Franklin St	Michigan City	IN	46360	**800-634-2650**	219-872-5055	207
LaPorte Savings Bank, The						
710 Indiana Ave	LaPorte	IN	46350	**866-362-7511**	219-362-7511	69
Laramie Area Chamber of Commerce						
800 S Third St	Laramie	WY	82070	**866-876-1012**	307-745-7339	137
Laramie County Community College						
1400 E College Dr	Cheyenne	WY	82007	**800-522-2993**	307-778-5222	160
Albany County						
1125 Boulder Dr	Laramie	WY	82070	**800-522-2993**	307-721-5138	160
Laramie River Dude Ranch						
25777 County Rd 103	Jelm	WY	82063	**800-551-5731**	970-435-5716	239
Larchmont Engineering & Irrigation Co						
11 Larchmont Ln PO Box 66	Lexington	MA	02420	**877-862-2550**	781-862-2550	274
Larco						
210 NE Tenth Ave PO Box 547	Brainerd	MN	56401	**800-523-6996***	218-829-9797	253
*Cust Svc						
Laredo Morning Times						
111 Esperanza Dr	Laredo	TX	78041	**800-232-7907**	956-728-2500	525-2
Laredo-Webb County Chamber of Commerce						
2310 San Bernardo Ave	Laredo	TX	78042	**800-292-2122**	956-722-9895	137
Larksfield Place						
7373 E 29th St N	Wichita	KS	67226	**866-232-8484**	316-858-3910	663
LARL (Lake Agassiz Regional Library)						
118 Fifth St S PO Box 900	Moorhead	MN	56560	**800-247-0449**	218-233-3757	431-3

	City	State	ZIP	Toll-Free	Phone	Class
LARON Inc						
4255 Santa Fe Dr	Kingman	AZ	86401	**800-248-3430**	928-757-8424	256
Larsen Farms						
2650 N 2375 E	Hamer	ID	83425	**800-767-6104***	208-662-5501	295-18
*Sales						
Larson Boats						
700 Paul Larson Memorial Dr	Little Falls	MN	56345	**800-336-2628***	320-632-5481	89
*General						
Larson Contracting Inc						
508 West Main St	Lake Mills	IA	50450	**800-765-1426**	641-592-5800	190-3
Larson Design Group Inc						
1000 Commerce Pk Dr Ste 201						
PO Box 487	Williamsport	PA	17701	**877-323-6603**	570-323-6603	261
Larson Distributing Co Inc						
5925 Broadway	Denver	CO	80216	**800-999-8115**	303-296-7253	358
Larson King LLP						
30 E Seventh St Ste 2800	Saint Paul	MN	55101	**877-373-5501**	651-312-6500	425
Larson Manufacturing Co						
2333 Eastbrook Dr	Brookings	SD	57006	**800-352-3360***	605-692-6115	235
*Cust Svc						
LarsonAllen LLP						
220 S Sixth St Ste 300	Minneapolis	MN	55402	**888-529-2648**	612-376-4500	2
Larson-Juhl						
3900 Steve Reynolds Blvd	Norcross	GA	30093	**800-221-4123**		308
Larue Coffee						
2631 S 156th Cir	Omaha	NE	68130	**800-658-4498**	402-333-9099	296-8
Las Cruces Convention & Visitors Bureau						
211 N Water St	Las Cruces	NM	88001	**800-429-9488**	575-541-2444	207
Las Cruces Public Schools						
505 S Main St Ste 249	Las Cruces	NM	88001	**888-222-1498**	575-527-5800	676
Las Cruces Sun-News						
256 W Las Cruces Ave	Las Cruces	NM	88005	**877-827-7200**	575-541-5400	525-2
LAS Enterprises Inc						
2413 L & A Rd	Metairie	LA	70001	**800-264-1527**	504-887-1515	188
Las Vegas Chamber of Commerce						
575 Symphony Park Ave Ste 100	Las Vegas	NV	89105	**888-635-7272**	702-641-5822	137
Las Vegas Club Hotel & Casino (LVC)						
18 E Fremont St	Las Vegas	NV	89101	**800-634-6532**	702-385-1664	132
Las Vegas Convention & Visitors Authority						
3150 Paradise Rd	Las Vegas	NV	89109	**877-847-4858**	702-892-0711	207
Las Vegas Convention Ctr						
3150 Paradise Rd	Las Vegas	NV	89109	**877-847-4858**	702-892-0711	206
Las Vegas Motor Speedway						
7000 Las Vegas Blvd N	Las Vegas	NV	89115	**800-644-4444**	702-644-4444	508
LaSalle County						
707 E Etna Rd	Ottawa	IL	61350	**800-247-5243**	815-433-3366	336
LaSalle Grill						
115 W Colfax Ave	South Bend	IN	46601	**800-382-9323**	574-288-1155	662
Lasco Fittings Inc						
414 Morgan St PO Box 116	Brownsville	TN	38012	**800-776-2756**	731-772-3180	589
Lasell College						
1844 Commonwealth Ave	Newton	MA	02466	**888-527-3554***	617-243-2225	166
*Admissions						
Laser Excel						
N6323 Berlin Rd PO Box 279	Green Lake	WI	54941	**800-285-6544**	920-294-6544	449
Laser Institute of America (LIA)						
13501 Ingenuity Dr Ste 128	Orlando	FL	32826	**800-345-2737**	407-380-1553	48-19
Laser Pros International						
One International Ln	Rhinelander	WI	54501	**888-558-5277**	715-369-5995	175
Laser Technology Inc						
7070 S Tucson Way	Englewood	CO	80112	**800-280-6113**	303-649-1000	490
Laserscope						
3070 Orchard Dr	San Jose	CA	95134	**800-878-3399**	408-943-0636	421
LaserVue Eye Ctr						
3540 Mendocino Ave Ste 200	Santa Rosa	CA	95403	**888-527-3745**	707-522-6200	786
Lasko Metal Products Inc						
820 Lincoln Ave	West Chester	PA	19380	**800-233-0268**	610-692-7400	36
LasscoWizer Inc						
485 Hague St	Rochester	NY	14606	**800-854-6595**	585-436-1934	621
Lassen County Chamber of Commerce						
75 N Weatherlow St	Susanville	CA	96130	**877-686-7878**	530-257-4323	137
LassoSoft LLC						
PO Box 33	Manchester	WA	98353	**888-286-7753**	954-302-3526	179-7
Lassus BROS Handy Dandy						
1800 Magnavox Way	Fort Wayne	IN	46804	**800-686-2836***	260-436-1415	205
*General						
Lassus Bros Oil Inc						
1800 Magnavox Way	Fort Wayne	IN	46804	**800-686-2836**	260-436-1415	323
LastMinuteTravel.com Inc						
220 E Central Pkwy						
Ste 4000	Altamonte Springs	FL	32701	**800-442-0568**	407-667-8700	763
Latah Creek Winery						
13030 E Indiana Ave	Spokane	WA	99216	**800-528-2427**	509-926-0164	49-6
Latham Hotel, The						
135 S 17th St	Philadelphia	PA	19103	**877-528-4261**	215-563-7474	376
Latham Seed Co						
131 180th St	Alexander	IA	50420	**877-465-2842**	641-692-3258	685
Lathem Time Corp						
200 Selig Dr SW	Atlanta	GA	30336	**800-241-4990**	404-691-0400	110
Laticrete International Inc						
91 Amity Rd	Bethany	CT	06524	**800-243-4788**	203-393-0010	3
Latigo Ranch						
PO Box 237	Kremmling	CO	80459	**800-227-9655**	970-724-9008	239
Latin Business Assn (LBA)						
120 S San Pedro St Ste 530	Los Angeles	CA	90012	**877-551-7778**	213-628-8510	48-12
Latina Media Ventures LLC						
625 Madison Ave 3rd Fl	New York	NY	10022	**888-489-7753**	212-642-0200	452-11
Latitude Consulting Group Inc						
100 E Michigan Ave Ste 200	Saline	MI	48176	**888-577-2797**		458
Latta's School Supply						
1502 Fourth Ave	Huntington	WV	25701	**800-624-3501**	304-523-8400	528
Latter Day Saints Business College						
95 North 300 West	Salt Lake City	UT	84101	**800-999-5767**	801-524-8100	788
Lattice Inc						
1751 S Naperville Rd Ste 100	Wheaton	IL	60189	**800-444-4309***	630-949-3250	179-12
*Sales						
Lattice Semiconductor Corp						
5555 NE Moore Ct	Hillsboro	OR	97124	**800-528-8423**	503-268-8000	687
NASDAQ: LSCC						
Laughing Elephant						
3645 Interlake Ave N	Seattle	WA	98103	**800-354-0400**		129
Laughlin Air Force Base						
561 Liberty Dr Ste 3	Laughlin AFB	TX	78843	**866-966-1020**	830-298-5988	492-1

Name / Address	City	State	ZIP	Toll-Free	Phone	Class
Laughlin Memorial Hospital 1420 Tuscolum Blvd	Greeneville	TN	37745	**800-852-7157**	423-787-5000	371-3
Laughlin River Lodge. 2700 S Casino Dr	Laughlin	NV	89029	**800-835-7903**	702-298-2242	132
Laughlin/Constable Inc 207 E Michigan St	Milwaukee	WI	53202	**800-432-8747**	414-272-2400	4
LaughStub LLC 2038 Armacost Ave	Los Angeles	CA	90025	**800-927-0939**		384
Launch Pad 18130 Jorene Rd	Odessa	FL	33556	**888-920-3450**		180
Laura Ingalls Wilder Museum & Home 3068 Hwy A	Mansfield	MO	65704	**877-924-7126**		513
Laureate Education Inc 650 S Exeter Street	Baltimore	MD	21202	**866-452-8732**	410-843-6100	242
Laurel Grocery Co Inc 129 Barbourville Rd	London	KY	40744	**800-467-6601**		296-8
Laurel Highlands Visitors Bureau 120 E Main St	Ligonier	PA	15658	**800-333-5661**	724-238-5661	207
Laurel Ink 911 N 145th St *Cust Svc	Seattle	WA	98133	**800-850-0081***		129
Laurel Inn 444 Presidio Ave	San Francisco	CA	94115	**800-738-7477**	415-567-8467	376
Laurel Lake Retirement Community 200 Laurel Lk Dr	Hudson	OH	44236	**866-650-2100**		663
Laurel Park Rt 198 & Racetrack Rd PO Box 130	Laurel	MD	20724	**800-638-1859**	301-725-0400	633
Laurel University 1215 Eastchester Dr	High Point	NC	27265	**855-528-7358**	336-887-3000	159
Laurelville Mennonite Church Ctr 941 Laurelville Ln	Mount Pleasant	PA	15666	**800-839-1021**	724-423-2056	664
Lauren Engineers & Constructors Inc PO Box 1761	Abilene	TX	79604	**800-433-7300**	325-670-9660	261
Lauren Mfg 2228 Reiser Ave SE	New Philadelphia	OH	44663	**855-989-9090**	330-339-3373	668
Laurens County Chamber of Commerce 291 Professional Pk Rd	Clinton	SC	29325	**866-548-9674**	864-833-2716	137
Laurens Electric Co-op Inc 2254 S Carolina 14	Laurens	SC	29360	**800-942-3141**		245
Laurent Clerc National Deaf Education Ctr 800 Florida Ave NE	Washington	DC	20002	**866-637-0102**	202-651-5050	47-17
Laurentian Bank of Canada 1981 McGill College Ave *TSE: LB*	Montreal	QC	H3A3K3	**800-252-1846**	514-284-4500	69
Laurentian University 935 Ramsey Lake Rd	Sudbury	ON	P3E2C6	**800-461-4030**	705-675-1151	773
Laurie Raphael 117 Dalhousie St	Quebec	QC	G1K9C8	**877-876-4555**	418-692-4555	662
Laurin Publishing Co Inc 100 West St	Pittsfield	MA	01202	**877-422-7300**	413-499-0514	628-9
LAUSD (Los Angeles Unified School District) 333 S Beaudry Ave	Los Angeles	CA	90017	**877-772-6273**	213-241-1000	676
Lauterbach Group Inc W222 N5710 Miller Way *Sales	Sussex	WI	53089	**800-841-7301***	262-820-8130	547
Lava Hot Springs State Foundation 430 E Main St PO Box 669	Lava Hot Springs	ID	83246	**800-423-8597**	208-776-5221	49-4
Laval University 2325 Rue University	Quebec	QC	G1V0A6	**877-785-2825**	418-656-2131	773
Lavanture Products Co 22825 Gallatin Way	Elkhart	IN	46514	**800-348-7625**	574-264-0658	593
Lavelle Industries Inc 665 McHenry St	Burlington	WI	53105	**800-528-3553**	262-763-2434	668
LaVezzi Precision Inc 999 Regency Dr	Glendale Heights	IL	60139	**800-323-1772**	630-582-1230	449
Law Enforcement Assoc Corp (LEA) 120 Penmarc Dr Ste 125 *OTC: LAWEQ*	Raleigh	NC	27616	**800-354-9669**	919-872-6210	51
Law Enforcement Technology Magazine 1233 Janesville Ave	Fort Atkinson	WI	53538	**800-547-7377**		452-5
Law Engine 7660-H Fay Avenue Ste 342	La Jolla	CA	92037	**800-894-2889**	858-456-1234	394
Law Officer's Bulletin 610 Opperman Dr	Eagan	MN	55123	**800-344-5008**	651-687-7000	524-2
Law Technology News 120 Broadway 5th Fl *Cust Svc	New York	NY	10271	**800-888-8300***	212-457-7905	452-7
Lawfinance Group Inc 1401 Los Gamos Dr Ste 140	San Rafael	CA	94903	**800-572-1986**	415-446-2300	216
Lawler Foods Ltd Inc PO Box 2558	Humble	TX	77347	**800-541-8285**	281-446-0059	295-1
Lawley Service Insurance 361 Delaware Ave *Cust Svc	Buffalo	NY	14202	**800-860-5741***	716-849-8618	387
Lawn & Golf Supply Co Inc 647 Nutt Rd PO Box 447	Phoenixville	PA	19460	**800-362-5650**	610-933-5801	426
Lawn Doctor Inc 142 SR 34	Holmdel	NJ	07733	**800-631-5660**		570
Lawn Equipment Parts Co 1475 River Rd	Marietta	PA	17547	**800-365-3726**	717-426-5200	426
Lawrence & Schiller Inc 3932 S Willow Ave	Sioux Falls	SD	57105	**800-356-9377**	605-338-8000	4
Lawrence Academy Powderhouse Rd PO Box 992	Groton	MA	01450	**800-977-4698**	978-448-6535	615
Lawrence Behr Assoc Inc 3400 Tupper Dr PO Box 8026	Greenville	NC	27834	**800-522-4464**	252-757-0279	197
Lawrence Companies (LTS) 872 Lee Hwy PO Box 7667	Roanoke	VA	24019	**800-336-9626**	540-966-4000	770
Lawrence County County Courthouse 430 Court St	New Castle	PA	16101	**855-564-6116**	724-658-2541	336
Lawrence County Chamber of Commerce 1609 N Locust Ave PO Box 86	Lawrenceburg	TN	38464	**877-388-4911**	931-762-4911	137
Lawrence County Tourist Promotion Agency 229 S Jefferson St	New Castle	PA	16101	**888-284-7599**	724-654-8408	207
Lawrence Daily Journal-World Co 609 New Hampshire St PO Box 888	Lawrence	KS	66044	**800-578-8748**	785-843-1000	628-8
Lawrence Equipment Inc 2034 Peck Rd	El Monte	CA	91733	**800-423-4500**	626-442-2894	297
Lawrence Hall Chevrolet Inc 1385 S Danville Dr	Abilene	TX	79605	**800-568-7158**	325-695-8800	56
Lawrence Journal-World 609 New Hampshire St	Lawrence	KS	66044	**800-578-8748**	785-843-1000	525-2
Lawrence Memorial Hospital (LMH) 325 Maine St	Lawrence	KS	66044	**800-749-4144**	785-505-5000	371-3
Lawrence Metal Products Inc 260 Spur Dr S PO Box 400	Bay Shore	NY	11706	**800-441-0019**		486
Lawrence Paper Co 2801 Lakeview Rd	Lawrence	KS	66049	**800-535-4553**	785-843-8111	99
Lawrence Public Library 707 Vermont St	Lawrence	KS	66044	**888-657-7323**	785-843-3833	431-3
Lawrence Public Schools 110 McDonald Dr	Lawrence	KS	66044	**800-772-1213**	785-832-5000	676
Lawrence Ragan Communications Inc 111 E Wacker Dr Ste 500	Chicago	IL	60601	**800-878-5331**	800-493-4867	628-9
Lawrence Technological University 21000 W 10-Mile Rd	Southfield	MI	48075	**800-225-5588**	248-204-3160	166
Lawrence University 115 S Drew St	Appleton	WI	54911	**888-959-2016**	920-832-7000	166
Lawrence University Mudd Library 711 E Boldt Way	Appleton	WI	54911	**888-300-4473**	920-832-6750	431-6
Lawrenceville School 2500 Main St PO Box 6008	Lawrenceville	NJ	08648	**800-735-2030**	609-896-0400	615
Lawry's Restaurants Inc 234 E Colorado Blvd Ste 500	Pasadena	CA	91101	**888-552-9797**	626-440-5234	661
Lawson State Community College *Bessemer* 1100 Ninth Ave SW	Bessemer	AL	35022	**800-373-4879**	205-925-2515	788
Lawton Industries Inc 4353 Pacific St	Rocklin	CA	95677	**800-692-2600**	916-624-7895	383
Lawton Public Library 110 SW Fourth St	Lawton	OK	73501	**855-895-8064**	580-581-3450	431-3
Lawton's Drug Stores Ltd 236 Brownlow Ave Ste 270	Dartmouth	NS	B3B1V5	**866-990-1599**	902-468-1000	231
Lawyers Diary & Manual 240 Mulberry St PO Box 50	Newark	NJ	07102	**800-444-4041**	973-642-1440	628-2
Lawyers' Committee for Civil Rights Under Law 1401 New York Ave NW Ste 400	Washington	DC	20005	**888-299-5227**	202-662-8600	48-10
Lawyers' Travel Service 71 Fifth Ave *General	New York	NY	10003	**800-431-1112***		761
lawyers.com Martindale-Hubbell 121 Chanlon Rd	New Providence	NJ	07974	**800-526-4902**	908-464-6800	172
Layer 3 Communications LLC 1555 Oakbrook Dr Ste 100	Norcross	GA	30093	**866-535-3924**	770-225-5300	252
Layne 4520 N State Rd 37 *All	Orleans	IN	47452	**855-529-6301***	812-865-3232	189-10
Layton Manufacturing Corp 825 Remsen Ave	Brooklyn	NY	11236	**800-545-8002**	718-498-6000	14
Lazard 30 Rockefeller Plz *NYSE: LAZ*	New York	NY	10112	**877-266-8601**	212-632-2685	681
Lazard Funds 30 Rockefeller Plz 57th Fl	New York	NY	10112	**800-823-6300**		521
La-Z-Boy Inc 1284 N Telegraph Rd *NYSE: LZB*	Monroe	MI	48162	**800-375-6890**	734-242-1444	318-2
Lazer Grant Inc 309 Mcdermot Ave	Winnipeg	MB	R3A1T3	**800-220-0005**	204-942-0300	2
Lazy L & B Ranch 1072 E Fork Rd *Cust Svc	Dubois	WY	82513	**800-453-9488***	307-455-2839	239
LB Foster Co 415 Holiday Dr *NASDAQ: FSTR*	Pittsburgh	PA	15220	**800-255-4500**		641
LB Furniture Industries LLC 99 S Third St	Hudson	NY	12534	**800-221-8752**	518-828-1501	318-3
L&B Transport LLC 708 US190 PO Box 74870	Port Allen	LA	70767	**800-545-9401**	225-387-0894	444
LB White Company Inc W 6636 LB White Rd	Onalaska	WI	54650	**800-345-7200**	608-783-5691	354
LBA (Latin Business Assn) 120 S San Pedro St Ste 530	Los Angeles	CA	90012	**877-551-7778**	213-628-8510	48-12
LBA Group Inc 3400 Tupper Dr	Greenville	NC	27834	**800-522-4464**	252-757-0279	261
LBI Eyewear 20801 Nordhoff St *Cust Svc	Chatsworth	CA	91311	**800-423-5175***	818-407-1890	535
LBJ Library & Museum 2313 Red River St	Austin	TX	78705	**800-874-6451**	512-721-0216	431-2
LBS (Library Binding Service) 1801 Thompson Ave	Des Moines	IA	50316	**800-247-5323**	515-262-3191	91
LBT Inc 11502 "I" St	Omaha	NE	68137	**888-528-7278**	402-333-4900	769
LBU Inc 217 Brook Ave	Passaic	NJ	07055	**800-678-4528**	973-773-4800	66
LC Doane Co 110 Pond Meadow Rd PO Box 700	Ivoryton	CT	06442	**800-447-5006**	860-767-8295	435
LC King Mfg Company Inc 24 Seventh St PO Box 367	Bristol	TN	37620	**800-826-2510**	423-764-5188	153-18
LCA-Vision Inc 7840 Montgomery Rd *NASDAQ: LCAV*	Cincinnati	OH	45236	**800-688-4550**	513-792-9292	786
LCCR (Leadership Conference on Civil Rights) 1629 K St NW Ste 1000	Washington	DC	20006	**888-460-0813**	202-466-3311	47-8
LCD Lighting Inc 37 Robinson Blvd	Orange	CT	06477	**800-826-9465**	203-795-1520	433
LCH Paper Tube & Core Co 11930 Larc Industrial Blvd	Burnsville	MN	55337	**800-472-3477**	952-358-3587	124
LCI (Lannett Company Inc) 13200 Townsend Rd *NYSE: LCI*	Philadelphia	PA	19154	**800-325-9994**	215-333-9000	474
LCMS (Lutheran Church Missouri Synod) 1333 S Kirkwood Rd	Saint Louis	MO	63122	**888-843-5267**	314-965-9000	47-20
LCNB National Bank 3209 W Galbraith Rd	Cincinnati	OH	45239	**800-344-2265**	513-932-1414	69
LCPS (Lenoir County Public School) 2017 W Vernon Ave PO Box 729	Kinston	NC	28504	**888-684-8404**	252-527-1109	676
LCS Technologies Inc 11230 Gold Express Dr Ste 310-140	Gold River	CA	95670	**855-277-5527**		616
LD Amory & Co Inc 101 S King St	Hampton	VA	23669	**800-552-9963**	757-722-1915	296-5
LDA (Learning Disabilities Assn of America) 4156 Library Rd	Pittsburgh	PA	15234	**888-300-6710**	412-341-1515	47-17

Name / Address	City	State	ZIP	Toll-Free	Phone	Class
LDP Inc						
75 Kiwanis Blvd PO Box O	West Hazleton	PA	18201	**800-522-8413**		179-3
LDR Industries Inc						
600 N Kilbourn Ave	Chicago	IL	60624	**800-545-5230**	773-265-3000	602
LDS Hospital						
8th Ave & C St	Salt Lake City	UT	84143	**888-301-3880**	801-408-1100	371-3
Le Chamois						
4557 Blackcomb Way	Whistler	BC	V0N1B4	**866-944-7853**	604-932-8700	376
Le Cirque						
3600 Las Vegas Blvd S	Las Vegas	NV	89109	**888-987-6667**	702-693-7111	662
Le Cordon Bleu College of Culinary Arts						
Atlanta						
1927 Lakeside Pkwy	Tucker	GA	30084	**888-549-8222**	770-938-4711	161
Le Creuset of America Inc						
114 Bob Gifford Blvd	Early Branch	SC	29916	**877-418-5547**	803-943-4308	481
Le Devoir						
2050 Bleury St Ninth Fl	Montreal	QC	H3A3M9	**800-463-7559**	514-985-3333	525-1
LE Johnson Products Inc						
2100 Sterling Ave	Elkhart	IN	46516	**800-837-5664**	574-293-5664	347
Le Mars Insurance Co						
PO Box 1608	Le Mars	IA	51031	**800-545-6480**		387
Le Meridian						
20 Sidney St	Cambridge	MA	02139	**800-543-4300**	617-577-0200	376
Le Meridien Chambers Minneapolis						
901 Hennepin Ave	Minneapolis	MN	55403	**866-961-2861***	612-767-6900	376
*General						
Le M,ridien Dallas, The Stoneleigh						
2927 Maple Ave	Dallas	TX	75201	**800-650-1458**	214-871-7111	376
Le Merigot - A JW Marriott Beach Hotel & Spa						
1740 Ocean Ave	Santa Monica	CA	90401	**888-539-7899**	310-395-9700	376
Le Montrose Suite Hotel						
900 Hammond St	West Hollywood	CA	90069	**800-776-0666**	310-855-1115	376
Le Moyne College						
1419 Salt Springs Rd	Syracuse	NY	13214	**800-333-4733***	315-445-4100	166
*Admissions						
Le Nouvel Montreal Hotel & Spa						
1740 Rene-Levesque Blvd W	Montreal	QC	H3H1R3	**800-363-6063**	514-931-8841	376
Le Parc Suite Hotel						
733 NW Knoll Dr	West Hollywood	CA	90069	**800-578-4837***	310-855-8888	376
*Resv						
Le Port-Royal Hotel & Suites						
144 St Pierre St	Quebec	QC	G1K8N8	**866-417-2777**	418-692-2777	376
Le Richelieu Hotel						
1234 Chartres St	New Orleans	LA	70116	**800-535-9653**	504-529-2492	376
Le Saint Sulpice						
414 Rue St Sulpice	Montreal	QC	H2Y2V5	**877-785-7423***	514-288-1000	376
*General						
Le Saint Tropez						
315 King St W	Toronto	ON	M5V1J5	**888-627-2357**	416-591-8600	662
Le Smith Co						
1030 E Wilson St	Bryan	OH	43506	**888-537-6484**	419-636-4555	347
Le Sueur Cheese Company Inc						
719 N Main St	Le Sueur	MN	56058	**800-247-0871**	507-665-3353	295-5
LEA (Law Enforcement Assoc Corp)						
120 Penmarc Dr Ste 125	Raleigh	NC	27616	**800-354-9669**	919-872-6210	51
OTC: LAWEQ						
Lea Regional Medical Ctr						
5419 N Lovington Hwy	Hobbs	NM	88240	**877-492-8001**	575-492-5000	371-3
Leach International Corp						
6900 Orangethorpe Ave	Buena Park	CA	90622	**800-232-7700**	714-736-7598	204
Leaders LLC						
Two Portland Fish Pier Ste 301	Portland	ME	04101	**888-583-7770**		681
Leadership Conference on Civil Rights (LCCR)						
1629 K St NW Ste 1000	Washington	DC	20006	**888-460-0813**	202-466-3311	47-8
Leadership Directories Inc						
104 Fifth Ave 3rd Fl	New York	NY	10011	**800-627-0311**	212-627-4140	628-2
Leadership Journal						
465 Gundersen Dr	Carol Stream	IL	60188	**800-777-3136**	630-260-6200	452-5
Leadership Management Inc						
4567 Lk Shore Dr	Waco	TX	76710	**800-568-1241**	254-776-2060	755
Leadership Performance Sustainability Laboratories						
4647 Hugh Howell Rd	Tucker	GA	30084	**800-241-8334**		534
Leader-Telegram						
701 S Farwell St	Eau Claire	WI	54701	**800-236-8808**	715-833-9200	525-2
Leading Age						
2519 Connecticut Ave NW	Washington	DC	20008	**866-702-3278**	202-783-2242	47-6
Leading Authorities Inc						
1990 M St Ste 800	Washington	DC	20036	**800-773-2537**	202-783-0300	699
Leading Hotels of the World						
99 Pk Ave	New York	NY	10017	**800-223-6800**	212-515-5600	373
Leading Lady						
24050 Commerce Pk	Beachwood	OH	44122	**800-321-4804***	216-464-5490	153-17
*Cust Svc						
Leadman Electronic USA Inc						
382 Laurelwood Dr	Santa Clara	CA	95054	**877-532-3626**	408-738-1751	175
LeadRival						
1207 S White Chapel Blvd						
Ste 250	Southlake	TX	76092	**800-332-8017**		5
League to Save Lake Tahoe						
2608 Lake Tahoe Blvd	South Lake Tahoe	CA	96150	**888-844-9904**	530-541-5388	47-13
Leahi Hospital						
3675 Kilauea Ave	Honolulu	HI	96816	**800-845-6733**	808-733-8000	371-7
Leaktite Corp						
40 Francis St	Leominster	MA	01453	**800-392-0039**	978-537-8000	601
Leamington District Chamber of Commerce						
318 Erie St S	Leamington	ON	N8H3C5	**800-393-3769**	519-326-2721	136
Leanin' Tree Museum of Western Art						
6055 Longbow Dr	Boulder	CO	80301	**800-525-0656**	303-530-1442	513
LeanLogistics Inc						
1351 S Waverly Rd	Holland	MI	49423	**866-584-7280**	616-738-6400	310
LeapFrog Enterprises Inc						
6401 Hollis St Ste 100	Emeryville	CA	94608	**800-701-5327**	510-420-5000	752
NYSE: LF						
Lear Capital Inc						
1990 S Bundy Dr Ste 600	Los Angeles	CA	90025	**800-576-9355**		251
Learning Care Group Inc						
21333 Haggerty Rd Ste 300	Novi	MI	48375	**877-817-3883**	248-697-9000	146
Learning Communications LLC						
5520 Trabuco Rd	Irvine	CA	92620	**800-622-3610**		506
Learning Disabilities Assn of America (LDA)						
4156 Library Rd	Pittsburgh	PA	15234	**888-300-6710**	412-341-1515	47-17
Learning Enhancement Corp						
200 S Wacker Dr Ste 3100	Chicago	IL	60606	**877-272-4610**	312-455-1758	225
Learning Express Inc						
29 Buena Vista St	Devens	MA	01434	**800-924-2296**	978-889-1000	751
Learning Research & Development Ctr (LRDC)						
University of Pittsburgh						
3939 O'Hara St	Pittsburgh	PA	15260	**800-397-0071**	412-624-7020	659
Learning Resources						
380 N Fairway Dr	Vernon Hills	IL	60061	**800-222-3909**	847-573-8400	243
Learning Tree International Inc						
1831 Michael Faraday Dr	Reston	VA	20190	**800-843-8733***	703-709-9119	754
OTC: LTRE *Cust Svc						
Learning Wrap-Ups Inc						
1660 W Gordon Ave Ste 4	Layton	UT	84041	**800-992-4966**	801-497-0050	243
LearningStation Inc						
8008 Corporate Ctr Dr Ste 210	Charlotte	NC	28226	**888-679-7058**		38
Lease Plan USA						
1165 Sanctuary Pkwy	Alpharetta	GA	30004	**800-457-8721**	770-933-9090	289
Leasing Assoc Inc						
12600 N Featherwood Dr Ste 400	Houston	TX	77034	**800-449-4807**	832-300-1300	289
Leather Industries of America (LIA)						
3050 K St NW Ste 400	Washington	DC	20007	**800-635-0617**	202-342-8497	48-4
Leathercraft						
102 Section House Rd	Hickory	NC	28601	**800-627-1561**		318-2
Leatherman Tool Group Inc						
12106 NE Ainsworth Cir	Portland	OR	97220	**800-847-8665**	503-253-7826	748
Leave No Trace Ctr for Outdoor Ethics Inc						
1830 17th St	Boulder	CO	80302	**800-332-4100**	303-442-8222	47-23
Leavenworth Convention & Visitors Bureau						
518 Shawnee St PO Box 44	Leavenworth	KS	66048	**800-844-4114**	913-682-4113	207
Leavenworth-Jefferson Electric Co-op Inc						
507 N Union St	McLouth	KS	66054	**888-796-6111**		245
leavitt group Enterprises						
216 S 200 W PO Box 130	Cedar City	UT	84720	**800-264-8085**	435-586-6553	387
Leavitt Tube						
1717 W 115th St	Chicago	IL	60643	**800-532-8488**	773-239-7700	485
Lebanon Area Chamber of Commerce						
186 N Adams St	Lebanon	MO	65536	**888-588-5710**	417-588-3256	137
Lebanon Seaboard Corp						
1600 E Cumberland St	Lebanon	PA	17042	**800-233-0628**	717-273-1685	280
Lebanon Valley College						
101 N College Ave	Annville	PA	17003	**866-582-4236**	717-867-6181	166
Lebenthal Wealth Advisors						
230 Park Ave Fl 32	New York	NY	10169	**877-425-6006**	212-425-6006	681
LEC (Lincoln Electric Co-op Inc)						
500 Osloski Rd PO Box 628	Eureka	MT	59917	**800-442-2994**	406-889-3301	245
Lechler Inc						
445 Kautz Rd	Saint Charles	IL	60174	**800-777-2926***	630-377-6611	482
*Cust Svc						
Leco Corp						
3000 Lakeview Ave	Saint Joseph	MI	49085	**800-292-6141**	269-985-5496	416
LeCroy Corp						
700 Chestnut Ridge Rd	Chestnut Ridge	NY	10977	**800-553-2769**	845-425-2000	248
NASDAQ: LCRY						
Lectrosonics Inc						
PO Box 15900	Rio Rancho	NM	87174	**800-821-1121**	505-892-4501	51
LED Supply Co						
747 Sheridan Blvd Unit 8E	Lakewood	CO	80214	**877-595-4769**		197
Ledalite Architectural Products						
19750-92A Ave	Langley	BC	V1M3B2	**800-665-5332**	604-888-6811	435
Ledger, The						
300 W Lime St	Lakeland	FL	33815	**888-431-7323**	863-802-7000	525-2
Ledtronics Inc						
23105 Kashiwa Ct	Torrance	CA	90505	**800-579-4875**	310-534-1505	433
Ledwell & Son Enterprises						
3300 Waco St	Texarkana	TX	75501	**888-533-9355**	903-838-6531	769
Lee & Cates Glass Inc						
5355 Shawland Rd	Jacksonville	FL	32254	**888-844-1989**	904-358-8555	190-6
Lee Brass Co						
1800 Golden Springs Rd	Anniston	AL	36207	**800-876-1811***		307
*General						
Lee Brick & Tile Co						
3704 Hawkins Ave PO Box 1027	Sanford	NC	27330	**800-672-7559**	919-774-4800	148
Lee Co Inc						
331 Mallory Stn Rd	Franklin	TN	37067	**888-567-7747**	615-567-1000	190-10
Lee Correctional Institution						
990 Wisacky Hwy	Bishopville	SC	29010	**877-846-3472**	803-428-2800	213
Lee County Electric Co-op Inc						
4980 Bayline Dr						
PO Box 3455	North Fort Myers	FL	33917	**800-282-1643**	239-995-2121	245
Lee County Visitors & Convention Bureau						
12800 University Dr Ste 550	Fort Myers	FL	33907	**800-237-6444**	239-338-3500	207
Lee Dan Communications Inc						
155 Adams Ave	Hauppauge	NY	11788	**800-231-1414**	631-231-1414	389
Lee Hecht Harrison LLC						
50 Tice Blvd	Woodcliff Lake	NJ	07677	**800-611-4544**		194
Lee Jeans						
9001 W 67th St	Merriam	KS	66202	**800-453-3348***	913-384-4000	153-10
*Cust Svc						
Lee Kum Kee Inc						
14841 Don Julian Rd	City of Industry	CA	91746	**800-654-5082***	626-709-1888	295-19
*Orders						
Lee Myles Auto Group						
847 Fern Ave	Reading	PA	19607	**800-533-6953**	201-262-0555	61-6
Lee Products Co						
800 E 80th St	Bloomington	MN	55420	**800-989-3544**	952-854-3544	527
Lee Silsby Compounding Pharmacy						
3216 Silsby Rd	Cleveland Heights	OH	44118	**800-918-8831**	216-321-4300	237
Lee Spring Company Inc						
140 58th St Ste 3C	Brooklyn	NY	11220	**800-110-2500**	718-236-2222	710
Lee Supply Corp						
6610 Guion Rd	Indianapolis	IN	46268	**800-873-1103**	317-290-2500	605
Lee University						
1120 N Ocoee St	Cleveland	TN	37311	**800-533-9930**	423-614-8000	166
Lee's Morvillo Group						
160 Niantic Ave	Providence	RI	02907	**800-821-1700**	401-353-1740	404
Lee's Summit Chamber of Commerce						
220 SE Main St	Lee's Summit	MO	64063	**888-816-5757**	816-524-2424	137
Leebaw Mfg Company Inc						
PO Box 553	Canfield	OH	44406	**800-841-8083**		465
Leech Lake Area Chamber of Commerce						
205 Minnesota Ave E	Walker	MN	56484	**800-833-1118**	218-547-1313	137
Leech Lake Tribal College						
6945 Little Wolf Rd						
PO Box 180	Cass Lake	MN	56633	**800-627-3529**	218-335-4200	163

Name / Address	City	State	ZIP	Toll-Free	Phone	Class
Leeches USA Ltd 300 Shames Dr	Westbury	NY	11590	**800-645-3569**	516-333-2570	470
Leelanau County 8527 E Government Ctr Dr	Suttons Bay	MI	49682	**866-256-9711**	231-256-9824	336
Leelanau Fruit Co 2900 SW Bay Shore Dr	Suttons Bay	MI	49682	**800-431-0718**	231-271-3514	295-21
Leer LP 206 Leer St *Cust Svc	New Lisbon	WI	53950	**800-766-5337***	608-562-7100	655
Leerink Swann & Co 1 Federal St 37th Fl	Boston	MA	02110	**800-808-7525**		398
Lees-McRae College 191 Main St W	Banner Elk	NC	28604	**800-280-4562**	828-898-5241	166
Leevac Shipyards Inc 111 Bunge St	Jennings	LA	70546	**800-244-3262**	337-824-2210	689
Leeward Community College 96-045 Ala Ike	Pearl City	HI	96782	**888-442-4551**	808-455-0011	160
Leff Electric 4700 Spring Rd	Cleveland	OH	44131	**800-686-5333**	216-432-3000	246
Leffler Energy Inc 15 Mt Joy St	Mount Joy	PA	17552	**800-984-1411**		572
LeFiell Manufacturing Co 13700 Firestone Blvd	Santa Fe Springs	CA	90670	**800-451-5971**	562-921-3411	485
Lefkowitz Garfinkel Champi & DeRienzo PC 10 Weybosset St	Providence	RI	02903	**800-927-5423**	401-421-4800	2
LeFleur's Bluff State Park 2140 Riverside Dr	Jackson	MS	39202	**800-237-6278**	601-987-3923	558
Legacy Bank 1580 E Cheyenne Mtn Blvd	Colorado Springs	CO	80906	**866-627-0800**	719-579-9150	69
Legacy Benefits Corp 350 Fifth Ave Ste 4320	New York	NY	10118	**800-875-1000**		784
Legacy Emanuel Hospital & Health Ctr 2801 N Gantenbein Ave	Portland	OR	97227	**888-598-4232**	503-413-2200	371-3
Legacy Golf Resort 6808 S 32nd St	Phoenix	AZ	85042	**888-828-3673**	602-305-5500	660
Legacy Good Samaritan Hospital 1015 NW 22nd Ave	Portland	OR	97210	**800-733-9959**	503-335-3500	371-3
Legacy Salmon Creek Hospital 2211 NE 139th St	Vancouver	WA	98686	**877-270-5566**	360-487-1000	371-3
Legal & General America Inc 1701 Research Blvd	Rockville	MD	20850	**800-638-8428**	301-279-4800	357-4
Legal Data Resources Inc 2816 W Summerdale Ave	Chicago	IL	60625	**844-732-2437**	773-561-2468	626
Legal Management: Journal of the Assn of Legal Administrators (ALA) 75 Tri State International Ste 222	Lincolnshire	IL	60069	**800-801-3830**	847-267-1252	452-15
Legal Sea Foods Inc 1 Seafood Way	Boston	MA	02210	**800-477-5342**	617-530-9000	661
LegalEase Inc 211 E 43rd St Ste 2203	New York	NY	10017	**800-393-1277**	212-393-9070	626
Legend Homes Corp 12755 SW 69th Ave Ste 100	Portland	OR	97223	**888-782-7937**	503-620-8080	644
Legend Power Systems Inc 8561 Commerce Ct	Burnaby	BC	V5A4N5	**866-772-8797**	604-420-1500	757
Legends of England 3520 Roberts Cut Off Rd	Fort Worth	TX	76114	**800-578-1065**	817-236-3141	358
Legends Theater 1600 W Hwy 76	Branson	MO	65616	**800-374-7469**	417-339-3003	565
Legg Company Inc 325 E Tenth St *Sales	Halstead	KS	67056	**800-835-1003***		367
Legg Mason Inc (LMI) 100 International Dr *NYSE: LM*	Baltimore	MD	21202	**800-822-5544**	410-539-0000	681
Leggett & Platt Inc Number 1 Leggett Rd PO Box 757 *NYSE: LEG*	Carthage	MO	64836	**800-888-4569**	417-358-8131	710
Leggett Wire Co One Leggett Rd	Carthage	MO	64836	**800-888-4569**	417-358-8131	800
Legion Lighting Company Inc 221 Glenmore Ave	Brooklyn	NY	11207	**800-453-4466**	718-498-1770	435
LEGO Systems Inc 555 Taylor Rd	Enfield	CT	06082	**877-518-5346**	860-763-6731	752
LEGOLAND California 1 Legoland Dr	Carlsbad	CA	92008	**877-534-6526**	760-438-5346	32
Lehigh Asphalt Paving & Construction Co Inc PO Box 549	Tamaqua	PA	18252	**877-222-5514**	570-668-4303	189-4
Lehigh Carbon Community College 4525 Education Pk Dr *General	Schnecksville	PA	18078	**800-414-3975***	610-799-2121	160
Morgan Ctr 234 High St	Tamaqua	PA	18252	**800-424-2460**	570-668-6880	160
Lehigh Fluid Power Inc 1413 Rt 179	Lambertville	NJ	08530	**800-257-9515**		632
Lehigh Inland Cement Ltd 12640 Inland Way *Orders	Edmonton	AB	T5V1K2	**800-252-9304***	780-420-2500	134
Lehigh Phoenix 18249 Phoenix Dr *General	Hagerstown	MD	21742	**800-632-4111***	301-733-0018	618
Lehigh Valley Health Network 700 E Broad St	Hazleton	PA	18201	**800-528-1234**	570-501-4000	371-3
Lehigh Valley Hospice 2166 S 12th St Ste 401	Allentown	PA	18103	**888-584-2273**	610-969-0300	368
Lehigh Valley International Airport 3311 Airport Rd	Allentown	PA	18109	**800-359-5842**	610-266-6000	27
Lehigh Valley Plastics Inc 187 N Commerce Way	Bethlehem	PA	18017	**800-354-5344**	484-893-5500	597
Lehigh Valley Visitor Ctr 840 Hamilton St Ste 200	Allentown	PA	18101	**800-747-0561**	610-882-9200	207
Lehman College 250 Bedford Pk Blvd W	Bronx	NY	10468	**800-311-5656**	718-960-8000	166
Lehman Hardware & Appliances Inc 4779 Kidron Rd	Dalton	OH	44618	**888-438-5346**		390
Lehman Millet Inc Two Atlantic Ave	Boston	MA	02110	**800-634-5315**		4
Lehman Trikes Inc 125 Industrial Dr *CVE: LHT*	Spearfish	SD	57783	**888-394-3357**	605-642-2111	510
Leica Geosystems Inc 3498 Kraft Ave SE *Sales	Grand Rapids	MI	49512	**800-367-9453***	616-977-4189	422
Leidenheimer Baking Co 1501 Simon Bolivar Ave	New Orleans	LA	70113	**800-259-9099**	504-525-1575	295-1
Leigh Baldwin & Company LLC One Hopper St	Utica	NY	13501	**800-659-8044**	315-734-1410	681
Leisure Sports Inc 7077 Koll Ctr Pkwy Ste 110	Pleasanton	CA	94566	**888-239-0930**	925-600-1966	376
Leisure Systems Inc 50 W Techne Ctr Dr Ste G	Milford	OH	45150	**866-928-9644**	513-831-2100	120
LeisureLink Inc 90 S 400 W Ste 300	Salt Lake City	UT	84101	**855-840-2249**		375
LEK Consulting 28 State St 16th Fl	Boston	MA	02109	**800-929-4535**	617-951-9500	195
LEKTRO Inc 1190 SE Flightline Dr	Warrenton	OR	97146	**800-535-8767**	503-861-2288	56
Lemay Auto Group 8220-75th St	Kenosha	WI	53142	**866-689-1492**	262-694-2000	56
Lemco Tool Corp 1850 Metzger Ave	Cogan Station	PA	17728	**800-233-8713**	570-494-0620	449
Lemon Peak Marketing Services 500 W Putnam Ave Ste 400	Greenwich	CT	06831	**888-253-7348**		5
Len-Co Lumber Corp 1445 Seneca St	Buffalo	NY	14210	**800-258-4585**	716-822-0243	361
LendingTree Inc 11115 Rushmore Dr	Charlotte	NC	28277	**800-555-8733**	704-541-5351	502
Lenexa Chamber of Commerce 11180 Lackman Rd	Lenexa	KS	66219	**800-679-0177**	913-888-1414	137
Lenexpo Inc 1293 Mtn View Alviso Rd Ste A	Sunnyvale	CA	94089	**877-536-3976**	408-962-0515	253
Lennox Industries Inc 2100 Lake Pk Blvd *Cust Svc	Richardson	TX	75080	**800-953-6669***		15
Lennox International Inc 2140 Lake Pk Blvd *NYSE: LII*	Richardson	TX	75080	**800-953-6669**	972-497-5000	15
Lenoir Community College PO Box 188	Kinston	NC	28502	**800-848-5497**	252-527-6223	160
Lenoir County Public School (LCPS) 2017 W Vernon Ave PO Box 729	Kinston	NC	28504	**888-684-8404**	252-527-1109	676
Lenoir Mirror Company Inc 401 Kincaid St	Lenoir	NC	28645	**800-438-8204**	828-728-3271	330
Lenoir-Rhyne University 625 Seventh Ave NE	Hickory	NC	28601	**800-277-5721**	828-328-7300	166
Lenox Corp PO Box 2006	Bristol	PA	19007	**800-223-4311**		721
Lenox Hotel 61 Exeter St	Boston	MA	02116	**800-225-7676**	617-536-5300	376
LENSAR Inc 2800 Discovery Dr	Orlando	FL	32826	**888-536-7271**		470
LensCrafters Inc 4000 Luxottica Pl	Mason	OH	45040	**877-753-6727**	513-765-4321	536
Lenze 630 Douglas St	Uxbridge	MA	01569	**800-217-9100**	508-278-9100	700
Leo Pharma Inc 123 Commerce Vly Dr E Ste 400 *General	Thornhill	ON	L3T7W8	**800-668-7234***	905-886-9822	84
Leo Wolleman Inc 45 W 45th St 10th Fl	New York	NY	10036	**800-223-5667**	212-840-1881	408
Leominster Credit Union 20 Adams St	Leominster	MA	01453	**800-649-4646**	978-537-8021	219
Leon Max Inc 3100 New York Dr	Pasadena	CA	91107	**888-334-4629**	626-797-9991	153-20
Leon S McGoogan Library of Medicine University of Nebraska Medical Ctr 986705 Nebraska Medical Ctr	Omaha	NE	68198	**866-800-5209**	402-559-6221	431-1
Leona Group LLC 4660 S Hagadorn Rd Ste 500	East Lansing	MI	48823	**800-656-6763**	517-333-9030	242
Leonard Paper Co 725 N Haven St *Cust Svc	Baltimore	MD	21205	**800-327-5547***		552
Leonard Valve Co 1360 Elmwood Ave	Cranston	RI	02910	**800-222-1208**	401-461-1200	777
Leppo Inc PO Box 154	Tallmadge	OH	44278	**800-453-7762**	330-633-3999	264-3
Leprino Foods Co 1830 W 38th Ave	Denver	CO	80211	**800-537-7466**	303-480-2600	295-5
Lerner Publishing Group 1251 Washington Ave N	Minneapolis	MN	55401	**800-328-4929**		628-2
Lerner Research Institute 9500 Euclid Ave	Cleveland	OH	44195	**800-223-2273**	216-444-3900	659
LES (Loyd's Electric Supply Inc) 838 Stonetree Dr	Branson	MO	65616	**800-492-4030**	417-334-2171	246
Les Stanford Chevrolet Inc 21730 Michigan Ave	Dearborn	MI	48124	**800-836-0972**	313-457-0364	56
Les Suites Hotel Ottawa 130 Besserer St	Ottawa	ON	K1N9M9	**866-682-0879**	613-232-2000	376
Les Trois Petits Cochons Inc 4223 First Ave Second Fl *General	Brooklyn	NY	11232	**800-537-7283***	212-219-1230	295-26
Lesaffre Yeast Corp 7475 W Main St *Cust Svc	Milwaukee	WI	53214	**877-677-7000***		295-42
LeSaint Logistics 868 W Crossroads Pkwy	Romeoville	IL	60446	**877-566-9375**	630-243-5950	444
LeSea Broadcasting Corp 61300 S Ironwood Rd	South Bend	IN	46614	**800-365-3732**	574-291-8200	728
Lesley University 29 Everett St	Cambridge	MA	02138	**800-999-1959**	617-868-9600	166
Leslie Controls Inc 12501 Telecom Dr	Tampa	FL	33637	**800-323-8366**	813-978-1000	777
Lesman Instrument Co 135 Bernice Dr	Bensenville	IL	60106	**800-953-7626**	630-595-8400	383
Leson Chevrolet Co Inc 1501 Westbank Express	Harvey	LA	70058	**877-496-2420**	504-366-4381	509
Lester Bldg Systems LLC 1111 Second Ave S	Lester Prairie	MN	55354	**800-826-4439**	320-395-2531	105
Lester Inc 19 Business Pk Dr	Branford	CT	06405	**800-999-5265**	203-488-5265	727
Lester Sales Co Inc 4312 W Minnesota St	Indianapolis	IN	46241	**800-544-6183**	317-244-7811	246
Lester's Florist Inc 2100 Bull St	Savannah	GA	31401	**800-841-1103**	912-233-6066	292
LeTourneau University 2100 S Mobberly Ave	Longview	TX	75602	**800-759-8811**	903-233-3000	166

				Toll-Free	Phone	Class
Level 3 Communications Inc						
1025 Eldorado Blvd	Broomfield	CO	80021	**877-453-8353**	720-888-1000	391
NYSE: LVLT						
Level Interactive						
241 Fourth Ave	Pittsburgh	PA	15222	**877-733-8625**		5
Levenger						
420 S Congress Ave	Delray Beach	FL	33445	**800-544-0880***	561-276-2436	454
*Cust Svc						
Leventhal Ltd						
PO Box 564	Fayetteville	NC	28302	**800-847-4095***		153-18
*General						
Levi Strauss & Co						
1155 Battery St	San Francisco	CA	94111	**866-290-6064**	415-501-6000	153-10
Levi Strauss Foundation						
1155 Battery St	San Francisco	CA	94111	**866-290-6064**	415-501-6000	303
Levinson Institute Inc						
28 Main St Ste 100	Jaffrey	NH	03452	**800-290-5735**	603-532-4700	755
Levolor Kirsch Window Fashions						
4110 Premier Dr	High Point	NC	27265	**800-752-9677**	336-812-8181	86
Lew A. Cummings Company Inc						
Four Peters Brook Dr	Hooksett	NH	03106	**800-647-0035**		619
Lewcott Corp						
86 Providence Rd	Millbury	MA	01527	**800-225-7725***	508-865-1791	598-2
*Sales						
Lewer Agency Inc						
4534 Wornall Rd	Kansas City	MO	64111	**800-821-7715**		387
Lewin Group						
3130 Fairview Pk Dr						
Ste 800	Falls Church	VA	22042	**877-227-5042**	703-269-5500	195
Lewis & Clark College						
0615 SW Palatine Hill Rd	Portland	OR	97219	**800-444-4111***	503-768-7040	166
*Admissions						
Lewis & Clark Library						
120 S Last Chance Gulch	Helena	MT	59601	**800-733-2767**	406-447-1690	431-3
Lewis & Clark State Recreation Site						
725 Summer St NE Ste C	Salem	OR	97301	**800-551-6949**	503-986-0707	558
Lewis & Clark Trail Heritage Foundation						
4201 Giant Springs Rd	Great Falls	MT	59405	**888-701-3434**	406-454-1234	47-23
Lewis & Michael Inc						
1827 Woodman Dr	Dayton	OH	45420	**800-543-3524**	937-252-6683	187
Lewis Bakeries Inc						
500 N Fulton Ave	Evansville	IN	47710	**800-365-2812**	812-425-4642	295-1
Lewis County						
499 US Hwy 33 E Ste 102	Weston	WV	26452	**800-296-7329**	304-269-7328	336
Lewis County Chamber of Commerce						
7576 S State St	Lowville	NY	13367	**800-724-0242**	315-376-2213	137
Lewis County Rural Electric Co-op						
18256 Hwy 16 PO Box 68	Lewistown	MO	63452	**888-454-4485**	573-215-4000	245
Lewis Direct Marketing						
325 E Oliver St	Baltimore	MD	21202	**800-533-5394**	410-539-5100	5
Lewis Electric Supply Company Inc						
1306 Second St						
PO Box 2237	Muscle Shoals	AL	35662	**800-239-0681**	256-383-0681	246
Lewis Goetz & Company Inc						
1571 Grandview Ave	Paulsboro	NJ	08066	**800-257-6239**	856-579-1421	382
Lewis M Carter Mfg Co						
PO Box 428	Donalsonville	GA	39845	**800-332-8232**	229-524-2197	297
Lewis S. Mills High School						
24 Lyon Rd	Burlington	CT	06013	**800-673-2411**	860-673-0423	676
Lewis Tree Service Inc						
300 Lucius Gordon Dr	West Henrietta	NY	14586	**800-333-1593**	585-436-3208	766
Lewis University						
One University Pkwy Unit 297	Romeoville	IL	60446	**800-897-9000**	815-836-5250	166
Lewis-Clark State College						
500 Eigth Ave	Lewiston	ID	83501	**800-933-5272**	208-792-5272	166
Lewis-Gale Medical Ctr						
1900 Electric Rd	Salem	VA	24153	**800-722-4673**	540-776-4000	371-3
Lewis-Goetz & Co Inc						
650 Washington Rd Ste 210	Pittsburgh	PA	15228	**888-327-8882**	412-341-7100	382
Lewiston Sales Inc						
21241 Dutchmans Crossing Rd	Lewiston	MN	55952	**800-732-6334**	507-523-2112	441
Lewistown Hospital						
400 Highland Ave	Lewistown	PA	17044	**800-248-0505**	717-248-5411	371-3
Lexar Media Inc						
47300 Bayside Pkwy	Fremont	CA	94538	**877-747-4031**	510-413-1200	288
Lexel Imaging Systems Inc						
1501 Newtown Pike	Lexington	KY	40511	**800-397-8121**	859-243-5500	253
Lexicon Marketing Corp						
6380 Wilshire Blvd	Los Angeles	CA	90048	**800-650-4444**	323-782-7400	727
Lexicon Pharmaceuticals Inc						
8800 Technology Forest Pl	The Woodlands	TX	77381	**855-828-4651**	281-863-3000	84
NASDAQ: LXRX						
Lexington Chamber of Commerce						
321 S Lake Dr	Lexington	SC	29072	**866-851-3000**	803-359-6113	137
Lexington Convention & Visitors Bureau						
301 E Vine St	Lexington	KY	40507	**800-845-3959**	859-233-7299	207
Lexington Corporate Properties Trust						
One Penn Plz Ste 4015	New York	NY	10119	**800-850-3948**	212-692-7200	646
Lexington Herald-Leader						
100 Midland Ave	Lexington	KY	40508	**800-999-8881**	859-231-3100	525-2
Lexington Home Brands						
1300 National Hwy	Thomasville	NC	27360	**800-952-5210**	336-474-5300	318-2
Lexington Philharmonic						
161 N Mill St	Lexington	KY	40507	**888-494-4226**	859-233-4226	566-3
Lexington Theological Seminary						
631 S Limestone St	Lexington	KY	40508	**866-296-6087**	859-252-0361	167-3
Lexington Veteran Affairs Medical Center						
1101 Veterans Dr	Lexington	KY	40502	**877-222-8387**	859-233-4511	388-3
LexisNexis Martindale-Hubbell						
121 Chanlon Rd	New Providence	NJ	07974	**800-526-4902**		384
LexisNexis Matthew Bender						
744 Broad St	Newark	NJ	07102	**800-252-9257**	973-820-2000	628-2
LexJet Corp						
1680 Fruitville Rd 3rd Fl	Sarasota	FL	34236	**800-453-9538**	941-330-1210	620
Lexmark Carpet Mills Inc						
285 Kraft Dr	Dalton	GA	30721	**800-871-3211**		130
Lexmark International Inc						
740 W New Cir Rd	Lexington	KY	40550	**800-539-6275***	859-232-2000	174-6
NYSE: LXK ■ *Cust Svc						
Lexus of Memphis Inc						
2600 Ridgeway Rd	Memphis	TN	38119	**877-876-9996***	901-362-8833	56
*Sales						

				Toll-Free	Phone	Class
LFA (Lupus Foundation of America Inc)						
2000 L St NW Ste 410	Washington	DC	20036	**800-558-0121**	202-349-1155	47-17
LFCU (Lockheed Federal Credit Union)						
2340 Hollywood Way	Burbank	CA	91505	**800-328-5328**	818-565-2020	219
LFL (Lady Foot Locker)						
112 W 34th St	New York	NY	10120	**800-991-6686**		300
LG Barcus & Sons Inc						
1430 State Ave	Kansas City	KS	66102	**800-255-0180**	913-621-1100	189-2
LG Electronics USA Inc						
1000 Sylvan Ave	Englewood Cliffs	NJ	07632	**800-180-9999***	201-816-2000	174-4
*Tech Supp						
LG Everist Inc						
300 S Phillips Ave Ste 200	Sioux Falls	SD	57117	**800-843-7992**	605-334-5000	498-4
LG2 Environmental Solutions Inc						
88 Riberia St	St Augustine	FL	32084	**800-435-0072**	904-824-8633	643
LGInternational						
6700 SW Bradbury Ct	Portland	OR	97224	**800-345-0534**	503-620-0520	410
LHC Group LLC						
420 W Pinhook Rd	Lafayette	LA	70503	**866-542-4768**	337-289-8188	360
NASDAQ: LHCG						
Li Cor Inc						
PO Box 4425	Lincoln	NE	68504	**800-447-3576**	402-467-3576	416
LIA (Laser Institute of America)						
13501 Ingenuity Dr Ste 128	Orlando	FL	32826	**800-345-2737**	407-380-1553	48-19
LIA (Leather Industries of America)						
3050 K St NW Ste 400	Washington	DC	20007	**800-635-0617**	202-342-8497	48-4
Liacouras Ctr						
1776 N Broad St	Philadelphia	PA	19121	**800-298-4200**	215-204-2400	565
Libbey Inc						
300 Madison Ave PO Box 10060	Toledo	OH	43699	**888-794-8469**	419-325-2100	332
NYSE: LBY						
Liberman Broadcasting, INC						
1845 Empire Ave	Burbank	CA	91504	**866-576-5353**	818-729-5300	730
Libertarian Party						
2600 Virginia Ave NW Ste 200	Washington	DC	20037	**800-353-2887**	202-333-0008	609
Liberty Bank						
315 Main St	Middletown	CT	06457	**800-622-6732**	800-354-8950	69
Liberty Bank & Trust Co						
PO Box 60131	New Orleans	LA	70160	**800-883-3943**	504-240-5100	69
Liberty Brass Turning Company Inc						
38-01 Queens Blvd	Long Island City	NY	11101	**800-345-5939**	718-784-2911	614
Liberty Ch						
1971 University Blvd	Lynchburg	VA	24506	**800-332-1883**	434-582-2000	729
Liberty County Chamber of Commerce						
425 W Oglethorpe Hwy	Hinesville	GA	31313	**855-766-2466**	912-368-4445	137
Liberty Diversified International Inc						
5600 Hwy 169 N	New Hope	MN	55428	**800-421-1270**	763-536-6600	357-3
Liberty Drug & Surgical Inc						
195 Main St	Chatham	NJ	07928	**877-816-0111**	973-635-6200	237
Liberty Forge Inc						
PO Box 1210	Liberty	TX	77575	**800-231-2377**	936-336-5785	478
Liberty Fund Inc						
8335 Allison Pt Trial						
Ste 300	Indianapolis	IN	46250	**800-955-8335**	317-842-0880	304
Liberty Hardware Mfg Corp						
140 Business Pk Dr	Winston-Salem	NC	27107	**800-542-3789**		347
Liberty Hospital						
2525 Glenn Hendren Dr	Liberty	MO	64068	**800-344-3829**	816-781-7200	371-3
Liberty Life Insurance Co						
2000 Wade Hampton Blvd	Greenville	SC	29615	**855-428-4363**	864-609-1000	388-2
Liberty Pumps Inc						
7000 Apple Tree Ave	Bergen	NY	14416	**800-543-2550**	585-494-1817	632
Liberty Safe & Security Products Inc						
1199 W Utah Ave	Payson	UT	84651	**800-247-5625**	801-925-1000	482
Liberty Savings Bank FSB						
2251 Rombach Ave	Wilmington	OH	45177	**800-627-7890**	800-436-6300	69
Liberty Tax Service Inc						
1716 Corporate Landing Pkwy	Virginia Beach	VA	23454	**800-790-3863***	757-493-8855	724
*Cust Svc						
Liberty Toyota Scion						
4397 Rt 130 S	Burlington	NJ	08016	**888-809-7798**	609-386-6300	509
Liberty Travel Inc						
69 Spring St	Ramsey	NJ	07446	**888-271-1584**	201-934-3500	761
Liberty Tree Mall						
100 Independence Way	Danvers	MA	01923	**877-746-6642**	978-777-0794	455
Liberty University						
1971 University Blvd	Lynchburg	VA	24502	**800-543-5317**	434-582-2000	166
LibertyTree						
100 Swan Way	Oakland	CA	94621	**800-927-8733**	510-632-1366	95
Libman Co						
220 N Sheldon St	Arcola	IL	61910	**800-646-6262**		102
Libra Industries Inc						
7770 Div Dr	Mentor	OH	44060	**800-825-1674**	440-974-7770	617
Library & Information Technology Assn (LITA)						
50 E Huron St	Chicago	IL	60611	**800-545-2433**	312-280-4270	48-11
Library Binding Service (LBS)						
1801 Thompson Ave	Des Moines	IA	50316	**800-247-5323**	515-262-3191	91
Library Hotel						
299 Madison Ave	New York	NY	10017	**877-793-7323**	212-983-4500	376
Library Journal						
160 Varick St 11th Fl	New York	NY	10013	**800-588-1030**	646-380-0700	452-8
Library Leadership & Management Assn (LLAMA)						
50 E Huron St	Chicago	IL	60611	**800-545-2433**		48-11
Library of Congress						
National Library Service for the Blind & Physically Handicapped						
1291 Taylor St NW	Washington	DC	20011	**888-657-7323**	202-707-5100	340
Library of Congress Information Bulletin						
101 Independence Ave SE	Washington	DC	20540	**888-371-5848**	202-707-2905	524-4
Library Reproduction Service						
14214 S Figueroa St	Los Angeles	CA	90061	**800-255-5002**	310-354-2610	618
Libyan Arab Jamahiriya						
309-315 E 48th St	New York	NY	10017	**800-253-9646**	212-752-5775	
LICH (Long Island College Hospital)						
339 Hicks St	Brooklyn	NY	11201	**800-227-8922**	718-780-1000	371-3
Licking Valley Oil Inc						
PO Box 246	Butler	KY	41006	**800-899-9449**	859-472-7111	572
LICT Corp						
401 Theodore Fremd Ave	Rye	NY	10580	**800-690-6903**	914-921-8821	726
Lido Van & Storage Co Inc						
2152 Alton Pkwy Ste N	Irvine	CA	92606	**800-339-5436**	949-863-9000	512
Liebherr-America Inc						
4100 Chestnut Ave	Newport News	VA	23607	**866-879-6312**	757-245-5251	191

Name / Address	Toll-Free	Phone	Class
Liechty Farm Equipment Inc 1701 S Defiance St ... Archbold OH 43502	800-272-5898	419-445-1565	274
Lied Ctr for Performing Arts 301 N 12th St ... Lincoln NE 68588	800-432-3231	402-472-4700	565
Life Alert 16027 Ventura Blvd ... Encino CA 91436	800-920-3410	818-700-7000	568
Life Flight Network LLC 22285 Yellow Gate Ln NE ... Aurora OR 97002	800-232-0911	503-678-4364	13
Life Force International Corp 495 Raleigh Ave ... El Cajon CA 92064	800-531-4877	858-218-3200	342
Life Insurance Co of Alabama 302 Broad St ... Gadsden AL 35901	800-226-2371	256-543-2022	388-2
Life Insurance Company of the Southwest 15455 Dallas Pkwy Ste 800 ... Addison TX 75001	800-579-2878		388-2
Life of the South Insurance Co 10151 Deerwood Pk Blvd Bldg 100 ... Jacksonville FL 32256	800-888-2738	904-350-9660	388-5
Life Pacific College 1100 W Covina Blvd ... San Dimas CA 91773	877-886-5433	909-599-5433	159
Life Partners Inc (LPI) 204 Woodhew Dr ... Waco TX 76712	800-368-5569	254-751-7797	784
Life Settlement Solutions Inc 9201 Spectrum Ctr Blvd Ste 105 ... San Diego CA 92123	800-762-3387	858-576-8067	784
Life Technologies Corp 3175 Staley Rd ... Grand Island NY 14072	800-955-6288		568
Life-Assist Inc 11277 Sunrise Park Dr ... Rancho Cordova CA 95742	800-824-6016		470
LifeBanc 4775 Richmond Rd Ste 350 ... Cleveland OH 44128	888-558-5433	216-752-5433	538
Lifeblood Mid-South Regional Blood Ctr 1040 Madison Ave ... Memphis TN 38104	888-543-3256	901-522-8585	88
LifeCell Corp One Millennium Way ... Branchburg NJ 08876	800-226-2714		538
LifeCore Biomedical LLC 3515 Lyman Blvd ... Chaska MN 55318 *Cust Svc	800-752-2663*	952-368-4300	84
LifeCourse Associates Inc 9080 Eaton Park Rd ... Great Falls VA 22066	866-537-4999		194
LifeFone 16 Yellowstone Ave ... White Plains NY 10607	888-687-0451		568
Lifeline Medical Assoc LLC 99 Cherry Hill Rd Ste 220 ... Parsippany NJ 07054	800-845-2785	973-316-0307	371-3
Lifeline of Ohio 770 Kinnear Rd Ste 200 ... Columbus OH 43212	800-525-5667	614-291-5667	538
Lifelink Foundation Inc 409 Bayshore Blvd ... Tampa FL 33606	800-262-5775	813-253-2640	360
LifeLink Tissue Bank 8510 Sunstate St ... Tampa FL 33634	800-683-2400	813-886-8111	538
LifeNet 1864 Concert Dr ... Virginia Beach VA 23453	800-847-7831	757-464-4761	538
LifeNet Health Northwest 501 SW 39th St ... Renton WA 98057	800-858-2282		538
Lifepath Hospice 3010 W Azeele St ... Tampa FL 33609	800-209-2200	813-877-2200	368
LifePoint Health 330 Seven Springs Way ... Brentwood TN 37027 NASDAQ: LPNT	888-982-9144	615-920-7000	350
LifePoint Inc 3950 Faber Pl Dr ... Charleston SC 29405	800-462-0755	843-763-7755	269
LifeRing Secular Recovery 1440 Broadway Ste 312 ... Oakland CA 94612	800-811-4142	510-763-0779	47-21
LifeScan Inc 1000 Gibraltar Dr ... Milpitas CA 95035	800-227-8862	408-263-9789	231
LifeScan Laboratory Inc 5255 W Golf ... Skokie IL 60077	800-270-0037		412
LifeServe Blood Ctr 431 E Locust St ... Des Moines IA 50309	800-287-4903		88
LifeShare Blood Centers 8910 Linwood Ave ... Shreveport LA 71106	800-256-4483	318-222-7770	88
LifeShare Community Blood Services 105 Cleveland St ... Elyria OH 44035	800-317-5412	440-322-5700	88
LifeShare of the Carolinas 1200 Ridgefield Blvd Ste 150 ... Asheville NC 28806	800-932-4483	828-665-0107	269
LifeShare Transplant Donor Services of Oklahoma 4705 NW Expy ... Oklahoma City OK 73132	888-580-5680	405-840-5551	538
LifeSize Communications Inc 1601 S Mopac Expwy Ste 100 ... Austin TX 78746	877-543-3749	512-347-9300	51
LifeSource Blood Services 2764 Aurora Ave ... Naperville IL 60540	877-543-3768		88
LifeSouth Community Blood Centers 4039 Newberry Rd ... Gainesville FL 32607	888-795-2707		88
LifeSouth Community Blood Centers Atlanta 4891 Ashford Dunwoody Rd ... Atlanta GA 30338	888-795-2707	404-329-1994	88
Lifespire 350 Fifth Ave Ste 301 ... New York NY 10118	800-221-5594	212-741-0100	47-17
Lifespring Inc 460 Spring St ... Jeffersonville IN 47130	800-456-2117	812-280-2080	350
Life-tech Inc PO Box 1849 ... Stafford TX 77497	800-231-9841	281-491-6600	471
Lifetime Brands Inc 1000 Steward Ave ... Garden City NY 11530 NASDAQ: LCUT	800-252-3390	516-683-6000	481
Lifetime Brands Inc Farberware Div 1000 Stewart Ave ... Garden City NY 11530	800-999-2811	516-683-6000	481
Lifetime Brands Inc Hoffritz Div 1000 Stewart Ave ... Garden City NY 11530	800-252-3390	516-683-6000	481
Lifetime Healthcare Cos, The 165 Ct St ... Rochester NY 14647	800-847-1200	585-454-1700	357-4
Lifetime Products Inc Freeport Ctr Bldg D-11 PO Box 160010 ... Clearfield UT 84016	800-242-3865	801-776-1532	701
Lifetouch Church Directories 1371 Portland Way N ... Galion OH 44833	800-521-4611	419-468-4739	628-10
Lifeway Foods Inc 6431 W Oakton St ... Morton Grove IL 60053 NASDAQ: LWAY	877-281-3874	847-967-1010	295-27
Lifewings Partners LLC 9198 Crestwyn Hills Dr ... Memphis TN 38125	800-290-9314		458
Lift-All Company Inc 1909 McFarland Dr ... Landisville PA 17538	800-909-1964	717-898-6615	465
Lifts West Condominium Resort Hotel PO Box 330 ... Red River NM 87558	800-221-1859	505-754-2778	660
Ligature, The 4909 Alcoa Ave ... Los Angeles CA 90058	800-944-5440	323-585-6000	771
Light Fabrications Inc 40 Hytec Cir ... Rochester NY 14606	800-836-6920	585-426-5330	3
Light for Life Foundation International PO Box 644 ... Westminster CO 80036	800-273-8255	303-429-3530	47-17
Light Impressions 2340 Brighton Henrietta Town Line Rd ... Rochester NY 14623	800-975-6429		620
Light Metals Corp 2740 Prairie St SW ... Wyoming MI 49509	888-363-8257	616-538-3030	480
Light Sources Inc 37 Robinson Blvd ... Orange CT 06477	800-826-9465	203-799-7877	433
LightEdge Solutions Inc 215 10th St Ste 1000 ... Des Moines IA 50309	877-771-3343	515-471-1000	795
Lighthouse Club Hotel 201 60th St ... Ocean City MD 21842	888-371-5400	410-524-5400	376
Lighthouse Computer Services Inc 6 Blackstone Valley Pl Ste 205 ... Lincoln RI 02865	888-542-8030	401-334-0799	181
Lighthouse Electric Co-op Inc PO Box 600 ... Floydada TX 79235	800-657-7192	806-983-2814	245
Lighthouse Hospice 1040 Kings Hwy N Ste 100 ... Cherry Hill NJ 08034 *General	888-467-7423*	856-414-1155	368
Lighthouse International 111 E 59th St ... New York NY 10022	800-829-0500	212-821-9200	47-17
Lighthouse Lodge & Suites 1150 Lighthouse Ave ... Pacific Grove CA 93950	800-858-1249		376
Lighting Quotient, The 114 Boston Post Rd ... West Haven CT 06516	800-222-0193	203-931-4455	435
Lightnin 135 Mt Read Blvd ... Rochester NY 14611	877-247-3797	585-436-5550	383
Lightning Source 1246 Heil Quaker Blvd ... La Vergne TN 37086	800-509-4156	615-213-5815	628-2
Lightning Transportation Inc 16820 Blake Rd ... Hagerstown MD 21740	800-233-0624	301-582-5700	770
Lightower Fiber Networks 80 Central St ... Boxborough MA 01719	888-583-4237	978-264-6000	726
Lightriver Technologies Inc 2150 John Glenn Dre Ste 200 ... Concord CA 94520	888-544-4825	941-552-9410	672
Lights of America 611 Reyes Dr ... Walnut CA 91789 *Cust Svc	800-321-8100*	909-594-7883	435
Lil' Drug Store Products Inc 1201 Continental Pl Ne ... Cedar Rapids IA 52402	800-553-5022		238
Lila Cockrell Theatre 200 E Market St ... San Antonio TX 78205 *General	877-504-8895*	210-207-8500	565
Lilleys' Landing Resort 367 River Ln ... Branson MO 65616	866-545-5397	417-334-6380	660
Lillie's Asian Cuisine 129 E Fremont St ... Las Vegas NV 89101	800-634-3454	702-385-7111	662
Lima Estates 411 N Middletown Rd ... Media PA 19063	888-398-2287	610-565-7020	663
Lima Memorial Hospital 1001 Bellefontaine Ave ... Lima OH 45804	800-252-3337	419-228-3335	371-3
Lima News 3515 Elida Rd ... Lima OH 45807	800-686-9924	419-223-1010	525-2
Lima/Allen County Convention & Visitors Bureau 144 S Main St Ste 101 ... Lima OH 45801	888-222-6075	419-222-6075	207
Lime Rock Park 60 White Hollow Rd ... Lakeville CT 06039	800-722-3577	860-435-5000	508
Limestone College 1115 College Dr ... Gaffney SC 29340	800-795-7151	864-489-7151	166
Limoneira Co 1141 Cummings Rd ... Santa Paula CA 93060 NASDAQ: LMNR	866-321-8953	805-525-5541	314-2
Limpert Bros Inc 202 NW Blvd PO Box 1480 ... Vineland NJ 08362	800-691-1353	856-691-1353	295-15
LIMRA International Inc 300 Day Hill Rd ... Windsor CT 06095	866-540-4505	860-688-3358	48-9
Lincoln Botanical Garden & Arboretum (BGA) University of Nebraska 1309 N 17th St ... Lincoln NE 68588	800-742-8800	402-472-2679	96
Lincoln Christian College Seminary 100 Campus View Dr ... Lincoln IL 62656	888-522-5228	217-732-3168	167-3
Lincoln City Visitor & Convention Bureau 801 SW Hwy 101 Ste 401 ... Lincoln City OR 97367	800-452-2151	541-996-1274	207
Lincoln College 300 Keokuk St ... Lincoln IL 62656	800-569-0556	217-732-3155	160
Lincoln College of Technology 7225 Winton Dr Bldg 128 ... Indianapolis IN 46268	800-228-6232	317-632-5553	788
Lincoln Convention & Visitors Bureau 1135 M St Ste 300 ... Lincoln NE 68508	800-423-8212	402-434-5335	207
Lincoln County 300 Central Ave ... Carrizozo NM 88301	800-687-2705	575-648-2385	336
LINCOLN EDUCATIONAL SERVICES 85 Sigourney St ... Hartford CT 06105	800-762-4337	800-254-0547	161
Suffield 8 PROGRESS DR ... Shelton CT 06484	800-254-0547	203-929-0592	161
Lincoln Electric Co 22801 St Clair Ave ... Cleveland OH 44117	888-935-3878	216-481-8100	798
Lincoln Electric Co-op Inc (LEC) 500 Osloski Rd PO Box 628 ... Eureka MT 59917	800-442-2994	406-889-3301	245
Lincoln Electric Holdings Inc 22801 St Clair Ave ... Cleveland OH 44117 NASDAQ: LECO	800-833-9353	216-481-8100	357-3
Lincoln FSB 1101 N St 68508 PO Box 80038 ... Lincoln NE 68501	800-333-2158	402-474-1400	70
Lincoln General Insurance Co 3501 Concord Rd ... York PA 17402	800-876-3350	717-757-0000	387
Lincoln Heritage Life Insurance Co PO Box 29045 ... Phoenix AZ 85038	800-433-8181		388-2
Lincoln Journal-Star 926 P St ... Lincoln NE 68508	800-742-7315	402-475-4200	525-2
Lincoln Laboratory Massachusetts Institute of Technology 244 Wood St ... Lexington MA 02420	800-445-8667	781-981-5500	659
Lincoln Land Community College 5250 Shepherd Rd PO Box 19256 ... Springfield IL 62794	800-727-4161	217-786-2200	160
Lincoln Land Oil Co PO Box 4307 ... Springfield IL 62708	800-238-4912	217-523-5050	315
Lincoln Memorial University 6965 Cumberland Gap Pkwy ... Harrogate TN 37752	800-325-0900	423-869-3611	166

Entry	Toll-Free	Phone	Class
Lincoln National Corp (LNC) 150 N Radnor-Chester Rd Radnor PA 19087 *NYSE: LNC*	**877-275-5462**	484-583-1400	357-4
Lincoln National Life Insurance Co 1300 S Clinton St Fort Wayne IN 46802	**800-454-6265**	260-455-2000	388-2
Lincoln Trail College 11220 State Hwy 1 Robinson IL 62454	**866-582-4322**	618-544-8657	160
Lincoln University 820 Chestnut St B-7 Young Hall Jefferson City MO 65102 *Admissions	**800-521-5052***	573-681-5599	166
Lincoln Wood Products Inc 1400 W Taylor St PO Box 375 Merrill WI 54452	**800-967-2461**		236
Lincoln-Mercury Co PO Box 6128 Dearborn MI 48121	**800-521-4140**		58
Linda Hall Library 5109 Cherry St Kansas City MO 64110	**800-662-1545**	816-363-4600	431-3
Lindal Cedar Homes Inc 4300 S 104th Pl Seattle WA 98178 *Prod Info	**800-426-0536***	206-725-0900	105
Lindblad Expeditions 96 Morton St Ninth Fl New York NY 10014	**800-397-3348**	212-765-7740	750
Lindeblad Piano Restoration 101 Us 46 Pine Brook NJ 07058	**888-587-4266**		520
Linden Hall School for Girls 212 E Main St Lititz PA 17543	**800-258-5778**	717-626-8512	615
Linden Publishing 2006 S Mary St Fresno CA 93721 *Sales	**800-345-4447***	559-233-6633	628-2
Linden Row Inn 100 E Franklin St Richmond VA 23219	**800-348-7424**	804-783-7000	376
Linden Warehouse & Distribution Co Inc 1300 Lower Rd Linden NJ 07036	**800-333-2855**	908-862-1400	770
Lindenmeyr Book Publishing Papers 521 Fifth Ave 6th Fl New York NY 10175	**800-221-3042**	212-551-3900	546
Lindenmeyr Central Three Manhattanville Rd Purchase NY 10577	**800-221-3042**	914-696-9300	546
Lindenmeyr Munroe 14 Research Pkwy Wallingford CT 06492	**800-842-8480**		546
Lindenmeyr Munroe Paper Corp 115 Moonachie Ave Moonachie NJ 07074	**800-221-3042**	201-440-6491	546
Lindenwood University 209 S Kingshighway Saint Charles MO 63301	**877-615-8212**	636-949-2000	166
Lindey's Prime Steak House 3600 N Snelling Ave Arden Hills MN 55112	**866-491-0538**	651-633-9813	662
LINDO Systems Inc 1415 N Dayton St Chicago IL 60622 *Sales	**800-441-2378***	312-988-7422	179-5
Lindquist Steels Inc 1050 Woodend Rd Stratford CT 06615	**800-243-9637**		487
Lindsay Corp 2222 N 111th St Omaha NE 68164 *NYSE: LNN*	**866-404-5049**	402-829-6800	273
Lindsay Manufacturing Inc PO Box 1708 Ponca City OK 74602	**800-546-3729**	580-762-2457	776
Lindsay Stone & Briggs Inc One South Pinckney St Suite 500 Madison WI 53703	**866-403-8838**	608-251-7070	4
Lindsey & Company Inc 2302 Llama Dr Searcy AR 72143	**800-890-7058**	501-268-5324	175
Lindsey Wilson College 210 Lindsey Wilson St Columbia KY 42728	**800-264-0138**	270-384-2126	166
Lindt & Sprungli USA 1 Fine Chocolate Pl Stratham NH 03885	**877-695-4638**	603-778-8100	295-8
Lineage Power Corp 601 Shiloh Rd Plano TX 75074	**877-546-3243**	972-244-9288	775
Lineagen Inc 423 Wakara Way Ste 200 Salt Lake City UT 84108	**888-888-6736**	801-931-6200	659
Linear Laboratories 42025 Osgood Rd Fremont CA 94539	**800-536-0262**	510-226-0488	202
Linear Technology Corp 1630 McCarthy Blvd Milpitas CA 95035 *NASDAQ: LLTC*	**888-500-6973**	408-432-1900	687
Linemaster Switch Corp 29 Plaine Hill Rd Woodstock CT 06281	**800-974-3668**	860-974-1000	480
Linen Chest Inc 4455 AutoRt Des Laurentides Laval QC H7L5X8	**800-363-3832**	514-341-7077	361
Linetec 725 S 75th Ave Wausau WI 54401	**888-717-1472**	715-843-4100	475
Linfield College 900 SE Baker St McMinnville OR 97128 *Admissions	**800-640-2287***	503-883-2213	166
Lingo Inc 7901 Jones Branch Dr Ninth Fl Mclean VA 22102	**888-546-4699**		384
Lingo Manufacturing Co 7400 Industrial Rd Florence KY 41042 *Cust Svc	**800-354-9771***	859-371-2662	233
Lingua School Inc 225 E Las Olas Blvd Sixth Fl Fort Lauderdale FL 33301	**888-654-6482**	954-577-9955	420
Linguistics Systems Inc 201 Broadway Cambridge MA 02139	**877-654-5006**		758
Link Electronics Inc 2137 Rust Ave Cape Girardeau MO 63703	**800-776-4411**	573-334-4433	115
Linn Gear Co 100 N Eigth St PO Box 397 Lebanon OR 97355	**800-547-2471**	541-259-1211	613
LINQ Services 6679 Santa Barbara Rd Ste D Elkridge MD 21075	**800-421-5467**		384
Lintern Corp 8685 Stn St Mentor OH 44060	**800-321-3638**	440-255-9333	14
Linville Caverns Inc 19929 US 221 N Marion NC 28752	**800-419-0540**		49-4
Lion Apparel Inc 7200 Poe Ave Ste 400 Dayton OH 45414	**800-548-6614**	937-898-1949	153-18
Lion Brand Yarn Co 135 Kero Rd Carlstadt NJ 07072	**800-795-5466**	212-243-8995	734-9
Lion Brewery Inc 700 N Pennsylvania Ave Wilkes-Barre PA 18705	**888-295-2337**	570-823-8801	101
Lion Bros Company Inc 10246 Reisterstown Rd Owings Mills MD 21117 *Cust Svc	**800-365-6543***	410-363-1000	258
Lion Inc 4700 42nd Ave SW Ste 430 Seattle WA 98116	**800-546-6463**	206-577-1440	502
Lion Magazine 300 W 22nd St Oak Brook IL 60523 *Circ	**800-710-7822***	630-571-5466	452-10

Entry	Toll-Free	Phone	Class
Lion Square Lodge & Conference Ctr 660 W Lionshead Pl Vail CO 81657	**800-525-1943**	970-476-2281	660
Lionel .com LLC 26750 23 Mile Rd Chesterfield MI 48051	**800-454-6635**	586-949-4100	752
Lionetti Assoc 450 S Front St Elizabeth NJ 07202	**800-734-0910**	908-820-8800	677
Lions Eye Bank of Manitoba & Northwest Ontario Inc 691 Wolseley Ave Winnipeg MB R3G1C3	**800-552-6820**	204-788-8507	269
Lions Eye Bank of Nebraska Inc *University of Nebraska Medical Ctr* UNMC 985541 Omaha NE 68198	**800-225-7244**	402-559-4039	269
Lions Eye Bank of North Dakota 410 E Thayer Ave Ste 201 Bismarck ND 58501	**800-372-3751**	701-250-9390	269
Lions Eye Bank of Wisconsin 2401 American Ln Madison WI 53704	**877-233-2354**	608-233-2354	269
Lions Gate Entertainment Corp Lions Gate Television Div 2700 Colorado Ave Ste 200 Santa Monica CA 90404	**800-322-2885**	310-449-9200	507
Lions Gate Hospital 231 E 15th St North Vancouver BC V7L2L7	**800-984-1131**	604-988-3131	371-2
Lions Medical Eye Bank & Research Ctr of Eastern Virginia Inc 600 Gresham Dr Norfolk VA 23507	**800-453-6059**		269
LiphaTech Inc 3600 W Elm St Milwaukee WI 53209	**888-331-7900**		84
Lipinski Landscape & Irrigation Contractors Inc 100 Sharp Rd Marlton NJ 08053	**800-644-6035**		419
LipoScience Inc 2500 Sumner Blvd Raleigh NC 27616	**877-547-6837**	919-212-1999	231
Lipper International Inc 235 Washington St Wallingford CT 06492	**800-243-3129**	203-269-8588	721
Lipscomb University 3901 Granny White Pk Nashville TN 37204	**800-333-4358**	615-966-1000	166
Lipten Company LLC 28054 Ctr Oaks Ct Wixom MI 48393	**800-860-0790**	248-374-8910	382
Liquid Transport Corp 8470 Allison Pt Blvd Ste 400 Indianapolis IN 46250	**800-942-3175**	317-841-4200	770
Liquidity Services Inc 1920 L St NW Sixth Fl Washington DC 20036 *NASDAQ: LQDT*	**800-310-4604**	202-467-6868	50
Liquidmetal Technologies Inc (LQMT) 30452 Esperanza Rancho Santa Margarita CA 92688 *OTC: LQMT*	**888-203-1112**	949-635-2100	477
Lisa Motor Lines 1145 Empire Central Pl PO Box 655888 Dallas TX 75247	**800-569-9200**	214-630-8090	770
Lisle Convention & Visitors Bureau 925 Burlington Ave Lisle IL 60532	**800-733-9811**	630-769-1000	207
List Industries Inc 401 Jim Moran Blvd Deerfield Beach FL 33442	**800-776-1342**	954-429-9155	318-3
Lista International Corp 106 Lowland St Holliston MA 01746 *Cust Svc	**800-722-3020***	508-429-1350	286
Listel Hotel, The 1300 Robson St Vancouver BC V6E1C5	**800-663-5491**	604-684-8461	376
Listo Pencil Corp 1925 Union St Alameda CA 94501	**800-547-8648**	510-522-2910	564
LITA (Library & Information Technology Assn) 50 E Huron St Chicago IL 60611	**800-545-2433**	312-280-4270	48-11
Litchfield Beach & Golf Resort 14276 Ocean Hwy Pawleys Island SC 29585	**888-766-4633**	843-237-3000	660
Litehouse Inc 1109 N Ella Ave Sandpoint ID 83864	**800-669-3169**	208-263-7569	295-19
Litetronics International Inc 4101 W 123rd St Alsip IL 60803	**800-860-3392**	708-389-8000	433
Lithia Motors Inc 360 E Jackson St Medford OR 97501 *NYSE: LAD*	**866-318-9660**		56
Lithographix Inc 12250 Crenshaw Blvd Hawthorne CA 90250 *General	**800-848-2449***	323-770-1000	619
Litho-Krome Co 5700 Old Brim Dr Midland GA 31820	**800-572-8028**	706-562-7900	619
Lithonia Lighting One Lithonia Way Conyers GA 30012	**800-858-7763**	770-922-9000	435
Lith-O-Roll Corp 9521 Telstar Ave El Monte CA 91731	**800-423-4176**	626-579-0340	449
Lititz Mutual Insurance Co Two N Broad St PO Box 900 Lititz PA 17543	**800-626-4751**	717-626-4751	388-4
Littau Harvester Inc 855 Rogue Ave Stayton OR 97383	**866-262-2495**	503-769-5953	274
Littelfuse Inc 8755 W Higgins Rd Ste 500 Chicago IL 60631 *NASDAQ: LFUS* ■ *Sales	**800-227-0029***	773-628-1000	720
Little America Hotel & Resort Cheyenne 2800 W Lincolnway Cheyenne WY 82009	**800-445-6945**	307-775-8400	376
Little America Hotel & Towers Salt Lake City 555 S Main St Salt Lake City UT 84101	**800-453-9450**	801-258-6568	376
Little America Hotel Flagstaff 2515 E Butler Ave Flagstaff AZ 86004	**800-352-4386**	928-779-7900	376
Little America Hotels & Resorts 500 S Main St Salt Lake City UT 84101	**800-281-7899**	801-596-5700	376
Little Bank Inc, The 804 Carey Rd Kinston NC 28501 *OTC: LTLB*	**855-449-0975**	252-939-9990	69
Little Brown & Co 237 Pk Ave New York NY 10017 *Cust Svc	**800-759-0190***	212-364-1100	628-2
Little Caesars Inc 2211 Woodward Ave Detroit MI 48201	**800-722-3727**	313-983-6409	661
Little Creek Casino Resort 91 W State Rt 108 Shelton WA 98584	**800-667-7711**	360-427-7711	660
Little Falls Granite Works 10802 Hwy 10 PO Box 240 Little Falls MN 56345	**800-862-2417**	320-632-9277	715
Little Gym International Inc 7001 N Scottsdale Rd Paradise Valley AZ 85253 *General	**888-228-2878***		351
Little Kids Inc 225 Chapman St Ste 202 Providence RI 02905	**800-545-5437**	401-454-7600	601
Little Lady Foods Inc 2323 Pratt Blvd Elk Grove Village IL 60007	**800-439-1440**	847-631-3500	295-36
Little Nell, The 675 E Durant Ave Aspen CO 81611	**888-843-6355**	970-920-4600	376

Company / Address	City	State	ZIP	Toll-Free	Phone	Class
Little Palm Island Resort & Spa 28500 Overseas Hwy MM 28.5	Little Torch Key	FL	33042	**800-343-8567**	305-872-2524	660
Little Pee Dee State Park 1298 State Pk Rd	Dillon	SC	29536	**800-491-1764**	843-774-8872	558
Little Rapids Corp 2273 Larsen Rd	Green Bay	WI	54303	**800-496-3040**	920-496-3040	569
Little River Electric Co-op Inc (LRECI) PO Box 220	Abbeville	SC	29620	**800-459-2141**	864-366-2141	245
Little Rock Air Force Base 1250 Thomas Ave	Little Rock AFB	AR	72099	**800-557-6815**	501-987-1110	492-1
Little Rock Convention & Visitors Bureau 426 W Markham St PO Box 3232	Little Rock	AR	72203	**800-844-4781**	501-376-4781	207
Little Talbot Island State Park 12157 Heckscher Dr	Jacksonville	FL	32226	**800-326-3521**	904-251-2320	558
Little Tikes Co, The 2180 Barlow Rd *Cust Svc	Hudson	OH	44236	**800-321-0183***		752
Little White House State Historic Site 401 Little White House Rd	Warm Springs	GA	31830	**800-864-7275**	706-655-5870	558
Littlefield Feedyard Farm to Market 37	Littlefield	TX	79339	**800-658-6014**	806-385-5141	10-1
Littleford Day Inc 7451 Empire Dr	Florence	KY	41042	**800-365-8555**	859-525-7600	383
Littler Mendelson PC 650 California St 20th Fl	San Francisco	CA	94108	**888-548-8537**	415-433-1940	425
Littlestown Foundry Inc 150 Charles St PO Box 69	Littlestown	PA	17340	**800-471-0844**	717-359-4141	307
Littleton Coin Company LLC 1309 Mt Eustis Rd	Littleton	NH	03561	**800-645-3122**	603-444-5386	49-3
Liturgical Publications Inc 2875 S James Dr	New Berlin	WI	53151	**800-876-4574**	262-785-1188	628-9
Live Design 249 W 17th St *Sales	New York	NY	10011	**866-505-7173***	212-204-4272	452-9
LiveMocha Inc 1011 Western Ave, Ste 1000	Seattle	WA	98104	**800-399-6212**	206-257-2500	384
Livengrin Foundation 4833 Hulmeville Rd	Bensalem	PA	19020	**800-245-4746**	215-638-5200	717
Livestock Marketing Assn (LMA) 10510 N Ambassador Dr	Kansas City	MO	64153	**888-484-8477**	816-891-0502	47-2
Living Assistance Services Inc 937 Haverford Rd Ste 200	Bryn Mawr	PA	19010	**800-365-4189**	610-924-0630	309
Living Bank PO Box 6725	Houston	TX	77027	**800-528-2971**	713-961-9431	47-17
Living Earth Crafts 3210 Executive Ridge Dr	Vista	CA	92081	**800-358-8292**	760-597-2155	75
Living Spa at El Monte Sagrado 317 Kit Carson Rd	Taos	NM	87571	**888-213-4419**	575-758-3502	698
Living Spaces Furniture LLC 14501 Artesia Blvd	La Mirada	CA	90638	**877-266-7300**		320
Livingston County Chamber of Commerce 4635 Millennium Dr	Geneseo	NY	14454	**800-538-7365**	585-243-2222	137
Livingston County Daily Press & Argus 323 E Grand River Ave	Howell	MI	48843	**888-999-1288**	517-548-2000	628-8
Livingston Memorial Visiting Nurse Assn Hospice 1996 Eastman Ave Ste 101	Ventura	CA	93003	**800-830-8881**	805-642-1608	368
Livingston Pipe & Tube Inc 1612 Rt 4 N PO Box 300	Staunton	IL	62088	**800-548-7473**	618-635-8700	487
Livingstone College 701 W Monroe St	Salisbury	NC	28144	**800-835-3435**	704-216-6963	166
LJ Gonzer Assoc Inc 14 Commerce Dr Ste 305	Cranford	NJ	07016	**866-692-4538**	908-709-9494	712
LJB Inc 2500 Newmark Dr PO Box 20246	Miamisburg	OH	45342	**866-552-3536**	937-259-5000	261
LK Industries 1357 W Beaver St	Jacksonville	FL	32209	**800-531-4975**	904-354-8882	297
LKQ Corp 120 N LaSalle St Ste 3300 *NASDAQ: LKQX*	Chicago	IL	60602	**877-557-2677**	312-621-1950	60
LL Bean Inc 15 Casco St	Freeport	ME	04033	**800-341-4341**	207-552-3080	454
LLAMA (Library Leadership & Management Assn) 50 E Huron St	Chicago	IL	60611	**800-545-2433**		48-11
Llano Estacado Winery 3426 E FM 1585 PO Box 3487	Lubbock	TX	79404	**800-634-3854**	806-745-2258	49-6
LLEC (Lyon-Lincoln Electric Co-op Inc) 205 W Hwy 14 PO Box 639	Tyler	MN	56178	**800-927-6276**	507-247-5505	245
Llewellyn Worldwide Inc 2143 Wooddale Dr	Woodbury	MN	55125	**800-843-6666**	651-291-1970	628-2
LLLI (La Leche League International Inc) 957 N Plum Grove Rd	Schaumburg	IL	60173	**800-525-3243**	847-519-7730	47-17
Lloyd Inc 604 W Thomas Ave PO Box 130	Shenandoah	IA	51601	**800-831-0004**	712-246-4000	575
Lloyd Laboratories Inc 24 Fitch Ct	Wakefield	MA	01880	**800-361-6766**	781-224-0083	143
Lloyd's Florist 9216 Preston Hwy	Louisville	KY	40229	**800-264-1825**	502-968-5428	292
LMA (Livestock Marketing Assn) 10510 N Ambassador Dr	Kansas City	MO	64153	**888-484-8477**	816-891-0502	47-2
LMG Inc PO Box 770429	Orlando	FL	32877	**888-226-3100**	407-850-0505	264-2
LMH (Lawrence Memorial Hospital) 325 Maine St	Lawrence	KS	66044	**800-749-4144**	785-505-5000	371-3
LMI (Legg Mason Inc) 100 International Dr *NYSE: LM*	Baltimore	MD	21202	**800-822-5544**	410-539-0000	681
LN Curtis & Sons 1800 Peralta St	Oakland	CA	94607	**800-443-3556**	510-839-5111	670
LNB Bancorp Inc 457 Broadway *NASDAQ: LNBB*	Lorain	OH	44052	**800-860-1007**	440-989-3348	357-2
LNC (Lincoln National Corp) 150 N Radnor-Chester Rd *NYSE: LNC*	Radnor	PA	19087	**877-275-5462**	484-583-1400	357-4
LNI Custom Manufacturing Inc 12536 Chadron Ave	Hawthorne	CA	90250	**800-338-3387**	310-978-2000	692
Load Rite Trailers Inc 265 Lincoln Hwy	Fairless Hills	PA	19030	**800-562-3783**	215-949-0500	753
Loaf N' Jug Mini Mart 442 Keeler Pkwy	Pueblo	CO	81001	**866-562-3658**	719-948-3071	205
loanDepot 26642 Towne Centre Dr	Foothill Ranch	CA	92610	**888-337-6888**		502
Loblaw Cos Ltd One President's Choice Cir	Brampton	ON	L6Y5S5	**888-495-5111**	905-459-2500	342
Lobster Sports Inc 7340 Fulton Ave	North Hollywood	CA	91605	**800-210-5992**	818-764-6000	701
LoBue & Majdalany Management Group 572B Ruger St PO Box 29920	San Francisco	CA	94129	**800-820-4690**	415-561-6110	46
Local Government Federal Credit Union 323 W Jones St Ste 600	Raleigh	NC	27603	**888-732-8562**	919-857-2150	219
LocBox 400 Second St Ste 400	San Francisco	CA	94107	**855-256-2269**		196
Lochinvar Corp 300 Maddox Simpson Pkwy	Lebanon	TN	37090	**800-722-2101**	615-889-8900	35
Lochmueller Group 6200 Vogel Rd	Evansville	IN	47715	**800-423-7411**	812-479-6200	256
Lock Haven University 401 N Fairview St	Lock Haven	PA	17745	**800-233-8978**	570-484-2011	166
Lock Joint Tube Inc 515 W Ireland Rd	South Bend	IN	46614	**800-257-6859**	574-299-5326	485
Lockheed Federal Credit Union (LFCU) 2340 Hollywood Way	Burbank	CA	91505	**800-328-5328**	818-565-2020	219
Lockheed Martin Corp 6801 Rockledge Dr *NYSE: LMT*	Bethesda	MD	20817	**866-562-2363**	301-897-6000	20
Lockheed Martin Space Systems Co Michoud Operations 13800 Old Gentilly Rd	New Orleans	LA	70129	**866-562-2363**	504-257-3311	499
Lockheed Window Corp Rt 100 PO Box 166	Pascoag	RI	02859	**800-537-3061**	401-568-3061	234
Lockmasters Security Institute 2101 John C Watts Dr	Nicholasville	KY	40356	**800-654-0637**	859-885-6041	347
Lockwood Advisors Inc 760 Moore Rd	King Of Prussia	PA	19406	**800-200-3033**		68
Lockwood Products Inc 5615 Willow Ln	Lake Oswego	OR	97035	**800-423-1625**	503-635-8113	367
Lodal Inc 620 N Hooper St PO Box 2315	Kingsford	MI	49802	**800-435-3500**	906-779-1700	509
LoDan Electronics Inc 3311 N Kennicott Ave	Arlington Heights	IL	60004	**800-401-4995**	847-398-5311	803
Lodge & Club at Ponte Vedra Beach 607 Ponte Vedra Blvd	Ponte Vedra Beach	FL	32082	**800-243-4304**	888-839-9145	660
Lodge & Spa at Cordillera 2205 Cordillera Way	Edwards	CO	81632	**800-877-3529**	970-926-2200	376
Lodge At Breckenridge, The 112 Overlook Dr	Breckenridge	CO	80424	**800-736-1607**	970-453-9300	376
Lodge at Pebble Beach 1700 17-Mile Dr	Pebble Beach	CA	93953	**800-654-9300**	831-624-3811	660
Lodge at Sonoma - A Renaissance Resort & Spa 1325 Broadway	Sonoma	CA	95476	**866-263-0758**	707-935-6600	660
Lodge at the Mountain Village 1415 Lowell Ave	Park City	UT	84060	**800-453-1360**	435-649-0800	376
Lodge at Ventana Canyon - A Wyndham Luxury Resort 6200 N Clubhouse Ln	Tucson	AZ	85750	**800-828-5701**	520-577-1400	660
Lodge Hotel & Conference Ctr 900 Spruce Hills Dr	Bettendorf	IA	52722	**866-690-4006**	563-359-7141	376
Lodge of Four Seasons 315 Four Seasons Dr PO Box 215 *Resv	Lake Ozark	MO	65049	**888-265-5500***	573-365-3000	660
Lodge on the Desert 306 N Alvernon Way	Tucson	AZ	85711	**877-498-6776**	520-320-2000	376
Lodgian Inc 2002 Summit Blvd Ste 300 *NYSE: LGN*	Atlanta	GA	30319	**888-750-5834**	404-364-9400	376
Lodging Magazine 385 Oxford Vly Rd Ste 420	Yardley	PA	19067	**800-394-5157**	215-321-9662	452-5
Lodi Conference & Visitors Bureau 115 S School St Ste 5	Lodi	CA	95240	**800-798-1810**	209-365-1195	207
Lodi Irrigation 1301 E Armstrong Rd	Lodi	CA	95242	**800-634-7272**		426
Lodi Memorial Hospital 975 S Fairmont Ave	Lodi	CA	95240	**800-323-3360**	209-334-3411	371-3
Lodi News-Sentinel 125 N Church St	Lodi	CA	95240	**800-407-7653**	209-369-2761	525-2
Loeber Motors Inc 4255 W Touhy Ave	Lincolnwood	IL	60712	**888-211-4485**	847-675-1000	56
Loews Coronado Bay Resort 4000 Coronado Bay Rd	Coronado	CA	92118	**800-815-6397**	619-424-4000	660
Loews Corp 667 Madison Ave	New York	NY	10065	**800-235-6397**	212-521-2000	186
Loews Ventana Canyon Resort 7000 N Resort Dr	Tucson	AZ	85750	**800-234-5117**	520-299-2020	660
Loftness Specialized Farm Equipment Inc 650 S Main St PO Box 337	Hector	MN	55342	**800-828-7624**	320-848-6266	273
Lofton Label Inc 6290 Claude Way	Inver Grove Heights	MN	55076	**877-447-8118**	651-552-6257	545-1
Lofts Hotel & Suites 55 E Nationwide Blvd *General	Columbus	OH	43215	**877-902-9022***	614-461-2663	376
Logan Capital Management Inc Six Coulter Ave Ste 2000	Ardmore	PA	19003	**800-215-1100**		398
Logan Clay Products Co 201 S Walnut St	Logan	OH	43138	**800-848-2141**		148
Logan Corp 555 Seventh Ave	Huntington	WV	25701	**888-853-4751**	304-526-4700	382
Logan County Chamber of Commerce 100 S Main St	Bellefontaine	OH	43311	**877-360-3608**	937-599-5121	137
Logan Farms Honey Glazed Hams 10560 Westheimer Rd	Houston	TX	77042	**800-833-4267**	713-781-4335	334
Logan Regional Medical Ctr 20 Hospital Dr	Logan	WV	25601	**888-982-9144**	304-831-1101	371-3
Logan Trucking Inc 3224 Navarre Rd SW	Canton	OH	44706	**800-683-0142**	330-478-1404	187
Logansport Financial Corp 723 E Broadway PO Box 569 *OTC: LOGN*	Logansport	IN	46947	**800-541-9154**	574-722-3855	357-2
Logansport Juvenile Correctional Facility 1118 S St Rd 25	Logansport	IN	46947	**800-800-5556**	574-753-7571	409
Logic Devices Inc 1375 Geneva Dr *OTC: LOGC*	Sunnyvale	CA	94089	**800-233-2518**	408-542-5400	687
Logicease Solutions Inc 1 Bay Plaza Ste 520	Burlingame	CA	94010	**866-212-3273**	650-373-1111	181
Logility Inc 470 E Paces Ferry Rd	Atlanta	GA	30305	**800-762-5207**	404-261-9777	179-1

Name / Address	City	State	ZIP	Toll-Free	Phone	Class
Logistics Plus Inc 1406 Peach St	Erie	PA	16501	**866-564-7587**	814-461-7600	310
Logitech Inc 6505 Kaiser Dr	Fremont	CA	94555	**800-231-7717*** *Sales	510-795-8500	174-2
Logos Christian College 9000 Regency Sq Blvd	Jacksonville	FL	32211	**800-252-4253**	904-745-3311	166
LOMA 2300 Windy Ridge Pkwy Ste 600	Atlanta	GA	30339	**800-275-5662**	770-951-1770	48-9
Loma Linda University Medical Ctr 11234 Anderson St	Loma Linda	CA	92354	**877-558-6248**	909-558-4000	371-3
Loma Linda University School of Medicine 11175 Campus St	Loma Linda	CA	92350	**800-422-4558**	909-558-4467	167-2
Lomanco Inc 2101 W Main St	Jacksonville	AR	72076	**800-643-5596**	501-982-6511	14
Lombardi's 401 Biscayne Blvd	Miami	FL	33132	**888-286-3792**		662
Lompoc Valley Chamber of Commerce & Visitors Bureau PO Box 626	Lompoc	CA	93438	**800-240-0999**	805-736-4567	137
London Drugs Ltd 12251 Horseshoe Way	Richmond	BC	V7A4X5	**888-991-2299**	604-272-7400	238
London Fog 1615 Kellogg Dr	Douglas	GA	31535	**877-588-8189**	912-384-8189	153-5
London Free Press 369 York St PO Box 2280	London	ON	N6A4G1	**866-541-6757**	519-679-1111	525-1
London Life Insurance Co 255 Dufferin Ave	London	ON	N6A4K1	**800-990-6654**	519-432-5281	388-2
London West Hollywood Hotel 1020 N San Vicente Blvd	West Hollywood	CA	90069	**866-282-4560**		375
London/Laurel County Tourist Commission 140 Faith Assembly Church Rd	London	KY	40741	**800-348-0095**	606-878-6900	207
Lone Mountain Ranch 750 Lone Mtn Ranch Rd PO Box 160069	Big Sky	MT	59716	**800-514-4644**	406-995-4644	239
Lone Oak Lodge 2221 N Fremont St	Monterey	CA	93940	**800-283-5663*** *General	831-372-4924	376
Lone Star Circuits 901 Hensley Ln	Wylie	TX	75098	**800-303-9266**	214-291-1427	617
Lone Star Container Corp 700 N Wildwood Dr	Irving	TX	75061	**800-552-6937**		99
Lone Star Lions Eye Bank 102 E Wheeler St PO Box 347	Manor	TX	78653	**800-977-3937**	512-457-0638	269
Lonely Planet Online 150 Linden St	Oakland	CA	94607	**800-275-8555**	510-250-6400	763
Lonely Planet Publications 50 Linden St	Oakland	CA	94607	**800-275-8555**	510-893-8555	628-2
Long & Foster Realtors 14501 George Carter Way	Chantilly	VA	20151	**800-237-8800**	703-653-8500	643
Long Beach Airport LGB 4100 Donald Douglas Dr	Long Beach	CA	90808	**800-331-1212**	562-570-2600	27
Long Beach City College 4901 E Carson St	Long Beach	CA	90808	**888-442-4551**	562-938-4111	160
Long Beach Convention & Visitors Bureau 301 E Ocean Blvd	Long Beach	CA	90802	**800-452-7829**	562-436-3645	207
Long Hollow Ranch 71105 Holmes Rd	Sisters	OR	97759	**877-923-1901**	541-923-1901	239
Long House Alaskan Hotel 4335 Wisconsin St	Anchorage	AK	99517	**888-243-2133**	907-243-2133	376
Long Island College Hospital (LICH) 339 Hicks St	Brooklyn	NY	11201	**800-227-8922**	718-780-1000	371-3
Long Island Convention & Visitors Bureau & Sports Commission 330 Motor Pkwy Ste 203	Hauppauge	NY	11788	**877-386-6654**		207
Long Island MacArthur Airport 100 Arrival Ave Ste 100	Ronkonkoma	NY	11779	**888-542-4776**	631-467-3300	27
Long Island Power Authority 333 Earle Ovington Blvd Ste 403	Uniondale	NY	11553	**877-275-5472*** *Cust Svc	516-222-7700	775
Long Island Press 575 Underhill Blvd Ste 210	Syosset	NY	11791	**800-545-6683**	516-284-3300	525-5
Long Island University *Brooklyn* One University Plz	Brooklyn	NY	11201	**800-548-7526**	718-488-1011	166
Long Painting Co 21414 68th Ave S	Kent	WA	98032	**800-678-5664**	253-234-8050	190-8
Long Prairie Packing Co 10 Riverside Dr	Long Prairie	MN	56347	**800-996-6440**	320-732-2171	468
Long View Systems Corp 3100 255 Fifth Ave SW	Calgary	AB	T2P3G6	**866-515-6900**	403-515-6900	175
Long Wharf Theatre 222 Sargent Dr	New Haven	CT	06511	**800-782-8497**	203-787-4282	565
Longacre Theatre 220 W 48th St	New York	NY	10036	**800-447-7400**	212-239-6200	736
Longboat Key Club 220 Sands Point Rd	Longboat Key	FL	34228	**800-237-8821**	941-383-8821	660
Longfellow-Evangeline State Historic Site 1200 N Main St	Saint Martinville	LA	70582	**888-677-2900**	337-394-3754	558
Longistics Transportation Inc 10900 World Trade Blvd	Raleigh	NC	27617	**800-289-0082**	919-872-7626	791-1
Long-Lewis Hardware Co 430 Ninth St N	Birmingham	AL	35203	**800-322-0492**	205-322-2561	348
Longust Distributing Inc 2432 W Birchwood Ave	Mesa	AZ	85202	**800-352-0521**	480-820-6244	358
Longview News-Journal 320 E Methvin St	Longview	TX	75601	**800-825-9799**	903-757-3311	525-2
Longview Partnership 410 N Ctr St	Longview	TX	75601	**800-338-7232**	903-237-4000	137
Longview School District 2715 Lilac St	Longview	WA	98632	**800-533-7881**	360-575-7000	676
Longview Solutions 100 Matsonford Rd Ste 230	Radnor	PA	19087	**888-456-6484**	610-977-0995	179-1
Longwood Gardens PO Box 501	Kennett Square	PA	19348	**800-737-5500**	610-388-1000	96
Longwood University 201 High St	Farmville	VA	23909	**800-281-4677**	434-395-2060	166
Lonsdale Quay Hotel 123 Carrie Cates Ct	North Vancouver	BC	V7M3K7	**800-836-6111**	604-986-6111	376
Lonseal Inc 928 E 238th St	Carson	CA	90745	**800-832-7111**	310-830-7111	358
Lookout Inn 6901 Lookout Rd	Boulder	CO	80301	**800-530-1513**	303-530-1513	376
Loomis Armored US Inc 2500 Citywest Blvd Ste 900	Houston	TX	77042	**866-383-5069**	713-435-6700	684
Loomis Co 850 N Pk Rd	Wyomissing	PA	19610	**800-782-0392**	610-374-4040	387
Loomis Communities 246 N Main St	South Hadley	MA	01075	**800-865-7655**	413-532-5325	663
Loomis Fargo & Co 2500 Citywest Blvd Ste 900	Houston	TX	77042	**866-383-5069**	713-435-6700	683
Loomis Sayles & Company Inc LP PO Box 219594	Kansas City	MO	64121	**800-343-2029**	800-633-3330	398
Loomis Sayles Funds One Financial Ctr	Boston	MA	02111	**800-633-3330**	617-482-2450	521
Loop Capital Markets LLC 111 W Jackson Blvd Ste 1901	Chicago	IL	60604	**888-294-8898**	312-913-4900	681
Loop-Loc Ltd 390 Motor Pkwy	Hauppauge	NY	11788	**800-562-5667**	631-582-2626	723
LOPA (Louisiana Organ Procurement Agency) 3545 N I-10 Service Rd Ste 300	Metairie	LA	70002	**800-521-4483**		538
Lorain Correctional Institution 2075 Avon Belden Rd	Grafton	OH	44044	**888-988-4768**	440-748-1049	213
Lorain County Community College 1005 N Abbe Rd	Elyria	OH	44035	**800-995-5222**	440-365-5222	160
Lorain County Visitors Bureau 8025 Leavitt Rd	Amherst	OH	44001	**800-334-1673**	440-984-5282	207
Lorain Public Library System 351 W Sixth St	Lorain	OH	44052	**800-322-7323**	440-244-1192	431-3
Lorain-Medina Rural Electric Co-op Inc 22898 W Rd	Wellington	OH	44090	**800-222-5673**	440-647-2133	245
Loram Maintenance of Way 3900 Arrowhead Dr PO Box 188	Hamel	MN	55340	**800-328-1466**	763-478-6014	641
Loras College 1450 Alta Vista St	Dubuque	IA	52001	**800-245-6727**	563-588-7100	166
Lord & Taylor 424 Fifth Ave	New York	NY	10018	**800-223-7440**	212-391-3344	229
Lord Abbett & Co 90 Hudson St	Jersey City	NJ	07302	**888-522-2388**	201-827-2000	398
Lord Corp 111 Lord Dr	Cary	NC	27511	**877-275-5673**	919-468-5979	3
Lord Elgin Hotel 100 Elgin St	Ottawa	ON	K1P5K8	**800-267-4298**	613-235-3333	376
Lord Fairfax Community College *Middletown* 173 Skirmisher Ln	Middletown	VA	22645	**800-906-5322**	540-868-7000	160
Lord Nelson Hotel & Suites 1515 S Pk St	Halifax	NS	B3J2L2	**800-565-2020**	902-423-6331	376
Lord Stanley Suites on the Park 1889 Alberni St	Vancouver	BC	V6G3G7	**888-767-7829**	604-688-9299	376
Lordco Parts Ltd 22866 Dewdney Trunk Rd	Maple Ridge	BC	V2X3K6	**877-591-1581**	604-467-1581	56
Lorenz Corp 501 E Third St	Dayton	OH	45402	**800-444-1144**	937-228-6118	628-7
Lorin Industries 1960 S Roberts St	Muskegon	MI	49443	**800-654-1159**	231-722-1631	476
Loroco Industries Inc 5000 Creek Rd	Cincinnati	OH	45242	**800-215-9474**	513-891-9544	548
Lorraine Travel Bureau Inc 377 Alhambra Cir	Coral Gables	FL	33134	**800-666-8911**	305-446-4433	761
Los Abrigados Resort 160 Portal Ln	Sedona	AZ	86336	**877-374-2582**	928-282-1777	660
Los Adaes State Historic Site 6354 Hwy 485	Robeline	LA	71469	**888-677-5378**	318-472-9449	558
Los Alamitos Medical Ctr 3751 Katella Ave	Los Alamitos	CA	90720	**800-540-4000**	562-598-1311	371-3
Los Alamos National Laboratory (LANL) PO Box 1663	Los Alamos	NM	87545	**877-723-4101**	505-667-7000	659
Los Alamos Technical Assoc Inc 999 Central Ave Ste 300	Los Alamos	NM	87544	**800-888-1745**	505-662-9080	193
Los Angeles Athletic Club 431 W Seventh St	Los Angeles	CA	90014	**800-421-8777**	213-625-2211	376
Los Angeles Biomedical Research Institute 1124 W Carson St	Torrance	CA	90502	**877-452-2674**		659
Los Angeles City College 855 N Vermont Ave	Los Angeles	CA	90029	**800-266-6883**	323-953-4000	160
Los Angeles Clippers Staples Ctr 1111 S Figueroa St Ste 1100	Los Angeles	CA	90015	**855-895-0872**	213-742-7100	705-1
Los Angeles Confidential Magazine 8530 Wilshire Blvd Ste 500	Beverly Hills	CA	90211	**866-891-3144**	310-289-7300	452-22
Los Angeles County Fairplex 1101 W McKinley Ave	Pomona	CA	91768	**877-859-9909**	909-623-3111	508
Los Angeles County Metropolitan Transportation Authority One Gateway Plz	Los Angeles	CA	90012	**800-621-7828**	213-922-6000	463
Los Angeles County Public Library 7400 E Imperial Hwy	Downey	CA	90242	**888-794-9466**	562-940-8462	431-3
Los Angeles Downtown News 1264 W First St	Los Angeles	CA	90026	**877-338-1010**	213-481-1448	525-4
Los Angeles Federal Credit Union PO Box 53032	Los Angeles	CA	90053	**877-695-2328**	818-242-8640	219
Los Angeles Galaxy Home Depot Ctr 18400 Avalon Blvd Ste 200	Carson	CA	90746	**877-342-5299**	310-630-2200	708
Los Angeles Kings Staples Ctr 1111 S Figueroa St	Los Angeles	CA	90015	**888-546-4752**	213-742-7100	707
Los Angeles Lakers 555 N Nash St	El Segundo	CA	90245	**866-648-4668**	310-426-6000	705-1
Los Angeles Magazine 5900 Wilshire Blvd 10th Fl	Los Angeles	CA	90036	**800-876-5222*** *Cust Svc	323-801-0100	452-22
Los Angeles Police Federal Credit Union PO Box 10188	Van Nuys	CA	91410	**877-695-2732**	818-787-6520	219
Los Angeles Sparks 865 S Figueroa St Ste 104	Los Angeles	CA	90017	**888-694-3278**	213-929-1300	705-2
Los Angeles Times 202 W First St	Los Angeles	CA	90012	**800-528-4637**	213-237-5000	525-2
Los Angeles Times Festival of Books Los Angeles Times 202 W First St	Los Angeles	CA	90012	**800-528-4637**	213-237-2335	281
Los Angeles Times-Washington Post News Service Inc 1150 15th St NW	Washington	DC	20071	**800-627-1150**	202-334-6000	523
Los Angeles Unified School District (LAUSD) 333 S Beaudry Ave	Los Angeles	CA	90017	**877-772-6273**	213-241-1000	676
Los Medanos College 2700 E Leland Rd	Pittsburg	CA	94565	**800-677-6337**	925-439-2181	160
LOSFA (Louisiana Office of Student Financial Assistance) 602 N Fifth St PO Box 91202	Baton Rouge	LA	70802	**800-259-5626**	225-219-1012	716

	City	St	Zip	Toll-Free	Phone	Class
Losi 4710 E Guasti Rd	Ontario	CA	91761	**888-899-5674**	909-390-9595	752
Lost River Caverns						
726 Durham St PO Box M	Hellertown	PA	18055	**888-529-1907**	610-838-8767	49-4
Lotus Cars USA Inc						
2402 Tech Ctr Pkwy NE	Lawrenceville	GA	30043	**800-245-6887***	770-476-6540	58
*Cust Svc						
Lou Bachrodt Auto Group						
7070 Cherryvale N Blvd	Rockford	IL	61112	**866-635-2349**	815-332-3000	56
LOUD Technologies Inc						
16220 Wood Red Rd NE	Woodinville	WA	98072	**866-858-5832**	425-892-6500	51
OTC: LTEC						
Loudoun House						
209 Castlewood Dr	Lexington	KY	40505	**866-945-7920**	859-254-7024	49-2
Loudoun Times-Mirror						
PO Box 359	Leesburg	VA	20178	**888-351-1660**	703-777-1111	525-4
Louhelen Baha'i School						
3208 S State Rd	Davison	MI	48423	**800-894-9716**	810-653-5033	664
Louie's Finer Meats Inc						
PO Box 774	Cumberland	WI	54829	**800-270-4297**	715-822-4728	295-26
Louis A Johnson Veterans Affairs Medical Ctr						
1 Medical Ctr Dr	Clarksburg	WV	26301	**800-733-0512**	304-623-3461	371-8
Louis Boston						
60 Northern Ave	Boston	MA	02210	**800-225-5135**	617-262-6100	155-3
Louis Ferre Inc						
302 Fifth Ave Ste 10	New York	NY	10001	**800-695-1061**	212-239-1600	345
Louis M Gerson Company Inc						
15 Sproat St	Middleboro	MA	02346	**800-225-8623**	508-947-4000	569
Louis M Martini Winery						
254 S St Helena Hwy	Saint Helena	CA	94574	**866-549-2582**		79-3
Louis Padnos Iron & Metal Co						
PO Box 1979	Holland	MI	49422	**800-442-3509**	616-396-6521	677
Louis Stokes Cleveland Veterans Affairs Medical Ctr						
10701 E Blvd	Cleveland	OH	44106	**888-838-6446**	216-791-3800	371-8
Louis Vuitton NA Inc						
One E 57th St	New York	NY	10022	**866-884-8866***	212-758-8877	155-6
*Cust Svc						
Louisburg College						
501 N Main St	Louisburg	NC	27549	**800-775-0208**	919-496-2521	160
Community Services Office						
627 N 4th St	Baton Rouge	LA	70802	**888-524-3578**		337-19
Consumer Protection Office						
PO Box 94095	Baton Rouge	LA	70804	**800-351-4889**		337-19
Department of Education						
1201 N Third St						
PO Box 94064	Baton Rouge	LA	70802	**877-453-2721**		337-19
Education Dept						
PO Box 94064	Baton Rouge	LA	70804	**877-453-2721**		337-19
Environmental Quality Dept						
602 N Fifth St	Baton Rouge	LA	70802	**866-896-5337**	225-219-5337	337-19
Housing Finance Agency						
2415 Quail Dr	Baton Rouge	LA	70808	**888-454-2001**	225-763-8700	337-19
Insurance Dept						
PO Box 94214	Baton Rouge	LA	70804	**800-259-5300**	225-342-5900	337-19
Legislature						
PO Box 94062	Baton Rouge	LA	70804	**800-256-3793**	225-342-2456	337-19
Louisiana						
Office of the Governor						
PO Box 94004	Baton Rouge	LA	70804	**866-366-1121**	225-342-7015	337-19
Public Service Commission						
PO Box 91154	Baton Rouge	LA	70821	**800-256-2397**	225-342-4404	337-19
Real Estate Commission						
PO Box 14785	Baton Rouge	LA	70898	**800-821-4529**	225-765-0191	337-19
State Parks Office						
PO Box 44426	Baton Rouge	LA	70804	**888-677-1400**	225-342-8111	337-19
Veterans Affairs Dept						
PO Box 94095	Baton Rouge	LA	70804	**877-432-8982**	225-219-5000	337-19
Wildlife & Fisheries Dept						
PO Box 98000	Baton Rouge	LA	70898	**800-442-2511**	225-765-2800	337-19
Louisiana Assn For, The Blind, The						
1750 Claiborne Ave	Shreveport	LA	71103	**877-913-6471**	318-635-6471	545-2
Louisiana Assn of Business & Industry						
3113 Vly Creek Dr						
PO Box 80258	Baton Rouge	LA	70898	**888-816-5224**	225-928-5388	138
Louisiana Association of Educators						
8322 One Kalais Ave	Baton Rouge	LA	70809	**800-256-4523**	225-343-9243	452-8
Louisiana College						
1140 College Dr	Pineville	LA	71359	**800-487-1906**	318-487-7011	166
Louisiana Culinary Institute						
10550 Airline Hwy	Baton Rouge	LA	70816	**877-533-3198**		161
Louisiana Delta Community College						
7500 Millhaven Rd	Monroe	LA	71203	**866-500-5322**	318-345-9000	160
Louisiana Dental Assn						
7833 Office Pk Blvd	Baton Rouge	LA	70809	**800-388-6642**	225-926-1986	227
Louisiana Ethics Board						
617 N Third St						
LaSalle Bldg Ste 10-36	Baton Rouge	LA	70802	**800-842-6630**	225-219-5600	337-19
Louisiana Medical Mutual Insurance Co						
1 Galleria Blvd Ste 700	Metairie	LA	70001	**800-452-2120**		388-5
Louisiana Office of Student Financial Assistance (LOSFA)						
602 N Fifth St PO Box 91202	Baton Rouge	LA	70802	**800-259-5626**	225-219-1012	716
Louisiana Organ Procurement Agency (LOPA)						
3545 N I-10 Service Rd Ste 300	Metairie	LA	70002	**800-521-4483**		538
Louisiana Pharmacists Assn						
450 Laurel St Ste 1400	Baton Rouge	LA	70801	**877-252-5100**	225-346-6883	578
Louisiana Public Broadcasting						
7733 Perkins Rd	Baton Rouge	LA	70810	**800-973-7246**	225-767-5660	624
Louisiana State Arboretum						
4213 Chicot Pk Rd	Ville Platte	LA	70586	**888-677-6100**	337-363-6289	558
Louisiana State Bar Assn (LSBA)						
601 St Charles Ave	New Orleans	LA	70130	**800-421-5722**	504-566-1600	71
Louisiana State Medical Society						
6767 Perkins Rd Ste 100	Baton Rouge	LA	70808	**800-375-9508**	225-763-8500	469
Louisiana State Museum						
751 Chartres St	New Orleans	LA	70116	**800-568-6968**	504-568-6968	513
Louisiana State Nurses Assn, The (LSNA)						
5713 Superior Dr Ste A-6	Baton Rouge	LA	70816	**800-457-6378**	225-201-0993	526
Louisiana State University						
Alexandria						
8100 US Hwy 71 S	Alexandria	LA	71302	**888-473-6417***	318-445-3672	166
*Admissions						
Baton Rouge						
110 Thomas Boyd Hall	Baton Rouge	LA	70803	**888-846-6810**	225-578-3202	166
Eunice PO Box 1129	Eunice	LA	70535	**888-367-5783**	337-457-7311	160

	City	St	Zip	Toll-Free	Phone	Class
Louisiana State University School of Medicine in New Orleans						
433 Bolivar St	New Orleans	LA	70112	**844-503-7283**	504-568-6262	167-2
Louisiana State University School of Medicine in Shreveport						
1501 Kings Hwy PO Box 33932	Shreveport	LA	71130	**800-337-3627**	318-675-5069	167-2
Louisiana State University System						
125 E Boyd Dr	Baton Rouge	LA	70803	**800-227-3002**	225-578-3357	774
Louisiana Tech University						
305 Wisteria St	Ruston	LA	71272	**800-528-3241***	318-257-2000	166
*Admissions						
Louisiana Tech University Prescott Memorial Library						
PO Box 10408	Ruston	LA	71272	**877-557-2575**	318-257-3555	431-6
Louisiana Veterinary Medical Assn						
8550 United Plz Blvd						
Ste 1001	Baton Rouge	LA	70809	**800-524-2996**	225-928-5862	783
Louisiana Workforce Commission						
1001 N 23rd St	Baton Rouge	LA	70802	**877-529-6757**	225-342-3111	259
Louisiana-Pacific Corp						
414 Union St Ste 2000	Nashville	TN	37219	**888-820-0325**	615-986-5600	674
NYSE: LPX						
Louisville & Jefferson County Convention & Visitors Bureau						
401 W Main St Ste 2300	Louisville	KY	40202	**800-626-5646**	502-584-2121	207
Louisville Ballet						
315 E Main St	Louisville	KY	40202	**800-775-7777**	502-583-3150	566-1
Louisville Bedding Co						
10400 Bunsen Way	Louisville	KY	40299	**800-626-2594**	502-491-3370	735
Louisville Bible College						
PO Box 91046	Louisville	KY	40291	**888-676-7458**	502-231-5221	166
Louisville Golf Club Co						
2320 Watterson Trail	Louisville	KY	40299	**800-456-1631**	502-491-5490	701
Louisville Magazine						
137 W Muhammad Ali Blvd						
Ste 102	Louisville	KY	40202	**866-832-0011**	502-625-0100	452-22
Louisville Presbyterian Theological Seminary						
1044 Alta Vista Rd	Louisville	KY	40205	**800-264-1839**	502-895-3411	167-3
Louisville Science Ctr						
727 W Main St	Louisville	KY	40202	**800-591-2203**	502-561-6100	513
Louisville Slugger Museum						
800 W Main St	Louisville	KY	40202	**877-775-8443**	502-585-5226	515
Louisville Technical Institute						
Sullivan College of Technology & Design						
3901 Atkinson Sq Dr	Louisville	KY	40218	**800-844-6528**	502-456-6509	788
Louisville Zoo						
1100 Trevilian Way	Louisville	KY	40213	**866-229-0502**	502-459-2181	810
Loup Public Power District (LPPD)						
2404 15th St PO Box 988	Columbus	NE	68602	**866-869-2087**	402-564-3171	245
Lourdes College						
6832 Convent Blvd	Sylvania	OH	43560	**800-878-3210**	419-885-5291	166
Lourdes Homecare & Hospice						
2855 Jackson St	Paducah	KY	42003	**800-870-7460**	270-444-2262	368
Lou-Rich Machine Tool Inc						
505 W Front St	Albert Lea	MN	56007	**800-893-3235**	507-377-8910	747
Love & Quiches Desserts						
178 Hanse Ave	Freeport	NY	11520	**800-525-5251**	516-623-8800	296-11
Love Envelopes Inc						
10733 E Ute St	Tulsa	OK	74116	**800-532-9747**	918-836-3535	263
Love's Travel Stops & Country Stores Inc						
10601 N Pennsylvania Ave	Oklahoma City	OK	73120	**800-388-0983**		205
Lovegreen Industrial Services Inc						
2280 Sibley Ct	Eagan	MN	55122	**800-262-8284**	651-890-1166	465
Lovejoy Hospice						
939 SE Eigth St	Grants Pass	OR	97526	**888-758-8569**	541-474-1193	368
Lovejoy Tool Company Inc						
133 Main St	Springfield	VT	05156	**800-843-8376**	802-885-2194	488
Lovelace Medical Ctr						
5400 Gibson Blvd SE	Albuquerque	NM	87108	**888-281-6531**	505-262-7000	371-3
Loveland Daily Reporter-Herald						
201 E Fifth St	Loveland	CO	80537	**800-244-5613**	970-669-5050	525-2
Loveman Steel Corp						
5455 Perkins Rd	Bedford Heights	OH	44146	**800-568-3626**		487
Lovers Key State Park						
8700 Estero Blvd	Fort Myers Beach	FL	33931	**800-326-3521**	239-463-4588	558
Loveshaw Corp						
2206 Easton Tpke	South Canaan	PA	18459	**800-747-1586***	570-937-4921	540
*Cust Svc						
Lovitt & Touche Inc						
7202 E Rosewood St Ste 200						
PO Box 32702	Tucson	AZ	85710	**800-426-2756**	520-722-3000	387
Lowe Boats						
2900 Industrial Dr	Lebanon	MO	65536	**800-641-4372**	417-532-9101	89
Lowe Electric Supply Co						
1525 Forsyth St PO Box 4767	Macon	GA	31208	**800-868-8661**	478-743-8661	246
Lowe's Cos Inc						
1000 Lowe's Blvd	Mooresville	NC	28117	**800-445-6937**	704-758-1000	361
NYSE: LOW						
Lowe's Home Centers Inc						
PO Box 1111	North Wilkesboro	NC	28656	**800-445-6937**		361
Lowell Health Care Ctr						
19 Varnum St	Lowell	MA	01850	**800-811-3535**	978-454-5644	445
Lowell Manufacturing Co						
100 Integram Dr	Pacific	MO	63069	**800-325-9660**	636-257-3400	51
Lowell Sun Publishing Co						
491 Dutton St	Lowell	MA	01854	**800-359-1300***	978-458-7100	628-8
*Cust Svc						
Lowen Corp						
PO Box 1528	Hutchinson	KS	67504	**800-835-2365**	620-663-2161	619
Lower Bucks County Chamber of Commerce						
409 Hood Blvd	Fairless Hills	PA	19030	**800-786-2234**	215-943-7400	137
Lower Cape Fear Hospice & Life Care						
1414 Physicians Dr	Wilmington	NC	28401	**800-733-1476**	910-796-7900	368
Lower Columbia College						
1600 Maple St PO Box 3010	Longview	WA	98632	**866-900-2311**	360-442-2301	160
Lower East Side Business Improvement District						
54 Orchard St	New York	NY	10002	**866-224-0206**	212-226-9010	455
Lower Keys Chamber of Commerce						
31020 Overseas Hwy	Big Pine Key	FL	33043	**800-872-3722**	305-872-2411	137
Lower Keys Medical Ctr						
5900 College Rd	Key West	FL	33040	**800-355-2470**	305-294-5531	371-3
Lower Valley Energy						
236 N Washington PO Box 188	Afton	WY	83110	**800-882-5875**	307-885-3175	245
Lower Wekiva River Preserve State Park						
1800 Wekiwa Cir	Apopka	FL	32712	**800-326-3521**	407-884-2008	558
Lowes Food Stores Inc						
1381 Old Mill Cir Ste 200	Winston-Salem	NC	27103	**800-669-5693**	336-659-0180	342

	Toll-Free	Phone	Class
Lowrance Electronics Inc			
12000 E Skelly Dr . . . . . Tulsa OK 74128	**800-628-4487**	918-437-6881	522
Lowrey Organ Co			
847 N Church Ct . . . . . Elmhurst IL 60126	**800-451-5940**	800-451-5939	520
Loxahatchee River Historical Museum			
500 Captian Armours Way			
Burt Reynolds Pk . . . . . Jupiter FL 33469	**800-435-7352**	561-747-8380	513
Loxcreen Co Inc, The			
1630 Old Dunbar Rd			
PO Box 4004 . . . . . West Columbia SC 29172	**800-330-5699**	803-822-8200	480
Loyal American Life Insurance Co			
Great American Financial Resources Inc			
PO Box 26580 . . . . . Austin TX 78755	**800-315-5522**	800-545-4269	388-2
Loyd's Aviation Services Inc			
1601 Skyway Dr Ste 100			
PO Box 80958 . . . . . Bakersfield CA 93308	**800-284-1334**	661-393-1334	62
Loyd's Electric Supply Inc (LES)			
838 Stonetree Dr . . . . . Branson MO 65616	**800-492-4030**	417-334-2171	246
Loyola College			
4501 N Charles St . . . . . Baltimore MD 21210	**800-221-9107**	410-617-5012	166
Loyola Marymount University			
One LMU Dr . . . . . Los Angeles CA 90045	**800-568-4636**	310-338-2700	166
Loyola University			
New Orleans			
6363 St Charles Ave CB 18 . . . . . New Orleans LA 70118	**800-456-9652***	504-865-3240	166
*Admissions			
School of Law			
25 E Pearson St . . . . . Chicago IL 60611	**866-596-7890**	312-915-7120	167-1
Loyola University Chicago			
Water Tower			
820 N Michigan Ave . . . . . Chicago IL 60611	**800-262-2373***	312-915-6500	166
*Admissions			
Loyola University Medical Ctr			
2160 S First Ave . . . . . Maywood IL 60153	**888-584-7888**		371-3
Lozier Corp			
6336 John J Pershing Dr . . . . . Omaha NE 68110	**800-228-9882**	402-457-8000	286
Lozier's Box R Ranch			
552 Willow Creek Rd PO Box 100 . . . . . Cora WY 82925	**800-822-8466**	307-367-4868	239
LP (Lakeland Plastics Inc)			
1550 McCormick Blvd . . . . . Mundelein IL 60060	**800-454-4006**	847-680-1550	592
LPCH (Lucile Packard Children's Hospital)			
725 Welch Rd . . . . . Palo Alto CA 94304	**800-995-5724**	650-497-8000	371-1
LPH (La Porte Hospital)			
1007 Lincolnway PO Box 250 . . . . . La Porte IN 46350	**800-235-6204**	219-326-1234	371-3
LPI (Life Partners Inc)			
204 Woodhew Dr . . . . . Waco TX 76712	**800-368-5569**	254-751-7797	784
LPL Financial Services			
75 State St 24th Fl . . . . . Boston MA 02109	**800-877-7210**		681
LPMC (Lake Pointe Medical Ctr)			
6800 Scenic Dr . . . . . Rowlett TX 75088	**866-525-5762**	972-412-2273	371-3
LPPD (Loup Public Power District)			
2404 15th St PO Box 988 . . . . . Columbus NE 68602	**866-869-2087**	402-564-3171	245
LPS Industries Inc			
10 Caesar Pl . . . . . Moonachie NJ 07074	**800-275-6577***	201-438-3515	541
*Sales			
LQ Management LLC			
La Quinta Inn & Suites			
909 Hidden Ridge Ste 600 . . . . . Irving TX 75038	**800-753-3757**	214-492-6600	376
LQMT (Liquidmetal Technologies Inc)			
30452 Esperanza . . . . . Rancho Santa Margarita CA 92688	**888-203-1112**	949-635-2100	477
OTC: LQMT			
LR Services			
602 Hayden Cir . . . . . Allentown PA 18109	**888-675-9650**	610-266-2500	13
LRCC (Lakes Region Community College)			
379 Belmont Rd . . . . . Laconia NH 03246	**800-357-2992**	603-524-3207	160
LRDC (Learning Research & Development Ctr)			
University of Pittsburgh			
3939 O'Hara St . . . . . Pittsburgh PA 15260	**800-397-0071**	412-624-7020	659
LRECI (Little River Electric Co-op Inc)			
PO Box 220 . . . . . Abbeville SC 29620	**800-459-2141**	864-366-2141	245
LRF (Lymphoma Research Foundation)			
115 Broadway Ste 1301 . . . . . New York NY 10006	**800-500-9976**	212-349-2910	47-17
LRP Publications			
360 Hiatt Dr . . . . . Palm Beach Gardens FL 33418	**800-341-7874**		524-2
LS Starrett Co			
121 Crescent St . . . . . Athol MA 01331	**800-482-8710**	978-249-3551	673
NYSE: SCX			
LSBA (Louisiana State Bar Assn)			
601 St Charles Ave . . . . . New Orleans LA 70130	**800-421-5722**	504-566-1600	71
LSI (Lake Shore Industries Inc)			
1817 Poplar St PO BOX 3427 . . . . . Erie PA 16508	**800-458-0463**		692
LSI Logic Corp			
1320 Ridder Park Dr . . . . . San Jose CA 95131	**800-372-2447**	408-433-8000	687
NASDAQ: LSI			
LSNA (Louisiana State Nurses Assn, The)			
5713 Superior Dr Ste A-6 . . . . . Baton Rouge LA 70816	**800-457-6378**	225-201-0993	526
LSP Products Group Inc			
3689 Arrowhead Dr . . . . . Carson City NV 89706	**800-854-3215**		601
LSQ Funding Group LC			
2600 Lucien Way Ste 100 . . . . . Maitland FL 32751	**800-474-7606**		272
LSS (Lutheran Social Services of The South Inc)			
8305 Cross Pk Dr PO Box 140767 . . . . . Austin TX 78754	**800-938-5777**	512-459-1000	47-20
LTI Trucking Services Inc			
411 N 10th St Ste 500 . . . . . St. Louis MO 63101	**800-642-7222**		313
LTS (Lawrence Companies)			
872 Lee Hwy PO Box 7667 . . . . . Roanoke VA 24019	**800-336-9626**	540-966-4000	770
LUA (Lumbermen's Underwriting Alliance)			
1905 NW Corporate Blvd			
PO Box 3061 . . . . . Boca Raton FL 33431	**800-327-0630**	561-994-1900	388-4
Lubbock Avalanche-Journal			
710 Ave J . . . . . Lubbock TX 79401	**800-692-4021**	806-762-8844	525-2
Lubbock Christian University			
5601 19th St . . . . . Lubbock TX 79407	**800-933-7601**	806-720-7151	166
Lubbock Convention & Visitors Bureau			
1500 Broadway St Sixth Fl . . . . . Lubbock TX 79401	**800-692-4035**	806-747-5232	207
Lubbock Municipal Auditorium/Coliseum			
1625 13th St . . . . . Lubbock TX 79415	**800-735-2989**	806-775-2242	711
Luberski Inc			
310 N Harbor Blvd Ste 205 . . . . . Fullerton CA 92832	**800-326-3220**	714-680-3447	296-4
Lubrication Engineers Inc			
300 Bailey Ave . . . . . Fort Worth TX 76107	**800-537-7683**	817-834-6321	534
Lubrication Technologies Inc			
900 Mendelssohn Ave N . . . . . Golden Valley MN 55427	**800-328-5573**	763-545-0707	534

	Toll-Free	Phone	Class
Lubrizol Corp			
29400 Lakeland Blvd . . . . . Wickliffe OH 44092	**800-380-5397**	440-943-4200	143
NYSE: LZ			
Luby's Inc			
13111 NW Fwy Ste 600 . . . . . Houston TX 77040	**800-886-4600**	713-329-6800	661
NYSE: LUB			
Lucas Assoc Inc			
3384 Peachtree Rd Ste 900 . . . . . Atlanta GA 30326	**800-515-0819**	800-466-4489	712
Lucasey Manufacturing Corp			
2744 E 11th St PO Box 14023 . . . . . Oakland CA 94601	**800-582-2739**	510-534-1435	477
Lucas-Milhaupt Inc			
5656 S Pennsylvania Ave . . . . . Cudahy WI 53110	**800-558-3856**	414-769-6000	480
Lucchese Boot Co			
20 ZANE GREY . . . . . El Paso TX 79906	**800-637-6888**	888-582-1883	300
Lucile Packard Children's Hospital (LPCH)			
725 Welch Rd . . . . . Palo Alto CA 94304	**800-995-5724**	650-497-8000	371-1
Lucks Co, The			
3003 S Pine St . . . . . Tacoma WA 98409	**800-426-9778**	253-383-4815	295-8
Lucky Eagle Casino			
12888 188th Ave SW . . . . . Rochester WA 98579	**800-720-1788**	360-273-2000	132
Lucky Inc 4 Times Sq . . . . . New York NY 10036	**888-959-5203**	800-405-8085	452-11
Lucta USA Inc			
Pine Meadow Corporate Ctr 950 Technology Way			
Ste 110 . . . . . Libertyville IL 60048	**800-323-5341**	847-996-3400	442
Lucy Robbins Welles Library			
95 Cedar St . . . . . Newington CT 06111	**800-842-1423**	860-665-8700	431-3
Ludlow Composites Corp			
2100 Commerce Dr . . . . . Fremont OH 43420	**800-628-5463**		667
Ludlum Measurements Inc			
501 Oak St . . . . . Sweetwater TX 79556	**800-622-0828**	325-235-5494	467
Ludowici Roof Tile Inc			
4757 Tile Plant Rd			
PO Box 69 . . . . . New Lexington OH 43764	**800-945-8453***	740-342-1995	148
*Cust Svc			
Lufkin Daily News			
300 Ellis Ave . . . . . Lufkin TX 75904	**888-664-8792**	936-632-6631	525-2
Lufkin/Angelina County Chamber of Commerce			
1615 S Chestnut St . . . . . Lufkin TX 75901	**800-409-5659**	936-634-6644	137
Luitpold Pharmaceuticals Inc			
One Luitpold Dr PO Box 9001 . . . . . Shirley NY 11967	**800-645-1706**	631-924-4000	575
Luke Air Force Base			
14185 W Falcon St . . . . . Luke AFB AZ 85309	**800-321-1080**	623-856-5853	492-1
Lumbee River Electric Membership Corp			
PO Box 830 . . . . . Red Springs NC 28377	**800-683-5571**	910-843-4131	245
Lumber Liquidators Inc			
1455 VFW Pkwy . . . . . West Roxbury MA 02132	**800-227-0332**	617-327-1222	290
Lumbermen's Underwriting Alliance (LUA)			
1905 NW Corporate Blvd			
PO Box 3061 . . . . . Boca Raton FL 33431	**800-327-0630**	561-994-1900	388-4
Lumberton Area Visitors Bureau			
3431 Lackey St . . . . . Lumberton NC 28360	**800-359-6971**	910-739-9999	207
Lumedx Corp			
555 12th St Ste 2060 . . . . . Oakland CA 94607	**800-966-0699**	510-419-1000	179-10
Lumen Legal			
1025 N Campbell Rd . . . . . Royal Oak MI 48067	**877-933-1330**	248-597-0400	712
Lumenis Ltd			
2033 Gateway Pl Ste 200 . . . . . San Jose CA 95110	**877-586-3647**	408-764-3000	421
Lumens Light & Living			
2028 K St . . . . . Sacramento CA 95811	**877-445-4486**	916-444-5585	802
Lumension Security Inc			
8660 E Hartford Dr Ste 300 . . . . . Scottsdale AZ 85255	**888-725-7828**		225
Lumex Inc			
290 E Helen Rd . . . . . Palatine IL 60067	**800-278-5666**	847-359-2790	253
Lumina Foundation for Education			
30 S Meridian St Ste 700 . . . . . Indianapolis IN 46204	**800-834-5756**	317-951-5300	304
Luminator 900 Klein Rd . . . . . Plano TX 75074	**800-388-8205**	972-424-6511	434
Luminex Corp			
12212 Technology Blvd . . . . . Austin TX 78727	**888-219-8020**	512-219-8020	416
NASDAQ: LMNX			
Luminex Software Inc			
871 Marlborough Ave . . . . . Riverside CA 92507	**888-586-4639***	951-781-4100	179-12
*Sales			
Lumitex Inc			
8443 Dow Cir . . . . . Strongsville OH 44136	**800-969-5483**	440-243-8401	720
Lummus Corp			
225 Bourne Blvd PO Box 929 . . . . . Savannah GA 31408	**800-458-6687**	912-447-9000	733
Lumos & Assoc Inc			
800 E College Pkwy . . . . . Carson City NV 89706	**800-621-7155**	775-883-7077	261
Luna Community College			
366 Luna Dr . . . . . Las Vegas NM 87701	**800-588-7232**	505-454-2500	160
Lund International Holdings Inc			
4325 Hamilton Mill Rd Ste 400 . . . . . Buford GA 30518	**800-241-7219**	678-804-3912	59
Lunday-Thagard Co			
9302 Garfield Ave . . . . . South Gate CA 90280	**800-266-6551**	562-928-7000	45
Lupus Foundation of America Inc (LFA)			
2000 L St NW Ste 410 . . . . . Washington DC 20036	**800-558-0121**	202-349-1155	47-17
Lurie Besikof Lapidus & Co LLP			
2501 Wayzata Blvd . . . . . Minneapolis MN 55405	**877-322-8228**	612-377-4404	2
Lurleen B Wallace Community College			
Andalusia			
1000 Dannelly Blvd			
PO Box 1418 . . . . . Andalusia AL 36420	**877-382-4357**	334-222-6591	160
MacAurthur			
1708 N Main St PO Box 910 . . . . . Opp AL 36467	**877-382-4357**	334-493-3573	788
Luster Products Inc			
1104 W 43rd St . . . . . Chicago IL 60609	**800-621-4255**	773-579-1800	215
Luther Brookdale Chevrolet			
6701 Brooklyn Blvd . . . . . Brooklyn Center MN 55429	**800-716-1271**		509
Luther Burbank Savings			
804 Fourth St . . . . . Santa Rosa CA 95404	**888-407-9904**	707-578-9216	69
Luther College			
700 College Dr . . . . . Decorah IA 52101	**800-458-8437**	563-387-2000	166
Luther L Smith & Son Inc			
PO Box 67 . . . . . Atlantic NC 28511	**800-328-8313**	252-225-3341	295-14
Luther Luckett Correctional Complex			
Dawkins Rd PO Box 6 . . . . . LaGrange KY 40031	**800-511-1670**	502-222-0363	213
Luther Seminary			
2481 Como Ave . . . . . Saint Paul MN 55108	**800-588-4373**	651-641-3456	167-3
Lutheran Church Missouri Synod (LCMS)			
1333 S Kirkwood Rd . . . . . Saint Louis MO 63122	**888-843-5267**	314-965-9000	47-20
Lutheran Community at Telford			
12 Lutheran Home Dr . . . . . Telford PA 18969	**877-343-7518**	215-723-9819	663
Lutheran Community Foundation			
625 Fourth Ave S Ste 200 . . . . . Minneapolis MN 55415	**800-365-4172**	612-340-4110	303

Company	Address	City	State	ZIP	Toll-Free	Phone	Class
Lutheran Disaster Response	8765 W Higgins Rd	Chicago	IL	60631	**800-638-3522**		47-5
Lutheran Home at Hollidaysburg, The	916 Hickory St	Hollidaysburg	PA	16648	**800-400-2285**	814-696-4527	47-20
Lutheran Homes Society Inc	2021 N McCord Rd	Toledo	OH	43615	**877-646-4050**	419-861-4990	47-15
Lutheran Hospital of Indiana	7950 W Jefferson Blvd	Fort Wayne	IN	46804	**800-444-2001**	260-435-7001	371-3
Lutheran Magazine	8765 W Higgins Rd	Chicago	IL	60631	**800-638-3522**		452-18
Lutheran School of Theology at Chicago	1100 E 55th St	Chicago	IL	60615	**800-635-1116**	773-256-0700	167-3
Lutheran Social Services of Illinois	1001 E Touhy Ave Ste 50	Des Plaines	IL	60018	**888-671-0300**	847-635-4600	47-15
Lutheran Social Services of The South Inc (LSS)	8305 Cross Pk Dr PO Box 140767	Austin	TX	78754	**800-938-5777**	512-459-1000	47-20
Lutheran Theological Seminary at Gettysburg	61 Seminary Ridge	Gettysburg	PA	17325	**800-658-8437**	717-334-6286	167-3
Lutheran Theological Seminary at Philadelphia	7301 Germantown Ave	Philadelphia	PA	19119	**800-286-4616**	215-248-4616	167-3
Luthi Machinery Co Inc	1 Magnuson Ave	Pueblo	CO	81003	**800-227-0682**	719-948-1110	297
Lutron Electronics Company Inc	7200 Suter Rd *Tech Supp	Coopersburg	PA	18036	**800-523-9466***	610-282-6280	204
Lutsen Resort	5700 W Hwy 61 PO Box 9	Lutsen	MN	55612	**800-258-8736**	218-663-7212	660
Lutz Frey Corp	1195 Ivy Dr	Lancaster	PA	17601	**800-280-6794**	717-898-6808	190-10
Luv N' Care Ltd	3030 Aurora Ave	Monroe	LA	71201	**800-588-6227**		258
Luvata Appleton LLC	553 Carter Ct	Kimberly	WI	54136	**866-488-0217**	920-749-3820	480
Lux Bond & Green Inc	46 Lasalle Rd	West Hartford	CT	06107	**800-524-7336**		407
Luxe Hotel Rodeo Drive	360 N Rodeo Dr	Beverly Hills	CA	90210	**800-468-3541**	310-273-0300	376
Luxe Hotel Sunset Blvd	11461 Sunset Blvd	Los Angeles	CA	90049	**800-468-3541**	310-476-6571	376
Luxe Worldwide Hotels	11461 W Sunset Blvd	Los Angeles	CA	90049	**866-589-3411**	310-440-3090	376
Luxfer Gas Cylinders	3016 Kansas Ave	Riverside	CA	92507	**800-764-0366**	951-684-5110	223
Luxo Corp	Five Westchester Plz	Elmsford	NY	10523	**800-222-5896**	914-345-0067	435
Luxor Div EBSCO Industries Inc	2245 Delany Rd	Waukegan	IL	60087	**800-323-4656**	847-244-1800	318-1
Luxor Hotel & Casino	3900 Las Vegas Blvd S *Resv	Las Vegas	NV	89119	**800-288-1000***	702-262-4000	132
Luxury Retreats International Inc	5530 St Patrick St Ste 2210	Montreal	QC	H4E1A8	**877-993-0100**	514-393-8844	500
Luzerne County Community College	1333 S Prospect St	Nanticoke	PA	18634	**800-377-5222**		160
LV Lomas Ltd	99 Summerlea Rd	Brampton	ON	L6T4V2	**800-575-3382**	905-458-1555	144
LVC (Las Vegas Club Hotel & Casino)	18 E Fremont St	Las Vegas	NV	89101	**800-634-6532**	702-385-1664	132
LW Robbins Assoc	201 Summer St	Holliston	MA	01746	**800-229-5972**		316
LWS (Laminated Wood Systems Inc)	1327 285th Rd PO Box 386	Seward	NE	68434	**800-949-3526**	402-643-4708	804
LXE Inc	125 Technology Pkwy	Norcross	GA	30092	**800-664-4593**	770-447-4224	174-1
Lyceum Theatre	149 W 45th St	New York	NY	10036	**800-432-7780**	212-239-6200	736
Lycoming College	700 College Pl	Williamsport	PA	17701	**800-345-3920**	570-321-4000	166
Lycoming Engines	652 Oliver St	Williamsport	PA	17701	**800-258-3279**	570-323-6181	522
Lycon Inc	1110 Harding St PO Box 427	Janesville	WI	53547	**800-955-8758**	608-754-7701	183
LycoRed Corp	377 Crane St	Orange	NJ	07051	**877-592-6733**	973-882-0322	474
Lykes Insurance Inc	400 N Tampa St	Tampa	FL	33602	**800-243-0491**	813-223-3911	388-4
Lyman Products Corp	475 Smith St	Middletown	CT	06457	**800-225-9626**	860-632-2020	284
Lyman-Richey Corp	4315 Cuming St	Omaha	NE	68131	**800-727-8432**	402-558-2727	192-1
Lymphoma Research Foundation (LRF)	115 Broadway Ste 1301	New York	NY	10006	**800-500-9976**	212-349-2910	47-17
Lynchburg College	1501 Lakeside Dr	Lynchburg	VA	24501	**800-426-8101**	434-544-8100	166
Lynches River Electric Co-op Inc	1104 W McGregor St	Pageland	SC	29728	**800-922-3486**	843-672-6111	245
Lynda.com Inc	6410 Via Real	Carpinteria	CA	93013	**888-335-9632**	805-477-3900	195
Lynden Air Cargo LLC	6441 S Airpark Pl	Anchorage	AK	99502	**888-243-7248**	907-243-7248	12
Lynden Inc	18000 International Blvd Ste 800	Seattle	WA	98188	**888-596-3361**	206-241-8778	310
Lynden Transport Inc	3027 Rampart Dr	Anchorage	AK	99501	**800-327-9390**		770
Lynde-Ordway Company Inc	3308 W Warner Ave	Santa Ana	CA	92704	**800-762-7057**	714-957-1311	110
Lyndon State College	1001 College Rd PO Box 919	Lyndonville	VT	05851	**800-225-1998**	802-626-6413	166
Lynn Ladder & Scaffolding Company Inc	20 Boston St	Lynn	MA	01904	**800-225-2510**	781-598-6010	418
Lynn University	3601 N Military Trl *Admissions	Boca Raton	FL	33431	**800-888-5966***	561-237-7900	166
LynuxWorks Inc	855 Embedded Way	San Jose	CA	95138	**800-255-5969**	408-979-3900	179-10
Lynx Medical Systems Inc	15325 SE 30th Pl Ste 200	Bellevue	WA	98007	**800-767-5969**	425-641-4451	178
Lyon & Healy Harps Inc	168 N Ogden Ave	Chicago	IL	60607	**800-621-3881**	312-786-1881	520
Lyon Rural Electric Co-op	116 S Marshall St	Rock Rapids	IA	51246	**800-658-3976**	712-472-2506	245
Lyon Work Space Products	420 N Main St	Montgomery	IL	60538	**800-433-8488**	630-892-8941	286
Lyon-Coffey Electric Co-op Inc	1013 N 4th PO Box 229	Burlington	KS	66839	**800-748-7395**	620-364-2116	245
Lyon-Lincoln Electric Co-op Inc (LLEC)	205 W Hwy 14 PO Box 639	Tyler	MN	56178	**800-927-6276**	507-247-5505	245
Lyons Magnus Inc	3158 E Hamilton Ave	Fresno	CA	93702	**800-344-7130**		295-20
Lyric Opera House	110 W Mt Royal Ave	Baltimore	MD	21201	**800-872-7245**	410-685-5086	565
LZ Truck Equipment Inc	1881 Rice St	Saint Paul	MN	55113	**800-247-1082**	651-488-2571	509

M

Company	Address	City	State	ZIP	Toll-Free	Phone	Class
M & A Technology Inc	2045 Chenault Dr	Carrollton	TX	75006	**800-225-1452**	972-490-5803	175
M & C Specialties Co	90 James Way *Cust Svc	SouthHampton	PA	18966	**800-441-6996***	215-322-1600	722
M & J Transportation	3536 Nicholson Ave	Kansas City	MO	64120	**866-298-3858**	816-231-6733	444
M & L Industries Inc	1210 St Charles St *General	Houma	LA	70360	**800-969-0068***	985-876-2280	382
M & M Designs Inc	1981 Quality Blvd PO Box 1049	Huntsville	TX	77320	**800-627-0656**		678
M & M Innovations	7424 Blythe Island Hwy	Brunswick	GA	31523	**800-688-3384**	912-265-7110	228
M & M Supply Co	909 W Peach Ave PO Box 548	Duncan	OK	73534	**800-424-9300**	580-252-7879	530
M & Q Plastic Products Inc	1120 Welsh Rd Ste 170	North Wales	PA	19454	**800-600-3068**	267-498-4000	597
M & R Sales & Service Inc	1n 372 Main St	Glen Ellyn	IL	60137	**800-736-6431**	630-858-6101	619
M at Miranova	2 Miranova PL Ste 100	Columbus	OH	43215	**877-491-1267**	614-629-0000	662
M Block & Sons Inc	5020 W 73rd St	Bedford Park	IL	60638	**800-621-8845**	708-728-8400	358
M Conley Co	1312 Fourth St SE	Canton	OH	44707	**800-362-6001**	330-456-8243	552
M Floyd John & Assoc Inc (JMFA)	125 N Burnett Dr	Baytown	TX	77520	**800-809-2307**		195
M Holland Co	400 Skokie Blvd Ste 600	Northbrook	IL	60062	**800-872-7370**	847-272-7370	596
M K Products Inc	16882 Armstrong Ave	Irvine	CA	92606	**800-787-9707**	949-863-1234	798
M R L Equipment Company Inc	PO Box 31154	Billings	MT	59107	**877-788-2907**	406-869-9900	355
M. H. Eby Inc	PO Box 127	Blue Ball	PA	17506	**800-292-4752**	717-354-4971	509
M. Lee Smith Publishers LLC	PO Box 5094	Brentwood	TN	37024	**800-274-6774**	615-373-7517	619
M.d.m. Commercial Enterprises Inc	1102 A1a N Ste 205	Ponte Vedra	FL	32082	**800-359-6741**		37
M.E.G. LLC	502 S Green St PO Box 240 *Cust Svc	Cambridge City	IN	47327	**800-645-3315***		286
M/A/R/C Research	1660 Westridge Cir	Irving	TX	75038	**800-884-6272**	972-983-0400	461
M/A-COM Technology Solutions Inc	100 Chelmsford St	Lowell	MA	01851	**800-366-2266**	978-656-2500	687
M/I Homes Inc	Three Easton Oval *NYSE: MHO*	Columbus	OH	43219	**888-644-4111**	614-418-8700	644
M2 Technology Inc	21702 Hardy Oak Ste 100	San Antonio	TX	78258	**800-267-1760**	210-566-3773	179-1
MA Gedney Co	2100 Stoughton Ave	Chaska	MN	55318	**888-244-0653**	952-448-2612	295-19
MA Reich & Co Inc	481 Franklin St	Buffalo	NY	14202	**800-746-7062**	716-856-4085	408
MAA (Mathematical Assn of America)	1529 18th St NW	Washington	DC	20036	**800-331-1622**	202-387-5200	48-19
MAA FOCUS	1529 18th St NW	Washington	DC	20036	**800-741-9415**	202-387-5200	452-8
Maaco LLC	440 S Church St Ste 700	Charlotte	NC	28202	**800-523-1180**	704-377-8855	61-4
Maas-Hansen Steel Corp	2435 E 37th St PO Box 58364	Vernon	CA	90058	**800-647-8335**	323-586-0171	487
Maas-Rowe Carillons Inc	2255 Meyers Ave	Escondido	CA	92029	**800-854-2023**		520
Maax Corp	160 St Joseph Blvd	Lachine	QC	H8S2L3	**888-957-7816**	877-438-6229	603
Mabis Healthcare Inc	1931 Norman Dr	Waukegan	IL	60085	**800-526-4753**		470
Mac Haik Auto Group	11711 Katy Fwy	Houston	TX	77079	**888-877-1748**	281-596-6261	56
Mac Papers	3300 Phillips Hwy PO Box 5369	Jacksonville	FL	32207	**800-622-2968**	904-348-3300	546
Mac Tools Inc	505 N Cleveland Ave	Westerville	OH	43082	**800-622-8665**	614-755-7000	748
Mac Trailer Mfg Inc	14599 Commerce St NE	Alliance	OH	44601	**800-795-8454**	330-823-9900	769
Mac Valves Inc	30569 Beck Rd	Wixom	MI	48393	**800-622-8587**	248-624-7700	777
Mac's Convenience Stores Inc	305 Milner Ave Ste 400 4th Fl	Toronto	ON	M1B3V4	**800-268-5574**		205
Macalester College	1600 Grand Ave *Admissions	Saint Paul	MN	55105	**800-231-7974***	651-696-6357	166
MacAllister Machinery Company Inc	7515 E 30th St	Indianapolis	IN	46219	**800-227-3228**	317-545-2151	355
Macally USA Mace Group Inc	4601 E Airport Dr	Ontario	CA	91761	**800-644-1132**	909-230-6888	174-2
MacArthur Co	2400 Wycliff St	Saint Paul	MN	55114	**800-777-7507**	651-646-2773	192-4

	Toll-Free	Phone	Class
MacArthur Place			
29 E MacArthur St ....Sonoma CA 95476	**800-722-1866**	707-938-2929	376
Macatawa Bank Corp			
10753 Macatawa Dr PO Box 3119 ....Holland MI 49424	**877-820-2265**	616-820-1444	357-2
NASDAQ: MCBC			
Macaulay-Brown Inc			
4021 Executive Dr ....Dayton OH 45430	**800-669-4000**	937-426-3421	261
MACC (Murray Area Chamber of Commerce)			
5250 S Commerce Dr Ste 180 ....Murray UT 84107	**877-209-0068**	801-263-2632	137
Macdonald Realty			
203 5188 Wminster Hwy ....Richmond BC V7C5S7	**877-278-3888**	604-279-9822	643
MacDonald-Miller Facility Solutions Inc			
7717 Detroit Ave SE ....Seattle WA 98106	**800-962-5979**	206-763-9400	190-10
MacDuffie School			
66 School St ....Granby MA 01033	**877-477-6217**	413-255-0000	615
Macerich Co, The			
401 Wilshire Blvd Ste 700 .....Santa Monica CA 90401	**800-421-7237**	310-394-6000	646
NYSE: MAC			
MACFS (Mid-America College of Funeral Science)			
3111 Hamburg Pk ....Jeffersonville IN 47130	**800-221-6158**	812-288-8878	788
Mac-Gray Corp			
404 Wyman St Ste 400...............Waltham MA 02451	**888-622-4729**	781-487-7600	382
NYSE: TUC			
Machias Savings Bank			
4 Ctr St PO Box 318 ....Machias ME 04654	**800-982-7179**	207-255-3347	69
Machine Specialty & Manufacturing Inc			
215 Rousseau Rd ....Youngsville LA 70592	**800-256-1292**	337-837-0020	478
Machinery Dealers NA (MDNA)			
315 S Patrick St ....Alexandria VA 22314	**800-872-7807**	703-836-9300	48-18
Machinery Sales Co			
17253 Chestnut St ....City of Industry CA 91748	**800-588-8111**	626-581-9211	382
Machinery Systems Inc			
614 E State Pkwy ....Schaumburg IL 60173	**888-650-5424**	847-882-8085	382
Mackay Communications Inc			
3691 Trust Dr ....Raleigh NC 27616	**877-462-2529**	919-850-3000	522
Mackay Envelope Corp			
2100 Elm St SE ....Minneapolis MN 55414	**800-622-5299**		263
Mack-Cali Realty Corp			
343 Thornall St ....Edison NJ 08837	**800-317-4445**	732-590-1000	646
NYSE: CLI			
Mackenzie Financial Corp			
180 Queen St W ....Toronto ON M5V3K1	**888-653-7070**	416-922-5322	398
MacKenzie-Childs LLC			
3260 SR- 90 ....Aurora NY 13152	**888-665-1999**	315-364-7123	320
Mackie Research Capital Corp			
308-4th Ave SW Ste 2700 ....Calgary AB T2P0H7	**888-292-0980**	403-292-0970	681
Mackinaw Area Visitors Bureau			
10800 US 23 ....Mackinaw City MI 49701	**800-666-0160**	231-436-5664	207
Mackinnon Transport Inc			
405 Laird Rd ....Guelph ON N1G4P7	**800-265-9394**	519-821-2311	791-1
MacKissic Inc			
PO Box 111 ....Parker Ford PA 19457	**800-348-1117**	610-495-7181	426
MacLean Power Systems			
11411 Addison St ....Franklin Park IL 60131	**855-677-7447**	847-455-0014	803
Maclean's Magazine			
One Mt Pleasant Rd 11th Fl ....Toronto ON M4Y2Y5	**800-268-9119**	416-764-1300	452-17
MacLean-Fogg Co			
1000 Allanson Rd ....Mundelein IL 60060	**800-323-4536**	847-566-0010	59
MacMurray College			
447 E College Ave ....Jacksonville IL 62650	**800-252-7485**	217-479-7056	166
MacNeal Hospital			
3249 S Oak Pk Ave ....Berwyn IL 60402	**888-622-6325**	708-783-9100	371-3
MacNeill Engineering Company Inc			
140 Locke Dr PO Box 735 ......Marlborough MA 01752	**800-652-4267**	508-481-8830	701
Macomb Area Chamber of Commerce & Downtown Development Corp			
214 N Lafayette St ....Macomb IL 61455	**800-232-0270**	309-837-4855	137
Macomb Community College			
Center			
44575 Garfield Rd ......Clinton Township MI 48038	**866-622-6621**	586-445-7999	160
South			
14500 E 12-Mile Rd ....Warren MI 48088	**866-622-6621**	586-445-7000	160
Macomb County Chamber			
28 First St Ste B ....Mount Clemens MI 48043	**800-564-3136**	586-493-7600	137
Macomb Journal			
203 N Randolph St ....Macomb IL 61455	**800-747-5401**	309-833-2114	525-2
Macon Centreplex Coliseum			
200 Coliseum Dr ....Macon GA 31217	**877-532-6144**	478-751-9152	711
Macon City Auditorium			
415 First St ....Macon GA 31201	**877-532-6144**	478-751-9152	565
Macon Electric Co-op			
31571 Bus Hwy 36 E PO Box 157......Macon MO 63552	**800-553-6901**	660-385-3157	245
Macon State College			
100 College Stn Dr ....Macon GA 31206	**800-272-7619**	478-471-2700	166
Macon Telegraph			
120 Broadway ....Macon GA 31201	**800-679-6397**	478-744-4200	525-2
Macon-Bibb County Convention/Visitors Bureau			
450 Martin Luther King Jr Blvd ....Macon GA 31201	**800-768-3401**	478-743-1074	207
MacPherson's Property Management Inc			
18551 Aurora Ave N Ste 301 ....Seattle WA 98133	**800-962-6473**	206-542-6363	643
MACS (Mobile Air Conditioning Society Worldwide)			
225 S Broad St ....Lansdale PA 19446	**800-641-1133**	215-631-7020	48-21
Macula Foundation Inc			
210 E 64th St 8th Fl ....New York NY 10065	**800-622-8524**	212-605-3777	47-17
Macworld Magazine			
501 Second St Ste 600..........San Francisco CA 94107	**800-288-6848***	415-243-0505	452-7
*Cust Svc			
Macy's Inc			
Seven W Seventh St ....Cincinnati OH 45202	**800-261-5385**	513-579-7000	229
NYSE: M			
Macy's Travel			
700 Nicollet Mall ....Minneapolis MN 55402	**800-316-6166**		750
Mad Catz Interactive Inc			
7480 Mission Vly Rd Ste 101 ....San Diego CA 92108	**800-659-2287**	619-683-9830	174-2
NYSE: MCZ			
Mad Science Group			
8360 Bougainville St Ste 201 ....Montreal QC H4P2G1	**800-586-5231**	514-344-4181	309
Mada Medical Products Inc			
625 Washington Ave ....Carlstadt NJ 07072	**800-526-6370**	201-460-0454	470
MADD (Mothers Against Drunk Driving)			
511 E John Carpenter Fwy Ste 700........Irving TX 75062	**877-275-6233**	214-744-6233	47-6
Madden Manufacturing Inc			
PO Box 387 ....Elkhart IN 46515	**800-369-6233**	574-295-4292	632
Madden's on Gull Lake			
11266 Pine Beach Peninsula ....Brainerd MN 56401	**800-642-5363**	218-829-2811	660
Madelaine Chocolate Novelties Inc			
9603 Beach Ch Dr ....Rockaway Beach NY 11693	**800-322-1505**	718-945-1500	295-8
Madera District Chamber of Commerce			
120 NE St ....Madera CA 93638	**866-382-7822**	559-673-3563	137
Madera Unified School District			
1902 HowaRd Rd ....Madera CA 93637	**800-322-6384**	559-675-4500	676
Madico Inc			
64 Industrial Pkwy ....Woburn MA 01801	**800-456-4331**	781-935-7850	592
Madison Cable Corp			
125 Goddard Memorial Dr ....Worcester MA 01603	**877-623-4766**	508-752-2884	801
Madison Chemical Company Inc			
3141 Clifty Dr ....Madison IN 47250	**800-345-1915**	812-273-6000	149
Madison Concourse Hotel & Governors Club			
1 W Dayton St ....Madison WI 53703	**800-356-8293**	608-257-6000	376
Madison Convention & Visitors Bureau			
115 E Jefferson St ....Madison GA 30650	**800-709-7406**	706-342-4454	207
Madison County			
248 SW Range Ave PO Box 237 ....Madison FL 32340	**877-272-3642**	850-973-2788	336
Madison Cutting Die Inc			
2547 Progress Rd ....Madison WI 53716	**800-395-9405**	608-221-3422	548
Madison Gas & Electric Co			
133 S Blair St ....Madison WI 53703	**800-245-1125**	608-252-7000	775
Madison Hotel, The			
One Convent Rd ....Morristown NJ 07960	**800-526-0729**	973-285-1800	376
Madison Investment Advisors Inc			
550 Science Dr ....Madison WI 53711	**800-767-0300**	608-274-0300	398
Madison National Life Insurance Company Inc			
PO Box 5008 ....Madison WI 53705	**800-356-9601**	608-830-2000	388-2
Madison Newspapers Inc			
1901 Fish Hatchery Rd ....Madison WI 53713	**800-252-7723***	608-252-6200	628-8
*Sales			
Madison the - A Loews Hotel			
667 Madison Ave ....New York NY 10065	**800-235-6397**	212-521-2000	376
Madison-Kipp Corp			
201 Waubesa St ....Madison WI 53704	**800-356-6148**		307
Madisonville Community College			
2000 College Dr ....Madisonville KY 42431	**866-227-4812**	270-821-2250	160
Madonna Rehabilitation Hospital			
5401 S St ....Lincoln NE 68506	**800-676-5448**	402-489-7102	371-6
Madonna University			
36600 Schoolcraft Rd ....Livonia MI 48150	**800-852-4951**	734-432-5339	166
MAF (Mission Aviation Fellowship)			
112 N Pilatus Ln ....Nampa ID 83687	**800-359-7623**	208-498-0800	47-20
Mafcote Industries Inc			
108 Main St ....Norwalk CT 06851	**800-221-3056***	203-847-8500	547
*Cust Svc			
MAG (Medical Assn of Georgia)			
1849 The Exchange Ste 200 ....Atlanta GA 30339	**800-282-0224**	678-303-9290	469
Mag Instrument Inc			
2001 S Hillman Ave ....Ontario CA 91761	**800-289-6241**	909-947-1006	435
Magazine Publishers of America (MPA)			
810 Seventh Ave 24th Fl ....New York NY 10019	**800-234-3368**	212-872-3700	48-16
Magee Rehabilitation Hospital			
1513 Race St ....Philadelphia PA 19102	**800-966-2433**	215-587-3000	371-6
Magellan Health Services Inc			
55 Nod Rd ....Avon CT 06001	**800-424-4399**	860-507-1900	457
NASDAQ: MGLN			
Magellan Medicaid Administration Inc			
4300 Cox Rd ....Glen Allen VA 23060	**800-884-2822**	804-965-7400	458
Magellan Midstream Partners LP			
One Williams Ctr ....Tulsa OK 74172	**800-574-6671**	918-574-7000	590
NYSE: MMP			
Maggie Valley Resort & Country Club			
1819 Country Club Dr ....Maggie Valley NC 28751	**800-438-3861**	828-926-1616	660
MaggieMoo's International LLC			
1346 Oakbrook Dr Ste 170 ....Norcross GA 30093	**877-639-2361**		309
Magic American Corp			
26901 Cannon Rd Ste 190 ....Bedford Heights OH 44146	**800-729-9029***		149
*Cust Svc			
Magic Plastics Inc			
25215 Ave Stanford ....Valencia CA 91355	**800-369-0303**	661-257-4485	601
Magic Tilt Trailers Inc			
2161 Lions Club Rd ....Clearwater FL 33764	**800-998-8458**	727-535-5561	769
Magic Valley Electric Co-op Inc			
1 3/4 Mile W Hwy 83 PO Box 267 ......Mercedes TX 78570	**866-225-5683**	956-903-3048	245
Magic Valley Newspapers			
132 Fairfield St W ....Twin Falls ID 83301	**800-658-3883**	208-733-0931	628-8
Magid Glove & Safety Manufacturing Co			
2060 N Kolmar Ave ....Chicago IL 60639	**800-444-8010**	773-384-2070	153-7
Magline Inc			
1205 W Cedar St ....Standish MI 48658	**800-624-5463**		465
Magna Chek Inc			
32701 Edward Ave ....Madison Heights MI 48071	**800-582-8947**	248-597-0089	732
Magna Design Inc			
26246 Twelve Trees Ln NW ....Poulsbo WA 98370	**800-426-1202**	360-394-1300	318-1
Magna Visual Inc			
9400 Watson Rd ....Saint Louis MO 63126	**800-843-3399**		527
Magnat-Fairview Inc			
1102 Sheridan St ....Chicopee MA 01022	**800-636-3433**	413-593-5742	480
Magnet Sales & Mfg Company Inc			
11248 Playa Ct ....Culver City CA 90230	**800-421-6692**	310-391-7213	433
Magnetech Industrial Services Inc			
800 Nave Rd SE ....Massillon OH 44646	**800-837-1614***	330-830-3500	480
*General			
MagneTek Inc			
N49 W13650 Campbell Dr .....Menomonee Falls WI 53051	**800-288-8178**		253
NASDAQ: MAG			
Magnetic Analysis Corp			
103 Fairview Park Dr ....Elmsford NY 10523	**800-463-8622**	914-699-9450	467
Magnetic Component Engineering Inc			
2830 Lomita Blvd ....Torrance CA 90505	**800-989-5656**		453
Magnetic Metals Corp			
1900 Hayes Ave ....Camden NJ 08105	**800-257-8174**	856-964-7842	476
Magnetrol International Inc			
5300 Belmont Rd ....Downers Grove IL 60515	**800-624-8765**	630-969-4000	202
Magnets.com			
51 Pacific Ave Ste 4 ....Jersey City NJ 07304	**866-229-8237**		363
Magnetsigns Adv Inc			
4225 38th St ....Camrose AB T4V3Z3	**800-219-8977**	780-672-8720	309
Mag-Nif Inc 8820 E Ave ....Mentor OH 44060	**800-869-5463**		752
Magnifying Ctr			
10086 W McNab Rd ....Tamarac FL 33321	**800-364-1612**	954-722-1580	536
Magnolia Brush Mfg Ltd			
1000 N Cedar PO Box 932 ....Clarksville TX 75426	**800-248-2261**	903-427-2261	102

				Toll-Free	Phone	Class
Magnolia Financial Inc						
187 W Broad St	Spartanburg	SC	29306	**866-573-0611**	864-573-9900	272
Magnolia Forest Products Inc						
13252 I- 55 S PO Box 99	Terry	MS	39170	**800-366-6374**		192-3
Magnolia Hotel & Spa, The						
623 Courtney St	Victoria	BC	V8W1B8	**877-624-6654**	250-381-0999	376
Magnolia Hotel Dallas						
1401 Commerce St	Dallas	TX	75201	**888-915-1110**	214-915-6500	376
Magnolia Hotel Denver						
818 17th St	Denver	CO	80202	**888-915-1110**	303-607-9000	376
Magnolia Hotel Houston						
1100 Texas Ave	Houston	TX	77002	**888-915-1110**	713-221-0011	376
Magnolia Metal Corp						
10675 Bedford Ave Ste 200	Omaha	NE	68134	**800-228-4043**	402-455-8760	307
Magnolia Plantation & Gardens						
3550 Ashley River Rd	Charleston	SC	29414	**800-367-3517**	843-571-1266	96
Magnotta Winery Corp						
271 Chrislea Rd	Vaughan	ON	L4L8N6	**800-461-9463**	905-738-9463	79-3
Magnum Hunter Resources						
120 Prosperous Pl Ste 201	Lexington	KY	40509	**877-778-5463**	859-263-3948	529
Magnum Integrated Technologies Inc						
200 First Gulf Blvd	Brampton	ON	L6W4T5	**800-830-0642**	905-595-1998	665
Magnum Magnetics Corp						
801 Masonic Pk Rd	Marietta	OH	45750	**800-258-0991**	740-373-7770	453
Magtrol Inc						
70 Gardenville Pkwy W	Buffalo	NY	14224	**800-828-7844**	716-668-5555	613
Magyar Bank						
400 Somerset St	New Brunswick	NJ	08901	**800-472-3272**	732-342-7600	69
Mahaffey Theater for the Performing Arts						
400 First St S	Saint Petersburg	FL	33701	**800-435-7352**	727-892-5798	565
Mahar Tool Supply Co Inc						
112 Williams St	Saginaw	MI	48605	**800-456-2427**	989-799-5530	382
Maharishi University of Management						
1000 N Fourth St	Fairfield	IA	52557	**800-369-6480**	641-472-1110	166
MAHLE Industries Inc						
2020 Sanford St	Muskegon	MI	49444	**888-255-1942**	231-722-1300	127
Mahoning County Convention & Visitors Bureau						
21 W Boardman St	Youngstown	OH	44503	**800-447-8201**	330-740-2130	207
Mahr Federal Inc						
1144 Eddy St	Providence	RI	02905	**800-343-2050***	401-784-3100	202
*Orders						
MAI (Medical Action Industries Inc)						
500 Expy Dr S	Brentwood	NY	11717	**800-645-7042**	631-231-4600	472
NASDAQ: MDCI						
Maid Brigade USA/Minimaid Canada						
Four Concourse Pkwy Ste 200	Atlanta	GA	30328	**800-722-6243**	770-551-9630	150
MaidPro Corp						
180 Canal St	Boston	MA	02114	**888-624-3776**	617-742-8787	309
Maid-Rite Steak Company Inc						
105 Keystone Industrial Pk	Dunmore	PA	18512	**800-233-4259**	570-343-4748	295-26
Maids International						
9394 W Dodge Rd Ste 140	Omaha	NE	68114	**800-843-6243**	402-558-8600	150
Mail Boxes Etc						
6060 Cornerstone Ct W	San Diego	CA	92121	**800-789-4623**	858-455-8800	112
Mail Shark						
4125 New Holland Rd	Mohnton	PA	19540	**888-457-4275**		363
Mailbox Bookbag Magazine						
3515 W Market St Ste 200	Greensboro	NC	27403	**800-714-7991**	336-854-0309	452-8
Mailender Inc						
9500 Glades Dr	Hamilton	OH	45011	**800-998-5453**	513-942-5453	681
Mailman Research Ctr						
McLean Hospital						
115 Mill St	Belmont	MA	02478	**800-333-0338**	617-855-2000	659
Main Street America Group						
55 W St	Keene	NH	03431	**800-258-5310**	603-352-4000	388-4
Main Street Capital Corp						
1300 Post Oak Blvd	Houston	TX	77056	**800-966-1559**	713-350-6000	402
NYSE: MAIN						
Main Street Gourmet Inc						
170 Muffin Ln	Cuyahoga Falls	OH	44223	**800-678-6246**	330-929-0000	295-2
Main Street Station Hotel & Casino						
200 N Main St	Las Vegas	NV	89101	**800-713-8933**	702-387-1896	376
Main-Care Energy						
PO Box 11029	Albany	NY	12211	**800-542-5552**		572
Maine						
Consumer Protection Unit						
6 State House Stn	Augusta	ME	04333	**800-436-2131**	207-626-8849	337-20
Economic & Community Development Dept						
59 State House Stn	Augusta	ME	04333	**800-541-5872**	207-624-9800	337-20
Elder Services Office						
11 Statehouse Stn	Augusta	ME	04333	**800-624-8404**		337-20
Environmental Protection Dept						
17 State House Stn	Augusta	ME	04333	**800-452-1942**	207-287-7688	337-20
Financial Institutions Bureau						
35 Anthony Ave 11 State House Stn	Augusta	ME	04333	**800-452-1926**	207-624-8090	337-20
Governor						
1 State House Stn	Augusta	ME	04333	**888-577-6690**	207-287-3531	337-20
Insurance Bureau						
34 State House Stn	Augusta	ME	04333	**800-300-5000**	207-624-8475	337-20
Rehabilitation Services Bureau						
150 State House Stn	Augusta	ME	04333	**800-698-4440**		337-20
State Government Information						
26 Edison Dr	Augusta	ME	04330	**888-577-6690**	207-624-9494	337-20
Maine Bar Journal						
124 State St PO Box 788	Augusta	ME	04332	**800-475-7523**	207-622-7523	452-15
Maine Biotechnology Services Inc						
1037 R Forest Ave	Portland	ME	04103	**800-925-9476**	207-797-5454	231
Maine College of Art						
97 Spring St	Portland	ME	04101	**800-639-4808**	207-775-3052	162
Maine Educator Magazine						
35 Community Dr	Augusta	ME	04330	**800-332-8529**	207-622-5866	452-8
Maine Finance Authority of Maine (FAME)						
5 Community Dr PO Box 949	Augusta	ME	04332	**800-228-3734**	207-623-3263	716
Maine Instrument Flight Inc						
PO Box 2	Augusta	ME	04332	**888-643-3597**	207-622-1211	62
Maine Lobster Direct						
48 Union Wharf	Portland	ME	04101	**800-556-2783**		296-5
Maine Maritime Academy						
66 Pleasant St	Castine	ME	04420	**800-227-8465***	207-326-4311	166
*Admissions						
Maine Medical Assn						
30 Assn Dr	Manchester	ME	04351	**800-772-0815**	207-622-3374	469
Maine Medical Ctr (MMC)						
22 Bramhall St	Portland	ME	04102	**877-339-3107**	207-662-0111	371-3
Maine Oxy						
22 Albiston Way	Auburn	ME	04210	**800-639-1108**	207-784-5788	798
Maine Public Broadcasting Network (MPBN)						
65 Texas Ave	Bangor	ME	04401	**800-884-1717**	207-941-1010	624
Maine State Bar Assn						
124 State St	Augusta	ME	04330	**800-475-7523**	207-622-7523	71
Maine Veterans Home-Augusta						
310 Cony Rd	Augusta	ME	04330	**888-684-4664**		781
Maine Veterans Home-Bangor						
44 Hogan Rd	Bangor	ME	04401	**888-684-4665**	207-942-2333	781
Maine Veterans Home-Caribou						
163 Van Buren Rd Ste 2	Caribou	ME	04736	**888-684-4667**	207-498-6074	781
Maine Veterans Home-Scarborough						
290 US Rt 1	Scarborough	ME	04074	**888-684-4666**	207-883-7184	781
Maine Veterans Home-South Paris						
477 High St	South Paris	ME	04281	**888-684-4668**	207-743-6300	781
Maine Veterinary Medical Assn (MVMA)						
97A Exchange St Ste 305	Portland	ME	04101	**800-448-2772**		783
Maine Windjammer Cruises						
PO Box 617	Camden	ME	04843	**800-736-7981**	207-236-2938	220
Maines Paper & Food Service Co						
101 Broome Corporate Pkwy	Conklin	NY	13748	**800-366-3669**	607-779-1200	296-8
Mainline Information Systems Inc						
1700 Summit Lk Dr	Tallahassee	FL	32317	**866-490-6246**	850-219-5000	181
Mainship Corp						
255 Diesel Rd	St Augustine	FL	32084	**800-771-5556**	904-827-2007	89
Mainstay						
1320 Flynn Rd Ste 401	Camarillo	CA	93012	**800-362-2605***	805-484-9400	179-12
*Orders						
Maintenx						
2202 N Howard Ave	Tampa	FL	33607	**855-751-0075**	813-254-1656	603
Mairs & Power Funds						
332 Minnesota St Ste W-1520	Saint Paul	MN	55101	**800-304-7404**	651-222-8478	521
Maison Dupuy Hotel						
1001 Toulouse St	New Orleans	LA	70112	**800-535-9177**	504-586-8000	376
Maitland Art Ctr						
231 W Packwood Ave	Maitland	FL	32751	**800-435-7352**	407-539-2181	49-1
Majestic Investor Holdings LLC						
One Buffington Harbor Dr	Gary	IN	46406	**800-522-4700**		131
Majestic Star Casino & Hotel						
One Buffington Harbor Dr	Gary	IN	46406	**800-522-4700**	219-977-7777	132
Majestic Steel USA						
5300 Majestic Pkwy	Cleveland	OH	44146	**800-321-5590**	440-786-2666	487
Majestic Theatre						
245 W 44th St	New York	NY	10036	**800-447-7400**	212-239-6200	736
Major Custom Cable Inc						
281 Lotus Dr	Jackson	MO	63755	**800-455-6224**		800
Major League Baseball (Office of the Commissioner)						
245 Pk Ave 31st Fl	New York	NY	10167	**866-800-1275***	212-931-7800	704
*Cust Svc						
Major Pharmaceutical Co						
31778 Enterprise Dr	Livonia	MI	48150	**800-875-0123**	734-743-6161	576
Make-A-Wish Foundation of America						
4742 N 24th St Ste 400	Phoenix	AZ	85016	**800-722-9474**	602-279-9474	47-5
MakeMusic! Inc						
7615 Golden Triangle Dr Ste M	Eden Prairie	MN	55344	**800-843-2066**	952-937-9611	179-6
NASDAQ: MMUS						
Makino						
7680 Innovation Way	Mason	OH	45040	**888-625-4661**	513-573-7200	450
Makita USA Inc						
14930 Northam St Ste C	La Mirada	CA	90638	**800-462-5482**	714-522-8088	749
Malaco Music Group Inc						
3023 W Northside Dr	Jackson	MS	39213	**800-272-7936***	601-982-4522	648
*Cust Svc						
Malaga Financial Corp						
2514 Via Tejon	Palos Verdes Estates	CA	90274	**888-562-5242**	310-375-9000	357-2
OTC: MLGF						
Malaga Inn						
359 Church St	Mobile	AL	36602	**800-235-1586**	251-438-4701	376
Malarkey Roofing Products						
PO Box 17217	Portland	OR	97217	**800-545-1191**	503-283-1191	45
Malaysia Airlines						
100 N Sepulveda Blvd Ste 1710	El Segundo	CA	90245	**800-552-9264***	310-535-9288	25
*Resv						
Malbar Vision Ctr						
409 N 78th St	Omaha	NE	68114	**800-701-3937**	402-391-6600	536
Malco Products Inc						
14080 State Hwy 55 NW PO Box 400	Annandale	MN	55302	**800-328-3530**	320-274-8246	748
Malcolm Drilling Co Inc						
3503 Breakwater Ct	Hayward	CA	94545	**800-523-2200**	510-780-9181	189-2
Malcolm Wiener Ctr for Social Policy						
John F Kennedy School of Government Harvard University 79 John F Kennedy St	Cambridge	MA	02138	**866-845-6596**	617-496-4082	625
Malcolm X College						
1900 W Van Buren St	Chicago	IL	60612	**877-542-0285**	312-850-7000	160
Malcom Randall VAMC NF/SGVHS						
1601 SW Archer Rd	Gainesville	FL	32608	**800-324-8387**	352-376-1611	371-8
Male Survivor						
5505 Connecticut Ave NW PO Box 103	Washington	DC	20015	**800-738-4181**		47-17
Malema Engineering Corp						
1060 S Rogers Cir	Boca Raton	FL	33487	**800-637-6418**	561-995-0595	202
Malibu Chamber of Commerce						
23805 Stuart Ranch Rd Ste 210	Malibu	CA	90265	**800-442-4988**	310-456-9025	137
Mallet & Company Inc						
51 Arch St Ext	Carnegie	PA	15106	**800-245-2757**	412-276-9000	295-23
Malleys Chocolates						
13400 Brookpark Rd	Cleveland	OH	44135	**800-835-5684**	216-362-8700	295-8
Mallin Casual Furniture						
One Minson Way	Montebello	CA	90640	**800-251-6537**		318-4
Mallinckrodt Inc						
675 McDonnell Blvd	Hazelwood	MO	63042	**800-778-7898**	314-654-2000	231
Malmstrom Air Force Base						
7410 Flightline Dr Bldg 300	Malmstrom AFB	MT	59402	**866-731-4633**	406-731-1110	492-1
Malnati Organization Inc						
3685 Woodhead Dr	Northbrook	IL	60062	**800-568-8646**	847-562-1814	661
Malnove Inc 13434 F St	Omaha	NE	68137	**800-228-9877**	402-330-1100	100

	City	State	ZIP	Toll-Free	Phone	Class
Malone College						
515 25th St NW	Canton	OH	44709	**800-521-1146**	330-471-8100	166
Maloney Technical Products						
1300 E Berry St	Fort Worth	TX	76119	**800-231-7236**	817-923-3344	589
Malt Products Corp						
88 Market St	Saddle Brook	NJ	07663	**800-526-0180**	201-845-4420	101
Maltby Electric Supply Company Inc						
336 Seventh St	San Francisco	CA	94103	**800-339-0668**	415-863-5000	246
Maltz Jupiter Theatre						
1001 E Indiantown Rd	Jupiter	FL	33477	**800-445-1666**	561-743-2666	738
Malvern Institute						
940 W King Rd	Malvern	PA	19355	**888-643-3869**	610-647-0330	717
Malvern Systems Inc						
81 Lancaster Ave Ste 219	Malvern	PA	19355	**800-296-9642**		179-1
MAMAC Systems Inc						
8189 Century Blvd	Minneapolis	MN	55317	**800-843-5116**	952-556-4900	202
Mammoth Mountain Resort						
One Minaret Rd PO Box 24	Mammoth Lakes	CA	93546	**800-626-6684**	760-934-2571	660
Mammoth Times, The						
PO Box 3929	Mammoth Lakes	CA	93546	**800-427-7623**	760-934-3929	525-4
Mana Products Inc						
32-02 Queens Blvd	Long Island City	NY	11101	**800-221-3071***	718-361-2550	215
*Cust Svc						
Manafort Bros Inc						
414 New Britain Ave	Plainville	CT	06062	**888-626-2367**	860-229-4853	190-5
Managed Care of America Inc						
1910 Cochran Rd Ste 605	Pittsburgh	PA	15220	**800-922-4966**	412-922-2803	387
Managed Health Network Inc						
1600 Los Gamos Dr Ste 300	San Rafael	CA	94903	**800-327-2133**		457
Managed HealthCare Northwest Inc						
422 East Burnside St Suite 215						
P.O. Box 4629	Portland	OR	97208	**800-648-6356**	503-413-5800	387
Management Consulting Inc						
1961 Diamond Springs Rd	Virginia Beach	VA	23455	**877-624-8090**	757-460-0879	261
Management Information Control Systems Inc (MICS)						
2025 Ninth St	Los Osos	CA	93402	**800-838-6427**	805-543-7000	179-10
Management Recruiters International Worldwide Inc						
1717 Arch St 36th Fl	Philadelphia	PA	19103	**800-875-4000**		266
Management Science Assoc Inc						
6565 Penn Ave	Pittsburgh	PA	15206	**800-672-4636**	412-362-2000	179-12
Manager's Intelligence Report (MIR)						
316 N Michigan Ave Ste 400	Chicago	IL	60601	**800-878-5331**		524-2
Manatee Convention Ctr						
1 Haben Blvd	Palmetto	FL	34221	**800-822-2017**	941-722-3244	206
Manatee Memorial Hospital						
206 Second St E	Bradenton	FL	34208	**844-854-9613**	941-746-5111	371-3
Manatron Inc						
510 E Milham Ave	Portage	MI	49002	**866-471-2900***	269-567-2900	179-11
*Cust Svc						
Manatt's Inc						
1775 Old 6 Rd	Brooklyn	IA	52211	**800-532-1121**	641-522-9206	189-4
Manchester College						
604 E College Ave	North Manchester	IN	46962	**800-852-3648***	260-982-5000	166
*Admissions						
Manchester Community College						
PO Box 1046	Manchester	CT	06045	**888-999-5545**	860-512-2800	160
Manchester Financial Inc						
2815 Townsgate Rd						
Ste 100	Westlake Village	CA	91361	**800-492-1107**		398
Manchester Tank						
1000 Corp Centre Dr Ste 300	Franklin	TN	37067	**800-399-5628**	615-370-6300	173
Manda Fine Meats						
2445 Sorrel Ave	Baton Rouge	LA	70802	**800-343-2642**	225-344-7636	296-9
Mandalay Bay Resort & Casino						
3950 Las Vegas Blvd S	Las Vegas	NV	89119	**877-632-7800**	702-632-7777	660
Mandarin Oriental Hotel Group (USA)						
345 California St						
Ste 1250	San Francisco	CA	94104	**800-526-6566**	415-772-8800	376
Mandarin Oriental Miami						
500 Brickell Key Dr	Miami	FL	33131	**800-526-6566**	305-913-8288	376
Mandarin Oriental New York						
80 Columbus Cir	New York	NY	10023	**866-801-8880**	212-805-8800	376
Mandarin Oriental San Francisco						
222 Sansome St	San Francisco	CA	94104	**800-526-6566**	415-276-9888	376
Mandarin Oriental Washington DC						
1330 Maryland Ave SW	Washington	DC	20024	**888-888-1778**	202-554-8588	376
Mandee Shop						
12 Vreeland Ave	Totowa	NJ	07512	**877-756-1958***	973-890-0021	155-6
*Cust Svc						
Mandel Scientific Company Inc						
Two Admiral Pl	Guelph	ON	N1G4N4	**888-883-3636**	519-763-9292	416
Manhasset Specialty Co						
3505 Fruitvale Blvd	Yakima	WA	98902	**800-795-0965**	509-248-3810	520
Manhattan Area Chamber of Commerce						
501 Poyntz Ave	Manhattan	KS	66502	**800-759-0134**	785-776-8829	137
Manhattan Assoc Inc						
2300 Windy Ridge Pkwy 10th Fl	Atlanta	GA	30339	**877-756-7435**	770-955-7070	179-10
NASDAQ: MANH						
Manhattan Bagel Co Inc						
555 Zang St Ste 300	Lakewood	CO	80228	**800-224-3563**	303-568-8000	67
Manhattan Beach State Recreation Site						
725 Summer St NE Ste C	Salem	OR	97301	**800-551-6949**	503-986-0707	558
Manhattan Chamber of Commerce						
1375 Broadway 3rd F	New York	NY	10018	**855-868-7692**	212-479-7772	137
Manhattan Christian College						
1415 Anderson Ave	Manhattan	KS	66502	**877-246-4622**	785-539-3571	159
Manhattan College						
4513 Manhattan College Pkwy	Bronx	NY	10471	**800-622-9235**	718-862-8000	166
Manhattan Convention & Visitors Bureau						
501 Poyntz Ave	Manhattan	KS	66502	**800-759-0134**	785-776-8829	207
Manhattan Public Library						
629 Poyntz Ave	Manhattan	KS	66502	**800-432-2796**	785-776-4741	431-3
Manhattan Toy						
300 First Ave N Suite 200	Minneapolis	MN	55401	**800-541-1345**	612-337-9600	63
Manhattanville College						
2900 Purchase St	Purchase	NY	10577	**800-328-4553**	914-323-5464	166
Manildra Group USA						
4210 Shawnee Mission Pkwy						
Ste 312A	Shawnee Mission	KS	66205	**800-323-8435**	913-362-0777	295-23
Manitex Inc						
3000 S Austin Ave	Georgetown	TX	78626	**877-314-3390**	512-942-3000	465
Manitou Cliff Dwellings Museum						
10 Cliff Rd	Manitou Springs	CO	80829	**800-354-9971**	719-685-5242	513

	City	State	ZIP	Toll-Free	Phone	Class
Manitowoc Area Visitor & Convention Bureau						
PO Box 966	Manitowoc	WI	54221	**800-627-4896**		207
Manitowoc Beverage Equipment						
2100 Future Dr	Sellersburg	IN	47172	**800-367-4233**	812-246-7000	297
Manitowoc Ice						
2110 S 26th St	Manitowoc	WI	54220	**800-545-5720**	920-682-0161	655
Manitowoc-Two Rivers Area Chamber of Commerce						
1515 Memorial Dr	Manitowoc	WI	54220	**866-727-5575**	920-684-5575	137
Manke Lumber Company Inc						
1717 Marine View Dr	Tacoma	WA	98422	**800-426-8488**	253-572-6252	674
Manko Window Systems Inc						
800 Hayes Dr	Manhattan	KS	66502	**800-642-1488**	785-776-9643	475
Mann & Parker Lumber Company Inc, The						
335 N Constitution Ave	New Freedom	PA	17349	**800-632-9098**	717-235-4834	494
Mann Packing Company Inc						
PO Box 690	Salinas	CA	93902	**800-285-1002**	831-422-7405	11-1
Manna Pro Corp						
707 Spirit 40 Pk Dr						
Ste 150	Chesterfield	MO	63005	**800-690-9908**		442
Mannington Mills Inc						
75 Mannington Mills Rd	Salem	NJ	08079	**800-356-6787***	856-935-3000	291
*Cust Svc						
Manns Bait Co						
1111 State Docks Rd	Eufaula	AL	36027	**800-841-8435**		701
Manoir du Lac Delage						
40 Ave du Lac	Lac Delage	QC	G3C5C4	**888-202-3242**	418-848-2551	660
Manor House Inn						
106 W St	Bar Harbor	ME	04609	**800-437-0088**	207-288-3759	376
Manor Industries Inc						
24400 Maplehurst	Clinton Township	MI	48036	**800-921-1007**	586-463-4604	451
Manor Park Inc						
2208 N Loop 250 W	Midland	TX	79707	**800-523-9898**	432-689-9898	663
Manor Vail Lodge						
595 E Vail Vly Dr	Vail	CO	81657	**800-950-8245**	970-476-5000	660
ManorCare Health Services - Mountainside						
1180 Rt 22 W	Mountainside	NJ	07092	**800-366-1232**	908-654-0020	445
Manpower Demonstration Research Corp						
16 E 34th St 19th Fl	New York	NY	10016	**800-221-3165**	212-532-3200	625
Mansfield Oil Co						
1025 Airport Pkwy SW	Gainesville	GA	30501	**800-695-6626**		532
Mansfield Plumbing Products Inc						
150 E First St	Perrysville	OH	44864	**877-850-3060**	419-938-5211	604
Mansfield State Historic Site						
15149 Hwy 175	Mansfield	LA	71052	**888-677-6267**	318-872-1474	558
Mansfield University						
Alumni Hall	Mansfield	PA	16933	**800-577-6826***	570-662-4000	166
*Admissions						
Mansfield, The						
12 W 44th St	New York	NY	10036	**800-255-5167**	212-277-8700	376
Mansfield/Richland County Convention & Visitors Bureau						
124 N Main St	Mansfield	OH	44902	**800-642-8282**	419-525-1300	207
Mansfield-Richland County Public Library						
43 W Third St	Mansfield	OH	44902	**877-795-2111**	419-521-3100	431-3
Mansion on Forsyth Park						
700 Drayton St	Savannah	GA	31401	**888-213-3671**	912-238-5158	376
Mansion View Inn & Suites						
529 S Fourth St	Springfield	IL	62701	**800-252-1083**	217-544-7411	376
Manson Construction Co						
5209 E Marginal Way S	Seattle	WA	98134	**800-262-6766***	206-762-0850	189-5
*General						
MantelsDirect						
217 N Seminary St	Florence	AL	35630	**888-493-8898**		184
Manton Industrial Cork Products Inc						
415 Oser Ave Unit U	Hauppauge	NY	11788	**800-663-1921**	631-273-0700	210
Mantros-Haeuser & Company Inc						
1175 Post Rd E	Westport	CT	06880	**800-344-4229***	203-454-1800	543
*General						
Mantua Mfg Co						
7900 Northfield Rd	Walton Hills	OH	44146	**800-333-8333***		318-2
*Orders						
Manual Woodworkers & Weavers Inc						
3737 HowaRd Gap Rd	Hendersonville	NC	28792	**800-542-3139**	828-692-7333	735
Manuel Lujan Insurance Inc						
4801 Indian School Rd NE	Albuquerque	NM	87110	**888-652-7771**	505-266-7771	388-4
Manufactured Housing Enterprises Inc						
09302 St Rt 6 Rt 6	Bryan	OH	43506	**800-821-0220**	419-636-4511	500
Manufactured Housing Institute (MHI)						
2101 Wilson Blvd Ste 610	Arlington	VA	22201	**800-505-5500**	703-558-0400	48-3
Manufactured Housing Institute PAC (MHI PAC)						
1655 N Ft Myer Dr Ste 104	Arlington	VA	22209	**800-505-5500**	703-558-0400	608
Manufactured Structures Corp (MSC)						
3089 E Fort Wayne Rd						
PO Box 350	Rochester	IN	46975	**800-662-5344**	574-223-4794	105
Manufacturing Jewelers & Suppliers of America Inc (MJSA)						
57 John L Dietsch Sq	Attleboro Falls	MA	02763	**800-444-6572**	401-274-3840	48-4
Manulife Financial Corp						
200 Bloor St E	Toronto	ON	M4W1E5	**800-795-9767**	416-926-3000	357-4
NYSE: MFC						
Manulife Mutual Funds						
200 Bloor St E N Twr 3	Toronto	ON	M4W1E5	**888-588-7999**		388-2
MAP (Mississippi Action For Progress Inc)						
1751 Morson Rd	Jackson	MS	39209	**800-924-4615**	601-923-4100	145
MAP International						
4700 Glynco Pkwy	Brunswick	GA	31525	**800-225-8550**	912-265-6010	47-5
MAPEI Corp						
1144 E Newport Ctr Dr	Deerfield Beach	FL	33442	**800-426-2734**	954-246-8888	3
Mapes Panels LLC						
2929 Cornhusker Hwy						
PO Box 80069	Lincoln	NE	68504	**800-228-2391**		688
MAPFRE USA Corp						
211 Main St	Webster	MA	01570	**800-922-8276**		388-4
Maple City Ice Co Inc						
371 Cleveland Rd	Norwalk	OH	44857	**877-762-9119***	419-668-2531	80-1
*Cust Svc						
Maple City Rubber Co						
55 Newton St PO Box 587	Norwalk	OH	44857	**800-841-9434**	419-668-8261	752
Maple Donuts Inc						
3455 E Market St	York	PA	17402	**800-627-5348**	717-757-7826	67
Maple Grove Farms of Vermont						
1052 Portland St	Saint Johnsbury	VT	05819	**800-525-2540**	802-748-5141	295-39
Maple Grove Raceway						
30 Stauffer Pk Ln	Mohnton	PA	19540	**877-814-2538**	610-856-7812	508
Maple Hill Farm Bed & Breakfast Inn						
11 Inn Rd	Hallowell	ME	04347	**800-622-2708**	207-622-2708	376

	Toll-Free	Phone	Class

Maple Island Inc
2497 Seventh Ave E
Ste 105 . . . . North Saint Paul MN 55109 | **800-369-1022** | 651-773-1000 | 295-10

Maple Knoll Communities Inc
11100 Springfield Pk . . . . Cincinnati OH 45246 | **800-272-3900** | 513-782-2400 | 663

Maple Leaf Farms Inc
PO Box 308 . . . . Milford IN 46542 | **800-348-2812** | 574-658-4121 | 10-7

Maplehurst Inc
50 Maplehurst Dr . . . . Brownsburg IN 46112 | **800-344-4235** | 317-858-9000 | 295-2

Maples Industries Inc
2210 Moody Ridge Rd . . . . Scottsboro AL 35768 | **800-537-5447*** | 256-259-1327 | 130
*Hum Res

MAQUET Cardiac Assist
15 Law Dr . . . . Fairfield NJ 07004 | **800-777-4222** | 973-244-6100 | 250

Maquoketa Valley Rural Electric Co-op
109 N Huber St . . . . Anamosa IA 52205 | **800-927-6068** | 319-462-3542 | 245

MARAD (Maritime Administration)
1200 New Jersey Ave SE . . . . Washington DC 20590 | **800-996-2723*** | 202-366-5807 | 338-15
*Hotline

Maradyne Corp
4540 W 160th St . . . . Cleveland OH 44135 | **800-537-7444** | 216-362-0755 | 14

Maranatha Baptist Bible College
745 W Main St . . . . Watertown WI 53094 | **800-622-2947** | 920-206-2330 | 166

Marathon Coach
91333 Coburg Industrial Way . . . . Coburg OR 97408 | **800-234-9991** | 541-343-9991 | 61-7

Marathon Enterprises Inc
Nine Smith St . . . . Englewood NJ 07631 | **800-722-7388** | 201-935-3330 | 295-26

Marathon Equipment Co
PO Box 1798 . . . . Vernon AL 35592 | **800-633-8974** | 205-695-9105 | 383

Maravia Corp of Idaho
602 E 45th St . . . . Boise ID 83714 | **800-223-7238** | 208-322-4949 | 701

Marble Institute of America (MIA)
28901 Clemens Rd Ste 100 . . . . Westlake OH 44145 | **800-433-4903** | 440-250-9222 | 48-3

Marbles Kids Museum
201 E Hargett St . . . . Raleigh NC 27601 | **800-745-3000** | 919-834-4040 | 513

Marborg Industries
728 E Yanonali St . . . . Santa Barbara CA 93103 | **800-798-1852** | 805-963-1852 | 651

Marburger Farm Dairy Inc
1506 Mars Evans City Rd . . . . Evans City PA 16033 | **800-331-1295** | 724-538-4800 | 10-2

Marc Publishing Co
600 Germantown Pk Ste B . . . . Lafayette Hill PA 19444 | **800-432-5478** | 610-834-8585 | 628-6

Marchex Inc
520 Pike St Ste 2000 . . . . Seattle WA 98101 | **800-840-1012** | 206-331-3300 | 7
NASDAQ: MCHX

Marco Beach Ocean Resort
480 S Collier Blvd . . . . Marco Island FL 34145 | **800-715-8517** | 239-393-1400 | 660

Marco Crane & Rigging Co
221 S 35th Ave . . . . Phoenix AZ 85009 | **800-668-2671** | 602-272-2671 | 264-3

MARCO Global
4259 22nd Ave W . . . . Seattle WA 98199 | **866-966-2726** | 206-285-3200 | 689

Marco Island Chamber of Commerce
1102 N Collier Blvd . . . . Marco Island FL 34145 | **800-788-6272** | 239-394-7549 | 137

Marco Promotional Products
2640 Commerce Dr . . . . Harrisburg PA 17110 | **877-545-9322** | | 9

Marco Rubber
35 Woodworkers Way . . . . Seabrook NH 03874 | **800-775-6525** | 603-468-3600 | 325

MARCOA Publishing Inc
9955 Black Mtn Rd . . . . San Diego CA 92126 | **800-854-2935** | 858-695-9600 | 628-1

Marcus Bros Textiles Inc
980 Ave of the Americas . . . . New York NY 10018 | **800-548-8295** | 212-354-8700 | 587

Marcus Corp
100 E Wisconsin Ave . . . . Milwaukee WI 53202 | **800-461-9330** | 414-905-1000 | 376
NYSE: MCS

Marcus Ctr for the Performing Arts
929 N Water St . . . . Milwaukee WI 53202 | **888-612-3500** | 414-273-7206 | 565

Marcus Dairy Inc
Four Eagle Rd . . . . Danbury CT 06810 | **800-243-2511** | 203-748-5611 | 295-27

Marcus Hotels & Resorts
100 E Wisconsin Ave Ste 1950 . . . . Milwaukee WI 53202 | **800-294-2812** | 414-905-1200 | 376

Marcus Theatres Corp
100 E Wisconsin Ave Ste 19 . . . . Milwaukee WI 53202 | **800-274-0099*** | 414-905-1000 | 737
*Cust Svc

Mares America Corp
One Selleck St . . . . Norwalk CT 06855 | **800-874-3236** | 203-855-0631 | 701

Margaret Chase Smith Policy Ctr
University of Maine
York Complex Ste 4 . . . . Orono ME 04469 | **877-486-2364** | 207-581-1648 | 625

Marian Heath Greeting Cards Inc
Nine Kendrick Rd . . . . Wareham MA 02571 | **800-688-9998*** | 508-291-0766 | 129
*Sales

Marian Koshland Science Museum
Sixth & E Sts NW . . . . Washington DC 20001 | **888-567-4526** | 202-334-1201 | 513

Marian University
3200 Cold Spring Rd . . . . Indianapolis IN 46222 | **800-772-7264*** | 317-955-6038 | 166
*Admissions

Mariani Packing Company Inc
500 Crocker Dr . . . . Vacaville CA 95688 | **800-231-1287** | 707-452-2800 | 11-1

Marianjoy Rehabilitation Hospital
26 W 171 Roosevelt Rd . . . . Wheaton IL 60187 | **800-462-2366** | 630-462-4000 | 371-6

Marianna Industries Inc
11222 "I" St . . . . Omaha NE 68137 | **800-228-9060** | 402-593-0211 | 231

Maricopa Medical Ctr
2601 E Roosevelt St . . . . Phoenix AZ 85008 | **866-749-2876** | 602-344-5011 | 371-3

Marie Callender Restaurant & Bakery
27101 Puerta Real Ste 260 . . . . Mission Viejo CA 92691 | **800-776-7437** | | 661

Marie Claire Magazine
300 W 57th St 34th Fl . . . . New York NY 10019 | **800-925-0485** | | 452-11

Marietta College
215 Fifth St . . . . Marietta OH 45750 | **800-331-7896*** | 740-376-4000 | 166
*Admissions

Marietta Conference Ctr & Resort
500 Powder Springs St . . . . Marietta GA 30064 | **888-685-2500** | 770-427-2500 | 374

Marietta Drapery & Window Coverings Company Inc
22 Trammel St PO Box 569 . . . . Marietta GA 30064 | **800-762-4774*** | 770-428-3335 | 735
*Mktg

Marietta Hospitality
37 Huntington St . . . . Cortland NY 13045 | **800-950-7772** | 607-753-6746 | 9

Marietta Memorial Hospital
401 Matthew St . . . . Marietta OH 45750 | **800-523-3977** | 740-374-1400 | 371-3

Marietta National Cemetery
500 Washington Ave . . . . Marietta GA 30060 | **866-236-8159** | | 135

Marijuana Anonymous World Services (MAWS)
PO Box 7807 . . . . Torrance CA 90504 | **800-766-6779** | | 47-21

Marin Convention & Visitors Bureau
1 Mitchell Blvd Ste B . . . . San Rafael CA 94903 | **866-925-2060** | 415-925-2060 | 207

Marin General Hospital
250 Bon Air Rd . . . . Greenbrae CA 94904 | **888-996-9644** | 415-925-7000 | 371-3

Marin Independent Journal
150 Alameda Del Prado . . . . Novato CA 94949 | **877-229-8655** | 415-883-8600 | 525-2

Marina Inn at Grande Dunes
8121 Amalfi Pl . . . . Myrtle Beach SC 29572 | **877-913-1333*** | 843-913-1333 | 376
*Resv

Marinco
2655 Napa Valley Corp Dr . . . . Napa CA 94558 | **800-307-6702** | 707-226-9600 | 802

Marine Biological Laboratory (MBL)
7 MBL St . . . . Woods Hole MA 02543 | **800-222-1222** | 508-548-3705 | 659

Marine Corps Assn (MCA)
PO Box 1775 . . . . Quantico VA 22134 | **800-336-0291** | 703-640-6161 | 47-19

Marine Corps Community Services
3044 Catlin Ave . . . . Quantico VA 22134 | **866-400-8753** | 703-784-3809 | 229

Marine Room, The
2000 Spindrift Dr . . . . La Jolla CA 92037 | **866-644-2351** | 858-459-7222 | 662

Marine Systems Corp
70 Fargo St Seaport Ctr . . . . Boston MA 02210 | **800-559-9293** | 617-542-3345 | 261

Marineland of Florida
9600 Ocean Shore Blvd . . . . Saint Augustine FL 32080 | **877-933-3402** | 904-460-1275 | 39

Marinelife Ctr of Juno Beach
14200 US Hwy 1 Loggerhead Pk . . . Juno Beach FL 33408 | **800-843-5451** | 561-627-8280 | 39

Mariners' Museum
100 Museum Dr . . . . Newport News VA 23606 | **800-581-7245** | 757-596-2222 | 513

Mario Pastega Guest House
3505 NW Samaritan Dr . . . . Corvallis OR 97330 | **888-872-0760** | 541-768-4650 | 369

Marion Ceramics Inc
PO Box 1134 . . . . Marion SC 29571 | **800-845-4010** | 843-423-1311 | 148

Marion County
200 S Third St Ste 104 . . . . Marion KS 66861 | **800-305-8851** | 620-382-2185 | 336

Marion County Chamber of Commerce
110 Adams St . . . . Fairmont WV 26554 | **800-975-8379** | 304-363-0442 | 137

Marion Military Institute
1101 Washington St . . . . Marion AL 36756 | **800-664-1842** | 334-683-2306 | 160

Marion Public Library
600 S Washington St . . . . Marion IN 46953 | **877-275-7673** | 765-668-2900 | 431-3

Marion Star, The
163 E Center St . . . . Marion OH 43302 | **877-987-2782** | 740-387-0400 | 525-2

Marion Technical College
1467 Mt Vernon Ave . . . . Marion OH 43302 | **800-772-1213** | 740-389-4636 | 788

Marion-Grant County Convention & Visitors Bureau
428 S Washington St Ste 261 . . . . Marion IN 46953 | **800-662-9474** | 765-668-5435 | 207

Marist College
3399 N Rd . . . . Poughkeepsie NY 12601 | **800-436-5483** | 845-575-3000 | 166

Maritime Administration (MARAD)
1200 New Jersey Ave SE . . . . Washington DC 20590 | **800-996-2723*** | 202-366-5807 | 338-15
*Hotline

Maritime Energy Inc
234 Pk St PO Box 485 . . . . Rockland ME 04841 | **800-333-4489** | 207-594-4487 | 572

Maritz Research Inc
1355 N Hwy Dr . . . . Fenton MO 63099 | **877-462-7489** | 636-827-4000 | 461

MarJam Supply Co Inc
20 Rewe St . . . . Brooklyn NY 11211 | **800-848-8407*** | 718-388-6465 | 361
*All

Marjorie Barrick Museum
4505 S Maryland Pkwy . . . . Las Vegas NV 89154 | **877-895-0334** | 702-895-3381 | 513

Mark Andy Inc
18081 Chesterfield Airport Rd . . . . . . Chesterfield MO 63005 | **800-700-6275** | 636-532-4433 | 621

Mark Hershey Farms Inc
479 Horseshoe Rd . . . . Lebanon PA 17042 | **888-801-3301** | 717-867-4624 | 442

Mark Morris Dance Group
3 Lafayette Ave . . . . Brooklyn NY 11217 | **800-957-1046** | 718-624-8400 | 566-1

Mark Sand & Gravel Co
525 Kennedy Pk Rd
PO Box 458 . . . . Fergus Falls MN 56537 | **800-427-8316** | 218-736-7523 | 498-4

Mark Spencer Hotel
409 SW 11th Ave . . . . Portland OR 97205 | **800-548-3934** | 503-224-3293 | 376

Mark Twain Hotel
225 NE Adams St . . . . Peoria IL 61602 | **866-325-6351** | 309-676-3600 | 376

Mark's Work Warehouse
30-1035 64th Ave SE . . . . Calgary AB T2H2J7 | **800-663-6275** | 403-255-9220 | 155-5

Mark/Space Softworks
1999 S Bascom Ave Ste 325 . . . . Campbell CA 95008 | **800-799-1718** | 408-293-7299 | 179-7

Markel Corp
4521 Highwoods Pkwy . . . . Glen Allen VA 23060 | **877-566-6323** | 800-431-1270 | 357-4
NYSE: MKL

Markel Specialty Commercial
4600 Cox Rd . . . . Glen Allen VA 23060 | **800-416-4364** | | 388-4

Markem-Imaje Inc
5448 Timberlea Blvd . . . . Mississauga ON L4W2T7 | **800-267-5108** | | 355

Market America Inc
1302 Pleasant Ridge Rd . . . . Greensboro NC 27409 | **866-420-1709** | 336-605-0040 | 113

Market Contractors Ltd of Oregon
10250 NE Marx St . . . . Portland OR 97220 | **800-793-1448** | 503-255-0977 | 187

Market Data Retrieval
Six Armstrong Rd . . . . Shelton CT 06484 | **800-333-8802** | 203-926-4800 | 5

Market Day Corp
555 W Pierce Rd Ste 200 . . . . Itasca IL 60143 | **877-632-7753** | 630-285-1470 | 342

Market Decisions LLC
75 Washington Ave Ste 206 . . . . Portland ME 04101 | **800-293-1538** | 207-767-6440 | 461

Market Forge Industries Inc
35 Garvey St . . . . Everett MA 02149 | **866-698-3188** | 617-387-4100 | 297

Market Pavilion Hotel
225 E Bay St . . . . Charleston SC 29401 | **877-440-2250** | 843-723-0500 | 376

Market Probe Inc
2655 N Mayfair Rd . . . . Milwaukee WI 53226 | **800-282-1376** | 414-778-6000 | 659

Market Scan Information Systems Inc
811 Camarillo Springs Ste B . . . . Camarillo CA 93012 | **800-658-7226** | | 179-10

Market Transport Ltd
110 N Marine Dr . . . . Portland OR 97217 | **800-547-0781** | 503-283-2405 | 770

Market Wire Inc
100 N Sepulveda Blvd Ste 325 . . . . El Segundo CA 90245 | **800-774-9473*** | 310-765-3200 | 523
*General

MarketBridge
4350 East-West Hwy Sixth Fl . . . . Bethesda MD 20814 | **888-468-6658** | 240-752-1800 | 196

Marketing Innovators International Inc
9701 W Higgins Rd . . . . Rosemont IL 60018 | **800-543-7373** | | 381

Marketing Library Services
143 Old Marlton Pk . . . . Medford NJ 08055 | **800-300-9868** | 609-654-6266 | 524-10

				Toll-Free	Phone	Class
Marketing News						
311 S Wacker Dr Ste 5800	Chicago	IL	60606	**800-262-1150**	312-542-9000	452-5
MarketingProfs LLC						
419 N Larchmont Blvd #295	Los Angeles	CA	90004	**866-557-9625**		196
Marketlab Inc						
6850 Southbelt Dr	Caledonia	MI	49316	**866-237-3722**		470
MarketLauncher Inc						
1800 Pembroke Dr Ste 300	Orlando	FL	32810	**800-901-3803**		7
Marketocracy Inc						
1208 W Magnolia Ste 236	Fort Worth	TX	76104	**877-462-4180**		398
Marketstar Corp						
2475 Washington Blvd	Ogden	UT	84401	**800-877-8259**	801-393-1155	712
MarketVision Research Inc						
10300 Alliance Rd Ste 200	Cincinnati	OH	45242	**800-232-4250**	513-791-3100	461
Markley Motors						
3325 S College Ave	Fort Collins	CO	80525	**888-480-5167**	970-226-2214	56
Marksville State Historic Site						
837 ML King Dr	Marksville	LA	71351	**888-253-8954**	318-253-8954	558
MarkWest Energy Partners LP						
1515 Arapahoe St Tower 1						
Ste 1600	Denver	CO	80202	**800-730-8388**	303-925-9200	590
NYSE: MWE						
Marland Clutch						
485 S Frontage Rd Ste 330	Burr Ridge	IL	60527	**800-216-3515**		613
Marlboro College						
2582 S Rd PO Box A	Marlboro	VT	05344	**800-343-0049**	802-257-4333	166
Marlen International Inc						
9202 Barton St	Overland Park	KS	66214	**800-862-7536**		297
Marley Engineered Products						
470 Beauty Spot Rd E	Bennettsville	SC	29512	**800-452-4179**	843-479-4006	36
Marlin Business Services Inc						
300 Fellowship Rd Ste 170	Mount Laurel	NJ	08054	**888-479-9111**		264-2
NASDAQ: MRLN						
Marlin Firearms Co						
PO Box 1871	Madison	NC	27025	**800-544-8892***		284
*Cust Svc						
Marlow Industries Inc						
10451 Vista Pk Rd	Dallas	TX	75238	**877-627-5691**	214-340-4900	253
Marmon/Keystone Corp						
PO Box 992	Butler	PA	16003	**800-544-1748**	724-283-3000	487
Marmon-Herrington Co						
13001 Magisterial Dr	Louisville	KY	40223	**800-227-0727**	502-253-0277	59
Maroon Inc						
1390 Jaycox Rd	Avon	OH	44011	**877-627-6661***	440-937-1000	144
*General						
Marotta Controls Inc						
78 Boonton Ave PO Box 427	Montville	NJ	07045	**888-627-6882**	973-334-7800	777
Marposs Corp						
3300 Cross Creek Pkwy	Auburn Hills	MI	48326	**888-627-7677**	248-370-0404	467
Marq Packaging Systems Inc						
3801 W Washington Ave	Yakima	WA	98903	**800-998-4301**	509-966-4300	550
Marquesa Hotel						
600 Fleming St	Key West	FL	33040	**800-869-4631**	305-292-1919	376
Marquette Asset Management						
60 S Sixth St Ste 3900	Minneapolis	MN	55402	**866-661-3770**	612-661-3770	398
Marquette Bank						
10000 W 151st St	Orland Park	IL	60462	**888-254-9500**	708-226-8026	69
Marquette Country Convention & Visitors Bureau						
337 W Washington St	Marquette	MI	49855	**800-544-4321**	906-228-7749	207
Marquette Hotel, The						
710 Marquette Ave	Minneapolis	MN	55402	**800-328-4782**	612-333-4545	376
Marquette Savings Bank						
920 Peach St	Erie	PA	16501	**866-672-3743**	814-455-4481	69
Marquette Transportation Company LLC						
5525 Mounes St PO Box 23521	New Orleans	LA	70123	**800-735-5845**	504-733-5845	460
Marquette University						
1217 W Wisconsin Ave	Milwaukee	WI	53233	**800-222-6544***	414-288-7302	166
*Admissions						
Marquette University Raynor Memorial Library						
1355 W Wisconsin Ave	Milwaukee	WI	53233	**800-876-1715**	414-288-7556	431-6
Marquez Bros International Inc						
5801 Rue Ferrari	San Jose	CA	95138	**800-858-1119**	408-960-2700	296-8
Marquis Spas Corp						
596 Hoffman Rd	Independence	OR	97351	**800-275-0888**	503-838-0888	372
Marquis Who's Who						
300 Connell Dr						
Ste 2000	Berkeley Heights	NJ	07922	**800-473-7020**	908-673-1000	628-2
Marriott Charleston Hotel						
170 Lockwood Blvd	Charleston	SC	29403	**888-236-2427**	843-723-3000	376
Marriott Columbus						
800 Front Ave	Columbus	GA	31901	**800-455-9261**	706-324-1800	376
Marriott International Inc						
10400 Fernwood Road	Bethesda	MD	20817	**800-450-4442**	301-380-3000	376
NASDAQ: MAR						
ExecuStay Corp						
2222 Corinth Ave	Los Angeles	CA	90064	**800-990-9292**		211
Ritz-Carlton Hotel Co LLC						
4445 Willard Ave Ste 800	Chevy Chase	MD	20815	**800-241-3333**	301-547-4700	376
Marriott Kaua'i Resort & Beach Club						
3610 Rice St Kalapaki Beach	Lihue	HI	96766	**800-220-2925**	808-245-5050	660
Marriott Montgomery Prattville at Capitol Hill						
2500 Legends Cir	Prattville	AL	36066	**800-593-6429***	334-290-1235	374
*Resv						
Marriott Vacation Club International						
6649 Westwood Blvd Ste 500	Orlando	FL	32821	**800-307-7312**	407-206-6000	743
Mars Electric Co						
38868 Mentor Ave	Willoughby	OH	44094	**800-288-6277**	440-946-2250	246
Mars Snack Food						
800 High St	Hackettstown	NJ	07840	**800-551-0895**	908-852-1000	295-8
Marsh & McLennan Cos Inc						
1166 Ave of the Americas	New York	NY	10036	**866-374-2662**	212-345-5000	357-3
NYSE: MMC						
Marsh Bellofram Corp						
8019 Ohio River Blvd	Newell	WV	26050	**800-727-5646**	304-387-1200	202
Marsh Berry & Company Inc						
4420 Sherwin Rd	Willoughby	OH	44094	**800-426-2774**	440-354-3230	195
Marsh Electronics Inc						
1563 S 101st St	Milwaukee	WI	53214	**800-236-8327***	414-475-6000	246
*Cust Svc						
Marsh Furniture Co						
PO Box 870	High Point	NC	27261	**800-696-2774**	336-884-7363	114
Marshall & Sterling Inc						
110 Main St	Poughkeepsie	NY	12601	**800-333-3766**	845-454-0800	387
Marshall & Stevens Inc						
355 S Grand Ave Ste 1750	Los Angeles	CA	90071	**800-950-9588**	213-612-8000	195
Marshall & Swift						
777 S Figueroa St 12th Fl	Los Angeles	CA	90017	**800-544-2678**	213-683-9000	179-10
Marshall Durbin Co						
2830 Commerce Blvd	Birmingham	AL	35210	**800-245-8204***	205-380-3251	612
*Sales						
Marshall Independent						
508 W Main St PO Box 411	Marshall	MN	56258	**877-276-6070**	507-537-1551	628-8
Marshall Pottery						
4901 Elysian Fields Rd	Marshall	TX	75672	**888-768-8721**	903-927-5400	332
Marshall Screw Products Co						
3820 Chandler Dr Ne	Minneapolis	MN	55421	**800-321-6727**		449
Marshall University						
One John Marshall Dr	Huntington	WV	25755	**800-642-3463**	304-696-3170	166
Marshalltown Area Chamber of Commerce						
709 S Ctr St PO Box 1000	Marshalltown	IA	50158	**800-725-5301**	641-753-6645	137
Marshalltown Co						
104 S Eigth Ave	Marshalltown	IA	50158	**800-888-0127**	641-753-5999	748
Marshalltown Community College						
3700 S Ctr St	Marshalltown	IA	50158	**866-622-4748**	641-752-7106	160
Marshfield Convention & Visitors Bureau						
700 S Central Ave PO Box 868	Marshfield	WI	54449	**800-422-4541**	715-384-3454	207
Martec Group Inc, The						
105 W Adams St Ste 2125	Chicago	IL	60603	**888-811-5755**	312-606-9690	659
Marten Transport Ltd						
129 Marten St	Mondovi	WI	54755	**800-395-3000**	715-926-4216	770
NASDAQ: MRTN						
Martha Jefferson Hospital (MJH)						
500 Martha Jefferson Dr	Charlottesville	VA	22902	**888-652-6663**	434-982-7000	371-3
Martha Stewart Living Magazine						
11 W 42nd St 25th Fl	New York	NY	10036	**800-999-6518**		452-11
Martha Washington Hotel & Spa, The						
150 W Main St	Abingdon	VA	24210	**888-999-8078**	276-628-3161	376
Martin & Bayley Inc						
1311 A W Main	Carmi	IL	62821	**800-876-2511**	618-382-2334	342
Martin Archery Inc						
3134 Heritage Rd	Walla Walla	WA	99362	**800-541-8902**	509-529-2554	701
Martin Asphalt Co						
Three Riverway Ste 400	South Houston	TX	77056	**800-662-0987**	713-350-6800	45
Martin County Travel & Tourism Authority						
100 E Church St PO Box 382	Williamston	NC	27892	**800-776-8566**	252-792-6605	207
Martin Door Manufacturing Inc						
2828 South 900 West	Salt Lake City	UT	84119	**800-388-9310**	801-973-9310	361
Martin Eagle Oil Company Inc						
2700 James St	Denton	TX	76205	**800-316-6148**	940-383-2351	572
Martin Engineering						
One Martin Pl	Neponset	IL	61345	**800-544-2947**	309-594-2384	208
Martin Enterprises Inc						
4315 Meyer Rd	Fort Wayne	IN	46806	**800-348-4759**	260-447-5591	770
Martin Furniture						
2345 Britannia Blvd	San Diego	CA	92154	**800-268-5669***		318-1
*Cust Svc						
Martin Glass Co						
25 Ctr Plz	Belleville	IL	62220	**800-325-1946**	618-277-1946	61-2
Martin Luther College						
1995 Luther Ct	New Ulm	MN	56073	**877-652-1995**	507-354-8221	166
Martin Marietta Magnesia Specialties Inc						
8140 Corporate Dr Ste 220	Nottingham	MD	21236	**800-648-7400**	410-780-5500	141
Martin Memorial Health Systems (MMHS)						
200 SE Hospital Ave PO Box 9010	Stuart	FL	34994	**800-368-3375**	772-287-5200	371-3
Martin Methodist College						
433 W Madison St	Pulaski	TN	38478	**800-467-1273**	931-363-9804	166
Martin Midstream Partners LP						
4200 Stone Rd	Kilgore	TX	75662	**800-256-6644**	903-983-6200	572
NASDAQ: MMLP						
Martin Resource Management Corp (MRMC)						
PO Box 191	Kilgore	TX	75663	**888-334-7473**	903-983-6200	315
Martin Supply Co						
200 Appleton Ave	Sheffield	AL	35660	**800-828-8116**	256-383-3131	382
Martin Wells Industries						
PO Box 01406	Los Angeles	CA	90001	**800-421-6000**	323-581-6266	127
Martin Wheel Company Inc						
342 W Ave	Tallmadge	OH	44278	**800-462-7846**	330-633-3278	744
Martin Yale Industries Inc						
251 Wedcor Ave	Wabash	IN	46992	**800-225-5644**	260-563-0641	110
Martin's Famous Pastry Shoppe Inc						
1000 Potato Roll Ln	Chambersburg	PA	17201	**800-548-1200***	717-263-9580	295-1
*Cust Svc						
Martin's Potato Chips Inc						
5847 Lincoln Hwy W						
PO Box 28	Thomasville	PA	17364	**800-272-4477**	717-792-3565	295-35
Martin/F Weber Co						
2727 Southampton Rd	Philadelphia	PA	19154	**800-876-8076**	215-677-5600	42
Martina's Flowers & Gifts						
3830 Washington Rd	Martinez	GA	30907	**800-927-1204**	706-863-7172	292
MartinAire Aviation LLC						
4553 Glenn Curtiss Dr	Addison	TX	75001	**866-557-1861**	972-349-5700	12
Martindale Electric Co						
1375 Hird Ave	Lakewood	OH	44107	**800-344-9191**	216-521-8567	511
Martinez Area Chamber of Commerce						
603 Marina Vista	Martinez	CA	94553	**877-855-5506**	925-228-2345	137
Martinique Promotion Bureau						
444 Madison Ave 16th Fl	New York	NY	10022	**800-391-4909**		765
Martinizing Dry Cleaning						
8944 Columbia Rd Ste J	Loveland	OH	45140	**800-827-0207**		309
Martins Run						
100 Halcyon Dr	Media	PA	19063	**877-824-3935**	610-353-7660	663
Martinsburg-Berkeley County Chamber of Commerce						
198 Viking Way	Martinsburg	WV	25401	**800-332-9007**	304-267-4841	137
Martinsville Bulletin						
PO Box 3711	Martinsville	VA	24115	**800-234-6575**	276-638-8801	525-2
Martinsville-Henry County Chamber of Commerce						
115 Broad St	Martinsville	VA	24112	**800-811-6302**	276-632-6401	137
Martin-Williams Adv						
150 S 5th st Ste 900	Minneapolis	MN	55402	**800-632-1388**	612-340-0800	4
Martrex Inc						
1107 Hazeltine Blvd Ste 535	Minnetonka	MN	55345	**800-328-3627**	952-933-5000	276
Marts & Lundy Inc						
1200 Wall St W	Lyndhurst	NJ	07071	**800-526-9005**	201-460-1660	775
Marty's Shoe Outlet Inc						
121 Carver Ave	Westwood	NJ	07675	**888-662-7897***	201-497-6637	300
*General						

				Toll-Free	Phone	Class
Martz First Class Coach Company Inc						
4783 37th St N	Saint Petersburg	FL	33714	**800-282-8020**	727-526-9086	106
Maruka USA Inc						
400 Commons Way	Rockaway	NJ	07866	**800-631-0426**	973-983-1000	383
Maruson Technology Corp						
18557 Gale Ave	City Of Industry	CA	91748	**888-627-8766**	626-912-8388	757
Marvel Abrasive Products Inc						
6230 S Oak Pk Ave	Chicago	IL	60638	**800-621-0673**		1
Marvel Consultants Inc						
28601 Chagrin Blvd Ste 210	Cleveland	OH	44122	**800-338-1257**	216-292-2855	623
Marvel Group Inc						
3843 W 43rd St	Chicago	IL	60632	**800-621-8846***		318-1
*Cust Svc						
Marvel Mfg Company Inc						
3501 Marvel Dr	Oshkosh	WI	54902	**800-472-9464**	920-236-7200	673
Marvell Semiconductor Inc						
5488 Marvell Ln	Santa Clara	CA	95054	**855-627-8355***	408-222-2500	177
*Cust Svc						
Marvelwood School						
476 Skiff Mountain Rd	Kent	CT	06757	**800-440-9107**	860-927-0047	615
Marvin Windows & Doors						
PO Box 100	Warroad	MN	56763	**888-537-7828**	218-386-1430	236
MARX Software Security Inc						
2900 Chamblee-Tucker Rd						
Bldg 9 Ste 100	Atlanta	GA	30341	**800-627-9468**	770-986-8887	179-12
Mary Ann Liebert Publishers Inc						
140 Huguenot St Third Fl	New Rochelle	NY	10801	**800-654-3237**	914-740-2100	628-9
Mary Baldwin College						
318 Prospect St	Staunton	VA	24401	**800-468-2262***	540-887-7019	166
*Admissions						
Mary Bridge Children's Hospital & Health Ctr						
317 Martin Luther King Jr Way	Tacoma	WA	98405	**800-552-1419**	253-403-1400	371-1
Mary Free Bed Rehabilitation Hospital						
235 Wealthy St SE	Grand Rapids	MI	49503	**800-528-8989**	616-242-0300	371-6
Mary Jane Thurston State Park						
1466 State Rt 65	McClure	OH	43534	**866-644-6727**	419-832-7662	558
Mary Kay Inc						
PO Box 799045	Dallas	TX	75379	**800-627-9529***	972-687-6300	215
*Cust Svc						
Mary Maxim Inc						
2001 Holland Ave PO Box 5019	Port Huron	MI	48061	**800-962-9504**	810-987-2000	454
Mary Maxim Ltd						
75 Scott Ave	Paris	ON	N3L3G5	**888-442-2266**		751
Mary Washington Hospice						
5012 Southpoint Pkwy	Fredericksburg	VA	22407	**800-257-1667**	540-741-1667	368
Mary Washington Hospital						
1001 Sam Perry Blvd	Fredericksburg	VA	22401	**800-395-2455**	540-741-1100	371-3
Marygrove College						
8425 W McNichols Rd	Detroit	MI	48221	**866-313-1927***	313-927-1200	166
*Admissions						
Maryland						
Assessments & Taxation Dept						
301 W Preston St 8th Fl	Baltimore	MD	21201	**888-246-5941**	410-767-1184	337-21
Court of Appeals						
361 Rowe Blvd 4th Fl	Annapolis	MD	21401	**800-926-2583**	410-260-1500	337-21
Criminal Injuries Compensation Board						
6776 Reisterstown Rd Ste 206	Baltimore	MD	21215	**888-679-9347**	410-585-3010	337-21
Department of Budget & Management						
45 Calvert St	Annapolis	MD	21401	**800-705-3493**		337-21
Education Dept						
200 W Baltimore St	Baltimore	MD	21201	**888-246-0016**	410-767-0100	337-21
Emergency Management Agency						
5401 Rue St Lo Dr	Reisterstown	MD	21136	**877-636-2872**	410-517-3600	337-21
Environment Dept						
1800 Washington Blvd	Baltimore	MD	21230	**800-633-6101**	410-537-3000	337-21
Higher Education Commision						
839 Bestgate Rd Ste 400	Annapolis	MD	21401	**800-974-0203**	410-260-4500	337-21
Housing & Community Development Dept						
100 Community Pl	Crownsville	MD	21032	**800-756-0119**		337-21
Insurance Administration						
525 St Paul Pl	Baltimore	MD	21202	**800-492-6116**	410-468-2000	337-21
Natural Resources Dept						
580 Taylor Ave	Annapolis	MD	21401	**877-620-8367**	410-260-8021	337-21
Parole & Probation Div						
6776 Reisterstown Rd	Baltimore	MD	21215	**877-227-8031**	410-585-3500	337-21
Physician Quality Assurance Board						
4201 Patterson Ave	Baltimore	MD	21215	**800-492-6836**	410-764-4777	337-21
Public Service Commission						
6 St Paul St 16th Fl	Baltimore	MD	21202	**800-492-0474**	410-767-8000	337-21
State Forest & Park Service						
580 Taylor Ave Rm E-3	Annapolis	MD	21401	**877-620-8367***	410-260-8186	337-21
*Campground Resv						
State Government Information						
State House	Annapolis	MD	21401	**800-811-8336**	410-974-3901	337-21
State Police						
1201 Reisterstown Rd	Pikesville	MD	21208	**800-525-5555**	410-653-4200	337-21
Teacher Certification & Accreditation Div						
200 W Baltimore St	Baltimore	MD	21201	**866-772-8922**	410-767-0412	337-21
Tourism Development Office						
217 E Redwood St 9th Fl	Baltimore	MD	21202	**800-543-1036**	410-767-3400	337-21
Treasurer						
80 Calvert St Rm 109	Annapolis	MD	21401	**800-974-0468**	410-260-7533	337-21
Veterans Affairs Dept						
31 Hopkins Plaza Rm 1231	Baltimore	MD	21201	**800-446-4926**	410-230-4444	337-21
Vital Records Div						
6550 Reisterstown Rd	Baltimore	MD	21215	**800-832-3277**	410-764-3038	337-21
Maryland & Virginia Milk Producers Co-op Assn Inc						
1985 Isaac Newton Sq W	Reston	VA	20190	**800-552-1976**	703-742-6800	296-4
Maryland Assn of Realtors						
2594 Riva Rd	Annapolis	MD	21401	**800-638-6425**	410-841-6080	647
Maryland Bar Journal						
520 W Fayette St	Baltimore	MD	21201	**800-492-1964**	410-685-7878	452-15
Maryland Cork Co Inc						
505 Blue Ball Rd PO Box 126	Elkton	MD	21922	**800-662-2675**	410-398-2955	210
Maryland Dept of Legislative Services						
90 State Cir	Annapolis	MD	21401	**800-492-7122**	410-946-5400	430
Maryland Ethics Commission						
45 Calvert St 3rd Fl	Annapolis	MD	21401	**877-669-6085**	410-260-7770	265
Maryland Hall for the Creative Arts						
801 Chase St	Annapolis	MD	21401	**866-438-3808**	410-263-5544	565
Maryland Historical Society Museum & Library						
201 W Monument St	Baltimore	MD	21201	**800-537-5487**	410-685-3750	513
Maryland Inn						
16 Church Cir	Annapolis	MD	21401	**800-847-8882**	410-263-2641	376

				Toll-Free	Phone	Class
Maryland Match Corp						
605 Alluvion St	Baltimore	MD	21230	**800-423-0013**	410-752-8164	464
Maryland Pharmacists Assn						
1800 Washington Blvd Ste 333	Baltimore	MD	21201	**800-833-7587**	410-727-0746	578
Maryland Plastics Inc						
251 E Central Ave	Federalsburg	MD	21632	**800-544-5582***	410-754-5566	600
*Cust Svc						
Maryland Public Television (MPT)						
11767 Owings Mills Blvd	Owings Mills	MD	21117	**800-223-3678**	410-581-4201	624
Maryland Renaissance Festival						
PO Box 315	Crownsville	MD	21032	**800-296-7304**	410-266-7304	147
Maryland State Bar Assn Inc						
520 W Fayette St	Baltimore	MD	21201	**800-492-1964**	410-685-7878	71
Maryland State Medical Society						
1211 Cathedral St	Baltimore	MD	21201	**800-492-1056**	410-539-0872	469
Maryland Student Financial Assistance Office						
839 Bestgate Rd Ste 400	Annapolis	MD	21401	**800-974-0203**	410-260-4565	716
Maryland Veterinary Medical Assn						
8015 Corporate Dr Ste A	Baltimore	MD	21236	**888-884-6862**	410-931-3332	783
Marylhurst University						
17600 Pacific Hwy 43						
PO Box 261	Marylhurst	OR	97036	**800-634-9982**	503-636-8141	166
Marymount Hospital						
12300 McCracken Rd	Garfield Heights	OH	44125	**800-801-2273**	216-581-0500	371-3
Marymount Manhattan College						
221 E 71st St	New York	NY	10021	**866-667-6572**	212-517-0400	166
Marymount University						
2807 N Glebe Rd	Arlington	VA	22207	**800-548-7638**	703-522-5600	166
Maryville College						
502 E Lamar Alexander Pkwy	Maryville	TN	37804	**800-597-2687**	865-981-8000	166
Marywood University						
2300 Adams Ave	Scranton	PA	18509	**866-279-9663**	570-348-6234	166
MAS Capital Inc						
2715 Coney Island Ave	Brooklyn	NY	11235	**866-553-7493**		682
Masco Cabinetry LLC						
5353 W US 223 PO Box 1946	Adrian	MI	49221	**866-850-8557**	517-263-0771	114
Masco Corp						
21001 Van Born Rd	Taylor	MI	48180	**888-627-6397**	313-274-7400	602
NYSE: MAS						
Masergy Communications Inc						
2740 N Dallas Pkwy Ste 260	Plano	TX	75093	**866-588-5885**	214-442-5700	224
Masimo Corp 40 Parker	Irvine	CA	92618	**800-326-4890**	949-297-7000	250
Masland Carpets Inc						
716 Bill Myles Dr	Saraland	AL	36571	**800-633-0468**		130
Mason City Convention & Visitors Bureau						
2021 Fourth St SW Hwy 122 W	Mason City	IA	50401	**800-423-5724**	641-422-1663	207
Mason Contractors Assn of America (MCAA)						
33 S Roselle Rd	Schaumburg	IL	60193	**800-536-2225**	224-678-9709	48-3
Mason Structural Steel Inc						
7500 Northfield Rd	Walton Hills	OH	44146	**800-686-1223**	440-439-1040	359
Masonic Service Assn of North America (MSANA)						
8120 Fenton St Ste 203	Silver Spring	MD	20910	**855-476-4010**	301-588-4010	47-15
Masonite International Corp						
201 N Franklin St Ste 300	Tampa	FL	33602	**800-895-2723**	813-877-2726	236
Mason-McDuffie Real Estate Inc						
5724 W Las Positas Blvd	Pleasanton	CA	94588	**888-971-4636**	925-924-4600	643
Maspeth Federal Savings						
56-18 69th St	Maspeth	NY	11378	**888-558-1300**	718-335-1300	69
Massa Products Corp						
280 Lincoln St	Hingham	MA	02043	**800-962-7543**	781-749-4800	659
Massachusetts						
Banks Div						
1000 Washington St Ste 710	Boston	MA	02118	**800-495-2265**	617-956-1501	337-22
Child Support Enforcement Div						
51 Sleeper St 4th Fl	Boston	MA	02205	**800-332-2733**	617-660-1234	337-22
Executive Office of Transportation						
10 Pk Plaza Ste 3170	Boston	MA	02116	**800-219-9936**	617-973-7000	337-22
Insurance Div						
1000 Washington St Ste 810	Boston	MA	02118	**877-563-4467**	617-521-7794	337-22
Parole Board						
12 Mercer Rd	Natick	MA	01760	**888-298-6272**	508-650-4500	337-22
Revenue Dept						
PO Box 7010	Boston	MA	02204	**800-392-6089**	617-626-2201	337-22
Travel & Tourism Office						
10 Pk Plaza Ste 4510	Boston	MA	02116	**800-227-6277**	617-973-8500	337-22
Massachusetts Assn of Realtors						
256 Second Ave	Waltham	MA	02451	**800-725-6272**	781-890-3700	647
Massachusetts Bay Community College						
Wellesley Hills						
50 Oakland St	Wellesley Hills	MA	02481	**800-233-3182**	781-239-3000	160
Massachusetts Bill Status						
1 Ashburton Pl Rm 1611	Boston	MA	02108	**800-392-6090**	617-727-7030	430
Massachusetts Board of Library Commissioners						
98 N Washington St	Boston	MA	02114	**800-952-7403**	617-725-1860	431-5
Massachusetts College of Art						
621 Huntington Ave	Boston	MA	02115	**800-834-3242**	617-879-7222	166
Massachusetts College of Pharmacy & Health Sciences						
179 Longwood Ave	Boston	MA	02115	**800-225-5506**	617-732-2850	166
Massachusetts Correctional Industries						
1 Industries Dr Bldg A						
PO Box 188	Norfolk	MA	02056	**800-222-2211**	508-850-1070	622
Massachusetts Dental Society						
Two Willow St Ste 200	Southborough	MA	01745	**800-342-8747**	508-480-9797	227
Massachusetts Maritime Academy						
101 Academy Dr	Buzzards Bay	MA	02532	**800-544-3411***	508-830-5000	166
*Admissions						
Massachusetts Medical Society (MMS)						
860 Winter St	Waltham	MA	02451	**800-322-2303**	781-893-4610	469
Massachusetts National Cemetery						
Conery Rd	Bourne	MA	02532	**800-827-1000**	508-563-7113	135
Massachusetts Nurses Assn (MNA)						
340 Tpke St	Canton	MA	02021	**800-882-2056**	781-821-4625	526
Massachusetts Pharmacists Assn						
500 W Cummings Pk Ste 3475	Woburn	MA	01801	**888-772-7227**	781-933-1107	578
Massage Ctr at Mohonk Mountain House						
1000 Mtn Rest Rd	New Paltz	NY	12561	**800-772-6646**	845-255-1000	698
Massanutten Military Academy						
614 S Main St	Woodstock	VA	22664	**877-466-6222**	540-459-2167	615
Massey Cancer Ctr						
Virginia Commonwealth University						
401 College St PO Box 980037	Richmond	VA	23298	**877-462-7739**	804-828-0450	659
Massey Services Inc						
315 Groveland St E	Orlando	FL	32804	**888-262-7739**	407-645-2500	570

	City	State	ZIP	Toll-Free	Phone	Class
MassMutual PAC 1295 State St	Springfield	MA	01111	**800-272-2216**	413-788-8411	608
MAST Vacation Partners Inc 635 Butterfield Rd Ste 150	Oakbrook Terrace	IL	60181	**888-778-4722**	630-889-9817	762
MasTec Inc 800 Douglas Rd 12th Fl *NYSE: MTZ*	Coral Gables	FL	33134	**800-531-5000**	305-599-1800	189-1
Master Appliance Corp 2420 18th St	Racine	WI	53403	**800-558-9413**	262-633-7791	749
Master Brewers Assn of the Americas (MBAA) 3340 Pilot Knob Rd	Saint Paul	MN	55121	**800-328-7560**	651-454-7250	48-6
Master Builders Solutions by BASF 23700 Chagrin Blvd	Cleveland	OH	44122	**800-628-9990**	216-839-7500	143
Master Cutlery Inc 700 Penhorn Ave	Secaucus	NJ	07094	**888-271-7229**	201-271-7600	222
Master Finish Co 2020 Nelson SE PO Box 7505	Grand Rapids	MI	49510	**877-590-5819**		476
Master Halco Inc 1321 Greenway Dr	Irving	TX	75038	**800-883-8384**	972-714-7300	279
Master Lock Company LLC 137 W Forest Hill Ave PO Box 927	Oak Creek	WI	53154	**800-464-2088**		347
Master Mark Plastics 210 Ampe Dr *Cust Svc	Paynesville	MN	56362	**800-535-4838***	320-845-2111	426
Master Mfg Co 747 N Yale Ave	Villa Park	IL	60181	**800-864-1649**	630-833-7060	173
Master Package Corp 200 Madson St	Owen	WI	54460	**800-396-8425**	715-229-2156	124
Master Spas Inc 6927 Lincoln Pkwy	Fort Wayne	IN	46804	**800-860-7727**	260-436-9100	372
MASTER Teacher Inc, The 2600 Leadership Ln	Manhattan	KS	66505	**800-669-9633**		521
Master's College 21726 Placerita Canyon Rd.	Santa Clarita	CA	91321	**800-568-6248**	661-259-3540	166
Master-Bilt Products 908 Hwy 15 N	New Albany	MS	38652	**800-647-1284**	662-534-9061	14
MasterCard Inc 2000 Purchase St *NYSE: MA*	Purchase	NY	10577	**800-100-1087**	914-249-2000	217
Masterchem Industries LLC 3135 Old Hwy M	Imperial	MO	63052	**866-774-6371**		543
MasterCraft Boat Co 100 Cherokee Cove Dr	Vonore	TN	37885	**800-443-8774**	423-884-2221	89
Mastercraft Industries Inc 777 S St	Newburgh	NY	12550	**800-835-7812**	845-565-8850	114
Mastercraft Mold Inc 3301 W Vernon Ave	Phoenix	AZ	85009	**800-628-1672**	602-484-4520	601
Masters Gallery Foods Inc 328 County Hwy PP PO Box 170 *General	Plymouth	WI	53073	**800-236-8431***	920-893-8431	296-4
Masters Gallery Ltd 2115 Fourth St SW	Calgary	AB	T2S1W8	**866-245-0616**	403-245-2064	41
Masters Inc 5741 NW Cornelius Pass Road	Hillsboro	OR	97124	**877-652-5656**	503-531-3308	229
Mastodon State Historic Site 1050 Charles J Becker Dr	Imperial	MO	63052	**800-334-6946**	636-464-2976	558
Matco Tools 4403 Allen Rd	Stow	OH	44224	**800-368-6651**	330-926-5332	748
Matco-Norca Inc Rt 22	Brewster	NY	10509	**800-431-2082**	845-278-7570	603
Mate Precision Tooling Inc 1295 Lund Blvd	Anoka	MN	55303	**800-328-4492**	763-421-0230	747
Matenaer Corp 810 Schoenhaar Dr	West Bend	WI	53090	**800-254-0873**	262-338-0700	487
Material Handling Industry of America (MHIA) 8720 Red Oak Blvd Ste 201	Charlotte	NC	28217	**800-345-1815**	704-676-1190	48-13
Materials Transportation Co (MTC) 1408 S Commerce PO Box 1358	Temple	TX	76503	**800-433-3110**	254-298-2900	383
Materion Corp 6070 Parkland Blvd *NYSE: MTRN*	Mayfield Heights	OH	44124	**800-321-2076**	216-486-4200	497
Mathematical Assn of America (MAA) 1529 18th St NW	Washington	DC	20036	**800-331-1622**	202-387-5200	48-19
Matheson Trucking Inc 9785 Goethe Rd	Sacramento	CA	95827	**800-455-7678**	916-685-2330	770
Matheus Lumber Company Inc 15800 Woodinville-Redmond Rd NE PO Box 2260	Woodinville	WA	98072	**800-284-7501**	425-489-3000	192-3
Mathews Assoc Inc 220 Power Ct	Sanford	FL	32771	**800-871-5262**	407-323-3390	73
Mathews Bros Co 22 Perkins Rd	Belfast	ME	04915	**800-615-2004**	207-338-6490	236
Mathews Co 500 Industrial Ave	Crystal Lake	IL	60012	**800-323-7045**	815-459-2210	273
Mathias Ham House Historic Site 2241 Lincoln Ave	Dubuque	IA	52001	**800-226-3369**	563-557-9545	49-2
Mathis Bros Furniture Inc 6611 S 101 St E Ave *Cust Svc	Tulsa	OK	74133	**800-329-3434***	918-461-7785	320
Mathnasium LLC 5120 W Goldleaf Cir Ste 300	Los Angeles	CA	90056	**877-601-6284**	323-421-8000	309
Mathy Construction Co Inc 920 Tenth Ave N	Onalaska	WI	54650	**800-822-5246**	608-783-6411	189-4
Matich Corp 1596 Harry Sheppard Blvd	San Bernardino	CA	92408	**800-404-4975**	909-382-7400	189-4
Matot Inc 2501 Van Buren St	Bellwood	IL	60104	**800-369-1070**	708-547-1888	256
Matrix Energy Services Inc 3221 Ramos Cir	Sacramento	CA	95827	**800-556-2123**	916-363-9283	256
Matrix Hotel 10640-100 Ave	Edmonton	AB	T5J3N8	**866-465-8150**	780-429-2861	376
Matrix LLC 19 Ave D	Johnson City	NY	13790	**800-338-5603**	607-766-0700	256
Matrix Service Co 5100 E Skelly Dr 74135 *NASDAQ: MTRX*	Tulsa	OK	74135	**866-367-6879**		532
Matrix Systems Inc 1041 Byers Rd	Miamisburg	OH	45342	**800-562-8749**	937-438-9033	683
Matson Logistics Inc 555 12th St	Oakland	CA	94607	**800-492-8766**	510-628-4000	444
Matson Navigation Co 555 12th St *Cust Svc	Oakland	CA	94607	**800-462-8766***	510-628-4000	311
Matsui International Company Inc 1501 W 178th St	Gardena	CA	90248	**800-359-5679**	310-767-7812	385
Matsui Nursery Inc 1645 Old Stage Rd	Salinas	CA	93908	**800-793-6433**	831-422-6433	366
Matt Castrucci Auto Mall of Dayton 3013 Mall Pk Dr	Dayton	OH	45459	**855-204-5293**	513-248-3431	509
Mattel Inc 333 Continental Blvd *NASDAQ: MAT*	El Segundo	CA	90245	**800-524-8697**	310-252-2000	752
Mattersight Corp 200 S Wacker Ste 820	Chicago	IL	60606	**877-235-6925**		458
Matthaei Botanical Gardens 1800 N Dixboro Rd	Ann Arbor	MI	48105	**800-666-8693**	734-647-7600	96
Matthews Book Co 11559 Rock Island Ct	Maryland Heights	MO	63043	**800-633-2665**	314-432-1400	95
Matthews International Corp Marking Products Div 6515 Penn Ave	Pittsburgh	PA	15206	**800-775-7775**	412-665-2500	462
Matthews Studio Equipment Group 2405 W Empire Ave	Burbank	CA	91504	**800-237-8263**	818-843-6715	584
Matthijssen Inc 14 Rt 10	East Hanover	NJ	07936	**800-845-2200**	973-887-1100	176
Mattress Firm Inc 5815 Gulf Fwy	Houston	TX	77023	**800-821-6621**	713-923-1090	359
Mattson Spray Equipment 230 W Coleman St	Rice Lake	WI	54868	**800-877-4857**	715-234-1617	173
Mattson Technology Inc 47131 Bayside Pkwy *NASDAQ: MTSN*	Fremont	CA	94538	**800-315-6607**	510-657-5900	686
Maui Community College 310 W Kaahumanu Ave	Kahului	HI	96732	**800-479-6692**	808-984-3267	160
Maui Divers of Hawaii 1520 Liona St	Honolulu	HI	96814	**800-462-4454**	808-946-7979	406
Maui Jim Inc 721 Wainee St	Lahaina	HI	96761	**888-352-2001**	808-661-8841	535
Maui Memorial Hospital 221 Mahalani St	Wailuku	HI	96793	**800-427-5940**	808-244-9056	371-3
Maui News 100 Mahalani St	Wailuku	HI	96793	**888-683-1115**	808-244-3981	525-2
Maui Ocean Ctr 192 Maalaea Rd	Wailuku	HI	96793	**800-350-5634**	808-270-7000	39
Maui Tacos International Inc 2001 Palmer Ave. Ste 105	Larchmont	NY	10538	**866-388-3758**		661
Mauldin & Jenkins Certified Public Accountants LLC 200 Galleria Pkwy SE	Atlanta	GA	30339	**800-277-0080**	770-955-8600	2
Maumee Bay Lodge & Conference Ctr 1750 Pk Rd Ste 2	Oregon	OH	43616	**800-282-7275**	419-836-1466	376
Mauna Kea Beach Hotel 62-100 Maunakea Beach Dr	Island of Hawaii	HI	96743	**866-977-4589**	808-882-7222	660
Mauna Lani Bay Hotel & Bungalows 68-1400 Mauna Lani Dr	Kohala Coast	HI	96743	**800-367-2323**	808-885-6622	660
Mauna Loa Macadamia Nut Corp 16-701 Macadamia Rd *Cust Svc	Keaau	HI	96749	**888-628-6256***	808-966-8618	10-9
Maupin Travel Inc 2501 Blue Ridge Rd	Raleigh	NC	27607	**800-786-2738**	919-821-2146	761
Maupintour Inc 2690 Weston Rd Ste 200	Weston	FL	33331	**800-255-4266**	954-653-3820	750
Maurer Mfg 1300 38th Ave W PO Box 160	Spencer	IA	51301	**888-274-6010**	712-262-2992	769
Maurey Manufacturing Corp 410 Industrial Pk Rd	Holly Springs	MS	38635	**800-284-2161**		613
Maurice's Gourmet Barbeque PO Box 6847	West Columbia	SC	29171	**800-628-7423**	803-791-5887	295-19
Maurices Inc 105 W Superior St	Duluth	MN	55802	**866-977-1542**	218-727-8431	155-4
Mauritzon Inc 3939 W Belden Ave	Chicago	IL	60647	**800-621-4352**	773-235-6000	723
Mautino Distributing Co 500 N Richards St *Cust Svc	Spring Valley	IL	61362	**800-851-2756***	815-664-4311	80-1
MavenWire LLC 630 Freedom Business Ctr Third Fl	King Of Prussia	PA	19406	**866-343-4870**		458
Maverick Technologies 265 Admiral Trost Rd PO Box 470	Columbia	IL	62236	**888-917-9109**	618-281-9100	179-1
Maverick USA Inc 13301 Valentine Rd	North Little Rock	AR	72117	**800-289-6600**	501-955-1255	770
Maverik Inc 880 W Center St *Cust Svc	North Salt Lake	UT	84054	**800-789-4455***	877-936-5557	205
MAWS (Marijuana Anonymous World Services) PO Box 7807	Torrance	CA	90504	**800-766-6779**		47-21
Mawson & Mawson Inc 1800 Old Lincoln Hwy PO Box 248	Langhorne	PA	19047	**800-262-9766**	215-750-1100	770
Max Credit Union 400 Eastdale Cir	Montgomery	AL	36117	**800-776-6776**	334-260-2600	69
Max Group Corp 17011 Green Dr	City of Industry	CA	91745	**800-256-9040**	626-935-0050	175
Max International Converters Inc 2360 Dairy Rd	Lancaster	PA	17601	**800-233-0222**		547
Max Tool Inc 119b Citation Ct	Birmingham	AL	35209	**800-783-6298**	205-942-2466	348
Maxcess International, Inc. 222 W Memorial Rd PO Box 26508	Oklahoma City	OK	73114	**800-333-3433**	405-755-1600	204
Maxell Corp of America 3 Garret Mountain Plaza 3rd Fl Ste 300	Woodland Park	NJ	07424	**800-533-2836**	973-653-2400	649
Maxim Crane Works 1225 Washington Pk	Bridgeville	PA	15017	**877-629-5438**	412-504-0200	264-3
Maxim Integrated Products Inc 120 San Gabriel Dr *NASDAQ: MXIM*	Sunnyvale	CA	94086	**888-629-4642**	408-737-7600	687
Maxim Technologies Inc 1607 Derwent Way	Delta	BC	V3M6K8	**800-663-9925**		149
Maxima Technologies Stewart Warner 1811 Rohrerstown Rd	Lancaster	PA	17601	**800-676-1837**	717-581-1000	490

	Toll-Free	Phone	Class
Maximum Human Performance Inc (MHP Inc)			
21 Dwight Pl .... Fairfield NJ 07004	**888-783-8844**	973-785-9055	787
MAXIMUS Inc			
11419 Sunset Hills Rd .... Reston VA 20190	**800-629-4687**	703-251-8500	195
NYSE: MMS			
MaxLinear Inc			
2051 Palomar Airport Rd			
Ste 100 .... Carlsbad CA 92011	**888-505-4369**	760-692-0711	686
NYSE: MXL			
Maxon Furniture Inc			
660 SW 39th St Ste 150 .... Renton WA 98057	**800-876-4274***		318-1
*Cust Svc			
Maxon Industries Inc			
11921 Slauson Ave .... Santa Fe Springs CA 90670	**800-227-4116**	562-464-0099	465
Maxor National Pharmacy Services Corp			
320 S Polk St Ste 100 .... Amarillo TX 79101	**800-658-6146**	806-324-5400	579
MaxPoint Interactive Inc			
3020 Carrington Mill Blvd			
Ste 300 .... Morrisville NC 27560	**800-916-9960**		178
Maxtex Inc			
3620 Francis Cir .... Alpharetta GA 30004	**800-241-1836**	770-772-6757	358
MaxVision Corp			
495 Production Ave .... Madison AL 35758	**800-533-5805**	256-772-3058	174-1
Maxwell Air Force Base			
55 Le May Plaza S .... Maxwell AFB AL 36112	**877-353-6807**	334-953-2014	492-1
Maxwell Museum of Anthropology			
University of New Mexico ...... Albuquerque NM 87131	**855-227-6231**	505-277-4405	513
Maxwell Technologies Inc			
5271 Viewridge Ct Ste 100 .... San Diego CA 92123	**877-511-4324**	858-503-3300	253
NASDAQ: MXWL			
Maxxam Analytics Inc			
335 LaiRd Rd Unit 2 .... Guelph ON N1G4P7	**877-706-7678**	905-288-2150	414
MaxYield Co-op			
313 Third Ave NE PO Box 49 .... West Bend IA 50597	**800-383-0003**	515-887-7211	275
May Institute Inc			
41 Pacella Pk Dr .... Randolph MA 02368	**800-778-7601**	781-440-0400	47-6
May Trucking Co			
4185 Brooklake Rd PO Box 9039 .... Salem OR 97305	**800-547-9169**		770
Maybelline New York			
575 Fifth Ave PO Box 1010. ...... New York NY 10017	**800-944-0730**		215
Mayco Industries LLC			
18 W Oxmoor Rd .... Birmingham AL 35209	**800-749-6061**	205-942-4242	688
Mayer Electric Supply Co			
3405 Fourth Ave S			
PO Box 1328. .... Birmingham AL 35222	**866-637-1255**	205-583-3500	246
Mayer Laboratories Inc			
1950 Addison St Ste 101 .... Berkeley CA 94704	**800-426-3633**	510-229-5300	732
Mayer Pollock Steel Corp			
Industrial Hwy .... Pottstown PA 19464	**855-773-2848***	610-323-5500	677
*General			
Mayesh Wholesale Florist Inc			
5401 W 104th St .... Los Angeles CA 90045	**888-462-9374**	310-348-4921	292
Mayfair Hotel & Spa			
3000 Florida Ave .... Coconut Grove FL 33133	**800-433-4555**	305-441-0000	376
Mayfield Paper Co			
1115 S Hill St .... San Angelo TX 76903	**800-725-1441**	325-653-1444	552
Mayfield Transfer Company Inc			
3200 W Lake St .... Melrose Park IL 60160	**800-222-2959**	708-681-4440	770
Mayflower Inn			
118 Woodbury Rd Rt 47 .... Washington CT 06793	**800-585-7198**	860-868-9466	376
Mayflower Park Hotel			
405 Olive Way .... Seattle WA 98101	**800-426-5100**	206-623-8700	376
Mayflower Retirement Community			
1620 Mayflower Ct .... Winter Park FL 32792	**800-228-6518**	407-672-1620	663
Mayflower Tours Inc			
1225 Warren Ave			
PO Box 490. .... Downers Grove IL 60515	**800-323-7604**	630-435-8500	750
Mayflower Transit LLC			
1 Mayflower Dr .... Fenton MO 63026	**800-325-3924**	636-305-4000	512
Mayhew Steel Products Inc			
199 Industrial Blvd .... Turners Falls MA 01376	**800-872-0037**	413-863-4860	748
Mayland Community College			
200 Mayland Dr PO Box 547 .... Spruce Pine NC 28777	**800-462-9526**	828-765-7351	160
Mayline Group			
619 N Commerce St PO Box 728 ...... Sheboygan WI 53082	**800-822-8037**	920-457-5537	318-1
May-mcconville Insurance Brokers Ltd			
123 St George St Ste 100 .... London ON N6A3A1	**877-629-6226**	519-673-0880	388-2
Mayo Aviation Inc			
7735 S Peoria St .... Englewood CO 80112	**800-525-0194**	303-792-4020	13
Mayo Civic Ctr			
30 Civic Ctr Dr SE .... Rochester MN 55904	**800-422-2199**	507-328-2220	206
Mayo Clinic Health System Austin			
1000 First Dr NW .... Austin MN 55912	**888-609-4065**	507-433-7351	371-3
Mayo Clinic Health System Southwest Minnesota			
1025 Marsh St .... Mankato MN 56001	**800-327-3721**	507-625-4031	371-3
Mayo Clinic Proceedings Magazine			
200 First St SW			
Siebens Bldg 7-70 .... Rochester MN 55905	**800-654-2452***	507-284-2094	452-16
*Cust Svc			
Mayo Foundation for Medical Education and Research			
200 First St SW .... Rochester MN 55902	**800-679-9084**	507-284-4002	368
Maysville Community & Technical College			
1755 US 68 .... Maysville KY 41056	**888-452-7322**	606-759-7141	160
Maytag Appliances			
403 W Fourth St N .... Newton IA 50208	**800-344-1274***		35
*Cust Svc			
Mayville Products Corp			
403 Degner Ave .... Mayville WI 53050	**800-230-0136**	920-387-3000	688
Mayville State University			
330 Third St NE .... Mayville ND 58257	**800-437-4104**		166
Mazda North American Operations			
7755 Irvine Ctr Dr PO Box 19734. .... Irvine CA 92618	**800-222-5500***	949-727-1990	58
*Cust Svc			
Mazel & Company Inc			
4300 W Ferdinand St .... Chicago IL 60624	**800-525-4023**	773-533-1600	487
Mazon Assoc Inc			
800 W Airport Fwy Ste 900. .... Irving TX 75062	**800-442-2740**	972-554-6967	272
Mazza Vineyards			
11815 E Lake Rd .... North East PA 16428	**800-796-9463**	814-725-8695	49-6
Mazzella Lifting Technologies			
21000 Aerospace Pkwy .... Cleveland OH 44142	**800-362-4601**	440-239-7000	465
MB Financial Inc			
6111 N River Rd .... Rosemont IL 60018	**888-422-6562**		357-2
NASDAQ: MBFI			

	Toll-Free	Phone	Class
MBA (Military Benefit Assn)			
14605 Avion Pkwy			
PO Box 221110. .... Chantilly VA 20153	**800-336-0100**	703-968-6200	47-19
MBA (Mortgage Bankers Assn)			
1919 M St NW 5th Fl .... Washington DC 20036	**800-793-6222**	202-557-2700	48-2
MBAA (Master Brewers Assn of the Americas)			
3340 Pilot Knob Rd .... Saint Paul MN 55121	**800-328-7560**	651-454-7250	48-6
MBC (Memorial Blood Centers)			
737 Pelham Blvd .... Saint Paul MN 55114	**888-448-3253***	651-332-7000	88
*Cust Svc			
MBC (Mc Kenzie Banking Co)			
676 N Main St .... McKenzie TN 38201	**866-321-7063**	731-352-2262	69
MBIA Insurance Corp			
113 King St .... Armonk NY 10504	**800-765-6242**	914-273-4545	388-5
MBL (Marine Biological Laboratory)			
7 MBL St .... Woods Hole MA 02543	**800-222-1222**	508-548-3705	659
MBL International Corp			
Four H Constitution Way .... Woburn MA 01801	**800-200-5459**	781-939-6964	195
MBM (MBM Corp)			
3134 Industry Dr .... North Charleston SC 29418	**800-223-2508***	843-552-2700	110
*Cust Svc			
MBM Corp (MBM)			
3134 Industry Dr .... North Charleston SC 29418	**800-223-2508***	843-552-2700	110
*Cust Svc			
MBNA (Monument Builders of North America)			
136 S Keowee St .... Dayton OH 45402	**800-233-4472**		48-3
MBP (McDonough Bolyard Peck Inc)			
3040 Williams Dr Williams Plz 1			
Ste 300. .... Fairfax VA 22031	**800-898-9088**	703-641-9088	261
MBS Assoc Inc			
10148 Commerce Pk Dr .... Cincinnati OH 45246	**888-469-9301**	513-645-1600	261
MBS Textbook Exchange Inc			
2711 W Ash St .... Columbia MO 65203	**800-325-0530***	573-445-2243	94
*Cust Svc			
MBT Financial Corp			
102 E Front St .... Monroe MI 48161	**800-321-0032**	734-241-3431	357-2
NASDAQ: MBTF			
MBTC (Mifflinburg Bank & Trust Co)			
250 E Chestnut St			
PO Box 186. .... Mifflinburg PA 17844	**888-966-3131**	570-966-1041	69
MC & A Inc			
615 Piikoi St Ste 1000 .... Honolulu HI 96814	**877-589-5589***	808-589-5500	761
*General			
MC Healthcare Products Inc			
4658 Ontario St .... Beamsville ON L0R1B4	**800-268-8671**		470
Mc Kenzie Banking Co (MBC)			
676 N Main St .... McKenzie TN 38201	**866-321-7063**	731-352-2262	69
MC Sports			
3070 Shaffer Ave SE .... Grand Rapids MI 49512	**800-626-1762**	616-942-2600	702
MCA (Marine Corps Assn)			
PO Box 1775 .... Quantico VA 22134	**800-336-0291**	703-640-6161	47-19
MCAA (Mason Contractors Assn of America)			
33 S Roselle Rd .... Schaumburg IL 60193	**800-536-2225**	224-678-9709	48-3
MCAA (Mechanical Contractors Assn of America)			
1385 Piccard Dr .... Rockville MD 20850	**800-556-3653**	301-869-5800	48-3
McAdams Wright Ragen Inc			
925 Fourth Ave Ste 3900 .... Seattle WA 98104	**888-212-8843**	206-664-8850	398
McAfee Inc			
2821 Mission College Blvd .... Santa Clara CA 95054	**888-847-8766***	408-988-3832	179-12
*Cust Svc			
McAllister Towing & Transportation Co Inc			
17 Battery Pl Ste 1200 .... New York NY 10004	**888-774-0400**	212-269-3200	460
MCAP Service Corp			
400-200 King St W .... Toronto ON M5H3T4	**800-387-4405**	416-598-2665	643
McArthur Dairy			
456 Flamingo Dr .... West Palm Beach FL 33401	**800-432-4872**	561-659-4811	295-27
McBee Assoc Inc			
997 Old Eagle School Rd Ste 205. .... Wayne PA 19087	**800-767-6203**	610-964-9680	195
MCC (Mennonite Central Committee)			
21 S 12th St PO Box 500 .... Akron PA 17501	**888-563-4676**	717-859-1151	47-5
McCabe Software Inc			
3300 N Ridge Rd .... Ellicott City MD 21043	**800-638-6316**	410-381-3710	179-12
McCain Foods Ltd			
181 Bay St Ste 3600. .... Toronto ON M5J2T3	**800-938-7799**	416-955-1700	295-21
McCain Foods USA Inc			
2275 Cabot Dr .... Lisle IL 60532	**800-938-7799**		295-21
McCall Aviation			
300 Deinhard Ln .... McCall ID 83638	**800-992-6559**	208-634-7137	62
McCall Handling Co			
8801 Wise Ave Ste 200. .... Dundalk MD 21222	**888-870-0685**	410-388-2600	382
McCall Pattern Co			
615 McCall Rd .... Manhattan KS 66502	**800-255-2762**		561
McCall Service Inc			
2861 College St .... Jacksonville FL 32205	**800-342-6948**	904-389-5561	570
McCall's Quilting Magazine			
741 Corporate Cir Ste A .... Golden CO 80401	**800-944-0736**	303-215-5600	452-14
McCallie School			
500 Dodds Ave .... Chattanooga TN 37404	**800-234-2163**	423-624-8300	615
McCallum Theatre			
73000 Fred Waring Dr .... Palm Desert CA 92260	**866-889-2787**	760-340-2787	565
McCann's Engineering & Manufacturing Co			
4570 W Colorado Blvd .... Los Angeles CA 90039	**800-423-2429**	818-637-7200	655
McCarran International Airport			
5757 Wayne Newton Blvd			
PO Box 11005. .... Las Vegas NV 89119	**888-261-4414**	702-261-5211	27
McClancy Seasoning Co			
One Spice Rd .... Fort Mill SC 29707	**800-843-1968**	803-548-2366	342
McClard's Bar-B-Q			
505 Albert Pike Rd .... Hot Springs AR 71901	**866-622-5273**	501-623-9665	662
McClarin Plastics Inc			
15 Industrial Dr .... Hanover PA 17331	**800-233-3189**	717-637-2241	599
McClatchy Co			
2100 Q St .... Sacramento CA 95816	**866-807-2200**	916-321-1855	628-8
NYSE: MNI			
McClatchy Newspapers			
2100 Q St .... Sacramento CA 95816	**866-807-2200**	916-321-1000	628-8
McCloskey Motors Inc			
6710 N Academy Blvd ...... Colorado Springs CO 80918	**877-389-6671**	719-594-9400	56
McClure Co			
4101 N Sixth St .... Harrisburg PA 17110	**800-382-1319**	717-232-9743	190-10
McClure-Johnston Co			
201 Corey Ave .... Braddock PA 15104	**800-232-0018**	412-351-4300	192-4
McCollister's Transportation Group Inc			
1800 Rt 130 N PO Box 9. .... Burlington NJ 08016	**800-257-9595**	609-386-0600	512

	Toll-Free	Phone	Class
McCone Electric Co-op Inc			
110 Main St ....Circle MT 59215	**800-684-3605**	406-485-3430	245
McConkey Co			
1615 Puyallup St PO Box 1690 ....Sumner WA 98390	**800-426-8124**	253-863-8111	200
McConnell Air Force Base			
57837 Coffeyville St			
Ste 271 ....McConnell AFB KS 67221	**877-272-7337**	316-759-6100	492-1
McConnell Jones Lanier & Murphy LLP			
The Lakes On Post Oak 3040 Post Oak Blvd			
Ste 1600 ....Houston TX 77056	**866-908-4650**	713-968-1600	2
McCook Community College			
1205 E Third St ....McCook NE 69001	**800-658-4348**	308-345-8100	160
McCook Public Power District			
1510 N Hwy 83 ....McCook NE 69001	**800-658-4285**	308-345-2500	245
McCormick & Co Inc			
18 Loveton Cir ....Sparks MD 21152	**800-632-5847**	410-771-7244	295-37
NYSE: MKC			
McCormick & Company Inc Food Service Div			
226 Schilling Cir ....Hunt Valley MD 21031	**800-322-7742**	410-771-7500	295-37
McCormick & Company Inc McCormick Flavor Div			
226 Schilling Cir ....Hunt Valley MD 21031	**800-322-7742**	410-771-7500	295-37
McCormick & Schmick's			
200 S Tryon St ....Charlotte NC 28202	**800-552-6379**	704-377-0201	662
McCormick & Schmick's Harborside			
0309 SW Montgomery ....Portland OR 97201	**888-262-4386***	503-220-1865	662
*Resv			
McCormick Ingredients			
18 Loveton Cir ....Sparks MD 21152	**800-632-5847**	410-771-7301	295-37
McCormick Theological Seminary			
5460 S University Ave ....Chicago IL 60615	**800-228-4687**	773-947-6300	167-3
McCorvey Sheet Metal Works LP			
8610 Wallisville Rd ....Houston TX 77029	**800-580-7545**	713-672-7545	688
McCourt Label Co			
20 Egbert Ln ....Lewis Run PA 16738	**800-458-2390**	814-362-3851	410
McCowan Design & Mfg Ltd			
1760 Birchmount Rd ....Toronto ON M1P2H7	**888-782-5189**	416-291-7111	528
McCoy-Ellison Inc			
1101 Curtis St PO Box 967 ....Monroe NC 28111	**800-811-5348**	704-289-5413	733
Mc-Coy-Mills			
700 W Commonwealth ....Fullerton CA 92832	**888-640-9266***	888-434-3145	509
*Sales			
McCrea Equipment Company Inc			
4463 Beech Rd ....Temple Hills MD 20748	**800-597-0091**	301-423-4585	190-10
McCrometer Inc			
3255 W Stetson Ave ....Hemet CA 92545	**800-220-2279**	951-652-6811	202
McCullagh Coffee			
245 Swan St ....Buffalo NY 14204	**800-753-3473**		295-7
McCullough & Assoc			
1746 NE Expy PO Box 29803 ....Atlanta GA 30329	**800-969-1606**	404-325-1606	144
McDaniel College			
2 College Hill ....Westminster MD 21157	**800-638-5005***	410-857-2230	166
*Admissions			
McDaniel Motor Co			
1111 Mt Vernon Ave ....Marion OH 43302	**888-350-3802**	740-389-2355	509
McDevitt Trucks Inc			
One Mack Ave PO Box 4640 ....Manchester NH 03108	**800-370-6225**	603-668-1700	56
McDonald Publishing			
567 Hanley Industrial Ct ....Saint Louis MO 63144	**800-722-8080**	314-781-7400	243
McDonald Wholesale Co			
2350 W Broadway St ....Eugene OR 97402	**877-722-5503**	541-345-8421	296-3
McDonald's Corp			
One McDonald's Plz ....Oak Brook IL 60523	**800-244-6227**	630-623-3000	661
NYSE: MCD			
McDonough Bolyard Peck Inc (MBP)			
3040 Williams Dr Williams Plz 1			
Ste 300 ....Fairfax VA 22031	**800-898-9088**	703-641-9088	261
McDowell County Tourism Development Authority			
25 W Main St ....Old Fort NC 28762	**888-233-6111**	828-668-4282	207
McDowell-Craig Office Furniture			
13146 Firestone Blvd ....Norwalk CA 90650	**877-921-2100**	562-921-4441	318-1
MCE (Medical Ctr Enterprise)			
400 N Edwards St ....Enterprise AL 36330	**800-994-6610**	334-347-0584	371-3
McElroy Metal Inc			
1500 Hamilton Rd ....Bossier City LA 71111	**800-562-3576**	318-747-8097	475
McElroy Truck Lines Inc			
111 80 Spur PO Box 104 ....Cuba AL 36907	**800-992-7863**	205-392-5579	444
Mcenearney Assoc Inc			
109 S Pitt St ....Alexandria VA 22314	**877-624-9322**	703-549-9292	643
McFarland & Company Inc			
960 NC Hwy 88 W PO Box 611 ....Jefferson NC 28640	**800-253-2187**	336-246-4460	628-2
McFarland Cascade			
1640 E Marc St PO Box 1496 ....Tacoma WA 98421	**800-426-8430***	253-572-3033	805
*Cust Svc			
McFarlane Mfg Company Inc			
1259 Water St PO Box 100 ....Sauk City WI 53583	**800-627-8569**	608-643-3321	276
MCG Capital Corp			
1100 Wilson Blvd Ste 3000 ....Arlington VA 22209	**888-748-3526**	703-247-7500	780
NASDAQ: MCGC			
McGard LLC			
3875 California Rd ....Orchard Park NY 14127	**800-444-5847**	716-662-8980	60
McGean-Rohco Inc			
2910 Harvard Ave ....Cleveland OH 44105	**800-932-7006***	216-441-4900	143
*Orders			
MCGG (Morrow County Grain Growers Inc)			
350 N Main St ....Lexington OR 97839	**800-452-7396**	541-989-8221	10-4
McGill Electrical Product Group			
9377 W Higgins Rd ....Rosemont IL 60018	**800-621-1506**	847-268-6000	802
McGough Construction Co Inc			
2737 Fairview Ave N ....Saint Paul MN 55113	**800-552-7670**	651-633-5050	187
McGraphics Inc			
601 Hagan St ....Nashville TN 37203	**888-280-8200**	615-242-8779	548
McGrath Auto Group			
4610 Ctr Pt Rd NE ....Cedar Rapids IA 52402	**888-902-8414**		56
McGrath RentCorp			
5700 Las Positas Rd ....Livermore CA 94551	**800-962-4284**	925-606-9200	500
NASDAQ: MGRC			
McGraw-Hill Cos Inc CTB/McGraw-Hill Div			
20 Ryan Ranch Rd ....Monterey CA 93940	**800-538-9547**	831-393-0700	244
McGraw-Hill Cos Inc SRA/McGraw-Hill Div			
8787 Orion Pl ....Columbus OH 43240	**800-334-7344**		243
McGraw-Hill Higher Education Group			
1333 Burr Ridge Pkwy ....Burr Ridge IL 60527	**800-634-3963**	630-789-4000	628-2
McGraw-Hill Professional Publishing Group			
Two Penn Plz 11th Fl ....New York NY 10121	**877-833-5524**		628-2

	Toll-Free	Phone	Class
McGriff Seibels & Williams Inc			
2211 Seventh Ave S			
PO Box 10265 ....Birmingham AL 35233	**800-476-2211**	205-252-9871	387
McGuire			
W194 N11481 McCormick Dr			
PO Box 309 ....Germantown WI 53022	**800-624-8473**	518-828-7652	465
McGuire Cadillac Inc			
910 Rt 1 N ....Woodbridge NJ 07095	**866-552-4208**		509
McGuire Furniture Co			
1201 Bryant St ....San Francisco CA 94103	**800-662-4847**	415-626-1414	318-2
McGuireWoods LLP			
901 E Cary St 1 James Ctr ....Richmond VA 23219	**877-712-8778**	804-775-1000	425
McHenry County College			
8900 US Hwy 14 ....Crystal Lake IL 60012	**888-977-4847**	815-455-3700	160
McIlhenny Co			
Hwy 329 ....Avery Island LA 70513	**800-634-9599***	337-365-8173	295-19
*Orders			
McIntire Co			
745 Clark Ave ....Bristol CT 06010	**800-437-9247**	860-585-0050	18
McIntosh Laboratory Inc			
Two Chambers St ....Binghamton NY 13903	**800-538-6576**	607-723-3512	51
McKay Nursery Company Inc			
750 S Monroe St PO Box 185 ....Waterloo WI 53594	**800-236-4242**	920-478-2121	322
McKean County			
500 W Main St ....Smethport PA 16749	**800-482-1280**	814-887-5571	336
McKee Foods Corp			
PO Box 750 ....Collegedale TN 37315	**800-522-4499***	423-238-7111	295-1
*Cust Svc			
McKee Surfaces			
PO Box 230 ....Muscatine IA 52761	**800-553-9662***	563-263-2421	587
*Cust Svc			
McKendree College			
701 College Rd ....Lebanon IL 62254	**800-232-7228**	618-537-4481	166
McKenna Long & Aldridge LLP			
303 Peachtree St Ste 5300 ....Atlanta GA 30308	**866-643-2933**	404-527-4000	425
McKenna Pro Imaging			
2800 Falls Ave ....Waterloo IA 50701	**800-238-3456***	319-235-6265	581
*General			
McKenney's Inc			
1056 Moreland Industrial			
Blvd SE ....Atlanta GA 30316	**877-440-4204**	404-622-5000	190-10
McKenzie County			
PO Box 699 ....Watford City ND 58854	**800-701-2804**	701-444-2804	336
McKenzie Tank Lines Inc			
975 Appleyard Dr ....Tallahassee FL 32304	**800-828-6495**	850-576-1221	770
McKeon Door Co			
44 Sawgrass Dr ....Bellport NY 11713	**800-266-9392**	631-803-3000	234
McKesson Corp			
One Post St ....San Francisco CA 94104	**800-482-3784**	415-983-8300	357-3
NYSE: MCK			
McKesson Information Solutions			
5995 Windward Pkwy ....Alpharetta GA 30005	**800-981-8601**	404-338-6000	179-10
McKesson Medical Group Extended Care			
8121 Tenth Ave N ....Golden Valley MN 55427	**800-328-8111**		470
McKesson Medical-Surgical			
8741 Landmark Rd ....Richmond VA 23228	**800-446-3008**	415-983-8300	470
McKesson Pharmaceutical			
One Post St ....San Francisco CA 94104	**800-571-2889**	415-983-8300	580
McKinley Air Transport Inc			
5430 Lauby Rd ....North Canton OH 44720	**800-225-6446***	330-499-3316	24
*General			
McKinley Equipment Corp			
17611 Armstrong Ave ....Irvine CA 92614	**800-770-6094**	949-261-9222	382
McKinley Grand Hotel			
320 Market Ave S ....Canton OH 44702	**877-454-5008**	330-454-5000	376
McKinstry Co			
5005 Third Ave S ....Seattle WA 98134	**800-669-6223**	206-762-3311	190-10
McKnight's Long-Term Care News			
One Northfield Plz Ste 521 ....Northfield IL 60093	**800-558-1703**	847-784-8706	628-9
MCL Inc			
501 S Woodcreek Rd ....Bolingbrook IL 60440	**800-743-4625***	630-759-9500	638
*Support			
McLane Company Inc			
4747 McLane Pkwy ....Temple TX 76504	**800-299-1401**	254-771-7500	296-8
McLane Foodservice Inc			
2085 Midway Rd ....Carrollton TX 75006	**800-299-1401**	972-364-2000	296-8
McLaren Regional Medical Ctr			
401 S Ballenger Hwy ....Flint MI 48532	**800-821-6517**	810-342-2000	371-3
McLaughlin & Moran Inc			
40 Slater Rd ....Cranston RI 02920	**800-423-0156**	401-463-5454	80-1
McLaughlin Research Corp			
132 Johnnycake Hill Rd ....Middletown RI 02842	**800-556-7154**	401-849-4010	261
McLaughlin Youth Ctr			
2600 Providence Dr ....Anchorage AK 99508	**800-478-2221**	907-261-4399	409
McLean Electric Co-op Inc			
4031 Hwy 37 Bypass NW ....Garrison ND 58540	**800-263-4922**	701-463-2291	245
Mclean Implement Inc			
793 Illinois Rte 130 ....Albion IL 62806	**888-720-4440**	618-445-3676	56
McLean Inc			
3409 E Miraloma Ave ....Anaheim CA 92806	**800-451-2424***	714-996-5451	450
*Cust Svc			
McLellan Botanicals			
2352 San Juan Rd ....Aromas CA 95004	**800-467-2443**		366
McLellan Equipment Inc			
251 Shaw Rd ....South San Francisco CA 94080	**800-848-8449**	650-873-8100	191
McLennan Community College			
1400 College Dr ....Waco TX 76708	**866-339-5555**	254-299-8000	160
McLennan County Electric Co-op			
1111 Johnson Dr PO Box 357 ....McGregor TX 76657	**800-840-2957**	254-840-2871	245
McLeod Co-op Power Assn			
1231 Ford Ave N ....Glencoe MN 55336	**800-494-6272**	320-864-3148	245
McLeod Express LLC			
5002 Cundiff Ct ....Decatur IL 62526	**800-709-3936***		676
*General			
McLeod Hospice			
1203 E Cheves St ....Florence SC 29506	**800-768-4556**	843-777-2564	368
McLoone			
75 Sumner St ....La Crosse WI 54603	**800-624-6641**	608-784-1260	692
MCM Elegante Suites			
4250 Ridgemont Dr ....Abilene TX 79606	**888-897-9644**	325-698-1234	376
MCM Management Corp			
35980 Woodward Ave			
Ste 210 ....Bloomfield Hills MI 48304	**800-843-7512**	248-932-9600	658

				Toll-Free	Phone	Class
MCM Services Group						
1300 Corporate Ctr Curve	Eagan	MN	55121	**888-507-6262**		197
McMenamins						
430 N Killingsworth	Portland	OR	97217	**800-669-8610**	503-223-0109	101
McMurry University						
1 McMurry University						
1400 Sayles Blvd	Abilene	TX	79697	**800-460-2392**	325-793-4700	166
McNally Industries LLC						
340 W Benson Ave	Grantsburg	WI	54840	**800-366-1410**	715-463-8300	632
McNaughton-McKay Electric Company Inc						
1357 E Lincoln Ave	Madison Heights	MI	48071	**888-626-2785**	248-399-7500	246
MCNB Bank & Trust Co						
PO Box 549	Welch	WV	24801	**800-532-9553**	304-436-4112	69
McNeal Enterprises Inc						
2031 Ringwood Ave	San Jose	CA	95131	**800-562-6325**	408-922-7290	595
McNear Brick & Block						
One McNear BrickyaRd Rd						
PO Box 151380	San Rafael	CA	94901	**888-442-6811**	415-453-7702	148
McNeely Pigott & Fox						
611 Commerce St Ste 2800	Nashville	TN	37203	**800-818-6953**	615-259-4000	627
McNeese State University						
4205 Ryan St	Lake Charles	LA	70609	**800-622-3352**	337-475-5000	166
McNeil & NRM Inc						
96 E Crosier St	Akron	OH	44311	**800-669-2525**	330-253-2525	383
McNeil Consumer & Specialty Pharmaceuticals						
7050 Camp Hill Rd	Fort Washington	PA	19034	**800-962-5357**	215-273-7000	576
McNeilus Cos Inc						
524 County Rd 34 E						
PO Box 70	Dodge Center	MN	55927	**800-265-1098**	507-374-6321	509
McNichols Co						
9401 Corporate Lake Dr	Tampa	FL	33634	**877-884-4653**		487
McNulty's Tea & Coffee Company Inc						
109 Christopher St	New York	NY	10014	**800-356-5200**	212-242-5351	157
McPherson College						
PO Box 1402	McPherson	KS	67460	**800-365-7402**	620-241-0731	166
MCR Safety						
5321 E Shelby Dr	Memphis	TN	38118	**800-955-6887**	901-795-5810	153-7
MCS Healthcare Public Relations						
1420 US Hwy 206 Ste 100	Bedminster	NJ	07921	**888-652-8200**	908-234-9900	627
McShan Lumber Company Inc						
PO Box 27	McShan	AL	35471	**800-882-3712**	205-375-6277	742
McShares Inc						
PO Box 1460	Salina	KS	67402	**800-234-7174**	785-825-2181	295-23
MCT Industries Inc						
7451 Pan American Fwy	Albuquerque	NM	87109	**800-876-8651**	505-345-8651	769
MCT Transportation LLC						
1600 E Benson Rd	Sioux Falls	SD	57104	**800-843-9904***	605-339-8400	770
*Cust Svc						
MCVB (Merced Conference & Visitors Bureau)						
710 W 16th St	Merced	CA	95340	**800-446-5353**	209-384-2791	207
MCW Energy Group Ltd						
344 Mira Loma Ave	Glendale	CA	91204	**800-979-1897**		529
McWane Inc						
2900 Hwy 280 Ste 300	Birmingham	AL	35223	**877-231-0904**	205-414-3100	588
McWane Science Center						
200 19th St N	Birmingham	AL	35203	**877-462-9263**	205-714-8300	513
MD Anderson Cancer Ctr						
1515 Holcombe Blvd	Houston	TX	77030	**800-889-2094**	713-792-2121	371-7
M-D Bldg Products Inc						
4041 N Santa Fe Ave	Oklahoma City	OK	73118	**800-654-8454***	405-528-4411	234
*Cust Svc						
MDA (Muscular Dystrophy Assn)						
3300 E Sunrise Dr	Tucson	AZ	85718	**800-572-1717**	520-529-2000	47-17
MDA Information Systems Inc						
6011 Executive Blvd	Rockville	MD	20852	**800-642-1687**	240-833-8200	261
MDC Holdings Inc						
4350 S Monaco St Ste 500	Denver	CO	80237	**888-500-7060**	303-773-1100	357-3
NYSE: MDC						
MDI (Molecular Devices Inc)						
1311 Orleans Dr Ste 408	Sunnyvale	CA	94089	**800-635-5577**	408-747-1700	416
MDI Achieve						
10900 Hampshire Ave South						
Ste 100	Bloomington	MN	55438	**800-869-1322**	952-995-9800	179-10
MDI Security Systems Inc						
12500 Network Dr Ste 303	San Antonio	TX	78249	**866-435-7634**	210-477-5400	683
MDI Worldwide						
38271 W 12-Mile Rd	Farmington Hills	MI	48331	**800-228-8925***	248-553-1900	233
*Sales						
Mdm Supply Inc						
PO Box 6018	Helena	MT	59604	**800-949-0005**	406-443-4012	605
MDNA (Machinery Dealers NA)						
315 S Patrick St	Alexandria	VA	22314	**800-872-7807**	703-836-9300	48-18
MDRT (Million Dollar Round Table)						
325 W Touhy Ave	Park Ridge	IL	60068	**877-883-4865***	847-692-6378	48-9
*General						
MDS (Mennonite Disaster Service)						
583 Airport Rd	Lititz	PA	17543	**800-241-8111**	717-735-3536	47-5
MDS						
N30 W22377 Green Rd	Waukesha	WI	53186	**888-523-2611**		358
MDT Labor LLC						
2325 Paxton Church Rd Ste B	Harrisburg	PA	17110	**888-454-9202**		260
MDU (Montana-Dakota Utilities Co)						
400 N Fourth St	Bismarck	ND	58501	**800-638-3278**	701-222-7900	775
MDU Communications International Inc						
60 D Commerce Way	Totowa	NJ	07512	**866-286-9638**	973-237-9499	672
OTC: MDTV						
MDU Resources Group Inc						
1200 W Century Ave PO Box 5650	Bismarck	ND	58506	**866-760-4852**	701-530-1000	186
NYSE: MDU						
ME Heuck Co						
1600 Beech St	Terre Haute	IN	47804	**866-634-3825***	812-238-5000	481
*Cust Svc						
ME Tile						
447 Atlas Dr	Nashville	TN	37211	**888-348-8453**		741
MEA Voice Magazine						
1216 Kendale Blvd						
PO Box 2573	East Lansing	MI	48826	**800-292-1934**	517-332-6551	452-8
Mead Clark Lumber Co						
Hearn Ave & Dowd Dr						
PO Box 529	Santa Rosa	CA	95402	**800-585-9663**	707-576-3333	192-3
Mead Fluid Dynamics Inc						
4114 N Knox Ave	Chicago	IL	60641	**877-632-3872***	773-685-6800	778
*Cust Svc						

				Toll-Free	Phone	Class
Meade Instruments Corp						
27 Hubble	Irvine	CA	92618	**800-626-3233**	949-451-1450	537
NASDAQ: MEAD						
Meadow Brook Dairy						
2365 Buffalo Rd	Erie	PA	16510	**800-352-4010**	814-899-3191	295-27
Meadow Lake Resort						
100 St Andrews Dr	Columbia Falls	MT	59912	**800-321-4653**	406-892-8700	660
Meadowbrook Insurance Group Inc						
26255 American Dr	Southfield	MI	48034	**800-482-2726**	248-358-1100	357-4
NYSE: MIG						
Meadowlands Exposition Ctr						
355 Plaza Dr	Secaucus	NJ	07094	**888-560-3976**	201-330-7773	206
Meadowood Napa Valley						
900 Meadowood Ln	Saint Helena	CA	94574	**800-458-8080**	707-963-3646	660
Meadows Foundation Inc						
3003 Swiss Ave	Dallas	TX	75204	**800-826-9431**	214-826-9431	304
Meadows Museum of Art at Centenary College						
2911 Centenary Blvd	Shreveport	LA	71104	**800-234-4448**	318-869-5169	513
Meadows Psychiatric Ctr						
132 The Meadows Dr	Centre Hall	PA	16828	**800-641-7529**	814-364-2161	371-5
Meadville Lombard Theological School						
5701 S Woodlawn Ave	Chicago	IL	60637	**800-848-0979**	773-256-3000	167-3
Meadville Medical Ctr (MMC)						
751 Liberty St	Meadville	PA	16335	**800-254-5164**	814-333-5000	371-3
Meadville Tribune						
947 Federal Ct	Meadville	PA	16335	**800-879-0006**	814-724-6370	525-2
Meadville-Western Crawford County Chamber of Commerce						
908 Diamond Pk	Meadville	PA	16335	**800-332-2338**	814-337-8030	137
MEAG Power						
1470 Riveredge Pkwy NW	Atlanta	GA	30328	**800-333-6324**	770-563-0300	775
Meaher State Park						
5200 Battleship Pkwy	Spanish Fort	AL	36577	**800-252-7275**	251-626-5529	558
Mears Group Inc						
4500 N Mission Rd	Rosebush	MI	48878	**800-632-7727**	989-433-2929	189-10
Mears Transportation Group						
324 W Gore St	Orlando	FL	32806	**800-759-5219**	407-422-4561	437
Measurement Specialties Inc						
1000 Lucas Way	Hampton	VA	23666	**800-745-8008**	757-766-1500	675
NASDAQ: MEAS						
MECA Sportswear						
1120 Townline Rd	Tomah	WI	54660	**800-729-6322**	608-374-6450	153-5
Mechanical Contractors Assn of America (MCAA)						
1385 Piccard Dr	Rockville	MD	20850	**800-556-3653**	301-869-5800	48-3
Mechanical Contractors Assn of America PAC						
1385 Piccard Dr	Rockville	MD	20850	**877-457-6482**	301-869-5800	608
Mechanical Inc						
2283 US Rt 20 E	Freeport	IL	61032	**877-426-6628**	815-235-2200	190-10
Mechanical Servants Inc						
2755 Thomas St	Melrose Park	IL	60160	**800-351-2000**	708-615-9439	238
Mechanical Technology Inc						
431 New Karner Rd	Albany	NY	12205	**800-937-5449**	518-533-2200	659
NASDAQ: MKTY						
Mechanics Savings Bank						
100 Minot Ave PO Box 400	Auburn	ME	04210	**877-886-1020**	207-786-5700	69
Mechanicsville Local						
6400 Mechanicsville Tpke	Mechanicsville	VA	23111	**800-468-3382**	804-746-1235	525-4
Mecklenburg Electric Co-op						
11633 Hwy Ninety Two	Chase City	VA	23924	**800-989-4161**	434-372-6100	245
Meckley Services Inc						
5701 General Washington Dr						
Ste O	Alexandria	VA	22312	**877-632-5539**	703-333-2040	603
Meclabs LLC						
1300 Marsh Landing Pkwy						
Ste 106	Jacksonville Beach	FL	32250	**800-517-5531**		
Meco Corp						
1500 Industrial Rd	Greeneville	TN	37745	**800-251-7558**		318-3
Mecosta-Osceola Intermediate School District						
15760 190th Ave	Big Rapids	MI	49307	**877-211-5253**	231-796-3543	676
Medaille College						
18 Agassiz Cir	Buffalo	NY	14214	**800-292-1582**	716-880-2200	166
Medallion Cabinetry						
1 Medallion Way	Waconia	MN	55387	**800-543-4074**	952-442-5171	114
Medallion Financial Corp						
437 Madison Ave 38th Fl	New York	NY	10022	**877-633-2554**	212-328-2100	216
NASDAQ: TAXI						
Medallion Laboratories						
9000 Plymouth Ave N	Minneapolis	MN	55427	**800-245-5615**	763-764-4453	193
Medart Inc						
124 Manufacturers Dr	Arnold	MO	63010	**800-888-7181***	636-282-2300	382
*Cust Svc						
MedCath Inc						
10720 Sikes Pl Ste 300	Charlotte	NC	28277	**800-461-9330**	704-708-6600	350
NASDAQ: MDTH						
Medcenter One Hospital						
300 N Seventh St	Bismarck	ND	58501	**800-932-8758**	701-323-6000	371-3
Medcom Trainex						
6060 Phyllis Dr	Cypress	CA	90630	**800-877-1443***		506
*Cust Svc						
Medcor Inc						
4805 W Prime Pkwy	McHenry	IL	60050	**877-696-6775**	815-363-9500	458
Medeco Security Locks Inc						
3625 Alleghany Dr	Salem	VA	24153	**800-839-3157**	540-380-5000	347
Medford Leas						
One Medford Leas Way	Medford	NJ	08055	**800-331-4302**	609-654-3000	663
Medford Mail Tribune						
PO Box 1108	Medford	OR	97501	**800-452-4011**	541-776-4411	525-2
Medford Public Library						
111 High St	Medford	MA	02155	**800-392-6089**	781-395-7950	431-3
Medgar Evers College						
1650 Bedford Ave	Brooklyn	NY	11225	**866-277-5719**	718-270-4900	166
Media 100 Inc						
450 Donald Lynch Blvd	Marlborough	MA	02210	**888-772-6747**	508-460-1600	179-8
Media Coalition Inc						
275 Seventh Ave Ste 1504	New York	NY	10001	**866-512-1600**	212-587-4025	48-14
Media Cybernetics Inc						
4340 E W Hwy Ste 400	Bethesda	MD	20814	**800-263-2088***	301-495-3305	179-10
*Sales						
Media General Broadcast Group						
111 N Fourth St	Richmond	VA	23219	**800-937-5449**	804-649-6000	728
Media Industry Newsletter (MIN)						
110 William St 11th Fl	New York	NY	10038	**888-707-5814**	212-621-4880	524-11
Media Law Reporter						
1801 S Bell St	Arlington	VA	22202	**800-372-1033**		524-11

Listing	Toll-Free	Phone	Class
Media Logic USA LLC			
59 Wolf Rd . . . . . Albany NY 12205	866-353-3011	518-456-3015	4
Media Relations Report			
316 N Michigan Ave Ste 400 . . . . . Chicago IL 60601	800-878-5331	312-960-4100	524-11
Media Services			
500 S Sepulveda Blvd 4th Fl. . . . . Los Angeles CA 90049	800-738-0409	310-440-9600	563
Media Space Solutions			
904 MainSt . . . . . Hopkins MN 55343	888-672-2100	612-253-3900	6
Media Temple Inc			
8520 National Blvd Bldg A . . . . . Culver City CA 90232	877-578-4000		392
Media Watch			
PO Box 618 . . . . . Santa Cruz CA 95061	800-631-6355	831-423-6355	47-8
Media/Professional Insurance Inc			
1201 Walnut Ste 1800 . . . . . Kansas City MO 64106	866-282-0565	816-471-6118	388-5
Media3 Technologies LLC			
33 Riverside Dr			
N River Commerce Pk. . . . . Pembroke MA 02359	800-903-9327	781-826-1213	795
Mediacom Communications Corp			
100 Crystal Run Rd . . . . . Middletown NY 10941	800-479-2082*	845-695-2600	115
*General			
Mediagrif Interactive Technologies Inc			
1111 St-Charles St W			
E Tower Ste 255 . . . . . Longueuil QC J4K5G4	877-677-9088	450-449-0102	179-1
TSE: MDF			
MEDICA			
401 Carlson Pkwy . . . . . Minnetonka MN 55305	800-952-3455*	952-992-2900	388-3
*Cust Svc			
Medical Action Industries Inc (MAI)			
500 Expy Dr S . . . . . Brentwood NY 11717	800-645-7042	631-231-4600	472
NASDAQ: MDCI			
Medical Analysis Systems Inc			
46360 Fremont Blvd . . . . . Fremont CA 94538	800-232-3342	510-979-5000	231
Medical Assn of Georgia (MAG)			
1849 The Exchange Ste 200 . . . . . Atlanta GA 30339	800-282-0224	678-303-9290	469
Medical Assurance Inc			
100 Brookwood Pl Ste 300 . . . . . Birmingham AL 35209	800-282-6242*	205-877-4400	388-5
*Cust Svc			
Medical Benefits Mutual Life Insurance Co			
1975 Tamarack Rd . . . . . Newark OH 43058	800-423-3151	740-522-8425	388-3
Medical City Hospital Transplant Ctr			
7777 Forest Ln Bldg A 12 S . . . . . Dallas TX 75230	800-348-4318	972-566-7000	759
Medical Coaches Inc			
399 County Hwy 58 . . . . . Oneonta NY 13820	800-432-1339	607-432-1333	509
Medical College of Georgia			
1120 15th St . . . . . Augusta GA 30912	800-736-2273	706-721-0211	166
Medical College of Georgia Hospital & Clinics			
1120 15th St . . . . . Augusta GA 30912	800-736-2273	706-721-0211	371-3
Medical College of Georgia School of Medicine			
1120 15th St . . . . . Augusta GA 30912	800-736-2273	706-721-0211	167-2
Medical Ctr at Princeton Home Care			
905 Herrontown Rd . . . . . Princeton NJ 08540	877-932-8395	609-497-4900	360
Medical Ctr Enterprise (MCE)			
400 N Edwards St . . . . . Enterprise AL 36330	800-994-6610	334-347-0584	371-3
Medical Ctr for Federal Prisoners Springfield			
1900 W Sunshine St . . . . . Springfield MO 65807	877-623-8426	417-862-7041	
Medical Ctr of Southeastern Oklahoma			
1800 University Blvd . . . . . Durant OK 74701	888-280-6276	580-924-3080	371-3
Medical Diagnostic Laboratories LLC			
2439 Kuser Rd . . . . . Hamilton NJ 08690	877-269-0090	609-570-1000	415
Medical Doctor Assoc Inc			
145 Technology Pkwy NW . . . . . Norcross GA 30092	800-780-3500	770-246-9191	195
Medical Education Technologies Inc (METI)			
6300 Edgelake Dr . . . . . Sarasota FL 34240	866-462-7920	941-377-5562	250
Medical Eye Bank of Maryland			
815 Pk Ave . . . . . Baltimore MD 21201	800-756-4824	410-752-2020	269
Medical Genetics Consultants			
819 DeSoto St . . . . . Ocean Springs MS 39564	800-362-4363		414
Medical Graphics Corp			
350 Oak Grove Pkwy . . . . . Saint Paul MN 55127	800-950-5597	651-484-4874	250
NASDAQ: ANGN			
Medical Group Management Assn (MGMA)			
104 Inverness Terr E . . . . . Englewood CO 80112	877-275-6462	303-799-1111	48-8
Medical Library Assn (MLA)			
65 E Wacker Pl Ste 1900 . . . . . Chicago IL 60601	800-523-1850	312-419-9094	48-11
Medical Mutual Group			
700 Spring Forest Rd . . . . . Raleigh NC 27609	800-662-7917	919-872-7117	388-5
Medical Mutual Insurance Company of Maine			
One City Ctr Ste 9 . . . . . Portland ME 04101	800-942-2791	207-775-2791	388-5
Medical Mutual Liability Insurance Society of Maryland			
225 International Cir			
PO Box 8016 . . . . . Hunt Valley MD 21030	800-492-0193	410-785-0050	388-5
Medical Mutual of Ohio			
2060 E Ninth St . . . . . Cleveland OH 44115	800-700-2583	216-687-7000	388-3
Medical Products Laboratories Inc			
9990 Global Rd			
PO Box 14366 . . . . . Philadelphia PA 19115	800-523-0191	215-677-2700	576
Medical Protective Co			
5814 Reed Rd . . . . . Fort Wayne IN 46835	800-463-3776	260-485-9622	388-5
Medical Research Law & Policy Report			
1801 S Bell St . . . . . Arlington VA 22202	800-372-1033		524-7
Medical Resources Inc			
1455 Broad St . . . . . Bloomfield NJ 07003	800-537-7272	973-707-1100	380
Medical Services of America Inc (MSA)			
171 Monroe Ln . . . . . Lexington SC 29072	800-845-5850	803-957-0500	360
Medical Staffing Assoc Inc			
6731 Whittier Ave 3rd Fl. . . . . McLean VA 22101	800-235-5105		712
Medical Staffing Network Holdings Inc			
901 Yamato Rd Ste 110 . . . . . Boca Raton FL 33431	800-676-8326		712
Medical Teams International (MTI)			
PO Box 10 . . . . . Portland OR 97207	800-959-4325	503-624-1000	47-5
Medical University of South Carolina			
41 Bee St MSC 203 . . . . . Charleston SC 29425	800-424-6872	843-792-3281	166
Medical University of South Carolina Medical Ctr			
171 Ashley Ave . . . . . Charleston SC 29425	800-424-6872	843-792-2300	371-3
MedicAlert Foundation International			
2323 Colorado Ave . . . . . Turlock CA 95382	800-432-5378*	209-668-3333	47-17
*Cust Svc			
Medicap Pharmacies Inc			
1 Rider Trail Plaza Dr . . . . . Earth City MO 63045	800-407-8055	314-993-6000	237
Medicare Compliance Alert			
11300 Rockville Pk Ste 1100 . . . . . Rockville MD 20852	800-929-4824	301-287-2700	524-7
Medicare Rights Ctr (MRC)			
520 Eigth Ave N Wing Third Fl . . . . . New York NY 10018	800-333-4114*	212-869-3850	47-17
*Hotline			
Medicines Co			
Eight Sylvan Way . . . . . Parsippany NJ 07054	800-388-1183	973-290-6000	84
NASDAQ: MDCO			
Medicis Pharmaceutical Corp			
7720 N Dobson Rd . . . . . Scottsdale AZ 85256	855-396-2084*	800-321-4576	576
Medico Group			
1515 S 75th St . . . . . Omaha NE 68124	800-228-6080	402-391-6900	388-2
Medico Industries Inc			
1500 Hwy 315 . . . . . Wilkes-Barre PA 18711	800-633-0027	570-825-7711	264-3
Medicomp Inc			
7845 Ellis Rd . . . . . Melbourne FL 32904	800-234-3278	321-676-0010	630
Medifast Inc			
11445 Cronhill Dr . . . . . Owings Mills MD 21117	800-209-0878		295-11
NYSE: MED			
Medifit Corporate Services Inc			
25 Hanover Rd . . . . . Florham Park NJ 07932	888-723-6334	973-593-9000	195
MedImpact Healthcare Systems Inc			
10680 Treena St Ste 500 . . . . . San Diego CA 92131	800-788-2949	858-566-2727	579
Medina Electric Co-op Inc			
PO Box 370 . . . . . Hondo TX 78861	866-632-3532	830-741-3334	245
Medina Gazette			
885 W Liberty St . . . . . Medina OH 44256	800-633-4623	330-725-4166	525-2
MediRevv Inc			
2600 University Pkwy . . . . . Coralville IA 52241	888-665-6310		197
Mediterranean Inn			
425 Queen Anne Ave N . . . . . Seattle WA 98109	866-525-4700	206-428-4700	376
Medivo Inc			
55 Broad St 16th Fl. . . . . New York NY 10004	888-362-4321		178
Mediware Information Systems Inc			
11711 W 79th St . . . . . Lenexa KS 66214	800-255-0026	913-307-1000	179-11
NASDAQ: MEDW			
MedjetAssist			
3500 Colonnade Pkwy Ste 500			
PO Box 43099 . . . . . Birmingham AL 35243	800-527-7478	205-595-6626	30
Medler Eelectric Company Inc			
2155 Redman Dr . . . . . Alma MI 48801	800-229-5740		249
Medley Communications Inc			
560-6 Birch St . . . . . Lake Elsinore CA 92530	888-551-7208	951-245-5200	775
Medline Industries Inc			
1 Medline Pl . . . . . Mundelein IL 60060	800-351-1512*	847-949-5500	569
*Cust Svc			
MedlinePlus			
National Library of Medicine			
8600 Rockville Pk . . . . . Bethesda MD 20894	888-346-3656	301-594-5983	353
Medovations Inc			
102 E Keefe Ave . . . . . Milwaukee WI 53212	800-558-6408	414-265-7620	471
MedPlus Inc			
4690 Pkwy Dr . . . . . Mason OH 45040	800-444-6235	513-229-5500	179-10
MedStar Health			
5565 Sterrett Pl 5th Fl. . . . . Columbia MD 21044	877-772-6505	410-772-6500	350
MEDTOX Diagnostics Inc			
1238 Anthony Rd . . . . . Burlington NC 27215	800-334-1116	336-226-6311	231
MEDTOX Scientific Inc			
402 W County Rd D . . . . . Saint Paul MN 55112	800-832-3244	651-636-7466	413
NASDAQ: MTOX			
Medtronic Inc			
710 Medtronic Pkwy NE . . . . . Minneapolis MN 55432	800-328-2518*	763-514-4000	250
NYSE: MDT ■ *Cust Svc			
Medtronic Inc Heart Valve Div			
710 Medtronic Pwy . . . . . Minneapolis MN 55432	800-633-8766	763-514-4000	472
Medtronic Microelectronics Ctr (MMC)			
710 Medtronic Pkwy . . . . . Minneapolis MN 55432	800-633-8766	763-514-4000	687
Medtronic MiniMed Inc			
18000 Devonshire St . . . . . Northridge CA 91325	800-646-4633		472
Medtronic Neurosurgery			
125 Cremona Dr . . . . . Goleta CA 93117	800-468-9710*	800-633-8766	471
*Cust Svc			
Medtronic of Canada Ltd			
6733 Kitimat Rd . . . . . Mississauga ON L5N1W3	800-268-5346	905-826-6020	250
Medtronic Perfusion Systems			
7611 Northland Dr . . . . . Brooklyn Park MN 55428	800-328-3320	763-391-9000	250
Medtronic Powered Surgical Solutions			
4620 N Beach St . . . . . Fort Worth TX 76137	800-643-2773	817-788-6400	472
Medtronic Surgical Technologies			
6743 Southpoint Dr N . . . . . Jacksonville FL 32216	800-874-5797	904-296-9600	472
Medvantx Inc			
5626 Oberlin Dr Ste 110 . . . . . San Diego CA 92121	866-744-0621	858-625-2990	712
Meeder Equipment Co			
12323 Sixth St . . . . . Rancho Cucamonga CA 91739	800-423-3711	909-463-0600	354
Meeker Co-op Light & Power Assn			
1725 E US Hwy 12 PO Box 68 . . . . . Litchfield MN 55355	800-232-6257	320-693-3231	245
Meet Minneapolis			
250 Marquette Ave Ste 1300 . . . . . Minneapolis MN 55401	800-445-7412	612-767-8000	207
Meeting Connection Inc, The			
893 High St . . . . . Worthington OH 43085	800-398-2568	614-888-2568	185
Meeting Professionals International (MPI)			
3030 LBJ Fwy Ste 1700 . . . . . Dallas TX 75234	866-748-9561	972-702-3000	48-12
Meeting Street Inn			
173 Meeting St . . . . . Charleston SC 29401	800-842-8022	843-723-1882	376
Meetings & Conventions Magazine			
100 Lighting Way . . . . . Secaucus NJ 07094	877-705-8889	201-902-2000	452-5
Megadyne Medical Products Inc			
11506 S State St . . . . . Draper UT 84020	800-747-6110	801-576-9669	471
Mega-Pro International Inc			
251 W Hilton Dr . . . . . Saint George UT 84770	800-541-9469	435-673-1001	787
Megger 4271 Bronze Way . . . . . Dallas TX 75237	800-723-2861	214-333-3201	248
Meggitt Training Systems Inc			
296 Brogdon Rd . . . . . Suwanee GA 30024	800-813-9046	678-288-1090	694
MEGTEC Systems Inc			
830 Prosper Rd . . . . . De Pere WI 54115	800-558-5535*	920-336-5715	383
*Cust Svc			
Meguiar's Inc			
17991 Mitchell S . . . . . Irvine CA 92614	800-347-5700*	949-752-8000	149
*Cust Svc			
Meherrin Agricultural & Chemical Co Inc			
413 Main St . . . . . Severn NC 27877	800-775-0333	252-585-1744	276
Meier Supply Company Inc			
530 Bloomingburg Rd . . . . . Middletown NY 10940	800-418-3216	845-733-5666	603
Meijer Inc			
2929 Walker Ave NW . . . . . Grand Rapids MI 49544	800-543-3704	616-453-6711	342
Meijer Stores Inc			
2929 Walker Ave NW . . . . . Grand Rapids MI 49544	800-543-3704	616-453-6711	342
Meisel Visual Imaging			
2019 McKenzie Dr . . . . . Carrollton TX 75006	800-527-5186	214-688-4950	581

Name / Address	City	State	ZIP	Toll-Free	Phone	Class
Meister Media Worldwide						
37733 Euclid Ave	Willoughby	OH	44094	**800-572-7740***	440-942-2000	628-9
*Orders						
Mel Bay Publications Inc						
Four Industrial Dr	Pacific	MO	63069	**800-863-5229**	636-257-3970	628-2
Melaleuca Inc						
3910 S Yellowstone Hwy	Idaho Falls	ID	83402	**800-282-3000***	208-522-0700	363
*Sales						
Melbourne Regional Chamber of East Central Florida						
1005 E Strawbridge Ave	Melbourne	FL	32901	**855-894-4673**	321-724-5400	207
Mele & Co						
2007 Beechgrove Pl	Utica	NY	13501	**800-635-6353**	315-733-4600	201
Melin Tool Co						
5565 Venture Dr Unit C	Cleveland	OH	44130	**800-521-1078**	216-362-4230	488
Melissa's/World Variety Produce Inc						
5325 S Soto St	Vernon	CA	90058	**800-588-0151**		296-7
Melitta Canada Inc						
10-6201 Hwy Ste 7	Vaughan	ON	L4H0K7	**800-565-4882**	905-851-9375	295-7
Mellano & Co						
766 Wall St	Los Angeles	CA	90014	**888-635-5266**	213-622-0796	292
Melnor Inc						
109 Tyson Dr	Winchester	VA	22603	**877-283-0697**	540-722-5600	426
Melting Pot of Annapolis, The						
2348 Solomons Island Rd	Annapolis	MD	21401	**800-783-0867**	410-266-8004	662
Melting Pot of Charlotte, The						
901 S Kings Dr Ste 140B	Charlotte	NC	28204	**800-783-0867**	704-334-4400	662
Melting Pot of Columbia, The						
1410 Colonial Life Blvd	Columbia	SC	29210	**800-783-0867**	803-731-8500	662
Melting Pot of Indianapolis, The						
5650 E 86th St Ste A	Indianapolis	IN	46250	**800-783-0867**	317-841-3601	662
Melting Pot of Pensacola, The						
418 Gregory St Ste 500	Pensacola	FL	32501	**800-783-0867**	850-438-4030	662
Melting Pot of San Antonio, The						
14855 Blanco Rd Ste 110	San Antonio	TX	78216	**800-783-0867**	210-479-6358	662
Melting Pot of Tampa, The						
13164 N Dale Mabry Hwy	Tampa	FL	33618	**800-783-0867**	813-962-6936	662
Melting Pot Restaurants Inc						
8810 Twin Lakes Blvd	Tampa	FL	33614	**800-783-0867**	813-881-0055	661
Melting Pot, The						
1601 Concord Pike						
Ste 43-47 Independence Mall	Wilmington	DE	19803	**800-783-0867**	302-652-6358	662
Melton Truck Lines Inc						
808 N 161 E Ave	Tulsa	OK	74116	**800-545-6651***	918-234-8000	770
*General						
Members Trust Co						
14025 Riveredge Dr Ste 280	Tampa	FL	33637	**888-727-9191**	813-631-9191	69
Memorial Blood Centers (MBC)						
737 Pelham Blvd	Saint Paul	MN	55114	**888-448-3253***	651-332-7000	88
*Cust Svc						
Memorial Health Partners						
4700 Waters Ave Ste 13	Savannah	GA	31404	**800-537-0690**	912-350-8000	388-3
Memorial Health System (MHS)						
Central						
80 W Lucerne Cir	Orlando	FL	32801	**800-416-2612**	407-841-1310	663
Memorial Health System (MHS)						
Central						
1400 E Boulder St	Colorado Springs	CO	80909	**877-422-3648**	719-365-5000	371-3
Memorial Healthcare Ctr						
826 W King St	Owosso	MI	48867	**800-206-8706**	989-723-5211	371-3
Memorial Hermann Memorial City Hospital						
921 Gessner Rd	Houston	TX	77024	**800-526-2121**	713-242-3000	371-3
Memorial Hermann Prevention & Recovery Ctr (MHPARC)						
3043 Gessner	Houston	TX	77080	**800-464-7272**	713-939-7272	371-5
Memorial Hospital						
715 S Taft Ave	Fremont	OH	43420	**800-971-8203**	419-332-7321	371-3
Memorial Hospital of Rhode Island (MHRI)						
111 Brewster St	Pawtucket	RI	02860	**800-647-4362**	401-729-2000	371-3
Memorial Hospital of South Bend						
615 N Michigan St	South Bend	IN	46601	**800-850-7913**	574-647-1000	371-3
Memorial Hospital of Sweetwater County						
1200 College Dr	Rock Springs	WY	82901	**866-571-0944***	307-362-3711	371-3
*General						
Memorial Medical Ctr						
1615 Maple Ln	Ashland	WI	54806	**877-611-1988**	715-685-5500	371-3
Memorial Sloan-Kettering Cancer Ctr						
1275 York Ave	New York	NY	10065	**800-525-2225**	212-639-2000	371-7
Memorial Sloan-Kettering Cancer Ctr Bone Marrow Transplant Service						
1275 York Ave	New York	NY	10065	**800-525-2225**	212-639-6009	759
Memphis Botanic Garden						
750 Cherry Rd	Memphis	TN	38117	**877-829-5500**	901-576-4100	96
Memphis Brooks Museum of Art						
1934 Poplar Ave Overton Pk	Memphis	TN	38104	**877-829-5500**	901-544-6200	513
Memphis College of Art						
1930 Poplar Ave	Memphis	TN	38104	**800-727-1088**	901-272-5100	162
Memphis Convention & Visitors Bureau						
47 Union Ave	Memphis	TN	38103	**888-633-9099**	901-543-5300	207
Memphis Flyer						
460 Tennessee St	Memphis	TN	38103	**800-581-5156**	901-521-9000	525-5
Memphis Machinery & Supply Co Inc						
2881 Directors Cove	Memphis	TN	38131	**800-388-4485**	901-527-4443	808
Memphis Magazine						
460 Tennessee St Ste 200	Memphis	TN	38103	**800-288-9999**	901-521-9000	452-22
Memphis Publishing Co						
495 Union Ave	Memphis	TN	38103	**800-444-6397***	901-529-2666	628-8
*Cust Svc						
Memry Corp						
Three Berkshire Blvd	Bethel	CT	06801	**866-466-3679**	203-739-1100	480
Men's Health Magazine						
400 S Tenth St	Emmaus	PA	18098	**800-666-2303**	610-967-5171	452-13
Men's Journal LLC						
1290 Ave of the Americas						
2nd Fl	New York	NY	10104	**800-677-6367**		452-11
Men's Wearhouse Inc						
6380 Rogerdale Rd	Houston	TX	77072	**877-986-9669**	281-776-7000	155-3
NYSE: MW						
Menard Electric Co-op						
14300 State Hwy 97						
PO Box 200	Petersburg	IL	62675	**800-872-1203**	217-632-7746	245
Menardi						
One Maxwell Dr	Trenton	SC	29847	**800-321-3218**	803-663-6551	66
Menasha Corp						
1645 Bergstrom Rd	Neenah	WI	54956	**800-558-5073**	920-751-1000	99
Menasha Packaging Co						
1645 Bergstrom Rd	Neenah	WI	54956	**800-558-5073**	920-751-1000	99
MENC: NA for Music Education						
1806 Robert Fulton Dr	Reston	VA	20191	**800-336-3768**	703-860-4000	48-5
Menches Tool & Die Inc						
30995 San Benito St	Hayward	CA	94544	**877-592-2328**	510-476-1160	688
Mended Hearts Inc, The						
8150 N Central Expy M2075	Dallas	TX	75206	**888-432-7899**	214-296-9252	47-17
Mendocino Coast Chamber of Commerce						
217 S Main St PO Box 1141	Fort Bragg	CA	95437	**800-382-7244**	707-961-6300	137
Mendocino Coast District Hospital						
700 River Dr	Fort Bragg	CA	95437	**866-767-3224**	707-961-1234	371-3
Mendocino Wine Co						
501 PaRducci Rd	Ukiah	CA	95482	**800-362-9463**	707-463-5350	79-3
Menger Hotel						
204 Alamo Plz	San Antonio	TX	78205	**800-345-9285**	210-223-4361	376
Menke Marking Devices						
13253 Alondra Blvd						
PO Box 2986	Santa Fe Springs	CA	90670	**800-231-6023**	562-921-1380	462
Menlo College						
1000 El Camino Real	Atherton	CA	94027	**800-556-3656**	650-543-3753	166
Menlo Worldwide Inc						
Con-Way Inc						
2855 Campus Dr Ste 300	San Mateo	CA	94403	**800-426-6929**	650-378-5200	444
Mennel Milling Co						
128 W Crocker St	Fostoria	OH	44830	**800-688-8151**	419-435-8151	295-23
Menninger Clinic						
2801 Gessner Dr PO Box 809045	Houston	TX	77080	**800-351-9058**	713-275-5000	371-5
Mennonite Brethren Biblical Seminary						
4824 E Butler Ave	Fresno	CA	93727	**800-251-6227**	559-453-2000	167-3
Mennonite Central Committee (MCC)						
21 S 12th St PO Box 500	Akron	PA	17501	**888-563-4676**	717-859-1151	47-5
Mennonite Disaster Service (MDS)						
583 Airport Rd	Lititz	PA	17543	**800-241-8111**	717-735-3536	47-5
Mental Health America (MHA)						
2000 N Beauregard St						
Sixth Fl	Alexandria	VA	22311	**800-969-6642***	703-684-7722	47-17
*Help Line						
Mentholatum Company Inc						
707 Sterling Dr	Orchard Park	NY	14127	**800-688-7660**	716-677-2500	576
Mentor Chamber of Commerce						
6972 Spinach Dr	Mentor	OH	44060	**800-825-6755**	440-255-1616	137
Mentor Corp						
201 Mentor Dr	Santa Barbara	CA	93111	**800-525-0245**	805-879-6000	472
NASDAQ: MENT						
Mentor Graphics Corp						
8005 SW Boeckman Rd	Wilsonville	OR	97070	**800-592-2210**	503-685-7000	179-5
NASDAQ: MENT						
MENTOR Network, The						
313 Congress St 5th Fl	Boston	MA	02210	**800-388-5150**	617-790-4800	457
MENTOR/National Mentoring Partnership						
1600 Duke St Ste 300	Alexandria	VA	22314	**877-333-2464**	703-224-2200	47-6
Menzner Lumber & Supply Co						
PO Box 217	Marathon	WI	54448	**800-257-1284**		494
Mera Pharmaceuticals Inc						
73-4460 Queen Kaahumanu Hwy						
Ste 110	Kailua-Kona	HI	96740	**800-480-6515**	808-326-9301	84
Meramec Valley R-3 School District						
126 N Payne St	Pacific	MO	63069	**866-632-9992**	636-271-1400	676
Mercantil Commercebank NA						
220 Alhambra Cir	Coral Gables	FL	33134	**888-629-0810**	305-460-8701	69
Mercantile Bank						
200 N 33rd St PO Box 3455	Quincy	IL	62305	**800-405-6372**	217-223-7300	357-2
NYSE: MBCR						
Mercantile Bank Corp						
310 Leonard St NW	Grand Rapids	MI	49504	**888-345-6296**	616-406-3000	357-2
NASDAQ: MBWM						
Merced College						
3600 M St	Merced	CA	95348	**800-784-2433**	209-384-6000	160
Merced Conference & Visitors Bureau (MCVB)						
710 W 16th St	Merced	CA	95340	**800-446-5353**	209-384-2791	207
Merced County Library						
2100 O St	Merced	CA	95340	**866-249-0773**	209-385-7643	431-3
Merced Irrigation District						
PO Box 2288	Merced	CA	95344	**855-800-2267**	209-722-5761	187
Mercedes-Benz Financial Services USA LLC						
PO Box 685	Roanoke	TX	76262	**800-654-6222**		214
Mercedes-Benz of San Francisco						
500 Eigth St	San Francisco	CA	94103	**877-554-6016**	415-673-2000	56
Mercedes-Benz USA LLC						
one Mercedes Dr	Montvale	NJ	07645	**800-367-6372***	201-573-0600	58
*Cust Svc						
Mercer Arboretum & Botanic Gardens						
22306 Aldine Westfield Rd	Humble	TX	77338	**877-321-2652**	281-443-8731	96
Mercer County						
704 Bland St PO Box 4088	Bluefield	WV	24701	**800-221-3206**	304-325-8438	336
Mercer County Community College						
PO Box B	Trenton	NJ	08690	**800-982-9491**	609-586-4800	160
Kerney Ctr						
N Broad & Academy St	Trenton	NJ	08608	**800-982-9491**	609-586-4800	160
West Windsor						
1200 Old Trenton Rd	West Windsor	NJ	08550	**800-982-9491**	609-586-4800	160
Mercer County Convention & Visitors Bureau						
704 Bland St PO Box 4088	Bluefield	WV	24701	**800-221-3206**	304-325-8438	207
Mercer County Joint Township Community Hospital						
800 W Main St	Coldwater	OH	45828	**888-844-2341**	419-678-2341	371-3
Mercer Forge Corp						
200 Brown St	Mercer	PA	16137	**800-558-5075**	724-662-2750	478
Mercer Hotel						
147 Mercer St	New York	NY	10012	**888-918-6060**	212-966-6060	376
Mercer Insurance Group Inc						
10 N Hwy 31 PO Box 278	Pennington	NJ	08534	**800-223-0534**	609-737-0426	388-4
Mercer LLC						
400 W Market St	Louisville	KY	40202	**800-333-3070**	502-561-4500	194
Mercer Transportation Co						
1128 W Main St PO Box 35610	Louisville	KY	40232	**800-626-5375**	502-584-2301	770
Mercer University						
1400 Coleman Ave	Macon	GA	31207	**800-637-2378**	478-301-2650	166
Cecil B Day						
3001 Mercer University Dr	Atlanta	GA	30341	**800-840-8577**	678-547-6089	166
Mercersburg Academy						
300 E Seminary St	Mercersburg	PA	17236	**800-588-2550**	717-328-6173	615
Merchandise Mart						
222 Merchandise Mart Plz						
Ste 470	Chicago	IL	60654	**800-677-6278**	312-527-4141	206

Company / Address	City	State	ZIP	Toll-Free	Phone	Class
Merchant Factors Corp						
1441 Broadway 22nd Fl	New York	NY	10018	**800-929-3293***	212-840-7575	272
*All						
Merchant One Payment Systems Inc						
524 Arthur Godfrey Rd						
3rd Fl	Miami Beach	FL	33140	**888-854-0347**	305-534-1666	95
Merchants Bancshares Inc						
PO Box 1009	Burlington	VT	05402	**800-322-5222**	802-658-3400	357-2
NASDAQ: MBVT						
Merchants Co						
1100 Edwards St	Hattiesburg	MS	39401	**800-451-8346**	601-583-4351	296-8
Merchants Credit Bureau						
955 Green St	Augusta	GA	30901	**800-426-5265**	706-823-6246	218
Merchants Grocery Co						
800 Maddox Dr PO Box 1268	Culpeper	VA	22701	**877-897-9893**	540-825-0786	342
Merchants Insurance Group						
250 Main St	Buffalo	NY	14202	**800-462-1077**	716-849-3333	388-4
Merchants Metals Inc						
900 Ashwood Pkwy Ste 600	Atlanta	GA	30338	**866-888-5611**	678-731-8077	279
Merchants Solutions Co						
4422 Roosevelt Rd	Hillside	IL	60162	**800-486-3214**	708-449-6650	111
Merck & Company Inc						
One Merck Dr						
PO Box 100	Whitehouse Station	NJ	08889	**800-672-6372***	908-423-1000	576
NYSE: MRK ■ *Cust Svc						
Mercom Inc						
313 Commerce Dr	Pawleys Island	SC	29585	**877-223-8330**	843-979-9957	181
Merco-Savory Inc						
1111 N Hadley Rd	Fort Wayne	IN	46804	**888-417-5462***	260-459-8200	297
*Cust Svc						
Mercury Computer Systems Inc						
201 Riverneck Rd	Chelmsford	MA	01824	**866-627-6951**	978-967-1401	174-1
NASDAQ: MRCY						
Mercury Insurance Group						
4484 Wilshire Blvd	Los Angeles	CA	90010	**800-956-3728**	323-937-1060	388-4
NYSE: MCY						
Mercury Lighting Products Company Inc						
20 Audrey Pl	Fairfield	NJ	07004	**800-637-2584**	973-244-9444	435
Mercury Luggage Manufacturing Co						
4843 Victor St	Jacksonville	FL	32207	**800-874-1885**	904-334-8801	448
Mercury Medical						
11300 49th St N	Clearwater	FL	33762	**800-237-6418**	727-573-0088	471
Mercury Wireless LLC						
2825 se california ave	Topeka	KS	66605	**800-354-4915**		726
Mercury Z						
1150 Se Maynard Rd Ste 140	Cary	NC	27511	**877-548-4052**		197
Mercy						
1235 E Cherokee	Springfield	MO	65804	**800-909-8326**	417-820-2000	371-3
Mercy College						
555 Broadway	Dobbs Ferry	NY	10522	**800-637-2969**	914-693-4500	166
Manhattan						
66 W 35th St	New York	NY	10001	**800-637-2969**	212-615-3313	166
White Plains						
277 Martine Ave	White Plains	NY	10601	**888-464-6737**	914-948-3666	166
Yorktown Heights						
2651 Strang Blvd	Yorktown Heights	NY	10598	**877-637-2946**	914-245-6100	166
Mercy Corps						
3015 SW First Ave	Portland	OR	97201	**800-292-3355**	503-796-6800	47-5
Mercy Hospital						
144 State St	Portland	ME	04101	**800-293-6583**	207-879-3000	371-3
Mercy Hospital & Trauma Ctr						
1000 Mineral Pt Ave	Janesville	WI	53548	**800-756-4147**	608-756-6000	371-3
Mercy Housing Inc						
1999 Broadway Ste 1000	Denver	CO	80202	**866-338-0557**	303-830-3300	188
Mercy Iowa City						
500 E Market St	Iowa City	IA	52245	**800-637-2942**	319-339-0300	371-3
Mercy Medical Ctr						
1111 Sixth Ave	Des Moines	IA	50314	**800-637-2993**	515-247-3121	371-3
Mercy Medical Ctr North Iowa						
1000 Fourth St SW	Mason City	IA	50401	**800-433-3883**	641-428-7000	371-3
Mercy Medical Ctr Redding						
2175 Rosaline Ave	Redding	CA	96001	**800-521-6377**	530-225-6000	371-3
Mercy Memorial Health Ctr (MMHC)						
1011 14th Ave NW	Ardmore	OK	73401	**888-637-2937**	580-223-5400	371-3
Mercyhurst College						
501 E 38th St	Erie	PA	16546	**800-825-1926**	814-824-2202	166
Mercy-USA for Aid & Development Inc (M-USA)						
44450 Pinetree Dr Ste 201	Plymouth	MI	48170	**800-556-3729**	734-454-0011	47-5
Meredith Collection						
1201 Millerton St SE	Canton	OH	44707	**888-325-3945**	330-484-1656	741
Meredith College						
3800 Hillsborough St	Raleigh	NC	27607	**800-637-3348***	919-760-8581	166
*All						
Meredith Village Savings Bank (MVSB)						
24 State Rt 25 PO Box 177	Meredith	NH	03253	**800-922-6872**	603-279-7986	69
Mereen-Johnson Machine Co						
4401 Lyndale Ave N	Minneapolis	MN	55412	**888-465-7297**	612-529-7791	808
Merfish Pipe & Supply Co						
PO Box 15879	Houston	TX	77220	**800-869-5731**	713-869-5731	487
Merge Helathcare						
350 N Orleans St First Fl	Chicago	IL	60654	**877-446-3743**	312-565-6868	379
Mergent FIS Inc						
580 Kingsley Pk Dr	Fort Mill	SC	29715	**800-342-5647**		628-10
Mergent Inc						
477 Madison Ave Ste 410	New York	NY	10022	**800-937-1398**	212-413-7700	628-9
Mergenthaler Transfer & Storage						
1414 N Montana Ave	Helena	MT	59601	**800-826-5463***	406-442-9470	770
*General						
Mergers & Acquisitions Law Report						
1801 S Bell St	Arlington	VA	22202	**800-372-1033**		524-7
Mergers & Acquisitions Magazine						
One State St Plz	New York	NY	10004	**888-807-8667***	212-803-6051	452-5
*Cust Svc						
Meri Meri						
63 Leonard St	Belmont	MA	02478	**800-638-2881**	617-484-5571	129
Merial Ltd						
3239 Satellite Blvd Bldg 500	Duluth	GA	30096	**888-637-4251**	678-638-3000	575
Mericon Industries Inc						
8819 N Pioneer Rd	Peoria	IL	61615	**800-242-6464**	309-693-2150	577
Meriden Public Library						
105 Miller St	Meriden	CT	06450	**800-567-0902**	203-238-2344	431-3
Meridian Bioscience Inc						
3471 River Hills Dr	Cincinnati	OH	45244	**800-543-1980***	513-271-3700	231
NASDAQ: VIVO ■ *Cust Svc						
Meridian Chamber of Commerce						
215 E Franklin Rd	Meridian	ID	83642	**866-833-3330**	208-888-2817	137
Meridian Community College						
910 Hwy 19 N	Meridian	MS	39307	**800-622-8431**	601-483-8241	160
Meridian Display & Merchandising Inc						
162 York Ave E	St Paul	MN	55117	**800-786-2501**	651-227-3020	5
Meridian Gold Co						
9670 Gateway Dr Ste 200	Reno	NV	89521	**888-231-8191**	775-850-3777	497
Meridian IQ						
11501 Outlook St Ste 500	Overland Park	KS	66211	**877-246-4909**		444
Meridian Mattress Factory Inc						
200 Rubush Rd PO Box 5127	Meridian	MS	39301	**800-844-3875**	601-693-3875	466
Meridian Medical Technologies Inc						
6350 Stevens Forest Rd Ste 301	Columbia	MD	21046	**800-638-8093**	443-259-7800	471
Meridian Plaza Resort						
2310 N Ocean Blvd	Myrtle Beach	SC	29577	**800-323-3011**	843-626-4734	376
Meridian Star Inc						
814 22nd Ave	Meridian	MS	39301	**800-232-2525***	601-693-1551	628-8
*Cust Svc						
Meridian Star, The						
PO Box 1591	Meridian	MS	39302	**800-232-2525**	601-693-1551	525-2
Meridian Systems						
1720 Prairie City Rd Ste 120	Folsom	CA	95630	**800-850-2660**	916-294-2000	179-1
Meridian Technology Group Inc						
12909 SW 68th Pkwy Ste 340	Portland	OR	97223	**800-755-1038**	503-697-1600	178
Meridian Title Corp						
202 S Michigan St	South Bend	IN	46601	**800-777-1574**	574-232-5845	388-6
Meridian/Lauderdale County Tourism Bureau						
212 Constitution Ave						
PO Box 5313	Meridian	MS	39301	**888-868-7720**	601-482-8001	207
Meridian-Lauderdale County Public Library						
2517 Seventh St	Meridian	MS	39301	**800-318-2596**	601-693-6771	431-3
Merion Publications Inc						
2900 Horizon Dr	King of Prussia	PA	19406	**800-355-1088**	610-278-1400	628-9
Merit Electric Company Inc						
6520 125th Ave N	Largo	FL	33773	**800-330-5945**	727-536-5945	190-4
Merit Medical Systems Inc						
1600 W Merit Pkwy	South Jordan	UT	84095	**800-356-3748**	801-253-1600	471
NASDAQ: MMSI						
Merit Resources Inc						
4410 114th St	Des Moines	IA	50322	**800-336-1931**	515-278-1931	623
Merit Systems Protection Board (MSPB)						
1615 M St NW	Washington	DC	20419	**800-209-8960**	202-653-7200	338-18
Merit Systems Protection Board Regional Offices (MSPB)						
Atlanta Region						
401 W Peachtree St NW 10th Fl	Atlanta	GA	30308	**800-209-8960**	404-730-2755	338-18
Merit Travel Group Inc						
111 Peter St Ste 200	Toronto	ON	M5V2H1	**800-268-5940**	416-364-3775	761
Merit USA						
620 Clark Ave	Pittsburg	CA	94565	**800-445-6374**		487
Meritus Health						
11116 Medical Campus Rd	Hagerstown	MD	21742	**800-735-2258**	301-790-8000	371-3
Meriwest Credit Union						
PO Box 530953	San Jose	CA	95153	**877-637-4937**		219
Merkle Wildlife Sanctuary						
580 Taylor Ave	Annapolis	MD	21401	**877-620-8367**		558
Merle Norman Cosmetics Inc						
9130 Bellanca Ave	Los Angeles	CA	90045	**800-421-6648**	310-641-3000	215
Merle's Automotive Supply Inc						
33 W University Blvd	Tucson	AZ	85705	**800-546-6040**	520-622-3526	53
Merlin Corp						
3815 E Main St Ste D	Saint Charles	IL	60174	**800-652-9910**	630-513-8200	309
Merrell Footwear						
9341 Courtland Dr NE	Rockford	MI	49351	**800-288-3124***	616-866-5500	300
*Cust Svc						
Merriam-Webster Inc						
PO Box 281	Springfield	MA	01102	**800-828-1880***	413-734-3134	628-2
*Cust Svc						
Merrick & Co						
2450 S Peoria St	Aurora	CO	80014	**800-544-1714**	303-751-0741	261
Merrick Systems Inc						
55 Waugh Dr Ste 400	Houston	TX	77007	**800-842-8389**	713-579-3400	179-10
Merrick's Inc						
2415 Parview Rd PO Box 620307	Middleton	WI	53562	**800-637-7425**	608-831-3440	442
Merrill Area Chamber of Commerce						
705 N Ctr Ave	Merrill	WI	54452	**877-907-2757**	715-536-9474	137
Merrill Corp						
1 Merrill Cir	Saint Paul	MN	55108	**800-688-4400**	651-646-4501	619
Merrill DataSite						
225 Varick St	New York	NY	10014	**866-399-3770**		384
Merrill Mfg Corp						
236 S Genesee St	Merrill	WI	54452	**800-831-6962**	715-536-5533	798
Merrimack Valley Chamber of Commerce						
264 Essex St	Lawrence	MA	01840	**800-966-3375**	978-686-0900	137
Merrimack Valley Distributing Co						
50 Prince St	Danvers	MA	01923	**800-698-0250**	978-777-2213	80-1
Merrimack Valley Hospice						
360 Merrimack St Bldg 9	Lawrence	MA	01843	**800-933-5593**		368
Merritt Equipment Co						
9339 Hwy 85	Henderson	CO	80640	**800-634-3036**	303-289-2286	769
Merry Maids						
3839 Forrest Hill-Irene Rd	Memphis	TN	38125	**866-212-5846**	800-776-4663	150
Mersen USA BN Corp						
400 Myrtle Ave	Boonton	NJ	07005	**800-526-0877***		126
*General						
Mertz Mfg LLC						
1701 N Waverly St	Ponca City	OK	74601	**800-654-6433**	580-762-5646	273
Mervis Industries Inc						
3295 E Main St	Danville	IL	61834	**800-637-3016**	217-442-5300	677
Mesa Arizona Temple						
101 S LeSueur	Mesa	AZ	85204	**855-537-4357**	480-833-1211	49
Mesa Arts Ctr						
1 E Main St PO Box 1466	Mesa	AZ	85201	**800-647-5463**	480-644-6501	49-1
Mesa Community College						
1833 W Southern Ave	Mesa	AZ	85202	**866-532-4983**	480-461-7000	160
Mesa Laboratories Inc						
12100 W Sixth Ave	Lakewood	CO	80228	**800-992-6372***	303-987-8000	470
NASDAQ: MLAB ■ *Sales						
Mesa State College						
1100 N Ave	Grand Junction	CO	81501	**800-982-6372**	970-248-1020	166
Mesa Systems Inc						
681 Railroad Blvd	Grand Junction	CO	81505	**800-654-3225**	888-229-1409	357-2

Listing	Toll-Free	Phone	Class
Mesabi Range Community & Technical College 1100 Industrial Pk Dr PO Box 648 ... Eveleth MN 55734	**800-657-3860**	218-741-3095	160
Mesco Bldg Solutions 5244 Bear Creek Ct ... Irving TX 75061	**800-556-3726**	214-687-9999	104
MESDA (Museum of Early Southern Decorative Arts) 924 S Main St ... Winston-Salem NC 27101	**800-441-5303**	336-721-7360	513
Mesirow Financial Inc 350 N Clark St ... Chicago IL 60610	**888-681-0082**	312-595-6000	681
Mesirow Financial Private Equity 350 N Clark St ... Chicago IL 60610	**800-453-0600**	312-595-6000	780
Meskwaki Bingo Hotel Casino 1504 305th St ... Tama IA 52339	**800-728-4263**		132
Mesquite Chamber of Commerce 617 N Ebrite St ... Mesquite TX 75149	**800-541-2355**	972-285-0211	137
Mesquite Public Library 300 W Grubb Dr ... Mesquite TX 75149	**866-797-8268**	972-216-6220	431-3
MessageBank LLC 250 W 57Th St Ste 1001 ... New York NY 10107	**800-989-8001**	212-333-9300	384
Messenger, The 713 Central Ave ... Fort Dodge IA 50501	**800-622-6613**	515-573-2141	525-2
Messiah College PO Box 3005 ... Grantham PA 17027	**800-233-4220**	717-691-6000	166
Mesta Electronics Inc 11020 Parker Dr ... North Huntingdon PA 15642	**800-535-6798**	412-754-3000	757
MET (Michigan Education Trust) PO Box 30198 ... Lansing MI 48909 *General	**800-638-4543***	517-335-4767	716
Meta Health Technology Inc 330 Seventh Ave 14th Fl ... New York NY 10001	**800-334-6840**	212-695-5870	179-11
Metafile Information Systems Inc 2900 43rd St NW ... Rochester MN 55901 *Sales	**800-638-2445***	507-286-9232	179-11
Metal Box International 11600 W King St ... Franklin Park IL 60131 *General	**800-622-2697***	847-455-8500	483
Metal Cladding Inc 230 S Niagara St ... Lockport NY 14094	**800-432-5513**		476
Metal Koting - Continuous Colour Coat Ltd 1430 Martin Grove Rd ... Rexdale ON M9W4Y1	**855-656-8464**	416-743-7980	476
Metal Marketplace International (MMI) 718 Sansom St ... Philadelphia PA 19106	**800-523-9191**	215-592-8777	408
Metal Powder Industries Federation (MPIF) 105 College Rd E ... Princeton NJ 08540	**800-443-4862**	609-452-7700	48-13
Metal Supermarkets IP Inc 520 Abilene Dr Second Fl ... Mississauga ON L5T2H7	**866-867-9344**	905-362-8226	487
Metalex Corp 1530 Artaius Pkwy PO Box 399 ... Libertyville IL 60048	**800-323-0792**	847-362-8300	714
Metal-Fab Inc 3025 May St ... Wichita KS 67213	**800-835-2830**	316-943-2351	688
Metalico Annaco Inc 943 Hazel St ... Akron OH 44305	**800-966-1499**	330-376-1400	677
Metallic Arts Inc 914 N Lake Rd ... Spokane WA 99212	**800-541-3200**	509-489-7173	767
Metals Week 2 Penn Plaza ... New York NY 10121	**800-752-8878**		524-13
Metalworking Group Inc 9070 Pippin Rd ... Cincinnati OH 45251	**800-476-9409**	513-521-4114	482
Metalworking Lubricants Co 25 Silverdome Industrial Park ... Pontiac MI 48342	**800-394-5494**	248-332-3500	534
Metcut Research Inc 3980 Rosslyn Dr ... Cincinnati OH 45209	**800-966-2888**	513-271-5100	732
Meteor Crater & Museum of Astrogeology Exit 233 Off I-40 Meteor Crater Rd ... Winslow AZ 86047	**800-289-5898**		513
Metglas Inc 440 Allied Dr ... Conway SC 29526	**800-581-7654**	843-349-7319	480
Methanex Corp 1800 Waterfront Centre 200 Burrard St ... Vancouver BC V6C3M1 *TSE: MX*	**800-661-8851**	604-661-2600	142
Methanol Institute (MI) 4100 Fairfax Dr Ste 740 ... Arlington VA 22203	**888-275-0768**	703-248-3636	47-12
Methapharm Inc 11772 W Sample Rd ... Coral Springs FL 33065	**800-287-7686**	954-341-0795	238
Methode Electronics Inc 7401 W Wilson Ave ... Chicago IL 60706 *NYSE: MEI*	**877-316-7700**	708-867-6777	253
Methodist Alliance Hospice 6400 Shelby View Dr Ste 101 ... Memphis TN 38134	**800-541-8277**	901-516-1999	368
Methodist ElderCare Services 5155 N High St ... Columbus OH 43214	**855-636-2225**	614-396-4990	663
Methodist Healthcare Ministries of South Texas Inc 4507 Medical Dr ... San Antonio TX 78229	**800-959-6673**	210-692-0234	350
Methodist Hospital 1305 N Elm St ... Henderson KY 42420	**888-318-1498**	270-827-7700	371-3
Methodist Hospital of Southern California 300 W Huntington Dr ... Arcadia CA 91007	**888-388-2838**	626-898-8000	371-3
Methodist Hospitals of Dallas 1441 N Beckley Ave ... Dallas TX 75203	**800-725-9664**	214-947-8181	350
Methodist Manor House 1001 Middleford Rd ... Seaford DE 19973	**800-775-4593**	302-629-4593	663
Methodist Rehabilitation Ctr 1350 E Woodrow Wilson Dr ... Jackson MS 39216	**800-223-6672**	601-981-2611	371-6
Methodist Theological School in Ohio 3081 Columbus Pk ... Delaware OH 43015	**800-333-6876**	740-363-1146	167-3
Methodist University 5400 Ramsey St ... Fayetteville NC 28311	**800-488-7110**	910-630-7000	166
METI (Medical Education Technologies Inc) 6300 Edgelake Dr ... Sarasota FL 34240	**866-462-7920**	941-377-5562	250
MetLife Inc 200 Pk Ave ... New York NY 10166 *NYSE: MET*	**800-638-5433**	212-578-2211	388-2
MetLife Investors Insurance Co Five Pk Plz Ste 1900 ... Irvine CA 92614	**800-848-3854**		388-2
Metl-Span LLC 1720 Lakepointe Dr Ste 101 ... Lewisville TX 75057	**877-585-9969**	972-221-6656	104
Met-Pro Corp Fybroc Div 700 Emlen Way ... Telford PA 18969	**800-392-7621**	215-723-8155	632
Met-Pro Corp Sethco Div 800 Emlen Way ... Telford PA 18969	**800-645-0500**	215-799-2577	632
Met-Pro Corp Systems Div 160 Cassell Rd PO Box 144 ... Harleysville PA 19438	**800-621-0734**	215-723-9300	18
Metra Electronics Corp 460 Walker St ... Holly Hill FL 32117 *Sales	**800-221-0932***	386-257-1186	51
MetraPark PO Box 2514 ... Billings MT 59103	**800-366-8538**	406-256-2400	206
MetraPark Arena 308 Sixth Ave N ... Billings MT 59101	**800-366-8538**	406-256-2400	711
Metric Machining Co 1425 S Vineyard Ave ... Ontario CA 91761	**800-937-9311**	909-947-9222	614
Metrix Instrument Co 8824 Fallbrook Dr ... Houston TX 77064	**800-638-7494**	713-461-2131	467
Metro - Sales Inc 1640 E 78th St ... Minneapolis MN 55423	**800-862-7414**	612-861-4000	111
Metro Creative Graphics Inc 519 Eigth Ave ... New York NY 10018	**800-223-1600**	212-947-5100	341
Metro Energy Group 1011 Hudson Ave ... Ridgefield NJ 07657	**800-951-2941**	201-941-3470	315
Metro Ford Inc 9000 NW Seventh Ave ... Miami FL 33150	**877-811-9402**		56
Metro Health Hospital 5900 Byron Ctr Ave ... Wyoming MI 49519	**800-968-0051**	616-252-7200	371-3
Metro Jackson Convention & Visitors Bureau 111 E Capitol St Ste 102 ... Jackson MS 39202	**800-354-7695**	601-960-1891	207
Metro Metals Northwest 5611 NE Columbia Blvd ... Portland OR 97218	**800-610-5680**	503-287-8861	677
Metro North Chamber of Commerce 14583 Orchard Pkwy Ste 300 ... Westminster CO 80023	**877-888-8811**	303-288-1000	137
Metro Pavia Health System Inc MaraMar Plz Bldg Avenida San Patricio Ste 950-960 ... Guaynabo PR 00968	**888-882-0882**		360
Metro Pulse 602 S Gay St Ste Mezzanine ... Knoxville TN 37902	**800-686-4208**	865-522-5399	525-5
Metro South Chamber of Commerce 60 School St ... Brockton MA 02301	**877-777-4414**	508-586-0500	137
Metro Storage LLC 13528 Boulton Blvd ... Lake Forest IL 60045 *Cust Svc	**888-498-1660***	847-235-8900	791-3
Metro Times 733 St Antoine St ... Detroit MI 48226	**866-501-3627**	313-961-4060	525-5
Metro West Chamber of Commerce 1671 Worcester Rd Ste 201 ... Framingham MA 01701	**866-709-9401**	508-879-5600	137
Metro Wire & Cable Co 6636 Metropolitan Pkwy ... Sterling Heights MI 48312	**800-633-1432**	586-264-3050	246
MetroHealth Medical Ctr 2500 MetroHealth Dr ... Cleveland OH 44109	**800-554-5251**	216-778-7800	371-3
Metrolina Greenhouses Inc 16400 Huntersville-Concord Rd ... Huntersville NC 28078	**800-543-3915**	704-875-1371	366
Metrolina Steel Inc 2601 Westinghouse Blvd ... Charlotte NC 28273	**800-849-7935**	704-598-7007	487
Metromedia Energy Inc 6 Industrial Way W ... Eatontown NJ 07724	**800-828-9427**	732-542-7575	775
Metromont Corp PO Box 2486 ... Greenville SC 29602	**888-295-0383**	864-295-0295	184
Metroplex Hospital 2201 S Clear Creek Rd ... Killeen TX 76549	**800-926-7664**	254-526-7523	371-3
Metropolis Magazine 61 W 23rd St Fourth Fl ... New York NY 10010	**800-344-3046**	212-627-9977	452-2
Metropolitan Ceramics 1201 Millerton St SE ... Canton OH 44707	**800-325-3945**		741
Metropolitan College of New York 431 Canal St ... New York NY 10013	**800-338-4465**	212-343-1234	166
Metropolitan Community College PO Box 3777 ... Omaha NE 68103	**800-228-9553**	402-457-2400	160
Metropolitan Community College Penn Valley 3201 SW Trafficway ... Kansas City MO 64111	**866-676-6224**	816-759-4000	160
Metropolitan Correctional Ctr *Chicago* 71 W Van Buren St ... Chicago IL 60605	**877-623-8426**	312-322-0567	
Metropolitan Health Networks Inc 777 Yamato Rd Ste 510 ... Boca Raton FL 33431 *NYSE: MDF*	**800-221-5487**	561-805-8500	458
Metropolitan Hotel Vancouver 645 Howe St ... Vancouver BC V6C2Y9	**800-667-2300**	604-687-1122	376
Metropolitan Milwaukee Assn of Commerce 756 N Milwaukee St ... Milwaukee WI 53202	**800-362-9472**	414-287-4100	137
Metropolitan Museum of Art 1000 Fifth Ave ... New York NY 10028	**800-468-7386**	212-879-5500	513
Metropolitan Nashville Public Schools (MNPS) 2601 Bransford Ave ... Nashville TN 37204	**800-848-0298**	615-259-8531	676
Metropolitan Plant & Flower Exchange 2125 Fletcher Ave ... Fort Lee NJ 07024	**800-638-7613**	201-944-1050	292
Metropolitan Poultry & Seafood Co 1920 Stanford Ct ... Landover MD 20785	**800-522-0060**	301-772-0060	296-10
Metropolitan State University 700 E Seventh St ... Saint Paul MN 55106	**888-234-2690**	651-793-1300	166
Metropolitan Trucking Inc (MRTK) 299 Market St Ste 300 ... Saddle Brook NJ 07663	**800-967-3278**		444
Metropolitan Tucson Convention & Visitors Bureau 100 S Church Ave ... Tucson AZ 85701	**800-638-8350**	520-624-1817	207
Metropolitan Vacuum Cleaner Co Inc one Ramapo Ave PO Box 149 ... Suffern NY 10901	**800-822-1602**	845-357-1600	776
Metrosonics 1060 Corporate Ctr Dr ... Oconomowoc WI 53066	**800-245-0779**	262-567-9157	467
Metrotech Corp 3251 Olcott St ... Santa Clara CA 95054	**800-446-3392**	408-734-1400	467
Metro-Tel Corp 11640 Arbor St Ste 100 ... Omaha NE 68144	**888-998-8300**	402-498-2964	725
MetroWest Medical Ctr 115 Lincoln St ... Framingham MA 01702	**800-357-6060**	508-383-1000	371-3
Metterra Hotel on Whyte 10454 82nd Ave ... Edmonton AB T6E4Z7	**866-465-8150**	780-465-8150	376
Mettler Electronics Corp 1333 S Claudina St ... Anaheim CA 92805	**800-854-9305**	714-533-2221	472
Mettler-Toledo International Inc 5 Barr Rd ... Ithaca NY 14850	**800-836-0836**		675
Metzgar Conveyor Co Inc 901 Metzgar Dr NW ... Comstock Park MI 49321	**888-266-8390**	616-784-0930	208
Mexican Restaurants Inc 1135 Edgebrook St ... Houston TX 77034 *OTC: CASA*	**800-444-2090**	713-943-7574	661
Mexico 2 UN Plaza 28th Fl ... New York NY 10017	**800-553-3210**	212-752-0220	

	Toll-Free	Phone	Class
Consulate General			
4506 Carolinas St Houston TX 77004	**877-639-4835**	713-271-6800	257
Mexico Plastics Company (Inc)			
2000 W Blvd Mexico MO 65265	**800-325-0216**		65
Mexico Tourism Board (CSTM)			
225 N Michigan Ave Ste 1800 Chicago IL 60601	**800-446-3942***		765
*General			
Meyer & Lundahl			
2345 W Lincoln St Phoenix AZ 85009	**800-264-9286**	602-254-9286	190-2
Meyer & Najem Inc			
13099 Parkside Dr Fishers IN 46038	**888-578-5131**	317-577-0007	187
Meyer Assoc Inc			
14 Seventh Ave N Saint Cloud MN 56303	**800-676-9233**	320-259-4000	727
Meyer Corp 1 Meyer Pl Vallejo CA 94590	**800-888-3883***	707-551-2800	481
*Cust Svc			
Meyer Jabara Hotels			
1601 Belvedere Rd			
Ste 407 S West Palm Beach FL 33406	**877-696-8671**	561-689-6602	376
Meyer Plastics Inc			
5167 E 65th St Indianapolis IN 46220	**800-968-4131**	317-259-4131	595
Meyerland Plaza			
420 Meyerland Plaza Houston TX 77096	**888-675-2275**	713-349-0245	455
Meyers Printing Cos Inc, The			
7277 Boone Ave N Minneapolis MN 55428	**800-927-9709**	763-533-9730	619
Meziere Enterprises Inc			
220 S Hale Ave Escondido CA 92029	**800-208-1755**	760-746-3273	476
MF Cachat Co			
14725 Detroit Ave Ste 300 Lakewood OH 44107	**800-729-8900**	216-228-8900	144
MFJ Enterprises Inc			
300 Industrial Pk Rd Starkville MS 39759	**800-647-1800**	662-323-5869	638
MFS Investment Management			
500 Boylston St Boston MA 02116	**877-960-6077**	617-954-5000	398
MGA Entertainment Inc			
16300 Roscoe Blvd Ste 150 Van Nuys CA 91406	**800-222-4685**	818-894-2525	751
MGBW (Mitchell Gold & Bob Williams Co)			
135 One Comfortable Pl Taylorsville NC 28681	**800-789-5401**	828-632-9200	318-2
MGM Grand Detroit			
1777 Third St Detroit MI 48226	**877-888-2121**	313-465-1400	132
MGM Grand Garden Arena			
3799 Las Vegas Blvd S Las Vegas NV 89109	**800-646-9143**	702-891-1111	711
MGM Grand Hotel & Casino			
3799 Las Vegas Blvd S Las Vegas NV 89109	**877-880-0880**	702-891-1111	660
MGM Mirage Design Group Inc			
3260 Industrial Rd Las Vegas NV 89109	**800-929-1111**	702-650-7400	187
MGM Transformer Co			
5701 Smithway St Commerce CA 90040	**800-423-4366**	323-726-0888	757
MGMA (Medical Group Management Assn)			
104 Inverness Terr E Englewood CO 80112	**877-275-6462**	303-799-1111	48-8
MGP Ingredients Inc			
100 Commercial St PO Box 130 Atchison KS 66002	**800-255-0302**	913-367-1480	295-23
NASDAQ: MGPI			
Mgs Inc			
178 Muddy Creek Church Rd Denver PA 17517	**800-952-4228**	717-336-7528	90
MHA (Mental Health America)			
2000 N Beauregard St			
Sixth Fl Alexandria VA 22311	**800-969-6642***	703-684-7722	47-17
*Help Line			
MHC Kenworth			
1524 N Corrington Ave Kansas City MO 64120	**888-259-4826**	816-483-7035	768
MHI (Manufactured Housing Institute)			
2101 Wilson Blvd Ste 610 Arlington VA 22201	**800-505-5500**	703-558-0400	48-3
MHI PAC (Manufactured Housing Institute PAC)			
1655 N Ft Myer Dr Ste 104 Arlington VA 22209	**800-505-5500**	703-558-0400	608
MHIA (Material Handling Industry of America)			
8720 Red Oak Blvd Ste 201 Charlotte NC 28217	**800-345-1815**	704-676-1190	48-13
MHM Services Inc			
1593 Spring Hill Rd Ste 600 Vienna VA 22182	**800-416-3649**	703-749-4600	458
MHNet Behavioral Health			
9606 N MoPac Exwy Ste 600 Austin TX 78759	**888-646-6889**		457
MHP Inc (Maximum Human Performance Inc)			
21 Dwight Pl Fairfield NJ 07004	**888-783-8844**	973-785-9055	787
MHPARC (Memorial Hermann Prevention & Recovery Ctr)			
3043 Gessner Houston TX 77080	**800-464-7272**	713-939-7272	371-5
MHRI (Memorial Hospital of Rhode Island)			
111 Brewster St Pawtucket RI 02860	**800-647-4362**	401-729-2000	371-3
MHS (Memorial Health System)			
1400 E Boulder St Colorado Springs CO 80909	**877-422-3648**	719-365-5000	371-3
MI (Methanol Institute)			
4100 Fairfax Dr Ste 740 Arlington VA 22203	**888-275-0768**	703-248-3636	47-12
MI Windows & Doors Inc			
650 W Market St Gratz PA 17030	**800-727-0835**	717-365-3300	234
MIA (Marble Institute of America)			
28901 Clemens Rd Ste 100 Westlake OH 44145	**800-433-4903**	440-250-9222	48-3
Miami Beach Chamber of Commerce			
1920 Meridian Ave 3rd Fl Miami Beach FL 33139	**800-501-0401**	305-672-1270	137
Miami Beach Resort & Spa			
4833 Collins Ave Miami Beach FL 33140	**866-765-9090**	305-532-3600	660
Miami Children's Hospital			
3100 SW 62nd Ave Miami FL 33155	**800-432-6837**	305-666-6511	371-1
Miami City Ballet			
2200 Liberty Ave Miami Beach FL 33139	**877-929-7010**	305-929-7000	566-1
Miami Corp, The			
720 Anderson Ferry Rd Cincinnati OH 45238	**800-543-0448**	513-451-6700	587
Miami County Chamber of Commerce			
13 E Main St Peru IN 46970	**800-521-9945**	765-472-1923	137
Miami International Airport Hotel			
NW 20th St & Le Jeune Rd Miami FL 33122	**800-327-1276**	305-871-4100	376
Miami International University of Art & Design			
1501 Biscayne Blvd Miami FL 33132	**800-225-9023**	305-428-5700	162
Miami Project to Cure Paralysis			
1095 NW 14th Terr			
Lois Pope LIFE Ctr Miami FL 33136	**800-782-6387***	305-243-6001	659
*General			
Miami Today			
710 Brickell Ave Miami FL 33131	**800-283-2707**	305-358-2663	525-4
Miami University			
501 E High St Oxford OH 45056	**866-426-4643**	513-529-1809	166
Middletown			
4200 E University Blvd Middletown OH 45042	**877-898-4656**	513-727-3200	166
Miami Valley Hospital			
One Wyoming St Dayton OH 45409	**800-544-0630***	937-208-8000	371-3
*All			
Miami-Cass County Rural Electric Membership Corp			
3086 W 100 N PO Box 168 Peru IN 46970	**800-844-6668***	765-473-6668	245
*General			
MIBRO Group			
111 Sinnott Rd Toronto ON M1L4S6	**866-941-9006**	416-285-9000	748
MIC (Micro Instrument Corp)			
1199 Emerson St PO Box 60619 Rochester NY 14606	**800-200-3150**	585-458-3150	449
Micah Group			
389 Waller Ave Ste 210 Lexington KY 40504	**877-260-7760**	859-260-7760	193
Micato Safaris			
15 W 26th St 11th Fl New York NY 10010	**800-642-2861**	212-545-7111	750
Michael Angelo's Gourmet Foods Inc			
200 Michael Angelo Way Austin TX 78728	**877-482-5426**	512-218-3500	295-36
Michael Baker Corp			
100 Airsite Dr			
Airsite Business Pk Moon Township PA 15108	**800-553-1153**	412-269-6300	261
NYSE: BKR			
Michael C Fina Inc			
545 Fifth Ave New York NY 10022	**800-289-3462**	212-557-2500	359
Michael C. Fina Corporate Sales			
3301 Hunters Point Ave Long Island City NY 11101	**800-999-3462**		194
Michael Foods Inc			
301 Carlson Pkwy Ste 400 Minnetonka MN 55305	**800-328-5474**	952-258-4000	612
Michael Gibson Gallery			
157 Carling St London ON N6A1H5	**866-644-2766**	519-439-0451	41
Michael J Fox Foundation for Parkinson's Research			
Grand Central Stn PO Box 4777 New York NY 10163	**800-708-7644**		304
Michael Lewis Co			
8900 W 50th St McCook IL 60525	**800-323-8808**	708-688-2200	85
Michael Ramey & Assoc Inc			
PO Box 744 Danville CA 94526	**800-321-0505**		397
Michael Weining Inc			
124 Crosslake Pk Dr			
PO Box 3158 Mooresville NC 28117	**877-548-0929**	704-799-0100	808
Michael's Finer Meats & Seafoods			
3775 Zane Trace Dr Columbus OH 43228	**800-282-0518**	614-527-4900	296-9
Michael's Transportation Service Inc			
140 Yolano Dr Vallejo CA 94589	**800-295-2448***	707-643-2099	108
*Cust Svc			
Michaels Stores Inc			
8000 Bent Branch Dr Irving TX 75063	**800-642-4235***	972-409-1300	44
*Cust Svc			
Michelangelo Hotel			
152 W 51st St New York NY 10019	**800-237-0990**	212-765-1900	376
Michelin North America Inc			
1 PkwyS PO Box 19001 Greenville SC 29602	**800-847-3435***	864-458-5000	744
*Cust Svc			
Michels Corp			
817 W Main St Brownsville WI 53006	**877-297-8663**	920-583-3132	189-10
Michel-schlumberger Partners LP			
4155 Wine Creek Rd Healdsburg CA 95448	**800-447-3060**	707-433-7427	79-3
Michigan			
Attorney General			
525 W Ottawa St Lansing MI 48933	**877-765-8388**	517-373-1110	337-23
Child Support Office			
235 S Grand Ave PO Box 30037 Lansing MI 48933	**866-661-0005**		337-23
Civil Service Dept			
Capitol Commons Ctr			
400 S Pine St Lansing MI 48913	**800-788-1766**	517-373-3030	337-23
Community Health Dept			
Capitol View Bldg			
201 Townsend St Lansing MI 48913	**800-649-3777**	517-373-3740	337-23
Crime Victims Services Commission			
320 S Walnut St Garden Level			
Lewis Cass Bldg Lansing MI 48913	**877-251-7373**		337-23
Economic Development Corp (MEDC)			
300 N Washington Sq Lansing MI 48913	**888-522-0103**	517-373-9808	337-23
eLibrary Information			
702 W Kalamazoo St PO Box 30007 Lansing MI 48909	**877-479-0021**	517-373-4331	337-23
Financial & Insurance Regulation			
PO Box 30220 Lansing MI 48909	**877-999-6442**	517-373-0220	337-23
Parks & Recreation Div			
PO Box 30257 Lansing MI 48909	**800-447-2757***	517-373-9900	337-23
*Campground Resv			
Travel Michigan			
300 N Washington Sq Lansing MI 48913	**888-784-7328**	517-373-0670	337-23
Michigan Assn of Realtors			
720 N Washington Ave Lansing MI 48906	**800-454-7842**	517-372-8890	647
Michigan Bar Journal			
306 Townsend St Lansing MI 48933	**888-726-3678**	517-346-6300	452-15
Michigan Career Education & Workforce Programs			
201 N Washington Sq			
Victor Office Center Lansing MI 48913	**888-253-6855**	517-335-5858	337-23
Michigan Chamber of Commerce			
600 S Walnut St Lansing MI 48933	**800-748-0266**	517-371-2100	138
Michigan Community Blood Centers			
1036 Fuller Ave NE Grand Rapids MI 49503	**866-642-5663**	616-774-2300	88
Michigan Community Blood Centers Northwest			
2575 Aero Pk Dr Traverse City MI 49686	**866-642-5663***	231-935-3030	88
*General			
Michigan Dental Assn			
3657 Okemos Rd Ste 200 Okemos MI 48864	**800-589-2632**	517-372-9070	227
Michigan Education Trust (MET)			
PO Box 30198 Lansing MI 48909	**800-638-4543***	517-335-4767	716
*General			
Michigan Fluid Power Inc			
4556 Spartan Industrial Dr SW Grandville MI 49418	**800-635-0289**	616-538-5700	383
Michigan Insurance Co			
1700 E Beltline Ne			
P.O. Box 152120, Suite 100 Grand Rapids MI 49515	**888-606-6426**	616-447-3600	387
Michigan International Speedway			
12626 US 12 Brooklyn MI 49230	**800-354-1010**	517-592-6666	508
Michigan Mfg Technology Ctr			
47911 Halyard Dr Plymouth MI 48170	**888-414-6682**		659
Michigan Millers Mutual Insurance Co			
2425 E Grand River Ave			
PO Box 30060 Lansing MI 48912	**800-888-1914**		388-4
Michigan Municipal League			
1675 Green Rd PO Box 1487 Ann Arbor MI 48105	**800-653-2483**	734-662-3246	47-5
Michigan Nurses Assn (MNA)			
2310 Jolly Oak Rd Okemos MI 48864	**888-646-8773**	517-349-5640	526

Name / Address	City	State	Zip	Toll-Free	Phone	Class
Michigan Out-of-Doors Magazine (MOOD) 2101 Wood St PO Box 30235	Lansing	MI	48912	**800-777-6720**	517-371-1041	452-22
Michigan Pharmacists Assn 815 N Washington Ave	Lansing	MI	48906	**866-226-2952**	517-484-1466	578
Michigan Stadium 1201 S Main St University of Michigan	Ann Arbor	MI	48104	**866-296-6849**	734-647-2583	711
Michigan State University College of Law 368 Law College Bldg	East Lansing	MI	48824	**800-844-9352**	517-432-6810	167-1
Michigan State University Library 100 Library	East Lansing	MI	48824	**800-500-1554**	517-353-8700	431-6
Michigan Student Financial Services Bureau Austin Bldg 430 W Allegan *General	Lansing	MI	48922	**800-642-5626***	888-447-2687	716
Michigan Technological University 1400 Townsend Dr	Houghton	MI	49931	**888-688-1885**	906-487-2335	166
Michigan Technological University J R Van Pelt Library 1400 Townsend Dr	Houghton	MI	49931	**877-688-2586**	906-487-2507	431-6
Michigan Theater 603 E Liberty St	Ann Arbor	MI	48104	**800-745-3000**	734-668-8397	565
Michigan Theological Seminary 41550 E Ann Arbor Trail	Plymouth	MI	48170	**800-356-6639**	734-207-9581	167-3
Michigan Wheel Corp 1501 Buchanan Ave SW	Grand Rapids	MI	49507	**800-369-4335**	616-452-6941	383
Mickey Thompson Tires 4600 Prosper Dr	Stow	OH	44224	**800-222-9092**	330-928-9092	744
Mickey Truck Bodies Inc 1305 Trinity Ave PO Box 2044	High Point	NC	27261	**800-334-9061**	336-882-6806	769
Mico Inc 1911 Lee Blvd	North Mankato	MN	56003	**800-477-6426**	507-625-6426	383
Micrel Inc 2180 Fortune Dr *NASDAQ: MCRL*	San Jose	CA	95131	**800-538-8450**	408-944-0800	687
Micro 100 Tool Corp 1410 E Pine Ave	Meridian	ID	83642	**800-421-8065**	208-888-7310	488
Micro Care Corp 595 John Downey Dr	New Britain	CT	06051	**800-638-0125**	860-827-0626	149
Micro Control Co 7956 Main St NE	Minneapolis	MN	55432	**800-328-9923**	763-786-8750	248
Micro Electronics, Inc. 2701 Charter St Ste A	Columbus	OH	43228	**877-636-9793**	614-326-8500	174-1
Micro Express Inc Eight Hammond Dr Ste 105	Irvine	CA	92618	**800-989-9900**	949-460-9911	174-1
Micro Industries Corp 8399 Green Meadow Dr N	Westerville	OH	43081	**800-722-1842**	740-548-7878	617
Micro Instrument Corp (MIC) 1199 Emerson St PO Box 60619	Rochester	NY	14606	**800-200-3150**	585-458-3150	449
Micro Matic USA Inc 10726 N Second St	Machesney Park	IL	61115	**866-291-5756**	815-968-7557	655
Micro Motion Inc 7070 Winchester Cir	Boulder	CO	80301	**800-522-6277**	303-530-8400	202
Micro Plastics Inc 11 Industry Ln Hwy 178 N PO Box 149	Flippin	AR	72634	**800-466-1467**	870-453-2261	601
Micro Power Electronics Inc 13955 SW Millikan Way	Beaverton	OR	97005	**866-233-4553**	503-693-7600	73
Micro Solutions Enterprises (MSE) 8201 Woodley Ave	Van Nuys	CA	91406	**800-673-4968**	818-407-7500	620
Micro Surface Engr Inc 1550 E Slauson Ave	Los Angeles	CA	90011	**800-322-5832**	323-582-7348	480
MicroAire Surgical Instruments Inc 3590 Grand Forks Blvd	Charlottesville	VA	22911	**800-722-0822**		471
MicroBilt Corp 1640 Airport Rd Ste 115	Kennesaw	GA	30144	**800-884-4747**		179-10
MicroBiz Corp 655 Oak Grove Ave Ste 493 Ste 493	Menlo Park	CA	94025	**800-937-2289**	702-749-5353	179-1
Microboards Technology LLC 8150 Mallory Ct PO Box 846	Chanhassen	MN	55317	**800-646-8881**	952-556-1600	174-8
Microchip Technology Inc 2355 West Chandler Blvd *NASDAQ: MCHP*	Chandler	AZ	85224	**877-860-3951**	480-792-7200	687
Micro-coax Inc 206 Jones Blvd	Pottstown	PA	19464	**800-223-2629**	610-495-0110	253
MicroFinancial Inc 16 New England Executive Pk Ste 200 *NASDAQ: MFI*	Burlington	MA	01803	**877-868-3800**	781-994-4800	216
Microfluidics International Corp 30 Ossipee Rd PO Box 9101	Newton	MA	02464	**800-370-5452**	617-969-5452	297
MicroGroup Inc Seven Industrial Pk Rd	Medway	MA	02053	**800-255-8823**	508-533-4925	588
Microlink Enterprise Inc 20955 Pathfinder Rd Ste 100	Diamond Bar	CA	91765	**800-829-3688**	562-205-1888	179-1
Micromatic LLC 525 Berne St	Berne	IN	46711	**800-333-5752**	260-589-2136	223
Micromeritics Instrument Corp 1 Micromeritics Dr	Norcross	GA	30093	**800-229-5052**	770-662-3620	416
MicroMetl Corp 3035 N Shadeland Ave Ste 300	Indianapolis	IN	46226	**800-662-4822**		655
MicroMod Automation Inc 75 Town Centre Dr	Rochester	NY	14623	**800-480-1975**	585-321-9200	202
Micron Technology Inc 8000 S Federal Way *NASDAQ: MU*	Boise	ID	83707	**888-363-2589**	208-368-4000	617
Micronesia *Consulate* 1725 N St NW Ste 910	Washington	DC	20036	**877-730-9753**	202-223-4383	257
Microphor Inc 452 E Hill Rd *Orders	Willits	CA	95490	**800-358-8280***	707-459-5563	604
Micro-Poise Measurment Systems LLC 1624 Englewood Ave	Akron	OH	44305	**800-428-3812**	330-784-1251	383
Micropump Inc 1402 NE 136th Ave *Sales	Vancouver	WA	98684	**800-222-9565***	360-253-2008	632
Micros Systems Inc 7031 Columbia Gateway Dr *NASDAQ: MCRS*	Columbia	MD	21046	**800-937-2211**	443-285-6000	607
Microsemi Corp 2381 Morse Ave *NASDAQ: MSCC*	Irvine	CA	92614	**800-713-4113**	949-221-7100	687
Microsoft Great Plains Business Solutions 3900 Great Plains Dr S	Fargo	ND	58104	**888-477-7877**	701-281-6500	179-1
Microsoft Press one Microsoft Wy *Cust Svc	Redmond	WA	98052	**800-642-7676***	425-882-8080	628-2
MicroStrategy 1850 Towers Crescent Plz *NASDAQ: MSTR*	Tysons Corner	VA	22182	**888-266-0321**	703-848-8600	179-11
Microtech Computers Inc 4921 Legends Dr *Tech Supp	Lawrence	KS	66049	**800-828-9533***	785-841-9513	174-1
Microtek Medical Holdings Inc 13000 Deerfield Pkwy Ste 300	Alpharetta	GA	30004	**800-777-7977**	678-896-4400	472
Microtek Medical Inc 512 N Lehmberg Rd	Columbus	MS	39702	**800-824-3027**	662-327-1863	472
MicroVention Inc 1311 Valencia Ave	Tustin	CA	92780	**800-990-8368**	714-247-8000	472
MicroVision Development Inc 5541 Fermi Ct Ste 120	Carlsbad	CA	92008	**800-998-4555**	760-438-7781	179-8
Microvision Inc 6222 185th Ave NE *NASDAQ: MVIS*	Redmond	WA	98052	**888-822-6847**	425-936-6847	537
MicroVote General Corp 6366 Guilford Ave	Indianapolis	IN	46220	**800-257-4901**	317-257-4900	789
MICS (Management Information Control Systems Inc) 2025 Ninth St	Los Osos	CA	93402	**800-838-6427**	805-543-7000	179-10
Mid America Computer Corp PO Box 700	Blair	NE	68008	**800-622-2502**	402-426-6222	225
Mid America Motorworks 17082 N Us Hwy 45 PO Box 1368	Effingham	IL	62401	**866-350-4543**	217-540-4200	60
Mid Coast Hospital 123 Medical Ctr Dr	Brunswick	ME	04011	**800-994-6610**	207-729-0181	371-3
Mid Ohio Energy Co-op Inc 555 W Franklin St	Kenton	OH	43326	**888-382-6732**	419-673-7289	245
Mid Penn Bancorp Inc 349 Union St *NASDAQ: MPB*	Millersburg	PA	17061	**866-642-7736**	717-692-2133	357-2
Mid Pines Inn & Golf Club 1010 Midland Rd	Southern Pines	NC	28387	**800-747-7272**	910-692-2114	660
Mid Seven Transportation Co 2323 Delaware Ave	Des Moines	IA	50317	**800-247-7448**	515-266-5181	770
MID-AM Bldg Supply Inc 1615 Omar Bradley Dr PO Box 645	Moberly	MO	65270	**800-892-5850**	660-263-2140	192-3
Midamar Corp PO Box 218	Cedar Rapids	IA	52406	**800-362-3711**	319-362-3711	296-9
Mid-America Charter Lines 2513 E Higgins Rd	Elk Grove Village	IL	60007	**800-323-0312**	847-437-3779	106
Mid-America College of Funeral Science (MACFS) 3111 Hamburg Pk	Jeffersonville	IN	47130	**800-221-6158**	812-288-8878	788
Mid-America Merchandising Inc 204 W Third St	Kansas City	MO	64105	**800-333-6737**	816-471-5600	9
Midamerica National Bancshares 100 W Elm St	Canton	IL	61520	**877-647-5050**	309-647-5000	69
MidAmerica Nazarene University 2030 E College Way	Olathe	KS	66062	**800-800-8887**	913-782-3750	166
Mid-America Publishing Corp 9 Second St NW	Hampton	IA	50441	**800-558-1244**	641-456-2585	628-8
Mid-America Reformed Seminary 229 Seminary Dr	Dyer	IN	46311	**888-440-6277**	219-864-2400	167-3
Mid-America Transplant Services (MTS) 1110 Highlands Plz Dr E Ste 100	Saint Louis	MO	63110	**888-376-4854**	314-735-8200	538
Mid-American Coaches Inc 4530 Hwy 47	Washington	MO	63090	**866-944-8687**		750
Midas International Corp 1300 Arlington Heights Rd	Itasca	IL	60143	**800-621-8545**	630-438-3000	61-3
Mid-Atlantic Christian Universit 715 N Poindexter St	Elizabeth City	NC	27909	**866-996-6228**	252-334-2070	159
Mid-Atlantic Convenience Stores LLC 1011 Boulder Springs Dr Ste 100	Richmond	VA	23225	**877-468-7797**	804-706-4702	323
Mid-Atlantic PenFed Realty Berkshire Hathaway HomeServices (PCR) 3050 Chain Bridge Rd	Fairfax	VA	22030	**800-550-2364**	703-691-7653	646
Mid-Carolina Electric Co-op Inc PO Box 669 *Cust Svc	Lexington	SC	29071	**888-813-8000***	803-749-6555	245
Midcom Corp 1275 N Manassero St Ste 200	Anaheim	CA	92807	**800-737-1632**	714-630-1999	712
Midcontinent Communications PO Box 5010	Sioux Falls	SD	57117	**800-888-1300**	605-274-9810	115
Mid-Continent Concrete Co PO Box 3878	Tulsa	OK	74102	**800-225-5422**	918-582-8111	183
Mid-Continent Group 1437 S Boulder Ave W PO Box 1409	Tulsa	OK	74119	**800-722-4994**	918-587-7221	388-4
Mid-Continent Public Library 15616 E 24 Hwy	Independence	MO	64050	**800-318-2596**	816-836-5200	431-3
Mid-Continent Safety 8225 E 35th St N *General	Wichita	KS	67226	**800-776-0956***	316-522-0900	670
Mid-Continent University 99 Powell Rd E	Mayfield	KY	42066	**888-628-4723**	270-247-8521	166
Mid-Continental Restoration Company Inc 401 E Hudson Rd PO Box 429	Fort Scott	KS	66701	**800-835-3700**	620-223-3700	190-7
Middle Bass Island State Park 1719 Fox Rd	Middle Bass Island	OH	43446	**866-644-6727**	419-285-0311	558
Middle Georgia Electric Membership Corp 600 Tippettville Rd	Vienna	GA	31092	**800-342-0144**	229-268-2671	245
Middle River Aircraft Systems (MRAS) 103 Chesapeake Pk Plaza	Baltimore	MD	21220	**877-432-3272**	410-682-1500	22
Middle Tennessee Medical Ctr 1700 Medical Center Pkwy *General	Murfreesboro	TN	37129	**800-400-5800***	615-396-4100	371-3
Middle Tennessee Mental Health Institute 221 Stewarts Ferry Pike	Nashville	TN	37214	**800-770-8277**	615-902-7400	371-5
Middle Tennessee Natural Gas Utility District (MTNG) 1036 W Broad St PO Box 670	Smithville	TN	37166	**800-880-6373**	615-597-4300	775
Middle Tennessee State University 1301 E Main St *Admissions	Murfreesboro	TN	37132	**800-433-6878***	615-898-2111	166
Middlebury College 131 S Main St	Middlebury	VT	05753	**877-214-3330**	802-443-3000	166
Middlebury College Library 110 Storrs Ave	Middlebury	VT	05753	**800-829-1040**	802-443-5494	431-6

	Toll-Free	Phone	Class
Middlebury Community Schools			
57853 Northridge Dr . . . . Middlebury IN 46540	**866-632-9992**	574-825-9425	676
Middleby Corp			
1400 Toastmaster Dr . . . . Elgin IL 60120	**800-331-5842**	847-741-3300	297
NASDAQ: MIDD			
Middlesboro Coca-Cola Bottling Works Inc			
1324 Cumberland Ave			
PO Box 1485. . . . . Middlesboro KY 40965	**800-442-0102**	877-692-4679	79-2
Middlesex County College			
2600 Woodbridge Ave PO Box 3050. . . . . . . Edison NJ 08818	**888-442-4551**	732-548-6000	160
Middlesex Hospital			
28 Crescent St . . . . Middletown CT 06457	**800-548-2394**	860-358-6000	371-3
Middlesex Mutual Assurance Co			
213 Ct St PO Box 891. . . . . Middletown CT 06457	**800-622-3780**		388-4
Middlesex Research Mfg Company Inc			
27 Apsley St . . . . Hudson MA 01749	**800-424-5188**	978-562-3697	734-2
Middlesex Savings Bank			
120 Flanders Rd . . . . Westborough MA 01581	**877-463-6287**	508-653-0300	69
Middlesex Water Co			
1500 Ronson Rd PO Box 1500. . . . . Iselin NJ 08830	**800-549-3802**	732-634-1500	775
NASDAQ: MSEX			
Middlesex West Chamber of Commerce			
179 Great Road Suite 104B. . . . . Acton MA 01720	**800-439-0183**	978-263-0010	137
Middleton Place			
4300 Ashley River Rd . . . . Charleston SC 29414	**800-782-3608**	843-556-6020	662
MidFirst Bank			
PO Box 76149. . . . . Oklahoma City OK 73147	**888-643-3477**	405-943-8002	69
Mid-Island Electrical Supply			
59 Mall Dr . . . . Commack NY 11725	**877-324-2636**	631-864-4242	246
Mid-Kansas Co-op Assn (MKC)			
117 N Edwards Ave . . . . Moundridge KS 67107	**800-864-4428**	620-345-6361	47-2
Mid-Lakes Distributing Inc			
1029 W Adams St . . . . Chicago IL 60607	**888-733-2700**	312-733-1033	605
Midland Area Chamber of Commerce			
300 Rodd St Ste 101. . . . . Midland MI 48640	**800-715-0074**	989-839-9901	137
Midland Chamber of Commerce			
109 N Main St . . . . Midland TX 79701	**800-624-6435**	432-683-3381	137
Midland Co			
7000 Midland Blvd . . . . Amelia OH 45102	**800-759-9008**	800-543-2644	357-4
Midland County Convention & Visitors Bureau			
300 Rodd St Ste 101. . . . . Midland MI 48640	**800-444-9979**	989-839-0340	207
Midland Daily News			
124 McDonald St . . . . Midland MI 48640	**877-411-2762**	989-835-7171	525-2
Midland Hospice Care			
200 SW Frazier Cir . . . . Topeka KS 66606	**800-491-3691**	785-232-2044	368
Midland Industries Inc			
1424 N Halsted St . . . . Chicago IL 60642	**800-662-8228**	312-664-7300	480
Midland Information Resources Co			
5440 Corporate Pk Dr . . . . Davenport IA 52807	**800-232-3696**	563-359-3696	619
Midland Memorial Hospital			
2200 W Illinois Ave . . . . Midland TX 79701	**800-833-2916**	432-685-1111	371-3
Midland Mortgage Co			
PO Box 26648 . . . . Oklahoma City OK 73126	**800-654-4566**		502
Midland National Bank			
527 N Main . . . . Newton KS 67114	**800-810-9457**	316-283-1700	69
Midland National Life Insurance Co			
One Sammons Plz . . . . Sioux Falls SD 57193	**800-923-3223**	605-335-5700	388-2
Midland Paper			
101 E Palatine Rd . . . . Wheeling IL 60090	**800-323-8522**	847-777-2700	546
Midland Power Co-op			
1005 E Lincolnway PO Box 420 . . . . Jefferson IA 50129	**800-833-8876**	515-386-4111	245
Midland Reporter-Telegram			
PO Box 1650 . . . . Midland TX 79702	**800-542-3952**	432-682-5311	525-2
Midland University			
900 N Clarkson St . . . . Fremont NE 68025	**800-642-8382**	402-941-6270	166
Midlands Technical College			
PO Box 2408 . . . . Columbia SC 29202	**800-922-8038**	803-738-1400	160
MidMichigan Home Care			
3007 N Saginaw Rd . . . . Midland MI 48640	**800-852-9350**	989-633-1400	368
Midnight Rose Hotel & Casino			
256 E Bennett Ave . . . . Cripple Creek CO 80813	**800-635-5825**	719-689-2446	132
Midnight Sun Adventure Travel			
1027 Pandora Ave . . . . Victoria BC V8V3P6	**800-255-5057**	250-480-9409	750
Mid-Ohio Aviation			
6250 N Honeytown Rd . . . . Smithville OH 44677	**800-669-4243**	330-669-2671	62
Mid-Ohio Sports Car Course			
7721 Steam Corners Rd			
PO Box 3108. . . . . Lexington OH 44904	**800-643-6446**	419-884-4000	508
Midrange Software Inc			
12716 Riverside Dr . . . . Studio City CA 91607	**800-737-6766**	818-762-8539	179-10
MidSouth Bancorp Inc			
102 Versailles Blvd . . . . Lafayette LA 70501	**800-213-2265**	337-237-8343	357-2
NYSE: MSL			
Mid-South Wire Company Inc			
1070 Visco Dr . . . . Nashville TN 37210	**800-714-7800**	615-743-2850	800
Midstate College			
411 W Northmoor Rd . . . . Peoria IL 61614	**800-251-4299**	309-692-4092	788
Midstate Electric Co-op Inc			
16755 Finley Butte Rd . . . . La Pine OR 97739	**800-722-7219**	541-536-2126	245
Mid-State Equipment Inc			
W 1115 Bristol Rd . . . . Columbus WI 53925	**877-677-4020**	920-623-4020	274
Mid-State Machine Products Inc			
83 Verti Dr . . . . Winslow ME 04901	**800-341-4672**	207-873-6136	747
Mid-States Bolt & Screw Co			
4126 Somers Dr . . . . Burton MI 48529	**800-482-0867**	810-744-0123	278
Mid-States Supply Co			
1716 Guinotte Ave . . . . Kansas City MO 64120	**800-825-1410**	816-842-4290	605
Midtown Hotel			
220 Huntington Ave . . . . Boston MA 02115	**800-343-1177**	617-262-1000	376
Midway College			
512 E Stephens St . . . . Midway KY 40347	**800-755-0031**	859-846-5346	166
Midwesco Filter Resources Inc			
385 Battaile Dr . . . . Winchester VA 22601	**800-336-7300**	540-667-8500	18
Midwest America Federal Credit Union			
1104 Medical Pk Dr . . . . Fort Wayne IN 46825	**800-348-4738**	260-482-3334	219
Midwest Bank			
105 E Soo St PO Box 40. . . . . . Parkers Prairie MN 56361	**877-365-5155**	218-338-6054	69
Midwest Canvas Corp			
4635 W Lake St . . . . Chicago IL 60644	**800-433-4701***	773-287-4400	723
*General			
Midwest Communications Inc			
904 Grand Ave . . . . Wausau WI 54403	**877-945-4236**	715-842-1437	634
Midwest Corporate Aviation			
3512 N Webb Rd . . . . Wichita KS 67226	**800-435-9622**	316-636-9700	62
Midwest Dental Equipment Services & Supplies			
2700 Commerce St . . . . Wichita Falls TX 76301	**800-766-2025**		228
Midwest EAP Solutions Inc			
1015 W St Germain St			
Ste 440 . . . . Saint Cloud MN 56301	**800-383-1908**	320-253-1909	457
Midwest Elastomers Inc			
700 Industrial Dr PO Box 412. . . . . . Wapakoneta OH 45895	**800-786-3539**	419-738-8844	598-3
Midwest Electric Co-op Corp			
104 Washington Ave . . . . Grant NE 69140	**800-451-3691**	308-352-4356	245
Midwest Employers Casualty Co			
14755 N Outer 40 Dr			
Ste 300 . . . . Chesterfield MO 63017	**877-975-2667**	636-449-7000	388-4
Midwest Energy Co-op			
901 E State St . . . . Cassopolis MI 49031	**800-492-5989**		245
Midwest Energy Inc			
1330 Canterbury Dr . . . . Hays KS 67601	**800-222-3121**	785-625-3437	245
Midwest Eye Banks			
4889 Venture Dr . . . . Ann Arbor MI 48108	**800-247-7250**	734-780-2100	269
Midwest Folding Products Inc			
1414 S Western Ave . . . . Chicago IL 60608	**800-621-4716**	312-666-3366	318-3
Midwest Helicopter Airways Inc			
525 Executive Dr . . . . Willowbrook IL 60527	**800-323-7609**	630-325-7860	356
MIDWEST Homes for Pets			
3142 S Cowan Rd PO Box 1031. . . . . . . Muncie IN 47302	**800-428-8560**	765-289-3355	571
Midwest Industries Inc			
122 E State Hwy 175 . . . . Ida Grove IA 51445	**800-859-3028**	712-364-3365	753
Midwest Library Service Inc			
11443 St Charles Rock Rd . . . . Bridgeton MO 63044	**800-325-8833**	314-739-3100	94
Midwest Living Magazine			
1716 Locust St . . . . Des Moines IA 50309	**800-678-8093**	515-284-3808	452-22
Midwest Mechanical Group			
801 Parkview Blvd . . . . Lombard IL 60148	**800-214-3680**	630-850-2300	190-10
Midwest Metal Products Co			
2100 W Mt Pleasant Rd . . . . Muncie IN 47302	**888-741-1044**		475
Midwest Motor Express Inc			
5015 E Main Ave . . . . Bismarck ND 58502	**800-741-4097**	701-223-1880	770
Midwest Plan Service			
122 Davidson Hall ISU . . . . Ames IA 50011	**800-562-3618**	515-294-4337	628-2
Midwest Pro Painting Inc			
12845 Farmington Rd . . . . Livonia MI 48150	**800-860-6757**	734-427-1040	190-8
Midwest Products Company Inc			
400 S Indiana St . . . . Hobart IN 46342	**800-348-3497***	219-942-1134	752
*Orders			
Midwest Quality Gloves Inc			
835 Industrial Rd . . . . Chillicothe MO 64601	**800-821-3028**	660-646-2165	153-7
Midwest Regional Medical Ctr			
2825 Parklawn Dr . . . . Midwest City OK 73110	**877-456-9617**	405-610-4411	371-3
Midwest Sales & Service Inc			
917 S Chapin St . . . . South Bend IN 46601	**800-772-7262**	574-287-3365	37
Midwest Specialized Transportation Inc			
PO Box 6418 . . . . Rochester MN 55903	**800-927-8007**		444
Mid-West Spring & Stamping Co			
1404 Joliet Rd Unit C . . . . Romeoville IL 60446	**800-619-0909**	630-739-3800	710
Mid-West Steel Bldg Co			
7301 Fairview . . . . Houston TX 77041	**800-777-9378**	713-466-7788	104
Midwest Systems			
5911 Hall St . . . . Saint Louis MO 63147	**800-383-6281**	314-389-6280	769
Midwest Tile & Concrete Products Inc			
4309 Webster Rd . . . . Woodburn IN 46797	**800-359-4701**	260-749-5173	184
Midwest Tool & Cutlery Co Inc			
1210 Progress St PO Box 160 . . . . Sturgis MI 49091	**800-782-4659**	269-651-7964	222
Midwest Towers Inc			
1156 Hwy 19 East . . . . Chickasha OK 73018	**800-900-2190**	405-224-4622	14
Midwest Truck & Auto Parts Inc			
1001 W Exchange . . . . Chicago IL 60609	**800-934-2727**	773-247-3400	60
Midwest Walnut Co			
1914 Postevin St . . . . Council Bluffs IA 51503	**800-592-5688**	712-325-9191	443
Midwest Wire Products Inc			
800 Woodward Heights . . . . Ferndale MI 48220	**800-989-9881**	248-399-5100	72
Midwest Wire Products LLC			
649 S Lansing Ave			
PO Box 770. . . . . Sturgeon Bay WI 54235	**800-445-0225**	920-743-6591	483
Midwestern Baptist Theological Seminary			
5001 N Oak Trafficway . . . . Kansas City MO 64118	**877-414-3720**	816-414-3700	167-3
Midwestern Industries Inc			
915 Oberlin Rd SW . . . . Massillon OH 44647	**877-474-9464***	330-837-4203	191
*Cust Svc			
Midwestern Intermediate Unit Iv			
453 Maple St . . . . Grove City PA 16127	**800-942-8035**	724-458-6700	676
Midwestern Regional Medical Ctr (MRMC)			
2520 Elisha Ave . . . . Zion IL 60099	**800-615-3055**	847-872-4561	371-7
Midwestern State University			
3410 Taft Blvd . . . . Wichita Falls TX 76308	**800-842-1922***	940-397-4000	166
*Admissions			
MidWestOne Financial Group Inc			
102 S Clinton St PO Box 1700 . . . . . . Iowa City IA 52240	**800-247-4418***	319-356-5800	357-2
*NASDAQ: MOFG ■ *Cust Svc			
Miele Inc			
9 Independence Way . . . . Princeton NJ 08540	**800-843-7231**	609-419-9898	35
MIF (Milk Industry Foundation)			
1250 H St NW Ste 900 . . . . Washington DC 20005	**866-225-4821**	202-737-4332	47-2
Mifflinburg Bank & Trust Co (MBTC)			
250 E Chestnut St			
PO Box 186. . . . . Mifflinburg PA 17844	**888-966-3131**	570-966-1041	69
Mighty Distributing System of America Inc			
650 Engineering Dr . . . . Norcross GA 30092	**800-829-3900**	770-448-3900	60
Mii Amo at Enchantment Resort			
525 Boynton Canyon Rd . . . . Sedona AZ 86336	**888-749-2137**	928-203-8500	698
Mijac Alarm			
9339 Charles Smith Ave			
Ste 100 . . . . Rancho Cucamonga CA 91730	**800-982-7612**	909-982-7612	684
Mikart Inc			
1750 Chattahoochee Ave NW . . . . Atlanta GA 30318	**888-464-5278**	404-351-4510	576
Mike Castrucci Ford Sales Inc			
1020 SR- 28 . . . . Milford OH 45150	**855-971-6897**	513-831-7010	509
Mike Durfee State Prison			
1412 Wood St . . . . Springfield SD 57062	**800-537-0025**	605-369-2201	213
Mike Murach & Assoc Inc			
4340 N Knoll . . . . Fresno CA 93722	**800-221-5528**	559-440-9071	628-2
Mike Reed Chevrolet			
1559 E Oglethorpe . . . . Hinesville GA 31313	**877-228-3943**		56
Mike Rose's Auto Body Inc			
2260 Via de Marcardos . . . . Concord CA 94520	**855-340-1739**	925-689-1739	61-4

Alphabetical Section

	Toll-Free	Phone	Class
Mike's Famous Harley-Davidson of Groton			
951 Bank St ....New London CT 06320	**800-326-6874**	860-574-9200	513
Miken Builders Inc			
32782 Cedar Dr Unit 1 ....Millville DE 19967	**800-888-7501**	302-537-4444	676
Mike-Sell's Potato Chip Co			
333 Leo St PO Box 115 ....Dayton OH 45404	**800-257-4742**	937-228-9400	295-35
Mikimoto (America) Company Ltd			
680 Fifth Ave Fourth Fl ......New York NY 10019	**800-223-4008**	212-457-4500	408
Mil Corp			
4000 Mitchellville Rd ....Bowie MD 20716	**800-875-0867**	301-805-8500	178
Mila Displays Inc			
1315B Broadway Ste 108 ......Hewlett NY 11557	**800-295-6452**	516-791-2643	5
Milaeger's Inc			
4838 Douglas Ave ....Racine WI 53402	**800-669-1229**	262-639-2040	322
Milan Express Company Inc			
1091 Ketauver Dr PO Box 699 ....Milan TN 38358	**800-231-7303**	731-686-7428	770
Milbank Tweed Hadley & McCloy LLP			
1 Chase Manhattan Plaza .....New York NY 10005	**800-229-0543**	212-530-5000	425
Milbar Hydro-Test Inc			
651 Aero Dr ....Shreveport LA 71107	**800-259-8210**	318-227-8210	532
Mile Marker International Inc			
2121 BLOUNT Rd ....Pompano Beach FL 33069	**800-886-8647**		60
Miles & More			
PO Box 946 ....Santa Clarita CA 91380	**800-581-6400**		26
Miles College			
5500 Myron Massey Blvd ....Fairfield AL 35064	**800-445-0708***	205-929-1000	166
*Admissions			
Miles Community College			
2715 Dickinson St ....Miles City MT 59301	**800-541-9281**	406-874-6100	160
Miles Kimball Co			
250 City Ctr Bldg ....Oshkosh WI 54906	**855-202-7394***	920-231-3800	454
*Cust Svc			
Miles Media Group Inc			
6751 Professional Pkwy W			
Ste 200 ....Sarasota FL 34240	**877-342-2424**	941-342-2300	628-9
MilesTek Corp			
1506 Interstate 35 W ....Denton TX 76207	**800-958-5173**	940-484-9400	195
Milestone Scientific Inc			
220 S Orange Ave ....Livingston NJ 07039	**800-862-1125**	973-535-2717	472
OTC: MLSS			
Milford Bank			
33 Broad St ....Milford CT 06460	**800-340-4862**	203-783-5700	69
Milford Daily News Co			
159 S Main St ....Milford MA 01757	**800-281-6498**	508-634-7522	628-8
Milford Federal Savings & Loan Assn			
PO Box 210 ....Milford MA 01757	**800-478-6990**	508-634-2500	70
Milford Mirror			
1000 Bridgeport Ave ....Shelton CT 06484	**800-372-2790***	203-402-2315	525-4
*Advestisement			
Milford-Miami Township Chamber of Commerce			
983 Lila Ave ....Milford OH 45150	**877-723-0513**	513-831-2411	137
Military & Aerospace Electronics Magazine			
98 Spit Brook Rd ....Nashua NH 03062	**866-423-4837**	847-763-9540	452-12
Military Benefit Assn (MBA)			
14605 Avion Pkwy			
PO Box 221110. ....Chantilly VA 20153	**800-336-0100**	703-968-6200	47-19
Military Engineer Magazine			
607 Prince St ....Alexandria VA 22314	**800-336-3097***	703-549-3800	452-12
*Cust Svc			
Military Officer Magazine			
201 N Washington St ....Alexandria VA 22314	**800-234-6622**	703-549-2311	452-12
Military Officers Assn of America (MOAA)			
201 N Washington St ....Alexandria VA 22314	**800-234-6622**	703-549-2311	47-19
Milk Industry Foundation (MIF)			
1250 H St NW Ste 900 ......Washington DC 20005	**866-225-4821**	202-737-4332	47-2
Milk Products LLC			
PO Box 150 ....Chilton WI 53014	**800-657-0793**	920-849-2348	295-10
Milk Specialties Co			
260 S Washington St .....Carpentersville IL 60110	**800-323-4274**	952-942-7310	442
Milkco Inc			
220 Deaverview Rd ....Asheville NC 28806	**800-842-8021**	828-254-9560	295-27
Mill Creek Mall			
654 Millcreek Mall ....Erie PA 16565	**800-615-3535**	814-868-9000	455
Mill Ridge Farm			
2800 Bowman Mill Rd ....Lexington KY 40513	**800-950-6397**	859-231-0606	365
Mill Steel Co			
5116 36th St SE ....Grand Rapids MI 49512	**800-247-6455**		714
Mill Street Inn			
75 Mill St ....Newport RI 02840	**800-392-1316**	401-849-9500	376
Mill Supply Div			
266 Morse St ....Hamden CT 06517	**888-585-9354***	203-777-7668	86
*General			
Millard Lumber Inc			
12900 I St PO Box 45445 ....Omaha NE 68145	**800-228-9260**	402-896-2800	192-3
Millcraft Paper Co			
6800 Grant Ave ....Cleveland OH 44105	**800-860-2482**	216-441-5500	546
Mille Lacs Band of Ojibwe			
43408 Oodena Dr ....Onamia MN 56359	**800-709-6445**	320-532-4181	131
Mille Lacs Electric Co-op			
PO Box 230 ....Aitkin MN 56431	**800-450-2191**	218-927-2191	245
Mille Lacs Health System			
200 Elm St N ....Onamia MN 56359	**877-535-3154**	320-532-3154	371-3
Millenium Aviation			
2365 Bernville Rd			
Reading Regional Airport ....Reading PA 19605	**800-366-9419**	610-372-4728	62
Millennium Broadway Hotel New York			
145 W 44th St ....New York NY 10036	**800-622-5569**	212-768-4400	374
Millennium Resort Scottsdale McCormick Ranch			
7401 N Scottsdale Rd ....Scottsdale AZ 85253	**800-243-1332**	716-681-2400	660
Miller & Chevalier Chartered			
655 15th St NW Ste 900 ....Washington DC 20005	**866-628-4282**	202-626-5800	425
Miller & Co LLC			
9700 W Higgins Rd Ste 1000 ....Rosemont IL 60018	**800-727-9847**	847-696-2400	495
Miller Bros Express LC			
560 West 400 North ....Hyrum UT 84319	**800-366-6239**	435-245-6025	444
Miller Chemical & Fertilizer Corp			
120 Radio Rd PO Box 333 ....Hanover PA 17331	**800-233-2040**	717-632-8921	280
Miller Electric Co			
2251 Rosselle St ....Jacksonville FL 32204	**877-540-2160***	904-513-2818	190-4
*Sales			
Miller Electric Mfg Co			
1635 W Spencer St ....Appleton WI 54914	**888-843-7693**	920-734-9821	798

	Toll-Free	Phone	Class
Miller Industries Inc			
8503 Hilltop Dr ....Ooltewah TN 37363	**800-292-0330**	423-238-4171	509
NYSE: MLR			
Miller Johnson Snell & Cummiskey PLC			
250 Monroe Ave NW Ste 800			
PO Box 306. ....Grand Rapids MI 49503	**866-667-6572**	616-831-1700	425
Miller Oil Co			
1000 E City Hall Ave ....Norfolk VA 23504	**800-333-4645**	757-623-6600	572
Miller Packing Co			
1122 Industrial Way PO Box 1390 ....Lodi CA 95241	**800-624-2328**	209-339-2310	295-26
Miller Pipeline Corp			
8850 Crawfordsville Rd ....Indianapolis IN 46234	**800-428-3742**	317-293-0278	189-10
Miller Products Company Inc			
2511 S Tricenter Blvd ....Durham NC 27713	**800-782-7437**	919-313-2100	569
Miller Saint Nazianz Inc			
511 E Main St ....Saint Nazianz WI 54232	**800-247-5557**	920-773-2121	273
Miller Transporters Inc			
5500 Hwy 80 W ....Jackson MS 39209	**800-645-5378***	601-922-8331	770
*Cust Svc			
Miller Travel Services Inc			
4380 W 12th St ....Erie PA 16505	**800-989-8747**	814-833-8888	761
Miller Valentine Group			
4000 Miller Valentine Ct ....Dayton OH 45439	**877-684-7687**	937-293-0900	646
Miller-Eads Company Inc			
4125 N Keystone Ave			
PO Box 55234. ....Indianapolis IN 46205	**800-530-0684**	317-545-7101	775
Miller-Lewis Benefit Consultants			
121 E Sixth Ave ....Lancaster OH 43130	**800-734-3198**	740-654-4055	387
Millers First Insurance Co			
111 E Fourth St ....Alton IL 62002	**800-558-0500**	618-463-3636	388-4
Miller-Stephenson Chemical Co			
55 Backus Ave ....Danbury CT 06810	**800-992-2424***	203-743-4447	143
*Tech Supp			
Millersville University of Pennsylvania			
One S George St			
PO Box 1002. ....Millersville PA 17551	**800-682-3648**	717-872-3011	166
Milligan College			
PO Box 500 ....Milligan College TN 37682	**800-262-8337**	423-461-8730	166
Milliken & Co KEX Div			
201 Lukken Industrial Dr W			
MS 801. ....LaGrange GA 30240	**800-241-4826**	706-880-5511	130
Milliken Millwork Inc			
6361 Sterling Dr N ....Sterling Heights MI 48312	**800-686-9218**	586-264-0950	494
Millikin University			
1184 W Main St ....Decatur IL 62522	**800-373-7733**	217-424-6211	166
Million Air			
4300 Westgrove Dr ....Addison TX 75001	**800-248-1602**	972-248-1600	62
Million Air Interlink Inc			
8501 Telephone Rd ....Houston TX 77061	**888-589-9059**	713-640-4000	24
Million Dollar Round Table (MDRT)			
325 W Touhy Ave ....Park Ridge IL 60068	**877-883-4865***	847-692-6378	48-9
*General			
Mill-Max Mfg Corp			
190 Pine Hollow Rd ....Oyster Bay NY 11771	**800-333-4237**	516-922-6000	802
Mill-Rose Co			
7995 Tyler Blvd ....Mentor OH 44060	**800-321-3533**	440-255-9171	102
Mills at Jersey Gardens, The			
651 Kapkowski Rd ....Elizabeth NJ 07201	**877-789-2327**	908-354-5900	455
Mills College			
5000 MacArthur Blvd ....Oakland CA 94613	**877-746-4557***	510-430-2135	166
*Admissions			
Mills House Hotel			
115 Meeting St ....Charleston SC 29401	**800-874-9600**	843-577-2400	376
Mills Iron Works Inc			
14834 Maple Ave ....Gardena CA 90248	**800-421-2281**	323-321-6520	588
Millsaps College			
1701 N State St ....Jackson MS 39210	**800-352-1050***	601-974-1000	166
*Admissions			
Millsite State Park			
Ferron Canyon Rd PO Box 1343 ......Huntington UT 84528	**800-322-3770**	435-384-2552	558
Milner Hotel Boston			
78 Charles St S ....Boston MA 02116	**877-645-6377**	617-426-6220	376
Milner Hotels Inc			
1538 Centre St ....Detroit MI 48226	**877-645-6377**	313-963-3950	376
Milner Technologies Inc			
5125 Peachtree Industrial Blvd ....Norcross GA 30092	**800-592-3766**	770-734-5300	179-1
Milpitas Post			
59 Marylinn Dr ....Milpitas CA 95035	**800-870-6397**	408-262-2454	525-4
Milsco Mfg Co			
9009 N 51st St ....Milwaukee WI 53223	**800-255-0337**	414-354-0500	680
Milton Academy			
170 Centre St ....Milton MA 02186	**866-645-8661**	617-898-1798	615
Milton Hershey School			
PO Box 830 ....Hershey PA 17033	**800-322-3248**	717-520-2100	615
Milton Transportation Inc			
5505 State Rt 405 PO Box 355 ....Milton PA 17847	**800-776-1150**	570-742-8774	770
Miltons Inc			
250 Granite St ....Braintree MA 02184	**800-645-8673**	781-848-1880	155-3
Milwaukee Area Technical College			
700 W State St ....Milwaukee WI 53233	**866-211-3380**	414-297-6600	788
Milwaukee Art Museum			
700 N Art Museum Dr ....Milwaukee WI 53202	**888-322-3326**	414-224-3200	513
Milwaukee Ballet			
504 W National Ave ....Milwaukee WI 53204	**888-612-3500**	414-643-7677	566-1
Milwaukee Brewers			
Miller Pk 1 Brewers Way ....Milwaukee WI 53214	**877-722-6458**	414-902-4452	704
Milwaukee Coast Guard Base			
2420 S Lincoln Memorial Dr ....Milwaukee WI 53207	**866-772-8724**	414-747-7100	156
Milwaukee Electric Tool Corp			
13135 W Lisbon Rd ....Brookfield WI 53005	**800-729-3878**	262-781-3600	749
Milwaukee Institute of Art & Design			
273 E Erie St ....Milwaukee WI 53202	**888-749-6423**	414-276-7889	166
Milwaukee Journal Sentinel			
333 W State St ....Milwaukee WI 53201	**800-456-5943**	414-224-2000	525-2
Milwaukee Magazine			
126 N Jefferson St ....Milwaukee WI 53202	**800-662-4818**	414-273-1101	452-22
Milwaukee Marble & Granite Co			
4535 W Mitchell St ....Milwaukee WI 53214	**877-645-6272**	414-645-0305	715
Milwaukee Public Library			
814 W Wisconsin Ave ....Milwaukee WI 53233	**866-947-7363**	414-286-3000	431-3
Milwaukee School of Engineering			
1025 N Broadway St ....Milwaukee WI 53202	**800-332-6763**	414-277-6763	166

	City	State	ZIP	Toll-Free	Phone	Class
Milwaukee Symphony Orchestra						
929 N Water St Ste 700	Milwaukee	WI	53202	**888-367-8101**	414-220-8322	566-3
Milwaukee Valve Company Inc						
16550 W Stratton Dr	New Berlin	WI	53151	**800-348-6544**	262-432-2800	777
Milwaukee Wave LLC						
510 W Kilbourn Ave	Milwaukee	WI	53203	**800-745-3000**	414-224-9283	708
Milwhite Inc						
5487 S Padre Island Hwy	Brownsville	TX	78521	**800-442-0082**	956-547-1970	498-2
MiMedx Group Inc						
1775 W Oak Commons Ct Ne	Marietta	GA	30062	**888-543-1917**		471
MIN (Media Industry Newsletter)						
110 William St 11th Fl	New York	NY	10038	**888-707-5814**	212-621-4880	524-11
Minam State Recreation Area						
72214 Marina Ln						
c/o Wallowa Lk Management Unit	Joseph	OR	97846	**800-551-6949**		558
Minco Inc						
510 Midway Cir	Midway	TN	37809	**800-525-9753**	423-422-6051	654
MindEdge Inc						
465 Waverley Oaks Rd Ste 202	Waltham	MA	02452	**877-592-8000**	781-250-1805	394
MindLeaders.com Inc						
5500 Glendon Ct Ste 200	Dublin	OH	43016	**800-223-3732**	614-781-7300	754
MindPlay Educational Software						
440 S Williams Blvd Ste 206	Tucson	AZ	85711	**800-221-7911**	520-888-1800	179-3
Mine & Mill Industrial Supply Company Inc						
2500 S Combee Rd	Lakeland	FL	33801	**800-282-8489**	863-665-5601	187
Mine Safety & Health Administration (MSHA)						
1100 Wilson Blvd	Arlington	VA	22209	**800-746-1553**	202-693-9400	338-13
Miner Enterprises Inc						
1200 E State St PO Box 471	Geneva	IL	60134	**888-822-5334**	630-232-3000	641
Mineral Resources International						
1990 W 3300 S	Ogden	UT	84401	**800-731-7866**	801-731-7040	296-8
Mineral Wells Area Chamber of Commerce						
511 E Hubbard St	Mineral Wells	TX	76067	**800-252-6989**	940-325-2557	137
Minerals Metals & Materials Society (TMS)						
184 Thorn Hill Rd	Warrendale	PA	15086	**800-759-4867**	724-776-9000	48-13
Minerva Networks Inc						
2150 Gold St	Santa Clara	CA	95002	**800-806-9594**	408-567-9400	638
Mingan Archipelago National Park Reserve of Canada						
1340 de la Digue St	Havre-Saint-Pierre	QC	G0G1P0	**877-737-3783**	418-538-3331	556
Mini-Circuits Laboratories Inc						
13 Neptune Ave	Brooklyn	NY	11235	**800-654-7949**	718-934-4500	687
Minka Group						
1151 W Bradford Ct	Corona	CA	92882	**800-221-7977**	951-735-9220	435
Minn-Dak Yeast Company Inc						
18175 Red River Rd W	Wahpeton	ND	58075	**800-348-0991**	701-642-3300	295-42
Minneapolis College of Art & Design						
2501 Stevens Ave	Minneapolis	MN	55404	**800-874-6223**	612-874-3760	162
Minneapolis Community & Technical College						
1501 Hennepin Ave	Minneapolis	MN	55403	**800-247-0911**	612-659-6200	160
Minneapolis Foundation						
80 S Eigth St 800 IDS Ctr	Minneapolis	MN	55402	**866-305-0543**	612-672-3878	302
Minneapolis Grain Exchange						
400 S Fourth St						
130 Grain Exchange Bldg	Minneapolis	MN	55415	**800-827-4746**	612-321-7101	682
Minneapolis Institute of Arts						
2400 Third Ave S	Minneapolis	MN	55404	**888-642-2787**	612-870-3000	513
Minneapolis Northwest						
6200 Shingle Creek Pkwy						
Ste 130	Brooklyn Center	MN	55430	**800-541-4364**	763-852-7500	207
Minneapolis Public Schools						
3345 Chicago Ave	Minneapolis	MN	55407	**800-543-7709**	612-668-0000	676
Minneapolis/St. Paul City Pages						
401 N Third St Ste 550	Minneapolis	MN	55401	**844-387-6962**	612-375-1015	525-5
Minneapolis-Saint Paul Magazine						
220 S Sixth St Ste 500	Minneapolis	MN	55402	**800-999-5589**	612-339-7571	452-22
Aging Board						
540 Cedar St	Saint Paul	MN	55155	**800-882-6262**	651-431-2500	337-24
Arts Board						
400 Sibley St Ste 200	Saint Paul	MN	55101	**800-866-2787**	651-215-1600	337-24
Minnesota						
Attorney General						
1400 Bremer Tower						
445 Minnesota St	Saint Paul	MN	55101	**800-657-3787**	651-296-3353	337-24
Attorney General's Office						
445 Minnesota St Ste 1400	Saint Paul	MN	55101	**800-657-3787**	651-296-3353	337-24
Employment & Economic Development Dept (DEED)						
1st National Bank Bldg 332 Minnesota St						
Ste E200	Saint Paul	MN	55101	**800-657-3858**	651-259-7114	337-24
Finance Dept						
658 Cedar St Ste 400	Saint Paul	MN	55155	**800-627-3529**	651-201-8000	337-24
Governor						
130 State Capitol						
75 Rev Dr Martin Luther King Jr Blvd	Saint Paul	MN	55155	**800-657-3717**	651-201-3400	337-24
Health Dept						
PO Box 64975	Saint Paul	MN	55164	**888-345-0823**	651-201-5000	337-24
Historical Society						
345 Kellogg Blvd W	Saint Paul	MN	55102	**800-657-3773**	651-259-3000	337-24
Housing Finance Authority						
400 Sibley St Ste 300	Saint Paul	MN	55101	**800-657-3769**	651-296-7608	337-24
Labor & Industry Dept						
443 Lafayette Rd N	Saint Paul	MN	55155	**800-342-5354**	651-284-5005	337-24
Legislature						
75 Constitution Ave						
State Capitol	Saint Paul	MN	55155	**800-657-3550**	651-296-2146	337-24
Medical Practice Board						
2829 University Ave SE						
Ste 500	Minneapolis	MN	55414	**800-657-3709**	612-617-2130	337-24
Natural Resources Dept						
500 Lafayette Rd	Saint Paul	MN	55155	**888-646-6367**	651-296-6157	337-24
Parks & Recreation Div						
500 Lafayette Rd	Saint Paul	MN	55155	**888-646-6367**	651-296-6157	337-24
Public Utilities Commission						
121 Seventh Pl E Ste 350	Saint Paul	MN	55101	**800-657-3782**	651-296-7124	337-24
Revenue Dept						
600 N Roberts St	Saint Paul	MN	55101	**800-652-9094**	651-296-3403	337-24
Transportation Dept						
395 John Ireland Blvd	Saint Paul	MN	55155	**800-657-3774**	651-296-3000	337-24
Workers" Compensation Div						
443 Lafayette Rd	Saint Paul	MN	55155	**800-342-5354**	651-284-5005	337-24
Minnesota Assn of Realtors						
5750 Lincoln Dr	Minneapolis	MN	55436	**800-862-6097**	952-935-8313	647
Minnesota Ballet						
301 W First St Ste 800	Duluth	MN	55802	**800-627-3529**	218-529-3742	566-1
Minnesota Campaign Finance & Public Disclosure Board						
658 Cedar St Ste 190	Saint Paul	MN	55155	**800-657-3889**	651-296-5148	265
Minnesota Chamber of Commerce						
400 Robert St N Ste 1500	Saint Paul	MN	55101	**800-821-2230**	651-292-4650	138
Minnesota Chemical Co						
2285 Hampden Ave	Saint Paul	MN	55114	**800-328-5689**	651-646-7521	424
Minnesota Conway						
575 Minnehaha Ave W St	Saint Paul	MN	55103	**800-223-2587**	651-251-1880	670
Minnesota Correctional Facility-Fairbault						
1101 Linden Ln	Faribault	MN	55021	**800-657-3830**	507-334-0700	213
Minnesota Dental Assn						
1335 Industrial Blvd						
Ste 200	Minneapolis	MN	55413	**800-950-3368**	612-767-8400	227
Minnesota Discovery Ctr						
1005 Discovery Dr	Chisholm	MN	55719	**800-372-6437**	218-254-7959	513
Minnesota Educator Magazine						
41 Sherburne Ave	Saint Paul	MN	55103	**800-652-9073**	651-227-9541	452-8
Minnesota Electric Supply Co						
1209 E Hwy 12	Willmar	MN	56201	**800-992-8830**	320-235-2255	246
Minnesota Eye Consultants PA						
710 E 24th St Ste 100	Minneapolis	MN	55404	**800-526-7632**	612-813-3600	786
Minnesota Historical Society History Ctr Museum						
345 Kellogg Blvd W	Saint Paul	MN	55102	**800-657-3773**	651-259-3001	513
Minnesota Lawyers Mutual Insurance Co						
333 S Seventh St Ste 2200	Minneapolis	MN	55402	**800-422-1370**		387
Minnesota Library Assn (MLA)						
1821 University Ave W						
Ste S256	Saint Paul	MN	55104	**877-867-0982**	651-999-5343	432
Minnesota Lions Eye Bank						
1000 Westgate Dr Ste 260	Saint paul	MN	55114	**866-887-4448***	612-625-5159	269
*Cust Svc						
Minnesota Medical Assn						
1300 Godward St NE Ste 2500	Minneapolis	MN	55413	**800-342-5662**	612-378-1875	469
Minnesota Medicine Magazine						
1300 Godward St NE Ste 2500	Minneapolis	MN	55413	**800-342-5662**	612-378-1875	452-16
Minnesota Nurses Assn (MNA)						
345 Randolph Ave Ste 200	Saint Paul	MN	55102	**800-536-4662**	651-646-4807	526
Minnesota Office of Higher Education						
1450 Energy Pk Dr Ste 350	Saint Paul	MN	55108	**800-657-3866**	651-642-0567	716
Minnesota Opera						
620 N First St	Minneapolis	MN	55401	**800-676-6737**	612-333-2700	566-2
Minnesota Orchestra						
1111 Nicollet Mall						
Orchestra Hall	Minneapolis	MN	55403	**800-292-4141**	612-371-5600	566-3
Minnesota Pharmacists Assn (MPhA)						
1935 W County Rd B2	Roseville	MN	55113	**800-451-8349**	651-697-1771	578
Minnesota Power						
30 W Superior St	Duluth	MN	55802	**800-228-4966**	218-722-2625	775
Minnesota Public Radio (MPR)						
480 Cedar St	Saint Paul	MN	55101	**800-228-7123**	651-290-1212	624
Minnesota State Bar Assn						
600 Nicollet Mall Ste 380	Minneapolis	MN	55402	**800-882-6722**	612-333-1183	71
Detroit Lakes						
900 Hwy 34E	Detroit Lakes	MN	56501	**800-492-4836**	218-846-3700	160
Minnesota State Community & Technical College						
Fergus Falls						
1414 College Way	Fergus Falls	MN	56537	**877-450-3322**	218-736-1500	160
Moorhead						
1900 28th Ave S	Moorhead	MN	56560	**800-426-5603**	218-299-6500	160
Mankato						
122 Taylor Ctr	Mankato	MN	56001	**800-722-0544***	507-389-1822	166
*Admissions						
Minnesota State University						
Moorhead						
1104 Seventh Ave S	Moorhead	MN	56563	**800-593-7246**	218-477-2161	166
Minnesota State University Mankato						
Memorial Library						
PO Box 8419	Mankato	MN	56002	**800-722-0544**	507-389-5952	431-6
Minnesota State University Moorhead Regional Science Ctr						
1104 Seventh Ave S	Moorhead	MN	56563	**800-593-7246**	218-477-2920	513
Minnesota Supply Company Inc						
6470 Flying Cloud Dr	Eden Prairie	MN	55344	**800-869-1028**	952-828-7300	382
Minnesota Timberwolves						
Target Ctr 600 First Ave N	Minneapolis	MN	55403	**855-895-0872**	612-673-1600	705-1
Minnesota Twins						
Metrodome						
34 Kirby Puckett Pl	Minneapolis	MN	55415	**800-338-9467**	612-375-1366	704
Minnesota Valley Co-op Light & Power Assn						
501 S First St	Montevideo	MN	56265	**800-247-5051**	320-269-2163	245
Minnesota Valley Electric Co-op						
125 Minnesota Vly Electric Dr						
PO Box 77024	Jordan	MN	55352	**800-282-6832**	952-492-2313	245
Minnesota Veterans Home-Minneapolis						
5101 Minnehaha Ave S	Minneapolis	MN	55407	**877-838-6757**	612-721-0600	781
Minnesota Veterans Home-Silver Bay						
45 Banks Blvd	Silver Bay	MN	55614	**877-729-8387**	218-226-6300	781
Minnesota Veterinary Medical Assn						
101 Bridgepoint Way						
Ste 100	South Saint Paul	MN	55075	**888-933-5363**	651-645-7533	783
Minnesota Vikings						
9520 Viking Dr	Eden Prairie	MN	55344	**877-722-6458**	952-828-6500	706-3
Minnesota West Community & Technical College						
1450 Collegeway	Worthington	MN	56187	**800-657-3966**	507-372-3400	160
Minnesota Wild						
317 Washington St	Saint Paul	MN	55102	**866-242-5006**	651-602-6000	707
Minnesota Wire & Cable Co						
1835 Energy Pk Dr	Saint Paul	MN	55108	**800-258-6922**	651-642-1800	802
Minnesota Zoo						
13000 Zoo Blvd	Apple Valley	MN	55124	**800-366-7811**	952-431-9200	810
Minntech Corp						
14605 28th Ave N	Minneapolis	MN	55447	**800-328-3345**	763-553-3300	471
Minor Rubber Company Inc						
49 Ackerman St	Bloomfield	NJ	07003	**800-433-6886**	973-338-6800	668
Minority Business Development Agency Regional Offices						
Chicago Region						
105 W Adams St Ste 2300	Chicago	IL	60603	**888-324-1551**	312-353-0182	338-2
Minot Convention & Visitors Bureau						
1020 S Broadway	Minot	ND	58701	**800-264-2626**	701-857-8206	207
Minot Daily News						
301 Fourth St SE	Mohall	ND	58761	**800-735-3119**	701-857-1900	525-2
Minot State University						
500 University Ave W	Minot	ND	58707	**800-777-0750**	701-858-3000	166
Minot State University Bottineau						
105 Simrall Blvd	Bottineau	ND	58318	**800-542-6866**	701-228-5451	160

	Toll-Free	Phone	Class
Minova USA Inc			
150 Carley Ct ....Georgetown KY 40324	800-626-2948	502-863-6800	598-2
Minskoff Theatre			
200 W 45th St ....New York NY 10036	800-714-8452	212-869-0550	736
Minson Corp			
1 Minson Way ....Montebello CA 90640	800-251-6537	323-513-1041	318-4
Minto Place Suite Hotel			
185 Lyons St N ....Ottawa ON K1R7X5	800-267-3377	613-232-2200	376
Minute Maid Park			
501 Crawford St ....Houston TX 77002	877-927-8767	713-259-8000	711
Minute Men Staffing Services			
3740 Carnegie Ave ....Cleveland OH 44115	877-873-8856	216-426-9675	712
Minuteman International Inc			
111 S Rohlwing Rd ....Addison IL 60101	800-323-9420	630-627-6900	383
Minuteman Press International Inc			
61 Executive Blvd ....Farmingdale NY 11735	800-645-3006	631-249-1370	309
Minuteman Trucks Inc			
2181 Providence Hwy ....Walpole MA 02081	800-231-8458	508-668-3112	770
Minwax Co			
10 Mountainview Rd ...Upper Saddle River NJ 07458	800-523-9299		543
MIR (Manager's Intelligence Report)			
316 N Michigan Ave Ste 400 ....Chicago IL 60601	800-878-5331		524-2
Mira Monte Inn & Suites			
69 Mt Desert St ....Bar Harbor ME 04609	800-553-5109		376
Mirabeau Park Hotel			
1100 N Sullivan Rd ......Spokane Valley WA 99037	866-584-4674	509-924-9000	376
Mirabito Fuel Group Inc			
49 Ct St PO Box 5306..........Binghamton NY 13902	800-934-9480	607-352-2800	315
Miracle Method US Corp			
4239 N Nevada Ave			
Ste 115..............Colorado Springs CO 80907	800-444-8827	719-594-9091	190-11
Miracle Mile Shops at Planet Hollywood			
3663 Las Vegas Blvd S ....Las Vegas NV 89109	888-800-8284	702-866-0703	49-5
Miracle Recreation Equipment Co			
878 Hwy 60 ....Monett MO 65708	800-523-4202	417-235-6917	343
Miracle-Ear Inc			
5000 Cheshire Pkwy N Ste 1 ....Minneapolis MN 55446	800-464-8002		472
Oceanside			
One Barnard Dr Ste 7 ....Oceanside CA 92056	888-201-8480	760-757-2121	160
MiraCosta College			
San Elijo			
3333 Manchester Ave ....Cardiff CA 92007	888-201-8480	760-944-4449	160
Mirage, The			
3400 Las Vegas Blvd S ....Las Vegas NV 89109	800-627-6667	702-791-7111	660
Miramar Federal Credit Union			
PO Box 261370 ....San Diego CA 92196	800-640-1228	858-695-9494	219
Miramont Castle Museum			
9 Capitol Hill Ave ....Manitou Springs CO 80829	888-685-1011	719-685-1011	513
Miramonte Resort & Spa			
45000 Indian Wells Ln ......Indian Wells CA 92210	800-237-2926	760-341-2200	660
Miraval AZ Resort & Spa			
5000 E Via Estancia Miraval ....Tucson AZ 85739	800-232-3969		697
Mirbeau Inn & Spa			
851 W Genesee St ....Skaneateles NY 13152	877-647-2328	315-685-5006	376
Mircom Technologies Ltd			
25 Interchange Way ....Vaughan ON L4K5W3	888-660-4655	905-660-4655	684
Mirror Image Internet Inc			
2 Highwood Dr ....Tewksbury MA 01876	800-353-2923	781-376-1100	179-7
Mirrotek International LLC			
90 Dayton Ave ....Passaic NJ 07055	888-659-3030	973-472-1400	537
Misericordia University			
301 Lake St ....Dallas PA 18612	866-262-6363	570-674-6400	166
Miss Elaine Inc			
8430 Valcour Ave ....Saint Louis MO 63123	800-458-1422	314-631-1900	153-14
MISS Foundation			
PO Box 5333 ....Peoria AZ 85385	888-455-6477	623-979-1000	47-21
Mission Ambulance			
1055 E Third St ....Corona CA 92879	800-899-9100		30
Mission Aviation Fellowship (MAF)			
112 N Pilatus Ln ....Nampa ID 83687	800-359-7623	208-498-0800	47-20
Mission Essential Personnel LLC			
4343 Easton Commons Ste 100 ....Columbus OH 43219	888-542-3447	614-416-2345	756
Mission Federal Credit Union			
PO Box 919023 ....San Diego CA 92121	800-500-6328	858-524-2850	219
Mission Foods			
1159 Cottonwood Ln Ste 200 ....Irving TX 75038	800-443-7994	972-232-5200	295-35
Mission Inn			
3649 Mission Inn Ave ....Riverside CA 92501	800-843-7755	951-784-0300	376
Mission Inn Resort & Club			
10400 County Rd 48 ....Howey in the Hills FL 34737	800-874-9053	352-324-3101	660
Mission Landscape Services Inc			
536 E Dyer Rd ....Santa Ana CA 92707	800-545-9963		419
Mission Mill Museum			
1313 Mill St SE ....Salem OR 97301	800-782-6724	503-585-7012	49-2
Mission of Nombre de Dios & Shrine of Our Lady of La Leche			
27 Ocean Ave ....Saint Augustine FL 32084	800-342-6529	904-824-2809	49
Mission Petroleum Carriers Inc			
8450 Mosley ....Houston TX 77075	800-737-9911	713-943-8250	463
Mission Pharmacal			
PO Box 786099 ....San Antonio TX 78278	800-531-3333	210-696-8400	576
Mission Pharmacy Services LLC			
201 N Jefferson St Ste 300 ....Kittanning PA 16201	877-758-2039		237
Mission Point Resort			
6633 Main St ....Mackinac Island MI 49757	800-833-7711		660
Mission Produce Inc			
2500 Vineyard Ave Ste 300..............Oxnard CA 93036	800-549-3420	805-981-3650	314-4
Mission Valley Ford Truck Sales Inc			
780 E Brokaw Rd PO Box 611150..San Jose CA 95112	888-284-7471	408-933-2300	56
Banking & Consumer Finance Dept			
PO Box 23729 ....Jackson MS 39225	800-844-2499	601-359-1031	337-25
Child Support Enforcement Div			
750 N State St ....Jackson MS 39202	800-345-6347	601-359-4929	337-25
Consumer Protection Div			
PO Box 22947 ....Jackson MS 39225	800-281-4418	601-359-4230	337-25
Contractors Board			
215 Woodline Dr Ste B..............Jackson MS 39232	800-880-6161	601-354-6161	337-25
Emergency Management Agency			
PO Box 5644 ....Pearl MS 39288	800-222-6362	601-933-6362	337-25
Family & Children Services Div			
750 N State St ....Jackson MS 39202	800-345-6347	601-359-4570	337-25
Higher Learning Institutions Board of Trustees			
3825 Ridgewood Rd Ste 915 ....Jackson MS 39211	800-327-2980	601-432-6198	337-25

	Toll-Free	Phone	Class
Mississippi			
Insurance Dept			
1001 Woolfolk State Office Bldg 501 NW St			
PO Box 79 ....Jackson MS 39201	800-562-2957	601-359-3569	337-25
Rehabilitation Services Dept			
1281 Highway 51 PO Box 1698.......Madison MS 39110	800-443-1000		337-25
State Government Information			
200 S Lamar St ....Jackson MS 39201	877-290-9487	601-351-5023	337-25
Mississippi Action For Progress Inc (MAP)			
1751 Morson Rd ....Jackson MS 39209	800-924-4615	601-923-4100	145
Mississippi Agriculture & Forestry Museum/National Agricultural Aviation Museum			
1150 Lakeland Dr ....Jackson MS 39216	800-844-8687	601-359-1100	513
Mississippi Assn of Realtors			
4274 Lakeland Dr PO Box 321000 ....Jackson MS 39232	800-747-1103	601-932-9325	647
Mississippi Authority for Educational Television			
3825 Ridgewood Rd ....Jackson MS 39211	800-850-4406	601-432-6565	624
Mississippi Blood Services			
115 Tree St ....Flowood MS 39232	888-902-5663	601-981-3232	88
Mississippi Business Journal			
200 N Congress St ....Jackson MS 39201	800-283-4625	601-364-1000	452-5
Mississippi Coast Coliseum & Convention Ctr			
2350 Beach Blvd ....Biloxi MS 39531	800-726-2781	228-594-3700	206
Mississippi College			
200 S Capitol St PO Box 4026 ....Clinton MS 39058	800-738-1236	601-925-3000	166
Mississippi County Electric Co-op			
510 N Broadway St ....Blytheville AR 72315	800-439-4563	870-763-4563	245
Mississippi Dental Assn			
2630 Ridgewood Rd Ste C ....Jackson MS 39216	866-982-0442	601-982-0442	227
Mississippi Economic Council			
PO Box 23276 ....Jackson MS 39225	800-748-7626	601-969-0022	138
Mississippi Employment Security Commission			
1235 Echelon Pkwy PO Box 1699.......Jackson MS 39215	888-844-3577	601-321-6000	259
Jackson County			
2300 Hwy 90 PO Box 100 ....Gautier MS 39553	866-735-1122	228-497-9602	160
Mississippi Gulf Coast Community College			
Jefferson Davis			
2226 Switzer Rd ....Gulfport MS 39507	866-735-1122	228-896-3355	160
Mississippi Gulf Coast Convention & Visitors Bureau			
2350 Beach Blvd Ste A ....Biloxi MS 39531	888-467-4853	228-896-6699	207
Mississippi Museum of Natural Science			
2148 Riverside Dr ....Jackson MS 39202	800-467-2757	601-576-6000	513
Mississippi Music Inc			
222 N Main St ....Hattiesburg MS 39401	800-844-5821	601-544-5821	518
Mississippi Pharmacists Assn			
341 Edgewood Terr Dr ....Jackson MS 39206	800-421-2408	601-981-0416	578
Mississippi River Museum			
125 N Front St ....Memphis TN 38103	800-507-6507	901-576-7241	513
Mississippi Sports Hall of Fame & Museum			
1152 Lakeland Dr ....Jackson MS 39216	800-280-3263	601-982-8264	515
Mississippi State Penitentiary			
Hwy 49 W PO Box 1057 ....Parchman MS 38738	800-844-0898	662-745-6611	213
Mississippi State Port Authority at Gulfport			
2510 14th St Ste 1450 ....Gulfport MS 39501	877-881-4367	228-865-4300	611
Mississippi State Veterans' Home Collins			
3261 Hwy 49 S ....Collins MS 39428	877-203-5632	601-765-0403	781
Mississippi State Veterans' Home Kosciusko			
310 Autumn Ridge Dr ....Kosciusko MS 39090	877-203-5632	662-289-7044	781
Mississippi Student Financial Aid Office			
3825 Ridgewood Rd ....Jackson MS 39211	800-327-2980	601-432-6997	716
Mississippi University for Women			
1100 College St MUW-1613 ....Columbus MS 39701	877-462-8439	662-329-4750	166
Mississippi Valley Equipment Company Inc			
1198 Pershall Rd ....Saint Louis MO 63137	800-325-8001	314-869-8600	355
Mississippi Valley Regional Blood Ctr			
5500 Lakeview Pkwy ....Davenport IA 52807	800-747-5401	563-359-5401	88
Mississippi Valley State University			
14000 Hwy 82 ....Itta Bena MS 38941	800-844-6885	662-254-9041	166
Mississippi Valley Title Insurance Co			
315 Tom Bigbee St ....Jackson MS 39201	800-647-2124	601-969-0222	388-6
Mississippi Welders Supply Co			
5150 W Sixth St PO Box 1036 ....Winona MN 55987	800-657-4422	507-454-5231	383
Missman Inc			
1011 27th Ave PO Box 6040.........Rock Island IL 61201	800-969-3029	309-788-7644	261
Missoula Area Chamber of Commerce			
825 E Front St ....Missoula MT 59802	800-814-2342	406-543-6623	137
Missoula Electric Co-op Inc			
1700 W Broadway ....Missoula MT 59808	800-352-5200	406-541-4433	245
Missoulian			
PO Box 8029 ....Missoula MT 59807	800-366-7102	406-523-5200	525-2
Child Support Enforcement Div			
PO Box 109002 ....Jefferson City MO 65102	800-859-7999		337-26
Consumer Protection Div			
207 W High St PO Box 899 ......Jefferson City MO 65102	800-392-8222	573-751-3321	337-26
Elementary & Secondary Education Dept			
205 Jefferson St			
PO Box 480 ....Jefferson City MO 65101	800-735-2966	573-751-4212	337-26
Finance Div			
PO Box 716 ....Jefferson City MO 65102	888-246-7225	573-751-3242	337-26
Missouri			
Higher Education Dept			
3515 Amazonas Dr ....Jefferson City MO 65109	800-473-6757	573-751-2361	337-26
Natural Resources Dept			
PO Box 176 ....Jefferson City MO 65102	800-361-4827*	573-751-3443	337-26
*Cust Svc			
Professional Registration Div			
3605 Missouri Blvd			
PO Box 1335 ....Jefferson City MO 65102	800-735-2966	573-751-0293	337-26
Public Service Commission			
200 Madison St			
PO Box 360 ....Jefferson City MO 65102	800-819-3180	573-751-3234	337-26
Securities Div			
600 W Main St			
PO Box 1276 ....Jefferson City MO 65102	800-721-7996	573-751-4704	337-26
State Courts Administrator			
PO Box 104480 ....Jefferson City MO 65110	888-541-4894		337-26
State Parks Div			
PO Box 176 ....Jefferson City MO 65102	800-334-6946	573-751-2479	337-26
Supreme Court			
207 W High St ....Jefferson City MO 65101	888-541-4894	573-751-4144	337-26
Tourism Div			
PO Box 1055 ....Jefferson City MO 65102	800-519-2100	573-751-4133	337-26
Transportation Dept			
105 W Capitol Ave ....Jefferson City MO 65102	888-275-6636	573-751-2551	337-26

	Toll-Free	Phone	Class
Vocational & Adult Education Div			
3024 Dupont Cir			
PO Box 480 .... Jefferson City MO 65109	**877-222-8963**	573-751-3251	337-26
Workers Compensation Div			
PO Box 58 .... Jefferson City MO 65102	**800-775-2667**	573-751-4231	337-26
Missouri Assn of Realtors			
2601 Bernadette Pl ....Columbia MO 65203	**800-403-0101**	573-445-8400	647
Missouri Baptist Hospital of Sullivan			
751 Sappington Bridge Rd .... Sullivan MO 63080	**866-888-8918**	573-468-4186	371-3
Missouri Baptist Medical Ctr			
3015 N Ballas Rd .... Saint Louis MO 63131	**800-392-0936**	314-996-5000	371-3
Missouri Baptist University			
One College Pk Dr .... Saint Louis MO 63141	**877-434-1115**	314-434-1115	166
Missouri Botanical Garden			
4344 Shaw Blvd .... Saint Louis MO 63110	**800-642-8842**	314-577-5100	96
Missouri Dental Assn			
3340 American Ave .... Jefferson City MO 65109	**800-688-1907**	573-634-3436	227
Missouri Enterprise			
1706 E 10th St .... Rolla MO 65401	**800-956-2682**		196
Missouri Fox Trotting Horse Breed Assn Inc			
PO Box 1027 .... Ava MO 65608	**877-663-4203**	417-683-2468	47-3
Missouri Gas Energy			
3420 Broadway .... Kansas City MO 64111	**800-582-1234**	816-756-5252	775
Missouri Lawyers Media			
319 N Fourth St .... Saint Louis MO 63102	**800-635-5297**	314-421-1880	628-8
Missouri Medicine Magazine			
PO Box 1028 .... Jefferson City MO 65102	**800-869-6762**	573-636-5151	452-16
Missouri River Regional Library			
214 Adams St .... Jefferson City MO 65101	**800-949-7323**	573-634-2464	431-3
Missouri Southern State University			
3950 Newman Rd .... Joplin MO 64801	**866-818-6778**	417-625-9300	166
Missouri Sports Hall of Fame			
3861 E Stan Musial Dr ....Springfield MO 65809	**800-498-5678**	417-889-3100	515
Missouri State Medical Assn			
113 Madison St .... Jefferson City MO 65101	**800-869-6762**	573-636-5151	469
Missouri State Parks			
PO Box 176 .... Jefferson City MO 65102	**800-334-6946**		558
Missouri State Teachers Assn			
407 S Sixth St ....Columbia MO 65201	**800-392-0532***	573-442-3127	452-8
General			
Missouri State University (MSU)			
901 S National Ave ....Springfield MO 65897	**800-492-7900**	417-836-5000	166
Missouri University of Science & Technology			
Rolla			
1870 Miner Cir G2 Parker Hall .... Rolla MO 65409	**800-522-0938**	573-341-4111	166
Missouri Valley College			
500 E College St .... Marshall MO 65340	**800-999-8219**	660-831-4000	166
Missouri Veterans Home-Cape Girardeau			
2400 Veterans Memorial Dr .... Cape Girardeau MO 63701	**800-392-0210**	573-290-5870	781
Missouri Veterinary Medical Assn			
2500 Country Club Dr .... Jefferson City MO 65109	**800-632-6900**	573-636-8612	783
Missouri Veterinary Medical Foundation Museum			
2500 Country Club Dr .... Jefferson City MO 65109	**800-632-6900**	573-636-8612	513
Missouri Vocational Enterprises			
1717 Industrial Dr			
PO Box 1898............... Jefferson City MO 65102	**800-392-8486***	573-751-6663	622
Sales			
Missouri Western State University			
4525 Downs Dr .... Saint Joseph MO 64507	**800-662-7041**	816-271-4266	166
Missourian Publishing Co			
14 W Main St .... Washington MO 63090	**888-239-7701**	636-239-7701	628-8
Mister Car Wash			
3561 E Sunrise Dr Ste 125 .... Tucson AZ 85718	**866-254-3229***	520-615-4000	61-1
Cust Svc			
Mister Money Investment			
2057 Vermont Dr .... Fort Collins CO 80525	**888-336-0403**	970-493-0574	139
Mister Safety Shoes Inc			
6-2300 Finch Ave W .... Toronto ON M9M2Y3	**800-707-0051**	416-746-3000	355
Misty Harbor & Barefoot Beach Resort			
118 Weirs Rd .... Gilford NH 03249	**800-336-4789**	603-293-4500	376
MIT International			
77 Massachusetts Ave ....Cambridge TX 02139	**800-228-9290***	617-253-1000	386
General			
MIT Museum			
265 Massachusetts Ave ....Cambridge MA 02139	**800-228-9000**	617-253-4444	513
Mitchell 1			
14145 Danielson St Ste A........... Poway CA 92064	**888-724-6742**	858-391-5000	628-11
Mitchell College			
437 Pequot Ave .... New London CT 06320	**800-443-2811***	860-701-5000	166
Admitting			
Mitchell Electric Membership Corp			
475 Cairo Rd .... Camilla GA 31730	**800-479-6034**	229-336-5221	245
Mitchell Furniture Systems Inc			
1700 W St Paul Ave .... Milwaukee WI 53201	**800-290-5960**	414-342-3111	318-3
Mitchell Gold & Bob Williams Co (MGBW)			
135 One Comfortable Pl .... Taylorsville NC 28681	**800-789-5401**	828-632-9200	318-2
Mitchell Industrial Tire Co			
2915 Eigth Ave PO Box 71839 .... Chattanooga TN 37407	**800-251-7226**	423-698-4442	744
Mitchell International Inc			
6220 Greenwich Dr .... San Diego CA 92122	**800-854-7030**	858-578-6550	628-11
Mitchell Metal Products Inc			
19250 Hwy 12 E PO Box 789 .... Kosciusko MS 39090	**800-258-6137**	662-289-7110	688
Mitchell Rubber Products Inc			
10220 San Sevaine Way .... Mira Loma CA 91752	**800-453-7526**		667
Mitchell Supreme Fuel Co			
532 Freeman St .... Orange NJ 07050	**800-832-7090**	973-678-1800	315
Mitchell Technical Institute			
821 N Capital St .... Mitchell SD 57301	**800-952-0042**	800-675-1969	160
MiTek Industries Inc			
14515 N Outer 40 Rd			
Ste 300 .... Chesterfield MO 63017	**800-325-8075**	314-434-1200	90
Mitel Networks Corp			
350 Legget Dr PO Box 13089 ....Kanata ON K2K2W7	**800-722-1301**	613-592-2122	725
Mitem Corp			
640 Menlo Ave .... Menlo Park CA 94025	**800-826-4836***	650-323-1500	179-12
Sales			
Mitsubishi Digital Electronics America Inc			
9351 Jeronimo Rd .... Irvine CA 92618	**800-332-2119**	949-465-6000	51
Mitsubishi Polyester Film LLC			
2001 Hood Rd .... Greer SC 29650	**800-334-1934**	864-879-5000	593
Mitsubishi Power Systems Inc			
100 Colonial Ctr Pkwy .... Lake Mary FL 32746	**800-445-9723**	407-688-6201	195
Mitsui & Co (USA) Inc			
200 Pk Ave .... New York NY 10166	**877-248-4237**	212-878-4000	444
Mitsui Chemicals America Inc			
800 Westchester Ave .... Rye Brook NY 10573	**800-972-7252**	914-701-5245	142
Mity-Lite Inc			
1301 West 400 North .... Orem UT 84057	**800-909-8034**	801-224-0589	318-3
Mix Software Inc			
1203 Berkeley Dr .... Richardson TX 75081	**800-333-0330**	972-231-0949	179-2
Miyako Hotel Los Angeles			
328 E First St ....Los Angeles CA 90012	**800-228-6596**	213-617-2000	376
Mizkan Americas Inc			
1661 Feehanville Dr			
Ste 300 .... Mount Prospect IL 60056	**800-323-4358**	847-590-0059	295-41
Mizuho Securities USA			
1251 Sixth Ave .... New York NY 10020	**866-216-1851***	212-282-3000	681
Sales			
Mizuno USA			
4925 Avalon Ridge Pkwy .... Norcross GA 30071	**800-966-1211**	770-441-5553	701
MJ Soffe Co			
1 Soffe Dr ....Fayetteville NC 28312	**888-257-8673**		153-1
MJH (Martha Jefferson Hospital)			
500 Martha Jefferson Dr .... Charlottesville VA 22902	**888-652-6663**	434-982-7000	371-3
MJM Electric Co-op Inc (MJMEC)			
264 NE St PO Box 80 .... Carlinville IL 62626	**800-648-4729**	217-854-3137	245
MJMEC (MJM Electric Co-op Inc)			
264 NE St PO Box 80 .... Carlinville IL 62626	**800-648-4729**	217-854-3137	245
MJSA (Manufacturing Jewelers & Suppliers of America Inc)			
57 John L Dietsch Sq .... Attleboro Falls MA 02763	**800-444-6572**	401-274-3840	48-4
MK Diamond Products Inc			
1315 Storm Pkwy ....Torrance CA 90501	**800-421-5830**	310-539-5221	673
MK Morse Co			
1101 11th St SE .... Canton OH 44707	**800-733-3377**	330-453-8187	673
MKC (Mid-Kansas Co-op Assn)			
117 N Edwards Ave ....Moundridge KS 67107	**800-864-4428**	620-345-6361	47-2
MKS Instruments Inc			
2 Tech Dr Ste 201 .... Andover MA 01810	**800-428-9401**	978-645-5500	202
ML McDonald LLC			
50 Oakland St PO Box 315 .... Watertown MA 02471	**800-733-6243**	617-923-0900	190-8
MLA (Minnesota Library Assn)			
1821 University Ave W			
Ste S256 .... Saint Paul MN 55104	**877-867-0982**	651-999-5343	432
MLA (Medical Library Assn)			
65 E Wacker Pl Ste 1900 .... Chicago IL 60601	**800-523-1850**	312-419-9094	48-11
MLA (Modern Language Assn)			
26 Broadway 3rd Fl. .... New York NY 10004	**800-323-4900**	646-576-5000	48-5
MLP Seating Corp			
2125 Lively Blvd .... Elk Grove Village IL 60007	**800-723-3030**	847-956-1700	318-3
MLQ Attorney Services			
2000 River Edge Pkwy Ste 885 .... Atlanta GA 30328	**800-446-8794**	770-984-7007	626
MM Systems Corp			
50 MM Way .... Pendergrass GA 30567	**800-241-3460**	706-824-7500	234
MMA Capital Management LLC (MuniMae)			
621 E Pratt St Ste 600. .... Baltimore MD 21202	**855-650-6932**	443-263-2900	502
OTC: MMAB			
MMC (Maine Medical Ctr)			
22 Bramhall St ....Portland ME 04102	**877-339-3107**	207-662-0111	371-3
MMC (Medtronic Microelectronics Ctr)			
710 Medtronic Pkwy ....Minneapolis MN 55432	**800-633-8766**	763-514-4000	687
MMC (Meadville Medical Ctr)			
751 Liberty St ....Meadville PA 16335	**800-254-5164**	814-333-5000	371-3
MMD Equipment			
121 High Hill Rd .... Swedesboro NJ 08085	**800-433-1382**	856-467-3200	478
MMF Industries			
1111 S Wheeling Rd .... Wheeling IL 60090	**800-323-8181**		683
MMG Ventures LP			
826 E Baltimore St .... Baltimore MD 21202	**800-248-1960**	410-333-2548	400
MMG Works/Status Promotions			
4601 Madison Ave .... Kansas City MO 64112	**800-945-4044**	816-472-5988	9
MMHC (Mercy Memorial Health Ctr)			
1011 14th Ave NW ....Ardmore OK 73401	**888-637-2937**	580-223-5400	371-3
MMHS (Martin Memorial Health Systems)			
200 SE Hospital Ave PO Box 9010 .... Stuart FL 34994	**800-368-3375**	772-287-5200	371-3
MMI (Metal Marketplace International)			
718 Sansom St .... Philadelphia PA 19106	**800-523-9191**	215-592-8777	408
MMR Group Inc			
15961 Airline Hwy .... Baton Rouge LA 70817	**800-880-5090**	225-756-5090	190-4
MMS (Massachusetts Medical Society)			
860 Winter St .... Waltham MA 02451	**800-322-2303**	781-893-4610	469
MNA (Massachusetts Nurses Assn)			
340 Tpke St .... Canton MA 02021	**800-882-2056**	781-821-4625	526
MNA (Michigan Nurses Assn)			
2310 Jolly Oak Rd .... Okemos MI 48864	**888-646-8773**	517-349-5640	526
MNA (Minnesota Nurses Assn)			
345 Randolph Ave Ste 200 .... Saint Paul MN 55102	**800-536-4662**	651-646-4807	526
MNPS (Metropolitan Nashville Public Schools)			
2601 Bransford Ave .... Nashville TN 37204	**800-848-0298**	615-259-8531	676
MOAA (Military Officers Assn of America)			
201 N Washington St .... Alexandria VA 22314	**800-234-6622**	703-549-2311	47-19
Moai Technologies Inc			
100 First Ave 9th Fl .... Pittsburgh PA 15222	**800-814-1548**	412-454-5550	179-7
Moberly Area Community College			
101 College Ave .... Moberly MO 65270	**800-622-2070**	660-263-4110	160
MOBI Wireless Management LLC			
6100 W 96th St Ste 150 .... Indianapolis IN 46278	**855-259-6624**		197
Mobile Air Conditioning Society Worldwide (MACS)			
225 S Broad St .... Lansdale PA 19446	**800-641-1133**	215-631-7020	48-21
Mobile Area Chamber of Commerce			
451 Government St .... Mobile AL 36602	**800-422-6951**	251-433-6951	137
Mobile Climate Control Corp			
17103 State Rd 4 E PO Box 150 .... Goshen IN 46528	**800-450-2211**	574-534-1516	14
Mobile County Public Schools			
1 Magnum Pass PO Box 180069 ...... Mobile AL 36618	**800-605-1033**	251-221-4000	676
Mobile National Cemetery			
1202 Virginia St .... Mobile AL 36604	**800-827-1000**	850-453-4108	135
Mobile Nations			
3151 E Thomas St .... Inverness FL 34453	**888-599-8998**	352-400-4400	155-5
Mobile Paint Manufacturing Co			
4775 Hamilton Blvd .... Theodore AL 36582	**800-621-6952**	251-443-6110	543
Mobile Parts Inc			
2472 Evans Rd .... Val Caron ON P3N1P5	**800-461-4055**	705-897-4955	355
Mobile Public Library			
701 Government St .... Mobile AL 36602	**877-322-8228**	251-208-7073	431-3

Name	Address	City	State	ZIP	Toll-Free	Phone	Class
Mobile Regional Airport	8400 Airport Blvd	Mobile	AL	36608	**800-357-5373**	251-633-4510	27
MobileIQ Inc	4800 Baseline Rd Ste E104-247	Boulder	CO	80303	**866-261-8600**		384
Mobivity Inc	58 W Buffalo Ste 200	Chandler	AZ	85225	**877-282-7660**		5
MOCAP Inc	409 Parkway Dr	Park Hills	MO	63601	**800-633-6775**	314-543-4000	601
MODA Hotel	900 Seymour St	Vancouver	BC	V6B3L9	**877-683-5522**	604-683-4251	376
Modal Shop Inc, The	1776 Mentor Ave	Cincinnati	OH	45212	**800-860-4867**	513-351-9919	416
MODCOMP Inc	1500 S Powerline Rd	Deerfield Beach	FL	33442	**800-940-1111**	954-571-4600	179-7
Model Airplane News	20 Westport Rd	Wilton	CT	06897	**800-827-0323**	203-431-9000	452-14
Model Coverall Service Inc	100 28th St SE	Grand Rapids	MI	49548	**800-968-6491**	616-241-6491	438
Modell's Sporting Goods	498 Seventh Ave 20th Fl	New York	NY	10018	**888-645-8667**	800-275-6633	155-5
Modern Art Museum of Fort Worth	3200 Darnell St	Fort Worth	TX	76107	**866-824-5566**	817-738-9215	513
Modern Chevrolet of Winston-Salem	5955 University Pkwy *General	Winston Salem	NC	27105	**888-306-0825***	336-722-4191	56
Modern Corp	4746 Model City Rd	Model City	NY	14107	**800-662-0012**	716-754-8226	792
Modern Dental Laboratory USA LLC	13228 SE 30th St Ste C-6	Bellevue	WA	98005	**877-711-8778**		412
Modern Group	2501 Durham Rd	Bristol	PA	19007	**877-879-4188**		264-3
Modern Group Ltd	2501 Durham Rd	Bristol	PA	19007	**800-223-3827**	215-943-9100	382
Modern Ice Equipment & Supply Co	5709 Harrison Ave	Cincinnati	OH	45248	**800-543-1581**	513-367-2101	656
Modern Inc/Environmental & Wastewater	210 Durham Rd	Ottsville	PA	18942	**888-965-3227**	610-847-5112	184
Modern Language Assn (MLA)	26 Broadway 3rd Fl	New York	NY	10004	**800-323-4900**	646-576-5000	48-5
Modern Machine Shop Magazine	6915 Valley Ave	Cincinnati	OH	45244	**800-950-8020**	513-527-8800	452-21
Modern Management Inc	253 Commerce Dr Ste 105	Grayslake	IL	60030	**800-323-1331**	847-945-7400	194
Modern Welding Company Inc	2880 New Hartford Rd	Owensboro	KY	42303	**800-922-1932**	270-685-4400	90
Modern Woodmen of America	1701 First Ave	Rock Island	IL	61201	**800-447-9811**	309-786-6481	388-2
Modernfold Inc	215 W New Rd	Greenfield	IN	46140	**800-869-9685**		286
Modesto Bee	1325 H St	Modesto	CA	95354	**800-776-4233**	209-578-2000	525-2
Modesto City Schools	426 Locust St	Modesto	CA	95351	**800-942-3767**	209-576-4011	676
Modesto Convention & Visitors Bureau	1150 Ninth St Ste C	Modesto	CA	95354	**888-640-8467**	209-526-5588	207
Modesto Symphony Orchestra	911 13th St	Modesto	CA	95354	**877-488-3380**	209-523-4156	566-3
Modis Inc	10201 Centurion Pkwy N Ste 400	Jacksonville	FL	32256	**800-372-2788**	904-360-2300	458
MOD-PAC Corp	1801 Elmwood Ave *NASDAQ: MPAC* ■ *Cust Svc	Buffalo	NY	14207	**866-216-6193***	716-873-0640	100
Mod-U-Kraf Homes LLC	260 Weaver St PO Box 573	Rocky Mount	VA	24151	**888-663-5723**	540-483-0291	105
Moeller Mfg Company Inc Punch & Die Div	43938 Plymouth Oaks Blvd	Plymouth	MI	48170	**800-521-7613**	734-416-0000	747
Moen Inc	25300 Al Moen Dr *Cust Svc	North Olmsted	OH	44070	**800-289-6636***	440-962-2000	602
Moen Inc CSI Bath Accessories Div	25300 Al Moen Dr	North Olmsted	OH	44070	**800-289-6636**	440-962-2000	602
Moews Seed Co Inc	9821 IL Hwy 89	Granville	IL	60640	**800-663-9795**	815-339-2201	10-4
Moffatt & Nichol Engineers	3780 Kilroy Airport Way # 750	Long Beach	CA	90806	**888-399-6609**	562-590-6500	261
Moffitt Corp Inc	1351 13th Ave S Ste 130	Jacksonville Beach	FL	32250	**800-474-3267**	904-241-9944	256
MOGL Loyalty Services Inc	9645 Scranton Rd Ste 110	San Diego	CA	92121	**888-664-5669**		384
Mohair Council of America	233 W Twohig Rd	San Angelo	TX	76903	**800-583-3161**	325-655-3161	47-2
Bullhead City	3400 Hwy 95	Bullhead City	AZ	86442	**866-664-2832**	928-758-3926	160
Lake Havasu	1977 W Acoma Blvd	Lake Havasu City	AZ	86403	**866-664-2832**	928-855-7812	160
Mohave Community College *North Mohave*	PO Box 980	Colorado City	AZ	86021	**800-678-3992**	928-875-2799	160
Mohawk Fine Papers Inc	465 Saratoga St	Cohoes	NY	12047	**800-843-6455**	518-237-1740	545-2
Mohawk Industries Inc	160 S Industrial Blvd *NYSE: MHK*	Calhoun	GA	30703	**800-241-4494**	706-629-7721	130
Mohawk Industries Inc Karastan Div	508 E Morris St	Dalton	GA	30721	**800-234-1120**		130
Mohawk Industries Inc Lees Carpets Div	160 S Industrial Blvd Ste 300	Calhoun	GA	30701	**800-241-4494**	706-629-7721	130
Mohawk Valley Psychiatric Ctr	1400 Noyes St	Utica	NY	13502	**800-597-8481**	315-738-3800	371-5
Mohegan Sun Resort & Casino	One Mohegan Sun Blvd	Uncasville	CT	06382	**888-226-7711**	860-862-8150	132
Mohegan Tribal Gaming Authority	One Mohegan Sun Blvd	Uncasville	CT	06382	**888-226-7711**		76
Mohonk Mountain House	1000 Mtn Rest Rd	New Paltz	NY	12561	**800-772-6646**	845-255-1000	660
Mohr Corp	PO Box 1600	Brighton	MI	48114	**800-223-6647**	810-225-9494	453
Mohr Power Solar Inc	1452 Pomona Rd	Corona	CA	92882	**800-637-6527**	951-736-2000	603
Mojave A Desert Resort	73721 Shadow Mtn Dr *Resv	Palm Desert	CA	92260	**800-391-1104***	760-346-6121	376

Name	Address	City	State	ZIP	Toll-Free	Phone	Class
Mokara Hotel & Spa	212 W Crockett St	San Antonio	TX	78205	**866-605-1212**	210-396-5800	698
Molalla Communications Co	211 Robbins St PO Box 360	Molalla	OR	97038	**800-332-2344**	503-829-1100	726
Mold Base Industries Inc	7501 Derry St	Harrisburg	PA	17111	**800-241-6656**		747
Mold-A-Matic Corp	147 River St	Oneonta	NY	13820	**866-886-2626**	607-433-2121	747
Molded Fiber Glass Cos	2925 MFG Pl PO Box 675	Ashtabula	OH	44005	**800-860-0196**	440-997-5851	597
Molded Fiber Glass Tray Co	6175 US Hwy 6 *Sales	Linesville	PA	16424	**800-458-6050***	814-683-4500	200
Moldex Metric Inc	10111 W Jefferson Blvd	Culver City	CA	90232	**800-421-0668**	310-837-6500	569
Molding Corp of America	10349 Norris Ave	Pacoima	CA	91331	**800-423-2747**	818-890-7877	597
Mold-Masters Injectioneering LLC	103 Peyerk Ct Ste E	Romeo	MI	48065	**800-387-2483**	586-752-6551	614
Mold-Rite Plastics LLC	1 Plant St PO Box 160	Plattsburgh	NY	12901	**800-432-5277**	518-561-1812	601
Mole Hollow Candles Ltd	208 Charlton Rd Rt 20 PO Box 223 *Cust Svc	Sturbridge	MA	01566	**800-445-6653***		326
Molecular Devices Inc (MDI)	1311 Orleans Dr Ste 408	Sunnyvale	CA	94089	**800-635-5577**	408-747-1700	416
Molecular Imaging Services Inc	10 Whitaker Ct	Bear	DE	19701	**866-937-8855**		412
Molecular Pathology Laboratory Network Inc	250 E Broadway	Maryville	TN	37804	**800-932-2943**	865-380-9746	414
Molex Inc	2222 Wellington Ct *NASDAQ: MOLX* ■ *Cust Svc	Lisle	IL	60532	**800-786-6539***	630-969-4550	253
Molex Premise Networks	2222 Wellington Ct	Lisle	IL	60532	**866-733-6659**	630-969-4550	725
Molin Concrete Products Co	415 Lilac St	Lino Lakes	MN	55014	**800-336-6546**	651-786-7722	184
Molina Healthcare Inc	200 Oceangate Ste 100 *NYSE: MOH*	Long Beach	CA	90802	**888-562-5442**	562-435-3666	388-3
Moline Dispatch Publishing Co	1720 Fifth Ave	Moline	IL	61265	**800-660-2472**	309-764-4344	628-8
Molle Toyota Inc	601 W 103rd St	Kansas City	MO	64114	**888-510-7705**	816-942-5200	56
Molloy College	1000 Hempstead Ave PO Box 5002 *Admissions	Rockville Centre	NY	11571	**888-466-5569***	516-678-5000	166
Molon Motor & Coil Corp	300 N Ridge Ave	Arlington Heights	IL	60005	**800-526-6867**	847-253-6000	511
Molpus Co, The	502 Vly View Dr PO Box 59	Philadelphia	MS	39350	**800-535-5434**	601-656-3373	804
Molson Coors Brewing Co	1225 17th St Ste 3200 *NYSE: TAP*	Denver	CO	80202	**800-645-5376**	303-927-2337	101
Momar Inc	1830 Ellsworth Industrial Dr	Atlanta	GA	30318	**800-556-3967**	404-355-4580	143
Moment Magazine	4115 Wisconsin Ave NW Ste 10	Washington	DC	20016	**800-777-1005**	202-363-6422	452-18
Momentum Bmw Ltd	10002 SW Fwy	Houston	TX	77074	**800-731-8114**		509
Momentum Systems Ltd	41 Twosome Dr Ste 9	Moorestown	NJ	08057	**800-279-1384**	856-727-0777	179-7
Momentum Technologies Inc (MTI)	1507 Boettler Rd	Uniontown	OH	44685	**800-720-0261**	330-896-5900	596
Monaco Coach Corp	91320 Coburg Industrial Way	Coburg	OR	97408	**888-327-4236**	877-466-6226	119
Monaco Government Tourist Office	565 Fifth Ave 23rd Fl	New York	NY	10017	**800-753-9696**	212-286-3330	765
Monadnock Paper Mills Inc	117 Antrim Rd *Orders	Bennington	NH	03442	**800-221-2159***	603-588-3311	550
Monarch Beverage Co	1123 Zonolite Rd NE Ste 10	Atlanta	GA	30306	**800-408-3590**	404-262-4040	79-2
Monarch Hotel & Conference Ctr	12566 SE 93rd Ave	Clackamas	OR	97015	**800-492-8700**	503-652-1515	376
Mondrian Hotel	8440 Sunset Blvd	West Hollywood	CA	90069	**800-525-8029**	323-650-8999	376
Monell Chemical Senses Ctr	3500 Market St	Philadelphia	PA	19104	**800-732-0999**	267-519-4700	659
Monetta Family of Mutual Funds	1776A S Naperville Rd Ste 100	Wheaton	IL	60189	**800-241-9772**	630-462-9800	521
Money & Politics Report	1801 S Bell St	Arlington	VA	22202	**800-372-1033**		524-7
Money Mailer LLC	12131 Western Ave	Garden Grove	CA	92841	**800-468-5865**	714-889-3800	5
Money Tree Software Ltd	2430 NW Professional Wy	Corvallis	OR	97330	**877-421-9815**	541-754-3701	178
MoneyGram International Inc	2828 N Harwood Fl 15 *NASDAQ: MGI*	Dallas	TX	75201	**800-666-3947**		68
Moneytree Inc	6720 Ft Dent Way	Seattle	WA	98188	**877-613-6669**	206-246-3500	68
Mongolia Casing Corp	4706 Grand Ave	Maspeth	NY	11378	**800-472-2197**	718-628-3800	295-26
Monical Pizza Corp	530 N Kinzie Ave	Bradley	IL	60915	**800-929-3227**	815-937-1890	661
Monitor, The	1400 E Nolana Loop	McAllen	TX	78504	**800-366-4343**	956-683-4000	525-2
Monitronics International Inc	2350 Valley View Ln Ste 100 *Cust Svc	Dallas	TX	75234	**800-290-0709***	972-243-7443	683
Monmouth College	700 E Broadway Ave	Monmouth	IL	61462	**888-827-8268**	309-457-2311	166
Monmouth Medical Ctr	300 Second Ave	Long Branch	NJ	07740	**888-724-7123**	732-222-5200	371-3
Monmouth Plantation	36 Melrose Ave	Natchez	MS	39120	**800-828-4531**	601-442-5852	376
Monmouth University	400 Cedar Ave	West Long Branch	NJ	07764	**800-543-9671**	732-571-3456	166
Monobind Inc	100 N Pt Dr	Lake Forest	CA	92630	**800-854-6265**	949-951-2665	231

Name / Address	City	State	ZIP	Toll-Free	Phone	Class
Monogram Biosciences Inc						
345 Oyster Pt Blvd	South San Francisco	CA	94080	**800-777-0177**	650-635-1100	416
Monograms						
5301 S Federal Cir	Littleton	CO	80123	**866-270-9841**		750
Monongalia General Hospital						
1200 JD Anderson Dr	Morgantown	WV	26505	**800-992-7600**	304-598-1200	371-3
Monro Muffler Brake Inc						
200 Holleder Pkwy	Rochester	NY	14615	**800-876-6676**	585-647-6400	61-3
NASDAQ: MNRO						
Monroe Bank & Trust						
102 E Front St	Monroe	MI	48161	**800-321-0032**	734-241-3431	69
Monroe Chamber of Commerce						
212 Walnut St Ste 100	Monroe	LA	71201	**888-677-5200**	318-323-3461	137
Monroe Clinic Hospital						
515 22nd Ave	Monroe	WI	53566	**800-338-0568**	608-324-2000	371-3
Monroe College						
2501 Jerome Ave	Bronx	NY	10468	**800-556-6676**	718-933-6700	788
Monroe County Chamber of Commerce						
1645 N Dixie Hwy Ste 20	Monroe	MI	48162	**855-386-1280**	734-384-3366	137
Monroe County Community College						
1555 S Raisinville Rd	Monroe	MI	48161	**877-937-6222**	734-242-7300	160
Monroe County Electric Power Assn						
601 N Main St	Amory	MS	38821	**866-656-2962**	662-256-7196	245
Monroe County Library System						
3700 S Custer Rd	Monroe	MI	48161	**800-462-2050**	734-241-5277	431-3
Monroe County Public Library System						
700 Fleming St	Key West	FL	33040	**877-772-8346**	305-292-3595	431-3
Monroe County Tourist Development Council						
1201 White St Ste 102	Key West	FL	33040	**800-242-5229**	305-296-1552	207
Monroe County Water Authority						
475 Norris Dr PO Box 10999	Rochester	NY	14610	**866-426-6292**	585-442-2000	775
Monroe Electronics Inc						
100 Housel Ave	Lyndonville	NY	14098	**800-821-6001**	585-765-2254	248
Monroe Environmental Corp						
810 W Front St	Monroe	MI	48161	**800-992-7707**	734-242-7654	383
Monroe Financial Partners Inc						
100 N Riverside Plz Ste 1620	Chicago	IL	60606	**800-766-5560**	312-327-2530	195
Monroe Fluid Technology Inc						
36 Draffin Rd PO Box 810	Hilton	NY	14468	**800-828-6351**	585-392-3434	143
Monroe Hardware Co						
101 N Sutherland Ave	Monroe	NC	28110	**800-222-1974**	704-289-3121	348
Monroe Oil Co						
519 E Franklin St PO Box 1109	Monroe	NC	28111	**800-452-2717***	704-289-5438	323
*General						
Monroe Title Insurance Corp						
47 W Main St	Rochester	NY	14614	**800-966-6763**	585-232-4950	388-6
Monroe Truck Equipment Inc						
1051 W Seventh St	Monroe	WI	53566	**800-356-8134**	608-328-8127	509
Monroeville Area Chamber of Commerce						
4268 Northern Pike	Monroeville	PA	15146	**800-527-8941**	412-856-0622	137
Monroe-West Monroe Convention & Visitors Bureau						
601 Constitution Dr						
PO Box 1436	West Monroe	LA	71292	**800-843-1872**	318-387-5691	207
Monrovia Public Library						
321 S Myrtle Ave	Monrovia	CA	91016	**888-620-1749**	626-256-8274	431-3
Monsoon Commerce Solutions Inc						
1250 45th St Ste 100	Emeryville	CA	94608	**800-520-2294**	510-594-4500	791-1
Monster Cable Products Inc						
455 Valley Dr	Brisbane	CA	94005	**877-800-8989**	415-840-2000	51
Montage Resort & Spa						
30801 S Coast Hwy	Laguna Beach	CA	92651	**866-271-6953**	949-715-6000	660
Montana						
Arts Council						
PO Box 202201	Helena	MT	59620	**800-282-3092**	406-444-6430	337-27
Banking & Financial Institutions Div						
Rm 155 Mitchell Bldg 125 N Roberts St						
PO Box 200101	Helena	MT	59620	**800-914-8423**	406-841-2920	337-27
Child & Family Services Div						
PO Box 8005	Helena	MT	59604	**866-820-5437**	406-841-2400	337-27
Consumer Protection Office						
POBox 200151	Helena	MT	59620	**800-481-6896**	406-444-4500	337-27
Information Technology Services Div						
125 N Roberts St	Helena	MT	59601	**800-628-4917**	406-444-2700	337-27
Revenue Dept						
PO Box 5805	Helena	MT	59604	**866-859-2254**	406-444-6900	337-27
Securities Dept						
840 Helena Ave	Helena	MT	59601	**800-332-6148**	406-444-2040	337-27
Victim Services Office						
2225 11th Ave PO Box 201410	Helena	MT	59620	**800-498-6455**	406-444-1907	337-27
Vital Records Bureau						
111 N Sanders St	Helena	MT	59604	**888-877-1946**	406-444-4228	337-27
Montana Assn of Realtors						
One S Montana Ave Ste M1	Helena	MT	59601	**800-477-1864**	406-443-4032	647
Montana Chamber of Commerce						
900 Gibbon St PO 1730	Helena	MT	59624	**888-442-6668**	406-442-2405	138
Montana Coffee Traders Inc						
5810 Hwy 93 S	Whitefish	MT	59937	**800-345-5282**	406-862-7633	157
Montana Dental Assn						
17 1/2 S Last Chance Gulch						
PO Box 1154	Helena	MT	59624	**800-257-4988**	406-443-2061	227
Montana Higher Education Board of Regents						
2500 Broadway St PO Box 203201	Helena	MT	59620	**877-501-1722**	406-444-6570	716
Montana Historical Society Museum						
225 N Roberts St	Helena	MT	59620	**800-243-9900**	406-444-2694	513
Montana Lawyer Magazine						
7 W Sixth Ave Ste 2B	Helena	MT	59601	**888-385-9119**	406-442-7660	452-15
Montana Lottery						
2525 N Montana Ave	Helena	MT	59601	**800-425-1435**	406-444-5825	447
Montana Medical Assn						
2021 11th Ave Ste 1	Helena	MT	59601	**877-443-4000**	406-443-4000	469
Montana Public Radio						
32 Campus Dr						
University of Montana	Missoula	MT	59812	**800-325-1565**	406-243-4931	624
Montana Public Television						
183 Visual Communications Bldg	Bozeman	MT	59717	**800-426-8243**	866-832-0829	624
Montana Rail Link Inc						
101 International Way	Missoula	MT	59808	**800-338-4750**	406-523-1500	639
Montana River Outfitters						
923 Tenth Ave N	Great Falls	MT	59401	**800-800-8218**	406-761-1677	750
Montana Standard						
25 W Granite St	Butte	MT	59701	**800-877-1074**	406-496-5500	525-2
Montana State Prison						
400 Conley Lk Rd	Deer Lodge	MT	59722	**888-739-9122**	406-846-1320	213
Montana State University						
Bozeman PO Box 172190	Bozeman	MT	59717	**888-678-2287***	406-994-2452	166
*Admissions						
Northern PO Box 7751	Havre	MT	59501	**800-662-6132**	406-265-3700	166
Montana Tech of the University of Montana						
1300 W Pk St	Butte	MT	59701	**800-445-8324***	406-496-4101	166
*Admissions						
Montana Veterans Home						
400 Veterans Dr	Columbia Falls	MT	59912	**888-279-7532**	406-892-3256	781
Montana Wilderness Assn (MWA)						
30 S Ewing St	Helena	MT	59601	**855-406-4483**	406-443-7350	47-13
Montana World Trade Ctr						
Gallagher Business Bldg University of Montana						
Ste 257	Missoula	MT	59812	**888-442-6668**	406-243-6982	809
Montana-Dakota Utilities Co (MDU)						
400 N Fourth St	Bismarck	ND	58501	**800-638-3278**	701-222-7900	775
Montauk Yacht Club Resort & Marina						
32 Star Island Rd	Montauk	NY	11954	**888-692-8668**	631-668-3100	660
MontaVista Software Inc						
2929 Patrick Henry Dr	Santa Clara	CA	95054	**888-624-4846**	408-572-8000	175
Montclair State University						
1 Normal Ave	Montclair	NJ	07043	**800-331-9205***	973-655-4000	166
*Admissions						
Monte Carlo Inn-Airport Suites						
7035 Edwards Blvd	Mississauga	ON	L5T2H8	**800-363-6400**	905-564-8500	376
Monte Carlo Resort & Casino						
3770 Las Vegas Blvd S	Las Vegas	NV	89109	**800-311-8999**	702-730-7777	660
Monte Package Company Inc						
3752 Riverside Rd	Riverside	MI	49084	**800-653-2807**	269-849-1722	201
Monte Sano State Park						
5105 Nolen Ave	Huntsville	AL	35801	**800-252-7275**	256-534-3757	558
Montello Inc						
6106 E 32nd Pl Ste 100	Tulsa	OK	74135	**800-331-4628**		143
Monterey Bay Aquarium						
886 Cannery Row	Monterey	CA	93940	**866-963-9645**	831-648-4800	39
Monterey Bay Inn						
242 Cannery Row	Monterey	CA	93940	**800-424-6242**	831-373-6242	376
Monterey Conference Ctr						
One Portola Plz	Monterey	CA	93940	**800-742-8091***	831-646-3770	206
*Sales						
Monterey County Convention & Visitors Bureau						
PO Box 1770	Monterey	CA	93942	**888-221-1010**	831-657-6400	207
Monterey County Herald						
Eight Upper Ragsdale Dr	Monterey	CA	93940	**800-688-1808**	831-372-3311	525-2
Monterey Hotel						
406 Alvarado St	Monterey	CA	93940	**800-727-0960**	831-375-3184	376
Monterey Inn Resort & Conference Centre						
2259 Prince of Wales Dr	Ottawa	ON	K2E6Z8	**800-565-1311**	613-288-3500	376
Monterey Mills Inc						
1725 E Delavan Dr	Janesville	WI	53546	**800-255-9665**	608-754-2866	734-4
Monterey Mushrooms Inc						
260 Westgate Dr	Watsonville	CA	95076	**800-333-6874**	831-763-5300	10-6
Monterey Pasta Co						
2315 Moore Ave	Fullerton	CA	92833	**800-588-7782**		295-31
Monterey Peninsula College						
980 Fremont St	Monterey	CA	93940	**877-663-5433**	831-646-4000	160
Monterey Plaza Hotel & Spa						
400 Cannery Row	Monterey	CA	93940	**800-334-3999**	831-646-1700	376
Monterey Public Library						
625 Pacific St	Monterey	CA	93940	**800-338-0505**	831-646-3932	431-3
Montesi Motors Inc						
444 State St	North Haven	CT	06473	**866-598-2263**	203-281-0481	56
Montesquieu Winery						
8221 Arjons Dr	San Diego	CA	92126	**800-860-2378**		627
Montfort Bros Inc						
44 Elm St	Fishkill	NY	12524	**800-724-1777**	845-896-6225	184
Montfort Group, The						
44 Elm St	Fishkill	NY	12524	**800-724-1777**	845-896-6225	184
Montgomery Advertiser						
425 Molton St	Montgomery	AL	36104	**877-424-0007**	334-262-1611	525-2
Montgomery Area Chamber of Commerce Convention & Visitor Bureau						
300 Water St	Montgomery	AL	36104	**800-240-9452**	334-261-1100	207
Montgomery Aviation Corp						
4525 Selma Hwy	Montgomery	AL	36108	**800-392-8044**	334-288-7334	62
Montgomery Botanical Ctr						
11901 Old Cutler Rd	Miami	FL	33156	**800-435-7352**	305-667-3800	96
Montgomery County Visitors & Convention Bureau						
218 E Pike St	Crawfordsville	IN	47933	**800-866-3973**	765-362-5200	207
Montgomery Hospice						
1355 Piccard Dr Ste 100	Rockville	MD	20850	**800-994-6610**	301-921-4400	368
Montgomery Mutual Insurance Co						
13830 Ballantyne Corporate Pl						
Ste 300	Charlotte	NC	28277	**800-561-0178**	704-759-7661	388-4
Montgomery Truss & Panel Inc						
803 W Main St	Grove City	PA	16127	**800-942-8010**	724-458-7500	804
Monticello						
931 Thomas Jefferson Pkwy						
PO Box 316	Charlottesville	VA	22902	**800-243-1743**	434-984-9822	49-2
Monticello Central School District						
237 Forestburgh Rd	Monticello	NY	12701	**866-805-0990**	845-794-7700	676
Montpelier Glove Co Inc						
129 N Main St	Montpelier	IN	47359	**800-645-3931**	765-728-2481	153-7
Montreal Canadiens						
Bell Centre						
1260 de la Gauchetiere St W	Montreal	QC	H3B5E8	**800-363-8162**	514-989-2841	707
Montreal Exchange						
800 Victoria Sq Third Fl						
PO Box 61	Montreal	QC	H4Z1A9	**800-361-5353**	514-871-2424	682
Montreal Inn						
Beach Dr & Madison Ave	Cape May	NJ	08204	**800-525-7011**	609-884-7011	660
Montreal Maine & Atlantic Railway Ltd						
15 Iron Rd	Hermon	ME	04401	**800-635-9449**	800-222-1433	639
Montreat College						
310 Gaither Cir PO Box 1267	Montreat	NC	28757	**800-622-6968**	828-669-8011	166
Montrose Chamber of Commerce						
1519 E Main St	Montrose	CO	81401	**800-923-5515**	970-249-5000	137
Montrose Travel						
2355 Honolulu Ave	Montrose	CA	91020	**800-766-4687**		761
Montrose Visitor & Convention Bureau						
1519 E Main St	Montrose	CO	81401	**888-212-8294**	970-249-5000	207
Montserrat College of Art						
23 Essex St PO Box 26	Beverly	MA	01915	**800-836-0487**	978-921-4242	166
Monument Builders of North America (MBNA)						
136 S Keowee St	Dayton	OH	45402	**800-233-4472**		48-3

Name / Address	City	State	ZIP	Toll-Free	Phone	Class
Monumental Sales Inc 537 22nd Ave N PO Box 667	Saint Cloud	MN	56302	**800-442-1660**	320-251-6585	715
MOOD (Michigan Out-of-Doors Magazine) 2101 Wood St PO Box 30235	Lansing	MI	48912	**800-777-6720**	517-371-1041	452-22
Moodie Implement Co 80335 US Hwy 87 W	Lewistown	MT	59457	**800-823-3373**	406-538-5433	355
Moody Bible Institute 820 N La Salle St	Chicago	IL	60610	**800-967-4624**	312-329-4400	159
Moody Dunbar Inc 2000 Waters Edge Dr Ste 21	Johnson City	TN	37604	**800-251-8202**	423-952-0100	295-20
Moody Gardens Convention Ctr Seven Hope Blvd	Galveston	TX	77554	**888-388-8484**	409-741-8484	206
Moody Gardens Hotel Seven Hope Blvd	Galveston	TX	77554	**888-388-8484**	409-741-8484	376
Moody Medical Library 914 Market st	Galveston	TX	77555	**866-235-5223**	409-772-2371	431-1
Moody Nolan Inc 300 Spruce St Ste 300	Columbus	OH	43215	**877-530-4984**	614-461-4664	261
Moody-Price LLC 18320 Petroleum Dr	Baton Rouge	LA	70809	**800-272-9832**		383
Moog Inc Jamison Rd; *NYSE: MOG/A*	East Aurora	NY	14052	**800-336-2112**	716-652-2000	204
Mooney Aircraft Corp 165 Al Mooney Rd	Kerrville	TX	78028	**800-456-3033**		20
Mooney General Paper Co 1451 Chestnut Ave PO Box 3800	Hillside	NJ	07205	**800-882-8846**	973-926-3800	540
Moonstruck Chocolate Co 6600 N Baltimore Ave	Portland	OR	97203	**800-557-6666**	503-247-3448	295-8
Moonworks 1137 Park E Dr	Woonsocket	RI	02895	**800-975-6666**		742
Moore College of Art & Design 20th St & the Pkwy	Philadelphia	PA	19103	**800-523-2025**	215-965-4000	162
Moore Food Distributors Co 9910 Page Ave	Saint Louis	MO	63132	**800-467-7878**	314-426-1300	296-7
Moore Industries International Inc 16650 Schoenborn St	North Hills	CA	91343	**800-999-2900**	818-894-7111	202
Moore Medical Corp 389 John Downey Dr; *Sales	New Britain	CT	06050	**800-234-1464***	860-826-3600	470
Moore Regional Hospital 155 Memorial Dr PO Box 3000	Pinehurst	NC	28374	**866-415-2778**	910-715-1000	371-3
Moore Stephens Lovelace PA 1201 S Orlando Ave Ste 400	Winter Park	FL	32789	**800-683-5401**	407-740-5400	2
Mooresville Graded School District 305 N Main St	Mooresville	NC	28115	**800-222-1222**	704-658-2530	676
Moorings Park 120 Moorings Pk Dr	Naples	FL	34105	**866-802-4302**	239-643-9111	663
Moors & Cabot Inc 111 Devonshire St	Boston	MA	02109	**800-426-0501**	617-426-0500	402
MOPS International 2370 S Trenton Way; *General	Denver	CO	80231	**888-910-6677***	303-733-5353	47-6
Morabito Baking Company Inc 757 Kohn St	Norristown	PA	19401	**800-525-7747**	610-275-5419	295-1
Moraine Park Technical College 235 N National Ave	Fond du Lac	WI	54935	**800-472-4554**	920-922-8611	788
Moran Printing Inc 5425 Florida Blvd	Baton Rouge	LA	70806	**800-211-8335**	225-923-2550	618
Mora-San Miguel Electric Co-op PO Box 240	Mora	NM	87732	**800-421-6773**	575-387-2205	245
Moravian Theological Seminary 1200 Main St	Bethlehem	PA	18018	**800-843-6541**	610-861-1516	167-3
More Hawaii for Less Inc 1200 Quail St Ste 290	Newport Beach	CA	92660	**800-967-6687**	949-724-5050	761
Moreau-Grand Electric Co-op Inc 405 Ninth St	Timber Lake	SD	57656	**800-952-3158**	605-865-3511	245
Morehead State University 100 Admissions Ctr	Morehead	KY	40351	**800-585-6781**	606-783-2000	166
Moretrench American Corp 100 Stickle Ave PO Box 316	Rockaway	NJ	07866	**800-394-6673**	973-627-2100	190-5
Moretz Inc 514 W 21st St	Newton	NC	28658	**866-714-8486**	828-464-0751	153-9
Morey's Seafood International LLC 1218 Hwy 10 S	Motley	MN	56466	**800-808-3474**	218-352-6345	295-14
Morgan Adhesives Co 4560 Darrow Rd	Stow	OH	44224	**866-262-2822**	330-688-1111	3
Morgan Bldg Systems Inc 2800 McCree Rd	Garland	TX	75041	**800-935-0321**	972-864-7300	105
Morgan Community College 920 Barlow Rd	Fort Morgan	CO	80701	**800-622-0216**	970-542-3100	160
Morgan Corp 111 Morgan Way PO Box 588	Morgantown	PA	19543	**800-666-7426**	610-286-5025	509
Morgan County 1226 Knoxville Hwy	Wartburg	TN	37887	**888-205-5017**		336
Morgan County Rural Electric Assn 20169 US Hwy 34	Fort Morgan	CO	80701	**877-495-6487**	970-867-5688	245
Morgan Foods Inc 90 W Morgan St	Austin	IN	47102	**888-430-1780**	812-794-1170	295-20
Morgan Lewis & Bockius LLP 1701 Market St	Philadelphia	PA	19103	**866-963-7137**	215-963-5000	425
Morgan Olson Corp 1801 S Nottawa Rd	Sturgis	MI	49091	**800-233-4823**		509
Morgan Run Natural Environment Area Benros Ln	Eldersburg	MD	21784	**800-830-3974**	410-461-5005	558
Morgan Run Resort & Club 5690 Cancha de Golf; *Resv	Rancho Santa Fe	CA	92091	**800-378-4653***	858-756-2471	660
Morgan Services Inc 323 N Michigan Ave	Chicago	IL	60601	**888-966-7426**	312-346-3181	438
Morgan Stanley 1585 Broadway; *NYSE: MS* ■ *General	New York	NY	10036	**800-223-2440***	212-761-4000	681
Morgan Stanley Family of Funds 1585 Broadway	New York	NY	10036	**800-223-2440**	212-761-4000	521
Morgan Stanley Investment Management 1221 Ave of the Americas 5th Fl; *General	New York	NY	10020	**800-223-2440***	212-296-6600	681
Morgan Stanley Venture Partners 1585 Broadway 38th Fl	New York	NY	10036	**866-722-7310**	212-761-4000	780
Morgan State University 1700 E Cold Spring Ln	Baltimore	MD	21251	**800-319-4678**	443-885-3333	166

Name / Address	City	State	ZIP	Toll-Free	Phone	Class
Morgans Hotel 237 Madison Ave	New York	NY	10016	**800-606-6090**	212-686-0300	376
Morgans Hotel Group Co 475 Tenth Ave; *NASDAQ: MHGC*	New York	NY	10018	**800-606-6090**	212-277-4100	376
Morgantown Area Chamber of Commerce 1029 University Ave Ste 101; *General	Morgantown	WV	26505	**800-618-2525***	304-292-3311	137
Mor-Gran-Sou Electric Co-op Inc 202 Sixth Ave W	Flasher	ND	58535	**800-750-8212**	701-597-3301	245
Moritz Embroidery Works Inc 1455 Industrial Pk PO Box 187	Mount Pocono	PA	18344	**800-533-4183**	570-839-9600	258
Morley Candy Makers Inc 23770 Hall Rd	Clinton Township	MI	48036	**800-651-7263**	586-468-4300	295-8
Morley Company Inc 2717 Schust	Saginaw	MI	48603	**800-323-1492**	989-791-2565	195
Morley Pedals 325 Cary Pt Dr	Cary	IL	60013	**800-284-5172**	847-639-4646	520
Morley-Murphy Co 200 S Washington St Ste 305	Green Bay	WI	54301	**877-499-3171**	920-499-3171	605
Morning Call PO Box 1260	Allentown	PA	18105	**800-666-5492**	610-820-6500	525-2
Morning Call Inc 101 N Sixth St	Allentown	PA	18101	**800-666-5492**	610-820-6500	628-8
Morning Sentinel 31 Front St	Waterville	ME	04901	**800-287-1945**	207-873-3341	525-2
Morningside College 1501 Morningside Ave	Sioux City	IA	51106	**800-831-0806**	712-274-5000	166
Morningside of Fullerton 800 Morningside Dr	Fullerton	CA	92835	**800-803-7597**	714-256-8000	663
Morningstar Inc 22 W Washington St; *NASDAQ: MORN* ■ *Orders	Chicago	IL	60606	**800-735-0700***	312-696-6000	398
Moro Bay State Park 6071 US Hwy 600	Jersey	AR	71651	**888-742-8701**	870-463-8555	558
Morongo Casino Resort & Spa 49500 Seminole Dr	Cabazon	CA	92230	**800-252-4499**	951-849-3080	660
MORPACE International Inc 31700 Middlebelt Rd Ste 200; *General	Farmington Hills	MI	48334	**800-881-1723***	248-737-5300	461
MorphoTrak Inc 113 S Columbus St 4th Fl	Alexandria	VA	22314	**800-601-6790**	703-797-2600	82
MorphoTrust USA Inc 296 Concord Rd	Billerica	MA	01821	**888-245-1114**	978-215-2400	683
Morrill Motors Inc 229 S Main Ave	Erwin	TN	37650	**888-743-7001**		511
Morrilton Packing Company Inc 51 Blue Diamond Dr	Morrilton	AR	72110	**800-264-2475**	501-354-2474	468
Morris & Dickson Co Ltd 410 Kay Ln	Shreveport	LA	71115	**800-388-3833**	318-797-7900	238
Morris College 100 W College St; *Admissions	Sumter	SC	29150	**866-853-1345***	803-934-3200	166
Morris Communications Company LLC 725 Broad St	Augusta	GA	30901	**800-622-6358**	706-724-0851	628-8
Morris Coupling Co 2240 W 15th St	Erie	PA	16505	**800-426-1579**	814-459-1741	485
Morris Hospital 150 W High St	Morris	IL	60450	**877-743-3123**	815-942-2932	371-3
Morris Industries Inc 777 Rt 23 PO Box 278	Pompton Plains	NJ	07444	**800-835-0777**	973-835-6600	530
Morris Material Handling Inc 315 W Forest Hill Ave	Oak Creek	WI	53154	**800-933-3001**	414-764-6200	465
Morris Performing Arts Ctr 211 N Michigan St	South Bend	IN	46601	**800-537-6415**	574-235-9190	565
Morrisette Paper Company Inc 5925 Summit Ave PO Box 20768	Browns Summit	NC	27214	**800-822-8882**	336-375-1515	546
Morrison Bros Co 570 E Seventh St	Dubuque	IA	52001	**800-553-4840**	563-583-5701	530
Morrison Brown Argiz & Farra LLP 1001 Brickell Bay Dr Ninth Fl	Miami	FL	33131	**800-239-3843**	305-373-5500	2
Morrison County 213 SE First Ave	Little Falls	MN	56345	**866-401-1111**	320-632-2941	336
Morrison County Record 216 SE First St	Little Falls	MN	56345	**888-637-2345**	320-632-2345	525-4
Morrison House 116 S Alfred St	Alexandria	VA	22314	**866-834-6628**	703-838-8000	662
Morrison Management Specialists Inc 5801 Peachtree Dunwoody Rd; *General	Atlanta	GA	30342	**800-367-5690***	800-225-4368	298
Morrison Milling Co 319 E Prairie St	Denton	TX	76201	**800-531-7912**	940-387-6111	295-23
Morrison-Clark Historic Inn & Restaurant 1015 L St NW	Washington	DC	20001	**800-332-7898**	202-898-1200	376
Morrisville State College 80 Eaton St PO Box 901; *Admissions	Morrisville	NY	13408	**800-258-0111***	315-684-6000	166
Morro Bay State Park 60 State Pk Rd Morro Bay State Pk Rd	Morro Bay	CA	93442	**800-777-0369**		558
Morrow & Co LLC 470 W Ave	Stamford	CT	06902	**800-662-5200**	203-658-9400	398
Morrow County Grain Growers Inc (MCGG) 350 N Main St	Lexington	OR	97839	**800-452-7396**	541-989-8221	10-4
Morse Industries Inc 25811 74th Ave S	Kent	WA	98032	**800-325-7513**		688
Morse Operations Inc 3790 W Blue Herron Blvd	Riviera Beach	FL	33404	**800-755-2593**		509
Mortara Instrument Inc 7865 N 86th St	Milwaukee	WI	53224	**800-231-7437**	414-354-1600	250
Mortgage Bankers Assn (MBA) 1919 M St NW 5th Fl	Washington	DC	20036	**800-793-6222**	202-557-2700	48-2
Mortgage Builders Software 24370 NW Hwy Ste 200	Southfield	MI	48075	**800-850-8060**		179-10
Mortgage Guaranty Insurance Corp 270 E Kilbourn Ave	Milwaukee	WI	53202	**800-558-9900**	414-347-6480	388-5
Mortgage Investors Group 8320 E Walker Springs Ln	Knoxville	TN	37923	**800-489-8910**	865-691-8910	502
Mortgage Resources Inc (MRI) 425 S Woods Mill Rd Ste 100	Chesterfield	MO	63017	**800-965-9910**	314-576-5577	502

Name / Address	City	State	Zip	Toll-Free	Phone	Class
Mortgageflex Systems Inc						
1200 Riverplace Blvd						
Ste 650	Jacksonville	FL	32207	**800-326-3539***	904-356-2490	178
*General						
Morton Buildings Inc						
252 W Adams St PO Box 399	Morton	IL	61550	**800-447-7436**	309-263-7474	104
Morton Grove Pharmaceuticals Inc						
6451 Main St	Morton Grove	IL	60053	**800-346-6854**	847-967-5600	577
Morton Salt Inc						
123 N Wacker Dr	Chicago	IL	60606	**800-725-8847**	312-807-2000	671
Morton's The Steakhouse						
5000 Westheimer Rd	Houston	TX	77056	**800-552-6379**	713-629-1946	662
Mosaic Hotel						
125 S Spalding Dr	Beverly Hills	CA	90212	**800-463-4466**	310-278-0303	376
Moscow Chamber of Commerce						
411 S Main St	Moscow	ID	83843	**855-202-0973**	208-882-1800	137
Moser Corp						
601 N 13th St	Rogers	AR	72756	**800-632-4564**	479-636-3481	320
Moses H Cone Memorial Hospital						
1200 N Elm St	Greensboro	NC	27401	**866-391-2734**	336-832-7000	371-3
Moses Lake Area Chamber of Commerce						
324 S Pioneer Way	Moses Lake	WA	98837	**800-992-6234**	509-765-7888	137
Moss Inc PO Box 189	Pasadena	MD	21123	**800-932-6677**	410-768-3442	231
Moss Supply Company Inc						
5001 N Graham St	Charlotte	NC	28269	**800-438-0770**	704-596-8717	234
Mossberg & Company Inc						
301 E Sample St	South Bend	IN	46601	**800-428-3340**	574-289-9253	618
Mosser Construction						
122 S Wilson Ave	Fremont	OH	43420	**800-589-3801**	419-334-3801	187
Mosser Hotel						
54 Fourth St	San Francisco	CA	94103	**800-227-3804**	415-986-4400	376
MoSys Inc						
3301 Olcott St	Santa Clara	CA	95054	**877-360-6690**	408-418-7500	687
Motel 6						
Red Roof Inn						
4001 International Pkwy	Carrollton	TX	75007	**800-466-8356**	972-360-9000	376
Motel 6 Wichita						
465 S Webb Rd	Wichita	KS	67207	**800-466-8356**	316-684-6363	376
Mother Jones Magazine						
222 Sutter St Ste 600	San Francisco	CA	94108	**800-438-6656**	415-321-1700	452-17
Mother Murphy's Labs Inc						
2826 S Elm St PO Box 16846	Greensboro	NC	27416	**800-849-1277**	336-273-1737	295-15
Mother's Polishes Waxes & Cleaners						
5456 Industrial Dr	Huntington Beach	CA	92649	**800-221-8257**	714-891-3364	149
Motherhood Maternity						
456 N Fifth St	Philadelphia	PA	19123	**800-291-7800**	215-873-2200	155-6
Mothers Against Drunk Driving (MADD)						
511 E John Carpenter Fwy Ste 700	Irving	TX	75062	**877-275-6233**	214-744-6233	47-6
Motion Control Engineering Inc						
11380 White Rock Rd	Rancho Cordova	CA	95742	**800-444-7442**	916-463-9200	256
Motion Industries Inc						
1605 Alton Rd	Birmingham	AL	35210	**800-526-9328**	205-956-1122	382
Motista Inc						
1777 Borel Pl Ste 500	San Mateo	CA	94402	**877-966-8478**		384
Motiva Enterprises LLC						
700 Milam St	Houston	TX	77002	**877-668-4825**	713-277-8000	573
MotivAction						
16355 36th Ave N Ste 100	Minneapolis	MN	55446	**866-277-3420**	763-412-3000	381
Motivano Inc						
5810 W Cypress St Ste H	Tampa	FL	33607	**866-664-4621**		195
Motivation Through Incentives Inc						
10400 W 103 St Ste 10	Overland Park	KS	66214	**800-826-3464**		381
MotivePower						
4600 Apple St	Boise	ID	83716	**800-445-8667**	208-947-4800	641
Motlow State Community College						
PO Box 8500	Lynchburg	TN	37352	**800-654-4877**	931-393-1500	160
Motor Appliance Corp						
555 Spirit of St Louis Blvd	Saint Louis	MO	63005	**800-622-3406**	636-532-3406	511
Motor Coach Industries International Co						
1700 E Golf Rd Ste 300	Schaumburg	IL	60173	**800-743-3624**	847-285-2000	509
Motor Products Owosso Corp						
201 S Delaney Rd	Owosso	MI	48867	**800-248-3841**		511
Motor Service Inc						
130 Byassee Dr	Hazelwood	MO	63042	**800-966-5080**	314-731-4111	187
Motor Trend Magazine						
6420 Wilshire Blvd						
Seventh Fl	Los Angeles	CA	90048	**800-800-6848**	323-782-2000	452-3
Motorcar Parts & Accessories						
2929 California St	Torrance	CA	90503	**800-890-9988**	310-212-7910	247
Motorcars International						
3015 E Cairo St	Springfield	MO	65802	**866-970-6800**	417-831-9999	56
MotorCity Casino Hotel						
2901 Grand River Ave	Detroit	MI	48201	**866-752-9622**	313-237-7711	132
Motorcycle Consumer News Magazine						
Three Burroughs	Irvine	CA	92618	**888-333-0354**	949-855-8822	452-3
Motorcycle Hall of Fame Museum						
13515 Yarmouth Dr	Pickerington	OH	43147	**800-262-5646**	614-856-2222	515
MotorHome Magazine						
2750 Park View Ct Ste 240	Oxnard	CA	93036	**800-678-1201***	805-667-4100	452-22
*Cust Svc						
Motorlease Corp						
1506 New Britain Ave	Farmington	CT	06032	**800-243-0182**	860-677-9711	289
Motson Graphics Inc						
1717 Bethlehem Pk	Flourtown	PA	19031	**800-972-1986**	215-233-0500	678
Mott Corp						
84 Spring Ln	Farmington	CT	06032	**800-289-6688**	860-747-6333	471
Mott's LLP						
PO Box 869077	Plano	TX	75086	**800-426-4891***		295-20
*Consumer Info						
Moultrie Feeders						
150 Industrial Rd	Alabaster	AL	35007	**800-653-3334**	205-664-6700	701
Moultrie-Colquitt County Chamber of Commerce						
116 First Ave SE	Moultrie	GA	31768	**888-408-4748**	229-985-2131	137
Mount Aloysius College						
7373 Admiral Perry Hwy	Cresson	PA	16630	**888-823-2220**	814-886-6383	166
Mount Bachelor Village Resort & Conference Ctr						
19717 Mt Bachelor Dr	Bend	OR	97702	**800-547-5204**	541-389-5900	660
Mount Carmel Public Utility Co						
316 Market St PO Box 220	Mount Carmel	IL	62863	**877-262-7036**	618-262-5151	775
Mount Carmel West Hospital						
793 W State St	Columbus	OH	43222	**800-346-1009**	614-234-5000	371-3
Mount Holyoke College						
50 College St	South Hadley	MA	01075	**800-642-4483**	413-538-2000	166
Mount Holyoke College Williston Memorial Library						
50 College St	South Hadley	MA	01075	**800-642-4483**	413-538-2000	431-6
Mount Joy Wire Corp						
1000 E Main St	Mount Joy	PA	17552	**800-321-2305**	717-653-1461	800
Mount Laurel Library						
100 Walt Whitman Ave	Mount Laurel	NJ	08054	**888-576-5529**	856-234-7319	431-3
Mount Marty College						
1105 W Eigth St	Yankton	SD	57078	**800-658-4552***	605-668-1545	166
*Admissions						
Mount Mary College						
2900 N Menomonee River Pkwy	Milwaukee	WI	53222	**800-321-6265***	414-256-1219	166
*Admissions						
Mount Mercy College						
1330 Elmhurst Dr NE	Cedar Rapids	IA	52402	**800-248-4504**	319-368-6460	166
Mount Miguel Covenant Village						
325 Kempton St	Spring Valley	CA	91977	**877-407-4790**	619-479-4790	663
Mount Nittany Medical Ctr						
1800 E Pk Ave	State College	PA	16803	**866-686-6171**	814-231-7000	371-3
Mount Olive College						
634 Henderson St	Mount Olive	NC	28365	**800-653-0854**	919-658-2502	166
Mount Prospect Chamber of Commerce						
107 S Main St	Mount Prospect	IL	60056	**800-584-4452**	847-398-6616	137
Mount Regis Ctr						
405 Kimball Ave	Salem	VA	24153	**877-217-3447**		717
Mount Revelstoke National Park of Canada						
PO Box 350	Revelstoke	BC	V0E2S0	**866-787-6221**	250-837-7500	556
Mount Royal College						
4825 Mt Royal Gate SW	Calgary	AB	T3E6K6	**877-440-5001**	403-440-6111	773
Mount Saint Mary College						
330 Powell Ave	Newburgh	NY	12550	**888-937-6762**	845-569-3248	166
Mount Saint Mary' s University						
12001 Chalon Rd	Los Angeles	CA	90049	**800-999-9893***	310-954-4250	166
*Admissions						
Mount Saint Mary's University						
16300 Old Emmitsburg Rd	Emmitsburg	MD	21727	**800-448-4347***	301-447-5214	166
*Admissions						
Mount Saint Mary's University Doheny						
10 Chester Pl	Los Angeles	CA	90007	**800-999-9893***	213-477-2500	160
*Admissions						
Mount Saint Vincent University						
166 Bedford Hwy	Halifax	NS	B3M2J6	**877-733-6788**	902-457-6117	773
Mount San Jacinto College						
1499 N State St	San Jacinto	CA	92583	**800-624-5561**	951-487-6752	160
Mount Shasta Resort						
1000 Siskiyou Lk Blvd	Mount Shasta	CA	96067	**800-958-3363**	530-926-3030	660
Mount Sinai Hospital Bone Marrow Transplant Program						
19 E 98th St Ste 4B	New York	NY	10029	**866-682-9380**	212-241-6021	759
Mount Sinai Hospital Medical Ctr of Chicago						
California Ave 15th St	Chicago	IL	60608	**877-448-7848**	773-542-2000	371-3
Mount Sinai Medical Ctr, The						
1 Gustave L Levy Pl	New York	NY	10029	**800-637-4627**	212-241-6500	371-3
Mount Union College						
1972 Clark Ave	Alliance	OH	44601	**800-334-6682***	330-823-2590	166
*Admissions						
Mount Vernon Convention & Visitors Bureau						
200 Potomac Blvd	Mount Vernon	IL	62864	**800-252-5464**	618-242-3151	207
Mount Vernon Mills Inc						
503 S Main St PO Box 100	Mauldin	SC	29662	**800-845-8857**	864-688-7100	734-1
Mount Vernon Nazarene University						
800 Martinsburg Rd	Mount Vernon	OH	43050	**800-766-8206***	740-392-6868	166
*Admissions						
Mount View Hotel & Spa						
1457 Lincoln Ave	Calistoga	CA	94515	**800-816-6877**	707-942-6877	376
Mount Washington Hotel & Resort						
Rt 302	Bretton Woods	NH	03575	**800-314-1752**	603-278-1000	660
Mountain America Credit Union						
PO Box 9001	West Jordan	UT	84084	**800-748-4302**	801-325-6228	219
Mountain Bike Magazine						
400 S Tenth St	Emmaus	PA	18098	**800-666-2806**		452-14
Mountain Electric Co-op Inc						
PO Box 180	Mountain City	TN	37683	**800-638-3788***	423-727-1800	245
*Cust Svc						
Mountain Haus						
292 E Meadow Dr	Vail	CO	81657	**800-237-0922**	970-476-2434	376
Mountain Home Air Force Base						
366 Gunfighter Ave						
Ste 314	Mountain Home AFB	ID	83648	**855-366-0140**	208-828-6800	492-1
Mountain Home Area Chamber of Commerce						
1023 Hwy 62	Mountain Home	AR	72653	**800-822-3536**	870-425-5111	137
Mountain Home National Cemetery						
PO Box 8	Mountain Home	TN	37684	**800-827-1000**	423-979-3535	135
Mountain Lake Hotel						
115 Hotel Cir	Pembroke	VA	24136	**800-346-3334**	540-626-7121	376
Mountain Laurel Resort & Spa						
Rt 940 PO Box 9	White Haven	PA	18661	**888-243-9300**	570-443-8411	660
Mountain Laurel Spa at Stonewall Resort						
940 Resort Dr	Roanoke	WV	26447	**888-278-8150**	304-269-8881	698
Mountain Lion Foundation						
PO Box 1896	Sacramento	CA	95812	**800-319-7621**	916-442-2666	47-3
Mountain Lodge at Telluride						
457 Mtn Village Blvd	Telluride	CO	81435	**866-368-6867**	970-369-5000	660
Mountain Ltd						
19 Yarmouth Dr Ste 301	New Gloucester	ME	04260	**800-322-8627**	207-688-6200	623
Mountain Manor Treatment Ctr						
9701 Keysville Rd	Emmitsburg	MD	21727	**800-537-3422**	301-447-2361	717
Mountain Parks Electric Inc						
321 W Agate Ave	Granby	CO	80446	**877-887-3378**	970-887-3378	245
Mountain Sky Guest Ranch						
PO Box 1219	Emigrant	MT	59027	**800-548-3392**	406-333-4911	239
Mountain States Pipe & Supply Co						
111 W Las Vegas St	Colorado Springs	CO	80903	**800-777-7173**	719-634-5555	605
Mountain Travel Sobek						
1266 66th St Ste 4	Emeryville	CA	94608	**888-831-7526**	510-594-6000	750
Mountain Valley Bank						
317 DAVIS Ave	Elkins	WV	26241	**800-555-3503**	304-637-2265	69
Mountain Valley Spring Co						
150 Central Ave	Hot Springs	AR	71901	**800-828-0836**	501-624-1635	793
Mountain View Electric Assn Inc						
1655 Fifth St	Limon	CO	80828	**800-388-9881**	719-775-2861	245
Mountain Villas						
9525 W Skyline Pkwy	Duluth	MN	55810	**866-688-4552**	218-624-5784	376
Mountain West Bank of Helena						
1225 Cedar St	Helena	MT	59604	**888-752-3341**	406-449-2265	69

Name / Address	City	State	Zip	Toll-Free	Phone	Class
Mountaineers, The 7700 Sand Pt Way NE	Seattle	WA	98115	**800-573-8484**	206-521-6000	47-23
Mountaire Corp PO Box 1320	Millsboro	DE	19966	**877-887-1490**	302-934-1100	442
Mountaire Farms 17269 NC Hwy 71 N	Lumber Bridge	NC	28357	**877-887-1490**	910-843-5942	612
Mountrail-Williams Electric Co-op 218 58th St W PO Box 1346	Williston	ND	58802	**800-279-2667**	701-577-3765	245
Mountz Inc 1080 N 11th St	San Jose	CA	95112	**888-925-2763**	408-292-2214	347
Mouser Custom Cabinetry 2112 N Hwy 31 W	Elizabethtown	KY	42701	**800-345-7537**	270-737-7477	114
Mouser Electronics Corp 1000 N Main St	Mansfield	TX	76063	**800-346-6873**	817-804-3888	246
Movado Group Inc 650 From Rd Ste 375 *NYSE: MOV* ■ *Cust Svc	Paramus	NJ	07652	**800-810-2311***	201-267-8000	151
Movie Colony Hotel 726 N Indian Canyon Dr	Palm Springs	CA	92262	**888-953-5700**	760-320-6340	376
Movies Unlimited Inc 3015 Darnell Rd	Philadelphia	PA	19154	**800-668-4344**	215-637-4444	454
Movius Interactive 11360 Lakefield Dr *Tech Supp	Duluth	GA	30097	**800-688-4001***	770-283-1000	725
Moyer & Son Inc 113 E Reliance Rd	Souderton	PA	18964	**866-669-3747**	215-799-2000	442
Moyno Inc 1895 W Jefferson St	Springfield	OH	45506	**877-486-6966**	937-327-3111	632
MP Biomedicals LLC Three Hutton Ctr Dr Ste 100	Santa Ana	CA	92707	**800-633-1352**	949-833-2500	472
MP Husky Corp 204 Old Piedmont Hwy PO Box 16749	Greenville	SC	29605	**800-277-4810**	864-234-4800	803
MP Metal Products Inc W1250 Elmwood Ave	Ixonia	WI	53036	**800-824-6744**	920-261-9650	477
MP Pumps Inc 34800 Bennett Dr	Fraser	MI	48026	**800-563-8006**	586-293-8240	632
MPA (Magazine Publishers of America) 810 Seventh Ave 24th Fl	New York	NY	10019	**800-234-3368**	212-872-3700	48-16
MPBN (Maine Public Broadcasting Network) 65 Texas Ave	Bangor	ME	04401	**800-884-1717**	207-941-1010	624
MPC Promotions 4300 Produce Rd PO Box 34336	Louisville	KY	40232	**800-331-0989**	502-451-4900	153-8
MPD Inc 316 E Ninth St	Owensboro	KY	42303	**866-225-5673**	270-685-6200	416
MPhA (Minnesota Pharmacists Assn) 1935 W County Rd B2	Roseville	MN	55113	**800-451-8349**	651-697-1771	578
MPI (Meeting Professionals International) 3030 LBJ Fwy Ste 1700	Dallas	TX	75234	**866-748-9561**	972-702-3000	48-12
MPI Label Systems Inc 450 Courtney Rd	Sebring	OH	44672	**800-423-0442**	330-938-2134	410
MPI Media Group 16101 108th Ave	Orland Park	IL	60467	**800-323-0442**	708-460-0555	504
MPI Technologies 37 E St	Winchester	MA	01890	**888-674-8088**	781-729-8300	593
MPIF (Metal Powder Industries Federation) 105 College Rd E	Princeton	NJ	08540	**800-443-4862**	609-452-7700	48-13
MPM Capital Offices 200 Clarendon St 54th Fl	Boston	MA	02116	**888-286-8010**	617-425-9200	780
MPM Medical Inc 2301 Crown Ct	Irving	TX	75038	**800-232-5512**	972-893-4090	471
MPR (Minnesota Public Radio) 480 Cedar St	Saint Paul	MN	55101	**800-228-7123**	651-290-1212	624
MPS Group Inc 2920 Scotten St	Detroit	MI	48210	**800-741-8779**	313-841-7588	193
MPT (Maryland Public Television) 11767 Owings Mills Blvd	Owings Mills	MD	21117	**800-223-3678**	410-581-4201	624
MPW Industrial Services Group Inc 9711 Lancaster Rd SE PO Box 10	Hebron	OH	43025	**800-827-8790**	740-927-8790	150
Mr Appliance Corp 1020 N University Parks Dr	Waco	TX	76707	**888-998-2011**	256-415-5069	309
Mr Crane Inc 647 N Hariton St	Orange	CA	92868	**800-672-7263**	714-633-2100	191
Mr Goodcents Franchise Systems Inc 8997 Commerce Dr	DeSoto	KS	66018	**800-648-2368**		661
Mr Handyman International LLC 3796 Plz Dr Ste 1C *Cust Svc	Ann Arbor	MI	48108	**800-289-4600***		309
Mr Hero Restaurants 7010 Engle Rd Ste 100	Middleburg Heights	OH	44130	**888-860-5082**	440-625-3080	661
Mr Jim's Pizza Inc 2521 Pepperwood St	Dallas	TX	75234	**800-583-5960**	972-267-5467	661
Mr Rooter Corp 1010 N University Parks Dr	Waco	TX	76707	**877-766-8305**	800-583-8003	190-10
M-R Sign Company Inc 1706 First Ave N	Fergus Falls	MN	56537	**800-231-5564**	218-736-5681	692
Mr Tire Auto Service Centers Inc 200 Holleder Pkwy	Rochester	NY	14615	**800-876-6676**		61-5
Mr Transmission 9675 Yonge St Second Fl	Richmond Hill	ON	L4C1V7	**800-373-8432**	905-884-1511	61-6
MRAS (Middle River Aircraft Systems) 103 Chesapeake Pk Plaza	Baltimore	MD	21220	**877-432-3272**	410-682-1500	22
MRC (Medicare Rights Ctr) 520 Eigth Ave N Wing Third Fl *Hotline	New York	NY	10018	**800-333-4114***	212-869-3850	47-17
MRC Global Inc Two Houston Ctr	Houston	TX	77010	**877-294-7574**		775
MRI (Mortgage Resources Inc) 425 S Woods Mill Rd Ste 100	Chesterfield	MO	63017	**800-965-9910**	314-576-5577	502
MRMC (Midwestern Regional Medical Ctr) 2520 Elisha Ave	Zion	IL	60099	**800-615-3055**	847-872-4561	371-7
MRMC (Martin Resource Management Corp) PO Box 191	Kilgore	TX	75663	**888-334-7473**	903-983-6200	315
MRTK (Metropolitan Trucking Inc) 299 Market St Ste 300	Saddle Brook	NJ	07663	**800-967-3278**		444
MRV Communications Inc 20415 Nordhoff St *OTC: MRVC* ■ *Sales	Chatsworth	CA	91311	**800-338-5316***	818-773-0900	780
Ms Aerospace Inc 13928 Balboa Blvd	Sylmar	CA	91342	**866-487-2365**	818-833-9095	278
Ms Magazine 1600 Wilson Blvd Ste 801	Arlington	VA	22209	**866-672-6363**	703-522-4201	452-11
MSA (Medical Services of America Inc) 171 Monroe Ln	Lexington	SC	29072	**800-845-5850**	803-957-0500	360
MSANA (Masonic Service Assn of North America) 8120 Fenton St Ste 203	Silver Spring	MD	20910	**855-476-4010**	301-588-4010	47-15
MSB Financial Corp (MSBF) 1902 Long Hill Rd *NASDAQ: MSBF*	Millington	NJ	07946	**844-265-9680**	908-647-4000	69
MSBF (MSB Financial Corp) 1902 Long Hill Rd *NASDAQ: MSBF*	Millington	NJ	07946	**844-265-9680**	908-647-4000	69
MSC (Manufactured Structures Corp) 3089 E Fort Wayne Rd PO Box 350	Rochester	IN	46975	**800-662-5344**	574-223-4794	105
MSC (Murray Supply Co) 102 W Third St	Winston Salem	NC	27101	**800-926-0457**	336-765-9480	605
MSC Filtration Technologies 198 Freshwater Blvd *Cust Svc	Enfield	CT	06082	**800-237-7359***	860-745-7475	794
MSC Industrial Direct Co 75 Maxess Rd *NYSE: MSM*	Melville	NY	11747	**800-645-7270**	516-812-2000	382
MSC.Software Corp Two MacArthur Pl	Santa Ana	CA	92707	**800-345-2078**	714-540-8900	179-5
MSE (Micro Solutions Enterprises) 8201 Woodley Ave	Van Nuys	CA	91406	**800-673-4968**	818-407-7500	620
MSF (Multiple Sclerosis Foundation) 6350 N Andrews Ave	Fort Lauderdale	FL	33309	**800-225-6495**	954-776-6805	47-17
Msf Electric Inc 10455 Fountaingate Dr	Stafford	TX	77477	**866-366-7943**	281-494-4700	190-4
MSHA (Mine Safety & Health Administration) 1100 Wilson Blvd	Arlington	VA	22209	**800-746-1553**	202-693-9400	338-13
MSI Benefits Group Inc 245 Townpark Dr Ste 100	Kennesaw	GA	30144	**800-580-1629**	770-425-1231	387
MSI Inventory Service Corp PO Box 320129	Flowood	MS	39232	**800-820-1460**	601-939-0130	396
MSK Precision Products Inc 10101 NW 67th St	Tamarac	FL	33321	**800-992-5018**	954-776-0770	614
MSM Industries Inc 802 Swan Dr	Smyrna	TN	37167	**800-648-6648**	615-355-4355	667
MSM Transportation Inc 124 Commercial Rd	Bolton	ON	L7E1K4	**800-667-4175**	905-951-6800	310
MSPB (Merit Systems Protection Board) 1615 M St NW	Washington	DC	20419	**800-209-8960**	202-653-7200	338-18
MSPB (Merit Systems Protection Board Regional Offices) 401 W Peachtree St NW 10th Fl	Atlanta	GA	30308	**800-209-8960**	404-730-2755	338-18
MSRB (Municipal Securities Rulemaking Board) 1900 Duke St Ste 600	Alexandria	VA	22314	**888-475-8376**	703-797-6600	48-2
MSU (Missouri State University) 901 S National Ave	Springfield	MO	65897	**800-492-7900**	417-836-5000	166
MSU-DOE Plant Research Laboratory Michigan State University 106 Plant Biology	East Lansing	MI	48824	**800-875-5090**	517-353-2270	659
M&T Bank One M & T Plz 13th Fl *NYSE: MTB*	Buffalo	NY	14203	**800-724-2440**	716-842-4470	69
Mt. Lebanon School District 7 Horsman Dr	Pittsburgh	PA	15228	**800-587-3257**	412-344-2000	676
MTA Today Magazine 20 Ashburton Pl	Boston	MA	02108	**800-392-6175**	617-878-8000	452-8
MTC (Materials Transportation Co) 1408 S Commerce PO Box 1358	Temple	TX	76503	**800-433-3110**	254-298-2900	383
MTD Products Inc 5965 Grafton Rd	Valley City	OH	44280	**800-800-7310**	330-225-2600	426
MTE Corp PO Box 9013	Menomonee Falls	WI	53051	**800-455-4683**	262-253-8200	757
MTI (Momentum Technologies Inc) 1507 Boettler Rd	Uniontown	OH	44685	**800-720-0261**	330-896-5900	596
MTI (Medical Teams International) PO Box 10	Portland	OR	97207	**800-959-4325**	503-624-1000	47-5
MTI America POBox 667140	Pompano Beach	FL	33066	**800-553-2155**		390
MTI Inc 1050 NW 229th Ave	Hillsboro	OR	97124	**800-426-6844**	503-648-6500	607
MTI Systems Inc 59 Interstate D	West Springfield	MA	01089	**800-644-4318**	413-733-1972	179-12
Mtm Recognition Corp 3201 SE 29th St	Oklahoma City	OK	73115	**877-686-7464**	405-670-4545	406
MTN/ATC Teleports 3044 N Commerce Pkwy	Miramar	FL	33025	**877-464-4686**	954-538-4000	672
MTNA (Music Teachers NA) 441 Vine St Ste 3100	Cincinnati	OH	45202	**888-512-5278**	513-421-1420	48-5
MTNG (Middle Tennessee Natural Gas Utility District) 1036 W Broad St PO Box 670	Smithville	TN	37166	**800-880-6373**	615-597-4300	775
MtronPTI 1703 E Hwy 50	Yankton	SD	57078	**800-762-8800**	605-665-9321	253
MTS (Mid-America Transplant Services) 1110 Highlands Plz Dr E Ste 100	Saint Louis	MO	63110	**888-376-4854**	314-735-8200	538
MTS (MTS Safety Products Inc) PO Box 204 *General	Golden	MS	38847	**800-647-8168***		569
MTS Medication Technologies Inc 2003 Gandy Blvd N *General	Saint Petersburg	FL	33702	**800-845-0053***		540
MTS Safety Products Inc (MTS) PO Box 204 *General	Golden	MS	38847	**800-647-8168***		569
MTS Systems Corp 14000 Technology Dr *NASDAQ: MTSC* ■ *Cust Svc	Eden Prairie	MN	55344	**800-328-2255***	952-937-4000	467
MTT-S (IEEE Microwave Theory & Techniques Society) IEEE Operations Ctr 445 Hoes Ln	Piscataway	NJ	08555	**800-678-4333**	732-562-5400	48-19
MTU Onsite Energy Corp 100 Power Dr	Mankato	MN	56001	**800-325-5450**	507-625-7973	511
Mu Phi Epsilon International Music Fraternity 4705 N Sonora Ave Ste 114	Fresno	CA	93722	**888-259-1471**	559-277-1898	47-16
Mueller Brass Co 2199 Lapeer Ave	Port Huron	MI	48060	**800-553-3336**	810-987-7770	480
Mueller Co 500 W Eldorado St	Decatur	IL	62522	**800-423-1323**	217-423-4471	777
Mueller Inc 1913 Hutchins Ave	Ballinger	TX	76821	**877-268-3553**	325-365-3555	104

Name / Address	City	State	ZIP	Toll-Free	Phone	Class
Mueller Industries Inc 8285 Tournament Dr Ste 150 *NYSE: MLI*	Memphis	TN	38125	**800-348-8464**	901-753-3200	480
Mueller Plastics Corp 3070 E Cedar	Ontario	CA	91761	**800-348-8464**	909-930-2060	589
Mueller Refrigeration Co Inc 121 Rogers St *Cust Svc	Hartsville	TN	37074	**800-937-5449***	615-374-2124	777
Mueller Steam Specialty 1491 NC Hwy 20 W	Saint Pauls	NC	28384	**800-334-6259**	910-865-8241	383
Muir Enterprises Inc 3575 West 900 South PO Box 26775	Salt Lake City	UT	84104	**877-268-2002**	801-363-7695	296-7
Muir Glen Organic Tomato Products PO Box 18932	Denver	CO	80218	**800-832-6345**	800-248-7310	295-20
Mule Creek State Prison 4001 Hwy 104	Ione	CA	95640	**877-256-6877**	209-274-4911	213
Mule Lighting Inc 46 Baker St	Providence	RI	02905	**800-556-7690**	401-941-4446	435
Mulhern Belting Inc 148 Bauer Dr	Oakland	NJ	07436	**800-253-6300**	201-337-5700	367
Muller Martini Mailroom Systems Inc 40 Rabro Dr	Hauppauge	NY	11788	**800-331-5674**	631-582-4343	540
MultAlloy Inc 8511 Monroe St	Houston	TX	77061	**800-568-9551**		487
Multax Systems Inc 505 N Sepulveda Blvd Ste 7	Manhattan Beach	CA	90266	**800-888-0199**	310-379-8398	261
Multi-Ad Inc 1720 W Detweiller Dr	Peoria	IL	61615	**800-348-6485**	309-692-1530	179-1
Multichannel News 28 E 28th St 12th Fl *Cust Svc	New York	NY	10016	**888-343-5563***	917-281-4700	452-9
Multicoat Corp 23331 Antonio Pkwy	Rancho Santa Margarita	CA	92688	**877-685-8426**	949-888-7100	495
Multifilm Packaging Corp 1040 N McLean Blvd	Elgin	IL	60123	**800-837-9727**	847-695-7600	541
Multimatic Products Inc 390 Oser Ave	Hauppauge	NY	11788	**800-767-7633**	631-231-1515	614
Multimedia Games Inc 206 Wild Basin Rd Bldg B 4th Fl *NASDAQ: MGAM*	Austin	TX	78746	**800-833-7110**	512-334-7500	321
MultiMedia Schools Magazine 143 Old Marlton Pk	Medford	NJ	08055	**800-300-9868**	609-654-6266	452-7
Multipet International Inc 265 W Commercial Ave	Moonachie	NJ	07074	**800-900-6738**	201-438-6600	571
Multiplan inc 115 Fifth Ave	New York	NY	10003	**800-922-4362**	212-780-2000	387
Multiple Sclerosis Foundation (MSF) 6350 N Andrews Ave	Fort Lauderdale	FL	33309	**800-225-6495**	954-776-6805	47-17
Multiquip Inc 18910 Wilmington Ave	Carson	CA	90746	**800-421-1244**	310-537-3700	382
Multi-Tech Systems 2205 Woodale Dr *Cust Svc	Mounds View	MN	55112	**800-328-9717***	763-785-3500	174-3
Multnomah Bible College & Biblical Seminary 8435 NE Glisan St	Portland	OR	97220	**800-275-4672**	503-255-0332	167-3
Muncie Star-Press 345 S High St	Muncie	IN	47305	**800-783-7827**	765-747-5700	525-2
Muncie Visitors Bureau 3700 S Madison St	Muncie	IN	47302	**800-568-6862**	765-284-2700	207
Muncie-Delaware County Chamber of Commerce 401 S High St	Muncie	IN	47305	**800-336-1373**	765-288-6681	137
Municipal Auditorium Arena 301 W 13th St	Kansas City	MO	64105	**800-821-7060**	816-513-5000	711
Municipal Credit Union PO Box 3205	New York	NY	10007	**866-512-6109**	212-693-4900	219
Municipal Litigation Reporter 590 Dutch Vly Rd NE	Atlanta	GA	30324	**800-926-7926**	404-881-1141	524-7
Municipal Securities Rulemaking Board (MSRB) 1900 Duke St Ste 600	Alexandria	VA	22314	**888-475-8376**	703-797-6600	48-2
MuniMae (MMA Capital Management LLC) 621 E Pratt St Ste 600 *OTC: MMAB*	Baltimore	MD	21202	**855-650-6932**	443-263-2900	502
Munro & Co Inc 3770 Malvern Rd 71901 PO Box 6048	Hot Springs	AR	71902	**800-819-1901**	501-262-6000	300
Munsch Hardt Kopf Harr Pc 500 N Akard St	Dallas	TX	75201	**800-321-6742**	214-855-7500	425
Munson Healthcare 1105 Sixth St	Traverse City	MI	49684	**800-468-6766**	231-935-5000	368
Munson's Candy Kitchen Inc 174 Hop River Rd	Bolton	CT	06043	**888-686-7667**	860-649-4332	295-8
Munters Corp 210 Sixth St PO Box 6428	Fort Myers	FL	33907	**800-843-5360**	239-936-1555	14
Munters Corp DHI 79 Monroe St *Sales	Amesbury	MA	01913	**800-843-5360***	978-241-1100	14
Muralo Company Inc 148 E Fifth St	Bayonne	NJ	07002	**800-631-3440**	201-437-0770	543
Murata Electronics North America Inc 2200 Lake Pk Dr	Smyrna	GA	30080	**800-704-6079**	770-436-1300	253
Murata Machinery USA Inc 2120 Queen City Dr	Charlotte	NC	28208	**800-428-8469**		451
Murdock Industrial Supply 1111 E 1st	Wichita	KS	67202	**800-362-2422**	316-262-4476	246
Murdock Webbing Co 27 Foundry St	Central Falls	RI	02863	**800-375-2052**	401-724-3000	734-5
Murnane Paper Corp 345 Fischer Farm Rd	Elmhurst	IL	60126	**855-632-8191**	630-530-8222	546
Murphy & Nolan Inc 340 Peat St PO Box 6689	Syracuse	NY	13217	**800-836-6385**	315-474-8203	487
Murphy Co Mechanical Contractors & Engineers 1233 N Price Rd	Saint Louis	MO	63132	**888-838-4038**	314-997-6600	190-10
Murphy Hardwood Plywood 2350 Prairie Rd	Eugene	OR	97402	**888-461-4545**	541-461-4545	606
Murphy Oil Corp 200 Peach St	El Dorado	AR	71730	**888-289-9314**	870-862-6411	573
Murphy Plywood Co 2350 Prairie Rd	Eugene	OR	97402	**888-461-4545**	541-461-4545	606
Murray Area Chamber of Commerce (MACC) 5250 S Commerce Dr Ste 180	Murray	UT	84107	**877-209-0068**	801-263-2632	137
Murray Bank, The 405 S 12th St	Murray	KY	42071	**877-965-1122**	270-753-5626	69
Murray Co 1807 Pk 270 Dr Ste 460	Saint Louis	MO	63146	**888-323-5560**	314-576-2818	676
Murray Guard Inc 58 Murray Guard Dr	Jackson	TN	38305	**800-238-3830**	731-668-3400	684
Murray Sheet Metal Co Inc 3112 Seventh St	Parkersburg	WV	26104	**800-464-8801**	304-422-5431	688
Murray State College One Murray Campus	Tishomingo	OK	73460	**800-342-0698**	580-371-2371	160
Murray State University 102 Curris Ctr	Murray	KY	42071	**800-272-4678**	270-809-3741	166
Murray Supply Co (MSC) 102 W Third St	Winston Salem	NC	27101	**800-926-0457**	336-765-9480	605
Murrays Ford Inc 3007 Blinker Pkwy	Du Bois	PA	15801	**800-371-6601**	814-371-6600	509
Murrey International Inc 14150 S Figueroa St	Los Angeles	CA	90061	**800-421-1022**	310-532-6091	701
Murrows Transfer Inc PO Box 4095 *Cust Svc	High Point	NC	27263	**800-669-2928***	336-475-6101	770
M-USA (Mercy-USA for Aid & Development Inc) 44450 Pinetree Dr Ste 201	Plymouth	MI	48170	**800-556-3729**	734-454-0011	47-5
Muscatine Community College 152 Colorado St	Muscatine	IA	52761	**888-336-3907**	563-288-6001	160
Muscle & Fitness Magazine 21100 Erwin St *Orders	Woodland Hills	CA	91367	**866-688-7679***	818-884-6800	452-13
Musco Sports Lighting LLC 100 First Ave W PO Box 808	Oskaloosa	IA	52577	**800-825-6020**	641-673-0411	435
Muscular Dystrophy Assn (MDA) 3300 E Sunrise Dr	Tucson	AZ	85718	**800-572-1717**	520-529-2000	47-17
Musculoskeletal Transplant Foundation 125 May St Ste 300	Edison	NJ	08837	**800-946-9008**	732-661-0202	538
Muse, The 130 W 46th St	New York	NY	10036	**877-692-6873**	212-485-2400	376
Musee Conti Historical Wax Museum of New Orleans 917 Rue Conti French Quarter	New Orleans	LA	70112	**800-233-5405**	504-525-2605	513
Museum Facsimiles 117 Fourth St	Pittsfield	MA	01201	**877-499-0020**	413-499-0020	129
Museum of Anthropology Wake Forest University Wingate Rd PO Box 7267	Winston-Salem	NC	27109	**888-925-3622**	336-758-5282	513
Museum of Art & Archaeology 1 Pickard Hall	Columbia	MO	65211	**866-447-9821**	573-882-3591	513
Museum of Contemporary Religious Art 221 N Grand Blvd	Saint Louis	MO	63103	**800-442-1142**	314-977-7170	513
Museum of Discovery 500 President Clinton Ave Ste 150	Little Rock	AR	72201	**800-880-6475**	501-396-7050	513
Museum of Early Southern Decorative Arts (MESDA) 924 S Main St	Winston-Salem	NC	27101	**800-441-5303**	336-721-7360	513
Museum of Flight 9404 E Marginal Way S	Seattle	WA	98108	**877-217-6379**	206-764-5700	513
Museum of Geology 501 E St Joseph St S Dakota School of Mines & Technology	Rapid City	SD	57701	**800-544-8162**	605-394-2467	513
Museum of Glass 1801 Dock St *General	Tacoma	WA	98402	**866-468-7386***	253-284-4750	513
Museum of History & Art 1100 Orange Ave	Coronado	CA	92118	**866-599-7242**	619-435-7242	513
Museum of International Folk Art 706 Camino Lejo	Santa Fe	NM	87505	**888-670-3655**	505-476-1200	513
Museum of Making Music 5790 Armada Dr	Carlsbad	CA	92008	**877-551-9976**	760-438-5996	513
Museum of Natural History & Science 1301 Western Ave Cincinnati Museum Ctr	Cincinnati	OH	45203	**800-733-2077**	513-287-7000	513
Museum of Nebraska History 15th & P St PO Box 82554	Lincoln	NE	68508	**800-833-6747**	402-471-4754	513
Museum of Northern Arizona 3101 N Ft Valley Rd	Flagstaff	AZ	86001	**800-423-1069**	928-774-5211	513
Museum of Science & Industry 5700 S Lk Shore Dr	Chicago	IL	60637	**800-468-6674**	773-684-1414	513
Museum of the Mountain Man 700 E Hennick St	Pinedale	WY	82941	**877-686-6266**	307-367-4101	513
Museum of Tolerance 9786 W Pico Blvd	Los Angeles	CA	90035	**800-900-9036**	310-553-8403	513
Museums at 18th & Vine 1616 E 18th St	Kansas City	MO	64108	**800-734-3447**	816-474-8463	513
Museums of Oglebay Institute 1330 National Rd	Wheeling	WV	26003	**800-624-6988**	304-242-7272	513
Musgrave Pencil Company Inc 701 W Ln St	Shelbyville	TN	37160	**800-736-2450**	931-684-3611	564
Music & Arts Centers Inc 4626 Wedgewood Blvd	Frederick	MD	21703	**888-731-5396**		519
Music for All 39 W Jackson Pl Ste 150	Indianapolis	IN	46225	**800-848-2263**	317-636-2263	47-11
Music People Inc 154 Woodlawn Rd Ste C	Berlin	CT	06037	**800-289-8889**		246
Music Teachers NA (MTNA) 441 Vine St Ste 3100	Cincinnati	OH	45202	**888-512-5278**	513-421-1420	48-5
Musician's Friend Inc PO Box 7479	Westlake Village	CA	91359	**800-391-8762**	801-501-8110	519
Musiciansbuy.com Inc 7830 Byron Dr Ste 1	West Palm Beach	FL	33404	**877-778-7845**	561-842-7451	519
Musicorp 2456 Remount Rd	North Charleston	SC	29406	**800-845-1922**	843-745-8501	520
Muskegon Area Chamber of Commerce 380 W Western Ste 202	Muskegon	MI	49440	**800-659-2955**	231-722-3751	137
Muskegon Area District Library 4845 Airline Rd	Muskegon	MI	49444	**877-569-4801**	231-737-6248	431-3
Muskegon Chronicle 981 Third St	Muskegon	MI	49440	**800-783-3161**	231-722-3161	525-2
Muskegon Community College 221 S Quarterline Rd	Muskegon	MI	49442	**866-711-4622**	231-773-9131	160
Muskegon County Convention & Visitors Bureau 610 W Western Ave	Muskegon	MI	49440	**800-250-9283**	231-724-3100	207
Muskingum College 163 Stormont St *Admissions	New Concord	OH	43762	**800-752-6082***	740-826-8211	166

	Toll-Free	Phone	Class
Musselman & Hall Contractors LLC			
4922 E Blue Banks			
PO Box 300858..............Kansas City MO 64130	800-257-4255	816-861-1234	190-3
Musson Rubber Company Inc			
1320 E Archwood Ave...............Akron OH 44306	800-321-2381*	330-773-7651	667
*Cust Svc			
Musson Theatrical Inc			
890 Walsh Ave...............Santa Clara CA 95050	800-843-2837	408-986-0210	713
Mustang Dynamometer			
2300 Pinnacle Pkwy.............Twinsburg OH 44087	888-468-7826	330-963-5400	467
Mustang Engineering LP			
16001 Pk Ten Pl................Houston TX 77084	866-313-0052	713-215-8000	261
Mustang Fuel Corp			
9800 N Oklahoma Ave.........Oklahoma City OK 73114	800-332-9400	405-748-9400	531
Mustang Tractor & Equipment Co			
12800 NW Fwy................Houston TX 77040	800-256-1001	713-460-2000	355
Mustek Inc			
15271 Barranca Pkwy............Irvine CA 92618	800-308-7226	949-790-3800	584
Muth Electric Inc			
1717 N Sanborn PO Box 1400..........Mitchell SD 57301	800-888-1597	605-996-3983	190-4
Mutiny Hotel			
2951 S Bayshore Dr................Miami FL 33133	888-868-8469	305-441-2100	376
Mutoh America Inc			
2602 S 47th St Ste 102...........Phoenix AZ 85034	800-996-8864	480-968-7772	174-6
Mutual Benefit Group			
409 Penn St PO Box 577..........Huntingdon PA 16652	800-283-3531	814-643-3000	521
Mutual Industries Inc			
707 W Grange St..............Philadelphia PA 19120	800-523-0888	215-927-6000	734-3
Mutual Insurance Company of Arizona			
PO Box 33180................Phoenix AZ 85067	800-352-0402	602-956-5276	388-2
Mutual Liquid Gas & Equipment Co Inc			
17117 S Broadway St.............Gardena CA 90248	800-633-3574	323-321-3771	315
Mutual Materials Co			
605 119th Ave NE..............Bellevue WA 98005	800-477-3008	425-452-2300	148
Mutual of America Life Insurance Co			
320 Pk Ave................New York NY 10022	800-468-3785	212-224-1600	388-2
Mutual of Enumclaw Insurance Co			
1460 Wells St...............Enumclaw WA 98022	800-366-5551	360-825-2591	388-4
Mutual of Omaha Bank			
3333 Farnam St................Omaha NE 68131	866-351-5646	877-471-7896	69
Mutual of Omaha Co			
Mutual of Omaha Plz.............Omaha NE 68175	800-775-6000	402-342-7600	357-4
Mutual of Omaha Insurance Co			
Mutual of Omaha Plaza.............Omaha NE 68175	800-775-6000	402-342-7600	388-2
Mutual Telecom Services Inc			
250 First Ave Ste 301............Needham MA 02494	800-687-2848		190-4
Mutual Trust Life Insurance Co			
1200 Jorie Blvd..............Oak Brook IL 60522	800-323-7320	630-990-1000	388-2
Mutual Wheel Co Inc			
2345 Fourth Ave................Moline IL 61265	800-798-6926	309-757-1200	60
MutualFirst Financial Inc			
110 E Charles St................Muncie IN 47305	800-382-8031	765-747-2800	357-2
NASDAQ: MFSF			
Muzak LLC			
3318 Lakemont Blvd............Fort Mill SC 29708	888-689-2559		517
Muzea Insider Consulting Services LLC			
1575 Delucchi Ln Ste 204..........Reno NV 89502	866-642-6427	775-850-9480	195
MVC Capital Inc			
287 Bowman Ave 2nd Fl............Purchase NY 10577	800-322-2885	914-510-9400	780
NYSE: MVC			
MVM Products LLC			
940 Calle Amanecer Ste K.....San Clemente CA 92673	888-246-5832	949-366-1470	584
MVMA (Maine Veterinary Medical Assn)			
97A Exchange St Ste 305..........Portland ME 04101	800-448-2772		783
MVP Health Care			
625 State St...............Schenectady NY 12305	800-777-4793	518-370-4793	388-3
MVP Laboratories Inc			
4805 G St.................Omaha NE 68117	800-856-4648	402-331-5106	575
MVRBC			
5500 Lakeview Pkwy............Davenport IA 52501	800-747-5401	641-682-8149	88
MVSB (Meredith Village Savings Bank)			
24 State Rt 25 PO Box 177..........Meredith NH 03253	800-922-6872	603-279-7986	69
MWA (Montana Wilderness Assn)			
30 S Ewing St................Helena MT 59601	855-406-4483	406-443-7350	47-13
Mwh Global Inc			
380 Interlocken Crescent			
Ste 200................Broomfield CO 80021	866-257-5984	303-533-1900	193
Mx Group, The			
7020 High Grove Blvd............Burr Ridge IL 60527	800-827-0170		195
MXL Industries Inc			
1764 Rohrerstown Rd............Lancaster PA 17601	800-233-0159	717-569-8711	597
My Alarm Center LLC			
3803 W Chester Pike			
Ste 100............Newtown Square PA 19073	866-484-4800		684
My Favorite Muffin			
500 Lk Cook Rd Ste 475............Deerfield IL 60015	800-251-6101	847-948-7520	309
My Receptionist			
800 Wisconsin St PO Box 109........Eau Claire WI 54703	800-686-0162		727
Myakka River State Park			
13208 SR 72................Sarasota FL 34241	800-326-3521	941-361-6511	558
Myers Container Corp			
8435 NE Killingsworth............Portland OR 97220	800-406-9377	503-501-5830	199
myFreightWorld LLC			
7133 W 95th St............Overland Park KS 66211	877-549-9438		390
Mylan			
2751 Napa Valley Corporate Dr.........Napa CA 94558	800-527-4278	707-224-3200	576
Mylan Pharmaceuticals Inc			
781 Chestnut Ridge Rd..........Morgantown WV 26505	800-796-9526		576
Mylan Pharmaceuticals ULC			
85 Advance Rd.............Etobicoke ON M8Z2S6	800-575-1379	416-236-2631	577
Mylan Technologies Inc			
1000 Mylan Blvd.............Canonsburg PA 15317	800-294-1322	724-514-1800	601
MyLLC.com Inc			
5716 Corsa Ave Ste 110.....Westlake Village CA 91362	888-886-9552		458
Mynelle Gardens			
4736 Clinton Blvd..............Jackson MS 39209	800-354-7695	601-960-1894	96
Myotronics-noromed Inc			
5870 S 194th St................Kent WA 98032	800-426-0316	206-243-4214	228
Myre-Big Island State Park			
19499 780th Ave.............Albert Lea MN 56007	888-646-6367	507-379-3403	558
Myriad Genetics Inc			
320 Wakara Way..........Salt Lake City UT 84108	800-469-7423	801-584-3600	84
NASDAQ: MYGN			

	Toll-Free	Phone	Class
Myrmo & Sons Inc			
3600 Franklin Blvd................Eugene OR 97403	800-683-7040	541-747-4565	449
Myron Corp			
205 Maywood Ave................Maywood NJ 07607	877-803-3358		9
Myrtle Beach Area Chamber of Commerce			
1200 N Oak St.............Myrtle Beach SC 29577	800-356-3016	843-626-7444	137
Myrtle Beach Area Convention Bureau			
1200 N Oak St.............Myrtle Beach SC 29577	800-356-3016	843-626-7444	207
Myrtle Beach Convention Ctr			
2101 N Oak St.............Myrtle Beach SC 29577	800-537-1690	843-918-1225	206
Myrtle Beach Resort Vacations			
5905 S Kings Hwy			
PO Box 3936.............Myrtle Beach SC 29578	888-627-3767	843-238-1559	660
Mysql Inc			
20400 Stevens Creek Blvd...........Cupertino CA 95014	866-221-0634	408-213-6600	178
Mystic Chamber of Commerce			
12 Roosevelt Ave,2nd Fl			
PO Box 143................Mystic CT 06355	866-572-9578	860-572-9578	137
Mystic Lake Casino Hotel			
2400 Mystic Lk Blvd............Prior Lake MN 55372	800-262-7799	952-445-9000	132
Mystic Sea Resort			
2105 S Ocean Blvd............Myrtle Beach SC 29577	800-443-7050	843-448-8446	660
Mystic Seaport -- The Museum of America & the Sea			
75 Greenmanville Ave PO Box 6000........Mystic CT 06355	888-973-2767	860-572-0711	513
Mystic Stamp Co			
9700 Mill St................Camden NY 13316	866-660-7147	315-245-2690	454
Mystique Casino			
1855 Greyhound Pk Dr............Dubuque IA 52001	800-373-3647	563-582-3647	633
MyUSACorporation.com Inc			
One Radisson Plz Ste 800.........New Rochelle NY 10801	877-330-2677		316
Mzinga			
10 Burlington Mall Rd			
Ste 111................Burlington MA 01803	888-694-6428		195
Mzinga Inc			
230 Third Ave................Waltham MA 02451	888-694-6428	781-930-5430	179-10

N

	Toll-Free	Phone	Class
N J R Corp			
125 Nicholson Ln................San Jose CA 95134	800-800-5441	408-321-0200	686
N Tepperman Ltd			
2595 Ouellette Ave...............Windsor ON N8X4V8	800-265-5062	519-969-9700	320
N Wasserstrom & Sons Inc			
2300 Lockbourne Rd.............Columbus OH 43207	800-444-4697	614-228-5550	299
N.b.c. Truck Equipment Inc			
28130 Groesbeck Hwy............Roseville MI 48066	800-778-8207	586-774-4900	60
N.E.T. Inc			
5651 Palmer Way Ste C............Carlsbad CA 92010	800-888-4638	760-929-5980	84
NA for the Advancement of Colored People (NAACP)			
4805 Mt Hope Dr..............Baltimore MD 21215	877-622-2798	410-580-5777	47-8
NA for the Exchange of Industrial Resources (NAEIR)			
560 McClure St................Galesburg IL 61401	800-562-0955	309-343-0704	47-5
NA for Uniformed Services (NAUS)			
5535 Hempstead Way.............Springfield VA 22151	800-842-3451	703-750-1342	47-19
Na Ho'ola Spa at Hyatt Regency Waikiki Resort			
2424 Kalakaua Ave..............Honolulu HI 96815	800-233-1234	808-923-1234	698
NA of Chain Drug Stores (NACDS)			
413 N Lee St..............Alexandria VA 22314	800-678-6223	703-549-3001	48-18
NA of College Stores (NACS)			
500 E Lorain St................Oberlin OH 44074	800-622-7498	440-775-7777	48-18
NA of Colleges & Employers (NACE)			
62 Highland Ave.............Bethlehem PA 18017	800-544-5272	610-868-1421	48-5
NA of Collegiate Directors of Athletics (NACDA)			
24651 Detroit Rd..............Westlake OH 44145	877-887-2261	440-892-4000	47-22
NA of Congregational Christian Churches (NACCC)			
8473 S Howell Ave............Oak Creek WI 53154	800-262-1620	414-764-1620	47-20
NA of Conservation Districts (NACD)			
509 Capitol Ct NE.............Washington DC 20002	888-695-2433	202-547-6223	48-7
NA of Convenience Stores (NACS)			
1600 Duke St..............Alexandria VA 22314	800-966-6227*	703-684-3600	48-18
*Cust Svc			
NA of Credit Management (NACM)			
8840 Columbia 100 Pkwy............Columbia MD 21045	800-955-8815	410-740-5560	48-2
NA of Electrical Distributors Inc (NAED)			
1181 Corporate Lk Dr............Saint Louis MO 63132	888-791-2512	314-991-9000	48-18
NA of Elementary School Principals (NAESP)			
1615 Duke St..............Alexandria VA 22314	800-386-2377	703-684-3345	48-5
NA of Federal Credit Unions (NAFCU)			
3138 Tenth St N...............Arlington VA 22201	800-336-4644	703-522-4770	48-2
NA of Free Will Baptists (NAFWB)			
5233 Mt View Rd................Antioch TN 37013	877-767-7659	615-731-6812	47-20
NA of Home Builders (NAHB)			
1201 15th St NW..............Washington DC 20005	800-368-5242	202-266-8200	48-3
NA of Home Builders PAC			
1201 15th St NW..............Washington DC 20005	800-368-5242	202-266-8200	608
NA of Housing & Redevelopment Officials (NAHRO)			
630 'I' St NW.............Washington DC 20001	877-866-2476	202-289-3500	48-7
NA of Insurance & Financial Advisors (NAIFA)			
2901 Telestar Ct.............Falls Church VA 22042	877-866-2432*	703-770-8100	48-9
*Sales			
NA of Neonatal Nurses (NANN)			
4700 W Lk Ave...............Glenview IL 60025	800-451-3795	847-375-3660	48-8
NA of Parliamentarians (NAP)			
213 S Main St.............Independence MO 64050	888-627-2929	816-833-3892	48-12
NA of People with AIDS (NAPWA)			
8401 Colesville Rd			
Ste 505.............Silver Spring MD 20910	866-846-9366	240-247-0880	47-17
NA of REALTORS			
430 N Michigan Ave..............Chicago IL 60611	800-874-6500	312-329-8200	48-17
NA of Retired Federal Employees			
606 N Washington St.............Alexandria VA 22314	800-627-3394	703-838-7760	608
NA of Women in Construction (NAWIC)			
327 S Adams St..............Fort Worth TX 76104	800-552-3506	817-877-5551	48-3
NAA (National Apartment Assn)			
4300 Wilson Blvd Ste 400.........Arlington VA 22203	800-632-3007	703-518-6141	48-17
NAA (National Auctioneers Assn)			
8880 Ballentine St.........Overland Park KS 66214	877-657-1990	913-541-8084	48-18

Name / Address	City	State	ZIP	Toll-Free	Phone	Class
NAAA (National Auto Auction Assn)						
5320 Spectrum Dr Ste D	Frederick	MD	21703	**800-232-5411**	301-696-0400	48-18
NAACP (NA for the Advancement of Colored People)						
4805 Mt Hope Dr	Baltimore	MD	21215	**877-622-2798**	410-580-5777	47-8
NAADAC PAC						
901 N Washington St Ste 600	Alexandria	VA	22314	**800-377-1136**	703-741-7686	608
Nabco Entrances Inc						
S82W18717 Gemini Dr	Muskego	WI	53150	**888-679-3319**	262-679-0045	475
Nabors Drilling International Ltd						
515 W Greens Rd Ste 1000	Houston	TX	77067	**877-344-7529**	281-874-0035	533
NACAC (North American Council on Adoptable Children)						
970 Raymond Ave Ste 106	Saint Paul	MN	55114	**877-823-2237**	651-644-3036	47-6
NACB Group Inc						
10 Starwood Dr	Hampstead	NH	03841	**800-370-2737**	603-329-4551	246
NACCAS (National Accrediting Commission of Cosmetology Arts & Sciences)						
4401 Ford Ave Ste 1300	Alexandria	VA	22302	**877-212-5752**	703-600-7600	47-1
NACCC (NA of Congregational Christian Churches)						
8473 S Howell Ave	Oak Creek	WI	53154	**800-262-1620**	414-764-1620	47-20
NACCO Industries Inc						
5875 Landerbrook Dr Ste 300	Cleveland	OH	44124	**877-756-5118**	440-449-9600	186
NYSE: NC						
NACD (NA of Conservation Districts)						
509 Capitol Ct NE	Washington	DC	20002	**888-695-2433**	202-547-6223	48-7
NACDA (NA of Collegiate Directors of Athletics)						
24651 Detroit Rd	Westlake	OH	44145	**877-887-2261**	440-892-4000	47-22
NACDS (NA of Chain Drug Stores)						
413 N Lee St	Alexandria	VA	22314	**800-678-6223**	703-549-3001	48-18
NACE (NA of Colleges & Employers)						
62 Highland Ave	Bethlehem	PA	18017	**800-544-5272**	610-868-1421	48-5
NACE International: Corrosion Society						
1440 S Creek Dr	Houston	TX	77084	**800-797-6223**	281-228-6200	48-13
NACHA - Electronic Payments Assn						
13665 Dulles Technology Dr Ste 300	Herndon	VA	20171	**800-487-9180**	703-561-1100	48-2
Nachi America Inc						
715 Pushville Rd	Greenwood	IN	46143	**888-340-2747**	317-530-1001	74
Na-Churs/Alpine Solutions						
421 Leader St	Marion	OH	43302	**800-622-4877**	740-382-5701	280
NACM (NA of Credit Management)						
8840 Columbia 100 Pkwy	Columbia	MD	21045	**800-955-8815**	410-740-5560	48-2
Nacogdoches Convention & Visitors Bureau						
200 E Main St	Nacogdoches	TX	75961	**888-653-3788**	936-564-7351	207
Nacogdoches Medical Ctr						
4920 NE Stallings Dr	Nacogdoches	TX	75965	**866-898-8446**	936-569-9481	371-3
Nacogdoches Public Library						
1112 N St	Nacogdoches	TX	75961	**800-252-5400**	936-559-2970	431-3
NACS (NA of College Stores)						
500 E Lorain St	Oberlin	OH	44074	**800-622-7498**	440-775-7777	48-18
NACS (NA of Convenience Stores)						
1600 Duke St	Alexandria	VA	22314	**800-966-6227***	703-684-3600	48-18
*Cust Svc						
NADA (National Automobile Dealers Assn)						
8400 Westpark Dr	McLean	VA	22102	**800-252-6232**	703-821-7000	48-18
NADCA (North American Die Casting Assn)						
241 Holbrook Dr	Wheeling	IL	60090	**800-275-8373**	847-279-0001	48-13
NAEA (National Art Education Assn)						
1806 Robert Fulton Dr	Reston	VA	20191	**800-299-8321**	703-860-8000	48-5
NAED (NA of Electrical Distributors Inc)						
1181 Corporate Lk Dr	Saint Louis	MO	63132	**888-791-2512**	314-991-9000	48-18
NAEDA (North American Equipment Dealers Assn)						
1195 Smizer Mill Rd	Fenton	MO	63026	**866-532-7653**	636-349-5000	48-18
NAEIR (NA for the Exchange of Industrial Resources)						
560 McClure St	Galesburg	IL	61401	**800-562-0955**	309-343-0704	47-5
NAESP (NA of Elementary School Principals)						
1615 Duke St	Alexandria	VA	22314	**800-386-2377**	703-684-3345	48-5
NAF (National Abortion Federation)						
1755 Massachusetts Ave NW	Washington	DC	20036	**800-772-9100**	202-667-5881	48-8
NAFCU (NA of Federal Credit Unions)						
3138 Tenth St N	Arlington	VA	22201	**800-336-4644**	703-522-4770	48-2
NAFEM (North American Assn of Food Equipment Manufacturers)						
161 N Clark St Ste 2020	Chicago	IL	60601	**888-493-5961**	312-821-0201	48-13
NAFWB (NA of Free Will Baptists)						
5233 Mt View Rd	Antioch	TN	37013	**877-767-7659**	615-731-6812	47-20
Nagel Chase Inc						
2323 Delaney Rd	Gurnee	IL	60031	**800-323-4552**		347
NAHB (NA of Home Builders)						
1201 15th St NW	Washington	DC	20005	**800-368-5242**	202-266-8200	48-3
NAHB Research Ctr						
400 Prince Georges Blvd	Upper Marlboro	MD	20774	**800-638-8556**	301-249-4000	659
NAHRO (NA of Housing & Redevelopment Officials)						
630 'I' St NW	Washington	DC	20001	**877-866-2476**	202-289-3500	48-7
NAICS (North American Industry Classification System)						
US Census Bureau						
4600 Silver Hill Rd	Washington	DC	20233	**800-923-8282**	301-763-4636	338-2
NAIFA (NA of Insurance & Financial Advisors)						
2901 Telestar Ct	Falls Church	VA	22042	**877-866-2432***	703-770-8100	48-9
*Sales						
NAIHC (National American Indian Housing Council)						
50 F St NW Ste 3300	Washington	DC	20001	**800-284-9165**	202-789-1754	48-7
Nailpro Magazine						
7628 Densmore Ave	Van Nuys	CA	91406	**800-442-5667**	818-782-7328	452-21
Nails Magazine						
3520 Challenger St	Torrance	CA	90503	**888-624-5744**	310-533-2400	452-21
Naismith Memorial Basketball Hall of Fame						
1000 W Columbus Ave	Springfield	MA	01105	**877-446-6752**	413-781-6500	515
Najarian Furniture Company Inc						
17560 Rowland St	City of Industry	CA	91748	**888-781-3088**	626-839-8700	319
Nakase Bros Wholesale Nursery						
9441 Krepp Dr	Huntington Beach	CA	92646	**800-747-4388**	714-962-6604	292
Nalco Co						
1601 W Diehl Rd	Naperville	IL	60563	**800-288-0879**	630-305-1000	143
Nalge Nunc International						
75 Panorama Creek Dr	Rochester	NY	14625	**800-625-4327**	585-586-8800	417
Nalley Lexus Smyrna						
2750 Cobb Pkwy SE	Smyrna	GA	30080	**877-454-4206**		56
NAMA (National Agri-Marketing Assn)						
11020 King St Ste 205	Overland Park	KS	66210	**800-530-5646**	913-491-6500	48-18
NAMCA (North America Missing Children Assn Inc)						
201 Brownlow Ave	Dartmouth	NS	B3B1W2	**800-260-0753**	902-494-2449	47-6
Namco Controls Corp						
2100 W Broad St	Elizabethtown	NC	28337	**800-390-6405**	910-862-2511	253
Name Maker Inc						
4450 Commerce Cir PO Box 43821	Atlanta	GA	30336	**800-241-2890**	404-691-2237	734-5
Name.com LLC						
2500 E Second Ave 2nd Fl	Denver	CO	80206	**800-365-0006**	720-249-2374	393
NAMI (National Alliance on Mental Illness)						
3803 N Fairfax Dr Ste 100	Arlington	VA	22203	**800-950-6264**	703-524-7600	47-17
NAMM - International Music Products Assn						
5790 Armada Dr	Carlsbad	CA	92008	**800-767-6266**	760-438-8001	48-18
NAMP (North American Meat Processors Assn)						
1910 Assn Dr	Reston	VA	20191	**800-535-4555**	703-758-1900	48-6
NANN (NA of Neonatal Nurses)						
4700 W Lk Ave	Glenview	IL	60025	**800-451-3795**	847-375-3660	48-8
NanoHorizons Inc						
270 Rolling Ridge Dr Ste 100	Bellefonte	PA	16823	**866-584-6235**	814-355-4700	160
Nanotechnology Research Ctr						
Georgia Institute of Technology						
791 Atlantic Dr	Atlanta	GA	30332	**800-424-9300**	404-894-5100	659
Nantucket Accommodations						
Two Windy Way	Nantucket	MA	02554	**866-743-3330**	508-228-9559	373
Nantucket Bank						
104 Pleasant St	Nantucket	MA	02554	**800-533-9313**	508-228-0580	69
Nantze Springs Inc						
156 W Carroll St	Dothan	AL	36301	**800-239-7873**	334-794-4218	296-11
Nanz & Kraft Florists Inc						
141 Breckenridge Ln	Louisville	KY	40207	**800-897-6551**	502-897-6551	292
NAO Inc						
1284 E Sedgley Ave	Philadelphia	PA	19134	**800-523-3495***	215-743-5300	18
*Cust Svc						
NAP (NA of Parliamentarians)						
213 S Main St	Independence	MO	64050	**888-627-2929**	816-833-3892	48-12
NAPA (National Automotive Parts Assn)						
2999 Circle 75 Pkwy	Atlanta	GA	30339	**800-538-6272**	770-953-1700	60
Napa Chamber of Commerce						
1556 First St	Napa	CA	94559	**877-807-2249**	707-226-7455	137
Napa City-County Library						
580 Coombs St	Napa	CA	94559	**877-848-7030**	707-253-4241	431-3
Napa River Inn						
500 Main St	Napa	CA	94559	**877-251-8500**	707-251-8500	376
Napa State Hospital						
2100 Napa-Vallejo Hwy	Napa	CA	94558	**866-762-0972**	707-253-5000	371-5
Napa Valley College						
2277 Napa-Vallejo Hwy	Napa	CA	94558	**800-826-1077**	707-256-7000	160
NAPCO (North American Publishing Co)						
1500 Springarden St 12th Fl	Philadelphia	PA	19130	**800-627-2689**	215-238-5300	628-9
NAPCO Inc						
120 Trojan Ave	Sparta	NC	28675	**800-854-8621**	336-372-5228	85
Napco Ply Gem Inc						
5020 Weston Pkwy Ste 400	Cary	MO	27153	**800-786-2726**	888-975-9436	688
NAPCO Security Systems Inc						
333 Bayview Ave	Amityville	NY	11701	**800-645-9445**	631-842-9400	683
NASDAQ: NSSC						
Napco Steel Inc						
1800 Arthur Dr	West Chicago	IL	60185	**800-292-8010**	630-293-1900	487
Napili Kai Beach Club						
5900 Honoapiilani Rd	Lahaina	HI	96761	**800-367-5030**	808-669-6271	660
NAPL (Epicomm)						
1 Meadowlands Plaza Ste 1511	East Rutherford	NJ	07073	**800-642-6275**	201-634-9600	48-16
Naples Bay Resort						
1500 Fifth Ave S	Naples	FL	34102	**866-605-1199**	239-530-1199	660
Naples Beach Hotel & Golf Club						
851 Gulf Shore Blvd N	Naples	FL	34102	**800-237-7600**	239-261-2222	660
Naples Daily News						
1075 Central Ave	Naples	FL	34102	**800-404-7343**	239-262-3161	525-2
Naples Museum of Art						
5833 Pelican Bay Blvd	Naples	FL	34108	**800-597-1900**	239-597-1111	513
Napoleon/Henry County Chamber of Commerce						
611 N Perry St	Napoleon	OH	43545	**800-322-6849**	419-592-1786	137
NAPWA (NA of People with AIDS)						
8401 Colesville Rd Ste 505	Silver Spring	MD	20910	**866-846-9366**	240-247-0880	47-17
NARA (National Archives & Records Administration)						
8601 Adelphi Rd	College Park	MD	20740	**866-272-6272**		338-18
NARBHA (Northern Arizona Regional Behavioral Health Authority Inc)						
1300 S Yale St	Flagstaff	AZ	86001	**877-923-1400**	928-774-7128	48-15
Narcolepsy Network Inc						
129 Waterwheel Ln	North Kingstown	RI	02852	**888-292-6522**	401-667-2523	47-17
Nardini Fire Equipment Company Inc						
405 County Rd E W	Saint Paul	MN	55126	**888-627-3464**	651-483-6631	670
Nardone Bros Baking Company Inc						
420 New Commerce Blvd	Wilkes-Barre	PA	18706	**800-822-5320**	570-823-0141	295-36
NARF (Native American Rights Fund)						
1506 Broadway	Boulder	CO	80302	**888-280-0726**	303-447-8760	48-10
NARIC (National Rehabilitation Information Ctr)						
8201 Corporate Dr Ste 600	Landover	MD	20785	**800-346-2742**	301-459-5900	47-17
Naropa University						
2130 Arapahoe Ave	Boulder	CO	80302	**800-772-6951**	303-444-0202	166
Narrow Fabric Industries Corp						
701 Reading Ave	Reading	PA	19611	**877-523-6373**	610-376-2891	734-5
NARSA (National Automotive Radiator Service Assn)						
3000 Village Run Rd Ste 103 221	Wexford	PA	15090	**800-551-3232**	724-799-8415	48-21
NAS (National Audubon Society)						
225 Varick St	New York	NY	10014	**800-274-4201**	212-979-3000	47-13
NAS Recruitment Communications						
9700 Rockside Rd Ste 170	Cleveland	OH	44125	**866-627-7327**		4
NASA TV						
300 E St SW	Washington	DC	20546	**877-546-1574**	202-358-0000	729
NASAA (North American Securities Administrators Assn)						
750 First St NE Ste 1140	Washington	DC	20002	**800-222-1253**	202-737-0900	48-2
NASB (North American Savings Bank)						
12520 S 71 Hwy	Grandview	MO	64030	**800-677-6272**	816-765-2200	69
NASB Financial Inc						
12520 S 71 Hwy	Grandview	MO	64030	**800-677-6272**	816-765-2200	357-2
NASDAQ: NASB						
NASBIC PAC						
1100 H St NW Ste 610	Washington	DC	20005	**800-471-6153**	202-628-5055	608
NASCO International Inc						
901 Janesville Ave	Fort Atkinson	WI	53538	**800-558-9595***	920-563-2446	454
*Orders						
NASFAA (National Assn of Student Financial Aid Administrators)						
1101 Connecticut Ave Ste 1100	Washington	DC	20036	**800-877-8339**	202-785-0453	48-5
Nash Produce Co						
6160 S N Carolina 58	Nashville	NC	27856	**800-334-3032**	252-443-6011	10-10

	Toll-Free	Phone	Class
Nashoba Valley Chamber of Commerce			
100 Sherman Ave ....Devens MA 01434	**877-322-8228**	978-772-6976	137
Nashotah House			
2777 Mission Rd ....Nashotah WI 53058	**800-627-4682**	262-646-6500	167-3
Nashua Corp			
11 Trafalgar Sq 2nd Fl ....Nashua NH 03063	**800-430-7488**	603-880-2323	545-1
Nashua Homes of Idaho Inc			
PO Box 170008 ....Boise ID 83717	**855-766-0222**	208-345-0222	500
Nashville Convention & Visitors Bureau (NCVB)			
150 Fourth Ave N Ste G250 ....Nashville TN 37219	**800-657-6910**	615-259-4730	207
Nashville Display			
306 Hartman Dr ....Lebanon TN 37087	**800-251-1150**	615-743-2900	233
Nashville General Hospital			
1818 Albion St ....Nashville TN 37208	**800-318-2596**	615-341-4000	371-3
Nashville Jet			
635 Hangar Ln ....Nashville TN 37217	**800-824-4778**	615-350-8400	13
Nashville Office Interiors			
1621 Church St ....Nashville TN 37203	**877-342-0294**	615-329-1811	320
Nashville Scene			
210 12th Ave S Ste 100 ....Nashville TN 37203	**800-577-3917**	615-244-7989	525-5
Nashville State Community College (NSCC)			
120 White Bridge Rd ....Nashville TN 37209	**800-272-7363**	615-353-3333	788
Nashville Wire Products Manufacturing Co			
199 Polk Ave ....Nashville TN 37210	**800-448-2125**	615-743-2500	72
NaSPA (Network & Systems Professionals Assn Inc)			
7044 S 13th St ....Oak Creek WI 53154	**877-777-3520**	414-768-8000	47-9
NASS (National Agricultural Statistics Service)			
1400 Independence Ave SW ....Washington DC 20250	**800-727-9540**	202-720-2707	338-1
NASS (North American Spine Society)			
7075 Veterans Blvd ....Burr Ridge IL 60527	**877-774-6337**	630-230-3600	48-8
Nassau County			
PO Box 870 ....Fernandina Beach FL 32035	**888-615-4398**	904-491-7300	336
Nassau Financial Federal Credit Union			
1325 Franklin Ave Ste 500 ....Garden City NY 11530	**800-216-2328**	516-742-4900	219
Nassau Inn, The			
10 Palmer Sq ....Princeton NJ 08542	**800-862-7728**	609-921-7500	376
Nassau Library System			
900 Jerusalem Ave ....Uniondale NY 11553	**800-662-1220**	516-292-8920	431-3
Nassau Valley Vineyards			
32165 Winery Way ....Lewes DE 19958	**800-425-2355**	302-645-9463	49-6
Nassau Veterans Memorial Coliseum			
1255 Hempstead Tpke ....Uniondale NY 11553	**800-745-3000**	516-794-9300	711
NASW News			
750 First St NE Ste 700 ....Washington DC 20002	**800-227-3590**	202-408-8600	452-16
NATA (National Air Transportation Assn)			
4226 King St ....Alexandria VA 22302	**800-808-6282**	703-845-9000	48-21
NATA (National Athletic Trainers Assn)			
2952 N Stemmons Fwy Ste 200 ....Dallas TX 75247	**800-879-6282**	214-637-6282	47-22
NATCA (National Air Traffic Controllers Assn)			
1325 Massachusetts Ave NW ....Washington DC 20005	**800-266-0895**	202-628-5451	411
NATCA PAC (National Air Traffic Controllers Assn PAC)			
1325 Massachusetts Ave NW ....Washington DC 20005	**800-266-0895**	202-628-5451	608
Natchez Convention & Visitors Bureau			
640 S Canal St ....Natchez MS 39120	**800-647-6724**	601-446-6345	207
Natchez Convention Ctr			
211 Main St ....Natchez MS 39120	**888-475-9144**	601-442-5880	206
Natchez Newspapers Inc			
503 N Canal St ....Natchez MS 39120	**877-896-0974**	601-442-9101	628-8
Natchez Trace Parkway			
2680 Natchez Trace Pkwy ....Tupelo MS 38804	**800-305-7417**	662-680-4025	557
Natchitoches Area Chamber of Commerce			
550 Second St ....Natchitoches LA 71457	**877-646-6689**	318-352-6894	137
NAT-COM Inc			
2622 Audubon Rd ....Eagleville PA 19403	**800-486-7947**	610-666-7947	189-1
NATE (National Association of Tower Erectors)			
Eight Second St SE ....Watertown SD 57201	**888-882-5865**	605-882-5865	48-3
Natel Engineering Co Inc			
9340 Owensmouth Ave ....Chatsworth CA 91311	**800-590-5774**	818-734-6500	617
Nathan's Famous Inc			
One Jericho Plz Second Fl ....Jericho NY 11753	**800-628-4267**	516-338-8500	661
NASDAQ: NATH			
Nation Magazine			
33 Irving Pl Eighth Fl ....New York NY 10003	**800-333-8536***	212-209-5400	452-17
*Cust Svc			
National Abortion Federation (NAF)			
1755 Massachusetts Ave NW ....Washington DC 20036	**800-772-9100**	202-667-5881	48-8
National Academies			
500 Fifth St NW ....Washington DC 20001	**800-624-6242**	202-334-2138	48-19
National Academy of Public Administration			
900 Seventh St NW Ste 600 ....Washington DC 20001	**800-883-3190**	202-347-3190	48-7
National Academy of Recording Arts & Sciences			
3030 Olympic Blvd ....Santa Monica CA 90404	**800-423-2017**	310-392-3777	47-4
National Academy Press			
500 Fifth St NW PO Box 285 ....Washington DC 20055	**800-624-6242**	202-334-3313	628-2
National Accrediting Commission of Cosmetology Arts & Sciences (NACCAS)			
4401 Ford Ave Ste 1300 ....Alexandria VA 22302	**877-212-5752**	703-600-7600	47-1
National Aeronautic Assn			
Hanger 7 1 S Smith Blvd			
Ste 202 ....Arlington VA 22202	**800-644-9777**	703-416-4888	47-22
National Afro-American Museum & Cultural Ctr			
1350 Brush Row Rd			
PO Box 578. ....Wilberforce OH 45384	**800-752-2603**	937-376-4944	513
National Agricultural Statistics Service (NASS)			
1400 Independence Ave SW ....Washington DC 20250	**800-727-9540**	202-720-2707	338-1
National Agri-Marketing Assn (NAMA)			
11020 King St Ste 205 ....Overland Park KS 66210	**800-530-5646**	913-491-6500	48-18
National Air Traffic Controllers Assn (NATCA)			
1325 Massachusetts Ave NW ....Washington DC 20005	**800-266-0895**	202-628-5451	411
National Air Traffic Controllers Assn PAC (NATCA PAC)			
1325 Massachusetts Ave NW ....Washington DC 20005	**800-266-0895**	202-628-5451	608
National Air Transportation Assn (NATA)			
4226 King St ....Alexandria VA 22302	**800-808-6282**	703-845-9000	48-21
National Alliance for Youth Sports			
2050 Vista Pkwy ....West Palm Beach FL 33411	**800-729-2057**	561-684-1141	47-22
National Alliance on Mental Illness (NAMI)			
3803 N Fairfax Dr Ste 100 ....Arlington VA 22203	**800-950-6264**	703-524-7600	47-17
National Alliance to End Homelessness			
1518 K St NW Ste 410 ....Washington DC 20005	**800-657-3769**	202-638-1526	47-5
National Alpha Lambda Delta			
328 Orange St ....Macon GA 31201	**800-925-7421**	478-744-9595	47-16
National AMBUCS Inc (AMBUCS)			
4285 Regency Ct PO Box 5127. ......High Point NC 27265	**800-838-1845**	336-852-0052	47-5
National American Indian Housing Council (NAIHC)			
50 F St NW Ste 3300 ....Washington DC 20001	**800-284-9165**	202-789-1754	48-7

	Toll-Free	Phone	Class
National American University			
321 Kansas City St ....Rapid City SD 57701	**800-843-8892**	605-394-4800	166
Sioux Falls			
5801 S Kiwanis Ave ....Sioux Falls SD 57108	**800-388-5430**	605-336-4600	166
National American University Colorado Springs			
1915 Jamboree Dr			
Ste 185 ....Colorado Springs CO 80920	**855-448-2318**	316-448-5400	166
National American University Independence			
3620 Arrowhead Ave ....Independence MO 64057	**866-628-1288**	816-412-7700	166
National Anti-Vivisection Society (NAVS)			
53 W Jackson Blvd Ste 1552 ....Chicago IL 60604	**800-888-6287**	312-427-6065	47-3
National Apartment Assn (NAA)			
4300 Wilson Blvd Ste 400 ....Arlington VA 22203	**800-632-3007**	703-518-6141	48-17
National Arbitration & Mediation			
990 Stewart Ave ....Garden City NY 11530	**800-358-2550**	516-794-8950	40
National Arbor Day Foundation			
100 Arbor Ave ....Nebraska City NE 68410	**888-448-7337**	402-474-5655	47-13
National Archives & Records Administration (NARA)			
8601 Adelphi Rd ....College Park MD 20740	**866-272-6272**		338-18
Archival Research Catalog			
8601 Adelphi Rd ....College Park MD 20740	**866-272-6272**		338-18
National Archives & Records Administration Regional Offices			
Northeast Region			
380 Trapelo Rd ....Waltham MA 02452	**866-406-2379**	781-663-0130	338-18
Pacific Alaska Region			
6125 Sand Pt Way NE ....Seattle WA 98115	**866-325-7208**	206-336-5115	338-18
National Art Education Assn (NAEA)			
1806 Robert Fulton Dr ....Reston VA 20191	**800-299-8321**	703-860-8000	48-5
National Art Materials Trade Assn			
15806 Brookway Dr Ste 300 ....Huntersville NC 28078	**877-970-0832**	704-892-6244	48-18
National Art Shop			
509 S National Ave ....Springfield MO 65802	**800-949-3743**	417-866-3743	44
National Artcraft Supply Co			
300 Campus Dr ....Aurora OH 44202	**888-937-2723**	330-562-3500	42
National Assn of Credit Management			
8840 Columbia 100 Pkwy ....Columbia MD 21045	**800-955-8815**	410-740-5560	452-5
National Assn of Student Financial Aid Administrators (NASFAA)			
1101 Connecticut Ave			
Ste 1100 ....Washington DC 20036	**800-877-8339**	202-785-0453	48-5
National Association of Landscape Professionals Inc (PLANET)			
950 Herndon Pkwy Ste 450 ....Herndon VA 20170	**800-395-2522**	703-736-9666	47-2
National Association of Nonprofit Accountants & Consultants (NSA)			
624 Grassmere Park Dr Ste 15 ....Nashville TN 37211	**800-231-2524**	615-373-9880	48-1
National Association of Theatre Owners. (NATO)			
750 First St NE Ste 1130 ....Washington DC 20002	**800-365-5701***	202-962-0054	47-4
*General			
National Association of Tower Erectors (NATE)			
Eight Second St SE ....Watertown SD 57201	**888-882-5865**	605-882-5865	48-3
National Athletic Trainers Assn (NATA)			
2952 N Stemmons Fwy Ste 200 ....Dallas TX 75247	**800-879-6282**	214-637-6282	47-22
National Auctioneers Assn (NAA)			
8880 Ballentine St ....Overland Park KS 66214	**877-657-1990**	913-541-8084	48-18
National Audubon Society (NAS)			
225 Varick St ....New York NY 10014	**800-274-4201**	212-979-3000	47-13
National Australia Bank Americas			
245 Pk Ave Ste 2800 ....New York NY 10167	**866-706-0509**	212-916-9500	69
National Auto Auction Assn (NAAA)			
5320 Spectrum Dr Ste D. ....Frederick MD 21703	**800-232-5411**	301-696-0400	48-18
National Automatic Sprinkler Industries			
8000 Corporate Dr ....Landover MD 20785	**800-638-2603**	301-577-1700	190-13
National Automobile Dealers Assn (NADA)			
8400 Westpark Dr ....McLean VA 22102	**800-252-6232**	703-821-7000	48-18
National Automotive Parts Assn (NAPA)			
2999 Circle 75 Pkwy ....Atlanta GA 30339	**800-538-6272**	770-953-1700	60
National Automotive Radiator Service Assn (NARSA)			
3000 Village Run Rd Ste 103 221.......Wexford PA 15090	**800-551-3232**	724-799-8415	48-21
National Aviation Academy			
150 Hanscom Dr ....Bedford MA 01730	**800-659-2080**	781-274-8448	788
National Bank of Arizona			
335 N Wilmot Rd Ste 100 ....Tucson AZ 85711	**800-497-8168**	520-571-1500	69
National Bank of Blacksburg			
PO Box 90002 ....Blacksburg VA 24062	**800-552-4123**	540-552-2011	69
National Bank of Kansas City (NBOFKC)			
3510 W 95th St ....Leawood KS 66206	**888-431-0097**	913-341-1144	69
National Bank, The			
852 Middle Rd ....Bettendorf IA 52722	**877-321-4347**	563-344-3935	69
National Bankshares Inc			
101 Hubbard St ....Blacksburg VA 24060	**800-552-4123**	540-951-6300	357-2
NASDAQ: NKSH			
National Banner Co			
11938 Harry Hines Blvd ....Dallas TX 75234	**800-527-0860**	972-241-2131	287
National Baptist Convention USA Inc			
1700 Baptist World Ctr Dr ....Nashville TN 37207	**866-531-3054**	615-228-6292	47-20
National Baseball Hall of Fame & Museum			
25 Main St ....Cooperstown NY 13326	**888-425-5633**	607-547-7200	515
National Beef Packing Co LLC			
12200 Ambassador Dr Ste 500			
PO Box 20046. ....Kansas City MO 64163	**800-449-2333**		468
National Beer Wholesalers Assn (NBWA)			
1101 King St Ste 600 ....Alexandria VA 22314	**800-300-6417**	703-683-4300	48-6
National Billiard Manufacturing Co			
3315 Eugenia Ave ....Covington KY 41015	**800-543-0880**	859-431-4129	701
National Biodynamics Laboratory (NBDL)			
University of New Orleans College of Engineering			
2000 Lakeshore Dr ....New Orleans LA 70148	**888-514-4275**		659
National Biodynamics Laboratory (NBDL)			
University of New Orleans College of Engineering			
453 Chestnut St ....Nashville TN 37203	**866-407-3165**	615-259-9396	618
National Board of Boiler & Pressure Vessel Inspectors			
1055 Crupper Ave ....Columbus OH 43229	**877-682-8772**	614-888-8320	48-7
National Book Festival			
Library of Congress			
101 Independence Ave SE. ....Washington DC 20540	**888-714-4696**	202-707-2777	281
National Border Patrol Museum			
4315 Woodrow Bean TransMtn Rd ....El Paso TX 79924	**877-276-8738**	915-759-6060	513
National Braille Press Inc			
88 St Stephen St ....Boston MA 02115	**888-965-8965**	617-266-6160	628-2
National Breast Cancer Coalition (NBCC)			
1101 17th St NW Ste 1300 ....Washington DC 20036	**800-622-2838**	202-296-7477	47-17
National Bureau of Economic Research			
1050 Massachusetts Ave ....Cambridge MA 02138	**800-621-8476**	617-868-3900	659
National Business Assn (NBA)			
5151 Beltline Rd Ste 1150 ....Dallas TX 75254	**800-456-0440**	972-458-0900	48-12

Alphabetical Section

Listing	City	State	ZIP	Toll-Free	Phone	Class
National Business Aviation Assn (NBAA)						
1200 18th St NW Ste 400	Washington	DC	20036	**800-394-6222**	202-783-9000	48-21
National Business Coalition on Health (NBCH)						
1015 18th St NW Ste 730	Washington	DC	20036	**800-223-4139**	202-775-9300	48-12
National Business Furniture Inc						
735 N Water St Ste 440	Milwaukee	WI	53202	**800-558-1010***	414-276-8511	319
*Sales						
National Business Incubation Assn (NBIA)						
40 W St Ste 25	Athens	OH	45701	**800-766-3782**	740-593-4331	48-12
National Business Services						
1601 Magoffin Ave	El Paso	TX	79901	**800-777-7807***	915-544-1271	318-1
*Sales						
National Businesswomen's Leadership Assn						
PO Box 419107	Kansas City	MO	64141	**800-258-7246**	913-432-7755	755
National Cable Television Co-op Inc (NCTC)						
11200 Corporate Ave	Lenexa	KS	66219	**800-720-5850**	913-599-5900	48-14
National Cancer Registrars Assn (NCRA)						
1340 Braddock Pl Ste 203	Alexandria	VA	22314	**800-621-4111**	703-299-6640	47-17
National Captioning Institute (NCI)						
3725 Concorde Pkwy Ste 100	Chantilly	VA	20151	**800-825-6758**	703-917-7600	624
National Caregiving Foundation						
801 N Pitt St	Alexandria	VA	22314	**800-930-1357**	703-299-9300	47-6
National Carriers Inc						
1501 E Eigth St	Liberal	KS	67901	**800-835-9180**	620-624-1621	770
National Catholic Educational Assn (NCEA)						
1077 30th St NW Ste 100	Washington	DC	20007	**800-711-6232**	202-337-6232	48-5
National Catholic Reporter Publishing Co						
115 E Armour Blvd	Kansas City	MO	64111	**800-333-7373**	816-531-0538	628-9
National Cattlemen's Beef Assn (NCBA)						
9110 E Nichols Ave Ste 300	Centennial	CO	80112	**866-233-3872**	303-694-0305	47-2
National Chemical Laboratories Inc						
401 N Tenth St	Philadelphia	PA	19123	**800-628-2436**	215-922-1200	149
National Chemicals Inc						
105 Liberty St PO Box 32	Winona	MN	55987	**800-533-0027***	507-454-5640	149
*Cust Svc						
National Child Care Assn (NCCA)						
1325 G St NW Ste 500	Washington	DC	20005	**866-536-1945**		47-6
National Child Care Information & Technical Assistance Ctr (NCCIC)						
9300 Lee Hwy	Fairfax	VA	22031	**877-296-2250**		338-8
National Children's Ctr Inc						
6200 Second St NW	Washington	DC	20011	**866-632-9992**	202-722-2300	676
National Church Residences Inc						
2335 N Bank Dr	Columbus	OH	43220	**800-388-2151**		643
National Church Supply Co, The						
PO Box 269	Chester	WV	26034	**800-627-9900**	304-387-5200	263
National Cigar Corp						
407 N Main St PO Box 97	Frankfort	IN	46041	**800-321-0247**		746
National Cleaners Assn						
252 W 29th St Second Fl	New York	NY	10001	**800-888-1622***	212-967-3002	48-4
*General						
National Clearinghouse for Alcohol & Drug Information						
11426 Rockville Pk						
PO Box 2345	Rockville	MD	20847	**800-729-6686**		338-8
National Club Assn (NCA)						
1201 15th St NW Ste 450	Washington	DC	20005	**800-625-6221**	202-822-9822	47-23
National Coalition Against Domestic Violence (NCADV)						
One Broadway Ste B210	Denver	CO	80203	**800-799-7233**	303-839-1852	47-6
National Coalition for Cancer Survivorship (NCCS)						
1010 Wayne Ave Ste 315	Silver Spring	MD	20910	**877-622-7937**		47-17
National Coalition for the Homeless (NCH)						
2201 P St NW	Washington	DC	20037	**877-243-1576**	202-462-4822	47-5
National Coalition of Black Meeting Planners (NCBMP)						
700 N. Fairfax St Suite 510	Alexandria	VA	22314	**800-551-9369**	571-527-3110	48-12
National Coatings Inc						
3520 Rennie School Rd	Traverse City	MI	49685	**888-947-2557**	231-943-2557	476
National Coffee Assn of USA Inc (NCA)						
45 Broadway Ste 1140	New York	NY	10006	**800-247-6755**	212-766-4007	48-6
National Coil Coating Assn (NCCA)						
1300 Sumner Ave	Cleveland	OH	44115	**800-532-0500**	216-241-7333	48-13
National College of Business & Technology						
Roanoke Valley						
1813 E Main St	Salem	VA	24153	**800-664-1886**	540-986-1800	788
National College of Business & Technology Bristol						
1328 Hwy 11 W	Bristol	TN	37620	**888-956-2732**	423-878-4440	788
National College of Business & Technology Florence						
8095 Connector Dr	Florence	KY	41042	**888-956-2732**	859-525-6510	788
National College of Business & Technology Nashville						
1638 Bell Rd	Nashville	TN	37211	**855-800-1715**	615-333-3344	788
National College of Business & Technology Pikeville						
50 National College Blvd	Pikeville	KY	41501	**800-664-1886**	606-478-7200	788
National Commerce Bank Services Inc						
80 Monroe Ave Ste 250	Memphis	TN	38103	**800-264-2609**		681
National Committee for Employer Support of the Guard & Reserve (ESGR)						
1555 Wilson Blvd Ste 319	Arlington	VA	22209	**800-336-4590**	703-696-1386	47-19
National Committee for Quality Assurance (NCQA)						
1100 13th St	Washington	DC	20005	**888-275-7585**	202-955-3500	47-10
National Committee to Preserve Social Security & Medicare (NCPSSM)						
10 G St NE Ste 600	Washington	DC	20002	**800-966-1935**	202-216-0420	47-7
National Community Pharmacists Assn (NCPA)						
100 Daingerfield Rd	Alexandria	VA	22314	**800-544-7447**	703-683-8200	48-8
National Confectioners Assn (NCA)						
1101 30th St NW Ste 200	Washington	DC	20007	**800-433-1200**	202-534-1440	48-6
National Confectioners Assn PAC (NCA)						
8320 Old Courthouse Rd Ste 300	Vienna	VA	22182	**800-433-1200**	703-790-5750	608
National Conference of State Legislatures						
7700 E First Pl	Denver	CO	80230	**866-229-2386**	303-364-7700	48-7
National Conference on Citizenship (NCOC)						
1875 K St NW 5th Fl	Washington	DC	20006	**800-745-7275**	202-729-8038	47-8
National Congress of American Indians (NCAI)						
1516 P St NW	Washington	DC	20005	**800-503-3330**	202-466-7767	47-14
National Constitution Ctr						
525 Arch St						
Independence Mall	Philadelphia	PA	19106	**866-917-1787**	215-409-6600	513
National Construction Rentals Inc						
15319 Chatsworth St	Mission Hills	CA	91345	**800-352-5675**	818-221-6000	264-3
National Consumers League (NCL)						
1701 K St NW Ste 1200	Washington	DC	20006	**800-388-2227**	202-835-3323	47-10
National Contract Management Assn (NCMA)						
21740 Beaumeade Cir Ste 125	Ashburn	VA	20147	**800-344-8096**	571-382-0082	48-12
National Co-op Business Assn (NCBA)						
1401 New York Ave NW						
Ste 1100	Washington	DC	20005	**800-356-9655**	202-638-6222	48-12
National Corporate Housing						
365 Herndon Pkwy Ste 111	Herndon	VA	20170	**866-229-4720**		373
National Corvette Museum						
350 Corvette Dr	Bowling Green	KY	42101	**800-538-3883**	270-781-7973	513
National Cotton Council of America						
7193 Goodlett Farms Pkwy	Memphis	TN	38016	**888-232-1738**	901-274-9030	48-18
National Council for Accreditation of Teacher Education (NCATE)						
2010 Massachusetts Ave NW						
Ste 500	Washington	DC	20036	**800-255-8664**	202-466-7496	47-1
National Council for Air & Stream Improvement Inc (NCASI)						
PO Box 13318	Research Triangle Park	NC	27709	**888-448-2473**	919-941-6400	47-13
National Council for Prescription Drug Programs (NCPDP)						
9240 E Raintree Dr	Scottsdale	AZ	85260	**888-665-2600**	480-477-1000	48-9
National Council for the Social Studies (NCSS)						
8555 16th St Ste 500	Silver Spring	MD	20910	**800-683-0812***	301-588-1800	48-5
*Orders						
National Council of Examiners for Engineering & Surveying (NCEES)						
280 Seneca Creek Rd	Seneca	SC	29678	**800-250-3196**	864-654-6824	48-3
National Council of Jewish Women (NCJW)						
475 Riverside Dr Ste 1901	New York	NY	10115	**800-829-6259**	212-645-4048	47-24
National Council of Juvenile & Family Court Judges (NCJFCJ)						
Univ of Nevada PO Box 8970	Reno	NV	89507	**800-527-3223**	775-784-6012	48-10
National Council of La Raza (NCLR)						
1126 16th St NW 6th Fl	Washington	DC	20036	**800-821-7060**	202-785-1670	47-14
National Council of Negro Women Inc (NCNW)						
633 Pennsylvania Ave NW	Washington	DC	20004	**800-462-6420**	202-737-0120	47-24
National Council of State Boards of Nursing (NCSBN)						
111 E Wacker Dr Ste 2900	Chicago	IL	60601	**866-293-9600**	312-525-3600	48-8
National Council of Teachers of English (NCTE)						
1111 W Kenyon Rd	Urbana	IL	61801	**877-369-6283**	217-328-3870	48-5
National Council of Teachers of Mathematics (NCTM)						
1906 Assn Dr	Reston	VA	20191	**800-235-7566***	703-620-9840	48-5
*Orders						
National Council of Textile Organizations (NCTO)						
910 17th St NW Ste 1020	Washington	DC	20006	**800-238-7192**	202-822-8028	48-13
National Council on Alcoholism & Drug Dependence Inc (NCADD)						
217 Broadway Ste 712	New York	NY	10007	**800-622-2255**	212-269-7797	47-17
National Council on Crime & Delinquency (NCCD)						
1970 Broadway Ste 500	Oakland	CA	94612	**800-306-6223**	510-208-0500	47-8
National Council on Economic Education (NCEE)						
122 E 42nd St Ste 2600	New York	NY	10168	**800-338-1192**	212-730-7007	48-5
National Council on Family Relations (NCFR)						
1201 W River Pkwy Ste 200	Minneapolis	MN	55454	**888-781-9331**		47-6
National Council on Problem Gambling Inc						
730 11th St NW Ste 601	Washington	DC	20001	**800-522-4700**	202-547-9204	48-8
National Council on Public History (NCPH)						
425 University Blvd						
327 Cavanaugh Hall	Indianapolis	IN	46202	**800-554-5542**	317-274-2716	47-7
National Council on Radiation Protection & Measurements (NCRP)						
7910 Woodmont Ave Ste 400	Bethesda	MD	20814	**800-462-3683**	301-657-2652	48-19
National Council on the Aging (NCOA)						
1901 L St NW Fourth Fl	Washington	DC	20036	**800-677-1116**	202-479-1200	47-6
National Court Appointed Special Advocate Assn (CASA)						
100 W Harrison St N Twr Ste 500	Seattle	WA	98119	**800-628-3233**	206-270-0072	47-6
National Court Reporters Assn (NCRA)						
8224 Old Courthouse Rd	Vienna	VA	22182	**800-272-6272**	703-556-6272	48-10
National Court Reporters Assn PAC						
8224 Old Courthouse Rd	Vienna	VA	22182	**800-272-6272**	703-556-6272	608
National Cowgirl Museum & Hall of Fame						
1720 Gendy St	Fort Worth	TX	76107	**800-476-3263**	817-336-4475	513
National CPA Health Care Advisors Assn (HCAA)						
624 Grassmere Pk Ste 15	Nashville	TN	37211	**800-231-2524**	615-373-9880	48-1
National Credit Union Administration						
1775 Duke St	Alexandria	VA	22314	**800-827-9650***	703-518-6300	338-18
*Fraud Hotline						
National Crop Insurance Services (NCIS)						
8900 Indian Creek Pkwy						
Ste 600	Overland Park	KS	66210	**800-951-6247**	913-685-2767	47-2
National Ctr for Employee Development (NCED)						
2701 E Imhoff Rd	Norman	OK	73071	**866-438-6233**	405-366-4420	374
National Ctr for Family Literacy (NCFL)						
325 W Main St Ste 300	Louisville	KY	40202	**877-326-5481**	502-584-1133	47-11
National Ctr for Genome Resources						
2935 Rodeo Pk Dr E	Santa Fe	NM	87505	**800-450-4854**	505-995-4451	659
National Ctr for Mfg Sciences (NCMS)						
3025 Boardwalk	Ann Arbor	MI	48108	**800-222-6267**	734-995-0300	659
National Ctr for Missing & Exploited Children (NCMEC)						
699 Prince St	Alexandria	VA	22314	**800-843-5678**	703-274-3900	47-6
National Ctr for Neighborhood Enterprise (NCNE)						
1625 K St Ste 1200	Washington	DC	20006	**866-518-1263**	202-518-6500	47-7
National Ctr for Retirement Benefits Inc						
666 Dundee Rd Ste 1200	Northbrook	IL	60062	**800-666-1000**		194
National Ctr for State Courts (NCSC)						
300 Newport Ave	Williamsburg	VA	23185	**800-616-6164**	757-259-1525	48-7
National Ctr for Victims of Crime, The						
2000 M St NW Ste 480	Washington	DC	20036	**800-394-2255**	202-467-8700	47-8
National Cycle Inc						
2200 Maywood Dr	Maywood	IL	60153	**877-972-7336**	708-343-0400	510
National Diagnostics Inc						
305 Patton Dr	Atlanta	GA	30336	**800-526-3867**	404-699-2121	231
National Disaster Search Dog Foundation						
501 E Ojai Ave	Ojai	CA	93023	**888-459-4376**	805-646-1015	47-3
National Discount Cruise Co						
1401 N Cedar Crest Blvd						
Ste 56	Allentown	PA	18104	**800-788-8108**	610-439-4883	761
National Disease Research Interchange (NDRI)						
1628 John F Kennedy Blvd						
8 Penn Ctr 8th Fl	Philadelphia	PA	19103	**800-222-6374**	215-557-7361	269
National Dissemination Ctr for Children with Disabilities						
1825 Connecticut Ave	Washington	DC	20009	**800-695-0285**	202-884-8200	47-17
National Distributors Inc						
1517 Avco Blvd	Sellersburg	IN	47172	**800-334-9677**	812-246-6306	444
National District Attorneys Assn (NDAA)						
99 Canal Ctr Plaza Ste 510	Alexandria	VA	22314	**888-325-9943**	703-549-9222	48-7
National Diversity Newspaper Job Bank						
c/o Morris Communications						
725 Broad St	Augusta	GA	30901	**800-622-6358**	706-724-0851	260
National Domestic Violence Hotline (NDVH)						
PO Box 161810	Austin	TX	78716	**800-799-7233**	512-794-1133	47-6
National Down Syndrome Congress (NDSC)						
1370 Ctr Dr Ste 102	Atlanta	GA	30338	**800-232-6372**	770-604-9500	47-17
National Down Syndrome Society (NDSS)						
666 Broadway 8th Fl	New York	NY	10012	**800-221-4602**		47-17
National Eating Disorders Assn						
603 Stewart St Ste 803	Seattle	WA	98101	**800-931-2237**		47-17

Alphabetical Section

				Toll-Free	Phone	Class
National Education Assn (NEA)						
1201 16th St NW	Washington	DC	20036	**888-552-0624**	202-833-4000	48-5
National Educational Telecommunications Assn (NETA)						
939 S Stadium Rd	Columbia	SC	29201	**866-270-5141**	803-799-5517	624
National Electrical Carbon						
251 Forrester Dr	Greenville	SC	29607	**800-471-7842**	864-284-9728	126
National Electrical Contractors Assn (NECA)						
3 Bethesda Metro Ctr Ste 1100	Bethesda	MD	20814	**800-214-0585**	301-657-3110	48-3
National Electrical Manufacturers Assn (NEMA)						
1300 N 17th St Ste 1752	Rosslyn	VA	22209	**888-236-2427**	703-841-3200	48-13
National Electrical Manufacturers Representatives Assn (NEMRA)						
28 Deer St Ste 302	Portsmouth	NH	03801	**800-446-3672**	914-524-8650	48-18
National Electronics Service Dealers Assn (NESDA)						
3608 Pershing Ave	Fort Worth	TX	76107	**800-946-0201**	817-921-9061	48-18
National Emblem Inc						
17036 S Avalon Blvd	Carson	CA	90746	**800-877-6185**	310-515-5055	258
National Employee Assistance Services Inc						
N 17 W 24100 Riverwood Dr						
Ste 300	Waukesha	WI	53188	**800-634-6433**	262-574-2500	457
National Endowment for the Humanities (NEH)						
400 7th St SW	Washington	DC	20506	**800-634-1121**	202-606-8400	338-18
National Energy Research Scientific Computing Ctr (NERSC)						
Lawrence Berkeley National						
Laboratory	Berkeley	CA	94720	**800-666-3772**	510-486-5849	659
National Energy Technology Laboratory (NETL)						
3610 Collins Ferry Rd	Morgantown	WV	26505	**800-432-8330**	304-285-4764	659
National Engineering Service Corp						
72 Mirona Rd	Portsmouth	NH	03801	**800-562-3463**	603-431-9740	712
National Environmental Balancing Bureau (NEBB)						
8575 Grovemont Cir	Gaithersburg	MD	20877	**866-497-4447**	301-977-3698	48-19
National Environmental Health Assn (NEHA)						
720 S Colorado Blvd Ste 1000-N	Denver	CO	80246	**866-956-2258**	303-756-9090	48-7
National Environmental Satellite Data & Information Service						
National Coastal Data Development Ctr						
Bldg 1100 Ste 101	Stennis Space Center	MS	39529	**866-732-2382**	228-688-2936	338-2
National Enzyme Co Inc						
15366 US Hwy 160	Forsyth	MO	65653	**800-825-8545**	417-546-4796	142
National Excelsior Co						
1999 N Ruby St	Melrose Park	IL	60160	**855-373-9235**	708-343-4225	588
National Exchange Club						
3050 W Central Ave	Toledo	OH	43606	**800-924-2643**	419-535-3232	47-15
National Fallen Firefighters Foundation						
PO Box 498	Emmitsburg	MD	21727	**888-744-6513**	301-447-1365	47-19
National Family Caregivers Assn (NFCA)						
10400 Connecticut Ave						
Ste 500	Kensington	MD	20895	**800-896-3650**	301-942-6430	47-6
National Farm Life Insurance Co						
6001 Bridge St	Fort Worth	TX	76112	**800-772-7557**	817-451-9550	387
National Farm Toy Museum						
1110 16th Ave SE	Dyersville	IA	52040	**877-475-2727**	563-875-2727	513
National Farmers Organization (NFO)						
528 Billy Sunday Rd Ste 100						
PO Box 2508	Ames	IA	50010	**800-247-2110**	515-292-2000	47-2
National Farmers Union Property & Casualty Co						
5619 DTC Pkwy Ste 300	Greenwood Village	CO	80111	**800-347-1961**	303-337-5500	388-4
National Federation of Community Development Credit Unions (NFCDCU)						
39 Broadway Ste 2140	New York	NY	10006	**800-437-8711**	212-809-1850	48-2
National Federation of Paralegal Assn (NFPA)						
23607 Hwy 99 Ste 2-C	Edmonds	WA	98020	**888-525-3675**	425-967-0045	48-10
National Federation of Republican Women (NFRW)						
124 N Alfred St	Alexandria	VA	22314	**800-373-9688**	703-548-9688	47-7
National Federation of State High School Assn (NFHS)						
PO Box 690	Indianapolis	IN	46206	**800-776-3462***	317-972-6900	47-22
*Cust Svc						
National Federation of the Blind (NFB)						
1800 Johnson St	Baltimore	MD	21230	**800-392-5671**	410-659-9314	47-17
National FFA Organization						
6060 FFA Dr	Indianapolis	IN	46268	**800-772-0939**	317-802-6060	47-2
National Fiber Technology LLC						
300 Canal St	Lawrence	MA	01840	**800-842-2751***	978-686-2964	345
*Cust Svc						
National Fibromyalgia Partnership Inc (NFP)						
140 Zinn Way	Linden	VA	22642	**866-725-4404**		47-17
National Filter Media Corp						
691 North 400 West	Salt Lake City	UT	84103	**800-777-4248**	801-363-6736	18
National Fingerprint Inc						
6999 Dolan Rd	Glouster	OH	45732	**888-823-7873**	740-767-3853	683
National Fire & Marine Insurance Co						
3024 Harney St	Omaha	NE	68131	**866-720-7861**	402-536-3000	388-4
National Fire Protection Assn (NFPA)						
One Batterymarch Pk	Quincy	MA	02169	**800-344-3555**	617-770-3000	47-17
National Fisherman Magazine						
121 Free St	Portland	ME	04101	**800-959-5073**	207-842-5600	452-21
National Fitness Trade Journal						
PO Box 2490	White City	OR	97503	**877-867-7835**	541-830-0400	452-21
National Floral Supply Inc						
3825 LeonaRdtown Rd Ste 4	Waldorf	MD	20601	**800-932-2772**	301-932-7600	292
National Forest Recreation Assn (NFRA)						
PO Box 488	Woodlake	CA	93286	**800-282-2444**	559-564-2365	47-23
National Foundation for Cancer Research (NFCR)						
4600 E W Hwy Ste 525	Bethesda	MD	20814	**800-321-2873**	301-654-1250	304
National Frame Builders Assn (NFBA)						
8735 W Higgins Rd Ste 300	Chicago	IL	60631	**800-557-6957**		48-3
National Fraternity of Kappa Delta Rho (KDR)						
331 S Main St	Greensburg	PA	15601	**800-536-5371**	724-838-7100	47-16
National Fraud Information Ctr (NFIC)						
1701 K St NW Ste 1200	Washington	DC	20006	**800-333-4636**	202-835-3323	47-10
National Freedom of Information Coalition						
Univ of Missouri	Columbia	MO	65211	**866-682-6663**	573-882-4856	47-8
National Freight Inc (NFI)						
1515 Burnt Mill Rd	Cherry Hill	NJ	08003	**877-634-3777***		444
*General						
National Fresh Water Fishing Hall of Fame						
10360 Hall of Fame Dr						
PO Box 690	Hayward	WI	54843	**866-268-4333**	715-634-4440	515
National Fruit Product Co Inc						
701 Fairmont Ave PO Box 2040	Winchester	VA	22601	**800-655-4022**	540-723-9614	314-3
National Fuel Gas Co						
6363 Main St	Williamsville	NY	14221	**800-365-3234***	716-857-7000	357-5
NYSE: NFG ■ *Cust Svc						
National Fuel Gas Distribution Corp						
6363 Main St	Williamsville	NY	14221	**800-365-3234**	716-857-7000	775
National Fuel Gas Supply Corp						
6363 Main St	Williamsville	NY	14221	**800-365-3234***	716-857-7000	775
*Cust Svc						
National Fuel Resources Inc						
165 Lawrence Bell Dr						
Ste 120	Williamsville	NY	14221	**800-839-9993**	716-630-6778	775
National Funeral Directors & Morticians Assn (NFDMA)						
6290 Shannon Pkwy	Union City	GA	30291	**800-434-0958**	770-969-0064	48-4
National Funeral Directors Assn (NFDA)						
13625 Bishop's Dr	Brookfield	WI	53005	**800-228-6332**	262-789-1880	48-4
National Funeral Directors Assn PAC						
13625 Bishop S Dr	Brookfield	WI	53005	**800-228-6332**	262-789-1880	608
National Futures Assn (NFA)						
300 S Riverside Plz Ste 1800	Chicago	IL	60606	**800-621-3570**	312-781-1300	48-2
National Garden Clubs Inc (NGC)						
4401 Magnolia Ave	Saint Louis	MO	63110	**800-550-6007**	314-776-7574	47-18
National Gardening Assn (NGA)						
1100 Dorset St	South Burlington	VT	05403	**800-538-7476**	802-863-5251	47-18
National Gaucher Foundation (NGF)						
2227 Idlewood Rd Ste 6	Tucker	GA	30084	**800-504-3189**	770-934-2910	47-17
National Genealogical Society (NGS)						
3108 Columbia Pk Ste 300	Arlington	VA	22204	**800-473-0060**	703-525-0050	47-18
National Genetics Institute						
2440 S Blvd Ste 235	Los Angeles	CA	90064	**800-352-7788**	310-996-0036	415
National Geographic Adventure Magazine						
1145 17th St NW	Washington	DC	20036	**800-647-5463**	202-857-7000	452-11
National Geographic Kids Magazine						
1145 17th St NW	Washington	DC	20036	**800-647-5463**	202-857-7000	452-6
National Geographic Magazine						
1145 17th St NW	Washington	DC	20036	**800-647-5463**	202-857-7000	452-11
National Geographic Society						
1145 17th St NW	Washington	DC	20036	**800-647-5463**	202-857-7000	48-19
National Geographic Society Explorers Hall						
1145 17th St NW	Washington	DC	20036	**800-647-5463**		513
National Geographic Traveler Magazine						
1145 17th St NW	Washington	DC	20036	**800-647-5463**	202-857-7000	452-22
National Glass Assn (NGA)						
8200 Greensboro Dr Ste 302	McLean	VA	22102	**866-342-5642**	703-442-4890	48-13
National Glass Ltd						
5744 198th St	Langley	BC	V3A7J2	**800-663-8168**	604-530-2311	358
National Golf Course Owners Assn (NGCOA)						
291 Seven Farms Dr Second Fl	Charleston	SC	29492	**800-933-4262**	843-881-9956	47-23
National Golf Foundation (NGF)						
1150 S US Hwy 1 Ste 401	Jupiter	FL	33477	**800-733-6006**	561-744-6006	47-22
National Grange						
1616 H St NW	Washington	DC	20006	**888-447-2643**	202-628-3507	47-2
National Grange Mutual Insurance Co						
55 W St	Keene	NH	03431	**800-258-5310**	603-352-4000	388-4
National Grid USA Service Company Inc						
25 Research Dr	Westborough	MA	01582	**800-548-8000**	508-389-2000	357-5
National Ground Water Assn (NGWA)						
601 Dempsey Rd	Westerville	OH	43081	**800-551-7379**	614-898-7791	47-12
National Ground Water Assn PAC						
601 Dempsey Rd	Westerville	OH	43081	**800-551-7379**	614-898-7791	608
National Guard Assn of the US (NGAUS)						
One Massachusetts Ave NW						
Ste 200	Washington	DC	20001	**888-226-4287**	202-789-0031	47-19
National Guard Products Inc						
4985 E Raines Rd	Memphis	TN	38118	**800-647-7874**		234
National Guardian Life Insurance Co (NGL)						
2 E Gilman St	Madison	WI	53703	**800-548-2962**	608-257-5611	388-2
National Gypsum Co						
2001 Rexford Rd	Charlotte	NC	28211	**800-628-4662**	704-365-7300	344
National Hansen's Disease Program (NHDP)						
1770 Physicians Pk Dr	Baton Rouge	LA	70816	**800-642-2477**	225-756-3700	659
National Hardwood Lumber Assn (NHLA)						
6830 Raleigh-LaGrange Rd	Memphis	TN	38134	**800-933-0318**	901-377-1818	48-3
National Head Start Assn (NHSA)						
1651 Prince St	Alexandria	VA	22314	**866-677-8724**	703-739-0875	47-11
National Headache Foundation (NHF)						
820 N Orleans St Ste 217	Chicago	IL	60610	**888-643-5552**		47-17
National Hearing Conservation Assn (NHCA)						
3030 W 81st Ave	Westminster	CO	80031	**800-445-8667**	303-224-9022	47-17
National Hemophilia Foundation (NHF)						
116 W 32nd St 11th Fl	New York	NY	10001	**800-424-2634**	212-328-3700	47-17
National Heritage Academies						
3850 Broadmoor Ave SE						
Ste 201	Grand Rapids	MI	49512	**877-223-6402***		242
*General						
National Herpes Resource Ctr (HRC)						
PO Box 13827	Research Triangle Park	NC	27709	**877-478-5868**	919-361-8400	47-17
National Highway Express Co						
971 Old Henderson St						
PO Box 20262	Columbus	OH	43220	**800-837-5700**	614-459-4900	770
National Center for Statistics & Analysis						
1200 New Jersey Ave SE	Washington	DC	20590	**800-934-8517**	202-366-1503	338-15
National Highway Traffic Safety Administration						
Vehicle Research & Test Ctr						
10820 SR 347 PO Box B37	East Liberty	OH	43319	**800-262-8309**	937-666-4511	338-15
National Highway Traffic Safety Administration Regional Offices						
NHTSA Region 3						
1200 New Jersey Ave Ste 6700	Washington	DC	20590	**888-327-4236**		338-15
National Hispanic Council on Aging (NHCOA)						
734 15th St NW Ste 1050	Washington	DC	20005	**800-633-4227**	202-347-9733	47-6
National Hispanic University						
14271 Story Rd	San Jose	CA	95127	**877-762-9801**	408-254-6900	166
National Home Furnishings Assn (NHFA)						
3910 Tinsley Dr Ste 101	High Point	NC	27265	**800-422-3778**	336-886-6100	48-4
National Home Health Care Corp						
700 White Plains Rd Ste 275	Scarsdale	NY	10583	**800-422-4661**	914-722-9000	360
National Homeland Security Research Ctr						
US Environmental Protection Agency						
26 W Martin Luther King Dr	Cincinnati	OH	45268	**888-372-7341**	513-569-7907	659
National Honor Society (NHS)						
1904 Assn Dr	Reston	VA	20191	**800-253-7746**	703-860-0200	47-11
National Hospice & Palliative Care Organization (NHPCO)						
1700 Diagonal Rd Ste 625	Alexandria	VA	22314	**800-658-8898***	703-837-1500	48-8
*Help Line						
National Hotel						
1677 Collins Ave	Miami Beach	FL	33139	**800-327-8370**	305-532-2311	376
National HVAC Service Ltd						
101 Bradford Rd Ste 340	Wexford	PA	15090	**800-281-3608**	724-935-9390	190-10
National Independent Automobile Dealers Assn (NIADA)						
2521 Brown Blvd	Arlington	TX	76006	**800-682-3837**	817-640-3838	48-18

Listing	Toll-Free	Phone	Class
National Indian Gaming Assn (NIGA) 224 Second St SE .... Washington DC 20003	866-694-3937	202-546-7711	47-23
National Industrial Lumber Co 1 Chicago Ave .... Elizabeth PA 15037	800-289-9352		192-3
National Industries for the Blind (NIB) 1310 Braddock Pl .... Alexandria VA 22314 *Cust Svc	800-433-2304*	703-310-0500	47-17
National Information Standards Organization (NISO) 3600 Clipper Mill Road Suite 302 .... Baltimore MD 21211	877-375-2160	301-654-2512	48-16
National Inhalant Prevention Coalition (NIPC) 318 Lindsay St .... Chattanooga TN 37403	800-269-4237	423-265-4662	47-17
National Institute for Literacy (NIFL) 1775 'I' St NW Ste 730 .... Washington DC 20006	800-228-8813	202-233-2025	338-6
National Institute of Governmental Purchasing Inc (NIGP) 151 Spring St .... Herndon VA 20170	800-367-6447	703-736-8900	48-7
National Institute of Standards & Technology (NIST) 100 Bureau Dr Sp 1070 .... Gaithersburg MD 20899	800-877-8339	301-975-6478	338-2
National Institutes of Health			
National Cancer Institute Public Inquiries Office 6116 Executive Blvd Rm 3036A .... Bethesda MD 20892	800-422-6237	301-435-3848	659
National Center for Complementary & Alternative Medicine National Institutes of Health 31 Ctr Dr Bldg 31 .... Bethesda MD 20892	888-644-6226	301-594-7103	338-8
National Institute of Mental Health 6001 Executive Blvd Rm 8184 MSC 9663 .... Bethesda MD 20892	866-615-6464	301-443-4513	338-8
National Institute of Neurological Disorders & Stroke PO Box 5801 .... Bethesda MD 20824	800-352-9424	301-496-5751	338-8
National Institute on Deafness & Other Communication Disorders 31 Ctr Dr Bldg 31 Rm 3C35 .... Bethesda MD 20892	800-241-1044	301-496-7243	659
National Library of Medicine National Institutes of Health 8600 Rockville Pike Bldg 38 .... Bethesda MD 20894	888-346-3656	301-594-5983	338-8
National Instrument LLC 4119 Fordleigh Rd .... Baltimore MD 21215	866-258-1914	410-764-0900	540
National Instruments Corp 11500 N Mopac Expy .... Austin TX 78759 *NASDAQ: NATI* ■ *Cust Svc	800-433-3488*	512-794-0100	179-5
National Insulation Assn (NIA) 99 Canal Ctr Plz Ste 222 .... Alexandria VA 22314	877-968-7642	703-683-6422	48-3
National Insurance Crime Bureau (NICB) 1111 E Touhy Ave Ste 400 .... Des Plaines IL 60018	800-447-6282	847-544-7002	48-9
National International Roofing Corp 11317 Smith Dr .... Huntley IL 60142	800-221-7663	847-669-3444	190-12
National Interstate Corp 3250 I- Dr .... Richfield OH 44286 *NASDAQ: NATL*	800-929-1500	330-659-8900	388-4
National Inventors Hall of Fame 3701 Highland Park NW Inventure Pl .... North Canton OH 44720	800-968-4332		513
National Investment Co Service Assn (NICSA) 8400 Westpark Dr 2nd Fl .... McLean VA 22102	800-426-1122	508-485-1500	48-2
National Jets 3495 SW Ninth Ave PO Box 22460 .... Fort Lauderdale FL 33315	800-327-3710	954-359-9900	62
National Jewish Medical & Research Ctr 1400 Jackson St PO Box 17169 .... Denver CO 80206	877-225-5654	303-388-4461	371-7
National Journal 600 New Hampshire Ave NW .... Washington DC 20037	800-613-6701	202-739-8400	452-17
National Jurist Magazine 7670 Opportunity Rd Ste 105 .... San Diego CA 92111	800-296-9656	858-300-3201	452-15
National Kappa Kappa Iota Inc 1875 E 15th St .... Tulsa OK 74104	800-678-0389	918-744-0389	47-16
National Kidney Foundation (NKF) 30 E 33rd St Eighth Fl .... New York NY 10016	800-622-9010	212-889-2210	47-17
National Kitchen & Bath Assn (NKBA) 687 Willow Grove St .... Hackettstown NJ 07840	800-843-6522		48-3
National Labor College 10000 New Hampshire Ave .... Silver Spring MD 20903	888-427-8100	301-431-6400	788
National Labor Relations Board (NLRB) 1099 14th St NW .... Washington DC 20570	866-667-6572	202-273-1991	338-18
National Labor Relations Board Regional Offices			
Region 1 10 Cswy St 6th Fl .... Boston MA 02222	866-667-6572	617-565-6700	338-18
Region 3 Niagara Ctr Bldg 130 S Elmwood Ave Ste 630 .... Buffalo NY 14202	866-667-6572	716-551-4931	338-18
Region 8 1240 E Ninth St Rm 1695 .... Cleveland OH 44199	866-667-6572	216-522-3715	338-18
Region 9 550 Main St Rm 3003 .... Cincinnati OH 45202	866-667-6572	513-684-3686	338-18
Region 11 4035 University Pkwy Ste 200 .... Winston-Salem NC 27106	866-667-6572	336-631-5201	338-18
Region 14 1222 Spruce St Rm 8.302 .... Saint Louis MO 63103	866-667-6572	314-539-7770	338-18
Region 16 Federal Bldg 819 Taylor St Rm 8A24 .... Fort Worth TX 76102	866-667-6572	817-978-2921	338-18
Region 18 330 Second Ave S Ste 790 .... Minneapolis MN 55401	866-667-6572	612-348-1757	338-18
Region 20 901 Market St Ste 400 .... San Francisco CA 94103	866-667-6572	415-356-5130	338-18
Region 25 575 N Pennsylvania St Ste 238 .... Indianapolis IN 46204	866-667-6572	317-226-7381	338-18
Region 31 11150 W Olympic Blvd Ste 700 .... Los Angeles CA 90064	866-667-6572	310-235-7352	338-18
National League for Nursing (NLN) 61 Broadway 33rd Fl .... New York NY 10006	800-669-1656	212-363-5555	48-8
National Legal Aid & Defender Assn (NLADA) 1140 Connecticut Ave NW Ste 900 .... Washington DC 20036	800-725-4513	202-452-0620	48-10
National Liberty Museum 321 Chestnut St .... Philadelphia PA 19106	800-732-0999	215-925-2800	513
National Little Britches Rodeo Assn (NLBRA) 5050 Edison Ave Ste 105 .... Colorado Springs CO 80915	800-763-3694	719-389-0333	47-22
National Lumber 71 Maple St .... Mansfield MA 02048	800-370-9663	508-339-8020	361
National Mail Order Assn LLC (NMOA) 2807 Polk St NE .... Minneapolis MN 55418	800-992-1377	612-788-1673	48-18
National Marfan Foundation (NMF) 22 Manhasset Ave .... Port Washington NY 11050	800-862-7326	516-883-8712	47-17
National Marine Electronics Assn (NMEA) Seven Riggs Ave .... Severna Park MD 21146	800-808-6632	410-975-9425	48-13
National Marine Fisheries Service Regional Offices			
Pacific Islands Region 1601 Kapiolani Blvd Rm 1110 .... Honolulu HI 96814	888-674-7411	808-944-2200	338-2
National Marine Representatives Assn (NMRA) PO Box 360 .... Gurnee IL 60031	800-890-3819	847-662-3167	48-18
National Marrow Donor Program (NMDP) 3001 Broadway St NE Ste 100 .... Minneapolis MN 55413	800-526-7809	612-627-5800	47-17
National Medical Assn (NMA) 8403 Colesville Rd Ste 920 .... Silver Spring MD 20910	800-662-0554	202-347-1895	48-8
National Mental Health Information Ctr PO Box 42557 .... Washington DC 20015	800-487-4889		338-8
National Metal Fabricators 2395 Greenleaf Ave .... Elk Grove Village IL 60007	800-323-8849	847-439-5321	688
National Meter & Automation 7220 S Fraser St .... Centennial CO 80112	877-212-8340	303-339-9100	603
National Middle School Assn (NMSA) 4151 Executive Pkwy Ste 300 .... Westerville OH 43081	800-528-6672	614-895-4730	48-5
National Milk Producers Federation (NMPF) 2101 Wilson Blvd Ste 400 .... Arlington VA 22201	888-723-3366	703-243-6111	48-6
National Mississippi River Museum & Aquarium 350 E Third St .... Dubuque IA 52001	800-226-3369	563-557-9545	513
National Model Railroad Assn (NMRA) 4121 Cromwell Rd .... Chattanooga TN 37421	800-654-2256	423-892-2846	47-18
National Motor Club of America Inc (NMC) 130 E John Carpenter Fwy .... Irving TX 75062	800-523-4582	972-999-1099	52
National Motorists Assn (NMA) 402 W Second St .... Waunakee WI 53597	800-882-2785	608-849-6000	48-21
National Multi Housing Council PAC 1850 M St NW Ste 540 .... Washington DC 20036	866-987-7367	202-974-2300	608
National Multiple Sclerosis Society 733 Third Ave Third Fl .... New York NY 10017	800-344-4867	212-986-3240	47-17
National Museum of Dentistry 31 S Greene St .... Baltimore MD 21201	866-787-8637	410-706-0600	513
National Museum of Natural History (Smithsonian Institution) 10th St & Constitution Ave NW .... Washington DC 20560	866-868-7774	202-633-1000	513
National Museum of Naval Aviation 1750 Radford Blvd Ste C .... Pensacola FL 32508 *General	800-247-6289*	850-452-3604	513
National Museum of Racing & Hall of Fame 191 Union Ave .... Saratoga Springs NY 12866	800-562-5394	518-584-0400	515
National Museum of the American Indian (Smithsonian Institution) One Bowling Green .... New York NY 10004	800-242-6624	212-514-3700	513
National Museum of the Marine Corps 18900 Jefferson Davis Hwy .... Triangle VA 22172	877-635-1775	703-221-1581	513
National Museum of Wildlife Art 2820 Rungius Rd PO Box 6825 .... Jackson WY 83002	800-313-9553	307-733-5771	513
National Museum of Women in the Arts 1250 New York Ave NW .... Washington DC 20005	866-875-4627	202-783-5000	513
National Music Museum 414 E Clark St .... Vermillion SD 57069	877-225-0027	605-677-5306	513
National Mutual Benefit 6522 Grand Teton Plaza .... Madison WI 53719	800-779-1936	608-833-1936	388-2
National NeedleArts Assn, The (TNNA) 1100-H Brandywine Blvd .... Zanesville OH 43701	800-889-8662	740-455-6773	47-18
National Newspaper Assn (NNA) PO Box 7540 .... Columbia MO 65205	800-829-4662	573-777-4980	48-14
National Niemann-Pick Disease Foundation Inc (NNPDF) 401 Madison Ave Ste B PO Box 49 .... Fort Atkinson WI 53538	877-287-3672	920-563-0930	47-17
National Nonwovens PO Box 150 .... EastHampton MA 01027	800-333-3469	413-527-3445	734-6
National Notary Assn (NNA) 9350 DeSoto Ave .... Chatsworth CA 91313	800-876-6827	818-739-4000	48-12
National Notary Magazine 9350 DeSoto Ave .... Chatsworth CA 91311 *Cust Svc	800-876-6827*	818-739-4000	452-5
National Nursing Staff Development Organization (NNSDO) 330 N Wabash Ave Ste 2000 .... Chicago IL 60611	800-489-1995	312-321-5135	48-8
National Ocean Industries Assn (NOIA) 1120 G St NW Ste 900 .... Washington DC 20005	800-558-9994	202-347-6900	47-12
National Office Furniture 1205 Kimball Blvd .... Jasper IN 47549	800-482-1717		318-1
National Oil & Gas Inc 409 N Main St .... Bluffton IN 46714	800-322-8454	260-824-2220	572
National Oilwell Varco (NOV) 7909 Parkwood Cir Dr .... Houston TX 77036 *NYSE: NOV*	888-262-8645	713-375-3700	184
National Optical Astronomy Observatories 950 N Cherry Ave .... Tucson AZ 85719	888-809-4012	520-318-8163	659
National Oral Health Information Clearinghouse (NIDCR) One NOHIC Way .... Bethesda MD 20892	866-232-4528	301-496-4261	47-17
National Organization for Albinism & Hypopigmentation (NOAH) PO Box 959 .... East Hampstead NH 03826	800-648-2310	603-887-2310	47-17
National Organization for Rare Disorders (NORD) 55 Kenosia Ave PO Box 1968 .... Danbury CT 06813	800-999-6673	203-744-0100	47-17
National Organization for the Reform of Marijuana Laws (NORML) 1600 K St NW Ste 501 .... Washington DC 20006	888-676-6765	202-483-5500	47-8
National Organization for Victim Assistance (NOVA) 510 King St Ste 424 .... Alexandria VA 22314	800-879-6682	703-535-6682	47-8
National Organization for Women (NOW) 1100 H St NW 3rd Fl .... Washington DC 20005	855-212-0212	202-628-8669	47-24
National Organization of Circumcision Information Resource Centers (NOCIRC) PO Box 2512 .... San Anselmo CA 94979	800-727-8622	415-488-9883	47-17
National Ornamental Metal Museum 374 Metal Museum Dr .... Memphis TN 38106	877-881-2326	901-774-6380	513
National Osteoporosis Foundation (NOF) 1232 22nd St NW .... Washington DC 20037	800-231-4222	202-223-2226	47-17
National Outdoor Leadership School 284 Lincoln St .... Lander WY 82520	800-710-6657	307-332-5300	676
National Ovarian Cancer Coalition (NOCC) 2501 Oak Lawn Ave Ste 435 .... Dallas TX 75219	888-682-7426		47-17
National Paint & Coatings Assn (NPCA) 1500 Rhode Island Ave NW .... Washington DC 20005	800-431-7900	202-462-6272	48-13
National Paper & Sanitary Supply 2511 S 156th Cir .... Omaha NE 68130	800-647-2737	402-330-5507	552

	Toll-Free	Phone	Class
National Park Community College			
101 College Dr ....Hot Springs AR 71913	800-760-1825	501-760-4222	160
National Parking Assn (NPA)			
1112 16th St NW Ste 840 ....Washington DC 20036	800-647-7275	202-296-4336	48-3
National Parks Conservation Assn (NPCA)			
1300 19th St NW Ste 300 ....Washington DC 20036	800-628-7275	202-223-6722	47-13
National Parks Magazine			
777 Sixth St NW Ste 700 ....Washington DC 20001	800-628-7275*	202-223-6722	452-19
*General			
National Partitions			
10300 Goldenfern Ln ....Knoxville TN 37931	888-818-5749	865-670-2100	286
National Peace Corps Assn (NPCA)			
1900 L St NW Ste 610 ....Washington DC 20036	800-424-8580	202-293-7728	47-5
National Pen Corp (NPC)			
12121 Scripps Summit Dr			
Ste 200 ....San Diego CA 92131	800-854-1000	858-675-3000	9
National Penn Bancshares Inc			
PO Box 547 ....Boyertown PA 19512	800-822-3321		357-2
NASDAQ: NPBC			
National Pesticide Information Ctr (NPIC)			
333 Weniger Hall ....Corvallis OR 97331	800-858-7378		47-17
National Pipe & Plastics Inc			
3421 Old Vestal Rd ....Vestal NY 13850	800-836-4350		589
National Pork Producers Council PAC			
122 C St NW Ste 875 ....Washington DC 20001	800-392-5705	202-347-3600	608
National Post			
1450 Don Mills Rd Ste 300 ....Toronto ON M3B3R5	800-267-6568	416-383-2300	525-1
National Precast Concrete Assn (NPCA)			
10333 N Meridian St			
Ste 272 ....Indianapolis IN 46290	800-366-7731	317-571-9500	48-3
National Press Foundation (NPF)			
1211 Connecticut Ave NW			
Ste 310 ....Washington DC 20036	877-472-3779	202-663-7280	48-16
National Presto Industries Inc			
3925 N Hastings Way ....Eau Claire WI 54703	800-877-0441	715-839-2121	36
NYSE: NPK			
National Printing Converters Inc			
18 S Murphy Ave ....Brazil IN 47834	800-877-6724	812-448-2555	410
National Processing Co			
5100 Interchange Way ....Louisville KY 40229	877-300-7757*	800-683-2289	255
*General			
National Propane Gas Assn PAC (NPGAPAC)			
1899 L St NW Ste 350 ....Washington DC 20036	888-445-1404	202-466-7200	608
National Property Inspections Inc (NPI)			
9375 Burt St Ste 201 ....Omaha NE 68114	800-333-9807	402-333-9807	362
National Psoriasis Foundation (NPF)			
6600 SW 92nd Ave Ste 300 ....Portland OR 97223	800-723-9166	503-244-7404	47-17
National Psychological Assn for Psychoanalysis (NPAP)			
40 W 13th St Ste 1 ....New York NY 10011	800-365-7006	212-924-7440	48-15
National Pump Company LLC			
7706 N 71st Ave ....Glendale AZ 85303	800-966-5240	623-979-3560	632
National Railroad Museum			
2285 S Broadway St ....Green Bay WI 54304	866-468-7630	920-437-7623	513
National Railroad Passenger Corp			
60 Massachusetts Ave NE ....Washington DC 20002	800-872-7245	202-906-3741	640
National Railway Equipment Co (NREC)			
14400 Robey Ave Ste 2 ....Dixmoor IL 60426	800-253-2905	708-388-6002	641
National Ready Mixed Concrete Assn (NRMCA)			
900 Spring St ....Silver Spring MD 20910	888-846-7622	301-587-1400	48-3
National Real Estate Investor Magazine			
6151 Powers Ferry Rd NW Ste 200.......Atlanta GA 30339	877-829-2782	770-955-2500	452-5
National Realty & Development Corp			
3 Manhattanville Rd ....Purchase NY 10577	800-932-7368	914-694-4444	646
National Recreation & Park Assn			
22377 Belmont Ridge Rd ....Ashburn VA 20148	800-626-6772	703-858-0784	47-1
National Recreation and Park Association (NSPR)			
22377 Belmont Ridge Rd ....Ashburn VA 20148	800-626-6772	703-858-0784	47-23
National Recreation Reservation Service (NRRS)			
PO Box 140 ....Ballston Spa NY 12020	877-444-6777	518-885-3639	763
National Register Publishing Co			
430 Mountain Ave			
Suite 400 ....New Providence NJ 07974	800-473-7020		628-2
National Rehabilitation Assn (NRA)			
633 S Washington St ....Alexandria VA 22314	888-258-4295	703-836-0850	47-17
National Rehabilitation Information Ctr (NARIC)			
8201 Corporate Dr Ste 600 ....Landover MD 20785	800-346-2742	301-459-5900	47-17
National Research Corp			
1245 Q St ....Lincoln NE 68508	800-388-4264	402-475-2525	461
NASDAQ: NRCI			
National Research Ctr for Coal & Energy (NRCCE)			
West Virginia University			
385 Evansdale Dr PO Box 6064 ....Morgantown WV 26506	800-624-8301	304-293-2867	659
National Research Ctr for Coal & Energy (NRCCE)			
West Virginia University			
10370 Richmond Ave Ste 1100			
PO Box 421879 ....Houston TX 77042	800-324-4327	713-781-3364	457
National Resource Ctr on Domestic Violence (NRCDV)			
6400 Flank Dr Ste 1300 ....Harrisburg PA 17112	800-799-7233		47-6
National Resource Ctr on Native American Aging (NRCNAA)			
501 N Columbia Rd Rm 4535.......Grand Forks ND 58202	800-896-7628	701-777-6780	47-6
National Restaurant Assn (NRA)			
2055 L St NW Ste 700 ....Washington DC 20036	800-424-5156	202-331-5900	48-6
National Restaurant Assn PAC			
2055 L St NW Ste 700 ....Washington DC 20036	888-804-0001	202-331-5900	608
National Retail Federation (NRF)			
325 Seventh St NW Ste 1100 ....Washington DC 20004	800-673-4692	202-783-7971	48-18
National Retail Hardware Assn (NRHA)			
5822 W 74th St ....Indianapolis IN 46278	800-772-4424*	317-290-0338	48-18
*Cust Svc			
National Reye's Syndrome Foundation (NRSF)			
426 N Lewis St ....Bryan OH 43506	800-233-7393	419-924-9000	47-17
National Right to Work Committee (NRTWC)			
8001 Braddock Rd Ste 500 ....Springfield VA 22160	800-325-7892	703-321-8510	48-12
National Rivet & Manufacturing Co			
21 E Jefferson St ....Waupun WI 53963	888-324-5511	920-324-5511	278
National Roofing Contractors Assn (NRCA)			
10255 W Higgins Rd Ste 600 ....Rosemont IL 60018	800-323-9545*	847-299-9070	48-3
*Cust Svc			
National Rosacea Society			
800 S NW Hwy Ste 200 ....Barrington IL 60010	888-662-5874	847-382-8971	47-17
National Rubber Technologies Corp			
35 Cawthra Ave ....Toronto ON M6N5B3	800-387-8501	416-657-1111	667

	Toll-Free	Phone	Class
National Runaway Switchboard (NRS)			
3080 N Lincoln Ave ....Chicago IL 60657	800-786-2929	773-880-9860	47-6
National Rural Electric Co-op Assn (NRECA)			
4301 Wilson Blvd ....Arlington VA 22203	866-759-2619	703-907-5939	47-12
National Rural Utilities Co-op Finance Corp			
2201 Co-op Way ....Herndon VA 20171	800-424-2954	703-709-6700	502
National Safety Apparel Inc (NSA)			
3865 W 150th St ....Cleveland OH 44111	800-553-0672		569
National Safety Council (NSC)			
1121 Spring Lk Dr ....Itasca IL 60143	800-621-7615	630-285-1121	47-17
National Salon Resources Inc			
3109 Louisiana Ave N ....Minneapolis MN 55427	800-622-0003	763-541-1000	75
National School Products			
1523 Old Niles Ferry Rd ....Maryville TN 37803	800-627-9393	865-984-3960	243
National School Supply & Equipment Assn (NSSEA)			
8380 Colesville Rd			
Ste 250 ....Silver Spring MD 20910	800-395-5550	301-495-0240	48-18
National Science Foundation (NSF)			
4201 Wilson Blvd ....Arlington VA 22230	800-877-8339	703-292-5111	338-18
National Science Teachers Assn (NSTA)			
1840 Wilson Blvd ....Arlington VA 22201	800-722-6782*	703-243-7100	48-5
*Sales			
National Scouting Museum			
1329 W Walnut Hill Ln ....Irving TX 75038	800-303-3047	972-580-2100	513
National Securities Corp			
410 Park Ave 14th Fl ....New York NY 10022	800-742-7730	212-417-8000	681
National Seminars Training			
6901 W 63rd St 3rd Fl ....Overland Park KS 66202	800-258-7246	913-432-7755	755
National Senior Golf Assn (NSGA)			
200 Perrine Rd Ste 201............Old Bridge NJ 08857	800-282-6772		47-22
National Serv-All Inc			
6231 McBeth Rd ....Fort Wayne IN 46809	800-876-9001	260-747-4117	792
National Services Group Inc			
1682 Langley Ave ....Irvine CA 92614	800-394-6000	714-564-7900	190-8
National Sheriffs' Assn (NSA)			
1450 Duke St ....Alexandria VA 22314	800-424-7827	703-836-7827	48-7
National Shoe Retailers Assn (NSRA)			
7386 N La Cholla Blvd ....Tucson AZ 85741	800-673-8446	520-209-1710	48-18
National Shrine of Our Lady of the Snows			
442 S De Mazenod Dr ....Belleville IL 62223	800-682-2879	618-397-6700	49
National Slovak Society of the USA (NSS)			
351 Vly Brook Rd ....McMurray PA 15317	800-488-1890	724-731-0094	47-14
National Small Business Assn (NSBA)			
1156 15th St NW Ste 1100 ....Washington DC 20005	800-345-6728	202-293-8830	48-12
National Soccer Coaches Assn of America (NSCAA)			
800 Ann Ave ....Kansas City KS 66101	800-458-0678	913-362-1747	47-22
National Society of Accountants (NSA)			
1010 N Fairfax St ....Alexandria VA 22314	800-966-6679	703-549-6400	48-1
National Society of Professional Engineers (NSPE)			
1420 King St ....Alexandria VA 22314	888-285-6773	703-684-2800	48-19
National Softball Hall of Fame & Museum			
2801 NE 50th St ....Oklahoma City OK 73111	800-654-8337	405-424-5266	515
National Space Society (NSS)			
1620 'I' St NW Ste 615 ....Washington DC 20006	888-624-8373	202-429-1600	48-19
National Speakers Bureau			
1177 W Bdwy Ste 300 ....Vancouver BC V6H1G3	800-661-4110	604-734-3663	699
National Speakers Bureau Inc			
14047 W Petronalla Dr			
Ste 102 ....Libertyville IL 60048	800-323-9442	847-295-1122	699
National Specialty Alloys LLC			
18250 Keith Harrow Blvd ....Houston TX 77084	800-847-5653*	281-345-2115	487
*General			
National Speed Sport News Magazine			
142 F S Cardigan Way ....Mooresville NC 28117	866-455-2531	704-489-5231	452-3
National Spinal Cord Injury Assn (NSCIA)			
75-20 Astoria Blvd			
Ste 120 ....East Elmhurst NY 11370	800-962-9629	718-512-0010	47-17
National Sporting Goods Assn (NSGA)			
1601 Feehanville Dr			
Ste 300 ....Mount Prospect IL 60056	800-815-5422	847-296-6742	48-4
National Sprint Car Hall of Fame & Museum			
One Sprint Capital Pl ....Knoxville IA 50138	800-874-4488	641-842-6176	515
National Staff Development Council (NSDC)			
504 S Locust St ....Oxford OH 45056	800-727-7288	513-523-6029	48-5
National Standard Parts Assoc Inc			
4400 Mobile Hwy ....Pensacola FL 32506	800-874-6813	850-456-5771	56
National Starch & Chemical Co			
10 Finderne Ave ....Bridgewater NJ 08807	866-961-6285		143
National Stock Exchange (NSX)			
440 S LaSalle St Ste 2600 ....Chicago IL 60605	800-843-3924	201-499-3700	682
National Stock Sign Co			
1040 El Dorado Ave ....Santa Cruz CA 95062	800-462-7726	831-476-2020	692
National Stone Sand & Gravel Assn (NSSGA)			
1605 King St ....Alexandria VA 22314	800-342-1415	703-525-8788	48-3
National Stone Sand & Gravel Assn PAC			
1605 King St ....Alexandria VA 22314	866-722-6959	703-525-8788	608
National Strength & Conditioning Assn (NSCA)			
1885 Bob Johnson Dr ....Colorado Springs CO 80906	800-815-6826	719-632-6722	47-22
National Stroke Assn (NSA)			
9707 E Easter Ln ....Centennial CO 80112	800-787-6537*		47-17
*Cust Svc			
National Stuttering Assn (NSA)			
119 W 40th St 14th Fl. ....New York NY 10018	800-937-8888	212-944-4050	47-17
National Sunflower Assn PAC			
2401 46th Ave SE Ste 206 ....Mandan ND 58554	888-718-7033	701-328-5100	608
National Super Service Company Inc			
3115 Frenchman Rd ....Toledo OH 43607	800-677-1663*	419-531-2121	383
*Cust Svc			
National Symphony Orchestra			
2700 F St NW ....Washington DC 20566	800-444-1324	202-416-8000	566-3
National System of Garage Ventilation Inc			
714 N Church St PO Box 1186.........Decatur IL 62525	800-728-8368	217-423-7314	15
National Taxpayers Union (NTU)			
108 N Alfred St ....Alexandria VA 22314	800-680-7289	703-683-5700	47-7
National Tay-Sachs & Allied Diseases Assn (NTSAD)			
2001 Beacon St Ste 204 ....Brighton MA 02135	800-906-8723	617-277-4463	47-17
National Technical Information Service (NTIS)			
5285 Port Royal Rd ....Springfield VA 22161	800-553-6847*	703-605-6000	659
*Orders			
National Technical Systems Inc			
24007 Ventura Blvd Ste 200 ....Calabasas CA 91302	800-879-9225	818-591-0776	732
NASDAQ: NTSC			
National Thoroughbred Racing Assn (NTRA)			
2525 Harrodsburg Rd Ste 500 ....Lexington KY 40504	800-792-6872	859-223-5444	47-22

Name / Address	City	State	ZIP	Toll-Free	Phone	Class
National Tire & Wheel Five Garden Ct	Wheeling	WV	26003	**800-847-3287**	304-233-7917	56
National Tobacco Company LP 5201 Interchange Way *Cust Svc	Louisville	KY	40229	**800-579-0975***	502-778-4421	746
National Tooling & Machining Assn (NTMA) 6363 Oak Tree Blvd	Independence	OH	44131	**800-248-6862**		48-13
National Tour Assn (NTA) 546 E Main St	Lexington	KY	40508	**800-682-8886**	859-226-4444	47-23
National Trade Productions Inc 313 S Patrick St	Alexandria	VA	22314	**800-687-7469**	703-683-8500	185
National Truck Equipment Assn (NTEA) 37400 Hills Tech Dr	Farmington Hills	MI	48331	**800-441-6832**	248-489-7090	48-21
National Truck Leasing System 450 S Summit Ave	Oakbrook	IL	60181	**800-729-6857**	630-953-8878	768
National Trust for Historic Preservation 1785 Massachusetts Ave NW	Washington	DC	20036	**800-944-6847**	202-588-6000	47-13
National Tube Supply Co 925 Central Ave	University Park	IL	60466	**800-229-6872**	708-534-2700	487
National Turkey Federation (NTF) 1225 New York Ave NW Ste 400	Washington	DC	20005	**866-536-7593**	202-898-0100	47-2
National Undersea Research Ctr for Hawaii & the Western Pacific University of Hawaii at Manoa	Honolulu	HI	96822	**888-800-0460**	808-956-6335	659
National Undersea Research Ctr for the Mid-Atlantic Bight Institute of Marine & Coastal Sciences Rutgers University 71 Dudley Rd	New Brunswick	NJ	08901	**888-776-6537**	732-932-6555	659
National Underwriter Co 5081 Olympic Blvd	Erlanger	KY	41018	**800-543-0874**		628-2
National University 11255 N Torrey Pines Rd	La Jolla	CA	92037	**800-628-8648**	858-642-8000	166
National University of Health Sciences 200 E Roosevelt Rd	Lombard	IL	60148	**800-826-6285**	630-629-2000	166
National Urban Technology Ctr 80 Maiden Ln Ste 606	New York	NY	10038	**800-998-3212**	212-528-7350	47-6
National Van Lines Inc 2800 W Roosevelt Rd	Broadview	IL	60155	**877-590-2810**	708-450-2900	512
National Vinyl LLC Seven Coburn St	Chicopee	MA	01013	**800-424-5300**	413-420-0548	236
National Vision Inc 296 Grayson Hwy *Cust Svc	Lawrenceville	GA	30045	**800-637-3597***	770-822-3600	536
National Volunteer Fire Council (NVFC) 7852 Walker Dr Ste 450	Greenbelt	MD	20770	**888-275-6832**	202-887-5700	48-4
National Watch & Clock Museum 514 Poplar St	Columbia	PA	17512	**800-368-6511**	717-684-8261	513
National Water Resources Assn (NWRA) 3800 Fairfax Dr # 4	Arlington	VA	22203	**800-468-3533**	703-524-1544	47-12
National Waterways Conference Inc (NWC) 4650 Washington Blvd Ste 608	Arlington	VA	22201	**866-371-1390**	703-243-4090	48-21
National Wellness Institute (NWI) 1300 College Ct PO Box 827	Stevens Point	WI	54481	**877-800-2729**	715-342-2969	47-17
National Western Life Insurance Co 850 E Anderson Ln *NASDAQ: NWLI*	Austin	TX	78752	**800-531-5442**	512-836-1010	388-2
National Wholesale Company Inc 400 National Blvd	Lexington	NC	27292	**800-480-4673**		454
National WIC Assn (NWA) 2001 S St NW Ste 580	Washington	DC	20009	**866-782-6246**	202-232-5492	47-6
National Wild Turkey Federation (NWTF) 770 Augusta Rd PO Box 530 *Cust Svc	Edgefield	SC	29824	**800-843-6983***	803-637-3106	47-3
National Wildlife Federation (NWF) 11100 Wildlife Ctr Dr	Reston	VA	20190	**800-822-9919**	703-438-6000	47-3
National Wildlife Health Ctr 6006 Schroeder Rd	Madison	WI	53711	**800-232-4636**	608-270-2400	659
National Wildlife Magazine 11100 Wildlife Ctr Dr *Cust Svc	Reston	VA	20190	**800-822-9919***	703-438-6000	452-19
National Women's Health Information Ctr 200 Independence Ave S.W	Washington	DC	20201	**800-994-9662**		338-8
National Wood Flooring Assn (NWFA) 111 Chesterfield Industrial Blvd	Chesterfield	MO	63005	**800-422-4556**	636-519-9663	48-3
National Woodland Owners Assn (NWOA) 374 Maple Ave E Ste 310	Vienna	VA	22180	**800-476-8733**	703-255-2700	47-2
National Youth Sports Coaches Assn (NYSCA) 2050 Vista Pkwy	West Palm Beach	FL	33411	**800-729-2057**	561-684-1141	47-22
National/AZON 1148 Rochester Rd	Troy	MI	48083	**800-325-5939**		545-1
National-Louis University 1000 Capitol Dr	Wheeling	IL	60090	**800-443-5522**	847-947-5718	166
Chicago 122 S Michigan Ave	Chicago	IL	60603	**800-443-5522**	888-658-8632	166
NationJob Inc 920 Morgan St Ste T	Des Moines	IA	50309	**800-292-7731**		260
Nationwide Arena 200 W Nationwide Blvd	Columbus	OH	43215	**800-645-2657**	614-246-2000	711
Nationwide Biweekly Administration Inc 855 Lower Bellbrook Rd	Xenia	OH	45385	**888-802-1296**		5
Nationwide Credit Inc (NCI) 2002 Summit Blvd Ste 600	Atlanta	GA	30319	**800-456-4729**		158
Nationwide Custom Homes 1100 Rives Rd	Martinsville	VA	24115	**800-216-7001**		105
Nationwide Life & Annuity Insurance Co One Nationwide Pl	Columbus	OH	43215	**800-882-2822**	614-249-7111	388-2
Nationwide Lift Trucks Inc 3900 N 28th Terr	Hollywood	FL	33020	**800-327-4431**	954-922-4645	56
Nationwide Magazine & Book Distributors Inc 3000 E Grauwyler Rd PO Box 170427 *General	Irving	TX	75017	**800-777-9068***	972-438-7852	676
Nationwide Mutual Fire Insurance Co 1 Nationwide Plaza	Columbus	OH	43215	**877-669-6877**	614-249-7111	388-4
Nationwide Mutual Insurance Co 1 Nationwide Plaza	Columbus	OH	43215	**877-669-6877**	614-249-7111	388-4
Nationwide Mutual Insurance Company 5100 Rings Rd	Dublin	OH	43017	**800-543-3747**	877-669-6877	388-2
Nationwide Recovery Systems Inc (NRS) 4635 McEwen Rd	Dallas	TX	75244	**800-458-6357**	972-798-1000	158
Nationwide Truck Brokers Inc (NTB) 4203 Roger B Chaffee Memorial Blvd SE Ste 2	Grand Rapids	MI	49548	**800-446-0682**	616-878-5554	770
Nationwide Van Lines Inc 1421 NW 65th Ave	Plantation	FL	33313	**800-310-0056**	954-585-3945	512
Native American Rights Fund (NARF) 1506 Broadway	Boulder	CO	80302	**888-280-0726**	303-447-8760	48-10
Native American Times PO Box 411	Tahlequah	OK	74465	**800-367-5390**	918-708-5838	628-8
Nativo Lodge Hotel 6000 Pan American Fwy NE	Albuquerque	NM	87109	**888-628-4861**	505-798-4300	376
NATO (National Association of Theatre Owners.) 750 First St NE Ste 1130 *General	Washington	DC	20002	**800-365-5701***	202-962-0054	47-4
NATSO Inc 1737 King St Ste 200	Alexandria	VA	22314	**800-956-9160**	703-549-2100	48-21
Naturade Products Inc 2030 Main St Ste 630	Irvine	CA	92614	**800-421-1830**		787
Natural Alternatives International Inc 1185 Linda Vista Dr *NASDAQ: NAII*	San Marcos	CA	92078	**800-848-2646**	760-744-7340	787
Natural Bridge Battlefield Historic State Park 7502 Natural Bridge Rd	Tallahassee	FL	32305	**800-326-3521**	850-922-6007	558
Natural Bridge State Resort Park 2135 Natural Bridge Rd	Slade	KY	40376	**800-325-1710**		558
Natural Casing Co 410 E Railroad St PO Box A	Peshtigo	WI	54157	**877-515-0270**		295-26
Natural Factors Nutritional Products Ltd 1550 United Blvd	Coquitlam	BC	V3K6Y7	**800-663-8900**	604-777-1757	787
Natural Habitat Adventures PO Box 3065	Boulder	CO	80307	**800-543-8917**	303-449-3711	750
Natural Life Pet Products Inc 205 E 29th St	Pittsburg	KS	66762	**800-367-2391**	620-230-0888	571
Natural Organics Inc 548 Broadhollow Rd	Melville	NY	11747	**800-645-9500**		787
Natural Resource Partners LP 601 Jefferson St Ste 3600 *NYSE: NRP*	Houston	TX	77002	**888-334-7102**	713-751-7507	496
Natural Resources Research Institute (NRRI) *University of Minnesota Duluth* 5013 Miller Trunk Hwy	Duluth	MN	55811	**800-234-0054**	218-720-4294	659
NaturaLawn of America Inc One E Church St	Frederick	MD	21701	**800-989-5444**	301-694-5440	570
Naturally Vitamins 4404 E Elwood St	Phoenix	AZ	85040	**800-899-4499**	480-991-0200	787
Nature National Press Bldg 529 14th St NW Ste 968	Washington	DC	20045	**800-524-0384**	202-737-2355	452-19
Nature Conservancy 4245 N Fairfax Dr Ste 100 *Cust Svc	Arlington	VA	22203	**800-628-6860***	703-841-5300	47-13
Nature Conservancy of Canada 36 Eglinton Ave W Ste 400	Toronto	ON	M4R1A1	**800-465-8005**	416-932-3202	47-13
Nature's Best 6 Pt Dr Ste 300	Brea	CA	92821	**800-800-7799**	714-255-4600	342
Nature's Way Products Inc 3051 W Maple Loop Dr Ste 125	Lehi	UT	84043	**800-962-8873**		787
Natus Medical Inc 1501 Industrial Rd *NASDAQ: BABY*	San Carlos	CA	94070	**800-255-3901**	650-802-0400	250
Natvar 8720 US Hwy 70 W	Clayton	NC	27520	**800-395-6288**	919-553-4151	593
Naugatuck Savings Bank 251 Church St PO Box 370	Naugatuck	CT	06770	**877-729-4442**	203-729-5291	70
Naugatuck Valley Financial Corp 333 Church St *NASDAQ: NVSL*	Naugatuck	CT	06770	**800-251-2161**	203-720-5000	69
NAUS (NA for Uniformed Services) 5535 Hempstead Way	Springfield	VA	22151	**800-842-3451**	703-750-1342	47-19
Nautel Ltd 10089 Peggy'S Cove Rd	Hackett'S Cove	NS	B3Z3J4	**877-662-8835**	902-823-3900	638
NAUTICUS the National Maritime Ctr One Waterside Dr	Norfolk	VA	23510	**800-664-1080**	757-664-1000	513
Nautilus Inc 16400 SE Nautilus Dr *NYSE: NLS*	Vancouver	WA	98684	**800-628-8458**	360-694-7722	267
Nautilus Insurance Group LLC 7233 E Butherus Dr	Scottsdale	AZ	85260	**800-842-8972**	480-951-0905	388-4
NAV CANADA 77 Metcalfe St PO Box 3411 Stn D	Ottawa	ON	K1P5L6	**800-876-4693**	613-563-5588	19
NAV Canada Training & Conference Ctr 1950 Montreal Rd	Cornwall	ON	K6H6L2	**877-832-6416**	613-936-5800	374
Navajo Express Inc 1400 W 64 Ave	Denver	CO	80221	**800-525-1969**	303-287-3800	770
Naval Air Station Jacksonville 6801 Roosevelt Blvd	Jacksonville	FL	32212	**800-849-6024**	904-542-2338	492-3
Naval Air Station Joint Reserve Base New Orleans 301 Russell Ave	New Orleans	LA	70143	**800-729-7327**	504-678-3254	492-3
Naval Air Station Patuxent River 22268 Cedar Point Road Bldg 409	Patuxent River	MD	20670	**877-995-5247**	301-342-3000	492-3
Naval Base San Diego 3455 Senn Rd	San Diego	CA	92136	**877-995-5247**	619-556-1011	492-3
Naval Enlisted Reserve Assn (NERA) 6703 Farragut Ave	Falls Church	VA	22042	**800-776-9020**	703-534-1329	47-19
Naval Hospital Bremerton One Boone Rd	Bremerton	WA	98312	**800-422-1383**	360-475-4000	371-4
Naval Institute Press 291 Wood Rd	Annapolis	MD	21402	**800-233-8764**	410-268-6110	628-4
Naval Station Mayport PO Box 280032	Mayport	FL	32228	**800-872-7245**	904-270-5401	492-3
Naval Surface Warfare Ctr *Dahlgren Div* 6149 Welsh Rd Ste 203	Dahlgren	VA	22448	**877-845-5656**		659
Navarro College 3200 W Seventh Ave	Corsicana	TX	75110	**800-628-2776**	903-874-6501	160
Navarro County Electric Co-op Inc 3800 Texas 22 PO Box 616	Corsicana	TX	75110	**800-771-9095**	903-874-7411	245
Navarro Research & Engineering Inc 669 Emory Valley Rd	Oak Ridge	TN	37830	**866-681-5265**	865-220-9650	193
Navasota Valley Electric Co-op Inc 2281 E US Hwy 79 PO Box 848	Franklin	TX	77856	**800-443-9462**	979-828-3232	245
Navellier Securities Corp 1 E Liberty St Ste 504	Reno	NV	89501	**800-887-8671**	775-785-2300	398
Navigant Consulting Inc 30 S Wacker Dr Ste 3100 *NYSE: NCI*	Chicago	IL	60606	**888-461-9425**	312-583-5700	195

				Toll-Free	Phone	Class
Navigators Group Inc						
One Penn Plz 32nd Fl	New York	NY	10119	**800-942-6906**	212-244-2333	357-4
NASDAQ: NAVG						
Navigators of Canada						
11 St John'S Dr	Arva	ON	N0M1C0	**866-202-6287**	519-660-8300	47-20
Navigators, The						
3820 N 30th St						
PO Box 6000	Colorado Springs	CO	80934	**866-568-7827**	719-598-1212	47-20
Navis Logistics Network						
6551 S Revere Pkwy Ste 250	Centennial	CO	80111	**800-344-3528**		542
Navis Pack & Ship Centers						
6551 S Revere Pkwy Ste 250	Centennial	CO	80111	**800-344-3528**		112
Navitaire Inc						
333 S Seventh St Ste 500	Minneapolis	MN	55402	**877-216-6787**	612-317-7000	195
Navitar Inc						
200 Commerce Dr	Rochester	NY	14623	**800-828-6778***	585-359-4000	584
*Cust Svc						
Navopache Electric Co-op Inc						
1878 W White Mtn Blvd	Lakeside	AZ	85929	**800-543-6324**	928-368-5118	245
NavPress						
351 Executive Dr	Carol Stream	CO	60188	**800-366-7788**	855-277-9400	628-3
NAVS (National Anti-Vivisection Society)						
53 W Jackson Blvd Ste 1552	Chicago	IL	60604	**800-888-6287**	312-427-6065	47-3
Navy Exchange Service Command (NEXCOM)						
3280 Virginia Beach Blvd	Virginia Beach	VA	23452	**800-628-3924**	757-463-6200	779
Navy League of the US						
2300 Wilson Blvd	Arlington	VA	22201	**800-356-5760**	703-528-1775	47-19
Navy Personnel Command (NPC)						
5720 Integrity Dr	Millington	TN	38055	**866-827-5672**	901-874-3165	338-5
Navy Pier						
600 E Grand Ave	Chicago	IL	60611	**800-595-7437**	312-595-5400	206
Navy Times Magazine						
6883 Commercial Dr	Springfield	VA	22159	**800-368-5718***	703-750-7400	452-12
*Cust Svc						
Navy-Marine Corps Relief Society (NMCRS)						
875 N Randolph St Ste 225	Arlington	VA	22203	**800-654-8364**	703-696-4904	47-19
NAWIC (NA of Women in Construction)						
327 S Adams St	Fort Worth	TX	76104	**800-552-3506**	817-877-5551	48-3
Naxos of America Inc						
1810 Columbia Ave	Franklin	TN	37064	**877-629-6723**	615-771-9393	648
Nazarene Theological Seminary						
1700 E Meyer Blvd	Kansas City	MO	64131	**800-831-3011**	816-333-6254	167-3
Nazareth Area Chamber of Commerce						
201 N Main St PO Box 173	Nazareth	PA	18064	**866-776-8240**	610-759-9188	137
Nazareth College of Rochester						
4245 E Ave	Rochester	NY	14618	**800-860-6942**	585-389-2525	166
Nazdar						
8501 Hedge Ln Terr	Shawnee	KS	66227	**800-767-9942**	913-422-1888	385
NBA (National Business Assn)						
5151 Beltline Rd Ste 1150	Dallas	TX	75254	**800-456-0440**	972-458-0900	48-12
NBA Entertainment						
450 Harmon Meadow Blvd	Secaucus	NJ	07094	**866-648-4668**	201-865-1500	507
NBAA (National Business Aviation Assn)						
1200 18th St NW Ste 400	Washington	DC	20036	**800-394-6222**	202-783-9000	48-21
NBBC (Northland Baptist Bible College)						
W10085 Pike Plains Rd	Dunbar	WI	54119	**800-425-9385**	715-324-6900	166
NBC15 615 Forward Dr	Madison	WI	53711	**800-894-4222**	608-274-1515	730-41
NBCC (National Breast Cancer Coalition)						
1101 17th St NW Ste 1300	Washington	DC	20036	**800-622-2838**	202-296-7477	47-17
NBCH (National Business Coalition on Health)						
1015 18th St NW Ste 730	Washington	DC	20036	**800-223-4139**	202-775-9300	48-12
NBDL (National Biodynamics Laboratory)						
2000 Lakeshore Dr	New Orleans	LA	70148	**888-514-4275**		659
NBFPL (New Bedford Free Public Library)						
613 Pleasant St	New Bedford	MA	02740	**877-336-2627**	508-991-6275	431-3
NBIA (National Business Incubation Assn)						
40 W St Ste 25	Athens	OH	45701	**800-766-3782**	740-593-4331	48-12
NBMDA (North American Bldg Material Distribution Assn)						
330 N Wabash Ave Ste 2000	Chicago	IL	60611	**888-747-7862**	312-321-6845	48-18
NBOFKC (National Bank of Kansas City)						
3510 W 95th St	Leawood	KS	66206	**888-431-0097**	913-341-1144	69
NBT Bancorp Inc						
52 S Broad St	Norwich	NY	13815	**800-628-2265**	607-337-2265	357-2
NASDAQ: NBTB						
NBT Bank NA						
PO Box 351	Norwich	NY	13815	**800-628-2265**	607-337-2265	69
NBWA (National Beer Wholesalers Assn)						
1101 King St Ste 600	Alexandria	VA	22314	**800-300-6417**	703-683-4300	48-6
NC Machinery Co						
17025 W Valley Hwy	Tukwila	WA	98188	**800-562-4735**	425-251-9800	382
NC Products Corp						
920 Withers Rd PO Box 27077	Raleigh	NC	27603	**888-965-3227**	919-772-6301	184
NCA (National Club Assn)						
1201 15th St NW Ste 450	Washington	DC	20005	**800-625-6221**	202-822-9822	47-23
NCA (National Confectioners Assn PAC)						
8320 Old Courthouse Rd Ste 300	Vienna	VA	22182	**800-433-1200**	703-790-5750	608
NCA (National Coffee Assn of USA Inc)						
45 Broadway Ste 1140	New York	NY	10006	**800-247-6755**	212-766-4007	48-6
NCA (National Confectioners Assn)						
1101 30th St NW Ste 200	Washington	DC	20007	**800-433-1200**	202-534-1440	48-6
NCA CASI (North Central Assn Commission on Accreditation & School Improvement)						
9115 Westside Pkwy	Alpharetta	GA	30009	**888-413-3669**		47-1
NCADD (National Council on Alcoholism & Drug Dependence Inc)						
217 Broadway Ste 712	New York	NY	10007	**800-622-2255**	212-269-7797	47-17
NCADV (National Coalition Against Domestic Violence)						
One Broadway Ste B210	Denver	CO	80203	**800-799-7233**	303-839-1852	47-6
NCAE News Bulletin						
PO Box 27347	Raleigh	NC	27611	**800-662-7924**	919-832-3000	452-8
NCAI (National Congress of American Indians)						
1516 P St NW	Washington	DC	20005	**800-503-3330**	202-466-7767	47-14
NCAL Bancorp						
12121 Wilshire Blvd	Los Angeles	CA	90025	**866-453-4042**	310-882-4800	69
OTC: NCAL						
NCASI (National Council for Air & Stream Improvement Inc)						
PO Box 13318	Research Triangle Park	NC	27709	**888-448-2473**	919-941-6400	47-13
NCATE (National Council for Accreditation of Teacher Education)						
2010 Massachusetts Ave NW						
Ste 500	Washington	DC	20036	**800-255-8664**	202-466-7496	47-1
NCBA (National Cattlemen's Beef Assn)						
9110 E Nichols Ave Ste 300	Centennial	CO	80112	**866-233-3872**	303-694-0305	47-2
NCBA (National Co-op Business Assn)						
1401 New York Ave NW						
Ste 1100	Washington	DC	20005	**800-356-9655**	202-638-6222	48-12

				Toll-Free	Phone	Class
NCBMP (National Coalition of Black Meeting Planners)						
700 N. Fairfax St Suite 510	Alexandria	VA	22314	**800-551-9369**	571-527-3110	48-12
NCCA (National Child Care Assn)						
1325 G St NW Ste 500	Washington	DC	20005	**866-536-1945**		47-6
NCCA (National Coil Coating Assn)						
1300 Sumner Ave	Cleveland	OH	44115	**800-532-0500**	216-241-7333	48-13
NCCD (National Council on Crime & Delinquency)						
1970 Broadway Ste 500	Oakland	CA	94612	**800-306-6223**	510-208-0500	47-8
NCCI Holdings Inc						
901 Peninsula Corporate Cir	Boca Raton	FL	33487	**800-622-4123***	561-893-1000	387
*Cust Svc						
NCCIC (National Child Care Information & Technical Assistance Ctr)						
9300 Lee Hwy	Fairfax	VA	22031	**877-296-2250**		338-8
NCCS (National Coalition for Cancer Survivorship)						
1010 Wayne Ave Ste 315	Silver Spring	MD	20910	**877-622-7937**		47-17
NCE Computer Group						
1866 Friendship Dr	El Cajon	CA	92020	**800-767-2587***	619-212-3000	176
*Cust Svc						
NCEA (National Catholic Educational Assn)						
1077 30th St NW Ste 100	Washington	DC	20007	**800-711-6232**	202-337-6232	48-5
NCED (National Ctr for Employee Development)						
2701 E Imhoff Rd	Norman	OK	73071	**866-438-6233**	405-366-4420	374
NCEE (National Council on Economic Education)						
122 E 42nd St Ste 2600	New York	NY	10168	**800-338-1192**	212-730-7007	48-5
NCEES (National Council of Examiners for Engineering & Surveying)						
280 Seneca Creek Rd	Seneca	SC	29678	**800-250-3196**	864-654-6824	48-3
NCFL (National Ctr for Family Literacy)						
325 W Main St Ste 300	Louisville	KY	40202	**877-326-5481**	502-584-1133	47-11
NCFR (National Council on Family Relations)						
1201 W River Pkwy Ste 200	Minneapolis	MN	55454	**888-781-9331**		47-6
NCH (National Coalition for the Homeless)						
2201 P St NW	Washington	DC	20037	**877-243-1576**	202-462-4822	47-5
NCH Corp						
2727 Chemsearch Blvd	Irving	TX	75062	**800-527-9919**	972-438-0211	149
NCI (Nissan Canada Inc)						
5290 Orbitor Dr	Mississauga	ON	L4W4Z5	**800-387-0122**		58
NCI (Nationwide Credit Inc)						
2002 Summit Blvd Ste 600	Atlanta	GA	30319	**800-456-4729**		158
NCI (National Captioning Institute)						
3725 Concorde Pkwy Ste 100	Chantilly	VA	20151	**800-825-6758**	703-917-7600	624
NCIC (Network Communications International Corp)						
PO Box 551	Longview	TX	75601	**800-382-2887**	903-757-4455	726
nCircle Network Security Inc						
101 Second St Ste 400	Portland	OR	94105	**866-897-8776**	503-276-7500	178
NCIS (National Crop Insurance Services)						
8900 Indian Creek Pkwy						
Ste 600	Overland Park	KS	66210	**800-951-6247**	913-685-2767	47-2
NCJFCJ (National Council of Juvenile & Family Court Judges)						
Univ of Nevada PO Box 8970	Reno	NV	89507	**800-527-3223**	775-784-6012	48-10
NCJW (National Council of Jewish Women)						
475 Riverside Dr Ste 1901	New York	NY	10115	**800-829-6259**	212-645-4048	47-24
NCL (National Consumers League)						
1701 K St NW Ste 1200	Washington	DC	20006	**800-388-2227**	202-835-3323	47-10
NCLR (National Council of La Raza)						
1126 16th St NW 6th Fl	Washington	DC	20036	**800-821-7060**	202-785-1670	47-14
NCM 404 N Berry St	Brea	CA	92821	**800-283-2933**	714-672-3500	190-16
NCMA (National Contract Management Assn)						
21740 Beaumeade Cir Ste 125	Ashburn	VA	20147	**800-344-8096**	571-382-0082	48-12
NCMEC (National Ctr for Missing & Exploited Children)						
699 Prince St	Alexandria	VA	22314	**800-843-5678**	703-274-3900	47-6
NCMIC Insurance Co						
14001 University Ave	Clive	IA	50325	**800-769-2000**	515-313-4500	388-5
NCMS (National Ctr for Mfg Sciences)						
3025 Boardwalk	Ann Arbor	MI	48108	**800-222-6267**	734-995-0300	659
NCNA (North Carolina Nurses Assn)						
103 Enterprise St PO Box 12025	Raleigh	NC	27605	**800-626-2153**	919-821-4250	526
NCNE (National Ctr for Neighborhood Enterprise)						
1625 K St Ste 1200	Washington	DC	20006	**866-518-1263**	202-518-6500	47-7
NCNW (National Council of Negro Women Inc)						
633 Pennsylvania Ave NW	Washington	DC	20004	**800-462-6420**	202-737-0120	47-24
NCOA (National Council on the Aging)						
1901 L St NW Fourth Fl	Washington	DC	20036	**800-677-1116**	202-479-1200	47-6
NCOA (Non Commissioned Officers Assn)						
9330 Corporate Dr Ste 701	Selma	TX	78154	**800-662-2620**	210-653-6161	47-19
NCOC (National Conference on Citizenship)						
1875 K St NW 5th Fl	Washington	DC	20006	**800-745-7275**	202-729-8038	47-8
NCPA (National Community Pharmacists Assn)						
100 Daingerfield Rd	Alexandria	VA	22314	**800-544-7447**	703-683-8200	48-8
NCPDP (National Council for Prescription Drug Programs)						
9240 E Raintree Dr	Scottsdale	AZ	85260	**888-665-2600**	480-477-1000	48-9
NCPH (National Council on Public History)						
425 University Blvd						
327 Cavanaugh Hall	Indianapolis	IN	46202	**800-554-5542**	317-274-2716	47-7
NCPSSM (National Committee to Preserve Social Security & Medicare)						
10 G St NE Ste 600	Washington	DC	20002	**800-966-1935**	202-216-0420	47-7
NCQA (National Committee for Quality Assurance)						
1100 13th St	Washington	DC	20005	**888-275-7585**	202-955-3500	47-10
NCRA (National Cancer Registrars Assn)						
1340 Braddock Pl Ste 203	Alexandria	VA	22314	**800-621-4111**	703-299-6640	47-17
NCRA (National Court Reporters Assn)						
8224 Old Courthouse Rd	Vienna	VA	22182	**800-272-6272**	703-556-6272	48-10
NCRP (National Council on Radiation Protection & Measurements)						
7910 Woodmont Ave Ste 400	Bethesda	MD	20814	**800-462-3683**	301-657-2652	48-19
NCSBN (National Council of State Boards of Nursing)						
111 E Wacker Dr Ste 2900	Chicago	IL	60601	**866-293-9600**	312-525-3600	48-8
NCSC (National Ctr for State Courts)						
300 Newport Ave	Williamsburg	VA	23185	**800-616-6164**	757-259-1525	48-7
NCSD (Nye County School District Inc)						
PO Box 113	Tonopah	NV	89049	**800-796-6273**	775-482-6258	676
NCSD (Niskayuna Central School District)						
1239 Van Antwerp Rd	Schenectady	NY	12309	**866-893-6337**	518-377-4666	676
NCSEAA (North Carolina State Education Assistance Authority)						
PO Box 14103	Research Triangle Park	NC	27709	**800-700-1775**	919-549-8614	716
NCSS (National Council for the Social Studies)						
8555 16th St Ste 500	Silver Spring	MD	20910	**800-683-0812***	301-588-1800	48-5
*Orders						
NCTC (National Cable Television Co-op Inc)						
11200 Corporate Ave	Lenexa	KS	66219	**800-720-5850**	913-599-5900	48-14
NCTE (National Council of Teachers of English)						
1111 W Kenyon Rd	Urbana	IL	61801	**877-369-6283**	217-328-3870	48-5
NCTM (National Council of Teachers of Mathematics)						
1906 Assn Dr	Reston	VA	20191	**800-235-7566***	703-620-9840	48-5
*Orders						

	Toll-Free	Phone	Class
NCTM News Bulletin			
1906 Assn Dr...............Reston VA 20191	800-235-7566	703-620-9840	452-8
NCTO (National Council of Textile Organizations)			
910 17th St NW Ste 1020..........Washington DC 20006	800-238-7192	202-822-8028	48-13
NCVB (Nashville Convention & Visitors Bureau)			
150 Fourth Ave N Ste G250..........Nashville TN 37219	800-657-6910	615-259-4730	207
NCVMA (North Carolina Veterinary Medical Assn)			
1611 Jones Franklin Rd Ste 108........Raleigh NC 27606	800-446-2862	919-851-5850	783
Nd Industries Inc			
1000 N Crooks Rd ....Clawson MI 48017	800-471-5000	248-288-0000	476
NDA (AMOA-National Dart Assn)			
9100 PuRdue Rd Ste 200 ....Indianapolis IN 46268	800-808-9884	317-387-1299	47-22
NDAA (National District Attorneys Assn)			
99 Canal Ctr Plaza Ste 510..........Alexandria VA 22314	888-325-9943	703-549-9222	48-7
NDRI (National Disease Research Interchange)			
1628 John F Kennedy Blvd			
8 Penn Ctr 8th Fl..............Philadelphia PA 19103	800-222-6374	215-557-7361	269
NDS Americas			
3500 Highland Ave ....Costa Mesa CA 92626	866-398-8749	714-434-2100	725
NDSC (National Down Syndrome Congress)			
1370 Ctr Dr Ste 102 ....Atlanta GA 30338	800-232-6372	770-604-9500	47-17
NDSL (North Dakota State Library)			
604 E Blvd Ave Dept 250 ....Bismarck ND 58505	800-472-2104	701-328-4622	431-5
NDSS (National Down Syndrome Society)			
666 Broadway 8th Fl..............New York NY 10012	800-221-4602		47-17
NDVH (National Domestic Violence Hotline)			
PO Box 161810 ....Austin TX 78716	800-799-7233	512-794-1133	47-6
NEA (National Education Assn)			
1201 16th St NW ....Washington DC 20036	888-552-0624	202-833-4000	48-5
Neace Lukens Inc			
2305 River Rd ....Louisville KY 40206	888-499-8092	502-894-2100	195
Nealanders International Inc			
6980 Creditview Rd ....Mississauga ON L5N8E2	800-263-1939	905-812-7300	571
Neapco Inc			
740 Queen St PO Box 399 ....Pottstown PA 19464	800-821-2374	610-323-6000	59
Nearfield Systems Inc			
19730 Magellan Dr ....Torrance CA 90502	800-334-7384	310-525-7000	202
NEBB (National Environmental Balancing Bureau)			
8575 Grovemont Cir ....Gaithersburg MD 20877	866-497-4447	301-977-3698	48-19
Nebraska			
Arts Council			
1004 Farnam St ....Omaha NE 68131	800-341-4067	402-595-2122	337-28
Child Support Enforcement Div			
PO Box 95026 ....Lincoln NE 68509	877-631-9973	402-471-3121	337-28
Economic Development Dept			
301 Centennial Mall S			
PO Box 94666 ....Lincoln NE 68509	800-426-6505	402-471-3747	337-28
Emergency Management Agency			
1300 Military Rd ....Lincoln NE 68508	877-297-2368	402-471-7421	337-28
Environmental Quality Dept			
1200 N St Ste 400 ....Lincoln NE 68508	877-253-2603	402-471-2186	337-28
Health & Human Services Dept			
301 Centennial Mall S ....Lincoln NE 68508	800-430-3244	402-471-3121	337-28
Historical Society			
1500 R St ....Lincoln NE 68501	800-833-6747	402-471-3270	337-28
Insurance Dept			
941 O St Ste 400 ....Lincoln NE 68508	877-564-7323	402-471-2201	337-28
Investment Finance Authority			
1230 'O' St Ste 200..............Lincoln NE 68508	800-204-6432	402-434-3900	337-28
Public Service Commission			
1200 N St Ste 300 ....Lincoln NE 68508	800-526-0017	402-471-3101	337-28
Travel & Tourism Div			
PO Box 98907 ....Lincoln NE 68509	877-632-7275	402-471-3796	337-28
Vocational Rehabilitation Services Div			
3901 N 27th St Ste 6 ....Lincoln NE 68521	800-472-3382	402-471-3231	337-28
Workers' Compensation Court			
1010 Lincoln Mall Ste 100 ....Lincoln NE 68508	800-599-5155	402-471-6468	337-28
Nebraska Book Co			
4700 S 19th St ....Lincoln NE 68512	800-869-0366	402-421-7300	94
Nebraska College of Technical Agriculture			
404 E 7th ....Curtis NE 69025	800-328-7847	308-367-4124	788
Nebraska Community Blood Bank			
100 N 84th St ....Lincoln NE 68505	877-486-9414	402-486-9414	88
Nebraska Correctional Ctr for Women			
1107 Recharge Rd ....York NE 68467	877-634-8463	402-362-3317	213
Nebraska Dental Assn			
7160 S 29th St Ste 1..............Lincoln NE 68516	888-789-2614	402-476-1704	227
Nebraska Educational Telecommunications (NET)			
1800 N 33rd St ....Lincoln NE 68503	800-868-1868		624
Nebraska Furniture Mart Inc			
700 S 72nd St ....Omaha NE 68114	800-336-9136	402-397-6100	320
Nebraska House			
983285 Nebraska Medical Ctr ....Omaha NE 68198	800-401-4444	402-559-5000	369
Nebraska Indian Community College			
PO Box 428 ....Macy NE 68039	844-440-6422	402-837-5078	163
Nebraska Library Commission			
1200 N St Ste 120 ....Lincoln NE 68508	800-307-2665	402-471-2045	431-5
Nebraska Lottery			
1800 "O" St PO Box 98901..........Lincoln NE 68509	800-587-5200	402-471-6100	447
Nebraska Machinery Co Inc			
3501 S Jeffers St			
PO Box 809..............North Platte NE 69101	800-494-9560	308-532-3100	382
Nebraska Nurses Assn (NNA)			
PO Box 3107 ....Kearney NE 68848	800-582-3014	402-475-3859	526
Nebraska Pharmacists Assn			
6221 S 58th St Ste A ....Lincoln NE 68516	866-365-7472	402-420-1500	578
Nebraska Plastics Inc			
PO Box 45 ....Cozad NE 69130	800-445-2887	308-784-2500	589
Nebraska Printing Company Inc			
4411 W Tampa Bay Blvd ....Tampa FL 33614	800-683-2056	813-873-7117	619
Nebraska Public Power District			
1414 15th St PO Box 499..........Columbus NE 68602	877-275-6773	402-564-8561	245
Nebraska Realtors Assn			
800 S 13th St Ste 200..............Lincoln NE 68508	800-777-5231	402-323-6500	647
Nebraska Repertory Theatre			
12th & R Sts 215 Temple Bldg ....Lincoln NE 68588	800-432-3231	402-472-2072	566-4
Nebraska State Bar Assn			
635 S 14th St Ste 200..........Lincoln NE 68501	800-927-0117	402-475-7091	71
Nebraska State Penitentiary			
4201 S 14th St ....Lincoln NE 68502	877-634-8463	402-471-3161	213
Nebraska Wesleyan University			
5000 St Paul Ave ....Lincoln NE 68504	800-541-3818	402-466-2371	166
NEC (Nueces Electric Co-op)			
709 E Main St PO Box 260970........Robstown TX 78380	800-632-9288	361-387-2581	245
NEC America Inc			
6555 N State Hwy 161 ....Irving TX 75039	866-632-3226*	214-262-2000	725
*Cust Svc			
NEC Corp of America			
10850 Gold Ctr Dr			
Ste 200 ....Rancho Cordova CA 95670	800-632-4636	916-463-7000	174-4
NEC Display Solutions of America Inc			
500 Pk Blvd Ste 1100..............Itasca IL 60143	800-632-4662*	630-467-3000	174-4
*Cust Svc			
NEC Electronics America Inc			
2801 Scott Blvd ....Santa Clara CA 95050	800-366-9782*	408-588-6000	687
*Tech Supp			
NECA (National Electrical Contractors Assn)			
3 Bethesda Metro Ctr Ste 1100..........Bethesda MD 20814	800-214-0585	301-657-3110	48-3
Neci 334 Hecla St ....Lake Linden MI 49945	888-648-7283	906-296-1000	231
NECR (New England Central Railroad)			
7411 Fullerton St Ste 300..........Jacksonville FL 32256	877-777-4778	904-596-1045	639
NED Corp			
31 Town Forest Rd ....Oxford MA 01540	800-343-6086		488
Nedco Electronics			
594 American Way ....Payson UT 84651	800-605-2323	801-465-1790	246
Needham & Co Inc			
445 Pk Ave 3rd Fl ....New York NY 10022	800-903-3268	212-371-8300	681
Needham Capital Partners			
445 Pk Ave ....New York NY 10022	800-625-7071	212-371-8300	780
Neel-Schaffer Inc			
125 S Congress St Ste 1100..........Jackson MS 39201	800-264-6335	601-948-3178	261
Neenah Foundry Co			
2121 Brooks Ave ....Neenah WI 54956	800-558-5075	920-725-7000	306
Negro Leagues Baseball Museum			
1616 E 18th St ....Kansas City MO 64108	888-221-6526	816-221-1920	515
NEH (National Endowment for the Humanities)			
400 7th St SW ....Washington DC 20506	800-634-1121	202-606-8400	338-18
NEHA (National Environmental Health Assn)			
720 S Colorado Blvd Ste 1000-N ....Denver CO 80246	866-956-2258	303-756-9090	48-7
Nehring Electric Works Inc			
1005 E Locust St ....DeKalb IL 60115	800-435-4481	815-756-2741	801
Neighborhood Health Partnership Inc			
7600 NW 19th St Ste 200 ....Miami FL 33126	877-972-8845		388-3
Neighbors Federal Credit Union			
PO Box 2831 ....Baton Rouge LA 70821	866-819-2178	225-819-2178	219
Neil Enterprises Inc			
450 E Bunker Ct ....Vernon Hills IL 60061	800-621-5584	847-549-7627	601
Neil Medical Group Inc			
2545 Jetport Rd ....Kinston NC 28504	800-735-9111		238
NELCO Inc			
Three Gill St Unit D..............Woburn MA 01801	800-635-2613	781-933-1940	472
NELLA Oil Co			
2360 Lindbergh St ....Auburn CA 95602	800-995-0401	530-885-0401	323
Nellie Mae Education Foundation			
1250 Hancock St Ste 205N..............Quincy MA 02169	877-635-5436	781-348-4200	304
Nelnet Inc			
121 S 13th St Ste 201..............Lincoln NE 68501	888-486-4722	402-458-2370	214
NYSE: NNI			
Nelson & Kennard			
2180 Harvard St Ste 160			
PO Box 13807..............Sacramento CA 95853	866-920-2295		425
Nelson & Small Inc			
212 Canco Rd ....Portland ME 04103	800-341-0780	207-775-5666	37
Nelson Crab Inc			
3088 Kindred Ave ....Tokeland WA 98590	800-262-0069	360-267-2911	295-13
Nelson Dewey State Park			
PO Box 658 ....Cassville WI 53806	888-936-7463	608-725-5374	558
Nelson Electric Supply Co Inc			
926 State St ....Racine WI 53404	800-806-3576	262-635-5050	246
Nelson Mullins Riley & Scarborough LLP			
1320 Main St 17th Fl ....Columbia SC 29201	800-237-2000	803-799-2000	425
Nelson Publishing			
2500 Tamiami Trl N ....Nokomis FL 34275	800-226-6113	941-966-9521	628-9
Nelson Tree Service Inc			
3300 Office Pk Dr Ste 205 ....Dayton OH 45439	800-522-4311	937-294-1313	766
Nelson Westerberg Inc			
1500 Arthur Ave			
Ste 200 ....Elk Grove Village IL 60007	800-245-2080	847-437-2080	512
Nelson-Jameson Inc			
2400 E Fifth St PO Box 647 ....Marshfield WI 54449	800-826-8302	715-387-1151	382
NEMA (National Electrical Manufacturers Assn)			
1300 N 17th St Ste 1752 ....Rosslyn VA 22209	888-236-2427	703-841-3200	48-13
Nemacolin Woodlands Resort & Spa			
1001 Lafayette Dr ....Farmington PA 15437	800-422-2736	724-329-8555	660
Nemaha-Marshall Electric Co-op			
402 Prairie St PO Box O ....Axtell KS 66403	866-736-2347*	785-736-2345	245
*Cust Svc			
Nemetschek North America			
7150 Riverwood Dr ....Columbia MD 21046	888-646-4223	410-290-5114	179-8
NEMRA (National Electrical Manufacturers Representatives Assn)			
28 Deer St Ste 302 ....Portsmouth NH 03801	800-446-3672	914-524-8650	48-18
Nemschoff Healthcare Furniture and Clinic Furniture			
909 N Eigth St ....Sheboygan WI 53081	800-203-8916*		318-3
*Cust Svc			
Neo Corp			
289 Silkwood Dr ....Canton NC 28716	800-822-1247		193
Neogard Div Jones-blair Co			
2728 Empire Central St ....Dallas TX 75235	800-492-9400	214-353-1600	543
Neogen Corp			
620 Lesher Pl ....Lansing MI 48912	800-234-5333	517-372-9200	231
NASDAQ: NEOG			
Neopost Inc Canada			
150 Steelcase Rd W ....Markham ON L3R3J9	800-636-7678	905-475-3722	110
Neos Therapeutics			
2940 N Hwy 360 Ste 100 ....Grand Prairie TX 75050	844-375-8324	972-408-1300	576
NEP Electronics Inc			
805 Mittel Dr ....Wood Dale IL 60191	800-284-7470	630-595-8500	246
Nephron Pharmaceuticals Corp			
4121 SW 34th St ....Orlando FL 32811	800-443-4313	407-999-2225	577
Nephros Inc			
41 Grand Ave ....River Edge NJ 07661	800-732-0330	201-343-5202	471
OTC: NEPH			
Neptco Inc			
30 Hamlet St ....Pawtucket RI 02861	800-354-5445	401-722-5500	722
Neptune Chemical Pump Co			
PO Box 247 ....Lansdale PA 19446	800-255-4017	215-699-8700	632
Neptune Society			
4312 Woodman Ave Third Fl ....Sherman Oaks CA 91423	888-637-8863		503

Name / Address	City	State	ZIP	Toll-Free	Phone	Class
Neptune-Benson Inc						
Six Jefferson Dr	Coventry	RI	02816	800-832-8002	401-821-2200	632
NER Data Products Inc						
307 S Delsea Dr	Glassboro	NJ	08028	888-637-3282		620
NERA (Naval Enlisted Reserve Assn)						
6703 Farragut Ave	Falls Church	VA	22042	800-776-9020	703-534-1329	47-19
NERC (North American Electric Reliability Council)						
1325 G St NW Ste 600	Washington	DC	20005	877-668-4493	609-452-8060	47-12
NERSC (National Energy Research Scientific Computing Ctr)						
Lawrence Berkeley National Laboratory	Berkeley	CA	94720	800-666-3772	510-486-5849	659
Nesco/American Harvest						
1700 Monroe St PO Box 237	Two Rivers	WI	54241	800-288-4545*	920-793-1368	36
*Cust Svc						
NESDA (National Electronics Service Dealers Assn)						
3608 Pershing Ave	Fort Worth	TX	76107	800-946-0201	817-921-9061	48-18
Neskowin Beach State Recreation Site						
198 NE 123rd St	Newport	OR	97365	800-551-6949		558
Nespelem Valley Electric Co-op Inc						
1009 F St	Nespelem	WA	99155	866-377-8642	509-634-4571	245
NestFamily						
1461 S Beltline Rd Ste 500	Coppell	TX	75019	800-596-7386	972-402-7100	33
Nestle Purina PetCare Co						
801 Chouteau Ave	Saint Louis	MO	63102	800-778-7462	314-982-1000	571
NET (Nebraska Educational Telecommunications)						
1800 N 33rd St	Lincoln	NE	68503	800-868-1868		624
Net Access Corp						
Nine Wing Dr	Cedar Knolls	NJ	07927	800-638-6336	973-590-5000	726
Net Driven						
280 Eureka St	Batesville	MS	38606	800-647-6133	662-563-1143	745
NET Radio						
1800 N 33rd St	Lincoln	NE	68503	800-868-1868		730-38
Net2Phone Inc						
520 Broad St	Newark	NJ	07102	800-386-6438	973-438-3111	726
Net32 Inc						
250 Towne Village Dr	Cary	NC	27513	800-517-1997	919-468-1177	228
NETA (National Educational Telecommunications Assn)						
939 S Stadium Rd	Columbia	SC	29201	866-270-5141	803-799-5517	624
Netchannel Inc						
8310 Rio Grande Blvd NW	Albuquerque	NM	87114	888-843-8282	505-843-8282	130
Netcracker Technology Corp						
95 Sawyer Rd University Ofc Pk III	Waltham	MA	02453	800-477-5785	781-419-3300	458
NetFlix Inc						
100 Winchester Cir	Los Gatos	CA	95032	800-290-8191	408-540-3700	785
NASDAQ: NFLX						
Netherland Rubber Co						
2931 Exon Ave	Cincinnati	OH	45241	800-582-1877	513-733-0883	325
Netherlands						
Consulate General						
666 Third Ave 19th Fl	New York	NY	10017	877-388-2443		257
Consulate General						
303 E Wacker Dr Ste 2600	Chicago	IL	60601	877-388-2443	312-856-0110	257
Embassy						
4200 Linnean Ave NW	Washington	DC	20008	877-388-2443		257
NetIQ Corp						
1233 W Loop S	Houston	TX	77027	888-323-6768*	713-548-1700	179-12
*Sales						
NETL (National Energy Technology Laboratory)						
3610 Collins Ferry Rd	Morgantown	WV	26505	800-432-8330	304-285-4764	659
Netlink Software Group America Inc						
999 Tech Row	Madison Heights	MI	48071	800-485-4462		197
Netmark.com						
1930 N Woodruff Ave	Idaho Falls	ID	83401	800-935-5133		196
NetMotion Wireless Inc						
701 N 34th St Ste 250	Seattle	WA	98103	877-818-7626	206-691-5500	179-1
NetNation Communications Inc						
550 Burrard St Ste 200	Vancouver	BC	V6C2B5	888-277-0000	604-688-8946	795
Neto Sausage Co Inc						
1313 Franklin St	Santa Clara	CA	95050	888-482-6386	408-296-0818	295-26
Netplanner Systems Inc						
3145 Northwoods Pkwy Ste 800	Norcross	GA	30071	800-795-1975	770-662-5482	177
Netrition Inc						
25 Corporate Cir Ste 118	Albany	NY	12203	888-817-2411	518-464-0765	352
NetScout Systems Inc						
310 Littleton Rd	Westford	MA	01886	800-357-7666	978-614-4000	179-7
NASDAQ: NTCT						
Netsertive Inc						
2400 Perimeter Park Dr Ste 100	Research Triangle Region	NC	27560	800-940-4351		196
NetShape Technologies Inc						
31005 Solon Rd	Solon	OH	44139	866-429-5724	440-248-5456	480
Netsmart Technologies Inc						
3500 Sunrise Hwy Ste D-122	Great River	NY	11739	800-421-7503	631-968-2000	179-11
Netsville Inc						
72 Cascade Dr	Rochester	NY	14614	888-638-7845	585-232-5670	190-4
Net-Temps Inc						
55 Middlesex St Ste 220	North Chelmsford	MA	01863	800-307-0062	978-251-7272	260
NetVillage.com LLC						
342 Main St	Laurel	MD	20707	888-638-8455	301-498-7797	179-7
Network & Systems Professionals Assn Inc (NaSPA)						
7044 S 13th St	Oak Creek	WI	53154	877-777-3520	414-768-8000	47-9
Network America Inc						
118 107th Ave	Treasure Island	FL	33706	877-624-8311		181
Network Appliance Inc						
495 E Java Dr	Sunnyvale	CA	94089	800-443-4537*	408-822-6000	177
NASDAQ: NTAP ■ *Sales						
Network Communications International Corp (NCIC)						
PO Box 551	Longview	TX	75601	800-382-2887	903-757-4455	726
Network Dynamics Inc						
640 Brooker Creek Blvd Ste 410	Oldsmar	FL	34677	877-818-8597	813-818-8597	177
Network Earth Inc						
14 Cambridge Ct	Wappingers Falls	NY	12590	888-201-5160		224
Network Global Logistics (NGL)						
320 Interlocken Pkwy Ste 100	Broomfield	CO	80021	866-938-1870		539
Network Infrastructure Corp						
8945 S Harl Ave Ste 102	Tempe	AZ	85284	866-456-4422	480-850-5050	190-4
Network Innovations Inc						
4424 Manilla Rd SE	Calgary	AB	T2G4B7	888-466-2772	403-287-5000	195
Network Multi-Family Security Corp						
4221 W John Carpenter Fwy	Irving	TX	75063	800-541-3138	972-490-9902	684
Network Solutions LLC						
13861 Sunrise Valley Dr Ste 300	Herndon	VA	20171	800-361-5712	703-668-4600	393
Network Telephone Services Inc						
21135 Erwin St	Woodland Hills	CA	91367	800-742-5687	818-992-4300	252
Network World Inc						
492 Old Connecticut Path	Framingham	MA	01701	800-622-1108		524-3
Network World Magazine						
492 Old Connecticut Path Ste 200 PO Box 9208	Framingham	MA	01701	800-622-1108		452-7
Networld Media Group LLC						
13100 Eastpoint Park Blvd Ste 100	Louisville	KY	40223	877-441-7545		390
NetZero Inc						
21301 Burbank Blvd	Woodland Hills	CA	91367	800-638-9376	818-287-3000	395
Neuberger Berman Funds						
PO Box 8403	Boston	MA	02266	800-877-9700	212-476-8800	521
Neuberger Berman LLC						
605 Third Ave	New York	NY	10158	800-223-6448		398
Neudesic LLC						
8105 Irvine Ctr Dr	Irvine	CA	92618	800-805-1805	949-754-4500	178
Neuisys LLC						
1500 Pinecroft Rd Ste 212	Greensboro	NC	27407	877-299-9052		732
Neumann College						
1 Neumann Dr	Aston	PA	19014	855-563-8626	610-459-0905	166
Neumayer Equipment Company Inc						
5060 Arsenal St	Saint Louis	MO	63139	800-843-4563	314-772-4501	383
NeuroMetrix						
62 Fourth Ave	Waltham	MA	02451	888-786-7287	781-890-9989	250
NASDAQ: NURO						
Neuromonics Inc						
2810 Emrick Blvd	Bethlehem	PA	18020	866-606-3876		250
Neuro-Tec Inc						
975 Cobb Pl Blvd Ste 301	Kennesaw	GA	30144	800-554-3407		470
NeuStar Inc						
21575 Ridgetop Cir	Sterling	VA	20166	855-638-2677	571-434-5400	46
Neutral Posture Inc						
3904 N Texas Ave	Bryan	TX	77803	800-446-3746	979-778-0502	318-1
Neutrogena Corp						
5760 W 96th St	Los Angeles	CA	90045	800-582-4048	310-642-1150	215
Nevada						
Child Support Enforcement Office						
1470 College Pkwy	Carson City	NV	89706	800-992-0900	775-684-0500	337-29
Economic Development Commission						
808 W Nye Ln	Carson City	NV	89703	800-336-1600	775-687-9900	337-29
Motor Vehicles Dept						
555 Wright Way	Carson City	NV	89711	877-368-7828	775-684-4368	337-29
Secretary of State						
101 N Carson St Ste 3	Carson City	NV	89701	800-450-8594	775-684-5708	337-29
Tourism Commission						
401 N Carson St	Carson City	NV	89701	800-237-0774	775-687-4322	337-29
Welfare Div						
1470 College Pkwy	Carson City	NV	89706	800-992-0900	775-684-0500	337-29
Nevada Appeal						
580 Mallory Way	Carson City	NV	89701	877-689-3249*	775-882-2111	525-2
*General						
Nevada Assn of Realtors						
760 Margrave Dr Ste 200	Reno	NV	89502	800-748-5526	775-829-5911	647
Nevada Bill Status						
401 S Carson St	Carson City	NV	89701	800-978-2878	775-684-3360	430
Nevada Dental Assn						
8863 W Flamingo Rd Ste 102	Las Vegas	NV	89147	800-962-6710	702-255-4211	227
Nevada Donor Network Inc						
2061 E Sahara Ave	Las Vegas	NV	89104	855-683-6667	702-796-9600	538
Nevada Irrigation District (NID)						
1036 W Main St	Grass Valley	CA	95945	800-222-4102	530-273-6185	775
Nevada Magazine						
401 N Carson St	Carson City	NV	89701	855-729-7117	775-687-5416	452-22
Nevada Power Co						
6226 W Sahara Ave	Las Vegas	NV	89146	800-331-3103*	702-367-5000	775
NYSE: NVE ■ *Cust Svc						
Nevada State Bank						
PO Box 990	Las Vegas	NV	89125	800-727-4743	702-383-0009	69
Nevada State Library & Archives (NSLA)						
100 N Stewart St	Carson City	NV	89701	800-922-2880	775-684-3360	431-5
Neville Chemical Co						
2800 Neville Rd	Pittsburgh	PA	15225	877-704-4200*	412-331-4200	598-2
*Cust Svc						
New Acton Mobile Industries LLC						
809 Gleneagles Ct	Baltimore	MD	21286	800-251-1600		105
New Age Health Spa						
PO Box 658	Neversink	NY	12765	800-682-4348	845-985-7600	697
New Balance Athletic Shoe Inc						
20 Guest St Brighton Landing	Brighton	MA	02135	800-595-9138	617-783-4000	300
New Bedford Free Public Library (NBFPL)						
613 Pleasant St	New Bedford	MA	02740	877-336-2627	508-991-6275	431-3
New Bern Area Chamber of Commerce						
316 S Front St	New Bern	NC	28560	877-811-1776	252-637-3111	137
New Bern National Cemetery						
1711 National Ave	New Bern	NC	28560	800-827-1000	252-637-2912	135
New Braunfels Chamber of Commerce						
390 S Seguin St	New Braunfels	TX	78130	800-572-2626	830-625-2385	137
New Braunfels Public Library						
700 E Common St	New Braunfels	TX	78130	800-434-8013	830-221-4300	431-3
New Brighton Area School District						
3225 43rd St	New Brighton	PA	15066	866-950-1040	724-843-1795	676
New Brunswick Museum						
One Market Sq	Saint John	NB	E2L4Z6	888-268-9595	506-643-2300	513
New Brunswick Scientific Company Inc						
44 Talmadge Rd PO Box 4005	Edison	NJ	08818	800-631-5417*	732-287-1200	417
*Cust Svc						
New Brunswick Theological Seminary						
17 Seminary Pl	New Brunswick	NJ	08901	800-445-6287	732-247-5241	167-3
New Canaan Library						
151 Main St	New Canaan	CT	06840	800-545-2433	203-594-5000	431-3
New Castle County Detention Ctr						
963 Centre Rd	Wilmington	DE	19805	800-969-4357	302-633-3100	409
New Castle County Library						
750 Library Ave	Newark	DE	19711	877-225-7351	302-731-7550	431-3
New Castle Hotels & Resorts						
2 Corporate Dr	Shelton	CT	06484	800-321-2211	203-925-8370	376
New Castle Industries Inc						
1399 Countyline Rd	New Castle	PA	16101	800-897-2830	724-656-5620	614
New Castle Public Library						
424 Delaware St	New Castle	DE	19720	877-225-7351	302-328-1995	431-3
New Castle Refractories Co Inc						
915 Industrial St	New Castle	PA	16102	888-396-3566	724-654-7711	654

Name / Address	Toll-Free	Phone	Class
New Century Education Foundation			
PO Box 43052 ....Upper Montclair NJ 07043	**866-326-1133**		179-1
New College of Florida			
5800 Bay Shore Rd ....Sarasota FL 34243	**800-435-7352**	941-487-5000	166
NEW Co-op Inc			
2626 First Ave S ....Fort Dodge IA 50501	**800-362-2233**	515-955-2040	275
New Country Volkswagen of Greenwich			
200 W Putnam Ave ....Greenwich CT 06830	**866-584-6747**		56
New Dimensions Radio Broadcasting Network			
PO Box 7847 ....Santa Rosa CA 95407	**800-935-8273**	707-468-5215	637
New Dimensions Research Corp			
260 Spagnoli Rd ....Melville NY 11747	**800-637-8870**	631-694-1356	233
New Directions Behavioral Health LLC			
PO Box 6729 ....Leawood KS 66206	**800-528-5763**	913-982-8200	457
New Directions Inc			
30800 Chagrin Blvd ....Cleveland OH 44124	**800-750-6709**	216-591-0324	717
New Edge Networks			
3000 Columbia House Blvd			
Ste 106 ....Vancouver WA 98661	**877-725-3343**	360-693-9009	395
New England Airlines Inc			
56 Airport Rd ....Westerly RI 02891	**800-243-2460**		25
New England Art Publisher			
10 Railroad St ....North Abington MA 02351	**800-333-0405**	781-616-2508	129
New England Baptist Hospital			
125 Parker Hill Ave ....Boston MA 02120	**800-370-6324**	617-754-5000	371-3
New England Bible College			
879 Sawyer St			
PO Box 2886..................South Portland ME 04116	**800-286-1859**	207-799-5979	166
New England Central Railroad (NECR)			
7411 Fullerton St Ste 300..........Jacksonville FL 32256	**877-777-4778**	904-596-1045	639
New England Coffee Co			
100 Charles St ....Malden MA 02148	**800-225-3537**		295-7
New England College			
98 Bridge St.......................Henniker NH 03242	**800-521-7642***	603-428-2223	166
*Admissions			
New England College of Business & Finance			
10 High St Ste 204....................Boston MA 02110	**888-357-7332**	617-951-2350	788
New England Computer Services Inc			
168 Boston Post Rd Stes 6 & 7 ....Madison CT 06443	**800-766-6327***	203-245-3999	179-10
*Sales			
New England Culinary Institute			
56 College St.....................Montpelier VT 05602	**877-223-6324**	802-223-6324	161
New England Federal Credit Union			
PO Box 527 ....Williston VT 05495	**800-400-8790**	802-879-8790	219
New England Garage Door			
15 Campanelli Cir ....Canton MA 02021	**800-676-7734**	781-821-2737	494
New England Homes			
270 Ocean Rd ....Greenland NH 03840	**800-800-8831**	603-436-8830	105
New England Institute of Art			
10 Brookline Pl W ....Brookline MA 02445	**800-903-4425**	617-739-1700	162
New England Institute of Technology			
2500 Post Rd ....Warwick RI 02886	**800-736-7744**	401-467-7744	788
New England Journal of Medicine			
10 Shattuck St ....Boston MA 02115	**800-843-6356**	617-734-9800	452-16
New England Life Flight Inc			
1727 Robins St Hangar ....Bedford MA 01730	**800-233-8998**	781-863-2213	13
New England Natural Bakers			
74 Fairview St E ....Greenfield MA 01301	**800-910-2884**	413-772-2239	295-4
New England Organ Bank			
60 First Ave ....Waltham MA 02451	**800-446-6362**	617-244-8000	538
New England Revolution			
Gillette Stadium 1 Patriot Pl ....Foxboro MA 02035	**877-438-7387**		708
New England Ropes Inc			
848 Airport Rd ....Fall River MA 02720	**800-333-6679**	508-678-8200	209
New England Security Inc			
10 Industrial Dr ....Westerly RI 02891	**800-556-7395**	401-596-0660	683
New England Wild Flower Society			
180 Hemenway Rd ....Framingham MA 01701	**888-636-0033**	508-877-7630	47-13
New England Wooden Ware Corp			
205 School St Ste 201 ....Gardner MA 01440	**800-252-9214**	978-632-3600	99
New Enterprise Rural Electric Co-op Inc			
3596 Brumbaugh Rd ....New Enterprise PA 16664	**800-270-3177**	814-766-3221	245
New Era Cap Company Inc			
160 Delaware Ave ....Buffalo NY 14202	**877-632-5950***	716-604-9000	153-8
*General			
New Era Life Insurance Co			
PO Box 4884 ....Houston TX 77210	**800-552-7879**		388-4
New Fairfield Free Public Library			
2 Brush Hill Rd PO Box F..........New Fairfield CT 06812	**877-227-7487**	203-312-5679	431-3
New Generation Mechanical			
1133 Empire Central Dr ....Dallas TX 75247	**877-235-5898**	972-830-9900	603
New Generation Research Inc			
225 Friend St Ste 801.................Boston MA 02114	**800-468-3810**	617-573-9550	628-2
New Germany State Park			
349 Headquarters Ln ....Grantsville MD 21536	**800-830-3974**	301-895-5453	558
New Hampshire			
Banking Dept			
53 Regional Dr Ste 200 ....Concord NH 03301	**800-437-5991**	603-271-3561	337-30
Child Support Services			
129 Pleasant St ....Concord NH 03301	**800-852-3345**	603-271-4427	337-30
Division of Vital Records Administration			
71 S Fruit St ....Concord NH 03301	**800-735-2964**	603-271-4650	337-30
Environmental Services Dept			
29 Hazen Dr PO Box 95 ....Concord NH 03301	**800-735-2964**	603-271-3503	337-30
Housing Finance Authority			
PO Box 5087 ....Manchester NH 03108	**800-439-7247**	603-472-8623	337-30
Public Utilities Commission			
21 S Fruit St Ste 10 ....Concord NH 03301	**800-852-3793***	603-271-2431	337-30
*Consumer Assistance			
Travel & Tourism Development Office			
PO Box 1856 ....Concord NH 03302	**800-262-6660**	603-271-2665	337-30
Victims' Assistance Commission			
33 Capitol St ....Concord NH 03301	**800-300-4500**	603-271-1284	337-30
Vocational Rehabilitation Office			
21 S Fruit St Ste 20 ....Concord NH 03301	**800-299-1647**	603-271-3471	337-30
New Hampshire Assn of Realtors			
115A Airport Rd.....................Concord NH 03301	**800-335-4862**	603-225-5549	647
New Hampshire Bar News			
2 Pillsbury St Ste 300.................Concord NH 03301	**800-868-1212**	603-224-6942	452-15
New Hampshire Catholic Charities Inc			
215 Myrtle St PO Box 686 ....Manchester NH 03104	**800-562-5249**	603-669-3030	47-20
New Hampshire Distributors Inc			
65 Regional Dr......................Concord NH 03301	**800-852-3781**	603-224-9991	80-1
New Hampshire Div of Travel & Tourism Development			
172 Pembroke Rd PO Box 1856........Concord NH 03302	**800-262-6660**	603-271-2665	207
New Hampshire Educator Magazine			
9 S Spring St ....Concord NH 03301	**866-556-3264**	603-224-7751	452-8
New Hampshire Electric Co-op			
579 Tenney Mtn Hwy ....Plymouth NH 03264	**800-698-2007**	603-536-1800	245
New Hampshire Employment Security (NHES)			
32 S Main St ....Concord NH 03301	**800-852-3400**	603-224-3311	259
New Hampshire Institute of Art			
148 Concord St ....Manchester NH 03104	**866-241-4918**	603-623-0313	513
New Hampshire Lottery Commission			
14 Integra Dr ....Concord NH 03301	**800-852-3324**	603-271-3391	447
New Hampshire Medical Society			
Seven N State St ....Concord NH 03301	**800-564-1909**	603-224-1909	469
New Hampshire Plastics Inc			
One Bouchard St ....Manchester NH 03103	**800-258-3036**	603-669-8523	593
New Hampshire Postsecondary Education Commission			
64 South Street Ste 300 ....Concord NH 03301	**800-735-2964**	603-271-2555	716
New Hampshire Public Television (NHPTV)			
268 Mast Rd ....Durham NH 03824	**800-639-8408**	603-868-1100	624
New Hampshire State Prison for Women			
317 Mast Rd ....Goffstown NH 03045	**800-639-1122**	603-668-6137	213
New Hampshire Veterans Home			
139 Winter St ....Tilton NH 03276	**800-735-2964**	603-527-4400	781
New Hanover Regional Medical Ctr			
2131 S 17th St...................Wilmington NC 28401	**877-228-8135**	910-343-7000	371-3
New Haven Hotel			
229 George St ....New Haven CT 06510	**800-644-6835**	203-498-3100	376
New Haven Premier Suites Hotel			
Three Long Wharf Dr ....New Haven CT 06511	**866-458-0232**	203-777-5337	376
New Haven Register			
40 Sargent Dr ....New Haven CT 06511	**800-925-2509**	203-789-5200	525-2
New Holland Church Furniture			
313 Prospect St PO Box 217 ....New Holland PA 17557	**800-648-9663**		318-3
New Horizon Kids Quest Inc			
3405 Annapolis Ln N Ste 100..........Plymouth MN 55447	**800-941-1007**		146
New Horizons Computer Learning Centers Inc			
1900 S State College Blvd			
Ste 450...........................Anaheim CA 92806	**888-236-3625**	714-940-8000	754
New Horizons Diagnostics Corp			
9110 Red Branch Rd ....Columbia MD 21045	**800-888-5015**	410-992-9357	231
New Horizons RV Corp			
2401 Lacy Dr ....Junction City KS 66441	**800-235-3140**	785-238-7575	119
New ICM LP			
PO Box 1060 ....El Campo TX 77437	**800-987-9008**	979-578-0543	153-4
New Jersey			
Banking & Insurance Dept			
20 W State St PO Box 325 ....Trenton NJ 08625	**800-446-7467**	609-292-7272	337-31
Child Support Office			
175 S Broad St PO Box 8068..........Trenton NJ 08650	**877-655-4371**		337-31
Mental Health Services Div			
PO Box 272 ....Trenton NJ 08625	**800-382-6717**	609-777-0700	337-31
Military & Veterans' Affairs Dept			
101 Eggert Crossing Rd ....Lawrenceville NJ 08648	**800-624-0508**	609-530-4600	337-31
Motor Vehicle Commission			
225 E State St PO Box 160............Trenton NJ 08666	**888-486-3339**	609-292-6500	337-31
Securities Bureau			
153 Halsey St Sixth Fl			
PO Box 47029 ....Newark NJ 07101	**866-446-8378**	973-504-3600	337-31
Travel & Tourism Div			
225 W State St PO Box 460 ....Trenton NJ 08625	**800-847-4865**	609-599-6540	337-31
Victims of Crime Compensation Board			
50 Pk Pl...........................Newark NJ 07102	**877-658-2221**	973-648-2107	337-31
New Jersey Bill Status			
State House Annex PO Box 068.........Trenton NJ 08625	**800-792-8630**	609-292-4840	430
New Jersey Bureau of State Use Industries			
163 N Olden Ave PO Box 867...........Trenton NJ 08625	**800-321-6524**		622
New Jersey Business Forms Manufacturing Co			
55 W Sheffield Ave ....Englewood NJ 07631	**800-466-6523**	201-569-4500	109
New Jersey City University			
2039 JFK Blvd ....Jersey City NJ 07305	**888-441-6528**	201-200-2000	166
New Jersey Convention & Exposition Ctr			
97 Sunfield Ave ....Edison NJ 08837	**800-367-0070**	732-417-1400	206
New Jersey Higher Education Student Assistance Authority			
4 Quakerbridge Plaza PO Box 540 ....Trenton NJ 08625	**800-792-8670**	609-584-4480	716
New Jersey Institute of Technology			
University Heights ....Newark NJ 07102	**800-925-6548**	973-596-3000	166
New Jersey Machine Inc			
56 Etna Rd ....Lebanon NH 03766	**800-432-2990***	603-448-0300	540
*Sales			
New Jersey Manufacturers Insurance Co			
301 Sullivan Way ....West Trenton NJ 08628	**800-232-6600**	609-883-1300	388-4
New Jersey Medical Society			
2 Princess Rd ....Lawrenceville NJ 08648	**800-706-7893**	609-896-1766	469
New Jersey Monthly Magazine			
55 Pk Pl PO Box 920 ....Morristown NJ 07963	**888-419-0419**	973-539-8230	452-22
New Jersey Natural Gas Co			
1415 Wyckoff Rd ....Wall NJ 07719	**800-221-0051**	732-938-1480	531
New Jersey Nets			
Nets Champion Ctr			
390 Murray Hill Pkwy...........East Rutherford NJ 07073	**800-346-6387**	201-935-8888	705-1
New Jersey Performing Arts Ctr			
1 Ctr St ....Newark NJ 07102	**888-466-5722**	973-642-8989	565
New Jersey State Nurses Assn (NJSNA)			
1479 Pennington Rd ....Trenton NJ 08618	**888-876-5762**	609-883-5335	526
New Jersey Transit Corp			
One Penn Plz E ....Newark NJ 07105	**800-772-3606***	973-491-7000	463
*Cust Svc			
New Leaf Publishing Group			
PO Box 726 ....Green Forest AR 72638	**800-999-3777**	870-438-5288	628-3
New Method Steel Stamps Inc			
31313 Kendall Ave ....Fraser MI 48026	**800-582-0199**	586-293-0200	462
Children Youth & Families Dept			
PO Drawer 5160 ....Santa Fe NM 87502	**800-610-7610**	800-432-2075	337-32
Crime Victims Reparation Commission			
8100 Mountain Rd NE Ste 106....Albuquerque NM 87110	**800-306-6262**	505-841-9432	337-32
Department of Veterans Services			
490 Old SF Trail ....Santa Fe NM 87504	**866-433-8387**	505-827-6300	337-32
Economic Development Dept			
PO Box 20003 ....Santa Fe NM 87504	**800-374-3061**	505-827-0300	337-32
Environment Dept			
1190 St Francis Dr Ste 4050 ....Santa Fe NM 87502	**800-219-6157**	505-827-2855	337-32

Listing	Toll-Free	Phone	Class
Highway & Transportation Dept (NMDOT)			
1120 Cerrillos Rd PO Box 1149 .... Santa Fe NM 87504	800-432-4269*	505-827-5100	337-32
*General			
Lieutenant Governor			
490 Old Santa Fe Trail Rm 417 .... Santa Fe NM 87501	800-432-4406	505-476-2250	337-32
Mortgage Finance Authority			
344 Fourth St SW .... Albuquerque NM 87102	800-444-6880	505-843-6880	337-32
New Mexico			
Secretary of State			
325 Don Gaspar Ave Ste 300 .... Santa Fe NM 87503	800-477-3632	505-827-3600	337-32
Tourism Dept			
491 Old Santa Fe Trail .... Santa Fe NM 87503	800-545-2070		337-32
Vital Records & Health Statistics Bureau			
1105 S St Francis Dr .... Santa Fe NM 87502	866-534-0051	505-827-0121	337-32
Vocational Rehabilitation Div			
435 St Michaels Dr Bldg D........... Santa Fe NM 87505	800-224-7005	505-954-8500	337-32
Workers' Compensation Admin			
2410 Ctr Ave SE			
PO Box 27198 .... Albuquerque NM 87125	800-255-7965	505-841-6000	337-32
New Mexico Behavioral Health Institute			
3695 Hot Springs Blvd .... Las Vegas NM 87701	800-446-5970	505-454-2100	371-5
New Mexico Democratic Party (DPNM)			
8214 Second St NW ste A.......... Albuquerque NM 87114	800-624-2457	505-830-3650	609-1
New Mexico Dental Assn			
9201 Montgomery Blvd NE			
Ste 601 .... Albuquerque NM 87111	888-997-2583	505-294-1368	227
New Mexico Ethics Administration			
325 Don Gaspar St Ste 300 .... Santa Fe NM 87501	800-477-3632	505-827-3600	265
New Mexico Financial Aid & Student Services Unit			
2048 Galisteo St .... Santa Fe NM 87505	800-279-9777	505-476-8400	716
New Mexico Higher Education Dept			
2048 Galisteo St .... Santa Fe NM 87505	800-279-9777	505-476-8400	337-32
New Mexico Highlands University			
901 University Ave .... Las Vegas NM 87701	877-850-9064	505-425-7511	166
New Mexico Institute of Mining & Technology (NMT)			
801 Leroy Pl .... Socorro NM 87801	800-428-8324*	505-835-5434	166
*Admissions			
New Mexico Junior College			
One Thunderbird Cir .... Hobbs NM 88240	800-657-6260	505-392-4510	160
New Mexico Lions Eye Bank			
2501 Yale Blvd SE Ste 100......... Albuquerque NM 87106	888-616-3937	505-266-3937	269
New Mexico Magazine			
PO Box 12002 .... Santa Fe NM 87504	800-898-6639		452-22
New Mexico Medical Society (NMMS)			
316 Osuna Rd NE Ste 501 .... Albuquerque NM 87107	800-748-1596	505-828-0237	469
New Mexico Museum of Art			
107 W Palace Ave .... Santa Fe NM 87501	877-567-7380	505-476-5072	513
New Mexico Museum of Space History			
Top of Hwy 2001 .... Alamogordo NM 88311	877-333-6589	575-437-2840	513
New Mexico Mutual Casualty Co			
PO Box 27825 .... Albuquerque NM 87125	800-788-8851	505-345-7260	388-4
New Mexico Newspapers Inc			
PO Box 450 .... Farmington NM 87499	866-272-3622	505-325-4545	628-8
New Mexico State University (NMSU)			
MSC-3A PO Box 30001 .... Las Cruces NM 88003	800-662-6678*	575-646-3121	166
*Admissions			
Carlsbad			
1500 University Dr .... Carlsbad NM 88220	888-888-2199	505-234-9200	160
New Mexico State Veterans Ctr			
992 S Broadway St .... Truth or Consequences NM 87901	800-964-3976	575-894-4200	781
New Milford Block & Supply			
574 Danbury Rd .... New Milford CT 06776	800-724-1888	860-355-1101	184
New Moon Magazine			
PO Box 161287 .... Duluth MN 55816	800-381-4743	218-878-9673	452-6
New Orleans Baptist Theological Seminary			
3939 Gentilly Blvd .... New Orleans LA 70126	800-662-8701	504-282-4455	167-3
New Orleans Cold Storage & Warehouse Company Inc (NOCS)			
3411 JouRdan Rd .... New Orleans LA 70126	800-782-2653	504-944-4400	791-2
New Orleans Firemens Federal Credit Union			
PO Box 689 .... Metairie LA 70004	800-647-1689	504-889-9090	219
New Orleans Jazz National Historical Park			
419 Decatur St .... New Orleans LA 70130	877-520-0677	504-589-4806	557
New Orleans Magazine			
110 Veterans Blvd Ste 123 .... Metairie LA 70005	877-221-3512*	504-828-1380	452-22
*Edit			
New Orleans Metropolitan Convention & Visitors Bureau			
2020 St Charles Ave .... New Orleans LA 70130	800-672-6124	504-566-5011	207
New Otani Kaimana Beach Hotel			
2863 Kalakaua Ave .... Honolulu HI 96815	800-356-8264	808-923-1555	376
New Otani North America Reservation Ctr			
120 S Los Angeles St .... Los Angeles CA 90012	800-421-8795*	213-629-1200	373
*Cust Svc			
New Penn Motor Express Inc			
625 S Fifth Ave .... Lebanon PA 17042	800-285-5000*	717-274-2521	770
*Cust Svc			
New Pig Corp			
One Pork Ave .... Tipton PA 16684	800-468-4647	814-684-0101	149
NEW Plastics Corp			
112 Fourth St .... Luxemburg WI 54217	800-666-5207	920-845-2326	97
New Process Steel Corp			
5800 Westview Dr .... Houston TX 77055	800-392-4989	713-686-9631	487
New Readers Press			
1320 Jamesville Ave .... Syracuse NY 13210	800-448-8878	315-422-9121	628-2
New Republic, The			
1331 H St NW Ste 700 .... Washington DC 20005	800-827-1289	202-508-4444	452-17
New River Community College			
5251 College PO Box 1127 .... Dublin VA 24084	866-462-6722	540-674-3600	160
New Riverside Ochre Co			
75 Old River Rd SE .... Cartersville GA 30121	800-248-0176*	770-382-4568	498-1
*Orders			
New Seabury Resort			
20 Red Brook Rd .... Mashpee MA 02649	877-687-3228	508-539-8200	660
New Tribes Mission (NTM)			
1000 E First St .... Sanford FL 32771	800-321-5375	407-323-3430	47-20
New Ulm Telecom Inc			
27 N Minnesota St .... New Ulm MN 56073	888-873-6853	507-354-4111	726
OTC: NULM			
New Venture Communications			
28 E Third Ave Ste 201 .... San Mateo CA 94401	800-307-0762	650-343-2735	48-17
New Ventures West			
3502 Geary Blvd Fl 2 .... San Francisco CA 94118	800-332-4618		458
New Vitality			
260 Smith St .... Farmingdale NY 11735	888-997-2941		779

Listing	Toll-Free	Phone	Class
New Washington State Bank			
402 E Main St PO Box 10 .... New Washington IN 47162	800-883-0131	812-293-3321	69
New Way Packaging Machinery Inc			
210 Blettner Ave .... Hanover PA 17331	844-801-3711	717-637-2133	540
New West Health Services			
130 Neill Ave .... Helena MT 59601	888-500-3355	406-457-2200	47-17
New World Library			
14 Pamaron Way .... Novato CA 94949	800-972-6657	415-884-2100	628-3
New World Pasta Co			
85 Shannon Rd .... Harrisburg PA 17112	800-730-5957*	717-526-2200	295-31
*Sales			
New World Symphony			
500 17th St .... Miami Beach FL 33139	800-597-3331	305-673-3330	566-3
New Year Tech Inc			
12330 Pinecrest Rd Ste 100 .... Reston VA 20191	800-525-7767	703-564-0290	179-12
New York			
Aging Office			
2 Empire State Plaza .... Albany NY 12223	800-342-9871		337-33
Banking Dept			
1 State St .... New York NY 10004	877-226-5697	800-342-3736	337-33
Division of Consumer Protection			
5 Empire State Plaza Ste 2101 .... Albany NY 12223	800-697-1220	518-474-3514	337-33
Empire State Development			
30 S Pearl St .... Albany NY 12245	800-782-8369	518-292-5100	337-33
Health Dept			
Empire State Plaza			
Corning II Tower .... Albany NY 12237	866-881-2809		337-33
Historic Preservation Div			
PO Box 189 .... Waterford NY 12188	800-456-2267	518-237-8643	337-33
Mental Health Office			
44 Holland Ave .... Albany NY 12229	800-597-8481	518-474-4403	337-33
Motor Vehicles Dept			
6 Empire State Plaza .... Albany NY 12228	800-368-1186	518-473-5595	337-33
Office of Court Admin			
25 Beaver St Rm 852 .... New York NY 10004	800-268-7869	212-428-2100	337-33
Parks Recreation & Historic Preservation Office			
1 Empire State Plaza .... Albany NY 12238	800-456-2267*	518-474-0456	337-33
*Campground Resv			
Taxation & Finance Dept			
WA Harriman Campus Bldg 9........... Albany NY 12227	800-225-5829	518-457-5149	337-33
Temporary & Disability Assistance Office			
40 N Pearl St 16th Fl .... Albany NY 12243	800-342-3009	518-473-1090	337-33
Tourism Div			
PO Box 2603 .... Albany NY 12223	800-225-5697	518-473-1064	337-33
Veterans' Affairs Div			
333 E Washington St Ste 430........... Albany NY 12223	888-838-7697	315-428-4046	337-33
Vital Records Office			
PO Box 2602 .... Albany NY 12220	877-854-4481	518-474-3077	337-33
Workers' Compensation Board			
328 State St .... Schenectady NY 12305	877-632-4996	518-462-8880	337-33
New York & Co			
330 W 34th St 5th Fl .... New York NY 10001	800-961-9906		155-6
New York Academy of Sciences			
250 Greenwich St 40th Fl .... New York NY 10007	800-843-6927	212-298-8600	48-19
New York Air Brake Co			
748 Starbuck Ave .... Watertown NY 13601	888-836-6922	315-786-5200	641
New York Athletic Commission			
123 William St 20th Fl .... New York NY 10038	866-269-3769	212-417-5700	703
New York Barbells			
160 Home St .... Elmira NY 14904	800-446-1833	607-733-8038	267
New York Bill Status			
202 Legislative Office Bldg .... Albany NY 12248	800-342-9860	518-455-4218	430
New York Business Development Corp (NYBDC)			
50 Beaver St Sixth Fl .... Albany NY 12207	800-923-2504	518-463-2268	216
New York Central Art Supply			
62 Third Ave .... New York NY 10003	800-950-6111		44
New York Central Mutual Fire Insurance Co (NYCM)			
1899 Central Plz E .... Edmeston NY 13335	800-234-6926		388-4
New York City Children's Ctr-Queens Campus (NYCCC)			
74-03 Commonwealth Blvd .... Bellerose NY 11426	800-597-8481	718-264-4500	371-1
New York City College of Technology			
300 Jay St .... Brooklyn NY 11201	855-492-3633	718-260-5000	166
New York Community Bancorp Inc			
615 Merrick Ave .... Westbury NY 11590	877-786-6560	516-683-4100	357-2
NYSE: NYCB			
New York Community Trust			
909 Third Ave 22nd Fl .... New York NY 10022	877-829-5500	212-686-0010	302
New York Correctional Industries			
550 Broadway .... Albany NY 12204	800-436-6321	518-436-6321	622
New York Daily News			
450 W 33rd St Third Fl.............. New York NY 10001	800-692-6397	212-210-2100	525-2
New York Education Law Report			
360 Hiatt Dr .... Palm Beach FL 33418	800-341-7874	561-622-6520	524-4
New York Eye & Ear Infirmary			
310 E 14th St .... New York NY 10003	800-522-4582	212-979-4000	371-7
New York Graphic Society Ltd			
129 Glover Ave .... Norwalk CT 06850	800-677-6947		628-10
New York Health Care Inc			
20 E Sunrise Hwy Ste 201 .... Valley Stream NY 11581	888-978-6942	718-375-6700	360
OTC: BBAL			
New York Higher Education Services Corp			
99 Washington Ave .... Albany NY 12255	888-697-4372	518-473-1574	716
New York Institute of Technology			
New York Institute of Technology Northern Blvd			
PO Box 8000.................... Old Westbury NY 11568	800-345-6948	516-686-1000	166
Islip			
PO Box 9029 .... Central Islip NY 11722	800-345-6948	516-686-1000	166
Manhattan			
1855 Broadway .... New York NY 10023	800-345-6948	212-261-1500	166
New York Islanders			
1535 Old Country Rd .... Plainview NY 11803	800-843-5678	516-501-6700	707
New York Labor Dept			
WA Harriman Campus Bldg 12........... Albany NY 12240	888-469-7365	518-457-9000	259
New York Law Journal			
120 Broadway Fifth Fl............... New York NY 10271	877-256-2472		452-15
New York Life Insurance & Annuity Corp			
51 Madison Ave .... New York NY 10010	800-598-2019	212-576-7000	388-2
New York Magazine			
75 Varick St .... New York NY 10013	800-678-0900	212-508-0700	452-22
New York Merchants Protective Company Inc			
75 W Merrick Rd .... Freeport NY 11520	888-696-7911	516-561-5210	684
New York Mets			
Shea Stadium 123-01			
Roosevelt Ave .... Flushing NY 11368	888-652-7467	718-507-6387	704

Name / Address	City	State	Zip	Toll-Free	Phone	Class
New York Military Academy						
78 Academy Ave	Cornwall On Hudson	NY	12520	**888-275-6962**	845-534-3710	615
New York Mortgage Trust Inc (NYMT)						
52 Vanderbilt Ave Ste 403	New York	NY	10017	**800-937-5449**	212-792-0107	645
NASDAQ: NYMT						
New York New York Hotel & Casino						
3790 Las Vegas Blvd S	Las Vegas	NV	89109	**800-689-1797**	702-740-6969	132
New York Palace Hotel						
455 Madison Ave	New York	NY	10022	**800-697-2522**	212-888-7000	376
New York Post						
1211 Ave of the Americas	New York	NY	10036	**800-552-7678**	212-930-8000	525-2
New York Red Bulls						
600 Cape May St Eighth Fl	Harrison	NJ	07029	**877-727-6223**		708
New York Replacement Parts Corp						
19 School St	Yonkers	NY	10701	**800-228-4718**	914-965-0122	605
New York Review of Books						
435 Hudson St Third Fl	New York	NY	10014	**800-354-0050**	212-757-8070	452-11
New York School of Interior Design						
170 E 70th St	New York	NY	10021	**800-336-9743**	212-472-1500	166
New York State Assn of Realtors						
130 Washington Ave	Albany	NY	12210	**800-462-7585**	518-463-0300	647
New York State Bar Assn						
1 Elk St	Albany	NY	12207	**800-342-3661**	518-463-3200	71
New York State Bridge Authority						
PO Box 1010	Highland	NY	12528	**800-333-8655**	845-691-7245	271
New York State Canal Corp						
200 Southern Blvd PO Box 189	Albany	NY	12201	**800-422-6254**	518-436-2700	460
New York State Dental Assn						
20 Corporate Woods Blvd #602	Albany	NY	12211	**800-255-2100**	518-465-0044	227
New York State Electric & Gas Corp						
Corporate Dr PO Box 5240	Binghamton	NY	13902	**800-572-1111**		775
New York State Medical Society						
865 Merrick Ave PO Box 5404	Westbury	NY	11590	**800-523-4405**	516-488-6100	469
New York State Nurses Assn (NYSNA)						
11 Cornell Rd	Latham	NY	12110	**800-724-6976**	518-782-9400	526
New York State Office of Parks Recreation & Historic Preservation						
Empire State Plaza Agency Bldg 1	Albany	NY	12238	**800-456-2267**	716-354-9101	49-4
New York State Society of Certified Public Accountant (FAE)						
14 Wall St 19th Fl	New York	NY	10005	**800-537-3635***	212-719-8300	48-1
*General						
New York State Veterinary Medical Society						
100 Great Oaks Blvd Ste 127	Albany	NY	12203	**800-876-9867**	518-869-7867	783
New York Susquehanna & Western Railway Corp (NYSW)						
One Railroad Ave	Cooperstown	NY	13326	**800-366-6979***	607-547-2555	639
*General						
New York Teacher Magazine						
800 Troy-Schenectady Rd	Latham	NY	12110	**800-342-9810**	518-213-6000	452-8
New York Times News Service Div						
620 Eigth Ave 9th Fl	New York	NY	10018	**800-698-4637**	212-556-7652	523
New York University						
22 Washington Sq N	New York	NY	10011	**888-243-2358**	212-998-4500	166
New York University School of Law						
110 W Third St	New York	NY	10012	**800-522-0925**	212-998-6100	167-1
New York University School of Medicine						
560 First Ave	New York	NY	10016	**855-698-2220**	212-263-7300	167-2
New York's Hotel Pennsylvania						
401 Seventh Ave	New York	NY	10001	**800-223-8585**	212-736-5000	376
New Yorker Boiler Company Inc						
PO Box 10	Hatfield	PA	19440	**800-535-4679**	215-855-8055	354
New Zealand						
Embassy						
37 Observatory Cir NW	Washington	DC	20008	**855-844-2835**	202-328-4800	257
NewAge Industries Inc						
145 James Way	SouthHampton	PA	18966	**800-506-3924**	215-526-2300	367
NewAgeSys Inc						
231 Clarksville Rd Ste 200	Princeton Junction	NJ	08550	**888-863-9243**	609-919-9800	181
Newark Group						
20 Jackson Dr	Cranford	NJ	07016	**800-777-7890**	908-276-4000	554
Newark Liberty International Airport						
One Hotel Rd	Newark	NJ	07114	**888-397-4636**	973-961-6007	27
Newark Museum						
49 Washington St	Newark	NJ	07102	**888-370-6765**	973-596-6550	513
Newark Paperboard Products Inc						
20 Jackson Dr	Cranford	NJ	07016	**800-777-7890**	908-276-4000	547
Newark Regional Business Partnership						
744 Broad St 26th Fl	Newark	NJ	07102	**800-662-6878**	973-522-0099	137
Newark School District						
100 E Miller St 4th Fl	Newark	NY	14513	**877-789-2613**	315-332-3230	770
Newberry Area Tourism Assn, The						
PO Box 308	Newberry	MI	49868	**800-831-7292**	906-293-5562	207
Newberry College						
2100 College St	Newberry	SC	29108	**800-845-4955**	803-276-5010	166
Newberry Electric Co-op Inc						
882 Wilson Rd	Newberry	SC	29108	**800-479-8838**	803-276-1121	245
Newbold Corp						
450 Weaver St	Rocky Mount	VA	24151	**800-552-3282**	540-489-4400	110
Newbury College						
129 Fisher Ave	Brookline	MA	02445	**800-755-7071**	617-730-7000	166
Newburyport Five Cents Savings Bank Inc, The						
63 State St PO Box 350	Newburyport	MA	01950	**877-462-3136**	978-462-3136	69
NewCloud Networks						
160 Inverness Dr W	Englewood	CO	80112	**855-255-5001**		384
Newcomb College Institute for Women						
43 Newcomb Pl	New Orleans	LA	70118	**888-327-0009**	504-865-5422	166
Newcomb Spring Corp						
235 Spring St	Southington	CT	06489	**888-579-3051**	860-621-0111	710
Newcon Optik						
105 Sparks Ave	North York	ON	M2H2S5	**877-368-6666**	416-663-6963	522
Newegg Inc						
16839 E Gale Ave	City of Industry	CA	91745	**800-390-1119**	626-271-9700	180
Newell Coach Corp						
6411 S Hwy 69 PO Box 511	Miami	OK	74354	**888-363-9355**	918-542-3344	119
Newell Paper Co						
1212 Grand Ave PO Box 631	Meridian	MS	39301	**800-844-8894**	601-693-1783	546
Newell Rubbermaid Inc						
Three Glenlake Pkwy	Atlanta	GA	30328	**800-752-9677**	770-418-7000	186
NYSE: NWL						
Newell Rubbermaid Inc Irwin Tools Div						
8935 Northpointe Executive Dr	Huntersville	NC	28078	**800-866-5740**	704-987-4555	748
Newell Rubbermaid Inc Tools & Hardware Group						
8935 NorthPointe Executive Dr	Huntersville	NC	28078	**800-464-7946**	704-987-4555	347
Newfield Exploration Co						
363 N Sam Houston Pkwy E Ste 100	Houston	TX	77060	**866-902-0562**	281-847-6000	529
NYSE: NFX						
Newkirk Products Inc						
15 Corporate Cir	Albany	NY	12203	**800-525-4237**	518-862-3200	628-2
NewlineNoosh Inc						
625 Ellis St Ste 300	Mountain View	CA	94043	**888-286-6674**	650-637-6000	179-1
Newly Weds Foods Inc						
4140 W Fullerton Ave	Chicago	IL	60639	**800-621-7521**	773-489-7000	295-37
Newman & Company Inc						
6101 Tacony St	Philadelphia	PA	19135	**800-523-3256**	215-333-8700	554
Newman University						
3100 McCormick Ave	Wichita	KS	67213	**877-639-6268**	316-942-4291	166
Newman's Inc						
3003 Texas 225	Pasadena	TX	77503	**800-231-3505**	713-675-8631	382
Newmar Corp						
355 Delaware St	Nappanee	IN	46550	**800-731-8300**	574-773-7791	119
NewMarket Corp						
330 S Fourth St	Richmond	VA	23219	**800-625-5191**	804-788-5000	357-3
NYSE: NEU						
Newpark Mats & Integrated Services LLC						
2700 Research Forest Dr Ste 100	The Woodlands	TX	77381	**877-628-7623**	281-362-6800	532
Newport Aquarium						
One Aquarium Way	Newport	KY	41071	**800-406-3474**	859-261-7444	39
Newport Beach Conference & Visitors Bureau						
1200 Newport Ctr Dr Ste 120	Newport Beach	CA	92660	**800-942-6278**	949-719-6100	207
Newport Beach Hotel & Suites						
One Wave Ave	Middletown	RI	02842	**800-655-1778**	401-846-0310	376
Newport Beachside Hotel & Resort						
16701 Collins Ave	Miami Beach	FL	33160	**800-327-5476**	305-949-1300	376
Newport Corp						
1791 Deere Ave	Irvine	CA	92606	**800-222-6440***	949-863-3144	537
NASDAQ: NEWP ■ *Sales						
Newport County Convention & Visitors Bureau						
23 America's Cup Ave	Newport	RI	02840	**800-976-5122**	401-849-8048	207
Newport Electronics Inc						
2229 S Yale St	Santa Ana	CA	92704	**800-639-7678***	714-540-4914	248
*Cust Svc						
Newport Grand Jai Alai						
150 Admiral Kalbfus Rd	Newport	RI	02840	**800-451-2500**	401-849-5000	132
Newport Harbor Hotel & Marina						
49 America's Cup Ave	Newport	RI	02840	**800-955-2558**	401-847-9000	376
Newport Leasing Inc						
4750 Von Karman Ave	Newport Beach	CA	92660	**800-274-0042***	949-476-8476	264-1
*Cust Svc						
Newport News Industrial Corp						
182 Enterprise Dr	Newport News	VA	23603	**800-627-0353**	757-380-7053	777
Newport News Tourism Development Office						
700 Town Ctr Dr Ste 320	Newport News	VA	23606	**888-493-7386**	757-926-1400	207
Newport on the Levee						
One Levee Way Ste 1113	Newport	KY	41071	**866-538-3359**	859-291-0550	49-5
Newport State Park						
475 County Rd NP	Ellison Bay	WI	54210	**800-847-9367**	920-854-2500	558
Newport Wave Inc						
15 McLean	Irvine	CA	92620	**800-999-2611**	949-651-1099	179-1
NewRetirement LLC						
1933 Davis St Ste 205	San Leandro	CA	94111	**866-441-0246**	415-738-2435	523
News & Advance						
PO Box 10129	Lynchburg	VA	24506	**800-275-8830**	434-385-5555	525-2
News & Observer						
215 S McDowell St	Raleigh	NC	27602	**800-522-4205**	919-829-4500	525-2
News & Record						
200 E Market St	Greensboro	NC	27401	**800-553-6880**	336-373-7000	525-2
News America Marketing						
1185 Ave of the Americas 27	New York	NY	10036	**800-462-0852**	212-782-8000	5
News Journal						
70 W Fourth St	Mansfield	OH	44903	**800-472-5547**	419-522-3311	525-2
News Leader						
11 N Central Ave	Staunton	VA	24401	**800-793-2459**	540-885-7281	525-2
News Tribune						
1950 S State St	Tacoma	WA	98405	**800-388-8742**	253-597-8742	525-2
News10						
400 Broadway	Sacramento	CA	95818	**866-397-9884**	916-441-2345	730-64
Newsbank Inc						
5801 Pelican Bay Blvd Ste 600	Naples	FL	34108	**800-243-7694**	239-263-6004	384
Newsday Inc						
235 Pinelawn Rd	Melville	NY	11747	**800-639-7329**	631-843-2700	525-2
News-Enterprise						
408 W Dixie Ave	Elizabethtown	KY	42701	**877-246-2322**	270-769-1200	525-2
News-Herald						
7085 Mentor Ave	Willoughby	OH	44094	**800-947-2737**	440-951-0000	525-2
NewsHub						
100 Lombard St Suite 203	Toronto	ON	M5C1M3	**800-889-9487**	416-536-4827	394
Newsome House Museum & Cultural Ctr						
2803 Oak Ave	Newport News	VA	23607	**888-493-7386**	757-247-2360	513
News-Review						
345 NE Winchester St	Roseburg	OR	97470	**888-459-3830**	541-672-3321	525-2
News-Sentinel						
600 W Main St	Fort Wayne	IN	46802	**800-444-3303**	260-461-8439	525-2
News-Star						
411 N Fourth St	Monroe	LA	71201	**800-259-7788**	318-322-5161	525-2
NewStar Fresh Foods LLC						
900 Work St	Salinas	CA	93901	**888-782-7220**	831-758-7800	295-19
News-Tribune						
426 Second St	La Salle	IL	61301	**800-892-6452**	815-223-3200	525-2
Newsweek Magazine						
Seven Hanover Sq	New York	NY	10004	**800-631-1040***		452-17
*Cust Svc						
Newtek Business Services Inc						
1440 Broadway 17th Fl	New York	NY	10018	**866-820-8902***	212-356-9500	780
NASDAQ: NEWT ■ *Sales						
NewTek Inc						
5131 Beckwith Blvd	San Antonio	TX	78249	**800-862-7837***	210-370-8000	179-8
*Cust Svc						
Newtex Industries Inc						
8050 Victor Mendon Rd	Victor	NY	14564	**800-836-1001**	585-924-9135	734-3
Newton Convention & Visitor Bureau						
300 E 17th St S Ste 400	Newton	IA	50208	**800-798-0299**	641-792-0299	207
Newton County						
201 N 3rd St	Kentland	IN	47951	**888-663-9866**	219-474-6081	336

Name / Address	City	State	ZIP	Toll-Free	Phone	Class
Newton County Chamber of Commerce 2101 Clark St	Covington	GA	30014	**866-462-6873**	770-786-7510	137
Newton Mfg Co 1123 First Ave E	Newton	IA	50208	**800-500-7227**	641-792-4121	9
Newtown Savings Bank Foundation Inc 39 Main St PO Box 497	Newtown	CT	06470	**800-461-0672**	203-426-2563	69
Nexcess.net LLC 21700 Melrose Ave	Southfield	MI	48075	**866-639-2377**		225
NEXCOM (Navy Exchange Service Command) 3280 Virginia Beach Blvd	Virginia Beach	VA	23452	**800-628-3924**	757-463-6200	779
Nexen Group Inc 560 Oak Grove Pkwy	Vadnais Heights	MN	55127	**800-843-7445**	651-484-5900	383
Nexion 6225 N State Hwy 161 Ste 450	Irving	TX	75038	**800-949-6410**	408-280-6410	762
Nexlan 28 W N St	Danville	IL	61832	**877-263-9526**	217-431-7236	178
Next Day Flyers 18711 S Broadwick St	Rancho Dominguez	CA	90220	**800-251-9948**		5
Next Net Media LLC 316 California Ave Ste 804	Reno	NV	89509	**800-737-5820**		384
Next Step Living Inc 21 Drydock Ave Second Fl	Boston	MA	02210	**866-867-8729**		193
NextEra Energy Resources LLC *NextEra Energy Resources LLC* 700 Universe Blvd PO Box 14000	Juno Beach	FL	33408	**888-867-3050**	561-691-7171	775
nextPoint Inc 4043 N Ravenswood Ave	Chicago	IL	60613	**888-929-6398**		178
Nextran Corp 1986 W Beaver St	Jacksonville	FL	32209	**800-347-6225**	904-354-3721	56
NextWave Wireless Inc 10350 Science Ctr Dr Ste 210 *OTC: WAVE*	San Diego	CA	92121	**800-461-9330**	858-731-5300	357-3
Nexus Corp 10983 Leroy Dr	Northglenn	CO	80233	**800-228-9639**	303-457-9199	105
Nexxtworks Inc 30798 Us Hwy 19 N	Palm Harbor	FL	34684	**888-533-8353**		384
Ney Oil Company Inc 145 S Water St PO Box 155	Ney	OH	43549	**800-962-9839**	419-658-2324	323
Neyra Industries 10700 Evendale Dr	Cincinnati	OH	45241	**800-543-7077**	513-733-1000	45
NF Smith & Assoc LP 5306 Hollister Rd	Houston	TX	77040	**800-468-7866**	713-430-3000	246
NFA (National Futures Assn) 300 S Riverside Plz Ste 1800	Chicago	IL	60606	**800-621-3570**	312-781-1300	48-2
NFB (National Federation of the Blind) 1800 Johnson St	Baltimore	MD	21230	**800-392-5671**	410-659-9314	47-17
NFBA (National Frame Builders Assn) 8735 W Higgins Rd Ste 300	Chicago	IL	60631	**800-557-6957**		48-3
NFCA (National Family Caregivers Assn) 10400 Connecticut Ave Ste 500	Kensington	MD	20895	**800-896-3650**	301-942-6430	47-6
NFCDCU (National Federation of Community Development Credit Unions) 39 Broadway Ste 2140	New York	NY	10006	**800-437-8711**	212-809-1850	48-2
NFCR (National Foundation for Cancer Research) 4600 E W Hwy Ste 525	Bethesda	MD	20814	**800-321-2873**	301-654-1250	304
NFDA (National Funeral Directors Assn) 13625 Bishop's Dr	Brookfield	WI	53005	**800-228-6332**	262-789-1880	48-4
NFDMA (National Funeral Directors & Morticians Assn) 6290 Shannon Pkwy	Union City	GA	30291	**800-434-0958**	770-969-0064	48-4
NFHS (National Federation of State High School Assn) PO Box 690 *Cust Svc	Indianapolis	IN	46206	**800-776-3462***	317-972-6900	47-22
NFI (National Freight Inc) 1515 Burnt Mill Rd *General	Cherry Hill	NJ	08003	**877-634-3777***		444
NFIC (National Fraud Information Ctr) 1701 K St NW Ste 1200	Washington	DC	20006	**800-333-4636**	202-835-3323	47-10
NFL Network 345 Park Avenue	New York	NY	10154	**800-724-3377**	212-450-2000	729
NFO (National Farmers Organization) 528 Billy Sunday Rd Ste 100 PO Box 2508	Ames	IA	50010	**800-247-2110**	515-292-2000	47-2
NFP (National Fibromyalgia Partnership Inc) 140 Zinn Way	Linden	VA	22642	**866-725-4404**		47-17
NFPA (National Federation of Paralegal Assn) 23607 Hwy 99 Ste 2-C	Edmonds	WA	98020	**888-525-3675**	425-967-0045	48-10
NFPA (National Fire Protection Assn) One Batterymarch Pk	Quincy	MA	02169	**800-344-3555**	617-770-3000	47-17
NFR (North Fork Ranch) 55395 Hwy 285 PO Box B	Shawnee	CO	80475	**800-843-7895**	303-838-9873	239
NFRA (National Forest Recreation Assn) PO Box 488	Woodlake	CA	93286	**800-282-2444**	559-564-2365	47-23
nFrame Inc 701 Congressional Blvd Ste 100	Carmel	IN	46032	**877-570-7827**	317-805-3759	391
NFRW (National Federation of Republican Women) 124 N Alfred St	Alexandria	VA	22314	**800-373-9688**	703-548-9688	47-7
NGA (National Gardening Assn) 1100 Dorset St	South Burlington	VT	05403	**800-538-7476**	802-863-5251	47-18
NGA (National Glass Assn) 8200 Greensboro Dr Ste 302	McLean	VA	22102	**866-342-5642**	703-442-4890	48-13
NGAUS (National Guard Assn of the US) One Massachusetts Ave NW Ste 200	Washington	DC	20001	**888-226-4287**	202-789-0031	47-19
NGC (National Garden Clubs Inc) 4401 Magnolia Ave	Saint Louis	MO	63110	**800-550-6007**	314-776-7574	47-18
NGCOA (National Golf Course Owners Assn) 291 Seven Farms Dr Second Fl	Charleston	SC	29492	**800-933-4262**	843-881-9956	47-23
NGF (National Gaucher Foundation) 2227 Idlewood Rd Ste 6	Tucker	GA	30084	**800-504-3189**	770-934-2910	47-17
NGF (National Golf Foundation) 1150 S US Hwy 1 Ste 401	Jupiter	FL	33477	**800-733-6006**	561-744-6006	47-22
NGK Metals Corp 917 Hwy 11 S	Sweetwater	TN	37874	**800-523-8268**	423-337-5500	307
NGK Spark Plugs Inc 46929 Magellan	Wixom	MI	48393	**877-473-6767**	248-926-6900	247
NGL (National Guardian Life Insurance Co) 2 E Gilman St	Madison	WI	53703	**800-548-2962**	608-257-5611	388-2
NGL (Network Global Logistics) 320 Interlocken Pkwy Ste 100	Broomfield	CO	80021	**866-938-1870**		539
NGS (National Genealogical Society) 3108 Columbia Pk Ste 300	Arlington	VA	22204	**800-473-0060**	703-525-0050	47-18
NGWA (National Ground Water Assn) 601 Dempsey Rd	Westerville	OH	43081	**800-551-7379**	614-898-7791	47-12
NH Yates & Company Inc 117 Church Ln # C	Cockeysville	MD	21030	**800-878-8181**		632
NHCA (National Hearing Conservation Assn) 3030 W 81st Ave	Westminster	CO	80031	**800-445-8667**	303-224-9022	47-17
NHCOA (National Hispanic Council on Aging) 734 15th St NW Ste 1050	Washington	DC	20005	**800-633-4227**	202-347-9733	47-6
NHDP (National Hansen's Disease Program) 1770 Physicians Pk Dr	Baton Rouge	LA	70816	**800-642-2477**	225-756-3700	659
NHES (New Hampshire Employment Security) 32 S Main St	Concord	NH	03301	**800-852-3400**	603-224-3311	259
NHF (National Headache Foundation) 820 N Orleans St Ste 217	Chicago	IL	60610	**888-643-5552**		47-17
NHF (National Hemophilia Foundation) 116 W 32nd St 11th Fl	New York	NY	10001	**800-424-2634**	212-328-3700	47-17
NHFA (National Home Furnishings Assn) 3910 Tinsley Dr Ste 101	High Point	NC	27265	**800-422-3778**	336-886-6100	48-4
NHK Laboratories Inc 12230 E Florience Ave	Santa Fe Springs	CA	90670	**866-645-5227**	562-944-5400	474
NHLA (National Hardwood Lumber Assn) 6830 Raleigh-LaGrange Rd	Memphis	TN	38134	**800-933-0318**	901-377-1818	48-3
NHPCO (National Hospice & Palliative Care Organization) 1700 Diagonal Rd Ste 625 *Help Line	Alexandria	VA	22314	**800-658-8898***	703-837-1500	48-8
NHPTV (New Hampshire Public Television) 268 Mast Rd	Durham	NH	03824	**800-639-8408**	603-868-1100	624
NHS (National Honor Society) 1904 Assn Dr	Reston	VA	20191	**800-253-7746**	703-860-0200	47-11
NHSA (National Head Start Assn) 1651 Prince St	Alexandria	VA	22314	**866-677-8724**	703-739-0875	47-11
NHTI Concord's Community College 31 College Dr	Concord	NH	03301	**800-247-0179**	603-271-6484	160
NIA (National Insulation Assn) 99 Canal Ctr Plz Ste 222	Alexandria	VA	22314	**877-968-7642**	703-683-6422	48-3
NIA Group Inc / Ste 400	Saddle Brook	NJ	07663	**800-669-6330**	201-845-6600	387
Niacet Corp 400 47th St	Niagara Falls	NY	14304	**800-828-1207**	716-285-1474	142
NIADA (National Independent Automobile Dealers Assn) 2521 Brown Blvd	Arlington	TX	76006	**800-682-3837**	817-640-3838	48-18
Niagara Blower Co Inc 673 Ontario St	Buffalo	NY	14207	**800-426-5169**	716-875-2000	14
Niagara Corp 667 Madison Ave	New York	NY	10021	**877-289-2277**	212-317-1000	714
Niagara County Community College 3111 Saunders Settlement Rd	Sanborn	NY	14132	**800-875-6269**	716-614-6222	160
Niagara Cutter Inc 200 John James Audubon Pkwy	Amherst	NY	14228	**888-689-8400**	716-689-8400	488
Niagara Duty Free Shop 5726 Falls Ave	Niagara Falls	ON	L2G7T5	**877-642-4337**	905-374-3700	241
Niagara Frontier Transit Metro System Inc 181 Ellicott St Ste 1	Buffalo	NY	14203	**877-294-9434**	716-855-7300	463
Niagara Hospice 4675 Sunset Dr	Lockport	NY	14094	**800-662-1220**	716-439-4417	368
Niagara Parks Botanical Gardens 2565 Niagara Pkwy N PO Box 150	Niagara Falls	ON	L2E6T2	**877-642-7275**	905-356-8554	96
Niagara Tourism & Convention Corp 10 Rainbow Blvd	Niagara Falls	NY	14303	**877-325-5787**	716-282-8992	207
Niagara Transformer Corp 1747 Dale Rd	Buffalo	NY	14225	**800-817-5652**	716-896-6500	757
Niagara University 5795 Lewiston Rd PO Box 2011	Niagara University	NY	14109	**800-462-2111**	716-286-8700	166
NIB (National Industries for the Blind) 1310 Braddock Pl *Cust Svc	Alexandria	VA	22314	**800-433-2304***	703-310-0500	47-17
NIBCO Inc 1516 Middlebury St	Elkhart	IN	46515	**800-234-0227**	574-295-3000	588
NIC Inc 25501 W Valley Pkwy Ste 300 *NASDAQ: EGOV*	Olathe	KS	66061	**877-234-3468**		179-10
NICB (National Insurance Crime Bureau) 1111 E Touhy Ave Ste 400	Des Plaines	IL	60018	**800-447-6282**	847-544-7002	48-9
NICE Systems Inc 301 Rt 17 N 10th Fl	Rutherford	NJ	07070	**800-994-4498**	201-964-2600	725
Nice-Pak Products Inc Two Nice-Pak Pk	Orangeburg	NY	10962	**800-999-6423**	845-365-1700	551
Niche Directories LLC 909 N Sepulveda Blvd 11th Fl	El Segundo	CA	90026	**877-242-9330**		384
Nicholas Family of Funds 700 N Water St Ste 1010	Milwaukee	WI	53202	**800-227-5987**	414-272-6133	521
Nicholas Financial Inc 2454 McMullen Booth Rd Bldg C *NASDAQ: NICK*	Clearwater	FL	33759	**800-237-2721**	727-726-0763	214
Nicholls State University 906 E First St *Admissions	Thibodaux	LA	70310	**877-446-0561***	985-448-4507	166
Nichols College 124 Ctr Rd	Dudley	MA	01571	**800-470-3379**	508-213-1560	166
Nichols Paper & Supply Company Inc PO Box 291	Muskegon	MI	49443	**800-442-0213**	231-799-2120	552
Nichols Wire 1547 Helton Dr	Florence	AL	35630	**800-633-3156**	256-764-4271	800
Nicholson Construction Co 12 McClane St	Cuddy	PA	15031	**800-388-2340**	412-221-4500	190-5
Nick Strimbu Inc 3500 PkwyRd	Brookfield	OH	44403	**800-446-8785**	330-448-4046	770
Nickelodeon Family Suites by Holiday Inn 14500 Continental Gateway	Orlando	FL	32821	**877-642-5111**	407-387-5437	660
Nickers International Ltd PO Box 50066	Staten Island	NY	10305	**800-642-5377**	718-448-6283	787
Nicor Gas 1844 Ferry Rd	Naperville	IL	60563	**888-642-6748**	630-983-8888	775
NICSA (National Investment Co Service Assn) 8400 Westpark Dr 2nd Fl	McLean	VA	22102	**800-426-1122**	508-485-1500	48-2
NID (Nevada Irrigation District) 1036 W Main St	Grass Valley	CA	95945	**800-222-4102**	530-273-6185	775
Nida Corp 300 S John Rodes Blvd	Melbourne	FL	32904	**800-327-6432**	321-727-2265	694
NIDCR (National Oral Health Information Clearinghouse) One NOHIC Way	Bethesda	MD	20892	**866-232-4528**	301-496-4261	47-17
Nidec Motor Corp 8050 W Florissant Ave	Saint Louis	MO	63136	**888-637-7333**		511

Listing	City	State	ZIP	Toll-Free	Phone	Class
Nielsen-Massey Vanillas Inc						
1550 S Shields Dr	Waukegan	IL	60085	**800-525-7873**	847-578-1550	295-15
NIFL (National Institute for Literacy)						
1775 'I' St NW Ste 730	Washington	DC	20006	**800-228-8813**	202-233-2025	338-6
NIGA (National Indian Gaming Assn)						
224 Second St SE	Washington	DC	20003	**866-694-3937**	202-546-7711	47-23
Night Optics USA Inc						
15182 Triton Ln Ste 101	Huntington Beach	CA	92649	**800-306-4448**	714-899-4475	535
Nightingale-Conant Corp						
6245 W Howard St	Niles	IL	60714	**800-557-1660***		506
*Cust Svc						
Nightscaping						
1705 E Colton Ave	Redlands	CA	92374	**800-544-4840**	909-794-2121	435
NIGP (National Institute of Governmental Purchasing Inc)						
151 Spring St	Herndon	VA	20170	**800-367-6447**	703-736-8900	48-7
NIH Osteoporosis & Related Bone Diseases-National Resource Ctr						
2 AMS Cir	Bethesda	MD	20892	**800-624-2663**	202-223-0344	338-8
Nihon Kohden America Inc						
90 Icon	Foothill Ranch	CA	92610	**800-325-0283**	949-580-1555	470
Nike Inc						
One Bowerman Dr	Beaverton	OR	97005	**800-344-6453***	503-671-6453	300
NYSE: NKE ■ *Cust Svc						
Nik-O-Lok Co						
3130 N Mitthoeffer Rd	Indianapolis	IN	46235	**800-428-4348**	317-899-6955	347
Nikon Inc						
1300 Walt Whitman Rd	Melville	NY	11747	**800-645-6687***	631-547-4200	584
*Cust Svc						
Niles Audio Corp						
1969 Kellog Ave	Carlsbad	CA	92008	**800-289-4434**	760-710-0992	253
Niles Community School						
111 Spruce St	Niles	MI	49120	**877-622-2321**	269-683-0732	676
Nilfisk-Advance Inc						
14600 21st Ave N	Plymouth	MN	55447	**800-989-2235***		383
*Cust Svc						
Nina Enterprises						
1350 S Leavitt St	Chicago	IL	60608	**800-886-8688**	312-733-6400	527
Nine Zero Hotel						
90 Tremont St	Boston	MA	02108	**866-906-9090**	617-772-5800	376
Nines Hotel, The						
525 SW Morrison	Portland	OR	97204	**877-229-9995**		40
Ninety-Nines Inc						
4300 Amelia Earhart Rd	Oklahoma City	OK	73159	**800-994-1929**	405-685-7969	47-24
Nintendo of America Inc						
4820 150th Ave NE	Redmond	WA	98052	**800-255-3700***	425-882-2040	752
*Cust Svc						
Ninyo & Moore						
5710 Ruffin Rd	San Diego	CA	92123	**800-427-0401**	858-576-1000	261
NIPC (National Inhalant Prevention Coalition)						
318 Lindsay St	Chattanooga	TN	37403	**800-269-4237**	423-265-4662	47-17
Nishnabotna Valley Rural Electric Co-op						
1317 Chatburn Ave	Harlan	IA	51537	**800-234-5122**	712-755-2166	245
Niskayuna Central School District (NCSD)						
1239 Van Antwerp Rd	Schenectady	NY	12309	**866-893-6337**	518-377-4666	676
NISO (National Information Standards Organization)						
3600 Clipper Mill Road Suite 302	Baltimore	MD	21211	**877-375-2160**	301-654-2512	48-16
Nissan Canada Inc (NCI)						
5290 Orbitor Dr	Mississauga	ON	L4W4Z5	**800-387-0122**		58
Nissan Motor Corp USA Infiniti Div						
One Nissan Way PO Box 685003	Franklin	TN	37067	**800-662-6200**		58
Nissan North America Inc						
25 Vantage way	Nashville	TN	37228	**800-647-7261**		58
NIST (National Institute of Standards & Technology)						
100 Bureau Dr Sp 1070	Gaithersburg	MD	20899	**800-877-8339**	301-975-6478	338-2
Nitel Inc						
1101 W Lk St Sixth Fl	Chicago	IL	60607	**888-450-2100**		224
Nitrous Express Inc						
5411 Seymour Hwy	Wichita Falls	TX	76310	**888-463-2781**	940-767-7694	56
Nitta Casings Inc						
141 Southside Ave PO Box 858	Bridgewater	NJ	08807	**800-526-3970***	908-218-4400	297
*Cust Svc						
Nitta Gelatin Inc						
598 Airport Blvd Ste 900	Morrisville	NC	27560	**888-648-8287**	919-238-3300	295-22
Nittany Lion Inn						
200 W Pk Ave	State College	PA	16803	**800-233-7505**	814-865-8500	376
Niver Western Wear Inc						
PO Box 101224	Fort Worth	TX	76185	**800-433-5752***	817-924-4299	153-19
*Orders						
NJSNA (New Jersey State Nurses Assn)						
1479 Pennington Rd	Trenton	NJ	08618	**888-876-5762**	609-883-5335	526
NJTV						
825 Eighth Avenue	New York	NY	10019	**800-882-6622**	609-777-0031	636-114
NKBA (National Kitchen & Bath Assn)						
687 Willow Grove St	Hackettstown	NJ	07840	**800-843-6522**		48-3
NKC of America Inc						
1584 E Brooks Rd	Memphis	TN	38116	**800-532-6727**	901-396-5353	208
NKF (National Kidney Foundation)						
30 E 33rd St Eighth Fl	New York	NY	10016	**800-622-9010**	212-889-2210	47-17
NKS Distributors Inc						
399 Churchmans Rd	New Castle	DE	19720	**800-310-5099**	302-322-1811	80-3
NKYCVB (Northern Kentucky Convention & Visitors Bureau)						
50 E RiverCenter Blvd Ste 200	Covington	KY	41011	**877-659-8474**	859-261-4677	207
NL Industries						
16801 Greenspoint Pk Dr	Houston	TX	77060	**800-866-5600**	281-423-3300	141
NYSE: NL						
NLADA (National Legal Aid & Defender Assn)						
1140 Connecticut Ave NW Ste 900	Washington	DC	20036	**800-725-4513**	202-452-0620	48-10
NLBRA (National Little Britches Rodeo Assn)						
5050 Edison Ave Ste 105	Colorado Springs	CO	80915	**800-763-3694**	719-389-0333	47-22
NLC Inc 319 W Main St	Jackson	MO	63755	**800-594-3958***	573-243-3141	798
*Sales						
NLN (National League for Nursing)						
61 Broadway 33rd Fl	New York	NY	10006	**800-669-1656**	212-363-5555	48-8
NLRB (National Labor Relations Board)						
1099 14th St NW	Washington	DC	20570	**866-667-6572**	202-273-1991	338-18
NMA (National Motorists Assn)						
402 W Second St	Waunakee	WI	53597	**800-882-2785**	608-849-6000	48-21
NMA (National Medical Assn)						
8403 Colesville Rd Ste 920	Silver Spring	MD	20910	**800-662-0554**	202-347-1895	48-8
NMC (National Motor Club of America Inc)						
130 E John Carpenter Fwy	Irving	TX	75062	**800-523-4582**	972-999-1099	52
NMCRS (Navy-Marine Corps Relief Society)						
875 N Randolph St Ste 225	Arlington	VA	22203	**800-654-8364**	703-696-4904	47-19
NMC-Wollard Inc						
2021 Truax Blvd	Eau Claire	WI	54703	**800-656-6867**	715-835-3151	465
NMDP (National Marrow Donor Program)						
3001 Broadway St NE Ste 100	Minneapolis	MN	55413	**800-526-7809**	612-627-5800	47-17
NMEA (National Marine Electronics Assn)						
Seven Riggs Ave	Severna Park	MD	21146	**800-808-6632**	410-975-9425	48-13
NMF (National Marfan Foundation)						
22 Manhasset Ave	Port Washington	NY	11050	**800-862-7326**	516-883-8712	47-17
NMHC (North Mississippi Medical Ctr Hospice)						
830 S Gloster St	Tupelo	MS	38801	**800-882-6274**	662-377-3000	368
NMMS (New Mexico Medical Society)						
316 Osuna Rd NE Ste 501	Albuquerque	NM	87107	**800-748-1596**	505-828-0237	469
NMOA (National Mail Order Assn LLC)						
2807 Polk St NE	Minneapolis	MN	55418	**800-992-1377**	612-788-1673	48-18
NMPF (National Milk Producers Federation)						
2101 Wilson Blvd Ste 400	Arlington	VA	22201	**888-723-3366**	703-243-6111	48-6
NMRA (National Marine Representatives Assn)						
PO Box 360	Gurnee	IL	60031	**800-890-3819**	847-662-3167	48-18
NMRA (National Model Railroad Assn)						
4121 Cromwell Rd	Chattanooga	TN	37421	**800-654-2256**	423-892-2846	47-18
NMS Capital Group LLC						
433 N Camden Dr Fourth Fl	Beverly Hills	CA	90210	**800-716-2080**		682
NMS Labs						
3701 Welsh Rd	Willow Grove	PA	19090	**800-522-6671**	215-657-4900	415
NMSA (National Middle School Assn)						
4151 Executive Pkwy Ste 300	Westerville	OH	43081	**800-528-6672**	614-895-4730	48-5
NMSU (New Mexico State University)						
MSC-3A PO Box 30001	Las Cruces	NM	88003	**800-662-6678***	575-646-3121	166
*Admissions						
NMT (New Mexico Institute of Mining & Technology)						
801 Leroy Pl	Socorro	NM	87801	**800-428-8324***	505-835-5434	166
*Admissions						
NN Inc						
2000 Waters Edge Dr Bldg 3 Ste 12	Johnson City	TN	37604	**877-888-0002**	423-743-9151	480
NASDAQ: NNBR						
NNA (Nebraska Nurses Assn)						
PO Box 3107	Kearney	NE	68848	**800-582-3014**	402-475-3859	526
NNA (National Newspaper Assn)						
PO Box 7540	Columbia	MO	65205	**800-829-4662**	573-777-4980	48-14
NNA (National Notary Assn)						
9350 DeSoto Ave	Chatsworth	CA	91313	**800-876-6827**	818-739-4000	48-12
NNM Peterson Manufacturing Co						
24133 W 143rd St	Plainfield	IL	60544	**800-826-9086**	815-436-9201	286
NNPDF (National Niemann-Pick Disease Foundation Inc)						
401 Madison Ave Ste B PO Box 49	Fort Atkinson	WI	53538	**877-287-3672**	920-563-0930	47-17
NNSDO (National Nursing Staff Development Organization)						
330 N Wabash Ave Ste 2000	Chicago	IL	60611	**800-489-1995**	312-321-5135	48-8
NNT Corp						
1320 Norwood Ave	Itasca	IL	60143	**800-556-9999**	630-875-9600	450
No Starch Press Inc						
38 Ringold St	San Francisco	CA	94103	**800-420-7240**	415-863-9900	628-2
NOAH (National Organization for Albinism & Hypopigmentation)						
PO Box 959	East Hampstead	NH	03826	**800-648-2310**	603-887-2310	47-17
Nob Hill						
3799 Las Vegas Blvd S MGM Grand Hotel	Las Vegas	NV	89109	**800-929-1111***	702-891-1111	662
*Resv						
Nob Hill Gazette						
5 Third St Ste 222	San Francisco	CA	94103	**866-617-4578**	415-227-0190	452-22
Nobel Biocare USA Inc						
22715 Savi Ranch Pkwy	Yorba Linda	CA	92887	**800-993-8100**	714-282-4800	228
NobelClad						
5405 Spine Rd	Boulder	CO	80301	**800-821-2666***	303-665-5700	477
NASDAQ: BOOM ■ *General						
Nobility Homes Inc						
3741 SW Seventh St	Ocala	FL	34474	**800-476-6624**	352-732-5157	500
OTC: NOBH						
Noble Corp						
13135 S Dairy Ashford Rd Ste 800	Sugar Land	TX	77478	**877-285-4162**	281-276-6100	533
NYSE: NE						
Noble Energy Inc						
100 Glenborough Dr Ste 100	Houston	TX	77067	**800-220-5824**	281-872-3100	529
NYSE: NBL						
Noble REMC						
300 Weber Rd PO Box 137	Albion	IN	46701	**800-933-7362**	260-636-2113	245
Nobles Co-op Electric						
22636 US Hwy 59 PO Box 788	Worthington	MN	56187	**800-776-0517**	507-372-7331	245
NobleWorks Inc						
500 Paterson Plank Rd	Union City	NJ	07087	**800-346-6253**	201-420-0095	129
NOCC (National Ovarian Cancer Coalition)						
2501 Oak Lawn Ave Ste 435	Dallas	TX	75219	**888-682-7426**		47-17
NOCIRC (National Organization of Circumcision Information Resource Centers)						
PO Box 2512	San Anselmo	CA	94979	**800-727-8622**	415-488-9883	47-17
NOCO Energy Corp						
2440 Sheridan Dr	Tonawanda	NY	14150	**800-500-6626**	716-833-6626	572
NOCS (New Orleans Cold Storage & Warehouse Company Inc)						
3411 JouRdan Rd	New Orleans	LA	70126	**800-782-2653**	504-944-4400	791-2
Nodak Electric Co-op Inc						
4000 32nd Ave S	Grand Forks	ND	58201	**800-732-4373**	701-746-4461	245
Noe Restaurant & Bar						
4 Riverway	Houston	TX	77056	**800-809-6664**	713-871-8177	662
Noetix Corp						
5010 148th Ave NE Ste 100	Redmond	WA	98052	**866-466-3849**	425-372-2699	178
Noevir USA Inc						
1095 Main St	Irvine	CA	92614	**800-872-8817**	949-660-1111	363
NOF (National Osteoporosis Foundation)						
1232 22nd St NW	Washington	DC	20037	**800-231-4222**	202-223-2226	47-17
NOIA (National Ocean Industries Assn)						
1120 G St NW Ste 900	Washington	DC	20005	**800-558-9994**	202-347-6900	47-12
Nolan Co						
1016 Ninth St SW	Canton	OH	44707	**800-297-1383**	330-453-7922	641
Nolo.com						
950 Parker St	Berkeley	CA	94710	**800-728-3555**		179-9
Nomanco Inc						
501 Nmc Dr	Zebulon	NC	27597	**800-345-7279**	919-269-6500	318-1
Non Commissioned Officers Assn (NCOA)						
9330 Corporate Dr Ste 701	Selma	TX	78154	**800-662-2620**	210-653-6161	47-19

Name / Address	City	State	ZIP	Toll-Free	Phone	Class
non-linear creations Inc						
987 Wellington St Ste 201	Ottawa	ON	K1Y2Y1	**866-915-2997**	613-241-2067	7
Nonpareil Corp						
40 N 400 W	Blackfoot	ID	83221	**800-522-2223**	208-785-5880	295-18
Nook Industries						
4950 E 49th St	Cleveland	OH	44125	**800-321-7800**	216-271-7900	613
Noon Hour Food Products Inc						
215 N Des Plaines	Chicago	IL	60661	**888-463-6332***	312-596-4225	295-13
*Cust Svc						
Nora Lighting Inc						
6505 Gayhart St	Commerce	CA	90040	**800-686-6672**	323-767-2600	246
NorAm Capital Holdings Inc						
15303 N Dallas Pkwy Ste 1030	Addison	TX	75001	**888-886-6726**		316
Noranda Aluminum Inc						
801 Crescent Ctr Dr Ste 600	Franklin	TN	37067	**800-325-8112**	615-771-5700	480
Norandex Bldg Materials Distribution Inc						
300 Executive Pkwy W Ste 100	Hudson	OH	44236	**800-528-0942**		192-4
Norben Import Corp						
99 S Newman St	Hackensack	NJ	07601	**800-526-4652***	201-487-0855	293
*General						
Norberg-ies						
4237 S 74th E Ave	Tulsa	OK	74145	**800-739-9145**	918-665-6888	720
Norbest Inc PO Box 890	Moroni	UT	84646	**800-453-5327**		296-10
Norbord Inc						
One Toronto St Ste 600	Toronto	ON	M5C2W4	**888-667-2673**	416-365-0705	606
TSE: NBD						
Norcal Mutual Insurance Company Inc						
560 Davis St	San Francisco	CA	94111	**800-652-1051**	415-397-9700	388-5
Nor-Cal Products Inc						
1967 S Oregon St	Yreka	CA	96097	**800-824-4166**	530-842-4457	588
Norcal Rental Group LLC						
318 Stealth Ct	Livermore	CA	94551	**800-649-6629**	925-961-0130	264-3
Norcold Inc						
600 S Kuther Rd	Sidney	OH	45365	**800-543-1219**	937-493-0033	655
Nor-Cote International Inc						
506 Lafayette Ave	Crawfordsville	IN	47933	**800-488-9180**	765-362-9180	385
Norcraft cabinetry						
3020 Denmark Ave	Eagan	MN	55121	**877-888-0002**	651-234-3300	114
NORD (National Organization for Rare Disorders)						
55 Kenosia Ave PO Box 1968	Danbury	CT	06813	**800-999-6673**	203-744-0100	47-17
NORD Drivesystems						
800 Nord Dr	Waunakee	WI	53597	**888-314-6673**		53
Nordaas American Homes Company Inc						
10091 State Hwy 22	Minnesota Lake	MN	56068	**800-658-7076**	507-462-3331	188
Nordic Ware						
5005 Hwy 7	Minneapolis	MN	55416	**877-466-7342**	952-920-2888	481
Nordion 447 March Rd	Ottawa	ON	K2K1X8	**800-465-3666**	613-592-2790	84
NYSE: NDZ						
Nordson Corp						
28601 Clemens Rd	Westlake	OH	44145	**800-321-2881**	440-892-1580	383
NASDAQ: NDSN						
Nordson MEDICAL						
3325 S Timberline Rd	Fort Collins	CO	80525	**888-404-5837**	970-267-5200	601
Nordyne Inc						
8000 Phoenix Pkwy	O'Fallon	MO	63368	**800-422-4328**	636-561-7300	14
Norfolk Convention & Visitors Bureau						
232 E Main St	Norfolk	VA	23510	**800-368-3097**	757-664-6620	207
Norfolk Daily News						
PO Box 977	Norfolk	NE	68702	**877-371-1020**	402-371-1020	525-2
Norfolk Public Schools						
800 E City Hall Ave	Norfolk	VA	23510	**800-846-4464**	757-628-3843	676
Norfolk Scope Arena						
201 E Brambleton Ave	Norfolk	VA	23510	**800-745-3000**	757-664-6464	711
Norfolk Southern Corp						
3 Commercial Pl	Norfolk	VA	23510	**800-635-5768***	855-667-3655	463
NYSE: NSC ■ *Cust Svc						
Norfolk Southern Railway Co						
Three Commercial Pl	Norfolk	VA	23510	**800-635-5768**	800-453-2530	639
Norfolk State University						
700 Pk Ave	Norfolk	VA	23504	**800-274-1821**	757-823-8600	166
Norforge & Machining Inc						
195 N Dean St	Bushnell	IL	61422	**800-839-3706**	309-772-3124	478
Norgren						
5400 S Delaware St	Littleton	CO	80120	**800-514-0129**	303-794-5000	778
Nor-Lake Inc						
727 Second St PO Box 248	Hudson	WI	54016	**800-388-5253**	715-386-2323	655
Norm Thompson Outfitters Inc						
3188 NW Aloclek Dr	Hillsboro	OR	97124	**800-547-1160**	503-614-4600	454
Norman Convention & Visitors Bureau						
309 E Main St	Norman	OK	73069	**800-767-7260**	405-366-8095	207
Norman Data Defense Systems Inc						
9302 Lee Hwy	Fairfax	VA	22031	**888-466-6762**	703-267-6109	179-12
Norman Frede Chevrolet Co						
16801 Feather Craft Ln	Houston	TX	77058	**888-307-1703**	281-486-2200	56
Norman W Paschall Co Inc						
1 Paschall Rd	Peachtree City	GA	30269	**800-849-1820**	770-487-7945	734-8
Normand's						
11639 A Jasper Ave	Edmonton	AB	T5K2S7	**866-308-4438**	780-482-2600	662
Normandale Community College						
9700 France Ave S	Bloomington	MN	55431	**866-880-8740**	952-487-8200	160
NorMed 4310 S 131 Pl	Seattle	WA	98168	**800-288-8200**		472
Norment Security Group Inc						
3224 Mobile Hwy	Montgomery	AL	36108	**800-466-3007**		683
NORML (National Organization for the Reform of Marijuana Laws)						
1600 K St NW Ste 501	Washington	DC	20006	**888-676-6765**	202-483-5500	47-8
NORPAC Foods Inc						
930 W Washington St	Stayton	OR	97383	**800-733-9311**	503-769-2101	295-21
Norris Cylinder Co						
4818 W Loop 281	Longview	TX	75603	**800-527-8418**	903-757-7633	223
Norris Electric Co-op						
8543 N State Hwy 130 PO Box 6000	Newton	IL	62448	**877-783-8765**	618-783-8765	245
Norris Ford						
901 Merritt Blvd	Baltimore	MD	21222	**866-460-5275***	410-285-0200	56
*Sales						
Norris Public Power District						
606 Irving St PO Box 399	Beatrice	NE	68310	**800-858-4707**	402-223-4038	245
Norris School District						
6940 Calloway Dr	Bakersfield	CA	93312	**800-877-8339**	661-387-7000	189-5
Norsat International Inc						
110-4020 Viking Way	Richmond	BC	V6V2N2	**800-644-4562**	604-821-2800	725
TSE: NII						
Norscot Group Inc						
1000 W Donges Bay Rd PO Box 998	Mequon	WI	53092	**800-653-3313**	262-241-3313	9
Norse Dairy Systems						
1740 Joyce Ave	Columbus	OH	43219	**800-637-2663**	614-294-4931	295-9
Nor-Son Inc						
7900 Hastings Rd	Baxter	MN	56425	**800-858-1722**	218-828-1722	187
Nortech Systems Inc						
1120 Wayzata Blvd E Ste 201	Wayzata	MN	55391	**800-237-9576**	952-345-2244	253
NASDAQ: NSYS						
Nortek Security & Control LLC						
1950 Camino Vida Roble Ste 150	Carlsbad	CA	92008	**800-421-1587***	760-438-7000	683
*Cust Svc						
North Adams Common Nursing Home						
175 Franklin St	North Adams	MA	01247	**800-445-4560**	413-664-4041	445
North Alabama Electric Co-op						
41103 US Hwy 72	Stevenson	AL	35772	**800-572-2900**	256-437-2281	245
North America Missing Children Assn Inc (NAMCA)						
201 Brownlow Ave	Dartmouth	NS	B3B1W2	**800-260-0753**	902-494-2449	47-6
North American Assn of Food Equipment Manufacturers (NAFEM)						
161 N Clark St Ste 2020	Chicago	IL	60601	**888-493-5961**	312-821-0201	48-13
North American Bldg Material Distribution Assn (NBMDA)						
330 N Wabash Ave Ste 2000	Chicago	IL	60611	**888-747-7862**	312-321-6845	48-18
North American Communications Resource Inc						
3344 Hwy 149	Eagan	MN	55121	**888-321-6227**	651-994-6800	246
North American Container Corp						
1811 W Oak Pkwy Ste D	Marietta	GA	30062	**800-929-0610**	770-431-4858	99
North American Council on Adoptable Children (NACAC)						
970 Raymond Ave Ste 106	Saint Paul	MN	55114	**877-823-2237**	651-644-3036	47-6
North American Development Bank						
203 S St Mary'S Ste 300	San Antonio	TX	78205	**800-499-6232**	210-231-8000	69
North American Die Casting Assn (NADCA)						
241 Holbrook Dr	Wheeling	IL	60090	**800-275-8373**	847-279-0001	48-13
North American Electric Reliability Council (NERC)						
1325 G St NW Ste 600	Washington	DC	20005	**877-668-4493**	609-452-8060	47-12
North American Enclosures Inc						
65 Jetson Ln	Central Islip	NY	11722	**800-645-9209**	631-234-9500	308
North American Equipment Dealers Assn (NAEDA)						
1195 Smizer Mill Rd	Fenton	MO	63026	**866-532-7653**	636-349-5000	48-18
North American Industries Inc						
80 Holton St	Woburn	MA	01801	**800-847-8470**	781-897-4100	465
North American Industry Classification System (NAICS)						
US Census Bureau						
4600 Silver Hill Rd	Washington	DC	20233	**800-923-8282**	301-763-4636	338-2
North American Meat Processors Assn (NAMP)						
1910 Assn Dr	Reston	VA	20191	**800-535-4555**	703-758-1900	48-6
North American Mission Board SBC						
4200 N Pt Pkwy	Alpharetta	GA	30022	**800-634-2462**	770-410-6000	47-5
North American Pipe Corp						
2801 Post Oak Blvd Ste 600	Houston	TX	77056	**800-370-5247**	713-840-7473	589
North American Plywood Corp						
12343 Hawkins St	Santa Fe Springs	CA	90670	**800-421-1372***	562-941-7575	606
*Sales						
North American Products Corp						
1180 Wernsing Rd	Jasper	IN	47546	**800-457-7468***	812-482-2000	450
*Cust Svc						
North American Publishing Co (NAPCO)						
1500 Springarden St						
12th Fl	Philadelphia	PA	19130	**800-627-2689**	215-238-5300	628-9
North American Roofing Services Inc						
41 Dogwood Rd	Asheville	NC	28806	**800-876-5602**	828-687-7767	190-12
North American Savings Bank (NASB)						
12520 S 71 Hwy	Grandview	MO	64030	**800-677-6272**	816-765-2200	69
North American Science Assoc Inc						
6750 Wales Rd	Northwood	OH	43619	**866-666-9455**	419-666-9455	659
North American Securities Administrators Assn (NASAA)						
750 First St NE Ste 1140	Washington	DC	20002	**800-222-1253**	202-737-0900	48-2
North American Specialty Glass						
2175 Kumry Rd PO Box 70	Trumbauersville	PA	18970	**888-785-5962**	215-536-0333	330
North American Specialty Insurance Co						
650 Elm St Ste 600	Manchester	NH	03101	**800-542-9200**	603-644-6600	388-4
North American Spine Society (NASS)						
7075 Veterans Blvd	Burr Ridge	IL	60527	**877-774-6337**	630-230-3600	48-8
North American Stainless Inc						
6870 Hwy 42 East	Ghent	KY	41045	**800-499-7833**	502-347-6000	357-3
North American Steel Co						
18300 Miles Ave	Cleveland	OH	44128	**800-321-9310**	216-475-7300	487
North American Title Co						
1855 Gateway Blvd Ste 600	Concord	CA	94520	**800-566-0370**	925-935-5599	388-6
North American Tool Corp						
215 Elmwood Ave	South Beloit	IL	61080	**800-872-8277**	815-389-2300	488
North Arkansas College						
1515 Pioneer Dr	Harrison	AR	72601	**800-679-6622**	870-743-3000	160
North Bay & District Chamber of Commerce						
1375 Seymour St PO Box 747	North Bay	ON	P1B8J8	**888-249-8998**	705-472-8480	136
North Bay Nissan Inc						
1250 Auto Ctr Dr	Petaluma	CA	94952	**877-818-6866**	707-769-7700	56
North Bay Produce Inc						
PO Box 988	Traverse City	MI	49685	**800-678-1941**		296-7
North Bend Rail Trail						
Rt 1 PO Box 221	Cairo	WV	26337	**800-225-5982**	304-643-2931	558
North Canton Area Chamber of Commerce						
121 S Main St	North Canton	OH	44720	**888-263-3423**	330-499-5100	137
North Carolina						
Marine Fisheries Div						
PO Box 769	Morehead City	NC	28557	**800-682-2632**	252-726-7021	337-34
Parks & Recreation Div						
217 W Jones St 1615 MSC	Raleigh	NC	27604	**877-722-6762**	919-707-9300	337-34
Tourism Div						
301 N Wilmington St	Raleigh	NC	27601	**800-847-4862**	919-733-4171	337-34
Transportation Dept						
1 S Wilmington St	Raleigh	NC	27611	**877-368-4968**		337-34
Utilities Commission						
4325 Mail Service Ctr	Raleigh	NC	27699	**866-380-9816**	919-733-7328	337-34
Victims Compensation Services Div						
4232 Mail Service Ctr	Raleigh	NC	27699	**800-826-6200**	919-733-7974	337-34
North Carolina A & T State University						
1601 E Market St	Greensboro	NC	27411	**800-443-8964***	336-334-7946	166
*Admissions						
North Carolina Aquarium at Fort Fisher						
900 Loggerhead Rd	Kure Beach	NC	28449	**800-832-3474**	910-458-8257	39
North Carolina Aquarium on Roanoke Island						
374 Airport Rd PO Box 967	Manteo	NC	27954	**866-332-3475**	252-473-3493	39
North Carolina Assn of Realtors Inc						
4511 Weybridge Ln	Greensboro	NC	27407	**800-443-9956**	336-294-1415	647

Name / Address	City	State	Zip	Toll-Free	Phone	Class
North Carolina Central University						
1801 Fayetteville St	Durham	NC	27707	**877-667-7533***	919-530-6100	166
*Admissions						
North Carolina Central University Art Museum						
1801 Fayetteville St	Durham	NC	27707	**877-667-7533**	919-530-6211	513
North Carolina Democratic Party						
220 Hillsborough St	Raleigh	NC	27603	**800-229-3367**	919-821-2777	609-1
North Carolina Dental Society						
1600 Evans Rd	Cary	NC	27513	**800-662-8754**	919-677-1396	227
North Carolina Eye Bank Inc						
3900 Westpoint Blvd Ste F	Winston-Salem	NC	27103	**800-552-9956**	336-765-0932	269
North Carolina Foam Industries Inc						
1515 Carter St	Mount Airy	NC	27030	**800-346-8229**	336-789-9161	192-4
North Carolina Granite Corp						
151 Granite Quarry Trl						
PO Box 151	Mount Airy	NC	27030	**800-227-6242**	336-786-5141	715
North Carolina High Country Host						
1700 Blowing Rock Rd	Boone	NC	28607	**800-438-7500**	828-264-1299	207
North Carolina Medical Society						
222 N Person St	Raleigh	NC	27601	**800-722-1350**	919-833-3836	469
North Carolina Mutual Life Insurance Co						
411 W Chapel Hill St	Durham	NC	27701	**800-626-1899**	919-682-9201	388-2
North Carolina Mutual Wholesale Drug Co						
816 Ellis Rd	Durham	NC	27703	**800-800-8551**	919-596-2151	238
North Carolina Nurses Assn (NCNA)						
103 Enterprise St PO Box 12025	Raleigh	NC	27605	**800-626-2153**	919-821-4250	526
North Carolina Sports Hall of Fame						
5 E Edenton St						
NC Museum of History	Raleigh	NC	27601	**877-627-6724**	919-807-7900	515
North Carolina State Bar						
217 E Edenton St PO Box 25996	Raleigh	NC	27601	**800-662-7407**	919-828-4620	71
North Carolina State Education Assistance Authority (NCSEAA)						
PO Box 14103	Research Triangle Park	NC	27709	**800-700-1775**	919-549-8614	716
North Carolina State Ports Authority						
2202 Burnett Blvd						
PO Box 9002	Wilmington	NC	28402	**800-334-0682**	910-763-1621	611
North Carolina State University						
2200 Hillsborough St	Raleigh	NC	27695	**800-662-7301**	919-515-2011	166
North Carolina State University Libraries						
CB 7111	Raleigh	NC	27695	**877-601-0590**	919-515-2843	431-6
North Carolina Veterinary Medical Assn (NCVMA)						
1611 Jones Franklin Rd Ste 108	Raleigh	NC	27606	**800-446-2862**	919-851-5850	783
North Carolina Wesleyan College						
3400 N Wesleyan Blvd	Rocky Mount	NC	27804	**800-488-6292***	252-985-5100	166
*Admissions						
North Carolina Zoological Park						
4401 Zoo Pkwy	Asheboro	NC	27205	**800-488-0444**	336-879-7000	810
North Central Assn Commission on Accreditation & School Improvement (NCA CASI)						
9115 Westside Pkwy	Alpharetta	GA	30009	**888-413-3669**		47-1
North Central Assn Higher Learning Commission						
230 S LaSalle St	Chicago	IL	60604	**800-621-7440**	312-263-0456	48-5
North Central Bronx Hospital						
3424 Kossuth Ave	Bronx	NY	10467	**877-207-2134**	718-519-5000	371-3
North Central College						
30 N Brainard St	Naperville	IL	60540	**800-411-1861**	630-637-5800	166
North Central Electric Co-op Inc						
538 11th St W	Bottineau	ND	58318	**800-247-1197**	701-228-2202	245
North Central Michigan College						
1515 Howard St	Petoskey	MI	49770	**888-298-6605**	231-348-6605	160
North Central Missouri College						
1301 Main St	Trenton	MO	64683	**800-880-6180**	660-359-3948	160
North Central Pennsylvania Regional Planning & Development Commission						
651 Montmorenci Rd	Ridgway	PA	15853	**800-942-9467**	814-773-3162	195
North Central Public Power District						
1409 Main St PO Box 90	Creighton	NE	68729	**800-578-1060**	402-358-5112	245
North Central State College						
2441 Kenwood Cir	Mansfield	OH	44906	**888-755-4899**	419-755-4800	788
North Central Telephone Co-op Corp						
PO Box 70	Lafayette	TN	37083	**888-882-1693**	615-666-2151	726
North Central University						
910 Elliot Ave S	Minneapolis	MN	55404	**800-289-6222***	612-343-4460	166
*Admissions						
North Coast Brewing Company Inc						
455 N Main St	Fort Bragg	CA	95437	**866-955-4190**	707-964-2739	101
North Coast Clinical Laboratory Inc						
2215 Cleveland Rd	Sandusky	OH	44870	**800-325-5737**	419-626-6012	415
North Country Business Products Inc						
1112 S Railroad St SE	Bemidji	MN	56619	**800-937-4140**	218-751-4140	319
North Country Community College						
23 Santanoni Ave	Saranac Lake	NY	12983	**888-879-6222**	518-891-2915	160
North Country Federal Credit Union Inc						
69 Swift St Ste 100	South Burlington	VT	05403	**800-660-3258**	802-657-6847	219
North Country Trail Assn						
229 E Main St	Lowell	MI	49331	**866-445-3628**	616-897-5987	47-23
Accountancy Board						
2701 S Columbia Rd	Grand Forks	ND	58201	**800-532-5904**	701-775-7100	337-35
Agriculture Dept						
600 E Blvd Ave Dept 602	Bismarck	ND	58505	**800-242-7535**	701-328-2231	337-35
Attorney General						
600 E Blvd Ave Dept 125	Bismarck	ND	58505	**800-366-6888**	701-328-2210	337-35
Child Support Enforcement Div						
1600 E Century Ave Ste 7	Bismarck	ND	58501	**800-231-4255**	701-328-3582	337-35
Consumer Protection Div						
1050 E Interstate Ave Ste 200	Bismarck	ND	58503	**800-472-2600**	701-328-3404	337-35
Crime Victims Compensation Program						
PO Box 5521	Bismarck	ND	58506	**800-445-2322**	701-328-6195	337-35
North Dakota						
Economic Development & Finance Div						
1600 E Century Ave Ste 200-B	Bismarck	ND	58503	**866-432-5682**	701-328-5300	337-35
Financial Institutions Dept						
2000 Schafer St Ste G	Bismarck	ND	58501	**800-366-6888**	701-328-9933	337-35
Housing Finance Agency						
PO Box 1535	Bismarck	ND	58502	**800-292-8621**	701-328-8080	337-35
Insurance Dept						
600 E Blvd Ave Dept 401	Bismarck	ND	58505	**800-247-0560**	701-328-2440	337-35
Parks & Recreation Dept						
1600 E Century Ave Ste 3	Bismarck	ND	58503	**800-807-4723**	701-328-5357	337-35
Secretary of State						
600 E Blvd Ave Dept 108	Bismarck	ND	58505	**800-352-0867**	701-328-2900	337-35
Tourism Div						
1600 Eentury Ave Ste 200S	Bismarck	ND	58502	**800-435-5663**	701-328-2525	337-35
Veterans Affairs Dept						
4201 38th St S Ste 104	Fargo	ND	58104	**866-634-8387**	701-239-7165	337-35
Vocational Rehabilitation Div						
1237 W Divide Ave Ste 2	Bismarck	ND	58501	**800-755-2745**	701-328-8800	337-35
Workers Compensation						
1600 E Century Ave Ste 1000	Bismarck	ND	58503	**800-777-5033**	701-328-3800	337-35
North Dakota Assn of Realtors						
318 W Apollo Ave	Bismarck	ND	58503	**800-279-2361**	701-355-1010	647
North Dakota Chamber of Commerce						
2000 Schafer St PO Box 2639	Bismarck	ND	58502	**800-382-1405**	701-222-0929	138
North Dakota Dental Assn						
PO Box 1332	Bismarck	ND	58502	**800-444-1330**	701-223-8870	227
North Dakota Game & Fish Dept						
100 N Bismarck Expy	Bismarck	ND	58501	**800-406-6409**	701-328-6300	513
North Dakota Legislative Council Services						
State Capitol Bldg						
600 E Blvd Ave	Bismarck	ND	58505	**800-366-6888**	701-328-2916	430
North Dakota Mill & Elevator						
1823 Mill Rd	Grand Forks	ND	58203	**800-538-7721**	701-795-7000	295-23
North Dakota State College of Science						
800 Sixth St N	Wahpeton	ND	58076	**800-342-4325**	701-671-2401	160
North Dakota State Hospital						
2605 Cir Dr	Jamestown	ND	58401	**888-862-7342**	701-253-3650	371-5
North Dakota State Library (NDSL)						
604 E Blvd Ave Dept 250	Bismarck	ND	58505	**800-472-2104**	701-328-4622	431-5
North Dakota State University						
1301 12th Ave N	Fargo	ND	58105	**800-488-6378**	701-231-8643	166
North East Mall						
1101 Melbourne St Ste 1000	Hurst	TX	76053	**877-746-6642**	817-284-3427	455
North East MS EPA						
10 PR 2050 PO Box 1037	Oxford	MS	38655	**877-234-6331**	662-234-6331	245
North European Oil Royalty Trust						
43 W Front St Ste 19A	Red Bank	NJ	07701	**800-368-5948**	732-741-4008	666
NYSE: NRT						
North Face, The						
14450 Doolittle Dr	San Leandro	CA	94577	**855-500-8639**	877-992-0111	701
North Florida Community College						
325 NW Turner Davis Dr	Madison	FL	32340	**877-501-0956**	850-973-2288	160
North Florida Lincoln Mercury						
4620 Southside Blvd	Jacksonville	FL	32216	**888-579-9646**		509
North Fork Ranch (NFR)						
55395 Hwy 285 PO Box B	Shawnee	CO	80475	**800-843-7895**	303-838-9873	239
North Fulton Hospital						
3000 Hospital Blvd	Roswell	GA	30076	**877-228-3638**	770-751-2500	371-3
North Greenville University						
7801 N Tigerville Rd						
PO Box 1892	Tigerville	SC	29688	**800-468-6642**	864-977-7000	160
North Hennepin Community College						
7411 85th Ave N	Brooklyn Park	MN	55445	**800-818-0395**	763-424-0702	160
North Idaho College						
1000 W Garden Ave	Coeur d'Alene	ID	83814	**877-404-4536**	208-769-3300	160
North Iowa Area Community College						
500 College Dr	Mason City	IA	50401	**888-466-4222**	641-423-1264	160
North Island Credit Union						
5898 Copley Dr	San Diego	CA	92111	**800-848-5654***	619-656-6525	219
*Cust Svc						
North Itasca Electric Co-op Inc						
301 Main Ave PO Box 227	Bigfork	MN	56628	**800-762-4048**	218-743-3131	245
North Lake Tahoe Resort Assn						
100 N Lake Blvd	Tahoe City	CA	96145	**800-824-6348**	530-581-6900	207
North Lake Tahoe Visitors & Convention Bureau						
PO Box 1757	Tahoe City	CA	96145	**800-462-5196**	530-581-8700	207
North Los Angel County Regional Ctr						
15400 Sherman Way Ste 170	Van Nuys	CA	91406	**800-430-4263**	818-778-1900	360
North Middlesex Savings Bank Inc						
Seven Main St PO Box 469	Ayer	MA	01432	**800-762-3306**	978-772-3306	69
North Mississippi Medical Ctr Hospice (NMHC)						
830 S Gloster St	Tupelo	MS	38801	**800-882-6274**	662-377-3000	368
North Museum of Natural History & Science						
400 College Ave	Lancaster	PA	17603	**800-732-0999**	717-291-3941	513
North Olympic Peninsula Visitor & Convention Bureau						
338 W First St Ste 104						
PO Box 670	Port Angeles	WA	98362	**800-942-4042**	360-452-8552	207
North Park Lincoln						
9207 San Pedro St	San Antonio	TX	78216	**888-696-5480**	210-341-8841	56
North Park Theological Seminary						
3225 W Foster Ave	Chicago	IL	60625	**800-964-0101**	773-244-6210	167-3
North Park University						
3225 W Foster Ave	Chicago	IL	60625	**800-888-6728**	773-244-5500	166
North Plains Electric Co-op Inc						
14585 Hwy 83 N PO Box 1008	Perryton	TX	79070	**800-272-5482**	806-435-5482	245
North Platte Community College						
North						
1101 Halligan Dr	North Platte	NE	69101	**800-658-4308**	308-535-3601	160
South						
601 W State Farm Rd	North Platte	NE	69101	**800-658-4348**		160
North Ridgeville City School District						
5490 Mills Creek Ln	North Ridgeville	OH	44039	**877-644-6457**	440-327-4444	676
North Rose-Wolcott Central School District						
11631 Salter Colvin Rd	Wolcott	NY	14590	**855-707-2267**	315-594-3141	676
North Sails Group LLC						
125 Old Gate Ln	Milford	CT	06460	**866-427-4747**	203-877-7621	723
North San Antonio Chamber of Commerce						
12930 Country Pkwy	San Antonio	TX	78216	**877-495-5888**	210-344-4848	137
North Santiam State Recreation Area						
PO Box 549	Detroit	OR	97342	**800-551-6949**		558
North Seattle Community College						
9600 College Way N	Seattle	WA	98103	**877-299-3593**	206-527-3600	160
North Shore Bank FSB						
15700 W Bluemound Rd	Brookfield	WI	53005	**800-236-4672**	262-797-3858	69
North Shore Gas Co						
3001 Grand Ave	Waukegan	IL	60085	**866-556-6004**	847-263-3200	775
North Shore Medical Ctr						
1100 NW 95th St	Miami	FL	33150	**800-984-3434**	305-835-6000	371-3
North Shore Recycled Fibers Inc						
53 Jefferson Ave	Salem	MA	01970	**800-225-2369**	978-744-4330	651
North Shore Steel						
1566 Miles St	Houston	TX	77015	**877-453-3533**	713-453-3533	487
North Shore University Hospital						
300 Community Dr	Manhasset	NY	11030	**888-214-4065**	516-562-0100	371-3
North Shore-Long Island Jewish Health System						
Bone Marrow & Blood Cell Transplant Program						
300 Community Dr	Manhasset	NY	11030	**888-321-3627**	516-562-8973	759
North Star Electric Co-op						
441 State Hwy 172 NW						
PO Box 719	Baudette	MN	56623	**888-634-2202**	218-634-2202	245

	Toll-Free	Phone	Class

North Star Glove Co
2916 S Steele St .... Tacoma WA 98409 | 800-423-1616 | 253-627-7107 | 153-7
North Star Lighting Inc
2150 Parkes Dr .... Broadview IL 60155 | 800-229-4330 | 708-681-4330 | 435
North State Bank Inc
6204 Falls of Neuse Rd .... Raleigh NC 27609 | 877-357-2265 | 919-787-9696 | 357-2
North States Industries Inc
1507 92nd Ln NE .... Blaine MN 55449 | 800-848-8421 | 763-486-1756 | 571
North Suburban Medical Ctr (NSMC)
9191 Grant St .... Thornton CO 80229 | 877-647-7440 | 303-451-7800 | 371-3
North Toledo Bend State Park
2907 N Toledo Pk Rd .... Zwolle LA 71486 | 888-677-6400 | 318-645-4715 | 558
North West REC
1505 Albany Pl SE
PO Box 435. .... Orange City IA 51041 | 800-383-0476 | 712-707-4935 | 245
North Western Electric Co-op Inc
04125 State Rt 576 PO Box 391 .... Bryan OH 43506 | 800-647-6932 | 419-636-5051 | 245
North Winds Investigations Inc
119 S Second St PO Box 1654. .... Rogers AR 72756 | 800-530-4514 | 479-925-1612 | 397
Northampton Community College
3835 Green Pond Rd .... Bethlehem PA 18020 | 877-543-0998 | 610-861-5300 | 160
Monroe
Three Old Mill Rd
PO Box 530 .... Tannersville PA 18372 | 877-543-0998 | 570-620-9221 | 160
Northbridge Financial Corp
105 Adelaide St W Ste 700 .... Toronto ON M5H1P9 | 855-620-6262 | 416-350-4400 | 357-2
Northbrook Chamber of Commerce & Industry
2002 Walters Ave .... Northbrook IL 60062 | 855-354-3337 | 847-498-5555 | 137
Northcentral Technical College
1000 W Campus Dr .... Wausau WI 54401 | 888-682-7144 | 715-675-3331 | 788
Northeast Airmotive Inc
1011 Westbrook St .... Portland ME 04102 | 877-354-7881 | 207-774-6318 | 62
Northeast Alabama Community College
PO Box 159 .... Rainsville AL 35986 | 866-572-5433 | 256-228-6001 | 160
Northeast Bancorp
500 Canal St .... Lewiston ME 04240 | 800-284-5989 | 207-786-3245 | 357-2
NASDAQ: NBN
Northeast Battery & Alternator Inc
240 Washington St .... Auburn MA 01501 | 800-441-8824 | 508-832-2700 | 60
Northeast Data Services
1316 College Ave .... Elmira NY 14901 | 800-699-5636* | 607-733-5541 | 410
*Cust Svc
Northeast Indiana Bancorp Inc
648 N Jefferson St .... Huntington IN 46750 | 800-550-3372 | 260-356-3311 | 357-2
OTC: NIDB
Northeast Iowa Community College
Calmar
1625 Hwy 150 S PO Box 400 .... Calmar IA 52132 | 800-728-2256 | 563-562-3263 | 160
Peosta
10250 Sundown Rd .... Peosta IA 52068 | 800-728-7367 | 563-556-5110 | 160
Northeast Mississippi Community College
101 Cunningham Blvd .... Booneville MS 38829 | 800-555-2154 | 662-728-7751 | 160
Northeast Mississippi Daily Journal
1242 S Green St .... Tupelo MS 38804 | 800-264-6397 | 662-842-2611 | 525-2
Northeast Nebraska Public Power District
1410 W Seventh St PO Box 350 .... Wayne NE 68787 | 800-750-9277 | 402-375-1360 | 245
Northeast Ohio Medical University
4209 State Rt 44 PO Box 95 .... Rootstown OH 44272 | 800-686-2511 | 330-325-2511 | 167-2
Northeast Oklahoma Electric Co-op Inc
443857 E Hwy 60 PO Box 948 .... Vinita OK 74301 | 800-256-6405 | 918-256-6405 | 245
Northeast Power Report
Two Penn Plz 25th Fl .... New York NY 10121 | 800-752-8878 | | 524-5
Northeast Rehabilitation Hospital
70 Butler St .... Salem NH 03079 | 800-439-2370 | 603-893-2900 | 371-6
Northeast Remsco Construction Inc
1433 Hwy 34 S Bldg B1 .... Farmingdale NJ 07727 | 800-879-8204 | 732-557-6100 | 189-7
Northeast State Technical Community College
2425 Hwy 75 PO Box 246. .... Blountville TN 37617 | 800-836-7822 | 423-323-3191 | 788
Northeast Texas Community College
1735 Chapel Hill Rd .... Mount Pleasant TX 75455 | 800-870-0142 | 903-572-1911 | 160
Northeast Times
2512 Metropolitan Dr .... Trevose PA 19053 | 800-556-3655 | 215-355-9009 | 525-4
Northeast Utilities Service Company Inc
56 Prospect St .... Hartford CT 06103 | 800-286-5000 | | 458
Northeast Wisconsin Technical College
PO Box 19042 .... Green Bay WI 54307 | 800-422-6982 | 920-498-5400 | 788
Northeastern Illinois University
5500 N St Louis Ave .... Chicago IL 60625 | 800-393-0865 | 773-442-4050 | 166
Northeastern Illinois University Williams Library
5500 N St Louis Ave .... Chicago IL 60625 | 800-393-0865 | 773-442-4470 | 431-6
Northeastern Junior College
100 College Ave .... Sterling CO 80751 | 800-626-4637 | 970-521-6600 | 160
Northeastern Log Homes Inc
10 Ames Rd .... Kenduskeag ME 04450 | 800-624-2797 | 207-884-7000 | 105
Muskogee
2400 W Shawnee .... Muskogee OK 74401 | 800-722-9614 | 918-683-0040 | 166
Northeastern State University
Tahlequah
600 N Grand Ave .... Tahlequah OK 74464 | 800-722-9614 | 918-456-5511 | 166
Northeastern Technical College
1201 Chesterfield Hwy .... Cheraw SC 29520 | 800-921-7399 | 843-921-6900 | 160
Northeastern University
360 Huntington Ave .... Boston MA 02115 | 855-476-3391 | 617-373-2000 | 166
Northeastern University School of Law
400 Huntington Ave .... Boston MA 02115 | 800-732-3400 | 617-373-2395 | 167-1
Northeastern Wisconsin Zoo
305 E Walnut St Rm 102
PO Box 23600. .... Green Bay WI 54301 | 888-844-8070 | 920-448-6242 | 810
Northern Arizona Regional Behavioral Health Authority Inc (NARBHA)
1300 S Yale St .... Flagstaff AZ 86001 | 877-923-1400 | 928-774-7128 | 48-15
Northern Arizona University
PO Box 4084 .... Flagstaff AZ 86011 | 888-628-2968* | 928-523-5511 | 166
*Admissions
Northern Arizona VA Health Care System
500 Hwy 89 N .... Prescott AZ 86313 | 800-949-1005 | 928-445-4860 | 371-8
Northern Business Products Inc
PO Box 16127 .... Duluth MN 55816 | 800-647-8775 | 218-726-0167 | 528
Northern California World Trade Ctr
One Capitol Mall Ste 300 .... Sacramento CA 95814 | 855-667-2259 | | 809
Northern Contours Inc
1355 Mendota Heights Rd
Ste 100. .... Mendota Heights MN 55120 | 866-344-8132 | 651-695-1698 | 114
Northern Electric Co-op Inc
39456 133nd St .... Bath SD 57427 | 800-529-0310 | 605-225-0310 | 245

Northern Electric Inc
1275 W 124th Ave .... Denver CO 80234 | 877-265-0794 | 303-428-6969 | 775
Northern Essex Community College
100 Elliott St .... Haverhill MA 01830 | 800-422-4453 | 978-556-3000 | 160
Northern Exposure Greeting Cards
2301 Circadian Way Ste 300 .... Santa Rosa CA 95407 | 800-237-3524 | 707-546-2153 | 129
Northern Factory Sales Inc
PO Box 660 .... Willmar MN 56201 | 800-328-8900 | 320-235-2288 | 60
Northern Funds
PO Box 75986 .... Chicago IL 60675 | 800-595-9111 | | 521
Northern Highland - American Legion State Forest
4125 County Hwy M .... Boulder Junction WI 54512 | 800-847-9367 | 715-385-2727 | 558
Northern Illinois University
1425 W Lincoln Hwy .... DeKalb IL 60115 | 800-892-3050 | 815-753-1000 | 166
Northern Illinois University College of Law
Swen Parson Hall .... DeKalb IL 60115 | 800-892-3050 | 815-753-9655 | 167-1
Northern Indiana Commuter Transportation District
33 E US Hwy 12 .... Chesterton IN 46304 | 800-323-5281 | 219-926-5744 | 463
Northern Industrial Sales Ltd
3526 Opie Cres .... Prince George BC V2N2P9 | 800-668-3317 | 250-562-4435 | 681
Northern Institutional Funds
801 S Canal St C5S .... Chicago IL 60607 | 800-637-1380 | | 521
Northern Kentucky Convention & Visitors Bureau (NKYCVB)
50 E RiverCenter Blvd Ste 200 .... Covington KY 41011 | 877-659-8474 | 859-261-4677 | 207
Northern Kentucky University
Nunn Dr .... Highland Heights KY 41099 | 800-637-9948* | 859-572-5220 | 166
*Admissions
Northern Kentucky Water District
2835 Crescent Springs Rd
PO Box 18640. .... Erlanger KY 41018 | 800-772-4636 | 859-578-9898 | 775
Northern Labs Inc
5800 W Dr PO Box 850 .... Manitowoc WI 54220 | 800-558-7621 | 920-684-7137 | 149
Northern Lights Inc
4420 14th Ave NW .... Seattle WA 98107 | 800-762-0165 | 206-789-3880 | 262
Northern Michigan University
1401 Presque Isle Ave .... Marquette MI 49855 | 800-682-9797 | 906-227-2650 | 166
Northern Natural Gas Co
1111 S 103rd St .... Omaha NE 68124 | 877-654-0646 | 402-398-7000 | 324
Northern Neck Electric Co-op Inc
85 St Johns St PO Box 288 .... Warsaw VA 22572 | 800-243-2860 | 804-333-3621 | 245
Northern New Mexico College
921 Paseo de Onate .... Espanola NM 87532 | 800-477-3632 | 505-747-2100 | 160
Northern Oklahoma College
1220 E Grand St PO Box 310 .... Tonkawa OK 74653 | 866-278-7134 | 580-628-6200 | 160
Northern Palm Beach County Chamber of Commerce
800 N US Hwy 1 .... Jupiter FL 33477 | 800-482-8293 | 561-746-7111 | 137
Northern Plains Electric Co-op
1515 W Main St .... Carrington ND 58421 | 800-882-2500 | 701-652-3156 | 245
Northern Power Systems Inc
29 Pitman Rd .... Barre VT 05641 | 877-906-6784 | 802-461-2955 | 659
Northern Precision Casting Co
300 Interchange N
PO Box 580. .... Lake Geneva WI 53147 | 800-934-4903 | 262-248-4461 | 305
Northern Quest Casino
100 N Hayford Rd .... Airway Heights WA 99001 | 877-871-6772 | 509-242-7000 | 132
Northern Regional Correctional Facility
112 Northern Regional
Correctional Dr. .... Moundsville WV 26041 | 866-984-8463 | 304-843-4067 | 213
Northern Security Insurance Co
PO Box 188 .... Montpelier VT 05601 | 800-451-5000 | 802-223-2341 | 388-4
Northern Seminary
660 E Butterfield Rd .... Lombard IL 60148 | 800-937-6287 | 630-620-2180 | 167-3
Northern Star Broadcasting LLC
3250 Racquet Club Dr .... Traverse City MI 49684 | 888-847-2346 | 231-922-4981 | 634
Northern State University
1200 S Jay St .... Aberdeen SD 57401 | 800-678-5330 | 605-626-3011 | 166
Northern States Financial Corp
1601 N Lewis Ave .... Waukegan IL 60085 | 800-339-4432 | 847-244-6000 | 357-2
OTC: NSFC
Northern Tool & Equipment Co
2800 Southcross Dr W .... Burnsville MN 55306 | 800-222-5381* | 952-894-9510 | 361
*Cust Svc
Northern Transportation Co Ltd
42003 Mackenzie Hwy .... Hay River NT X0E0R9 | 866-935-6825 | 867-587-2442 | 312
Northern Trust Co
50 S LaSalle St .... Chicago IL 60603 | 888-289-6542 | 312-630-6000 | 69
NASDAQ: NTRS
Northern Trust Company of Connecticut
300 Atlantic St Ste 400 .... Stamford CT 06901 | 866-876-9944 | 312-630-0779 | 398
Northern Video Systems Inc
3625 Cincinnati Ave .... Rocklin CA 95765 | 800-366-4472 | 916-543-4000 | 246
Alexandria
3001 N Beauregard St .... Alexandria VA 22311 | 855-259-1019 | 703-845-6200 | 160
Northern Virginia Community College
Annandale
8333 Little River Tpke .... Annandale VA 22003 | 877-408-2028 | 703-323-3000 | 160
Manassas
6901 Sudley Rd .... Manassas VA 20109 | 855-259-1019 | 703-257-6600 | 160
Northern Virginia Electric Co-op
PO Box 2710 .... Manassas VA 20108 | 888-335-0500 | 703-335-0500 | 245
Northern Waters Library Service
3200 E Lakeshore Dr .... Ashland WI 54806 | 800-228-5684 | 715-682-2365 | 431-3
Northfield an Oldcastle Co
2200 S Main St .... West Bend WI 53095 | 800-227-6512 | 262-338-5700 | 184
Northfield Block Co
One Hunt Ct .... Mundelein IL 60060 | 800-358-3003 | 847-949-3600 | 715
Northfield Lines Inc
32611 Northfield Blvd .... Northfield MN 55057 | 888-670-8068 | 507-645-5267 | 106
Northfield Mount Hermon School
206 Main St .... Northfield MA 01360 | 866-664-4483 | 413-498-3227 | 615
Northfield Savings Bank (NSB)
PO Box 347 .... Northfield VT 05663 | 800-672-2274 | 802-485-5871 | 69
Northgate Mall
401 NE Northgate Way Ste 210. .... Seattle WA 98125 | 877-789-2327 | 206-362-4777 | 455
Northland Baptist Bible College (NBBC)
W10085 Pike Plains Rd .... Dunbar WI 54119 | 800-425-9385 | 715-324-6900 | 166
Northland College
1411 Ellis Ave .... Ashland WI 54806 | 800-753-1840 | 715-682-1224 | 166
Northland Community & Technical College
1101 US Hwy 1 E .... Thief River Falls MN 56701 | 800-959-6282 | 218-681-0701 | 160
East Grand Forks
2022 Central Ave NE .... East Grand Forks MN 56721 | 800-451-3441 | 218-773-3441 | 160
Northland Corp
1260 E Van Deinse St .... Greenville MI 48838 | 800-223-3900 | | 35

Name / Address	City	State	ZIP	Toll-Free	Phone	Class
Northland Inn & Executive Conference Ctr, The						
7025 Northland Dr	Minneapolis	MN	55428	**800-441-6422**	763-536-8300	374
Northland Insurance Co						
385 Washington St	Saint Paul	MN	55102	**800-237-9334**		388-4
Northland Pioneer College						
PO Box 610	Holbrook	AZ	86025	**800-266-7845**	928-532-6111	160
Northland Plastics Inc						
1420 S 16th St PO Box 290	Sheboygan	WI	53081	**800-776-7163**		593
Northland Services Inc						
6700 W Marginal Way SW	Seattle	WA	98106	**800-426-3113**	206-763-3000	311
Northland Trucking Inc						
1515 S 22nd Ave	Phoenix	AZ	85009	**800-214-5564**	602-254-0007	770
Northleaf Capital Partners						
79 Wellington St W Sixth Fl						
PO Box 120	Toronto	ON	M5K1N9	**866-964-4141**		780
Northlight Theatre						
9501 Skokie Blvd	Skokie	IL	60077	**800-356-9377**	847-673-6300	738
Northpoint Escrow & Title LLC						
10800 NE Eighth St Ste 200	Bellevue	WA	98004	**877-678-1678**	425-453-8880	388-6
Northport Medical Ctr						
2700 Hospital Dr	Northport	AL	35476	**866-840-0750**	205-333-4500	371-3
Northrim BanCorp Inc						
3111 C St	Anchorage	AK	99503	**800-478-3311**	907-562-0062	69
NASDAQ: NRIM						
Northrop Grumman Newport News						
13560 Jefferson Ave	Newport News	VA	23603	**888-493-7386**	757-886-7777	689
Northshire Information Inc						
4869 Main St	Manchester Center	VT	05255	**800-437-3700**	802-362-2200	95
Northstar Aerospace Inc						
6006 W 73rd St	Bedford Park	IL	60638	**800-362-3907**	708-728-2000	21
TSE: NAS						
Northstar Cruises						
80 Bloomfield Ave Ste 102	Caldwell	NJ	07006	**800-249-9360**		761
NorthStar Moving Corp						
9120 Mason Ave	Chatsworth	CA	91311	**800-275-7767**	818-727-0128	512
Northstar Travel Media LLC						
100 Lighting Way	Secaucus	NJ	07094	**800-742-7076**	201-902-2000	628-9
Northstar-at-Tahoe						
PO Box 129	Truckee	CA	96160	**800-466-6784**		660
Northumberland County						
201 Market St 2nd Fl	Sunbury	PA	17801	**800-692-7208**	570-988-4167	336
Northview Public School						
4451 Hunsberger NE	Grand Rapids	MI	49525	**866-632-9992**	616-363-4857	676
Northway Toyota						
727 New Loudon Rd	Latham	NY	12110	**877-525-3488**	518-783-1951	56
Northwest Administrators Inc						
2323 Eastlake Ave E	Seattle	WA	98102	**877-304-6702**	206-329-4900	387
NorthWest Arkansas Community College						
One College Dr	Bentonville	AR	72712	**800-995-6922**	479-636-9222	160
Northwest Bancorp Inc						
PO Box 128	Warren	PA	16365	**800-859-1000**	814-728-7263	357-2
Northwest Bedding						
6102 S Hayford Rd	Spokane	WA	99224	**800-456-7686**	509-244-3000	466
Northwest Christian College						
828 E 11th Ave	Eugene	OR	97401	**877-463-6622**	541-343-1641	166
Northwest College						
231 W Sixth St	Powell	WY	82435	**800-560-4692**	307-754-6000	160
Northwest Community Bank						
86 Main St PO Box 1019	Winsted	CT	06098	**800-455-6668**	860-379-7561	69
Northwest Designs Ink Inc						
13456 SE 27th Pl Ste 200	Bellevue	WA	98005	**800-925-9327**		155-5
Northwest Florida Daily News						
PO Box 2949	Fort Walton Beach	FL	32549	**800-755-1185**	850-863-1111	525-2
Northwest Georgia Bank						
5063 Alabama Hwy PO Box 789	Ringgold	GA	30736	**800-528-2273**	706-965-3000	69
Northwest Georgia Trade & Convention Ctr						
2211 Dug Gap Battle Rd	Dalton	GA	30720	**800-824-7469**	706-272-7676	206
Northwest Grain Growers Inc						
850 N Fourth Ave	Walla Walla	WA	99362	**800-994-4290**	509-525-6510	275
Northwest Herald Inc						
PO Box 250	Crystal Lake	IL	60039	**800-589-8910**	815-459-4040	628-8
Northwest Hospital & Medical Ctr						
1550 N 115th St	Seattle	WA	98133	**877-694-4677**	206-364-0500	371-3
Northwest Hospital Ctr						
5401 Old Ct Rd	Randallstown	MD	21133	**800-876-1175**	410-521-2200	371-3
Northwest Indian College						
2522 Kwina Rd	Bellingham	WA	98226	**866-676-2772**	360-676-2772	163
Northwest Iowa Community College						
603 W Pk St	Sheldon	IA	51201	**800-352-4907**	712-324-5061	160
Northwest Local School District (NWLSD)						
3240 Banning Rd	Cincinnati	OH	45239	**800-374-2806**	513-923-1000	676
Northwest Missouri Psychiatric Rehabilitation Ctr						
3505 Frederick Ave	Saint Joseph	MO	64506	**800-273-8255**	816-387-2300	371-5
Northwest Missouri State University						
800 University Dr	Maryville	MO	64468	**800-633-1175**	660-562-1148	166
Northwest Natural Gas Co						
220 NW Second Ave	Portland	OR	97209	**800-422-4012**	503-226-4211	775
NYSE: NWN						
Northwest Nazarene University						
623 Holly St	Nampa	ID	83686	**877-668-4968***	208-467-8000	166
*Admissions						
Northwest Pennsylvania's Great Outdoors Visitors Bureau						
2801 Maplevale Rd	Brookville	PA	15825	**800-348-9393**	814-849-5197	207
Northwest Pipe Co						
12005 N Burgard	Portland	OR	97203	**800-824-9824**	503-285-1400	485
NASDAQ: NWPX						
Northwest Pipe Fittings Inc						
33 S Eigth St W	Billings	MT	59101	**800-937-4737**	406-252-0142	605
Northwest Protective Service Inc						
801 S Fidalgo 2nd Fl	Seattle	WA	98108	**866-877-1965**	206-448-4040	684
Northwest Rural Public Power District						
5613 State Hwy 87						
PO Box 249	Hay Springs	NE	69347	**800-847-0492**	308-638-4445	245
Northwest Savings Bank						
100 Liberty St PO Box 128	Warren	PA	16365	**800-822-2009**	814-726-2140	69
Northwest School						
1415 Summit Ave	Seattle	WA	98122	**800-426-7127**	206-682-7309	615
Northwest Texas Hospital						
1501 S Coulter	Amarillo	TX	79106	**800-887-1114**	806-354-1000	371-3
Northwest University						
5520 108th Ave NE	Kirkland	WA	98033	**800-669-3781***	425-822-8266	166
*Admissions						
Northwest Wholesale Inc						
1567 N Wenatchee Ave	Wenatchee	WA	98801	**800-874-6607**	509-662-2141	276
Northwestern College						
101 Seventh St SW	Orange City	IA	51041	**800-747-4757**	712-707-7000	166
Northwestern College Chicago Campus						
4829 N Lipps Ave	Chicago	IL	60630	**888-205-2283**	773-777-4220	788
Northwestern Corp						
PO Box 490	Morris	IL	60450	**800-942-1316**	815-942-1300	54
Northwestern Counseling Support & Services Inc						
107 Fisher Pond Rd	Saint Albans	VT	05478	**800-834-7793**	802-524-6554	350
Northwestern Electric Co-op Inc						
2925 William Ave	Woodward	OK	73802	**800-375-7423**	580-256-7425	245
Northwestern Industries Inc						
2500 W Jameson St	Seattle	WA	98199	**800-426-2771**	206-285-3140	328
Northwestern Michigan College						
1701 E Front St	Traverse City	MI	49686	**800-748-0566**	231-995-1000	160
Northwestern Mutual Investment Services LLC						
611 E Wisconsin Ave Ste 300	Milwaukee	WI	53202	**866-664-7737**		398
Northwestern Ohio Security Systems Inc						
121 E High St	Lima	OH	45801	**800-833-6416**	614-527-7037	684
Northwestern Pacific Indemnity Co						
15 Mtn View Rd	Warren	NJ	07059	**800-252-4670***	908-903-2000	388-4
*Claims						
Northwestern Polytechnic University						
47671 Westinghouse Dr	Fremont	CA	94539	**877-878-8883**	510-657-5913	166
Northwestern Publishing House						
1250 N 113th St	Milwaukee	WI	53226	**800-662-6022***	414-475-6600	628-3
*Orders						
Northwestern Rural Electric Co-op Assn Inc						
22534 State Rte						
Ste 86	Cambridge Springs	PA	16403	**800-352-0014**	800-472-7910	245
Northwestern State University						
200 Central Ave	Natchitoches	LA	71497	**800-767-8115**	318-357-6361	166
Northwestern State University Watson Memorial Library						
913 University Pkwy	Natchitoches	LA	71497	**888-540-9657**	318-357-4477	431-6
Northwestern Tools Inc						
3130 Valleywood Dr	Dayton	OH	45429	**800-236-3956**	937-298-9994	747
Northwestern University						
1801 Hinman Ave	Evanston	IL	60208	**800-227-7368**	847-491-7271	166
Northwestern University School of Law						
357 E Chicago Ave	Chicago	IL	60611	**800-229-2032**	312-503-3100	167-1
Northwest-Shoals Community College						
Phil Campbell						
2080 College Rd	Phil Campbell	AL	35581	**800-645-8967**	256-331-6200	160
Northwood University						
Texas						
1114 W FM 1382	Cedar Hill	TX	75104	**800-927-9663**	972-291-1541	166
Northwood University Florida						
2600 N Military Trl	West Palm Beach	FL	33409	**800-458-8325***	561-478-5500	166
*Admissions						
Northwood University Michigan						
4000 Whiting Dr	Midland	MI	48640	**800-622-9000**	989-837-4200	166
Norton's Flowers & Gifts						
2900 Washtenaw Ave	Ypsilanti	MI	48197	**800-682-8667**	734-434-2700	292
Norvell Electronics Inc						
PO Box 701027	Dallas	TX	75370	**800-893-0593**	972-858-3713	246
Norwalk Chamber of Commerce						
12040 Foster Rd	Norwalk	CA	90650	**800-427-2200**	562-864-7785	137
Norwalk Community College						
188 Richards Ave	Norwalk	CT	06854	**800-565-3036**	203-857-7060	160
Norwalk Compressor Co						
1650 Stratford Ave	Stratford	CT	06615	**800-556-5001**	203-386-1234	173
Norwalk Concert Hall						
125 E Ave	Norwalk	CT	06851	**800-357-9577**	203-854-7900	565
Norwalk Furniture Corp						
100 Furniture Pkwy	Norwalk	OH	44857	**800-837-2565***	419-744-3200	318-2
*Orders						
Norwalk Hospital						
34 Maple St	Norwalk	CT	06856	**800-789-4584**	203-852-2000	371-3
Norwegian-American Hospital						
1044 N Francisco St	Chicago	IL	60622	**877-624-9333**	773-292-8200	371-3
Norwell Manufacturing Inc						
82 Stevens St	East Taunton	MA	02718	**800-822-2831**	508-823-1751	435
Norwich University						
158 Harmon Dr	Northfield	VT	05663	**800-468-6679**	802-485-2001	166
Norwin Chamber of Commerce						
321 Main St	Irwin	PA	15642	**800-480-2265**	724-863-0888	137
Norwood Hotel						
112 Marion St	Winnipeg	MB	R2H0T1	**888-888-1878**	204-233-4475	376
Norwood Marking Systems						
2538 Wisconsin Ave	Downers Grove	IL	60515	**800-626-3464**	630-968-0646	462
Norwood Promotional Products Inc						
14421 Myerlake Cir	Clearwater	IN	33760	**877-555-2223**	727-538-3527	9
Notre Dame de Namur University						
1500 Ralston Ave	Belmont	CA	94002	**800-263-0545**	650-508-3600	166
Nottoway Plantation						
31025 Louisiana Hwy 1	White Castle	LA	70788	**866-527-6884**	225-545-2730	513
Notus Career Management						
Five Centerpointe Dr						
Ste 400	Lake Oswego	OR	97035	**800-431-1990**		40
Nouvelles Images Inc						
68 Morgan Ave	Danbury	CT	06810	**800-345-1383**	203-730-1004	129
NOV (National Oilwell Varco)						
7909 Parkwood Cir Dr	Houston	TX	77036	**888-262-8645**	713-375-3700	184
NYSE: NOV						
NOVA (National Organization for Victim Assistance)						
510 King St Ste 424	Alexandria	VA	22314	**800-879-6682**	703-535-6682	47-8
Nova Biomedical Corp						
200 Prospect St	Waltham	MA	02454	**800-458-5813***	781-894-0800	416
*Sales						
NOVA Chemicals Corp						
1000 Seventh Ave SW PO Box 2518	Calgary	AB	T2P5C6	**866-289-6682**	403-750-3600	598-2
Nova Fisheries						
2532 Yale Ave E	Seattle	WA	98102	**888-458-6682**	206-781-2000	285
Nova Internet Services Inc						
PO Box 703696 Ste 230	Dallas	TX	75370	**877-668-2663**	214-904-9600	395
Nova Scotia Dept of Tourism & Culture						
1800 Argyle St PO Box 456	Halifax	NS	B3J2R5	**800-565-0000**	902-425-5781	764
Nova Scotia Power Inc						
PO Box 910	Halifax	NS	B3J2W5	**800-428-6230**	902-428-6230	775
Nova Solutions Inc						
421 Industrial Ave	Effingham	IL	62401	**800-730-6682**	217-342-7070	318-1
Nova Southeastern University						
3301 College Ave	Fort Lauderdale	FL	33314	**800-541-6682**	954-262-8000	166
Nova Southeastern University Shepard Broad Law Ctr						
3305 College Ave	Fort Lauderdale	FL	33314	**800-986-6529**	954-262-6100	167-1

Alphabetical Section

	Toll-Free	Phone	Class
Novacel 21 Third St . . . . Palmer MA 01069	877-668-2235	413-283-3468	541
Novacoast Inc			
1505 Chapala St . . . . Santa Barbara CA 93101	800-949-9933		181
Novacopy Inc			
5520 Shelby Oaks Dr . . . . Memphis TN 38134	800-264-0637	901-388-3399	528
Novagard Solutions Inc			
5109 Hamilton Ave . . . . Cleveland OH 44114	800-380-0138	216-881-8111	325
NovaGold Resources Inc			
200 Grandville St Ste 2300			
PO Box 24 . . . . Vancouver BC V6C1S4	866-699-6227	604-669-6227	497
NYSE: NG			
Novar Controls Corp			
6060 Rockside Woods Blvd			
Ste 400 . . . . Cleveland OH 44131	800-348-1235		203
Novartis Pharmaceuticals Canada Inc			
385 boul Bouchard . . . . Dorval QC H9S1A9	800-465-2244	514-631-6775	576
Novartis Pharmaceuticals Co			
10401 Cornhusker Hwy . . . . Waverly NE 68462	888-669-6682	402-464-6311	576
Novartis Pharmaceuticals Corp			
1 Health Plaza . . . . East Hanover NJ 07936	888-669-6682*	862-778-8300	576
*Cust Svc			
Novartis Vaccines & Diagnostics			
One Health Plz Bldg 122 . . . . East Hanover NJ 07936	888-644-8585	862-778-8300	84
NYSE: NVS			
Novastar Financial Inc			
2114 Central Ste 600 . . . . Kansas City MO 64108	800-591-1137	816-237-7000	645
Novatec Inc			
222 Thomas Ave . . . . Baltimore MD 21225	800-237-8379	410-789-4811	317
Novatel Wireless Inc			
9645 Scranton Rd Ste 205 . . . . San Diego CA 92121	888-888-9231		174-3
NASDAQ: NVTL			
Novato Chamber of Commerce			
807 DeLong Ave . . . . Novato CA 94945	800-897-1164	415-897-1164	137
Novavax Inc			
9920 Belward Campus Dr . . . . Rockville MD 20850	800-642-1687	240-268-2000	84
NASDAQ: NVAX			
Novell Design Studio			
129 Chestnut St . . . . Roselle NJ 07203	888-668-3551		406
Novell Inc			
1800 S Novell Pl . . . . Provo UT 84606	800-529-3400	801-861-4272	179-1
Noveo Technologies Inc			
9655 A Ignace St . . . . Brossard QC J4Y2P3	877-314-2044	450-444-2044	603
Novi Chamber of Commerce, The			
41875 W 11 Mile Rd Ste 201 . . . . Novi MI 48375	888-440-7325	248-349-3743	137
Novo Nordisk of North America Inc			
100 College Rd W . . . . Princeton NJ 08540	800-727-6500	609-987-5800	576
Novo Nordisk Pharmaceuticals Inc			
800 Scudders Mill Rd . . . . Princeton NJ 08536	800-727-6500*	609-987-5800	576
*Cust Svc			
Novosci			
2021 Airport Rd . . . . Conroe TX 77301	800-854-0567	281-363-4950	471
Novotus LLC			
5508 Parkcrest Ste 100 . . . . Austin TX 78731	800-856-0143	512-733-2244	195
NOVUS Auto Glass			
12800 Hwy 13 S Ste 500 . . . . Savage MN 55378	800-776-6887	952-736-7843	61-2
Novus Inc			
655 Calle Cubitas . . . . Guaynabo PR 00969	888-530-4546	787-272-4546	300
NOW (National Organization for Women)			
1100 H St NW 3rd Fl . . . . Washington DC 20005	855-212-0212	202-628-8669	47-24
Now Courier Inc			
PO Box 6066 . . . . Indianapolis IN 46206	800-543-6066		454
NowDocs International Inc			
1985 Lookout Dr . . . . North Mankato MN 56003	888-669-3627		178
Nox-Crete Inc			
1444 S 20th St . . . . Omaha NE 68108	800-669-2738	402-341-2080	143
Noxubee County			
503 S Washington St PO Box 308 . . . . Macon MS 39341	800-487-0165		336
Noyes Museum of Art			
733 Lily Lake Rd . . . . Oceanville NJ 08231	800-852-7899	609-652-8848	513
NP Dodge Real Estate			
8701 W Dodge Rd Ste 300 . . . . Omaha NE 68114	800-642-5008	402-397-4900	643
NPA (National Parking Assn)			
1112 16th St NW Ste 840 . . . . Washington DC 20036	800-647-7275	202-296-4336	48-3
NPAP (National Psychological Assn for Psychoanalysis)			
40 W 13th St Ste 1 . . . . New York NY 10011	800-365-7006	212-924-7440	48-15
NPC (Navy Personnel Command)			
5720 Integrity Dr . . . . Millington TN 38055	866-827-5672	901-874-3165	338-5
NPC (National Pen Corp)			
12121 Scripps Summit Dr			
Ste 200 . . . . San Diego CA 92131	800-854-1000	858-675-3000	9
NPC International Inc			
7300 W 129th St . . . . Overland Park KS 66213	866-299-1148	913-327-5555	661
NPCA (National Precast Concrete Assn)			
10333 N Meridian St			
Ste 272 . . . . Indianapolis IN 46290	800-366-7731	317-571-9500	48-3
NPCA (National Paint & Coatings Assn)			
1500 Rhode Island Ave NW . . . . Washington DC 20005	800-431-7900	202-462-6272	48-13
NPCA (National Parks Conservation Assn)			
1300 19th St NW Ste 300 . . . . Washington DC 20036	800-628-7275	202-223-6722	47-13
NPCA (National Peace Corps Assn)			
1900 L St NW Ste 610 . . . . Washington DC 20036	800-424-8580	202-293-7728	47-5
NPD Group Inc			
900 W Shore Rd . . . . Port Washington NY 11050	866-444-1411	516-625-0700	461
NPES: Assn for Suppliers of Printing Publishing & Converting Technologies			
1899 Preston White Dr . . . . Reston VA 20191	866-381-9839	703-264-7200	48-16
NPF (National Psoriasis Foundation)			
6600 SW 92nd Ave Ste 300 . . . . Portland OR 97223	800-723-9166	503-244-7404	47-17
NPF (National Press Foundation)			
1211 Connecticut Ave NW			
Ste 310 . . . . Washington DC 20036	877-472-3779	202-663-7280	48-16
NPGAPAC (National Propane Gas Assn PAC)			
1899 L St NW Ste 350 . . . . Washington DC 20036	888-445-1404	202-466-7200	608
NPI (National Property Inspections Inc)			
9375 Burt St Ste 201 . . . . Omaha NE 68114	800-333-9807	402-333-9807	362
NPIC (National Pesticide Information Ctr)			
333 Weniger Hall . . . . Corvallis OR 97331	800-858-7378		47-17
NPSS (IEEE Nuclear & Plasma Sciences Society)			
445 Hoes Ln . . . . Piscataway NJ 08854	800-678-4333	732-981-0060	48-19
NPTA Alliance			
330 N Wabash Ave Ste 2000 . . . . Chicago IL 60611	800-355-6782	312-321-4092	48-18
nQueue Inc			
7890 S Hardy Dr Ste 105 . . . . Tempe AZ 85284	800-299-5933		181
NRA (National Rehabilitation Assn)			
633 S Washington St . . . . Alexandria VA 22314	888-258-4295	703-836-0850	47-17
NRA (National Restaurant Assn)			
2055 L St NW Ste 700 . . . . Washington DC 20036	800-424-5156	202-331-5900	48-6
NRA Institute for Legislative Action			
11250 Waples Mill Rd . . . . Fairfax VA 22030	800-392-8683		608
NRC Sports Inc			
603 Pleasant St . . . . Paxton MA 01612	800-243-5033		454
NRCA (National Roofing Contractors Assn)			
10255 W Higgins Rd Ste 600 . . . . Rosemont IL 60018	800-323-9545*	847-299-9070	48-3
*Cust Svc			
NRCCE (National Research Ctr for Coal & Energy)			
385 Evansdale Dr PO Box 6064 . . . Morgantown WV 26506	800-624-8301	304-293-2867	659
NRCDV (National Resource Ctr on Domestic Violence)			
6400 Flank Dr Ste 1300 . . . . Harrisburg PA 17112	800-799-7233		47-6
NRCNAA (National Resource Ctr on Native American Aging)			
501 N Columbia Rd Rm 4535 . . . . . . Grand Forks ND 58202	800-896-7628	701-777-6780	47-6
NRD LLC			
2937 Alt Blvd PO Box 310 . . . . Grand Island NY 14072	800-525-8076	716-773-7634	202
NREC (National Railway Equipment Co)			
14400 Robey Ave Ste 2 . . . . Dixmoor IL 60426	800-253-2905	708-388-6002	641
NREC Power Systems			
5222 Hwy 311 . . . . Houma LA 70360	800-851-6732	985-872-5480	262
NRECA (National Rural Electric Co-op Assn)			
4301 Wilson Blvd . . . . Arlington VA 22203	866-759-2619	703-907-5939	47-12
NRF (National Retail Federation)			
325 Seventh St NW Ste 1100 . . . . . . Washington DC 20004	800-673-4692	202-783-7971	48-18
NRG Energy Inc			
211 Carnegie Ctr . . . . Princeton NJ 08540	866-735-1214	609-524-4500	775
NYSE: NRG			
NRHA (National Retail Hardware Assn)			
5822 W 74th St . . . . Indianapolis IN 46278	800-772-4424*	317-290-0338	48-18
*Cust Svc			
NRMCA (National Ready Mixed Concrete Assn)			
900 Spring St . . . . Silver Spring MD 20910	888-846-7622	301-587-1400	48-3
NRRI (Natural Resources Research Institute)			
5013 Miller Trunk Hwy . . . . Duluth MN 55811	800-234-0054	218-720-4294	659
NRRS (National Recreation Reservation Service)			
PO Box 140 . . . . Ballston Spa NY 12020	877-444-6777	518-885-3639	763
NRS (National Runaway Switchboard)			
3080 N Lincoln Ave . . . . Chicago IL 60657	800-786-2929	773-880-9860	47-6
NRS (Nationwide Recovery Systems Inc)			
4635 McEwen Rd . . . . Dallas TX 75244	800-458-6357	972-798-1000	158
NRSF (National Reye's Syndrome Foundation)			
426 N Lewis St . . . . Bryan OH 43506	800-233-7393	419-924-9000	47-17
NRTA/AARP Bulletin			
601 E St NW . . . . Washington DC 20049	888-867-2277	202-434-2277	524-6
NRTWC (National Right to Work Committee)			
8001 Braddock Rd Ste 500 . . . . Springfield VA 22160	800-325-7892	703-321-8510	48-12
NRV Inc			
N8155 American St . . . . Ixonia WI 53036	800-558-0002	920-261-7000	442
NSA (National Stroke Assn)			
9707 E Easter Ln . . . . Centennial CO 80112	800-787-6537*		47-17
*Cust Svc			
NSA (National Association of Nonprofit Accountants & Consultants)			
624 Grassmere Park Dr Ste 15 . . . . Nashville TN 37211	800-231-2524	615-373-9880	48-1
NSA (National Safety Apparel Inc)			
3865 W 150th St . . . . Cleveland OH 44111	800-553-0672		569
NSA (National Stuttering Assn)			
119 W 40th St 14th Fl. . . . . New York NY 10018	800-937-8888	212-944-4050	47-17
NSA (National Sheriffs' Assn)			
1450 Duke St . . . . Alexandria VA 22314	800-424-7827	703-836-7827	48-7
NSA (National Society of Accountants)			
1010 N Fairfax St . . . . Alexandria VA 22314	800-966-6679	703-549-6400	48-1
NSB (Northfield Savings Bank)			
PO Box 347 . . . . Northfield VT 05663	800-672-2274	802-485-5871	69
NSBA (National Small Business Assn)			
1156 15th St NW Ste 1100 . . . . Washington DC 20005	800-345-6728	202-293-8830	48-12
NSC (National Safety Council)			
1121 Spring Lk Dr . . . . Itasca IL 60143	800-621-7615	630-285-1121	47-17
NSC International			
7090 Central Ave . . . . Hot Springs AR 71913	800-643-1520	501-525-0133	382
NSCA (National Strength & Conditioning Assn)			
1885 Bob Johnson Dr . . . . Colorado Springs CO 80906	800-815-6826	719-632-6722	47-22
NSCAA (National Soccer Coaches Assn of America)			
800 Ann Ave . . . . Kansas City KS 66101	800-458-0678	913-362-1747	47-22
NSCC (Nashville State Community College)			
120 White Bridge Rd . . . . Nashville TN 37209	800-272-7363	615-353-3333	788
NSCIA (National Spinal Cord Injury Assn)			
75-20 Astoria Blvd			
Ste 200 . . . . East Elmhurst NY 11370	800-962-9629	718-512-0010	47-17
NSDC (National Staff Development Council)			
504 S Locust St . . . . Oxford OH 45056	800-727-7288	513-523-6029	48-5
NSEA Voice Magazine			
605 S 14th St Ste 200 . . . . Lincoln NE 68508	800-742-0047	402-475-7611	452-8
NSF (National Science Foundation)			
4201 Wilson Blvd . . . . Arlington VA 22230	800-877-8339	703-292-5111	338-18
NSGA (National Senior Golf Assn)			
200 Perrine Rd Ste 201 . . . . Old Bridge NJ 08857	800-282-6772		47-22
NSGA (National Sporting Goods Assn)			
1601 Feehanville Dr			
Ste 300 . . . . Mount Prospect IL 60056	800-815-5422	847-296-6742	48-4
NSK Corp			
4200 Goss Rd . . . . Ann Arbor MI 48105	888-446-5675	800-675-9930	613
NSLA (Nevada State Library & Archives)			
100 N Stewart St . . . . Carson City NV 89701	800-922-2880	775-684-3360	431-5
NSMC (North Suburban Medical Ctr)			
9191 Grant St . . . . Thornton CO 80229	877-647-7440	303-451-7800	371-3
NSPE (National Society of Professional Engineers)			
1420 King St . . . . Alexandria VA 22314	888-285-6773	703-684-2800	48-19
Nspire Health Inc			
1830 Lefthand Cir . . . . Longmont CO 80501	800-574-7374	303-666-5555	471
NSPR (National Recreation and Park Association)			
22377 Belmont Ridge Rd			
22377 Belmont Ridge Rd . . . . Ashburn VA 20148	800-626-6772	703-858-0784	47-23
NSRA (National Shoe Retailers Assn)			
7386 N La Cholla Blvd . . . . Tucson AZ 85741	800-673-8446	520-209-1710	48-18
NSS (National Space Society)			
1620 'I' St NW Ste 615 . . . . Washington DC 20006	888-624-8373	202-429-1600	48-19
NSS (National Slovak Society of the USA)			
351 Vly Brook Rd . . . . McMurray PA 15317	800-488-1890	724-731-0094	47-14
NSSEA (National School Supply & Equipment Assn)			
8380 Colesville Rd			
Ste 250 . . . . Silver Spring MD 20910	800-395-5550	301-495-0240	48-18
NSSGA (National Stone Sand & Gravel Assn)			
1605 King St . . . . Alexandria VA 22314	800-342-1415	703-525-8788	48-3

				Toll-Free	Phone	Class
NSTA (National Science Teachers Assn)						
1840 Wilson Blvd	Arlington	VA	22201	**800-722-6782***	703-243-7100	48-5
*Sales						
NSTAR 800 Boylston St	Boston	MA	02199	**800-592-2000**	617-424-2000	357-5
NYSE: NST						
NSTAR Gas						
One N Star Way	Westwood	MA	02090	**800-592-2000**		775
NSTAR Global Services Inc						
120 Partlo St	Garner	NC	27529	**877-678-2766**		260
NSX (National Stock Exchange)						
440 S LaSalle St Ste 2600	Chicago	IL	60605	**800-843-3924**	201-499-3700	682
Nsync Services Inc						
850 Greenview Dr	Grand Prairie	TX	75050	**866-706-7962**	972-641-7426	246
NTA (National Tour Assn)						
546 E Main St	Lexington	KY	40508	**800-682-8886**	859-226-4444	47-23
NTB (Nationwide Truck Brokers Inc)						
4203 Roger B Chaffee Memorial Blvd SE						
Ste 2	Grand Rapids	MI	49548	**800-446-0682**	616-878-5554	770
NTEA (National Truck Equipment Assn)						
37400 Hills Tech Dr	Farmington Hills	MI	48331	**800-441-6832**	248-489-7090	48-21
NTELOS Holdings Corp						
1154 Shenandoah Village Dr						
PO Box 1990	Waynesboro	VA	22980	**877-468-3567**	540-946-3500	726
NASDAQ: NTLS						
NTF (National Turkey Federation)						
1225 New York Ave NW Ste 400	Washington	DC	20005	**866-536-7593**	202-898-0100	47-2
NTIS (National Technical Information Service)						
5285 Port Royal Rd	Springfield	VA	22161	**800-553-6847***	703-605-6000	659
*Orders						
NTM (New Tribes Mission)						
1000 E First St	Sanford	FL	32771	**800-321-5375**	407-323-3430	47-20
NTMA (National Tooling & Machining Assn)						
6363 Oak Tree Blvd	Independence	OH	44131	**800-248-6862**		48-13
NTN Bearing Corp of America						
1600 E Bishop Ct	Mount Prospect	IL	60056	**800-323-2358**	847-298-7500	613
NTP Distribution Inc						
27150 SW Kinsman Rd	Wilsonville	OR	97070	**800-242-6987**	503-570-0171	60
NTP Software						
20A NW Blvd Ste 136	Nashua	NH	03063	**800-226-2755**	603-622-4400	179-12
NTRA (National Thoroughbred Racing Assn)						
2525 Harrodsburg Rd Ste 500	Lexington	KY	40504	**800-792-6872**	859-223-5444	47-22
NTSAD (National Tay-Sachs & Allied Diseases Assn)						
2001 Beacon St Ste 204	Brighton	MA	02135	**800-906-8723**	617-277-4463	47-17
NTT DATA, Inc						
100 City Sq	Boston	MA	02129	**800-745-3263**		181
NTT DoCoMo USA Inc						
757 Third Ave 16th Fl	New York	NY	10017	**888-362-6661**		726
NTU (National Taxpayers Union)						
108 N Alfred St	Alexandria	VA	22314	**800-680-7289**	703-683-5700	47-7
Nu Horizons Electronics Corp						
70 Maxess Rd	Melville	NY	11747	**800-432-5742**	631-396-5000	246
Nu Way Co-op Inc						
PO Box Q	Trimont	MN	56176	**800-445-4118**	507-639-2311	276
Nuance Communications Inc						
One Wayside Rd	Burlington	MA	01803	**800-654-1187**	781-565-5000	179-7
NASDAQ: NUAN						
NuCare Pharmaceuticals Inc						
622 W Katella Ave	Orange	CA	92867	**888-482-9545**		577
Nuclear Regulatory Commission Regional Offices						
Region 1						
2100 Renaissance Blvd	King of Prussia	PA	19406	**800-432-1156**	610-337-5000	338-18
Region 2						
61 Forsyth St SW Ste 23T85	Atlanta	GA	30303	**800-577-8510**	404-562-4400	338-18
Region 3						
2443 Warrenville Rd Ste 210	Lisle	IL	60532	**800-522-3025**	630-829-9500	338-18
Region 4						
1600 E Lamar Blvd	Arlington	TX	76011	**800-952-9677**	817-860-8100	338-18
NuclearFuel						
1200 G St NW Ste 1000	Washington	DC	20005	**800-228-9290**	202-383-2000	524-5
Nucleonics Week						
2 Penn Plaza 25th Fl	New York	NY	10121	**800-752-8878**	212-904-3070	524-5
NuCo2 Inc						
2800 SE Marketplace	Stuart	FL	34997	**800-472-2855**	772-221-1754	144
Nucor Corp						
1915 Rexford Rd	Charlotte	NC	28211	**800-294-1322**	704-366-7000	475
NYSE: NUE						
Nucor Corp Cold Finish Div						
2800 N Governor Williams Hwy	Darlington	SC	29540	**800-333-0590**	704-366-7000	714
Nucor Corp Steel Div						
1455 Hagan Ave	Huger	SC	29450	**800-424-9300**	843-336-6000	714
Nucor Steel Memphis Inc						
3601 Paul R Lowry Rd	Memphis	TN	38109	**888-682-6786**		487
Nucor-Yamato Steel Co						
5929 E State Hwy 18	Blytheville	AR	72315	**800-289-6977**	870-762-5500	714
Nucraft Furniture Co						
5151 W River Dr	Comstock Park	MI	49321	**877-682-7238**	616-784-6016	320
Nudo Products Inc						
1500 Taylor Ave	Springfield	IL	62703	**800-826-4132**	217-528-5636	741
Nueces Electric Co-op (NEC)						
709 E Main St PO Box 260970	Robstown	TX	78380	**800-632-9288**	361-387-2581	245
nuherbs co						
3820 Penniman Ave	Oakland	CA	94619	**800-233-4307**	510-534-4372	296-8
Nu-Life Environmental Inc						
PO Box 1527	Easley	SC	29641	**800-654-1752**	864-855-5155	382
Nu-Lite Electrical Wholesalers						
850 Edwards Ave	Harahan	LA	70123	**800-256-1603**	504-733-3300	246
Numara Software Inc						
2202 NW Shore Blvd Ste 650	Tampa	FL	33607	**800-557-3031***	813-227-4500	179-12
*Sales						
Numark Laboratories Inc						
164 Northfield Ave	Edison	NJ	08837	**800-338-8079**		576
Numerex Corp						
1600 Parkwood Cir Fifth Fl	Atlanta	GA	30339	**800-665-5686**	770-693-5950	725
NASDAQ: NMRX						
Numeridex Inc						
632 S Wheeling Rd	Wheeling	IL	60090	**800-323-7737**		111
Numonics Corp						
101 Commerce Dr						
PO Box 1005	Montgomeryville	PA	18936	**800-523-6716**	215-362-2766	174-2
Nunhems USA Inc						
1200 Anderson Corner Rd	Parma	ID	83660	**800-733-9505***	208-674-4000	685
*Cust Svc						

				Toll-Free	Phone	Class
Nuo Therapeutics Inc						
207A Perry Pkwy Ste 1	Gaithersburg	MD	20877	**866-298-6633**		84
OTC: NUOT						
Nupla Corp						
11912 Sheldon St	Sun Valley	CA	91352	**800-872-7661**	818-768-6800	603
Nursefinders Inc						
524 E Lamar Blvd Ste 300	Arlington	TX	76011	**800-445-0459**	817-460-1181	712
Nurserymen's Exchange						
2651 N Cabrillo Hwy	Half Moon Bay	CA	94019	**800-227-5229***	650-712-4195	366
*General						
Nursing Ctr						
323 Norristown Rd Ste 200	Ambler	PA	19002	**800-346-7844**	800-787-8985	394
Nursing Spectrum Greater New York/New Jersey Metro Magazine						
1721 Moon Lk Blvd						
Ste 540	Hoffman Estates	IL	60169	**800-770-0866**		452-16
Nushagak Electric & Telephone Co-op Inc						
557 Kenny Wren Rd	Dillingham	AK	99576	**800-478-5296**	907-842-5251	245
Nussbaum Trucking Inc						
19336 N 1425 East Rd	Normal	IL	61748	**800-322-7305**	309-452-4426	770
Nustar GP Holdings LLC						
PO Box 781609	San Antonio	TX	78248	**800-866-9060**	210-918-2000	357-3
NYSE: NSH						
Nutra Pharma Corp						
12502 W Atlantic Blvd	Coral Springs	FL	33071	**877-895-5647**	954-509-0911	474
Nutra-Blend Inc						
3200 Second St	Neosho	MO	64850	**800-657-5657**		575
Nutraceutical International Corp						
1400 Kearns Blvd	Park City	UT	84060	**800-669-8877**	435-655-6000	787
NASDAQ: NUTR						
Nutraceutix Inc						
9609 153rd Ave NE	Redmond	WA	98052	**800-548-3222**	425-883-9518	474
Nutramax Laboratories Inc						
2208 Lakeside Blvd	Edgewood	MD	21040	**800-925-5187**	410-776-4000	215
Nutrifaster Inc						
209 S Bennett St	Seattle	WA	98108	**800-800-2641**	206-767-5054	97
NutriSystem Inc						
300 Welsh Rd Bldg 1	Horsham	PA	19044	**800-585-5483**	215-706-5300	797
NASDAQ: NTRI						
Nuts & Volts Magazine						
430 Princeland Ct	Corona	CA	92879	**800-783-4624***	951-371-8497	452-14
*Orders						
Nuttall Gear LLC						
2221 Niagra Falls Blvd	Niagara Falls	NY	14304	**800-724-6710**	716-298-4100	700
Nutting						
450 Pheasant Ridge Dr	Watertown	SD	57201	**800-533-0337**	605-882-3000	465
NuUnion Credit Union						
501 S Capitol Ave	Lansing	MI	48933	**888-267-7200**	517-267-7200	219
NuVasive Inc						
7475 Lusk Blvd	San Diego	CA	92121	**800-475-9131**	858-909-1800	471
NASDAQ: NUVA						
Nuveen Investments Inc						
333 W Wacker Dr	Chicago	IL	60606	**800-257-8787**	312-917-7700	681
Nuvite Chemical Compounds Corp						
213 Freeman St	Brooklyn	NY	11222	**800-394-8351**	718-383-8351	149
Nuvo Research Inc						
7560 Airport Rd Unit 10	Mississauga	ON	L4T4H4	**888-398-3463**	905-673-6980	84
TSE: NRI						
Nu-Wa Industries Inc						
3701 Johnson Rd	Chanute	KS	66720	**800-835-0676**	620-431-2088	119
Nu-Way Industries Inc						
555 Howard Ave	Des Plaines	IL	60018	**888-488-5631**	847-298-7710	688
Nu-Wool Company Inc						
2472 Port Sheldon Rd	Jenison	MI	49428	**800-748-0128**	616-669-0100	386
Nu-Yale Cleaners						
6300 Hwy 62	Jeffersonville	IN	47130	**888-644-7400**	812-285-7400	423
NV5						
2525 Natomas Pk Dr Ste 300	Sacramento	CA	95833	**877-941-2068**	916-641-9100	261
NVE Corp						
11409 Vly View Rd	Eden Prairie	MN	55344	**800-467-7141**	952-829-9217	687
NASDAQ: NVEC						
NVFC (National Volunteer Fire Council)						
7852 Walker Dr Ste 450	Greenbelt	MD	20770	**888-275-6832**	202-887-5700	48-4
N-Viro International Corp						
2254 Centennial Rd	Toledo	OH	43606	**800-336-2225**	419-535-6374	792
OTC: NVIC						
NW Natural						
220 NW Second Ave PO Box 6017	Portland	OR	97209	**800-422-4012**	503-226-4211	529
NWA (National WIC Assn)						
2001 S St NW Ste 580	Washington	DC	20009	**866-782-6246**	202-232-5492	47-6
NWC (National Waterways Conference Inc)						
4650 Washington Blvd Ste 608	Arlington	VA	22201	**866-371-1390**	703-243-4090	48-21
NWF (National Wildlife Federation)						
11100 Wildlife Ctr Dr	Reston	VA	20190	**800-822-9919**	703-438-6000	47-3
NWFA (National Wood Flooring Assn)						
111 Chesterfield Industrial Blvd	Chesterfield	MO	63005	**800-422-4556**	636-519-9663	48-3
NWI (National Wellness Institute)						
1300 College Ct						
PO Box 827	Stevens Point	WI	54481	**877-800-2729**	715-342-2969	47-17
NWL Transformers Inc						
312 Rising Sun Rd	Bordentown	NJ	08505	**800-742-5695**	609-298-7300	253
NWLSD (Northwest Local School District)						
3240 Banning Rd	Cincinnati	OH	45239	**800-374-2806**	513-923-1000	676
NWOA (National Woodland Owners Assn)						
374 Maple Ave E Ste 310	Vienna	VA	22180	**800-476-8733**	703-255-2700	47-2
NWRA (National Water Resources Assn)						
3800 Fairfax Dr # 4	Arlington	VA	22203	**800-468-3533**	703-524-1544	47-12
NWT Tourism						
PO Box 610	Yellowknife	NT	X1A2N5	**800-661-0788**	867-873-7200	764
NWTF (National Wild Turkey Federation)						
770 Augusta Rd PO Box 530	Edgefield	SC	29824	**800-843-6983***	803-637-3106	47-3
*Cust Svc						
NxStage Medical Inc						
439 S Union St Fifth Fl	Lawrence	MA	01843	**866-697-8243**	978-687-4700	471
NASDAQ: NXTM						
NYACK						
350 N Highland Ave	Nyack	NY	10960	**800-541-6891**	845-353-2020	167-3
Nyack College						
One S Blvd	Nyack	NY	10960	**800-336-9225***	845-358-1710	166
*Admissions						
NYBDC (New York Business Development Corp)						
50 Beaver St Sixth Fl	Albany	NY	12207	**800-923-2504**	518-463-2268	216
NYCCC (New York City Children's Ctr-Queens Campus)						
74-03 Commonwealth Blvd	Bellerose	NY	11426	**800-597-8481**	718-264-4500	371-1

Alphabetical Section

	Toll-Free	Phone	Class
NYCE Corp			
400 Plaza Dr ....Secaucus NJ 07094	888-323-0310	904-438-6000	68
NYCM (New York Central Mutual Fire Insurance Co)			
1899 Central Plz E ....Edmeston NY 13335	800-234-6926		388-4
NYDJ Apparel LLC			
5401 S Soto St ....Vernon CA 90058	800-407-6001	323-581-9040	155-6
Nye County School District Inc (NCSD)			
PO Box 113 ....Tonopah NV 89049	800-796-6273	775-482-6258	676
NYLIFE Securities Inc			
51 Madison Ave Rm 251 ....New York NY 10010	800-695-4785		681
Nylok Corp			
15260 Hallmark Dr ....Macomb MI 48042	800-826-5161	586-786-0100	3
Nylon Corp of America			
333 Sundial Ave ....Manchester NH 03103	800-851-2001	603-627-5150	598-1
NYMT (New York Mortgage Trust Inc)			
52 Vanderbilt Ave Ste 403........New York NY 10017	800-937-5449	212-792-0107	645
NASDAQ: NYMT			
NYP Corp			
805 E Grand St ....Elizabeth NJ 07201	800-524-1052	908-351-6550	66
Nysarc Inc			
393 Delaware Ave ....Delmar NY 12054	800-735-8924	518-439-8311	425
NYSCA (National Youth Sports Coaches Assn)			
2050 Vista Pkwy ......West Palm Beach FL 33411	800-729-2057	561-684-1141	47-22
NYSE Arce			
115 Samsone St ....San Francisco CA 94104	877-729-7291		682
NYSE Euronext			
11 Wall St ....New York NY 10005	866-873-7422	212-656-3000	682
NYSE: NYX			
NYSNA (New York State Nurses Assn)			
11 Cornell Rd ....Latham NY 12110	800-724-6976	518-782-9400	526
Nystrom Inc			
9300 73rd Ave N ....Minneapolis MN 55428	800-547-2635	763-488-9200	234
NYSW (New York Susquehanna & Western Railway Corp)			
One Railroad Ave ....Cooperstown NY 13326	800-366-6979*	607-547-2555	639
General			
Nytef Plastics Ltd Inc			
6643 42nd Terr N ......West Palm Beach FL 33407	800-646-9833	561-840-9499	596

O

	Toll-Free	Phone	Class
O & S Trucking Inc			
3769 E Evergreen St ....Springfield MO 65803	800-509-2021	417-864-4780	770
O Berk Co 3 Milltown Ct ....Union NJ 07083	800-631-7392	908-851-9500	382
O E C Graphics Inc			
555 W Waukau Ave PO Box 2443.......Oshkosh WI 54902	800-388-7770	920-235-7770	476
O Henry Hotel			
624 Green Vly Rd ....Greensboro NC 27408	800-965-8259	336-854-2000	376
O S F Flavors Inc			
40 Baker Hollow Rd ....Windsor CT 06095	800-466-6015	860-298-8350	296-11
O'Brien International			
14615 NE 91st St ....Redmond WA 98052	800-662-7436	425-202-2100	701
O'Connell Oil Assoc Inc			
545 Merrill Rd ....Pittsfield MA 01201	800-464-4894	413-499-4800	323
O'Connor Davies Munns & Dobbins LLP			
665 Fifth Ave ....New York NY 10022	800-397-0249	212-286-2600	2
O'Connor Woods			
3400 Wagner Heights Rd ....Stockton CA 95209	800-957-3308	209-956-3400	663
O'Day Equipment Inc			
1301 40th St NW ....Fargo ND 58102	800-654-6329	701-282-9260	630
O'Gara Coach Company LLC			
8833 W Olympic Blvd ......Beverly Hills CA 90211	888-291-5533		56
O'Halloran Adv Inc			
270 Saugatuck Ave ....Westport CT 06880	877-466-6616	203-341-9400	5
O'halloran International Inc			
PO Box 1804 ....Des Moines IA 50305	800-800-6503	515-967-3300	760
O'Hare International Airport			
Dept of Aviation			
PO Box 66142 ....Chicago IL 60666	800-832-6352	773-686-3700	27
O'Keeffe's Inc			
325 Newhall St ....San Francisco CA 94124	888-653-3333	415-822-4222	234
O'Leary Paint			
300 E Oakland Ave ....Lansing MI 48906	800-477-2066	517-487-2066	543
O'More College of Design			
423 S Margin St ....Franklin TN 37064	888-662-1970	615-794-4254	166
O'neal Flat Rolled Metals			
1229 S Fulton Ave ....Brighton CO 80601	800-336-3365	303-654-0300	487
O'Neal Steel Inc			
744 41st St N ....Birmingham AL 35222	800-861-8272	205-599-8000	487
O'Reilly & Assoc Inc			
1005 Gravenstein Hwy N ....Sebastopol CA 95472	800-998-9938	707-829-0515	628-11
O'Reilly Automotive Inc			
233 S Patterson ....Springfield MO 65802	888-327-7153	417-862-6708	53
NASDAQ: ORLY			
O'Rourke Wrecking Co			
660 Lunken Pk Dr ....Cincinnati OH 45226	800-354-9850	513-871-1400	190-16
O'Ryan Group Inc			
4010 Pilot Ste 108 ....Memphis TN 38118	800-253-0750	901-794-4610	692
O1 Communications Inc			
1515 K St Ste 100.........Sacramento CA 95814	888-444-1111		726
OA (Overeaters Anonymous Inc)			
PO Box 44020 ....Rio Rancho NM 87174	866-505-4966	505-891-2664	47-21
OAAA (Outdoor Adv Assn of America Inc)			
1850 M St NW Ste 1040...........Washington DC 20036	800-537-0983	202-833-5566	608
OAG Worldwide			
3025 Highland Pkwy			
Ste 200 ....Downers Grove IL 60515	800-342-5624	630-515-5300	628-10
OAGI (Open Applications Group Inc)			
PO Box 4897 ....Marietta GA 30061	800-236-4600	404-402-1962	48-13
OAH (Organization of American Historians)			
112 N Bryan Ave ....Bloomington IN 47408	888-737-7006	812-855-7311	48-5
Oahe Electric Co-op Inc			
102 S Cranford St PO Box 216...........Blunt SD 57522	800-640-6243	605-962-6243	245
Oak Assoc Funds			
PO Box 8233 ....Denver CO 80201	888-462-5386		521
Oak Brook Hills Marriott Resort			
3500 Midwest Rd ....Oak Brook IL 60523	800-228-9290	630-850-5555	374

	Toll-Free	Phone	Class
Oak Forest - Crestwood Area Chamber of Commerce			
15440 S Central Ave ....Oak Forest IL 60452	800-526-7879	708-687-4600	137
Oak Hall Industries			
840 Union St ....Salem VA 24153	800-223-0429	540-387-0000	153-13
Oak Hills Christian College			
1600 Oak Hills Rd SW ....Bemidji MN 56601	888-751-8670	218-751-8670	159
Oak Mountain State Park			
200 Terr Dr PO Box 278 ....Pelham AL 35124	800-252-7275	205-620-2520	558
Oak Park Area Convention & Visitors Bureau			
1118 Westgate ....Oak Park IL 60301	888-625-7275	708-524-7800	207
Oak Plantation Resort & Suites Condominium Association Inc			
4090 Enchanted Oaks Cir ....Kissimmee FL 34741	888-411-4141		375
Oak Ridge Convention & Visitors Bureau			
102 Robertsville Rd Ste C..........Oak Ridge TN 37830	800-887-3429	865-482-7821	207
Oak Ridge Financial			
701 Xenia Ave S Ste 100 ....Minneapolis MN 55416	800-231-8364	763-923-2200	68
Oak Ridge Hotel & Conference Ctr			
1 Oak Ridge Dr ....Chaska MN 55318	800-737-9588*	952-368-3100	374
Sales			
Oakdale Electric Co-op			
PO Box 128 ....Oakdale WI 54649	800-241-2468	608-372-4131	245
Oakgrove Construction Inc			
6900 Seneca St ....Elma NY 14059	866-435-1499	716-652-2200	189-4
Oakhurst Dairy			
364 Forest Ave ....Portland ME 04101	800-482-0718	207-772-7468	295-27
Oakland Ballet Co			
2201 Broadway Ste 206 ....Oakland CA 94612	866-711-6037	510-893-3132	566-1
Oakland City University			
138 N Lucretia St ....Oakland City IN 47660	800-737-5125	812-749-4781	166
Oakland Community College			
2480 Opdyke Rd ....Bloomfield Hills MI 48304	800-829-1040	248-341-2000	160
Highland Lakes			
7350 Cooley Lake Rd ....Waterford MI 48327	800-829-1040	248-942-3100	160
Southfield			
2480 Opdyke Rd ....Bloomfield Hills MI 48304	800-829-1040	248-341-2000	160
Oakland Convention Ctr			
1001 Broadway ....Oakland CA 94607	800-228-9290	510-451-4000	206
Oakland Museum of California			
1000 Oak St ....Oakland CA 94607	888-625-6873*	510-238-2200	513
General			
Oakland Press			
48 W Huron St ....Pontiac MI 48342	888-977-3677	248-332-8181	628-8
Oakland Raiders			
1220 Harbor Bay Pkwy ....Alameda CA 94502	800-724-3377	510-864-5000	706-3
Oakland Unified School District			
1025 Second Ave ....Oakland CA 94606	888-604-4636	510-879-8582	676
Oakland University			
2200 Squirrel Rd ....Rochester MI 48309	800-625-8648*	248-370-2100	166
Admissions			
Oaklawn Park			
2705 Central Ave ....Hot Springs AR 71901	800-625-5296*	501-623-4411	633
General			
Oakleaf Waste Management LLC			
415 Day Hill Rd ....Windsor CT 06095	888-625-5323	713-512-6200	792
Oakley Inc			
1 Icon ....Foothill Ranch CA 92610	800-403-7449*	949-951-0991	535
Cust Svc			
Oakley Transport Inc			
101 ABC Rd PO Box 4170 ....Lake Wales FL 33859	800-969-8265	863-638-1435	444
Oakmark Family of Funds			
330 W nineth St ....Kansas City MO 64105	800-625-6275	617-483-8327	521
Oak-Mitsui Inc			
80 First St ....Hoosick Falls NY 12090	800-424-8802	518-686-4961	294
Oaks at Ojai			
122 E Ojai Ave ....Ojai CA 93023	800-753-6257	805-646-5573	697
Oakton Community College			
Skokie Campus			
7701 N Lincoln Ave ....Skokie IL 60077	877-823-2378	847-635-1600	160
Oakwood Annapolis Hospital			
33155 Annapolis Rd ....Wayne MI 48184	800-543-9355	734-467-4000	371-3
Oakwood College			
7000 Adventist Blvd ....Huntsville AL 35896	800-824-5312	256-726-7356	166
Oakwood Crystal City			
400 15th St S ....Arlington VA 22202	877-969-5142	703-920-9550	211
Oakwood Friends School			
22 Spackenkill Rd ....Poughkeepsie NY 12603	800-843-3341	845-462-4200	615
Oakwood Healthcare Inc			
18101 Oakwood Blvd PO Box 2500 ......Dearborn MI 48124	800-543-9355	313-593-7000	350
Oakwood Heritage Hospital			
10000 Telegraph Rd ....Taylor MI 48180	800-543-9355	313-295-5000	371-3
Oakwood Hospital & Medical Ctr			
18101 Oakwood Blvd ....Dearborn MI 48124	800-543-9355	313-593-7000	371-3
Oakwood Laboratories LLC			
7670 First Pl Ste A ......Oakwood Village OH 44146	888-625-9352	440-359-0000	84
Oakwood Products Inc			
1741 Old Dunbar Rd ....West Columbia SC 29172	800-467-3386	803-739-8800	142
Oakwood Southshore Medical Ctr			
5450 Fort St ....Trenton MI 48183	800-543-9355	734-671-3800	371-3
Oakwood Worldwide			
2222 Corinth Ave ....Los Angeles CA 90064	800-888-0808	310-478-1021	211
Oakworks Inc			
923 E Wellspring Rd ....New Freedom PA 17349	800-558-8850	717-235-6807	470
OANDA Corp			
140 Broadway 46th Fl..........New York NY 10005	800-826-8164	416-593-9436	68
OAS (Organization of American States)			
1889 F St NW ....Washington DC 20006	888-442-4887	202-458-3000	47-7
Oasis Outsourcing			
4511 Woodland Corporate Blvd ....Tampa FL 33614	866-709-9401	813-864-8321	623
Oasis Outsourcing Inc			
2054 Vista Pkwy Ste 300 ......West Palm Beach FL 33411	888-627-4735*		623
General			
Oatey Co			
4700 W 160th St ....Cleveland OH 44135	800-321-9532*	216-267-7100	602
Cust Svc			
O-AT-KA Milk Products Co-op Inc			
700 Ellicott St ....Batavia NY 14020	800-828-8152	585-343-0536	295-3
OATSystems Inc			
309 Waverley Oaks Rd Ste 306 ....Waltham MA 02452	877-628-7877	781-907-6100	179-10
OB Macaroni Co			
PO Box 53 ....Fort Worth TX 76101	800-553-4336*	817-335-4629	295-31
Orders			
Obagi Medical Products Inc			
3760 Kilroy Airport Way			
Ste 500 ....Long Beach CA 90806	800-636-7546	562-628-1007	215

Name / Address	City	State	ZIP	Toll-Free	Phone	Class
OBCI (Ocean Bio-Chem Inc)						
4041 SW 47th Ave	Fort Lauderdale	FL	33314	**800-327-8583**	954-587-6280	149
NASDAQ: OBCI						
Oberbeck Grain Co						
700 Walnut St	Highland	IL	62249	**800-632-2012**	618-654-2387	442
Oberfields LLC						
1165 Alum Creek Dr	Columbus	OH	43209	**800-845-7644**	614-252-0955	192-4
Oberg Industries Inc						
2301 Silverville Rd PO Box 368	Freeport	PA	16229	**866-487-2365**	724-295-2121	747
Oberlin Inn						
Seven N Main St	Oberlin	OH	44074	**800-376-4173**	440-775-1111	376
oberoSPM						
7560 Airport Rd Unit 12	Mississauga	ON	L4T4H4	**888-815-2996**		316
Oberto Sausage Co						
7060 S 238th St	Kent	WA	98032	**877-453-7591**	253-854-7056	295-26
Oberweis Securities Inc						
3333 Warrenville Rd Ste 500	Lisle	IL	60532	**800-323-6166**	630-577-2300	681
OBI (Ocean Breeze International)						
3910 Via Real	Carpinteria	CA	93013	**888-715-8888**	805-684-1747	366
OBI (Oklahoma Blood Institute)						
1001 N Lincoln Blvd	Oklahoma City	OK	73104	**866-708-4995**	405-278-3100	88
Objectivity Inc						
640 W California Ave Ste 210	Sunnyvale	CA	94086	**800-767-6259**	408-992-7100	179-1
Obs Inc						
1324 WTuscarawas St PO Box 6210	Canton	OH	44706	**800-362-9592**	330-453-3725	509
Observer & Eccentric Newspapers						
615 W Lafayette Second Level	Detroit	MI	48226	**866-887-2737**		628-8
Observer Publishing Co						
122 S Main St	Washington	PA	15301	**800-222-6397**	724-222-2200	628-8
Observer-Reporter						
122 S Main St	Washington	PA	15301	**800-222-6397**	724-222-2200	525-2
OC Tanner Co						
1930 S State St	Salt Lake City	UT	84115	**800-453-7490**		406
Ocala-Marion County Chamber of Commerce						
310 SE Third St	Ocala	FL	34471	**800-466-5055**	352-629-8051	137
OCC (Optical Cable Corp)						
5290 Concourse Dr	Roanoke	VA	24019	**800-622-7711**	540-265-0690	801
NASDAQ: OCC						
OCCC (Orange County Convention Ctr)						
9800 International Dr	Orlando	FL	32819	**800-345-9845**	407-685-9800	206
Occidental College						
1600 Campus Rd	Los Angeles	CA	90041	**800-825-5262***	323-259-2700	166
*Admissions						
Occoneechee State Park						
1192 Occoneechee Pk Rd	Clarksville	VA	23927	**800-933-7275**	434-374-2210	558
Occupational Safety & Health Administration (OSHA)						
200 Constitution Ave NW	Washington	DC	20210	**800-321-6742**	202-693-1999	338-13
Occupational Safety & Health Administration Regional Offices						
Region 1						
JFK Federal Bldg Rm E-340	Boston	MA	02203	**800-321-6742**	617-565-9860	338-13
Region 2						
201 Varick St Ste 670	New York	NY	10014	**800-321-6742**	212-337-2378	338-13
Region 3						
Curtis Ctr 170 S Independence Mall W Ste 740W	Philadelphia	PA	19106	**800-321-6742**	215-861-4900	338-13
Region 10						
300 Fifth Ave Ste 1280	Seattle	WA	98104	**800-321-6742***	206-757-6700	338-13
*Help Line						
Occupational Safety & Health Review Commission Regional Offices						
Atlanta Region						
100 Alabama St SW Rm 2R90	Atlanta	GA	30303	**800-321-6742**	404-562-1640	338-18
OC&E Woods Line State Trail						
46000 Hwy 97 N 46000 Hwy 97 N	Chiloquin	OR	97624	**800-551-6949**	541-883-5558	558
Ocean Bank						
780 NW 42nd Ave	Miami	FL	33126	**877-688-2265**	305-442-2660	69
Ocean Beauty Seafoods Inc						
1100 W Ewing St	Seattle	WA	98119	**800-365-8950**	206-285-6800	295-14
Ocean Bio-Chem Inc (OBCI)						
4041 SW 47th Ave	Fort Lauderdale	FL	33314	**800-327-8583**	954-587-6280	149
NASDAQ: OBCI						
Ocean Breeze International (OBI)						
3910 Via Real	Carpinteria	CA	93013	**888-715-8888**	805-684-1747	366
Ocean City City Hall						
301 Baltimore Ave	Ocean City	MD	21842	**800-626-2326**	410-289-8931	335
Ocean City Convention & Visitors Bureau						
4001 Coastal Hwy	Ocean City	MD	21842	**800-626-2326**	410-289-8181	207
Ocean City Hotel-Motel-Restaurant Assn						
PO Box 340	Ocean City	MD	21843	**800-626-2326**	410-289-6733	373
Ocean Conservancy						
1300 19th St NW Eighth Fl	Washington	DC	20036	**800-519-1541**	202-429-5609	47-13
Ocean Ctr						
101 N Atlantic Ave	Daytona Beach	FL	32118	**800-858-6444**	386-254-4500	206
Ocean Edge Resort & Golf Club						
2907 Main St	Brewster	MA	02631	**800-343-6074**	508-896-9000	660
Ocean Five Hotel						
436 Ocean Dr	Miami Beach	FL	33139	**877-666-0505***	305-532-7093	376
*Resv						
Ocean Forest Plaza						
5523 N Ocean Blvd	Myrtle Beach	SC	29577	**800-845-6701***	843-497-0044	376
*General						
Ocean Futures Society						
325 Chapala St	Santa Barbara	CA	93101	**800-477-7500**	805-899-8899	47-13
Ocean Kayak						
125 Gilman Falls Ave Bldg B	Old Town	ME	04468	**800-852-9257**		701
Ocean Key Resort						
424 Atlantic Ave	Virginia Beach	VA	23451	**800-955-9700**	757-425-2200	376
Ocean Key Resort & Spa						
0 Duval St	Key West	FL	33040	**800-328-9815**	305-296-7701	660
Ocean Manor Resort						
4040 Galt Ocean Dr	Fort Lauderdale	FL	33308	**800-955-0444**	954-566-7500	660
Ocean Medical Ctr (OMC)						
425 Jack Martin Blvd	Brick	NJ	08724	**800-560-9990**	732-840-2200	371-3
Ocean Mist Resort						
97 S Shore Dr	South Yarmouth	MA	02664	**800-655-1972**	508-398-2633	660
Ocean One Cruise Outlet						
3264 Marilynn St	Lancaster	CA	93536	**888-353-1922**	661-949-2873	761
Ocean Place Resort & Spa						
One Ocean Blvd	Long Branch	NJ	07740	**800-411-6493**	732-571-4000	660
Ocean Pointe Suites at Key Largo						
500 Burton Dr	Tavernier	FL	33070	**800-882-9464**	305-853-3000	376
Ocean Reef Resort						
7100 N Ocean Blvd	Myrtle Beach	SC	29572	**888-322-6411**	843-449-4441	660
Ocean Resort Hotel Waikiki						
175 Paoakalani Ave	Honolulu	HI	96815	**877-367-1912**	808-922-3861	376
Ocean Sands Resort & Spa						
1350 N Ocean Blvd	Pompano Beach	FL	33062	**800-721-7033**	954-590-1000	660
Ocean Shores Convention Ctr						
120 W Chance a La Mer Ave	Ocean Shores	WA	98569	**800-874-6737**	360-289-4411	206
Ocean Sky Hotel & Resort						
4060 Galt Ocean Dr	Fort Lauderdale	FL	33308	**800-678-9022**	954-565-6611	376
Ocean Speedway Inc						
8070 Soquel Dr Ste 120	Aptos	CA	95003	**800-925-9925**	831-662-9466	508
Ocean Spray Cranberries Inc						
1 Ocean Spray Dr	Lakeville-Middleboro	MA	02349	**800-662-3263**	508-946-1000	295-20
Ocean Walk Resort						
300 N Atlantic	Daytona Beach	FL	32118	**888-743-2561**	386-323-4800	376
Ocean Waters Spa						
600 N Atlantic Ave	Daytona Beach	FL	32118	**844-284-2685**	386-267-1660	697
Oceaneering International Inc						
11911 FM 529	Houston	TX	77041	**877-680-5478**	713-329-4500	532
NYSE: OII						
OceanFirst Bank						
975 Hooper Ave PO Box 2009	Toms River	NJ	08753	**888-623-2633**	732-240-4500	69
OceanFirst Financial Corp						
975 Hooper Ave	Toms River	NJ	08753	**888-623-2633**	732-240-4500	357-2
NASDAQ: OCFC						
Oceania Cruises Inc						
8300 NW 33rd St Ste 308	Miami	FL	33122	**800-531-5619**	305-514-2300	220
Oceanic USA						
2002 Davis St	San Leandro	CA	94577	**800-435-3483**	510-562-0500	701
Oceanside Beach State Recreation Site						
13000 Whiskey Creek Rd W	Tillamook	OR	97141	**800-551-6949**		558
Oceanus Partners						
16540 Pointe Village Dr Ste 208	Lutz	FL	33558	**888-496-1117**		197
Ocenco Inc						
10225 82nd Ave	Pleasant Prairie	WI	53158	**800-932-2293**	262-947-9000	669
Oce-USA Inc						
5450 N Cumberland Ave Sixth Fl	Chicago	IL	60656	**800-877-6232**	773-714-8500	582
OCF (Omaha Community Foundation)						
302 S 36th St Ste 100	Omaha	NE	68131	**800-794-3458**	402-342-3458	302
Ochsner Clinic Foundation Hospital						
1514 Jefferson Hwy	New Orleans	LA	70121	**800-343-0269**	504-842-3000	371-3
Ochsner Medical Ctr West Bank						
2500 Belle Chasse Hwy	Gretna	LA	70056	**800-231-5257**	504-391-5454	371-3
OCLC (Online Computer Library Ctr Inc)						
6565 Kilgour Pl	Dublin	OH	43017	**800-848-5878**		48-11
OCM (One Call Medical Inc)						
20 Waterview Blvd PO Box 614	Parsippany	NJ	07054	**800-872-2875**	973-257-1000	379
OCMC (Ouachita County Medical Ctr)						
PO Box 797	Camden	AR	71711	**877-836-2472**	870-836-1000	371-3
OCMMC (Orange Coast Memorial Medical Ctr)						
9920 Talbert Ave	Fountain Valley	CA	92708	**877-597-4777**	714-378-7000	371-3
Ocmulgee Electric Membership Corp						
5722 Eastman St	Eastman	GA	31023	**800-342-5509**	478-374-7001	245
Oconee Electric Membership Corp						
3445 US Hwy 80 W	Dudley	GA	31022	**800-522-2930**	478-676-3191	245
Oconomowoc Convention & Visitors Bureau						
174 E Wisconsin Ave	Oconomowoc	WI	53066	**888-936-7463**	262-569-2186	207
Oconomowoc Memorial Hospital						
791 Summit Ave	Oconomowoc	WI	53066	**800-242-0313**	262-569-9400	371-3
Oconto Electric Co-op						
7478 Rea Rd PO Box 168	Oconto Falls	WI	54154	**800-472-8410**	920-846-2816	245
OCP (Oregon Catholic Press)						
5536 NE Hassalo St	Portland	OR	97213	**877-596-1653**	503-281-1191	628-3
Octagon Capital Corp						
181 University Ave Ste 400	Toronto	ON	M5H3M7	**888-478-8888**	416-368-3322	681
October Company Inc						
51 Ferry St	EastHampton	MA	01027	**800-628-9346**	413-527-9380	294
Ocwen Federal Bank FSB						
1661 Worthington Rd Ste 100	West Palm Beach	FL	33409	**800-280-3863**	561-682-8000	69
Ocwen Financial Corp						
1661 Worthington Rd Ste 100 PO Box 24737	West Palm Beach	FL	33409	**800-746-2936**	561-681-8000	357-2
NYSE: OCN						
Odan Laboratories Ltd						
325 Stillview Ave	Pointe-Claire	QC	H9R2Y6	**800-387-9342**	514-428-1628	231
Odebrecht Construction Inc						
201 Alhambra Cir Ste 1400	Coral Gables	FL	33134	**800-771-0001**	305-341-8800	187
Odell Brewing Co						
800 E Lincoln Ave	Fort Collins	CO	80524	**888-887-2797**	970-498-9070	101
Odessa American						
PO Box 2952	Odessa	TX	79760	**800-592-4433**	432-337-4661	525-2
Odessa Chamber of Commerce						
700 N Grant St Ste 200	Odessa	TX	79761	**800-780-4678**	432-332-9111	137
Odessa College						
201 W University Blvd	Odessa	TX	79764	**866-968-2862**	432-335-6400	160
Odessa Convention & Visitors Bureau						
700 N Grant Ave Ste 200	Odessa	TX	79761	**800-780-4678**	432-333-7871	207
Odessa Regional Medical Ctr						
520 E Sixth St	Odessa	TX	79761	**877-898-6080**	432-582-8000	371-7
ODG (Ontario Drive & Gear Ltd)						
220 Bergey Ct	New Hamburg	ON	N3A2J5	**877-274-6288**	519-662-2840	29
ODL Inc						
215 E Roosevelt Ave	Zeeland	MI	49464	**800-253-3900**	616-772-9111	328
Odlum Brown Ltd						
250 Howe St Ste 1100	Vancouver	BC	V6C3S9	**866-636-8222**	604-669-1600	398
Odom's Tennessee Pride Sausage Inc						
1201 Neelys Bend Rd	Madison	TN	37115	**866-484-8641**	615-868-1360	295-26
Odon Wagner Gallery						
196 Davenport Rd	Toronto	ON	M5R1J2	**800-551-2465**	416-962-0438	41
Odor Management Inc						
18-6 E Dundee Rd Ste 101	Barrington	IL	60010	**800-662-6367**	847-304-9111	576
ODS Cos						
601 SW Second Ave	Portland	OR	97204	**888-221-0802**	503-228-6554	388-3
ODW Logistics Inc						
1580 Williams Rd	Columbus	OH	43207	**800-743-7062**	614-497-1660	444
Odyssey HealthCare Inc						
717 N Harwood St	Dallas	TX	75201	**888-922-9711**	214-922-9711	446
Odyssey Healthcare of Kansas City						
4911 S Arrowhead Dr	Independence	MO	64055	**800-944-4357**	816-795-1333	368
Odyssey Magazine						
30 Grove St Ste C	Peterborough	NH	03458	**800-821-0115**	603-924-7209	452-6
Odyssey Marine Exploration Inc						
5215 W Laurel St	Tampa	FL	33607	**800-458-4646**	813-876-1776	460
NASDAQ: OMEX						
Odyssey Re Holdings Corp						
300 First Stamford Pl	Stamford	CT	06902	**866-745-4440**	203-977-8000	388-4

Name / Address	City	State	ZIP	Toll-Free	Phone	Class
OEA (Ohio Education Assn)						
225 E Broad St PO Box 2550	Columbus	OH	43216	**800-282-1500**	614-228-4526	452-8
OEA (Oregon Education Magazine)						
6900 SW Atlanta St Bldg 1	Portland	OR	97223	**800-858-5505**	503-684-3300	452-8
Oeconnection LLC						
4205 Highlander Pkwy	Richfield	OH	44286	**888-776-5792**	330-523-1830	178
OF Mossberg & Sons Inc						
Seven Grasso Ave	North Haven	CT	06473	**800-363-3555**	203-230-5300	284
OFA (Orphan Foundation of America)						
21351 Gentry Dr Ste 130	Sterling	VA	20166	**800-950-4673**	571-203-0270	47-6
Off the Beaten Path						
Seven E Beall St	Bozeman	MT	59715	**800-445-2995**	406-586-1311	750
Office Chairs Inc						
14815 Radburn Ave	Santa Fe Springs	CA	90670	**866-624-4968**	562-802-0464	318-1
Office Depot Inc						
2200 Old Germantown Rd	Delray Beach	FL	33445	**800-937-3600**	561-438-4800	528
NASDAQ: ODP						
Office Environments Inc						
11407 Granite St	Charlotte	NC	28273	**888-861-2525**	704-714-7200	319
Office Movers Inc						
6500 Kane Way	Elkridge	MD	21075	**800-331-4025**	410-799-7704	463
Office of Disability Employment Policy						
200 Constitution Ave NW						
Ste S1303	Washington	DC	20210	**866-633-7365**	202-693-7880	338-13
Office of General Services						
Corning Tower						
41st Fl Empire State Plz	Albany	NY	12242	**877-426-6006**	518-474-3899	206
Office of Justice Programs						
Bureau of Justice Statistics						
810 Seventh St NW	Washington	DC	20531	**800-851-3420**	202-307-0765	338-12
Office of National Drug Control Policy						
PO Box 6000	Rockville	MD	20849	**800-666-3332**		338
Office of Special Counsel						
1730 M St NW Ste 218	Washington	DC	20036	**800-872-9855**	202-254-3600	338-18
Office of Special Counsel for Immigration-Related Unfair Employment Practices						
950 Pennsylvania Ave NW	Washington	DC	20038	**800-255-7688**	202-616-5594	338-12
Office of Special Counsel Regional Offices						
Dallas Field Office						
525 Griffin St Rm 824 PO Box 103	Dallas	TX	75202	**800-872-9855**	214-747-1519	338-18
San Francisco Bay Area Field Office						
Federal Bldg						
1301 Clay St Ste 1220-N	Oakland	CA	94612	**800-872-9855**	510-637-3460	338-18
Office Star Products						
1901 S Archibald PO Box 3520	Ontario	CA	91761	**800-950-7262**	909-930-2000	319
Official Payments Corp						
3550 Engineering Dr	Norcross	GA	30092	**877-754-4413**	770-325-3100	181
Off-Road Magazine						
2400 E Katella Ave Ste 1100	Anaheim	CA	92806	**877-462-6752**	714-848-8880	452-3
OG & E Electric Services						
PO Box 24990	Oklahoma City	OK	73124	**800-272-9741**	405-553-3000	775
Ogden Eccles Conference Ctr						
2415 Washington Blvd	Ogden	UT	84401	**866-472-4627**	801-689-8600	206
Ogden Regional Medical Ctr						
5475 Adams Ave Pkwy	Ogden	UT	84405	**877-870-3745**	801-479-2111	371-3
Ogden/Weber Convention & Visitors Bureau						
2438 Washington Blvd	Ogden	UT	84401	**800-255-8824**	801-778-6250	207
OGE Energy Corp						
321 N Harvey St	Oklahoma City	OK	73102	**800-272-9741**	405-553-3000	357-5
NYSE: OGE						
Oglebay Institute's Stifel Fine Arts Ctr						
1330 National Rd	Wheeling	WV	26003	**800-624-6988**	304-242-7700	49-1
Oglebay Resort & Conference Ctr						
Rt 88 N Oglebay Pk	Wheeling	WV	26003	**800-624-6988**	304-243-4000	660
Oglethorpe University						
3000 Woodrow Way NE	Atlanta	GA	30319	**800-428-4484**	404-364-8307	166
Ogontz Corp						
2835 Terwood Rd	Willow Grove	PA	19090	**800-523-2478**	215-657-4770	777
OGR (International Order of the Golden Rule)						
3520 Executive Ctr Dr Ste 300	Austin	TX	78731	**800-637-8030**	512-334-5504	48-4
OHANA Waikiki Beachcomber Hotel						
2300 Kalakaua Ave	Honolulu	HI	96815	**866-956-4262**	808-922-4646	376
Ohaus Corp						
19-A Chapin Rd PO Box 2033	Pine Brook	NJ	07058	**800-672-7722**	973-377-9000	675
Ohel Children's Home & Family Services Inc						
4510 16th Ave	Brooklyn	NY	11204	**800-603-6435**	718-851-6300	360
Agriculture Dept						
8995 E Main St	Reynoldsburg	OH	43068	**800-282-1955**	614-728-6201	337-36
Consumer Protection Section						
30 E Broad St 14th Fl	Columbus	OH	43215	**800-282-0515**	614-466-8831	337-36
Education Dept						
25 S Front St	Columbus	OH	43215	**877-644-6338**	614-995-1545	337-36
Financial Institutions Div						
77 S High St 21st Fl	Columbus	OH	43266	**866-278-0003**	614-728-8400	337-36
Highway Patrol (OSHP)						
1970 W Broad St PO Box 182074	Columbus	OH	43223	**877-772-8765**	614-466-2660	337-36
Insurance Dept						
50 W Town St Third Fl Ste 300	Columbus	OH	43215	**800-686-1526**	614-644-2658	337-36
Mental Health Dept						
30 E Broad St 8th Fl	Columbus	OH	43215	**888-636-4889**	614-466-2596	337-36
Parks & Recreation Div						
2045 Morse Rd Bldg C-3	Columbus	OH	43229	**800-282-7275**	614-265-6561	337-36
Taxation Dept						
30 E Broad St 22nd Fl						
PO Box 530	Columbus	OH	43215	**888-405-4089**	614-466-2166	337-36
Travel & Tourism Div						
PO Box 1001	Columbus	OH	43216	**800-282-5393**	614-466-8844	337-36
Ohio						
Wildlife Div						
2045 Morse Rd Bldg G	Columbus	OH	43229	**800-945-3543**	614-265-6300	337-36
Workers' Compensation Bureau						
30 W Spring St	Columbus	OH	43215	**800-644-6292**	614-644-6292	337-36
Ohio Art Co 1 Toy St	Bryan	OH	43506	**800-800-3141**	419-636-3141	752
OTC: OART						
Ohio Associated Enterprises LLC						
1382 W Jackson St	Painesville	OH	44077	**888-637-4832**	440-354-3148	802
Ohio Casualty Insurance Co						
9450 SewaRd Rd	Fairfield	OH	45014	**800-843-6446**	513-603-2400	388-4
Ohio Chamber of Commerce						
230 E Town St PO Box 15159	Columbus	OH	43215	**800-622-1893**	614-228-4201	138
Ohio Dental Assn						
1370 Dublin Rd	Columbus	OH	43215	**800-497-6076**	614-486-2700	227
Ohio Desk Co						
1122 Prospect Ave E	Cleveland	OH	44115	**800-334-4922**	216-623-0600	319
Ohio Dominican University						
1216 Sunbury Rd	Columbus	OH	43219	**800-955-6446**	614-251-4500	166
Ohio Edison Co						
76 S Main St PO Box 3637	Akron	OH	44308	**800-736-3402**		775
Ohio Education Assn (OEA)						
225 E Broad St PO Box 2550	Columbus	OH	43216	**800-282-1500**	614-228-4526	452-8
Ohio Gas Co PO Box 528	Bryan	OH	43506	**800-331-7396**	419-636-1117	529
Ohio Gasket & Shim Company Inc						
976 Evans Ave	Akron	OH	44305	**800-321-2438**	330-630-2030	325
Ohio Historical Society						
1982 Velma Ave	Columbus	OH	43211	**800-686-6124**	614-297-2300	513
Ohio Indemnity Co						
250 E Broad St 7th Fl	Columbus	OH	43215	**800-628-8581**	614-228-2800	388-4
Ohio Lottery Commission						
615 W Superior Ave	Cleveland	OH	44113	**800-686-4208**	216-787-3200	447
Ohio Machinery Co						
3993 E Royalton Rd	Broadview Heights	OH	44147	**800-837-6200**	440-526-6200	355
Ohio Magazine						
1422 Euclid Ave Ste 730	Cleveland	OH	44115	**800-210-7293**	216-771-2833	452-22
Ohio Magnetics Inc						
5400 Dunham Rd	Maple Heights	OH	44137	**800-486-6446**	216-662-8484	465
Ohio Medical Transportation Inc						
2827 W Dblin Granville Rd	Columbus	OH	43235	**877-633-3598**	614-734-8001	13
Ohio Medicine Magazine						
3401 Mill Run Dr	Hilliard	OH	43026	**800-766-6762**	614-527-6762	452-16
Ohio Northern University						
525 S Main St	Ada	OH	45810	**888-408-4668***	419-772-2000	166
*Admissions						
Ohio Northern University Claude W Pettit College of Law						
525 S Main St	Ada	OH	45810	**877-452-9668**	419-772-2211	167-1
Ohio Northern University Heterick Memorial Library						
525 S Main St	Ada	OH	45810	**866-943-5787**	419-772-2181	431-6
Ohio Nut & Bolt Co						
5250 W 164th St	Brook Park	OH	44142	**800-362-0291**	216-267-2240	278
Ohio Penal Industries (OPI)						
1221 McKinley Ave	Columbus	OH	43222	**800-237-3454**	614-752-0287	622
Ohio State Bar Assn (OSBA)						
1700 Lk Shore Dr	Columbus	OH	43204	**800-282-6556**	614-487-2050	71
Ohio State Life Insurance Co						
PO Box 410288	Kansas City	MO	64141	**800-752-1387**		388-2
Ohio State Medical Assn						
3401 Mill Run Dr	Hilliard	OH	43026	**800-766-6762**	614-527-6762	469
Ohio State University						
154 W 12th Ave	Columbus	OH	43210	**800-426-5046**	614-292-3980	166
Libraries						
1858 Neil Ave Mall	Columbus	OH	43210	**800-555-1212**	614-292-6175	431-6
Lima 4240 Campus Dr	Lima	OH	45804	**800-228-1102**	419-995-8391	166
Newark						
1179 University Dr	Newark	OH	43055	**800-963-9275**	740-366-3321	166
Ohio State University Police, The						
1680 Madison Ave	Wooster	OH	44691	**800-358-4678**	330-287-0111	659
Ohio Tuition Trust Authority						
580 S High St Ste 208	Columbus	OH	43215	**800-233-6734***	614-752-9400	716
*Cust Svc						
Ohio University						
Chillicothe						
101 University Dr	Chillicothe	OH	45601	**877-462-6824**	740-774-7200	166
Eastern						
45425 National Rd	Saint Clairsville	OH	43950	**800-648-3331**	740-695-1720	166
Lancaster						
1570 Granville Pike	Lancaster	OH	43130	**800-444-2910**	740-654-6711	166
Southern						
1804 Liberty Ave	Ironton	OH	45638	**800-626-0513**	740-533-4600	166
Ohio University Press						
19 Cir Dr The Ridges	Athens	OH	45701	**800-621-2736***	740-593-1154	628-4
*Sales						
Ohio Valley Banc Corp						
420 Third Ave	Gallipolis	OH	45631	**800-468-6682**	740-446-2631	357-2
NASDAQ: OVBC						
Ohio Valley Supply Co						
3512 Spring Grove Ave	Cincinnati	OH	45223	**800-696-5608**	513-681-8300	192-3
Ohio Valley University						
One Campus View Dr	Vienna	WV	26105	**877-446-8668***	304-865-6000	166
*Admissions						
Ohio Veterans Home						
3416 Columbus Ave	Sandusky	OH	44870	**800-572-7934***	419-625-2454	781
*Admissions						
Ohio Veterinary Medical Assn (OVMA)						
3168 Riverside Dr	Columbus	OH	43221	**800-662-6862**	614-486-7253	783
Ohio Workforce Developement Office						
4020 E Fifth Ave PO Box 1618	Columbus	OH	43219	**888-296-7541**		337-36
Ohly Americas						
3388 Bacon St	Rhinelander	WI	54501	**800-321-2689**	320-587-2481	295-42
OHM (Orchard Hiltz & McCliment Inc)						
34000 Plymouth Rd	Livonia	MI	48150	**888-522-6711**	734-522-6711	261
Ohmart/VEGA Corp						
4241 Allendorf Dr	Cincinnati	OH	45209	**800-367-5383**	513-272-0131	467
Ohmite Manufacturing Co						
1600 Golf Rd Ste 850	Rolling Meadows	IL	60008	**866-964-6483**	847-258-0300	253
Ohmstede						
895 N Main St	Beaumont	TX	77704	**800-568-2328**	409-833-6375	90
OI Corp						
151 Graham Rd						
PO Box 9010	College Station	TX	77842	**800-653-1711**	979-690-1711	416
OIC International						
1500 Walnut St Ste 1304	Philadelphia	PA	19102	**800-653-6424**	215-842-0220	47-5
Oil & Gas Equipment Corp						
Eight Rd 350	Flora Vista	NM	87415	**800-868-9624**	505-333-2300	383
Oil & Gas Journal						
PO Box 2002	Tulsa	OK	74101	**800-633-1656**	918-831-9423	452-21
Oil Creek Plastics Inc						
45619 State Hwy 27						
PO Box 385	Titusville	PA	16354	**800-537-3661**	814-827-3661	589
Oil Ctr Research LLC						
106 Montrose Ave	Lafayette	LA	70503	**800-256-8977**	337-993-3559	534
Oil Price Information Service						
3349 Hwy 138 Bldg D Ste D	Wall	NJ	07719	**888-301-2645***	732-901-8800	524-5
*Cust Svc						
Oil-Dri Corp of America						
410 N Michigan Ave Ste 400	Chicago	IL	60611	**800-645-3747**	312-321-1515	495
NYSE: ODC						
Ojai Valley Inn & Spa						
905 Country Club Rd	Ojai	CA	93023	**800-422-6524**	805-640-2068	660

	Toll-Free	Phone	Class
Ojo Caliente Mineral Springs Resort			
50 Los Banos Dr PO Box 68 .... Ojo Caliente NM 87549	800-222-9162	505-583-2233	697
OK Foods Inc			
PO Box 1787 .... Fort Smith AR 72902	800-635-9441		612
OK International			
12151 Monarch St .... Garden Grove CA 92841	800-495-1775	714-799-9910	253
Okeechobee Correctional Institution			
3420 NE 168th St .... Okeechobee FL 34972	800-574-5729	863-462-5400	213
Okefenoke Rural Electric Membership Corp (REMC)			
14384 Cleveland St PO Box 602 .... Nahunta GA 31553	800-262-5131	912-462-5131	245
Oki Data Americas Inc			
2000 Bishops Gate Blvd .... Mount Laurel NJ 08054	800-654-3282*	856-235-2600	174-6
*Cust Svc			
OKI Developments Inc			
1416 112th Ave NE .... Bellevue WA 98004	877-465-3654	425-454-2800	357-3
Child Support Enforcement Div			
PO Box 248822 .... Oklahoma City OK 73124	800-522-2922	405-522-2273	337-37
Oklahoma			
Commerce Dept			
900 N Stiles Ave .... Oklahoma City OK 73104	800-879-6552	405-815-6552	337-37
Environmental Quality Dept			
707 N Robinson Ave			
PO Box 1677 .... Oklahoma City OK 73101	800-869-1400	405-702-1000	337-37
Housing Finance Agency			
100 NW 63rd St Ste 200 .... Oklahoma City OK 73116	800-256-1489	405-848-1144	337-37
Insurance Dept (OID)			
3625 NW 56th Ste 100 .... Oklahoma City OK 73152	800-522-0071	405-521-2828	337-37
Parks Div			
PO Box 52002 .... Oklahoma City OK 73152	800-654-8240	405-230-8300	337-37
Rehabilitative Services Dept			
5501 N Portland Ave .... Oklahoma City OK 73112	800-845-8476	405-951-3400	337-37
Wildlife Conservation Dept (ODWC)			
PO Box 53465 .... Oklahoma City OK 73152	800-522-8039	405-521-4660	337-37
Oklahoma Assn of Realtors			
9807 N Broadway .... Oklahoma City OK 73114	800-375-9944	405-848-9944	647
Oklahoma Baptist University			
500 W University St .... Shawnee OK 74804	800-654-3285	405-275-2850	166
Oklahoma Bar Assn			
1901 N Lincoln Blvd			
PO Box 53036 .... Oklahoma City OK 73105	800-522-8065	405-416-7000	71
Oklahoma Blood Institute (OBI)			
1001 N Lincoln Blvd .... Oklahoma City OK 73104	866-708-4995	405-278-3100	88
Oklahoma Christian University			
PO Box 11000 .... Oklahoma City OK 73136	800-877-5010	405-425-5000	166
Oklahoma City Convention & Visitors Bureau			
123 Pk Ave .... Oklahoma City OK 73102	800-225-5652	405-297-8912	207
Oklahoma City Museum of Art			
415 Couch Dr .... Oklahoma City OK 73102	800-579-9278	405-236-3100	513
Oklahoma City National Memorial & Memorial Ctr Museum			
620 N Harvey Ave .... Oklahoma City OK 73102	888-542-4673	405-235-3313	513
Oklahoma City University			
2501 N Blackwelder Ave .... Oklahoma City OK 73106	800-633-7242*	405-208-5050	166
*Admissions			
Oklahoma City University School of Law			
2501 N Blackwelder Ave .... Oklahoma City OK 73106	800-230-3012	405-208-5000	167-1
Oklahoma City Zoological Park & Botanical Gardens			
2101 NE 50th St .... Oklahoma City OK 73111	800-891-2917	405-424-3344	810
Oklahoma Correctional Industries			
3402 N Martin Luther King Ave ..... Oklahoma City OK 73111	800-522-3565	405-425-7500	622
Oklahoma Dental Assn			
317 NE 13th St .... Oklahoma City OK 73104	800-876-8890	405-848-8873	227
Oklahoma Dept of Libraries			
200 NE 18th St .... Oklahoma City OK 73105	800-522-8116	405-521-2502	431-5
Oklahoma Education Association			
323 E Madison			
PO Box 18485 .... Oklahoma City OK 73154	800-522-8091	405-528-7785	452-8
Oklahoma Federal Credit Union			
517 NE 36th St .... Oklahoma City OK 73105	800-522-8510	405-524-6467	219
Oklahoma Medical Research Foundation (OMRF)			
825 NE 13th St .... Oklahoma City OK 73104	800-522-0211	405-271-6673	659
Oklahoma Natural Gas Co			
401 N Harvey PO Box 401 .... Oklahoma City OK 73101	800-664-5463		775
Oklahoma Panhandle State University			
323 Eagle Blvd .... Goodwell OK 73939	800-664-6778	580-349-2611	166
Oklahoma State University			
219 Student Union Bldg .... Stillwater OK 74078	800-852-1255	405-744-5000	166
Oklahoma City			
900 N Portland Ave .... Oklahoma City OK 73107	800-560-4099	405-947-4421	160
Okmulgee			
1801 E Fourth St .... Okmulgee OK 74447	800-722-4471	918-293-4678	788
Tulsa			
700 N Greenwood Ave .... Tulsa OK 74106	800-522-4002	918-594-8000	166
Oklahoma Telephone & Telegraph Inc			
26 N Otis Ave .... Dustin OK 74839	800-869-1989		384
Oklahoma Veterans Ctr Ardmore			
1015 S Commerce .... Ardmore OK 73401	800-941-2160	580-223-2266	781
Oklahoma Veterans Ctr Norman			
1776 E Robinson St .... Norman OK 73071	800-782-5218	405-360-5600	445
Oklahoma Veterans Ctr Talihina			
10014 SE 1138th Ave			
PO Box 1168 .... Talihina OK 74571	800-941-2160	918-567-2251	781
Oklahoma Veterinary Medical Assn			
PO Box 14521 .... Oklahoma City OK 73113	800-248-2862	405-478-1002	783
Oklahoman, The			
9000 N Broadway .... Oklahoma City OK 73114	800-375-6397	405-475-3311	525-2
OLA (Optical Laboratories Assn)			
225 Reinekers Ln Ste 700 .... Alexandria VA 22314	800-477-5652	703-548-6619	48-8
OLCC (Orange Lake Country Club Inc)			
8505 W Irlo Bronson Memorial Hwy .... Kissimmee FL 34747	800-877-6522	407-239-0000	660
Old Alabama Town			
301 Columbus St .... Montgomery AL 36104	888-240-1850	334-240-4500	49-2
Old American Insurance Co			
3520 Broadway .... Kansas City MO 64111	800-733-6242	816-753-7000	388-2
Old Bridge Chemicals Inc			
PO Box 175 .... Old Bridge NJ 08857	800-275-3924	732-727-2225	141
Old Bridge Public Library			
One Old Bridge Plz .... Old Bridge NJ 08857	800-829-1040	732-721-5600	431-3
Old Colony Hospice			
1 Credit Union Way .... Randolph MA 02368	800-370-1322	781-341-4145	368
Old Dominion Freight Line Inc			
500 Old Dominion Way .... Thomasville NC 27360	800-432-6335	336-889-5000	770
NASDAQ: ODFL			
Old Dominion Insurance Co			
4601 Touchton Rd E Ste 330			
Ste 3400 .... Jacksonville FL 32246	800-226-0875	904-642-3000	388-4
Old Dominion University			
Rollins Hall .... Norfolk VA 23529	800-348-7926	757-683-3685	166
Old Dutch Foods Inc			
2375 Terminal Rd .... Roseville MN 55113	800-989-2447	651-633-8810	296-3
Old Exchange & Provost Dungeon			
122 E Bay St .... Charleston SC 29401	888-763-0448	843-727-2165	49-2
Old Florida Museum			
259 San Marco Ave .... Saint Augustine FL 32084	800-813-3208	904-824-8874	513
Old House			
309 W San Francisco St .... Santa Fe NM 87501	800-955-4455	505-988-4455	662
Old Idaho Penitentiary State Historic Site			
2445 Old Penitentiary Rd .... Boise ID 83712	877-653-4367	208-334-2844	49-2
Old Line Bank			
1525 Pointer Ridge Pl .... Bowie MD 20716	800-416-6373	301-430-2500	69
NASDAQ: WSB			
Old Mansion Foods			
3811 Corporate Rd			
PO Box 1838 .... Petersburg VA 23805	800-476-1877	804-862-9889	295-7
Old Mill Toronto			
21 Old Mill Rd .... Toronto ON M8X1G5	866-653-6455	416-236-2641	376
Old Mill Winery			
403 S Broadway .... Geneva OH 44041	800-227-6972		79-3
Old National Bank			
1 Main St PO Box 718 .... Evansville IN 47705	800-731-2265		69
Old Newbury Crafters			
36 Main St Ste 2 .... Amesbury MA 01913	800-343-1388		693
Old Point Financial Corp			
One W Mellen St PO Box 3392 .... Hampton VA 23663	800-952-0051	757-728-1200	357-2
NASDAQ: OPOF			
Old Republic Insured Automotive Services Inc			
8282 S Memorial Dr .... Tulsa OK 74133	800-331-3780	918-307-1000	388-5
Old Republic National Title Insurance Co (ORTIG)			
400 Second Ave S .... Minneapolis MN 55401	800-328-4441	612-371-1111	388-6
Old Republic Surety			
445 S Moorlands Rd Ste 200 .... Brookfield WI 53005	800-217-1792	262-797-2640	388-5
Old Salem			
600 S Main St .... Winston-Salem NC 27101	800-441-5305	336-721-7300	513
Old Second Bancorp Inc			
37 S River St .... Aurora IL 60506	888-892-6565	630-892-0202	357-2
NASDAQ: OSBC			
Old Town Canoe Co			
125 Gilman Falls Ave Bldg B			
PO Box 548 .... Old Town ME 04468	800-343-1555	207-827-5513	701
Old Town San Diego State Historic Park			
4002 Wallace St .... San Diego CA 92110	800-777-0369	619-220-5422	558
Old Virginia Brick Co			
2500 W Main St .... Salem VA 24153	800-879-8227	540-389-2357	148
Old Wisconsin Sausage Co			
5030 PlaybiRd Rd .... Sheboygan WI 53083	877-451-7988		295-26
Oldcastle BuildingEnvelope			
4161 S Morgan St .... Chicago IL 60609	866-653-2278	773-523-8400	328
Oldcastle Inc			
900 Ashwood Pkwy Ste 600 .... Atlanta GA 30338	800-899-8455	770-804-3363	184
Oldcastle Precast Bldg Systems Div			
1401 Trimble Rd .... Edgewood MD 21040	800-523-9144		190-3
Olde Country Reproductions Inc			
722 W Market St .... York PA 17405	800-358-3997*	717-848-1859	693
*Cust Svc			
Oldfields School			
1500 Glencoe Rd .... Glencoe MD 21152	800-767-0700	410-472-4800	615
Olds Products Co			
10700 88th Ave .... Pleasant Prairie WI 53158	800-233-8064	262-947-3500	295-19
Olean Times-Herald			
639 Norton Dr .... Olean NY 14760	800-722-8812	716-372-3121	525-2
Olean Wholesale Grocery Co-op Inc			
1587 Haskell Rd PO Box 1070 .... Olean NY 14760	866-774-9751	716-372-2020	296-8
Oleta River State Park			
3400 NE 163rd St .... North Miami Beach FL 33160	800-326-3521	305-919-1846	558
Oley Foundation			
214 Hun Memorial MC-28			
Albany Medical Ctr .... Albany NY 12208	800-776-6539	518-262-5079	47-17
Olgoonik Development LLC			
3201 C St Ste 700 .... Anchorage AK 99503	855-763-2613	907-562-8728	188
Olin Corp Winchester Div			
427 N Shamrock St .... East Alton IL 62024	800-356-2666	618-258-2000	284
Olis Inc			
130 Conway Dr Ste A B & C .... Bogart GA 30622	800-852-3504	706-353-6547	416
Oliver Inlet State Marine Park			
400 Willoughby Ave PO Box 111071 ...... Juneau AK 99801	855-277-4491	907-465-4563	558
Oliver M Dean Inc			
125 Brooks St .... Worcester MA 01606	800-648-3326	508-856-9100	426
Oliver Machinery Co			
6902 S 194th St .... Kent WA 98032	800-559-5065	253-867-0334	808
Oliver of Adrian Inc			
1111 E Beecher St PO Box 189 .... Adrian MI 49221	877-668-0885	517-263-2132	450
Oliver Products Co			
445 Sixth St NW .... Grand Rapids MI 49504	800-253-3893	616-456-7711	297
Oliver Trucking Corp			
1101 Harding Ct .... Indianapolis IN 46217	888-561-4449	317-787-1101	770
Oliver Winery			
8024 N SR-37 .... Bloomington IN 47404	800-258-2783	812-876-5800	49-6
Olivet College			
320 S Main St .... Olivet MI 49076	800-456-7189	269-749-7000	166
Olivet Nazarene University			
One University Ave .... Bourbonnais IL 60914	800-648-1463	815-939-5011	166
Olivia Cruises & Resorts			
434 Brannan St .... San Francisco CA 94107	800-631-6277	415-962-5700	750
OLM LLC			
Four Trefoil Dr .... Trumbull CT 06611	800-741-6813	203-445-7700	795
Olney Central College			
305 NW St .... Olney IL 62450	866-622-4322	618-395-7777	160
Olney Friends School			
61830 Sandy Ridge Rd .... Barnesville OH 43713	800-303-4291	740-425-3655	615
Olon Industries Inc			
42 Armstrong Ave .... Georgetown ON L7G4R9	800-387-2319	905-877-7300	592
Olson Precast Co (OPC)			
2750 Marion Dr .... Las Vegas NV 89115	800-876-8374	702-643-4371	184
Olson Research Assoc Inc			
10290 Old Columbia Rd .... Columbia MD 21046	888-657-6680	410-290-6999	179-10
Olsson Assoc			
1111 Lincoln Mall Ste 111 .... Lincoln NE 68508	877-831-6389	402-474-6311	261

	Toll-Free	Phone	Class
Olsun Electrics Corp			
10901 Commercial St .... Richmond IL 60071	800-336-5786		757
Olum's of Binghamton Inc			
3701 Vestal Pkwy E .... Vestal NY 13850	855-264-8674*	607-729-5775	320
*Cust Svc			
Olymel LP			
2200 Pratte Ave Pratte .... Saint-Hyacinthe QC J2S4B6	800-361-7990	450-771-0400	612
Olympia Lacey Tumwater Visitor & Convention Bureau			
103 Sid Snyder Ave SW .... Olympia WA 98501	877-704-7500	360-704-7544	207
Olympia Medical Ctr			
5900 W Olympic Blvd .... Los Angeles CA 90036	800-874-4325	310-657-5900	371-3
Olympia Resort & Spa			
1350 Royale Mile Rd .... Oconomowoc WI 53066	800-558-9573	262-369-4999	660
Olympia School District			
1113 Legion Way SE .... Olympia WA 98501	855-846-8376	360-596-6100	676
Olympia Tile International Inc			
1000 Lawrence Ave W .... Toronto ON M6A1C6	800-268-1613	416-785-6666	192-4
Olympic College			
1600 Chester Ave .... Bremerton WA 98337	800-259-6718	360-792-6050	160
Shelton			
937 W Alpine Way .... Shelton WA 98584	800-259-6718	360-427-2119	160
Olympic Ctr Arena			
2634 Main St .... Lake Placid NY 12946	800-462-6236	518-523-1655	711
Olympic Medical Ctr			
939 Caroline St .... Port Angeles WA 98362	888-362-6260	360-417-7000	371-3
Olympic Steel Inc			
5096 Richmond Rd .... Bedford Heights OH 44146	800-321-6290	216-292-3800	487
NASDAQ: ZEUS			
Olympus Flag & Banner			
9000 W Heather Ave .... Milwaukee WI 53224	800-558-9620	414-355-2010	287
OM Group Inc			
811 Sharon Dr .... Westlake OH 44145	800-519-0083	440-899-2950	143
NYSE: OMG			
OMA (Oregon Medical Assn)			
11740 SW 68th Pkwy Ste 100 .... Portland OR 97223	877-605-3229	503-619-8000	469
Omaha Bedding Co			
4011 S 60th St .... Omaha NE 68117	800-279-9018	402-733-8600	466
Omaha Community Foundation (OCF)			
302 S 36th St Ste 100 .... Omaha NE 68131	800-794-3458	402-342-3458	302
Omaha Community Playhouse			
6915 Cass St .... Omaha NE 68132	888-782-4338	402-553-0800	566-4
Omaha Standard Inc			
3501 S 11th St Ste 1 .... Council Bluffs IA 51501	800-279-2201	712-328-7444	509
Omaha Truck Center Inc			
10710 I St PO Box 27379 .... Omaha NE 68127	800-866-2204	402-592-2440	125
Omaha Wholesale Hardware Co			
PO Box 3628 .... Omaha NE 68102	800-238-4566	402-444-1673	348
Omaha World-Herald			
1314 Douglas St .... Omaha NE 68102	800-284-6397	402-444-1000	525-2
OMAX Corp			
21409 72nd Ave S .... Kent WA 98032	800-838-0343	253-872-2300	688
OMB Watch			
1742 Connecticut Ave NW ...... Washington DC 20009	866-483-5137	202-234-8494	47-1
OMC (Ocean Medical Ctr)			
425 Jack Martin Blvd .... Brick NJ 08724	800-560-9990	732-840-2200	371-3
OMCO Inc 214 E Mill St .... Odon IN 47562	800-525-0272	812-636-7362	442
OMD Corp			
3705 Missouri Blvd .... Jefferson City MO 65109	866-440-8664	573-893-8930	179-1
Omega Engineering Inc			
One Omega Dr PO Box 4047 .... Stamford CT 06907	800-826-6342	203-359-1660	202
Omega Flex Inc			
451 Creamery Way .... Exton PA 19341	800-355-1039	610-524-7272	778
NASDAQ: OFLX			
Omega Healthcare Investors Inc			
200 International Cir			
Ste 3500 .... Hunt Valley MD 21030	877-511-2891	410-427-1700	646
NYSE: OHI			
Omega Institute for Holistic Studies			
150 Lake Dr .... Rhinebeck NY 12572	800-944-1001	845-266-4444	664
Omega Medical Health Systems Inc			
1200 E High St Ste 106 .... Pottstown PA 19464	866-716-6342		470
Omega Optical			
13515 N Stemmons Fwy .... Dallas TX 75234	800-366-6342	972-241-4141	535
Omega Products International			
1681 California Ave .... Corona CA 92881	800-600-6634	951-737-7447	192-3
Omega Shielding Products Inc			
1384 Pompton Ave .... Cedar Grove NJ 07009	800-828-5784	973-890-7455	325
Omega World Travel Inc			
3102 Omega Office Pk Dr .... Fairfax VA 22031	800-756-6342	703-359-0200	761
Omgeo LLC			
55 Thomson Pl .... Boston MA 02210	866-496-6436		196
OMHS (Owensboro Medical Health Systems)			
811 E Parish Ave PO Box 20007 ...... Owensboro KY 42303	877-888-6647	270-688-2000	371-3
Omnetics Connector Corp			
7260 Commerce Cir E .... Minneapolis MN 55432	800-343-0025*	763-572-0656	802
*Cust Svc			
Omni Barton Creek Resort & Spa			
8212 Barton Club Dr .... Austin TX 78735	800-336-6158	512-329-4000	660
Omni Cubed Inc			
1390 Broadway Ste B155 .... Placerville CA 95667	877-311-1976		226
OMNI HOMESTEAD RESORT, THE			
7696 Sam Snead Hwy .... Hot Springs VA 24445	800-838-1766	540-839-1766	660
Omni Hotels			
4001 Maple Ave .... Dallas TX 75219	800-843-6664	402-952-6664	376
Omni Hotels Select Guest Loyalty Program			
11819 Miami St Third Fl .... Omaha NE 68164	800-843-6664*		375
*Cust Svc			
Omni Interlocken Resort			
500 Interlocken Blvd .... Broomfield CO 80021	800-843-6664	303-438-6600	660
Omni International Inc			
435 12th St SW PO Box 1409 .... Vernon AL 35592	800-844-6664	205-695-9173	318-1
Omni La Mansion del Rio			
112 College St .... San Antonio TX 78205	800-292-7300	210-518-1000	376
Omni Orlando Resort at Championsgate			
1500 Masters Blvd .... Champions Gate FL 33896	800-843-6664	407-390-6664	660
Omni Rancho Las Palmas Resort & Spa			
41000 Bob Hope Dr .... Rancho Mirage CA 92270	866-423-1195	760-568-2727	698
Omnicare Inc			
201 E 4th St Ste 1900 .... Cincinnati OH 45202	800-342-5627	800-990-6664	580
NYSE: OCR			
Omnicell Inc			
1201 Charleston Rd .... Mountain View CA 94043	800-850-6664	650-251-6100	417
NASDAQ: OMCL			

	Toll-Free	Phone	Class
Omnigraphics Inc			
PO Box 31-1640 .... Detroit MI 48231	800-234-1340		628-2
Omni-Lite Industries Canada Inc			
17210 Edwards Rd .... Cerritos CA 90703	800-577-6664	562-404-8510	614
OMNIPLEX World Services Corp			
14151 Pk Meadow Dr Ste 300 .... Chantilly VA 20151	800-356-3406	703-652-3100	271
OmniSource Corp			
7575 W Jefferson Blvd .... Fort Wayne IN 46804	800-666-4789	260-422-5541	677
Omnitracs LLC			
10290 Campus Point Dr .... San Diego CA 92121	800-647-3325		726
Omnitronics LLC			
6573 Cochran Rd .... Solon OH 44139	800-762-9266	440-349-4900	51
OMNOVA Solutions Inc Performance Chemicals Div			
165 S Cleveland Ave .... Mogadore OH 44260	888-253-5454	330-628-6536	143
OMRF (Oklahoma Medical Research Foundation)			
825 NE 13th St .... Oklahoma City OK 73104	800-522-0211	405-271-6673	659
OMRON Corp			
One Commerce Dr .... Schaumburg IL 60173	800-556-6766	847-843-7900	204
Omron Healthcare Inc			
1925 W Field Ct .... Lake Forest IL 60045	877-216-1333	847-680-6200	470
OMRON Scientific Technologies Inc			
6550 Dumbarton Cir .... Fremont CA 94555	888-510-4357	510-608-3400	204
OMT Inc			
1-1717 Dublin Ave .... Winnipeg MB R3H0H2	888-665-0501	204-786-3994	392
OmTool Ltd			
Six Riverside Dr .... Andover MA 01810	800-886-7845	978-327-5700	179-7
OTC: OMTL			
OMYA Inc 39 Main St .... Proctor VT 05765	800-451-4468	802-459-3311	141
On Assignment Inc			
26745 Malibu Hills Rd .... Calabasas CA 91301	800-426-9196	818-878-7900	712
NYSE: ASGN			
ON Semiconductor Corp			
5005 E McDowell Rd .... Phoenix AZ 85008	800-282-9855	602-244-6600	687
NASDAQ: ON			
ONA (Oregon Nurses Assn)			
18765 SW Boones Ferry Rd .... Tualatin OR 97062	800-634-3552	503-293-0011	526
Ona Beach State Park			
5580 S Coast Hwy .... Newport OR 97366	800-551-6949		558
Onalaska Ctr for Commerce & Tourism			
1101 Main St .... Onalaska WI 54650	800-873-1901	608-781-9570	207
Onboard Systems International			
13915 NW Third Ct .... Vancouver WA 98685	800-275-0883	360-546-3072	522
OnCard Marketing Inc			
276 Fifth Ave Ste 608 .... New York NY 10001	866-996-8729		461
Oncenter Complex			
800 S State St .... Syracuse NY 13202	800-776-7548	315-435-8000	206
Oncology Nursing Society (ONS)			
125 Enterprise Dr .... Pittsburgh PA 15275	866-257-4667	412-859-6100	48-8
Oncology Plus Inc			
1070 E Brandon Blvd .... Brandon FL 33511	877-410-0779		237
Oncolytics Biotech Inc			
1167 Kensington Crescent NW			
Ste 210 .... Calgary AB T2N1X7	800-731-5319	403-670-7377	84
TSE: ONC			
Oncor			
1616 Woodall Rodgers Fwy			
Ste 2M-012 .... Dallas TX 75202	888-313-6862	214-486-2000	775
Ondine Biomedical Inc			
1100 Melville St Ste 910 .... Vancouver BC V6E4A6	800-564-6253	604-669-0555	231
Onduline North America Inc			
4900 Ondura Dr .... Fredericksburg VA 22407	800-777-7663	540-898-7000	192-4
One Call Medical Inc (OCM)			
20 Waterview Blvd PO Box 614 ...... Parsippany NJ 07054	800-872-2875	973-257-1000	379
One Lambda Inc			
21001 Kittridge St .... Canoga Park CA 91303	800-822-8824	818-702-0042	474
One Liberty Properties Inc			
60 Cutter Mill Rd Ste 303 .... Great Neck NY 11021	800-937-5449	516-466-3100	646
NYSE: OLP			
One Napili Way			
5355 Lower Honoapiilani Hwy .... Lahaina HI 96761	800-841-6284*	808-669-2007	743
*Cust Svc			
One Source Industries LLC			
185 Technology Dr .... Irvine CA 92618	800-899-4990		539
One Southern Indiana			
4100 Charlestown Rd .... New Albany IN 47150	800-521-2232	812-945-0266	137
One Touch Systems Inc			
2346 Bering Dr .... San Jose CA 95131	800-721-8682	408-436-4600	179-7
One Washington Cir Hotel			
One Washington Cir NW .... Washington DC 20037	800-424-9671	202-872-1680	376
One World Theatre			
7701 Bee Caves Rd .... Austin TX 78746	888-616-0522	512-330-9500	565
OneAmerica Financial Partners Inc (PML)			
PO Box 368 .... Indianapolis IN 46206	800-249-6269	317-285-1877	388-2
OneBeacon Insurance Group			
601 Carlson Pkwy Ste 600 ...... Minnetonka MN 55305	877-434-3900	781-332-7000	388-4
OneClass			
415 Yonge St Unit 1205 .... Toronto ON M5B2E7	855-392-6946		384
OneCoast Network LLC			
230 Spring St Ste 1800 .... Atlanta GA 30303	866-592-5514		358
Oneida County Convention & Visitors Bureau			
PO Box 551 .... Utica NY 13503	800-426-3132	315-724-7221	207
Oneida Financial Corp			
182 Main St .... Oneida NY 13421	800-211-0564	315-363-2000	357-2
NASDAQ: ONFC			
Oneida-Madison Electric Co-op Inc			
6630 State Rt 20 .... Bouckville NY 13310	866-632-9992	315-893-1851	245
OneLegacy Transplant Donor Network			
221 S Figueroa St Ste 500 ...... Los Angeles CA 90012	800-786-4077	213-229-5600	538
OneMorePallet.com			
9891 Montgomery Rd Ste 122 .... Cincinnati OH 45242	855-438-1667		384
Oneonta Trading Corp			
1 Oneonta Way .... Wenatchee WA 98801	800-688-2191	509-663-2191	296-7
OneSCM			
6805 Capital of Texas Hwy			
Ste 370 .... Austin TX 78731	800-324-5143	512-231-8191	179-1
OneSource Information Services Inc			
300 Baker Ave .... Concord MA 01742	800-433-0287	978-318-4300	628-10
ONESPRING LLC			
980 Birmingham Rd			
Ste 501-165 .... Alpharetta GA 30004	888-472-1840		181
OneTouch Direct LLC			
4902 W Sligh Ave .... Tampa FL 33634	866-948-4005		40
ONGUARD Industries			
1850 Clark Rd .... Havre de Grace MD 21078	800-365-2282	410-272-2000	300

Name / Address	City	State	ZIP	Toll-Free	Phone	Class
Onity Inc						
2232 Northmont Pkwy Ste 100	Duluth	GA	30096	800-424-1433		348
Onix Networking Corp						
18519 Detroit Ave	Lakewood	OH	44107	800-664-9638		175
Online Computer Library Ctr Inc (OCLC)						
6565 Kilgour Pl	Dublin	OH	43017	800-848-5878		48-11
Online Copy Corp						
48815 Kato Rd	Fremont	CA	94539	800-833-4460	510-226-6810	240
Online Transport System Inc						
6311 W Stoner Dr	Greenfield	IN	46140	866-543-1235	317-894-2159	770
OnlineMetals.com						
1138 W Ewing	Seattle	WA	98119	800-533-6350		487
Onondaga Coach Corp						
PO Box 277	Auburn	NY	13021	800-451-1570	315-255-2216	106
Onondaga Community College						
4941 Onondaga Rd	Syracuse	NY	13215	800-827-1000	315-498-2622	160
onProject Inc						
PO Box 104	Franklin Lakes	NJ	07417	877-936-6776	973-971-9970	38
ONS (Oncology Nursing Society)						
125 Enterprise Dr	Pittsburgh	PA	15275	866-257-4667	412-859-6100	48-8
Onset Computer Corp						
PO Box 3450	Pocasset	MA	02559	800-564-4377	508-759-9500	202
Onslow County Public Library						
58 Doris Ave E	Jacksonville	NC	28540	800-351-1697	910-455-7350	431-3
Onslow County Tourism						
1099 Gum Branch Rd	Jacksonville	NC	28540	800-932-2144		207
Onsrud Cutter LP						
800 Liberty Dr	Libertyville	IL	60048	800-234-1560	847-362-1560	488
Ontario Centres of Excellence Inc						
156 Front St W Ste 200	Toronto	ON	M5J2L6	866-759-6014	416-861-1092	214
Ontario Clean Water Agency						
1 Yonge St	Toronto	ON	M5E1E5	800-515-2759	416-314-5600	193
Ontario Convention & Visitors Bureau						
2000 E Convention Ctr Way	Ontario	CA	91764	800-455-5755	909-937-3000	207
Ontario Convention Ctr						
2000 E Convention Ctr Way	Ontario	CA	91764	800-455-5755	909-937-3000	206
Ontario Die Co of America						
2735 20th St	Port Huron	MI	48060	800-763-8272	810-987-5060	747
Ontario Drive & Gear Ltd (ODG)						
220 Bergey Ct	New Hamburg	ON	N3A2J5	877-274-6288	519-662-2840	29
Ontario Knife Co						
26 Empire St	Franklinville	NY	14737	800-222-5233	716-676-5527	222
Ontario Medical Supply Ltd						
1100 Algoma Rd	Ottawa	ON	K1B0A3	800-804-1112	613-244-8620	360
Ontario Real Estate Assn						
99 Duncan Mill Rd	Don Mills	ON	M3B1Z2	866-444-5557	416-445-9910	643
Ontario State Recreation Site						
23751 Old Hwy 30	Huntington	OR	97907	800-551-6949		558
Ontario Tourism Marketing Partnership Corp						
10 Dundas St E Ste 900	Toronto	ON	M7A2A1	800-668-2746	905-282-1721	764
Onyx EMS LLC						
2920 Kelly Ave	Watertown	SD	57201	800-258-7989	605-886-2519	253
Onyx Hotel						
155 Portland St	Boston	MA	02114	866-660-6699	617-557-9955	376
Onyx Pharmaceuticals Inc						
249 E Grand Av	South San Francisco	CA	94080	877-669-9121	650-266-0000	84
NASDAQ: ONXX						
OOIDA (Owner-Operator Independent Drivers Assn Inc)						
One NW OOIDA Dr	Grain Valley	MO	64029	800-444-5791	816-229-5791	48-21
OPC (Olson Precast Co)						
2750 Marion Dr	Las Vegas	NV	89115	800-876-8374	702-643-4371	184
OPCMIA (Operative Plasterers' & Cement Masons' International Assn of the US & Canada)						
11720 Beltsville Dr Ste 700	Beltsville	MD	20705	888-379-1558	301-623-1000	48-3
Open Applications Group Inc (OAGI)						
PO Box 4897	Marietta	GA	30061	800-236-4600	404-402-1962	48-13
Open Arms Hospice						
1836 W Georgia Rd	Simpsonville	SC	29680	866-473-6276	864-688-1700	368
Open Court Publishing Co						
70 E Lake St Ste 800	Chicago	IL	60601	800-815-2280		628-2
Open Group						
44 Montgomery St Ste 960	San Francisco	CA	94104	800-433-6611	415-374-8280	47-9
Open Kitchen Inc						
1161 W 21st St	Chicago	IL	60608	800-339-5334	312-666-5335	298
Open Pantry Food Marts						
10505 Corporate Dr						
Ste 101	Pleasant Prairie	WI	53158	800-242-3358	262-857-1156	205
Open Plan Systems Inc						
4700 Deepwater Terminal Rd	Richmond	VA	23234	888-869-4681	804-275-2468	318-1
Open Storage Solutions Inc						
2 Castleview Dr	Toronto	ON	L6T5S9	800-387-3419	905-790-0660	175
Open Systems Inc						
4301 Dean Lakes Blvd	Shakopee	MN	55379	800-328-2276*		179-1
*Sales						
Open Systems of Cleveland Inc						
22999 Forbes Rd Ste A	Cleveland	OH	44146	888-881-6660	440-439-2332	175
Open Text Corp						
275 Frank Tompa Dr	Waterloo	ON	N2L0A1	800-499-6544*	519-888-7111	179-7
TSE: OTC ■ *General						
Open Text Corp (USA)						
100 Tri-State International Pkwy						
3rd Fl	Lincolnshire	IL	60069	800-507-5777*	847-267-9330	179-7
TSE: OTC ■ *Sales						
OpenConnect Systems Inc						
2711 LBJ Fwy Ste 700	Dallas	TX	75234	800-551-5881	972-484-5200	179-7
OPENonline						
1650 Lk Shore Dr Ste 350	Columbus	OH	43204	888-381-5656	614-481-6999	626
OpenTable Inc						
One Montgomery St						
Fourth Fl	San Francisco	CA	94103	800-673-6822	415-344-4200	179-10
NASDAQ: OPEN						
OpenText Corp						
8600 W Bryn Mawr Ave Ste 710 N	Chicago	IL	60631	800-499-6544	773-632-1400	179-1
OpenWorks						
4742 N 24th St Ste 450	Phoenix	AZ	85016	800-777-6736	602-224-0440	309
Opera Omaha						
1625 Farnam St Ste 100	Omaha	NE	68102	877-346-7372	402-346-4398	566-2
Opera San Jose						
2149 Paragon Dr	San Jose	CA	95131	800-745-3000	408-437-4450	566-2
Operation USA						
3617 Hayden Ave Ste A	Culver City	CA	90232	800-678-7255	310-838-3455	47-5
Operational Technologies Corp						
4100 NW Loop 410 Ste 230	San Antonio	TX	78229	855-276-6136	210-731-0000	261
Operative Plasterers' & Cement Masons' International Assn of the US & Canada (OPCMIA)						
11720 Beltsville Dr Ste 700	Beltsville	MD	20705	888-379-1558	301-623-1000	48-3
Opex Corp						
305 Commerce Dr	Moorestown	NJ	08057	800-835-2362	856-727-1100	179-10
OPGI (Original Parts Group Inc)						
1770 Saturn Way	Seal Beach	CA	90740	800-243-8355	562-594-1000	53
OPI (Ohio Penal Industries)						
1221 McKinley Ave	Columbus	OH	43222	800-237-3454	614-752-0287	622
Opinion Research Corp (ORC)						
902 Carnegie Ctr Ste 220	Princeton	NJ	08540	800-444-4672		461
OPIS						
9737 Washingtonian Blvd						
Ste 100	Gaithersburg	MD	20878	888-301-2645	301-287-2645	524-5
Oppenheimer Cos Inc						
877 W Main Ste 700	Boise	ID	83702	800-727-9939	208-343-4883	296-8
OppenheimerFunds Inc						
225 Liberty St	New York	NY	10281	800-525-7048		521
Opsource Inc						
5201 Great America Pkwy						
Ste 120	Santa Clara	CA	95054	800-664-9973	408-567-2000	795
Optek Technology Inc						
1645 Wallace Dr	Carrollton	TX	75006	800-341-4747	972-323-2200	687
Optex Inc						
13661 Benson Ave Bldg C	Chino	CA	91710	800-966-7839	909-993-5770	683
Opti Care Eye Health Center						
87 Grandview Ave	Waterbury	CT	06708	800-334-3937	203-574-2020	536
Optical Cable Corp (OCC)						
5290 Concourse Dr	Roanoke	VA	24019	800-622-7711	540-265-0690	801
NASDAQ: OCC						
Optical Disc Solutions Inc						
1767 Sheridan St	Richmond	IN	47374	888-987-6334	765-935-7574	649
Optical Gaging Products Inc						
850 Hudson Ave	Rochester	NY	14621	800-647-4243	585-544-0450	537
Optical Laboratories Assn (OLA)						
225 Reinekers Ln Ste 700	Alexandria	VA	22314	800-477-5652	703-548-6619	48-8
Optical Society of America (OSA)						
2010 Massachusetts Ave NW	Washington	DC	20036	800-843-6664	202-223-8130	48-8
Opti-Com Mfg Network Co Inc						
259 Plauche St	New Orleans	LA	70123	800-345-8774	504-736-0331	803
Optimist International						
4494 Lindell Blvd	Saint Louis	MO	63108	800-500-8130	314-371-6000	47-15
Optimum Health Institute						
6970 Central Ave	Lemon Grove	CA	91945	800-993-4325	619-464-3346	697
Optimum Resource Inc						
18 Hunter Rd	Hilton Head Island	SC	29926	888-784-2592	843-689-8000	179-3
OPTIO LLC						
390 Spaulding Ave SE	Ada	MI	49301	888-981-3282		197
Option Advisor						
5151 Pfeiffer Rd Ste 250	Cincinnati	OH	45242	800-448-2080	513-589-3800	524-9
OptionsXpress Inc						
311 W Monroe Ste 1000	Chicago	IL	60606	888-280-8020	312-630-3300	170
Opus Bank						
19900 MacArthur Blvd 12th Fl	Irvine	CA	92612	855-678-7226	949-250-9800	357-2
Opus Framing Ltd						
3445 Cornett Rd	Vancouver	BC	V5M2H3	800-663-6953	604-435-9991	528
Opus Hotel						
322 Davie St	Vancouver	BC	V6B5Z6	866-642-6787		376
OPW Engineered Systems						
2726 Henkle Dr	Lebanon	OH	45036	800-547-9393*	513-932-9114	613
*Cust Svc						
OPW Fuel Management Systems						
6900 Santa Fe Dr	Hodgkins	IL	60525	800-547-9393	708-485-4200	202
Oracle Corp						
500 Oracle Pkwy	Redwood Shores	CA	94065	800-392-2999*	650-506-7000	179-1
NYSE: ORCL ■ *Sales						
Oracle Magazine						
500 Oracle Pkwy MS OPL3	Redwood Shores	CA	94065	800-392-2999	650-506-7000	452-7
Oracle USA						
500 Oracle Pkwy	Redwood Shores	CA	94065	800-392-2999	650-506-7000	179-1
Oral Health America						
410 N Michigan Ave Ste 352	Chicago	IL	60611	800-523-3438	312-836-9900	47-17
Oral Roberts University						
7777 S Lewis Ave	Tulsa	OK	74171	800-678-8876	918-495-6161	166
Oral Roberts University Library						
7777 S Lewis Ave	Tulsa	OK	74171	800-678-8876	918-495-6723	431-6
Oral-B Laboratories						
600 Clipper Dr Ste 200	Belmont	CA	94002	800-566-7252		470
Orange & Rockland Utilities Inc						
One Blue Hill Plz	Pearl River	NY	10965	877-434-4100*		775
*Cust Svc						
Orange Belt Stages						
PO Box 949	Visalia	CA	93292	800-266-7433	559-733-4408	750
Orange Chamber of Commerce						
439 E Chapman Ave	Orange	CA	92866	866-273-9817	714-538-3581	137
Orange City Area Health System						
1000 Lincoln Cir SE	Orange City	IA	51041	800-808-6264	712-737-4984	371-3
Orange Coast Magazine						
3701 Birch St Ste 100	Newport Beach	CA	92660	800-397-8179	949-862-1133	452-22
Orange Coast Memorial Medical Ctr (OCMMC)						
9920 Talbert Ave	Fountain Valley	CA	92708	877-597-4777	714-378-7000	371-3
Orange County Convention Ctr (OCCC)						
9800 International Dr	Orlando	FL	32819	800-345-9845	407-685-9800	206
Orange County Industrial Plastics Inc						
4811 E La Palma Ave	Anaheim	CA	92807	800-974-6247	714-632-9450	596
Orange County Public Schools						
445 W Amelia St	Orlando	FL	32801	800-378-9264	407-317-3200	676
Orange County Regional History Ctr						
65 E Central Blvd	Orlando	FL	32801	800-965-2030	407-836-8500	513
Orange County Register						
625 N Grand Ave	Santa Ana	CA	92701	877-469-7344	714-796-7000	525-2
Orange County Rural Electric Membership Corp						
7133 N State Rd 337 PO Box 208	Orleans	IN	47452	888-337-5900	812-865-2229	245
Orange County Trust Co						
PO Box 790	Middletown	NY	10940	888-341-5100	845-341-5000	69
Orange County's Credit Union						
PO Box 11777	Santa Ana	CA	92711	888-354-6228	714-755-5900	219
Orange Julius of America						
7505 Metro Blvd	Minneapolis	MN	55439	866-793-7582	952-830-0200	661
Orange Lake Country Club Inc (OLCC)						
8505 W Irlo Bronson Memorial Hwy	Kissimmee	FL	34747	800-877-6522	407-239-0000	660
Orange Line Oil Company Inc						
404 E Commercial St	Pomona	CA	91767	800-492-6864	909-623-0533	572
Orange Regional Medical Ctr						
60 Prospect Ave	Middletown	NY	10940	888-321-6762	845-343-2424	371-3

Name / Address	City	State	Zip	Toll-Free	Phone	Class
Orange Research Inc						
140 Cascade Blvd	Milford	CT	06460	**800-989-5657**	203-877-5657	202
Orange Tree Employment Screening						
7275 Ohms Ln	Minneapolis	MN	55439	**800-886-4777**	952-941-9040	626
Orange Tree Golf & Conference Resort						
10601 N 56th St	Scottsdale	AZ	85254	**866-729-7159**	480-948-6100	660
Orangeburg County Chamber of Commerce						
155 Riverside Dr SW						
PO Box 328	Orangeburg	SC	29116	**800-545-6153**	803-534-6821	137
Orangeburg Pecan Company Inc						
761 Russell St	Orangeburg	SC	29115	**800-845-6970**	803-534-4277	276
OraSure Technologies Inc						
220 E First St	Bethlehem	PA	18015	**800-869-3538**	610-882-1820	231
NASDAQ: OSUR						
ORBCOMM						
22265 Pacific Blvd Ste 200	Dulles	VA	20166	**877-538-7764***	703-433-6300	672
*Cust Svc						
ORBIS Corp						
1055 Corporate Ctr Dr	Oconomowoc	WI	53066	**800-999-8683**	262-560-5000	200
ORBIS International Inc						
520 Eigth Ave 11th Fl	New York	NY	10018	**800-672-4787**	646-674-5500	47-5
ORC (Opinion Research Corp)						
902 Carnegie Ctr Ste 220	Princeton	NJ	08540	**800-444-4672**		461
Orchard Garden Hotel						
466 Bush St	San Francisco	CA	94108	**888-717-2881**	415-399-9807	376
Orchard Hiltz & McCliment Inc (OHM)						
34000 Plymouth Rd	Livonia	MI	48150	**888-522-6711**	734-522-6711	261
Orchard Hotel						
665 Bush St	San Francisco	CA	94108	**888-717-2881**	415-362-8878	376
Orchard Software Corp						
701 Congressional Blvd Ste 360	Carmel	IN	46032	**800-856-1948**	317-573-2633	178
Orchards Hotel, The						
222 Adams Rd	Williamstown	MA	01267	**800-225-1517**	413-458-9611	376
Orchards Inn of Sedona						
254 Hwy N 89 A	Sedona	AZ	86336	**855-474-7719**		376
Orchestra Hall						
1111 Nicollet Mall	Minneapolis	MN	55403	**800-292-4141**	612-371-5600	565
Orchestra New England						
PO Box 200123	New Haven	CT	06520	**800-595-4849**	203-777-4690	566-3
Orchestre Symphonique de Montreal						
260 de Maisonneuve Blvd W						
Second Fl	Montreal	QC	H2X1Y9	**888-842-9951**	514-842-9951	566-3
Orco Block Co Inc						
11100 Beach Blvd	Stanton	CA	90680	**800-473-6726**	714-527-2239	184
Orcon Corp						
1570 Atlantic St	Union City	CA	94587	**800-227-0505***	510-489-8100	593
*General						
Orcutt/Winslow						
3003 N Central Ave	Phoenix	AZ	85012	**800-331-5842**	602-257-1764	187
Order Sons of Italy in America (OSIA)						
219 E St NE	Washington	DC	20002	**800-552-6742**	202-547-2900	47-14
Order-Matic Corp						
340 S Eckroat St						
PO Box 25463	Oklahoma City	OK	73129	**800-767-6733**	405-672-1487	174-7
Oreck Corp						
1400 Salem Rd	Cookeville	TN	38506	**800-289-5888**		776
Oregon						
Crime Victims Service Div						
1162 Ct St NE	Salem	OR	97301	**877-877-9392**	503-378-4400	337-38
Dept of Transportation						
355 Capitol St NE Ste 135 Rm 222	Salem	OR	97301	**888-275-6368**	503-986-4000	337-38
Financial Fraud/Consumer Protection Section						
1162 Ct St NE	Salem	OR	97301	**877-877-9392**	503-378-4400	337-38
Fish & Wildlife Dept (ODFW)						
3406 Cherry Ave NE	Salem	OR	97303	**800-720-6339**	503-947-6000	337-38
Legislative Assembly						
900 Ct St NE	Salem	OR	97301	**800-332-2313**		337-38
Oregon Business Development Dept (OBDD)						
775 Summer St NE Ste 200	Salem	OR	97301	**800-735-2900***	503-986-0123	337-38
*General						
Parks & Recreation Dept (OPRD)						
725 Summer St NE Ste C	Salem	OR	97301	**800-551-6949**	503-986-0707	337-38
Vocational Rehabilitation Services Office (OVRS)						
700 Summer St NE E-87	Salem	OR	97301	**877-277-0513**	800-692-9666	337-38
Oregon Aero Inc						
34020 Skyway Dr	Scappoose	OR	97056	**800-888-6910**	503-543-7399	522
Oregon Assn of Realtors						
2110 Mission St SE	Salem	OR	97308	**800-252-9115**	503-362-3645	647
Oregon Catholic Press (OCP)						
5536 NE Hassalo St	Portland	OR	97213	**877-596-1653**	503-281-1191	628-3
Oregon Caves National Monument						
19000 Caves Hwy	Cave Junction	OR	97523	**877-245-9022**	541-592-2100	557
Oregon Cherry Growers Inc						
1520 Woodrow NE	Salem	OR	97301	**800-367-2536**	503-364-8421	314-3
Oregon Coast Aquarium						
2820 SE Ferry Slip Rd	Newport	OR	97365	**800-452-7888**	541-867-3474	39
Oregon Coast Magazine						
4969 Hwy 101 Ste 2	Florence	OR	97439	**800-348-8401**	541-997-8401	452-22
Oregon Connection						
1125 S First St	Coos Bay	OR	97420	**800-255-5318**	541-267-7804	326
Oregon Convention Ctr						
777 NE Martin Luther King Jr						
Blvd	Portland	OR	97232	**800-791-2250**	503-235-7575	206
Oregon Dental Assn						
PO Box 3710	Wilsonville	OR	97070	**800-452-5628**	503-620-3230	227
Oregon Education Magazine (OEA)						
6900 SW Atlanta St Bldg 1	Portland	OR	97223	**800-858-5505**	503-684-3300	452-8
Oregon Food Bank Inc						
PO Box 55370	Portland	OR	97238	**888-398-8702**	503-282-0555	47-5
Oregon Freeze Dry Inc						
PO Box 1048	Albany	OR	97321	**800-547-4060**	541-926-6001	295-18
Oregon Garden, The						
879 W Main St PO Box 155	Silverton	OR	97381	**877-674-2733**	503-874-8100	96
Oregon Health & Science University						
Bone Marrow Transplant Program (OHSU)						
3181 SW Sam Jackson Pk Rd	Portland	OR	97239	**800-799-7233**	503-494-1617	759
School of Medicine						
3181 SW Sam Jackson Pk Rd						
L-109	Portland	OR	97239	**800-775-5460**	503-494-7800	167-2
Oregon Health & Science University Hospital						
3181 SW Sam Jackson Pk Rd	Portland	OR	97239	**800-292-4466**	503-494-8311	166
Oregon Institute of Technology						
3201 Campus Dr	Klamath Falls	OR	97601	**800-422-2017**	541-885-1150	166

Name / Address	City	State	Zip	Toll-Free	Phone	Class
Oregon International Port of Coos Bay						
125 Central Ave Ste 300						
PO Box 1215	Coos Bay	OR	97420	**800-463-3339**	541-267-7678	611
Oregon Lions Sight & Hearing Foundation						
1010 NW 22nd Ave Ste 144	Portland	OR	97210	**800-635-4667**	503-413-7399	269
Oregon Medical Assn (OMA)						
11740 SW 68th Pkwy Ste 100	Portland	OR	97223	**877-605-3229**	503-619-8000	469
Oregon Museum of Science & Industry						
1945 SE Water Ave	Portland	OR	97214	**800-955-6674**	503-797-4000	513
Oregon Mutual Insurance Co						
PO Box 808	McMinnville	OR	97128	**800-888-2141**	503-472-2141	388-4
Oregon Nurses Assn (ONA)						
18765 SW Boones Ferry Rd	Tualatin	OR	97062	**800-634-3552**	503-293-0011	526
Oregon Potato Co						
PO Box 3110	Pasco	WA	99302	**800-336-6311**	509-545-4545	295-18
Oregon State Bar Assn						
16037 SW Upper Boones Ferry Rd	Tigard	OR	97224	**800-452-8260**	503-620-0222	71
Oregon State Bar Bulletin, The						
16037 SW Upper Boones Ferry Rd						
PO Box 231935	Tigard	OR	97281	**800-452-8260**	503-620-0222	452-15
Oregon State University						
104 Kerr Admin Bldg	Corvallis	OR	97331	**800-291-4192**	541-737-4411	166
Oregon State University Press						
121 The Vly Library	Corvallis	OR	97331	**800-426-3797***	541-737-3166	628-4
*Orders						
Oregon Symphony Orchestra						
921 SW Washington St Ste 200	Portland	OR	97205	**800-228-7343**	503-228-4294	566-3
Oregon Veterans' Home						
700 Veterans Dr	The Dalles	OR	97058	**800-846-8460**	541-296-7190	781
Oregon Veterinary Medical Assn						
1880 Lancaster Dr NE Ste 118	Salem	OR	97305	**800-235-3502**	503-399-0311	783
Oregon-California Trails Assn						
524 S Osage St PO Box 1019	Independence	MO	64051	**888-811-6282**	816-252-2276	47-23
Oregonian						
1320 SW Broadway	Portland	OR	97201	**800-723-3638***	503-221-8100	525-2
*News Rm						
Orelube Corp, The						
20 Sawgrass Dr	Bellport	NY	11713	**800-645-9124**	631-205-9700	534
Orfila Vineyards & Winery						
13455 San Pasqual Rd	Escondido	CA	92025	**800-868-9463**	760-738-6500	49-6
Organ Supply Industries Inc						
2320 W 50th St	Erie	PA	16506	**800-458-0289**	814-835-2244	520
Organic Milling Co						
505 W Allen Ave	San Dimas	CA	91773	**800-638-8686**	909-599-0961	295-4
Organic Valley Family of Farms						
One Organic Way	LaFarge	WI	54639	**888-444-6455**		296-7
Organization for Tropical Studies (OTS)						
410 Swift Ave PO Box 90630	Durham	NC	27705	**877-572-4484**	919-684-5774	48-5
Organization of American Historians (OAH)						
112 N Bryan Ave	Bloomington	IN	47408	**888-737-7006**	812-855-7311	48-5
Organization of American States (OAS)						
1889 F St NW	Washington	DC	20006	**888-442-4887**	202-458-3000	47-7
Organizational Dynamics Inc						
790 Boston Rd Ste 201	Billerica	MA	01821	**800-634-4636**	978-671-5454	195
Orgill Inc						
3742 Tyndale Dr	Memphis	TN	38125	**800-347-2860**	901-754-8850	348
Orient Express Hotels Inc						
1114 Ave of the Americas	New York	NY	10036	**800-237-1236**	212-302-5055	376
NYSE: OEH						
Oriental Institute Museum						
1155 E 58th St						
University of Chicago	Chicago	IL	60637	**800-791-9354**	773-702-9514	513
Oriental Trading Company Inc						
5455 S 90th St	Omaha	NE	68127	**800-875-8480**	402-596-1200	454
Oriental Weavers of America						
3252 Lower Dug Gap Rd SW	Dalton	GA	30720	**800-832-8020**	706-277-9666	130
Original Cake Candle Co, The						
102 Sundale Rd PO Box 97	Norwich	OH	43767	**800-288-2340**	740-872-3248	121
Original Hartstone Pottery, The						
1719 Dearborn St	Zanesville	OH	43701	**800-339-4278**	740-452-9000	721
Original Lincoln Logs Ltd						
Five Riverside Dr						
PO Box 135	Chestertown	NY	12817	**800-833-2461**		105
Original Parts Group Inc (OPGI)						
1770 Saturn Way	Seal Beach	CA	90740	**800-243-8355**	562-594-1000	53
Origins Natural Resources Inc						
767 Fifth Ave	New York	NY	10153	**800-674-4467***		215
*Cust Svc						
Oriole Park at Camden Yards						
333 Camden St	Baltimore	MD	21201	**888-848-2473**	410-547-6100	711
Orion Instruments LLC						
2105 Oak Villa Blvd	Baton Rouge	LA	70815	**866-556-7466**	225-906-2343	202
Orion International Consulting Group Inc						
912 Capital of Texas Hwy S						
Ste 220	Austin	TX	78746	**800-336-7466**	512-327-7111	712
Orion Magazine						
187 Main St	Great Barrington	MA	01230	**888-909-6568**	413-528-4422	452-19
Orion Mobility LLC						
4 Mountainview Terrace Ste 101	Danbury	CT	06810	**800-476-7787**	203-762-0365	195
Orion Township Public Library						
825 Joslyn Rd	Lake Orion	MI	48362	**877-924-7467**	248-693-3000	431-3
Oritani Financial Corp						
370 Pascack Rd						
PO Box 1329	Washington Township	NJ	07676	**888-674-8264**	201-664-5400	69
NASDAQ: ORIT						
Orkin Exterminating Co Inc						
2170 Piedmont Rd NE	Atlanta	GA	30324	**844-498-7458**	877-250-1652	570
Orland Square						
288 Orland Sq	Orland Park	IL	60462	**877-746-6642**	708-349-1646	455
Orlando Baking Company Inc						
7777 Grand Ave	Cleveland	OH	44104	**800-362-5504**	216-361-1872	295-1
Orlando Magazine						
801 N Magnolia Ave Ste 201	Orlando	FL	32803	**866-356-3075**	407-423-0618	452-22
Orlando Museum of Art						
2416 N Mills Ave	Orlando	FL	32803	**800-435-7352**	407-896-4231	513
Orlando Regional Medical Ctr (ORMC)						
1414 Kuhl Ave	Orlando	FL	32806	**800-424-6998**	321-841-5111	371-3
Orlando Science Ctr						
777 E Princeton St	Orlando	FL	32803	**888-672-4386**	407-514-2000	513
Orlando Sentinel						
633 N Orange Ave	Orlando	FL	32801	**800-347-6868**	407-420-5000	525-2
Orlando Weekly						
1505 E Colonial Dr St Ste 200	Orlando	FL	32803	**800-474-7576**	407-377-0400	525-5

	Toll-Free	Phone	Class
Orlando, The			
8384 W Third St ....Los Angeles CA 90048	800-624-6835	323-658-6600	376
Orlando/Orange County Convention & Visitors Bureau Inc			
6700 Forum Dr Ste 100 ....Orlando FL 32821	800-972-3304	407-363-5872	207
Orleans Las Vegas Hotel & Casino			
4500 W Tropicana Ave ....Las Vegas NV 89103	800-675-3267	702-365-7111	132
ORMC (Orlando Regional Medical Ctr)			
1414 Kuhl Ave ....Orlando FL 32806	800-424-6998	321-841-5111	371-3
ORMCO Corp			
1717 W Collins Ave ....Orange CA 92867	800-854-1741*	714-516-7400	228
*Cust Svc			
Ormec Systems Corp			
19 Linden Pk ....Rochester NY 14625	800-656-7632	585-385-3520	204
Oro-Cal Mfg Company Inc			
1720 Bird St ....Oroville CA 95965	800-367-6225	530-533-5065	406
Oroville Area Chamber of Commerce			
1789 Montgomery St ....Oroville CA 95965	800-655-4653	530-538-2542	137
Orphan Foundation of America (OFA)			
21351 Gentry Dr Ste 130 ....Sterling VA 20166	800-950-4673	571-203-0270	47-6
Orpheum Theatre			
409 S 16th St ....Omaha NE 68102	866-434-8587	402-345-0202	565
Orr Safety Corp			
11601 Interchange Dr ....Louisville KY 40229	800-726-6789	502-774-5791	670
Orrco Inc			
515 Collins Blvd PO Box 147 ......Orrville OH 44667	800-321-3085	330-683-5015	571
Orrick Herrington & Sutcliffe LLP			
666 Fifth Ave ....New York NY 10103	866-342-5259	212-506-5000	425
Orscheln Farm & Home LLC			
1800 Overcenter Dr PO Box 698......Moberly MO 65270	800-498-5090	660-263-4377	276
ORT American Inc			
75 Maiden Ln 10th Fl ....New York NY 10038	800-519-2678	212-505-7700	47-5
Orthman Manufacturing Inc			
75765 Rd 435 PO Box 638.......Lexington NE 68850	800-658-3270	308-324-4654	273
Ortho Development Corp			
12187 S Business Pk Dr ....Draper UT 84020	800-429-8339	801-553-9991	472
Ortho Technology Inc			
17401 Commerce Park Blvd ....Tampa FL 33647	800-999-3161	813-991-5896	471
Ortho-Clinical Diagnostics Inc			
1001 US Rt 202 N PO Box 350.........Raritan NJ 08869	800-828-6316		471
Orthodox Union (OU)			
11 Broadway ....New York NY 10004	855-505-7500	212-563-4000	47-20
Orthofix Inc			
1720 Bray Central Dr ....McKinney TX 75069	800-527-0404	469-742-2500	472
ORTIG (Old Republic National Title Insurance Co)			
400 Second Ave S ....Minneapolis MN 55401	800-328-4441	612-371-1111	388-6
Orvis International Travel			
178 Conservation Way ....Sunderland VT 05250	800-547-4322	802-362-8790	701
OSA (Optical Society of America)			
2010 Massachusetts Ave NW ....Washington DC 20036	800-843-6664	202-223-8130	48-8
Osage Hills State Park			
2131 Osage Hills State Pk Rd .....Pawhuska OK 74056	800-622-6317	918-336-4141	558
Osage Valley Electric Co-op Assn			
1321 N Orange St ....Butler MO 64730	800-889-6832	660-679-3131	245
OSBA (Ohio State Bar Assn)			
1700 Lk Shore Dr ....Columbus OH 43204	800-282-6556	614-487-2050	71
Osborn International			
5401 Hamilton Ave ....Cleveland OH 44114	800-720-3358*	216-361-1900	102
*Cust Svc			
Osborn Transportation Inc			
1245 West Grand Ave ....Rainbow City AL 35902	866-215-3659	256-442-2514	770
Osborne Industries Inc			
120 N Industrial Ave ....Osborne KS 67473	800-255-0316	785-346-2192	273
Oscar Scherer State Park			
1843 S Tamiami Trail ....Osprey FL 34229	800-326-3521	941-483-5956	558
Oscar Wilson Engines & Parts Inc			
826 Lone Star Dr ....O Fallon MO 63366	800-233-3723	636-978-1313	383
Osceola Electric Co-op Inc			
1102 Egret Dr PO Box 127 ....Sibley IA 51249	888-754-2519	712-754-2519	245
Osceola News-Gazette			
108 Church St ....Kissimmee FL 34741	800-281-5303	407-846-7600	525-4
Oscor Inc			
3816 DeSoto Blvd ....Palm Harbor FL 34683	800-726-7267*	727-937-2511	250
*Cust Svc			
OSF HealthCare			
1100 E Norris Dr ....Ottawa IL 61350	800-635-1440	815-433-3100	371-3
OSF Hospice			
2265 W Altorfer Dr ....Peoria IL 61615	800-673-5288		368
OSF Saint Anthony Medical Ctr			
5666 E State St ....Rockford IL 61108	800-343-3185	815-226-2000	371-3
OSF Saint Francis Medical Ctr			
530 NE Glen Oak Ave ....Peoria IL 61637	888-627-5673	309-655-2000	371-3
OSF Saint Mary Medical Ctr			
3333 N Seminary St ....Galesburg IL 61401	877-795-0416	309-344-3161	371-3
OSG Tap & Die Inc			
676 E Fullerton Ave ......Glendale Heights IL 60139	800-837-2223	630-790-1400	488
OSHA (Occupational Safety & Health Administration)			
200 Constitution Ave NW ....Washington DC 20210	800-321-6742	202-693-1999	338-13
OSHA Up-to-Date Newsletter			
1121 Spring Lk Dr ....Itasca IL 60143	800-621-7615*	630-285-1121	524-8
*Cust Svc			
Oshkosh Convention & Visitors Bureau			
2401 W Waukau Ave ....Oshkosh WI 54904	877-303-9200	920-303-9200	47-20
Oshkosh Northwestern Co			
224 State St ....Oshkosh WI 54901	800-924-6168	920-235-7700	628-8
Oshkosh Truck Corp			
2307 Oregon St ....Oshkosh WI 54903	800-392-9921	920-235-9150	509
OSI Security Devices Inc			
1580 Jayken Way ....Chula Vista CA 91911	800-711-6814	619-628-1000	684
OSIA (Order Sons of Italy in America)			
219 E St NE ....Washington DC 20002	800-552-6742	202-547-2900	47-14
Osmose Inc			
980 Ellicott St ....Buffalo NY 14209	800-877-7653	716-882-5905	805
OSRAM Sylvania Glass Technologies			
131 Portsmouth Ave ....Exeter NH 03833	800-258-8290	603-772-4331	433
Ossid Corp			
PO Drawer 1968			
4000 College Rd..........Rocky Mount NC 27802	800-334-8369	252-446-6177	540
Ossining Union Free School District			
190 Croton Ave ....Ossining NY 10562	877-769-7447	914-941-7700	676
Ossur			
27412 Aliso Viejo Pkwy ....Aliso Viejo CA 92656	800-233-6263		110
Ostbye & Anderson Inc			
10055 51st Ave N ....Minneapolis MN 55442	866-553-1515	763-553-1515	406
Osteomed Corp			
3885 Arapaho Rd ....Addison TX 75001	800-456-7779*	972-677-4600	471
*Cust Svc			
Osteotech Inc			
710 Medtronic Pkwy ....Minneapolis MN 55432	800-633-8766	763-514-4000	84
Osteria Del Circo			
3600 Las Vegas Blvd S ....Las Vegas NV 89109	866-259-7111	888-987-6667	662
Osthoff Resort, The			
101 Osthoff Ave PO Box 151 ....Elkhart Lake WI 53020	800-876-3399	920-876-3366	660
Oswald Cos			
1100 Superior Ave Ste 1500..........Cleveland OH 44114	800-975-9468	216-367-8787	387
Oswego County Opportunities Inc			
239 Oneida St ....Fulton NY 13069	877-342-7618	315-598-4717	47-15
Otelco Inc			
505 Third Ave E ....Oneonta AL 35121	800-344-7483	205-625-3574	726
NASDAQ: OTT			
Otero County Electric Co-op Inc			
202 Burro Ave PO Box 227 .....Cloudcroft NM 88317	800-548-4660	575-682-2521	245
Otesaga, The			
60 Lake St ....Cooperstown NY 13326	800-348-6222	607-547-9931	660
Otis College of Art & Design			
9045 Lincoln Blvd ....Los Angeles CA 90045	800-527-6847	310-665-6820	162
Otis-Magie Insurance Agency Inc			
332 W Superior St Ste 700 ....Duluth MN 55802	800-241-2425	218-722-7753	387
Otomix Inc			
747 Glasgow Ave ....Inglewood CA 90301	800-701-7867	310-215-6100	300
OTS (Organization for Tropical Studies)			
410 Swift Ave PO Box 90630 ....Durham NC 27705	877-572-4484	919-684-5774	48-5
OTS			
3924 Clock Pointe Trl ....Stow OH 44224	877-445-2058		40
Otsego Club			
696 M-32 E Main St PO Box 556 ....Gaylord MI 49734	800-752-5510	989-732-5181	660
Ottawa Citizen			
1101 Baxter Rd PO Box 5020 ....Ottawa ON K2C3M4	800-267-6100	613-829-9100	525-1
Ottawa City Hall			
110 Laurier Ave W ....Ottawa ON K1P1J1	866-261-9799	613-580-2400	335
Ottawa Macdonald-Cartier International Airport			
1000 Airport PkwyPrivate			
Ste 2500...............Ottawa ON K1V9B4	888-901-6222	613-248-2000	27
Ottawa Senators			
1000 Palladium Dr Scotia Bank Pl ......Kanata ON K2V1A5	800-444-7367	613-599-0100	707
Ottawa Sun PO Box 9729 ....Ottawa ON K1G5H7	877-624-1463	613-739-7000	525-1
Ottawa Tourism & Convention Authority			
130 Albert St Ste 1800 ....Ottawa ON K1P5G4	800-363-4465	613-237-5150	207
Ottawa University			
1001 S Cedar St ....Ottawa KS 66067	800-755-5200*	785-242-5200	166
*Admissions			
Ottawa University Phoenix			
10020 N 25th Ave ....Phoenix AZ 85021	800-235-9586	602-371-1188	166
Ottawa Visitors Ctr			
106 W Lafayette St ....Ottawa IL 61350	888-688-2924	815-434-2737	207
Ottawa-AM 1200 (Sports)			
87 George St ....Ottawa ON K1N9H7	877-670-1200	613-789-2486	636-79
Ottens Flavors			
7800 Holstein Ave ....Philadelphia PA 19153	800-523-0767	215-365-7800	295-15
Otter Crest State Scenic Viewpoint			
198 NE 123rd St ....Newport OR 97365	800-551-6949		558
Otter Point State Recreation Site			
PO Box 1345 ....Port Orford OR 97465	800-551-6949		558
Otter Tail Corp			
4334 18th Ave SW PO Box 9156 ....Fargo ND 58106	866-410-8780	218-739-8479	357-3
NASDAQ: OTTR			
Otter Tail Power Co			
215 S Cascade St ....Fergus Falls MN 56537	800-257-4044	218-739-8200	775
Otter Tail Telcom			
230 W Lincoln Ave ....Fergus Falls MN 56537	800-247-2706	218-826-6161	115
Otterbein College			
One S Grove St ....Westerville OH 43081	800-488-8144*	614-823-1500	166
*Admissions			
Otterbein Retirement Living Communities			
580 N SR 741 ....Lebanon OH 45036	888-513-9131	513-933-5400	663
Otterbine Barebo Inc			
3840 Main Rd E ....Emmaus PA 18049	800-237-8837	610-965-6018	320
Otto Bock Healthcare North America Inc			
Two Carlson Pkwy N Ste 100 ....Minneapolis MN 55447	800-328-4058	763-553-9464	470
Otto Brehm Inc			
PO Box 249 ....Yonkers NY 10710	800-272-6886	914-968-6100	296-11
Otto Engineering Inc			
2 E Main St ....Carpentersville IL 60110	888-234-6886	847-428-7171	720
Ottumwa Courier			
213 E Second St ....Ottumwa IA 52501	800-532-1504	641-684-4611	525-2
OTZ Telephone Co-op Inc			
PO Box 324 ....Kotzebue AK 99752	800-478-3111	907-442-3114	726
OU (Orthodox Union)			
11 Broadway ....New York NY 10004	855-505-7500	212-563-4000	47-20
Ouachita Baptist University			
410 Ouachita St ....Arkadelphia AR 71998	800-342-5628*	870-245-5000	166
*Admissions			
Ouachita County Medical Ctr (OCMC)			
PO Box 797 ....Camden AR 71711	877-836-2472	870-836-1000	371-3
Our Lady of Fatima Retreat House			
5353 E 56th St ....Indianapolis IN 46226	800-480-2520	317-545-7681	664
Our Lady of Holy Cross College			
4123 Woodland Dr ....New Orleans LA 70131	800-259-7744	504-394-7744	166
Our Lady of Lourdes Medical Ctr			
1600 Haddon Ave ....Camden NJ 08103	888-568-7337	856-757-3500	371-3
Our Lady of the Lake College			
7434 Perkins Rd ....Baton Rouge LA 70808	877-242-3509*	225-768-1700	166
*Admissions			
Our Lady of the Lake University			
411 SW 24th St ....San Antonio TX 78207	800-436-6558	210-434-6711	166
Our Sunday Visitor Inc			
200 Noll Plaza ....Huntington IN 46750	800-348-2440	260-356-8400	628-8
OurParents Inc			
8521 Leesburg Pk Ste 310 ....Vienna VA 22182	866-629-1634		384
Outdoor Adv Assn of America Inc (OAAA)			
1850 M St NW Ste 1040......Washington DC 20036	800-537-0983	202-833-5566	608
Outdoor Ch			
43445 Business Pk Dr Ste 103........Temecula CA 92590	800-770-5750	951-699-6991	729
NASDAQ: OUTD			
Outdoor Photographer Magazine			
12121 Wilshire Blvd 12th Fl.......Los Angeles CA 90025	800-283-4410*	310-820-1500	452-14
*Cust Svc			

	Toll-Free	Phone	Class
Outdoor Ventures			
10579 S Main St ....Hayward WI 54843	**866-710-2846**	715-634-4447	702
Outer Banks Visitors Bureau			
One Visitor Ctr Cir .... Manteo NC 27954	**877-629-4386**	252-473-2138	207
Outerlink Corp			
187 Ballardvale St Ste A260 .... Wilmington MA 01887	**877-688-3770**	978-284-6070	672
OUTFRONT Media Inc			
405 Lexington Ave .... New York NY 10174	**800-926-8834**	212-297-6400	8
Outlets at Anthem			
4250 W Anthem Way .... Phoenix AZ 85086	**888-482-5834**	623-465-9500	455
Outokumpu Stainless Pipe Inc			
1101 N Main St .... Wildwood FL 34785	**800-731-7473**	352-748-1313	485
Outreach International			
129 W Lexington PO Box 210. ..... Independence MO 64050	**888-833-1235**	816-833-0883	47-5
Outrigger Enterprises Group			
2375 Kuhio Ave .... Honolulu HI 96815	**800-462-6262**	808-921-6941	376
OHANA Hotels & Resorts			
2375 Kuhio Ave .... Honolulu HI 96815	**866-254-1605**		376
Outrigger Hotels & Resorts			
2375 Kuhio Ave .... Honolulu HI 96815	**800-688-7444**	808-921-6941	376
Outrigger Kanaloa at Kona			
78-261 Manukai St ....Kailua-Kona HI 96740	**800-688-7444**	808-322-9625	660
Outrigger Reef on the Beach			
2169 Kalia Rd .... Honolulu HI 96815	**800-688-7444**	808-923-3111	660
Outrigger Waikiki on the Beach			
2335 Kalakaua Ave .... Honolulu HI 96815	**800-688-7444**	808-923-0711	376
Outside Magazine			
400 Market St ....Santa Fe NM 87501	**888-909-2382***	505-989-7100	452-14
General			
Outstart Inc			
745 Atlantic Ave 4th Fl .... Boston MA 02111	**877-971-9171**	617-897-6800	38
Outward Bound			
910 Jackson St ....Golden CO 80401	**866-467-7651**	207-510-7533	756
Ovation Instore			
57-13 49th Pl ....Maspeth NY 11378	**800-553-2202**	718-628-2600	233
Overcomers in Christ			
PO Box 34460 ....Omaha NE 68134	**866-573-0966**	402-573-0966	47-21
Overcomers Outreach			
PO Box 922950 ....Sylmar CA 91392	**800-310-3001**	818-833-1803	47-21
Overeaters Anonymous Inc (OA)			
PO Box 44020 ....Rio Rancho NM 87174	**866-505-4966**	505-891-2664	47-21
Overhead Door Company of Sacramento Inc			
6756 Franklin Blvd .... Sacramento CA 95823	**800-929-3667**	916-421-3747	190-2
Overhead Door Corp			
2501 S State Hwy 121 Bus			
Ste 200 ....Lewisville TX 75067	**800-275-3290**	469-549-7100	234
Overhill Farms Inc			
2727 E Vernon Ave ....Vernon CA 90058	**800-859-6406**	323-582-9977	295-36
NYSE: OFI			
Overland Express Co			
5539 Harvey Wilson			
PO Box 262322. ....Houston TX 77207	**800-929-7402**	713-672-6161	770
Overland Park Convention & Visitors Bureau			
9001 W 110th St Ste 100 ..... Overland Park KS 66210	**800-262-7275**	913-491-0123	207
Overland Sheepskin Company Inc			
2096 Nutmeg Ave .... Fairfield IA 52556	**800-683-7526**	641-472-8434	155-5
Overland Storage Inc			
4820 Overland Ave .... San Diego CA 92123	**800-729-8725**	858-571-5555	177
NASDAQ: OVRL			
Overlook Press			
141 Wooster St ....New York NY 10012	**800-527-9703**	212-673-2210	628-2
Overly Manufacturing Co			
574 W Otterman St .... Greensburg PA 15601	**800-979-7300**	724-834-7300	486
Overseas Adventure Travel			
347 Congress St ....Boston MA 02210	**800-221-0814**		750
Overseas Shipholding Group Inc			
666 Third Ave ....New York NY 10017	**800-851-9677**	212-953-4100	312
Overstock.com Inc			
6350 South 3000 East ....Salt Lake City UT 84121	**800-843-2446***	801-947-3100	779
*NASDAQ: OSTK ■ *Cust Svc*			
Overton Brooks Veterans Affairs Medical Ctr			
510 E Stoner Ave .... Shreveport LA 71101	**800-863-7441**	318-221-8411	371-8
Overton Power District # 5			
615 N Moapa Vly Blvd PO Box 395 .... Overton NV 89040	**888-409-6735**	702-397-2512	245
Overwaitea Food Group			
19855 92A Ave .... Langley BC V1M3B6	**800-242-9229**	604-888-1213	342
Ovid Technologies Inc			
333 Seventh Ave 20th Fl. ....New York NY 10001	**800-950-2035**	646-674-6300	384
OVMA (Ohio Veterinary Medical Assn)			
3168 Riverside Dr .... Columbus OH 43221	**800-662-6862**	614-486-7253	783
OW Lee Company Inc			
1822 E Francis St ....Ontario CA 91761	**800-776-9533**	909-947-3771	318-4
Owatonna Area Chamber of Commerce & Tourism			
320 Hoffman Dr .... Owatonna MN 55060	**800-423-6466**	507-451-7970	137
Owatonna Public Library			
105 N Elm St ....Owatonna MN 55060	**800-657-3864**	507-444-2460	431-3
Owen Community Bank			
279 E Morgan St PO Box 187. ....Spencer IN 47460	**800-690-2095**	812-829-2095	357-2
Owen Electric Co-op Inc			
8205 Hwy 127 N PO Box 400. ....Owenton KY 40359	**800-372-7612**	502-484-3471	245
Owen Industries Inc			
501 Ave H ....Carter Lake IA 51510	**800-831-9252**	712-347-5500	487
Owens & Assoc Investigations			
8765 Aero Dr Ste 306. .... San Diego CA 92123	**800-297-1343**		397
Findlay			
3200 Bright Rd ....Findlay OH 45840	**800-466-9367**		160
Owens Community College			
Toledo			
30335 Oregon Rd .... Perrysburg OH 43551	**800-466-9367**	419-661-7000	160
Owensboro Community & Technical College			
4800 New Hartford Rd .... Owensboro KY 42303	**866-755-6282**	270-686-4400	788
Owensboro Federal Credit Union			
717 Harvard Dr PO Box 1189. ....Owensboro KY 42302	**800-264-1054**	270-683-1054	219
Owensboro Grain Co			
822 E Second St ....Owensboro KY 42303	**800-874-0305**	270-926-2032	295-29
Owensboro Medical Health Systems (OMHS)			
811 E Parrish Ave PO Box 20007. ....Owensboro KY 42303	**877-888-6647**	270-688-2000	371-3
Owensboro-Davies County Tourist Commission			
215 E Second St .... Owensboro KY 42303	**800-489-1131**	270-926-1100	207
Owl Magazine			
10 Lower Spadina Ave Ste 400. .... Toronto ON M5V2Z2	**800-551-6957**	416-340-2700	452-6
Owl Wire & Cable Inc			
3127 Seneca Tpke ....Canastota NY 13032	**800-765-9473**	315-697-2011	800

	Toll-Free	Phone	Class
Owner-Operator Independent Drivers Assn Inc (OOIDA)			
One NW OOIDA Dr .... Grain Valley MO 64029	**800-444-5791**	816-229-5791	48-21
OX Paper Tube & Core Inc			
331 Maple Ave ....Hanover PA 17331	**800-414-2476**		124
Oxbow Meadows Environmental Learning Ctr			
3535 S Lumpkin Rd .... Columbus GA 31903	**866-264-2035**	706-507-8550	49-4
Oxfam America			
226 Cswy St Fifth Fl .... Boston MA 02114	**800-776-9326**	617-482-1211	47-5
Oxford Bank			
PO Box 129 ....Addison IL 60101	**800-236-2442**	630-629-5000	69
Oxford Biomedical Research Inc			
2165 Avon Industrial Dr .... Rochester Hills MI 48309	**800-692-4633**	248-852-8815	231
Oxford Convention & Visitors Bureau			
102 Ed Perry Blvd ....Oxford MS 38655	**800-758-9177**	662-232-2367	207
Oxford Global Resources Inc			
100 Cummings Ctr Ste 206L ....Beverly MA 01915	**800-426-9196**	978-236-1182	712
Oxford Health Plans LLC			
48 Monroe Tpke ....Trumbull CT 06611	**800-444-6222**	203-459-9100	388-3
Oxford Health Plans (NJ) Inc			
111 Wood Ave S Ste 2 .... Iselin NJ 08830	**800-201-6920**	732-623-1000	388-3
Oxford Hotel			
1600 17th St ....Denver CO 80202	**800-228-5838**	303-628-5400	376
Oxford Instruments Measurement Systems			
300 Bake Ave Ste 150. ....Concord MA 01742	**800-447-4717**		467
Oxford Life Insurance Co			
2721 N Central Ave .... Phoenix AZ 85004	**800-308-2318***	602-263-6666	388-2
Cust Svc			
Oxford Palace			
745 S Oxford Ave .... Los Angeles CA 90005	**800-532-7887**	213-389-8000	376
Oxford Suites Boise			
1426 S Entertainment Ave .... Boise ID 83709	**888-322-8001***	208-322-8000	376
General			
Oxford Suites Spokane Valley			
15015 E Indiana Ave .... Spokane Valley WA 99216	**866-668-7848**	509-847-1000	376
Oxford Suites Spokane-Downtown			
115 W N River Dr .... Spokane WA 99201	**800-774-1877**	509-353-9000	376
Oxford University Press			
198 Madison Ave .... New York NY 10016	**800-445-9714***	212-726-6000	628-2
Orders			
Oxford-Lafayette County Chamber of Commerce			
299 W Jackson Ave .... Oxford MS 38655	**800-880-6967**	662-234-4651	137
Oxiem LLC			
One S Limestone ....Springfield OH 45502	**866-432-8235**		7
Oxnard Convention & Visitors Bureau			
1000 Town Ctr Dr Ste 130 .... Oxnard CA 93036	**800-269-6273**	805-385-7545	207
Oyster Point Hotel, The			
146 Bodman Pl ....Red Bank NJ 07701	**800-345-3484**	732-530-8200	376
O-Z/Gedney			
9377 W Higgins Rd .... Rosemont IL 60018	**800-621-1506**	847-268-6000	803
Ozark Area Chamber of Commerce			
294 Painter Ave ....Ozark AL 36360	**800-582-8497**	334-774-9321	137
Ozark Border Electric Co-op			
3281 S Westwood .... Poplar Bluff MO 63901	**800-392-0567**	573-785-4631	245
Ozark Christian College			
1111 N Main St ....Joplin MO 64801	**800-299-4622**	417-624-2518	159
Ozark Folk Ctr State Park			
1032 Pk Ave ....Mountain View AR 72560	**800-264-3655**	870-269-3851	558
Ozark Motor Lines Inc			
3934 Homewood Rd .... Memphis TN 38118	**800-264-4100**	901-251-9711	770
Ozark National Scenic Riverways			
404 Watercress Dr PO Box 490 .... Van Buren MO 63965	**877-444-6777**	573-323-4236	557
Ozark Regional Transit			
2423 E Robinson Ave .... Springdale AR 72764	**800-865-5901**	479-756-5901	107
Ozarka College			
218 College Dr ....Melbourne AR 72556	**800-821-4335**	870-368-7371	160
Ozarks Coca-Cola Dr Pepper Bottling Co			
1777 N Packer Rd .... Springfield MO 65803	**866-223-4498**	417-865-9900	97
Ozarks Electric Co-op Corp			
3641 W Wedington Dr .... Fayetteville AR 72704	**800-521-6144**	479-521-2900	245

P

	Toll-Free	Phone	Class
P & F Industries Inc			
445 Broadhollow Rd .... Melville NY 11747	**800-327-9403**	631-694-9800	749
NASDAQ: PFIN			
P A Landers Inc			
351 Winter St ....Hanover MA 02339	**800-660-6404**	781-826-8818	187
P E La Moreaux & Assoc Inc			
PO Box 2310 ....Tuscaloosa AL 35403	**800-682-6338**	205-752-5543	193
P J Noyes Company Inc			
89 Bridge St ....Lancaster NH 03584	**800-522-2469**	603-788-4952	296-8
P. T. M. Corp			
6560 Bethuy Rd ....Fair Haven MI 48023	**800-486-2212**	586-725-2211	59
P1 Group Inc			
2151 Haskell Ave Bldg 1. .... Lawrence KS 66046	**800-376-2911**	785-843-2910	190-10
Paasche Airbrush Co			
4311 N Normandy ....Chicago IL 60634	**800-621-1907***	773-867-9191	42
Sales			
PABCO Gypsum			
37851 Cherry St ....Newark CA 94560	**877-449-7786**	510-792-9555	344
Pabst Brewing Co, The			
10635 Santa Monica Blvd			
Ste 350 ....Los Angeles CA 90025	**800-947-2278**		101
Pabst Theater			
144 E Wells St ....Milwaukee WI 53202	**800-523-7117**	414-286-3205	565
PAC Paper Inc			
6416 NW Whitney Rd .... Vancouver WA 98665	**800-223-4981**	360-695-7771	547
Pac Tec			
12365 Haynes St ....Clinton LA 70722	**877-554-2544**	225-683-8602	601
PACCAR Leasing Corp			
777 106th Ave NE .... Bellevue WA 98004	**800-759-2979**	425-468-7877	768
Pace Mechanical Services Inc			
301 Merritt Seven ....Norwalk CT 06851	**866-890-7794**	203-849-7800	190-10
Pace Products Inc			
4510 W 89th St Ste 110 .... Prairie Village KS 66207	**888-389-8203**		45

Name / Address	City	State	ZIP	Toll-Free	Phone	Class
Pace University						
One Pace Plz	New York	NY	10038	**866-722-3338**	212-346-1200	166
Pleasantville/Briarcliff						
861 Bedford Rd	Pleasantville	NY	10570	**866-722-3338**	914-773-3200	166
pace-edwards						
2400 Commercial Rd	Centralia	WA	98531	**800-338-3697**	360-736-9991	119
Pacer International Inc						
2300 Clayton Rd Ste 1200	Concord	CA	94520	**877-917-2237**	925-887-1400	357-3
NYSE: XPO						
Pacesetter Claims Service Inc						
2871 N Hwy 167	Catoosa	Ok	74015	**888-218-4880**	918-665-8887	387
Pacesetter Steel Service Inc						
1045 Big Shanty Rd	Kennesaw	GA	30144	**800-749-6505**	770-919-8000	487
Pacific & Western Credit Corp						
140 Fullarton St Ste 2002	London	ON	N6A5P2	**866-979-1919**	519-645-1919	357-2
TSE: PWC						
Pacific Alaska Freightways Inc						
2812 70th Ave E	Fife	WA	98424	**800-426-9940**	253-926-3292	310
Pacific Bag Inc						
15300 Woodinville Redmond Rd NE Ste A	Woodinville	WA	98072	**800-562-2247**	425-455-1128	64
Pacific Beach Hotel						
2490 Kalakaua Ave	Honolulu	HI	96815	**800-367-6060**	808-922-1233	376
Pacific Biometrics Inc						
645 Elliott Ave W Ste 300	Seattle	WA	98119	**800-767-9151**	206-298-0068	231
Pacific Bioscience Laboratories Inc						
16275 NE 67th Ct Suite 112	Redmond	WA	98052	**888-525-2747**	425-283-5700	471
Pacific Building Systems (PBS)						
2100 N Pacific Hwy	Woodburn	OR	97071	**800-727-7844***	503-981-9581	104
*General						
Pacific Cataract & Laser Institute						
2517 NE Kresky Ave	Chehalis	WA	98532	**800-888-9903**	360-748-8632	786
Pacific Coast Container Inc						
432 Estudillo Ave	San Leandro	CA	94577	**800-458-4788**	510-346-6100	641
Pacific Coast Feather Co						
1964 Fourth Ave S	Seattle	WA	98134	**888-297-1778**	206-624-1057	735
Pacific Coast Fruit Co						
201 NE Second Ave Ste 100	Portland	OR	97232	**800-423-4945**	503-234-6411	296-7
Pacific Coast Jet Charter Inc						
10600 White Rock Rd	Rancho Cordova	CA	95670	**800-655-3599**	916-631-6507	13
Pacific Coast Lighting						
20238 Plummer St	Chatsworth	CA	91311	**800-709-9004**	818-886-9751	435
Pacific Coast Producers						
631 N Cluff Ave	Lodi	CA	95240	**877-618-4776**	209-367-8800	295-20
Pacific Combustion Engineering Co						
2107 Border Ave	Torrance	CA	90501	**800-342-4442**	310-212-6300	417
Pacific Continental Corp						
111 W Seventh Ave PO Box 10727	Eugene	OR	97440	**877-231-2265**	541-686-8685	69
NASDAQ: PCBK						
Pacific Crest Securities Inc						
111 SW Fifth Ave 42nd Fl	Portland	OR	97204	**800-314-9837**	503-248-0721	681
Pacific Crest Trail Assn (PCTA)						
1331 Garden Hwy	Sacramento	CA	95833	**888-728-7245**	916-285-1846	47-23
Pacific Disaster Ctr						
1305 N Holopono St Ste 2	Kihei	HI	96753	**888-808-6688**	808-891-0525	659
Pacific Ethanol Corp						
400 Capitol Mall Ste 2060	Sacramento	CA	95814	**866-508-4969**	916-403-2123	143
NASDAQ: PEIX						
Pacific Fibre & Rope Company Inc						
903 Flint St PO Box 187	Wilmington	CA	90744	**800-825-7673**	310-834-4567	209
Pacific Fisherman Inc						
5351 24th Ave NW	Seattle	WA	98107	**877-644-6148**	206-784-2562	689
Pacific Fixture Company Inc						
12860 San Fernando Rd Unit B	Sylmar	CA	91342	**800-272-2349**	818-362-2130	286
Pacific Gas & Electric Co						
77 Beale St	San Francisco	CA	94105	**800-743-5000***	415-973-7000	775
*Cust Svc						
Pacific Grain Products International Inc						
351 Hanson Way PO Box 2060	Woodland	CA	95776	**800-333-0110***	530-662-5056	295-23
*Cust Svc						
Pacific Guardian Life Insurance Company Ltd						
1440 Kapiolani Blvd Ste 1700	Honolulu	HI	96814	**800-367-5354**	808-955-2236	388-2
Pacific Handy Cutter Inc						
17819 Gillette Ave	Irvine	CA	92614	**800-229-2233***	714-662-1033	222
*Cust Svc						
Pacific Health Laboratories Inc						
100 Matawan Rd Ste 150	Matawan	NJ	07747	**877-363-8769***	732-739-2900	787
*General						
Pacific Inn						
600 Marina Dr	Seal Beach	CA	90740	**866-466-0300**	562-493-7501	376
Pacific Inn Resort & Conference Centre						
1160 King George Hwy	Surrey	BC	V4A4Z2	**800-667-2248**	604-535-1432	376
Pacific Institute						
1709 Harbor Ave SW	Seattle	WA	98126	**800-426-3660**	206-628-4800	755
Pacific International Rice Mills Inc						
845 Kentucky Ave	Woodland	CA	95695	**800-747-4764**	530-661-6028	295-23
Pacific Internet						
105 W Clay St	Ukiah	CA	95482	**888-722-8638**	707-468-1005	795
Pacific Investment Management Company LLC						
840 Newport Ctr Dr	Newport Beach	CA	92660	**800-387-4626**	949-720-6000	398
Pacific Life Insurance Co						
700 Newport Ctr Dr	Newport Beach	CA	92660	**800-800-7646**	949-219-3011	388-2
Pacific Lutheran Theological Seminary						
2770 Marin Ave	Berkeley	CA	94708	**800-235-7587**	510-524-5264	167-3
Pacific Lutheran University						
1010 122nd St S	Tacoma	WA	98444	**800-274-6758**	253-531-6900	166
Pacific Marine Credit Union						
M C X Complex	Camp Pendleton	CA	92055	**800-736-4500**	760-430-7511	219
Pacific Medical Inc						
1700 N Chrisman Rd	Tracy	CA	95304	**800-726-9180**		472
Pacific Mercantile Bancorp						
949 S Coast Dr Ste 105	Costa Mesa	CA	92626	**877-450-2265***	714-438-2600	357-2
NASDAQ: PMBC ■ *General						
Pacific Modern Homes Inc (PMHI)						
9723 Railroad St	Elk Grove	CA	95624	**800-395-1011**	916-685-9514	105
Pacific Mutual Holding Co						
700 Newport Ctr Dr	Newport Beach	CA	92660	**800-347-7787**	949-219-3011	357-4
Pacific Northwest Ballet						
301 Mercer St	Seattle	WA	98109	**800-225-7635**	206-441-2424	566-1
Pacific Northwest College of Art						
1241 NW Johnson St	Portland	OR	97209	**888-390-7499**	503-226-4391	166
Pacific Northwest Inlander						
9 S Washington St	Spokane	WA	99201	**888-431-9911**	509-325-0634	525-5

Name / Address	City	State	ZIP	Toll-Free	Phone	Class
Pacific Northwest National Laboratory (PNNL)						
902 Battelle Blvd PO Box 999	Richland	WA	99352	**888-375-7665**	509-375-2121	659
Pacific NW Federal Credit Union (PNWFCU)						
12106 NE Marx St	Portland	OR	97220	**866-692-8669**	503-256-5858	219
Pacific Packaging Products Inc						
24 Industrial Way	Wilmington	MA	01887	**800-777-0300**	978-657-9100	552
Pacific Palms Conference Resort						
1 Industry Hills Pkwy	City of Industry	CA	91744	**800-524-4557***	626-810-4455	660
*Cust Svc						
Pacific Paper Tube Inc						
1025 98th Ave	Oakland	CA	94603	**888-377-8823**	510-562-8823	124
Pacific Polymers Inc						
12271 Monarch St	Garden Grove	CA	92841	**800-888-8340**	714-898-0025	3
Pacific Power & Light						
825 NE Multnomah St	Portland	OR	97232	**888-221-7070***	503-813-7100	775
*Cust Svc						
Pacific Power Group						
600 S 56th Pl	Ridgefield	WA	98642	**800-882-3860**	360-887-7400	382
Pacific Premier Bancorp Inc						
1600 Sunflower Ave	Costa Mesa	CA	92626	**888-388-5433**	714-431-4000	357-2
NASDAQ: PPBI						
Pacific Press						
1350 N Kings Rd	Nampa	ID	83687	**800-765-6955***	208-465-2500	628-9
*Cust Svc						
Pacific Press Technologies						
714 Walnut St	Mount Carmel	IL	62863	**800-851-3586**	618-262-8666	451
Pacific Repertory Theater						
PO Box 222035	Carmel	CA	93922	**866-622-0709**	831-622-0700	566-4
Pacific Rim Mechanical						
7655 Convoy Ct	San Diego	CA	92111	**800-891-4822**	858-974-6500	14
Pacific Rim Mining Corp						
625 Howe St Ste 1050	Vancouver	BC	V6C2T6	**888-775-7097**	604-689-1976	497
OTC: PFRMF						
Pacific School of Religion						
1798 Scenic Ave	Berkeley	CA	94709	**800-999-0528**	510-848-0528	167-3
Pacific Science Ctr						
200 Second Ave N	Seattle	WA	98109	**800-664-8775**	206-443-2001	513
Pacific Service Federal Credit Union						
PO Box 8191	Walnut Creek	CA	94596	**888-858-6878**	925-296-6200	219
Pacific Shores Inn						
4802 Mission Blvd	San Diego	CA	92109	**888-478-7829**	858-483-6300	376
Pacific Source Inc						
PO Box 2323	Woodinville	WA	98072	**888-343-1515**		192-3
Pacific Specialty Insurance Co						
3601 Haven Ave	Menlo Park	CA	94025	**800-962-1172**		388-4
Pacific States Felt & Mfg Company Inc						
23850 Clawiter Rd	Hayward	CA	94545	**800-566-8866**	510-783-0277	325
Pacific Steel & Recycling						
1401 Third St NW	Great Falls	MT	59404	**800-889-6264**	406-771-7222	487
Pacific Storage Co						
PO Box 334	Stockton	CA	95201	**888-823-5467**	209-320-6600	791-1
Pacific Sunwear of California Inc						
3450 E Miraloma Ave	Anaheim	CA	92806	**800-444-6770**	714-414-4000	155-4
NASDAQ: PSUN						
Pacific Terrace Hotel						
610 Diamond St	San Diego	CA	92109	**800-344-3370**	858-581-3500	376
Pacific Title Archives						
10717 Vanowen St	North Hollywood	CA	91605	**800-968-9111**	818-760-4223	507
Pacific Transit System						
216 N Second St	Raymond	WA	98577	**800-833-6388**	360-875-9418	107
Pacific Union College						
One Angwin Ave	Angwin	CA	94508	**800-862-7080**	707-965-6336	166
Pacific University						
2043 College Way	Forest Grove	OR	97116	**800-677-6712***	503-352-2007	166
*Admissions						
Pacific University Library						
2043 College Way	Forest Grove	OR	97116	**800-677-6712**	503-352-1400	431-6
Pacific Western Transportation Ltd						
6999 ordan Dr	Mississauga	ON	L5T1K6	**800-387-6787**	905-564-3232	106
Pacific Wings						
One Keolani Pl Ste 30	Kahului	HI	96732	**888-575-4546**	808-873-0877	25
Pacificare of Texas						
6200 NW Pkwy	San Antonio	TX	78249	**800-624-7272**	210-474-5000	388-3
PacifiCorp						
825 NE Multnomah St	Portland	OR	97232	**888-221-7070**	503-813-5000	775
Package Industries Inc						
15 Harback Rd	Sutton	MA	01590	**800-225-7242**	508-865-5871	104
Package Pavement Company Inc						
PO Box 408	Stormville	NY	12582	**800-724-8193**	845-221-2224	45
Packaging Corp of America						
1955 W Field Ct	Lake Forest	IL	60045	**800-456-4725**		99
NYSE: PKG						
Packaging Distribution Services Inc (PDS)						
2308 Sunset Rd	Des Moines	IA	50321	**800-747-2699**	515-243-3156	552
Packaging Machinery Manufacturers Institute (PMMI)						
4350 N Fairfax Dr Ste 600	Arlington	VA	22203	**888-275-7664**	703-243-8555	48-13
Packaging Services of Maryland Inc						
16461 Elliott Pkwy	Williamsport	MD	21795	**800-223-6255**	301-223-6200	542
Packaging Specialties Inc						
300 Lake Rd	Medina	OH	44256	**800-344-9271**	330-723-6000	199
Packaging Systems International Inc						
4990 Acoma St	Denver	CO	80216	**800-525-6110**	303-296-4445	540
Packard Industries Inc						
1515 US 31 N	Niles	MI	49120	**800-253-0866**	269-684-2550	286
Packard Transport Inc						
24021 S Municipal Dr PO Box 380	Channahon	IL	60410	**800-467-9260**	815-467-9260	463
Packer Country Visitor & Convention Bureau						
1901 S Oneida St	Green Bay	WI	54304	**888-867-3342**	920-494-9507	207
Packerland Rent-a-mat Inc						
12580 W Rohr Ave	Butler	WI	53007	**800-472-9339**	262-781-5321	130
Packing House						
900 E Layton Ave	Milwaukee	WI	53207	**800-727-9477**	414-483-5054	662
PackLate.com Inc						
100 Four Falls Corporate Ctr Ste 104	West Conshohocken	PA	19428	**877-472-2552**		384
Packless Metal Hose Inc						
PO Box 20668	Waco	TX	76702	**800-347-4859**	254-666-7700	14
Pacon Corp						
2525 N Casaloma Dr	Appleton	WI	54912	**800-333-2545**		547
Pacrim Hospitality Services Inc						
30 Damascus Rd	Bedford	NS	B4A0C1	**877-680-7666**	902-404-7474	195
Pactiv Corp						
1900 W Field Ct	Lake Forest	IL	60045	**888-828-2850**	847-482-2000	554

Name / Address	City	State	Zip	Toll-Free	Phone	Class
Pact-One Solutions Inc						
8215 S Eastern Ave Ste 101	Las Vegas	NV	89123	**866-722-8663**		175
Padco Inc						
2220 Elm St SE	Minneapolis	MN	55414	**800-328-5513**	612-378-7270	102
PADF (Pan American Development Foundation)						
1889 F St NW 2nd Fl	Washington	DC	20006	**877-572-4484**	202-458-3969	47-5
Padgett Business Services						
160 Hawthorne Pk	Athens	GA	30606	**800-723-4388**		2
PADI (Professional Assn of Diving Instructors International)						
30151 Tomas St	Rancho Santa Margarita	CA	92688	**800-729-7234***	949-858-7234	47-22
*Sales						
PADI Americas						
30151 Tomas St	Rancho Santa Margarita	CA	92688	**888-725-4801**	949-858-7234	506
PAFA (Pennsylvania Academy of the Fine Arts Museum)						
118 N Broad St	Philadelphia	PA	19102	**800-799-7233**	215-972-7600	513
Page & Assoc Inc						
1979 Lakeside Pkwy Ste 200	Tucker	GA	30084	**800-252-5282**		784
Page One Bookstore						
11018 Montgomery Blvd NE	Albuquerque	NM	87111	**800-521-4122**	505-294-2026	95
Paige Electric Company LP						
1160 Springfield Rd	Union	NJ	07083	**800-327-2443**	908-687-7810	246
PAII (Professional Assn of Innkeepers International)						
207 White Horse Pk	Haddon Heights	NJ	08035	**800-468-7244**	856-310-1102	48-4
Pain.com						
Dannemiller Memorial Educational Foundation						
5711 NW Pkwy Ste 100	San Antonio	TX	78246	**800-328-2308**	210-572-2512	353
Paine College						
1235 15th St	Augusta	GA	30901	**800-476-7703**	706-821-8200	166
Paint & Decorating Retailers Assn (PDRA)						
1401 Triad Ctr Dr	Saint Peters	MO	63376	**800-737-0107**	636-326-2636	48-18
Paint Creek State Park						
280 Taylor Rd	Bainbridge	OH	45612	**866-644-6727**	937-981-7061	558
Painted Buffalo Inn						
400 W Broadway PO Box 2547	Jackson	WY	83001	**800-288-3866**	307-733-4340	376
Painters Supply & Equipment Co						
25195 Brest Rd	Taylor	MI	48180	**800-589-8100**	734-946-8119	543
Painting & Decorating Contractors of America (PDCA)						
2316 Millpark Dr						
Ste 220	Maryland Heights	MO	63043	**800-332-7322***	314-514-7322	48-3
*Cust Svc						
Paisano Publications LLC						
28210 Dorothy Dr	Agoura Hills	CA	91301	**800-323-3484**	818-889-8740	628-9
Pak Mail Centers of America Inc						
7173 S Havana St Ste 600	Centennial	CO	80112	**800-778-6665***	303-957-1000	112
*Cust Svc						
Pak West Paper & Packaging						
4042 W Garry Ave	Santa Ana	CA	92704	**800-927-7299**	714-557-7420	541
Pakistan International Airlines Corp (PIA)						
1200 New Jersey Ave SE	Washington	DC	20590	**800-578-6786**		25
PakSense Inc						
6223 N Discovery Pl	Boise	ID	83713	**877-832-0720**	208-489-9010	202
Pala Casino Resort & Spa						
35008 Pala-Temecula Rd	Pala	CA	92059	**877-946-7252**	760-510-5100	660
Pala Mesa Resort						
2001 Old Hwy 395	Fallbrook	CA	92028	**800-722-4700**	760-728-5881	660
Palace Casino						
158 Howard Ave	Biloxi	MS	39530	**800-725-2239**	228-432-8888	131
Palace Hotel						
2 New Montgomery St	San Francisco	CA	94105	**866-716-8136**	415-512-1111	376
Palace Station Hotel & Casino						
2411 W Sahara Ave	Las Vegas	NV	89102	**800-634-3101***	702-367-2411	132
*Resv						
Palace, The						
601 Vine St	Cincinnati	OH	45202	**800-942-9000**	513-381-6006	662
Palace, Theatre, The						
1420 Celebrity Cir						
Broadway at the Beach	Myrtle Beach	SC	29577	**888-841-2787**	843-448-9224	565
Paladin Data Systems Corp						
19362 Powder Hill Pl NE	Poulsbo	WA	98370	**800-532-8448**	360-779-2400	178
Paladin Labs Inc						
100 Blvd Alexis Nihon						
Ste 600	St-Laurent	QC	H4M2P2	**888-376-7830**	514-340-1112	84
TSE: PLB						
Palais Royal						
10201 S Main St	Houston	TX	77025	**800-743-8730**	713-346-2430	155-2
Palestine Regional Medical Ctr						
2900 S Loop 256	Palestine	TX	75801	**800-222-1222**	903-731-1000	371-3
PALHACC (President Abraham Lincoln Hotel & Conference Ctr)						
701 E Adams St	Springfield	IL	62701	**855-610-8733**	217-544-8800	376
Palisade Corp						
798 Cascadilla St	Ithaca	NY	14850	**800-432-7475**	607-277-8000	179-1
Pall Corp						
2200 Northern Blvd	East Hills	NY	11548	**800-645-6532**	516-484-5400	383
NYSE: PLL						
Pall Life Sciences						
600 S Wagner Rd	Ann Arbor	MI	48103	**800-521-1520**	734-665-0651	416
PALLAB (Physician's Automated Laboratory Inc)						
9830 Brimhall Rd	Bakersfield	CA	93312	**800-675-2271**	661-829-2260	415
Palladium Group Inc						
55 Old Bedford Rd Ste 100	Lincoln	MA	01773	**800-773-2399**	781-259-3737	195
Pallet Consultants Corp						
PO Box 1692	Pompano Beach	FL	33061	**888-782-2909**	954-946-2212	544
Pallet Masters Inc						
655 E Florence Ave	Los Angeles	CA	90001	**800-675-2579**	323-758-6559	544
Pallet Services Inc						
12926 Farm to Market Rd	Mount Vernon	WA	98273	**800-769-2245**		201
PalletOne Inc						
1470 US Hwy 17 S	Bartow	FL	33830	**800-771-1148**	863-533-1147	544
Palm						
5800 Universal Blvd						
Hard Rock Hotel	Orlando	FL	32819	**866-333-7256**	407-503-7256	662
Palm Automotive Group						
1801 Tamiami Trail						
PO Box 512049	Punta Gorda	FL	33950	**800-643-2112***	941-639-1155	56
*General						
Palm Beach Atlantic University						
PO Box 24708	West Palm Beach	FL	33416	**888-468-6722**	561-803-2000	166
Lake Worth						
4200 Congress Ave	Lake Worth	FL	33461	**866-576-7222**	561-868-3350	160
Palm Beach Community College						
Palm Beach Gardens						
3160 PGA Blvd	Palm Beach Gardens	FL	33410	**866-576-7222**	561-207-5340	160
Palm Beach County Convention & Visitors Bureau						
1555 Palm Beach Lakes Blvd						
Ste 800	West Palm Beach	FL	33401	**800-554-7256**	561-233-3000	207
Palm Beach County School District, The						
3300 Forest Hill Blvd	West Palm Beach	FL	33406	**866-930-8402**	561-434-8000	676
Palm Beach Daily Business Review						
324 Datura St Ste 140	West Palm Beach	FL	33401	**800-777-7300**	561-820-2060	452-5
Palm Beach Illustrated Magazine						
1000 N Dixie Hwy Ste C	West Palm Beach	FL	33401	**800-308-7346**	561-659-6160	452-22
Palm Beach Newspapers Inc						
PO Box 24700	West Palm Beach	FL	33416	**800-432-7595**	561-820-4100	628-8
Palm Beach Opera						
415 S Olive Ave	West Palm Beach	FL	33401	**800-435-7352**	561-833-7888	566-2
Palm Beach Post						
2751 S Dixie Hwy	West Palm Beach	FL	33405	**800-432-7595**	561-820-4100	525-2
Palm Management Corp						
1730 Rhode Island Ave NW						
Ste 900	Washington	DC	20036	**800-388-7256**	202-775-7256	661
Palm Mountain Resort & Spa						
155 S BelaRdo Rd	Palm Springs	CA	92262	**800-622-9451**	760-325-1301	660
Palm Press Inc						
1442A Walnut St PO Box 120	Berkeley	CA	94709	**800-322-7256**	510-486-0502	129
Palm Restaurant						
837 Second Ave	New York	NY	10017	**866-333-7256**	212-687-2953	662
Palm Springs Chamber of Commerce						
190 W Amado Rd	Palm Springs	CA	92262	**888-947-6667**	760-325-1577	137
Palm Springs Convention Ctr						
277 N Avenida Caballeros	Palm Springs	CA	92262	**800-898-7256**	760-325-6611	206
Palm Springs Desert Resorts Convention & Visitors Authority						
70-100 Hwy 111	Rancho Mirage	CA	92270	**800-967-3767**	760-770-9000	207
Palm Springs International Airport						
3200 E Tahquitz Canyon Way	Palm Springs	CA	92262	**800-847-4389**	760-318-3800	27
Palm, The						
200 Dartmouth St	Boston	MA	02116	**866-333-7256**	617-867-9292	662
Palmer Asphalt Co						
196 W Fifth St PO Box 58	Bayonne	NJ	07002	**800-352-9898**	201-339-0855	45
Palmer Correctional Ctr						
PO Box 919	Palmer	AK	99645	**877-741-0741**	907-745-5054	213
Palmer Holland Inc						
25000 Country Club Blvd						
Ste 444	North Olmsted	OH	44070	**800-635-4822**		144
Palmer House Hilton						
17 E Monroe St	Chicago	IL	60603	**800-445-8667**	312-726-7500	376
Palmer Investigative Services						
624 W Gurley St Ste A	Prescott	AZ	86304	**800-280-2951**	928-778-2951	397
Palmer Moving & Storage						
24660 Dequindre Rd	Warren	MI	48091	**800-521-3954**	586-436-3804	512
Palmer Paving Corp						
25 Blanchard St	Palmer	MA	01069	**800-244-8354**	413-283-8354	189-4
Palmer Theological Seminary						
588 N Gulph Rd	King Of Prussia	PA	19406	**800-220-3287**	610-896-5000	167-3
Palmer-Donavin Manufacturing Co						
1200 Steelwood Rd	Columbus	OH	43212	**800-589-4412**	614-486-9657	192-3
Palmerton Area School District						
680 Fourth St	Palmerton	PA	18071	**800-732-0999**	610-826-7101	676
Palmetto Brick Co						
3501 BrickyaRd Rd	Wallace	SC	29596	**800-922-4423**	843-537-7861	148
Palmetto Dunes Resort						
4 Queen Folly Rd	Hilton Head Island	SC	29928	**866-380-1778**		660
Palmetto Health Home Care & Hospice						
1400 Pickens St	Columbia	SC	29202	**800-238-1884**	803-296-3100	368
Palmetto Island State Park						
19501 Pleasant Rd	Abbeville	LA	70510	**888-677-3668**	337-893-3930	558
Palmetto State Transportation Company Inc						
1050 Pk W Blvd	Greenville	SC	29611	**800-269-0175**	864-672-3800	770
Palms Casino Resort						
4321 W Flamingo Rd	Las Vegas	NV	89103	**866-942-7777**	702-942-7777	132
Palms Resort						
2500 N Ocean Blvd	Myrtle Beach	SC	29577	**800-300-1198**	843-626-8334	660
Palms West Chamber of Commerce						
13901 Southern Blvd	Loxahatchee	FL	33470	**800-790-2364**	561-790-6200	137
Palms West Hospital (PWH)						
13001 Southern Blvd	Loxahatchee	FL	33470	**877-549-9337**	561-798-3300	371-3
Palms, The						
3025 Collins Ave	Miami Beach	FL	33140	**800-550-0505**	305-534-0505	660
Palmyra Bologna Company Inc						
230 N College St	Palmyra	PA	17078	**800-282-6336**	717-838-6336	295-26
Palo Alto Weekly						
450 Cambridge Ave	Palo Alto	CA	94306	**800-766-4466**	650-326-8210	525-5
Paloma Systems Inc						
11250 Waples Mill Rd	Fairfax	VA	22030	**855-300-2686**	703-626-5024	796
Palomar Pomerado Health						
15615 Pomerado Rd	Poway	CA	92064	**800-628-2880**	858-613-4000	350
Palomar Technologies						
2728 Loker Ave W	Carlsbad	CA	92010	**800-854-3467**	760-931-3600	798
Palos Verdes Inn						
1700 S Pacific Coast Hwy	Redondo Beach	CA	90277	**800-421-9241**	310-316-4211	376
Palos Verdes Peninsula News						
609 Deep Valley Dr						
Ste 200	Rolling Hills Estates	CA	90274	**877-512-6397**	310-372-0388	525-4
PAM Transportation Services Inc						
297 W Henri De Tonti Blvd	Tontitown	AR	72770	**800-879-7261**	479-361-9111	770
NASDAQ: PTSI						
Pamarco						
171 E Marquardt Dr	Wheeling	IL	60090	**800-323-7735***	847-459-6000	668
*Sales						
Pamarco Global Graphics						
235 E 11th Ave	Roselle	NJ	07203	**800-526-2180**	908-241-1200	621
Pamlab LLC						
4099 Hwy 190 E Service Rd	Covington	LA	70433	**844-639-9725**	985-893-4097	238
Pampered Chef Ltd						
1 Pampered Chef Ln	Addison	IL	60101	**888-687-2433**		363
Pan Abode Cedar Homes Inc						
1100 Maple Ave SW	Renton	WA	98057	**800-782-2633**	425-255-8260	105
Pan American Development Foundation (PADF)						
1889 F St NW 2nd Fl	Washington	DC	20006	**877-572-4484**	202-458-3969	47-5
Pan American Screw Inc						
630 Reese Dr SW	Conover	NC	28613	**800-951-2222***	828-466-0060	278
*Cust Svc						
Pan Pacific Hotel Vancouver						
999 Canada Pl Ste 300	Vancouver	BC	V6C3B5	**800-937-1515**	604-662-8111	376
Pan Pacific Whistler Mountainside						
4320 Sundial Crescent	Whistler	BC	V0N1B4	**888-905-9995**	604-905-2999	660

	Toll-Free	Phone	Class
Pan Western Corp			
4910 Donovan Way Ste A . . . . . North Las Vegas NV 89081	800-443-1560	702-632-2931	770
Panalpina			
1776 On-the-Green 67 E Pk Pl . . . . . . Morristown NJ 07960	866-202-0377	973-683-9000	444
Panama City Beach Convention & Visitors Bureau			
17001 Panama City			
Beach Pkwy . . . . Panama City Beach FL 32413	800-722-3224	850-233-5070	207
Panamax Inc			
1690 Corporate Cir . . . . Petaluma CA 94954	800-472-5555	707-283-5900	253
Pan-American Life Insurance Co			
601 Poydras St . . . . New Orleans LA 70130	877-939-4550*		388-2
*Life Ins			
Panasas Inc			
969 W Maude Ave . . . . Sunnyvale CA 94085	800-726-2727	408-215-6800	178
Panasonic Avionics Corp			
26200 Enterprise Way . . . . Lake Forest CA 92630	877-627-2300	949-672-2000	51
Panasonic Consumer Electronics Co			
1 Panasonic Way . . . . Secaucus NJ 07094	800-103-1333	888-762-2097	51
NYSE: PC			
Panasonic Corp of North America			
1 Panasonic Way . . . . Secaucus NJ 07094	800-211-7262*	888-762-2097	51
*Cust Svc			
Panasonic Corporation of North America			
Two Riverfront Plaza . . . . Newark NJ 07102	888-223-1012		174-1
Panasonic Electric Works Corp of America			
629 Central Ave . . . . New Providence NJ 07974	800-276-6289	908-464-3550	204
Panavise Products Inc			
7540 Colbert Dr . . . . Reno NV 89511	800-759-7535	775-850-2900	688
Panavision Inc			
6219 DeSoto Ave . . . . Woodland Hills CA 91367	800-260-1846	818-316-1000	584
Panchero's Mexican Grill			
2475 Coral Ct Ste B . . . . Coralville IA 52241	888-639-2378	319-545-6565	661
Panda Express			
1717 Walnut Grove Ave . . . . Rosemead CA 91770	800-877-8988	626-312-5401	661
Panda Restaurant Group Inc			
1683 Walnut Grove Ave . . . . Rosemead CA 91770	800-877-8988	626-799-9898	661
Pandel Inc			
21 River Dr . . . . Cartersville GA 30120	800-537-3868	770-382-1034	361
Panduit Corp			
17301 Ridgeland Ave . . . . Tinley Park IL 60477	888-506-5400	708-532-1800	802
Panel Prints Inc			
1001 Moosic Rd . . . . Old Forge PA 18518	800-557-2635	570-457-8334	619
Panel Processing Inc			
120 N Industrial Hwy . . . . Alpena MI 49707	800-433-7142	989-356-9007	806
Panelfold Inc			
10700 NW 36th Ave . . . . Miami FL 33167	800-433-3222	305-688-3501	286
Paneloc Corp			
PO Drawer 547 . . . . Farmington CT 06034	800-394-6711	860-677-6711	347
Panera Bread Co			
3630 S Geyer Rd . . . . Saint Louis MO 63127	800-301-5566	314-984-1000	67
NASDAQ: PNRA			
Panhandle Co-op Assn			
401 S Beltline Hwy W . . . . Scottsbluff NE 69361	800-732-4546*	308-632-5301	276
*Cust Svc			
Panhandle Royalty Co			
5400 N Grand Blvd			
Grand Ctr Bldg Ste 300 . . . . Oklahoma City OK 73112	800-884-4225	405-948-1560	531
Panhandle Telecommunication Systems Inc (PTSI)			
2222 NW Hwy . . . . Guymon OK 73942	800-562-2556	580-338-2556	726
Panhandle-Plains Higher Education Authority Inc (PPHEA)			
1303 23rd St PO Box 839 . . . . Canyon TX 79015	877-629-3669	806-324-4100	47-11
Pannell Kerr Forster Of Texas Pc			
5847 San Felipe St . . . . Houston TX 77057	800-829-3676	713-860-1400	2
Pannier Corp			
207 Sandusky St . . . . Pittsburgh PA 15212	877-726-6437	412-323-4900	489
Pannier Graphics			
345 Oak Rd . . . . Gibsonia PA 15044	800-544-8428	724-265-4900	692
Pan-O-Gold Baking Co			
444 E St Germain . . . . Saint Cloud MN 56304	800-444-7005	320-251-9361	295-1
Panola Partnership Inc			
150-A Public Sq . . . . Batesville MS 38606	888-872-6652	662-563-3126	137
Panola-Harrison Electric Co-op			
410 E Houston St PO Box 1058 . . . . Marshall TX 75670	800-972-1093	903-935-7936	245
Panolam Industries International Inc			
20 Progress Dr . . . . Shelton CT 06484	800-672-6652	203-925-1556	806
Panorama Balloon Tours			
2683 Via De La Valle 625G . . . . Del Mar CA 92014	800-455-3592		750
Panorama City			
1751 Cir Ln SE . . . . Lacey WA 98503	800-999-9807	360-456-0111	663
Panoramic Corp			
4321 Goshen Rd . . . . Fort Wayne IN 46818	800-654-2027		747
Panoramic Inc			
1500 N Parker Dr . . . . Janesville WI 53545	800-333-1394	608-754-8850	100
Pan-Osten Co			
6944 Louisville Rd . . . . Bowling Green KY 42101	800-472-6678	270-783-3900	286
Pantages Hotel			
200 Victoria St . . . . Toronto ON M5B1V8	866-852-1777	416-362-1777	376
Pantages Theater			
901 Broadway . . . . Tacoma WA 98402	800-291-7593	253-591-5890	565
Pantagraph			
PO Box 2907 . . . . Bloomington IL 61702	800-747-7323	309-829-9000	525-2
Panther State Forest			
HC 63 PO Box Box 923 . . . . Panther WV 24872	800-225-5982	304-938-2252	558
Pantry Inc			
305 Gregson Dr . . . . Cary NC 27511	877-798-4792	919-774-6700	205
NASDAQ: PTRY			
Panzer Nursery Inc			
17980 W Baseline Rd . . . . Beaverton OR 97006	888-212-5327	503-645-1185	366
Paoli Inc			
201 E Martin St . . . . Orleans IN 47452	800-472-8669		318-1
Papa Gino's Inc			
600 Providence Hwy . . . . Dedham MA 02026	800-727-2446	781-461-1200	661
Papa John's International Inc			
PO Box 99900 . . . . Louisville KY 40269	877-547-7272		295-36
NASDAQ: PZZA			
Papa Murphy's International Inc			
8000 NE Pkwy Dr Ste 350 . . . . Vancouver WA 98662	800-778-7879	360-260-7272	661
Paper Crafts Magazine			
14850 Pony Express Rd . . . . Bluffdale UT 84065	800-727-2387	801-816-8300	452-14
Paper Pak Industries (PPI)			
1941 N White Ave . . . . La Verne CA 91750	888-293-6529	909-392-1750	296-9
Paper Systems Inc			
185 S Pioneer Blvd . . . . Springboro OH 45066	888-564-6774	937-746-6841	547

	Toll-Free	Phone	Class
Paper Tigers, The			
2201 Waukegan Rd Ste 180 . . . . Bannockburn IL 60015	800-621-1774	847-919-6500	651
Paper Transport Inc			
2701 Executive Dr . . . . Green Bay WI 54304	800-317-3650		770
Paperclip Software Inc			
One University Plz . . . . Hackensack NJ 07601	800-929-3503	201-525-1221	179-1
Papercone Corp			
3200 Fern Vly Rd . . . . Louisville KY 40213	800-626-5308	502-961-9493	263
PaperDirect Inc			
1005 E Woodmen Rd . . . . Colorado Springs CO 80920	800-272-7377		546
Paperdoll Co			
4944 Encino Ave . . . . Encino CA 91316	866-223-1145	818-906-8411	129
Papers Inc			
206 S Main St . . . . Milford IN 46542	800-733-4111	574-658-4111	628-8
Papers, The			
206 S Main St PO Box 188 . . . . Milford IN 46542	800-733-4111	574-658-4111	525-4
Pappas Restaurants Inc			
13939 NW Fwy . . . . Houston TX 77040	877-277-2748	713-869-0151	661
Pappas Seafood House			
13939 NW Fwy . . . . Houston TX 77040	877-277-2748	713-869-0151	661
Papyrus Franchise Corp			
500 Chadbourne Rd . . . . Fairfield CA 94533	800-789-1649		128
Par Pharmaceutical Cos Inc			
300 Tice Blvd . . . . Woodcliff Lake NJ 07677	800-828-9393	201-802-4000	577
NYSE: PRX			
Par Pharmaceutical Inc			
One Ram Ridge Rd . . . . Spring Valley NY 10977	800-828-9393	201-802-4000	577
PAR Technology Corp			
8383 Seneca Tpke . . . . New Hartford NY 13413	800-448-6505	315-738-0600	607
NYSE: PAR			
Para Systems Inc			
Minuteman UPS			
1455 LeMay Dr . . . . Carrollton TX 75007	800-238-7272	972-446-7363	253
Para-Chem Southern Inc			
863 SE Main St PO Box 127 . . . . Simpsonville SC 29681	800-763-7272	864-967-7691	3
Par-A-Dice Hotel			
21 Blackjack Blvd . . . . East Peoria IL 61611	800-727-2342	309-699-7711	376
Paradigm Medical Industries Inc			
4273 South 590 West . . . . Salt Lake City UT 84123	800-742-0671	801-977-8970	250
OTC: PDMI			
Paradise Chamber of Commerce			
5550 Sky Way Ste 1 . . . . Paradise CA 95969	800-838-3006	530-877-9356	137
Paradise Inc			
1200 W MLK Blvd PO Box Y . . . . Plant City FL 33563	800-330-8952		295-8
OTC: PARF			
Paradise Island Vacations			
1000 S Pine Island Rd			
Ste 800 . . . . Plantation FL 33324	888-877-7525*	954-809-2000	761
*Resv			
Paradise Point Resort & Spa			
1404 W Vacation Rd . . . . San Diego CA 92109	800-344-2626	858-274-4630	660
Paradise Point State Recreation Site			
PO Box 1345 . . . . Port Orford OR 97465	800-551-6949		558
Paradise Post			
5399 Clark Rd . . . . Paradise CA 95969	855-857-7247	530-877-4413	525-4
Parago Inc			
700 State Hwy 121 Bypass			
Ste 200 . . . . Lewisville TX 75067	866-219-7533		224
Paragon Casino Resort			
711 Paragon Pl . . . . Marksville LA 71351	800-946-1946		132
Paragon Development Systems Inc			
1823 Executive Dr . . . . Oconomowoc WI 53066	800-966-6090		175
Paragon Industries Inc			
2011 S Town E Blvd . . . . Mesquite TX 75149	800-876-4328	972-288-7557	317
Paragon Laboratories			
20433 Earl St . . . . Torrance CA 90503	800-231-3670	310-370-1563	787
Paragon Packaging Inc			
7700 Centerville Rd . . . . Ferndale CA 95536	888-615-0065	707-786-4004	100
Paragon Sporting Goods Corp			
867 Broadway 18th St . . . . New York NY 10003	800-961-3030	212-255-8889	702
Paragon Steel Enterprises LLC			
4211 County Rd 61 . . . . Butler IN 46721	800-411-5677	260-868-1100	487
Paragould Light Water & Cable (PLWC)			
1901 Jones Rd . . . . Paragould AR 72450	800-482-8998	870-239-7700	115
Parallax Inc			
599 Menlo Dr Ste 100 . . . . Rocklin CA 95765	888-512-1024	916-624-8333	617
Parametric Technology Corp (PTC)			
140 Kendrick St . . . . Needham MA 02494	800-613-7535	781-370-5000	179-5
NASDAQ: PTC			
Paramount Apparel International Inc			
One Paramount Dr . . . . Bourbon MO 65441	800-255-4287	573-732-4411	153-8
Paramount Builders Inc			
501 Central Dr . . . . Virginia Beach VA 23454	888-340-9002	757-340-9000	361
Paramount Chemical Specialties Inc			
14750 NE 95th St . . . . Redmond WA 98052	877-846-7826	425-882-2673	149
Paramount Cosmetics Inc			
93 Entin Rd Ste 4 . . . . Clifton NJ 07014	800-522-9880	973-472-2323	215
Paramount Fitness Corp			
6450 E Bandini Blvd . . . . Los Angeles CA 90040	800-721-2121	323-721-2121	267
Paramount Health Care			
1901 Indian Wood Cir . . . . Maumee OH 43537	800-462-3589	419-887-2525	388-3
Paramount Hotel			
235 W 46th St . . . . New York NY 10036	855-234-2074*	212-764-5500	376
*Resv			
Paramount Industries Inc			
304 N Howard St . . . . Croswell MI 48422	800-521-5405	810-679-2551	435
Paramount Technologies Inc			
1374 EW Maple Rd . . . . Walled Lake MI 48390	800-725-4408	248-960-0909	38
Paramount Theatre			
123 Third Ave SE . . . . Cedar Rapids IA 52401	800-369-8863	319-398-5226	565
Paramount's Kings Dominion			
16000 Theme Pkwy . . . . Doswell VA 23047	800-367-7623	804-876-5000	32
Parasec Inc			
2804 Gateway Oaks Dr Ste 200			
PO Box 160568 . . . . Sacramento CA 95833	800-533-7272*		626
*General			
Parc Aquarium du Quebec			
1675 des Hotels Ave . . . . Quebec QC G1W4S3	866-659-5264	418-659-5264	39
Parcel Plus Inc			
13121 Louetta Rd . . . . Cypress TX 77429	888-280-2053	281-376-0054	112
Parchem Trading Ltd			
415 Huguenot St . . . . New Rochelle NY 10801	800-282-3982	914-654-6800	231
Parents Helping Parents (PHP)			
1400 Parkmoor Ave Ste 100 . . . . San Jose CA 95126	855-727-5775	408-727-5775	47-6

	Toll-Free	Phone	Class
Parents of Murdered Children (POMC)			
4960 Ridge Ave Ste 2 ....Cincinnati OH 45209	**888-818-7662**	513-721-5683	47-6
PAREXEL International Corp			
195 W St ....Waltham MA 02451	**800-301-5033**	781-487-9900	659
NASDAQ: PRXL			
Parfums de Coeur Ltd			
85 Old Kings Hwy N ....Darien CT 06820	**800-887-2738**		567
Paris Business Products			
800 Highland Dr ....Westampton NJ 08060	**800-523-6454***	609-265-9200	109
*Cust Svc			
Paris Farmers' Union			
PO Box D ....South Paris ME 04281	**800-639-3603**	207-743-8976	276
Paris Gourmet of New York Inc			
145 Grand St ....Carlstadt NJ 07072	**800-727-8791**		296-8
Paris Junior College			
2400 Clarksville St ....Paris TX 75460	**800-232-5804**	903-785-7661	160
Paris Las Vegas			
3655 Las Vegas Blvd S ....Las Vegas NV 89109	**800-342-7724**	800-522-4700	376
Paris Mountain State Park			
2401 State Pk Rd ....Greenville SC 29609	**866-345-7275**	864-244-5565	558
Paris-Henry County Chamber of Commerce			
2508 Eastwood St ....Paris TN 38242	**800-345-1103**	731-642-3431	137
Park 'N Fly			
2060 Mt Paran Rd Ste 207 ....Atlanta GA 30327	**800-325-4863***		555
*Cust Svc			
Park 100 Foods Inc			
326 E Adams St ....Tipton IN 46072	**800-854-6504**	765-675-3480	295-26
Park Avenue Auto Group			
250 W Passaic St ....Maywood NJ 07607	**800-269-2891***	201-843-7900	289
*General			
Park Bancorp Inc			
5400 S Pulaski Rd ....Chicago IL 60632	**888-727-5333**	773-582-8616	357-2
OTC: PFED			
Park Cities Limousine			
7129 Harry Hines Blvd ....Dallas TX 75235	**888-559-0708**	214-824-0011	437
Park City Chamber of Commerce/Convention & Visitors Bureau			
1910 Prospector Ave			
PO Box 1630. ....Park City UT 84060	**800-453-1360**	435-649-6100	207
Park City Mountain Resort (PCMR)			
1345 Lowell Ave PO Box 39 ....Park City UT 84060	**800-222-7275**	435-649-8111	660
Park Community Federal Credit Union			
PO Box 18630 ....Louisville KY 40261	**800-626-2870**	502-968-3681	216
Park County			
1002 Sheridan Ave ....Cody WY 82414	**800-786-2844**	307-527-8510	336
Park County Travel Council (PCTC)			
836 Sheridan Ave PO Box 2454 ....Cody WY 82414	**800-393-2639**	307-587-2297	207
Park Electric Co-op Inc			
5706 US Hwy 89 S PO Box 1119 ...Livingston MT 59047	**888-298-0657**	406-222-3100	245
Park Hyatt Beaver Creek Resort & Spa			
136 E Thomas Pl ....Avon CO 81620	**800-233-1234***	970-949-1234	660
*Cust Svc			
Park National Bank			
50 N Third St PO Box 3500 ....Newark OH 43058	**888-791-8633**	740-349-8451	357-2
NYSE: PRK			
Park Place Technologies Inc			
5910 Landerbrook Dr ....Cleveland OH 44124	**877-778-8707**		178
Park Seed Co			
One Parkton Ave ....Greenwood SC 29647	**800-845-3369***		685
*Orders			
Park Shore Resort			
600 Neapolitan Way ....Naples FL 34103	**800-548-2077**	239-263-2222	660
Park Shore Waikiki Hotel			
2586 Kalakaua Ave ....Honolulu HI 96815	**866-536-7975**	808-954-7426	376
Park South Hotel			
124 E 28th St ....New York NY 10016	**800-315-4642**	212-448-0888	376
Park To Fly Inc			
7800 Narcoossee Rd ....Orlando FL 32822	**888-851-8875**	407-851-8875	555
Park University			
8700 NW River Pk Dr ....Parkville MO 64152	**800-745-7275**	816-741-2000	166
Park Vista Resort Hotel			
705 Cherokee OrchaRd Rd			
PO Box 30. ....Gatlinburg TN 37738	**800-227-5622***	865-436-9211	376
*Sales			
Park Water Co			
9750 Washburn Rd ....Downey CA 90241	**800-727-5987**	562-923-0711	775
Parkdale Mills Inc			
531 Cotton Blossom Cir ....Gastonia NC 28054	**800-331-1843**	704-874-5000	734-9
Parke County Rural Electric Membership Corp			
119 W High St ....Rockville IN 47872	**800-537-3913**	765-569-3133	245
Parke-Bell Ltd Inc			
709 W 12th St ....Huntingburg IN 47542	**800-457-7456**	812-683-3707	113
Parker Drilling Co			
1401 Enclave Pkwy Ste 600 ....Houston TX 77077	**800-468-9716**	281-406-2000	533
NYSE: PKD			
Parker Fluid Connectors Group			
6035 Parkland Blvd ....Cleveland OH 44124	**800-272-7537***	216-896-3000	367
*General			
Parker Furniture			
10375 SW Beaverton-Hillsdale Hwy ....Beaverton OR 97005	**866-515-9673**	503-644-0155	320
Parker Hannifin Corp			
6035 Parkland Blvd ....Cleveland OH 44124	**800-272-7537***	216-896-3000	223
*NYSE: PH ▧ *Cust Svc			
Parker Hannifin Corp Automation Actuator Div			
135 Quadral Dr ....Wadsworth OH 44281	**800-272-7537**	330-336-3511	223
Parker Hannifin Corp Brass Products Div			
100 Parker Dr ....Otsego MI 49078	**800-272-7537**	269-694-9411	778
Parker Hannifin Corp Cylinder Div			
500 S Wolf Rd ....Des Plaines IL 60016	**800-272-7537**	847-298-2400	223
Parker Hannifin Corp Daedal Div			
1140 Sandy Hill Rd ....Irwin PA 15642	**800-245-6903**	724-861-8200	537
Parker Hannifin Corp Electromechanical Automation Div			
5500 Business Pk Dr ....Rohnert Park CA 94928	**800-358-9068**	707-584-7558	204
Parker Hannifin Corp Finite Filtratio & Separation Div			
500 Glaspie St ....Oxford MI 48371	**800-521-4357**	248-628-6400	18
Parker Hannifin Corp General Valve Div			
26 Clinton Dr Unit 103 ....Hollis NH 03049	**800-272-7537**		778
Parker Hannifin Corp Hydraulic Valve Div			
520 Ternes Ave ....Elyria OH 44035	**800-272-7537**	440-366-5200	777
Parker Hannifin Corp Skinner Valve Div			
95 Edgewood Ave ....New Britain CT 06051	**800-825-8305**	860-827-2300	778
Parker Hannifin Corp Veriflo Div			
250 Canal Blvd ....Richmond CA 94804	**800-272-7537**	510-235-9590	202

	Toll-Free	Phone	Class
Parker Instrumentation Group			
6035 Parkland Blvd ....Cleveland OH 44124	**800-272-7537**	216-896-3000	223
Parker Lumber Co of Port Arthur Inc			
2948 Gulfway Dr ....Port Arthur TX 77642	**855-828-9792**	409-983-2745	192-3
Parker Majestic Inc			
300 N Pike Rd ....Sarver PA 16055	**866-572-7537**	724-352-1551	450
Parker McCrory Manufacturing Co			
2000 Forest Ave ....Kansas City MO 64108	**800-662-1038**	816-221-2000	204
Parker Paint Mfg Co Inc			
3003 S Tacoma Way ....Tacoma WA 98409	**855-862-6639**		543
Parker Powis Inc			
775 Heinz Ave ....Berkeley CA 94710	**800-321-2463**	510-848-2463	91
Parker Rose Design Inc			
10075 Mesa Rim Rd Ste A ....San Diego CA 92121	**800-403-2711**		40
Parker Smith & Feek Inc			
2233 112th Ave NE ....Bellevue WA 98004	**800-457-0220***	425-709-3600	387
*Cust Svc			
Parker Steel Co			
PO Box 2883 ....Toledo OH 43606	**800-333-4140**	419-473-2481	487
Parker-Hannifin Corp			
1160 Ctr Rd ....Avon OH 44011	**800-272-5464**	440-937-6211	760
Parkersburg & Wood County Public Library			
3100 Emerson Ave ....Parkersburg WV 26104	**800-642-8674**	304-420-4587	431-3
ParkerVision Inc			
7915 Baymeadows Way ....Jacksonville FL 32256	**800-532-8034**	904-737-1367	638
NASDAQ: PRKR			
Parkhill Smith & Cooper Inc			
4222 85th St ....Lubbock TX 79423	**800-400-6646**	806-473-2200	261
Parkhurst Manufacturing Co			
18999 Hwy Y ....Sedalia MO 65301	**800-821-7380**	660-826-8685	509
Parking Panda Corp			
3422 Fait Ave ....Baltimore MD 21224	**800-232-6415**		555
Parkinson's Disease Foundation (PDF)			
1359 Broadway ....New York NY 10018	**800-457-6676**	212-923-4700	47-17
Parkland College			
2400 W Bradley Ave ....Champaign IL 61821	**888-467-6065**	217-351-2200	160
Parkland College Theatre			
2400 W Bradley Ave ....Champaign IL 61821	**800-346-8089**	217-351-2528	565
Parkland Plastics Inc			
104 Yoder Dr PO Box 339. ....Middlebury IN 46540	**800-835-4110**	574-825-4336	652
Parkland School District			
1210 Springhouse Rd ....Allentown PA 18104	**866-632-9992**	610-351-5503	676
Parkline Inc			
PO Box 65 ....Winfield WV 25213	**800-786-4855**	304-586-2113	104
Parkridge East Hospital			
941 Spring Creek Rd ....Chattanooga TN 37412	**800-605-1527**	423-894-7870	371-3
Parks Assoc Inc			
5310 Harvest Hill Rd Ste 235			
PO Box 162. ....Dallas TX 75230	**800-727-5711**	972-490-1113	659
Parks Bros Farm Inc			
6733 Parks Rd ....Van Buren AR 72956	**800-334-5770**	479-474-1125	366
Parks Canada			
25-7-N Eddy St ....Gatineau QC K1A0M5	**888-773-8888**	613-860-1251	556
Parksite Inc			
1563 Hubbard Ave ....Batavia IL 60510	**800-338-3355**	630-761-9490	192-3
Parkson Corp			
1401 W Cyperess Creek Rd ....Fort Lauderdale FL 33309	**888-727-5766**		383
Parkview Hospital			
2200 Randallia Dr ....Fort Wayne IN 46805	**888-737-9311**	260-373-4000	371-3
Parkview Medical Ctr			
400 W 16th St ....Pueblo CO 81003	**800-543-4046**	719-584-4000	371-3
Parkville Insurances Services Inc			
15242 E Whittier Blvd			
PO Box 1275. ....Whittier CA 90603	**800-350-2702**	562-945-2702	387
Parkway Clinical Laboratories Inc			
3494 Progress Dr ....Bensalem PA 19020	**800-327-2764**	215-245-5112	415
Parkway Construction & Assoc LP			
1000 Civic Cir ....Lewisville TX 75067	**800-869-4567**	972-221-1979	187
Parkway Electric Inc			
11952 James St ....Holland MI 49424	**800-574-9553**	616-392-2788	775
Parkway Inn			
125 N Jackson St PO Box 494 ....Jackson WY 83001	**800-247-8390**		376
Parkway Properties Inc			
188 E Capitol St Ste 1000. ....Jackson MS 39201	**800-748-1667**	601-948-4091	646
NYSE: PKY			
Parmalat Canada Ltd			
405 the W Mall 10th Fl ....Toronto ON M9C5J1	**800-563-1515**		295-27
Parmed Pharmaceuticals Inc			
4220 Hyde Pk Blvd ....Niagara Falls NY 14305	**800-727-6331**	716-284-5666	238
Parr Instrument Co			
211 53rd St ....Moline IL 61265	**800-872-7720**	309-762-7716	417
Parrish & Heimbecker Ltd (P&H)			
201 Portage Ave Ste 1400 ....Winnipeg MB R3B3K6	**800-665-8937**	204-956-2030	275
Parrish Tire Company Inc			
5130 Indiana Ave ....Winston-Salem NC 27106	**800-849-8473**	336-767-0202	61-5
Parsons Buick Co, The			
151 E St ....Plainville CT 06062	**877-274-2613**	860-747-1693	56
Parsons Child & Family Ctr			
60 Academy Rd ....Albany NY 12208	**800-342-3009**	518-426-2600	47-6
Parsons Corp			
100 W Walnut St ....Pasadena CA 91124	**800-883-7300***	626-440-2000	261
*All			
Parsons Electric LLC			
5960 Main St NE ....Minneapolis MN 55432	**800-403-4832**	763-571-8000	190-4
Parsons Infrastructure & Technology			
100 W Walnut St ....Pasadena CA 91124	**800-300-0287**	626-440-4000	261
Parsons New School for Design			
65 Fifth Ave Rm 103 ....New York NY 10003	**800-252-0852***	212-229-8989	166
*Admissions			
Parter Medical Products Inc			
17015 Kingsview Ave ....Carson CA 90746	**800-666-8282**	310-327-4417	417
Particle Dynamics International LLC			
2629 S Hanley Rd ....Saint Louis MO 63144	**800-452-4682**	314-968-2376	576
Particle Measuring Systems Inc			
5475 Airport Blvd ....Boulder CO 80301	**800-238-1801***	303-443-7100	416
*Cust Svc			
Partner Assessment Corp			
2154 Torrance Blvd Ste 200 ....Torrance CA 90501	**800-419-4923**		193
Partner Reinsurance Co of the US			
1 Greenwich Plaza ....Greenwich CT 06830	**800-831-9146**	203-485-4200	388-2
PARTNERS A Tasteful Choice Co			
20232 72nd Ave ....South Kent WA 98032	**800-632-7477**	253-867-1580	67

	Toll-Free	Phone	Class
Partners Benefit Group Inc			
Five Crystal Pond Rd ....Southborough MA 01772	877-993-5600		458
Partners of the Americas			
1424 K St NW Ste 700 ....Washington DC 20005	800-322-7844	202-628-3300	47-5
Partnership for a Drug-Free America			
405 Lexington Ave Ste 1601 ....New York NY 10174	855-378-4373	212-922-1560	47-17
Partnerships In Community Living Inc			
480 Main St E PO Box 129..........Monmouth OR 97361	800-222-1222	503-838-2403	47-15
Parton Lumber Company Inc			
251 Parton Rd ....Rutherfordton NC 28139	800-624-1501	828-287-4257	674
Partridge Inn			
2110 Walton Way ....Augusta GA 30904	800-476-6888	706-737-8888	376
Parts Assoc Inc			
12420 Plz Dr ....Parma OH 44130	800-321-1128	216-433-7700	348
Parts Central Inc			
3243 Whitfield St ....Macon GA 31204	800-226-9396	478-745-0878	60
PartsBase Inc			
905 Clint Moore Rd ....Boca Raton FL 33487	888-322-6896*	561-953-0700	760
*Cust Svc			
Partschannel Inc			
119 Regal Row Rd Ste B ....Dallas TX 75247	800-562-2126	214-688-0018	56
PartsRiver Inc			
3155 Kearney St Ste 210 ....Fremont CA 94538	855-700-7278		179-7
Party City Corp			
25 Green Pond Rd Ste 1 ....Rockaway NJ 07866	800-727-8924	973-453-8600	559
Partylite Gifts Inc			
59 Armstrong Rd ....Plymouth MA 02360	888-999-5706	508-830-3100	363
Par-Way Tryson Co			
107 Bolte Ln ....Saint Clair MO 63077	800-844-4554	636-629-4545	295-30
PAS (Percussive Arts Society)			
110 W Washington St ....Indianapolis IN 46204	888-990-6663	317-974-4488	47-4
Pasadena Convention & Visitors Bureau			
300 E Green St ....Pasadena CA 91101	800-307-7977	626-795-9311	207
Pasadena Playhouse, The			
39 S El Molino Ave ....Pasadena CA 91101	800-733-2767	626-356-7529	738
Pasadena Star-News			
911 E Colorado Blvd ....Pasadena CA 91106	800-788-1200	626-578-6300	525-2
Pasco-Hernando Community College			
North			
11415 Ponce de Leon Blvd ....Brooksville FL 34601	877-879-7422	352-796-6726	160
Pasek Corp			
Nine W Third St ....South Boston MA 02127	800-628-2822	617-269-7110	684
Paslin Co			
25303 Ryan Rd ....Warren MI 48091	877-972-7546	586-758-0200	747
Paslode			
888 Forest Edge Dr ....Vernon Hills IL 60061	800-682-3428*	847-634-1900	749
*Cust Svc			
PASNAP (Pennsylvania Assn of Staff Nurses & Allied Professionals)			
One Fayette St Ste 475 ....Conshohocken PA 19428	800-500-7850	610-567-2907	526
Paso Robles Inn			
1103 Spring St ....Paso Robles CA 93446	800-676-1713	805-238-2660	376
Pason Systems Inc			
6130 Third St SE ....Calgary AB T2H1K4	877-255-3158	403-301-3400	179-10
TSE: PSI			
Passaic Valley Water Commission			
1525 Main Ave ....Clifton NJ 07011	877-772-7077	973-340-4300	775
Passavant Retirement Community			
401 S Main St ....Zelienople PA 16063	888-498-7753	724-452-5400	663
Passenger Vessel Assn (PVA)			
103 Oronoco St Ste 200 ....Alexandria VA 22314	800-807-8360	703-518-5005	48-21
Passkey International			
180 Old Colony Ave Third Fl ....Quincy MA 02170	866-649-1539		38
Passport Corp			
85 Chestnut Ridge Rd ....Montvale NJ 07645	800-926-6736	201-573-0038	179-1
Passport Health Communications Inc			
720 Cool Springs Blvd Ste 200 ....Franklin TN 37067	888-661-5657	615-661-5657	179-10
Boston Agency			
10 Cswy St Rm 247			
Tip O'Neill Federal Bldg ....Boston MA 02222	877-487-2778		338-14
Connecticut Agency			
850 Canal Street ....Stamford CT 06902	877-487-2778		338-14
Honolulu Agency			
300 Ala Moana Bldg Ste 1-330 ......Honolulu HI 96850	877-487-2778		338-14
Passport Services Regional Offices			
Los Angeles Agency			
11000 Wilshire Blvd			
Ste 1000..................Los Angeles CA 90024	877-487-2778		338-14
New Orleans Agency			
365 Canal St Ste 1300 ....New Orleans LA 70130	877-487-2778		338-14
New York Agency			
376 Hudson St 10th Fl..............New York NY 10014	877-487-2778		338-14
Philadelphia Agency			
US Custom House			
200 Chesnut St Rm 103 ....Philadelphia PA 19106	877-487-2778		338-14
San Francisco Agency			
95 Hawthorne St 5th Fl..........San Francisco CA 94105	877-487-2778		338-14
Washington (DC) Agency			
600 19th St NW			
First Floor Sidewalk Level ....Washington DC 20006	877-487-2778		338-14
Pastel Journal			
4700 E Galbraith Rd ....Cincinnati OH 45236	800-422-2550	513-531-2222	452-2
Pastorelli Food Products Inc			
162 N Sangamon St ....Chicago IL 60607	800-767-2829	312-666-2041	295-36
Pat Catan's Craft Centers			
21160 Drake Rd ....Strongsville OH 44149	800-321-1494	440-238-7318	44
Pat O'Brien's International Inc			
718 St Peter St ....New Orleans LA 70116	800-597-4823	504-525-4823	661
Patagonia Inc			
259 W Santa Clara St PO Box 150 ....Ventura CA 93001	800-638-6464*	805-643-8616	155-4
*Cust Svc			
Patch Products Inc			
1400 E Inman Pkwy ....Beloit WI 53511	800-524-4263	608-362-6896	752
Patent Trademark & Copyright Law Daily			
1801 S Bell St ....Arlington VA 22202	800-372-1033		524-7
Paternity Testing Corp (PTC)			
300 Portland St ....Columbia MO 65201	888-837-8323	573-442-9948	414
Paterson Pacific Parchment Co			
625 Greg St ....Sparks NV 89431	800-678-8104	775-353-3000	552
Path Logic Inc			
950 Riverside Pkwy			
Ste 90 ....West Sacramento CA 95605	855-291-4528		415
Path Master Inc			
1960 Midway Dr ....Twinsburg OH 44087	855-738-2722	330-425-4994	246
Patheon Inc			
2100 Syntex Ct ....Mississauga ON L5N7K9	866-529-2922	905-821-4001	474
Pathfinder Bancorp Inc			
214 W First St ....Oswego NY 13126	800-811-5620	315-343-0057	357-2
NASDAQ: PBHC			
Patient Advocate Foundation Inc			
700 Thimble Shoals Blvd			
Ste 200 ....Newport News VA 23606	800-532-5274		304
Patients Rights Council (PRC)			
PO Box 760 ....Steubenville OH 43952	800-958-5678	740-282-3810	47-8
Patioshoppers Inc			
41188 Sandalwood Cir ....Murrieta CA 92562	800-940-6123	951-696-1700	320
Patni Americas Inc			
116 Pine St Ste 320 ....Harrisburg PA 17101	877-209-0463	617-914-8000	178
Patricia Grand Resort			
2710 N Ocean Blvd ....Myrtle Beach SC 29577	800-255-4763	843-448-8453	660
Patricia Seybold Group			
210 Commercial St ....Boston MA 02109	855-310-0101	617-742-5200	458
Patrick Engineering Inc			
4970 Varsity Dr ....Lisle IL 60532	800-799-7050	630-795-7200	261
Patrick Henry Community College			
645 Patriot Ave			
PO Box 5311 ....Martinsville VA 24112	855-874-6692	276-638-8777	160
Patrick Industries Inc			
107 W Franklin St PO Box 638 ....Elkhart IN 46515	800-331-2151	574-294-7511	114
NASDAQ: PATK			
Patrick Industries Inc Patrick Metals Div			
5020 Lincolnway E ....Mishawaka IN 46544	800-922-9692	574-255-9692	480
Patrick James Inc			
780 W Shaw Ave ....Fresno CA 93704	888-427-6003	559-224-5500	155-3
Patriot Flooring Supply Inc			
110 Commerce Way ....Woburn MA 01801	866-444-4433		681
Patriot Ledger			
400 Crown Colony Dr			
PO Box 699159................Quincy MA 02269	888-782-2267	617-786-7000	525-2
Patriot National Bancorp Inc			
900 Bedford St ....Stamford CT 06901	888-728-7468	203-251-7200	357-2
NASDAQ: PNBK			
Patriot Technologies Inc			
5108 Pegasus Ct Ste F ....Frederick MD 21704	888-417-9899	301-695-7500	178
Patriot Transportation Holding Inc			
501 Riverside Ave Ste 500 ....Jacksonville FL 32202	877-704-1776	904-396-5733	770
NASDAQ: PATI			
Patriot-News			
812 Market St ....Harrisburg PA 17101	800-692-7207	717-255-8100	525-2
Patriots Point Naval & Maritime Museum			
40 Patriots Pt Rd ....Mount Pleasant SC 29464	800-248-3508	843-884-2727	513
Patriots Theater			
Memorial Dr ....Trenton NJ 08608	866-847-7682	609-984-8484	565
Patten Industries Inc			
635 W Lake St ....Elmhurst IL 60126	877-688-2228	630-279-4400	355
Patten University			
2433 Coolidge Ave ....Oakland CA 94601	877-472-8836	510-261-8500	166
Pattern Insight Inc			
465 Fairchild Dr Ste 209........Mountain View CA 94043	866-582-2655		178
Patterson Cos Inc			
1031 Mendota Heights Rd ....Saint Paul MN 55120	800-328-5536	651-686-1600	470
NASDAQ: PDCO			
Patterson Office Supplies			
3310 N Duncan Rd ....Champaign IL 61822	800-637-1140	217-351-5400	109
Patterson-Schwartz & Assoc Inc			
7234 Lancaster Pike Ste 100A ....Hockessin DE 19707	877-456-4663	302-234-5270	643
Patterson-UTI Energy Inc			
450 Gears Rd Ste 500................Houston TX 77067	866-387-1933	281-765-7100	533
NASDAQ: PTEN			
Pattison Sign Group			
555 Ellesmere Rd ....Scarborough ON M1R4E8	800-268-6536	416-759-1111	692
Patuxent Cos			
2124 Priest Bridge Dr Ste 18 ....Crofton MD 21114	800-628-4942	410-793-0181	190-16
Paul Brown Stadium			
1 Paul Brown Stadium ....Cincinnati OH 45202	866-621-8383	513-621-3550	711
Paul C Buff Inc			
2725 Bransford Ave ....Nashville TN 37204	800-443-5542	615-383-3982	435
Paul Casket Co			
505 S Green St ....Cambridge City IN 47327	800-521-8202	765-478-3991	133
Paul D Camp Community College			
100 N College Dr PO Box 737 ....Franklin VA 23851	866-933-0508	757-569-6700	160
Hobbs Suffolk			
271 Kenyon Rd ....Suffolk VA 23434	855-877-3918	757-925-6300	160
Paul deLima Co Inc			
7546 Morgan Rd ....Liverpool NY 13090	800-962-8864	315-457-3725	295-7
Paul Fredrick Menstyle			
223 W Poplar St ....Fleetwood PA 19522	800-247-1417	610-944-0909	155-3
Paul H Gesswein & Co			
255 Hancock Ave ....Bridgeport CT 06605	800-544-2043	203-366-5400	404
Paul Heuring Motors Inc			
720 N Hobart Rd ....Hobart IN 46342	888-851-9702	219-942-3673	56
Paul Laurence Dunbar House			
219 N Paul Laurence Dunbar St ....Dayton OH 45402	800-860-0148	937-224-7061	49-2
Paul M. Grist State Park			
1546 Grist Rd ....Selma AL 36701	800-252-7275	334-872-5846	558
Paul Moak Automotive Inc			
740 Larson St ....Jackson MS 39202	888-804-2108	601-352-2700	56
Paul Mueller Co			
1600 W Phelps St ....Springfield MO 65802	800-683-5537	417-831-3000	383
OTC: MUEL			
Paul Quinn College			
3837 Simpson Stuart Rd ....Dallas TX 75241	800-433-3243	214-376-1000	166
Paul Sawyier Public Library			
319 Wapping St ....Frankfort KY 40601	800-829-3676	502-352-2665	431-3
Paul Smith's College			
Rt 30 & 86 PO Box 265 ....Paul Smiths NY 12970	800-421-2605*	518-327-6227	166
*Admissions			
Paul Stuart Inc			
Madison Ave & 45th St ....New York NY 10017	800-678-8278*	212-682-0320	155-4
*Orders			
Paul W Bryant Museum			
300 Paul W Bryant Dr ....Tuscaloosa AL 35487	866-772-2327*	205-348-4668	515
*General			
Paulding-Putman Electric Co-op			
910 N Williams St ....Paulding OH 45879	800-686-2357	419-399-5015	245
Pauline Books & Media			
50 St Paul's Ave ....Boston MA 02130	800-876-4463*	617-522-8911	628-3
*Sales			

	Toll-Free	Phone	Class
Pavco Inc			
1935 John Crosland Jr Dr . . . . Charlotte NC 28208	800-321-7735*	704-496-6800	143
*Orders			
Pawleys Plantation			
70 Tanglewood Dr . . . . Pawleys Island SC 29585	800-367-9959	843-237-6000	660
Pawling Corp			
32 Nelson Hill Rd PO Box 200 . . . . Wassaic NY 12592	800-431-3456		667
PAWS (Performing Animal Welfare Society)			
11435 Simmerhorn Rd . . . . Galt CA 95632	800-513-6560	209-745-2606	47-3
Pax World Fund Family			
30 Penhallow St Ste 400. . . . . Portsmouth NH 03801	800-767-1729	603-431-8022	521
Paxton & Vierling Steel Co			
501 Ave H . . . . Carter Lake IA 51510	800-831-9252		475
Paxton Co			
1111 Ingleside Rd . . . . Norfolk VA 23502	800-234-7290	757-853-6781	760
Paxton Van Lines Inc			
5300 Port Royal Rd . . . . Springfield VA 22151	800-336-4536	703-321-7600	512
Pay Plus Benefits Inc			
1110 N Ctr Pkwy Ste B . . . . Kennewick WA 99336	888-531-5781	509-735-1143	623
Paychex Inc			
911 Panorama Trl S . . . . Rochester NY 14625	800-828-4411	585-385-6666	563
NASDAQ: PAYX			
Paycom			
7501 W Memorial Rd . . . . Oklahoma City OK 73142	800-580-4505		724
Payden & Rygel			
333 S Grand Ave . . . . Los Angeles CA 90071	800-572-9336	213-625-1900	398
Payless Drug Stores Inc			
16100 SW 72nd Ave			
PO Box 230969. . . . . Portland OR 97224	800-330-3665	503-626-9436	577
Payless ShoeSource Inc			
3231 SE Sixth Ave . . . . Topeka KS 66607	877-452-7500	785-233-5171	300
Payment Services Corp Inc			
360 Albert St Ste 1220 . . . . Ottawa ON K1R7X7	866-972-0616		316
Paymetric Inc			
1225 Northmeadow Pkwy Ste 110 . . . . Roswell GA 30076	888-445-4901	678-242-5281	2
Payne Engineering Co			
Rt 29 PO Box 70. . . . . Scott Depot WV 25560	800-331-1345*	304-757-7353	204
*Orders			
Payne Theological Seminary			
1230 Wilberforce Clifton Rd . . . . Wilberforce OH 45384	888-816-8933	937-376-2946	167-3
Paynes Creek Historic State Park			
888 Lake Branch Rd . . . . Bowling Green FL 33834	800-326-3521	863-375-4717	558
Pay-O-Matic Corp			
160 Oak Dr . . . . Syosset NY 11791	888-545-6311	516-496-4900	139
PayReel Inc			
24928 Genesee Trl Rd . . . . Golden CO 80401	800-352-7397	303-526-4900	507
Payroll Practitioner's Monthly			
Three Bethesda Metro Ctr			
Ste 250 . . . . Bethesda MD 20814	800-372-1033		524-2
Payson Casters Inc			
2323 N Delaney Rd . . . . Gurnee IL 60031	800-323-4552	847-336-6200	347
Payspan Inc			
7751 Belfort Pkwy Ste 200 . . . . Jacksonville FL 32256	877-331-7154		179-1
Payworks Inc			
1565 Willson Pl . . . . Winnipeg MB R3T4H1	866-788-3500		724
PB & H Moulding Corp			
124 Pickard Dr E . . . . Syracuse NY 13211	800-746-9724	315-455-5602	308
PBA (Professional Bowlers Assn)			
719 Second Ave Ste 701. . . . . Seattle WA 98104	877-910-2695	206-332-9688	47-22
PBA (Professional Beauty Assn)			
15825 N 71st St Ste 100. . . . . Scottsdale AZ 85254	800-468-2274	480-281-0424	48-18
PBCVB (Pine Bluff Convention & Visitors Bureau)			
One Convention Ctr Plz . . . . Pine Bluff AR 71601	800-536-7660	870-536-7600	207
PBEC (Polk-Burnett Electric Co-op)			
1001 State Rd 35 . . . . Centuria WI 54824	800-421-0283	715-646-2191	245
PBI Market Equipment Inc			
2667 Gundry Ave . . . . Signal Hill CA 90755	800-421-3753	562-595-4785	299
PBI/Gordon Corp			
1217 W 12th St			
PO Box 014090. . . . . Kansas City MO 64101	800-821-7925	816-421-4070	280
PBM Corp			
20600 Chagrin Blvd Ste 450. . . . . Cleveland OH 44122	800-341-5809	216-283-7999	38
PBM Graphics Inc			
3700 S Miami Blvd . . . . Durham NC 27703	800-849-8100	919-544-6222	619
PBM Inc			
1070 Sandy Hill Rd . . . . Irwin PA 15642	800-967-4726	724-863-0550	778
PBR (Professional Bull Riders Inc)			
101 W Riverwalk . . . . Pueblo CO 81003	800-366-8538	719-242-2800	47-15
PBS (Pacific Building Systems)			
2100 N Pacific Hwy . . . . Woodburn OR 97071	800-727-7844*	503-981-9581	104
*General			
PBS Supply Company Inc			
7013 S 216th St . . . . Kent WA 98032	877-727-7515	253-395-5550	527
PBSP (Pelican Bay State Prison)			
5905 Lake Earl Dr			
PO Box 7000. . . . . Crescent City CA 95531	877-256-6877	707-465-1000	213
PC Connection Inc			
730 Milford Rd Rt 101A . . . . Merrimack NH 03054	888-213-0607	603-683-2000	180
NASDAQ: PCCC			
PC Connection Inc MacConnection Div			
730 Milford Rd Rt 101A . . . . Merrimack NH 03054	888-213-0260		180
PC Gamer Magazine			
4000 Shoreline Ct			
Ste 400 . . . . South San Francisco CA 94080	877-404-1337	650-238-2505	452-14
PC Magazine			
28 E 28th St . . . . New York NY 10016	800-289-0429	212-503-3500	452-7
PC Mall Inc			
2555 W 190th St . . . . Torrance CA 90504	800-555-6255	310-354-5600	180
NASDAQ: PCMI			
PC Richard & Son Inc			
150 Price Pkwy . . . . Farmingdale NY 11735	800-696-2000	631-843-4300	34
PC World Communications Inc			
501 Second St . . . . San Francisco CA 94107	800-234-3498*	415-243-0505	628-9
*General			
PC/Nametag			
124 Horizon Dr PO Box 8604 . . . . Verona WI 53593	877-626-3824		179-8
PCA Engineering Inc			
57 Cannonball Rd			
PO Box 196. . . . . Pompton Lakes NJ 07442	800-666-7221	973-616-4501	261
PCB Group Inc			
3425 Walden Ave . . . . Depew NY 14043	800-828-8840	716-684-0001	253
PCBE Inc PO Box 1575 . . . . Tacoma WA 98401	800-540-8322	253-404-0891	452-5

	Toll-Free	Phone	Class
PCCA (Portable Computer & Communications Assn)			
PO Box 680 . . . . Hood River OR 97031	877-323-8888	541-490-5140	47-9
PCF (Prevent Cancer Foundation)			
1600 Duke St Ste 500. . . . . Alexandria VA 22314	800-227-2732	703-836-4412	47-17
PCGH (UH Parma Medical Center)			
7007 Powers Blvd . . . . Parma OH 44129	855-292-4292	440-743-3000	371-3
PCI (Project Concern International)			
5151 Murphy Canyon Rd Ste 320. . . . . San Diego CA 92123	877-724-4673	858-279-9690	47-5
PCMA (Professional Convention Management Assn)			
35 E Wacker Dr Ste 500 . . . . Chicago IL 60601	877-827-7262	312-423-7262	48-12
PCMR (Park City Mountain Resort)			
1345 Lowell Ave PO Box 39 . . . . Park City UT 84060	800-222-7275	435-649-8111	660
PCOM (Philadelphia College of Osteopathic Medicine)			
4170 City Ave . . . . Philadelphia PA 19131	800-999-6998*	215-871-6100	788
*Admissions			
PCR (Mid-Atlantic PenFed Realty Berkshire Hathaway HomeServices)			
3050 Chain Bridge Rd . . . . Fairfax VA 22030	800-550-2364	703-691-7653	646
PCRM (Physicians Committee for Responsible Medicine)			
5100 Wisconsin Ave NW			
Ste 400 . . . . Washington DC 20016	866-416-7276	202-686-2210	48-8
PCS (Precision Computer Services Inc)			
175 Constitution Blvd S . . . . Shelton CT 06484	800-340-9890	203-929-0000	176
PCS Co 34488 Doreka Dr . . . . Fraser MI 48026	800-521-0546	586-294-7780	747
PCTA (Pacific Crest Trail Assn)			
1331 Garden Hwy . . . . Sacramento CA 95833	888-728-7245	916-285-1846	47-23
PCTC (Park County Travel Council)			
836 Sheridan Ave PO Box 2454 . . . . Cody WY 82414	800-393-2639	307-587-2297	207
PDA (Presbyterian Disaster Assistance)			
100 Witherspoon St . . . . Louisville KY 40202	800-728-7228		47-5
PDA (Property Damage Appraisers Inc)			
6100 SW Blvd Ste 200 . . . . Fort Worth TX 76109	800-749-7324		309
PDC (Petroleum Development Corp)			
120 Genesis Blvd PO Box 26 . . . . Bridgeport WV 26330	800-624-3821	303-860-5800	529
NASDAQ: PDCE			
PDC Facilities Inc			
700 Walnut Ridge Dr . . . . Hartland WI 53029	800-545-5998	262-367-7700	187
PDCA (Painting & Decorating Contractors of America)			
2316 Millpark Dr			
Ste 220 . . . . Maryland Heights MO 63043	800-332-7322*	314-514-7322	48-3
*Cust Svc			
PDEMC (Pee Dee Electric Membership Corp)			
575 US Hwy 52 S . . . . Wadesboro NC 28170	800-992-1626	704-694-2114	245
PDF (Parkinson's Disease Foundation)			
1359 Broadway . . . . New York NY 10018	800-457-6676	212-923-4700	47-17
PDI (Pearlstine Distributors Inc)			
1600 Chrlston Rgonal Pkwy . . . . Charleston SC 29492	800-922-1048	843-388-6800	439
PDI Financial Group			
601 N Lynndale Dr . . . . Appleton WI 54914	800-234-7341	920-739-2303	681
PDI Inc			
300 Interpace Pkwy			
Morris Corp Ctr 1 Bldg A . . . . Parsippany NJ 07054	800-242-7494		196
NASDAQ: PDII			
PDK (Phi Delta Kappa International)			
408 N Union St . . . . Bloomington IN 47407	800-766-1156	812-339-1156	47-16
PDMA (Product Development & Management Assn)			
330 N Wabash Ave Ste 2000. . . . . Chicago IL 60611	800-232-5241	312-321-5145	48-12
PdMA Corp			
5909-C Hampton Oaks Pkwy . . . . Tampa FL 33610	800-476-6463	813-621-6463	202
PDQ Manufacturing Inc			
1698 Scheuring Rd . . . . De Pere WI 54115	800-227-3373	920-983-8333	383
PDRA (Paint & Decorating Retailers Assn)			
1401 Triad Ctr Dr . . . . Saint Peters MO 63376	800-737-0107	636-326-2636	48-18
PDS (Personnel Data Systems Inc)			
470 Norrifftown Rd Ste 202 . . . . Blue Bell PA 19422	800-243-8737	610-238-4600	179-1
PDS (Packaging Distribution Services Inc)			
2308 Sunset Rd . . . . Des Moines IA 50321	800-747-2699	515-243-3156	552
PDS Gaming Corp			
6280 Annie Oakley Dr . . . . Las Vegas NV 89120	800-479-3612	702-736-0700	216
PDSINC (Productive Data Solutions Inc)			
6160 S Syracuse Way			
Ste B160 . . . . Greenwood Village CO 80111	800-404-7165	303-220-7165	712
Pea River Electric Co-op			
1311 W Roy Parker Rd PO Box 969 . . . . Ozark AL 36360	800-264-7732	334-774-2545	245
Peabody Energy Corp			
Peabody Plz 701 Market St. . . . . St. Louis MO 63101	866-470-4500	314-342-3400	496
Peabody Institute of the Johns Hopkins University			
Peabody Conservatory of Music			
One E Mt Vernon Pl . . . . Baltimore MD 21202	800-368-2521	410-659-8110	166
Peabody Memphis			
149 Union Ave . . . . Memphis TN 38103	800-732-2639	901-529-4000	376
Peabody Supply Co Inc			
PO Box 669 . . . . Peabody MA 01960	800-445-5816	978-532-2200	605
Peace Bridge Duty Free Inc			
One Peace Bridge Plz			
PO Box 339. . . . . Fort Erie ON L2A5N1	800-361-1302		241
Peace Corps			
1111 20th St NW . . . . Washington DC 20526	800-424-8580	202-692-1040	338-18
Peace Corps Regional Offices			
Atlanta Regional Office			
1111 20th Street NW . . . . Washington DC 20526	855-855-1961	404-562-3456	338-18
Chicago Regional Office			
55 W Monroe St Ste 450 . . . . Chicago IL 60603	800-424-8580	312-353-4990	338-18
Dallas Regional Office			
1100 Commerce St Ste 427 . . . . Dallas TX 75242	855-855-1961		338-18
Los Angeles Regional Office			
2361 Rosecrans Ave Ste 155 . . . El Segundo CA 90245	800-424-8580	310-356-1100	338-18
Mid-Atlantic Regional Office			
1525 Wilson Blvd Ste 100 . . . . Arlington VA 22209	800-424-8580	202-692-1040	338-18
New York Regional Office			
201 Varick St Ste 1025. . . . . New York NY 10014	800-424-8580	212-352-5440	338-18
Northwest Regional Office			
1601 Fifth Ave Ste 605 . . . . Seattle WA 98101	800-424-8580	206-553-5490	338-18
San Francisco Regional Office			
1301 Clay St Ste 620-N . . . . Oakland CA 94610	800-424-8580	510-452-8444	338-18
Peace River Electric Co-op Inc			
210 Metheny Rd PO Box 1310 . . . . Wauchula FL 33873	800-282-3824		245
Peace River Regional Medical Ctr			
2500 Harbor Blvd . . . . Port Charlotte FL 33952	888-941-2495	941-766-4122	371-3
Peaceable Kingdom Press			
950 Gilman St Ste 200 . . . . Berkeley CA 94710	877-444-5195	510-558-2051	129
Peaceful Valley Ranch			
475 Peaceful Vly Rd . . . . Lyons CO 80540	800-955-6343	303-747-2881	239
PeaceHealth St Joseph Medical Ctr			
2901 Squalicum Pkwy . . . . Bellingham WA 98225	800-541-7209	360-734-5400	371-3

Name / Address	City	State	ZIP	Toll-Free	Phone	Class
Peach County School District Inc						
523 Vineville St	Fort Valley	GA	31030	**866-632-9992**	478-825-5933	676
Peach State Integrated Technologies Inc						
3005 Business Pk Dr	Norcross	GA	30071	**800-998-6517**	678-327-2000	383
Peach State Labs Inc (PSL)						
180 Burlington Rd PO Box 1087	Rome	GA	30162	**800-634-1653**	706-291-8743	143
Peachtree Planning Corp						
5040 Roswell Rd NE	Atlanta	GA	30342	**800-366-0839**	404-260-1600	112
Peacock Suites						
1745 S Anaheim Blvd	Anaheim	CA	92805	**800-522-6401**	714-535-8255	376
Peak 10						
752 Barret Ave	Louisville	KY	40204	**866-732-5836**	502-315-6015	177
Peak Nutrition Inc						
1097 11th St PO Box 87	Syracuse	NE	68446	**800-600-2069***	402-269-2825	787
*Sales						
Peak of the Market						
1200 King Edward St	Winnipeg	MB	R3H0R5	**888-289-7325**	204-632-7325	296-7
Peak Technical Services Inc						
583 Epsilon Dr	Pittsburgh	PA	15238	**888-888-7325**	412-696-1080	712
Peak Technologies Inc						
10330 Old Columbia Rd	Columbia	MD	21046	**800-926-9212**		175
Peaks Resort & Golden Door Spa						
136 Country Club Dr	Telluride	CO	81435	**800-789-2220**		660
Peapack-Gladstone Bank						
500 Hills Dr Ste 300						
PO Box 700	Bedminster	NJ	07921	**800-742-7595**	908-234-0700	357-2
NASDAQ: PGC						
Peapod LLC						
9933 Woods Dr	Skokie	IL	60077	**800-573-2763**	847-583-9400	342
Pearce Bevill Leesburg & Moore Pc						
110 Office Pk Dr	Birmingham	AL	35223	**800-654-1654**	205-323-5440	2
Pearl Harbor Federal Credit Union (PHFCU)						
94-449 Ukee St	Waipahu	HI	96797	**800-987-5583**		219
Pearl Hotel, The						
1410 Rosecrans St	San Diego	CA	92106	**877-732-7573**	619-226-6100	376
Pearl Meat Packing Company Inc						
27 York Ave	Randolph	MA	02368	**800-462-3022**	781-228-5100	468
Pearl River Community College						
101 Hwy 11 N	Poplarville	MS	39470	**877-772-2338**	601-403-1000	160
Pearl River Valley Electric Power Assn						
1422 Hwy 13 N PO Box 1217	Columbia	MS	39429	**855-277-8372**	601-736-2666	245
Pearland Area Chamber of Commerce						
6117 Broadway St	Pearland	TX	77581	**888-604-5888**	281-485-3634	137
Pearlstine Distributors Inc (PDI)						
1600 Chrlston Rgonal Pkwy	Charleston	SC	29492	**800-922-1048**	843-388-6800	439
Pearpoint Inc						
72055 Corporate Way	Thousand Palms	CA	92276	**800-688-8094**	760-343-7350	202
Pearson Co						
1420 Progress Ave	High Point	NC	27260	**800-225-0265**	336-882-8135	318-2
Pearson Dental Supplies Inc						
13161 Telfair Ave	Sylmar	CA	91342	**800-535-4535**	818-362-2600	470
Pearson Education Inc						
One Lake St	Upper Saddle River	NJ	07458	**800-922-0579***	201-236-6716	628-2
*Cust Svc						
Pearson Education School Div						
1900 E Lk Ave Ofc Ste B-110A	Glenview	IL	60025	**800-348-4474**		628-2
Pearson Packaging Systems						
8120 W Sunset Hwy	Spokane	WA	99224	**800-732-7766**	509-838-6226	540
Pearson's Candy Co						
2140 W Seventh St	Saint Paul	MN	55116	**800-328-6507***	651-698-0356	295-8
*Cust Svc						
Peavey Electronics Corp						
5022 Hartley Peavey Dr	Meridian	MS	39305	**877-732-8391**	601-483-5365	51
Pechanga Resort & Casino						
45000 Pechanga Pkwy	Temecula	CA	92592	**877-711-2946**	951-693-1819	660
Pecora Corp						
165 Wambold Rd	Harleysville	PA	19438	**800-523-6688**	215-723-6051	3
Peddinghaus Corp						
300 N Washington Ave	Bradley	IL	60915	**800-786-2448**	815-937-3800	450
Pedernales Electric Co-op Inc						
PO Box 1	Johnson City	TX	78636	**888-554-4732**	830-868-7155	245
Pediatric Services of America Inc						
310 Technology Pkwy	Norcross	GA	30092	**800-408-4442**	770-441-1580	360
Pediatrix Medical Group Inc						
1301 Concord Terr	Sunrise	FL	33323	**800-243-3839**	954-384-0175	458
Pedorthic Footwear Assn (PFA)						
2025 M St NW Ste 800	Washington	DC	20036	**800-673-8447**	202-367-1145	47-17
Pedowitz Group, The						
810 Mayfield Rd	Milton	GA	30009	**855-738-6584**		196
Pee Dee Electric Membership Corp (PDEMC)						
575 US Hwy 52 S	Wadesboro	NC	28170	**800-992-1626**	704-694-2114	245
Peebles Inc						
1 Peebles St	South Hill	VA	23970	**800-723-4548**	434-447-5200	229
Peelle Co						
373 Nesconset Hwy Ste 311	Hauppauge	NY	11788	**800-787-5020**	905-846-4545	234
Peer Bearing Co						
2200 Norman Dr S	Waukegan	IL	60085	**800-433-7337**	847-578-1000	74
Peer Foods Group Inc						
1200 W 35th St Ste 5E	Chicago	IL	60609	**800-365-5644**	773-927-1440	295-26
Peerless Chain Co						
1416 E Sanborn St	Winona	MN	55987	**800-533-8056**	507-457-9100	669
Peerless Cleaners Inc						
519 N Monroe St	Decatur	IL	62522	**800-879-7056**	217-423-7703	83
Peerless Electronics Inc						
700 Hicksville Rd	Bethpage	NY	11714	**800-285-2121**	516-594-3500	246
Peerless Food Equipment						
500 S Vandemark Rd	Sidney	OH	45365	**800-999-3327**	937-492-4158	297
Peerless Industrial Group						
PO Box 949	Clackamas	OR	97015	**800-547-6806**	800-873-1916	669
Peerless Insurance Co						
62 Maple Ave	Keene	NH	03431	**800-542-5385**	603-352-3221	388-4
Peerless Machinery Corp						
500 S Vandenmark Rd PO Box 769	Sidney	OH	45365	**877-795-7377**	937-492-4158	297
Peerless Manufacturing Co						
14651 N Dallas Pkwy Ste 500	Dallas	TX	75254	**877-879-7634**	214-357-6181	383
NASDAQ: PMFG						
Peerless Pottery Inc						
319 S Fifth St	Rockport	IN	47635	**800-457-5765**	800-457-5785	604
Peerless Premier Appliance Co						
119 S 14th St	Belleville	IL	62222	**800-858-5844**	941-763-3915	35
Peerless Products Inc						
2403 S Main St	Fort Scott	KS	66701	**800-279-9999**	620-223-4610	234
Peerless Pump Co						
2005 ML King Jr St						
PO Box 7026	Indianapolis	IN	46207	**800-879-0182**	317-925-9661	632
Peerless Steel Corp						
2450 Austin	Troy	MI	48083	**800-482-3947**	248-528-3200	487
Peerless Tire Co						
5000 Kingston St	Denver	CO	80239	**800-999-7810**	303-371-4300	53
Peery Hotel						
110 West 300 South	Salt Lake City	UT	84101	**800-331-0073**	801-521-4300	376
Peet Frate Line Inc						
650 S Eastwood Dr PO Box 1129	Woodstock	IL	60098	**800-435-6909**	815-338-5500	770
Peet's Coffee & Tea Inc						
1400 Pk Ave	Emeryville	CA	94608	**800-999-2132***	510-594-2100	157
NASDAQ: GMCR ■ *Orders						
Pegasus International Hotel						
501 Southard St	Key West	FL	33040	**800-397-8148**	305-294-9323	376
Pegasus Logistics Group Inc						
615 Freeport Pkwy Ste 100	Coppell	TX	75019	**800-997-7226**	469-671-0300	444
Pegasus Solutions Inc						
5430 LBJ Fwy Ste 1100	Dallas	TX	75240	**800-843-4343**	214-234-4000	333
Peggy Knight Solutions Inc						
1750 Bridgeway	Sausalito	CA	94965	**800-997-7753**	415-289-1777	345
Peg-Perego USA Inc						
3625 Independence Dr	Fort Wayne	IN	46808	**800-671-1701***	260-482-8191	63
*Cust Svc						
PEI-Genesis						
2180 Hornig Rd	Philadelphia	PA	19116	**800-675-1214**	215-673-0400	246
Peirce College						
1420 Pine St	Philadelphia	PA	19102	**888-467-3472**	215-545-6400	166
Peirce-Phelps Inc						
2000 N 59th St	Philadelphia	PA	19131	**800-222-2742**	215-879-7000	37
Pekin Insurance (FAIA)						
2505 Ct St	Pekin	IL	61558	**800-322-0160**	309-346-1161	388-4
Pekin Life Insurance Co						
2505 Ct St	Pekin	IL	61558	**800-322-0160**	309-346-1161	388-2
OTC: PKIN						
Peking Handicraft Inc						
1388 San Mateo Ave	South San Francisco	CA	94080	**800-872-6888**	650-871-3788	358
Peking Noodle Co Inc						
1514 N San Fernando Rd	Los Angeles	CA	90065	**877-735-4648**	323-223-2023	295-31
Pelco 3500 Pelco Way	Clovis	CA	93612	**800-289-9100**	559-292-1981	638
Pelham Hotel						
444 Common St	New Orleans	LA	70130	**888-856-4486**	504-522-4444	376
Pelican Bay State Prison (PBSP)						
5905 Lake Earl Dr						
PO Box 7000	Crescent City	CA	95531	**877-256-6877**	707-465-1000	213
Pelican Products Inc						
147 N Main St	South Deerfield	MA	01373	**800-542-7344**	413-665-2163	200
Pelican Rope Works Inc						
4001 W Carriage Dr	Santa Ana	CA	92704	**800-464-7673**	714-545-0116	209
Pelivan Transit						
333 S Oak St PO Box B	Big Cabin	OK	74332	**800-482-4594**	918-783-5793	107
Pella Co-op Electric Assn						
2615 Washington St	Pella	IA	50219	**800-619-1040**	641-628-1040	245
Pella Corp 102 Main St	Pella	IA	50219	**877-473-5527***	641-621-1000	236
*Cust Svc						
Pellettieri Rabstein & Altman						
100 Nassau Pk Blvd	Princeton	NJ	08540	**800-432-5297**	609-520-0900	425
Pembina Pipeline Corp						
700 Ninth Ave SW	Calgary	AB	T2P3V4	**888-428-3222**	403-231-7500	402
TSE: PPL						
Pembroke Hospital						
199 Oak St	Pembroke	MA	02359	**800-222-2237**	781-829-7000	371-5
Pembrooke Occupational Health Inc						
2307 N Parham Rd	Richmond	VA	23229	**888-378-4832**	804-346-1010	194
Pemco Inc						
3333 Crocker Ave	Sheboygan	WI	53082	**888-310-1898**	920-458-2500	549
Pemiscot-Dunklin Electric Co-op						
Hwy 412 W PO Box 509	Hayti	MO	63851	**800-558-6641**	573-757-6641	245
Pemko Mfg Company Inc						
4226 Transport St	Ventura	CA	93003	**800-283-9988**	805-642-2600	325
PEN Products						
2010 E New York St	Indianapolis	IN	46201	**800-736-2550**	317-955-6800	622
Penasco Valley Telecommunications (PVT)						
4011 W Main St	Artesia	NM	88210	**800-505-4844**		726
Pencco Inc						
831 Bartlett Rd PO Box 600	San Felipe	TX	77473	**800-864-1742**	979-885-0005	142
Pence Kelly Construction LLC						
2747 Pence Loop SE	Salem	OR	97302	**800-434-6654**	503-399-7223	187
Penco Products Inc						
99 Brower Ave	Oaks	PA	19456	**800-562-1000**	610-666-0500	318-1
Pencom Systems Inc						
152 Remsen St	Brooklyn	NY	11201	**800-736-2664**	718-923-1111	623
Penda Corp PO Box 449	Portage	WI	53901	**800-356-7704**		59
Pender Memorial Hospital						
507 E Fremont St	Burgaw	NC	28425	**888-468-5474**	910-259-5451	371-3
Pendle Hill						
338 Plush Mill Rd	Wallingford	PA	19086	**800-742-3150**	610-566-4507	664
Pendleton Grain Growers Inc						
1000 SW Dorian St PO Box 1248	Pendleton	OR	97801	**800-422-7611**	541-276-7611	275
Pendleton Woolen Mills Inc						
220 NW Broadway	Portland	OR	97209	**800-760-4844**	503-226-4801	153-5
PendoPharm Inc						
6111 Royalmount	Montreal	QC	H4P2T4	**866-926-7653***	514-340-5045	474
*Cust Svc						
Pendu Manufacturing Inc						
718 N Shirk Rd	New Holland	PA	17557	**800-233-0471**	717-354-4348	808
Pengo Corp						
500 E Hwy 10	Laurens	IA	50554	**800-599-0211***	712-845-2540	191
*Cust Svc						
Pengrowth Energy Trust						
222 Third Ave SW Ste 2100	Calgary	AB	T2P0B4	**800-223-4122**	403-233-0224	666
NYSE: PGH						
Penguin Group (USA) Inc						
375 Hudson St	New York	NY	10014	**800-847-5515***	212-366-2000	628-2
*Sales						
Penguin Hotel						
1418 Ocean Dr	Miami Beach	FL	33139	**800-499-7964**	305-534-9334	376
Penguin Point Franchise Systems Inc						
2691 E US 30 PO Box 975	Warsaw	IN	46580	**800-577-5755**	574-267-3107	661
Penguin Random House						
1745 Broadway	New York	NY	10019	**800-733-3000**	212-782-9000	628-2

Listing	City	State	Zip	Toll-Free	Phone	Class
Penguin Random House Inc						
Bantam Dell Publishing Group						
1745 Broadway 10th Fl	New York	NY	10019	**888-523-9292**	212-782-9000	628-2
Peninsula Airways Inc						
6100 Boeing Ave	Anchorage	AK	99502	**800-448-4226**	907-771-2500	25
Peninsula Asset Management Inc						
1111 Third Ave W Ste 340	Bradenton	FL	34205	**800-269-6417**		398
Peninsula Beverly Hills						
9882 S Santa Monica Blvd	Beverly Hills	CA	90212	**800-462-7899**	310-551-2888	376
Peninsula Chicago						
108 E Superior St	Chicago	IL	60611	**866-288-8889**	312-337-2888	376
Peninsula Daily News						
305 W First St PO Box 1330	Port Angeles	WA	98362	**800-826-7714**	360-452-2345	525-2
Peninsula Fine Arts Ctr						
101 Museum Dr	Newport News	VA	23606	**800-227-2788**	757-596-8175	49-1
Peninsula Hospital						
2347 Jones Bend Rd	Louisville	TN	37777	**800-526-8215**	865-970-9800	371-5
Peninsula Light Co						
13315 Goodnough Dr NW	Gig Harbor	WA	98332	**888-809-8021**	253-857-5950	245
Peninsula New York						
700 Fifth Ave	New York	NY	10019	**800-262-9467**	212-956-2888	376
Peninsula Regional Medical Ctr						
100 E Carroll St	Salisbury	MD	21801	**800-543-7780**	410-546-6400	371-3
Penn Aluminum International Inc						
1117 N Second St PO Box 490	Murphysboro	IL	62966	**800-445-7366***	618-684-2146	480
*All						
Penn Color Inc						
400 Old Dublin Pk	Doylestown	PA	18901	**866-617-7366**	215-345-6550	543
Penn Commercial Inc						
242 Oak Spring Rd	Washington	PA	15301	**888-309-7484**	724-222-5330	788
Penn Emblem Co						
10909 Dutton Rd	Philadelphia	PA	19154	**800-793-7366**		258
Penn Fibre Plastics						
2434 Bristol Rd	Bensalem	PA	19020	**800-662-7366***		593
*Cust Svc						
Penn Insurance & Annuity Co						
600 Dresher Rd	Horsham	PA	19044	**800-523-0650***	215-956-8000	388-2
*Cust Svc						
Penn Line Service Inc						
300 Scottdale Ave	Scottdale	PA	15683	**800-448-9110***	724-887-9110	189-10
*All						
Penn Machine Co						
106 Stn St	Johnstown	PA	15905	**800-736-6872**	814-288-1547	588
Penn Millers Insurance Co						
72 N Franklin St PO Box P	Wilkes-Barre	PA	18773	**800-233-8347**		388-4
Penn Mutual Life Insurance Co						
600 Dresher Rd	Horsham	PA	19044	**800-523-0650***	215-956-8000	388-2
*Cust Svc						
Penn National Gaming Inc						
825 Berkshire Blvd Ste 200	Wyomissing	PA	19610	**877-565-2112**		633
NASDAQ: PENN						
Penn National Insurance Co						
2 N Second St PO Box 2361	Harrisburg	PA	17101	**800-388-4764**	717-234-4941	388-4
Penn Presbyterian Medical Ctr (PPMC)						
39th & Market Sts	Philadelphia	PA	19104	**800-789-7366**	215-662-8000	371-3
Penn Stater Conference Ctr Hotel						
215 Innovation Blvd	State College	PA	16803	**800-233-7505**	814-863-5000	374
Penn Treaty American Corp						
3440 Lehigh St	Allentown	PA	18103	**800-362-0700**		357-4
Penn Treaty Network America Insurance Co						
3440 Lehigh St	Allentown	PA	18103	**800-362-0700**		388-2
Penn United Technology Inc						
799 N Pike Rd	Cabot	PA	16023	**866-572-7537**	724-352-1507	747
Penn Virginia Corp						
100 Matsonford Rd Ste 200	Radnor	PA	19087	**877-316-5288**	610-687-8900	529
NYSE: PVA						
Penn West Energy Trust						
425 First St SW Ste 2200	Calgary	AB	T2P3L8	**866-693-2707**	403-777-2500	666
Penn West Petroleum Ltd						
Ninth Ave SW Ste 200	Calgary	AB	T2P1K3	**866-693-2707**	403-777-2500	529
TSE: PWT						
Penn's Best Inc						
PO Box 128	Meshoppen	PA	18630	**800-852-3243**		770
Penn's View Hotel						
14 N Front St	Philadelphia	PA	19106	**800-331-7634**	215-922-7600	376
Pennco Tech						
3815 Otter St	Bristol	PA	19007	**844-226-0975***	215-785-0111	788
*General						
Penncorp Servicegroup Inc						
600 N Second St Ste 401	Harrisburg	PA	17101	**800-544-9050**	717-234-2300	626
PennEngineering & Manufacturing Corp						
5190 Old Easton Rd	Danboro	PA	18916	**800-237-4736**	215-766-8853	278
Pennichuck Corp						
25 Manchester St	Merrimack	NH	03054	**800-553-5191**	603-882-5191	775
NASDAQ: PNNW						
Pennington Seed Inc						
1280 AtlantaHwy	Madison	GA	30650	**800-285-7333**	706-342-1234	685
Penn-Plax Inc						
35 Marcus Blvd	Hauppauge	NY	11788	**800-645-6055**	631-273-3787	571
Penns Grove-Carneys Point Regional Board of Education						
100 Iona Ave	Penns Grove	NJ	08069	**877-652-7624**	856-299-4250	676
PennSuburban Chamber of Commerce						
34 Susquehanna Ave	Lansdale	PA	19446	**800-847-9772**	215-362-9200	137
Pennsylvania						
Banking Dept						
17 N Second St						
Market Square Plz	Harrisburg	PA	17101	**800-722-2657**	717-783-4721	337-39
Insurance Dept						
1326 Strawberry Sq	Harrisburg	PA	17120	**877-881-6388**		337-39
Public Utility Commission						
400 N St Keystone Bldg						
PO Box 3265	Harrisburg	PA	17120	**800-692-7380**	717-783-1740	337-39
State Parks Bureau						
PO Box 8551	Harrisburg	PA	17105	**888-727-2757**	717-787-6640	337-39
Transportation Dept						
400 N St	Harrisburg	PA	17120	**800-932-4600**	717-787-2838	337-39
Vocational Rehabilitation Office (OVR)						
1521 N Sixth St	Harrisburg	PA	17102	**800-442-6351**	717-787-5244	337-39
Workers Compensation Bureau						
1171 S Cameron St Rm 324	Harrisburg	PA	17104	**800-482-2383**	717-783-5421	337-39
Pennsylvania Academy of the Fine Arts						
School of Fine Arts						
118 N Broad St	Philadelphia	PA	19102	**800-799-7233**	215-972-7600	162

Listing	City	State	Zip	Toll-Free	Phone	Class
Pennsylvania Academy of the Fine Arts Museum (PAFA)						
118 N Broad St	Philadelphia	PA	19102	**800-799-7233**	215-972-7600	513
Pennsylvania Anthracite Heritage Museum						
RR1 Bald Mountain Rd	Scranton	PA	18504	**800-732-0999**	570-963-4804	513
Pennsylvania Assn of Realtors						
4501 Chambers Hill Rd	Harrisburg	PA	17111	**800-555-3390**	717-561-1303	647
Pennsylvania Assn of Staff Nurses & Allied Professionals (PASNAP)						
One Fayette St Ste 475	Conshohocken	PA	19428	**800-500-7850**	610-567-2907	526
Pennsylvania Ballet						
1819 John F Kennedy Blvd	Philadelphia	PA	19103	**800-732-0999**	215-551-7000	566-1
Pennsylvania Bar Assn						
100 S St	Harrisburg	PA	17101	**800-932-0311**	717-238-6715	71
Pennsylvania Bar News						
100 S St	Harrisburg	PA	17101	**800-932-0311**	717-238-6715	452-15
Pennsylvania Chamber of Business & Industry						
417 Walnut St	Harrisburg	PA	17101	**800-225-7224**	717-255-3252	138
Pennsylvania College of Technology						
One College Ave	Williamsport	PA	17701	**800-367-9222***	570-326-3761	788
*Admissions						
Pennsylvania Convention Ctr						
1101 Arch St	Philadelphia	PA	19107	**800-428-9000**	215-418-4700	206
Pennsylvania Correctional Industries						
PO Box 47	Camp Hill	PA	17001	**877-673-3724***	717-425-7292	622
*General						
Pennsylvania Democratic Party						
300 N Second St 8th Fl	Harrisburg	PA	17101	**800-437-7439**	717-920-8470	609-1
Pennsylvania Dutch Candies						
1250 Slate Hill Rd	Camp Hill	PA	17011	**800-233-7082**	717-761-5440	295-8
Pennsylvania Higher Education Assistance Agency						
1200 N Seventh St	Harrisburg	PA	17102	**800-233-0557**		716
Pennsylvania Hospital						
800 Spruce St	Philadelphia	PA	19107	**800-789-7366**	215-829-3000	371-3
Pennsylvania Institute of Technology (PIT)						
800 Manchester Ave	Media	PA	19063	**800-422-0025***	610-892-1500	788
*Admissions						
Pennsylvania Manufacturers Assn Co						
380 Sentry Pkwy	Blue Bell	PA	19422	**800-222-2749**		388-4
Pennsylvania Medical Society Liability Insurance Co (PMSLIC)						
1700 Bent Creek Blvd						
PO Box 2080	Mechanicsburg	PA	17050	**800-445-1212**	717-791-1212	388-5
Pennsylvania Real Estate Investment Trust						
200 S Broad St Third Fl	Philadelphia	PA	19102	**866-875-0700**	215-875-0700	646
NYSE: PEI						
Pennsylvania State Employees Credit Union						
One Credit Union Pl	Harrisburg	PA	17110	**800-237-7328**	717-234-8484	219
Pennsylvania State Ethics Commission						
309 Finance Bldg						
PO Box 11470	Harrisburg	PA	17108	**800-932-0936**	717-783-1610	265
Pennsylvania State System of Higher Education						
2986 N Second St	Harrisburg	PA	17110	**800-732-0999**	717-720-4000	337-39
Pennsylvania State University						
Altoona						
3000 Ivyside Pk	Altoona	PA	16601	**800-848-9843**	814-949-5466	166
Beaver						
100 University Dr	Monaca	PA	15061	**877-564-6778**	724-773-3500	160
DuBois One College Pl	Du Bois	PA	15801	**800-346-7627**	814-375-4700	160
Fayette						
2201 University Dr	Lemont Furnace	PA	15456	**877-568-4130**	724-430-4100	160
Harrisburg						
777 W Harrisburg Pk	Middletown	PA	17057	**800-222-2056**	717-948-6250	166
Hazleton						
76 University Dr	Hazleton	PA	18202	**800-279-8495**	570-450-3000	160
Mont Alto						
One Campus Dr	Mont Alto	PA	17237	**800-392-6173**	717-749-6000	160
Schuylkill						
200 University Dr	Schuylkill Haven	PA	17972	**800-243-2374**	570-385-6000	160
Shenango						
147 Shenango Ave	Sharon	PA	16146	**888-275-7009**	724-983-2803	160
York 1031 Edgecomb Ave	York	PA	17403	**800-778-6227**	717-771-4000	160
Pennsylvania State University at Erie						
Behrend College						
4701 College Dr	Erie	PA	16563	**866-374-3378**	814-898-6000	166
Pennsylvania State University Dickinson School of Law						
150 S College St	Carlisle	PA	17013	**800-840-1122**	717-240-5000	167-1
Pennsylvania State University Press						
820 N University Dr						
USB1 Ste C	University Park	PA	16802	**800-326-9180**	814-865-1327	628-4
Pennsylvania Tool & Gages Inc						
PO Box 534	Meadville	PA	16335	**877-827-8285**	814-336-3136	747
Pennsylvania Trust Co						
Five Radnor Corp Ctr Ste 450	Radnor	PA	19087	**800-975-4316**	610-975-4300	681
Penny Laine Papers						
2211 Century Ctr Blvd Ste 110	Irving	TX	75062	**800-456-6484**	972-812-3000	129
Pennyrile Forest State Resort Park						
20781 Pennyrile Lodge Rd	Dawson Springs	KY	42408	**800-325-1711**		558
Pennyrile Rural Electric Co-op Corp						
2000 Harrison St						
PO Box 2900	Hopkinsville	KY	42241	**800-297-4710***	270-886-2555	245
*Cust Svc						
Penobscot Marine Museum						
Five Church St PO Box 498	Searsport	ME	04974	**800-268-8030**	207-548-2529	513
Penobscot McCrum LLC						
28 Pierce St	Belfast	ME	04915	**800-435-4456**	207-338-4360	295-21
Penray Cos Inc						
440 Denniston Ct	Wheeling	IL	60090	**800-373-6729**	847-459-5000	143
Penrod Co						
2809 S Lynnhaven Rd						
Ste 350	Virginia Beach	VA	23452	**800-537-3497**	757-498-0186	192-2
Pensacola Aviation Ctr Inc						
4145 Jerry L MayGarden Rd	Pensacola	FL	32504	**800-874-6580**	850-434-0636	62
Pensacola Christian College						
250 Brent Ln	Pensacola	FL	32503	**800-722-4636**	850-478-8496	166
Pensacola Convention & Visitors Bureau						
1401 E Gregory St	Pensacola	FL	32502	**800-874-1234**	850-434-1234	207
Pensacola Greyhound Track						
951 Dog Track Rd	Pensacola	FL	32506	**800-345-3997**	850-455-8595	633
Pensacola Gulf Coast Regional Airport						
2430 Airport Blvd Ste 225	Pensacola	FL	32504	**800-874-6580**	850-436-5000	27
Pensacola Junior College						
Warrington						
5555 W Hwy 98	Pensacola	FL	32507	**888-897-3605**	850-484-2200	160

Name / Address	City	State	ZIP	Toll-Free	Phone	Class
Pension Benefit Guaranty Corp						
1200 K St NW	Washington	DC	20005	800-400-7242*	202-326-4000	338-18
*Cust Svc						
Pension Rights Ctr						
1350 Connecticut Ave NW						
Ste 206	Washington	DC	20036	866-735-7737	202-296-3776	47-6
Pensions & Investments Magazine						
711 Third Ave	New York	NY	10017	888-446-1422*	212-210-0100	452-5
*Cust Svc						
Penske Vehicle Services Inc						
1225 E Maple Rd	Troy	MI	48083	877-210-5290	248-729-5400	195
Pentagon 2000 Software Inc						
15 W 34th St Fifth Fl	New York	NY	10001	800-643-1806	212-629-7521	179-1
Pentagon Federal Credit Union						
2930 Eisenhower Ave	Alexandria	VA	22314	800-247-5626		219
Pentagroup Financial LLC						
5959 Corp Dr Ste 1400	Houston	TX	77036	800-385-9060	832-615-2100	158
Pentair						
7433 Harwin Dr	Houston	TX	77036	800-545-6258		202
Pentair Ltd						
1351 Rt 55	Lagrangeville	NY	12540	888-711-7487	845-463-7200	701
Pentair Residential Filtration LLC						
20580 Enterprise Ave	Brookfield	WI	53008	888-784-9065	262-784-4490	90
Pentair Water Pool & Spa						
1620 Hawkins Ave	Sanford	NC	27330	800-831-7133		632
Pentastar Aviation						
7310 Highland Rd	Waterford	MI	48327	800-662-9612	248-666-3630	13
Pentax Imaging Co						
633 17th St Ste 2600	Denver	CO	80202	800-877-0155	303-799-8000	174-6
Pentecostal Assemblies						
3214 S Service Rd	Burlington	ON	L7N3J2	800-295-6368	905-637-7558	47-20
Pentecostal Theological Seminary						
900 Walker St NE	Cleveland	TN	37311	800-228-9126	423-478-1131	167-3
PenTeleData						
540 Delaware Ave PO Box 197	Palmerton	PA	18071	800-281-3564		225
Penticton & Wine Country Chamber of Commerce						
553 Railway St	Penticton	BC	V2A8S3	800-663-5052	250-492-4103	136
Pentron Clinical Technologies LLC						
53 N Plains Industrial Rd	Wallingford	CT	06492	800-243-3969		228
Pentwater Wire Products Inc (PWP)						
474 Carroll St PO Box 947	Pentwater	MI	49449	877-869-6911	231-869-6911	286
People for the American Way (PFAW)						
2000 M St NW Ste 400	Washington	DC	20036	800-326-7329	202-467-4999	47-7
People for the Ethical Treatment of Animals (PETA)						
501 Front St	Norfolk	VA	23510	800-248-7729	757-622-7382	47-3
People Lease Inc						
689 Town Ctr Blvd Ste B	Ridgeland	MS	39157	800-723-3025	601-987-3025	623
People Magazine						
Rockefeller Ctr						
Time & Life Bldg	New York	NY	10020	800-541-9000	212-522-3347	452-11
People's Energy Co-op						
1775 Lk Shady Ave S	Oronoco	MN	55960	800-214-2694	507-367-7000	245
People's Light & Theatre Co						
39 Conestoga Rd	Malvern	PA	19355	800-732-0999	610-647-1900	738
People's Mutual Holdings						
850 Main St	Bridgeport	CT	06604	800-392-3009	203-338-7171	357-2
People's Securities Inc						
850 Main St	Bridgeport	CT	06601	800-772-4400	203-338-0800	681
People's United Bank						
850 Main St Bridgeport Ctr	Bridgeport	CT	06604	800-772-1090	203-338-7171	69
Peoples Bancorp Inc						
138 Putnam St	Marietta	OH	45750	800-374-6123	740-373-3155	357-2
NASDAQ: PEBO						
Peoples Bancorp of North Carolina Inc						
518 W 'C' St	Newton	NC	28658	800-948-7195	828-464-5620	357-2
NASDAQ: PEBK						
Peoples Educational Holdings Inc						
299 Market St	Saddle Brook	NJ	07663	800-822-1080	201-712-0090	628-2
OTC: PEDH						
Peoples Financial Services Corp						
82 Franklin Ave	Hallstead	PA	18822	888-868-3858	570-879-2175	69
NASDAQ: PFIS						
Peoples Gas Light & Coke Co						
130 E Randolph Dr	Chicago	IL	60601	866-556-6001*	312-240-4000	775
*Cust Svc						
Peoples National Bank						
5175 N Academy Blvd	Colorado Springs	CO	80918	800-862-6696	719-528-4000	69
Peoples Savings Bank (PSB)						
414 N Adams PO Box 248	Wellsburg	IA	50680	877-493-3799	641-869-3721	69
PeopleStrategy Inc						
5883 Glenridge Dr Ste 200	Atlanta	GA	30328	855-488-4100		179-1
People-to-People Health Foundation						
255 Carter Hall Ln	Millwood	VA	22646	800-544-4673	540-837-2100	47-5
Peoria Area Convention & Visitors Bureau						
456 Fulton St Ste 300	Peoria	IL	61602	800-747-0302	309-676-0303	207
Peoria Journal Star						
One News Plz	Peoria	IL	61643	800-225-5757	309-686-3000	525-2
PEP Filters Inc						
322 Rolling Hill Rd	Mooresville	NC	28117	800-243-4583	704-662-3133	794
PEPCO (Professional Electric Products Co)						
33210 Lakeland Blvd	Eastlake	OH	44095	800-872-7000	440-946-3790	246
Pepco Energy Services Inc						
1300 N 17th St Ste 1600	Arlington	VA	22209	800-424-8028	703-253-1800	775
Pepperball Technologies Inc						
6540 Lusk Blvd Ste C137	San Diego	CA	92121	877-887-3773	858-638-0236	752
Pepperidge Farm Inc						
595 Westport Ave	Norwalk	CT	06851	888-737-7374*	203-846-7000	295-1
*PR						
Peppermill Hotel & Casino						
2707 S Virginia St	Reno	NV	89502	800-648-6992	775-826-2121	132
Pepsi Bottling Ventures LLC						
4141 Parklake Ave Ste 600	Raleigh	NC	27612	800-662-8792	919-865-2300	295-37
PepsiCo Inc						
700 Anderson Hill Rd	Purchase	NY	10577	800-433-2652*	914-253-2000	186
NYSE: PEP ▦ *PR						
Peptides International Inc						
11621 Electron Dr	Louisville	KY	40299	800-777-4779	502-266-8787	231
Per Mar Security						
1910 E Kimberly Rd	Davenport	IA	52807	800-473-7627	563-359-3200	683
Perceptics Corp						
9737 Cogdill Rd Ste 200	Knoxville	TN	37932	800-448-8544		179-12
Percival Scientific Inc						
505 Research Dr	Perry	IA	50220	800-695-2743	515-465-9363	417
Percussion Software Inc						
600 Unicorn Pk Dr	Woburn	MA	01801	800-283-0800	781-438-9900	179-1
Percussive Arts Society (PAS)						
110 W Washington St	Indianapolis	IN	46204	888-990-6663	317-974-4488	47-4
Perdido Beach Resort						
27200 Perdido Beach Blvd	Orange Beach	AL	36561	800-634-8001	251-981-9811	660
Perdue Farms Inc						
31149 Old Ocean City Rd	Salisbury	MD	21804	800-473-7383	410-543-3000	612
Peregrine Pharmaceuticals Inc						
14282 Franklin Ave Ste 100	Tustin	CA	92780	800-987-8256	714-508-6000	84
NASDAQ: PPHM						
Perennial Public Power District						
2122 S Lincoln Ave	York	NE	68467	800-289-0288	402-362-3355	245
Perfecseal Inc						
3500 N Main St PO Box 2968	Oshkosh	WI	54903	888-871-8574	920-303-7000	541
Perfect Commerce Inc						
One Compass Way Ste 120	Newport News	VA	23606	877-871-3788*	757-766-8211	38
*Sales						
Perfect Shutters Inc						
12213 Rte 173	Hebron	IL	60034	800-548-3336	815-648-2401	690
Perfect Turf Inc						
622 Sandpebble Dr	Schaumburg	IL	60193	888-796-8873		594
PerfectData Corp						
1323 Conshohocken Rd	Plymouth Meeting	PA	19462	800-973-7332		527
Perfection Clutch Co						
100 Perfection Way	Timmonsville	SC	29161	800-258-8312	843-326-5544	59
Performance Contracting Group Inc						
16400 College Blvd	Lenexa	KS	66219	800-255-6886	913-888-8600	190-10
Performance Inc						
One Performance Way	Chapel Hill	NC	27514	800-727-2453*		702
*Cust Svc						
Performance Office Papers						
21565 Hamburg Ave	Lakeville	MN	55044	800-458-7189		109
Performing Animal Welfare Society (PAWS)						
11435 Simmerhorn Rd	Galt	CA	95632	800-513-6560	209-745-2606	47-3
Pergo Inc						
3128 Highwoods Blvd Ste 100	Raleigh	NC	27604	800-337-3746	919-773-6000	291
Pericom Semiconductor Corp						
3545 N First St	San Jose	CA	95134	800-435-2336	408-435-0800	687
NASDAQ: PSEM						
Perillo Tours						
577 Chestnut Ridge Rd	Woodcliff Lake	NJ	07677	800-431-1515	201-307-1234	750
Peripheral Dynamics Inc						
5150 Campus Dr						
Whitemarsh Industrial Pk	Plymouth Meeting	PA	19462	800-523-0253	610-825-7090	174-7
Peripheral Manufacturing Inc						
4775 Paris St	Denver	CO	80239	800-468-6888	303-371-8651	649
Perkasie Industries Corp						
PO Box 179	Perkasie	PA	18944	800-523-6747*	215-257-6581	595
*Sales						
Perkins Coie LLP						
1201 Third Ave Ste 4800	Seattle	WA	98101	888-720-8382	206-359-8000	425
Perkins Equipment Div						
630 John Hancock Rd	Taunton	MA	02780	800-733-5708	508-824-2800	299
Perkins Restaurant & Bakery						
6075 Poplar Ave Ste 800	Memphis	TN	38119	800-877-7375	901-766-6400	661
Perkiomen School						
200 Seminary St PO Box 130	Pennsburg	PA	18073	866-966-9998	215-679-9511	615
Perkiomen Valley Chamber of Commerce						
351 E Main St	Collegeville	PA	19426	800-349-7623	610-489-6660	137
Perley-Halladay Assn Inc						
1037 Andrew Dr	West Chester	PA	19380	800-248-5800	610-296-5800	791-2
Perlick Corp						
8300 W Good Hope Rd	Milwaukee	WI	53223	800-558-5592	414-353-7060	655
Perma-Bound						
617 E Vandalia Rd	Jacksonville	IL	62650	800-637-6581	217-243-5451	91
Permadur Industries Inc						
186 Rt 206 S	Hillsborough	NJ	08844	800-392-0146	908-359-9767	383
Perma-Fix Environmental Services Inc						
8302 Dunwoody Pl Ste 250	Atlanta	GA	30350	800-365-6066	770-587-9898	658
NASDAQ: PESI						
Perma-Glaze Inc						
1638 Research Loop Rd Ste 160	Tucson	AZ	85710	800-332-7397	520-722-9718	190-11
Permatron Group						
2020 Touhy Ave	Elk Grove Village	IL	60007	800-882-8012	847-434-1421	17
Permco Inc						
1500 Frost Rd	Streetsboro	OH	44241	800-628-2801	330-626-2801	631
Pernod Ricard USA						
100 Manhattanville Rd	Purchase	NY	10577	800-847-5949	914-848-4800	80-3
Perreca Electric Co						
520 Broadway	Newburgh	NY	12550	800-973-7732	845-562-4080	190-4
Perrigo Co						
515 Eastern Ave	Allegan	MI	49010	800-719-9260	269-673-8451	577
NYSE: PRGO						
Perry County						
333 7th St	Tell City	IN	47586	888-343-6262	812-547-7933	336
Perry Homes						
PO Box 34306	Houston	TX	77234	800-247-3779	713-947-1750	188
Perry's Ice Cream Company Inc						
One Ice Cream Plz	Akron	NY	14001	800-873-7797	716-542-5492	295-25
Perseus Books Group, The						
210 American Dr	Jackson	TN	38301	800-343-4499	731-426-6061	628-2
Perseverance Theatre						
914 Third St	Douglas	AK	99824	855-462-8497	907-364-2421	566-4
Persimmon Press						
PO Box 297	Belmont	CA	94002	800-910-5080	650-802-8325	129
Person & Covey Inc						
616 Allen Ave	Glendale	CA	91201	800-423-2341		215
Person County Public Schools						
304 S Morgan St	Roxboro	NC	27573	866-724-6650	336-599-2191	676
Personal Capital Corp						
726 Main St	Redwood City	CA	94063	855-855-8005		398
Personal Finance Newsletter						
7600A Leesburg Pk						
W Bldg Ste 300	Falls Church	VA	22043	800-832-2330	703-394-4931	524-9
PersonalizeDx						
17500 Red Hill Ave Ste 210	Irvine	CA	92614	877-429-6643		412
Personal-Touch Home Care Inc						
186-18 Hillside Ave	Jamaica	NY	11432	888-275-4147	718-468-2500	360
Personnel Data Systems Inc (PDS)						
470 Norristown Rd Ste 202	Blue Bell	PA	19422	800-243-8737	610-238-4600	179-1
Personnel Decisions International Corp						
33 S Sixth St Ste 4900	Minneapolis	MN	55402	800-344-2415	612-339-0927	194

Alphabetical Section

	Toll-Free	Phone	Class
Personnel Management Inc			
PO Box 6657 ....Shreveport LA 71136	**800-259-4126**	318-869-4555	623
Persons Majestic Mfg Co			
PO Box 370 ....Huron OH 44839	**800-772-2453**	419-433-9057	510
Perspectives Ltd			
20 N Clark St Ste 2650 ....Chicago IL 60602	**800-866-7556**	312-558-5318	457
Perstorp Polyols Inc			
600 Matzinger Rd ....Toledo OH 43612	**800-537-0280***	419-729-5448	142
*Cust Svc			
Perteet Inc			
2707 Colby Ave Ste 900 Ste900 ....Everett WA 98201	**800-615-9900**	425-252-7700	261
Peru			
Consulate General			
5177 Richmond Ave Ste 695 ....Houston TX 77056	**800-444-1027**	713-355-9517	257
Consulate General			
870 Market St Ste 1067 ....San Francisco CA 94102	**877-714-7378**	415-362-7136	257
Consulate General			
100 Hamilton Plaza ....Paterson NJ 07505	**877-714-7378**	973-278-3324	257
Consulate General			
3450 Wilshire Blvd Ste 800 ....Los Angeles CA 90010	**800-444-1027**	213-252-5910	257
Consulate General			
444 Brickell Ave Ste M135 ....Miami FL 33131	**877-714-7378**		257
Consulate General			
180 N Michigan Ave Ste 1830 ....Chicago IL 60601	**877-714-7378**	312-782-1599	257
Peru State College			
600 Hoyt St PO Box 10...........Peru NE 68421	**800-742-4412**	402-872-3815	166
Pervasive Software Inc			
12365 Riata Trace Pkwy Bldg B ....Austin TX 78727	**800-287-4383**	512-231-6000	179-12
NASDAQ: PVSW			
Peryam & Kroll Research Corp			
6323 N Avondale Ave ....Chicago IL 60631	**800-747-5522**	800-281-3155	659
PES (IEEE Power Engineering Society)			
IEEE Operations Ctr			
445 Hoes Ln ....Piscataway NJ 08854	**800-678-4333**	732-562-3883	48-19
Pet Industry Joint Advisory Council (PIJAC)			
1220 19th St NW Ste 400..........Washington DC 20036	**800-553-7387**	202-452-1525	48-4
Pet Safe International			
10427 Electric Ave ....Knoxville TN 37932	**800-732-2677***	865-777-5404	571
*Cust Svc			
Pet Sitters International (PSI)			
201 E King St ....King NC 27021	**800-325-7353**	336-983-9222	47-3
Pet Supermarket Inc			
1100 International Pkwy ....Sunrise FL 33323	**866-434-1990**	954-351-0834	571
Pet Supplies Inc			
Customer Service Return Ctr			
1 Maplewood Dr ....Hazleton PA 18202	**800-738-7877**		779
Pet Valu Canada Inc			
225 Royal Crest Crt ....Markham ON L3R9X6	**800-845-4759**	905-946-1200	571
Pet's Health Plan			
3840 Greentree Ave SW ....Canton OH 44706	**800-807-6724**	330-484-8080	388-1
PETA (People for the Ethical Treatment of Animals)			
501 Front St ....Norfolk VA 23510	**800-248-7729**	757-622-7382	47-3
PETCO Animal Supplies Inc			
9125 Rehco Rd ....San Diego CA 92121	**877-738-6742**	858-453-7845	571
Petco Park			
100 Pk Blvd ....San Diego CA 92101	**866-800-1275**	619-795-5000	711
Pete Gross House			
525 Minor Ave N ....Seattle WA 98109	**800-331-3131**	206-262-1000	369
Peter Gillhams Natural Vitality			
4879 Fountain Ave ....Los Angeles CA 90029	**888-324-9904**		296-8
Peter Glenn Ski & Sports			
2901 W Oakland Pk Blvd ....Fort Lauderdale FL 33311	**800-818-0946**	954-484-3606	702
Peter Pan Bus Lines			
PO Box 1776 ....Springfield MA 01102	**800-343-9999**		106
Peter Pan Bus Lines Inc			
1776 Main St ....Springfield MA 01103	**800-237-8747**	413-786-9300	107
Peter Pan Seafoods Inc			
2200 Sixth Ave Ste 1000 ....Seattle WA 98121	**800-331-3522**	206-728-6000	295-13
Peter Paul Electronics Co Inc			
480 John Downey Dr ....New Britain CT 06051	**800-825-8377**	860-229-4884	777
Peter Pepper Products Inc			
17929 S Susana Rd ....Compton CA 90221	**800-496-0204**	310-639-0390	584
Peter Piper Inc			
950 W Behrend Dr Ste 102.........Phoenix AZ 85027	**800-899-3425**	480-609-6400	661
Peter White Public Library			
217 N Front St ....Marquette MI 49855	**800-992-9012**	906-228-9510	431-3
Petersburg Fisheries			
PO Box 1147 ....Petersburg AK 99833	**877-772-4294**	907-772-4294	295-13
Petersen Aluminum Corp			
1005 Tonne Rd ....Elk Grove Village IL 60007	**800-323-1960**	847-228-7150	688
Petersen Automotive Museum			
6060 Wilshire Blvd ....Los Angeles CA 90036	**800-546-7866**	323-930-2277	513
Petersen Inc			
1527 North 2000 West ....Ogden UT 84404	**800-410-6789**	801-732-2000	355
Peterson Industries Inc			
616 E Hwy 36 ....Smith Center KS 66967	**800-368-3759**	785-282-6825	119
Peterson Machine Tool Inc			
1100 N Union St ....Council Grove KS 66846	**800-835-3528**		383
Peterson Manufacturing Co			
4200 E 135th St ....Grandview MO 64030	**800-821-3490**	816-765-2000	434
Peterson Steel Corp			
61 W Mountain St ....Worcester MA 01606	**800-325-3245**	508-853-3630	487
Peterson Tractor Co			
955 Marina Blvd ....San Leandro CA 94577	**800-590-5945**	510-357-6200	274
Peterson's Nelnet LLC			
121 S 13th St Ste 201...........Lincoln NE 68508	**877-338-7772**	609-896-8669	260
PetFoodDirect.com			
189 Main St ....Harleysville PA 19438	**877-738-3663***	215-513-1999	571
*Cust Svc			
Petit Jean Electric Co-op			
270 Quality Dr PO Box 37...........Clinton AR 72031	**800-786-7618**	501-745-2493	245
Petland Inc			
250 Riverside St ....Chillicothe OH 45601	**800-221-5935**	740-775-2464	571
PetMed Express Inc			
1441 SW 29th Ave ....Pompano Beach FL 33069	**800-738-6337**	954-979-5995	571
NASDAQ: PETS			
Petoskey Area Visitors Bureau			
401 E Mitchell St ....Petoskey MI 49770	**800-845-2828**	231-348-2755	207
Petoskey Plastics Inc			
One Petoskey St ....Petoskey MI 49770	**800-999-6556**	231-347-2602	593
Petra 3602 W Lake Rd ....Erie PA 16505	**866-906-2931**	814-838-7197	662
Petro Plastics Company Inc			
450 S Ave ....Garwood NJ 07027	**800-486-4738**	908-789-1200	592

	Toll-Free	Phone	Class
Petrocco Farms			
14110 Brighton Rd ....Brighton CO 80601	**888-876-2207**	303-659-6498	10-10
Petroleum & Resources Corp			
Seven St Paul St Ste 1140 ....Baltimore MD 21202	**800-638-2479**	410-752-5900	402
NYSE: PEO			
Petroleum Development Corp (PDC)			
120 Genesis Blvd PO Box 26 ....Bridgeport WV 26330	**800-624-3821**	303-860-5800	529
NASDAQ: PDCE			
Petroleum Marketers Assn of America's Small Business Community			
1901 N Fort Myer Dr Ste 500 ....Arlington VA 22209	**888-372-7341**	703-351-8000	608
PetroLiance LLC			
739 N State St ....Elgin IL 60123	**800-628-7231**	877-738-7699	572
Petrotech Inc			
151 Brookhollow Esplanade ....New Orleans LA 70123	**800-486-8850**	504-620-6600	511
PETsMART Inc			
19601 N 27th Ave ....Phoenix AZ 85027	**800-738-1385***	623-580-6100	571
NASDAQ: PETM ■ *Cust Svc			
Pettibone Michigan			
1100 Superior Ave ....Baraga MI 49908	**800-467-3884**	906-353-4800	465
Peugeot Motors of America Inc			
150 Clove Rd Ste 3...........Little Falls NJ 07424	**800-223-0587**	973-812-4444	58
Pew Charitable Trusts			
2005 Market St			
1 Commerce Sq Ste 1700...........Philadelphia PA 19103	**800-595-4889**	215-575-9050	304
PF Chang's China Bistro Inc			
7676 E Pinnacle Peak Rd ....Scottsdale AZ 85255	**866-732-4264**	480-888-3000	661
NASDAQ: PFCB			
PFA (Pedorthic Footwear Assn)			
2025 M St NW Ste 800 ....Washington DC 20036	**800-673-8447**	202-367-1145	47-17
Pfaltzgraff Co			
PO Box 21769 ....York PA 17402	**800-999-2811**		721
PFAW (People for the American Way)			
2000 M St NW Ste 400...........Washington DC 20036	**800-326-7329**	202-467-4999	47-7
Pfeiffer University			
48380 Hwy 52 N ....Misenheimer NC 28109	**800-338-2060**	704-463-1360	166
PFERD Milwaukee Brush Company Inc			
30 Jytek Dr ....Leominster MA 01453	**800-342-9015**	978-840-6420	102
Pfister Hotel			
424 E Wisconsin Ave ....Milwaukee WI 53202	**800-558-8222**	414-273-8222	376
Pfizer Canada Inc			
17300 TransCanada Hwy ....Kirkland QC H9J2M5	**800-463-6001**	514-695-0500	576
Pfizer Inc			
235 E 42nd St ....New York NY 10017	**800-879-3477**	212-733-2323	576
NYSE: PFE			
Pfizer Inc Animal Health Group			
235 E 42nd St ....New York NY 10017	**800-879-3477**	212-573-2323	575
PFSweb Inc			
505 Millennium Dr Ste 500 ....Allen TX 75013	**888-330-5504**	972-881-2900	458
NASDAQ: PFSW			
PG & E Corp			
77 Beale St 24th Fl ....San Francisco CA 94105	**800-743-5000**	415-267-7000	357-5
NYSE: PCG			
PG Life Link Inc			
167 Gap Way ....Erlanger KY 41018	**800-287-4123**	859-283-5900	253
PG Publishing Co			
34 Blvd of the Allies ....Pittsburgh PA 15222	**800-228-6397***	412-263-1100	628-8
*Cust Svc			
PGA National Resort & Spa			
400 Ave of the Champions ...Palm Beach Gardens FL 33418	**800-633-9150**	561-627-2000	660
PGA of America			
100 Ave of the Champions ...Palm Beach Gardens FL 33418	**800-477-6465**	561-624-8400	47-22
PGI (Premiere Global Services Inc)			
3280 Peachtree Rd NE			
Ste 1000 Terminus Bldg ....Atlanta GA 30305	**866-548-3203**	719-457-6901	38
NYSE: PGI			
PGI International			
16101 Vallen Dr ....Houston TX 77041	**800-231-0233**	713-466-0056	777
PGT Industries			
1070 Technology Dr ....Nokomis FL 34275	**800-282-6019**	941-480-1600	234
P&H (Parrish & Heimbecker Ltd)			
201 Portage Ave Ste 1400 ....Winnipeg MB R3B3K6	**800-665-8937**	204-956-2030	275
Phadia US Inc			
4169 Commercial Ave ....Portage MI 49002	**800-346-4364**	269-492-1940	231
Phantom Laboratory Inc, The			
2727 SR- 29 ....Greenwich NY 12834	**800-525-1190**	518-692-1190	659
Pharmaceutical Assoc Inc			
1700 Perimeter Rd ....Greenville SC 29605	**888-233-2334**	864-277-7282	231
Pharmaceutical Calibrations & Instrumentation LLC			
8100 Brownleigh Dr Ste 100-A...........Raleigh NC 27617	**877-724-2257**		577
Pharmaceutical Law & Industry Report			
1801 S Bell St ....Arlington VA 22202	**800-372-1033**		524-7
Pharmacists Mutual Insurance Co			
808 Hwy 18 W PO Box 370 ....Algona IA 50511	**800-247-5930***		388-4
*General			
Pharmacy Today Magazine			
2215 Constitution Ave NW ....Washington DC 20037	**800-237-2742**	202-628-4410	452-16
Pharmacyclics Inc			
995 E Arques Ave ....Sunnyvale CA 94085	**800-458-0330**	408-774-0330	84
NASDAQ: PCYC			
Pharmalucence Inc			
29 Dunham Rd ....Billerica MA 01821	**800-221-7554**	781-275-7120	231
Pharmascience Inc			
6111 Royalmount Ave Ste 100 ....Montreal QC H4P2T4	**866-853-1178**	514-340-9800	231
Pharmetics Inc			
3695 AutoRt Des Laurentides ....Laval QC H7L3H7	**877-472-4433**	450-682-8580	231
Phase Matrix Inc			
109 Bonaventura Dr ....San Jose CA 95134	**877-447-2736**	408-428-1000	248
Phase One Inc			
200 Broadhollow Rd Ste 312 ....Melville NY 11747	**888-742-7366**	631-757-0400	584
Phase Technology			
6400 Youngerman Cir ....Jacksonville FL 32244	**888-742-7385**	904-777-0700	51
PHCC (Plumbing-Heating-Cooling Contractors NA)			
180 S Washington St ....Falls Church VA 22040	**800-533-7694**	703-237-8100	48-3
PHD Inc			
9009 Clubridge Dr ....Fort Wayne IN 46809	**800-624-8511**	260-747-6151	223
PhDx Systems Inc			
1001 University Blvd SE			
Ste 103 ....Albuquerque NM 87106	**888-999-7439**	505-764-0174	38
Phelps School			
583 Sugartown Rd ....Malvern PA 19355	**800-344-8328**	610-644-1754	615
Phenix City-Russell County Chamber of Commerce			
1107 Broad St ....Phenix City AL 36867	**800-892-2248**	334-298-3639	137

	Toll-Free	Phone	Class
PHF (Phoenix House Foundation Inc) 164 W 74th St 4th Fl. . . . New York NY 10023	800-378-4435	888-671-9392	717
PHFCU (Pearl Harbor Federal Credit Union) 94-449 Ukee St . . . Waipahu HI 96797	800-987-5583		219
PHH (Port Huron Hospital) 1221 Pine Grove Ave . . . Port Huron MI 48060	888-327-0671	810-987-5000	371-3
PHH Mortgage Corp 3000 Leadenhall Rd . . . Mount Laurel NJ 08054	800-210-8849		502
Phi Alpha Theta *National History Honor Society* 4202 E Fowler Ave SOC 107 . . . Tampa FL 33620	800-394-8195		47-16
Phi Delta Kappa International (PDK) 408 N Union St . . . Bloomington IN 47407	800-766-1156	812-339-1156	47-16
Phi Delta Kappan Magazine 408 N Union St . . . Bloomington IN 47407	800-766-1156	812-339-1156	452-10
Phi Delta Phi International Legal Fraternity 1426 21st St NW . . . Washington DC 20036	800-368-5606	202-223-6801	47-16
Phi Delta Theta 2 S Campus Ave . . . Oxford OH 45056	888-373-9855	513-523-6345	47-16
PHI Inc 2001 SE Evangeline Thwy . . . Lafayette LA 70508 *NASDAQ: PHII*	866-815-7101	337-235-2452	356
Phi Kappa Psi 5395 Emerson Way . . . Indianapolis IN 46226	800-486-1852	317-632-1852	47-16
Phi Kappa Tau 5221 Morning Sun Rd . . . Oxford OH 45056	800-758-1906	513-523-4193	47-16
Phi Mu Alpha Sinfonia Fraternity of America Inc 10600 Old State Rd . . . Evansville IN 47711	800-473-2649	812-867-2433	47-16
Phi Sigma Kappa International 2925 E 96th St . . . Indianapolis IN 46240	888-846-6851	317-573-5420	47-16
Phi Sigma Pi National Honor Fraternity Inc 2119 Ambassador Cir . . . Lancaster PA 17603	800-366-1916	717-299-4710	47-16
Phi Theta Kappa International Honor Society 1625 Eastover Dr . . . Jackson MS 39211	800-946-9995	601-984-3504	47-16
Phibro Animal Health Corp 300 Frank W Burr Blvd Ste 21 . . . Teaneck NJ 07660	800-223-0434	201-329-7300	141
Phifer Inc 4400 Kauloosa Ave PO Box 1700. . . Tuscaloosa AL 35401	800-633-5955	205-345-2120	410
Phil Long Dealerships 1212 Motor City Dr . . . Colorado Springs CO 80905	866-644-1378		56
Phil Smart Inc 600 E Pike St . . . Seattle WA 98122	877-241-4528	206-324-5959	56
Philadelphia College of Osteopathic Medicine (PCOM) 4170 City Ave . . . Philadelphia PA 19131 *Admissions	800-999-6998*	215-871-6100	788
Philadelphia Consolidated Holding Corp 231 Saint Asaph's Rd Ste 100 . . . Bala Cynwyd PA 19004	888-647-8639	610-617-7900	388-4
Philadelphia Contributionship Insurance Co 212 S Fourth St . . . Philadelphia PA 19106 *Cust Svc	888-627-1752*	215-627-1752	388-4
Philadelphia Inquirer 801 Market St Ste 300 PO Box 8263. . . Philadelphia PA 19107	800-341-3413	215-854-2000	525-2
Philadelphia International Airport 8000 Essington Ave . . . Philadelphia PA 19153	800-514-0301	215-937-6937	27
Philadelphia Mixing Solutions, Ltd 1221 E Main St . . . Palmyra PA 17078	800-956-4937	717-832-2800	297
Philadelphia Museum of Art 2600 Benjamin Franklin Pkwy. . . Philadelphia PA 19130	800-732-0999	215-763-8100	513
Philadelphia Regional Port Authority 3460 N Delaware Ave 2nd Fl. . . Philadelphia PA 19134	800-449-7575	215-426-2600	611
Philadelphia Reserve Supply Co 200 Mack Dr . . . Croydon PA 19021	800-347-7726	215-785-3141	192-4
Philadelphia University 4201 Henry Ave . . . Philadelphia PA 19144 *Admissions	800-951-7287*	215-951-2800	166
Philander Smith College 900 Daisy Bates Dr . . . Little Rock AR 72202	800-446-6772	501-370-5221	166
Philanthropic Research Inc 4801 Courthouse St Ste 220. . . Williamsburg VA 23188	800-784-9378	757-229-4631	47-10
Philharmonic Ctr for the Arts 5833 Pelican Bay Blvd . . . Naples FL 34108	800-597-1900	239-597-1111	565
Philip Crosby Assoc 306 Dartmouth St . . . Boston MA 02116	877-276-7295		195
Philip Morris USA 2325 Bells Rd . . . Richmond VA 23234	800-343-0975	804-274-2000	746
Philippi-Hagenbuch Inc 7424 W Plank Rd . . . Peoria IL 61604	800-447-6464	309-697-9200	484
Philippines *Consulate General* 447 Sutter St 6th Fl Philippine Ctr Bldg. . . San Francisco CA 94108	877-700-0669	415-433-6666	257
Consulate General 30 N Michigan Ave Ste 2100 . . . Chicago IL 60602	888-259-7838	312-332-6458	257
Consulate General 3600 Wilshire Blvd Ste 500 . . . Los Angeles CA 90010	800-527-2820	213-639-0980	257
Consulate General 556 Fifth Ave . . . New York NY 10036	866-589-1878	212-764-1330	257
Embassy 1600 Massachusetts Ave NW . . . Washington DC 20036	888-373-7888	202-467-9300	257
Philips Advance Light Electro 10275 W Higgins Rd . . . Rosemont IL 60018	800-322-2086	847-390-5000	757
Philips Canlyte, Inc 3015 Louis Amos . . . Lachine QC H8T1C4 *All	800-668-2770*	514-636-0670	435
Philips Day-Brite 776 S Green St . . . Tupelo MS 38804	800-234-1890		435
Philips Global PACS 5000 Marina Blvd Ste 100 . . . Brisbane CA 94005 *Cust Svc	877-328-2808*	650-228-5555	379
Philips Holding USA Inc 1251 Ave of the Americas . . . New York NY 10020	800-453-6860	212-536-0500	435
Philips Lighting Co 200 Franklin Sq Dr . . . Somerset NJ 08873	800-555-0050		433
Philips Medical Systems 3000 Minuteman Rd . . . Andover MA 01810	800-934-7372	978-659-3000	379
Phillip's Flower Shops Inc 524 N Cass Ave . . . Westmont IL 60559	800-356-7257	630-719-5200	292
Phillips & Johnston Inc 21w179 Hill Ave . . . Glen Ellyn IL 60137	877-411-8823	630-469-8150	487
Phillips & Jordan Inc 6621 Wilbanks Rd . . . Knoxville TN 37912	800-955-0876	865-688-8342	190-5
Phillips & Temro Industries 9700 W 74th St . . . Eden Prairie MN 55344	800-328-6108	952-941-9700	59
Phillips Academy 180 Main St . . . Andover MA 01810	877-445-5477	978-749-4000	615
Phillips Beach Plaza Hotel 1301 Atlantic Ave . . . Ocean City MD 21842	800-492-5834	410-289-9121	376
Phillips Bros Electrical Contractors Inc 235 Sweet Spring Rd . . . Glenmoore PA 19343	800-220-5051	610-458-8578	190-4
Phillips Buick-Pontiac-Gmc Truck Inc 2160 US Hwy 441 . . . Fruitland Park FL 34731	888-664-7454	352-728-1212	56
Phillips Corp 7390 Coca Cola Dr . . . Hanover MD 21076	800-878-4242	410-564-2929	488
Phillips Distributing Corp 3010 Nob Hill Rd . . . Madison WI 53713	800-236-7269	608-222-9177	80-3
Phillips Distribution Inc 3000 E Houston St Ste B . . . San Antonio TX 78220	800-580-2397	210-227-2397	552
Phillips Exeter Academy 20 Main St . . . Exeter NH 03833	800-245-2525	603-772-4311	615
Phillips Group 501 Fulling Mill Rd . . . Middletown PA 17057	800-538-7500	717-944-0400	528
Phillips Machine Service Inc 367 George St . . . Beckley WV 25801	800-733-1521	304-255-0537	383
Phillips Mushroom Farms Inc 1011 Kaolin Rd . . . Kennett Square PA 19348	800-722-8818	610-925-0520	10-6
Phillips Plywood Company Inc 13599 Desmond St . . . Pacoima CA 91331 *Cust Svc	800-649-6410*	818-897-7736	606
Phillips Theological Seminary 901 N Mingo Rd . . . Tulsa OK 74116	800-843-4675	918-610-8303	167-3
Phillips-Van Heusen Corp 200 Madison Ave . . . New York NY 10016 *NYSE: PVH*	866-214-6694	212-381-3500	153-11
Philosophy Inc 3809 E Watkins . . . Phoenix AZ 85034	800-568-3151		215
Philotechnics Ltd 201 Renovare Blvd . . . Oak Ridge TN 37830	888-723-9278	865-483-1551	271
Phoebe Putney Memorial Hospital 417 W Third Ave . . . Albany GA 31702	877-312-1167	229-312-1000	371-3
Phoenician, The 6000 E Camelback Rd . . . Scottsdale AZ 85251	800-888-8234	480-941-8200	660
Phoenix American Inc 2401 Kerner Blvd . . . San Rafael CA 94901	866-895-5050		216
Phoenix Children's Hospital 1919 E Thomas Rd . . . Phoenix AZ 85016	888-908-5437	602-546-1000	371-1
Phoenix Convention Ctr 100 N Third St . . . Phoenix AZ 85004	800-282-4842	602-262-6225	206
Phoenix Cos Inc, The One American Row PO Box 5056 . . . Hartford CT 06102 *NYSE: PNX*	800-628-1936	860-403-5000	357-4
Phoenix Coyotes 6751 N Sunset Blvd Ste 200 . . . Glendale AZ 85305	877-448-4483	623-772-3200	707
Phoenix Flower Shops 5733 E Thomas Rd Ste 4 . . . Scottsdale AZ 85251	888-311-0404	480-289-4000	292
Phoenix Footwear Group Inc 5937 Darwin Ct Ste 109 . . . Carlsbad CA 92008 *OTC: PXFG*	888-218-7275	760-602-9688	300
Phoenix Forging Company Inc 800 Front St . . . Catasauqua PA 18032	800-444-3674	610-264-2861	478
Phoenix Grand Hotel Salem 201 Liberty St SE . . . Salem OR 97301	877-540-7800	503-540-7800	376
Phoenix Growth Capital Corp 2401 Kerner Blvd . . . San Rafael CA 94901	866-895-5050		216
Phoenix Hotel 601 Eddy St . . . San Francisco CA 94109	800-248-9466	415-776-1380	376
Phoenix House Foundation Inc (PHF) 164 W 74th St 4th Fl. . . New York NY 10023	800-378-4435	888-671-9392	717
Phoenix International Freight Services Ltd 14701 Charlson Rd . . . Eden Prairie MN 55347	855-229-6128	952-937-6761	310
Phoenix Leasing Inc 2401 Kerner Blvd . . . San Rafael CA 94901	866-895-5050		216
Phoenix Magazine 15169 N Scottsdale Ste C10. . . Scottsdale AZ 85254	866-481-6970	480-664-3960	452-22
Phoenix Manufacturing Inc 3655 E Roeser Rd . . . Phoenix AZ 85040 *Cust Svc	800-325-6952*	602-437-1034	14
Phoenix Media Communications Group 126 Brookline Ave . . . Boston MA 02215	888-536-7464	617-536-5390	628-8
Phoenix Metals Co 4685 Buford Hwy . . . Norcross GA 30071	800-241-2290	770-447-4211	487
Phoenix Park 'n Swap 3801 E Washington St . . . Phoenix AZ 85034	800-772-0852	602-273-1250	271
Phoenix Park Hotel 520 N Capitol St . . . Washington DC 20001	800-824-5419	202-638-6900	376
Phoenix Pharmaceuticals Inc 330 Beach Rd . . . Burlingame CA 94010	800-988-1205	650-558-8898	231
Phoenix Seminary 4222 E Thomas Rd Ste 400 . . . Phoenix AZ 85018	888-443-1020	602-850-8000	167-3
Phoenix Society for Burn Survivors Inc 1835 RW Berends Dr SW . . . Grand Rapids MI 49519	800-888-2876	616-458-2773	47-17
Phoenix Suns US Airways Ctr 201 E Jefferson St . . . Phoenix AZ 85004	866-648-4668	602-379-7900	705-1
Phoenix Symphony One N First St Ste 200 . . . Phoenix AZ 85004	800-776-9080	602-495-1117	566-3
Phoenix Technologies Ltd 915 Murphy Ranch Rd . . . Milpitas CA 95035	800-677-7305	408-570-1000	179-12
Phoenix Transportation Services LLC 335 E Yusen Dr . . . Georgetown KY 40324	800-860-0889	502-863-0108	770
Phoenix Vintners LLC Four S Main St Ste 2 . . . Ipswich MA 01938	877-340-9869		454
Phonic Ear Inc 2080 Lakeville Hwy . . . Petaluma CA 94954	800-227-0735	707-769-1110	472
Photo Marketing Assn International (PMA) 3000 Picture Pl . . . Jackson MI 49201	800-762-9287	517-788-8100	48-18
Photo Research Inc 9731 Topanga Canyon Pl . . . Chatsworth CA 91311	877-424-6423	818-341-5151	416
Photo Researchers Inc 307 Fifth Ave Third Fl. . . New York NY 10016	800-833-9033	212-758-3420	586
Photo Resource Hawaii 111 Hekili St Ste 241 . . . Kailua HI 96734	888-599-7773	808-599-7773	586
Photo USA 2140 Colonial Ave . . . Roanoke VA 24015	888-234-6320	540-344-0961	581

	Toll-Free	Phone	Class
PhotoMedex Inc 147 Keystone Dr ....Montgomeryville PA 18936 NASDAQ: PHMD	800-366-4758	215-619-3600	421
PhotoSource 5106 Louetta Rd ....Spring TX 77379	800-786-6277	281-370-2220	524-13
Photosource International 1910 35th Rd ....Osceola WI 54020	800-786-6277	715-248-3800	628-9
PHP (Parents Helping Parents) 1400 Parkmoor Ave Ste 100 ....San jose CA 95126	855-727-5775	408-727-5775	47-6
Phunware Inc 7800 Shoal Creek Blvd ....Austin TX 78757	855-521-8485		178
Phybridge Inc 3495 Laird Rd Ste 12 ....Mississauga ON L5L5S5	888-901-3633	905-901-3633	603
Phygen LLC 2301 Dupont Ave Ste 510..........Irvine CA 92612	800-939-7008		472
Physical Electronics Inc 18725 Lake Dr E ....Chanhassen MN 55317	800-328-7515	952-828-6100	416
Physician's Automated Laboratory Inc (PALLAB) 9830 Brimhall Rd............Bakersfield CA 93312	800-675-2271	661-829-2260	415
Physicians Committee for Responsible Medicine (PCRM) 5100 Wisconsin Ave NW Ste 400 ....Washington DC 20016	866-416-7276	202-686-2210	48-8
Physicians for Social Responsibility (PSR) 1875 Connecticut Ave NW Ste 1012 ....Washington DC 20009	800-459-1887	202-667-4260	48-8
Physicians Life Insurance Co 2600 Dodge St....................Omaha NE 68131	800-228-9100	402-633-1000	388-2
Physicians Mutual Insurance Co 2600 Dodge St....................Omaha NE 68131	800-228-9100	402-633-1000	388-2
Physicians Plus Insurance Corp 2650 Novation Pkwy Ste 200 ....Madison WI 53713	800-545-5015	608-282-8900	388-3
Physicians Weight Loss Centers of America Inc 395 Springside Dr ....Akron OH 44333	800-205-7887	330-666-7952	797
Physics Today Magazine One Physics Ellipse ....College Park MD 20740	800-344-6902	301-209-3040	452-19
Physio-Control Inc 11811 Willows Rd NE..........Redmond WA 98052	800-442-1142	425-867-4000	250
Physmark Inc 101 E Pk Blvd Ste 600 ....Plano TX 75074	800-922-7060	972-231-8000	180
PI Inc 213 Dennis St ....Athens TN 37303	800-894-4876	423-745-6213	601
Pi Lambda Phi Fraternity Inc 60 Newtown Rd Ste 118 ....Danbury CT 06810	800-395-4724	203-740-1044	47-16
PIA (Pakistan International Airlines Corp) 1200 New Jersey Ave SE ......Washington DC 20590	800-578-6786		25
PIA (Pittsburgh Institute of Aeronautics) Five Allegheny County Airport ....West Mifflin PA 15122	800-444-1440	412-346-2100	788
PIA/GATF (Printing Industries of America/Graphic Arts Technical Foundation) 200 Deer Run Rd ....Sewickley PA 15143	800-910-4283	412-741-6860	48-16
Piad Precision Casting Corp 112 Industrial Pk Rd ....Greensburg PA 15601	800-441-9858	724-838-5500	307
PianoDisc 4111 N Fwy Blvd ....Sacramento CA 95834	800-566-3472	916-567-9999	520
Piantedosi Baking Company Inc 240 Commercial St ....Malden MA 02148	800-339-0080	781-321-3400	295-1
Pibbs Industries 133-15 32nd Ave ....Flushing NY 11354	800-551-5020	718-445-8046	75
Pic Design Corp 86 Benson Rd PO Box 1004 ....Middlebury CT 06762	800-243-6125	203-758-8272	613
PIC Skate 22 Village Dr ....Riverside RI 02915	800-882-3448	401-490-9334	701
PIC USA 100 Bluegrass Commons Blvd Ste 2200..............Hendersonville TN 37075	800-325-3398	615-265-2700	10-5
Picacho State Recreation Area 1416 Ninth St PO Box 942896 ....Sacramento CA 95814	800-777-0369	916-653-6995	558
Piccadilly Cafeterias Inc 3332 S Sherwood Forest Blvd ......Baton Rouge LA 70816	800-552-7422	225-293-4853	661
Piccadilly Circus Pizza 1007 Okoboji Ave PO Box 188............Milford IA 51351	800-338-4340		661
Piccadilly Inn Hotels 2305 W Shaw Ave ....Fresno CA 93711	888-286-2645	559-348-5520	376
Pickaway County District Public Library 1160 N Ct St ....Circleville OH 43113	888-268-3756	740-477-1644	431-3
Pickaway County Visitors Bureau 325 W Main St ....Circleville OH 43113	800-283-4678	740-474-3636	207
Pickens-Kane Moving Co 410 N Milwaukee Ave ....Chicago IL 60610	888-871-9998	312-942-0330	512
Pickett County 1 Courthouse Sq Ste 200 ....Byrdstown TN 38549	888-406-4704	931-864-3798	336
Pickwick Electric Co-op 530 Mulberry Ave ....Selmer TN 38375	800-372-8258	731-645-3411	245
PICO Holdings Inc 7979 Ivanhoe Ave Ste 301 ......La Jolla CA 92037 NASDAQ: PICO	888-389-3222	858-456-6022	357-4
Pico Macom Inc 8880 Rehco Rd ....San Diego CA 92121	800-421-6511	858-546-5050	638
Pics Telecom International Corp 1920 Lyell Ave ....Rochester NY 14606	800-521-7427	585-295-2000	725
Pidilite USA Inc 902 South US Highway 1 Ste 18........Jupiter FL 33477	800-843-7813	561-775-9600	144
Piedmont Airlines Inc 5443 Airport Terminal Rd ....Salisbury MD 21804	800-354-3394	410-742-2996	25
Piedmont Baptist College 420 S Broad St ....Winston-Salem NC 27101 *Admissions	800-937-5097*	336-725-8344	166
Piedmont College 165 Central Ave ....Demorest GA 30535	800-277-7020	706-776-0103	166
Piedmont Mechanical Inc 116 John Dodd Rd ....Spartanburg SC 29303	800-849-5725	864-578-9114	190-10
Piedmont Medical Ctr 222 S Herlong Ave ....Rock Hill SC 29732	800-222-4218	803-329-1234	371-3
Piedmont Natural Gas 4720 Piedmont Row Dr PO Box 33068............Charlotte NC 28210 NYSE: PNY	800-752-7504	704-364-3120	775
Piedmont Technical College 620 N Emerald Rd ....Greenwood SC 29646	800-868-5528	864-941-8324	788
Piedmont Truck Tires Inc PO Box 18228 ....Greensboro NC 27419	800-274-8473	336-668-0091	745
Pieper Electric Inc 5070 N 35th St ....Milwaukee WI 53209	800-424-8802	414-462-7700	190-4

	Toll-Free	Phone	Class
Pier 1 Imports Inc 100 Pier 1 Pl ....Fort Worth TX 76102 NYSE: PIR	800-245-4595	817-252-8000	359
Pier 1 Kids 100 Pier 1 Pl ....Fort Worth TX 76102	800-433-4035	817-252-8000	320
Pier 5 Hotel 711 Eastern Ave ....Baltimore MD 21202	866-583-4162	410-539-2000	376
Pier House Resort Caribbean Spa One Duval St ....Key West FL 33040	800-723-2791	305-296-4600	660
Pieratt's 110 Mt Tabor Rd ....Lexington KY 40517	855-743-7288	859-268-6000	34
Pierce College Puyallup 1601 39th Ave SE ......Puyallup WA 98374	877-353-6763	253-840-8400	160
Pierce County Library System 3005 112th St E ....Tacoma WA 98446	800-346-0995	253-536-6500	431-3
Pierce County Security Inc 2002 99th St E ....Tacoma WA 98445	800-773-4432	253-535-4433	684
Pierce Distribution Services Co PO Box 15600 ....Loves Park IL 61132	800-466-7397		444
Pierce Mfg Inc 2600 American Dr ....Appleton WI 54914 *Cust Svc	888-974-3723*	920-832-3000	509
Pierce Pacific Manufacturing Inc 4424 NE 158th PO Box 30509 ....Portland OR 97294	800-760-3270	503-808-9110	191
Pierce Pepin Co-op Services W7725 US Hwy 10 PO Box 420 ......Ellsworth WI 54011	800-924-2133	715-273-4355	245
Pierce Transit 3701 96th St SW PO Box 99070.......Lakewood WA 98499	800-562-8109	253-581-8000	463
Piercey Automotive Group 16901 Millikan Ave ....Irvine CA 92606	877-280-1044	949-396-6000	56
Pierre Area Chamber of Commerce 800 W Dakota Ave ....Pierre SD 57501	800-962-2034	605-224-7361	137
Pigeon Forge Dept of Tourism P.O. Box 1390 ....Pigeon Forge TN 37868	800-251-9100	865-453-8574	207
Piggly Wiggly Carolina Company Inc PO Box 118047 ....Charleston SC 29423	800-243-9880	843-554-9880	342
PIIRS (Princeton Institute for International & Regional Studies) Princeton University Bendheim Hall ....Princeton NJ 08544	888-486-3339	609-258-4852	625
PIJAC (Pet Industry Joint Advisory Council) 1220 19th St NW Ste 400 ....Washington DC 20036	800-553-7387	202-452-1525	48-4
Pike County Chamber of Commerce & Economic Development District 112 N Railroad Blvd ....McComb MS 39648	800-844-2653	601-684-2291	137
Pike Electric Corp 100 Pike Way PO Box 868 ....Mount Airy NC 27030 NYSE: PIKE	800-424-7453	336-789-2171	190-4
Pike Industries Inc 3 Eastgate Pk Rd ....Belmont NH 03220	800-283-0803	603-527-5100	189-4
Pike Lumber Company Inc PO Box 247 ....Akron IN 46910	800-356-4554	574-893-4511	674
Pikes Peak Community College Centennial 5675 S Academy Blvd ......Colorado Springs CO 80906	800-456-6847	719-502-2000	160
Downtown Studio 100 W Pikes Peak Ave ......Colorado Springs CO 80903	800-456-6847	719-502-2000	160
Rampart Range 11195 Hwy 83 ......Colorado Springs CO 80921	800-456-6847	719-502-2000	160
Pikes Peak Ctr 190 S Cascade Ave ......Colorado Springs CO 80903	866-464-2626	719-477-2100	565
Pikeville College 147 Sycamore St ....Pikeville KY 41501	866-232-7700	606-218-5250	166
Pilgrim Plastic Products Co 1200 W Chestnut St ....Brockton MA 02301	877-343-7810	508-583-9046	9
Pilgrim Psychiatric Ctr 998 Crooked Hill Rd ....West Brentwood NY 11717	800-597-8481	631-761-3500	371-5
Pilgrim Tours & Travel Inc 3071 Main St PO Box 268 ......Morgantown PA 19543	800-322-0788	610-286-0788	750
Pilgrim's Corp 1770 Promontory Cir ....Greeley CO 80634 NASDAQ: PPC	800-321-1470		612
Pillar Induction Co 21905 Gateway Rd ....Brookfield WI 53045	800-558-7733	262-317-5300	317
Pillars Hotel at New River Sound 111 N Birch Rd ....Fort Lauderdale FL 33304	800-241-3333	954-467-9639	376
Piller Inc 45 Turner Rd ....Middletown NY 10941	800-597-6937		511
Pilling Surgical 2917 Weck Dr ......Research Triangle Park NC 27709 *Cust Svc	866-246-6990*	919-544-8000	471
Pillsbury Winthrop Shaw Pittman LLP 50 Fremont St ....San Francisco CA 94105	800-477-0770	415-983-1000	425
Pilot Travel Centers LLC PO Box 10146 ....Knoxville TN 37939	800-562-6210	865-938-1439	323
Pilot Tribune PO Box 1187 ....Storm Lake IA 50588	800-447-1985	712-732-3130	525-2
Pima Community College West 2202 W Anklam Rd ....Tucson AZ 85709	800-860-7462	520-206-6600	160
Pima County Public Library 101 N Stone Ave ....Tucson AZ 85701	877-705-5437	520-594-5600	431-3
PIMCO Institutional Funds PO Box 219024 ....Kansas City MO 64121	800-927-4648		521
Pine Bluff Convention & Visitors Bureau (PBCVB) One Convention Ctr Plz ....Pine Bluff AR 71601	800-536-7660	870-536-7600	207
Pine Bluff Cotton Belt Federal Credit Union 1703 River Pines Blvd ....Pine Bluff AR 71601	888-249-1904	870-535-6365	219
Pine Butte Guest Ranch 351 S Fork Rd ....Choteau MT 59422	877-812-3698	406-466-2158	239
Pine Cone Hill Inc 125 Pecks Rd ....Pittsfield MA 01201	877-586-4771	413-496-9700	587
Pine County 635 Northridge Dr NW ....Pine City MN 55063	800-450-7463	320-591-1400	336
Pine Crest Inn 85 Pine Crest Ln ....Tryon NC 28782	800-633-3001	828-859-9135	376
Pine Grove Furnace State Park 1100 Pine Grove Rd ....Gardners PA 17324	888-727-2757	717-486-7174	558
Pine Hall Brick Co 2701 Shorefair Dr ....Winston-Salem NC 27116	800-334-8689		148
Pine Manor College 400 Heath St ....Chestnut Hill MA 02467	800-762-1357	617-731-7104	166
Pine Mountain State Resort Park 1050 State Pk Rd ....Pineville KY 40977	800-325-1712		558
Pine Needles Lodge & Golf Club PO Box 88 ....Southern Pines NC 28388	800-747-7272	910-692-7111	660

	Toll-Free	Phone	Class
Pine Pointe Hospice & Palliative Care			
6261 Peak Rd ....Macon GA 31210	800-211-1084	478-633-5660	368
Pine Rest Christian Mental Health Services			
300 68th St SE PO Box 165 ....Grand Rapids MI 49501	800-678-5500	616-455-5000	371-5
Pine Ridge Winery LLC			
5901 Silverado Trail ....Napa CA 94558	800-575-9777		79-3
Pine Run Community			
777 Ferry Rd ....Doylestown PA 18901	888-992-8992	215-345-9000	663
Pine State Trading Co			
8 Ellis Ave ....Augusta ME 04330	800-873-3825	207-622-3741	80-1
Pinehurst Resort & Country Club			
80 Carolina Vista Dr ....Pinehurst NC 28374	800-487-4653	910-295-6811	660
Pinelands Regional School District			
PO Box 248 ....Tuckerton NJ 08087	866-850-0511	609-296-3106	676
Pines Lodge			
141 Scott Hill Rd ....Beaver Creek CO 81620	800-859-8242*	970-429-5043	376
*Resv			
Pines Resort, The			
103 Shore Rd PO Box 70 ....Digby NS B0V1A0	800-667-4637	902-245-2511	660
Pines Technology			
30505 Clemens Rd ....Westlake OH 44145	800-207-2840	440-835-5553	489
Pinestone Resort			
4252 County Rd Ste 21...............Haliburton ON K0M1S0	800-461-0357	705-457-1800	660
Ping Inc			
2201 W Desert Cove Ave			
PO Box 82000...............................Phoenix AZ 85071	800-474-6434		701
Pinnacle Business Finance Inc			
615 Commerce St Ste 101 ....Tacoma WA 98402	800-566-1993	253-284-5600	216
Pinnacle Business Systems Inc			
3824 S Blvd St Ste 200...............Edmond OK 73013	800-311-0757		225
Pinnacle Data Systems Inc			
6600 Port Rd Ste 100 ....Groveport OH 43125	800-882-8282	614-748-1150	174-1
Pinnacle Entertainment Inc			
3980 Howard Hughes Pkwy ....Las Vegas NV 89169	877-764-8750	702-541-7777	131
NYSE: PNK			
Pinnacle Foods Corp			
399 Jefferson Rd ....Parsippany NJ 07054	866-266-7596	973-541-6620	295-39
Pinnacle Health Hospital at Community General			
4300 Londonderry Rd ....Harrisburg PA 17109	888-782-5678	717-652-3000	371-3
Pinnacle Inn Resort			
301 Pinnacle Inn Rd ....Beech Mountain NC 28604	800-405-7888	828-387-2231	660
Pinnacle Management Systems Inc			
8500 North Stemmons Freeway			
Ste 6010 ....Dallas TX 75247	888-975-1119	703-382-9161	195
Pinnacle Motor Club			
130 E John Carpenter Fwy ....Irving TX 75062	800-446-1289		52
Pinnacle Performance Improvement Worldwide (PPIW)			
101 Main St ....Pepperell MA 01463	800-368-3408	978-925-9797	195
Pinnacle West Capital Corp			
400 N Fifth St ....Phoenix AZ 85004	800-457-2983	602-250-1000	357-5
NYSE: PNW			
Pinnacles National Monument			
5000 Hwy 146 ....Paicines CA 95043	877-444-6777	831-389-4485	557
Pinnacol Assurance			
7501 E Lowry Blvd ....Denver CO 80230	800-873-7242	303-361-4000	388-4
Pinova Holdings Inc			
2801 Cook St ....Brunswick GA 31520	888-807-2958		594
Pintoresco Advisors LLC			
466 Foothill Blvd			
Ste 333 ....La Canada Flintridge CA 91011	866-217-1140	213-223-2070	69
Pioneer Bank			
21 Second St PO Box 1048 ....Troy NY 12181	866-873-9573	518-274-4800	70
Pioneer Broach Co			
6434 Telegraph Rd ....Los Angeles CA 90040	800-621-1945	323-728-1263	450
Pioneer Electric Co-op			
344 W US Rt 36 PO Box 1307 ....Piqua OH 45356	800-762-0997	937-773-2523	245
Pioneer Electric Co-op Inc			
1850 W Oklahoma St PO Box 368 ....Ulysses KS 67880	800-794-9302	620-356-1211	245
Pioneer Electronics (USA) Inc			
1925 E Dominguez St ....Long Beach CA 90810	800-421-1404	310-952-2000	51
Pioneer Funds			
60 State St ....Boston MA 02109	800-225-6292	617-742-7825	521
Pioneer Hi-Bred International Inc			
PO Box 1000 ....Johnston IA 50131	800-247-6803	515-535-3200	10-4
Pioneer Long Distance Inc			
PO Box 539 ....Kingfisher OK 73750	888-782-2667		726
Pioneer Metal Finishing LLC			
486 Globe Ave ....Green Bay WI 54304	877-721-1100		476
Pioneer Mfg			
4529 Industrial Pkwy ....Cleveland OH 44135	800-877-1500	216-671-5500	543
Pioneer National Latex Co			
5000 E 29th St N ....Wichita KS 67220	800-386-4438	316-685-2266	752
Pioneer Paper Stock			
155 Irving Ave N ....Minneapolis MN 55405	800-821-8512	612-374-2280	651
Pioneer Steel Corp			
7447 Intervale St ....Detroit MI 48238	800-999-9440	313-933-9400	487
Pioneer Telephone Assn Inc			
PO Box 707 ....Ulysses KS 67880	800-308-7536	620-356-3211	726
Pioneer Tool & Forge Inc			
101 Sixth St ....New Kensington PA 15068	800-359-6408	724-337-4700	749
Pioneer Transfer LLC			
2034 S St Aubin St			
PO Box 2567 ....Sioux City IA 51106	800-325-4650		310
Pioneer Wholesale Co			
500 W Bagley Rd ....Berea OH 44017	888-234-5400	440-234-5400	43
Pioneer/Eclipse Corp			
One Eclipse Rd ....Sparta NC 28675	800-367-3550*	336-372-8080	383
*Cust Svc			
Pioneers			
10123 William Carey Dr ....Orlando FL 32832	800-359-9297	407-382-6000	47-20
Pipe & Tube Supply Inc			
1407 N Cypress ....North Little Rock AR 72114	800-770-8823	501-372-6556	383
Pipe Welders Inc			
2965 W State Rd 84 ....Fort Lauderdale FL 33312	800-787-8401	954-587-8400	475
Pipeline & Hazardous Materials Safety Administration			
Office of Hazardous Materials Safety			
1200 New Jersey Ave SE ....Washington DC 20590	800-467-4922	202-366-4433	338-15
Piper Jaffray Cos			
800 Nicollet Mall Ste 800 ....Minneapolis MN 55402	800-333-6000	612-303-6000	681
NYSE: PJC			
Piper Products Inc			
300 S 84th Ave ....Wausau WI 54401	800-544-3057	715-842-2724	297
Pipestone Publishing Co			
PO Box 277 ....Pipestone MN 56164	800-325-6440	507-825-3333	628-8
Pipestone Veterinary Clinic LLC			
1300 Hwy 75 S PO Box 188 ....Pipestone MN 56164	800-658-2523	507-825-4211	782
Piping & Equipment Inc			
9100 Canniff St ....Houston TX 77017	888-889-9683	713-947-9393	382
Piping Technology & Products Inc			
3701 Holmes Rd PO Box 34506 ....Houston TX 77051	866-746-9172	713-422-2271	588
PIT (Pennsylvania Institute of Technology)			
800 Manchester Ave ....Media PA 19063	800-422-0025*	610-892-1500	788
*Admissions			
Pitco Frialator Inc			
PO Box 501 ....Concord NH 03302	800-258-3708	603-225-6684	297
Pitmar Tours			
7549 140th St Ste 9 ....Surrey BC V3W5J9	877-596-9670	604-596-9670	750
Pitney Bowes Group 1 Software			
4200 Parliament Pl Ste 600 ....Lanham MD 20706	800-367-6950	301-731-2300	179-1
Pitney Bowes Inc			
One Elmcroft Rd ....Stamford CT 06926	800-672-6937	203-356-5000	110
NYSE: PBI			
Pitney Bowes Management Services			
90 Pk Ave ....New York NY 10016	800-322-8000	212-808-3800	458
Pitt Ohio Express			
15 27th St ....Pittsburgh PA 15222	800-366-7488*	412-232-3015	770
*Cust Svc			
Pitt Plastics Inc			
1400 Atkinson Ave ....Pittsburg KS 66762	800-835-0366		65
Pitts Toyota Inc			
210 N Jefferson St PO Box 4013 ....Dublin GA 31021	888-561-8030	478-272-3244	56
Pittsburg Area Chamber of Commerce			
117 W Fourth St ....Pittsburg KS 66762	800-794-4780	620-231-1000	137
Pittsburg State University			
1701 S Broadway St ....Pittsburg KS 66762	800-854-7488	620-235-4251	166
Pittsburg Tank & Tower Co Inc			
1 Watertank Pl ....Henderson KY 42420	800-222-5555	270-826-9000	190-14
Pittsburgh Ballet Theatre			
2900 Liberty Ave ....Pittsburgh PA 15201	800-441-1414	412-281-0360	566-1
Pittsburgh Cut Flower Co			
1901 Liberty Ave ....Pittsburgh PA 15222	800-837-2837	412-355-7000	293
Pittsburgh Institute of Aeronautics (PIA)			
Five Allegheny County Airport ....West Mifflin PA 15122	800-444-1440	412-346-2100	788
Pittsburgh Institute of Mortuary Science Inc			
5808 Baum Blvd ....Pittsburgh PA 15206	800-933-5808	412-362-8500	788
Pittsburgh International Airport			
Landside Terminal Fourth Fl Mezz			
PO Box 12370 ....Pittsburgh PA 15231	888-429-5377	412-472-3525	27
Pittsburgh Penguins			
1001 Fifth Avenue ....Pittsburgh PA 15219	800-642-7367	412-642-1300	707
Pittsburgh Pirates			
115 Federal St PO Box 7000 ....Pittsburgh PA 15212	800-289-2827	412-321-2827	704
Pittsburgh Plumbing Heating & Industrial (PPHI)			
434 Melwood Ave ....Pittsburgh PA 15213	800-445-4155	412-622-8100	14
Pittsburgh Public Theater			
621 Penn Ave ....Pittsburgh PA 15222	800-732-0999	412-316-8200	566-4
Pittsburgh Supercomputing Ctr			
300 S Craig St ....Pittsburgh PA 15213	800-221-1641	412-268-4960	659
Pittsburgh Symphony Orchestra			
600 Penn Ave			
Heinz Hall for the Performing Arts...... Pittsburgh PA 15222	800-743-8560	412-566-7366	566-3
Pittsburgh Technical Institute (PTI)			
1111 McKee Rd ....Oakdale PA 15071	800-784-9675	412-809-5100	788
Pittsburgh Theological Seminary			
616 N Highland Ave ....Pittsburgh PA 15206	800-451-4194	412-362-5610	167-3
Pittsburgh Tribune-Review			
503 Martindale St 3rd Fl...............Pittsburgh PA 15212	800-909-8742	412-321-6460	525-2
Pittsburgh Zoo & PPG Aquarium			
1 Wild Pl ....Pittsburgh PA 15206	800-732-0999	412-665-3640	810
Pittsylvania County School Board			
39 Bank St SE PO Box 232 ....Chatham VA 24531	888-440-6520	434-432-2761	676
Pitzer College			
1050 N Mills Ave ....Claremont CA 91711	800-748-9371	909-621-8129	166
Pizza Boli's			
5721 Falls Rd 5725 Falls Rd...............Baltimore MD 21209	800-234-2654	410-323-3278	661
Pizza Factory Inc			
49430 Rd 426 ....Oakhurst CA 93644	800-654-4840	559-683-3377	661
Pizza Inn Inc			
3551 Plano Pkwy ....The Colony TX 75056	800-880-9955	469-384-5000	661
NASDAQ: RAVE			
Pizza Plus Pizza Inc			
299 Franklin Dr ....Blountville TN 37617	800-675-1220	423-279-9335	661
Pizza Pro Inc			
2107 N Second St PO Box 1285...............Cabot AR 72023	800-777-7554	501-605-1175	661
Pizza Ranch Inc			
204 19th St SE ....Orange City IA 51041	800-321-3401		661
PJ Keating Co			
998 Reservoir Rd ....Lunenburg MA 01462	800-441-4119	978-582-5200	189-4
PK (Promise Keepers)			
PO Box 11798 ....Denver CO 80211	866-776-6473		47-20
PK Safety Supply			
2005 Clement Ave Bldg 9...............Alameda CA 94501	800-829-9580	510-337-8880	670
PK4 Media Inc			
1600 E Franklin Ave Ste C ....El Segundo CA 90245	888-320-6281		384
PKC Corp			
One Mill St C13 Ste 355...............Burlington VT 05401	800-752-5351	802-658-5351	179-10
PKM Electric Co-op Inc			
406 N Minnesota St ....Warren MN 56762	800-552-7366	218-745-4711	245
PLA (Public Library Assn)			
50 E Huron St ....Chicago IL 60611	800-545-2433	312-280-5752	48-11
Place D'Armes Hotel			
625 St Ann St ....New Orleans LA 70116	800-366-2743	504-524-4531	376
Place Louis Riel All-Suite Hotel			
190 Smith St ....Winnipeg MB R3C1J8	800-665-0569	204-947-6961	376
Placentia Chamber of Commerce			
201 E Yorba Linda Blvd Ste C...............Placentia CA 92870	844-730-0418	714-528-1873	137
Placentia-Linda Hospital			
1301 N Rose Dr ....Placentia CA 92870	888-754-9729	714-993-2000	371-3
Placer County Library			
350 Nevada St ....Auburn CA 95603	800-488-4308	530-886-4500	431-3
Placon Corp			
6096 McKee Rd ....Madison WI 53719	800-541-1535	608-271-5634	595
Plaid Enterprises Inc			
3225 Westech Dr ....Norcross GA 30092	800-842-4197	678-291-8100	42
Plaid Pantries Inc			
10025 SW Allen Blvd ....Beaverton OR 97005	800-677-5243	503-646-4246	205

Name / Address	City	State	Zip	Toll-Free	Phone	Class
Plain Dealer 1801 Superior Ave	Cleveland	OH	44114	**800-362-0727**	216-999-5000	525-2
Plains All American Pipeline LP 333 Clay St Ste 1600 *NYSE: PAA* ■ *Mktg	Houston	TX	77002	**866-753-3619***	713-646-4100	590
Plains Cotton Co-op Assn 3301 E 50th St PO Box 2827	Lubbock	TX	79408	**800-333-8011**	806-763-8011	275
Plains Dairy Products 300 N Taylor St	Amarillo	TX	79107	**800-365-5608**	806-374-0385	296-4
Plains Grain & Agronomy LLC 109 Third Ave PO Box 6	Enderlin	ND	58027	**800-950-2219**	701-437-2400	10-3
Plains Hotel, The 1600 Central Ave	Cheyenne	WY	82001	**866-275-2467**	307-638-3311	376
Plains Regional Medical Ctr 2100 N ML King Blvd	Clovis	NM	88101	**800-923-6980**	505-769-2141	371-3
Plains Reporter PO Box 1447	Williston	ND	58802	**800-950-2165**	701-572-2165	525-4
PlainsCapital Corp 2323 Victory Ave Ste 1400	Dallas	TX	75219	**866-762-8392**	214-252-4100	357-2
Plainview Milk Products Co-Op 130 Second St SW	Plainview	MN	55964	**800-356-5606**	507-534-3872	295-3
Plan USA 155 Plan Way	Warwick	RI	02886	**800-556-7918**	401-738-5600	47-6
Planar Systems Inc 1195 NW Compton Dr *NASDAQ: PLNR*	Beaverton	OR	97006	**866-475-2627**	503-748-1100	174-4
Plane & Pilot Magazine 12121 Wilshire Blvd 12th Fl	Los Angeles	CA	90025	**800-283-4330**	310-820-1500	452-14
Planemasters Ltd 32 W 611 Tower Rd DuPage Airport	West Chicago	IL	60185	**800-994-6400**	630-513-2100	13
Planesmart! Aviation LLC Addison Airport 15841 Addison Rd	Addison	TX	75001	**888-228-4283**	972-380-8004	681
PLANET (National Association of Landscape Professionals Inc) 950 Herndon Pkwy Ste 450	Herndon	VA	20170	**800-395-2522**	703-736-9666	47-2
Planet Hollywood Resort & Casino 3667 Las Vegas Blvd S	Las Vegas	NV	89109	**866-919-7472**	702-785-5555	660
Planit Solutions Inc 3800 Palisades Dr	Tuscaloosa	AL	35405	**800-280-6932**	205-556-9199	179-5
Planned Parenthood Action Fund Inc 1110 Vermont Ave NW	Washington	DC	20005	**800-430-4907**	202-973-4800	608
Planned Parenthood Federation of America 434 W 33rd St	New York	NY	10001	**800-230-7526**	212-541-7800	47-6
Planned Systems International Inc 10632 Lttle Patuxent Pkwy	Columbia	MD	21044	**800-275-7749**	410-964-8000	181
Plano Convention & Visitors Bureau 2000 E Spring Creek Pkwy	Plano	TX	75074	**800-817-5266**	972-941-5840	207
Plano Molding Co 431 E S St	Plano	IL	60545	**800-226-9868**	630-552-3111	200
Plant Maintenance Service Corp 3000 Fite Rd	Memphis	TN	38168	**800-459-9131**	901-353-9880	90
Plant Services Magazine 555 W Pierce Rd Ste 301	Itasca	IL	60143	**800-872-9141**	630-467-1300	452-21
Plantation Inn & Golf Resort 9301 W Ft Island Trl	Crystal River	FL	34429	**800-632-6262**	352-795-4211	660
Plante & Moran PLLC 27400 NW Hwy	Southfield	MI	48034	**866-639-9991**	248-352-2500	2
Planters Cotton Oil Mill Inc 2901 Planters Dr	Pine Bluff	AR	71601	**800-264-7070**	870-534-3631	295-29
Planters Electric Membership Corp 1740 Hwy 25 N PO Box 979	Millen	GA	30442	**888-397-3742**	478-982-4722	245
Planters Inn 112 N Market St	Charleston	SC	29401	**800-845-7082**	843-722-2345	376
Plantronics Inc 345 Encinal St *NYSE: PLT*	Santa Cruz	CA	95060	**800-544-4660**	831-426-5858	725
Plants of the Southwest 3095 Agua Fria Rd	Santa Fe	NM	87507	**800-788-7333**	505-438-8888	322
Planview Inc 8300 N Mopac Ste 300	Austin	TX	78759	**800-856-8600**	512-346-8600	179-1
Plaquemine Lock State Historic Site 57730 Main St	Plaquemine	LA	70764	**877-987-7158**	225-687-7158	513
Plaquemines Parish School Board 557 F Edward Hebert Blvd	Belle Chasse	LA	70037	**877-453-2721**	504-595-6400	676
Plascore Inc 615 N Fairview St	Zeeland	MI	49464	**800-630-9257**	616-772-1220	687
Plaskolite Inc 1770 Joyce Ave	Columbus	OH	43219	**800-848-9124**	614-294-3281	593
Plasma Ruggedized Solutions Inc 2284 Ringwood Ave Ste A	San Jose	CA	95131	**800-994-7527**	408-954-8405	476
Plaspros Inc 1143 Ridgeview Dr	McHenry	IL	60050	**800-752-7776**	815-430-2300	597
Plas-Tanks Industries Inc 39 Standen Dr	Hamilton	OH	45015	**800-247-6709**	513-942-3800	200
Plastatech Engineering Ltd 725 Morley Dr	Saginaw	MI	48601	**800-892-9358**	989-754-6500	192-4
Plastic Card Systems Inc 31 Pierce St	Northborough	MA	01532	**800-742-2273**	508-351-6210	174-6
Plastic Components Inc N 116 W 18271 Morse Dr	Germantown	WI	53022	**877-253-1496**		597
Plastic Development Co Inc 75 Palmer Industrial Rd PO Box 4007	Williamsport	PA	17701	**800-451-1420**		372
Plastic Forming Company Inc 20 S Bradley Rd	Woodbridge	CT	06525	**800-732-2060**	203-397-1338	200
Plastic Packaging Inc 1246 Main Ave SE	Hickory	NC	28602	**800-333-2466**	828-328-2466	65
Plastic Recycling of Iowa Falls Inc 10252 Hwy 65	Iowa Falls	IA	50126	**800-338-1438**	641-648-5073	652
Plastic Safety Systems Inc 2444 Baldwin Rd	Cleveland	OH	44104	**800-662-6338**		669
Plasticolors Inc 2600 Michigan Ave PO Box 816	Ashtabula	OH	44005	**888-661-7675**	440-997-5137	141
Plasticrest Products Inc 4519 W Harrison St	Chicago	IL	60624	**800-828-2163**	773-826-2163	286
Plastics Color & Compounding Inc 14201 Paxton Ave	Calumet City	IL	60409	**800-922-9936**		598-2
Plastikon Industries Inc 688 Sandoval Way	Hayward	CA	94544	**800-370-0858**	510-400-1010	601
Plastiques Cascades Re-Plast 1350 Ch Quatre- Saisons	Notre-Dame-du-Bon-Conseil	QC	J0C1A0	**800-567-5813**	819-336-2440	652
Plast-O-Matic Valves Inc 1384 Pompton Ave	Cedar Grove	NJ	07009	**800-323-2710**	973-256-3000	777

Name / Address	City	State	Zip	Toll-Free	Phone	Class
Plastpro Inc 5200 W Century Blvd 9F	Los Angeles	CA	90045	**800-779-0561**	310-693-8600	601
Plastronics Socket Co Inc 2601 Texas Dr *Cust Svc	Irving	TX	75062	**800-582-5822***	972-258-2580	253
Platform Computing Inc 3760 14th Ave	Markham	ON	L3R3T7	**877-528-3676**	905-948-8448	179-1
Platinum Hotel 211 E Flamingo Rd *General	Las Vegas	NV	89169	**877-211-9211***	702-365-5000	376
Platinum Select LP 5001 Statesman Dr	Irving	TX	75201	**866-953-0011**		387
Plato Woodwork Inc 200 Third St SW	Plato	MN	55370	**800-328-5924**	320-238-2193	114
Plato's Closet 23021 Outer Dr	Allen Park	MI	48101	**800-592-8049**	313-278-2300	309
Platon Digital Graphics 136 Oregon St	El Segundo	CA	90245	**800-499-0292**		619
Platt & Labonia Co 70 Stoddard Ave	North Haven	CT	06473	**800-505-9099**	203-239-5681	688
Platt Electric Supply 10605 SW Allen Blvd	Beaverton	OR	97005	**800-257-5288**	503-641-6121	246
Platt Luggage Inc 4051 W 51st St	Chicago	IL	60632	**800-222-1555**	773-838-2000	448
Plattco Corp 7 White St	Plattsburgh	NY	12901	**800-352-1731**	518-563-4640	777
Platte-Clay Electric Co-op Inc 1000 W Hwy 92 PO Box 100	Kearney	MO	64060	**800-431-2131**	816-628-3121	245
Platts Two Penn Plz 25th Fl	New York	NY	10121	**800-752-8878**	212-904-3070	628-9
Playbill Magazine 525 Seventh Ave Ste 1801	New York	NY	10018	**800-533-4330**	212-557-5757	452-9
PlayCore Inc 401 Chestnut St Ste 410	Chattanooga	TN	37402	**877-762-7563**		343
Player's Club Resort 35 Deallyon Ave	Hilton Head Island	SC	29928	**800-497-7529**	843-785-3355	660
Playhouse Square 1501 Euclid Ave Ste 200	Cleveland	OH	44115	**866-546-1353**	216-771-4444	565
PlayNetwork Inc 8727 148th Ave NE *Sales	Redmond	WA	98052	**888-964-8274***	425-497-8100	517
Playscripts 450 Seventh Ave Ste 809	New York	NY	10123	**866-639-7529**		779
Playworld Systems Inc 1000 Buffalo Rd	Lewisburg	PA	17837	**800-233-8404**	570-522-9800	343
Plaza Art 633 Middleton St	Nashville	TN	37203	**866-668-6714**	615-254-3368	44
Plaza Artists Materials of the MidAtlantic Inc 1990 K Str NW	Washington	DC	20006	**866-668-6714**	202-331-7090	44
Plaza Bank 7460 W Irving Pk Rd *General	Norridge	IL	60706	**877-714-9599***	708-456-3440	69
Plaza Fleet Parts Inc 1520 S Broadway	Saint Louis	MO	63104	**800-325-7618**	314-231-5047	60
Plaza Group Inc 10375 Richmond Ave Ste 1620	Houston	TX	77042	**800-876-3738**	713-266-0707	144
Plaza Home Mortgage Inc 5090 Shoreham Pl Ste 206	San Diego	CA	92122	**866-260-2529**	858-346-1208	502
Plaza Hotel & Casino One Main St PO Box 760	Las Vegas	NV	89101	**800-634-6575**	702-386-2110	376
Plaza Hotel, The 5th Ave at Central Park S	New York	NY	10019	**888-850-0909**	212-759-3000	375
Plaza Live, The 425 N Bumby Ave	Orlando	FL	32803	**877-435-9849**	407-228-1220	565
Plaza on the River Resort Club Hotel 121 W St	Reno	NV	89501	**800-628-5974**	775-786-2200	376
Plaza Resort & Spa 600 N Atlantic Ave	Daytona Beach	FL	32118	**800-429-8662**	386-255-4471	660
Plaza Suite Hotel Resort 620 S Peters St	New Orleans	LA	70130	**800-770-6721**		376
Plaza Suites Silicon Valley 3100 Lakeside Dr	Santa Clara	CA	95054	**800-345-1554**	408-748-9800	376
Plaza Tire Service 2075 Corporate Cr	Cape Girardeau	MO	63702	**877-787-1691**		61-5
PLB Sports Inc Penn Ctr W Bldg 3 Ste 411	Pittsburgh	PA	15276	**877-752-7778**	412-787-8800	295-8
Pleasant Excavating Co Inc 24024 Frederick Rd Ste 200	Clarksburg	MD	20871	**800-842-1180**	301-428-0800	190-5
Pleasant Holidays LLC 2404 Townsgate Rd	Westlake Village	CA	91361	**800-742-9244**	818-991-3390	761
Pleasant Trucking Inc 2250 Industrial Dr PO Box 778	Connellsville	PA	15425	**800-245-2402**		770
Pleasant Valley State Prison 24863 W Jayne Ave PO Box 8500	Coalinga	CA	93210	**877-256-6877**	559-935-4900	213
Pleasant View Gardens Inc 7316 Pleasant St	Loudon	NH	03307	**866-862-2974**	603-435-8361	322
Pleasanton Chamber of Commerce 777 Peters Ave	Pleasanton	CA	94566	**877-807-2249**	925-846-5858	137
Please Touch Museum Memorial Hall Fairmount Pk 4231 Ave of the Republic	Philadelphia	PA	19131	**800-732-0999**	215-963-0667	514
Pleiger Plastics Co PO Box 1271	Washington	PA	15301	**800-753-4437**	724-228-2244	601
Pleora Technologies Inc 340 Terry Fox Dr Suite 300	Kanata	ON	K2K3A2	**888-687-6877**	613-270-0625	659
PLF (Public Lands Foundation) PO Box 7226	Arlington	VA	22207	**866-985-9636**	703-790-1988	47-13
PLI (Practising Law Institute) 810 Seventh Ave 26th Fl	New York	NY	10019	**800-260-4754**	212-824-5700	48-10
Plitek LLC 69 Rawls Rd	Des Plaines	IL	60018	**800-966-1250**		601
PLRB (Property Loss Research Bureau) 3025 Highland Pkwy Ste 800	Downers Grove	IL	60515	**888-711-7572**	630-724-2200	48-9
Plug Power Inc 968 Albany-Shaker Rd *NASDAQ: PLUG*	Latham	NY	12110	**877-474-1993**	518-782-7700	253
Plum Creek Timber Company Inc 601 Union St Ste 3100 *NYSE: PCL*	Seattle	WA	98101	**800-858-5347**	206-467-3600	742
Plumas County Visitors Bureau 550 Crescent St	Quincy	CA	95971	**800-326-2247**	530-283-6345	207

Name / Address	City	State	ZIP	Toll-Free	Phone	Class
Plumas-Sierra Rural Electric Co-op						
73233 SR 70 Ste A	Portola	CA	96122	**800-555-2207**	530-832-4261	245
Plumb Supply Co						
1622 NE 51st Ave	Des Moines	IA	50313	**800-483-9511**	515-262-9511	605
Plumbers Supply Co						
1000 E Main St	Louisville	KY	40206	**800-626-5133**	502-582-2261	605
Plumbing Distributors Inc						
1025 Old Norcross Rd	Lawrenceville	GA	30046	**800-262-9231**	770-963-9231	605
Plumbing-Heating-Cooling Contractors NA (PHCC)						
180 S Washington St	Falls Church	VA	22040	**800-533-7694**	703-237-8100	48-3
Plump Jack's Squaw Valley Inn						
1920 Squaw Vly Rd						
PO Box 2407	Olympic Valley	CA	96146	**800-323-7666**	530-583-1576	376
Plumrose USA Inc						
1901 Butterfield Rd						
Ste 305	Downers Grove	IL	60515	**800-526-4909**	732-624-4040	468
PLWC (Paragould Light Water & Cable)						
1901 Jones Rd	Paragould	AR	72450	**800-482-8998**	870-239-7700	115
PLX Technology Inc						
870 W Maude Ave	Sunnyvale	CA	94085	**800-759-3735**	408-774-9060	687
NASDAQ: PLXT						
PlymKraft Inc						
479 Export Cir	Newport News	VA	23601	**800-992-0854**	757-595-0364	209
Plymouth State University						
17 High St	Plymouth	NH	03264	**800-842-6900**	603-535-2237	166
Plymouth Tube Co						
29 W 150 Warrenville Rd	Warrenville	IL	60555	**800-323-9506***	630-393-3550	485
*Mktg						
Plymouth Village						
900 Salem Dr	Redlands	CA	92373	**800-391-4552**	909-793-9195	663
Plywood Supply Inc						
7036 NE 175th St	Kenmore	WA	98028	**888-774-9663**	425-485-8585	606
PM Beef Group LLC						
2850 Hwy 60 E	Windom	MN	56101	**800-622-5213**	507-831-2761	10-1
PM Co						
9220 Glades Dr	Fairfield	OH	45011	**800-327-4359**	513-825-7626	547
PM Construction Co Inc						
PO Box 728	Saco	ME	04072	**800-646-0068**	207-282-7697	187
PMA (Polish Museum of America)						
984 N Milwaukee Ave	Chicago	IL	60642	**800-535-2071**	773-384-3352	513
PMA (Photo Marketing Assn International)						
3000 Picture Pl	Jackson	MI	49201	**800-762-9287**	517-788-8100	48-18
PMA (Produce Marketing Assn)						
1500 Casho Mill Rd	Newark	DE	19711	**800-872-7245**	302-738-7100	48-6
PMC Commercial Trust						
17950 Preston Rd Ste 600	Dallas	TX	75252	**800-486-3223**	972-349-3200	216
NASDAQ: CMCT						
PMC Specialties Group Inc						
501 Murray Rd	Cincinnati	OH	45217	**800-543-2466**	513-242-3300	142
PMC-Sierra Inc						
1380 Bordeaux Dr	Sunnyvale	CA	94089	**866-268-7116**	408-239-8000	687
NASDAQ: PMCS						
PMHI (Pacific Modern Homes Inc)						
9723 Railroad St	Elk Grove	CA	95624	**800-395-1011**	916-685-9514	105
PMI (Project Management Institute)						
14 Campus Blvd	Newtown Square	PA	19073	**866-276-4764**	610-356-4600	48-12
PMI Group Inc						
3003 Oak Rd	Walnut Creek	CA	94597	**800-288-1970**		357-4
OTC: PMI						
PMI Mortgage Insurance Co						
3003 Oak Rd	Walnut Creek	CA	94597	**800-288-1970**	925-658-7878	388-5
PML (OneAmerica Financial Partners Inc)						
PO Box 368	Indianapolis	IN	46206	**800-249-6269**	317-285-1877	388-2
PMMI (Packaging Machinery Manufacturers Institute)						
4350 N Fairfax Dr Ste 600	Arlington	VA	22203	**888-275-7664**	703-243-8555	48-13
PMP Corp 25 Security Dr	Avon	CT	06001	**800-243-6628***	860-677-9656	490
*Cust Svc						
PMPA (Precision Machined Products Assn)						
6700 W Snowville Rd	Brecksville	OH	44141	**800-233-1234**	440-526-0300	48-13
PMS Systems Corp						
2800 28th St Ste 109	Santa Monica	CA	90405	**800-755-3968**	310-450-2566	179-5
PMSLIC (Pennsylvania Medical Society Liability Insurance Co)						
1700 Bent Creek Blvd						
PO Box 2080	Mechanicsburg	PA	17050	**800-445-1212**	717-791-1212	388-5
PNBC (Progressive National Baptist Convention Inc)						
601 50th St NE	Washington	DC	20019	**800-876-7622**	202-396-0558	47-20
PNC Arena						
1400 EdwaRds Mill Rd	Raleigh	NC	27607	**800-745-3000**	919-861-2300	711
PNC Bank						
600 Grant St	Pittsburgh	PA	15219	**888-762-2265**		69
NYSE: PNC-L						
PNC Bank Delaware						
300 Delaware Ave	Wilmington	DE	19899	**888-762-2265**	302-429-1361	69
PNC Bank NA						
249 Fifth Ave 1 PNC Plaza	Pittsburgh	PA	15222	**888-762-2265**	412-762-2000	69
PNC Financial Services Group Inc						
249 Fifth Ave 1 PNC Plz	Pittsburgh	PA	15222	**877-762-2000**	412-762-2000	357-2
NYSE: PNC						
PNC Park						
115 Federal St	Pittsburgh	PA	15212	**866-800-1275**	412-321-2827	711
Pneumech Systems Mfg LLC						
201 Pneu Mech Dr	Statesville	NC	28625	**800-358-7374**	704-873-2475	18
Pneutek 17 Friars Dr	Hudson	NH	03051	**800-431-8665**	603-883-1660	749
PNM Resources Inc						
Alvarado Sq	Albuquerque	NM	87158	**888-342-5766**	505-241-2700	357-5
NYSE: PNM						
PNNL (Pacific Northwest National Laboratory)						
902 Battelle Blvd PO Box 999	Richland	WA	99352	**888-375-7665**	509-375-2121	659
PNWFCU (Pacific NW Federal Credit Union)						
12106 NE Marx St	Portland	OR	97220	**866-692-8669**	503-256-5858	219
PNY Technologies Inc						
299 Webro Rd	Parsippany	NJ	07054	**800-769-7079**	973-515-9700	288
Poblocki Sign Company LLC						
922 S 70th St	West Allis	WI	53214	**800-776-7064**	414-453-4010	692
Pocahontas County						
PO Box 275	Marlinton	WV	24954	**800-336-7009**		336
Pocahontas State Park						
10301 State Pk Rd	Chesterfield	VA	23832	**800-933-7275**	804-796-4255	558
Pocino Foods Co						
14250 Lomitas Ave	City of Industry	CA	91746	**800-345-0150**	626-968-8000	295-26
Pocomoke River State Park						
3461 Worcester Hwy	Snow Hill	MD	21863	**877-620-8367**	410-632-2566	558
Pocomoke State Forest						
580 Taylor Ave	Annapolis	MD	21401	**877-620-8367**		558
Pocono Manor Golf Resort & Spa						
one Manor Dr Rt 314	Pocono Manor	PA	18349	**800-233-8150**	570-839-7111	660
Pocono Mountains Vacation Bureau						
1004 Main St	Stroudsburg	PA	18360	**800-722-9199**	570-421-5791	207
Pocono Raceway						
Long Pond Rd PO Box 500	Long Pond	PA	18334	**800-722-3929**	570-646-2300	508
Pocono Record						
511 Lenox St	Stroudsburg	PA	18360	**800-530-6310**	570-421-3000	525-2
Podiatry Insurance Company of America						
3000 Meridian Blvd Ste 400	Franklin	TN	37067	**800-251-5727**	615-984-2005	388-5
POH Regional Medical Ctr						
50 N Perry St	Pontiac	MI	48342	**888-327-0671**	248-338-5000	371-3
Pohly Co						
867 Boylston St 5th Fl	Boston	MA	02116	**800-383-0888**	617-451-1700	628-9
Point Loma Nazarene University						
3900 Lomaland Dr	San Diego	CA	92106	**800-733-7770***	619-849-2200	166
*Admissions						
Point Park University						
201 Wood St	Pittsburgh	PA	15222	**800-321-0129***	412-391-4100	166
*Admissions						
Point Pelee National Park of Canada						
407 Monarch Ln RR 1	Leamington	ON	N8H3V4	**888-773-8888**	519-322-2365	556
Point Plaza Suites & Conference Hotel						
950 J Clyde Morris Blvd	Newport News	VA	23601	**800-841-1112**	757-599-4460	376
Point Reyes National Seashore						
1 Bear Valley Rd	Point Reyes Station	CA	94956	**877-874-2478**	415-464-5100	557
Point, The						
PO Box 1327	Saranac Lake	NY	12983	**800-255-3530**	518-891-5674	660
Pointe Coupee Electric Membership Corp						
2506 False River Dr						
PO Box 160	New Roads	LA	70760	**800-738-7232**	225-638-3751	245
Pointe Hilton at Squaw Peak Resort						
7677 N 16th St	Phoenix	AZ	85020	**800-685-0550**	602-997-2626	660
Pointe Hilton Resort at Tapatio Cliffs						
11111 N Seventh St	Phoenix	AZ	85020	**800-947-9784**	602-866-7500	660
Pointe Scientific Inc						
5449 Research Dr PO Box 87188	Canton	MI	48188	**800-445-9853**	734-487-8300	231
Pointe Technology Group Inc						
7272 Pk Cir Dr Ste 200	Hanover	MD	21076	**800-730-6171**	410-712-9425	181
Points of Light Foundation & Volunteer Ctr National Network						
1400 'I' St NW Ste 800	Washington	DC	20005	**866-269-0510**	202-729-8000	47-5
Poisoned Pen Bookstore						
4014 N Goldwater Blvd	Scottsdale	AZ	85251	**888-560-9919**	480-947-2974	95
Polar Beverages Inc						
1001 Southbridge St	Worcester	MA	01610	**800-734-9800***	508-753-4300	79-2
*Cust Svc						
Polar Service Centers						
7600 E Sam Houston Pkwy N	Houston	TX	77049	**800-955-8558**	281-459-6400	769
Polar Tank Trailer Inc						
12810 County Rd 17	Holdingford	MN	56340	**800-826-6589**	320-746-2255	769
Polar Ware Co 502 Hwy 67	Kiel	WI	53042	**800-237-3655***		482
*Cust Svc						
Polaris Pool Systems Inc						
2620 Commerce Way	Vista	CA	92081	**800-822-7933**	760-599-9600	794
Polaris Technologies Inc						
500 Victoria Rd	Austintown	OH	44515	**800-783-2179**		494
Police & Fire Federal Credit Union						
901 Arch St	Philadelphia	PA	19107	**800-228-8801**	215-931-0300	219
Polish Museum of America (PMA)						
984 N Milwaukee Ave	Chicago	IL	60642	**800-535-2071**	773-384-3352	513
Politics & Prose Bookstore						
5015 Connecticut Ave NW	Washington	DC	20008	**800-722-0790**	202-364-1919	95
Polk Audio Inc						
5601 Metro Dr	Baltimore	MD	21215	**800-377-7655**	410-358-3600	51
Polk County Rural Public Power District						
115 W 3rd St PO Box 465	Stromsburg	NE	68666	**888-242-5265**	402-764-4381	245
Polk County Travel & Tourism						
20 E Mills St PO Box 308	Columbus	NC	28722	**800-440-7848**	828-894-2324	207
Polk-Burnett Electric Co-op (PBEC)						
1001 State Rd 35	Centuria	WI	54824	**800-421-0283**	715-646-2191	245
Pollock Paper & Packaging						
One Pollock Pl	Grand Prairie	TX	75050	**800-843-7320***	972-263-2126	552
*Cust Svc						
Pollstar						
4697 W Jacquelyn Ave	Fresno	CA	93722	**800-344-7383**	559-271-7900	452-9
Pollution Control Corp						
500 W Country Club Rd	Chickasha	OK	73018	**800-966-1265**		197
Polsinelli Shalton Flanigan Suelthaus PC						
700 W 47th St Ste 1000	Kansas City	MO	64112	**888-572-7025**	816-753-1000	425
Polsinello Fuels Inc						
41 Riverside Ave	Rensselaer	NY	12144	**800-334-5823**	518-463-0084	315
POLY (POLY Languages Institute Inc)						
5757 Wilshire Blvd Ste 510	Los Angeles	CA	90036	**877-738-5787**	323-933-9399	420
Poly Cycle Inc						
5501 Campbells Run Rd	Pittsburgh	PA	15205	**800-394-4333**	412-747-1101	449
Poly Foam Inc						
116 Pine St S	Lester Prairie	MN	55354	**844-446-4339**	320-395-2551	594
POLY Languages Institute Inc (POLY)						
5757 Wilshire Blvd Ste 510	Los Angeles	CA	90036	**877-738-5787**	323-933-9399	420
Poly Molding LLC						
96 Fourth Ave	Haskell	NJ	07420	**800-229-7161**	973-835-7161	594
Poly-America Inc						
2000 W Marshall Dr	Grand Prairie	TX	75051	**800-527-3322**	972-337-7100	65
Polycom Inc						
4750 Willow Rd	Pleasanton	CA	94588	**800-765-9266**		725
PolyConversions Inc						
505 Condit Dr	Rantoul	IL	61866	**888-893-3330**	217-893-3330	569
Polygon Co						
103 Industrial Pk Dr						
PO Box 176	Walkerton	IN	46574	**800-918-9261**	574-586-3145	595
Polygon Network						
PO Box 4806	Dillon	CO	80435	**800-221-4435**		390
Polygon Northwest Co						
11624 SE Fifth St Ste 200	Bellevue	WA	98005	**800-765-9466**	425-586-7700	644
Polymedco Inc						
510 Furnace Dock Rd	Cortlandt Manor	NY	10567	**800-431-2123**	914-739-5400	231
Polynesian Adventure Tours Inc						
2880 Kilihau St	Honolulu	HI	96819	**800-622-3011**	808-833-3000	750
Polynesian Cultural Ctr						
55-370 Kamehameha Hwy	Laie	HI	96762	**800-367-7060**	808-293-3005	513
Polynesian Resort, The						
615 Ocean Shores Blvd NW	Ocean Shores	WA	98569	**800-562-4836**	360-289-3361	660

	Toll-Free	Phone	Class
PolyOne Corp			
33587 Walker Rd . . . . Avon Lake OH 44012	**866-765-9663**	440-930-1000	598-2
NYSE: POL			
Poly-Pak Industries Inc			
125 Spagnoli Rd . . . . Melville NY 11747	**800-969-1993**		65
PolyPeptide Laboratories Inc			
365 Maple Ave . . . . Torrance CA 90503	**800-338-4965**	310-782-3569	231
Polysciences Inc			
400 Valley Rd . . . . Warrington PA 18976	**800-523-2575***	215-343-6484	231
*Cust Svc			
Polyspede Electronics Company Inc			
6770 Twin Hills Ave . . . . Dallas TX 75231	**888-476-5944**	214-363-7245	511
Polytechnic University			
Long Island			
105 Maxess Rd . . . . Melville NY 11747	**877-503-7659***	631-755-4300	166
*Admissions			
Polytron Corp			
4400 Wyland Dr . . . . Elkhart IN 46516	**888-228-0246**	574-522-0246	204
Polyvinyl Films Inc			
PO Box 753 . . . . Sutton MA 01590	**800-343-6134**	508-865-3558	593
PolyVision Corp			
3970 Johns Creek Ct Ste 325 . . . . Suwanee GA 30024	**800-620-7659**	678-542-3100	174-2
POM Inc			
200 S Elmira Ave			
PO Box 430 . . . . Russellville AR 72802	**800-331-7275**	479-968-2880	490
POMC (Parents of Murdered Children)			
4960 Ridge Ave Ste 2 . . . . Cincinnati OH 45209	**888-818-7662**	513-721-5683	47-6
POMCO 2425 James St . . . . Syracuse NY 13206	**800-934-2459**	315-432-9171	387
Pomeroy IT Solutions Inc			
1020 Petersburg Rd . . . . Hebron KY 41048	**800-846-8727**	859-586-0600	181
Pomperaug Woods			
80 Heritage Rd . . . . Southbury CT 06488	**866-817-8935**	203-262-6555	663
Pomps Tire Service Inc			
1123 Cedar St . . . . Green Bay WI 54301	**800-236-8911**	920-435-8301	745
Ponca City Library			
515 E Grand Ave . . . . Ponca City OK 74601	**800-522-8165**	580-767-0345	431-3
Ponca City Medical Ctr			
1900 N 14th St . . . . Ponca City OK 74601	**800-222-1222**	580-765-3321	371-3
Ponca City Publishing Inc			
PO Box 191 . . . . Ponca City OK 74602	**866-765-3311**	580-765-3311	628-8
Ponca City Tourism			
420 E Grand Ave PO Box 1109 . . . . . . Ponca City OK 74602	**866-763-8092**	580-765-4400	207
Ponce de Leon's Fountain of Youth			
11 Magnolia Ave . . . . Saint Augustine FL 32084	**800-356-8222**	904-829-3168	49-2
Pontarelli Limousine Service			
2225 W Hubbard St . . . . Chicago IL 60612	**800-322-5466**	312-226-5466	437
Pontchartrain Ctr			
4545 Williams Blvd . . . . Kenner LA 70065	**800-745-3000**	504-465-9985	206
Pontchartrain Hotel			
2031 St Charles Ave . . . . New Orleans LA 70130	**800-777-6193**	504-524-0581	376
Ponte Vedra Inn & Club			
200 Ponte Vedra Blvd . . . . . Ponte Vedra Beach FL 32082	**800-234-7842**	904-285-1111	660
Pontifical College Josephinum			
7625 N High St . . . . Columbus OH 43235	**888-252-5812**	614-885-5585	167-3
Ponvia Technology Inc			
49-T Sherwood Ter . . . . Lake Bluff IL 60045	**877-217-0875**		444
PONY Baseball/Softball Inc			
1951 Pony Pl PO Box 225 . . . . Washington PA 15301	**800-321-4473**	724-225-1060	47-22
Pony Express National Museum			
914 Penn St . . . . Saint Joseph MO 64503	**800-530-5930**	816-279-5059	513
Poof-Slinky Inc			
4280 S Haggerty Rd PO Box 701394 . . . . . . Canton MI 48188	**800-829-9502**	734-454-9552	752
Poolmaster Inc			
770 Del Paso Rd . . . . Sacramento CA 95834	**800-854-1492**	916-567-9800	701
Pop Warner Little Scholars Inc			
586 Middletown Blvd Ste C-100 . . . . . Langhorne PA 19047	**800-257-4268**	215-752-2691	47-22
Poplar Bluff Regional Medical Ctr			
2620 N Westwood Blvd . . . . Poplar Bluff MO 63901	**800-327-0275**	573-785-7721	371-3
Poplar Bluff Regional Medical Ctr South Campus			
621 WPine Blvd . . . . Poplar Bluff MO 63901	**800-327-0275**	573-686-4111	371-3
Poplar Springs Hospital			
350 Poplar Dr PO Box 3060 . . . . Petersburg VA 23805	**866-546-2229**	804-733-6874	371-5
Popular Woodworking Magazine			
4700 E Galbraith Rd . . . . Cincinnati OH 45236	**877-860-9140***	513-531-2690	452-14
*Cust Svc			
Population Connection			
2120 L St NW Ste 500 . . . . Washington DC 20037	**800-767-1956**	202-332-2200	47-5
Population Reference Bureau (PRB)			
1875 Connecticut Ave NW			
Ste 520 . . . . Washington DC 20009	**800-877-9881**	202-483-1100	47-7
Population-Environment Balance Inc			
2000 P St NW Ste 600 . . . . Washington DC 20036	**800-866-6269**	202-955-5700	47-7
Porex Technologies Corp			
500 Bohannon Rd . . . . Fairburn GA 30213	**800-241-0195***	770-964-1421	601
*Cust Svc			
Pork Report			
1776 NW 114th St PO Box 9114 . . . . . Des Moines IA 50325	**800-456-7675**	515-223-2600	452-1
Porky Products Corp			
400 Port Carteret Dr . . . . Carteret NJ 07008	**800-952-0265***	732-541-0200	296-9
*General			
Porsche Cars North America Inc			
980 Hammond Dr Ste 1000 . . . . Atlanta GA 30328	**800-505-1041**	770-290-3500	58
Porsche of Maplewood			
2780 Maplewood Dr . . . . Maplewood MN 55109	**888-693-6579**	888-679-1698	56
Port Arthur Convention & Visitors Bureau			
3401 Cultural Ctr Dr . . . . Port Arthur TX 77642	**800-235-7822**	409-985-7822	207
Port Canaveral			
445 Challanger Rd . . . . Cape Canaveral FL 32920	**888-767-8226**	321-783-7831	611
Port Freeport			
PO Box 615 . . . . Freeport TX 77542	**800-362-5743**	979-233-2667	611
Port Hudson State Historic Site			
236 Hwy 61 . . . . Jackson LA 70748	**888-677-3400**	225-654-3775	558
Port Huron Hospital (PHH)			
1221 Pine Grove Ave . . . . Port Huron MI 48060	**888-327-0671**	810-987-5000	371-3
Port Jervis City School District			
PO Box 1104 . . . . Port Jervis NY 12771	**877-544-6664**	845-858-3100	187
Port Metro Vancouver			
999 Canada Pl . . . . Vancouver BC V6C3T4	**888-767-8826**	604-665-9000	611
Port of Anchorage			
2000 Anchorage Port Rd . . . . Anchorage AK 99501	**877-650-8400**	907-343-6200	611
Port of Astoria			
422 Gateway Ave . . . . Astoria OR 97103	**800-860-4093**	503-325-4521	611
Port of Baltimore			
Maryland Port Administration			
401 E Pratt St . . . . Baltimore MD 21202	**800-638-7519***		611
*General			
Port of Brownsville			
1000 Foust Rd . . . . Brownsville TX 78521	**800-378-5395**	956-831-4592	611
Port of Corpus Christi			
222 Power St . . . . Corpus Christi TX 78401	**800-580-7110**	361-882-5633	611
Port of Duluth			
Duluth Seaway Port Authority			
1200 Port Terminal Dr . . . . Duluth MN 55802	**800-232-0703**	218-727-8525	611
Port of Everett			
2911 Bond St Ste 202 . . . . Everett WA 98201	**800-729-7678**	425-259-3164	611
Port of Lake Charles			
150 Marine St . . . . Lake Charles LA 70601	**800-845-7678**	337-439-3661	611
Port of Milwaukee			
2323 S Lincoln Memorial Dr . . . . Milwaukee WI 53207	**800-367-5690**	414-286-3511	611
Port of New Orleans			
1350 Port of New Orleans Pl . . . . New Orleans LA 70130	**800-776-6652**	504-522-2551	611
Port of Orange			
Orange County Navigation Port District			
1201 Childers Rd . . . . Orange TX 77630	**800-368-3749**	409-883-4363	611
Port of Palm Beach			
1 E 11th St Ste 400 . . . . Riviera Beach FL 33404	**877-377-1737**	561-842-4201	611
Port of Pensacola			
700 S Barracks St . . . . Pensacola FL 32502	**800-711-1712**	850-436-5070	611
Port of Port Lavaca-Point Comfort			
Calhoun Port Authority			
PO Box 397 . . . . Point Comfort TX 77978	**800-933-3643**	361-987-2813	611
Port of Portland			
7200 NE Airport Way			
PO Box 3529 . . . . Portland OR 97218	**800-547-8411**	503-415-6000	611
Port of Richmond Commission			
900 E Broad St . . . . Richmond VA 23219	**800-467-4943**	804-646-6335	611
Port of San Diego			
3165 Pacific Hwy . . . . San Diego CA 92101	**800-854-2757**	619-686-6200	611
Port of San Francisco			
Pier 1 The Embarcadero . . . . San Francisco CA 94111	**800-479-5314**	415-274-0400	611
Port of Seattle			
PO Box 1209 . . . . Seattle WA 98111	**800-426-7817**	206-728-3000	611
Port of Seward			
PO Box 167 . . . . Seward AK 99664	**855-445-7131**	907-224-3138	611
Port of South Louisiana			
171 Belle Terre Blvd PO Box 909 . . . . . . LaPlace LA 70068	**866-536-8300**	985-652-9278	611
Port of Stockton			
2201 W Washington St . . . . Stockton CA 95203	**800-344-3213**	209-946-0246	611
Port of Vancouver			
3103 NW Lower River Rd . . . . Vancouver WA 98660	**800-475-8012**	360-693-3611	611
Port Plastics Inc			
15325 Fairfield Ranch Rd			
Ste 150 . . . . Chino Hills CA 91709	**800-800-0039**	480-813-6118	596
Port Townsend Marine Science Ctr			
532 Battery Way . . . . Port Townsend WA 98368	**800-566-3932**	360-385-5582	513
Portable Computer & Communications Assn (PCCA)			
PO Box 680 . . . . Hood River OR 97031	**877-323-8888**	541-490-5140	47-9
Portable Technology Solutions LLC			
221 David Ct . . . . Calverton NY 11933	**877-640-4152**		178
Porta-Bote International			
1074 Independence Ave . . . . Mountain View CA 94043	**800-227-8882**	650-961-5334	89
Porta-Fab Corp			
18080 Chesterfield Airport Rd . . . . . . Chesterfield MO 63005	**800-325-3781**	636-537-5555	104
Portage County			
449 S Meridian St 7th Fl . . . . Ravenna OH 44266	**800-772-3799**	330-297-3600	336
Portage County District Library			
10482 S St . . . . Garrettsville OH 44231	**800-500-5179**	330-527-4378	431-3
Portage Electric Products Inc			
7700 Freedom Ave NW . . . . North Canton OH 44720	**888-464-7374**	330-499-2727	203
Porta-King Building Systems			
4133 Shoreline Dr . . . . Earth City MO 63045	**800-284-5346**		187
Porter Capital Corp			
2112 First Ave N . . . . Birmingham AL 35203	**800-737-7344**	205-322-5442	272
Porter Inc			
2200 W Monroe St . . . . Decatur IN 46733	**800-736-7685**	260-724-9111	89
Porter Instrument Company Inc			
245 Township Line Rd			
PO Box 907 . . . . Hatfield PA 19440	**888-723-4001**	215-723-4000	202
Porter Medical Ctr Inc			
115 Porter Dr . . . . Middlebury VT 05753	**800-994-6610**	802-388-4701	458
Porter Precision Products Inc			
2734 Banning Rd . . . . Cincinnati OH 45239	**800-543-7041**	513-923-3777	747
Porter Truck Sales LP			
135 McCarty St . . . . Houston TX 77029	**800-956-2408**	713-672-2400	509
PorterCorp			
4240 136th Ave . . . . Holland MI 49424	**800-354-7721**	616-399-1963	104
Porters of Racine			
301 Sixth St . . . . Racine WI 53403	**800-558-3245**	262-633-6363	320
Portfolio Recovery Assoc LLC			
120 Corporate Blvd			
Ste 100 Reverside Commerce Ctr . . . . Norfolk VA 23502	**888-772-7326**		158
NASDAQ: PRAA			
Portland Baroque Orchestra			
1020 SW Taylor St Ste 200 . . . . Portland OR 97205	**800-494-8497**	503-222-6000	566-3
Portland Business Alliance			
200 SW Market St Ste 150 . . . . Portland OR 97201	**800-224-1180**	503-224-8684	137
Portland General Electric			
121 SW Salmon St . . . . Portland OR 97204	**800-542-8818**	503-464-8000	775
NYSE: POR			
Portland Harbor Hotel			
468 Fore St . . . . Portland ME 04101	**888-798-9090**	207-775-9090	376
Portland International Airport			
7000 NE Airport Way . . . . Portland OR 97218	**800-547-8411**	503-460-4234	27
Portland Opera			
211 SE Caruthers St . . . . Portland OR 97214	**866-739-6737**	503-241-1407	566-2
Portland Public Schools			
501 N Dixon St . . . . Portland OR 97227	**800-766-8206**	503-916-2000	676
Portland Regency Hotel			
20 Milk St . . . . Portland ME 04101	**800-727-3436**	207-774-4200	376
Portland State University			
1825 SW Broadway . . . . Portland OR 97201	**800-547-8887**	503-725-3000	166
Portland Teachers Credit Union			
PO Box 3750 . . . . Portland OR 97208	**800-527-3932**	503-228-7077	219

Listing	Toll-Free	Phone	Class
Port-O-Call Hotel 1510 Boardwalk ... Ocean City NJ 08226	800-334-4546	609-399-8812	376
Portofino Bay Hotel at Universal Orlando - A Loews Hotel 5601 Universal Blvd ... Orlando FL 32819	800-235-6397	407-503-1000	660
Portofino Hotel & Yacht Club 260 Portofino Way ... Redondo Beach CA 90277	800-468-4292	310-379-8481	376
Portofino Inn & Suites Anaheim 1831 S Harbor Blvd ... Anaheim CA 92802 *Resv	800-398-3963*	714-782-7600	376
Portofino Spa at Portofino Island Resort 10 Portofino Dr ... Pensacola FL 32561	866-849-0223	850-916-5000	698
Portola Plaza Hotel 2 Portola Plaza ... Monterey CA 93940	888-222-5851	831-649-4511	376
Portrait Software Inc 125 Summer St 16th Fl ... Boston MA 02110	800-327-8627	617-457-5200	179-1
Portsmouth Area Chamber of Commerce 342 Second St PO Box 509 ... Portsmouth OH 45662	800-648-2574	740-353-7647	137
Portsmouth Daily Times PO Box 581 ... Portsmouth OH 45662	866-430-8358	740-353-3101	525-2
Portsmouth Regional Hospital 333 Borthwick Ave ... Portsmouth NH 03801	800-685-8282	603-436-5110	371-3
Posca Bros Dental Laboratory Inc 641 W Willow St ... Long Beach CA 90806	800-537-6722	562-427-1811	412
Posey Co 5635 Peck Rd ... Arcadia CA 91006	800-447-6739	626-443-3143	472
Positech Corp 191 N Rush Lk Rd ... Laurens IA 50554	800-831-6026	712-841-4548	465
Positively Cleveland Visitors Ctr 100 Public Sq Ste 100 ... Cleveland OH 44113	800-321-1001	216-875-6680	207
Positronic Industries Inc 423 N Campbell Ave PO Box 8247 ... Springfield MO 65801	800-641-4054	417-866-2322	253
Posner Industries Inc 8641 Edgeworth Dr ... Capitol Heights MD 20743	888-767-6377	301-350-1000	487
Post Gardens Inc 21189 Huron River Dr ... Rockwood MI 48173	800-834-4630	734-379-9688	366
Post Glover Resistors Inc 4750 Olympic Blvd Bldg B ... Erlanger KY 41018 *Cust Svc	800-537-6144*	859-283-0778	253
Post Hotel, The 200 Pipestone Rd PO Box 69 ... Lake Louise AB T0L1E0	800-661-1586	403-522-3989	376
Post Publishing Co 131 W Innes St ... Salisbury NC 28144	800-546-5664	704-633-8950	628-8
Post University 800 Country Club Rd ... Waterbury CT 06723	800-345-2562	203-596-4500	166
Postal Connections of America 6136 Frisco Sq Blvd Ste 400 ... Frisco TX 75034	800-767-8257		309
PostalAnnex+ Inc 7580 Metropolitan Dr Ste 200 ... San Diego CA 92108	800-456-1525	619-563-4800	112
Post-Journal 15 W Second St ... Jamestown NY 14701	866-756-9600	716-487-1111	525-2
Postler & Jaeckle Corp 615 S Ave ... Rochester NY 14620	800-724-4252	585-546-7450	190-10
PostNet International Franchise Corp 1819 Wazee St ... Denver CO 80202	800-841-7171	303-771-7100	112
Postpartum Support International 2200 Pacific Coast Hwy Ste 304A ... Hermosa Beach CA 90254	800-944-4773		47-17
Post-Register PO Box 1800 ... Idaho Falls ID 83403	800-574-6397	208-522-1800	525-2
Post-Standard PO Box 4915 ... Syracuse NY 13221	866-447-3787	315-470-0011	525-2
Post-Star 76 Lawrence St ... Glens Falls NY 12801	800-724-2543	518-792-3131	525-2
Posty Cards 1600 Olive St ... Kansas City MO 64127	800-821-7968	816-231-2323	129
Potash Corp 1101 Skokie Blvd ... Northbrook IL 60062	800-667-0403	847-849-4200	280
Potash Corp of Saskatchewan Inc 122 First Ave S Ste 500 ... Saskatoon SK S7K7G3 NYSE: POT	800-667-3930	306-933-8500	280
Potawatomi Bingo Casino 1721 W Canal St ... Milwaukee WI 53233	800-729-7244	414-645-6888	132
Potawatomi Inn Pokagan State Pk 6 Ln 100A Lk James ... Angola IN 46703	877-768-2928	260-833-1077	660
Potawatomi State Park 3740 County Rd PD ... Sturgeon Bay WI 54235	800-847-9367*	920-746-2890	558
Potomac Conference Corp of Seventh Day Adventists 606 Greenville Ave ... Staunton VA 24401	800-732-1844	540-886-0771	47-20
Potomac Mills 2700 Potomac Mills Cir Ste 307 ... Woodbridge VA 22192	877-746-6642	703-496-9301	455
Potomac State College 101 Ft Ave ... Keyser WV 26726	800-262-7332	304-788-6800	160
Potomac Supply Corp 1398 Kinsale Rd ... Kinsale VA 22488 *Sales	800-365-3900*	804-472-2527	544
Potter Distributing Inc 4037 Roger B Chaffee Blvd ... Grand Rapids MI 49548	800-748-0568	616-531-6860	37
Potter Electric Signal Company Inc 5757 Phantom Dr Ste 125 ... Hazelwood MO 63042	800-325-3936	314-878-4321	283
5757 Phantom Dr Ste 125 ... Hazelwood MO 63042	800-325-3936	314-878-4321	739
Potter-Roemer 17451 Hurley St ... City of Industry CA 91744	800-366-3473	626-855-4890	669
Poudre Valley Hospital 1024 S Lemay Ave ... Fort Collins CO 80524	800-994-6610	970-495-7000	371-3
Poudre Valley Rural Electric Assn Inc 7649 Rea Pkwy ... Fort Collins CO 80528	800-432-1012	970-226-1234	245
Poughkeepsie Journal 85 Civic Ctr Plz ... Poughkeepsie NY 12601	800-765-1120	845-437-4800	525-2
Pounding Mill Quarry Corp 171 St Clair S Crossing ... Bluefield VA 24605	888-661-7625	276-326-1145	498-5
Poverty Point National Monument c/o Poverty Pt State Historic Site PO Box 276 ... Epps LA 71237	888-926-5492	318-926-5492	557
Poverty Point Reservoir State Park 1500 Poverty Pt Pkwy ... Delhi LA 71232	800-474-0392	318-878-7536	558
Poverty Point State Historic Site 6859 Hwy 577 ... Pioneer LA 71266	888-926-5492	318-926-5492	558
Powder River Energy Corp (PRE) 221 Main St PO Box 930 ... Sundance WY 82729	800-442-3630		245
Powder River Transportation 1700 U S 14 ... Gillette WY 82716	888-970-7233	307-682-0960	107
Powel House 244 S Third St ... Philadelphia PA 19106	877-426-8056	215-627-0364	49-2
Powell Electronics Inc 200 Commodore Dr ... Swedesboro NJ 08085	800-235-7880	856-241-8000	246
Powell Industries Inc 8550 Mosely Dr ... Houston TX 77075 NASDAQ: POWL	800-480-7273	713-944-6900	720
Powell Skate One Corp 30 S La Patera Ln ... Santa Barbara CA 93117	800-288-7528	805-964-1330	701
Powell Symphony Hall 718 N Grand Blvd ... Saint Louis MO 63103	800-232-1880	314-533-2500	565
Powell's Books Inc Seven NW Ninth Ave ... Portland OR 97209	800-878-7323	503-228-0540	95
Powell's City of Books 40 NW Tenth Ave ... Portland OR 97209	800-878-7323	503-228-4651	95
Power & Motoryacht Magazine 260 Madison Ave Fourth Fl ... New York NY 10016	800-284-8036	860-767-3200	452-4
Power & Telephone Supply Company Inc 2673 Yale Ave ... Memphis TN 38112 *Cust Svc	800-238-7514*	901-866-3300	246
Power Battery Co Inc 25 McLean Blvd ... Paterson NJ 07514	800-455-0054	973-523-8630	73
Power Distribution Inc 4200 Oakleys Ct ... Richmond VA 23223	800-225-4838	804-737-9880	720
Power Engineering Corp PO Box 766 ... Wilkes-Barre PA 18703	800-626-0903	570-823-8822	261
Power Motive Corp 5000 Vasquez Blvd ... Denver CO 80216	800-627-0087	303-355-5900	355
Power Organics 301 S Old Stage Rd ... Mount Shasta CA 96067	866-277-3420	530-926-6684	787
Power Service Products Inc PO Box 1089 ... Weatherford TX 76086	800-643-9089	817-599-9486	531
Power Surge Web Solutions 1171 South Robertson Blvd Ste 194 ... Los Angeles CA 90035	800-867-5055	312-492-4053	795
Powercon Corp PO Box 477 ... Severn MD 21144	800-638-5055	410-551-6500	720
Powerex Inc 173 Pavilion Ln ... Youngwood PA 15697	800-451-1415	724-925-7272	687
Powerfilm Inc 2337 230th St ... Ames IA 50014	888-354-7773	515-292-7606	687
Powernail Co 1300 Rose Rd ... Lake Zurich IL 60047	800-323-1653	847-634-3000	749
Powers Fasteners Inc Two Powers Ln ... Brewster NY 10509	800-524-3244	914-235-6300	488
PowerScore Inc 57 Hasell St ... Charleston SC 29401	800-545-1750		754
PowerSecure International Inc 1609 Heritage Commerce Ct ... Wake Forest NC 27587 NYSE: POWR	866-347-5455	919-556-3056	775
Powersteering Software Inc 25 First St ... Cambridge MA 02141	866-390-9088	617-492-0707	179-7
Powrmatic Inc 2906 Baltimore Blvd PO Box 439 ... Finksburg MD 21048	800-966-9100	410-833-9100	354
Pozas Bros Trucking Company Inc 8130 Enterprise Dr ... Newark CA 94560	800-874-8383	510-742-9939	770
PPA (Professional Photographers of America Inc) 229 Peachtree St NE Ste 2200 ... Atlanta GA 30303	800-786-6277	404-522-8600	47-4
PPAI (Promotional Products Assn International) 3125 Skyway Cir N ... Irving TX 75038	888-426-7724	972-252-0404	48-18
PPC Mechanical Seals 2769 Mission Dr ... Baton Rouge LA 70805	800-731-7325	225-356-4333	325
PPFA (Professional Picture Framers Assn) 2282 Springport Rd Ste F ... Jackson MI 49202	800-762-9287	517-788-8100	47-4
PPG Industries Inc 17451 Von Karman Ave ... Irvine CA 92614	800-544-3338	949-474-0400	543
PPHEA (Panhandle-Plains Higher Education Authority Inc) 1303 23rd St PO Box 839 ... Canyon TX 79015	877-629-3669	806-324-4100	47-11
PPHI (Pittsburgh Plumbing Heating & Industrial) 434 Melwood Ave ... Pittsburgh PA 15213	800-445-4155	412-622-8100	14
PPI (Paper Pak Industries) 1941 N White Ave ... La Verne CA 91750	888-293-6529	909-392-1750	296-9
PPII (Pinnacle Performance Improvement Worldwide) 101 Main St ... Pepperell MA 01463	800-368-3408	978-925-9797	195
PPL Corp Two N Ninth St ... Allentown PA 18101 NYSE: PPL	800-342-5775	610-774-5151	357-5
PPL Electric Utilities Corp Two N Ninth St ... Allentown PA 18101 *Cust Svc	800-342-5775*	610-774-5151	775
PPL Global LLC Two N Ninth St ... Allentown PA 18101 NYSE: PPL	800-342-5775	610-774-5151	775
PPM Consultants Inc 2508 Ticheli Rd ... Monroe LA 71202	800-761-8675	318-323-7270	261
PPMC (Penn Presbyterian Medical Ctr) 39th & Market Sts ... Philadelphia PA 19104	800-789-7366	215-662-8000	371-3
PPPL (Princeton Plasma Physics Laboratory) James Forrestal Campus Princeton University PO Box 451 ... Princeton NJ 08543	800-772-2222	609-243-2750	659
PR Photos 4521 Pga Blvd ... Palm Beach Gardens FL 33418	866-551-7827		523
Prab Inc 5944 E Kilgore Rd ... Kalamazoo MI 49048	800-968-7722	269-382-8200	208
Practising Law Institute (PLI) 810 Seventh Ave 26th Fl ... New York NY 10019	800-260-4754	212-824-5700	48-10
Prader-Willi Syndrome Assn (USA) 8588 Potter Pk Dr Ste 500 ... Sarasota FL 34238	800-926-4797	941-312-0400	47-17
Pragma Systems Inc 13809 Research Blvd Ste 675 ... Austin TX 78750	800-224-1675	512-219-7270	179-12
Pragmatek Consulting Group 8500 Normandale Lake Blvd Ste 1060 ... Bloomington MN 55437	800-833-3164	612-333-3164	195
Prairie Band Casino & Resort 12305 150th Rd ... Mayetta KS 66509	888-727-4946	785-966-7777	132
Prairie Bible Institute 330 Fifth Ave NE PO Box 4000 ... Three Hills AB T0M2N0	800-661-2425	403-443-5511	773
Prairie Farms Dairy Inc 1100 N Broadway St ... Carlinville IL 62626	800-654-2547	217-854-2547	295-27
Prairie Group Inc 7601 W 79th St ... Bridgeview IL 60455 *Sales	800-649-3690*	708-458-0400	183

	Toll-Free	Phone	Class
Prairie Knights Casino & Resort			
7932 Hwy 24 ....Fort Yates ND 58538	**800-425-8277**	701-854-7777	132
Prairie Lakes Hospital & Care Ctr			
401 Ninth Ave NW ....Watertown SD 57201	**877-917-7547**	605-882-7000	371-3
Prairie Land Electric Co-op Inc			
14935 US Hwy 36 ....Norton KS 67654	**800-577-3323**	785-877-3323	245
Prairie Livestock LLC			
2139 Barton Ferry Rd			
PO Box 636. ....West Point MS 39773	**800-647-6350**	662-494-5651	441
Prairie Meadows Racetrack & Casino			
1 Prairie Meadows Dr			
PO Box 1000. ....Altoona IA 50009	**800-325-9015**	515-967-1000	132
Prairie Public Broadcasting Inc			
207 N Fifth St ....Fargo ND 58102	**800-359-6900**	701-241-6900	624
Prairie State College			
202 S Halsted St ....Chicago Heights IL 60411	**866-255-5437**	708-709-3500	160
Prairie View A & M University			
PO Box 519 ....Prairie View TX 77446	**800-787-7826**	936-857-2626	166
Prasco LLC			
6125 Commerce Ct ....Mason OH 45040	**866-469-1414**	513-618-3333	231
Pratt & Whitney Canada Inc			
1000 Marie-Victorin Blvd ....Longueuil QC J4G1A1	**800-268-8000**	450-677-9411	21
Pratt Communications			
2913 Tech Ctr ....Santa Ana CA 92705	**800-980-2323***	714-540-6840	775
*General			
Pratt Industries USA			
1800C Sarasota Pkwy ....Conyers GA 30013	**800-835-2088**	770-918-5678	541
Pratt Institute			
200 Willoughby Ave ....Brooklyn NY 11205	**800-331-0834**	718-636-3669	166
Pratt Regional Medical Ctr Corp			
200 Commodore St ....Pratt KS 67124	**877-572-2787**	620-672-7451	371-3
Praxair Inc			
39 Old Ridgebury Rd ....Danbury CT 06810	**800-772-9247**	203-837-2000	141
NYSE: PX			
Praxis Series Online Educational Testing Service Teaching & Learning Div (ETS)			
PO Box 6051 ....Princeton NJ 08541	**800-772-9476**	609-771-7395	244
PRB (Population Reference Bureau)			
1875 Connecticut Ave NW			
Ste 520 ....Washington DC 20009	**800-877-9881**	202-483-1100	47-7
PRC (Patients Rights Council)			
PO Box 760 ....Steubenville OH 43952	**800-958-5678**	740-282-3810	47-8
PRE (Powder River Energy Corp)			
221 Main St PO Box 930 ....Sundance WY 82729	**800-442-3630**		245
PreCash Inc			
1800 W Loop S Ste 1400 ....Houston TX 77027	**800-773-2274**	713-600-2200	214
Pre-Cast Specialties Inc			
1380 NE 48th St ....Pompano Beach FL 33064	**800-749-4041**	954-781-4040	184
Precept Medical Products Inc			
370 Airport Rd PO Box 2400 ....Arden NC 28704	**800-851-4431**	828-681-0209	569
Precision Assoc Inc			
3800 N Washington Ave ......Minneapolis MN 55412	**800-394-6590**	612-333-7464	668
Precision Auto Care Inc			
748 Miller Dr SE ....Leesburg VA 20175	**800-438-8863**	703-777-9095	61-5
OTC: PACI			
Precision Computer Services Inc (PCS)			
175 Constitution Blvd S ....Shelton CT 06484	**800-340-9890**	203-929-0000	176
Precision Devices Inc			
8840 N Greenview Dr ....Middleton WI 53562	**800-274-9825**	608-831-4445	253
Precision Dynamics Corp			
13880 Del Sur St ....San Fernando CA 91340	**800-847-0670**	818-897-1111	472
Precision Electronic Glass Inc			
1013 Hendee Rd ....Vineland NJ 08360	**800-982-4734**	856-691-2234	330
Precision Fabrics Group Inc			
301 N Elm St Ste 600 ....Greensboro NC 27401	**800-284-8001**	336-510-8000	734-1
Precision Foods Inc			
11457 Olde Cabin Rd Ste 100 ....Saint Louis MO 63141	**800-442-5242**	314-567-7400	295-37
Precision H2O Inc			
6328 E Utah Ave ....Spokane WA 99212	**800-425-2098**	509-536-9214	1
Precision IBC Inc			
8054 Mcgowin Dr ....Fairhope AL 36532	**800-544-7069**	251-990-6789	681
Precision Interconnect Corp			
10025 SW Freeman Ct ....Wilsonville OR 97070	**800-522-6752**	503-685-9300	253
Precision Laboratories Inc			
1429 S Shields Dr ....Waukegan IL 60085	**800-323-6280**	847-596-3001	143
Precision Machined Products Assn (PMPA)			
6700 W Snowville Rd ....Brecksville OH 44141	**800-233-1234**	440-526-0300	48-13
Precision Optics Corp Inc			
22 E Broadway ....Gardner MA 01440	**800-447-2812**	978-630-1800	379
OTC: PEYE			
Precision Parts & Remanufacturing Co			
4411 SW 19th St ....Oklahoma City OK 73108	**800-654-3846**	405-681-2592	247
Precision Products Inc			
316 Limit St ....Lincoln IL 62656	**800-225-5891***	217-735-1590	426
*Cust Svc			
Precision Shooting Equipment Inc			
2727 N Fairview Ave ....Tucson AZ 85705	**800-477-7789**	520-884-9065	701
Precision Solar Controls Inc			
2985 Market St ....Garland TX 75041	**800-686-7414**	972-278-0553	692
Precision Specialties Co			
1201 East Pecan St ....Sherman TX 75090	**800-527-3295**		404
Precision Steel Warehouse Inc			
3500 Wolf Rd ....Franklin Park IL 60131	**800-323-0740**	847-455-7000	487
Precision Tank & Equipment Company Inc			
3503 Conover Rd ....Virginia IL 62691	**800-258-4197**	217-452-7228	273
Precision Thermoplastic Components Inc			
PO Box 1296 ....Lima OH 45802	**800-860-4505**	419-227-4500	601
Precision Valve Corp			
800 Westchester Ave ....Rye Brook NY 10573	**866-686-8464**	914-969-6500	482
Precision Walls Inc			
1230 NE MaynaRd Rd ....Cary NC 27513	**800-849-9255**	919-832-0380	190-9
Precisionform Inc			
148 W Airport Rd ....Lititz PA 17543	**800-233-3821**	717-560-7610	614
Preco Electronics Inc			
10335 W Emerald St ....Boise ID 83704	**866-977-7326**	208-323-1000	467
Precor Inc			
20031 142nd Ave NE ....Woodinville WA 98072	**800-786-8404**	425-486-9292	267
Predator Trucking Co			
3181 Trumbull Ave ....McDonald OH 44437	**888-773-3875**		770
Preferred Bank Los Angeles			
601 S Figueroa St 29th Fl. ......Los Angeles CA 90017	**888-673-1808**	213-891-1188	69
NASDAQ: PFBC			
Preferred CommunityChoice PPO			
218 W Sixth St ....Tulsa OK 74119	**800-884-4776**	918-594-5200	388-3

	Toll-Free	Phone	Class
Preferred Employers Insurance Co			
PO Box 85478 ....San Diego CA 92186	**888-472-9001***	866-472-9602	388-4
*Cust Svc			
Preferred Health Systems Inc			
8535 E 21st St N ....Wichita KS 67206	**800-990-0345**	316-609-2345	388-3
Preferred Hotel Group			
Preferred Hotels & Resorts Worldwide Inc			
311 S Wacker Dr Ste 1900 ....Chicago IL 60606	**800-650-1281**	312-913-0400	376
Summit Hotels & Resorts			
311 S Wacker Dr Ste 1900 ....Chicago IL 60606	**800-650-1281**	312-913-0400	376
Preferred Meal Systems Inc			
5240 St Charles Rd ....Berkeley IL 60163	**800-886-6325***	708-318-2500	295-36
*Cust Svc			
Preferred Mutual Insurance Co			
One Preferred Way ....New Berlin NY 13411	**800-333-7642**	607-847-6161	388-4
Preferred Properties of Venice Inc			
325 W Venice Ave ....Venice FL 34285	**877-640-7653**	941-485-9602	643
Preformed Line Products			
660 Beta Dr ....Cleveland OH 44143	**800-622-6757**	440-461-5200	802
NASDAQ: PLPC			
Preload Inc			
49 Wireless Blvd STE 200 ....Hauppauge NY 11788	**888-773-5623**	631-231-8100	184
Premera Blue Cross			
7001 220th St SW ....Mountlake Terrace WA 98043	**800-722-1471***	425-918-4000	388-3
*Cust Svc			
Premera Blue Cross Blue Shield of Alaska			
2550 Denali St Ste 1404. ....Anchorage AK 99503	**800-508-4722***	907-258-5065	388-3
*Cust Svc			
Premier & Curzons Fitness Clubs			
5100 Dixie Rd ....Mississauga ON L4W1C9	**866-371-7307**	905-602-9912	351
Premier America Credit Union			
19867 Prairie St PO Box 2178 ....Chatsworth CA 91313	**800-772-4000**	818-772-4000	219
Premier Bank & Trust			
600 S Main St Ste C ....North Canton OH 44720	**855-728-6010**	330-499-1900	69
Premier Beverage Company of Florida			
9801 Premier Pkwy ....Miramar FL 33025	**800-432-2002**	954-436-9200	80-3
Premier Coach Company Inc			
946 Rte 7 S ....Milton VT 05468	**800-532-1811**	802-655-4456	106
Premier Colors Inc			
100 Industrial Dr ....Union SC 29379	**800-245-6944**	864-427-0338	143
Premier Dental Products Co			
1710 Romano Dr			
PO Box 4500 ....Plymouth Meeting PA 19462	**888-773-6872**	610-239-6000	228
Premier Die Casting Co			
1177 Rahway Ave ....Avenel NJ 07001	**800-394-3006**	732-634-3000	307
Premier Equipment LLC			
2025 US Hwy 14 W ....Huron SD 57350	**800-627-5469**	605-352-7100	274
Premier Golf			
4355 River Green Pkwy ....Duluth GA 30096	**866-260-4409**	770-291-4202	761
Premier Inc			
12255 El Camino Real ....San Diego CA 92130	**877-777-1552**	858-481-2727	350
Premier Jets			
2140 NE 25th Ave ....Hillsboro OR 97124	**800-635-8583**	503-640-2927	13
Premier Malt Products Inc			
25760 Groesbeck Hwy Ste 103. ....Warren MI 48089	**800-521-1057***	586-443-3355	456
*Cust Svc			
Premier Members Federal Credit Union			
5495 Arapahoe Ave ....Boulder CO 80303	**800-468-0634**	303-657-7000	219
Premier Pyrotechnics Inc			
25255 Hwy K ....Richland MO 65556	**888-647-6863**		44
Premier Realty Group			
Two N Sewalls Point Rd ....Stuart FL 34996	**800-915-8517**	772-287-1777	643
Premier Safety & Service Inc			
Two Industrial Pk Dr ....Oakdale PA 15071	**800-828-1080**	724-693-8699	383
Premier Salons Inc			
8341 Tenth Ave N			
Golden Vly ....Golden Valley MN 55427	**800-542-4247**		76
Premier Subaru LLC			
150 N Main St PO Box 3366. ....Branford CT 06405	**800-411-4551**	203-481-0687	56
Premier Tool & Die Cast Corp			
9886 N Tudor Rd ....Berrien Springs MI 49103	**800-417-8717**	269-471-7715	307
Premier Tours			
21 S 12th St Ninth Fl ....Philadelphia PA 19107	**800-545-1910**		750
Premier Valley Bank			
255 E River Pk Cir Ste 180 ....Fresno CA 93720	**877-438-2002**	559-438-2002	69
Premiere Global Services Inc (PGI)			
3280 Peachtree Rd NE			
Ste 1000 Terminus Bldg ....Atlanta GA 30305	**866-548-3203**	719-457-6901	38
NYSE: PGI			
Premiere Lock Co			
8301 E 81st St ....Tulsa OK 74133	**800-575-2658**	918-294-8179	347
Premiere Radio Networks Inc			
15260 Ventura Blvd Ste 400 ....Sherman Oaks CA 91403	**800-276-4431***	818-377-5300	637
*All			
PremierGarage Systems LLC			
21405 N 15th Ln ....Phoenix AZ 85027	**866-590-9411**	480-483-3030	309
Premio Foods Inc			
50 Utter Ave ....Hawthorne NJ 07506	**800-864-7622**	973-427-1106	295-26
Premium Distributors			
3500 Fort Lincoln Dr NE ....Washington DC 20018	**800-827-4020**	202-526-3900	80-1
Prentke Romich Co			
1022 Heyl Rd ....Wooster OH 44691	**800-848-8008**	330-262-1984	203
Pre-Paid Legal Services Inc			
one Pre-Paid Way ....Ada OK 74820	**800-654-7757**	580-436-1234	388-5
Presagis			
1301 W George Bush Fwy			
Ste 120 ....Richardson TX 75080	**800-361-6424**		179-8
Presbyterian Childrens Services Inc			
1220 N Lindbergh Blvd ....St. Louis MO 63132	**800-383-8147**	314-989-9727	47-20
Presbyterian Church (USA)			
100 Witherspoon St ....Louisville KY 40202	**888-728-7228**	502-569-5000	47-20
Presbyterian College			
503 S Broad St ....Clinton SC 29325	**800-476-7272**	864-833-2820	166
Presbyterian Disaster Assistance (PDA)			
100 Witherspoon St ....Louisville KY 40202	**800-728-7228**		47-5
Presbyterian Homes Inc, The			
2109 Sandy Ridge Rd ....Colfax NC 27235	**800-225-9573**	336-886-6553	47-15
Presbyterian Homes of SC			
2817 Ashland Rd ....Columbia SC 29210	**888-842-4855**	803-772-5885	663
Presbyterian Hospital			
1100 Central Ave SE ....Albuquerque NM 87106	**888-977-2333**	505-841-1234	371-3
Presbyterian Kaseman Hospital			
8300 Constitution Ave NE ....Albuquerque NM 87110	**800-432-4600**	505-291-2000	371-3

	Toll-Free	Phone	Class
Presbyterian SeniorCare-Westminster Place			
1215 Hulton Rd .... Oakmont PA 15139	877-772-6500	412-828-5600	445
Presbyterians Today Magazine			
100 Witherspoon St .... Louisville KY 40202	800-728-7228	800-872-3283	452-18
Prescolite Inc			
701 Millennium Blvd .... Greenville SC 29607	888-777-4832	864-678-1000	435
Prescott Chamber of Commerce			
117 W Goodwin St .... Prescott AZ 86303	800-266-7534	928-445-2000	137
Prescott College			
220 Grove Ave .... Prescott AZ 86301	877-350-2100		166
Prescott Hotel			
545 Post St .... San Francisco CA 94102	866-271-3632	415-563-0303	376
Prescott National Cemetery			
500 Hwy 89 N .... Prescott AZ 86301	800-827-1000	928-717-7569	135
Prescott Valley Chamber of Commerce			
3001 N Main St Ste 2A .... Prescott Valley AZ 86314	800-355-0843	928-772-8857	137
Prescription Solutions			
3515 Harbor Blvd .... Costa Mesa CA 92626	800-788-4863		579
Prescriptives Inc			
767 Fifth Ave .... New York NY 10153	866-290-6471		215
Presentation College			
1500 N Main St .... Aberdeen SD 57401	800-437-6060	605-225-1634	166
President Abraham Lincoln Hotel & Conference Ctr (PALHACC)			
701 E Adams St .... Springfield IL 62701	855-610-8733	217-544-8800	376
Presidential Life Insurance Co			
69 Lydecker St .... Nyack NY 10960	800-926-7599	845-358-2300	388-2
Presidential Online Bank			
4520 East-West Hwy .... Bethesda MD 20814	800-383-6266	301-652-0700	69
Presidio Group Inc, The			
5295 South 300 West			
Ste 550 .... Salt Lake City UT 84107	800-924-1404	801-924-1400	195
Presidio Networked Solutions Inc			
7601 Ora Glen Dr Ste 100 .... Greenbelt MD 20770	800-452-6926	301-313-2000	181
Presley Tours Inc			
16 Presley Pk Dr PO Box 58 .... Makanda IL 62958	800-621-6100	618-549-0704	750
Presque Isle Electric & Gas Co-op			
PO Box 308 .... Onaway MI 49765	800-423-6634	989-733-8515	245
Presque Isle State Park			
301 Peninsula Dr Ste 1............... Erie PA 16505	888-727-2757	814-833-7424	558
Press Democrat			
427 Mendocino Ave .... Santa Rosa CA 95401	800-675-5056	707-546-2020	525-2
Press Ganey Associates Inc			
404 Columbia Pl .... South Bend IN 46601	800-232-8032		195
Press Journal			
14522 S Outer 40 Dr .... Chesterfield MO 63017	800-545-6953	314-821-1110	525-4
Presscut Industries Inc			
1730 Briercroft Ct .... Carrollton TX 75006	800-442-4924	972-389-0615	325
Pressed4Time Inc			
Eight Clock Tower Pl Ste 110 .... Maynard MA 01754	800-423-8711		423
Press-Enterprise			
3450 14th St .... Riverside CA 92501	877-473-6397	951-684-1200	525-2
Press-Enterprise Co			
PO Box 792 .... Riverside CA 92502	800-794-6397	951-684-1200	628-8
Press-Enterprise Inc			
3185 Lackawanna Ave .... Bloomsburg PA 17815	888-484-6345	570-784-2121	628-8
Presses Inc			
6360 W 73rd St .... Chicago IL 60638	800-927-9393	708-496-7400	451
Pressley Ridge			
5500 Corporate Dr Ste 400 .... Pittsburgh PA 15237	800-718-0356	412-872-9400	47-6
Pressman Toy Corp			
121 New England Ave .... Piscataway NJ 08854	800-800-0298*	732-562-1590	752
*Cust Svc			
Press-Republican			
170 Margaret St PO Box 459 .... Plattsburgh NY 12901	800-288-7323	518-561-2300	525-2
Press-Seal Gasket Corp			
2424 W State Blvd .... Fort Wayne IN 46808	800-348-7325	260-436-0521	325
Presstek Inc			
55 Executive Dr .... Hudson NH 03051	800-422-3616	603-595-7000	771
NASDAQ: PRST			
Pressure Profile Systems Inc			
5757 Century Blvd Ste 600 .... Los Angeles CA 90045	888-249-2464	310-641-8100	202
Prestera Trucking			
19129 US Rt 52 .... South Point OH 45680	855-761-7943	740-894-4770	770
Prestige Accommodations International			
1231 E Dyer Rd Ste 240 .... Santa Ana CA 92705	800-321-6338	714-957-9100	185
Prestige Chrysler Dodge Inc			
200 Alpine St .... Longmont CO 80501	866-439-1926	303-651-3000	56
Prestige Cosmetics Corp			
1601 Green Rd .... Pompano Beach FL 33064	800-722-7488*	954-480-9202	215
*General			
Prestige Financial Services Inc			
1420 S 500 W .... Salt Lake City UT 84115	888-822-7422	801-844-2100	214
Prestige Travel & Cruises Inc			
6175 Spring Mountain Rd .... Las Vegas NV 89146	800-758-5693	702-251-5552	761
Prestini Musical Instruments Inc			
2020 N Aurora Dr .... Nogales AZ 85628	800-528-6569*	520-287-4931	520
*General			
Presto Products Co			
670 N Perkins St PO Box 2399 .... Appleton WI 54912	800-558-3525	920-739-9471	65
Presto Tape Inc			
1626 Bridgewater Rd .... Bensalem PA 19020	800-331-1373	215-245-8555	722
Prestolite Wire Corp			
200 Galleria Officentre			
Ste 212 .... Southfield MI 48034	800-498-3132	248-355-4422	801
Preston Industries Inc			
6600 W Touhy Ave .... Niles IL 60714	800-229-7569	847-647-0611	417
Presto-X Co			
10421 Portal Rd Ste 101 .... Gretna NE 68028	800-759-1942		570
Pretzelmaker			
1346 Oakbrook Dr Ste 170 .... Norcross GA 30093	877-639-2361		661
Pretzels Inc			
123 Harvest Rd PO Box 503 .... Bluffton IN 46714	800-456-4838	260-824-4838	295-9
Prevent Blindness America			
211 W Wacker Dr Ste 1700 .... Chicago IL 60606	800-331-2020		47-17
Prevent Cancer Foundation (PCF)			
1600 Duke St Ste 500 .... Alexandria VA 22314	800-227-2732	703-836-4412	47-17
Prevention Magazine			
400 S Tenth St .... Emmaus PA 18098	800-813-8070	212-697-2040	452-13
Prevue Pet Products Inc			
224 N Maplewood Ave .... Chicago IL 60612	800-243-3624	312-243-3624	571
PRG-Schultz International Inc			
600 Galleria Pkwy Ste 100 .... Atlanta GA 30339	800-752-5894	770-779-3900	2
Price Books & Forms Inc			
531 E Sierra Madre Ave .... Glendora CA 91741	800-423-8961		628-2
Price Canyon Ranch			
PO Box 39 .... Rodeo NM 88056	800-727-0065	520-558-2383	239
Price Electric Co-op			
508 N Lake Ave PO Box 110 .... Phillips WI 54555	800-884-0881	715-339-2155	245
Price Pfister Inc			
19701 Da Vinci St .... Lake Forest CA 92610	800-732-8238	949-672-4000	602
Priceline.com LLC			
800 Connecticut Ave .... Norwalk CT 06854	800-774-2354		50
NASDAQ: PCLN			
PriceWaiter LLC			
426 Market St .... Chattanooga TN 37421	855-671-9889		384
PricewaterhouseCoopers LLP			
300 Madison Ave .... New York NY 10017	800-993-9971	646-471-4000	2
PRIDE (Prison Rehabilitative Industries & Diversified Enterprises Inc)			
223 Morrison Rd Ste 200 .... Brandon FL 33511	877-283-6819	813-324-8700	622
Pride International Inc			
5847 San Felipe St Ste 3300 .... Houston TX 77057	877-736-3772	713-789-1400	532
Pride Mobility Products Corp			
182 Susquehanna Ave .... Exeter PA 18643	800-800-8586		472
Pride Products Corp			
4333 Veterans Memorial Hwy ... Ronkonkoma NY 11779	800-898-5550	631-737-4444	779
Pride Solvents & Chemical Co of New York Inc			
6 Long Island Ave .... Holtsville NY 11742	800-424-8802	631-758-0200	144
Pride Transport Inc			
5499 W 2455 S .... Salt Lake City UT 84120	800-877-1320	801-972-8890	770
Priest Lake State Park			
314 Indian Creek Pk Rd .... Coolin ID 83821	888-922-6743*	208-443-2200	558
*Resv			
Priester Aviation			
1061 S Wolf Rd .... Wheeling IL 60090	888-323-7887	847-537-1133	24
Priester Pecan Company Inc			
PO Box 381 .... Fort Deposit AL 36032	800-277-3226	334-227-4301	295-28
Prima Tech USA			
279 Faison McGowan Rd Ste 2 .... Kenansville NC 28349	888-833-7099	910-296-6116	470
Primacy			
1577 New Britain Ave .... Farmington CT 06032	866-497-3725	860-679-9332	7
Primary Global Research LLC			
1975 W El Camino Real			
Ste 300 .... Mountain View CA 94040	888-893-1688		398
Primary Packaging Inc			
10810 Industrial Pkwy NW .... Bolivar OH 44612	800-774-2247	330-874-3131	87
Prime Contractors Inc			
525 N Sam Houston Pkwy E .... Houston TX 77060	800-692-8378	281-999-0875	187
Prime Inc			
PO Box 4208 .... Springfield MO 65808	800-848-4560*	417-866-0001	770
*Cust Svc			
Prime Management Services			
3416 Primm Ln .... Birmingham AL 35216	866-609-1599	205-823-6106	46
Prime Outlets San Marcos			
3939 S IH-35 .... San Marcos TX 78666	866-888-5530	512-396-2200	455
Prime Rate Premium Finance Corp			
2141 Enterprise Dr			
PO Box 100507 .... Florence SC 29501	800-777-7458*	843-669-0937	214
*Cust Svc			
Prime Resources Corp			
1100 Boston Ave .... Bridgeport CT 06610	800-621-5463	203-331-9100	9
Prime Therapeutics Inc			
1305 Corporate Ctr Dr .... Eagan MN 55121	800-858-0723	612-777-4000	579
PrimeArray Systems Inc			
127 Riverneck Rd .... Chelmsford MA 01824	800-433-5133	978-654-6250	177
PRIMEDIA Inc & Consumer Source Inc			
3585 Engineering Dr Ste 100 .... Norcross GA 30092	800-216-1423	678-421-3000	628-9
Primera Technology Inc			
Two Carlson Pkwy N Ste 375 .... Plymouth MN 55447	800-797-2772	763-475-6676	174-6
Primerica Financial Services			
3120 Breckinridge Blvd .... Duluth GA 30099	800-257-4725	770-381-1000	398
Primeritus Financial Services Inc			
440 Metroplex Dr .... Nashville TN 37211	888-833-4238		390
Primex Plastics Corp			
1235 N 'F' St .... Richmond IN 47374	800-222-5116	765-966-7774	593
Primm Valley Resort & Casino			
31900 S Las Vegas Blvd .... Primm NV 89019	800-926-4455		660
Primo Microphones Inc			
1805 Couch Dr .... McKinney TX 75069	800-767-7463	972-548-9807	51
Primorigen Biosciences Inc			
510 Charmany Dr .... Madison WI 53719	866-372-7442	608-441-8332	84
Primrose Oil Company Inc			
11444 Benton Dr PO Box 29665 .... Dallas TX 75229	800-275-2772	972-241-1100	534
Primrose School Franchising Co			
3660 Cedarcrest Rd .... Acworth GA 30101	800-745-0677	770-529-4100	146
Primus Telecommunications (PTGi)			
7901 Jones Ranch Dr Ste 900 .... McLean VA 22102	866-385-3360	703-902-2800	726
NYSE: PTGI			
Prince Albert National Park of Canada			
Northern Prairies Field Unit			
PO Box 100 .... Waskesiu Lake SK S0J2Y0	877-737-3783*	306-663-4522	556
*Campground Resv			
Prince Castle Inc			
355 E Kehoe Blvd .... Carol Stream IL 60188	800-722-7853	630-462-8800	297
Prince Conti Hotel			
830 Conti St .... New Orleans LA 70112	800-366-2743	504-529-4172	376
Prince Corp			
8351 County Rd H .... Marshfield WI 54449	800-777-2486	715-384-3105	571
Prince Edward Island National Park of Canada			
2 Palmers Ln .... Charlottetown PE C1A5V8	800-663-7192*	902-672-6350	556
*Campground Resv			
Prince Edward Island Tourism			
PO Box 2000 .... Charlottetown PE C1A7N8	800-463-4734	902-368-4000	764
Prince George Hotel, The			
1725 Market St .... Halifax NS B3J3N9	800-565-1567	902-425-1986	376
Prince Global Sports LLC			
One Advantage Ct .... Bordentown NJ 08505	800-283-6647*	609-291-5800	701
*All			
Prince Lionheart Inc			
2421 Westgate Rd .... Santa Maria CA 93455	800-544-1132	805-922-2250	63
Prince Preferred Guest Program			
100 Holomoana St .... Honolulu HI 96815	800-774-6234		375
Prince Resorts Hawaii			
100 Holomoana St .... Honolulu HI 96815	888-977-4623	808-956-1111	660
Prince William County-Greater Manassas Chamber of Commerce			
9720 Capital Ct Ste 203 .... Manassas VA 20110	877-867-3853	703-368-6600	137
Prince William Regional Chamber of Commerce			
9720 Capital Ct Suite 203 .... Manassas VA 20110	877-867-3853	703-368-6600	137

Company / Address	City	State	ZIP	Toll-Free	Phone	Class
Princess Bayside Beach Hotel & Golf Ctr						
4801 Coastal Hwy	Ocean City	MD	21842	**888-622-9743***	410-723-2900	376
*General						
Princess Cruises						
24844 Rockefeller Ave	Santa Clarita	CA	91355	**800-774-6237**	661-753-0000	220
Princess House Inc						
470 Miles Standish Blvd	Taunton	MA	02780	**800-622-0039***	508-823-0711	363
*Sales						
Princess Royale Oceanfront Hotel & Conference Ctr						
9100 Coastal Hwy	Ocean City	MD	21842	**800-476-9253**	410-524-7777	376
Princeton Excess & Surplus Lines Insurance Co						
555 College Rd E	Princeton	NJ	08543	**800-544-2378**	609-243-4200	388-4
Princeton Institute for International & Regional Studies (PIIRS)						
Princeton University						
Bendheim Hall	Princeton	NJ	08544	**888-486-3339**	609-258-4852	625
Princeton Insurance Co						
746 Alexander Rd PO Box 5322	Princeton	NJ	08540	**800-334-0588**	609-452-9404	388-4
Princeton National Bancorp Inc						
606 S Main St	Princeton	IL	61356	**888-897-2276**	309-662-4444	357-2
OTC: PNBC						
Princeton Packet, The						
300 Witherspoon St PO Box 350	Princeton	NJ	08542	**888-747-1122**	609-924-3244	628-8
Princeton Plasma Physics Laboratory (PPPL)						
James Forrestal Campus Princeton University						
PO Box 451	Princeton	NJ	08543	**800-772-2222**	609-243-2750	659
Princeton Regional School District						
25 Valley Rd						
Administration Bldg	Princeton	NJ	08540	**877-652-2873**	609-806-4200	676
Princeton Theological Seminary						
64 Mercer St	Princeton	NJ	08540	**800-622-6767**	609-921-8300	167-3
Princeton University						
33 Washington Rd	Princeton	NJ	08544	**877-609-2273**	609-258-3000	166
Princeton University Press						
41 William St	Princeton	NJ	08540	**800-777-4726**	609-258-4900	628-4
Principal Financial Group Foundation Inc						
711 High St	Des Moines	IA	50392	**800-986-3343**	515-247-7227	303
Principal Financial Group Inc						
711 High St	Des Moines	IA	50392	**800-986-3343**	515-247-5111	357-4
NYSE: PFG						
Principal Technical Services Inc						
9960 Research Dr Ste 200	Irvine	CA	92618	**888-787-3711**		712
Principia College						
One Maybeck Pl	Elsah	IL	62028	**800-277-4648**	618-374-2131	166
Principle Business Enterprises Inc						
PO Box 129	Dunbridge	OH	43414	**800-467-3224**	419-352-1551	551
Prinsco Inc						
108 W Hwy 7 PO Box 265	Prinsburg	MN	56281	**800-992-1725**	320-978-4116	593
Print Direction Inc						
1600 Indian Brook Way	Norcross	GA	30093	**877-435-1672**	770-446-6446	619
Print Magazine						
10151 Carver Rd Ste 200	Blue Ash	OH	45242	**877-860-9145**	513-531-2690	452-5
Print Services & Distribution Assn (PSDA)						
330 N. Wabash Ave Ste 2000	Chicago	IL	60611	**800-336-4641**	800-230-0175	47-9
Printed Systems						
1265 Gillingham Rd	Neenah	WI	54956	**800-352-2332***		410
*Sales						
PrintEdd Products of North America						
2641 N Forum Dr	Grand Prairie	TX	75052	**800-367-6728**	972-660-3800	109
Printek Inc						
1517 Townline Rd	Benton Harbor	MI	49022	**800-368-4636**	269-925-3200	174-6
Printers & Stationers Inc						
113 N Ct St	Florence	AL	35630	**800-624-5334**	256-764-8061	528
Printfection LLC						
3700 Quebec St Unit 100-136	Denver	CO	80207	**866-459-7990**		196
Printing House Ltd, The						
1403 Bathurst St	Toronto	ON	M5R3H8	**800-874-0870**	416-536-6113	341
Printing Industries of America/Graphic Arts Technical Foundation (PIA/GATF)						
200 Deer Run Rd	Sewickley	PA	15143	**800-910-4283**	412-741-6860	48-16
Printing Prep Inc						
12 E Tupper St	Buffalo	NY	14203	**877-878-7114**	716-852-5011	771
PrintingForLess.com Inc						
100 PFL Way	Livingston	MT	59047	**800-930-6040**		619
Printmail Systems Inc						
23 Friends Ln	Newtown	PA	18940	**800-910-4844**	215-860-4250	225
Print-O-Stat Inc						
1011 W Market St	York	PA	17404	**800-711-8014**	717-854-7821	718
Print-O-Tape Inc						
755 Tower Rd	Mundelein	IL	60060	**800-346-6311**	847-362-1476	410
Printpack Inc						
2800 Overlook PkwyNE	Atlanta	GA	30339	**800-669-6820**	404-460-7000	541
Printronix Inc						
14600 Myford Rd	Irvine	CA	92606	**800-665-6210**	714-368-2300	174-6
Prior Aviation Service Inc						
50 N Airport Dr	Buffalo	NY	14225	**800-621-2923**	716-633-1000	62
Prior Lake-Savage Area Public School District 719						
4540 Tower St SE	Prior Lake	MN	55372	**855-346-1650**	952-226-0000	676
Priority Capital Inc						
174 Green St	Melrose	MA	02176	**800-761-2118**	781-321-8778	216
Priority Chevrolet of Chesapeake						
1495 S Military Hwy	Chesapeake	VA	23320	**855-315-0212**	757-424-1811	56
Priority Express Courier						
Five Chelsea Pkwy	Boothwyn	PA	19061	**800-526-4646**	610-364-3300	539
Priority Health						
1231 E Beltline NE	Grand Rapids	MI	49525	**800-942-0954**	616-942-0954	388-3
Priority Wire & Cable Inc						
PO Box 398	North Little Rock	AR	72115	**800-945-5542***	501-372-5444	246
*General						
Prism Plastics Inc						
1544 Hwy 65	New Richmond	WI	54017	**877-246-7535**	715-246-7535	601
Prisma Graphic Corp						
2937 E Broadway Rd	Phoenix	AZ	85040	**800-379-5777**	602-243-5777	619
Prismaflex Inc						
1645 Queens Way E	Mississauga	ON	L4X3A3	**888-454-2244**	905-279-9793	692
PRISMHR						
50 Resnik Rd Ste 200	Plymouth	MA	02360	**877-837-4311**	508-747-7261	225
Prison Rehabilitative Industries & Diversified Enterprises Inc (PRIDE)						
223 Morrison Rd Ste 200	Brandon	FL	33511	**877-283-6819**	813-324-8700	622
Pritchett LLC						
13355 Noel Rd Ste 1650	Dallas	TX	75240	**800-992-5922**	214-239-9600	195
Pritchett Trucking Inc						
1050 SE Sixth St PO Box 311	Lake Butler	FL	32054	**800-486-7504**	386-496-2630	770
Pritikin Longevity Ctr & Spa						
8755 NW 36th St	Doral	FL	33178	**800-327-4914**	305-935-7131	697

Company / Address	City	State	ZIP	Toll-Free	Phone	Class
Privacy & Security Law Report						
1801 S Bell St	Arlington	VA	22202	**800-372-1033**		524-7
Private Capital Management						
8889 Pelican Bay Blvd Ste 500	Naples	FL	34108	**800-763-0337**	239-254-2500	780
Private Citizen Inc						
PO Box 233	Naperville	IL	60566	**888-382-1222**	630-393-1555	47-10
Private Security Case Law Reporter						
590 Dutch Vly Rd NE						
PO Box 13729	Atlanta	GA	30324	**800-926-7926**	404-881-1141	524-7
PrivateBancorp Inc						
120 S LaSalle St	Chicago	IL	60603	**800-662-7748**		357-2
NASDAQ: PVTB						
PRN Health Services Inc						
4321 W College Ave Ste 200	Appleton	WI	54914	**888-830-8811**		260
Pro Assurance Corp						
1250 23rd St NW Ste 250	Washington	DC	20037	**800-613-3615**	202-969-1866	388-2
Pro Farmer						
6612 Chancellor Dr Ste 300	Cedar Falls	IA	50613	**800-772-0023***	319-277-1278	524-13
*Cust Svc						
Pro Lights & Staging News Magazine						
6000 S Eastern Ste 14-J	Las Vegas	NV	89119	**888-667-7438***	702-932-5585	452-21
*General						
Pro Performance Sports LLC						
2081 Faraday Ave	Carlsbad	CA	92008	**877-225-7275**		702
Pro Petroleum Inc						
4985 N Sloan Ln	Las Vegas	NV	89115	**877-791-4900**		572
Pro Products LLC						
7201 Engle Rd	Fort Wayne	IN	46804	**866-357-5063**	260-490-5970	794
Pro Star Sports Inc						
1133 Winchester Ave	Kansas City	MO	64126	**800-821-8482**	816-241-9737	267
Pro Tapes & Specialties						
PO Box 53026	Newark	NJ	07101	**800-345-0234**	732-346-0900	722
PrO Unlimited Inc						
301 Yamato Rd Ste3199	Boca Raton	FL	33431	**800-291-1099**		724
Proair LLC						
28731 County Rd 6	Elkhart	IN	46514	**800-338-8544**	574-264-5494	14
ProAssurance Corp						
100 Brookwood Pl Ste 300	Birmingham	AL	35209	**800-282-6242**	205-877-4400	357-4
NYSE: PRA						
ProCard Inc						
1819 Denver W Dr						
Bldg 26 Ste 300	Lakewood	CO	80401	**800-469-6578**	303-279-2255	179-10
Proceedings of the IEEE Magazine						
445 Hoes Ln	Piscataway	NJ	08855	**800-678-4333**	732-562-5478	452-21
Process Equipment Inc						
2770 Welborn St PO Box 1607	Pelham	AL	35124	**888-663-2028**	205-663-5330	18
Process Software Corp						
959 Concord St	Framingham	MA	01701	**800-722-7770**	508-879-6994	179-12
Proco Products Inc						
PO Box 590	Stockton	CA	95201	**800-344-3246**	209-943-6088	667
ProCom Inc						
28838 US Hwy 69 PO Box 27	Lamoni	IA	50140	**800-433-9893**	641-784-8841	727
Procter & Gamble Pharmaceuticals Canada Inc						
PO Box 355 Stn A	Toronto	ON	M5W1C5	**800-668-0150**	416-730-4711	576
Proctor Academy						
204 Main St PO Box 500	Andover	NH	03216	**800-626-4907**	603-735-6000	615
Prodata Systems Inc						
11007 Slater Ave NE	Kirkland	WA	98033	**866-582-7485**	425-296-4168	38
Pro-Dex Inc						
2361 McGaw Ave	Irvine	CA	92614	**800-562-6204**		357-3
NASDAQ: PDEX						
Prodigy Diabetes Care LLC						
2701-A Hutchison McDonald Rd						
PO Box 481928	Charlotte	NC	28269	**800-366-5901**		471
Produce Marketing Assn (PMA)						
1500 Casho Mill Rd	Newark	DE	19711	**800-872-7245**	302-738-7100	48-6
Produce Source Partners						
13167 Telcourt Rd	Ashland	VA	23005	**800-344-4728**	804-262-8300	296-7
Producers Dairy Foods Inc						
250 E Belmont Ave	Fresno	CA	93701	**800-660-1171**	559-264-6583	295-27
Producers Livestock Marketing Assn						
4809 S 114th St	Omaha	NE	68137	**800-257-4046**	402-597-9189	441
Producers Peanut Company Inc						
PO Box 250	Suffolk	VA	23434	**800-847-5491**	757-539-7496	295-32
Producers Rice Mill Inc						
PO Box 1248	Stuttgart	AR	72160	**800-369-7675**	870-673-4444	295-23
Product Development & Management Assn (PDMA)						
330 N Wabash Ave Ste 2000	Chicago	IL	60611	**800-232-5241**	312-321-5145	48-12
Production Equipment Co						
401 Liberty St	Meriden	CT	06450	**800-758-5697**	203-235-5795	465
Production Management Industries LLC						
9761 Hwy 90 E	Morgan City	LA	70380	**888-229-3837**	985-631-3837	532
Production Press Inc						
307 E Morgan St	Jacksonville	IL	62650	**800-231-3880**	217-243-3353	619
Production Products Co						
6176 E Molloy Rd	East Syracuse	NY	13057	**800-800-6652**	315-431-7200	614
Production Tool Supply						
8655 E Eight Mile Rd	Warren	MI	48089	**800-366-3600**	586-755-7770	382
Productive Alternatives Inc						
1205 N Tower Rd	Fergus Falls	MN	56537	**800-627-3529**	218-998-5630	230
Productive Data Solutions Inc (PDSINC)						
6160 S Syracuse Way						
Ste B160	Greenwood Village	CO	80111	**800-404-7165**	303-220-7165	712
Productivity Inc						
Four Armstrong Rd Third Fl	Shelton	CT	06484	**800-966-5423**	203-225-0451	755
Producto Machine Co						
800 Union Ave	Bridgeport	CT	06607	**800-722-2606***	203-367-8675	747
*Cust Svc						
Professional Assn of Diving Instructors International (PADI)						
30151 Tomas St	Rancho Santa Margarita	CA	92688	**800-729-7234***	949-858-7234	47-22
*Sales						
Professional Assn of Innkeepers International (PAII)						
207 White Horse Pk	Haddon Heights	NJ	08035	**800-468-7244**	856-310-1102	48-4
Professional Bank Services Inc						
6200 Dutchmans Ln Ste 305	Louisville	KY	40205	**800-523-4778**	502-451-6633	195
Professional Beauty Assn (PBA)						
15825 N 71st St Ste 100	Scottsdale	AZ	85254	**800-468-2274**	480-281-0424	48-18
Professional Bowlers Assn (PBA)						
719 Second Ave Ste 701	Seattle	WA	98104	**877-910-2695**	206-332-9688	47-22
Professional Bull Riders Inc (PBR)						
101 W Riverwalk	Pueblo	CO	81003	**800-366-8538**	719-242-2800	47-15
Professional Community Management Inc						
23726 Birtcher Dr	Lake Forest	CA	92630	**800-369-7260**		646

Alphabetical Section

	Toll-Free	Phone	Class
Professional Convention Management Assn (PCMA)			
35 E Wacker Dr Ste 500 ....Chicago IL 60601	**877-827-7262**	312-423-7262	48-12
Professional Cutlery Direct LLC			
242 Branford Rd ....North Branford CT 06471	**800-792-6650**		222
Professional Electric Products Co (PEPCO)			
33210 Lakeland Blvd ....Eastlake OH 44095	**800-872-7000**	440-946-3790	246
Professional Liability Underwriting Society			
5353 Wayzata Blvd Ste 600 ......Minneapolis MN 55416	**800-845-0778**	952-746-2580	48-9
Professional Photographers of America Inc (PPA)			
229 Peachtree St NE Ste 2200 ....Atlanta GA 30303	**800-786-6277**	404-522-8600	47-4
Professional Picture Framers Assn (PPFA)			
2282 Springport Rd Ste F...........Jackson MI 49202	**800-762-9287**	517-788-8100	47-4
Professional Research Consultants Inc			
11326 P St ....Omaha NE 68137	**800-428-7455**	402-592-5656	195
Professional Service Industries Inc (PSI)			
1901 S Meyers Rd			
Ste 400 ....Oakbrook Terrace IL 60181	**800-548-7901**	630-691-1490	261
Professional Services Council (PSC)			
4401 Wilson Blvd Ste 1110 ....Arlington VA 22203	**800-353-9118**	703-875-8059	48-12
Professional Shorthand Reporters Inc (PSR)			
601 Poydras St Ste 1615 ....New Orleans LA 70130	**800-536-5255**	504-529-5255	440
Professional Software Engineering Inc			
780 Lynnhaven Pkwy			
Ste 350 ....Virginia Beach VA 23452	**800-924-1091**	757-431-2400	181
Professional Staff Management Inc			
6801 Lake Plaza Dr			
Suite D-405 ....Indianapolis IN 46220	**800-967-5515**	317-816-7007	623
Professional Tennis Registry			
PO Box 4739 ....Hilton Head Island SC 29938	**800-421-6289**	843-785-7244	47-22
Professional Travel Inc			
25000 Great Northern Corporate Ctr			
Ste 170 ....Cleveland OH 44070	**800-247-0060**	440-734-8800	761
Profile Bank			
45 Wakefield St PO Box 1808...........Rochester NH 03866	**800-554-8969**	603-332-2610	69
Profiles International Inc			
5205 Lk Shore Dr ....Waco TX 76710	**866-751-1644**	254-751-1644	712
Profit Sharing/401(k) Council of America (PSCA)			
20 N Wacker Dr Ste 3700 ....Chicago IL 60606	**866-614-8407**	312-419-1863	48-12
Profitable Investing			
9201 Corporate Blvd ....Rockville MD 20850	**800-219-8592**	301-250-2200	524-9
Proflowers.com			
4840 Eastgate Mall ....San Diego CA 92121	**800-580-2913**		292
ProForma			
8800 E Pleasant Vly Rd ....Independence OH 44131	**800-825-1525**	216-520-8400	619
Progenics Pharmaceuticals Inc			
777 Old Saw Mill River Rd ....Tarrytown NY 10591	**866-644-7188**	914-789-2800	84
NASDAQ: PGNX			
Program Planning Professionals			
1340 Eisenhower Pl ....Ann Arbor MI 48108	**877-728-2331**	734-741-7770	195
Programmer's Paradise Inc			
1157 Shrewsbury Ave Ste C ....Shrewsbury NJ 07702	**800-441-1511**	732-389-8950	175
Progress Energy Inc			
410 S Wilmington St PO Box 2041.......Raleigh NC 27601	**800-452-2777**	919-546-6111	357-5
NYSE: PGN			
Progress Printing Co			
2677 Waterlick Rd ....Lynchburg VA 24502	**800-572-7804**		619
Progress Rail Services			
1600 Progress Dr			
PO Box 1037...........Albertville AL 35950	**800-476-8769**	256-505-6600	677
Progress Software Corp			
14 Oak Pk ....Bedford MA 01730	**800-477-6473**	781-280-4000	179-1
NASDAQ: PRGS			
Progressive Bank NA			
1090 E Bethlehem Blvd ....Wheeling WV 26003	**866-235-1923**	304-238-0040	69
Progressive Casualty Insurance Co			
6300 Wilson Mills Rd			
Campus E...........Mayfield Village OH 44143	**800-776-4737**	440-461-5000	388-4
Progressive Employer Services			
6407 Parkland Dr ....Sarasota FL 34243	**888-925-2990**	941-925-2990	623
Progressive Impressions			
1 Hardman Dr ....Bloomington IL 61701	**800-644-0444**	309-664-0444	628-9
Progressive Mktg Products Inc			
3130 E Miraloma Ave ....Anaheim CA 92806	**800-368-9700**	714-632-7100	195
Progressive National Baptist Convention Inc (PNBC)			
601 50th St NE ....Washington DC 20019	**800-876-7622**	202-396-0558	47-20
Progressive Plastics Inc			
14801 Emery Ave ....Cleveland OH 44135	**800-252-0053**	216-252-5595	97
Progressive Produce Co			
5790 Peachtree St ....Los Angeles CA 90040	**800-900-0757**	323-890-8100	296-7
Project Concern International (PCI)			
5151 Murphy Canyon Rd Ste 320......San Diego CA 92123	**877-724-4673**	858-279-9690	47-5
Project Inform			
273 Ninth St ....San Francisco CA 94103	**877-435-7443**	415-558-8669	47-17
Project Management Institute (PMI)			
14 Campus Blvd ....Newtown Square PA 19073	**866-276-4764**	610-356-4600	48-12
Project Safe Neighborhoods			
Office of Justice Programs			
810 Seventh St NW ....Washington DC 20531	**888-744-6513**	202-616-6500	198
Project Vote			
1350 I St NW Ste 1250 ....Washington DC 20005	**888-546-4173**	202-546-4173	47-7
Projection Presentation Technology			
5803 Rolling Rd ....Springfield VA 22152	**800-377-7650**	703-912-1334	264-2
Projections Unlimited Inc			
15311 Varrenca Pkwy ....Irvine CA 92618	**800-551-4405***	714-544-2700	246
Cust Svc			
Prolab Nutrition			
21411 Prairie St ....Chatsworth CA 91311	**800-776-5221**	818-739-6000	787
Prolifics			
114 W 47th St 20th Fl. ....New York NY 10036	**800-458-3313**	212-267-7722	179-2
ProLiteracy Worldwide			
1320 Jamesville Ave ....Syracuse NY 13210	**800-448-8878**	315-422-9121	47-5
ProLogis			
4545 Airport Way ....Denver CO 80239	**800-566-2706**	303-375-9292	646
NYSE: PLD			
Prolon Inc			
305 Industrial Ave ....Port Gibson MS 39150	**800-628-7749**	601-437-4211	600
Promark Technology Inc			
10900 Pump House Rd			
Ste B. ....Annapolis Junction MD 20701	**800-634-0255**	240-280-8030	175
Promega Corp			
2800 Woods Hollow Rd ....Madison WI 53711	**800-356-9526**	608-274-4330	231
Promera Health			
61 accord park dr ....Norwell MA 02061	**888-878-9058**		360

	Toll-Free	Phone	Class
Prometheus Laboratories Inc			
9410 Carroll Pk Dr ....San Diego CA 92121	**888-892-8391**		576
Prometric			
1501 S Clinton St ....Baltimore MD 21224	**866-776-6387**	443-455-8000	244
Promise Keepers (PK)			
PO Box 11798 ....Denver CO 80211	**866-776-6473**		47-20
Promise Regional Medical Ctr-Hutchinson			
1701 E 23rd Ave ....Hutchinson KS 67502	**800-267-6891**	620-665-2000	371-3
Promise Technology Inc			
580 Cottonwood Dr ....Milpitas CA 95035	**800-888-0245***	408-228-1400	617
Sales			
Promodel Corp			
3400 Bath Pike Ste 200 ....Bethlehem PA 18017	**888-900-3090**	801-223-4600	179-10
Promotional Products Assn International (PPAI)			
3125 Skyway Cir N ....Irving TX 75038	**888-426-7724**	972-252-0404	48-18
Promotions Unlimited			
7601 Durand Ave ....Mount Pleasant WI 53177	**800-992-9307**	262-681-7000	5
Prompton State Park			
c/o Lackawanna ....North Abington Township PA 18414	**888-727-2757**	570-945-3239	558
ProMutual Group			
101 Arch St 4th Fl. ....Boston MA 02110	**800-225-6168**		388-5
ProPacificfresh			
70 Pepsi Way PO Box 1069 ....Durham CA 95938	**888-232-0908**	530-893-0596	296-7
Propel Software Corp			
1010 Rincon Cir ....San Jose CA 95131	**866-799-4767**	408-571-6300	179-7
Property Damage Appraisers Inc (PDA)			
6100 SW Blvd Ste 200 ....Fort Worth TX 76109	**800-749-7324**		309
Property Loss Research Bureau (PLRB)			
3025 Highland Pkwy			
Ste 800 ....Downers Grove IL 60515	**888-711-7572**	630-724-2200	48-9
Property Owners Exchange Inc			
6630 Baltimore National Pk			
Ste 208 ....Catonsville MD 21228	**800-869-3200**	410-719-0100	626
Property-Owners Insurance Co			
PO Box 30660 ....Lansing MI 48909	**800-288-8740**	517-323-1200	388-2
Propet USA Inc			
2415 W Valley Hwy N ....Auburn WA 98001	**800-877-6738**	253-854-7600	300
ProPhase Labs Inc			
621 Shady Retreat Rd ....Doylestown PA 18901	**800-505-2653**	215-345-0919	576
NASDAQ: PRPH			
ProPhotonix Inc			
32 Hampshire Rd ....Salem NH 03079	**877-941-8631**	603-893-8778	537
OTC: STKR			
Propper Mfg Company Inc			
36-04 Skillman Ave ....Long Island City NY 11101	**800-832-4300***	718-392-6650	471
Cust Svc			
Proserv Anchor Crane Group			
455 Aldine Bender PO Box 670965 ......Houston TX 77060	**800-835-2223**	281-405-9048	465
Proshot Concrete Inc			
4158 Musgrove Dr ....Florence AL 35630	**800-633-3141**	256-764-5941	190-3
Proskauer Rose LLP			
1585 Broadway ....New York NY 10036	**866-444-3272**	212-969-3000	425
Prosoco Inc			
3741 Greenway Cir ....Lawrence KS 66046	**800-255-4255**		149
ProSource Solutions LLC			
4199 Kinross Lakes Pkwy			
Ste 150 ....Richfield OH 44286	**866-549-0279**		197
Prospect Medical Holdings Inc			
10780 Santa Monica Blvd			
Ste 400 ....Los Angeles CA 90025	**800-708-3230**	310-943-4500	458
Prospector Hotel			
375 Whittier St ....Juneau AK 99801	**800-331-2711**	907-586-3737	376
Prospectr Marketing			
3508 W 22nd St ....Minneapolis MN 55416	**800-908-3523**		5
Prosperity Bancshares Inc			
1301 N Mechanic ....El Campo TX 77437	**800-862-9098**	979-578-8181	357-2
NYSE: PB			
Prostar Computer Inc			
837 Lawson St ....City of Industry CA 91748	**888-576-4742**	626-839-6472	175
Prostrollo Motor Sales Inc			
PO Box 1415 ....Huron SD 57350	**866-466-4515**		56
Prosum technology services			
2321 Rosecrans Ave Ste 4225 ....El Segundo CA 90245	**888-477-6786**	310-426-0600	38
Protect-All Inc			
109 Badger Pkwy ....Darien WI 53114	**888-432-8526**		547
Protected Investors of America Inc			
235 Montgomery St			
Ste 1050 ....San Francisco CA 94104	**800-786-2559**		195
protection One Alarm Monitoring			
1035 N Third St Ste 101 ....Lawrence KS 66044	**800-438-4357**	877-776-1911	683
Protection Services Inc			
635 Lucknow Rd ....Harrisburg PA 17110	**866-489-1234**	717-236-9307	692
Protective Insurance Co			
111 Congressional Blvd Ste 500 ....Carmel IN 46032	**800-644-5501**	317-636-9800	388-5
Protective Life & Annuity Insurance Co			
2801 Hwy 280 S ....Birmingham AL 35223	**844-733-5433**	205-268-1000	388-2
Protective Life Corp			
2801 Hwy 280 S ....Birmingham AL 35223	**800-333-3418**	205-268-1000	357-4
NYSE: PL			
Protectoseal Co			
225 W Foster Ave ....Bensenville IL 60106	**800-323-2268**	630-595-0800	123
Protegrity Services Inc			
260 Wekiva Springs Rd Ste 1040 ..Longwood FL 32779	**800-883-4000**	407-551-3962	387
Protein Sciences Corp			
1000 Research Pkwy ....Meriden CT 06450	**800-488-7099**	203-686-0800	84
Protel Inc			
4150 Kidron Rd ....Lakeland FL 33811	**800-925-8882**	863-644-5558	725
Protestant Episcopal Theological Seminary in Virginia			
3737 Seminary Rd ....Alexandria VA 22304	**800-941-0083**	703-370-6600	167-3
Protide Pharmaceuticals Inc			
505 Oakwood Rd Ste 200 ....Lake Zurich IL 60047	**800-552-3569**	847-726-3100	576
Protocol Networks Inc			
15 Shore Dr ....Johnston RI 02919	**877-676-0146**		181
ProtoSource Network			
2511 W Shaw Ave Ste 102 ....Fresno CA 93711	**866-490-8600**		395
Protravel International Inc			
515 Madison Ave 10th Fl ....New York NY 10022	**800-227-1059**	212-755-4550	761
Provantage Corp			
7249 Whipple Ave NW ....North Canton OH 44720	**800-336-1166**	330-494-8715	175
Provell Inc			
855 Village Center Drive			
Suite 116 ....North Oaks MN 55127	**800-624-2946**	952-258-2000	458
Provena Covenant Medical Ctr			
1400 W Pk St ....Urbana IL 61801	**800-245-6697**	217-337-2000	371-3

	Toll-Free	Phone	Class
Provena Saint Mary's Hospital			
500 W Ct St ....Kankakee IL 60901	**888-740-4111**	815-937-2400	371-3
Provia Door Inc			
2150 SR- 39 ....Sugarcreek OH 44681	**800-669-4711***	330-852-4711	235
*General			
Provide Commerce Inc			
4840 Eastgate Mall ....San Diego CA 92121	**800-776-3569***	858-638-4900	292
*Cust Svc			
Providence & Worcester Railroad Co			
75 Hammond St ....Worcester MA 01610	**877-373-6374**	508-755-4000	639
NASDAQ: PWX			
Providence Behavioral Health Hospital			
1233 Main St ....Holyoke MA 01040	**800-274-7724**	413-536-5111	717
Providence Biltmore Hotel			
11 Dorrance St ....Providence RI 02903	**800-294-7709**		376
Providence Centralia Hospital			
914 S Scheuber Rd ....Centralia WA 98531	**877-736-2803***	360-736-2803	371-3
*Help Line			
Providence College			
One Cunningham Sq ....Providence RI 02918	**800-721-6444***	401-865-1000	166
*Admissions			
Providence College & Seminary			
10 College Crescent ....Otterburne MB R0A1G0	**800-668-7768**	204-433-7488	167-3
Providence Health & Services (JWCI)			
2200 Santa Monica Blvd ....Santa Monica CA 90404	**800-262-6259**	310-582-7450	659
Providence Homes Inc			
4901 Belfort Rd Ste 140 ....Jacksonville FL 32256	**866-836-0981**	904-262-9898	188
Providence Hospice of Seattle			
425 Pontius Ave N Ste 300 ....Seattle WA 98109	**888-782-4445**	206-320-4000	368
Providence Hospitals			
2435 Forest Dr ....Columbia SC 29204	**877-256-5381**	803-256-5300	371-3
Providence Journal			
75 Fountain St ....Providence RI 02902	**888-697-7656**	401-277-7303	525-2
Providence Life Services			
18601 N Creek Dr ....Tinley Park IL 60477	**800-509-2800**	708-342-8100	663
Providence Medford Medical Ctr			
1111 Crater Lk Ave ....Medford OR 97504	**877-541-0588**	541-732-5000	371-3
Providence Medical Ctr			
8929 Parallel Pkwy ....Kansas City KS 66112	**800-281-7777**	913-596-4000	371-3
Providence Mountains State Recreation Area			
1416 Ninth St ....Sacramento CA 95814	**800-777-0369**		558
Providence Mutual Fire Insurance Co			
340 E Ave ....Warwick RI 02886	**877-763-1800**	401-827-1800	388-4
Providence Portland Medical Ctr			
4805 NE Glisan St ....Portland OR 97213	**800-833-8899**	503-215-1111	371-3
Providence Sacred Heart Medical Ctr			
101 W Eigth Ave ....Spokane WA 99204	**800-442-8534**	509-474-3170	371-3
Providence Saint Peter Hospital (PSPH)			
413 Lilly Rd NE ....Olympia WA 98506	**888-492-9480**	360-491-9480	371-3
Providence Saint Vincent Medical Ctr			
9205 SW Barnes Rd Ste 20 ....Portland OR 97225	**800-677-6752**	503-216-2401	371-3
Providence Service Corp			
64 E Broadway ....Tucson AZ 85701	**800-747-6950**	520-748-7108	457
NASDAQ: PRSC			
Providence Sound Home Care & Hospice			
3432 S Bay Rd NE ....Olympia WA 98506	**800-869-7062**	360-459-8311	368
Providence St Mary Medical Ctr			
401 W Poplar St PO Box 1477 ....Walla Walla WA 99362	**877-215-7833**	509-525-3320	371-3
Providence Warwick Convention & Visitors Bureau			
10 Memorial Blvd ....Providence RI 02903	**800-233-1636**	401-456-0200	207
Provident Bank			
3756 Central Ave ....Riverside CA 92506	**800-442-5201**	951-686-6060	357-2
NASDAQ: PROV			
Provident Central Credit Union			
303 Twin Dolphin Dr ....Redwood City CA 94065	**800-632-4600**	650-508-0300	219
Provident Community Bancshares Inc			
2700 Celanese Rd ....Rock Hill SC 29732	**800-933-3030**	803-325-9400	357-2
OTC: PCBS			
Provident Savings Bank FSB			
3756 Central Ave ....Riverside CA 92506	**800-442-5201**	951-686-6060	69
PROVIDENT TRAVEL			
11309 Montgomery Rd ....Cincinnati OH 45249	**800-354-8108**	513-247-1100	381
Providge Consulting LLC			
2207 Concord Pike Ste 537 ....Wilimington DE 19803	**888-927-6583**		178
Provimi North America Inc			
10 Collective Way ....Brookville OH 45309	**888-522-2420**	937-770-2400	442
Provision Ministry Group			
PO Box 19700 ....Irvine CA 92623	**800-233-3880**		676
Provo City Library			
550 N University Ave ....Provo UT 84601	**800-914-8931**	801-852-6650	431-3
Proxim Wireless Corp			
1561 Buckeye Dr ....Milpitas CA 95035	**800-229-1630**	408-383-7600	725
OTC: PRXM			
Proximo Consulting Services Inc			
2500 Plz Five ....Jersey City NJ 07311	**800-236-9250**		178
Prozyme Inc			
3832 Bay Ctr Pl ....Hayward CA 94545	**800-457-9444**	510-638-6900	231
PRSA (Public Relations Society of America)			
33 Maiden Ln 11th Fl ....New York NY 10038	**800-350-0111**	212-460-1400	48-18
Prudential Financial Inc			
751 Broad St ....Newark NJ 07102	**800-843-7625**	973-802-6000	398
NYSE: PRU			
Prudential Overall Supply			
PO Box 11210 ....Santa Ana CA 92711	**800-767-5536**	949-250-4855	438
Prudential Savings Bank			
1834 W Oregon Ave ....Philadelphia PA 19145	**800-554-8969**	215-755-1500	69
Prym-Dritz Corp			
950 Brisack Rd ....Spartanburg SC 29303	**800-255-7796***	864-576-5050	587
*Cust Svc			
PS Business Parks Inc			
701 Western Ave ....Glendale CA 91201	**888-299-3246***	818-244-8080	646
NYSE: PSB ■ *Cust Svc			
PS Energy Group Inc			
2987 Clairmont Rd Ste 500 ....Atlanta GA 30329	**800-334-7548**	404-321-5711	775
PSA Airlines Inc			
3400 Terminal Dr ....Vandalia OH 45377	**800-235-0986***	937-454-1116	25
*Resv			
PSB (Peoples Savings Bank)			
414 N Adams PO Box 248 ....Wellsburg IA 50680	**877-493-3799**	641-869-3721	69
PSC (Professional Services Council)			
4401 Wilson Blvd Ste 1110 ....Arlington VA 22203	**800-353-9118**	703-875-8059	48-12
PSC			
5151 San Felipe Ste 1100 ....Houston TX 77056	**800-726-1300**		193

	Toll-Free	Phone	Class
PSCA (Profit Sharing/401(k) Council of America)			
20 N Wacker Dr Ste 3700 ....Chicago IL 60606	**866-614-8407**	312-419-1863	48-12
PSDA (Print Services & Distribution Assn)			
330 N. Wabash Ave Ste 2000 ....Chicago IL 60611	**800-336-4641**	800-230-0175	47-9
PSEG Power LLC			
80 Pk Plz ....Newark NJ 07101	**800-436-7734**	973-430-7000	775
PSF Industries Inc			
65 S Horton St ....Seattle WA 98134	**800-426-1204***	206-622-1252	190-10
*General			
PSI (Pet Sitters International)			
201 E King St ....King NC 27021	**800-325-7353**	336-983-9222	47-3
PSI (Professional Service Industries Inc)			
1901 S Meyers Rd			
Ste 400 ....Oakbrook Terrace IL 60181	**800-548-7901**	630-691-1490	261
PSI Upsilon Fraternity			
3003 E 96th St ....Indianapolis IN 46240	**800-394-1833**	317-571-1833	47-16
PSL (Peach State Labs Inc)			
180 Burlington Rd PO Box 1087 ....Rome GA 30162	**800-634-1653**	706-291-8743	143
PSPH (Providence Saint Peter Hospital)			
413 Lilly Rd NE ....Olympia WA 98506	**888-492-9480**	360-491-9480	371-3
PSR (Physicians for Social Responsibility)			
1875 Connecticut Ave NW			
Ste 1012 ....Washington DC 20009	**800-459-1887**	202-667-4260	48-8
PSR (Professional Shorthand Reporters Inc)			
601 Poydras St Ste 1615 ....New Orleans LA 70130	**800-536-5255**	504-529-5255	440
Psychemedics Corp			
125 Nagog Pk Ste 200 ....Acton MA 01720	**800-628-8073**	978-206-8220	84
NASDAQ: PMD			
Psychiatric Institute of Washington			
4228 Wisconsin Ave NW ....Washington DC 20016	**800-369-2273**	202-885-5600	371-5
Psychology Today Magazine			
115 E 23 St 9th Fl ....New York NY 10010	**800-931-2237**	212-260-7210	452-11
Psychotherapy Networker			
5135 MacArthur Blvd NW ....Washington DC 20016	**888-883-3782**	202-537-8950	452-16
PTC (Paternity Testing Corp)			
300 Portland St ....Columbia MO 65201	**888-837-8323**	573-442-9948	414
PTC (Parametric Technology Corp)			
140 Kendrick St ....Needham MA 02494	**800-613-7535**	781-370-5000	179-5
NASDAQ: PTC			
PTGi (Primus Telecommunications)			
7901 Jones Ranch Dr Ste 900 ....McLean VA 22102	**866-385-3360**	703-902-2800	726
NYSE: PTGI			
PTI (Pittsburgh Technical Institute)			
1111 McKee Rd ....Oakdale PA 15071	**800-784-9675**	412-809-5100	788
PTI Technologies Inc			
501 Del Norte Blvd ....Oxnard CA 93030	**800-331-2701**	805-604-3700	383
PTR Baler & Compactor Co			
2207 E Ontario St ....Philadelphia PA 19134	**800-523-3654**	215-533-5100	465
PTSI (Panhandle Telecommunication Systems Inc)			
2222 NW Hwy ....Guymon OK 73942	**800-562-2556**	580-338-2556	726
Pubco Corp			
3830 Kelley Ave ....Cleveland OH 44114	**800-878-3399**	216-881-5300	110
Public Belt Railroad Commission			
4822 Tchoupitulas St ....New Orleans LA 70115	**800-524-3421***	504-896-7410	642
*Cust Svc			
Public Broadcasting Council of Central New York			
506 Old Liverpool Rd			
PO Box 2400 ....Syracuse NY 13220	**800-451-9269**	315-453-2424	624
Public Broadcasting Northwest Pennsylvania			
8425 Peach St ....Erie PA 16509	**800-727-8854**	814-864-3001	624
Public Consulting Group Inc			
148 State St ....Boston MA 02109	**800-210-6113**		195
Public Employee Magazine			
1625 L St NW ....Washington DC 20036	**800-792-0045**	202-429-1130	452-12
Public Health Institute			
555 12th St 10th Fl ....Oakland CA 94607	**866-632-9992**	510-285-5500	47-17
Public Lands Foundation (PLF)			
PO Box 7226 ....Arlington VA 22207	**866-985-9636**	703-790-1988	47-13
Public Library Assn (PLA)			
50 E Huron St ....Chicago IL 60611	**800-545-2433**	312-280-5752	48-11
Public Radio 89.5			
800 Tucker Dr ....Tulsa OK 74104	**888-594-5947**	918-631-2577	636-115
Public Relations Society of America (PRSA)			
33 Maiden Ln 11th Fl ....New York NY 10038	**800-350-0111**	212-460-1400	48-18
Public Service Enterprise Group Inc			
80 Pk Plz ....Newark NJ 07102	**800-436-7734***	973-430-7000	357-5
NYSE: PEG ■ *Cust Svc			
Public Service of New Hampshire			
780 N Commercial St ....Manchester NH 03105	**800-662-7764**	603-669-4000	775
Public Storage Inc			
701 Western Ave ....Glendale CA 91201	**800-567-0759***	818-244-8080	791-3
NYSE: PSA ■ *Cust Svc			
Public Welfare Foundation			
1200 U St NW ....Washington DC 20009	**800-275-7934**	202-965-1800	304
Public Works Commission of The City of Fayetteville North Carolina			
955 Old Wilmington Rd			
PO Box 1089 ....Fayetteville NC 28301	**877-687-7921**	910-483-1382	775
Publication Printers Corp			
2001 S Platte River Dr ....Denver CO 80223	**888-824-0303**	303-936-0303	619
Publications & Communications Inc			
13552 Hwy 183 N Ste A ....Austin TX 78750	**800-678-9724**	512-250-9023	628-9
Publications International Ltd			
7373 N Cicero Ave ....Lincolnwood IL 60712	**800-777-5582***	847-676-3470	628-2
*General			
Publick House Historic Resort			
277 Main St Rt 131 ....Sturbridge MA 01566	**800-782-5425***	508-347-3313	376
*Cust Svc			
Publishers Press Inc			
100 Frank E Simon Ave ....Shepherdsville KY 40165	**800-627-5801**	502-955-6526	618
Publishers Printing Co			
100 Frank E Simon Ave ....Shepherdsville KY 40165	**800-627-5801**	502-955-6526	619
Publishers' Warehouse			
2700 Crestwood Blvd ....Irondale AL 35210	**800-653-2726**	205-956-2078	94
Publix Super Markets Inc			
3300 Publix Corporate Pkwy ....Lakeland FL 33811	**800-242-1227***	863-688-1188	342
*PR			
PubMed			
US National Library of Medicine			
8600 Rockville Pike ....Bethesda MD 20894	**888-346-3656**		353
Pucel Enterprises Inc			
1440 E 36th St ....Cleveland OH 44114	**800-336-4986**	216-881-4604	465
Pueblo Chieftain			
825 W Sixth St PO Box 440 ....Pueblo CO 81003	**800-279-6397**	719-544-3520	525-2

	Toll-Free	Phone	Class

Pueblo Community College
900 W Orman Ave ....Pueblo CO 81004 | 888-642-6017 | 719-549-3200 | 160

Pueblo Grande Museum & Archaeological Park
4619 E Washington St ....Phoenix AZ 85034 | 877-706-4408 | 602-495-0901 | 513

Puerto Rico Convention Bureau
100 Convention Blvd ....San Juan PR 00907 | 800-214-0420 | 787-725-2110 | 207

Puerto Rico Farm Credit Aca
PO Box 363649 ....San Juan PR 00936 | 800-981-3323 | 787-753-0579 | 216

Puerto Rico Tourism Co
Paseo La Princesa ....Old San Juan PR 00902 | 800-866-7827 | 787-721-2400 | 765

Puerto Rico Veterinary Medical Assn
352 San Claudio Ave Ste 248 ....San Juan PR 00926 | 888-791-1856 | 787-283-0565 | 783

Puffin Inn
4400 SpenaRd Rd ....Anchorage AK 99517 | 800-478-3346 | 907-243-4044 | 376

Puget Sound Blood Ctr
921 Terry Ave ....Seattle WA 98104 | 800-366-2831 | 206-292-6500 | 88

Puget Sound Educational Service District
800 Oakesdale Ave SW ....Renton WA 98057 | 800-664-4549 | 425-917-7600 | 676

Puget Sound Energy Inc
10885 NE Fourth St ....Bellevue WA 98004 | 888-225-5773 | 425-452-1234 | 775

Puget Sound Rope Corp
1012 Second St ....Anacortes WA 98221 | 888-525-8488 | 360-293-8488 | 209

Pulaski Financial Corp
12300 Olive Blvd ....Saint Louis MO 63141 | 888-649-3320 | 314-878-2210 | 357-2
NASDAQ: PULB

Pullman Chamber of Commerce
415 N Grand Ave ....Pullman WA 99163 | 800-365-6948 | 509-334-3565 | 137

Pullman/Holt Corp
10702 N 46th St ....Tampa FL 33617 | 800-237-7582 | 813-971-2223 | 383

PULSE
1301 McKinney St Ste 2500 ....Houston TX 77010 | 800-420-2122 | 713-223-1400 | 68

Pulse Communications Inc
2900 Towerview Rd ....Herndon VA 20171 | 800-381-1997* | 703-471-2900 | 725
*Cust Svc

Puma North America Inc
10 Lyberty Way ....Westford MA 01886 | 888-565-7862* | 978-698-1000 | 300
*General

Pumpkin Hollow Farm
1184 Rt 11 ....Craryville NY 12521 | 877-325-3583 | 518-325-3583 | 664

Punchbowl Inc
50 Speen St Ste 202 ....Framingham MA 01701 | 877-570-4340 | 508-589-4486 | 106

Purafil Inc
2654 Weaver Way ....Doraville GA 30340 | 800-222-6367 | 770-662-8545 | 18

Puratos Corp
1941 Old Cuthbert Rd ....Cherry Hill NJ 08034 | 800-654-0036* | 856-428-4300 | 295-16
*All

Purcell Tire & Rubber Co
301 N Hall St ....Potosi MO 63664 | 888-878-2355 | 573-438-2131 | 744

Purchase College
735 Anderson Hill Rd ....Purchase NY 10577 | 800-553-8118 | 914-251-6000 | 166

Purchasing Magazine
225 Wyman St ....Waltham MA 02451 | 888-393-5000 | | 452-5

Purdue University
Calumet 2200 169th St ....Hammond IN 46323 | 800-447-8738 | 219-989-2400 | 166

Purdue University Press
504 W State St Stewart Ctr 370 .....West Lafayette IN 47907 | 800-247-6553* | 765-494-2038 | 628-4
*Orders

Purdy Corp
101 Prospect Ave ....Cleveland OH 44115 | 800-547-0780 | | 347

Pure & Secure LLC
4120 NW 44th St ....Lincoln NE 68524 | 800-875-5915* | 402-467-9300 | 794
*Cust Svc

Pure Auto LLC
164 Market St Ste 250 ....Charleston SC 29401 | 877-860-7873 | | 384

Pure-Flo Water Co
7737 Mission Gorge Rd ....Santee CA 92071 | 800-787-3356* | 619-448-5120 | 793
*Cust Svc

PureWorks Inc
5000 Meridian Blvd Ste 600 ....Franklin TN 37067 | 888-202-3016 | 615-367-4404 | 38

Puritan of Cape Cod
408 Main St ....Hyannis MA 02601 | 800-924-0606 | 508-775-2400 | 155-2

PuriTec
4705 S Durango Dr Ste 100-102 .... Las Vegas NV 89147 | 888-491-4100 | 610-268-5420 | 17

Purity Wholesale Grocers Inc
5400 Broken Sound Blvd NW ....Boca Raton FL 33487 | 800-323-6838 | 561-994-9360 | 296-8

Purnell School
51 Pottersville Rd
PO Box 500 ....Pottersville NJ 07979 | 800-228-9290 | 908-439-2154 | 615

Purolator Inc
5995 Avebury Rd ....Mississauga ON L5R3T8 | 888-744-7123 | 905-712-8101 | 539

Purple Communications Inc
595 Menlo Dr ....Rocklin CA 95765 | 800-900-9478 | | 384

Purple Sage Motel
1501 E Coliseum Dr ....Snyder TX 79549 | 800-388-8255 | 325-573-5491 | 375

Pursuit Boats
3901 St Lucie Blvd ....Fort Pierce FL 34946 | 800-947-8778 | 772-465-6006 | 89

Putman Media Inc
555 W Pierce Rd ....Itasca IL 60143 | 866-666-6033 | 630-467-1301 | 628-9

Putnam County
130 Orie Griffin Blvd
PO Box 1578...................Palatka FL 32178 | 800-426-9975 | 386-329-0800 | 336

Putnam County Convention & Visitors Bureau
12 W Washington St ....Greencastle IN 46135 | 800-829-4639 | 765-653-8743 | 207

Putnam Family of Funds
PO Box 41203 ....Providence RI 02940 | 800-225-1581 | | 521

Putnam Investments
30 Dan Rd PO Box 8383 ....Canton MA 02021 | 888-478-8626 | 617-292-1000 | 398

Putnam Valley School District Inc
146 Peekskill Hollow Rd ......Putnam Valley NY 10579 | 800-666-5327 | 845-528-8143 | 676

Putney School
418 Houghton Brook Rd ....Putney VT 05346 | 800-999-9080 | 802-387-5566 | 615

Putzmeister America
1733 90th St ....Sturtevant WI 53177 | 800-553-3414 | | 191

Puyallup Public Library
324 S Meridian ....Puyallup WA 98371 | 866-862-4232 | 253-841-5454 | 431-3

PV Labs Inc
1074 Cooke Blvd Ste 400A ....Burlington ON L7T4A8 | 888-667-7202 | 905-667-7202 | 683

PVA (Passenger Vessel Assn)
103 Oronoco St Ste 200 ....Alexandria VA 22314 | 800-807-8360 | 703-518-5005 | 48-21

PVA Tepla America Inc
251 Corporate Terr ....Corona CA 92879 | 800-527-5667* | 951-371-2500 | 204
*Sales

PVG Asset Management Corp
24918 Genesee Trl Rd ....Golden CO 80401 | 800-777-0818 | 303-526-0548 | 398

PVI Industries LLC
3209 Galvez Ave PO Box 7124 ....Fort Worth TX 76111 | 800-784-8326 | 817-335-9531 | 90

PVS Chemicals Inc
10900 Harper Ave ....Detroit MI 48213 | 800-932-8860 | 313-921-1200 | 143

PVT (Penasco Valley Telecommunications)
4011 W Main St ....Artesia NM 88210 | 800-505-4844 | | 726

PW Minor & Son Inc
3 Tread Easy Ave PO Box 678 ....Batavia NY 14020 | 800-333-4067 | 585-343-1500 | 300

PW Stephens Inc
15201 Pipeline Ln
Unit B ....Huntington Beach CA 92649 | 800-750-7733 | 714-892-2028 | 658

PWH (Palms West Hospital)
13001 Southern Blvd ....Loxahatchee FL 33470 | 877-549-9337 | 561-798-3300 | 371-3

PWP (Pentwater Wire Products Inc)
474 Carroll St PO Box 947 ....Pentwater MI 49449 | 877-869-6911 | 231-869-6911 | 286

PWR LLC
6402 Deere Rd Ste 3 ....Syracuse NY 13206 | 800-342-0878 | 315-701-0210 | 757

Pyramid Interiors Distributors Inc
PO Box 181058 ....Memphis TN 38181 | 800-456-0592 | 901-375-4197 | 192-3

Pyramid Point Post-Acute Rehabilitation Ctr
8530 Township Line Rd ....Indianapolis IN 46260 | 800-861-0086 | 317-876-9955 | 445

Pyramid Technologies Inc
45 Gracey Ave ....Meriden CT 06451 | 888-479-7264 | 203-238-0550 | 151

Q

	Toll-Free	Phone	Class

Q Carriers Inc
1415 Maras St ....Shakopee MN 55379 | 800-800-4755 | 952-445-8718 | 770

QACVB (Quincy Area Convention & Visitors Bureau)
532 Gardner Expy ....Quincy IL 62301 | 800-978-4748 | 217-214-3700 | 207

QAD Inc
100 Innovation Pl ....Santa Barbara CA 93108 | 888-641-4141 | 805-684-6614 | 179-1
NASDAQ: QADB

Qantas Airways Cargo
6555 W Imperial Hwy ....Los Angeles CA 90045 | 800-227-0290* | 310-665-2280 | 12
*General

Qantas Airways Ltd
6080 Ctr Dr Ste 400 ....Los Angeles CA 90045 | 800-227-4500 | 310-726-1400 | 25

QBE Holdings Inc
Wall St Plz 88 Pine St ....New York NY 10005 | 800-456-1626 | 212-422-1212 | 388-4

QC Holdings Inc
9401 Indian Creek Pkwy
Ste 1500 ....Overland Park KS 66210 | 866-660-2243 | | 139
NASDAQ: QCCO

QCI Asset Management
40A Grove St ....Pittsford NY 14534 | 800-836-3960 | 585-218-2060 | 398

QED Inc
1661 W Third Ave ....Denver CO 80223 | 800-700-5011 | 303-825-5011 | 246

QEP Co Inc
1001 Broken Sound Pkwy NW
Ste A ....Boca Raton FL 33487 | 800-777-8665* | 561-994-5550 | 748
OTC: QEPC ■ *Sales

QlikTech International AB
150 N Radnor Chester Rd Ste E220 ....Radnor PA 19087 | 888-828-9768 | | 179-10
NASDAQ: QLIK

QLogic Corp
26650 Aliso Viejo Pkwy ....Aliso Viejo CA 92656 | 800-662-4471 | 949-389-6000 | 687
NASDAQ: QLGC

QLT Inc
887 Great Northern Way
Ste 101 ....Vancouver BC V5T4T5 | 800-663-5486 | 604-707-7000 | 84
NASDAQ: QLT

QLT USA Inc
2579 Midpoint Dr ....Fort Collins CO 80525 | 800-901-5241 | 970-482-5868 | 576

QMI (Quality Mfg Company Inc)
PO Box 616 ....Winchester KY 40392 | 866-460-6459 | 859-744-0420 | 449

QNB Corp
15 N Third St PO Box 9005 ....Quakertown PA 18951 | 800-491-9070 | 215-538-5600 | 69
OTC: QNBC

QSA ToolWorks LLC
3100 47th Ave ....Long Island City NY 11101 | 800-784-7018 | 516-935-9151 | 179-7

QSC Audio Products LLC
1675 MacArthur Blvd ....Costa Mesa CA 92626 | 800-854-4079 | 714-754-6175 | 51

QSI (Quality Systems Inc)
18111 Von Karman Ave Ste 600 ....Irvine CA 92612 | 800-888-7955* | 949-255-2600 | 179-10
NASDAQ: QSII ■ *Cust Svc

Quad Cities Convention & Visitors Bureau
1601 River Dr Ste 110 ....Moline IL 61265 | 800-747-7800 | 309-277-0937 | 207

Quad City Bank & Trust
3551 Seventh St ....Moline IL 61265 | 866-676-0551 | 309-736-3580 | 357-2
NASDAQ: QCRH

Quad City Conservation Alliance Expo Ctr
2621 Fourth Ave ....Rock Island IL 61201 | 877-734-1565 | 309-788-5912 | 206

Quad-City Peterbilt Inc
8100 N Fairmount St ....Davenport IA 52806 | 866-601-8607 | | 509

Quad-City Times
500 E Third St ....Davenport IA 52801 | 800-437-4641 | 563-383-2200 | 525-2

Quadel Consulting
1200 G St NW Ste 700 ....Washington DC 20005 | 866-640-1019 | 202-789-2500 | 195

Quadra Chemicals Ltd
3901 Fixtessier ....Vaudreuil-Dorion QC J7V5V5 | 800-665-6553 | 450-424-0161 | 144

Quadrant Engineering Plastic Products USA
2120 Fairmont Ave PO Box 14235 ....Reading PA 19612 | 800-366-0300 | 610-320-6600 | 595

Quadrex Corp
PO Box 3881 ....Woodbridge CT 06525 | 800-275-7033* | 203-393-3112 | 331
*Sales

Quail Lodge Resort & Golf Club
8205 Valley Greens Dr ....Carmel CA 93923 | 866-675-1101 | 831-624-2888 | 660

Quaker Chemical Corp
901 Hector St ....Conshohocken PA 19428 | 800-523-7010 | 610-832-4000 | 143
NYSE: KWR

Quaker Oats Co
555 W Monroe St ....Chicago IL 60661 | 800-367-6287 | 312-821-1000 | 295-36

Quaker Window Products Inc
504 S Hwy 63 PO Box 128 ....Freeburg MO 65035 | 800-347-0438 | | 234

Name / Address	City	State	ZIP	Toll-Free	Phone	Class
Qualcomm Stadium 9449 Friars Rd	San Diego	CA	92108	800-400-7115	619-641-3100	711
Qual-Craft Industries PO Box 559	Stoughton	MA	02072	800-231-5647	781-344-1000	347
Quali Tech Inc 318 Lake Hazeltine Dr	Chaska	MN	55318	800-328-5870	952-448-5151	442
Qualicaps Inc 6505 Franz Warner Pkwy	Whitsett	NC	27377	800-227-7853	336-449-3900	576
Qualico Steel Co Inc PO Box 149	Webb	AL	36376	866-234-5382	334-793-1290	475
Qualified Remodeler Magazine 1233 Janesville Ave	Fort Atkinson	WI	53538	800-547-7377	920-563-6388	452-21
Qualified Resources International LLC 78 Kenwood St	Cranston	RI	02907	866-421-9840	401-946-1002	623
Qualis Health PO Box 33400	Seattle	WA	98133	800-949-7536	206-364-9700	371-3
Qualitel Corp 11831 Beverly Pk Rd	Everett	WA	98204	800-647-7706	425-423-8388	253
QualiTest Ltd 1139 Post Rd	Fairfield	CT	06824	877-882-9540		390
Qualitest Pharmaceuticals 130 Vintage Dr	Huntsville	AL	35811	800-444-4011		576
Quality Biological Inc 7581 Lindbergh Dr	Gaithersburg	MD	20879	800-443-9331	301-840-9331	231
Quality Books Inc 1003 W Pines Rd *Cust Svc	Oregon	IL	61061	800-323-4241*	815-732-4450	94
Quality Containers of New England 247 Portland St Ste 300	Yarmouth	ME	04096	800-639-1550	207-846-5420	97
Quality Customs Broker Inc 4464 S Whitnall Ave	Saint Francis	WI	53235	888-813-4647	414-482-9447	310
Quality Dining Inc 4220 Edison Lakes Pkwy	Mishawaka	IN	46545	800-589-3820	574-271-4600	661
Quality Distribution Inc 4041 Pk Oaks Blvd Ste 200 *NASDAQ: QLTY*	Tampa	FL	33610	800-282-2031		770
Quality Inn & Suites Naples Golf Resort 4100 Golden Gate Pkwy	Naples	FL	34116	800-277-0017	239-455-1010	660
Quality Inn Halifax Airport Hotel 60 Sky Blvd Halifax International Airport	Goffs	NS	B2T1K3	800-667-3333	902-873-3000	376
Quality Inn West Harvest 17803 Stony Plain Rd	Edmonton	AB	T5S1B4	800-661-2133	780-484-8000	376
Quality Liquid Feeds Inc PO Box 240	Dodgeville	WI	53533	800-236-2345	608-935-2345	276
Quality Management Solutions LLC 146 Lowell St Ste 300B	Wakefield	MA	01889	800-645-6430		197
Quality Manufacturing Inc 969 Labore Industrial Ct	Saint Paul	MN	55110	800-243-5473	651-483-5473	692
Quality Meats & Seafoods 700 Ctr St	West Fargo	ND	58078	800-342-4250	701-282-0202	468
Quality Mfg Company Inc (QMI) PO Box 616	Winchester	KY	40392	866-460-6459	859-744-0420	449
Quality Perforating Inc 166 Dundaff St	Carbondale	PA	18407	800-872-7373	570-282-4344	483
Quality Plywood Specialties Inc 4500 110th Ave N	Clearwater	FL	33762	888-722-1181	727-572-0500	192-3
Quality Progress Magazine 600 N Plankinton Ave PO Box 3005 *Cust Svc	Milwaukee	WI	53201	800-248-1946*	414-272-8575	452-21
Quality Systems Inc (QSI) 18111 Von Karman Ave Ste 600 *NASDAQ: QSII* ■ *Cust Svc	Irvine	CA	92612	800-888-7955*	949-255-2600	179-10
Quality Transportation 36-40 37th St Ste 201	Long Island City	NY	11101	800-677-2838	212-308-6333	310
Qualstar Corp 3990-B Heritage Oak Ct *NASDAQ: QBAK*	Simi Valley	CA	93063	800-468-0680	805-583-7744	174-8
Qualys Inc 1600 Bridge Pkwy	Redwood Shores	CA	94065	866-801-6161	650-801-6100	683
Quam-Nichols Company Inc 234 E Marquette Rd	Chicago	IL	60637	800-633-3669	773-488-5800	51
Quanex Building Products 2270 Woodale Dr	Mounds View	MN	55112	800-233-4383	763-231-4000	494
Quanex Building Products Corp 1900 W Loop S Ste 1500 *Cust Svc	Houston	TX	77027	888-475-0633*	713-961-4600	235
Quantimetrix Corp 2005 Manhattan Beach Blvd	Redondo Beach	CA	90278	800-624-8380	310-536-0006	231
Quantum Analytics 3400 East Third Ave	Foster City	CA	94404	800-992-4199	650-312-0900	264-3
Quantum Audio Designs Inc 6408 State Hwy 77	Benton	MO	63736	888-545-4404	573-545-4404	519
Quantum Corp 224 Airport Pkwy Ste 300 *NYSE: QTM* ■ *Tech Supp	San Jose	CA	95110	800-677-6268*	408-944-4000	174-8
Quantum Corporate Funding Ltd 1140 Ave of the Americas 16th Fl	New York	NY	10036	800-352-2535	212-768-1200	272
Quantum Dental Technologies Inc 748 Briar Hill Ave	Toronto	ON	M6B1L3	866-993-9910		228
Quantum/ATL 141 Innovation Dr	Irvine	CA	92617	800-677-6268	949-856-7800	174-8
Quantum3D Inc 6330 San Ignacio Ave	San Jose	CA	95119	888-747-1020	408-361-9999	174-1
Quantus Software 32-62 Scurfield Blvd	Winnipeg	MB	R3Y1M5	866-478-1308		194
Quark Inc 1800 Grant St *Cust Svc	Denver	CO	80203	800-676-4575*		179-8
Quarles & Brady LLP 411 E Wisconsin Ave Ste 2040	Milwaukee	WI	53202	800-654-2200	414-277-5000	425
Quarterpath Inn & Suites 614 York St	Williamsburg	VA	23185	800-581-7245	757-220-0960	376
Quartz Mountain Resort & Conference Ctr 22469 Lodge Rd	Lone Wolf	OK	73655	877-999-5567	580-563-2424	660
Quatech Inc 5675 Hudson Industrial Pkwy	Hudson	OH	44236	800-553-1170	330-655-9000	617
Quatred LLC 532 Fourth Range Rd	Pembroke	NH	03275	888-395-8534		40
Quebec Inn 7175 Blvd Hamel Ouest	Quebec City	QC	G2G1B6	800-567-5276	418-872-9831	376
Queen & Crescent Hotel 535 Tchoupitoulas St	New Orleans	LA	70130	800-455-3417		376
Queen Anne Hotel 1590 Sutter St	San Francisco	CA	94109	800-227-3970	415-441-2828	376
Queen City TV & Appliance Company Inc 2430 Queen City Dr *All	Charlotte	NC	28208	800-365-6665*	704-391-6000	34
Queen Cutlery Co 507 Chestnut St *Sales	Titusville	PA	16354	800-222-5233*	814-827-3673	222
Queen Kapiolani Hotel 150 Kapahulu Ave	Honolulu	HI	96815	866-970-4164	808-922-1941	376
Queen's College Faculty of Theology 210 Prince Philip Dr Ste 3000	Saint John's	NL	A1B3R6	877-753-0116	709-753-0116	167-3
Queens Chamber of Commerce 75-20 Astoria Blvd Ste 140	Jackson Heights	NY	11370	877-256-5556	718-898-8500	137
Queens College 65-30 Kissena Blvd	Flushing	NY	11367	888-888-0606	718-997-5000	166
Queens Courier 38-15 Bell Blvd	Bayside	NY	11361	800-275-8777	718-224-5863	525-4
Queens Hospital Ctr 82-68 164th St	Jamaica	NY	11432	888-692-6116	718-883-3000	371-3
Queens Museum of Art New York City Bldg	Queens	NY	11368	866-867-9665	718-592-9700	513
Queens University of Charlotte 1900 Selwyn Ave	Charlotte	NC	28274	800-849-0202	704-337-2212	166
Queensboro Co 113 E Broad St PO Box 467	Louisville	GA	30434	800-236-2442	478-625-2000	770
Queensborough Community College 222-05 56th Ave	Bayside	NY	11364	877-253-7122	718-631-6262	160
Queenstown Bank of Maryland 7101 Main St PO Box 120	Queenstown	MD	21658	888-827-4300	410-827-8881	69
Quest Companies Inc 8011 N Point Blvd Ste 201	Winston-salem	NC	27106	800-467-9409		7
Quest Diagnostics at Nichols Institute 33608 Ortega Hwy	San Juan Capistrano	CA	92675	800-642-4657	949-728-4000	415
Quest Diagnostics Inc Three Giralda Farms *NYSE: DGX*	Madison	NJ	07940	800-222-0446	201-393-5000	415
Quest Software Inc Five Polaris Way *NASDAQ: QSFT*	Aliso Viejo	CA	92656	800-306-9329	949-754-8000	179-1
Questar Assessment Inc 5550 Upper 147th St W PO Box 382 *OTC: QUSA* ■ *Cust Svc	Apple Valley	MN	55124	800-800-2598*	800-471-5448	243
Questar Capital Corp 5701 Golden Hills Dr	Minneapolis	MN	55416	888-446-5872		681
Questar Corp 333 S State St PO Box 45433 *NYSE: STR*	Salt Lake City	UT	84145	800-323-5517	801-324-5000	357-5
Questar Gas Co PO Box 45841	Salt Lake City	UT	84139	800-323-5517	801-324-5111	775
Questar Gas Management Co PO Box 45360	Salt Lake City	UT	84145	800-323-5517	801-324-5111	324
Questar InfoComm Inc 180 East 100 South PO Box 45433	Salt Lake City	UT	84145	800-729-6790	801-324-5856	726
Questcor Pharmaceuticals Inc 1300 N Kellogg Ste D *NASDAQ: QCOR*	Anaheim Hills	CA	92807	888-435-2284	714-786-4200	84
Questel Orbit 1725 Duke St Ste 625	Alexandria	VA	22314	800-456-7248	703-519-1820	626
Questex LLC 275 Grove St Ste 2-130	Newton	MA	02466	888-552-4346	617-219-8300	524-13
Questia Media America Inc 1 N State St Ste 900	Chicago	IL	60602	800-759-4726	800-889-0097	384
Questica Inc 980 Fraser Dr Ste 105	Burlington	ON	L7L5P5	877-707-7755		180
Queue Inc 80 Hathaway Dr	Stratford	CT	06615	800-232-2224		179-3
Quicken Loans Arena One Ctr Ct	Cleveland	OH	44115	888-894-9424	216-420-2000	711
Quicksilver Resources Inc 777 W Rosedale St Ste 300 *OTC: KWKAQ*	Fort Worth	TX	76104	877-665-8600	817-665-5000	531
Quidel Corp 10165 McKellar Ct *NASDAQ: QDEL*	San Diego	CA	92121	800-874-1517	858-552-1100	231
Quikbook 381 Pk Ave S 3rd Fl	New York	NY	10016	800-789-9887	212-686-7666	373
Quikey Manufacturing Co 1500 Industrial Pkwy	Akron	OH	44310	877-901-1200	330-633-8106	9
QUIKRETE Cos 3490 Piedmont Rd Ste 1300	Atlanta	GA	30305	800-282-5828	404-634-9100	184
Quikstik Labels 220 Broadway	Everett	MA	02149	800-225-3496	617-389-7570	410
QuikTrip Corp 4705 S 129th E Ave	Tulsa	OK	74134	800-441-0253	918-615-7700	205
Quilter's Newsletter Magazine 741 Corporate Cir Ste A	Golden	CO	80401	800-477-6089	303-215-5600	452-14
Quiltmaker Magazine 741 Corporate Cir Ste A	Golden	CO	80401	800-388-7023	800-881-6634	452-14
Quimby House Inn 109 Cottage St	Bar Harbor	ME	04609	800-344-5811	207-288-5811	376
Quincy Area Convention & Visitors Bureau (QACVB) 532 Gardner Expy	Quincy	IL	62301	800-978-4748	217-214-3700	207
Quincy College 150 Newport Ave Ext Ste 1	Quincy	MA	02171	800-698-1700	617-984-1700	160
Quincy Herald-Whig 130 S Fifth St	Quincy	IL	62301	800-373-9444	217-223-5100	525-2
Quincy Hotel 1823 L St NW	Washington	DC	20036	800-424-2970	202-223-4320	376
Quincy Mutual Fire Insurance Co 57 Washington St	Quincy	MA	02169	800-899-1116		388-4
Quincy Newspapers Inc 130 S Fifth St	Quincy	IL	62301	800-373-9444	217-223-5100	628-8
Quincy Street Inc 13350 Quincy St	Holland	MI	49424	800-784-6290	616-399-3330	468
Quincy University 1800 College Ave	Quincy	IL	62301	866-703-4004	217-222-8020	166

Name / Address	City	State	ZIP	Toll-Free	Phone	Class
Quinnipiac University 275 Mt Carmel Ave *Admissions	Hamden	CT	06518	**800-462-1944***	203-582-8600	166
Quinnipiac University School of Law 275 Mt Carmel Ave	Hamden	CT	06518	**800-462-1944**	203-582-3400	167-1
Quintiles Canada Inc 100 Alexis-Nihon Ste 800 *General	Saint Laurent	QC	H4M2P4	**866-267-4479***	514-855-0888	576
Quintiles Transnational Corp 4820 Emperor Blvd	Durham	NC	27703	**866-267-4479**	919-998-2000	576
Quirch Foods Co 7600 NW 82nd Pl	Miami	FL	33166	**800-458-5252**	305-691-3535	296-9
Quiznos Corp 1275 Grant St Ste 200	Denver	CO	80203	**866-486-2783**	720-359-3300	661
QUMAS 66 York St *Sales	Jersey City	NJ	07302	**800-577-1545***	973-805-8600	179-10
QVC Inc 1200 Wilson Dr	West Chester	PA	19380	**800-367-9444**	484-701-1000	729
Qvidian Corp 175 Cabot St Ste 210	Lowell	MA	01854	**800-272-0047**	513-631-1155	179-10
Qwest Arena 233 S Capitol Blvd	Boise	ID	83702	**888-330-8497**	208-424-2200	711

R

Name / Address	City	State	ZIP	Toll-Free	Phone	Class
R & B Wagner Inc PO Box 423	Butler	WI	53007	**888-243-6914**	414-214-0444	588
R & D Batteries Inc 3300 Corporate Ctr Dr PO Box 5007	Burnsville	MN	55306	**800-950-1945**	952-890-0629	73
R & D Magazine 100 Enterprise Dr Ste 600	Rockaway	NJ	07866	**866-885-9794**	973-920-7000	452-19
R & D Systems Inc 614 McKinley Pl NE	Minneapolis	MN	55413	**800-343-7475**	612-379-2956	231
R & K Industrial Products Co 1945 Seventh St	Richmond	CA	94801	**800-842-7655**	510-234-7212	667
R & M Energy Systems 301 Premier Rd *Sales	Borger	TX	79007	**888-262-8645***	806-274-5293	382
R & M Office Furniture 9615 Oates Dr	Sacramento	CA	95827	**800-660-1756**	916-362-1756	319
R & R Limousine 4403 Kiln Ct	Louisville	KY	40218	**800-582-5576**	502-458-1862	437
R & R Marketing LLC 10 Patton Dr	West Caldwell	NJ	07006	**800-772-2096**	973-228-5100	80-3
R & R Trucking Inc 302 Thunder Rd PO Box 545	Duenweg	MO	64841	**800-625-6885**	417-623-6885	770
R & S/Godwin Truck Body Co LLC 5168 S US Hwy 23 PO Box 420	Ivel	KY	41642	**800-826-7413**	606-874-2151	509
R B M Co 2700 Texas Ave PO Box 12	Knoxville	TN	37921	**800-521-5656**	865-524-8621	382
R E I Consultants Inc PO Box 286	Beaver	WV	25813	**800-999-0105**	304-255-2500	193
R J Schinner Company Inc 16950 W Lincoln Ave PO Box 510470	New Berlin	WI	53151	**800-234-1460**	262-797-7180	779
R K Allen Oil Inc 36002 AL Hwy 21	Talladega	AL	35161	**800-445-5823**	256-362-4261	572
R K Electric Inc 42021 Osgood Rd	Fremont	CA	94539	**800-400-4418**	510-770-5660	190-4
R Kidd Fuels Corp 1172 Twinney Dr	Newmarket	ON	L3Y9E2	**866-274-2315**		572
R Seelaus & Company Inc 25 Deforest Ave Ste 304	Summit	NJ	07901	**800-922-0584**		681
R W Mercer Co 2322 Brooklyn Rd PO Box 180	Jackson	MI	49204	**877-763-7237**	517-787-2960	187
RA (Ruotolo Assoc Inc) 29 Broadway Ste 210	Cresskill	NJ	07626	**800-786-8656**	201-568-3898	316
RA Miller Industries Inc 14500 168th Ave PO Box 858	Grand Haven	MI	49417	**888-845-9450**	616-842-9450	638
RAB (Radio Adv Bureau) 125 W 55th St 21st Fl	New York	NY	10019	**800-252-7234**	212-681-7200	48-18
RAB Lighting 170 Ludlow Ave	Northvale	NJ	07647	**888-722-1000**	201-784-8600	435
Raba-Kistner Consultants Inc 12821 W Golden Ln	San Antonio	TX	78249	**866-722-2547**	210-699-9090	190-15
Rabbit Hill Inn 48 Lower Waterford Rd PO Box 55	Lower Waterford	VT	05848	**800-626-3215**	802-748-5168	376
Rabo Bank 1026 E Grand Ave	Arroyo Grande	CA	93420	**800-942-6222**	805-473-7710	69
Rabun County School District 963 Tiger Connector	Tiger	GA	30576	**866-632-9992**	706-212-4350	676
Rabun Gap-Nacoochee School 339 Nacoochee Dr	Rabun Gap	GA	30568	**800-543-7467**	706-746-7467	615
Raccoon Mountain Caverns 319 W Hills Dr	Chattanooga	TN	37419	**800-823-2267**	423-821-9403	49-4
Raccoon Valley Electric Co-op 28725 Hwy 30 PO Box 486	Glidden	IA	51443	**800-253-6211**	712-659-3649	245
Race Face Components Inc 100 Braid St Unit 100	New Westminster	BC	V3L3P4	**800-527-9244**	604-527-9996	153-1
RaceTrac Petroleum Inc 3225 Cumberland Blvd Ste 100	Atlanta	GA	30339	**888-636-5589**	770-431-7600	323
Racine County Convention & Visitors Bureau 14015 Washington Ave	Sturtevant	WI	53177	**800-272-2463**	262-884-6400	207
Racine Public Library 75 Seventh St	Racine	WI	53403	**888-529-0061**	262-636-9241	431-3
Racks Inc PO Box 530840	San Diego	CA	92153	**877-920-7225**	619-661-0987	286
RACVB (Ridgecrest Area Convention & Visitors Bureau) 139 Balsam St Ste 1700	Ridgecrest	CA	93555	**800-847-4830**	760-375-8202	207
RAD Data Communications Ltd 900 Corporate Dr	Mahwah	NJ	07430	**800-444-7234**	201-529-1100	725
Rada Manufacturing Co PO Box 838	Waverly	IA	50677	**800-311-9691**	319-352-5454	222
Radar Industries 27101 Grosbeck Hwy	Warren	MI	48089	**800-779-0301**		484
Radel Trey (Rep R - FL) 1123 Longworth Bldg	Washington	DC	20515	**866-264-0957**	202-225-2536	
Radford University 801 E Main St *Admissions	Radford	VA	24142	**800-890-4265***	540-831-5371	166
Radiac Abrasives Inc 1015 S College Ave	Salem	IL	62881	**800-851-1095**	618-548-4200	1
Radialpoint 2050 Bleury St Ste 300	Montreal	QC	H3A2J5	**866-286-2636**	514-286-2636	179-9
Radian Asset Assurance Inc *Radian Group Inc, The* 335 Madison Ave 25th Fl	New York	NY	10017	**877-723-4261**	212-983-3100	388-5
Radian Group Inc 1601 Market St *NYSE: RDN*	Philadelphia	PA	19103	**800-523-1988**	215-564-6600	388-5
Radiant Communications Corp 1600-1050 W Pender St *CVE: RCN*	Vancouver	BC	V6E4T3	**888-219-2111**		795
Radiant Electric Co-op Inc 100 N 15th St	Fredonia	KS	66736	**800-821-0956**	620-378-2161	245
Radiant Pools Div Trojan Leisure Products LLC 440 N Pearl St	Albany	NY	12207	**866-697-5870**	518-434-4161	719
Radiant Research Inc 11500 Northlake Dr Ste 320	Cincinnati	OH	45249	**866-232-8484**	513-247-5500	659
Radiation Therapy Services Inc 2270 Colonial Blvd	Fort Myers	FL	33907	**800-437-1619**	239-931-7275	349
Radiator Specialty Co 1900 Wilkinson Blvd	Charlotte	NC	28208	**877-464-4865**	704-688-2405	143
Radio Adv Bureau (RAB) 125 W 55th St 21st Fl	New York	NY	10019	**800-252-7234**	212-681-7200	48-18
Radio America 1100 N Glebe Rd Ste 900	Arlington	VA	22201	**800-807-4703**	703-302-1000	635
Radio Control Boat Modeler 88 Danbury Rd	Wilton	CT	06897	**888-235-2021**	203-431-9000	452-14
Radio Distributing Company Inc 27015 Trolley Industrial Dr	Taylor	MI	48180	**800-462-1544**	313-295-4500	37
Radio Flyer Inc 6515 W Grand Ave	Chicago	IL	60707	**800-621-7613**	773-637-7100	752
Radiocat 32-A Mellor Ave	Baltimore	MD	21228	**800-323-9729**		782
Radiodetection Corp 154 Portland Rd	Bridgton	ME	04009	**877-247-3797**	207-647-9495	248
Radiological Society of North America (RSNA) 820 Jorie Blvd	Oak Brook	IL	60523	**800-381-6660**	630-571-2670	48-8
Radiology Business Management Assn (RBMA) 10300 Eaton Pl Ste 460	Fairfax	VA	22030	**888-224-7262**	703-621-3355	48-8
RadioShack Corp 300 RadioShack Cir *NYSE: RSH*	Fort Worth	TX	76102	**800-843-7422**	800-442-7221	34
Radisson Butler Blvd 4700 Salisbury Rd	Jacksonville	FL	32256	**888-201-1718**	904-281-9700	376
Radisson Chicago-O'Hare Hotel 1450 E Touhy Ave	Des Plaines	IL	60018	**888-201-1718**	847-296-8866	376
Radisson Hotel Bloomington Mall of America 1700 American Blvd E *Resv	Bloomington	MN	55425	**800-967-9033***	952-854-8700	376
Radisson Milwaukee North Shore 7065 N Port Washington Rd	Milwaukee	WI	53217	**800-395-7046**	414-351-6960	376
Radisson Palm Beach Shores Resort & Vacation Villas 11340 Blondo S Ste 100	Omaha	NE	68164	**800-615-7253**		660
Radisson Resort Parkway 2900 PkwyBlvd	Kissimmee	FL	34747	**800-333-3333**	407-396-7000	660
RadiSys Corp 5445 NE Dawson Creek Dr *NASDAQ: RSYS*	Hillsboro	OR	97124	**800-950-0044**	503-615-1100	617
RADIUS 7700 Wisconsin Ave Ste 400	Bethesda	MD	20814	**800-989-3059**	301-718-9500	762
RadView Software Inc 111 Deerwood Rd Ste 200	San Ramon	CA	94583	**888-723-8439**	908-526-7756	179-12
Radware Inc 575 Corporate Dr Lobby 2	Mahwah	NJ	07430	**888-234-5763**	201-512-9771	179-11
Rady Children's Hospital (RCH) 3020 Children's Way MC 5101	San Diego	CA	92123	**800-788-9029**	858-576-1700	371-1
Radyne Corp 211 W Boden St	Milwaukee	WI	53207	**800-236-8360**	414-481-8360	317
RAE Corp 4615 Prime Pkwy	McHenry	IL	60050	**800-323-7049**	815-385-3500	511
RAE Systems 3775 N First St	San Jose	CA	95134	**877-723-2878**	408-952-8200	202
Raf Technologies Inc 200 Lexington Ave	Deland	FL	32724	**888-876-6424**	386-736-1698	757
Raft River Rural Electric Co-op Inc 155 N Main St PO Box 617	Malta	ID	83342	**800-342-7732**	208-645-2211	245
Ragan Communications Inc 316 N Michigan Ave Ste 400	Chicago	IL	60601	**800-878-5331**	312-960-4100	524-2
Rail Link Inc 13901 Sutton Pk Dr S Ste 125	Jacksonville	FL	32224	**877-777-4778**	904-223-1110	642
Railroad Pass Hotel & Casino 2800 S Boulder Hwy	Henderson	NV	89002	**800-654-0877**	702-294-5000	132
Railroad Retirement Board 844 N Rush St	Chicago	IL	60611	**877-772-5772**	312-751-4300	338-18
Rails Co 101 Newark Way	Maplewood	NJ	07040	**800-217-2457**	973-763-4320	760
Railserve Inc 1691 Phoenix Blvd Ste 110	Atlanta	GA	30349	**800-345-7245**	770-996-6838	642
Railway Supply Institute Inc (RSI) 425 Third St Ste 920	Washington	DC	20024	**800-995-3579**	202-347-4664	48-21
Rain Creek Baking Co, The 2401 W Almond Ave	Madera	CA	93637	**800-530-0505**	559-674-4445	296-11
Rainbow Art Glass Inc 1761 Rt 34 S	Farmingdale	NJ	07727	**800-526-2356**	732-681-6003	328
Rainbow International 1010 N University Pk Dr	Waco	TX	76707	**855-724-6269**	254-756-5463	150
Rainbow Light Nutritional Sys Inc 100 Ave Tea	Santa Cruz	CA	95060	**800-635-1233**		474
Rainbow Trout Ranch (RTR) 1484 FDR 250 PO Box 458	Antonito	CO	81120	**800-633-3397**	719-376-5659	239
Rainbows 1360 Hamilton Pkwy	Itasca	IL	60143	**800-266-3206**	847-952-1770	47-6
Raindance Spa at the Lodge at Sonoma Renaissance Resort 1325 Broadway	Sonoma	CA	95476	**866-263-0758**	707-935-6600	698
Rainforest Action Network (RAN) 221 Pine St Fifth Fl	San Francisco	CA	94104	**800-368-1819**	415-398-4404	47-13

Name / Address	City	State	ZIP	Toll-Free	Phone	Class
Rainier Industries Ltd 18375 Olympic Ave S	Tukwila	WA	98188	800-869-7162	425-251-1800	723
Rainier Investment Management Mutual Funds 601 Union St Ste 2801	Seattle	WA	98101	800-536-4640		521
RainMaker Software Inc 1777 Sentry Pkwy W	Blue Bell	PA	19422	800-336-0339	610-567-3409	179-10
RAINN (Rape Abuse & Incest National Network) 2000 L St NW Ste 406	Washington	DC	20036	800-656-4673	202-544-1034	47-6
Rainwater, Holt & Sexton PA 6315 Ranch Dr	Little Rock	AR	72223	800-434-4800		425
Rainwise Inc 25 Federal St	Bar Harbor	ME	04609	800-762-5723	207-288-5169	404
Rainy River Community College 1501 Hwy 71	International Falls	MN	56649	800-456-3996	218-285-7722	160
Raj, The 1734 Jasmine Ave	Fairfield	IA	52556	800-248-9050	641-472-9580	697
Rakuten Marketing LLC 215 Pk Ave S 9th Fl	New York	NY	10003	888-880-8430	646-943-8200	7
Ralco Nutrition Inc 1600 Hahn Rd	Marshall	MN	56258	800-533-5306		442
Raleigh America Inc 6004 S 190th St Ste 101	Kent	WA	98032	800-222-5527		81
Raleigh Studios Worldwide 5300 Melrose Ave	Hollywood	CA	90038	888-960-3456	323-466-3111	505
Raleigh USA 6004 S 190th St Ste 101	Kent	WA	98032	800-222-5527	253-395-1100	81
Raleigh-Durham International Airport PO Box 80001	Raleigh	NC	27623	800-252-7522	919-840-2123	27
Raley's 500 W Capitol Ave PO Box 15618	Sacramento	CA	95852	800-925-9989	916-373-3333	342
Ralls County Electric Co-op 17594 Hwy 19 PO Box 157	New London	MO	63459	877-985-8711	573-985-8711	245
Rally House & Kansas Sampler 9750 Quivira Rd	Lenexa	KS	66215	800-645-5394		779
Rallyorg 580 Howard St Ste 402	San Francisco	CA	94105	888-648-2220		384
Ralph Pill Electrical Supply Co 50 Von Hillern Street	Boston	MA	02125	800-897-1769	617-265-8800	246
Ralph Rosenberg Court Reporters Inc 1001 Bishop St Ste 2460	Honolulu	HI	96813	888-524-5888		440
Ralphs Grocery Co 1014 Vine Street *Cust Svc	Cincinnati,	OH	45202	800-576-4377*		342
Ralston Metal Products Ltd 50 Watson Rd S	Guelph	ON	N1L1E2	800-265-7611		475
Ram Graphics Inc 2408 S Pk Ave	Alexandria	IN	46001	800-531-4656		678
RAM Nationwide Inc 240 W N Bend Rd	Cincinnati	OH	45216	800-837-0110	513-821-0010	770
RAMA (Retail Adv & Marketing Assn) 325 Seventh St NW Ste 1100	Washington	DC	20004	800-673-4692	202-783-7971	48-18
Rama Corp 600 W Esplanade Ave	San Jacinto	CA	92583	800-472-5670	951-654-7351	14
Ramada Middletown 425 E Main Rd	Middletown	RI	02842	800-854-9517	401-846-3555	376
Ramada Plaza & Conference Ctr 4900 Sinclair Rd	Columbus	OH	43229	800-272-6232	614-846-0300	376
Ramapo Catskill Library System 619 Rt 17-M	Middletown	NY	10940	800-327-7343	845-343-1131	431-3
Ramco Systems Corp 3150 Brunswick Pk Ste 130	Lawrenceville	NJ	08648	800-472-6261	609-620-4800	225
Ramona Chamber of Commerce 960 Main St	Ramona	CA	92065	800-411-7343	760-789-1311	137
Ramos Oil Company Inc 1515 S River Rd *Cust Svc	West Sacramento	CA	95691	800-477-7266*	916-371-2570	572
Rampart Brokerage Corp 1983 Marcus Ave Ste C130	New Hyde Park	NY	11042	800-772-6727	516-538-7000	387
Ramsey County 15 W Kellogg Blvd Rm 250	Saint Paul	MN	55102	866-520-7225	651-266-8000	336
Ramsey County Public Library 4570 N Victoria St	Shoreview	MN	55126	888-335-9632	651-486-2200	431-3
Ramsey Winch Company Inc 1600 N Garnett Rd	Tulsa	OK	74116	800-777-2760	918-438-2760	191
Ramtech Bldg Systems Inc 1400 Hwy 287 S	Mansfield	TX	76063	855-887-1888		187
Ramtron International Corp 1850 Ramtron Dr *NASDAQ: RMTR*	Colorado Springs	CO	80921	800-541-4736	719-481-7000	687
RAN (Rainforest Action Network) 221 Pine St Fifth Fl	San Francisco	CA	94104	800-368-1819	415-398-4404	47-13
Ranch at Steamboat 1800 Ranch Rd	Steamboat Springs	CO	80487	888-686-8075	970-879-3000	376
Ranch Inn 45 E Pearl St	Jackson	WY	83001	800-348-5599	307-733-6363	376
Rancho Cucamonga Chamber of Commerce 9047 Arrow Route Suite 180	Rancho Cucamonga	CA	91730	800-677-5434	909-987-1012	137
Rancho Cucamonga Public Library 7368 Archibald Ave	Rancho Cucamonga	CA	91730	800-655-4555	909-477-2720	431-3
Rancho de la Osa Guest Ranch PO Box 1	Sasabe	AZ	85633	800-872-6240	520-823-4257	239
Rancho de los Caballeros 1551 S Vulture Mine Rd	Wickenburg	AZ	85390	800-684-5030	928-684-5484	660
Rancho Los Amigos National Rehabilitation Ctr 7601 E Imperial Hwy	Downey	CA	90242	877-726-2461	562-401-7111	371-6
Rancho Valencia Resort 5921 Valencia Cir PO Box 9126	Rancho Santa Fe	CA	92067	800-548-3664	858-756-1123	660
Rancho Viejo Resort & Country Club One Rancho Viejo Dr	Rancho Viejo	TX	78575	800-531-7400	956-350-4000	660
Rancocas Metals Corp 35 Indel Ave	Rancocas	NJ	08073	800-762-6382	609-267-4120	487
RAND Corp 1776 Main St	Santa Monica	CA	90401	877-584-8642	310-393-0411	625
Rand McNally 9855 Woods Dr PO Box 7600	Skokie	IL	60077	800-275-7263		628-1
Randall Bearings Inc 1046 Greenlawn Ave PO Box 1258	Lima	OH	45802	800-626-7071	419-223-1075	478
Randall Bros Inc 665 Marietta St NW *Cust Svc	Atlanta	GA	30313	800-476-4539*	404-892-6666	494
Randall County Feedyard 15000 FM 2219	Amarillo	TX	79119	800-658-6014	806-499-3701	10-1
Randall Museum 199 Museum Way	San Francisco	CA	94114	866-807-7148	415-554-9600	513
Randall-Reilly Publishing Co 3200 Rice Mine Rd NE *Cust Svc	Tuscaloosa	AL	35406	800-633-5953*		628-9
Randolph College 2500 Rivermont Ave *Admissions	Lynchburg	VA	24503	800-745-7692*	434-947-8000	166
Randolph Community College 629 Industrial Pk Ave	Asheboro	NC	27205	800-433-3243	336-633-0200	160
Randolph County 1302 N Randolph Ave	Elkins	WV	26241	800-422-3304	304-636-2780	336
Randolph Electric Membership Corp 879 McDowell Rd PO Box 40	Asheboro	NC	27204	800-672-8212	336-625-5177	245
Randolph Packing Co 275 Roma Jean Pkwy	Streamwood	IL	60107	800-451-1607	630-830-3100	295-26
Randolph Savings Bank 129 N Main St PO Box 354	Randolph	MA	02368	877-963-2100	781-963-2100	69
Randolph-Brooks Federal Credit Union PO Box 2097	Universal City	TX	78148	800-580-3300	210-945-3300	219
Randolph-Macon Academy 200 Academy Dr	Front Royal	VA	22630	800-272-1172	540-636-5200	615
Randolph-Macon College PO Box 5005	Ashland	VA	23005	800-888-1762	804-752-7200	166
Rane Corp 10802 47th Ave W	Mukilteo	WA	98275	877-764-0093	425-355-6000	51
R-Anell Custom Homes Inc 235 Anthony Grave Rd *Cust Svc	Crouse	NC	28033	800-951-5511*	704-483-5511	500
Rangam Consultants Inc 370 Campus Dr Ste 103	Somerset	NJ	08873	877-583-7054	908-704-8843	225
Rangen Inc 115 13th Ave S *Cust Svc	Buhl	ID	83316	800-657-6446*	208-543-6421	442
Ranger College 1100 College Cir	Ranger	TX	76470	800-772-1213	254-647-3234	160
Ranger Construction Industries Inc 101 Sansbury's Way	West Palm Beach	FL	33411	800-969-9402	561-793-9400	189-4
Rangeview Library District 5877 E 120th Ave	Thornton	CO	80602	800-222-3937	303-288-2001	431-3
Rankin County Chamber of Commerce 101 Service Dr	Brandon	MS	39043	800-987-8280	601-825-2268	137
Ranor Inc One Bella Dr	Westminster	MA	01473	800-225-9552	978-874-0591	475
Ransom & Randolph Co 3535 Briarfield Blvd	Maumee	OH	43537	800-800-7496	419-865-9497	654
Rapat Corp 919 Odonnel St	Hawley	MN	56549	800-325-6377	218-483-3344	208
Rape Abuse & Incest National Network (RAINN) 2000 L St NW Ste 406	Washington	DC	20036	800-656-4673	202-544-1034	47-6
Raphael Kansas City 325 Ward Pkwy	Kansas City	MO	64112	800-821-5343	816-756-3800	376
Rapid Chevrolet Company Inc 2090 Deadwood Ave PO Box 1765	Rapid City	SD	57702	800-456-2105	605-343-1282	509
Rapid City Convention & Visitors Bureau 444 Mt Rushmore Rd N	Rapid City	SD	57701	800-487-3223	605-718-8484	207
Rapid City Journal 507 Main St	Rapid City	SD	57701	800-843-2300	605-394-8300	525-2
Rapid City Regional Airport 4550 Terminal Rd Ste 102	Rapid City	SD	57703	800-357-9998	605-393-9924	27
Rapid Displays 4300 W 47th St	Chicago	IL	60632	800-356-5775	773-927-1091	233
Rapid Engineering Inc 1100 7-Mile Rd NW	Comstock Park	MI	49321	800-536-3461	616-784-0500	317
Rapid Focus Security LLC 253 Summer St Ste 303	Boston	MA	02210	855-793-1337		684
Rapid Industries 4003 Oaklawn Dr	Louisville	KY	40219	800-727-4381	502-968-3645	208
Rapid Insight Inc 53 Technology Ln Ste 112	Conway	NH	03818	888-585-6511		178
Rapid Response Monitoring Services Inc 400 W Division St	Syracuse	NY	13204	800-558-7767		684
RAPIDS Wholesale Equipment Co 6201 S Gateway Dr	Marion	IA	52302	800-472-7431	319-447-1670	299
Rappahannock Community College *Glenns* 12745 College Dr	Glenns	VA	23149	800-836-9381	804-758-6700	160
Warsaw 52 Campus Dr	Warsaw	VA	22572	800-836-9381	804-333-6700	160
Raptim Humanitarian Travel 6420 Inducon Dr W Ste A	Sanborn	NY	14132	800-272-7846	716-754-9232	762
Raritan Computer Inc 400 Cottontail Ln	Somerset	NJ	08873	800-724-8090	732-764-8886	253
Raritan Valley Community College PO Box 3300	Somerville	NJ	08876	888-326-4058	908-526-1200	160
Rasmussen Equipment Co 3333 West 2100 South	Salt Lake City	UT	84119	800-453-8032	801-972-5588	355
Rasmussen Iron Works Inc 12028 E Philadelphia St	Whittier	CA	90601	888-301-0440	562-696-8718	354
RateHub.ca 103 Balliol St	Toronto	ON	M4S1C8	800-679-9622		461
Rath & Strong Inc 1666 Massachusetts Ave PO Box 170	Lexington	MA	02420	800-622-2025	781-861-1700	195
Raulerson Hospital 1796 Hwy 441 N	Okeechobee	FL	34972	800-449-8642	863-763-2151	371-3
Ravalli County Fair 100 Old Corvallis Rd	Hamilton	MT	59840	800-225-6779	406-363-3411	633
Rave Computer Assn Inc 7171 Sterling Ponds Ct	Sterling Heights	MI	48312	800-966-7283	586-939-8230	175
Raven Industries Inc 205 E Sixth St *NASDAQ: RAVN*	Sioux Falls	SD	57104	800-243-5435	605-336-2750	593
Ravenswood Winery Inc 18701 Gehricke Rd	Sonoma	CA	95476	888-669-4679		79-3
Ravine Gardens State Park 1600 Twigg St	Palatka	FL	32177	800-326-3521	386-329-3721	558
Rawah Ranch 11447 N County Rd 103	Glendevey	CO	82063	800-820-3152		239

				Toll-Free	Phone	Class
Raxco Software Inc						
Six Montgomery Village Ave						
Ste 500	Gaithersburg	MD	20879	800-546-9728*	301-527-0803	179-12
*Tech Supp						
Ray Products Company Inc						
1700 Chablis Ave	Ontario	CA	91761	800-423-7859	909-390-9906	595
Raybestos Powertrain LLC						
711 Tech Dr	Crawfordsville	IN	47933	800-729-7763		59
Raybourn Group International						
9100 PuRdue Rd Ste 200	Indianapolis	IN	46268	800-362-2546	317-328-4636	46
Raymarine Inc						
21 Manchester St	Merrimack	NH	03054	800-539-5539	603-881-5200	522
Raymond Bldg Supply Corp						
7751 Bayshore Rd	North Fort Myers	FL	33917	877-731-7272	239-731-8300	192-3
Raymond Corp						
22 S Canal St	Greene	NY	13778	800-235-7200*	607-656-2311	465
*General						
Raymond Excavating Co Inc						
800 Gratiot Blvd	Marysville	MI	48040	800-837-6770	810-364-6881	190-5
Raymond F Kravis Ctr for the Performing Arts						
701 Okeechobee Blvd	West Palm Beach	FL	33401	800-572-8471	561-832-7469	565
Raymond Gary State Park						
Hwy 70	Fort Towson	OK	74735	800-622-6317	580-873-2307	558
Raymond Handling Concepts Corp						
41400 Boyce Rd	Fremont	CA	94538	800-675-2500	510-745-7500	264-3
Raymond James Financial Inc						
880 Carillon Pkwy	Saint Petersburg	FL	33716	800-248-8863	727-567-1000	681
NYSE: RJF						
Raymond James (USA) Ltd						
2200 - 925 W Georgia St	Vancouver	BC	V6C3L2	877-570-7558		682
Raymond R Andy Guest Jr Shenandoah River State Park						
350 Daughter of Stars Dr	Bentonville	VA	22610	800-933-7275	540-622-6840	558
Raymond Vineyard						
849 Zinfandel Ln	Saint Helena	CA	94574	800-525-2659	707-963-6941	79-3
Rayner Covering Systems Inc						
665 Schneider Dr	South Elgin	IL	60177	800-648-0757	847-695-2264	601
Raynor Garage Doors						
1101 E River Rd	Dixon	IL	61021	800-472-9667	815-288-1431	234
Raypak Inc						
2151 Eastman Ave	Oxnard	CA	93030	800-438-4328	805-278-5300	354
Raytech Industries						
475 Smith St	Middletown	CT	06457	800-243-7163*	860-632-2020	1
*Cust Svc						
Raytek Inc						
1201 Shaffer Rd Bldg 2	Santa Cruz	CA	95061	800-227-8074	831-458-3900	687
Raytheon Company						
10 Moulton St	Cambridge	MA	02138	866-230-1307	617-873-8000	179-10
Raytheon Intelligence & Information Systems						
1200 S Jupiter Rd	Garland	TX	75042	800-423-0210	972-205-5100	522
Rayven Inc						
431 Griggs St N	Saint Paul	MN	55104	800-878-3776*	651-642-1112	620
*Cust Svc						
R-B Financial-mortgages Inc						
44028 Mound Rd Ste 3	Sterling Heights	MI	48314	800-566-4663*	586-254-8435	502
*General						
RB Royal Industries Inc						
1350 S Hickory St						
PO Box 1168	Fond du Lac	WI	54936	800-892-1550	920-921-1550	614
RBC Bearings Inc						
3131 W Segerstrom Ave						
PO Box 1953	Santa Ana	CA	92704	866-722-2376	714-546-3131	613
RBC Capital Markets						
1 Liberty Plaza	New York	NY	10006	800-387-1122	212-428-6200	681
RBC Centura Banks Inc						
PO Box 1220	Rocky Mount	NC	27802	800-769-2553		357-2
RBC Liberty Insurance						
PO Box 789	Greenville	SC	29602	800-551-8354	864-609-8111	388-2
RBC Royal Bank						
PO Box 6001 Ste A	Montreal	QC	H3C3A9	800-769-2599		69
RBC Trust Company (Delaware) Ltd						
4550 New Linden Hill Rd						
Ste 200	Wilmington	DE	19808	800-441-7698	302-892-6976	69
RBCM (Royal British Columbia Museum)						
675 Belleville St	Victoria	BC	V8W9W2	888-447-7977	250-356-7226	513
RBF Consulting						
14725 Alton Pkwy	Irvine	CA	92618	800-479-3808	949-472-3505	261
RBG (Royal Botanical Gardens)						
680 Plains Rd W	Burlington	ON	L7T4H4	800-694-4769	905-527-1158	96
RBI Corp						
10201 Cedar Ridge Dr	Ashland	VA	23005	800-444-7370		355
RBMA (Radiology Business Management Assn)						
10300 Eaton Pl Ste 460	Fairfax	VA	22030	888-224-7262	703-621-3355	48-8
RBN Energy LLC						
2323 S Shepherd Dr Ste 1010	Houston	TX	77019	888-400-9838		458
Rbx Inc						
PO Box 2118	Springfield	MO	65802	877-450-2200	800-245-5507	770
RC Fine Foods						
PO Box 236	Belle Mead	NJ	08502	800-526-3953	908-359-5500	295-11
RC Knox & Co						
One Goodwin Sq 24th Fl	Hartford	CT	06103	800-742-2765	860-524-7600	387
RC Smith Co						
14200 Southcross Dr W	Burnsville	MN	55306	800-747-7648	952-854-0711	286
RCA Rubber Co						
1833 E Market St	Akron	OH	44305	800-321-2340	330-784-1291	291
RCH (Rady Children's Hospital)						
3020 Children's Way MC 5101	San Diego	CA	92123	800-788-9029	858-576-1700	371-1
RCI (Resort Condominiums International)						
9998 N Michigan Rd	Carmel	IN	46032	800-338-7777	317-805-8000	743
RCI (Retail Confectioners International)						
2053 S Waverly Ste C	Springfield	MO	65804	800-545-5381	417-883-2775	48-6
RCI Custom Products						
801 NE St Ste 2A	Frederick	MD	21701	800-546-4724	301-620-9130	204
RCM Technologies Inc						
2500 McClellan Ave Ste 350	Pennsauken	NJ	08109	800-322-2885	856-356-4500	712
NASDAQ: RCMT						
RCMA (Religious Conference Management Assn Inc)						
7702 Woodland Dr Ste 120	Indianapolis	IN	46278	800-221-8235	317-632-1888	48-12
RCMC (Rush-Copley Medical Ctr)						
2000 Ogden Ave	Aurora	IL	60504	866-426-7539	630-978-6200	371-3
RCMP Heritage Ctr						
5907 Dewdney Ave	Regina	SK	S4T0P4	866-567-7267	306-522-7333	513
RCP (Rubbermaid Commercial Products)						
3124 Valley Ave	Winchester	VA	22601	800-347-9800	540-667-8700	601
RCP Block & Brick Inc						
8240 Broadway	Lemon Grove	CA	91945	800-794-4727	619-460-7250	184
RDA Corp						
303 International Cir						
Ste 340	Hunt Valley	MD	21030	888-441-1278	410-308-9300	178
RDA Group						
450 Enterprise Ct	Bloomfield Hills	MI	48302	800-669-7324	248-332-5000	461
RDC (Roche Diagnostics Corp)						
9115 Hague Rd PO Box 50457	Indianapolis	IN	46250	800-428-5076*	317-521-2000	231
*Cust Svc						
RDI Marketing Services						
4350 Glendale Milford Rd						
Ste 250	Cincinnati	OH	45242	800-388-7636	513-984-5927	5
Rdk Truck Sales Inc						
3214 E Adamo Dr	Tampa	FL	33605	877-735-4636	813-241-0711	509
RDO Equipment Co						
3401 38th St S	Fargo	ND	58104	800-342-4643	701-282-5400	274
RE Lewis Refrigeration Inc						
803 S Lincoln St PO Box 92	Creston	IA	50801	800-264-0767*	641-782-8183	656
*Cust Svc						
RE/MAX International Inc						
5075 S Syracuse St	Denver	CO	80237	800-525-7452*	303-770-5531	643
*Cust Svc						
RE/MAX LLC						
5075 S Syracuse St	Denver	CO	80237	800-525-7452		657
RE/MAX of Western Canada Inc						
1060 Manhattan Dr Ste 340	Kelowna	BC	V1Y9X9	800-563-3622	250-860-3628	643
RE/MAX Ontario-Atlantic						
7101 Syntex Dr	Mississauga	ON	L5N6H5	888-542-2499	905-542-2400	643
RE/MAX Quebec Inc						
1500 Cunard St	Laval	QC	H7S2B7	800-361-9325	450-668-7743	643
REA Energy Co-op Inc						
75 Airport Rd	Indiana	PA	15701	800-211-5667	724-349-4800	245
Rea Magnet Wire Company Inc						
3600 E Pontiac St	Fort Wayne	IN	46803	800-732-9473	260-421-7321	800
Reach Resort						
1435 Simonton St	Key West	FL	33040	888-318-4316	305-296-5000	660
Reader's Digest Association Inc						
44 S Bdwy	White Plains	NY	10601	800-457-4708	914-244-2293	628-9
Readerlink Distribution Services LLC						
1420 Kensington Rd Ste 300	Oak Brook	IL	60523	800-549-5389	708-547-4400	94
Reading & Berks County Visitors Bureau						
2525 N 12th St Ste 101	Reading	PA	19605	800-443-6610	610-375-4085	207
Reading Area Community College						
10 S Second St PO Box 1706	Reading	PA	19603	800-626-1665	610-372-4721	160
Reading Is Fundamental Inc (RIF)						
1825 Connecticut Ave NW						
Ste 400	Washington	DC	20009	877-743-7323	202-536-3400	47-11
Reading Precast Inc						
5494 Pottsville Pike	Leesport	PA	19533	800-724-4881	610-926-5000	184
Reading Rock Inc						
4600 Devitt Dr	Cincinnati	OH	45246	800-482-6466	513-874-2345	184
Reading Truck Body Inc						
201 Hancock Blvd	Reading	PA	19611	800-458-2226*		509
*All						
Ready Pac Produce Inc						
4401 Foxdale Ave	Irwindale	CA	91706	800-800-7822		295-33
ReadyPulse						
1600 A El Camino Real	San Carlos	CA	94070	888-998-7412		5
Reagan Wireless Corp						
720 S Powerline Rd						
Ste D	Deerfield Beach	FL	33442	877-724-3266	954-596-2355	246
Reagent Chemical & Research Inc						
115 Rt 202	Ringoes	NJ	08551	800-231-1807	908-284-2800	144
Real Estate Buyer's Agent Council (REBAC)						
430 N Michigan Ave	Chicago	IL	60611	800-648-6224		48-17
Real Estate Institute of Bc						
1750 - 355 Burrard St	Vancouver	BC	V6C2G8	800-667-2166	604-685-3702	643
Real Estate Law Report						
610 Opperman Dr	Eagan	MN	55123	800-328-4880*	651-687-7000	524-7
*Cust Svc						
Real Estate One Inc						
25800 NW Hwy Ste 100	Southfield	MI	48075	800-521-0508	248-304-6700	643
Real Goods Solar						
833 W S Boulder Rd	Louisville	CO	80027	888-567-6527		613
NASDAQ: RSGE						
Real Living First Service Realty						
13155 SW 42nd St Ste 200	Miami	FL	33175	800-899-8477	305-551-9400	643
Real Living Inc						
77 E Nationwide Blvd	Columbus	OH	43215	800-848-7400	614-459-7400	309
Realestateexpresscom						
12977 N 40 Dr Ste 108	Saint Louis	MO	63141	866-739-7277		643
RealNetworks Inc						
2601 Elliott Ave Ste 1000	Seattle	WA	98121	888-484-8256*	206-674-2700	179-8
NASDAQ: RNWK ■ *Cust Svc						
Realtime Software Corp						
24 Deane Rd	Bernardston	MA	01337	800-323-1143	847-803-1100	179-1
Realtor Magazine						
430 N Michigan Ave Ninth Fl	Chicago	IL	60611	800-874-6500	312-329-8458	452-5
Realtors Assn of New Mexico						
2201 Bros Rd	Santa Fe	NM	87505	800-224-2282	505-982-2442	647
Realty Executives International Inc						
7600 N 16th St Ste 100	Phoenix	AZ	85020	800-252-3366	602-957-0747	643
Realty Income Corp						
600 La Terraza Blvd	Escondido	CA	92025	877-924-6266	760-741-2111	646
NYSE: O						
RealtyBid International Inc						
3225 Rainbow Dr Ste 248	Rainbow City	AL	35906	877-518-5600		390
Reaslo Inc						
5214F Diamond Heights Blvd						
Ste 217	San Francisco	CA	94131	888-870-7889		384
Reason Magazine						
3415 S Sepulveda Blvd						
Ste 400	Los Angeles	CA	90034	888-732-7668*	310-391-2245	452-17
*Cust Svc						
Reason Public Policy Institute						
3415 S Sepulveda Blvd						
Ste 400	Los Angeles	CA	90034	888-732-7668	310-391-2245	625
Reaxis Inc						
941 Robinson Hwy	Mcdonald	PA	15057	800-426-7273		385
REBAC (Real Estate Buyer's Agent Council)						
430 N Michigan Ave	Chicago	IL	60611	800-648-6224		48-17
Re-Bath LLC						
16879 N 75th Ave Ste 101	Peoria	AZ	85382	800-426-4573		190-11

Alphabetical Section

	Toll-Free	Phone	Class
Rebco Inc			
1171-1225 Madison Ave . . . . Paterson NJ 07509	**800-777-0787**	973-684-0200	234
Rebel State Historic Site			
1260 Hwy 1221 . . . . Marthaville LA 71450	**888-677-3600**	318-472-6255	558
Rebuilding Together Inc			
1899 L St NW Ste 1000 . . . . Washington DC 20036	**800-473-4229**		47-5
REC (Rural Electric Co-op Inc)			
801 N Industrial Heights			
PO Box 609. Lindsay OK 73052	**800-259-3504**	405-756-3104	245
Recall Inc			
180 Technology Pkwy NW			
180 Technology Pkwy. . . . . Norcross GA 30092	**888-732-2556**		791-1
Reciprocal of America			
4200 Innslake Dr Ste 102 . . . . Glen Allen VA 23060	**800-284-8847**	804-747-8600	388-5
Reckitt Benckiser Inc			
399 Interpace Pkwy			
PO Box 225. . . . . Parsippany NJ 07054	**800-333-3899***	973-404-2600	149
*Cust Svc			
Reco Equipment Inc			
41245 Reco Rd . . . . Belmont OH 41245	**800-686-7326**	740-782-1314	191
RECON Dynamics LLC			
2300 Carillon Point . . . . Kirkland WA 98033	**877-480-3551**		684
Recon Management Services Inc			
3649 S Beglis Pkwy . . . . Sulphur LA 70665	**888-301-4662**	337-583-4662	623
Reconditioned Systems Inc (RSI)			
2636 S Wilson St Ste 105. . . . . Tempe AZ 85282	**800-280-5000**	480-968-1772	318-1
Record Play Tek Inc			
110 E Vistula St . . . . Bristol IN 46507	**800-809-5233**	574-848-5233	51
Record Searchlight			
PO Box 492397. . . . . Redding CA 96049	**800-666-1331**	530-243-2424	525-2
Record USA			
4324 Phil Hargett Ct . . . . Monroe NC 28105	**800-438-1937***	704-289-9212	253
*Sales			
Record, The			
160 King St E . . . . Kitchener ON N2G4E5	**800-265-8261**	519-894-2231	525-1
Record-Courier			
1050 W Main St PO Box 5199 . . . . Kent OH 44240	**800-560-9657**	330-541-9400	525-2
Recording for the Blind & Dyslexic (RFB&D)			
20 Roszel Rd . . . . Princeton NJ 08540	**800-221-4792**		47-17
Record-Journal			
11 Crown St . . . . Meriden CT 06450	**800-228-6915**	203-235-1661	525-2
Recreation Vehicle Dealers Assn (RVDA)			
3930 University Dr Third Fl . . . . Fairfax VA 22030	**800-336-0355**	703-591-7130	48-18
Recreation Vehicle Industry Assn (RVIA)			
1896 Preston White Dr . . . . Reston VA 20191	**800-336-0154**	703-620-6003	48-21
Recreation.gov			
1849 C St NW . . . . Washington DC 20240	**877-444-6777**	202-208-4743	198
Recreational Equipment Inc (REI)			
6750 S 228th St . . . . Kent WA 98032	**800-426-4840***	253-395-3780	702
*Orders			
Recreatives Industries Inc			
60 Depot St . . . . Buffalo NY 14206	**800-255-2511**	716-855-2226	29
Recursion Software Inc			
2591 Dallas Pkwy Ste 200 . . . . Frisco TX 75034	**800-727-8674**	972-731-8800	180
Recycled Paper Greetings Inc			
111 N Canal St Ste 700 . . . . Chicago IL 60606	**800-777-3331**		129
Red Ball Oxygen Co Inc			
609 N Market . . . . Shreveport LA 71107	**800-551-8150**	318-425-3211	382
Red Bud Industries			
200 B & E Industrial Dr . . . . Red Bud IL 62278	**800-851-4612***	618-282-3801	489
*Cust Svc			
Red Carpet Charters			
4820 SW 20th . . . . Oklahoma City OK 73128	**888-878-5100**	405-672-5100	106
Red Devil Inc			
1437 S Boulder . . . . Tulsa OK 74119	**800-423-3845**		3
Red Diamond Inc			
400 Park Ave . . . . Moody AL 35004	**800-292-4651**	205-577-4000	295-7
Red Dot Corp			
1209 W Corsicana St . . . . Athens TX 75751	**800-657-2234***		104
*Cust Svc			
Red Ewald Inc			
2669 US 181 . . . . Karnes City TX 78118	**800-242-3524**	830-780-3304	599
Red Fleet State Park			
8750 North Hwy 191 . . . . Vernal UT 84078	**800-322-3770**	435-789-4432	558
Red Foundry Inc			
1608 S Ashland Ave . . . . Chicago IL 60608	**888-406-1099**		623
Red Hat Inc			
1801 Varsity Dr . . . . Raleigh NC 27606	**888-733-4281**	919-754-3700	179-12
NYSE: RHT			
Red Hill Patrick Henry National Memorial			
1250 Red Hill Rd . . . . Brookneal VA 24528	**800-514-7463**	434-376-2044	557
Red Hot & Blue Restaurants Inc			
1600 Wilson Blvd . . . . Arlington VA 22209	**888-509-7100**	703-276-7427	661
Red Inn			
15 Commercial St . . . . Provincetown MA 02657	**866-473-3466**	508-487-7334	662
Red Jacket Beach Resort			
39 Todd Rd . . . . South Yarmouth MA 02664	**800-227-3263**	508-398-6941	376
Red Lake Electric Co-op Inc			
412 International Dr			
PO Box 430. . . . . Red Lake Falls MN 56750	**800-245-6068**	218-253-2168	245
Red Lake Gaming Enterprises Inc			
PO Box 543 . . . . Red Lake MN 56671	**888-679-2501**	218-679-2111	131
Red Lion Hotels Corp			
201 W N River Dr Ste 100. . . . . Spokane WA 99201	**800-733-5466***		376
NYSE: RLH ■ *Resv			
Red Lion Templin's Hotel on the River			
414 E First Ave . . . . Post Falls ID 83854	**800-733-5466**	208-773-1611	660
Red River Commodities Inc			
501 42nd St N . . . . Fargo ND 58102	**800-437-5539**	701-282-2600	685
Red River Specialties Inc			
PO Box 7241 . . . . Shreveport LA 71137	**800-256-3344**	318-425-5944	276
Red River Valley Co-op Power Assn			
109 Second Ave E . . . . Halstad MN 56548	**800-788-7784**	218-456-2139	245
Red Robin Gourmet Burgers Inc			
6312 S Fiddlers Green Cir			
Ste 200-N. . . . . Greenwood Village CO 80111	**877-733-6543**	303-846-6000	661
NASDAQ: RRGB			
Red Rock Distributing Co			
One NW 50th St . . . . Oklahoma City OK 73118	**800-323-7109**	405-677-3373	444
Red Rock Resort Spa & Casino			
11011 W Charleston Blvd . . . . Las Vegas NV 89135	**866-767-7773**	702-797-7777	376
Red Spot Interactive			
1001 jupiter park dr . . . . Jupiter FL 33458	**800-401-7931**		458
Red Spot Paint & Varnish Co Inc			
1107 E Louisiana St . . . . Evansville IN 47711	**877-777-4778**	812-428-9100	543
Red Star Oil			
802 Purser Dr . . . . Raleigh NC 27603	**800-774-6033**	919-772-1944	444
Red Thread			
300 E River Dr . . . . East Hartford CT 06108	**800-334-4922**	860-528-9981	319
Red Wind Casino			
12819 Yelm Hwy . . . . Olympia WA 98513	**866-946-2444**	360-412-5000	132
Red Wing Shoe Company Inc			
314 Main St . . . . Red Wing MN 55066	**800-733-9464***	651-388-8211	300
*Cust Svc			
Red Wing Software Inc			
491 Hwy 19 . . . . Red Wing MN 55066	**800-732-9464**	651-388-1106	179-1
Redco Foods Inc			
One Hansen Island . . . . Little Falls NY 13365	**800-556-6674**	315-823-1300	295-40
Redd Paper Co			
3851 Ctr Loop . . . . Orlando FL 32808	**800-961-6656**	407-299-6656	546
Reddy Ice Holdings Inc			
8750 N Central Expy Ste 1800 . . . . Dallas TX 75231	**800-683-4423**	214-526-6740	377
OTC: RDDYQ			
Redeemer University College			
777 Garner Rd E . . . . Ancaster ON L9K1J4	**877-779-0913**	905-648-2131	773
Redemtech Inc			
4115 Leap Rd . . . . Hilliard OH 43026	**800-393-7627**	614-850-3366	179-1
Redfin			
9890 S Maryland Pkwy Ste 200 . . . . . . Las Vegas NV 89183	**800-561-5463**	877-973-3346	5
Redico Inc			
1850 S Lee Ct . . . . Buford GA 30518	**800-242-3920**		656
Rediker Software Inc			
2 Wilbraham Rd . . . . Hampden MA 01036	**800-213-9860**	413-566-3463	178
Redland Brick Inc			
15718 Clear Spring Rd . . . . Williamsport MD 21795	**800-366-2742**	301-223-7700	148
Redlands Chamber of Commerce			
1 E Redlands Blvd . . . . Redlands CA 92373	**800-966-6428**	909-793-2546	137
Redlands Community College			
1300 S Country Club Rd . . . . El Reno OK 73036	**866-415-6367**	405-262-2552	160
Redlands Community Hospital Foundation			
PO Box 3391 . . . . Redlands CA 92373	**888-397-4999**	909-335-5500	371-3
RedLegg			
902 S Randall Rd Ste C 319 . . . . St. Charles IL 60174	**877-811-5040**		197
Redlon & Johnson			
172 St John St Ste 174. . . . . Portland ME 04102	**800-905-5250**	207-773-4755	605
Redman Equipment & Mfg Co			
19800 Normandie Ave . . . . Torrance CA 90502	**888-733-2602**	310-329-1134	90
Redneck Trailer Supplies			
2100 NW By-Pass . . . . Springfield MO 65803	**877-973-3632**	417-864-5210	769
Redner's Markets Inc			
3 Quarry Rd . . . . Reading PA 19605	**888-673-4663**	610-926-3700	342
Red-Ray Mfg Co Inc			
10-22 County Line Rd . . . . Branchburg NJ 08876	**800-883-9218**	908-722-0040	317
Redstone College			
Denver			
10851 W 120th Ave . . . . Broomfield CO 80021	**800-888-3995**	303-466-1714	788
Redstone Federal Credit Union			
220 Wynn Dr NW . . . . Huntsville AL 35893	**800-234-1234**	256-837-6110	219
Redstone Highlands Health Care Ctr			
6 Garden Ctr Dr . . . . Greensburg PA 15601	**800-732-0999**	724-832-8400	445
Redwood Credit Union			
PO Box 6104 . . . . Santa Rosa CA 95406	**800-479-7928**	707-545-4000	214
Redwood Trust Inc			
One Belvedere Pl Ste 300 . . . . Mill Valley CA 94941	**866-269-4976**	415-389-7373	502
NYSE: RWT			
Reebok International Ltd			
1895 JW Foster Blvd . . . . Canton MA 02021	**866-870-1743**	781-401-5000	300
Reed 28 Sword St . . . . Auburn MA 01501	**800-343-6068**	508-753-6530	451
Reed College			
3203 SE Woodstock Blvd . . . . Portland OR 97202	**800-547-4750***	503-777-7511	166
*Admissions			
Reed Gold Mine State Historic Site			
9621 Reed Mine Rd . . . . Midland NC 28107	**877-628-6386**	704-721-4653	49-2
Reed Manufacturing Co			
1425 W Eighth St . . . . Erie PA 16502	**800-456-1697**	814-452-3691	748
Reed Mfg Co Inc			
1321 S Veterans Blvd . . . . Tupelo MS 38804	**800-466-1154**	662-842-4472	153-10
Reeder Distributors Inc			
5450 Wilbarger St . . . . Fort Worth TX 76119	**800-722-3103**	817-429-5957	572
Reedley College			
995 N Reed Ave . . . . Reedley CA 93654	**866-245-3276**	559-638-3641	160
Reeds Jewelers Inc			
PO Box 2229 . . . . Wilmington NC 28402	**877-406-3266***	910-350-3100	407
*Orders			
Reedsville Co-op Assn Inc			
PO Box 460 . . . . Reedsville WI 54230	**800-236-4047**	920-754-4321	276
Reef Industries Inc			
9209 Almeda Genoa Rd . . . . Houston TX 77075	**800-231-6074**	713-507-4200	592
Reef Resort			
2101 S Ocean Blvd . . . . Myrtle Beach SC 29577	**800-845-1212***	843-448-1765	660
*Cust Svc			
Reese Enterprises Inc			
16350 Asher Ave . . . . Rosemount MN 55068	**800-328-0953**	651-423-1126	234
Reese Pharmaceutical Co			
10617 Frank Ave . . . . Cleveland OH 44106	**800-321-7178**		238
Reeve Store Equipment Co			
9131 Bermudez St PO Box 276. . . . . . Pico Rivera CA 90660	**800-927-3383**	562-949-2535	286
Reeves Construction Co Inc			
101 Sheraton Ct . . . . Macon GA 31210	**800-743-0593**	478-474-9092	189-4
Reeves-Wiedeman Co Inc			
14861 W 100th St . . . . Lenexa KS 66215	**800-365-0024**	913-492-7100	605
Reference & User Services Assn (RUSA)			
50 E Huron St . . . . Chicago IL 60611	**800-545-2433**	312-280-4398	48-11
Reflexite Corp			
120 Darling Dr . . . . Avon CT 06001	**800-654-7570**	860-676-7100	734-2
Reflexite North America			
315 S St . . . . New Britain CT 06051	**800-654-7570**	860-223-9297	669
Reformed Church in America			
475 Riverside Dr 18th Fl. . . . . New York NY 10115	**800-722-9977**	212-870-3071	47-20
Reformed Theological Seminary			
5422 Clinton Blvd . . . . Jackson MS 39209	**800-543-2703**	601-923-1600	167-3
Refrigerated Food Express Inc			
57 Littlefield St . . . . Avon MA 02322	**800-342-8822**	508-587-4600	770
Refrigeration Sales Corp			
9450 Allen Dr Ste A . . . . Valley View OH 44125	**866-894-8200**	216-881-7800	605
Refrigeration Service Engineers Society (RSES)			
1666 Rand Rd . . . . Des Plaines IL 60016	**800-297-5660**	847-297-6464	48-3

	Toll-Free	Phone	Class
RefrigiWear Inc			
54 Breakstone Dr . . . . .Dahlonega GA 30533	800-645-3744*	706-864-5757	153-5
*Cust Svc			
Refugees International (RI)			
2001 S St NW Ste 700-K . . . . Washington DC 20009	800-733-8433	202-828-0110	47-5
Regal Entertainment Group			
7132 Regal Ln . . . . .Knoxville TN 37918	877-835-5734*	865-922-1123	737
NYSE: RGC ▥ *Cust Svc			
Regal Marine Industries Inc			
2300 Jetport Dr . . . . .Orlando FL 32809	800-877-3425	407-851-4360	89
Regal Plastic Supply Co			
111 E Tenth Ave . . . . . . North Kansas City MO 64116	800-627-2102	816-421-6290	596
Regal Press Inc, The			
129 Guild St . . . . .Norwood MA 02062	800-447-3425	781-769-3900	619
Regal Travel			
615 Piikoi St Ste 104 . . . . .Honolulu HI 96814	800-799-0865	808-566-7620	761
Regal-Beloit Corp			
200 State St . . . . .Beloit WI 53511	800-672-6495	608-364-8800	613
NYSE: RBC			
Regal-Beloit Corp Durst Div			
PO Box 298 . . . . .Beloit WI 53512	800-356-0775	608-365-2563	700
Regalia Manufacturing Co			
2018 Fourth Ave . . . . .Rock Island IL 61201	800-798-7471	309-788-7471	767
Regatta Travel Solutions Inc			
325 Winding River Ln			
Ste 201B . . . . .Charlottesville VA 22911	800-605-5093		390
Regence Blue Cross Blue Shield of Oregon			
PO Box 1071 .Portland OR 97207	888-734-3623	503-225-5351	388-3
Regence BlueCross BlueShield of Utah			
2890 E Cottonwood Pkwy . . . . .Salt Lake City UT 84121	800-624-6519*	801-333-2100	388-3
*Cust Svc			
Regency Centers			
One Independent Dr Ste 114 . . . . .Jacksonville FL 32202	800-950-6333	904-598-7000	646
NYSE: REG			
Regency Fairbanks Hotel			
95 Tenth Ave . . . . .Fairbanks AK 99701	800-478-1320	907-459-2700	376
Regency Infographics Inc (SED)			
2867 E Allegheny Ave . . . . .Philadelphia PA 19134	800-829-0020	215-425-8800	771
Regency Lighting Co			
9261 Jordan Ave . . . . Chatsworth CA 91311	800-284-2024		246
Regency Limousine International			
83-03 24th Ave . . . . East Elmhurst NY 11370	866-302-2201	718-507-4000	437
Regency Suites Calgary			
610 Fourth Ave SW . . . . .Calgary AB T2P0K1	800-468-4044	403-231-1000	376
Regency Suites Hotel Midtown Atlanta			
975 W Peachtree St . . . . .Atlanta GA 30309	800-642-3629	404-876-5003	376
Regeneron Pharmaceuticals Inc			
777 Old Saw Mill River Rd . . . . .Tarrytown NY 10591	800-637-8322	914-847-7000	84
NASDAQ: REGN			
Regent College			
5800 University Blvd . . . . .Vancouver BC V6T2E4	800-663-8664	604-224-3245	167-3
Regent University			
Library			
1000 Regent University Dr . . . . . .Virginia Beach VA 23464	888-249-1822	757-352-4916	431-6
Regents Bank NA			
PO Box 9137 .La Jolla CA 92038	866-395-5800	858-729-7700	69
Regents Point			
19191 Harvard Ave . . . . .Irvine CA 92612	800-347-3735*	949-988-0849	663
*General			
Regional Acceptance Corp			
1424 E Fire Tower Rd . . . . .Greenville NC 27858	877-722-7299	252-321-7700	214
Regional Hospital of Jackson			
367 Hospital Blvd . . . . .Jackson TN 38305	800-454-9970	731-661-2000	371-3
Regional International Corp			
1007 Lehigh Stn Rd . . . . .Henrietta NY 14467	800-836-0409	585-359-2011	60
Regional Jet Ctr			
12344 Tower Dr . . . . .Bentonville AR 72712	866-962-3835	479-205-1100	62
Regional Medical Ctr, The			
3000 St Matthews Rd . . . . .Orangeburg SC 29118	800-476-3377	803-395-2200	371-3
Regional Tissue Bank QEII Health Sciences Centre			
5788 University Ave			
Rm 431 MacKenzie Bldg. . . . . .Halifax NS B3H1V7	800-314-6515	902-473-4171	538
Regional Transportation Commission of Southern Nevada (RTC)			
600 S Grand Central Pkwy			
Ste 350 . . . . .Las Vegas NV 89106	800-228-3911	702-676-1500	463
Regional Transportation District (RTD)			
1600 Blake St .Denver CO 80202	800-366-7433	303-628-9000	463
Regions Bank			
1900 Fifth Ave N . . . . .Birmingham AL 35203	800-734-4667		69
Regions Financial Corp			
1900 Fifth Ave N . . . . .Birmingham AL 35203	866-688-0658		357-2
NYSE: RF			
Regions Mortgage Inc			
215 Forrest St . . . . .Hattiesburg MS 39401	800-986-2462		502
Regis College			
235 Wellesley St . . . . .Weston MA 02493	866-438-7344	781-768-7000	166
Regis Corp			
7201 Metro Blvd . . . . .Minneapolis MN 55439	888-888-7778	952-947-7777	76
NYSE: RGS			
Regis Corp MasterCuts Div			
7201 Metro Blvd . . . . .Minneapolis MN 55439	877-857-2070	952-947-7777	76
Regis Corp Pro-Cuts Div			
7201 Metro Blvd . . . . .Minneapolis MN 55439	877-857-2070	952-947-7777	76
Regis Corp Regis Hairstylists Div			
7201 Metro Blvd . . . . .Minneapolis MN 55439	877-857-2070	952-947-7777	76
Regis Corp SmartStyle Div			
7201 Metro Blvd . . . . .Minneapolis MN 55439	877-857-2070	952-947-7777	76
Regis Corp Trade Secret Div			
7201 Metro Blvd . . . . .Minneapolis MN 55439	888-888-7778	952-947-7777	76
Regis Technologies Inc			
8210 Austin Ave . . . . .Morton Grove IL 60053	800-323-8144	847-967-6000	576
Regis University			
Colorado Springs			
7450 Campus Dr Ste 100 . . . . Colorado Springs CO 80920	800-568-8932		166
Register Tapes Unlimited Inc			
1445 Langham Creek . . . . .Houston TX 77084	800-247-4793	281-206-2500	4
Register.com Inc			
575 Eigth Ave Eighth Fl . . . . .New York NY 10018	888-734-4783		393
Register-Herald			
801 N Kanawha St . . . . .Beckley WV 25801	800-950-0250	304-255-4400	525-2
Register-Mail			
140 S Prairie St PO Box 310 . . . . .Galesburg IL 61401	877-732-8258	309-343-7181	525-2

	Toll-Free	Phone	Class
Register-Star			
364 Warren St . . . . .Hudson NY 12534	800-836-1616	518-828-1616	525-2
Regitar USA Inc			
2575 Container Dr . . . . .Montgomery AL 36109	877-734-4827	334-244-1885	348
Regnery Publishing Inc			
300 New Jersey Ave NW . . . . .Washington DC 20001	888-219-4747	202-216-0600	628-2
Regreen Inc			
2928 N Main St . . . . .Los Angeles CA 90031	855-573-4733		193
Regupol America			
33 Keystone Dr . . . . .Lebanon PA 17042	800-537-8737		291
Rehabilitation Hospital of Indiana			
4141 Shore Dr . . . . .Indianapolis IN 46254	866-510-2273	317-329-2000	371-6
Rehabilitation Hospital of New Mexico			
4441 E Lohman Ave . . . . .Las Cruces NM 88011	888-659-3952	575-521-6400	371-6
Rehabilitation Hospital of the Pacific			
226 N Kuakini St . . . . .Honolulu HI 96817	800-973-4226	808-531-3511	371-6
Rehabilitation Institute of Chicago			
345 E Superior St . . . . .Chicago IL 60611	800-354-7342*	312-238-1000	371-6
*Admitting			
Rehau Inc			
1501 EdwaRds Ferry Rd NE . . . . .Leesburg VA 20176	800-247-9445	703-777-5255	235
Rehmann Group			
5800 Gratiot St Ste 201 . . . . .Saginaw MI 48638	866-799-9580	989-799-9580	2
Rehoboth Beach Convention Ctr			
229 Rehoboth Ave . . . . .Rehoboth Beach DE 19971	888-743-3628	302-227-4641	207
Rehoboth Beach-Dewey Beach Chamber of Commerce			
501 Rehoboth Ave . . . . .Rehoboth Beach DE 19971	800-441-1329	302-227-2233	137
Rehrig Pacific Co			
4010 E 26th St . . . . .Los Angeles CA 90023	800-421-6244	323-262-5145	200
REI 1700 45th St E . . . . .Sumner WA 98352	800-426-4840	253-891-2500	63
REI (Recreational Equipment Inc)			
6750 S 228th St . . . . .Kent WA 98032	800-426-4840*	253-395-3780	702
*Orders			
REI Adventures			
PO Box 1938 . . . . .Sumner WA 98390	800-622-2236	253-437-1100	750
Reichhold Inc			
2400 Ellis Rd . . . . .Durham NC 27703	800-448-3482	919-990-7500	598-2
Reid Jones McRorie & Williams Inc			
PO Box 18527 . . . . .Charlotte NC 28218	800-785-2604	704-537-0012	387
Reidler Decal Corp			
264 Industrial Pk Rd			
PO Box 8. . . . . .Saint Clair PA 17970	800-628-7770		410
Reiff & Nestor Co			
50 Reiff St PO Box 147 . . . . .Lykens PA 17048	800-521-3422	717-453-7113	488
Reily Foods Co			
640 Magazine St . . . . .New Orleans LA 70130	800-535-1961	504-524-6131	295-7
Reimers Electra Steam Inc			
4407 Martinsburg Pk			
PO Box 37. . . . . .Clear Brook VA 22624	800-872-7562	540-662-3811	354
Reindl Bindery Company Inc			
W194 N11381 McCormick Dr . . . . . .Germantown WI 53022	800-878-1121	262-293-1444	91
Reinhardt College			
7300 Reinhardt College Cir . . . . .Waleska GA 30183	877-346-4273	770-720-5526	166
Reinhart Food Service			
7735 Westside Industrial Dr . . . . .Jacksonville FL 32219	888-781-5464	904-781-9888	299
Reinke Mfg Co Inc			
5325 Reinke Rd . . . . .Deshler NE 68340	866-365-7381	402-365-7251	273
Reinsurance Group of America Inc			
1370 Timberlake Manor Pkwy. . . . . . .Chesterfield MO 63017	800-985-4326	636-736-7000	357-4
NYSE: RGA			
Reis Inc			
530 Fifth Ave Fifth Fl . . . . .New York NY 10036	800-366-7347	212-921-1122	461
NASDAQ: REIS			
Reisterstown Lumber Co, The			
PO Box 337 . . . . .Reisterstown MD 21136	800-289-8739	410-833-1300	361
REITPAC			
1875 'I' St NW Ste 600 . . . . .Washington DC 20006	800-362-7348	202-739-9400	608
Rejuvenation Inc			
2550 NW Nicolai St . . . . .Portland OR 97210	888-401-1900	503-231-1900	435
Relais & Chateaux Assn			
10 E 53rd St . . . . .New York NY 10022	800-735-2478	212-319-4880	47-23
Relais International			
1690 Woodward Dr Ste 215 . . . . .Ottawa ON K2C3R8	888-294-5244	613-226-5571	179-12
Relco Systems Inc			
7310 Chestnut Ridge Rd . . . . .Lockport NY 14094	800-262-1020	716-434-8100	770
Relevant Radio			
1496 Bellevue St Ste 202			
PO Box 10707. . . . . .Green Bay WI 54311	877-291-0123	920-884-1460	635
Reliable Carriers Inc			
41555 Koppernick Rd . . . . .Canton MI 48187	800-521-6393	734-453-6677	463
Reliable Castings Corp			
3530 Spring Grove Ave . . . . .Cincinnati OH 45223	866-722-2278	513-541-2627	307
Reliable Contracting Co Inc			
1 Church View Rd . . . . .Millersville MD 21108	800-492-4357	410-987-0313	189-4
Reliable Life Insurance Co			
100 King St W PO Box 557. . . . . .Hamilton ON L8N3K9	800-465-0661	905-523-5587	388-2
Reliable of Milwaukee Inc			
6737 W Washington Ste 3200 . . . . .Milwaukee WI 53214	800-336-6876	414-272-5084	153-17
Reliable Tire Co			
805 N Blackhorse Pk . . . . .Blackwood NJ 08012	800-342-3426*		745
*All			
Reliable Wholesale Lumber Inc			
7600 Redondo Cir . . . . .Huntington Beach CA 92648	877-795-4638	714-848-8222	192-3
Reliance Controls Corp			
2001 Young Ct . . . . .Racine WI 53404	800-634-6155	262-634-6155	720
Reliance Standard Life Insurance			
2001 Market St Ste 1500 . . . . .Philadelphia PA 19103	800-351-7500	267-256-3500	388-2
Reliant Energy Retail Services LLC			
1201 Fannin St. . . . . .Houston TX 77002	866-660-4900	866-222-7100	775
Religion News Service (RNS)			
529 14th St NW Ste 425. . . . . .Washington DC 20045	800-767-6781	202-463-8777	523
Religious Conference Management Assn Inc (RCMA)			
7702 Woodland Dr Ste 120 . . . . .Indianapolis IN 46278	800-221-8235	317-632-1888	48-12
Relios Inc			
6815 Academy Pkwy W NE . . . . .Albuquerque NM 87109	800-827-6543	505-345-5304	406
Reliv International Inc			
136 Chesterfield Industrial Blvd . . . . . .Chesterfield MO 63005	800-735-4887	636-537-9715	363
NASDAQ: RELV			
RELM Wireless Corp			
7100 Technology Dr . . . . .West Melbourne FL 32904	800-648-0947*	321-984-1414	638
NYSE: RWC ▥ *Cust Svc			

	Toll-Free	Phone	Class
RELO Direct Inc			
161 N Clark St Ste 1250 .....Chicago IL 60601	800-621-7356	312-384-5900	657
Relocation America			
25800 NW Hwy Ste 210 .....Southfield MI 48075	877-500-4466		657
Relocation Center Inc, The			
1042 E Juneau Ave .....Milwaukee WI 53202	800-783-5337	414-226-4200	643
Relton Corp			
317 Rolyn Dr PO Box 60019 .....Arcadia CA 91066	800-423-1505*	323-681-2551	748
*Cust Svc			
Rem Sales Inc			
910 Gay Hill Rd .....Windsor CT 06095	877-689-1860	860-687-3400	382
REMC (Okefenoke Rural Electric Membership Corp)			
14384 Cleveland St PO Box 602 .....Nahunta GA 31553	800-262-5131	912-462-5131	245
Remedy Temp Inc			
3820 State St .....Santa Barbara CA 93105	800-688-6162	805-882-2200	712
Remet Corp			
210 Commons Rd .....Utica NY 13502	877-939-0171	315-797-8700	305
Reminder Press Inc			
130 Old Town Rd PO Box 27 .....Vernon CT 06066	888-456-2211	860-875-3366	628-8
Reminder, The			
PO Box 210 .....Vernon CT 06066	888-456-2211	860-875-3366	525-4
Reminger & Reminger Company LPa			
101 W Prospect Ave .....Cleveland OH 44115	800-486-1311	216-687-1311	425
Remington Arms Company Inc			
870 Remington Dr PO Box 700 .....Madison NC 27025	800-243-9700	336-548-8700	284
Remington College Largo			
6302 E Dr Martin Luther King Jr Blvd Ste 400 .....Tampa FL 33619	800-560-6192		788
Remington College Tampa			
6302 E MLK Blvd Ste 400 .....Tampa FL 33619	800-323-8122*	813-935-5700	788
*General			
Remington Park Race Track			
One Remington Pl .....Oklahoma City OK 73111	866-456-9880	405-424-1000	633
Remington Suite Hotel			
220 Travis St .....Shreveport LA 71101	800-444-6750	318-425-5000	376
Reminisce Magazine			
750 Third Ave Third Fl .....New York WI 10017	888-859-7838	414-423-0100	452-11
Remmele Engineering Inc			
10 Old Hwy 8 SW .....New Brighton MN 55112	800-733-6198*	651-635-4100	747
*General			
Remo Inc			
28101 Industry Dr .....Valencia CA 91355	800-525-5134	661-294-5600	520
Remstar International Inc			
41 Eisenhower Dr .....Westbrook ME 04092	800-639-5805		382
Remy Cointreau USA Inc			
1290 Ave of the Americas .....New York NY 10104	800-858-9898*	212-399-4200	80-3
*General			
Remy International Inc			
600 Corp Dr .....Pendleton IN 46064	800-372-3555	765-778-6499	59
NYSE: REMY			
Renaissance Esmeralda Resort			
44-400 Indian Wells Ln .....Indian Wells CA 92210	888-236-2427	760-773-4444	660
Renaissance Group			
981 Worcester St .....Wellesley MA 02482	800-514-2667		387
Renaissance Learning Inc			
2911 Peach St .....Wisconsin Rapids WI 54494	800-338-4204	715-424-3636	179-3
Renaissance Orlando Resort at SeaWorld			
6677 Sea Harbor Dr .....Orlando FL 32821	800-327-6677	407-351-5555	660
Renaissance Portsmouth Hotel & Waterfront Conference Ctr			
425 Water St .....Portsmouth VA 23704	888-839-1775	757-673-3000	374
Renaissance Resort at World Golf Village			
500 S Legacy Trl .....Saint Augustine FL 32092	888-740-7020	904-940-8000	660
Renaissance Vinoy Resort & Golf Club			
501 Fifth Ave NE .....Saint Petersburg FL 33701	800-468-3571	727-894-1000	660
Renasant Bank			
209 Troy St PO Box 709 .....Tupelo MS 38802	800-680-1601	662-680-1001	69
Renasant Corp			
209 Troy St PO Box 709 .....Tupelo MS 38802	800-680-1601*	662-680-1001	357-2
NASDAQ: RNST *Cust Svc			
Renco Corp			
116 Third Ave N .....Minneapolis MN 55401	800-359-8181	612-338-6124	575
Renco Electronics Inc			
595 International Pl .....Rockledge FL 32955	800-645-5828	321-637-1000	246
Rend Lake College			
468 N Ken Gray Pkwy .....Ina IL 62846	800-369-5321	618-437-5321	160
Renee's Garden Seeds Inc			
7389 W Zayante Rd .....Felton CA 95018	888-880-7228	831-335-7228	685
Renegade/Kibbi LLC			
52216 State Rd 15 .....Bristol IN 46507	888-522-1126	574-848-1126	119
Renew Data Corp			
9500 Arboretum Blvd .....Austin TX 78759	888-811-3789	512-276-5500	225
ReNew Life Formulas Inc			
2076 Sunnydale Blvd .....Clearwater FL 33765	800-830-1800	727-450-1061	296-11
Renew Plastics			
112 Fourth St PO Box 480 .....Luxemburg WI 54217	800-666-5207	920-845-2326	652
Renewable Fuels Assn (RFA)			
425 Third St SW .....Washington DC 20024	800-433-8850	202-289-3835	47-12
Renfro Corp			
661 Linville Rd .....Mount Airy NC 27030	800-334-9091	336-719-8000	153-9
Renfrow Bros Inc			
855 Gossett Rd PO Box 4786 .....Spartanburg SC 29307	888-522-5958	864-579-0558	187
Renkus-heinz Inc			
19201 Cook St .....Foothill Ranch CA 92610	855-411-2364	949-588-9997	51
Rennco LLC 300 Elm St .....Homer MI 49245	800-409-5225		779
Rennoc Corp			
645 Pine St .....Greenville OH 45331	800-372-7100		153-5
Reno Gazette-Journal			
PO Box 22000 .....Reno NV 89520	800-648-5048	775-788-6200	525-2
Reno News & Review			
708 N Ctr St .....Reno NV 89501	866-703-3873	916-498-1234	525-5
RENO Refractories Inc			
601 Reno Dr .....Morris AL 35116	800-741-7366	205-647-0240	654
RENO Refractories Inc Reftech Div			
601 Reno Dr .....Morris AL 35116	800-741-7366*		654
*General			
Renold Ajax Inc			
100 Bourne St .....Westfield NY 14787	800-251-9012	716-326-3121	613
Renold Jeffrey			
2307 Maden Dr .....Morristown TN 37813	800-251-9012	423-586-1951	208
Reno-Sparks Convention & Visitors Authority			
PO Box 837 .....Reno NV 89504	800-443-1482	775-827-7600	207
Reno-Sparks Convention Ctr			
4590 S Virginia St .....Reno NV 89502	800-367-7366	775-827-7600	206
Reno-Tahoe International Airport			
2001 E Plumb Ln .....Reno NV 89502	877-736-6359	775-328-6400	27
Renova Lighting Systems Inc			
20 Middlesex St .....Mansfield MA 02048	800-635-6682	401-682-1850	435
Renovator's Supply Inc			
Renovators Old Ml .....Millers Falls MA 01349	800-659-2211	413-423-3300	347
Rensselaer County Regional Chamber of Commerce			
255 River St .....Troy NY 12180	800-822-2400	518-274-7020	137
Rent-A-Center Inc			
5501 Headquarters Dr .....Plano TX 75024	800-422-8186		264-2
NASDAQ: RCII			
Rental Research Services Inc			
7525 Mitchell Rd Ste 301 .....Eden Prairie MN 55344	800-328-0333	952-935-5700	626
Rentals Inc			
3585 Engineering Dr .....Norcross GA 30092	888-501-7368		384
Rent-A-PC Inc			
265 Oser Ave .....Hauppauge NY 11788	800-800-8686	631-273-8888	264-1
Rentenbach Engineering Co			
2400 Sutherland Ave .....Knoxville TN 37919	877-546-2440	865-546-2440	261
RentPath Inc			
3585 Engineering Dr Ste 100 .....Norcross GA 30092	800-216-1423	678-421-3000	628-9
Rentrak Corp			
7700 NE Ambassador Pl Third Fl .....Portland OR 97220	800-929-0070	503-284-7581	179-1
NASDAQ: RENT			
Renville-Sibley Co-op Power Assn			
103 Oak St PO Box 68 .....Danube MN 56230	800-826-2593	320-826-2593	245
Repairclinic.com Inc			
48600 Michigan Ave .....Canton MI 48188	800-269-2609	734-495-3079	348
Repligen Corp			
41 Seyon St .....Waltham MA 02453	800-622-2259*	781-250-0111	84
NASDAQ: RGEN *Sales			
Reply Inc			
12667 Alcosta Blvd Ste 200 .....San Ramon CA 94583	888-466-8677	925-983-3400	4
Reporter			
12247 S Harlem Ave .....Palos Heights IL 60463	800-633-4227	708-448-6161	525-2
Reproduction Enterprises Inc			
908 N Prairie Rd .....Stillwater OK 74075	866-734-2855	405-377-8037	11-2
Reprographics One Inc			
36060 Industrial Rd .....Livonia MI 48150	800-333-2600	734-542-8800	584
Republic Airways Holdings Inc			
8909 PuRdue Rd Ste 300 .....Indianapolis IN 46268	800-433-7300	317-484-6000	357-1
NASDAQ: RJET			
Republic Bancorp Inc			
601 W Market St .....Louisville KY 40202	888-540-5363	502-584-3600	357-2
NASDAQ: RBCAA			
Republic Bank & Trust Co			
601 W Market St .....Louisville KY 40202	888-584-3600	502-584-3600	69
Republic Financial Corp			
3300 S Parker Rd Ste 500 .....Aurora CO 80014	888-822-8766	303-751-3501	216
Republic First Bancorp Inc			
50 S 16th St Ste 2400 .....Philadelphia PA 19102	888-875-2265	215-735-4422	357-2
NASDAQ: FRBK			
Republic Industries Inc			
1400 Warren Dr .....Marshall TX 75672	866-284-0941	903-935-3680	114
Republic Mortgage Insurance Co			
101 N Cherry St Ste 101 .....Winston-Salem NC 27101	800-999-7642		388-5
Republic Plumbing Supply Company Inc			
890 Providence Hwy .....Norwood MA 02062	800-696-3900		605
Republic Powdered Metals Inc			
2628 Pearl Rd .....Medina OH 44256	800-382-1218		543
Republic Services of Southern Nevada			
770 E Sahara Ave .....Las Vegas NV 89193	800-752-4092	702-735-5151	792
Republic Storage Systems LLC			
1038 Belden Ave NE .....Canton OH 44705	800-477-1255*	330-438-5800	286
*Sales			
Republic Western Insurance Co			
2721 N Central Ave .....Phoenix AZ 85004	800-528-7134*		388-4
*Claims			
Republic, The			
333 Second St .....Columbus IN 47201	800-876-7811	812-372-7811	525-2
Republican Co			
1860 Main St .....Springfield MA 01103	800-828-5597	413-788-1000	628-8
Republican National Committee (RNC)			
310 First St SE .....Washington DC 20003	800-445-5768	202-863-8500	609
Republican-American Inc			
389 Meadow St .....Waterbury CT 06702	800-992-3232	203-574-3636	628-8
Reputation Rhino LLC			
711 Third Ave 12th Fl .....New York NY 10017	888-975-3331		384
Request Foods Inc			
PO Box 2577 .....Holland MI 49422	800-748-0378*	616-786-0900	295-36
*Sales			
ReQuest Inc			
100 Saratoga Village Blvd Ste 45 .....Ballston Spa NY 12020	800-236-2812*	518-899-1254	51
*Sales			
RES Mfg Company Inc			
7801 N 73rd St .....Milwaukee WI 53223	800-334-8044	414-354-4530	483
Rescar Inc			
1101 31st St Ste 250 .....Downers Grove IL 60515	800-851-5196	630-963-1114	642
Resco Plastics Inc			
93783 Newport Ln .....Coos Bay OR 97420	800-266-5097	541-269-5485	652
Resco Products Inc			
Two Penn Ctr W Ste 430 .....Pittsburgh PA 15276	888-283-5505	412-494-4491	653
Rescuecom Corp			
2560 Burnet Ave .....Syracuse NY 13206	800-737-2837		309
Research & Diagnostic Antibodies			
2645 W Cheyenne Ave .....North Las Vegas NV 89032	800-858-7322	702-638-7800	231
Research & Innovative Technology Administration			
Bureau of Transportation Statistics			
1200 New Jersey Ave SE .....Washington DC 20590	800-853-1351	202-366-1270	338-15
Office of Research Development & Technology			
1200 New Jersey Ave SE .....Washington DC 20590	800-853-1351		338-15
Research Assoc Inc			
27999 Clemens Rd .....Cleveland OH 44145	800-255-9693	440-892-9439	397
Research Pharmaceutical Services Inc			
520 Virginia Dr .....Fort Washington PA 19034	866-777-1151*	215-540-0700	712
*General			
Research Products Corp			
1015 E Washington Ave .....Madison WI 53703	800-334-6011	608-257-8801	17
Research Technology International Inc			
4700 W Chase Ave .....Lincolnwood IL 60712	800-323-7520*	847-677-3000	584
*Sales			
Research to Prevent Blindness Inc (RPB)			
645 Madison Ave 21st Fl .....New York NY 10022	800-621-0026	212-752-4333	47-17

	Toll-Free	Phone	Class
Research Triangle Institute			
3040 Cornwallis Rd			
PO Box 12194 . . . . Research Triangle Park NC 27709	800-334-8571	919-541-6000	659
Reser's Fine Foods Inc			
15570 SW Jenkins Rd . . . . Beaverton OR 97006	800-333-6431	503-643-6431	295-33
Reserve Casino Hotel			
321 Gregory St . . . . Central City CO 80427	800-924-6646	303-582-0800	132
Reserve Officers Assn of the US (ROA)			
One Constitution Ave NE . . . . Washington DC 20002	800-809-9448	202-479-2200	47-19
Reserve Telephone Company Inc			
PO Box T . . . . Reserve LA 70084	888-611-6111	985-536-1111	726
ReserveAmerica Holdings Inc			
2480 Meadowvale Blvd			
Ste 120 . . . . Mississauga ON L5N8M6	877-444-6777		763
Reserves Network, The			
22021 Brookpark Rd . . . . Cleveland OH 44126	866-876-2020	440-779-6681	623
Residence & Conference Centre - Toronto			
1760 Finch Ave E . . . . Toronto ON M2J5G3	877-225-8664	416-491-8811	376
Residential Control Systems			
11481 Sunrise Gold Cir			
Ste 1 . . . . Rancho Cordova CA 95742	888-727-4822	916-635-6784	203
Residential Mortgage LLC			
100 Calais Dr . . . . Anchorage AK 99503	888-357-2707	907-222-8800	502
Resilite Sports Products			
PO Box 764 . . . . Sunbury PA 17801	800-843-6287	570-473-3529	701
Resinall Corp			
PO Box 195 . . . . Severn NC 27877	800-421-0561		598-2
ResMed Inc			
9001 Spectrum Ctr Blvd . . . . San Diego CA 92123	800-424-0737	858-836-5000	471
NYSE: RMD			
Resolute Systems Inc			
1550 N Prospect Ave . . . . Milwaukee WI 53202	800-776-6060	414-276-4774	40
RESOLVE: National Infertility Assn			
1760 Old Meadow Rd Ste 500 . . . . McLean VA 22102	888-592-4449	703-556-7172	47-17
Resort 2 Me			
975 Cass St . . . . Monterey CA 93940	800-757-5646	831-642-6622	373
Resort at Port Arrowhead, The			
3080 Bagnell Dam Blvd			
PO Box 1930 . . . . Lake Ozark MO 65049	800-532-3575	573-365-2334	660
Resort at Singer Island			
3800 N Ocean Dr . . . . Riviera Beach FL 33404	800-721-7033	561-340-1700	660
Resort at Squaw Creek			
400 Squaw Creek Rd			
PO Box 3333 . . . . Olympic Valley CA 96146	800-327-3353	530-583-6300	660
Resort at the Mountain			
68010 E Fairway Ave . . . . Welches OR 97067	877-439-6774	503-622-3101	660
Resort Condominiums International (RCI)			
9998 N Michigan Rd . . . . Carmel IN 46032	800-338-7777	317-805-8000	743
Resort Semiahmoo			
9565 Semiahmoo Pkwy . . . . Blaine WA 98230	855-917-3767	360-318-2000	660
Resort Sports Network			
Outside Television			
33 Riverside Ave 4th Fl . . . . Westport CT 06880	888-795-9488	203-221-9240	729
Resorts Casino Hotel			
1133 Boardwalk . . . . Atlantic City NJ 08401	800-334-6378		660
Resource & Financial Management Systems Inc			
3073 Palisades Ct . . . . Tuscaloosa AL 35405	800-701-7367		178
Resource Connection Inc			
161 S Main St . . . . Middleton MA 01949	800-649-5228	978-777-9333	185
Resource Development Corp			
280 Daines St Ste 200 . . . . Birmingham MI 48009	800-360-7222	248-646-2300	38
Resource Management Inc			
281 Main St Ste 5 . . . . Fitchburg MA 01420	800-508-0048*		623
*Cust Svc			
Resource Management Service LLC			
31 Inverness Ctr Pkwy			
Ste 360 . . . . Birmingham AL 35242	800-995-9516		301
Resource Plus			
9636 Heckscher Dr . . . . Jacksonville FL 32226	888-678-8966		342
Resources Global Professionals			
17101 Armstrong Ave . . . . Irvine CA 92614	800-900-1131	714-430-6400	712
NASDAQ: RECN			
Respec Inc			
3824 Jet Dr . . . . Rapid City SD 57703	877-737-7321	605-394-6400	261
Respironics Novametrix LLC			
Five Technology Dr . . . . Wallingford CT 06492	800-345-6443	724-387-4000	250
Response Biomedical Corp			
1781 75th Ave W . . . . Vancouver BC V6P6P2	888-591-5577	604-456-6010	416
TSE: RBM			
Response Envelope Inc			
1340 S Baker Ave . . . . Ontario CA 91761	800-750-0046	909-923-5855	263
Rest Haven-York			
1050 S George St . . . . York PA 17403	800-368-1019	717-843-9866	445
Restaurant & Stores Equipment Co			
230 West 700 South . . . . Salt Lake City UT 84101	800-877-0087	801-364-1981	299
Restaurant Developers Corp			
7010 Engle Rd Ste 100 . . . . Cleveland OH 44130	888-860-5082	440-625-3080	661
Restaurant Technologies Inc			
2250 Pilot Knob Rd			
Ste 100 . . . . Mendota Heights MN 55120	888-796-4997	651-796-1600	299
Restaurants Unlimited Inc			
411 First Ave S Ste 200 . . . . Seattle WA 98104	877-855-6106	206-634-0550	661
Restless Legs Syndrome Foundation Inc			
1610 14th St NW Ste 300 . . . . Rochester MN 55901	877-463-6757	507-287-6465	47-17
Reston Hospital Ctr			
1850 Town Ctr Pkwy . . . . Reston VA 20190	888-327-8882*	703-689-9000	371-3
*General			
Restonic Mattress			
201 James E Casey Dr . . . . Buffalo NY 14206	800-898-6075	716-895-1414	466
Restonic Mattress Corp			
737 Main St . . . . Buffalo NY 14203	800-898-6075		466
Restoration Hardware Inc			
2900 N MacArthur Dr Ste 100 . . . . Tracy CA 95376	800-910-9836		359
Results Travel			
701 Carlson Pkwy . . . . Minnetonka MN 55305	800-456-4000	763-212-5000	309
RESUMate Inc			
2500 Packard St Ste 200 . . . . Ann Arbor MI 48104	800-530-9310*	734-477-9402	179-10
*Cust Svc			
Retail Adv & Marketing Assn (RAMA)			
325 Seventh St NW Ste 1100 . . . . Washington DC 20004	800-673-4692	202-783-7971	48-18
Retail Confectioners International (RCI)			
2053 S Waverly Ste C . . . . Springfield MO 65804	800-545-5381	417-883-2775	48-6

	Toll-Free	Phone	Class
Retail Pro International LLC			
400 Plz Dr Ste 200 . . . . Folsom CA 95630	800-738-2457	916-605-7200	179-10
OTC: RTPRQ			
Retail Solutions Providers Assn (RSPA)			
10130 Perimeter Pkwy Ste 420 . . . . Charlotte NC 28216	800-782-2693	704-357-3124	48-18
Retama Park			
1 Retama Pkwy . . . . Selma TX 78154	800-473-8262	210-651-7000	633
Retif Oil & Fuel Inc			
527 Destrehan Ave PO Box 52679 . . . . Harvey LA 70058	800-349-9000	504-349-9000	572
Retired & Senior Volunteer Program (RSVP)			
1201 New York Ave NW . . . . Washington DC 20525	800-833-3722	202-606-5000	198
Retirement Advantage Inc, The			
47 Park Pl Ste 850 . . . . Appleton WI 54914	888-872-2364		458
Retractable Technologies Inc			
511 Lobo Ln . . . . Little Elm TX 75068	888-806-2626	972-294-1010	472
NYSE: RVP			
Retreat Hospital			
2621 Grove Ave . . . . Richmond VA 23220	800-888-3627	804-254-5100	371-3
Rettew Assoc Inc			
3020 Columbia Ave . . . . Lancaster PA 17603	800-738-8395	717-394-3721	261
Reusable Industrial Packaging Assn (RIPA)			
8401 Corporate Dr Ste 450 . . . . Landover MD 20785	800-441-8780	301-577-3786	48-13
Rev.com Inc			
251 Kearny St Eighth Fl . . . . . . San Francisco CA 94108	888-369-0701		390
Revcom Inc			
251 E Edwards Ave . . . . Carpentersville IL 60110	800-323-8261	847-428-4412	18
Revelation Software			
99 Kinderkamack Rd . . . . Westwood NJ 07675	800-262-4747	201-594-1422	179-2
Revels Tractor Company Inc			
2217 N Main St . . . . Fuquay-Varina NC 27526	800-849-5469	919-552-5697	274
Revention Inc			
1315 W Sam Houston Pkwy North			
Ste 100 . . . . Houston TX 77043	877-738-7444		197
Revere Control Systems Inc			
2240 Rocky Ridge Rd . . . . Birmingham AL 35216	800-536-2525	205-824-0004	720
Revere Copper Products Inc			
One Revere Pk . . . . Rome NY 13440	800-448-1776	315-338-2022	480
Revere Group, The			
325 N LaSalle Ste 325 . . . . Chicago IL 60654	800-745-3263	312-873-3400	195
Revere Mills Inc			
2860 S River Rd Ste 250 . . . . Des Plaines IL 60018	800-367-8258	847-759-6800	358
Review & Herald Publishing Assn			
55 W Oak Ridge Dr . . . . Hagerstown MD 21740	800-456-3991	301-393-3000	628-9
Revive Spa at the JW Marriott Desert Ridge Resort Phoenix			
5350 E Marriott Dr . . . . Phoenix AZ 85054	800-845-5279	480-293-3700	698
Revlon Consumer Products Corp			
1501 Williamsport St . . . . Oxford NC 27565	800-473-8566	212-527-4000	215
Revlon Foundation Inc			
237 Pk Ave . . . . New York NY 10017	800-473-8566*		303
*Cust Svc			
Revlon Inc			
237 Pk Ave . . . . New York NY 10017	800-473-8566	212-527-4000	357-3
NYSE: REV			
Revue & News, The			
319 N Main St . . . . Alpharetta GA 30004	800-864-5960	770-442-3278	525-4
Rewards Network			
2 N Riverside Plaza Suite 200 . . . . Chicago IL 60606	877-392-7313	866-559-3463	217
Rex Artist Supplies			
3160 SW 22 St . . . . Miami FL 33145	800-739-2782	305-445-1413	44
Rex Heat Treat			
951 W Eigth St PO Box 270 . . . . Lansdale PA 19446	800-220-4739	215-855-1131	479
Rex Lumber Co			
840 Main St . . . . Acton MA 01720	800-343-0567	978-263-0055	806
Rex Moore Electrical Contractors & Engineers			
6001 Outfall Cir . . . . Sacramento CA 95828	800-266-1922	916-372-1300	190-4
Rex Oil Co Inc			
814 & 1000 Lexington Ave . . . . Thomasville NC 27360	800-843-0572	336-472-3368	572
Rex Supply Co			
3715 Harrisburg Blvd . . . . Houston TX 77003	800-369-0669	713-222-2251	382
Rexam Inc			
4201 Congress St Ste 340 . . . . Charlotte NC 28209	800-944-2217	704-551-1500	541
Rexel Ryall Electrical Supplies			
11775 E 45th Ave . . . . Denver CO 80239	888-739-3577	303-629-7721	246
Rexhall Industries Inc			
46147 Seventh St W . . . . Lancaster CA 93534	800-765-7500	661-726-0565	119
OTC: REXLQ			
Reynolda House Museum of American Art			
2250 Reynolda Rd . . . . Winston-Salem NC 27106	888-663-1149	336-758-5150	513
Reynolds & Reynolds Co			
One Reynolds Way . . . . Dayton OH 45430	800-767-0080	937-485-2000	179-10
Reynolds American Inc			
401 N Main St PO Box 2990 . . . . Winston-Salem NC 27101	877-703-0386	336-741-2000	746
NYSE: LO			
Reynolds Plantation			
100 Linger Longer Rd . . . . Greensboro GA 30642	800-800-5250	706-467-0600	660
Reynolds Smith & Hills Inc			
10748 Deerwood Pk Blvd . . . . Jacksonville FL 32256	800-741-2014	904-256-2500	261
Reynolds-Alberta Museum			
6426 40 Ave PO Box 6360 . . . . Wetaskiwin AB T9A2G1	800-661-4726	780-361-1351	513
Reynoldsburg This Week			
7801 N Central Dr . . . . Lewis Center OH 43035	888-837-4342	740-888-6100	525-4
RF Industries			
7610 Miramar Rd Bldg 6000 . . . . . . San Diego CA 92126	800-233-1728	858-549-6340	253
NASDAQ: RFIL			
RF Micro Devices Inc			
7628 Thorndike Rd . . . . Greensboro NC 27409	800-937-5449	336-664-1233	687
NASDAQ: RFMD			
RF Murray & Co CPAs PC			
3741 Wilder Rd . . . . Bay City MI 48706	800-929-3556	989-686-7740	2
RFA (Renewable Fuels Assn)			
425 Third St SW . . . . Washington DC 20024	800-433-8850	202-289-3835	47-12
RFB&D (Recording for the Blind & Dyslexic)			
20 Roszel Rd . . . . Princeton NJ 08540	800-221-4792		47-17
RFI Communications & Security Systems			
360 Turtle Creek Ct . . . . San Jose CA 95125	800-341-9292	408-298-5400	190-4
RG Barry Corp			
13405 Yarmouth Dr NW . . . . Pickerington OH 43147	800-848-7560	614-864-6400	300
NASDAQ: DFZ			
RGFCC Corp			
8507 Oxon Hill Rd			
Ste 301 . . . . Fort Washington MD 20744	888-389-1230		458
Rgh Enterprises Inc			
1810 Summit Commerce Pk . . . . Twinsburg OH 44087	800-307-5930	330-963-6998	470

	City	State	ZIP	Toll-Free	Phone	Class
RGHS (Rochester General Health System)						
1425 Portland Ave	Rochester	NY	14621	**877-922-5465**	585-922-4000	371-3
RGS (Ruffed Grouse Society)						
451 McCormick Rd	Coraopolis	PA	15108	**888-564-6747**	412-262-4044	47-3
RH Donnelley Corp						
1001 Winstead Dr	Cary	NC	27513	**844-339-6334**	919-297-1600	628-6
RHA Health Services Inc						
17 Church St	Asheville	NC	28801	**866-742-2428**	828-232-6844	458
RheTech Inc						
1500 E N Territorial Rd	Whitmore Lake	MI	48189	**800-869-1230**	734-769-0585	598-2
Rhett House Inn						
1009 Craven St	Beaufort	SC	29902	**888-480-9530**	843-524-9030	376
RHIMR (Robert Half Management Resources)						
2884 Sand Hill Rd Ste 200	Menlo Park	CA	94025	**888-400-7474**	650-234-6000	195
Rhino Foods Inc						
79 Industrial Pkwy	Burlington	VT	05401	**800-542-3463**	802-862-0252	295-2
Rhino Records						
3400 W Olive Ave	Burbank	CA	91505	**800-827-4466**	800-546-3670	648
Rhode Island						
Higher Education Assistance Authority (RIHEAA)						
560 Jefferson Blvd	Warwick	RI	02886	**800-922-9855**	401-736-1100	716
Tourism Div						
315 Iron Horse Way Ste 101	Providence	RI	02908	**800-556-2484**		337-40
Rhode Island Airport Corp						
2000 Post Rd Warwick	Warwick	RI	02886	**888-268-7222**	401-691-2000	27
Rhode Island Assn of Realtors						
100 Bignall St	Warwick	RI	02888	**866-438-8345**	401-785-9898	647
Rhode Island Bar Assn						
115 Cedar St	Providence	RI	02903	**877-659-0801**	401-421-5740	71
Rhode Island Bar Journal						
115 Cedar St	Providence	RI	02903	**800-335-5701**	401-421-5740	452-15
Rhode Island Blood Ctr						
405 Promenade St	Providence	RI	02908	**800-283-8385**	401-453-8360	88
Rhode Island College						
600 Mt Pleasant Ave	Providence	RI	02908	**800-669-5760**	401-456-8000	166
Rhode Island Medical Society						
235 Promenade St Ste 500	Providence	RI	02908	**800-343-7776**	401-331-3207	469
Rhode Island School of Design						
Two College St	Providence	RI	02903	**800-364-7473**	401-454-6100	162
Rhode Island State Employees Credit Union						
160 Francis St	Providence	RI	02903	**855-322-7428**	401-751-7440	219
Rhode Island Textile Co						
211 Columbus Ave	Pawtucket	RI	02861	**800-556-6488**	401-722-3700	734-5
Rhoden Auto Ctr Inc						
3400 S Expy St	Council Bluffs	IA	51501	**866-562-6248**	712-309-4000	56
Rhodes College						
2000 N Pkwy	Memphis	TN	38112	**800-844-5969**	901-843-3700	166
Rhodes International Inc						
PO Box 25487	Salt Lake City	UT	84125	**800-876-7333***	801-972-0122	295-16
*Cust Svc						
Rhododendron Species Botanical Garden						
2525 S 336th St PO Box 3798	Federal Way	WA	98063	**877-242-2528**	253-838-4646	96
RHR International LLP						
233 S Wacker Dr 95th Fl	Chicago	IL	60606	**800-892-4496**	312-924-0800	195
Rhythm City Casino						
101 W River Dr	Davenport	IA	52801	**844-852-4386**	563-328-8000	132
RI (Refugees International)						
2001 S St NW Ste 700-K	Washington	DC	20009	**800-733-8433**	202-828-0110	47-5
RI Lampus Co						
816 RI Lampus Ave PO Box 167	Springdale	PA	15144	**800-872-7310**	412-362-3800	184
Rialto Chamber of Commerce						
120 N Riverside Ave	Rialto	CA	92376	**800-597-4955**	909-875-5364	137
Rialto Theater						
310 S Ninth St	Tacoma	WA	98402	**800-291-7593**	253-591-5890	565
Rib Crib Corp						
4535 S Harvard Ave	Tulsa	OK	74135	**800-275-9677**	918-712-7427	661
Ribbon Technology Corp						
825 Taylor Stn Rd PO Box 30758	Gahanna	OH	43230	**800-848-0477**	614-864-5444	800
Ribelin Sales Inc						
3857 Miller Pk Dr	Garland	TX	75042	**800-374-1594**	972-272-1594	144
Ricart Automotive Group						
4255 S Hamilton Rd	Columbus	OH	43125	**888-225-6783**	888-631-9726	56
Rice Fruit Co						
2760 Carlisle Rd PO Box 66	Gardners	PA	17324	**800-627-3359**	717-677-8131	314-3
Rice Packaging Inc						
356 Somers Rd	Ellington	CT	06029	**800-367-6725**	860-872-8341	100
Rice University						
6100 Main St	Houston	TX	77005	**800-527-6957**	713-348-0000	166
Ricerca Biosciences LLC						
7528 Auburn Rd PO Box 1000	Concord	OH	44077	**888-742-3722**	440-357-3300	659
RiceTec Inc						
1925 FM 2917 PO Box 1305	Alvin	TX	77511	**877-580-7423**	281-393-3502	295-23
Rich Mountain Electric Co-op Inc						
515 Janssen PO Box 897	Mena	AR	71953	**877-828-4074**	479-394-4140	245
Rich Ranch						
939 Cottonwood Lakes Rd	Seeley Lake	MT	59868	**800-532-4350**	406-677-2317	239
Rich Worldwide Travel Inc						
500 Mamaroneck Ave	Harrison	NY	10528	**800-431-1130**	914-835-7600	761
Richard King Mellon Foundation						
500 Grant St Ste 4106	Pittsburgh	PA	15219	**800-424-9836**	412-392-2800	304
Richard L. Roudebush VA Medical Ctr						
1481 W Tenth St	Indianapolis	IN	46202	**888-878-6889**	317-988-4498	371-8
Richard Rodgers Theatre						
226 W 46th St	New York	NY	10036	**866-755-3075**	212-221-1211	736
Richard Wolf Medical Instruments Corp						
353 Corporate Woods Pkwy	Vernon Hills	IL	60061	**800-323-9653**	847-913-1113	250
Richard Young's Intelligence Report						
700 Indian Springs Dr	Lancaster	PA	17601	**800-219-8592***		524-9
*Cust Svc						
Richards Graphic Communications Inc						
2700 Van Buren St	Bellwood	IL	60104	**866-827-3686**	708-547-6000	771
Richards Industries Inc						
3170 Wasson Rd	Cincinnati	OH	45209	**800-543-7311***	513-533-5600	588
*Cust Svc						
Richards Maple Products Inc						
545 Water St	Chardon	OH	44024	**800-352-4052**		295-39
Richardson Convention & Visitors Bureau						
411 W Arapaho Rd Ste 105	Richardson	TX	75080	**888-690-7287**	972-744-4034	207
Richardson Electronics Ltd						
40 W 267 Keslinger Rd PO Box 393	LaFox	IL	60147	**800-348-5580***	630-208-2200	246
NASDAQ: RELL ■ *Sales						
Richardson Public Library						
900 Civic Ctr Dr	Richardson	TX	75080	**800-735-2989**	972-744-4350	431-3

	City	State	ZIP	Toll-Free	Phone	Class
Richards-Wilcox Inc						
600 S Lake St	Aurora	IL	60506	**800-253-5668**		208
Richland Electric Co-op						
1027 N Jefferson St	Richland Center	WI	53581	**800-242-8511**	608-647-3173	245
Richland Glass Company Inc						
1640 SW Blvd	Vineland	NJ	08360	**800-959-0312**	856-691-1697	330
Richland Hospital Inc, The						
333 E Second St	Richland Center	WI	53581	**888-467-7485**	608-647-6321	371-3
Richman Group of Cos						
340 Pemberwick Rd	Greenwich	CT	06831	**800-333-3509**	203-869-0900	644
Richmond American Homes Inc						
4350 S Monaco St	Denver	CO	80237	**888-402-4663**	303-773-2727	644
Richmond Chamber of Commerce						
3925 Macdonald Ave	Richmond	CA	94805	**800-921-1117**	510-234-3512	137
Richmond Coliseum						
601 E Leigh St	Richmond	VA	23219	**800-228-9290**	804-780-4970	711
Richmond Community College						
PO Box 1189	Hamlet	NC	28345	**800-908-9946**	910-410-1700	160
Richmond County Hospice						
1119 N US Hwy 1	Rockingham	NC	28379	**800-322-2997**	910-997-4464	368
Richmond Gear						
PO Box 238	Liberty	SC	29657	**800-934-2727***	864-843-9231	700
*Sales						
Richmond International Forest Products Inc						
4050 Innslake Dr Ste 100	Glen Allen	VA	23060	**800-767-0111**	804-747-0111	192-3
Richmond Metropolitan Convention & Visitors Bureau						
401 N Third St	Richmond	VA	23219	**800-370-9004**	804-782-2777	207
Richmond National Battlefield Park						
3215 E Broad St	Richmond	VA	23223	**866-733-7768**	804-226-1981	513
Richmond Public Library						
325 Civic Ctr Plaza	Richmond	CA	94804	**800-833-2900**	510-620-6555	431-3
Richmond Times-Dispatch						
PO Box 85333	Richmond	VA	23293	**800-468-3382**	804-649-6000	628-8
Richmond Tours						
1828 Hylan Blvd	Staten Island	NY	10305	**800-766-3868**	718-979-3111	750
Richmond, The						
1757 Collins Ave	Miami Beach	FL	33139	**855-627-3767**	305-538-2331	376
Richmond/Wayne County Convention & Tourism Bureau						
5701 National Rd E	Richmond	IN	47374	**800-828-8414**	765-935-8687	207
Richmor Aviation Inc						
1142 Rt 9 H						
Columbia County Airport	Hudson	NY	12534	**800-331-6101**	518-828-9461	62
Rick Johnson & Assoc of Colorado						
1649 Downing St	Denver	CO	80218	**800-530-2300**	303-296-2200	397
Rickard Circular Folding Co						
325 N Ashland Ave	Chicago	IL	60607	**800-747-1389**	312-243-6300	91
Ricklin-Echikson Assoc						
374 Millburn Ave	Millburn	NJ	07041	**800-544-2317**	973-376-2020	194
Ricks Barbecue Inc						
2367 Hwy 43 S	Leoma	TN	38468	**800-544-5864**	931-852-2324	187
Rickwood Caverns State Park						
370 Rickwood Pk Rd	Warrior	AL	35180	**800-252-7275**	205-647-9692	558
Ricoh Americas Corp						
Five Dedrick Pl	West Caldwell	NJ	07006	**800-727-1885**	973-882-2000	111
Ricon Corp						
7900 Nelson Rd	Panorama City	CA	91402	**800-322-2884**	818-267-3000	256
Riddle Memorial Hospital						
1068 W Baltimore Pike	Media	PA	19063	**866-225-5654**	484-227-9400	371-3
Rideau Inc						
473 Deslauriers	Montreal	QC	H4N1W2	**800-363-6464**		458
Rideout Memorial Hospital						
726 Fourth St	Marysville	CA	95901	**888-923-3800**	530-749-4300	371-3
Rider University						
Westminster Choir College						
101 Walnut Ln	Princeton	NJ	08540	**800-962-4647**	609-921-7100	166
Ridewell Corp						
PO Box 4586	Springfield	MO	65808	**877-434-8088**	417-833-4565	59
Ridge Behavioral Health System						
3050 Rio Dosa Dr	Lexington	KY	40509	**800-753-4673**	859-269-2325	371-5
Ridge Tahoe						
400 Ridge Club Dr PO Box 5790	Stateline	NV	89449	**800-334-1600**	775-588-3553	660
Ridgecrest Area Convention & Visitors Bureau (RACVB)						
139 Balsam St Ste 1700	Ridgecrest	CA	93555	**800-847-4830**	760-375-8202	207
Ridgeview Medical Ctr (RMC)						
500 S Maple St	Waconia	MN	55387	**800-967-4620**	952-442-2191	371-3
Ridgewater College						
Hutchinson						
Two Century Ave SE	Hutchinson	MN	55350	**800-722-1151**	320-234-8500	788
Willmar						
2101 15th Ave NW PO Box 1097	Willmar	MN	56201	**800-722-1151**	320-222-5200	788
Ridgewood Savings Bank						
71-02 Forest Ave	Ridgewood	NY	11385	**800-250-4832**	718-240-4800	69
RidgeWorth Funds						
50 Hurt Plaza Ste 1400	Atlanta	GA	30305	**866-595-2470**		521
Ridg-U-Rak Inc						
120 S Lake St PO Box 150	North East	PA	16428	**866-479-7225**	814-725-8751	286
Riechmann Transport Inc						
3328 W Chain of Rocks Rd	Granite City	IL	62040	**800-844-4225**	618-797-6700	770
Riedell Shoes Inc						
122 Cannon River Ave	Red Wing	MN	55066	**800-698-6893**	651-388-8251	701
Riegel Consumer Products						
51 Riegel Rd PO Box E	Johnston	SC	29832	**800-845-3251**	803-275-2541	735
Riekes Equipment Co						
PO Box 3392	Omaha	NE	68103	**800-856-0931**	402-593-1181	382
Riel House National Historic Site of Canada						
330 River Rd	Winnipeg	MB	R2M3Z8	**877-852-3100**	204-257-1783	556
RIF (Reading Is Fundamental Inc)						
1825 Connecticut Ave NW						
Ste 400	Washington	DC	20009	**877-743-7323**	202-536-3400	47-11
Right at Home Inc						
6464 Crt St Ste 150	Omaha	NE	68106	**877-697-7537**	402-697-7537	309
Right Management Consultants Inc						
1818 Market St 33rd Fl	Philadelphia	PA	19103	**800-237-4448**	215-988-1588	194
Right Systems Inc						
2600 Willamette Dr NE Ste C	Lacey	WA	98516	**800-571-1717**	360-956-0414	225
Righteous Babe Records						
341 Delaware Ave PO Box 95	Buffalo	NY	14202	**800-664-3769**	716-852-8020	648
Rigid Bldg Systems Ltd						
18933 Aldine Westfield Rd	Houston	TX	77073	**888-467-4443**	281-443-9065	104
Rigid Hitch Inc						
3301 W Burnsville Pkwy	Burnsville	MN	55337	**800-624-7630***	952-895-5001	753
*Cust Svc						
Rim Country Regional Chamber of Commerce						
100 W Main St	Payson	AZ	85547	**800-249-2678**	928-474-4515	137

	Toll-Free	Phone	Class
RIM Logistics Ltd			
200 N Gary Ave Ste B . . . . .Roselle IL 60172	888-275-0937	630-595-0610	444
Rimage Corp			
7725 Washington Ave S . . . . .Minneapolis MN 55439	800-553-8312	952-944-8144	174-8
Rimrock Foundation			
1231 N 29th St . . . . .Billings MT 59101	800-227-3953	406-248-3175	717
Rimrock Resort Hotel, The			
300 Mountain Ave PO Box 1110. . . . . Banff AB T1L1J2	888-746-7625	403-762-3356	660
Rimrock Stages Inc			
1660 W Broadway St . . . . .Missoula MT 59808	800-255-7655	406-549-2339	107
Rinchem Company Inc			
6133 Edith Blvd NE . . . . .Albuquerque NM 87107	888-375-2436	505-345-3655	444
Ring Container Technology			
65 Industrial Park Rd . . . . Oakland TN 38060	800-280-6333		123
Ringdale Inc			
101 Halmar Cove . . . . .Georgetown TX 78628	888-288-9080	512-288-9080	177
Ringling College of Art & Design			
2700 N Tamiami Trl . . . . .Sarasota FL 34234	800-255-7695	941-351-5100	162
Rink Systems Inc			
1103 Hershey St . . . . .Albert Lea MN 56007	800-944-7930	507-373-9175	14
Rinker Materials Corp Concrete Pipe Div			
8311 W Carder Ct . . . . .Littleton CO 80125	800-909-7763	303-791-1600	184
Rio Grande Electric Co-op Inc			
Hwy 90 & State Hwy 131			
PO Box 1509. . . . . .Brackettville TX 78832	800-749-1509	830-563-2444	245
Rio Grande Valley Chamber of Commerce			
322 S Missouri St . . . . .Weslaco TX 78596	800-628-5115	956-968-3141	137
Rio Verde Development Inc			
25609 N Danny Ln . . . . .Rio Verde AZ 85263	800-233-7103	480-471-1962	188
RioCan Real Estate Investment Trust			
2300 Yonge St Ste 500			
PO Box 2386. . . . . .Toronto ON M4P1E4	800-465-2733	416-866-3033	645
TSE: REI.UN.CA			
Rip Griffin Truck Travel Ctr Inc			
4710 Fourth St . . . . .Lubbock TX 79416	800-333-9330	806-795-8785	323
RIPA (Reusable Industrial Packaging Assn)			
8401 Corporate Dr Ste 450. . . . . .Landover MD 20785	800-441-8780	301-577-3786	48-13
Ripley Co			
46 Nooks Hill Rd . . . . .Cromwell CT 06416	800-528-8665	860-635-2200	748
Ripley's Aquarium			
1110 Celebrity Cir . . . . .Myrtle Beach SC 29577	800-734-8888	843-916-0888	39
Ripon College			
300 Seward St PO Box 248. . . . . .Ripon WI 54971	800-947-4766*		166
*Admissions			
Risdall Adv Agency			
550 Main St . . . . .New Brighton MN 55112	888-747-3255	651-286-6700	4
Rising Star Casino Resort			
777 Rising Star Dr . . . . .Rising Sun IN 47040	800-472-6311	812-438-1234	132
Risk Management Assn (RMA)			
1801 Market St Ste 300 . . . . .Philadelphia PA 19103	800-677-7621*	215-446-4000	48-2
*Cust Svc			
RiskWatch (RWI)			
1237 N Gulfstream Ave . . . . .Sarasota Fl 34236	800-360-1898		179-10
RISO Inc			
Eight New England Executive Park			
Ste 390 . . . . .Burlington MA 01803	800-942-7476*	978-777-7377	174-6
*General			
Ritchie Tractor			
1746 W Lmar Alxander Pkwy . . . . .Maryville TN 37801	888-319-0282	865-981-3199	322
Rite Aid Corp			
30 Hunter Ln .Camp Hill PA 17011	800-748-3243	717-761-2633	237
NYSE: RAD			
Rite-Hite Corp			
8900 N Arbon Dr . . . . .Milwaukee WI 53224	800-456-0600	414-355-2600	669
Rite-Style Optical Co			
12240 Emmet St . . . . .Omaha NE 68164	800-373-3200	402-492-8822	536
Riteway Bus Service Inc Motorcoach Div			
W201 N13900 Fond du Lac Ave . . . . . . .Richfield WI 53076	800-776-7026	262-677-3282	106
Ritrama			
800 Kasota Ave SE . . . . .Minneapolis MN 55414	800-328-5071	612-378-2277	3
Rittal Corp			
One Rittal Pl . . . . .Springfield OH 45504	800-477-4000	937-399-0500	803
Rittenhouse Book Distributors Inc			
511 Feheley Dr . . . . .King of Prussia PA 19406	800-345-6425*		94
*Cust Svc			
Rittenhouse Hotel			
210 W Rittenhouse Sq . . . . .Philadelphia PA 19103	800-635-1042	215-546-9000	376
Ritz Camera & Image			
2 Bergen Turnpike . . . . .Ridgefield Park NJ 07660	855-622-7489*	201-881-1900	118
*Cust Svc			
Ritz-Carlton Amelia Island			
4750 Amelia Island Pkwy . . . . .Amelia Island FL 32034	800-241-3333	904-277-1100	660
Ritz-Carlton Bachelor Gulch			
0130 Daybreak Ridge .Avon CO 81620	800-241-3333	970-748-6200	660
Ritz-Carlton Dallas			
2121 McKinney Ave . . . . .Dallas TX 75201	800-960-7082*	214-922-0200	376
*Resv			
Ritz-Carlton Half Moon Bay			
One Miramontes Pt Rd . . . . .Half Moon Bay CA 94019	800-241-3333*	650-712-7000	660
*General			
Ritz-Carlton Hotel Co LLC, The			
4445 Willard Ave Ste 800. . . . . .Chevy Chase MD 20815	800-241-3333	301-547-4700	660
Ritz-Carlton Hotel Company, The			
1111 Ritz-Carlton Dr . . . . .Sarasota FL 34236	800-241-3333	866-922-6882	698
Ritz-Carlton Huntington Hotel & Spa			
4445 Willard Ave Ste 800 . . . . .Chevy Chase MD 20815	800-241-3333	301-547-4700	660
Ritz-Carlton Kapalua			
1 Ritz-Carlton Dr Kapalua. . . . . .Maui HI 96761	800-262-8440*	808-669-6200	660
*Resv			
Ritz-Carlton Key Biscayne			
455 Grand Bay Dr . . . . .Key Biscayne FL 33149	800-241-3333	305-365-4500	660
Ritz-Carlton Laguna Niguel, The			
One Ritz Carlton Dr . . . . .Dana Point CA 92629	800-542-8680	949-240-2000	660
Ritz-Carlton Lodge Reynolds Plantation			
One Lk Oconee Trl . . . . .Greensboro GA 30642	800-826-1945	706-467-0600	660
Ritz-Carlton Naples Golf Resort			
2600 Tiburon Dr . . . . .Naples FL 34109	888-856-2164*	239-593-2000	660
*Resv			
Ritz-Carlton Orlando Grande Lakes			
4012 Central Florida Pkwy . . . . .Orlando FL 32837	800-576-5760	407-206-2400	660
Ritz-Carlton Phoenix			
2401 E Camelback Rd . . . . .Phoenix AZ 85016	800-241-3333	602-468-0700	660
Ritz-Carlton San Juan, The			
6961 Ave of the Governors			
Isla Verde . . . . .Carolina PR 00979	800-241-3333	787-253-1700	660
Ritz-Carlton Sarasota			
1111 Ritz-Carlton Dr . . . . .Sarasota FL 34236	800-241-3333	941-309-2000	660
Ritz-Carlton Tysons Corner, The			
1700 Tysons Blvd . . . . .McLean VA 22102	800-241-3333	703-506-4300	698
Ritz-Craft Corp of Pennsylvania Inc			
15 Industrial Pk Rd . . . . .Mifflinburg PA 17844	800-326-9836	570-966-1053	500
Riu Hotel Florida Beach			
3101 Collins Ave .Miami FL 33140	888-666-8816	305-673-5333	376
Rivco Products Inc			
440 S Pine St . . . . .Burlington WI 53105	888-801-8222	262-763-8222	510
River Bend Industries			
2421 16th Ave S . . . . .Moorhead MN 56560	800-365-3070	218-236-1818	200
River Birch Homes Inc			
400 River Birch Dr . . . . .Hackleburg AL 35564	888-760-3314	205-935-1997	500
River City Bank			
PO Box 15247 . . . . .Sacramento CA 95851	800-564-7144*	916-567-2899	69
OTC: RCBC ▩ *Cust Svc			
River City Brass Band Inc			
500 Grant St Ste 2720 . . . . .Pittsburgh PA 15219	800-292-7222	412-434-7222	566-3
River Country Tourism Bureau			
PO Box 214 . . . . .Three Rivers MI 49093	800-447-2821		207
River Garden Hebrew Home for the Aged			
11401 Old St Augustine Rd . . . . .Jacksonville FL 32258	800-468-3571	904-260-1818	445
River Oaks Ctr			
96 River Oaks Ctr Dr . . . . .Calumet City IL 60409	877-746-6642	708-868-0600	455
River Oaks Hospital			
1525 River Oaks Rd W . . . . .New Orleans LA 70123	800-366-1740	504-734-1740	371-3
River Parishes Hospital			
500 Rue De Sante . . . . .Laplace LA 70068	800-231-5275	985-652-7000	371-3
River Park Hospital			
1230 Sixth Ave . . . . .Huntington WV 25701	800-621-2673	304-526-9111	371-5
River Ranch Fresh Foods			
1156 Abbott St . . . . .Salinas CA 93901	800-538-5868	831-758-1390	11-1
River Region West Campus			
2100 Highway 61 North/1111 N			
Frontage Road. . . . . .Vicksburg MS 39183	800-843-2131	601-883-5000	371-3
River Rock Casino Resort			
8811 River Rd . . . . .Richmond BC V6X3P8	866-748-3718	604-247-8900	660
River Valley Bancorp			
430 Clifty Dr .Madison IN 47250	800-994-4849	812-273-4949	357-2
NASDAQ: RIVR			
River Walk			
110 Broadway Ste 500 . . . . .San Antonio TX 78204	800-417-4139	210-227-4262	49-5
River's Edge Resort Cottages			
4200 Boat St . . . . .Fairbanks AK 99709	800-770-3343	907-474-0286	376
Riverbend Maximum Security Institution			
7475 Cockrill Bend Blvd . . . . .Nashville TN 37243	800-770-8277	615-350-3100	213
Riverdale Mills Corp			
130 Riverdale St PO Box 200 . . . . .Northbridge MA 01534	800-762-6374	508-234-8715	279
Riveredge Nature Ctr			
4458 W Hawthorne Dr PO Box 26. . . . . .Newburg WI 53060	800-287-8098	262-375-2715	49-4
Riveredge Resort Hotel			
17 Holland St . . . . .Alexandria Bay NY 13607	800-365-6987	315-482-9917	376
Riverhead Bldg Supply Corp			
1093 Pulaski St . . . . .Riverhead NY 11901	800-378-3650	631-727-3650	192-3
Riverland Community College			
1900 Eigth Ave NW . . . . .Austin MN 55912	800-247-5039	507-433-0600	160
Riverland Energy Co-op			
N28988 State Rd 93 PO Box 277 . . . . . . .Arcadia WI 54612	800-411-9115	608-323-3381	245
RiverMead Retirement Community			
150 RiverMead Rd . . . . .Peterborough NH 03458	800-200-5433	603-924-0062	663
RiverPoint Group LLC			
2200 E Devon Ave Ste 385 . . . . .Des Plaines IL 60018	800-297-5601	847-233-9600	181
Rivers Oceans & Mountains Adventures Inc (ROAM)			
2485 Hwy 3A . . . . .Nelson BC V1L6K7	888-639-1114		750
Riverside City Public Library			
3581 Mission Inn Ave . . . . .Riverside CA 92501	888-225-7377	951-826-5201	431-3
Riverside Clay Co Inc			
201 Truss Ferry Rd . . . . .Pell City AL 35128	800-924-0637	205-338-3366	498-2
Riverside Convention & Visitors Bureau			
3750 University Ave Ste 175. . . . . .Riverside CA 92501	888-748-7733	951-222-4700	207
Riverside Foods Inc			
2520 Wilson St . . . . .Two Rivers WI 54241	800-678-4511	920-793-4511	295-14
Riverside Ford			
1419 Ludington St . . . . .Escanaba MI 49829	877-326-5326	906-786-1130	56
Riverside Ford Inc			
2089 Riverside Dr PO Box 225 . . . . .Macon GA 31204	800-395-6210*	478-464-2900	56
*Sales			
Riverside Forest Products Inc			
2912 Professional Pkwy . . . . .Augusta GA 30907	888-855-8733	706-855-5500	192-3
Riverside Group			
655 Driving Pk Ave . . . . .Rochester NY 14613	800-777-2463	585-458-2090	91
Riverside Hotel			
620 E Las Olas Blvd . . . . .Fort Lauderdale FL 33301	800-325-3280	954-467-0671	376
Riverside Manufacturing Co			
301 Riverside Dr . . . . .Moultrie GA 31768	800-841-8677	229-985-5210	153-18
Riverside Marine Inc			
11051 Pulaski Hwy . . . . .White Marsh MD 21162	800-448-6872	410-335-1500	89
Riverside Mattress Co			
225 Dunn Rd . . . . .Fayetteville NC 28312	888-288-5195	910-483-0461	466
Riverside Methodist Hospital			
3535 Olentangy River Rd . . . . .Columbus OH 43214	800-837-7555	614-566-5000	371-3
Riverside Military Academy			
2001 Riverside Dr . . . . .Gainesville GA 30501	800-462-2338	770-532-6251	615
Riverside Publishing Co			
3800 Golf Rd Ste 200 . . . . .Rolling Meadows IL 60008	800-323-9540*	630-467-7000	244
*Cust Svc			
Riverside Refractories Inc			
201 Truss Ferry Rd . . . . .Pell City AL 35128	800-924-0637	205-338-3366	653
Riverside Transit Agency (RTA)			
1825 Third St PO Box 59968 . . . . .Riverside CA 92517	800-800-7821	951-565-5000	463
Riverstone Billings Inn			
880 N 29th St . . . . .Billings MT 59101	800-231-7782	406-252-6800	376
RiverStone Group Inc			
1701 Fifth Ave . . . . .Moline IL 61265	800-906-2489	309-757-8250	183
Riverton Memorial Hospital LLC			
2100 W Sunset Dr . . . . .Riverton WY 82501	888-982-9144	307-856-4161	371-3
Rivertown Newspaper Group			
2760 N Service Dr PO Box 15. . . . . .Red Wing MN 55066	800-535-1660	651-388-8235	628-8
Rivervalley Behavioral Health Hospital			
1000 Industrial Dr . . . . .Owensboro KY 42301	800-755-8477	270-689-6800	717

	Toll-Free	Phone	Class
Riverview Community Bank			
900 Washington St Ste 100 .... Vancouver WA 98660	800-822-2076	360-693-6650	69
Riverview Hospital			
395 Westfield Rd ....Noblesville IN 46060	800-523-6001	317-773-0760	371-3
Riverview Psychiatric Ctr			
250 Arsenal St			
11 State House Stn....................Augusta ME 04330	888-261-6684	207-624-4600	371-5
Rivier College			
420 S Main St ....Nashua NH 03060	800-447-4843	603-888-1311	166
Riviera Finance			
220 Ave I ....Redondo Beach CA 90277	800-872-7484		272
Riviera Hotel			
1431 Robson St ....Vancouver BC V6G1C3	888-699-5222	604-685-1301	376
Riviera Hotel & Casino			
2901 Las Vegas Blvd S ....Las Vegas NV 89109	866-275-6030*	702-734-5110	660
*Resv			
RJ Donovan Correctional Facility at Rock Mountain			
480 Alta Rd ....San Diego CA 92179	877-256-6877	619-661-6500	213
RJ Marshall Co			
26776 W 12-Mile Rd ....Southfield MI 48034	888-514-8600*	248-353-4100	715
*Cust Svc			
RJ O'Brien & Assoc			
222 S Riverside Plz Ste 900 ....Chicago IL 60606	866-438-7564	312-373-5000	170
RJN Group Inc			
200 W Front St ....Wheaton IL 60187	800-227-7838	630-682-4700	193
RK Mechanical Inc			
3800 Xanthia St ....Denver CO 80238	877-576-9696	303-355-9696	190-10
RKI Inc			
2301 Central Pkwy ....Houston TX 77092	800-346-8988	713-688-4414	465
RL Adams Plastics Inc			
5955 Crossroads Commerce ....Wyoming MI 49519	800-968-2241	616-261-4400	594
RL Drake Co			
9900 Springboro Pike ....Miamisburg OH 45342	800-777-8876	937-746-4556	638
RLI Corp			
9025 N Lindbergh Dr ....Peoria IL 61615	800-331-4929*	309-692-1000	357-4
NYSE: RLI ■ *Cust Svc			
RLI Insurance Co			
9025 N Lindbergh Dr ....Peoria IL 61615	800-331-4929	309-692-1000	388-4
RMA (Risk Management Assn)			
1801 Market St Ste 300 ....Philadelphia PA 19103	800-677-7621*	215-446-4000	48-2
*Cust Svc			
RMA (Rubber Manufacturers Assn)			
1400 K St NW Ste 900 ....Washington DC 20005	800-220-7622	202-682-4800	48-13
RMC (Ridgeview Medical Ctr)			
500 S Maple St ....Waconia MN 55387	800-967-4620	952-442-2191	371-3
RMCF (Rocky Mountain Chocolate Factory Inc)			
265 Turner Dr ....Durango CO 81303	888-525-2462*	970-259-0554	122
NASDAQ: RMCF ■ *Cust Svc			
RME360			
4805 Independence Pkwy Ste 250 ....Tampa FL 33634	888-383-8770		5
RMF Engineering Inc			
5520 Research Pk Dr Third Fl.........Baltimore MD 21228	800-938-5760	410-576-0505	261
RMH (Ross Memorial Hospital)			
10 Angeline St N ....Lindsay ON K9V4M8	800-510-7365	705-324-6111	371-2
RMH (Rockingham Memorial Hospital)			
2010 Health Campus Dr ....Harrisonburg VA 22801	800-736-8272	540-689-1000	371-3
RMHC (Ronald McDonald House Charities)			
1 Kroc Dr Dept 014..............Oak Brook IL 60523	855-670-4787	630-623-7048	47-5
RMLEB (Rocky Mountain Lions Eye Bank)			
1675 Aurora Crt Ste El2049			
PO Box 6026.......................Aurora CO 80045	800-444-7479	720-848-3937	269
RMO Inc (Rocky Mountain Orthodontics Inc)			
650 W Colfax Ave ....Denver CO 80204	800-525-6375	303-592-8200	228
RMPB (Rocky Mountain Public Broadcasting Network)			
1089 Bannock St ....Denver CO 80204	800-274-6666	303-892-6666	624
RMPersonnel Inc			
4707 Montana Ave ....El Paso TX 79903	866-333-7176	915-565-7674	623
Rmx Global Logistics			
35715 US Hwy 40 Bldg B ....Evergreen CO 80439	888-824-7365		310
RNC (Republican National Committee)			
310 First St SE ....Washington DC 20003	800-445-5768	202-863-8500	609
RNC Genter Capital Management			
11601 Wilshire Blvd 25th Fl.........Los Angeles CA 90025	800-877-7624	310-477-6543	398
Rnk Inc			
333 Elm St Ste 310.................Dedham MA 02026	877-323-2486	781-613-6000	726
RnR RV Ctr			
23203 E Knox Ave ....Liberty Lake WA 99019	866-386-4875		56
RNS (Religion News Service)			
529 14th St NW Ste 425..........Washington DC 20045	800-767-6781	202-463-8777	523
ROA (Reserve Officers Assn of the US)			
One Constitution Ave NE ....Washington DC 20002	800-809-9448	202-479-2200	47-19
Road & Track Magazine			
1499 Monrovia Ave ....Newport Beach CA 92663	800-835-6422	949-720-5300	452-3
Road America			
N 7390 Hwy 67 ....Elkhart Lake WI 53020	800-365-7223	920-892-4576	508
Road Atlanta Raceway			
5300 Winder Hwy ....Braselton GA 30517	800-849-7223	770-967-6143	508
Road King Inn Columbia Mall			
3300 30th Ave S ....Grand Forks ND 58201	800-707-1391		376
Road Runner Group			
60 Columbus Cir			
60 Columbus Cir ....New York NY 10023	866-689-3678	703-345-3422	395
Roadrunner Transportation Systems Inc			
4900 S Pennsylvania Ave ....Cudahy WI 53110	800-831-4394	414-615-1500	642
NYSE: RRTS			
Roadtec Inc			
800 Manufacturers Rd			
PO Box 180515.................Chattanooga TN 37405	800-272-7100	423-265-0600	191
Roadtex Transportation Corp			
13 Jensen Dr ....Somerset NJ 08873	800-762-3839		770
ROAM (Rivers Oceans & Mountains Adventures Inc)			
2485 Hwy 3A ....Nelson BC V1L6K7	888-639-1114		750
Roam Mobility Inc			
400 – 311 Water St ....Vancouver BC V6B1B8	888-762-6487		224
Roaman's			
2300 SE Ave ....Indianapolis IN 46283	800-677-0229		454
Roane State Community College			
276 Patton Ln ....Harriman TN 37748	800-343-9104	865-354-3000	160
Roanoke Civic Ctr			
710 Williamson Rd ....Roanoke VA 24016	877-482-8496	540-853-2241	711
Roanoke College			
221 College Ln ....Salem VA 24153	800-388-2276*	540-375-2270	166
*Admissions			
Roanoke Electric Co-op			
518 NC 561 W ....Aulander NC 27805	800-433-2236	252-539-4600	245
Roanoke Regional Chamber of Commerce			
210 S Jefferson St ....Roanoke VA 24011	800-506-0489	540-983-0700	137
Roanoke Times			
201 W Campbell Ave SW ....Roanoke VA 24011	800-346-1234	540-981-3340	525-2
Roanoke Valley Convention & Visitors Bureau			
101 Shenandoah Ave NE ....Roanoke VA 24016	800-635-5535	540-342-6025	207
Roaring Brook Ranch & Tennis Resort			
Rte 9N S ....Lake George NY 12845	800-882-7665	518-668-5767	660
Roaring Spring Blank Book Co			
740 Spang St ....Roaring Spring PA 16673	800-441-1653	814-224-5141	85
Roasterie Inc, The			
1204 W 27th St ....Kansas City MO 64108	800-376-0245	816-931-4000	342
Robbers Cave State Park			
Hwy 2 N ....Wilburton OK 74578	800-654-8240	918-465-2565	558
Robbie Manufacturing Inc			
10810 Mid America Ave ....Lenexa KS 66219	800-255-6328	913-492-3400	594
Robbins Inc			
4777 Eastern Ave ....Cincinnati OH 45226	800-543-1913	513-871-8988	674
Robbins LLC			
3415 Thompson St ....Muscle Shoals AL 35661	800-633-3312	256-383-5441	744
Robbins Mfg Co			
13001 N Nebraska Ave ....Tampa FL 33612	888-558-8199	813-971-3030	805
Robern Inc			
701 N Wilson Ave ....Bristol PA 19007	800-877-2376	215-826-9800	318-2
Roberson Motors Inc			
3100 Ryan Dr SE ....Salem OR 97301	888-281-6220	503-363-4117	56
Roberson Museum & Science Ctr			
30 Front St ....Binghamton NY 13905	888-269-5325	607-772-0660	513
Robert Allen Fabrics Inc			
225 Foxboro Blvd ....Foxboro MA 02035	800-333-3777		587
Robert Bearden Inc			
2601 Industrial Pk Dr PO Box 870 ....Cairo GA 39828	888-298-6928	229-377-6928	770
Robert Bosch LLC			
38000 Hills Tech Dr ....Farmington Hills MI 48331	800-893-6342*	248-876-1000	51
*Sales			
Robert Bosch Tool Corp			
1800 W Central Rd ....Mount Prospect IL 60056	877-267-2499	224-232-2000	749
Robert C Williams American Museum of Papermaking			
500 Tenth St NW ....Atlanta GA 30318	800-558-6611	404-894-7840	513
Robert Dietrick Co Inc			
PO Box 605 ....Fishers IN 46038	866-767-1888	317-842-1991	382
Robert E Morris Co			
910 Gay Hill Rd ....Windsor CT 06095	877-689-1860	860-687-3300	382
Robert E Nolan Company Inc			
92 Hopmeadow St ....Weatogue CT 06089	800-653-1941	860-658-1941	195
Robert H Wager Co			
570 Montroyal Rd ....Rural Hall NC 27045	800-562-7024	336-969-6909	777
Robert Half Management Resources (RHIMR)			
2884 Sand Hill Rd Ste 200 ....Menlo Park CA 94025	888-400-7474	650-234-6000	195
Robert Hull Fleming Museum			
61 Colchester Ave			
University of Vermont..............Burlington VT 05405	888-382-1222	802-656-0750	513
Robert J Dole VA Medical Center			
5500 E Kellogg St ....Wichita KS 67218	888-878-6881	316-685-2221	371-3
Robert Kaufman Company Inc			
PO Box 59266 ....Los Angeles CA 90059	800-877-2066	310-538-3482	587
Robert Mondavi Co			
7801 St Helena Hwy ....Oakville CA 94562	888-766-6328	707-226-1395	79-3
Chicago			
401 S State St ....Chicago IL 60605	800-762-5960	312-935-6800	166
DuPage			
905 Meridian Lk Dr ....Aurora IL 60504	800-762-5960*	630-375-8100	166
*Admissions			
Robert Morris College			
Orland Park			
43 Orland Sq Dr ....Orland Park IL 60462	800-225-1520	708-226-3800	166
Springfield			
3101 Montvale Dr ....Springfield IL 62704	800-762-5960	217-793-2500	166
Robert Morris University			
6001 University Blvd ....Moon Township PA 15108	800-762-0097	412-262-8200	166
Robert Morris University Institute of Culinary Arts			
401 S State St ....Chicago IL 60605	800-762-5960	312-935-4100	161
Dupage			
905 Meridian Lk Dr ....Aurora IL 60504	800-762-5960		161
Robert N Karpp Company Inc			
480 E First St ....Boston MA 02127	800-244-5886	617-269-5880	192-2
Robert Packer Hospital			
One Guthrie Sq ....Sayre PA 18840	888-448-8474	570-888-6666	371-3
Robert R McCormick Tribune Foundation			
205 N Michigan Ave Ste 4300 ....Chicago IL 60611	800-435-7352	312-445-5000	304
Robert S Fisher & Company Inc			
280 Sheffield St ....Mountainside NJ 07092	800-526-8052	908-928-0002	406
Robert Treat Hotel			
50 Pk Pl ....Newark NJ 07102	800-569-2300	973-622-1000	376
Robert W Baird & Company Inc			
PO Box 672 ....Milwaukee WI 53201	800-792-2473	414-765-3500	681
Robert Wood Johnson University Hospital			
1 Robert Wood Johnson Pl ....New Brunswick NJ 08901	888-637-9584	732-828-3000	371-3
Roberts Automatic Products Inc			
880 Lake Dr ....Chanhassen MN 55317	800-879-9837	952-949-1000	614
Roberts Dairy Co			
2901 Cuming St ....Omaha NE 68131	800-779-4321	402-344-4321	296-4
Roberts Hawaii Inc			
680 Iwilei Rd Ste 700 ....Honolulu HI 96817	800-831-5541	808-523-7750	750
Roberts Wesleyan College			
2301 Westside Dr ....Rochester NY 14624	800-777-4792*	585-594-6000	166
*Admissions			
Roberts-Gordon Inc			
1250 William St PO Box 44 ....Buffalo NY 14240	800-828-7450	716-852-4400	354
Roberts-Hamilton			
6601 Pkwy Cir Ste A..........Brooklyn Center MN 55430	800-888-2222	763-315-0100	605
Robertshaw Industrial Products			
1602 Mustang Dr ....Maryville TN 37801	800-228-7429	865-981-3100	202
Robertson Furniture Company Inc			
890 Elberton St ....Toccoa GA 30577	800-241-0713	706-886-1494	318-1
Robertson Heating Supply Co			
2155 W Main St ....Alliance OH 44601	800-433-9532	330-821-9180	605
Robertson Inc			
97 Bronte St N ....Milton ON L9T2N8	800-268-5090	905-878-2861	278
Robertson Manufacturing Inc			
112 Woodland Ave ....West Grove PA 19390	800-260-5423	610-869-9600	723

	Toll-Free	Phone	Class
Robertson Transformer Co			
13611 Thornton Rd ....Blue Island IL 60406	800-323-5633	708-388-2315	191
Robinson Ctr			
101 S. Spring St			
PO Box 3232 ....Little Rock AR 72201	800-844-4781	501-376-4781	565
Robinson Helicopter Co			
2901 Airport Dr ....Torrance CA 90505	800-905-0655	310-539-0508	20
Robinson Industries Inc			
3051 W Curtis Rd ....Coleman MI 48618	877-465-4055	989-465-6111	541
Robinson Mfg Company Inc			
798 Market St PO Box 338 ....Dayton TN 37321	800-251-7286	423-775-2212	153-17
Robishaw Engineering Inc			
10106 Matheson Ln ....Houston TX 77043	800-877-1706	713-468-1706	689
Robotics Institute			
Carnegie Mellon University			
5000 Forbes Ave. ....Pittsburgh PA 15213	800-767-8483	412-268-3818	659
Robson Communities			
9532 E Riggs Rd ....Sun Lakes AZ 85248	800-732-9949		644
Robson Forensic Inc			
354 N Prince St ....Lancaster PA 17603	800-813-6736	717-293-9050	195
ROC (Rutgers Organics Corp)			
201 Struble Rd ....State College PA 16801	888-469-2188	814-238-2424	141
Roche Diagnostics Corp (RDC)			
9115 Hague Rd PO Box 50457.......Indianapolis IN 46250	800-428-5076*	317-521-2000	231
*Cust Svc			
Roche Palo Alto LLC			
4300 Hacienda Dr ....Pleasanton CA 94588	866-796-1569	925-730-8000	84
Rochester College			
800 W Avon Rd ....Rochester Hills MI 48307	800-521-6010	248-218-2011	166
Rochester Community & Technical College			
851 30th Ave SE ....Rochester MN 55904	800-247-1296	507-285-7210	160
Rochester Convention & Visitors Bureau			
30 Civic Ctr Dr SE Ste 200 ......Rochester MN 55904	800-634-8277	507-288-4331	207
Rochester Eye & Tissue Bank			
524 White Spruce Blvd ....Rochester NY 14623	800-568-4321	585-272-7890	269
Rochester Gas & Electric Corp			
89 E Ave ....Rochester NY 14649	800-743-2110		775
Rochester Gauges Inc of Texas			
11616 Harry Hines Blvd ....Dallas TX 75229	800-821-1829	972-241-2161	202
Rochester General Health System (RGHS)			
1425 Portland Ave ....Rochester NY 14621	877-922-5465	585-922-4000	371-3
Rochester Medical Corp			
1 Rochester Medical Dr ....Stewartville MN 55976	800-243-3315	507-533-9600	471
NASDAQ: ROCM			
Rochester Midland Corp			
333 Hollenbeck St ....Rochester NY 14621	800-836-1627	585-336-2200	143
Rock & Gem Magazine			
290 Maple Ct Ste 232 ....Ventura CA 93003	866-377-4666	805-644-3824	452-14
Rock 'N Learn Inc			
105 Commercial Cir ....Conroe TX 77304	800-348-8445	936-539-2731	243
Rock 103			
2650 Thousand Oaks Blvd			
Ste 4100 ....Memphis TN 38118	800-444-9347	901-259-1300	636-66
Rock Bridge Memorial State Park			
5901 S Hwy 163 ....Columbia MO 65203	800-334-6946	573-449-7402	558
Rock City Gardens			
1400 Patten Rd ....Lookout Mountain GA 30750	800-854-0675	706-820-2531	49-4
Rock Creek Resort			
6380 US Hwy 212 ....Red Lodge MT 59068	800-667-1119	406-446-1111	660
Rock Island Argus			
1724 Fourth Ave ....Rock Island IL 61201	800-660-2472	309-786-6441	525-2
Rock of Ages Corp			
560 Graniteville Rd ....Graniteville VT 05654	800-421-0166	802-476-3119	715
Rock River Lumber & Grain Co			
5502 Lyndon Rd PO Box 68 ....Prophetstown IL 61277	800-605-4333	815-537-5131	295-23
Rock River Valley Blood Ctr			
3065 N Perryville Rd Ste 105 ....Rockford IL 61114	877-778-2299*	815-965-8751	88
*General			
Rock Springs Chamber of Commerce			
1897 Dewar Dr ....Rock Springs WY 82901	800-463-8637	307-362-3771	137
Rock Springs National Bank			
200 Second St PO Box 880 ......Rock Springs WY 82902	800-469-8801	307-362-8801	68
Rock Springs Run State Reserve			
30601 CR 433 ....Sorrento FL 32776	800-326-3521	407-884-2008	558
Rock TENN			
1415 W 44th St ....Chicago IL 60609	877-643-5414	773-254-1030	99
Rock Valley College			
3301 N Mulford Rd ....Rockford IL 61114	800-973-7821	815-921-7821	160
Rock View Resort			
1049 Parkview Dr ....Hollister MO 65672	800-375-9530	417-334-4678	376
Rock Wool Manufacturing Co			
1400 Seventh Ct PO Box 506 ....Leeds AL 35094	800-874-7625*	205-699-6121	386
*Sales			
Rocket Box Inc			
125 E 144th St ....Bronx NY 10451	800-762-5521	718-292-5370	200
Rocket Supply Corp			
404 N Rt 115 PO Box 98.........Roberts IL 60962	800-252-6871		509
Rockford Area Convention & Visitors Bureau			
102 N Main St ....Rockford IL 61101	800-521-0849	815-963-8111	207
Rockford Art Museum			
711 N Main St ....Rockford IL 61103	800-521-0849	815-968-2787	513
Rockford Chamber of Commerce			
308 W State St Ste 190 ....Rockford IL 61101	888-375-3000	815-987-8100	137
Rockford College			
5050 E State St ....Rockford IL 61108	800-892-2984	815-226-4000	166
Rockford Corp			
600 S Rockford Dr ....Tempe AZ 85281	800-903-2897	480-967-3565	51
OTC: ROFO			
Rockford Industrial Welding Supply Inc			
4646 Linden Rd ....Rockford IL 61109	800-226-1904	815-226-1900	383
Rockford Institute			
928 N Main St ....Rockford IL 61103	800-383-0680	815-964-5053	625
Rockford MetroCentre			
300 Elm St ....Rockford IL 61101	800-745-3000	815-968-5600	711
Rockford Process Control Inc			
2020 Seventh St ....Rockford IL 61104	800-228-3779	815-966-2000	347
Rockford Register Star			
99 E State St ....Rockford IL 61104	800-383-7827	815-987-1200	525-2
Rockford Systems Inc			
4620 Hydraulic Rd ....Rockford IL 61109	800-922-7533*	815-874-7891	204
*Cust Svc			
Rockhill-York County Convention & Visitors Bureau			
452 S Anderson Rd ....Rock Hill SC 29730	888-702-1320	803-329-5200	207

	Toll-Free	Phone	Class
Rockhurst University			
1100 Rockhurst Rd ....Kansas City MO 64110	800-842-6776	816-501-4000	166
Rockhurst University Continuing Education Ctr Inc			
PO Box 419107 ....Kansas City MO 64141	800-258-7246	913-432-7755	755
Rocking Horse Ranch Resort			
600 Rt 44-55 ....Highland NY 12528	800-647-2624	845-691-2927	660
Rockingham Memorial Hospital (RMH)			
2010 Health Campus Dr ....Harrisonburg VA 22801	800-736-8272	540-689-1000	371-3
Rockingham New Holland Inc			
600 W Market St ....Harrisonburg VA 22802	888-864-5503	540-434-6791	274
Rock-It Cargo USA Inc			
5438 W 104th St			
PO Box 90519. ....Los Angeles CA 90045	800-973-1727	310-410-0935	310
Rockland Community College			
145 College Rd ....Suffern NY 10901	800-722-7666	845-574-4000	160
Rockland Federal Credit Union			
241 Union St ....Rockland MA 02370	800-562-7328	781-878-0232	219
Rockland Immunochemicals Inc			
PO Box 326 ....Gilbertsville PA 19525	800-656-7625	610-369-1008	231
Rocklin Area Chamber of Commerce			
3700 Rocklin Rd ....Rocklin CA 95677	800-228-3380	916-624-2548	137
Rocklin Park Hotel			
5450 China Garden Rd ....Rocklin CA 95677	888-630-9400	916-630-9400	376
Rockmount Ranch Wear Manufacturing Co			
1626 Wazee St ....Denver CO 80202	800-776-2566	303-629-7777	153-19
Rockport Company Inc			
1895 JW Foster Blvd ....Canton MA 02021	800-828-0545	781-401-5000	300
Rockport Schooner Cruises			
PO Box 272 ....Belfast ME 04915	866-732-2473	207-338-3088	220
Rock-Tenn Co			
504 Thrasher St ....Norcross GA 30071	877-643-5414	770-448-2193	99
NYSE: RKT			
Rockview Dairies Inc			
7011 Stewart & Gray Rd ....Downey CA 90241	800-423-2479	562-927-5511	296-4
Rockwell Collins Inc			
400 Collins Rd NE ....Cedar Rapids IA 52498	888-721-3094	319-295-1000	522
NYSE: COL			
Rockwell Farms Inc			
332 Rockwell Farms Rd ....Rockwell NC 28138	800-635-6576		366
Rockwell Medical Inc			
30142 Wixom Rd ....Wixom MI 48393	800-449-3353	248-960-9009	250
NASDAQ: RMTI			
Rockwood Retaining Walls Inc			
7200 Hwy 63 N ....Rochester MN 55906	800-535-2375	888-288-4045	184
Rockwood Retirement Community			
2903 E 25th Ave ....Spokane WA 99223	800-727-6650	509-536-6650	663
Rocky Mount Area Chamber of Commerce			
100 Coastline St Ste 200 ....Rocky Mount NC 27804	800-682-6746	252-446-0323	137
Rocky Mount Cord Co			
381 N Grace St ....Rocky Mount NC 27804	800-342-9130*	252-977-9130	209
*Orders			
Rocky Mount Museum			
200 Hyder Hill Rd			
PO Box 160. ....Piney Flats TN 37686	888-538-1791	423-538-7396	513
Rocky Mountain Chocolate Factory Inc (RMCF)			
265 Turner Dr ....Durango CO 81303	888-525-2462*	970-259-0554	122
NASDAQ: RMCF ▪ *Cust Svc			
Rocky Mountain College			
1511 Poly Dr ....Billings MT 59102	800-877-6259	406-657-1000	166
Rocky Mountain Fabrication Inc			
PO Box 16409 ....Salt Lake City UT 84116	888-763-5307	801-596-2400	90
Rocky Mountain Hardware Inc			
1020 Airport Way PO Box 4108 ....Hailey ID 83333	888-788-2013	208-788-2013	347
Rocky Mountain Health Foundation			
2775 Crossroads Blvd ....Grand Junction CO 81506	800-843-0719	970-248-5027	47-17
Rocky Mountain Health Plans			
2775 Crossroads Blvd			
PO Box 10600. ....Grand Junction CO 81502	800-843-0719	970-244-7760	388-3
Rocky Mountain Lions Eye Bank (RMLEB)			
1675 Aurora Crt Ste E|2049			
PO Box 6026. ....Aurora CO 80045	800-444-7479	720-848-3937	269
Rocky Mountain Orthodontics Inc (RMO Inc)			
650 W Colfax Ave ....Denver CO 80204	800-525-6375	303-592-8200	228
Rocky Mountain Public Broadcasting Network (RMPB)			
1089 Bannock St ....Denver CO 80204	800-274-6666	303-892-6666	624
Rocky Mountain Tissue Bank			
2993 S Peoria St Ste 390 ....Aurora CO 80014	800-424-5169	303-337-3330	538
Rocky Rococo			
105 E Wisconsin Ave ....Oconomowoc WI 53066	800-888-7625	262-569-5580	661
Rocky Shoes & Boots Inc			
39 E Canal St ....Nelsonville OH 45764	877-795-2410	740-753-3130	300
NASDAQ: RCKY			
Rodey Dickason Sloan Akin & Robb P A			
201 Third St NW Ste 2200 ....Albuquerque NM 87102	800-226-2935	505-765-5900	425
Rodney Hunt Co			
46 Mill St ....Orange MA 01364	800-448-8860	978-544-2511	475
Rodney Strong Vineyards			
11455 Old Redwood Hwy ....Healdsburg CA 95448	800-678-4763	707-431-1533	79-3
Roe Dental Laboratory Inc			
9565 Midwest Ave ....Garfield Heights OH 44125	800-228-6663	216-663-2233	412
Roeder Implement Inc			
2550 Rockdale Rd ....Dubuque IA 52003	800-557-1184	563-557-1184	274
Roeder Travel Ltd			
9805 York Rd ....Cockeysville MD 21030	800-379-9887	410-667-6090	761
Roehl Transport Inc			
1916 E 29th St PO Box 750 ....Marshfield WI 54449	800-826-8367	715-591-3795	770
Roesch Inc			
100 N 24th St ....Belleville IL 62222	800-423-6243		476
Roffman Miller Assoc Inc			
1835 Market St Ste 500 ....Philadelphia PA 19103	800-995-1030	215-981-1030	398
Rogan Corp			
3455 Woodhead Dr ....Northbrook IL 60062	800-584-5662	847-498-2300	601
Roger Dean Chevrolet Inc			
2235 Okeechobee Blvd ....West Palm Beach FL 33409	877-827-4705	561-683-8100	56
Roger Dean Stadium			
4751 Main St ....Jupiter FL 33458	800-926-7678	561-775-1818	711
Roger Smith Hotel			
501 Lexington Ave ....New York NY 10017	800-445-0277	212-755-1400	376
Roger Ward Inc			
17275 Green Mtn Rd ....San Antonio TX 78247	888-909-3147*	210-655-8623	770
*General			
Roger Williams University			
One Old Ferry Rd ....Bristol RI 02809	800-458-7144	401-254-3500	166

Company / Address	City	State	ZIP	Toll-Free	Phone	Class
Roger Williams University Ralph R Papitto School of Law						
10 Metacom Ave	Bristol	RI	02809	**800-633-2727**	401-254-4500	167-1
Rogers Bros Corp						
100 Orchard St	Albion	PA	16401	**800-441-9880**	814-756-4121	769
Rogers Corp						
One Technology Dr	Rogers	CT	06263	**800-227-6437**	860-774-9605	598-2
Rogers Jewelry Co						
PO Box 3151	Modesto	CA	95353	**800-877-4221**		407
Rogers Memorial Hospital Inc						
34700 Valley Rd	Oconomowoc	WI	53066	**800-767-4411**	262-646-4411	371-5
Rogers Printing Inc						
PO Box 215	Ravenna	MI	49451	**800-622-5591**	231-853-2244	619
Rogers State University						
1701 W Will Rogers Blvd	Claremore	OK	74017	**800-256-7511**	918-343-7546	166
Rogers State University Bartlesville						
1701 W Will Rogers Blvd	Claremore	OK	74107	**800-256-7511**	918-343-7777	160
Rogers State University Pryor						
421 S Elliott St	Pryor	OK	74361	**800-256-7511**	918-825-6117	160
Rogers Supply Company Inc						
PO Box 740	Champaign	IL	61824	**800-252-0406**	217-356-0166	656
Rogers Wireless Communications Inc						
333 Bloor St. E, 4th Fl	Toronto	ON	M4W1G9	**800-575-9090**	888-764-3771	726
Rogers-Lowell Area Chamber of Commerce						
317 W Walnut St	Rogers	AR	72756	**800-364-1240**	479-636-1240	137
Rogue Community College						
3345 Redwood Hwy	Grants Pass	OR	97527	**800-411-6508**	541-956-7500	160
Rogue Valley Manor						
1200 Mira Mar Ave	Medford	OR	97504	**800-848-7868**	541-857-7214	663
Rogue Wave Software Inc						
5500 Flatiron Pkwy	Boulder	CO	80301	**800-487-3217**	303-473-9118	179-2
Rohnert Park Chamber of Commerce						
101 Golf Course Dr Ste C-7	Rohnert Park	CA	94928	**888-364-7379**	707-584-1415	137
Rohrer Corp						
717 Seville Rd PO Box 1009	Wadsworth	OH	44282	**800-243-6640**	330-335-1541	601
Ro-Lab American Rubber Co Inc						
8830 W Linne Rd	Tracy	CA	95304	**800-678-0726**	209-836-0965	367
Roland Cooper State Park						
285 Deer Run Dr	Camden	AL	36726	**800-252-7275**	334-682-4838	558
Roland DGA Corp						
15363 Barranca Pkwy	Irvine	CA	92618	**800-542-2307**	949-727-2100	174-6
Roland Machinery Co						
816 N Dirksen Pkwy	Springfield	IL	62702	**800-252-2926**	217-789-7711	355
Roland's Electric Inc						
307 Suburban Ave Ste A	Deer Park	NY	11729	**800-981-8010**	631-242-8080	775
Rolf C. Hagen Corp						
305 Forbes Blvd	Mansfield	MA	02048	**800-724-2436***	508-339-9531	571
*Cust Svc						
Rolf Institute of Structural Integration						
5055 Chaparral Ct Ste 103	Boulder	CO	80301	**800-530-8875**	303-449-5903	47-17
Roll Call						
77 K St NE	Washington	DC	20002	**800-432-2250**	202-650-6500	524-7
Roll Shutter Systems Inc						
21633 N 14th Ave	Phoenix	AZ	85027	**800-551-7655**	623-869-7057	690
Rolla Area Chamber of Commerce						
1311 KingsHwy	Rolla	MO	65401	**888-809-3817**	573-364-3577	137
Roll-A-Way Inc						
1661 Glenlake Ave	Itasca	IL	60143	**866-749-5424**		690
Rolled Alloys Inc						
125 W Sterns Rd	Temperance	MI	48182	**800-521-0332**	734-847-0561	487
Rolled Steel Products Corp						
2187 Garfield Ave	Los Angeles	CA	90040	**800-400-7833**	323-723-8836	487
Rollex Corp						
800 Chasa Ave	Elk Grove Village	IL	60007	**800-251-3300***	847-437-3000	688
*Cust Svc						
Rolling Hills Electric Co-op Inc						
122 W Main St PO Box 307	Mankato	KS	66956	**877-906-5903**	785-378-3151	245
Rolling Oaks Mall						
6909 N Loop 1604 E	San Antonio	TX	78247	**877-746-6642**	210-651-5513	455
Rolling Shield Inc						
2500 NW 74th Ave	Miami	FL	33122	**800-474-9404**		690
Rolling Stone Magazine						
1290 Ave of the Americas						
2nd Fl	New York	NY	10104	**800-283-1549**		452-9
Rollins College						
1000 Holt Ave	Winter Park	FL	32789	**800-799-2586**	407-646-2000	166
Rollprint Packaging Products Inc						
320 S Stewart Ave	Addison	IL	60101	**800-276-7629**	630-628-1700	541
Rolls-Royce Engine Services Inc						
7200 Earhart Rd	Oakland	CA	94621	**866-793-4273**	510-613-1000	24
Rolls-Royce North America						
1875 Explorer St Ste 200	Reston	VA	20190	**888-269-2377**	703-834-1700	21
Rollstock Inc						
5720 Brighton Ave	Kansas City	MO	64130	**800-295-2949**	616-570-0430	540
Rollx Vans						
6591 Hwy 13 W	Savage	MN	55378	**800-956-6668**	952-890-7851	61-7
Rolta Tusc Inc						
333 E Butterfield Rd Ste 900	Lombard	IL	60148	**800-755-8872**	630-960-2909	181
Romac Industries Inc						
21919 20th Ave SE	Bothell	WA	98021	**800-426-9341**	425-951-6200	588
Roman Research Inc						
800 Franklin St	Hanson	MA	02341	**800-225-8652**		412
Romanoff International Supply Corp						
Nine Deforest St	Amityville	NY	11701	**800-221-7448***	631-842-2400	404
*Cust Svc						
Romar Transportation Systems Inc						
3500 S Kedzie Ave	Chicago	IL	60632	**800-621-5416**	773-376-8800	310
Rome Specialty Company Inc Rosco Div						
501 W Embargo St	Rome	NY	13440	**800-794-8357**	315-337-8200	701
Rome Tool & Die Company Inc						
113 Hemlock St	Rome	GA	30161	**800-241-3369**	706-234-6743	747
Romeo Community School District						
316 N Main St	Romeo	MI	48065	**888-427-6818**	586-752-0200	676
Romero Mazda						
1307 Kettering Dr	Ontario	CA	91761	**888-317-2233**	909-390-8484	56
Romika USA LLC						
3405 Del Webb Ave NE	Salem	OR	97301	**888-777-4174**	503-485-1848	300
Ron Carter Automotive Group						
3205 FM 528	Alvin	TX	77511	**800-531-8285**	281-331-3111	56
Ron Foth Adv						
8100 N High St	Columbus	OH	43235	**888-766-3684**	614-888-7771	4
Ron Jon Surf Shop						
3850 S Banana River Blvd	Cocoa Beach	FL	32931	**888-757-8737**	321-799-8888	702
Ron Kendall Masonry Inc						
101 Benoist Farms Rd	West Palm Beach	FL	33411	**866-844-1404**	561-793-5924	190-7

Company / Address	City	State	ZIP	Toll-Free	Phone	Class
RONA Inc						
220 Ch du Tremblay	Boucherville	QC	J4B8H7	**877-599-5900**	514-599-5100	361
TSE: RON						
Ronald Blue & Company LLC						
300 Colonial Ctr Pkwy Ste 300	Roswell	GA	30076	**800-841-0362**	770-280-6000	398
Akron 245 Locust St	Akron	OH	44302	**800-262-0333**	330-253-5400	370
Albany 139 S Lake Ave	Albany	NY	12208	**866-244-8464**	518-438-2655	370
Ronald McDonald House						
Albuquerque						
1011 Yale Ave NE	Albuquerque	NM	87106	**877-842-8960**	505-842-8960	370
Ann Arbor						
1600 Washington Heights	Ann Arbor	MI	48104	**800-544-8684**	734-994-4442	370
Camden 550 Mickle Blvd	Camden	NJ	08103	**877-858-3539**	856-966-4663	370
Chapel Hill						
101 Old Mason Farm Rd	Chapel Hill	NC	27517	**800-835-5479**	919-913-2040	370
Chattanooga						
200 Central Ave	Chattanooga	TN	37403	**855-670-4787**	423-778-4300	370
Cleveland						
10415 Euclid Ave	Cleveland	OH	44106	**800-223-2273**	216-229-5758	370
Detroit 3911 Beaubien	Detroit	MI	48201	**800-426-7667**	313-745-5909	370
Durham						
506 Alexander Ave	Durham	NC	27705	**866-244-8464**	919-286-9305	370
Falls Church						
3312 Gallows Rd	Falls Church	VA	22042	**855-227-7435**	703-698-7080	370
Fort Myers						
16100 Roserush Ct	Fort Myers	FL	33908	**800-435-7352**	239-437-0202	370
Galveston						
301 14th St	Galveston	TX	77550	**800-275-2946**	409-762-8770	370
Hershey						
745 W Governor Rd	Hershey	PA	17033	**800-732-0999**	717-533-4001	370
Huntington						
1500 17th St	Huntington	WV	25701	**855-227-7435**	304-529-1122	370
Kansas City						
2502 Cherry St	Kansas City	MO	64108	**888-353-4537**	816-842-8321	370
Las Vegas						
2323 Potosi St	Las Vegas	NV	89146	**888-248-1561**	702-252-4663	370
Philadelphia						
3925 Chestnut St	Philadelphia	PA	19104	**800-723-0999**	215-387-8406	370
Providence						
45 Gay St	Providence	RI	02905	**888-353-4537**	401-274-4447	370
Richmond						
2330 Monument Ave	Richmond	VA	23220	**800-368-3472**	804-355-6517	370
Scranton						
332 Wheeler Ave	Scranton	PA	18510	**800-775-9610**	570-969-8998	370
Seattle						
5130 40th Ave NE	Seattle	WA	98105	**866-987-9330**	206-838-0600	370
Wilmington						
1901 Rockland Rd	Wilmington	DE	19803	**888-656-4847**	302-656-4847	370
Winston-Salem						
419 S Hawthorne Rd	Winston-Salem	NC	27103	**855-227-7435**	336-723-0228	370
Ronald McDonald House Charities (RMHC)						
1 Kroc Dr Dept 014	Oak Brook	IL	60523	**855-670-4787**	630-623-7048	47-5
Gainesville						
1600 SW 14th St	Gainesville	FL	32608	**800-435-7352**	352-374-4404	370
Ronald Reagan Bldg & International Trade Ctr						
1300 Pennsylvania Ave NW	Washington	DC	20004	**800-734-7393**	202-312-1300	809
Ronald Reagan Presidential Library & Museum						
40 Presidential Dr	Simi Valley	CA	93065	**800-410-8354**	805-577-4000	431-2
Ronan Engineering Co						
21200 Oxnard St	Woodland Hills	CA	91367	**800-327-6626**		202
Ronis Bros						
39 Harriet Pl	Lynbrook	NY	11563	**888-555-1234**	516-887-5266	459
Roofing Wholesale Co Inc						
1918 W Grant St	Phoenix	AZ	85009	**800-528-4532***	602-258-3794	192-4
*Cust Svc						
Rooftop Media Inc						
530 Howard St Ste 400	San Francisco	CA	94105	**800-860-0293**		115
Room & Board Inc						
4600 Olson Memorial Hwy	Golden Valley	MN	55422	**800-301-9720**	763-521-4431	318-2
Room 214 Inc						
3390 Valmont Rd Ste 214	Boulder	CO	80301	**866-624-1851**		7
Roosevelt & Cross Inc						
One Exchange Plz 55 Broadway						
22nd Fl	New York	NY	10006	**800-348-3426**	212-344-2500	681
Roosevelt Field Mall						
630 Old Country Rd	Garden City	NY	11530	**877-746-6642**	516-742-8001	455
Roosevelt Hotel						
45 E 45th St	New York	NY	10017	**888-833-3969**	212-661-9600	376
Roosevelt Paper Co						
One Roosevelt Dr	Mount Laurel	NJ	08054	**800-523-3470**	856-303-4100	546
Roosevelt University						
430 S Michigan Ave	Chicago	IL	60605	**877-277-5978***	312-341-3500	166
*Admissions						
Albert A Robin						
1400 N Roosevelt Blvd	Schaumburg	IL	60173	**877-277-5978***	847-619-8600	166
*Admissions						
Root Candles Co						
623 W Liberty St	Medina	OH	44256	**800-289-7668**	330-725-6677	121
Root Inc						
5470 Main St	Sylvania	OH	43560	**800-852-1315**		197
Root-Lowell Manufacturing Co						
1000 Foreman Rd PO Box 289	Lowell	MI	49331	**800-748-0098**	616-897-9211	273
RootsWeb.com						
360 W 4800 N	Provo	UT	84604	**800-262-3787**	801-705-7000	394
Roper Industries Inc						
6901 Professional Pkwy Ste 200	Sarasota	FL	34240	**888-227-3565**	941-556-2601	202
NYSE: ROP						
Roper Pump Co						
3475 Old Maysville Rd	Commerce	GA	30529	**800-944-6769***	706-335-5551	632
*Sales						
Roplast Industries Inc						
3155 S Fifth Ave	Oroville	CA	95965	**800-767-5278**	530-532-9500	65
Roppe Corp						
1602 N Union St	Fostoria	OH	44830	**800-537-9527**	419-435-8546	291
Rorke Data Inc						
7626 Golden Triangle Dr	Eden Prairie	MN	55344	**800-328-8147**	952-829-0300	175
Rosalind Franklin University of Medicine & Science						
3333 Green Bay Rd	North Chicago	IL	60064	**800-254-0460**	847-578-3205	167-2
Rosamond Gifford Zoo at Burnet Park						
1 Conservation Pl	Syracuse	NY	13204	**800-724-5006**	315-435-8511	810
Rosario Resort & Spa						
1400 Rosario Rd	Eastsound	WA	98245	**800-562-8820**	360-376-2222	660
Rosback Co						
125 Hawthorne Ave	Saint Joseph	MI	49085	**800-542-2420**	269-983-2582	621

	Toll-Free	Phone	Class
Rosco Laboratories Inc			
52 Harbor View Ave . . . . Stamford CT 06902	800-767-2669	203-708-8900	713
Roscoe Co			
3535 W Harrison St . . . . Chicago IL 60624	888-476-7263*	773-722-5000	438
*Cust Svc			
Roscoe Village			
600 N Whitewoman St . . . . Coshocton OH 43812	800-877-1830	740-622-7644	513
Rose & Kiernan Inc			
99 Troy Rd . . . . East Greenbush NY 12061	866-488-6582	518-244-4245	388-5
Rose Assoc Inc			
200 Madison Ave . . . . New York NY 10016	888-475-8860	212-210-6666	643
Rose City Printing & Packaging Inc			
900 SE Tech Crt Dr . . . . Vancouver WA 98683	800-704-8693		100
Rose Displays Ltd			
35 Congress St . . . . Salem MA 01970	800-631-9707	978-219-8100	195
Rose Hotel			
807 Main St . . . . Pleasanton CA 94566	800-843-9540	925-846-8802	376
Rose Medical Ctr			
4567 E Ninth Ave . . . . Denver CO 80220	866-746-4282	303-320-2121	371-3
Rose Packing Company Inc			
65 S Barrington Rd . . . . South Barrington IL 60010	800-323-7363	847-381-5700	468
Rose Printing Company Inc			
2503 Jackson Bluff Rd . . . . Tallahassee FL 32304	800-227-3725	850-576-4151	618
Rose Products & Services Inc			
545 Stimmel Rd . . . . Columbus OH 43223	800-264-1568	614-443-7647	403
Roseau Electric Co-op Inc			
1107 Third St NE . . . . Roseau MN 56751	888-847-8840	218-463-1543	245
Rosebud Mfg Co Inc			
701 SE 12th St . . . . Madison SD 57042	800-256-4561	605-256-4561	114
Roseburg Forest Products Co			
PO Box 1088 . . . . Roseburg OR 97470	800-245-1115	541-679-3311	674
Roseburg National Cemetery			
1770 Harvard Blvd . . . . Roseburg OR 97470	800-535-1117	541-826-2511	135
Rosecroft Raceway			
6336 Rosecroft Dr . . . . . Fort Washington MD 20744	877-818-9467	301-567-4500	132
Rosedale on Robson Suite Hotel			
838 Hamilton St . . . . Vancouver BC V6B6A2	800-661-8870	604-689-8033	376
Rosedown Plantation State Historic Site			
12501 Hwy 10 . . . . Saint Francisville LA 70775	888-376-1867	225-635-3332	49-2
Rose-Hulman Institute of Technology			
5500 Wabash Ave . . . . Terre Haute IN 47803	800-248-7448*	812-877-1511	166
*Admissions			
Rosellen Suites at Stanley Park			
2030 Barclay St . . . . Vancouver BC V6G1L5	888-317-6648	604-689-4807	376
Rosemont College			
1400 Montgomery Ave . . . . Rosemont PA 19010	800-331-0708*	610-527-0200	166
*Admissions			
Rosemount Analytical Inc Process Analytical Div			
6565 P Davis Industrial Pkwy . . . . Solon OH 44139	800-433-6076	440-914-1261	202
Rosen Centre Hotel			
9840 International Dr . . . . Orlando FL 32819	800-204-7234	407-996-9840	376
Rosen Hotels & Resorts Inc			
9840 International Dr . . . . Orlando FL 32819	800-204-7234	407-996-9840	376
Rosen Plaza Hotel			
9700 International Dr . . . . Orlando FL 32819	800-366-9700	407-996-9700	376
Rosen Publishing Group Inc, The			
29 E 21st St . . . . New York NY 10010	800-237-9932		628-2
Rosen Shingle Creek			
9939 Universal Blvd . . . . Orlando FL 32819	866-996-9939	407-996-9939	376
Rosenbaum Family House			
1 Medical Ctr Dr PO Box 8228 . . . Morgantown WV 26506	855-988-2273	304-598-6094	369
Rosenberg-Richmond Area Chamber of Commerce			
4120 Ave H . . . . Rosenberg TX 77471	877-382-7414	281-342-5464	137
Rosencrantz-Bemis Water Well Co			
1105 Hwy 281 Bypass . . . . Great Bend KS 67530	800-466-2467	620-793-5512	190-15
Rosendin Electric Inc			
880 N Mabury Rd . . . . San Jose CA 95133	800-540-4734*	408-286-2800	190-4
*General			
Rosenthal & Rosenthal Inc			
1370 Broadway . . . . New York NY 10018	800-999-4800	212-356-1400	272
Rosetta Resources Inc			
717 Texas Ste 2800 . . . . Houston TX 77002	800-526-2112	713-335-4000	531
NASDAQ: ROSE			
Rosetta Stone Ltd			
1919 N Lynn St 7th Fl. . . . . Arlington VA 22209	800-788-0822		676
NYSE: RST			
Rosewood Hotels & Resorts			
500 Crescent Ct Ste 300. . . . . Dallas TX 75201	888-767-3966	214-880-4200	376
Rosewood Retirement Community			
1301 New Stine Rd . . . . Bakersfield CA 93309	800-984-4216	661-834-0620	663
Roslyn Claremont Hotel			
1221 Old Northern Blvd . . . . Roslyn NY 11576	800-626-9005	516-625-2700	376
Rosner Auto Group			
3507 Jefferson Davis Hwy. . . . . . Fredericksburg VA 22408	855-271-7618*	855-265-5075	56
*Sales			
Ross & Wallace Paper Products Inc			
204 Old Covington Hwy . . . . Hammond LA 70403	800-854-2300		64
Ross Controls			
1250 Stephenson Hwy . . . . Troy MI 48083	800-438-7677	248-764-1800	778
Ross Industries Inc			
5321 Midland Rd . . . . Midland VA 22728	800-336-6010	540-439-3271	297
Ross Matthews Mills Inc			
657 Quarry St . . . . Fall River MA 02723	800-753-7677	508-677-0601	734-5
Ross Memorial Hospital (RMH)			
10 Angeline St N . . . . Lindsay ON K9V4M8	800-510-7365	705-324-6111	371-2
Ross Metals Corp			
27 W 47th St . . . . New York NY 10036	800-334-7191		480
Ross Optical Industries Inc			
1410 Gail Borden Pl . . . . El Paso TX 79935	800-880-5417	915-595-5417	537
Ross Realty Investments Inc			
3325 S University Dr Ste 210 . . . . Davie FL 33328	800-370-4202	954-452-5000	643
Ross Reels			
11 Ponderosa Ct . . . . Montrose CO 81401	866-587-6747	970-249-0606	701
Ross Simons Jewelers Inc			
Nine Ross Simons Dr . . . . Cranston RI 02920	800-835-0919		407
Ross Smith Asset Management Inc			
601 10th Ave S W Ste 155 . . . . Calgary AB T2R0B2	888-494-6893		521
Ross Technology Corp			
104 N Maple Ave . . . . Leola PA 17540	800-345-8170	717-656-2200	90
Ross Valley School District			
110 Shaw Dr . . . . San Anselmo CA 94960	800-322-6384	415-454-2162	676
Rostra Precision Controls Inc			
2519 Dana Dr . . . . Laurinburg NC 28352	800-782-3379*	910-276-4853	522
*Cust Svc			
Roswell Bookbinding Co			
2614 N 29th Ave . . . . Phoenix AZ 85009	888-803-8883	602-272-9338	91
Roswell Chamber of Commerce			
131 W Second St . . . . Roswell NM 88202	877-849-7679	575-623-5695	137
Roswell Park Cancer Institute			
Elm and Carlton St . . . . Buffalo NY 14263	877-275-7724	716-845-2300	371-7
Roswell Park Cancer Institute Blood & Marrow Transplantation Program			
Elm & Carlton Sts . . . . Buffalo NY 14263	800-685-6825	716-845-3516	759
Rotary Forms Press Inc			
835 S High St . . . . Hillsboro OH 45133	800-654-2876	937-393-3426	109
Rotary Foundation, The			
1560 Sherman Ave . . . . Evanston IL 60201	800-435-7352	847-866-3000	47-5
Rotary Lift			
2700 Lanier Dr . . . . Madison IN 47250	800-445-5438	812-273-1622	383
Rotek Inc			
1400 S Chillicothe Rd PO Box 312. . . . . . . Aurora OH 44202	800-221-8043	330-562-4000	74
Roth Bros Inc			
PO Box 4209 . . . . Youngstown OH 44515	800-872-7684	330-793-5571	190-10
Roth Distributing Co			
11300 W 47th St . . . . Minnetonka MN 55343	800-363-3818	952-933-4428	37
Roth Pump Co			
PO Box 4330 . . . . Rock Island IL 61204	888-444-7684	309-787-1791	632
Rothbury Farms			
PO Box 202 . . . . Grand Rapids MI 49501	877-684-2879		295-1
Rothenberger USA			
4455 Boeing Dr . . . . Rockford IL 61109	800-545-7698	815-397-7617	450
Rothschild North America Inc			
1251 Ave of the Americas			
51st Fl. . . . . New York NY 10020	844-726-3863	212-403-3500	398
Rotmans Furniture & Carpet			
725 Southbridge St . . . . Worcester MA 01610	800-768-6267	508-755-5276	320
RotoMetrics Group			
800 Howerton Ln . . . . Eureka MO 63025	800-325-3851	636-587-3600	747
Rotor Clip Company Inc			
187 Davidson Ave . . . . Somerset NJ 08873	800-557-6867*	732-469-7333	325
*Cust Svc			
Roto-Rooter Inc			
255 E Fifth St			
2500 Chemed Ctr . . . . Cincinnati OH 45202	800-768-6911	513-762-6690	190-10
Rottler Mfg			
8029 S 200th St . . . . Kent WA 98032	800-452-0534	253-872-7050	450
Rough Creek Lodge			
5165 County Rd 2013 . . . . Glen Rose TX 76043	877-907-0754	254-965-3700	376
Rough Notes Company Inc, The			
11690 Technology Dr . . . . Carmel IN 46032	800-428-4384	317-582-1600	452-5
Rough Rider Industries			
3303 E Main Ave . . . . Bismarck ND 58506	800-732-0557	701-328-6161	622
Rough River Dam State Resort Park			
450 Lodge Rd . . . . Falls of Rough KY 40119	800-325-1713		558
Round Butte Seed Growers Inc			
505 C St . . . . Culver OR 97734	866-385-7001	541-546-5222	322
Round Lake Area Chamber of Commerce & Industry			
2007 Civic Ctr Way . . . . Round Lake Beach IL 60073	800-334-7661	847-546-2002	137
Round Rock Chamber of Commerce			
212 E Main St . . . . Round Rock TX 78664	800-227-7776	512-255-5805	137
Rountree Transport & Rigging Inc			
2640 N Ln Ave . . . . Jacksonville FL 32254	800-342-5036	904-781-1033	770
Roush Manufacturing Inc			
12068 Market St . . . . Livonia MI 48150	800-215-9658	734-779-7028	59
Rousseau Metal Inc			
105 Ave De Gasp Ouest . . . St Jean-Port-Joli QC G0R3G0	866-463-4270	418-598-3381	347
Route 66 Casino Hotel			
14500 Central Ave . . . . Albuquerque NM 87121	866-352-7866	505-352-7866	132
Roux Assoc Inc			
209 Shafter St . . . . Islandia NY 11749	800-322-7689	631-232-2600	194
Rowan County Convention & Visitors Bureau			
204 E Innes St Ste 120 . . . . Salisbury NC 28144	800-332-2343	704-638-3100	207
Rowan International Inc			
2800 Post Oak Blvd Ste 5450. . . . . . . Houston TX 77056	888-385-2663	713-621-7800	533
Rowan Regional Medical Ctr (RRMC)			
612 Mocksville Ave . . . . Salisbury NC 28144	888-844-0080	704-210-5000	371-3
Rowan University			
201 Mullica Hill Rd . . . . Glassboro NJ 08028	877-787-6926*	856-256-4200	166
*Admissions			
Rowe Machinery & Automation Inc			
76 Hinckley Rd . . . . Clinton ME 04927	800-247-2645	207-426-2351	489
Rowell Chemical Corp			
15 Salt Creek Ln Ste 205 . . . . Hinsdale IL 60521	888-261-7963	630-920-8833	144
Rowman & Littlefield Publishers Inc			
4501 Forbes Blvd Ste 200 . . . . Lanham MD 20706	800-462-6420	301-459-3366	628-2
Rowmark Inc			
2040 Industrial Dr . . . . Findlay OH 45840	800-243-3339	419-425-2407	592
Roxane Laboratories Inc			
1809 Wilson Rd . . . . Columbus OH 43228	800-520-1631*	614-276-4000	576
*Cust Svc			
Roy Anderson Corp			
11400 Reichold Rd . . . . Gulfport MS 39503	800-688-4003	228-896-4000	187
Roy Bros Inc			
764 Boston Rd . . . . Billerica MA 01821	800-225-0830*	978-667-1921	770
*Cust Svc			
Roy E Hanson Jr Mfg			
1600 E Washington Blvd . . . . Los Angeles CA 90021	800-421-9395	213-747-7514	90
Roy J Carver Biotechnology Ctr			
1206 W Gregory . . . . Urbana IL 61801	800-550-3033	217-333-1695	659
Royal & SunAlliance Insurance Co of Canada (RSA)			
18 York Street Suite 800 . . . . Toronto ON M5J2T8	800-268-8406	416-366-7511	388-4
Royal Alliance Assoc Inc			
One World Financial Ctr			
14th Fl . . . . New York NY 10281	800-821-5100		681
Royal Aloha Vacation Club			
1505 Dillingham Blvd Ste 212 . . . . . . Honolulu HI 96817	800-367-5212	808-847-8050	743
Royal Bank of Canada			
200 Bay St Ninth Fl S Twr . . . . Toronto ON M5J2J5	800-769-2599	416-955-7806	69
TSE: RY			
Royal Baths Manufacturing Co			
14635 Chrisman Rd . . . . Houston TX 77039	800-826-0074	281-442-3400	372
Royal Botanical Gardens (RBG)			
680 Plains Rd W . . . . Burlington ON L7T4H4	800-694-4769	905-527-1158	96
Royal British Columbia Museum (RBCM)			
675 Belleville St . . . . Victoria BC V8W9W2	888-447-7977	250-356-7226	513

	Toll-Free	Phone	Class
Royal Business Forms Inc			
3301 Ave E E ....Arlington TX 76011	800-255-9303	817-640-5248	109
Royal Canadian Military Institute			
426 University Ave ....Toronto ON M5G1S9	800-585-1072	416-597-0286	513
Royal Caribbean International			
1050 Caribbean Way ....Miami FL 33132	800-327-6700	305-539-6000	220
Royal Chemical Co			
1755 Enterprise Pkwy Ste 600 ....Twinsburg OH 44087	800-468-2975	330-467-1300	143
Royal Coach Tours			
630 Stockton Ave ....San Jose CA 95126	800-927-6925	408-279-4801	750
Royal Coachman Worldwide			
88 Ford Rd Ste 26..................Denville NJ 07834	800-472-7433	973-400-3200	437
Royal Concrete Pipe Inc			
PO Box 430 ....Stacy MN 55079	800-817-3240	651-462-2130	184
Royal Consumer Information Products Inc			
379 Campus Dr 2nd Fl ....Somerset NJ 08873	888-261-4555*	732-627-9977	110
*Sales			
Royal Crest Dairy Inc			
350 S Pearl St ....Denver CO 80209	888-226-6455	303-777-2227	295-27
Royal Cup Coffee			
160 Cleage Dr ....Birmingham AL 35217	800-366-5836*		295-7
*Cust Svc			
Royal Garden at Waikiki Hotel			
440 Olohana St ....Honolulu HI 96815	800-989-0971	808-943-0202	376
Royal Group, The			
30 Royal Group Crescent ....Woodbridge ON L4H1X9	800-263-2353	905-264-0701	235
Royal Holiday Beach Resort			
1988 Beach Blvd ....Biloxi MS 39531	800-874-0402*	228-388-7553	376
*Resv			
Royal Ice Cream Co			
6200 Euclid Ave ....Cleveland OH 44103	888-645-6606	216-432-1144	295-25
Royal Lahaina Resort			
2780 Kekaa Dr ....Lahaina HI 96761	800-222-5642	808-661-3611	660
Royal Mouldings Ltd			
135 Bearcreek Rd PO Box 610 ....Marion VA 24354	800-368-3117	276-783-8161	308
Royal Neighbor Magazine			
230 16th St ....Rock Island IL 61201	800-627-4762	309-788-4561	452-10
Royal Oak Foundation, The			
35 W 35th St Ste 1200 ....New York NY 10001	800-913-6565	212-480-2889	47-13
Royal Pacific Resort at Universal Orlando - A Loews Hotel			
6300 Hollywood Way ....Orlando FL 32819	800-232-7827	407-503-3000	660
Royal Palms Resort & Spa			
5200 E Camelback Rd ....Phoenix AZ 85018	800-672-6011	602-840-3610	660
Royal Regency Hotel			
165 Tuckahoe Rd ....Yonkers NY 10710	800-215-3858		376
Royal Roads University			
2005 Sooke Rd ....Victoria BC V9B5Y2	800-788-8028	250-391-2511	773
Royal Roads University Botanical Garden			
2005 Sooke Rd ....Victoria BC V9B5Y2	800-788-8028	250-391-2511	96
Royal Seating Ltd			
1110 Industrial Blvd ....Cameron TX 76520	888-388-3224*	254-605-5500	318-3
*Cust Svc			
Royal Securities Co			
4095 Chicago Dr SW Ste 120.........Grandville MI 49418	800-421-3518	616-538-2550	681
Royal Sonesta Hotel Boston			
40 Edwin H Land Blvd ....Cambridge MA 02142	800-766-3782	617-806-4200	376
Royal Sonesta Hotel New Orleans			
300 Bourbon St ....New Orleans LA 70130	800-766-3782	504-586-0300	376
Royal Sun Inn			
1700 S Palm Canyon Dr ....Palm Springs CA 92264	800-619-4786	760-327-1564	376
Royal Textile Mills Inc			
929 Firetower Rd ....Yanceyville NC 27379	800-334-9361		153-1
Royal Tractor Co Inc			
109 Overland Pk Pl ....New Century KS 66031	888-782-7278	913-782-2598	465
Royal Trucking Co			
1323 Eshman Ave N PO Box 387 ......West Point MS 39773	800-321-1293	662-494-1637	770
Royal Tyrrell Museum of Palaeontology			
Hwy 838			
Midland Provincial Pk..............Drumheller AB T0J0Y0	888-440-4240	403-823-7707	513
Royalton Hotel			
44 W 44th St ....New York NY 10036	800-606-6090	212-869-4400	376
Royalty Carpet Mills Inc			
17111 Red Hill Ave ....Irvine CA 92614	800-854-8331	949-474-4000	130
Royce & Assoc LLC			
745 Fifth Ave 24th Fl ....New York NY 10151	800-221-4268		398
Roylco Inc			
3251 Abbeville Hwy			
PO Box 13409......................Anderson SC 29624	800-362-8656	864-296-0043	243
Roysons Corp			
40 Vanderhoof Ave ....Rockaway NJ 07866	888-769-7667	973-625-7923	290
Rozelle Cosmetics			
4260 Loop Rd ....Westfield VT 05874	800-451-4216	802-744-2270	215
RP International			
PO Box 900 ....Woodland Hills CA 91365	877-999-8322	818-992-0500	47-17
RPB (Research to Prevent Blindness Inc)			
645 Madison Ave 21st Fl ....New York NY 10022	800-621-0026	212-752-4333	47-17
RPC Inc			
2801 Buford Hwy Ste 520...............Atlanta GA 30324	800-776-9437	404-321-2140	532
NYSE: RES			
Rpl Supplies Inc			
141 Lanza Ave Bldg 3A................Garfield NJ 07026	800-524-0914	973-767-0880	175
RPM Industries Inc			
26 Aurelius Ave ....Auburn NY 13021	800-669-3676	315-255-1105	200
RPM International Inc			
2628 Pearl Rd ....Medina OH 44256	800-776-4488	330-273-5090	543
NYSE: RPM			
RPS Products Inc			
281 Keyes Ave ....Hampshire IL 60140	800-683-7030	847-683-3400	18
RR Bowker LLC			
630 Central Ave ....New Providence NJ 07974	888-269-5372	908-286-1090	628-2
RR Donnelley			
111 S Wacker Dr ....Chicago IL 60606	800-742-4455		618
RR Donnelley Logistics			
1000 Windham Pkwy ....Bolingbrook IL 60490	888-744-7773	630-226-6100	5
RR Donnelley Response Marketing Services			
4101 Winfield Rd ....Warrenville IL 60555	800-722-9001	630-963-9494	5
R&R Products Inc			
3334 E Milber St ....Tucson AZ 85714	800-528-3446	520-889-3593	383
RREEF			
101 California St 26th Fl..........San Francisco CA 94111	800-222-5885*	415-781-3300	398
*All			
RRMC (Rowan Regional Medical Ctr)			
612 Mocksville Ave ....Salisbury NC 28144	888-844-0080	704-210-5000	371-3

	Toll-Free	Phone	Class
RS (IEEE Reliability Society)			
IEEE Operations Ctr			
445 Hoes Ln ....Piscataway NJ 08854	800-678-4333	732-981-0060	48-19
RS Corcoran Co			
500 N Vine St ....New Lenox IL 60451	800-637-1067	815-485-2156	632
RS Electronics Inc			
34443 Schoolcraft Rd ....Livonia MI 48150	866-600-6040	734-525-1155	246
RS Hughes Company Inc			
10639 Glenoaks Blvd ....Pacoima CA 91331	877-774-8443	818-686-9111	382
RS Hughes Company Inc Saunders Div			
975 N Todd Ave ....Azusa CA 91702	888-932-8836*	626-691-1111	449
*Sales			
RS Owens & Co			
5535 N Lynch Ave ....Chicago IL 60630	800-282-6200	773-282-6000	767
RSA (Royal & SunAlliance Insurance Co of Canada)			
18 York Street Suite 800 ....Toronto ON M5J2T8	800-268-8406	416-366-7511	388-4
RSA Security Inc			
174 Middlesex Tpke ....Bedford MA 01730	800-995-5095	781-515-5000	179-12
RSES (Refrigeration Service Engineers Society)			
1666 Rand Rd ....Des Plaines IL 60016	800-297-5660	847-297-6464	48-3
RSI (Reconditioned Systems Inc)			
2636 S Wilson St Ste 105...............Tempe AZ 85282	800-280-5000	480-968-1772	318-1
RSI (Railway Supply Institute Inc)			
425 Third St Ste 920...............Washington DC 20024	800-995-3579	202-347-4664	48-21
RSI Home Products Inc			
400 E Orangethorpe Ave ....Anaheim CA 92801	888-774-8062	714-449-2200	114
RSNA (Radiological Society of North America)			
820 Jorie Blvd ....Oak Brook IL 60523	800-381-6660	630-571-2670	48-8
RSPA (Retail Solutions Providers Assn)			
10130 Perimeter Pkwy Ste 420.........Charlotte NC 28216	800-782-2693	704-357-3124	48-18
RSR Group Inc			
4405 Metric Dr ....Winter Park FL 32792	800-541-4867	407-677-1000	701
RSVP (Retired & Senior Volunteer Program)			
1201 New York Ave NW ....Washington DC 20525	800-833-3722	202-606-5000	198
RSVP Publications			
6730 W Linebaugh Ave Ste 201 ....Tampa FL 33625	800-360-7787	813-960-7787	309
RSVP Vacations			
2535 25th Ave S ....Minneapolis MN 55406	800-328-7787	310-432-2300	750
RT Vanderbilt Company Inc			
30 Winfield St ....Norwalk CT 06855	800-243-6064*	203-853-1400	142
*Cust Svc			
RTA (Riverside Transit Agency)			
1825 Third St PO Box 59968 ....Riverside CA 92517	800-800-7821	951-565-5000	463
RTC (Regional Transportation Commission of Southern Nevada)			
600 S Grand Central Pkwy			
Ste 350 ....Las Vegas NV 89106	800-228-3911	702-676-1500	463
RTD (Regional Transportation District)			
1600 Blake St ....Denver CO 80202	800-366-7433	303-628-9000	463
RTEA (Cloud Peak Energy Inc)			
505 S Gillette Ave PO Box 3009...........Gillette WY 82717	866-470-4300	307-687-6000	496
RTEC (Rural Transit Enterprises Coordinated Inc)			
100 E Main St ....Mount Vernon KY 40456	800-321-7832	606-256-9835	107
RTI Biologics Inc			
11621 Research Cir ....Alachua FL 32615	877-343-6832	386-418-8888	84
NASDAQ: RTIX			
RTN Federal Credit Union			
600 Main St Ste 3.................Waltham MA 02452	800-338-0221	781-736-9900	219
RTP Co 580 E Front St ....Winona MN 55987	800-433-4787	507-454-6900	598-2
RTR (Rainbow Trout Ranch)			
1484 FDR 250 PO Box 458.............Antonito CO 81120	800-633-3397	719-376-5659	239
RTS Financial Service			
8601 Monrovia ....Lenexa KS 66215	877-242-4390		272
RTS Packaging LLC			
504 Thrasher St ....Norcross GA 30071	800-558-6984		100
RTW Inc			
8500 Normandale Lk Blvd Ste 1400			
PO Box 390327....................Bloomington MN 55437	800-789-2242*	952-893-0403	388-4
*Sales			
RUAN Transportation Management Systems			
666 Grand Ave 3200 Ruan Ctr ....Des Moines IA 50309	866-782-6669	515-245-2500	289
Ruane Cunniff & Goldfarb Inc			
9 W 57th St Ste 5000 ....New York NY 10019	800-686-6884	212-832-5280	398
RubbAir Door Div Eckel Industries Inc			
100 Groton Shirley Rd ....Ayer MA 01432	800-966-7822	978-772-0480	235
Rubber Manufacturers Assn (RMA)			
1400 K St NW Ste 900 ....Washington DC 20005	800-220-7622	202-682-4800	48-13
Rubbermaid Commercial Products (RCP)			
3124 Valley Ave ....Winchester VA 22601	800-347-9800	540-667-8700	601
Rubberset Co			
101 W Prospect Ave ....Cleveland OH 44115	800-345-4939		102
Rubenstein Bros Inc			
102 St Charles Ave ....New Orleans LA 70130	800-102-7862	504-581-6666	155-3
Rubicon Minerals Corp			
800 W Pender St Ste 1540 ......Vancouver BC V6C2V6	866-365-4706	604-623-3333	497
NYSE: RBY			
Rubio's Restaurants Inc			
1902 Wright Pl Ste 300 ....Carlsbad CA 92008	800-354-4199	760-929-8226	661
Ruby Falls			
1720 S Scenic Hwy ....Chattanooga TN 37409	800-755-7105	423-821-2544	49-4
Ruby Tuesday Inc			
150 W Church Ave ....Maryville TN 37801	800-325-0755	865-379-5700	661
NYSE: RT			
Rudd Equipment Co			
4344 Poplar Level Rd ....Louisville KY 40213	800-527-2282	502-456-4050	355
Rudolph Foods Company Inc			
6575 Bellefontaine Rd ....Lima OH 45804	800-241-7675	419-648-3611	295-9
Rudolph Technologies Inc			
One Rudolph Rd PO Box 1000 ....Flanders NJ 07836	877-467-8365	973-691-1300	467
NASDAQ: RTEC			
rue21 Inc			
800 Commonwealth Dr Ste 100 ... Warrendale PA 15086	888-871-2744	724-776-9780	155-6
NASDAQ: RUE			
Ruffed Grouse Society (RGS)			
451 McCormick Rd ....Coraopolis PA 15108	888-564-6747	412-262-4044	47-3
Ruffin Bldg Systems Inc			
6914 Louisiana 2 ....Oak Grove LA 71263	800-421-4232	318-428-2305	104
Rug Doctor LP			
4701 Old Shepard Pl ....Plano TX 75093	800-784-3628	972-673-1400	264-2
Rug Hooking Magazine			
5067 Ritter Rd ....Mechanicsburg PA 17055	866-375-8626	717-796-0411	452-14
Rugg Mfg Company Inc			
105 Newton St ....Greenfield MA 01302	800-633-8772	413-773-5471	426
Ruiz Foods Inc			
PO Box 37 ....Dinuba CA 93618	800-477-6474	559-591-5510	295-36

	City	State	ZIP	Toll-Free	Phone	Class
Rules-based Medicine Inc						
3300 Duval Rd	Austin	TX	78759	**866-726-6277**	512-835-8026	576
Rumble Tuff Inc						
865 North 1430 West	Orem	UT	84057	**855-228-8388**	801-609-8168	318-2
Rumpke						
10795 Hughes Rd	Cincinnati	OH	45251	**800-582-3107**		792
Rumsey Electric Co						
15 Colwell Ln	Conshohocken	PA	19428	**800-462-2402**	610-832-9000	246
Run Consultants LLC						
925 N Point Pkwy Ste 160	Alpharetta	GA	30005	**866-457-2193**		260
Rundle-Spence Manufacturing Co						
PO Box 510008	New Berlin	WI	53151	**800-783-6060**	262-782-3000	605
Runge Conservation Nature Ctr						
2901 W Truman Blvd	Jefferson City	MO	65109	**800-392-1111**	573-751-4115	49-4
Runner's World Magazine						
400 S Tenth St	Emmaus	PA	18098	**800-666-2828***	610-967-5171	452-13
*Cust Svc						
Runzheimer International						
Runzheimer Pk	Rochester	WI	53167	**800-558-1702**	262-971-2200	194
Ruotolo Assoc Inc (RA)						
29 Broadway Ste 210	Cresskill	NJ	07626	**800-786-8656**	201-568-3898	316
Rural Electric Convenience Co-op Co						
3973 W SR 104 PO Box 19	Auburn	IL	62615	**800-245-7322**	217-438-6197	245
Rural Electric Co-op Inc (REC)						
801 N Industrial Heights						
PO Box 609	Lindsay	OK	73052	**800-259-3504**	405-756-3104	245
Rural Housing Service						
1400 Independence Ave SW						
Rm 5014	Washington	DC	20250	**800-414-1226**	202-690-1533	338-1
Rural Mutual Insurance Company Inc						
1241 John Q Hammons Dr						
PO Box 5555	Madison	WI	53705	**800-362-7881**	608-836-5525	388-4
Rural Resources Community Action						
956 S Main St Ste A	Colville	WA	99114	**800-538-7659**	509-684-8421	146
Rural Telephone Service Company Inc						
PO Box 158	Lenora	KS	67645	**877-625-7872**	785-567-4281	726
Rural Transit Enterprises Coordinated Inc (RTEC)						
100 E Main St	Mount Vernon	KY	40456	**800-321-7832**	606-256-9835	107
Rural/Metro Corp						
9221 E Via de Ventura	Scottsdale	AZ	85258	**800-352-2309**		30
Ruritan National						
5451 Lyons Rd PO Box 487	Dublin	VA	24084	**877-787-8727**	540-674-5431	47-15
RUSA (Reference & User Services Assn)						
50 E Huron St	Chicago	IL	60611	**800-545-2433**	312-280-4398	48-11
Rusch Inc						
2917 Weck Dr						
PO Box 12600	Research Triangle Park	NC	27709	**866-246-6990**	919-544-8000	472
Rush Enterprises Inc						
555 IH 35 S Ste 500	New Braunfels	TX	78130	**800-973-7874**	830-626-5200	264-3
NASDAQ: RUSHA						
Rush Gears Inc						
550 Virginia Dr	Fort Washington	PA	19034	**800-523-2576**	215-542-9000	700
Rush Industries Inc						
118 N Wrenn St	High Point	NC	27260	**800-524-0258**	336-886-7700	318-2
Rush Shelby Energy Inc						
2777 S 840 W PO Box 55	Manilla	IN	46150	**800-706-7362***	765-544-2600	245
*General						
Rush Truck Center - Whittier						
2450 Kella Ave	Whittier	CA	90601	**877-605-7623**	562-551-5000	56
Rush-Copley Medical Ctr (RCMC)						
2000 Ogden Ave	Aurora	IL	60504	**866-426-7539**	630-978-6200	371-3
Rushmore Forest Products						
23848 Hwy 385 PO Box 619	Hill City	SD	57745	**866-466-5254**	605-574-2512	674
Rushmore Plaza Civic Ctr						
444 Mt Rushmore Rd N	Rapid City	SD	57701	**800-468-6463**	605-394-4115	206
Rusken Packaging Inc						
PO Box 2100	Cullman	AL	35056	**800-232-8108**	256-734-0092	100
Russ Bassett Co						
8189 Byron Rd	Whittier	CA	90606	**800-350-2445**	562-945-2445	286
Russ' Restaurants Inc						
390 E Eigth St	Holland	MI	49423	**800-521-1778**	616-396-6571	661
Russel Metals Inc						
6600 Financial Dr	Mississauga	ON	L5N7J6	**800-268-0750**	905-819-7777	487
TSE: RUS						
Russelectric Inc						
99 Industrial Pk Rd	Hingham	MA	02043	**800-225-5250**	781-749-6000	720
Russell Florist Inc						
5001 Gravois Ave	Saint Louis	MO	63116	**800-351-9003**	314-351-4676	292
Russell Investment Group						
909 A St	Tacoma	WA	98402	**800-787-7354**		398
Russell Investments						
1301 Second Ave 18th Fl	Seattle	WA	98101	**800-426-7969**	206-505-7877	398
Russell Karting Specialties Inc						
PO Box 1220	Raymore	MO	64083	**800-821-3359**	816-322-3330	56
Russell Reynolds Assoc Inc						
200 Pk Ave 23rd Fl	New York	NY	10166	**800-259-0470**	212-351-2000	266
Russell Sage College						
45 Ferry St	Troy	NY	12180	**888-837-9724***	518-244-2217	166
*Admissions						
Russell Standard Corp						
285 Kappa Dr Ste 300	Pittsburgh	PA	15238	**800-323-3053***		45
*General						
Russell Stover Candies Inc						
4900 Oak St	Kansas City	MO	64112	**800-477-8683**	816-842-9240	295-8
Russellville Area Chamber of Commerce						
708 W Main St	Russellville	AR	72801	**855-678-2447**	479-968-2530	137
Russian National Tourist Office						
224 W 30th St Ste 701	New York	NY	10001	**877-221-7120**	646-473-2233	765
Russin Lumber Corp						
21 Leonards Dr	Montgomery	NY	12549	**800-724-0010**	845-457-4000	192-3
Rust College						
150 Rust Ave	Holly Springs	MS	38635	**888-886-8492**	662-252-8000	166
Rustler Lodge						
10380 East Hwy 210 PO Box 8030	Alta	UT	84092	**888-532-2582**	801-742-2200	660
Rust-Oleum Corp						
11 E Hawthorn Pkwy	Vernon Hills	IL	60061	**800-323-3584**	847-367-7700	543
Ruston/Lincoln Chamber of Commerce						
211 N Trenton	Ruston	LA	71270	**800-392-9032**	318-255-2031	137
Rusty Parrot Lodge & Spa						
PO Box 1657	Jackson	WY	83001	**800-458-2004**	307-733-2000	660
Rutgers Organics Corp (ROC)						
201 Struble Rd	State College	PA	16801	**888-469-2188**	814-238-2424	141
Rutgers the State University of New Jersey						
School of Law Camden						
217 N Fifth St	Camden	NJ	08102	**800-466-7561**	856-225-6375	167-1
Rutgers University Press						
106 Somerset St 3rd Fl	New Brunswick	NJ	08901	**800-272-6817**	732-745-4935	628-4
Ruth Eckerd Hall						
1111 McMullen Booth Rd	Clearwater	FL	33759	**800-875-8682**	727-791-7060	565
Ruth Lilly Medical Library						
975 W Walnut St IB 100	Indianapolis	IN	46202	**877-952-1988**	317-274-7182	431-1
Ruth's Hospitality Group Inc						
1030 W Canton Ave Ste 100	Winter Park	FL	32789	**800-544-0808***	407-333-7440	661
NASDAQ: RUTH ■ *Sales						
Rutherford B Hayes Presidential Ctr						
Spiegel Grove	Fremont	OH	43420	**800-998-7737**	419-332-2081	431-2
Rutherford County Chamber of Commerce						
501 Memorial Blvd	Murfreesboro	TN	37129	**800-716-7560**	615-893-6565	137
Rutherford Electric Membership Corp						
186 Hudlow Rd PO Box 1569	Forest City	NC	28043	**800-521-0920**	828-245-1621	245
Rutherford Institute						
PO Box 7482	Charlottesville	VA	22906	**800-225-1791**	434-978-3888	47-8
Rutland Herald						
PO Box 668	Rutland	VT	05702	**800-498-4296**		525-2
Rutland Plastic Technologies						
10021 Rodney St	Pineville	NC	28134	**800-438-5134**	704-553-0046	598-2
Rutland Region Chamber of Commerce						
50 Merchants Row	Rutland	VT	05701	**800-756-8880**	802-773-2747	336
Ruttger's Bay Lake Lodge						
25039 Tame Fish Lk Rd						
PO Box 400	Deerwood	MN	56444	**800-450-4545**	218-678-2885	660
RV World Inc of Nokomis						
2110 Tamiami Trl N	Nokomis	FL	34275	**800-262-2182**	941-966-2182	56
RVDA (Recreation Vehicle Dealers Assn)						
3930 University Dr Third Fl	Fairfax	VA	22030	**800-336-0355**	703-591-7130	48-18
RVIA (Recreation Vehicle Industry Assn)						
1896 Preston White Dr	Reston	VA	20191	**800-336-0154**	703-620-6003	48-21
RW Beckett Corp						
PO Box 1289	Elyria	OH	44036	**800-645-2876**	440-327-1060	354
RW Screw Products Inc						
999 Oberlin Rd SW	Massillon	OH	44647	**866-797-2739**	330-837-9211	614
RW Warner Inc						
217 Monroe Ave	Frederick	MD	21701	**800-854-5387**	301-662-5387	190-10
RWH Trucking Inc						
2970 Old Oakwood Rd	Oakwood	GA	30566	**800-256-8119**		770
RWI (RiskWatch)						
1237 N Gulfstream Ave	Sarasota	Fl	34236	**800-360-1898**		179-10
RWM Casters Co						
PO Box 668	Gastonia	NC	28053	**800-634-7704**		347
Rx Optical						
1700 S Pk St	Kalamazoo	MI	49001	**800-792-2737**	269-342-0003	536
RX Worldwide Meetings Inc						
3060 Communications Pkwy Ste 200	Plano	TX	75093	**800-562-1713**	214-291-2920	185
Rx&D (Canada's Research-Based Pharmaceutical Cos)						
55 Metcalfe St Ste 1220	Ottawa	ON	K1P6L5	**800-363-0203**	613-236-0455	48-8
Rxusa Inc						
81 Seaview Blvd	Port Washington	NY	11050	**800-764-3648**	516-467-2500	237
Ryan Herco Products Corp						
3010 N San Fernando Blvd	Burbank	CA	91504	**800-848-1141**	818-841-1141	596
Rycon Construction Inc						
2525 Liberty Ave	Pittsburgh	PA	15222	**800-883-1901**	412-392-2525	187
Rydell Chevrolet Inc						
1325 E San Marnan Dr	Waterloo	IA	50702	**866-697-5167**	319-234-4601	509
Ryder System Inc						
11690 NW 105th St	Miami	FL	33178	**800-297-9337**	305-500-3726	768
NYSE: R						
Rydex Funds						
805 King Farm Blvd Ste 600	Rockville	MD	20850	**800-820-0888***	301-296-5100	521
*Cust Svc						
Ryerson University						
350 Victoria St	Toronto	ON	M5B2K3	**866-592-8882**	416-979-5000	773
Ryman Auditorium						
116 Fifth Ave N	Nashville	TN	37219	**800-733-6779**	615-458-8700	565
Rynone Mfg Corp						
PO Box 128	Sayre	PA	18840	**800-839-1654**	570-888-5272	114
Ryobi Technologies Inc						
1428 Pearman Dairy Rd	Anderson	SC	29625	**800-525-2579**		348
Ryokan College						
11965 Venice Blvd Ste 304	Los Angeles	CA	90066	**866-796-5261**	310-390-7560	166
Rytex Co 100 N Pk Ave	Peru	IN	46970	**800-277-5458**		545-2

S

	City	State	ZIP	Toll-Free	Phone	Class
S & C Electric Co						
6601 N Ridge Blvd	Chicago	IL	60626	**800-621-5546**	773-338-1000	720
S & D Coffee Inc						
300 Concord Pkwy PO Box 1628	Concord	NC	28026	**800-933-2210***	704-782-3121	295-7
*Cust Svc						
S & H Express Inc						
400 Mulberry St PO Box 20219	York	PA	17403	**800-637-9782**	717-848-5015	444
S & M Machine Service Inc						
109 E Highland Dr	Oconto Falls	WI	54154	**800-323-1579**	920-846-8130	450
S & M Moving Systems Inc						
12128 Burke St	Santa Fe Springs	CA	90670	**800-528-4561**	562-567-2100	512
S & ME Inc						
3201 Spring Forest Rd	Raleigh	NC	27616	**800-849-2517***	919-872-2660	193
*Cust Svc						
S & S Industries Inc						
115 Clemmons Rd	Mount Juliet	TN	37122	**800-762-4104**	615-754-8000	386
S & S Mills Inc						
414 C N Pk Dr	Dalton	GA	30720	**800-241-4013**	706-277-3677	130
S & S Technology						
10625 Telge Rd	Houston	TX	77095	**800-231-1747**	281-815-1300	379
S & S Tire & Auto Service Center						
1475 Jingle Bell Ln	Lexington	KY	40509	**800-685-6794**		53
S & S Transport Inc						
PO Box 12579	Grand Forks	ND	58208	**800-726-8022**		770

	Toll-Free	Phone	Class

S & S Worldwide Inc
75 Mill St .... Colchester CT 06415 **800-243-9232*** 860-537-3451 454
*Orders

S Abraham & Sons Inc
PO Box 1768 .... Grand Rapids MI 49501 **866-248-3163*** 616-453-6358 296-8
*General

S E A Consultants Inc
215 First St Ste 320 .... Cambridge MA 02142 **855-746-4849** 617-497-7800 261

S Howes Company Inc
25 Howard St .... Silver Creek NY 14136 **888-255-2611** 716-934-2611 297

S K C Communication Products Inc
8320 Hedge Ln Terr .... Shawnee Mission KS 66227 **800-882-7779** 913-422-4222 246

S Lichtenberg & Co Inc
295 Fifth Ave Rm 918 .... New York NY 10016 **800-682-1959*** 212-689-4510 735
*Cust Svc

S Parker Hardware Manufacturing Corp
PO Box 9882 .... Englewood NJ 07631 **800-772-7537** 201-569-1600 347

S R C Corp
PO Box 30676 .... Salt Lake City UT 84130 **800-888-4545** 801-268-4500 276

S R Snodgrass AC
2100 Corporate Dr .... Wexford PA 15090 **800-580-7738** 724-934-0344 2

S Schwab Co Inc
12101 Upper Potomac
Industrial Pk St .... Cumberland MD 21502 **800-638-2937** 301-729-4488 153-4

S T Bunn Construction
1904 University Blvd
PO Box 20109 .... Tuscaloosa AL 35401 **800-297-6302** 205-752-8195 770

S. Freedman & Sons Inc
3322 Pennsy Dr .... Landover MD 20785 **800-545-7277** 301-322-5000 552

S.l.c. Meter Service Inc
10375 Dixie Hwy .... Davisburg MI 48350 **800-433-4332** 248-625-0667 382

SA (Sexaholics Anonymous)
PO Box 3565 .... Brentwood TN 37024 **866-424-8777** 615-370-6062 47-21

SA Comunale Company Inc
2900 Newpark Dr .... Barberton OH 44203 **800-776-7181** 330-706-3040 190-13

SA Day Mfg Co Inc
1489 Niagara St .... Buffalo NY 14213 **800-747-0030** 716-881-3030 143

SA Healy Co
1910 S Highland Ave Ste 300 ...... Lombard IL 60148 **888-724-3259** 630-678-3110 261

SA Recycling LLC
2411 N Glassell St .... Orange CA 92865 **800-468-7272** 714-632-2000 677

SAA (Society of American Archivists)
17 N State St Ste 1425 .... Chicago IL 60602 **866-722-7858** 312-606-0722 47-4

SAA (Sex Addicts Anonymous)
PO Box 70949 .... Houston TX 77270 **800-477-8191** 713-869-4902 47-21

SAA (Society for American Archaeology)
900 Second St NE Ste 12 .... Washington DC 20002 **800-759-5219** 202-789-8200 48-5

Saags Products Inc
1799 Factor Ave .... San Leandro CA 94577 **800-352-7224** 510-352-8000 295-26

Saba Software Inc
2400 Bridge Pkwy ..... Redwood Shores CA 94065 **877-722-2101** 650-581-2500 179-3
OTC: SABA

Sabert Corp
2288 Main St Ext .... Sayreville NJ 08872 **800-722-3781**   541

Sabin Corp
3800 Constitution Ave
PO Box 788 .... Bloomington IN 47403 **800-457-4500** 812-339-2235 592

Sabre Industries Inc
8653 E Hwy 67 .... Alvarado TX 76009 **866-254-3707** 817-852-1700 261

SAC (Smith Affiliated Capital)
800 Third Ave 12th Fl .... New York NY 10022 **888-387-3298** 212-644-9440 400

SAC Federal Credit Union (SAFCU)
11515 S 39th St PO Box 1149 .... Bellevue NE 68123 **800-228-0392** 402-292-8000 219

Sac Osage Electric Co-op Inc
4815 E Hwy 54
PO Box 111 .... El Dorado Springs MO 64744 **800-876-2701** 417-876-2721 245

Sacor Financial Inc
1911 Douglas Blvd 85-126 .... Roseville CA 95661 **866-556-0231**   390

Sacramento Bag Manufacturing Co
440 N Pioneer Ave Ste 300 .... Woodland CA 95776 **800-287-2247** 530-662-6130 66

Sacramento Ballet
1631 K St .... Sacramento CA 95814 **800-925-9989** 916-552-5800 566-1

Sacramento Bee
PO Box 15779 .... Sacramento CA 95852 **800-284-3233*** 916-321-1000 525-2
*Cust Svc

Sacramento Convention & Visitors Bureau
1608 'I' St .... Sacramento CA 95814 **800-292-2334** 916-808-7777 207

Sacramento Kings
ARCO Arena 1 Sports Pkwy .... Sacramento CA 95834 **866-746-7622** 916-928-0000 705-1

Sacramento Monarchs
ARCO Arena 1 Sports Pkwy .... Sacramento CA 95834 **877-329-9622** 916-928-6900 705-2

Sacramento Theatre Co
1419 H St .... Sacramento CA 95814 **888-478-2849** 916-443-6722 566-4

Sacred Heart HealthCare System
421 Chew St .... Allentown PA 18102 **800-994-6610** 610-776-4500 371-3

Sacred Heart Hospital
900 W Clairemont Ave .... Eau Claire WI 54701 **888-445-4554** 715-717-4121 371-3

Sacred Heart Hospital of Pensacola
5151 N Ninth Ave .... Pensacola FL 32504 **800-874-1026** 850-416-7000 371-3

Sacred Heart Medical Ctr
1255 Hilyard St .... Eugene OR 97401 **800-288-7444** 541-686-7300 371-3

SADD (Students Against Destructive Decisions)
255 Main St .... Marlborough MA 01752 **877-723-3462** 508-481-3568 47-6

Saddle Mountain State Natural Area
9500 Sandpiper Ln c/o Nehalem Bay Management Unit
PO Box 366 .... Nehalem OR 97138 **800-551-6949**   558

Sadler's Smokehouse Ltd
PO Box 1088 .... Henderson TX 75653 **800-777-5581** 903-655-7262 295-26

Sadoff & Rudoy Industries LLP
240 W Arndt St .... Fond du Lac WI 54936 **877-972-3633*** 920-921-2070 677
*General

SAE (Sigma Alpha Epsilon Fraternity)
1856 Sheridan Rd .... Evanston IL 60201 **800-233-1856** 847-475-1856 47-16

SAE (Society of Automotive Engineers Inc)
400 Commonwealth Dr ...... Warrendale PA 15096 **877-606-7323** 724-776-4841 48-21

SAE Circuits Colorado Inc
4820 N 63rd St .... Boulder CO 80301 **800-234-9001** 303-530-1900 617

Saebo Inc
2725 Water Ridge Pkwy
Ste 320 Six LakePointe Plaza ...... Charlotte NC 28217 **888-284-5433**   470

SAEC (South Alabama Electric Co-op)
PO Box 449 .... Troy AL 36081 **800-556-2060** 334-566-2060 245

SAF (Santa Fe Municipal Airport)
121 Aviation Dr PO Box 909 .... Santa Fe NM 87504 **866-773-2587** 505-955-2900 27

SAF (Society of American Florists)
1601 Duke St .... Alexandria VA 22314 **800-336-4743** 703-836-8700 48-4

Safari Circuits Inc
411 Washington St .... Otsego MI 49078 **888-694-7230** 269-694-9471 177

Safari West Wildlife Preserve & Tent Camp
3115 Porter Creek Rd ...... Santa Rosa CA 95404 **800-616-2695** 707-579-2551 810

Safariland LLC
13386 International Pkwy .... Jacksonville FL 32218 **800-347-1200**   534

Safco Products Co
9300 W Research Ctr Rd ..... New Hope MN 55428 **800-328-3020*** 763-536-6700 318-1
*Cust Svc

SAFCU (SAC Federal Credit Union)
11515 S 39th St PO Box 1149 .... Bellevue NE 68123 **800-228-0392** 402-292-8000 219

Safe 1 Credit Union
PO Box 2203 .... Bakersfield CA 93303 **800-322-4529** 661-327-3818 219

Safe Auto Insurance Co
Four Easton Oval PO Box 182109 ..... Columbus OH 43219 **800-723-3288** 614-231-0200 388-4

SAFE Credit Union
3720 Madison Ave ...... North Highlands CA 95660 **800-733-7233** 916-979-7233 219

Safeamerica Credit Union
6001 Gibraltar Dr .... Pleasanton CA 94588 **800-972-0999** 925-734-4111 219

Safeguard Business Systems Inc
8585 N Stemmons Fwy Ste 600 N ..... Dallas TX 75247 **800-523-2422**   140

Safeguard Chemical Corp
411 Wales Ave .... Bronx NY 10454 **800-536-3170** 718-585-3170 280

SafeGuard Health Enterprises Inc
95 Enterprise Ste 100 .... Aliso Viejo CA 92656 **800-880-1800** 949-425-4300 388-3

Safeguard Properties Inc
7887 Safeguard Cir ...... Valley View OH 44125 **800-852-8306** 216-739-2900 502

Safeguard Scientifics Inc
435 Devon Pk Dr Ste 800 .... Wayne PA 19087 **877-506-7371** 610-293-0600 780
NYSE: SFE

Safeguard Security & Communications Inc
8454 N 90th St .... Scottsdale AZ 85258 **800-426-6060** 480-609-6200 684

Safelite Group Inc
2400 Farmers Dr .... Columbus OH 43235 **877-664-8931**   61-2

SafeNet Inc
4690 Millennium Dr .... Belcamp MD 21017 **800-533-3958*** 410-931-7500 177
*Sales

Safetec of America Inc
887 Kensington Ave .... Buffalo NY 14215 **800-456-7077** 716-895-1822 149

Safe-T-Gard Corp
12105 W Cedar Dr .... Lakewood CO 80228 **800-356-9026*** 303-763-8900 569
*Cust Svc

Safety Harbor Resort & Spa
105 N Bayshore Dr ...... Safety Harbor FL 34695 **888-237-8772** 727-726-1161 660

Safety Products Inc
3517 Craftsman Blvd .... Lakeland FL 33803 **800-248-6860** 863-665-3601 670

Safety Sam Inc
2626 S Roosevelt St Ste 2 .... Tempe AZ 85282 **866-478-6980**   755

Safety Seal Piston Ring Co
4000 Airport Rd .... Marshall TX 75672 **800-962-3631*** 903-938-9241 127
*Sales

Safety Speed Cut Mfg Co Inc
13943 Lincoln St NE .... Ham Lake MN 55304 **800-772-2327** 763-755-1600 808

Safety Supply South Inc
100 Centrum Dr .... Irmo SC 29063 **800-522-8344***   670
*Cust Svc

Safety Technology International Inc
2306 Airport Rd .... Waterford MI 48327 **800-888-4784** 248-673-9898 601

Safety-Kleen Systems Inc
2600 N Central Expwy Ste 400 ...... Richardson TX 75080 **800-669-5740** 800-323-5040 658

Safeware Inc
3200 HubbaRd Rd .... Landover MD 20785 **800-331-6707*** 301-683-1234 670
*Cust Svc

Safeway Insurance Group
790 Pasquinelli Dr .... Westmont IL 60559 **800-273-0300** 630-887-8300 388-4

Safeway Sign Co
9875 Yucca Rd .... Adelanto CA 92301 **800-637-7233** 760-246-7070 692

SAFH (Sutter Auburn Faith Community Hospital)
11815 Education St .... Auburn CA 95602 **800-478-8837** 530-888-4500 371-3

SAFLOK
31750 Sherman Ave ..... Madison Heights MI 48071 **800-999-6213** 248-837-3700 683

Saf-T-Cab Inc
PO Box 2587 .... Fresno CA 93745 **800-344-7491** 559-268-5541 509

Saf-T-Gard International Inc
205 Huehl Rd .... Northbrook IL 60062 **800-548-4273** 847-291-1600 670

Safway Services Inc
N 19 W 24200 Riverwood Dr ...... Waukesha WI 53188 **800-558-4772** 262-523-6500 264-3

SAG (Screen Actors Guild)
5757 Wilshire Blvd .... Los Angeles CA 90036 **800-724-0767** 323-954-1600 411

Sag Harbor Industries Inc
1668 Sag Harbor Tpke ..... Sag Harbor NY 11963 **800-724-5952** 631-725-0440 511

Saga Communications Inc
73 Kercheval Ave .... Grosse Pointe Farms MI 48236 **800-777-3674** 313-886-7070 634
NYSE: SGA

Sagamore Health Network
11555 N Meridian St Ste 400 .... Carmel IN 46032 **800-364-3469** 317-573-2886 388-3

Sagamore Insurance Co
111 Congressional Blvd Ste 500 ...... Carmel IN 46032 **800-317-9402**   388-4

Sagamore, The
110 Sagamore Rd ...... Bolton Landing NY 12814 **866-384-1944** 518-644-9400 660

Sage College of Albany
140 New Scotland Ave .... Albany NY 12208 **888-837-9724*** 518-292-1730 166
*Admissions

Sage Fixed Assets
2325 Dulles Corner Blvd Ste 700 ...... Herndon VA 20171 **800-368-2405** 8.0-036-8e+009 179-1

Sage Publications Inc
2455 Teller Rd .... Thousand Oaks CA 91320 **800-818-7243** 805-499-9774 628-2

Sage Telecom Inc
3300 E Renner Rd
Ste 350 Bldg 2 .... Richardson TX 75082 **877-742-5622** 214-495-4700 726

Sagebrush Steakhouse
129 Fast Ln .... Mooresville NC 28117 **877-704-5939** 704-660-5939 661

SagePoint Financial Inc
2800 N Central Ave Ste 2100 .... Phoenix AZ 85004 **800-552-3319**   681

Sager Electronics Inc
19 Lorena Dr .... Middleboro MA 02346 **800-724-3780** 508-947-8888 246

Sagestone Spa & Salon
Red Mountain Resort
1275 East Red Mtn Cir .... Ivins UT 84738 **877-246-4453** 435-673-4905 697

Saginaw Chippewa Tribal College
2274 Enterprise Dr ...... Mount Pleasant MI 48858 **800-225-8172** 989-775-4123 163

Name / Address	City	State	ZIP	Toll-Free	Phone	Class
Saginaw Control & Engineering Inc						
95 Midland Rd	Saginaw	MI	48638	**800-234-6871**	989-799-6871	803
Saginaw County Chamber of Commerce						
515 N Washington Ave 2nd Fl	Saginaw	MI	48607	**888-609-8342**	989-752-7161	137
Saginaw News						
203 S Washington Ave	Saginaw	MI	48607	**800-875-6397**	989-752-7171	525-2
Saginaw Pipe Company Inc						
1980 Hwy 31 S PO Box 8	Saginaw	AL	35137	**800-433-1374**	205-664-3670	487
Saginaw Valley State University						
7400 Bay Rd	University Center	MI	48710	**800-968-9500**	989-964-4200	166
Saginaw Valley State University Zahnow Library						
7400 Bay Rd	University Center	MI	48710	**800-968-9500**	989-964-4240	431-6
Sahlen Packing Company Inc						
318 Howard St	Buffalo	NY	14206	**800-466-8165**	716-852-8677	295-26
SAIC Inc (Science Application International Corp Inc)						
1710 SAIC Dr	McLean	VA	22102	**866-400-7242**	703-676-4300	179-5
SAIL Magazine						
98 N Washington St Ste 107	Boston	MA	02114	**877-388-7761**	617-720-8600	452-4
Sailboats Inc						
250 Marina Dr	Superior	WI	54880	**800-826-7010**	715-392-7131	756
Sailing World Magazine						
55 Hammarlund Way	Middletown	RI	02842	**866-436-2460***	401-845-5100	452-4
*Cust Svc						
Saint Agnes HealthCare						
900 S Caton Ave	Baltimore	MD	21229	**800-875-8750**	410-368-6000	371-3
Saint Alexius Hospital						
Broadway Campus						
3933 S Broadway	Saint Louis	MO	63118	**800-245-1431**	314-865-7000	371-3
Saint Alphonsus Regional Medical Ctr						
1055 N Curtis Rd	Boise	ID	83706	**877-401-3627**	208-367-2121	371-3
Saint Ambrose University						
518 W Locust St	Davenport	IA	52803	**800-383-2627***	563-333-6000	166
*Admissions						
Saint Andrew's College						
15800 Yonge St	Aurora	ON	L4G3H7	**877-378-1899**	905-727-3178	615
Saint Andrew's School						
3900 Jog Rd	Boca Raton	FL	33434	**888-357-7332**	561-210-2000	615
Saint Andrews Estates						
6152 Verde Trail N	Boca Raton	FL	33433	**866-897-3490***	561-487-4728	663
*Mktg						
Saint Andrews Presbyterian College						
1700 Dogwood Mile	Laurinburg	NC	28352	**800-763-0198**	910-277-5555	166
Saint Anselm College						
100 St Anselm Dr	Manchester	NH	03102	**888-426-7356**	603-641-7500	166
Saint Anthony Hospital						
1000 N Lee St	Oklahoma City	OK	73101	**800-227-6964**	405-272-7000	371-3
Saint Anthony the - A Wyndham Historic Hotel						
300 E Travis St	San Antonio	TX	78205	**800-996-3426**	210-227-4392	376
Saint Anthony's Hospice						
2410 S Green St	Henderson	KY	42420	**866-380-2326**	270-826-2326	368
Saint Augustine National Cemetery						
104 Marine St	Saint Augustine	FL	32084	**800-273-8255**	352-793-7740	135
Saint Augustine's College						
1315 Oakwood Ave	Raleigh	NC	27610	**800-948-1126***	919-516-4016	166
*Admissions						
Saint Barnabas Medical Ctr						
94 Old Short Hills Rd	West Orange	NJ	07052	**888-724-7123**	973-322-5000	371-3
Saint Bernard Preparatory School						
1600 St Bernard Dr SE	Cullman	AL	35055	**800-722-0999**	256-739-6682	615
Saint Bernard State Park						
501 St Bernard Pkwy	Braithwaite	LA	70040	**888-677-7823**	504-682-2101	558
Saint Catherine's School						
6001 Grove Ave	Richmond	VA	23226	**800-648-4982**	804-288-2804	615
Saint Charles Mercy Hospital						
2600 Navarre Ave	Oregon	OH	43616	**888-987-6372**	419-696-7200	371-3
Saint Clair County Library System						
210 McMorran Blvd	Port Huron	MI	48060	**877-987-7323**	810-987-7323	431-3
Saint Cloud Area Convention & Visitors Bureau						
525 Hwy 10 S Ste 1	Saint Cloud	MN	56304	**800-264-2940**	320-251-4170	207
Saint Cloud Hospital						
1406 Sixth Ave	Saint Cloud	MN	56303	**800-835-6652**	320-251-2700	371-3
Saint Cloud Technical & Community College						
1540 Northway Dr	Saint Cloud	MN	56303	**800-222-1009**	320-308-5089	788
Saint Cloud Times						
3000 7th Street North						
PO Box 768	Saint Cloud	MN	56303	**877-922-1274**	320-255-8700	525-2
Saint Croix Electric Co-op						
1925 Ridgeway St	Hammond	WI	54015	**800-924-3407**	715-796-7000	245
Saint Croix Forge Inc						
5195 Scandia Trl	Forest Lake	MN	55025	**866-668-7642**	651-464-8967	478
Saint Croix Press Inc						
1185 S Knowles Ave	New Richmond	WI	54017	**800-826-6622**	715-246-5811	628-9
Saint Croix State Park						
30065 St Croix Pk Rd	Hinckley	MN	55037	**888-646-6367**	320-384-6591	558
Saint Elizabeth Hospital						
1506 S Oneida St	Appleton	WI	54915	**800-223-7332**	920-738-2000	371-3
Saint Francis Health Ctr						
1700 SW Seventh St	Topeka	KS	66606	**855-578-3726**	785-295-8000	371-3
Saint Francis Hospital & Medical Ctr						
114 Woodland St	Hartford	CT	06105	**800-993-4312**	860-714-4000	371-3
Saint Francis Medical Ctr						
601 Hamilton Ave	Trenton	NJ	08629	**888-216-3293**	609-599-5000	371-3
Saint Francis Xavier University						
PO Box 5000	Antigonish	NS	B2G2W5	**877-867-7839***	902-863-3300	773
*Admissions						
Saint George Library Ctr						
5 Central Ave	Staten Island	NY	10301	**800-342-3688**	718-442-8560	431-3
Saint Gregory Luxury Hotel & Suites						
2033 M St NW	Washington	DC	20036	**800-821-4367**	202-530-3600	376
Saint Gregory's University						
1900 W MacArthur St	Shawnee	OK	74804	**888-784-7347***	405-878-5100	166
*Admissions						
Saint John's Hospital						
1575 Beam Ave	Maplewood	MN	55109	**888-477-4221**	651-232-7000	371-3
Saint John's Northwestern Military Academy						
1101 N Genesee St	Delafield	WI	53018	**800-752-2338**	262-646-7115	615
Saint John's Preparatory School						
1857 Watertower Rd						
PO Box 4000	Collegeville	MN	56321	**800-525-7737**	320-363-3321	615
Saint John's University						
PO Box 2000	Collegeville	MN	56321	**800-544-1489***	320-363-2196	166
*Admissions						
Saint John's University Alcuin Library						
2835 Abbey Plaza						
PO Box 2500	Collegeville	MN	56321	**800-544-1489**	320-363-2122	431-6
Saint John's-Ravenscourt School						
400 S Dr	Winnipeg	MB	R3T3K5	**800-437-0040**	204-477-2400	615
Saint Johns River Community College						
5001 St Johns Ave	Palatka	FL	32177	**888-757-2293**	386-312-4200	160
Saint Joseph Area Chamber of Commerce						
3003 Frederick Ave	Saint Joseph	MO	64506	**800-748-7856**	816-232-4461	137
Saint Joseph Convention & Visitors Bureau						
109 S Fourth St	Saint Joseph	MO	64501	**800-785-0360**	816-233-6688	207
Saint Joseph Hospital						
700 Broadway	Fort Wayne	IN	46802	**800-258-0974**	260-425-3000	371-3
Saint Joseph Mercy Ann Arbor						
5301 McAuley Dr	Ypsilanti	MI	48197	**866-522-8268**	734-712-3456	371-3
Saint Joseph Mercy Home Care & Hospice						
5301 McAuley Dr	Ypsilanti	MI	48197	**888-884-6569**	734-712-3456	368
Saint Joseph Mercy Oakland						
44405 Woodward Ave	Pontiac	MI	48341	**800-396-1313**	248-858-3000	371-3
Saint Joseph's College of Maine						
278 Whites Bridge Rd	Standish	ME	04084	**800-338-7057***	207-893-7746	166
*Admissions						
Saint Joseph's Hospital						
2661 County Hwy I	Chippewa Falls	WI	54729	**877-723-1811**	715-723-1811	371-3
Saint Joseph's Hospital Health Ctr						
301 Prospect Ave	Syracuse	NY	13203	**888-785-6371**	315-448-5111	371-3
Saint Joseph's University						
5600 City Ave	Philadelphia	PA	19131	**888-232-4295**	610-660-1000	166
Saint Jude Children's Research Hospital Stem Cell Transplantation Div						
262 Danny Thomas Pl	Memphis	TN	38105	**800-822-6344**	901-595-3300	759
Saint Jude Medical						
St Jude Medical Inc	St Paul	MN	55117	**800-328-9634**	651-756-2000	471
NYSE: STJ						
Saint Lawrence Seaway Development Corp						
1200 New Jersey Ave SE	Washington	DC	20590	**800-785-2779**	202-366-0091	338-15
Saint Lawrence University						
23 Romoda Dr	Canton	NY	13617	**800-285-1856***	315-229-5261	166
*Admissions						
Saint Leo University						
33701 State Rd 52	Saint Leo	FL	33574	**800-334-5532**	352-588-8200	166
Palatka Ctr						
33701 State Rd 52 PO Box 6665	Saint Leo	FL	33574	**800-334-5532**	352-588-8200	166
Saint Louis Children's Hospital						
One Children's Pl	Saint Louis	MO	63110	**800-427-4626**	314-454-6000	371-1
Saint Louis Christian College						
1360 Grandview Dr	Florissant	MO	63033	**800-887-7522***	314-837-6777	159
*Admissions						
Saint Louis College of Pharmacy						
4588 Parkview Pl	Saint Louis	MO	63110	**800-278-5267**	314-367-8700	166
Saint Louis Embroidery						
1759 Scherer Pkwy	Saint Charles	MO	63303	**800-457-6676**	636-724-2200	258
Saint Louis Executive Conference Ctr						
701 Convention Plz	Saint Louis	MO	63101	**800-325-7962**	314-342-5050	206
Saint Louis Music Inc						
1400 Ferguson Ave	Saint Louis	MO	63133	**800-727-4512**	314-727-4512	520
Saint Louis Paper & Box Co						
3843 Garfield Ave	Saint Louis	MO	63113	**800-779-7901**	314-531-7900	552
Saint Louis Science Ctr						
5050 Oakland Ave	Saint Louis	MO	63110	**800-456-4491**	314-289-4400	513
Saint Louis Symphony Orchestra						
718 N Grand Blvd	Saint Louis	MO	63103	**800-232-1880**	314-533-2500	566-3
Saint Louis University						
221 N Grand Blvd	Saint Louis	MO	63103	**800-758-3678**	314-977-7288	166
Saint Louis University Cancer Ctr Hematology & Oncology Div						
3655 Vista Ave	Saint Louis	MO	63110	**866-977-4440**	314-977-4440	759
Saint Louis University School of Law						
3700 Lindell Blvd	Saint Louis	MO	63108	**800-758-3678**	314-977-2766	167-1
Saint Louis University School of Medicine						
One North Grand Rm17	Saint Louis	MO	63103	**800-758-3678**		167-2
Saint Lucia						
Embassy						
3216 New Mexico Ave NW	Washington	DC	20016	**800-456-3984**	202-364-6792	257
Saint Lucia Tourist Board						
800 Second Ave Ninth Fl	New York	NY	10017	**800-456-3984**	212-867-2950	765
Saint Luke's Hospital & Regional Trauma Ctr						
915 E First St	Duluth	MN	55805	**866-261-5915**	218-249-5555	371-3
Saint Luke's Hospital of New Bedford						
101 Page St	New Bedford	MA	02740	**800-497-1727**	508-997-1515	371-3
Saint Luke's Regional Medical Ctr						
2720 Stone Pk Blvd	Sioux City	IA	51104	**800-352-4660**	712-279-3500	371-3
Saint Martin's University						
5300 Pacific Ave SE	Lacey	WA	98503	**800-368-8803***	360-438-4311	166
*Admissions						
Saint Mary Mercy Hospital						
36475 Five-Mile Rd	Livonia	MI	48154	**800-464-7492**	734-655-4800	371-3
Saint Mary's College						
Le Mans Hall Rm 122	Notre Dame	IN	46556	**800-551-7621***	574-284-4587	166
*Admissions						
Saint Mary's College of California						
1928 St Mary's Rd	Moraga	CA	94556	**800-800-4762***	925-631-4000	166
*Admissions						
Saint Mary's College of Maryland						
18952 E Fisher Rd	Saint Marys City	MD	20686	**800-492-7181***	240-895-2000	166
*Admissions						
Saint Mary's Health Care System						
1230 Baxter St	Athens	GA	30606	**800-233-7864**	706-389-3000	371-3
Saint Mary's Health Ctr						
6420 Clayton Rd	Richmond Heights	MO	63117	**877-783-4193**	314-768-8000	371-3
Saint Mary's Hospital						
2251 N Shore Dr	Rhinelander	WI	54501	**800-578-0840***	715-361-2000	371-3
*Cust Svc						
Saint Mary's Hospital & Regional Medical Ctr						
2635 N Seventh St	Grand Junction	CO	81502	**800-458-3888**		371-3
Saint Mary's Hospital Medical Ctr						
1726 Shawano Ave	Green Bay	WI	54303	**800-666-5606**	920-498-4200	371-3
Saint Mary's River State Park						
c/o Pt Lookout State Pk						
11175 Pt Lookout Rd	Scotland	MD	20687	**800-830-3974**	301-872-5688	558
Saint Mary's School						
900 Hillsborough St	Raleigh	NC	27603	**800-948-2557**	919-424-4000	615
Saint Mary's University						
One Camino Santa Maria	San Antonio	TX	78228	**800-367-7868***	210-436-3126	166
*Admissions						

	City	State	ZIP	Toll-Free	Phone	Class
Saint Mary's University of Minnesota						
700 Terr Heights	Winona	MN	55987	**800-635-5987**	507-452-4430	166
Saint Mary-Corwin Medical Ctr						
1008 Minnequa Ave	Pueblo	CO	81004	**800-228-4039**	719-557-4000	371-3
Saint Mary-of-the-Woods College						
3301 St Mary Rd	Saint Mary Of The Woods	IN	47876	**800-926-7692**	812-535-5106	166
Saint Meinrad Archabbey						
200 Hill Dr	Saint Meinrad	IN	47577	**800-682-0988**	812-357-6585	664
Saint Michael's College						
One Winooski Pk	Colchester	VT	05439	**800-762-8000**	802-654-2000	166
Saint Michael's Hospital						
30 Bond St	Toronto	ON	M5B1W8	**866-797-0000**	416-360-4000	371-2
Saint Michael's University School						
3400 Richmond Rd	Victoria	BC	V8P4P5	**800-661-5199**	250-592-2411	615
Saint Michaels Harbour Inn & Marina						
101 N Harbor Rd	Saint Michaels	MD	21663	**800-955-9001**	410-745-9001	376
Saint Norbert College						
100 Grant St	De Pere	WI	54115	**800-236-4878***	920-403-3005	166
*Admissions						
Saint Paul College						
235 Marshall Ave	Saint Paul	MN	55102	**800-227-6029**	651-846-1600	788
Saint Paul Foundation						
55 E Fifth St Ste 600	Saint Paul	MN	55101	**800-875-6167**	651-224-5463	302
Saint Paul Hotel						
350 Market St	Saint Paul	MN	55102	**800-292-9292**	651-292-9292	376
Saint Paul Public Library						
90 W Fourth St	Saint Paul	MN	55102	**888-335-9632**	651-266-7000	431-3
Saint Paul School of Theology						
5123 Truman Rd	Kansas City	MO	64127	**800-825-0378**		167-3
Saint Paul University						
223 Main St	Ottawa	ON	K1S1C4	**800-637-6859**	613-236-1393	773
Saint Regis Aspen						
315 E Dean St	Aspen	CO	81611	**888-627-7198***	970-920-3300	698
*General						
Saint Regis Culvert Inc						
202 Morrell St	Charlotte	MI	48813	**800-527-4604**	517-543-3430	688
Saint Regis Hotel						
602 Dunsmuir St	Vancouver	BC	V6B1Y6	**800-770-7929**	604-681-1135	376
Saint Regis Hotel Winnipeg						
285 Smith St	Winnipeg	MB	R3C1K9	**800-663-7344**	204-942-0171	376
Saint Regis Monarch Beach Resort & Spa						
One Monarch Beach Resort	Dana Point	CA	92629	**800-722-1543**	949-234-3200	660
Saint Regis Resort Aspen						
315 E Dean St	Aspen	CO	81611	**888-627-7198**	970-920-3300	660
Saint Rita's Medical Ctr (SRMC)						
730 W Market St	Lima	OH	45801	**800-232-7762**	419-227-3361	371-3
Saint Tammany Parish Tourist & Convention Commission						
68099 Hwy 59	Mandeville	LA	70471	**800-634-9443**	985-892-0520	207
Saint Thomas Hospital						
4220 HaRding Rd	Nashville	TN	37205	**800-400-5800**	615-222-2111	371-3
Saint Thomas University						
16401 NW 37th Ave	Miami Gardens	FL	33054	**800-367-9010**	305-628-6546	166
Saint Thomas University School of Law						
16401 NW 37th Ave	Miami Gardens	FL	33054	**800-245-4569**	305-623-2310	167-1
Saint Tropez Hotel						
Rumor						
455 E Harmon Ave	Las Vegas	NV	89109	**877-997-8667**	702-369-5400	376
Saint Vincent & the Grenadines Tourist Information Office						
801 Second Ave 21st Fl	New York	NY	10017	**800-729-1726**	212-687-4981	765
Saint Vincent Charity Hospital (SVCH)						
2351 E 22nd St	Cleveland	OH	44115	**800-750-0750**	216-861-6200	371-3
Saint Vincent College						
300 Fraser Purchase Rd	Latrobe	PA	15650	**800-782-5549**	724-532-6600	166
Saint Vincent Hospital						
835 S Van Buren St	Green Bay	WI	54301	**800-236-3030**	920-433-0111	371-3
Saint Vincent Hospital-Worcester Medical Ctr						
123 Summer St	Worcester	MA	01608	**877-633-2368**	508-363-5000	371-3
Saint Vincent Women's Hospital						
8111 Township Line Rd	Indianapolis	IN	46260	**800-582-8258**	317-415-8111	371-7
Saint Vincent's Medical Ctr						
2800 Main St	Bridgeport	CT	06606	**877-255-7847**	203-576-6000	371-3
Saint Xavier University						
3700 W 103rd St	Chicago	IL	60655	**800-462-9288**	773-298-3000	166
Saint-Gobain Abrasives Inc						
2770 W Washington St	Stephenville	TX	76401	**800-561-9490**	254-918-2310	1
Saint-Gobain Advanced Ceramics Latrobe						
4702 Rt 982	Latrobe	PA	15650	**800-438-7237**	724-539-6000	249
Saint-Gobain Corp						
750 E Swedesford Rd	Valley Forge	PA	19482	**800-506-7427**	610-341-7000	328
SAISD (San Antonio Independent School District)						
141 Lavaca St	San Antonio	TX	78210	**800-943-6422**	210-554-2200	676
Sakatah Lake State Park						
50499 Sakatah Lake State Pk Rd	Waterville	MN	56096	**888-646-6367**	507-362-4438	558
Sakonnet Vineyards						
162 W Main Rd	Little Compton	RI	02837	**800-919-4637**	401-635-8486	49-6
Sakura Finetek USA Inc						
1750 W 214th St	Torrance	CA	90501	**800-725-8723**	310-972-7800	416
Saladmaster Inc						
230 Westway Pl Ste 101	Arlington	TX	76018	**800-765-5795**	817-633-3555	481
Salco Products Inc						
1385 101st St Ste A	Lemont	IL	60439	**800-535-8990**	630-783-2570	641
Saleen Automotive Inc						
2735 Wardlow Rd	Corona	CA	92882	**800-888-8945**		58
Salem College						
601 S Church St	Winston-Salem	NC	27101	**800-327-2536***	336-721-2600	166
*Admissions						
Salem Conference Ctr						
200 Commercial St SE	Salem	OR	97301	**877-589-1700***	503-589-1700	206
*Sales						
Salem Convention & Visitors Assn						
181 High St NE	Salem	OR	97301	**800-874-7012**	503-581-4325	207
Salem Five & Savings Bank						
210 Essex St	Salem	MA	01970	**800-850-5000***	978-745-5555	69
*Cust Svc						
Salem Hospital						
665 Winter St SE	Salem	OR	97301	**800-876-1718**		371-3
Salem International University						
223 W Main St	Salem	WV	26426	**800-283-4562**	304-326-1109	166
Salem Museum						
801 E Main St	Salem	VA	24153	**888-827-2536**	540-389-6760	513
Salem Tools Inc						
1602 Midland Rd	Salem	VA	24153	**800-390-4348**	540-389-0233	383

	City	State	ZIP	Toll-Free	Phone	Class
Salem Witch Museum						
19 1/2 Washington Sq N	Salem	MA	01970	**800-392-6100**	978-744-1692	513
Salem-Keizer Public Schools						
2450 Lancaster Dr NE	Salem	OR	97305	**877-293-1090**	503-399-3000	676
Salem-Republic Rubber Co						
475 W California Ave	Sebring	OH	44672	**800-686-4199**	330-938-9801	367
Sales Benchmark Index						
1595 Peachtree Pkwy Ste 204-328	Cumming	GA	30041	**888-556-7338**		5
Sales Leader						
2222 Sedwick Dr Ste 101	Durham	NC	27713	**800-223-8720**		524-10
Sales Readiness Group Inc						
8015 SE 28th St Ste 206	Mercer Island	WA	98040	**800-490-0715**		196
Salesforce.Com Foundation						
The Landmark @ One Market						
Ste 300	San Francisco	CA	94105	**800-667-6389**		304
Salesforce.com Inc						
One Market St						
The Landmark Ste 300	San Francisco	CA	94105	**800-667-6389**	415-901-7000	38
NYSE: CRM						
Salesnet						
3296 Summit Ridge Pkwy Ste 210	Duluth	GA	30096	**866-732-8632**		38
Salice America Inc						
2123 Crown Centre Dr	Charlotte	NC	28227	**800-222-9652**	704-841-7810	347
Salin Bank						
8455 Keystone Xing	Indianapolis	IN	46240	**800-320-7536**	317-452-8000	676
Salinas Valley Chamber of Commerce						
119 E Alisal St	Salinas	CA	93901	**888-678-2871**	831-751-7725	137
Salinas Valley Memorial Hospital (SVMH)						
450 E Romie Ln	Salinas	CA	93901	**800-722-4673**	831-757-4333	371-3
Salisbury Bancorp Inc						
Five Bissell St PO Box 1868	Lakeville	CT	06039	**800-222-9801**	860-435-9801	357-2
NASDAQ: SAL						
Salisbury Hotel						
123 W 57th St	New York	NY	10019	**888-692-5757**	212-246-1300	376
Salisbury Inc						
29085 Airpark Dr	Easton	MD	21601	**855-255-5309**	410-770-4901	693
Salisbury University						
1200 Camden Ave	Salisbury	MD	21801	**888-543-0148**	410-543-6000	166
Salish Kootenai College						
PO Box 70	Pablo	MT	59855	**877-752-6553**	406-275-4800	163
Salish Lodge & Spa						
6501 Railroad Ave DE						
PO Box 1109	Snoqualmie	WA	98065	**800-272-5474**	425-888-2556	660
Salishan Lodge & Golf Resort						
PO Box 118	Gleneden Beach	OR	97388	**800-452-2300**		660
Salix Pharmaceuticals Inc						
8510 Colonnade Ctr Dr	Raleigh	NC	27615	**800-508-0024**	919-862-1000	576
NASDAQ: SLXP						
Salk Institute for Biological Studies						
PO Box 85800	San Diego	CA	92186	**800-245-9757**	858-453-4100	659
Sallie Mae						
12061 Bluemont Way	Reston	VA	20190	**888-272-5543***	703-810-3000	214
*Cust Svc						
Sally Beauty Company Inc						
3001 Colorado Blvd	Denton	TX	76210	**800-777-5706**	940-898-7500	75
Salmon River Electric Co-op Inc						
1130 Main St PO Box 384	Challis	ID	83226	**877-806-2283**	208-879-2283	245
Salon Media Group Inc						
101 Spear St Ste 203	San Francisco	CA	94105	**800-257-8650**	415-645-9200	795
Salsbury Industries Inc						
1010 E 62nd St	Los Angeles	CA	90001	**800-624-5299**	323-846-6700	286
Salt Lake City International Airport						
776 N Terminal Dr						
PO Box 145550	Salt Lake City	UT	84116	**800-595-2442**	801-575-2400	27
Salt Lake Convention & Visitors Bureau						
90 SW Temple	Salt Lake City	UT	84101	**800-541-4955**	801-534-4900	207
Salt Lake Temple						
50 W N Temple St	Salt Lake City	UT	84150	**800-453-3860**	801-240-2640	49
Salt River Electric Co-op Corp						
111 W Brashear Ave	Bardstown	KY	40004	**800-221-7465**	502-348-3931	245
Salt River Project (SRP)						
1521 N Project Dr	Tempe	AZ	85281	**800-258-4777**	602-236-5900	775
Salt Springs State Park						
c/o Lackawanna	North Abington Twp	PA	18414	**888-727-2757**	570-945-3239	558
Salt Water Sportsman Magazine						
460 N Orlando Ave Ste 200	Winter Park	FL	32789	**800-759-2127**	407-628-4802	452-20
Salter Bus Lines Inc						
212 Hudson Ave	Jonesboro	LA	71251	**800-223-8056**	318-259-2522	106
Salter Labs						
100 Sycamore Rd	Arvin	CA	93203	**800-421-0024**	661-854-3166	471
Salty Dog Cafe, The						
232 S Sea Pines Dr	Hilton Head Island	SC	29928	**877-725-8936**	843-671-5199	662
Salus Group Benefits Inc						
37525 Mound Rd	Sterling Heights	MI	48310	**866-991-9907**		260
Salvatore's Italian Gardens						
6461 Transit Rd	Depew	NY	14043	**877-456-4097**	716-683-7990	662
Salve Regina University						
100 Ochre Pt Ave	Newport	RI	02840	**888-467-2583**	401-847-6650	166
Sam Clar Office Furniture Inc						
1221 Diamond Way	Concord	CA	94520	**800-726-2527**	925-602-3900	320
Sam Hausman Meat Packer Inc						
4261 Beacon	Corpus Christi	TX	78403	**800-364-5521**	361-883-5521	468
Sam Houston Electric Co-op Inc						
1157 E Church St	Livingston	TX	77351	**800-458-0381**	936-327-5711	245
Sam Houston Jones State Park						
107 Sutherland Rd	Lake Charles	LA	70611	**888-677-7264**	337-855-2665	558
Sam Houston Race Park						
7575 N Sam Houston Pkwy W	Houston	TX	77064	**800-807-7223**	281-807-8700	633
Sam Houston State University						
1903 University Ave	Huntsville	TX	77340	**866-232-7528**	936-294-1111	166
Sam Kane Beef Processors Inc						
9001 Leopard St	Corpus Christi	TX	78409	**800-242-4142**	361-241-5000	468
Sam Swope Volkswagen of Clarksville						
125 W Lewis & Clark Pkw	Clarksville	IN	47129	**866-308-0592**	812-948-1541	56
Sam's Town Hotel & Casino Shreveport						
315 Clyde Fant Pkwy	Shreveport	LA	71101	**877-770-7867**		132
Sam's Town Hotel & Gambling Hall						
5111 Boulder Hwy	Las Vegas	NV	89122	**800-897-8696**	702-456-7777	132
Samaritan Hospice						
Five Eves Dr Ste 300	Marlton	NJ	08053	**800-229-8183**	856-596-1600	368
Samaritan Medical Ctr						
830 Washington St	Watertown	NY	13601	**877-888-6138**	315-785-4000	371-3
Samaritan Village						
138-02 Queens Blvd	Briarwood	NY	11435	**800-532-4357**	718-206-2000	717

	Toll-Free	Phone	Class
Sambazon Inc			
1160 Calle Cordillera . . . . San Clemente CA 92673	**877-726-2296**	949-498-8618	296-7
Samco Scientific Corp			
81 WYMAN ST PO Box 9046 . . . . Waltham MA 02451	**800-522-3359**	781-622-1000	417
SAME (Society of American Military Engineers)			
607 Prince St . . . . Alexandria VA 22314	**800-336-3097**	703-549-3800	47-19
Samford University			
800 Lakeshore Dr . . . . Birmingham AL 35229	**800-888-7218***	205-726-3673	166
*Admissions			
SAMHSA (Substance Abuse & Mental Health Services Administration)			
1 Choke Cherry Rd . . . . Rockville MD 20857	**877-726-4727**	240-276-2000	338-8
Sammann Co Inc			
9935 N Us Hwy 12 E . . . . Michigan City IN 46360	**800-348-2508**	219-872-4413	231
Sammons Trucking			
3665 W Broadway . . . . Missoula MT 59808	**800-548-9276**	406-728-2600	770
Samoset Resort			
220 Warrenton St . . . . Rockport ME 04856	**800-341-1650**	207-594-2511	660
Sampco Inc			
651 W Washington Blvd Ste 300 . . . . Chicago IL 60661	**800-767-0689**	312-346-1506	296-9
SAMPE (Society for the Advancement of Material & Process Engineering)			
1161 Pk View Dr Ste 200 . . . . Covina CA 91724	**800-562-7360**	626-331-0616	48-19
Sampson-Bladen Oil Co Inc			
510 Commerce St PO Box 469 . . . . Clinton NC 28329	**800-849-4177**	910-592-4177	323
SAMS (Society of Accredited Marine Surveyors Inc)			
7855 Argyle Forest Blvd			
Ste 203 . . . . Jacksonville FL 32244	**800-344-9077**	904-384-1494	47-1
Sams Technical Publishing			
9850 E 30th St . . . . Indianapolis IN 46229	**800-428-7267***		628-2
*Cust Svc			
Samsill Corp			
5740 Hartman Rd . . . . Fort Worth TX 76119	**800-255-1100**	817-536-1906	85
Samson Rope Technologies Inc			
2090 Thornton Rd . . . . Ferndale WA 98248	**800-227-7673***	360-384-4669	209
*Cust Svc			
Samsung Semiconductors Inc			
3655 N First St . . . . San Jose CA 95134	**800-726-7864***	408-544-4000	687
*General			
Samsung Telecommunications America LLP			
1301 E Lookout Dr . . . . Richardson TX 75082	**800-726-7864**	972-761-7000	725
Samtec Inc			
520 Parkeast Blvd . . . . New Albany IN 47150	**800-726-8329**	812-944-6733	253
Samuel A Ramirez & Co Inc			
61 Broadway Ste 2924 . . . . New York NY 10006	**800-888-4086**		681
Samuel Cabot Inc			
100 Hale St . . . . Newburyport MA 01950	**800-877-8246**	978-465-1900	543
Samuel Mahelona Memorial Hospital			
4800 Kawaihau Rd . . . . Kapaa HI 96746	**800-845-6733**	808-822-4961	371-7
Samuel Merritt College			
370 Hawthorne Ave . . . . Oakland CA 94609	**800-607-6377***	510-869-6576	166
*Admissions			
Samuels Jewelers			
9607 Research Blvd			
Ste 100 Bldg F . . . . Austin TX 78759	**877-202-2870**	512-369-1400	407
Samy's Camera Inc			
431 S Fairfax Ave . . . . Los Angeles CA 90036	**800-321-4726**	323-938-2420	118
San Angelo Chamber of Commerce			
418 W Ave B . . . . San Angelo TX 76903	**800-252-1381**	325-655-4136	207
San Angelo Standard Times Inc			
PO Box 5111 . . . . San Angelo TX 76902	**800-588-1884**	325-653-1221	628-8
San Angelo Standard-Times			
34 W Harris Ave . . . . San Angelo TX 76903	**800-588-1884**	325-659-8200	525-2
San Antonio Convention & Visitors Bureau			
203 S St Marys St Ste 200 . . . . San Antonio TX 78205	**800-447-3372**	210-207-6700	207
San Antonio Express-News			
Ave E & Third St . . . . San Antonio TX 78205	**800-555-1551**	210-250-3000	525-2
San Antonio Federal Credit Union			
PO Box 1356 . . . . San Antonio TX 78295	**800-234-7228**	210-258-1234	219
San Antonio Independent School District (SAISD)			
141 Lavaca St . . . . San Antonio TX 78210	**800-943-6422**	210-554-2200	676
San Antonio International Airport (SAT)			
9800 Airport Blvd Rm 2041 . . . . . . San Antonio TX 78216	**800-237-6639**	210-207-3411	27
San Antonio Missions National Historical Park			
2202 Roosevelt Ave . . . . San Antonio TX 78210	**866-945-7920**	210-534-8833	557
San Antonio Municipal Auditorium			
200 E Market St PO Box 1809 . . . . . San Antonio TX 78205	**877-504-8895**	210-207-8500	565
San Benito Public Library			
101 W Rose St . . . . San Benito TX 78586	**800-444-1187**	956-361-3860	431-3
San Bernard Electric Co-op Inc			
309 W Main St . . . . Bellville TX 77418	**800-364-3171**	979-865-3171	245
San Bernardino Area Chamber of Commerce			
PO Box 658 . . . . San Bernardino CA 92402	**800-928-5091**	909-885-7515	137
San Bernardino Convention & Visitors Bureau			
1955 Hunts Ln Ste 102 . . . . San Bernardino CA 92408	**800-867-8366**	909-891-1151	207
San Bernardino County			
385 N Arrowhead Ave Fl 5 . . . . . . San Bernardino CA 92415	**888-818-8988**	909-387-8306	336
San Carlos Hotel			
150 E 50th St . . . . New York NY 10022	**800-722-2012**	212-755-1800	376
San Clemente Chamber of Commerce			
1100 N El Camino Real . . . . San Clemente CA 92672	**877-411-3662**	949-492-1131	137
San Diego Blood Bank			
440 Upas St . . . . San Diego CA 92103	**800-479-3902**	619-296-6393	88
San Diego Business Journal			
4909 Murphy Canyon Rd Ste 200 . . . . . . San Diego CA 92123	**888-425-7325**	858-277-6359	452-5
San Diego Chargers			
4020 Murphy Canyon Rd . . . . San Diego CA 92123	**877-242-7437**	858-874-4500	706-3
San Diego Christian College			
2100 Greenfield Dr . . . . El Cajon CA 92019	**800-676-2242**	619-441-2200	166
San Diego Concierge			
4379 30th St Ste 4 . . . . San Diego CA 92104	**800-979-9091**	619-280-4121	373
San Diego Convention Ctr			
111 W Harbor Dr . . . . San Diego CA 92101	**800-525-7322**	619-525-5000	206
San Diego County Credit Union			
6545 Sequence Dr . . . . San Diego CA 92121	**877-732-2848**		219
San Diego Daily Transcript			
2131 Third Ave . . . . San Diego CA 92101	**800-697-6397**	619-232-4381	525-2
San Diego Eye Bank (SDEB)			
9246 Lightwave Ave Ste 120 . . . . . . San Diego CA 92123	**800-393-2265**	858-694-0400	269
San Diego Gas & Electric Co			
101 Ash St . . . . San Diego CA 92101	**800-411-7343**	619-696-2000	775
San Diego Public Library			
820 E St . . . . San Diego CA 92101	**866-470-1308**	619-236-5800	431-3
San Diego Union-Tribune			
350 Camino De La Reina . . . . San Diego CA 92108	**800-244-6397**	619-299-3131	525-2
San Diego Zoo Safari Park			
15500 San Pasqual Valley Rd . . . . Escondido CA 92027	**877-363-6237***	760-747-8702	810
*Cust Svc			
San Dieguito Printers			
1880 Diamond St . . . . San Marcos CA 92078	**800-321-5794**	760-744-0910	628-10
San Francisco Art Institute			
800 Chestnut St . . . . San Francisco CA 94133	**800-345-7324**	415-771-7020	162
San Francisco Ballet			
455 Franklin St . . . . San Francisco CA 94102	**888-622-2108**	415-865-2000	566-1
San Francisco Chamber of Commerce			
235 Montgomery St 12th Fl . . . . . San Francisco CA 94104	**888-834-3040**	415-392-4520	137
San Francisco Chronicle			
901 Mission St . . . . San Francisco CA 94103	**866-732-4766**	415-777-1111	525-2
San Francisco Conservatory of Music			
50 Oak St . . . . San Francisco CA 94102	**800-999-8219**	415-864-7326	166
San Francisco Convention & Visitors Bureau			
201 Third St Ste 900 . . . . San Francisco CA 94103	**855-847-6272**	415-974-6900	207
San Francisco Federal Credit Union			
770 Golden Gate Ave . . . . San Francisco CA 94102	**800-852-7598**	415-775-5377	219
San Francisco General Hospital Medical Ctr			
1001 Potrero Ave Ste 1E21 . . . . . San Francisco CA 94110	**800-723-7140**	415-206-8426	371-3
San Francisco International Airport			
PO Box 8097 . . . . San Francisco CA 94128	**800-435-9736**	650-821-8211	27
San Francisco Magazine			
243 Vallejo St . . . . San Francisco CA 94111	**866-736-2499**	415-398-2800	452-22
San Francisco Museum of Modern Art			
151 Third St . . . . San Francisco CA 94103	**800-792-0754**	415-357-4000	513
San Francisco Music Box Co			
5370 W 95th St . . . . Prairie Village KS 66207	**800-227-2190**		326
San Francisco Theological Seminary			
105 Seminary Rd . . . . San Anselmo CA 94960	**800-447-8820**	415-451-2800	167-3
San Gabriel Valley Tribune			
1210 N Azusa Canyon Rd . . . . West Covina CA 91790	**800-788-1200**	626-962-8811	525-2
San Isabel Electric			
893 E Enterprise Dr . . . . Pueblo West CO 81007	**800-279-7432**	719-547-2160	245
San Joaquin Hotel			
1309 W Shaw Ave . . . . Fresno CA 93711	**800-775-1309***	559-225-1309	376
*General			
San Jose Convention & Visitors Bureau			
408 Almaden Blvd . . . . San Jose CA 95110	**800-726-5673**	408-295-9600	207
San Jose Convention Center (SJC)			
150 W San Carlos St . . . . San Jose CA 95110	**800-726-5673**	408-792-4194	206
San Jose Ctr for the Performing Arts			
255 Almaden Blvd . . . . San Jose CA 95113	**800-726-5673**	408-792-4111	565
San Jose Sharks			
HP Pavilion at San Jose			
525 W Santa Clara St . . . . San Jose CA 95113	**800-755-5050**	408-287-7070	707
San Jose State University			
1 Washington Sq . . . . San Jose CA 95192	**800-273-8255**	408-924-1000	166
San Jose Unified School District			
855 Lenzen Ave . . . . San Jose CA 95126	**800-433-3243**	408-535-6000	676
San Juan Airlines Co			
4000 Airport Rd Ste A . . . . Anacortes WA 98221	**800-874-4434**	360-293-4691	13
San Juan College			
4601 College Blvd . . . . Farmington NM 87402	**866-426-1233**	*505-326-3311	160
San Luis Obispo New Times			
505 Higuera St . . . . San Luis Obispo CA 93401	**800-546-4219**	805-546-8208	525-5
San Luis Resort Spa & Conference Ctr			
5222 Seawall Blvd . . . . Galveston Island TX 77551	**800-445-0090***	409-744-1500	660
*Cust Svc			
San Luis Valley Rural Electric Co-op			
3625 US Hwy 160 W . . . . Monte Vista CO 81144	**800-332-7634**	719-852-3538	245
San Manuel Indian Bingo & Casino			
777 San Manuel Blvd . . . . Highland CA 92346	**800-359-2464**		132
San Marcos Academy			
2801 Ranch to Market 12 . . . . San Marcos TX 78666	**800-428-5120***	512-353-2400	615
*Admissions			
San Marcos Area Chamber of Commerce			
202 N CM Allen Pkwy . . . . San Marcos TX 78666	**888-200-5620**	512-393-5900	137
San Marcos Chamber of Commerce			
939 Grand Ave . . . . San Marcos CA 92078	**800-814-7241**	760-744-1270	137
San Mateo County Convention & Visitors Bureau			
111 Anza Blvd Ste 410 . . . . Burlingame CA 94010	**800-288-4748**	650-348-7600	207
San Mateo County Times			
477 Ninth Ave Ste 110 . . . . San Mateo CA 94402	**800-870-6397**	650-348-4321	525-2
San Mateo County Transit District			
1250 San Carlos Ave			
PO Box 3006 . . . . San Carlos CA 94070	**800-660-4287**	650-508-6200	463
San Miguel Power Assn Inc			
170 W Tenth Ave . . . . Nucla CO 81424	**800-864-7256**	970-864-7311	245
San Miguel Produce Inc			
4444 Naval Air Rd . . . . Oxnard CA 93033	**888-347-3367**	805-488-0981	10-10
San Patricio Electric Co-op Inc			
402 E Sinton St . . . . Sinton TX 78387	**888-740-2220**	361-364-2220	245
San Rafael Chamber of Commerce			
817 Mission Ave . . . . San Rafael CA 94901	**888-378-0777**	415-454-4163	137
San Sebastian Winery			
157 King St . . . . Saint Augustine FL 32084	**888-352-9463**	904-826-1594	49-6
San Vicente Inn & Golf Course			
24157 San Vicente Rd . . . . Ramona CA 92065	**800-776-1289**	760-789-3788	660
Sancap Abrasives			
16123 Armour St NE . . . . Alliance OH 44601	**800-433-6663**	330-821-3510	1
Sanctuary on Camelback Mountain			
5700 E McDonald Dr . . . . Paradise Valley AZ 85253	**800-245-2051**	480-948-2100	660
Sand Dunes Resort Hotel			
201 74th Ave N . . . . Myrtle Beach SC 29572	**800-726-3783**	843-449-3313	660
Sand Mountain Electric Co-op			
402 Main St W . . . . Rainsville AL 35986	**877-843-2512**	256-638-2153	245
Sand Seed Service Inc			
4765 Hwy 143 . . . . Marcus IA 51035	**800-352-2228**	712-376-4135	685
Sand Technology Inc			
4115 Rue Sherbrooke Ouest . . . . Westmount QC H3Z1B1	**877-468-2538**	514-939-3477	179-1
NYSE: SNDTF			
Sandals Life Style			
4950 SW 72nd Ave . . . . Miami FL 33155	**888-726-3257**	876-952-5510	375
Sandals Resorts International			
4950 SW 72nd Ave . . . . Miami FL 33155	**888-726-3257**	305-284-1300	660
Sandata Technologies Inc			
26 Harbor Pk Dr . . . . Port Washington NY 11050	**800-544-7263***	516-484-4400	179-11
*Sales			
Sandel Avionics Inc			
2401 Dogwood Way . . . . Vista CA 92081	**877-726-3357**	760-727-4900	21
Sandelman & Assoc Inc			
257 La Paloma Ste 1 . . . . San Clemente CA 92672	**888-897-7881**	949-388-5600	659

Name / Address	City	State	ZIP	Toll-Free	Phone	Class
Sanderling Resort & Spa						
1461 Duck Rd	Duck	NC	27949	**800-701-4111**	252-261-4111	660
Sanders Ford Inc						
1135 Lejeune Blvd	Jacksonville	NC	28540	**888-897-8527***	910-455-1911	509
*General						
Sanderson-MacLeod Inc						
1199 S Main St PO Box 50	Palmer	MA	01069	**866-522-3481**	413-283-3481	102
Sandestin Golf & Beach Resort						
9300 Emerald Coast Pkwy W	Sandestin	FL	32550	**800-277-0800**	850-267-8000	660
Sandhills Community College						
3395 Airport Rd	Pinehurst	NC	28374	**800-338-3944**	910-692-6185	160
Sandhills Publishing						
120 W Harvest Dr	Lincoln	NE	68521	**800-331-1978**	402-479-2181	628-9
Sandia Resort & Casino						
30 Rainbow Rd NE	Albuquerque	NM	87113	**800-526-9366**	505-796-7500	132
Sandler O'Neill + Partners LP						
1251 Avenue of the Americas						
6th Fl	New York	NY	10020	**800-635-6851**	212-466-7800	681
Sandler Sales Institute						
10411 Stevenson Rd	Stevenson	MD	21153	**800-669-3537**	410-653-1993	755
Sandmeyer Steel Co						
One Sandmeyer Ln	Philadelphia	PA	19116	**800-523-3663**	215-464-7100	714
Sandridge Food Corp (SFC)						
133 Commerce Dr	Medina	OH	44256	**800-672-2523**	330-725-2348	295-33
Sands Casino Resort Bethlehem						
77 Sands Blvd	Bethlehem	PA	18015	**877-726-3777**		376
Sands Ocean Club Resort						
9550 Shore Dr	Myrtle Beach	SC	29572	**888-999-8485***		376
*General						
Sands Regency Casino Hotel						
345 N Arlington Ave	Reno	NV	89501	**866-337-1555***	775-348-2200	376
*Resv						
Sandusky Cabinets Inc						
16125 Widmere Rd PO Box 517	Arvin	CA	93203	**800-886-8688***	661-854-5551	286
*Cust Svc						
Sandusky Electric Inc						
1513 Sycamore Line PO Box 2353	Sandusky	OH	44870	**800-356-1243**	419-625-4915	246
Sandusky Register						
314 W Market St	Sandusky	OH	44870	**800-466-1243**	419-625-5500	525-2
Sandusky-Chicago Abrasive Wheel Co						
1100 W Barker Ave	Michigan City	IN	46360	**800-843-4980**	219-879-6601	1
Sandvik Coromant Co						
1702 Nevins Rd	Fair Lawn	NJ	07410	**800-726-3845***	201-794-5000	450
*Cust Svc						
Sandvik Inc						
1702 Nevins Rd	Fair Lawn	NJ	07410	**800-726-3845**	201-794-5000	357-3
Sandwich Lodge & Resort						
54 Rt 6A - Old King's Hwy						
PO Box 1038	Sandwich	MA	02563	**800-282-5353**	508-888-2275	376
Sandy Corp						
300 E Big Beaver Rd Ste 500	Troy	MI	48083	**866-876-0606**	248-729-4628	195
Sandy Point State Park						
1100 E College Pkwy	Annapolis	MD	21409	**877-620-8836**	410-974-2149	558
Sandy Sansing Chevrolet						
6200 N Pensacola Blvd	Pensacola	FL	32505	**888-885-1844***	850-476-2480	56
*Sales						
Sandy Spring Bancorp Inc						
17801 Georgia Ave	Olney	MD	20832	**800-399-5919**	301-774-6400	357-2
NASDAQ: SASR						
Sandy Spring National Bank of Maryland						
17801 Georgia Ave	Olney	MD	20832	**800-399-5919**	301-774-6400	69
Sanford Aircraft Services Inc						
701 Rod Sullivan Rd	Sanford	NC	27330	**888-871-1947**	919-708-5549	62
Sanford-Brown College						
Boston 126 Newbury St	Boston	MA	02116	**877-809-2444**	617-578-7100	788
Sangre de Cristo Electric Assn						
29780 US Hwy 24	Buena Vista	CO	81211	**800-933-3823**	719-395-2412	245
Sanibel Harbour Marriott Resort & Spa						
17260 Harbour Pt Dr	Fort Myers	FL	33908	**800-767-7777**	239-466-4000	660
Sanibel Inn						
937 E Gulf Dr	Sanibel	FL	33957	**866-565-5480**	239-472-3181	376
SaniServ Inc						
451 E County Line Rd	Mooresville	IN	46158	**800-733-8073**	317-831-7030	297
Sanitary Services Co Inc						
21 Bellwether Way Ste 404	Bellingham	WA	98225	**888-333-9882**	360-734-3490	792
Sanofi Pasteur Inc						
Discovery Dr	Swiftwater	PA	18370	**800-822-2463***	570-839-7187	84
*Orders						
Sanofi-Aventis Canada						
2150 St Elzear Blvd W	Laval	QC	H7L4A8	**800-363-6364**	514-331-9220	84
S-Anon International Family Groups Inc						
PO Box 111242	Nashville	TN	37222	**800-210-8141**	615-833-3152	47-21
Sanrio Inc						
570 Eccles Ave	South San Francisco	CA	94080	**800-759-6454**	650-952-2880	327
Santa Barbara Inn						
901 E Cabrillo Blvd	Santa Barbara	CA	93103	**800-231-0431**	805-966-2285	376
Santa Barbara News-Press Publishing Co						
715 Anacapa St	Santa Barbara	CA	93101	**800-654-3292**	805-564-5200	628-8
Santa Barbara Visitors Bureau & Film Commission						
1601 Anacapa St	Santa Barbara	CA	93101	**800-676-1266**	805-966-9222	207
Santa Clara Convention/Visitors Bureau						
1850 Warburton Ave	Santa Clara	CA	95050	**800-272-6822**	408-244-9660	207
Santa Clara County Library						
14600 Winchester Blvd	Los Gatos	CA	95032	**800-286-1991**	408-293-2326	431-3
Santa Clara Valley Transportation Authority (VTA)						
3331 N First St	San Jose	CA	95134	**800-894-9908**	408-321-5555	463
Santa Cruz Chamber of Commerce						
611 Ocean St Ste 1	Santa Cruz	CA	95060	**866-282-5900**	831-457-3713	137
Santa Cruz County Conference & Visitors Council						
303 Water St Ste 100	Santa Cruz	CA	95060	**800-833-3494**	831-425-1234	207
Santa Cruz County Fair & Rodeo						
3142 Arizona 83 PO Box 85	Sonoita	AZ	85637	**866-394-0121**	520-455-5553	633
Santa Fe Convention Ctr						
201 W Marcy St	Santa Fe	NM	87501	**800-777-2489**	505-955-6200	207
Santa Fe County						
102 Grant Ave	Santa Fe	NM	87504	**877-607-0741**	505-986-6200	336
Santa Fe Municipal Airport (SAF)						
121 Aviation Dr PO Box 909	Santa Fe	NM	87504	**866-773-2587**	505-955-2900	27
Santa Fe Opera, The						
301 Opera Dr	Santa Fe	NM	87506	**800-280-4654**	505-986-5900	566-2
Santa Fe Station						
4949 N Rancho Dr	Las Vegas	NV	89130	**888-786-7389***	702-658-4900	132
*Resv						
Santa Fe Symphony Orchestra & Chorus Inc						
551 W Cordova Rd Ste D Ste D	Santa Fe	NM	87505	**800-480-1319**	505-983-3530	566-3
Santa Fe University of Art & Design						
1600 St Michaels Dr	Santa Fe	NM	87505	**800-456-2673**		166
Santa Gertrudis Breeders International						
PO Box 1257	Kingsville	TX	78364	**800-500-8242**	361-592-9357	47-2
Santa Maria Inn						
801 S Broadway	Santa Maria	CA	93454	**800-462-4276**	805-928-7777	376
Santa Maria Valley Chamber of Commerce						
614 S Broadway	Santa Maria	CA	93454	**800-331-3779**	805-925-2403	137
Santa Monica Civic Auditorium						
1855 Main St	Santa Monica	CA	90401	**866-728-3229**	310-458-8551	206
Santa Monica Convention & Visitors Bureau						
1920 Main St Ste B	Santa Monica	CA	90405	**800-544-5319**	310-319-6263	207
Santa Monica Mountains National Recreation Area						
401 W Hillcrest Dr	Thousand Oaks	CA	91360	**888-275-8747**	805-370-2300	557
Santa Rosa County Chamber of Commerce						
5247 Stewart St	Milton	FL	32570	**800-239-8732**	850-623-2339	137
Santa Rosa Junior College						
1501 Mendocino Ave	Santa Rosa	CA	95401	**800-564-7752**	707-527-4011	160
Santarus Inc						
3721 Vly Centre Dr						
Ste 400 Fourth Fl	San Diego	CA	92130	**888-778-0887***	858-314-5700	84
NASDAQ: SNTS ■ *Cust Svc						
Santee Electric Co-op Inc						
424 Sumter Hwy	Kingstree	SC	29556	**800-922-1604**	843-355-6187	245
Santillana USA Publishing Co						
2023 NW 84th Ave	Doral	FL	33122	**800-245-8584**	305-591-9522	628-2
Santinelli International Inc						
325 Oser Ave	Hauppauge	NY	11788	**800-644-3343**	631-435-3343	449
Sanyo Mfg Corp						
3333 Sanyo Rd	Forrest City	AR	72335	**800-100-3003**	870-633-5030	51
SAP						
100 Consilium Pl	Scarborough	ON	M1H3E3	**888-777-1727**	416-791-7100	179-1
SAP America Inc						
1721 Moon Lake Blvd						
Ste 300	Hoffman Estates	IL	60169	**800-872-1727**	847-230-3800	178
Sapa Inc						
7933 NE 21st Ave	Portland	OR	97211	**800-547-0790**	503-802-3000	476
Sapiens International Corp						
4000 CentreGreen Way Ste 150	Cary	NC	27513	**888-281-1167**	919-405-1500	179-10
NASDAQ: SPNS						
Sapient Corp						
131 Dartmouth St 3rd Fl	Boston	MA	02116	**866-796-6860**	617-621-0200	796
NASDAQ: SAPE						
Sarah Bush Lincoln Health Ctr (SBLHC)						
1000 Health Ctr Dr PO Box 372	Mattoon	IL	61938	**800-345-3191**	217-258-2525	371-3
Sarah Lawrence College						
One Meadway	Bronxville	NY	10708	**800-888-2858**		166
Saranac Glove Co						
999 LOmbardi Ave	Green Bay	WI	54304	**800-727-2622**	920-435-3737	153-7
Sarasota Film Festival						
332 Cocoanut Ave	Sarasota	FL	34236	**866-575-3456**	941-364-9514	282
Sarasota Herald-Tribune						
1741 Main St	Sarasota	FL	34236	**866-284-7102**	941-953-7755	525-2
Sarasota Jungle Gardens						
3701 Bay Shore Rd	Sarasota	FL	34234	**877-681-6547**	941-355-5305	810
Sarasota Memorial Hospital						
1700 S Tamiami Trl	Sarasota	FL	34239	**800-764-8255**	941-917-9000	371-3
Sarasota Opera						
61 N Pineapple Ave	Sarasota	FL	34236	**866-951-0111**	941-366-8450	566-2
Sarasota Orchestra						
709 N Tamiami Trl	Sarasota	FL	34236	**866-508-0611**	941-953-4252	566-3
Sarasota-Bradenton International Airport						
6000 Airport Cir	Sarasota	FL	34243	**800-711-1712**	941-359-5200	27
Saratoga County Chamber of Commerce						
28 Clinton St	Saratoga Springs	NY	12866	**855-765-7873**	518-584-3255	137
Saratoga Eagle Sales & Service Inc						
45 Duplainville Rd	Saratoga Springs	NY	12866	**800-310-5099**	518-581-7377	80-1
Saratoga Hilton						
534 Broadway	Saratoga Springs	NY	12866	**800-445-8667**	518-584-4000	376
SARCOM Inc						
8337 Green Meadows Dr N						
Ste A	Lewis Center	OH	43035	**800-700-1000**	614-854-1300	177
SARCOM Inc AEP Colloids Div						
6299 Rt 9N	Hadley	NY	12835	**800-848-0658**	518-696-9900	144
Sargent & Greenleaf Inc						
One Security Dr	Nicholasville	KY	40356	**800-826-7652**	859-885-9411	347
Sargent Art Inc						
100 E Diamond Ave	Hazleton	PA	18201	**800-424-3596**	570-454-3596	42
Sargent Controls & Aerospace						
5675 W Burlingame Rd	Tucson	AZ	85743	**800-230-0359**	520-744-1000	223
Sargent Corp						
378 Bennoch Rd	Stillwater	ME	04489	**800-533-1812**	207-827-4435	189-4
Sargent Manufacturing Co						
100 Sargent Dr	New Haven	CT	06511	**800-727-5477**		347
Sargento Foods Inc						
1 Persnickety Pl	Plymouth	WI	53073	**800-243-3737**	920-893-8484	295-5
Sartomer Co						
502 Thomas Jones Way	Exton	PA	19341	**800-345-8247**	610-363-4100	598-2
Sartori Food Corp						
107 Pleasant View Rd	Plymouth	WI	53073	**800-558-5888***	920-893-6061	295-5
*Cust Svc						
SAS (Scandinavian Airlines System)						
301 Route 17 N Ste 500	Rutherford	NJ	07070	**800-221-2350**	800-437-5807	25
SAS Institute Inc						
100 SAS Campus Dr	Cary	NC	27513	**800-727-0025**	919-677-8000	179-1
Sas Safety Corp						
3031 Gardenia Ave	Long Beach	CA	90807	**800-262-0200**	562-427-2775	472
SAS Shoemakers						
1717 SAS Dr	San Antonio	TX	78224	**877-782-7463**		300
Sashco Inc						
720 S Rochester Ave Ste D	Ontario	CA	91761	**800-600-3232**	909-937-8222	190-6
Saskatchewan Indian Gaming Authority						
250 - 103 C Packham Ave	Saskatoon	SK	S7N4K4	**800-306-6789**	306-477-7777	132
Saskatchewan Roughriders						
1910 Piffles Taylor Way						
PO Box 1966	Regina	SK	S4P3E1	**888-474-3377**	306-569-2323	706-2
Sassy Inc						
2305 Breton Industrial Pk Dr	Kentwood	MI	49508	**800-323-6336**	616-243-0767	63
SAT (San Antonio International Airport)						
9800 Airport Blvd Rm 2041	San Antonio	TX	78216	**800-237-6639**	210-207-3411	27

Name / Address	Toll-Free	Phone	Class
Satchidananda Ashram Yogaville (SAYVA) 108 Yogaville Way ....Buckingham VA 23921 *Resv	**800-858-9642***	434-969-3121	664
SATCOM Technologies 1500 Prodelin Dr PO Box 850 .... Newton NC 28658	**888-874-7646**	828-464-4141	638
Satellite Broadcasting & Communications Assn (SBCA) 1730 M St NW Ste 600............. Washington DC 20036	**800-541-5981**	202-349-3620	48-14
Satellite Hotel 411 Lakewood Cir .... Colorado Springs CO 80910	**800-423-8409**	719-596-6800	376
Satellite Industries Inc 2530 Xenium Ln N ....Minneapolis MN 55441	**800-328-3332**		500
Satellite Logistics Group Inc 12621 Featherwood Ste 390...........Houston TX 77034	**877-795-7540**	281-902-5500	310
Satellite Store 7412 Preston Hwy ....Louisville KY 40219	**800-693-9393**	502-966-0045	189-10
Satin American Corp 40 Oliver Terr .... Shelton CT 06484	**877-356-5050**		720
SatisfYd 47 E Chicago Ave Ste 310 .... Naperville IL 60540	**800-562-9557**		197
Satmetrix Systems Inc 1100 Pk Pl ....San Mateo CA 94403	**888-800-2313**	650-227-8300	178
Sato America Inc 10350A Nations Ford Rd .... Charlotte NC 28273	**888-871-8741**	704-644-1650	174-6
Satori Software Inc 1301 5th Ave Ste 2200 .... Seattle WA 98101	**800-553-6477**	206-357-2900	179-1
Saturday Evening Post, The 1100 Waterway Blvd ....Indianapolis IN 46202	**800-829-5576**	317-634-1100	452-11
Saturn Fasteners Inc 425 S Varney St ....Burbank CA 91502	**800-947-9414**	818-846-7145	347
Saturn Industries Inc 157 Union Tpke .... Hudson NY 12534	**800-775-1651**	518-828-9956	126
Saucon Valley School District 2097 Polk Vly Rd ....Hellertown PA 18055	**866-632-9992**	610-838-7026	676
Saucony Inc 191 Spring St ....Lexington MA 02420	**800-282-6575**		300
Sauder Village 22611 SR 2 PO Box 235............... Archbold OH 43502	**800-590-9755**	419-446-2541	513
Sauder Woodworking Co 502 Middle St PO Box 156............ Archbold OH 43502 *Cust Svc	**800-523-3987***	419-446-2711	318-2
Sault Sainte Marie Convention & Visitors Bureau 1808 Ashmun St ....Sault Sainte Marie MI 49783	**800-647-2858**	906-632-3366	207
Saunders Archery Co 1874 14th Ave PO Box 1707.......... Columbus NE 68601 *Cust Svc	**800-228-1408***	402-564-7176	701
Saunders Manufacturing Co 65 Nickerson Hill Rd .... Readfield ME 04355	**800-341-4674**	207-685-9860	483
Sause Bros 3710 NW Front Ave ....Portland OR 97210	**800-488-4167**	503-222-1811	460
Savage Arms Inc 100 Springdale Rd .... Westfield MA 01085	**800-243-3220**	413-568-7001	284
Savanna Portage State Park 55626 Lake Pl .... McGregor MN 55760	**888-646-6367**	218-426-3271	558
Savannah Area Chamber of Commerce 101 E Bay St ....Savannah GA 31401	**877-728-2662**	912-644-6400	137
Savannah Area Convention & Visitors Bureau 101 E Bay St ....Savannah GA 31401	**877-728-2662**	912-644-6400	207
Savannah Civic Ctr 301 W Oglethorp Ave ....Savannah GA 31401	**800-337-1101**	912-651-6550	565
Savannah College of Art & Design *Atlanta* 1600 Peachtree St PO Box 77300....... Atlanta GA 30357	**877-722-3285**	404-253-2700	162
Savannah Distributing Co Inc 2425 W Gwinnett St PO Box 1388 ......Savannah GA 31415 *General	**800-551-0777***	912-233-1167	80-1
Savannah International Trade & Convention Ctr One International Dr ....Savannah GA 31421	**888-644-6822**	912-447-4000	206
Savannah Technical College 5717 White Bluff Rd ....Savannah GA 31405	**800-769-6362**	912-443-5700	788
Savant Manufacturing Inc 2930 Hwy 383 PO Box 520.............. Kinder LA 70648	**800-326-6880**	337-738-5896	347
SAVE - Suicide Awareness Voices of Education 8120 Penn Ave S Ste 470.......... Bloomington MN 55431	**888-511-7283**	952-946-7998	48-15
Save America's Forests 4 Library Ct SE ....Washington DC 20003	**800-729-1363**	202-544-9219	47-13
Save the Manatee Club (SMC) 500 N Maitland Ave Ste 210........... Maitland FL 32751	**800-432-5646**	407-539-0990	47-3
Save-A-Lot Ltd 100 Corporate Office Dr ....Earth City MO 63045 *General	**800-346-3808***	314-592-9100	342
Savers Property & Casualty Insurance Co 26255 American Dr .... Southfield MI 48034	**800-482-2726**	248-204-8299	388-4
Savoy Suites Georgetown 2505 Wisconsin Ave NW ....Washington DC 20007	**877-301-0002**	202-337-9700	376
SAVVIS Inc One Savvis Pkwy ....Town & Country MO 63017	**800-728-8471**	314-628-7000	391
Sawgrass Marriott Resort & Beach Club 1000 PGA Tour Blvd ....Ponte Vedra Beach FL 32082	**800-228-9290**	904-285-7777	660
Sawmill Creek Resort 400 Sawmill Creek Dr .... Huron OH 44839	**800-729-6455**	419-433-3800	660
Sawyer County 10610 Main St Ste 10.................Hayward WI 54843	**877-699-4110**	715-634-4866	336
Saxon Shoes Inc 11800 W Broad St Ste 2750.......... Richmond VA 23233 *General	**800-686-5616***	804-285-3473	300
Saybrook Point Inn & Spa Two Bridge St ....Old Saybrook CT 06475	**800-243-0212**	860-395-2000	660
Sayers Group LLC 825 Corporate Woods Pkwy ....Vernon Hills IL 60061	**800-323-5357**		181
Saylor Beall Mfg Company Inc 400 N Kibbee St.................. Saint Johns MI 48879	**800-248-9001**	989-224-2371	173
SAYVA (Satchidananda Ashram Yogaville) 108 Yogaville Way ....Buckingham VA 23921 *Resv	**800-858-9642***	434-969-3121	664
SB Whistler & Sons Inc PO Box 270 .... Medina NY 14103	**800-828-1010**	585-318-4630	747
Sb1 Federal Credit Union PO Box 7480 ....Philadelphia PA 19101	**800-806-9465**	215-569-3700	219
SBA (Small Business Administration) 409 Third St SW ....Washington DC 20416	**800-827-5722**	202-205-6600	338-18
SBA Communications Corp 5900 Broken Sound Pkwy NW .... Boca Raton FL 33487 *NASDAQ: SBAC*	**800-487-7483**	561-995-7670	171

Name / Address	Toll-Free	Phone	Class
SBAA (Spina Bifida Assn) 4590 MacArthur Blvd NW Ste 250..........................Washington DC 20007	**866-546-8372**	202-944-3285	47-17
Sbar's Inc 14 Sbar Blvd ....Moorestown NJ 08057	**800-989-7227**	856-234-8220	43
SBC Foundation 130 E Travis St Ste 350.............San Antonio TX 78205	**800-591-9663**		303
SBCA (Satellite Broadcasting & Communications Assn) 1730 M St NW Ste 600............. Washington DC 20036	**800-541-5981**	202-349-3620	48-14
SBCC (South Baldwin Chamber of Commerce) 112 W Laurel Ave PO Box 1117 .... Foley AL 36535	**877-461-3712**	251-943-3291	137
SBE (Society of Broadcast Engineers Inc) 9102 N Meridian St Ste 150.........Indianapolis IN 46260	**800-237-1776**	317-846-9000	48-14
SBL (Society of Biblical Literature) The Luce Ctr 825 Houston Mill Rd................... Atlanta GA 30329	**866-727-9955**	404-727-3100	47-20
SBLHC (Sarah Bush Lincoln Health Ctr) 1000 Health Ctr Dr PO Box 372 ....Mattoon IL 61938	**800-345-3191**	217-258-2525	371-3
SBM (Society of Behavioral Medicine) 555 E Wells St Ste 1100............. Milwaukee WI 53202	**800-784-8669**	414-918-3156	48-15
SBS (Storage Battery Systems Inc) N56 W16665 Ridgewood Dr.... Menomonee Falls WI 53051	**800-554-2243**	262-703-5800	246
SBSO (South Bend Symphony Orchestra) 127 N Michigan St .... South Bend IN 46601	**800-537-6415**	574-232-6343	566-3
SC Johnson & Son Inc 1525 Howe St .... Racine WI 53403	**800-494-4855**	262-260-2154	149
SCA (Student Conservation Assn) 689 River Rd PO Box 550...........Charlestown NH 03603	**888-722-9675**	603-543-1700	47-13
SCA Americas 2929 Arch St Ste 2600 ....Philadelphia PA 19104 *Cust Svc	**800-328-9043***	610-499-3700	551
SCAA (Specialty Coffee Assn of America) 330 Golden Shore Ave Ste 50........ Long Beach CA 90802	**800-995-9019**	562-624-4100	48-6
Scalamandre Silks Inc 350 Wireless Blvd .... Hauppauge NY 11788	**800-932-4361**	631-467-8800	734-1
Scale Auto Magazine 21027 Crossroads Cir .... Waukesha WI 53186 *Cust Svc	**800-533-6644***	262-796-8776	452-14
Scales Air Compressor Corp 110 Voice Rd .... Carle Place NY 11514	**877-798-0454**	516-248-9096	173
SCAN (Sports Cardiovascular & Wellness Nutritionists) 4500 Rockside Rd Ste 400 ....Cleveland OH 44131 *General	**800-249-2875***	216-503-0053	48-8
SCAN Health Plan 3800 Kilroy Airport Way Ste 100.......................... Long Beach CA 90806	**800-247-5091**	562-989-5100	349
SCANA Corp 220 Operation Way ....Cayce SC 29033 *NYSE: SCG*	**800-251-7234**	803-217-9000	357-5
SCANA Energy Marketing Inc 220 Operation Way MC 092 ....Cayce SC 29033	**800-472-1051**	803-217-9000	775
Scandinavian Airlines System (SAS) 301 Route 17 N Ste 500 .... Rutherford NJ 07070	**800-221-2350**	800-437-5807	25
Scania USA Inc 121 Interpark Blvd Ste 601 ....San Antonio TX 78216	**800-272-2642**	210-403-0007	509
Scan-Optics Inc 169 Progress Dr .... Manchester CT 06042	**800-543-8681**	860-645-7878	179-8
ScanSource Inc Six Logue Ct .... Greenville SC 29615 *NASDAQ: SCSC*	**800-944-2432**	864-288-2432	175
Scantron Corp 34 Parker ....Irvine CA 92618	**800-722-6876**	949-639-7500	174-7
Scarsdale Union Free School District 2 Brewster Rd ....Scarsdale NY 10583	**888-837-6437**	914-721-2410	676
Scattergood Friends School 1951 Delta Ave .... West Branch IA 52358	**888-737-4636**	319-643-7628	615
SCB (Shipowners Claims Bureau) 1 Battery Pk Plaza 31st Fl............. New York NY 10004	**800-774-8724**	212-847-4500	48-21
SCB Bancorp Inc 1501 E Eldorado St .... Decatur IL 62521	**888-769-2265**	217-428-7781	69
SCBT Financial Corp 950 John C Calhoun Dr .... Orangeburg SC 29115 *NASDAQ: SCBT*	**800-277-2175**	803-534-2175	357-2
SCC Soft Computer Inc 5400 Tech Data Dr .... Clearwater FL 33760	**800-763-8352**	727-789-0100	181
SCCA (Sports Car Club of America) 6700 SW Topeka Blvd Ste 300 ....Topeka KS 66619	**800-770-2055**	785-357-7222	47-18
SCDAA (Sickle Cell Disease Assn of America) 3700 Koppers St Ste 570 ....Baltimore MD 21202	**800-421-8453**	410-528-1555	47-17
Scelzi Equipment Inc 1030 W Gladstone St....................Azusa CA 91702	**866-972-3594**	626-334-0573	509
Scene 1468 W Ninth St Ste 805 ....Cleveland OH 44113	**877-598-8703**	216-241-7550	525-5
Scenic Airlines Inc 3900 Paradise Rd Ste 223 .... Las Vegas NV 89169	**866-235-9422**	702-638-3300	750
Scenic Rivers Energy Co-op 231 N Sheridan St ....Lancaster WI 53813	**800-236-2141**	608-723-2121	245
SCG (Southern Connecticut Gas) 60 Marsh Hill Rd ....Orange CT 06477	**866-268-2887**		775
SC&H Group LLC 910 Ridgebrook Rd ....Sparks MD 21152	**800-832-3008**	410-403-1500	2
Schaefer Pyrotechnics Inc 376 Hartman Bridge Rd .... Ronks PA 17572	**877-598-2264**	717-687-0647	268
Schaefer Systems International Inc 10021 Westlake Dr .... Charlotte NC 28241	**800-876-6000**	704-944-4500	200
Schaeffer Mfg Company Inc 102 Barton St..................... Saint Louis MO 63104 *Cust Svc	**800-325-9962***	314-865-4100	534
Schaeffer's Investment Research Inc 5151 Pfeiffer Rd Ste 250............. Cincinnati OH 45242	**800-448-2080**	513-589-3800	628-9
Schaeffler Group USA Inc 308 Springhill Farm Rd ....Fort Mill SC 29715	**800-361-5841**	803-548-8500	74
Schaff Piano Supply Co 451 Oakwood Rd .... Lake Zurich IL 60047	**800-747-4266**	847-438-4556	520
Schaller & Weber Inc 22-35 46th St ....Astoria NY 11105 *Orders	**800-847-4115***	718-721-5480	295-26
Schatten Properties Management Company Inc 1514 S St.........................Nashville TN 37212	**800-892-1315**	615-329-3011	644
Schatz Bearing Corp 10 Fairview Ave .... Poughkeepsie NY 12601	**800-554-1406**	845-452-6000	74
Schaumburg Specialties Co 550 Albion Ave Unit 30 .... Schaumburg IL 60193	**800-834-8125**		110

				Toll-Free	Phone	Class
Schawbel Corp						
26 Crosby Dr	Bedford	MA	01730	**866-753-3837**	781-541-6900	36
Schawk Inc						
1695 S River Rd	Des Plaines	IL	60018	**800-621-1909**	847-827-9494	619
NYSE: SGK						
Scheirer Machine Company Inc						
3200 Industrial Blvd	Bethel Park	PA	15102	**800-448-4590**	412-833-6500	449
Schenck Business Solutions						
200 E Washington St	Appleton	WI	54911	**800-236-2246**	920-731-8111	2
Schenck Trebel Corp						
535 Acorn St	Deer Park	NY	11729	**800-873-2357**	631-242-4010	675
Schendel Pest Services						
1035 SE Quincy St	Topeka	KS	66612	**800-591-7378**	785-232-9357	570
Schetky Northwest Sales Inc						
8430 NE Killingsworth St	Portland	OR	97220	**800-255-8341**	503-287-4141	509
Scheurer Hospital Inc						
170 N Caseville Rd	Pigeon	MI	48755	**800-208-9060**	989-453-3223	371-3
Schick Shadel Hospital						
12101 Ambaum Blvd SW	Seattle	WA	98146	**800-500-6395**		717
Schilli Transportation Services Inc						
6358 W US Hwy 24	Remington	IN	47977	**800-759-2101**	219-261-2100	770
Schindler Elevator Corp						
20 Whippany Rd	Morristown	NJ	07960	**800-225-3123**	973-397-6500	256
Schlager Group Inc						
325 N Saint Paul Ste 3425	Dallas	TX	75201	**888-416-5727**		93
Schlegel Systems Inc						
1555 Jefferson Rd	Rochester	NY	14623	**888-924-7694**	585-427-7200	325
Schlenner Wenner & Co						
630 Roosevelt Rd	Saint Cloud	MN	56301	**877-616-0286**	320-251-0286	2
Schlessman Seed Co						
11513 US Rt 250	Milan	OH	44846	**888-534-7333**	419-499-2572	685
Schleuniger Inc						
87 Colin Dr	Manchester	NH	03103	**877-902-1470***	603-668-8117	451
*Tech Supp						
Schlueter Co						
310 N Main St	Janesville	WI	53545	**800-359-1700**	608-755-5444	297
Schmidt Baking Company Inc						
7801 Fitch Ln	Baltimore	MD	21236	**800-456-2253**	410-668-8200	295-1
Schmidt-Goodman Office Products						
1920 N Broadway	Rochester	MN	55906	**800-247-0663**	507-282-3870	320
Schmiede Corp						
1865 Riley Creek Rd						
PO Box 1630	Tullahoma	TN	37388	**800-535-1851**	931-455-4801	449
Schnadig International Corp						
4200 Tudor Ln	Greensboro	NC	27410	**800-468-8730**		318-2
Schneck Medical Ctr						
411 W Tipton St	Seymour	IN	47274	**800-234-9222**	812-522-2349	371-3
Schneider Corp						
8901 Otis Ave	Indianapolis	IN	46216	**866-973-7100**	317-826-7100	261
Schneider Electric Buildings LLC						
1354 Clifford Ave	Loves Park	IL	61111	**888-444-1311**		187
Schneider National Inc						
3101 S Packerland Dr						
PO Box 2545	Green Bay	WI	54306	**800-558-6767**	920-592-2000	444
Schneider Optics Century Div						
7701 Haskell Ave	Van Nuys	CA	91406	**800-228-1254**	818-766-3715	584
Schneider Valley Farms Dairy						
1860 E Third St	State College	PA	17701	**800-516-1750**	814-237-3426	295-27
Schnitzer Steel Industries Inc						
3200 NW Yeon Ave	Portland	OR	97210	**800-562-9876**	503-224-9900	714
NASDAQ: SCHN						
Schnuck Markets Inc						
11420 Lackland Rd	Saint Louis	MO	63146	**800-264-4400**	314-994-9900	342
Schoepfle Garden						
12882 Diagonal Rd	La Grange	OH	44050	**800-526-7275**	440-458-5121	96
Schoharie Crossing State Historic Site						
129 Schoharie St PO Box 140	Fort Hunter	NY	12069	**800-456-2267**	518-829-7516	558
Scholars Inn Gourmet Cafe						
717 N College Ave	Bloomington	IN	47404	**800-765-3466**	812-332-1892	662
Scholarship America						
One Scholarship Way						
PO Box 297	Saint Peter	MN	56082	**800-537-4180**	507-931-1682	47-11
Scholastic Arrow Book Club						
555 Broadway	New York	NY	10012	**800-724-6527***	212-343-6100	92
*Orders						
Scholastic Book Fairs Inc						
1080 Greenwood Blvd	Lake Mary	FL	32746	**800-874-4809**	407-829-7300	94
Scholastic Coach & Athletic Director Magazine						
557 Broadway	New York	NY	10012	**800-724-6527***	212-343-6100	452-8
*General						
Scholastic Corp						
557 Broadway	New York	NY	10012	**800-724-6527***	212-343-6100	628-9
Scholastic News						
557 Broadway	New York	NY	10012	**800-724-6527***	212-343-6100	243
*Orders						
Schonbek Worldwide Lighting Inc						
61 Industrial Blvd	Plattsburgh	NY	12901	**800-836-1892**	518-563-7500	435
School Annual Publishing Co						
2568 Park Ctr Blvd Ste B	State College	PA	16801	**800-436-6030**		628-2
School Board of Highlands County Florida						
PO Box 9300	Sebring	FL	33871	**877-357-7456**	863-471-5555	676
School District of The Chathams						
58 Meyersville Rd	Chatham	NJ	07928	**800-225-5425**	973-457-2500	676
School Law News						
360 Hiatt Dr	Palm Beach Gardens	FL	33418	**800-341-7874**		524-4
School Nutrition Assn (SNA)						
700 S Washington St Ste 300	Alexandria	VA	22314	**800-877-8822**	703-739-3900	48-6
School of the Art Institute of Chicago						
36 S Wabash Ave	Chicago	IL	60603	**800-232-7242***	312-629-6100	166
*Admissions						
School of the Museum of Fine Arts						
230 The Fenway	Boston	MA	02115	**800-643-6078***	617-369-3626	166
*Admissions						
School of Visual Arts						
209 E 23rd St	New York	NY	10010	**800-436-4204**	212-592-2000	162
School Specialty Inc						
PO Box 1579	Appleton	WI	54912	**888-388-3224**	920-734-5712	243
NASDAQ: SCHS						
Schoolcraft College						
18600 Haggerty Rd	Livonia	MI	48152	**844-727-6763**	734-462-4400	160
SchoolDocs LLC						
5944 Luther Ln Ste 600	Dallas	TX	75225	**866-311-2293**		384
Schools Financial Credit Union						
1485 Response Rd Ste 126	Sacramento	CA	95815	**800-962-0990**	916-569-5400	219

				Toll-Free	Phone	Class
School-Tech Inc						
745 State Cir PO Box 1941	Ann Arbor	MI	48106	**800-521-2832**		343
Schoolwires Inc						
330 Innovation Blvd						
Ste 301	State College	PA	16803	**877-427-9413**		242
Schott International Inc						
2850 Gilchrist Rd	Akron	OH	44305	**877-661-2121**	330-794-2121	587
Schott North America Inc						
555 Taxter Rd	Elmsford	NY	10523	**877-261-2100**	914-831-2200	328
Schramm Inc						
800 E Virginia Ave	West Chester	PA	19380	**888-737-9438**	610-696-2500	530
Schreiber Corp						
29945 Beck Rd	Wixom	MI	48393	**800-558-2706**	248-926-1500	190-12
Schreiber Foods International Inc						
600 E Crescent Ave						
Ste 103	Upper Saddle River	NJ	07458	**800-631-7070**	201-327-3535	296-11
Schreiner University						
2100 Memorial Blvd	Kerrville	TX	78028	**800-343-4919**	830-792-7217	166
Schreiner's Iris Gardens						
3625 Quinaby Rd NE	Salem	OR	97303	**800-525-2367**	503-393-3232	96
Schroder Investment Management North America Inc (SIMNA)						
875 Third Ave 22nd Fl	New York	NY	10022	**800-730-2932**		681
Schroeder Industries LLC						
580 W Pk Rd	Leetsdale	PA	15056	**800-722-4810**	724-318-1100	208
Schroeder's Flowerland Inc						
1530 S Webster Ave	Green Bay	WI	54301	**800-236-4769**	920-436-6363	292
Schroer Manufacturing Co						
511 Osage Ave	Kansas City	KS	66105	**800-444-1579**	913-281-1500	416
Schuff Steel Co						
420 S 19th Ave	Phoenix	AZ	85009	**800-435-8528**	602-252-7787	190-14
Schuff Steel Inc						
1920 Ledo Rd	Albany	GA	31707	**800-248-5367**	229-883-4506	475
Schukei Chevrolet Inc						
721 S Monroe PO Box 1525	Mason City	IA	50401	**866-918-6497**	641-423-5402	56
Schulmerich Carillons Inc						
Carillon Hill	Sellersville	PA	18960	**800-772-3557**	215-257-2771	520
Schulte Building Systems Inc						
17600 Badtke Rd	Hockley	TX	77447	**877-257-2534**	281-304-6111	105
Schultz Collins Lawson Chambers Inc						
455 Market St Ste 1250	San Francisco	CA	94105	**877-291-2205**	415-291-3000	398
Schumacher Electric Corp						
801 E Business Ctr Dr	Mount Prospect	IL	60056	**800-621-5485**		253
Schumacher Elevator Co						
One Schumacher Way PO Box 393	Denver	IA	50622	**800-779-5438**	319-984-5676	256
Schumacher Group						
200 Corporate Blvd Ste 201	Lafayette	LA	70508	**800-893-9698**	337-354-1332	350
Schurman Fine Papers						
500 Chadbourne Rd PO Box 6030	Fairfield	CA	94533	**800-789-1649***		545-2
*Sales						
Schust Engineering Inc						
701 North St	Auburn	IN	46706	**800-686-9297**		190-12
Schuster Electronics Inc						
2057-D E Aurora Rd	Twinsburg	OH	44087	**800-521-1358**		246
Schuyler Mansion State Historic Site						
32 Catherine St	Albany	NY	12202	**800-456-2267**	518-434-0834	558
Schuylkill Chamber of Commerce						
91 S Progress Ave	Pottsville	PA	17901	**800-755-1942**	570-622-1942	137
Schuylkill Valley School District						
929 Lakeshore Dr	Leesport	PA	19533	**888-883-8237**	610-926-1706	676
Schwaab Inc						
11415 W Burleigh St	Milwaukee	WI	53222	**800-935-9877**	414-771-4150	462
Schwan Food Co						
115 W College Dr	Marshall	MN	56258	**800-533-5290**	507-532-3274	295-36
Schwank Inc						
Two Schwank Way at Hwy 56N	Waynesboro	GA	30830	**877-446-3727**		354
Schwarz						
8338 Austin Ave	Morton Grove	IL	60053	**800-323-4903**		552
Schwebel Baking Co						
PO Box 6018	Youngstown	OH	44501	**800-860-2867**	330-783-2860	295-1
Schweitzer E O Mfg Company Inc						
450 Enterprise Pkwy	Lake Zurich	IL	60047	**888-870-7350**	847-362-8304	248
Schweitzer-Mauduit International Inc						
100 N Pt Ctr E Ste 600	Alpharetta	GA	30022	**800-514-0186**	770-569-4271	550
NYSE: SWM						
Schweizer Emblem Co						
1022 Busse Hwy	Park Ridge	IL	60068	**800-942-5215***	847-292-1022	258
*Cust Svc						
Schwend Inc						
28945 Johnston Rd	Dade City	FL	33523	**800-243-7757**	352-588-2220	769
Schwerdtle Stamp Co						
166 Elm St	Bridgeport	CT	06604	**800-535-0004**	203-330-2750	462
SCI Infrastructure LLC						
2825 S 154th St	Seatac,	WA	98188	**800-255-0633**	206-242-0633	603
SciClone Pharmaceuticals Inc						
950 Tower Ln Ste 900	Foster City	CA	94404	**800-724-2566**	650-358-3456	576
NASDAQ: SCLN						
SCI-Coal Township						
1 Kelley Dr	Coal Township	PA	17866	**800-322-4472**	570-644-7890	213
Scicom Data Services Ltd						
10101 Bren Rd E	Minnetonka	MN	55343	**800-488-9087**	952-933-4200	225
Science Application International Corp Inc (SAIC Inc)						
1710 SAIC Dr	McLean	VA	22102	**866-400-7242**	703-676-4300	179-5
Science Central						
1950 N Clinton St	Fort Wayne	IN	46805	**866-776-2673**	260-424-2400	513
Science Magazine						
1200 New York Ave NW	Washington	DC	20005	**800-731-4939**	202-326-6500	452-19
Science Museum of Minnesota						
120 W Kellogg Blvd	Saint Paul	MN	55102	**800-221-9444**	651-221-9444	513
Science Museum Oklahoma						
2100 NE 52nd St	Oklahoma City	OK	73111	**800-532-7652**	405-602-6664	513
Science News						
1719 N St NW	Washington	DC	20036	**800-552-4412***	202-785-2255	452-19
*Cust Svc						
ScienceCare Inc						
21410 N 19th Ave Ste 126	Phoenix	AZ	85027	**800-417-3747**	602-331-3641	538
Scientech Inc						
5649 Arapahoe Ave	Boulder	CO	80303	**800-525-0522**	303-444-1361	675
Scientific Equipment & Furniture Assn (SEFA)						
65 Hilton Avenue	Garden City	NY	11530	**877-294-5424**	516-294-5424	48-19
Scientific Games Corp						
750 Lexington Ave 25th Fl	New York	NY	10022	**800-827-2946**	212-754-2233	321
NASDAQ: SGMS						
Scientific Industries Inc						
70 Orville Dr	Bohemia	NY	11716	**888-850-6208**	631-567-4700	416

	Toll-Free	Phone	Class
Scientific Learning Corp			
300 Frank H Ogawa Plz Ste 600 . . . . Oakland CA 94612	**888-665-9707**	510-444-3500	179-3
OTC: SCIL			
Scientific Protein Laboratories Inc			
700 E Main St PO Box 158 . . . . Waunakee WI 53597	**800-334-4775**	608-849-5944	474
Sciforma Corp			
985 University Ave Ste 5. . . . . Los Gatos CA 95032	**800-533-9876***	408-354-0144	179-1
Sales			
SCIMEDX Corp			
100 Ford Rd . . . . Denville NJ 07834	**800-221-5598**	973-625-8822	231
Scion Steel Inc			
21555 Mullin Ave . . . . Warren MI 48089	**800-288-2127**	586-755-4000	714
Scioto Sign Company Inc			
6047 US Rt 68 N . . . . Kenton OH 43326	**800-572-4686**	419-673-1261	692
Scioto Trail State Park			
144 Lake Rd . . . . Chillicothe OH 45601	**866-644-6727**		558
SCIP (Society of Competitive Intelligence Professionals)			
1700 Diagonal Rd Ste 600 . . . . Alexandria VA 22314	**877-463-7678**	703-739-0696	48-12
Sci-Port Discovery Ctr			
820 Clyde Fant Pkwy . . . . Shreveport LA 71101	**877-724-7678**	318-424-3466	513
SciQuest Inc			
6501 Weston Pkwy Ste 200 . . . . Cary NC 27513	**888-638-7322**	919-659-2100	179-4
Scivantage Inc			
10 Exchange Pl Unit 13 . . . . Jersey City NJ 07302	**866-724-8268**	646-452-0050	175
Sclafani's Cooking School Inc			
107 Gennaro Pl . . . . Metairie LA 70001	**800-583-1282**	504-833-7861	161
Scleroderma Foundation			
300 Rosewood Dr Ste 105 . . . . Danvers MA 01923	**800-722-4673**	978-463-5843	47-17
Scolari's Food & Drug Co			
950 Holman Way . . . . Sparks NV 89431	**800-219-7401**	775-575-1381	342
Scolding Locks Corp			
1520 W Rogers Ave . . . . Appleton WI 54914	**800-537-9707**	920-733-5561	215
Scoot & Doodle Inc			
2625 Middlefield Rd Ste 223 . . . . Palo Alto CA 94306	**888-563-9224**		384
SCORE American Soccer Company Inc			
726 E Anaheim St . . . . Wilmington CA 90744	**800-626-7774**		153-18
SCORE Assn			
1175 Herndon Pkwy Ste 900 . . . . Herndon VA 20170	**800-634-0245**		48-12
Scot Forge Co			
8001 Winn Rd PO Box 8. . . . . Spring Grove IL 60081	**800-435-6621**	847-587-1000	478
Scot Pump			
6437 Pioneer Rd PO Box 286 . . . . Cedarburg WI 53012	**888-835-0600**	262-377-7000	632
Scotch Gulf Lumber			
1850 Conception St Rd . . . . Mobile AL 36610	**800-496-3307**	251-457-6872	674
Scotch Lumber Co			
119 W Main St PO Box 38 . . . . Fulton AL 36446	**800-936-4424**	334-636-4424	674
Scotchman Industries Inc			
180 E Hwy 14 . . . . Philip SD 57567	**800-843-8844**	605-859-2542	488
Scotia Capital Markets			
One Liberty Plz . . . . New York NY 10006	**877-294-3435**	212-225-5000	681
Scotsman Ice Systems			
775 Corporate Woods Pkwy . . . . Vernon Hills IL 60061	**800-726-8762***	847-215-4500	655
Cust Svc			
Scotsman Inn West			
5922 W Kellogg St . . . . Wichita KS 67209	**800-950-7268**	316-943-3800	376
Scott & White Health Plan			
2401 S 31st St . . . . Temple TX 76508	**800-321-7947**	254-298-3000	388-3
Scott & White Memorial Hospital			
2401 S 31st St . . . . Temple TX 76508	**800-792-3710**	254-724-2111	371-3
Scott Community College			
500 Belmont Rd . . . . Bettendorf IA 52722	**888-336-3907**	563-441-4001	160
Scott Construction Inc			
560 Munroe Ave . . . . Lake Delton WI 53940	**800-843-1556**	608-254-2555	189-4
Scott County Library System			
13090 Alabama Ave S . . . . Savage MN 55378	**877-772-8346**	952-707-1770	431-3
Scott Danahy Naylon Company Inc (SDN)			
300 Spindrift Dr . . . . Williamsville NY 14221	**800-728-6362**	716-633-3400	387
Scott Electric			
1000 S Main St PO Box S. . . . . Greensburg PA 15601	**800-442-8045**	724-834-4321	246
Scott Enterprises Inc			
2225 Downs Dr Sixth Fl Exce Stes . . . . Erie PA 16509	**877-866-3445**	814-868-9500	384
Scott Family of Dealerships			
3333 Lehigh St . . . . Allentown PA 18103	**800-274-1039**		56
Scott Fetzer Company Scot Laboratories Div			
16841 Pk Cir Dr . . . . Chagrin Falls OH 44023	**800-486-7268**	440-543-3033	149
Scott Fly Rod Co			
2355 Air Pk Way . . . . Montrose CO 81401	**800-728-7208**		701
Scott Health & Safety			
4320 Goldmine Rd PO Box 569 . . . . Monroe NC 28110	**800-247-7257**	704-291-8300	569
Scott Industrial Systems Inc			
4433 Interpoint Blvd PO Box 1387 . . . . . . Dayton OH 45401	**800-416-6023**	937-233-8146	465
Scott Industries Inc			
1573 Hwy 136 W PO Box 7 . . . . Henderson KY 42419	**800-951-9276**	270-831-2037	386
Scott Logistics Corp			
PO Box 391 . . . . Rome GA 30162	**800-893-6689**	706-234-1184	310
Scott Madden & Assoc Inc			
2626 Glenwood Ave Ste 480. . . . . Raleigh NC 27608	**800-321-9774**	919-781-4191	195
Scott Sign Systems Inc			
7525 Pennsylvania Ave Ste 101 . . . . Sarasota FL 34243	**800-237-9447**	941-355-5171	692
Scott Tim (Sen R - SC)			
520 Hart Senate Office Bldg . . . . Washington DC 20510	**855-425-6324**	202-224-6121	
Scott USA Inc			
PO Box 2030 . . . . Sun Valley ID 83353	**800-292-5874**	208-622-1000	701
Scott's Liquid Gold Inc			
4880 Havana St . . . . Denver CO 80239	**800-447-1919**	303-373-4860	149
OTC: SLGD			
Scottdel Inc			
400 Church St . . . . Swanton OH 43558	**800-446-2341**	419-825-2341	130
Scott-Gross Company Inc			
664 Magnolia Ave . . . . Lexington KY 40505	**800-967-6874**		323
Scotts Lawn Service			
14111 Scottslawn Rd . . . . Marysville OH 43040	**888-270-3714***	937-644-0011	570
Cust Svc			
Scotts Miracle Gro Products Inc			
14111 Scottslawn Rd . . . . Marysville OH 43041	**888-270-3714**	937-644-0011	280
Scotts Miracle-Gro Co			
14111 Scottslawn Rd . . . . Marysville OH 43041	**800-543-8873***	937-644-0011	280
*NYSE: SMG ■ *Cust Svc*			
Scottsdale Camelback Resort			
6302 E Camelback Rd . . . . Scottsdale AZ 85251	**800-891-8585**	480-947-3300	660
Scottsdale Community College			
9000 E Chaparral Rd . . . . Scottsdale AZ 85256	**800-784-2433**	480-423-6000	160
Scottsdale Convention & Visitors Bureau			
4343 N Scottsdale Rd Ste 170 . . . . Scottsdale AZ 85251	**800-782-1117**	480-421-1004	207

	Toll-Free	Phone	Class
Scottsdale Ctr for the Performing Arts			
7380 E Second St . . . . Scottsdale AZ 85251	**800-309-8532**	480-994-2787	565
Scottsdale Culinary Institute			
8100 E Camelback Rd Ste 1001 . . . . Scottsdale AZ 85251	**888-557-4222**	480-990-3773	161
Scottsdale Insurance Co			
8877 N Gainey Ctr Dr . . . . Scottsdale AZ 85258	**800-423-7675**	480-365-4000	388-4
Scottsdale Plaza Resort			
7200 N Scottsdale Rd . . . . Scottsdale AZ 85253	**800-832-2025**	480-948-5000	660
Scottsdale Resort & Conference Ctr			
7700 E McCormick Pkwy . . . . Scottsdale AZ 85258	**800-528-0293**	480-991-9000	374
Scottsdale Stadium			
7408 E Osborn Rd . . . . Scottsdale AZ 85251	**877-229-5042**	480-312-2856	711
Scoular Co			
2027 Dodge St . . . . Omaha NE 68102	**800-488-3500**	402-342-3500	275
Scout Stuff			
PO Box 7143 . . . . Charlotte NC 28241	**800-323-0736**		779
Scovill Fasteners Inc			
1802 Scovill Dr . . . . Clarkesville GA 30523	**888-726-8455***	706-754-1000	587
Cust Svc			
SCPPD (South Central Public Power District)			
275 S Main St PO Box 406. . . . . Nelson NE 68961	**800-557-5254**	402-225-2351	245
Scranton Mfg Company Inc			
101 State St PO Box 336 . . . . Scranton IA 51462	**800-831-1858**	712-652-3396	273
Scranton Times-Tribune			
149 Penn Ave . . . . Scranton PA 18503	**800-228-4637**	570-348-9100	525-2
SCREC (Sullivan County Rural Electric Co-op Inc)			
5675 Rt 87 PO Box 65 . . . . Forksville PA 18616	**800-570-5081**	570-924-3381	245
Screen Actors Guild (SAG)			
5757 Wilshire Blvd . . . . Los Angeles CA 90036	**800-724-0767**	323-954-1600	411
Screen Graphics of Florida Inc			
1801 N Andrews Ave . . . . Pompano Beach FL 33069	**800-346-4420**		678
Screen Works			
2201 W Fulton St . . . . Chicago IL 60612	**800-294-8111***	312-243-8265	713
Cust Svc			
Screeningone Inc			
2233 W 190th St . . . . Torrance CA 90504	**888-327-6511**		218
ScripNet			
10050 Banburry Cross Dr			
Ste 290 . . . . Las Vegas NV 89144	**888-880-8562**	702-248-2692	579
Scripps College			
1030 Columbia Ave . . . . Claremont CA 91711	**800-770-1333**	909-621-8149	166
Scripps Green Hospital			
10666 N Torrey Pines Rd . . . . La Jolla CA 92037	**800-727-4777**	858-455-9100	371-3
Scripps Health			
4275 Campus Pt Ct . . . . San Diego CA 92121	**800-727-4777**		350
Scripps Howard Foundation			
312 Walnut St PO Box 5380 . . . . Cincinnati OH 45201	**800-888-3000**	513-977-3035	303
Scripps Howard Inc			
PO Box 5380 . . . . Cincinnati OH 45202	**800-888-3000**	513-977-3000	628-8
Script Care Inc			
6380 Folsom Dr . . . . Beaumont TX 77706	**800-880-9988**		579
ScriptLogic Corp			
6000 Broken Sound Pkwy NW . . . . Boca Raton FL 33487	**800-306-9329**	561-886-2400	179-12
ScriptSave			
4911 E Broadway Blvd Ste 200. . . . . Tucson AZ 85711	**800-347-5985**		579
Scruggs Company Inc			
PO Box 2065 . . . . Valdosta GA 31604	**800-230-7263**	229-242-2388	189-4
SCS (Structural Component Systems Inc)			
1255 Front St . . . . Fremont NE 68026	**800-844-5622**	402-721-5622	188
SCS Engineers			
3900 Kilroy Airport Way			
Ste 100 . . . . Long Beach CA 90806	**800-326-9544**	562-426-9544	261
SCTE (Society of Cable Telecommunications Engineers)			
140 Philips Rd . . . . Exton PA 19341	**800-542-5040**	610-363-6888	48-19
Scully Signal Co			
70 Industrial Way . . . . Wilmington MA 01887	**800-272-8559**	617-692-8600	202
SCUP (Society for College & University Planning)			
339 E Liberty St Ste 300. . . . . Ann Arbor MI 48104	**800-257-2578**	734-669-3270	48-5
SD Ireland Co			
193 Industrial Ave . . . . Williston VT 05495	**800-339-4565**	802-863-6222	184
SD Richman Sons Inc			
2435 Wheatsheaf Ln . . . . Philadelphia PA 19137	**800-648-3576**	215-535-5100	677
SDEB (San Diego Eye Bank)			
9246 Lightwave Ave Ste 120. . . . . San Diego CA 92123	**800-393-2265**	858-694-0400	269
SDI Chicago			
33 West Monroe Ste 400 . . . . Chicago IL 60603	**888-968-7734**	312-580-7500	684
SDI Technologies Inc			
1299 Main St . . . . Rahway NJ 07065	**800-333-3092**		51
SDMS (Society of Diagnostic Medical Sonography)			
2745 Dallas Pkwy . . . . Plano TX 75093	**800-229-9506**	214-473-8057	48-8
SDN (Scott Danahy Naylon Company Inc)			
300 Spindrift Dr . . . . Williamsville NY 14221	**800-728-6362**	716-633-3400	387
SDPB (South Dakota Public Broadcasting)			
555 N Dakota St PO Box 5000 . . . . Vermillion SD 57069	**800-456-0766**	605-677-5861	624
SEA (Software Engineering of America Inc)			
1230 Hempstead Tpke . . . . Franklin Square NY 11010	**800-272-7322**	516-328-7000	179-12
Sea Blue			
1 Borgata Way . . . . Atlantic City NJ 08401	**877-786-9900***	609-317-1000	662
Cust Svc			
Sea Breeze Inc			
441 Rt 202 . . . . Towaco NJ 07082	**800-732-2733**	973-334-7777	295-15
Sea Cloud Cruises Inc			
282 Grand Ave Ste 3 . . . . Englewood NJ 07631	**888-732-2568**	201-227-9404	220
Sea Crest Resort & Conference Ctr			
350 Quaker Rd . . . . North Falmouth MA 02556	**800-225-3110**	508-540-9400	660
Sea Eagle Boats Inc			
19 N Columbia St Ste 1 . . . . Port Jefferson NY 11777	**800-748-8066**	631-473-7308	701
Sea Gull Lighting Products LLC A Generations Brands Co			
301 W Washington St . . . . Riverside NJ 08075	**800-347-5483**	856-764-0500	435
Sea Harvest Packing Co			
PO Box 818 . . . . Brunswick GA 31521	**800-627-4300**	912-264-3212	295-14
Sea Island Co			
PO Box 30351 . . . . Sea Island GA 31561	**800-732-4752**	912-638-3611	646
Sea Life Park			
41-202 Kalanianaole Hwy . . . . Waimanalo HI 96795	**866-365-7446**	808-259-2500	39
SEA Ltd			
7349 Worthington-Galena Rd . . . . Columbus OH 43085	**800-782-6851**		458
Sea Magazine			
17782 Cowan St Ste C . . . . Irvine CA 92614	**800-873-7327**	949-660-6150	452-4
Sea Mar Community Health Ctr			
1040 S Henderson St . . . . Seattle WA 98108	**855-289-4503**	206-763-5277	350
Sea Mist Resort			
1200 S Ocean Blvd . . . . Myrtle Beach SC 29577	**800-793-6507**	843-448-1551	660

	City	State	ZIP	Toll-Free	Phone	Class
Sea Palms Golf & Tennis Resort 5445 Frederica Rd	Saint Simons Island	GA	31522	**800-841-6268**	912-638-3351	660
Sea Pines Resort, The 32 Greenwood Dr	Hilton Head Island	SC	29928	**866-561-8802**	843-785-3333	644
Sea Ranch Lodge 60 Sea Walk Dr PO Box 44	The Sea Ranch	CA	95497	**800-732-7262**	707-785-2371	376
Sea Spa at Loews Coronado Bay Resort 4000 Loews Coronado Bay Rd	Coronado	CA	92118	**800-815-6397**	619-424-4000	698
Sea Star Line LLC 10550 Deerwood Pk Blvd Ste 509	Jacksonville	FL	32256	**877-775-7447**	904-855-1260	311
Sea Tow Services International Inc 1560 Youngs Ave PO Box 1178	Southold	NY	11971	**800-473-2869**	631-765-3660	460
Sea Trail Corp 75A Clubhouse Rd	Sunset Beach	NC	28468	**888-321-9076**	910-287-1100	644
Sea Venture Resort 100 Ocean View Ave	Pismo Beach	CA	93449	**800-443-7778**	805-773-4994	660
Sea View Hotel 9909 Collins Ave	Bal Harbour	FL	33154	**800-447-1010**	305-866-4441	376
Seaboard Asphalt Products Co 3601 Fairfield Rd	Baltimore	MD	21226	**800-536-0332**	410-355-0330	45
Seaboard Corp 9000 W 67th St *NYSE: SEB*	Shawnee Mission	KS	66202	**866-676-8886**	913-676-8800	186
Seaboard Folding Box Co Inc 35 Daniels St	Fitchburg	MA	01420	**800-225-6313**	978-342-8921	100
Seaboard Foods 9000 W 67th St Ste 200	Shawnee Mission	KS	66202	**800-262-7907**	913-261-2600	10-5
Seaboard International Forest Products LLC 22F Cotton Rd Ste F	Nashua	NH	03063	**800-669-6800**	603-881-3700	192-3
Seaboard Marine 8001 NW 79th Ave	Miami	FL	33166	**866-676-8886**	305-863-4444	312
SeaChange International Inc 50 Nagog Pk *NASDAQ: SEAC*	Acton	MA	01720	**844-855-8324**	978-897-0100	638
Seacoast Banking Corp of Florida 815 Colorado Ave PO Box 9012 *NASDAQ: SBCF* ■ *All	Stuart	FL	34994	**800-706-9991***	772-287-4000	357-2
Seacomm Erectors Inc 32527 SR 2 PO Box 1740	Sultan	WA	98294	**800-497-8320**	360-793-6564	189-1
SEACOR Holdings Inc 2200 Eller Dr PO Box 13038 *NYSE: CKH*	Fort Lauderdale	FL	33316	**800-516-6203**	954-523-2200	658
Seacrest Oceanfront Resort on the South Beach 803 S Ocean Blvd	Myrtle Beach	SC	29577	**888-889-8113**		660
SeaDream Yacht Club 601 Brickell Key Dr Ste 1050	Miami	FL	33131	**800-707-4911**	305-631-6110	220
Seafarers International Union 5201 Auth Way	Camp Springs	MD	20746	**800-252-4674**	301-899-0675	411
Seagull Book & Tape Inc 1720 S Redwood Rd	Salt Lake City	UT	84104	**800-999-6257**		95
Seal Methods Inc 11915 Shoemaker Ave	Santa Fe Springs	CA	90670	**800-423-4777**	562-944-0291	325
Sealed Unit Parts Company Inc 2230 Landmark Pl	Allenwood	NJ	08720	**800-333-9125**	732-223-6644	14
Sealing Devices Inc 4400 Walden Ave *Cust Svc	Lancaster	NY	14086	**800-727-3257***	716-684-7600	325
Sealing Equipment Products Co Inc 123 Airpark Industrial Rd *Cust Svc	Alabaster	AL	35007	**800-633-4770***		325
Seaman Corp 1000 Venture Blvd	Wooster	OH	44691	**800-927-8578**	330-262-1111	734-2
Seamen's Bank 221 Commercial St PO Box 659	Provincetown	MA	02657	**855-227-5347**	508-487-0035	69
Seaport Hotel & World Trade Ctr One Seaport Ln	Boston	MA	02210	**877-732-7678**	617-385-4000	376
Seaport World Trade Ctr Boston 200 Seaport Blvd	Boston	MA	02210	**800-440-3318**	617-385-4212	809
SEARAC (Southeast Asia Resource Action Ctr) 1628 16th St NW Third Fl	Washington	DC	20009	**888-907-1485**	202-667-4690	47-5
Search Company International 1535 Grant St Ste 140	Denver	CO	80203	**800-727-2120**	303-863-1800	626
Search Network Ltd 1503 42nd St Ste 210	West Des Moines	IA	50266	**800-383-5050**	515-223-1153	626
Searcher: The Magazine for Database Professionals 143 Old Marlton Pk	Medford	NJ	08055	**800-300-9868**	609-654-6266	452-7
SearchTec Inc 314 N 12th St Ste 100	Philadelphia	PA	19107	**877-273-2724**	215-963-0888	626
Searles Valley Minerals 9401 Indian Creek Pkwy Ste 1000	Overland Park	KS	66210	**800-637-2775**	913-344-9500	498-1
Sears Canada Inc 290 Yonge St Ste 700 *TSE: SCC*	Toronto	ON	M5B2C3	**877-987-3277**	416-362-1711	229
Sears Imported Autos Inc 13500 Wayzata Blvd *Sales	Minnetonka	MN	55305	**800-493-1720***	952-546-5301	56
Sears Manufacturing Co 1718 S Concord St PO Box 3667 *Cust Svc	Davenport	IA	52808	**800-553-3013***	563-383-2800	680
Sears Tower 233 S Wacker Dr	Chicago	IL	60606	**877-759-3325**	312-875-9447	49-2
Seaside Civic & Convention Ctr 415 First Ave	Seaside	OR	97138	**800-394-3303**	503-738-8585	206
Seaside Golf Vacations 218 Main St	North Myrtle Beach	SC	29582	**877-732-6999**		761
Seaside Inn 541 E Gulf Dr	Sanibel Island	FL	33957	**866-565-5092**	239-472-1400	376
Seasons Hospice & Palliative Care of California-Orange 750 The City Dr	Orange	CA	92868	**877-508-0644**	714-980-0900	368
Seasons-4 Inc 4500 Industrial Access Rd	Douglasville	GA	30134	**800-888-9900**	770-489-0716	14
Seastrom Mfg Company Inc 456 Seastrom St	Twin Falls	ID	83301	**800-634-2356**	208-737-4300	347
Seat of the Soul Foundation PO Box 3310	Ashland	OR	97520	**877-733-4279**	541-482-1515	47-20
Seats Inc 1515 Industrial St	Reedsburg	WI	53959	**800-443-0615**	608-524-8261	680
Seattle Cancer Care Alliance 825 Eastlake Ave E PO Box 19023	Seattle	WA	98109	**800-804-8824**	206-288-1024	759
Seattle Children's Hospital 4800 Sand Pt Way NE	Seattle	WA	98105	**866-987-2000**	206-987-2000	371-1
Seattle Convention Ctr Pike Street 1011 Pike St	Seattle	WA	98101	**800-225-5466**	206-682-8282	376
Seattle Lighting Fixture Co 222 Second Ave Ext S *Cust Svc	Seattle	WA	98104	**800-689-1000***	206-622-4736	359
Seattle Manufacturing Corp 6930 Salashan Pkwy	Ferndale	WA	98248	**800-426-6251**	360-366-5534	569
Seattle Mariners Safeco Field 1250 First Ave S	Seattle	WA	98134	**800-255-7932**	206-346-4000	704
Seattle Opera PO Box 9248 *Sales	Seattle	WA	98109	**800-426-1619***	206-389-7600	566-2
Seattle Pacific University 3307 Third Ave W	Seattle	WA	98119	**800-366-3344**	206-281-2000	166
Seattle Post-Intelligencer 101 Elliott Ave W Second Fl	Seattle	WA	98119	**800-542-0820**	206-448-8000	525-2
Seattle Repertory Theatre (SRT) 155 Mercer St PO Box 900923	Seattle	WA	98109	**877-900-9285**	206-443-2210	566-4
Seattle Seahawks 12 Seahawks Way	Renton	WA	98056	**888-635-4295**		706-3
Seattle Storm 351 Elliott Ave W Ste 500	Seattle	WA	98119	**877-329-9622**	206-281-5800	705-2
Seattle SuperSonics 1201 Third Ave Ste 1000	Seattle	WA	98101	**800-743-7021**	206-281-5800	705-1
Seattle University 901 12th Ave	Seattle	WA	98122	**800-426-7123**	206-296-6000	166
Seattle University Lemieux Library 901 12th Ave	Seattle	WA	98122	**800-426-7123**	206-296-6210	431-6
Seattle's Best Coffee Co PO Box 3717	Seattle	WA	98124	**800-611-7793**		157
Seattle's Convention & Visitors Bureau 701 Pike St Ste 800	Seattle	WA	98101	**866-732-2695**	206-461-5800	207
SeaWorld Orlando 7007 Sea World Dr	Orlando	FL	32821	**800-327-2424**	407-351-3600	32
SeaWorld San Diego 500 SeaWorld Dr	San Diego	CA	92109	**800-257-4268**	619-226-3901	32
Sebago Inc 9341 Courtland Dr	Rockford	MI	49351	**866-699-7367**	616-866-5500	300
Sebasco Harbor Resort 29 Keynon Rd	Phippsburg	ME	04562	**800-225-3819**	207-389-1161	660
Sebastiani Vineyards Inc 389 Fourth St E	Sonoma	CA	95476	**855-232-2338**	707-933-3230	79-3
Sebesta Blomberg & Assoc Inc 1450 Energy Park Dr Ste 300	St Paul	MN	55108	**877-706-6858**	651-634-0775	261
Sebring International Raceway 113 Midway Dr	Sebring	FL	33870	**800-626-7223**	863-655-1442	508
SEC (Shelby Electric Co-op) Rt 128 N Sixth St PO Box 560	Shelbyville	IL	62565	**800-677-2612**	217-774-3986	245
SEC (Securities & Exchange Commission) 100 F St NE	Washington	DC	20549	**800-732-0330**	202-942-8088	338-18
Secap USA Inc 10 Clipper Rd	Conshohocken	PA	19428	**800-523-0320**	610-825-6205	111
Sechrist Industries Inc 4225 E La Palma Ave	Anaheim	CA	92807	**800-732-4747**	714-579-8400	471
SECO (Southeast Electric Co-op Inc) 110 S Main St	Ekalaka	MT	59324	**888-485-8762**	406-775-8762	245
Secoa Inc 8650 109th Ave N	Champlin	MN	55316	**800-328-5519**	763-506-8800	713
Seco-Larm USA Inc 16842 Millikan Ave	Irvine	CA	92606	**800-662-0800**	949-261-2999	683
Second Amendment Foundation 12500 NE Tenth Pl	Bellevue	WA	98005	**800-426-4302**	425-454-7012	47-8
Second Cup Ltd 6303 Airport Rd	Mississauga	ON	L4V1R8	**877-212-1818**		157
Secova Inc 5000 Birch St W Tower Ste 1400	Newport Beach	CA	92660	**800-257-0011**	714-384-0530	195
SECPA (Southeast Colorado Power Assn) 901 W 3rd	La Junta	CO	81050	**800-332-8634**	719-384-2551	245
Secret Garden Spa at the Prince of Wales Hotel Six Picton St PO Box 46	Niagara-on-the-Lake	ON	L0S1J0	**888-669-5566**	905-468-3246	698
Secretary of Education 400 Maryland Ave SW	Washington	DC	20202	**800-872-5327**	202-401-3000	338-6
Secretary of Labor 200 Constitution Ave NW Rm S2018	Washington	DC	20210	**866-487-2365**	202-693-6000	338-13
Board of Veterans' Appeals 810 Vermont Ave NW	Washington	DC	20420	**800-923-8387**		338-17
Center for Veterans Enterprise 810 Vermont Ave	Washington	DC	20420	**800-273-8255**	800-827-1000	338-17
Secretary of Veterans Affairs *Center for Women Veterans* 810 Vermont Ave NW	Washington	DC	20420	**800-827-1000**		338-17
SECU (State Employees' Credit Union) PO Box 29606	Raleigh	NC	27626	**888-732-8562**	919-857-2150	219
Secura Insurance Cos PO Box 819	Appleton	WI	54912	**800-558-3405**	920-739-3161	388-4
Securance LLC 6922 W Linebaugh Ave Ste 101	Tampa	FL	33625	**877-578-0215**		181
Secure Communication Systems Inc 1740 E Wilshire Ave	Santa Ana	CA	92705	**866-926-2940**	714-547-1174	638
Secure First Credit Union PO Box 170070	Birmingham	AL	35217	**877-520-2115**	205-520-2115	219
SecureInfo Corp 211 N Loop 1604 E Ste 200	San Antonio	TX	78232	**888-677-9351**	210-403-5600	181
Securitas Security Services USA Inc 2 Campus Dr	Parsippany	NJ	07054	**800-555-0906**	973-267-5300	683
Securitech Inc 8230 E Broadway Blvd Ste E-10	Tucson	AZ	85710	**888-792-4473**	520-721-0305	626
Securities & Exchange Commission (SEC) 100 F St NE	Washington	DC	20549	**800-732-0330**	202-942-8088	338-18
Securities Industry & Financial Markets Assn (SIFMAA) 120 Broadway 35th Fl	New York	NY	10271	**888-367-7966**	212-313-1200	48-2
Securities Law Daily 1801 S Bell St	Arlington	VA	22202	**800-372-1033**		524-7
Securities Regulation & Law Report 1801 S Bell St	Arlington	VA	22202	**800-372-1033**		524-7
Securities Service Network Inc 9729 Cogdill Rd Ste 301	Knoxville	TN	37932	**866-843-4635**		681

Name / Address	City	State	ZIP	Toll-Free	Phone	Class
Securitron Magnalock Corp						
10027 S 51st St Ste 102	Phoenix	AZ	85044	**800-624-5625***	623-582-4626	347
*Sales						
Security Bank of Pulaski County						
110 Lynn St PO Box S	Waynesville	MO	65583	**800-264-4274**	573-774-6417	69
Security Benefit Group of Cos						
One Security Benefit Pl	Topeka	KS	66636	**800-888-2461**	785-438-3000	357-4
Security Benefit Life Insurance Co						
One Security Benefit Pl	Topeka	KS	66636	**800-888-2461**	785-438-3000	388-2
Security Corp						
22325 Roethel Dr	Novi	MI	48375	**877-374-5700**		683
Security Defense Systems Corp						
160 Pk Ave	Nutley	NJ	07110	**800-325-6339**		683
Security Engineered Machinery Company Inc						
Five Walkup Dr PO Box 1045	Westborough	MA	01581	**800-225-9293***	508-366-1488	110
*Sales						
Security Federal Bank (SFB)						
238 Richland Ave W	Aiken	SC	29801	**866-851-3000**	803-641-3000	70
Security Finance Corp						
PO Box 811	Spartanburg	SC	29304	**800-395-8195***	864-582-8193	214
*All						
Security Fire Protection Co Inc						
4495 Mendenhall Rd S	Memphis	TN	38141	**888-274-8595**	901-362-6250	190-13
Security Funds						
One Security Benefit Pl	Topeka	KS	66636	**800-888-2461**	785-438-3000	521
Security Industry Assn (SIA)						
635 Slaters Ln Ste 110	Alexandria	VA	22314	**866-817-8888**	703-683-2075	48-4
Security Life Insurance Co of America						
10901 Red Cir Dr	Minnetonka	MN	55343	**800-328-4667**	952-544-2121	388-2
Security Mutual Life Insurance Co of New York						
100 Court St PO Box 1625	Binghamton	NY	13901	**800-927-8846**	607-723-3551	388-2
Security National Financial Corp (SNFC)						
5300 South 360 West Ste 250						
PO Box 57250	Salt Lake City	UT	84123	**800-574-7117**	801-264-1060	388-2
NASDAQ: SNFCA						
Security Service Federal Credit Union						
16211 La Cantera Pkwy	San Antonio	TX	78256	**800-527-7328**	210-476-4000	219
Security Signal Devices Inc						
1740 N Lemon St	Anaheim	CA	92801	**800-888-0444**		683
Security Storage Co						
1701 Florida Ave NW	Washington	DC	20009	**800-736-6825**	202-234-5600	512
Security Supply Corp						
196 Maple Ave	Selkirk	NY	12158	**800-333-2226**	518-767-2226	605
Security Van Lines LLC						
100 W Airline Dr PO Box 830	Kenner	LA	70062	**800-218-6915**	800-794-5961	770
Securus Technologies Inc						
14651 Dallas Pkwy	Dallas	TX	75254	**800-844-6591**	972-277-0300	726
SED (Regency Infographics Inc)						
2867 E Allegheny Ave	Philadelphia	PA	19134	**800-829-0020**	215-425-8800	771
SED International Inc						
4916 N Royal Atlanta Dr	Tucker	GA	30084	**800-444-8962***	770-491-8962	175
*Sales						
Seda France Inc						
8301 Springdale Rd Ste 800	Austin	TX	78724	**800-474-0854**	512-206-0105	94
Sedgwick County Electric Co-op						
1355 S 383rd St W PO Box 220	Cheney	KS	67025	**866-542-4732**	316-542-3131	245
Sedgwick Detert Moran & Arnold LLP						
One Market Plz						
Steuart Twr Eighth Fl	San Francisco	CA	94105	**800-826-3262**	415-781-7900	425
Sedlak Interiors Inc						
34300 Solon Rd	Solon	OH	44139	**800-260-2949**	440-248-2424	320
See Water Inc						
121 N Dillon St	San Jacinto	CA	92583	**888-733-9283**	951-487-8073	202
See's Candies Inc						
210 El Camino Real	South San Francisco	CA	94080	**800-877-7337***	650-761-2490	295-8
*Cust Svc						
Seedway LLC						
1734 Railroad Pl	Hall	NY	14463	**800-836-3710**	585-526-6391	685
SEEK Careers/Staffing Inc						
PO Box 148	Grafton	WI	53024	**800-870-7181**	262-377-8888	712
Seelbach Hilton Louisville						
500 S Fourth St	Louisville	KY	40202	**800-333-3399**	502-585-3200	376
Seelye Plastics Inc						
9700 Newton Ave S	Bloomington	MN	55431	**800-328-2728**		596
SeePoint Technology LLC						
2619 Manhattan Beach Blvd	Redondo Beach	CA	90278	**888-587-1777**	310-725-9660	607
SEER Technology Inc						
2681 Parleys Way Ste 201	Salt Lake City	UT	84109	**877-505-7337**	801-746-7888	416
SEFA (Scientific Equipment & Furniture Assn)						
65 Hilton Avenue	Garden City	NY	11530	**877-294-5424**	516-294-5424	48-19
Sefar Printing Solutions Inc						
111 Calumet St	Depew	NY	14043	**800-995-0531**	716-683-4050	734-3
Seguin Area Chamber of Commerce						
116 N Camp St	Seguin	TX	78155	**888-674-7224**	830-379-6382	137
Seguin Independent School District						
1221 E Kingsbury St	Seguin	TX	78155	**866-632-9992**	830-372-5771	676
Segway Inc						
14 Technology Dr	Bedford	NH	03110	**866-473-4929**	603-222-6000	509
SEI One Freedom Vly Dr	Oaks	PA	19456	**800-342-5734**	610-676-1000	521
NASDAQ: SEIC						
SEI (Software Engineering Institute)						
4500 Fifth Ave	Pittsburgh	PA	15213	**888-201-4479**	412-268-5800	659
SEI (Stephenson Equipment Inc)						
7201 Paxton St	Harrisburg	PA	17111	**800-325-6455**	717-564-3434	264-3
SEI (System Engineering International Inc)						
5115 Pegasus Ct Ste Q	Frederick	MD	21704	**800-765-4734**	301-694-9601	775
Seiko Corp of America						
1111 MacArthur Blvd	Mahwah	NJ	07430	**800-545-2783***	201-529-5730	151
*Cust Svc						
Seiko Instruments USA Inc						
21221 S Western Ave Ste 250	Torrance	CA	90501	**800-688-0817***	310-517-7700	151
*Sales						
Seiko Instruments USA Inc Micro Printer Div						
2990 Lomita Blvd	Torrance	CA	90505	**800-688-0817**	310-517-7778	174-6
Seiler Instrument & Mfg Company Inc						
3433 Tree Court Industrial Blvd	Saint Louis	MO	63122	**800-489-2282**	314-968-2282	537
Seitz LLC						
212 Industrial Ln	Torrington	CT	06790	**800-261-2011**	860-489-0476	597
Seize The Deal LLC						
1851 N Greenville Ave						
Ste 100	Richardson	TX	75081	**866-210-0881**		384

Name / Address	City	State	ZIP	Toll-Free	Phone	Class
SEJ (Society of Environmental Journalists)						
115 W Ave	Jenkintown	PA	19046	**866-208-3372**	215-884-8174	48-14
SEK Genetics						
9525 70th Rd	Galesburg	KS	66740	**800-443-6389**		11-2
Sekisui America Corp						
333 Meadowlands Pkwy 4th Fl	Secaucus	NJ	07094	**866-260-5851***	201-423-7960	596
*General						
Sekisui Voltek LLC						
100 Shepard St	Lawrence	MA	01843	**800-225-0668**	978-685-2557	594
Seko Worldwide Inc						
1100 Arlington Heights Rd						
Ste 600	Itasca	IL	60143	**800-323-1235**	630-919-4800	444
Selas Heat Technology Company LLC						
130 Keystone Dr	Montgomeryville	PA	18936	**800-523-6500**	215-646-6600	317
Selby Furniture Hardware Company Inc						
321 Rider Ave	Bronx	NY	10451	**800-224-0058**	718-993-3700	347
Selden's Home Furnishings						
1802 62nd Ave E	Tacoma	WA	98424	**800-870-7880**	253-922-5700	320
Select Engineered Systems						
7991 W 26th Ave	Hialeah	FL	33016	**800-342-5737**	305-823-5410	684
Select Medical Corp						
4714 Gettysburg Rd	Mechanicsburg	PA	17055	**888-735-6332**	717-972-1100	458
Select Portfolio Servicing Inc						
3815 SW Temple	Salt Lake City	UT	84115	**800-258-8602**		214
Select Staffing						
3820 State St	Santa Barbara	CA	93105	**800-688-6162**	805-882-2200	712
Select-A-Ticket Inc						
25 Rt 23 S	Riverdale	NJ	07457	**800-735-3288**	973-839-6100	740
Selected Funds						
PO Box 8243	Boston	MA	02266	**800-243-1575**		521
Selected Independent Funeral Homes						
500 Lake Cook Rd Ste 205	Deerfield	IL	60015	**800-323-4219**	847-236-9401	48-4
Selectica Inc						
2121 S. El Camino Rl 10th Fl	San Mateo	CA	94403	**877-712-9560**	650-532-1500	179-1
NASDAQ: SLTC						
Selective Enterprises Inc						
10701 Texland Blvd	Charlotte	NC	28273	**800-334-1207**	704-588-3310	358
Selective Insurance Company of America						
40 Wantage Ave	Branchville	NJ	07890	**800-777-9656**	973-948-3000	388-4
Selective Insurance Group Inc						
40 Wantage Ave	Branchville	NJ	07890	**800-777-9656**	973-948-3000	357-4
NASDAQ: SIGI						
Region 1						
PO Box 94638	Palatine	IL	60094	**888-655-1825**	847-688-6888	338-18
Selective Service System Regional Offices						
Region 2						
PO Box 94638	Palatine	IL	60094	**888-655-1825**	847-688-6888	338-18
Select-O-Hits Inc						
1981 Fletcher Creek Dr	Memphis	TN	38133	**800-346-0723**	901-388-1190	516
Selectquote Insurance Services						
595 Market St 10th Fl	San Francisco	CA	94105	**800-670-3213**	415-543-7338	387
Selee Corp						
700 Shepherd St	Hendersonville	NC	28792	**800-842-3818**	828-697-2411	142
SELEX Inc						
11300 W 89th St	Overland Park	KS	66214	**800-765-0861**	913-495-2600	522
Self Magazine						
4 Times Sq	New York	NY	10036	**800-274-6111**	212-286-2860	452-11
Self Storage Assn (SSA)						
1900 N Beauregard St Ste 450	Alexandria	VA	22311	**888-735-3784**	703-575-8000	48-21
Self-Employed America Magazine						
PO Box 241	Annapolis Junction	MD	20701	**800-649-6273**		452-5
Selfhelp Community Services Inc						
520 Eigth Ave Fifth Fl	New York	NY	10018	**866-735-1234**		360
Self-Seal Container Corp						
401 E Fourth St	Bridgeport	PA	19405	**800-334-1428**	610-275-2300	124
Sellars						
6565 N 60th St	Milwaukee	WI	53223	**800-237-8454**	414-353-5650	734-6
Selling Power Magazine						
1140 International Pkwy	Fredericksburg	VA	22406	**800-752-7355**	540-752-7000	452-5
Selling Source LLC						
325 E Warm Springs Rd Ste 200	Las Vegas	NV	89119	**800-251-6147**	702-407-0707	195
Sellstrom Manufacturing Co						
2050 Hammond Dr	Schaumburg	IL	60173	**800-323-7402**	847-358-2000	569
Selma-Dallas County Chamber of Commerce						
912 Selma Ave	Selma	AL	36701	**800-457-3562**	334-875-7241	137
Selmer Co						
2200 Woodale Ave	Green Bay	WI	54313	**800-992-6538**	920-434-0230	188
SEM (Society for Experimental Mechanics Inc)						
7 School St	Bethel	CT	06801	**800-627-8258**	203-790-6373	48-19
SEM (Society for Ethnomusicology)						
Indiana University						
1165 E 3rd St Morrison Hall 005	Bloomington	IN	47405	**800-933-9330**	812-855-6672	47-4
SEMA Equipment Inc						
11555 Hwy 60 Blvd	Wanamingo	MN	55983	**800-569-1377**	507-824-2256	274
Semasys Inc						
702 Ashland St	Houston	TX	77007	**800-231-1425***	713-869-8331	286
*Cust Svc						
SEMCO ENERGY Gas Co						
1411 Third St Ste A	Port Huron	MI	48060	**800-624-2019**		573
Semiconductor Environmental Safety & Health Assn (SESHA)						
1313 Dolley Madison Blvd Ste 402	McLean	VA	22101	**800-433-1790**	703-790-1745	48-19
Semiconductor Equipment & Materials International						
3081 Zenker Rd	San Jose	CA	95134	**877-746-7788**	408-943-6900	48-19
Seminole Casino Hollywood						
4150 N State Rd 7	Hollywood	FL	33021	**866-222-7466**	954-961-3220	132
Seminole Casino Immokalee						
506 S First St	Immokalee	FL	34142	**800-218-0007**		132
Seminole Coconut Creek Casino						
5550 NW 40th St	Coconut Creek	FL	33073	**866-222-7466**	954-977-6700	132
Seminole County Convention & Visitors Bureau						
1515 International Pkwy						
Suite 1013	Lake Mary	FL	32746	**800-800-7832**	407-665-2900	207
Seminole Feed						
335 NE Watula Ave PO Box 940	Ocala	FL	34470	**800-683-1881**	352-732-4143	442
Seminole Hard Rock Hotel & Casino Hollywood						
1 Seminole Way	Hollywood	FL	33314	**888-236-4848**	954-327-7625	660
Seminole Hard Rock Hotel & Casino Tampa (SHRH & C)						
5223 N Orient Rd	Tampa	FL	33610	**866-222-7466***	813-627-7625	132
*General						
Seminole Herald						
PO Box 1667	Sanford	FL	32772	**800-955-8770**	407-322-2611	525-2
Seminole State College						
2701 Boren Blvd PO Box 351	Sanford	FL	32773	**877-738-6365**	405-382-9950	160

	Toll-Free	Phone	Class
Seminole Towne Ctr			
200 Towne Ctr Cir .... Sanford FL 32771	877-746-6642	407-323-2262	455
Semling-Menke Company Inc			
PO Box 378 .... Merrill WI 54452	800-333-2206	715-536-9411	236
Semonin Realtors			
4967 US Hwy 42 Ste 200 .... Louisville KY 40222	800-548-1650	502-425-4760	643
Sempra Energy Corp			
101 Ash St .... San Diego CA 92101	800-411-7343	619-696-2000	357-5
NYSE: SRE			
Senate House State Historic Site			
296 Fair St .... Kingston NY 12401	800-456-2267	845-338-2786	558
Senate Luxury Suites			
900 SW Tyler St .... Topeka KS 66612	800-488-3188	785-233-5050	376
Senator Inn & Spa of Augusta			
284 Western Ave .... Augusta ME 04330	877-772-2224	207-622-8800	698
SENCO Products Inc			
4270 Ivy Pt Blvd .... Cincinnati OH 45245	800-543-4596*		749
*Tech Supp			
Sendec Corp			
72 Perinton Pkwy .... Fairport NY 14450	800-295-8000	585-425-3390	204
Senderex Cargo Inc			
5451 104th St .... Los Angeles CA 90045	800-421-5846	310-342-2900	310
Sendmail Inc			
6475 Christie Ave Ste 350 .... Emeryville CA 94608	888-594-3150	510-594-5400	179-7
Sen-Dure Products Inc			
6785 NW 17th Ave .... Fort Lauderdale FL 33309	800-394-5112	954-973-1260	90
Seneca Fouts Memorial State Natural Area			
Wygant Trail .... Hood River OR 97014	800-551-6949		558
Seneca Niagara Casino			
310 Fourth St .... Niagara Falls NY 14303	877-873-6322	716-299-1100	132
Seneca Resources Corp			
1201 Louisiana St Ste 400 .... Houston TX 77002	800-365-3234	713-654-2600	529
Seneca Tank Inc			
5585 NE 16th St .... Des Moines IA 50313	800-362-2910	515-262-5900	56
Senergy Petroleum LLC			
622 S 56th Ave .... Phoenix AZ 85043	800-964-0076	602-272-6795	572
Senior Aerospace Ketema Div			
790 Greenfield Dr .... El Cajon CA 92021	800-669-6820	619-442-3451	21
Senior Corps			
1201 New York Ave NW .... Washington DC 20525	800-833-3722	202-606-5000	198
Senior Housing Properties Trust			
255 Washington St .... Newton MA 02458	866-511-5038	617-796-8350	646
NYSE: SNH			
Senior Market Sales Inc (SMS)			
8420 W Dodge Rd Fifth Fl .... Omaha NE 68114	800-786-5566	402-397-3311	387
Senior Settlements LLC			
1000 S Lenola Rd			
Bldg 1 Ste 202 .... Maple Shade NJ 08052	800-834-0628	856-235-2133	784
Senior Softball USA			
2701 K St Ste 101A .... Sacramento CA 95816	888-244-9499	916-326-5303	47-22
Senior Whole Health LLC (SWH)			
58 Charles St 2nd Fl .... Cambridge MA 02141	888-794-7268	617-494-5353	350
Senior-Living.com Inc			
8521 Leesburg Pk Ste 310 .... Vienna VA 22182	866-342-4297		384
Seniorsplus			
Eight Falcon Rd PO Box 659. .... Lewiston ME 04243	800-427-1241	207-795-4010	663
Sennheiser Electronics Corp			
One Enterprise Dr .... Old Lyme CT 06371	877-736-6434	860-434-9190	246
Sensidyne Inc			
16333 Bay Vista Dr .... Clearwater FL 33760	800-451-9444	727-530-3602	202
Sensient Technologies Corp			
777 E Wisconsin Ave 11th Fl .... Milwaukee WI 53202	800-558-9892	414-271-6755	295-15
NYSE: SXT			
Sensitech Inc			
800 Cummings Ctr Ste 258x .... Beverly MA 01915	800-843-8367	978-927-7033	172
Sensormatic Electronics Corp			
6600 Congress Ave .... Boca Raton FL 33487	800-327-1765	561-912-6000	683
SensorMedics Corp			
22745 Savi Ranch Pkwy .... Yorba Linda CA 92887	800-231-2466	714-283-2228	250
SensoryEffects Flavor Co			
231 Rock Industrial Park Dr .... Bridgeton MO 63044	800-422-5444	314-291-5444	295-37
Sentara Careplex Hospital			
3000 Colliseum Dr .... Hampton VA 23666	800-736-8272	757-736-1000	371-3
Sentara Obici Hospital			
2800 Godwin Blvd .... Suffolk VA 23434	800-736-8272	757-934-4000	371-3
Sentara Virginia Beach General Hospital			
1060 First Colonial Rd ..... Virginia Beach VA • 23454	800-736-8272	757-395-8000	371-3
Sentient Jet LLC			
100 Grossman Dr Ste 400 .... Braintree MA 02184	866-602-0044	781-763-0200	13
Sentinel Hotel			
614 SW 11th Ave .... Portland OR 97205	888-246-5631	503-224-3400	376
Sentinel Process			
3265 Sunset Ln .... Hatboro PA 19040	800-345-3569	919-462-7108	329
Sentinel, The			
457 E N St .... Carlisle PA 17013	800-829-5570	717-243-2611	525-2
Sentry Group			
900 Linden Ave .... Rochester NY 14625	800-828-1438*	585-381-4900	683
*Cust Svc			
Sentry Insurance Co			
2 Technology Park Dr .... Westford MA 01886	800-373-6879	978-392-7119	388-4
Sentry Insurance Group			
1800 N Pt Dr .... Stevens Point WI 54481	800-373-6879	715-346-6000	357-4
Sentry Life Insurance Co			
1800 N Pt Dr .... Stevens Point WI 54481	800-373-6879	715-346-6000	388-2
Sentry Security LLC			
339 Egidi Dr .... Wheeling IL 60090	888-272-7080	847-353-7200	684
Sentry Technology Corp			
1881 Lakeland Ave .... Ronkonkoma NY 11779	800-645-4224		683
OTC: SKVY			
SEOP Inc			
1720 E Garry St Ste 103 .... Santa Ana CA 92705	877-231-1557		7
sephora.com Inc			
525 Market St			
First Market Twr 32nd Fl. .... San Francisco CA 94105	877-737-4672*	415-284-3300	215
*Cust Svc			
SEPLSO (Southeastern Library System of Oklahoma)			
401 N Second St .... McAlester OK 74501	800-215-6494	918-426-0456	431-3
SEPM (Society for Sedimentary Geology)			
4111 S Darlington Ste 100 .... Tulsa OK 74135	800-865-9765	918-610-3361	48-19
Sepp Leaf Products Inc			
381 Pk Ave S Ste 1301 .... New York NY 10016	800-971-7377	212-683-2840	43
Septagon Construction			
113 E Third St .... Sedalia MO 65301	800-733-5999	660-827-2115	187
Sequachee Valley Electric Co-op			
512 Cedar Ave PO Box 31 ..... South Pittsburg TN 37380	800-923-2203	423-837-8605	245
Sequatchie Concrete Service Inc			
406 Cedar Ave .... South Pittsburg TN 37380	800-824-0824	423-837-7913	184
Sequenom Inc			
3595 John Hopkins Ct .... San Diego CA 92121	877-821-7266	858-202-9000	84
NASDAQ: SQNM			
Sequoia Fund Inc			
767 Fifth Ave Ste 4701 .... New York NY 10153	800-686-6884	212-832-5280	521
Sequoyah Bay State Park			
6237 E 100th St N .... Wagoner OK 74467	800-622-6317	918-683-0878	558
SeraCare Life Sciences Inc			
37 Birch St .... Milford MA 01757	800-676-1881	508-244-6400	88
NASDAQ: SRLS			
Serco Inc			
1818 Library St Ste 1000 .... Reston VA 20190	866-628-6458	703-939-6000	24
SERENA Software Inc			
1900 Seaport Blvd			
Second Fl. .... Redwood City CA 94063	800-457-3736	650-481-3400	179-1
Serengeti Eyewear Inc			
9200 Cody St .... Overland Park KS 66214	800-423-3537*	913-752-3400	535
*Cust Svc			
Serengeti Systems Inc			
812 W 11th St Third Fl .... Austin TX 78701	800-634-3122	512-345-2211	179-12
Serenity Lane			
616 E 16th Ave .... Eugene OR 97401	800-543-9905	541-687-1110	717
Sererra Consulting Group LLC			
5430 Trabuco Rd Ste 150 .... Irvine CA 92620	877-276-3774		197
Serfilco Ltd			
2900 MacArthur Blvd .... Northbrook IL 60062	800-323-5431	847-559-1777	632
SERI (Society for Ecological Restoration International)			
1017 O St NW .... Washington DC 20001	866-895-4735	202-299-9518	47-13
Sericol Inc			
1101 W Cambridge Dr .... Kansas City KS 66103	800-737-4265	913-342-4060	385
Serrano Hotel			
405 Taylor St .... San Francisco CA 94102	866-575-9941	415-885-2500	376
Serta Mattress/AW Inc			
8415 ARdmore Rd .... Landover MD 20785	888-557-3782	301-322-1000	466
Sertoma International			
1912 E Meyer Blvd .... Kansas City MO 64132	800-593-5646	816-333-8300	47-5
Serv-a-lite Products Inc			
3451 Morton Dr .... East Moline IL 61244	800-800-4900		348
Servall Co			
6761 E Ten Mile Rd .... Center Line MI 48015	800-856-9874	586-754-9985	37
SERVE			
5900 Summit Ave Ste 201 .... Browns Summit NC 27214	800-755-3277	336-315-7400	659
Serve You Custom Prescription Management			
10201 Innovation Dr Ste 600 .... Milwaukee WI 53226	888-243-6890	414-410-8100	579
Server Products Inc			
3601 Pleasant Hill Rd			
PO Box 98. .... Richfield WI 53076	800-558-8722	262-628-5600	297
Server Technology Inc			
1040 Sandhill Dr .... Reno NV 89521	800-835-1515	775-284-2000	177
Service by Air Inc			
222 Crossways Pk Dr .... Woodbury NY 11797	800-243-5545		12
Service Communications Inc			
10675 Willows Rd NE Ste 100 .... Redmond WA 98052	800-488-0468		180
Service Construction Supply Inc			
PO Box 13405 .... Birmingham AL 35202	866-729-4968	205-252-3158	192-3
Service Electric Cable TV & Communications			
2260 Ave A .... Bethlehem PA 18017	800-232-9100	610-865-9100	115
Service Employees International Union			
1800 Massachusetts Ave NW .... Washington DC 20036	800-424-8592	202-730-7000	411
Service Ideas Inc			
2354 Ventura Dr .... Woodbury MN 55125	800-328-4493	651-730-8800	299
Service Intelligence Inc			
1061 Red Venture Dr Ste 175 .... Fort Mill SC 29707	800-263-2980		458
Service King Collision Repair Centers			
808 S Central Expy .... Richardson TX 75080	866-730-5464	972-960-7595	61-4
Service Spring Corp			
4370 Moline Martin Rd .... Millbury OH 43447	800-752-8522	419-838-6081	709
Service Steel Aerospace Corp			
4609 70th St E .... Fife WA 98424	800-426-9794		487
ServiceMaster Clean			
3839 Forrest Hill Irene Rd .... Memphis TN 38125	800-255-9687*	800-245-4622	150
*General			
Servo Products Co			
34940 Lakeland Blvd .... Eastlake OH 44095	800-521-7359	440-942-9999	450
Servpro Industries Inc			
801 Industrial Blvd .... Gallatin TN 37066	800-826-9586	615-451-0600	150
SESAC Inc			
55 Music Sq E .... Nashville TN 37203	800-826-9996	615-320-0055	47-4
SESHA (Semiconductor Environmental Safety & Health Assn)			
1313 Dolley Madison Blvd Ste 402 .... McLean VA 22101	800-433-1790	703-790-1745	48-19
Sesquicentennial State Park			
9564 Two Notch Rd .... Columbia SC 29223	888-245-9300	803-788-2706	558
SESRC (Social & Economic Sciences Research Ctr)			
Wilson Hall Rm 133			
PO Box 644014. .... Pullman WA 99164	800-932-5393	509-335-1511	659
SETA (Southeast Tissue Alliance)			
6241 NW 23rd St Ste 400. .... Gainesville FL 32653	866-432-1164	352-248-2114	538
Setai, The			
2001 Collins Ave .... Miami Beach FL 33139	888-625-7500	305-520-6000	376
Setco Sales Co			
5880 Hillside Ave .... Cincinnati OH 45233	800-543-0470	513-941-5110	450
SETEL UC			
5121 Maryland Way Ste 300. .... Brentwood TN 37027	800-743-1340	615-874-6000	775
Sethness Products Co			
3422 W Touhy Ave .... Lincolnwood IL 60712	888-772-1880	847-329-2080	295-15
Setina Manufacturing Company Inc			
2926 Yelm Hwy Se .... Olympia WA 98501	800-426-2627		390
Seton Hall University			
400 S Orange Ave .... South Orange NJ 07079	800-992-4723	973-761-9332	166
Seton Hill University			
One Seton Hill Dr .... Greensburg PA 15601	800-826-6234	724-838-4255	166
Seton Medical Ctr			
1900 Sullivan Ave .... Daly City CA 94015	800-371-2176	650-992-4000	371-3
Setra Systems Inc			
159 Swanson Rd .... Boxborough MA 01719	800-257-3872	978-263-1400	467
Settlers Life Insurance Co			
1969 Lee Hwy Ste U1 .... Bristol VA 24203	800-523-2650	276-645-4300	388-2
Seven Falls Co			
2850 S Cheyenne Canyon Rd ... Colorado Springs CO 80906	855-923-7272	719-632-0765	49-4

	Toll-Free	Phone	Class
Seven Oaks Capital Assoc LLC			
7854 Anselmo Ln			
PO Box 82360 . . . . Baton Rouge LA 70810	**800-511-4588**	225-757-1919	272
Seven Pines National Cemetery			
400 E Williamsburg Rd . . . . Sandston VA 23150	**800-535-1117**	804-795-2031	135
Seven Springs Mountain Resort			
777 Waterwheel Dr . . . . Champion PA 15622	**800-452-2223**	814-352-7777	660
Sevenson Environmental Services Inc			
2749 Lockport Rd . . . . Niagara Falls NY 14305	**800-777-3836**	716-284-0431	658
Seventh Generation Inc			
60 Lake St . . . . Burlington VT 05401	**800-456-1191**	802-658-3773	149
Seventh Mountain Resort			
18575 SW Century Dr . . . . Bend OR 97702	**800-452-6810**	541-382-8711	660
Seventh-day Adventist World Church			
12501 Old Columbia Pike . . . . . . Silver Spring MD 20904	**800-226-1119**	301-680-6000	47-20
Severance Hall			
11001 Euclid Ave . . . . .Cleveland OH 44106	**800-686-1411**	216-231-7300	565
Severn Bancorp Inc			
200 Westgate Cir Ste 200 . . . . Annapolis MD 21401	**800-752-5854**	410-260-2000	69
NASDAQ: SVBI			
Severn Trent Services			
580 Virginia Dr Ste 300 . . . . . . Fort Washington PA 19034	**866-646-9201**	215-646-9201	794
Seward County Community College			
1801 N Campus Ave PO Box 1137 . . . . Liberal KS 67905	**800-373-9951**	620-624-1951	160
Seward Motor Freight Inc			
PO Box 126 . . . . Seward NE 68434	**800-786-4468**	402-643-4503	770
Sewing Source Inc, The			
PO Box 639 . . . . Spring Hope NC 27882	**800-849-6945**	252-478-3900	358
Sex Addicts Anonymous (SAA)			
PO Box 70949 . . . . Houston TX 77270	**800-477-8191**	713-869-4902	47-21
Sexaholics Anonymous (SA)			
PO Box 3565 . . . . Brentwood TN 37024	**866-424-8777**	615-370-6062	47-21
Seymour Johnson Air Force Base			
1510 Wright Bros Ave . . . . . Seymour Johnson AFB NC 27531	**800-525-0102**	919-722-0027	492-1
Seymour Mfg Co Inc			
PO Box 248 . . . . Seymour IN 47274	**800-815-7253**	812-522-2900	748
Seymour of Sycamore Inc			
917 Crosby Ave . . . . .Sycamore IL 60178	**800-435-4482**	815-895-9101	543
SFB (Security Federal Bank)			
238 Richland Ave W . . . . .Aiken SC 29801	**866-851-3000**	803-641-3000	70
SFC (Sandridge Food Corp)			
133 Commerce Dr . . . . Medina OH 44256	**800-672-2523**	330-725-2348	295-33
SFC Graphics			
110 E Woodruff Ave . . . . Toledo OH 43604	**800-537-1130**	419-255-1283	692
SFPA (Southern Forest Products Assn)			
2900 Indiana Ave . . . . Kenner LA 70065	**866-574-4155**	504-443-4464	47-2
SFS intec Inc			
Spring St & Van Reed Rd . . . . Wyomissing PA 19610	**800-234-4533**	610-376-5751	614
SFSP (Society of Financial Service Professionals)			
19 Campus Blvd Ste 100 . . . . Newtown Square PA 19073	**800-392-6900**	610-526-2500	48-9
SG Wholesale Roofing Supplies Inc			
1101 E Sixth St . . . . Santa Ana CA 92701	**888-747-8500***	714-568-1906	192-4
*Cust Svc			
SGH (Sharp Grossmont Hospital)			
5555 Grossmont Ctr Dr . . . . .La Mesa CA 91942	**800-827-4277**	619-740-6000	371-3
SGH (Southwest General Hospital)			
7400 Barlite Blvd . . . . .San Antonio TX 78224	**877-215-9355**	210-921-2000	371-3
SGH Golf Inc			
9403 Kenwood Rd Ste C110 . . . . Cincinnati OH 45242	**800-284-8884**	513-984-0414	761
SGIA (Specialty Graphic Imaging Assn)			
10015 Main St . . . . Fairfax VA 22031	**888-385-3588**	703-385-1335	48-16
SGL Carbon LLC			
307 Jamestown Rd . . . . .Morganton NC 28655	**800-828-6601**	828-437-3221	126
SGNA (Society of Gastroenterology Nurses & Assoc Inc)			
401 N Michigan Ave . . . . Chicago IL 60611	**800-245-7462**	312-321-5165	48-8
SGS Canada Inc			
6490 Vipond Dr . . . . Mississauga ON L5T1W8	**877-887-4163***	905-364-3757	732
*General			
SGS North America Inc			
201 State Rt 17 N . . . . Rutherford NJ 07070	**800-645-5227**	201-508-3000	357-3
SH (Shive-Hattery Inc)			
316 Second St SE Ste 500			
PO Box 1599. . . . . .Cedar Rapids IA 52406	**800-798-0227**	319-362-0313	261
Shades of Green on Walt Disney World Resort			
1950 W Magnolia Palm Dr . . . . . . Lake Buena Vista FL 32830	**888-593-2242**	407-824-3400	376
Shadin LP			
6831 Oxford St . . . . .St Louis Park MN 55426	**800-328-0584**	952-927-6500	522
Shadow Mountain Resort & Club			
45-750 San Luis Rey . . . . Palm Desert CA 92260	**800-472-3713**	760-346-6123	660
Shadyside Nursing & Rehabilitation Ctr			
5609 Fifth Ave . . . . Pittsburgh PA 15232	**800-366-1232**	412-362-3500	371-6
Shafer's Tour & Charter			
500 N St . . . . Endicott NY 13760	**800-287-8986**	607-797-2006	106
Shaffer Trucking Inc			
49 E Main St PO Box 418 . . . . New Kingstown PA 17072	**800-742-3337***	717-766-4708	770
*Cust Svc			
Shaffstall Corp			
8531 Bash St . . . . .Indianapolis IN 46250	**800-357-6250**	317-842-2077	174-8
Shaker Group Inc, The			
862 Albany Shaker Rd . . . . .Latham NY 12110	**800-267-0314**	518-786-9286	444
Shaker Recruitment Adv & Communications			
1100 Lake St Third Fl . . . . .Oak Park IL 60301	**800-323-5170**	708-383-5320	4
Shaker Village of Pleasant Hill			
3501 Lexington Rd . . . . Harrodsburg KY 40330	**800-734-5611**	859-734-5411	513
Shakespeare Fishing Tackle Co			
7 Science Ct . . . . Columbia SC 29203	**800-466-5643***	803-754-7000	701
*Cust Svc			
Shakespeare Monofilaments & Specialty Polymers			
6111 Shakespeare Rd . . . . Columbia SC 29223	**800-845-2110**	803-754-7011	601
Shakespeare Theatre			
516 Eigth St SE . . . . Washington DC 20003	**877-487-8849**	202-547-3230	566-4
Shakey's USA			
2200 W Valley Blvd . . . . .Alhambra CA 91803	**888-444-6686**	626-576-0616	661
Shaklee Corp			
4747 Willow Rd . . . . .Pleasanton CA 94588	**800-742-5533**	925-924-2000	363
Shambaugh & Son LP			
7614 Opportunity Dr . . . . Fort Wayne IN 46825	**866-890-7794**	260-487-7777	190-10
Shambhala Mountain Ctr			
151 Shambhala Wy . . . . . Red Feather Lakes CO 80545	**888-788-7221**	970-881-2184	664
Shamrock Communications Inc			
149 Penn Ave . . . . Scranton PA 18503	**800-228-4637**	570-348-9100	634

	Toll-Free	Phone	Class
Shamrock Foods			
3900 E Camelback Rd Ste 300 . . . . Phoenix AZ 85018	**800-289-3663**	602-477-2500	295-27
Shamrock Scientific Specialty Systems Inc			
34 Davis Dr . . . . .Bellwood IL 60104	**800-323-0249**	708-547-9005	410
Shamrock Steel Sales Inc			
238 W County Rd S . . . . .Odessa TX 79763	**800-299-2317**	432-337-2317	487
Shamrock Technologies Inc			
Foot Of Pacific St . . . . Newark NJ 07114	**800-349-1822**	973-242-2999	144
Shands Hospital at the University of Florida			
1600 SW Archer Rd . . . . Gainesville FL 32610	**855-483-7546**	352-265-0111	371-3
Shands Hospital at the University of Florida Blood & Bone Marrow Transplant Program			
1600 SW Archer Rd			
PO Box 100403. . . . . Gainesville FL 32610	**800-749-7424**	352-733-0972	759
Shane Co			
9790 E Arapahoe Rd . . . . Greenwood Village CO 80112	**866-467-4263**		407
Shanks Extracts Inc			
350 Richardson Dr . . . . .Lancaster PA 17603	**800-346-3135**	717-393-4441	296-8
Shannon Diversified Inc			
1190 N Del Rio Pl . . . . .Ontario CA 91764	**800-794-2345**		103
Shannon Medical Ctr (SMC)			
120 E Harris Ave . . . . San Angelo TX 76903	**888-657-5202**	325-653-6741	371-3
Shanty Creek Resort			
5780 Shanty Creek Rd . . . . Bellaire MI 49615	**800-678-4111**	231-533-8621	660
Shape LLC			
2105 Corporate Dr . . . . .Addison IL 60101	**800-367-5811**	630-620-8394	757
Share Corp			
7821 N Faulkner Rd . . . . Milwaukee WI 53224	**800-776-7192**	414-355-4000	149
Share Our Strength			
1730 M St NW Ste 700. . . . . Washington DC 20036	**800-969-4767**	202-393-2925	47-5
SHARE Pregnancy & Infant Loss Support Inc			
402 Jackson St . . . . .Saint Charles MO 63301	**800-821-6819**	636-947-6164	47-21
Shari's Restaurant & Pies			
9400 SW Gemini Dr . . . . .Beaverton OR 97008	**800-433-5334**	503-605-4299	661
Sharon Coating LLC			
277 Sharpsville Ave . . . . .Sharon PA 16146	**800-456-1794**	724-981-3545	306
Sharonville Convention Ctr			
11355 Chester Rd . . . . Sharonville OH 45246	**800-294-3179**	513-771-7744	206
Sharp Bros Seed Co			
1005 S Sycamore . . . . Healy KS 67850	**800-462-8483**	620-398-2231	685
Sharp Decisions Inc			
1040 Ave of the A . . . . New York NY 10018	**800-742-7792**	212-481-5533	112
Sharp Electronics Corp			
One Sharp Plz . . . . .Mahwah NJ 07430	**800-237-4277**	201-529-8200	51
Sharp Grossmont Hospital (SGH)			
5555 Grossmont Ctr Dr . . . . .La Mesa CA 91942	**800-827-4277**	619-740-6000	371-3
Sharp Water Culligan			
129 Columbia Rd . . . . .Salisbury MD 21801	**800-439-3853**	410-742-3333	794
Shasta Beverages Inc			
26901 Industrial Blvd . . . . .Hayward CA 94545	**800-834-9980**	510-783-3200	79-2
Shattuck-Saint Mary's School			
1000 Shumway Ave PO Box 218 . . . . . . Faribault MN 55021	**800-421-2724**	507-333-1616	615
Shaw Air Force Base			
517 Lance Ave Ste 106 . . . . Shaw AFB SC 29152	**800-235-7776**	803-895-2019	492-1
Shaw Communications Inc			
630 Third Ave SW . . . . Calgary AB T2P4L4	**888-472-2222**	403-750-4500	115
TSE: SJR/B			
Shaw Group Inc, The			
4171 Essen Ln . . . . Baton Rouge LA 70809	**866-235-5687***	832-513-1000	588
NYSE: SHAW ■ *General			
Shaw Industries Inc			
616 E Walnut Ave . . . . Dalton GA 30722	**800-441-7429**		130
Shaw University			
118 E S St . . . . Raleigh NC 27601	**800-214-6683***	919-546-8275	166
*Admissions			
Shawano Country Chamber of Commerce			
1263 S Main St . . . . Shawano WI 54166	**800-235-8528**	715-524-2139	137
ShawCor Ltd			
25 Bethridge Rd . . . . Toronto ON M9W1M7	**800-668-4842**	416-743-7111	530
TSE: SCL/A			
Shawnee Milling Company Inc			
201 S Broadway PO Box 1567 . . . . Shawnee OK 74802	**800-654-2600**	405-273-7000	295-23
Shawnee State University			
940 Second St . . . . Portsmouth OH 45662	**800-959-2778**	740-351-3221	166
Shawnee Telephone Co			
PO Box 69 . . . . Equality IL 62934	**800-461-3956**	618-276-4211	726
Shawver & Son Inc			
144 NE 44th St . . . . .Oklahoma City OK 73105	**800-320-5121**	405-525-9451	190-4
SHDR (Stanley Hunt DuPree & Rhine Inc)			
7701 Airport Ctr Dr . . . . Greensboro NC 27409	**888-999-4701**	800-768-4873	194
Shea's Performing Arts Ctr			
646 Main St . . . . .Buffalo NY 14202	**866-341-5945**	716-847-1410	565
Shealy's Truck Ctr Inc			
1340 Bluff Rd . . . . Columbia SC 29201	**800-951-8580**	803-771-0176	509
Sheboygan County Chamber of Commerce			
621 S Eigth St . . . . Sheboygan WI 53081	**800-457-9497**	920-457-9491	137
Sheboygan Paint Company Inc			
1439 N 25th St PO Box 417 . . . . Sheboygan WI 53082	**800-773-7801**	920-458-2157	543
Sheboygan Press			
632 Center Ave PO Box 358 . . . . Sheboygan WI 53081	**800-686-3900**	920-457-7711	525-2
Shee Atika Inc			
315 Lincoln St Ste 300 . . . . Sitka AK 99835	**800-478-3534**	907-747-3534	112
Sheet Metal Workers International Assn (SMWIA)			
1750 New York Ave NW			
Sixth Fl . . . . Washington DC 20006	**800-251-7045**	202-783-5880	48-3
Sheetz Inc			
5700 Sixth Ave . . . . Altoona PA 16602	**800-487-5444**	814-941-5106	205
Sheffield Plastics Inc			
119 Salisbury Rd . . . . Sheffield MA 01257	**800-254-1707***	413-229-8711	593
*Cust Svc			
Shelburne Farms			
1611 Harbor Rd . . . . Shelburne VT 05482	**800-286-6022**	802-985-8686	47-13
Shelburne Murray Hill			
303 Lexington Ave . . . . .New York NY 10016	**866-233-4642**	212-689-5200	376
Shelby County			
612 Ct St . . . . Harlan IA 51537	**800-735-3942**	712-755-3831	336
Shelby County Chamber of Commerce			
501 N Harrison St . . . . Shelbyville IN 46176	**800-318-4083**	317-398-6647	137
Shelby County Office of Tourism			
315 E Main St . . . . Shelbyville IL 62565	**800-874-3529**	217-774-2244	207
Shelby Elastics Inc			
639 N Post Rd PO Box 2405. . . . . .Shelby NC 28150	**800-562-4507**	704-487-4301	734-5
Shelby Electric Co-op (SEC)			
Rt 128 N Sixth St			
PO Box 560. . . . . .Shelbyville IL 62565	**800-677-2612**	217-774-3986	245

Name / Address	City	State	Zip	Toll-Free	Phone	Class
Shelby Energy Co-op Inc						
620 Old Finchville Rd	Shelbyville	KY	40065	**800-292-6585**	502-633-4420	245
Shelby Materials						
PO Box 280	Shelbyville	IN	46176	**800-548-9516**		183
Shelby Williams Industries Inc						
810 W Hwy 25/70	Newport	TN	37821	**800-873-3252***	423-623-0031	318-3
*General						
Shelbyville Daily Union						
100 W Main St	Shelbyville	IL	62565	**800-772-1213**	217-774-2161	525-2
Shelbyville-Bedford County Chamber of Commerce						
100 N Cannon Blvd	Shelbyville	TN	37160	**888-662-2525**	931-684-3482	137
Shelbyville-Shelby County Public Library						
57 W Broadway	Shelbyville	IN	46176	**866-466-I438**	317-398-7121	431-3
Sheldahl Inc						
1150 Sheldahl Rd	Northfield	MN	55057	**800-927-3580**	507-663-8000	687
Sheldon Jackson Museum						
104 College Dr	Sitka	AK	99835	**800-587-0430**	907-747-8981	513
Shell Lubricants						
PO Box 2463 909 Fannin St	Houston	TX	77252	**888-743-5586***	713-241-6161	534
*Cust Svc						
Shell Oil Co						
910 Louisanna St	Houston	TX	77002	**888-467-4355**	713-241-6161	529
Shell Point Village						
15101 Shell Pt Blvd	Fort Myers	FL	33908	**800-780-1131***	239-466-1131	663
*Mktg						
Shelly Automotive Group						
Irvine BMW						
9881 Research Dr	Irvine	CA	92618	**888-853-7429**		56
SheltAir Aviation Services Fort Lauderdale						
4860 NE 12th Ave	Fort Lauderdale	FL	33334	**800-700-2210**	954-771-2210	62
ShelterLogic Corp						
150 Callendar Rd	Watertown	CT	06795	**800-932-9344**	860-945-6442	104
Shelton-Mason County Chamber of Commerce						
215 W Railroad Ave PO Box 2389	Shelton	WA	98584	**800-576-2021**	360-426-2021	137
Shelving Inc						
32 S Squirrel Rd	Auburn Hills	MI	48326	**800-637-9508**	248-852-8600	358
Shenandoah County Library						
514 Stoney Creek Blvd	Edinburg	VA	22824	**800-829-5137**	540-984-8200	431-3
Shenandoah Life Insurance Co						
2301 Brambleton Ave	Roanoke	VA	24015	**800-848-5433**	540-985-4400	388-2
Shenandoah National Park						
3655 US Hwy 211E	Luray	VA	22835	**800-732-0911**	540-999-3500	557
Shenandoah Telecommunications Co						
500 Shentel Way	Edinburg	VA	22824	**800-743-6835**	540-984-5224	357-3
NASDAQ: SHEN						
Shenandoah University						
1460 University Dr	Winchester	VA	22601	**800-432-2266**	540-665-4581	166
Shenandoah Valley Westminster-Canterbury						
300 Westminster-Canterbury Dr	Winchester	VA	22603	**800-492-9463**	540-665-5914	663
Shenango Valley Chamber of Commerce						
41 Chestnut St	Sharon	PA	16146	**800-732-0993**	724-981-5880	137
Shenvalee Golf Resort						
9660 Fairway Dr PO Box 930	New Market	VA	22844	**888-339-3181**	540-740-3181	660
Shepard Niles						
220 N Genesee St	Montour Falls	NY	14865	**800-481-2260**	607-535-7111	465
Shephard's Beach Resort						
619 S Gulfview Blvd	Clearwater Beach	FL	33767	**800-237-8477**	727-441-6875	376
Shepherd CE Company Inc						
2221 Canada Dry St	Houston	TX	77023	**800-324-6733**	713-924-4300	593
Shepherd Electric Supply						
7401 Pulaski Hwy	Baltimore	MD	21237	**800-253-1777***	410-866-6000	246
*Sales						
Shepherd of the Hills Homestead & Outdoor Theatre						
5586 W Hwy 76	Branson	MO	65616	**800-653-6288**	417-334-4191	565
Shepherd University						
301 N King St	Shepherdstown	WV	25443	**800-344-5231**	304-876-5000	166
Shepherdsville-Bullitt County Tourist & Convention Commission						
395 Paroquet Springs Dr	Shepherdsville	KY	40165	**800-526-2068**	502-543-8687	207
Sheplers Inc						
6501 W Kellogg Dr	Wichita	KS	67209	**888-835-4004**		155-5
Sheppard Air Force Base						
419 G Ave Ste 3	Sheppard AFB	TX	76311	**877-676-1847**	940-676-2511	492-1
Sheppard Motors						
2300 W Seventh Ave	Eugene	OR	97402	**877-362-1865***	541-343-8811	56
*Sales						
Sheppard Pratt Health System (SPHS)						
6501 N Charles St	Baltimore	MD	21285	**800-627-0330**	410-938-3000	371-5
Sheraton Delfina Santa Monica						
530 W Pico Blvd	Santa Monica	CA	90405	**888-627-8532**	310-399-9344	376
Sheraton Gateway Hotel Los Angeles						
6101 W Century Blvd	Los Angeles	CA	90045	**888-627-7104**	310-642-1111	376
Sheraton Kauai Resort						
2440 Hoonani Rd	Koloa	HI	96756	**800-325-3535***	808-742-1661	660
*Resv						
Sheraton Maui Resort						
2605 Kaanapali Pkwy	Lahaina	HI	96761	**866-716-8109**	808-661-0031	660
Sheraton Sand Key Resort						
1160 Gulf Blvd	Clearwater Beach	FL	33767	**800-456-7263**	727-595-1611	660
Sheraton Waikiki						
2255 Kalakaua Ave	Honolulu	HI	96815	**800-325-3535**	808-922-4422	660
Sheraton Wild Horse Pass Resort & Spa						
5594 W Wild Horse Pass Blvd	Chandler	AZ	85226	**800-325-3535**	602-225-0100	660
Shercon Inc						
6262 Katella Ave	Cypress	CA	90630	**888-227-5847**	714-548-3999	667
Sheridan College						
Gillette						
300 W Sinclair St	Gillette	WY	82718	**800-913-9139**	307-686-0254	160
Sheridan County Chamber of Commerce						
1517 E Fifth St	Sheridan	WY	82801	**800-453-3650**	307-672-2485	137
Sheridan Electric Co-op Inc						
PO Box 227	Medicine Lake	MT	59247	**800-553-4344**	406-789-2231	245
Sheridan Group						
11311 McCormick Rd Ste 260	Hunt Valley	MD	21031	**800-352-2210**	410-785-7277	618
Sheridan Healthcare Inc						
1613 NW 136th Ave Ste 200	Sunrise	FL	33323	**800-437-2672**		458
Sherman & Reilly Inc						
400 W 33rd St	Chattanooga	TN	37401	**800-251-7780***	423-756-5300	465
*Sales						
Sherman Bros Trucking						
32921 Diamond Hill Dr						
PO Box 706	Harrisburg	OR	97446	**800-547-8980**	541-995-7751	770
Sherritt International Corp						
1133 Yonge St	Toronto	ON	M4T2Y7	**800-704-6698**	416-924-4551	497
TSE: S						
Sherrod Vans Inc						
3151 Industrial Blvd	Waycross	GA	31503	**800-824-6333**		61-7
Sherry Matthews Inc						
200 S Congress Ave	Austin	TX	78704	**877-478-4397**	512-478-4397	4
Sherry Mfg						
3287 NW 65th St	Miami	FL	33147	**800-741-4750**	305-693-7000	153-3
Sherry-Netherland Hotel						
781 Fifth Ave	New York	NY	10022	**877-743-7710**	212-355-2800	376
Sherwood						
2200 North Main St	Washington	PA	15301	**888-508-2583**	724-225-8000	777
Sherwood Oaks						
100 Norman Dr	Cranberry Township	PA	16066	**800-642-2217**	724-776-8100	663
Shetler Moving & Storage Inc						
1253 E Diamond Ave	Evansville	IN	47711	**800-321-5069**	812-421-7750	770
SHI (Software House International)						
290 Davidson Ave	Somerset	NJ	08873	**888-764-8888**		175
Shibuya Hoppmann Corp						
13129 Airpark Dr Ste 120	Elkwood	VA	22718	**800-368-3582***	540-829-2564	540
*Cust Svc						
Shick Tube Veyor Corp						
4346 Clary Blvd	Kansas City	MO	64130	**877-744-2587**	816-861-7224	208
Shield Air Solutions Inc						
3708 Greenhouse Rd	Houston	TX	77084	**800-237-2095**	281-944-4300	14
Shield Pack LLC						
411 Downing Pines Rd	West Monroe	LA	71292	**800-551-5185**	318-387-4743	593
Shields Bag & Printing Co						
1009 Rock Ave	Yakima	WA	98902	**800-541-8630**	509-248-7500	65
SHIFT Communications LLC						
275 Washington St Ste 410	Newton	MA	02458	**800-494-8477**	617-779-1800	627
ShiftCentral Inc						
210 John St Ste 100	Moncton	NB	E1C0B8	**866-551-5533**		5
Shilo Inn Hotel Salt Lake City						
206 SW Temple	Salt Lake City	UT	84101	**800-222-2244**		376
Shilo Inn Suites Hotel Portland Airport						
117707 NE Airport Way	Portland	OR	97220	**800-222-2244**	503-252-7500	376
Shilo Inn Suites Salem						
3304 Market St	Salem	OR	97301	**800-222-2244**	503-581-4001	376
Shilo Inns Suites Hotels						
11600 SW Shilo Ln	Portland	OR	97225	**800-222-2244**	503-641-6565	376
Shimadzu Medical Systems						
20101 S Vermont Ave	Torrance	CA	90502	**800-477-1227***	310-217-8855	379
*General						
Shimadzu Scientific Instruments Inc						
7102 Riverwood Dr	Columbia	MD	21046	**800-477-1227**	410-381-1227	416
Shimer College						
3424 S State St	Chicago	IL	60616	**800-215-7173**	312-235-3506	166
Shinano Kenshi Corp						
5737 Mesmer Ave	Culver City	CA	90230	**800-755-0752**	818-889-5028	511
Shin-Etsu Silicones of America						
1150 Damar Dr	Akron	OH	44305	**800-544-1745**	330-630-9860	142
Shipley Energy						
415 Norway St	York	PA	17403	**800-839-1849**	717-848-4100	315
Shipowners Claims Bureau (SCB)						
1 Battery Pk Plaza 31st Fl	New York	NY	10004	**800-774-8724**	212-847-4500	48-21
Shippensburg University						
1871 Old Main Dr	Shippensburg	PA	17257	**800-822-8028**	717-477-1231	166
Shippers Express Co						
1651 Kerr Dr	Jackson	MS	39204	**800-647-2480**	601-948-4251	770
Shipshewana/LaGrange County Convention & Visitors Bureau						
350 S Van Buren St Ste H	Shipshewana	IN	46565	**800-254-8090**	260-768-4008	207
Shirley Plantation						
501 Shirley Plantation Rd	Charles City	VA	23030	**800-232-1613**	804-829-5121	49-2
Shirtcliff Oil Co						
PO Box 6003	Myrtle Creek	OR	97457	**800-422-0536**	541-863-5268	323
Shive-Hattery Inc (SH)						
316 Second St SE Ste 500						
PO Box 1599	Cedar Rapids	IA	52406	**800-798-0227**	319-362-0313	261
Shively Bros Inc						
2919 S Grand Travers St						
PO Box 1520	Flint	MI	48501	**800-530-9352**	810-232-7401	382
Shively Labs						
188 Harrison Rd PO Box 389	Bridgton	ME	04009	**888-744-8359**	207-647-3327	638
Shivvers Inc						
614 W English St	Corydon	IA	50060	**800-245-9093**	641-872-1005	273
Sho-Air International						
5401 Argosy Ave	Huntington Beach	CA	92649	**800-227-9111**	949-476-9111	310
Shoals Chamber of Commerce						
20 Hightower Pl PO Box 1331	Florence	AL	35630	**877-764-4661**	256-764-4661	137
Shoe Carnival Inc						
7500 E Columbia St	Evansville	IN	47715	**800-430-7463***	812-867-6471	300
NASDAQ: SCVL ■ *Cust Svc						
Shoe Show of Rocky Mountain Inc						
2201 Trinity Church Rd	Concord	NC	28027	**888-557-4637***	704-782-4143	300
*Cust Svc						
Shook & Fletcher Insulation Co						
4625 Valleydale Rd	Birmingham	AL	35242	**888-829-2575**	205-991-7606	192-4
Shook Builder Supply Co						
1400 16th St NE	Hickory	NC	28601	**800-968-0758**	828-328-2051	804
Shook Construction						
4977 Northcutt Pl	Dayton	OH	45414	**800-664-1844**	937-276-6666	189-7
Shook Hardy & Bacon LLP						
2555 Grand Blvd	Kansas City	MO	64108	**800-821-7962**	816-474-6550	425
Shop 'n Save						
10461 Manchester Rd	Kirkwood	MO	63122	**800-428-6974**	314-984-0900	342
Shop Hobby Lobby						
7717 SW 44th St	Oklahoma City	OK	73179	**800-888-0321**	405-745-1275	43
Shoplet.com						
39 Broadway Ste 2030	New York	NY	10006	**800-757-3015**	212-619-3353	779
Shopper Local						
2222 Sedwick Rd # 102	Durham	NC	27713	**877-251-4592**		411
Shoppers Food & Pharmacy						
10501 Martin Luther King Jr Hwy	Bowie	MD	20720	**800-866-0514**	240-544-0180	342
Shopping Centers Today						
1221 Ave of the Americas	New York	NY	10020	**888-427-2885**	646-728-3800	524-13
Shopping Ch, The						
Credit Card Dept						
59 Ambassador Dr	Mississauga	ON	L5T2P9	**888-202-0888**	905-362-2020	729
ShopRite PO Box 7812	Edison	NJ	08818	**800-746-7748**		342
ShopRite Supermarkets Inc						
600 York St	Elizabeth	NJ	07207	**800-746-7748**	908-527-3300	342

Listing	City	State	ZIP	Toll-Free	Phone	Class
Shops at Carolina Furniture of Williamsburg						
5425 Richmond Rd	Williamsburg	VA	23188	**800-582-8916**	757-565-3000	320
Shops at Woodlake						
725 Woodlake Rd	Kohler	WI	53044	**855-444-2838**	920-459-1713	455
Shopsmith Inc						
6530 Poe Ave	Dayton	OH	45414	**800-543-7586***	937-898-6070	749
OTC: SSMH ▪ *Cust Svc						
Shop-Vac Corp						
2323 Reach Rd	Williamsport	PA	17701	**800-356-0783**	570-326-0502	383
ShopVisible LLC						
945 East Paces Ferry Rd Ste 1475	Atlanta	GA	30326	**866-493-7037**		384
Shore Memorial Hospital						
9507 Hospital Ave PO Box 17	Nassawadox	VA	23413	**800-834-7035**	757-414-8000	371-3
Shoreline Community College						
16101 Greenwood Ave N	Shoreline	WA	98133	**866-427-4747**	206-546-4101	160
Shoreline Container Inc						
4450 N 136th Ave PO Box 1993	Holland	MI	49422	**800-968-2088**	616-399-2088	99
Shoreline Star Greyhound Park & Entertainment Complex LLC						
255 Kossuth St	Bridgeport	CT	06608	**888-463-6446**		633
Shorr Packaging Inc						
800 N Commerce St	Aurora	IL	60504	**888-885-0055**	630-978-1000	552
Short Freight Lines Inc						
459 S River Rd PO Box 357	Bay City	MI	48707	**800-248-0625**	989-893-3505	770
Short Hills Tours						
46 Chatham Rd PO Box 310	Short Hills	NJ	07078	**800-348-6871**	973-467-2113	750
Short-Elliott-Hendrickson Inc						
3535 Vadnais Ctr Dr	Saint Paul	MN	55110	**800-325-2055**	651-490-2000	261
Shorter University						
315 Shorter Ave	Rome	GA	30165	**800-868-6980**	706-233-7319	166
Showalter Flying Service						
600 Herndon Ave PO Box 140753	Orlando	FL	32803	**800-894-7331**	407-326-6062	62
Showcase Honda						
1333 E Camelback Rd	Phoenix	AZ	85014	**855-788-5798**	866-956-6481	56
SHPTV (Smoky Hills Public Television)						
604 Elm St	Bunker Hill	KS	67626	**800-362-9347**	785-483-6990	624
Shreve Memorial Library						
424 Texas St	Shreveport	LA	71101	**866-783-5462**	318-226-5897	431-3
Shreveport-Bossier Convention & Tourist Bureau						
629 Spring St	Shreveport	LA	71101	**800-551-8682**	318-222-9391	207
SHRH & C (Seminole Hard Rock Hotel & Casino Tampa)						
5223 N Orient Rd	Tampa	FL	33610	**866-222-7466***	813-627-7625	132
*General						
Shriners Hospitals for Children						
2900 N Rocky Pt Dr	Tampa	FL	33607	**800-237-5055**	813-281-0300	350
Shriners Hospitals for Children Boston						
51 Blossom St	Boston	MA	02114	**800-255-1916**	617-722-3000	371-1
Shriners Hospitals for Children Cincinnati						
3229 Burnet Ave	Cincinnati	OH	45229	**800-875-8580**	513-872-6000	371-1
Shriners Hospitals for Children Erie						
1645 W Eigth St	Erie	PA	16505	**800-873-5437**	814-875-8700	371-1
Shriners Hospitals for Children Greenville						
950 W Faris Rd	Greenville	SC	29605	**800-361-7256**	864-271-3444	371-1
Shriners Hospitals for Children Honolulu						
1310 Punahou St	Honolulu	HI	96826	**888-888-6314**	808-941-4466	371-1
Shriners Hospitals for Children Lexington						
1900 Richmond Rd	Lexington	KY	40502	**800-668-4634**	859-266-2101	371-1
Shriners Hospitals for Children Los Angeles						
3160 Geneva St	Los Angeles	CA	90020	**888-486-5437**	213-388-3151	371-1
Shriners Hospitals for Children Salt Lake City						
Fairfax Rd & Virginia St	Salt Lake City	UT	84103	**800-313-3745**	801-536-3500	371-1
Shriners Hospitals for Children Tampa						
12502 N Pine Dr	Tampa	FL	33612	**800-237-5055**	813-972-2250	371-1
SHRM (Society for Human Resource Management)						
1800 Duke St	Alexandria	VA	22314	**800-283-7476**	703-548-3440	48-12
SHRM Global Forum						
1800 Duke St	Alexandria	VA	22314	**800-283-7476**	703-548-3440	172
SHSMD (Society for Healthcare Strategy & Market Development)						
155 N Wacker Dr Ste 400	Chicago	IL	60606	**800-242-2626**	312-422-3888	48-8
Shubert Theater						
247 College St	New Haven	CT	06510	**866-889-8061**	203-624-1825	565
Shubert Theatre						
225 W 44th St	New York	NY	10036	**800-432-7250**	212-239-6200	736
Shumsky Enterprises Inc						
811 E Fourth St	Dayton	OH	45402	**800-223-2203**	937-223-2203	4
Shur-Co Inc						
2309 Shur-Lok St PO Box 713	Yankton	SD	57078	**800-474-8756**	605-665-6000	723
Shure Inc						
5800 W Touhy Ave	Niles	IL	60714	**800-257-4873**	847-866-2200	51
Shure Manufacturing Corp						
1901 W Main St	Washington	MO	63090	**800-227-4873**	636-390-7100	318-1
SHURflo Pump Mfg Company Inc						
5900 Katella Ave Ste A	Cypress	CA	90630	**800-854-3218**	562-795-5200	632
Shurtape Technologies LLC						
1712 Eigth St Dr SE	Hickory	NC	28602	**888-442-8273**	828-322-2700	722
Shuster's Bldg Components						
2920 Clay Pk	Irwin	PA	15642	**800-676-0640**	724-446-7000	494
Shutter Mill Inc						
8517 S Perkins Rd	Stillwater	OK	74074	**800-416-6455**	405-377-6455	690
Shutterbug Magazine						
1419 Chaffee Dr Ste 1	Titusville	FL	32780	**800-829-3340**	386-447-6318	452-14
Shutters on the Beach						
One Pico Blvd	Santa Monica	CA	90405	**800-334-9000**	310-458-0030	376
Shuttleworth Inc						
10 Commercial Rd	Huntington	IN	46750	**800-444-7412**	260-356-8500	208
SI Jacobson Mfg Co						
1414 Jacobson Dr	Waukegan	IL	60085	**800-621-5492**	847-623-1414	541
SIA (Security Industry Assn)						
635 Slaters Ln Ste 110	Alexandria	VA	22314	**866-817-8888**	703-683-2075	48-4
SIAM (Society for Industrial & Applied Mathematics)						
3600 Market St 6th Fl	Philadelphia	PA	19104	**800-447-7426**	215-382-9800	48-19
Siano Appliance Distributors Inc						
5372 Pleasant View Rd	Memphis	TN	38134	**800-742-6699**	901-382-5833	37
Sibley State Park						
800 Sibley Pk Rd	New London	MN	56273	**888-646-6367**	320-354-2055	558
SICB (Society for Integrative & Comparative Biology)						
1313 Dolley Madison Blvd Ste 402	McLean	VA	22101	**800-955-1236**	703-790-1745	48-19
Sickle Cell Disease Assn of America (SCDAA)						
3700 Koppers St Ste 570	Baltimore	MD	21202	**800-421-8453**	410-528-1555	47-17
Sico North America Inc						
7525 Cahill Rd	Minneapolis	MN	55439	**800-328-6138**	952-941-1700	318-3
Sidewinder Conversions						
44658 Yale Rd W	Chilliwack	BC	V2R0G5	**888-266-2299**	604-792-2082	61-7
Sidley Austin LLP						
1 S Dearborn St	Chicago	IL	60603	**800-306-5230**	312-853-7000	425
Sidney Transportation Services						
777 W Russell Rd PO Box 748	Sidney	OH	45365	**800-743-6391**	937-498-2323	676
Sidran Inc						
1050 Venture Ct Ste 100	Carrollton	TX	75006	**800-969-5015**	214-352-7979	153-19
Sidwell Co Inc						
675 Sidwell Ct	Saint Charles	IL	60174	**877-743-9355**	630-549-1000	718
Siebert Brandford Shank & Co LLC						
100 Wall St 18th Fl	New York	NY	10005	**800-334-6800**	646-775-4850	681
Siebert Financial Corp						
885 Third Ave	New York	NY	10022	**877-327-8379**	212-644-2400	357-3
NASDAQ: SIEB						
Siegel & Gale						
625 Ave of the Americas 4th Fl	New York	NY	10011	**800-356-9377**	212-453-0400	7
Siegel & Stockman USA						
126 W 25th St	New York	NY	10001	**888-515-8949**	212-633-0138	459
Siegel Display Products						
300 Sixth Ave N	Minneapolis	MN	55401	**800-626-0322**	612-340-1493	232
Siegers Seed Co						
13031 Reflections Dr	Holland	MI	49424	**800-962-4999**	616-786-4999	276
Siegfried USA LLC						
33 Industrial Pk Rd	Pennsville	NJ	08070	**877-763-8630***	856-678-3601	474
*Cust Svc						
Siegwerk USA Co						
3535 SW 56th St	Des Moines	IA	50321	**800-728-8200**	515-471-2100	385
Siemens Bldg Technologies Inc						
1000 Deerfield Pkwy	Buffalo Grove	IL	60089	**800-877-7545***	847-215-1000	203
*General						
Siemens Bldg Technologies Inc Fire Safety Div						
8 Fernwood Rd	Florham Park	NJ	07932	**888-303-3353**	973-593-2600	283
8 Fernwood Rd	Florham Park	NJ	07932	**888-303-3353**	973-593-2600	739
Siemens Corp						
527 Madison Ave Ste 8	New York	NY	10022	**800-743-6367**	212-258-4000	186
Siemens Financial Services Inc						
170 Wood Ave S	Iselin	NJ	08830	**800-327-4443**	732-590-6500	216
Siemens Foundation						
170 Wood Ave S	Iselin	NJ	08830	**877-822-5233**		303
Siemens Hearing Instruments Inc						
10 Constitution Ave PO Box 1397	Piscataway	NJ	08855	**800-766-4500**		472
Siemens Medical Solutions Inc						
51 Valley Stream Pkwy	Malvern	PA	19355	**800-888-7436**	800-225-5336	379
Siemens Product Lifecycle Management Software Inc						
5800 Granite Pkwy Ste 600	Plano	TX	75024	**800-498-5351**	972-987-3000	179-10
Siemens Water Technologies						
181 Thorn Hill Rd	Warrendale	PA	15086	**800-424-9300**	724-772-0044	794
Siemer Milling Co						
111 W Main St PO Box 670	Teutopolis	IL	62467	**800-826-1065**	217-857-3131	295-23
Siemon Co						
101 Siemon Co Dr	Watertown	CT	06795	**866-548-5814**	860-945-4200	801
Siena College						
515 Loudon Rd	Loudonville	NY	12211	**888-287-4362***	518-783-2300	166
*Admissions						
Siena Heights University						
1247 E Siena Heights Dr	Adrian	MI	49221	**800-521-0009**	517-263-0731	166
Siena Hotel						
1505 E Franklin St	Chapel Hill	NC	27514	**800-223-7379**	919-929-4000	376
Sierra Club Canada						
412-1 Nicholas St	Ottawa	ON	K1N7B7	**888-810-4204**	613-241-4611	47-13
Sierra College						
Nevada County						
250 Sierra College Dr	Grass Valley	CA	95945	**800-242-4004**	530-274-5300	160
Sierra Donor Services						
1760 Creekside Oak Dr Ste 200	Sacramento	CA	95833	**877-401-2546**	916-567-1600	538
Sierra Energy						
1020 Winding Creek Rd Ste 100	Roseville	CA	95678	**800-576-2264**	916-218-1600	572
Sierra Industries Ltd						
122 Howard Langford Dr	Uvalde	TX	78801	**888-835-9377**	830-278-4481	24
Sierra Instruments Inc						
Five Harris Ct Bldg L	Monterey	CA	93940	**800-866-0200**	831-373-0200	202
Sierra Magazine						
85 Second St 2nd Fl	San Francisco	CA	94105	**866-338-1015**	415-977-5500	452-19
Sierra Medical Ctr						
1625 Medical Ctr Dr	El Paso	TX	79902	**800-994-6610**	915-747-4000	371-3
Sierra Monitor Corp						
1991 Tarob Ct	Milpitas	CA	95035	**888-509-1970**	408-262-6611	467
OTC: SRMC						
Sierra Nevada College						
999 Tahoe Blvd	Incline Village	NV	89451	**866-412-4636**	775-831-1314	166
Sierra NV Healthcare Systems (VA Medical Ctr)						
975 Kirman Ave	Reno	NV	89502	**888-838-6256**	775-786-7200	371-8
Sierra Providence Physical Rehabilitation Hospital						
1740 Curie Dr	El Paso	TX	79902	**800-252-5400**	915-544-3399	371-6
Sierra Tucson Inc						
39580 S Lago Del Oro Pkwy	Tucson	AZ	85739	**800-842-4487**	520-624-4000	717
Sierra Vista Regional Medical Ctr (SVRMC)						
1010 Murray Ave	San Luis Obispo	CA	93405	**866-904-6871**	805-546-7600	371-3
Sierra Volkswagen Inc						
510 E Norris Dr PO Box 456	Ottawa	IL	61350	**866-308-5670**		56
SIFMAA (Securities Industry & Financial Markets Assn)						
120 Broadway 35th Fl	New York	NY	10271	**888-367-7966**	212-313-1200	48-2
SIG Mfg Company Inc						
401 S Front St	Montezuma	IA	50171	**800-247-5008***	641-623-5154	752
*Sales						
SIG SAUER Inc						
18 Industrial Dr	Exeter	NH	03833	**866-345-6744**	603-772-2302	284
Sight Society of Northeastern New York Inc						
Lions Eye Bank at Albany						
6 Executive Pk Dr	Albany	NY	12203	**888-615-3937**	518-489-7606	269
SightLife						
221 Yale Ave N Ste 450	Seattle	WA	98109	**800-847-5786**	206-682-8500	269
Sigma Alpha Epsilon Fraternity (SAE)						
1856 Sheridan Rd	Evanston	IL	60201	**800-233-1856**	847-475-1856	47-16
Sigma Chi Fraternity						
1714 Hinman Ave	Evanston	IL	60201	**877-829-5500**	847-869-3655	47-16
Sigma Corp of America						
15 Fleetwood Ct	Ronkonkoma	NY	11779	**800-896-6858**	631-585-1144	535
Sigma Design						
5521 Jackson St	Alexandria	LA	71303	**888-990-0900***	318-449-9900	179-8
*Sales						
Sigma Electronics Inc						
1027 Commercial Ave	East Petersburg	PA	17520	**866-569-2681**	717-569-2926	253

Name / Address	City	State	ZIP	Toll-Free	Phone	Class
Sigma Gamma Rho Sorority Inc						
1000 Southhill Dr Ste 200	Cary	NC	27513	**888-747-1922**	919-678-9720	47-16
Sigma Phi Epsilon Fraternity						
310 S Blvd	Richmond	VA	23220	**800-767-1901**	804-353-1901	47-16
Sigma Pi Fraternity						
106 N Castle Heights Ave	Lebanon	TN	37087	**800-332-1897**	615-373-5728	47-16
Sigma Systems Inc						
201 Boston Post Rd Ste 201	Marlborough	MA	01752	**888-867-4462**	508-925-3200	712
Sigma Theta Tau International						
550 W N St	Indianapolis	IN	46202	**888-634-7575**	317-634-8171	47-16
Sigma Xi Scientific Research Society						
3106 E NC Hwy 54						
PO Box 13975	Research Triangle Park	NC	27709	**800-243-6534**	919-549-4691	47-16
Sigma-Aldrich Corp						
3050 Spruce St	Saint Louis	MO	63103	**800-325-3010**	314-771-5765	143
NASDAQ: SIAL						
Sigma-Tau Pharmaceutical Inc						
9841 Washingtonian Blvd						
Ste 500	Gaithersburg	MD	20878	**800-447-0169**	301-948-1041	576
SigmaTron International Inc						
2201 Landmeier Rd	Elk Grove Village	IL	60007	**800-700-9095**	847-956-8000	617
NASDAQ: SGMA						
Sign Builders Inc						
4800 Jefferson Ave						
PO Box 28380	Birmingham	AL	35228	**800-222-7330**		692
Sign Designs Inc						
204 Campus Way	Modesto	CA	95350	**800-421-7446**	209-524-4484	692
Signal Magazine						
4400 Fair Lakes Ct	Fairfax	VA	22033	**800-336-4583**	703-631-6100	452-5
Signal Transformer Company Inc						
500 Bayview Ave	Inwood	NY	11096	**866-239-5777**	516-239-5777	253
Signalert Corp						
150 Great Neck Rd Ste 301	Great Neck	NY	11021	**800-829-6229**	516-829-6444	398
SignalPoint Communications Corp						
433 Hackensack Ave						
Continental Plz 6th Fl	Hackensack	NJ	07601	**877-928-3292**	201-968-9797	726
Sign-A-Rama						
2121 Vista Pkwy	West Palm Beach	FL	33411	**800-776-8105***	561-640-5570	692
*All						
Signator Investors Inc						
197 Clarendon St C-8	Boston	MA	02116	**800-543-6611**		398
Signature Bank						
565 Fifth Ave 12th Fl	New York	NY	10017	**866-744-5463**	646-822-1500	69
NASDAQ: SBNY						
Signature Breads Inc						
100 Justin Dr	Chelsea	MA	02150	**888-602-6533**		295-1
Signature Eyewear Inc						
498 N Oak St	Inglewood	CA	90302	**800-765-3937**	310-330-2700	535
OTC: SEYE						
Signature Graphics Inc						
1000 Signature Dr	Porter	IN	46304	**800-356-3235**	219-926-4994	341
Signature Hardware						
2700 Crescent Springs Pike	Erlanger	KY	41017	**866-855-2284**	859-647-7564	347
Signature Services Corp						
2705 Hawes Ave PO Box 35885	Dallas	TX	75235	**800-929-5519**	214-353-2661	298
Signe's Bakery & Cafe						
93 Arrow Rd	Hilton Head Island	SC	29928	**866-807-4463**	843-785-9118	662
Signet Marking Devices						
3121 Red Hill Ave	Costa Mesa	CA	92626	**800-421-5150**	714-549-0341	462
Signs by Tomorrow USA Inc						
8681 Robert Fulton Dr	Columbia	MD	21046	**800-765-7446**	410-312-3600	692
Signs First Corp						
720 Wildwood Trace	Winchester	TN	37398	**800-598-5845**	931-636-4031	692
Signs Now						
5368 Dixie Hwy Ste 1	Waterford	MI	48329	**800-356-3373**	248-596-8600	692
Signtech Electrical Adv Inc						
4444 Federal Blvd	San Diego	CA	92102	**877-885-1135**	619-527-6100	692
Signtronix						
1445 W Sepulveda Blvd	Torrance	CA	90501	**800-729-4853**		692
Sika Corp						
201 Polito Ave	Lyndhurst	NJ	07071	**800-933-7452**	201-933-8800	143
Sika Sarnafil Inc						
100 Dan Rd	Canton	MA	02021	**800-451-2504**	781-828-5400	45
Sikich LLP						
1415 W Diehl Rd Ste 400	Naperville	IL	60563	**877-279-1900**	630-566-8400	2
Silberline Mfg Company Inc						
130 Lincoln Dr PO Box B	Tamaqua	PA	18252	**800-348-4824**	570-668-6050	141
Silbrico Corp						
6300 River Rd	Hodgkins	IL	60525	**800-323-4287**	708-354-3350	495
Silent Knight						
7550 Meridian Cir Ste 100	Maple Grove	MN	55369	**800-328-0103**	763-493-6400	283
7550 Meridian Cir Ste 100	Maple Grove	MN	55369	**800-328-0103**	763-493-6400	739
Silgan Plastics Corp						
14515 N Outer Forty						
Ste 210	Chesterfield	MO	63017	**800-274-5426**		97
Silicon Image Inc						
1060 E Arques Ave	Sunnyvale	CA	94085	**800-633-8284**	408-616-4000	687
Silicon Laboratories Inc						
400 W Cesar Chavez	Austin	TX	78701	**877-444-3032**	512-416-8500	687
NASDAQ: SLAB						
Silicon Valley Assn of Realtors						
19400 Stevens Creek Blvd						
Ste 100	Cupertino	CA	95014	**877-699-6787**	408-200-0100	643
Silicon Valley Staffing						
2200 Powell St Ste 510	Emeryville	CA	94608	**877-660-6000**	510-923-9898	712
Silipos Inc						
7049 Williams Rd	Niagara Falls	NY	14304	**800-229-4404**	716-283-0700	576
Silks						
222 Sansome St	San Francisco	CA	94104	**800-526-6566**	415-986-2020	662
Siltronic Corp						
7200 NW Front Ave	Portland	OR	97210	**800-922-5371**	503-243-2020	687
Silver Airways Corp						
1100 Lee Wagener Blvd						
Ste 201	Fort Lauderdale	FL	33315	**844-674-5837**	954-985-1500	25
Silver City-Grant County Chamber of Commerce						
201 N Hudson St	Silver City	NM	88061	**800-548-9378**	575-538-3785	137
Silver Cloud Hotel Seattle Broadway						
1100 Broadway	Seattle	WA	98122	**800-590-1801**	206-325-1400	376
Silver Cloud Inn Seattle-Lake Union						
1150 Fairview Ave N	Seattle	WA	98109	**800-330-5812***	206-447-9500	376
*General						
Silver Cloud Inn University District						
5036 25th Ave NE	Seattle	WA	98105	**800-205-6940**	206-526-5200	376
Silver Diner Inc						
12276 Rockville Pk	Rockville	MD	20852	**866-561-0518**	301-770-0333	661
Silver Eagle Distributors LP						
7777 Washington Ave	Houston	TX	77007	**855-332-2110**	713-869-4361	80-1
Silver Edge Co-op						
39999 Hilton Rd	Edgewood	IA	52042	**800-632-5953**	563-928-6419	276
Silver Fox Tours & Motorcoaches						
Three Silver Fox Dr	Millbury	MA	01527	**800-342-5998**	508-865-6000	750
Silver King Hotel						
1485 Empire Ave	Park City	UT	84060	**888-667-2775**	435-649-5500	376
Silver King Refrigeration Inc						
1600 Xenium Ln N	Minneapolis	MN	55441	**800-328-3329**	763-923-2441	655
Silver Lake College						
2406 S Alverno Rd	Manitowoc	WI	54220	**800-236-4752**	920-686-6175	166
Silver Lake Cookie Company Inc						
141 Freeman Ave	Islip	NY	11751	**800-645-9048**	631-581-4000	295-9
Silver Legacy Capital Corp						
407 N Virginia St	Reno	NV	89501	**800-687-8733**		681
Silver Legacy Resort & Casino						
407 N Virginia St	Reno	NV	89501	**800-687-8733**	775-325-7401	132
Silver Line Bldg Products						
1 Silver Line Dr	North Brunswick	NJ	08902	**800-234-4228***	732-247-2030	234
*Sales						
Silver Smith Hotel & Suites						
10 S Wabash Ave	Chicago	IL	60603	**800-979-0084**	312-372-7696	376
Silver Springs Bottled Water Company Inc						
PO Box 926	Silver Springs	FL	34489	**800-556-0334**		296-11
Silver Springs Citrus Inc						
25411 N Mare Ave	Howey in the Hills	FL	34737	**800-940-2277**	352-324-2101	314-2
Silver Standard Resources Inc						
999 W Hastings St Ste 1180	Vancouver	BC	V6C2W2	**888-338-0046**	604-689-3846	497
TSE: SSO						
Silver Star Automotive Group						
Lotus of Thousand Oaks						
3601 Auto Mall Dr	Thousand Oaks	CA	91362	**800-472-5450**		56
Silver Star Meats Inc						
1720 Middletown Rd						
PO Box 393	McKees Rocks	PA	15136	**800-548-1321**	412-771-5539	295-26
Silver Towne LP						
120 E Union City Pike						
PO Box 424	Winchester	IN	47394	**800-788-7481**	765-584-7481	326
Silverado Resort & Spa						
1600 Atlas Peak Rd	Napa	CA	94558	**800-532-0500**	707-257-0200	660
Silverado Stages Inc						
241 Prado Rd	San Luis Obispo	CA	93401	**888-383-8109**	805-545-8400	750
SilverBirch Hotels & Resorts						
1600 - 1030 W Georgia St	Vancouver	BC	V6E2Y3	**800-661-1232**	604-646-2447	376
Silverdale Beach Hotel						
3073 NW Bucklin Hill Rd	Silverdale	WA	98383	**800-544-9799**	360-698-1000	376
Silvergate Bank						
4275 Executive Sq Ste 800	La Jolla	CA	92037	**800-595-5856**	858-362-6300	69
Silverleaf Resorts Inc						
1221 Riverbend Dr Ste 120	Dallas	TX	75247	**800-613-0310**	214-631-1166	743
Silversea Cruises						
110 E Broward Blvd	Fort Lauderdale	FL	33301	**800-722-9955**	954-522-4477	220
SilverSky						
440 Wheelers Farms Rd Ste 202	Milford	CT	06461	**800-234-2175**		795
SilverStone Group						
11516 Miracle Hills Dr Ste 100	Omaha	NE	68154	**800-288-5501**	402-964-5400	387
Silverton Hotel & Casino						
3333 Blue Diamond Rd	Las Vegas	NV	89139	**866-722-4608**	702-263-7777	132
Silverton Marine Corp						
301 Riverside Dr	Millville	NJ	08332	**800-524-2804**	856-825-4117	89
Silvestri Studio Inc						
8125 Beach St	Los Angeles	CA	90001	**800-647-8874**	323-277-4420	459
Silvi Concrete Products Inc						
355 Newbold Rd	Fairless Hills	PA	19030	**800-426-6273**	215-295-0777	183
Silvon Software Inc						
900 Oakmont Ln Ste 400	Westmont	IL	60559	**800-874-5866**	630-655-3313	179-1
SIM (Society for Information Management)						
401 N Michigan Ave Ste 2400	Chicago	IL	60611	**800-387-9746**	312-527-6734	47-9
Sim USA Inc						
PO Box 7900	Charlotte	NC	28241	**800-521-6449**		47-20
Sima Products Corp						
120 Pennsylvania Ave	Oakmont	PA	15139	**800-345-7462**	412-828-3700	51
Simba Information						
60 Long Ridge Rd Ste 300	Stamford	CT	06902	**888-297-4622**	203-325-8193	628-9
Simco Drilling Equipment Inc						
PO Box 448	Osceola	IA	50213	**855-222-8570**	641-342-2166	191
Simco Electronics						
1178 Bordeaux Dr	Sunnyvale	CA	94089	**866-299-6029**	408-734-9750	732
SIMKAR Corp						
700 Ramona Ave	Philadelphia	PA	19120	**800-523-3602**	215-831-7700	435
Simmons College						
300 The Fenway	Boston	MA	02115	**800-345-8468**	617-521-2000	166
Simmons College Beatley Library						
300 The Fenway	Boston	MA	02115	**800-831-4284**	617-521-2780	431-6
Simmons First National Corp						
501 Main St	Pine Bluff	AR	71601	**866-246-2400**	870-541-1000	357-2
NASDAQ: SFNC						
Simmons Pet Foods Inc						
316 N Hico	Siloam Springs	AR	72761	**866-463-6738**		571
Simmons-Boardman Publishing Corp						
55 Broad St 26th fl 12th Fl	New York	NY	10004	**800-895-4389**	212-620-7200	628-9
Simms Fishing Products Corp						
101 Evergreen Dr	Bozeman	MT	59715	**800-217-4667**	406-585-3557	701
SIMNA (Schroder Investment Management North America Inc)						
875 Third Ave 22nd Fl	New York	NY	10022	**800-730-2932**		681
Simon & Schuster						
1230 Ave of the Americas	New York	NY	10020	**800-223-2336***	212-698-7000	628-2
*Cust Svc						
Simon & Schuster Interactive						
1230 Ave of the Americas	New York	NY	10020	**800-223-2336**	212-698-7000	628-1
Simon Metals LLC						
2202 E River St	Tacoma	WA	98421	**800-562-8464**	253-272-9364	677
Simon Roofing & Sheet Metal Corp						
70 Karago Ave	Youngstown	OH	44512	**800-523-7714**	330-629-7663	45
Simon Wiesenthal Ctr						
1399 Roxbury Dr Ste 100	Los Angeles	CA	90035	**800-900-9036**	310-553-9036	47-8
Simonds International						
135 Intervale Rd	Fitchburg	MA	01420	**800-343-1616**		673
Simoniz USA						
201 Boston Tpke	Bolton	CT	06043	**800-227-5536**	860-646-0172	149

	Toll-Free	Phone	Class
Simons Trucking Inc			
920 Simon Dr PO Box 8 ....Farley IA 52046	800-373-2580	563-744-3304	770
Simonsen Industries Inc			
500 Iowa 31 ....Quimby IA 51049	800-831-4860	712-445-2211	273
Simonton Court Historic Inn & Cottages			
320 Simonton St ....Key West FL 33040	800-944-2687		376
Simple & Delicious			
5400 S 60th St ....Greendale WI 53129	800-344-6913	414-423-0100	452-11
Simplex Homes			
1 Simplex Dr ....Scranton PA 18504	800-233-4233	570-346-5113	105
Simplex Inc			
5300 Rising Moon Rd ....Springfield IL 62711	800-637-8603	217-483-1600	253
Simplicity Consulting Inc			
11250 Kirkland Way Ste 203 ....Kirkland WA 98033	888-252-0385		197
Simplicity Manufacturing Inc			
PO Box 702 ....Milwaukee WI 53201	800-837-6836		426
Simply Orange Juice Co			
2659 Orange Ave ....Apopka FL 32703	800-871-2653		295-20
Simpson College			
701 N 'C' St ....Indianola IA 50125	800-362-2454	515-961-6251	166
Simpson Dura-Vent Inc			
877 Cotting Ct ....Vacaville CA 95688	800-835-4429	707-446-1786	688
Simpson Gumpertz & Heger Inc			
41 Seyon St Bldg 1 Ste 500 ....Waltham MA 02453	800-729-7429	781-907-9000	261
Simpson Mfg Company Inc			
5956 W Las Positas Blvd ......Pleasanton CA 94588	800-925-5099	925-560-9000	15
NYSE: SSD			
Simpson Norton Corp			
4144 S Bullard Ave ....Goodyear AZ 85338	877-859-8676	623-932-5116	274
Simpson Strong-Tie Company Inc			
5956 W Las Positas Blvd ......Pleasanton CA 94588	800-925-5099	925-560-9000	347
Simpson University			
2211 College View Dr ....Redding CA 96003	888-974-6776	530-226-4606	166
Simpson's Eggs Inc			
5015 Hwy 218 E ....Monroe NC 28110	800-726-1330	704-753-1478	10-7
Sims Bros Inc			
1011 S Prospect St PO Box 1170 .....Marion OH 43301	800-536-7465	740-387-9041	677
Simtrol Inc			
520 Guthridge Ct ....Norcross GA 30092	800-423-0769	678-533-1200	179-12
Simulations Plus Inc			
42505 Tenth St W ....Lancaster CA 93534	888-266-9294	661-723-7723	179-10
NASDAQ: SLP			
Sinai Grace Hospital			
6071 W Outer Dr ....Detroit MI 48235	888-362-2500	313-966-3300	371-3
Sinai Hospital of Baltimore			
2401 W Belvedere Ave ....Baltimore MD 21215	800-444-8233	410-601-9000	371-3
Sinclair Marketing			
550 E S Temple St ....Salt Lake City UT 84102	800-325-3265	801-524-2700	572
Singapore Airlines KrisFlyer			
380 World Way Ste 336B ....Los Angeles CA 90045	800-742-3333	310-646-6221	26
Singapore Airlines Ltd			
222 N Sepulveda Blvd			
Ste 1600 ....El Segundo CA 90245	800-742-3333	310-647-1922	25
Singer Lewak Greenbaum & Goldstein LLP			
10960 Wilshire Blvd 7th Fl ......Los Angeles CA 90024	877-754-4557	310-477-3924	2
Singer Sewing Co			
1224 Hill Quaker Blvd			
PO Box 7017 ....La Vergne TN 37086	877-738-9869	615-213-0880	36
Singing Machine Company Inc, The			
6601 Lyons Rd Bldg A-7 ....Coconut Creek FL 33073	866-670-6888	954-596-1000	246
OTC: SMDM			
Sinton Dairy Foods Co LLC			
3801 Sinton Rd ....Colorado Springs CO 80907	800-388-4970	719-633-3821	295-10
Sioux Automation Ctr Inc			
877 First Ave NW ....Sioux Center IA 51250	866-722-1488	712-722-1488	274
Sioux City Convention Ctr			
801 Fourth St ....Sioux City IA 51101	800-593-2228	712-279-4800	206
Sioux City Foundry Co			
801 Div St ....Sioux City IA 51102	800-831-0874	712-252-4181	306
Sioux City Journal			
515 Pavonia St ....Sioux City IA 51101	800-397-3530	712-293-4300	525-2
Sioux City Tourism Bureau			
801 Fourth St ....Sioux City IA 51101	800-593-2228	712-279-4800	207
Sioux Falls Arena			
1201 NW Ave ....Sioux Falls SD 57104	800-338-3177	605-367-7288	711
Sioux Falls Convention & Visitors Bureau			
200 N Phillips Ave Ste 102 ......Sioux Falls SD 57104	800-333-2072	605-336-1620	207
Sioux Falls Seminary			
2100 S Summit ....Sioux Falls SD 57105	800-440-6227	605-336-6588	167-3
Sioux Honey Assn Co-op			
301 Lewis Blvd ....Sioux City IA 51101	888-270-6956	712-258-0638	295-24
Sioux Steel Co			
196 1/2 E Sixth St ....Sioux Falls SD 57104	800-557-4689	605-336-1750	273
Sioux Tools Inc			
250 Snap-on Dr ....Murphy NC 28906	800-722-7290*	828-835-9765	749
*Orders			
Sioux Valley-Southwestern Electric Co-op Inc			
47092 SD Hwy 34 PO Box 216 .....Colman SD 57017	800-234-1960	605-534-3535	245
Sioux-Preme Packing Co			
4241 US 75th Ave ....Sioux Center IA 51250	800-735-7675*		468
*General			
SIPA (Specialized Information Publishers Assn)			
8229 Boone Blvd Ste 260 ....Vienna VA 22182	800-356-9302	703-992-9339	48-14
SIR (Society of Interventional Radiology)			
3975 Fair Rdige Dr Ste 400 N ......Fairfax VA 22033	800-488-7284	703-691-1805	48-8
Sir Francis Drake Hotel			
450 Powell St ....San Francisco CA 94102	800-795-7129	415-392-7755	376
Sir Speedy Inc			
26722 Plaza Dr ....Mission Viejo CA 92691	800-854-8297	949-348-5000	619
Sir Winston's Restaurant & Lounge			
1126 Queens Hwy ....Long Beach CA 90802	877-342-0738	562-435-3511	662
SIRCHIE Finger Print Laboratories Inc			
100 Hunter Pl ....Youngsville NC 27596	800-356-7311	919-554-2244	82
Sirius Solution LLC			
1233 W Loop S ....Houston TX 77027	800-585-1085	713-888-0488	195
Sirsi Corp			
3300 N Ashton Blvd Ste 500 ....Lehi UT 84043	800-288-8020		178
SIRVA Inc			
700 Oakmont Ln ....Terrace IL 60181	888-444-4765	630-570-8900	657
SIS (Software Information Systems Inc)			
165 Barr St ....Lexington KY 40507	800-337-6914	859-977-4747	181
Sisbarro Dealerships			
425 W Boutz Rd ....Las Cruces NM 88005	888-241-1007	575-524-7707	56

	Toll-Free	Phone	Class
Siskin Hospital for Physical Rehabilitation			
1 Siskin Plaza ....Chattanooga TN 37403	800-994-6610	423-634-1200	371-6
Siskin Steel & Supply Co Inc			
1901 Riverfront Pkwy ....Chattanooga TN 37408	800-756-3671	423-756-3671	487
Sisters Network Inc			
2922 Rosedale St ....Houston TX 77004	866-781-1808	713-781-0255	47-21
Sita World Travel Inc			
16250 Ventura Blvd ....Encino CA 91436	800-421-5643	818-990-9530	761
SITEL Corp			
2 American Ctr			
3102 W End Ave Ste 1000 ....Nashville TN 37203	866-957-4835	615-301-7100	727
Siteman Cancer Ctr			
4921 Parkview Pl ....Saint Louis MO 63110	800-600-3606	314-362-5196	659
Sitex Corp			
1300 Commonwealth Dr ......Henderson KY 42420	800-278-3537	270-827-3537	438
Sitka Convention & Visitors Bureau			
303 Lincoln St Ste 4 ....Sitka AK 99835	800-557-4852	907-747-5940	207
Sitka Harbor			
617 Katlian St ....Sitka AK 99835	866-948-8683	907-747-3439	611
Sitka National Cemetery			
803 Sawmill Creek Rd ....Sitka AK 99835	800-273-8255	907-384-7075	135
Sitrick & Co			
1840 Century Pk E Ste 800 ....Los Angeles CA 90067	800-288-8809	310-788-2850	627
Sitton Buick GMC			
2640 Laurens Rd ....Greenville SC 29607	888-484-8009	864-288-5600	56
Sivaco Wire Group			
800 Rue Ouellette ....Marieville QC J3M1P5	800-876-9473	450-658-8741	800
Six Flags Fiesta Texas			
17000 IH-10 W ....San Antonio TX 78257	800-370-7488	210-697-5000	32
Six Flags Great Adventure			
One Six Flags Blvd ....Jackson NJ 08527	800-772-2287	732-928-1821	32
Six Flags New England			
1623 Main St ....Agawam MA 01001	800-370-7488	413-786-9300	32
Six Flags Wild Safari			
One Six Flags Blvd ....Jackson NJ 08527	800-772-2287	732-928-1821	32
Six Robblees' Inc			
11010 Tukwila International Blvd .....Tukwila WA 98168	800-275-7499	206-767-7970	60
Six States Distributors Inc			
247 West 1700 South ....Salt Lake City UT 84115	800-453-5703*	801-488-4666	60
*Cust Svc			
Sixth Floor Museum			
411 Elm St Ste 120 Dealey Plz ....Dallas TX 75202	888-485-4854	214-747-6660	513
Sizemore Inc			
2116 Walton Way ....Augusta GA 30904	800-445-1748	706-736-1456	683
S-j Transportation Co Inc			
PO Box 169 ....Woodstown NJ 08098	800-524-2552	856-769-2741	770
SJC (San Jose Convention Center)			
150 W San Carlos St ....San Jose CA 95110	800-726-5673	408-792-4194	206
SJE-Rhombus			
22650 County Hwy 6			
PO Box 1708 ....Detroit Lakes MN 56502	800-746-6287	218-847-1317	202
SJF Material Handling Equipment			
211 Baker Ave ....Winsted MN 55395	800-598-5532	320-485-2824	383
SJMH (Stonewall Jackson Memorial Hospital)			
230 Hospital Plaza ....Weston WV 26452	866-637-0471	304-269-8000	371-3
SK Food Group Inc			
4600 37th Ave SW ....Seattle WA 98126	800-722-6290	206-935-8100	363
Skaggs Community Health Ctr			
545 Branson Landing Blvd			
PO Box 650. ....Branson MO 65615	800-994-6610	417-335-7000	371-3
Skagit Valley Casino Resort			
5984 N Darrk Ln ....Bow WA 98232	877-275-2448	360-724-7777	132
Skagit Valley College			
2405 E College Way ....Mount Vernon WA 98273	877-385-5360	360-416-7600	160
Skagit Valley Herald			
1000 E College Way			
PO Box 578. ....Mount Vernon WA 98273	800-683-3300	360-424-3251	525-2
Skagway Visitor Information			
245 Broadway PO Box 1029 ....Skagway AK 99840	888-762-1898	907-983-2855	207
Skamania Lodge			
1131 SW Skamania Lodge Way			
PO Box 189. ....Stevenson WA 98648	800-221-7117	509-427-7700	374
SKB Corp			
434 W Levers Pl ....Orange CA 92867	800-410-2024*	714-637-1252	448
*Sales			
Skechers USA Inc			
228 Manhattan Beach Blvd			
Ste 200 ....Manhattan Beach CA 90266	800-746-3411*	310-318-3100	300
NYSE: SKX ■ *Cust Svc			
Ski Bromont			
150 Champlain ....Bromont QC J2L1A2	866-276-6668	450-534-2200	376
Ski Magazine			
5720 Flatiron Pkwy ....Boulder CO 80301	888-444-8151	303-253-6300	452-20
Skidmore College			
815 N Broadway ....Saratoga Springs NY 12866	800-867-6007	518-580-5000	166
Skilled Care Pharmacy Inc			
6175 Hi Tek Ct ....Mason OH 45040	800-334-1624	513-459-7455	577
Skillforce Inc			
405 Williams Court Ste 100 ......Baltimore MD 21220	866-581-8989		260
SkillSoft PLC			
107 NE Blvd ....Nashua NH 03062	877-545-5763	603-324-3000	755
SkillsUSA			
14001 James Monroe Hwy ....Leesburg VA 20176	800-321-8422	703-777-8810	47-11
SkinMedica Inc			
5770 Armada Dr ....Carlsbad CA 92008	866-577-3072	760-448-3600	215
Skinner Transfer Corp			
PO Box 438 ....Reedsburg WI 53959	800-356-9350	608-524-2326	770
Skuttle Manufacturing Co			
101 Margaret St ....Marietta OH 45750	800-848-9786	740-373-9169	14
Sky & Telescope Magazine			
90 Sherman St ....Cambridge MA 02140	800-253-0245	617-864-7360	452-19
Sky Bird Travel & Tours Inc			
24701 Swanson ....Southfield MI 48033	888-759-2473	248-372-4800	16
Sky Bright			
65 Aviation Dr ....Gilford NH 03249	800-639-6012	603-528-6818	62
Sky Hotel			
709 E Durant Ave ....Aspen CO 81611	800-882-2582	970-925-6760	376
Sky Publishing Corp			
90 Sherman St ....Cambridge MA 02140	800-253-0245	617-864-7360	628-9
Sky Sox Stadium			
4385 Tutt Blvd			
Security Service Field ....Colorado Springs CO 80922	866-698-4253	719-597-1449	711

	Toll-Free	Phone	Class
Sky Ute Casino			
14324 US Hwy 172 N ....Ignacio CO 81137	**888-842-4180**	970-563-7777	132
Skybank Financial Services Corp			
1444 Biscayne Blvd Ste 309...........Miami FL 33132	**800-617-9980**		225
Skybooks Inc			
1310 Tradeport Dr ....Jacksonville FL 32218	**866-929-8700**	904-741-8700	56
Skyline Chili Inc			
4180 Thunderbird Ln ....Fairfield OH 45014	**800-443-4371***	513-874-1188	661
*General			
Skyline Corp			
2520 By-Pass Rd ....Elkhart IN 46514	**800-348-7469**	574-294-6521	119
NYSE: SKY			
Skyline Medical Ctr			
3441 Dickerson Pike ....Nashville TN 37207	**800-242-5662**	615-769-2000	371-3
Skyline Steel LLC			
Eight Woodhollow Rd Ste 102 ....Parsippany NJ 07054	**866-875-9546**		487
Skyline Telephone Membership Corp			
PO Box 759 ....West Jefferson NC 28694	**877-475-9546**	336-877-3111	726
Skylink Travel			
980 Ave of the Americas ....New York NY 10018	**800-247-6659**	212-573-8980	16
SkyMall Inc			
1520 E Pima St ....Phoenix AZ 85034	**800-759-6255**		454
Skyservice Airlines Inc			
9785 Ryan Ave ....Dorval QC H9P1A2	**888-985-1402**	514-636-3300	13
Skystone Ryan			
Skystone Partners LLC			
635 W Seventh St Ste 107 ......Cincinnati OH 45203	**800-883-0801**	513-241-6778	316
SkyTech Inc			
550 Airport Rd ....Rock Hill SC 29732	**888-386-3596**	803-366-5108	62
SkyTel Corp			
PO Box 2469 ....Jackson MS 39225	**800-759-8737***		726
*Cust Svc			
Skytop Lodge			
One Skytop ....Skytop PA 18357	**800-345-7759**	570-595-7401	660
Skywalker Communications Inc			
9390 Veterans Memorial Pkwy ....O'Fallon MO 63366	**800-844-9555**	636-272-8025	246
Skyward Inc			
5233 Coye Dr ....Stevens Point WI 54481	**800-236-0001**	715-341-9406	179-12
Skyworks LLC			
100 Thielman Dr ....Buffalo NY 14206	**866-983-1184**	716-822-5438	264-3
SL Power Electronics Inc			
6050 King Dr Bldg A............Ventura CA 93003	**800-235-5929**	805-486-4565	253
SLA (Special Libraries Assn)			
331 S Patrick St ....Alexandria VA 22314	**866-446-6069**	703-647-4900	48-11
Slack Inc			
6900 Grove Rd ....Thorofare NJ 08086	**800-257-8290**	856-848-1000	628-9
Slade Gorton Company Inc			
225 Southampton St ....Boston MA 02118	**800-225-1573**	617-442-5800	296-5
Slay Industries Inc			
1441 Hampton Ave ....Saint Louis MO 63139	**800-852-7529**	314-647-7529	444
SLB (South Louisiana Bank)			
1362 W Tunnel Blvd PO Box 1718 ....Houma LA 70361	**877-275-3342**	985-851-3434	69
Sledd Co			
100 E Cove Ext ....Wheeling WV 26003	**800-333-0374***	304-243-1820	746
*General			
Sleep Train Inc			
2205 Plz Dr ....Rocklin CA 95765	**800-919-2337**		466
SLH (Solheim Lutheran Home)			
2236 Merton Ave ....Los Angeles CA 90041	**888-257-7518**	323-257-7518	663
SlickEdit Inc			
3000 Aerial Ctr Pkwy			
Ste 120 ....Morrisville NC 27560	**800-934-3348**	919-473-0070	179-2
S-Line Cargo Control & Safety Products			
11414 Mathis ....Dallas TX 75234	**800-687-9900**		760
Slippery Rock University			
One Morrow Way ....Slippery Rock PA 16057	**800-929-4778**	724-738-9000	166
SLM Corp			
12061 Bluemont Way ....Reston VA 20190	**888-272-5543***	703-810-3000	214
NASDAQ: SLM ■ *Cust Svc			
SLM Manufacturing Corp			
215 Davidson Ave ....Somerset NJ 08873	**800-526-3708**	732-469-7500	593
Sloan Implement Co			
120 N Business 51 ....Assumption IL 62510	**800-745-4020**	217-226-4411	274
Sloan Management Review			
77 Massachusetts Ave E60-100 ....Cambridge MA 02139	**800-876-5764**	617-253-7170	452-5
Sloan Valve Co			
10500 Seymour Ave ....Franklin Park IL 60131	**800-982-5839**	847-671-4300	602
Slomin's Inc			
125 Lauman Ln ....Hicksville NY 11801	**800-252-7663**	516-932-7000	683
Slope Electric Co-op Inc			
116 E 12th St PO Box 338 ....New England ND 58647	**800-559-4191**	701-579-4191	245
Sly Inc			
8300 Dow Cir ....Strongsville OH 44136	**800-334-2957**	440-891-3200	18
SM Arnold Inc			
7901 Michigan Ave ....Saint Louis MO 63111	**800-325-7865***	314-544-4103	102
*Cust Svc			
SMA (Southern Medical Assn)			
35 W Lakeshore Dr ....Birmingham AL 35209	**800-423-4992**	205-945-1840	48-8
Small Business Administration (SBA)			
409 Third St SW ....Washington DC 20416	**800-827-5722**	202-205-6600	338-18
Small Business Administration Regional Offices			
Region 6 1301 Young St ....Dallas TX 75202	**800-772-1213**	214-767-9401	338-18
Region 10			
701 Fifth Ave Ste 2900..............Seattle WA 98104	**800-772-1213**	206-615-2236	338-18
Small Planet Foods Inc			
106 Woodworth St ....Sedro Woolley WA 98284	**800-624-4123**	360-855-0100	295-18
Small Station Assn			
KRWG-TV			
PO Box 30001 MSCPB 22 ....Las Cruces NM 88003	**877-308-2408**	575-646-2222	624
Small Tube Products Company Inc			
PO Box 1017 ....Duncansville PA 16635	**800-458-3493**	814-695-4491	485
SMART (Special Military Active Retired Travel Club)			
600 University Office Blvd			
Ste 1A..............Pensacola FL 32504	**800-354-7681**	850-478-1986	47-23
SMART (Suburban Mobility Authority for Regional Transportation)			
535 Griswold St			
Ste 600 Buhl Bldg..............Detroit MI 48226	**866-962-5515**	313-223-2100	463
Smart & Final Inc			
600 Citadel Dr ....Commerce CA 90040	**800-894-0511**	323-869-7500	342
Smart Card Alliance Inc			
191 Clarkville Rd ....Princeton Junction NJ 08550	**800-556-6828**	609-799-5654	48-2
Smart City Networks			
5795 W Badura Ave Ste 110..........Las Vegas NV 89118	**888-446-6911**	702-943-6000	726

	Toll-Free	Phone	Class
Smart Furniture Inc			
430 Market St ....Chattanooga TN 37402	**888-467-6278**	423-267-7007	320
Smart Industries Corp			
1626 Delaware Ave ....Des Moines IA 50317	**800-553-2442**	515-265-9900	321
Smart LLC			
Smart TuitionOne Woodbridge Ctr			
Ste 800..............Woodbridge NJ 07095	**866-395-2986**		390
SMART Modular Technologies Inc			
39870 Eureka Dr ....Newark CA 94560	**800-956-7627**	510-623-1231	174-2
NASDAQ: SMOD			
Smart Online Inc			
4505 Emperor Blvd Ste 320 ....Durham NC 27703	**800-578-9000**		38
Smart Power Systems Inc			
1760 Stebbins Dr ....Houston TX 77043	**800-241-6880**	713-464-8000	253
SMART Recovery			
7304 Mentor Ave Ste F..............Mentor OH 44060	**866-951-5357**	440-951-5357	47-21
SMART Technologies Inc			
3636 Research Road NW ....Calgary AB T2L1Y1	**888-427-6278**	403-245-0333	174-2
TSE: SMA			
SmartBargains Inc			
101 S State Rd 7 Ste 201 ....Hollywood FL 33023	**877-222-6660**		229
SmarTire Systems Inc			
13151 Vanier Pl Ste 150............Richmond BC V5V2J1	**800-247-2725**	604-276-9884	59
Smartpak Equine LLC			
40 Grissom Rd Ste 500............Plymouth MA 02360	**888-752-5171**	774-773-1000	363
Smartronix Inc			
44150 Smartronix Way ....Hollywood MD 20636	**866-442-7767**	301-373-6000	178
SmartScrubs LLC			
3400 E Mcdowell Rd ....Phoenix AZ 85008	**800-800-5788**		470
Smarty Ants Inc			
1400 Rollins Rd ....Burlingame CA 94010	**877-905-2687**		384
SMC (Southwestern Michigan College)			
58900 Cherry Grove Rd ....Dowagiac MI 49047	**800-456-8675**	269-782-1000	160
SMC (Shannon Medical Ctr)			
120 E Harris Ave ....San Angelo TX 76903	**888-657-5202**	325-653-6741	371-3
SMC (Save the Manatee Club)			
500 N Maitland Ave Ste 210 ....Maitland FL 32751	**800-432-5646**	407-539-0990	47-3
SMCC (Southern Maine Community College)			
Two Ft Rd ....South Portland ME 04106	**877-282-2182**	207-741-5500	788
SMD (Surface Mount Distribution Inc)			
1 Oldfield ....Irvine CA 92618	**800-820-7634**	949-470-7700	246
SME (Society of Mfg Engineers)			
One SME Dr ....Dearborn MI 48128	**800-733-4763***	313-425-3000	48-13
*Cust Svc			
SME (Society for Mining Metallurgy & Exploration Inc)			
8307 Shaffer Pkwy ....Littleton CO 80127	**800-763-3132**	303-973-9550	48-13
SMH (Southeast Missouri Hospital)			
1701 Lacey St ....Cape Girardeau MO 63701	**800-800-5123**	573-334-4822	371-3
SMI (Speedway Motorsports Inc)			
5555 Concord Pkwy S..............Concord NC 28027	**800-461-9330**	704-455-3239	182
NYSE: TRK			
SMI (Spring Manufacturers Institute)			
2001 Midwest Rd Ste 106..............Oak Brook IL 60523	**866-482-5569**	630-495-8588	48-13
Smile Train Inc			
41 Madison Ave Ste 28..............New York NY 10010	**877-543-7645**	212-689-9199	47-5
Smith & Butterfield Co Inc			
2800 Lynch Rd ....Evansville IN 47711	**800-321-6543**	812-422-3261	528
Smith & Greene Co			
19015 66th Ave S ....Kent WA 98032	**800-232-8050**	425-656-8000	299
Smith & Nephew Inc			
970 Lk Carillon Dr 310 ....Saint Petersburg FL 33716	**800-876-1261***	727-392-1261	472
*Cust Svc			
Smith & Nephew Inc Endoscopy Div			
150 Minuteman Rd ....Andover MA 01810	**800-343-5717**	978-749-1000	471
Smith & Nephew Inc Orthopaedic Div			
1450 Brooks Rd ....Memphis TN 38116	**800-821-5700**	901-396-2121	472
Smith & Richardson Manufacturing Co			
PO Box 589 ....Geneva IL 60134	**800-426-0876**	630-232-2581	614
Smith & Wesson Corp			
2100 Roosevelt Ave ....Springfield MA 01104	**800-331-0852***	413-781-8300	284
*Cust Svc			
Smith & Wesson Holding Corp			
2100 Roosevelt Ave ....Springfield MA 01104	**800-372-6454**	413-781-8300	284
NASDAQ: SWHC			
Smith Affiliated Capital (SAC)			
800 Third Ave 12th Fl..............New York NY 10022	**888-387-3298**	212-644-9440	400
Smith Bros Co			
3501 W 48th Pl ....Chicago IL 60632	**800-621-0225**	773-927-3737	295-35
Smith College			
Seven College Ln ....NortHampton MA 01063	**800-383-3232**	413-584-2700	166
Smith Dairy			
1381 Dairy Ln ....Orrville OH 44667	**800-776-7076**	330-683-8710	295-27
Smith Dray Line			
320 Frontage Rd ....Greenville SC 29611	**866-642-6389**		512
Smith Equipment Mfg Co			
2601 Lockheed Ave ....Watertown SD 57201	**866-931-9730***	605-882-3200	798
*Cust Svc			
Smith Gardens Inc			
4164 Meridian St Ste 400...........Bellingham WA 98226	**800-755-6256**	360-733-4671	366
Smith Graham & Co			
600 Travis St Ste 6900..............Houston TX 77002	**800-739-4470**	713-227-1100	398
Smith McDonald Corp			
1270 Niagara St ....Buffalo NY 14213	**800-753-8548**	716-684-7200	601
SMITH Mfg Company Inc			
1610 S Dixie Hwy..........Pompano Beach FL 33060	**800-653-9311**	954-941-9744	81
Smith Motors Inc of Hammond			
6405 Indianapolis Blvd ....Hammond IN 46320	**877-392-2689**	219-845-4000	56
Smith Power Products Inc			
3065 W California Ave ....Salt Lake City UT 84104	**800-658-5352**	801-415-5000	382
Smith Pump Co Inc			
301 M B Industrial ....Woodway TX 76712	**800-299-8909**	254-776-0377	632
Smith Ranch Homes			
400 Deer Vly Rd Ste L..............San Rafael CA 94903	**800-772-6264**	415-491-4918	663
Smith Ready Mix Inc			
251 W Lincolnway ....Valparaiso IN 46383	**888-632-5656**	219-462-3191	183
Smith Robertson Museum & Cultural Ctr			
528 Bloom St ....Jackson MS 39202	**800-354-7695**	601-960-1457	513
Smith System Driver Improvement Institute Inc			
2201 Brookhollow Plz Dr			
Ste 200 ....Arlington TX 76006	**800-777-7648**	817-652-6969	160
Smithco Inc 34 W Ave ....Wayne PA 19087	**877-833-7648**	610-688-4009	426
Smith-Edwards-Dunlap Co			
2867 E Allegheny Ave ....Philadelphia PA 19134	**800-829-0020**	215-425-8800	618

	Toll-Free	Phone	Class
Smithereen Exterminators Inc 7400 N Melvina Ave .... Niles IL 60714	800-336-3500	847-647-0010	570
Smithfield Foods Inc 200 Commerce St .... Smithfield VA 23430 *NYSE: SFD*	800-276-6158	757-365-3000	468
Smiths Medical ASD Inc 160 Weymouth St .... Rockland MA 02370	800-258-5361	781-878-8011	472
Smiths Medical MD Inc 1265 Grey Fox Rd .... Saint Paul MN 55112	800-258-5361	651-633-2556	472
Smiths Medical Respiratory Support Products 5200 Upper Metro Pl Ste 200 .... Dublin OH 43017	800-258-5361	214-618-0218	472
Smithsonian Air & Space Magazine PO Box 37012 .... Washington DC 20013 *Cust Svc	800-766-2149*	202-633-6070	452-19
Smithsonian Folkways Recordings 600 Maryland Ave SW Ste 200 .... Washington DC 20024	800-410-9815	202-633-6450	648
Smithsonian Institution Business Ventures Div 600 Maryland Ave SW Ste 6000 .... Washington DC 20024	800-521-5330	202-633-6080	628-9
Smithsonian Magazine 600 Maryland Ave Ste 6001 .... Washington DC 20024	800-766-2149	202-633-6090	452-11
Smitty's Supply Inc 63399 Hwy 51 N PO Box 530 .... Roseland LA 70456	800-256-7575	985-748-9687	534
SMO (Southern Maryland Oil Co Inc) 109 N Maple Ave .... La Plata MD 20646	888-222-3720		572
Smoke Magazine 26 Broadway .... New York NY 10004	800-766-2633	212-391-2060	452-14
Smoker Craft PO Box 65 .... New Paris IN 46553	866-719-7873		89
Smoky Hills Public Television (SHPTV) 604 Elm St .... Bunker Hill KS 67626	800-362-9347	785-483-6990	624
Smoky Mountain Truck Ctr LLC 841 Eastern Star Rd PO Box 5729 .... Kingsport TN 37663	800-451-1508	423-349-3000	56
Smoky Mountain Visitors Bureau 7906 E Lamar Alexander Pkwy .... Townsend TN 37882	800-525-6834	865-448-6134	207
Smooth-On Inc 2000 St John St .... Easton PA 18042	800-766-6841	610-252-5800	42
SMPS (Society for Marketing Professional Services) 99 Canal Ctr Plz .... Alexandria VA 22314	800-292-7677	703-549-6117	48-18
SMR Technologies Inc 93 Nettie Fenwick Rd .... Fenwick WV 26202	800-767-6899	304-846-6636	667
SMS (Systems Maintenance Services Inc) 10420 Harris Oaks Blvd Suite C .... Charlotte NC 28269	877-405-0330		176
SMS (Senior Market Sales Inc) 8420 W Dodge Rd Fifth Fl .... Omaha NE 68114	800-786-5566	402-397-3311	387
SMS Data Products Group Inc 1751 Pinnacle Dr 12th Fl .... McLean VA 22102	800-331-1767		181
Smugglers' Notch Resort 4323 Vermont Rt 108 S .... Jeffersonville VT 05464	800-451-8752	802-644-8851	660
Smulekoff's Fine Home Furnishings PO Box 74090 .... Cedar Rapids IA 52407	888-384-6995	319-362-2181	320
SMWIA (Sheet Metal Workers International Assn) 1750 New York Ave NW Sixth Fl .... Washington DC 20006	800-251-7045	202-783-5880	48-3
Smyth Cos Inc 1085 Snelling Ave N .... Saint Paul MN 55108	800-473-3464	651-646-4544	410
SNA (School Nutrition Assn) 700 S Washington St Ste 300 .... Alexandria VA 22314	800-877-8822	703-739-3900	48-6
Snack Food Assn 1600 Wilson Blvd Ste 650 .... Arlington VA 22209	800-628-1334	703-836-4500	48-6
Snacks Unlimited One General Mills Blvd .... Minneapolis MN 55426	800-248-7310	763-764-7600	295-35
SNAP (Survivors Network of Those Abused by Priests) PO Box 6416 .... Chicago IL 60680	877-762-7432	312-455-1499	47-21
Snap-on Credit LLC 950 Technology Way Ste 301 .... Libertyville IL 60048	877-777-8455		216
Snap-on Diagnostics 420 Barclay Blvd .... Lincolnshire IL 60069	800-424-7226	847-478-0700	248
Snap-on Inc 2801 80th St .... Kenosha WI 53143 *NYSE: SNA*	877-762-7664	262-656-5200	748
Snapping Shoals Electric Membership Corp 14750 Brown Bridge Rd .... Covington GA 30016	888-999-1416	770-786-3484	245
Snappy Tomato Pizza Co 6111 A Burgundy Hill Dr .... Burlington KY 41005	888-463-7627	859-525-4680	661
Snap-Tite Autoclave Engineers Div 8325 Hessinger Dr .... Erie PA 16509	800-458-0409	814-838-5700	90
SNBC (Sun Bancorp Inc) 226 Landis Ave .... Vineland NJ 08360 *NASDAQ: SNBC*	800-786-9066		357-2
SNC Mfg Company Inc 101 W Waukau Ave .... Oshkosh WI 54902	800-558-3325	920-231-7370	253
SNE Enterprises Inc 880 Southview Dr .... Mosinee WI 54455	800-826-5509	715-693-7000	236
Snell & Wilmer LLP One Arizona Ctr 400 E Van Buren St Ste 1900 .... Phoenix AZ 85004	800-322-0430	602-382-6000	425
Snell House 21 Atlantic Ave .... Bar Harbor ME 04609	866-763-5524	207-288-8004	376
Snethkamp Chrysler Dodge Jeep Ram 11600 Telegraph Rd .... Redford MI 48239	888-455-6146	313-255-2700	509
SNFC (Security National Financial Corp) 5300 South 360 West Ste 250 PO Box 57250 .... Salt Lake City UT 84123 *NASDAQ: SNFCA*	800-574-7117	801-264-1060	388-2
SNK America Inc 1150 Feehanville Dr .... Mount Prospect IL 60056	888-765-6224	847-364-0801	450
SNM (Society of Nuclear Medicine) 1850 Samuel Morse Dr .... Reston VA 20190	888-633-5343	703-708-9000	48-8
SNMP Research International Inc 3001 Kimberlin Heights Rd .... Knoxville TN 37920	877-644-5866	865-579-3311	179-12
Snohomish Flying Service Inc 9900 Airport Way .... Snohomish WA 98296	800-827-1000	360-568-1541	62
Snow College 150 College Ave PO Box 1028 .... Ephraim UT 84627	800-848-3399	435-283-7000	160
Snow Goer Magazine 3300 Fernbrook Ln N Ste 200 .... Plymouth MN 55447	800-710-5249		452-20
Snow King Resort 400 E Snow King Ave Jackson Hole .... Jackson WY 83001	800-522-5464	307-733-5200	660
Snow Valley Mountain Resort 35100 State Hwy 18 PO Box 2337 .... Running Springs CA 92382	800-680-7669	909-867-2751	660

	Toll-Free	Phone	Class
Snowbasin Ski Resort 3925 E Snowbasin Rd .... Huntsville UT 84317	888-437-5488	801-620-1100	660
Snowbird Mountain Lodge 4633 Santeetlah Rd .... Robbinsville NC 28771	800-941-9290	828-479-3433	376
Snowbird Ski & Summer Resort Hwy 210 PO Box 929000 .... Snowbird UT 84092	800-453-3000	801-742-2222	660
Snowdale State Park 501 S 439 .... Salina OK 74361	800-622-6317	918-434-2651	558
Snowshoe Mountain Resort 10 Snowshoe Dr .... Snowshoe WV 26209	877-441-4386	304-572-1000	660
Snowy Owl Inn 41 Village Rd .... Waterville Valley NH 03215	800-766-9969	603-236-8383	376
Snyder & Assoc Inc PO Box 1159 .... Ankeny IA 50023 *General	888-964-2020*	515-964-2020	261
Snyder Chevrolet 524 N Perry St .... Napoleon OH 43545	800-569-3957	419-599-1015	56
Snyder Langston Inc 17962 Cowan St .... Irvine CA 92614	800-899-4122	949-863-9200	187
Snyder of Berlin 1313 Stadium Dr .... Berlin PA 15530	800-374-7949	814-267-4641	295-35
Snyder Paper Corp 250 26th St Dr SE .... Hickory NC 28602	800-222-8562	828-328-2501	552
Snyder Tire 401 Cadiz Rd .... Steubenville OH 43953	800-967-8473	740-264-5543	745
Snyder's of Hanover 1250 York St PO Box 6917 .... Hanover PA 17331	800-233-7125	717-632-4477	295-9
SOAR (Soar Corp) 5200 Constitution Ave NE .... Albuquerque NM 87110	866-616-4450	505-268-6110	648
Soar Corp (SOAR) 5200 Constitution Ave NE .... Albuquerque NM 87110	866-616-4450	505-268-6110	648
Soaring Eagle Casino & Resort 6800 E Soaring Eagle Blvd .... Mount Pleasant MI 48858	888-732-4537		132
Sobel Westex Inc 2670 Western Ave .... Las Vegas NV 89109	888-887-6235		358
Social & Economic Sciences Research Ctr (SESRC) *Washington State University* Wilson Hall Rm 133 PO Box 644014 .... Pullman WA 99164	800-932-5393	509-335-1511	659
Social Annex Inc 5301 Beethoven St Ste 260 .... Los Angeles CA 90066	866-802-8806		384
Social Security Administration (SSA) 6401 Security Blvd .... Baltimore MD 21235	800-772-1213	410-965-8904	338-18
Social Security Administration Regional Offices *Region 2* 26 Federal Plaza Rm 40-102 .... New York NY 10278	800-772-1213	212-264-4036	338-18
Region 4 61 Forsyth St SW Ste 23T30 .... Atlanta GA 30303	800-772-1213		338-18
Region 5 600 W Madison St PO Box 8280 .... Chicago IL 60680	800-772-1213	312-575-4050	338-18
Social Studies School Service 10200 Jefferson Blvd PO Box 802 .... Culver City CA 90232	800-421-4246	310-839-2436	95
Social Work Magazine 750 First St NE Ste 700 .... Washington DC 20002	800-227-3590	202-408-8600	452-16
Society for American Archaeology (SAA) 900 Second St NE Ste 12 .... Washington DC 20002	800-759-5219	202-789-8200	48-5
Society for Biomaterials 15000 Commerce Pkwy Ste C .... Mount Laurel NJ 08054	800-337-9255	856-439-0826	48-19
Society for College & University Planning (SCUP) 339 E Liberty St Ste 300 .... Ann Arbor MI 48104	800-257-2578	734-669-3270	48-5
Society for Ecological Restoration International (SERI) 1017 O St NW .... Washington DC 20001	866-895-4735	202-299-9518	47-13
Society for Ethnomusicology (SEM) Indiana University 1165 E 3rd St Morrison Hall 005 .... Bloomington IN 47405	800-933-9330	812-855-6672	47-4
Society for Experimental Mechanics Inc (SEM) 7 School St .... Bethel CT 06801	800-627-8258	203-790-6373	48-19
Society for Healthcare Epidemiology of America 1300 Wilson Blvd Ste 300 .... Arlington VA 22209	877-734-2726	703-684-1006	48-8
Society for Healthcare Strategy & Market Development (SHSMD) 155 N Wacker Dr Ste 400 .... Chicago IL 60606	800-242-2626	312-422-3888	48-8
Society for Human Resource Management (SHRM) 1800 Duke St .... Alexandria VA 22314	800-283-7476	703-548-3440	48-12
Society for Industrial & Applied Mathematics (SIAM) 3600 Market St 6th Fl .... Philadelphia PA 19104	800-447-7426	215-382-9800	48-19
Society for Information Management (SIM) 401 N Michigan Ave Ste 2400 .... Chicago IL 60611	800-387-9746	312-527-6734	47-9
Society for Integrative & Comparative Biology (SICB) 1313 Dolley Madison Blvd Ste 402 .... McLean VA 22101	800-955-1236	703-790-1745	48-19
Society for Marketing Professional Services (SMPS) 99 Canal Ctr Plz .... Alexandria VA 22314	800-292-7677	703-549-6117	48-18
Society for Mining Metallurgy & Exploration Inc (SME) 8307 Shaffer Pkwy .... Littleton CO 80127	800-763-3132	303-973-9550	48-13
Society for Protective Coatings (SSPC) 40 24th St Sixth Fl .... Pittsburgh PA 15222	877-281-7772	412-281-2331	48-13
Society for Risk Analysis (SRA) 1313 Dolley Madison Blvd Ste 402 .... McLean VA 22101	800-364-5800	703-790-1745	48-19
Society for Sedimentary Geology (SEPM) 4111 S Darlington Ste 100 .... Tulsa OK 74135	800-865-9765	918-610-3361	48-19
Society for Social Work Leadership in Health Care 100 N 20th St Fourth Fl .... Philadelphia PA 19103	866-237-9542	215-599-6134	48-15
Society for Surgery of the Alimentary Tract (SSAT) 900 Cummings Ctr Ste 221-U .... Beverly MA 01915	866-849-5866	978-927-8330	48-8
Society for the Advancement of Material & Process Engineering (SAMPE) 1161 Pk View Dr Ste 200 .... Covina CA 91724	800-562-7360	626-331-0616	48-19
Society for Vascular Surgery (SVS) 633 N St Clair St 22nd Fl .... Chicago IL 60611	800-258-7188	312-334-2300	48-8
Society of Accredited Marine Surveyors Inc (SAMS) 7855 Argyle Forest Blvd Ste 203 .... Jacksonville FL 32244	800-344-9077	904-384-1494	47-1
Society of American Archivists (SAA) 17 N State St Ste 1425 .... Chicago IL 60602	866-722-7858	312-606-0722	47-4
Society of American Florists (SAF) 1601 Duke St .... Alexandria VA 22314	800-336-4743	703-836-8700	48-4
Society of American Florists PAC 1601 Duke St .... Alexandria VA 22314	800-336-4743	703-836-8700	608
Society of American Military Engineers (SAME) 607 Prince St .... Alexandria VA 22314	800-336-3097	703-549-3800	47-19
Society of Automotive Engineers Inc (SAE) 400 Commonwealth Dr .... Warrendale PA 15096	877-606-7323	724-776-4841	48-21
Society of Behavioral Medicine (SBM) 555 E Wells St Ste 1100 .... Milwaukee WI 53202	800-784-8669	414-918-3156	48-15

	Toll-Free	Phone	Class
Society of Biblical Literature (SBL) The Luce Ctr 825 Houston Mill Rd. ...... Atlanta GA 30329	866-727-9955	404-727-3100	47-20
Society of Broadcast Engineers Inc (SBE) 9102 N Meridian St Ste 150 ...... Indianapolis IN 46260	800-237-1776	317-846-9000	48-14
Society of Cable Telecommunications Engineers (SCTE) 140 Philips Rd ...... Exton PA 19341	800-542-5040	610-363-6888	48-19
Society of Competitive Intelligence Professionals (SCIP) 1700 Diagonal Rd Ste 600 ...... Alexandria VA 22314	877-463-7678	703-739-0696	48-12
Society of Diagnostic Medical Sonography (SDMS) 2745 Dallas Pkwy ...... Plano TX 75093	800-229-9506	214-473-8057	48-8
Society of Environmental Journalists (SEJ) 115 W Ave ...... Jenkintown PA 19046	866-208-3372	215-884-8174	48-14
Society of Financial Service Professionals (SFSP) 19 Campus Blvd Ste 100 ...... Newtown Square PA 19073	800-392-6900	610-526-2500	48-9
Society of Gastroenterology Nurses & Assoc Inc (SGNA) 401 N Michigan Ave ...... Chicago IL 60611	800-245-7462	312-321-5165	48-8
Society of Interventional Radiology (SIR) 3975 Fair Rdige Dr Ste 400 N. ...... Fairfax VA 22033	800-488-7284	703-691-1805	48-8
Society of Mfg Engineers (SME) One SME Dr ...... Dearborn MI 48128 *Cust Svc	800-733-4763*	313-425-3000	48-13
Society of Nuclear Medicine (SNM) 1850 Samuel Morse Dr ...... Reston VA 20190	888-633-5343	703-708-9000	48-8
Society of Petroleum Engineers (SPE) 222 Palisades Creek Dr ...... Richardson TX 75080	800-456-6863	972-952-9393	47-12
Society of Professional Journalists (SPJ) 3909 N Meridian St ...... Indianapolis IN 46208	800-331-1212	317-927-8000	48-14
Society of Saint Andrew (SoSA) 3383 Sweet Hollow Rd ...... Big Island VA 24526	800-333-4597	434-299-5956	47-5
Society of Teachers of Family Medicine (STFM) 11400 Tomahawk Creek Pkwy Ste 540 ...... Leawood KS 66211	800-274-7928	913-906-6000	48-8
Society of Telecommunications Consultants (STC) 13275 California 89 ...... Old Station CA 96071	800-782-7670	530-335-7313	48-20
Society of Thoracic Surgeons (STS) 633 N St Clair St Ste 2320 ...... Chicago IL 60611	877-865-5321	312-202-5800	48-8
Society of Toxicology (SOT) 1767 Business Ctr Dr ...... Reston VA 20190	800-826-6762	703-438-3115	48-8
Society of Vacuum Coaters (SVC) 71 Pinon Hill Pl NE ...... Albuquerque NM 87122	800-777-4643	505-856-7188	48-13
Society of Women Engineers (SWE) 120 S La Salle St Ste 1515 ...... Chicago IL 60603	877-793-4636	312-596-5223	48-19
Socorro Electric Co-op Inc 215 Manzanares Ave PO Box H ...... Socorro NM 87801	800-351-7575	575-835-0560	245
Socrates Media LLC 111 S Wacker Dr ...... Chicago IL 60606	877-860-4649		109
Sodexo Inc 9801 Washingtonian Blvd ...... Gaithersburg MD 20878	800-763-3946		298
Sof Tec Solutions Inc 384 Inverness Pkwy # 211 ...... Englewood CO 80112	888-376-3832	303-662-1010	225
Soffront Software Inc 45437 Warm Springs Blvd ...... Fremont CA 94539	800-763-3766	510-413-9000	179-1
Sofia Hotel 150 W Broadway ...... San Diego CA 92101	800-826-0009	619-234-9200	376
Sofradir EC Inc 373 Rt 46W ...... Fairfield NJ 07004	800-759-9577	973-882-0211	683
Softchalk LLC 22 S Auburn Ave ...... Richmond VA 23221	877-638-2425		178
Softerware Inc 132 Welsh Rd Ste 140 ...... Horsham PA 19044	800-220-8111	215-628-0400	178
Softlayer Technologies Inc 4849 Alpha Rd ...... Dallas TX 75244 *Sales	866-398-7638*	214-442-0600	225
Soft-Lite LLC 10250 Philipp Pkwy ...... Streetsboro OH 44241	800-551-1953	330-528-3400	235
Softmart Inc 450 Acorn Ln ...... Downingtown PA 19335 *Cust Svc	800-328-1319*	610-518-4000	175
Softomate LLC 104 Sixth St Unit B ...... Lynden WA 98264	877-243-8735		523
SoftPress Systems Inc 3020 Bridgeway Ste 408 ...... Sausalito CA 94965	800-853-6454	415-331-4820	179-8
Software AG USA 11700 Plz America Dr Ste 700 ...... Reston VA 20190	877-724-4965	703-860-5050	179-1
Software Engineering Institute (SEI) 4500 Fifth Ave ...... Pittsburgh PA 15213	888-201-4479	412-268-5800	659
Software Engineering of America Inc (SEA) 1230 Hempstead Tpke ...... Franklin Square NY 11010	800-272-7322	516-328-7000	179-12
Software Engineering Services Corp 1311 Ft Crook Rd S ...... Bellevue NE 68005	800-244-1278	402-292-8660	659
Software House International (SHI) 290 Davidson Ave ...... Somerset NJ 08873	888-764-8888		175
Software Information Systems Inc (SIS) 165 Barr St ...... Lexington KY 40507	800-337-6914	859-977-4747	181
Software Pursuits Inc 1900 S Norfolk St ...... San Mateo CA 94403	800-367-4823	650-372-0900	179-12
Software Technology Group 555 S 300 E ...... Salt Lake City UT 84111	888-595-1001	801-595-1000	181
Softworld Inc 281 Winter St Ste 301. ...... Waltham MA 02451	877-899-1166	781-466-8882	712
SOG Specialty Knives & Tools LLC 6521 212th St SW ...... Lynnwood WA 98036	888-405-6433	425-771-6230	358
SoHo Grand Hotel 310 W Broadway ...... New York NY 10013	800-965-3000	212-965-3000	376
SoHo Metropolitan Hotel 318 Wellington St W ...... Toronto ON M5V3T4	866-764-6638	416-599-8800	376
SOHOware Inc 1250 Oakmead Pkwy Ste 210 ...... Sunnyvale CA 94085	800-632-1118	408-565-9888	177
Soil & Water Conservation Society (SWCS) 945 SW Ankeny Rd ...... Ankeny IA 50023	800-843-7645	515-289-2331	47-13
Soilmoisture Equipment Corp 801 S Kellogg Ave ...... Goleta CA 93117	888-964-0040	805-964-3525	416
Sojourner-Douglass College 200 N Central Ave ...... Baltimore MD 21202	800-732-2630	410-276-0306	166
Sokol & Co 5315 Dansher Rd ...... Countryside IL 60525 *Cust Svc	800-328-7656*	708-482-8250	295-1
Solano County Fair 900 Fairgrounds Dr ...... Vallejo CA 94589	800-700-2482	707-551-2000	633
Solar Industries Inc PO Box 27337 ...... Tucson AZ 85726	800-449-2323	520-519-8258	192-3
Solar Solutions & Distribution LLC 2500 W Fifth Ave ...... Denver CO 80204	855-765-3478	303-948-6300	687
Solar Tours 1629 K St NW Ste 604 ...... Washington DC 20006	800-388-7652	202-861-5864	16
Solarus 440 E Grand Ave ...... Wisconsin Rapids WI 54494	800-421-9282	715-421-8111	726
Solatube International Inc 2210 Oak Ridge Way ...... Vista CA 92081	888-765-2882	760-477-1120	687
Solazyme Inc 225 Gateway Blvd ...... South San Francisco CA 94080 NASDAQ: SZYM	877-917-9075	650-780-4777	465
Soldier Field 1410 S Museum Campus Dr ...... Chicago IL 60605	800-322-5868	312-235-7000	711
Soldier of Fortune Magazine 2135 11th St ...... Boulder CO 80302	800-377-2789	303-449-3750	452-12
Soldiers & Sailors Memorial Auditorium 399 McCallie Ave ...... Chattanooga TN 37402	800-772-1213	423-757-5156	565
Soldiers + Sailors Memorial Hospital 32-36 Central Ave ...... Wellsboro PA 16901	800-808-5287	570-723-7764	371-3
Soldiers Delight Natural Environment Area 5100 Deer Park Rd ...... Owings Mills MD 21117	800-830-3974	410-461-5005	558
Solebury School 6832 Phillips Mill Rd ...... New Hope PA 18938	800-675-6900	215-862-5261	615
Solectek Corp 6370 Nancy Ridge Dr Ste 109. ...... San Diego CA 92121	888-299-8057	858-450-1220	177
Solheim Lutheran Home (SLH) 2236 Merton Ave ...... Los Angeles CA 90041	888-257-7518	323-257-7518	663
Soliant LLC 1872 Hwy 9 Bypass ...... Lancaster SC 29720	800-288-9401	803-285-9401	593
Solid Concepts Inc 28309 Ave Crocker ...... Valencia CA 91355	888-311-1017	661-295-4400	449
Solid Waste Assn of North America (SWANA) 1100 Wayne Ave Ste 700 ...... Silver Spring MD 20910	800-467-9262	301-585-2898	524-5
SolidBoss Worldwide Inc 200 Veterans Blvd ...... South Haven MI 49090	888-258-7252	269-637-6356	744
SolidWorks Corp 300 Baker Ave ...... Concord MA 01742	800-693-9000	978-371-5011	179-10
Soligenix Inc 29 Emmons Dr Ste C-10. ...... Princeton NJ 08540 OTC: SNGX	877-407-3974	609-538-8200	84
Solitude Ski Resort 12000 Big Cottonwood Canyon ...... Brighton UT 84121	800-748-4754	801-534-1400	660
Solo Printing Inc 7860 NW 66th St ...... Miami FL 33166	800-325-0118	305-594-8699	619
Soloflex Inc 22590 NW Badertscher Rd ...... Hillsboro OR 97124	800-547-8802		267
Solomon Corp 103 W Main PO Box 245 ...... Solomon KS 67480	800-234-2867	785-655-2191	613
Solomon Pond Mall 601 Donald Lynch Blvd ...... Marlborough MA 01752	877-746-6642	508-303-6255	455
Solomon R Guggenheim Museum 1071 Fifth Ave ...... New York NY 10128	800-329-6109	212-423-3500	513
Solta Medical Inc 25881 Industrial Blvd ...... Hayward CA 94545	877-782-2286		250
Solutek Corp 94 Shirley St ...... Boston MA 02119	800-403-0770	617-445-5335	143
Solutions AE Inc 236 Auburn Ave ...... Atlanta GA 30303	888-562-4441		458
Solvay America Inc 3333 Richmond Ave ...... Houston TX 77098 *General	800-365-6565*	713-525-6000	576
Solvay Chemicals Inc 3333 Richmond Ave ...... Houston TX 77098	800-765-8292	713-525-6800	498-1
Solvents & Chemicals Inc 4704 Shank Rd PO Box 490 ...... Pearland TX 77581	800-622-3990	281-485-5377	144
Somagen Diagnostics Inc 9220 25th Ave ...... Edmonton AB T6N1E1	800-661-9993	780-702-9500	470
Somers Cove Marina 715 Broadway PO Box 67 ...... Crisfield MD 21817	800-967-3474	410-968-0925	558
Somerset Capital Group Ltd 612 Wheelers Farms Rd ...... Milford CT 06461	877-282-9922	203-701-5100	264-2
Somerset Community College 808 Monticello St ...... Somerset KY 42501	877-629-9722	606-679-8501	160
Somerset County Library 1 Vogt Dr ...... Bridgewater NJ 08807	888-313-3532	908-526-4016	431-3
Somerset Door & Column Co 174 Sagamore St ...... Somerset PA 15501	800-242-7916	814-444-9427	494
Somerset Fine Arts PO Box 869 ...... Fulshear TX 77441 *Sales	800-444-2540*		628-10
Somerset Inn 2601 W Big Beaver Rd ...... Troy MI 48084	800-228-8769	248-643-7800	376
Somerset Rural Electric Co-op 223 Industrial Pk Rd PO Box 270. ...... Somerset PA 15501	800-443-4255	814-445-4106	245
Somerset Tire Services Inc PO Box 5936 ...... Bridgewater NJ 08807	800-445-1434	732-356-8500	61-5
Somerset Trust Co 151 W Main St PO Box 777 ...... Somerset PA 15501	800-972-1651	814-443-9200	69
Somerset Welding & Steel Inc 10558 Somerset Pk ...... Somerset PA 15501	800-777-2671	814-444-3400	509
Somerset-Pulaski County Chamber of Commerce 445 S Hwy 27 Ste 101 ...... Somerset KY 42501	877-629-9722	606-679-7323	137
Sommer Electric Corp 818 Third St NE ...... Canton OH 44704	800-766-6373	330-455-9454	246
Sommer Metalcraft Corp 315 Poston Dr PO Box 688. ...... Crawfordsville IN 47933	888-876-6637	765-362-6201	477
Sommer's Automotive 7211 W Meq PO Box 37 ...... Mequon WI 53092	888-494-4193	262-242-0100	56
Sompo Japan Insurance Co of America 777 Third Ave 28th Fl ...... New York NY 10017	800-208-3614	212-416-1200	388-4
Sonalysts Inc 215 Waterford Pkwy N ...... Waterford CT 06385	800-526-8091	860-442-4355	261
Sonesta Hotel & Suites Coconut Grove 2889 McFarlane Rd ...... Miami FL 33133	800-766-3782	305-529-2828	376
Sonetics Corp 7340 SW Durham Rd ...... Portland OR 97224	800-833-4558		638
Soniat House 1133 Chartres St ...... New Orleans LA 70116	800-544-8808	504-522-0570	376
Sonic Air Systems Inc 1050 Beacon St ...... Brea CA 92821	800-827-6642	714-255-0124	18
Sonic Corp 300 Johnny Bench Dr ...... Oklahoma City OK 73104 NASDAQ: SONC	877-828-7868	405-225-5000	661
Sonic Drive-in Restaurants 300 Johnny Bench Dr ...... Oklahoma City OK 73104	877-828-7868	405-225-5000	661

	Toll-Free	Phone	Class
Sonic Innovations Inc			
2501 Cottontail Ln Ste 300 . . . . Somerset NJ 08873	**888-678-4327**	888-423-7834	472
Sonicor Inc			
82 Otis St . . . . West Babylon NY 11704	**800-864-5022**	631-920-6555	772
Sonics & Materials Inc			
53 Church Hill Rd . . . . Newtown CT 06470	**800-745-1105**	203-270-4600	772
OTC: SIMA			
SonicWALL Inc			
2001 Logic Dr . . . . San Jose CA 95124	**888-557-6642**	408-745-9600	177
Sonnenalp Resort of Vail			
20 Vail Rd . . . . Vail CO 81657	**800-654-8312**	970-476-5656	660
Sonobond Ultrasonics Inc			
1191 McDermott Dr . . . . West Chester PA 19380	**800-323-1269**	610-696-4710	798
Sonoco			
One N Second St . . . . Hartsville SC 29550	**800-377-2692**		594
NYSE: SON			
Sonoma County Fairgrounds			
1350 Bennett Valley Rd . . . . Santa Rosa CA 95404	**866-487-9243**	707-545-4200	633
Sonoma County Transit			
355 W Robles Ave . . . . Santa Rosa CA 95407	**800-345-7433**	707-585-7516	463
Sonoma Developmental Ctr			
15000 Arnold Dr . . . . Eldridge CA 95431	**800-862-0007**	707-938-6000	230
Sonoma Raceway			
Hwy S 37 & 121 . . . . Sonoma CA 95476	**800-870-7223**	707-938-8448	508
Sonoma Technical Support Services			
8840 210th St Ste 342 . . . . Langley BC V1M2Y2	**866-898-3123**		197
Sonora Regional Medical Ctr (SRMC)			
1000 Greenly Rd . . . . Sonora CA 95370	**877-336-3566***	209-536-5000	371-3
*Compliance			
SonoSite Inc			
21919 30th Dr SE . . . . Bothell WA 98021	**888-482-9449**	425-951-1200	379
NASDAQ: SONO			
Sons of Norway			
1455 W Lake St Second Fl . . . . Minneapolis MN 55408	**800-945-8851**	612-827-3611	47-14
Sonstegard Foods Co			
1911 W 57th St Ste 102 . . . . Sioux Falls SD 57108	**800-533-3184**		612
Sony Corp of America			
550 Madison Ave . . . . New York NY 10022	**800-282-2848**	212-833-6800	51
Sony Creative Software			
1617 Sherman Ave . . . . Madison WI 53704	**800-577-6642**	608-256-3133	179-9
Sony Electronics Inc			
One Sony Dr . . . . Park Ridge NJ 07656	**800-222-7669***	201-930-1000	51
*Cust Svc			
Sony Pictures Entertainment Inc			
10202 W Washington Blvd . . . . Culver City CA 90232	**855-327-7669**	310-244-4000	507
Sony Pictures Television			
10202 W Washington Blvd . . . . Culver City CA 90232	**888-476-6972**	310-244-4000	507
Sooner Pipe LLC			
1331 Lamar St			
Ste 970 4 Houston Ctr . . . . Houston TX 77010	**800-888-9161**	713-759-1200	382
Sopark Corp			
3300 S Pk Ave . . . . Buffalo NY 14218	**866-576-7275**	716-822-0434	617
Sopheon Corp			
3001 Metro Dr Ste 460 . . . . Bloomington MN 55425	**800-367-8358**	952-851-7500	384
Sophie Station Suites			
1717 University Ave . . . . Fairbanks AK 99709	**800-528-4916**		376
Sophos Inc			
3 Van de Graaff Dr 2nd Fl . . . . Burlington MA 01803	**866-866-2802**		179-1
SOR Inc			
14685 W 105th St . . . . Lenexa KS 66215	**800-676-6794**	913-888-2630	202
Sorbee International Ltd			
9990 Global Rd . . . . Philadelphia PA 19115	**800-654-3997**	215-645-1111	295-8
Sorenson Media Inc			
13961 Minuteman Dr Ste 100 . . . . Draper UT 84020	**888-767-3676**	801-501-8650	537
Sorin Group USA Inc			
14401 W 65th Way . . . . Arvada CO 80004	**800-289-5759**	303-424-0129	471
Sorrento Electronics Inc			
4949 Greencraig Ln . . . . San Diego CA 92123	**800-252-1180**	858-522-8300	467
SOS (Store Opening Solutions)			
800 Middle Tennessee Blvd . . . . Murfreesboro TN 37129	**877-388-9262**		444
SOS Children's Villages-USA			
1001 Connecticut Ave NW			
Ste 1250 . . . . Washington DC 20036	**888-767-4543***	202-347-7920	47-6
*General			
SoSA (Society of Saint Andrew)			
3383 Sweet Hollow Rd . . . . Big Island VA 24526	**800-333-4597**	434-299-5956	47-5
SOT (Society of Toxicology)			
1767 Business Ctr Dr . . . . Reston VA 20190	**800-826-6762**	703-438-3115	48-8
Sotheby's International Realty			
38 E 61st St . . . . New York NY 10065	**866-899-4747**	212-606-7660	643
Sothys USA Inc			
1500 NW 94th Ave . . . . Miami FL 33172	**800-325-0503**	305-594-4222	238
Soudan Underground Mine State Park			
1302 McKinley Park Rd . . . . Soudan MN 55782	**888-646-6367**	218-753-2245	558
Sound Com Corp			
227 Depot St . . . . Berea OH 44017	**800-628-8739**	440-234-2604	51
Sound Glass Sales Inc			
5501 75th St W . . . . Tacoma WA 98499	**800-468-9949**	253-473-7477	190-6
Sound Impressions Music Marketing L.L.C			
14290 Gillis Rd Ste A . . . . Dallas TX 75244	**888-512-9119**		196
Sound Shore Fund			
3435 Stelzer Rd . . . . Columbus OH 43219	**800-754-8758**		521
SoundBite Communications Inc			
22 Crosby Dr . . . . Bedford MA 01730	**888-436-3797**	877-768-6324	726
NASDAQ: SDBT			
Soundcoat Co			
One Burt Dr . . . . Deer Park NY 11729	**800-394-8913**	631-242-2200	386
SoundConnect LLC			
One Batterymarch Park Ste 104 . . . . Quincy MA 02169	**888-827-4462**		224
Source Intelligence LLC			
1921 Palomar Oaks Way Ste 205 . . . . Carlsbad CA 92008	**877-916-6337**		193
Source Media Inc			
One State St Plz 27th Fl . . . . New York NY 10004	**800-221-1809**	212-803-8200	628-9
Source Technologies			
2910 Whitehall Pk Dr . . . . Charlotte NC 28273	**800-922-8501**	704-969-7500	179-1
Sourcebooks Inc			
1935 Brookdale Rd Ste 139 . . . . Naperville IL 60563	**800-432-7444**	630-961-3900	628-2
SourceGas			
655 E Millsap Dr . . . . Fayetteville AR 72703	**800-563-0012**		775
SourceLink Inc			
500 Pk Blvd Ste 415 . . . . Itasca IL 60143	**866-947-6872**		5
SourceMedical Solutions Inc			
100 Grandview Pl Ste 400 . . . . Birmingham AL 35243	**866-245-8093**		225

	Toll-Free	Phone	Class
South African Airways			
515 E Las Olas Blvd			
16th Fl . . . . Fort Lauderdale FL 33301	**800-722-9675**	954-769-5000	25
South Alabama Electric Co-op (SAEC)			
PO Box 449 . . . . Troy AL 36081	**800-556-2060**	334-566-2060	245
South Arkansas Arboretum			
PO Box 7010 . . . . El Dorado AR 71731	**888-287-2757**		558
South Arkansas Community College			
PO Box 7010 . . . . El Dorado AR 71731	**800-955-2289**	870-862-8131	160
South Baldwin Chamber of Commerce (SBCC)			
112 W Laurel Ave PO Box 1117 . . . . Foley AL 36535	**877-461-3712**	251-943-3291	137
South Bay Correctional Facility			
600 US Hwy 27 S . . . . South Bay FL 33493	**800-574-5729**	561-992-9505	213
South Baylo University			
1126 N Brookhurst St . . . . Anaheim CA 92801	**888-642-2956**	714-533-1495	166
South Beach Marina Inn & Vacation Rentals			
232 S Sea Pines Dr . . . . Hilton Head Island SC 29928	**800-367-3909**	843-671-6498	376
South Beach State Park			
5580 S Coast Hwy . . . . South Beach OR 97366	**800-452-5687**	541-867-4715	558
South Bend Medical Foundation			
530 N Lafayette Blvd . . . . South Bend IN 46601	**800-544-0925**	574-234-4176	415
South Bend Symphony Orchestra (SBSO)			
127 N Michigan St . . . . South Bend IN 46601	**800-537-6415**	574-232-6343	566-3
South Bend Tribune			
225 W Colfax Ave . . . . South Bend IN 46626	**800-220-7378**	574-235-6464	525-2
South Bend/Mishawaka Convention & Visitors Bureau			
401 E Colfax Ave Ste 310 . . . . South Bend IN 46617	**800-519-0577**	574-234-0051	207
South Boston Speedway			
1188 James D Hagood Hwy			
PO Box 1066 . . . . South Boston VA 24592	**877-440-1540**	434-572-4947	508
South Broadway Cultural Ctr			
1025 Broadway Blvd SE . . . . Albuquerque NM 87102	**866-441-6075**	505-848-1320	49-1
South Carolina			
Child Support Enforcement Office			
3150 Harden St Ext . . . . Columbia SC 29203	**800-768-5858**	803-898-9210	337-41
Commerce Dept			
1201 Main St Ste 1600 . . . . Columbia SC 29201	**800-868-7232**	803-737-0400	337-41
State Government Information			
1301 Gervais St Ste 710 . . . . Columbia SC 29201	**866-340-7105**	803-771-0131	337-41
Veterans Affairs Div			
1205 Pendleton St Ste 463 . . . . Columbia SC 29201	**800-827-1000**	803-734-0200	337-41
Vocational Rehabilitation Dept			
1410 Boston Ave PO Box 15 . . . . West Columbia SC 29171	**800-832-7526**	803-896-6500	337-41
South Carolina Aquarium			
100 Aquarium Wharf . . . . Charleston SC 29401	**800-722-6455**	843-577-3474	39
South Carolina Assn of Realtors			
3780 Fernandina Rd . . . . Columbia SC 29210	**800-233-6381**	803-772-5206	647
South Carolina Assn of Veterinarians			
PO Box 11766 . . . . Columbia SC 29211	**800-441-7228**	803-254-1027	783
South Carolina Bar			
950 Taylor St . . . . Columbia SC 29201	**877-797-2227**	803-799-6653	71
South Carolina Chamber of Commerce			
1201 Main St Ste1100 . . . . Columbia SC 29201	**800-799-4601**	803-799-4601	138
South Carolina Democratic Party			
PO Box 5965 . . . . Columbia SC 29250	**800-841-1817**	803-799-7798	609-1
South Carolina Dental Assn			
120 Stonemark Ln . . . . Columbia SC 29210	**800-327-2598**	803-750-2277	227
South Carolina Electric & Gas Co			
PO Box 100255 . . . . Columbia SC 29202	**800-251-7234**	803-635-4444	775
South Carolina Federal Credit Union			
PO Box 190012 . . . . North Charleston SC 29419	**800-845-0432**	843-797-8300	219
South Carolina Higher Education Tuition Grants Commission			
115 Atrium Wy Ste 102 . . . . Columbia SC 29203	**877-382-4357**	803-896-1120	716
South Carolina Medical Assn			
132 W Pk Blvd . . . . Columbia SC 29210	**800-327-1021**	803-798-6207	469
South Carolina Press Services Inc			
106 Outlet Pointe Blvd			
PO Box 11429 . . . . Columbia SC 29210	**888-727-7377**	803-750-9561	616
South Carolina State Ports Authority			
176 Concord St . . . . Charleston SC 29401	**800-845-7106**	843-723-8651	611
South Carolina State University			
300 College St NE			
PO Box 7127 . . . . Orangeburg SC 29117	**800-260-5956***	803-536-7000	166
*Admissions			
South Central Arkansas Electric Co-op			
1140 Main St . . . . Arkadelphia AR 71923	**800-814-2931**	870-246-6701	245
Faribault			
1225 Third St . . . . Faribault MN 55021	**800-422-0391**	507-332-5800	160
South Central College			
Mankato			
1920 Lee Blvd . . . . North Mankato MN 56003	**800-722-9359**	507-389-7200	160
South Central Correctional Facility			
555 Forest Ave PO Box 279 . . . . Clifton TN 38425	**800-251-3589**	931-676-5372	213
South Central Electric Assn			
71176 Tiell Dr PO Box 150 . . . . Saint James MN 56081	**888-805-7232**	507-375-3164	245
South Central Indiana Rural Electric Membership Corp			
300 Morton Ave PO Box 3100 . . . . Martinsville IN 46151	**800-264-7362**	765-342-3344	245
South Central Power Company Inc			
2780 Coon Path Rd . . . . Lancaster OH 43130	**800-282-5064**	740-653-4422	245
South Central Public Power District (SCPPD)			
275 S Main St PO Box 406 . . . . Nelson NE 68961	**800-557-5254**	402-225-2351	245
South Central Rural Telephone Co-op Corp Inc			
PO Box 159 . . . . Glasgow KY 42142	**877-678-2111**	270-678-2111	726
South Charlotte Nissan			
9215 S Blvd . . . . Charlotte NC 28273	**888-411-1423**	704-552-9191	56
South Coast Plaza			
3333 Bristol St . . . . Costa Mesa CA 92626	**800-782-8888**		455
South College			
3904 Lonas Dr . . . . Knoxville TN 37909	**877-557-2575**	865-251-1800	788
South Dakota			
Child Support Div			
700 Governors Dr . . . . Pierre SD 57501	**800-286-9145**	605-773-3641	337-42
Crime Victims' Compensation Program			
700 Governors Dr . . . . Pierre SD 57501	**800-696-9476**	605-773-6317	337-42
Department of Health			
600 E Capitol Ave . . . . Pierre SD 57501	**800-738-2301**	605-773-4961	337-42
Economic Development Office			
711 E Wells Ave . . . . Pierre SD 57501	**800-872-6190**	605-773-3301	337-42
Parks & Recreation Div			
523 E Capitol Ave . . . . Pierre SD 57501	**800-710-2267***	605-773-3391	337-42
*Campground Resv			
Rehabilitation Services Div			
500 E Capitol Ave . . . . Pierre SD 57501	**800-265-9684**	605-773-3195	337-42

	Toll-Free	Phone	Class
Tourism Office			
711 E Wells Ave ....Pierre SD 57501	**800-952-3625**	605-773-3301	337-42
South Dakota Assn of Realtors			
204 N Euclid Ave ....Pierre SD 57501	**800-227-5877**	605-224-0554	647
South Dakota Chamber of Commerce & Industry			
108 N Euclid Ave ....Pierre SD 57501	**800-742-8112**	605-224-6161	138
South Dakota Dental Assn			
804 N Euclid Ave Ste 103 ....Pierre SD 57501	**866-551-8023**	605-224-9133	227
South Dakota Lions Eye Bank			
4501 W 61st St N ....Sioux Falls SD 57107	**800-245-7846**	605-373-1008	269
South Dakota Newspaper Services			
1125 32nd Ave Ste 202 ....Brookings SD 57006	**800-658-3697**	605-692-4300	616
South Dakota Public Broadcasting (SDPB)			
555 N Dakota St PO Box 5000 ....Vermillion SD 57069	**800-456-0766**	605-677-5861	624
South Dakota School of Mines & Technology			
501 E St Joseph St ....Rapid City SD 57701	**800-544-8162**	605-394-2414	166
South Dakota State Library			
800 Governors Dr ....Pierre SD 57501	**800-423-6665**	605-773-3131	431-5
South Dakota State University			
PO Box 2201 ....Brookings SD 57007	**800-952-3541**	605-688-4121	166
South Dakota State University Briggs Library			
N Campus Dr PO Box 2115 ....Brookings SD 57007	**800-786-2038**	605-688-5106	431-6
South Dakota Wheat Growers Assn			
908 Lamont St SE ....Aberdeen SD 57401	**888-429-4902**	605-225-5500	275
South Florida Sun-Sentinel			
200 E Las Olas Blvd ....Fort Lauderdale FL 33301	**800-548-6397***	954-356-4000	525-2
*Cust Svc			
South Georgia Pecan Co			
309 S Lee St ....Valdosta GA 31601	**800-627-6630**	229-244-1321	295-28
South Jersey Healthcare HospiceCare			
2848 S Delsea Dr Bldg 1 ....Vineland NJ 08360	**800-770-7547**		368
South Kentucky Rural Electrical Co-op			
925 N Main St PO Box 910 ....Somerset KY 42502	**800-264-5112**	606-678-4121	245
South Louisiana Bank (SLB)			
1362 W Tunnel Blvd PO Box 1718 ....Houma LA 70361	**877-275-3342**	985-851-3434	69
South Mountain Community College			
7050 S 24th St ....Phoenix AZ 85042	**855-622-2332**	602-243-8000	160
South Nassau Communities Hospital			
1 Healthy Way ....Oceanside NY 11572	**877-768-8462**	516-632-3000	371-3
South Oklahoma City Chamber of Commerce			
701 SW 74 St ....Oklahoma City OK 73139	**877-309-2070**	405-634-1436	137
South Padre Island Convention & Visitors Bureau			
7355 Padre Blvd ....South Padre Island TX 78597	**800-767-2373**	956-761-6433	207
South Padre Island Convention Centre			
7355 Padre Blvd ....South Padre Island TX 78597	**800-657-2373**	956-761-3000	206
South Piedmont Community College			
680 Hwy 74 ....Polkton NC 28135	**800-766-0319**	704-272-5300	160
South Pier Inn on the Canal			
701 Lake Ave S ....Duluth MN 55802	**800-430-7437**	218-786-9007	376
South Plains Electric Co-op Inc			
PO Box 1830 ....Lubbock TX 79408	**800-658-2655**	806-775-7766	245
South Point Hotel & Casino			
9777 Las Vegas Blvd S ....Las Vegas NV 89183	**866-796-7111**	702-796-7111	376
South River Electric Membership Corp			
17494 US 421 S PO Box 931 ....Dunn NC 28335	**800-338-5530**	910-892-8071	245
South Seas Island Resort			
5400 Plantation Rd ....Captiva FL 33924	**866-565-5089**	239-472-5111	660
South Shore Harbour Resort & Conference Ctr			
2500 S Shore Blvd ....League City TX 77573	**800-442-5005***	281-334-1000	660
*Resv			
South Shore Hospital			
55 Fogg Rd ....South Weymouth MA 02190	**800-439-2370**	781-340-8000	371-3
South Shore Plaza			
250 Granite St ....Braintree MA 02184	**877-746-6642**	781-843-8200	455
South Shore Transportation Inc			
4010 Columbus Ave ....Sandusky OH 44870	**888-428-0879**	419-626-6267	770
South Sioux City Convention & Visitors Bureau			
3900 Dakota Ave Ste 11 ....South Sioux City NE 68776	**866-494-1307**	402-494-1307	207
South Tacoma Honda			
7802 S Tacoma Way ....Tacoma WA 98409	**888-497-2416**	253-472-2300	56
South Texas Blood & Tissue Ctr			
6211 IH-10 W ....San Antonio TX 78201	**800-292-5534**	210-731-5555	88
South Toledo Bend State Park			
120 Bald Eaglel Rd ....Anacoco LA 71403	**888-398-4770**	337-286-9075	558
South University			
Montgomery			
5355 Vaughn Rd ....Montgomery AL 36116	**866-629-2962**	334-395-8800	166
South University Columbia			
Nine Science Ct ....Columbia SC 29203	**800-688-0932**	803-799-9082	166
South University Savannah			
709 Mall Blvd ....Savannah GA 31406	**800-688-0932**	912-201-8000	166
South University West Palm Beach			
9801 Belvedere Rd			
University Ctr ....West Palm Beach FL 33411	**800-688-0932**	561-273-6500	166
Southampton Inn			
91 Hill St ....SouthHampton NY 11968	**800-832-6500**	631-283-6500	376
Southbend Inc			
1100 Old Honeycutt Rd ....Fuquay-Varina NC 27526	**800-755-4777**	919-762-1000	297
Southbridge Savings Bank Inc			
253-257 Main St PO Box 370 ....Southbridge MA 01550	**800-939-9103**	508-765-9103	69
Southco Distributing Co			
2201 S John St ....Goldsboro NC 27530	**800-969-3172**	919-735-8012	296-8
Southdale Ctr			
10 Southdale Ctr ....Edina MN 55435	**877-746-6642**	952-925-7874	455
Southeast Alabama Medical Ctr			
1108 Ross Clark Cir ....Dothan AL 36301	**800-507-7262**	334-793-8111	371-3
Southeast Arkansas College			
1900 Hazel St ....Pine Bluff AR 71603	**888-732-7582**	870-543-5915	160
Southeast Asia Resource Action Ctr (SEARAC)			
1628 16th St NW Third Fl ....Washington DC 20009	**888-907-1485**	202-667-4690	47-5
Southeast Colorado Power Assn (SECPA)			
901 W 3rd ....La Junta CO 81050	**800-332-8634**	719-384-2551	245
Beatrice			
4771 W Scott Rd ....Beatrice NE 68310	**800-233-5027**	402-228-3468	160
Southeast Community College			
Lincoln 8800 'O' St ....Lincoln NE 68520	**800-642-4075**	402-471-3333	160
Milford 600 State St ....Milford NE 68405	**800-933-7223**	402-761-2131	788
Southeast Electric Co-op Inc (SECO)			
110 S Main St ....Ekalaka MT 59324	**888-485-8762**	406-775-8762	245
Southeast Georgia Health System Brunswick Campus			
2415 Parkwood Dr ....Brunswick GA 31520	**844-882-7227**	912-466-7000	371-3
Southeast Industrial Equipment Inc			
12200 Steele Creek Rd			
PO Box 39110 ....Charlotte NC 28273	**800-752-6368**	704-399-9700	465

	Toll-Free	Phone	Class
Southeast Kentucky Community & Technical College			
Cumberland			
700 College Rd ....Cumberland KY 40823	**888-274-7322**	606-589-2145	160
Middlesboro			
1300 Chichester Ave ....Middlesboro KY 40965	**888-274-7322**	606-242-2145	160
Whitesburg			
Two Long Ave ....Whitesburg KY 41858	**888-274-7322**	606-633-0279	160
Southeast Milk Inc			
1950 SE Hwy 484 PO Box 3790 ....Belleview FL 34420	**800-598-7866**		295-27
Southeast Missouri Hospital (SMH)			
1701 Lacey St ....Cape Girardeau MO 63701	**800-800-5123**	573-334-4822	371-3
Southeast Missouri State University			
1 University Plaza ....Cape Girardeau MO 63701	**866-562-6801**	573-651-2000	166
Southeast Missourian			
301 Broadway St ....Cape Girardeau MO 63701	**800-879-1210**	573-335-6611	525-2
Southeast Technical Institute			
2320 N Career Ave ....Sioux Falls SD 57107	**800-247-0789**	605-367-8355	788
Southeast Tissue Alliance (SETA)			
6241 NW 23rd St Ste 400 ....Gainesville FL 32653	**866-432-1164**	352-248-2114	538
Southeastern Aluminum Products Inc			
6701 Suemac Pl ....Jacksonville FL 32254	**800-243-8200***	904-781-8200	234
*Sales			
Southeastern Baptist Theological Seminary			
120 S Wingate St ....Wake Forest NC 27587	**800-284-6317**	919-556-3101	167-3
Southeastern Community College North			
1500 W Agency Rd ....West Burlington IA 52655	**866-722-4692**	319-752-2731	160
Southeastern Community College South			
335 Messenger Rd ....Keokuk IA 52632	**866-722-4692**	319-524-3221	160
Southeastern Electric Co-op Inc			
1514 E Hwy 70 PO Box 1370 ....Durant OK 74702	**866-924-1315**	580-924-2170	245
Southeastern Equipment Company Inc			
10874 E Pike Rd ....Cambridge OH 43725	**800-798-5438**	740-432-6303	355
Southeastern Freight Lines Inc			
420 Davega Rd ....Lexington SC 29073	**800-637-7335**	803-794-7300	770
Southeastern Illinois College			
3575 College Rd ....Harrisburg IL 62946	**866-338-2742**	618-252-6376	160
SouthEastern Illinois Electric Co-op			
585 Hwy 142 S PO Box 251 ....Eldorado IL 62930	**800-833-2611**	618-273-2611	245
Southeastern Indiana Rural Electric Membership Corp			
712 S Buckeye St ....Osgood IN 47037	**800-737-4111**	812-689-4111	245
Southeastern Library System of Oklahoma (SEPLSO)			
401 N Second St ....McAlester OK 74501	**800-215-6494**	918-426-0456	431-3
Southeastern Louisiana University			
500 Western Ave ....Hammond LA 70402	**800-222-7358**	985-549-2062	166
Southeastern Metals Mfg Company Inc			
11801 Industry Dr ....Jacksonville FL 32218	**800-874-0335**	904-757-4200	234
Southeastern Oklahoma State University			
1405 N Fourth St ....Durant OK 74701	**800-435-1327**	580-745-2000	166
Southeastern University			
1000 Longfellow Blvd ....Lakeland FL 33801	**800-500-8760**	863-667-5000	166
Southeastern Wholesale Tire Co			
4721 Trademark Dr ....Raleigh NC 27610	**800-849-9215***	919-832-3900	745
*General			
Southerland Inc			
1973 Southerland Dr ....Nashville TN 37207	**800-443-1183***	615-226-9650	466
*Cust Svc			
Southern Accents Magazine			
2100 Lakeshore Dr ....Birmingham AL 35209	**877-262-5866**	205-445-6000	452-22
Southern Adventist University			
4881 Taylor Cir ....Collegedale TN 37315	**800-768-8437**	423-236-2000	166
Southern Air Inc			
2655 Lakeside Dr ....Lynchburg VA 24501	**800-743-1214**	434-385-6200	190-10
Southern Arizona Veterans Healthcare System			
3601 S Sixth Ave ....Tucson AZ 85723	**800-470-8262**	520-792-1450	371-8
Southern Arkansas University			
100 E University St ....Magnolia AR 71753	**800-332-7286**	870-235-4000	166
Southern Assn of Colleges & Schools			
1866 Southern Ln ....Decatur GA 30033	**888-413-3669**	404-679-4500	48-5
Southern Audio Services			
14763 Florida Blvd ....Baton Rouge LA 70819	**800-843-8823***	225-272-7135	51
*Cust Svc			
Southern Baptist Theological Seminary			
2825 Lexington Rd ....Louisville KY 40280	**800-626-5525**	502-897-4011	167-3
Southern Biotechnology Assoc Inc			
160A Oxmoor Blvd ....Birmingham AL 35209	**800-722-2255**	205-945-1774	231
Southern California Boiler Inc			
5331 Business Dr ....Huntington Beach CA 92649	**800-775-2645**	714-891-0701	188
Southern California Edison Co			
2244 Walnut Grove Ave ....Rosemead CA 91770	**800-655-4555**	626-302-1212	775
Southern California Gas Co			
555 W Fifth St ....Los Angeles CA 90013	**800-427-2200**	562-733-1852	775
Southern California Regional Rail Authority			
700 S Flower St Ste 2600 ....Los Angeles CA 90017	**800-371-5465**	213-452-0200	463
Southern Centrifugal Inc			
4180 S Creek Rd ....Chattanooga TN 37406	**800-634-8176**	423-622-4131	307
Southern Chester County Chamber of Commerce			
217 W State St ....Kennett Square PA 19348	**800-343-6583**	610-444-0774	137
Southern Communications Services Inc			
5555 Glenridge Connector			
Ste 500 ....Atlanta GA 30342	**800-818-5462**		726
Southern Company Inc			
3101 Carrier St ....Memphis TN 38116	**800-264-7626**	901-345-2531	530
Southern Components Inc			
7360 Julie Frances Dr			
PO Box 29010 ....Shreveport LA 71129	**800-256-2144**	318-687-3330	804
Southern Connecticut Gas (SCG)			
60 Marsh Hill Rd ....Orange CT 06477	**866-268-2887**		775
Southern Connecticut Newspapers Inc			
9 Riverbend Dr S Bldg 9-A ....Stamford CT 06907	**800-542-2517**	203-964-2200	628-8
Southern Connecticut State University			
501 Crescent St ....New Haven CT 06515	**888-500-7278**	203-392-5200	166
Southern Controls Inc			
3511 Wetumpka Hwy ....Montgomery AL 36110	**800-392-5770**		246
Southern Farm Bureau Casualty Insurance Co			
1800 E County Line Rd Ste 400 ....Ridgeland MS 39157	**800-272-7977**	601-957-7777	388-4
Southern Film Extruders Inc			
2319 English Rd ....High Point NC 27262	**800-334-6101**	336-885-8091	593
Southern Folger Detention Equipment Co			
4634 S Presa St ....San Antonio TX 78223	**888-745-0530**	210-533-1231	683
Southern Forest Products Assn (SFPA)			
2900 Indiana Ave ....Kenner LA 70065	**866-574-4155**	504-443-4464	47-2
Southern FS Inc			
2002 E Main St PO Box 728 ....Marion IL 62959	**800-492-7684**	618-993-2833	276

Listing	Toll-Free	Phone	Class
Southern Glove Mfg Company Inc			
749 AC Little Dr ..... Newton NC 28658	**800-222-1113***	828-464-4884	153-7
*Cust Svc			
Southern Graphic Systems Inc			
502 N Willow Ave ..... Tampa FL 33606	**800-777-6789**	813-253-3427	771
Southern Graphics Systems			
7435 Empire Dr ..... Florence KY 41042	**800-777-6789**	859-525-1190	771
Southern Grouts & Mortars Inc			
1502 SW Second Pl ..... Pompano Beach FL 33069	**800-641-9247**	954-943-2288	3
Southern Illinois Electric Co-op			
7420 US Hwy 51 S ..... Dongola IL 62926	**800-762-1400**	618-827-3555	245
Southern Illinois Healthcare			
1239 E Main St ..... Carbondale IL 62902	**866-744-2468**	618-457-5200	350
Southern Illinois University			
Edwardsville			
SR 157 ..... Edwardsville IL 62026	**888-328-5168**	618-650-2000	166
Southern Illinois University Edwardsville			
Lovejoy Library			
30 Hairpin Dr PO Box 1063 ..... Edwardsville IL 62026	**888-328-5168**	618-650-4636	431-6
Southern Illinois University School of Law			
1209 W Chautauqua Rd ..... Carbondale IL 62901	**800-739-9187**	618-453-8858	167-1
Southern Illinois University School of Medicine			
520 N Fourth St			
PO Box 19670 ..... Springfield IL 62702	**800-342-5748**	217-545-8000	167-2
Southern Illinoisan			
710 N Illinois Ave			
PO Box 2108 ..... Carbondale IL 62902	**800-228-0429**	618-529-5454	525-2
Southern Imperial Inc			
1400 Eddy Ave ..... Rockford IL 61103	**800-747-4665***	815-877-7041	286
*Cust Svc			
Southern Indiana Rehabilitation Hospital			
3104 Blackiston Blvd ..... New Albany IN 47150	**800-737-7090**	812-941-8300	371-6
Southern Indiana Rural Electric Co-op Inc			
1776 Tenth St PO Box 219 ..... Tell City IN 47586	**800-323-2316**	812-547-2316	245
Southern Industrial Constructors Inc			
6101 Triangle Dr ..... Raleigh NC 27617	**866-890-7794**	919-782-4600	190-10
Southern Ionics Inc			
201 Commerce St ..... West Point MS 39773	**800-953-3585**	662-494-3055	141
Southern Iowa Electric Co-op Inc			
22458 Hwy 2 PO Box 70 ..... Bloomfield IA 52537	**800-607-2027**	641-664-2277	245
Southern Living Magazine			
2100 Lakeshore Dr ..... Birmingham AL 35209	**800-366-4712**	205-445-6000	452-22
Southern Maine Community College (SMCC)			
Two Ft Rd ..... South Portland ME 04106	**877-282-2182**	207-741-5500	788
Southern Maryland Oil Co Inc (SMO)			
109 N Maple Ave ..... La Plata MD 20646	**888-222-3720**		572
Southern Medical Assn (SMA)			
35 W Lakeshore Dr ..... Birmingham AL 35209	**800-423-4992**	205-945-1840	48-8
Southern Medical Journal			
35 Lakeshore Dr ..... Birmingham AL 35209	**800-423-4992**	205-945-1840	452-16
Southern Methodist University			
6425 Boaz Ln ..... Dallas TX 75205	**800-323-0672**	214-768-2000	166
Southern Methodist University Dedman School of Law			
3300 University Blvd ..... Dallas TX 75205	**888-768-5291**	214-768-2550	167-1
Southern Michigan Bank & Trust			
51 W Pearl St PO Box 309 ..... Coldwater MI 49036	**800-379-7628**	517-279-5500	69
Southern Midcoast Maine Chamber			
Two Main St			
Border Trust Business Ctr ..... Topsham ME 04086	**877-725-8797**	207-725-8797	137
Southern Nazarene University			
6729 NW 39th Expy ..... Bethany OK 73008	**800-648-9899**	405-789-6400	166
Southern New Hampshire University			
2500 N River Rd ..... Manchester NH 03106	**800-668-1249**	603-668-2211	166
Southern Ocean County Chamber of Commerce			
265 W Ninth St ..... Ship Bottom NJ 08008	**800-292-6372**	609-494-7211	137
Southern Ocean Medical Ctr			
1140 Rt 72 W ..... Manahawkin NJ 08050	**888-864-4203**	609-978-8900	371-3
Southern Optical Company Inc			
1909 N Church St ..... Greensboro NC 27405	**800-888-8842**	336-272-8146	535
Southern Oregon University			
1250 Siskiyou Blvd Britt Hall ..... Ashland OR 97520	**800-482-7672**	541-552-6411	166
Southern Pan Services Co (SPS)			
2385 Lithonia Industrial Blvd			
PO Box 679 ..... Lithonia GA 30058	**800-334-9145**	678-301-2400	770
Southern Park Mall			
7401 Market St ..... Youngstown OH 44512	**877-746-6642**	330-758-4511	455
Southern Petroleum Lab Inc			
8850 Interchange Dr ..... Houston TX 77054	**877-775-5227**	713-660-0901	732
Southern Pine Electric Power Assn			
110 Risher St PO Box 60 ..... Taylorsville MS 39168	**800-231-5240**	601-785-6511	245
Southern Polytechnic State University			
1100 S Marietta Pkwy ..... Marietta GA 30060	**800-635-3204***	678-915-4188	166
*Admissions			
Southern Public Power District (SPPD)			
4550 W Husker Hwy			
PO Box 1687 ..... Grand Island NE 68803	**800-652-2013**	308-384-2350	245
Southern Pump & Tank Co			
4800 N Graham St ..... Charlotte NC 28269	**800-477-2826***	704-596-4373	382
*Cust Svc			
Southern Refrigeration Corp			
3140 Shenandoah Ave ..... Roanoke VA 24017	**800-763-4433**	540-342-3493	656
Southern Regional High School District Board of Education			
105 Cedar Bridge Rd ..... Manahawkin NJ 08050	**866-850-0511**	609-597-9481	676
Southern Research Company Inc			
2850 Centenary Blvd ..... Shreveport LA 71104	**888-772-6952**	318-227-9700	397
Southern Research Institute			
2000 Ninth Ave S ..... Birmingham AL 35205	**800-967-6774**	205-581-2000	659
Southern Spring & Stamping Inc			
401 Sub Stn Rd ..... Venice FL 34285	**800-450-5882**	941-488-2276	709
Southern Staircase Inc			
6025 Shiloh Rd Ste E ..... Alpharetta GA 30005	**800-874-8408**	770-888-7333	494
Southern State Community College			
North			
1850 Davids Dr ..... Wilmington OH 45177	**877-644-6562**	937-382-6645	160
South 12681 US Rt 62 ..... Sardinia OH 45171	**877-644-6562**	937-695-0307	160
Southern States Chemical Co			
1600 E President St ..... Savannah GA 31404	**888-337-8922**	912-232-1101	280
Southern States Co-op Inc			
6606 W Broad St ..... Richmond VA 23230	**866-372-8272**	804-281-1000	276
Southern States Frederick Co-op Inc			
500 E South St ..... Frederick MD 21705	**866-633-5747**	301-663-6164	276
Southern States Packaging Co			
PO Box 650 ..... Spartanburg SC 29304	**800-621-2051**		542
Southern Tile Distributors Inc			
4590 Village Ave ..... Norfolk VA 23502	**800-333-8970**	757-855-8041	358
Southern Union State Community College			
Opelika			
1701 Lafayette Pkwy ..... Opelika AL 36801	**800-707-0057**	334-745-6437	160
Valley			
321 Fob James Dr ..... Valley AL 36854	**800-707-0057**	334-756-4151	160
Southern University & A & M College			
156 Elton C Harrison Dr			
PO Box 9757 ..... Baton Rouge LA 70813	**800-256-1531***	225-771-5180	166
*Admissions			
Southern University Law Ctr			
Two Roosevelt Steptoe Dr			
PO Box 9294 ..... Baton Rouge LA 70813	**800-537-1135**	225-771-6297	167-1
Southern University Museum of Art (SUSLA)			
3050 Martin Luther King Jr Dr ..... Shreveport LA 71107	**800-458-1472**	318-670-6000	513
Southern Vermont Cable Co			
PO Box 166 ..... Bondville VT 05340	**800-544-5931**		115
Southern Vermont College			
982 Manison Dr ..... Bennington VT 05201	**800-378-2782**	802-442-5427	166
Southern Virginia University			
One University Hill Dr ..... Buena Vista VA 24416	**800-229-8420**	540-261-8400	166
Southern Weaving Co			
1005 W Bramlett Rd ..... Greenville SC 29611	**800-849-8962**	864-233-1635	734-5
Southern Wesleyan University			
907 Wesleyan Dr ..... Central SC 29630	**800-282-8798**	864-644-5000	166
Southern West Virginia Convention & Visitors Bureau			
1406 Harper Rd ..... Beckley WV 25801	**800-847-4898**	304-252-2244	207
Southern Wholesale Flooring Company Inc			
955B Cobb Pl Blvd			
PO Box 440069 ..... Kennesaw GA 30144	**800-282-7590**	770-514-7110	359
Southern Wine & Spirits of America Inc			
1600 NW 163rd St ..... Miami FL 33169	**800-776-0180**	305-625-4171	80-3
Southern Wine & Spirits of Colorado			
5270 Fox St PO Box 5603 ..... Denver CO 80216	**800-332-9956**	303-292-1711	80-3
Southern Wine & Spirits of Illinois			
300 E Crossroads Pkwy			
Bolingbrook Corp Ctr ..... Bolingbrook IL 60440	**800-776-0180**	630-685-3000	80-3
Southernmost Illinois Tourism Bureau			
PO Box 378 ..... Anna IL 62906	**800-248-4373**	618-833-9928	207
Southernmost On the Beach			
508 S St ..... Key West FL 33040	**800-354-4455**		376
Southfield Dodge Chrysler Jeep Ram			
28100 Telegraph Rd ..... Southfield MI 48034	**888-388-0451***	248-354-2950	56
*Sales			
SouthFirst Bancshares Inc			
126 N Norton Ave PO Box 167 ..... Sylacauga AL 35150	**800-239-1492**	256-245-4365	357-2
OTC: SZBI			
Southfork Hotel			
1600 N Central Expy ..... Plano TX 75074	**877-386-4383**	972-578-8555	376
Southgate Community School District			
13305 Reeck Rd ..... Southgate MI 48195	**888-263-5897**	734-246-4600	676
Southland Tube Inc			
3525 Richard Arrington Blvd N ..... Birmingham AL 35234	**800-543-9024**	205-251-1884	485
SouthPark Mall			
4400 Sharon Rd ..... Charlotte NC 28211	**888-726-5930**	704-364-4411	455
SouthPointe Pavilions			
2910 Pine Lake Rd Ste Q ..... Lincoln NE 68516	**800-733-2767**	402-421-2114	455
Southside Bancshares Inc			
1201 S Beckham Ave ..... Tyler TX 75701	**877-639-3511**	903-531-7111	357-2
NASDAQ: SBSI			
Southside Electric Co-op Inc			
2000 W Virgina Ave ..... Crewe VA 23930	**800-552-2118**	434-645-7721	245
Southside Virginia Community College			
109 Campus Dr ..... Alberta VA 23821	**888-220-7822**	434-949-1000	160
Southwark Metal Mfg Company Inc			
2800 Red Lion Rd ..... Philadelphia PA 19114	**800-523-1052**	215-735-3401	688
Southway Inn			
2431 Bank St ..... Ottawa ON K1V8R9	**877-688-4929**	613-737-0811	376
Southwest Airlines Air Cargo			
2702 Love Field Dr ..... Dallas TX 75235	**800-533-1222**		12
Southwest Airlines Co			
2702 Love Field Dr PO Box 36611 ..... Dallas TX 75235	**800-435-9792**	214-792-4000	25
NYSE: LUV			
Southwest Airport Services Inc			
11811 N Brantly Ave Ste 500 ..... Houston TX 77034	**888-362-6738**	281-484-6551	62
Southwest Art Magazine			
10901 W 120th Ave Ste 350 ..... Broomfield CO 80021	**877-212-1938**	303-442-0427	452-2
Southwest Bancorp Inc			
608 S Main St PO Box 1988 ..... Stillwater OK 74076	**888-762-4762**		357-2
NASDAQ: OKSB			
Southwest Baptist University			
1600 University Ave ..... Bolivar MO 65613	**800-526-5859**		166
SouthWest Capital Bank			
622 Douglas Ave ..... Las Vegas NM 87701	**800-748-2406**	505-425-7565	69
Southwest Florida International Airport			
11000 Terminal Access Rd			
Ste 8671 ..... Fort Myers FL 33913	**800-359-6786**	239-590-4800	27
Southwest Freightlines			
11991 Transpark Dr Horizon City ..... El Paso TX 79927	**800-776-5799***	915-860-8592	770
*General			
Southwest Gas Corp			
5241 Spring Mtn Rd			
PO Box 98510 ..... Las Vegas NV 89193	**800-748-5539**	702-876-7237	775
NYSE: SWX			
Southwest Gas Corp Northern Nevada Div			
400 Eagle Stn Ln ..... Carson City NV 89701	**877-860-6020**		775
Southwest Gas Corp Southern Arizona Div			
3401 E Gas Rd ..... Tucson AZ 85714	**877-860-6020**		775
Southwest Gas Corp Southern California Div			
13471 Mariposa Rd ..... Victorville CA 92395	**877-860-6020**		775
Southwest Gas Corp Southern Nevada Div			
5241 Spring Mtn Rd ..... Las Vegas NV 89150	**877-860-6020**	702-876-7011	775
Southwest General Hospital (SGH)			
7400 Barlite Blvd ..... San Antonio TX 78224	**877-215-9355**	210-921-2000	371-3
Southwest Georgia Financial Corp			
201 First St SE ..... Moultrie GA 31768	**888-683-2265**	229-985-1120	357-2
NYSE: SGB			
Southwest Institute of Healing Arts			
1100 E Apache Blvd ..... Tempe AZ 85281	**888-504-9106**	480-994-9244	788
Southwest Iowa Rural Electric Co-op			
1801 Grove Ave ..... Corning IA 50841	**888-591-1261**	641-322-3165	245

	Toll-Free	Phone	Class
Southwest King County Chamber of Commerce			
14220 Interurban Ave S Ste 134 .... Tukwila WA 98168	800-638-8613	206-575-1633	137
Southwest Louisiana Convention & Visitors Bureau			
1205 N Lakeshore Dr .... Lake Charles LA 70601	800-456-7952	337-436-9588	207
Southwest Louisiana Electric Membership Corp			
3420 NE Evangeline Thruway .... Lafayette LA 70509	888-275-3626	337-896-5384	245
Southwest Medical Assoc Inc			
638 E Market St PO Box 2168 .... Rockport TX 78382	800-929-4854		712
Southwest Minnesota State University			
1501 State St .... Marshall MN 56258	800-642-0684		166
Southwest Mississippi Electric Power Assn			
18671 Hwy 61 PO Box 5............... Lorman MS 39096	800-287-8564		245
Southwest Missouri Bank			
2417 S Grand Ave .... Carthage MO 64836	800-943-8488	417-358-1770	69
Southwest Plastic Binding Co			
109 Millwell Ct .... Maryland Heights MO 63043	800-325-3628	314-739-4400	85
Southwest Public Power District			
221 S Main St PO Box 289.............Palisade NE 69040	800-379-7977	308-285-3295	245
Southwest Rural Electric Assn			
700 N Broadway PO Box 310............ Tipton OK 73570	800-256-7973	580-667-5281	245
Southwest Tennessee Community College			
PO Box 780 ....Memphis TN 38101	877-717-7822	901-333-5000	160
Southwest Tennessee Electric Membership Corp			
1009 E Main St .... Brownsville TN 38012	800-772-0472	731-772-1322	245
Southwest Texas Electric Co-op Inc			
101 E Gillis St PO Box 677............ Eldorado TX 76936	800-643-3980	325-853-2544	245
Southwest Texas Junior College			
2401 Garner Field Rd ....Uvalde TX 78801	888-886-8490	830-278-4401	160
Southwest Virginia Community College			
724 Community College Rd ....Cedar Bluff VA 24609	855-877-3944	276-964-2555	160
Southwest Washington Convention & Visitors Bureau			
1220 Main S Ste 220 .... Vancouver WA 98660	877-600-0800	360-750-1553	207
Southwest Wisconsin Library System			
1775 Fourth St....................Fennimore WI 53809	866-866-3393	608-822-3393	431-3
Southwest Wisconsin Technical College (SWTC)			
1800 Bronson Blvd ....Fennimore WI 53809	800-362-3322	608-822-3262	788
Southwestern Adventist University			
100 W Hillcrest Dr PO Box 567 ....Keene TX 76059	888-732-7928*	817-645-3921	166
*Admissions			
Southwestern Assemblies of God University			
1200 Sycamore St ....Waxahachie TX 75165	888-937-7248	972-937-4010	166
Southwestern Baptist Theological Seminary			
PO Box 22740 ....Fort Worth TX 76122	877-467-9287	817-923-1921	167-3
Southwestern Christian College			
PO Box 10 .... Terrell TX 75160	800-925-9357	972-524-3341	166
Southwestern Christian University			
7210 NW 39th Expy PO Box 340 .... Bethany OK 73008	888-418-9272	405-789-7661	166
Southwestern College			
900 Otay Lakes Rd .... Chula Vista CA 91910	866-262-9881	619-421-6700	160
Southwestern Community College			
1501 W Townline St.................. Creston IA 50801	800-247-4023	641-782-7081	160
Southwestern Electric Co-op Inc			
525 US Rt 40 PO Box 549 .... Greenville IL 62246	800-637-8667		245
Southwestern Energy Co			
2350 N Sam Houston Pkwy E			
Ste 300............................Houston TX 77032	866-322-0801	832-796-1000	775
NYSE: SWN			
Southwestern Eye Ctr			
2610 E University Dr .... Mesa AZ 85213	800-224-3339*	480-892-8400	786
*General			
Southwestern Illinois College			
2500 Carlyle Ave .... Belleville IL 62221	800-222-5131	618-235-2700	160
Southwestern Indian Polytechnic Institute			
9169 Coors Blvd NW			
PO Box 10146................... Albuquerque NM 87120	800-586-7474	505-346-2306	163
Southwestern Industries Inc			
2615 Homestead Pl .... Rancho Dominguez CA 90220	800-421-6875	310-608-4422	450
Southwestern Medical Ctr (SWMC)			
5602 SW Lee Blvd ....Lawton OK 73505	877-707-1780	580-531-4700	371-3
Southwestern Michigan College (SMC)			
58900 Cherry Grove Rd ....Dowagiac MI 49047	800-456-8675	269-782-1000	160
Niles Area 2229 US 12 .... Niles MI 49120	800-456-8675	269-782-1233	160
Southwestern Motor Transport Inc			
4600 Goldfield ....San Antonio TX 78218	800-531-1071	210-661-6791	770
Southwestern Oregon Community College			
1988 Newmark Ave ....Coos Bay OR 97420	800-962-2838	541-888-2525	160
Southwestern Petroleum Corp			
PO Box 961005 .... Fort Worth TX 76161	800-877-9372	817-332-2336	534
Southwestern University			
PO Box 770 ....Georgetown TX 78627	800-252-3166	512-863-1200	166
Southwestern Vermont Medical Ctr			
100 Hospital Dr .... Bennington VT 05201	800-543-1624	802-442-6361	371-3
Southwestern Wire Inc			
PO Box CC .... Norman OK 73070	800-348-9473	405-447-6900	800
Southwestern/Great American			
2451 Atrium Way .... Nashville TN 37214	888-602-7867*		94
*Cust Svc			
Southwick Inc			
2400 Shattuck Ave ....Berkeley CA 94704	888-686-0046	510-845-2530	56
Southwire Co			
1 Southwire Dr..................... Carrollton GA 30119	800-444-1700	770-832-4242	480
Southwire Company Machinery Div			
One Southwire Dr .... Carrollton GA 30119	800-444-1700	770-832-4242	477
Southworth Co			
265 Main St ....Agawam MA 01001	800-225-1839	413-789-1200	545-2
Southworth Products Corp			
PO Box 1380 ....Portland ME 04104	800-743-1000	207-878-0700	465
Souvenirs Gifts & Novelties Trade Assn			
588 Sutter St Ste 140............ San Francisco CA 19003	800-284-5451	610-645-6940	48-18
Sovereign Bank FSB			
PO Box 12646 ....Reading PA 19612	877-768-2265*		69
*Cust Svc			
Sovereign Pharmaceuticals Ltd			
7590 Sand St ....Fort Worth TX 76118	877-248-0228	817-284-0429	576
Sovereign Society, The			
98 S E Sixth Ave Ste 2 ....Delray Beach FL 33483	888-358-8125		398
Sovran Self Storage Inc			
6467 Main St ....Buffalo NY 14221	800-242-1715	716-633-1850	791-3
NYSE: SSS			
Soybean Digest			
7900 International Dr			
Ste 300..........................Minneapolis MN 55425	800-722-5334*	952-851-4667	452-1
*Cust Svc			

	Toll-Free	Phone	Class
SP Systems Inc			
7500 Greenway Ctr Dr Ste 850.........Greenbelt MD 20770	877-327-8732	301-614-1322	179-1
Spa & Fitness Club at the Four Seasons Hotel Washington			
2800 Pennsylvania Ave NW ....Washington DC 20007	800-819-5053	202-944-2022	698
Spa at Big Cedar Lodge			
612 Devil's Pool Rd ....Ridgedale MO 65739	800-225-6343	417-339-5201	698
Spa at Coeur d'Alene			
115 S Second St .... Coeur d'Alene ID 83814	800-684-0514	208-765-4000	697
Spa at Eagle Crest Resort			
1522 Cline Falls Hwy			
PO Box 1215.......................Redmond OR 97756	800-682-4786	541-923-9647	698
Spa at Le Merigot JW Marriott Beach Hotel Santa Monica			
1740 Ocean Ave ....Santa Monica CA 90401	888-236-2427	310-395-9700	698
Spa at Pebble Beach			
1518 Cypress Dr ....Pebble Beach CA 93953	800-654-9300	831-649-7615	698
Spa at Peninsula Beverly Hills			
9882 S Santa Monica Blvd .... Beverly Hills CA 90212	800-462-7899	310-551-2888	697
Spa at Pinehurst Resort			
80 Carolina Vista Dr			
PO Box 4000.......................Pinehurst NC 28374	800-487-4653	910-235-8320	698
Spa at the Beverly Wilshire, The			
9500 Wilshire Blvd .... Beverly Hills CA 90212	800-545-4000	310-385-7023	698
Spa at the Bodega Bay Lodge			
103 Coast Hwy 1 .... Bodega Bay CA 94923	888-875-2250	707-875-3525	698
Spa at the Breakers			
One S County Rd ....Palm Beach FL 33480	888-273-2537	561-653-6656	698
Spa at the Broadmoor			
One Lake Ave .... Colorado Springs CO 80906	800-634-7711	719-634-7711	698
Spa at the Buena Vista Palace Resort in the Walt Disney World Resort			
1900 Buena Vista Dr			
PO Box 22206................Lake Buena Vista FL 32830	866-397-6516	407-827-3200	698
Spa at the Camelback Inn JW Marriott Resort Golf Club & Spa			
5402 E Lincoln Dr .... Scottsdale AZ 85253	800-922-2635	480-596-7040	698
Spa at the Chattanoogan			
1201 S Broad St .... Chattanooga TN 37402	800-619-0018	423-424-3779	698
Spa at the Equinox Resort			
3567 Main St Rt 7-A......... Manchester Village VT 05254	800-362-4747		698
Spa at the Fairmont Inn Sonoma Mission Inn			
100 Boyes Blvd ....Sonoma CA 95476	877-289-7354	707-938-9000	698
Spa at the Hotel Hershey			
100 Hotel Rd ....Hershey PA 17033	877-772-9988	717-520-5888	698
Spa at the JW Marriott Desert Springs Resort Palm Desert			
74855 Country Club Dr ....Palm Desert CA 92260	800-845-5279	760-341-2211	698
Spa at the Norwich Inn			
607 W Thames St ....Norwich CT 06360	800-275-4772	860-886-2401	698
Spa at the PGA National Resort			
450 Ave of			
the Champions............ Palm Beach Gardens FL 33418	800-633-9150	561-627-3111	698
Spa at the Ponte Vedra Inn & Club			
200 Ponte Vedra Blvd ....Ponte Vedra Beach FL 32082	800-234-7842	904-273-7700	698
Spa at the Ritz-Carlton Amelia Island			
4750 Amelia Island Pkwy ....Amelia Island FL 32034	800-241-3333	904-277-1087	698
Spa at the Ritz-Carlton Bachelor Gulch			
0130 Daybreak Ridge .... Avon CO 81620	800-241-3333	970-748-6200	698
Spa at the Ritz-Carlton Half Moon Bay			
One Miramontes Pt Rd ....Half Moon Bay CA 94019	800-241-3333	650-712-7040	698
Spa at the Ritz-Carlton New Orleans			
921 Canal St .... New Orleans LA 70112	800-241-3333	504-670-2929	698
Spa at the Saddlebrook Resort			
5700 Saddlebrook Way ....Wesley Chapel FL 33543	800-729-8383	813-907-4419	698
Spa at the Sagamore			
110 Sagamore Rd .... Bolton Landing NY 12814	866-384-1944	518-743-6081	698
Spa at the Sanderling Resort			
1461 Duck Rd .... Duck NC 27949	855-412-7866	252-261-7744	698
Spa at the Vail Marriott Mountain Resort			
715 W Lionshead Cir .... Vail CO 81657	800-648-0720	970-479-5004	698
Spa at the Villagio Inn			
6481 Washington St ....Yountville CA 94599	800-351-1133	707-948-5050	698
Spa at White Oaks Conference Resort			
253 Taylor Rd .... Niagara-on-the-Lake ON L0S1J0	800-263-5766	905-641-2599	698
Spa Esmeralda at the Renaissance Esmeralda Resort			
44400 Indian Wells Ln ....Indian Wells CA 92210	800-845-5279	760-836-1265	698
Spa Gaucin at the Saint Regis Monarch Beach			
One Monarch Beach Resort ....Dana Point CA 92629	800-722-1543	949-234-3367	698
Spa Grande at the Grand Wailea Resort Maui			
3850 Wailea Alanui Dr .... Wailea HI 96753	800-772-1933	808-875-1234	698
Spa La Quinta at La Quinta Resort			
49499 Eisenhower Dr ....La Quinta CA 92253	877-527-7721	760-777-4800	698
Spa Manufacturers			
6060 Ulmerton Rd ....Clearwater FL 33760	877-530-9493	727-530-9493	372
Spa Moana at the Hyatt Regency Maui Resort & Spa			
200 Nohea Kai Dr .... Lahaina HI 96761	800-233-1234	808-667-4725	698
Spa Resort Casino			
401 E Amado Rd ....Palm Springs CA 92262	888-999-1995		132
Spa Resort, The			
100 N Indian Canyon Dr ....Palm Springs CA 92262	800-854-1279		660
Spa Shiki at the Lodge of Four Seasons			
315 Horseshoe Bend Pkwy ....Lake Ozark MO 65049	800-843-5253	573-365-8108	698
Spa Suites at Kahala Hotel & Resort			
5000 Kahala Ave ....Honolulu HI 96816	800-367-2525	808-739-8938	698
Spa Terre at Paradise Point Resort			
1404 Vacation Rd .... San Diego CA 92109	800-344-2626	858-581-5998	698
Spa Terre at the Hotel Viking			
One Bellevue Ave ....Newport RI 02840	800-556-7126	401-847-3300	698
Spa Terre at the Inn & Spa at Loretto			
211 Old Santa Fe Trl ....Santa Fe NM 87501	800-727-5531	505-984-7997	698
Spa Toccare at Borgata Hotel Casino			
1 Borgata Way ....Atlantic City NJ 08401	877-448-5833	609-317-7555	698
Spa Torrey Pines at the Lodge at Torrey Pines			
11480 N Torrey Pines Rd .... La Jolla CA 92037	800-656-0087	858-453-4420	698
Space Coast Credit Union			
8045 N Wickham Rd			
PO Box 419001....................Melbourne FL 32941	800-447-7228	321-752-2222	219
Space Coast Jet Ctr			
7003 Challenger Ave .... Titusville FL 32780	800-559-5473	321-267-8355	62
Space Dynamics Laboratory			
1695 N Research Pkwy ....North Logan UT 84341	866-487-2365	435-797-4600	659
Space Needle LLC			
203 Sixth Ave N .... Seattle WA 98109	800-937-9582	206-905-2200	49-3
Space Science & Engineering Ctr			
University of Wisconsin			
1225 W Dayton St.................. Madison WI 53706	866-391-1753	608-262-0544	659
Space Systems/Loral			
3825 Fabian Way .... Palo Alto CA 94303	800-332-6490	650-852-4000	638

	Toll-Free	Phone	Class
Space Transit Planetarium			
3280 S Miami Ave .... Miami FL 33129	**866-268-0250**	305-646-4200	591
SPACECO Inc			
9575 W Higgins Rd Ste 700 .... Rosemont IL 60018	**888-772-2326**	847-696-4060	261
SpaceGuard Products Inc			
711 S Commerce Dr .... Seymour IN 47274	**800-841-0680**	812-523-3044	286
Spacelabs Health Care			
35301 SE Center St .... Snoqualmie WA 98065	**800-522-7025**	425-396-3300	250
Spacesaver Corp			
1450 Janesville Ave .... Fort Atkinson WI 53538	**800-492-3434**	800-255-8170	286
Spago			
3500 Las Vegas Blvd S Ste G1 ..... Las Vegas NV 89109	**800-241-3333**	702-369-6300	662
SpaHalekulani at the Halekulani Hotel			
2199 Kalia Rd .... Honolulu HI 96815	**800-367-2343**	808-931-5322	698
Spalding			
PO Box 90015 .... Bowling Green KY 42103	**855-253-4533**		701
Spalding Regional Medical Ctr			
601 S Eigth St .... Griffin GA 30224	**866-717-5826**	770-228-2721	371-3
Spalding Rehabilitation Hospital			
900 Potomac St .... Aurora CO 80011	**800-367-3309**	303-367-1166	371-6
Spalding University			
851 S Fourth St .... Louisville KY 40203	**800-896-8941**	502-585-9911	166
Span-America Medical Systems Inc			
70 Commerce Ctr .... Greenville SC 29615	**800-888-6752**	864-288-8877	472
NASDAQ: SPAN			
Spangler Candy Co			
400 N Portland St PO Box 71 .... Bryan OH 43506	**888-636-4221***	419-636-4221	295-8
*Sales			
Spanish Cove			
11 Palm Ave .... Yukon OK 73099	**800-965-2683**		663
Spanlink Communications Inc			
605 Hwy 169 N Ste 900 .... Minneapolis MN 55441	**800-303-1239***	763-971-2000	726
*Sales			
Spansion Inc			
915 DeGuigne Dr .... Sunnyvale CA 94085	**866-772-6746**	408-962-2500	288
NYSE: CODE			
SPAR Group Inc			
560 White Plains Rd .... Tarrytown NY 10591	**800-314-7727**	914-332-4100	4
NASDAQ: SGRP			
Spark Energy Gas LP			
2105 Citywest Blvd .... Houston TX 77042	**877-547-7275**		324
Sparks Belting Co			
3800 Stahl Dr SE .... Grand Rapids MI 49546	**800-451-4537**	616-949-2750	367
Sparks Marketing Group Inc			
2828 Charter Rd .... Philadelphia PA 19154	**800-925-7727**	215-676-1100	286
Sparling Instruments Company Inc			
4097 N Temple City Blvd .... El Monte CA 91731	**800-800-3569***	626-444-0571	490
*Sales			
Sparrow Health System			
1215 E Michigan Ave .... Lansing MI 48912	**800-772-7769**	517-364-1000	371-3
Sparta Systems Inc			
Holmdel Corporate Plz 2137			
Hwy 35 .... Holmdel NJ 07733	**888-261-5948**	732-203-0400	178
Spartan Chemical Company Inc			
1110 Spartan Dr .... Maumee OH 43537	**800-537-8990**	419-531-5551	143
Spartan College of Aeronautics & Technology			
8820 E Pine St PO Box 582833 .... Tulsa OK 74115	**800-331-1204***	918-836-6886	788
*Admissions			
Spartan Distributors Inc			
487 W Div St .... Sparta MI 49345	**800-822-2216**	616-887-7301	274
Spartan Motors Inc			
1541 Reynolds Rd .... Charlotte MI 48813	**800-937-5449**	517-543-6400	509
NASDAQ: SPAR			
Spartanburg Community College			
800 Brisack Rd PO Box 4386 .... Spartanburg SC 29305	**866-591-3700**	864-592-4800	788
Spartanburg Herald-Journal			
189 W Main St .... Spartanburg SC 29306	**800-922-4158**	864-582-4511	525-2
Spartanburg Methodist College			
1000 Powell Mill Rd .... Spartanburg SC 29301	**800-772-7286**	864-587-4000	160
Spartanburg Regional Medical Ctr (SRMC)			
101 E Wood St .... Spartanburg SC 29303	**800-318-2596**	864-560-6000	371-3
Spartanburg Steel Products Inc			
1290 New Cut Rd PO Box 6428 ...... Spartanburg SC 29304	**888-974-7500**	864-585-5211	484
Sparton			
27 Hale Spring Rd .... Plaistow NH 03865	**800-443-4132**	603-382-3840	204
Spaulding Composites Co			
55 Nadeau Dr .... Rochester NH 03867	**800-801-0560**	603-332-0555	592
Spaulding Composites Company Fab Div			
55 Nadeau Dr .... Rochester NH 03867	**800-801-0560**	603-332-0555	595
Spavinaw State Park			
555 S Main .... Spavinaw OK 74366	**800-622-6317**	918-589-2651	558
SpawGlass Construction Corp			
13800 W Rd .... Houston TX 77041	**800-771-0422**	281-970-5300	458
SPE (Society of Petroleum Engineers)			
222 Palisades Creek Dr .... Richardson TX 75080	**800-456-6863**	972-952-9393	47-12
SpeakerCraft Inc			
940 Columbia Ave .... Riverside CA 92507	**800-448-0976**	951-787-0543	174-5
Speakers Unlimited			
PO Box 27225 .... Columbus OH 43227	**888-333-6676**	614-864-3703	699
Speakman Co			
400 Anchor Mill Rd .... New Castle DE 19720	**800-537-2107**		602
Spear Inc			
5510 Courseview Dr .... Mason OH 45040	**800-627-7327**	513-459-1100	410
Spearfish Canyon Resort			
10619 Roughlock Falls Rd .... Lead SD 57754	**877-975-6343**	605-584-3435	660
Spears Manufacturing Co			
PO Box 9203 .... Sylmar CA 91392	**800-862-1499**	818-364-1611	601
Spec Bldg Materials Inc			
4300 W Ave .... San Antonio TX 78213	**800-588-3892**	210-342-2727	192-4
Spec's Wines Spirits & Finer Foods			
2410 Smith St .... Houston TX 77006	**888-526-8787**	713-526-8787	439
Specco Industries Inc			
13087 Main St .... Lemont IL 60439	**800-441-6646**	630-257-5060	143
Special Counsel Inc			
10201 Centurion Pkwy N			
Ste 400 .... Jacksonville FL 32256	**800-737-3436**	904-737-3436	712
Special Devices Inc			
14370 White Sage Rd .... Moorpark CA 93021	**888-782-0082**	805-553-1200	268
Special Education Report			
360 Hiatt St .... Palm Beach Gardens FL 33418	**800-621-5463***	561-622-6520	524-4
*Sales			
Special Libraries Assn (SLA)			
331 S Patrick St .... Alexandria VA 22314	**866-446-6069**	703-647-4900	48-11
Special Metals Corp			
4317 Middle Settlement Rd ...... New Hartford NY 13413	**800-334-8351**	315-798-2900	480
Special Military Active Retired Travel Club (SMART)			
600 University Office Blvd			
Ste 1A .... Pensacola FL 32504	**800-354-7681**	850-478-1986	47-23
Special Olympics Inc			
1133 19th St NW 11th Fl .... Washington DC 20036	**800-700-8585**	202-628-3630	47-22
Special Wish Foundation Inc			
1250 Memory Ln N Ste B .... Columbus OH 43209	**800-486-9474**	614-258-3186	47-5
Specialized Bicycle Components			
15130 Concord Cir .... Morgan Hill CA 95037	**877-808-8154**	408-779-6229	81
Specialized Information Publishers Assn (SIPA)			
8229 Boone Blvd Ste 260 .... Vienna VA 22182	**800-356-9302**	703-992-9339	48-14
Specialized Printed Forms Inc			
352 Ctr St .... Caledonia NY 14423	**800-688-2381**	585-538-2381	109
Special-Lite Inc			
PO Box 6 .... Decatur MI 49045	**800-821-6531**	269-423-7068	234
Specialty Bolt & Screw Inc			
235 Bowles Rd .... Agawam MA 01001	**800-322-7878**	413-789-6700	348
Specialty Brands Of America Inc			
1400 Old Country Rd .... Westbury NY 11590	**877-795-3599**	516-997-6969	296-8
Specialty Catalog Corp			
400 Manley St .... West Bridgewater MA 02379	**800-364-9060**	508-638-7000	454
Specialty Coffee Assn of America (SCAA)			
330 Golden Shore Ave Ste 50 .... Long Beach CA 90802	**800-995-9019**	562-624-4100	48-6
Specialty Design & Mfg Co			
PO Box 4039 .... Reading PA 19606	**800-720-0867**	610-779-1357	747
Specialty Graphic Imaging Assn (SGIA)			
10015 Main St .... Fairfax VA 22031	**888-385-3588**	703-385-1335	48-16
Specialty Hearse & Ambulance Sale Corp			
60 Engineers Ln E .... Farmingdale NY 11735	**800-349-6102***	516-349-7700	56
*General			
Specialty Laboratories Inc			
27027 Tourney Rd .... Valencia CA 91355	**800-421-7110***	661-799-6543	415
*Sales			
Specialty Loose Leaf Inc			
One Cabot St .... Holyoke MA 01040	**800-227-3623**	413-532-0106	545-2
Specialty Merchandise Corp			
996 Flower Glen St .... Simi Valley CA 93065	**800-345-4762***	805-578-5500	363
*Orders			
Specialty Motors Inc			
25060 Ave Tibbitts .... Valencia CA 91355	**800-232-2612**	661-257-7388	511
Specialty Pipe & Tube Inc			
PO Box 516 .... Mineral Ridge OH 44440	**800-842-5839**	330-505-8262	487
Specialty Plastic Fabricators Inc			
9658 196th St .... Mokena IL 60448	**800-747-9509**	708-479-5501	200
Specialty Products & Insulation Co (SPI)			
1650 Manheim Pk Ste 202 .... Lancaster PA 17601	**800-788-7764**	717-569-3900	192-4
Specialty Retailers Inc			
10201 S Main St .... Houston TX 77025	**800-579-2302**		155-4
Specialty Silicone Fabricators			
3077 Rollie Gates Dr .... Paso Robles CA 93446	**800-394-4284**	805-239-4284	471
Specialty Tires of America Inc			
1600 Washington St .... Indiana PA 15701	**800-622-7327**	724-349-9010	744
Specialty Tools & Fasteners Distributors Assn (STAFDA)			
500 Elm Grove Rd Ste 210			
PO Box 44. .... Elm Grove WI 53122	**800-352-2981**	262-784-4774	48-18
Specialty Vehicle Institute of America (SVIA)			
Two Jenner St Ste 150 .... Irvine CA 92618	**800-887-2887**	949-727-3727	48-21
Specification Rubber Products Inc			
1568 First St N .... Alabaster AL 35007	**800-633-3415**	205-663-2521	325
Specified Technologies Inc			
200 Evans Way Ste 2 .... Somerville NJ 08876	**800-992-1180**	908-526-8000	144
Specmo Auto Sound & Speed			
G3189 S Dort Hwy .... Burton MI 48529	**800-545-7910**		53
Speco Technologies			
200 New Hwy .... Amityville NY 11701	**800-645-5516**	631-957-8700	37
Spectator, The			
44 Frid St .... Hamilton ON L8N3G3	**800-263-6902**	905-526-3333	525-1
Spectera Inc			
6220 Old Dobbin Ln			
Liberty 6, Ste 200 .... Columbia MD 21045	**800-638-3120**		388-3
Spectra Colors Corp			
25 Rizzolo Rd .... Kearny NJ 07032	**800-527-8588**	201-997-0606	144
Spectra Energy Corp			
5400 Westheimer Ct .... Houston TX 77056	**800-700-8744**	713-627-5400	775
Spectra Integrated Systems Inc			
8100 Arrowridge Blvd .... Charlotte NC 28273	**800-443-7561**	704-525-7099	246
Spectra Merchandising International Inc			
4230 N Normandy Ave .... Chicago IL 60634	**800-777-5331**	773-202-8408	246
Spectranetics Corp			
9965 Federal Dr .... Colorado Springs CO 80921	**800-231-0978**	719-447-2000	421
NASDAQ: SPNC			
Spectraserv Inc			
75 Jacobus Ave .... South Kearny NJ 07032	**800-445-4436**	973-589-0277	770
Spectrolab Inc			
12500 Gladstone Ave .... Sylmar CA 91342	**800-936-4888**	818-365-4611	687
Spectronics Corp			
956 Brush Hollow Rd .... Westbury NY 11590	**800-274-8888**		202
Spectrum Analytical Inc			
830 Silver St .... Agawam MA 01001	**800-789-9115**	413-789-9018	732
Spectrum Brands			
3001 Deming Way .... Middleton WI 53711	**800-566-7899**	608-275-3340	280
Spectrum Corp			
10048 Easthaven Blvd .... Houston TX 77075	**800-392-5050**	713-944-6200	692
Spectrum Financial System Inc			
163 McKenzie Rd .... Mooresville NC 28115	**800-525-0555**	704-663-4466	195
Spectrum Glass Co			
PO Box 646 .... Woodinville WA 98072	**800-426-3120**	425-483-6699	328
Spectrum Health Blodgett Campus			
100 Michigan St NE .... Grand Rapids MI 49503	**866-989-7999**	616-774-7444	371-3
Spectrum Health Systems Inc			
10 Mechanic St Ste 302 .... Worcester MA 01608	**800-464-9555**	508-792-5400	47-15
Spectrum Healthcare Resources Inc			
12647 Olive Blvd Ste 600 .... Saint Louis MO 63141	**800-325-3982**		458
Spectrum Industries Inc			
925 First Ave .... Chippewa Falls WI 54729	**800-235-1262**	715-723-6750	286
Spectrum Laboratories Inc			
18617 Broadwick St .... Rancho Dominguez CA 90220	**800-634-3300**	310-885-4600	416
Spectrum Laboratory Products Inc			
14422 S San Pedro St PO Box 290. ...... Gardena CA 90248	**800-772-8786***	310-516-8000	474
*General			

	Toll-Free	Phone	Class
Spectrum Pharmaceuticals Inc			
11500 S Eastern Ave Ste 240 ....Henderson NV 89052	**800-332-1088**	702-835-6300	84
NASDAQ: SPPI			
Spectrum Signal Processing by Vecima			
2700 Production Way Ste 300 ....Burnaby BC V5A4X1	**800-663-8986**	604-676-6700	617
Spectrum Systems Inc			
3410 W Nine-Mile Rd ....Pensacola FL 32526	**800-432-6119**	850-944-3392	416
Speechwriter's Newsletter			
316 N Michigan Ave Ste 400 ....Chicago IL 60601	**800-878-5331**	312-960-4100	524-11
Speedie & Assoc Inc			
3331 E Wood St ....Phoenix AZ 85040	**800-628-6221**	602-997-6391	732
Speedling Inc			
4447 Old 41 Hwy S ....Ruskin FL 33570	**800-881-4769***		366
*Cust Svc			
Speedway LLC			
500 Speedway Dr .... Enon OH 45323	**800-643-1948***	937-864-3001	323
*Cust Svc			
Speedway Motorsports Inc (SMI)			
5555 Concord Pkwy S ....Concord NC 28027	**800-461-9330**	704-455-3239	182
NYSE: TRK			
Speedway Redi Mix Inc			
1201 N Taylor Rd ....Garrett IN 46738	**800-227-5649**	260-357-6885	183
Spellman Hardwoods Inc			
4645 N 43rd Ave ....Phoenix AZ 85031	**800-624-5401**	602-272-2313	192-3
Spelman College			
350 Spelman Ln SW ....Atlanta GA 30314	**800-982-2411***	404-681-3643	166
*Admissions			
Spence Law Firm LLC			
15 S Jackson St ....Jackson WY 83001	**800-967-2117**	307-733-7290	425
Spencer Cos Inc			
120 Woodson St PO Box 18128 ....Huntsville AL 35801	**800-633-2910**	256-533-1150	572
Spencer Industries Inc			
19308 68th Ave S ....Kent WA 98032	**800-367-5646**	253-796-1100	760
Spencer Recovery Centers Inc			
1316 S Coast Hwy ....Laguna Beach CA 92651	**800-334-0394**		717
Spencer Reed Group Inc			
6900 College Blvd Ste 1 ....Overland Park KS 66211	**800-477-5035**	913-663-4400	266
Spencer Savings Bank			
PO Box 912 ....Spencer MA 01562	**800-547-2885**	508-885-5313	69
Spencer Savings Bank SLA			
611 River Dr ....Elmwood Park NJ 07407	**800-363-8115**	973-772-6700	69
Spencer Turbine Co			
600 Day Hill Rd ....Windsor CT 06095	**800-232-4321**	860-688-8361	18
Spenco Medical Corp			
PO Box 2501 ....Waco TX 76702	**800-877-3626**	254-772-6000	472
Sperry & Rice Mfg Company LLC			
9146 US Hwy 52 ....Brookville IN 47012	**800-541-9277**	765-647-4141	668
SPFPA (International Union Security Police & Fire Professionals of America)			
25510 Kelly Rd ....Roseville MI 48066	**800-228-7492**	586-772-7250	411
SPG International			
11230 Harland Dr ....Covington GA 30014	**877-503-4774**		286
Spherix Inc			
6430 Rockledge Dr Ste 503 ....Bethesda MD 20817	**855-816-0624**	301-897-2540	193
NASDAQ: SPEX			
SPHS (Sheppard Pratt Health System)			
6501 N Charles St ....Baltimore MD 21285	**800-627-0330**	410-938-3000	371-5
SPI (Specialty Products & Insulation Co)			
1650 Manheim Pk Ste 202 ....Lancaster PA 17601	**800-788-7764**	717-569-3900	192-4
SPI Pharma			
Rockwood Office Park Fl 2 ....Wilmington DE 19809	**800-789-9755**	302-576-8567	474
SPI/Mobile Pulley Works Inc			
905 S Ann St ....Mobile AL 36605	**866-334-6325**	251-653-0606	261
Spice Hunter Inc			
184 Suburban Rd			
PO Box 8110. ....San Luis Obispo CA 93403	**800-444-3061**		295-37
Spice World Inc			
8101 Presidents Dr ....Orlando FL 32809	**800-433-4979**		295-37
Spicers Paper Inc			
12310 Slauson Ave ....Santa Fe Springs CA 90670	**800-774-2377**	562-698-1199	546
Spider Staging Corp			
365 Upland Dr ....Tukwila WA 98188	**877-774-3370**	206-575-6445	486
Spillman Technologies Inc			
4625 Lake Pk Blvd ....Salt Lake City UT 84120	**800-860-8026***	801-902-1200	179-10
*General			
Spilltech Environmental Inc			
1627 Odonoghue St ....Mobile AL 36615	**800-228-3877**		601
Spin Master Ltd			
450 Front St W ....Toronto ON M5V1B6	**800-622-8339**	416-364-6002	752
Spina Bifida Assn (SBAA)			
4590 MacArthur Blvd NW			
Ste 250 ....Washington DC 20007	**866-546-8372**	202-944-3285	47-17
Spindrift Inn			
652 Cannery Row ....Monterey CA 93940	**800-841-1879**	831-646-8900	376
SpinGo Solutions Inc			
14193 S Minuteman Dr Ste 100 ....Draper UT 84020	**877-377-4646**		384
Spinnaker Coating Inc			
518 E Water St ....Troy OH 45373	**800-543-9452**	937-332-6500	547
Spiral Binding Company Inc			
One Maltese Dr ....Totowa NJ 07511	**800-631-3572**	973-256-0666	85
Spiralock Corp			
25235 Dequindre Rd ....Madison Heights MI 48071	**800-521-2688**	248-543-7800	488
Spirax Sarco Inc			
1150 Northpoint Blvd ....Blythewood SC 29016	**800-883-4411**	803-714-2000	202
Spire Corp			
1 Patriots Pk ....Bedford MA 01730	**800-510-4815**	781-275-6000	686
OTC: SPIR			
Spire Inc 65 Bay St ....Boston MA 02125	**877-350-8837**	617-350-8837	341
Spirit Airlines Inc			
2800 Executive Way ....Miramar FL 33025	**800-772-7117**		25
NASDAQ: SAVE			
Spirit Manufacturing Inc			
2601 Commerce Dr ....Jonesboro AR 72402	**800-258-4555**	870-935-1107	267
Spirite Industries Inc			
150 S Dean St ....Englewood NJ 07631	**800-272-6897**	201-871-4910	153-17
Spiritled Woman - Charisma Magazine			
600 Rinehart Rd ....Lake Mary FL 32746	**866-776-6473**	407-333-0600	452-18
Spiritual Life Ctr			
7100 E 45th St N ....Wichita KS 67226	**800-348-2440**	316-744-0167	664
SPJ (Society of Professional Journalists)			
3909 N Meridian St ....Indianapolis IN 46208	**800-331-1212**	317-927-8000	48-14
SPL Integrated Solutions			
6301 Benjamin Rd Ste 101 ....Tampa FL 33634	**800-292-4125**	813-884-7168	725
Splendora Independent School District			
23419 FM 2090 Rd ....Splendora TX 77372	**866-861-2010**	281-689-3128	676

	Toll-Free	Phone	Class
Split Rock Creek State Park			
50th Ave ....Jasper MN 56144	**888-646-6367**	507-348-7908	558
Split Rock Lighthouse State Park			
3755 Split Rock Lighthouse Rd...... Two Harbors MN 55616	**800-366-8917**	218-595-7625	558
Split Rock Resort			
100 Moseywood Rd ....Lake Harmony PA 18624	**800-255-7625**	570-722-9111	660
Spokane Art Supply Inc			
1303 N Monroe St ....Spokane WA 99201	**800-556-5568**	509-327-6622	44
Spokane Civic Theatre			
1020 N Howard St ....Spokane WA 99201	**800-325-7328**	509-325-1413	565
Spokane Community College			
1810 N Greene St ....Spokane WA 99217	**800-248-5644**	509-533-7000	160
Spokane Convention & Visitors Bureau			
801 W Riverside Ste 301 ....Spokane WA 99201	**800-662-0084**	509-624-1341	207
Spokane Falls Community College			
3410 W Ft George Wright Dr ....Spokane WA 99224	**888-509-7944**	509-533-3500	160
Spokane Hardware Supply Inc			
2001 E Trent Ave ....Spokane WA 99202	**800-888-1663**	509-535-1663	347
Spokane International Airport			
9000 W Airport Dr ....Spokane WA 99224	**855-787-2227**	509-455-6455	27
Spokane Public Radio			
2319 N Monroe St ....Spokane WA 99205	**800-328-5729**	509-328-5729	636-104
Spokane Symphony			
PO Box 365 ....Spokane WA 99210	**800-899-1482**	509-624-1200	566-3
Spokane Valley Mall			
14700 E Indiana Ave ....Spokane WA 99216	**800-326-3264**	509-926-3700	455
Spoon River College (SRC)			
23235 N County Hwy 22 ....Canton IL 61520	**800-334-7337**	309-647-4645	160
Spoon River Electric Co-op Inc (SREC)			
930 S Fifth Ave PO Box 340 ....Canton IL 61520	**877-404-2572**	309-647-2700	245
Sport Chalet Inc			
One Sport Chalet Dr ....La Canada CA 91011	**888-801-9162**	818-949-5300	702
NASDAQ: SPCHB			
Sport Clips Inc			
110 Briarwood Dr ....Georgetown TX 78628	**800-872-4247**	512-869-1201	309
Sport Obermeyer Ltd USA Inc			
115 AABC ....Aspen CO 81611	**800-525-4203**	970-925-5060	153-5
Sport Supply Group Inc			
1901 Diplomat Dr ....Dallas TX 75234	**800-527-7510**	972-484-9484	701
Sport-Haley Inc			
200 Union Blvd Ste 400 ....Denver CO 80228	**800-627-9211**	303-320-8800	153-3
SportPharma Inc			
Three Terminal Rd ....New Brunswick NJ 08901	**800-872-0101**	732-545-3130	787
Sports Afield Magazine			
15621 Chemical Ln .... Huntington Beach CA 92649	**800-451-4788**	714-373-4910	452-20
Sports Business Daily			
120 W Morehead St Ste 310..........Charlotte NC 28202	**800-829-9839**	704-973-1410	452-20
Sports Car Club of America (SCCA)			
6700 SW Topeka Blvd Ste 300 ....Topeka KS 66619	**800-770-2055**	785-357-7222	47-18
Sports Car Magazine			
16842 Von Karman Ave Ste 125 ....Irvine CA 92606	**800-722-7140**	949-417-6700	452-3
Sports Cardiovascular & Wellness Nutritionists (SCAN)			
4500 Rockside Rd Ste 400 ....Cleveland OH 44131	**800-249-2875***	216-503-0053	48-8
*General			
Sports Creek Raceway			
4290 Morrish Rd ....Swartz Creek MI 48473	**844-635-4708**	810-635-3333	633
Sports Empire			
PO Box 6169 ....Lakewood CA 90714	**800-255-5258**	562-920-2350	761
Sports Leisure Vacations			
9812 Old Winery Pl ....Sacramento CA 95827	**800-951-5556**	916-361-2051	750
Sports Promotion Network			
PO Box 200548 ....Arlington TX 76006	**800-460-9989**		702
Sports Spectrum Magazine			
105 Corporate Blvd Ste 2 ....Indian Trail NC 28079	**866-821-2971**	704-821-2971	452-20
Sports Travel Inc			
60 Main St PO Box 50 ....Hatfield MA 01038	**800-662-4424**	413-247-7678	750
Sports Turf Managers Assn (STMA)			
805 New Hampshire Ste E ....Lawrence KS 66044	**800-323-3875**	785-843-2549	47-22
Sportservice Corp			
40 Fountain Plz ....Buffalo NY 14202	**800-828-7240**	716-858-5000	298
SportsPlay Equipment Inc			
5642 Natural Bridge Ave ....Saint Louis MO 63120	**800-727-8180**	314-389-4140	343
Spotlight 29 Casino			
46-200 Harrison Pl ....Coachella CA 92236	**800-655-1330**	760-775-5566	132
Spotnails			
1100 Hicks Rd ....Rolling Meadows IL 60008	**800-873-2239**	847-259-1620	800
SpotOn Inc			
2350 Kerner Blvd Ste 380.............San Rafael CA 94901	**877-814-4102**		384
SPPD (Southern Public Power District)			
4550 W Husker Hwy			
PO Box 1687............. Grand Island NE 68803	**800-652-2013**	308-384-2350	245
Spradling International Inc			
200 Cahaba Vly Pkwy PO Box 1668 ...... Pelham AL 35124	**800-333-0955**	205-985-4206	587
Sprague Energy			
185 International Dr Ste 200.........Portsmouth NH 03801	**800-225-1560**	603-431-1000	572
Sprayway Inc			
500 S Vista Ave ....Addison IL 60101	**800-332-9000**	630-628-3000	143
Sprecher + Schuh			
15910 International Plaza Dr ....Houston TX 77032	**877-721-5913**	281-442-9000	204
Spring Arbor Distributors			
One Ingram Blvd ....La Vergne TN 37086	**800-395-4340**	615-793-5000	94
Spring Arbor University			
106 E Main St ....Spring Arbor MI 49283	**800-968-9103***	517-750-1200	166
*Admissions			
Spring Creek Barbeque			
2340 W I- 20 Ste 100 ....Arlington TX 76017	**888-467-0505**	817-467-0505	662
Spring Creek Ranch			
1800 Spirit Dance Rd ....Jackson WY 83001	**800-443-6139**	307-733-8833	376
Spring Dynamics Inc			
7378 Research Dr ....Almont MI 48003	**888-274-8432**	810-798-2622	710
Spring Engineers Inc			
9740 Tanner Rd ....Houston TX 77041	**800-899-9488**	713-690-9488	710
Spring Glen Fresh Foods Inc			
314 Spring Glen Dr PO Box 518.............Ephrata PA 17522	**800-641-2853**	717-733-2201	295-19
Spring Grove Cemetery			
4521 Spring Grove Ave ....Cincinnati OH 45232	**888-853-2230**	513-681-7526	503
Spring Grove Hospital Ctr			
55 Wade Ave ....Catonsville MD 21228	**866-734-3337***	410-402-6000	371-5
*General			
Spring Harbor Hospital			
123 Andover Rd ....Westbrook ME 04092	**888-524-0080**	207-761-2200	371-5

	Toll-Free	Phone	Class
Spring Hill College			
4000 Dauphin St .... Mobile AL 36608	800-742-6704*	251-380-4000	166
*Admissions			
Spring House Estates			
728 Norristown Rd .... Lower Gwynedd PA 19002	888-365-2287	215-628-8110	663
Spring Manufacturers Institute (SMI)			
2001 Midwest Rd Ste 106. .... Oak Brook IL 60523	866-482-5569	630-495-8588	48-13
Spring Mountain Vineyards			
2805 Spring Mtn Rd .... Saint Helena CA 94574	877-769-4637	707-967-4188	314-5
Springer Electric Co-op Inc			
408 Maxwell Ave PO Box 698. .... Springer NM 87747	800-288-1353	505-483-2421	245
Springfield Armory			
420 W Main St .... Geneseo IL 61254	800-680-6866	309-944-5631	284
Springfield Chamber of Commerce			
101 S 'A' St .... Springfield OR 97477	866-346-1651	541-746-1651	137
Springfield College			
263 Alden St .... Springfield MA 01109	800-343-1257*	413-748-3136	166
*Admissions			
Springfield College in Illinois - Benedictine University			
1500 N Fifth St .... Springfield IL 62702	800-635-7289	217-525-1420	160
Springfield Conservation Nature Ctr			
4600 S Chrisman Ave .... Springfield MO 65804	800-392-1111	417-888-4237	49-4
Springfield Convention & Visitors Bureau			
109 N Seventh St .... Springfield IL 62701	800-545-7300	217-789-2360	207
Springfield Electric Supply Co			
700 N Ninth St .... Springfield IL 62702	800-747-2101	217-788-2100	246
Springfield Hospital Ctr			
6655 Sykesville Rd .... Sykesville MD 21784	800-333-7564	410-970-7000	371-5
Springfield Missouri Convention & Visitors Bureau			
815 E St Louis St Ste 100. .... Springfield MO 65806	800-678-8767	417-881-5300	207
Springfield Museums			
21 Edwards St .... Springfield MA 01103	800-625-7738	413-263-6800	513
Springfield News Leader			
651 N Boonville Ave .... Springfield MO 65806	800-695-2005	417-836-1100	525-2
Springfield News-Sun			
202 N Limestone St .... Springfield OH 45503	800-441-6397	937-328-0300	525-2
Springfield Public School District #186			
1900 W Monroe St .... Springfield IL 62704	877-632-7753	217-525-3000	676
Springfield ReManufacturing Corp			
650 N Broadview Pl .... Springfield MO 65802	800-772-7733	417-862-3501	262
Springfield Technical Community College			
1 Armory Sq PO Box 900 .... Springfield MA 01102	800-326-6142	413-781-7822	160
Spring-Green Lawn Care Corp			
11909 Spaulding School Dr .... Plainfield IL 60585	800-435-4051	815-436-8777	570
Springmaid Beach Resort			
3200 S Ocean Blvd .... Myrtle Beach SC 29577	866-764-8501		698
Springs Window Fashions LP			
7549 Graber Rd .... Middleton WI 53562	877-792-0002	608-836-1011	358
Sprocket Staffing Services			
35 Colby Ave .... Manasquan NJ 08736	800-269-1441		260
SPROUT Wellness Solutions Inc			
366 Adelaide St W Ste 301. .... Toronto ON M5V1R9	866-535-5027		224
SPS (Southern Pan Services Co)			
2385 Lithonia Industrial Blvd			
PO Box 679. .... Lithonia GA 30058	800-334-9145	678-301-2400	770
Spurlin Industries Inc			
625 Main St .... Palmetto GA 30268	800-749-4475	770-463-1644	372
SPX Cooling Technologies			
7401 W 129th St .... Overland Park KS 66213	800-462-7539	913-664-7400	90
SPX Corp			
13515 Ballantyne Corporate Pl .... Charlotte NC 28277	877-247-3797	704-752-4400	186
NYSE: SPW			
SPX Corp OTC Div			
655 Eisenhower Dr .... Owatonna MN 55060	800-533-6127	507-455-7000	747
SPX Corp Robinair Div			
655 Eisenhower Dr .... Owatonna MN 55060	800-628-6496	507-455-7000	203
SQN Banking Systems			
65 Indel Ave Second Fl. .... Rancocas NJ 08073	888-744-7226	609-261-5500	179-10
Square Books			
160 Courthouse Sq .... Oxford MS 38655	800-648-4001*	662-236-2262	95
Square One Mall			
1201 Broadway .... Saugus MA 01906	877-746-6642	781-233-8787	455
Squaw Valley USA			
PO Box 2007 .... Olympic Valley CA 96146	800-403-0206	530-583-6955	660
Squire Patton Boggs			
127 Public Sq 4900 Key Tower. .... Cleveland OH 44114	800-743-2773	216-479-8500	425
SRA (Society for Risk Analysis)			
1313 Dolley Madison Blvd Ste 402 ..... McLean VA 22101	800-364-5800	703-790-1745	48-19
SRA International Inc			
4300 Fair Lakes Ct .... Fairfax VA 22033	800-511-6398	703-803-1500	181
SRAM Corp			
1333 N Kingsbury St 4th Fl .... Chicago IL 60622	800-346-2928	312-664-8800	81
SRC (Spoon River College)			
23235 N County Hwy 22 .... Canton IL 61520	800-334-7337	309-647-4645	160
SRC (Syracuse Research Corp)			
7502 Round Pond Rd .... North Syracuse NY 13212	800-724-0451	315-452-8000	659
SRDS			
1700 Higgins Rd .... Des Plaines IL 60018	800-851-7737	847-375-5000	628-2
SREC (Spoon River Electric Co-op Inc)			
930 S Fifth Ave PO Box 340 .... Canton IL 61520	877-404-2572	309-647-2700	245
SriLankan Airlines			
379 Thornall St 6th Fl. .... Edison NJ 08837	877-915-2652	732-205-0017	25
SriLankan Travel Inc			
379 Thornall St Sixth Fl .... Edison NJ 08837	877-915-2652	732-205-0017	26
SRMC (Saint Rita's Medical Ctr)			
730 W Market St .... Lima OH 45801	800-232-7762	419-227-3361	371-3
SRMC (Spartanburg Regional Medical Ctr)			
101 E Wood St .... Spartanburg SC 29303	800-318-2596	864-560-6000	371-3
SRMC (Sonora Regional Medical Ctr)			
1000 Greenly Rd .... Sonora CA 95370	877-336-3566*	209-536-5000	371-3
*Compliance			
SRP (Salt River Project)			
1521 N Project Dr .... Tempe AZ 85281	800-258-4777	602-236-5900	775
SRS Labs Inc			
2909 Daimler St .... Santa Ana CA 92705	800-243-2733*	949-442-1070	687
NASDAQ: SRSL ■ *General			
SRT (Seattle Repertory Theatre)			
155 Mercer St PO Box 900923. .... Seattle WA 98109	877-900-9285	206-443-2210	566-4
SS & C Technologies Inc			
80 Lamberton Rd .... Windsor CT 06095	800-234-0556	860-298-4500	179-11
SS Nesbitt & Co Inc			
3500 Blue Lake Dr .... Birmingham AL 35243	800-422-3223	205-262-2700	388-4
S&S Public Relations Inc			
One Northfield Plz Ste 400 .... Northfield IL 60093	800-287-2279		627
SSA (Self Storage Assn)			
1900 N Beauregard St Ste 450 .... Alexandria VA 22311	888-735-3784	703-575-8000	48-21
SSA (Social Security Administration)			
6401 Security Blvd .... Baltimore MD 21235	800-772-1213	410-965-8904	338-18
SSA Marine			
1131 SW Klickitat Way .... Seattle WA 98134	800-422-3505	206-623-0304	460
SSAI (Support Systems Assoc Inc)			
709 S Harbor City Blvd			
Ste 350 .... Melbourne FL 32901	877-234-7724	321-724-5566	261
SSAT (Society for Surgery of the Alimentary Tract)			
900 Cummings Ctr Ste 221-U .... Beverly MA 01915	866-849-5866	978-927-8330	48-8
Ssci			
3065 Kent Ave .... West Lafayette IN 47906	800-375-2179	765-463-0112	195
SSCS (IEEE Solid State Circuits Society)			
445 Hoes Ln .... Piscataway NJ 08854	800-678-4333	732-981-3400	48-19
SSgA Funds			
One Lincoln St .... Boston MA 02111	800-997-7327	617-786-3000	521
SSIT (IEEE Society on Social Implications of Technology)			
IEEE Operations Ctr			
445 Hoes Ln .... Piscataway NJ 08854	800-678-4333	732-981-0060	48-19
SSJCPL (Stockton-San Joaquin County Public Library)			
605 N El Dorado St .... Stockton CA 95202	866-805-7323	209-937-8416	431-3
SSM Health			
620 E Monroe St .... Mexico MO 65265	844-776-9355	573-582-5000	371-3
SSM Healthy			
1000 N. Lee St .... Oklahoma City OK 73102	866-203-5846	618-242-4600	350
SSM Hospice			
2 Harbor Bend Ct .... Lake Saint Louis MO 63367	800-835-1212	636-695-2050	368
SSM Rehabilitation Hospital			
6420 Clayton Rd .... Saint Louis MO 63117	800-818-9494	314-768-5300	371-6
SSPC (Society for Protective Coatings)			
40 24th St Sixth Fl .... Pittsburgh PA 15222	877-281-7772	412-281-2331	48-13
SSS Co			
71 University Ave PO Box 4447 .... Atlanta GA 30315	800-237-3843	404-521-0857	576
SST Corp			
635 Brighton Rd .... Clifton NJ 07012	800-222-0921	973-473-4300	474
SSW (Episcopal Theological Seminary of the Southwest)			
501 E 32nd PO Box 2247 .... Austin TX 78705	800-252-5400	512-472-4133	167-3
St Agnes Hospital			
430 E Div St .... Fond du Lac WI 54935	800-922-3400	920-929-2300	371-3
St Alexius Medical Ctr			
900 E Broadway Ave .... Bismarck ND 58501	877-530-5550	701-530-7755	371-3
S&T Bancorp Inc			
800 Philadelphia St .... Indiana PA 15701	800-325-2265	724-349-1800	357-2
NASDAQ: STBA			
S&T Bank			
800 Philadelphia St PO Box 190. .... Indiana PA 15701	800-325-2265*	724-349-1800	69
*Cust Svc			
S-T Industries Inc			
301 Armstrong Blvd N .... Saint James MN 56081	800-326-2039	507-375-3211	488
St James Hotel			
406 Main St .... Red Wing MN 55066	800-252-1875	651-388-2846	376
St John Providence Health System			
28000 Dequindre .... Warren MI 48092	866-501-3627		371-3
ST Johnson Co			
925 Stanford Ave .... Oakland CA 94608	800-225-1348	510-652-6000	317
St Joseph Communications			
50 MacIntosh Blvd .... Concord ON L4K4P3	877-660-3111*	905-660-3111	619
*General			
St Julien Hotel & Spa			
900 Walnut St .... Boulder CO 80302	877-303-0900	720-406-9696	376
St Lawrence County Chamber of Commerce			
101 Main St .... Canton NY 13617	877-228-7810	315-386-4000	137
St Mary's County Maryland Libraries			
23250 Hollywood Rd .... Leonardtown MD 20650	800-783-3625	301-475-2846	431-3
St Moritz Security Services Inc			
4600 Clairton Blvd .... Pittsburgh PA 15236	800-218-9156	412-885-3144	684
St Paul Flight Ctr			
270 Airport Rd .... Saint Paul MN 55107	800-368-0107	651-227-8108	62
St Petersburg General Hospital			
6500 38th Ave N .... Saint Petersburg FL 33710	800-733-0610	727-384-1414	371-3
St Renatus LLC			
1000 Centre Ave .... Fort Collins CO 80526	888-686-2314	970-282-0156	231
St.Vincent Health			
2001 W 86th St .... Indianapolis IN 46260	866-338-2345	317-338-2345	445
STA (Student Transportation of America Inc)			
3349 Hwy 138 Bldg B Ste D. .... Wall NJ 07719	888-942-2250	732-280-4200	108
Sta International			
1400 Old Country Rd Ste 411. .... Westbury NY 11590	866-970-9882	516-997-2400	216
STA Overlaminations			
100 S Puente St .... Brea CA 92821	800-235-8273	714-255-7888	722
STAAR Surgical Co			
1911 Walker Ave .... Monrovia CA 91016	800-352-7842	626-303-7902	535
NASDAQ: STAA			
Stabila Inc			
332 Industrial Dr			
P.O. Box 402. .... South Elgin IL 60177	800-869-7460		748
Stackbin Corp			
29 Powderhill Rd .... Lincoln RI 02865	800-333-1603*	401-333-1600	199
*Sales			
Stack-On Products Co			
1360 N Old Rand Rd .... Wauconda IL 60084	800-323-9601	847-526-1611	483
Stackpole Books			
5067 Ritter Rd . ... Mechanicsburg PA 17055	800-732-3669*	717-796-0411	628-2
*Sales			
Stafast Products Inc			
505 Lk Shore Blvd .... Painesville OH 44077	800-782-3278	440-357-5546	278
STAFDA (Specialty Tools & Fasteners Distributors Assn)			
500 Elm Grove Rd Ste 210			
PO Box 44. .... Elm Grove WI 53122	800-352-2981	262-784-4774	48-18
Staff Management Inc			
5919 Spring Creek Rd .... Rockford IL 61114	800-535-3518*	815-282-3900	623
*General			
Staff One Inc			
8111 LBJ Fwy .... Dallas TX 75251	800-771-7823		623
Staffdigest Magazine			
PO Box 384 Ste H3. .... Alief TX 77411	800-444-0674*	281-498-2913	452-5
*General			
Stafford-Smith Inc			
3414 S Burdick St .... Kalamazoo MI 49001	800-968-2442	269-343-1240	656
Staffworks Group			
20505 W 12 Mile Rd .... Southfield MI 48076	877-304-9690		260

Name / Address	City	State	Zip	Toll-Free	Phone	Class
Stage Neck Inn						
Eight Stage Neck Rd Rt 1A						
PO Box 70	York Harbor	ME	03911	**800-222-3238**	207-363-3850	660
Stahl Specialty Co						
11 E Pacific PO Box 6	Kingsville	MO	64061	**800-821-7852**	816-597-3322	307
STAHL/A Scott Fetzer Co						
3201 W Old Lincoln Way	Wooster	OH	44691	**800-277-8245**	330-264-7441	509
Sta-Home Hospice						
406 Briarwood Dr Bldg 200	Jackson	MS	39206	**800-782-4663**	601-956-5100	360
Staker Parson Cos						
2350 South 1900 West	Ogden	UT	84401	**888-672-7766**	801-731-1111	189-4
Staley Inc						
8101 Fourche Rd	Little Rock	AR	72209	**877-616-0661**	501-565-3006	190-4
Stallings Crop Insurance Corp						
PO Box 6100	Lakeland	FL	33807	**800-721-7099**	863-647-2747	387
Stamas Yacht Inc						
300 Pampas Ave	Tarpon Springs	FL	34689	**800-782-6271***	727-937-4118	89
*Sales						
Stamats Communications Inc						
615 Fifth St SE	Cedar Rapids	IA	52401	**800-553-8878**	319-364-6167	628-9
Stambaugh Auditorium						
1000 Fifth Ave	Youngstown	OH	44504	**866-516-2269**	330-747-5175	565
Stamford Chamber of Commerce						
733 Summer St Ste 104	Stamford	CT	06901	**866-262-4548**	203-359-4761	137
Stamford Suites						
720 Bedford St	Stamford	CT	06901	**866-394-4365**	203-359-7300	376
Stampede Meat Inc						
7351 S 78th Ave	Bridgeview	IL	60455	**800-353-0933**		295-26
Stamper Black Hills Gold Jewelry						
7201 S Hwy 16	Rapid City	SD	57702	**800-843-8753***	605-342-0751	406
*Cust Svc						
Stamp-Rite Inc						
154 S Larch St	Lansing	MI	48912	**800-328-1988**	517-487-5071	462
Stamps.com Inc						
1990 E Grand Ave	El Segundo	CA	90245	**855-889-7867**		179-1
NASDAQ: STMP						
Stan Houston Equipment Co						
501 S Marion Rd	Sioux Falls	SD	57106	**800-952-3033**	605-336-3727	355
Stan Hywet Hall & Gardens						
714 N Portage Path	Akron	OH	44303	**888-836-5533**	330-836-5533	513
Stan's Lumber Inc						
226 E Main St	Twin Lakes	WI	53181	**800-535-2890**	262-877-2181	192-3
Stanadyne Corp						
92 Deerfield Rd	Windsor	CT	06095	**888-336-3473**	860-525-0821	59
Stanbio Laboratory LP						
1261 N Main St	Boerne	TX	78006	**800-531-5535**	830-249-0772	231
Stanbury Uniforms Inc						
108 Stanbury Industrial Dr						
PO Box 100	Brookfield	MO	64628	**800-826-2246**	660-258-2246	153-18
Stancil Corp						
2644 S Croddy Way	Santa Ana	CA	92704	**800-290-4103**	714-546-2002	51
Standard & Poor's Corp						
55 Water St	New York	NY	10041	**877-772-5436**	212-438-1000	628-2
Standard Air & Lite Corp						
2406 Woodmere Dr	Pittsburgh	PA	15205	**800-472-2458**	412-920-6505	605
Standard Alloys & Mfg						
PO Box 969	Port Arthur	TX	77640	**800-231-8240**	409-983-3201	632
Standard Bank & Trust Co						
7800 W 95th St	Hickory Hills	IL	60457	**866-499-2265**	708-598-7400	69
Standard Digital Imaging						
4426 S 108th St	Omaha	NE	68137	**800-642-8062**	402-592-1292	240
Standard Duplicating Machines Corp						
10 Connector Rd	Andover	MA	01810	**800-526-4774**	978-470-1920	111
Standard Electric Co						
2650 Trautner Dr PO Box 5289	Saginaw	MI	48603	**800-322-0215**	989-497-2100	246
Standard Electric Supply Co						
222 N Emmber Ln PO Box 651	Milwaukee	WI	53233	**800-776-8222**	414-272-8100	246
Standard Filter Corp						
5928 Balfour Ct	Carlsbad	CA	92008	**800-634-5837**	760-929-8559	18
Standard Furniture Mfg Company Inc						
801 Hwy 31 S	Bay Minette	AL	36507	**877-788-1899***	251-937-6741	318-2
*General						
Standard Imaging Inc						
3120 Deming Way	Middleton	WI	53562	**800-261-4446**	608-831-0025	630
Standard Knapp Inc						
63 Pickering St	Portland	CT	06480	**800-628-9565***	860-342-1100	540
*Cust Svc						
Standard Life Insurance Company of Indiana						
10689 N Pennsylvania St	Indianapolis	IN	46280	**800-222-3216**	317-574-6201	388-2
Standard Locknut Inc						
1045 E 169th St	Westfield	IN	46074	**800-783-6887**	317-867-0100	449
Standard Meat Company LP						
5105 Investment Dr	Dallas	TX	75236	**866-859-6313**	214-561-0561	295-26
Standard Mfg Company Inc						
750 Second Ave	Troy	NY	12182	**800-227-1056***	518-235-2200	153-5
*Cust Svc						
Standard Motors Ltd						
44 Second Ave NW	Swift Current	SK	S9H3V6	**800-268-3131**	306-773-3131	56
Standard Parking Corp						
900 N Michigan Ave Ste 1600	Chicago	IL	60611	**888-700-7275**	312-274-2000	555
Standard Publishing Co						
8805 Governors Hill Dr						
Ste 400	Cincinnati	OH	45249	**800-543-1353***	513-931-4050	628-9
*Orders						
Standard Register Co						
600 Albany St	Dayton	OH	45417	**800-755-6405**	937-221-1825	109
OTC: SRCTQ						
Standard Roofing Co						
516 N McDonough St						
PO Box 1309	Montgomery	AL	36102	**800-239-5705**	334-265-1262	190-12
Standard Sales Co Inc						
4800 E 42nd St Ste 400	Odessa	TX	79762	**800-331-5453**	432-367-7662	80-1
Standard Textile Company Inc						
One Knollcrest Dr	Cincinnati	OH	45237	**800-999-0400**	513-761-9255	472
Standard Textile Company Inc Decorative Products						
One Knollcrest Dr	Cincinnati	OH	45237	**800-999-0400***	513-761-9255	735
*General						
Standard, The						
40 Island Ave	Miami Beach	FL	33139	**800-327-8363**	305-673-1717	660
Standard-Examiner						
332 Standard Way	Ogden	UT	84404	**800-234-5505**	801-625-4200	525-2
Standards Council of Canada						
270 Albert St Ste 200	Ottawa	ON	K1P6N7	**800-844-6790**	613-238-3222	461
Standex Electronics Inc						
4538 Camberwell Rd	Cincinnati	OH	45209	**866-782-6339**	513-871-3777	253
Standex International Corp						
11 Keewaydin Dr	Salem	NH	03079	**800-514-5275**	603-893-9701	186
NYSE: SXI						
Standex International Corp Consumer Group						
11 Keewaydin Dr	Salem	NH	03079	**800-514-5275**	603-893-9701	628-3
NYSE: SXI						
Standex International Corp Custom Hoists Div						
771 County Rd 30A W						
PO Box 98	Hayesville	OH	44838	**800-837-4668**	419-368-4721	223
Standex International Corp Food Service Equipment Group						
11 Keewaydin Dr	Salem	NH	03079	**800-647-1284**	603-893-9701	299
NYSE: SXI						
Stanford Cancer Ctr						
875 Lake Blake Wilbur Dr	Stanford	CA	94305	**800-422-6237**	650-498-6000	659
Stanford Federal Credit Union						
1860 Embarcadero Rd	Palo Alto	CA	94303	**888-723-7328**	650-723-2509	219
Stanford University						
450 Serra Mall	Stanford	CA	94305	**877-407-9529**	650-723-2091	166
Stanford University Green Library						
557 Escondido Mall	Stanford	CA	94305	**800-521-0600**	650-723-2300	431-6
Stanford University Press						
1450 Page Mill Rd	Palo Alto	CA	94304	**800-621-2736**	650-723-9434	628-4
Stanford University School of Medicine Blood & Marrow Transplant Program						
300 Pasteur Dr						
Rm H-3249 MC 5623	Stanford	CA	94305	**888-275-5724**	650-723-0822	759
Stanion Wholesale Electric Co						
812 S Main St PO Box F	Pratt	KS	67124	**866-782-6466**	620-672-5678	246
Stanislaus Farm Supply Co						
624 E Service Rd	Modesto	CA	95358	**800-323-0725**	209-538-7070	276
Stanislaus Food Products Co						
1202 D St	Modesto	CA	95354	**800-327-7201**		295-20
Stanley Access Technologies						
65 Scott Swamp Rd	Farmington	CT	06032	**800-722-2377**	860-677-2861	234
Stanley Assembly Technologies Div						
5335 Avion Pk Dr	Cleveland	OH	44143	**877-787-7830**	440-461-5500	749
Stanley Consultants Inc						
225 Iowa Ave	Muscatine	IA	52761	**800-553-9694**	563-264-6600	261
Stanley Creations Inc						
1414 Willow Ave	Melrose Park	PA	19027	**800-220-1414**	215-635-6200	406
Stanley Hotel						
333 Wonderview Ave	Estes Park	CO	80517	**800-976-1377**	970-586-3371	376
Stanley Hunt DuPree & Rhine Inc (SHDR)						
7701 Airport Ctr Dr	Greensboro	NC	27409	**888-999-4701**	800-768-4873	194
Stanley Korshak						
500 Crescent Ct Ste 100	Dallas	TX	75201	**855-749-9539**	214-871-3600	155-4
Stanley Martin Cos						
11111 Sunset Hills Rd Ste 200	Reston	VA	20190	**800-446-4807**	703-964-5000	644
Stanley Supply & Services Inc						
335 Willow St	North Andover	MA	01845	**888-887-9473***	978-682-2000	748
*Cust Svc						
Stanley Tools Inc						
480 Myrtle St	New Britain	CT	06053	**800-262-2161***	860-225-5111	748
*Cust Svc						
Stanley Vidmar Storage Technologies						
11 Grammes Rd	Allentown	PA	18103	**800-523-9462**		286
Stanly Community College						
141 College Dr	Albemarle	NC	28001	**877-275-4219**	704-982-0121	788
Stant Corp						
1620 Columbia Ave	Connersville	IN	47331	**800-822-3121**	765-825-3121	601
Stantec Inc						
400 E Vine St Ste 300	Lexington	KY	40507	**866-782-6832**	859-233-2100	261
NYSE: STN						
Stanton Carpet Corp						
211 Robbins Ln	Syosset	NY	11791	**888-809-2989**	516-822-5878	361
Stanton County Public Power District						
807 Douglas St	Stanton	NE	68779	**877-439-2300**	402-439-2228	245
Stanton's Sheet Music						
330 S Fourth St	Columbus	OH	43215	**800-426-8742**	614-224-4257	519
Staplcotn Co-op Assn Inc						
214 W Market St	Greenwood	MS	38930	**800-293-6231**	662-453-6231	275
Staples Business Advantage						
500 Staples Dr	Framingham	MA	01702	**877-826-7755**		527
Staples Construction Company Inc						
1501 Eastman Ave	Ventura	CA	93003	**800-881-4650**	805-658-8786	458
Staples Promotional Products						
7500 W 110th St	Overland Park	KS	66210	**800-369-4669**	913-319-3100	9
Stapleton Technologies Inc						
1350 W 12th St	Long Beach	CA	90813	**800-266-0541**	562-437-0541	143
Stapleton-Spence Packing Co						
1530 The Alameda Ste 320	San Jose	CA	95126	**800-297-8815**	408-297-8815	295-20
Staplex Co						
777 Fifth Ave	Brooklyn	NY	11232	**800-221-0822***	718-768-3333	110
*Cust Svc						
Star 92.9						
265 Hegeman Ave	Colchester	VT	05446	**866-865-7827**	802-655-0093	636
Star Beacon						
PO Box 2100	Ashtabula	OH	44005	**800-554-6768**	440-998-2323	525-2
Star Bldg Systems						
8600 S I-35	Oklahoma City	OK	73149	**800-879-7827**		104
Star Casualty Insurance Company Inc						
PO Box 451037	Miami	FL	33134	**877-782-7210**		387
Star Clippers Inc						
760 NW 107th Ave	Miami	FL	33172	**800-442-0556***	305-442-0550	220
*Resv						
Star Cutter Co						
23461 Industrial Pk Dr	Farmington	MI	48335	**877-635-3488**	248-474-8200	488
Star Democrat						
29088 Airpark Dr PO Box 600	Easton	MD	21601	**800-734-3158**	410-822-1500	525-2
Star Distributors Inc						
460 Frontage Rd	West Haven	CT	06516	**877-922-3501**	203-932-3636	80-1
Star Fleet Inc						
PO Box 769	Goshen	IN	46527	**877-805-9547**	888-281-8727	770
Star Ford Lincoln						
1100 S Brand Blvd	Glendale	CA	91204	**800-239-0755**	818-956-0977	56
Star Furniture Company Inc						
16666 Barker Springs Rd	Houston	TX	77084	**800-364-6661**	281-492-6661	320
Star Gas Partners LP						
2187 Atlantic St	Stamford	CT	06902	**877-237-3063**	203-328-7310	315
NYSE: SGU						
Star Insurance Co						
26255 American Dr	Southfield	MI	48034	**800-482-2726**	248-204-8299	388-4

	City	State	ZIP	Toll-Free	Phone	Class
Star Island Resort						
5000 Ave of the Stars	Kissimmee	FL	34746	**800-513-2820**	407-997-8000	376
Star Leasing Co						
4080 Business Pk Dr	Columbus	OH	43204	**888-771-1004**	614-278-9999	768
Star Micronics America Inc						
1150 King George's Post Rd	Edison	NJ	08837	**800-782-7636**	732-623-5500	174-6
Star Milling Co						
24067 Water St	Perris	CA	92570	**800-733-6455**	951-657-3143	442
Star Multi Care Services Inc						
115 Broad Hollow Rd Ste 275	Melville	NY	11747	**877-920-0600**	631-424-7827	360
Star Nail Products Inc						
29120 Ave Paine	Valencia	CA	91355	**800-762-6245**	661-257-7827	215
Star of the West Milling Co						
121 E Tuscola St	Frankenmuth	MI	48734	**888-281-4161**	989-652-9971	10-3
Star One Federal Credit Union						
PO Box 3643	Sunnyvale	CA	94088	**866-543-5202**	408-543-5202	219
Star Pipe LLC						
4018 Westhollow Pkwy	Houston	TX	77082	**800-999-3009**	281-558-3000	588
Star Rentals Inc						
1919 Fourth Ave S	Seattle	WA	98134	**800-825-7880**	206-622-7880	264-3
Star Sales & Distributing Corp						
29 Commerce Way	Woburn	MA	01801	**800-222-8118**	781-933-8830	192-2
Star Sales Company Inc						
1803 N Central St	Knoxville	TN	37917	**800-347-9494**	865-524-0771	327
Star Trac by Unisen Inc						
14410 Myford Rd	Irvine	CA	92606	**800-228-6635**	714-669-1660	267
Star Transportation Inc						
PO Box 100925	Nashville	TN	37224	**800-333-3060***	615-256-4336	770
*Cust Svc						
Star Travel Services Inc						
1025 Acuff Rd Fourth Fl	Bloomington	IN	47404	**800-542-1687**	812-336-6811	761
Star Tribune						
425 Portland Ave	Minneapolis	MN	55488	**800-827-8742**	612-673-4000	525-2
Star Truck Rentals Inc						
3940 Eastern Ave SE	Grand Rapids	MI	49508	**800-748-0468**	616-243-7033	768
Star, The						
106 E Buena Vista Ave	North Augusta	SC	29841	**888-397-3742**	803-279-2793	525-4
Starboard Cruise Services Inc						
8400 NW 36th St	Miami	FL	33166	**800-540-4785**	786-845-7300	241
Starbucks Coffee Co						
2401 Utah Ave S	Seattle	WA	98134	**800-782-7282**	206-447-1575	157
Starco Impex Inc						
2710 S 11th St	Beaumont	TX	77701	**866-740-9601**		342
Starcraft Marine LLC						
68143 Clunette St PO Box 65	New Paris	IN	46553	**800-535-5722**	574-831-2103	89
Stardock Systems Inc						
15090 N Beck Rd Ste 300	Plymouth	MI	48170	**888-782-7362**	734-927-0677	175
Star-Gazette						
201 Baldwin St	Elmira	NY	14902	**800-836-8970**	607-734-5151	525-2
Stark & Stark						
993 Lenox Dr Bldg 2	Lawrenceville	NJ	08648	**800-535-3425**	609-896-9060	425
Stark State College of Technology						
6200 Frank Ave NW	North Canton	OH	44720	**800-797-8275**	330-494-6170	788
Starkey Laboratories Inc						
6700 Washington Ave S	Eden Prairie	MN	55344	**800-328-8602**	952-941-6401	472
Starkweather & Shepley Inc						
60 Catamore Blvd	East Providence	RI	02914	**800-854-4625**	401-435-3600	387
Star-Ledger, The						
One Star Ledger Plz	Newark	NJ	07102	**800-501-2100**	973-877-4141	525-2
Starlight Theatre						
4600 Starlight Rd Swope Pk	Kansas City	MO	64132	**800-776-1730**	816-363-7827	565
Starlite Limousines LLC						
PO Box 13542	Scottsdale	AZ	85267	**800-875-4104**	480-422-3619	437
Starmark Cabinetry						
600 E 48th St N	Sioux Falls	SD	57104	**800-755-7789**	800-594-9444	114
Star-News						
PO Box 840	Wilmington	NC	28402	**800-272-1277**	910-343-2000	525-2
Starr Bus Charter & Tours						
2531 E State St	Trenton	NJ	08619	**800-782-7703**	609-587-0626	106
Starr Commonwealth						
13725 Starr Commonwealth Rd	Albion	MI	49224	**800-837-5591**	517-629-5591	47-15
Starr King School for the Ministry						
2441 LeConte Ave	Berkeley	CA	94709	**866-727-4894**	510-845-6232	167-3
STARR Life Sciences Corp						
333 Allegheny Ave Ste 300	Oakmont	PA	15139	**866-978-2779**		416
Starrett Tru-Stone Technologies Div						
1101 Prosper Dr PO Box 430	Waite Park	MN	56387	**800-959-0517**	320-251-7171	715
Starrett Webber Gage Div						
24500 Detroit Rd	Cleveland	OH	44145	**800-255-3924**	440-835-0001	488
Startec Global Communications Corp						
11300 Rockville Pike Ste 900	Rockville	MD	20852	**800-827-3374**	301-610-4300	726
Starvin' Artist Supplies						
802 S Oak Pk	Oak Park	IL	60304	**800-427-8478**	708-358-3600	44
Starving Students Moving & Storage Co						
1850 Sawtelle Blvd Ste 300	Los Angeles	CA	90025	**888-931-6683**		512
Starwest Botanicals Inc						
11253 Trade Ctr Dr	Rancho Cordova	CA	95742	**800-800-4372***	916-638-8100	474
*General						
Starwood Hotels & Resorts Worldwide Inc						
Saint Regis Hotels & Resorts						
1111 Westchester Ave	White Plains	NY	10604	**888-625-4988**	914-640-8100	376
Westin Hotels & Resorts						
1111 Westchester Ave	White Plains	NY	10604	**888-625-5144**	914-640-8100	376
Starwood Hotels Preferred Guest Program						
111 Westchester Ave	White Plains	NY	10604	**888-625-4988**	512-834-2426	375
Starwood Vacation Ownership Inc						
Sheraton Vistana Resort						
8800 Vistana Ctr Dr	Orlando	FL	32821	**800-847-8262***	407-239-3100	743
*Resv						
State Auto National Insurance Co						
518 E Broad St	Columbus	OH	43215	**800-444-9950**	614-464-5000	388-4
State Auto Property & Casualty Insurance Co						
518 E Broad St	Columbus	OH	43215	**800-444-9950**	614-464-5000	388-4
State Automobile Mutual Insurance Co						
518 E Broad St	Columbus	OH	43215	**800-444-9950**	614-464-5000	388-4
State Bank						
175 N Leroy St	Fenton	MI	48430	**800-535-0517**	810-629-2263	69
State Bank of Waterloo						
PO Box 148	Waterloo	IL	62298	**800-367-7576**	618-939-7194	69
State Bar Assn of North Dakota						
504 N Washington St						
PO Box 2136	Bismarck	ND	58502	**800-472-2685**	701-255-1404	71
State Bar of Arizona						
4201 N 24th St Ste 200	Phoenix	AZ	85016	**866-482-9227**	602-252-4804	71
State Bar of Georgia						
104 Marietta St NW Ste 100	Atlanta	GA	30303	**800-334-6865**	404-527-8700	71
State Bar of Michigan						
306 Townsend St	Lansing	MI	48933	**800-968-1442**	517-346-6300	71
State Bar of Nevada						
600 E Charleston Blvd	Las Vegas	NV	89104	**800-254-2797**	702-382-2200	71
State Bar of New Mexico						
5121 Masthead St NE						
PO Box 92860	Albuquerque	NM	87109	**800-876-6227**	505-797-6000	71
State Bar of Texas						
1414 Colorado St	Austin	TX	78701	**800-204-2222**	512-427-1463	71
State Bar of Wisconsin						
5302 Eastpark Blvd	Madison	WI	53718	**800-728-7788**	608-257-3838	71
State Compensation Insurance Fund						
1275 Market St	San Francisco	CA	94103	**866-721-3498**	415-565-1234	388-4
State Electric Supply Company Inc						
2010 Second Ave	Huntington	WV	25703	**800-624-3417***	304-523-7491	246
*Cust Svc						
State Employees Credit Union of Maryland Inc						
971 Corporate Blvd	Linthicum	MD	21090	**800-879-7328**	410-487-7328	219
State Employees Federal Credit Union						
700 Patroon Creek Blvd						
Patroon Creek Corporate Ctr	Albany	NY	12206	**800-727-3328**	518-452-8234	219
State Employees' Credit Union (SECU)						
PO Box 29606	Raleigh	NC	27626	**888-732-8562**	919-857-2150	219
State Environment Daily						
1801 S Bell St	Arlington	VA	22202	**800-372-1033**		524-5
State Fair Community College						
3201 W 16th St	Sedalia	MO	65301	**877-311-7322**	660-530-5800	160
State Farm Financial Services FSB						
PO Box 2316	Bloomington	IL	61702	**877-734-2265**		69
State Farm Insurance						
One State Farm Plz	Bloomington	IL	61710	**800-447-4930**	309-766-2311	388-2
State Farm Mutual Funds						
PO Box 219548	Kansas City	MO	64121	**800-447-4930**		521
State Forest State Park						
56750 Hwy 14	Walden	CO	80480	**866-265-6447**	970-723-8366	558
State Historical Society of Missouri, The						
1020 Lowry St	Columbia	MO	65201	**800-747-6366**	573-882-1187	513
State Industrial Products						
3100 Hamilton Ave	Cleveland	OH	44114	**877-747-6986**	216-861-7114	149
State Journal, The						
1216 Wilkinson Blvd	Frankfort	KY	40601	**800-621-3362**	502-227-4556	525-2
State Journal-Register						
PO Box 219	Springfield	IL	62705	**800-397-6397**	217-788-1300	525-2
State Library of Ohio						
274 E First Ave Ste 100	Columbus	OH	43201	**800-686-1532**	614-644-7061	431-5
State Life Insurance Co						
One American Sq PO Box 368	Indianapolis	IN	46206	**800-537-6442***	317-285-2300	388-2
*Cust Svc						
State of the Heart Home Health & Hospice						
1350 N Broadway	Greenville	OH	45331	**800-417-7535**	937-548-2999	368
State Pipe & Supply Inc						
9615 S Norwalk Blvd	Santa Fe Springs	CA	90670	**800-733-6410**	562-695-5555	487
State Plaza Hotel						
2117 E St NW	Washington	DC	20037	**800-424-2859**	202-861-8200	376
State Supply Co						
597 Seventh St E	Saint Paul	MN	55130	**877-775-7705**	651-774-5985	603
State Teachers Retirement System of Ohio						
275 E Broad St	Columbus	OH	43215	**888-227-7877**		521
State Telephone Regulation Report						
2115 Ward Ct NW	Washington	DC	20037	**800-771-9202**	202-872-9200	524-11
State Theatre						
15 Livingston Ave	New Brunswick	NJ	08901	**888-636-1133**	732-247-7200	565
State Training School						
3211 Edgington Ave	Eldora	IA	50627	**800-362-2178**	641-858-5402	409
State University of New York						
Brockport						
350 New Campus Dr	Brockport	NY	14420	**888-800-0029**	585-395-2751	166
Canton 34 Cornell Dr	Canton	NY	13617	**800-388-7123**	315-386-7011	160
College of Agriculture & Technology at Cobleskill						
Rt 7	Cobleskill	NY	12043	**800-295-8988**	518-255-5525	166
College of Environmental Science & Forestry						
One Forestry Dr	Syracuse	NY	13210	**800-777-7373***	315-470-6500	166
*Admissions						
College of Technology at Alfred						
10 Upper College Dr	Alfred	NY	14802	**800-425-3733**	607-587-4215	160
Delhi Two Main St	Delhi	NY	13753	**800-963-3544**	607-746-4000	160
Empire State College						
One Union Ave	Saratoga Springs	NY	12866	**800-847-3000**	518-587-2100	166
Geneseo 1 College Cir	Geneseo	NY	14454	**866-245-5211***	585-245-5571	166
*Admitting						
Institute of Technology						
PO Box 3050	Utica	NY	13504	**866-278-6948**	315-792-7500	166
Maritime College						
6 Pennyfield Ave Fort Schuyler	Bronx	NY	10465	**888-800-0029**	718-409-7200	166
New Paltz						
One Hawk Dr	New Paltz	NY	12561	**877-696-7411**	845-257-3212	166
Plattsburgh						
101 Broad St	Plattsburgh	NY	12901	**888-673-0012***	518-564-2040	166
*Admissions						
Potsdam						
44 Pierrpont Ave	Potsdam	NY	13676	**877-768-7326***	315-267-2180	166
*Admissions						
University at Buffalo						
12 Capen Hall	Buffalo	NY	14260	**888-822-3648**	716-645-2450	166
State University of New York at Buffalo						
Health Sciences Library (HSL)						
3435 Main St Abbott Hall Rm 102	Buffalo	NY	14214	**866-432-5849**	716-829-3900	431-1
State University of New York Press (SUNY)						
22 Corporate Woods Blvd Third Fl	Albany	NY	12211	**866-430-7869**	518-472-5000	628-4
State University of New York Upstate Medical University						
766 Irving Ave	Syracuse	NY	13210	**800-736-2171**	315-464-4570	167-2
State University of New York, The (SUNY)						
State University Plz	Albany	NY	12246	**800-342-3811**	518-320-1888	774
State Volunteer Mutual Insurance Co						
101 W Pk Dr Ste 300	Brentwood	TN	37027	**800-342-2239**	615-377-1999	388-5
State, The						
1401 Shop Rd	Columbia	SC	29201	**800-888-5353**	803-771-6161	525-2
Statehouse Convention Ctr						
426 W Markham PO Box 3232	Little Rock	AR	72203	**800-844-4781**	501-376-4781	206
Staten Island Hotel						
1415 Richmond Ave	Staten Island	NY	10314	**800-230-4134**	718-698-5000	376

Alphabetical Section

	Toll-Free	Phone	Class
States Industries Inc			
PO Box 7037 ....Eugene OR 97401	800-626-1981	541-688-7871	606
Statesboro-Bulloch Chamber of Commerce			
102 S Main St ....Statesboro GA 30458	855-478-5551	912-764-6111	137
Statesville Brick Co			
391 BrickyaRd Rd ....Statesville NC 28677	800-522-4716	704-872-4123	148
Statewide Remodeling Inc			
2940 N Hwy 360 Ste 300 ....Grand Prairie TX 75050	800-317-8283	214-677-9000	235
Static Control Components Inc			
3010 Lee Ave PO Box 152 ......Sanford NC 27331	800-488-2426	919-774-3808	175
Station Casinos Inc			
1505 S Pavilion Ctr Dr ....Las Vegas NV 89135	800-634-3101*	702-495-3000	131
*Resv			
Stationers Inc			
1945 Fifth Ave ....Huntington WV 25703	800-862-7200	304-528-2780	528
Staub Metals Corp			
7747 E Rosecrans Ave ....Paramount CA 90723	800-447-8282	562-602-2200	487
Staunton National Cemetery			
901 Richmond Ave ....Staunton VA 24401	800-273-8255	540-825-0027	135
Stavis Seafoods Inc			
212 Northern Ave Ste 305.........Boston MA 02210	800-390-5103	617-482-6349	296-5
Stay Aspen Snowmass			
425 Rio Grande Pl ....Aspen CO 81611	888-649-5982	970-925-9000	373
STC (Society of Telecommunications Consultants)			
13275 California 89 ....Old Station CA 96071	800-782-7670	530-335-7313	48-20
Steadmantech			
1153 Powderhouse Rd ....Vestal NY 13850	866-772-0882		178
Steadyhand Investment Funds Limited Partnership			
1747 W Third Ave ....Vancouver BC V6J1K7	888-888-3147		521
Steak N Shake Co			
3810 W Washington Holt Rd ....Indianapolis IN 46241	877-785-6745	317-241-0483	661
Stealth Computer Corp			
530 Rowntree Dairy Rd Bldg 4 ....Woodbridge ON L4L8H2	888-783-2584	905-264-9000	174-1
Stealth Monitoring Inc			
15182 Marsh Lane ....Dallas TX 75001	855-783-2584	214-341-0123	684
Steam Bros Inc			
2400 Vermont Ave ....Bismarck ND 58504	800-767-5064	701-222-1263	150
Steamatic Inc			
3333 Quorum Dr Ste 280 ....Fort Worth TX 76137	888-783-2628*	817-332-1575	150
*General			
Steamboat Grand Resort Hotel & Conference Ctr			
2300 Mt Werner Cir ....Steamboat Springs CO 80487	877-269-2628	970-871-5500	660
Steamboat Ski & Resort Corp			
2305 Mt Werner Cir .....Steamboat Springs CO 80487	877-237-2628	970-879-6111	660
Steamtown National Historic Site			
150 S Washington Ave ....Scranton PA 18503	888-693-9391	570-340-5200	557
Stearns ElectricAssn			
900 E Kraft Dr ....Melrose MN 56352	800-962-0655	320-256-4241	245
Stearns Packaging Corp			
4200 Sycamore Ave ....Madison WI 53714	800-655-5008	608-246-5150	149
Stearns Weaver Miller Weissler Alhadeff & Sitterson P.A.			
150 W Flagler St Ste 2200 ....Miami FL 33130	866-293-7866	305-789-3200	425
Steel & Pipe Supply Co			
555 Poyntz Ave ....Manhattan KS 66502	800-521-2345	785-587-5100	487
Steel Ceilings Inc			
451 E Coshocton St ....Johnstown OH 43031	800-848-0496	740-967-1063	486
Steel City Corp			
190 N Meridian Rd ....Youngstown OH 44501	800-321-0350	330-792-7663	483
Steel Dynamics Inc			
7575 W Jefferson Blvd			
Ste 200 ....Fort Wayne IN 46804	866-740-8700	260-969-3500	714
NASDAQ: STLD			
Steel Grip Inc			
700 Garfield St PO Box 747 ....Danville IL 61832	800-223-1595	217-442-6240	569
Steel House Inc			
3644 Eastham Dr ....Culver City CA 90232	888-978-3354		5
Steel King Industries Inc			
2700 Chamber St ....Stevens Point WI 54481	800-826-0203	715-341-3120	465
Steel of West Virginia Inc			
17th St & Second Ave ....Huntington WV 25703	800-624-3492	304-696-8200	714
Steel Service Corp			
2260 Flowood Dr PO Box 321425 .....Jackson MS 39232	800-844-9222	601-939-9222	306
Steel Supply Co, The			
5101 Newport Dr ....Rolling Meadows IL 60008	800-323-7571		487
Steel Warehouse Company Inc			
2722 W Tucker Dr ....South Bend IN 46619	800-348-2529	574-236-5100	487
Steelcase Inc			
801 44th St SE PO Box 1967 ....Grand Rapids MI 49501	888-783-3522	616-247-2710	318-1
NYSE: SCS			
SteelCloud Inc			
20110 Ashbrook Pl Ste 270 ....Ashburn VA 20147	800-296-3866	703-674-5500	177
OTC: SCLD			
Steelcraft Mfg Co			
9017 Blue Ash Rd ....Cincinnati OH 45242	877-613-8766*	513-745-6400	234
*Cust Svc			
Steele Canvas Basket Corp			
201 William St PO Box 6267 IMCN ......Chelsea MA 02150	800-541-8929	617-889-0202	723
Steele Inc			
26112 Iowa Ave NE PO Box 7304.......Kingston WA 98346	888-783-3538	360-297-4555	569
Steele Truck Ctr Inc			
2150 Rockfill Rd ....Fort Myers FL 33916	888-806-4839	239-334-7300	56
Steele-Waseca Co-op Electric (SWCE)			
2411 W Bridge St PO Box 485 ....Owatonna MN 55060	800-526-3514	507-451-7340	245
Steelman Industries Inc			
2800 Hwy 135 N PO Box 1461........Kilgore TX 75662	800-287-6633	903-984-3061	317
Steelman Transportation			
2160 N Burton ....Springfield MO 65803	800-488-6287	417-831-6300	770
Steere Enterprises Inc			
285 Commerce St ....Tallmadge OH 44278	800-875-4926	330-633-4926	597
Stefanini TechTeam Inc			
27335 W Eleven-Mile Rd ....Southfield MI 48034	800-522-4451	248-357-2866	181
Steiff North America			
24 Albion Rd Ste 220 ....Lincoln RI 02865	888-978-3433	401-312-0080	752
Stein Eriksen Lodge			
7700 Stein Way ....Park City UT 84060	800-453-1302	435-649-3700	660
Stein Hospice Service			
1912 Hayes Ave Ste 3..........Sandusky OH 44870	800-625-5269	419-625-5269	368
Steinaker State Park			
4335 N Hwy 191 ....Vernal UT 84078	800-322-3770	435-789-4432	558
Steiner Electric Co			
1250 Touhy Ave ....Elk Grove Village IL 60007	800-783-4637	847-228-0400	246
Steiner Industries			
5801 N Tripp Ave ....Chicago IL 60646	800-621-4515	773-588-3444	569
Steinhafels			
W 231 N 1013 County Hwy F ....Waukesha WI 53186	866-351-4600*	262-436-4600	320
*Cust Svc			
Steinwall Inc			
1759 116th Ave NW ....Coon Rapids MN 55448	800-229-9199	763-767-7060	601
Steinway & Sons			
1 Steinway Pl ....Long Island City NY 11105	800-783-4692	718-721-2600	520
Stellar Group			
2900 Hartley Rd ....Jacksonville FL 32257	800-488-2900	904-260-2900	187
StellArt			
2012 Waltzer Rd ....Santa Rosa CA 95403	866-621-1987	707-569-1378	129
Stemco LP			
300 Industrial Blvd			
PO Box 1989....................Longview TX 75606	800-527-8492	903-758-9981	59
Sten Corp			
13828 Lincoln St NE ....Ham Lake MN 55304	800-328-7958	952-545-2776	186
Stenograph LLC			
1500 Bishop Ct ....Mount Prospect IL 60056	800-323-4247	847-803-1400	178
Stenotype Institute of Jacksonville			
3563 Phillips Hwy			
Bldg E Ste 501 ....Jacksonville FL 32207	800-273-5090	904-398-4141	788
Stens Corp			
2424 Cathy Ln ....Jasper IN 47546	800-457-7444	812-482-2526	426
Step2 Co			
10010 Aurora-Hudson Rd ....Streetsboro OH 44241	800-347-8372*	330-656-0440	63
*Cust Svc			
Stepan Co			
22 W Frontage Rd ....Northfield IL 60093	800-745-7837*	847-446-7500	143
*Cust Svc			
Stephen Gould Corp			
35 S Jefferson Rd ....Whippany NJ 07981	800-456-7896	973-428-1500	99
Stephens Inc			
111 Ctr St ....Little Rock AR 72201	800-643-9691	501-377-2000	681
Stephenson Equipment Inc (SEI)			
7201 Paxton St ....Harrisburg PA 17111	800-325-6455	717-564-3434	264-3
Stereotaxis Inc			
4320 Forest Pk Ave ....Saint Louis MO 63108	866-646-2346	314-678-6100	379
NASDAQ: STXS			
Stericycle Inc			
28161 N Keith Dr ....Lake Forest IL 60045	866-783-7422	847-367-5910	792
NASDAQ: SRCL			
Sterigenics			
2015 Spring Rd Ste 650 ....Oak Brook IL 60523	800-472-4508	630-928-1700	772
Sterilite Corp			
PO Box 524 ....Townsend MA 01469	800-225-1046		600
STERIS Corp			
5960 Heisley Rd ....Mentor OH 44060	800-548-4873	440-354-2600	471
NYSE: STE			
Sterling Bank & Trust FSB			
1 Town Sq 19th Fl.................Southfield MI 48076	866-619-2265	248-351-3442	69
Sterling Business Forms			
PO Box 2486 ....White City OR 97503	800-759-3676*		109
*Cust Svc			
Sterling College			
PO Box 72 ....Craftsbury Common VT 05827	800-648-3591	802-586-7711	788
Sterling Computer Corp			
600 Stevens Port Dr			
Ste 200 ....Dakota Dunes SD 57049	877-242-4074	605-242-4000	712
Sterling Cruises & Travel			
8700 W Flagler St Ste 105 ....Miami FL 33174	800-435-7967	305-592-2522	761
Sterling Cut Glass Company Inc			
3233 Mineola Pk ....Erlanger KY 41018	800-368-1158	859-283-2333	358
Sterling Electric Inc			
7997 Allison Ave ....Indianapolis IN 46268	800-654-6220*	317-872-0471	511
*Cust Svc			
Sterling Fibers Inc			
5005 Sterling Way ....Pace FL 32571	800-342-3779*	850-994-5311	598-2
*Cust Svc			
Sterling Inc			
2900 S 160th St ....New Berlin WI 53151	800-783-7835*	262-641-8600	202
*Cust Svc			
Sterling Optical			
520 Eigth Ave 23rd Fl ....New York NY 10018	800-393-7789	516-390-2117	536
Sterling Paper Co			
2155 E Castor Ave ....Philadelphia PA 19134	800-745-5350	215-744-5350	100
Sterling Plumbing			
444 Highland Dr ....Kohler WI 53044	888-783-7546*	920-457-4441	604
*Cust Svc			
Sterling Production Control Units			
2280 W Dorothy Ln ....Dayton OH 45439	800-968-7728	937-299-5594	383
Sterling Publishing Company Inc			
387 Pk Ave S Fifth Fl ....New York NY 10016	800-367-9692*	212-532-7160	628-2
*Cust Svc			
Sterling Savings Bank			
105 W Simpson Ave ....Mccleary WA 98557	800-650-7141		69
Sterling Truck Corp			
12120 Telegraph Rd ....Redford Township MI 48239	800-385-4357*	800-785-4357	509
*Cust Svc			
Sterling-Clark-Lurton Corp			
PO Box 130 ....Norwood MA 02062	800-225-9872	781-762-5400	543
Stern Oil Company Inc			
PO Box 218 ....Freeman SD 57029	800-477-2744	605-925-7999	572
Sterne Agee & Leach Inc			
800 Shades Creek Pkwy			
Ste 700 ....Birmingham AL 35209	800-240-1438	205-949-3500	681
Stetson University			
421 N Woodland Blvd Unit 8378 ....DeLand FL 32723	800-688-0101*	386-822-7100	166
*Admissions			
Stetson University DuPont-Ball Library			
421 N Woodland Blvd ....DeLand FL 32723	800-688-0101	386-822-7183	431-6
Steuben County Rural Electric Membership Corp			
1212 S Wayne St ....Angola IN 46703	888-233-9088	260-665-3563	245
Steuben County Tourism Bureau			
430 N Wayne St Ste 1B.............Angola IN 46703	888-665-5668	260-665-5386	207
Steuben Rural Electric Co-op Inc			
Nine Wilson Ave ....Bath NY 14810	800-843-3414	607-776-4161	245
Steve Barry Buick Inc			
16000 Detroit Ave ....Lakewood OH 44107	866-327-5818	216-920-0866	56
Steve Hopkins Inc			
2499 Auto Mall Pkwy ....Fairfield CA 94533	877-873-3913	707-427-1000	509
Steve Landers Toyota			
10825 Colonel Glenn Rd ....Little Rock AR 72204	888-314-4350	501-568-5800	509
Steve Millen Sportparts Inc			
3176 Airway Ave ....Costa Mesa CA 92626	866-250-5542	714-540-5566	56

	Toll-Free	Phone	Class
Steven Barclay Agency			
12 Western Ave .... Petaluma CA 94952	888-965-7323	707-773-0654	699
Steven Engineering Inc			
230 Ryan Way .... South San Francisco CA 94080	800-258-9200	650-588-9200	246
Steven's Hope for Children Inc			
1014 W Foothill Blvd Ste B............ Upland CA 91786	866-378-3836	909-373-0678	369
Stevens Aviation Inc			
600 Delaware St			
Donaldson Industrial Pk .... Greenville SC 29605	800-359-7838	864-678-6000	62
Stevens Creek Software			
PO Box 2126 ....Cupertino CA 95015	800-823-4279	408-725-0424	179-9
Stevens Henager College			
1890 South 1350 West .... Ogden UT 84401	800-622-2640		160
Stevens Institute of Technology			
Castle Pt on the Hudson .... Hoboken NJ 07030	800-458-5323	201-216-5194	166
Stevens Marine Inc			
9180 SW Burnham St .... Tigard OR 97223	800-225-7023	503-620-7023	89
Stevens Transport			
PO Box 279010 .... Dallas TX 75227	800-233-9369	866-551-0337	770
Stevens Travel Management Inc			
119 W 40th St 14th Fl. .... New York NY 10018	800-275-7400	212-696-4300	761
Stevens Water Monitoring Systems			
12067 NE Glenn Widing Dr			
Ste 106................Portland OR 97220	800-452-5272	503-469-8000	537
Stevens Worldwide Van Lines			
527 W Morley Dr .... Saginaw MI 48601	888-860-4566	800-678-3836	512
Steves & Sons Inc			
203 Humble Ave ....San Antonio TX 78225	800-617-8586*	210-924-5111	236
*Sales			
Steves Homestead Museum			
509 King William St ....San Antonio TX 78204	800-523-5077	210-225-5924	513
Stewart & Assoc Inc			
50 W Douglas St Ste 1200 .... Freeport IL 61032	888-310-2840	815-235-3807	397
Stewart Directories Inc			
100 W Pennsylvania Ave			
PO Box 20250. .... Towson MD 21204	800-311-0786		628-6
Stewart EFI LLC			
45 Old Waterbury Rd ....Thomaston CT 06787	800-393-5387	860-283-8213	484
Stewart Engineering Supply Inc			
3221 E Pioneer Pkwy .... Arlington TX 76010	800-533-1265	817-640-1767	111
Stewart Enterprises Inc			
1333 S Clearview Pkwy .... New Orleans LA 70121	877-239-3264	713-522-5141	503
NASDAQ: STEI			
Stewart Environmental Consultants LLC			
3801 Automation Way			
Ste 200....................Fort Collins CO 80525	800-373-1348	970-226-5500	195
Stewart Filmscreen Corp			
1161 W Sepulveda Blvd ....Torrance CA 90502	800-762-4999	310-784-5300	584
Stewart Information Services Corp			
1980 Post Oak Blvd Ste 800 ....Houston TX 77056	800-729-1900	713-625-8100	388-6
NYSE: STC			
Stewart REI Data Inc			
1980 Post Oak Blvd Ste 800 ....Houston TX 77056	800-729-1900	212-922-0050	388-6
Stewart School of Cosmetology			
604 NW Ave ....Sioux Falls SD 57104	800-537-2625	605-336-2775	76
Stewart Sutherland Inc			
5411 E 'V' Ave .... Vicksburg MI 49097	800-253-1034	269-649-0530	64
Stewart Systems			
808 Stewart Ave .... Plano TX 75074	800-966-5808	972-422-5808	208
Stewart Title Guaranty Co			
1980 Post Oak Blvd Ste 800 ....Houston TX 77056	800-729-1900	713-625-8100	388-6
Stewart Title Insurance Co			
300 E 42nd St 10th Fl................New York NY 10017	800-913-4170	212-922-0050	60
STFM (Society of Teachers of Family Medicine)			
11400 Tomahawk Creek Pkwy			
Ste 540................Leawood KS 66211	800-274-7928	913-906-6000	48-8
Stg International Inc			
4900 Seminary Rd Ste 1100.........Alexandria VA 22311	855-507-0660	703-578-6030	181
STI (Superconductor Technologies Inc)			
460 Ward Dr ....Santa Barbara CA 93111	800-727-3648	805-690-4500	253
NASDAQ: SCON			
STI Electronics Inc			
261 Palmer Rd .... Madison AL 35758	888-650-3006	256-461-9191	383
Stickk.com LLC			
39 E 30th St Ste 4.............New York NY 10016	866-578-4255		384
Sticky Fingers			
235 Meeting St ....Charleston SC 29401	800-784-2597	843-853-7427	662
Stidham Trucking Inc			
PO Box 308 .... Yreka CA 96097	800-827-9500	530-842-4161	187
Stifel Financial Corp			
501 N Broadway .... Saint Louis MO 63102	800-679-5446		681
NYSE: SF			
Stifel Nicolaus & Co Inc			
501 N Broadway .... Saint Louis MO 63102	800-679-5446	314-342-2000	681
Stihl Inc			
536 Viking Dr .... Virginia Beach VA 23452	800-467-8445*	757-486-9100	749
*Cust Svc			
Stillman Bancorp NA			
PO Box 150 .... Stillman Valle IL 61084	877-275-3342	815-645-2000	69
Stillman College			
3601 Stillman Blvd ....Tuscaloosa AL 35401	800-841-5722	205-349-4240	166
Stillwater Chamber of Commerce			
409 S Main St .... Stillwater OK 74075	800-593-5573	405-372-5573	137
Stillwater Spa at the Hyatt Regency Newport			
One Goat Island .... Newport RI 02840	800-233-1234	401-851-3225	698
Stilson Products			
15935 Sturgeon St .... Roseville MI 48066	888-400-5978	586-778-1100	488
Stimple & Ward Co			
3400 Babcock Blvd .... Pittsburgh PA 15237	800-792-6457	412-364-5200	511
Stimson Lumber Co			
520 SW Yamhill St Ste 700. ....Portland OR 97204	800-445-9758	503-222-1676	674
Stirling Properties			
109 Northpark Blvd Ste 300 .... Covington LA 70433	888-261-2022	985-898-2022	646
STMA (Sports Turf Managers Assn)			
805 New Hampshire Ste E ....Lawrence KS 66044	800-323-3875	785-843-2549	47-22
STMicroelectronics NV			
Pmb #192 134 Vintage Park Blvd			
Ste A....................Houston TX 77070	888-356-1766	281-469-2035	687
Stock Bldg Supply			
8020 Arco Corporate Dr .... Raleigh NC 27617	877-734-6365	919-431-1000	192-3
Stock Car Racing Magazine			
PO Box 420235 ....Palm Coast FL 32142	800-333-2633		452-3
Stock Drive Products/Sterling Instrument			
2101 Jericho Tpke .... New Hyde Park NY 11040	800-737-7436	516-328-3300	613
Stock Equipment Co			
16490 Chillicothe Rd ....Chagrin Falls OH 44023	888-742-1249	440-543-6000	273
Stock Seed Farms			
28008 Mill Rd .... Murdock NE 68407	800-759-1520	402-867-3771	685
Stock Transportation Ltd			
128 Wellington St W Ste 201 ......Barrie ON L4N1K9	888-952-0878		108
Stock Yards Packing Co Inc			
2457 W North Ave .... Melrose Park IL 60160	877-785-9273		295-26
StockCap			
123 Manufacturers Dr .... Arnold MO 63010	800-827-2277	636-282-6800	152
Stockmen's Livestock Market Inc			
1200 E Hwy 50 PO Box 528 .... Yankton SD 57078	800-532-0952	605-665-9641	441
Stockton-San Joaquin County Public Library (SSJCPL)			
605 N El Dorado St .... Stockton CA 95202	866-805-7323	209-937-8416	431-3
Stockwatch			
700 W Georgia St PO Box 10371 ...... Vancouver BC V7Y1J6	800-268-6397	604-687-1500	401
Stockyards Hotel			
109 E Exchange Ave .... Fort Worth TX 76164	800-423-8471	817-625-6427	376
Stoelting LLC 502 Hwy 67 .... Kiel WI 53042	800-558-5807	920-894-2293	297
Stoever Glass & Company Inc			
30 Wall St ....New York NY 10005	800-223-3881		398
Stokes Electric Company Inc			
1701 McCalla Ave .... Knoxville TN 37915	800-999-0351	865-525-0351	246
Stolle Machinery Co LLC			
6949 S Potomac St .... Centennial CO 80112	800-433-8333	303-708-9044	540
Stoller Fisheries			
1301 18th St PO Box B.......... Spirit Lake IA 51360	800-831-5174	712-336-1750	295-14
Stoller USA			
4001 W Sam Houston Pkwy N			
Ste 100..................Houston TX 77043	800-539-5283	713-461-1493	280
Stonco Lighting			
2345 Vauxhall Rd ....Union NJ 07083	800-334-2212	908-964-7000	435
Stone Castle Hotel & Conference Ctr, The			
3050 Green Mtn Dr ....Branson MO 65616	800-677-6906	417-335-4700	376
Stone Mountain State Park			
3042 Frank Pkwy ....Roaring Gap NC 28668	877-722-6762	336-957-8185	558
Stonebridge Inn			
300 Carriage Way			
PO Box 5008. .... Snowmass Village CO 81615	800-922-7242	970-923-2420	376
Stonebridge Press Inc			
25 Elm St ....Southbridge MA 01550	800-536-5836	508-764-4325	628-8
StoneFly Inc			
21353 Cabot Blvd ....Hayward CA 94545	888-786-6335	510-265-1616	177
Stoneridge Shopping Ctr			
1 Stoneridge Mall ....Pleasanton CA 94588	877-746-6642	925-463-2778	455
Stonestown Galleria			
3251 20th Ave .... San Francisco CA 94132	800-326-3264	415-564-8848	455
Stonewall Jackson Hotel & Conference Ctr			
24 S Market St .... Staunton VA 24401	866-880-0024	540-885-4848	376
Stonewall Jackson Memorial Hospital (SJMH)			
230 Hospital Plaza .... Weston WV 26452	866-637-0471	304-269-8000	371-3
Stonewall Resort			
940 Resort Dr ....Roanoke WV 26447	888-278-8150	304-269-7400	660
Stoneway Electric Supply Co			
402 N Perry St ....Spokane WA 99202	800-841-1408	509-535-2933	246
Stoney Creek Inn			
101 Mariner's Way ....East Peoria IL 61611	800-659-2220	309-694-1300	376
Stonhard Inc			
1000 E Pk Ave .... Maple Shade NJ 08052	800-854-0310*	856-779-7500	291
*Cust Svc			
Stonyfield Farm Inc			
10 Burton Dr .... Londonderry NH 03053	800-776-2697	603-437-4040	295-25
STOPS Inc			
8855 Grissom Pkwy ....Titusville FL 32780	866-632-2161	321-383-4111	388-4
Storage Battery Systems Inc (SBS)			
N56 W16665 Ridgewood Dr .... Menomonee Falls WI 53051	800-554-2243	262-703-5800	246
Storage Engine Inc			
One Sheila Dr Bldg 6A .... Tinton Falls NJ 07724	866-734-8899	732-747-6995	177
Stor-All Storage			
1375 W Hillsboro Blvd ...... Deerfield Beach FL 33442	877-786-7255	954-421-7888	791-3
Storck USA LP			
325 N LaSalle St Ste 400 ....Chicago IL 60654	800-852-5542	312-467-5700	295-8
Store Opening Solutions (SOS)			
800 Middle Tennessee Blvd ....Murfreesboro TN 37129	877-388-9262		444
Storer Coachways			
3519 McDonald Ave .... Modesto CA 95358	800-621-3383	209-521-8250	106
Storey Publishing LLC			
210 Mass Moca Way .... North Adams MA 01247	800-827-7444	413-346-2100	628-2
Stork News of America Inc			
1305 Hope Mills Rd Ste A ....Fayetteville NC 28304	800-633-6395	910-429-2229	309
Storkcraft Baby			
7433 Nelson Rd .... Richmond BC V6W1G3	877-274-0277	604-274-5121	318-2
Storm King School			
314 Mountain Rd .... Cornwall On Hudson NY 12520	800-225-9144	845-534-9860	615
Storm Products Inc			
165 South 800 West .... Brigham City UT 84302	800-369-4402	435-723-0403	701
Stormont-Vail Regional Health Ctr			
1500 SW Tenth Ave .... Topeka KS 66604	800-432-2951	785-354-6000	371-3
Stornoway Diamond Corp			
980 W First St Ste 118 ... N.Vancouver BC V7P3N4	877-331-2232	604-983-7750	498-3
TSE: SWY			
Storopack Inc			
12007 S Woodruff Ave .... Downey CA 90241	800-829-1491	562-803-5582	594
Storr Tractor Co			
3191 Rt 22 ....Branchburg NJ 08876	800-526-3802	908-722-9830	426
Stoughton Hospital			
900 Ridge St .... Stoughton WI 53589	888-816-3831	608-873-6611	371-3
Stow Co, The			
3311 Windquest Dr .... Holland MI 49424	800-562-4257	616-399-3311	804
Stowe Mountain Resort			
5781 Mountain Rd ....Stowe VT 05672	800-253-4754	802-253-3000	660
Stoweflake Mountain Resort & Spa			
1746 Mountain Rd PO Box 369 ......Stowe VT 05672	800-253-2232	802-253-7355	660
Strafford Publications Inc			
PO Box 13729 ....Atlanta GA 30324	800-926-7926	404-881-1141	628-9
Straight A Tours & Travel			
6881 Kingspointe Pkwy Ste 18 ....Orlando FL 32819	800-237-5440	407-896-1242	750
Straight Arrow Products Inc			
2020 Highland Ave .... Bethlehem PA 18020	800-827-9815	610-882-9606	231
Straight North LLC			
1001 W 31st St .... Downers Grove IL 60515	866-353-3953		7
Strait Music Co			
2428 W Ben White Blvd .... Austin TX 78704	800-725-8877	512-476-6927	519

Company / Address	City	State	ZIP	Toll-Free	Phone	Class
Straith Hospital for Special Surgery						
23901 Lahser Rd	Southfield	MI	48034	**800-994-6610**	248-357-3360	371-7
Stranahan House Museum Inc						
335 SE Sixth Ave	Fort Lauderdale	FL	33301	**800-435-7352**	954-524-4736	513
Stranahan Theater						
4645 Heatherdowns Blvd	Toledo	OH	43614	**866-381-7469**	419-381-8851	565
Strand Lighting						
10911 Petal St	Dallas	TX	75238	**800-733-0564**	214-647-7880	435
Strand Media Group						
3955 Hwy 17 Bypass Ste D						
PO Box 1389	Murrells Inlet	SC	29576	**877-844-1722**	843-626-8911	637
Strand Theatre						
619 Louisiana Ave	Shreveport	LA	71101	**800-313-6373**	318-226-1481	565
Strange's Florist Inc						
3313 Mechanicsville Pk	Richmond	VA	23223	**800-421-4070**	804-321-2200	292
StrataCare Inc						
17838 Gillette Ave	Irvine	CA	92614	**800-277-6512**		179-1
Stratasys Inc						
7665 Commerce Way	Eden Prairie	MN	55344	**800-937-3010**	952-937-3000	261
NASDAQ: SSYS						
Stratcor Inc						
1180 Omega Dr Ste 1180	Pittsburgh	PA	15205	**800-573-6052**	412-787-4500	497
Strategic Air & Space Museum						
28210 W Pk Hwy	Ashland	NE	68003	**800-358-5029**	402-944-3100	513
Strategic Diagnostics Inc						
111 Pencader Dr	Newark	DE	19702	**800-544-8881**	302-456-6789	231
NASDAQ: SDIX						
Strategic Distribution Inc						
1414 Radcliffe St Ste 300	Bristol	PA	19007	**800-322-2644**	215-633-1900	382
Strategic Finance Magazine						
10 Paragon Dr Ste 1	Montvale	NJ	07645	**800-638-4427**	201-573-9000	452-5
Strategy Institute						
401 Richmond St W Ste 401	Toronto	ON	M5V3A8	**866-298-9343**	416-944-9200	461
Strater Hotel						
699 Main Ave	Durango	CO	81301	**800-247-4431**	970-247-4431	376
Stratford Court						
45 Katherine Blvd	Palm Harbor	FL	34684	**888-434-4648**	727-787-1500	663
Stratford Homes LP						
402 S Weber Ave	Stratford	WI	54484	**800-448-1524**	715-687-3133	105
Stratford Hotel						
242 Powell St	San Francisco	CA	94102	**888-688-0038**	415-397-7080	376
Stratford Star						
1000 Bridgeport Ave	Shelton	CT	06484	**800-372-2790***	203-402-2319	525-4
*Advestisement						
Stratford University School of Culinary Arts						
7777 Leesburg Pk	Falls Church	VA	22043	**800-444-0804**	703-821-8570	161
Strathcona Hotel						
60 York St	Toronto	ON	M5J1S8	**800-268-8304**	416-363-3321	376
Strathcona Hotel, The						
919 Douglas St	Victoria	BC	V8W2C2	**800-663-7476**	250-383-7137	376
Stratix						
4920 Avalon Ridge Pkwy	Norcross	GA	30071	**800-883-8300**	770-326-7580	174-7
Stratos Global Corp						
6550 Rock Spring Dr Ste 650	Bethesda	MD	20817	**800-563-2255**	301-214-8800	672
Stratosphere Multimedia LLC						
551 Madison Ave Seventh Fl	New York	NY	10022	**888-212-0700**	212-702-0700	195
Stratosphere Tower Hotel & Casino						
2000 S Las Vegas Blvd	Las Vegas	NV	89104	**800-998-6937**	702-380-7777	132
Strattec Security Corp						
3333 W Good Hope Rd	Milwaukee	WI	53209	**877-251-8799***	414-247-3333	59
NASDAQ: STRT ■ *General						
Stratton Equity Co-op Co Inc						
98 Colorado Ave PO Box 25	Stratton	CO	80836	**800-438-7070**	719-348-5326	275
Stratton Hats Inc						
3200 Randolph St	Bellwood	IL	60104	**877-453-3777**	708-544-5220	153-8
Stratton Seed Co						
1530 Hwy 79 S	Stuttgart	AR	72160	**800-264-4433**	870-673-4433	685
Stratton Veterans Affairs Medical Ctr						
113 Holland Ave	Albany	NY	12208	**800-223-4810**	518-626-5000	371-8
Stratus Properties Inc						
212 Lavaca St Ste 300	Austin	TX	78701	**800-690-0315**	512-478-5788	644
NYSE: STRS						
Stratus Technologies						
111 Powdermill Rd	Maynard	MA	01754	**800-787-2887**	978-461-7000	179-12
Straub Clinic & Hospital						
888 S King St	Honolulu	HI	96813	**800-232-9491**	808-522-4000	371-3
Straub International Inc						
214 SW 40th Ave PO Box 1606	Great Bend	KS	67530	**800-658-1706**	620-792-5256	274
Strayer University						
Takoma Park						
6830 Laurel St NW	Washington	DC	20012	**888-311-0355**	202-722-8100	166
Strayer University Alexandria						
2730 Eisenhower Ave	Alexandria	VA	22314	**888-311-0355**		166
Strayer University Arlington						
2121 15th St N	Arlington	VA	22201	**888-478-7293**	703-892-5100	166
Strayer University Fredericksburg						
150 Riverside Pkwy						
Ste 100	Fredericksburg	VA	22406	**888-311-0355**	540-374-4300	166
Strayer University Prince George's						
4710 Auth Pl Ste 100	Suitland	MD	20746	**866-344-3297**	888-311-0355	166
Stream Gas & Electric Ltd						
1950 Stemmons Fwy Ste 3000	Dallas	TX	75207	**866-447-8732**		775
Streamlight Inc						
30 Eagleville Rd	Eagleville	PA	19403	**800-523-7488**	610-631-0600	435
Streamline Health Solutions Inc						
10200 Alliance Rd Ste 200	Cincinnati	OH	45242	**800-878-5269**	513-794-7100	38
NASDAQ: STRM						
Streamwood Behavioral Health Ctr						
1400 E Irving Pk Rd	Streamwood	IL	60107	**800-272-7790**	630-837-9000	371-1
Streater Inc						
411 S First Ave	Albert Lea	MN	56007	**800-527-4197**		286
Streator Dependable Manufacturing Co						
1705 N Shabbona St	Streator	IL	61364	**800-795-0551**	815-672-0551	465
Streck Inc						
7002 S 109th St	Omaha	NE	68128	**800-228-6090**	402-333-1982	231
Streeter Assoc Inc						
101 E Woodlawn Ave PO Box 118	Elmira	NY	14902	**866-493-1640**	607-734-4151	187
Streimer Sheet Metal Works Inc						
740 N Knott St	Portland	OR	97227	**888-288-3828**	503-288-9393	688
Strem Chemicals Inc						
Seven Mulliken Way	Newburyport	MA	01950	**800-647-8736**	978-499-1600	144
Stretch Inc						
1322 Orleans Dr	Sunnyvale	CA	94089	**800-468-6853**	408-543-2700	687
Stretch-N-Grow International Inc						
PO Box 7599	Seminole	FL	33775	**800-348-0166**		309
Strictly Business Computer Systems Inc						
848 Fourth Ave Ste 200	Huntington	WV	25701	**888-529-0401**		177
Stride Rite Corp						
191 Spring St	Lexington	MA	02420	**800-299-6575***	617-824-6000	300
*Cust Svc						
Stride Tool Inc Imperial Div						
30333 Emerald Vly Pkwy	Glenwillow	OH	44139	**888-467-8665**	440-247-4600	748
StrikoDynarad						
501 E Roosevelt Ave	Zeeland	MI	49464	**855-787-4561**	616-772-3705	317
Stripes Convenience Stores						
4525 Ayers St	Corpus Christi	TX	78415	**800-569-3585**	361-884-2464	205
NYSE: SUSS						
Strippit Inc/LVD						
12975 Clarence Ctr Rd	Akron	NY	14001	**800-828-1527**	716-542-4511	451
Strong Enterprises Inc						
11236 Satellite Blvd	Orlando	FL	32837	**800-344-6319**	407-859-9317	569
Strong Memorial Hospital						
University of Rochester Medical Ctr						
601 Elmwood Ave	Rochester	NY	14642	**800-999-6673**	585-275-2100	371-3
Stronghaven Inc						
5090 McDougall Dr SW	Atlanta	GA	30336	**866-374-9148**	404-699-1952	99
Strother Ventures II Inc						
2929 Breezewood Ave						
Ste 200	Fayetteville	NC	28303	**855-753-6143**	910-864-2327	643
Structural Component Systems Inc (SCS)						
1255 Front St	Fremont	NE	68026	**800-844-5622**	402-721-5622	188
Structural Concepts Corp						
888 Porter Rd	Muskegon	MI	49441	**800-433-9489**	231-798-8888	286
Structural Wood Corp						
4000 Labore Rd	Saint Paul	MN	55110	**800-652-9058**	651-426-8111	804
Structure House						
3017 Pickett Rd	Durham	NC	27705	**800-553-0052**	919-493-4205	697
Structures Unlimited Inc						
88 Pine St	Manchester	NH	03103	**800-225-3895**	603-645-6539	688
Struktol Company of America Inc						
PO Box 1649	Stow	OH	44224	**800-327-8649**	330-928-5188	142
Stryker Corp						
2825 Airview Blvd	Kalamazoo	MI	49002	**800-616-1406**	269-385-2600	471
NYSE: SYK						
Stry-Lenkoff Co Inc						
1100 W Broadway	Louisville	KY	40232	**800-626-8247**	502-587-6804	109
STS (Society of Thoracic Surgeons)						
633 N St Clair St Ste 2320	Chicago	IL	60611	**877-865-5321**	312-202-5800	48-8
STS Component Solutions LLC						
2910 SW 42 Ave	Palm City	FL	34990	**888-777-2960**		22
Stuart Anderson's Black Angus						
4410 El Camino Real	Los Altos	CA	94022	**800-382-3852**		661
Stuart C Irby Co						
815 S President St	Jackson	MS	39201	**866-687-4729**	601-960-7346	189-10
Stuart Hall School						
235 W Frederick St PO Box 210	Staunton	VA	24402	**888-306-8926**	540-885-0356	615
Stuart Jet Ctr LLC						
2501 Aviation Way	Stuart	FL	34996	**877-735-9538**	772-288-6700	62
Stuart-Martin County Chamber of Commerce						
1650 S Kanner Hwy	Stuart	FL	34994	**800-962-2873**	772-287-1088	137
Stubbe's Precast						
30 Muir Line	Harley	ON	N0E1E0	**866-355-2183**	519-424-2183	184
StubHub Inc						
199 Fremont St Fl 4	San Francisco	CA	94105	**866-788-2482**	415-222-8400	454
Stuckey's Corp						
8555 16th St Ste 850	Silver Spring	MD	20910	**800-423-6171**	301-585-8222	661
Studebaker National Museum						
201 Chapin St	South Bend	IN	46601	**888-391-5600**	574-235-9714	513
Student Advantage LLC						
280 Summer St	Boston	MA	02210	**800-333-2920**		381
Student Conservation Assn (SCA)						
689 River Rd PO Box 550	Charlestown	NH	03603	**888-722-9675**	603-543-1700	47-13
Student Tours Inc						
60 W Ave	Vineyard Haven	MA	02568	**800-331-7093**	508-693-5078	750
Student Transportation of America Inc (STA)						
3349 Hwy 138 Bldg B Ste D	Wall	NJ	07719	**888-942-2250**	732-280-4200	108
Student Travel Services Inc						
1413 Madison Pk Dr	Glen Burnie	MD	21061	**800-648-4849**		750
Studentcity.com Inc						
8 Essex Ctr Dr	Peabody	MA	01960	**888-777-4642**		761
Students Against Destructive Decisions (SADD)						
255 Main St	Marlborough	MA	01752	**877-723-3462**	508-481-3568	47-6
Studio City Chamber of Commerce						
4024 Radford Ave						
Edit 2 Ste F	Studio City	CA	91604	**877-227-0088**	818-655-5916	137
Stuecker & Assoc Inc						
1930 Bishop Ln Watterson Towers						
Ste 1001	Louisville	KY	40218	**800-799-9327**	502-452-9227	457
Stuller Settings Inc						
PO Box 87777	Lafayette	LA	70598	**800-877-7777**		404
Stupp Bros Inc						
3800 Weber Rd	Saint Louis	MO	63125	**800-899-1856**	314-638-5000	475
Stupp Corp						
12555 Ronaldson Rd	Baton Rouge	LA	70807	**800-535-9999**	225-775-8800	485
Sturbridge Host Hotel & Conference Ctr						
366 Main St	Sturbridge	MA	01566	**800-582-3232**	508-347-7393	376
Sturdisteel Co						
PO Box 2655	Waco	TX	76702	**800-433-3116**		318-3
Sturdy Corp						
1822 Carolina Beach Rd	Wilmington	NC	28401	**800-721-3282**	910-763-2500	204
Sturm Foods Inc						
PO Box 287	Manawa	WI	54949	**800-347-8876**	920-596-2511	296-11
Stuttering Foundation of America						
3100 Walnut Grove Rd Ste 603	Memphis	TN	38111	**800-992-9392**	901-452-7343	47-17
Styer Transportation Co						
7870 215th St W	Lakeville	MN	55044	**800-548-9149**	952-469-4491	770
Style Crest Inc						
2450 Enterprise St	Fremont	OH	43420	**800-925-4440**	419-332-7369	103
Stylex PO Box 5038	Delanco	NJ	08075	**800-257-5742**		318-1
Stylmark Inc						
PO Box 32008	Minneapolis	MN	55432	**800-328-2495**	763-574-7474	286
Suarez Corp Industries						
7800 Whipple Ave NW	North Canton	OH	44720	**800-764-0008**	330-494-5504	196
Subaru of America Inc						
2235 Marlton Pike W	Cherry Hill	NJ	08002	**800-782-2783**	856-488-8500	58
Subco Foods Inc						
4350 S Taylor Dr	Sheboygan	WI	53081	**800-473-0757**	920-457-7761	295-16

	City	State	ZIP	Toll-Free	Phone	Class
Subia Corp						
6612 Gulton Ct NE	Albuquerque	NM	87109	**800-275-2636**	505-345-2636	341
Substance Abuse & Mental Health Services Administration (SAMHSA)						
1 Choke Cherry Rd	Rockville	MD	20857	**877-726-4727**	240-276-2000	338-8
Center for Mental Health Services						
1 Choke Cherry Ln	Rockville	MD	20857	**877-726-4727**		338-8
Center for Substance Abuse Prevention						
1 Choke Cherry Rd	Rockville	MD	20857	**877-726-4727**	240-276-2420	338-8
Center for Substance Abuse Treatment						
1 Choke Cherry Rd PO Box 2345	Rockville	MD	20857	**877-726-4727**	240-276-2130	338-8
Substance Abuse Foundation						
3125 E Seventh St	Long Beach	CA	90804	**888-476-2743**	562-987-5722	717
Suburban Collection						
1810 Maplelawn Dr	Troy	MI	48084	**877-471-7100**		56
Suburban Life Publications						
1101 W 31st St Ste 100	Downers Grove	IL	60515	**800-397-9397**	630-368-1100	628-8
Suburban Mobility Authority for Regional Transportation (SMART)						
535 Griswold St						
Ste 600 Buhl Bldg	Detroit	MI	48226	**866-962-5515**	313-223-2100	463
Suburban Press & Metro Press						
1550 Woodville Rd	Millbury	OH	43447	**800-300-6158**	419-836-2221	525-4
Suburban Propane LP						
One Suburban Plz 240 Rt 10 W						
PO Box 206	Whippany	NJ	07981	**800-776-7263**	973-887-5300	315
Suburban Transit Corp						
750 Somerset St	New Brunswick	NJ	08901	**800-222-0492**	732-249-1100	107
Suby Von Haden & Assoc SC						
1221 John Q Hammons Dr	Madison	WI	53717	**800-279-2616**	608-831-8181	2
Sucampo Pharmaceuticals Inc						
4520 East-West Hwy						
3rd Fl Ste 300	Bethesda	MD	20814	**800-332-1088**	301-961-3400	576
NASDAQ: SCMP						
Success Motivation International Inc						
4567 Lakeshore Dr	Waco	TX	76710	**888-391-0050***	254-776-9966	363
*Sales						
Successfactors Inc						
1500 Fashion Island Blvd						
Ste 300	San Mateo	CA	94404	**800-809-9920**	650-645-2000	179-11
NYSE: SFSF						
Successories Inc						
1040 Holland Dr	Boca Raton	FL	33487	**800-535-2773**		309
Succor Creek State Natural Area						
1298 Lk Owyhee Dam Rd	Adrian	OR	97901	**800-551-6949**		558
Suddath Cos						
815 S Main St	Jacksonville	FL	32207	**800-395-7100**	904-352-2577	512
Suddenlink Communications						
6151 Paluxy Dr	Tyler	TX	75703	**877-694-9474**		115
Sudenga Industries Inc						
2002 Kingbird Ave	George	IA	51237	**888-783-3642**	712-475-3301	273
Suffolk County Community College						
Grant						
1001 Crooked Hill Rd	Brentwood	NY	11717	**800-621-3362**	631-851-6700	160
Suffolk Downs						
111 Waldemar Ave	East Boston	MA	02128	**800-225-3460**	617-567-3900	132
Suffolk University						
Eight Ashburton Pl	Boston	MA	02108	**800-678-3365**	617-573-8460	166
Sugar Creek Foods International						
301 N El Paso St	Russellville	AR	72801	**800-445-2715**		295-25
Sugar Creek Packing Co						
2101 Kenskill Ave	Washington Court House	OH	43160	**800-848-8205**	740-335-7440	295-26
Sugar Creek Scrap Inc						
1201 W National Ave	West Terre Haute	IN	47885	**800-466-7462**	812-533-2147	677
Sugar Foods Corp						
950 Third Ave 21st Fl	New York	NY	10022	**800-732-8963**	212-753-6900	296-11
Sugarbush Resort & Inn						
1840 Sugarbush Access Rd	Warren	VT	05674	**800-537-8427**	802-583-6300	660
Sugarloaf/USA						
5092 Access Rd	Carrabassett Valley	ME	04947	**800-843-5623**	207-237-2000	660
SuiteAmerica						
4970 Windplay Dr						
Ste C-1	El Dorado Hills	CA	95762	**800-410-4305**	916-941-7970	211
Suites at Fisherman's Wharf						
2655 Hyde St	San Francisco	CA	94109	**800-227-3608**	415-771-0200	376
Suites Hotel in Canal Park, The						
325 Lake Ave S	Duluth	MN	55802	**877-766-2665**	218-727-4663	376
Suit-Kote Corp						
1911 Lorings Crossing Rd	Cortland	NY	13045	**800-622-5636**	607-753-1100	45
Sukut Construction Inc						
4010 W Chandler Ave	Santa Ana	CA	92704	**888-785-8801**	714-540-5351	189-4
Sul Ross State University						
E Hwy 90	Alpine	TX	79832	**888-722-7778**	432-837-8011	166
Sullair Corp						
3700 E Michigan Blvd	Michigan City	IN	46360	**800-785-5247**	219-879-5451	173
Sullivan County Rural Electric Co-op Inc (SCREC)						
5675 Rt 87 PO Box 65	Forksville	PA	18616	**800-570-5081**	570-924-3381	245
Sullivan Curtis Monroe						
1920 Main St	Irvine	CA	92614	**800-427-3253**	949-250-7172	387
Sullivan International Group Inc						
2750 Womble Rd	San Diego	CA	92106	**888-744-1432**	619-260-1432	261
Sullivan Tire Co Inc						
PO Box 370	Rockland	MA	02370	**877-855-4826**	781-871-2299	61-5
Sullivan University						
3101 BaRdstown Rd	Louisville	KY	40205	**800-844-1354**	502-456-6505	166
Sullivan-Palatek Inc						
1201 W US Hwy 20	Michigan City	IN	46360	**800-438-6203**	219-874-2497	173
Sulphur Springs Valley Electric Co-op Inc						
PO Box 820	Willcox	AZ	85644	**877-877-6861**	520-384-2221	245
Sultana Distribution Services Inc						
600 Food Ctr Dr	Bronx	NY	10474	**877-617-5500**	718-617-5500	296-3
Sulzer Metco US Inc						
1101 Prospect Ave	Westbury	NY	11590	**877-280-2342**	516-334-1300	173
Sumitomo Corp of America						
600 Third Ave 42nd Fl	New York	NY	10016	**877-980-3283**	212-207-0700	357-3
Sumitomo Machinery Corp of America						
4200 Holland Blvd	Chesapeake	VA	23323	**800-762-9256**	757-485-3355	700
Sumitomo Metal Industries Ltd						
1815 Sandusky St	Fostoria	OH	44830	**866-877-2020**	419-436-4499	614
Summa Barberton Hospital						
155 Fifth St NE	Barberton	OH	44203	**888-905-6071**	330-615-3000	371-3
Summerwood Corp						
14 Balligomingo Rd	Conshohocken	PA	19428	**800-760-0950**	610-520-1000	661
Summit Aviation Inc						
4200 Summit Bridge Rd						
PO Box 258	Middletown	DE	19709	**800-441-9343**	302-834-5400	24
Summit Bank						
2969 Broadway	Oakland	CA	94611	**800-380-9333**	510-839-8800	69
Summit Chemical Co						
235 S Kresson St	Baltimore	MD	21224	**800-227-8664**	410-522-0661	280
Summit Christian College						
2025 21st St	Gering	NE	69341	**888-305-8083**	308-632-6933	166
Summit Electric Supply Co						
2900 Stanford NE	Albuquerque	NM	87107	**800-824-4400**	505-346-9000	246
Summit Energy Services Inc						
10350 Ormsby Pk Pl Ste 400	Louisville	KY	40223	**866-907-8664**	502-429-3800	458
Summit Food Service Distributors Inc						
580 Industrial Rd	London	ON	N5V1V1	**800-265-9267**	519-453-3410	298
Summit Holding Southeast Inc						
PO Box 600	Gainesville	GA	30503	**800-971-2667**	678-450-5825	357-4
Summit Industries Inc						
PO Box 7329	Marietta	GA	30065	**800-241-6996**		149
Summit Lodge & Spa						
4359 Main St	Whistler	BC	V0N1B4	**888-913-8811**	604-932-2778	376
Summit Motorsports Park						
1300 Ohio 18	Norwalk	OH	44857	**800-729-6455**	419-668-5555	508
Summit Partners						
222 Berkeley St 18th Fl	Boston	MA	02116	**800-503-4611**	617-824-1000	780
Summit Pet Product Distributors Inc						
420 N Chimney Rock Rd	Greensboro	NC	27410	**800-323-2963**	336-294-3200	782
Summit Plastics Inc						
107 S Laurel St	Summit	MS	39666	**800-790-7117**	601-276-7500	593
Summit Security Services Inc						
390 Rexcorp Plz W Tower -						
Lobby Level	Uniondale	NY	11556	**800-615-5888**	516-240-2400	684
Summit State Bank						
500 Bicentennial Way						
PO Box 6188	Santa Rosa	CA	95406	**800-428-5008**	707-568-6000	70
NASDAQ: SSBI						
Summit Technical Services Inc						
355 Centerville Rd	Warwick	RI	02886	**800-643-7372**	401-736-8323	623
Summit Trailer Sales Inc						
One Summit Plz	Summit Station	PA	17979	**800-437-3729**	570-754-3511	769
Summitt Trucking LLC						
1800 Progress Way	Clarksville	IN	47129	**866-999-7799**	812-285-7777	770
Sumner Regional Medical Ctr						
555 Hartsville Pike	Gallatin	TN	37066	**888-863-6198**	615-328-8888	371-3
Sumner School District						
1202 Wood Ave	Sumner	WA	98390	**866-548-3847**	253-891-6000	676
Sumner-Cowley Electric Co-op Inc						
2223 N A St PO Box 220	Wellington	KS	67152	**888-326-3356**	620-326-3356	245
Sumter Electric Co-op Inc						
PO Box 301	Sumterville	FL	33585	**800-732-6141**	352-793-3801	245
Sumter Electric Membership Corp						
1120 Felder St	Americus	GA	31709	**800-342-6978**	229-924-8041	245
Sun Bancorp Inc (SNBC)						
226 Landis Ave	Vineland	NJ	08360	**800-786-9066**		357-2
NASDAQ: SNBC						
Sun Chemical Corp						
35 Waterview Blvd	Parsippany	NJ	07054	**800-543-2323**	973-404-6000	385
Sun Circle Inc						
286 S G St	Arcata	CA	95521	**800-458-6543**	707-822-5777	273
Sun Coast Resources Inc						
6922 Cavalcade St	Houston	TX	77028	**800-677-3835**	713-429-8492	572
Sun Control Products Window Shades						
1908 Second St SW	Rochester	MN	55902	**800-533-0010**	507-282-2620	86
Sun Country Airlines Inc						
1300 Mendota Heights Rd	Mendota Heights	MN	55120	**800-359-6786**	651-681-3900	25
Sun Devil Fire Equipment Inc						
2929 W Clarendon Ave	Phoenix	AZ	85017	**800-536-3845**	623-245-0636	670
Sun Devil Stadium						
500 E Veterans Way						
Arizona State University	Tempe	AZ	85281	**888-786-3857**	480-965-3482	711
Sun Drilling Products Corp						
503 Main St PO Box 129	Belle Chasse	LA	70037	**800-962-6490**	504-393-2778	534
Sun Ergoline Inc						
1 Walter Kratz Dr	Jonesboro	AR	72401	**888-771-0996**		433
Sun Healthcare Group Inc						
18831 Von Karman Ste 400	Irvine	CA	92612	**800-729-6600**	949-255-7100	446
NASDAQ: SUNH						
SUN Home Health Services Inc						
61 Duke St PO Box 232	Northumberland	PA	17857	**888-478-6227**	570-473-8320	368
Sun Life Assurance Company of Canada						
One Sun Life Executive Pk						
PO Box 9133	Wellesley Hills	MA	02481	**800-786-5433**	781-237-6030	388-2
Sun Life Financial Inc						
150 King St W	Toronto	ON	M5H1J9	**877-786-5433**	416-979-9966	357-4
TSE: SLF						
Sun Magazine						
8815 Conroy Windermere Rd						
Ste 130	Orlando	FL	32835	**888-218-9968**	407-477-2815	452-11
Sun Mountain Lodge						
604 Patterson Lk Rd						
PO Box 1000	Winthrop	WA	98862	**800-572-0493**	509-996-2211	660
Sun National Bank						
350 Fellowship Road						
Ste. 101	Mount Laurel	NJ	08054	**800-786-9066**		69
Sun News						
914 Frontage Rd E	Myrtle Beach	SC	29578	**800-568-1800**	843-626-8555	525-2
Sun Newspapers						
5510 Cloverleaf Pkwy	Cleveland	OH	44125	**800-362-8008**	216-999-3900	628-8
Sun Orchard Inc						
1198 W Fairmont Dr	Tempe	AZ	85282	**800-505-8423**		295-20
Sun River Electric Co-op Inc						
310 First Ave S PO Box 309	Fairfield	MT	59436	**800-452-7516**	406-467-2527	245
Sun Valley Area Chamber of Commerce						
11501 Strathern St						
PO Box 308	Sun Valley	CA	91352	**877-834-7064**	818-768-2014	137
Sun Valley Floral Farms Inc						
3160 Upper Bay Rd	Arcata	CA	95521	**800-747-0396**		366
Sun Valley Resort						
1 Sun Valley Rd	Sun Valley	ID	83353	**800-786-8259**	208-622-4111	660
Sun Valley/Ketchum Chamber & Visitors Bureau						
491 Sun Vly Rd	Ketchum	ID	83340	**800-634-3347**	208-726-3423	137

Company / Address	City	State	ZIP	Toll-Free	Phone	Class
Sun Viking Lodge 2411 S Atlantic Ave	Daytona Beach Shores	FL	32118	800-874-4469	386-252-6252	376
Sun, The 4030 N Georgia Blvd	San Bernardino	CA	92407	800-922-0922	909-889-9666	525-2
Sunbelt Furniture Express Inc PO Box 487	Hickory	NC	28603	800-766-1117	828-464-7240	770
Sunbelt Rentals Inc 2341 Deerfield Dr *General	Fort Mill	SC	29715	800-667-9328*	704-348-2676	264-3
Sunbelt Transfomer Ltd 1922 S Martin Luther King Jr Dr	Temple	TX	76504	800-433-3128	254-771-3777	249
Sunburst Shutters 6480 W Flamingo Rd Ste D	Las Vegas	NV	89103	877-786-2877	702-367-1600	690
Suncast Corp 701 N Kirk Rd	Batavia	IL	60510	800-444-3310	630-879-2050	318-2
Sunchaser Vacation Villas 5129 Riverview Gate Rd *Resv	Fairmont Hot Springs	BC	V0B1L1	877-451-1250*	250-345-4545	743
Sunco Carriers Inc 1025 N Chestnut Rd	Lakeland	FL	33805	800-237-8288	863-688-1948	770
Suncoast Hotel & Casino 9090 Alta Dr	Las Vegas	NV	89145	877-677-7111	702-636-7111	376
Suncoast Post-Tension LP 509 N Sam Houston Pkwy Ste 400 E	Houston	TX	77060	800-847-8886	281-668-1840	190-3
Suncor Energy Inc 150 - 6 Ave SW PO Box 2844 *NYSE: SU*	Calgary	AB	T2P3E3	800-558-9071	403-296-8000	529
Sundance Trail Guest Ranch 17931 Red Feather Lakes Rd	Red Feather Lakes	CO	80545	800-357-4930	970-224-1222	239
Sunday River Ski Resort 15 S Ridge Rd PO Box 4500	Newry	ME	04261	800-543-2754	207-824-3500	660
Sundial Beach & Golf Resort 1451 Middle Gulf Dr	Sanibel	FL	33957	866-717-2323	239-472-4151	660
Sundial Boutique Hotel 4340 Sundial Crescent	Whistler	BC	V0N1B4	800-661-2321	604-932-2321	376
Sundowner Trailers Inc 9805 S State Hwy 48	Coleman	OK	73432	800-654-3879	580-937-4255	753
Sundt Construction 2620 S 55th St	Tempe	AZ	85282	800-280-3000	480-293-3000	190-2
Sundt Construction Inc 2015 W River Rd Ste 101	Tucson	AZ	85704	800-467-5544	520-750-4600	187
Sunex International Inc 100 Roe Rd	Travelers Rest	SC	29690	800-833-7869	864-834-8759	347
SunGard Availability Services 680 E Swedesford Rd	Wayne	PA	19087	800-468-7483	484-582-2000	391
SunGard Data Systems Inc 680 E Swedesford Rd	Wayne	PA	19087	866-264-4829	800-468-7483	225
SunGard Pentamation Inc 1000 Business Ctr Dr Ste 1 *Cust Svc	Lake mary	FL	32746	866-965-7732*	610-691-3616	179-11
Sun-Journal PO Box 4400	Lewiston	ME	04243	800-482-0759	207-784-5411	525-2
Sunland Group Inc 1033 La Posada Dr Ste 370	Austin	TX	78752	866-732-8500	512-494-0208	261
Sunland Park Racetrack & Casino 1200 Futurity Dr	Sunland Park	NM	88063	800-572-1142	575-874-5200	633
Sunnen Products Co 7910 Manchester Ave	Saint Louis	MO	63143	800-325-3670	314-781-2100	450
Sunny 107.9 Radio *Palm Beach Broadcasting* 701 Northpoint Pkwy Ste 500	West Palm Beach	FL	33407	800-919-1079	561-616-4777	636-118
Sunny Land Tours Inc 21 Old Kings Rd N Ste B-212	Palm Coast	FL	32137	800-783-7839	386-449-0059	750
Sunnyland Farms Inc PO Box 8200	Albany	GA	31706	800-999-2488		454
Sunoco Chemicals 1735 Market St Ste LL	Philadelphia	PA	19103	800-786-6261	215-977-3000	142
Sunoco Inc 1735 Market St Ste LL *NYSE: SUN*	Philadelphia	PA	19103	800-786-6261	215-977-3000	529
Sunovion Pharmaceuticals Inc 84 Waterford Dr	Marlborough	MA	01752	888-394-7377	508-481-6700	231
SunPower Corp 77 Rio Robles *NASDAQ: SPWR*	San Jose	CA	95134	800-786-7693	408-240-5500	687
SunQuest Vacations 77-6435 Kuakini Hwy	Kailua-Kona	HI	96740	800-367-5168	808-329-6438	761
Sunray Co-op 201 N Main PO Box 430	Sunray	TX	79086	800-621-3570	806-948-4121	10-4
Sunrich LLC 3824 SW 93rd St PO Box 128	Hope	MN	56046	800-297-5997	507-451-6030	79-1
Sunrider International 1625 Abalone Ave *Orders	Torrance	CA	90501	888-278-6743*	310-781-3808	363
Sunrise Medical Inc 2842 Business Pk Ave	Fresno	CA	93727	800-333-4000		472
Sunrise Medical Laboratories Inc 250 Miller Pl *Cust Svc	Hicksville	NY	11801	800-782-0282*	631-435-1515	415
Sunrise Senior Living Inc 7902 Westpark Dr Ste T-900 *NYSE: SRZ*	McLean	VA	22102	800-929-4124	703-273-7500	446
Sunrise Specialty Co 930 98th Ave	Oakland	CA	94603	800-444-4280	510-729-7277	604
Sunriver Resort 17600 Ctr Dr PO Box 3609	Sunriver	OR	97707	800-547-3922	541-593-1000	660
Sunsational Cruises 2470 E Glen Canyon Rd	Green Valley	AZ	85614	800-239-6252	480-491-6248	761
Sunset Beach Resort 3287 W Gulf Dr	Sanibel Island	FL	33957	866-565-5091	239-472-1700	660
Sunset Inn Travel Apartments 1111 Burnaby St	Vancouver	BC	V6E1P4	800-786-1997	604-688-2474	376
Sunset Marquis Hotel & Villas 1200 N Alta Loma Rd	West Hollywood	CA	90069	800-858-9758	310-657-1333	376
Sunset Publishing Corp 80 Willow Rd	Menlo Park	CA	94025	800-227-7346	650-321-3600	628-9
Sunset Ridge School District 29 525 Sunset Ridge Rd	Northfield	IL	60093	888-331-2195	847-881-9400	676
Sunset Station Hotel & Casino 1301 W Sunset Rd	Henderson	NV	89014	888-786-7389	702-547-7777	376
Sunset Transportation Inc 11325 Concord Village Ave	St Louis	MO	63123	800-849-6540		310
Sunshine Artist Magazine 4075 LB McLeod Rd Ste E	Orlando	FL	32811	800-597-2573	407-648-7479	452-2
Sunshine Business Class 150 Kingswood Rd PO Box 8465	Mankato	MN	56001	800-873-7681		129
Sunshine Dairy Foods Inc 801 NE 21st Ave	Portland	OR	97232	800-544-0554	503-234-7526	296-4
Sunshine Makers Inc 15922 Pacific Coast Hwy	Huntington Harbour	CA	92649	800-228-0709	562-795-6000	149
Sunshine Mills Inc 500 Sixth St SW	Red Bay	AL	35582	800-633-3349	256-356-9541	571
Sunshine Minting Inc 7600 Mineral Dr Ste 700	Coeur d'Alene	ID	83815	800-274-5837	208-772-9592	406
Sunstar Americas Inc 4635 W Foster Ave	Chicago	IL	60630	888-777-3101		228
Sunstore Solar Energy Solutions 3090 S Hwy 14	Greer	SC	29650	800-571-8310	864-297-6776	603
Sunsweet Growers Inc 901 N Walton Ave	Yuba City	CA	95993	800-417-2253	530-674-5010	295-18
Sunteck Transport Group 6413 Congress Ave Ste 260 *PINK: AUTO*	Boca Raton	FL	33487	800-759-7910	561-988-9456	444
Suntron Corp 2401 W Grandview Rd	Phoenix	AZ	85023	800-690-6903	602-298-4939	617
Suntrust Bank PO Box 4418 *NYSE: STI*	Atlanta	GA	30302	800-786-8787		69
SunTrust Banks Inc 303 Peachtree St NE *NYSE: STI*	Atlanta	GA	30308	800-786-8787	404-588-7711	357-2
SunTrust Mortgage Inc 1001 Semmes Ave	Richmond	VA	23224	800-634-7928		502
SunTrust Robinson Humphrey Capital Markets 3333 Peachtree Rd NE	Atlanta	GA	30326	800-634-7928	404-926-5000	681
Sunwest Silver Company Inc 324 Lomas Blvd NW	Albuquerque	NM	87102	800-771-3781	505-243-3781	292
SUNY (State University of New York Press) 22 Corporate Woods Blvd Third Fl	Albany	NY	12211	866-430-7869	518-472-5000	628-4
SUNY (State University of New York, The) State University Plz	Albany	NY	12246	800-342-3811	518-320-1888	774
Supelco Inc 595 N Harrison Rd	Bellefonte	PA	16823	800-247-6628	814-359-3441	416
Super Color Digital LLC 16761 Hale Ave	Irvine	CA	92606	800-979-4446	949-622-0010	619
Super Glue Corp 9420 Santa Anita Ave	Rancho Cucamonga	CA	91730	800-538-3091	909-987-0550	3
Super H Mart Inc 2550 Pleasant Hill Rd	Duluth	GA	30096	877-427-7386	678-543-4000	342
Super Holiday Tours 116 Gatlin Ave	Orlando	FL	32806	800-327-2116		750
Super Products LLC 17000 W Cleveland Ave	New Berlin	WI	53151	800-837-9711	262-784-7100	383
Super Sack Manufacturing Corp 11510 Data Dr	Dallas	TX	75218	800-331-9200	214-340-7060	66
Super Sky Products Inc 10301 N Enterprise Dr	Mequon	WI	53092	800-558-0467	262-242-2000	234
Super Store Industries 16888 McKinley Ave PO Box 549	Lathrop	CA	95330	888-292-8004	209-858-2010	296-8
Super Talk 1270 4303 Memorial Hwy	Mandan	ND	58554	844-255-7886	701-663-1270	636
Superb Internet Corp 999 Bishop St Ste 1850	Honolulu	HI	96813	888-354-6128	808-544-0387	795
Superbag Corp 9291 Baythrone Dr	Houston	TX	77041	888-842-1177	713-462-1173	65
Superchips Inc 1790 E Airport Blvd	Sanford	FL	32773	888-227-2447	407-585-7000	174-1
Superconductor Technologies Inc (STI) 460 Ward Dr *NASDAQ: SCON*	Santa Barbara	CA	93111	800-727-3648	805-690-4500	253
SuperCoups 350 Revolutionary Dr	East Taunton	MA	02718	800-626-2620	508-977-2000	5
Supercuts 7201 Metro Blvd	Minneapolis	MN	55439	877-857-2070		76
SuperFlow Technologies Group 4747 Centennial Blvd	Colorado Springs	CO	80919	800-471-7701	719-471-1746	467
SuperGlass Windshield Repair Inc 6101 Chancellor Dr Ste 200	Orlando	FL	32809	866-557-7497	407-240-1920	61-2
Superheat Fgh Services Inc 680 Industrial Pk Dr	Evans	GA	30809	888-508-3226		224
Superior Abrasives Inc 4800 Wadsworth Rd	Dayton	OH	45414	800-235-9123	937-278-9123	1
Superior Air Parts Inc 621 S Royal Ln Ste 100	Coppell	TX	75019	800-420-4727	972-829-4600	522
Superior Aluminum Products Inc 555 E Main St PO Box 430	Russia	OH	45363	800-548-8656	937-526-4065	486
Superior Boiler Works Inc 3524 E Fourth St PO Box 1527	Hutchinson	KS	67504	800-444-6693	620-662-6693	90
Superior Carriers Inc 711 Jory Blvd Ste 101-N	Oak Brook	IL	60523	800-654-7707	630-573-2555	770
Superior Clay Corp 6566 Superior Rd SE	Uhrichsville	OH	44683	800-848-6166	740-922-4122	148
Superior Dairy Inc 4719 Navarre Rd SW	Canton	OH	44706	800-597-5460	330-477-4515	295-27
Superior Die Set Corp 900 W Drexel Ave	Oak Creek	WI	53154	800-558-6040	414-764-4900	747
Superior Die Tool & Machine Co 2301 Fairwood Ave	Columbus	OH	43207	800-292-2181	614-444-2181	747
Superior Electric 28 Spring Ln Ste 3	Farmington	CT	06032	800-390-6405	860-507-2025	720
Superior Energy Services Inc 601 Poydras St Ste 2400 *NYSE: SPN*	New Orleans	LA	70130	800-259-7774	504-587-7374	531
Superior Environmental Corp 1128 Franklin Ct	Marne	MI	49435	877-667-4142	616-667-4000	194
Superior Essex Communications LP 6120 Powers Ferry Rd Ste 150	Atlanta	GA	30339	800-551-8948	770-657-6000	725
Superior Essex Inc 6120 Powers Ferry Rd Ste 150 *NASDAQ: SPSX*	Atlanta	GA	30339	800-551-8948	770-657-6000	801

Company / Address	City	State	ZIP	Toll-Free	Phone	Class
Superior Essex Inc Magnet Wire/Winding Wire Div 1601 Wall St PO Box 1601	Fort Wayne	IN	46802	**800-551-8948**	260-461-4550	800
Superior Farms 1480 Drew Ave Ste 100	Davis	CA	95618	**800-228-5262**	530-297-7299	468
Superior Gearbox Co 803 W Hwy 32	Stockton	MO	65785	**800-346-5745**	417-276-5191	700
Superior Graphite 10 S Riverside Plaza Ste 1470 *Cust Svc	Chicago	IL	60606	**800-327-0337***	312-559-2999	126
Superior Information Services Inc 300 Phillips Blvd Ste 500	Trenton	NJ	08618	**800-792-8888**	609-883-7000	626
Superior Medical Supply Inc 11005 Dover St Unit 1100	Broomfield	CO	80021	**877-460-1411**		319
Superior Mfg Group 5655 W 73rd St	Chicago	IL	60638	**800-621-2802**	708-458-4600	291
Superior Oil Co Inc 1402 N Capitol Ave Ste 100	Indianapolis	IN	46202	**800-553-5480**	317-781-4400	596
Superior Packaging Solutions 26858 Almond Ave	Redlands	CA	92374	**800-680-2393**		554
Superior Plus Income Fund 840-7 Ave SW Ste 1400	Calgary	AB	T2P3G2	**866-490-7587**	403-218-2970	402
Superior Press Inc 11930 Hamden Pl *Cust Svc	Santa Fe Springs	CA	90670	**888-590-7998***	562-948-1866	85
Superior Products Inc 3786 Ridge Rd	Cleveland	OH	44144	**800-651-9490**	216-651-9400	614
Superior Public Library 1530 Tower Ave	Superior	WI	54880	**866-894-4899**	715-394-8860	431-3
Superior Shores Resort 1521 Superior Shores Dr	Two Harbors	MN	55616	**800-242-1988**	218-834-5671	660
Superior Software Inc 16055 Ventura Blvd Ste 650	Encino	CA	91436	**800-421-3264**	818-990-1135	179-1
Superior Technical Resources Inc 250 International Dr	Williamsville	NY	14221	**800-568-8310**	716-929-1400	712
Superior Tire & Rubber Corp 1818 Pennsylvania Ave W PO Box 308 *Cust Svc	Warren	PA	16365	**800-289-1456***	814-723-2370	744
Superior Tool Co 100 Hayes Dr Unit C *Cust Svc	Cleveland	OH	44131	**800-533-3244***	216-398-8600	748
Superior Trailer Sales Co 501 Hwy 80	Sunnyvale	TX	75182	**800-637-0324**	972-226-3893	509
Superior Uniform Group Inc 10055Seminole Blvd *NASDAQ: SGC* ■ *Cust Svc	Seminole	FL	33772	**800-727-8643***	727-397-9611	153-18
Superior Water Light & Power 2915 Hill Ave PO Box 519	Superior	WI	54880	**800-227-7957**	715-394-2200	775
Superior/Douglas County Convention & Visitors Bureau 305 Harborview Pkwy	Superior	WI	54880	**800-942-5313**	715-392-7151	207
Superior-Douglas County Chamber of Commerce 205 Belknap St	Superior	WI	54880	**800-942-5313**	715-394-7716	137
Superlite Block Co Inc 4150 W Turney Ave	Phoenix	AZ	85019	**800-366-7877**	602-352-3500	184
Supermarket Systems Inc 6419 Bannington Rd	Charlotte	NC	28226	**800-553-1905**	704-542-6000	656
Superseal Mfg Co Inc PO Box 795	South Plainfie	NJ	07080	**800-433-4873**	908-561-5910	235
SuperTalk 99.7 WTN 10 Music Cir E	Nashville	TN	37203	**800-618-7445**	615-321-1067	636-74
SUPERVALU Inc 7075 Flying Cloud Dr *NYSE: SVU* ■ *Cust Svc	Eden Prairie	MN	55344	**877-322-8228***	952-828-4000	296-8
Superwinch Inc 359 Lake Rd	Dayville	CT	06241	**800-323-2031**	860-928-7787	191
Supply Room Cos Inc 14140 N Washington Hwy	Ashland	VA	23005	**800-849-7239**	804-412-1200	528
Supply Technologies LLC 6065 Parkland Blvd	Cleveland	OH	44124	**800-695-8650**	440-947-2100	348
Support Services of America Inc 12440 Firestone Blvd Ste 312	Norwalk	CA	90650	**888-564-0005**	562-868-3550	150
Support Systems Assoc Inc (SSAI) 709 S Harbor City Blvd Ste 350	Melbourne	FL	32901	**877-234-7724**	321-724-5566	261
Support.com Inc 900 Chesapeake Dr 2nd Fl *NASDAQ: SPRT*	Redwood City	CA	94063	**877-493-2778**	650-556-9440	179-7
Supra Alloys Inc 351 Cortez Cir	Camarillo	CA	93012	**800-647-8772**	805-388-2138	487
Supreme Corp 325 Spence Rd	Conover	NC	28613	**888-604-6975**	828-322-6975	734-9
Supreme Mfg Company Inc Five Connerty Ct	East Brunswick	NJ	08816	**800-772-7632**	732-254-0087	342
Supreme Oil Co 2109 W Monte Vista Rd	Phoenix	AZ	85009	**800-752-7888**		532
Sur La Table 5701 Sixth Ave S Ste 486	Seattle	WA	98108	**800-243-0852**		359
Sure Winner Foods Inc Two Lehner Rd	Saco	ME	04072	**800-640-6447**	207-282-1258	296-4
Surefire LLC 18300 Mt Baldy Cir	Fountain Valley	CA	92708	**800-828-8809**	714-545-9444	73
SurePayroll 2350 Ravine Way Ste 100	Glenview	IL	60025	**877-954-7873**	847-676-8420	563
Surety Group Inc 3715 Northside Pkwy NW Ste 1-315	Atlanta	GA	30327	**800-486-8211**	404-352-8211	388-5
Surety LLC 12020 Sunrise Vly Dr Ste 250	Reston	VA	20191	**800-298-3115**	571-748-5800	179-7
Surf & Sand Resort 1555 S Coast Hwy	Laguna Beach	CA	92651	**888-869-7569**	949-497-4477	376
Surface Combustion Inc 1700 Indian Wood Cir	Maumee	OH	43537	**800-537-8980**	419-891-7150	317
Surface Mount Distribution Inc (SMD) 1 Oldfield	Irvine	CA	92618	**800-820-7634**	949-470-7700	246
Surface Shields Inc 10457 163rd Pl	Orland Park	IL	60467	**800-913-5667**	708-226-9810	291
Surfsand Resort 148 W Gower Rd	Cannon Beach	OR	97110	**800-547-6100**	503-436-2274	376
Surfside Inn 1211 Atlantic Ave	Virginia Beach	VA	23451	**800-437-2497**	757-428-1183	376
Surgical Appliance Industries Inc 3960 Rosslyn Dr	Cincinnati	OH	45209	**800-888-0867**		472
Surgical Principals Inc 1625 S Tacoma Way	Tacoma	WA	98409	**888-801-9251**		470
Surgical Staff Inc 120 St Matthews Ave	San Mateo	CA	94401	**800-339-9599**	650-558-3999	712
SurModics Inc 9924 W 74th St *NASDAQ: SRDX*	Eden Prairie	MN	55344	**866-787-6639**	952-829-2700	231
Surprise Valley Electric Co-op 22595 US 395	Alturas	CA	96101	**866-843-2667**	530-233-3511	245
Surrey Hotel 20 E 76th St	New York	NY	10021	**866-233-4642**	212-288-3700	376
Surry-Yadkin Electric Membership Corp 510 S Main St	Dobson	NC	27017	**800-682-5903**	336-356-8241	245
Sur-Seal Gasket & Packing Inc 6156 Wesselman Rd	Cincinnati	OH	45248	**800-345-8966**		325
Survivors Network of Those Abused by Priests (SNAP) PO Box 6416	Chicago	IL	60680	**877-762-7432**	312-455-1499	47-21
Susan G Komen for the Cure 5005 LBJ Fwy Ste 250	Dallas	TX	75244	**800-227-2345**	972-855-1600	47-17
Susan Schein Automotive 3171 Pelham Pkwy PO Box 215	Pelham	AL	35124	**800-845-1578**	205-664-1491	56
SUSLA (Southern University Museum of Art) 3050 Martin Luther King Jr Dr	Shreveport	LA	71107	**800-458-1472**	318-670-6000	513
Susquehanna Bancshares Inc 26 N Cedar St PO Box 1000 *NASDAQ: SUSQ*	Lititz	PA	17543	**800-311-3182**	717-626-4721	357-2
Susquehanna Bank 26 N Cedar St PO Box 100	Lititz	PA	17543	**800-311-3182**	717-626-4721	69
Susquehanna University 514 University Ave	Selinsgrove	PA	17870	**800-326-9672**	570-374-0101	166
Suss Consulting 801 Old York Rd Noble Plz Ste 305	Jenkintown	PA	19046	**888-984-5900**	215-884-5900	196
Sussex Bank 200 Munsonhurst Rd *NASDAQ: SBBX*	Franklin	NJ	07416	**800-511-9900**	973-827-2914	357-2
Sussex County Chamber of Commerce 120 Hampton House Rd	Newton	NJ	07860	**844-256-7328**	973-579-1811	137
Sussex County Library 125 Morris Tpke	Newton	NJ	07860	**800-318-2596**	973-948-3660	431-3
Sussex Rural Electric Co-op 64 County Rt 639 PO Box 346	Sussex	NJ	07461	**877-504-6463**	973-875-5101	245
Sussman Automatic Corp 43-20 34th St	Long Island City	NY	11101	**800-727-8326**	718-937-4500	90
Suter Company Inc 258 May St	Sycamore	IL	60178	**800-435-6942**	815-895-9186	295-36
Sutherland Asbill & Brennan LLP 999 Peachtree St NE	Atlanta	GA	30309	**855-857-9769**	404-853-8000	425
Sutphen Corp PO Box 158	Amlin	OH	43002	**800-726-7030**	614-889-1005	509
Sutter Auburn Faith Community Hospital (SAFH) 11815 Education St	Auburn	CA	95602	**800-478-8837**	530-888-4500	371-3
Sutter County Library 750 Forbes Ave	Yuba City	CA	95991	**800-533-2873**	530-822-7137	431-3
Sutter Health 2200 River Plaza	Sacramento	CA	95833	**888-888-6044**	916-733-8800	350
Sutter Medical Ctr of Santa Rosa 3325 Chanate Rd	Santa Rosa	CA	95404	**800-651-5111**	707-576-4006	371-3
Suttle 1001 E Hwy 212	Hector	MN	55342	**800-852-8662**	320-848-6711	725
Sutton Ford Inc 21315 S Central Ave	Matteson	IL	60443	**866-232-2966**	708-720-8115	56
Sutton Place Hotel Edmonton 10235 101st St	Edmonton	AB	T5J3E9	**866-378-8866**	780-428-7111	376
Suwannee Valley Electric Co-op PO Box 160	Live Oak	FL	32064	**800-752-0025**	386-362-2226	245
Suzuki Musical Instrument Corp PO Box 261030 *Cust Svc	San Diego	CA	92196	**800-854-1594***	619-258-1896	520
Svam International Inc 233 E Shore Rd Ste 201	Great Neck	NY	11023	**800-903-6716**	516-466-6655	181
SVB Financial Group 3005 Tasman Dr *NASDAQ: SIVB*	Santa Clara	CA	95054	**800-760-9644**	408-654-7400	357-2
SVC (Society of Vacuum Coaters) 71 Pinon Hill Pl NE	Albuquerque	NM	87122	**800-777-4643**	505-856-7188	48-13
SVCH (Saint Vincent Charity Hospital) 2351 E 22nd St	Cleveland	OH	44115	**800-750-0750**	216-861-6200	371-3
Svenhard's Swedish Bakery Inc 335 Adeline St	Oakland	CA	94607	**800-705-3379**	510-834-5035	295-1
SVIA (Specialty Vehicle Institute of America) Two Jenner St Ste 150	Irvine	CA	92618	**800-887-2887**	949-727-3727	48-21
SVMH (Salinas Valley Memorial Hospital) 450 E Romie Ln	Salinas	CA	93901	**800-722-4673**	831-757-4333	371-3
SVRMC (Sierra Vista Regional Medical Ctr) 1010 Murray Ave	San Luis Obispo	CA	93405	**866-904-6871**	805-546-7600	371-3
SVS (Society for Vascular Surgery) 633 N St Clair St 22nd Fl	Chicago	IL	60611	**800-258-7188**	312-334-2300	48-8
SVS Vision 140 Macomb Pl	Mount Clemens	MI	48043	**800-787-4600**	586-468-7612	536
SW Steakhouse 3131 Las Vegas Blvd S	Las Vegas	NV	89109	**888-320-7198**	702-770-9966	662
Swag, The 2300 Swag Rd	Waynesville	NC	28785	**800-789-7672**	828-926-0430	376
SWANA (Solid Waste Assn of North America) 1100 Wayne Ave Ste 700	Silver Spring	MD	20910	**800-467-9262**	301-585-2898	524-5
Swaner Hardwood Co Inc 5 W Magnolia Blvd PO Box 4200	Burbank	CA	91503	**800-368-1108**	818-953-5350	674
Swank Motion Pictures Inc 10795 Watson Rd	St Louis	MO	63127	**888-248-8757**	314-984-6000	507
Swans Candles 8933 Gravelly Lk Dr SW	Lakewood	WA	98499	**888-848-7926**	253-584-4666	121
Swanson Contracting Co 11701 S Mayfield Ave	Alsip	IL	60803	**800-622-6850**	708-388-0623	189-8
Swanson Health Products Inc PO Box 2803	Fargo	ND	58108	**800-824-4491**	701-356-2700	787
Swany America Corp 115 Corp Dr	Johnstown	NY	12095	**800-237-9269**	518-725-3333	153-7
Swarovski North America Ltd One Kenney Dr	Cranston	RI	02920	**800-289-4900**	401-463-6400	332
Swarthmore College 500 College Ave *Admissions	Swarthmore	PA	19081	**800-667-3110***	610-328-8300	166
Swarthout Coaches Inc 115 Graham Rd	Ithaca	NY	14850	**800-772-7267**	607-257-2277	106
Swatch Group 1200 Harbor Blvd 7th Fl	Weehawken	NJ	07086	**800-456-5354**	201-271-1400	151

Name	Address	City	State	ZIP	Toll-Free	Phone	Class
SWCA Inc	3033 N Central Ave Ste 145	Phoenix	AZ	85012	**800-828-8517**	602-274-3831	193
SWCE (Steele-Waseca Co-op Electric)	2411 W Bridge St PO Box 485	Owatonna	MN	55060	**800-526-3514**	507-451-7340	245
SWCS (Soil & Water Conservation Society)	945 SW Ankeny Rd	Ankeny	IA	50023	**800-843-7645**	515-289-2331	47-13
SWE (Society of Women Engineers)	120 S La Salle St Ste 1515	Chicago	IL	60603	**877-793-4636**	312-596-5223	48-19
Swedish Council of America	2600 Pk Ave	Minneapolis	MN	55407	**800-380-2711**	612-871-0593	47-14
SwedishAmerican Hospital	1401 E State St	Rockford	IL	61104	**800-322-4724**	815-968-4400	371-3
Sweed Machinery Inc	653 Second Ave PO Box 228 *Sales	Gold Hill	OR	97525	**800-888-1352***	541-855-1512	489
Sweeney Buick	7997 Market St	Youngstown	OH	44512	**877-360-4928**		509
Sweepster Inc	2800 N Zeeb Rd	Dexter	MI	48130	**800-456-7100**	734-996-9116	102
Sweet Adelines International	9110 S Toledo Ave	Tulsa	OK	74137	**800-992-7464**	918-622-1444	47-18
Sweet Briar College	134 Chappel Rd *Admissions	Sweet Briar	VA	24595	**800-381-6142***	434-381-6100	166
Sweet Candy Co Inc	3780 W Directors Row	Salt Lake City	UT	84104	**800-669-8669**	801-886-1444	295-8
Sweet Mfg Company Inc	2000 E Leffel Ln *Cust Svc	Springfield	OH	45505	**800-334-7254***	937-325-1511	208
Sweet Ovations	1741 Tomlinson Rd	Philadelphia	PA	19116	**800-280-9387**	215-676-3900	295-21
Sweetwater Authority	PO Box 2328	Chula Vista	CA	91912	**866-275-3772**	619-420-1413	775
Sweetwater Sound Inc	5501 US Hwy 30 W	Fort Wayne	IN	46818	**800-222-4700**	260-432-8176	519
Swenson Spreader Co	127 Walnut St	Lindenwood	IL	61049	**888-825-7323**	815-393-4455	191
SWEPCo	One Riverside Plz	Columbus	OH	43215	**888-216-3523**		775
SWF Cos	1949 E Manning Ave	Reedley	CA	93654	**800-344-8951**	559-638-8484	540
SWH (Senior Whole Health LLC)	58 Charles St 2nd Fl	Cambridge	MA	02141	**888-794-7268**	617-494-5353	350
SWH Supply Co	242 E Main St	Louisville	KY	40202	**800-321-3598**	502-589-9287	656
Swibco Inc	4810 Venture Rd	Lisle	IL	60532	**877-794-2261**	630-968-8900	752
Swift Energy Co	16825 Northchase Dr Ste 400 *NYSE: SFY*	Houston	TX	77060	**800-777-2412**	281-874-2700	529
Swift Glass Company Inc	131 W 22nd St	Elmira Heights	NY	14903	**800-537-9438**	607-733-7166	330
Swift Spinning Inc	16 Corporate Ridge Pkwy PO Box 8767	Columbus	GA	31907	**800-849-1252**	706-323-6303	734-9
Swift Transportation Company Inc	2200 S 75th Ave *NYSE: SWFT*	Phoenix	AZ	85043	**800-800-2200**	602-269-9700	770
Swiger Coils Systems Inc	4677 Mfg Rd	Cleveland	OH	44135	**800-321-3310**	216-362-7500	511
Swim 'n Sport Retail Inc	2396 NW 96th Ave	Miami	FL	33172	**800-497-2111**		155-6
Swineford National Bank	1255 N Susquehanna Trial PO Box 241	Hummels Wharf	PA	17831	**866-762-1903**	570-743-7786	69
Swintec Corp	320 W Commercial Ave	Moonachie	NJ	07074	**800-225-0867**	201-935-0115	110
Swire Coca-Cola USA	12634 S 265 W	Draper	UT	84020	**800-497-2653**	801-816-5300	80-2
Swisher County Cattle Co	Farm Market 214 Rd	Tulia	TX	79088	**800-658-6014**	806-627-4231	10-1
Swisher Electric Co-op Inc	401 SW Second St PO Box 67	Tulia	TX	79088	**800-530-4344**	806-995-3567	245
Swisher Hygiene Co	4725 Piedmont Row Dr	Charlotte	NC	28210	**800-444-4138**	704-364-7707	150
Swisher Mower & Machine Company Inc	1602 Corporate Dr	Warrensburg	MO	64093	**800-222-8183**	660-747-8183	426
Swiss Army Brands Inc	7 Victoria Dr PO Box 874 *Cust Svc	Monroe	CT	06468	**800-442-2706***	203-929-6391	222
Swiss Precision Instruments Inc	11450 Markon Dr	Garden Grove	CA	92841	**888-774-8200**	714-799-1555	383
Swiss Re Life & Health America Inc	175 King St	Armonk	NY	10504	**800-937-5449**	914-828-8000	357-4
Swiss Valley Farms	247 Research Pkwy PO Box 4493	Davenport	IA	52808	**800-747-6113**	563-468-6600	295-5
Swisslog	10825 E 47th Ave	Denver	CO	80239	**800-525-1841**	303-371-7770	208
Switzerland Tourism	608 Fifth Ave Ste 202	New York	NY	10020	**800-794-7795**	212-757-5944	765
SWMC (Southwestern Medical Ctr)	5602 SW Lee Blvd	Lawton	OK	73505	**877-707-1780**	580-531-4700	371-3
SWTC (Southwest Wisconsin Technical College)	1800 Bronson Blvd	Fennimore	WI	53809	**800-362-3322**	608-822-3262	788
SY Bancorp Inc	1040 E Main St *NASDAQ: SYBT*	Louisville	KY	40206	**800-625-9066**	502-582-2571	357-2
Syagen Technology Inc	1411 Warner Ave	Tustin	CA	92780	**877-258-8250**	714-258-4400	732
Sybase Inc	1 Sybase Dr	Dublin	CA	94568	**800-792-2735**	925-236-5000	179-1
Sycara Inc	6263 N Scottsdale Rd Ste 180	Scottsdale	AZ	85250	**855-479-2272**		623
Sycuan Casino & Resort	5469 Casino Way *General	El Cajon	CA	92019	**800-279-2826***	619-445-6002	132
Sydneys Closet	11840 Dorsett Rd	Maryland Heights	MO	63043	**888-479-3639**	314-344-5066	155-6
Sydnor Hydro Inc	2111 Magnolia St PO Box 27186	Richmond	VA	23261	**800-552-7714**	804-643-2725	794
SYGMA Network Inc	5550 Blazer Pkwy Ste 300	Dublin	OH	43017	**877-441-1144**		296-8
Sykes Enterprises Inc	400 N Ashley Dr Ste 2800 *NASDAQ: SYKE*	Tampa	FL	33602	**800-867-9537**	813-274-1000	181
Sylvan Dale Guest Ranch	2939 N County Rd 31 D	Loveland	CO	80538	**877-667-3999**	970-667-3915	239
Sylvan Inc	90 Glade Dr	Kittanning	PA	16201	**866-352-7520**	724-543-3900	10-6
Sylvan Learning Centers	1001 Fleet St	Baltimore	MD	21202	**888-338-2283**		242
Sylvania Steel Corp	4169 Holland Sylvania Rd *General	Toledo	OH	43623	**800-435-0986***	419-885-3838	487
Symantec Corp	350 Ellis St *NASDAQ: SYMC*	Mountain View	CA	94043	**800-441-7234**	650-527-8000	179-12
Symbolist	1090 Texan Trl	Grapevine	TX	76051	**800-498-6885**		196
Symmetricom Inc	2300 Orchard Pkwy *NASDAQ: SYMM*	San Jose	CA	95131	**888-367-7966**	408-433-0910	725
Symmons Industries Inc	31 Brooks Dr	Braintree	MA	02184	**800-796-6667**	781-848-2250	602
Symon Communications Inc	500 N Central Expy Ste 175	Plano	TX	75074	**800-827-9666**	972-578-8484	177
Symphony Ctr	220 S Michigan Ave *Cust Svc	Chicago	IL	60604	**800-223-7114***	312-294-3000	565
Symphony Nova Scotia	6101 University Ave Dalhousie Arts Ctr.	Halifax	NS	B3H4R2	**800-874-1669**	902-494-3820	566-3
Symrise Inc	300 N St *General	Teterboro	NJ	07608	**800-422-1559***	201-288-3200	143
Synagro Technologies Inc	435 Williams Ct Ste 100	Baltimore	MD	21220	**800-370-0035**	443-489-9017	792
Synalloy Corp	775 Spartan Blvd Ste 102 PO Box 5627 *NASDAQ: SYNL* ■ *Orders	Spartanburg	SC	29304	**800-937-5449***	864-585-3605	588
Synchronoss Technologies Inc	200 Crossing Blvd *NASDAQ: SNCR*	Bridgewater	NJ	08807	**866-620-3940**		224
Syndicate Sales Inc	PO Box 756	Kokomo	IN	46903	**800-428-0515**	765-457-7277	601
Syndication Networks Corp	8700 Waukegan Rd Ste 250	Morton Grove	IL	60053	**800-743-1988**	847-583-9000	637
Synergetics USA Inc	3845 Corporate Ctr Dr *NASDAQ: SURG*	O'Fallon	MO	63368	**800-600-0565**	636-939-5100	471
Synergex International Corp	2330 Gold Meadow Way	Rancho Cordova	CA	95670	**800-366-3472**	916-635-7300	179-10
Synergistics Inc	16 Tech Cir	Natick	MA	01760	**866-455-5222**	508-655-1340	179-11
Synergy Associates LLC	550 Clydesdale Trl	Medina	MN	55340	**888-763-9920**		181
Synergy Co of Utah LLC, The	2279 S Resource Blvd	Moab	UT	84532	**800-723-0277**		659
Syngenta Corp	3411 Silverside Rd Ste 100	Wilmington	DE	19810	**800-555-2470**	302-425-2000	280
Syngenta Crop Protection Inc	410 Swing Rd PO Box 18300	Greensboro	NC	27409	**800-797-5040**	336-632-6000	280
Synnex Corp	44201 Nobel Dr *NYSE: SNX* ■ *Cust Svc	Fremont	CA	94538	**800-756-1888***	510-656-3333	175
Synopsys Inc	700 E Middlefield Rd *NASDAQ: SNPS*	Mountain View	CA	94043	**800-541-7737**	650-584-5000	179-10
Synovis Life Technologies Inc	2575 University Ave *NASDAQ: SYNO*	Saint Paul	MN	55114	**800-255-4018**	651-796-7300	472
Synovus Financial Corp	1111 Bay Ave Ste 500 PO Box 120 *NYSE: SNV*	Columbus	GA	31902	**888-796-6887**	706-649-2311	357-2
Synrad Inc	4600 Campus Pl	Mukilteo	WA	98275	**800-796-7231**	425-349-3500	422
Syn-Tech Inc	3100 Ridgelake Dr Ste 101	Metairie	LA	70002	**800-535-7619**	504-835-7825	246
Syntellect Inc	16610 N Black Canyon Hwy Ste 100	Phoenix	AZ	85053	**800-788-9733**		725
Synutra International Inc	2275 Research Blvd Ste 500 *NASDAQ: SYUT*	Rockville	MD	20850	**866-405-2350**	301-840-3888	787
Synventive Molding Solutions Inc	10 Centennial Dr	Peabody	MA	01960	**800-367-5662**	978-750-8065	383
Sypris Electronics LLC	10901 N McKinley Dr	Tampa	FL	33612	**800-937-9220**	813-972-6000	253
Sypris Solutions Inc	101 Bullitt Ln Ste 450 *NASDAQ: SYPR*	Louisville	KY	40222	**800-588-9119**	502-329-2000	253
Syracuse New Times	1415 W Genesee St	Syracuse	NY	13204	**800-856-1900**	315-422-7011	525-5
Syracuse Research Corp (SRC)	7502 Round Pond Rd	North Syracuse	NY	13212	**800-724-0451**	315-452-8000	659
Syracuse Scenery & Stage Lighting Company Inc	101 Monarch Dr	Liverpool	NY	13088	**800-453-7775**	315-453-8096	713
Syracuse Stamping Co	1054 S Clinton St	Syracuse	NY	13202	**800-581-5555**	315-476-5306	484
Syracuse University	900 S Crouse Ave	Syracuse	NY	13244	**800-782-5867**	315-443-3611	166
Syracuse University Bird Library	222 Waverly Ave	Syracuse	NY	13244	**866-722-7858**	315-443-2093	431-6
Sysco Central Ohio Inc	2400 Harrison Rd	Columbus	OH	43204	**800-735-3341**	614-272-0655	296-8
Sysco Denver Inc	5000 Beeler St	Denver	CO	80238	**800-366-6696**	303-585-2000	296-8
Sysco Food Services of Idaho Inc	5710 Pan Am Ave	Boise	ID	83716	**800-747-9726**	208-345-9500	296-8
Sysco Grand Rapids	3700 Sysco Ct SE	Grand Rapids	MI	49512	**800-669-6967**	616-949-3700	296-8
Sysco Hampton Roads Inc	7000 Harbour View Blvd	Suffolk	VA	23435	**800-234-2451**	757-673-4000	296-8
Sysco Indianapolis LLC	4000 W 62nd St	Indianapolis	IN	46268	**800-347-3920**	317-291-2020	296-11

Name / Address	City	State	ZIP	Toll-Free	Phone	Class
Sysco Jacksonville Inc 1501 Lewis Industrial Dr PO Box 37045 *General	Jacksonville	FL	32254	**800-786-2611***	904-786-2600	298
Sysco Kansas City Inc 1915 E Kansas City Rd	Olathe	KS	66061	**800-735-3341**	913-829-5555	295-26
Syska & Hennessy Group 11 W 42nd St	New York	NY	10036	**800-328-1600**	212-921-2300	261
Sysmex America Inc One Nelson C White Pkwy	Mundelein	IL	60060	**800-379-7639**	847-996-4500	470
SYSPRO 959 S Coast Dr Ste 100	Costa Mesa	CA	92626	**800-369-8649**	714-437-1000	179-1
Systech Corp 16510 Via Esprillo	San Diego	CA	92127	**800-800-8970**	858-674-6500	177
Systel Business Equipment Company Inc 3756 Sycamore Dairy Rd	Fayetteville	NC	28303	**800-849-5900**	910-483-7114	111
System Automation 7110 Samuel Morse Dr Ste 100	Columbia	MD	21046	**800-839-4729**	301-837-8000	179-10
System Engineering International Inc (SEI) 5115 Pegasus Ct Ste Q	Frederick	MD	21704	**800-765-4734**	301-694-9601	775
System Innovators Inc 10550 Deerwood Pk Blvd Ste 700	Jacksonville	FL	32256	**800-963-5000**		179-10
System Sensor 3825 Ohio Ave *Tech Supp	Saint Charles	IL	60174	**800-736-7672***	630-377-6580	253
Systematic Financial Management LP 300 Frank W Burr Blvd Seventh Fl Glenpoint Ctr E 7th Fl	Teaneck	NJ	07666	**800-258-0497**	201-928-1982	398
Systematics Inc 1025 Saunders Ln PO Box 2429	West Chester	PA	19380	**800-222-9353**	610-696-9040	798
Systemax Inc 11 Harbor Pk Dr *NYSE: SYX*	Port Washington	NY	11050	**888-645-0878**	516-608-7000	174-1
Systems & Forecasts 150 Great Neck Rd Ste 301	Great Neck	NY	11021	**800-982-4372**	516-829-6444	524-9
Systems Maintenance Services Inc (SMS) 10420 Harris Oaks Blvd Suite C	Charlotte	NC	28269	**877-405-0330**		176
Systron Donner Inertial 355 Lennon Ln	Walnut Creek	CA	94598	**866-234-4976**	925-979-4400	522

T

Name / Address	City	State	ZIP	Toll-Free	Phone	Class
T & A Supply Company Inc 6821 S 216th St Bldg A PO Box 927	Kent	WA	98032	**800-562-2857**	253-872-3682	358
T & D Metal Products Co 602 E Walnut St	Watseka	IL	60970	**800-634-7267**	815-432-4938	483
T & E Industries Inc 215 Watchung Ave *Sales	Orange	NJ	07050	**800-245-7080***	973-672-5454	325
T & R Electric Supply Company Inc 308 SW Third St	Colman	SD	57017	**800-843-7994**	605-534-3555	757
T & S Brass & Bronze Works Inc PO Box 1088 *Cust Svc	Travelers Rest	SC	29690	**800-476-4103***	864-834-4102	602
T & T Trucking Inc 11396 N Hwy 99 *Cust Svc	Lodi	CA	95240	**800-692-3457***	209-931-6000	770
T Cook's 5200 E Camelback Rd	Phoenix	AZ	85018	**800-672-6011**	602-808-0766	662
T Cross Ranch LLC 82 Parque Creek Rd PO Box 638	Dubois	WY	82513	**877-827-6770**	307-455-2206	239
T G H Aviation 2389 Rickenbacker Way	Auburn	CA	95602	**800-843-4976**	530-823-6204	56
T Marzetti Co 1105 Schrock Rd	Columbus	OH	43229	**800-999-1835**	614-846-2232	295-19
T R Toppers Inc 320 Fairchild	Pueblo	CO	81001	**800-748-4635**	719-948-4902	295-8
T Rowe Price Assoc Inc 100 E Pratt St	Baltimore	MD	21202	**800-638-7890**	410-345-2000	398
T Rowe Price Group Inc 100 E Pratt St *NASDAQ: TROW*	Baltimore	MD	21202	**800-638-7890**	410-345-2000	357-3
T Rowe Price Mutual Funds 100 E Pratt St	Baltimore	MD	21202	**800-638-5660**	410-345-2000	521
T. Bruce Sales Inc Nine Carbaugh St	West Middlesex	PA	16159	**800-944-0738**	724-528-9961	475
T. Marzetti Company. P.O. Box 29163	Columbus	OH	43229	**800-999-1835**		295-9
T.u.c.s. Cleaning Service Inc 166 Central Ave	Orange	NJ	07050	**800-992-5998**	973-673-0700	150
T3 Expo LLC Eight Lakeville Business Park Unit 1	Lakeville	MA	02347	**888-698-3397**		185
TA Assoc Inc 200 Clarendon St 56th Fl	Boston	MA	02116	**800-836-8873**	617-574-6700	780
TAB Products Co 605 Fourth St	Mayville	WI	53050	**888-466-8228**		527
Tabb Brockenbrough & Ragland LLC 4905 Dickens Rd	Richmond	VA	23230	**800-296-0531**	804-355-7984	387
TABB Inc PO Box 10	Chester	NJ	07930	**800-887-8222**		626
Taber Extrusions LP 915 S Elmira Ave	Russellville	AR	72802	**800-563-6853**	479-968-1021	480
Table Mountain Casino 8184 Table Mountain Rd	Friant	CA	93626	**800-541-3637**	559-822-7777	132
Taboo Resort Golf & Spa 1209 Muskoka Beach Rd	Gravenhurst	ON	P1P1R1	**800-461-0236**		698
Tabor College 400 S Jefferson St *Admissions	Hillsboro	KS	67063	**800-822-6799***	620-947-3121	166
Tacala LLC 3750 Corporate Woods Dr	Vestavia Hills	AL	35242	**800-822-6235**	205-443-9600	661
Taco Cabana Inc 8918 Tesoro Dr Ste 200	San Antonio	TX	78217	**800-357-9924**	210-804-0990	661
Taco Inc 1160 Cranston St	Cranston	RI	02920	**888-778-2733**	401-942-8000	354
Taco Time International Inc 9311 E Via de Venutra	Scottsdale	AZ	85258	**866-452-4252**	480-362-4800	661
Tacoma Electric Supply Inc 1311 S Tacoma Way	Tacoma	WA	98409	**800-422-0540**	253-475-0540	246
Tacoma General Hospital 315 MLK Jr Way	Tacoma	WA	98405	**800-552-1419**	253-403-1000	371-3
Tacoma Inc 328 E Church St	Martinsville	VA	24112	**800-352-9417**	276-666-9417	661
Tacoma Mall 4502 S Steele St Ste 1177	Tacoma	WA	98409	**877-746-6642**	253-475-4565	455
Tacoma Regional Convention & Visitor Bureau 1516 Pacific Ave Ste 500	Tacoma	WA	98402	**800-272-2662**	253-627-2836	207
Tacoma Rubber Stamp & Sign 919 Market St	Tacoma	WA	98402	**800-544-7281**	253-383-5433	462
Taconic 136 Coonbrook Rd PO Box 69	Petersburg	NY	12138	**800-833-1805**	518-658-3202	734-2
Tadiran Batteries 2001 Marcus Ave Ste 125E	New Hyde Park	NY	11042	**800-537-1368**	516-621-4980	73
TAF (Taxpayers Against Fraud Education Fund) 1220 19th St NW Ste 501 *General	Washington	DC	20036	**800-873-2573***	202-296-4826	48-10
Taft College 29 Emmons Pk Dr	Taft	CA	93268	**800-379-6784**	661-763-7700	160
TAG (Tube Art Group) 11715 SE Fifth St	Bellevue	WA	98005	**800-562-2854**	206-223-1122	692
TAG Solutions LLC 12 Elmwood Rd	Albany	NY	12204	**800-724-0023**	518-292-6500	725
Tag-A-Long Expeditions 452 N Main St	Moab	UT	84532	**800-453-3292**	435-259-8946	750
Tag-It Pacific Inc 21900 Burbank Blvd Ste 270	Woodland Hills	CA	91367	**877-870-5176**	818-444-4100	410
Tahitian Noni International 333 W Riverpark Dr *Cust Svc	Provo	UT	84604	**800-445-2969***	801-234-1000	295-11
Tahoe Mountain Sports 11200 Donner Pass Rd Ste 5e	Truckee	CA	96161	**866-891-9177**		702
Tahoe Seasons Resort 3901 Saddle Rd PO Box 16300	South Lake Tahoe	CA	96151	**800-540-4874**	530-541-6700	660
Tahoma National Cemetery 18600 SE 240th St	Kent	WA	98042	**800-827-1000**	425-413-9614	135
Tailhook Assn 9696 Businesspark Ave	San Diego	CA	92131	**800-322-4665**	858-689-9223	47-19
Tailored Chemical Products Inc 700 12th St Dr NW	Hickory	NC	28601	**800-627-1687**	828-322-6512	3
Tailored Living LLC 1927 N Glassell St	Orange	CA	92865	**866-675-8819**		358
Taitron Components Inc 28040 W Harrison Pkwy *NASDAQ: TAIT*	Valencia	CA	91355	**800-247-2232**	661-257-6060	246
Taiwan Semiconductor Mfg Company Ltd (TSMC) 2585 Junction Ave *NYSE: TSM*	San Jose	CA	95134	**877-248-4237**	408-382-8000	687
Taiyo Yuden (USA) Inc 1930 N Thoreau Dr Ste 190	Schaumburg	IL	60173	**800-348-2496**	847-925-0888	253
Taj Boston 15 Arlington St	Boston	MA	02116	**877-482-5267**	617-536-5700	376
Taj Campton Place 340 Stockton St	San Francisco	CA	94108	**866-969-1825**	415-781-5555	376
TAJ Technologies Inc 1168 Northland Dr	Mendota Heights	MN	55120	**877-825-2801**	651-688-2801	712
Takagi Industrial Company USA Inc Five Whatney	Irvine	CA	92618	**888-882-5244**	949-770-7171	15
Takara Belmont USA Inc 101 Belmont Dr	Somerset	NJ	08873	**877-283-1289**		75
Take 3 Trailers Inc 1808 Hwy 105	Brenham	TX	77833	**800-428-2533**	979-337-9568	753
Takeda Canada Inc 435 N Service Rd W Ste 101	Oakville	ON	L6M4X8	**888-367-3331**	905-469-9333	84
Talan Products Inc 18800 Cochran Ave	Cleveland	OH	44110	**877-419-2805**	216-458-0170	478
Talbott Hotel 20 E Delaware Pl	Chicago	IL	60611	**800-825-2688**	312-944-4970	376
Talbott Recovery Campus 5448 Yorktowne Dr	Atlanta	GA	30349	**800-445-4232**	770-994-0185	717
Talent Curve 14 Bridle Path	Pittsboro	NC	27312	**866-494-0248**		458
TalentLens Inc 19500 Bulverde Rd	San Antonio	TX	78259	**888-298-6227**		260
Taleo Corp 4140 Dublin Blvd Ste 400 *NYSE: ORCL*	Dublin	CA	94568	**800-672-2531**	925-452-3000	179-1
Talisma Corp 777 Yamato Rd	Boca Raton	FL	33431	**866-397-2537**	561-923-2500	38
Talk O'Texas Brands Inc 1610 Roosevelt St	San Angelo	TX	76905	**800-749-6572**	325-655-6077	295-20
Talk Radio Network (TRN) PO Box 3755	Central Point	OR	97502	**888-383-3733**		637
TalkPoint Communications Inc 100 William St	New York	NY	10038	**866-323-8660**	212-909-2900	177
Talladega Castings & Machine Co Inc 228 N Ct St	Talladega	AL	35160	**800-766-6708**	256-362-5550	306
Talladega College 627 W Battle St	Talladega	AL	35160	**866-540-3956**	256-362-0206	166
Talladega Machinery & Supply Co Inc 301 N Johnson Ave PO Box 736 *Cust Svc	Talladega	AL	35161	**800-289-8672***	256-362-4124	306
Tallan Inc 175 Capital Blvd Ste 401	Rocky Hill	CT	06067	**800-677-3693**	860-633-3693	178
Tallapoosa River Electric Co-op 15163 US Hwy 431 S PO Box 675	Lafayette	AL	36862	**800-332-8732**	334-864-9331	245
TallyGenicom 15345 Barranca Pkwy Ste 100	Irvine	CA	92618	**800-436-4266**	714-368-2300	174-6
Talquin Electric Co-op Inc 1640 W Jefferson St	Quincy	FL	32351	**888-271-8778**	850-627-7651	245
TALX Corp 11432 Lackland Dr	Saint Louis	MO	63146	**800-888-8277**	314-214-7000	38
T-A-M (Trace-A-Matic Inc) 1570 Commerce Ave	Brookfield	WI	53045	**877-375-0217**	262-797-7300	614
Tam International Inc 4620 Southerland Rd	Houston	TX	77092	**800-462-7617**	713-462-7617	530

	Toll-Free	Phone	Class
Tamarac Inc			
701 Fifth Ave 14th Fl .... Seattle WA 98104	866-525-8811		398
Tamco Inc			
1466 Delberts Dr .... Monongahela PA 15063	800-826-2672	724-258-6622	748
Tampa Armature Works Inc			
6312 78th St .... Riverview FL 33578	866-465-8905	813-621-5661	511
Tampa Bay & Co			
401 E Jackson St Ste 2100 .... Tampa FL 33602	877-230-0078	813-223-1111	207
Tampa Bay Beaches Chamber of Commerce			
6990 Gulf Blvd .... Saint Pete Beach FL 33706	855-344-5999	727-360-6957	137
Tampa Bay Downs Inc			
11225 Racetrack Rd .... Tampa FL 33626	800-200-4434	813-855-4401	633
Tampa Bay Fisheries Inc			
3060 Gallagher Rd .... Dover FL 33527	800-732-3663	813-752-8883	295-14
Tampa Bay History Ctr			
801 Old Water St .... Tampa FL 33602	800-352-3671	813-228-0097	513
Tampa Bay Lightning			
St Pete Times Forum			
401 Channelside Dr .... Tampa FL 33602	800-745-3000	813-301-6500	707
Tampa Convention Ctr			
333 S Franklin St .... Tampa FL 33602	866-790-4111	813-274-8511	206
Tampa International Airport			
4100 George J Bean Pkwy			
PO Box 22287 .... Tampa FL 33607	866-289-9673	813-870-8700	27
Tampa Marriott Waterside Hotel & Marina			
700 S Florida Ave .... Tampa FL 33602	888-268-1616	813-204-6300	698
Tampa Museum of Art			
120 W Gasparilla Plaza .... Tampa FL 33602	866-790-4111	813-274-8130	513
Tampa Port Authority			
1101 Channelside Dr .... Tampa FL 33602	800-741-2297	813-905-7678	611
Tamron USA Inc			
10 Austin Blvd .... Commack NY 11725	800-827-8880*	631-858-8400	584
*General			
Tandberg Data			
10225 Westmoor Dr Ste 125 .... Westminster CO 80021	800-392-2983	303-442-4333	174-8
Tandus Centiva			
311 Smith Industrial Blvd			
PO Box 1447. .... Dalton GA 30722	800-248-2878	706-259-9711	130
Tangent Inc			
191 Airport Blvd .... Burlingame CA 94010	800-342-9388	650-342-9388	174-1
Tanger Factory Outlet Centers Inc			
3200 Northline Ave Ste 360 .... Greensboro NC 27408	800-720-6728	336-292-3010	646
NYSE: SKT			
Tanger Outlet Ctr San Marcos			
4015 S IH-35 Ste 319. .... San Marcos TX 78666	800-408-8424	512-396-7446	455
Tanglewood Resort Hotel & Conference Ctr			
290 Tanglewood Cir .... Pottsboro TX 75076	800-833-6569	903-786-2968	660
Tangoe Inc			
35 Executive Blvd .... Orange CT 06477	877-571-4737	203-859-9300	178
NASDAQ: TNGO			
Tanimura & Antle Inc			
PO Box 4070 .... Salinas CA 93912	800-772-4542		10-10
Tanner Cos LLC			
581 Rock Rd .... Rutherfordton NC 28139	877-872-4578	828-287-4205	153-20
Tanner Electric Co			
45710 SE North Bend Way .... North Bend WA 98045	800-472-0208	425-888-0623	245
Tanner Industries Inc			
735 Davisville Rd Third Fl .... SouthHampton PA 18966	800-643-6226	215-322-1238	144
Tanner Research Inc			
825 S Myrtle Ave .... Monrovia CA 91016	877-325-2223	626-471-9700	175
Tanner Systems Inc			
625 19th Ave NE .... Saint Joseph MN 56374	800-461-6454	320-363-1800	141
Tanque Verde Guest Ranch			
14301 E Speedway Blvd .... Tucson AZ 85748	800-234-3833	520-296-6275	660
Tanque Verde Ranch			
14301 E Speedway .... Tucson AZ 85748	800-234-3833	520-296-6275	239
Tantalus Resort Lodge			
4200 Whistler Way .... Whistler BC V0N1B4	888-633-4046	604-932-4146	660
Tan-Tar-A Resort Golf Club & Spa			
494 Tantara Dr PO Box 188TT .... Osage Beach MO 65065	800-826-8272*	573-348-3131	660
*Resv			
TanTara Transportation Corp			
2420 Stewart Rd .... Muscatine IA 52761	800-650-0292	563-262-8621	770
Tap Packaging Solutions			
2160 Superior Ave .... Cleveland OH 44114	800-827-5679	216-781-6000	553
TAP Plastics Inc			
6475 Sierra Ln .... Dublin CA 94568	800-894-0827	925-829-4889	600
Tapatio Springs Golf Resort & Conference Ctr			
One Resort Way .... Boerne TX 78006	800-999-3299		660
Tapco Group			
29797 Beck Rd .... Wixom MI 48393	800-367-8741	248-668-6400	690
Tape & Label Converters Inc			
8231 Allport Ave .... Santa Fe Springs CA 90670	888-285-2462	562-945-3486	410
Tape Craft Corp			
200 Tape Craft Dr .... Oxford AL 36203	800-521-1783*		734-5
*Cust Svc			
Tapecon Inc			
10 Latta Rd .... Rochester NY 14612	800-333-2407	585-621-8400	410
TAPEMARK Co			
1685 Marthaler Ln .... West Saint Paul MN 55118	800-535-1998	651-455-1611	410
Tapeswitch Corp			
100 Schmitt Blvd .... Farmingdale NY 11735	800-234-8273	631-630-0442	720
Tapmatic Corp			
802 S Clearwater Loop .... Post Falls ID 83854	800-854-6019*	208-773-8048	488
*General			
TAPPI (Technical Assn of the Pulp & Paper Industry)			
15 Technology Pkwy S .... Norcross GA 30092	800-332-8686*	770-446-1400	48-13
*Sales			
Tapscott's			
1403 E 18th St .... Owensboro KY 42303	800-626-1922	270-684-2308	293
TAR (Tennessee Assn of Realtors)			
901 19th Ave S .... Nashville TN 37212	877-321-1477	615-321-1477	647
Tara Toy Corp			
40 Adams Ave .... Hauppauge NY 11788	800-899-8272	631-273-8697	752
Tarboro Edgecombe Chamber of Commerce			
509 Trade St .... Tarboro NC 27886	888-404-3424	252-823-7241	137
Target Corp			
1000 Nicollet Mall .... Minneapolis MN 55403	800-440-0680*	612-304-6073	229
NYSE: TGT *Cust Svc			
Targeted Job Fairs Inc			
4441 Glenway Ave .... Cincinnati OH 45205	800-695-1939		260
Targus Inc			
1211 N Miller St .... Anaheim CA 92806	877-482-7487	714-765-5555	448
Tarkett Inc			
1001 Yamaska St E .... Farnham QC J2N1J7	800-363-9276	450-293-3173	291
Tarleton State University			
1333 W Washington			
PO Box T-0030 .... Stephenville TX 76402	800-687-8236	254-968-9000	166
Taro Pharmaceuticals Inc			
130 E Dr .... Brampton ON L6T1C1	800-268-1975	905-791-8276	576
Taro Pharmaceuticals USA Inc			
3 Skyline Dr .... Hawthorne NY 10532	800-544-1449	914-345-9001	577
Tarr LLC			
2429 N Borthwick St .... Portland OR 97227	800-422-5069		144
Northeast			
828 W Harwood Rd .... Hurst TX 76054	800-799-7233	817-515-8223	160
Tarrant County College			
Northwest			
4801 Marine Creek Pkwy .... Fort Worth TX 76179	800-799-7233	817-515-7100	160
Tarryall River Ranch			
270015 County Rd 77 .... Lake George CO 80827	800-408-8407	719-748-1214	239
Tarrytown Music Hall			
13 Main St PO Box 686 .... Tarrytown NY 10591	877-840-0457	914-631-3390	565
TASC Technical Services LLC			
73 Newton Rd .... Plaistow NH 03865	877-304-8272		196
Task Force Tips Inc			
3701 Innovation Way .... Valparaiso IN 46383	800-348-2686	219-462-6161	283
3701 Innovation Way .... Valparaiso IN 46383	800-348-2686	219-462-6161	739
Taskstream LLC			
71 W 23rd St .... New York NY 10010	800-311-5656	212-868-2700	225
Tasler Inc			
1804 Tasler Dr .... Webster City IA 50595	800-482-7537	515-832-5200	544
Taste of Home Magazine			
5400 S 60th St .... Greendale WI 53129	800-344-6913	414-423-0100	452-11
Tasty Baking Co			
4300 S 26th St Ste 200. .... Philadelphia PA 19112	800-248-2789	215-221-8500	295-1
Tate Access Floors Inc			
7510 Montevideo Rd .... Jessup MD 20794	800-231-7788	410-799-4200	486
Tate Andale Inc			
1941 Lansdowne Rd .... Baltimore MD 21227	800-296-8283	410-247-8700	588
Tattered Cover Book Store Inc			
1628 16th St .... Denver CO 80202	800-833-9327	303-436-1070	95
Tatung Company of America Inc			
2850 El Presidio St .... Long Beach CA 90810	800-827-2850	310-637-2105	174-4
Tau Beta Pi Assn			
1512 Middle Dr .... Knoxville TN 37996	877-829-5500	865-546-4578	47-16
Tau Beta Sigma National Honorary Band Sorority			
PO Box 849 .... Stillwater OK 74076	800-543-6505*	405-372-2333	47-16
*Cust Svc			
Taubman Centers Inc			
200 E Long Lk Rd			
Ste 300 .... Bloomfield Hills MI 48303	800-297-6003	248-258-6800	646
NYSE: TCO			
Tauck World Discovery			
10 Norden Pl .... Norwalk CT 06855	800-468-2825	203-899-6500	750
Taunton Area Chamber of Commerce			
12 Taunton Green Ste 201 .... Taunton MA 02780	800-225-0394	508-824-4068	137
Taurus International Mfg Inc			
16175 NW 49th Ave .... Miami FL 33014	800-327-3776	305-624-1115	284
Tavaero Jet Charter			
7930 Airport Blvd .... Houston TX 77061	800-343-3771	713-644-6431	13
Tavistock Restaurants LLC			
35 Braintree Hill Office Pk .... Braintree MA 02184	800-424-2753	781-817-4400	661
Tax Executives Institute (TEI)			
1200 G St NW Ste 300 .... Washington DC 20005	877-244-7711	202-638-5601	48-1
Tax Management Inc			
1801 S Bell St .... Arlington VA 22202	800-372-1033	703-341-3000	628-9
Taxpayers Against Fraud Education Fund (TAF)			
1220 19th St NW Ste 501 .... Washington DC 20036	800-873-2573*	202-296-4826	48-10
*General			
Taycor LLC			
6065 Bristol Pkwy .... Culver City CA 90230	800-322-9738	310-895-7704	216
Taylor			
750 N Blackhawk Blvd .... Rockton IL 61072	800-255-0626	815-624-8333	297
Taylor & Francis Group			
270 Madison Ave .... New York NY 10016	800-797-3803	212-216-7855	628-2
Taylor & Fulton Inc			
932 Fifth Ave W .... Palmetto FL 34221	800-457-5577	941-729-3883	10-10
Taylor & Messick Inc			
325 Walt Messick Rd .... Harrington DE 19952	800-237-1272	302-398-3729	513
Taylor Bldg Products			
631 N First St .... West Branch MI 48661	800-248-3600	989-345-5110	234
Taylor Capital Group Inc			
9550 W Higgins Rd .... Rosemont IL 60018	866-750-9107	847-653-7978	357-2
NASDAQ: TAYC			
Taylor Corp			
1725 Roe Crest Dr .... North Mankato MN 56003	800-545-6620	507-625-2828	357-3
Taylor County RECC			
625 W Main St PO Box 100 .... Campbellsville KY 42719	800-931-4551	270-465-4101	245
Taylor Electric Co-op			
N1831 State Hwy 13 .... Medford WI 54451	800-862-2407	715-678-2411	245
Taylor Enterprises Inc (TEI)			
2586 Southport Rd .... Spartanburg SC 29302	800-922-3149	864-573-9518	572
Taylor Farms Inc			
PO Box 1649 .... Salinas CA 93902	866-675-6120	831-676-9765	296-7
Taylor Freezer Sales Company Inc			
2032 Atlantic Ave .... Chesapeake VA 23324	800-768-6945		656
Taylor Freezers of California			
221 Harris Ct .... South San Francisco CA 94080	877-978-4800		403
Taylor Law Offices Pc			
122 E Washington Ave .... Effingham IL 62401	800-879-2250		425
Taylor Precision Products LLC			
2311 W 22nd St .... Oak Brook IL 60523	866-843-3905		203
Taylor Technologies Inc			
31 Loveton Cir .... Sparks MD 21152	800-837-8548*	410-472-4340	794
*Cust Svc			
Taylor Truck Line Inc			
31485 Northfield Blvd .... Northfield MN 55057	800-962-5994	507-645-4531	770
Taylor University			
236 W Reade Ave .... Upland IN 46989	800-882-3456	765-998-2751	166
Fort Wayne			
915 W Rudisill Blvd .... Fort Wayne IN 46807	800-882-3456*	260-744-8790	166
*General			
Taylor University College & Seminary			
11525 23rd Ave .... Edmonton AB T6J4T3	800-567-4988	780-431-5200	167-3
Taylor-Dunn Manufacturing Co			
2114 W Ball Rd .... Anaheim CA 92804	800-688-8680	714-956-4040	465

Name / Address	City	State	ZIP	Toll-Free	Phone	Class
TaylorMade - Adidas Golf						
5545 Fermi Ct	Carlsbad	CA	92008	**800-555-1212***	760-918-6000	701
*Cust Svc						
Taylor-Winfield Inc						
PO Box 779	Youngstown	OH	44509	**800-523-4899**	330-259-8500	798
Tazewell Area Chamber of Commerce						
Tazewell Mall PO Box 6	Tazewell	VA	24651	**855-233-6362**	276-988-5091	137
TB Butler Publishing Co						
410 W Erwin St	Tyler	TX	75702	**800-333-9141**	903-597-8111	628-8
TB Wood's Inc						
440 N Fifth Ave	Chambersburg	PA	17201	**888-829-6637**	717-264-7161	613
TBA LLC						
6700 Enterprise Dr	Louisville	KY	40214	**800-626-3525**	502-367-0222	605
Tbb Global Logistics Inc						
802 Far Hills Dr	New Freedom	PA	17349	**800-937-8224**	717-227-5000	444
TBC (Teal Becker & Chiramonte)						
7 Washington Sq	Albany	NY	12205	**888-380-9660**	518-456-6663	2
TBC (Tom Barrow Co)						
2800 Plant Atkinson Rd	Smyrna	GA	30080	**800-229-8226**	404-351-1010	14
Tbm Consulting Group Inc						
4400 Ben Franklin Blvd	Durham	NC	27704	**866-532-6826**	919-471-5535	195
TBN (Trinity Broadcasting Network)						
PO Box A	Santa Ana	CA	92711	**888-731-1000**	714-832-2950	729
TBT (Transco Business Technologies)						
34 Leighton Rd	Augusta	ME	04330	**800-322-0003**	207-622-6251	111
TCA (Truckload Carriers Assn)						
555 E Braddock Rd	Alexandria	VA	22314	**800-666-2770**	703-838-1950	48-21
TCC (Customer Communicator, The)						
712 Main St Ste 187B	Boonton	NJ	07005	**800-232-4317**	973-265-2300	524-2
TCE Capital Corp						
505 Consumers Rd Ste 707	Toronto	ON	M2J4V8	**800-465-0400**	416-497-7400	272
TCI Aluminum/North Inc						
2353 Davis Ave	Hayward	CA	94545	**800-824-6197**	510-786-3750	487
TCI College of Technology						
320 W 31st St	New York	NY	10001	**800-878-8246**	212-594-4000	788
TCI International Inc						
3541 Gateway Blvd	Fremont	CA	94538	**800-827-2661**	510-687-6100	638
TCI Scales Inc						
PO Box 1648	Snohomish	WA	98291	**800-522-2206**	425-353-4384	675
TCIA (Tree Care Industry Assn)						
136 Harvey Rd Ste 101	Londonderry	NH	03053	**800-733-2622**	603-314-5380	47-13
TCK (Twin City Knitting Company Inc)						
104 Rock Barn Rd NE	Conover	NC	28613	**800-438-6884**	828-464-4830	153-9
TCM (Temp-Control Mechanical Corp)						
4800 N Ch Ave	Portland	OR	97217	**877-826-3828**	503-285-9851	14
TCT Ministries Inc						
11717 N Rt 37 PO Box 1010	Marion	IL	62959	**800-232-9855**	618-997-4700	729
TCU (Teachers Credit Union)						
PO Box 1395	South Bend	IN	46624	**800-552-4745**	574-284-6247	219
TCVB (Tyler Convention & Visitors Bureau)						
315 N Broadway	Tyler	TX	75702	**800-235-5712**	903-592-1661	207
TCW Group Inc						
865 S Figueroa St Ste 1800	Los Angeles	CA	90017	**800-386-3829**	213-244-0000	521
TD Bank NA						
1701 Rt 70 E	Cherry Hill	NJ	08034	**888-751-9000**	856-751-2739	69
TD Banknorth Massachusetts						
295 Pk Ave	Worcester	MA	01609	**800-747-7000***	508-752-2584	69
*Cust Svc						
TDECU (Texas Dow Employees Credit Union)						
1001 FM 2004	Lake Jackson	TX	77566	**800-839-1154**	979-297-1154	219
TDI-Transistor Devices Inc						
85 Horsehill Rd	Cedar Knolls	NJ	07927	**800-488-6724**	973-267-1900	253
TDK USA Corp						
525 RXR Plaza PO Box 9302	Uniondale	NY	11556	**800-285-2783***	516-535-2600	51
*General						
TDS (Texas Disposal Systems Inc)						
12200 Carl Rd	Creedmoor	TX	78610	**800-375-8375**	512-421-1300	792
TDS Telecommunications Corp						
525 Junction Rd	Madison	WI	53717	**866-571-6662**	608-664-4000	726
Tea Council of the USA Inc						
362 Fifth Ave Ste 801	New York	NY	10001	**877-212-5752**	212-986-9415	48-6
Teach For America						
315 W 36th St Seventh Fl	New York	NY	10018	**800-832-1230**	212-279-2080	48-5
Teacher Created Resources						
6421 Industry Way	Westminster	CA	92683	**888-343-4335**		243
Teacher Magazine						
6935 Arlington Rd Ste 100	Bethesda	MD	20814	**800-346-1834**	301-280-3100	452-8
Teachers Credit Union (TCU)						
PO Box 1395	South Bend	IN	46624	**800-552-4745**	574-284-6247	219
Teachers Federal Credit Union (TFCU)						
2410 N Ocean Ave						
PO Box 9029	Farmingville	NY	11738	**800-341-4333**	631-698-7000	219
Teachers of English to Speakers of Other Languages (TESOL)						
700 S Washington St Ste 200	Alexandria	VA	22314	**888-547-3369**	703-836-0774	48-5
Teachers Protective Mutual Life Insurance Co						
116-118 N Prince St	Lancaster	PA	17603	**800-555-3122**	717-394-7156	387
Teaching & Mentoring Communities (TMC)						
PO Box 2579	Laredo	TX	78044	**888-836-5151**	956-722-5174	48-5
Teal Becker & Chiramonte (TBC)						
7 Washington Sq	Albany	NY	12205	**888-380-9660**	518-456-6663	2
Teal's Express Inc						
22411 Teal Dr PO Box 6010	Watertown	NY	13601	**800-836-0369**	315-788-6437	770
Team Health Inc						
265 Brookview Ctr Way Ste 400	Knoxville	TN	37919	**800-342-2898**	865-693-1000	712
Team Inc 200 Hermann Dr	Alvin	TX	77511	**800-662-8326**	281-331-6154	532
NYSE: TISI						
Team Volkswagen of Hayward Corp						
25115 Mission Blvd	Hayward	CA	94544	**866-308-2825**		56
TeamQuest Corp						
One TeamQuest Way	Clear Lake	IA	50428	**800-551-8326**	641-357-2700	179-12
Teamwork Newsletter						
2222 Sedwick Dr	Durham	NC	27713	**800-223-8720**		524-2
Teaneck Public Library						
840 Teaneck Rd	Teaneck	NJ	07666	**800-245-1377**	201-837-4171	431-3
TEC (Thompson Electric Co)						
2300 Seventh St PO Box 207	Sioux City	IA	51105	**800-832-2936**	712-252-4221	775
Tec Laboratories Inc						
7100 Tec Labs Way SW	Albany	OR	97321	**800-482-4464**	541-926-4577	231
Tech Briefs Media Group						
261 Fifth Ave Ste 1901	New York	NY	10016	**888-456-3398**	212-490-3999	452-19
Tech Credit Union						
10951 Broadway	Crown Point	IN	46307	**800-276-8324**	219-663-5120	219
Tech Data Corp						
5350 Tech Data Dr	Clearwater	FL	33760	**800-237-8931**	727-539-7429	175
NASDAQ: TECD						
Tech International						
200 E Coshocton St	Johnstown	OH	43031	**800-336-8324**	740-967-9015	744
Tech Lighting LLC						
7400 Linda Ave	Skokie	IL	60077	**800-522-5315**	847-410-4400	435
Tech Museum of Innovation						
201 S Market St	San Jose	CA	95113	**800-660-4287**	408-294-8324	513
Tech Packaging Inc						
13241 Bartram Pk Blvd						
Ste 601	Jacksonville	FL	32258	**866-453-8324**	904-288-6403	542
Tech Usa Inc						
8334 Veterans Hwy	Millersville	MD	21108	**888-584-8181**	410-729-4328	195
Tech4Learning Inc						
10981 San Diego Mission Rd						
Ste 120	San Diego	CA	92108	**877-834-5453**	619-563-5348	454
Techalloy Company Inc Baltimore Wire Div						
2310 Chesapeake Ave	Baltimore	MD	21222	**800-638-1458**	410-633-9300	800
Techline USA LLC						
500 S Div St	Waunakee	WI	53597	**800-356-8400**		318-1
Techne Corp						
614 McKinley Pl NE	Minneapolis	MN	55413	**800-343-7475**	612-379-8854	231
NASDAQ: TECH						
Technetics Group						
3125 Damon Way	Burbank	CA	91505	**800-618-4701**	818-841-9667	601
Technical Assn of the Pulp & Paper Industry (TAPPI)						
15 Technology Pkwy S	Norcross	GA	30092	**800-332-8686***	770-446-1400	48-13
*Sales						
Technical Chemical Co						
3327 Pipeline Rd	Cleburne	TX	76033	**800-527-0885**	817-645-6088	143
Technical Communications Corp						
100 Domino Dr	Concord	MA	01742	**800-952-4082**	978-287-5100	725
NASDAQ: TCCO						
Technical Communities Inc						
1000 Cherry Ave Ste 100	San Bruno	CA	94066	**888-665-2765**	650-624-0525	196
Technical Consumer Products Inc						
325 Campus Dr	Aurora	OH	44202	**800-324-1496**		433
Technical Gas Products Inc						
66 Leonardo Dr	North Haven	CT	06473	**800-847-0745**		572
Technical Systems Integration Inc						
816 Greenbrier Cir Ste 208	Chesapeake	VA	23320	**800-566-8744**	757-424-5793	256
Technical Transportation Inc						
1701 W Northwest Hwy Ste 100	Grapevine	TX	76051	**800-852-8726**		444
Techni-Car Inc						
450 Commerce Blvd	Oldsmar	FL	34677	**800-886-0022**	813-855-0022	61-5
Techni-Cast Corp						
11220 Garfield Ave	South Gate	CA	90280	**800-923-4585**	562-923-4585	307
Technicote Westfield Inc						
222 Mound Ave	Miamisburg	OH	45342	**800-358-4448**	937-859-4448	545-1
Technidrill Systems Inc						
429 Portage Blvd	Kent	OH	44240	**800-914-5863**	330-678-9980	450
Techniform Industries Inc						
2107 Hayes Ave	Fremont	OH	43420	**800-691-2816**	419-332-8484	592
Techni-Tool Inc						
1547 N Trooper Rd PO Box 1117	Worcester	PA	19490	**800-832-4866***	610-941-2400	348
*Cust Svc						
Techno-Aide Inc						
7117 Centennial Blvd	Nashville	TN	37209	**800-251-2629**	615-350-7030	471
Technology Advancement Group Inc						
22355 Tag Way	Sterling	VA	20166	**800-824-7693**	703-406-3000	174-1
Technology Funding Inc						
460 St Michael's Dr Ste 1000	Santa Fe	NM	87505	**800-821-5323**		780
Technology Futures Inc (TFI)						
13740 Research Blvd (N Hwy 183)						
Ste C-1	Austin	TX	78750	**800-835-3887**	512-258-8898	197
Technology Integration Group (TIG)						
7810 Trade St	San Diego	CA	92121	**800-858-0549**	858-566-1900	177
Technology Marketing Corp						
One Technology Plz	Norwalk	CT	06854	**800-243-6002***	203-852-6800	628-2
*Cust Svc						
Technology Partners						
550 University Ave	Palo Alto	CA	94301	**800-747-3924**	650-289-9000	780
Technology Service Corp						
962 Wayne Ave Ste 800	Silver Spring	MD	20910	**800-324-7700**	301-565-2970	659
TechnoServe 49 Day St	Norwalk	CT	06854	**800-999-6757**	203-852-0377	47-5
TechServe Alliance						
1420 King St Ste 610	Alexandria	VA	22314	**888-421-1442**	703-838-2050	47-9
TechSmith Corp						
2405 Woodlake Dr	Okemos	MI	48864	**800-517-3001**	517-381-2300	179-8
TechTarget						
275 Grove St Ste 800	Newton	MA	02466	**888-274-4111**	617-431-9200	628-10
Techware Distribution Inc						
7720 W 78th St	Minneapolis	MN	55439	**800-295-0083**	952-944-0083	225
TechWorks						
4030 W Braker Ln	Austin	TX	78759	**800-688-7466***	512-794-8533	617
*Cust Svc						
Teck Cominco American Inc						
501 N Riverpoint Blvd Ste 300	Spokane	WA	99202	**888-767-7718**	509-747-6111	497
Tecnica USA						
19 Technology Dr	West Lebanon	NH	03784	**800-258-3897**	603-298-8032	701
Tecnicard Inc						
3191 Coral Way Ste 800	Miami	FL	33145	**800-317-6020**	305-442-0018	225
Tecnico Corp						
831 Industrial Ave	Chesapeake	VA	23324	**800-786-2207***	757-545-4013	689
*General						
Teco Diagnostics						
1268 N Lakeview Ave	Anaheim	CA	92807	**800-222-9880**	714-463-1111	231
Tecom Industries Inc						
375 Conejo Ridge Ave	Thousand Oaks	CA	91361	**866-840-8550**	805-267-0100	638
TECO-Westinghouse Motor Co						
5100 N IH-35	Round Rock	TX	78681	**800-451-8798**	512-255-4141	700
TECSYS Inc						
1 Pl Alexis Nihon Ste 800	Montreal	QC	H3Z3B8	**800-922-8649**	514-866-0001	179-1
Tectum Inc						
105 S Sixth St	Newark	OH	43055	**888-977-9691**	740-345-9691	806
Tedia Company Inc						
1000 Tedia Way	Fairfield	OH	45014	**800-787-4891**	513-874-5340	142
Teeco Products Inc						
16881 Armstrong Ave	Irvine	CA	92606	**800-854-3463**	949-261-6295	382
Teeter Irrigation Inc						
2729 W Oklahoma	Ulysses	KS	67880	**800-524-5497**	620-353-1111	274
Tegal Corp						
2201 S McDowell Blvd	Petaluma	CA	94954	**800-828-3425**	707-763-5600	686

	Toll-Free	Phone	Class
TEGAM Inc 10 Tegam Way ....Geneva OH 44041	800-666-1010	440-466-6100	248
Tegrant Corp 1401 Pleasant St ....DeKalb IL 60115	800-633-3962	815-756-8451	541
TEI (Taylor Enterprises Inc) 2586 Southport Rd ....Spartanburg SC 29302	800-922-3149	864-573-9518	572
TEI (Tax Executives Institute) 1200 G St NW Ste 300 ....Washington DC 20005	877-244-7711	202-638-5601	48-1
Tejas Inc 8226 Bee Caves Rd ....Austin TX 78746	800-846-6803	512-306-8222	681
Tejas Logistics System PO Box 1339 ....Waco TX 76703	800-535-9786	254-753-0301	791-1
Tekelec 5200 Paramount Pkwy ....Morrisville NC 27560 NASDAQ: TKLC	800-633-0738	919-460-5500	725
Teknon Corp 15443 NE 95th St ....Redmond WA 98052	800-338-6142	425-895-8535	190-4
Teknor Apex Co 505 Central Ave ....Pawtucket RI 02861	800-556-3864	401-725-8000	598-3
TEKPAK Inc 1410 Washington St ....Marion AL 36756	866-901-8073	334-683-6121	124
Tekra Corp 16700 W Lincoln Ave ....New Berlin WI 53151	800-448-3572	262-784-5533	596
Tekran Instruments Corp 230 Tech Ctr Dr ....Knoxville TN 37912	888-383-5726	865-688-0688	416
TEKsystems Inc 7437 Race Rd ....Hanover MD 21076	888-519-0776	410-540-7700	712
Tekworks Inc 13000 Gregg St Ste B ....Poway CA 92064	877-835-9675		177
Tel Electronics Inc 313 S 740 E St Suite 1 ......American Fork UT 84003	800-564-9424	801-756-9606	725
TeL Systems 7235 Jackson Rd ....Ann Arbor MI 48103	800-686-7235	734-761-4506	246
TelAlaska Inc 201 E 56th St ....Anchorage AK 99518	888-570-1792	907-563-2003	726
Telco Systems Inc 15 Berkshire Rd ....Mansfield MA 02048	800-227-0937	781-255-2120	725
Telcoe Federal Credit Union 820 Lousiana St ....Little Rock AR 72201	800-482-9009	501-375-5321	219
Tele Business USA 1945 Techny Rd Ste 3.............Northbrook IL 60062	877-315-8353		727
Tel-e Technologies 7 Kodiak Crescent ....Toronto ON M3J3E5	800-661-2340	416-631-1300	5
Telebyte Inc 355 Marcus Blvd ....Hauppauge NY 11788	800-835-3298	631-423-3232	177
Teleco Inc 430 Woodruff Rd Ste 300 ....Greenville SC 29607	800-800-6159	864-297-4400	246
Telecom AM 2115 Ward Ct NW ....Washington DC 20037	800-771-9202	202-872-9200	524-11
TeleCommunication Systems Inc 275 W St Ste 400 ....Annapolis MD 21401 NASDAQ: TSYS	800-810-0827	410-263-7616	224
Tele-Communications Inc 5125 W 140th St ....Brookpark OH 44142	877-841-8914	216-267-0800	246
TelecomPioneers 1801 California St 44th Fl..............Denver CO 80202	800-872-5995	303-571-1200	47-15
Telect Inc 23321 E Knox Ave ....Liberty Lake WA 99019 *Cust Svc	800-551-4567*	509-926-6000	725
Teledyne Advanced Pollution Instrumentation 9480 Carroll Pk Dr ....San Diego CA 92121	800-324-5190	858-657-9800	202
Teledyne Brown Engineering Inc 300 Sparkman Dr PO Box 070007..........Huntsville AL 35807	800-933-2091	256-726-1000	261
Teledyne Monitor Labs Inc (TML) 35 Inverness Dr E..........Englewood CO 80112	800-422-1499	303-792-3300	202
Teledyne Technologies Inc 1049 Camino Dos Rios ....Thousand Oaks CA 91360 NYSE: TDY	877-666-6968	805-373-4545	21
Teleflex Inc 155 S Limerick Rd ....Limerick PA 19468 NYSE: TFX	866-246-6990	610-948-5100	186
Teleflex Medical 2917 Weck Dr PO Box 12600..........Research Triangle Park NC 27709	866-246-6990	919-544-8000	59
TeleflexGFI Control Systems LP 100 Hollinger Crescent ....Kitchener ON N2K2Z3	800-667-4275	519-576-4270	59
Telegraph Herald 801 Bluff St ....Dubuque IA 52001	800-553-4801	563-588-5611	525-2
Telegraph, The PO Box 278 ....Alton IL 62002	866-299-9256	618-463-2500	525-2
Telelatino Network Inc (TLN) 5125 Steeles Ave W ....Toronto ON M9L1R5	800-551-8401	416-744-8200	729
Tele-Measurements Inc 145 Main Ave ....Clifton NJ 07014	800-223-0052	973-473-8822	195
Tele-Media Corp 804 Jacksonville Rd P.O. Box 39..........Bellefonte PA 16823	800-704-4254	814-353-2025	115
Telephone & Data Systems Inc 30 N La Salle St Ste 4000.............Chicago IL 60602 NYSE: TDS	877-337-1575	312-630-1900	357-3
Telephone Service Co 2 Willipie St ....Wapakoneta OH 45895	800-743-5707	419-739-2200	726
Telephonics Corp 815 Broad Hollow Rd ....Farmingdale NY 11735	877-517-2327	631-755-7000	638
Telerent Leasing Corp 4191 Fayetteville Rd ....Raleigh NC 27603	800-626-0682	919-772-8604	37
Telerx 723 Dresher Rd ....Horsham PA 19044	800-283-5379	267-942-3300	727
TeleSearch Staffing Solutions 251 Re 206 ....Flanders NJ 07836	800-499-8367	973-927-7870	623
TeleServices Direct 5305 Lakeview Pkwy S Dr ....Indianapolis IN 46268	888-646-6626	317-216-2240	727
Telesource Services LLC 1450 Highwood E ....Pontiac MI 48340	800-525-4300	248-335-3000	246
Telesouth Communications Inc 6311 Ridgewood Rd ....Jackson MS 39211	888-808-8637	601-957-1700	634
Telesta Therapeutics Inc 275 Labrosse Ave ....Pointe-Claire QC H9R1A3 TSE: TST	800-387-0825	514-697-6636	84
Telestream Inc 848 Gold Flat Rd Ste 1 ....Nevada City CA 95959	877-681-2088	530-470-1300	179-8
TeleTech Holdings Inc 9197 S Peoria St ....Englewood CO 80112 NASDAQ: TTEC ▦ *General	800-835-3832*	303-397-8100	727
Teletrac Inc 7391 Lincoln Way ....Garden Grove CA 92841	800-500-6009	714-897-0877	683
Tele-Track 5550 Peach Tree Pkwy Ste 600 ....Norcross GA 30092	800-729-6981	770-449-8809	218
Telex Communications Inc 12000 Portland Ave S ....Burnsville MN 55337	877-863-4169	952-884-4051	51
Teligent Inc 210 Brookwood Rd ....Atmore AL 36502	888-411-1175	251-368-8600	726
Telkonet Inc 10200 W Innovation Dr Ste 300 ..Milwaukee WI 53226 OTC: TKOI ▦ *Sales	888-703-9398*	414-223-0473	177
Tellurex Corp 1462 International Dr ....Traverse City MI 49686	877-774-7468	231-947-0110	687
Telmar Technology 901 Jupiter Rd ....Plano TX 75074	866-835-6276	972-836-0400	246
Telonic Berkeley Inc 1080 La Mirada Ct ....Vista CA 92081 *Sales	800-311-8805*	760-744-8350	253
Telpar Inc 187 Crosby Rd Ste 100...........Dover NH 03820	800-872-4886	603-750-7237	174-6
TelSpan Inc 101 W Washington St E Tower Ste 1200 ....Indianapolis IN 46204	800-800-1729		384
Telus 1000 Rue de Serigny ....Longueuil QC J4K5B1	888-709-8759	450-928-6000	795
Temecula Creek Inn 44501 Rainbow Canyon Rd ....Temecula CA 92592	877-517-1823	855-685-9299	660
Temecula Valley Chamber of Commerce (TVCC) 26790 Ynez Ct Ste A.............Temecula CA 92591	866-676-5090	951-676-5090	137
Temo Sunrooms Inc 20400 Hall Rd ....Clinton Township MI 48038	800-344-8366		104
Tempco Electric Heater Corp 607 N Central Ave ....Wood Dale IL 60191	888-268-6396	630-350-2252	317
Temp-Control Mechanical Corp (TCM) 4800 N Ch Ave ....Portland OR 97217	877-826-3828	503-285-9851	14
Tempe Convention & Visitors Bureau 51 W Third St Ste 105 ....Tempe AZ 85281	866-914-1052	480-894-8158	207
Temperature Systems Inc 5001 Voges Rd ....Madison WI 53718	800-366-0930	608-271-7500	605
Temple College 2600 S First St ....Temple TX 76504 *Admissions	800-460-4636*	254-298-8300	160
Temple Meridian 4312 S 31st St ....Temple TX 76502	855-444-7658	254-771-2350	663
Temple University James E Beasley School of Law 1719 N Broad St ....Philadelphia PA 19122	800-560-1428	215-204-7861	167-1
Temple University Press 1852 N 10th St USB 305 ....Philadelphia PA 19122	800-621-2736	215-926-2140	628-4
Templeton Unified School District 960 Old County Rd ....Templeton CA 93465	800-316-6142	805-434-5800	676
Temporary Solutions Inc 10550 Linden Lk Plz Ste 200 ....Manassas VA 20109	888-222-0457	703-361-2220	712
Temptronic Corp 41 Hampden Rd ....Mansfield MA 02048 *Tech Support	800-558-5080*	781-688-2300	416
Tempur-Pedic International Inc 1713 Jaggie Fox Way ....Lexington KY 40511 NYSE: TPX	800-821-6621		466
Tempus Resorts International 7380 Sand Lake Rd Ste 600 ....Orlando FL 32819	877-747-4747	407-226-1000	743
Ten-8 Fire Equipment Inc 2904 59th Ave Dr E ....Bradenton FL 34203	877-989-7660	941-756-7779	509
TenCate Geosynthetics North America 365 S Holland Dr ....Pendergrass GA 30567	888-795-0808	706-693-2226	734-3
TenCate Grass North America 1131 Broadway St ....Dayton TN 37321	800-251-1033	423-775-0792	598-1
TenCate Protective Fabrics USA 6501 Mall Blvd ....Union City GA 30291	800-241-8630		734-3
Tender Corp 106 Burndy Rd ....Littleton NH 03561	800-258-4696	603-444-5464	280
Tenenbaum's Vacation Stores Inc 300 Market St ....Kingston PA 18704	800-545-7099	570-288-8747	761
Tengasco Inc 11121 Kingston Pk Ste E ....Knoxville TN 37934 NYSE: TGC	888-669-0684	865-675-1554	529
Tennant Co 701 N Lilac Dr ....Minneapolis MN 55422 NYSE: TNC ▦ *Cust Svc	800-553-8033*	763-540-1200	383
Tenneco Inc 500 N Field Dr ....Lake Forest IL 60045 NYSE: TEN	866-839-3259	847-482-5000	59
Tennessean 1100 Broadway ....Nashville TN 37203	800-342-8237	615-259-8033	525-2
Tennessee *Child Support Services Div* 400 Deaderick St 12th Fl ....Nashville TN 37248	800-838-6911	615-313-4880	337-43
Economic & Community Development Dept (ECD) 312 Eigth Ave N 11th Fl ....Nashville TN 37243	877-768-6374	615-741-1888	337-43
Mental Health & Developmental Disabilities Dept 425 Fifth Ave N 3rd Fl ....Nashville TN 37243	800-669-1851	615-532-6500	337-43
Real Estate Commission 500 James Robertson Pkwy Ste 180 ....Nashville TN 37243	800-342-4031	615-741-2273	337-43
Securities Div 500 James Robertson Pkwy Ste 680 ....Nashville TN 37243	800-863-9117	615-741-2947	337-43
State Parks Div 401 Church St 7th Fl ....Nashville TN 37243	888-867-2757	615-532-0001	337-43
Supreme Court 511 Union St Nashville City Ctr Ste 600 ....Nashville TN 37219	800-448-7970	615-741-2687	337-43
Tennessee Aquarium 1 Broad St ....Chattanooga TN 37402	800-262-0695	423-802-6768	39
Tennessee Assn of Realtors (TAR) 901 19th Ave S ....Nashville TN 37212	877-321-1477	615-321-1477	647
Tennessee Baptist Convention 5001 Maryland Way ....Brentwood TN 37027	800-558-2090	615-371-2029	47-20
Tennessee Bar Assn 221 Fourth Ave N Ste 400..........Nashville TN 37219	800-899-6993	615-383-7421	71
Tennessee Farm Bureau News 147 Bear Creek Pike ....Columbia TN 38401	877-876-2222	931-388-7872	452-1
Tennessee Farmers Co-op 180 Old Nashville Hwy ......La Vergne TN 37086	800-366-2667	615-793-8011	276

				Toll-Free	Phone	Class
Tennessee Fitness Spa						
299 Natural Bridge Pk Rd	Waynesboro	TN	38485	**800-235-8365**	931-722-5589	697
Tennessee Performing Arts Ctr						
505 Deaderick St	Nashville	TN	37219	**866-455-2823**	615-782-4000	565
Tennessee Rehabilitative Initiative in Correction (TRICOR)						
240 Great Cir Rd Ste 310	Nashville	TN	37228	**800-958-7426**	615-741-5705	622
Tennessee State Library & Archives						
403 Seventh Ave N	Nashville	TN	37243	**877-850-4959**	615-741-2764	431-5
Tennessee State Museum						
505 Deaderick St	Nashville	TN	37243	**800-407-4324**	615-741-2692	513
Tennessee State University						
3500 John A Merritt Blvd						
PO Box 9609	Nashville	TN	37209	**888-463-6878***	615-963-5000	166
*Admissions						
Tennessee Steel Haulers Inc						
PO Box 78189	Nashville	TN	37207	**800-776-4004**	615-271-2400	770
Tennessee Technological University						
One William L Jones Dr	Cookeville	TN	38505	**800-255-8881**	931-372-3888	166
Tennessee Temple University						
1815 Union Ave	Chattanooga	TN	37404	**800-553-4050**	423-493-4100	166
Tennessee Titans						
460 Great Cir Rd	Nashville	TN	37228	**800-334-4628**	615-565-4000	706-3
Tennessee Valley Electric Co-op						
590 Florence Rd	Savannah	TN	38372	**866-925-4916**	731-925-4916	245
Tennessee Valley Printing Company Inc						
PO Box 2213	Decatur	AL	35609	**888-353-4612**	256-353-4612	628-8
Tennessee Veterinary Medical Assn						
PO Box 803	Fayetteville	TN	37334	**800-697-3587**	931-438-0070	783
Tennessee Wesleyan College						
204 E College St PO Box 40	Athens	TN	37371	**800-742-5892**	423-745-7504	166
Tennsco Corp						
201 Tennsco Dr PO Box 1888	Dickson	TN	37056	**866-446-8686***	615-446-8000	318-1
*Cust Svc						
Tenrox						
401 Congress Avenue	Austin	TX	78701	**855-944-7526**	626-796-6640	179-1
Tension Envelope Corp						
819 E 19th St	Kansas City	MO	64108	**800-388-5122**		263
Teo Technologies Inc						
11609 49th Pl W	Mukilteo	WA	98275	**800-524-0024**	425-349-1000	725
TEOCO Corp						
12150 Monument Dr Ste 400	Fairfax	VA	22033	**888-868-3626**	703-322-9200	780
Teradata Corp						
10000 Innovation Dr	Dayton	OH	45342	**866-548-8348**		225
NYSE: TDC						
TERATECH Corp						
77-79 Terr Hall Ave	Burlington	MA	01803	**866-837-2766**	781-270-4143	471
Terex Corp Crane Div						
202 Raleigh St	Wilmington	NC	28412	**877-794-5284**	910-395-8500	465
Terex-Telelect Inc						
500 Oakwood Rd PO Box 1150	Watertown	SD	57201	**800-982-8975**	605-882-4000	465
Terlato Wine Group, The (TWG)						
900 Armour Dr	Lake Bluff	IL	60044	**800-950-7676**	847-604-8900	80-3
Terminal City Club						
837 W Hastings St	Vancouver	BC	V6C1B6	**888-253-8777**	604-681-4121	376
Terminal Corp, The						
1657 S Highland Ave Ste A	Baltimore	MD	21224	**800-560-7207**		310
Terminix International Company LP						
860 Ridge Lk Blvd	Memphis	TN	38120	**866-399-0453**		570
Termnet Merchant Services Inc						
1601 Dodge St Ste 1600	Omaha	NE	68102	**800-228-2443**		195
Terra Community College						
2830 Napoleon Rd	Fremont	OH	43420	**800-334-3886**	419-334-8400	160
Terra Dotta LLC						
501 W Franklin St Ste 105	Chapel Hill	NC	27516	**877-368-8277**		178
Terraces at Phoenix, The						
7550 N 16th St	Phoenix	AZ	85020	**800-836-4281**	602-906-4024	663
Terracon						
18001 W 106th St	Olathe	KS	66061	**800-593-7777**	913-599-6886	261
Terre Haute Convention & Visitors Bureau						
5353 E Margaret Dr	Terre Haute	IN	47803	**800-366-3043**		207
Terre Haute Regional Hospital (THRH)						
3901 S Seventh St	Terre Haute	IN	47802	**866-270-2311**	812-232-0021	371-3
Terre Hill Silo Company Inc						
PO Box 10	Terre Hill	PA	17581	**800-242-1509**	717-445-3100	184
Terrebonne General Medical Ctr (TGMC)						
8166 Main St	Houma	LA	70360	**888-850-6270**	985-873-4141	371-3
Terros Inc						
3003 N Central Ave Ste 200	Phoenix	AZ	85012	**800-631-1314**	602-222-9444	350
Terry Laboratories Inc						
7005 Technology Dr	Melbourne	FL	32904	**800-367-2563**	321-259-1630	474
Terry Precision Bicycles for Women Inc						
47 Maple St	Burlington	VT	05401	**800-289-8379**		81
Terryberry Co						
2033 Oak Industrial Dr NE	Grand Rapids	MI	49505	**800-253-0882**	616-458-1391	406
Terry-Durin Co						
409 Seventh Ave SE	Cedar Rapids	IA	52401	**800-332-8114**	319-364-4106	246
Terumo Cardiovascular Systems Corp						
6200 Jackson Rd	Ann Arbor	MI	48103	**800-262-3304**	734-663-4145	471
Terumo Medical Corp						
2101 Cottontail Ln	Somerset	NJ	08873	**800-283-7866**	732-302-4900	471
TES (Total Energy Solutions LLC)						
100 International Dr Ste 260	Portsmouth	NH	03801	**877-436-9812**		112
Tesa Tape Inc						
5825 Carnegie Blvd	Charlotte	NC	28209	**800-426-2181**	704-554-0707	722
Tesco Industries LP						
1035 E Hacienda	Bellville	TX	77418	**800-699-5824**		318-3
Tesko Welding & Manufacturing Co						
7350 W Montrose Ave	Norridge	IL	60706	**800-621-4514**	708-452-0045	286
Tesla Motors Inc						
3500 Deer Creek Rd	Palo Alto	CA	94304	**888-518-3752**	650-681-5000	58
TESOL (Teachers of English to Speakers of Other Languages)						
700 S Washington St Ste 200	Alexandria	VA	22314	**888-547-3369**	703-836-0774	48-5
Tesoro Corp						
1225 17th Street	Denver	CO	80202	**800-299-0570**		572
TESSCO Technologies Inc						
11126 McCormick Rd	Hunt Valley	MD	21031	**800-472-7373**	410-229-1000	246
NASDAQ: TESS						
TestAmerica Laboratories Inc						
4625 E Cotton Ctr Blvd Ste 189	Phoenix	AZ	85040	**866-785-5227**	602-437-3340	732
Testing Machines Inc						
40 McCullough Dr	New Castle	DE	19720	**800-678-3221***	302-613-5600	467
*General						
Testor Corp						
440 Blackhawk Pk Ave	Rockford	IL	61104	**800-837-8677**	815-962-6654	752

				Toll-Free	Phone	Class
Teters Floral Products Inc						
1425 S Lillian Ave	Bolivar	MO	65613	**800-999-5996**	417-326-7654	293
Teton County Public Library						
125 Virginian Ln	Jackson	WY	83001	**800-878-2167**	307-733-2164	431-3
Teton Mountain Lodge & Spa						
3385 Cody Ln PO Box 564	Teton Village	WY	83025	**800-631-6271**	307-201-6066	376
Tetra Corporate Services LLC						
6995 Union Park Ctr						
Suite 360	Salt Lake City	UT	84047	**800-417-0548**	801-566-2600	264-3
Tetra Medical Supply Corp						
6364 W Gross Pt Rd	Niles	IL	60714	**800-621-4041***	847-647-0590	470
*Cust Svc						
Tetra Tech EC Inc						
1000 the American Rd	Morris Plains	NJ	07950	**800-580-3765**	973-630-8000	261
Tetra Tech/KCM						
3475 E Foothill Blvd	Pasadena	CA	91107	**888-288-8288**	626-351-4664	261
NASDAQ: TTEK						
TETRA Technologies Inc						
25025 I-45 N	The Woodlands	TX	77380	**800-327-7817**	281-367-1983	141
NYSE: TTI						
Tetrahedron Assoc Inc						
PO Box 710157	San Diego	CA	92171	**800-958-3872**	619-661-0552	451
Tettegouche State Park						
5702 Hwy 61	Silver Bay	MN	55614	**800-366-8917**	218-226-6365	558
Teufel Nursery Inc						
3431 NW John Olsen Pl	Hillsboro	OR	97124	**800-483-8335**	503-646-1111	293
Teva Pharmaceutical USA						
1090 Horsham Rd	North Wales	PA	19454	**800-545-8800**	215-591-3000	577
NYSE: TEVA						
Teva Sport Sandals						
123 N Leroux St	Flagstaff	AZ	86001	**800-367-8382***	928-779-5938	300
*General						
Texans Credit Union						
777 E Campbell Rd	Richardson	TX	75081	**800-843-5295**	972-348-2000	219
Texarkana College						
2500 N Robison Rd	Texarkana	TX	75599	**877-275-4377**	903-838-4541	160
Texarkana Gazette						
315 Pine St	Texarkana	TX	75501	**866-747-7424***	903-794-3311	525-2
*General						
Aging & Disability Services						
701 W 51st St Ste W253	Austin	TX	78751	**888-388-6332**	512-438-3011	337-44
Agriculture Dept						
PO Box 12847	Austin	TX	78711	**800-835-5832***	512-463-7476	337-44
*Cust Svc						
Arts Commission						
920 Colorado Ste 501						
PO Box 13406	Austin	TX	78701	**800-252-9415**	512-463-5535	337-44
Banking Dept						
2601 N Lamar Blvd	Austin	TX	78705	**877-276-5554**	512-475-1300	337-44
Child Support Div						
300 W 15th St	Austin	TX	78701	**800-252-8014**	512-460-6000	337-44
Comptroller of Public Accounts						
111 E 17th St	Austin	TX	78774	**800-531-5441**	512-463-4600	337-44
Consumer Protection Div						
PO Box 12548	Austin	TX	78711	**800-621-0508***		337-44
*General						
Crime Victims Services Div						
PO Box 12198	Austin	TX	78711	**800-983-9933**	512-936-1200	337-44
Environmental Quality Commission (TCEQ)						
12100 Pk 35 Cir PO Box 13087	Austin	TX	78711	**800-735-2989**	512-239-1000	337-44
General Land Office						
1700 N Congress Ave Ste 935	Austin	TX	78701	**800-998-4456**	512-463-5001	337-44
Governor PO Box 12428	Austin	TX	78711	**800-843-5789**	512-463-2000	337-44
Insurance Dept						
333 Guadalupe St PO Box 149104	Austin	TX	78714	**800-252-3439**	512-463-6169	337-44
Medical Board						
PO Box 2018	Austin	TX	78768	**800-248-4062***	512-305-7010	337-44
*Cust Svc						
Motor Vehicle Div						
4000 Jackson Ave PO Box 2293	Austin	TX	78731	**888-368-4689**		337-44
Parks & Wildlife Dept						
4200 Smith School Rd	Austin	TX	78744	**800-792-1112**	512-389-4800	337-44
Texas						
Public Utility Commission						
PO Box 13326	Austin	TX	78711	**888-782-8477**	512-936-7000	337-44
Railroad Commission						
PO Box 12967	Austin	TX	78711	**877-228-5740**	512-463-7131	337-44
State Government Information						
1501 N Congress Ste 4224	Austin	TX	78711	**877-452-9060**	512-936-9500	337-44
Veterans Commission						
PO Box 12277	Austin	TX	78711	**800-252-8387**	512-463-5538	337-44
Vital Statistics Bureau						
1100 W 49th St PO Box 12040	Austin	TX	78756	**888-963-7111**		337-44
Workers Compensation Commission						
7551 Metro Ctr Dr	Austin	TX	78744	**800-252-7031***	512-804-4000	337-44
*Cust Svc						
Texas A & M International University						
5201 University Blvd	Laredo	TX	78041	**888-489-2648**	956-326-2001	166
Texas A & M University						
Rudder Tower Ste 205	College Station	TX	77843	**888-890-5667**	979-845-8901	166
Galveston						
200 Seawolf Pkwy Bldg 3026	Galveston	TX	77553	**877-322-4443**	409-740-4428	166
Kingsville						
700 University Blvd MSC 128	Kingsville	TX	78363	**800-726-8192**	361-593-2111	166
Texarkana						
7101 University Ave	Texarkana	TX	75503	**866-791-9120**	903-223-3000	166
Texas A & M University Press						
John H Lindsey Bldg						
4354 TAMU	College Station	TX	77843	**800-826-8911***	979-845-1436	628-4
*Orders						
Texas Agriculture Magazine						
7420 Fish Pond Rd PO Box 2689	Waco	TX	76710	**800-772-6535**	254-772-3030	452-1
Texas Art Supply						
2001 Montrose Blvd	Houston	TX	77006	**800-888-9278**	713-526-5221	44
Texas Assn of Realtors						
1115 San Jacinto Blvd Ste 200	Austin	TX	78701	**800-873-9155**	512-480-8200	647
Texas Bar Journal						
1414 Colorado St Ste 902	Austin	TX	78701	**800-204-2222**	512-463-1463	452-15
Texas Basket Co						
100 Myrtle Dr	Jacksonville	TX	75766	**800-657-2200**	903-586-8014	201
Texas Book Festival						
610 Brazos St Ste 200	Austin	TX	78701	**800-222-8733**	512-477-4055	281
Texas Capital Bank						
2000 McKinney Ave Ste 700	Dallas	TX	75201	**877-839-2265**	214-932-6600	69

	Toll-Free	Phone	Class
Texas Children's Hospital			
6621 Fannin St ....Houston TX 77030	800-364-5437	832-824-1000	371-1
Texas Christian University			
TCU PO Box 297043 ....Fort Worth TX 76129	800-828-3764	817-257-7490	166
Texas Christian University Mary Couts Burnett Library			
2800 S University Dr ....Fort Worth TX 76129	866-321-7428	817-257-7000	431-6
Texas City-La Marque Chamber of Commerce			
9702 Emmett F Lowry Expy ...Texas City TX 77591	877-986-8719*	409-935-1408	137
*General			
Texas Coffee Co Inc			
3297 S M L King Jr Pkwy ......Beaumont TX 77705	800-259-3400	409-835-3434	295-7
Texas College			
2404 N Grand Ave ....Tyler TX 75702	800-306-6299	903-593-8311	166
Texas Crushed Stone Co			
5300 S IH-35 PO Box 1000 ......Georgetown TX 78627	800-772-8272	512-930-0106	498-5
Texas Ctr for Infectious Diseases			
2303 SE Military Dr ....San Antonio TX 78223	800-839-5864	210-534-8857	371-7
Texas Dental Assn			
1946 S IH-35 Ste 400 ....Austin TX 78704	800-832-1145	512-443-3675	227
Texas Disposal Systems Inc (TDS)			
12200 Carl Rd ....Creedmoor TX 78610	800-375-8375	512-421-1300	792
Texas Dow Employees Credit Union (TDECU)			
1001 FM 2004 ....Lake Jackson TX 77566	800-839-1154	979-297-1154	219
Texas Electric Co-ops Inc			
1122 Colorado St 24th Fl ....Austin TX 78701	800-301-2860	512-454-0311	245
Texas Enterprises Inc			
5005 E Seventh St ....Austin TX 78702	800-545-4412	512-385-2167	572
Texas Farm Bureau			
7420 Fish Pond Rd PO Box 2689 ......Waco TX 76710	800-488-7872	254-772-3030	452-1
Texas Farm Products Co			
915 S Fredonia St ....Nacogdoches TX 75964	800-392-3110	936-564-3711	571
Texas Healthcare PLLC			
2821 Lackland Rd Ste 300 ......Fort Worth TX 76116	800-844-8850	817-378-3640	371-3
Texas Hospital Insurance Exchange			
8310 N Capital of Texas Hwy			
Ste 250 ....Austin TX 78731	800-792-0060	512-451-5775	388-5
Texas Instruments Inc			
12500 TI Blvd ....Dallas TX 75243	800-336-5236*	972-995-3773	687
NASDAQ: TXN ▪ *Cust Svc			
Texas Land & Cattle Steak House			
9911 W IH- 10 ....San Antonio TX 78230	855-685-1622	210-699-8744	662
Texas Lawyers Insurance Exchange (TLIE)			
900 Congress Ave Ste 500 ....Austin TX 78701	800-252-9332	512-480-9074	388-5
Texas Lime Co			
15865 Farm Rd 1434 PO Box 851 ......Cleburne TX 76033	800-772-8000	817-641-4433	436
Texas Lutheran University			
1000 W Ct St ....Seguin TX 78155	800-771-8521	830-372-8000	166
Texas Medical Assn			
401 W 15th St ....Austin TX 78701	800-880-1300	512-370-1300	469
Texas Medicine Magazine			
401 W 15th St ....Austin TX 78701	800-880-1300	512-370-1300	452-16
Texas Memorial Museum			
2400 Trinity St ....Austin TX 78705	800-687-4132	512-471-1604	513
Texas Motorplex			
7500 W Hwy 287 ....Ennis TX 75119	800-668-6775	972-878-2641	508
Texas Mutual Insurance Co			
6210 E Hwy 290 ....Austin TX 78723	888-532-5246	512-224-3800	388-4
Texas Orthopedic Hospital			
7401 Main St ....Houston TX 77030	866-783-4549	713-799-8600	371-7
Texas Pacific Land Trust			
1700 Pacific Ave Ste 2770 ....Dallas TX 75201	877-231-7500	214-969-5530	666
NYSE: TPL			
Texas Pharmacy Assn			
12007 Research Blvd Ste 201........Austin TX 78759	800-505-5463	512-836-8350	578
Texas Pipe & Supply Co Inc			
2330 Holmes Rd ....Houston TX 77051	800-233-8736	713-799-9235	487
Texas Presbyterian Foundation			
3500 Oak Lawn Ave Ste 300 ....Dallas TX 75219	800-955-3155	214-522-3155	47-20
Texas Process Equipment Co			
5215 Ted St ....Houston TX 77040	800-828-4114	713-460-5555	382
Texas Public Radio (TPR)			
8401 Datapoint Dr Ste 800 ....San Antonio TX 78229	800-622-8977	210-614-8977	624
Texas Rangers			
Rangers Ballpark in Arlington			
1000 Ballpark Way ....Arlington TX 76011	866-800-1275	817-273-5222	704
Texas Refinery Corp			
840 N Main St ....Fort Worth TX 76164	800-827-0711	817-332-1161	534
Texas Republican Party			
1108 Lavaca Ste 500 ....Austin TX 78701	800-525-5555	512-477-9821	609-2
Texas Roadhouse Inc			
6040 Dutchmans Ln Ste 400 ....Louisville KY 40205	800-839-7623	502-426-9984	661
NASDAQ: TXRH			
Texas Scottish Rite Hospital for Children			
2222 Welborn St ....Dallas TX 75219	800-421-1121	214-559-5000	371-1
Texas Southern University			
3100 Cleburne St ....Houston TX 77004	800-252-5400	713-313-7011	166
Texas Southmost College			
80 Fort Brown St ....Brownsville TX 78520	800-850-0160	956-882-8200	160
Texas Sports Hall of Fame			
1108 S University Parks Dr ....Waco TX 76706	800-567-9561	254-756-1633	515
Texas Star Bank			
177 E Jefferson PO Box 608 ......Van Alstyne TX 75495	866-546-8273	903-482-5234	69
Texas State Aquarium			
2710 N Shoreline Blvd ....Corpus Christi TX 78402	800-477-4853*	361-881-1200	39
*General			
Texas State Cemetery			
909 Navasota St ....Austin TX 78702	877-673-6839	512-463-0605	49-3
Abilene 650 E Hwy 80 ....Abilene TX 79601	800-852-8784	325-672-7091	160
Harlingen			
1902 N Loop 499 ....Harlingen TX 78550	800-852-8784	956-364-4000	160
Texas State Technical College			
Sweetwater			
300 Homer K Taylor Dr ....Sweetwater TX 79556	877-450-3595	325-235-7300	160
Waco 3801 Campus Dr ....Waco TX 76705	800-792-8784	254-799-3611	160
Texas State University			
San Marcos			
601 University Dr ....San Marcos TX 78666	866-294-0987*	512-245-2340	166
*Admissions			
Texas Station Gambling Hall & Hotel			
2101 Texas Star Ln ....North Las Vegas NV 89032	800-654-8888*	702-631-1000	132
*Resv			
Texas Tech University			
PO Box 45005 ....Lubbock TX 79409	888-270-3369	806-742-1480	166
Texas Tech University Libraries			
18th & Boston Ave PO Box 40002 ....Lubbock TX 79409	888-270-3369	806-742-2265	431-6
Texas Tech University Press			
2903 Fourth St ....Lubbock TX 79409	800-832-4042	806-742-2982	628-4
Texas Transeastern Inc			
PO Box 5339 ....Pasadena TX 77508	800-866-8579	281-604-3100	770
Texas Transplant Institute			
7700 Floyd Curl Dr ....San Antonio TX 78229	800-298-7824	210-575-3817	759
Texas United Corp			
4800 San Felipe ....Houston TX 77056	800-554-8658	713-877-2600	141
Texas United Pipe Inc			
11627 N Houston Rosslyn Rd ....Houston TX 77086	800-966-8741*	281-448-3276	589
*Sales			
Texas Vet Lab Inc			
1702 N Bell St ....San Angelo TX 76903	800-284-8403		575
Texas Veterinary Medical Assn			
8104 Exchange Dr ....Austin TX 78754	800-711-0023	512-452-4224	783
Texas Wesleyan University			
1201 Wesleyan St ....Fort Worth TX 76105	800-580-8980	817-531-4444	166
Texas Wesleyan University School of Law			
1515 Commerce St ....Fort Worth TX 76102	800-733-9529	817-212-4000	167-1
Texas Woman's University			
304 Admin Dr PO Box 425589 ....Denton TX 76204	866-809-6130	940-898-3188	166
Texas-New Mexico Power Co (TNMP)			
577 N Garden Ridge Blvd ....Lewisville TX 75067	888-866-7456	972-420-4189	775
Tex-Tech Industries Inc			
1 City Ctr 11th Fl ....Portland ME 04101	800-441-7089	207-933-4404	734-3
Textile Care Services Inc			
225 Wood Lk Dr SE ....Rochester MN 55904	800-422-0945		438
Textile Rental Services Assn (TRSA)			
1800 Diagonal Rd Ste 200 ....Alexandria VA 22314	877-770-9274	703-519-0029	48-4
Textile Rubber & Chemical Company Inc			
1300 Tiarco Dr SW ....Dalton GA 30721	800-727-8453	706-277-1300	598-3
Tex-Tube Co			
1503 N Post Oak Rd ....Houston TX 77055	800-839-7473	713-686-4351	485
Textured Coatings Of America			
2422 E 15th St ....Panama City FL 32405	800-454-0340	850-769-0347	543
TF Financial Corp			
3 Penns Trail ....Newtown PA 18940	800-822-3321	215-579-4000	357-2
NASDAQ: THRD			
TF Kinnealey & Company Inc			
1100 Pearl St ....Brockton MA 02301	800-225-4950	508-638-7700	295-26
TFB (Fauquier Bank, The)			
10 Courthouse Sq PO Box 561........Warrenton VA 20186	800-638-3798	540-347-2700	69
TFC (Franchise Co, The)			
5399 Eglinton Ave W Ste 110 ....Etobicoke ON M9C5K9	800-294-5591	416-620-3960	458
TFC USA			
150 Shoreline Dr ....Redwood City CA 94065	800-345-2465	650-508-6000	729
TFCU (Teachers Federal Credit Union)			
2410 N Ocean Ave			
PO Box 9029.................Farmingville NY 11738	800-341-4333	631-698-7000	219
TFH Publications Inc			
One TFH Plz PO Box 427 ....Neptune NJ 07754	800-631-2188*	732-988-8400	628-2
*General			
TFI (Technology Futures Inc)			
13740 Research Blvd (N Hwy 183)			
Ste C-1 ....Austin TX 78750	800-835-3887	512-258-8898	197
Tforce Energy Services			
6143 S Willow Ste 320.......Greenwood Village CO 80111	877-234-1444		676
TFS Capital LLC			
10 N High St Ste 500 ....West Chester PA 19380	888-837-4446		521
TFT (Trees for Tomorrow)			
519 Sheridan St E			
PO Box 609.................Eagle River WI 54521	800-838-9472	715-479-6456	48-5
TFX Medical Inc			
50 Plantation Dr ....Jaffrey NH 03452	800-548-6600	603-532-7706	471
TGC Industries Inc			
101 E Pk Blvd Ste 955 ....Plano TX 75074	800-223-7470	972-881-1099	531
NASDAQ: TGE			
Tgi Direct			
5365 Hill 23 Dr ....Flint MI 48507	800-337-2237		5
TGMC (Terrebonne General Medical Ctr)			
8166 Main St ....Houma LA 70360	888-850-6270	985-873-4141	371-3
TH Properties			
345 Main St ....Harleysville PA 19438	800-225-5847*	215-513-4270	188
*Sales			
Thaddeus Stevens College of Technology (TSCT)			
750 E King St ....Lancaster PA 17602	800-842-3832	717-299-7701	788
Thai Airways International Ltd			
222 N Sepulveda Blvd Ste 100 ......El Segundo CA 90245	800-426-5204	310-640-0097	25
Thales Communications Inc			
22605 Gateway Ctr Dr ....Clarksburg MD 20871	800-258-4420	240-864-7000	638
Thales e-Security Inc			
2200 N Commerce Pkwy Ste 200 ....Weston FL 33326	888-744-4976	954-888-6200	179-12
Tharco Inc			
2222 Grant Ave ....San Lorenzo CA 94580	800-772-2332		99
Thayer Hotel			
674 Thayer Rd ....West Point NY 10996	800-247-5047	845-446-4731	376
Thayer Scale Corp			
91 Schoosett St ....Pembroke MA 02359	800-225-0450	781-826-8101	675
Thayers Natural Pharmaceuticals Inc			
PO Box 56 ....Westport CT 06881	888-842-9371		787
Theatre Development Fund			
1501 Broadway 21st Fl...........New York NY 10036	888-424-4685	212-221-0885	740
Theatre For A New Audience			
154 Christopher St Ste 3D ....New York NY 10014	866-811-4111	212-229-2819	738
Theatre IV			
114 W Broad St ....Richmond VA 23220	800-235-8687	804-783-1688	566-4
Theda Care at Home			
3000 E College Ave ....Appleton WI 54915	800-984-5554	920-969-0919	368
Theda Clark Medical Ctr			
130 Second St ....Neenah WI 54956	800-236-3122	920-729-3100	371-3
Theodore Presser Co			
588 N Gulph Rd ....King of Prussia PA 19406	800-854-6764	610-592-1222	628-7
TheraCare			
116 W 32nd St 8th Fl ....New York NY 10001	800-505-7000	212-564-2350	350
Theragenics Corp			
5203 Bristol Industrial Way ....Buford GA 30518	800-458-4372	770-271-0233	231
NYSE: TGX			
Therapedic International			
1375 Jersey Ave ....North Brunswick NJ 08902	800-233-7467		466
Theriault's			
PO Box 151 ....Annapolis MD 21404	800-966-3655	410-224-3655	50

	Toll-Free	Phone	Class
Thermafiber Inc			
3711 W Mill St ....Wabash IN 46992	888-834-2371	260-563-2111	386
Thermal Care Inc			
7720 N Lehigh Ave ....Niles IL 60714	888-828-7387	847-966-2260	14
Thermal Circuits Inc			
One Technology Way ....Salem MA 01970	800-808-4328	978-745-1162	317
Thermal Corp			
1264 Slaughter Rd ....Madison AL 35758	800-633-2962	256-837-1122	605
Thermal Dynamics Corp			
82 Benning St ....West Lebanon NH 03784	800-752-7621	603-298-5711	450
Thermal Engineering Corp			
2741 The Blvd ....Columbia SC 29209	800-331-0097	803-783-0750	317
Thermal Engineering of Arizona Inc			
2250 W Wetmore Rd ....Tucson AZ 85705	866-832-7278	520-888-4000	424
Thermal Industries Inc			
3700 Haney C ....Murrysville PA 15668	800-245-1540	724-733-3880	235
Thermal Product Solutions			
3827 Riverside Rd ....Riverside MI 49084	800-873-4468	269-849-2700	317
Thermal Solutions LLC			
PO Box 3244 ....Lancaster PA 17604	800-860-5726	717-239-7642	354
ThermaSys Corp			
2776 Gunter Pk Dr E Ste RS ....Montgomery AL 36109	877-274-4328	334-244-9240	90
Therma-Tru Corp			
1750 Indian Wood Cir ....Maumee OH 43537	800-537-8827	419-891-7400	234
Thermionics Laboratory			
1842 Sabre St ....Hayward CA 94545	800-962-2310	510-538-3304	173
Thermo Fisher Scientific Inc			
81 Wyman St PO Box 9046 ....Waltham MA 02454	800-678-5599	781-622-1000	467
NYSE: TMO			
Thermo Fluids Inc			
4301 W Jefferson St ....Phoenix AZ 85043	800-350-7565	602-272-2400	677
Thermo Scientific			
12076 Santa Fe Dr PO Box 14428 ....Lenexa KS 66215	800-255-6730	913-888-0939	231
Thermo Spas Inc			
155 E St ....Wallingford CT 06492	800-876-0158		372
Thermodyn Corp			
3550 Silica Rd ....Sylvania OH 43560	800-654-6518	419-841-7782	668
Thermodynetics Inc			
651 Day Hill Rd ....Windsor CT 06095	800-394-1633	860-683-2005	90
OTC: TDYT			
ThermoElectric Cooling America Corp			
4048 W Schubert Ave ....Chicago IL 60639	888-832-2872	773-342-4900	14
ThermoGenesis Corp			
2711 Citrus Rd ....Rancho Cordova CA 95742	800-783-8357	916-858-5100	417
NASDAQ: KOOL			
Thermopatch Corp			
2204 Erie Blvd E ....Syracuse NY 13224	800-252-6555	315-446-8110	733
Thermoplastic Processes Inc			
1268 Valley Rd ....Stirling NJ 07980	888-554-6400	908-561-3000	593
Thermos Co			
475 N Martingale Rd Ste 1100 ......Schaumburg IL 60173	800-243-0745	847-439-7821	600
ThermoSafe Brands			
3930 N Ventura Dr			
Ste 450 ....Arlington Heights IL 60004	800-323-7442	847-398-0110	594
ThermoServ			
3901 Pipestone Rd ....Dallas TX 75212	800-635-5559	214-631-0307	594
Thermo-Twin Industries Inc			
1155 Allegheny Ave ....Oakmont PA 15139	800-641-2211	412-826-1000	234
Thermwell Products Co			
420 Rt 17 S ....Mahwah NJ 07430	800-526-5265	201-684-4400	386
Thermwood Corp			
904 Buffaloville Rd ....Dale IN 47523	800-533-6901*	812-937-4476	808
*OTC: TOOD ◼ *Mktg*			
Thern Inc			
5712 Industrial Pk Rd PO Box 347 ......Winona MN 55987	800-843-7648	507-454-2996	465
TheStreet.com Inc			
14 Wall St 15th Fl ....New York NY 10005	800-562-9571	212-321-5000	401
NASDAQ: TST			
Theta Delta Chi Inc			
214 Lewis Wharf ....Boston MA 02110	800-999-1847	617-742-8886	47-16
Theta Tau Professional Engineering Fraternity			
1011 San Jacinto Ste 205................Austin TX 78701	800-264-1904	512-472-1904	47-16
Thetford Corp			
7101 Jackson Ave PO Box 1285........Ann Arbor MI 48106	800-521-3032	734-769-6000	603
Thetford Corp Recreational Vehicle Group			
2901 E Bristol St Ste B................Elkhart IN 46514	800-831-1076	574-266-7980	603
Thibaut Inc			
480 Frelinghuysen Ave ....Newark NJ 07114	800-223-0704	973-643-1118	790
Thibodaux Regional Medical Ctr (TRMC)			
602 N Acadia Rd ....Thibodaux LA 70301	800-822-8442	985-447-5500	371-3
Thief River Falls Convention & Visitors Bureau (TRFCVB)			
102 Main Ave N ....Thief River MN 56701	800-657-3700	218-686-9785	207
Thiel College			
75 College Ave ....Greenville PA 16125	800-248-4435	724-589-2000	166
Thiele Technologies			
315 27th Ave NE ....Minneapolis MN 55418	800-932-3647	612-782-1200	540
Think Computer Corp			
3260 Hillview Ave ....Palo Alto CA 94304	888-815-8599	415-670-9350	175
thinkASG			
15265 Alton Pkwy Ste 300 ....Irvine CA 92618	800-991-9274		197
ThinkTV			
110 S Jefferson St ....Dayton OH 45402	800-247-1614	937-220-1600	624
Third Federal Savings & Loan Assn of Cleveland			
7007 Broadway Ave ....Cleveland OH 44105	888-844-7333	216-429-5228	69
Thirstystone Resources Inc			
1304 Corporate Dr ....Gainesville TX 76240	800-829-6888	940-668-6793	292
Thistledown Racing Club Inc			
21501 Emery Rd ....Cleveland OH 44128	866-503-3792	216-662-8600	633
Thobe Group Inc			
2727 Raintree Dr ....Carrollton TX 75006	888-462-3477	972-245-9444	196
Thomas Aquinas College			
10000 Ojai Rd ....Santa Paula CA 93060	800-634-9797	805-525-4417	166
Thomas B Finan Ctr			
10102 Country Club Rd SE			
PO Box 1722................Cumberland MD 21502	888-854-0035	301-777-2405	371-5
Thomas C Wilson Inc			
21-11 44th Ave ....Long Island City NY 11101	800-230-2636	718-729-3360	749
Thomas College			
180 W River Rd ....Waterville ME 04901	800-339-7001*	207-859-1111	166
*Admissions			
Thomas Conveyor Co			
555 N Burleson Blvd ....Burleson TX 76028	800-433-2217	817-295-7151	208
Thomas Creative Apparel Inc			
One Harmony Pl ....New London OH 44851	800-537-2575	419-929-1506	153-13

	Toll-Free	Phone	Class
Thomas E Creek Veterans Affairs Medical Ctr			
6010 Amarillo Blvd W ....Amarillo TX 79106	800-687-8262	806-355-9703	371-8
Thomas Edison State College			
101 W State St ....Trenton NJ 08608	888-442-8372		166
Thomas Engineering Inc			
575 W Central Rd ....Hoffman Estates IL 60192	800-634-9910	847-358-5800	383
Thomas G Faria Corp			
385 Norwich-New London Tpke ......Uncasville CT 06382	800-473-2742	860-848-9271	490
Thomas H Lee Partners			
100 Federal St 35th Fl ....Boston MA 02110	877-456-3427	617-227-1050	402
Thomas Hospital			
750 Morphy Ave ....Fairhope AL 36532	800-422-2027	251-928-2375	371-3
Thomas Jefferson School of Law			
1155 Island Ave ....San Diego CA 92101	877-318-6901	619-297-9700	167-1
Thomas Jefferson University			
1020 Walnut St ....Philadelphia PA 19107	866-594-4722	215-955-6000	166
Thomas Jefferson University Hospital			
111 S 11th St ....Philadelphia PA 19107	800-533-3669	215-955-6000	371-3
Thomas More College			
333 Thomas More Pkwy ....Crestview Hills KY 41017	800-825-4557	859-344-3332	166
Thomas Nelson Inc			
501 Nelson Pl PO Box 141000........Nashville TN 37214	800-251-4000	615-889-9000	628-3
Thomas Publishing Co			
5 Penn Plaza ....New York NY 10001	800-733-1127	212-695-0500	628-2
Thomas Reprographics			
600 N Central Expy ....Richardson TX 75080	800-877-3776	972-231-7227	240
Thomas Scientific			
1654 High Hill Rd PO Box 99........Swedesboro NJ 08085	800-345-2100	856-467-2000	417
Thomas Transcription Services Inc			
PO Box 26613 ....Jacksonville FL 32226	888-878-2889	904-751-5058	473
Thomas University			
1501 Millpond Rd ....Thomasville GA 31792	800-538-9784	229-226-1621	166
Thomas Weisel Partners Group LLC			
One Montgomery St ....San Francisco CA 94104	888-267-3700	415-364-2500	780
Thomaston Savings Bank			
203 Main St PO Box 907 ....Thomaston CT 06787	855-344-1874*	860-283-1874	69
*General			
Thomasville Medical Ctr			
207 Old Lexington Rd ....Thomasville NC 27360	888-844-0080	336-472-2000	371-3
Thombert Inc			
316 E Seventh St N ....Newton IA 50208	800-433-3572		601
Thompson Electric Co (TEC)			
2300 Seventh St PO Box 207 ......Sioux City IA 51105	800-832-2936	712-252-4221	775
Thompson Hine LLP			
127 Public Sq 3900 Key Ctr ....Cleveland OH 44114	877-257-3382	216-566-5500	425
Thompson Hospitality			
505 Huntmar Pk Dr Ste 350 ....Herndon VA 20170	800-842-2737	703-964-5500	661
Thompson Industrial Services LLC			
104 N Main ....Sumter SC 29150	800-849-8040	803-773-8005	603
Thompson International Inc			
PO Box 656 ....Henderson KY 42420	800-626-7054	270-826-3751	383
Thompson Olde Inc			
3250 Camino Del Sol ....Oxnard CA 93030	800-827-1565	805-983-0388	358
Thompson Packers Inc			
550 Carnation St ....Slidell LA 70460	800-989-6328	985-641-6640	468
Thompson Publishing Group Inc			
805 15th St NW Third Fl ....Washington DC 20005	800-677-3789*	202-872-4000	628-9
*Cust Svc			
Thompson Pump & Mfg Company Inc			
4620 City Ctr Dr			
PO Box 291370................Port Orange FL 32129	800-767-7310	386-767-7310	632
Thompson Rivers University			
900 McGill Rd PO Box 3010.........Kamloops BC V2C5N3	800-663-1663	250-828-5000	773
Thompson Siegel & Walmsley Inc			
6806 Paragon Pl Ste 300 ....Richmond VA 23230	800-697-1056	804-353-4500	398
Thompson Technologies Inc			
114 Townpark Dr Ste 100 ....Kennesaw GA 30144	888-794-7947	770-794-8380	712
Thoms Proestler Co			
8001 TPC Rd ....Rock Island IL 61204	800-747-1234	309-787-1234	296-8
Thomsen Group LLC			
1303 43rd St ....Kenosha WI 53140	800-558-4018		295
Thomson CenterWatch Inc			
100 N Washington St Ste 301................Boston MA 02114	800-765-9647*	617-948-5100	628-10
*Cust Svc			
Thomson CompuMark			
500 Victory Rd ....North Quincy MA 02171	800-692-8833	617-479-1600	626
Thomson Elite			
800 Corporate Pointe			
Ste 150................Los Angeles CA 90230	800-354-8337*	424-243-2100	179-10
*Cust Svc			
Thomson Financial			
22 Thomson Pl ....Boston MA 02210	888-216-1929	617-856-2000	384
Thomson ISI ResearchSoft			
2141 Palomar Airport Rd			
Ste 350 ....Carlsbad CA 92009	800-722-1227	760-438-5526	195
Thomson Safaris			
14 Mt Auburn St ....Watertown MA 02472	800-235-0289	617-923-0426	627
Thomson Tax & Acctg			
7322 Newman Blvd ....Dexter MI 48130	800-968-8900*		179-1
*Cust Svc			
Thomson-Hood Veterans Ctr			
100 Veterans Dr ....Wilmore KY 40390	800-928-4838	859-858-2814	781
Thomson-Macconnell Cadillac Inc			
2820 Gilbert Ave ....Cincinnati OH 45206	877-472-0738		509
Thomsons Art Supply Inc			
184 Mamaroneck Ave ....White Plains NY 10601	800-287-4885	914-949-4885	44
Thor Inc			
1280 W 2550 S St ....Ogden UT 84401	888-846-7462	801-393-3312	296-8
Thoratec Corp			
6035 Stoneridge Dr ....Pleasanton CA 94588	800-528-2577	925-847-8600	250
NASDAQ: THOR			
Thorco Industries Inc			
1300 E 12th St ....Lamar MO 64759	800-445-3375	417-682-3375	233
Thorlabs Quantum Electronics Inc			
10335 Guilford Rd ....Jessup MD 20794	877-226-8342	240-456-7100	687
Thor-Lo Inc			
2210 Newton St ....Statesville NC 28677	888-846-7567	704-872-6522	153-9
Thornburg Investment Management Funds			
2300 N Ridgetop Rd ....Santa Fe NM 87506	800-533-9337	505-984-0200	521
Thorndike Press			
10 Water St Ste 310 ....Waterville ME 04901	800-223-1244	207-861-7500	628-2
Thorneloe University			
935 Ramsey Lake Rd ....Sudbury ON P3E2C6	800-461-4030*	705-673-1730	773
*General			

Name / Address	City	State	ZIP	Toll-Free	Phone	Class
Thornton Oil Corp						
10101 Linn Stn Rd Ste 200	Louisville	KY	40223	**800-928-8022**	502-425-8022	323
Thornton W Burgess Society						
6 Discovery Hill Rd	East Sandwich	MA	02537	**800-844-4542**	508-888-6870	47-13
Thoro'Bred Inc						
5020 E La Palma Ave	Anaheim	CA	92807	**877-585-5152**	714-779-2581	478
Thoroughbred Direct Intermodal Services						
5165 Campus Dr Ste 400	Plymouth Meeting	PA	19462	**877-250-2902**	610-567-3360	444
Thoroughbred Owners & Breeders Assn (TOBA)						
PO Box 910668	Lexington	KY	40591	**888-606-8622**	859-276-2291	47-3
Thoroughbred Software International Inc						
285 Davidson Ave Ste 302	Somerset	NJ	08873	**800-524-0430**	732-560-1377	179-2
Thorp Reed & Armstrong LLP						
301 Grant St 14th Fl	Pittsburgh	PA	15219	**800-949-3120**	412-394-7711	425
Thousand Hills Golf Resort						
245 S Wildwood Dr	Branson	MO	65616	**877-262-0430**	417-336-5873	660
Thread Check Inc						
390 Oser Ave	Hauppauge	NY	11788	**800-767-7633**	631-231-1515	488
Threads Magazine						
63 S Main St PO Box 5506	Newtown	CT	06470	**800-283-7252***	203-426-8171	452-14
*General						
Three Bars Cattle & Guest Ranch						
9500 Wycliffe Perry Creek Rd	Cranbrook	BC	V1C7C7	**877-426-5230**	250-426-5230	239
Three D Graphics Inc						
11340 W Olympic Blvd Ste 352	Los Angeles	CA	90064	**800-913-0008**	310-231-3330	179-8
Three Hands Corp						
13259 Ralston Ave	Sylmar	CA	91342	**800-443-5443**	818-833-1200	358
Three Island Crossing State Park						
1083 S Three Island Pk Dr	Glenns Ferry	ID	83623	**866-634-3246**	208-366-2394	558
Three Lakes Information Bureau						
1704 Superior St PO Box 268	Three Lakes	WI	54562	**800-972-6103**	715-546-3344	207
Three Notch Electric Membership Corp						
PO Box 295	Donalsonville	GA	39845	**800-239-5377**	229-524-5377	245
Three Rivers Community College						
2080 Three Rivers Blvd	Poplar Bluff	MO	63901	**877-879-8722**	573-840-9600	160
Threshold Financial Technologies Inc						
3269 American Dr	Mississauga	ON	L4V1X5	**888-414-3733**	905-678-7373	253
Threshold Pharmaceuticals Inc						
170 Harbor Way Suite 300	South San Francisco	CA	94080	**866-276-9886**	650-474-8200	84
NASDAQ: THLD						
THRH (Terre Haute Regional Hospital)						
3901 S Seventh St	Terre Haute	IN	47802	**866-270-2311**	812-232-0021	371-3
Thrifty Car Rental						
5330 E 31st St	Tulsa	OK	74135	**888-400-8877**	918-665-3930	125
Thrifty White Stores						
6055 Nathan Lane N Ste 200	Plymouth	MN	55442	**800-642-3275**	763-513-4300	237
Thrivent Financial for Lutherans						
4321 N BallaRd Rd	Appleton	WI	54919	**800-847-4836**	920-684-3225	388-2
Thumb Correctional Facility						
3225 John Conley Dr	Lapeer	MI	48446	**855-444-3911**	810-667-2045	213
Thunder Valley Casino						
1200 Athens Ave	Lincoln	CA	95648	**877-468-8777**	916-408-7777	132
Thunderbird Rural Public Transportation System						
2801 W Loop 306 Ste A PO Box 60050	San Angelo	TX	76904	**877-947-8729**	325-944-9666	107
Thunderbird School of Global Management						
One Global Pl	Glendale	AZ	85306	**800-848-9084**	602-978-7000	676
Thurgood Marshall Scholarship Fund						
80 Maiden Ln Ste 2204	New York	NY	10038	**866-632-9992**	212-573-8888	716
Thybar Corp						
913 S Kay Ave	Addison	IL	60101	**800-666-2872**	630-543-5300	688
Thyme on the Creek						
1345 28th St	Boulder	CO	80302	**866-866-8086**	303-998-3835	662
Thyssen Krupp Hearn						
59 I- Dr	Wentzville	MO	63385	**877-854-7178**	636-332-1772	195
ThyssenKrupp Access Inc						
4001 E 138th St	Grandview	MO	64030	**800-669-9047**	816-763-3100	256
ThyssenKrupp Elevator						
9280 Crestwyn Hills Dr	Memphis	TN	38125	**877-230-0303**		357-3
ThyssenKrupp Materials NA						
22355 W 11 Mile Rd	Southfield	MI	48033	**800-926-2600**	248-233-5600	487
TIA (Tire Industry Assn)						
1532 Pointer Ridge Pl Ste G	Bowie	MD	20716	**800-876-8372**	301-430-7280	48-4
TIA (Transportation Intermediaries Assn)						
1625 Prince St Ste 200	Alexandria	VA	22314	**800-435-1791**	703-299-5700	48-21
TIAA-CREF						
730 Third Ave	New York	NY	10017	**866-842-2442**	212-490-9000	388-2
TIAW (International Alliance for Women)						
1101 Pennsylvania Ave NW Fl 6	Washington	DC	20004	**888-712-5200**		47-24
TIB Financial Corp						
121 Alhambra Plz Ste 1601	Coral Gables	FL	33134	**800-639-5111**		357-2
NASDAQ: TIBB						
TIBCO Software Inc						
1700 Westlake Ave N Ste 500	Seattle	WA	98109	**866-247-8182**	206-283-8802	179-3
Ticket Source Inc						
5516 E Mockingbird Ln Ste 100	Dallas	TX	75206	**800-557-6872**	214-821-9011	740
Tickets.com Inc						
555 Anton Blvd 11th Fl	Costa Mesa	CA	92626	**800-352-0212**	714-327-5400	740
TicketWeb Inc						
PO Box 77250	San Francisco	CA	94103	**866-777-8932***		740
*Cust Svc						
Tickfaw State Park						
27225 Patterson Rd	Springfield	LA	70462	**888-981-2020**	225-294-5020	558
Tickle Pink Inn at Carmel Highlands						
155 Highland Dr	Carmel	CA	93923	**800-635-4774**	831-624-1244	376
Ticona LLC						
8040 Dixie Hwy	Florence	KY	41042	**800-833-4882**	859-372-3244	598-2
Tidel Engineering Inc						
2025 W Belt Line Rd Ste 114	Carrollton	TX	75006	**800-678-7577**	972-484-3358	55
Tideland Electric Membership Corp						
25831 Hwy 264 E	Pantego	Nc	27860	**800-637-1079**	252-943-3046	245
Tidewater Barge Lines Inc						
6305 NW Old Lower River Rd	Vancouver	WA	98660	**800-562-1607**	360-693-1491	313
Chesapeake						
1428 Cedar Rd	Chesapeake	VA	23322	**800-371-0898**	757-822-5100	160
Norfolk 315 Granby St	Norfolk	VA	23510	**800-371-0898**	757-822-1110	160
Tidewater Community College						
Portsmouth						
7000 College Dr	Portsmouth	VA	23703	**800-371-0898**	757-822-2124	160
Virginia Beach						
1700 College Crescent	Virginia Beach	VA	23453	**800-371-0898**	757-822-7100	160
Tidewater Grill						
1060 Charleston Town Ctr	Charleston	WV	25389	**888-456-3463**	304-345-2620	662
Tidewater Inc						
601 Poydras St Ste 1900	New Orleans	LA	70130	**800-678-8433**	504-568-1010	460
NYSE: TDW						
Tidewater Inn & Conference Ctr						
101 E Dover St	Easton	MD	21601	**800-237-8775**	410-822-1300	376
Tidewell Hospice						
5955 Rand Blvd	Sarasota	FL	34238	**800-959-4291**	941-552-7500	368
TIDI Products LLC						
570 Enterprise Dr	Neenah	WI	54956	**800-521-1314**		472
Tie Down Engineering Inc						
255 Villanova Dr SW	Atlanta	GA	30336	**800-241-1806**	404-344-0000	475
Tier One LLC						
31 Pecks Ln	Newtown	CT	06470	**877-251-2228**	203-426-3030	449
TierraNet Inc						
14284 Dani Elson St	Poway	CA	92064	**877-843-7721**	858-560-9416	795
Tietex International						
3010 N Blackstock Rd	Spartanburg	SC	29301	**800-843-8390**	864-574-0500	734-6
Tiffany & Co						
727 Fifth Ave	New York	NY	10022	**800-526-0649***	212-755-8000	407
NYSE: TIF ■ *Orders						
Tiffen Company LLC						
90 Oser Ave	Hauppauge	NY	11788	**800-645-2522**	631-273-2500	584
Tiffin University						
155 Miami St	Tiffin	OH	44883	**800-968-6446**	419-447-6442	166
Tift Regional Medical Ctr						
1641 Madison Ave	Tifton	GA	31794	**800-648-1935**	229-382-7120	371-3
Tifton-Tift County Chamber of Commerce						
100 Central Ave	Tifton	GA	31794	**800-550-8438**	229-382-6200	137
TIG (Technology Integration Group)						
7810 Trade St	San Diego	CA	92121	**800-858-0549**	858-566-1900	177
Tiger Button Company Inc						
307 W 38th St Fourth Fl	New York	NY	10018	**800-223-2754**	212-594-0570	587
Tiger Financial News Network						
601 Cleveland St Ste 618	Clearwater	FL	33755	**877-518-9190**	727-467-9190	635
Tiger Lines LLC Lodi						
927 Black Diamond Way	Lodi	CA	95241	**800-967-8443**	209-334-4100	770
TigerDirect Inc						
7795 W Flagler St Ste 35	Miami	FL	33144	**800-800-8300**		175
TigerLogic Corp						
25-A Technology Dr	Irvine	CA	92618	**800-367-7425**	949-442-4400	179-12
NASDAQ: TIGR						
Tihati Productions Ltd						
3615 Harding Ave Ste 507	Honolulu	HI	96816	**877-846-5554**	808-735-0292	566-4
TII Network Technologies Inc						
141 Rodeo Dr	Edgewood	NY	11717	**888-844-4720**	631-789-5000	631
NASDAQ: TIII						
Tilcon Connecticut Inc						
PO Box 1357	New Britain	CT	06050	**888-845-2666**	860-224-6010	45
Tilcon NY Inc						
162 Old Mill Rd	West Nyack	NY	10994	**800-872-7762**	845-358-4500	498-5
Tillamook Bay Community College						
4301 Third St	Tillamook	OR	97141	**888-306-8222**	503-842-8222	160
Tillamook People's Utility District						
1115 Pacific Ave	Tillamook	OR	97141	**800-422-2535**	503-842-2535	245
Tilley Chemical Company Inc						
501 Chesapeake Pk Plz	Baltimore	MD	21220	**800-638-6968**	410-574-4500	144
Tilson HR Inc						
1530 American Way Ste 200	Greenwood	IN	46143	**800-276-3976**	317-885-3838	623
Tim Hortons Inc						
874 Sinclair Rd	Oakville	ON	L6K2Y1	**888-601-1616**	905-845-6511	661
NYSE: THI						
Tim's Cascade Snacks						
1150 Industry Dr N	Algona	WA	98001	**800-533-8467**	253-833-0255	295-35
TimBar Packaging & Display						
148 N Penn St PO Box 449	Hanover	PA	17331	**800-572-6061**	717-632-4727	99
Timber Products Co						
305 S Fourth St PO Box 269	Springfield	OR	97477	**800-547-9520**	541-747-4577	192-3
Timberland Bancorp Inc						
624 Simpson Ave	Hoquiam	WA	98550	**800-562-8761**	360-533-4747	357-2
NASDAQ: TSBK						
Timberland Co, The						
200 Domain Dr	Stratham	NH	03885	**800-258-0855**	603-772-9500	300
NYSE: VFC						
Timberland Homes Inc						
1201 37th St NW	Auburn	WA	98001	**800-488-5036**	253-735-3435	105
Timberland Regional Library						
415 Tumwater Blvd SW	Tumwater	WA	98501	**877-284-6237**	360-943-5001	431-3
Timberlawn Mental Health System						
4600 Samuell Blvd	Dallas	TX	75228	**800-426-4944**	214-381-7181	371-5
Timberline Lodge						
27500 E Timberline Rd	Government Camp	OR	97028	**800-547-1406**	503-272-3311	660
Timberwolf Tours Ltd						
51404 RR 264 Ste 34	Spruce Grove	AB	T7Y1E4	**888-467-9697**	780-470-4966	750
Timco Services Inc						
1724 E Milton Rd	Lafayette	LA	70508	**800-749-2054**	337-233-5185	264-3
Time Definite Services Inc						
1360 Madeline Ln Ste 300	Elgin	IL	60124	**800-466-8040**		310
Time Mark Corp						
11440 E Pine St	Tulsa	OK	74116	**800-862-2875**	918-438-1220	204
Time, The						
224 W 49th St	New York	NY	10019	**877-846-3692**	212-246-5252	376
Timely Inc						
10241 Norris Ave	Pacoima	CA	91331	**800-247-6242**	818-492-3500	286
TimeMed Labeling Systems Inc						
144 Tower Dr	Burr Ridge	IL	60527	**800-323-4840***	630-986-1800	547
*Cust Svc						
Time-O-Matic Inc						
1015 Maple St	Danville	IL	61832	**800-637-2645**	217-442-0611	204
Times 222 Lake St	Shreveport	LA	71101	**800-551-8892**	318-459-3200	525-2
Times Fiber Communications Inc						
358 Hall Ave PO Box 384	Wallingford	CT	06492	**800-677-2288**	203-265-8500	800
Times Herald						
911 Military St	Port Huron	MI	48060	**800-462-4057**	810-985-7171	525-2
Times Herald Inc						
410 Markley St PO Box 591	Norristown	PA	19404	**888-933-4233**	610-272-2500	628-8
Times Herald-Record						
40 Mulberry St PO Box 2046	Middletown	NY	10940	**800-295-2181**	845-341-1100	525-2
Times Leader						
200 S Fourth St	Martins Ferry	OH	43935	**800-244-5671**	740-633-1131	525-2
Times Leader, The						
15 N Main St	Wilkes-Barre	PA	18711	**800-427-8649**	570-829-7101	525-2

Company / Address	City	State	ZIP	Toll-Free	Phone	Class
Times Microwave Systems Inc						
PO Box 5039	Wallingford	CT	06492	**800-867-2629**	203-949-8400	253
Times News Publishing Co						
707 S Main St	Burlington	NC	27215	**800-488-0085**	336-227-0131	628-8
Times of Acadiana						
1100 Bertrand Dr	Lafayette	LA	70506	**877-289-2216**	337-289-6300	525-4
Times Printing Company Inc						
100 Industrial Dr	Random Lake	WI	53075	**800-236-4396**	920-994-4396	619
Times Record						
219 S College Ave	Aledo	IL	61231	**800-784-6776**	309-582-5112	525-4
Times Record News						
PO Box 120	Wichita Falls	TX	76307	**800-627-1646**	940-767-8341	525-2
Times Recorder						
34 S Fourth St	Zanesville	OH	43701	**844-265-6246**	740-452-4561	525-2
Times Reporter						
629 Wabash Ave NW	New Philadelphia	OH	44663	**800-686-5577**	330-364-5577	525-2
Times Union						
645 Albany Shaker Rd						
PO Box 15000	Albany	NY	12212	**877-263-7995**	518-454-5420	525-2
Times Union Ctr						
51 S Pearl St	Albany	NY	12207	**866-308-3394**	518-487-2000	711
Times, The						
601 W 45th Ave	Munster	IN	46321	**800-837-3232**	219-933-3200	525-2
Timesavers Inc						
11123 89th Ave N	Maple Grove	MN	55369	**800-537-3611**	763-488-6600	383
Times-Citizen Communications Inc						
406 Stevens St PO Box 640	Iowa Falls	IA	50126	**800-798-2691**	641-648-2521	628-8
Times-News						
PO Box 481	Burlington	NC	27216	**800-488-0085**	336-227-0131	525-2
Times-Picayune						
3800 Howard Ave	New Orleans	LA	70125	**800-925-0000**	504-826-3279	525-2
Times-Standard						
930 Sixth St	Eureka	CA	95501	**800-514-0301**	707-498-1817	525-2
Times-Tribune, The						
201 N Kentucky Ave	Corbin	KY	40701	**877-629-9722**	606-528-2464	525-2
TIMET (Titanium Metals Corp)						
224 Vly Creek Blvd Ste 200	Exton	PA	19341	**800-753-1550**	610-968-1300	480
NYSE: TIE						
TimeValue Software						
22 Mauchly	Irvine	CA	92618	**800-426-4741***	949-727-1800	179-11
*Sales						
Timex Group USA Inc						
555 Christian Rd PO Box 310	Middlebury	CT	06762	**800-448-4639**	203-346-5000	151
Timken Co						
1835 Dueber Ave SW	Canton	OH	44706	**800-223-1954**	330-438-3000	74
NYSE: TKR						
Timpte Inc						
1827 Industrial Dr	David City	NE	68632	**888-256-4884**	402-367-3056	769
Tindall Corp						
3076 N Blackstock Rd						
PO Box 1778	Spartanburg	SC	29301	**800-849-4521**	864-576-3230	184
Tingley Rubber Corp						
1551 S Washington Ave Ste 403						
Ste 403	Piscataway	NJ	08854	**800-631-5498***		569
*Cust Svc						
Tinsley Adv						
2000 S Dixie Hwy	Miami	FL	33133	**800-432-2242**	305-856-6060	4
Tioga County Visitors Bureau						
2053 Rt 660 PO Box 139	Wellsboro	PA	16901	**888-846-4228**	570-724-0635	207
Tioga Pipe Supply Company Inc						
2450 Wheatsheaf Ln	Philadelphia	PA	19137	**800-523-3678**	215-831-0700	487
Tiorco Inc						
2452 S Trenton Way Ste M	Denver	CO	80231	**800-525-0578**	303-923-6440	532
TIP Rural Electric Co-op						
612 W Des Moines St PO Box 534	Brooklyn	IA	52211	**800-934-7976**	641-522-9221	245
Tip Top Canning Co						
505 S Second St PO Box 126	Tipp City	OH	45371	**800-352-2635**	937-667-3713	295-20
Tip Top Poultry Inc						
327 Wallace Rd	Marietta	GA	30062	**800-241-5230**	770-973-8070	612
TIPAC (Title Industry PAC)						
1828 L St NW Ste 705	Washington	DC	20036	**800-787-2582**	202-296-3671	608
Tipmont Rural Electric Membership Corp						
403 S Main St	Linden	IN	47955	**800-726-3953**		245
Tippecanoe County Public Library						
627 S St	Lafayette	IN	47901	**800-542-7818**	765-429-0100	431-3
Tipper Tie Inc						
2000 Lufkin Rd	Apex	NC	27502	**800-331-2905**	919-362-8811	152
Tire Centers LLC						
310 Inglesby Pkwy	Duncan	SC	29334	**800-603-2430**	864-329-2700	745
Tire Industry Assn (TIA)						
1532 Pointer Ridge Pl Ste G	Bowie	MD	20716	**800-876-8372**	301-430-7280	48-4
Tire Rack						
7101 Vorden Pkwy	South Bend	IN	46628	**888-541-1777**	574-287-2345	745
Tire Warehouse						
200 Holleder Pkwy	Rochester	NY	14615	**800-876-6676**		53
Tire Warehouse Inc						
7500 NW 35 Terr	Miami	FL	33122	**877-235-0102**	305-696-0096	745
Tire Wholesalers Co Inc						
1783 E 14-Mile Rd	Troy	MI	48083	**800-577-3353**	248-589-9910	745
Tire's Warehouse Inc						
240 Teller St	Corona	CA	92879	**800-655-8851**	951-808-0111	745
Tire-Rama Inc						
1401 Industrial Ave						
PO Box 23509	Billings	MT	59104	**800-828-1642**	406-245-4006	745
Tires Plus Total Car Care						
2021 Sunnydale Blvd	Clearwater	FL	33765	**800-440-4167**	727-441-3727	61-5
TIRR Memorial Hermann Hospital						
1333 Moursund St	Houston	TX	77030	**800-447-3422**	713-799-5000	371-6
Tishcon Corp						
50 Sylvester St	Westbury	NY	11590	**800-848-8442**	516-333-3050	787
Titan America Inc						
1151 Azalea Garden Rd	Norfolk	VA	23502	**800-468-7622**	757-858-6500	183
Titan International Inc						
2701 Spruce St	Quincy	IL	62301	**800-872-2327**	217-228-6011	59
NYSE: TWI						
Titan Laboratories						
1380 Zuni St PO Box 40567	Denver	CO	80204	**800-848-4826**		572
Titan Lenders Corp						
5353 W Dartmouth Ave Ste 50	Denver	CO	80227	**866-412-9180**		178
Titan Pharmaceuticals Inc						
400 Oyster Pt Blvd						
Ste 505	South San Francisco	CA	94080	**888-417-8516**	650-244-4990	84
OTC: TTNP						
Titan Specialties Inc						
11785 Hwy 152	Pampa	TX	79065	**800-692-4486***	806-665-3781	530
*Sales						
Titan Tire Co						
2345 E Market St	Des Moines	IA	50317	**800-872-2327**	515-265-9200	744
Titan Wheel Corp						
2701 Spruce St	Quincy	IL	62301	**800-872-2327**	217-228-6011	59
Titanium Metals Corp (TIMET)						
224 Vly Creek Blvd Ste 200	Exton	PA	19341	**800-753-1550**	610-968-1300	480
NYSE: TIE						
Titeflex Corp						
603 Hendee St	Springfield	MA	01139	**800-765-2525**	413-739-5631	367
Title Guaranty of Hawaii Inc						
235 Queen St	Honolulu	HI	96813	**800-222-3229**	808-533-6261	388-6
Title Industry PAC (TIPAC)						
1828 L St NW Ste 705	Washington	DC	20036	**800-787-2582**	202-296-3671	608
Title Resources Guaranty Co (TRGC)						
8111 LBJ Fwy Ste 1200	Dallas	TX	75251	**800-526-8018**	972-644-6500	388-6
Titonka Bancshares Inc						
PO Box 309	Titonka	IA	50480	**866-985-3247**	515-928-2142	357-2
Titusville Area Chamber of Commerce						
2000 S Washington Ave	Titusville	FL	32780	**800-435-7352**	321-267-3036	137
TiVo Inc 2160 Gold St	Alviso	CA	95002	**877-367-8486**	408-519-9100	115
NASDAQ: TIVO						
Tivoli Lodge						
386 Hanson Ranch Rd	Vail	CO	81657	**800-451-4756**	970-476-5615	376
Tizbi Inc						
800 Saint Mary's St Ste 402	Raleigh	NC	27605	**888-729-0951**		178
TJ Cope Inc						
11500 Norcom Rd	Philadelphia	PA	19154	**800-483-3473**	215-961-2570	803
TJ Hale Co						
W 139 N 9499 Hwy 145						
PO Box 250	Menomonee Falls	WI	53051	**800-236-4253**	262-255-5555	286
TJ Maxx						
770 Cochituate Rd	Framingham	MA	01701	**800-926-6299***	508-390-1000	155-2
*Cust Svc						
TJ Samson Community Hospital						
1301 N Race St	Glasgow	KY	42141	**800-651-5635**	270-651-4444	371-3
Tjernlund Products Inc						
1601 Ninth St	White Bear Lake	MN	55110	**800-255-4208**	651-426-2993	18
TJX Cos Inc						
770 Cochituate Rd	Framingham	MA	01701	**800-926-6299**	508-390-1000	155-4
NYSE: TJX						
TK Stanley Inc						
6739 Hwy 184	Waynesboro	MS	39367	**800-477-2855**		532
T-I Irrigation Co						
151 E Hwy 6 AB Rd PO Box 1047	Hastings	NE	68902	**800-330-4264**	402-462-4128	273
TLC Engineering for Architecture						
255 S Orange Ave # 1600	Orlando	FL	32801	**800-835-9926**	407-841-9050	261
TLC Vision Corp						
50 Burnhamthorpe Rd W						
Ste 101	Mississauga	ON	L5B3C2	**877-852-2020**		786
TLIE (Texas Lawyers Insurance Exchange)						
900 Congress Ave Ste 500	Austin	TX	78701	**800-252-9332**	512-480-9074	388-5
TLN (Telelatino Network Inc)						
5125 Steeles Ave W	Toronto	ON	M9L1R5	**800-551-8401**	416-744-8200	729
Tm Deer Park Services LP						
2525 Battleground Rd						
PO Box 1914	Deer Park	TX	77536	**800-488-0648**	281-930-2525	144
TM Smith Tool International Corp						
360 Hubbard Ave	Mount Clemens	MI	48043	**800-521-4894**	586-468-1465	488
TMA (Tobacco Merchants Assn)						
PO Box 8019	Princeton	NJ	08543	**888-672-4991**	609-275-4900	47-2
TMA Systems LLC						
5100 E Skelly Dr Ste 900	Tulsa	OK	74135	**800-862-1130**	918-858-6600	179-11
TMC (Teaching & Mentoring Communities)						
PO Box 2579	Laredo	TX	78044	**888-836-5151**	956-722-5174	48-5
TMC (Tufts Medical Ctr)						
800 Washington St	Boston	MA	02111	**866-220-3699**	617-636-5000	371-3
TMC (Tulane Medical Ctr)						
1415 Tulane Ave	New Orleans	LA	70112	**800-588-5800**	504-588-5108	371-3
TMG Company LLC						
1718 Briarcrest Dr Ste 100	Bryan	TX	77802	**800-720-1563**	979-774-4492	2
TMI Coatings Inc						
3291 Terminal Dr	Saint Paul	MN	55121	**800-328-0229**	651-452-6100	190-8
TMI LLC						
5350 Campbells Run Rd	Pittsburgh	PA	15205	**800-888-9750**	412-787-9750	601
TMI Systems Design Corp						
50 S Third Ave W	Dickinson	ND	58601	**800-456-6716**	701-456-6716	318-3
TML (Teledyne Monitor Labs Inc)						
35 Inverness Dr E	Englewood	CO	80112	**800-422-1499**	303-792-3300	202
T-Mobile USA Inc						
12920 SE 38th St	Bellevue	WA	98006	**800-318-9270**	425-383-4000	726
TMS (Tube City IMS Corp)						
12 Monongahela Ave	Glassport	PA	15045	**800-860-2442**	412-678-6141	677
NYSE: TMS						
TMS (Minerals Metals & Materials Society)						
184 Thorn Hill Rd	Warrendale	PA	15086	**800-759-4867**	724-776-9000	48-13
TMW Systems Inc						
21111 Chagrin Blvd	Beachwood	OH	44122	**800-401-6682**	216-831-6606	179-10
TNCI (Trans National Communications International Inc)						
2 Charlesgate W Ste 500	Boston	MA	02215	**800-800-8400**	617-369-1000	726
Tnemec Company Inc						
6800 Corporate Dr	Kansas City	MO	64120	**800-863-6321**	816-483-3400	543
TNMP (Texas-New Mexico Power Co)						
577 N Garden Ridge Blvd	Lewisville	TX	75067	**888-866-7456**	972-420-4189	775
TNNA (National NeedleArts Assn, The)						
1100-H Brandywine Blvd	Zanesville	OH	43701	**800-889-8662**	740-455-6773	47-18
TNR Technical Inc						
301 Central Pk Dr	Sanford	FL	32771	**800-346-0601**	407-321-3011	73
OTC: TNRK						
TNS Inc						
11480 Commerce Pk Dr Ste 600	Reston	VA	20191	**800-240-2824**	703-453-8300	726
NYSE: TNS						
TO Haas Tire Co Inc						
2400 'O' St PO Box 81067	Lincoln	NE	68510	**866-393-5204**	402-261-2854	745
TOAST.net						
4841 Monroe St Ste 307	Toledo	OH	43623	**888-862-7863**	419-292-2200	395
Toastmasters International						
23182 Arroyo Vista	Rancho Santa Margarita	CA	92688	**877-738-8118**	949-858-8255	47-15
TOBA (Thoroughbred Owners & Breeders Assn)						
PO Box 910668	Lexington	KY	40591	**888-606-8622**	859-276-2291	47-3

Name	Address	City	State	ZIP	Toll-Free	Phone	Class
Tobacco Merchants Assn (TMA)	PO Box 8019	Princeton	NJ	08543	**888-672-4991**	609-275-4900	47-2
Tobe Direct	9700 Park Plz Ave Ste 210	Louisville	KY	40241	**866-820-7313**		7
Toccoa Falls College	107 Kincaid Dr *General	Toccoa Falls	GA	30598	**800-868-3257***	706-886-6831	159
Today's Christian Woman Magazine	465 Gundersen Dr *Orders	Carol Stream	IL	60188	**877-247-4787***	630-260-6200	452-18
Todd-Wadena Electric Co-op	550 Ash Ave NE PO Box 431	Wadena	MN	56482	**800-321-8932**	218-631-3120	245
TodoCast Inc	31831 Camino Capistrano Ste 301	San Juan Capistrano	CA	92675	**866-510-7889**		384
Tog Shop Inc	30 Tozer Rd	Beverly	MA	01915	**800-767-6666**	978-922-2040	454
Togus National Cemetery	VA Regional Office Ctr	Togus	ME	04330	**800-273-8255**	508-563-7113	135
Tokatee Klootchman State Natural Site	93111 Hwy 101 N	Florence	OR	97439	**800-551-6949**		558
Tokio Marine Life	230 Pk Ave	New York	NY	10169	**800-628-2796**	212-297-6600	388-4
Tokyo Electron America Inc	2400 Grove Blvd	Austin	TX	78741	**800-828-6596**	512-424-1000	686
Toledo Edison Co	PO Box 3687	Akron	OH	44309	**800-447-3333**		775
Toledo Express Airport	11013 Airport Hwy	Swanton	OH	43558	**888-381-8294**	419-865-2351	27
Toledo Museum of Art	2445 Monroe St	Toledo	OH	43620	**800-644-6862**	419-255-8000	513
Toledo Opera	425 Jefferson Ave Ste 601	Toledo	OH	43604	**866-860-9048**	419-255-7464	566-2
Toledo Symphony	1838 Parkwood Ave	Toledo	OH	43604	**800-348-1253**	419-246-8000	566-3
Toledo Zoo	2700 Broadway	Toledo	OH	43609	**866-900-1146**	419-385-5721	810
Toledo-Lucas County Port Authority	1 Maritime Plaza	Toledo	OH	43604	**800-969-4700**	419-243-8251	611
Toll Bros Inc	250 Gibraltar Rd *NYSE: TOL*	Horsham	PA	19044	**855-897-8655**	215-938-8000	644
Tolland County Chamber of Commerce	30 Lafayette Sq	Vernon	CT	06066	**800-243-3174**	860-872-0587	137
Tollgrade Communications Inc	3120 Unionville Rd Ste 400 *Cust Svc	Cranberry Township	PA	16066	**800-878-3399***	412-820-1400	725
Tol-O-Matic Inc	3800 County Rd 116	Hamel	MN	55340	**800-328-2174**	763-478-8000	223
Tom Barrow Co (TBC)	2800 Plant Atkinson Rd	Smyrna	GA	30080	**800-229-8226**	404-351-1010	14
Tom Bensen Chevrolet Co Inc	9400 San Pedro	San Antonio	TX	78216	**866-635-6971**	210-341-3311	56
Tom Duffy Co	5200 Watt Ct Ste B	Fairfield	CA	94534	**800-479-5671**		290
Tom Hassenfritz Equipment Co	1300 W Washington St	Mount Pleasant	IA	52641	**800-634-4885**	319-385-3114	274
Tom James Co	263 Seaboard Ln	Franklin	TN	37067	**800-236-9023**	615-771-0795	153-11
Tom McCall & Assoc Inc	20180 Governors Hwy Ste 100	Olympia Fields	IL	60461	**800-715-5474**	708-747-5707	195
Tom Roush Inc	525 W David Brown Dr	Westfield	IN	46074	**877-349-0851**	317-896-5561	509
Tom Snyder Productions Inc	100 Talcott Ave	Watertown	MA	02472	**800-342-0236**	617-926-6000	179-3
Tom Sturgis Pretzels Inc	2267 Lancaster Pk	Reading	PA	19607	**800-817-3834**	610-775-0335	295-9
Tom's of Maine Inc	302 Lafayette Ctr	Kennebunk	ME	04043	**800-367-8667**	800-985-3874	215
Tomah Convention & Visitors Bureau	901 Kilbourn Ave PO Box 625	Tomah	WI	54660	**800-948-6624**	608-372-2166	207
Tomah Veterans Affairs Medical Ctr	500 E Veterans St	Tomah	WI	54660	**800-872-8662**	608-372-3971	371-8
Tomball Independent School District	221 W Main St	Tomball	TX	77375	**877-382-4357**	281-357-3100	676
Tombigbee Electric Co-op Inc	7686 US Hwy PO Box 610	Guin	AL	35563	**800-621-8069**	205-468-3325	245
Tombigbee State Park	264 Cabin Dr	Tupelo	MS	38804	**800-467-2757**	662-842-7669	558
Tomco2 Equipment Co	3340 Rosebud Rd	Loganville	GA	30052	**800-832-4262**	770-979-8000	794
Tomlinson Industries	13700 Broadway Ave	Cleveland	OH	44125	**800-945-4589**	216-587-3400	297
Tommy Tape	378 Four Rod Rd	Berlin	CT	06037	**888-866-8273**	860-378-0111	722
Tompkins Cortland Community College	170 N St	Dryden	NY	13053	**888-567-8211**	607-844-8211	160
Tompkins County Public Library	101 E Green St	Ithaca	NY	14850	**800-772-7267**	607-272-4557	431-3
Tompkins International	6870 Perry Creek Rd	Raleigh	NC	27616	**800-789-1257**	919-876-3667	195
Tompkins Trust Co	PO Box 460 *NYSE: TMP*	Ithaca	NY	14851	**888-273-3210**	607-273-3210	69
Toms Truck Ctr Inc	1008 E Fourth St PO Box 88	Santa Ana	CA	92701	**800-638-1015**	714-338-6060	56
Tomson Steel Co (Inc)	PO Box 940	Middletown	OH	45042	**800-837-3001**		487
TOMY International Inc	1111 W 22nd St Ste 320	Oak Brook	IL	60523	**800-704-8697**		752
Tongass Trading Co	201 Dock St	Ketchikan	AK	99901	**800-235-5102**	907-225-5101	229
Toni & Guy USA Inc	2311 Midway Rd	Carrollton	TX	75006	**800-256-9391**		76
Tonix Corp	40910 Encyclopedia Cir	Fremont	CA	94538	**800-227-2072**	510-651-8050	153-3
Tonner Doll Co	301 Wall St PO Box 4410	Kingston	NY	12402	**800-794-2107**	845-339-9537	752
Tony Packo's	1902 Front St	Toledo	OH	43605	**866-472-2567**	419-691-1953	662
Toobs Inc	347 Quintana Rd	Morro Bay	CA	93442	**800-795-8662**		701
Tooele County Chamber of Commerce	154 S Main	Tooele	UT	84074	**800-378-0690**	435-882-0690	137
Tool Smith Company Inc	1300 Fourth Ave S PO Box 2384	Birmingham	AL	35233	**800-317-8665**	205-323-2576	383
Tool-Flo Mfg Inc	7803 Hansen Rd	Houston	TX	77061	**800-345-2815**	713-941-1080	450
Tools for Bending Inc	194 W Dakota Ave *Cust Svc	Denver	CO	80223	**800-873-3305***	303-777-7170	451
Toolwire Inc	7031 Koll Ctr Pkwy Ste 220	Pleasanton	CA	94566	**866-935-8665**	925-227-8500	38
Tootsie Roll Industries Inc	7401 S Cicero Ave *NYSE: TR*	Chicago	IL	60629	**866-972-6879**	773-838-3400	295-8
Top Air Sprayers	601 S Broad St	Kalida	OH	45853	**800-322-6301**	419-532-3121	273
Top Flight Inc	1300 Central Ave	Chattanooga	TN	37408	**800-777-3740**	423-266-8171	263
Top Producer Magazine	1818 Market St 31st Fl	Philadelphia	PA	19103	**800-320-7992**		452-1
Top Producer Systems Inc	10651 Shellbridge Way Ste 155	Richmond	BC	V6X2W8	**800-821-3657**		180
Topa Insurance Corp	1800 Ave of the Stars	Los Angeles	CA	90067	**800-949-6505**	310-201-0451	388-4
Topaz Hotel	1733 N St NW	Washington	DC	20036	**800-546-7866**	202-393-3000	376
Topco Assoc LLC	7711 Gross Pt Rd	Skokie	IL	60077	**888-423-0139**	847-676-3030	296-8
TopCoder Inc	95 Glastonbury Blvd	Glastonbury	CT	06033	**866-867-2633**	860-633-5540	178
Topcon Medical Systems Inc	111 Bauer Dr	Oakland	NJ	07436	**800-223-1130**	201-599-5100	379
Topeka Capital-Journal	616 SE Jefferson St	Topeka	KS	66607	**800-777-7171**	785-295-1111	525-2
Topeka Correctional Facility	815 SE Rice Rd	Topeka	KS	66603	**888-317-8204**	785-296-3317	213
Topica Inc	1 Post Street Suite 875	San Francisco	CA	94104	**888-728-2465**	415-344-0800	7
Topnotch at Stowe Resort & Spa	4000 Mountain Rd	Stowe	VT	05672	**800-451-8686**		660
Topp Industries Inc	420 N State Rd 25 PO Box 420	Rochester	IN	46975	**800-354-4534**	574-223-3681	594
Toppenish School District 202	306 Bolin Dr	Toppenish	WA	98948	**888-730-1101**	509-865-4455	676
Topps Company Inc	One Whitehall St	New York	NY	10004	**800-489-9149**	212-376-0300	295-6
Topps Safety Apparel Inc	2516 E State Rd 14	Rochester	IN	46975	**800-348-2990**	574-223-4311	153-18
TOPS Club Inc	4575 S Fifth St	Milwaukee	WI	53207	**800-932-8677**	414-482-4620	47-17
Toptica Photonics Inc	1286 Blossom Dr Ste 1	Victor	NY	14564	**877-277-9897**	585-657-6663	416
Torchmark Corp	3700 S Stonebridge Dr *NYSE: TMK*	McKinney	TX	75070	**877-577-3899**	972-569-4000	357-4
Torian Plum Condo Resort	1855 Ski Time Sq Dr	Steamboat Springs	CO	80487	**800-228-2458**	970-879-8811	660
Torke Coffee Roasting Company Inc	3455 Paine Ave PO Box 694	Sheboygan	WI	53081	**800-242-7671**	920-458-4114	295-7
Toro Co	8111 Lyndale Ave *NYSE: TTC*	Bloomington	MN	55420	**888-384-9939**		426
Toro Co Irrigation Div	5825 Jasmine St	Riverside	CA	92504	**800-654-1882**		273
Toro Company Commercial Products Div	8111 Lyndale Ave *Cust Svc	Bloomington	MN	55420	**800-348-2424***	952-888-8801	426
Toronto Aerospace Museum	65 Carl Hall Rd PO Box 1	Toronto	ON	M3K2E1	**866-585-2227**	416-638-6078	513
Toronto Blue Jays	One Blue Jays Way Ste 3200	Toronto	ON	M5V1J1	**888-654-6529**	416-341-1000	704
Toronto Convention & Visitors Assn	207 Queen's Quay W Ste 405 PO Box 126	Toronto	ON	M5J1A7	**800-499-2514**	416-203-2600	207
Toronto International Film Festival Inc	Reitman Sq 350 King St W	Toronto	ON	M5V3X5	**888-599-8433**		282
Toronto Star	One Yonge St	Toronto	ON	M5E1E6	**800-268-9756**	416-869-4949	525-1
Toronto Stock Exchange	130 King St W	Toronto	ON	M5X1J2	**888-873-8392**	416-947-4670	682
Toronto Sun	333 King St E	Toronto	ON	M5A3X5	**888-786-7821**	416-947-2222	525-1
Torrance Memorial Medical Ctr	3330 Lomita Blvd	Torrance	CA	90505	**866-843-2572**	310-325-9110	371-3
Torrance State Hospital	121 Longview Dr PO Box 111	Torrance	PA	15779	**866-816-9212**	724-459-8000	371-5
Torray Fund	7501 Wisconsin Ave Ste 750 W	Bethesda	MD	20814	**800-443-3036**	301-493-4600	521
Torrey Pines State Reserve	c/o San Diego Coast District 4477 Pacific Hwy	San Diego	CA	92110	**866-240-4655**	858-755-2063	558
Tortoise Energy Capital Corp	11550 Ash St Ste 300 *NYSE: TYY*	Leawood	KS	66211	**866-362-9331**	913-981-1020	780
Toshiba America Electronic Components Inc	19900 MacArthur Blvd Ste 400	Irvine	CA	92612	**800-879-4963**	949-623-2900	687
Toshiba America Inc	1251 Ave of the Americas Ste 4100	New York	NY	10020	**800-457-7777**	212-596-0600	51
Toshiba America Information Systems Inc	9740 Irvine Blvd *Cust Svc	Irvine	CA	92618	**800-457-7777***	949-583-3000	174-1
Toshiba America Medical Systems Inc	2441 Michelle Dr *Cust Svc	Tustin	CA	92780	**800-521-1968***	714-730-5000	379
Toshiba International Corp	13131 W Little York Rd	Houston	TX	77041	**800-231-1412**	713-466-0277	511
Toski & Co PC	300 Essjay Rd Ste 115	Williamsville	NY	14221	**800-546-7556**	716-634-0700	2
Total Energy Services Ltd	2550 300-5th Ave SW Ste 2550 *NYSE: TOT*	Calgary	AB	T2P3C4	**877-818-6825**	403-216-3939	533

Company	Address	City	State	Zip	Toll-Free	Phone	Class
Total Energy Solutions LLC (TES)	100 International Dr Ste 260	Portsmouth	NH	03801	**877-436-9812**		112
Total Lubricants USA	5 N Stiles St	Linden	NJ	07036	**800-323-3198**	908-862-9300	534
Total Management Solutions Inc	55 Harristown Rd	Glen Rock	NJ	07452	**866-544-0707**	201-447-0707	46
Total Package Express Inc	5871 Cheviot Rd	Cincinnati	OH	45247	**800-420-5505**	513-741-5500	770
Total Plastics Inc	3316 Pagosa Ct	Indianapolis	IN	46226	**800-382-4635**	317-543-3540	595
Total Quality Logistics Inc (TQL)	4289 Ivy Pointe Blvd	Cincinnati	OH	45245	**800-580-3101**	513-831-2600	310
Total Resource Management Inc	510 King St Ste 300	Alexandria	VA	22314	**877-548-5100**	703-548-4285	194
Total Seal Inc	22642 N 15th Ave	Phoenix	AZ	85027	**800-874-2753**	623-587-7400	127
Total Technologies Ltd	Nine Studebaker	Irvine	CA	92618	**800-669-4885**	949-465-0200	253
Total Telcom Inc	540 1632 Dickson Ave	Kelowna	BC	V1Y7T2	**877-860-3762**		726
Totem Ocean Trailer Express Inc	32001 32nd Ave S Ste 200	Federal Way	WA	98001	**800-426-0074**	253-449-8100	311
Toter Inc	PO Box 5338	Statesville	NC	28677	**800-424-0422**	704-872-8171	200
Totes Isotoner Corp	9655 International Blvd	Cincinnati	OH	45246	**800-762-8712**	513-682-8200	153-7
Toto Tours Ltd	1326 W Albion Ave	Chicago	IL	60626	**800-565-1241**	773-274-8686	750
Toto USA Inc	1155 Southern Rd	Morrow	GA	30260	**888-295-8134**	770-282-8686	604
TouchAmerica	1403 S Third Street Ext	Hillsborough	NC	27278	**800-678-6824**	919-732-6968	75
TouchLogic Corp	30 Kinnear Ct Ste 602	Richmond Hill	ON	L4B1K8	**877-707-0207**		384
TouchPoint Technologies LLC	2319 Oak Myrtle Ln Ste 104	Wesley Chapel	FL	33544	**877-898-6824**		363
Touchstorm LLC	355 Lexington Ave 12th Fl	New York	NY	10017	**877-794-6101**		384
TouchSystems Corp	220 Tradesmen Dr	Hutto	TX	78634	**800-320-5944**	512-846-2424	607
Tougaloo College	500 W County Line Rd *Admissions	Tougaloo	MS	39174	**888-424-2566***	601-977-7700	166
Tough Traveler Ltd	1012 State St *Cust Svc	Schenectady	NY	12307	**800-468-6844***	518-377-8526	63
Tourette Syndrome Assn Inc	42-40 Bell Blvd Ste 205	Bayside	NY	11361	**888-486-8738**	718-224-2999	47-17
Touring & Tasting	125 S Quarantina St	Santa Barbara	CA	93103	**800-850-4370**	805-965-2813	439
Tourism Bureau Southwestern Illinois	10950 Lincoln Trail	Fairview Heights	IL	62208	**800-442-1488**	618-397-1488	207
Tourism Calgary	200 238 11th Ave SE	Calgary	AB	T2G0X8	**800-661-1678**	403-263-8510	207
Tourism Malaysia	818 W Seventh St Ste 970	Los Angeles	CA	90017	**800-336-6842**	213-689-9702	765
Tourism New Brunswick	PO Box 12345	Campbellton	NB	E3N3T6	**800-561-0123**		764
Tourism Saskatchewan	1621 Albert St	Regina	SK	S4P2S5	**877-237-2273**	306-787-9600	764
Tourism Yukon	PO Box 2703	Whitehorse	YT	Y1A2C6	**800-661-0494**		764
Touro College	27-33 W 23rd St	New York	NY	10010	**888-247-1387**	212-463-0400	166
Touvelle State Recreation Site	8598 Table Rock Rd 3792 N River Rd	Central Point	OR	97502	**800-551-6949**	541-983-2277	558
Tower Federal Credit Union	7901 Sandy Spring Rd	Laurel	MD	20707	**800-787-8328**	301-497-7000	219
Tower Financial Corp	116 E Berry St *NASDAQ: TOFC*	Fort Wayne	IN	46802	**800-731-2265**	317-706-9500	357-2
Tower Group Inc	120 Broadway 14th Fl *NASDAQ: TWGP*	New York	NY	10271	**877-883-6599**	212-655-2000	388-4
Tower Innovations	3266 Tower Dr	Newburgh	IN	47630	**800-664-8222**	812-853-0595	171
Tower Sales Inc	936 E Grand Ave PO Box 36	Tower City	PA	17980	**800-839-1849**	717-647-2100	572
Tower Travel Management	53 Ogden Ave Ste 2520	Clarendon Hills	IL	60514	**800-542-9700**		761
Towmaster Inc	61381 US Hwy 12	Litchfield	MN	55355	**800-462-4517**	320-693-7900	769
Town & Country Inn	20 State RT 2 PO Box 220 *General	Gorham	NH	03581	**800-325-4386***	603-466-3315	376
Town & Country Inn & Conference Ctr	2008 Savannah Hwy	Charleston	SC	29407	**800-334-6660**	843-571-1000	376
Town & Country Resort Hotel	500 Hotel Cir N	San Diego	CA	92108	**800-772-8527**	619-291-7131	660
Town Bank	850 W N Shore Dr	Hartland	WI	53029	**800-433-3076**	262-367-1900	69
Town Fair Tire Company Inc	460 Coe Ave	East Haven	CT	06512	**800-972-2245**		53
Town Food Service Equipment Co	72 Beadel St	Brooklyn	NY	11222	**800-221-5032**	718-388-5650	297
Town Inn Suites	620 Church St	Toronto	ON	M4Y2G2	**800-387-2755**	416-964-3311	376
Town Pump Inc	600 S Main St	Butte	MT	59701	**800-823-4931**	406-497-6700	323
Town Talk Inc	6310 Cane Run Rd PO Box 58157	Louisville	KY	40258	**800-626-2220**	502-933-7575	153-8
Towne Air Freight	24805 US 20 W	South Bend	IN	46628	**800-468-6963**	574-233-3183	310
Towne Technologies Inc	6-10 Bell Ave PO Box 460	Somerville	NJ	08876	**800-837-2515**	908-722-9500	476
TowneBank	4501 Cox Rd PO Box 5310	Glen Allen	VA	23060	**800-372-4445**	804-967-7000	69
TownHouse Inn	1411 Tenth Ave S	Great Falls	MT	59405	**800-442-4667**	406-761-4600	376
Towns County	1411 Jack Dayton Cir	Young Harris	GA	30582	**800-984-1543**	706-896-4966	336
Townsend Hotel	100 Townsend St	Birmingham	MI	48009	**800-548-4172**	248-642-7900	376
Townsend Press	439 Kelley Dr	West Berlin	NJ	08091	**800-772-6410**	856-753-0554	628-2
Towson University	8000 York Rd	Towson	MD	21252	**866-301-3375**	410-704-2113	166
Toxics Law Reporter	1801 S Bell St	Arlington	VA	22202	**800-372-1033**		524-5
Toxikon Corp	15 Wiggins Ave	Bedford	MA	01730	**800-458-4141**	781-275-3330	732
Toy Industry Assn	1115 Broadway Ste 400	New York	NY	10010	**800-541-1345**	212-675-1141	48-4
Toyo Ink America LLC	1225 N Michael Dr *General	Wood Dale	IL	60191	**866-969-8696***		385
Toyo Tire USA Corp	6261 Katella Ave Ste 2B	Cypress	CA	90630	**800-678-3250**		744
Toyoda Machinery USA Inc	316 W University Dr	Arlington Heights	IL	60004	**800-257-2985**	847-253-0340	450
Toyota Canada Inc	One Toyota Pl *Cust Svc	Scarborough	ON	M1H1H9	**888-869-6828***	416-438-6320	58
Toyota Ctr	1510 Polk St	Houston	TX	77002	**866-446-8849**	713-758-7200	711
Toyota Financial Services	19001 S Western Ave *Cust Svc	Torrance	CA	90501	**800-874-8822***	212-715-7386	214
Toyota Motor North America Inc	601 Lexington Ave 49th Fl	New York	NY	10022	**800-331-4331**		357-3
Toyota Motor Sales USA Inc	19001 S Western Ave *Cust Svc	Torrance	CA	90501	**800-331-4331***	310-468-4000	58
Toyota Motor Sales USA Inc Lexus Div	19001 S Western Ave *Cust Svc	Torrance	CA	90501	**800-255-3987***		58
Toyota Tsusho America Inc	805 Third Ave 16th Fl	New York	NY	10022	**800-883-0100**	212-355-3600	487
TP Orthodontics Inc	100 Ctr Plz	La Porte	IN	46350	**800-348-8856**	219-785-2591	228
TP Trucking LLC	5630 Table Rock Rd	Central Point	OR	97502	**800-777-1121**	541-664-4776	770
TPI Corp	PO Box 4973	Johnson City	TN	37602	**800-682-3398**	423-477-4131	15
TPL (Trust for Public Land)	116 New Montgomery St Fourth Fl	San Francisco	CA	94105	**800-714-5263**	415-495-4014	47-13
TPL Communications	3370 San Fernando Rd Unit 206	Los Angeles	CA	90065	**800-447-6937**	323-256-3000	638
TPR (Texas Public Radio)	8401 Datapoint Dr Ste 800	San Antonio	TX	78229	**800-622-8977**	210-614-8977	624
TQL (Total Quality Logistics Inc)	4289 Ivy Pointe Blvd	Cincinnati	OH	45245	**800-580-3101**	513-831-2600	310
TR Miller Mill Company Inc	215 Deer St PO Box 708	Brewton	AL	36427	**800-633-6740**	251-867-4331	674
Trabert & Hoeffer	111 E Oak St	Chicago	IL	60611	**800-539-3573**	312-787-1654	407
TRAC Media Services	3961 E Speedway Blvd Ste 410	Tucson	AZ	85712	**888-299-1866**	520-299-1866	624
Trace-A-Matic Inc (T-A-M)	1570 Commerce Ave	Brookfield	WI	53045	**877-375-0217**	262-797-7300	614
TracFone Wireless Inc	9700 NW 112th Ave	Miami	FL	33178	**800-876-5753**	305-640-2000	726
Trachte Bldg Systems Inc	314 Wilburn Rd	Sun Prairie	WI	53590	**800-356-5824**		104
Tracie Martyn Salon	59 Fifth Ave Ste 1	New York	NY	10003	**866-862-7896**	212-206-9333	697
TRACO	71 Progress Ave	Cranberry Township	PA	16066	**800-992-4444**	724-776-7000	234
TRACS (TransNational Assn of Christian Colleges & Schools)	15935 Forest Rd PO Box 328	Forest	VA	24551	**800-669-4000**	434-525-9539	47-1
Tractor Supply Co	200 Powell Pl *NASDAQ: TSCO*	Brentwood	TN	37027	**877-718-6750**		274
Tracy-Luckey Company Inc	110 N Hicks St PO Box 880	Harlem	GA	30814	**800-476-4796**	706-556-6216	11-1
Trada Inc	1023 Walnut St	Boulder	CO	80302	**877-871-1835**		384
Trade Products Corp	12124 Popes Head Rd	Fairfax	VA	22030	**888-352-3580**	703-502-9000	319
Trade Service Company LLC	15092 Ave of Science	San Diego	CA	92128	**800-854-1527**		224
Tradescape Inc	520 S El Camino Real Ste 640	San Mateo	CA	94402	**800-697-6068**		197
TradeStation Group Inc	8050 SW Tenth St Ste 2000	Plantation	FL	33324	**800-871-3577**	954-652-7000	179-10
TradeStation Securities Inc	8050 SW Tenth St Ste 2000	Plantation	FL	33324	**800-808-9336**	954-652-7000	681
Trading Direct	160 Broadway E Bldg Seventh Fl	New York	NY	10038	**800-925-8566**	212-766-0230	681
Traditional Bank	49 W Main St PO Box 326	Mount Sterling	KY	40353	**800-498-0414**	859-498-0414	69
Traditional Home Magazine	1716 Locust St *Circ	Des Moines	IA	50309	**800-374-8791***	515-284-3762	452-11
Traffic Control Service Inc	2435 Lemon Ave	Signal Hill	CA	90755	**800-763-3999**		264-3
Trail King Industries Inc	147 Industrial Pk Rd	Brookville	PA	15825	**800-545-1549**	814-849-2342	769
Trailer Bridge Inc	10405 New Berlin Rd E *OTC: TRBRQ*	Jacksonville	FL	32226	**800-554-1589**	904-751-7100	311
Trailer Transit Inc	1130 E US 20	Porter	IN	46304	**800-423-3647**	219-926-2111	770
Trailercraft Inc	1301 E 64th Ave	Anchorage	AK	99518	**800-478-3238**	907-563-3238	509
Trailiner Corp	PO Box 5270	Springfield	MO	65801	**800-833-8209**	417-866-7258	769
Trailstar Mfg Corp	20700 Harrisburg-Westville Rd PO Box 2086	Alliance	OH	44601	**800-235-5635**	330-821-9900	769
Trailways Transportation System Inc	3554 Chain Bridge Rd Ste 301	Fairfax	VA	22030	**877-467-3346**	703-691-3052	106

	Toll-Free	Phone	Class
Training & Development Magazine			
1640 King St ....Alexandria VA 22313	800-628-2783	703-683-8100	452-5
Training Assoc Corp, The			
289 Tpke Rd ....Westborough MA 01581	800-241-8868	508-890-8500	623
Training Industry Inc			
401 Harrison Oaks Blvd Ste 300............Cary NC 27513	866-298-4203		390
TRAK Microwave Corp			
4726 Eisenhower Blvd ....Tampa FL 33634	888-283-8444	813-901-7200	253
Tramex Travel Inc			
4505 Spicewood Springs Rd			
Ste 200 ....Austin TX 78759	800-527-3039	512-343-2201	761
Trana Discovery Inc			
2054-260 Kildare Farm Rd ....Cary NC 27518	866-390-3452		231
Trans Am Travel			
4222 King St Ste 130 ....Alexandria VA 22302	800-822-7600	703-998-7676	16
Trans Med USA Inc			
31 Progress Ave ....Tyngsboro MA 01879	800-442-1142	978-649-1970	470
Trans National Communications International Inc (TNCI)			
2 Charlesgate W Ste 500 ....Boston MA 02215	800-800-8400	617-369-1000	726
Trans World Corp (TWC)			
545 Fifth Ave Ste 940 ....New York NY 10017	877-407-9037	212-983-3355	376
OTC: TWOC			
Trans1 Inc			
301 Government Ctr Dr ....Wilmington NC 28403	866-256-1206	910-332-1700	471
TransAct Technologies Inc			
one Hamden Ctr 2319 Whitney Ave			
Ste 3B...........................Hamden CT 06518	800-243-8941	203-859-6800	174-6
NASDAQ: TACT			
Transaction Network Services Inc.			
10740 Parkridge Blvd Ste 100 ....Reston VA 20191	800-240-2824	703-453-8300	217
TransAm Trucking Inc			
15910 S 169th Hwy ....Olathe KS 66062	800-800-5945	913-782-5300	770
Transamerica			
4333 Edgewood Rd NE ....Cedar Rapids IA 52499	800-852-4678	319-355-8511	388-5
Transamerica Corporation			
4333 Edgewood Rd NE ....Cedar Rapids IA 52499	800-797-2643*	319-355-3985	388-2
*Cust Svc			
Transamerica Occidental Life Insurance Co			
1150 S Olive St ....Los Angeles CA 90015	800-852-4678*	213-742-2111	388-2
*Cust Svc			
Transat AT Inc			
300 Leo-Pariseau St Ste 600 ....Montreal QC H2X4C2	800-387-0825	514-987-1616	761
TSE: TRZ.B			
Trans-Border Global Freight Systems Inc			
2103 Route 9 ....Round Lake NY 12151	800-493-9444	518-785-6000	310
Trans-Bridge Lines Inc			
2012 Industrial Dr ....Bethlehem PA 18017	800-962-9135	610-868-6001	107
TransCanada Pipelines Ltd			
450 First St SW ....Calgary AB T2P5H1	800-661-3805	403-920-2000	324
Trans-Carriers Inc			
5135 US Hwy 78 ....Memphis TN 38118	800-999-7383	901-368-2900	770
Transcat Inc			
35 Vantage Pt Dr ....Rochester NY 14624	800-800-5001	585-352-9460	202
NASDAQ: TRNS			
TransChemical Inc			
419 De Soto Ave ....Saint Louis MO 63147	888-873-6481	314-231-6905	144
Transco Business Technologies (TBT)			
34 Leighton Rd ....Augusta ME 04330	800-322-0003	207-622-6251	111
Transco Industries Inc			
5534 NE 122nd Ave PO Box 20429 ......Portland OR 97230	800-545-9991	503-256-1955	208
Transco Railway Products Inc			
820 Hopley Ave ....Bucyrus OH 44820	800-472-4592	419-562-1031	641
TransCon Builders Inc			
25250 Rockside Rd ....Cleveland OH 44146	800-451-2608	440-439-2100	644
Transcontinental Inc			
1100 Rene-Levesque Blvd W			
24th Fl ....Montreal QC H3B4X9	800-361-5479	514-392-9000	628-9
Transcontinental Insurance Co			
333 S Wabash Ave CNA Ctr ....Chicago IL 60604	800-437-8854	312-822-5000	388-4
Transcontinental Realty Investors Inc			
1603 Lyndon B Johnson Fwy			
Ste 800 ....Dallas TX 75234	800-400-6407	469-522-4200	645
NYSE: TCI			
Trans-Continental Systems Inc			
10801 Evendale Dr ....Cincinnati OH 45241	800-525-8726	513-769-4774	639
TransCore Holdings Inc			
8158 Adams Dr ....Hummelstown PA 17036	800-923-4824	717-561-2400	261
Transentric			
1400 Douglas St Ste 0840 ....Omaha NE 68179	800-877-0328	402-544-6000	179-10
TRANSFLO Terminal Services Inc			
500 Water St Ste J975 ....Jacksonville FL 32202	866-872-6735		444
Transforce Inc			
6551 Loisdale Ct Ste 801 ....Springfield VA 22150	800-308-6989	703-838-5580	712
Transgenomic Inc			
12325 Emmet St ....Omaha NE 68164	888-233-9283	402-452-5400	416
OTC: TBIO			
Transhield Inc			
2932 Thorne Dr ....Elkhart IN 46514	888-731-7700	574-266-4118	587
TRANSInternational System Inc			
130 E Wilson Bridge Rd Ste 150			
Ste 150 ....Worthington OH 43085	800-340-7540	614-891-4942	310
Transition Networks Inc			
10900 Red Cir Dr ....Minnetonka MN 55343	800-526-9267	952-941-7600	177
Transitions Optical Inc			
9251 Belcher Rd ....Pinellas Park FL 33782	800-533-2081	727-545-0400	535
Translations.com Inc			
Three Pk Ave 39th Fl. ....New York NY 10016	800-688-7205	212-689-1616	180
Trans-Lux Corp			
26 Pearl St ....Norwalk CT 06850	800-243-5544	203-853-4321	174-4
OTC: TNLX			
Trans-Lux Fair-Play Inc			
1700 Delaware Ave ....Des Moines IA 50317	800-247-0265	515-265-5305	174-4
Transmedia			
719 Battery St ....San Francisco CA 94111	800-229-7234	415-956-3118	637
TransNational Assn of Christian Colleges & Schools (TRACS)			
15935 Forest Rd PO Box 328 ....Forest VA 24551	800-669-4000	434-525-9539	47-1
Transocean Inc			
4 Greenway Plaza ....Houston TX 77046	877-440-0173	713-232-7500	533
NYSE: RIG			
Transource Computers Corp			
2405 W Utopia Rd ....Phoenix AZ 85027	800-486-3715	623-879-8882	174-1
Transparent Language Inc			
12 Murphy Dr ....Nashua NH 03062	800-538-8867		179-3
Trans-Phos Inc			
PO Box 9004 ....Bartow FL 33831	800-940-1575	863-534-1575	770
Transplace			
3010 Gaylord Pkwy Ste 200 ....Frisco TX 75034	866-413-9266		444
Transpo Electronics Inc			
2150 Brengle Ave ....Orlando FL 32808	800-327-6903		247
Transport Corp of America Inc			
1715 Yankee Doodle Rd ....Eagan MN 55121	800-328-3927	651-686-2500	770
Transport Distribution Co			
PO Box 306 ....Joplin MO 64802	800-866-7709	417-624-3814	770
Transport Inc			
2225 Main Ave SE ....Moorhead MN 56560	800-598-7267	218-236-6300	770
Transport Refrigeration Inc			
301 Lawrence Dr ....De Pere WI 54115	888-502-3569	920-339-5700	656
Transport Service Co			
2001 Spring Rd Ste 400 ....Oak Brook IL 60523	800-323-5561*	630-472-5900	770
*Sales			
Transport Workers Union of America			
501 Third St NW 9th Fl. ....Washington DC 20001	888-565-6898	202-719-3900	48-21
Transportation Communications International Union			
3 Research Pl ....Rockville MD 20850	877-772-5772	301-948-4910	411
Transportation Insurance Co			
333 S Wabash Ave ....Chicago IL 60604	800-437-8854	312-822-5000	388-4
Transportation Intermediaries Assn (TIA)			
1625 Prince St Ste 200..............Alexandria VA 22314	800-435-1791	703-299-5700	48-21
Transportation Management Assoc Inc			
344 Oak Grove Church Rd ....Mocksville NC 27028	800-745-8292		310
Transportation Research Board (TRB)			
500 Fifth St NW ....Washington DC 20001	866-233-4642	202-334-2934	48-21
Transportation Research Ctr Inc (TRC Inc)			
10820 State Rt 347			
PO Box B-67. ....East Liberty OH 43319	800-837-7872	937-666-2011	659
Transportation Security Administration (TSA)			
601 S 12th St ....Arlington VA 22202	866-289-9673	202-282-8000	338-9
Federal Air Marshal Service			
601 S 12th St ....Arlington VA 22202	866-289-9673		338-9
Trans-Tel Central Inc (TTC)			
2805 Broce Dr ....Norman OK 73072	800-729-4636	405-447-5025	775
TransUnion LLC			
555 W Adams St ....Chicago IL 60661	866-922-2100		218
Transwest			
20770 I-76 Frontage Rd ....Brighton CO 80603	800-289-3161	303-289-3161	56
TransWood Carriers Inc			
PO Box 189 ....Omaha NE 68101	888-346-8092		770
TransWorks			
9910 Dupont Cir Dr E Ste 200 ....Fort Wayne IN 46825	800-435-4691	260-487-4400	179-10
TransWorld Business			
2052 Corte Del Nogal Ste 100 ....Carlsbad CA 92011	800-788-7072*	760-722-7777	628-9
*General			
Transworld Systems Inc			
2235 Mercury Way Ste 275 ....Santa Rosa CA 95407	888-446-4733	707-236-3800	158
Transylvania University			
300 N Broadway ....Lexington KY 40508	800-872-6798	859-233-8242	166
Tranter Inc			
1900 Old Burk Hwy ....Wichita Falls TX 76306	800-414-6908	940-723-7125	90
Tranzonic Cos			
26301 Curtiss Wright Pkwy			
Ste 200 ....Cleveland OH 44143	800-553-7979	216-535-4300	551
Trapp Family Lodge			
700 Trapp Hill Rd PO Box 1428 ....Stowe VT 05672	800-826-7000	802-253-8511	660
Trattoria Del Lupo			
3950 Las Vegas Blvd S ....Las Vegas NV 89119	800-275-8273	702-740-5522	662
Traulsen & Company Inc			
4401 Blue Mound Rd ....Fort Worth TX 76106	800-825-8220		14
Travaasa Hana			
5031 Hana Hwy ....Hana HI 96713	855-868-7282	808-248-8211	660
Travcoa			
100 N Sepulveda Blvd			
Ste 1700 ....El Segundo CA 90245	800-992-2003	310-649-7104	750
Travel & Transport Inc			
2120 S 72nd St ....Omaha NE 68124	800-228-2545	402-399-4500	761
Travel + Leisure Magazine			
1120 Ave of the Americas			
10th Fl ....New York NY 10036	800-452-9292	212-382-5600	452-20
Travel Agent Magazine			
757 Third Ave 5th Fl. ....New York NY 10017	855-424-6247	212-895-8200	452-22
Travel Authority Inc			
702 N Shore Dr Ste 300 ....Jeffersonville IN 47130	888-501-7010	812-206-5100	761
Travel Destinations Management Group Inc			
110 Painters Mill Rd ....Owings Mills MD 21117	800-635-7307	410-363-3111	761
Travel Dynamics International			
132 E 70th St ....New York NY 10021	800-257-5767	212-517-7555	220
Travel Focus			
First Class International			
8111 LBJ Fwy Ste 900 ....Dallas tx 75251	800-222-9968	214-915-9000	761
Travel Impressions Ltd			
465 Smith St ....Farmingdale NY 11735	800-284-0044	631-845-8000	761
Travel Institute			
148 Linden St Ste 305 ....Wellesley MA 02482	800-542-4282	781-237-0280	47-23
Travel Insured International			
52-S Oakland Ave			
PO Box 280568. ....East Hartford CT 06128	800-243-3174		388-7
Travel Lane County			
PO Box 10286 ....Eugene OR 97440	800-547-5445	541-484-5307	207
Travel Manitoba			
155 Carlton St Seventh Fl. ....Winnipeg MB R3C3H8	800-665-0040	204-927-7800	764
Travel Planners Inc			
381 Pk Ave S ....New York NY 10016	800-221-3531	212-532-1660	373
Travel Portland			
1000 SW Broadway Ste 2300 ....Portland OR 97205	800-962-3700	503-275-9750	207
Travel Team Inc			
2495 Main St ....Buffalo NY 14214	800-245-8326	716-862-7600	761
TravelCenters of America			
24601 Ctr Ridge Rd Ste 200 ....Westlake OH 44145	800-632-9240	440-808-9100	323
Travelclick			
Seven Times Sq 38th Fl ....New York NY 10036	866-674-4549	212-817-4800	195
Travelennium Inc			
556 Colonial Rd ....Memphis TN 38117	800-844-4924	901-767-0761	761
Travelers Cos Inc			
385 Washington St ....Saint Paul MN 55102	800-328-2189	651-310-7911	357-4
NYSE: TRV			
Travelers Motor Club			
720 NW 50th St ....Oklahoma City OK 73154	800-654-9208	405-848-1711	52

Company / Address	City	State	ZIP	Toll-Free	Phone	Class
Travelex International Inc						
2061 N Barrington Rd	Hoffman Estates	IL	60169	**800-882-0499**	847-882-0400	762
Travelhost Inc						
10701 N Stemmons Fwy	Dallas	TX	75220	**800-527-1782**	972-556-0541	628-9
Travelhost Magazine						
10701 N Stemmons Fwy	Dallas	TX	75220	**800-527-1782**	972-556-0541	452-22
Traveline Travel Agencies Inc						
4074 Erie St	Willoughby	OH	44094	**888-700-8747**	440-602-8090	761
Travelocity.com LP						
3150 Sabre Dr	Southlake	TX	76092	**888-872-8356**		373
Travelodge Virginia Beach						
1909 Atlantic Ave	Virginia Beach	VA	23451	**800-578-7878**	757-425-0650	376
Travelong Inc						
225 W 35th St Ste 1501	New York	NY	10001	**800-537-6043**	212-736-2166	761
Travelpro USA						
700 Banyan Trl	Boca Raton	FL	33431	**800-741-7471**	561-998-2824	448
TravelSmith Outfitters						
773 San Marin Dr Ste 2300	Novato	CA	94945	**800-770-3387**		454
TravelStore Inc						
11601 Wilshire Blvd	Los Angeles	CA	90025	**800-850-3224**	310-575-5540	761
Travers Tool Company Inc						
128-15 26th Ave	Flushing	NY	11354	**800-221-0270***	718-886-7200	382
*Cust Svc						
Traverse City Area Chamber of Commerce						
202 E Grandview Pkwy	Traverse City	MI	49684	**800-942-5322**	231-947-5075	137
Traverse City Convention & Visitors Bureau						
101 W Grandview Pkwy	Traverse City	MI	49684	**800-940-1120**	231-947-1120	207
Traverse Electric Co-op Inc						
1618 Broadway PO Box 66	Wheaton	MN	56296	**800-927-5443**	320-563-8616	245
Travis & Beverly Cross Guest Housing Ctr						
9320 SW Barnes Rd	Portland	OR	97225	**888-550-1575**	503-216-1575	369
Travis Body & Trailer Inc						
13955 FM529	Houston	TX	77041	**800-535-4372**	713-466-5888	769
Travis Federal Credit Union						
One Travis Way	Vacaville	CA	95687	**800-877-8328**	707-449-4000	219
Travis Meats Inc						
7210 Clinton Hwy PO Box 670	Powell	TN	37849	**800-247-7606**	865-938-9051	468
Travizon Meeting Management						
275 Mishawum Rd Ste 300	Woburn	MA	01801	**800-423-2500**	888-781-5200	185
Traylor Bros Inc						
835 N Congress Ave	Evansville	IN	47715	**866-895-1491**	812-477-1542	189-4
TRB (Transportation Research Board)						
500 Fifth St NW	Washington	DC	20001	**866-233-4642**	202-334-2934	48-21
TRC Cos Inc						
21 Griffin Rd N	Windsor	CT	06095	**800-365-8254**	860-298-9692	193
TRC Inc (Transportation Research Ctr Inc)						
10820 State Rt 347						
PO Box B-67	East Liberty	OH	43319	**800-837-7872**	937-666-2011	659
Treasure Bay Casino & Hotel						
1980 Beach Blvd	Biloxi	MS	39531	**800-747-2839***	228-385-6000	660
*General						
Treasure Chest Casino						
5050 Williams Blvd	Kenner	LA	70065	**800-298-0711**	504-443-8000	132
Treasure Coast Hospice						
1201 SE Indian St	Stuart	FL	34997	**800-299-4677**	772-403-4500	368
Treasure Island Hotel & Casino						
3300 Las Vegas Blvd S	Las Vegas	NV	89109	**800-288-7206**	702-894-7111	660
Treasure Valley Community College						
650 College Blvd	Ontario	OR	97914	**888-292-5247**	541-881-8822	160
Treats International Franchise Corp						
1550-A Laperriere Ave Ste 201	Ottawa	ON	K1Z7T2	**800-461-4003**	613-563-4073	67
Tredegar Corp						
1100 Boulders Pkwy Ste 200	Richmond	VA	23225	**800-411-7441**	804-330-1000	357-3
NYSE: TG						
Tredegar Corp Film Products Div						
1100 Boulders Pkwy	Richmond	VA	23225	**855-330-1001**	804-330-1000	593
Tree Care Industry Assn (TCIA)						
136 Harvey Rd Ste 101	Londonderry	NH	03053	**800-733-2622**	603-314-5380	47-13
Tree Island Industries						
3933 Boundary Rd PO Box 50	Richmond	BC	V6V1T8	**800-663-0955**	604-524-3744	480
Tree Island Steel						
12459 Arrow Rt	Rancho Cucamonga	CA	91739	**800-255-6974**	909-594-7511	800
Tree Top Inc						
220 E Second Ave	Selah	WA	98942	**800-237-0515**	509-697-7251	295-20
Trees for Tomorrow (TFT)						
519 Sheridan St E						
PO Box 609	Eagle River	WI	54521	**800-838-9472**	715-479-6456	48-5
Trees Inc						
650 N Sam Houston Pkwy E						
Ste 209	Houston	TX	77060	**866-865-9617**	281-447-1327	766
Treetops Resort						
3962 Wilkinson Rd	Gaylord	MI	49735	**866-348-5249**	989-732-6711	660
Trefethen Vineyards Winery Inc						
1160 Oak Knoll Ave	Napa	CA	94558	**866-895-7696**	707-255-7700	79-3
Trego County						
18001 283 Hwy	WaKeeney	KS	67672	**877-962-7248**	785-743-6385	336
Trehel Corp						
PO Box 1707	Clemson	SC	29633	**800-319-7006**	864-654-6582	187
Trek Inc						
11601 Maple Ridge Rd	Medina	NY	14103	**800-367-8735**	585-798-3140	248
Trelleborg Automotive Americas						
400 Aylworth Ave	South Haven	MI	49090	**800-635-9331**	269-637-2116	59
Trelleborg Coated Systems US Inc						
790 Reeves St	Spartanburg	SC	29301	**800-344-0714**		734-1
Tremco Inc Roofing Div						
3735 Green Rd	Beachwood	OH	44122	**800-852-6013**	216-292-5000	3
Tremont Chicago						
100 E Chestnut St	Chicago	IL	60611	**888-627-8281**	312-751-1900	376
Trench Plate Rental Co						
13217 Laureldale Ave	Downey	CA	90242	**800-821-4478**		23
TREND Enterprises Inc						
300 Ninth Ave SW	New Brighton	MN	55112	**800-860-6762***	651-631-2850	243
*Cust Svc						
Trendex Inc						
240 E Maryland Ave	Saint Paul	MN	55117	**800-328-9200**	651-489-4655	85
TrendMicro Inc						
10101 N De Anza Blvd	Cupertino	CA	95014	**800-228-5651**	408-257-1500	179-12
Trends International LLC						
5188 W 74th St	Indianapolis	IN	46268	**866-406-7771**	317-388-1212	327
Trendware International Inc						
20675 Manhattan Pl	Torrance	CA	90501	**888-326-6061**	310-961-5500	177
Trendway Corp						
13467 Quincy St PO Box 9016	Holland	MI	49422	**800-968-5344**	616-399-3900	318-1

Company / Address	City	State	ZIP	Toll-Free	Phone	Class
Trenholm State Technical College						
1225 Air Base Blvd	Montgomery	AL	36108	**800-917-2081**	334-420-4200	788
Trent Inc						
201 Leverington Ave	Philadelphia	PA	19127	**800-544-8736**	215-482-5000	317
Trent University						
1600 W Bank Dr	Peterborough	ON	K9J7B8	**888-739-8885**	705-748-1011	773
Trenwyth Industries Inc						
One Connely Rd PO Box 438	Emigsville	PA	17318	**800-233-1924***	717-767-6868	184
*Cust Svc						
Trevecca Nazarene University						
333 Murfreesboro Rd	Nashville	TN	37210	**888-210-4868**	615-248-1200	166
Trex Enterprises Corp						
10455 Pacific Ctr Ct	San Diego	CA	92121	**800-626-5885**	858-646-5300	659
TRFCVB (Thief River Falls Convention & Visitors Bureau)						
102 Main Ave N	Thief River	MN	56701	**800-657-3700**	218-686-9785	207
TRGC (Title Resources Guaranty Co)						
8111 LBJ Fwy Ste 1200	Dallas	TX	75251	**800-526-8018**	972-644-6500	388-6
Tri County Area Chamber of Commerce						
152 E High St Ste 360	Pottstown	PA	19464	**800-869-5566**	610-326-2900	137
Tri County Ford Mercury Inc						
5101 W Hwy 146 PO Box 425	Buckner	KY	40010	**800-945-2520**	502-241-7333	56
TRI MAP International Inc						
111 Val Dervin Pkwy	Stockton	CA	95206	**888-687-4627**	209-234-0100	254
Tri Star Freight System Inc						
5407 Mesa Dr	Houston	TX	77028	**800-229-1095**	713-631-1095	770
Tri State Distribution Inc						
600 Vista Dr	Sparta	TN	38583	**800-392-9824**		470
Tri Tool Inc						
3041 Sunrise Blvd	Rancho Cordova	CA	95742	**800-345-5015**	916-288-6100	614
Tri Union Express Inc						
1939 N Lafayette Ct	Griffith	IN	46319	**800-228-9098**	219-838-5400	791-1
Triad Guaranty Insurance Corp						
101 S Stratford Rd	Winston-Salem	NC	27104	**888-691-8074***	336-723-1282	388-5
*Cust Svc						
Triad Isotopes Inc						
4205 Vineland Rd Ste L1	Orlando	FL	32811	**866-310-0086**	407-455-6700	231
Triad Products Co						
1801 W 'B' St	Hastings	NE	68901	**888-253-4227***	402-462-2181	601
*General						
Triad Transport Inc						
PO Box 818	McAlester	OK	74502	**800-324-1139**	918-426-4751	770
Triad's 105.7 Man Up, The						
2-B PAI Pk	Greensboro	NC	27409	**800-950-2482**	336-822-2000	636
Triangle Brick Co						
6523 NC Hwy 55	Durham	NC	27713	**800-672-8547**	919-544-1796	148
Triangle C Dude Ranch						
3737 Hwy 26	Dubois	WY	82513	**800-661-4928**	307-455-2225	239
Triangle Fastener Corp						
1925 Preble Ave	Pittsburgh	PA	15233	**800-486-1832***	412-321-5000	348
*General						
Triangle Orthopedic Assoc PA						
120 William Penn Plz	Durham	NC	27704	**800-359-3053**	919-220-5255	371-3
Triangle Package Machinery Co						
6655 W Diversey Ave	Chicago	IL	60707	**800-621-4170**	773-889-0200	540
Triangle Suspension Systems Inc						
47 E Maloney Rd	Du Bois	PA	15801	**800-458-6077**	814-375-7211	59
Triangle Tech Inc						
Du Bois PO Box 551	Du Bois	PA	15801	**800-874-8324**	814-371-2090	788
Erie 2000 Liberty St	Erie	PA	16502	**800-874-8324**	814-453-6016	788
Greensburg						
222 E Pittsburgh St	Greensburg	PA	15601	**800-874-8324**	724-832-1050	788
Trianon Old Naples						
955 Seventh Ave S	Naples	FL	34102	**877-482-5228**	239-435-9600	376
Tri-basin Natural Resources District						
1723 Burlington St	Holdrege	NE	68949	**877-995-6688**		197
Triboro Quilt Mfg Inc						
172 S Broadway	White Plains	NY	10605	**800-227-2077**	914-428-7551	63
Tribridge						
4830 W Kennedy Blvd Ste 890	Tampa	FL	33609	**877-744-1360**		179-1
Tribune Chronicle						
240 Franklin St SE	Warren	OH	44482	**888-550-8742**	330-841-1600	525-2
Tribune Newspapers of Snohomish County						
127 Ave C Ste B PO Box 499	Snohomish	WA	98291	**877-894-4663**	360-568-4121	525-4
Tribune Review Publishing Co						
622 Cabin Hill Dr	Greensburg	PA	15601	**800-524-5700**	724-834-1151	628-8
Tribune, The						
3825 S Higuera St	San Luis Obispo	CA	93401	**800-477-8799**	805-781-7800	525-2
Tribune-Democrat						
425 Locust St	Johnstown	PA	15907	**855-255-5975**	814-532-5050	525-2
Tribune-Star						
PO Box 149	Terre Haute	IN	47808	**800-783-8742**	812-231-4200	525-2
Tri-Campbell Farms						
15111 Hwy 17	Grafton	ND	58237	**800-222-7783**	701-352-3116	10-10
Trican Well Service Ltd						
645 Seventh Ave SW Ste 2900	Calgary	AB	T2P4G8	**877-587-4226**	403-266-0202	532
TSE: TCW						
Tri-Cities Chaplaincy						
2108 W Entiat Ave	Kennewick	WA	99336	**800-783-0544**	509-783-7416	368
Tri-Cities Visitor & Convention Bureau						
7130 W Grandridge Blvd Ste B	Kennewick	WA	99336	**800-254-5824**	509-735-8486	207
Tri-City Electrical Contractors Inc						
430 W Dr	Altamonte Springs	FL	32714	**800-768-2489**	407-788-3500	190-4
Tri-City Herald						
333 W Canal Dr	Kennewick	WA	99336	**800-874-0445**	509-582-1500	525-2
Tri-City Meats Inc						
1346 N Hickory Ave	Meridian	ID	83642	**800-747-9726**	208-884-2600	296-9
Trickle Up Program Inc						
104 W 27th St 12th Fl	New York	NY	10001	**866-246-9980**	212-255-9980	47-5
TriCo Bancshares						
63 Constitution Dr	Chico	CA	95973	**800-922-8742**	530-898-0300	357-2
NASDAQ: TCBK						
Tricomm Services Corp						
1247 N Church St Ste 8	Moorestown	NJ	08057	**800-872-2401**	856-914-9001	775
TRICOR (Tennessee Rehabilitative Initiative in Correction)						
240 Great Cir Rd Ste 310	Nashville	TN	37228	**800-958-7426**	615-741-5705	622
Tricor America Inc						
717 Airport Blvd	South San Francisco	CA	94080	**800-669-7874**	650-877-3650	539
Tri-County Electric						
302 E Glaydas St PO Box 880	Hooker	OK	73945	**800-522-3315**	580-652-2418	245
Tri-County Electric Co-op						
6473 Old State Rd						
PO Box 217	Saint Matthews	SC	29135	**877-874-1215**	803-874-1215	245
Tri-County Electric Co-op Inc						
600 NW Pkwy	Azle	TX	76020	**800-367-8232**	817-444-3201	245

	Toll-Free	Phone	Class
Tri-County Electric Membership Corp			
PO Box 487 . . . . Gray GA 31032	866-254-8100	478-986-8100	245
Tri-County Mall			
11700 Princeton Pike . . . . Cincinnati OH 45246	866-905-4675	513-671-0120	455
Tri-County Rural Electric Co-op Inc			
22 N Main St PO Box 526 . . . . Mansfield PA 16933	800-343-2559	570-662-2175	245
Tri-County Technical College			
7900 Hwy 76 . . . . Pendleton SC 29670	866-269-5677	864-646-8361	788
Trident Medical Ctr			
9330 Medical Plz Dr . . . . Charleston SC 29406	866-492-9085	843-797-7000	371-3
Trident Seafood Corp			
5303 Shilshole Ave NW . . . . Seattle WA 98107	800-426-5490	206-783-3818	295-14
Trident Technical College (TTC)			
7000 Rivers Ave			
PO Box 118067 . . . . North Charleston SC 29406	877-349-7184	843-574-6111	788
Tri-Dim Filter Corp			
93 Industrial Dr Bldg 2 . . . . Louisa VA 23093	800-458-9835	540-967-2600	18
Tri-Ed Distribution Inc			
135 Crossways Pk Dr W . . . . Woodbury NY 11797	888-874-3336	516-941-2800	246
Tri-Gas & Oil Company Inc			
3941 Federalsburg Hwy			
PO Box 465 . . . . Federalsburg MD 21632	800-638-7802	410-754-8184	324
Tri-K Industries Inc			
Two Stewart Ct PO Box 10 . . . . Denville NJ 07834	800-526-0372	973-298-8850	474
Tri-line Carriers L.p			
235185 Ryan Rd . . . . Rocky View AB T1X0K1	800-661-9191		313
TriLink BioTechnologies Inc			
9955 Mesa Rim Rd . . . . San Diego CA 92121	800-863-6801	858-546-0004	732
Tri-Lite Inc			
1642 N Besly Ct . . . . Chicago IL 60642	800-322-5250	773-384-7765	435
Trilithic Inc			
9710 Pk Davis Dr . . . . Indianapolis IN 46235	800-344-2412	317-895-3600	248
Trilogy Communications Inc			
2910 Hwy 80 E . . . . Pearl MS 39208	888-713-1414	601-932-4461	801
Trimac Panel Products			
5201 SW Westgate Dr Ste 200 . . . . Portland OR 97221	800-237-8765*	503-297-1826	606
*General			
Trimaco LLC			
2300 Gateway Centre Blvd			
Ste 200 . . . . Morrisville NC 27560	800-325-7356	919-674-3460	723
Trimark Corp			
PO Box 350 . . . . New Hampton IA 50659	800-447-0343	641-394-3188	347
TriMark USA Inc			
505 Collins St . . . . South Attleboro MA 02703	800-755-5580	508-399-2400	299
Trimble Navigation Ltd			
935 Stewart Dr . . . . Sunnyvale CA 94085	800-827-8000	408-481-8000	522
NASDAQ: TRMB			
Trimco/Builders Brass Works			
3528 Emery St . . . . Los Angeles CA 90023	800-637-8746	323-262-4191	347
Trimedyne Inc			
15091 Bake Pkwy . . . . Irvine CA 92618	800-733-5273	949-559-5300	421
OTC: TMED			
Trimfit Inc			
1900 Frost Rd Ste 111 . . . . Bristol PA 19007	800-347-7697	215-781-0600	153-9
Trimfoot Co LLC			
115 Trimfoot Terr . . . . Farmington MO 63640	800-325-6116		300
TrimMaster			
4860 N Fifth St Hwy . . . . Temple PA 19560	800-356-4237	610-921-0203	733
Trim-Rite Food Corp			
801 Commerce Pkwy . . . . Carpentersville IL 60110	800-626-9442	847-649-3400	296-9
TriNet Group Inc			
1100 San Leandro Blvd			
Ste 300 . . . . San Leandro CA 94577	888-874-6388	510-352-5000	623
Trinidad State Junior College			
600 Prospect St . . . . Trinidad CO 81082	800-621-8752	719-846-5011	160
Trinity Bible College			
50 Sixth Ave N . . . . Ellendale ND 58436	800-523-1603	701-349-3621	159
Trinity Biotech PLC			
5919 Farnsworth Ct . . . . Carlsbad CA 92008	800-331-2291	760-929-0500	231
NASDAQ: TRIB			
Trinity Broadcasting Network (TBN)			
PO Box A . . . . Santa Ana CA 92711	888-731-1000	714-832-2950	729
Trinity College of Florida			
2430 Welbilt Blvd . . . . Trinity FL 34655	800-388-0869	727-376-6911	159
Trinity Episcopal School for Ministry			
311 11th St . . . . Ambridge PA 15003	800-874-8754	724-266-3838	167-3
Trinity Fiduciary Partners LLC			
106 Decker Court Ste 226 . . . . Irving TX 75062	877-334-1283		521
Trinity Hardwood Distributors Inc			
110 East Oregon . . . . Dallas TX 75203	800-492-9856	214-948-3001	319
Trinity Hospital of Augusta			
2803 Wrightsboro Rd Ste 38 . . . . Augusta GA 30909	800-999-6673	706-729-6000	368
Trinity Hospital Saint Joseph's			
One W Burdick Expy . . . . Minot ND 58701	800-247-1316	701-857-5000	371-3
Trinity Industries Inc			
2525 Stemmons Fwy . . . . Dallas TX 75207	800-631-4420	214-631-4420	186
NYSE: TRN			
Trinity International University			
2065 Half Day Rd . . . . Deerfield IL 60015	800-822-3225	847-945-8800	166
Trinity International University South Florida			
8190 W SR 84 . . . . Davie FL 33324	800-822-3225	954-382-6400	166
Trinity Lutheran Seminary			
2199 E Main St . . . . Columbus OH 43209	866-610-8571	614-235-4136	167-3
Trinity Marine Products Inc			
2525 N Stemmons Fwy . . . . Dallas TX 75207	877-876-5463	214-589-8446	689
Trinity Medical Ctr West			
4000 Johnson Rd . . . . Steubenville OH 43952	877-271-4176	740-264-8000	371-3
Trinity Mining Service			
109 48th St . . . . Pittsburgh PA 15201	800-264-2583	412-682-4700	641
Trinity Rail Group LLC			
2525 N Stemmons Fwy . . . . Dallas TX 75207	800-631-4420	214-631-4420	641
Trinity Systems Technologies Inc			
5885 Cumming Hwy Ste 108-273 . . . Sugar Hill GA 30518	888-828-5655		197
Trinity Trailer Manufacturing Inc			
8200 S Eisenman Rd . . . . Boise ID 83716	800-235-6577	208-336-3666	769
Trinity University			
One Trinity Pl . . . . San Antonio TX 78212	800-874-6489	210-999-7011	166
Trinity Valley Community College			
Athens 100 Cardinal Dr . . . . Athens TX 75751	866-882-2937	903-675-6200	160
Trinity Valley Electric Co-op Inc (TVEC)			
1800 Hwy 243 E PO Box 888 . . . . . . Kaufman TX 75142	800-766-9576	972-932-2214	245
Trinity Western University			
7600 Glover Rd . . . . Langley BC V2Y1Y1	888-468-6898	604-888-7511	773

	Toll-Free	Phone	Class
Trintech Inc			
15851 Dallas Pkwy Ste 900 . . . . Addison TX 75001	800-416-0075	972-701-9802	179-1
Trion Industries Inc			
297 Laird St . . . . Wilkes-Barre PA 18702	800-444-4665	570-824-1000	286
Triple Creek Ranch			
5551 W Fork Rd . . . . Darby MT 59829	800-654-2943	406-821-4600	660
Triple Crown Corp			
5351 Jaycee Ave . . . . Harrisburg PA 17112	877-822-4663	717-657-5729	188
Triple Crown Nutrition Inc			
319 Barry Ave S Ste 303 . . . . Wayzata MN 55391	800-451-9916		442
Triple Crown Services			
2720 Dupont Commerce Ct			
Ste 200 . . . . Fort Wayne IN 46825	800-325-6510	260-416-3600	639
Triple J Wilderness Ranch			
91 Mortimer Rd PO Box 310 . . . . Augusta MT 59410	800-826-1300	406-562-3653	239
Triple Play Products LLC			
904 Main St Ste 330 . . . . Hopkins MN 55343	800-829-1625	952-938-0531	63
Triple/S Dynamics Inc			
1031 S Haskell Ave PO Box 151027 . . . . Dallas TX 75315	800-527-2116	214-828-8600	465
Tripler Army Medical Ctr			
1 Jarrett White Rd Tripler AMC . . . . . Honolulu HI 96859	877-880-2184	808-433-6661	371-4
Triple-S Steel Supply LLC			
PO Box 21119 . . . . Houston TX 77226	800-231-1034	713-697-7105	487
Triplett Office Essentials Corp			
3553 109th St . . . . Urbandale IA 50322	800-437-5034	515-270-9150	528
Tripos Inc			
1699 S Hanley Rd . . . . Saint Louis MO 63144	800-323-2960	314-647-1099	179-5
Tripwire Inc			
101 SW Main St Ste 1500 . . . . Portland OR 97204	800-874-7947*	503-276-7500	179-12
*General			
TriQuint Semiconductor Inc			
2300 NE Brookwood Pkwy . . . . Hillsboro OR 97124	855-367-8768	503-615-9000	687
NASDAQ: TQNT			
TriSports.com			
4495 S Coach Dr . . . . Tucson AZ 85714	888-293-3934		702
Tristar Southern Hills Medical Ctr			
391 Wallace Rd . . . . Nashville TN 37211	800-242-5662	615-781-4000	371-3
Tri-State Armature & Electrical Works Inc			
330 GE Patterson PO Box 466 . . . . . . Memphis TN 38126	800-238-7654	901-527-8412	246
Tri-State Better Business Bureau			
5401 Vogel Rd Ste 410 . . . . Evansville IN 47715	800-359-0979	812-473-0202	78
Tri-State Bible College			
506 Margaret St . . . . South Point OH 45680	800-333-3243	740-377-2520	159
Tri-State Chamber of Commerce			
5 S Broome St . . . . Port Jervis NY 12771	800-707-6925	845-856-6694	137
Tri-State Drilling Inc			
16940 Hwy 55 W . . . . Plymouth MN 55446	800-383-1033	763-553-1234	190-15
Tri-State Electric Membership Corp (TSEMC)			
2310 Blue Ridge Dr . . . . Blue Ridge GA 30513	800-351-1111	706-492-3251	245
Tri-state Fabricators Inc			
1146 Ferris Rd . . . . Amelia OH 45102	888-523-1488	513-752-5005	603
Tri-state Forest Products Inc			
2105 Sheridan Ave . . . . Springfield OH 45505	800-949-6325	937-323-6325	192-3
Tri-State Iron & Metal Co			
1725 E Ninth St . . . . Texarkana AR 71854	800-773-8409	870-773-8409	677
Tri-State Travel			
4349 Industrial Pk Dr . . . . Galena IL 61036	800-779-4869	815-777-0820	750
Tri-State Utility Products Inc			
1030 Atlanta Industrial Dr . . . . Marietta GA 30066	800-282-7985	770-427-3119	246
Tri-State Video Services Inc			
1379 Pittsburgh Rd . . . . Valencia PA 16059	888-382-7768	724-898-1630	37
Triton Systems Inc			
21405 B St . . . . Long Beach MS 39560	866-787-4866	228-575-3100	253
Triton-Tek Inc			
445 W Erie St Ste 208 . . . . Chicago IL 60654	866-387-4866	312-467-9201	225
Triumph Controls Inc			
205 Church Rd . . . . North Wales PA 19454	800-322-2885	215-699-4861	204
Triumph Learning			
136 Madison Ave . . . . New York NY 10016	800-221-9372		628-2
Triumph Pet Industries Inc			
500 Sixth St SW . . . . Red Bay AL 35582	800-633-3349	256-356-9541	571
Triumph Twist Drill Co Inc			
1 SW 7th St . . . . Chisholm MN 55719	800-942-1501	218-263-3891	748
Triumvirate Environmental			
61 Innerbelt Rd . . . . Somerville MA 02143	800-966-9282	617-628-8098	792
TriZetto Corporation			
501 N Broadway 3rd Fl . . . . Sacramento CA 95814	800-969-3666		178
TRMC (Thibodaux Regional Medical Ctr)			
602 N Acadia Rd . . . . Thibodaux LA 70301	800-822-8442	985-447-5500	371-3
TRN (Talk Radio Network)			
PO Box 3755 . . . . Central Point OR 97502	888-383-3733		637
Trojan Battery Co			
12380 Clark St . . . . Santa Fe Springs CA 90670	800-423-6569*	562-236-3000	73
*Cust Svc			
Trojan Inc			
198 Trojan St PO Box 850 . . . . Mount Sterling KY 40353	800-264-0526	859-498-0526	433
Tronair Inc			
1740 Eber Rd Ste E . . . . Holland OH 43528	800-426-6301	419-866-6301	22
Trone			
1823 Eastchester Dr . . . . High Point NC 27265	877-493-3043	336-886-1622	4
Tronox Inc			
3301 NW 150th St . . . . Oklahoma City OK 73134	866-775-5009	405-775-5000	141
Trophy Nut Company Inc			
320 N Second St . . . . Tipp City OH 45371	800-729-6887	937-667-8478	295-28
Trophyland USA Inc			
7001 W 20th Ave . . . . Hialeah FL 33014	800-327-5820		767
Tropical Cheese Industries Inc			
450 Fayette St PO Box 1357 . . . . . . Perth Amboy NJ 08861	888-874-4928	732-442-4898	295-5
Tropical Everglades Visitor Assn			
160 US Hwy Ste 1 . . . . Florida City FL 33034	800-272-6232	305-245-9180	207
Tropical Ford			
9900 S Orange Blossom Trial . . . . . . Orlando FL 32837	800-790-7137*	407-851-3800	56
*Sales			
Tropical Shipping			
Five E 11th St . . . . Riviera Beach FL 33404	800-367-6200	561-881-3900	312
Tropical Winds Oceanfront Hotel			
1398 N Atlantic Ave . . . . Daytona Beach FL 32118	800-245-6099	386-258-1016	376
Tropicana Entertainment			
2831 Boardwalk . . . . Atlantic City NJ 08401	800-843-8767		660
OTC: TPCA			
Tropicana Express			
2121 S Casino Dr . . . . Laughlin NV 89029	800-243-6846	702-298-4200	132
Tropicana Field			
One Tropicana Dr . . . . Saint Petersburg FL 33705	888-326-7297	727-825-3137	711

	Toll-Free	Phone	Class
Tropicana Inn & Suites			
1540 S Harbor Blvd .... Anaheim CA 92802	**800-828-4898**	714-635-4082	376
Tropicana Resort & Casino			
3801 Las Vegas Blvd S .... Las Vegas NV 89109	**800-462-8767***	702-739-2222	660
*Resv			
Tropitone Furniture Co Inc			
5 Marconi .... Irvine CA 92618	**800-654-7000***	949-951-2010	318-4
*All			
Trout Unlimited (TU)			
1300 N 17th St Ste 500 .... Arlington VA 22209	**800-834-2419**	703-522-0200	47-3
TrouveMoiUnPro Inc			
736 Wellington Ste 100 .... Montreal QC H3C1T4	**855-360-1390**		224
Trouw Nutrition			
115 Executive Dr .... Highland IL 62249	**800-365-1357**	618-654-2070	442
Troxler Electronic Laboratories Inc			
3008 E Cornwallis Rd			
PO Box 12057........... Research Triangle Park NC 27709	**877-876-9537**	919-549-8661	202
Troy Corp			
8 Vreeland Rd PO Box 955 .... Florham Park NJ 07932	**800-448-2843**	973-443-4200	543
Troy Public Library			
510 W Big Beaver Rd .... Troy MI 48084	**855-203-5274**	248-524-3538	431-3
Troy Sunshade Co			
607 Riffle Ave .... Greenville OH 45331	**800-833-8769**	937-548-2466	723
Troy University			
600 University Ave .... Troy AL 36082	**800-551-9716**	334-670-3100	166
Montgomery			
231 Montgomery St			
PO Box 4419 .... Montgomery AL 36104	**888-357-8843**		166
Troy-CSL Lighting Inc			
14508 Nelson Ave .... City of Industry CA 91744	**800-533-8769**	626-336-4511	435
Troyer Foods Inc			
17141 State Rd 4 .... Goshen IN 46528	**800-876-9377**	574-533-0302	296-10
TRSA (Textile Rental Services Assn)			
1800 Diagonal Rd Ste 200 .... Alexandria VA 22314	**877-770-9274**	703-519-0029	48-4
TRU TECH Systems Inc			
24550 N River Rd			
PO Box 46965.................. Mount Clemens MI 48046	**877-878-8324**	586-469-2700	450
Tru Vue Inc			
9400 W 55th St .... McCook IL 60525	**800-621-8339**	708-485-5080	328
Truck Equipment Service Co			
800 Oak St .... Lincoln NE 68521	**800-869-0363**	402-476-3225	769
Truck Sales & Service Inc			
PO Box 262 .... Midvale OH 44653	**800-282-6100**	740-922-3412	56
Truck Utilities Inc			
2370 English St .... Saint Paul MN 55109	**800-869-1075**	651-484-3305	509
Truck Works Inc			
3220 W Sherman St .... Phoenix AZ 85009	**877-894-8757**	602-233-3713	56
Truckin Movers Corp			
1031 Harvest St .... Durham NC 27704	**800-334-1651**	919-682-2300	512
Truck-Lite Company Inc			
310 E Elmwood Ave .... Falconer NY 14733	**800-562-5012***	716-665-6214	434
*Cust Svc			
Truckload Carriers Assn (TCA)			
555 E Braddock Rd .... Alexandria VA 22314	**800-666-2770**	703-838-1950	48-21
True Blue Inc			
PO Box 2910 .... Tacoma WA 98401	**800-610-8920**	253-383-9101	712
NYSE: TBI			
True Fitness Technology Inc			
865 Hoff Rd .... O'Fallon MO 63366	**800-426-6570**	636-272-7100	267
True Manufacturing Co			
2001 E Terra Ln .... O'Fallon MO 63366	**800-325-6152**	636-240-2400	655
True Temper Sports			
8275 Tournament Dr Ste 200 .... Memphis TN 38125	**800-355-8783**	901-746-2000	701
TrueCloud			
2147 E Baseline Rd .... Tempe AZ 85283	**866-990-8783**		197
Truett-McConnell College			
100 Alumni Dr .... Cleveland GA 30528	**800-226-8621**	706-865-2134	166
Truevance Management Inc			
7666 Blanding Blvd			
PO Box 440879.................... Jacksonville FL 32244	**800-285-2028**	904-777-9052	261
Tru-Flex Metal Hose Corp			
2391 S State Rd 263			
PO Box 247.................... West Lebanon IN 47991	**800-255-6291**	765-893-4403	588
TruGreen ChemLawn			
860 Ridge Lk Blvd .... Memphis TN 38120	**866-369-9539**		570
Truheat Inc			
700 Grand St .... Allegan MI 49010	**800-879-6199**	269-673-2145	317
Truitt Bros Inc			
1105 Front St NE .... Salem OR 97301	**800-547-8712**	503-362-3674	295-20
Truliant Federal Credit Union			
3200 Truliant Way .... Winston-Salem NC 27103	**800-822-0382**	336-659-1955	219
Truline Corp			
9390 Redwood St .... Las Vegas NV 89139	**800-634-6489**	702-362-7495	770
Tru-Link Fence Co			
5440 Touhy Ave .... Skokie IL 60077	**800-568-9300**	847-568-9300	279
Trulioo Inc			
300 - 420 W Hastings St .... Vancouver BC V6B1L1	**888-773-0179**		224
Truly Nolen of America Inc			
3636 E Speedway Blvd .... Tucson AZ 85716	**800-468-7859**	800-528-3442	570
Trumaker Inc			
701 Sutter St Fl 5 .... San Francisco CA 94109	**855-623-3878**		681
Truman Hotel & Conference Ctr			
1510 Jefferson St .... Jefferson City MO 65109	**800-392-0202**	573-635-7171	376
Truman State University			
100 E Normal St .... Kirksville MO 63501	**800-892-7792**	660-785-4000	166
Trumbull Industries Inc			
400 Dietz Rd NE .... Warren OH 44482	**800-477-1799**	330-393-6624	1
Trump International Hotel & Tower			
725 Fifth Ave .... New York NY 10022	**888-448-7867**	312-588-8000	376
Trump International Sonesta Beach Resort			
18001 Collins Ave .... Sunny Isles Beach FL 33160	**800-766-3782**	305-692-5600	660
Trump Taj Mahal Casino Resort			
1000 Boardwalk & Virginia Ave ...... Atlantic City NJ 08401	**800-426-2537**	609-449-1000	660
TruSignal LLC			
25 6th Ave N .... St. Cloud MN 56303	**855-569-0426**		384
Trust Bank			
600 E Main St PO Box 158 .... Olney IL 62450	**800-766-3451**	618-395-4311	69
Trust for Public Land (TPL)			
116 New Montgomery St			
Fourth Fl...................... San Francisco CA 94105	**800-714-5263**	415-495-4014	47-13
Trustco Bank Corp NY			
PO Box 1082 .... Schenectady NY 12301	**800-670-3110**	518-377-3311	357-2
NASDAQ: TRST			

	Toll-Free	Phone	Class
Trustees of the University of Pennsylvania			
Bone Marrow & Stem Cell Transplant Program			
3400 Spruce St .... Philadelphia PA 19104	**800-417-9391**	215-662-4533	759
Trustile Doors LLC			
1780 E 66th Ave .... Denver CO 80229	**866-442-5302**	303-286-3931	236
Trustmark Insurance Co			
400 Field Dr .... Lake Forest IL 60045	**888-246-9949**	847-615-1500	388-2
Trustmark National Bank			
248 E Capitol St PO Box 291 .... Jackson MS 39201	**800-243-2524***	601-208-5111	357-2
NASDAQ: TRMK ■ *Cust Svc			
Truth Hardware Inc			
700 W Bridge St .... Owatonna MN 55060	**800-866-7884***	507-451-5620	347
*Cust Svc			
Truth Publishing Company Inc			
421 S Second St .... Elkhart IN 46516	**800-585-5416**	574-294-1661	628-8
Truth, The PO Box 487 .... Elkhart IN 46515	**800-585-5416**	574-294-1661	525-2
TruTouch Technologies Inc			
73 Carriage Way .... Sudbury MA 01776	**866-721-6221**		577
Trutrak Flight Systems Inc			
1500 S Old Missouri Rd .... Springdale AR 72764	**866-878-8725**	479-751-0250	522
Truwest Credit Union			
PO Box 3489 .... Scottsdale AZ 85271	**855-878-9378**	480-441-5900	502
Tryon Trucking Inc			
PO Box 68 .... Fairless Hills PA 19030	**800-523-5254**	215-295-6622	770
TSA (Transportation Security Administration)			
601 S 12th St .... Arlington VA 22202	**866-289-9673**	202-282-8000	338-9
TSC Apparel LLC			
12080 Mosteller Rd .... Cincinnati OH 45241	**800-543-7230**	513-771-1138	154
TSCT (Thaddeus Stevens College of Technology)			
750 E King St .... Lancaster PA 17602	**800-842-3832**	717-299-7701	788
TSE Industries Inc			
4370 112th Terr N .... Clearwater FL 33762	**800-237-7634**	727-573-7676	601
TSEMC (Tri-State Electric Membership Corp)			
2310 Blue Ridge Dr .... Blue Ridge GA 30513	**800-351-1111**	706-492-3251	245
TSI Global Cos			
700 Fountain Lakes Blvd .... Saint Charles MO 63301	**800-875-5605**	636-949-8889	725
TSI Health Sciences Inc			
305 S Fourth St E Ste 101 .... Missoula MT 59801	**877-549-9123**	406-549-9123	474
TSI Inc			
500 CaRdigan Rd .... Shoreview MN 55126	**800-874-2811**	651-483-0900	202
TSI Power Corp			
1103 W Pierce Ave .... Antigo WI 54409	**800-874-3160**	715-623-0636	253
TSMC (Taiwan Semiconductor Mfg Company Ltd)			
2585 Junction Ave .... San Jose CA 95134	**877-248-4237**	408-382-8000	687
NYSE: TSM			
TSN Inc			
4001 Salazar Way PO Box 679 .... Frederick CO 80530	**888-997-5959***	303-530-0600	552
*General			
TSO3 Inc			
2505 Dalton Ave .... Quebec QC G1P3S5	**866-715-0003**	418-651-0003	472
TST/Impreso Inc			
652 Southwestern Blvd .... Coppell TX 75019	**800-527-2878**	972-462-0100	545-1
TSTA Advocate Magazine			
316 W 12th St .... Austin TX 78701	**877-275-8782**	512-476-5355	452-8
Abilene 650 E Hwy 80 .... Abilene TX 79601	**800-852-8784**	325-672-7091	160
TT Group Inc			
702 Carnation Dr .... Aurora MO 65605	**800-445-0886***	417-678-2181	300
*General			
TTC (Trans-Tel Central Inc)			
2805 Broce Dr .... Norman OK 73072	**800-729-4636**	405-447-5025	775
TTC (Trident Technical College)			
7000 Rivers Ave			
PO Box 118067............... North Charleston SC 29406	**877-349-7184**	843-574-6111	788
TTC Marketing Solutions			
3945 N Neenah .... Chicago IL 60634	**800-530-7189**		727
TTI Inc			
2441 NE Pkwy .... Fort Worth TX 76106	**800-225-5884***	817-740-9000	246
*Sales			
TTSG (Twinless Twins Support Group International)			
PO Box 980481 .... Ypsilanti MI 48198	**888-205-8962**		47-21
TTX Co			
101 N Wacker Dr .... Chicago IL 60606	**800-889-4357**	312-853-3223	264-5
TU (Trout Unlimited)			
1300 N 17th St Ste 500 .... Arlington VA 22209	**800-834-2419**	703-522-0200	47-3
Tub Springs State Wayside			
12845 Green Springs Hwy			
3792 N River Rd .... Ashland OR 97520	**800-551-6949**		558
Tubbys Grilled Submarines			
31920 Groesbeck Hwy .... Fraser MI 48026	**800-752-0644**		661
Tube Art Group (TAG)			
11715 SE Fifth St .... Bellevue WA 98005	**800-562-2854**	206-223-1122	692
Tube City IMS Corp (TMS)			
12 Monongahela Ave .... Glassport PA 15045	**800-860-2442**	412-678-6141	677
NYSE: TMS			
Tube Processing Corp			
604 E Le Grande Ave .... Indianapolis IN 46203	**800-295-4119**	317-787-1321	485
Tubelite Inc			
4878 Mackinaw Trl .... Reed City MI 49677	**800-866-2227**		234
Tube-Mac Industries Ltd			
853 Arvin Ave .... Stoney Creek ON L8E5N8	**877-643-8823**	905-643-8823	598-2
Tubular Steel Inc			
1031 Executive Pkwy Dr .... Saint Louis MO 63141	**800-388-7491**	314-851-9200	487
Tubular Textile Machinery			
113 Woodside Dr PO Box 2097 .... Lexington NC 27292	**800-531-3715**	336-956-6444	733
Tucker County Convention & Visitors Bureau			
410 William Ave .... Davis WV 26260	**800-782-2775**	304-259-5315	207
Tucows Inc			
96 Mowat Ave .... Toronto ON M6K3M1	**800-371-6992**	416-535-0123	394
TSE: TC			
Tucson Electric Power Co			
1 S Church Ave Ste 100 .... Tucson AZ 85701	**800-430-4046**	520-571-4000	775
Tucson International Airport			
7250 S Tucson Blvd .... Tucson AZ 85706	**800-758-1874**	520-573-8100	27
Tucson Medical Ctr			
5301 E Grant Rd .... Tucson AZ 85712	**800-526-5353**	520-327-5461	371-3
Tudi Mechanical Systems of Tampa Inc			
343 Munson Ave .... Mc Kees Rocks PA 15136	**877-367-8834**	412-771-4100	603
Tuesday Morning Corp			
6250 LBJ Fwy .... Dallas TX 75240	**800-457-0099**	972-387-3562	326
NASDAQ: TUES			
Tufco Technologies Inc			
PO Box 23500 .... Green Bay WI 54305	**800-558-8145**	920-336-0054	547
NASDAQ: TFCO			

	Toll-Free	Phone	Class
Tuff Torq Corp			
5943 Commerce Blvd .... Morristown TN 37814	**866-572-3441**	423-585-2000	426
Tuffaloy Products Inc			
1400 S Batesville Rd .... Greer SC 29650	**800-521-3722**	864-879-0763	798
TuffStuff Fitness Equipment Inc			
13971 Norton Ave .... Chino CA 91710	**888-884-8275**	909-629-1600	351
Tuffy Assoc Corp			
7150 Granite Cir .... Toledo OH 43617	**800-228-8339**	419-865-6900	61-5
Tuftco Corp			
2318 S Holtzclaw Ave .... Chattanooga TN 37408	**800-288-3826**	423-698-8601	733
Tuftco Finishing Systems Inc			
100 W Industrial Blvd .... Dalton GA 30720	**800-288-3826**	706-277-1110	733
Tufts Associated Health Plans			
705 Mt Auburn Street .... Watertown MA 02472	**800-462-0224**	617-972-9400	388-3
Tufts Library			
46 Broad St .... Weymouth MA 02188	**888-283-3757**	781-337-1402	431-3
Tufts Medical Ctr (TMC)			
800 Washington St .... Boston MA 02111	**866-220-3699**	617-636-5000	371-3
Tufts University			
4 Colby St .... Medford MA 02155	**800-326-4001**	617-628-5000	166
Tugboat Inn			
80 Commercial St			
PO Box 267. .... Boothbay Harbor ME 04538	**800-248-2628**	207-633-4434	376
Tulalip Resort Casino			
10200 Quil Ceda Blvd .... Tulalip WA 98271	**888-272-1111**		698
Tulane Medical Ctr (TMC)			
1415 Tulane Ave .... New Orleans LA 70112	**800-588-5800**	504-588-5108	371-3
Tulane University			
6823 St Charles Ave .... New Orleans LA 70118	**800-873-9283***	504-865-5000	166
*Admissions			
Tulane University Law School			
6329 Freret St			
Weinmann Hall .... New Orleans LA 70118	**800-328-6819**	504-865-5930	167-1
Tulare Joint Union High School District			
426 N Blackstone Ave .... Tulare CA 93274	**800-942-3767**	559-688-2021	676
Tulco Oils Inc			
5240 E Pine PO Box 582410 .... Tulsa OK 74115	**800-375-2347**	918-838-3354	572
Tulip City Air Service Inc			
1581 S Washington Ave .... Holland MI 49423	**800-748-0515**	616-392-7831	13
Tulsa Ballet			
1212 E 45th Pl .... Tulsa OK 74105	**800-722-9942**	918-749-6030	566-1
Tulsa Community College			
Metro 909 S Boston Ave .... Tulsa OK 74119	**866-970-0233**	918-595-7000	160
Tulsa Convention & Visitors Bureau			
One W Third Ste 100 .... Tulsa OK 74103	**800-558-3311**		207
Tulsa Convention Ctr			
100 Civic Ctr .... Tulsa OK 74103	**800-678-7177**	918-894-4350	206
Tulsa Metro Chamber			
One West Third St Ste 100 .... Tulsa OK 74103	**888-424-9411**	918-585-1201	137
Tulsa Opera			
1610 S Boulder Ave .... Tulsa OK 74119	**866-298-2530**	918-582-4035	566-2
Tulsa Public Schools			
3027 S New Haven Ave .... Tulsa OK 74114	**866-632-9992**	918-746-6800	676
Tulsa World			
315 S Boulder Ave .... Tulsa OK 74103	**800-897-3557**	918-583-2161	525-2
Tulsair Beechcraft Inc			
3207 N Sheridan Rd .... Tulsa OK 74115	**800-331-4071**	918-835-7651	24
Tumbling River Ranch			
3715 Pk County Rd 62 PO Box 30 .... Grant CO 80448	**800-654-8770**	303-838-5981	239
Tundra Lodge Resort & Waterpark			
865 Lombardi Ave .... Green Bay WI 54304	**877-886-3725**	920-405-8700	660
Tunica County Convention & Visitors Bureau			
13625 Hwy 61 N ....Robinsonville MS 38664	**888-488-6422**		207
Tunnel Duty Free Shop Inc			
465 Goyeau St ....Windsor ON N9A1H1	**800-669-2105**	519-252-2713	241
Tuohy Furniture Corp			
42 St Albans Pl .... Chatfield MN 55923	**800-533-1696***	507-867-4280	318-1
*Cust Svc			
Tuolumne County Chamber of Commerce			
222 S Shepherd St .... Sonora CA 95370	**877-532-4212**	209-532-4212	137
Tupelo Buffalo Park & Zoo			
2272 N Coley Rd .... Tupelo MS 38803	**866-272-4766**	662-844-8709	810
Tupelo National Battlefield			
2680 Natchez Trace Pkwy .... Tupelo MS 38804	**800-305-7417**	662-680-4025	557
Tupelo Regional Airport			
105 Lemons Dr .... Tupelo MS 38801	**877-777-4778**	662-823-4359	27
Tupperware Corp			
14901 S Orange Blossom Trail .... Orlando FL 32837	**800-468-9716***	407-826-5050	600
NYSE: TUP ■ *Cust Svc			
Turbo Refrigerating			
1000 W Ormsby Ave .... Louisville KY 40210	**800-853-8648**	502-635-3000	655
Turbomeca USA Inc			
2709 N Forum Dr .... Grand Prairie TX 75052	**800-662-6322**	972-606-7600	21
Turf Paradise Racetrack			
1501 W Bell Rd .... Phoenix AZ 85023	**800-639-8783**	602-942-1101	633
Consulate General			
1990 Post Oak Blvd Ste 1300........ Houston TX 77056	**888-566-7656**	713-622-5849	257
Consulate General			
6300 Wilshire Blvd Ste 2010 ......Los Angeles CA 90048	**800-874-8875**	323-655-8832	257
Turkey			
Embassy			
2525 Massachusetts Ave NW .... Washington DC 20008	**877-367-8875**	202-612-6700	257
Turkey Hill Dairy Inc			
2601 River Rd ....Conestoga PA 17516	**800-693-2479**	717-872-5461	295-25
Turks & Caicos Islands Tourism Office			
60 E 42nd St Ste 2817 .... New York NY 10165	**800-241-0824**	646-375-8830	765
Turlock Chamber of Commerce			
115 S Golden State Blvd .... Turlock CA 95380	**800-834-0401**	209-632-2221	137
Turner County			
PO Box 191 ....Ashburn GA 31714	**800-436-7442**	229-567-2011	336
Turner Dairy Farms Inc			
1049 Jefferson Rd .... Pittsburgh PA 15235	**800-892-1039**	412-372-2211	295-25
Turner Gas Company Inc			
PO Box 26554 ....Salt Lake City UT 84126	**800-932-4277**	801-973-6886	572
Turner Industries Group LLC			
8687 United Plaza Blvd			
Ste 500. .... Baton Rouge LA 70809	**800-288-6503**	225-922-5050	189-9
Turning Point Hospital			
3015 Veterans Pkwy PO Box 1177 ....Moultrie GA 31776	**800-342-1075**	229-985-4815	717
Turning Point of Tampa			
6227 Sheldon Rd .... Tampa FL 33615	**800-397-3006**	813-882-3003	717
Turning Stone Resort Casino LLC			
5218 Patrick Rd .... Verona NY 13478	**800-771-7711**	315-361-7711	132

	Toll-Free	Phone	Class
Turpin Sales & Marketing Inc			
330 Cold Spring Ave .... West Springfield MA 01089	**877-377-7573**		458
Turret Steel Industries Inc			
105 Pine St .... Imperial PA 15126	**800-245-4800**	724-218-1014	487
Turtle Bay Exploration Park			
840 Auditorium Dr .... Redding CA 96001	**800-887-8532**	530-243-8850	513
Turtle Bay Resort			
57-091 Kamehameha Hwy .... Kahuku HI 96731	**866-475-2567**	808-293-6000	660
Turtle Cay Resort			
600 Atlantic Ave .... Virginia Beach VA 23451	**888-989-7788**	757-437-5565	660
Turtle Magazine			
1100 Waterway Blvd ....Indianapolis IN 46202	**800-558-2376**	317-634-1100	452-6
Turtle Mountain Community College			
10145 BIA Rd 7 .... Belcourt ND 58316	**800-827-1100**	701-477-7862	163
Tuscaloosa News			
315 28th Ave ....Tuscaloosa AL 35401	**800-888-8639**	205-345-0505	525-2
Tuscaloosa VA Medical Ctr			
3701 Loop Rd E ....Tuscaloosa AL 35404	**888-269-3045**	205-554-2000	371-8
Tuscany Suites & Casino			
255 E Flamingo Rd .... Las Vegas NV 89169	**877-887-2261***	702-893-8933	376
*Resv			
Tuscarora Yarns Inc			
8760 E Franklin St .... Mount Pleasant NC 28124	**800-849-6527**	704-436-6527	734-9
Tusculum College			
60 Shiloh Rd Hwy 107 ....Greeneville TN 37743	**800-729-0256**	423-636-7300	166
Tuskegee University			
1200 W Montgomery Rd .... Tuskegee AL 36088	**800-622-6531***	334-727-8011	166
*Admissions			
Tuskegee University Ford Motor Co Library/Learning Resource Ctr			
Hollis Burke Frissell Library Bldg........ Tuskegee AL 36088	**800-622-6531**	334-727-8894	431-6
Tustin Nissan			
30 Auto Ctr Dr ....Tustin CA 92782	**888-468-1391***	714-669-8282	56
*Sales			
Tutco Inc			
500 Gould Dr .... Cookeville TN 38506	**877-262-4533**	931-432-4141	14
Tuthill Corp			
8500 S Madison St .... Burr Ridge IL 60527	**800-634-2695**	630-382-4900	632
Tuthill Corp Plastics Group			
2050 Sunnydale Blvd .... Clearwater FL 33765	**800-634-2695**	727-446-8593	597
Tuthill Vacuum & Blower Systems			
4840 W Kearney St ....Springfield MO 65803	**800-825-6937**	417-865-8715	18
Tuthill Vacuum Systems			
4840 W Kearney St ....Springfield MO 65803	**800-634-2695**	417-865-8715	173
Tuttle Publishing			
364 Innovation Dr			
Airport Industrial Pk .... North Clarendon VT 05759	**800-526-2778***	802-773-8930	628-2
*Sales			
TV Guide Magazine LLC			
11 West 42nd St 16th Fl .... New York NY 10036	**800-866-1400**	212-852-7500	452-9
TVCC (Temecula Valley Chamber of Commerce)			
26790 Ynez Ct Ste A.............. Temecula CA 92591	**866-676-5090**	951-676-5090	137
TVEC (Trinity Valley Electric Co-op Inc)			
1800 Hwy 243 E PO Box 888 .... Kaufman TX 75142	**800-766-9576**	972-932-2214	245
T-w Transport Inc			
7405 S Hayford Rd .... Cheney WA 99004	**800-356-4070**	509-623-4004	770
TWC (Trans World Corp)			
545 Fifth Ave Ste 940 .... New York NY 10017	**877-407-9037**	212-983-3355	376
OTC: TWOC			
TWC Aviation			
1162 Aviation Ave .... San Jose CA 95110	**800-359-7060**	408-286-3832	62
Tweed Museum of Art			
1201 ordean Ct .... Duluth MN 55812	**866-999-6995**	218-726-8222	513
Twentieth Century Fox Home Entertainment Inc			
2121 Ave of the Stars			
Suite 100 ....Los Angeles CA 90067	**877-369-7867**	310-369-3900	504
Twenty-First Century Assoc			
266 Summit Ave .... Hackensack NJ 07601	**888-760-5052**	201-678-1144	158
TWG (Terlato Wine Group, The)			
900 Armour Dr ....Lake Bluff IL 60044	**800-950-7676**	847-604-8900	80-3
Twin Bridges State Park			
14801 Hwy 137 S .... Fairland OK 74343	**800-622-6317**	918-540-2545	558
Twin Cities Air Service			
81 Airport Dr .... Auburn ME 04210	**800-564-3882**		13
Twin Cities Public Television Inc			
172 E Fourth St .... Saint Paul MN 55101	**866-229-1300**	651-222-1717	624
Twin City EDM			
7940 Rancher Rd NE .... Fridley MN 55432	**800-397-0338**	763-783-7808	449
Twin City Knitting Company Inc (TCK)			
104 Rock Barn Rd NE ....Conover NC 28613	**800-438-6884**	828-464-4830	153-9
Twin City Testing			
662 Cromwell Ave .... Saint Paul MN 55114	**888-645-8378**	651-645-3601	732
Twin County Regional Hospital			
200 Hospital Dr .... Galax VA 24333	**800-295-3342**	276-236-8181	371-3
Twin Falls Area Chamber of Commerce			
858 Blue Lakes Blvd N .... Twin Falls ID 83301	**866-734-3838**	208-733-3974	137
Twin Falls School District 411			
201 Main Ave W .... Twin Falls ID 83301	**800-726-0003**	208-733-6900	676
Twin Farms			
452 Royalton Tpke PO Box 115 .... Barnard VT 05031	**800-894-6327**	802-234-9999	376
Twin Lakes State Park			
788 Twin Lakes Rd .... Green Bay VA 23942	**800-933-7275**	434-392-3435	558
Twin Lakes Telephone Co-op			
200 Telephone Ln .... Gainesboro TN 38562	**800-644-8582***	931-268-2151	726
*Cust Svc			
Twin Oaks Hammocks			
138 Twin Oaks Rd .... Louisa VA 23093	**800-688-8946**	540-894-5125	318-4
Twin River Casino			
100 Twin River Rd .... Lincoln RI 02865	**877-827-4837**	401-475-8505	633
Twin River National Bank			
1507 G St .... Lewiston ID 83501	**877-743-4948**	208-746-4848	69
Twin Rivers Unified School District			
3222 Winona Way .... North Highlands CA 95660	**888-674-6854**	916-566-1628	676
Twin Valley Electric Co-op Inc			
501 S Huston Ave PO Box 385 ...... Altamont KS 67330	**866-784-5500**	620-784-5500	245
Twin Valleys Public Power District			
1145 Nasby St ....Cambridge NE 69022	**800-658-4266**	308-697-3315	245
Twin-Boro News			
210 Knickerbocker Rd .... Cresskill NJ 07626	**888-473-2673**	201-894-6715	525-4
Twinco Romax			
4635 Willow Dr .... Hamel MN 55340	**800-682-3800***	763-478-2360	60
*Cust Svc			

				Toll-Free	Phone	Class
Twinhead Corp						
48303 Fremont Blvd	Fremont	CA	94538	**800-995-8946***		174-1
*Sales						
Twinlab						
600 E Quality Dr	American Fork	UT	84003	**800-645-5626**	801-763-0700	787
Twinless Twins Support Group International (TTSG)						
PO Box 980481	Ypsilanti	MI	48198	**888-205-8962**		47-21
Twitchell Corp						
4031 Ross Clark Cir	Dothan	AL	36303	**800-633-7550***	334-792-0002	734-2
*General						
Two Bunch Palms Resort & Spa						
67425 Two Bunch						
Palms Trl	Desert Hot Springs	CA	92240	**800-472-4334**	760-329-8791	660
Two Men & A Truck International Inc						
3400 Belle Chase Way	Lansing	MI	48911	**800-345-1070**	517-394-7210	512
TWP Inc						
2831 Tenth St	Berkeley	CA	94710	**800-227-1570**	510-548-4434	679
TXU Electric						
1601 Bryan St	Dallas	TX	75201	**800-242-9113**	214-486-2534	775
Tyco Electronics Federal Credit Union						
PO Box 3449	Redwood City	CA	94064	**888-673-3288**		219
Tyco International Ltd						
Nine Roszel Rd	Princeton	NJ	08540	**800-685-4509**	609-720-4200	683
NYSE: TYC						
Tyco SimplexGrinnell						
50 Technology Dr	Westminster	MA	01441	**800-746-7539**	978-731-2500	283
50 Technology Dr	Westminster	MA	01441	**800-746-7539**	978-731-2500	739
Tyger Scientific Inc						
324 Stokes Ave	Ewing	NJ	08638	**888-329-8990**	609-434-0143	231
TYK America Inc						
301 BrickyaRd Rd	Clairton	PA	15025	**800-569-9359**	412-384-4259	654
Tyler & Co						
400 Northridge Rd Ste 1250	Atlanta	GA	30350	**800-989-6789**	770-396-3939	266
Tyler Area Chamber of Commerce						
315 N Broadway Ave	Tyler	TX	75702	**800-235-5712**	903-592-1661	137
Tyler Convention & Visitors Bureau (TCVB)						
315 N Broadway	Tyler	TX	75702	**800-235-5712**	903-592-1661	207
Tyler Equipment Corp						
251 Shaker Rd						
PO Box 544	East Longmeadow	MA	01028	**800-292-6351**	413-525-6351	355
Tyler Junior College						
PO Box 9020	Tyler	TX	75711	**800-687-5680**	903-510-2523	160
Tyler Morning Telegraph						
PO Box 2030	Tyler	TX	75710	**800-772-1213**	903-597-8111	525-2
Tyler Pipe Co						
11910 CR 492	Tyler	TX	75706	**800-527-8478**	903-882-5511	306
Tyler Technologies Inc						
5949 Sherry Ln Ste 1400	Dallas	TX	75225	**800-431-5776**		179-10
NYSE: TYL						
Tymco Inc						
225 E Industrial Blvd PO Box 2368	Waco	TX	76703	**800-258-9626**	254-799-5546	509
Tyndale House Publishers Inc						
351 Executive Dr	Carol Stream	IL	60188	**800-323-9400**		628-3
Tyndale University College & Seminary						
25 Ballyconnor Ct	Toronto	ON	M2M4B3	**877-896-3253**	416-226-6380	167-3
Tyndall Air Force Base						
445 Suwannee Rd 101	Tyndall AFB	FL	32403	**800-356-5273**	850-283-1110	492-1
Tyndall Federal Credit Union Inc						
PO Box 59760	Panama City	FL	32412	**888-896-3255**	850-769-9999	216
Tyonek Mfg Group Inc						
229 Palmer Rd	Madison	AL	35758	**877-258-6200**	256-258-6200	522
TYR Sport						
1790 Apollo Ct	Seal Beach	CA	90740	**800-252-7878**	714-897-0799	153-16
Tyson Events Ctr						
401 Gordon Dr	Sioux City	IA	51101	**800-593-2228**	712-279-4850	206
Tyson Foods Inc						
2210 W Oaklawn Dr						
PO Box 2020	Springdale	AR	72762	**800-643-3410**	479-290-4000	612
NYSE: TSN						
Tyson Fresh Meats Inc						
800 Stevens Port Dr	Dakota Dunes	SD	57049	**800-416-2269**	605-235-2061	468
Tyson Prepared Foods Inc						
5701 McNutt Rd	Santa Teresa	NM	88008	**888-301-7304**	575-589-0100	295-26
Tysons Corner Ctr						
1961 Chain Bridge Rd	McLean	VA	22102	**877-247-5223**	703-847-7300	455

U

				Toll-Free	Phone	Class
U S Cavalry Inc						
2855 Centennial Ave	Radcliff	KY	40160	**800-777-7172**	270-351-1164	155-5
U S Employees O C Federal Credit Union						
PO Box 44000	Oklahoma City	OK	73144	**800-227-6366**	405-685-6200	219
U S Risk Insurance Group Inc						
10210 N Central Expy	Dallas	TX	75231	**800-926-9155**	214-265-7090	387
U W Provision Company Inc						
PO Box 620038	Middleton	WI	53562	**800-832-0517**	608-836-7421	296-9
U.S. Bankcard Services Inc						
17171 E Gale Ave						
Ste 110	City Of Industry	CA	91745	**888-888-8872**		251
U.S. Department of Veterans Affairs						
325 E 'H' St	Iron Mountain	MI	49801	**800-215-8262**	906-774-3300	371-8
U.S. Facilities Inc						
30 N 41 St Ste 400	Philadelphia	PA	19104	**800-236-6241**		193
U.S. Fleet Forces Command						
1562 Mitscher Ave Ste 250	Norfolk	VA	23551	**800-473-3549**	757-836-3630	492-3
U.S. National Ski Hall of Fame						
610 Palms Ave	Ishpeming	MI	49849	**800-648-0720**	906-485-6323	515
UAB Comprehensive Cancer Ctr						
University of Alabama at Birmingham						
1824 Sixth Ave S	Birmingham	AL	35294	**800-294-7780**	205-934-4011	659
UAB Medical West						
995 Ninth Ave SW	Bessemer	AL	35022	**800-994-6610**	205-481-7000	371-3
UAFC (Universal American Corp)						
44 S Broadway Ste 1200	White Plains	NY	10601	**866-249-8668**	914-934-5200	357-4
NYSE: UAM						
UAMS Medical Ctr						
4301 W Markham St	Little Rock	AR	72205	**877-467-6560**	501-686-7000	371-3
UAS (United Air Specialists Inc)						
4440 Creek Rd	Cincinnati	OH	45242	**800-252-4647**	513-891-0400	18
Ubics Inc						
333 Technology Dr Ste 210	Canonsburg	PA	15317	**800-441-0077**	724-746-6001	112
OTC: UBIX						
uBid Inc						
740 Hilltop Dr	Itasca	IL	60143	**866-946-8243**		50
UBS Financial Services Inc						
1285 Ave of the Americas	New York	NY	10019	**800-221-3260**	212-713-2000	681
UBS Warburg LLC						
677 Washington Blvd	Stamford	CT	06901	**800-221-3260**	203-719-3000	681
UC Davis Cancer Ctr						
4501 X St	Sacramento	CA	95817	**800-362-5566**	916-734-5800	371-7
UC Irvine Healthcare						
101 the City Dr S	Orange	CA	92868	**877-824-3627**	714-456-7890	371-3
UCare Minnesota						
500 Stinson Blvd NE						
PO Box 52	Minneapolis	MN	55413	**866-457-7144**	612-676-6500	47-17
UCB Pharma Inc						
1950 Lake Pk Dr	Smyrna	GA	30080	**800-477-7877**	770-970-7500	576
UCC (United Church of Christ)						
700 Prospect Ave	Cleveland	OH	44115	**866-822-8224**	216-736-2100	47-20
UCG Holdings						
11300 Rockville Pike Ste 1100	Rockville	MD	20852	**800-929-4824**	301-287-2700	524-7
Uchee Pines Lifestyle Ctr						
30 Uchee Pines Rd PO Box 75	Seale	AL	36875	**877-824-3374**	334-855-4764	697
UCIT Online Security						
6441 Northam Dr	Mississauga	ON	L4V1J2	**866-756-7847**	905-405-9898	684
UCLA (University of California)						
110 Sproul Hall MC Ste 5800	Berkeley	CA	94720	**866-740-1260**	510-642-6000	166
UCM (United Color Manufacturing Inc)						
PO Box 480	Newtown	PA	18940	**800-852-5942**	215-860-2165	143
UCS (Utica Community Schools)						
11303 Greendale Dr	Sterling Heights	MI	48312	**800-877-8339**	586-797-1000	676
UCS (Union of Concerned Scientists)						
Two Brattle Sq Sixth Fl	Cambridge	MA	02238	**800-666-8276**	617-547-5552	47-13
UDASD (Upper Dauphin Area School District)						
5668 State Rt 209	Lykens	PA	17048	**866-632-9992**	717-362-8134	676
UDL Laboratories Inc						
1718 Northrock Ct	Rockford	IL	61103	**800-435-5272**	800-848-0462	577
UFC (United Farmers Co-op)						
705 E Fourth St PO Box 461	Winthrop	MN	55396	**866-998-3266**	507-647-6600	10
UFCW (United Food & Commercial Workers International Union)						
1775 K St NW	Washington	DC	20006	**800-551-4010**	202-223-3111	411
UFP Technologies Inc						
172 E Main St	Georgetown	MA	01833	**800-372-3172**	978-352-2200	594
NASDAQ: UFPT						
UFPI (Universal Forest Products Inc)						
2801 E Beltline Ave NE	Grand Rapids	MI	49525	**800-598-9663**	616-364-6161	674
NASDAQ: UFPI						
UGC (United Guaranty Corp)						
230 N Elm St	Greensboro	NC	27401	**800-334-8966**		388-5
UGI (United-Guardian Inc)						
230 Marcus Blvd PO Box 18050	Hauppauge	NY	11788	**800-645-5566**	631-273-0900	474
NASDAQ: UG						
UH Parma Medical Center (PCGH)						
7007 Powers Blvd	Parma	OH	44129	**855-292-4292**	440-743-3000	371-3
U-Haul International Inc						
2727 N Central Ave	Phoenix	AZ	85004	**800-528-0361**		768
UHMS (Undersea & Hyperbaric Medical Society)						
21 W Colony Pl Ste 280	Durham	NC	27705	**877-533-8467**	919-490-5140	47-17
UIC (Universal Instruments Corp)						
33 Broome Corporate Pk	Conklin	NY	13748	**800-842-9732**	607-779-7522	686
UIL Holdings Corp						
157 Church St	New Haven	CT	06506	**800-722-5584**	203-499-2000	357-5
NYSE: UIL						
Uintah County						
147 E Main St	Vernal	UT	84078	**800-966-4680**	435-781-0770	336
UK (Underwater Kinetics)						
13400 Danielson St	Poway	CA	92064	**800-852-7483**	858-513-9100	701
Ukiah-Dale Forest State Scenic Corridor						
Ukiah-Dale Forest State Scenic Corridor						
PO Box 85	Ukiah	OR	97880	**800-551-6949**	541-983-2277	558
Ukrainian NA Inc (UNA)						
2200 Rt 10	Parsippany	NJ	07054	**800-253-9862**		47-14
Ukrainian National Federal Credit Union						
215 Second Ave PO Box 160	New York	NY	10003	**866-859-5848**	212-533-2980	219
UL LLC 10 Water St	Enfield	CT	06082	**800-903-5660**	860-749-8371	732
Ulbrich Stainless Steels & Special Metals Inc (USSM)						
57 Dodge Ave	North Haven	CT	06473	**800-243-1676**	203-239-4481	714
ULC (Universal Lending Corp)						
6775 E Evans Ave	Denver	CO	80224	**800-758-4063**		502
ULI (Urban Land Institute)						
1025 Thomas Jefferson St NW						
Ste 500W	Washington	DC	20007	**800-321-5011***	202-624-7000	47-8
*Orders						
U-line Corp						
PO Box 245040	Milwaukee	WI	53224	**800-779-2547**	414-354-0300	779
ULLICO Casualty Co						
1625 I St NW	Washington	DC	20006	**800-431-5425**		388-5
ULLICO Inc						
1625 Eye St NW	Washington	DC	20006	**800-431-5425**		357-4
Ullman Devices Corp						
664 Danbury Rd	Ridgefield	CT	06877	**800-784-7796**	203-438-6577	748
Ullman Oil Inc						
PO Box 23399	Chagrin Falls	OH	44023	**800-543-5195**	440-543-5195	572
Ulster County Community College						
Cottekill Rd	Stone Ridge	NY	12484	**800-724-0833**	845-687-5000	160
ULTA Beauty						
1000 Remington Blvd Ste 120	Bolingbrook	IL	60440	**866-983-8582**	630-410-4800	215
Ulteig Engineers Inc						
3350 38th Ave S PO Box 9615	Fargo	ND	58104	**888-858-3441**	701-280-8500	261
Ultera Systems Inc						
26081 Merit Cir Ste 125	Laguna Hills	CA	92653	**877-462-7362**	949-367-8800	177
Ultimate Software Group Inc						
2000 Ultimate Way	Weston	FL	33326	**800-432-1729**	954-331-7000	179-1
NASDAQ: ULTI						
Ultimate Support Systems Inc						
5836 Wright Dr	Loveland	CO	80538	**800-525-5628**		520
Ultra Electronics Flightline Systems Inc						
7625 Omni Tech Pl	Victor	NY	14564	**888-959-9001**	585-924-4000	638
Ultra Electronics-DNE Technologies Inc						
50 Barnes Pk N	Wallingford	CT	06492	**800-370-4485**	203-265-7151	638

	Toll-Free	Phone	Class
UltraBac Software			
15015 Main St Ste 200 . . . . Bellevue WA 98007	866-554-8562	425-644-6000	179-12
Ultracraft Co			
6163 Old 421 Rd . . . . Liberty NC 27298	800-262-4046		114
Ultrafabrics LLC			
303 S Broadway . . . . Tarrytown NY 10591	888-361-9216	914-460-1730	734-3
Ultralife Batteries Inc			
2000 Technology Pkwy . . . . Newark NY 14513	800-332-5000	315-332-7100	73
NASDAQ: ULBI			
Ultramar Travel Management International			
14 E 47th St Fifth Fl . . . . New York NY 10017	888-856-2929		761
Ultra-Poly Corp			
102 Demi Rd PO Box 330 . . . . Portland PA 18351	800-932-0619	570-897-7500	601
UltraStaff			
1818 Memorial Dr Ste 200 . . . . Houston TX 77007	800-522-7707	713-522-7100	712
Ultra-tech Enterprises Inc			
4701 Taylor Rd . . . . Punta Gorda FL 33950	800-293-2001	941-575-2000	476
Ultratech Inc			
3050 Zanker Rd . . . . San Jose CA 95134	800-222-1213	408-321-8835	686
NASDAQ: UTEK			
UMA (United Motorcoach Assn)			
113 SW St Fourth Fl . . . . Alexandria VA 22314	800-424-8262	703-838-2929	48-21
Uman Pharma Inc			
100 De L'Industrie Blvd . . . . Candiac QC J5R1J1	877-444-9989	450-444-9989	231
UMass Hotel at the Campus Ctr			
1 Campus Ctr Way . . . . Amherst MA 01003	877-822-2110	413-549-6000	376
UMB Bank NA			
1010 Grand Blvd . . . . Kansas City MO 64106	800-821-2171	816-860-7000	69
UMB Capital Corp			
1010 Grand Blvd . . . . Kansas City MO 64106	800-821-2171	816-860-7000	399
UMB Financial Corp			
1010 Grand Blvd . . . . Kansas City MO 64106	800-821-2171	816-860-7000	357-2
NASDAQ: UMBF			
UMCES (University of Maryland Ctr for Environmental Science)			
2020 Horn Pt Rd . . . . Cambridge MD 21613	866-842-2520	410-228-9250	659
UMCP (University Medical Ctr at Princeton)			
253 Witherspoon St . . . . Princeton NJ 08540	877-932-8935	609-497-4304	371-3
UmeVoice Inc			
20C Pimentel Ct Ste 1 . . . . Novato CA 94949	888-230-3300	415-883-1500	179-7
UMF Medical			
1316 Eisenhower Blvd . . . . Johnstown PA 15904	800-638-5322	814-266-8726	318-3
UMHC (University of Miami Hospital & Clinics)			
1475 NW 12th Ave . . . . Miami FL 33136	800-545-2292	305-243-1000	759
Umpqua Bank			
PO Box 1820 . . . . Roseburg OR 97470	866-486-7782	503-973-5945	69
Umpqua Community College			
1140 Umpqva College Rd			
PO Box 967 . . . . Roseburg OR 97470	800-820-5161	541-440-4600	160
Umpqua Dairy Products Co			
333 SE Sykes Ave PO Box 1306 . . . . Roseburg OR 97470	888-672-6455	541-672-2638	295-27
Umpqua Holdings Corp			
One SW Columbia St Ste 1200 . . . . Portland OR 97258	866-486-7782	503-727-4100	357-2
NASDAQ: UMPQ			
Umpqua Lighthouse State Park			
84505 Hwy 101 S . . . . Florence OR 97439	800-551-6949		558
UMSL (University of Missouri)			
104 Jesse Hall . . . . Columbia MO 65211	800-856-2181	573-882-6333	166
Umstead Hotel & Spa			
100 Woodland Pond . . . . Cary NC 27513	866-877-4141	919-447-4000	376
UMW (Utah Metal Works Inc)			
805 Everett Ave			
PO Box 1073 . . . . Salt Lake City UT 84116	877-221-0099	877-364-5679	651
UNA (Utah Nurses Assn)			
4505 S Wastch Blvd			
Ste 330B . . . . Salt Lake City UT 84124	800-338-7657	801-272-4510	526
UNA (Ukrainian NA Inc)			
2200 Rt 10 . . . . Parsippany NJ 07054	800-253-9862		47-14
Unaflex LLC			
1350 S Dixie Hwy E . . . . Pompano Beach FL 33064	800-327-1286	954-943-5002	367
Unarco Material Handling Inc			
701 16th Ave E . . . . Springfield TN 37172	800-862-7261		286
UNC Neuroscience Ctr			
University of N Carolina			
115 Mason Farm Rd CB 7250 . . . . Chapel Hill NC 27599	800-862-4938	919-843-8536	659
Uncle Milton Industries Inc			
29209 Canwood St Ste 120 . . . . Agoura CA 91301	800-869-7555*	818-707-0800	752
*General			
Uncle Ray's LLC			
14245 Birwood St . . . . Detroit MI 48238	800-800-3286	313-834-0800	295-35
UNC-TV (University of North Carolina Ctr for Public Television)			
10 TW Alexander Dr			
PO Box 14900 . . . . Research Triangle Park NC 27709	800-906-5050	919-549-7000	624
UNC-TV Ch 4 (PBS)			
10 TW Alexander Dr			
PO Box 14900 . . . . Research Triangle Park NC 27709	800-906-5050	919-549-7000	730
Under Secretary for Political Affairs			
Bureau of South & Central Asian Affairs			
2201 C St NW . . . . Washington DC 20520	800-877-8339	202-647-4000	338-14
Underground Construction Company Inc			
5145 Industrial Way . . . . Benicia CA 94510	800-424-6521	707-746-8800	189-10
Undersea & Hyperbaric Medical Society (UHMS)			
21 W Colony Pl Ste 280 . . . . Durham NC 27705	877-533-8467	919-490-5140	47-17
Underwater Kinetics (UK)			
13400 Danielson St . . . . Poway CA 92064	800-852-7483	858-513-9100	701
Underwood Transfer Company LLC			
940 W Troy Ave . . . . Indianapolis IN 46225	800-428-2372	317-783-9235	770
UNFCU (United Nations Federal Credit Union)			
24-01 44th Rd Ct Sq Pl . . . . . Long Island City NY 11101	800-891-2471	347-686-6000	219
UNFI Specialty Distribution Services			
88 Huntoon Memorial Hwy . . . . Leicester MA 01524	877-476-8749	508-892-8171	238
Unger Co			
12401 Berea Rd . . . . Cleveland OH 44111	800-321-1418	216-252-1400	541
Unibank For Savings			
49 Church St . . . . Whitinsville MA 01588	800-578-4270	508-234-8112	69
Unibilt Industries Inc			
8005 Johnson Stn Rd PO Box 373 . . . . . . Vandalia OH 45377	800-777-9942		105
Unicell Body Co			
571 Howard St . . . . Buffalo NY 14206	800-628-8914*	716-853-8628	509
*Cust Svc			
Unicep Packaging Inc			
1702 Industrial Dr . . . . Sandpoint ID 83864	800-354-9396	208-265-9696	542
Unicircuit Inc			
8192 Southpark Ln . . . . Littleton CO 80120	800-648-6449	303-730-0505	617

	Toll-Free	Phone	Class
Unico American Corp			
23251 Mulholland Dr . . . . Woodland Hills CA 91364	800-669-9800	818-591-9800	388-4
Unicoi State Park & Lodge			
1788 Hwy 356 Rd . . . . Helen GA 30545	800-573-9659		558
UNICOM			
565 Brea Canyon Rd Ste A . . . . Walnut CA 91789	800-346-6668	626-964-7873	177
Unicor Medical Inc			
4160 Carmichael Rd . . . . Montgomery AL 36106	800-825-7421		95
UnicornHRO			
25 Hanover Rd Ste B . . . . Florham Park NJ 07932	800-368-8149	973-360-0688	38
Unicorp			
291 Cleveland St . . . . Orange NJ 07050	800-526-1389	973-674-1700	347
Unicorr			
455 Sackett Pt Rd . . . . North Haven CT 06473	800-877-6875*	203-248-2161	541
*General			
Unicover Corp			
One Unicover Ctr . . . . Cheyenne WY 82008	800-443-4225*	307-771-3000	454
*Cust Svc			
Uniden America Corp			
4700 Amon Carter Blvd . . . . Fort Worth TX 76155	800-297-1023*	817-858-3300	725
*Cust Svc			
Uniek Inc			
805 Uniek Dr . . . . Waunakee WI 53597	800-248-6435	608-849-9999	308
Unifab Corp			
5260 Lovers Ln . . . . Portage MI 49002	800-648-9569*	269-382-2803	477
*General			
Unified Brands			
1055 Mendell Davis Dr . . . . Jackson MS 39272	888-994-7636		383
Unified Grocers Inc			
5200 Sheila St . . . . Commerce CA 90040	800-724-7762	323-264-5200	296-8
Unified Industries Inc			
6551 Loisdale Ct Ste 400 . . . . Springfield VA 22150	800-666-1642	703-922-9800	261
Unified School District of Antigo			
120 S Dorr St . . . . Antigo WI 54409	800-795-3272	715-627-4355	676
Uniform & Textile Service Assn (UTSA)			
1300 N 17th St Ste 750 . . . . Arlington VA 22209	800-996-3426	703-247-2600	48-4
Uniform Commercial Code Law Letter			
610 Opperman Dr . . . . Eagan MN 55123	800-328-4880*	651-687-7000	524-13
*Cust Svc			
Unigen Corp			
45388 Warm Springs Blvd . . . . Fremont CA 94539	800-826-0808	510-668-2088	617
UNIGLOBE Travel USA LLC			
18662 MacArthur Blvd Ste 100 . . . . Irvine CA 92612	877-438-4338	949-623-9000	762
UniLect Corp			
PO Box 3026 . . . . Danville CA 94526	888-864-5328	925-833-8660	789
Unilux Inc			
59 N Fifth St . . . . Saddle Brook NJ 07663	800-522-0801	201-712-1266	467
Unimark Products			
9818 Pflumm Rd . . . . Lenexa KS 66215	800-255-6356*	913-649-2424	177
*Cust Svc			
Unimin Corp			
258 Elm St . . . . New Canaan CT 06840	800-223-2236	203-966-8880	498-4
Union Bank of California NA			
400 California St			
First Fl . . . . San Francisco CA 94104	800-238-4486	415-765-3434	69
Union Bankshares Inc			
20 Lower Main St . . . . Morrisville VT 05661	866-862-1891	802-888-6600	357-2
NASDAQ: UNB			
Union Church of Pocantico Hills			
555 Bedford Rd . . . . Sleepy Hollow NY 10591	800-638-7646	914-631-8200	49
Union College			
3800 S 48th St . . . . Lincoln NE 68506	800-228-4600*	402-486-2504	166
*Admissions			
Union County			
1103 S First St . . . . Clayton NM 88415	800-390-7858	575-374-9253	336
Union County Chamber of Commerce			
135 W Main St . . . . Union SC 29379	877-202-8755	864-427-9039	137
Union County College			
1033 Springfield Ave . . . . Cranford NJ 07016	877-468-3229	908-709-7000	160
Union Eyecare Centers			
4750 Beidler Rd . . . . Willoughby OH 44094	800-443-9699	216-986-9700	536
Union FSB			
1565 Mineral Spring Ave . . . . North Providence RI 02904	888-226-0819	401-353-8900	69
Union Group			
649 Alden St . . . . Fall River MA 02722	800-289-3523	508-675-4545	85
Union Institute & University			
440 E McMillan St . . . . Cincinnati OH 45206	800-486-3116	513-861-6400	166
Union Labor Report			
1801 S Bell St . . . . Arlington VA 22202	800-372-1033		524-13
Union Leader			
100 William Loeb Dr . . . . Manchester NH 03109	800-562-8218	603-668-4321	525-2
Union of American Physicians & Dentists			
180 Grand Ave Ste 1380 . . . . Oakland CA 94612	800-622-0909	510-839-0193	411
Union of Concerned Scientists (UCS)			
Two Brattle Sq Sixth Fl . . . . Cambridge MA 02238	800-666-8276	617-547-5552	47-13
Union Pacific Corp			
1400 Douglas St . . . . Omaha NE 68179	888-870-8777	402-544-5000	357-3
NYSE: UNP			
Union Pacific Railroad Co			
1400 Douglas St . . . . Omaha NE 68179	888-870-8777		639
Union Pacific Railroad Employees' Health Systems			
1040 North 2200 West . . . . Salt Lake City UT 84116	800-547-0421	801-595-4300	388-3
Union Power Co-op			
1525 N Rocky River Rd . . . . Monroe NC 28110	800-922-6840	704-289-3145	245
Union Rural Electric Co-op Inc			
15461 US 36E . . . . Marysville OH 43040	800-642-1826	937-642-1826	245
Union Standard Equipment Co			
801 E 141st St . . . . Bronx NY 10454	877-282-7333	718-585-0200	297
Union Standard Insurance Co			
122 W Carpenter Fwy Ste 350 . . . . Irving TX 75039	800-444-0049	972-719-2400	388-4
Union Station A Wyndham Historic Hotel			
PO Box 4090 . . . . Aberdeen SD 57401	800-996-3426		376
Union Tank Car Co			
175 W Jackson Blvd Ste 2100 . . . . Chicago IL 60604	866-535-7685	312-431-3111	641
Union Theological Seminary			
3041 Broadway . . . . New York NY 10027	800-251-9489	212-662-7100	167-3
Union Theological Seminary & Presbyterian School of Christian Education			
3401 Brook Rd . . . . Richmond VA 23227	800-229-2990	804-355-0671	167-3
Union University			
1050 Union University Dr . . . . Jackson TN 38305	800-338-6466	731-661-5210	166
Unipunch Products Inc			
311 Fifth St NW . . . . Clear Lake WI 54005	800-828-7061		747

Name / Address	City	State	ZIP	Toll-Free	Phone	Class
Unique Carpets Ltd						
7360 Jurupa Ave	Riverside	CA	92504	**800-547-8266**	951-352-8125	130
Unique Communications Inc						
3650 Coral Ridge Dr	Coral Springs	FL	33065	**800-881-8182**	954-735-4002	246
Unique Functional Products Corp						
135 Sunshine Ln	San Marcos	CA	92069	**800-854-1905**	760-744-1610	753
Unique Industries Inc						
4750 League Island Blvd	Philadelphia	PA	19112	**800-888-0559**	215-336-4300	327
Unique Lighting Systems Inc						
1240 Simpson Way	Escondido	CA	92029	**800-955-4831**		757
UniSea Inc						
15400 NE 90th St PO Box 97019	Redmond	WA	98073	**800-535-8509**	425-881-8181	295-14
Uniseal Inc						
1800 W Maryland St	Evansville	IN	47712	**800-443-9081**	812-436-4840	3
Unisearch Inc						
1780 Barnes Blvd SW	Tumwater	WA	98512	**800-722-0708**	360-956-9500	626
Unisec Inc						
2555 Nicholson St	San Leandro	CA	94577	**800-982-4587**		683
Unishippers Assn Inc						
746 E Winchester Ste 200	Salt Lake City	UT	84107	**800-999-8721**		539
Unisource Manufacturing Inc						
8040 NE 33rd Dr	Portland	OR	97211	**800-234-2566**	503-281-4673	449
Unisource NTC						
1560 Holly Court Ste 200	Thousand Oaks	CA	91360	**800-736-8470**		458
Unisource Worldwide Inc						
6600 Governors Lake Pkwy	Norcross	GA	30071	**800-864-7687**	770-447-9000	546
Unistar-Sparco Computers Inc						
7089 Ryburn Dr	Millington	TN	38053	**800-840-8400**	901-872-2272	454
Unistress Corp						
550 Cheshire Rd	Pittsfield	MA	01201	**800-927-9468**	413-499-1441	184
Unit Chemical Corp						
7360 Commercial Way	Henderson	NV	89015	**800-879-8648**	702-564-6454	149
Unit Corp						
7130 S Lewis Ave Ste 1000	Tulsa	OK	74136	**800-722-3612**	918-493-7700	533
NYSE: UNT						
Unitarian Universalist Service Committee (UUSC)						
689 Massachusetts Ave	Cambridge	MA	02139	**800-388-3920**	617-868-6600	47-5
Unitech Services Group						
295 Parker St	Springfield	MA	01151	**800-344-3824**	413-543-6911	438
United Air Specialists Inc (UAS)						
4440 Creek Rd	Cincinnati	OH	45242	**800-252-4647**	513-891-0400	18
United Airlines Cargo						
PO Box 66100	Chicago	IL	60666	**800-822-2746**		12
United American Bank						
101 S Ellsworth Ave	San Mateo	CA	94401	**877-275-3342**	650-579-1500	69
OTC: UABK						
United Bakery Equipment Co Inc						
15815 W 110th St	Lenexa	KS	66219	**888-823-2253**	913-541-8700	297
United Bancorp Inc						
201 S Fourth St	Martins Ferry	OH	43935	**888-275-5566**	740-633-0445	357-2
NASDAQ: UBCP						
United Bancshares Inc						
100 S High St PO Box 67	Columbus Grove	OH	45830	**800-837-8111**	419-659-2141	357-2
NASDAQ: UBOH						
United Bank						
11185 Fairfax Blvd	Fairfax	VA	22030	**800-327-9862**	703-219-4850	69
United Bankshares Inc						
514 Market St	Parkersburg	WV	26101	**800-327-9862**	304-424-8800	357-2
NASDAQ: UBSI						
United Behavioral Health Inc						
425 Market St 27th Fl	San Francisco	CA	94105	**800-888-2998**	415-547-5000	457
United Blood Services						
6210 E Oak St PO Box 1867	Scottsdale	AZ	85257	**800-288-2199**	480-946-4201	88
United Blood Services of Arizona						
Chandler						
6220 E Oak St Ste 33	Scottsdale	AZ	85252	**877-827-4376**		88
San Luis Obispo						
4119 Broad St Ste 100	San Luis Obispo	CA	93401	**877-827-4376**	805-543-4290	88
United Blood Services of Colorado						
146 Sawyer Dr	Durango	CO	81303	**800-288-2199**	970-385-4601	88
United Blood Services of Mississippi						
Meridian						
1115 25th Ave	Meridian	MS	39301	**877-827-4376**	601-482-2482	88
United Blood Services of Montana						
Billings						
1444 Grand Ave	Billings	MT	59102	**800-365-4450**	406-248-9168	88
Albuquerque						
1515 University Blvd NE	Albuquerque	NM	87102	**800-333-8037**		88
United Blood Services of New Mexico						
Farmington						
475 E 20th St	Farmington	NM	87401	**888-804-9913**		88
Las Cruces						
1200 Commerce Dr	Las Cruces	NM	88011	**800-582-3146***	575-527-1322	88
*General						
United Blood Services of North Dakota						
Bismarck						
517 S Seventh St	Bismarck	ND	58504	**800-456-6159**		88
Fargo 3231 S 11th St	Fargo	ND	58104	**800-288-2199***	701-293-9453	88
*General						
United Blood Services of Texas						
El Paso						
424 S Mesa Hills	El Paso	TX	79912	**877-827-4376**	915-544-5422	88
McAllen						
1400 S Sixth St	McAllen	TX	78501	**888-827-4376***	956-213-7500	88
*General						
San Angelo						
2020 W Beauregard Ave	San Angelo	TX	76901	**800-756-0024***	325-223-7500	88
*General						
United Brass Works Inc						
714 S Main St	Randleman	NC	27317	**800-334-3035**	336-498-2661	777
United Brotherhood of Carpenters & Joiners of America						
101 Constitution Ave NW	Washington	DC	20001	**800-530-5090**	202-546-6206	411
United Central Bank						
4555 W Walnut St	Garland	TX	75042	**855-773-8778**	972-487-1505	69
United Chemi-Con Inc						
9801 W Higgins Rd	Rosemont	IL	60018	**800-344-4539**	847-696-2000	253
United Church of Christ (UCC)						
700 Prospect Ave	Cleveland	OH	44115	**866-822-8224**	216-736-2100	47-20
United Color Manufacturing Inc (UCM)						
PO Box 480	Newtown	PA	18940	**800-852-5942**	215-860-2165	143
United Commercial Travellers						
1801 Watermark Dr Ste 100	Columbus	OH	43215	**800-848-0123**	614-228-3276	452-10
United Community Banks Inc						
PO Box 398	Blairsville	GA	30514	**866-270-7200**	706-781-2265	357-2
NASDAQ: UCBI						
United Community Financial Corp						
PO Box 1111	Youngstown	OH	44501	**877-272-7661**	330-742-0500	357-2
NASDAQ: UCFC						
United CoolAir Corp						
491 E Princess St	York	PA	17403	**877-905-1111**	717-843-4311	14
United Country Real Estate Inc						
2820 NW Barry Rd	Kansas City	MO	64154	**800-999-1020**	816-420-6200	643
United Dairy Farmers						
3955 Montgomery Rd	Cincinnati	OH	45212	**800-654-2809***	513-396-8700	295-27
*General						
United Dairy Inc						
300 N Fifth St	Martins Ferry	OH	43935	**800-252-1542**	740-633-1451	295-27
United Displaycraft						
333 E Touhy Ave	Des Plaines	IL	60018	**877-632-8767***	847-375-3800	233
*General						
United Drill Bushing Corp						
12200 Woodruff Ave	Downey	CA	90241	**800-486-3466**	562-803-1521	488
United Electric Co-op Inc						
1330 21st St	Heyburn	ID	83336	**800-342-1585**	208-679-2222	245
United Electric Supply Inc						
10 Bellecor Dr	New Castle	DE	19720	**800-322-3374**	302-322-3333	775
United Electrical Sales Ltd						
4496 36th St	Orlando	FL	32811	**800-432-5126**	407-246-1992	246
United Engine & Machine Company Inc						
1040 Corbett St	Carson City	NV	89706	**800-648-7970**	775-882-7790	127
United Farmers Co-op (UFC)						
705 E Fourth St PO Box 461	Winthrop	MN	55396	**866-998-3266**	507-647-6600	10
United Feather & Down Inc						
414 E Golf Rd	Des Plaines	IL	60016	**800-932-3696**	847-296-6610	735
United Federations of Security						
540 N State Rd	Briarcliff Manor	NY	10510	**800-227-4291**	914-941-4103	48-7
United Financial Bancorp Inc						
95 Elm St PO Box 9020	West Springfield	MA	01090	**866-959-2265**	413-787-1700	69
NASDAQ: UBNK						
United Fire & Casualty Co						
118 Second Ave SE	Cedar Rapids	IA	52407	**800-332-7977**	319-399-5700	388-4
NASDAQ: UFCS						
United Fire Equipment Co						
335 N Fourth Ave	Tucson	AZ	85705	**800-362-0150**	520-622-3639	670
United Fire Group						
118 Second Ave SE						
PO Box 73909	Cedar Rapids	IA	52407	**800-332-7977**	319-399-5700	357-4
United Food & Commercial Workers International Union (UFCW)						
1775 K St NW	Washington	DC	20006	**800-551-4010**	202-223-3111	411
United Freezer & Storage Co						
650 N Meridian Rd						
PO Box 2446	Youngstown	OH	44509	**800-716-1416**	330-792-1739	791-2
United Guaranty Corp (UGC)						
230 N Elm St	Greensboro	NC	27401	**800-334-8966**		388-5
United Heartland Inc						
PO Box 3026	Milwaukee	WI	53201	**866-206-5851**		388-4
United Heritage Life Insurance Co						
PO Box 7777	Meridian	ID	83680	**800-657-6351**	208-493-6100	388-2
United Hospice of Atlanta						
1626 Jeurgens Ct	Norcross	GA	30093	**800-222-0321**	770-279-6200	368
United Hospital						
333 N Smith Ave	Saint Paul	MN	55102	**800-869-1320**	651-241-8000	371-3
United Illuminating Co						
157 Church St	New Haven	CT	06510	**800-722-5584***	203-499-2000	775
*Cust Svc						
United Insurance Holdings Corp						
360 Central Ave						
Ste 900	Saint Petersburg	FL	33701	**800-861-4370**	800-295-8016	388-2
NASDAQ: UIHC						
United Investors Life Insurance Co						
2801 Hwy 280 S	Birmingham	AL	35223	**800-866-9933**	205-268-1000	388-2
United Laboratories Inc						
320 37th Ave	Saint Charles	IL	60174	**800-323-2594**		143
United Life Insurance Co						
PO Box 73909	Cedar Rapids	IA	52407	**800-332-7977**	319-399-5700	388-2
United Marketing Group LLC						
929 N Plum Grove Rd	Schaumburg	IL	60173	**800-513-7000**	847-240-2005	196
United Materials LLC						
The Woodlands Corporate Ctr E 3949 Forest Pkwy						
Ste 400	North Tonawanda	NY	14120	**888-918-6483**	716-213-5832	183
United Methodist News Service						
810 12th Ave S	Nashville	TN	37203	**800-251-8140**	615-742-5470	523
United Methodist Publishing House						
201 Eigth Ave S	Nashville	TN	37203	**800-672-1789**	615-749-6000	628-3
United Microelectronics Corp						
488 De Guigne Dr	Sunnyvale	CA	94085	**800-990-1135**	408-523-7800	687
NYSE: UMC						
United Motorcoach Assn (UMA)						
113 SW St Fourth Fl	Alexandria	VA	22314	**800-424-8262**	703-838-2929	48-21
United National Group						
Three Bala Plz E Ste 300	Bala Cynwyd	PA	19004	**800-333-0352**	610-664-1500	388-4
United National Insurance Co						
Three Bala Plz E Ste 300	Bala Cynwyd	PA	19004	**800-333-0352**	610-664-1500	388-4
United Nations Federal Credit Union (UNFCU)						
24-01 44th Rd Ct Sq Pl	Long Island City	NY	11101	**800-891-2471**	347-686-6000	219
United Network for Organ Sharing (UNOS)						
700 N Fourth St	Richmond	VA	23219	**888-894-6361**	804-782-4800	47-17
United Notions Inc						
13800 Hutton St	Dallas	TX	75234	**800-527-9447**	972-484-8901	587
United of Omaha Life Insurance Co						
Mutual of Omaha Plaza	Omaha	NE	68175	**800-775-6000**	402-342-7600	388-2
United Optical						
2111 Van Deman St	Baltimore	MD	21224	**888-267-8422**		536
United Pacific Pet						
12060 Cabernet Dr	Fontana	CA	92337	**800-979-3333**	951-360-8550	571
United Parcel Service Inc (UPS)						
55 Glenlake Pkwy NE	Atlanta	GA	30328	**800-742-5877***	404-828-6000	539
NYSE: UPS ■ *Cust Svc						
United Performance Metals						
3475 Symmes Rd	Hamilton	OH	45015	**888-282-3292**	513-860-6500	714
United Pharmacal Company of Missouri Inc						
3705 Pear St	Saint Joseph	MO	64503	**800-254-8726**	816-233-8800	571
United Pioneer Co						
2777 Summer St Ste 206	Stamford	CT	06905	**800-466-9823**		569
United Plastic Fabricating Inc						
165 Flagship Dr	North Andover	MA	01845	**800-638-8265**		598-1

	City	ST	Zip	Toll-Free	Phone	Class
United Plywood & Lumber Inc						
1640 Mims Ave SW	Birmingham	AL	35211	**800-272-6486**	205-925-7601	606
United Power Inc						
500 Co-op Way	Brighton	CO	80603	**800-468-8809**	303-659-0551	245
United Producers Inc						
8351 N High St Ste 250	Columbus	OH	43235	**800-456-3276**		441
United Recovery Systems LP						
5800 N Course Dr	Houston	TX	77072	**800-568-0399**	713-977-1234	158
United Refrigeration Inc						
11401 Roosevelt Blvd	Philadelphia	PA	19154	**888-578-9100***	215-698-9100	656
*General						
United Regional Chamber of Commerce						
42 Union St	Attleboro	MA	02703	**800-333-6624**	508-222-0801	137
United Rentals						
3266 E Washington St	Phoenix	AZ	85233	**800-624-1808**	602-267-3898	264-3
United Rentals Inc						
224 Selleck St	Stamford	CT	06902	**800-877-3687**	203-622-3131	264-3
NYSE: URI						
United Road Services Inc						
10701 Middlebelt Rd	Romulus	MI	48174	**866-470-0036**	734-947-7900	770
United Rural Electric Membership Corp						
4563 E Markle Rd	Markle	IN	46770	**800-542-6339**	260-758-3155	245
United Salt Corp						
4800 San Felipe St	Houston	TX	77056	**800-554-8658**	713-877-2600	498-1
United Scenic Artists						
29 W 38th St 15th Fl	New York	NY	10018	**800-456-3863**	212-581-0300	411
United Security Bancshares						
2126 Inyo St Dept 98	Fresno	CA	93721	**888-683-6030**	559-248-4943	69
NASDAQ: UBFO						
United Security Bancshares Inc						
PO Box 249	Thomasville	AL	36784	**866-546-8273**	334-636-5424	357-2
NASDAQ: USBI						
United Security Life Insurance Company of Illinois (Inc)						
6640 S Cicero Ave	Bedford Park	IL	60638	**800-875-4422**		388-2
United Services Automobile Assn (USAA)						
10750 McDermott Fwy	San Antonio	TX	78288	**800-531-8722**		186
United Soybean Board (USB)						
16305 Swingley Ridge Rd						
Ste 150	Chesterfield	MO	63017	**800-989-8721**	636-530-1777	47-2
United Space Alliance (USA)						
600 Gemini Ave	Houston	TX	77058	**800-367-5690**	281-212-6200	271
United States Aviation						
4141 N Memorial Dr	Tulsa	OK	74115	**800-897-5387**	918-836-7345	62
United States Brass & Copper Co Inc						
1401 Brook Dr	Downers Grove	IL	60515	**800-821-2854**	630-629-9340	487
United States Endoscopy Group Inc						
5976 Heisley Rd	Mentor	OH	44060	**800-769-8226**	440-639-4494	471
United States Information Systems Inc (USIS)						
35 W Jefferson Ave	Pearl River	NY	10965	**866-222-3778**	845-358-7755	775
United States Steel Corp						
600 Grant St	Pittsburgh	PA	15219	**866-433-4801**	412-433-1121	261
NYSE: X						
United Stationers Inc						
1 PkwyN Blvd Ste 100	Deerfield	IL	60015	**855-275-6947**	847-627-7000	527
United Stations Radio Network						
1065 Ave of the Americas						
3rd Fl	New York	NY	10018	**866-989-1975**	212-869-1111	635
United Sugars Corp						
7803 Glenroy Rd Ste 300	Bloomington	MN	55439	**800-984-3585**	952-896-0131	296-11
United Suppliers Inc						
30473 260th St PO Box 538	Eldora	IA	50627	**800-782-5123**	641-858-2341	276
United Systems & Software Inc						
300 Colonial Ctr Pkwy Ste 150						
PO Box 958444	Lake Mary	FL	32746	**800-522-8774**	407-875-2120	178
United Textile Company Inc						
751-143rd Ave	San Leandro	CA	94578	**800-233-0077***	510-276-2288	501
*General						
United Theological Seminary of the Twin Cities						
3000 Fifth St NW	New Brighton	MN	55112	**800-937-1316**	651-633-4311	167-3
United Therapeutics Corp						
1040 Spring St	Silver Spring	MD	20910	**877-864-8437**	301-608-9292	576
NASDAQ: UTHR						
United Titanium Inc						
3450 Old Airport Rd	Wooster	OH	44691	**800-321-4938**	330-264-2111	307
United Tool & Stamping Company of North Carolina Inc						
2817 Enterprise Ave	Fayetteville	NC	28306	**800-883-6087**	910-323-8588	688
United Transportation Union						
14600 Detroit Ave	Cleveland	OH	44107	**800-558-8842**	216-228-9400	411
United Trust Group Inc (UTGI)						
5250 S Sixth St	Springfield	IL	62705	**800-323-0050**	217-241-6410	357-4
OTC: UTGN						
United Utilities Inc						
5450 A St	Anchorage	AK	99509	**800-478-2020**	907-561-1674	726
United Utility Supply Co-op Inc						
4515 Bishop Ln	Louisville	KY	40218	**800-366-4887**	502-957-2568	246
United Van Lines Inc						
1 United Dr	St. Louis	MO	63026	**877-740-3040**	636-343-3900	512
United Way of America						
701 N Fairfax St	Alexandria	VA	22314	**800-892-2757**	703-836-7100	47-5
United Window & Door Manufacturing Inc						
24-36 Fadem Rd	Springfield	NJ	07081	**800-848-4550**	973-912-0600	475
United World Life Insurance Co						
Mutual of Omaha Plz	Omaha	NE	68175	**800-775-6000**	402-342-7600	388-2
United-Bilt Homes Inc						
8500 Line Ave	Shreveport	LA	71106	**800-551-8955**	318-861-4572	188
United-Guardian Inc (UGI)						
230 Marcus Blvd PO Box 18050	Hauppauge	NY	11788	**800-645-5566**	631-273-0900	474
NASDAQ: UG						
UnitedHealth Group Inc						
9900 Bren Rd E	Minnetonka	MN	55343	**800-328-5979**	952-936-1300	388-3
NYSE: UNH						
UnitedHealthcare						
9900 Bren Rd E	Minnetonka	MN	55343	**800-362-0655**	952-936-1300	388-3
Unitek Miyachi Corp						
1820 S Myrtle Ave	Monrovia	CA	91017	**866-751-7378**	626-303-5676	798
Unitel Inc PO Box 165	Unity	ME	04988	**888-760-1048**	207-948-3900	726
Unitil Corp						
Six Liberty Ln W	Hampton	NH	03842	**800-852-3339**	603-772-0775	357-5
NYSE: UTL						
Unitron LP						
10925 Miller Rd PO Box 38902	Dallas	TX	75238	**800-527-1279**	214-340-8600	511
Unitus Community Credit Union						
PO Box 1937	Portland	OR	97207	**800-452-0900**	503-227-5571	219

	City	ST	Zip	Toll-Free	Phone	Class
Unity Bancorp Inc						
64 Old Hwy 22	Clinton	NJ	08809	**800-618-2265**	908-730-7630	357-2
NASDAQ: UNTY						
Unity College						
90 Quaker Hill Rd	Unity	ME	04988	**800-624-1024**	207-948-3131	166
Unity Forest State Scenic Corridor						
US-26 23751 Old Hwy 30	Ironside	OR	97908	**800-551-6949**		558
Unity Health Insurance						
840 Carolina St	Sauk City	WI	53583	**800-362-3308**	608-643-2491	388-3
Unity Hospice						
2366 Oak Ridge Cir	De Pere	WI	54115	**800-990-9249**	920-338-1111	368
Unity Lake State Recreation Site						
18998 OR-245 59500 Hwy 26/395	Unity	OR	97884	**800-551-6949**	541-932-4453	558
Univar USA Inc						
17425 NE Union Hill Rd	Redmond	WA	98052	**855-888-8648**	425-889-3400	144
Univenture Inc						
13311 Industrial Pkwy	Marysville	OH	43040	**800-992-8262**		601
Univera Healthcare						
205 Pk Club Ln	Buffalo	NY	14221	**877-883-9577**	716-847-1480	388-3
Universal American Corp (UAFC)						
44 S Broadway Ste 1200	White Plains	NY	10601	**866-249-8668**	914-934-5200	357-4
NYSE: UAM						
Universal American Mortgage Co						
700 NW 107th Ave 3rd Fl	Miami	FL	33172	**800-741-8262**		502
Universal Audio Inc						
1700 Green Hills Rd	Scotts Valley	CA	95066	**877-698-2834**	831-440-1176	51
Universal Brush Manufacturing Co						
16200 Dixie Hwy	Markham	IL	60428	**800-323-3474**	708-331-1700	102
Universal Creative Concepts Corp						
10143 Royalton Rd Unit E	North Royalton	OH	44133	**800-876-8626**	440-230-1366	9
Universal Display & Fixtures Co						
726 E Hwy 121	Lewisville	TX	75057	**800-235-0701**	972-221-5022	233
Universal Enterprises Inc						
8030 SW Nimbus	Beaverton	OR	97008	**800-547-5740**	503-644-8723	357-2
Universal Fabric Structures Inc						
2200 Kumry Rd	Quakertown	PA	18951	**800-634-8368**	215-529-9921	723
Universal Forest Products Inc (UFPI)						
2801 E Beltline Ave NE	Grand Rapids	MI	49525	**800-598-9663**	616-364-6161	674
NASDAQ: UFPI						
Universal Health Services Inc						
367 S Gulph Rd	King of Prussia	PA	19406	**800-347-7750**	610-768-3300	350
NYSE: UHS						
Universal Hospital Services Inc						
7700 France Ave S Ste 275	Minneapolis	MN	55435	**800-847-7368**	952-893-3200	264-4
Universal Image						
PO Box 77090	Winter Garden	FL	34787	**800-553-5499**	407-352-5302	585
Universal Industries Inc						
5800 Nordic Dr	Cedar Falls	IA	50613	**800-553-4446**	319-277-7501	208
Universal Instruments Corp (UIC)						
33 Broome Corporate Pk	Conklin	NY	13748	**800-842-9732**	607-779-7522	686
Universal Lending Corp (ULC)						
6775 E Evans Ave	Denver	CO	80224	**800-758-4063**		502
Universal Manufacturing Co						
405 Diagonal St PO Box 190	Algona	IA	50511	**800-651-7445**	515-295-3557	59
OTC: UFMG						
Universal Mfg Co Inc						
5030 Mackey S	Overland Park	KS	66203	**800-524-5860**	913-815-6230	752
Universal Orlando						
6000 Universal Blvd	Orlando	FL	32819	**877-801-9720**	407-363-8000	32
Universal Overall Co						
1060 W Van Buren St	Chicago	IL	60607	**800-621-3344***	312-226-3336	153-18
*Cust Svc						
Universal Plastic Mold Inc						
13245 Los Angeles St	Baldwin Park	CA	91706	**888-893-1587**		597
Universal Polymer & Rubber Ltd						
15730 Madison Rd	Middlefield	OH	44062	**800-782-2375**	440-632-1691	668
Universal Security Instruments Inc						
11407 Cronhill Dr	Owings Mills	MD	21117	**800-390-4321**	410-363-3000	683
TSE: UUU						
Universal Service Administrative Co (USAC)						
2000 L St NW Ste 200	Washington	DC	20036	**888-641-8722**	202-776-0200	726
Universal Service Administrative Company Schools & Libraries Div						
2000 L St NW Ste 200	Washington	DC	20036	**888-203-8100**		726
Universal Services of America Inc						
1551 N Tustin Ave Ste 650	Santa Ana	CA	92705	**866-877-1965**	714-619-9700	684
Universal Sodexho						
5749 Susitna Dr	Harahan	LA	70123	**888-763-3967**	301-987-4000	298
Universal Steel Co						
6600 Grant Ave	Cleveland	OH	44105	**800-669-2645**	216-883-4972	487
Universal Studios Hollywood						
100 Universal City Plaza	Universal City	CA	91608	**800-864-8377**		32
Universal Truckload Services Inc						
12755 E Nine Mile Rd	Warren	MI	48089	**800-233-9445**	586-920-0100	770
NASDAQ: UACL						
Universal Tube Inc						
2607 Bond St	Rochester Hills	MI	48309	**800-394-8823**	248-853-5100	588
Universal Wilde						
26 Dartmouth St	Westwood	MA	02090	**866-825-5515**	781-251-2700	5
Universal Wire Cloth Co						
16 N Steel Rd	Morrisville	PA	19067	**800-523-0575**	215-736-8981	679
Universal's Islands of Adventure						
6000 Universal Studios Plz	Orlando	FL	32819	**877-801-9720**	407-363-8000	32
UniversalPegasus International Inc						
4848 Loop Central Dr	Houston	TX	77081	**800-966-1811***	713-977-7770	261
*General						
Universite de Moncton						
Campus Shippagan						
218 Blvd JD Gauthier	Shippagan	NB	E8S1P6	**800-363-8336**	506-336-3400	773
Edmundston						
165 Blvd Hebert	Edmundston	NB	E3V2S8	**888-736-8623**	506-737-5051	773
University & State Employees Credit Union						
10120 Pacific Heights Blvd						
Ste 100	San Diego	CA	92121	**866-873-2448**	858-795-6100	219
University at Albany						
1400 Washington Ave	Albany	NY	12222	**800-293-7869**	518-442-3300	166
University at Albany University Libraries						
1400 Washington Ave	Albany	NY	12222	**800-342-4146**	518-442-3600	431-6
University Behavioral Ctr						
2500 Discovery Dr	Orlando	FL	32826	**800-999-0807**	407-281-7000	371-5
University Directories						
88 VilCom Cir	Chapel Hill	NC	27514	**800-743-5556**		628-6

	City	State	Zip	Toll-Free	Phone	Class
University Galleries						
400 SW 13th St Fine Arts Bldg B						
PO Box 115803	Gainesville	FL	32611	**800-745-3000**	352-273-3000	513
University Games Corp						
2030 Harrison St	San Francisco	CA	94110	**800-347-4818**	415-503-1600	752
University Health Care System						
1350 Walton Way	Augusta	GA	30901	**866-591-2502**	706-722-9011	371-3
University Hospital						
4502 Medical Dr	San Antonio	TX	78229	**866-588-3301**	210-358-4000	371-3
University Hospital SUNY Upstate Medical University						
750 E Adams St	Syracuse	NY	13210	**877-464-5540**	315-464-5540	371-3
University Hospitals of Cleveland						
11100 Euclid Ave	Cleveland	OH	44106	**866-844-2273**	216-844-1000	371-3
University Inn Seattle						
4140 Roosevelt Way NE	Seattle	WA	98105	**800-733-3855**	206-632-5055	376
University Medical Ctr at Princeton (UMCP)						
253 Witherspoon St	Princeton	NJ	08540	**877-932-8935**	609-497-4304	371-3
University Medical Ctr Blood & Marrow Transplantation Program						
1501 N Campbell Ave						
PO Box 24-5176	Tucson	AZ	85724	**800-524-5928**	520-694-0111	759
University Moving & Storage Co						
23305 Commerce Dr	Farmington Hills	MI	48335	**800-448-6683**	248-615-7000	187
University Museum						
3219 Hudson Rd						
University of Northern Iowa	Cedar Falls	IA	50614	**800-772-2736**	319-273-2188	513
University of Akron						
277 E Buchtel Ave	Akron	OH	44325	**800-655-4884***	330-972-7100	166
*Admissions						
University of Akron School of Law						
150 University Ave	Akron	OH	44325	**800-655-4884**	330-972-7331	167-1
University of Akron Wayne College						
1901 Smucker Rd	Orrville	OH	44667	**800-221-8308**	330-683-2010	160
University of Alabama						
PO Box 870132	Tuscaloosa	AL	35487	**800-933-2262***	205-348-6010	166
*Admissions						
Birmingham						
1530 Third Ave S THT 647	Birmingham	AL	35294	**800-421-8743**	205-996-6670	166
Gorgas Library						
Information Ctr First Fl	Tuscaloosa	AL	35487	**888-764-5603**	205-348-6047	431-6
Huntsville						
301 Sparkman Dr	Huntsville	AL	35899	**800-824-2255**	256-824-1000	166
University of Alabama Press, The						
200 Hackberry Ln Second Fl						
PO Box 870380	Tuscaloosa	AL	35487	**800-621-2736***	205-348-5180	628-4
*Orders						
University of Alabama System						
401 Queen City Ave	Tuscaloosa	AL	35401	**800-638-6420**	205-348-5861	774
University of Alaska Anchorage						
3211 Providence Dr	Anchorage	AK	99508	**888-822-8973**	907-786-1800	166
University of Alaska Anchorage Kenai Peninsula College						
156 College Rd	Soldotna	AK	99669	**877-262-0330**		160
University of Alaska Anchorage Kodiak College						
117 Benny Benson Dr	Kodiak	AK	99615	**800-486-7660**	907-486-4161	160
University of Alaska Fairbanks						
Bristol Bay						
527 Seward St PO Box 1070	Dillingham	AK	99576	**800-478-5109**	907-842-5109	166
Northwest						
400 E Front St PO Box 400	Nome	AK	99762	**800-478-2202**	907-443-2201	160
University of Alaska Museum of the North						
907 Yukon Dr	Fairbanks	AK	99775	**866-478-2721**	907-474-7505	513
University of Alaska Press						
794 University Ave Ste 220	Fairbanks	AK	99709	**888-252-6657**	907-474-5831	628-4
University of Alaska Southeast						
11120 Glacier Hwy	Juneau	AK	99801	**877-465-4827**	907-296-6000	166
University of Alaska Southeast Ketchikan						
2600 Seventh Ave	Ketchikan	AK	99901	**877-465-6400**	907-225-6177	160
University of Alaska Southeast Sitka						
1332 Seward Ave	Sitka	AK	99835	**800-478-6653**	907-747-6653	160
University of Alberta						
Augustana						
4901-46th Ave	Camrose	AB	T4V2R3	**800-661-8714**	780-679-1100	773
University of Arizona Press, The						
1510 E University Blvd						
PO Box 210055	Tucson	AZ	85721	**800-426-3797**	520-621-1441	628-4
University of Arkansas						
232 Silas Hunt Hall	Fayetteville	AR	72701	**800-377-8632***	479-575-5346	166
*Admissions						
Monticello						
PO Box 3600	Monticello	AR	71656	**800-844-1826**	870-460-1026	166
Pine Bluff						
1200 N University Dr	Pine Bluff	AR	71601	**800-264-6585***	870-575-8000	166
*Admissions						
University of Arkansas Press						
McIlroy House 105 McIlroy	Fayetteville	AR	72701	**800-621-2736**	479-575-7258	628-4
University of Arkansas School of Law						
1045 W Maple St	Fayetteville	AR	72701	**800-295-9118**	479-575-5601	167-1
University of Baltimore						
1420 N Charles St	Baltimore	MD	21201	**877-277-5982***	410-837-4200	166
*Admitting						
University of Bridgeport						
126 Pk Ave	Bridgeport	CT	06604	**800-392-3582**	203-576-4000	166
University of British Columbia						
2016-1874 E Mall	Vancouver	BC	V6T1Z1	**877-272-1422**	604-822-9836	773
University of California (UCLA)						
Berkeley						
1117 Williston Rd	South Burlington	VT	05403	**800-445-8667**	802-660-7523	662
University of California (UCLA)						
Berkeley						
110 Sproul Hall MC Ste 5800	Berkeley	CA	94720	**866-740-1260**	510-642-6000	166
Merced PO Box 2039	Merced	CA	95344	**866-270-7301**	209-724-4400	166
Riverside						
900 University Ave						
1120 Hinderaker Hall	Riverside	CA	92521	**800-426-2586**	951-827-3411	166
Santa Barbara						
1210 Cheadle Hall	Santa Barbara	CA	93106	**888-488-8272**	805-893-8000	166
Santa Cruz						
1156 High St						
Hahn Bldg Rm 150	Santa Cruz	CA	95064	**800-933-7584**	831-459-2131	166
University of California Davis						
Shields Library						
100 NW Quad	Davis	CA	95616	**877-772-5772**	530-752-6561	431-6
University of California Davis School of Medicine						
4610 X St	Sacramento	CA	95817	**855-221-4673**	916-734-4800	167-2

	City	State	Zip	Toll-Free	Phone	Class
University of California Irvine						
Library PO Box 19557	Irvine	CA	92623	**800-848-4722**	949-824-6836	431-6
University of California Irvine School of Medicine						
1001 Health Sciences Rd						
252 Irvine Hall	Irvine	CA	92697	**800-824-5388**	949-824-6119	167-2
University of California Press						
2120 Berkeley Way	Berkeley	CA	94704	**800-777-4726**	510-642-4247	628-4
University of California San Diego Medical Ctr						
200 W Arbor Dr	San Diego	CA	92103	**800-926-8273**	619-543-6222	371-3
University of Central Arkansas						
201 Donaghey Ave	Conway	AR	72035	**888-407-4747***	501-450-5000	166
*Admissions						
University of Charleston						
2300 MacCorkle Ave SE	Charleston	WV	25304	**800-995-4682***	304-357-4800	166
*Admissions						
University of Chicago Medical Ctr						
5841 S Maryland Ave	Chicago	IL	60637	**888-824-0200**	773-702-1000	371-3
University of Chicago Press						
1427 E 60th St	Chicago	IL	60637	**800-621-2736***	773-702-7700	628-4
*Sales						
University of Chicago Press Journals Div						
PO Box 37005	Chicago	IL	60637	**877-705-1878**	773-702-7700	628-9
University of Cincinnati						
2600 Clifton Ave						
PO Box 210091	Cincinnati	OH	45221	**866-397-3382**	513-556-1100	166
University of Cincinnati Clermont College						
4200 Clermont College Dr	Batavia	OH	45103	**866-446-2822**	513-732-5200	160
University of Cincinnati Langsam Library						
PO Box 210033	Cincinnati	OH	45221	**866-397-3382**	513-556-1515	431-6
University of Colorado						
Colorado Springs						
PO Box 7150	Colorado Springs	CO	80933	**800-990-8227**	719-262-3000	166
University of Colorado at Colorado Springs						
Kraemer Family Library						
1420 Austin Bluffs Pkwy						
PO Box 7150	Colorado Springs	CO	80918	**800-990-8227**	719-255-3295	431-6
Avery Point						
1084 Shennecossett Rd	Groton	CT	06340	**888-247-5556**	860-405-9019	160
University of Connecticut						
Babbidge Library						
369 Fairfield Rd Unit 2005	Storrs	CT	06269	**888-603-9635**	860-486-2219	431-6
University of Connecticut Health Ctr						
John Dempsey Hospital						
263 Farmington Ave	Farmington	CT	06030	**800-535-6232**	860-679-2000	371-3
University of Connecticut School of Law						
45 Elizabeth St	Hartford	CT	06105	**800-633-7867**	860-570-5100	167-1
University of Dallas						
1845 E Northgate Dr	Irving	TX	75062	**800-628-6999***	972-721-5266	166
*Admissions						
University of Dayton						
300 College Pk	Dayton	OH	45469	**800-837-7433**	937-229-4411	166
University of Dayton School of Law						
300 College Pk	Dayton	OH	45469	**800-837-7433**	937-229-3211	167-1
University of Denver						
2199 S University Blvd	Denver	CO	80210	**800-525-9495**	303-871-2036	166
University of Detroit Mercy						
4001 W McNichols Rd	Detroit	MI	48221	**800-635-5020***	313-993-1000	166
*Admissions						
University of Detroit Mercy School of Law						
651 E Jefferson Ave	Detroit	MI	48226	**888-726-6921**	313-596-0264	167-1
University of Dubuque						
2000 University Ave	Dubuque	IA	52001	**800-722-5583**	563-589-3000	166
University of Dubuque Theological Seminary						
2000 University Ave	Dubuque	IA	52001	**800-369-8387**	563-589-3122	167-3
University of Evansville						
1800 Lincoln Ave	Evansville	IN	47722	**800-423-8633**	812-488-2000	166
University of Findlay						
1000 N Main St	Findlay	OH	45840	**800-472-9502**	419-422-8313	166
University of Florida						
219 Grinter Hall						
PO Box 115500	Gainesville	FL	32611	**866-876-4472**	352-392-3261	166
University of Florida Fredric G Levin College of Law						
2500 SW Second Ave	Gainesville	FL	32611	**877-429-1297**	352-273-0890	167-1
University of Florida Libraries						
PO Box 117001	Gainesville	FL	32611	**877-351-2377**	352-392-0342	431-6
University of Georgia Library						
320 S Jackson St	Athens	GA	30602	**877-314-5560**	706-542-0621	431-6
University of Great Falls						
1301 20th St S	Great Falls	MT	59405	**800-856-9544***		166
*Admissions						
University of Hartford						
200 Bloomfield Ave	West Hartford	CT	06117	**800-947-4303**	860-768-4296	166
University of Hawaii						
Hilo 200 W Kawili St	Hilo	HI	96720	**800-897-4456***	808-974-7414	166
*Admissions						
Manoa						
2600 Campus Rd Rm 001	Honolulu	HI	96822	**800-823-9771***	808-956-8975	166
*Admissions						
West Oahu						
96-129 Ala Ike	Pearl City	HI	96782	**866-299-8656**	808-454-4700	166
University of Hawaii Federal Credit Union						
PO Box 22070	Honolulu	HI	96823	**800-927-3397**	808-983-5500	219
University of Hawaii Foundation, The						
2444 Dole St Bachman Hall 105	Honolulu	HI	96822	**866-846-4262**	808-956-8849	219
University of Hawaii Press						
2840 Kolowalu St	Honolulu	HI	96822	**888-847-7377**	808-956-8255	628-4
University of Houston						
Victoria						
3007 N Ben Wilson St	Victoria	TX	77901	**877-970-4848**	361-570-4848	166
University of Houston Law Ctr						
100 Law Ctr	Houston	TX	77204	**800-252-9690**	713-743-2100	167-1
University of Idaho						
Boise						
322 E Front St Ste 190	Boise	ID	83702	**866-264-7384**	208-334-2999	166
University of Idaho College of Law						
Sixth & Rayburn St PO Box 442321	Moscow	ID	83844	**888-884-3246**	208-885-4977	167-1
University of Illinois						
Springfield						
One University Plz						
MS UHB 1080	Springfield	IL	62703	**888-977-4847**	217-206-4847	166
University of Illinois Chicago						
Daley Library						
801 S Morgan St Rm 1-280	Chicago	IL	60607	**866-904-5843**	312-996-2716	431-6

Alphabetical Section

	Toll-Free	Phone	Class
University of Illinois College of Law			
504 E Pennsylvania Ave .... Champaign IL 61820	**800-369-6151**	217-333-0930	167-1
University of Illinois Medical Ctr			
1740 W Taylor St .... Chicago IL 60612	**866-600-2273**	312-996-3900	371-3
University of Illinois Medical Ctr Stem Cell Transplant Unit			
1740 W Taylor St .... Chicago IL 60612	**866-600-2273**	312-996-3900	759
University of Illinois Press			
1325 S Oak St .... Champaign IL 61820	**866-244-0626**	217-333-0950	628-4
University of Indianapolis			
1400 E Hanna Ave .... Indianapolis IN 46227	**800-232-8634**	317-788-3368	166
University of Iowa			
107 Calvin Hall .... Iowa City IA 52242	**800-553-4692**	319-335-3847	166
University of Iowa Athletics Hall of Fame			
KHF Bldg 446 .... Iowa City IA 52242	**877-462-6342**	319-384-1031	515
University of Iowa College of Law			
130 Byington Rd .... Iowa City IA 52242	**800-553-4692**	319-335-9034	167-1
University of Iowa Press			
119 W Pk Rd 100 Kuhl House .... Iowa City IA 52242	**800-621-2736**	319-335-2000	628-4
University of Iowa Roy J & Lucille A Carver College of Medicine			
200 CMAB .... Iowa City IA 52242	**800-725-8460**	319-335-6707	167-2
University of Judaism			
15600 Mulholland Dr .... Los Angeles CA 90077	**888-853-6763**	310-476-9777	166
University of Kansas School of Law			
1535 W 15th St .... Lawrence KS 66045	**877-404-5823**	785-864-4550	167-1
University of Kentucky			
800 Rose St .... Lexington KY 40536	**866-900-4685**	859-257-9000	166
University of Kentucky College of Law			
620 S Limestone St .... Lexington KY 40506	**800-888-8189**	859-257-1678	167-1
University of Kentucky College of Medicine			
Office of Medical Education			
MN 104 UKMC .... Lexington KY 40536	**800-273-8255**	859-323-6161	167-2
University of La Verne			
1950 Third St .... La Verne CA 91750	**800-876-4858***	909-593-3511	166
Admissions			
Lafayette			
611 McKinley St .... Lafayette LA 70504	**800-752-6553**	337-482-1000	166
University of Louisiana			
Monroe			
700 University Ave .... Monroe LA 71209	**800-372-5127***	318-342-5430	166
Admissions			
University of Louisville			
2301 S Third St .... Louisville KY 40292	**800-334-8635**	502-852-5555	166
University of Louisville Hospital			
530 S Jackson St .... Louisville KY 40202	**800-891-0947**	502-562-3000	371-3
University of Louisville School of Medicine			
323 E Chestnut St			
Abell Bldg Rm 413 .... Louisville KY 40202	**800-334-8635**	502-852-5193	167-2
University of Maine			
5713 Chadbourne Hall .... Orono ME 04469	**877-486-2364***	207-581-1110	166
Admissions			
Fort Kent			
23 University Dr .... Fort Kent ME 04743	**888-879-8635***	207-834-7500	166
Admissions			
Machias			
Nine O'Brien Ave .... Machias ME 04654	**888-468-6866***	207-255-1200	166
Admissions			
University of Manitoba			
65 Chancellors Cir			
424 University Ctr .... Winnipeg MB R3T2N2	**800-224-7713***	204-474-8880	773
Admissions			
University of Mary			
7500 University Dr .... Bismarck ND 58504	**800-288-6279***	701-255-7500	166
Admissions			
University of Mary Hardin-Baylor			
900 College St PO Box 8004 .... Belton TX 76513	**800-727-8642**	254-295-8642	166
University of Mary Washington			
1301 College Ave .... Fredericksburg VA 22401	**800-468-5614***	540-654-2000	166
Admissions			
University of Maryland			
Baltimore County			
1000 Hilltop Cir .... Baltimore MD 21250	**800-810-0271**	410-455-1000	166
University of Maryland Ctr for Environmental Science (UMCES)			
2020 Horn Pt Rd .... Cambridge MD 21613	**866-842-2520**	410-228-9250	659
University of Maryland Greenebaum Cancer Ctr			
22 S Greene St Ste N9E17 .... Baltimore MD 21201	**800-888-8823**	410-328-7904	759
University of Maryland Medical Ctr			
22 S Greene St .... Baltimore MD 21201	**800-492-5538**	410-328-8667	371-3
University of Maryland Medical System			
22 S Greene St .... Baltimore MD 21201	**800-492-5538**	410-328-8667	350
University of Maryland University College Marriott Conference Ctr Hotel			
3501 University Blvd E .... Adelphi MD 20783	**800-721-7033**	301-985-7300	374
University of Massachusetts Press			
PO Box 429 .... Amherst MA 01004	**800-562-0112**	413-545-2217	628-4
University of Memphis Cecil C Humphreys School of Law			
3715 Central Ave .... Memphis TN 38152	**800-872-3728**	901-678-2421	167-1
University of Memphis McWherter Library			
126 Ned R McWherter Library ..... Memphis TN 38152	**866-670-6147**	901-678-2201	431-6
University of Miami Hospital & Clinics (UMHC)			
Sylvester Comprehensive Cancer Ctr			
1475 NW 12th Ave .... Miami FL 33136	**800-545-2292**	305-243-1000	759
University of Miami Richter Library			
PO Box 248214 .... Coral Gables FL 33124	**800-708-6754**	305-284-3551	431-6
University of Michigan			
Flint 303 E Kearsley St .... Flint MI 48502	**800-942-5636**	810-762-3000	166
University of Michigan Dearborn			
Mardigian Library			
4901 Evergreen Rd .... Dearborn MI 48128	**877-619-6650**	313-593-5445	431-6
University of Michigan Press			
839 Greene St .... Ann Arbor MI 48104	**866-804-0002**	734-764-4388	628-4
Crookston			
2900 University Ave			
170 Owen Hall .... Crookston MN 56716	**800-862-6466**	218-281-8569	166
Duluth			
1049 University Dr .... Duluth MN 55812	**800-232-1339**	218-726-8000	166
Morris 600 E Fourth St .... Morris MN 56267	**800-992-8863**	320-589-6035	166
University of Minnesota			
Twin Cities			
240 Williamson Hall			
231 Pillsbury Dr SE .... Minneapolis MN 55455	**800-752-1000**	612-625-2008	166
University of Minnesota Crookston			
UMC Library			
2900 University Ave .... Crookston MN 56716	**800-862-6466**	218-281-8399	431-6
University of Minnesota Duluth			
UMD Library			
416 Library Dr .... Duluth MN 55812	**866-999-6995**	218-726-8102	431-6
University of Minnesota Medical Ctr Fairview			
Riverside Campus			
2450 Riverside Ave .... Minneapolis MN 55454	**888-702-4073**	612-273-3000	371-3
University of Minnesota Medical Ctr Fairview - University Campus			
500 Harvard St .... Minneapolis MN 55455	**800-688-5252**	612-273-3000	371-3
University of Minnesota Medical School Twin Cities			
420 Delaware St SE			
Mayo MC 293 .... Minneapolis MN 55455	**800-752-1000**	612-624-5100	167-2
University of Mississippi			
Tupelo			
1918 Briar Ridge Rd .... Tupelo MS 38804	**888-846-5622**	662-844-5622	166
Williams Library			
1 Library Loop .... University MS 38677	**800-891-4596**	662-915-7091	431-6
University of Mississippi School of Medicine			
2500 N State St .... Jackson MS 39216	**888-815-2005**	601-984-1080	167-2
University of Missouri (UMSL)			
Columbia			
2810 Golf Rd .... Pewaukee WI 53072	**800-247-6640**	262-547-0201	374
University of Missouri (UMSL)			
Columbia			
104 Jesse Hall .... Columbia MO 65211	**800-856-2181**	573-882-6333	166
Kansas City			
5100 Rockhill Rd .... Kansas City MO 64110	**800-775-8652**	816-235-1000	166
Saint Louis			
One University Blvd .... Saint Louis MO 63121	**888-462-8675***	314-516-5000	166
Admissions			
University of Missouri Botanic Garden			
General Services Bldg .... Columbia MO 65211	**800-856-2181**	573-882-4240	96
University of Missouri Kansas City			
Nichols Library			
800 E 51st St .... Kansas City MO 64110	**800-775-8652**	816-235-1534	431-6
University of Missouri Press			
2910 LeMone Blvd .... Columbia MO 65201	**800-621-2736**	573-882-7641	628-4
University of Missouri System			
321 University Hall .... Columbia MO 65211	**800-225-6075**	573-882-2011	774
University of Missouri-Kansas City School of Medicine			
2411 Holmes St .... Kansas City MO 64108	**800-735-2466**	816-235-1111	167-2
University of Mobile			
5735 College Pkwy .... Mobile AL 36613	**800-946-7267**	251-675-5990	166
University of Moncton			
18 Ave Antonine-Maillet .... Moncton NB E1A3E9	**800-363-8336**	506-858-4000	773
University of Montana			
College of Technology			
909 S Ave W .... Missoula MT 59801	**800-542-6882**	406-243-7852	788
Helena College of Technology			
1115 N Roberts St .... Helena MT 59601	**800-827-1000**	406-444-6800	788
Western			
710 S Atlantic St .... Dillon MT 59725	**877-683-7331***	406-683-7011	166
Admissions			
University of Montana Missoula			
Mansfield Library			
32 Campus Dr .... Missoula MT 59812	**800-240-4939**	406-243-2053	431-6
University of Nebraska			
Kearney 905 W 25th St .... Kearney NE 68849	**800-532-7639**	308-865-8441	166
Lincoln 1410 Q St .... Lincoln NE 68588	**800-742-8800**	402-472-2023	166
Omaha 6001 Dodge St .... Omaha NE 68182	**800-858-8648**	402-554-2800	166
University of Nebraska Medical Ctr			
42nd and Emile .... Omaha NE 68198	**800-642-1095**	402-559-4000	371-3
University of Nebraska Medical Ctr Bone Marrow & Stem Cell Transplantation Program (Adults)			
987400 Nebraska Medical Ctr .... Omaha NE 68198	**800-922-0000**	402-559-2000	759
University of Nebraska Press			
1111 Lincoln Mall .... Lincoln NE 68508	**800-755-1105***	402-472-3581	628-4
Orders			
University of Nebraska School of Medicine			
985527 Nebraska Medical Ctr .... Omaha NE 68198	**800-626-8431**	402-559-2259	167-2
University of Nebraska System			
3835 Holdrege St Varner Hall .... Lincoln NE 68583	**800-542-1602**	402-472-2111	774
University of Nevada			
Reno 1664 N Virginia St .... Reno NV 89557	**866-263-8232**	775-784-1110	166
University of New England			
11 Hills Beach Rd .... Biddeford ME 04005	**800-477-4863***	207-283-0171	166
Admissions			
Westbrook College			
716 Stevens Ave .... Portland ME 04103	**800-477-4863***	207-797-7261	166
Admissions			
University of New Hampshire			
Manchester			
400 Commercial St .... Manchester NH 03101	**800-287-9793**	603-641-4321	166
University of New Haven			
300 Boston Post Rd .... West Haven CT 06516	**800-342-5864**	203-932-7319	166
University of New Mexico (UNM)			
One University of New Mexico ...... Albuquerque NM 87131	**800-225-5866**	505-277-0111	166
Gallup 200 College Rd .... Gallup NM 87301	**800-225-5866**	505-863-7500	166
Valencia			
280 La Entrada .... Los Lunas NM 87031	**800-225-5866**	505-925-8580	160
University of New Mexico School of Medicine			
1 University of New Mexico .... Albuquerque NM 87131	**877-977-2263**	505-272-4766	167-2
University of New Orleans			
Administrative Bldg			
Rm 103 Lakefront .... New Orleans LA 70148	**800-256-5866***	504-280-6000	166
Admissions			
University of North Alabama			
1 Harrison Plaza .... Florence AL 35632	**800-825-5862**	256-765-4608	166
University of North Carolina			
Asheville			
One University Heights			
CPO 1320 .... Asheville NC 28804	**800-531-9842**	828-251-6481	166
Greensboro			
1400 Spring Garden St .... Greensboro NC 27412	**877-862-4123**	336-334-5000	166
Pembroke PO Box 1510 .... Pembroke NC 28372	**800-949-8627**	910-521-6000	166
Wilmington			
601 S College Rd .... Wilmington NC 28403	**800-596-2880**	910-962-3000	166
University of North Carolina Ctr for Public Television (UNC-TV)			
10 TW Alexander Dr			
PO Box 14900 .... Research Triangle Park NC 27709	**800-906-5050**	919-549-7000	624
University of North Carolina Press			
116 S Boundary St .... Chapel Hill NC 27514	**800-848-6224**	919-966-3561	628-4
University of North Dakota			
PO Box 8357 .... Grand Forks ND 58202	**800-225-5863**	701-777-3000	166

	Toll-Free	Phone	Class

University of North Dakota School of Medicine & Health Sciences
501 N Columbia Rd . . . . . . Grand Forks ND 58203 — 800-225-5863 — 701-777-5046 — 167-2

University of North Florida
4567 St Johns Bluff Rd S . . . . Jacksonville FL 32224 — 866-697-7150 — 904-620-1000 — 166

University of North Texas
PO Box 311277 . . . . Denton TX 76203 — 800-868-8211 — 940-565-2681 — 166

University of North Texas Health Science Ctr
3500 Camp Bowie Blvd . . . . . Fort Worth TX 76107 — 800-687-7580 — 817-735-2000 — 414

University of North Texas Libraries
1155 Union Cir PO Box 305190 . . . . Denton TX 76203 — 877-872-0264 — 940-565-2413 — 431-6

University of North Texas Press
1155 Union Cir Ste 311336 . . . . . . Denton TX 76203 — 800-826-8911 — 940-565-2142 — 628-4

University of Northern Colorado
501 20th St CB 92 . . . . Greeley CO 80639 — 888-700-4862* — 970-351-2881 — 166
*Admissions

University of Northern Iowa
1222 W 27th St . . . . Cedar Falls IA 50614 — 800-772-2037* — 319-273-2281 — 166
*Admissions

University of Oklahoma
1000 Asp Ave . . . . Norman OK 73019 — 800-234-6868 — 405-325-0311 — 166

University of Oregon
1585 E 13th Ave . . . . Eugene OR 97403 — 800-232-3825* — 541-346-1000 — 166
*Admissions

University of Oregon Bookstore Inc
PO Box 3176 . . . . Eugene OR 97403 — 800-352-1733 — 541-346-4331 — 95

University of Ottawa
550 Cumberland St . . . . Ottawa ON K1N6N5 — 877-868-8292 — 613-562-5800 — 773

University of Ottawa Faculty of Medicine
451 Smyth Rd . . . . Ottawa ON K1H8M5 — 877-868-8292 — 613-562-5700 — 167-2

University of Pennsylvania
3451 Walnut St . . . . Philadelphia PA 19104 — 800-537-5487 — 215-898-5000 — 166

University of Pennsylvania Press
3902 Spruce St . . . . Philadelphia PA 19104 — 800-537-5487* — 215-898-6261 — 628-4
*Cust Svc

University of Pennsylvania Van Pelt Library
3420 Walnut St . . . . Philadelphia PA 19104 — 877-784-8379 — 215-898-7091 — 431-6
Bradford
300 Campus Dr . . . . Bradford PA 16701 — 800-872-1787 — 814-362-7555 — 166
Greensburg
150 Finoli Dr . . . . Greensburg PA 15601 — 888-843-4563 — 724-837-7040 — 166
Hillman Library
3960 Forbes Ave . . . . Pittsburgh PA 15260 — 888-465-4329 — 412-648-7710 — 431-6
Johnstown
157 Blackington Hall . . . . . . Johnstown PA 15904 — 800-765-4875 — 814-269-7050 — 166

University of Pittsburgh
Titusville
504 E Main St . . . . Titusville PA 16354 — 888-878-0462 — — 160

University of Pittsburgh Medical Ctr (UPMC)
Horizon
110 N Main St . . . . Greenville PA 16125 — 888-447-1122 — 724-588-2100 — 371-3
South Side
2000 Mary St . . . . Pittsburgh PA 15203 — 800-533-8762 — 412-488-5550 — 371-3

University of Pittsburgh Medical Ctr Health System
200 Lothrop St . . . . Pittsburgh PA 15213 — 800-533-8762 — 412-647-2345 — 350

University of Pittsburgh Press
3400 Forbes Ave 5th Fl . . . . . Pittsburgh PA 15261 — 800-621-2736* — 412-383-2456 — 628-4
*Sales

University of Portland
5000 N Willamette Blvd . . . . . . Portland OR 97203 — 888-627-5601 — 503-943-7147 — 166

University of Puget Sound
1500 N Warner St . . . . Tacoma WA 98416 — 800-396-7191 — 253-879-3100 — 166

University of Redlands
1200 E Colton Ave PO Box 3080 . . . . . . Redlands CA 92373 — 800-455-5064 — 909-793-2121 — 166

University of Regina
3737 Wascana Pkwy . . . . Regina SK S4S0A2 — 800-644-4756 — 306-585-4111 — 773

University of Richmond
Westhampton College
28 Westhampton Way
. . . . University Of Richmond VA 23173 — 800-700-1662 — 804-289-8000 — 166

University of Rio Grande
218 N College Ave . . . . Rio Grande OH 45674 — 800-282-7201 — 740-245-5353 — 166

University of Rio Grande Rio Grande Community College
218 N College Ave . . . . Rio Grande OH 45674 — 800-282-7201 — 740-245-5353 — 160

University of Rochester
Wallace Hall PO Box 270251 . . . . . . Rochester NY 14627 — 888-822-2256* — 585-275-2121 — 166
*Admissions

University of Rochester School of Medicine & Dentistry
601 Elmwood Ave . . . . Rochester NY 14642 — 888-661-6162 — 585-275-0017 — 167-2

University of Saint Francis
180 Remsen St . . . . Brooklyn Heights NY 11201 — 800-356-8329 — 718-522-2300 — 166

University of Saint Mary
4100 S Fourth St . . . . Leavenworth KS 66048 — 800-752-7043 — 913-682-5151 — 166

University of Saint Thomas
3800 Montrose Blvd . . . . Houston TX 77006 — 800-856-8565 — 713-522-7911 — 166

University of Saint Thomas O'Shaughnessy-Frey Library
2115 Summit Ave . . . . Saint Paul MN 55105 — 800-328-6819 — 651-962-5494 — 431-6

University of Saint Thomas School of Law
1000 LaSalle Ave . . . . Minneapolis MN 55403 — 800-328-6819 — 651-962-4892 — 167-1

University of San Diego
5998 Alcala Pk . . . . San Diego CA 92110 — 800-248-4873 — 619-260-4506 — 166

University of San Diego School of Law
5998 Alcala Pk . . . . San Diego CA 92110 — 800-248-4873 — 619-260-4528 — 167-1

University of San Francisco
2130 Fulton St . . . . San Francisco CA 94117 — 800-225-5873* — 415-422-5555 — 166
*Admissions

University of San Francisco Gleeson Library
2130 Fulton St . . . . San Francisco CA 94117 — 800-225-5873 — 415-422-5555 — 431-6

University of Saskatchewan
1121 College Dr . . . . Saskatoon SK S7N0W3 — 877-653-8501 — 306-966-8970 — 167-3
Saint Thomas More College
1437 College Dr . . . . Saskatoon SK S7N0W6 — 800-667-2019 — 306-966-8900 — 773

University of Sciences & Arts of Oklahoma
1727 W Alabama Ave . . . . Chickasha OK 73018 — 800-933-8726 — 405-224-3140 — 166

University of Scranton
800 Linden St St Thomas Hall . . . . . . Scranton PA 18510 — 888-727-2686 — 570-941-7400 — 166

University of Sioux Falls
1101 W 22nd St . . . . Sioux Falls SD 57105 — 800-888-1047 — 605-331-6600 — 166

University of South Alabama
2500 Meisler Hall . . . . Mobile AL 36688 — 800-872-5247 — 251-460-6141 — 166

University of South Carolina
1600 Hampton St . . . . Columbia SC 29208 — 800-868-5872 — 803-777-7000 — 166
Aiken
471 University Pkwy . . . . Aiken SC 29801 — 800-937-0762 — 803-648-6851 — 166

Beaufort
801 Carteret St . . . . Beaufort SC 29902 — 866-455-4753 — 843-521-4100 — 166
Sumter 200 Miller Rd . . . . Sumter SC 29150 — 888-872-7868 — 803-775-8727 — 166
Union 401 E Main St . . . . Union SC 29379 — 800-768-5566 — 864-429-8728 — 160
Upstate
800 University Way . . . . Spartanburg SC 29303 — 800-277-8727 — 864-503-5246 — 166

University of South Carolina McKissick Museum
University of S Carolina
816 Bull St . . . . Columbia SC 29208 — 888-825-9711 — 803-777-7251 — 513

University of South Carolina Press
1600 Hampton St Fifth Fl . . . . Columbia SC 29208 — 800-768-2500* — 803-777-5243 — 628-4
*Orders

University of South Dakota
414 E Clark St . . . . Vermillion SD 57069 — 877-269-6837 — 605-677-5341 — 166

University of South Dakota Foundation
1110 N Dakota St PO Box 5555 . . . . . . Vermillion SD 57069 — 800-521-3575 — 605-677-6703 — 774

University of South Dakota School of Law
414 E Clark St . . . . Vermillion SD 57069 — 877-269-6837 — 605-677-5443 — 167-1
Sarasota-Manatee
8350 N Tamiami Trail . . . . Sarasota FL 34243 — 866-974-1222 — 941-359-4200 — 166

University of South Florida
Tampa 4202 E Fowler Ave . . . . Tampa FL 33620 — 877-873-2855 — 813-974-2011 — 166

University of South Florida College of Medicine (USF)
12901 Bruce B Downs Blvd . . . . Tampa FL 33612 — 877-338-2577 — 813-974-2229 — 167-2

University of South Florida Polytechnic
Lakeland
3433 Winter Lake Rd . . . . Lakeland FL 33803 — 800-873-5636 — 863-667-7017 — 166

University of Southern California
Doheny Memorial Library
3550 Trousdale Pkwy
University Pk Campus . . . . Los Angeles CA 90089 — 800-775-7330 — 213-740-4039 — 431-6

University of Southern Indiana
8600 University Blvd . . . . Evansville IN 47712 — 800-467-1965 — 812-464-1765 — 166

University of Southern Maine
96 Falmouth St . . . . Portland ME 04103 — 800-800-4876 — 207-780-4141 — 166
Gorham 37 College Ave . . . . Gorham ME 04038 — 800-800-4876 — 207-780-5670 — 166
Lewiston-Auburn College
51 Westminster St . . . . Lewiston ME 04240 — 800-800-4876 — 207-753-6500 — 166

University of Southern Maine Arboretum
PO Box 9300 . . . . Portland ME 04104 — 800-800-4876 — — 96

University of Southern Mississippi
118 College Dr . . . . Hattiesburg MS 39406 — 800-446-0892 — 601-266-1000 — 166

University of St Francis
500 Wilcox St . . . . Joliet IL 60435 — 800-735-7500 — — 166

University of Tennessee
Chattanooga
615 McCallie Ave . . . . Chattanooga TN 37403 — 800-882-6627 — 423-425-4111 — 166
Martin
544 University St . . . . Martin TN 38238 — 800-829-8861 — 731-881-7020 — 166

University of Tennessee Health Science Ctr
Health Sciences Library & Biocommunications Ctr
877 Madison Ave . . . . Memphis TN 38103 — 877-747-0004 — 901-448-5634 — 431-1

University of Tennessee Knoxville
Hodges Library
1015 Volunteer Blvd . . . . Knoxville TN 37996 — 800-426-9119 — 865-974-4351 — 431-6
Brownsville
80 Fort Brown St . . . . Brownsville TX 78520 — 800-892-3348 — 956-882-8200 — 166
Dallas
800 W Campbell Rd Ste Be3204 . . . . Richardson TX 75080 — 800-889-2443 — 972-883-2111 — 166
El Paso
500 W University Ave . . . . El Paso TX 79968 — 800-551-0294* — 915-747-5000 — 166
*Admissions
Pan American
1201 W University Dr . . . . Edinburg TX 78539 — 866-441-8872 — 956-381-8872 — 166
Permian Basin
4901 E University Blvd . . . . Odessa TX 79762 — 866-552-8872* — 432-552-2020 — 166
*Admissions

University of Texas
San Antonio
6900 N Loop 1604 W . . . . San Antonio TX 78249 — 800-669-0919 — 210-458-4011 — 166
Tyler
3900 University Blvd . . . . Tyler TX 75799 — 800-888-9537 — 903-566-7000 — 166

University of Texas at Austin Performing Arts Ctr
E 23rd St & E Robert Dedman Dr . . . . Austin TX 78713 — 800-687-6010 — 512-471-1444 — 565

University of Texas Medical Branch
301 University Blvd . . . . Galveston TX 77555 — 800-228-1841 — 409-772-2618 — 167-2

University of Texas Medical Branch Hospitals
301 University Blvd . . . . Galveston TX 77555 — 800-201-0527 — 409-772-1011 — 371-3

University of Texas Press
2100 Comal St . . . . Austin TX 78722 — 800-252-3206* — 512-471-7233 — 628-4
*Sales

University of Texas Southwestern Medical Ctr at Dallas Library, The
5323 Harry Hines Blvd . . . . Dallas TX 75390 — 866-645-6455 — 214-648-2001 — 431-1
Hematopoietic Cell Transplant Program
2201 Inwood Rd Second Fl . . . . Dallas TX 75390 — 866-645-6455 — 214-645-4673 — 759

University of Texas Southwestern Medical Ctr Dallas
Southwestern Medical School
5323 Harry Hines Blvd . . . . Dallas TX 75390 — 866-648-2455 — 214-648-3111 — 167-2

University of Texas System
601 Colorado St . . . . Austin TX 78701 — 866-882-2034 — 512-499-4200 — 774

University of the Arts
320 S Broad St . . . . Philadelphia PA 19102 — 800-616-2787 — 215-717-6049 — 162

University of the Cumberlands
6191 College Stn Dr . . . . Williamsburg KY 40769 — 800-343-1609 — 606-539-4201 — 166

University of the Incarnate Word
4301 Broadway St . . . . San Antonio TX 78209 — 800-749-9673* — 210-829-6000 — 166
*Admissions

University of the Ozarks
415 N College Ave . . . . Clarksville AR 72830 — 800-264-8636* — 479-979-1227 — 166
*Admissions

University of the Pacific
3601 Pacific Ave . . . . Stockton CA 95211 — 800-959-2867 — 209-946-2211 — 166

University of the Sciences in Philadelphia
600 S 43rd St . . . . Philadelphia PA 19104 — 888-857-6264 — 215-596-8800 — 166

University of the South
735 University Ave . . . . Sewanee TN 37383 — 800-522-2234 — 931-598-1238 — 166

University of Toledo
2801 W Bancroft St . . . . Toledo OH 43606 — 800-586-5336 — 419-530-4636 — 166

University of Toledo Carlson Library
2801 W Bancroft St MS 509 . . . . Toledo OH 43606 — 800-586-5336 — 419-530-2324 — 431-6

University of Toledo College of Medicine
2801 W Bancroft . . . . Toledo OH 43606 — 800-586-5336 — 419-530-4636 — 167-2

University of Toledo Medical Center, The
3000 Arlington Ave . . . . Toledo OH 43614 — 800-321-8383 — 419-383-4000 — 371-3

	City	State	ZIP	Toll-Free	Phone	Class
University of Tulsa						
800 S Tucker Rd	Tulsa	OK	74104	**800-331-3050**	918-631-2307	166
University of Utah Hospital & Clinics (UUHSC)						
Blood & Marrow Transplant Program						
50 N Medical Dr	Salt Lake City	UT	84132	**800-824-2073***	801-581-2121	759
*General						
University of Utah Marriott Library						
Marriott Library 295 S 1500 E	Salt Lake City	UT	84112	**800-458-0145**	801-581-8558	431-6
University of Utah Press						
295 South 1500 East						
Ste 5400	Salt Lake City	UT	84112	**800-621-2736**	801-585-0082	628-4
University of Utah School of Medicine						
30 N 1900 E	Salt Lake City	UT	84132	**844-988-7284**	801-581-7201	167-2
University of Vermont						
85 S Prospect St	Burlington	VT	05405	**800-499-0113**	802-656-3131	166
University of Vermont College of Medicine						
89 Beaumont Ave						
E-126 Given Bldg	Burlington	VT	05405	**800-571-0668**	802-656-2156	167-2
University of Vermont Medical Center, The (FAHC)						
111 Colchester Ave	Burlington	VT	05401	**800-358-1144**	802-847-0000	371-3
University of Virginia Health System						
1215 Lee St	Charlottesville	VA	22908	**800-251-3627**	434-924-0211	371-3
University of Virginia Press						
210 Sprigg Ln						
PO Box 400318	Charlottesville	VA	22903	**800-831-3406***	434-924-3469	628-4
*Orders						
University of Virginia School of Law						
580 Massie Rd	Charlottesville	VA	22903	**877-307-0158**	434-924-7354	167-1
University of Virginia's College at Wise						
One College Ave	Wise	VA	24293	**888-282-9324***	276-328-0102	166
*Admissions						
University of Washington Press						
4333 Brooklyn Ave NE	Seattle	WA	98195	**800-537-5487**	206-543-4050	628-4
University of Washington School of Law						
William H Gates Hall						
PO Box 353020	Seattle	WA	98195	**866-866-0158**	206-543-4078	167-1
University of West Alabama						
Stn 200 UWA	Livingston	AL	35470	**800-621-8044***	205-652-3400	166
*Admissions						
University of West Florida Ctr for Fine & Performing Arts						
11000 University Pkwy Bldg 82	Pensacola	FL	32514	**800-263-1074**	850-474-2000	565
University of Western Ontario						
King's University College						
266 Epworth Ave	London	ON	N6A2M3	**800-265-4406**	519-433-3491	773
Baraboo/Sauk County						
1006 Connie Rd	Baraboo	WI	53913	**800-621-7440**	608-355-5200	160
Barron County						
1800 College Dr	Rice Lake	WI	54868	**800-608-4578**	715-234-8176	160
University of Wisconsin						
Eau Claire						
105 Garfield Ave PO Box 4004	Eau Claire	WI	54701	**800-473-2255**	715-836-2637	166
Fox Valley						
1478 Midway Rd	Menasha	WI	54952	**800-273-8255**	920-832-2600	160
Green Bay						
2420 Nicolet Dr	Green Bay	WI	54311	**800-465-4329**	920-465-2000	166
La Crosse						
1725 State St						
115 Graff Main Hall	La Crosse	WI	54601	**800-382-2150**	608-785-8000	166
Manitowoc						
705 Viebahn St	Manitowoc	WI	54220	**800-657-3866**	920-683-4700	160
Marathon County						
518 S Seventh Ave	Wausau	WI	54401	**888-367-8962**	715-261-6100	160
Marshfield/Wood County						
2000 W Fifth St	Marshfield	WI	54449	**800-273-8255**	715-389-6530	160
Platteville						
One University Plz	Platteville	WI	53818	**800-362-5515**	608-342-1125	166
Richland						
1200 Hwy 14 W	Richland Center	WI	53581	**800-947-3529**	608-647-6186	160
River Falls						
410 S Third St						
B3 E Hathorn Hall	River Falls	WI	54022	**800-852-5711**	715-425-3911	166
Stout						
802 S Broadway	Menomonie	WI	54751	**800-447-8688***	715-232-1232	166
*Admissions						
Superior						
Belknap & Catlin PO Box 2000	Superior	WI	54880	**877-345-3494**	715-394-8101	166
Washington County						
400 S University Dr	West Bend	WI	53095	**800-240-0276**	262-335-5200	160
University of Wisconsin Eau Claire						
McIntyre Library						
105 Garfield Ave	Eau Claire	WI	54702	**877-267-1384**	715-836-3715	431-6
University of Wisconsin Hospital & Clinics						
600 Highland Ave	Madison	WI	53792	**800-323-8942**	608-263-6400	371-3
University of Wisconsin Law School						
975 Bascom Mall	Madison	WI	53706	**866-301-1753**	608-262-2240	167-1
University of Wisconsin Stout						
Library						
315 Tenth Ave E	Menomonie	WI	54751	**866-716-6685**	715-232-1215	431-6
University of Wisconsin Superior						
Jim Dan Hill Library						
PO Box 2000	Superior	WI	54880	**877-232-1727**	715-394-8343	431-6
University of Wisconsin System						
1220 Linden Dr						
1720 Van Hise Hall	Madison	WI	53706	**800-442-6461**	608-262-2321	774
University of Wyoming						
1000 E University Ave Dept 3435	Laramie	WY	82071	**800-342-5996***	307-766-5160	166
*Admissions						
University of Wyoming College of Law						
1000 E University Ave Dept 3035	Laramie	WY	82071	**800-442-6757**	307-766-6416	167-1
University of Wyoming Libraries						
PO Box 3334	Laramie	WY	82071	**800-442-6757**	307-766-3190	431-6
University Park Mall						
6501 N Grape Rd	Mishawaka	IN	46545	**877-746-6642**	574-277-2223	455
University Place						
310 SW Lincoln St	Portland	OR	97201	**866-845-4647**	503-221-0140	376
University Press Books (UPB)						
2430 Bancroft Way	Berkeley	CA	94704	**800-676-8722**	510-548-0585	95
University Press of America						
4501 Forbes Blvd Ste 200	Lanham	MD	20706	**800-462-6420**	301-459-3366	628-2
University Press of Colorado						
5589 Arapahoe Ave Ste 206C	Boulder	CO	80303	**800-621-2736**	720-406-8849	628-4
University Press of Florida						
15 NW 15th St	Gainesville	FL	32611	**800-226-3822***	352-392-1351	628-4
*Sales						
University Press of Kentucky						
663 S Limestone St	Lexington	KY	40508	**800-537-5487***	859-257-8400	628-4
*Sales						
University Press of Mississippi						
3825 Ridgewood Rd	Jackson	MS	39211	**800-737-7788**	601-432-6205	628-4
University Press of New England (UPNE)						
One Ct St Ste 250	Lebanon	NH	03766	**800-421-1561***	603-448-1533	628-4
*Orders						
University Products Inc						
517 Main St	Holyoke	MA	01040	**800-628-1912**	413-532-3372	553
Univest Corp of Pennsylvania						
14 N Main St PO Box 64197	Souderton	PA	18964	**877-723-5571**		357-2
NASDAQ: UVSP						
Univex Corp						
Three Old Rockingham Rd	Salem	NH	03079	**800-258-6358**	603-893-6191	297
Univision Television Group Inc						
5999 Ctr Dr	Los Angeles	CA	90045	**800-594-5387**	310-846-2800	728
Uniweld Products Inc						
2850 Ravenswood Rd	Fort Lauderdale	FL	33312	**800-323-2111**	954-584-2000	798
Uniworld						
17323 Ventura Blvd	Encino	CA	91316	**800-733-7820**	818-382-7820	221
UniWorld Group Inc						
1 Metro Ctr N	Brooklyn	NY	11201	**800-900-2958**	212-219-1600	4
Unlimited Systems Corp Inc						
9530 Padgett St	San Diego	CA	92126	**800-275-6354**	858-537-5010	174-3
UNM (University of New Mexico)						
One University of New Mexico	Albuquerque	NM	87131	**800-225-5866**	505-277-0111	166
Uno Chicago Grill						
100 Charles Pk Rd	Boston	MA	02132	**866-600-8667**	617-323-9200	661
Uno Langmann Ltd						
2117 Granville St	Vancouver	BC	V6H3E9	**800-730-8825**	604-736-8825	41
Uno Restaurant Corp						
100 Charles Pk Rd	Boston	MA	02132	**866-600-8667**	617-323-9200	661
UNOS (United Network for Organ Sharing)						
700 N Fourth St	Richmond	VA	23219	**888-894-6361**	804-782-4800	47-17
UnumProvident Corp						
1 Fountain Sq	Chattanooga	TN	37402	**800-262-0018**	423-294-1011	357-4
Unverferth Mfg Company Inc						
601 S Broad St	Kalida	OH	45853	**800-322-6301**	419-532-3121	273
UOP LLC						
25 E Algonquin Rd	Des Plaines	IL	60017	**800-877-6184**	847-391-2000	141
Up With Paper						
6049 Hi-Tek Ct	Mason	OH	45040	**800-852-7677**	513-759-7473	129
Up With People						
6830 Broadway	Denver	CO	80221	**877-264-8856**	303-460-7100	47-15
UPAC (Imperial PFS)						
8245 Nieman Rd	Lenexa	KS	66214	**800-877-7848**	913-894-6150	216
UPB (University Press Books)						
2430 Bancroft Way	Berkeley	CA	94704	**800-676-8722**	510-548-0585	95
Upchurch Scientific Inc						
619 Oak St	Oak Harbor	WA	98277	**866-339-4653**		416
UPMC (University of Pittsburgh Medical Ctr)						
110 N Main St	Greenville	PA	16125	**888-447-1122**	724-588-2100	371-3
UPNE (University Press of New England)						
One Ct St Ste 250	Lebanon	NH	03766	**800-421-1561***	603-448-1533	628-4
*Orders						
Upper Bucks Chamber of Commerce						
2170 Portzer Rd	Quakertown	PA	18951	**888-942-8257**	215-536-3211	137
Upper Cumberland Electric Membership Corp						
138 Gordonsville Hwy	South Carthage	TN	37030	**800-261-2940**	615-735-2940	245
Upper Dauphin Area School District (UDASD)						
5668 State Rt 209	Lykens	PA	17048	**866-632-9992**	717-362-8134	676
Upper Deck Co LLC						
5909 Sea Otter Pl	Carlsbad	CA	92010	**800-873-7332***		752
*Cust Svc						
Upper Iowa University						
605 Washington St PO Box 1857	Fayette	IA	52142	**800-553-4150***	563-425-5200	166
*Admissions						
Upper Peninsula Telephone Co						
PO Box 86	Carney	MI	49812	**800-950-8506**	906-639-2111	726
Upper Room Chapel & Museum						
1908 Grand Ave	Nashville	TN	37212	**800-972-0433**	615-340-7200	513
Upper Sioux Agency State Park						
5908 Hwy 67	Granite Falls	MN	56241	**800-366-8917**	320-564-4777	558
Upper Valley Medical Ctr (UVMC)						
3130 N County Rd 25-A	Troy	OH	45373	**866-608-3463**	937-440-4000	371-3
UPS (United Parcel Service Inc)						
55 Glenlake Pkwy NE	Atlanta	GA	30328	**800-742-5877***	404-828-6000	539
NYSE: UPS ■ *Cust Svc						
UPS Capital Business Credit						
35 Glenlake Pkwy NE	Atlanta	GA	30328	**877-263-8772**		69
UPS Store, The						
6060 Cornerstone Ct W	San Diego	CA	92121	**800-789-4623**	858-455-8800	309
UPS Strategic Enterprise Fund						
55 Glenlake Pkwy NE						
Bldg 1 4th Fl	Atlanta	GA	30328	**800-742-5877**		780
UPS Supply Chain Solutions						
12380 Morris Rd	Alpharetta	GA	30005	**800-742-5727**	913-693-6151	444
Upsher-Smith Laboratories Inc						
6701 Evenstad Dr	Maple Grove	MN	55369	**800-654-2299**	763-315-2000	576
Upstate New York Transplant Services Inc						
110 Broadway	Buffalo	NY	14203	**800-227-4771**	716-853-6667	269
Upstate Shredding LLC						
1 Recycle Dr Tioga Industrial Pk	Owego	NY	13827	**800-245-3133**	607-687-7777	677
Upstate Tours & Travel						
207 Geyser Rd	Saratoga Springs	NY	12866	**800-237-5252**	518-584-5252	750
Urban Alternative						
PO Box 4000	Dallas	TX	75208	**800-800-3222**	214-943-3868	47-20
Urban Decay						
833 W 16th St	Newport Beach	CA	92663	**800-784-8722**	949-631-4504	215
Urban Foundation/Engineering LLC						
32-33 111th St	East Elmhurst	NY	11369	**800-843-6664**	718-478-3021	190-5
Urban Land Institute (ULI)						
1025 Thomas Jefferson St NW						
Ste 500W	Washington	DC	20007	**800-321-5011***	202-624-7000	47-8
*Orders						
Urban Outfitters Inc						
30 Industrial Pk Blvd	Trenton	SC	29847	**800-282-2200**		155-4
Urban Science						
400 Renaissance Ctr Ste 2900	Detroit	MI	48243	**800-321-6900**	313-259-9900	195

	Toll-Free	Phone	Class
Urologix Inc			
14405 21st Ave N ....Minneapolis MN 55447	**800-475-1403**	763-475-1400	471
URS			
7633 E 63rd Pl Ste 500.................. Tulsa OK 74133	**800-564-6253**	918-294-3030	189-10
URS Corp			
600 Montgomery St 26th Fl .... San Francisco CA 94111	**877-877-8970**	415-774-2700	261
NYSE: URS			
Urschel Laboratories Inc			
2503 Calumet Ave PO Box 2200....... Valparaiso IN 46384	**844-877-2435**	219-464-4811	297
Ursinus College			
601 E Main St PO Box 1000......... Collegeville PA 19426	**877-448-3282**	610-409-3200	166
Ursula of Switzerland Inc			
31 Mohawk Ave .... Waterford NY 12188	**800-826-4041**		153-20
Ursuline College			
2550 Lander Rd .... Pepper Pike OH 44124	**888-778-5463**	440-449-4200	166
Us Adventure Rv			
5120 n brady st .... Davenport IA 52806	**877-768-4678**		23
US Air Force 375th Medical Group			
310 W Losey St .... Scott AFB IL 62225	**866-683-2778**		371-4
US Air Force Academy (USAFA)			
2304 Cadet Dr			
Ste 2300 .... Air Force Academy CO 80840	**800-443-9266**	719-333-1110	493
US Airconditioning Distributors			
16900 Chestnut St .... City of Industry CA 91748	**800-937-7222**	626-854-4500	605
US Airways Express			
111 W Rio Salado Pkwy .... Tempe AZ 85281	**800-679-8215**	480-693-0800	25
US Airways Group Inc			
111 W Rio Salado Pkwy .... Tempe AZ 85281	**800-428-4322**	480-693-0800	357-1
NYSE: LCC			
US Alliance Federal Credit Union			
600 Midland Ave .... Rye NY 10580	**800-431-2754**		219
US Apple Assn			
8233 Old Courthouse Rd Ste 200......... Vienna VA 22182	**800-781-4443**	703-442-8850	47-2
US Army Aeromedical Research Laboratory			
MCMR-UAC Bldg 6901 .... Fort Rucker AL 36362	**888-386-7635**	334-255-6920	659
US Army Engineer Research & Development Ctr (ERDC)			
3909 Halls Ferry Rd .... Vicksburg MS 39180	**800-522-6937**	601-634-3188	659
US Army War College			
122 Forbes Ave .... Carlisle PA 17013	**800-453-0992**	717-245-3131	338-4
US Balloon Mfg Company Inc			
140 58th St .... Brooklyn NY 11220	**800-285-4000**		327
US Bancorp			
800 Nicollet Mall .... Minneapolis MN 55402	**800-872-2657***	651-466-3000	357-2
NYSE: USB *Cust Svc			
US Bank NA			
800 Nicollet Mall .... Minneapolis MN 55402	**800-872-2657**	651-466-3000	69
US Bankruptcy Court			
Alaska			
605 W Fourth Ave Ste 138 .... Anchorage AK 99501	**800-859-8059**	907-271-2655	339-1
Minnesota			
300 S Fourth St			
7W US Courthouse............. Minneapolis MN 55415	**866-260-7337**	612-664-5260	339-1
Missouri Eastern			
111 S Tenth St 4th Fl .... Saint Louis MO 63102	**866-803-9517**	314-244-4500	339-1
Pennsylvania Middle			
197 S Main St .... Wilkes-Barre PA 18701	**877-298-2053**	570-831-2500	339-1
Texas Northern			
1100 Commerce St Rm 1254........... Dallas TX 75242	**800-442-6850**	214-753-2000	339-1
Washington Eastern			
904 W Riverside Ave Ste 304......... Spokane WA 99201	**800-519-2549**	509-353-2404	339-1
Wisconsin Eastern			
US Courthouse			
517 E Wisconsin Ave Rm 126 ...... Milwaukee WI 53202	**877-781-7277**	414-297-3291	339-1
US Biathlon Assn			
49 Pineland Dr Ste 301-A........ New Gloucester ME 04260	**800-242-8456***	207-688-6500	47-22
*General			
US Bobsled & Skeleton Federation (USBSF)			
196 Old Military Rd .... Lake Placid NY 12946	**888-431-3598**	518-523-1842	47-22
US Bronze Powders Inc			
408 Rt 202 N .... Flemington NJ 08822	**800-544-0186***	908-782-5454	480
*General			
US Bronze Sign Co			
811 Second Ave .... New Hyde Park NY 11040	**800-872-5155**	516-352-5155	767
US Button Corp			
328 Kennedy Dr .... Putnam CT 06260	**800-243-1842**	860-928-2707	587
US Catholic Magazine			
205 W Monroe .... Chicago IL 60606	**800-328-6515***	312-236-7782	452-18
*Cust Svc			
US Cellular Corp (USCC)			
8410 W Bryn Mawr Ave Ste 700......... Chicago IL 60631	**888-944-9400**	773-399-8900	726
NYSE: USM			
US Cellular Ctr			
370 First Ave E .... Cedar Rapids IA 52401	**800-745-3000**	319-398-5211	206
US Census Bureau Regional Offices			
Atlanta			
101 Marietta St NW Ste 3200.......... Atlanta GA 30303	**800-424-6974**	404-730-3832	338-2
Boston			
4 Copley Pl Ste 301 .... Boston MA 02117	**800-562-5721**	617-424-4501	338-2
Chicago			
1111 W 22nd St Ste 400 .... Oak Brook IL 60523	**800-865-6384**	630-288-9200	338-2
Denver			
6900 W Jefferson Ave Ste 100......... Denver CO 80235	**800-852-6159**	303-264-0202	338-2
Los Angeles			
15350 Sherman Way Ste 300........ Van Nuys CA 91406	**800-992-3530**	818-267-1700	338-2
New York			
395 Hudson St Ste 800 .... New York NY 10014	**800-991-2520**	212-584-3400	338-2
Philadelphia			
833 Chestnut St Ste 504.......... Philadelphia PA 19107	**800-262-4236**	215-717-1800	338-2
US Chamber of Commerce			
1615 H St NW .... Washington DC 20062	**800-638-6582**	202-659-6000	138
US Chemical & Plastics			
600 Nova Dr SE PO Box 709 .... Massillon OH 44646	**800-321-0672**	330-830-6000	59
US Chess Federation (USCF)			
PO Box 3967 .... Crossville TN 38557	**800-903-8723**	931-787-1234	47-18
US Chrome Corp			
175 Garfield Ave .... Stratford CT 06615	**800-637-9019**		476
US Citizenship & Immigration Services Regional Offices			
Eastern Region			
70 Kimball Ave .... South Burlington VT 05403	**800-767-1833**		338-9
US Coachways Inc			
100 St Mary's Ave Ste 2B .... Staten Island NY 10305	**800-359-5991**	718-477-4242	437
US Coast Guard			
National Maritime Ctr			
100 Forbes Dr .... Martinsburg WV 25404	**888-427-5662**	304-433-3400	338-9

	Toll-Free	Phone	Class
US Coast Guard Academy			
15 Mohegan Ave .... New London CT 06320	**800-883-8724**	860-444-8500	166
US Coast Guard Air Station Detroit			
1461 N Perimeter Rd			
Selfridge ANGB.................... Selfridge MI 48045	**800-424-8802**		156
US Commission on Civil Rights Regional Offices			
Midwestern Regional Office			
55 W Monroe St Ste 410 .... Chicago IL 60603	**800-552-6843**	312-353-8311	338-18
US Conference of Catholic Bishops (USCCB)			
3211 Fourth St NE .... Washington DC 20017	**866-582-0943**	202-541-3000	47-20
US Council for International Business (USCIB)			
1212 Ave of the Americas			
18th Fl .... New York NY 10036	**866-768-5925**	212-354-4480	48-12
US Curling Assn (USCA)			
5525 Clem's Way .... Stevens Point WI 54482	**888-287-5377**	715-344-1199	47-22
US Customs & Border Protection			
1300 Pennsylvania Ave NW .... Washington DC 20229	**877-227-5511**	703-526-4200	338-9
US Dataworks Inc			
1 Sugar Creek Ctr Blvd			
5th Fl .... Sugar Land TX 77478	**888-254-8821**	281-504-8000	179-10
OTC: UDWK			
US Dept of Education			
Region 6			
1999 Bryan St Ste 1620.............. Dallas TX 75201	**877-521-2172**	214-661-9600	338-6
US Dept of Labor Women's Bureau			
200 Constitution Ave NW			
Rm S-3002 .... Washington DC 20210	**800-827-5335**	202-693-6710	198
US Diamond Wheel Co			
101 Kendall Pt Dr .... Oswego IL 60543	**800-223-0457**	800-851-1095	495
US Digital Corp			
1400 NE 136th Ave .... Vancouver WA 98684	**800-736-0194**	360-260-2468	179-10
US Digital Media Inc			
1929 W Lone Cactus Dr .... Phoenix AZ 85027	**877-992-3766**	623-587-4900	540
US District Court Colorado			
901 19th St .... Denver CO 80294	**800-359-8699**	303-844-3433	339-2
US District Court for the District of Alaska			
222 W Seventh Ave Ste 4 .... Anchorage AK 99513	**866-243-3814**	907-677-6100	339-2
US District Court Mississippi Southern			
PO Box 23552 .... Jackson MS 39225	**866-517-7682**	601-965-4439	339-2
US District Court Nebraska			
111 S 18th Plaza Ste 1152 .... Omaha NE 68102	**866-220-4381**	402-661-7350	339-2
US District Court North Carolina Western			
401 W Trade St .... Charlotte NC 28202	**866-851-1605**	704-350-7400	339-2
US District Court Oklahoma Northern			
333 W Fourth St .... Tulsa OK 74103	**866-213-1957**	918-699-4700	339-2
US District Court Texas Western			
655 E Durango Blvd Rm G65 .... San Antonio TX 78206	**800-659-2497**	210-472-6550	339-2
US District Court Vermont			
11 Elmwood Ave Rm 506			
PO Box 945....................... Burlington VT 05402	**800-837-8718**	802-951-6301	339-2
US Drug Testing Laboratories Inc			
1700 S Mt Prospect Rd .... Des Plaines IL 60018	**800-235-2367**	847-375-0770	413
US Ecology			
300 E Mallard Dr Ste 300................ Boise ID 83706	**800-590-5220**	208-331-8400	658
NASDAQ: ECOL			
US Election Assistance Commission			
1201 New York Ave NW Ste 300...... Washington DC 20005	**866-747-1471**	202-566-3100	338-18
US Energy Corp			
877 N Eigth W .... Riverton WY 82501	**800-776-9271**	307-856-9271	497
NASDAQ: USEG			
US Equipment Company Inc			
8311 Sorensen Ave .... Santa Fe Springs CA 90670	**800-255-4731**		355
US Fencing Assn (USFA)			
1 Olympic Plaza .... Colorado Springs CO 80909	**888-431-3598**	719-866-4511	47-22
US Fish & Wildlife Service (USFWS)			
1849 C St NW .... Washington DC 20240	**800-344-9453**	202-208-4717	338-11
US Fish & Wildlife Service Regional Offices			
Great Lakes/Big Rivers Region			
5600 American Blvd W			
Ste 900...................... Bloomington MN 55437	**800-877-8339**	612-713-5360	338-11
US Foods Culinary Equipment & Supplies			
2621 Fairview Ave N Ste 2 .... Roseville MN 55113	**866-636-2338**	651-638-8993	299
US Fund for UNICEF			
125 Maiden Ln .... New York NY 10038	**800-367-5437**		47-5
US General Services Administration			
1800 F St NW .... Washington DC 20405	**800-488-3111**		338-18
US Geological Survey			
Ask USGS			
12201 Sunrise Valley Dr .... Reston VA 20192	**888-275-8747**	703-648-5953	338-11
US Global Investors Inc			
7900 Callaghan Rd .... San Antonio TX 78229	**800-873-8637**	210-308-1234	398
NASDAQ: GROW			
US Golf Assn (USGA)			
77 Liberty Corner Rd .... Far Hills NJ 07931	**800-336-4446***	908-234-2300	47-22
*Orders			
US Government Printing Office Bookstore (GPO)			
732 N Capitol St NW .... Washington DC 20401	**866-512-1800**	202-512-1800	340
US Grant, The			
326 Broadway .... San Diego CA 92101	**800-237-5029**	619-232-3121	376
US Health & Human Services Department			
Region 9			
90 7th St Ste 4-100 .... San Francisco CA 94103	**800-368-1019**		338-8
Us Health Connect Inc			
500 Office Ctr Dr .... Fort Washington PA 19034	**800-889-4944**		160
US House of Representatives			
Permanent Select Committee on Intelligence			
Capitol Visitor Ctr HVC-304			
US Capitol Bldg .... Washington DC 20515	**877-858-9040**	202-225-4121	340-1
US Immigration & Customs Enforcement (ICE)			
425 'I' St NW .... Washington DC 20536	**866-347-2423**	202-514-1900	338-9
US Industries Inc			
1701 First Ave .... Evansville IN 47710	**800-456-8721**	812-425-2428	190-12
US Ink Corp			
651 Garden St .... Carlstadt NJ 07072	**800-423-8838**	201-935-8666	385
US Junior Chamber of Commerce			
7447 S Lewis Ave .... Tulsa OK 74136	**800-905-5499**	636-681-1857	47-7
US LABS Inc			
2601 Campus Dr .... Irvine CA 92612	**888-875-2270**	800-710-1800	415
US Lawns			
4700 Millenia Blvd Ste 240 .... Orlando FL 32839	**800-875-2967**		419
US Learning Inc			
516 Tennessee St Ste 219............. Memphis TN 38103	**800-647-9166**	901-767-5700	755

Alphabetical Section

	Toll-Free	Phone	Class
US Legal Support Inc			
363 N Sam Houston Pkwy E			
Ste 900 ....Houston TX 77060	800-567-8757	713-653-7100	440
US Marshals Service			
401 Courthouse Square ....Alexandria VA 22314	800-336-0102*	202-307-9100	338-12
*General			
US Merchant Marine Academy			
300 Steamboat Rd ....Kings Point NY 11024	866-546-4778	516-726-5800	166
Us Micro Corp			
7000 Highlnds Pkwy SE ....Smyrna GA 30082	888-876-4276	770-437-0706	175
US Mint			
801 Ninth St NW ....Washington DC 20220	800-872-6468*	202-756-6468	338-16
*Cust Svc			
San Francisco			
155 Hermann St ....San Francisco CA 94102	800-872-6468	415-575-8000	338-16
US Naval Academy			
121 Blake Rd ....Annapolis MD 21402	888-249-7707*	410-293-1000	493
*Admissions			
US Naval Institute			
291 Wood Rd ....Annapolis MD 21402	800-233-8764	410-268-6110	47-19
US New Mexico Federal Credit Union (USNMFCU)			
3939 Osuna Rd NE PO Box 129 .....Albuquerque NM 87109	888-342-8766	505-342-8888	219
US News & World Report			
1050 Thomas Jefferson St NW ......Washington DC 20007	800-836-6397	212-716-6800	452-17
US News University Connection LLC			
9417 Princess Palm Ave ....Tampa FL 33619	866-442-6587		384
US Olympic Training Ctr			
1750 E Boulder St ....Colorado Springs CO 80909	800-775-8762	719-866-4618	711
US PAACC (US Pan Asian American Chamber of Commerce)			
1329 18th St NW ....Washington DC 20036	800-696-7818	202-296-5221	47-14
US Pan Asian American Chamber of Commerce (US PAACC)			
1329 18th St NW ....Washington DC 20036	800-696-7818	202-296-5221	47-14
US Parachute Assn (USPA)			
5401 Southpoint Ctr Blvd ....Fredericksburg VA 22407	800-765-2336	540-604-9740	47-22
US Parole Commission			
5550 Friendship Blvd Rm 420 ......Chevy Chase MD 20815	888-585-9103	301-492-5990	338-12
US Patent & Trademark Office			
PO Box 1450 ....Alexandria VA 22313	800-786-9199	571-272-1000	338-2
US Penitentiary			
Atwater			
1 Federal Way PO Box 019001........Atwater CA 95301	877-623-8426	209-386-0257	
US Pharmacist Magazine			
100 Ave of the Americas			
Ninth Fl...................New York NY 10013	800-825-4696		452-16
US Pharmacopeia (USP)			
12601 Twinbrook Pkwy ....Rockville MD 20852	800-227-8772	301-881-0666	48-8
US Physical Therapy			
1300 W Sam Houston Pkwy S			
Ste 300 ....Houston TX 77042	800-580-6285	713-297-7000	349
NYSE: USPH			
US Pipe & Foundry Co			
Two Chase Corporate Drive			
Suite 200 ....Birmingham AL 35244	866-347-7473		306
US Plastic Corp			
1390 Newbrecht Rd ....Lima OH 45801	800-537-9724	419-228-2242	200
US Postal Service (USPS)			
475 L'Enfant Plaza W SW ....Washington DC 20260	800-275-8777*	202-268-2000	338-18
*Cust Svc			
US Potato Board (USPB)			
7555 E Hampden Ave Ste 412 ....Denver CO 80231	866-632-9992	303-369-7783	47-2
US Premium Beef LLC (USPB)			
12200 N Ambassador Dr			
PO Box 20103................Kansas City MO 64163	866-877-2525	816-713-8800	295-26
US Professional Tennis Assn (USPTA)			
3535 Briarpark Dr Ste 1 ....Houston TX 77042	800-877-8248	713-978-7782	47-22
US Recordings Inc			
2925 Country Dr ....Little Canada MN 55117	877-272-5250	651-765-6400	388-6
US Ring Binder			
6800 Arsenal St ....Saint Louis MO 63139	800-888-8772	314-645-7880	85
US Robotics Corp			
1300 E Woodfield Dr Ste 506 ....Schaumburg IL 60173	877-710-0884	847-874-2000	174-3
US Rowing Assn			
Two Wall St ....Princeton NJ 08540	800-314-4769	609-924-1578	47-22
US Security Assoc Inc			
200 Mansell Ct Fifth Fl..............Roswell GA 30076	800-730-9599	770-625-1500	684
US Security Inc			
4544 NW 10th St ....Oklahoma City OK 73127	877-917-5566	405-947-3377	684
US Shipping Corp			
399 Thornall St 8th Fl................Edison NJ 08837	866-942-6592	732-635-1500	311
US Silica Co			
106 Sand Mine Rd			
PO Box 187............Berkeley Springs WV 25411	800-243-7500	304-258-2500	498-4
US Soccer Federation			
1801 S Prairie Ave ....Chicago IL 60616	800-745-3000	312-808-1300	47-22
US Special Delivery Inc			
821 E Blvd ....Kingsford MI 49802	800-821-6389	906-774-1931	676
US Suites			
4970 Windplay Dr C1 ....El Dorado Hills CA 95762	800-877-8483*	916-941-7970	376
*Cust Svc			
US Synchronized Swimming			
132 E Washington St			
Ste 800 ....Indianapolis IN 46204	800-775-8762	317-237-5700	47-22
US Telecom Assn (USTA)			
607-14th St NW Ste 400............Washington DC 20005	877-869-6903	202-326-7300	48-20
US Tool Grinding Inc			
701 S Desloge Dr ....Desloge MO 63601	800-775-8665	573-431-3856	450
US Travel Assn			
1100 New York Ave NW Ste 450......Washington DC 20005	877-212-5752	202-408-8422	48-7
US Trotting Assn (USTA)			
750 Michigan Ave ....Columbus OH 43215	877-800-8782	614-224-2291	47-22
US Tsubaki Inc			
301 E Marquardt Dr ....Wheeling IL 60090	800-323-7790	847-459-9500	613
US Vision Inc			
1 Harmon Dr			
Glen Oaks Industrial Pk.............Glendora NJ 08029	800-524-0789	856-228-1000	536
US WorldMeds LLC			
4010 Dupont Cir Ste L-07 ....Louisville KY 40207	888-900-8796	502-815-8000	238
US Xpress Enterprises Inc			
4080 Jenkins Rd ....Chattanooga TN 37421	800-251-6291	423-510-3000	770
USA (United Space Alliance)			
600 Gemini Ave ....Houston TX 77058	800-367-5690	281-212-6200	271

	Toll-Free	Phone	Class
USA 800 Inc			
9808 E 66th Terr			
PO Box 16795.................Kansas City MO 64133	800-821-7539	816-358-1303	727
USA Baby			
793 Springer Dr ....Lombard IL 60148	800-767-9464	630-652-0600	320
USA Basketball			
5465 Mark Dabling			
Boulevard ....Colorado Springs CO 80918	888-284-5383	719-590-4800	47-22
USA Communications Inc			
920 E 56th St Ste B................Kearney NE 68847	877-234-0102		384
USA Container Company Inc			
1776 S Second St ....Piscataway NJ 08854	888-752-7722	732-752-7722	199
USA Datanet Corp			
109 S Warren St Ste 602 ....Syracuse NY 13202	800-566-8655		726
USA for UNHCR			
1775 K St NW Ste 580 ....Washington DC 20006	800-770-1100	202-296-1115	47-5
USA Freedom Corps			
1201 New York Ave NW ....Washington DC 20005	800-833-3722	202-606-5000	338
USA Gymnastics			
201 S Capitol Ave Ste 300 ....Indianapolis IN 46225	800-345-4719	317-237-5050	47-22
USA Hockey			
1775 Bob Johnson Dr ....Colorado Springs CO 80906	800-566-3288	719-576-8724	47-22
USA Judo Inc			
1 Olympic Plaza			
Ste 505 ....Colorado Springs CO 80909	800-775-8762	719-866-4730	47-22
USA Mobility Inc			
6677 Richmond Hwy ....Alexandria VA 22306	800-231-2556	703-660-6677	726
USA Student Travel			
5080 Robert J Mathews Pkwy.....El Dorado Hills CA 95762	800-448-4444	916-939-6805	750
USA Swimming			
1 Olympic Plaza ....Colorado Springs CO 80909	800-333-3333	719-866-4578	47-22
USA Table Tennis			
1 Olympic Plaza ....Colorado Springs CO 80909	800-775-8762	719-866-4583	47-22
USA Technologies Inc			
Ste 140 100 Deerfield Ln Chester ....Malvern PA 19355	800-633-0340		251
USA Today			
7950 Jones Branch Dr ....McLean VA 22108	800-872-0001*	703-854-3400	525-3
*Cust Svc			
USA Track & Field (USATF)			
132 E Washington St			
Ste 800 ....Indianapolis IN 46204	800-365-4663	317-261-0500	47-22
USA Truck Inc			
3200 Industrial Pk Rd ....Van Buren AR 72956	800-643-9691	479-471-2500	770
NASDAQ: USAK			
USA Water Polo			
2124 Main St Ste 210.........Huntington Beach CA 92648	888-712-2166	714-500-5445	47-22
USA Water Ski			
1251 Holy Cow Rd ....Polk City FL 33868	800-533-2972	863-324-4341	47-22
USA Weightlifting (USAW)			
1 Olympic Plaza ....Colorado Springs CO 80909	800-775-8762	719-866-4508	47-22
USA Workers' Injury Network			
1250 S Capital of Texas Hwy			
Bldg 3 Ste 500 ....Austin TX 78746	800-872-0020*		388-4
*Cust Svc			
USA Wrestling			
6155 Lehman Dr ....Colorado Springs CO 80918	888-431-3598	719-598-8181	47-22
USA.NET Inc			
1155 Kelly Johnson Blvd			
Ste 305 ....Colorado Springs CO 80920	800-234-2175	719-265-2930	38
USAA (United Services Automobile Assn)			
10750 McDermott Fwy ....San Antonio TX 78288	800-531-8722		186
USAA (USAA Life Insurance Co)			
9800 Fredericksburg Rd ....San Antonio TX 78288	800-531-8000	210-531-8722	388-2
USAA FSB (USAAFSB)			
10750 McDermott Fwy ....San Antonio TX 78288	800-531-8722		69
USAA Investment Management			
9800 Fredericksburg Rd			
PO Box 659453................San Antonio TX 78288	800-531-8722		398
USAA Life Insurance Co (USAA)			
9800 Fredericksburg Rd ....San Antonio TX 78288	800-531-8000	210-531-8722	388-2
USAA Property & Casualty Insurance Group			
9800 Fredericksburg Rd ....San Antonio TX 78288	800-531-8722	210-531-8722	388-4
USAA Real Estate Co			
9830 Colonnade Blvd Ste 600 ....San Antonio TX 78230	800-531-8182		646
USAAFSB (USAA FSB)			
10750 McDermott Fwy ....San Antonio TX 78288	800-531-8722		69
USAC (Universal Service Administrative Co)			
2000 L St NW Ste 200 ....Washington DC 20036	888-641-8722	202-776-0200	726
USAFA (US Air Force Academy)			
2304 Cadet Dr			
Ste 2300 ....Air Force Academy CO 80840	800-443-9266	719-333-1110	493
USANA Health Sciences Inc			
3838 West PkwyBlvd ....Salt Lake City UT 84120	888-950-9595	801-954-7100	787
NYSE: USNA			
US-Analytics Solutions Group LLC			
600 E Las Colinas Blvd Ste 2222 ....Irving TX 75039	877-828-8727*	214-630-0081	181
*General			
USATF (USA Track & Field)			
132 E Washington St			
Ste 800 ....Indianapolis IN 46204	800-365-4663	317-261-0500	47-22
U-Save Auto Rental of America Inc			
1052 Highland Colony Pkwy			
Ste 204 ....Ridgeland MS 39157	800-438-2300*	601-713-4333	125
*General			
USAW (USA Weightlifting)			
1 Olympic Plaza ....Colorado Springs CO 80909	800-775-8762	719-866-4508	47-22
USB (United Soybean Board)			
16305 Swingley Ridge Rd			
Ste 150 ....Chesterfield MO 63017	800-989-8721	636-530-1777	47-2
USBSF (US Bobsled & Skeleton Federation)			
196 Old Military Rd ....Lake Placid NY 12946	888-431-3598	518-523-1842	47-22
USCA (US Curling Assn)			
5525 Clem's Way ....Stevens Point WI 54482	888-287-5377	715-344-1199	47-22
USCC (US Cellular Corp)			
8410 W Bryn Mawr Ave Ste 700 ....Chicago IL 60631	888-944-9400	773-399-8900	726
NYSE: USM			
USCCB (US Conference of Catholic Bishops)			
3211 Fourth St NE ....Washington DC 20017	866-582-0943	202-541-3000	47-20
USCF (US Chess Federation)			
PO Box 3967 ....Crossville TN 38557	800-903-8723	931-787-1234	47-18

	Toll-Free	Phone	Class
USCIB (US Council for International Business)			
1212 Ave of the Americas			
18th Fl . . . New York NY 10036	**866-768-5925**	212-354-4480	48-12
USF (University of South Florida College of Medicine)			
12901 Bruce B Downs Blvd . . . Tampa FL 33612	**877-338-2577**	813-974-2229	167-2
USFA (US Fencing Assn)			
1 Olympic Plaza . . . Colorado Springs CO 80909	**888-431-3598**	719-866-4511	47-22
USFS (Forest Service)			
1400 Independence Ave SW . . . Washington DC 20050	**800-832-1355**	202-205-8333	338-1
USFWS (US Fish & Wildlife Service)			
1849 C St NW . . . Washington DC 20240	**800-344-9453**	202-208-4717	338-11
USG Corp			
550 W Adams St . . . Chicago IL 60661	**800-874-4968**	312-436-4000	344
NYSE: USG			
USGA (US Golf Assn)			
77 Liberty Corner Rd . . . Far Hills NJ 07931	**800-336-4446***	908-234-2300	47-22
*Orders			
USHEALTH Group Inc			
300 Burnett St Ste 200 . . . Fort Worth TX 76102	**800-387-9027**		388-6
Ushio America Inc			
5440 Cerritos Ave . . . Cypress CA 90630	**800-326-1960**	714-236-8600	433
uShip Inc			
205 Brazos St . . . Austin TX 78701	**800-698-7447**		384
Usi Electronics Inc			
2775 W Cypress Creek Rd . . . Fort Lauderdale FL 33309	**800-874-8111**	954-493-8111	253
USIS			
7799 Leesburg Pk			
Ste 1100-S . . . Falls Church VA 22043	**888-270-8978**	703-448-0178	626
USIS (United States Information Systems Inc)			
35 W Jefferson Ave . . . Pearl River NY 10965	**866-222-3778**	845-358-7755	775
USL Pharma			
301 S Cherokee St . . . Denver CO 80223	**800-654-2299**	303-607-4500	577
USM Corp			
32 Stevens St . . . Haverhill MA 01830	**800-361-2056**	978-374-0303	383
USM Inc			
1880 Markley St . . . Norristown PA 19401	**800-355-4000**	610-278-9000	187
US-Mexico Chamber of Commerce California Pacific Chapter			
2450 Colorado Ave Ste 400E . . . Santa Monica CA 90404	**800-997-9148**	310-586-7901	
USMotivation			
7840 Roswell Rd			
Bldg 100 Third Fl . . . Atlanta GA 30350	**866-885-4702**		381
USNMFCU (US New Mexico Federal Credit Union)			
3939 Osuna Rd NE PO Box 129 . . . Albuquerque NM 87109	**888-342-8766**	505-342-8888	219
USNR			
1981 Schurman Way PO Box 310 . . . Woodland WA 98674	**800-289-8767**	360-225-8267	674
USNR Inc			
558 Robinson Rd PO Box 310 . . . Woodland WA 98674	**800-289-8767**	360-225-8267	808
USP (US Pharmacopeia)			
12601 Twinbrook Pkwy . . . Rockville MD 20852	**800-227-8772**	301-881-0666	48-8
USPA (US Parachute Assn)			
5401 Southpoint Ctr Blvd . . . Fredericksburg VA 22407	**800-765-2336**	540-604-9740	47-22
USPB (US Premium Beef LLC)			
12200 N Ambassador Dr			
PO Box 20103 . . . Kansas City MO 64163	**866-877-2525**	816-713-8800	295-26
USPB (US Potato Board)			
7555 E Hampden Ave Ste 412 . . . Denver CO 80231	**866-632-9992**	303-369-7783	47-2
USPS (US Postal Service)			
475 L'Enfant Plaza W SW . . . Washington DC 20260	**800-275-8777***	202-268-2000	338-18
*Cust Svc			
USPTA (US Professional Tennis Assn)			
3535 Briarpark Dr Ste 1 . . . Houston TX 77042	**800-877-8248**	713-978-7782	47-22
USS Alabama Battleship Memorial Park			
2703 Battleship Pkwy PO Box 65 . . . Mobile AL 36602	**888-414-4448**	251-433-2703	49-3
USS Kidd Veterans Memorial & Museum			
305 S River Rd . . . Baton Rouge LA 70802	**800-638-0594**	225-342-1942	49-3
USS Lexington Museum on the Bay			
2914 N Shoreline Blvd . . . Corpus Christi TX 78402	**800-523-9539**	361-888-4873	513
USS Missouri Memorial Assn Inc			
63 Cowpens St . . . Honolulu HI 96818	**877-644-4896**	808-455-1600	49-3
USSM (Ulbrich Stainless Steels & Special Metals Inc)			
57 Dodge Ave . . . North Haven CT 06473	**800-243-1676**	203-239-4481	714
USS-POSCO Industries			
900 Loveridge Rd . . . Pittsburg CA 94565	**800-877-7672**	925-439-6000	714
USTA (US Telecom Assn)			
607-14th St NW Ste 400 . . . Washington DC 20005	**877-869-6903**	202-326-7300	48-20
USTA (US Trotting Assn)			
750 Michigan Ave . . . Columbus OH 43215	**877-800-8782**	614-224-2291	47-22
Aging & Adult Services Div			
195 N 1950 W Rm 325 . . . Salt Lake City UT 84116	**877-424-4640**	801-538-3910	337-45
Child & Family Services Div			
195 N 1950 W Rm 225 . . . Salt Lake City UT 84116	**855-323-3237**	801-538-4100	337-45
Community & Economic Development Dept			
60 E S Temple 3rd Fl . . . Salt Lake City UT 84111	**855-204-9046**	801-538-8680	337-45
Environmental Quality Dept			
195 N 1950 W . . . Salt Lake City UT 84116	**800-458-0145**	801-536-4400	337-45
Governor			
350 N State St Ste 200			
PO Box 142220 . . . Salt Lake City UT 84114	**800-705-2464**	801-538-1000	337-45
Labor Commission			
PO Box 146600 . . . Salt Lake City UT 84114	**800-530-5090**	801-530-6800	337-45
Lieutenant Governor			
PO Box 142325 . . . Salt Lake City UT 84114	**800-705-2464**		337-45
Motor Vehicle Div			
PO Box 30412 . . . Salt Lake City UT 84130	**800-368-8824**	801-297-7780	337-45
Occupational & Professional Licensing Div			
PO Box 146741 . . . Salt Lake City UT 84111	**866-275-3675**	801-530-6628	337-45
Office of Tourism			
300 N State St . . . Salt Lake City UT 84114	**800-200-1160**	801-538-1900	337-45
Parks & Recreation Div			
1594 W N Temple Ste 116 . . . Salt Lake City UT 84116	**800-322-3770**	801-538-7220	337-45
Rehabilitation Office			
250 E 500 S . . . Salt Lake City UT 84111	**800-473-7530**	801-538-7530	337-45
Utah			
Workers' Compensation Fund			
100 W Towne Ridge Pkwy . . . Sandy UT 84070	**800-446-2667**	385-351-8000	337-45
Utah Assn of Realtors			
230 W Towne Ridge Pkwy Ste 500 . . . Sandy UT 84070	**800-594-8933**	801-676-5200	647
Utah Business Magazine			
90 S 400 W Ste 650 . . . Salt Lake City UT 84101	**866-294-1660**	801-568-0114	452-5
Utah Higher Education Assistance Authority			
PO Box 145112 . . . Salt Lake City UT 84114	**877-336-7378**	801-321-7294	716
Utah Medical Products Inc			
7043 S 300 W . . . Midvale UT 84047	**866-754-9789**	801-566-1200	471
NASDAQ: UTMD			
Utah Metal Works Inc (UMW)			
805 Everett Ave			
PO Box 1073 . . . Salt Lake City UT 84116	**877-221-0099**	877-364-5679	651
Utah Nurses Assn (UNA)			
4505 S Wastch Blvd			
Ste 330B . . . Salt Lake City UT 84124	**800-338-7657**	801-272-4510	526
Utah State Bar			
645 S 200 E . . . Salt Lake City UT 84111	**877-752-2611**	801-531-9077	71
Utah State Library			
250 N 1950 W Ste A . . . Salt Lake City UT 84116	**800-662-9150**	801-715-6777	431-5
Utah State University			
1600 Old Main Hill . . . Logan UT 84322	**800-488-8108**	435-797-1116	166
Utah Transit Authority			
3600 S 700 W			
PO Box 30810 . . . Salt Lake City UT 84130	**888-743-3882**	801-262-5626	463
Utah Valley Convention & Visitors Bureau			
111 S University Ave . . . Provo UT 84601	**800-222-8824**	801-851-2100	207
Utah Valley State College			
800 W University Pkwy . . . Orem UT 84058	**800-952-8220**	801-863-4636	160
Utak Laboratories Inc			
25020 Ave Tibbitts . . . Valencia CA 91355	**800-235-3442**	661-294-3935	231
UTC RETAIL Inc			
100 Rawson Rd . . . Victor NY 14564	**800-349-0546**		607
Ute Mountain Casino			
Three Weeminuche Dr . . . Towaoc CO 81334	**800-258-8007**	970-565-8800	132
UTEX Industries Inc			
10810 Katy Fwy Ste 100 . . . Houston TX 77043	**800-359-9230**	713-467-1000	325
UTGI (United Trust Group Inc)			
5250 S Sixth St . . . Springfield IL 62705	**800-323-0050**	217-241-6410	357-4
OTC: UTGN			
Utica Boilers Inc			
PO Box 4729 . . . Utica NY 13504	**800-325-5479**	866-847-6656	354
Utica College			
1600 Burrstone Rd . . . Utica NY 13502	**800-782-8884***	315-792-3111	166
*Admissions			
Utica Community Schools (UCS)			
11303 Greendale Dr . . . Sterling Heights MI 48312	**800-877-8339**	586-797-1000	676
Utica First Insurance Co			
5981 Airport Rd . . . Oriskany NY 13424	**800-456-4556**	315-736-8211	388-4
Utica National Insurance Group			
180 Genesee St . . . New Hartford NY 13413	**800-274-1914**	315-734-2000	388-2
Utica School of Commerce			
201 Bleecker St . . . Utica NY 13501	**800-321-4872**	315-733-2307	788
Utilimaster Holding Co			
603 Earthway Blvd . . . Bristol IN 46507	**800-237-7806**		53
Utility Environment Report			
Two Penn Plz 25th Fl . . . New York NY 10121	**800-752-8878**		524-5
Utility Forecaster			
7600A Leesburg Pk			
W Bldg Ste 300 . . . Falls Church VA 22043	**800-832-2330**	703-394-4931	524-9
Utility Service Company Inc			
535 Courtney Hodges Blvd . . . Perry GA 31069	**855-526-4413**	478-987-0303	193
Utility Services Inc			
400 N Fourth St . . . Bismarck ND 58501	**800-638-3278**	701-222-7900	189-10
Utility Tool & Trailer Co			
151 E 16th St PO Box 360 . . . Clintonville WI 54929	**800-874-6807**	715-823-3167	769
Utility Trailer Mfg Co			
17295 E Railroad St . . . City of Industry CA 91748	**800-874-6807**	626-965-1541	769
Utility/Keystone Trailer Sales Inc			
1976 Auction Rd . . . Manheim PA 17545	**888-327-4236**	717-653-9444	56
Utne Reader Magazine			
12 N 12th St Ste 400 . . . Minneapolis MN 55403	**800-736-8863***	612-338-5040	452-11
*Cust Svc			
Utrecht Art Supplies			
PO Box 1769 . . . Galesburg IL 61402	**888-336-3114**	609-409-8001	42
UTSA (Uniform & Textile Service Assn)			
1300 N 17th St Ste 750 . . . Arlington VA 22209	**800-996-3426**	703-247-2600	48-4
UTStarcom Inc			
1732 North First St Ste 220 . . . San Jose CA 95112	**877-547-6340**	408-453-4557	725
NASDAQ: UTSI			
UTZ Quality Foods Co			
900 High St . . . Hanover PA 17331	**800-367-7629**	717-637-6644	295-35
UUHSC (University of Utah Hospital & Clinics)			
50 N Medical Dr . . . Salt Lake City UT 84132	**800-824-2073***	801-581-2121	759
*General			
UUSC (Unitarian Universalist Service Committee)			
689 Massachusetts Ave . . . Cambridge MA 02139	**800-388-3920**	617-868-6600	47-5
UVA Culpeper Hospital			
501 Sunset Ln . . . Culpeper VA 22701	**866-608-4749**	540-829-4100	371-3
Uvex Safety Inc			
900 Douglas Pk . . . Smithfield RI 02917	**800-682-0839***		569
*General			
UVMC (Upper Valley Medical Ctr)			
3130 N County Rd 25-A . . . Troy OH 45373	**866-608-3463**	937-440-4000	371-3
UVP Inc 2066 W 11th St . . . Upland CA 91786	**800-452-6788***	909-946-3197	433
*Cust Svc			
UXB International Inc			
2020 Kraft Dr Ste 2100 . . . Blacksburg VA 24060	**800-422-4892**	540-443-3700	658

V

	Toll-Free	Phone	Class
V & S Midwest Carriers Corp			
2001 Hyland Ave PO Box 107 . . . Kaukauna WI 54130	**800-876-4330**	920-766-9696	770
VA (Department of Veterans Affairs)			
810 Vermont Ave NW . . . Washington DC 20420	**800-827-1000***	202-461-7600	338-17
*Cust Svc			
Castle Point Campus			
41 Castle Pt Rd . . . Wappingers Falls NY 12590	**877-222-8387**	845-831-2000	371-8
VA Hudson Valley Health Care System			
Montrose Campus			
2094 Albany Post Rd PO Box 100 . . . Montrose NY 10548	**800-269-8749**	914-737-4400	371-8
VA Medical Ctr			
4500 S Lancaster Rd . . . Dallas TX 75216	**800-849-3597**	214-742-8387	371-8

	Toll-Free	Phone	Class
VA Puget Sound Health Care System - Seattle Div			
1660 S Columbian Way .... Seattle WA 98108	800-329-8387	206-762-1010	759
Vacation Co			
42 New Orleans Rd			
Ste 102 .... Hilton Head Island SC 29928	800-845-7018	843-686-6100	373
Vacation Internationale			
1417 116th Ave NE ....Bellevue WA 98004	800-444-6633	425-454-8429	743
Vacation.com Inc			
1650 King St Ste 450 ....Alexandria VA 22314	800-843-0733		762
Vacudyne Inc			
375 E Joe Orr Rd ....Chicago Heights IL 60411	800-459-9591	708-757-5200	383
Vail Cascade Resort & Spa			
1300 Westhaven Dr .... Vail CO 81657	800-420-2424	970-476-7111	660
Vail Mountain Lodge & Spa, The			
352 E Meadow Dr .... Vail CO 81657	888-794-0410	970-476-0700	698
Vail Resorts Management Co			
390 Interlocken Crescent			
Ste 1000 ....Broomfield CO 80021	800-842-8062	303-404-1800	660
NYSE: MTN			
Vail Valley Chamber of Commerce			
101 Fawcett Rd Ste 240 ....Avon CO 81620	800-525-3875	970-476-1000	137
Vail Valley Tourism Bureau			
PO Box 1130 .... Vail CO 81658	800-525-3875	970-476-1000	207
Vaisala Inc			
10-D Gill St ....Woburn MA 01801	888-824-7252	781-933-4500	467
Val Surf Inc			
4810 Whitsett Ave ....Valley Village CA 91607	888-825-7873	818-769-6977	702
Valassis Communications Inc			
19975 Victor Pkwy ....Livonia MI 48152	800-437-0479	734-591-3000	619
NYSE: VCI			
Valcom Inc			
5614 Hollins Rd ....Roanoke VA 24019	800-825-2661	540-563-2000	725
Valdese General Hospital (VGH)			
720 Malcolm Blvd Ste 200 ....Valdese NC 28690	800-994-6610	828-874-2251	371-3
Valdosta Daily Times			
PO Box 968 ....Valdosta GA 31603	800-600-4838	229-244-1880	525-2
Valdosta State University			
1500 N Patterson St ....Valdosta GA 31698	800-618-1878	229-333-5800	166
Valence Technology Inc			
12303 Technology Blvd Ste 950 ....Austin TX 78727	888-825-3623	512-527-2900	73
Valentino's			
2601 S 70th St ....Lincoln NE 68506	888-240-8257	402-434-9350	661
Valeo Pharma Inc			
16667 Hymus Blvd Kirkland ....Montreal QC H9H4R9	888-694-0865	514-694-0150	231
Valerie Wilson Travel Inc			
475 Pk Ave S ....New York NY 10016	800-776-1116	212-532-3400	761
Valeritas Inc			
750 Rt 202 S Ste 600 ....Bridgewater NJ 08807	855-384-8848	908-927-9920	470
Valero LP			
PO Box 696000 ....San Antonio TX 78269	800-333-3377	866-297-6093	590
Val-Fab Inc			
218 Jackson St ....Neenah WI 54956	888-482-5322	920-722-1009	475
Valiant Products Corp			
2727 Fifth Ave W ....Denver CO 80204	800-347-2727*	303-892-1234	438
*Cust Svc			
Valiant Steel & Equipment Inc			
6455 Old Peachtree Rd ....Norcross GA 30071	800-939-9905	770-417-1235	487
VALIC (Variable Annuity Life Insurance Co)			
2929 Allen Pkwy ....Houston TX 77019	800-448-2542		388-2
Validar Inc			
800 Maynard Ave S Ste 401 ....Seattle WA 98134	888-784-2929	206-264-9151	179-1
Valin Corp			
555 E California Ave ....Sunnyvale CA 94086	800-774-5630	408-730-9850	355
Valle Verde			
900 Calle de los Amigos .... Santa Barbara CA 93105	800-750-5089	805-883-4000	663
Vallejo Chamber of Commerce			
427 York St ....Vallejo CA 94590	877-397-7936	707-644-5551	137
Vallejo Convention & Visitors Bureau			
289 Mare Island Way ....Vallejo CA 94590	866-921-9277*	707-642-3653	207
*General			
Vallejo Times Herald			
440 Curtola Pkwy ....Vallejo CA 94590	800-600-1141	707-644-1141	525-2
Valley Blox Inc			
210 Stone Spring Rd ....Harrisonburg VA 22801	800-648-6725	540-434-6725	184
Valley Cabinet Inc			
845 Prosper Rd ....De Pere WI 54115	800-236-8981	920-336-3174	114
Valley City Mfg Co Ltd, The			
64 Hatt St ....Dundas ON L9H2G3	800-306-3319	905-628-2253	318-3
Valley City State University			
101 College St SW ....Valley City ND 58072	800-532-8641	701-845-7990	166
Valley Craft			
2001 S Hwy 61 ....Lake City MN 55041	800-328-1480	651-345-3386	465
Valley Electric Assn Inc			
800 E Hwy 372 PO Box 237 ....Pahrump NV 89048	800-742-3330	775-727-5312	245
Valley Electric Supply Corp			
1361 N State Rd PO Box 724 .... Vincennes IN 47591	800-825-7877	812-882-7860	246
Valley First Credit Union			
PO Box 1411 ....Modesto CA 95353	877-549-4567	209-549-8500	219
Valley Forge Christian College			
1401 Charlestown Rd ....Phoenixville PA 19460	800-432-8322	610-935-0450	166
Valley Forge Convention & Visitors Bureau			
1000 First Ave Ste 101 .... King of Prussia PA 19406	888-847-4883*	610-834-1550	207
*General			
Valley Forge Medical Ctr & Hospital			
1033 W Germantown Pk ....Norristown PA 19403	888-539-8500	610-539-8500	717
Valley Forge Military Academy & College			
1001 Eagle Rd ....Wayne PA 19087	800-234-8362	610-989-1300	160
Valley Freightliner Inc			
277 Stewart Rd SW ....Pacific WA 98047	800-523-8014		56
Valley Fresh Inc			
3600 E Linwood Ave ....Turlock CA 95380	800-523-4635	209-669-5600	612
Valley Health System			
223 N Van Dien Ave ....Ridgewood NJ 07450	800-825-5391	201-447-8000	371-3
Valley Hospice Inc			
380 Summit Ave ....Steubenville OH 43952	877-467-7423	740-284-4440	368
Valley Internet Inc			
102 Maple St East ....Fayetteville TN 37334	888-433-1924	931-433-1921	40
Valley Joist			
3019 Gault Ave N ....Fort Payne AL 35967	800-263-0324	256-845-2330	688
Valley Medical Ctr			
400 S 43rd St ....Renton WA 98055	855-923-4633	425-228-3450	371-3
Valley Morning Star			
PO Box 511 ....Harlingen TX 78551	877-786-7612	956-430-6200	525-2
Valley National Bancorp			
1455 Valley Rd ....Wayne NJ 07470	800-522-4100	973-305-8800	357-2
NYSE: VLY			
Valley National Bank			
615 Main Ave ....Passaic NJ 07055	800-522-4100	973-777-6768	69
Valley News			
24 Interchange Dr ....West Lebanon NH 03784	800-874-2226	603-298-8711	525-2
Valley News Dispatch			
210 Fourth Ave ....Tarentum PA 15084	877-698-2553	800-909-8742	525-2
Valley of the Sun United Way			
1515 E Osborn Rd ....Phoenix AZ 85014	877-322-8228	602-631-4800	47-21
Valley Power Systems Inc			
425 S Hacienda Blvd ....City of Industry CA 91745	800-924-4265	626-333-1243	760
Valley Regional Medical Ctr			
100-A E Alton Gloor Blvd ....Brownsville TX 78526	877-422-2030	956-350-7000	371-3
Valley River Inn			
1000 Vly River Way ....Eugene OR 97401	800-543-8266	541-743-1000	376
Valley Rural Electric Co-op Inc			
10700 Fairgrounds Rd			
PO Box 477..................Huntingdon PA 16652	800-432-0680	814-643-2650	245
Valley Telephone Co-op Inc			
752 E Maley St ....Willcox AZ 85643	800-421-5711	520-384-2231	726
Valley Town Crier			
1811 N 23rd St ....McAllen TX 78501	800-285-5667	956-682-2423	525-4
Valley View Casino Ctr			
3500 Sports Arena Blvd ....San Diego CA 92110	800-745-3000	619-224-4171	711
Valley Yellow Pages			
1850 N Gateway Blvd ....Fresno CA 93727	800-350-8887	559-251-8888	628-6
Valley-Dynamo			
7224 Burns Rd ....Richland Hills TX 76118	800-826-7856	972-595-5365	321
Valmark Industries Inc			
7900 National Dr ....Livermore CA 94550	800-770-7074	925-960-9900	410
Valmont Industries Inc			
One Valmont Plz ....Omaha NE 68154	800-825-6668	402-963-1000	273
NYSE: VMI			
Valor Brands LLC			
3159 Royal Dr Ste 360 ....Alpharetta GA 30022	866-949-9098	770-346-9250	155-1
Valor Oil			
1200 Alsop Ln ....Owensboro KY 42303	800-544-5823	270-683-2461	572
Valpak Direct Marketing Systems Inc			
8605 Largo Lakes Dr ....Largo FL 33773	800-237-6266		5
Valparaiso University			
1700 Chapel Dr ....Valparaiso IN 46383	888-468-2576	219-464-5011	166
Valparaiso University School of Law			
651 College Ave ....Valparaiso IN 46383	888-825-7652	219-465-7829	167-1
Valpey Fisher Corp			
75 S St ....Hopkinton MA 01748	800-982-5737	508-435-6831	253
Valspar Refinish Inc			
210 Crosby St ....Minneapolis MN 39466	800-844-3691*	800-845-2500	543
*Cust Svc			
Valtra Inc			
7141 Paramount Blvd ....Pico Rivera CA 90660	800-989-5244	562-949-8625	382
Value City Furniture			
4300 E Fifth Ave ....Columbus OH 43219	888-751-8552	888-672-2411	320
Value Drug Mart Assoc Ltd			
16504 - 121A Ave ....Edmonton AB T5V1J9	888-554-8258	780-453-1701	238
Value Line Asset Management			
220 E 42nd St ....New York NY 10017	800-634-3583	212-907-1500	398
Value Line Inc			
220 E 42nd St ....New York NY 10017	800-634-3583*	212-907-1500	628-9
NASDAQ: VALU ■ *Cust Svc			
ValueClick Inc			
30699 Russell Ranch Rd			
Ste 250 ....Westlake Village CA 91362	877-361-3316	818-575-4500	7
NASDAQ: VCLK			
ValueClick Media			
530 E Montecito St ....Santa Barbara CA 93103	877-361-3316	805-879-1600	7
ValueOptions Inc			
12369 Sunrise Vly Dr Ste C ....Reston VA 20191	877-334-0077	703-390-6800	457
Valve Manufacturers Assn of America (VMA)			
1050 17th St NW Ste 280 ....Washington DC 20036	800-468-3571	202-331-8105	48-13
Valvoline Co			
3499 Blazer Pkwy PO Box 14000 ....Lexington KY 40509	800-832-6825	859-357-7777	534
Vam USA LLC			
19210 Hardy Rd ....Houston TX 77041	800-634-6612	713-479-3200	225
Vamac Inc			
4201 Jacque St ....Richmond VA 23230	800-768-2622	804-353-7811	605
Van Air Systems Inc			
2950 Mechanic St ....Lake City PA 16423	800-840-9906	814-774-2631	383
Van Ausdall & Farrar Inc			
6430 E 75th St ....Indianapolis IN 46250	800-467-7474	317-634-2913	527
Van Bergen & Greener Inc			
1818 Madison St ....Maywood IL 60153	800-621-3889	708-343-4700	247
Van Bortel Aircraft Inc			
4912 S Collins ....Arlington TX 76018	800-759-4295	817-468-7788	760
Van Bortel Subaru			
6327 SR- 96 ....Victor NY 14564	800-724-8872	585-924-5230	56
Van Buren State Park			
12259 Township Rd 218 ....Van Buren OH 45889	866-644-6727	419-832-7662	558
Van Cleef & Arpels Inc			
744 Fifth Ave ....New York NY 10019	877-826-2533	212-896-9284	407
Van Conversions Inc			
925 S Trooper Rd ....Norristown PA 19403	800-884-8267*	610-666-9100	61-7
*Cust Svc			
Van Diest Supply Co			
1434 220th St PO Box 610 .... Webster City IA 50595	800-779-2424	515-832-2366	280
Van Doren Sales Inc			
10 NE Cascade Ave ....East Wenatchee WA 98802	866-886-1837	509-886-1837	297
Van Dyk Group Inc, The			
12800 Long Beach Blvd ....Beach Haven NJ 08008	800-222-0131	609-492-1511	387
Van Dyke Supply Co			
39771 SD Hwy 34 ....Woonsocket SD 57385	800-279-7985	704-279-7985	454
Van Eerden Foodservice Co			
650 Ionia Ave SW ....Grand Rapids MI 49503	800-833-7374	616-475-0900	770
Van Galder Bus Co			
715 S Pearl St ....Janesville WI 53548	800-747-0994	608-752-5407	106
Van Gilder Insurance Corp			
1515 Wine Coop ....Denver CO 80202	800-872-8500*	303-837-8500	387
*General			
Van Horn Inc			
PO Box 380 ....Cerro Gordo IL 61818	800-252-1615	217-677-2131	276
Van Meter Industrial Inc			
850 32nd Ave SW ....Cedar Rapids IA 52404	800-247-1410	319-366-5301	246

	City	State	ZIP	Toll-Free	Phone	Class
Van Roy Coffee Co, The						
4569 Spring Rd	Cleveland	OH	44131	**877-826-7669**	216-749-7069	295-7
Van Ru Credit Corp						
1350 E Touhy Ave Ste 300E	Des Plaines	IL	60018	**800-468-2678**		158
Van Well Nursery						
2821 Grant Rd	East Wenatchee	WA	98802	**800-572-1553**	509-886-8189	293
Van Wezel Performing Arts Ctr						
777 N Tamiami Trl	Sarasota	FL	34236	**800-826-9303**	941-953-3368	565
Van Wingerden International Inc						
4112 Haywood Rd	Mills River	NC	28759	**800-226-3597**	828-891-4116	366
Van Wyk Freight Lines Inc						
PO Box 70	Grinnell	IA	50112	**800-362-2595**	641-236-7551	770
Van Zandt Emrich & Cary Inc						
12401 Plantside Dr	Louisville	KY	40299	**800-928-7355**	502-456-2001	387
Van Zyverden Inc						
8079 Van Zyverden Rd	Meridian	MS	39305	**800-332-2852**	601-679-8274	293
Vanadium Group Corp						
134 Three Degree Rd	Pittsburgh	PA	15237	**800-685-0354**	412-367-6060	261
Vance Air Force Base						
246 Brown Pkwy	Vance AFB	OK	73705	**866-966-1020**	580-213-7476	492-1
Vance Birthplace State Historic Site						
911 Reems Creek Rd	Weaverville	NC	28787	**800-767-1560**	828-645-6706	49-2
Vance Bros Inc						
5201 Brighton PO Box 300107	Kansas City	MO	64130	**800-821-8549**	816-923-4325	45
Vance Publishing Corp						
400 Knightsbridge Pkwy	Lincolnshire	IL	60069	**800-621-2845**	847-634-2600	628-9
Vance-Granville Community College						
South PO Box 39	Creedmoor	NC	27522	**877-823-2378**	919-528-4737	160
Warren County						
PO Box 207	Warrenton	NC	27536	**877-823-2378**	252-257-1900	160
Vancouver Aquarium Marine Science Ctr						
845 Avison Way	Vancouver	BC	V6G3E2	**800-931-1186**	604-659-3474	39
Vancouver Canucks						
800 Griffiths Way	Vancouver	BC	V6B6G1	**877-788-3937**	604-899-7400	707
Vancouver Convention & Exposition Centre (VCEC)						
1055 Canada Pl	Vancouver	BC	V6C0C3	**866-785-8232**	604-689-8232	206
Vancouver Door Company Inc						
203 Fifth St NW	Puyallup	WA	98371	**800-999-3667**	253-845-9581	236
Vancouver School of Theology						
6040 Iona Dr	Vancouver	BC	V6T2E8	**866-822-9031**	604-822-9031	167-3
Vander Haag's Inc						
3809 Fourth Ave W	Spencer	IA	51301	**888-940-5030**	712-262-7000	60
Vanderbilt Beach Resort						
9225 Gulf Shore Dr N	Naples	FL	34108	**800-243-9076**	239-597-3144	660
Vanderbilt Grace						
41 Mary St	Newport	RI	02840	**888-826-4255**	401-846-6200	376
Vanderbilt Kennedy Ctr for Research on Human Development						
21st Ave S	Nashville	TN	37203	**800-772-1213**	615-322-8240	659
Vanderbilt Minerals Corp						
30 Winfield St	Norwalk	CT	06855	**800-243-6064**	203-853-1400	498-3
Vanderbilt Mortgage & Finance Inc						
500 Alcoa Trl	Maryville	TN	37804	**800-970-7250**		502
Vanderbilt University						
2201 W End Ave	Nashville	TN	37240	**800-288-0432**	615-322-7311	166
Vanderbilt University Medical Ctr						
1215 21st Ave S	Nashville	TN	37232	**877-936-8422**	615-322-5000	371-3
Vanderbilt University Press						
2014 Broadway Ste 320	Nashville	TN	37203	**800-627-7377**	615-322-3585	628-4
Vanderbilt University School of Medicine						
215 Light Hall	Nashville	TN	37232	**866-263-8263**	615-322-2145	167-2
VanDyke Software Inc						
4848 Tramway Ridge Dr NE						
Ste 101	Albuquerque	NM	87111	**800-952-5210**	505-332-5700	179-12
Vanee Foods Company Inc						
5418 McDermott Dr	Berkeley	IL	60163	**800-654-6647***	708-449-7300	295-36
*Cust Svc						
Vanguard Brokerage Services						
PO Box 2600	Valley Forge	PA	19482	**800-992-8327**	610-669-1000	681
Vanguard Cleaning Systems Inc						
655 Mariners Island Blvd						
Ste 303	San Mateo	CA	94404	**800-564-6422**	650-287-2400	150
Vanguard East						
1172 Azalea Garden Rd	Norfolk	VA	23502	**800-221-1264**		9
Vanguard Group						
455 Devon Pk Dr	Wayne	PA	19087	**800-662-7447**	610-669-1000	398
Vanguard Trucks Centers						
700 Ruskin Dr	Forest Park	GA	30297	**866-216-7925**		53
Vanguard University of Southern California						
55 Fair Dr	Costa Mesa	CA	92626	**800-722-6279***	714-556-3610	166
*Admissions						
Vanilla Forums Inc						
414 McGill St, Ste 800	Montreal	QC	H2Y1S1	**866-845-0815**		384
Vanir Construction Management Inc						
4540 Duckhorn Dr Ste 300	Sacramento	CA	95834	**888-912-1201**	916-575-8887	458
Vanity Fair Magazine						
Four Times Sq	New York	NY	10036	**800-365-0635**		452-11
Vanity Shop of Grand Forks Inc						
2410 Great Northern Dr	Fargo	ND	58102	**866-247-7920**	701-237-3330	155-6
Vans Inc						
15700 Shoemaker Ave	Santa Fe Springs	CA	90670	**855-909-8267**	562-565-8267	300
Vantage Credit Union (VCU)						
PO Box 4433	Bridgeton	MO	63044	**800-522-6009**	314-298-0055	219
Vantage Mobility International (VMI)						
5202 S 28th Pl	Phoenix	AZ	85040	**800-348-8267**	602-243-2700	61-7
Vantage Products Corp						
960 Almon Rd	Covington	GA	30014	**800-481-3303**	770-788-0136	690
Vantage Trailers Inc						
29335 Hwy Blvd	Katy	TX	77494	**800-826-8245**	281-391-2664	769
Vanteon Corp						
250 Cross Keys Office Pk						
Bldg 250	Fairport	NY	14450	**888-506-5677**	585-419-9555	261
VanTran Industries Inc						
7711 Imperial Dr	Waco	TX	76712	**800-433-3346**	254-772-9740	757
Van-Wall Equipment Inc						
22728 141st Dr PO Box 575	Perry	IA	50220	**800-568-2381**	515-465-5681	274
Vapor Bus International						
1010 Johnson Dr	Buffalo Grove	IL	60089	**866-375-4126**	847-777-6400	641
Varel International						
1625 W Crosby Dr Ste 124	Carrollton	TX	75006	**800-827-3526**	972-242-1160	191
Varflex Corp 512 W Ct St	Rome	NY	13440	**800-648-4014**	315-336-4400	803
Variable Annuity Life Insurance Co (VALIC)						
2929 Allen Pkwy	Houston	TX	77019	**800-448-2542**		388-2
Varian Medical Systems Inc						
3100 Hansen Way	Palo Alto	CA	94304	**800-544-4636**	650-493-4000	379
NYSE: VAR						
Varian Semiconductor Equipment Assoc Inc						
35 Dory Rd	Gloucester	MA	01930	**800-344-1111**	978-282-2000	686
Variety Distributors Inc						
609 Seventh St	Harlan	IA	51537	**800-274-1095**	712-755-2184	327
Variform Inc						
5020 Weston Pkwy Ste 400	Cary	NC	27513	**800-800-2244**	888-975-9436	192-4
Varscona Hotel						
8208 106th St	Edmonton	AB	T6E6R9	**866-465-8150**	780-434-6111	376
Vasamed Inc						
7615 Golden Triangle Dr						
Ste A	Eden Prairie	MN	55344	**800-695-2737**		471
Vascular Solutions Inc						
6464 Sycamore Ct	Minneapolis	MN	55369	**877-979-4300**	763-656-4300	471
NASDAQ: VASC						
Vasomedical Inc						
180 Linden Ave	Westbury	NY	11590	**800-455-3327**	516-997-4600	250
OTC: VASO						
Vassar Bros Medical Ctr						
45 Reade Pl	Poughkeepsie	NY	12601	**877-729-2444**	845-454-8500	371-3
Vassar College						
124 Raymond Ave	Poughkeepsie	NY	12604	**800-827-7270**	845-437-7000	166
Vatterott College Berkeley						
8580 Evans Ave	Berkeley	MO	63134	**888-202-2636**	314-264-1000	788
Vatterott College South County						
12970 Maurer Industrial Dr	Saint Louis	MO	63127	**866-312-8276**	314-843-4200	788
Vatterott College Springfield						
3850 S Campbell	Springfield	MO	65807	**844-244-3304**	417-831-8116	788
Vaughan & Bushnell Manufacturing Co						
11414 Maple Ave PO Box 390	Hebron	IL	60034	**800-435-6000**	815-648-2446	748
Vaughan Chamber of Commerce						
25 Edilcan Dr Ste 2	Vaughan	ON	L4K3S4	**888-943-8937**	905-761-1366	136
Vaughan Company Inc						
364 Monte-Elma Rd	Montesano	WA	98563	**888-249-2467**	360-249-4042	632
Vaughan Regional Medical Ctr						
1015 Medical Ctr Pkwy	Selma	AL	36701	**800-994-6610**	334-418-4100	371-3
Vaughn College of Aeronautics & Technology						
86-01 23rd Ave	East Elmhurst	NY	11369	**800-695-3317**	718-429-6600	166
Vaughn Manufacturing Corp						
26 Old Elm St PO Box 5431	Salisbury	MA	01952	**800-282-8446**	978-462-6683	35
VBCVB (Virginia Beach Convention & Visitor Bureau)						
2101 Parks Ave Ste 500	Virginia Beach	VA	23451	**800-700-7702**	757-385-4700	207
Vbrick Systems Inc						
12 Beaumont Rd	Wallingford	CT	06492	**866-827-4251**	203-265-0044	725
VBT Bicycling & Walking Vacations						
614 Monkton Rd	Bristol	VT	05443	**800-245-3868**	802-453-4811	750
VCA Antech Inc						
12401 W Olympic Blvd	Los Angeles	CA	90064	**800-966-1822**	310-571-6500	782
NASDAQ: WOOF						
VCEC (Vancouver Convention & Exposition Centre)						
1055 Canada Pl	Vancouver	BC	V6C0C3	**866-785-8232**	604-689-8232	206
VCF Films Inc						
1100 Sutton Ave	Howell	MI	48843	**888-905-7680**		593
VCG LLC						
1805 Old Alabama Rd	Roswell	GA	30076	**800-318-4983**	770-246-2300	179-12
VCU (Vantage Credit Union)						
PO Box 4433	Bridgeton	MO	63044	**800-522-6009**	314-298-0055	219
VDA (Virginia Dental Assn)						
3460 Mayland Ct Ste 110	Richmond	VA	23233	**877-726-0850**	804-288-5750	227
VEC (Victoria Electric Co-op Inc)						
102 S Ben Jordan St	Victoria	TX	77901	**800-344-8377**	361-573-2428	245
Vecellio & Grogan Inc						
2251 Robert C Byrd Dr	Beckley	WV	25802	**800-255-6575**	304-252-6575	189-4
Vectech Pharmaceutical Consultants Inc						
12501 E Grand River Ave	Brighton	MI	48116	**800-966-8832**	248-478-5820	261
Vector Marketing Co						
322 Houghton Ave	Olean	NY	14760	**800-828-0448**		363
Vector Security Inc						
2000 Ericsson Dr	Warrendale	PA	15086	**800-832-8575**		683
Vectorply Corp						
3500 Lakewood Dr	Phenix City	AL	36867	**800-577-4521**	334-291-7704	734-1
Vectra Bank Colorado NA						
2000 S Colorado Blvd Ste 2-1200	Denver	CO	80222	**800-232-8948**	720-947-7700	69
Vectra Fitness Inc						
7901 S 190th St	Kent	WA	98032	**800-283-2872**	425-291-9550	267
Vectra Visual						
3950 Business Pk Dr	Columbus	OH	43204	**800-862-2341**	614-351-6868	619
Vectren Corp						
211 NW Riverside Dr						
PO Box 209	Evansville	IN	47708	**800-227-1376**	812-491-4000	357-5
NYSE: VVC						
Vectus Inc						
18685 Main St 101 PMB 360	Huntington Beach	CA	92648	**866-483-2887**		384
Vee Bar Guest Ranch						
38 Vee Bar Ranch Rd	Laramie	WY	82070	**800-483-3227**	307-745-7036	239
Vee Neal Aviation Inc						
148 Aviation Ln Ste 109	Latrobe	PA	15650	**800-278-2710**	724-539-4533	62
Veeco Instruments Inc						
One Terminal Dr	Plainview	NY	11803	**888-248-3326**	516-677-0200	686
NASDAQ: VECO						
Veeder-Root						
125 Powder Forest Dr	Simsbury	CT	06070	**888-262-7539**	860-651-2700	202
Veeder-Root Red Jacket Div						
125 Powder Forest Dr						
PO Box 2003	Simsbury	CT	06070	**800-873-3313**	860-651-2700	632
Veenstra & Kimm Inc						
3000 Westown Pkwy	West Des Moines	IA	50266	**800-241-8000**	515-225-8000	261
Veetronix Inc						
1311 W Pacific Ave	Lexington	NE	68850	**800-445-0007***	308-324-6661	802
*General						
Vega Group						
7220 Washington Ave	New Orleans	LA	70125	**800-771-2979**	504-488-5222	185
Vegetable Juices Inc						
7400 S Narragansett Ave	Chicago	IL	60638	**888-776-9752***	708-924-9500	295-20
*General						
Vegetarian Times						
300 N Continental Blvd						
Ste 650	El Segundo	CA	90245	**800-573-1900**	310-356-4100	452-13
Vehicle Safety Mfg LLC						
408 Central Ave	Newark	NJ	07107	**800-832-7233***	973-643-3000	434
*General						

Company / Address	Toll-Free	Phone	Class
VehSmart Inc 12180 Ridgecrest Rd Ste 412 .... Victorville CA 92395	855-834-7627		638
Veka Inc 100 Veka Dr .... Fombell PA 16123	800-654-5589	724-452-1000	235
Velcro USA Inc 406 Brown Ave .... Manchester NH 03103	800-225-0180	603-669-4880	587
Veldkamp's Flowers 9501 W Colfax Ave .... Lakewood CO 80215	800-247-3730	303-232-2673	292
Vellano Bros Inc Seven Hemlock St .... Latham NY 12110	800-342-9855	518-785-5537	382
Vellumoid Inc 54 Rockdale St .... Worcester MA 01606	800-609-5558	508-853-2500	325
Velsicol Chemical Corp 10400 W Higgins Rd Ste 700 .... Rosemont IL 60018 *Cust Svc	877-847-8351*	847-813-7888	142
VELUX America Inc 450 Old BrickyaRd Rd .... Greenwood SC 29648	866-358-3589	864-941-4700	486
Velvac Inc 2405 S Calhoun Rd .... New Berlin WI 53151	800-783-8871	262-786-0700	59
Velvet Cloak Inn, The 1505 Hillsborough St .... Raleigh NC 27605	888-828-0335	919-828-0333	376
Venchurs Packaging 800 Liberty St .... Adrian MI 49221	855-264-4300	517-263-8937	542
Vendant Inc 26 Parker St .... Newburyport MA 01950	800-714-4900	978-462-0737	179-12
Vendome Group LLC 216 E 45th St Sixth Fl .... New York NY 10017	800-519-3692		628-9
Venetian Resort Hotel & Casino 3355 Las Vegas Blvd S .... Las Vegas NV 89109	866-659-9643	702-414-1000	660
Vengroff Williams & Assoc Inc (VWA) 2099 S State College Bvld .... Anaheim CA 92806	800-238-9655	866-737-4344	158
Venice Gondolier Sun 200 E Venice Ave .... Venice FL 34285	877-818-6204	941-207-1000	525-4
Venkel Ltd 5900 Shepherd Mtn Cove .... Austin TX 78730	800-950-8365	512-794-0081	246
Venoco Inc 370 17th St Ste 3900 .... Denver CO 80202 NYSE: VQ	877-777-4778	303-626-8300	150
VENSURE Employer Services Inc 4140 E Baseline Rd Ste 201 .... Mesa AZ 85206	800-409-8958		357-3
Ventamatic Ltd 100 Washington Rd .... Mineral Wells TX 76067	800-433-1626		15
Ventana Inn 48123 Hwy 1 .... Big Sur CA 93920	800-628-6500	831-667-2331	660
Ventana Medical Systems Inc 1910 Innovation Pk Dr .... Tucson AZ 85755	800-227-2155	520-887-2155	471
Ventas Inc 353 N Clark St Ste 3300 .... Chicago IL 60654 NYSE: VTR	877-483-6827		645
Ventura County Medical Center 3291 Loma Vista Rd .... Ventura CA 93003	800-369-7437	805-652-6000	371-3
Ventura County Star 550 Camarillo Ctr Dr .... Camarillo CA 93010	800-221-7827	805-437-0000	525-2
Ventura Foods LLC 40 Pt Dr .... Brea CA 92821	800-421-6257	714-257-3700	295-30
Ventura Visitors & Convention Bureau 101 S California St .... Ventura CA 93001	800-333-2989	805-648-2075	207
Ventura Youth Correctional Facility 3100 Wright Rd .... Camarillo CA 93010	866-232-5627	805-485-7951	409
Venture Lighting International Inc 32000 Aurora Rd .... Solon OH 44139	800-451-2606	440-248-3510	433
Venture Tape Corp 30 Commerce Rd .... Rockland MA 02370	800-343-1076	781-331-5900	722
VentureOut 575 Pierce St Ste 604 .... San Francisco CA 94117	888-431-6789	415-626-5678	750
Venuelabs 505 Fifth Ave S Ste 300 .... Seattle WA 98104	866-333-7328		390
Venus Swimwear 11711 Marco Beach Dr 1 Venus Plz. .... Jacksonville FL 32224	800-366-7946	904-645-6000	153-16
Venus Wafers Inc 100 Research Rd .... Hingham MA 02043	800-545-4538	781-740-1002	295-9
Vera Bradley Designs 2208 Production Rd .... Fort Wayne IN 46808	800-975-8372	260-482-4673	346
VeraData.com LLC 7680 Cambridge Manor Pl Ste 200 .... Fort Myers FL 33907	800-561-9927		196
Verant Identification Systems Inc 2496 Ridge Rd W Ste 203 .... Rochester NY 14626	866-257-4351	585-214-2451	684
Verbatim Americas LLC 1200 W WT Harris Blvd .... Charlotte NC 28262	800-538-8589	704-547-6500	649
Verdigris Valley Electric Co-op 8901 E 146th St N .... Collinsville OK 74021	800-870-5948	918-371-2584	245
Verdin Co, The 444 Reading Rd .... Cincinnati OH 45202	800-543-0488		151
Verecloud Inc 555 Eldorado Blvd Ste 200 .... Broomfield CO 80021	877-300-2158		178
Verendrye Electric Co-op Inc 615 Hwy 52 .... Velva ND 58790	800-472-2141	701-338-2855	245
Verhalen Inc 500 Pilgrim Way PO Box 11968 .... Green Bay WI 54304	800-895-0071	920-431-8900	192-3
Verichem Laboratories Inc 90 Narragansett Ave .... Providence RI 02907	800-552-5859	401-461-0180	732
Vericon Resources Inc 3550 Engineering Dr Ste 225 ...... Norcross GA 30092	800-795-3784	770-457-9922	397
Verified Audit Circulation Inc 900 Larkspur Landing Cir .... Larkspur CA 94939	800-775-3332	415-461-6006	724
Verified Credentials Inc 20890 Kenbridge Ct .... Lakeville MN 55044	800-473-4934	952-985-7200	626
VeriFone Inc 2099 Gateway Pl Ste 600 .... San Jose CA 95110 NYSE: PAY	800-837-4366	408-232-7800	607
VeriFone Systems Inc 2099 Gateway Pl Ste 600 .... San Jose CA 95110 NYSE: PAY	800-837-4366	408-232-7800	607
Veriforce LLC 19221 I-45 S Ste 200 .... Shenandoah TX 77385	800-426-1604		755
Verigent LLC 149 Plantation Ridge Dr Ste 100 .... Mooresville NC 28117	877-637-6422	704-658-3271	603
Verint Video Solutions 330 South Service Rd .... Melville NY 11747	800-638-5969	800-483-7468	683
Verio Inc 8005 S Chester St Ste 200 .... Centennial CO 80112 *Sales	800-438-8374*	561-912-2555	395
VeriSign Inc 350 Ellis St .... Mountain View CA 94043 NASDAQ: VRSN ■ *Sales	866-893-6565*	650-426-3100	726
VeriStor Systems Inc 3308 Peachtree Industrial Blvd .... Duluth GA 30096	866-956-2948	678-990-1593	174-8
Veritas DGC Inc 10300 Townpark Dr .... Houston TX 77072	800-344-4266	832-351-8300	531
Veritec Inc 2445 Winnetka Ave N .... Golden Valley MN 55427	866-546-1011	763-253-2670	687
Veritext LLC 290 W Mt Pleasant Ave Ste 3200 .... Livingston NJ 07039	800-567-8658		440
Verity Credit Union PO Box 75974 .... Seattle WA 98175	800-444-4589	206-440-9000	219
Verity International Ltd 200 King St W Ste 1301 .... Toronto ON M5H3T4	877-623-2396	416-862-8422	195
Verizon Arena One Verizon Arena Way. ...... North Little Rock AR 72114	800-745-3000	501-340-5660	711
Verizon Business 1 Verizon Way .... Basking Ridge NJ 07920 *Cust Svc	877-297-7816*	908-559-2000	726
Verizon Credit Inc 201 N Tampa St .... Tampa FL 33602	800-483-7988	813-229-6000	216
Verizon Wireless 180 Washington Valley Rd .... Bedminster NJ 07921	800-922-0204	908-306-7000	726
Vermeer Midsouth Inc 1200 Vermeer Cv .... Cordova TN 38018	800-264-4123	901-758-1928	383
Vermilion Community College 1900 E Camp St .... Ely MN 55731	800-657-3608	218-365-7200	160
Vermilion Energy Trust 3500 520 Third Ave SW .... Calgary AB T2P0R3 TSE: VET	866-895-8101	403-269-4884	533
Vermillion County 255 S Main St .... Newport IN 47966	800-340-8155	765-492-5345	336
Vermont Academy PO Box 500 .... Saxtons River VT 05154	800-698-8867	802-869-6229	615
Vermont Chamber of Commerce PO Box 37 .... Montpelier VT 05601	800-451-4279	802-223-3443	138
Vermont Children & Families Dept 103 S Main St 2nd Fl 5 N .... Waterbury VT 05671	800-786-3214	802-241-2100	337-46
Vermont Consumer Assistance Program 146 University Pl .... Burlington VT 05405	800-649-2424	802-656-3183	337-46
Vermont Convention Bureau 60 Main St Ste 100 .... Burlington VT 05401	877-264-3503	802-860-0606	207
Vermont Dept of Libraries 109 State St .... Montpelier VT 05609	888-350-0950	802-828-3261	431-5
Vermont Electric Co-op Inc 42 Wescom Rd .... Johnson VT 05656	800-832-2667	802-635-2331	245
Vermont Emergency Management Office 103 S Main St .... Waterbury VT 05671	800-347-0488	802-241-5000	337-46
Vermont Garden Park 1100 Dorset St .... South Burlington VT 05403	800-538-7476	802-863-5251	96
Vermont Gas Systems Inc 85 Swift St .... South Burlington VT 05403	800-639-8081	802-863-4511	323
Vermont Historic Preservation Div National Life Bldg 6th Fl .... Montpelier VT 05620	800-639-1522	802-828-3213	337-46
Vermont Law School 168 Chelsea St PO Box 96 ...... South Royalton VT 05068	800-227-1395	802-831-1239	167-1
Vermont Life One National Life Dr Sixth Fl. .... Montpelier VT 05620	800-284-3243	802-828-3241	452-22
Vermont Medical Society 134 Main St .... Montpelier VT 05601	800-640-8767	802-223-7898	469
Vermont Mutual Insurance Co 89 State St PO Box 188 .... Montpelier VT 05601	800-451-5000	802-223-2341	388-4
Vermont NEA Today Magazine 10 Wheelock St .... Montpelier VT 05602	800-649-6375	802-223-6375	452-8
Vermont Public Television (VPT) 204 Ethan Allen Ave .... Colchester VT 05446	800-639-7811	802-655-4800	624
Vermont State Dental Society 100 Dorset St Ste 18. .... South Burlington VT 05403	800-300-3046	802-864-0115	227
Vermont State Nurses Assn (VSNA) 100 Dorset St Ste 13. .... South Burlington VT 05403	800-540-9390	802-651-8886	526
Vermont Structural Slate Company Inc Three Prospect St PO Box 98 .... Fair Haven VT 05743	800-343-1900	802-265-4933	715
Vermont Student Assistance Corp (VSAC) PO Box 2000 .... Winooski VT 05404	800-642-3177	802-655-9602	716
Vermont Symphony Orchestra Two Church St Ste 19 .... Burlington VT 05401	800-876-9293	802-864-5741	566-3
Vermont Systems Inc 12 Market Pl .... Essex Junction VT 05452	877-883-8757	802-879-6993	179-10
Vermont Technical College PO Box 500 .... Randolph Center VT 05061	800-442-8821	802-728-1000	788
Vermont Teddy Bear Company Inc 6655 Shelburne Rd .... Shelburne VT 05482	800-988-8277	802-985-3001	752
Vermont Veterans Affairs Office 118 State St .... Montpelier VT 05602	888-666-9844	802-828-3379	337-46
Vermont Vocational Rehabilitation Div 103 S Main St .... Waterbury VT 05671	866-879-6757	802-241-2186	337-46
Vermont's North Country Chamber of Commerce 246 Cswy St .... Newport VT 05855	800-635-4643	802-334-7782	137
Verndale Corp, The 28 Damrell St Ste 300. .... Boston MA 02127	866-942-8376		363
Vernon College 4400 College Dr .... Vernon TX 76384	866-336-9371	940-552-6291	160
Vernon Electric Co-op 110 Saugstad Rd .... Westby WI 54667	800-447-5051	608-634-3121	245
Vernon Parish Library 1401 Nolan Trace .... Leesville LA 71446	800-737-2231	337-239-2027	431-3
Vernon Parish School Board 201 Belview Rd .... Leesville LA 71446	800-621-1742	337-239-3401	676
Vernon Tool Company Ltd 503 Jones Rd .... Oceanside CA 92054	800-452-1542	760-433-5860	450
Vero Beach Press-Journal PO Box 1268 .... Vero Beach FL 32961	866-894-9851	772-562-2315	525-2
Verologix LLC Ste 700 6 Centerpointe Dr .... La Palma CA 90623	800-403-8041		197
Veronica Foods Co 1991 Dennison St .... Oakland CA 94606	800-370-5554	510-535-6833	295-30
Versa Press Inc 1465 Springbay Rd .... East Peoria IL 61611	800-447-7829		618
Versalogic Corp 4211 W 11th Ave .... Eugene OR 97402	800-824-3163	541-485-8575	174-1

Name / Address	City	State	Zip	Toll-Free	Phone	Class
Versant Corp						
255 Shoreline Dr Ste 450	Redwood City	CA	94065	**888-446-4737**	650-232-2400	179-1
NASDAQ: VSNT						
Versar Inc						
6850 Versar Ctr	Springfield	VA	22151	**800-283-7727***	703-750-3000	261
NYSE: VSR ■ *Cust Svc						
Verso Corp						
6775 Lenox Ctr Ct Ste 400	Memphis	TN	38115	**877-837-7606**		550
NYSE: VRS						
Vertafore Inc						
11724 NE 195th St	Bothell	WA	98011	**800-444-4813**	425-402-1000	225
Vertex Engineering Services Inc						
400 Libbey Pkwy	Weymouth	MA	02189	**888-298-5162**	781-952-6000	193
Vertex Inc						
1041 Old Cassatt Rd	Berwyn	PA	19312	**800-355-3500**	610-640-4200	179-1
Vertical Communications Inc						
3940 Freedom Cr Ste 110	Santa Clara	CA	95054	**800-914-9985***	408-404-1600	179-7
OTC: VRCC ■ *Sales						
Vertical Management Systems Inc						
Seven N Fair Oaks Ave						
Second Fl	Pasadena	CA	91103	**800-867-4357**		178
Vertical Vision Financial Marketing LLC						
145 Towne Lk Pkwy	Woodstock	GA	30188	**866-984-1585**		5
Vescio Threading Co						
14002 Anson Ave	Santa Fe Springs	CA	90670	**800-361-4218**	562-802-1868	449
Vesco Oil Corp						
16055 W 12-Mile Rd	Southfield	MI	48076	**800-527-5358**		572
Vescom Corp						
705 Main Rd N	Hampden	ME	04444	**800-841-1769**	207-945-5051	684
Vessel Metrics LLC						
Three Church Cir Ste 325	Annapolis	MD	21401	**888-214-1710**		384
Vestra Resources Inc						
5300 Aviation Dr	Redding	CA	96002	**877-983-7872**	530-223-2585	301
Veteran's Truck Line Inc						
800 Black Hawk Dr	Burlington	WI	53105	**800-456-9476**	262-539-3400	357-2
Veterans Affairs Long Beach Medical Ctr						
5901 E Seventh St	Long Beach	CA	90822	**888-769-8387**	562-826-8000	371-8
Veterans Affairs Medical Ctr						
1700 S Lincoln Ave	Lebanon	PA	17042	**800-409-8771**		371-8
Veterans Affairs Outpatient Clinic						
1515 W Pleasant St Bldg 1	Knoxville	IA	50138	**800-816-8878**	641-842-3101	371-8
Veterans Affairs Puget Sound Medical Ctr						
1660 S Columbian Way	Seattle	WA	98108	**800-329-8387**	206-762-1010	371-8
Veterans Benefits Administration						
810 Vermont Ave NW	Washington	DC	20420	**800-827-1000**		338-17
Veterans for Peace Inc (VFP)						
216 S Meramec Ave	Saint Louis	MO	63105	**877-429-0678**	314-725-6005	47-5
Veterans Health Administration						
Office of Research & Development						
810 Vermont Ave NW MC 12	Washington	DC	20420	**800-827-1000**		338-17
Veterans Home of California-Barstow						
100 E Veterans Pkwy	Barstow	CA	92311	**800-746-0606**	760-252-6200	781
Veterans Home of California-Chula Vista						
700 E Naples Ct	Chula Vista	CA	91911	**800-952-5626**		781
Veterans Home of California-Yountville						
1227 O St	Sacramento	CA	95814	**800-952-5626**		781
Veterans Memorial Library						
301 S University Ave	Mount Pleasant	MI	48858	**888-520-8103**	989-773-3242	431-3
Veterans of Foreign Wars of the US (VFW)						
406 W 34th St	Kansas City	MO	64111	**800-963-3180**	816-756-3390	47-19
Veterinary Pet Insurance Inc						
PO Box 2344	Brea	CA	92822	**800-872-7387**		388-1
Veterinary Pharmacies of America Inc						
2854 Antoine Dr	Houston	TX	77092	**877-838-7979**		575
Vetoquinol Canada Inc						
2000 Ch Georges	Lavaltrie	QC	J5T3S5	**800-363-1700**	450-586-2252	575
VetSelect Animal Hospital						
2150 Old Novi Rd	Novi	MI	48377	**800-462-8749**	248-624-1100	782
VetStrategy						
780 Hwy 6 N	Waterdown	ON	L0R2H1	**866-901-6471**		458
Vetter Health Services Inc						
20220 Harney St	Elkhorn	NE	68022	**800-388-4264**	402-895-3932	458
Vetter Stone Co (VSC)						
23894 Third Ave	Mankato	MN	56001	**800-878-2850**	507-345-4568	715
VFA Inc 99 Bedford St	Boston	MA	02111	**800-693-3132**	617-451-5100	179-1
VFP (Veterans for Peace Inc)						
216 S Meramec Ave	Saint Louis	MO	63105	**877-429-0678**	314-725-6005	47-5
VFUC (Visions Federal Credit Union)						
24 McKinley Ave	Endicott	NY	13760	**800-242-2120**	607-754-7900	219
VFW (Veterans of Foreign Wars of the US)						
406 W 34th St	Kansas City	MO	64111	**800-963-3180**	816-756-3390	47-19
VGH (Valdese General Hospital)						
720 Malcolm Blvd Ste 200	Valdese	NC	28690	**800-994-6610**	828-874-2251	371-3
V&H Inc						
1505 S Central Ave	Marshfield	WI	54449	**800-826-2308**	715-486-8800	56
VHA Inc						
220 Las Colinas Blvd E						
PO Box 140909	Irving	TX	75039	**800-842-5146**	972-830-7845	458
Vi 71 S Wacker Dr	Chicago	IL	60606	**800-421-1442**	312-803-8800	663
VIA Metropolitan Transit						
800 W Myrtle St	San Antonio	TX	78212	**866-362-4200**	210-362-2000	463
VIA Rail Canada Inc						
Three Pl Ville-Marie Ste 500	Montreal	QC	H3B2C9	**800-681-2561**	514-871-6000	640
VIA Technologies Inc						
940 Mission Ct	Fremont	CA	94539	**888-524-9382**	510-683-3300	687
ViaSat Inc						
6155 El Camino Real	Carlsbad	CA	92009	**877-363-7396**	760-476-2200	672
NASDAQ: VSAT						
ViaTech Publishing Solutions						
1440 Fifth Ave	Bay Shore	NY	11706	**800-645-8558**	631-968-8500	85
Viatran Corp						
3829 Forest Pkwy Ste 500	Wheatfield	NY	14120	**800-688-0030**	716-629-3800	253
VIBAC Canada Inc						
12250 Industrial Blvd	Montreal	QC	H1B5M5	**800-557-0192**	514-640-0250	722
Vibro-Meter Inc						
144 Harvey Rd	Londonderry	NH	03053	**800-842-4291**	603-669-0940	22
Viceroy Palm Springs						
415 S BelaRdo Rd	Palm Springs	CA	92262	**866-781-9923**	760-320-4117	376
Viceroy Santa Monica						
1819 Ocean Ave	Santa Monica	CA	90401	**888-622-4567**	310-260-7500	376
Vi-Chem Corp						
55 Cottage Grove St SW	Grand Rapids	MI	49507	**800-477-8501**	616-247-8501	598-2

Name / Address	City	State	Zip	Toll-Free	Phone	Class
Vicon Industries Inc						
89 Arkay Dr	Hauppauge	NY	11788	**800-645-9116***	631-952-2288	638
NYSE: VII ■ *Sales						
Vicor Corp						
25 Frontage Rd	Andover	MA	01810	**800-869-5300**	978-470-2900	253
NASDAQ: VICR						
Victaulic Co						
4901 Kesslersville Rd	Easton	PA	18040	**800-742-5842***	610-559-3300	588
*Sales						
Victor Graphics Inc						
1211 Bernard Dr	Baltimore	MD	21223	**800-899-8303**	410-233-8300	618
Victor L Phillips Co						
4100 Gardner Ave	Kansas City	MO	64120	**800-878-9290**	816-241-9290	355
Victor O Schinnerer & Co Inc						
2 Wisconsin Cir Ste 200	Chevy Chase	MD	20815	**888-867-9327**	301-961-9800	388-5
Victor Printing Inc						
One Victor Way	Sharon	PA	16146	**800-443-2845**	724-342-2106	109
Victor Settings Inc						
25 Brook Ave	Maywood	NJ	07607	**800-322-9008**	201-845-4433	404
Victor Technology LLC						
175 E Crossroads Pkwy	Boling Brook	IL	60440	**800-628-2420**	630-754-4400	117
Victor Valley Community College						
18422 Bear Valley Rd	Victorville	CA	92392	**877-741-8532**	760-245-4271	160
Victoria Advocate						
PO Box 1518	Victoria	TX	77902	**800-234-8108**	361-575-1451	525-2
Victoria Cruises Inc						
57-08 39th Ave	Woodside	NY	11377	**800-348-8084***	212-818-1680	221
*Cust Svc						
Victoria Electric Co-op Inc (VEC)						
102 S Ben Jordan St	Victoria	TX	77901	**800-344-8377**	361-573-2428	245
Victoria Inn Winnipeg						
1808 Wellington Ave	Winnipeg	MB	R3H0G3	**877-842-4667**	204-786-4801	376
Victoria Insurance						
22901 Millcreek Blvd	Cleveland	OH	44122	**800-888-8424**	216-896-6990	388-4
Victoria International Airport						
1962 Canso Rd	North Saanich	BC	V8L5V5	**866-844-4354**	250-656-3987	356
Victoria Regent Hotel, The						
1234 Wharf St	Victoria	BC	V8W3H9	**800-663-7472**	250-386-2211	376
Victoria Theatre						
138 N Main St	Dayton	OH	45402	**888-228-3630**	937-228-3630	565
Victoria Vaudeville Theater						
1228 Market St	Wheeling	WV	26003	**800-505-7464**	304-233-7464	565
Victoria's Secret Stores						
4 Limited Pkwy	Reynoldsburg	OH	43068	**800-411-5116**		155-6
Victorian Condo-Hotel & Conference Ctr						
6300 Seawall Blvd	Galveston	TX	77551	**800-231-6363**	409-740-3555	376
Victorian Trading Co						
15600 W 99th St	Lenexa	KS	66219	**800-700-2035***	913-438-3995	454
*Cust Svc						
Victory Electric Co-op Assn Inc						
3230 N 14th Ave	Dodge City	KS	67801	**800-279-7915**	620-227-2139	245
Victory Funds						
4900 Tiedeman Rd PO Box 182593	Brooklyn	OH	44144	**800-539-3863**		521
Victory Pharma Inc						
11682 El Camino Real	San Diego	CA	92130	**866-427-6819**	858-720-4500	238
Victory Refrigeration Inc						
110 Woodcrest Rd	Cherry Hill	NJ	08003	**800-523-5008**	856-428-4200	655
Victory White Metal Co						
6100 Roland Ave	Cleveland	OH	44127	**800-635-5050**	216-271-1400	480
Victorystore.Com Inc						
5200 SW 30Th St	Davenport	IA	52802	**866-241-2295**		619
Vicwest Corp						
1296 S Service Rd W	Oakville	ON	L6L5T7	**800-265-6583**	905-825-2252	486
Video Display Corp						
1868 Tucker Industrial Rd	Tucker	GA	30084	**800-241-5005***	770-938-2080	174-4
NASDAQ: VIDE ■ *Cust Svc						
Video King Gaming Systems (VKGS LLC)						
2717 N 118 Cir Ste 210	Omaha	NE	68164	**800-635-9912**	402-951-2970	321
Video Symphony Entertraining Inc						
266 E Magnolia Blvd	Burbank	CA	91502	**888-370-7589**	818-557-6500	507
VideoGenie Inc						
314 Lytton Ave Ste 100	Palo Alto	CA	94301	**877-392-2235**		384
Videojet Technologies Inc						
1500 Mittel Blvd	Wood Dale	IL	60191	**800-843-3610***	630-860-7300	383
*Cust Svc						
Videoland Inc						
6808 Hornwood Dr	Houston	TX	77074	**800-877-2900**		34
Videomaker Magazine						
1350 E Ninth St PO Box 4591	Chico	CA	95927	**800-284-3226**	530-891-8410	452-9
VideoMining Corp						
403 S Allen St Ste 101	State College	PA	16801	**800-898-9950**		178
Videotex Systems Inc						
10255 Miller Rd	Dallas	TX	75238	**800-888-4336**	972-231-9200	179-8
Vie de France Yamazaki Inc						
2070 Chain Bridge Rd Ste 500	Vienna	VA	22182	**800-446-4404***	703-442-9205	67
*General						
Viejas Casino						
5000 Willows Rd	Alpine	CA	91901	**800-847-6537**	619-445-5400	132
Vienna Sausage Manufacturing Co						
2501 N Damen Ave	Chicago	IL	60647	**800-366-3647**	773-278-7800	295-26
Vietnam Women's Memorial Foundation Inc						
1735 Connecticut Ave NW						
Third Fl	Washington	DC	20009	**866-822-8963**		49-3
ViewCast Corp						
3701 W Plano Pkwy Ste 300	Plano	TX	75075	**800-540-4119**	972-488-7200	177
ViewCentral						
900 E Hamilton Ave	Campbell	CA	95008	**800-631-1545**	408-626-3800	196
OTC: RMKR						
ViewSonic Corp						
381 Brea Canyon Rd	Walnut	CA	91789	**800-888-8583**	909-444-8888	174-4
Vigilant Insurance Co						
15 Mtn View Rd	Warren	NJ	07059	**800-252-4670***	908-903-2000	388-4
*Claims						
Vignette Corp						
1301 S Mopac Expy Ste 100	Austin	TX	78746	**800-540-7292**	512-741-4300	179-1
Vi-Jon Labs Inc						
8515 Page Ave	Saint Louis	MO	63114	**800-424-9300**	314-427-1000	215
Viking Acoustical Corp						
21480 Heath Ave	Lakeville	MN	55044	**800-328-8385**	952-469-3405	318-1
Viking Corp						
210 N Industrial Pk Dr	Hastings	MI	49058	**800-968-9501**	269-945-9501	283
210 N Industrial Pk Dr	Hastings	MI	49058	**800-968-9501**	269-945-9501	739
Viking Drill & Tool Inc						
355 State St	Saint Paul	MN	55107	**800-328-4655**	651-227-8911	488

Alphabetical Section

	Toll-Free	Phone	Class
Viking Electric Supply Inc			
451 Industrial Blvd W ....Minneapolis MN 55413	800-435-3345	612-627-1300	246
Viking Forest Products LLC			
7615 Smetana Ln ....Eden Prairie MN 55344	800-733-3801	952-941-6512	192-3
Viking Magazine Service Inc			
PO Box 201059 ....Bloomington MN 55420	800-339-9492		363
Viking Materials Inc			
3225 Como Ave SE ....Minneapolis MN 55414	800-682-3942*	612-617-5800	487
*General			
Viking Metal Cabinet Co			
24047 W Lockport St Ste 209..........Plainfield IL 60544	800-776-7767		286
Viking Pools Inc			
121 Crawford Rd PO Box 96..........Williams CA 95987	800-854-7665	530-473-5319	719
Viking Pump Inc			
406 State St ....Cedar Falls IA 50613	800-123-1234	319-266-1741	632
Viking Range Corp			
111 Front St ....Greenwood MS 38930	888-845-4641	662-455-1200	297
Viking River Cruises			
5700 Canoga Ave Ste 200 ....Woodland Hills CA 91367	877-668-4546*	818-227-1234	221
*Cust Svc			
Viking Trailways			
201 Glendale Rd ....Joplin MO 64804	800-400-2779	417-781-2779	107
Viktor Incentives & Meetings			
4020 Copper View Ste 130.........Traverse City MI 49684	800-748-0478	231-947-0882	381
Villa Florence			
225 Powell St ....San Francisco CA 94102	866-980-9684	415-397-7700	376
Villa Gardens			
842 E Villa St ....Pasadena CA 91101	800-958-4552	626-463-5329	663
Villa Julie College			
1525 Green Spring Valley Rd ....Stevenson MD 21153	877-468-6852	410-486-7001	166
Villa Lighting Supply Inc			
2929 Chouteau Ave ....Saint Louis MO 63103	800-325-0963		390
Villa Pueblo Towers			
2501 E 104th Ave ....Thornton CO 80233	888-808-8828	303-255-4100	663
Villa Roma Resort & Conference Ctr			
356 Villa Roma Rd ....Callicoon NY 12723	800-533-6767	845-887-4880	660
Villa Royale Inn			
1620 Indian Trl ....Palm Springs CA 92264	800-245-2314	760-327-2314	376
Village Green Cos			
30833 NW Hwy ....Farmington Hills MI 48334	800-521-2220	248-851-9600	188
Village Green Resort & Gardens			
725 Row River Rd ....Cottage Grove OR 97424	800-343-7666	541-942-2491	660
Village Inn			
400 W 48th Ave ....Denver CO 80216	800-800-3644	303-296-2121	661
Village Latch Inn			
101 Hill St PO Box 3000..........SouthHampton NY 11968	800-545-2824	631-283-2160	376
Village Nurseries			
1589 N Main St ....Orange CA 92867	800-542-0209		322
Village on the Green			
500 Village Pl ....Longwood FL 32779	888-541-3443*	407-682-0230	663
*Mktg			
Village South Inc			
3050 Biscayne Blvd 9th Fl ....Miami FL 33137	800-443-3784	305-573-3784	717
Village Super Market Inc			
733 Mountain Ave ....Springfield NJ 07081	800-746-7748	973-467-2200	342
NASDAQ: VLGEA			
Village Vacances Valcartier			
1860 Valcartier Blvd ....Valcartier QC G0A4S0	888-384-5524	418-844-2200	32
Village, The			
2200 W Acacia Ave ....Hemet CA 92545	800-257-7888	951-658-3369	663
Villages of Lake Sumter Inc			
1000 Lk Sumter Landing ....The Villages FL 32162	800-245-1081	352-753-2270	644
Villagio Inn & Spa			
6481 Washington St ....Yountville CA 94599	800-351-1133	707-944-8877	376
Villas by the Sea Resort			
1175 N Beachview Dr ....Jekyll Island GA 31527	800-841-6262	912-635-2521	660
Villas of Grand Cypress Golf Resort			
One N Jacaranda ....Orlando FL 32836	800-835-7377	407-239-4700	660
Villaume Industries Inc			
2926 Lone Oak Cir ....Saint Paul MN 55121	800-488-3610*	651-454-3610	804
*Cust Svc			
Villere's Florist			
750 Martin Behrman Ave ....Metairie LA 70005	800-845-5373	504-833-3716	292
Villeroy & Boch Tableware Ltd			
Five Vaughn Dr ....Princeton NJ 08540	800-536-2284		359
Vimco Inc			
300 Hansen Access Rd ....King Of Prussia PA 19406	888-468-4626*	610-768-0500	192-1
*Cust Svc			
Vimich Traffic Logistics			
12201 Tecumseh Rd E ....Tecumseh ON N8N1M3	800-284-1045		444
Vin Devers Inc			
5570 Monroe St ....Sylvania OH 43560	888-847-9535	419-885-5111	56
Vincennes University			
1002 N First St ....Vincennes IN 47591	800-742-9198	812-888-4313	160
Jasper 850 College Ave ....Jasper IN 47546	800-809-8852	812-482-3030	160
Vincent Printing Company Inc			
1512 Sholar Ave ....Chattanooga TN 37406	800-251-7262		678
Vindicator, The			
107 Vindicator Sq PO Box 780.......Youngstown OH 44501	877-700-4647	330-747-1471	525-2
Vinely			
One Kendall Sq Bldg 400 B4202.......Cambridge MA 02139	888-294-1128		384
Vinson & Elkins LLP			
1001 Fannin St			
1st City Tower Ste 2500 ....Houston TX 77002	877-610-2009	713-758-2222	425
Vinson Guard Service Inc			
955 Howard Ave ....New Orleans LA 70113	800-441-7899	504-529-2260	684
Vintage Inn Napa Valley			
6541 Washington St ....Yountville CA 94599	800-351-1133*		376
*Cust Svc			
Vintners Inn			
4350 Barnes Rd ....Santa Rosa CA 95403	800-421-2584	707-575-7350	376
Vinylplex Inc			
1800 Atkinson Ave ....Pittsburg KS 66762	877-779-7473	620-231-8290	589
Vinyltech Corp			
201 S 61st Ave ....Phoenix AZ 85043	800-255-3924	602-233-0071	589
Viox Services Inc			
15 W Voorhees St ....Cincinnati OH 45215	888-846-9462	513-948-8469	271
VIP Tour & Charter Bus Co			
129-137 Fox St ....Portland ME 04101	800-231-2222*	207-772-4457	106
*General			
ViPS Inc			
1 W Pennsylvania Ave Ste 700 ....Towson MD 21204	800-242-0230	410-832-8300	179-10

	Toll-Free	Phone	Class
Viracon Inc			
800 Pk Dr ....Owatonna MN 55060	800-533-2080	507-451-9555	328
Virco Manufacturing Corp			
2027 Harpers Way ....Torrance CA 90501	800-448-4726*	310-533-0474	318-3
NASDAQ: VIRC ■ *Cust Svc			
Virgin Atlantic Airways Ltd			
747 Belden Ave ....Norwalk CT 06850	888-747-7474	800-821-5438	25
Virgin Atlantic Cargo			
JFK International Airport			
Bldg 15..............Jamaica NY 11430	800-828-6822	516-775-2600	12
Virgin Atlantic Flying Club			
747 Belden Ave ....Norwalk CT 06850	800-365-9500		26
Virgin Mobile USA Inc			
10 Independence Blvd ....Warren NJ 07059	888-322-1122	908-607-4000	726
Virginia			
Aging & Rehabilitative Services Dept			
8004 Franklin Farms Dr ....Richmond VA 23229	800-552-5019	804-662-7000	337-47
Child Support Enforcement Div			
730 E Broad St ....Richmond VA 23219	800-468-8894		337-47
Criminal Injuries Compensation Fund (CICF)			
PO Box 26927 ....Richmond VA 23261	800-552-4007		337-47
Governor			
1111 E Broad St PO Box 1475 ....Richmond VA 23219	800-828-1120	804-786-2211	337-47
Health Professions Dept			
9960 Mayland Dr Ste 300..........Henrico VA 23233	800-533-1560	804-367-4400	337-47
Housing Development Authority			
601 S Belvidere St ....Richmond VA 23220	800-968-7837	804-782-1986	337-47
Information Technologies Agency (VITA)			
11751 Meadowville Ln ....Chester VA 23836	866-637-8482		337-47
State Parks Div			
203 Governor St Ste 306 ....Richmond VA 23219	800-933-7275*		337-47
*Resv			
Vital Records Div			
2001 Maywill St PO Box 1000 ......Richmond VA 23230	877-572-6333	804-662-6200	337-47
Virginia Assn of Realtors			
10231 Telegraph Rd ....Glen Allen VA 23059	800-755-8271	804-264-5033	647
Virginia Ballet Theatre			
134 W Olney Rd ....Norfolk VA 23510	866-892-6990	757-622-4822	566-1
Virginia Beach Convention & Visitor Bureau (VBCVB)			
2101 Parks Ave Ste 500 ......Virginia Beach VA 23451	800-700-7702	757-385-4700	207
Virginia Beach Convention Ctr			
2101 Parks Ave Ste 500 ....Virginia Beach VA 23451	800-700-7702	757-385-4700	565
Virginia Beach Resort Hotel & Conference Ctr			
2800 Shore Dr ....Virginia Beach VA 23451	800-468-2722	757-481-9000	660
Virginia Chamber of Commerce			
919 E Main St ....Richmond VA 23219	800-847-4882	804-644-1607	138
Virginia College Savings Plan			
9001 Arboretum Pkwy PO Box 607.....Richmond VA 23236	888-567-0540	804-786-0719	716
Virginia Commonwealth University			
910 W Franklin St ....Richmond VA 23284	800-841-3638	804-828-0100	166
Virginia Commonwealth University Cabell Library			
901 Pk Ave PO Box 842033 ....Richmond VA 23284	844-352-7399	804-828-1105	431-6
Virginia Commonwealth University School of Medicine			
1101 E Marshall St			
PO Box 980565..............Richmond VA 23298	800-332-8813	804-828-9629	167-2
Virginia Credit Union			
7500 Boulders View Dr ....Richmond VA 23225	800-285-5051	804-323-6000	219
Virginia Crossings Resort			
1000 Virginia Ctr Pkwy ....Glen Allen VA 23059	888-444-6553	804-727-1400	660
Virginia Democratic Party			
1710 E Franklin St Second Fl ....Richmond VA 23223	800-322-1144	804-644-1966	609-1
Virginia Dental Assn (VDA)			
3460 Mayland Ct Ste 110 ....Richmond VA 23233	877-726-0850	804-288-5750	227
Virginia Dept of Taxation			
1957 Westmoreland St			
PO Box 1115..............Richmond VA 23230	800-828-1120	804-367-8037	524-7
Virginia Episcopal School			
400 VES Rd PO Box 408..........Lynchburg VA 24503	800-937-3582	434-385-3607	615
Virginia Gazette			
216 Ironbound Rd ....Williamsburg VA 23188	800-944-6908	757-220-1736	525-4
Virginia International Terminals Inc			
7737 Hampton Blvd Ste D224 ....Norfolk VA 23505	800-541-2431*	757-440-7000	460
*General			
Virginia Journal of Education			
116 S Third St ....Richmond VA 23219	800-552-9554	804-648-5801	452-8
Virginia Marti College of Art & Design			
11724 Detroit Ave ....Lakewood OH 44107	800-473-4350	216-221-8584	162
Virginia Medical News			
2924 Emerywood Pkwy Ste 300 ....Richmond VA 23294	800-746-6768		452-16
Virginia Medical Society			
4205 Dover Rd ....Richmond VA 23221	800-746-6768	804-353-2721	469
Virginia Military Institute			
319 Letcher Ave ....Lexington VA 24450	800-767-4207	540-464-7211	166
Virginia Mirror Co Inc			
300 Moss St S ....Martinsville VA 24112	800-368-3011	276-632-9816	328
Virginia Natural Gas Inc AGL Resources Inc			
PO Box 4569 ....Atlanta GA 30302	800-633-4236	404-584-4000	775
Virginia Peninsula Chamber of Commerce			
21 Enterprise Pkwy Ste 100 ....Hampton VA 23666	800-462-3204	757-262-2000	137
Virginia Plastics Co Inc			
3453 Aerial Way Dr PO Box 4577.......Roanoke VA 24018	877-351-1699	540-981-9700	803
Virginia Polytechnic Institute & State University			
112 Burruss Hall ....Blacksburg VA 24061	800-555-9292	540-231-6000	166
Virginia Press Services Inc			
11529 Nuckols Rd ....Glen Allen VA 23059	800-849-8717	804-521-7570	616
Virginia Railway Express (VRE)			
1500 King St Ste 202 ....Alexandria VA 22314	800-743-3873	703-684-1001	463
Virginia State Bar			
707 E Main St Ste 1500 ....Richmond VA 23219	800-552-7977	804-775-0500	71
Virginia State University			
One Hayden Dr ....Petersburg VA 23806	800-871-7611*	804-524-5000	166
*Admissions			
Virginia Symphony Orchestra			
861 Glenrock Rd Ste 200 ....Norfolk VA 23502	855-876-7677	757-466-3060	566-3
Virginia Tile Co			
28320 Plymouth Rd ....Livonia MI 48150	877-356-7461	734-762-2400	358
Virginia Transformer Corp			
220 Glade View Dr ....Roanoke VA 24012	800-882-3944	540-345-9892	757
Virginia Union University			
1500 N Lombardy St ....Richmond VA 23220	800-368-3227	804-342-3570	166
Virginia Veterinary Medical Assn (VVMA)			
3801 Westerre Pkwy Ste D ....Henrico VA 23233	800-937-8862	804-346-2611	783
Virginia War Museum			
9285 Warwick Blvd ....Newport News VA 23607	888-493-7386	757-247-8523	513

Name / Address	City	State	ZIP	Toll-Free	Phone	Class
Virginia Wesleyan College 1584 Wesleyan Dr	Norfolk	VA	23502	**800-737-8684**	757-455-3200	166
Virginia West Electric Supply Co (WVES) 250 12-th St W	Huntington	WV	25704	**800-624-3433**	304-525-0361	246
Virginia Western Community College 3094 Colonial Ave PO Box 14007	Roanoke	VA	24038	**855-874-6690**	540-857-8922	160
Virginian Lodge 750 W Broadway PO Box 1052	Jackson Hole	WY	83001	**800-262-4999**	307-733-2792	376
Virginian Suites 1500 Arlington Blvd	Arlington	VA	22209	**866-371-1446**	703-522-9600	376
Virginian-Pilot 150 W Bramelton Ave	Norfolk	VA	23510	**800-446-2004**	757-446-2000	525-2
ViroPharma Inc 730 Stockton Dr *NASDAQ: VPHM*	Exton	PA	19341	**877-841-4559**	610-458-7300	84
Virtela Technology Services Inc 5680 Greenwood Plz Blvd Ste 200	Greenwood Village	CO	80111	**877-803-9629**	720-475-4000	177
Virtexco Corp 977 Norfolk Sq	Norfolk	VA	23502	**800-766-1082**	757-466-1114	187
VirtualBank 3801 PGA Blvd Ste 700 PO Box 109638	Palm Beach Gardens	FL	33410	**877-998-2265**		69
Virtuoso 505 Main St Ste 5	Fort Worth	TX	76102	**800-401-4274**	817-870-0300	762
Visa Inc PO Box 8999 *NYSE: V*	San Francisco	CA	94128	**866-765-9644**	650-432-3200	217
Visalia Convention & Visitors Bureau PO Box 2734	Visalia	CA	93279	**800-524-0303**	559-334-0141	207
Visalia Convention Ctr 303 E Acequia Ave	Visalia	CA	93291	**800-640-4888**	559-713-4000	206
Visara International Inc 2700 Gateway Centre Blvd Ste 600	Morrisville	NC	27560	**888-334-4380**	919-882-0200	177
Viscount Gort Hotel 1670 Portage Ave	Winnipeg	MB	R3J0C9	**800-665-1122**	204-775-0451	376
Viscount Suite Hotel 4855 E Broadway Blvd *Resv	Tucson	AZ	85711	**800-527-9666***	520-745-6500	376
Vishay Intertechnology Inc 63 Lancaster Ave *NYSE: VSH*	Malvern	PA	19355	**800-567-6098**	610-644-1300	687
Visible Systems Corp 201 Spring St *Sales	Lexington	MA	02421	**888-850-9911***	781-778-0200	179-1
Vision Council, The 225 Reinekers Ln Ste 700	Alexandria	VA	22314	**866-826-0290**	703-548-4560	48-4
Vision Financial Corp PO Box 506	Keene	NH	03431	**800-793-0223**		388-5
Vision Ford Lincoln 1500 S White Sands Blvd	Alamogordo	NM	88310	**888-811-2921**	888-285-7516	56
Vision Global AR Ltee 80, Queen St Ste 301	Montreal	QC	H3C2N5	**800-667-7690**	514-879-0020	507
Vision Solutions Inc 15300 Barranca Pkwy	Irvine	CA	92618	**800-683-4667**	949-253-6500	179-12
Vision Technologies Inc 530 McCormick Dr Ste G	Glen Burnie	MD	21061	**866-746-1122**	410-424-2183	178
VisionAIR Inc 5601 Barbados Blvd	Castle Hayne	NC	28429	**800-882-2108**	910-675-9117	179-12
Visionaire Inc 502 Jesse St	Grand Prairie	TX	th St	**866-838-2810**	972-647-1056	56
Visionary Integration Professionals Inc 80 Iron Pt Cir Ste 100	Folsom	CA	95630	**800-434-2673**	916-985-9625	181
Vision-Ease Lens Inc 7000 Sunwood Dr NW *Cust Svc	Ramsey	MN	55303	**800-328-3449***	320-251-8140	535
Visions Federal Credit Union (VFUC) 24 McKinley Ave	Endicott	NY	13760	**800-242-2120**	607-754-7900	219
Vision-Sciences Inc 40 Ramland Rd S *NASDAQ: VSCI*	Orangeburg	NY	10962	**800-874-9975**	845-365-0600	379
Visionworks of America Inc 175 E Houston St	San Antonio	TX	78205	**800-669-1183**	210-340-3531	536
Visit Eau Claire 4319 Jeffers Rd Ste 201	Eau Claire	WI	54703	**888-523-3866**	715-831-2345	207
Visit Jacksonville 208 N Laura St Ste 1	Jacksonville	FL	32202	**800-733-2668**	904-798-9111	207
Visit MercerCounty PA 50 N Water Ave	Sharon	PA	16146	**800-637-2370**	724-346-3771	207
Visit Milledgeville 200 W Hancock St	Milledgeville	GA	31061	**800-653-1804**	478-452-4687	207
Visit Rochester 45 E Ave Ste 400	Rochester	NY	14604	**800-677-7282**	585-279-8300	207
Visit Sarasota County 1777 Main St Ste 302	Sarasota	FL	34236	**800-522-9799**	941-955-0991	207
Visit St Petersburg Clearwater 13805 58th St N Ste 2-200	Clearwater	FL	33760	**877-352-3224**	727-464-7200	207
Visit Topeka Inc 618 S Kansas Ave	Topeka	KS	66603	**800-235-1030**	785-234-1030	207
VisitErie 208 E Bayfront Pkwy Ste 103	Erie	PA	16507	**800-524-3743**	814-454-1000	207
Visiting Nurse Assn 12565 W Ctr Rd Ste 100	Omaha	NE	68144	**800-456-8869**	402-342-5566	368
Visiting Nurse Assn of Morris County (Inc) 175 South St	Morristown	NJ	07960	**800-938-4748**	973-539-1216	360
Visiting Nurse Assn of Ohio 2500 E 22nd St	Cleveland	OH	44115	**877-698-6264**	216-931-1400	368
Visiting Nurse Assn of the Treasure Coast 1110 35th Ln	Vero Beach	FL	32960	**800-749-5760**	772-567-5551	368
Visiting Nurse Assns of America (VNAA) 900 19th St NW Ste 200	Washington	DC	20006	**888-866-8773**	202-384-1420	48-8
Viskase Cos Inc 8205 S Cass Ste 115	Darien	IL	60561	**800-323-8562**	630-874-0700	541
VIST Financial Corp PO Box 6219 PO Box 6219 *NASDAQ: VIST*	Wyomissing	PA	19610	**888-238-3330**	610-926-7632	357-2
Vista Auto 21501 Ventura Blvd	Woodland Hills	CA	91364	**888-887-6530**	888-313-4252	56
Vista Color Lab Inc 2048 Fulton Rd	Cleveland	OH	44113	**800-890-0062**	216-651-2830	341
Vista del Monte 3775 Modoc Rd	Santa Barbara	CA	93105	**800-736-1333**	805-687-0793	663
Vista Grande Villa 2251 Springport Rd	Jackson	MI	49202	**800-889-8499**	517-787-0222	663
Vista Host Inc 10370 Richmond Ave Ste 150	Houston	TX	77042	**800-257-3000**	713-267-5800	376
Vista Metals Inc 65 Ballou Blvd	Bristol	RI	02809	**800-431-4113**	401-253-1772	487
Vista Verde Guest & Ski Ranch PO Box 770465	Steamboat Springs	CO	80477	**800-526-7433**	970-879-3858	239
Vista-pro Automotive LLC 15 Century Blvd Ste 600	Nashville	TN	37214	**888-250-2676**	615-622-2200	509
Vistar/VSA Corp 12650 E Arapahoe Rd Bldg D	Centennial	CO	80112	**800-880-9900**	303-662-7100	296-8
Visteon Corp 1 Village Ctr Dr *NYSE: VC*	Van Buren Township	MI	48111	**866-967-0260**	734-710-5000	59
Vistronix Inc 11091 Sunset Hills Rd Ste 700	Reston	VA	20190	**800-483-2434**	703-463-2059	181
Visual Departures Ltd 2001 W Main St Ste 195	Stamford	CT	06902	**800-628-2003**		584
Visual Learning Systems Inc PO Box 8226	Missoula	MT	59807	**866-968-7857**		178
Visual Marketing Inc 154 W Erie St	Chicago	IL	60654	**800-662-8640**	312-664-9177	233
Visual Planning Corp 71 Meadowbank Dr	Ottawa	NY	12919	**888-884-5444**	613-563-8727	482
Vita Food Products Inc 2222 W Lake St	Chicago	IL	60612	**800-989-8482**	312-738-4500	295-13
Vita Plus Corp 2514 Fish Hatchery Rd	Madison	WI	53713	**800-362-8334**	608-256-1988	442
Vitacost.com Inc 5400 Broken Sound Blvd NW Ste 500	Boca Raton	FL	33487	**800-381-0759**		237
VitaDigest.com 20687-2 Amar Rd Ste 258	Walnut	CA	91789	**877-848-2168**		342
Vital Images Inc 5850 Opus Pkwy Ste 300	Minnetonka	MN	55343	**800-208-3005**	952-487-9500	179-10
Vital Pharmaceuticals Inc 1600 N Pk Dr	Weston	FL	33326	**800-954-7904**	954-641-0570	80-2
Vital Signs Inc 20 Campus Rd	Totowa	NJ	07512	**800-932-0760**	973-790-1330	471
Vitamin Shoppe Inc 2101 91st St *NYSE: VSI*	North Bergen	NJ	07047	**800-223-1216**	201-868-5959	237
Vitaminerals Inc 1815 Flower St	Glendale	CA	91201	**800-432-1856**		295-11
Vita-Mix Corp 8615 Usher Rd	Cleveland	OH	44138	**800-848-2649**	440-235-4840	36
VITAS Healthcare Corp 100 S Biscayne Blvd Ste 400	Miami	FL	33131	**866-418-4827**	305-374-4143	360
VITAS Healthcare Corp of California 16830 Ventura Blvd Ste 315	Encino	CA	91436	**800-582-9533**	818-385-0273	368
VITAS Healthcare Corp of Pennsylvania 1787 Sentry Pk W Bldg 16 Ste 400	Blue Bell	PA	19422	**800-582-9533**	215-542-3000	368
VITAS Healthcare Corp of San Gabriel Cities 1343 N Grand Ave	Covina	CA	91724	**800-582-9533**	626-918-2273	368
VITAS Hospice Care 100 S Biscayne Blvd Ste 1300 *General	Miami	FL	33131	**800-582-9533***	305-374-4143	368
Vitasoy USA Inc 1 New England Way	Ayer	MA	01432	**800-848-2769**	800-462-7692	295-8
Viterbo University 900 Viterbo Dr	La Crosse	WI	54601	**800-848-3726**	608-796-3000	166
Vitesse Semiconductor Corp 741 Calle Plano	Camarillo	CA	93012	**800-642-1687**	805-388-3700	687
Vitran Express Canada Inc 1201 Creditstone Rd *NASDAQ: VTNC*	Concord	ON	L4K0C2	**800-263-9588**	416-798-4965	770
Vitran Express Inc 1600 W Oliver Ave	Indianapolis	IN	46221	**800-366-0150**	317-803-4000	770
Vitria Technology Inc 945 Stewart Dr Ste 200	Sunnyvale	CA	94085	**877-365-5935**		179-1
Vitro Seating Products Inc 201 Madison St *Cust Svc	Saint Louis	MO	63102	**800-325-7093***	314-241-2265	318-1
Viva Group Inc 11766 Wilshire Blvd Ste 300	Los Angeles	CA	90025	**866-432-7368**		384
VIVA Health Inc 1222 14th Ave S	Birmingham	AL	35205	**800-633-1542**	205-939-1718	387
Vivint Solar Inc 4931 North 300 West	Provo	UT	84604	**877-404-4129**		193
Vivitar Corp 195 Carter Dr	Edison	NJ	08817	**800-637-1090**	732-248-1306	584
Vivus Inc 1172 Castro St *NASDAQ: VVUS*	Mountain View	CA	94040	**888-367-6873**	650-934-5200	576
ViWo Inc 10801 National blvd 410	Los Angeles	CA	90064	**877-958-5174**		197
Viziflex Seels Inc 406 N Midland Ave	Saddle Brook	NJ	07663	**800-627-7752**		601
Vizza Wash Services LLC 2208 NW Loop 410 *Cust Svc	San Antonio	TX	78230	**866-493-8822***	210-493-8822	61-1
VJ Technologies Inc 89 Carlough Rd	Bohemia	NY	11716	**800-858-9729**	631-589-8800	732
VJV IT 96 Linwood Plz	Fort Lee	NJ	07024	**800-614-7561**		623
VKGS LLC (Video King Gaming Systems) 2717 N 118 Cir Ste 210	Omaha	NE	68164	**800-635-9912**	402-951-2970	321
VMA (Valve Manufacturers Assn of America) 1050 17th St NW Ste 280	Washington	DC	20036	**800-468-3571**	202-331-8105	48-13
VMC Consulting Corp 11611 Willows Rd NE	Redmond	WA	98052	**877-393-8622**	425-558-7700	712
VMI (Vantage Mobility International) 5202 S 28th Pl	Phoenix	AZ	85040	**800-348-8267**	602-243-2700	61-7
VML Inc 250 NW RichaRds Rd	Kansas City	MO	64116	**800-990-2468**	816-283-0700	4
VNA 154 Hindman Rd	Butler	PA	16001	**877-862-6659**	724-282-6806	368
VNA (VNA Hospice Care) 11440 Olive Blvd Ste 200	Creve Coeur	MO	63141	**800-392-4740**	314-918-7171	368
VNA & Hospice of Northern California 1900 Powell St Ste 300	Emeryville	CA	94608	**800-698-1273**	510-450-8596	368
VNA & Hospice of Southern California 150 W First St Ste 270	Claremont	CA	91711	**888-357-3574**	909-624-3574	368

Name	Address	City	State	ZIP	Toll-Free	Phone	Class
VNA Hospice & Home Health of Lackawanna County	301 Delaware Ave	Olyphant	PA	18447	**800-936-7671**	570-383-5180	368
VNA Hospice Care (VNA)	11440 Olive Blvd Ste 200	Creve Coeur	MO	63141	**800-392-4740**	314-918-7171	368
VNA of Central Jersey (VNACJ)	176 Riverside Ave	Red Bank	NJ	07701	**800-862-3330**		368
VNA of Greater St Louis *Hospice Care*	11440 Olive Blvd Ste 200	Creve Coeur	MO	63141	**800-392-4740**	314-918-7171	368
Vna of Rhode Island	475 Kilvert St	Warwick	RI	02886	**800-638-6274**	401-574-4900	360
VNAA (Visiting Nurse Assns of America)	900 19th St NW Ste 200	Washington	DC	20006	**888-866-8773**	202-384-1420	48-8
VNACJ (VNA of Central Jersey)	176 Riverside Ave	Red Bank	NJ	07701	**800-862-3330**		368
Vogt Ice	1000 W Ormsby Ave Ste 19	Louisville	KY	40210	**800-853-8648**	502-635-3000	655
Vogue Pool Products	7050 St Patrick St	LaSalle	QC	H8N1V2	**800-363-3232**	514-363-3232	719
Voice, The	51180 Bedford St	New Baltimore	MI	48047	**800-561-2248**	586-716-8100	525-4
Voicecom	5900 Windward Pkwy Ste 500	Alpharetta	GA	30005	**888-468-3554**		726
Voices of September 11th	161 Cherry St	New Canaan	CT	06840	**866-505-3911**	203-966-3911	47-5
VoIP Innovations Inc	Eight Penn Ctr W Ste 101	Pittsburgh	PA	15276	**877-478-6471**		384
Volcano Corp	3661 Vly Centre Dr Ste 200	San Diego	CA	92130	**800-228-4728**		472
Volk Corp	23936 Industrial Pk Dr *Cust Svc	Farmington Hills	MI	48335	**800-521-6799***	248-477-6700	462
Volkswagen Canada Inc	777 Bayly St W	Ajax	ON	L1S7G7	**800-822-8987**	905-428-6700	58
Volkswagen of America Inc	3800 Hamlin Rd	Auburn Hills	MI	48326	**800-822-8987**		58
Vollrath Co LLC, The	1236 N 18th St	Sheboygan	WI	53081	**800-624-2051**	920-457-4851	299
Vollwerth & Co	200 Hancock St PO Box 239	Hancock	MI	49930	**800-562-7620**	906-482-1550	295-26
Volt VIEWtech Inc	4761 E Hunter Ave	Anaheim	CA	92807	**888-396-9927**	714-695-3377	458
Volume Transportation Inc	6575 Marshall Blvd	Lithonia	GA	30058	**800-879-5565**	770-482-1400	770
Volunteer State Community College	1480 Nashville Pk	Gallatin	TN	37066	**888-335-8722**	615-452-8600	160
Volunteers of America	1660 Duke St	Alexandria	VA	22314	**800-899-0089**	703-341-5000	47-5
Volusia Speedway Park	1500 W State Rd	De Leon Springs	FL	32130	**800-275-4279**	386-985-4402	508
Volvo Cars of North America	One Volvo Dr *Cust Svc	Rockleigh	NJ	07647	**800-458-1552***	201-768-7300	58
Volvo Honolulu	704 Ala Moana Blvd	Honolulu	HI	96813	**888-892-2456**		509
Volvo Penta of the Americas Inc	1300 Volvo Penta Dr	Chesapeake	VA	23320	**800-522-1959**	757-436-2800	262
Vomela Specialty Co	274 E Fillmore Ave	Saint Paul	MN	55107	**800-645-1012**	651-228-2200	692
Von Duprin Inc	2720 Tobey Dr	Indianapolis	IN	46219	**800-999-0408**		199
Von Paris Enterprises Inc	8691 Larkin Rd	Savage	MD	20763	**800-866-6355**	410-888-8500	512
Von Roll Isola USA	200 Von Roll Dr	Schenectady	NY	12306	**800-654-7652**	518-344-7100	495
Vonage Holdings Corp	23 Main St *NYSE: VG*	Holmdel	NJ	07733	**877-862-2562**	732-528-2600	726
Vontobel Asset Management Inc	1540 Broad Way Ave 38th Fl *General	New York	NY	10036	**800-445-8872***	212-415-7000	398
Voorhees College	213 Wiggins Dr PO Box 678 *Admissions	Denmark	SC	29042	**800-446-6250***	803-780-1234	166
Voorhees Pediatric Facility	1304 Laurel Oak Rd	Voorhees	NJ	08043	**888-873-5437**	856-346-3300	445
Voorwood Co	2350 Barney St PO Box 1127	Anderson	CA	96007	**800-826-0089**	530-365-3311	808
Vornado Air Circulation Systems Inc	415 E 13th St	Andover	KS	67002	**800-234-0604**	316-733-0035	17
Vornado Realty Trust	888 Seventh Ave *NYSE: VNO*	New York	NY	10019	**800-294-1322**	212-894-7000	646
Vorwerk USA Company LP	1964 Corporate Sq	Longwood	FL	32750	**800-562-6726**	407-830-9988	363
Voss Belting & Specialty Co	6965 N Hamlin Ave	Lincolnwood	IL	60712	**800-323-3935**	847-673-8900	367
Voss Lighting	PO Box 22159	Lincoln	NE	68542	**866-292-0529**	402-328-2281	246
Voto Manufacturers Sales Co	500 N Third St PO Box 1299	Steubenville	OH	43952	**800-848-4010**	740-282-3621	382
Vox Medica Inc	601 Walnut St Ste 250-S	Philadelphia	PA	19106	**800-842-6482**	215-238-8500	4
Voya Services Company	1 Orange Way	Windsor	CT	06095	**855-663-8692**	860-580-4646	388-3
Voyageur Inn	200 Viking Dr	Reedsburg	WI	53959	**800-444-4493**	608-524-6431	376
Voyageur Lakewalk Inn	333 E Superior St	Duluth	MN	55802	**800-258-3911**	218-722-3911	376
Voyageurs National Park	360 Hwy 11 E	International Falls	MN	56649	**888-381-2873**	218-286-5258	557
VPI Corp	3123 S Ninth St *Orders	Sheboygan	WI	53081	**800-874-4240***	920-458-4664	593
VPOP Technologies Inc	1772J Avenida de los Arboles PO Box 372 *Sales	Thousand Oaks	CA	91362	**888-811-8767***	805-529-9374	795
VPSI Inc	1220 Rankin Dr	Troy	MI	48083	**800-826-7433**	248-597-3500	463
VPT (Vermont Public Television)	204 Ethan Allen Ave	Colchester	VT	05446	**800-639-7811**	802-655-4800	624
VRE (Virginia Railway Express)	1500 King St Ste 202	Alexandria	VA	22314	**800-743-3873**	703-684-1001	463
Vsa Inc	6929 Seward Ave	Lincoln	NE	68507	**800-888-2140**	402-467-3668	246
VSAC (Vermont Student Assistance Corp)	PO Box 2000	Winooski	VT	05404	**800-642-3177**	802-655-9602	716
VSC (Vetter Stone Co)	23894 Third Ave	Mankato	MN	56001	**800-878-2850**	507-345-4568	715
VSE Corp	2550 Huntington Ave *NASDAQ: VSEC*	Alexandria	VA	22303	**800-455-4873**	703-960-4600	261
VSM Abrasives	1012 E Wabash St *Cust Svc	O'Fallon	MO	63366	**800-737-0176***	636-272-7432	1
VSNA (Vermont State Nurses Assn)	100 Dorset St Ste 13	South Burlington	VT	05403	**800-540-9390**	802-651-8886	526
VT Inc	8500 Shawnee Mission Pkwy	Shawnee Mission	KS	66202	**800-747-4400**	913-895-0200	56
V-T Industries Inc	1000 Industrial Pk	Holstein	IA	51025	**800-827-1615**	712-368-4381	592
VTA (Santa Clara Valley Transportation Authority)	3331 N First St	San Jose	CA	95134	**800-894-9908**	408-321-5555	463
VTech Communications Inc	9590 SW Gemini Dr Ste 120	Beaverton	OR	97008	**800-595-9511**	503-596-1200	725
VTech Electronics North America LLC	1155 W Dundee St Ste 130	Arlington Heights	IL	60004	**800-521-2010**	847-400-3600	752
VTS Investigations LLC	PO Box 971	Elgin	IL	60121	**800-538-4464**		397
Vulcan Corp	30 Garfield Pl Ste 1040 *Sales	Cincinnati	OH	45202	**800-447-1146***	513-621-2850	667
Vulcan Inc	410 E Berry Ave	Foley	AL	36535	**888-846-2728**		151
Vulcan Industries Inc	300 Display Dr	Moody	AL	35004	**888-444-4417**	205-640-2400	233
Vulcan Materials Co	1200 Urban Ctr Dr PO Box 385014 *NYSE: VMC*	Birmingham	AL	35238	**800-615-4331**	205-298-3000	498-5
Vulcan Materials Company Western Div	3200 San Fernando Rd *NYSE: VMC*	Los Angeles	CA	90065	**800-615-4331**	323-258-2777	498-5
Vulcan Service	5724 Hwy 280 E	Birmingham	AL	35242	**800-841-9600**		94
Vutec Corp	11711 W Sample Rd	Coral Springs	FL	33065	**800-770-4700**	954-545-9000	584
VVMA (Virginia Veterinary Medical Assn)	3801 Westerre Pkwy Ste D	Henrico	VA	23233	**800-937-8862**	804-346-2611	783
VWA (Vengroff Williams & Assoc Inc)	2099 S State College Bvld	Anaheim	CA	92806	**800-238-9655**	866-737-4344	158
VWR International	100 Matsonford Rd Bldg 1 Ste 200	Radnorpa	PA	19087	**800-932-5000**	610-431-1700	470
Vystar Credit Union	1802 Kernan Blvd S	Jacksonville	FL	32246	**800-445-6289**	904-777-6000	219

W

Name	Address	City	State	ZIP	Toll-Free	Phone	Class
W & H Co-op Oil Co	407 13th St N	Humboldt	IA	50548	**800-392-3816**	515-332-2782	323
W & H Systems Inc	120 Asia Pl	Carlstadt	NJ	07072	**800-966-6993**	201-933-7840	208
W A Baum Company Inc	620 Oak St	Copiague	NY	11726	**888-281-6061**	631-226-3940	471
W Atlee Burpee Co	300 Pk Ave *Cust Svc	Warminster	PA	18974	**800-333-5808***	215-674-4900	685
W L Halsey Grocery Company Inc	PO Box 6485	Huntsville	AL	35824	**800-621-0240**	256-772-9691	296-8
W M Sprinkman Corp	4234 Courtney Rd PO Box 390	Franksville	WI	53126	**800-816-1610**	262-835-2390	383
W O W Logistics Co	3040 W Wisconsin Ave	Appleton	WI	54914	**800-236-3565**	920-734-9924	791-1
W. N. Morehouse Truck Line Inc	4010 Dahlman Ave	Omaha	NE	68107	**800-228-9378**	402-733-2200	676
W. R. Vernon Produce Co	PO Box 4054	Winston Salem	NC	27101	**800-222-6406**	336-725-9741	296-7
W.B. Nelson State Recreation Site	5580 S Coast Hwy	Newport	OR	97366	**800-551-6949**		558
W.F. Taylor Company Inc	11545 Pacific Ave	Fontana	CA	92337	**800-397-4583**	951-360-6677	3
W/M Display Group	1040 W 40th St	Chicago	IL	60609	**800-443-2000**	773-254-3700	286
WA Brown & Son Inc	209 Long Meadow Dr	Salisbury	NC	28147	**800-438-2316**	704-636-5131	655
WA Charnstrom Co	5391 12th Ave E *Cust Svc	Shakopee	MN	55379	**800-328-2962***		465
WA Roosevelt Co	2727 Commerce St	La Crosse	WI	54603	**800-279-2726**	608-781-2000	605
WAAY-TV Ch 31 (ABC)	1000 Monte Sano Blvd SE	Huntsville	AL	35801	**888-407-4747**	256-533-3131	730-34
Wabash College	410 W Wabash Ave PO Box 352	Crawfordsville	IN	47933	**800-345-5385**	765-361-6225	166
Wabash County Rural Electric Membership Corp	350 Wedcor Ave	Wabash	IN	46992	**800-563-2146**	260-563-2146	245
Wabash Electric Supply Inc	1400 S Wabash St	Wabash	IN	46992	**800-552-7777**	260-563-4146	246
Wabash National Corp	1000 Sagamore PkwyS PO Box 6129 *NYSE: WNC* ■ *Sales	Lafayette	IN	47903	**800-937-4784***	765-771-5300	769
Wabash Technologies	1375 Swan St PO Box 829	Huntington	IN	46750	**800-487-6865**	260-355-4100	223
Wabash Telephone Co-op Inc	PO Box 299	Louisville	IL	62858	**800-228-9824**	618-665-3311	726

Name	Address	City	State	ZIP	Toll-Free	Phone	Class
Wabash Valley Manufacturing Inc	505 E Main St	Silver Lake	IN	46982	**800-253-8619**	260-352-2102	318-4
Wabash Valley Service Company Inc	909 N Ct St	Grayville	IL	62844	**888-869-8127**	618-375-2311	276
WABC-AM 770 (N/T)	2 Penn Plaza 17th Fl	New York	NY	10121	**800-848-9222**	212-613-3800	636-76
WABCO Locomotive Products	1001 Air Brake Ave *Cust Svc	Wilmerding	PA	15148	**877-922-2627***	412-825-1000	641
Wabtec Corp	1001 Air Brake Ave *NYSE: WAB* ■ *Cust Svc	Wilmerding	PA	15148	**877-922-2627***	412-825-1000	641
WACG-FM 90.7 (NPR)	2500 Walton Way	Atlanta	GA	30904	**800-222-4788**	706-737-1661	636-8
Wachovia Bank	11601 Wilshire Blvd	Los Angeles	CA	90025	**800-225-5935**	310-477-8004	69
Wachter Inc	16001 W 99th St	Lenexa	KS	66219	**800-462-9638**	913-541-2500	775
Wachters' Organic Sea Products Corp	550 Sylvan St	Daly City	CA	94014	**800-682-7100**	650-757-9851	787
Wacker Chemical Corp	3301 Sutton Rd	Adrian	MI	49221	**888-922-5374**	517-264-8500	142
Wacker Neuson	N 92 W 15000 Anthony Ave	Menomonee Falls	WI	53051	**800-770-0957**	262-255-0500	191
Waco	2546 Gen Armistead Ave	Norristown	PA	19403	**800-928-7159**	610-630-4800	18
Waco Convention & Visitors Bureau	100 Washington Ave	Waco	TX	76701	**800-321-9226**	254-750-5810	207
Waco Tribune-Herald	900 Franklin Ave	Waco	TX	76701	**800-678-8742**	254-757-5757	525-2
Wacoal America	50 Polito Ave	Lyndhurst	NJ	07071	**800-922-6250**	212-743-9600	153-17
Wacoal Europe	65 Sprague St	Hyde Park	MA	02136	**800-733-8964**	617-361-7559	153-17
Wacom Technology Corp	1311 SE Cardinal Ct	Vancouver	WA	98683	**800-922-6613**	360-896-9833	174-2
Waco-McLennan County Library	1717 Austin Ave	Waco	TX	76701	**800-433-7300**	254-750-5941	431-3
Waddell & Reed Financial Inc	6300 Lamar Ave *NYSE: WDR*	Overland Park	KS	66201	**888-923-3355**	913-236-2000	398
Wade College	1950 N Stemmons Fwy Ste 2026	Dallas	TX	75207	**800-624-4850**	214-637-3530	788
Wade Tours Inc	797 Burdeck St	Schenectady	NY	12306	**800-955-9233**	518-355-4500	750
Wade-Trim Group Inc	500 Griswold Ave Ste 2500	Detroit	MI	48226	**800-482-2864**	313-961-3650	261
WAEV-FM 97.3 (AC)	245 Alfred St	Savannah	GA	31408	**800-543-3548**	912-964-7794	636-100
WAFB-TV Ch 9 (CBS)	844 Government St	Baton Rouge	LA	70802	**888-677-2900**	225-215-4700	730-8
Waffle House Inc	5986 Financial Dr	Norcross	GA	30071	**877-992-3353**	770-729-5700	661
Waggoners Trucking	5220 Midland Rd	Billings	MT	59101	**800-999-9097**	406-248-1919	770
Wagner College	1 Campus Rd *Admissions	Staten Island	NY	10301	**800-221-1010***	718-390-3400	166
Wagner Oil Co	500 Commerce St Ste 600	Fort Worth	TX	76102	**800-457-5332**	817-335-2222	529
Wagner Spray Tech Corp	1770 Fernbrook Ln	Plymouth	MN	55447	**800-328-8251**	763-553-7000	173
Wago Corp	N120 W19129 Freistadt Rd	Germantown	WI	53022	**800-346-7245**		204
Wah Chang	1600 Old Salem Rd NE	Albany	OR	97321	**888-926-4211**	541-926-4211	480
Wahl Clipper Corp	2900 Locust St	Sterling	IL	61081	**800-767-9245**	815-625-6528	215
Wahl Refractory Solutions LLC	767 OH-19	Fremont	OH	43420	**800-837-9245**	419-334-2658	654
Wahlco Inc	2722 S Fairview St	Santa Ana	CA	92704	**800-423-5432**	714-979-7300	449
Wahlcometroflex Inc	29 Lexington St	Lewiston	ME	04240	**800-272-6652**	207-784-2338	475
Wah-Sha-She State Park	HC 75 Hwy 60	Copan	OK	74022	**800-622-6317**	918-532-4334	558
WAIglobal	411 Eagleview Blvd Ste 100	Exton	PA	19341	**800-877-3340**	484-875-6600	60
Waikiki Gateway Hotel	2070 Kalakaua Ave	Honolulu	HI	96815	**866-444-4352**	808-955-3741	376
Waikiki Parc Hotel	2233 Helumoa Rd	Honolulu	HI	96815	**800-422-0450**	808-921-7272	376
Waikiki Resort Hotel	2460 Koa Ave	Honolulu	HI	96815	**800-367-5116**	808-922-4911	376
Wailea Beach Marriott Resort & Spa	3700 Wailea Alanui Dr	Wailea	HI	96753	**800-845-5279**	808-879-1922	660
WAIQ-TV Ch 26 (PBS)	1255 Madison Ave	Montgomery	AL	36107	**800-239-5239**	205-328-8756	730-44
Waisman Ctr	University of Wisconsin 1500 Highland Ave	Madison	WI	53705	**888-428-8476**	608-263-5940	659
WAKA-TV Ch 8 (CBS)	3020 Eastern Blvd	Montgomery	AL	36116	**800-467-0401**	334-271-8888	730-44
Wake Correctional Ctr	1000 Rock Quarry Rd	Raleigh	NC	27610	**866-719-0108**	919-733-7988	213
Wake Electric	100 S Franklin St PO Box 1229	Wake Forest	NC	27588	**800-474-6300**	919-863-6300	245
Wake Forest University School of Medicine	Medical Ctr Blvd	Winston-Salem	NC	27157	**800-445-2255**	336-716-4264	167-2
Wakefern Food Corp	600 York St	Elizabeth	NJ	07207	**800-746-7748**	908-527-3300	296-8
Wakefield's Inc	1212 Quintard Ave PO Box 400	Anniston	AL	36201	**800-333-1552**	256-237-9521	155-2
Wako Chemicals USA Inc	1600 Bellwood Rd	Richmond	VA	23237	**800-992-9256**	804-271-7677	231
WAKR-AM 1590 (N/T)	1795 W Market St	Akron	OH	44313	**888-723-9688**	330-869-9800	636-2
Wakunaga of America Company Ltd	23501 Madero	Mission Viejo	CA	92691	**800-421-2998**	949-855-2776	787
WAKW-FM 93.3 (Rel)	6275 Collegevue Pl PO Box 24126	Cincinnati	OH	45224	**888-542-9393**	513-542-9259	636-27
Walch Education	40 Walch Dr	Portland	ME	04103	**800-558-2846**	207-772-2846	628-2
Wald Relocation Services Ltd	8708 W Little York Rd Ste 190	Houston	TX	77040	**800-527-1408**	713-512-4800	512
Waldbaums	Two Paragon Dr	Montvale	NJ	07645	**866-443-7374**		342
Walden Farms	1209 W St Georges Ave	Linden	NJ	07036	**800-229-1706**		295-19
Walden Woods Project, The	44 Baker Farm Rd	Lincoln	MA	01773	**800-554-3569**	781-259-4700	47-13
Waldinger Corp	2601 Bell Ave	Des Moines	IA	50321	**800-473-4934**	515-284-1911	190-14
Waldoch Crafts Inc	13821 Lake Dr NE	Forest Lake	MN	55025	**800-328-9259**	651-464-3215	61-7
Waldon Mfg LLC	201 W Oklahoma Ave	Fiarview	OK	73737	**866-283-2759**	580-227-3711	465
Waldorf College	106 S Sixth St	Forest City	IA	50436	**800-292-1903**	641-585-2450	166
Waldorf Towers, The	100 E 50th St	New York	NY	10022	**800-925-3673**	212-355-3100	376
Wale Apparatus Co Inc	400 Front St	Hellertown	PA	18055	**800-334-9253**	610-838-7047	331
Walgreen Co	200 Wilmot Rd	Deerfield	IL	60015	**800-925-4733***	847-940-2500	237
Walker Art Ctr	1750 Hennepin Ave	Minneapolis	MN	55403	**888-339-4496**	612-375-7600	513
Walker Baptist Medical Ctr	3400 Hwy 78 E	Jasper	AL	35501	**877-474-4243**	205-387-4000	371-3
Walker County Board of Education	1710 Alabama Ave PO Box 311	Jasper	AL	35501	**866-276-7735**	205-387-0555	676
Walker County Chamber of Commerce	204 19th St E Ste 101 *General	Jasper	AL	35501	**800-384-4571***	205-384-4571	137
Walker Information Inc	301 Pennsylvania Pkwy	Indianapolis	IN	46280	**800-334-3939**	317-843-3939	461
Walker Magnetics Group Inc	20 Rockdale St	Worcester	MA	01606	**800-962-4638**	508-853-3232	488
Walker MS Inc	20 Third Ave	Somerville	MA	02143	**800-528-2787**	617-776-6700	79-1
Walker Process Equipment	840 N Russell Ave	Aurora	IL	60506	**800-992-5537**	630-892-7921	794
Walker Stainless Equipment Co LLC	625 W State St	New Lisbon	WI	53950	**800-356-5734**	608-562-7500	297
Walker Tool & Die Inc	2411 Walker Ave NW	Grand Rapids	MI	49544	**877-925-5378**	616-453-5471	747
Walker's Furniture Inc	2611 N Woodruff Rd	Spokane	WA	99206	**866-667-6655**	509-535-1995	320
WALK-FM 97.5 (AC)	66 Colonial Dr	Patchogue	NY	11772	**877-263-7995**	631-475-5200	636
Walking Adventures International	14612 NE Fourth Plain Rd Ste A	Vancouver	WA	98682	**800-779-0353**		750
WalkMed Infusion LLC	96 Inverness Dr E Ste J	Englewood	CO	80112	**800-578-0555**	303-420-9569	471
Wall Lenk Corp	1950 Dr Martin Luther King Jr *Cust Svc	Kinston	NC	28501	**888-527-4186***	252-527-4186	748
Wall Street Journal, The	1211 Ave of the Americas *General	New York	NY	10036	**800-568-7625***	212-416-2000	525-3
Walla Walla Community College	500 Tausick Way	Walla Walla	WA	99362	**877-992-9922**	509-522-2500	160
Walla Walla University	204 S College Ave	College Place	WA	99324	**800-541-8900**	509-527-2327	166
Walla Walla Valley Chamber of Commerce	29 E Sumach St	Walla Walla	WA	99362	**866-826-9422**	509-525-0850	137
Wallace Community College	1141 Wallace Dr	Dothan	AL	36303	**800-543-2426**	334-983-3521	160
Wallace Community College Selma	3000 Earl Goodwin Pkwy	Selma	AL	36703	**855-428-8313**	334-876-9227	788
Wallace Hardware Company Inc	5050 S Davy Crockett Pkwy PO Box 6004	Morristown	TN	37815	**800-776-0976**	423-586-5650	348
Wallace Roberts & Todd LLC	1700 Market St 28th Fl	Philadelphia	PA	19103	**800-978-4450**	215-732-5215	261
Wallace State Community College	801 Main St	Hanceville	AL	35077	**866-350-9722**	256-352-8000	160
Wallace Thomson Hospital	322 W S St *General	Union	SC	29379	**800-277-5633***	864-301-2000	371-3
Wallace Welch Willingham	300 First Ave S Fifth Fl	Saint Petersburg	FL	33701	**800-783-5085**	727-522-7777	387
Wallach & Company Inc	107 W Federal St	Middleburg	VA	20117	**800-237-6615**	540-687-3166	388-7
Wallco Inc	53 E Jackson St # 55	Wilkes Barre	PA	18701	**800-392-5526**	570-823-6181	687
Wallcoverings Assn	401 N Michigan Ave Ste 2200	Chicago	IL	60611	**800-575-8016**	312-644-6610	48-4
Waller Truck Company Inc	400 S McCleary Rd	Excelsior Springs	MO	64024	**800-821-2196**	816-629-3400	770
Wallick & Volk Mortgage	222 E 18th St	Cheyenne	WY	82001	**800-280-8655**	307-634-5941	214
Wallingford Buick GMC	1122 Old N Colony Rd *Cust Svc	Wallingford	CT	06492	**888-765-9107***	203-269-8741	56
Wallingford Coffee Mills Inc	11401 Rockfield Ct	Cincinnati	OH	45241	**800-533-3690**	513-771-4570	79-2
Wallis Oil Co	106 E Washington St	Cuba	MO	65453	**800-467-6652**	573-885-2277	323
Walls 360 Inc	5054 Bond St	Las Vegas	NV	89118	**888-244-9969**		390
Walman Optical Company Inc	801 12th Ave N	Minneapolis	MN	55411	**800-873-9256**	612-520-6000	535
Wal-Mart Foundation	702 SW Eigth St *NYSE: WMT*	Bentonville	AR	72716	**800-438-6278**	479-273-4000	303
Wal-Mart Stores Inc	702 SW Eigth St *NYSE: WMT* ■ *Cust Svc	Bentonville	AR	72716	**800-925-6278***	479-273-4000	229
Wal-Mart Stores Inc Supercenter Div	702 SW Eigth St	Bentonville	AR	72716	**800-925-6278**	479-273-4000	229
Walmart.com	7000 Marina Blvd	Brisbane	CA	94005	**800-925-6278**		229

Name / Address	City	State	ZIP	Toll-Free	Phone	Class
Walpole Co-op Bank Inc 982 Main St PO Box 350	Walpole	MA	02081	**877-322-8228**	508-668-1080	69
Walpole Inc PO Box 1177	Okeechobee	FL	34973	**800-741-6500**	863-763-5593	770
Walpole Woodworkers Inc 767 E St Rt 7 *Cust Svc	Walpole	MA	02081	**800-343-6948***	508-668-2800	318-4
Walsh Group Inc 929 W Adams St	Chicago	IL	60607	**800-957-1842**	312-563-5400	187
Walsh University 2020 E Maple St *Admissions	North Canton	OH	44720	**800-362-9846***	330-499-7090	166
Walsworth Publishing Co 306 N Kansas Ave	Marceline	MO	64658	**800-972-4968**	660-376-3543	628-2
Walt Disney World Dolphin 1500 Epcot Resorts Blvd	Lake Buena Vista	FL	32830	**888-828-8850**	407-934-4000	660
Walt Disney World Swan 1200 Epcot Resorts Blvd	Lake Buena Vista	FL	32830	**888-828-8850**	407-934-4000	660
Walt Whitman House State Historic Site 330 Mickle Blvd	Camden	NJ	08103	**800-843-6420**		558
Waltek Inc 14310 Sunfish Lk Blvd	Ramsey	MN	55303	**800-937-9496**	763-427-3181	305
Walter B Jones Alcohol & Drug Abuse Treatment Ctr 2577 W Fifth St	Greenville	NC	27834	**800-422-1884**	252-830-3426	717
Walter E Smithe Furniture Inc 1251 W Thorndale Ave	Itasca	IL	60143	**800-948-4263**	630-285-8000	318-2
Walter Haas & Sons Inc 123 W 23rd St	Hialeah	FL	33010	**800-552-3845**	305-883-2257	692
Walter Oil & Gas Corp 1100 Louisiana St Ste 200	Houston	TX	77002	**888-756-7880**	713-659-1221	531
Walter P Moore 1301 Mckinney St Ste 1100	Houston	TX	77010	**800-364-7300**	713-630-7300	261
Walter P Reuther Psychiatric Hospital 30901 Palmer Rd	Westland	MI	48186	**877-765-8388**	734-367-8400	371-5
Walter USA Inc N22 W23855 Ridgeview Pkwy W	Waukesha	WI	53188	**800-945-5554**		488
Walters State Community College 500 S Davy Crockett Pkwy	Morristown	TN	37813	**800-225-4770**	423-585-2600	160
Walters Wholesale Electric Co 2825 Temple Ave	Signal Hill	CA	90755	**800-700-5483**	562-988-3100	246
Waltham Services Inc 817 Moody St	Waltham	MA	02453	**866-974-7378**	781-893-1810	570
Walton Press (WP) 402 Mayfield Dr	Monroe	GA	30655	**800-354-0235**	770-267-2596	548
Walton-De Funiak Library 3 Cir Dr	DeFuniak Springs	FL	32435	**800-342-0141**	850-892-3624	431-3
WAMC/Northeast Public Radio 318 Central Ave	Albany	NY	12206	**800-323-9262**	518-465-5233	624
WAMC-FM 90.3 (NPR) 318 Central Ave	Albany	NY	12206	**800-323-9262**	518-465-5233	636-3
Wanke Cascade Co 6330 N Cutter Cir	Portland	OR	97217	**800-365-5053**	503-289-8609	358
Wanzek Construction Inc 2028 2nd Ave NW	West Fargo	ND	58078	**877-492-6935**	701-282-6171	187
WAPE-FM 95.1 (CHR) 8000 Belfort Pkwy Ste 100	Jacksonville	FL	32256	**800-475-9595**	904-245-8500	636-56
WAPS-FM 91.3 (AAA) 65 Steiner Ave	Akron	OH	44301	**877-411-3662**	330-761-3099	636-2
Wapusk National Park of Canada PO Box 127	Churchill	MB	R0B0E0	**888-773-8888**	204-675-8863	556
War Resisters League 339 Lafayette St	New York	NY	10012	**800-975-9688**	212-228-0450	47-5
Ward Cedar Log Homes 37 Bangor St PO Box 72 *Cust Svc	Houlton	ME	04730	**800-341-1566***		105
Ward Trucking Corp PO Box 1553	Altoona	PA	16603	**800-458-3625**	814-944-0803	770
Ward's Marine Electric Inc 617 SW Third Ave	Fort Lauderdale	FL	33315	**800-545-9273**	954-523-2815	775
Ward-Kraft Inc 2401 Cooper St	Fort Scott	KS	66701	**800-821-4021**	620-223-5500	109
Ware County Board of Education 1301 Bailey St PO Box 1789	Waycross	GA	31502	**800-419-3191**	912-283-8656	187
Warehouse Home Furnishings Distributors Inc 1851 Telfair St PO Box 1140	Dublin	GA	31021	**800-456-0424**		320
Warm Co 5529 186th Pl SW	Lynnwood	WA	98037	**800-234-9276**	425-248-2424	734-1
Warner Bros Entertainment Inc 4000 Warner Blvd	Burbank	CA	91522	**800-778-7879**	818-954-1853	507
Warner Electric 449 Gardner St	South Beloit	IL	61080	**800-825-6544**	815-389-3771	613
Warner Manufacturing Co 13435 Industrial Pk Blvd	Minneapolis	MN	55441	**800-444-0606**	763-559-4740	748
Warner Pacific College 2219 SE 68th Ave	Portland	OR	97215	**800-804-1510**	503-517-1020	166
Warner Southern College 13895 Hwy 27	Lake Wales	FL	33859	**800-309-9563**		166
Warner Theatre 811 State St	Erie	PA	16501	**800-352-0050**	814-452-4857	565
Warner Vineyards Inc 706 S Kalamazoo St	Paw Paw	MI	49079	**800-756-5357**	269-657-3165	79-3
Warnors Ctr for the Performing Arts 1400 Fulton St	Fresno	CA	93721	**800-320-1733**	559-264-2848	565
Warp Bros Flex-O-Glass Inc 4647 W Augusta Blvd	Chicago	IL	60651	**800-621-3345**	773-261-5200	541
Warrantech Corp Inc 2200 Hwy 121	Bedford	TX	76021	**800-833-8801**	817-785-6601	364
Warranty Group Inc, The 175 W Jackson 11th Fl	Chicago	IL	60604	**800-621-2130**	312-356-3000	388-5
Warranty Life Services Inc 4152 Meridian St Ste 105-29	Bellingham	WA	98226	**888-927-7269**		390
Warren Co, The 2201 Loveland Ave	Erie	PA	16506	**800-562-0357**		294
Warren Communications News Inc 2115 Ward Ct NW	Washington	DC	20037	**800-771-9202**	202-872-9200	628-9
Warren Correctional Institution 379 Collins Rd PO Box 728	Manson	NC	27553	**866-719-0108**	252-456-3400	213
Warren County Rural Electric Membership Corp 15 Midway St PO Box 37	Williamsport	IN	47993	**800-872-7319**	765-762-6114	245
Warren County Visitors Bureau 22045 Rt 6	Warren	PA	16365	**800-624-7802**	814-726-1222	207
Warren County-Vicksburg Public Library 700 Veto St	Vicksburg	MS	39180	**800-721-7222**	601-636-6411	431-3
Warren Electric Co-op Inc (WEC) 320 E Main St PO Box 208	Youngsville	PA	16371	**800-364-8640**	814-563-7548	245
Warren Equities Inc 27 Warren Way	Providence	RI	02905	**877-623-6765**	401-781-9900	357-3
Warren Fabricating & Machining 3240 Mahoning Ave NW	Warren	OH	44483	**800-827-0596**	330-847-0596	449
Warren Oil Company Inc PO Box 1507	Dunn	NC	28335	**800-779-6456**	910-892-6456	572
Warren Resources Inc 1114 Ave of the Americas 34th Fl *NASDAQ: WRES*	New York	NY	10036	**877-587-9494**	212-697-9660	529
Warren Rural Electric Co-op Corp 951 Fairview Ave	Bowling Green	KY	42101	**866-319-3234**	270-842-6541	245
Warren Transport Inc 210 Beck Ave *General	Waterloo	IA	50701	**800-553-2007***	319-233-6113	770
Warren Wilson College 701 Warren Wilson Rd *Admissions	Swannanoa	NC	28778	**800-934-3536***	828-298-3325	166
Warrior Custom Golf Inc 15 Mason Ste A	Irvine	CA	92618	**800-600-5113**	949-699-2499	702
Warsaw Chemical Company Inc Argonne Rd PO Box 858	Warsaw	IN	46580	**800-548-3396**	574-267-3251	149
Wartburg College 100 Wartburg Blvd	Waverly	IA	50677	**800-772-2085**	319-352-8264	166
Wartburg Theological Seminary 333 Wartburg Pl	Dubuque	IA	52003	**800-225-5987**	563-589-0200	167-3
Wartsila North America Inc 16330 Air Ctr Blvd	Houston	TX	77032	**877-927-8745**	281-233-6200	262
Warwick Denver Hotel 1776 Grant St	Denver	CO	80203	**800-203-3232**	303-861-2000	376
Warwick Melrose Hotel 3015 Oak Lawn Ave	Dallas	TX	75219	**800-521-7172**	214-521-5151	376
Warwick New York Hotel 65 W 54th St	New York	NY	10019	**800-223-4099**	212-247-2700	376
Warwick Seattle Hotel 401 Lenora St	Seattle	WA	98121	**800-426-9280**	206-443-4300	376
Warwick Valley Telephone Co 47 Main St PO Box 592 *NASDAQ: WWVY* ■ *Cust Svc	Warwick	NY	10990	**800-952-7642***	845-986-8080	726
Wasatch Academy 120 South 100 West	Mount Pleasant	UT	84647	**800-634-4690**	435-462-1400	615
Wasco Products Inc 22 Pioneer Ave PO Box 351	Sanford	ME	04073	**800-388-0293**	207-324-8060	328
Wash Depot Holdings Inc 14 Summer St	Malden	MA	02148	**800-339-3949**	781-324-2000	61-1
WASH Multifamily Laundry Systems 100 N Sepulveda Blvd 12th Fl *General	El Segundo	CA	90245	**800-421-6897***		37
Washburn University 1700 SW College Ave	Topeka	KS	66621	**800-736-9060**	785-670-1010	166
WASH-FM 97.1 (AC) 1801 Rockville Pk Fifth Fl	Rockville	MD	20852	**866-927-4361**	240-747-2700	636
Financial Institutions Dept PO Box 41200	Olympia	WA	98504	**877-746-4334**	360-902-8703	337-48
Health Dept PO Box 47890	Olympia	WA	98504	**800-525-0127**	360-236-4501	337-48
Historical Society 1911 Pacific Ave	Tacoma	WA	98402	**888-238-4373**	253-272-3500	337-48
Housing Finance Commission 1000 Second Ave Ste 2700	Seattle	WA	98104	**800-767-4663**	206-464-7139	337-48
Natural Resources Dept 1111 Washington St SE PO Box 47000	Olympia	WA	98504	**800-258-5990**	360-902-1000	337-48
Revenue Dept PO Box 47478	Olympia	WA	98504	**800-647-7706**	360-705-6714	337-48
Washington *Social & Health Services Dept* PO Box 45130	Olympia	WA	98504	**800-737-0617**	360-902-8400	337-48
State Parks & Recreation Commission 1111 Israel Rd SW *Campground Resv	Olympia	WA	98504	**888-226-7688***	360-902-8500	337-48
Utilities & Transportation Commission 1300 S Evergreen Pk Dr SW PO Box 47250	Olympia	WA	98504	**888-333-9882**	360-664-1160	337-48
Veterans Affairs Dept PO Box 41150	Olympia	WA	98504	**800-562-2308**	360-753-5586	337-48
Vocational Rehabilitation Div PO Box 45340	Olympia	WA	98504	**800-637-5627**	360-438-8000	337-48
Washington & Jefferson College 60 S Lincoln St	Washington	PA	15301	**888-926-3529**	724-222-4400	166
Washington & Lee University 204 W Washington St	Lexington	VA	24450	**800-221-3943**	540-458-8710	166
Washington Adventist University 7600 Flower Ave	Takoma Park	MD	20912	**800-835-4212**	301-891-4000	166
Washington Bible College/Capital Bible Seminary 6511 Princess Garden Pkwy	Lanham	MD	20706	**877-793-7227**	301-552-1400	159
Washington Bill Status PO Box 40600	Olympia	WA	98504	**800-562-6000**	360-786-7573	430
Washington Chain & Supply Inc 2901 Utah Ave S PO Box 3645	Seattle	WA	98124	**800-851-3429**	206-623-8500	760
Washington College 300 Washington Ave	Chestertown	MD	21620	**800-422-1782**	410-778-2800	166
Washington Convention Ctr Authority 801 Mt Vernon Pl NW	Washington	DC	20001	**800-368-9000**	202-249-3000	206
Washington Corp PO Box 16630	Missoula	MT	59808	**800-832-7329**	406-523-1300	261
Washington County Chamber of Commerce 314 S Austin St	Brenham	TX	77833	**888-273-6426**	979-836-3695	137
Washington County Library 8595 Central Pk Pl	Woodbury	MN	55125	**800-657-3750**	651-275-8500	431-3
Washington County Mental Health Services Inc (WCMHS) PO Box 647	Montpelier	VT	05601	**800-649-2642**	802-229-0591	350
Washington County Tractor Inc PO Box 1619	Brenham	TX	77834	**800-256-5655**	979-836-4591	274
Washington County Visitors Assn 11000 SW Stratus St Ste 170	Beaverton	OR	97008	**800-537-3149**	503-644-5555	207
Washington Court Hotel 525 New Jersey Ave NW	Washington	DC	20001	**800-321-3010**	202-628-2100	376

	Toll-Free	Phone	Class
Washington DC Accommodations 2201 Wisconsin Ave NW Ste C-120 ... Washington DC 20007	800-503-3330	202-293-8000	373
Washington DC Convention & Tourism Corp 901 Seventh St NW 4th Fl ... Washington DC 20001	800-422-8644	202-789-7000	207
Washington Dental Service 9706 Fourth Ave NE ... Seattle WA 98115	800-367-4104	206-522-1300	388-3
Washington Duke Inn & Golf Club 3001 Cameron Blvd ... Durham NC 27705	800-443-3853	919-490-0999	376
Washington Education Assn Inc 32032 Weyerhaeuser Way S PO Box 9100 ... Federal Way WA 98001	800-622-3393	253-941-6700	48-5
Washington Electric Co-op 40 Church Street ... East Montpelier VT 05602	800-932-5245	802-223-5245	245
Washington Electric Co-op Inc 406 Colegate Dr ... Marietta OH 45750	877-594-9324	740-373-2141	245
Washington Electric Membership Corp 258 N Harris St ... Sandersville GA 31082	800-552-2577	478-552-2577	245
Washington Express Service LLC 12240 Indian Creek Ct Ste 100 ... Beltsville MD 20705	800-939-5463	301-210-0899	539
Washington Federal Inc 425 Pike St ... Seattle WA 98101 *NASDAQ: WAFD*	800-324-9375	206-624-7930	357-2
Washington Gas & Light Co 6801 Industrial Rd ... Springfield VA 22151	800-752-7520	703-750-4440	775
Washington Gas Energy Services Inc (WGES) 13865 Sunrise Vly Dr Ste 200 ... Herndon VA 20171	888-884-9437	703-793-7500	775
Washington Group Consultants LLC PO Box A ... Fairfax VA 22031	800-236-7323	703-591-6600	195
Washington Internet Daily 2115 Ward Ct NW ... Washington DC 20037	800-771-9202	202-872-9200	524-3
Washington Lawyer Magazine 1101 K St NW Ste 200 ... Washington DC 20005	877-333-2227	202-737-4700	452-15
Washington Local Schools 3505 W Lincolnshire Blvd ... Toledo OH 43606	800-462-3589	419-473-8251	187
Washington Missourian 14 W Main St PO Box 336 ... Washington MO 63090	888-239-7701	636-239-7701	525-4
Washington Mystics 627 N Glebe Rd Ste 850 ... Arlington VA 22203	877-329-9622	202-266-2200	705-2
Washington National Insurance Co 11825 N Pennsylvania St ... Carmel IN 46032	866-595-2255		388-2
Washington Pavilion of Arts & Science 301 S Main PO Box 984 ... Sioux Falls SD 57104	877-927-4728	605-367-6000	513
Washington Plaza Hotel 10 Thomas Cir NW Massachusetts Ave at 14th St ... Washington DC 20005	800-424-1140	202-842-1300	376
Washington Post 1150 15th St NW ... Washington DC 20071	800-627-1150	202-334-6000	525-2
Washington Post Writers Group 1150 15th St NW ... Washington DC 20071	800-879-9794	202-334-6375	523
Washington Real Estate Investment Trust (WRIT) 6110 Executive Blvd Ste 800 ... Rockville MD 20852 *NYSE: WRE*	800-565-9748	301-984-9400	646
Washington School District Inc 201 Allison Ave ... Washington PA 15301	855-846-8376	724-223-5085	676
Washington Square Hotel 103 Waverly Pl ... New York NY 10011	800-222-0418	212-777-9515	376
Washington State Bar Assn 1325 Fourth Ave Ste 600 ... Seattle WA 98101	800-945-9722	206-727-8200	71
Washington State Bar News 1325 Fourth Ave Ste 600 ... Seattle WA 98101	800-945-9722		452-15
Washington State Employees Credit Union 400 E Union Ave ... Olympia WA 98501	800-562-0999	360-943-7911	219
Washington State Lottery PO Box 43000 ... Olympia WA 98504	800-732-5101	360-664-4720	447
Washington State Medical Assn 2033 Sixth Ave Ste 1100 ... Seattle WA 98121	800-552-0612	206-441-9762	469
Washington State Nurses Assn (WSNA) 575 Andover Pk W Ste 101 ... Seattle WA 98188	800-231-8482	206-575-7979	526
Washington State Pharmacy Assn 411 Williams Ave S ... Renton WA 98057	800-562-6000	425-228-7171	578
Washington State University PO Box 641040 ... Pullman WA 99164	888-468-6978	509-335-3564	166
Spokane 310 N Riverpoint Blvd PO Box 1495 ... Spokane WA 99210	800-233-3247	509-358-7978	166
Washington State Veterinary Medical Assn 8024 Bracken Pl SE ... Snoqualmie WA 98065	800-399-7862	425-396-3191	783
Washington Trust Bancorp Inc 23 Broad St ... Westerly RI 02891 *NASDAQ: WASH*	800-475-2265	401-348-1200	357-2
Washington University in Saint Louis One Brookings Dr ... Saint Louis MO 63130	800-638-0700	314-935-5000	166
Washington University in Saint Louis Olin Library 1 Brookings Dr PO Box 1061 ... Saint Louis MO 63130	800-779-3272	314-935-5400	431-6
Washington-Saint Tammany Electric Co-op 950 Pearl St PO Box N ... Franklinton LA 70438	866-672-9773	985-839-3562	245
Wasserstrom Co 477 S Front St ... Columbus OH 43215	866-634-8927	614-228-6525	299
Waste Industries USA Inc 3301 Benson Dr Ste 601 ... Raleigh NC 27609	800-647-9946	919-325-3000	792
Waste Management Inc 1001 Fannin St Ste 4000 ... Houston TX 77002 *NYSE: WM*	800-633-7871	713-512-6200	792
Wastecorp Inc PO Box 70 ... Grand Island NY 14072	888-829-2783		632
WatchGuard Technologies Inc 505 Fifth Ave S Ste 500 ... Seattle WA 98104	800-734-9905*	206-613-6600	177
Watco Companies LLC 315 W Third St ... Pittsburg KS 66762	866-386-9321	620-231-2230	641
Water Country USA 176 Water Country Pkwy ... Williamsburg VA 23185	800-343-7946		32
Water Environment Federation (WEF) 601 Wythe St ... Alexandria VA 22314	800-666-0206	703-684-2400	47-13
Water Furnace International Inc 9000 Conservation Way ... Fort Wayne IN 46809	800-222-5667	260-478-5667	354
Water Pik Inc 1730 E Prospect Rd ... Fort Collins CO 80553	800-525-2774		228
Water Saver Faucet Co 701 W Erie St 2nd Fl ... Chicago IL 60654 *Parts	800-973-7278*	312-666-5500	602
Water Street 131 N Water St ... Edgartown MA 02539	800-225-6005	508-627-7000	662
Water's Edge Resort & Spa 1525 Boston Post Rd PO Box 688 ... Westbrook CT 06498	800-222-5901	860-399-5901	660
Waterbury Button Co 1855 Peck Ln ... Cheshire CT 06410	800-928-1812		587
Waterco USA Inc 1864 Tobacco Rd ... Augusta GA 30906 *General	800-277-4150*	706-793-7291	794
Waterford Township Public Library 5168 Civic Ctr Dr ... Waterford MI 48329	800-318-2596	248-674-4831	431-3
Waterford, The 601 Universe Blvd ... Juno Beach FL 33408	888-335-1678	561-627-3800	663
Waterfront Hotel 10 Washington St ... Oakland CA 94607	888-842-5333	510-836-3800	376
Waterfront Playhouse 312 Wall St ... Key West FL 33040	800-435-7352	305-294-5015	565
Waterfront Warehouse Four Pinkney St ... Annapolis MD 21401	800-603-4020	410-267-7619	49-2
Waterloo Cedar Falls Courier PO Box 540 ... Waterloo IA 50701	800-798-1730	319-291-1421	525-2
Waterloo Convention & Visitor Bureau 500 Jefferson St ... Waterloo IA 50701	800-728-8431	319-233-8350	207
Waterloo Industries Inc 139 W Forest Hill Ave ... Oak Creek WI 53154 *Cust Svc	800-558-5528*		483
Watermark Learning Inc 7300 Metro Blvd Ste 207 ... Minneapolis MN 55439	800-646-9362	952-921-0900	195
Watermark Medical LLC 1641 Worthington Rd Ste 320 ... West Palm Beach FL 33409	877-710-6999		250
Waterous Co 125 Hardman Ave ... South Saint Paul MN 55075	800-488-1228	651-450-5000	632
Waters Corp 34 Maple St ... Milford MA 01757 *NYSE: WAT*	800-252-4752	508-478-2000	416
Waters Edge Hotel 25 Main St ... Tiburon CA 94920	888-662-9555	415-789-5999	376
Watersaver Company Inc 5870 E 56th Ave ... Commerce City CO 80022	800-525-2424	303-289-1818	593
Watertech Whirlpool Bath & Spa 2507 Plymouth Rd ... Johnson City TN 37601	800-289-8827	423-926-1470	372
Waterton Lakes Lodge Resort 101 Clematis Ave PO Box 4 ... Waterton Park AB T0K2M0	888-985-6343	403-859-2150	660
Watertown Daily Times 260 Washington St ... Watertown NY 13601	800-642-6222	315-782-1000	525-2
Watertown Free Public Library 123 Main St ... Watertown MA 02472	800-829-3676	617-972-6431	431-3
Watertown Public Library 100 S Water St ... Watertown WI 53094	800-829-3676	920-262-4090	431-3
Waterville Valley Resort One Ski Area Rd PO Box 540 ... Waterville Valley NH 03215	800-468-2553	603-236-8311	660
Waterworks Operating Company LLC 60 Backus Ave ... Danbury CT 06810	800-899-6757	203-546-6000	602
Watkins College of Art & Design 2298 Rose Parks Blvd ... Nashville TN 37228	866-877-6395	615-383-4848	162
Watkins Mfg Corp 1280 Pk Ctr Dr ... Vista CA 92081	800-999-4688		372
Watlow Winona 1241 Bundy Blvd ... Winona MN 55987	800-928-5692	507-454-5300	203
Watonwan Farm Service 233 W Ciro St ... Truman MN 56088	800-657-3282	507-776-2831	275
Watrous Nursing Ctr 9 Neck Rd ... Madison CT 06443	800-353-5368	203-245-9483	445
Watson Foods Company Inc 301 Heffernan Dr ... West Haven CT 06516	800-388-3481	203-932-3000	295-16
Watson Furniture Group Inc 26246 Twelve Trees Ln NW ... Poulsbo WA 98370	800-426-1202	360-394-1300	318-1
Watson Group Financial Corp 6501 Highland Rd ... Waterford MI 48327	800-666-1572	248-666-2700	216
Watson Label Products Corp 10616 Trenton Ave ... Saint Louis MO 63132	800-678-6715	314-493-9300	619
Watson Realty Co 9101 Camino Media ... Bakersfield CA 93311	800-777-0646	661-327-5161	643
Watson Rice & Co 301 Rt 17 N 4th Fl ... Rutherford NJ 07070	800-945-5985	201-460-4590	2
Watsontown Trucking Company Inc 60 Belford Blvd ... Milton PA 17847	800-344-0313	570-522-9820	770
Watts Fluidair Inc Nine Cutts Rd ... Kittery ME 03904	877-467-4323	207-439-9511	778
Watts Radiant Inc 4500 E Progress Pl ... Springfield MO 65803	800-276-2419	417-864-6108	14
Watts Towers of Simon Rodia State Historic Park 1765 East 107th Street 1925 Las Virgenes ... Calabasas CA 91302	866-240-4655	213-847-4646	558
WAUK-AM 540 (Sports) 310 W Wisconsin Ave Ste 100 ... Milwaukee WI 53203	800-990-3776	414-273-3776	636-68
Waukesha Bearings Corp W 231 N 2811 Roundy Cir E Ste 200 ... Pewaukee WI 53072	888-832-3517	262-506-3000	613
Waukesha Cherry-Burrell Corp (WCB) 611 Sugar Creek Rd ... Delavan WI 53115	800-252-5200	262-728-1900	632
Waukesha County Chamber of Commerce 2717 N Grandview Blvd Ste 204 ... Waukesha WI 53188	800-937-2965	262-542-4249	137
Waukesha County Freeman 801 N Barstow St PO Box 7 ... Waukesha WI 53187	800-762-6219	262-542-2501	525-2
Waukesha Foundry Company Inc 1300 Lincoln Ave ... Waukesha WI 53186	800-727-0741	262-542-0741	306
Waukesha Memorial Hospital 725 American Ave ... Waukesha WI 53188	800-326-2011	262-928-1000	371-3
Waupaca Elevator Co Inc 1726 N BallaRd Rd ... Appleton WI 54911	800-238-8739	920-991-9082	256
Waupaca Foundry 1955 Brunner Dr PO Box 249 ... Waupaca WI 54981	800-669-6820	715-258-6611	306
Wausau Central Wisconsin Convention & Visitors Bureau (CWCVB) 10204 Pk Plz Ste B ... Rothschild WI 54474	888-948-4748	715-355-8788	207
Wausau Chemical Corp 2001 N River Dr ... Wausau WI 54403	800-950-6656	715-842-2285	142
Wausau Daily Herald 800 Scott St ... Wausau WI 54403	800-477-4838	715-842-2101	525-2
Wausau Financial Systems Inc 875 Indianhead Dr PO Box 37 ... Mosinee WI 54455	800-937-0017	715-359-0427	179-10

	Toll-Free	Phone	Class
Wausau Paper Corp			
100 Paper Pl ....Mosinee WI 54455	**800-723-0008**	715-693-4470	545-1
NYSE: WPP			
Wausau Paper Corp Printing & Writing Paper Div			
One Clark's Island ....Wausau WI 54403	**800-723-0008**	715-675-3361	545-2
Wausau Paper Corp Specialty Paper Div			
100 Paper Pl ....Mosinee WI 54455	**800-723-0008**	715-693-4470	545-1
Wausau Tile Inc			
PO Box 1520 ....Wausau WI 54402	**800-388-8728**	715-359-3121	184
WaUSAu Window & Wall Systems			
7800 International Dr ....Wausau WI 54401	**877-678-2983**	715-845-2161	475
Wauwinet, The			
120 Wauwinet Rd PO Box 2580 ....Nantucket MA 02584	**800-426-8718**	508-228-0145	376
WAV Inc			
2380 Prospect Dr ....Aurora IL 60504	**800-678-2419**	630-818-1000	177
WAVA-AM 780 (Rel)			
1901 N Moore St Ste 200 ....Arlington VA 22209	**888-976-6924**	703-807-2266	636
WAVA-FM 105.1 (Rel)			
1901 N Moore St Ste 200 ....Arlington VA 22209	**888-293-9282**	703-807-2266	636
Wave Systems Corp			
480 Pleasant St ....Lee MA 01238	**800-928-3638**	413-243-1600	179-1
NASDAQ: WAVX			
Wavedivision Holdings LLC			
401 Kirkland Prk Pl Ste 500 ....Kirkland WA 98033	**866-928-3123**	425-576-8200	726
WaveLink Corp			
1011 Western Ave Ste 601 ....Seattle WA 98104	**888-697-9283***	206-274-4280	179-7
*Tech Supp			
Waverly Plastics Company Inc			
PO Box 801 ....Waverly IA 50677	**800-454-6377**	319-352-3333	65
WAVE-TV Ch 3 (NBC)			
725 S Floyd St PO Box 32970 ....Louisville KY 40203	**800-223-2579**	502-585-2201	
WAVV-FM 101.1 (AC)			
11800 Tamiami Trl E ....Naples FL 34113	**866-310-9288**	239-775-9288	636-73
Wawa Inc			
260 W Baltimore Pike ....Media PA 19063	**800-444-9292**	610-358-8000	205
Waxman Industries Inc			
24460 Aurora Rd ....Bedford Heights OH 44146	**800-201-7298**	440-439-1830	605
OTC: WXMN			
WAXN-TV Ch 64 (ABC)			
1901 N Tryon St ....Charlotte NC 28206	**888-664-6835**	704-335-4786	730-14
WAXQ-FM 104.3 (CR)			
32 Ave of the Americas ....New York NY 10013	**888-872-1043**	212-377-7900	636-76
Way Station Inc			
230 W Patrick St PO Box 3826 ....Frederick MD 21705	**888-549-0629**	301-662-0099	47-15
Wayest Safety Inc			
3750 N I-44 Service Rd ....Oklahoma City OK 73112	**800-256-1003**	405-942-7101	670
Wayland Academy			
101 N University Ave ....Beaver Dam WI 53916	**800-860-7725**	920-885-3373	615
Wayland Baptist University			
1900 W Seventh St ....Plainview TX 79072	**800-588-1928**	806-291-1000	166
Waymouth Farms Inc			
5300 Boone Ave ....New Hope MN 55428	**800-527-0094**	763-533-5300	295-8
Wayne Bank			
717 Main St ....Honesdale PA 18431	**800-598-5002**	570-253-1455	357-2
Wayne Combustion Systems			
801 Glasgow Ave ....Fort Wayne IN 46803	**855-929-6327**	260-425-9200	354
Wayne Community College			
3000 Wayne Memorial Dr			
PO Box 8002 ....Goldsboro NC 27533	**866-414-5064**	919-735-5151	160
Wayne County Boot Camp			
PO Box 182 ....Clifton TN 38425	**855-876-7283**	931-676-3345	213
Wayne County Convention & Visitors Bureau			
428 W Liberty St ....Wooster OH 44691	**800-362-6474**	330-264-1800	207
Wayne Farms Enterprises LLC			
1020 County Rd 114 ....Jack AL 36346	**800-241-3110**	334-897-3435	612
Wayne Farms LLC			
4110 Continental Dr ....Oakwood GA 30566	**800-392-0844**		10-7
Wayne Hummer Investments LLC			
222 S Riverside Pz 28th Fl ....Chicago IL 60606	**800-621-4477**	866-943-4732	681
Wayne J Griffin Electric Inc			
116 Hopping Brook Rd ....Holliston MA 01746	**800-421-0151**		190-4
Wayne Mills Co Inc			
130 W Berkley St ....Philadelphia PA 19144	**800-220-8053**	215-842-2134	734-5
Wayne Savings Bancshares Inc			
151 N Market St ....Wooster OH 44691	**800-414-1103**	330-264-5767	357-2
NASDAQ: WAYN			
Wayne State College			
1111 Main St ....Wayne NE 68787	**800-228-9972**	402-375-7000	166
Wayne State University			
42 W Warren ....Detroit MI 48202	**877-978-4636**	313-577-3577	166
Wayne-Dalton Corp			
One Door Dr PO Box 67 ....Mount Hope OH 44660	**800-827-3667**	330-674-7015	234
Waynesburg College			
51 W College St ....Waynesburg PA 15370	**800-225-7393***	724-627-8191	166
*Admissions			
Waynesville Inn Golf & Country Club, The			
176 Country Club Dr ....Waynesville NC 28786	**800-627-6250**	828-456-3551	660
Wayne-White Counties Electric Co-op			
1501 W Main St ....Fairfield IL 62837	**888-871-7695**	618-842-2196	245
Wayside Furniture Inc			
1367 Canton Rd ....Akron OH 44312	**877-499-3968**	330-733-6221	320
WAYZ-FM 104.7 (Ctry)			
10960 John Wayne Dr ....Greencastle PA 17225	**888-950-1047**	717-597-9200	636
WBAL-TV Ch 11 (NBC)			
3800 Hooper Ave ....Baltimore MD 21211	**800-622-4121**	410-467-3000	730-6
WBAY-TV Ch 2 (ABC)			
115 S Jefferson St ....Green Bay WI 54301	**800-261-9229**	920-432-3331	730-32
WBCT-FM 93.7 (Ctry)			
77 Monroe Ctr St NW			
Ste 1000 ....Grand Rapids MI 49503	**800-633-9393**	616-459-1919	636-47
WBG (Wright Business Graphics)			
18440 NE San Rafael St			
PO Box 20489. ....Portland OR 97230	**800-547-8397**		109
WBGL-FM 91.7 (Rel)			
4101 Fieldstone Road			
PO Box 111. ....Champaign IL 61822	**800-475-9245***	217-359-8232	636-23
*Cust Svc			
WBH (Baptist Health Paducah)			
2501 Kentucky Ave ....Paducah KY 42003	**877-271-4176**	270-575-2100	371-3
WBHM-FM 90.3 (NPR)			
650 11th St S ....Birmingham AL 35233	**800-444-9246**	205-934-2606	636-14
WBHY-FM 88.5 (Rel)			
PO Box 1328 ....Mobile AL 36633	**888-473-8488**	251-473-8488	636-70
WBI (Wirtz Beverage Illinois LLC)			
3333 S Laramie Ave 11th Fl ....Cicero IL 60804	**800-344-2838**	708-298-3333	80-3
WBI Energy			
1250 W Century Ave ....Bismarck ND 58503	**877-924-4677**	701-530-1064	324
WBI Holdings Inc			
1250 W Century Ave ....Bismarck ND 58503	**877-924-4677***		324
*General			
WBIG-FM 100.3 (Oldies)			
1801 Rockville Pk Fifth Fl. ....Rockville MD 20852	**800-493-1003**	240-747-2700	636
WBIQ-TV Ch 10 (PBS)			
2112 11th Ave S Ste 400 ....Birmingham AL 35205	**800-239-5233**	205-328-8756	730-9
WBKL-FM 92.7 (Rel)			
PO Box 2098 ....Omaha NE 68103	**800-525-5683**		636-12
WBNS-FM 97.1 (AC)			
605 S Front St Ste 300 ....Columbus OH 43215	**888-691-9710**	614-460-3850	636-32
WBNX-TV Ch 55 (CW)			
2690 State Rd ....Cuyahoga Falls OH 44223	**800-282-0515**	330-922-5500	730
WBRB-FM 101.3 (Ctry)			
1065 Radio Pk Dr ....Mount Clare WV 26408	**877-232-7121**	304-623-6546	636
WBRE-TV Ch 28 (NBC)			
62 S Franklin St ....Wilkes-Barre PA 18701	**800-367-9222**	570-823-2828	730
WBUR-FM 90.9 (NPR)			
890 Commonwealth Ave ....Boston MA 02215	**800-909-9287**	617-353-0909	636-16
WC McQuaide Inc			
153 Macridge Rd ....Johnstown PA 15904	**800-456-0292**	814-269-6000	770
WCAT-FM 102.3 (Ctry)			
728 N Hanover St ....Carlisle PA 17013	**800-932-0505**	717-243-1200	636
WCAX-TV Ch 3 (CBS)			
30 Joy Dr ....South Burlington VT 05403	**855-669-9657**	802-658-6300	730
WCB (Waukesha Cherry-Burrell Corp)			
611 Sugar Creek Rd ....Delavan WI 53115	**800-252-5200**	262-728-1900	632
WCBB-TV Ch 10 (PBS)			
1450 Lisbon St ....Lewiston ME 04240	**800-884-1717**	207-783-9101	730
WCBS-AM 880 (N/T)			
524 W 57th St 8th Fl. ....New York NY 10019	**800-242-6397**	212-975-4321	636-76
WCBU-FM 89.9 (NPR)			
1501 W Bradley Ave ....Peoria IL 61625	**888-488-9228**	309-677-3690	636-81
WCEC (Wharton County Electric Co-op Inc)			
1815 E Jackson St ....El Campo TX 77437	**800-460-6271**	979-543-6271	245
WCFT-TV Ch 33 (ABC)			
800 Concourse Pkwy Ste 200........Birmingham AL 35244	**800-819-0121**	205-403-3340	730-9
WCHS-TV Ch 8 (ABC)			
1301 Piedmont Rd ....Charleston WV 25301	**888-696-9247**	304-346-5358	730-13
WCI Communities Inc			
24301 Walden Ctr Dr ....Bonita Springs FL 34134	**800-924-4005**	239-498-8200	644
WCIA-TV Ch 3 (CBS)			
PO Box 20 ....Champaign IL 61824	**800-676-3382**	217-356-8333	730
WCIC-FM 91.5 (Rel)			
3902 W Baring Trace ....Peoria IL 61615	**877-692-9242**		636-81
WCLK-FM 91.9 (Jazz)			
111 James P Brawley Dr SW ....Atlanta GA 30314	**888-448-3925**	404-880-8273	636-8
WCLT-FM 100.3 (Ctry)			
PO Box 5150 ....Newark OH 43058	**800-837-9258**	740-345-4004	636
WCLV			
1375 Euclid Ave Idea Ctr ....Cleveland OH 44115	**877-399-3307**	216-916-6301	637
WCMHS (Washington County Mental Health Services Inc)			
PO Box 647 ....Montpelier VT 05601	**800-649-2642**	802-229-0591	350
WCMR-AM 1270 (Rel)			
PO Box 307 ....Elkhart IN 46515	**800-522-9376**	574-875-5166	636
WCNY-FM 91.3 (NPR)			
506 Old Liverpool Rd ....Liverpool NY 13088	**800-451-9269**	315-453-2424	636
WCNY-TV Ch 24 (PBS)			
506 Old Liverpool Rd			
PO Box 2400. ....Syracuse NY 13220	**800-638-5163**	315-453-2424	
WCOL-FM 92.3 (Ctry)			
2323 W Fifth Ave Ste 200 ....Columbus OH 43204	**800-899-9265**	614-486-6101	636-32
WCOS-FM 97.5 (Ctry)			
316 Greystone Blvd ....Columbia SC 29210	**800-570-9690**	803-343-1100	636-30
WCPX-TV Ch 38 (I)			
333 S Desplaines St Ste 101 ....Chicago IL 60661	**800-531-5000**	312-376-8520	
WCQR-FM 88.3 (Rel)			
2312 Oak St ....Gray TN 37615	**888-477-5676**	423-477-5676	636
WCQS-FM 88.1 (NPR)			
73 Broadway ....Asheville NC 28801	**866-448-3881**	828-210-4800	636-7
WCR (Women's Council of REALTORS)			
430 N Michigan Ave ....Chicago IL 60611	**800-245-8512**		48-17
WCSG-FM 91.3 (Rel)			
1159 E Beltline Ave NE ....Grand Rapids MI 49525	**800-968-4543**	616-942-1500	636-47
WCSH-TV Ch 6 (NBC)			
One Congress Sq ....Portland ME 04101	**800-464-1213**	207-828-6666	730-57
WCTL-FM 106.3 (Rel)			
10912 Peach St ....Waterford PA 16441	**800-568-8924**	814-796-6000	636
WCTV-TV Ch 6 (CBS)			
1801 Halstead Blvd ....Tallahassee FL 32309	**888-297-9461**	850-893-6666	730-75
WCU (Western Carolina University)			
One University Dr ....Cullowhee NC 28723	**877-928-4968**	828-227-7211	166
WCVE-TV Ch 23 (PBS)			
23 Sesame St ....Richmond VA 23235	**800-476-8440**	804-320-1301	730-61
WCWC (Western Canada Wilderness Committee)			
227 Abbott St ....Vancouver BC V6B2K7	**800-661-9453**	604-683-8220	47-13
WD-40 Co			
1061 Cudahy Pl ....San Diego CA 92110	**800-448-9340**	619-275-1400	534
NASDAQ: WDFC			
WDAE-AM 620 (Sports)			
4002 W Gandy Blvd ....Tampa FL 33611	**888-546-4620**	813-832-1000	636-111
WDAM-TV Ch 7 (NBC)			
PO Box 16269 ....Hattiesburg MS 39404	**800-844-9326**	601-544-4730	730
WDAS-FM 105.3 (Urban AC)			
111 Presidential Blvd			
Ste 100 ....Bala Cynwyd PA 19004	**800-745-3000**	610-784-3333	636
WDAY-FM 93.7 (CHR)			
1020 25th St S ....Fargo ND 58103	**877-478-5437**	701-237-5346	636-42
WDAZ-TV Ch 8 (ABC)			
2220 S Washington St ....Grand Forks ND 58201	**877-382-4357**	701-775-2511	730-27
WDCX-FM 99.5 (Rel)			
625 Delaware Ave Ste 308 ....Buffalo NY 14202	**800-684-2848**	716-883-3010	636-18
WDEL-AM 1150 (N/T)			
2727 Shipley Rd ....Wilmington DE 19810	**800-544-1150**	302-478-2700	636-119
WDIA-AM 1070 (Urban)			
2650 Thousand Oaks Blvd			
Ste 4100. ....Memphis TN 38118	**800-339-4673**	901-259-1300	636-66
WDIO-TV Ch 10 (ABC)			
10 Observation Rd ....Duluth MN 55811	**800-477-1013**	218-727-6864	730-22

Name / Address	City	State	ZIP	Toll-Free	Phone	Class
WDJA-AM 1420 (N/T)						
2710 W Atlantic Ave	Delray Beach	FL	33445	**877-278-1420**	561-278-1420	636
WDKS-FM 106.1 (CHR)						
117 SE Fifth St	Evansville	IN	47708	**888-454-5477**	812-425-4226	636-40
WDL Systems						
220 Chatham Business Dr	Pittsboro	NC	27312	**800-548-2319***	919-545-2500	175
*Sales						
WDLI-TV Ch 17 (TBN)						
PO Box A	Santa Ana	CA	92711	**888-731-1000**	714-832-2950	730-15
WDMA (Window & Door Manufacturers Assn)						
330 N Wabash Ave Ste 2000	Chicago	IL	60611	**800-223-2301**	847-299-5200	48-3
WDNA-FM 88.9 (Jazz)						
2921 Coral Way	Miami	FL	33145	**877-929-7001**	305-662-8889	636-67
WDRM-FM 102.1 (Ctry)						
26869 Peoples Rd	Madison	AL	35756	**866-302-0102**	256-309-2400	636
WDSC-TV						
1200 W International Speedway Blvd	Daytona Beach	FL	32114	**866-273-5825**	386-506-4415	730
WDSE-TV Ch 8 (PBS)						
632 Niagara Ct	Duluth	MN	55811	**888-563-9373**	218-788-2831	730-22
WDSU-TV Ch 6 (NBC)						
846 Howard Ave	New Orleans	LA	70113	**888-925-4127**	504-679-0600	730-47
WDUZ-AM 1400 (Sports)						
810 Victoria St	Green Bay	WI	54302	**855-724-1075**	920-468-4100	636-48
WDWS-AM 1400 (N/T)						
2301 S Neil St	Champaign	IL	61820	**800-223-9397**	217-351-5300	636-23
WDXB-FM 102.5 (Ctry)						
600 Beacon Pkwy W Ste 400	Birmingham	AL	35209	**877-541-1966**	205-439-9600	636-14
WE Aubuchon Company Inc						
95 Aubuchon Dr	Westminster	MA	01473	**800-431-2712**	978-874-0521	361
WE Bassett Co						
100 Trap Falls Rd Ext	Shelton	CT	06484	**800-394-8746**	203-929-8483	215
We Care Health Services Inc						
151 Bloor St W Ste 602	Toronto	ON	M5S1S4	**888-429-3227**	416-922-7601	360
WE Donoghue & Company Inc						
629 Washington St	Norwood	MA	02062	**800-642-4276**		398
We Energies						
231 W Michigan St PO Box 2046	Milwaukee	WI	53203	**800-242-9137**	414-221-2345	775
WE Yoder Inc						
41 S Maple St	Kutztown	PA	19530	**800-889-5149**	610-683-7383	189-8
WEAO-TV Ch 49 (PBS)						
1750 Campus Ctr Dr	Kent	OH	44240	**800-544-4549**	330-677-4549	730
WEAR-TV Ch 3 (ABC)						
4990 Mobile Hwy	Pensacola	FL	32506	**877-903-7867**	850-456-3333	730
Weather Ch Inc, The						
300 I N Pkwy Po Box 724554	Atlanta	GA	30339	**866-843-0392**	770-226-0000	729
Weather Services International						
400 Minuteman Rd	Andover	MA	01810	**800-872-2359**	978-983-6300	179-10
Weather Shield Manufacturing Inc						
One Weather Shield Plz						
PO Box 309	Medford	WI	54451	**800-222-2995**	715-748-2100	236
Weatherbank Inc						
1015 Waterwood Pkwy Ste J	Edmond	OK	73034	**800-687-3562**	405-359-0773	69
Weatherby Inc						
1605 Commerce Way	Paso Robles	CA	93446	**800-227-2016**	805-227-2600	284
Weatherchem Corp						
2222 Highland Rd	Twinsburg	OH	44087	**800-316-0072**	330-425-4206	152
Weatherford Chamber of Commerce						
401 Ft Worth St	Weatherford	TX	76086	**888-594-3801**	817-596-3801	137
Weatherford College						
225 College Pk Dr	Weatherford	TX	76086	**800-287-5471**	817-594-5471	160
Weatherford International Inc						
515 Post Oak Blvd Ste 600	Houston	TX	77027	**866-398-0010**	713-693-4000	530
NYSE: WFT						
Weatherford Public Library						
1014 Charles St	Weatherford	TX	76086	**800-489-0190**	817-598-4150	431-3
Weathermatic						
3301 W Kingsley Rd	Garland	TX	75041	**888-484-3776**	972-278-6131	426
Weatherproof Garment Co						
1071 Ave of the Americas	New York	NY	10018	**800-645-7788**	212-695-7716	153-11
Weatherspoon Art Museum						
500 Tate St	Greensboro	NC	27402	**877-862-4123**	336-334-5770	513
Weathervane Seafood Restaurant						
306 US Rt 1	Kittery	ME	03904	**800-914-1774**	207-439-0330	661
Weaver-Bailey Contractors Inc						
PO Box 60	El Paso	AR	72045	**800-253-3385**	501-796-2301	190-3
Weavertown Environmental Group						
Two Dorrington Rd	Carnegie	PA	15106	**800-746-4850**	724-746-4850	188
Web Age Solutions Inc						
439 University Ave Ste 820	Toronto	ON	M5G1Y8	**866-206-4644**		225
Web Equipment						
464 Central Rd	Fredericksburg	VA	22401	**800-225-3858**	540-657-5855	191
Web.com						
12808 Grand Bay Pkwy W	Jacksonville	FL	32258	**800-338-1771**	904-680-6600	796
Webb Institute						
298 Crescent Beach Rd	Glen Cove	NY	11542	**866-708-9322**	516-671-2213	166
Webb School						
PO Box 488	Bell Buckle	TN	37020	**888-733-9322**	931-389-9322	615
Webb Wheel Products Inc						
2310 Industrial Dr SW	Cullman	AL	35055	**800-633-3256**	256-739-6660	59
Webber International University						
1201 N Scenic Hwy	Babson Park	FL	33827	**800-741-1844**	863-638-2910	166
WEBCARGO Inc						
800 Pl Victoria						
Ste 2603 Tour de la bourse CP 329	Montreal	QC	H4Z1G8	**866-905-0123**		363
WEBE-FM 108 (AC)						
Two Lafayette Sq	Bridgeport	CT	06604	**800-932-3108**	203-333-9108	636-107
Weber County Library						
2464 Jefferson Ave	Ogden	UT	84401	**866-678-5342**	801-337-2632	431-3
Weber Logistics						
13530 Rosecrans Ave	Santa Fe Springs	CA	90670	**855-469-3237**		444
Weber Marking Systems Inc						
711 W Algonquin Rd	Arlington Heights	IL	60005	**800-843-4242***	847-364-8500	410
*Sales						
Davis						
2750 N University Pk Blvd	Layton	UT	84041	**800-848-7770**	801-395-3473	166
Weber State University						
Stewart Library						
2901 University Cir	Ogden	UT	84408	**877-306-3140**	801-626-6403	431-6
Weber's Inn						
3050 Jackson Rd	Ann Arbor	MI	48103	**800-443-3050***	734-769-2500	376
*Resv						
Weber-Knapp Co						
441 Chandler St	Jamestown	NY	14701	**800-828-9254**	716-484-9135	347
Weber-Stephen Products Co						
200 E Daniels Rd	Palatine	IL	60067	**800-446-1071***		35
*Cust Svc						
WebEyeCare Inc						
10 Canal St Ste 302	Bristol	PA	19007	**888-536-7480**		363
WebNet Services Inc						
247 Rt 100	Somers	NY	10589	**866-923-4811**	914-232-6900	178
Webroot Software Inc						
2560 55th St	Boulder	CO	80301	**800-772-9383**	303-442-3813	179-12
Websense Inc						
10240 Sorrento Vly Rd	San Diego	CA	92121	**800-723-1166**	858-320-8000	179-7
NASDAQ: WBSN						
Webster Bank Arena						
600 Main St Second St	Bridgeport	CT	06604	**800-745-3000**	203-345-2300	711
Webster City Federal Bancorp						
820 Des Moines St	Webster City	IA	50595	**866-519-4004**	515-832-3071	357-2
NYSE: WCFB						
Webster Electric Co-op						
1240 Spur Dr	Marshfield	MO	65706	**800-643-4305**	417-859-2216	245
Webster Financial Corp						
PO Box 10305	Waterbury	CT	06726	**800-325-2424**		357-2
NYSE: WBS						
Webster First Federal Credit Union						
271 Greenwood St	Worcester	MA	01607	**800-962-4452**	508-671-5000	70
Webster Industries Inc						
95 Chestnut Ridge Rd,	Montvale	NJ	07645	**800-955-2374**	800-999-2374	65
WEC (Warren Electric Co-op Inc)						
320 E Main St PO Box 208	Youngsville	PA	16371	**800-364-8640**	814-563-7548	245
Wedding Shoppe Inc, The						
1196 Grand Ave	Saint Paul	MN	55105	**877-294-4991**	651-298-1144	155-6
Wedge Community Co-Op Inc						
2105 Lyndale Ave S	Minneapolis	MN	55405	**800-535-4555**	612-871-3993	342
Wedgewood Hotel						
845 Hornby St	Vancouver	BC	V6Z1V1	**800-663-0666**	604-689-7777	376
Wedgewood Resort Hotel						
212 Wedgewood Dr	Fairbanks	AK	99701	**800-528-4916**		376
Wedgworth Farms Inc						
300 North Dixie Hwy						
Ste 471	West Palm Beach	FL	33401	**800-477-2077**	561-832-4164	10-8
Wedmore Place LLC						
5810 Wessex Hundred	Williamsburg	VA	23185	**866-933-6673**		375
WEDR-FM 99.1 (Urban)						
2741 N 29th Ave	Hollywood	FL	33020	**800-843-2677**	305-444-4404	636
Weed USA Inc						
5780 Harrow Glen Ct	Galena	OH	43021	**800-933-3758**	740-548-3881	701
WEEI-AM 850 (Sports)						
20 Guest St Third Fl	Brighton	MA	02135	**888-525-0850**	617-779-3500	636
Weeks Seed Company Inc						
1050 Moye Blvd	Greenville	NC	27834	**800-322-1234**	252-757-1234	685
Weeks-Lerman Group						
58-38 Page Pl	Maspeth	NY	11378	**800-544-5959**	718-803-5000	527
Weetabix Co Inc						
300 Nickerson Rd	Marlborough	MA	01752	**800-343-0590**	978-368-0991	295-4
WEF (Water Environment Federation)						
601 Wythe St	Alexandria	VA	22314	**800-666-0206**	703-684-2400	47-13
WEG (West Essex Graphics Inc)						
305 Fairfield Ave	Fairfield	NJ	07004	**800-221-5859**		771
Wege Pretzel Co						
PO Box 334	Hanover	PA	17331	**800-888-4646**	717-843-0738	295-9
Wegmans Food Markets Inc						
1500 Brooks Ave PO Box 30844	Rochester	NY	14603	**800-934-6267**	585-328-2550	342
WEHT-TV Ch 25 (ABC)						
800 Marywood Dr	Henderson	KY	42420	**800-879-8542**	270-826-6281	730
WEI (Wieland Electric Inc)						
49 International Rd	Burgaw	NC	28425	**800-943-5263**	910-259-5050	246
Weibel Vineyards						
One Winemaster Way	Lodi	CA	95240	**800-932-9463**	209-365-9463	79-3
Weidenhammer Systems Corp						
935 Berkshire Blvd	Reading	PA	19610	**866-497-2227**	610-378-1149	178
Weidmann Electrical Technology						
1 Gordon Mills Way						
PO Box 903	Saint Johnsbury	VT	05819	**800-242-6748**	802-748-8106	803
Weidmuller Inc						
821 Southlake Blvd	Richmond	VA	23236	**800-849-9343***	804-794-2877	802
*Cust Svc						
Weidner Ctr for the Performing Arts						
2420 Nicolet Dr						
University of Wisconsin at Green Bay	Green Bay	WI	54311	**800-895-0071**	920-465-2726	565
Weightech						
1649 Country Elite Dr	Waldron	AR	72958	**800-457-3720**	479-637-4182	358
Weiler Corp						
1 Wildwood Dr	Cresco	PA	18326	**800-835-9999***	570-595-7495	102
*Cust Svc						
Weinbrenner Shoe Co Inc						
108 S Polk St	Merrill	WI	54452	**800-569-6817***	715-536-5521	300
*General						
Weingarten Realty Investors						
2600 Citadel Plz Dr Ste 300	Houston	TX	77008	**800-688-8865**	713-866-6000	646
NYSE: WRI						
Weingartz Supply Co						
46061 Van Dyke Ave	Utica	MI	48317	**855-669-7278**	586-731-7240	322
WEIQ-TV Ch 42 (PBS)						
2112 11th Ave S Ste 400	Birmingham	AL	35205	**800-239-5233**	205-328-8756	730-9
Weirton Medical Ctr						
601 Colliers Way	Weirton	WV	26062	**800-994-6610**	304-797-6000	371-3
Weis Markets						
1000 S Second St PO Box 471	Sunbury	PA	17801	**866-999-9347**		342
NYSE: WMK						
Weiser Lock A Masco Co						
19701 Da Vinci	Lake Forest	CA	92610	**800-677-5625**		347
Weiss Research Inc						
15430 Endeavour Dr	Jupiter	FL	33478	**800-291-8545**		398
WEKU-FM 88.9 (Clas)						
521 Lancaster Ave						
102 Perkins Bldg-EKU	Richmond	KY	40475	**800-621-8890**		636
Wel Companies Inc						
1625 S Broadway PO Box 5610	De Pere	WI	54115	**800-333-4415**	920-339-0110	770
Welch Allyn Medical Products						
4341 State St Rd	Skaneateles Falls	NY	13152	**800-289-2500**	315-685-4100	250
Welch Allyn Monitoring Inc						
8500 SW Creekside Pl	Beaverton	OR	97008	**800-289-2500***	503-530-7500	250
*Cust Svc						
Welch Packaging Group						
1020 Herman St	Elkhart	IN	46516	**800-246-2475**	574-295-2460	99

Name / Address	City	State	Zip	Toll-Free	Phone	Class
Weld Mold Co 750 Rickett Rd	Brighton	MI	48116	**800-521-9755**	810-229-9521	798
Welder Training & Testing Institute 1144 N Graham St	Allentown	PA	18109	**800-223-9884**	610-820-9551	788
Weldmac Manufacturing Co 1451 N Johnson Ave	El Cajon	CA	92020	**800-252-1533**	619-440-2300	449
Weldon Williams & Lick Inc 711 N A St	Fort Smith	AR	72901	**800-242-4995**	479-783-4113	619
Welk Resort Branson 1984 State Hwy 165	Branson	MO	65616	**800-505-9355**	417-336-3575	660
Welk Resort San Diego 8860 Lawrence Welk Dr *Resv	Escondido	CA	92026	**800-932-9355***	760-749-3000	660
Well Spa at Miramonte Resort 45000 Indian Wells Ln	Indian Wells	CA	92210	**866-843-9355**	760-837-1652	698
Well Spouse Assn 63 W Main St Ste H	Freehold	NJ	07728	**800-838-0879**	732-577-8899	47-6
Wella Corp 6109 DeSoto Ave	Woodland Hills	CA	91367	**800-829-4422**	818-999-5112	215
Wellborn Forest Products Inc 2212 Airport Blvd	Alexander City	AL	35010	**800-846-2562**	256-234-7900	114
Wellbridge Co 6140 Greenwood Plaza Blvd Ste 200 *Acctg	Greenwood Village	CO	80111	**888-458-0489***	303-866-0800	351
WellCare Group Inc 8735 Henderson Rd Rm 3	Tampa	FL	33634	**866-765-4385**	813-290-6200	388-3
WellCare Health Plans Inc PO Box 31372	Tampa	FL	33631	**866-530-9491**		388-3
Welles-Turner Memorial Library 2407 Main St	Glastonbury	CT	06033	**800-411-9671**	860-652-7719	431-3
Welligent Inc 5205 Colley Ave	Norfolk	VA	23508	**888-317-5960**		178
Wellington Hotel 871 Seventh Ave	New York	NY	10019	**800-652-1212**	212-247-3900	376
Wellington Power Corp 40th & Butler Sts	Pittsburgh	PA	15201	**800-540-0017**	412-681-0103	190-4
Wellington Resort 551 Thames St	Newport	RI	02840	**800-228-2968**	401-849-1770	376
Wells Bloomfield Industries 10 Sunnen Dr	Saint Louis	MO	63143	**888-356-5362**		297
Wells Cargo Inc 1503 W McNaughton St	Elkhart	IN	46514	**800-348-7553**	574-264-9661	769
Wells College 170 Main St PO Box 500 *Admissions	Aurora	NY	13026	**800-952-9355***	315-364-3266	166
Wells College Long Library 170 Main St	Aurora	NY	13026	**800-952-9355**	315-364-3266	431-6
Wells Concrete Products Inc 835 Hwy 109 NE PO Box 308	Wells	MN	56097	**800-658-7049**	507-553-3138	184
Wells County Public Library 200 W Washington St	Bluffton	IN	46714	**800-824-6111**	260-824-1612	431-3
Wells Enterprises Inc 1 Blue Bunny Dr *All	Le Mars	IA	51031	**888-309-1742***	712-546-4000	295-25
Wells Fargo 420 Montgomery St NYSE: WFC	San Francisco	CA	94104	**800-877-4833**		216
Wells Fargo Bank 5622 Third St	Katy	TX	77493	**800-869-3557**	281-391-2101	69
Wells Fargo Bank Indiana NA 111 E Wayne St	Fort Wayne	IN	46802	**800-869-3557**	260-461-6430	69
Wells Fargo Bank NA 420 Montgomery St	San Francisco	CA	94104	**800-869-3557**	415-396-2619	69
Wells Fargo Bank Texas NA 707 Castroville Rd	San Antonio	TX	78237	**800-869-3557**	210-856-6224	69
Wells Fargo Education Financial Services PO Box 5185	Sioux Falls	SD	57117	**800-658-3567**		214
Wells Fargo Equipment Finance Inc 733 Marquette Ave Ste 700	Minneapolis	MN	55402	**877-322-8228**	612-667-9876	216
Wells Fargo Home Mortgage 2840 Ingersoll Ave	Des Moines	IA	50312	**800-869-3557**	515-237-5196	502
Wells Lamont Corp 6640 W Touhy Ave	Niles	IL	60714	**800-323-2830**	847-647-8200	153-7
Wells Lamont Industry Group 6640 W Touhy Ave	Niles	IL	60714	**800-247-3295**		153-7
Wells-Gardner Electronics Corp 9500 W 55th St Ste A NYSE: WGA	McCook	IL	60525	**800-336-6630**	708-290-2100	174-4
Welocalize Inc 241 E Fourth St Ste 207	Frederick	MD	21701	**800-370-9515**	301-668-0330	195
Welsbach Electric Corp 111-01 14th Ave	College Point	NY	11356	**866-890-7794**	718-670-7900	190-4
WEMU-FM 89.1 (NPR) PO Box 980350	Ypsilanti	MI	48198	**888-299-8910**	734-487-2229	636
Wenaas AGS Inc 12211 Parc Crest Dr Bldg Ste 100	Stafford	TX	77477	**888-576-2668**	281-931-4300	153-18
Wenatchee Valley Chamber of Commerce 2 S Mission St	Wenatchee	WA	98801	**800-572-7753**	509-662-2116	137
Wenatchee Valley College 1300 Fifth St	Wenatchee	WA	98801	**877-982-4968**	509-682-6800	160
Wenatchee World 14 N Mission St	Wenatchee	WA	98801	**800-572-4433**	509-663-5161	525-2
Wendell August Forge Inc 2074 Leesburg-Grove City Rd	Mercer	PA	16137	**866-354-5192**	724-748-9501	326
Wendell's Inc 6601 Bunker Lk Blvd NW PO Box 458	Ramsey	MN	55303	**800-936-3355**	763-576-8200	462
WEND-FM 106.5 (Alt) 801 Wood Ridge Ctr Dr	Charlotte	NC	28217	**800-934-1065**	704-714-9444	636-25
Wendle Motors Inc 9000 N Div	Spokane	WA	99218	**888-685-7177**		509
Wenger Corp 555 Pk Dr PO Box 448	Owatonna	MN	55060	**800-493-6437**	507-455-4100	520
Wenger North America Inc 15 Corporate Dr *Cust Svc	Orangeburg	NY	10962	**800-431-2996***	845-365-3500	222
Wenner Bread Products Inc 33 Rajon Rd	Bayport	NY	11705	**800-869-6262**	631-563-6262	295-1
Wentworth Hauser & Violich (WHV) 301 Battery St	San Francisco	CA	94111	**800-204-2650**	415-981-6911	398
Wentworth Institute of Technology 550 Huntington Ave	Boston	MA	02115	**800-556-0610**	617-989-4590	166
Wentworth Mansion 149 Wentworth St	Charleston	SC	29401	**888-466-1886**	843-853-1886	376
Wentworth-Douglass Hospital 789 Central Ave	Dover	NH	03820	**877-201-7100**	603-742-5252	371-3
WENZ-FM 107.9 (Urban) 2510 St Clair Ave NE	Cleveland	OH	44114	**800-440-1079**	216-579-1111	636-28
Werner Co 93 Werner Rd	Greenville	PA	16125	**888-523-3371**		418
Werner Electric Supply Co 2341 Industrial Dr	Neenah	WI	54956	**800-236-5026**	920-729-4500	246
Werner Enterprises Inc 14507 Frontier Rd NASDAQ: WERN	Omaha	NE	68138	**800-228-2240**	402-895-6640	770
Werner G Smith Inc 1730 Train Ave *General	Cleveland	OH	44113	**800-535-8343***	216-861-3676	295-12
Werner Tool & Mfg Co Inc 12301 E McNichols Rd	Detroit	MI	48205	**800-362-8491**	313-526-6020	692
WERN-FM 88.7 (NPR) 821 University Ave	Madison	WI	53706	**800-747-7444**		636-65
Werres Corp 807 E S St	Frederick	MD	21701	**800-638-6563**	301-620-4000	382
Wert Bookbinding Inc 9975 Allentown Blvd *Cust Svc	Grantville	PA	17028	**800-344-9378***	717-469-0629	91
Werthan Packaging Inc 605 HWY 76	White House	TN	37188	**800-467-0348**	615-672-3336	64
WERU-FM 89.9 (Var) 1186 Acadia Hwy	East Orland	ME	04431	**800-643-6273**	207-469-6600	636
Werzalit of America Inc 40 Holly Ave	Bradford	PA	16701	**800-999-3730**	814-362-3881	494
WesBanco Inc One Bank Plz NASDAQ: WSBC	Wheeling	WV	26003	**800-328-3369**	304-234-9000	69
Wescast Industries Inc 150 Savannah Oaks Dr TSE: WCS.A	Brantford	ON	N3T5V7	**800-564-6253**	519-750-0000	59
Wesco Cedar Inc PO Box 520	Creswell	OR	97426	**800-547-2511**	541-688-5020	192-4
Wesco Fabrics Inc 4001 Forest St	Denver	CO	80216	**800-950-9372**	303-388-4101	735
Wesco Inc 1460 Whitehall Rd	Muskegon	MI	49445	**800-968-0200**		323
Wescom Credit Union 123 S Marengo Ave PO Box 7058	Pasadena	CA	91101	**888-493-7266**	626-535-1000	219
Wes-Garde Components Group Inc 190 Elliott St	Hartford	CT	06114	**800-554-8866**	860-525-6907	246
Weslaco Area Chamber of Commerce 301 W Railroad	Weslaco	TX	78596	**800-700-2443**	956-968-2102	137
Wesley Homes 815 S 216th St	Des Moines	WA	98198	**866-937-5390**	206-824-5000	663
Wesley Long Community Hospital 501 N Elam Ave	Greensboro	NC	27403	**866-391-2734**	336-832-1000	371-3
Wesley Medical Ctr 5001 Hardy St	Hattiesburg	MS	39402	**800-622-8892**	601-268-8000	371-3
Wesley Theological Seminary 4500 Massachusetts Ave NW	Washington	DC	20016	**800-882-4987**	202-885-8600	167-3
Wesley Towers 700 Monterey Pl	Hutchinson	KS	67502	**888-663-9175**	620-663-9175	663
Wesleyan College 4760 Forsyth Rd	Macon	GA	31210	**800-447-6610**	478-477-1110	166
Wesleyan University Olin Library 252 Church St	Middletown	CT	06459	**800-421-1561**	860-685-2660	431-6
Wesleyan University Press 215 Long Ln	Middletown	CT	06459	**800-421-1561**	860-685-7711	628-4
Wesspur Tree Equipment 2121 Iron St	Bellingham	WA	98225	**800-268-2141**	360-734-5242	426
West Allis Public Library 7421 W National Ave	West Allis	WI	53214	**800-877-8339**	414-302-8500	431-3
West Allis-West Milwaukee Chamber of Commerce 6737 W Washington St Ste 2141	West Allis	WI	53214	**800-554-1448**	414-302-9901	137
West Bancorp Inc PO Box 65020 NASDAQ: WTBA	West Des Moines	IA	50265	**800-810-2301**	515-222-2300	357-2
West Baton Rouge Museum 845 N Jefferson Ave	Port Allen	LA	70767	**888-881-6811**	225-336-2422	513
West Bend Area Chamber of Commerce 304 S Main St	West Bend	WI	53095	**888-338-8666**	262-338-2666	137
West Bend Housewares LLC 2845 Wingate St PO Box 2780	West Bend	WI	53095	**866-290-1851**		36
West Bend Mutual Insurance Co 1900 S 18th Ave	West Bend	WI	53095	**800-236-5010**	262-334-5571	388-4
West Canadian Digital Imaging Inc 200 - 1601 Ninth Ave SE	Calgary	AB	T2G0H4	**800-267-2555**	403-245-2555	341
West Central Electric Co-op Inc 204 Main St PO Box 17	Murdo	SD	57559	**800-242-9232**	605-669-2472	245
West Central Illinois Educational Telecommunications Corp PO Box 6248	Springfield	IL	62708	**800-232-3605**	217-483-7887	624
West Central Steel Inc 110 19th St NW PO Box 1178	Willmar	MN	56201	**800-992-8853**	320-235-4070	487
West Central Tribune PO Box 839	Willmar	MN	56201	**800-450-1150**	320-235-1150	525-2
West Chester University 700 S High St	West Chester	PA	19383	**877-315-2165**	610-436-1000	166
West Chester University Green Library 700 S High St	West Chester	PA	19383	**800-886-9654**	610-436-1000	431-6
West Coast Aviation Services 19711 Campus Dr Ste 150	Santa Ana	CA	92707	**800-352-6153**	949-852-8340	13
West Coast Bank 506 SW Coast Hwy *Cust Svc	Newport	OR	97365	**800-895-3345***	877-272-3678	69
West Coast Club 21100 Pacific Coast Hwy Hilton Waterfront Beach Resort	Huntington Beach	CA	92648	**800-548-8690**	714-845-8000	662
West Coast Connection 1725 Main St Ste 215	Weston	FL	33326	**800-767-0227**	954-888-9780	750
West Coast Distributing Inc Commerce Pl 350 Main St	Boston	MA	02148	**800-235-3730**	781-665-9393	10-10
West Coast Industries Inc 10 Jackson St	San Francisco	CA	94111	**800-243-3150**	415-621-6656	318-1
West Coast Shoe Co 52828 NW Shoe Factory Ln PO Box 607	Scappoose	OR	97056	**800-326-2711**	503-543-7114	300

				Toll-Free	Phone	Class
West Coast Trends						
17811 Jamestown Ln	Huntington Beach	CA	92647	**800-736-4568**	714-843-9288	701
West Corp						
11808 Miracle Hills Dr	Omaha	NE	68154	**800-232-0900***		727
*Sales						
West Essex Graphics Inc (WEG)						
305 Fairfield Ave	Fairfield	NJ	07004	**800-221-5859**		771
West Fargo Pioneer						
PO Box 457	West Fargo	ND	58078	**888-382-1222**	701-282-2443	525-4
West Florida Electric Co-op						
5282 Peanut Rd	Graceville	FL	32440	**800-342-7400**	850-263-3231	245
West Florida Regional Library						
200 W Gregory St	Pensacola	FL	32501	**800-435-7352**	850-436-5060	431-3
West Group						
610 Opperman Dr	Eagan	MN	55123	**800-328-4880***	651-687-7000	628-2
*Cust Svc						
West Hills College						
Coalinga						
300 Cherry Ln	Coalinga	CA	93210	**800-266-1114**	559-934-2000	160
West Hollywood Convention & Visitors Bureau						
8687 Melrose Ave Ste M38	West Hollywood	CA	90069	**800-368-6020**	310-289-2525	207
West Islip Public Library						
3 Higbie Ln	West Islip	NY	11795	**866-833-1122**	631-661-7080	431-3
West Kentucky Community & Technical College						
4810 Alben Barkley Dr						
PO Box 7380	Paducah	KY	42001	**855-469-5282**	270-554-9200	160
West Kentucky Rural Electric Co-op Corp						
PO Box 589	Mayfield	KY	42066	**877-495-7322**	270-247-1321	245
West Liberty Foods LLC						
228 W Second St	West Liberty	IA	52776	**888-511-4500**	319-627-6000	612
West Linn Paper Co						
4800 Mill St	West Linn	OR	97068	**800-989-3608**	503-557-6500	550
West Marine Inc						
500 Westridge Dr	Watsonville	CA	95076	**800-262-8464**	831-728-2700	760
NASDAQ: WMAR						
West Metro Chamber of Commerce						
1006 12th St	Cayce	SC	29033	**866-720-5400**	803-794-6504	137
West Monroe Partners LLC						
222 W Adams St	Chicago	IL	60606	**800-828-6708**	312-602-4000	195
West Music Inc						
1212 Fifth St PO Box 5521	Coralville	IA	52241	**800-373-2000**	319-351-2000	519
West Nebraska Register						
PO Box 608	Grand Island	NE	68802	**800-652-2229**	308-382-4660	525-4
West Nottingham Academy						
1079 Firetower Rd	Colora	MD	21917	**866-381-3684**	410-658-5556	615
West Orange Chamber of Commerce						
12184 W Colonial Dr	Winter Garden	FL	34787	**877-999-9981**	407-656-1304	137
West Orange Public Library						
46 Mt Pleasant Ave	West Orange	NJ	07052	**800-345-7587**	973-736-0198	431-3
West Oregon Electric Co-op Inc						
652 Rose Ave PO Box 69	Vernonia	OR	97064	**800-777-1276**	503-429-3021	245
West Palm Beach Public Library						
411 Clematis St	West Palm Beach	FL	33401	**866-472-7275**	561-868-7700	431-3
West Penetone Corp						
700 Gotham Pkwy	Carlstadt	NJ	07072	**800-631-1652**	201-567-3000	149
West Penn Allegheny Health System						
4800 Friendship Ave	Pittsburgh	PA	15224	**800-994-6610**		350
West Pharmaceutical Services Inc						
101 Gordon Dr	Lionville	PA	19341	**800-345-9800**	610-594-2900	472
NYSE: WST						
West Point Market						
1711 W Market St	Akron	OH	44313	**800-838-2156**	330-864-2151	455
West River Electric Assn Inc						
1200 W Fourth Ave PO Box 412	Wall	SD	57790	**888-279-2135**		245
West River Telecommunications Co-op						
PO Box 467	Hazen	ND	58545	**800-748-7220**	701-748-2211	726
West Shore Chamber of Commerce						
2830 Aldwynd Rd	Victoria	BC	V9B3S7	**888-234-3566**	250-478-1130	136
West Shore Community College						
PO Box 277	Scottville	MI	49454	**800-848-9722**	231-845-6211	160
West Side Unlimited Corp						
4201 16th Ave SW	Cedar Rapids	IA	52404	**800-373-2957**	319-390-4466	357-2
West Star Aviation Inc						
796 Heritage Way	Grand Junction	CO	81506	**800-255-4193**	970-243-7500	24
West Suburban Bank						
711 Westmore Meyers Rd	Lombard	IL	60148	**800-258-4009**	630-652-2000	69
West Suburban Chamber of Commerce						
9440 Joliet Rd Ste B	Hodgkins	IL	60525	**800-796-9696**	708-387-7550	137
West Suburban Hospital Medical Ctr						
Three Erie Ct	Oak Park	IL	60302	**866-938-7256**	708-383-6200	371-3
West Texas A & M University						
2501 Fourth Ave	Canyon	TX	79016	**877-656-2065**	806-651-2020	166
West Tree Service Inc						
6300 Forbing Rd	Little Rock	AR	72209	**800-779-2967**	501-568-5111	766
West Valley Construction Company Inc						
580 McGlincey Ln	Campbell	CA	95008	**800-588-5510**		189-10
West Valley Medical Ctr						
1717 Arlington Ave	Caldwell	ID	83605	**866-270-2311**	208-459-4641	371-3
West Vancouver Chamber of Commerce						
1846 Marine Dr	West Vancouver	BC	V7V1J6	**888-471-9996**	604-926-6614	136
Child Support Enforcement Bureau						
231 Capitol St Ste 111	Charleston	WV	25301	**800-571-4864**	304-347-8688	337-49
Children & Families Bureau						
350 Capitol St Rm R-730	Charleston	WV	25301	**800-642-8589**	304-558-0628	337-49
Community Development Div						
1900 Kanawha Blvd E	Charleston	WV	25311	**800-982-3386**	304-558-2234	337-49
Consumer Protection Div						
812 Quarrier St 1st Fl	Charleston	WV	25301	**800-368-8808**	304-558-8986	337-49
Crime Victims Compensation Fund						
1900 Kanawha Blvd E Rm W-334	Charleston	WV	25305	**877-562-6878**	304-347-4850	337-49
Development Office						
1900 Kanawah Blvd E						
Bldg 6 Rm 525B	Charleston	WV	25305	**800-982-3386**	304-558-2234	337-49
Housing Development Fund						
814 Virginia St E	Charleston	WV	25301	**800-933-9843**	304-345-6475	337-49
Insurance Commission						
PO Box 50540	Charleston	WV	25305	**888-879-9842**	304-558-3354	337-49
Motor Vehicles Div						
5707 Maccorkle Ave SE						
Ste 400	Charleston	WV	25304	**800-642-9066**	304-558-3900	337-49
Public Service Commission						
208 Brooke St PO Box 812	Charleston	WV	25301	**800-344-5113**	304-340-0300	337-49
Rehabilitation Services Div						
107 Capitol St	Charleston	WV	25301	**800-642-8207**		337-49

				Toll-Free	Phone	Class
Secretary of State						
1900 Kanawha Blvd E						
Bldg 1 Ste 157K	Charleston	WV	25305	**866-767-8683**	304-558-6000	337-49
West Virginia						
Securities Div						
1900 Kanawha Blvd E						
Bldg 1 Rm W-100	Charleston	WV	25305	**877-982-9148**	304-558-2257	337-49
State Parks and Forests						
324 4th Ave	Charleston	WV	25305	**800-225-5982**	304-558-2764	337-49
Tourism Div						
90 MacCorkle Ave SW	Charleston	WV	25303	**800-225-5982**		337-49
Treasurer						
1900 Kanawha Blvd E						
Bldg 1 Ste E-145	Charleston	WV	25305	**800-422-7498**	304-558-5000	337-49
Veterans Affairs Div						
1321 Plaza E Ste 101	Charleston	WV	25301	**888-838-2332**	304-558-3661	337-49
West Virginia Assn of Realtors						
2110 Kanawha Blvd E	Charleston	WV	25311	**800-445-7600**	304-342-7600	647
West Virginia Bill Status						
State Capitol Complex						
Rm MB27 Bldg 1	Charleston	WV	25305	**877-565-3447**	304-347-4836	430
West Virginia Correctional Industries						
617 Leon Sullivan Way	Charleston	WV	25301	**800-525-5381**	304-558-6054	622
West Virginia Ethics Commission						
210 Brooks St Ste 300	Charleston	WV	25301	**866-558-0664**	304-558-0664	265
West Virginia Higher Education Policy Commission						
1018 Kanawha Blvd E Ste 700	Charleston	WV	25301	**888-825-5707**	304-558-2101	716
West Virginia Junior College						
Charleston						
1000 Virginia St E	Charleston	WV	25301	**800-924-5208**	304-345-2820	788
West Virginia Junior College - Bridgeport						
176 Thompson Dr	Bridgeport	WV	26330	**800-470-5627**	304-842-4007	788
West Virginia Library Commission						
1900 Kanawha Blvd E	Charleston	WV	25305	**800-642-9021**	304-558-2041	431-5
West Virginia Medical Journal						
PO Box 4106	Charleston	WV	25364	**800-257-4747**	304-925-0342	452-16
West Virginia National Cemetery						
42 Veterans Memorial Lane	Grafton	WV	26354	**800-273-8255**	304-265-2044	135
West Virginia Nurses Assn (WVNA)						
1007 Bigley Ave Ste 308	Charleston	WV	25302	**800-400-1226**	304-342-1169	526
West Virginia Press Association						
3422 Pennsylvania Ave	Charleston	WV	25302	**800-235-6881**	304-342-6908	616
West Virginia School Journal						
1558 Quarrier St	Charleston	WV	25311	**800-642-8261**	304-346-5315	452-8
West Virginia State Bar						
2000 Deitrick Blvd	Charleston	WV	25311	**866-989-8227**	304-553-7220	71
West Virginia State Medical Assn						
4307 MacCorkle Ave SE						
PO Box 4106	Charleston	WV	25364	**800-257-4747**	304-925-0342	469
West Virginia State Museum						
1900 Kanawha Blvd E						
The Cultural Ctr	Charleston	WV	25305	**800-120-4000**	304-558-0220	513
West Virginia State University						
Barron Dr Rt 25 E PO Box 1000	Institute	WV	25112	**800-987-2112**	304-766-3000	166
West Virginia University						
PO Box 6009	Morgantown	WV	26506	**800-344-9881**	304-293-2121	166
Institute of Technology						
405 Fayette Pk	Montgomery	WV	25136	**888-554-8324**	304-442-1000	166
Parkersburg						
300 Campus Dr	Parkersburg	WV	26104	**800-982-9887**	304-424-8000	160
West Virginia University School of Medicine						
Medical Ctr Dr						
Health Sciences Ctr N Rm 1146	Morgantown	WV	26506	**800-543-5650**	304-293-2408	167-2
West Virginia Wesleyan College						
59 College Ave	Buckhannon	WV	26201	**800-722-9933***	304-473-8000	166
*Admitting						
West Wind Inn						
3345 W Gulf Dr	Sanibel	FL	33957	**800-824-0476**	239-472-1541	660
West Window Corp						
226 Industrial Pk Dr	Martinsville	VA	24112	**800-446-4167**	276-638-2394	234
Westak Inc						
1225 Elko Dr	Sunnyvale	CA	94089	**800-387-3766**	408-734-8686	617
Westamerica Bancorp						
1108 Fifth Ave	San Rafael	CA	94901	**800-848-1088**	415-257-8000	69
NASDAQ: WABC						
Westar Energy						
PO Box 758500	Topeka	KS	66675	**800-544-4857**	785-575-6300	775
Westar Energy Inc						
818 S Kansas Ave	Topeka	KS	66612	**800-383-1183**	785-575-6300	357-5
NYSE: WR						
Westat Inc						
1600 Research Blvd	Rockville	MD	20850	**800-669-6820**	301-251-1500	461
Westcare Management Inc						
3155 River Rd S Ste 100	Salem	OR	97302	**800-541-3732**		195
Westchester Community College						
75 Grasslands Rd	Valhalla	NY	10595	**800-235-7267**	914-606-6600	160
Westchester Philharmonic						
123 Main St Lobby Level	White Plains	NY	10601	**800-553-0031**	914-682-3707	566-3
Westchester Toyota Service						
75 Vredenburgh Ave	Yonkers	NY	10704	**866-232-7662**	914-968-6500	56
Westchester, The						
125 Westchester Ave						
Ste 925	White Plains	NY	10601	**877-746-6642**	914-421-1333	455
West-Com Nurse Call Systems Inc						
2200 Cordelia Rd	Fairfield	CA	94534	**800-761-1180**	707-428-5900	175
Westcon Group Inc						
520 White Plains Rd 2nd Fl	Tarrytown	NY	10591	**800-527-9516**	914-829-7000	175
Westcon Group, Inc						
Westcon Convergence						
520 White Plains Rd Ste 100	Omaha	NE	68154	**877-642-7750**		175
WestEd						
730 Harrison St Fifth Fl	San Francisco	CA	94107	**877-493-7833**	415-565-3000	659
Westell Technologies Inc						
750 N Commons Dr	Aurora	IL	60504	**800-323-6883**	630-898-2500	725
NASDAQ: WSTL						
Westerbeke Corp						
150 John Hancock Rd						
Miles Standish Industrial Pk	Taunton	MA	02780	**800-582-7846**	508-823-7677	262
Westerly Hospital						
25 Wells St	Westerly	RI	02891	**800-933-5960**	401-596-6000	371-3
Western & Southern Financial Group						
400 Broadway	Cincinnati	OH	45202	**800-333-5222**	513-629-1800	357-4
Western & Southern Life Insurance Co						
400 Broadway	Cincinnati	OH	45202	**800-926-1993**		388-2

Name / Address	City	State	ZIP	Toll-Free	Phone	Class
Western Agcredit						
PO Box 95850	South Jordan	UT	84095	**800-824-9198**	801-571-9200	216
Western Aircraft Inc						
4300 S Kennedy St	Boise	ID	83705	**800-333-3442**	208-338-1800	62
Western Bagel Baking Corp						
7814 Sepulveda Blvd	Van Nuys	CA	91405	**800-555-0882**	818-786-5847	342
Western Bus Sales Inc						
30355 SE Hwy 212	Boring	OR	97009	**800-258-2473**	503-905-0002	56
Western Canada Wilderness Committee (WCWC)						
227 Abbott St	Vancouver	BC	V6B2K7	**800-661-9453**	604-683-8220	47-13
Western Cardinal Inc						
205 Durley Ave	Camarillo	CA	93010	**800-882-3018**	805-482-2586	62
Western Carolina University (WCU)						
One University Dr	Cullowhee	NC	28723	**877-928-4968**	828-227-7211	166
Western Consolidated Co-op						
520 Co Rd 9 PO Box 78	Holloway	MN	56249	**800-368-3310**	320-394-2171	276
Western Co-op Electric Assn Inc						
635 S 13th St	WaKeeney	KS	67672	**800-330-1025**	785-743-5561	245
Western Co-op Transport Assn						
4501 72nd St SW	Montevideo	MN	56265	**800-992-8817**	320-269-5531	770
Western Copper Corp						
1111 W Georgia St Ste 2050	Vancouver	BC	V6E4M3	**888-966-9995**	604-684-9497	497
Western Diesel Services Inc						
1100 Research Blvd	Saint Louis	MO	63132	**855-257-6937**	314-868-8620	262
Western Digital Corp						
3355 Michelson Dr Ste 100	Irvine	CA	92612	**800-832-4778**	949-672-7000	174-8
NASDAQ: WDC						
Western Electronics LLC						
1550 S Tech Ln	Meridian	ID	83642	**888-857-5775**	208-955-9700	617
Western Enterprises Inc						
875 Bassett Rd	Westlake	OH	44145	**800-783-7890**		798
Western Express Inc						
7135 Centennial Pl	Nashville	TN	37209	**800-316-7160**	615-259-9920	770
Western Exterminator Co						
305 N Crescent Way	Anaheim	CA	92801	**800-698-2440**	714-517-9000	570
Western Extralite Co						
1470 Liberty St	Kansas City	MO	64102	**800-279-8833**	816-421-8404	246
Western Forestry & Conservation Assn						
4033 SW Canyon Rd	Portland	OR	97221	**888-722-9416**	503-226-4562	47-12
Western Forge & Flange Co						
687 County Rd 2201	Cleveland	TX	77327	**800-352-6433**	281-727-7060	478
Western Fraternal Life Assn (WFLA)						
1900 First Ave NE	Cedar Rapids	IA	52402	**877-935-2467**	319-363-2653	388-2
Western Hoist Inc						
1839 Cleveland Ave	National City	CA	91950	**888-994-6478**	619-474-3361	465
Western Horizon Resorts (WHR)						
103 W Tomichi Ave Ste 201A	Gunnison	CO	81230	**800-378-3709**	970-641-5387	120
Western Hydro Corp						
3449 Enterprise Ave	Hayward	CA	94545	**800-972-5945**	510-783-9166	383
Western Illinois Electrical Co-op						
524 N Madison St PO Box 338	Carthage	IL	62321	**800-576-3125**	217-357-3125	245
Western Illinois University						
1 University Cir	Macomb	IL	61455	**877-742-5948***	309-298-1414	166
*Admissions						
Quad Cities						
3561 60th St	Moline	IL	61265	**877-742-5948**	309-762-9481	166
Western International Securities Inc						
70 S Lake Ave Ste 700	Pasadena	CA	91101	**888-793-7717**		681
Western International University						
9215 N Black Canyon Hwy	Phoenix	AZ	85021	**866-948-4636**	602-943-2311	166
Western Iowa Co-op						
3330 Moville St PO Box 106	Hornick	IA	51026	**800-488-3201**	712-874-3211	275
Western Iowa Power Co-op						
809 Iowa 39	Denison	IA	51442	**800-253-5189**	712-263-2943	245
Western Iowa Tech Community College						
4647 Stone Ave	Sioux City	IA	51102	**800-352-4649**	712-274-6400	788
Western Kentucky University						
1906 College Heights Blvd	Bowling Green	KY	42101	**800-495-8463***	270-745-0111	166
*Admissions						
Western Lime Corp						
206 N Sixth Ave PO Box 57	West Bend	WI	53095	**800-433-0036**	262-334-2874	436
Western Living Magazine						
2608 Granville St Ste 560	Vancouver	BC	V6H3V3	**800-363-3272**	604-877-7732	452-11
Western Lumber Cy LLC						
2240 Tower E Ste 200	Medford	OR	97504	**800-633-5554**	541-779-5121	192-3
WESTERN MASS NEWS						
1300 Liberty St	Springfield	MA	01104	**877-872-2756**	413-733-4040	
Western Massachusetts Electric Co						
1 Federal St Bldg 111-4	Springfield	MA	01105	**800-286-2000**	413-785-5871	775
Western Mental Health Institute						
11100 Hwy 64 W	Bolivar	TN	38008	**800-770-8277**	731-228-2000	371-5
Western Michigan University Waldo Library						
1903 W Michigan Ave MS 5353	Kalamazoo	MI	49008	**866-533-3438**	269-387-5202	431-6
Western Museum of Mining & Industry						
225 N Gate Blvd	Colorado Springs	CO	80921	**800-752-6558**	719-488-0880	513
Western National Mutual Insurance Co						
5350 W 78th St	Edina	MN	55439	**800-862-6070**	952-835-5350	388-4
Western Nebraska Community College						
1601 E 27th St	Scottsbluff	NE	69361	**800-348-4435**	308-635-3606	160
Western Nevada Community College (WNC)						
Douglas						
1680 Bently Pkwy S	Minden	NV	89423	**877-838-2778**	775-782-2413	160
Western Nevada Supply Co						
950 S Rock Blvd	Sparks	NV	89431	**800-648-1230**	775-359-5800	605
Western New England College School of Law						
1215 Wilbraham Rd	Springfield	MA	01119	**800-325-1122**	413-782-3111	167-1
Western New Mexico University						
1000 W College St						
PO Box 680	Silver City	NM	88061	**800-872-9668***	505-538-6011	166
*Admissions						
Western Oilfields Supply Co						
3404 State Rd	Bakersfield	CA	93308	**800-350-7246**	661-399-9124	264-3
Western Oklahoma State College						
2801 N Main St	Altus	OK	73521	**800-662-1113**	580-477-2000	160
Western Ophthalmics Corp						
19019 36th Ave W Ste G	Lynnwood	WA	98036	**800-426-9938**	425-672-9332	537
Western Oregon University						
345 Monmouth Ave N	Monmouth	OR	97361	**877-877-1593***	503-838-8000	166
*Admissions						
Western Outdoors Magazine						
185 Avenida La Pata	San Clemente	CA	92673	**800-290-2929**	949-366-0030	452-22
Western Pacific Storage Systems Inc						
300 E Arrow Hwy	San Dimas	CA	91773	**800-732-9777**		286
Western Partitions Inc						
8300 SW Hunziker Rd	Tigard	OR	97223	**800-783-0315**	503-620-1600	190-9
Western Petroleum Co						
9531 W 78th St	Eden Prairie	MN	55344	**800-972-3835**	952-941-9090	572
Western Pioneer Inc						
4601 Shilshole Ave NW	Seattle	WA	98107	**800-426-6783**	206-789-1930	311
Western Plastic Products Inc						
8441 Monroe Ave	Stanton	CA	90680	**800-453-1881**		9
Western Power Sports Inc						
601 E Gowen Rd	Boise	ID	83716	**800-999-3388**	208-376-8400	702
Western Reflections						
261 Commerce Way	Gallatin	TN	37066	**800-507-8302***	615-451-9700	435
*Cust Svc						
Western Reserve Academy						
115 College St	Hudson	OH	44236	**877-486-2048**	330-650-9717	615
Western Reserve Farm Co-op Inc						
14961 S State Ave						
PO Box 339	Middlefield	OH	44062	**888-427-6672**	440-632-1192	276
Western Reserve Group, The						
1685 Cleveland Rd	Wooster	OH	44691	**800-362-0426**	330-262-9060	388-4
Western Security Bank						
2812 First Ave N	Billings	MT	59101	**800-983-5537**	406-371-8200	69
Western Seminary						
5511 SE Hawthorne Blvd	Portland	OR	97215	**877-517-1800**	503-517-1800	167-3
Western Slope Auto Co						
2264 Hwy 6 & 50	Grand Junction	CO	81505	**888-461-3493**	970-243-0843	56
Western State College of Colorado						
600 N Adams St	Gunnison	CO	81231	**800-876-5309***	970-943-2119	166
*Admissions						
Western State Hospital						
9601 Steilacoom Blvd SW	Tacoma	WA	98498	**877-501-2233**	253-582-8900	371-5
Western State University College of Law						
1111 N State College Blvd	Fullerton	CA	92831	**800-978-4529**	714-459-1101	167-1
Western States Envelope & Label Co						
4480 N 132nd St	Butler	WI	53007	**800-558-0514**	262-781-5540	263
Western States Equipment Co						
500 E Overland Rd PO Box 38	Meridian	ID	83642	**800-836-4308**	208-888-2287	355
Western States Petroleum Inc						
450 S 15th Ave	Phoenix	AZ	85007	**800-220-1353**	602-252-4011	572
Western States Ticket Service						
143 W McDowell Rd	Phoenix	AZ	85003	**800-326-0331**	602-254-3300	740
Western States Weeklies Inc						
PO Box 600600	San Diego	CA	92160	**800-628-9466**	619-280-2985	628-8
Western Sugar Co-op						
7555 E Hampden Ave Ste 600	Denver	CO	80231	**800-523-7497**	303-830-3939	295-38
Western Syrup Co						
13766 Milroy Pl	Santa Fe Springs	CA	90670	**800-521-3888**	562-921-4485	295-15
Western Technical College						
400 Seventh St N	La Crosse	WI	54601	**800-322-9982**	608-785-9200	788
Western Technologies Inc						
3737 E Broadway Rd	Phoenix	AZ	85040	**800-580-3737**	602-437-3737	193
Western Telematic Inc						
5 Sterling	Irvine	CA	92618	**800-854-7226**	949-586-9950	174-3
Western Texas College						
6200 College Ave	Snyder	TX	79549	**888-468-6982**	325-573-8511	160
Western Texas Lions Eye Bank Alliance						
2030 Pullman St Ste 4	San Angelo	TX	76902	**866-226-7632**	325-653-8666	269
Western Theological Seminary						
101 E 13th St	Holland	MI	49423	**800-392-8554**	616-392-8555	167-3
Western Trailer Co						
251 W Gowen Rd	Boise	ID	83716	**888-344-2539**	208-344-2539	769
Western Truck Parts & Equip Co						
3801 Airport Way S	Seattle	WA	98108	**800-255-7383**	206-624-5099	60
Western Union Holdings Inc						
12500 E Belford Ave	Englewood	CO	80112	**800-325-6000***	720-332-1000	68
NYSE: WU ■ *Cust Svc						
Western United Life Assurance Co						
929 W Sprague Ave PO Box 2290	Spokane	WA	99210	**800-247-2045***	509-835-2500	388-2
*General						
Western Upper Peninsula Convention & Visitor Bureau						
405 N Lake St PO Box 706	Ironwood	MI	49938	**800-522-5657**	906-932-4850	207
Western Village Inn & Casino						
815 Nichols Blvd	Sparks	NV	89434	**800-648-1170**		132
Western Wood Preserving Co						
1310 Zehnder St PO Box 1250	Sumner	WA	98390	**800-472-7714**	253-863-8191	805
Western World Insurance Co						
400 Parson's Pond Dr	Franklin Lakes	NJ	07417	**888-847-8600**	201-847-8600	388-5
Western Wyoming Beverages Inc						
100 Reliance Rd	Rock Springs	WY	82901	**800-551-8244**	307-362-6332	80-2
Western Wyoming Community College						
2500 College Dr	Rock Springs	WY	82901	**800-226-1181**	307-382-1600	160
Western-Southern Life Assurance Co						
400 Broadway	Cincinnati	OH	45202	**866-832-7719**		388-2
Westerville Public Library						
126 S State St	Westerville	OH	43081	**800-816-0662**	614-882-7277	431-3
Westerville This Week						
7801 N Central Dr	Lewis Center	OH	43035	**888-837-4342**	740-888-6100	525-4
Westex Inc						
122 W 22nd St	Oak Brook	IL	60523	**866-493-7839**	773-523-7000	734-7
Westfalia Technologies Inc						
3655 Sandhurst Dr	York	PA	17406	**800-673-2522**	717-764-1115	208
Westfield Board of Education Inc						
302 Elm St	Westfield	NJ	07090	**800-355-2583**	908-789-4401	676
Westfield Financial Inc						
141 Elm St	Westfield	MA	01085	**800-995-5734**	413-568-1911	357-2
NASDAQ: WFD						
Westford Regency Inn & Conference Ctr						
219 Littleton Rd	Westford	MA	01886	**800-543-7801**	978-692-8200	376
Westgate Branson Woods						
2201 Roark Vly Rd	Branson	MO	65616	**877-253-8572**	417-334-2324	376
Westgate Hotel, The						
1055 Second Ave	San Diego	CA	92101	**800-522-1564**	619-238-1818	662
Westgate Painted Mountain Country Club						
6302 E McKellips Rd	Mesa	AZ	85215	**888-433-3707**	480-654-3611	376
Westglow Resort & Spa						
224 Westglow Cir	Blowing Rock	NC	28605	**800-562-0807**	828-295-4463	698
Westham Trade Co Ltd						
3620 NW 114th Ave	Doral	FL	33178	**888-852-5000**	305-717-5400	175
West-Herr Automotive Group Inc						
3448 McKinley Pkwy	Blasdell	NY	14219	**800-643-2112**	716-649-5640	56
Westin Automotive Products Inc						
5200 N Irwindale Ave Ste 220	Irwindale	CA	91706	**800-345-8476**	626-960-6762	60
Westin Houston Downtown, The						
1520 Texas Ave	Houston	TX	77002	**800-427-4697**	713-228-1520	376

	Toll-Free	Phone	Class
Westin Key West Resort & Marina			
245 Front St ....Key West FL 33040	**866-837-4250**	305-294-4000	660
Westin Kierland Resort & Spa			
6902 E Greenway Pkwy ......Scottsdale AZ 85254	**800-354-5892**	480-624-1000	698
Westin Maui Resort & Spa, The			
2365 Kaanapali Pkwy ....Lahaina HI 96761	**866-716-8112**	808-667-2525	698
Westin Resort & Spa			
4090 Whistler Way ....Whistler BC V0N1B4	**888-627-8979**	604-905-5000	698
Westin Resort Tremblant			
100 Ch Kandahar ....Mont-Tremblant QC J8E1E2	**800-937-8461**	819-681-8000	660
Westin San Francisco Market Street			
50 Third St ....San Francisco CA 94103	**888-627-8561**	415-974-6400	376
WestJet Airlines Ltd			
22 Aerial Pl NE ....Calgary AB T2E3J1	**888-293-7853**	403-444-2600	25
TSE: WJA			
Westlake Chemical Corp			
2801 Post Oak Blvd Ste 600 ....Houston TX 77056	**888-953-3623**	713-960-9111	598-2
NYSE: WLK			
Westlake Plastics Co			
PO Box 127 ....Lenni PA 19052	**800-999-1700**	610-459-1000	597
Westland Chamber of Commerce			
36900 Ford Rd ....Westland MI 48185	**800-737-4859**	734-326-7222	137
Westland Corp			
1735 S Maize Rd ....Wichita KS 67209	**800-247-1144**	316-721-1144	747
Westland Sales			
PO Box 427 ....Clackamas OR 97015	**800-356-0766**	503-655-2563	37
Westlaw Court Express			
1100 13th St NW Ste 300 ....Washington DC 20005	**877-362-7387**	202-423-2163	626
West-Lite Supply Company Inc			
12951 166th St ....Cerritos CA 90703	**800-660-6678**		246
Westman Freightliner Inc			
2200 Fourth Ave Mankato			
PO Box 699. ....Mankato MN 56001	**866-576-6914**	507-625-4118	56
Westmark Hotels Inc			
300 Elliott Ave W ....Seattle WA 98119	**800-544-0970**		376
Westminster Bradenton Manor			
1700 21st Ave W ....Bradenton FL 34205	**866-846-8046**	941-748-4161	663
Westminster Chamber of Commerce			
1025 Westminster Mall .....Westminster CA 92683	**800-929-3556**	714-898-2559	137
Westminster College			
501 Westminster Ave ....Fulton MO 65251	**800-475-3361***	573-592-5251	166
*Admissions			
Westminster Oaks			
4449 Meandering Way ....Tallahassee FL 32308	**866-937-6257**	850-878-1136	663
Westminster Place			
3200 Grant St ....Evanston IL 60201	**800-896-9095**	847-570-3422	663
Westminster School District			
14121 Cedarwood St .....Westminster CA 92683	**800-678-9133**	714-894-7311	676
Westminster Theological Seminary			
2960 Church Rd ....Glenside PA 19038	**800-373-0119**	215-887-5511	167-3
Westminster Village			
803 N Wahneta St ....Allentown PA 18109	**888-563-8147**	610-782-8300	663
Westminster-Canterbury of Lynchburg			
501 VES Rd ....Lynchburg VA 24503	**800-962-3520**	434-386-3500	663
Westminster-Canterbury on Chesapeake Bay			
3100 Shore Dr ....Virginia Beach VA 23451	**800-349-1722**	757-496-1100	663
Westminster-Canterbury Richmond			
1600 Westbrook Ave ....Richmond VA 23227	**800-445-9904**	804-264-6000	663
Westmont College			
955 La Paz Rd ....Santa Barbara CA 93108	**800-777-9011***	805-565-6000	166
*Admissions			
Westmoreland Chamber of Commerce			
241 Tollgate Hill Rd ....Greensburg PA 15601	**866-468-1231**	724-834-2900	137
Westmoreland Coal Co			
9540 S Maroon Cir Ste 200 ....Englewood CO 80112	**855-922-6463**	719-442-2600	496
NASDAQ: WLB			
Westmoreland County Community College			
145 Pavilion Ln ....Youngwood PA 15697	**800-262-2103**	724-925-4000	160
Westmoreland Mall			
5256 Rt 30 E ....Greensburg PA 15601	**800-333-7310**	724-836-5025	455
Weston & Sampson Inc			
Five Centennial Dr ....Peabody MA 01960	**800-726-7766**	978-532-1900	261
Westpac Banking Corp Americas Div			
575 Fifth Ave 39th Fl ....New York NY 10017	**888-269-2377**	212-551-1800	69
Westport Country Playhouse			
25 Powers Ct ....Westport CT 06880	**888-927-7529**	203-227-4177	565
Westville 1850's Village			
9294 Singer Pond Rd PO Box 1850 ..... Lumpkin GA 31815	**888-733-1850**	229-838-6310	513
Westward Look Resort			
245 E Ina Rd ....Tucson AZ 85704	**800-722-2500**	520-297-1151	660
West-Ward Pharmaceutical Corp			
401 Industrial Way W ....Eatontown NJ 07724	**800-631-2174***	732-542-1191	577
*Cust Svc			
Westwood College			
Denver 7350 N Broadway ....Denver CO 80221	**800-281-2978**	303-650-5050	788
Westwood College Atlanta Northlake			
2309 Parklake Dr NE ....Atlanta GA 30345	**866-821-6145**	770-743-3000	788
Westwood College Dallas			
8390 LBJ Fwy			
Ste 100 Executive Ctr 1. ....Dallas TX 75243	**800-331-4879**	800-281-2978	788
Westwood College Inland Empire			
20 W Seventh St ....Upland CA 91786	**866-221-5632**	909-931-7550	788
Westwood College Los Angeles			
3250 Wilshire Blvd Ste 400 .....Los Angeles CA 90010	**866-930-9256**	213-739-9999	788
Westwood College O'Hare Airport			
8501 W Higgins Rd Ste 100 ....Chicago IL 60631	**866-235-2457**	773-380-6800	788
Westwood College River Oaks			
80 River Oaks Ctr Ste 111. ....Calumet City IL 60409	**888-549-4960**	708-832-1988	788
Westwood Holdings Group Inc			
200 Crescent Ct Ste 1200. ....Dallas TX 75201	**800-687-0372**	214-756-6900	357-2
NYSE: WHG			
Westwood Lodge Hospital			
45 Clapboardtree St ....Westwood MA 02090	**800-222-2237**	781-762-7764	371-5
Wet 'n Wild Emerald Pointe			
3910 S Holden Rd ....Greensboro NC 27406	**800-555-5900**	336-852-9721	32
Wet 'n Wild Orlando			
6200 International Dr ....Orlando FL 32819	**800-992-9453***	407-351-1800	32
*General			
Wet Seal Inc			
26972 Burbank Ave ....Foothill Ranch CA 92610	**866-746-7938**	949-699-3900	155-6
NASDAQ: WTSLA			
WeTip Inc			
PO Box 1296 ....Rancho Cucamonga CA 91729	**800-782-7463**	909-987-5005	47-8
Wetsel Inc			
961 N Liberty St ....Harrisonburg VA 22802	**800-572-4018***	540-434-6753	685
*Cust Svc			
WETS-FM 89.5 (NPR)			
PO Box 70630 ....Johnson City TN 37614	**888-895-9387**	423-439-6440	636-57
WEVO-FM 89.1 (N/T)			
Two Pillsbury St Ste 600. ....Concord NH 03301	**800-639-4131**	603-228-8910	636
Weyerhaeuser Co			
33663 Weyerhaeuser Way S ....Federal Way WA 98003	**800-525-5440**	253-924-2345	186
NYSE: WY			
WF Meyers Co			
1008 13th St PO Box 426 ....Bedford IN 47421	**800-457-4055**	812-275-4485	450
WF Young Inc			
302 Benton Dr			
PO Box 1990. ....East Longmeadow MA 01028	**800-628-9653**	413-526-9999	576
WFAE-FM 90.7 (NPR)			
8801 JM Keynes Dr Ste 91 ....Charlotte NC 28262	**800-876-9323***	704-549-9323	636-25
*Cust Svc			
WFCA (World Floor Covering Assn)			
2211 Howell Ave ....Anaheim CA 92806	**800-624-6880**	714-978-6440	48-4
WFCF-FM 88.5 (Var)			
Flagler College			
PO Box 1027. ....Saint Augustine FL 32085	**800-304-4208**	904-819-6449	636
WFDD-FM 88.5 (NPR)			
1834 Wake Forest Rd			
Ste 8850 ....Winston-Salem NC 27109	**800-262-8850**	336-758-8850	636-120
WFDM-FM 95.9 (N/T)			
645 Industrial Dr ....Franklin IN 46131	**800-278-9200**	317-736-4040	636
WFFF-TV Ch 44 (Fox)			
298 Mountain View Dr ....Colchester VT 05446	**888-344-7233**	802-660-9333	730
WFHN-FM 107.1 (CHR)			
22 Sconticut Neck Rd ....Fairhaven MA 02719	**877-854-9467**	508-999-6690	636
WFI (Wireless Facilities Inc)			
4800 Westfields Blvd Ste 200 ....Chantilly VA 20151	**877-566-7277**	703-563-7100	197
NASDAQ: WFII			
WFIE-TV Ch 14 (NBC)			
1115 Mt Auburn Rd ....Evansville IN 47720	**800-832-0014**	812-426-1414	730-25
WFIR-AM 960 (N/T)			
3934 Electric Rd SW ....Roanoke VA 24018	**800-367-7623**	540-345-1511	636-90
WFIU-FM 103.7			
Indiana University			
1229 E Seventh St. ....Bloomington IN 47405	**877-285-9348**	812-855-1357	636
WFLA (Western Fraternal Life Assn)			
1900 First Ave NE ....Cedar Rapids IA 52402	**877-935-2467**	319-363-2653	388-2
WFLA-TV Ch 8 (NBC)			
PO Box 1410 ....Tampa FL 33601	**800-338-0808**	813-228-8888	730-76
WFMJ-TV Ch 21 (NBC)			
101 W Boardman St ....Youngstown OH 44503	**800-488-9365**	330-744-8611	730-83
WFNZ-AM 610 (Sports)			
1520 S Blvd Ste 300. ....Charlotte NC 28203	**866-570-9610**	704-319-9369	636-25
WFP (World Food Program USA)			
1725 Eye St NW Ste 510. ....Washington DC 20036	**888-454-0555**	202-530-1694	47-5
WFPG-FM 96.9 (AC)			
950 Tilton Rd Ste 200. ....Northfield NJ 08225	**800-969-9374**	609-645-9797	636
WFRE-FM 99.9 (Ctry)			
5966 Grove Hill Rd ....Frederick MD 21703	**877-999-9373**	301-663-4181	636
WFSQ-FM 91.5 (Clas)			
1600 Red Barber Plaza ....Tallahassee FL 32310	**866-321-9378**	850-487-3086	636-110
WFSU-FM 88.9 (NPR)			
1600 Red Barber Plaza ....Tallahassee FL 32310	**800-322-9378**	850-487-3086	636-110
WFSU-TV Ch 11 (PBS)			
1600 Red Barber Plz ....Tallahassee FL 32310	**800-322-9378**	850-487-3170	730-75
WFTS-TV Ch 28 (ABC)			
4045 N Himes Ave ....Tampa FL 33607	**877-833-2828**	813-354-2828	730-76
WFUV-FM 90.7 (Var)			
441 E Fordham Rd			
Fordham University. ....Bronx NY 10458	**888-400-5520**	718-817-4550	636
WFWA-TV Ch 39 (PBS)			
2501 E Coliseum Blvd ....Fort Wayne IN 46805	**888-484-8839**	260-484-8839	730-29
WFXC-FM 107.1 (Urban AC)			
8001-101 Creedmoor Rd ....Raleigh NC 27613	**800-467-3699**	919-848-9736	636-87
WFXK-FM 104.3 (Urban AC)			
8001-101 Creedmoor Rd ....Raleigh NC 27613	**800-321-5975**	919-848-9736	636-87
WG Bill Hefner Veterans Affairs Medical Ctr			
1601 Brenner Ave ....Salisbury NC 28144	**800-469-8262**	704-638-9000	371-8
WGAR-FM 99.5 (Ctry)			
6200 Oak Tree Blvd S			
4th Fl ....Independence OH 44131	**855-222-0995**	216-520-2600	636
WGAw (Writers Guild of America West)			
7000 W Third St ....Los Angeles CA 90048	**800-421-4182**	323-951-4000	411
WGBG-FM 98.5 (CR)			
20200 DuPont Blvd ....Georgetown DE 19947	**866-292-5483**	302-856-2567	636
WGBH-TV Ch 2 (PBS)			
1 Guest St ....Brighton MA 02135	**800-492-1111**	617-300-2000	730
WGCU-FM 90.1 (NPR)			
10501 FGCU Blvd S ....Fort Myers FL 33965	**888-824-0030**	239-590-2300	636
WGCU-TV Ch 30 (PBS)			
10501 FGCU Blvd S ....Fort Myers FL 33965	**888-824-0030***	239-590-2300	730-45
*General			
WGES (Washington Gas Energy Services Inc)			
13865 Sunrise Vly Dr Ste 200 ....Herndon VA 20171	**888-884-9437**	703-793-7500	775
WGGS-TV Ch 16 (Ind)			
3409 Rutherford Rd Ext ....Taylors SC 29687	**800-849-3683***	864-244-1616	730
*General			
WGHP-TV Ch 8 (Fox)			
2005 Francis St ....High Point NC 27263	**800-808-6397**	336-841-8888	730
WGI Heavy Minerals Inc			
810 E Sherman Ave ....Coeur d'Alene ID 83814	**888-542-7638**	208-666-6000	498-3
TSE: WG			
WGL Holdings Inc			
101 Constitution Ave NW ....Washington DC 20080	**800-645-3751**	703-750-2000	357-5
NYSE: WGL			
WGM (World Gospel Mission)			
3783 E State Rd 18 PO Box 948 ....Marion IN 46952	**800-426-0846**	765-664-7331	47-20
WGMD-FM 92.7 (N/T)			
PO Box 530 ....Rehoboth Beach DE 19971	**800-518-9292**	302-945-2050	636
WGNE-FM 99.9 (Ctry)			
6440 Atlantic Blvd ....Jacksonville FL 32211	**888-725-2345**	904-727-9696	636
WG&R Furniture Co			
900 Challenger Dr ....Green Bay WI 54311	**888-947-7782**	920-469-4880	320
WGRD-FM 97.9 (Rock)			
50 Monroe Ave NW Ste 500 ....Grand Rapids MI 49503	**800-947-3979**	616-451-4800	636-47
WGTS-FM 91.9 (Rel)			
7600 Flower Ave ....Takoma Park MD 20912	**877-948-7919**	301-891-4200	636

	Toll-Free	Phone	Class
WGTY-FM 107.7 (Ctry)			
1560 Fairfield Rd			
PO Box 3179............................Gettysburg PA 17325	**800-366-9489**	717-334-3101	636
WGVU-FM 88.5 (NPR)			
301 W Fulton St ....Grand Rapids MI 49504	**800-442-2771**	616-331-6666	636-47
WGVU-TV Ch 35 (PBS)			
301 W Fulton St ....Grand Rapids MI 49504	**800-442-2771**	616-331-6666	730-31
WGY-AM 810 (N/T)			
1203 Troy-Schenectady Rd			
Ste 201 Riverhill Dr.....................Latham NY 12110	**800-825-5949**	518-452-4800	636
WH Bagshaw Company Inc			
One Pine St Ext PO Box 766...........Nashua NH 03061	**800-343-7467**	603-883-7758	383
WH Freeman & Co			
41 Madison Ave ....New York NY 10010	**800-446-8923**	212-576-9400	628-2
WHA-AM 970 (NPR)			
821 University Ave ....Madison WI 53706	**800-747-7444**		636-65
WHAD-FM 90.7 (NPR)			
310 W Wisconsin Ave Ste 750-E .....Milwaukee WI 53203	**800-486-8655**	414-227-2040	636-68
WHAL-FM 95.7 (Rel)			
2650 Thousand Oaks Blvd			
Ste 4100...........................Memphis TN 38118	**888-302-6222**	901-259-1300	636-66
Wham-O Inc			
6301 Owensmouth Ave			
Ste 700..........................Woodland Hills CA 91367	**888-942-6650**		752
Wharf Resources USA Inc			
10928 Wharf Rd..............................Lead SD 57754	**800-567-6223**	605-584-1441	497
Wharton County Electric Co-op Inc (WCEC)			
1815 E Jackson St ....El Campo TX 77437	**800-460-6271**	979-543-6271	245
Wharton County Junior College			
911 Boling Hwy ....Wharton TX 77488	**800-561-9252**	979-532-4560	160
Sugar Land			
14004 University Blvd ....Sugar Land TX 77479	**800-561-9252**	281-243-8447	160
Wharton County Library			
1920 N Fulton St ....Wharton TX 77488	**800-244-5492**	979-532-8080	431-3
Wharton Ctr for the Performing Arts			
Michigan State University ....East Lansing MI 48824	**800-942-7866**	517-432-2000	565
Wharton Group			
101 S Livingston Ave ....Livingston NJ 07039	**800-521-2725**	973-992-5775	387
Wharton Independent School District			
2100 N Fulton St ....Wharton TX 77488	**800-818-3453**	979-532-3612	676
Wharton-Smith Inc			
PO Box 471028 ....Lake Monroe FL 32747	**888-393-0068***	407-321-8410	189-10
*Help Line			
WHAS-AM 840 (N/T)			
4000 One Radio Dr.................Louisville KY 40218	**800-444-8484**	502-479-2222	636-63
Whatcom Community College			
237 W Kellogg Rd ....Bellingham WA 98226	**855-767-9003**	360-676-2170	160
WHBM (White House/Black Market)			
11215 Metro Pkwy ....Fort Myers FL 33966	**877-948-2525**	239-277-6200	155-6
WHCF-FM 88.5 (Rel)			
PO Box 5000 ....Bangor ME 04402	**800-947-2577**	207-947-2751	636-11
Wheat Belt Public Power District			
2104 Illinois St ....Sidney NE 69162	**800-261-7114**	308-254-5871	245
Wheat Montana Farms Inc			
10778 US Hwy 287 ....Three Forks MT 59752	**800-535-2798**	406-285-3614	296-1
Wheat Ridge Ministries			
One Pierce Pl Ste 250E...................Itasca IL 60143	**800-762-6748**	630-766-9066	47-20
Wheatland Electric Co-op Inc			
101 S Main St ....Scott City KS 67871	**800-762-0436**	620-872-5885	245
Wheatland Rural Electric Assn			
2154 S St PO Box 1209 ....Wheatland WY 82201	**800-344-3351**	307-322-2125	245
Wheatland Tube Co			
700 S Dock St ....Sharon PA 16146	**800-257-8182**		485
Wheatmark Inc			
1760 E River Rd Ste 145..............Tucson AZ 85718	**888-934-0888**	520-798-0888	628-2
Wheaton College			
26 E Main St ....Norton MA 02766	**800-394-6003***	508-286-8200	166
*Admissions			
Wheaton Franciscan Healthcare			
All Saints			
3801 Spring St ....Racine WI 53405	**877-304-6332**	262-687-4011	371-3
Wheaton Van Lines Inc			
8010 Castleton Rd ....Indianapolis IN 46250	**800-932-7799**	317-849-7900	512
Wheaton-Kensington Chamber of Commerce			
2401 Blueridge Ave Ste 101 ....Wheaton MD 20902	**800-927-9061**	301-949-0080	137
Wheel & Sprocket Inc			
5722 S 108th St ....Hales Corners WI 53130	**866-892-6059**	414-529-6600	702
Wheelabrator Technologies Inc			
4 Liberty Ln W ....Hampton NH 03842	**800-682-0026**	603-929-3000	792
Wheeled Coach Industries Inc			
2737 Forsyth Rd ....Winter Park FL 32792	**800-342-0720**	407-677-7777	509
Wheeler Lumber LLC			
9330 James Ave S ....Bloomington MN 55431	**800-328-3986**	952-929-7854	192-3
Wheeler Mfg Co Inc			
107 Main Ave PO Box 629 ....Lemmon SD 57638	**800-843-1937**	605-374-3848	406
Wheeler Opera House			
320 E Hyman St ....Aspen CO 81611	**866-449-0464**	970-920-5770	565
Wheeler-Rex Inc			
3744 Jefferson Rd PO Box 688........Ashtabula OH 44005	**800-321-7950**	440-998-2788	748
Wheeling Convention & Visitors Bureau			
1401 Main St ....Wheeling WV 26003	**800-828-3097**	304-233-7709	207
Wheeling Island Gaming Inc			
One S Stone St ....Wheeling WV 26003	**877-943-3546**	304-232-5050	132
Wheeling Jesuit University			
316 Washington Ave ....Wheeling WV 26003	**800-624-6992**	304-243-2000	166
Wheeling Symphony Orchestra			
1025 Main St Ste 811................Wheeling WV 26003	**800-395-9241**	304-232-6191	566-3
Wheelock College			
200 The Riverway ....Boston MA 02215	**800-734-5212**	617-879-2206	166
Wheels Etc			
17521 Mesa St ....Hesperia CA 92345	**800-758-4737**	909-350-8200	745
Wheelwright Museum of the American Indian			
704 Camino Lejo ....Santa Fe NM 87505	**800-607-4636**	505-982-4636	513
Whelan Security Co			
1699 S Hanley Rd Ste 350 ....St Louis MO 63144	**888-494-3526**	314-644-3227	684
WHEMCO Inc			
5 Hot Metal St ....Pittsburgh PA 15203	**800-800-7686**	412-390-2700	665
WHEN-AM 620 (Sports)			
500 Plum St Ste 400...................Syracuse NY 13204	**800-582-7583**	315-472-9797	636-109
Whetstone Valley Electric Co-op			
1101 E Fourth Ave ....Milbank SD 57252	**800-568-6631**	605-432-5331	245
WHFS-AM 1580 (N/T)			
4200 Parliament Pl Ste 300 ....Lanham MD 20706	**888-432-1580**	301-731-1580	636

	Toll-Free	Phone	Class
WHIL-FM 91.3 (NPR)			
166 Reese Phifer Hall			
PO Box 870150........................Tuscaloosa AL 35487	**800-654-4262**	205-348-6644	636-70
WHIQ-TV Ch 24 (PBS)			
2112 11th Ave S Ste 400 ....Birmingham AL 35205	**800-239-5233**	205-328-8756	730-9
Whirl Air Flow Corp			
20055 177th St ....Big Lake MN 55309	**800-373-3461**	763-262-1200	208
Whirlpool Canada			
200-6750 Century Ave ....Mississauga ON L5N0B7	**800-807-6777**	905-821-6400	37
Whirlpool Corp			
2000 N M-63 ....Benton Harbor MI 49022	**800-253-1301**	269-923-5000	35
NYSE: WHR			
Whirlpool Corp KitchenAid Div			
553 Benson Rd ....Benton Harbor MI 49022	**800-422-1230**		36
Whirlpool Corp North American Region			
2000 N M-63 ....Benton Harbor MI 49022	**800-253-1301**	269-923-5000	35
Whirlpool Foundation			
2000 N M-63 ....Benton Harbor MI 49022	**800-952-9245**	269-923-5000	303
Whirlwind Steel			
8234 Hansen Rd...........................Houston TX 77075	**800-324-9992**	713-946-7140	104
Whistler Blackcomb Mountain Ski Resort			
4545 Blackcomb Way ....Whistler BC V0N1B4	**800-766-0449**	604-932-3434	660
Whistler Group Inc			
13016 N Walton Blvd ....Bentonville AR 72712	**800-531-0004***	479-273-6012	522
*Cust Svc			
Whitacre Greer Fireproofing Inc			
1400 S Mahoning Ave ....Alliance OH 44601	**800-947-2837***	330-823-1610	148
*Cust Svc			
Whitaker Buick Co			
131 19th St SW ....Forest Lake MN 55025	**877-324-8885**	651-674-3931	56
Whitaker House/Anchor Distributors			
1030 Hunt Vly Cir ....New Kensington PA 15068	**800-444-4484***	724-334-7000	628-3
*General			
Whitaker Oil Co			
1557 Marietta Rd NW ....Atlanta GA 30318	**888-895-3506**	404-355-8220	144
WHIT-AM 1550 (Nost)			
730 Rayovac Dr ....Madison WI 53711	**800-422-7128**	608-273-1000	636-65
White Bag Co Inc			
8027 Hwy 161 N			
PO Box 15357...................North Little Rock AR 72117	**800-527-1733**	501-835-1444	65
White Bison Inc			
701 N 20th St ....Colorado Springs CO 80904	**877-871-1495**	719-548-1000	47-21
White Bros Trucking Co			
4N793 School Rd ....Wasco IL 60183	**800-323-4762**	630-584-3810	770
White Cap Industries Inc			
1723 S Ritchie St ....Santa Ana CA 92705	**800-944-8322**	714-258-3300	192-3
White Coffee Corp			
18-35 Steinway Pl ....Astoria NY 11105	**800-221-0140**	718-204-7900	295-7
White County Chamber of Commerce			
122 N Main St ....Cleveland GA 30528	**800-392-8279**	706-865-5356	137
White County Medical Ctr			
3214 E Race Ave ....Searcy AR 72143	**888-562-7520**	501-268-6121	371-3
White County Rural Electric Membership Corp			
302 N Sixth St ....Monticello IN 47960	**800-844-7161**	574-583-7161	245
White Electrical Construction Co			
1730 Chattahoochee Ave ....Atlanta GA 30318	**888-519-4483**	404-351-5740	190-4
White Elephant Inn & Cottages			
50 Easton St ....Nantucket MA 02554	**800-475-2637**	508-228-2500	376
White Flower Farm Inc			
30 Irene St ....Torrington CT 06790	**800-411-6159***	860-496-9624	322
*Cust Svc			
White Glove Placement Inc			
85 Bartlett St ....Brooklyn NY 11206	**866-387-8100**	718-387-8181	712
White House/Black Market (WHBM)			
11215 Metro Pkwy ....Fort Myers FL 33966	**877-948-2525**	239-277-6200	155-6
White Knight Engineered Products			
9525 Monroe Rd Ste 100 ....Charlotte NC 28270	**888-743-4700**	704-542-6876	569
White Mountain Adventures			
131 Eagle Crescent PO Box 4259 ....Banff AB T1L1A6	**800-408-0005**	403-760-4403	750
White Mountain Hotel & Resort			
2560 W Side Rd PO Box 1828 .....North Conway NH 03860	**800-533-6301**	603-356-7100	660
White Mountains Community College (WMCC)			
2020 Riverside Dr ....Berlin NH 03570	**800-445-4525**	603-752-1113	160
White Mountains Insurance Group Ltd			
80 S Main St ....Hanover NH 03755	**866-295-3762**	603-640-2200	357-4
NYSE: WTM			
White Oak Manor Inc			
130 E Main St PO Box 3347 ....Spartanburg SC 29304	**800-826-6762**	864-582-7503	663
White Oaks Conference Resort & Spa			
253 Taylor Rd SS4 ....Niagara-on-the-Lake ON L0S1J0	**800-263-5766***	905-688-2550	374
*Resv			
White Paper Co			
9990 River Way ....Delta BC V4G1M9	**888-840-7300**	604-951-3900	546
White Plains Honda			
344 Central Ave ....White Plains NY 10606	**877-553-9292**	914-948-3305	56
White Plains Public Library			
100 Martine Ave ....White Plains NY 10601	**877-772-8346**	914-422-1400	431-3
White River Distributors Inc			
720 Ramsey ....Batesville AR 72501	**800-548-7219**	870-793-2374	477
White River Electric Assn (WREA)			
PO Box 958 ....Meeker CO 81641	**800-922-1987**	970-878-5041	245
White River Junction Veterans Affairs Medical Ctr			
215 N Main St ....White River Junction VT 05009	**866-687-8387**	802-295-9363	371-8
White River Paper Co			
1118 Rt 14 ....Hartford VT 05047	**800-461-7695**	802-281-4501	770
White River State Park			
801 W Washington St ....Indianapolis IN 46204	**800-665-9056**	317-233-2434	558
White River Valley Electric Co-op Inc			
2449 State Hwy 76 E ....Branson MO 65616	**800-879-4056**	417-335-9335	245
White Rock Products Corp			
141-07 20th Ave Ste 403 ....Whitestone NY 11357	**800-969-7625**	718-746-3400	79-2
White Sands Federal Credit Union			
2190 E Lohman Ave ....Las Cruces NM 88001	**800-658-9933**	575-647-4500	69
White Sands of La Jolla			
516 Burchett St ....Glendale CA 92037	**800-347-3735**	818-247-0420	663
White Stallion Ranch			
9251 W Twin Peaks Rd ....Tucson AZ 85743	**888-977-2624**	520-297-0252	239
White Star Tours			
26 E Lancaster Ave ....Reading PA 19607	**800-437-2323**	610-775-5000	750
White Swan Inn			
845 Bush St ....San Francisco CA 94108	**800-999-9570**	415-775-1755	376
White's Electronics Inc			
1011 Pleasant Valley Rd ....Sweet Home OR 97386	**800-999-9147***	800-547-6911	467
*Sales			

Name / Address	City	State	ZIP	Toll-Free	Phone	Class
White's Farm Supply Inc 4154 State Rt 31	Canastota	NY	13032	**800-633-4443**	315-697-2214	355
White's Inc 4614 Navigation Blvd PO Box 2344	Houston	TX	77011	**800-231-9559**	713-928-2632	274
White's Nursery & Greenhouses Inc 3133 Old Mill Rd	Chesapeake	VA	23323	**800-966-9969**	757-487-2300	366
Whiteface Club & Resort 373 Whiteface Inn Ln	Lake Placid	NY	12946	**800-422-6757**	518-523-2551	660
Whitehall Printing Co 4244 Corporate Sq	Naples	FL	34104	**800-321-9290**		618
Whiteman Air Force Base 1081 Arnold Ave Bldg 59 Ste 104	Whiteman AFB	MO	65305	**866-363-8667**	660-687-6123	492-1
Whitesell Corp 2703 Avalon Ave	Muscle Shoals	AL	35661	**800-826-3317*** *General	256-248-8500	481
Whitewater Grille 200 Lee St E	Charleston	WV	25301	**800-845-5279**	304-353-3636	662
Whitewater State Park 19041 Hwy 74	Altura	MN	55910	**800-366-8917**	507-932-3007	558
Whitewater Valley Rural Electric Membership Corp 101 Brownsville Ave	Liberty	IN	47353	**800-529-5557**	765-458-5171	245
Whiting Auditorium 1241 E Kearsley St	Flint	MI	48503	**888-823-6837**	810-237-7333	565
Whiting Corp 26000 Whiting Way	Monee	IL	60449	**800-861-5744**		465
Whiting-Turner Contracting Co 300 E Joppa Rd Eighth Fl	Towson	MD	21286	**800-638-4279**	410-821-1100	187
Whitlam Label Company Inc 24800 Sherwood Ave	Center Line	MI	48015	**800-755-2235**	586-757-5100	410
Whitlock Group 12820 W Creekk Pkwy Ste M	Richmond	VA	23238	**800-726-9843**	804-273-9100	246
Whitlock Packaging Corp 1701 S Lee St	Fort Gibson	OK	74434	**800-833-9382**	918-478-4300	295-20
Whitman College 345 Boyer Ave	Walla Walla	WA	99362	**877-462-9448*** *Admissions	509-527-5111	166
Whitmore Manufacturing Co PO Box 9300	Rockwall	TX	75087	**800-699-6318**	972-771-1000	543
Whitney Ctr 200 Leeder Hill Dr	Hamden	CT	06517	**800-237-3847**	203-848-2641	663
Whitney Museum of American Art 945 Madison Ave	New York	NY	10021	**800-944-8639**	212-570-3600	513
Whitney National Bank 228 St Charles Ave	New Orleans	LA	70130	**800-844-4450**	504-586-7456	69
Whitney the - A Wyndham Historic Hotel 610 Poydras St	New Orleans	LA	70130	**800-996-3426**	504-581-4222	376
Whitney Tool Company Inc 906 R St PO Box 545	Bedford	IN	47421	**800-536-1971**	812-275-4491	450
Whittier Hospital Medical Ctr 9080 Colima Rd	Whittier	CA	90605	**800-613-4291**	562-945-3561	371-3
Whittier Wood Products 3787 W First Ave PO Box 2827	Eugene	OR	97402	**800-653-3336**	541-687-0213	318-2
Whitworth College 300 W Hawthorne Rd	Spokane	WA	99251	**800-533-4668*** *Admissions	509-777-1000	166
WHLT-TV Ch 22 (CBS) 5912 Hwy 49 Cloverleaf Mall Ste A	Hattiesburg	MS	39401	**866-328-1987**	601-545-2077	730
WHNT-TV Ch 19 (CBS) PO Box 19	Huntsville	AL	35804	**800-533-8819**	256-533-1919	730-34
WhoKnows Inc 800 W El Camino Real Ste 180	Mountain View	CA	94040	**877-338-2763**		384
Whole Foods Market Inc 550 Bowie St *NASDAQ: WFM*	Austin	TX	78703	**888-992-6227**	512-477-4455	352
Wholeshare Inc 2431 Mission St	San Francisco	CA	94110	**800-625-4605**		384
WHO-TV Ch 13 (NBC) 1801 Grand Ave	Des Moines	IA	50309	**800-777-8398**	515-242-3500	730-21
WHP-AM 580 (N/T) 600 Corporate Cir	Harrisburg	PA	17110	**888-251-7797**	717-540-8800	636-50
WHPT-FM 102.5 (CR) 11300 Fourth St N Ste 300	Saint Petersburg	FL	33716	**800-771-1025**	727-579-2000	636-111
WHQG-FM 102.9 (Rock) 5407 W McKinley Ave	Milwaukee	WI	53208	**877-777-1029**	414-978-9000	636-68
WHR (Western Horizon Resorts) 103 W Tomichi Ave Ste 201A	Gunnison	CO	81230	**800-378-3709**	970-641-5387	120
WHTZ-FM 100.3 (CHR) 32 Ave of the Americas	New York	NY	10013	**800-242-0100**	212-377-7900	636-76
WHUR-FM 96.3 (Urban AC) 529 Bryant St NW	Washington	DC	20059	**877-550-0694**	202-806-3500	636-117
WHV (Wentworth Hauser & Violich) 301 Battery St	San Francisco	CA	94111	**800-204-2650**	415-981-6911	398
WHXT-FM 103.9 (Urban) 1900 Pineview Rd	Columbia	SC	29209	**877-874-1039**	803-695-8600	636-30
WHY (World Hunger Year Inc) 505 Eigth Ave Ste 2100	New York	NY	10018	**800-548-6479**	212-629-8850	47-5
WHYN-AM 560 (N/T) 1331 Main St Fourth Fl	Springfield	MA	01103	**800-345-9759**	413-781-1011	636-105
WHYN-FM 93.1 (AC) 1331 Main St Fourth Fl	Springfield	MA	01103	**888-293-9310**	413-781-1011	636-105
WI (Wilderness Inquiry) 808 14th Ave SE	Minneapolis	MN	55414	**800-728-0719**	612-676-9400	47-23
WIBB-FM 97.9 (Urban) 7080 Industrial Hwy	Macon	GA	31216	**800-813-8418**	478-781-1063	636-64
WIBC-FM 93.1 (N/T) 40 Monument Cir Ste 400	Indianapolis	IN	46204	**800-571-9422**	317-266-9422	636-54
Wichita Area Technical College 301 S Grove St Bldg A	Wichita	KS	67211	**866-296-4031**	316-677-9400	788
Wichita Convention & Visitors Bureau 515 Main St Ste 115	Wichita	KS	67202	**800-288-9424**	316-265-2800	207
Wichita Eagle, The 825 E Douglas Ave	Wichita	KS	67202	**800-200-8906**	316-268-6000	525-2
Wichita Falls CVB 1000 Fifth St	Wichita Falls	TX	76301	**800-799-6732**		565
Wichita Grand Opera 225 W Douglas Ave Century II Performing Arts Ctr	Wichita	KS	67202	**855-755-7328**	316-683-3444	566-2
Wichita Kenworth Inc 5115 N Broadway	Wichita	KS	67219	**800-825-5558**	316-838-0867	509

Name / Address	City	State	ZIP	Toll-Free	Phone	Class
Wichita State University 1845 Fairmount St	Wichita	KS	67260	**800-362-2594*** *Admissions	316-978-3456	166
Wick Buildings 405 Walter Rd	Mazomanie	WI	53560	**855-438-9425**		500
Wickaninnish Inn 500 Osprey Ln PO Box 250	Tofino	BC	V0R2Z0	**800-333-4604**	250-725-3100	376
Wicks Pipe Organ Co 1100 Fifth St	Highland	IL	62249	**877-654-2191*** *Cust Svc	618-654-2191	520
Wicomico County Convention & Visitors Bureau 8480 Ocean Hwy	Delmar	MD	21875	**800-332-8687**	410-548-4914	207
WICS-TV Ch 20 (ABC) 2680 E Cook St	Springfield	IL	62703	**800-263-9720**	217-753-5620	730-73
WideBand Corp 401 W Grand St	Gallatin	MO	64640	**888-663-3050**	660-663-3000	177
Widener University One University Pl	Chester	PA	19013	**888-943-3637*** *Admissions	610-499-4000	166
Widener University Commonwealth Law School 3800 Vartan Way	Harrisburg	PA	17110	**888-943-3637**	717-541-3900	167-1
Widener University School of Law Wilmington 4601 Concord Pk	Wilmington	DE	19803	**888-943-3637*** *General	302-477-2100	167-1
Wider Church Ministries 700 Prospect Ave Seventh Fl	Cleveland	OH	44115	**866-822-8224**	216-736-3200	47-20
Wieland 13737 Main St PO Box 1000	Grabill	IN	46741	**888-943-5263**	260-627-3686	318-3
Wieland Electric Inc (WEI) 49 International Rd	Burgaw	NC	28425	**800-943-5263**	910-259-5050	246
Wiers Farm Inc 4465 St Rt 103 S PO Box 385	Willard	OH	44890	**800-777-6243**	419-935-0131	10-10
Wiese Industries Inc 1501 Fifth St PO Box 39	Perry	IA	50220	**800-568-4391**	515-465-9854	273
Wieser & Cawley Furniture 1301 Colegate Dr	Marietta	OH	45750	**800-339-0094**	740-373-1676	320
Wieser Concrete Products Inc W3716 US Hwy 10	Maiden Rock	WI	54750	**800-325-8456**	715-647-2311	184
Wig America Co 27317 Industrial Blvd	Hayward	CA	94545	**800-338-7600**	510-887-9579	345
Wiggins Lift Company Inc 2571 Cortez St	Oxnard	CA	93031	**800-350-7821**	805-485-7821	465
Wigwam Golf Resort & Spa 300 E Wigwam Blvd	Litchfield Park	AZ	85340	**800-327-0396**	623-935-3811	660
Wigwam Mills Inc 3402 Crocker Ave	Sheboygan	WI	53082	**800-558-7760**	920-457-5551	153-9
Wika Instrument Corp 1000 Wiegand Blvd	Lawrenceville	GA	30043	**888-945-2872**	770-513-8200	202
WIKY-FM 104.1 (AC) 1162 Mt Auburn Rd	Evansville	IN	47720	**800-454-9459**	812-424-8284	636-40
Wilberforce University 1055 N Bickett Rd PO Box 1001	Wilberforce	OH	45384	**800-367-8568*** *Admissions	937-376-2911	166
Wilbur Curtis Company Inc 6913 Acco St	Montebello	CA	90640	**800-421-6150**	323-837-2300	297
Wilco Farmers 200 Industrial Way	Mount Angel	OR	97362	**800-382-5339**	503-845-6122	276
Wilcom Inc 73 Daniel Webster Hwy PO Box 508	Belmont	NH	03220	**800-222-1898**	603-524-2622	638
Wilcox Memorial Hospital (WMH) 3-3420 Kuhio Hwy	Lihue	HI	96766	**877-709-9355**	808-245-1100	371-3
Wilcoxon Research Inc 20511 Seneca Meadows Pkwy	Germantown	MD	20876	**800-945-2696**	301-330-8811	2
Wild Animal Baby Magazine 11100 Wildlife Ctr Dr	Reston	VA	20190	**800-822-9919**		452-6
Wild Animal Safari 1300 Oak Grove Rd	Pine Mountain	GA	31822	**800-367-2751**	706-663-8744	810
Wild Birds Unlimited Inc 11711 N College Ave Ste 146	Carmel	IN	46032	**800-326-4928**	317-571-7100	571
Wild Dunes Resort 5757 Palm Blvd	Isle of Palms	SC	29451	**800-845-8880**	843-886-6000	660
Wild Flavors Inc 1261 Pacific Ave	Erlanger	KY	41018	**800-263-5286**	859-342-3600	295-15
Wild Palms Hotel 910 E Fremont Ave	Sunnyvale	CA	94087	**800-738-7477**	408-738-0500	376
Wild Rice Electric Co-op Inc 502 N Main PO Box 438	Mahnomen	MN	56557	**800-244-5709**	218-935-2517	245
Wild Wings LLC 2101 S Hwy 61	Lake City	MN	55041	**800-445-4833**	651-345-5355	454
Wilde Automotive Management of Wisc Onsin Inc 1710 A Hwy 164	Waukesha	WI	53186	**888-379-5817**	262-513-2770	56
Wilderness Inquiry (WI) 808 14th Ave SE	Minneapolis	MN	55414	**800-728-0719**	612-676-9400	47-23
Wilderness Press c/o Keen Communications 2204 First Ave S Ste 102	Birmingham	AL	35233	**800-443-7227**		628-2
Wilderness Trails Ranch 1766 County Rd 302	Durango	CO	81303	**800-527-2624**	970-247-0722	239
Wilderness Travel 1102 Ninth St	Berkeley	CA	94710	**800-368-2794**	510-558-2488	750
WildPackets Inc 1340 Treat Blvd Ste 500	Walnut Creek	CA	94597	**800-466-2447**	925-937-3200	179-12
Wildwoods Convention Ctr 4501 Boardwalk	Wildwood	NJ	08260	**800-992-9732**	609-729-9000	206
Wiley College 711 Wiley Ave	Marshall	TX	75670	**800-658-6889*** *Admissions	903-927-3300	166
Wiley Publishing Inc 111 River St	Hoboken	NJ	07030	**800-225-5945**	201-748-6000	628-2
Wiley Sanders Truck Lines Inc PO Box 707	Troy	AL	36081	**800-633-8740**	334-566-5184	444
Wiley Waterski and Wakeboard Pro Shop 1417 S Trenton	Seattle	WA	98108	**800-962-0785**	206-762-1300	701
Wilheit Packaging LLC 1527 May Dr	Gainesville	GA	30507	**800-727-4421**	770-532-4421	444
Wilhelm Trucking & Rigging Co 3250 NW St Helens Rd PO Box 10363	Portland	OR	97210	**800-873-4285*** *Cust Svc	503-227-0561	770
Wilkes University 84 W S St	Wilkes-Barre	PA	18766	**800-945-5378**		166

Alphabetical Section

Name	Address	City	State	ZIP	Toll-Free	Phone	Class
Wilkes-Barre/Scranton International Airport	100 Terminal Dr Ste 1	Avoca	PA	18641	**877-235-9287**	570-602-2000	27
Wilkins-Rogers Inc	27 Frederick Rd *Cust Svc	Ellicott City	MD	21043	**877-438-4338***	410-465-5800	295-23
Will Rogers Memorial Museum	1720 W Will Rogers Blvd	Claremore	OK	74017	**800-324-9455**	918-341-0719	513
Will Vision & Laser Centers	8100 NE Pkwy Dr Ste 125	Vancouver	WA	98662	**877-542-3937**	360-885-1327	786
Willamette Stone State Heritage Site	11321 SW Terwilliger Blvd	Portland	OR	97219	**800-551-6949**		558
Willamette University	900 State St	Salem	OR	97301	**877-542-2787**	503-370-6303	166
Willamette University College of Law	245 Winter St SE	Salem	OR	97301	**844-232-7228**	503-370-6282	167-1
Willamette Valley Co	1075 Arrowsmith St	Eugene	OR	97402	**800-333-9826**	541-484-9621	543
Willamette Valley Hospice	1015 Third St NW	Salem	OR	97304	**800-555-2431**	503-588-3600	368
Willamette Valley Vineyards Inc	8800 Enchanted Way SE *NASDAQ: WVVI* ■ *Sales	Turner	OR	97392	**800-344-9463***	503-588-9463	79-3
Willamette View	12705 SE River Rd	Portland	OR	97222	**800-446-0670**	503-654-6581	663
Willard Bay State Park	900 West 650 North Ste A	Willard	UT	84340	**800-322-3770**	435-734-9494	558
Willbanks Metals Inc	1155 NE 28th St	Fort Worth	TX	76106	**800-772-2352**	817-625-6161	487
Willdan	2401 E Katella Ave Ste 300	Anaheim	CA	92806	**800-424-9144**	714-940-6300	261
Willert Home Products Inc	4044 Pk Ave	Saint Louis	MO	63110	**877-373-4858**	314-772-2822	149
William B Meyer Inc	255 Long Beach Blvd	Stratford	CT	06615	**800-727-5985**	203-375-5801	676
William Blair & Company LLC	222 W Adams St	Chicago	IL	60606	**800-621-0687**	312-236-1600	681
William Carey University	498 Tuscan Ave	Hattiesburg	MS	39401	**800-962-5991**	601-318-6051	166
William E Walter Inc	1917 Howard Ave	Flint	MI	48503	**800-681-3320**	810-232-7459	190-10
William F Renk & Sons Inc	6809 Wilburn Rd	Sun Prairie	WI	53590	**800-289-7365**		10-4
William H Harvey	4334 S 67th St	Omaha	NE	68117	**800-321-9532**	402-331-1175	325
William H Sadlier Inc	Nine Pine St *OTC: SADL*	New York	NY	10005	**800-221-5175**		628-2
William J Kline & Son Inc	One Venner Rd	Amsterdam	NY	12010	**800-453-6397**	518-843-1100	628-8
William Jessup University	333 Sunset Blvd	Rocklin	CA	95765	**800-355-7522**	916-577-2200	166
William Jewell College	500 College Hill WJC PO Box 1002	Liberty	MO	64068	**888-253-9355**	816-781-7700	166
William K Walthers Inc	5601 W Florist Ave	Milwaukee	WI	53218	**800-877-7171**	414-527-0770	752
William M. Tugman State Park	72549 Hwy 101	Lakeside	OR	97449	**800-551-6949**		558
William Marvy Company Inc	1540 St Clair Ave	Saint Paul	MN	55105	**800-874-2651**	651-698-0726	75
William Mitchell College of Law	875 Summit Ave	Saint Paul	MN	55105	**888-962-5529**	651-227-9171	167-1
William Morrow & Co	10 E 53rd St	New York	NY	10022	**800-242-7737**	212-207-7000	628-2
William Paterson University	300 Pompton Rd	Wayne	NJ	07470	**877-978-3923**	973-720-2000	166
William Peace University	15 E Peace St	Raleigh	NC	27604	**800-732-2347**	919-508-2000	166
William Penn Assn	709 Brighton Rd	Pittsburgh	PA	15233	**800-848-7366**	412-231-2979	387
William Penn Life Insurance Co of New York	100 Quentin Roosevelt Blvd	Garden City	NY	11530	**800-346-4773**	516-794-3700	388-2
William Penn University	201 Trueblood Ave	Oskaloosa	IA	52577	**800-779-7366**		166
William R Sharpe Jr Hospital	936 Sharpe Hospital Rd	Weston	WV	26452	**866-384-5250**	304-269-1210	371-5
William S Hein & Company Inc	1285 Main St	Buffalo	NY	14209	**800-828-7571**	716-882-2600	628-2
William V MacGill & Co	1000 N LombaRd Rd	Lombard	IL	60148	**800-323-2841**	630-889-0500	470
William Woods University	One University Ave *Admissions	Fulton	MO	65251	**800-995-3159***	573-592-4221	166
Williams & Williams Real Estate Auction	7120 S Lewis Ave Ste 200	Tulsa	OK	74136	**800-801-8003**	918-250-2012	643
Williams Baptist College	60 W Fulbright St	Walnut Ridge	AR	72476	**800-722-4434**	870-886-6741	166
Williams College	880 Main St	Williamstown	MA	01267	**877-374-7526**	413-597-3131	166
Williams Cos Inc	1 Williams Ctr *NYSE: WMB*	Tulsa	OK	74103	**800-945-5426**	918-573-2000	357-3
Williams Distributing Corp	880 Burnett Rd	Chicopee	MA	01020	**800-332-9634**	413-594-4900	80-1
Williams Gas Pipeline Gulfstream	1905 Intermodal Cir Ste 310	Palmetto	FL	34221	**800-440-8475**		324
Williams Gun Sight Co	7389 Lapeer Rd	Davison	MI	48423	**800-530-9028**	810-653-2131	284
Williams Industries Inc	2201 E Michigan Rd	Shelbyville	IN	46176	**800-383-4701**	317-392-4701	597
Williams Kitchen & Bath	658 Richmond NW	Grand Rapids	MI	49504	**800-968-3718**	616-771-0505	37
Williams Partners LP	One Williams Ctr *NYSE: WPZ*	Tulsa	OK	74172	**800-600-3782**	918-573-2000	324
Williams Performing Arts Ctr	*Abilene Christian University* 1600 Campus Ct	Abilene	TX	79601	**800-460-6228**	325-674-2199	565
Williams Records Management	1925 E Vernon Ave *Cust Svc	Los Angeles	CA	90058	**800-207-3267***	323-234-3453	225
Williams Sausage Company Inc	5132 Old Troy Hickman Rd	Union City	TN	38261	**800-844-4242**	731-885-5841	296-9
Williams Supply Inc	210 Seventh St	Roanoke	VA	24016	**800-533-6969**	540-343-9333	246
Williams White & Co	600 River Dr	Moline	IL	61265	**877-797-7650**		451
Williamsburg Area Chamber of Commerce	421 N Boundary St PO Box 3495	Williamsburg	VA	23187	**800-368-6511**	757-229-6511	137
Williamsburg Destination Marketing Committee	421 N Boundary St PO Box 3495	Williamsburg	VA	23187	**800-368-6511**	757-229-6511	207
Williamsburg Inn	136 E Francis St	Williamsburg	VA	23185	**800-447-8679**	757-229-1000	660
Williamsburg Landing	5700 Williamsburg Landing Dr	Williamsburg	VA	23185	**800-554-5517**	757-565-6505	663
Williamsburg Lodge	310 S England St *Cust Svc	Williamsburg	VA	23185	**800-447-8679***	757-229-1000	376
Williamsburg Technical College	601 MLK Jr Ave	Kingstree	SC	29556	**800-768-2021**	843-355-4110	160
Williamson ARH Hospital	260 Hospital Dr *General	South Williamson	KY	41503	**800-283-9375***	606-237-1700	371-3
Williamson Cadillac Co	7815 SW 104th St	Miami	FL	33156	**877-228-6093**	305-670-7100	57
Williamson County Tourism Bureau	1602 Sioux Dr *General	Marion	IL	62959	**800-433-7399***	618-997-3690	207
Williamson County-Franklin Chamber of Commerce	5005 Meridian Blvd Ste 150	Franklin	TN	37067	**800-356-3445**	615-771-1912	137
Williamson Free School of Mechanical Trades, The	106 S New Middletown Rd	Media	PA	19063	**888-565-1095**	610-566-1776	788
Williamson Law Book Co	790 Canning Pkwy	Victor	NY	14564	**800-733-9522**	585-924-3400	179
Williamson-Dickie Mfg Co	509 W Vickery Blvd	Fort Worth	TX	76104	**866-411-1501**		153-18
Williamsport Area School District	201 W Third St	Williamsport	PA	17701	**888-448-4642**	570-327-5500	676
Williamsport Sun-Gazette	252 W Fourth St	Williamsport	PA	17701	**800-339-0289**	570-326-1551	525-2
Williamsport/Lycoming Chamber of Commerce	100 W Third St	Williamsport	PA	17701	**800-732-2258**	570-326-1971	137
Williams-Sonoma Inc	3250 Van Ness Ave *NYSE: WSM*	San Francisco	CA	94109	**800-838-2589**	415-421-7900	359
Williamstown Commons Nursing & Rehabilitation Ctr	25 Adams Rd	Williamstown	MA	01267	**800-445-4560**	413-458-2111	445
Willingboro Public Library	220 Willingboro Pkwy	Willingboro	NJ	08046	**866-321-9571**	609-877-6668	431-3
Willington Cos	11 Middle River Dr	Stafford Springs	CT	06076	**877-892-2966**	860-684-4281	476
Willingway Hospital	311 Jones Mill Rd	Statesboro	GA	30458	**800-242-9455**	912-764-6236	717
Willis Group Holdings Ltd	200 Liberty St 1 World Financial Ctr *NYSE: WSH*	New York	NY	10281	**800-234-8596**	212-915-8888	387
Willis Shaw Express Inc	201 N Elm St	Elm Springs	AR	72728	**800-843-9904**	479-248-7261	770
Williston State College	1410 University Ave PO Box 1326	Williston	ND	58802	**888-863-9455**	701-774-4200	160
Willmar Poultry Co, The (WPC)	3735 County Rd 5 SW	Willmar	MN	56201	**800-328-8849**	320-235-8850	10-7
Willoughby Area Chamber of Commerce	28 Public Sq	Willoughby	OH	44094	**877-229-4361**	440-942-1632	137
Willow Creek Press Inc	9931 Hwy 70 W PO Box 147 *Cust Svc	Minocqua	WI	54548	**800-850-9453***	715-358-7010	129
Willow River State Park	1034 County Hwy A	Hudson	WI	54016	**800-847-9367**	715-386-5931	558
Willow Stream Spa at Fairmont Scottsdale Princess	7575 E Princess Dr	Scottsdale	AZ	85255	**800-908-9540**	480-585-2732	698
Willow Stream Spa at the Fairmont Banff Springs	405 Spray Ave	Banff	AB	T1L1J4	**800-404-1772**	403-762-1772	698
Willow Stream Spa at the Fairmont Empress	633 Humboldt St	Victoria	BC	V8W1A6	**866-854-7444**	250-995-4650	698
Willow Valley Lakes Manor	300 Willow Vly Lakes Dr	Willow Street	PA	17584	**800-770-5445**	717-464-0800	663
Willow Valley Resort & Conference Ctr	2400 Willow St Pike	Lancaster	PA	17602	**800-444-1714**	717-464-2711	660
Willows Chamber of Commerce	118 W Sycamore	Willows	CA	95988	**855-233-6362**	530-934-8150	137
Willows Historic Palm Springs Inn	412 W Tahquitz Canyon Way	Palm Springs	CA	92262	**800-966-9597**	760-320-0771	376
Willows Hotel	555 W Surf St	Chicago	IL	60657	**877-207-2111**	773-528-8400	376
Willows Lodge	14580 NE 145th St	Woodinville	WA	98072	**877-424-3930**	425-424-3900	376
Willows, The	1 Lyman St	Westborough	MA	01581	**800-464-8060**	508-366-4730	663
Willsie Cap & Gown Co	1220 S 13th St	Omaha	NE	68108	**800-234-4696**	402-341-6536	153-13
Wilma Theater	265 S Broad St	Philadelphia	PA	19107	**800-732-0999**	215-893-9456	565
Wilmer Service Line	515 W Sycamore St	Coldwater	OH	45828	**800-494-5637**		109
Wilmington College of Ohio	1870 Quaker Way	Wilmington	OH	45177	**800-341-9318**	937-382-6661	166
Wilmington Fibre Specialty Co	700 Washington St	New Castle	DE	19720	**800-220-5132**	302-328-7525	592
Wilmington National Cemetery	2011 Market St	Wilmington	NC	28403	**800-535-1117**	910-815-4877	135
Wilmington Treatment Ctr	2520 Troy Dr	Wilmington	NC	28401	**877-762-3750**	910-762-2727	717
Wilmington Trust Co	1100 N Market St	Wilmington	DE	19890	**800-441-7120**	302-651-1000	69
Wilmington University	320 N DuPont Hwy *Admissions	New Castle	DE	19720	**877-967-5464***	302-356-6739	166
Wilshire Enterprises Inc	100 Eagle Rock Ave Ste 100 *OTC: WLSE*	East Hanover	NJ	07936	**888-697-3962**	973-585-7770	529

Name / Address	Toll-Free	Phone	Class
Wilshire Mutual Funds Inc PO Box 219512, Kansas City MO 64121	888-200-6796		521
Wilshire State Bank 3200 Wilshire Blvd Ste 1400, Los Angeles CA 90010	866-886-2265	213-368-7700	69
Wilson Air Ctr 2930 Winchester Rd, Memphis International Airport, Memphis TN 38118	800-464-2992	901-345-2992	62
Wilson Bus Lines Inc 203 Patriots Rd PO Box 415, East Templeton MA 01438	800-253-5235	978-632-3894	106
Wilson Chamber of Commerce 200 Nash St NE, Wilson NC 27893	855-905-0604	252-237-0165	137
Wilson College 1015 Philadelphia Ave, Chambersburg PA 17201 *Admissions	800-421-8402*	717-264-4141	166
Wilson County Public Library 249 W Nash St, Wilson NC 27893	877-321-2652	252-237-5355	431-3
Wilson Hotel Management Company Inc 8700 Trl Lk Dr W Ste 300, Memphis TN 38125	800-945-7661	901-346-8800	376
Wilson Industrial Sales Company Inc 201 S Wilson, Brook IN 47922	800-633-5427	219-275-7333	144
Wilson Learning Corp 8000 W 78th St Ste 200, Edina MN 55439	800-328-7937	952-944-2880	755
Wilson Lines of Minnesota Inc 2131 Second Ave, Newport MN 55055 *General	800-525-3333*	651-459-2384	770
Wilson Memorial Hospital 915 W Michigan St, Sidney OH 45365	800-589-9641	937-498-2311	371-3
Wilson of Wallingford Inc 221 Rogers Ln PO Box 185, Wallingford PA 19086	888-607-2621	610-566-7600	315
Wilson Quarterly Magazine 1300 Pennsylvania Ave NW, 1 Woodrow Wilson Plaza, Washington DC 20004 *Orders	888-947-9018*	202-691-4000	452-11
Wilson Sporting Goods Co 8750 W Bryn Mawr Ave, Chicago IL 60631	800-874-5930	773-714-6400	701
Wilson Supply Co 1302 Conti St, Houston TX 77002	800-874-5930	713-237-3700	382
Wilson Tool International Inc 12912 Farnham Ave, White Bear Lake MN 55110	800-328-9646	651-286-6001	688
Wilson Trailer Co 4400 S Lewis Blvd, Sioux City IA 51106	800-798-2002	712-252-6500	769
Wilson Trophy Co 1724 Frienza Ave, Sacramento CA 95815	800-635-5005	916-927-9733	767
Wilson Trucking Corp 137 Wilson Blvd, Fishersville VA 22939	866-645-7405	540-949-3200	770
Wilson Visitors Bureau 209 Broad St, Wilson NC 27893	800-497-7398	252-243-8440	207
Wilson WindowWare Inc 5421 California Ave SW, Seattle WA 98136	800-762-8383	206-938-1740	179-12
Wilsonart International Inc 2400 Wilson Pl, Temple TX 76504 *Cust Svc	800-433-3222*	254-207-7000	592
Wilsons Leather Inc 7401 Boone Ave N, Brooklyn Park MN 55428	800-967-6270	763-391-4000	155-5
Wiltern Theatre 3790 Wilshire Blvd, Los Angeles CA 90010	800-348-8499	213-388-1400	565
Wilton Armetale Co PO Box 600, Mount Joy PA 17552	800-779-4586		481
Wilton Industries Inc 2240 W 75th St, Woodridge IL 60517	800-794-5866	630-963-7100	481
WILX-TV Ch 10 (NBC) 500 American Rd, Lansing MI 48911	866-653-4261	517-393-0110	730-36
Wimmer's Meat Products Inc 126 W Grant St, West Point NE 68788 *Cust Svc	800-762-9865*	402-372-2437	295-26
WIN Energy Rural Electric Membership Corp 3981 S US Hwy 41, Vincennes IN 47591	800-882-5140	812-882-5140	245
Winbco Tank Co 1200 E Main St PO Box 618, Ottumwa IA 52501	800-822-1855		90
Winchester Equipment Co 121 Indian Hollow Rd, Winchester VA 22603	800-323-3581		355
Winchester Star Two N Kent St, Winchester VA 22601	800-296-8639	540-667-3200	525-2
Winchester Systems Inc 101 Billerica Ave Bldg 5, North Billerica MA 01862 *Cust Svc	800-325-3700*	781-265-0200	177
Winchuck State Recreation Site 1655 Hwy 101 N, Brookings OR 97415	800-551-6949		558
WinCo Foods Inc PO Box 5756, Boise ID 83705	888-674-6854	208-377-0110	342
Winco Inc 5516 SW First Ln, Ocala FL 34474	800-237-3377	352-854-2929	318-3
WinCraft Inc 1124 W Fifth St, Winona MN 55987	800-533-8006	507-454-5510	327
WinCup 4640 Lewis Rd, Stone Mountain GA 30083	800-292-2877	770-938-5281	594
Wind River Ranch PO Box 3410, Estes Park CO 80517	800-523-4212	970-586-4212	239
Wind River Systems Inc 500 Wind River Way, Alameda CA 94501	800-545-9463	510-748-4100	179-12
Windermere Relocation Inc 5424 Sand Point Way NE, Seattle WA 98105	866-740-9589	206-527-3801	657
Windham Region Chamber of Commerce 1010 Main St, Willimantic CT 06226	800-635-9161	860-423-6389	137
Windings Inc PO Box 566, New Ulm MN 56073	800-795-8533	507-359-2034	449
Windmill Health Products Six Henderson Dr, West Caldwell NJ 07006	800-822-4320	973-575-6591	787
Window & Door Manufacturers Assn (WDMA) 330 N Wabash Ave Ste 2000, Chicago IL 60611	800-223-2301	847-299-5200	48-3
Window Gang 405 Arendell St, Morehead City NC 28557	877-946-4264	252-726-1463	150
Window Rama Enterprises Inc 71 Heartland Blvd, Edgewood NY 11717	800-897-7262	800-695-7262	192-3
Windsor Arms Hotel 18 St Thomas St, Toronto ON M5S3E7	877-999-2767	416-971-9666	376
Windsor Court Hotel 300 Gravier St, New Orleans LA 70130	888-596-0955	504-523-6000	376
Windsor Factory Supply Ltd 730 N Service Rd, Windsor ON N8X3J3	800-387-2659	519-966-2202	382
Windsor Foods 3355 W Alabama St Ste 730, Houston TX 77098	800-458-4054	713-843-5200	295-36
Windsor Inc 4533 Pacific Blvd, Vernon CA 90058	888-494-6376	323-282-9000	155-6
Windsor K,,rcher Group 1351 W Stanford Ave, Englewood CO 80110	800-444-7654	303-762-1800	383
Windsor Star, The 167 Ferry St, Windsor ON N9A4M5	800-265-5647	519-255-5711	525-1
Windsor Vineyards 205 Concourse Blvd, Santa Rosa CA 95403	800-289-9463		314-5
Windsor Windows & Doors 900 S 19th St, West Des Moines IA 50265	800-218-6186	515-223-6660	236
Windsor-Bertie Area Chamber of Commerce 121 Granville St PO Box 572, Windsor NC 27983	800-334-5010	252-794-4277	137
Windstar Cruises 2101 Fourth Ave Ste 210, Seattle WA 98121 *Resv	800-258-7245*	206-292-9606	220
Windstar Lines Inc 1903 US Hwy 71 N, Carroll IA 51401	888-494-6378	712-792-4221	187
Wine & Spirits Shippers Assn Inc (WSSA) 11800 Sunrise Vly Dr, Reston VA 20191 *General	800-368-3167*	703-860-2300	48-6
Wine Club, The 1431 S Village Way, Santa Ana CA 92705	800-966-5432	714-835-6485	439
Wine Spectator Magazine 387 Pk Ave S Eighth Fl, New York NY 10016 *Orders	800-752-7799*	212-684-4224	452-14
Wine.com Inc 114 Sansome St 3rd Fl, San Francisco CA 94104	800-592-5870	415-291-9500	439
WineAmerica 1015 18th St NW Ste 500, Washington DC 20036	800-824-5419	202-783-2756	48-1
Winebow Inc 75 Chestnut Ridge Rd, Montvale NJ 07645	800-859-0689	201-445-0620	80-3
Winebrenner Theological Seminary 950 N Main St, Findlay OH 45840	800-992-4987	419-434-4200	167-3
Winegard Co 3000 Kirkwood St, Burlington IA 52601 *Cust Svc	800-288-8094*	319-754-0600	638
Winery at Wolf Creek 2637 Cleveland Massillon Rd, Norton OH 44203	800-436-0426	330-666-9285	49-6
WineStyles Inc 5515 Mills Civic Pkwy Ste 110, West Des Moines IA 50266	866-424-9463		309
Winetasting Network, The 578 Gateway Dr, Napa CA 94558	800-435-2225		681
Wing Enterprises Inc 1198 N Spring Creek, Springville UT 84663	866-872-5901	801-489-3684	418
Wing Hing Foods Inc 2539 E Philadelphia St, Ontario CA 91761	855-734-2742		342
Wing Zone Franchise Corp 900 Cir 75 Pkwy Ste 930, Atlanta GA 30339	877-946-4966	404-875-5045	309
Wingate University 315 E Wilson St, Wingate NC 28174	800-755-5550	704-233-8000	166
Wingfoot Commercial Tire Systems LLC 1000 S 21st St, Fort Smith AR 72901	800-643-7330	479-788-6400	61-5
Wingra Stone Co 2975 Kapec Rd PO Box 44284, Madison WI 53744	800-249-6908	608-271-5555	184
WINGS (Wings Foundation) 7550 W Yale Ave Ste B 201, Denver CO 80227	800-373-8671	303-238-8660	47-21
Wings Financial Credit Union 14985 Glazier Ave Ste 100, Apple Valley MN 55124	800-692-2274	952-997-8000	219
Wings Foundation (WINGS) 7550 W Yale Ave Ste B 201, Denver CO 80227	800-373-8671	303-238-8660	47-21
Wings Tours Inc 11350 McCormick Rd Ste 703, Hunt Valley MD 21031	800-869-4647	410-771-0925	750
WinHolt Equipment Group 141 Eileen Way, Syosset NY 11791	800-444-3595	516-222-0335	465
Winkler Inc 535 E Medcalf St, Dale IN 47523	800-621-3843	812-937-4421	296-8
Winland Electronics Inc 1950 Excel Dr, Mankato MN 56001 NYSE: WEX	800-635-4269	507-625-7231	202
Winmark Corp 605 Hwy 169 N Ste 400, Minneapolis MN 55441 NASDAQ: WINA	800-433-2540	763-520-8500	155-1
Winn Transportation 1831 Westwood Ave, Richmond VA 23227	800-296-9466	804-358-9466	106
Winnebago Industries Inc 605 W Crystal Lk Rd PO Box 152, Forest City IA 50436 NYSE: WGO	800-643-4892	641-585-3535	119
Winnemucca Convention & Visitors Authority 50 W Winnemucca Blvd, Winnemucca NV 89445	800-962-2638	775-623-5071	207
Winner International LLC 32 W State St, Sharon PA 16146	800-258-2321	724-981-1152	683
Winner Livestock Auction Co 31690 Livestock Barn Rd, Winner SD 57580	800-201-0451	605-842-0451	441
Winner's Cir Resort 550 Via de la Valle, Solana Beach CA 92075	800-874-8770	858-755-6666	660
Winners Sports Haven 600 Long Wharf Dr, New Haven CT 06511	800-468-2260		132
Winnipeg Free Press 1355 Mountain Ave, Winnipeg MB R2X3B6	800-542-8900	204-697-7000	525-1
Winona Convention & Visitors Bureau 160 Johnson St, Winona MN 55987	800-657-4972	507-452-0735	207
Winona National Bankÿÿÿ PO Box 499, Winona MN 55987	800-546-4392	507-454-4320	357-2
Winona State University 175 W Mark St, Winona MN 55987	800-342-5978	507-457-5000	166
Winpak Ltd 100 Saulteaux Crescent, Winnipeg MB R3J3T3 TSE: WPK	800-841-2600	204-889-1015	541
Winship Cancer Institute of Emory University 1365 Clifton Rd NE, Atlanta GA 30322	888-946-7447	404-778-1900	759
Winslow BMW 730 N Cir Dr, Colorado Springs CO 80909	866-635-2349	719-473-1373	56
Winsted Precision Ball Corp 159 Colebrook River Rd, Winsted CT 06098	800-462-3075	860-379-2788	74
Winston Bros Inc 131 Newbury St, Boston MA 02116	800-457-4901	617-541-1100	292
Winston F2S Corp 1604 Cherokee Trace, White Oak TX 75693	800-527-8465	903-757-7341	530
Winston Industries LLC 2345 Carton Dr, Louisville KY 40299	800-234-5286	502-495-5400	297
Winston Resources Inc 122 E 42nd St Ste 320, New York NY 10168	800-494-6786	212-557-5000	712

Name / Address	City	State	ZIP	Toll-Free	Phone	Class
Winston-Salem Convention & Visitors Bureau						
200 Brookstown Ave	Winston-Salem	NC	27101	**866-728-4200**	336-728-4200	207
Winston-Salem Journal						
418 N Marshall St	Winston-Salem	NC	27101	**800-642-0925**	336-727-7211	525-2
Winston-Salem Southbound Railway Co						
4550 Overdale Rd	Winston-Salem	NC	27107	**888-780-7245**	336-788-9407	639
Winston-Salem State University						
601 S ML King Jr Dr						
206 Thompson Ctr	Winston-Salem	NC	27110	**800-257-4052***	336-750-2000	166
*Admissions						
Wintec Industries Inc						
675 Sycamore Dr	Milpitas	CA	95035	**866-989-4683**	408-856-0500	617
Winter Gardens Quality Foods Inc						
304 Commerce St PO Box 339	New Oxford	PA	17350	**800-242-7637**	717-624-4911	295-36
Winter Hill Bank						
342 Broadway	Somerville	MA	02145	**800-444-4300**	617-666-8600	69
Winter Park Chamber of Commerce						
151 W Lyman Ave	Winter Park	FL	32789	**877-972-4262***	407-644-8281	137
*Help Line						
Winter Park Resort						
85 Parsenn Rd	Winter Park	CO	80482	**800-903-7275***	970-726-5514	373
*Resv						
Winter Quarters State Historic Site						
4929 Hwy 608	Newellton	LA	71357	**888-677-9468**	318-467-9750	558
Wintergreen Resort						
Rt 664 PO Box 706	Wintergreen	VA	22958	**800-266-2444**	855-699-1858	698
Wintersilks Inc						
PO Box 196 4th Fl	Jessup	PA	18434	**800-648-7455**	800-718-3687	454
Winterthur Museum & Country Estate						
5105 Kennett Pk	Winterthur	DE	19735	**800-448-3883**	302-888-4600	513
Winthrop Realty Trust						
7 Bulfinch Pl Ste 500	Boston	MA	02114	**800-622-6757**	617-570-4614	646
NYSE: FUR						
Winward International Inc						
3089 Whipple Rd	Union City	CA	94587	**800-888-8898**	510-487-8686	292
Winware Inc						
1955 W Oak Cir	Marietta	GA	30062	**888-419-1399**	770-419-1399	178
WIOQ-FM 102.1 (CHR)						
111 Presidential Blvd						
Ste 100	Bala Cynwyd	PA	19004	**800-521-1021**	610-784-3333	636
Wipaire Inc						
1700 Henry Ave	South St Paul	MN	55075	**888-947-2473**	651-451-1205	522
Wipe-Tex International Corp						
110 E 153rd St	Bronx	NY	10451	**800-643-9607**	718-665-0787	501
Wire Belt Company of America						
154 Harvey Rd	Londonderry	NH	03053	**800-922-2637***	603-644-2500	208
*Cust Svc						
Wired News						
Wired 520 Third St						
Ste 305	San Francisco	CA	94107	**800-769-4733**		394
Wireless Analytics LLC						
230 N St Ste 4	Danvers	MA	01923	**888-588-5550**		224
Wireless Facilities Inc (WFI)						
4800 Westfields Blvd Ste 200	Chantilly	VA	20151	**877-566-7277**	703-563-7100	197
NASDAQ: WFII						
Wireless Toyz Ltd						
29155 NW Hwy	Southfield	MI	48034	**866-237-2624**	248-426-8200	309
Wireless Xcessories Group Inc						
1840 County Line Rd						
Ste 301	Huntingdon Valley	PA	19006	**800-233-0013**	215-322-4600	253
OTC: WIRX						
Wireless Zone						
34 Industrial Pk Pl	Middletown	CT	06457	**888-881-2622**	860-632-9494	34
Wiremasters Inc						
1788 N Pt Rd	Columbia	TN	38401	**800-635-5342**	615-791-0281	246
Wirerope Works Inc						
100 Maynard St	Williamsport	PA	17701	**800-541-7673***	570-326-5146	800
*Cust Svc						
Wirtz Beverage Illinois LLC (WBI)						
3333 S Laramie Ave 11th Fl	Cicero	IL	60804	**800-344-2838**	708-298-3333	80-3
WIS International						
9265 Sky Park Ct Ste 100	San Diego	CA	92123	**800-268-6848**	858-565-8111	396
Wisco Industries Inc						
736 Janesville St	Oregon	WI	53575	**800-999-4726**	608-835-3106	35
Wisco Products Inc						
109 Commercial St	Dayton	OH	45402	**800-367-6570**	937-228-2101	688
Wisco Supply Inc						
815 S Saint Vrain St	El Paso	TX	79901	**800-947-2689**	915-544-8294	603
Wisconsin						
Crime Victims Services Office						
PO Box 7951	Madison	WI	53707	**800-446-6564**	608-264-9497	337-50
Housing & Economic Development Authority						
201 W Washington Ave Ste 700	Madison	WI	53703	**800-334-6873**	608-266-7884	337-50
Insurance Commission						
PO Box 7873	Madison	WI	53707	**800-236-8517**	608-266-3585	337-50
Legislature						
State Capitol	Madison	WI	53702	**800-362-9472**	608-266-9960	337-50
Parks & Recreation Bureau						
101 S Webster St PO Box 7921	Madison	WI	53707	**888-936-7463**	608-266-2621	337-50
Public Instruction Dept						
125 S Webster St PO Box 7841	Madison	WI	53707	**800-441-4563**	608-266-3390	337-50
Teacher Education & Licensing Bureau						
125 S Webster St	Madison	WI	53703	**800-441-4563**	608-266-3390	337-50
Treasurer PO Box 2114	Madison	WI	53707	**855-375-2274**		337-50
Veterans Affairs Dept						
201 W Washington Ave						
PO Box 7843	Madison	WI	53703	**800-947-8387**	608-266-1311	337-50
Vocational Rehabilitation Div						
201 East Washington Avenue						
PO Box 7852	Madison	WI	53707	**800-442-3477**	608-261-0050	337-50
Wisconsin Aviation Inc						
1741 River Dr	Watertown	WI	53094	**800-657-0761**	920-261-4567	62
Wisconsin Bill Status						
1 E Main St	Madison	WI	53708	**800-362-9472**	608-266-9960	430
Wisconsin Box Company Inc						
929 Townline Rd	Wausau	WI	54402	**800-876-6658**	715-842-2248	201
Wisconsin Coach Lines Inc						
1520 Arcadian Ave	Waukesha	WI	53186	**877-324-7767**	262-542-8861	106
Wisconsin Dells Visitors & Convention Bureau						
701 Superior St						
PO Box 390	Wisconsin Dells	WI	53965	**800-223-3557**	608-254-8088	207
Wisconsin Dental Assn						
6737 W Washington St						
Ste 2360	West Allis	WI	53214	**800-364-7646**	414-276-4520	227
Wisconsin Department of Public Instruction						
125 S Webster St PO Box 7841	Madison	WI	53707	**800-441-4563**	608-266-3390	431-5
Wisconsin Educational Communications Board						
3319 W Beltline Hwy	Madison	WI	53713	**800-422-9707**	608-264-9600	624
Wisconsin Energy Corp						
231 W Michigan St	Milwaukee	WI	53203	**800-242-9137***	414-221-2345	357-5
NYSE: WEC ■ *General						
Wisconsin Film & Bag Inc						
3100 E Richmond St	Shawano	WI	54166	**800-765-9224**	715-524-2565	65
Wisconsin Historical Museum						
30 N Carroll St	Madison	WI	53703	**888-748-7479**	608-264-6555	513
Wisconsin Indianhead Technical College						
New Richmond Campus						
1019 S Knowles Ave	New Richmond	WI	54017	**800-243-9482**	715-246-6561	788
Rice Lake Campus						
1900 College Dr	Rice Lake	WI	54868	**800-243-9482**	715-234-7082	788
Superior Campus						
600 N 21 St	Superior	WI	54880	**800-243-9482**	715-394-6677	788
Wisconsin Lutheran College						
8800 W Bluemound Rd	Milwaukee	WI	53226	**800-765-4977**	414-443-8800	166
Wisconsin Machine Tool Corp						
3225 Gateway Rd Ste 100	Brookfield	WI	53045	**800-243-3078**	262-317-3048	450
Wisconsin Maritime Museum						
75 Maritime Dr	Manitowoc	WI	54220	**866-724-2356**	920-684-0218	513
Wisconsin National Primate Research Ctr						
1220 Capitol Ct	Madison	WI	53715	**800-833-7050**	608-263-3500	659
Wisconsin Power & Light Co						
4902 N Biltmore Ln PO Box 77007	Madison	WI	53718	**800-255-4268**		775
Wisconsin Public Radio (WPR)						
821 University Ave	Madison	WI	53706	**800-747-7444**		624
Wisconsin Public Service Corp						
PO Box 19001	Green Bay	WI	54307	**800-450-7260**		775
Wisconsin Public Television (WPT)						
821 University Ave	Madison	WI	53706	**800-422-9707**	608-263-2121	624
Wisconsin Realtors Assn						
4801 Forest Run Rd Ste 201	Madison	WI	53704	**800-279-1972**	608-241-2047	647
Wisconsin Reinsurance Corp						
2810 City View Dr	Madison	WI	53707	**800-939-9473**	608-242-4500	388-4
Wisconsin State Fair Park						
640 S 84th St	West Allis	WI	53214	**800-884-3247**	414-266-7033	513
Wisconsin State Journal						
1901 Fish Hatchery Rd	Madison	WI	53713	**800-362-8333**	608-252-6200	525-2
Wisconsin State Medical Society						
330 E Lakeside St	Madison	WI	53701	**866-442-3800**		469
Wisconsin Steel & Tube Corp						
1555 N Mayfair Rd	Milwaukee	WI	53226	**800-279-8335**	414-453-4441	487
Wisconsin Veterans Home						
N2665 County Rd QQ	King	WI	54946	**877-944-6667**	715-258-5586	781
Wisconsin Veterinary Medical Assn (WVMA)						
2801 Crossroads Dr Ste 1200	Madison	WI	53718	**888-254-5202**	608-257-3665	783
Wise Alloys LLC						
4805 Second St	Muscle Shoals	AL	35661	**855-287-1922***	256-386-6000	688
*Sales						
Wise Business Forms Inc						
555 McFarland 400 Dr	Alpharetta	GA	30004	**888-815-9473**	770-442-1060	109
Wise Electric Co-op Inc						
1900 N Trinity St	Decatur	TX	76234	**888-627-9326**	940-627-2167	245
Wise Foods Inc						
245 Townpark Dr Ste 75	Kennesaw	GA	30144	**888-759-4401**	770-426-5821	295-35
Wiseco Piston Inc						
7201 Industrial Pk Blvd	Mentor	OH	44060	**800-321-1364**	440-951-6600	127
Wiseway Motor Freight Inc						
PO Box 838	Hudson	WI	54016	**800-876-1660**		770
WISP (Women's Independence Scholarship Program Inc)						
4900 Randall Pkwy Ste H	Wilmington	NC	28403	**866-255-7742**	910-397-7742	304
Wiss Janney Elstner Assoc Inc						
330 Pfingsten Rd	Northbrook	IL	60062	**800-345-3199**	847-272-7400	261
Wist Office Products Co						
107 W Julie Dr	Tempe	AZ	85283	**800-999-9478**	480-921-2900	528
Wistar Institute						
3601 Spruce St	Philadelphia	PA	19104	**800-724-6633**	215-898-3700	659
WITF-FM 89.5 (NPR)						
4801 Lindle Rd	Harrisburg	PA	17111	**800-366-9483**	717-704-3000	636-50
Withers Broadcasting Co						
PO Box 1508	Mount Vernon	IL	62864	**800-333-1577**	618-242-3500	634
WithumSmith+Brown						
5 Vaughn Dr	Princeton	NJ	08540	**866-455-7438**	609-520-1188	2
WITI (Women in Technology International)						
13351-D Riverside Dr						
Ste 441	Sherman Oaks	CA	91423	**800-334-9484**	818-788-9484	48-19
Witmer's Inc						
39821 SR 14	Salem	OH	44460	**888-427-6025**	330-427-2147	274
Witt Industries Inc						
4600 Mason-Montgomery Rd	Mason	OH	45040	**800-543-7417**		652
Witt Lincoln						
588 Camino Del Rio N	San Diego	CA	92108	**877-245-6856**	619-358-5000	56
Witt Printing Company Inc						
301 Oak St	El Dorado Springs	MO	64744	**800-641-4342**	417-876-4721	109
Witt/Kieffer Ford Hadelman & Lloyd						
2015 Spring Rd Ste 510	Oak Brook	IL	60523	**888-281-1370**	630-990-1370	266
Wittek Golf Supply Co Inc						
3865 N Commercial Ave	Northbrook	IL	60062	**800-869-1800**	847-943-2399	701
Wittenberg University						
200 W Ward St PO Box 720	Springfield	OH	45501	**800-677-7558**	937-327-6314	166
Wittenberg University Thomas Library						
807 Woodlawn Ave						
PO Box 7207	Springfield	OH	45504	**800-677-7558**	937-327-7511	431-6
Witzco Trailers Inc						
6101 McIntosh Rd	Sarasota	FL	34238	**800-363-7237**	941-922-5301	769
WIVB-TV Ch 4 (CBS)						
2077 Elmwood Ave	Buffalo	NY	14207	**800-794-3687**	716-874-4410	730-11
WIVK-FM 107.7 (Ctry)						
4711 Old Kingston Pike	Knoxville	TN	37919	**877-995-9961**	865-588-6511	
Wixon Inc						
1390 E Bolivar Ave	Saint Francis	WI	53235	**800-841-5304**	414-769-3000	295
Wizards of the Coast Inc						
1600 Lind Ave SW Ste 400	Renton	WA	98057	**800-324-6496**	425-226-6500	752
Wizcom Technologies Inc						
Boston Post Rd W 33 Ste 320	Marlborough	MA	01752	**888-777-0552**	508-251-5388	174-7
WIZF-FM 101.1 (Urban)						
705 Central Ave	Cincinnati	OH	45202	**866-236-7588**	513-679-6000	636-27
WIZN-FM 106.7 (Rock)						
255 S Champlain St	Burlington	VT	05401	**888-873-9496**	802-860-2440	636-19

Name / Address	City	State	ZIP	Toll-Free	Phone	Class
WJAX-AM 1220 (Nost)						
5353 Arlington Expy	Jacksonville	FL	32211	**800-331-0176**	904-371-1184	636-56
WJGL-FM 96.9 (CR)						
8000 Belfort Pkwy	Jacksonville	FL	32256	**800-438-1601**	904-245-8500	636-56
WJHL-TV Ch 11 (CBS)						
338 E Main St	Johnson City	TN	37601	**800-861-5255**	423-926-2151	
WJHM-FM 102 (Urban)						
1800 Pembrook Dr Ste 400	Orlando	FL	32810	**866-438-0220**	407-919-1000	636-78
WJMZ-FM 107.3 (Urban)						
220 N Main St Ste 402	Greenville	SC	29601	**800-767-1073**	864-235-1073	636-49
WJQK-FM 99.3 (Rel)						
425 Centerstone Ct	Zeeland	MI	49464	**866-931-9936**	616-931-9930	636
WJSR-FM 91.1 (CR)						
Jefferson State Community College						
2601 Carson Rd	Birmingham	AL	35215	**800-767-4984**	205-856-7702	636-14
WJZY-TV Ch 46 (CW)						
3501 Performance Rd	Charlotte	NC	28214	**888-369-4762**	704-398-0046	730-14
WKBW-TV Ch 7 (ABC)						
7 Broadcast Plaza	Buffalo	NY	14202	**888-373-7888**	716-845-6100	730-11
WKCN-FM 99.3 (Ctry)						
1820 Wynnton Rd	Columbus	GA	31906	**800-628-2866**	706-327-1217	636-31
WKCQ-FM 98.1 (Ctry)						
2000 Whittier St	Saginaw	MI	48601	**800-262-0098**	989-752-8161	636
WKDD-FM 98.1 (AC)						
7755 Freedom Ave	North Canton	OH	44720	**888-533-4582**	330-836-4700	636
WKGR-FM 98.7 (CR)						
3071 Continental Dr	West Palm Beach	FL	33407	**877-541-1966**	561-616-6600	636-118
WKIS-FM 99.9 (Ctry)						
194 NW 187th St	Miami	FL	33169	**866-978-0800**	305-654-1700	636-67
WKJV-AM 1380						
70 Adams Hill Rd	Asheville	NC	28806	**800-809-9558**	828-252-1380	636-7
WKKT-FM 96.9 (Ctry)						
801 Wood Ridge Ctr Dr	Charlotte	NC	28217	**877-903-7867**	704-714-9444	636-25
WKLB-FM 102.5 (Ctry)						
55 Morrissey Blvd	Boston	MA	02125	**888-819-1025**	617-822-9600	636-16
WKMG-TV Ch 6 (CBS)						
4466 N John Young Pkwy	Orlando	FL	32804	**800-435-7352**	407-521-1200	730-52
WKMJ-TV Ch 68 (PBS)						
600 Cooper Dr	Lexington	KY	40502	**800-432-0951**	859-258-7000	730
WKNO-FM 91.1 (NPR)						
900 Getwell Rd	Memphis	TN	38111	**800-766-9566**	901-325-6544	636-66
WKNO-TV Ch 10 (PBS)						
7151 Cherry Farms Rd	Cordova	TN	38016	**877-717-7822**	901-729-8765	730
WKPC-TV Ch 15 (PBS)						
600 Cooper Dr	Lexington	KY	40502	**800-432-0951**	859-258-7000	730
WKPT-TV Ch 19 (ABC)						
222 Commerce St	Kingsport	TN	37660	**877-768-5048**	423-246-9578	730
WKRC-TV Ch 12 (CBS)						
1906 Highland Ave	Cincinnati	OH	45219	**877-889-5610**	513-763-5500	
WKRN-TV Ch 2 (ABC)						
441 Murfreesboro Rd	Nashville	TN	37210	**800-222-5555**	615-369-7222	730-46
WKRR-FM 92.3 (CR)						
192 E Lewis St	Greensboro	NC	27406	**800-762-5923**	336-274-8042	636
WKSF-FM 99.9 (Ctry)						
13 Summerlin Rd	Asheville	NC	28806	**800-303-5477**	828-257-2700	636-7
WKSU-FM 89.7 (NPR)						
1613 E Summit St	Kent	OH	44242	**800-672-2132**	330-672-3114	636
WKVV-FM 101.7						
PO Box 2098	Omaha	NE	68103	**800-525-5683**		636
WKXW-FM 101.5 (N/T)						
109 Walters Ave	Trenton	NJ	08638	**800-800-7822**	609-359-5300	636-114
WKYC-TV Ch 3 (NBC)						
1333 Lakeside Ave E	Cleveland	OH	44114	**877-790-7370**	216-344-3333	730-15
WKYL-FM 102.1 (NAC)						
102 Perkins Bldg						
521 Lancaster Ave.	Richmond	KY	40475	**800-621-8890**		636-60
WKZL-FM 107.5 (CHR)						
192 E Lewis St	Greensboro	NC	27406	**800-682-1075**	336-274-8042	636
WLAC-AM 1510 (N/T)						
55 Music Sq W	Nashville	TN	37203	**800-688-9522**	615-664-2400	636-74
WLBZ-TV Ch 2 (NBC)						
329 Mt Hope Ave	Bangor	ME	04401	**800-244-6306**	207-942-4821	730-7
WLDE-FM 101.7 (Oldies)						
347 W Berry St Ste 600	Fort Wayne	IN	46802	**888-450-1017**	260-423-3676	636-44
WLFJ-FM 89.3 (Rel)						
2420 Wade Hampton Blvd	Greenville	SC	29615	**800-447-7234**	864-292-6040	636-49
WLLL-AM 930 (Rel)						
PO Box 11375	Lynchburg	VA	24506	**888-224-9809***	434-385-9555	636
*Cust Svc						
WLOS-TV Ch 13 (ABC)						
110 Technology Dr	Asheville	NC	28803	**800-209-2293**	828-684-1340	730-4
WLPB-TV Ch 27 (PBS)						
7733 Perkins Rd	Baton Rouge	LA	70810	**800-272-8161**	225-767-5660	730-8
WLRH-FM 89.3 (NPR)						
University of Alabama-Huntsville						
John Wright Dr	Huntsville	AL	35899	**800-239-9574**	256-895-9574	636-53
WLTW-FM 106.7 (AC)						
32 Ave of the Americas 2nd Fl	New York	NY	10013	**800-222-1067**	212-377-7900	636-76
WLUK-TV Ch 11 (Fox)						
787 Lombardi Ave	Green Bay	WI	54304	**800-242-8067**	920-494-8711	730-32
WLVQ-FM 96.3 (Rock)						
2400 Corporate Exchange Dr						
Ste 200	Columbus	OH	43231	**877-736-9696**	614-227-9696	636-32
WLYF-FM 101.5 (AC)						
20450 NW Second Ave	Miami	FL	33169	**877-790-1015**		636-67
WM Barr & Company Inc						
2105 Ch Ave	Memphis	TN	38109	**800-238-2672**	901-775-0100	543
WMAE-FM 89.5 (NPR)						
3825 Ridgewood Rd	Jackson	MS	39211	**800-850-4406**	601-432-6565	636-55
WMAG-FM 99.5 (AC)						
2-B PAI Pk	Greensboro	NC	27409	**866-415-4158**	336-822-2000	636
WMBI-FM 90.1 (Rel)						
820 N LaSalle Blvd	Chicago	IL	60610	**877-376-2194**	312-329-4300	636-26
WMBM-AM 1490 (Rel)						
13242 NW Seventh Ave	North Miami	FL	33168	**800-721-9626**	305-769-1100	636-67
WMBX-FM 102.3 (Urban)						
701 Northpoint Pkwy						
Ste 500	West Palm Beach	FL	33407	**800-969-1023**		636-118
WMCC (White Mountains Community College)						
2020 Riverside Dr	Berlin	NH	03570	**800-445-4525**	603-752-1113	160
WMEH-FM 90.9 (NPR)						
63 Texas Ave	Bangor	ME	04401	**800-884-1717**	207-941-1010	636-11
WMF (World Monuments Fund)						
350 Fifth Ave Ste 2412	New York	NY	10118	**800-547-9171**	646-424-9594	47-4
WMF Americas Inc						
3512 Faith Church Rd	Indian Trail	NC	28079	**800-966-3009**	704-882-3898	358
WMGE-FM 94.9 (Span CHR)						
7601 Riviera Blvd	Miramar	FL	33023	**877-599-2946**	954-862-2000	636
WMH (Wilcox Memorial Hospital)						
3-3420 Kuhio Hwy	Lihue	HI	96766	**877-709-9355**	808-245-1100	371-3
WMIT-FM 106.9 (Rel)						
Three Porters Cove Rd	Asheville	NC	28805	**800-330-9648**	828-285-8477	636
WMK Inc 810 Moe Dr	Akron	OH	44310	**877-275-4912**	330-633-1118	56
WMLL-FM 96.5 (CR)						
500 Commercial St	Manchester	NH	03101	**800-666-0957**	603-669-5777	
WMMPA (Wood Moulding & Millwork Producers Assn)						
507 First St	Woodland	CA	95695	**800-550-7889**	530-661-9591	48-3
WMPI-FM 105.3 (Ctry)						
22 E McClain Ave	Scottsburg	IN	47170	**800-441-1053**	812-752-3688	636
WMS Gaming Inc						
800 S Northpoint Blvd	Waukegan	IL	60085	**800-522-4700**	847-785-3000	321
WMT-FM 96.5 (AC)						
600 Old Marion Rd NE	Cedar Rapids	IA	52402	**800-258-0096**	319-395-0530	636-22
WMTW-TV Ch 8 (ABC)						
99 Danville Corner Rd	Auburn	ME	04210	**800-248-6397**	207-782-1800	730
WMU (Woman's Missionary Union)						
100 Missionary Ridge	Birmingham	AL	35242	**800-968-7301**	205-991-8100	47-20
WMUM-FM 89.7 (NPR)						
243 Carey Salem Rd	Cochran	GA	31014	**800-222-4788**	478-301-5760	636
WMVP-AM 1000 (Sports)						
190 N State St 7th Fl	Chicago	IL	60601	**800-438-3776**	312-980-1000	636-26
WMXJ-FM 102.7 (Oldies)						
20450 NW Second Ave	Miami	FL	33169	**800-924-1027**	305-521-5100	636-67
WMYA-TV Ch 40 (MNT)						
33 Villa Rd	Greenville	SC	29615	**800-288-2413**	828-684-1340	730-4
WMYD-TV Ch 20 (MNT)						
2777 Franklin Rd Ste 1220	Southfield	MI	48034	**800-825-0770**	248-355-2020	730
WMYI-FM 102.5 (AC)						
101 N Main St Ste 1000						
PO Box 100	Greenville	SC	29601	**800-248-0863**	864-235-1025	636-49
WMZQ-FM 98.7 (Ctry)						
1801 Rockville Pk Fifth Fl	Rockville	MD	20852	**800-505-0098**	240-747-2700	636
WN (World Neighbors Inc)						
4127 NW 122nd St	Oklahoma City	OK	73120	**800-242-6387**	405-752-9700	47-5
WNC (Western Nevada Community College)						
1680 Bently Pkwy S	Minden	NV	89423	**877-838-2778**	775-782-2413	160
WNC Supply LLC						
37841 N 16th St	Phoenix	AZ	85086	**800-538-5108**	623-594-4602	620
WNCF-TV Ch 32 (ABC)						
3251 Harrison Rd	Montgomery	AL	36109	**800-467-0424**	334-270-2834	730-44
WNCW-FM 88.7 (AAA)						
PO Box 804	Spindale	NC	28160	**800-245-8870**	828-287-8000	636
WNCY-FM 100.3 (Ctry)						
PO Box 23333	Green Bay	WI	54305	**800-359-1003**	920-435-3771	636-48
WNDV-FM 92.9 (CHR)						
3371 Cleveland Rd Ste 300	South Bend	IN	46628	**800-242-0100**	574-273-9300	
WNEM-TV Ch 5 (CBS)						
107 N Franklin St	Saginaw	MI	48607	**800-522-9636**	989-755-8191	730
WNEP-TV Ch 16 (ABC)						
16 Montage Mtn Rd	Moosic	PA	18507	**800-982-4374**	570-346-7474	730
WNIN-FM 88.3 (NPR)						
405 Carpenter St	Evansville	IN	47708	**855-888-9646**	812-423-2973	636-40
WNIN-TV Ch 9 (PBS)						
405 Carpenter St	Evansville	IN	47708	**855-888-9646**	812-423-2973	730-25
WNIT-TV Ch 34.1 (PBS)						
300 W Jefferson Blvd						
PO Box 7034	South Bend	IN	46601	**877-411-3662**	574-675-9648	
WNKU-FM 105.9 (Ctry)						
301 Landrum Academic Ctr	Highland Heights	KY	41099	**855-897-7897**	859-572-6500	636
WNND-FM 103.5 (NAC)						
4401 Carriage Hill Ln	Columbus	OH	43220	**877-984-8786**	614-451-2191	636-32
WNNL-FM 103.9 (Rel)						
8001-101 Creedmoor Rd	Raleigh	NC	27613	**877-310-9665**	919-848-9736	636-87
WNYT-TV Ch 13 (NBC)						
715 N Pearl St	Albany	NY	12204	**800-999-9698**	518-436-4791	730-1
WO Grubb Steel Erection Inc						
5120 Jefferson Davis Hwy	Richmond	VA	23234	**866-964-7822**	804-271-9471	190-14
WOAI-AM 1200 (N/T)						
6222 NW IH-10	San Antonio	TX	78201	**800-707-5150**	210-736-9700	636-95
Woburn Public Library						
45 Pleasant St	Woburn	MA	01801	**800-392-6089**	781-933-0148	431-3
WOCL-FM 105.9 (Rock)						
1800 Pembrook Dr Ste 400	Orlando	FL	32810	**877-919-1059**	407-919-1000	636-78
WOCN (Wound Ostomy & Continence Nurses Society)						
15000 Commerce Pkwy Ste C	Mount Laurel	NJ	08054	**888-224-9626**		48-8
WODE-FM 99.9						
107 Paxinosa Rd W	Easton	PA	18040	**800-733-2767**	610-258-6155	636
WOGG-FM 94.9 (Ctry)						
123 Blaine Rd	Brownsville	PA	15417	**866-983-9898**	724-938-2000	636
WOGL-FM 98.1 (Oldies)						
Two Bala Plz Ste 800	Bala Cynwyd	PA	19004	**800-942-8998**	610-668-5998	636
WOIO-TV Ch 19 (CBS)						
1717 E 12th St	Cleveland	OH	44114	**877-929-1943**	216-771-1943	730-15
WOI-TV Ch 5 (ABC)						
3903 Westown Pkwy	West Des Moines	IA	50266	**800-858-5555**	515-457-9645	730
Wojan Window & Door Corp						
217 Stover Rd	Charlevoix	MI	49720	**800-632-9827**	231-547-2931	475
WOKO-FM 98.9 (Ctry)						
70 Joy Dr	South Burlington	VT	05403	**800-354-9890**	802-862-9890	636
Wolf Gordon Inc						
33-00 47th Ave	Long Island City	NY	11101	**800-347-0550**		543
Wolf Manufacturing Co						
1801 W Waco Dr PO Box 3100	Waco	TX	76707	**800-437-0940**	254-753-7301	153-3
Wolf Ridge Ski Resort						
578 Vly View Cir	Mars Hill	NC	28754	**800-817-4111**	828-689-4111	660
Wolf Robotics LLC						
4600 Innovation Dr	Fort Collins	CO	80525	**866-965-3911**	970-225-7600	486
Wolf Trap Foundation for the Performing Arts						
1645 Trap Rd	Vienna	VA	22182	**877-965-3872**	703-255-1900	565
Wolf X-Ray Corp						
100 W Industry Ct	Deer Park	NY	11729	**800-356-9729***	631-242-9729	379
*Cust Svc						
Wolferman's						
2500 S Pacific Hwy PO Box 9100	Medford	OR	97501	**800-999-0169**		295-1
Wolfgang Candy Co						
50 E Fourth Ave	York	PA	17404	**800-248-4273**	717-843-5536	295-8

				Toll-Free	Phone	Class
Wolfram Research Inc 100 Trade Ctr Dr	Champaign	IL	61820	800-965-3726	217-398-0700	178
Wolfson Casing Corp 700 S Fulton Ave	Mount Vernon	NY	10550	800-221-8042	914-668-9000	295-26
WOLL-FM 105.5 (AC) 3071 Continental Dr	West Palm Beach	FL	33407	888-415-1055	561-616-6600	636-118
Wolters Kluwer Financial Services Inc 100 S Fifth St Ste 700	Minneapolis	MN	55402	800-552-9408	612-656-7700	179-10
Wolverine Mutual Insurance Co One Wolverine Way	Dowagiac	MI	49047	800-733-3320	269-782-3451	387
Wolverine Power Systems Inc 3229 80th Ave	Zeeland	MI	49464	800-485-8068	616-879-0040	511
Woman's Life Insurance Society 1338 Military St PO Box 5020	Port Huron	MI	48061	800-521-9292	810-985-5191	388-2
Woman's Missionary Union (WMU) 100 Missionary Ridge	Birmingham	AL	35242	800-968-7301	205-991-8100	47-20
Women Alive 1566 Burnside Ave	Los Angeles	CA	90019	800-554-4876	323-965-1564	47-17
Women in Military Service for America Memorial Foundation Inc Dept 560	Washington	DC	20042	800-222-2294	703-533-1155	47-19
Women in Technology International (WITI) 13351-D Riverside Dr Ste 441	Sherman Oaks	CA	91423	800-334-9484	818-788-9484	48-19
Women Management 199 Lafayette St 7th Fl	New York	NY	10012	800-838-3006	212-334-7480	
Women's & Children's Hospital of Buffalo 219 Bryant St	Buffalo	NY	14222	800-462-7653	716-878-7000	371-1
Women's Bureau 200 Constitution Ave NW Rm S3002	Washington	DC	20210	800-827-5335	202-693-6710	338-13
Women's Bureau Regional Offices						
Region 2 201 Varick St Rm 602	New York	NY	10014	800-827-5335	212-337-2389	338-13
Region 3 200 Constitution Ave NW Ste 631E	Washington	DC	20210	800-827-5335	866-487-2365	338-13
Region 4 Sam Nunn Federal Ctr 61 Forsyth St SW Ste 6B75	Atlanta	GA	30303	800-827-5335	404-562-2336	338-13
Region 5 Federal Bldg 230 S Dearborn St Rm 1022	Chicago	IL	60604	800-827-5335	312-353-6985	338-13
Region 6 Federal Bldg 525 Griffin St Ste 735	Dallas	TX	75202	800-827-5335	972-850-4700	338-13
Region 7 2300 Main St Ste 1050	Kansas City	MO	64108	800-827-5335	816-285-7233	338-13
Region 8 1999 Broadway Ste 1620 PO Box 46550	Denver	CO	80201	800-827-5335	303-844-1286	338-13
Region 9 90 Seventh St Ste 2650	San Francisco	CA	94103	800-827-5335	415-625-2638	338-13
Region 10 1111 Third Ave Rm 925	Seattle	WA	98101	800-827-5335	206-553-1534	338-13
Women's Council of REALTORS (WCR) 430 N Michigan Ave	Chicago	IL	60611	800-245-8512		48-17
Women's Independence Scholarship Program Inc (WISP) 4900 Randall Pkwy Ste H	Wilmington	NC	28403	866-255-7742	910-397-7742	304
Women's International Pharmacy Inc PO Box 6468	Madison	WI	53716	800-279-5708	608-221-7800	454
Women's Sports Foundation 1899 Hempstead Tpke Ste 400 Eisenhower Pk	East Meadow	NY	11554	800-227-3988	516-542-4700	47-22
Women's Wear Daily Magazine 750 Third Ave Fifth Fl	New York	NY	10017	800-289-0273	212-630-4600	452-11
WOMX-FM 105.1 (AC) 1800 Pembrook Dr Ste 400	Orlando	FL	32810	877-919-1051	407-919-1000	636-78
Wonder View Inn & Suites 50 Eden St PO Box 25	Bar Harbor	ME	04609	888-439-8439	207-288-3358	376
Wonderland Amusement Park 2601 Dumas Dr	Amarillo	TX	79107	800-383-4712	806-383-0832	32
Wonderlic Inc 400 Lakeview Pkwy Ste 200	Vernon Hills	IL	60061	877-605-9496	847-680-4900	628-10
Wonders of Wildlife 500 W Sunshine St	Springfield	MO	65807	877-245-9453	417-890-9453	810
Won-Door Corp 1865 South 3480 West	Salt Lake City	UT	84104	800-453-8494	801-973-7500	234
WONE-FM 97.5 (Rock) 1795 W Market St	Akron	OH	44313	888-588-8436	330-869-9800	636-2
Wong & Knowles CPA PC 340 W Butterfield Rd	Elmhurst	IL	60126	866-966-4272	630-993-2223	2
Wood & Tait Inc 64-5249 Kauakea Rd	Kamuela	HI	96743	800-774-8585	808-885-5090	397
Wood County 1 Courthouse Sq	Bowling Green	OH	43402	866-860-4140	419-354-9000	336
Wood County Electric Co-op Inc 501 S Main St	Quitman	TX	75783	800-762-2203	903-763-2203	245
Wood Moulding & Millwork Producers Assn (WMMPA) 507 First St	Woodland	CA	95695	800-550-7889	530-661-9591	48-3
Wood National Cemetery 5000 W National Ave Bldg 1301	Milwaukee	WI	53295	888-878-3256	414-382-5300	135
Wood Preservers Inc 15939 Historyland Hwy PO Box 158	Warsaw	VA	22572	800-368-2536	804-333-4022	805
Wood Pro Inc 421 Washington St PO Box 363	Auburn	MA	01501	800-786-5577	508-832-3291	741
Wood Tobe-Coburn School Eight E 40th St	New York	NY	10016	800-394-9663	212-686-9040	788
Woodard & Curran 41 Hutchins Dr	Portland	ME	04102	800-426-4262	207-774-2112	261
Woodburn Co Stores 1001 N Arney Rd	Woodburn	OR	97071	866-888-5530	503-981-1900	455
Woodburn Nursery & Azaleas 13009 McKee School Rd NE *Sales	Woodburn	OR	97071	888-634-2232*	503-634-2231	366
Woodbury County Rural Electric Co-op Assn 1495 Humboldt Ave	Moville	IA	51039	800-469-3125	712-873-3125	245
Woodbury Pewterers Inc 860 Main St S	Woodbury	CT	06798	800-648-2014		693
Woodbury University 7500 Glenoaks Blvd	Burbank	CA	91510	800-784-9663	818-767-0888	166
Woodcliff Hotel & Spa 199 Woodcliff Dr	Fairport	NY	14450	800-365-3065	585-381-4000	660
Woodcraft Supply LLC 1177 Rosemar Rd PO Box 1686	Parkersburg	WV	26105	800-535-4482		44
Woodfield Inc 3161 Hwy 376 S	Camden	AR	71701	800-501-6020	870-231-6020	187
Woodford Manufacturing Co 2121 Waynoka Rd *Sales	Colorado Springs	CO	80915	800-621-6032*		602
Woodforest Financial Group Inc PO Box 7889	Spring	TX	77387	877-968-7962	832-375-2000	69
Wood-Fruitticher Grocery Company Inc 2900 Alton Rd	Birmingham	AL	35210	800-328-0026	205-836-9663	296-8
Woodgrain Distribution 80 Shelby St	Montevallo	AL	35115	800-756-0199	205-665-2546	308
Woodgrain Millworks Inc 300 NW 16th St PO Box 566	Fruitland	ID	83619	800-452-3801	208-452-3801	494
Woodharbor Doors & Cabinetry Inc 3277 Ninth St SW	Mason City	IA	50401	866-219-9786	641-423-0444	494
Woodhill Supply Inc 4665 Beidler Rd	Willoughby	OH	44094	800-362-6111	440-269-1100	605
Woodland Aviation Inc 25170 Aviation Ave	Davis	CA	95616	800-442-1333	530-759-6037	62
Woodland Chamber of Commerce 307 First St	Woodland	CA	95695	888-843-2636	530-662-7327	137
Woodland Heights Medical Ctr 505 S John Redditt Dr	Lufkin	TX	75904	800-222-1222	936-634-8311	371-3
Woodland Hills Chamber of Commerce 20121 Ventura Blvd Ste 309	Woodland Hills	CA	91364	877-527-3247	818-347-4737	137
Woodland Hills Youth Development Ctr 3965 Stewarts Ln	Nashville	TN	37218	855-418-1622	615-532-2000	409
Woodland Public Library 250 First St	Woodland	CA	95695	800-321-2752	530-661-5980	431-3
Woodlands Academy of the Sacred Heart 760 E Westleigh Rd	Lake Forest	IL	60045	888-234-3080	847-234-4300	615
Woodlands Inn, The 1073 Hwy 315	Wilkes-Barre	PA	18702	844-779-8472	570-824-9831	660
Woodlands Resort & Conference Ctr, The 2301 N Millbend Dr *Resv	The Woodlands	TX	77380	800-433-2624*	281-367-1100	374
Woodlawn National Cemetery 1825 Davis St	Elmira	NY	14901	877-907-8585	607-732-5411	135
Woodloch Pines Inc 731 Welcome Lk Rd	Hawley	PA	18428	800-966-3562	570-685-8000	376
Woodmark Hotel on Lake Washington 1200 Carillon Pt	Kirkland	WA	98033	800-822-3700	425-822-3700	376
WOODMEN Magazine 1700 Farnam St	Omaha	NE	68102	800-225-3108	402-342-1890	452-10
Woodmen of the World Life Insurance Society 1700 Farnam St	Omaha	NE	68102	877-664-3332		388-2
Woodridge Public Library 3 Plaza Dr	Woodridge	IL	60517	800-279-0400	630-964-7899	431-3
Woodrow Wilson National Fellowship Foundation 5 Vaughn Dr # 300	Princeton	NJ	08540	800-899-9963	609-452-7007	47-11
Woodrow Wilson Presidential Library 20 N Coalter St PO Box 24	Staunton	VA	24401	888-496-6376	540-885-0897	431-2
Woodruff Electric Co-op PO Box 1619	Forrest City	AR	72336	888-559-6400	870-633-2262	245
Woodruff Energy 73 Water St PO Box 777	Bridgeton	NJ	08302	800-557-1121	856-455-1111	315
Woods Equipment Co 2606 S Illinois Rt 2 PO Box 1000	Oregon	IL	61061	800-319-6637	815-732-2141	273
Woods Resort & Conference Ctr Mountain Lk Rd PO Box 5	Hedgesville	WV	25427	800-248-2222		660
Woodshop News 10 Bokum Rd	Essex	CT	06426	800-444-7686	860-767-8227	452-14
Woodside Fund 303 Twin Dolphin Dr Ste 600	Redwood Shores	CA	94065	888-368-5545	650-610-8050	780
Woodsmith Magazine 2200 Grand Ave *Cust Svc	Des Moines	IA	50312	800-333-5075*		452-14
Woodson & Bozeman Inc 3870 New Getwell Rd	Memphis	TN	38118	800-876-4243	901-362-1500	37
Woodstock Inn & Resort 14 The Green	Woodstock	VT	05091	800-448-7900	802-457-1100	660
Woodstream Corp 69 N Locust St *All	Lititz	PA	17543	800-800-1819*	717-626-2125	280
Woodsville Guaranty Savings Bank 10 Pleasant St PO Box 266	Woodsville	NH	03785	800-564-2735	603-747-2735	69
WoodTrust Financial Corp 181 Second St S	Wisconsin Rapids	WI	54494	800-716-3742	715-423-7600	69
Woodward Communications Inc 801 Bluff St	Dubuque	IA	52001	800-553-4801		636
Woodward Resource Ctr 1251 334th St	Woodward	IA	50276	888-229-9223	515-438-2600	230
Woodway USA W229 N591 Foster Ct	Waukesha	WI	53186	800-966-3929	262-548-6235	267
Woodwind & Brasswind 4004 Technology Dr	South Bend	IN	46628	800-348-5003	574-251-3500	519
Woody Bogler Trucking Co PO Box 229	Rosebud	MO	63091	800-899-4120	573-764-3700	770
Woolaroc Ranch Museum & Wildlife Preserve 1925 Woolaroc Ranch Rd	Bartlesville	OK	74003	888-966-5276	918-336-0307	513
Woolrich Inc 2 Mill St	Woolrich	PA	17779	800-995-1299	570-769-6464	153-5
Woonsocket Harris Public Library 303 Clinton St	Woonsocket	RI	02895	800-359-3090	401-769-9044	431-3
Wooster Brush Co 604 Madison Ave	Wooster	OH	44691	800-392-7246	330-264-4440	102
Wooster Products Inc 1000 Spruce St PO Box 6005	Wooster	OH	44691	800-321-4936	330-264-2844	486
Wooster Republican Printing Co 212 E Liberty St	Wooster	OH	44691	800-686-2958	330-264-1125	628-8
Woot Inc 4121 International Pkwy	Carrollton	TX	75007	866-551-6881	972-417-3959	175
Worcester Academy 81 Providence St	Worcester	MA	01604	800-235-6426	508-754-5302	615
Worcester County Convention & Visitors Bureau 30 Elm St Second Fl	Worcester	MA	01609	866-755-7439	508-755-7400	207
Worcester Envelope Co 22 Millbury St PO Box 406	Auburn	MA	01501	800-343-1398	508-832-5394	263
Worcester Telegram & Gazette Inc 20 Franklin St PO Box 15012	Worcester	MA	01615	800-678-6680	508-793-9100	628-8
Worden Bros Inc 4905 Pine Cone Dr	Durham	NC	27707	800-776-4940	919-408-0542	179-1

Company	Address	City	State	ZIP	Toll-Free	Phone	Class
Worden Company Inc	199 E 17th St	Holland	MI	49423	**800-748-0561**	616-392-1848	318-3
Wordsmart Corp	10025 Mesa Rim Rd	San Diego	CA	92121	**800-858-9673**	858-565-8068	179-3
Work 'n Gear Stores	2300 Crown Colony Dr Ste 300	Quincy	MA	02169	**800-987-0218**		155-5
Work Out World	762 SR- 18	Brunswick	NJ	08816	**888-564-6969**	732-390-7390	351
WorkCare.com	300 S Harbor Blvd Ste 600	Anaheim	CA	92805	**800-455-6155**		195
Workers' Credit Union	815 Main St PO Box 900	Fitchburg	MA	01420	**800-221-4020**	978-345-1021	219
Working Solutions	1820 Preston Pk Blvd Ste 2000	Plano	TX	75093	**866-857-4800**	972-964-4800	727
Working Together	360 Hiatt Dr	Palm Beach Gardens	FL	33418	**800-621-5463**	561-622-6520	524-2
Workman Publishing	225 Varick St	New York	NY	10014	**800-722-7202**	212-254-5900	628-2
Workmen's Circle/Arbeter Ring Inc	247 W 37th St Fifth Fl	New York	NY	10018	**800-922-2558**	212-889-6800	48-9
Workplace Answers LLC	3701 Executive Ctr Dr Ste 201	Austin	TX	78731	**866-861-4410**		398
Workplace Law Report	1801 S Bell St	Arlington	VA	22202	**800-372-1033**		524-7
Workplace Resource LLC	4400 NE Loop 410 Ste 130	San Antonio	TX	78218	**800-580-3000**	512-472-7300	320
Workplace Systems Inc	562 Mammoth Rd	Londonderry	NH	03053	**800-258-9700**	603-622-3727	318-1
Works Computing Inc	1801 American Blvd E Ste 12	Bloomington	MN	55425	**866-222-4077**	952-746-1580	174-3
Workscape Inc	123 Felton St	Marlborough	MA	01752	**888-605-9620**	508-861-5500	38
Worksman Trading Corp	94-15 100th St	Ozone Park	NY	11416	**800-962-2453**	718-322-2000	81
Worksoft Inc	15851 Dallas Pkwy Ste 855	Addison	TX	75001	**866-836-1773**	214-239-0400	179-10
World Animal Protection (WSPA)	450 Seventh Avenue 31st Floor	New York	NY	10123	**800-883-9772**		47-3
World Book Inc	233 N Michigan Ave Ste 2000	Chicago	IL	60601	**800-967-5325**	312-729-5800	628-2
World Cat	1090 W St James St	Tarboro	NC	27886	**866-485-8899**	252-641-8000	89
World Chamber of Commerce Directory Inc	446 E 29th St	Loveland	CO	80538	**888-883-3231**	970-663-3231	628-6
World Class Plastics Inc	7695 SR- 708	Russells Point	OH	43348	**800-954-3140**	937-843-4927	601
World Concern	19303 Fremont Ave N	Seattle	WA	98133	**800-755-5022**	206-546-7201	47-5
World Courier Inc	1313 Fourth Ave	New Hyde Park	NY	11040	**800-221-6600**	516-354-2600	539
World Currency USA Inc	16 W Main St	Marlton	NJ	08053	**888-593-7927**		682
World Data Products Inc	121 Cheshire Ln	Minnetonka	MN	55305	**888-210-7636**	952-476-9000	177
World Dryer Corp	5700 McDermott Dr	Berkeley	IL	60163	**800-323-0701**	708-449-6950	36
World Electronics Sales & Service Inc	3000 Kutztown Rd	Reading	PA	19605	**800-523-0427**	610-939-9800	253
World Energy Alternatives LLC	2 Constitution Ctr	Boston	MA	02129	**800-829-3676**	617-889-7300	202
World Floor Covering Assn (WFCA)	2211 Howell Ave	Anaheim	CA	92806	**800-624-6880**	714-978-6440	48-4
World Food Program USA (WFP)	1725 Eye St NW Ste 510	Washington	DC	20036	**888-454-0555**	202-530-1694	47-5
World Fuel Services Corp	9800 NW 41st St Ste 400 *NYSE: INT*	Miami	FL	33178	**800-345-3818**	305-428-8000	572
World Future Society	7910 Woodmont Ave Ste 450	Bethesda	MD	20814	**800-989-8274**	301-656-8274	48-19
World Gospel Mission (WGM)	3783 E State Rd 18 PO Box 948	Marion	IN	46952	**800-426-0846**	765-664-7331	47-20
World Health	7222 Edgemont Blvd NW	Calgary	AB	T3A2X7	**866-278-4131**	403-239-4048	351
World Hunger Year Inc (WHY)	505 Eigth Ave Ste 2100	New York	NY	10018	**800-548-6479**	212-629-8850	47-5
World Inspection Network International Inc	12345 Lk City Way NE Ste 365	Seattle	WA	98125	**800-309-6753**		362
World Learning	1 Kipling Rd PO Box 676	Brattleboro	VT	05302	**800-257-7751**	802-257-7751	47-5
World Learning International Development Programs	1015 15th St NW Ste 750	Washington	DC	20005	**800-345-2929**	202-408-5420	47-11
World Minerals Inc	130 Castilian Dr	Goleta	CA	93117	**800-893-4445**	805-562-0200	408
World Monuments Fund (WMF)	350 Fifth Ave Ste 2412	New York	NY	10118	**800-547-9171**	646-424-9594	47-4
World Neighbors Inc (WN)	4127 NW 122nd St	Oklahoma City	OK	73120	**800-242-6387**	405-752-9700	47-5
World of Coca-Cola Atlanta	121 Baker St NW	Atlanta	GA	30313	**888-855-5701**	404-676-5151	513
World of Watches	101 S State Rd 7 Ste 201	Hollywood	FL	33023	**866-961-8463**	954-983-2181	151
World of Wigs	2305 E 17th St	Santa Ana	CA	92705	**800-794-5572**	714-547-4461	345
World Policy Institute (WPI)	220 Fifth Ave 9th Fl	New York	NY	10001	**800-207-8354**	212-481-5005	625
World Publishing Co	315 S Boulder Ave	Tulsa	OK	74102	**800-444-6552**	918-583-2161	628-8
World Relief	Seven E Baltimore St	Baltimore	MD	21202	**800-535-5433**	443-451-1900	47-5
World Securities Law Report	1801 S Bell St	Arlington	VA	22202	**800-372-1033**		524-7
World Spice Inc	223 E Highland Pkwy	Roselle	NJ	07203	**800-234-1060**	908-245-0600	295-37
World Travel Bureau Inc	618 N Main St	Santa Ana	CA	92701	**800-899-3370**	714-835-8111	761
World Travel Holdings (WTH)	100 Fordham Rd Bldg C Bldg C	Wilmington	MA	01887	**877-958-7447**	617-424-7990	761
World Travel Inc	1724 W Schuylkill Rd	Douglassville	PA	19518	**800-341-2014**	610-327-9000	761
World University	107 N Ventura St PO Box 1567	Ojai	CA	93024	**888-370-7589**	805-646-1444	166
World Vision Inc	34834 Weyerhaeuser Way S PO Box 9716	Federal Way	WA	98001	**888-511-6548**	253-815-1000	47-5
World Wide Fittings Inc	7501 N Natchez Ave	Niles	IL	60714	**800-393-9894**	847-588-2200	588
World Wide Packaging LLC	15 Vreeland Rd Ste 4	Florham Park	NJ	07932	**800-950-0390**	973-805-6500	231
World Wildlife Fund (WWF)	1250 24th St NW PO Box 97180	Washington	DC	20090	**800-225-5993**	202-293-4800	47-3
World Wildlife Fund Canada (WWF)	245 Eglinton Ave E Ste 410	Toronto	ON	M4P3J1	**800-267-2632**	416-489-8800	47-3
World Wrapps	3023 80th Ave SE Ste 200	Mercer Island	WA	98040	**888-233-9727**	206-233-9727	661
World Wrestling Entertainment Inc	1241 E Main St *NYSE: WWE*	Stamford	CT	06902	**866-993-7467**	203-352-8600	182
World's Finest Chocolate Inc	4801 S Lawndale	Chicago	IL	60632	**888-821-8452**		295-8
World*Class Learning Materials	PO Box 639	Candler	NC	28715	**800-638-6470**		243
World, The	403 US Rt 302-Berlin	Barre	VT	05641	**800-639-9753**	802-479-2582	525-4
Worldata	3000 N Military Trl	Boca Raton	FL	33431	**800-331-8102**	561-393-8200	6
WorldatWork	14040 N Northsight Blvd	Scottsdale	AZ	85260	**877-951-9191**	202-315-5500	48-12
WorldClass Travel Network	7831 Southtown Ctr Ste A	Bloomington	MN	55431	**800-234-3576**	952-835-8636	762
Worldfest Houston International Film Festival	PO Box 56566	Houston	TX	77256	**866-965-9955**	713-629-3700	282
WorldMark the Club	9805 Willows Rd NE	Redmond	WA	98052	**800-722-3487**	425-498-1950	743
WorldMed Assist	1230 Mtn Side Ct	Concord	CA	94521	**866-999-3848**		360
WORLDPAC Inc	37137 Hickory St	Newark	CA	94560	**800-888-9982**	510-742-8900	60
WorldPass Travel Group LLC	5080 Robert J Matthews Pkwy	El Dorado Hills	CA	95762	**800-949-0650**	916-939-6805	750
Worlds.com Inc	11 Royal Rd	Brookline	MA	02445	**800-315-2580**	617-725-8900	179-8
WorldStrides	218 W Water St Ste 400 *General	Charlottesville	VA	22902	**800-999-7676***		750
WorldTEK Event & Travel Management	One Audubon Ste 400	New Haven	CT	06511	**800-233-5989**	203-772-0470	762
WorldVenture	1501 W Mineral Ave	Littleton	CO	80120	**800-487-4224**	720-283-2000	47-20
Worldwatch Institute	1776 Massachusetts Ave NW	Washington	DC	20036	**877-539-9946**	202-452-1999	625
Worldwide Express	2828 Routh St Ste 400	Dallas	TX	75201	**800-758-7447**	214-720-2400	539
Worldwide Golf Shops Inc	1430 S Village Way	Santa Ana	CA	92705	**888-216-5252**	714-543-8284	701
Worldwide Holidays Inc	7800 Red Rd Ste 112	South Miami	FL	33143	**800-327-9854**	305-665-0841	761
Worldwide Sign Systems	446 N Cecil St	Bonduel	WI	54107	**800-874-3334**		692
Worldwide Steel Buildings	PO Box 588	Peculiar	MO	64078	**800-825-0316**		104
Worldwide Travel & Cruise Assoc Inc	150 S University Dr Ste E	Plantation	FL	33324	**800-881-8484**	954-452-8800	761
Worley & Obetz Inc	85 White Oak Rd PO Box 429	Manheim	PA	17545	**800-697-6891**	717-665-6891	315
Wormser Corp	150 Coolidge Ave	Englewood	NJ	07631	**800-546-4040**		153-14
Worship Network	PO Box 428	Safety Harbor	FL	34695	**800-728-8723**		729
Wort Hotel	50 N Glenwood *Cust Svc	Jackson	WY	83001	**800-322-2727***	307-733-2190	376
Worth & Company Inc	6263 Kellers Church Rd	Pipersville	PA	18947	**800-220-5130**	267-362-1100	190-10
Worth Co, The	214 Sherman Ave PO Box 88	Stevens Point	WI	54481	**800-944-1899**	715-344-6081	701
Worthen Industries Inc	Three E Spit Brook Rd	Nashua	NH	03060	**800-444-5988**	603-888-5443	3
Worthington Biochemical Corp	730 Vassar Ave	Lakewood	NJ	08701	**800-445-9603**	732-942-1660	231
Worthington Direct Holdings LLC	6301 Gaston Ave Ste 670	Dallas	TX	75214	**800-599-6636**		357-3
Worthington Industries	200 Old E Wilson Bridge Rd	Columbus	OH	43085	**866-928-2657**	614-438-3013	90
Worthington Steel Co	1127 Dearborn Dr	Columbus	OH	43085	**800-944-3733**	614-438-3210	714
Wor-Wic Community College	32000 Campus Dr	Salisbury	MD	21804	**800-735-2258**	410-334-2800	160
Wound Ostomy & Continence Nurses Society (WOCN)	15000 Commerce Pkwy Ste C	Mount Laurel	NJ	08054	**888-224-9626**		48-8
WOWK-TV Ch 13 (CBS)	555 Fifth Ave	Huntington	WV	25701	**800-333-7636**	304-525-1313	730
WOWO-AM 1190 (N/T)	2915 Maples Rd	Fort Wayne	IN	46816	**800-333-1190**	260-447-5511	636-44
WOWT-TV Ch 6 (NBC)	3501 Farnam St	Omaha	NE	68131	**866-434-8587**	402-346-6666	730-51
Wozniak Industries Inc Commercial Forged Products Div	5757 W 65th St	Bedford Park	IL	60638	**800-637-2695**	708-458-1220	478
WP (Walton Press)	402 Mayfield Dr	Monroe	GA	30655	**800-354-0235**	770-267-2596	548
WP Carey & Company LLC	50 Rockefeller Plz Second Fl *NYSE: WPC*	New York	NY	10020	**800-972-2739**	212-492-1100	646
WP Stewart & Company Ltd	527 Madison Ave 20th Fl *OTC: WPSL*	New York	NY	10022	**888-695-4092**	212-750-8585	398
WPBT-TV Ch 2 (PBS)	14901 NE 20th Ave	Miami	FL	33181	**800-222-9728**	305-949-8321	730-42
WPC (Willmar Poultry Co, The)	3735 County Rd 5 SW	Willmar	MN	56201	**800-328-8849**	320-235-8850	10-7
WPCS-FM 89.5 (Rel)	PO Box 18000	Pensacola	FL	32523	**800-726-1191**	850-479-6570	636-80
WPCV-FM 97.5 (Ctry)	404 W Lime St	Lakeland	FL	33815	**800-227-9797**	863-682-8184	636
WPEG-FM 97.9 (Urban)	1520 S Blvd Ste 300	Charlotte	NC	28203	**800-525-0098**	704-342-2644	636-25
WPGC-FM 95.5 (CHR)	4200 Parliament Pl Ste 300	Lanham	MD	20706	**877-955-5267**		636

Name	Address	City	State	ZIP	Toll-Free	Phone	Class
WPI (World Policy Institute)	220 Fifth Ave 9th Fl	New York	NY	10001	**800-207-8354**	212-481-5005	625
WPLM-FM 99.1 (AC)	17 Columbus Rd	Plymouth	MA	02360	**877-327-9991**	508-746-1390	636
WPLN-FM 90.3 (NPR)	630 Mainstream Dr	Nashville	TN	37228	**877-760-2903**	615-760-2903	636-74
WPMT-TV Ch 43 (Fox)	2005 S Queen St	York	PA	17403	**866-976-8747**	717-843-0043	730
WPNE-FM 89.3 (NPR)	2420 Nicolet Dr	Green Bay	WI	54311	**800-654-6228**	920-465-2444	636-48
WPOC-FM 93.1 (Country)	711 W 40th St Ste 350	Baltimore	MD	21211	**866-962-5487**	410-366-7600	636-10
WPR (Wisconsin Public Radio)	821 University Ave	Madison	WI	53706	**800-747-7444**		624
WPRO-FM 92.3 (CHR)	1502 Wampanoag Trl	East Providence	RI	02915	**800-638-0092**	401-433-4200	636
WPRW-FM 107.7 (Urban)	2743 Perimeter Pkwy Bldg 100 Ste 300	Augusta	GA	30909	**800-650-2876**	706-396-6000	
WPST-FM 94.5 (AC)	619 Alexander Rd 3rd Fl	Princeton	NJ	08540	**800-248-9778**	609-419-0300	636
WPT (Wisconsin Public Television)	821 University Ave	Madison	WI	53706	**800-422-9707**	608-263-2121	624
WPTD-TV Ch 16 (PBS)	110 S Jefferson St	Dayton	OH	45402	**800-247-1614**	937-220-1600	730-19
WPTF-AM 680 (N/T)	3012 Highwoods Blvd Ste 201	Raleigh	NC	27604	**800-662-7979**	919-790-9392	636-87
WPX Delivery Solutions	3320 W Valley Hwy N Ste 111	Auburn	WA	98001	**800-562-1091**	253-876-2760	539
WPXD-TV Ch 31 (I)	3975 Varsity Dr	Ann Arbor	MI	48108	**888-467-2988**	734-973-7900	730
WPXI-TV Ch 11 (NBC)	4145 Evergreen Rd	Pittsburgh	PA	15214	**866-347-4434**	412-237-1100	730-55
WPXN-TV Ch 31 (I)	810 Seventh Ave 30th Fl	New York	NY	10019	**800-987-9936**	212-603-8419	730-48
WQBE-FM 97.5 (Ctry)	817 Suncrest Pl	Charleston	WV	25303	**800-222-3697**	304-344-9700	636-24
WQED-FM 89.3 (Clas)	4802 Fifth Ave	Pittsburgh	PA	15213	**800-876-1316**	412-622-1436	636-85
WQED-TV Ch 13 (PBS)	4802 Fifth Ave	Pittsburgh	PA	15213	**800-876-1316**	412-622-1370	730-55
WQFL-FM 100.9 (Rel)	PO Box 2118	Omaha	NE	68103	**888-937-2471**		636
WQHT-FM 97.1 (Urban)	395 Hudson St Seventh Fl	New York	NY	10014	**800-223-9797**	212-229-9797	636-76
WQLH-FM 98.5 (AC)	810 Victoria St	Green Bay	WI	54302	**855-782-7985**	920-468-4100	636-48
WQLN-FM 91.3 (NPR)	8425 Peach St	Erie	PA	16509	**800-727-8854**	814-864-3001	636-38
WQLN-TV Ch 54 (PBS)	8425 Peach St	Erie	PA	16509	**800-727-8854**	814-864-3001	730-24
WQMX-FM 94.9	1795 W Market St	Akron	OH	44313	**800-589-6499**	330-869-9800	636-2
WQN Inc	14911 Quorum Dr Ste 140 *OTC: WQNI*	Dallas	TX	75254	**866-661-6176**		726
WQQL-FM 101.9 (Oldies)	3501 E Sangamon Ave	Springfield	IL	62707	**877-984-8786**	217-753-5400	
WQSR-FM 102.7 (Var)	711 W 40th St	Baltimore	MD	21211	**888-410-1027**	410-366-7600	636-10
WQUN-AM 1220 (Nost)	3085 Whitney Ave	Hamden	CT	06518	**800-462-1944**	203-582-8984	636
WR Case & Sons Cutlery Co	50 Owens Way PO Box 4000	Bradford	PA	16701	**800-523-6350**		222
WR Grace & Co	7500 Grace Dr *NYSE: GRA*	Columbia	MD	21044	**800-638-6014**	410-531-4000	143
WR Hambrecht & Co	909 Montgomery St 3rd Fl *Cust Svc	San Francisco	CA	94133	**855-753-6484***	415-551-8600	681
Wragtime Air Freight Inc	596 W 135th St	Gardena	CA	90248	**800-586-9701**		770
WRAL-FM 101.5 (AC)	3100 Highwoods Blvd Ste 140	Raleigh	NC	27604	**800-745-3000**	919-890-6101	636-87
WRAL-TV Ch 5 (CBS)	2619 Western Blvd	Raleigh	NC	27606	**800-245-9725**	919-821-8555	730-60
Wrangell Harbor	PO Box 531	Wrangell	AK	99929	**800-347-4462**	907-874-3736	611
Wrap-On Company Inc	5550 W 70th Pl	Chicago	IL	60638	**800-621-6947**	708-496-2150	800
WRAZ-TV Ch 50 (Fox)	512 S Mangum St	Durham	NC	27701	**877-369-5050**	919-595-5050	730-60
WRBS-FM 95.1 (Rel)	3500 Commerce Dr	Baltimore	MD	21227	**800-965-9324**	410-247-4100	636-10
WRBT-FM 94.9 (Ctry)	600 Corporate Cir	Harrisburg	PA	17110	**800-682-3047**	717-540-8800	636-50
WRCH-FM 100.5 (AC)	10 Executive Dr	Farmington	CT	06032	**800-530-1005**	860-677-6700	636
WRDW-FM 96.5 (Urban)	555 City Line Ave Ste 330	Bala Cynwyd	PA	19004	**866-811-4111**	610-667-9000	636
WRDW-TV Ch 12 (CBS)	PO Box 1212	Augusta	GA	30903	**866-591-2502**	803-278-1212	
WREA (White River Electric Assn)	PO Box 958	Meeker	CO	81641	**800-922-1987**	970-878-5041	245
WRFX-FM 99.7 (CR)	801 Wood Ridge Ctr Dr	Charlotte	NC	28217	**800-766-9970**	704-714-9444	636-25
Wright & Lato	2100 Felver Ct	Rahway	NJ	07065	**800-724-1855**	973-674-8700	406
Wright Business Graphics (WBG)	18440 NE San Rafael St PO Box 20489	Portland	OR	97230	**800-547-8397**		109
Wright Color Graphics	9051 Sunland Blvd	Sun Valley	CA	91352	**877-246-8877**	818-246-8877	618
Wright Express Corp	97 Darling Ave *NYSE: WEX*	South Portland	ME	04106	**800-761-7181**	207-773-8171	217
Wright Global Graphics	5115 Prospect St	Thomasville	NC	27360	**800-678-9019**	336-472-4200	410
Wright Group, The	6428 Airport Rd	Crowley	LA	70526	**800-201-3096**	337-783-3096	576
Wright Investors' Service	440 Wheelers Farms Rd	Milford	CT	06461	**800-232-0013**	203-783-4400	398
Wright Line LLC	160 Gold Star Blvd	Worcester	MA	01606	**800-225-7348**	508-852-4300	318-1
Wright Medical Group Inc	5677 Airline Rd *NASDAQ: WMGI*	Arlington	TN	38002	**800-238-7188**	901-867-9971	472
Wright Medical Technology Inc	5677 Airline Rd	Arlington	TN	38002	**800-238-7188**	901-867-9971	472
Wright State University	3640 Colonel Glenn Hwy *Admissions	Dayton	OH	45435	**800-247-1770***	937-775-5740	166
Wright State University Boonshoft School of Medicine	3640 Col Glenn Hwy	Dayton	OH	45435	**800-338-4057**	937-775-2934	167-2
Wright State University Lake	7600 Lk Campus Dr	Celina	OH	45822	**800-237-1477**	419-586-0300	160
Wright Transportation Inc	2333 Dauphin Island Pkwy	Mobile	AL	36605	**800-342-4598**	251-432-6390	770
Wright Travel Inc	2505 21st Ave S Fifth Fl	Nashville	TN	37212	**800-577-0888**	615-783-1111	761
Wright-Hennepin Co-op Electric Assn	6800 Electric Dr PO Box 330	Rockford	MN	55373	**800-943-2667**	763-477-3000	245
Wright-Patt Credit Union Inc	2455 Executive Pk Blvd PO Box 286	Fairborn	OH	45324	**800-762-0047**	937-912-7000	219
Wrightsoft Corp	131 Hartwell Ave	Lexington	MA	02421	**800-225-8697**		225
Wrigley Co, The	410 N Michigan Ave	Chicago	IL	60611	**888-985-2064**	312-644-2121	295-6
Wrigley Field	1060 W Addison St	Chicago	IL	60613	**866-800-1275**	773-404-2827	711
Wrisco Industries Inc	355 Hiatt Dr Ste B	Palm Beach Gardens	FL	33418	**800-627-2646**	561-626-5700	487
WRIT (Washington Real Estate Investment Trust)	6110 Executive Blvd Ste 800 *NYSE: WRE*	Rockville	MD	20852	**800-565-9748**	301-984-9400	646
Writer's Digest	4700 E Galbraith Rd *Cust Svc	Cincinnati	OH	45236	**800-283-0963***	513-531-2690	452-21
Writer's Digest Book Club	4700 E Galbraith Rd *Cust Svc	Cincinnati	OH	45236	**800-759-0963***	513-531-2690	92
Writers Guild of America West (WGAw)	7000 W Third St	Los Angeles	CA	90048	**800-421-4182**	323-951-4000	411
WRKO-AM 680 (N/T)	20 Guest St Third Fl	Brighton	MA	02135	**877-469-4322**	617-779-3400	636
WRLK-TV Ch 35 (PBS)	1101 George Rogers Blvd	Columbia	SC	29201	**800-922-5437**	803-737-3200	730-16
WRNR-FM 103.1	112 Main St 3rd Fl	Annapolis	MD	21401	**877-762-1031**	410-626-0103	
WROQ-FM 101.1 (CR)	25 Garlington Rd	Greenville	SC	29615	**888-257-0058**	864-271-9200	636-49
Wrought Washer Manufacturing Inc	2100 S Bay St	Milwaukee	WI	53207	**800-558-5217**	414-744-0771	478
WRR Environmental Services	5200 Ryder Rd	Eau Claire	WI	54701	**800-727-8760**	715-834-9624	658
WRTI-FM 90.1 (NPR)	1509 Cecil B Moore Ave 3rd Fl	Philadelphia	PA	19121	**866-809-9784**	215-204-8405	636-82
WRTV-TV Ch 6 (ABC)	1330 N Meridian St	Indianapolis	IN	46202	**877-667-4265**	317-635-9788	
WRVE-FM 99.5 (AC)	1203 Troy-Schenectady Rd Riverhill Ctr Ste 201	Latham	NY	12110	**800-995-9783**	518-452-4800	636
WRVM-FM 102.7 (Rel)	PO Box 212	Suring	WI	54174	**888-225-9786**	920-842-2900	636
WS Badcock Corp (WSBC)	PO Box 497	Mulberry	FL	33860	**800-223-2625**		320
WS Emerson Co Inc	15 Acme Rd	Brewer	ME	04412	**800-789-6120**		154
WS Hampshire Inc	365 Keyes Ave	Hampshire	IL	60140	**800-541-0251**	847-683-4400	715
WS Packaging Group Inc	2571 S. Hemlock Rd	Green Bay	WI	54229	**800-236-3424**	800-818-5481	410
WSBC (WS Badcock Corp)	PO Box 497	Mulberry	FL	33860	**800-223-2625**		320
WSBE-TV Ch 36 (PBS)	50 Pk Ln	Providence	RI	02907	**866-438-0220**	401-222-3636	730-59
WSBT-TV Ch 22 (CBS)	1301 E Douglas Rd	Mishawaka	IN	46545	**877-634-7181**	574-232-6397	730
WSCB-FM 89.9 (Urban)	263 Alden St	Springfield	MA	01109	**800-727-0504**	413-748-3000	636-105
WSCN-FM 100.5 (NPR)	207 W Superior St Ste 224	Duluth	MN	55802	**800-228-7123**	218-722-9411	636-36
WSEE-TV Ch 35 (CBS)	3514 State St	Erie	PA	16508	**888-346-8982**	814-454-5201	730-24
WSEN-FM 92.1 (CR)	8456 Smokey Hollow Rd PO Box 1050	Baldwinsville	NY	13027	**866-890-6453**	315-635-3971	636
WSET-TV Ch 13 (ABC)	2320 Langhorne Rd	Lynchburg	VA	24501	**800-639-7847**	434-528-1313	730
WSF Industries Inc	Seven Hackett Dr	Tonawanda	NY	14150	**800-874-8265**	716-692-4930	475
WSFS Financial Corp	500 Delaware Ave *NASDAQ: WSFS*	Wilmington	DE	19801	**888-973-7226**	302-792-6000	357-2
WSHA-FM 88.9 (Jazz)	118 E S St	Raleigh	NC	27601	**800-241-0421**	919-546-8430	636-87
WSHU-FM 91.1 (NPR)	5151 Pk Ave	Fairfield	CT	06825	**800-937-6045**	203-365-0425	636
WSI Internet	5580 Explorer Dr Ste 600	Mississauga	ON	L4W4Y1	**888-678-7588**	905-678-7588	309
WSJV-TV Ch 28 (Fox)	PO Box 28	South Bend	IN	46624	**800-435-3803**	574-679-9758	
WSLS-TV Ch 10 (NBC)	PO Box 10	Roanoke	VA	24022	**800-800-9757**	540-981-9110	730-62
WSNA (Washington State Nurses Assn)	575 Andover Pk W Ste 101	Seattle	WA	98188	**800-231-8482**	206-575-7979	526
WSOC-TV Ch 9 (ABC)	1901 N Tryon St	Charlotte	NC	28206	**800-247-6299**	704-338-9999	730-14
WSPA (World Animal Protection)	450 Seventh Avenue 31st Floor	New York	NY	10123	**800-883-9772**		47-3
WSPA-TV Ch 7 (CBS)	250 International Dr	Spartanburg	SC	29303	**800-207-6397**	864-576-7777	730-4
WSPD-AM 1370 (N/T)	125 S Superior St	Toledo	OH	43604	**800-745-3000**	419-244-8321	636-112

	City	State	Zip	Toll-Free	Phone	Class
WSSA (Wine & Spirits Shippers Assn Inc)						
11800 Sunrise Vly Dr	Reston	VA	20191	**800-368-3167***	703-860-2300	48-6
*General						
WSTO-FM 96.1 (CHR)						
1162 Mt Auburn Rd	Evansville	IN	47720	**888-685-1961**	812-421-9696	636-40
WSTW-FM 93.7 (CHR)						
2727 Shipley Rd	Wilmington	DE	19810	**800-544-9370**	302-478-2700	636-119
WSUA-AM 1260 (Span)						
2100 Coral Way Ste 201	Miami	FL	33145	**877-453-5437**	305-285-1260	636-67
WSUN-FM 97.1 (Alt)						
11300 Fourth St N						
Ste 300	Saint Petersburg	FL	33716	**877-327-9797**	727-579-2000	636-111
WSVH-FM 91.1 (NPR)						
13040 Abercorn St Ste 8	Savannah	GA	31419	**877-472-1227**	912-344-3565	636-100
WSWT-FM 106.9 (AC)						
331 Fulton St Ste 1200	Peoria	IL	61602	**800-597-1069**	309-637-3700	636-81
WTBC-AM 1230 (N/T)						
2110 McFarland Blvd E Ste C	Tuscaloosa	AL	35404	**800-518-1977**	205-758-5523	636-116
WTEN-TV Ch 10 (ABC)						
341 Northern Blvd	Albany	NY	12204	**800-888-9836**	518-436-4822	730-1
WTFM-FM 98.5 (AC)						
222 Commerce St	Kingsport	TN	37660	**888-633-5452**	423-246-9578	636
WTH (World Travel Holdings)						
100 Fordham Rd Bldg C Bldg C	Wilmington	MA	01887	**877-958-7447**	617-424-7990	761
WTIU-TV Ch 30 (PBS)						
1229 E Seventh St	Bloomington	IN	47405	**800-662-3311**	812-855-5900	730
WTKR-TV Ch 3 (CBS)						
720 Boush St	Norfolk	VA	23510	**866-347-2423**	757-446-1000	730-49
WTKS-AM 1290 (N/T)						
245 Alfred St	Savannah	GA	31408	**877-263-7995**	912-964-7794	636-100
WTLY-FM 107.1 (AC)						
325 John Knox Rd Bldg G	Tallahassee	FL	32303	**855-274-2389**	850-422-3107	636-110
WTP Inc PO Box 937	Coloma	MI	49038	**800-521-0731**	269-468-3399	722
WTPT-FM 93.3 (Rock)						
25 Garlington Rd	Greenville	SC	29615	**800-774-0093**	864-271-9200	636-49
WTSP-TV Ch 10 (CBS)						
11450 Gandy Blvd N	Saint Petersburg	FL	33702	**877-762-7824**	727-577-1010	730-76
WTSU-FM 89.9 (NPR)						
Troy University Wallace Hall	Troy	AL	36082	**800-800-6616**		636
WTTG-TV Ch 5 (Fox)						
5151 Wisconsin Ave NW	Washington	DC	20016	**866-756-3587**	202-244-5151	730-79
WTTS-FM 92.3 (AAA)						
400 One City Centre	Bloomington	IN	47404	**800-923-9887**	812-332-3366	636
WTVD-TV Ch 11 (ABC)						
411 Liberty St	Durham	NC	27701	**855-324-8477**	919-683-1111	730-60
WTVP-TV Ch 47 (PBS)						
101 State St	Peoria	IL	61602	**800-837-4747**	309-677-4747	730-53
WUAL-FM 91.5 (NPR)						
166 Reese Phifer Hall						
PO Box 870150	Tuscaloosa	AL	35487	**800-654-4262**	205-348-6644	636-116
Wuesthoff Medical Ctr Rockledge						
110 Longwood Ave	Rockledge	FL	32955	**800-999-6673**	321-636-2211	371-3
WUMB-FM 91.9 (Folk)						
100 Morrissey Blvd	Boston	MA	02125	**800-573-2100**	617-287-6900	636-16
WUMP-AM 730 (Sports)						
3280 Peachtree Rd Ste 2300	Atlanta	GA	30305	**866-485-9867**	256-830-8300	636
WUNC-FM 91.5 (NPR)						
120 Friday Center Dr						
PO Box 0915	Chapel Hill	NC	27517	**800-962-9862**	919-445-9150	636
WUOM-FM 91.7 (NPR)						
535 W William St Ste 110	Ann Arbor	MI	48103	**888-258-9866**	734-764-9210	
WUOT-FM 91.9 (NPR)						
209 Communications Bldg						
University of Tennessee	Knoxville	TN	37996	**888-266-9868**	865-974-5375	
WURTH (Action Bolt & Tool Co)						
2051 E Blue Heron Blvd	Riviera Beach	FL	33404	**800-423-0700**		348
Wurth Service Supply Inc						
4935 W 86th St	Indianapolis	IN	46268	**877-999-8784**	317-704-1000	348
Wurth USA Inc						
93 Grant St	Ramsey	NJ	07446	**800-987-8487**	201-825-2710	60
WUSF-FM 89.7 (NPR)						
4202 E Fowler Ave TVB 100	Tampa	FL	33620	**800-741-9090**	813-974-8700	636-111
WUSF-TV Ch 16 (PBS)						
4202 E Fowler Ave	Tampa	FL	33620	**800-654-3703**	813-974-4000	730-76
WUTC-FM 88.1 (NPR)						
615 McCallie Ave						
104 Cadek Hall Dept 1151	Chattanooga	TN	37403	**800-272-3900**	423-425-4756	
WUWM-FM 89.7 (NPR)						
111 E Wisconsin Ave Ste 700	Milwaukee	WI	53202	**844-387-6926**	414-227-3355	636-68
WVCY-TV Ch 30 (Ind)						
3434 W Kilbourn Ave	Milwaukee	WI	53208	**800-729-9829**	414-935-3000	730-43
WVES (Virginia West Electric Supply Co)						
250 12-th St W	Huntington	WV	25704	**800-624-3433**	304-525-0361	246
WVEZ-FM 106.9 (AC)						
612 S 4th St	Louisville	KY	40202	**866-566-2456**	502-589-4800	636-63
WVII-TV Ch 7 (ABC)						
371 Target Industrial Cir	Bangor	ME	04401	**888-820-8458***	207-945-6457	730-7
*General						
WVIT-TV Ch 30 (NBC)						
1422 New Britain Ave	West Hartford	CT	06110	**800-523-9848**	860-521-3030	730
WVMA (Wisconsin Veterinary Medical Assn)						
2801 Crossroads Dr Ste 1200	Madison	WI	53718	**888-254-5202**	608-257-3665	783
WVMA (Wyoming Veterinary Medical Assn)						
1841 W Secluded Ct	Kuna	ID	83634	**800-272-1813**	208-922-9431	783
WVNA (West Virginia Nurses Assn)						
1007 Bigley Ave Ste 308	Charleston	WV	25302	**800-400-1226**	304-342-1169	526
WVOM-FM 103.9 (N/T)						
184 Target Industrial Cir	Bangor	ME	04401	**800-966-1039**	207-947-9100	636-11
WVPE-FM 88.1 (NPR)						
2424 California Rd	Elkhart	IN	46514	**888-399-9873**	574-262-5660	636
WVPS-FM 107.9 (NPR)						
365 Troy Ave	Colchester	VT	05446	**800-639-2192**	802-655-9451	636
WVTF-FM 89.1 (NPR)						
3520 Kingsbury Ln	Roanoke	VA	24014	**800-856-8900**	540-989-8900	636-90
WVTM-TV Ch 13 (NBC)						
1732 Valley View Dr	Birmingham	AL	35209	**844-248-7698**	205-933-1313	730-9
WW Grainger Inc						
100 Grainger Pkwy	Lake Forest	IL	60045	**888-361-8649**	847-535-1000	246
NYSE: GWW						
WW Norton & Company Inc						
500 Fifth Ave Sixth Fl	New York	NY	10110	**800-233-4830**	212-354-5500	628-2
WWDC-FM 101.1 (Rock)						
1801 Rockville Pk Fifth Fl	Rockville	MD	20852	**866-913-2101**	240-747-2701	636
WWF (World Wildlife Fund Canada)						
245 Eglinton Ave E Ste 410	Toronto	ON	M4P3J1	**800-267-2632**	416-489-8800	47-3
WWF (World Wildlife Fund)						
1250 24th St NW PO Box 97180	Washington	DC	20090	**800-225-5993**	202-293-4800	47-3
WWFG-FM 99.9 (Ctry)						
351 Tilghman Rd	Salisbury	MD	21804	**800-664-3764**	410-742-1923	636
WWGR-FM 101.9 (Ctry)						
10915 K-Nine Dr	Bonita Springs	FL	34135	**877-787-1019**	239-495-8383	636
WWKA-FM 92.3 (Ctry)						
4192 N John Young Pkwy	Orlando	FL	32804	**866-438-0220**	407-298-9292	636-78
WWMT-TV Ch 3 (CBS)						
590 W Maple St	Kalamazoo	MI	49008	**800-875-3333**		730
WWNO-FM 89.9 (NPR)						
University of New Orleans						
Lake Frnt Campus	New Orleans	LA	70148	**800-286-7002**	504-280-7000	636-75
WWPR-FM 105.1 (Urban)						
32 Ave of the Americas	New York	NY	10013	**800-585-1051**	212-377-7900	636-76
WWSW-FM 94.5 (Oldies)						
200 Fleet St 4th Fl	Pittsburgh	PA	15220	**800-653-2258**	412-937-1441	636-85
WXBM-FM 102.7 (Ctry)						
6085 Quintette Rd	Pace	FL	32571	**844-962-7436**	850-994-5357	636
WXEL-FM 90.7 (NPR)						
3401 S Congress Ave	West Palm Beach	FL	33426	**800-915-9935**	561-737-8000	636-118
WXEL-TV Ch 42 (PBS)						
PO Box 6607	West Palm Beach	FL	33405	**800-915-9935**	561-737-8000	730-80
WXGL-FM 107.3 (AC)						
11300 Fourth St N						
Ste 300	Saint Petersburg	FL	33716	**800-242-1073**	727-579-2000	636-111
WXKR-FM 94.5 (CR)						
3225 Arlington Ave	Toledo	OH	43614	**866-240-9945**	419-725-5700	636-112
WXLK-FM 92.3 (CHR)						
3934 Electric Rd SW	Roanoke	VA	24018	**800-468-9236**	540-774-9200	636-90
WXXJ-FM 102.9 (AC)						
8000 Belfort Pkwy	Jacksonville	FL	32256	**800-460-6394**	904-245-8500	636-56
WXYZ-TV Ch 7 (ABC)						
20777 W 10-Mile Rd	Southfield	MI	48037	**800-825-0770**	248-827-7777	730
Wyandot Inc						
135 Wyandot Ave	Marion	OH	43302	**800-992-6368**	740-383-4031	295-35
Wyatt Transfer Inc						
3035 Bells Rd PO Box 24326	Richmond	VA	23224	**800-552-5708**	804-743-3800	770
Wyatt-Quarles Seed Co						
730 US Hwy 70 W	Garner	NC	27529	**800-662-7591**	919-772-4243	274
Wycliffe Bible Translators						
11221 John Wycliffe Blvd	Orlando	FL	32832	**800-992-5433**	407-852-3600	47-20
Wyffels Hybrids Inc						
13344 US Hwy 6	Geneseo	IL	61254	**800-369-7833**	309-944-8334	10-4
WYFF-TV Ch 4 (NBC)						
505 Rutherford St	Greenville	SC	29609	**800-453-9933**	864-242-4404	730-4
WYGM-AM 740 (Span)						
2500 Maitland Ctr Pkwy Ste 401	Maitland	FL	32751	**800-729-8255**	407-916-7800	636
WYKZ-FM 98.7 (AC)						
245 Alfred St	Savannah	GA	31408	**800-473-8546**	912-964-7794	636-100
WYLD-AM 940 (Rel)						
929 Howard Ave	New Orleans	LA	70113	**800-899-9265**	504-679-7300	636-75
Wylie Spray Center						
702 E 40th St	Lubbock	TX	79404	**888-249-5162**	806-763-1335	273
Wynalda Packaging						
8221 Graphic Dr NE	Belmont	MI	49306	**800-952-8668***	616-866-1561	541
*General						
Wyndham ByRequest Program						
PO Box 4090	Aberdeen	SD	57401	**800-996-3426**		375
AmeriHost Inn						
8001 International Dr	Orlando	FL	32819	**877-999-3223***	407-351-2420	376
*Resv						
Baymont Inn & Suites						
PO Box 4090	Aberdeen	SD	57401	**866-464-2321**		376
Ramada						
949 Route 46	Parsippany	NJ	07054	**877-212-2733***		376
*Resv						
Wyndham Hotel Group						
Travelodge						
PO Box 4090	Aberdeen	SD	57041	**800-525-4055***	312-427-8000	376
*Resv						
Wyndham Vacation Resorts						
6277 Sea Harbor Dr	Orlando	FL	32821	**800-251-8736**		376
Wyndham Lake Buena Vista						
1850 Hotel Plaza Blvd	Lake Buena Vista	FL	32830	**800-624-4109**	407-828-4444	376
Wyndham Peachtree Conference Ctr						
2443 Hwy 54 W	Peachtree City	GA	30269	**800-996-3426**	770-487-2000	374
Wyndham Vacation Rentals						
14 Sylvan Way	Parsippany	NJ	07054	**800-467-3529**	973-753-6300	660
Wyndham Vacation Resorts King Cotton Villas						
One King Cotton Rd	Edisto Beach	SC	29438	**800-251-8736**	843-869-2561	660
Wynfrey Hotel						
1000 Riverchase Galleria	Birmingham	AL	35244	**800-633-7313**	205-987-1600	376
Wynn Las Vegas						
3131 Las Vegas Blvd S	Las Vegas	NV	89109	**877-321-9966**	702-770-7000	376
Wynne Transport Service Inc						
2222 N 11th St	Omaha	NE	68108	**800-383-9330**	402-342-4001	770
Wyo-Ben Inc						
1345 Discovery Dr	Billings	MT	59102	**800-548-7055***	406-652-6351	498-2
*Cust Svc						
Wyoming						
Aging Div						
6101 Yellowstone Rd N Rm 259B	Cheyenne	WY	82002	**800-442-2766**	307-777-7986	337-51
Highway Patrol (WHP)						
5300 Bishop Blvd	Cheyenne	WY	82009	**800-442-9090**	307-777-4301	337-51
State Parks & Historical Sites Div						
2301 Central Ave	Cheyenne	WY	82002	**877-996-7275**	307-777-6323	337-51
Tourism Div						
1520 Etchepare Cir	Cheyenne	WY	82007	**800-225-5996**	307-777-7777	337-51
Wyoming Assn of Realtors						
951 Werner Ct Ste 300	Casper	WY	82601	**800-676-4085**	307-237-4085	647
Wyoming Legislative Service Office						
3001 E Pershing Blvd	Cheyenne	WY	82002	**800-342-9570**	307-777-7881	430
Wyoming Machinery Co						
5300 Old W Yellowstone Hwy	Casper	WY	82604	**800-244-0527**	307-472-1000	355
Wyoming Medical Ctr						
1233 E Second St	Casper	WY	82601	**800-822-7201**	307-577-7201	371-3
Wyoming Medical Society						
122 E 17th St	Cheyenne	WY	82001	**888-879-3599**	307-635-2424	469
Wyoming Public Television						
2660 Peck Ave	Riverton	WY	82501	**800-495-9788**	307-856-6944	624

Alphabetical Section

Name / Address	Toll-Free	Phone	Class
Wyoming Republican Party 1821 Carey Ave PO Box 984 ..... Casper WY 82003	800-424-9530	307-234-9166	609-2
Wyoming Seminary 201 N Sprague Ave ..... Kingston PA 18704	877-996-7361	570-270-2160	615
Wyoming Tribune-Eagle 702 W Lincolnway ..... Cheyenne WY 82001	800-561-6268	307-634-3361	525-2
Wyoming Veterinary Medical Assn (WVMA) 1841 W Secluded Ct ..... Kuna ID 83634	800-272-1813	208-922-9431	783
Wyotech Sacramento 980 Riverside Pkwy ..... West Sacramento CA 95605	888-308-7158	916-376-8888	788
WYOU-TV Ch 22 (CBS) 62 S Franklin St ..... Wilkes-Barre PA 18701	855-241-5144	570-961-2222	730
WYPR-FM 88.1 (NPR) 2216 N Charles St ..... Baltimore MD 21218	866-789-8627	410-235-1660	636-10
Wyrulec Co 3978 US Hwy 26/85 ..... Torrington WY 82240	800-628-5266	307-837-2225	245
Wyse Meter Solutions Inc RPO Newmarket Court PO Box 95530 ..... Newmarket ON L3Y8J8	866-681-9465		390
WYSE Technology Inc 3471 N First St ..... San Jose CA 95134	800-800-9973	408-473-1200	174-1
Wysong Inc 4820 US 29 N ..... Greensboro NC 27405	800-299-7664	336-621-3960	451
WZPX-TV Ch 43 (I) 2610 Horizon Dr SE Ste E ..... Grand Rapids MI 49546	800-987-9936	616-222-4343	730-31
WZVN-TV Ch 26 (ABC) 3719 Central Ave ..... Fort Myers FL 33901	888-232-8635	239-939-2020	730-45

X

Name / Address	Toll-Free	Phone	Class
Xactware Solutions Inc One Xactware Plz ..... Orem UT 84097 *Sales	800-424-9228*	801-764-5900	179-11
Xaloy Inc 1399 Countyline Rd ..... New Castle PA 16101	800-897-2830		614
Xamax Industries Inc 63 Silvermine Rd ..... Seymour CT 06483	888-926-2988	203-888-7200	550
Xand Corp 11 Skyline Dr ..... Hawthorne NY 10532	800-522-2823	914-592-8282	458
Xante Corp 2800 Dauphin St Ste 100 ..... Mobile AL 36606	800-926-8839	251-473-6502	174-6
Xantech Corp 1969 Kellogg Ave ..... Carlsbad CA 92008 *Sales	800-843-5465*	818-362-0353	51
Xanterra Parks & Resorts 6312 S Fiddlers Green Cir Ste 600-N ..... Greenwood Village CO 80111	800-236-7916	303-600-3400	271
Xantrex Technology Inc 3700 Gilmore Way ..... Burnaby BC V5G4M1	800-670-0707	604-422-8595	253
XATA Corp 965 Prairie Ctr Dr ..... Eden Prairie MN 55344	800-745-9282	952-707-5600	522
Xavier University 3800 Victory Pkwy ..... Cincinnati OH 45207	800-344-4698	513-745-3000	166
Xavier University Library 3800 Victory Pkwy ..... Cincinnati OH 45207	877-382-2293	513-745-3881	431-6
Xavier University of Louisiana 1 Drexel Dr ..... New Orleans LA 70125	877-520-7388	504-486-7411	166
Xcaliber LP 5051 Fm 2920 ..... Spring TX 77388	866-620-8586	281-219-8100	191
Xcel Energy Inc PO Box 840 ..... Denver CO 80201 NYSE: XEL	877-322-8228	303-571-7511	775
X-Cel Optical Company Inc 806 S Benton Dr ..... Sauk Rapids MN 56379 *General	800-747-9235*	320-251-8404	535
Xcerra Corporation 1355 California Cir ..... Milpitas CA 95035 NASDAQ: XCRA	800-451-2400	408-635-4300	248
X-COM Systems LLC 12345-B Sunrise Vly Dr ..... Reston VA 20191	800-342-8408	703-390-1087	204
Xeris Pharmaceuticals Inc 3208 Red River St Ste 300 ..... Austin TX 78705	888-570-4781		231
Xerox Canada Ltd 5650 Yonge St ..... North York ON M2M4G7	800-939-3769		582
Xerox Corp 45 Glover Ave PO Box 4505 ..... Norwalk CT 06856 NYSE: XRX	800-327-9753	203-968-3000	582
Xerox Financial Services Inc 800 Long Ridge Rd ..... Stamford CT 06904	800-275-9376	203-968-3000	216
Xerox Foundation 45 Glover Ave ..... Norwalk CT 06856	800-275-9376		303
Xertrex International Inc 1530 W Glenlake Ave ..... Itasca IL 60143	800-822-2437	630-773-4020	553
Xertrex International Inc Tabbies Div 1530 W Glenlake Ave ..... Itasca IL 60143	800-822-2437	630-773-4160	553
XETV-TV Ch 6 (CW) 8253 Ronson Rd ..... San Diego CA 92111	866-700-6397	858-279-6666	730-68
X-Gen Pharmaceuticals Inc 300 Daniels Zenker Dr PO Box 445 ..... Horseheads NY 14845	866-390-4411		577
Xilinx Inc 2100 Logic Dr ..... San Jose CA 95124 NASDAQ: XLNX	800-594-5469	408-559-7778	687
XIOtech Corp 9950 Federal Dr Ste 100 ..... Colorado Springs CO 80921	866-472-6764	719-388-5500	179-12
XL Brands 198 Nexus Dr ..... Dalton GA 30721	800-367-4583	706-272-5800	143
XL Specialty Insurance Co 70 Seaview Ave ..... Stamford CT 06902	877-263-7995	203-964-5200	388-5
Xlibris Corp 1663 Liberty Dr Ste 200 ..... Bloomington IN 47403	888-795-4274		619
XO Communications Inc 13865 Sunrise Vly Dr ..... Herndon VA 20171	866-349-0134	703-547-2000	726
XOMA (US) LLC 2910 Seventh St ..... Berkeley CA 94710 NASDAQ: XOMA	800-468-9716	510-204-7200	84

Name / Address	Toll-Free	Phone	Class
Xora Inc 850 N Shoreline Blvd ..... Mountain View CA 94043	877-477-9672	650-314-6460	179-11
XP Power 990 Benicia Ave ..... Sunnyvale CA 94085	800-253-0490	408-732-7777	246
Xpedx 3351 W Addison St ..... Chicago IL 60618	800-678-8536	773-442-6200	528
XPO Logistics Inc 6805 Perimeter Dr ..... Dublin OH 43016	800-837-7584	614-923-1400	444
XS Smith Inc 932 Page Rd ..... Washington NC 27889	800-631-2226	252-940-5060	104
Xtek Inc 11451 Reading Rd ..... Cincinnati OH 45241	888-332-9835	513-733-7800	449
XTO Energy Inc 810 Houston St ..... Fort Worth TX 76102	800-299-2800	817-870-2800	529
XTRAC LLC 245 Summer St ..... Boston MA 02210	855-975-3569		384
Xtramart 221 Quinebaug Rd ..... North Grosvenordale CT 06255	800-243-6366		205
XtremeEDA Corp 201-1339 Wellington St W ..... Ottawa ON K1Y3B8	800-586-0280	613-728-5912	461
Xybernet Inc 10640 Scripps Ranch Blvd ..... San Diego CA 92131 *Cust Svc	800-228-9026*	858-530-1900	179-10
Xyron Inc 8465 N 90th St Ste 6 ..... Scottsdale AZ 85258	800-793-3523	480-443-9419	480

Y

Name / Address	Toll-Free	Phone	Class
Y-12 Federal Credit Union 501 Lafayette Dr PO Box 2512 ..... Oak Ridge TN 37830	800-482-1043	865-482-1043	219
Yachats Ocean Road State Natural Site 5580 S Coast Hwy ..... Newport OR 97366	800-551-6949		558
Yachting Magazine 55 Hammarlund Way ..... Middletown RI 02842	800-999-0869		452-4
Yacktman Asset Management Co 6300 Bridgepoint Pkwy Bldg 1 Ste 320 ..... Austin TX 78730	800-835-3879	512-767-6700	398
Yadkin Bank 1318 N Bridge St ..... Elkin NC 28621 NASDAQ: YDKN	866-867-9979	336-526-6371	69
Yaffe Cos Inc, The 1200 S G St ..... Muskogee OK 74403	800-759-2333	918-687-7543	677
Yahoo! Photos 701 First Ave ..... Sunnyvale CA 94089	888-267-7574	408-349-3300	581
Yak Communications Corp 48 Yonge St Ste 1200 ..... Toronto ON M5E1G6	877-925-4925		726
Yakima Bait Company Inc PO Box 310 ..... Granger WA 98932	800-527-2711	509-854-1311	701
Yakima Convention Ctr 10 N Eigth St ..... Yakima WA 98901	800-221-0751	509-575-6062	206
Yakima Federal Savings & Loan Assn 118 E Yakima Ave ..... Yakima WA 98901	800-331-3225	509-248-2634	69
Yakima Herald-Republic PO Box 9668 ..... Yakima WA 98909	800-343-2799	509-248-1251	525-2
Yale Appliance 296 Freeport St ..... Dorchester MA 02122	800-565-6435	617-825-9253	34
Yale Carolinas Inc (YCI) 9839 S Tryon St ..... Charlotte NC 28273	800-844-1454	704-588-6930	383
Yale Ctr for British Art 1080 Chapel St PO Box 208280 ..... New Haven CT 06510	877-274-8278	203-432-2800	513
Yale Divinity School Admissions Office 409 Prospect St ..... New Haven CT 06511	866-358-3806	203-432-5360	167-3
Yale Repertory Theatre 1120 Chapel St PO Box 1257 ..... New Haven CT 06505	800-973-2837	203-432-1234	566-4
Yale Residential Security Products Inc 100 Yale Ave ..... Lenoir City TN 37771 *Cust Svc	800-438-1951*		347
Yale Security Inc.ÿ 1902 Airport Rd ..... Monroe NC 28110	800-438-1951		347
Yale University Press 302 Temple St ..... New Haven CT 06511 *Sales	800-405-1619*	203-432-0960	628-4
Yale University School of Medicine 333 Cedar St ..... New Haven CT 06510	877-925-3637	203-785-2643	167-2
YALSA (Young Adult Library Services Assn) 50 E Huron St ..... Chicago IL 60611	800-545-2433	312-280-4390	48-11
Yamaha Electronics Corp 6660 Orangethorpe Ave ..... Buena Park CA 90620	800-292-2982	714-522-9888	51
Yamaha Motor Corp USA 6555 Katella Ave ..... Cypress CA 90630 *Cust Svc	800-656-7695*		510
Yamato Corp 1775 S Murray Blvd ..... Colorado Springs CO 80916	800-538-1762	719-591-1500	675
Yamazen Inc 735 E Remington Rd ..... Schaumburg IL 60173	800-882-8558	847-490-8130	382
Yampa Valley Electric Assn Inc 32 Tenth St ..... Steamboat Springs CO 80487	888-873-9832	970-879-1160	245
Yankee Candle Company Inc PO Box 110 ..... South Deerfield MA 01373	877-803-6890	413-665-8306	326
Yankee Gas Services Co 107 Selden St ..... Berlin CT 06037	800-989-0900		775
Yankee Magazine 1121 Main St PO Box 520 ..... Dublin NH 03444	800-288-4284	603-563-8111	452-22
Yankee Publishing Inc PO Box 520 ..... Dublin NH 03444	800-729-9265	603-563-8111	628-9
Yankton Press & Dakotan 319 Walnut St PO Box 56 ..... Yankton SD 57078	800-743-2968	605-665-7811	628-8
Yarde Metals Inc 45 Newell St ..... Southington CT 06489	800-444-9494	860-406-6061	485
Yardley Products Corp 10 W College Ave ..... Yardley PA 19067	800-457-0154	215-493-2723	347
Yarema Die & Engineering Co Inc 300 Minnesota Rd ..... Troy MI 48083	800-937-9311	248-585-2830	747
Yark Automotive Group Inc 6019 W Central Ave ..... Toledo OH 43615	866-390-8894		509
Yarrow Hotel & Conference Ctr 1800 Pk Ave ..... Park City UT 84060	800-445-8667	435-649-7000	376

Name / Address	City	State	ZIP	Toll-Free	Phone	Class
Yaskawa America Inc 2121 Norman Dr S	Waukegan	IL	60085	800-927-5292	847-887-7000	204
Yates-American Machine Company Inc 2880 Kennedy Dr	Beloit	WI	53511	800-752-6377	608-364-6333	808
Yavapai College 1100 E Sheldon St	Prescott	AZ	86301	800-922-6787	928-445-7300	160
Verde Valley 601 Black Hills Dr	Clarkdale	AZ	86324	800-922-6787	928-634-7501	160
Yavapai Regional Medical Ctr 1003 Willow Creek Rd	Prescott	AZ	86301	877-976-9762	928-445-2700	371-3
Yazoo County Chamber of Commerce 212 E Broadway Ste 7	Yazoo City	MS	39194	800-638-6582	662-746-1273	137
Yazoo Mills Inc PO Box 369 *Cust Svc	New Oxford	PA	17350	800-242-5216*	717-624-8993	124
Yazoo Valley Electric Power Assn PO Box 8	Yazoo City	MS	39194	800-281-5098	662-746-4251	245
YBP Library Services 999 Maple St	Contoocook	NH	03229	800-258-3774	603-746-3102	94
YCI (Yale Carolinas Inc) 9839 S Tryon St	Charlotte	NC	28273	800-844-1454	704-588-6930	383
Yeck Bros Co 2222 Arbor Blvd	Dayton	OH	45439	800-417-2767	937-294-4000	5
Yellow Book USA 398 RXR Plaza	Uniondale	NY	11556	877-237-6120	917-861-5858	628-6
YellowBrix Inc 200 North Glebe Rd Ste 1025	Arlington	VA	22203	888-325-9366	703-548-3300	179-7
Yellowhead Helicopters Ltd 3010 Selwyn Rd	Valemount	BC	V0E2Z0	888-566-4401	250-566-4401	356
YELLOWPAGES.com LLC 208 S Akard Ste 1825	Dallas	TX	75202	866-329-7118		394
Yellowstone Baptist College 1515 S Shiloh Rd	Billings	MT	59106	800-487-9950	406-656-9950	166
Yellowstone Valley Electric Co-op 150 Co-op Way	Huntley	MT	59037	800-736-5323	406-348-3411	245
Yenkin-Majestic Paint Corp 1920 Leonard Ave	Columbus	OH	43219	800-848-1898	614-253-8511	543
Yesmail 309 SW Sixth Ave Ste 700	Portland	OR	97204	877-937-6245	503-241-4185	7
Yesterday USA Radio Networks, The 2001 Plymouth Rock Dr	Richardson	TX	75081	800-624-2272	972-889-9872	635
Yesware Inc 75 Kneeland St Fl 15	Boston	MA	02111	855-937-9273		384
Yeti Coolers 3411 Hidalgo St	Austin	TX	78702	888-872-0227	512-394-9384	601
Yetter Manufacturing Inc 109 S McDonough St PO Box 358	Colchester	IL	62326	800-447-5777	309-776-4111	273
Yingling Aircraft Inc 2010 Airport Rd	Wichita	KS	67209	800-835-0083	316-943-3246	760
YK International Co 3246 W Montrose Ave	Chicago	IL	60618	800-266-5254	773-583-5270	345
YMCA (YMCA of the USA) 101 N Wacker Dr 14th Fl	Chicago	IL	60606	800-872-9622	312-977-0031	47-6
YMCA of the USA (YMCA) 101 N Wacker Dr 14th Fl	Chicago	IL	60606	800-872-9622	312-977-0031	47-6
YoCream International Inc 5858 NE 87th Ave	Portland	OR	97220	800-962-7326	503-256-3754	295-25
Yoder 4899 Commerce Pkwy	Cleveland	OH	44128	800-631-0520	216-292-4460	614
Yogo Inn 211 E Main St	Lewistown	MT	59457	800-860-9646	406-535-8721	376
Yokogawa Corp of America 12530 W Airport Blvd	Sugar Land	TX	77478	800-888-6400	281-340-3800	248
Yokohama Tire Corp 601 S Acacia Ave	Fullerton	CA	92831	800-423-4544	714-870-3800	744
Yonex Corp 20140 S Western Ave	Torrance	CA	90501	800-449-6639	310-793-3800	701
York Barbell Co Inc 3300 BoaRd Rd *Cust Svc	York	PA	17406	800-358-9675*	717-767-6481	267
York Bldg Products Co 950 Smile Way	York	PA	17404	800-673-2408	717-848-2831	184
York Building Services Inc 99 Grand St Ste 3	Moonachie	NJ	07074	855-443-9675		256
York College 1125 E Eigth St	York	NE	68467	800-950-9675	402-363-5600	166
York County Community College 112 College Dr	Wells	ME	04090	800-580-3820	207-646-9282	160
York County Transportation Authority 1230 Roosevelt Ave	York	PA	17404	800-632-9063	717-846-5562	463
York Dispatch 205 N George St	York	PA	17401	800-227-2345	717-854-1575	525-2
York Electric Co-op Inc PO Box 150	York	SC	29745	800-582-8810	803-684-4247	245
York Ford Inc 1481 Bwy	Saugus	MA	01906	888-874-0636	781-231-1945	56
York Group Inc 2 Northshore Ctr Ste 100	Pittsburgh	PA	15212	800-223-4964	412-995-1600	133
York Newspaper Co 1891 Loucks Rd	York	PA	17408	800-559-3520	717-767-6397	628-8
York Solutions LLC One Westbrook Corporate Ctr Ste 910	Westchester	IL	60154	877-700-9675	708-531-8362	712
York State Bank & Trust Co 700 N Lincoln AvE	York	NE	68467	888-295-5540	402-362-4411	69
York Sunday News 1891 Loucks Rd	York	PA	17408	800-483-5517	717-767-6397	525-4
York Technical College 452 S Anderson Rd	Rock Hill	SC	29730	800-922-8324	803-327-8000	160
York Telecom Corp 81 Corbett Way	Eatontown	NJ	07724	866-836-8463	732-413-6000	726
York University 4700 Keele St	Toronto	ON	M3J1P3	800-426-2255	416-736-2100	773
York Wallcoverings Inc 750 Linden Ave PO Box 5166	York	PA	17405	800-375-9675	717-846-4456	790
York Water Co, The 130 E Market St PO Box 15089 *NASDAQ: YORW*	York	PA	17405	800-750-5561	717-845-3601	775
Yorktowne Hotel 48 E Market St	York	PA	17401	800-233-9324	717-848-1111	376
Yosemite Assn *Yosemite Conservancy* 5020 El Portal Rd PO Box 230	El Portal	CA	95318	800-469-7275	209-379-2317	47-13
Yoshinoya Beef Bowl 991 Knox St	Torrance	CA	90502	800-576-8017	310-527-6060	661
Youghiogheny River Natural Resources Management Area c/o Deep Creek Lake State Pk 898 State Pk Rd	Swanton	MD	21561	877-620-8367	301-387-5563	558
YouMail Inc 43 Corporate Park Ste 200	Irvine	CA	92606	800-374-0013		181
Young Adult Library Services Assn (YALSA) 50 E Huron St	Chicago	IL	60611	800-545-2433	312-280-4390	48-11
Young America Corp 10 S 5th St 7th Fl	Minneapolis	MN	55402	800-533-4529		727
Young America's Foundation 110 Elden St	Herndon	VA	20170	800-292-9231	800-872-1776	47-7
Young at Art Children's Museum 751 SW 121st Ave	Davie	FL	33325	800-435-7352	954-424-0085	514
Young Bros Ltd PO Box 3288	Honolulu	HI	96801	800-572-2743	808-543-9311	311
Young Children Magazine 1313 L St NW Ste 500 PO Box 97156	Washington	DC	20005	800-424-2460	202-232-8777	452-8
Young Corp 3231 Utah Ave S	Seattle	WA	98134	800-321-9090	206-624-1071	191
Young Electric Sign Co 2401 Foothill Dr	Salt Lake City	UT	84109	888-959-3726	801-464-4600	692
Young Fashions Inc 10300 Perkins Rd	Baton Rouge	LA	70810	800-824-4154	225-766-1010	587
Young Harris College PO Box 116	Young Harris	GA	30582	800-241-3754	706-379-3111	160
Young Industries Inc 16 Painter St	Muncy	PA	17756	800-546-3165	570-546-3165	208
Young Israel of New Rochelle 1149 N Ave	New Rochelle	NY	10804	888-942-3638	914-636-2215	47-20
Young Living Essential Oils 3125 Executive Pkwy	Lehi	UT	84043	866-203-5666	801-418-8900	787
Young Manufacturing Inc 2331 N 42nd St	Grand Forks	ND	58203	800-451-9884	701-772-5541	478
Young Mfg Company Inc 521 S Main St PO Box 167	Beaver Dam	KY	42320	800-545-6595	270-274-3306	494
Young Pecan Co 1831 W Evans St Ste 200 *All	Florence	SC	29501	800-829-6864*	843-662-8591	295-28
Young Presidents' Organization (YPO) 600 E Las Colinas Blvd Ste 1000	Irving	TX	75039	800-773-7976	972-587-1500	48-12
Young Touchstone Inc 200 Smith Ln *Sales	Jackson	TN	38301	800-238-8230*	731-424-5045	15
Young Transportation & Tours 843 Riverside Dr	Asheville	NC	28804	800-622-5444	828-258-0084	106
Young's Commercial Transfer 2075 W Scranton Ave PO Box 871	Porterville	CA	93257	800-289-1639	559-784-6651	770
Young's Market Company LLC 500 S Central Ave	Los Angeles	CA	90013	800-627-2777	213-612-1248	80-3
Young's Plant Farm PO Box 3410	Auburn	AL	36830	800-304-8609		366
Younger Optics 2925 California St	Torrance	CA	90503	800-366-5367	310-783-1533	535
Youngsoft Inc 49197 Wixom Tech Dr	Wixom	MI	48393	888-470-4553	248-675-1200	178
Youngstown State University One University Plz *Admissions	Youngstown	OH	44555	877-468-6978*	330-941-3000	166
Youngstown Warren Regional Chamber 11 Central Sq Ste 1600	Youngstown	OH	44503	877-807-2249	330-744-2131	137
Youngstown-Warren Regional Airport 1453 Youngstown-Kingsville Rd NE	Vienna	OH	44473	800-444-1440	330-856-1537	27
Your Big Backyard Magazine 11100 Wildlife Ctr Dr	Reston	VA	20190	800-822-9919		452-6
Your Church Magazine 465 Gundersen Dr	Carol Stream	IL	60188	877-247-4787	630-260-6200	452-5
Your Community Bank 2323 Ring Rd	Elizabethtown	KY	42701	800-314-2265	270-765-2131	68
Yourga Trucking Inc 100 Shenango St	Wheatland	PA	16161	800-245-1722	724-981-3600	770
Youth For Understanding USA 6400 Goldsboro Rd Ste 100	Bethesda	MD	20817	800-424-3691	240-235-2100	47-11
Youth Villages Inner Harbour 4685 Dorsett Shoals Rd	Douglasville	GA	30135	800-255-8657	770-852-6333	371-1
YouVisit LLC 20533 Biscayne Blvd Ste 1322	Aventura	FL	33180	866-585-7158		384
YPO (Young Presidents' Organization) 600 E Las Colinas Blvd Ste 1000	Irving	TX	75039	800-773-7976	972-587-1500	48-12
YPO-WPO 600 E Las Colinas Blvd Ste 1000	Irving	TX	75039	800-773-7976	972-587-1500	48-12
Ypsilanti Area Convention & Visitors Bureau 106 W Michigan Ave	Ypsilanti	MI	48197	800-265-9045	734-483-4444	207
YRC Worldwide Inc 10990 Roe Ave *NASDAQ: YRCW*	Overland Park	KS	66211	800-846-4300	913-696-6100	357-3
Yrrid Software Inc 507 Monroe St	Chapel Hill	NC	27516	800-443-0065	919-968-7858	179-12
YSI Inc 1700-1725 Brannum Ln *Cust Svc	Yellow Springs	OH	45387	800-765-4974*	937-767-7241	202
Y-Tex Corp 1825 Big Horn Ave PO Box 1450	Cody	WY	82414	800-443-6401	307-587-5515	280
Yucaipa Valley Water District PO Box 730	Yucaipa	CA	92399	800-272-8869	909-797-5117	775
Yucca Valley Chamber of Commerce 56711 29 Palms Hwy	Yucca Valley	CA	92284	855-568-5348	760-365-6323	137
Yule Tree Farms LLC PO Box 429	Aurora	OR	97002	888-970-8733	503-651-2114	742
Yum! Brands Inc 1441 Gardiner Ln *NYSE: YUM*	Louisville	KY	40213	800-225-5532	502-874-8300	661
Yuma Civic Ctr 1440 W Desert Hills Dr	Yuma	AZ	85365	800-410-2554	928-373-5040	206
Yuma Convention & Visitors Bureau 201 N Fourth Ave	Yuma	AZ	85364	800-293-0071	928-783-0071	207
Yuma County Chamber of Commerce 180 W First St Ste A	Yuma	AZ	85364	877-782-0438	928-782-2567	137
Y-W Electric Assn Inc 250 Main Ave PO Box Y	Akron	CO	80720	800-660-2291	970-345-2291	245

Name / Address	City	State	ZIP	Toll-Free	Phone	Class
YWCA (YWCA USA)						
2025 M St NW Ste 550	Washington	DC	20036	**888-872-9259**	202-467-0801	47-6
YWCA USA (YWCA)						
2025 M St NW Ste 550	Washington	DC	20036	**888-872-9259**	202-467-0801	47-6

Z

Name / Address	City	State	ZIP	Toll-Free	Phone	Class
Z Communications Inc						
14118 Stowe Dr Ste B	Poway	CA	92064	**877-808-1226**	858-621-2700	253
Z Gallerie Inc						
1855 W 139th St	Gardena	CA	90249	**800-358-8288**	310-630-1200	359
Z57 Internet Solutions						
10045 Mesa Rim Rd	San Diego	CA	92121	**800-899-8148**		225
Z92 FM						
10714 Mockingbird Dr	Omaha	NE	68127	**800-955-9230**	402-592-5300	636-77
Zachary & Elizabeth Fisher House						
111 Rockville Pk Ste 420	Rockville	MD	20850	**888-294-8560**		369
Zachary Confections Inc						
2130 IN-28	Frankfort	IN	46041	**800-445-4222***		295-8
*Cust Svc						
Zachys Wine & Liquor Inc						
16 E Pkwy	Scarsdale	NY	10583	**800-723-0241**	914-723-0241	439
Zack Electronics Inc						
1070 Hamilton Rd	Duarte	CA	91010	**800-466-0449**	626-303-0655	246
Zacky Farms						
13200 Crossroads Pkwy N Ste 250	City of Industry	CA	91746	**800-888-0235**	562-641-2020	296-10
Zacky Farms Inc						
2020 SE Ave	Fresno	CA	93721	**800-888-0235**	562-641-2020	10-7
Zadro Products Inc						
5422 Argosy Ave	Huntington Beach	CA	92649	**800-468-4348**	714-892-9200	601
ZAGG Inc						
3855 South 500 West Ste J	Salt Lake City	UT	84115	**800-700-9244**	801-263-0699	601
Zale Corp						
Zales Jewelers Div						
901 W Walnut Hill Ln	Irving	TX	75038	**800-311-5393***	972-580-4000	407
*Cust Svc						
Zale Corp Bailey Banks & Biddle Div						
901 W Walnut Hill Ln	Irving	TX	75038	**800-468-9716***	866-249-2593	407
*Cust Svc						
Zampell Cos						
Nine Stanley Tucker Dr	Newburyport	MA	01950	**877-926-7355**	978-465-0055	603
Zane State College						
1555 Newark Rd	Zanesville	OH	43701	**800-686-8324**	740-454-2501	788
Zaner Group LLC						
150 S Wacker Dr Ste 2350	Chicago	IL	60606	**800-621-1414**	312-277-0050	170
Zaner-Bloser Inc						
1201 Dublin Rd	Columbus	OH	43215	**800-421-3018**	614-486-0221	628-2
Zanesville City School Board						
160 N Fourth St	Zanesville	OH	43701	**866-280-7377**	740-454-9751	676
Zanesville-Muskingum County Chamber of Commerce						
205 N Fifth St	Zanesville	OH	43701	**800-743-2303**	740-455-8282	137
Zanesville-Muskingum County Convention & Visitors Bureau						
205 N Fifth St	Zanesville	OH	43701	**800-743-2303**	740-455-8282	207
ZAP 501 Fourth St	Santa Rosa	CA	95401	**800-251-4555***	707-525-8658	760
OTC: ZAAP ■ *Orders						
Zappos.com						
400 E Stewart Ave Ste 104	Las Vegas	KY	89101	**800-927-7671**		454
Zasio Enterprises Inc						
12601 W Explorer Dr Ste 250	Boise	ID	83713	**800-513-1000**		178
ZaZa Energy Corp						
1301 McKinney St Ste 3000	Houston	TX	77010	**866-266-2502**	713-595-1900	529
NASDAQ: ZAZA						
ZBA Inc						
94 Old Camplain Rd	Hillsborough	NJ	08844	**800-750-4239**	908-359-2070	174-7
ZeaVision LLC						
Spirit Business Ctr Ii 680F Crown Industrial Ct	Chesterfield	MO	63005	**866-833-2800**	314-628-1000	342
Zebra Books						
Kensington Publishing Corp						
119 W 40th St	New York	NY	10018	**800-221-2647**	212-407-1500	628-2
Zebra Marketing						
7119 Laurel Canyon Blvd Suite 3	North Hollywood	CA	91605	**800-348-2422**	818-765-6442	9
Zebra Technologies Corp						
475 Half Day Rd Ste 500	Lincolnshire	IL	60069	**800-423-0422**	847-634-6700	174-6
NASDAQ: ZBRA						
Zee Medical Inc						
22 Corporate Pk	Irvine	CA	92606	**800-435-7763**		470
Zehnder America Inc						
540 Portsmouth Ave	Greenland	NH	03840	**888-778-6701**	603-422-6700	603
Zeigler Beverage Co						
1513 N Broad St	Lansdale	PA	19446	**800-854-6123***	215-855-5161	295-20
*Sales						
Zeigler Bros Inc						
400 GaRdner Stn Rd PO Box 95	Gardners	PA	17324	**800-841-6800**	717-677-6181	442
Zeks Compressed Air Solutions						
1302 Goshen Pkwy	West Chester	PA	19380	**800-888-2323**	610-692-9100	173
Zenith Cutter Co						
5200 Zenith Pkwy	Loves Park	IL	61111	**800-223-5202**	815-282-5200	488
Zenith Insurance Co						
PO Box 9055	Van Nuys	CA	91409	**800-440-5020**	818-713-1000	388-4
Zenith Products Corp						
400 Lukens Dr	New Castle	DE	19720	**800-892-3986**		318-2
Zenith Specialty Bag Company Inc						
17625 E Railroad St PO Box 8445	City of Industry	CA	91748	**800-962-2247**		64
Zenithstar Insurance Co						
Zenith Insurance Co						
1101 Capital of Texas Hwy S Bldg J PO Box 163510	Austin	TX	78746	**800-841-3987**	512-306-1700	388-4
Zenovia Digital Exchange Corp						
3141 Fairview Park Dr Ste 160	Falls Church	VA	22042	**855-936-6842**	703-813-6400	384
ZEP Inc						
1310 Seaboard Industrial Blvd NW	Atlanta	GA	30318	**877-428-9937**	404-352-1680	149
NYSE: ZEP						
Zephyr Egg Co Inc						
4622 Gall Blvd	Zephyrhills	FL	33542	**800-333-4415**	813-782-1521	10-7
Zephyr Environmental Corp						
2600 Via Fortuna Ste 450	Austin	TX	78746	**800-452-5558**	512-329-5544	261
Zephyr Mfg Company Inc						
201 Hindry Av	Inglewood	CA	90301	**800-624-3944**	310-410-4907	748
Zephyrhills Chamber of Commerce						
38550 Fifth Ave	Zephyrhills	FL	33542	**800-851-8754**	813-782-1913	137
Zepto Metrix Corp						
872 Main St	Buffalo	NY	14202	**800-274-5487***	716-882-0920	231
*Cust Svc						
Zero International Inc						
415 Concord Ave	Bronx	NY	10455	**800-635-5335**	718-585-3230	325
Zero Manufacturing Inc						
500 West 200 North	North Salt Lake	UT	84054	**800-959-5050**	801-298-5900	448
Zero-Max Inc						
13200 Sixth Ave N	Plymouth	MN	55441	**800-533-1731**	763-546-4300	613
Zerowait Corp						
707 Kirkwood Hwy	Wilmington	DE	19805	**888-811-0808**	302-996-9408	193
Zeta Phi Beta Sorority Inc						
1734 New Hampshire Ave NW	Washington	DC	20009	**800-393-2503**	202-387-3103	47-16
Zeta Psi Fraternity of North America						
15 S Henry St	Pearl River	NY	10965	**800-477-1847**	845-735-1847	47-16
Zetec Inc						
8226 Bracken Pl SE Ste 100	Snoqualmie	WA	98065	**800-643-1771**	425-974-2700	248
Zhone Technologies Inc						
7001 Oakport St	Oakland	CA	94621	**877-946-6320**	510-777-7000	725
NASDAQ: ZHNE						
Ziebart International Corp						
1290 E Maple Rd	Troy	MI	48083	**800-877-1312**	248-588-4100	61-1
Zieger & Sons Inc						
6215 Ardleigh St	Philadelphia	PA	19138	**800-752-2003**	215-438-7060	293
Zierick Manufacturing Corp						
131 Radio Cr	Mount Kisco	NY	10549	**800-882-8020**	914-666-2911	802
Zimmer Inc						
1800 W Ctr St PO Box 708	Warsaw	IN	46580	**800-613-6131**	574-267-6131	472
Zimmer Radio Group						
3215 Lemone Industrial Blvd Ste 200	Columbia	MO	65201	**800-455-1099**	573-875-1099	634
Zimmerman Auto Center						
4001 First Ave	Cedar Rapids	IA	52402	**855-877-4223**		56
Zingle Inc						
5235 Avenida Encinas Ste A	Carlsbad	CA	92008	**877-946-4536**		224
Zinkan Enterprises Inc						
1919 Case Pkwy N	Twinsburg	OH	44087	**800-229-6801**		143
Zion Bible College						
27 Middle Hwy	Barrington	RI	02806	**800-356-4014**	401-246-0900	159
Zions First National Bank						
1 S Main St	Salt Lake City	UT	84111	**800-974-8800**	801-974-8800	69
Zippertubing Co						
7150 W Erie St	Chandler	AZ	85226	**855-289-1874**	480-285-3990	593
ZipRealty Inc						
2000 Powell St Ste 300	Emeryville	CA	94608	**800-225-5947**	510-735-2600	643
NASDAQ: ZIPR						
Zix Corp						
2711 N Haskell Ave Ste 2300-LB	Dallas	TX	75204	**888-771-4049**	214-370-2000	179-12
NASDAQ: ZIXI						
ZK Celltest Inc						
256 Gibraltar Dr Ste 109	Sunnyvale	CA	94089	**800-837-8235**	408-752-0449	202
Z-Law Software Inc						
80 Upton Ave PO Box 40602	Providence	RI	02940	**800-526-5588**	401-331-3002	178
ZLB Behring LLC						
1020 First Ave PO Box 61501	King of Prussia	PA	19406	**800-683-1288**	610-878-4000	576
Zodiac Pool Systems Inc						
2620 Commerce Way	Vista	CA	92081	**800-822-7933**		794
Zoeller Co						
3649 Kane Run Rd	Louisville	KY	40211	**800-928-7867**	502-778-2731	632
OTC: ZOLR						
Zogenix Inc						
12400 High Bluff Dr Ste 650	San Diego	CA	92130	**866-964-3649**	858-259-1165	576
Zolato Inc						
2801 First Ave Ste 306	Seattle	WA	98121	**866-557-6716**		461
ZOLL Medical Corp						
269 Mill Rd	Chelmsford	MA	01824	**800-348-9011**	978-421-9655	250
Zonar Systems LLC						
18200 Cascade Ave S	Seattle	WA	98188	**877-843-3847**	206-878-2459	522
Zone Alarm						
800 Bridge Pkwy	Redwood City	CA	94065	**877-966-5221**	415-633-4500	179-7
Zoocheck Canada						
788 1/2 O'Connor Dr	Toronto	ON	M4B2S6	**888-801-3222**	416-285-1744	47-3
Zoom Information Inc						
307 Waverley Oaks Rd	Waltham	MA	02452	**800-949-7040**	781-693-7500	112
Zootoo LLC						
400 Plz Dr First Fl	Secaucus	NJ	07094	**877-580-7387**		384
Zortec International						
25 Century Blvd Ste 103	Nashville	TN	37214	**800-361-7005**	615-361-7000	179-2
Zotos International Inc						
100 Tokeneke Rd	Darien	CT	06820	**888-242-4247**	203-655-8911	215
ZT Group International Inc						
350 Meadowlands Pkwy	Secaucus	NJ	07094	**888-984-8899**	201-559-1000	177
ZTEST Electronics Inc						
523 Mcnicoll Ave	North York	ON	M2H2C9	**866-393-4891**	416-297-5155	617
Zuken USA						
238 Littleton Rd Ste 100	Westford	MA	01886	**800-447-7332**	978-692-4900	179-5
Zumar Industries Inc						
9719 Santa Fe Springs Rd	Santa Fe Springs	CA	90670	**800-654-7446**	562-941-4633	692
Zumiez Inc						
6300 Merrill Creek Pkwy Ste B	Everett	WA	98203	**877-828-6929**	425-551-1500	155-2
NASDAQ: ZUMZ						
Zurich North America						
1400 American Ln	Schaumburg	IL	60196	**800-382-2150**	847-605-6000	388-5
Zygo Corp						
Laurel Brook Rd	Middlefield	CT	06455	**800-994-6669**	860-347-8506	537
NASDAQ: ZIGO						
Zyme Solutions Inc						
240 Twin Dolphin Dr Ste E	Redwood Shores	CA	94065	**888-200-6629**		224

Alphabetical Section

	Toll-Free	Phone	Class
ZymoGenetics Inc			
1201 Eastlake Ave E .... Seattle WA 98102	**800-332-2056**	206-442-6600	84
ZyQuest Inc			
1385 W Main Ave Ste 101 .... De Pere WI 54115	**800-992-0533**	920-499-0533	181
ZyXEL Communications Inc			
1130 N Miller St .... Anaheim CA 92806	**800-255-4101**	714-632-0882	174-3

	Toll-Free	Phone	Class

Alphabetical Section

Classified Section

Listings in the Classified Section are organized alphabetically under subject headings denoting a business or organization type. These headings are fully outlined in the Index to Classified Headings located at the back of this book. "See" and "See Also" references are included in this section to help locate appropriate subject categories. Alphabetizing is on a word-by-word rather than letter-by-letter basis. For a detailed explanation of the scope and arrangement of listings in Toll-Free Phone Book USA, please refer to "How To Use This Directory" at the beginning of this book. An explanation of individual page elements is also provided under the "Sample Entry" on the back inside cover of the book.

1 ABRASIVE PRODUCTS

				Toll-Free	Phone
Basic Carbide Corp					
900 Main St	Lowber	PA	15660	800-426-4291	724-446-1630
Bullard Abrasives Inc					
Six Carol Dr	Lincoln	RI	02865	800-227-4469	401-333-3000
Camel Grinding Wheels					
7525 N Oak Pk Ave	Niles	IL	60714	800-447-4248	847-647-5994
Comco Inc 2151 N Lincoln St	Burbank	CA	91504	800-796-6626	818-841-5500
Composition Materials Company Inc					
249 Pepes Farm Rd	Milford	CT	06460	800-262-7763	203-874-6500
Ervin Industries Inc					
3893 Research Pk Dr	Ann Arbor	MI	48108	800-748-0055	734-769-4600
Formax Manufacturing Corp					
168 Wealthy St SW	Grand Rapids	MI	49503	800-242-2833	616-456-5458
Gemtex Abrasives					
60 Belfield Rd	Toronto	ON	M9W1G1	800-387-5100	416-245-5605
Glit/Microtron					
809 Broad St PO Box 709	Wrens	GA	30833	800-325-1051	314-739-8585
Marvel Abrasive Products Inc					
6230 S Oak Pk Ave	Chicago	IL	60638	800-621-0673	
Precision H2O Inc					
6328 E Utah Ave	Spokane	WA	99212	800-425-2098	509-536-9214
Radiac Abrasives Inc					
1015 S College Ave	Salem	IL	62881	800-851-1095	618-548-4200
Raytech Industries					
475 Smith St	Middletown	CT	06457	800-243-7163*	860-632-2020
*Cust Svc					
Saint-Gobain Abrasives Inc					
2770 W Washington St	Stephenville	TX	76401	800-561-9490	254-918-2310
Sancap Abrasives					
16123 Armour St NE	Alliance	OH	44601	800-433-6663	330-821-3510
Sandusky-Chicago Abrasive Wheel Co					
1100 W Barker Ave	Michigan City	IN	46360	800-843-4980	219-879-6601
Superior Abrasives Inc					
4800 Wadsworth Rd	Dayton	OH	45414	800-235-9123	937-278-9123
Trumbull Industries Inc					
400 Dietz Rd NE	Warren	OH	44482	800-477-1799	330-393-6624
VSM Abrasives					
1012 E Wabash St	O'Fallon	MO	63366	800-737-0176*	636-272-7432
*Cust Svc					

2 ACCOUNTING FIRMS

				Toll-Free	Phone
Active Captive Management					
16485 Laguna Canyon Rd Ste 200	Irvine	CA	92618	800-921-0155	949-727-0155
Ahola Corp, The					
6820 W Snowville Rd	Brecksville	OH	44141	800-727-2849	440-717-7620
Altera Payroll Inc					
2400 Northside Crossing	Macon	GA	31210	877-474-6060	478-477-6060
Beason & Nalley Inc					
101 Monroe St Ne	Huntsville	AL	35801	800-416-1946	256-533-1720
BenefitMall					
3450 Lakeside Dr Ste 400	Miramar	FL	33027	877-729-6299	954-874-4800
Berkowitz Dick Pollack & Brant LLP					
200 S Biscayne Blvd Sixth Fl	Miami	FL	33131	800-999-1272	305-379-7000
Berry Dunn Mcneil & Parker					
100 Middle St 4th Fl	Portland	ME	04101	800-908-4490	207-775-2387
Blackman Kallick					
10 S Riverside Plaza	Chicago	IL	60606	866-939-3921	312-207-1040
Blue & Co					
12800 N Meridian St Ste 400	Carmel	IN	46032	800-717-2583	317-848-8920
Blum Shapiro					
29 S Main St PO Box 272000	West Hartford	CT	06107	866-356-2586	860-561-4000
Bonadio Group, The					
171 Sully's Trail Ste 201	Pittsford	NY	14534	877-917-3077	585-381-1000
Burr Pilger & Mayer LLP (BPMLLP)					
600 California St Ste 1300	San Francisco	CA	94108	866-312-4390	415-421-5757
CBIZ Tofias PC					
500 Boylston St	Boston	MA	02116	888-761-8835	617-761-0600
Certified General Accountants Assn of British Columbia					
300-1867 W Broadway	Vancouver	BC	V6J5L4	800-565-1211	604-732-1211
Certipay					
199 Ave B NW Ste 270	Winter Haven	FL	33881	800-422-3782	863-299-2400
Clark Nuber PS					
10900 NE Fourth St Ste 1700	Bellevue	WA	98004	800-504-8747*	425-454-4919
*General					
CliftonLarsonAllen - CLA					
301 SW Adams St Ste 1000	Peoria	IL	61602	800-354-5849	309-671-4500
Complete Payroll Processing Inc					
7488 SR- 39 Po Box 190	Perry	NY	14530	888-237-5800	585-237-5800
Contingent Workforce Solutions Inc					
2430 Meadowpine Blvd Ste 101	Mississauga	ON	L5N6S2	866-837-8630	
Elliott Davis Decosimo LLC					
2 Union Sq Tallan Bldg Ste 1100	Chattanooga	TN	37402	800-782-8382	423-756-7100
Elliott Davis LLC					
200 E Broad St PO Box 6286	Greenville	SC	29606	800-503-4721	864-242-3370
Ernst & Young					
Ernst & Young Tower 222 Bay St PO Box 251	Toronto	ON	M5K1J7	800-291-3380	416-864-1234
Federal Management Systems Inc					
462 K St NW	Washington	DC	20001	877-637-8277	202-842-3003
Fiducial					
1370 Ave of the Americas 31st Fl	New York	NY	10019	866-343-8242	212-207-4700
Flex Checks Inc					
PO Box 141215	Grand Rapids	MI	49514	866-791-7900	616-791-7900
Friedberg Smith & Co PC					
855 Main St	Bridgeport	CT	06604	800-772-1213	203-366-5876
Friedman LLP 1700 Broadway	New York	NY	10019	800-372-1033	212-842-7000
Gallina LLP					
2870 Gold Tailings Crt 2nd Fl	Rancho Cordova	CA	95670	877-638-1188	916-638-1188
Gumbiner Savett Inc					
1723 Cloverfield Blvd	Santa Monica	CA	90404	800-989-9798	310-828-9798
Hacker Johnson & Smith PA					
500 N Wshore Blvd Ste 1000	Tampa	FL	33609	800-366-7126	813-286-2424
Hill Barth & King LLC					
7680 Market St	Youngstown	OH	44512	800-733-8613	330-758-8613
Honkamp Krueger & Company PC					
2345 JFK Rd PO Box 699	Dubuque	IA	52004	888-556-0123	563-556-0123
Huckstep & Assoc LLC					
3734 S Ave Ste E	Springfield	MO	65807	800-269-6466	417-889-8991
JH Cohn LLP					
Four Becker Farm Rd	Roseland	NJ	07068	877-704-3500	973-228-3500
Kahn Litwin Renza & Company Ltd					
951 N Main St	Providence	RI	02904	888-557-8557	401-274-2001
Kaufman Rossin & Co PA					
2699 S Bayshore Dr	Miami	FL	33133	866-357-9634	305-858-5600
LarsonAllen LLP					
220 S Sixth St Ste 300	Minneapolis	MN	55402	888-529-2648	612-376-4500
Lazer Grant Inc					
309 Mcdermot Ave	Winnipeg	MB	R3A1T3	800-220-0005	204-942-0300
Lefkowitz Garfinkel Champi & DeRienzo PC					
10 Weybosset St	Providence	RI	02903	800-927-5423	401-421-4800
Lurie Besikof Lapidus & Co LLP					
2501 Wayzata Blvd	Minneapolis	MN	55405	877-322-8228	612-377-4404
Mauldin & Jenkins Certified Public Accountants LLC					
200 Galleria Pkwy SE	Atlanta	GA	30339	800-277-0080	770-955-8600
McConnell Jones Lanier & Murphy LLP					
The Lakes On Post Oak 3040 Post Oak Blvd Ste 1600	Houston	TX	77056	866-908-4650	713-968-1600
Moore Stephens Lovelace PA					
1201 S Orlando Ave Ste 400	Winter Park	FL	32789	800-683-5401	407-740-5400
Morrison Brown Argiz & Farra LLP					
1001 Brickell Bay Dr Ninth Fl	Miami	FL	33131	800-239-3843	305-373-5500
O'Connor Davies Munns & Dobbins LLP					
665 Fifth Ave	New York	NY	10022	800-397-0249	212-286-2600
Padgett Business Services					
160 Hawthorne Pk	Athens	GA	30606	800-723-4388	
Pannell Kerr Forster Of Texas Pc					
5847 San Felipe St	Houston	TX	77057	800-829-3676	713-860-1400
Paymetric Inc					
1225 Northmeadow Pkwy Ste 110	Roswell	GA	30076	888-445-4901	678-242-5281
Pearce Bevill Leesburg & Moore Pc					
110 Office Pk Dr	Birmingham	AL	35223	800-654-1654	205-323-5440
Plante & Moran PLLC					
27400 NW Hwy	Southfield	MI	48034	866-639-9991	248-352-2500
PRG-Schultz International Inc					
600 Galleria Pkwy Ste 100	Atlanta	GA	30339	800-752-5894	770-779-3900
PricewaterhouseCoopers LLP					
300 Madison Ave	New York	NY	10017	800-993-9971	646-471-4000
Rehmann Group					
5800 Gratiot St Ste 201	Saginaw	MI	48638	866-799-9580	989-799-9580
RF Murray & Co CPAs PC					
3741 Wilder Rd	Bay City	MI	48706	800-929-3556	989-686-7740

				Toll-Free	Phone

S R Snodgrass AC
2100 Corporate Dr .... Wexford PA 15090 | 800-580-7738 | 724-934-0344

SC&H Group LLC
910 Ridgebrook Rd .... Sparks MD 21152 | 800-832-3008 | 410-403-1500

Schenck Business Solutions
200 E Washington St .... Appleton WI 54911 | 800-236-2246 | 920-731-8111

Schlenner Wenner & Co
630 Roosevelt Rd .... Saint Cloud MN 56301 | 877-616-0286 | 320-251-0286

Sikich LLP
1415 W Diehl Rd Ste 400 .... Naperville IL 60563 | 877-279-1900 | 630-566-8400

Singer Lewak Greenbaum & Goldstein LLP
10960 Wilshire Blvd 7th Fl .... Los Angeles CA 90024 | 877-754-4557 | 310-477-3924

Suby Von Haden & Assoc SC
1221 John Q Hammons Dr .... Madison WI 53717 | 800-279-2616 | 608-831-8181

Teal Becker & Chiramonte (TBC)
7 Washington Sq .... Albany NY 12205 | 888-380-9660 | 518-456-6663

TMG Company LLC
1718 Briarcrest Dr Ste 100 .... Bryan TX 77802 | 800-720-1563 | 979-774-4492

Toski & Co PC
300 Essjay Rd Ste 115 .... Williamsville NY 14221 | 800-546-7556 | 716-634-0700

Watson Rice & Co
301 Rt 17 N 4th Fl .... Rutherford NJ 07070 | 800-945-5985 | 201-460-4590

Wilcoxon Research Inc
20511 Seneca Meadows Pkwy .... Germantown MD 20876 | 800-945-2696 | 301-330-8811

WithumSmith+Brown
5 Vaughn Dr .... Princeton NJ 08540 | 866-455-7438 | 609-520-1188

Wong & Knowles CPA PC
340 W Butterfield Rd .... Elmhurst IL 60126 | 866-966-4272 | 630-993-2223

3   ADHESIVES & SEALANTS

				Toll-Free	Phone

Adhesives Research Inc
400 Seaks Run Rd PO Box 100........ Glen Rock PA 17327 | 800-445-6240 | 717-235-7979

Arlon Graphics
2811 S Harbor Blvd .... Santa Ana CA 92704 | 800-232-7161 | 714-540-2811

Atlas Minerals & Chemicals Inc
1227 Valley Rd .... Mertztown PA 19539 | 800-523-8269* | 610-682-7171
*Cust Svc

Avery Dennison Corp
207 Goode Ave .... Glendale CA 91203 | 888-567-4387* | 626-304-2000
NYSE: AVY ■ *Cust Svc

BASF Corp/Bldg Systems
889 Valley Pk Dr .... Shakopee MN 55379 | 800-433-9517* | 952-496-6000
*Cust Svc

Bestolife Corp
2777 Stemmons Fwy Ste 1800 .... Dallas TX 75207 | 855-243-9164 | 214-583-0271

Bostik Inc
11320 Watertown Plank Rd .... Wauwatosa WI 53226 | 800-726-7845 | 414-774-2250

BR 111 Exotic Hardwood Flooring
1 NE 40th St .... Miami FL 33137 | 800-525-2711

Brady Coated Products
6555 W Good Hope Rd .... Milwaukee WI 53223 | 800-662-1191 | 414-358-6600

CFC International Inc
500 State St .... Chicago Heights IL 60411 | 800-393-4505 | 708-891-3456

Colloid Environmental Technologies Co (CETCO)
2870 Forbs Ave .... Hoffman Estates IL 60192 | 800-527-9948 | 847-851-1899

Custom Bldg Products
13001 Seal Beach Blvd .... Seal Beach CA 90740 | 800-272-8786 | 562-598-8808

DAP Products Inc
2400 Boston St Ste 200 .... Baltimore MD 21224 | 800-543-3840* | 410-675-2100
*Cust Svc

Devcon Inc 30 Endicott St .... Danvers MA 01923 | 800-626-7226 | 855-489-7262

Dymax Corp
318 Industrial Ln Ste 2 .... Torrington CT 06790 | 877-396-2963 | 860-482-1010

Eclectic Products Inc
1075 Arrowsmith St PO Box 2280 .... Eugene OR 97402 | 800-693-4667 | 541-284-9621

Elmer's Products Inc
One Easton Oval .... Columbus OH 43219 | 888-435-6377

Euclid Chemical Co
19218 Redwood Rd .... Cleveland OH 44110 | 800-321-7628 | 216-531-9222

Foster Construction Products Inc
1105 S Frontenac St .... Aurora IL 60504 | 800-231-9541

Fox Industries Inc
3100 Falls Cliff Rd .... Baltimore MD 21211 | 888-760-0369 | 410-243-8856

Franklin International
2020 Bruck St .... Columbus OH 43207 | 800-877-4583 | 614-443-0241

Geocel Corp PO Box 398 .... Elkhart IN 46515 | 800-348-7615 | 574-264-0645

Grace Darex Packaging Technologies
62 Whittemore Ave .... Cambridge MA 02140 | 866-333-3726 | 617-498-4987

H B Fuller Construction Products Inc
1105 S Frontenac Rd .... Aurora IL 60504 | 800-832-9002

HB Fuller Co
1200 Willow Lk Blvd PO Box 64683........ Saint Paul MN 55164 | 888-423-8553 | 651-236-5900
NYSE: FUL

Henkel Corp
One Henkel Way .... Rocky Hill CT 06067 | 800-243-4874* | 860-571-5100
*Cust Svc

Hercules Chemical Company Inc
111 S St .... Passaic NJ 07055 | 800-221-9330 | 973-778-5000

Houghton International Inc
945 Madison Ave PO Box 930 .... Valley Forge PA 19482 | 888-459-9844 | 610-666-4000

Illinois Tool Works Inc TACC Div
56 Air Stn Industrial Pk .... Rockland MA 02370 | 888-751-0409*
*Hotline

Inovex Industries Inc
45681 Oakbrook Ct Ste 102 .... Sterling VA 20166 | 888-374-3366 | 703-421-9778

IPS Group Inc 455 W Victoria St .... Compton CA 90220 | 800-888-8312 | 310-898-3300

Laticrete International Inc
91 Amity Rd .... Bethany CT 06524 | 800-243-4788 | 203-393-0010

Light Fabrications Inc
40 Hytec Cir .... Rochester NY 14606 | 800-836-6920 | 585-426-5330

Lord Corp 111 Lord Dr .... Cary NC 27511 | 877-275-5673 | 919-468-5979

MAPEI Corp
1144 E Newport Ctr Dr .... Deerfield Beach FL 33442 | 800-426-2734 | 954-246-8888

Morgan Adhesives Co
4560 Darrow Rd .... Stow OH 44224 | 866-262-2822 | 330-688-1111

				Toll-Free	Phone

Nylok Corp 15260 Hallmark Dr .... Macomb MI 48042 | 800-826-5161 | 586-786-0100

Pacific Polymers Inc
12271 Monarch St .... Garden Grove CA 92841 | 800-888-8340 | 714-898-0025

Para-Chem Southern Inc
863 SE Main St PO Box 127 .... Simpsonville SC 29681 | 800-763-7272 | 864-967-7691

Pecora Corp
165 Wambold Rd .... Harleysville PA 19438 | 800-523-6688 | 215-723-6051

Red Devil Inc 1437 S Boulder .... Tulsa OK 74119 | 800-423-3845

Ritrama
800 Kasota Ave SE .... Minneapolis MN 55414 | 800-328-5071 | 612-378-2277

Southern Grouts & Mortars Inc
1502 SW Second Pl .... Pompano Beach FL 33069 | 800-641-9247 | 954-943-2288

Super Glue Corp
9420 Santa Anita Ave .... Rancho Cucamonga CA 91730 | 800-538-3091 | 909-987-0550

Tailored Chemical Products Inc
700 12th St Dr NW .... Hickory NC 28601 | 800-627-1687 | 828-322-6512

Tremco Inc Roofing Div
3735 Green Rd .... Beachwood OH 44122 | 800-852-6013 | 216-292-5000

Uniseal Inc
1800 W Maryland St .... Evansville IN 47712 | 800-443-9081 | 812-436-4840

W.F. Taylor Company Inc
11545 Pacific Ave .... Fontana CA 92337 | 800-397-4583 | 951-360-6677

Worthen Industries Inc
Three E Spit Brook Rd .... Nashua NH 03060 | 800-444-5988 | 603-888-5443

4   ADVERTISING AGENCIES

SEE ALSO Public Relations Firms

				Toll-Free	Phone

A Web That Works
2733 Concession Rd 7 .... Bowmanville ON L1C3K6 | 800-579-9253 | 905-263-2666

Alesco Data Group LLC
5276 Summerlin Commons Way ...... Fort Myers FL 33907 | 800-701-6531 | 239-275-5006

All-Ways Adv Co
1442 Broad St .... Bloomfield NJ 07003 | 800-255-9291 | 973-338-0700

Aspen Marketing Services
1240 N Ave .... West Chicago IL 60185 | 800-848-0212 | 630-293-9600

Bailey Lauerman & Assoc Inc
1248 O St Ste 900 .... Lincoln NE 68508 | 800-869-0411 | 402-475-2800

Bernard Hodes Group
220 E 42 St .... New York NY 10017 | 888-438-9911 | 212-999-9000

Cade & Assoc Adv Inc
1645 Metropolitan Blvd .... Tallahassee FL 32308 | 800-715-2233 | 850-385-0300

Commercial Mailing Accessories Inc
28220 Playmor Beach Rd .... Rocky Mount MO 65072 | 800-325-7303

Cotton & Co 633 SE Fifth St .... Stuart FL 34994 | 800-266-9076 | 772-287-6612

Creative Alliance Inc
437 W Jefferson St .... Louisville KY 40202 | 800-525-0294 | 502-584-8787

Davis Elen Adv
865 S Figueroa St Ste 1200 .... Los Angeles CA 90017 | 800-729-4322 | 213-688-7236

Dudnyk
5 Walnut Grove Dr Ste 280 .... Horsham PA 19044 | 800-767-3263 | 215-443-9406

Fahlgren Inc
4030 Easton Station Ste 300 .... Columbus OH 43219 | 800-731-8927 | 614-383-1500

Fallon
901 Marquette Ave Ste 2400 .... Minneapolis MN 55402 | 888-758-2345 | 612-758-2345

Hunter Barth Adv Inc
2043 Wcliff Dr Ste 303 .... Newport Beach CA 92660 | 877-524-2732 | 949-631-9900

Ideal Adv & Printing
116 N Winnebago St .... Rockford IL 61101 | 800-208-0294 | 815-965-1713

Innis Maggiore Group Inc
4715 Whipple Ave NW .... Canton OH 44718 | 800-460-4111 | 330-492-5500

Intermark Group Inc
101 25th St N .... Birmingham AL 35243 | 800-624-9239 | 205-803-0000

Kuno Creative Group LLC
36901 American Wy Ste 2A .... Avon OH 44011 | 800-303-0806

Laughlin/Constable Inc
207 E Michigan St .... Milwaukee WI 53202 | 800-432-8747 | 414-272-2400

Lawrence & Schiller Inc
3932 S Willow Ave .... Sioux Falls SD 57105 | 800-356-9377 | 605-338-8000

Lehman Millet Inc
Two Atlantic Ave .... Boston MA 02110 | 800-634-5315

Lindsay Stone & Briggs Inc
One South Pinckney St Suite 500 ..... Madison WI 53703 | 866-403-8838 | 608-251-7070

Martin-Williams Adv
150 S 5th St Ste 900 .... Minneapolis MN 55402 | 800-632-1388 | 612-340-0800

Media Logic USA LLC
59 Wolf Rd .... Albany NY 12205 | 866-353-3011 | 518-456-3015

NAS Recruitment Communications
9700 Rockside Rd Ste 170 .... Cleveland OH 44125 | 866-627-7327

Register Tapes Unlimited Inc
1445 Langham Creek .... Houston TX 77084 | 800-247-4793 | 281-206-2500

Reply Inc
12667 Alcosta Blvd Ste 200 .... San Ramon CA 94583 | 888-466-8677 | 925-983-3400

Risdall Adv Agency
550 Main St .... New Brighton MN 55112 | 888-747-3255 | 651-286-6700

Ron Foth Adv
8100 N High St .... Columbus OH 43235 | 888-766-3684 | 614-888-7771

Shaker Recruitment Adv & Communications
1100 Lake St Third Fl .... Oak Park IL 60301 | 800-323-5170 | 708-383-5320

Sherry Matthews Inc
200 S Congress Ave .... Austin TX 78704 | 877-478-4397 | 512-478-4397

Shumsky Enterprises Inc
811 E Fourth St .... Dayton OH 45402 | 800-223-2203 | 937-223-2203

Siegel & Gale
625 Ave of the Americas 4th Fl ...... New York NY 10011 | 800-356-9377 | 212-453-0400

SPAR Group Inc
560 White Plains Rd .... Tarrytown NY 10591 | 800-314-7727 | 914-332-4100
NASDAQ: SGRP

Tinsley Adv 2000 S Dixie Hwy .... Miami FL 33133 | 800-432-2242 | 305-856-6060

Trone
1823 Eastchester Dr .... High Point NC 27265 | 877-493-3043 | 336-886-1622

UniWorld Group Inc
1 Metro Ctr N .... Brooklyn NY 11201 | 800-900-2958 | 212-219-1600

VML Inc
250 NW Richards Rd .... Kansas City MO 64116 | 800-990-2468 | 816-283-0700

			Toll-Free	Phone

Vox Medica Inc
601 Walnut St Ste 250-S . . . . Philadelphia PA 19106 **800-842-6482** 215-238-8500

ADVERTISING DISPLAYS

SEE Signs ; Displays - Exhibit & Trade Show ; Displays - Point-of-Purchase

5   ADVERTISING SERVICES - DIRECT MAIL

			Toll-Free	Phone

29 Prime Inc
9701 Jeronimo Rd . . . . Irvine CA 92618 **888-513-7746**

3DShopping.com
28th Fl US Bank Tower . . . . Los Angeles CA 90071 **800-442-5299**

Accurate Mailings Inc
215 O'Neill Ave . . . . Belmont CA 94002 **800-732-3290** 650-508-8885

Acxiom Corp
601 E Third St . . . . Little Rock AR 72201 **888-337-7699** 501-342-7799
NASDAQ: ACXM

Adwerx Inc 307 W Main St . . . . Durham NC 27701 **888-746-5678**

Adzzup LLC
8240 S Kyrene Rd Ste 101 . . . . Tempe AZ 85284 **888-723-9987**

Agency Revolution 698 NW . . . . Bend OR 97701 **800-606-0477**

AKT Enterprises
6424 Forest City Rd . . . . Orlando FL 32810 **877-306-3651**

Americomm
804 Greenbrier Cir . . . . Chesapeake VA 23320 **800-527-6757** 757-622-2724

Ameripack Inc
107 N Gold Dr . . . . Robbinsville NJ 08691 **800-456-7963** 609-259-7004

BlueSpire Strategic Marketing
7650 Edinborough Way Ste 500 . . . . Minneapolis MN 55435 **800-727-6397**

Boostability Inc
2600 West Executive Pkwy Ste 200 . . . . Lehi UT 84043 **800-261-1537**

Brierley & Partners
5465 Legacy Dr Ste 300 . . . . Plano TX 75024 **800-899-8700** 214-760-8700

Bulldog Solutions LLC
7600 N Capital of Texas Hwy Bldg C
Ste 250 . . . . Austin TX 78731 **877-402-9199**

Cardlytics Inc
675 Ponce de Leon Ave NE Ste 6000 . . . . Atlanta GA 30308 **888-798-5802**

Catalina Marketing Corp
200 Carillon Pkwy . . . . Saint Petersburg FL 33716 **888-322-3814** 727-579-5000

Centron Data Services Inc
1175 Devin Dr . . . . Norton Shores MI 49441 **800-732-8787***
*Cust Svc

Comark Direct
507 S Main St . . . . Ft. Worth TX 76104 **888-742-0405**

DirectMailcom
201 Skipjack Rd . . . . Prince Frederick MD 20678 **866-284-5816** 301-855-1700

eLocal Listing LLC
28765 Single Oak Dr Ste 250 . . . . Temecula CA 92590 **800-285-0484**

FFF Enterprises Inc
41093 County Ctr Dr . . . . Temecula CA 92591 **800-843-7477** 951-296-2500

Focus Direct LLC
9707 Broadway . . . . San Antonio TX 78217 **800-555-1551** 210-805-9185

Funnel Science Internet Marketing LLC
1802 N Carson St . . . . Carson City NV 89701 **877-301-0001**

Haines & Company Inc
8050 Freedom Ave . . . . North Canton OH 44720 **800-843-8452**

Harte-Hanks Inc
9601 McAllister Fwy Ste 610 . . . . San Antonio TX 78216 **800-456-9748** 210-829-9000
NYSE: HHS

Heritage Co, The
2402 Wildwood Ave Ste 500. . . . . North Little Rock AR 72120 **800-643-8822** 501-835-5000

Hkm Direct Market Communications Inc
5501 Cass Ave . . . . Cleveland OH 44102 **800-860-4456***
*General

infoGroup Inc
1020 E First St . . . . Papillion NE 68046 **866-414-7848** 402-836-5290

LeadRival
1207 S White Chapel Blvd Ste 250. . . . . Southlake TX 76092 **800-332-8017**

Lemon Peak Marketing Services
500 W Putnam Ave Ste 400 . . . . Greenwich CT 06831 **888-253-7348**

Level Interactive
241 Fourth Ave . . . . Pittsburgh PA 15222 **877-733-8625**

Lewis Direct Marketing
325 E Oliver St . . . . Baltimore MD 21202 **800-533-5394** 410-539-5100

Market Data Retrieval
Six Armstrong Rd . . . . Shelton CT 06484 **800-333-8802** 203-926-4800

Meridian Display & Merchandising Inc
162 York Ave E . . . . St Paul MN 55117 **800-786-2501** 651-227-3020

Mila Displays Inc
1315B Broadway Ste 108 . . . . Hewlett NY 11557 **800-295-6452** 516-791-2643

Mobivity Inc
58 W Buffalo Ste 200 . . . . Chandler AZ 85225 **877-282-7660**

Money Mailer LLC
12131 Western Ave . . . . Garden Grove CA 92841 **800-468-5865** 714-889-3800

Nationwide Biweekly Administration Inc
855 Lower Bellbrook Rd . . . . Xenia OH 45385 **888-802-1296**

News America Marketing
1185 Ave of the Americas 27 . . . . New York NY 10036 **800-462-0852** 212-782-8000

Next Day Flyers
18711 S Broadwick St . . . . Rancho Dominguez CA 90220 **800-251-9948**

O'Halloran Adv Inc
270 Saugatuck Ave . . . . Westport CT 06880 **877-466-6616** 203-341-9400

Promotions Unlimited
7601 Durand Ave . . . . Mount Pleasant WI 53177 **800-992-9307** 262-681-7000

Prospectr Marketing
3508 W 22nd St . . . . Minneapolis MN 55416 **800-908-3523**

RDI Marketing Services
4350 Glendale Milford Rd Ste 250 . . . . Cincinnati OH 45242 **800-388-7636** 513-984-5927

ReadyPulse
1600 A El Camino Real . . . . San Carlos CA 94070 **888-998-7412**

Redfin
9890 S Maryland Pkwy Ste 200 . . . . Las Vegas NV 89183 **800-561-5463** 877-973-3346

RME360
4805 Independence Pkwy Ste 250 . . . . Tampa FL 33634 **888-383-8770**

RR Donnelley Logistics
1000 Windham Pkwy . . . . Bolingbrook IL 60490 **888-744-7773** 630-226-6100

RR Donnelley Response Marketing Services
4101 Winfield Rd . . . . Warrenville IL 60555 **800-722-9001** 630-963-9494

RSVP Publications
6730 W Linebaugh Ave Ste 201 . . . . Tampa FL 33625 **800-360-7787** 813-960-7787

Sales Benchmark Index
1595 Peachtree Pkwy Ste 204-328 . . . . Cumming GA 30041 **888-556-7338**

ShiftCentral Inc
210 John St Ste 100 . . . . Moncton NB E1C0B8 **866-551-5533**

SourceLink Inc
500 Pk Blvd Ste 415 . . . . Itasca IL 60143 **866-947-6872**

Steel House Inc
3644 Eastham Dr . . . . Culver City CA 90232 **888-978-3354**

SuperCoups
350 Revolutionary Dr . . . . East Taunton MA 02718 **800-626-2620** 508-977-2000

Tel-e Technologies
7 Kodiak Crescent . . . . Toronto ON M3J3E5 **800-661-2340** 416-631-1300

Tension Envelope Corp
819 E 19th St . . . . Kansas City MO 64108 **800-388-5122**

Tgi Direct 5365 Hill 23 Dr . . . . Flint MI 48507 **800-337-2237**

Universal Wilde
26 Dartmouth St . . . . Westwood MA 02090 **866-825-5515** 781-251-2700

Valpak Direct Marketing Systems Inc
8605 Largo Lakes Dr . . . . Largo FL 33773 **800-237-6266**

Vertical Vision Financial Marketing LLC
145 Towne Lk Pkwy . . . . Woodstock GA 30188 **866-984-1585**

Yeck Bros Co 2222 Arbor Blvd . . . . Dayton OH 45439 **800-417-2767** 937-294-4000

6   ADVERTISING SERVICES - MEDIA BUYERS

			Toll-Free	Phone

Ektron Inc
542 Amherst St (Rt 101A) . . . . Nashua NH 03063 **866-435-8766** 603-594-0249

Media Space Solutions
904 MainSt . . . . Hopkins MN 55343 **888-672-2100** 612-253-3900

Worldata
3000 N Military Trl . . . . Boca Raton FL 33431 **800-331-8102** 561-393-8200

7   ADVERTISING SERVICES - ONLINE

			Toll-Free	Phone

Absorbent Ink
5812 Trade Ctr Dr Ste 100 . . . . Austin TX 78744 **866-618-3471**

Access To Media
432 Front St . . . . Chicopee MA 01013 **866-612-0034**

Active Network
10182 Telesis Ct Ste 100 . . . . San Diego CA 92121 **888-543-7223** 858-964-3800

Blue Cat Design
Mastwoods Rd . . . . Welcome ON L1A3V5 **888-258-3228** 905-753-1017

Commission Junction Inc
530 E Montecito St . . . . Santa Barbara CA 93103 **800-761-1072** 805-730-8000

Creative Outdoor Advertising
2402 Stouffville Rd . . . . Gormley ON L0H1G0 **800-661-6088**

eBay Enterprise Inc
935 First Ave . . . . King of Prussia PA 19406 **877-255-2857** 610-491-7000
NASDAQ: EBAY

Faction Media LLP
1730 Blake St Ste 200 . . . . Denver CO 80202 **866-788-5306**

HelloWorld
One ePrize Dr . . . . Pleasant Ridge MI 48069 **877-837-7493**

Marchex Inc
520 Pike St Ste 2000 . . . . Seattle WA 98101 **800-840-1012** 206-331-3300
NASDAQ: MCHX

MarketLauncher Inc
1800 Pembroke Dr Ste 300. . . . . Orlando FL 32810 **800-901-3803**

non-linear creations inc
987 Wellington St Ste 201 . . . . Ottawa ON K1Y2Y1 **866-915-2997** 613-241-2067

Oxiem LLC
One S Limestone . . . . Springfield OH 45502 **866-432-8235**

Primacy
1577 New Britain Ave . . . . Farmington CT 06032 **866-497-3725** 860-679-9332

Quest Companies Inc
8011 N Point Blvd Ste 201 . . . . Winston-salem NC 27106 **800-467-9409**

Rakuten Marketing LLC
215 Pk Ave S 9th Fl . . . . New York NY 10003 **888-880-8430** 646-943-8200

Room 214 Inc
3390 Valmont Rd Ste 214. . . . . Boulder CO 80301 **866-624-1851**

SEOP Inc
1720 E Garry St Ste 103 . . . . Santa Ana CA 92705 **877-231-1557**

Siegel & Gale
625 Ave of the Americas 4th Fl . . . . New York NY 10011 **800-356-9377** 212-453-0400

Straight North LLC
1001 W 31st St . . . . Downers Grove IL 60515 **866-353-3953**

Tobe Direct
9700 Park Plz Ave Ste 210 . . . . Louisville KY 40241 **866-820-7313**

Topica Inc
1 Post Street Suite 875 . . . . San Francisco CA 94104 **888-728-2465** 415-344-0800

Transcontinental Inc
1100 Rene-Levesque Blvd W 24th Fl . . . . Montreal QC H3B4X9 **800-361-5479** 514-392-9000

ValueClick Inc
30699 Russell Ranch Rd
Ste 250 . . . . Westlake Village CA 91362 **877-361-3316** 818-575-4500
NASDAQ: VCLK

ValueClick Media
530 E Montecito St . . . . Santa Barbara CA 93103 **877-361-3316** 805-879-1600

Yesmail
309 SW Sixth Ave Ste 700 . . . . Portland OR 97204 **877-937-6245** 503-241-4185

8   ADVERTISING SERVICES - OUTDOOR ADVERTISING

			Toll-Free	Phone

Kubin-Nicholson Corp
8440 N 87th St . . . . Milwaukee WI 53224 **800-858-9557** 414-586-4300

	Toll-Free	Phone
Lamar Adv Co		
5321 Corporate Blvd ....Baton Rouge LA 70808	800-235-2627	225-926-1000
NASDAQ: LAMR		
OUTFRONT Media Inc		
405 Lexington Ave ....New York NY 10174	800-926-8834	212-297-6400

9   ADVERTISING SPECIALTIES

SEE ALSO Signs ; Smart Cards ; Trophies, Plaques, Awards

	Toll-Free	Phone
ADG Promotional Products		
2300 Main St ....Hugo MN 55038	800-852-5208	
AIA Corporation (AIA)		
800 Winneconne Ave ....Neenah WI 54956	800-460-7836	920-886-3700
Airmate Co Inc		
16280 County Rd D ....Bryan OH 43506	800-544-3614	419-636-3184
Alexander Mfg Co		
12978 Tesson Ferry Rd ....Sappington MO 63128	800-258-2743*	314-842-3344
*General		
Allen Co 712 E Main St ....Blanchester OH 45107	800-329-2491	937-783-2491
Americanna Co 29 Aldrin Rd ....Plymouth MA 02360	888-747-5550*	508-747-5550
*Cust Svc		
Amsterdam Printing & Litho Corp		
166 Wallins Corners Rd ....Amsterdam NY 12010	800-833-6231*	518-842-6000
*Cust Svc		
Arthur Blank & Co Inc		
225 Rivermoor St ....Boston MA 02132	800-776-7333	617-325-9600
Atlas Match LLC		
1801 S Airport Cir ....Euless TX 76040	800-628-2426	817-267-1500
Belaire Products Inc		
763 S Broadway St ....Akron OH 44311	800-886-3224	330-253-3116
Bergamot Inc		
820 E Wisconsin St ....Delavan WI 53115	800-922-6733*	262-728-5572
*Cust Svc		
Brown & Bigelow Inc		
345 Plato Blvd E ....Saint Paul MN 55107	800-628-1755*	651-293-7000
*Cust Svc		
Churchwell Co		
814 S Edgewood Ave ....Jacksonville FL 32205	877-537-6166	904-356-5721
Dunn Manufacturing Inc		
1400 Goldmine Rd ....Monroe NC 28110	800-868-7111	704-283-2147
EBSCO Creative Concepts		
3500 Blue Lake Dr Ste 150 ......Birmingham AL 35243	800-756-7023	205-262-2696
Flair Communications Agency Inc		
214 W Erie St ....Chicago IL 60654	800-621-8317	312-943-5959
Hit Promotional Products Inc		
7150 Bryan Dairy Rd ....Largo FL 33777	800-237-6305	727-541-5561
Instant Imprints		
5897 Oberlin Dr Ste 200...........San Diego CA 92121	800-542-3437	858-642-4848
Marco Promotional Products		
2640 Commerce Dr ....Harrisburg PA 17110	877-545-9322	
Marietta Hospitality		
37 Huntington St ....Cortland NY 13045	800-950-7772	607-753-6746
Maryland Match Corp		
605 Alluvion St ....Baltimore MD 21230	800-423-0013	410-752-8164
Mid-America Merchandising Inc		
204 W Third St ....Kansas City MO 64105	800-333-6737	816-471-5600
MMG Works/Status Promotions		
4601 Madison Ave ....Kansas City MO 64112	800-945-4044	816-472-5988
Myron Corp 205 Maywood Ave ....Maywood NJ 07607	877-803-3358	
National Pen Corp (NPC)		
12121 Scripps Summit Dr Ste 200...........San Diego CA 92131	800-854-1000	858-675-3000
Newton Mfg Co		
1123 First Ave E ....Newton IA 50208	800-500-7227	641-792-4121
Norscot Group Inc		
1000 W Donges Bay Rd PO Box 998 ....Mequon WI 53092	800-653-3313	262-241-3313
Norwood Promotional Products Inc		
14421 Myerlake Cir ....Clearwater IN 33760	877-555-2223	727-538-3527
Pilgrim Plastic Products Co		
1200 W Chestnut St ....Brockton MA 02301	877-343-7810	508-583-9046
Prime Resources Corp		
1100 Boston Ave ....Bridgeport CT 06610	800-621-5463	203-331-9100
Quikey Manufacturing Co		
1500 Industrial Pkwy ....Akron OH 44310	877-901-1200	330-633-8106
Staples Promotional Products		
7500 W 110th St ....Overland Park KS 66210	800-369-4669	913-319-3100
Universal Creative Concepts Corp		
10143 Royalton Rd Unit E............North Royalton OH 44133	800-876-8626	440-230-1366
Vanguard East		
1172 Azalea Garden Rd ....Norfolk VA 23502	800-221-1264	
Western Plastic Products Inc		
8441 Monroe Ave ....Stanton CA 90680	800-453-1881	
Zebra Marketing		
7119 Laurel Canyon Blvd		
Suite 3 ....North Hollywood CA 91605	800-348-2422	818-765-6442

AGRICULTURAL CHEMICALS

AGRICULTURAL MACHINERY & EQUIPMENT

SEE Farm Machinery & Equipment - Mfr ; Farm Machinery & Equipment - Whol

10   AGRICULTURAL PRODUCTS

SEE ALSO Seed Companies ; Fruit Growers ; Horse Breeders ; Horticultural Products Growers

	Toll-Free	Phone
United Farmers Co-op (UFC)		
705 E Fourth St PO Box 461 ......Winthrop MN 55396	866-998-3266	507-647-6600

10-1 Cattle Ranches, Farms, Feedlots (Beef Cattle)

	Toll-Free	Phone
Agri Beef Co		
1555 Shoreline Dr Ste 320 ....Boise ID 83702	800-657-6305	208-338-2500
AzTx Cattle Co PO Box 390 ......Hereford TX 79045	800-999-5065	806-364-8871
Cactus Feeders Inc		
2209 W Seventh Ave ....Amarillo TX 79106	877-698-7355	806-373-2333
Coyote Lake Feedyard Inc		
1287 FM 1731 ....Muleshoe TX 79347	800-299-3321	806-946-3321
Dean Cluck Feedyard Inc		
105 Dean Cluck Ave ....Gruver TX 79040	888-458-4787	806-733-5021
Dinklage Feedyards		
PO Box 274 ....Sidney NE 69162	888-343-5940	308-254-5940
Friona Feedyard 2370 FM 3140 ....Friona TX 79035	800-658-6014	806-265-3574
Friona Industries LP		
500 S Taylor St Ste 601 PO Box 15568 ....Amarillo TX 79101	800-658-6014	806-374-1811
Garden City Feed Yard		
1805 W Annie Scheer Rd ....Garden City KS 67846	800-272-4191	620-275-4191
JR Simplot Co		
999 W Main St Ste 1300................Boise ID 83702	800-832-8893	208-336-2110
Littlefield Feedyard		
Farm to Market 37 ....Littlefield TX 79339	800-658-6014	806-385-5141
PM Beef Group LLC		
2850 Hwy 60 E ....Windom MN 56101	800-622-5213	507-831-2761
Randall County Feedyard		
15000 FM 2219 ....Amarillo TX 79119	800-658-6014	806-499-3701
Swisher County Cattle Co		
Farm Market 214 Rd ....Tulia TX 79088	800-658-6014	806-627-4231

10-2 Dairy Farms

	Toll-Free	Phone
Hollandia Dairy Inc		
622 E Mission Rd ....San Marcos CA 92069	888-883-2479	760-744-3222
Kreider Farms		
1461 Lancaster Rd ....Manheim PA 17545	888-665-4415	717-665-4415
Marburger Farm Dairy Inc		
1506 Mars Evans City Rd ....Evans City PA 16033	800-331-1295	724-538-4800

10-3 General Farms

	Toll-Free	Phone
Agrex Inc		
10975 Grandview Dr St Ste 200 ....Overland Park KS 66210	800-334-6788	913-851-6300
Amana Colonies 622 46th Ave ....Amana IA 52203	800-579-2294	319-622-7622
farmers win coop (FFC)		
110 N Jefferson ....Fredericksburg IA 50630	800-562-8389	563-237-5324
FarmTek		
1440 Field of Dreams Way ....Dyersville IA 52040	800-327-6835	563-875-2288
Gold-eagle Co-op		
515 N Locust St PO Box 280 ....Goldfield IA 50542	800-825-3331	
Plains Grain & Agronomy LLC		
109 Third Ave PO Box 6 ....Enderlin ND 58027	800-950-2219	701-437-2400
Star of the West Milling Co		
121 E Tuscola St ....Frankenmuth MI 48734	888-281-4161	989-652-9971

10-4 Grain Farms

	Toll-Free	Phone
AgriNorthwest		
7404 W Hood Pl Ste B ....Kennewick WA 99336	888-632-5511	509-734-1195
Country Pride Co-op (CPC)		
648 W Second St PO Box 529 ....Winner SD 57580	888-325-7743	605-842-2711
Golden Grain Energy LLC		
1822 43rd St SW ....Mason City IA 50401	888-443-2676	641-423-8525
Hoegemeyer Hybrids Inc		
1755 Hoegemeyer Rd ....Hooper NE 68031	800-245-4631	402-654-3399
Moews Seed Co Inc		
9821 IL Hwy 89 ....Granville IL 60640	800-663-9795	815-339-2201
Morrow County Grain Growers Inc (MCGG)		
350 N Main St ....Lexington OR 97839	800-452-7396	541-989-8221
Pioneer Hi-Bred International Inc		
PO Box 1000 ....Johnston IA 50131	800-247-6803	515-535-3200
Sunray Co-op		
201 N Main PO Box 430................Sunray TX 79086	800-621-3570	806-948-4121
William F Renk & Sons Inc		
6809 Wilburn Rd ....Sun Prairie WI 53590	800-289-7365	
Wyffels Hybrids Inc		
13344 US Hwy 6 ....Geneseo IL 61254	800-369-7833	309-944-8334

10-5 Hog Farms

	Toll-Free	Phone
Cargill Inc		
15407 McGinty Rd W ....Wayzata MN 55391	800-227-4455	952-742-7575
Hog Slat Inc		
PO Box 300 ....Newton Grove NC 28366	800-949-4647	910-594-0219
PIC USA		
100 Bluegrass Commons Blvd		
Ste 2200 ....Hendersonville TN 37075	800-325-3398	615-265-2700
Seaboard Foods		
9000 W 67th St Ste 200 ....Shawnee Mission KS 66202	800-262-7907	913-261-2600
Smithfield Foods Inc		
200 Commerce St ....Smithfield VA 23430	800-276-6158	757-365-3000
NYSE: SFD		
Tyson Foods Inc		
2210 W Oaklawn Dr PO Box 2020 ....Springdale AR 72762	800-643-3410	479-290-4000
NYSE: TSN		

10-6 Mushroom Growers

			Toll-Free	Phone
Monterey Mushrooms Inc				
260 Westgate Dr ....Watsonville CA 95076			**800-333-6874**	831-763-5300
Phillips Mushroom Farms Inc				
1011 Kaolin Rd ....Kennett Square PA 19348			**800-722-8818**	610-925-0520
Sylvan Inc 90 Glade Dr ....Kittanning PA 16201			**866-352-7520**	724-543-3900

10-7 Poultry & Eggs Production

			Toll-Free	Phone
Amick Farms Inc				
2079 Batesburg Hwy ....Batesburg SC 29006			**800-926-4257**	803-532-1400
Aviagen Group				
5015 Bradford Dr ....Huntsville AL 35805			**800-826-9685**	256-890-3800
Cobb-Vantress Inc				
PO Box 1030 ....Siloam Springs AR 72761			**800-748-9719**	479-524-3166
Cooper Farms				
22348 County Rd 140 PO Box 547 .... Oakwood OH 45873			**800-423-2765**	419-594-3325
Culver Duck Farms Inc				
PO Box 910 ....Middlebury IN 46540			**800-825-9225**	574-825-9537
Foster Farms Inc				
1000 Davis St PO Box 457 .... Livingston CA 95334			**800-255-7227**	
Maple Leaf Farms Inc				
PO Box 308 ....Milford IN 46542			**800-348-2812**	574-658-4121
Michael Foods Inc				
301 Carlson Pkwy Ste 400 .... Minnetonka MN 55305			**800-328-5474**	952-258-4000
Perdue Farms Inc				
31149 Old Ocean City Rd .... Salisbury MD 21804			**800-473-7383**	410-543-3000
Pilgrim's Corp				
1770 Promontory Cir ....Greeley CO 80634			**800-321-1470**	
NASDAQ: PPC				
Simpson's Eggs Inc				
5015 Hwy 218 E ....Monroe NC 28110			**800-726-1330**	704-753-1478
Tyson Foods Inc				
2210 W Oaklawn Dr PO Box 2020 .... Springdale AR 72762			**800-643-3410**	479-290-4000
NYSE: TSN				
Wayne Farms LLC				
4110 Continental Dr ....Oakwood GA 30566			**800-392-0844**	
Willmar Poultry Co, The (WPC)				
3735 County Rd 5 SW ....Willmar MN 56201			**800-328-8849**	320-235-8850
Zacky Farms Inc 2020 SE Ave .... Fresno CA 93721			**800-888-0235**	562-641-2020
Zephyr Egg Co Inc				
4622 Gall Blvd ....Zephyrhills FL 33542			**800-333-4415**	813-782-1521

10-8 Sugarcane & Sugarbeets Growers

			Toll-Free	Phone
Wedgworth Farms Inc				
300 North Dixie Hwy Ste 471 .... West Palm Beach FL 33401			**800-477-2077**	561-832-4164

10-9 Tree Nuts Growers

			Toll-Free	Phone
Hammons Products Co				
105 Hammons Dr PO Box 140 .... Stockton MO 65785			**888-429-6887**	
Mauna Loa Macadamia Nut Corp				
16-701 Macadamia Rd ....Keaau HI 96749			**888-628-6256***	808-966-8618
*Cust Svc				
Sunnyland Farms Inc				
PO Box 8200 ....Albany GA 31706			**800-999-2488**	

10-10 Vegetable Farms

			Toll-Free	Phone
Barnes Farming Corp				
7840 Old Bailey Hwy ....Spring Hope NC 27882			**800-367-2799**	
Bolthouse Farms				
7200 E Brundage Ln ....Bakersfield CA 93307			**800-467-4683**	
Buurma Farms Inc				
3909 Kok Rd ....Willard OH 44890			**888-428-8762**	419-935-6411
Caruso Inc 3465 Hauck Rd ....Cincinnati OH 45241			**800-759-7659**	513-860-9200
Christopher Ranch				
305 Bloomfield Ave ....Gilroy CA 95020			**800-779-1156**	408-847-1100
CROPP Co-op One Organic Way ....LaFarge WI 54639			**888-444-6455**	
D'Arrigo Bros Company of California Inc				
PO Box 850 ....Salinas CA 93902			**800-995-5939***	831-455-4500
*Cust Svc				
Earthbound Farm				
1721 San Juan Hwy ....San Juan Bautista CA 95045			**800-690-3200**	831-623-7880
Fresh Express Inc				
550 South Caldwell St Ste 1212 ....Charlotte NC 28202			**800-242-5472***	
*Cust Svc				
Greenheart Farms Inc				
902 Zenon Way PO Box 1510 .... Arroyo Grande CA 93420			**800-549-5531**	805-481-2234
Grimmway Farms Inc				
PO Box 81498 ....Bakersfield CA 93380			**800-301-3101**	
Harris Farms Inc				
27366 W Oakland Ave ....Coalinga CA 93210			**800-311-6211**	559-884-2859
Hartung Bros Inc				
708 Heartland Trl Ste 2000 ....Madison WI 53717			**800-362-2522**	608-829-6000
Nash Produce Co				
6160 S N Carolina 58 ....Nashville NC 27856			**800-334-3032**	252-443-6011
Petrocco Farms				
14110 Brighton Rd ....Brighton CO 80601			**888-876-2207**	303-659-6498
San Miguel Produce Inc				
4444 Naval Air Rd ....Oxnard CA 93033			**888-347-3367**	805-488-0981
Tanimura & Antle Inc				
PO Box 4070 ....Salinas CA 93912			**800-772-4542**	

			Toll-Free	Phone
Taylor & Fulton Inc				
932 Fifth Ave W ....Palmetto FL 34221			**800-457-5577**	941-729-3883
Tri-Campbell Farms				
15111 Hwy 17 ....Grafton ND 58237			**800-222-7783**	701-352-3116
West Coast Distributing Inc				
Commerce Pl 350 Main St ....Boston MA 02148			**800-235-3730**	781-665-9393
Wiers Farm Inc				
4465 St Rt 103 S PO Box 385. ....Willard OH 44890			**800-777-6243**	419-935-0131

11	AGRICULTURAL SERVICES

11-1 Crop Preparation Services

			Toll-Free	Phone
Farmers Co-op Union, The				
225 S Broadway PO Box 159 ....Sterling KS 67579			**800-238-1843**	620-278-2141
Fresh Express Inc				
550 South Caldwell St Ste 1212 ....Charlotte NC 28202			**800-242-5472***	
*Cust Svc				
Gruma Corp				
1159 Cottonwood L Ste 200 ....Irving TX 75038			**800-627-3221**	972-232-5000
Haines City Citrus Growers Assn (HCCGA)				
Eight Railroad Ave PO Box 337. ......Haines City FL 33844			**800-327-6676***	863-422-1174
*Sales				
Hazelnut Growers of Oregon				
401 N 26th Ave ....Cornelius OR 97113			**800-273-4676**	503-648-4176
Index Fresh Inc				
18184 Slover Ave ....Bloomington CA 92316			**800-352-6931**	909-877-0999
Mann Packing Company Inc				
PO Box 690 ....Salinas CA 93902			**800-285-1002**	831-422-7405
Mariani Packing Company Inc				
500 Crocker Rd ....Vacaville CA 95688			**800-231-1287**	707-452-2800
River Ranch Fresh Foods				
1156 Abbott St ....Salinas CA 93901			**800-538-5868**	831-758-1390
Tracy-Luckey Company Inc				
110 N Hicks St PO Box 880 ....Harlem GA 30814			**800-476-4796**	706-556-6216

11-2 Livestock Improvement Services

			Toll-Free	Phone
ABS Global Inc				
1525 River Rd PO Box 459. ....DeForest WI 53532			**800-356-5331***	608-846-3721
*Cust Svc				
Accelerated Genetics				
E 10890 Penny Ln ....Baraboo WI 53913			**800-451-9275**	608-356-8357
Alta California				
N8350 High Road ....Watertown WI 53094			**800-932-2855**	920-261-5065
COBA/Select Sires Inc				
1224 Alton Darby Creek Rd ....Columbus OH 43228			**800-837-2621**	614-878-5333
Cobb-Vantress Inc				
PO Box 1030 ....Siloam Springs AR 72761			**800-748-9719**	479-524-3166
Dairy One 730 Warren Rd ....Ithaca NY 14850			**800-344-2697**	607-257-1272
Genex Co-op Inc/CRI				
117 E Green Bay St ....Shawano WI 54166			**888-333-1783**	715-526-2141
Reproduction Enterprises Inc				
908 N Prairie Rd ....Stillwater OK 74075			**866-734-2855**	405-377-8037
SEK Genetics 9525 70th Rd ....Galesburg KS 66740			**800-443-6389**	

12	AIR CARGO CARRIERS

			Toll-Free	Phone
ABX Air Inc				
145 Hunter Dr ....Wilmington OH 45177			**800-736-3973**	937-382-5591
Aeronet Worldwide				
42 Corporate Pk ....Irvine CA 92606			**800-552-3869**	949-474-3000
Ameriflight Inc				
4700 Empire Ave Hngr 1. ....Burbank CA 91505			**800-800-4538**	818-847-0000
Amerijet International Inc				
2800 S Andrews Ave .... Fort Lauderdale FL 33316			**800-927-6059**	954-320-5300
Atlas Air Worldwide Holdings Inc				
2000 Westchester Ave ....Purchase NY 10577			**866-434-1617**	914-701-8000
NASDAQ: AAWW				
Cathay Pacific Cargo				
6040 Avion Dr Ste 338 ....Los Angeles CA 90045			**800-628-6960**	310-417-0052
Cayman Airways Cargo Services				
6103 NW 72nd Ave ....Miami FL 33166			**800-252-2746**	305-526-3190
China Airlines Cargo Sales & Service				
11201 Aviation Blvd ....Los Angeles CA 90045			**800-778-4838**	310-646-4293
Delta Air Cargo				
PO Box 20559 Dept 670 ....Atlanta GA 30320			**800-352-2737**	
Kalitta Flying Service				
818 Willow Run Airport ....Ypsilanti MI 48198			**800-521-1590**	734-484-0088
Lynden Air Cargo LLC				
6441 S Airpark Pl ....Anchorage AK 99502			**888-243-7248**	907-243-7248
MartinAire Aviation LLC				
4553 Glenn Curtiss Dr ....Addison TX 75001			**866-557-1861**	972-349-5700
Qantas Airways Cargo				
6555 W Imperial Hwy ....Los Angeles CA 90045			**800-227-0290***	310-665-2280
*General				
Service by Air Inc				
222 Crossways Pk Dr ....Woodbury NY 11797			**800-243-5545**	
Southwest Airlines Air Cargo				
2702 Love Field Dr ....Dallas TX 75235			**800-533-1222**	
United Airlines Cargo				
PO Box 66100 ....Chicago IL 60666			**800-822-2746**	
Virgin Atlantic Cargo				
JFK International Airport Bldg 15 ....Jamaica NY 11430			**800-828-6822**	516-775-2600

Classified Section

	Toll-Free	Phone

13 — AIR CHARTER SERVICES

SEE ALSO Helicopter Transport Services ; Aviation - Fixed-Base Operations

		Toll-Free	Phone
Active Aero Group 2068 E St	Belleville MI 48111	800-872-5387*	734-547-7200
*Cust Svc			
Aero Air LLC 2050 NE 25th Ave	Hillsboro OR 97124	800-448-2376	503-640-3711
Air Charter Team 4151 N Mulberry Dr Ste 250	Kansas City MO 64116	800-205-6610	816-283-3280
Air Palm Springs 145 S Gene Autry Trl Ste 14	Palm Springs CA 92262	800-760-7774	760-322-1104
AirFlite Inc 3250 AirFlite Way	Long Beach CA 90807	800-241-3548	562-490-6200
American Air Charter Inc 577 Bell Ave	Chesterfield MO 63005	888-532-2710	636-532-2707
Avstar Aviation Ltd 12 N Haven Ln	East Northport NY 11731	800-575-2359	631-499-0048
Berry Aviation Inc 1807 Airport Dr	San Marcos TX 78666	800-229-2379	512-353-2379
Bluffton Flying Service Co 1080 Navajo Dr	Bluffton OH 45817	800-468-6359	419-358-7045
Charter Flight Inc 1928 S Blvd	Charlotte NC 28208	800-521-3148	704-359-9124
Chrysler Aviation Inc (CAI) 7120 Hayvenhurst Ave Ste 309	Van Nuys CA 91406	800-995-0825	818-989-7900
Clay Lacy Aviation 7435 Valjean Ave	Van Nuys CA 91406	800-423-2904	818-989-2900
CSI Aviation Services Inc 3700 Rio Grand Blvd NW	Albuquerque NM 87107	800-765-9464	505-761-9000
Era Helicopters LLC 600 Airport Service Rd PO Box 6550	Lake Charles LA 70606	800-256-2372	337-478-6131
Exec Air Montana Inc 2430 Airport Rd	Helena MT 59601	800-513-2190	406-442-2190
Executive Jet 4556 Airport Rd	Cincinnati OH 45226	877-356-5387	513-979-6600
Fair Winds Air Charter Inc 2525 SE Witham Field Hngr 7	Stuart FL 34996	800-989-9665	772-288-4130
Flightstar Corp Seven Airport Rd Willard Airport	Savoy IL 61874	800-747-4777	217-351-7700
Hop-A-Jet Inc 5525 NW 15th Ave Ste 150	Fort Lauderdale FL 33309	800-556-6633	954-771-5779
International Jet Aviation Services 8511 Aviator Ln	Centennial CO 80112	800-858-5891	303-790-0414
Jet Aviation Business Jets Inc 112 Charles A Lindbergh Dr	Teterboro NJ 07608	800-736-8538	201-462-4100
Jet Resource Inc 455 Wilmer Ave Lunken Airport Hngr 27	Cincinnati OH 45226	800-404-5387	513-871-1554
KaiserAir Inc 8735 Earhart Rd PO Box 2626	Oakland CA 94621	800-538-2625	510-569-9622
Key Air LLC Three Juliano Dr Ste 201	Oxford CT 06478	888-539-2471	203-264-0605
Life Flight Network LLC 22285 Yellow Gate Ln NE	Aurora OR 97002	800-232-0911	503-678-4364
LR Services 602 Hayden Cir	Allentown PA 18109	888-675-9650	610-266-2500
Mayo Aviation Inc 7735 S Peoria St	Englewood CO 80112	800-525-0194	303-792-4020
Million Air Interlink Inc 8501 Telephone Rd	Houston TX 77061	888-589-9059	713-640-4000
Nashville Jet 635 Hangar Ln	Nashville TN 37217	800-824-4778	615-350-8400
New England Life Flight Inc 1727 Robins St Hangar	Bedford MA 01730	800-233-8998	781-863-2213
Ohio Medical Transportation Inc 2827 W Dblin Granville Rd	Columbus OH 43235	877-633-3598	614-734-8001
Pacific Coast Jet Charter Inc 10600 White Rock Rd	Rancho Cordova CA 95670	800-655-3599	916-631-6507
Pentastar Aviation 7310 Highland Rd	Waterford MI 48327	800-662-9612	248-666-3630
Planemasters Ltd 32 W 611 Tower Rd DuPage Airport	West Chicago IL 60185	800-994-6400	630-513-2100
Premier Jets 2140 NE 25th Ave	Hillsboro OR 97124	800-635-8583	503-640-2927
Priester Aviation 1061 S Wolf Rd	Wheeling IL 60090	888-323-7887	847-537-1133
San Juan Airlines Co 4000 Airport Rd Ste A	Anacortes WA 98221	800-874-4434	360-293-4691
Sentient Jet LLC 100 Grossman Dr Ste 400	Braintree MA 02184	866-602-0044	781-763-0200
Skyservice Airlines Inc 9785 Ryan Ave	Dorval QC H9P1A2	888-985-1402	514-636-3300
Tavaero Jet Charter 7930 Airport Blvd	Houston TX 77061	800-343-3771	713-644-6431
Tulip City Air Service Inc 1581 S Washington Ave	Holland MI 49423	800-748-0515	616-392-7831
Twin Cities Air Service 81 Airport Dr	Auburn ME 04210	800-564-3882	
West Coast Aviation Services 19711 Campus Dr Ste 150	Santa Ana CA 92707	800-352-6153	949-852-8340

14 — AIR CONDITIONING & HEATING EQUIPMENT - COMMERCIAL/INDUSTRIAL

SEE ALSO Refrigeration Equipment - Mfr ; Air Conditioning & Heating Equipment - Residential

		Toll-Free	Phone
Absolut Aire Inc 5496 N Riverview Dr	Kalamazoo MI 49004	800-804-4000	269-382-1875

		Toll-Free	Phone
ACS Group 1100 E Woodfield Rd Ste 588	Schaumburg IL 60173	800-783-7835	847-273-7700
Advantage Engineering Inc 525 E S- 18 Rd	Greenwood IN 46142	800-669-1282	317-887-0729
Aitken Products Inc 566 N Eagle St PO Box 151	Geneva OH 44041	800-569-9341	440-466-5711
American Coolair Corp 3604 Mayflower St	Jacksonville FL 32205	877-250-2822	904-389-3646
Arctic Industries Inc 9731 NW 114th Way	Miami FL 33178	800-325-0123	305-883-5581
Armstrong International Inc 2081 SE Ocean Blvd 4th Fl	Stuart FL 34996	866-738-5125	772-286-7175
Auer Steel & Heating Supply Co 2935 W Silver Spring Dr	Milwaukee WI 53209	800-242-0406	414-463-1234
Blissfield Manufacturing Co 626 Depot St	Blissfield MI 49228	800-626-1772*	517-486-2121
*Cust Svc			
Brainerd Compressor Rebuilders Inc 3034 Sandbrook St	Memphis TN 38116	800-228-4138	
Brooks Automation Inc Polycold Systems 3800 Lakeville Hwy	Petaluma CA 94954	800-698-6149	707-769-7000
Bry-Air Inc 10793 SR 37 W	Sunbury OH 43074	877-427-9247	740-965-2974
Carrier Corp 1 Carrier Pl	Farmington CT 06034	800-227-7437	860-674-3000
CEI Enterprises Inc 245 WoodwaRd Rd SE	Albuquerque NM 87102	800-545-4034	
ClimateMaster Inc 7300 SW 44th St	Oklahoma City OK 73179	800-299-9747	405-745-6000
Colmac Coil Manufacturing Inc 370 N Lincoln St PO Box 571	Colville WA 99114	800-845-6778	509-684-2595
DiversiTech Inc 6650 Sugarloaf Pkwy Ste 100	Duluth GA 30097	800-995-2222	678-542-3600
Dometic Corp 2320 Industrial Pkwy PO Box 490	Elkhart IN 46516	800-544-4881	574-294-2511
Doucette Industries Inc (DII) 20 Leigh Dr	York PA 17406	800-445-7511	717-845-8746
Drink More Water Store 7595-A Rickenbacker Dr	Gaithersburg MD 20879	800-697-2070	
DRISTEEM Corp 14949 Technology Dr	Eden Prairie MN 55344	800-328-4447	952-949-2415
DRS Sustainment Systems Inc 7375 Industrial Rd	Florence KY 41042	800-694-5005	859-372-8204
Duro Dyne Corp 81 Spence St	Bay Shore NY 11706	800-899-3876	631-249-9000
EGS Electrical Group LLC EasyHeat Div 9377 W Higgins Rd	Rosemont IL 60018	800-621-1506	847-268-6000
Fidelity Engineering Corp 25 Loveton Cir PO Box 2500	Sparks MD 21152	800-787-6000	410-771-9400
Friedrich 10001 Reunion Pl Ste 500	San Antonio TX 78216	800-541-6645	210-546-0500
Hastings HVAC Inc 3606 Yost Ave PO Box 669	Hastings NE 68902	800-228-4243*	402-463-9821
*Cust Svc			
Henry Technologies 701 S Main St	Chatham IL 62629	800-964-3679	217-483-2406
ITW Vortec 10125 Carver Rd	Cincinnati OH 45242	800-441-7475	513-891-7485
Layton Manufacturing Corp 825 Remsen Ave	Brooklyn NY 11236	800-545-8002	718-498-6000
Lintern Corp 8685 Stn St	Mentor OH 44060	800-321-3638	440-255-9333
Lomanco Inc 2101 W Main St	Jacksonville AR 72076	800-643-5596	501-982-6511
Maradyne Corp 4540 W 160th St	Cleveland OH 44135	800-537-7444	216-362-0755
Master-Bilt Products 908 Hwy 15 N	New Albany MS 38652	800-647-1284	662-534-9061
Midwest Towers Inc 1156 Hwy 19 East	Chickasha OK 73018	800-900-2190	405-224-4622
Mobile Climate Control Corp 17103 State Rd 4 E PO Box 150	Goshen IN 46528	800-450-2211	574-534-1516
Munters Corp 210 Sixth St PO Box 6428	Fort Myers FL 33907	800-843-5360	239-936-1555
Munters Corp DHI 79 Monroe St	Amesbury MA 01913	800-843-5360*	978-241-1100
*Sales			
Niagara Blower Co Inc 673 Ontario St	Buffalo NY 14207	800-426-5169	716-875-2000
Nordyne Inc 8000 Phoenix Pkwy	O'Fallon MO 63368	800-422-4328	636-561-7300
Pacific Rim Mechanical 7655 Convoy Ct	San Diego CA 92111	800-891-4822	858-974-6500
Packless Metal Hose Inc PO Box 20668	Waco TX 76702	800-347-4859	254-666-7700
Phoenix Manufacturing Inc 3655 E Roeser Rd	Phoenix AZ 85040	800-325-6952*	602-437-1034
*Cust Svc			
Pittsburgh Plumbing Heating & Industrial (PPHI) 434 Melwood Ave	Pittsburgh PA 15213	800-445-4155	412-622-8100
Proair LLC 28731 County Rd 6	Elkhart IN 46514	800-338-8544	574-264-5494
Rama Corp 600 W Esplanade Ave	San Jacinto CA 92583	800-472-5670	951-654-7351
Rink Systems Inc 1103 Hershey St	Albert Lea MN 56007	800-944-7930	507-373-9175
Sealed Unit Parts Company Inc 2230 Landmark Pl	Allenwood NJ 08720	800-333-9125	732-223-6644
Seasons-4 Inc 4500 Industrial Access Rd	Douglasville GA 30134	800-888-9900	770-489-0716
Shield Air Solutions Inc 3708 Greenhouse Rd	Houston TX 77084	800-237-2095	281-944-4300
Skuttle Manufacturing Co 101 Margaret St	Marietta OH 45750	800-848-9786	740-373-9169
Temp-Control Mechanical Corp (TCM) 4800 N Ch Ave	Portland OR 97217	877-826-3828	503-285-9851
Thermal Care Inc 7720 N Lehigh Ave	Niles IL 60714	888-828-7387	847-966-2260
ThermoElectric Cooling America Corp 4048 W Schubert Ave	Chicago IL 60639	888-832-2872	773-342-4900

				Toll-Free	Phone
Tom Barrow Co (TBC) 2800 Plant Atkinson Rd	Smyrna	GA	30080	**800-229-8226**	404-351-1010
Traulsen & Company Inc 4401 Blue Mound Rd	Fort Worth	TX	76106	**800-825-8220**	
Tutco Inc 500 Gould Dr	Cookeville	TN	38506	**877-262-4533**	931-432-4141
United CoolAir Corp 491 E Princess St	York	PA	17403	**877-905-1111**	717-843-4311
Watts Radiant Inc 4500 E Progress Pl	Springfield	MO	65803	**800-276-2419**	417-864-6108

15 AIR CONDITIONING & HEATING EQUIPMENT - RESIDENTIAL

SEE ALSO Air Conditioning & Heating Equipment - Commercial/Industrial

				Toll-Free	Phone
Airefco Inc 18755 SW Teton Ave PO Box 1349	Tualatin	OR	97062	**800-869-1349**	503-692-3210
Allied Air Enterprises 215 Metropolitan Dr	West Columbia	SC	29170	**800-448-5872**	
Amana Appliances Inc 2800 220th Trl *Cust Svc	Amana	IA	52204	**800-843-0304***	319-622-5511
Bard Mfg Co Inc 1914 Randolph Dr	Bryan	OH	43506	**877-347-6456**	419-636-1194
Friedrich 10001 Reunion Pl Ste 500	San Antonio	TX	78216	**800-541-6645**	210-546-0500
International Comfort Products Corp (ICP) 650 Heil Quaker Ave	Lewisburg	TN	37091	**800-458-6650**	931-359-3511
Kim Hotstart Manufacturing Co 5723 E Alki Ave	Spokane	WA	99212	**800-224-5550**	509-536-8660
Lennox Industries Inc 2100 Lake Pk Blvd *Cust Svc	Richardson	TX	75080	**800-953-6669***	
Lennox International Inc 2140 Lake Pk Blvd *NYSE: LII*	Richardson	TX	75080	**800-953-6669**	972-497-5000
National System of Garage Ventilation Inc 714 N Church St PO Box 1186	Decatur	IL	62525	**800-728-8368**	217-423-7314
Simpson Mfg Company Inc 5956 W Las Positas Blvd *NYSE: SSD*	Pleasanton	CA	94588	**800-925-5099**	925-560-9000
Takagi Industrial Company USA Inc Five Whatney	Irvine	CA	92618	**888-882-5244**	949-770-7171
TPI Corp PO Box 4973	Johnson City	TN	37602	**800-682-3398**	423-477-4131
Ventamatic Ltd 100 Washington Rd	Mineral Wells	TX	76067	**800-433-1626**	
Whirlpool Corp 2000 N M-63 *NYSE: WHR*	Benton Harbor	MI	49022	**800-253-1301**	269-923-5000
Young Touchstone Inc 200 Smith Ln *Sales	Jackson	TN	38301	**800-238-8230***	731-424-5045

AIR CONDITIONING EQUIPMENT - AUTOMOTIVE

AIR CONDITIONING EQUIPMENT - WHOL

SEE Plumbing, Heating, Air Conditioning Equipment & Supplies - Whol

16 AIR FARE CONSOLIDATORS

				Toll-Free	Phone
Brazilian Travel Service (BTS) 16 W 46th St Second Fl	New York	NY	10036	**800-342-5746**	212-764-6161
C & H International 4751 Wilshire Blvd Ste 201	Los Angeles	CA	90010	**800-833-8888**	323-933-2288
Centrav Inc 511 E Travelers Trl	Burnsville	MN	55337	**800-874-2033**	952-886-7650
GTT Global 4100 Spring Valley Rd Ste 202	Dallas	TX	75244	**888-288-7182**	972-239-5069
International Travel Systems Inc 64 Madison Ave 2nd Fl	Wood-Ridge	NJ	07075	**800-258-0135**	201-727-0470
Sky Bird Travel & Tours Inc 24701 Swanson	Southfield	MI	48033	**888-759-2473**	248-372-4800
Skylink Travel 980 Ave of the Americas	New York	NY	10018	**800-247-6659**	212-573-8980
Solar Tours 1629 K St NW Ste 604	Washington	DC	20006	**800-388-7652**	202-861-5864
Trans Am Travel 4222 King St Ste 130	Alexandria	VA	22302	**800-822-7600**	703-998-7676

17 AIR PURIFICATION EQUIPMENT - HOUSEHOLD

SEE ALSO Appliances - Small - Mfr

				Toll-Free	Phone
Air Quality Engineering Inc 7140 Northland Dr N	Brooklyn Park	MN	55428	**800-328-0787**	763-531-9823
Airguard Industries Inc 100 River Ridge Cir	Jeffersonville	IN	47130	**800-999-3458**	866-247-4827
Dayton Reliable Air Filter Inc 2294 N Moraine Dr *Orders	Dayton	OH	45439	**800-699-0747***	
Gaylord Industries Inc 10900 SW Avery St	Tualatin	OR	97062	**800-547-9696**	503-691-2010
General Filters Inc 43800 Grand River Ave	Novi	MI	48375	**866-476-5101**	
Home Care Industries Inc ALFCO Div One Lisbon St *Cust Svc	Clifton	NJ	07013	**800-325-1908***	973-365-1600
Indoor Purification Systems Inc *Surround Air Div* 334 N Marshall Way Ste C	Layton	UT	84041	**888-812-1516**	801-547-1162
Koch Filter Corp 625 W Hill St	Louisville	KY	40208	**800-757-5624**	502-634-4796
Permatron Group 2020 Touhy Ave	Elk Grove Village	IL	60007	**800-882-8012**	847-434-1421
PuriTec 4705 S Durango Dr Ste 100-102	Las Vegas	NV	89147	**888-491-4100**	610-268-5420
Research Products Corp 1015 E Washington Ave	Madison	WI	53703	**800-334-6011**	608-257-8801
RPS Products Inc 281 Keyes Ave	Hampshire	IL	60140	**800-683-7030**	847-683-3400
Spencer Turbine Co 600 Day Hill Rd	Windsor	CT	06095	**800-232-4321**	860-688-8361
Tjernlund Products Inc 1601 Ninth St	White Bear Lake	MN	55110	**800-255-4208**	651-426-2993
United Air Specialists Inc (UAS) 4440 Creek Rd	Cincinnati	OH	45242	**800-252-4647**	513-891-0400
Vornado Air Circulation Systems Inc 415 E 13th St	Andover	KS	67002	**800-234-0604**	316-733-0035

18 AIR PURIFICATION EQUIPMENT - INDUSTRIAL

				Toll-Free	Phone
AAF International Corp 10300 Ormsby Pk Pl Ste 600	Louisville	KY	40223	**888-223-2003**	502-637-0011
Advantec MFS Inc 6723 Sierra Ct Ste A	Dublin	CA	94568	**800-334-7132**	925-479-0625
Aget Manufacturing Co 1408 E Church St	Adrian	MI	49221	**800-832-2438**	517-263-5781
Air Quality Engineering Inc 7140 Northland Dr N	Brooklyn Park	MN	55428	**800-328-0787**	763-531-9823
Airflow Systems Inc 11221 Pagemill Rd	Dallas	TX	75243	**800-818-6185**	214-503-8008
Airguard Industries Inc 100 River Ridge Cir	Jeffersonville	IN	47130	**800-999-3458**	866-247-4827
American Fan Company Inc 2933 Symmes Rd	Fairfield	OH	45014	**866-771-6266**	513-874-2400
Anguil Environmental Systems Inc 8855 N 55th St	Milwaukee	WI	53223	**800-488-0230**	414-365-6400
Baghouse & Industrial Sheet Metal Services Inc 1731 Pomona Rd	Corona	CA	92880	**888-224-4687**	951-272-6610
Beckett Air Inc 37850 Beckett Pkwy	North Ridgeville	OH	44039	**800-831-7839**	440-327-9999
Clarcor Inc 840 Crescent Ctr Dr Ste 600 *NYSE: CLC*	Franklin	TN	37067	**800-252-7267**	615-771-3100
Cleanroom Systems 7000 Performance Dr	North Syracuse	NY	13212	**800-825-3268**	315-452-7400
Clements National Co 6650 S Narragansett Ave	Chicago	IL	60638	**800-966-0016**	708-594-5890
Columbus Industries Inc 2938 SR-752	Ashville	OH	43103	**800-766-2552**	740-983-2552
CUNO Inc 400 Research Pkwy	Meriden	CT	06450	**800-243-6894**	203-237-5541
Disa Systems Inc 150 Transit Ave	Thomasville	NC	27360	**800-845-8508**	336-889-9187
Filtration Group Inc 912 E Washington St	Joliet	IL	60433	**800-739-4600**	815-726-4600
Flanders Corp 531 Flanders Filters Rd *OTC: FLDR*	Washington	NC	27889	**800-637-2803**	252-946-8081
Fuel Tech Inc 27601 Bella Vista Pkwy *NASDAQ: FTEK* ▪ *General	Warrenville	IL	60555	**800-666-9688***	630-845-4500
Gaylord Industries Inc 10900 SW Avery St	Tualatin	OR	97062	**800-547-9696**	503-691-2010
General Filters Inc 43800 Grand River Ave	Novi	MI	48375	**866-476-5101**	
Great Lakes Filters 301 Arch Ave	Hillsdale	MI	49242	**800-521-8565**	
Hartzell Fan Inc 910 S Downing St	Piqua	OH	45356	**800-336-3267**	937-773-7411
Home Care Industries Inc ALFCO Div One Lisbon St *Cust Svc	Clifton	NJ	07013	**800-325-1908***	973-365-1600
Honeyville Metal Inc 4200 S 900 W	Topeka	IN	46571	**800-593-8377**	260-593-2266
Houston Service Industries Inc 7901 Hansen Rd	Houston	TX	77061	**800-725-2291**	713-947-1623
King Engineering Corp 3201 S State St *Cust Svc	Ann Arbor	MI	48106	**800-242-8871***	734-662-5691
Koch Filter Corp 625 W Hill St	Louisville	KY	40208	**800-757-5624**	502-634-4796
McIntire Co 745 Clark Ave	Bristol	CT	06010	**800-437-9247**	860-585-0050
Met-Pro Corp Systems Div 160 Cassell Rd PO Box 144	Harleysville	PA	19438	**800-621-0734**	215-723-9300
Midwesco Filter Resources Inc 385 Battaile Dr	Winchester	VA	22601	**800-336-7300**	540-667-8500
NAO Inc 1284 E Sedgley Ave *Cust Svc	Philadelphia	PA	19134	**800-523-3495***	215-743-5300
National Filter Media Corp 691 North 400 West	Salt Lake City	UT	84103	**800-777-4248**	801-363-6736
Parker Hannifin Corp Finite Filtratio & Separation Div 500 Glaspie St	Oxford	MI	48371	**800-521-4357**	248-628-6400
Pneumech Systems Mfg LLC 201 Pneu Mech Dr	Statesville	NC	28625	**800-358-7374**	704-873-2475
Process Equipment Inc 2770 Welborn St PO Box 1607	Pelham	AL	35124	**888-663-2028**	205-663-5330
Purafil Inc 2654 Weaver Way	Doraville	GA	30340	**800-222-6367**	770-662-8545
Revcor Inc 251 E Edwards Ave	Carpentersville	IL	60110	**800-323-8261**	847-428-4412
RPS Products Inc 281 Keyes Ave	Hampshire	IL	60140	**800-683-7030**	847-683-3400
Sly Inc 8300 Dow Cir	Strongsville	OH	44136	**800-334-2957**	440-891-3200
Sonic Air Systems Inc 1050 Beacon St	Brea	CA	92821	**800-827-6642**	714-255-0124

					Toll-Free	Phone
Spencer Turbine Co						
600 Day Hill Rd	Windsor	CT	06095		800-232-4321	860-688-8361
Standard Filter Corp						
5928 Balfour Ct	Carlsbad	CA	92008		800-634-5837	760-929-8559
Tjernlund Products Inc						
1601 Ninth St	White Bear Lake	MN	55110		800-255-4208	651-426-2993
Tri-Dim Filter Corp						
93 Industrial Dr Bldg 2	Louisa	VA	23093		800-458-9835	540-967-2600
Tuthill Vacuum & Blower Systems						
4840 W Kearney St	Springfield	MO	65803		800-825-6937	417-865-8715
United Air Specialists Inc (UAS)						
4440 Creek Rd	Cincinnati	OH	45242		800-252-4647	513-891-0400
Waco						
2546 Gen Armistead Ave	Norristown	PA	19403		800-928-7159	610-630-4800

19   AIR TRAFFIC CONTROL SERVICES

The Federal Aviation Administration (a US government agency) and NAV CANADA (a private, not-for-profit Canadian firm) provide air traffic services nationwide in the US and Canada, respectively. The types of services provided include aircraft routing, approach and departure instruction, and weather information.

					Toll-Free	Phone
Federal Aviation Administration (FAA)						
800 Independence Ave SW	Washington	DC	20591		866-835-5322	
Federal Aviation Administration Northwest Mountain Region						
1601 Lind Ave SW	Renton	WA	98057		800-220-5715	425-227-2001
NAV CANADA						
77 Metcalfe St PO Box 3411 Stn D	Ottawa	ON	K1P5L6		800-876-4693	613-563-5588

20   AIRCRAFT

SEE ALSO Airships

					Toll-Free	Phone
AeroVironment Inc						
181 W Huntington Dr Ste 202	Monrovia	CA	91016		888-833-2148	626-357-9983
NASDAQ: AVAV						
Airbus Helicopters Inc						
2701 Forum Dr	Grand Prairie	TX	75052		800-873-0001	972-641-0000
Bell Helicopter Textron Inc						
600 E Hurst Blvd (State Hwy 10)	Hurst	TX	76053		888-874-5884	817-280-2011
Bombardier Aerospace						
400 Cote-Vertu Rd W	Dorval	QC	H4S1Y9		866-855-5001*	514-855-5000
*General						
Dassault Falcon Jet Corp						
PO Box 2000	South Hackensack	NJ	07606		800-527-2463	201-440-6700
Erickson Air-Crane Co						
5550 SW Macadam Ave Ste 200	Portland	OR	97239		800-424-2413	503-505-5800
Lockheed Martin Corp						
6801 Rockledge Dr	Bethesda	MD	20817		866-562-2363	301-897-6000
NYSE: LMT						
Mooney Aircraft Corp						
165 Al Mooney Rd	Kerrville	TX	78028		800-456-3033	
Robinson Helicopter Co						
2901 Airport Dr	Torrance	CA	90505		800-905-0655	310-539-0508

21   AIRCRAFT ENGINES & ENGINE PARTS

					Toll-Free	Phone
AAR Corp						
1100 N Wood Dale Rd 1 AAR Pl	Wood Dale	IL	60191		800-422-2213	630-227-2000
NYSE: AIR						
Abipa Canada Inc						
2000, Blvd Dagenais ouest	Laval	QC	H7L5W2		877-963-6888	450-963-6888
Beacon Industries Inc						
12300 Old Tesson Rd	Saint Louis	MO	63128		800-454-7159	314-487-7600
Continental Motors Inc						
2039 Broad St	Mobile	AL	36615		800-718-3411	251-438-3411
Engine Components Inc (ECI)						
9503 Middlex	San Antonio	TX	78217		800-324-2359	210-820-8101
Flight Dimensions International Inc						
4835 Cordell Ave Ste 150	Bethesda	MD	20814		866-235-6870	301-634-8201
Garsite LLC						
539 S Tenth St	Kansas City	KS	66105		888-427-7483	913-342-5600
Gros-Ite Industries						
1790 New Britain Ave	Farmington	CT	06032		877-777-4778	860-677-2603
Hartzell Engine Technologies LLC						
2900 Selma Hwy	Montgomery	AL	36108		877-359-5355	334-386-5400
Insight Technology Inc						
Nine Akira Way	Londonderry	NH	03053		866-509-2040	603-626-4800
Kalitta Charters LLC						
843 Willow Run Airport	Ypsilanti	MI	48198		800-525-4882	734-544-3400
Kelly Aerospace Turbine Rotables Inc						
3414 W 29th St S	Wichita	KS	67217		866-359-5287	316-943-6100
Kreisler Mfg Corp						
180 Van Riper Ave	Elmwood Park	NJ	07407		888-750-5834	201-791-0700
Northstar Aerospace Inc						
6006 W 73rd St	Bedford Park	IL	60638		800-362-3907	708-728-2000
TSE: NAS						
Parker Hannifin Corp						
6035 Parkland Blvd	Cleveland	OH	44124		800-272-7537*	216-896-3000
NYSE: PH ■ *Cust Svc						
Pratt & Whitney Canada Inc						
1000 Marie-Victorin Blvd	Longueuil	QC	J4G1A1		800-268-8000	450-677-9411
Rolls-Royce North America						
1875 Explorer St Ste 200	Reston	VA	20190		888-269-2377	703-834-1700
Sandel Avionics Inc						
2401 Dogwood Way	Vista	CA	92081		877-726-3357	760-727-4900
Senior Aerospace Ketema Div						
790 Greenfield Dr	El Cajon	CA	92021		800-669-6820	619-442-3451
Teledyne Technologies Inc						
1049 Camino Dos Rios	Thousand Oaks	CA	91360		877-666-6968	805-373-4545
NYSE: TDY						

					Toll-Free	Phone
Turbomeca USA Inc						
2709 N Forum Dr	Grand Prairie	TX	75052		800-662-6322	972-606-7600

22   AIRCRAFT PARTS & AUXILIARY EQUIPMENT

SEE ALSO Precision Machined Products

					Toll-Free	Phone
AAR Composites						
14201 Myerlake Cir	Clearwater	FL	33760		800-422-2213	727-539-8585
AAR Corp						
1100 N Wood Dale Rd 1 AAR Pl	Wood Dale	IL	60191		800-422-2213	630-227-2000
NYSE: AIR						
Advanced Technology Co						
2858 E Walnut St	Pasadena	CA	91107		800-447-2442	626-449-2696
Aerospace Products International (API)						
3778 Distriplex Dr N	Memphis	TN	38118		888-274-2497	901-365-3470
Arkwin Industries Inc						
686 Main St	Westbury	NY	11590		800-284-2551	516-333-2640
Avcorp Industries Inc						
10025 River Way	Delta	BC	V4G1M7		866-781-3111	604-582-6677
Avox Systems Inc						
225 Erie St	Lancaster	NY	14086		866-278-3237	716-683-5100
CEF Industries Inc						
320 S Church St	Addison	IL	60101		800-888-6419	630-628-2299
CRS Jet Spares Inc						
6701 NW 12th Ave	Fort Lauderdale	FL	33309		800-338-5387	954-972-2807
Curtiss-Wright Corp						
10 Waterview Blvd 2nd Fl	Parsippany	NJ	07054		855-449-0995	973-541-3700
NYSE: CW						
Esterline Interface Technologies						
600 W Wilbur Ave	Coeur d'Alene	ID	83815		800-444-5923	208-765-8000
Fairchild Controls Corp						
540 Highland St	Frederick	MD	21701		800-695-5378	301-228-3400
FletchAir Inc						
103 Turkey Run Ln	Comfort	TX	78013		800-329-4647	830-995-5900
Global Ground Support LLC						
540 Old Hwy 56	Olathe	KS	66061		888-780-0303	913-780-0300
Goodrich Corp Aircraft Interior Products Div						
3420 S Seventh St	Phoenix	AZ	85040		877-808-7575	602-243-2200
Honeywell Aerospace						
3520 Westmoor St	South Bend	IN	46628		800-707-4555	574-231-2000
L-3 Communications Integrated Systems						
10001 Jack Finney Blvd	Greenville	TX	75402		877-282-1168	903-455-3450
Middle River Aircraft Systems (MRAS)						
103 Chesapeake Pk Plaza	Baltimore	MD	21220		877-432-3272	410-682-1500
STS Component Solutions LLC						
2910 SW 42 Ave	Palm City	FL	34990		888-777-2960	
Tronair Inc						
1740 Eber Rd Ste E	Holland	OH	43528		800-426-6301	419-866-6301
Vibro-Meter Inc						
144 Harvey Rd	Londonderry	NH	03053		800-842-4291	603-669-0940

23   AIRCRAFT RENTAL

SEE ALSO Aviation - Fixed-Base Operations

					Toll-Free	Phone
AeroTurbine Inc						
2323 NW 82nd Ave	Miami	FL	33122		877-747-2370*	305-590-2600
*Cust Svc						
Jetscape Inc						
10 S New River Dr E Ste 200	Fort Lauderdale	FL	33301		800-355-5387	954-763-4737
Trench Plate Rental Co						
13217 Laureldale Ave	Downey	CA	90242		800-821-4478	
Us Adventure Rv						
5120 n brady st	Davenport	IA	52806		877-768-4678	

24   AIRCRAFT SERVICE & REPAIR

					Toll-Free	Phone
AAR Aircraft Component Services						
747 Zeckendorf Blvd	Garden City	NY	11530		800-422-2213	516-222-9000
AAR Corp						
1100 N Wood Dale Rd 1 AAR Pl	Wood Dale	IL	60191		800-422-2213	630-227-2000
NYSE: AIR						
AAR Landing Gear Services						
9371 NW 100th St	Miami	FL	33178		800-422-2213	305-887-4027
American Avionics						
7023 Perimeter Rd S	Seattle	WA	98108		800-518-5858*	206-763-8530
*Sales						
Barfield Inc 4101 NW 29th St	Miami	FL	33142		800-321-1039	305-894-5300
Cutter Aviation						
2802 E Old Tower Rd	Phoenix	AZ	85034		800-234-5382	602-273-1237
Duncan Aviation Inc						
3701 Aviation Rd	Lincoln	NE	68524		800-228-4277	402-475-2611
Elliott Aviation Inc						
6601 74th Ave PO Box 100	Milan	IL	61264		800-447-6711	309-799-3183
Emteq Inc						
5349 S Emmer Dr	New Berlin	WI	53151		888-679-6170	262-679-6170
Honeywell Aerospace						
3520 Westmoor St	South Bend	IN	46628		800-707-4555	574-231-2000
Jet Aviation						
112 Charles A Lindbergh Dr	Teterboro	NJ	07608		800-538-0832	201-288-8400
Kfs Inc						
1840 West Airfield Dr	Dallas	TX	75261		800-364-4115	817-488-4115
L-3 Communications Flight International Aviation LLC						
One Lear Dr	Newport News	VA	23602		800-358-4685	757-886-5500
McKinley Air Transport Inc						
5430 Lauby Rd	North Canton	OH	44720		800-225-6446*	330-499-3316
*General						
Million Air Interlink Inc						
8501 Telephone Rd	Houston	TX	77061		888-589-9059	713-640-4000
Priester Aviation						
1061 S Wolf Rd	Wheeling	IL	60090		888-323-7887	847-537-1133

				Toll-Free	Phone
Rolls-Royce Engine Services Inc 7200 Earhart Rd	Oakland	CA	94621	**866-793-4273**	510-613-1000
Serco Inc 1818 Library St Ste 1000	Reston	VA	20190	**866-628-6458**	703-939-6000
Sierra Industries Ltd 122 Howard Langford Dr	Uvalde	TX	78801	**888-835-9377**	830-278-4481
Summit Aviation Inc 4200 Summit Bridge Rd PO Box 258	Middletown	DE	19709	**800-441-9343**	302-834-5400
Tulsair Beechcraft Inc 3207 N Sheridan Rd	Tulsa	OK	74115	**800-331-4071**	918-835-7651
West Star Aviation Inc 796 Heritage Way	Grand Junction	CO	81506	**800-255-4193**	970-243-7500

25 AIRLINES - COMMERCIAL

SEE ALSO Air Cargo Carriers ; Air Charter Services ; Airlines - Frequent Flyer Programs

				Toll-Free	Phone
Aeroflot Russian International Airlines 10 Rockefeller Plaza Ste 1015	New York	NY	10020	**866-879-7647**	212-944-2300
Air India 570 Lexington Ave 15th Fl	New York	NY	10022	**800-223-7776**	
Air New Zealand Ltd 1960 E Grand Ave Ste 300	El Segundo	CA	90245	**800-262-1234**	310-648-7104
Air Sunshine Inc PO Box 22237	Fort Lauderdale	FL	33335	**800-435-8900**	954-434-8900
Air Tahiti Nui 1990 E Grand Ave *Cust Svc	El Segundo	CA	90245	**877-824-4846***	310-662-1860
All Nippon Airways Company Ltd 2050 W 190th St Ste 100	Torrance	CA	90504	**800-235-9262**	
American Airlines Inc 4333 Amon Carter Blvd	Fort Worth	TX	76155	**800-433-7300**	817-963-1234
Bearskin Airlines 1475 W Walsh St	Thunder Bay	ON	P7E4X6	**800-465-2327**	807-577-1141
Bering Air 1470 Sepalla Dr PO Box 1650	Nome	AK	99762	**800-478-5422**	907-443-5464
British Airways PLC (BA) 75-20 Astoria Blvd	Flushing	NY	11370	**800-403-0882**	347-418-4000
Bulloch & Bulloch Inc 309 Cash Memorial Blvd	Forest Park	GA	30297	**800-339-8177**	404-762-5063
Cape Air 660 Barnstable Rd	Hyannis	MA	02601	**866-227-3247**	508-771-6944
Cayman Airways Ltd 91 Owen Roberts Dr	Grand Cayman	KY	10092	**800-422-9626**	345-949-8200
Czech Airlines 1 Penn Plaza Ste 1416	New York	NY	10001	**855-359-2932**	
Delta Air Lines Inc 1030 Delta Blvd *NYSE: DAL*	Atlanta	GA	30354	**800-221-1212**	404-715-2600
El Al Israel Airlines Ltd 15 E 26th St Sixth Fl	New York	NY	10010	**800-223-6700**	212-852-0600
EVA Airways 200 N Sepulveda Blvd Ste 1600	El Segundo	CA	90245	**800-695-1188**	310-362-6600
Great Lakes Aviation Ltd 1022 Airport Pkwy *OTC: GLUX*	Cheyenne	WY	82001	**800-554-5111**	307-432-7000
Hawaiian Airlines Inc 3375 Koapaka St Ste G350	Honolulu	HI	96819	**800-367-5320**	808-835-3700
JetBlue Airways 29 Queens Blvd Ste 118 *NASDAQ: JBLU*	Forest Hills	NY	11375	**800-538-2583**	718-286-7900
Kenmore Air Harbor Inc 6321 NE 175th St	Kenmore	WA	98028	**866-435-9524**	425-486-1257
Korean Air 6101 W Imperial Hwy	Los Angeles	CA	90045	**800-438-5000**	310-417-5200
Malaysia Airlines 100 N Sepulveda Blvd Ste 1710 *Resv	El Segundo	CA	90245	**800-552-9264***	310-535-9288
New England Airlines Inc 56 Airport Rd	Westerly	RI	02891	**800-243-2460**	
Pacific Wings One Keolani Pl Ste 30	Kahului	HI	96732	**888-575-4546**	808-873-0877
Pakistan International Airlines Corp (PIA) 1200 New Jersey Ave SE	Washington	DC	20590	**800-578-6786**	
Peninsula Airways Inc 6100 Boeing Ave	Anchorage	AK	99502	**800-448-4226**	907-771-2500
Piedmont Airlines Inc 5443 Airport Terminal Rd	Salisbury	MD	21804	**800-354-3394**	410-742-2996
PSA Airlines Inc 3400 Terminal Dr *Resv	Vandalia	OH	45377	**800-235-0986***	937-454-1116
Qantas Airways Ltd 6080 Ctr Dr Ste 400	Los Angeles	CA	90045	**800-227-4500**	310-726-1400
Scandinavian Airlines System (SAS) 301 Route 17 N Ste 500	Rutherford	NJ	07070	**800-221-2350**	800-437-5807
Silver Airways Corp 1100 Lee Wagener Blvd Ste 201	Fort Lauderdale	FL	33315	**844-674-5837**	954-985-1500
Singapore Airlines Ltd 222 N Sepulveda Blvd Ste 1600	El Segundo	CA	90245	**800-742-3333**	310-647-1922
Skyservice Airlines Inc 9785 Ryan Ave	Dorval	QC	H9P1A2	**888-985-1402**	514-636-3300
South African Airways 515 E Las Olas Blvd 16th Fl	Fort Lauderdale	FL	33301	**800-722-9675**	954-769-5000
Southwest Airlines Co 2702 Love Field Dr PO Box 36611 *NYSE: LUV*	Dallas	TX	75235	**800-435-9792**	214-792-4000
Spirit Airlines Inc 2800 Executive Way *NASDAQ: SAVE*	Miramar	FL	33025	**800-772-7117**	
SriLankan Airlines 379 Thornall St 6th Fl	Edison	NJ	08837	**877-915-2652**	732-205-0017
Sun Country Airlines Inc 1300 Mendota Heights Rd	Mendota Heights	MN	55120	**800-359-6786**	651-681-3900
Thai Airways International Ltd 222 N Sepulveda Blvd Ste 100	El Segundo	CA	90245	**800-426-5204**	310-640-0097
US Airways Express 111 W Rio Salado Pkwy	Tempe	AZ	85281	**800-679-8215**	480-693-0800
Virgin Atlantic Airways Ltd 747 Belden Ave	Norwalk	CT	06850	**888-747-7474**	800-821-5438
WestJet Airlines Ltd 22 Aerial Pl NE *TSE: WJA*	Calgary	AB	T2E3J1	**888-293-7853**	403-444-2600

26 AIRLINES - FREQUENT FLYER PROGRAMS

				Toll-Free	Phone
Aer Lingus Airlines Gold Cir Club 300 Jericho Quad Ste 130	Jericho	NY	11753	**800-474-7424**	
Air Jamaica 7th Heaven 9200 S Dadeland Blvd	Miami	FL	33156	**800-523-5585**	305-670-3222
British Airways Executive Club PO Box 300743	Jamaica	NY	11430	**800-452-1201**	
Continental Airlines Inc 900 Grand Plz Dr	Houston	TX	77067	**800-621-7467**	713-952-1630
Czech Airlines OK Plus 147 W 35th St Ste 1505	New York	NY	10001	**855-359-2932**	
Hawaiian Airlines HawaiianMiles PO Box 30008	Honolulu	HI	96820	**877-426-4537**	
Icelandair North America 1900 Crown Colony Dr	Quincy	MA	02169	**800-223-5500**	
Korean Air Skypass 1813 Wilshire Blvd Ste 300	Los Angeles	CA	90057	**800-438-5000**	213-484-1900
Kuwait Airways Oasis Club 400 Kelby St	Fort Lee	NJ	07024	**800-458-9248**	201-582-9222
Miles & More PO Box 946	Santa Clarita	CA	91380	**800-581-6400**	
Singapore Airlines KrisFlyer 380 World Way Ste 336B	Los Angeles	CA	90045	**800-742-3333**	310-646-6221
SriLankan Travel Inc 379 Thornall St Sixth Fl	Edison	NJ	08837	**877-915-2652**	732-205-0017
Virgin Atlantic Flying Club 747 Belden Ave	Norwalk	CT	06850	**800-365-9500**	

27 AIRPORTS

SEE ALSO Ports & Port Authorities

Listings for airports in the US and Canada are organized by states and provinces, and then by city names within those groupings.

				Toll-Free	Phone
Akron-Canton Airport 5400 Lauby Rd NW	North Canton	OH	44720	**888-434-2359**	330-499-4221
Asheville Regional Airport 61 Terminal Dr Ste 1	Fletcher	NC	28732	**866-719-3910**	828-684-2226
Augusta Regional Airport - Bush Field (AGS) 1501 Aviation Way	Augusta	GA	30906	**866-289-9673**	706-798-3236
Augusta State Airport 75 Airport Rd	Augusta	ME	04330	**800-654-3131**	207-626-2306
Baltimore/Washington International Thurgood Marshall Airport (BWI) PO Box 8766	Baltimore	MD	21240	**800-435-9294**	410-859-7111
Bangor International Airport 287 Godfrey Blvd	Bangor	ME	04401	**866-359-2264**	207-992-4600
Baton Rouge Metropolitan Airport 9430 Jackie Cochran Dr Ste 300	Baton Rouge	LA	70807	**877-359-2538**	225-355-0333
Bishop International Airport G-3425 W Bristol Rd	Flint	MI	48507	**800-433-7300**	810-235-6560
Calgary International Airport 2000 Airport Rd NE	Calgary	AB	T2E6W5	**877-254-7427**	403-735-1200
Capital Region International Airport 4100 Capital City Blvd	Lansing	MI	48906	**866-841-4900**	517-321-6121
Chicago Midway Airport 5700 S Cicero Ave	Chicago	IL	60638	**800-832-6352**	773-838-0600
Columbia Metropolitan Airport 3000 Aviation Way W PO Box 280037	Columbia	SC	29170	**888-562-5002**	803-822-5010
Dallas-Fort Worth International Airport (DFW) 3200 E Airfield Dr PO Box 619428	Dallas	TX	75261	**800-252-7522**	972-973-8888
Dayton International Airport 3600 Terminal Dr Ste 300	Vandalia	OH	45377	**800-433-7300**	937-454-8200
Denver International Airport 8500 Pena Blvd	Denver	CO	80249	**800-247-2336**	303-342-2000
Des Moines International Airport 5800 Fleur Dr	Des Moines	IA	50321	**877-686-0029**	515-256-5050
Du Page Airport Authority 2700 International Dr Ste 200	West Chicago	IL	60185	**800-208-5690**	630-584-2211
Duluth International Airport 4701 Grinden Dr	Duluth	MN	55811	**855-787-2227**	218-727-2968
Edmonton International Airport 8340 Sparrow Crescent	Edmonton	AB	T9E8B7	**800-854-9517**	780-980-0986
Flagstaff Pulliam Airport 6200 S Pulliam Dr	Flagstaff	AZ	86001	**800-463-1389**	928-556-1234
Fort Lauderdale/Hollywood International Airport 100 Aviation Blvd	Fort Lauderdale	FL	33315	**866-682-2258**	954-359-1200
Fort Smith Regional Airport 6700 McKennon Blvd Ste 200	Fort Smith	AR	72903	**800-992-7433**	479-452-7000
Fresno Yosemite International Airport 5175 E Clinton Way	Fresno	CA	93727	**800-244-2359**	559-621-4500
Gerald R Ford International Airport 5500 44th St SE	Grand Rapids	MI	49512	**866-289-9673**	616-233-6000
Greater Rockford Airport 60 Airport Dr	Rockford	IL	61109	**800-517-2000**	815-969-4000
Greenville-Spartanburg Airport (GSP) 2000 GSP Dr Ste 1	Greer	SC	29651	**800-331-1212**	864-877-7426
Halifax Stanfield International Airport (HIAA) 1 Bell Blvd	Enfield	NS	B2T1K2	**800-565-5359**	902-873-4422
Harrisburg International Airport One Terminal Dr Ste 300	Middletown	PA	17057	**888-235-9442**	717-948-3900
Hartsfield-Jackson Atlanta International Airport 6000 N Terminal Pkwy Ste 4000	Atlanta	GA	30320	**800-897-1910**	404-530-6600
Hattiesburg-Laurel Regional Airport 1002 Terminal Dr	Moselle	MS	39459	**800-433-7300**	601-649-2444
Hot Springs Memorial Field 525 Airport Rd	Hot Springs	AR	71913	**800-992-7433**	501-321-6750

		Toll-Free	Phone
Jackson International Airport			
100 International Dr Ste 300 . . . . Jackson MS 39208		800-227-7368	601-939-5631
Juneau International Airport			
1873 Shell Simmons Dr Ste 200 . . . . Juneau AK 99801		800-478-4176	907-789-7821
Kahului Airport			
1 Kahului Airport Rd . . . . Kahului HI 96732		800-321-3712	808-872-3830
Kona International Airport			
73-200 Kupipi St . . . . Kailua-Kona HI 96740		800-321-3712	808-327-9520
Lambert Saint Louis International Airport			
10701 Lambert International Blvd			
PO Box 10212. . . . . Saint Louis MO 63145		855-787-2227	314-426-8000
Lehigh Valley International Airport			
3311 Airport Rd . . . . Allentown PA 18109		800-359-5842	610-266-6000
Long Beach Airport LGB			
4100 Donald Douglas Dr . . . . Long Beach CA 90808		800-331-1212	562-570-2600
Long Island MacArthur Airport			
100 Arrival Ave Ste 100 . . . . Ronkonkoma NY 11779		888-542-4776	631-467-3300
McCarran International Airport			
5757 Wayne Newton Blvd PO Box 11005 . . . . Las Vegas NV 89119		888-261-4414	702-261-5211
Mobile Regional Airport			
8400 Airport Blvd . . . . Mobile AL 36608		800-357-5373	251-633-4510
Newark Liberty International Airport			
One Hotel Rd . . . . Newark NJ 07114		888-397-4636	973-961-6007
O'Hare International Airport			
Dept of Aviation			
PO Box 66142 . . . . Chicago IL 60666		800-832-6352	773-686-3700
Ottawa Macdonald-Cartier International Airport			
1000 Airport PkwyPrivate Ste 2500 . . . . Ottawa ON K1V9B4		888-901-6222	613-248-2000
Palm Springs International Airport			
3200 E Tahquitz Canyon Way . . . . Palm Springs CA 92262		800-847-4389	760-318-3800
Pensacola Gulf Coast Regional Airport			
2430 Airport Blvd Ste 225 . . . . Pensacola FL 32504		800-874-6580	850-436-5000
Philadelphia International Airport			
8000 Essington Ave . . . . Philadelphia PA 19153		800-514-0301	215-937-6937
Pittsburgh International Airport			
Landside Terminal Fourth Fl Mezz			
PO Box 12370. . . . . Pittsburgh PA 15231		888-429-5377	412-472-3525
Portland International Airport			
7000 NE Airport Way . . . . Portland OR 97218		800-547-8411	503-460-4234
Raleigh-Durham International Airport			
PO Box 80001 . . . . Raleigh NC 27623		800-252-7522	919-840-2123
Rapid City Regional Airport			
4550 Terminal Rd Ste 102 . . . . Rapid City SD 57703		800-357-9998	605-393-9924
Reno-Tahoe International Airport			
2001 E Plumb Ln . . . . Reno NV 89502		877-736-6359	775-328-6400
Rhode Island Airport Corp			
2000 Post Rd Warwick . . . . Warwick RI 02886		888-268-7222	401-691-2000
Salt Lake City International Airport			
776 N Terminal Dr			
PO Box 145550. . . . . Salt Lake City UT 84116		800-595-2442	801-575-2400
San Antonio International Airport (SAT)			
9800 Airport Blvd Rm 2041 . . . . San Antonio TX 78216		800-237-6639	210-207-3411
San Francisco International Airport			
PO Box 8097 . . . . San Francisco CA 94128		800-435-9736	650-821-8211
Santa Fe Municipal Airport (SAF)			
121 Aviation Dr PO Box 909 . . . . Santa Fe NM 87504		866-773-2587	505-955-2900
Sarasota-Bradenton International Airport			
6000 Airport Cir . . . . Sarasota FL 34243		800-711-1712	941-359-5200
Southwest Florida International Airport			
11000 Terminal Access Rd Ste 8671 . . . . Fort Myers FL 33913		800-359-6786	239-590-4800
Spokane International Airport			
9000 W Airport Dr . . . . Spokane WA 99224		855-787-2227	509-455-6455
Tampa International Airport			
4100 George J Bean Pkwy PO Box 22287 . . . . Tampa FL 33607		866-289-9673	813-870-8700
Toledo Express Airport			
11013 Airport Hwy . . . . Swanton OH 43558		888-381-8294	419-865-2351
Tucson International Airport			
7250 S Tucson Blvd . . . . Tucson AZ 85706		800-758-1874	520-573-8100
Tupelo Regional Airport			
105 Lemons Dr . . . . Tupelo MS 38801		877-777-4778	662-823-4359
Wilkes-Barre/Scranton International Airport			
100 Terminal Dr Ste 1. . . . . Avoca PA 18641		877-235-9287	570-602-2000
Youngstown-Warren Regional Airport			
1453 Youngstown-Kingsville Rd NE . . . . Vienna OH 44473		800-444-1440	330-856-1537

28   AIRSHIPS

SEE ALSO Aircraft

		Toll-Free	Phone
Cameron Balloons US			
PO Box 3672 . . . . Ann Arbor MI 48106		866-423-6178	734-426-5525
ILC Dover Inc			
One Moonwalker Rd . . . . Frederica DE 19946		800-631-9567	302-335-3911

29   ALL-TERRAIN VEHICLES

SEE ALSO Sporting Goods

		Toll-Free	Phone
American Honda Motor Company Inc			
1919 Torrance Blvd . . . . Torrance CA 90501		800-999-1009	310-783-3170
Cycle Country Access Corp			
205 N Depot St PO Box 107 . . . . Fox Lake WI 53933		800-841-2222*	
*Sales			
Ontario Drive & Gear Ltd (ODG)			
220 Bergey Ct . . . . New Hamburg ON N3A2J5		877-274-6288	519-662-2840
Recreatives Industries Inc			
60 Depot St . . . . Buffalo NY 14206		800-255-2511	716-855-2226
Yamaha Motor Corp USA			
6555 Katella Ave . . . . Cypress CA 90630		800-656-7695*	
*Cust Svc			

30   AMBULANCE SERVICES

		Toll-Free	Phone
Abbott Ambulance Inc			
2500 Abbott Pl . . . . Saint Louis MO 63143		888-974-7035	314-768-1000
Acadian Ambulance Service Inc			
300 Hopkins St . . . . Lafayette LA 70501		800-259-3333	
American Medical Response (AMR)			
6200 S Syracuse Way Ste 200 . . . . Greenwood Village CO 80111		877-244-4890	303-495-1200
Global Air Response			
5919 Approach Rd . . . . Sarasota FL 34238		800-631-6565	
MedjetAssist			
3500 Colonnade Pkwy Ste 500			
PO Box 43099. . . . . Birmingham AL 35243		800-527-7478	205-595-6626
Mission Ambulance			
1055 E Third St . . . . Corona CA 92879		800-899-9100	
Rural/Metro Corp			
9221 E Via de Ventura . . . . Scottsdale AZ 85258		800-352-2309	
Skyservice Airlines Inc			
9785 Ryan Ave . . . . Dorval QC H9P1A2		888-985-1402	514-636-3300

31   AMUSEMENT PARK COMPANIES

SEE ALSO Circus, Carnival, Festival Operators

		Toll-Free	Phone
CAMELBACK MOUNTAIN			
301 Resort Dr . . . . Tannersville PA 18372		888-337-6966	570-629-1661
Island Windjammers Inc			
165 Shaw Dr . . . . Acworth GA 30102		877-772-4549	
Kennywood Entertainment Corp			
4800 Kennywood Blvd . . . . West Mifflin PA 15122		800-213-5861	412-461-8127

32   AMUSEMENT PARKS

		Toll-Free	Phone
Adventuredome			
2880 Las Vegas Blvd S . . . . Las Vegas NV 89109		866-456-8894	702-691-5861
Adventureland Park			
305 34th Ave NW . . . . Altoona IA 50009		800-532-1286	515-266-2121
Busch Gardens Williamsburg			
1 Busch Gardens Blvd . . . . Williamsburg VA 23185		800-343-7946	
Cedar Fair Parks			
14523 Carowinds Blvd . . . . Charlotte NC 28273		800-888-4386	704-588-2600
Darien Lake Theme Park Resort			
9993 Allegheny Rd PO Box 91 . . . . Darien Center NY 14040		866-640-0652	585-599-4641
Disney's California Adventure			
1313 S Disneyland Dr . . . . Anaheim CA 92802		800-225-2024	714-781-7290
Dollywood			
2700 Dollywood Parks Blvd. . . . . Pigeon Forge TN 37863		800-365-5996	
Dorney Park & Wildwater Kingdom			
3830 Dorney Pk Rd . . . . Allentown PA 18104		800-747-0561	610-395-3724
Dutch Wonderland Family Amusement Park			
2249 Lincoln Hwy E . . . . Lancaster PA 17602		866-386-2839	717-291-1888
Grand Harbor Resort & Waterpark			
350 Bell St . . . . Dubuque IA 52001		866-690-4006	563-690-4000
Hersheypark			
100 Hershey Pk Dr . . . . Hershey PA 17033		800-437-7439	717-534-3900
Holiday World & Splashin' Safari			
452 E Christmas Blvd . . . . Santa Claus IN 47579		877-463-2645	812-937-4401
Indiana Beach			
5224 E Indiana Beach Rd . . . . Monticello IN 47960		800-583-4306	574-583-4141
Knoebels Amusement Resort			
391 Knoebels Blvd . . . . Elysburg PA 17824		800-487-4386	570-672-2572
Knott's Berry Farm			
8039 Beach Blvd . . . . Buena Park CA 90620		800-742-6427	714-220-5220
Lagoon & Pioneer Village			
375 N Lagoon Dr . . . . Farmington UT 84025		800-748-5246	801-451-8000
LEGOLAND California			
1 Legoland Dr . . . . Carlsbad CA 92008		877-534-6526	760-438-5346
Paramount's Kings Dominion			
16000 Theme Pkwy . . . . Doswell VA 23047		800-367-7623	804-876-5000
SeaWorld Orlando			
7007 Sea World Dr . . . . Orlando FL 32821		800-327-2424	407-351-3600
SeaWorld San Diego			
500 SeaWorld Dr . . . . San Diego CA 92109		800-257-4268	619-226-3901
Six Flags Fiesta Texas			
17000 IH-10 W . . . . San Antonio TX 78257		800-370-7488	210-697-5000
Six Flags Great Adventure			
One Six Flags Blvd . . . . Jackson NJ 08527		800-772-2287	732-928-1821
Six Flags New England			
1623 Main St . . . . Agawam MA 01001		800-370-7488	413-786-9300
Six Flags Wild Safari			
One Six Flags Blvd . . . . Jackson NJ 08527		800-772-2287	732-928-1821
Universal Orlando			
6000 Universal Blvd . . . . Orlando FL 32819		877-801-9720	407-363-8000
Universal Studios Hollywood			
100 Universal City Plaza . . . . Universal City CA 91608		800-864-8377	
Universal's Islands of Adventure			
6000 Universal Studios Plz . . . . Orlando FL 32819		877-801-9720	407-363-8000
Village Vacances Valcartier			
1860 Valcartier Blvd . . . . Valcartier QC G0A4S0		888-384-5524	418-844-2200
Water Country USA			
176 Water Country Pkwy . . . . Williamsburg VA 23185		800-343-7946	
Wet 'n Wild Emerald Pointe			
3910 S Holden Rd . . . . Greensboro NC 27406		800-555-5900	336-852-9721
Wet 'n Wild Orlando			
6200 International Dr . . . . Orlando FL 32819		800-992-9453*	407-351-1800
*General			
Wonderland Amusement Park			
2601 Dumas Dr . . . . Amarillo TX 79107		800-383-4712	806-383-0832

33 ANIMATION COMPANIES

SEE ALSO Motion Picture Production - Special Interest ; Motion Picture & Television Production

				Toll-Free	Phone
NestFamily 1461 S Beltline Rd Ste 500	Coppell	TX	75019	**800-596-7386**	972-402-7100

34 APPLIANCE & HOME ELECTRONICS STORES

SEE ALSO Furniture Stores ; Home Improvement Centers ; Computer Stores ; Department Stores

				Toll-Free	Phone
ABC Appliance Inc 1 Silverdome Industrial Pk	Pontiac	MI	48343	**800-981-3866**	248-335-4222
Audio Direct 2004 E Irvington Rd Ste 264 *Cust Svc	Tucson	AZ	85714	**888-628-3467***	
Best Buy Company Inc 7601 Penn Ave S *NYSE: BBY*	Minneapolis	MN	55423	**888-237-8289**	612-291-1000
BrandsMart USA Corp 3200 SW 42nd St	Fort Lauderdale	FL	33312	**800-432-8579**	
Conn's Inc 3295 College St *NASDAQ: CONN* ■ *Cust Svc	Beaumont	TX	77701	**800-511-5750***	409-832-1696
Gregg Appliances Inc 4151 E 96th St *NYSE: HGG*	Indianapolis	IN	46240	**800-284-7344**	317-848-8710
Interbond Corp of America 3200 SW 42nd St	Fort Lauderdale	FL	33312	**800-432-8579**	
PC Richard & Son Inc 150 Price Pkwy	Farmingdale	NY	11735	**800-696-2000**	631-843-4300
Pieratt's 110 Mt Tabor Rd	Lexington	KY	40517	**855-743-7288**	859-268-6000
Queen City TV & Appliance Company Inc 2430 Queen City Dr *All	Charlotte	NC	28208	**800-365-6665***	704-391-6000
RadioShack Corp 300 RadioShack Cir *NYSE: RSH*	Fort Worth	TX	76102	**800-843-7422**	800-442-7221
Videoland Inc 6808 Hornwood Dr	Houston	TX	77074	**800-877-2900**	
Wireless Zone 34 Industrial Pk Pl	Middletown	CT	06457	**888-881-2622**	860-632-9494
Yale Appliance 296 Freeport St	Dorchester	MA	02122	**800-565-6435**	617-825-9253

35 APPLIANCES - MAJOR - MFR

SEE ALSO Air Conditioning & Heating Equipment - Residential

				Toll-Free	Phone
Anaheim Mfg Co 2680 Orbiter St PO Box 4146 *Cust Svc	Brea	CA	92821	**800-854-3229***	310-542-5259
AO Smith Corp 11270 W Pk Pl Ste 170 PO Box 245008 *NYSE: AOS*	Milwaukee	WI	53224	**800-359-4065**	414-359-4000
AO Smith Water Products Co 500 Tennessee Waltz Pkwy	Ashland City	TN	37015	**800-527-1953**	
ASKO Appliances Inc PO Box 44848	Madison	WI	53744	**800-898-1879**	
Atlanta Attachment Co Inc 362 Industrial Pk Dr	Lawrenceville	GA	30045	**877-206-5116**	770-963-7369
Bradford White Corp 725 Talamore Dr	Ambler	PA	19002	**800-523-2931**	215-641-9400
Brown Stove Works Inc 1422 Carolina Ave *All	Cleveland	TN	37320	**800-251-7485***	423-476-6544
Cemline Corp PO Box 55	Cheswick	PA	15024	**800-245-6268**	724-274-5430
Char-Broil 1442 Belfast Ave *Cust Svc	Columbus	GA	31902	**866-239-6777***	706-571-7000
CookTek LLC 156 N Jefferson St Ste 300	Chicago	IL	60661	**888-266-5835**	312-563-9600
Dwyer Products Corp 1226 Michael Dr Ste F	Wood Dale	IL	60191	**800-822-0092**	630-741-7900
Electric Heater Co 45 Seymour St	Stratford	CT	06615	**800-647-3165**	203-378-2659
Electrolux Appliances PO Box 212237	Augusta	GA	30907	**877-435-3287**	
Fisher & Paykel Appliances Inc 5900 Skylab Rd	Huntington Beach	CA	92647	**888-936-7872**	
In-Sink-Erator 4700 21st St	Racine	WI	53406	**800-558-5712**	262-554-5432
LG Electronics USA Inc 1000 Sylvan Ave *Tech Supp	Englewood Cliffs	NJ	07632	**800-180-9999***	201-816-2000
Lochinvar Corp 300 Maddox Simpson Pkwy	Lebanon	TN	37090	**800-722-2101**	615-889-8900
Maytag Appliances 403 W Fourth St N *Cust Svc	Newton	IA	50208	**800-344-1274***	
Miele Inc 9 Independence Way	Princeton	NJ	08540	**800-843-7231**	609-419-9898
Northland Corp 1260 E Van Deinse St	Greenville	MI	48838	**800-223-3900**	
Peerless Premier Appliance Co 119 S 14th St	Belleville	IL	62222	**800-858-5844**	941-763-3915
Sharp Electronics Corp One Sharp Plz	Mahwah	NJ	07430	**800-237-4277**	201-529-8200
Vaughn Manufacturing Corp 26 Old Elm St PO Box 5431	Salisbury	MA	01952	**800-282-8446**	978-462-6683
Weber-Stephen Products Co 200 E Daniels Rd *Cust Svc	Palatine	IL	60067	**800-446-1071***	
Whirlpool Corp 2000 N M-63 *NYSE: WHR*	Benton Harbor	MI	49022	**800-253-1301**	269-923-5000
Whirlpool Corp North American Region 2000 N M-63	Benton Harbor	MI	49022	**800-253-1301**	269-923-5000
Wisco Industries Inc 736 Janesville St	Oregon	WI	53575	**800-999-4726**	608-835-3106

36 APPLIANCES - SMALL - MFR

SEE ALSO Vacuum Cleaners - Household ; Air Purification Equipment - Household

				Toll-Free	Phone
Abatement Technologies 605 Satellite Blvd Ste 300	Suwanee	GA	30024	**800-634-9091**	678-889-4200
Andis Co 1800 County Rd H	Sturtevant	WI	53177	**800-558-9441**	262-884-2600
Broan-NuTone LLC 926 W State St PO Box 140 *Cust Svc	Hartford	WI	53027	**800-558-1711***	262-673-4340
Bunn-O-Matic Corp 1400 Stevenson Dr	Springfield	IL	62703	**800-637-8606**	217-529-6601
Cadet Mfg Company Inc 2500 W Fourth Plain Blvd	Vancouver	WA	98660	**800-442-2338**	360-693-2505
Casablanca Fan Co 761 Corporate Ctr Dr	Pomona	CA	91768	**888-227-2178**	909-689-1477
City of Chula Vista 276 Fourth Ave	Chula Vista	CA	91910	**877-478-5478**	619-691-5047
Conair Corp One Cummings Pt Rd *OTC: CNGA*	Stamford	CT	06902	**800-326-6247**	203-351-9000
Craftmade International Inc 650 S Royal Ln *OTC: CRFT*	Coppell	TX	75019	**800-486-4892**	972-393-3800
Cuisinart 1 Cummings Pt Rd	Stamford	CT	06902	**800-726-0190**	203-975-4609
El Electronics LLC 1800 Shames Dr	Westbury	NY	11590	**877-346-3837**	516-334-0870
Fan-Tastic Vent Corp 2083 S Almont Ave	Imlay City	MI	48444	**800-521-0298**	810-724-3818
Hamilton Beach/Proctor-Silex Inc 4421 Waterfront Dr *Cust Svc	Glen Allen	VA	23060	**800-851-8900***	804-273-9777
Hunter Fan Co 7130 Goodlett Farms Pkwy Ste 400	Memphis	TN	38016	**888-830-1326**	901-743-1360
Jarden Consumer Solutions 2381 Executive Ctr Dr	Boca Raton	FL	33431	**800-777-5452**	561-912-4100
KAZ Inc 250 Tpke Rd	Southborough	MA	01772	**800-477-0457**	
King Electrical Manufacturing Co 9131 Tenth Ave S	Seattle	WA	98108	**800-603-5464**	206-762-0400
Lasko Metal Products Inc 820 Lincoln Ave	West Chester	PA	19380	**800-233-0268**	610-692-7400
LG Electronics USA Inc 1000 Sylvan Ave *Tech Supp	Englewood Cliffs	NJ	07632	**800-180-9999***	201-816-2000
Lifetime Brands Inc Farberware Div 1000 Stewart Ave	Garden City	NY	11530	**800-999-2811**	516-683-6000
Marley Engineered Products 470 Beauty Spot Rd E	Bennettsville	SC	29512	**800-452-4179**	843-479-4006
National Presto Industries Inc 3925 N Hastings Way *NYSE: NPK*	Eau Claire	WI	54703	**800-877-0441**	715-839-2121
Nesco/American Harvest 1700 Monroe St PO Box 237 *Cust Svc	Two Rivers	WI	54241	**800-288-4545***	920-793-1368
Schawbel Corp 26 Crosby Dr	Bedford	MA	01730	**866-753-3837**	781-541-6900
Sharp Electronics Corp One Sharp Plz	Mahwah	NJ	07430	**800-237-4277**	201-529-8200
Singer Sewing Co 1224 Hill Quaker Blvd PO Box 7017	La Vergne	TN	37086	**877-738-9869**	615-213-0880
Vita-Mix Corp 8615 Usher Rd	Cleveland	OH	44138	**800-848-2649**	440-235-4840
West Bend Housewares LLC 2845 Wingate St PO Box 2780	West Bend	WI	53095	**866-290-1851**	
Whirlpool Corp KitchenAid Div 553 Benson Rd	Benton Harbor	MI	49022	**800-422-1230**	
World Dryer Corp 5700 McDermott Dr	Berkeley	IL	60163	**800-323-0701**	708-449-6950

37 APPLIANCES - WHOL

				Toll-Free	Phone
All Inc 185 Plato Blvd W	Saint Paul	MN	55107	**800-829-2127**	651-227-6331
Almo Corp 2709 Commerce Way	Philadelphia	PA	19154	**800-345-2566**	215-698-4000
Aves Audio Visual Systems Inc PO Box 500	Sugar Land	TX	77487	**800-365-2837**	281-295-1300
Blodgett Supply Co Inc 100 Ave D PO Box 759	Williston	VT	05495	**888-888-3424**	802-864-9831
Brady Marketing Co 1331N California Blvd Ste 320	Walnut Creek	CA	94596	**800-326-6080**	925-676-1300
Brooke Distributors Inc 16250 NW 52nd Ave	Hialeah	FL	33014	**800-275-8792**	305-624-9752
Bursma Electronic Distributing Inc 2851 Buchanan Ave SW	Grand Rapids	MI	49548	**800-777-2604**	616-831-0080
C & L Supply Co PO Box 578	Vinita	OK	74301	**800-256-6411**	918-256-6411
DAS Inc 724 Lawn Rd	Palmyra	PA	17078	**866-622-7979**	717-964-3642
Electrical Distributing Inc 4600 NW St Helens Rd	Portland	OR	97210	**800-877-4229**	503-226-4044
Gamla Enterprises North America Inc 875 Ave of The Americas Ste 205	New York	NY	10001	**800-442-6526**	212-947-3790
Gotham Sales Co 302 Main St	Millburn	NJ	07041	**800-292-7726**	973-912-8412

				Toll-Free	Phone

Hall Electric Supply Company Inc
263 Main St . . . . Stoneham MA 02180 **800-444-3726** 781-438-3800

HB Communications Inc
60 Dodge Ave . . . . North Haven CT 06473 **800-243-4414** 203-234-9246

Home Entertainment Distribution Inc
120 Shawmut Rd . . . . Canton MA 02021 **800-343-9619** 781-821-0087

M.d.m. Commercial Enterprises Inc
1102 A1a N Ste 205 . . . . Ponte Vedra FL 32082 **800-359-6741**

Midwest Sales & Service Inc
917 S Chapin St . . . . South Bend IN 46601 **800-772-7262** 574-287-3365

Nelson & Small Inc
212 Canco Rd . . . . Portland ME 04103 **800-341-0780** 207-775-5666

Peirce-Phelps Inc
2000 N 59th St . . . . Philadelphia PA 19131 **800-222-2742** 215-879-7000

Potter Distributing Inc
4037 Roger B Chaffee Blvd . . . . Grand Rapids MI 49548 **800-748-0568** 616-531-6860

Radio Distributing Company Inc
27015 Trolley Industrial Dr . . . . Taylor MI 48180 **800-462-1544** 313-295-4500

Roth Distributing Co
11300 W 47th St . . . . Minnetonka MN 55343 **800-363-3818** 952-933-4428

Servall Co
6761 E Ten Mile Rd . . . . Center Line MI 48015 **800-856-9874** 586-754-9985

Siano Appliance Distributors Inc
5372 Pleasant View Rd . . . . Memphis TN 38134 **800-742-6699** 901-382-5833

Speco Technologies
200 New Hwy . . . . Amityville NY 11701 **800-645-5516** 631-957-8700

Telerent Leasing Corp
4191 Fayetteville Rd . . . . Raleigh NC 27603 **800-626-0682** 919-772-8604

Tri-State Video Services Inc
1379 Pittsburgh Rd . . . . Valencia PA 16059 **888-382-7768** 724-898-1630

WASH Multifamily Laundry Systems
100 N Sepulveda Blvd 12th Fl . . . . El Segundo CA 90245 **800-421-6897***
*General

Westland Sales PO Box 427 . . . . Clackamas OR 97015 **800-356-0766** 503-655-2563

Whirlpool Canada
200-6750 Century Ave . . . . Mississauga ON L5N0B7 **800-807-6777** 905-821-6400

Williams Kitchen & Bath
658 Richmond NW . . . . Grand Rapids MI 49504 **800-968-3718** 616-771-0505

Woodson & Bozeman Inc
3870 New Getwell Rd . . . . Memphis TN 38118 **800-876-4243** 901-362-1500

38 APPLICATION SERVICE PROVIDERS (ASPS)

Application Service Providers rent, deliver, license, manage, and/or host proprietary and/ or third-party business software ("applications") and/or computer services to multiple users (customers). Included here are companies that host software applications as well as companies that provide the equipment necessary to do so.

				Toll-Free	Phone

AllMeds Inc
151 Lafayette Dr Ste 401 . . . . Oak Ridge TN 37830 **888-343-6337** 865-482-1999

Ariba Inc 807 11th Ave . . . . Sunnyvale CA 94089 **866-772-7422** 650-390-1000
NASDAQ: ARBA

Baillio's Inc
5301 Menaul Blvd NE . . . . Albuquerque NM 87110 **800-540-7511** 505-883-7511

BizLand Inc
70 BlanchaRd Rd . . . . Burlington MA 01803 **800-249-5263**

Cayenta Canada Corp
4200 N Fraser Way Ste 201 . . . . Burnaby BC V5J5K7 **866-229-3682** 604-570-4300

Chemical Safety Corp
5901 Christie Ave Ste 502 . . . . Emeryville CA 94608 **888-594-1100** 510-594-1000

Cision Inc
12051 Indian Creek Ct . . . . Beltsville MD 20705 **866-639-5087** 301-459-2590
NASDAQ: VOCS

CliniComp International
9655 Towne Ctr Dr . . . . San Diego CA 92121 **800-350-8202** 858-546-8202

Computer Programs & Systems Inc (CPSI)
6600 Wall St . . . . Mobile AL 36695 **800-711-2774** 251-639-8100
NASDAQ: CPSI

Connectria Corp
10845 Olive Blvd Ste 300 . . . . Saint Louis MO 63141 **800-781-7820** 314-587-7000

Critical Path Inc
2655 Campus Dr Ste 250 . . . . San Mateo CA 94403 **800-353-8437** 650-480-7300

Cyveillance Inc
11091 Sunset Hills Rd Ste 210 . . . . Reston VA 20190 **888-243-0097** 703-351-1000

Daptiv
1008 Western Ave Suite 700 . . . . Seattle WA 98101 **888-621-8361** 206-341-9117

Digital River Inc
10380 Bren Rd W Ste 150 . . . . Minnetonka MN 55343 **800-598-7450**
NASDAQ: DRIV

DigitalWork Inc
2345 S Alma School Rd Suite 105 . . . . Mesa AZ 85210 **877-496-7571**

DocMan Technologies
31300 Bainbridge Rd . . . . Cleveland OH 44122 **888-636-2626**

E-Builder Inc
1800 NW 69 Ave Ste 201 . . . . Plantation FL 33313 **800-580-9322** 954-556-6701

E-Markets Inc
807 Mountain Ave Ste 200 . . . . Berthoud CO 80513 **877-674-7419**

eGain Communications Corp
345 E Middlefield Rd . . . . Mountain View CA 94043 **888-603-4246** 650-230-7500
NASDAQ: EGAN

Electric Mail Company Inc
3999 Henning Dr Ste 300 . . . . Burnaby BC V5C6P9 **800-419-7463** 604-482-1111

ePlus Inc
13595 Dulles Technology Dr . . . . Herndon VA 20171 **888-482-1122** 703-984-8400
NASDAQ: PLUS

FinancialCAD Corp
13450 102nd Ave Ste 1750 . . . . Surrey BC V3T5X3 **800-304-0702** 604-957-1200

HealthMEDX
5100 N Towne Ctr Dr . . . . Ozark MO 65721 **877-875-1200** 417-582-1816

Intacct Corp
125 S Market St Ste 600 . . . . San Jose CA 95113 **877-437-7765** 408-878-0900

Internap Network Services Corp
250 Williams St Ste E-100 . . . . Atlanta GA 30303 **877-843-7627** 404-302-9700
NASDAQ: INAP

IntraLinks Inc
150 E 42nd St Ste 8 . . . . New York NY 10017 **888-546-5383** 212-543-7700

Journyx Inc
7600 Burnet Rd Ste. 300 . . . . Austin TX 78757 **800-755-9878** 512-834-8888

Kleinschmidt Inc
450 Lake Cook Rd . . . . Deerfield IL 60015 **800-824-2330** 847-945-1000

LearningStation Inc
8008 Corporate Ctr Dr Ste 210 . . . . Charlotte NC 28226 **888-679-7058**

onProject Inc
PO Box 104 . . . . Franklin Lakes NJ 07417 **877-936-6776** 973-971-9970

Oracle Corp
500 Oracle Pkwy . . . . Redwood Shores CA 94065 **800-392-2999*** 650-506-7000
NYSE: ORCL ■ *Sales

Outstart Inc
745 Atlantic Ave 4th Fl . . . . Boston MA 02111 **877-971-9171** 617-897-6800

Paramount Technologies Inc
1374 EW Maple Rd . . . . Walled Lake MI 48390 **800-725-4408** 248-960-0909

Passkey International
180 Old Colony Ave Third Fl . . . . Quincy MA 02170 **866-649-1539**

PBM Corp
20600 Chagrin Blvd Ste 450 . . . . Cleveland OH 44122 **800-341-5809** 216-283-7999

Perfect Commerce Inc
One Compass Way Ste 120 . . . . Newport News VA 23606 **877-871-3788*** 757-766-8211
*Sales

PhDx Systems Inc
1001 University Blvd SE Ste 103 . . . . Albuquerque NM 87106 **888-999-7439** 505-764-0174

Premiere Global Services Inc (PGI)
3280 Peachtree Rd NE
Ste 1000 Terminus Bldg . . . . Atlanta GA 30305 **866-548-3203** 719-457-6901
NYSE: PGI

Prodata Systems Inc
11007 Slater Ave NE . . . . Kirkland WA 98033 **866-582-7485** 425-296-4168

Prosum technology services
2321 Rosecrans Ave Ste 4225 . . . . El Segundo CA 90245 **888-477-6786** 310-426-0600

PureWorks Inc
5000 Meridian Blvd Ste 600 . . . . Franklin TN 37067 **888-202-3016** 615-367-4404

Radware Inc
575 Corporate Dr Lobby 2 . . . . Mahwah NJ 07430 **888-234-5763** 201-512-9771

Resource Development Corp
280 Daines St Ste 200 . . . . Birmingham MI 48009 **800-360-7222** 248-646-2300

Salesforce.com Inc
One Market St
The Landmark Ste 300 . . . . San Francisco CA 94105 **800-667-6389** 415-901-7000
NYSE: CRM

Salesnet
3296 Summit Ridge Pkwy Ste 210 . . . . Duluth GA 30096 **866-732-8632**

Smart Online Inc
4505 Emperor Blvd Ste 320 . . . . Durham NC 27703 **800-578-9000**

Streamline Health Solutions Inc
10200 Alliance Rd Ste 200 . . . . Cincinnati OH 45242 **800-878-5269** 513-794-7100
NASDAQ: STRM

Talisma Corp
777 Yamato Rd . . . . Boca Raton FL 33431 **866-397-2537** 561-923-2500

TALX Corp
11432 Lackland Dr . . . . Saint Louis MO 63146 **800-888-8277** 314-214-7000

Toolwire Inc
7031 Koll Ctr Pkwy Ste 220 . . . . Pleasanton CA 94566 **866-935-8665** 925-227-8500

UnicornHRO
25 Hanover Rd Ste B. . . . . Florham Park NJ 07932 **800-368-8149** 973-360-0688

USA.NET Inc
1155 Kelly Johnson Blvd
Ste 305 . . . . Colorado Springs CO 80920 **800-234-2175** 719-265-2930

Workscape Inc
123 Selton St . . . . Marlborough MA 01752 **888-605-9620** 508-861-5500

39 AQUARIUMS - PUBLIC

SEE ALSO Zoos & Wildlife Parks ; Botanical Gardens & Arboreta

				Toll-Free	Phone

Adventure Aquarium
1 Riverside Dr . . . . Camden NJ 08103 **800-616-5297** 856-365-3300

Audubon Aquarium of the Americas
6500 Magazine St . . . . New Orleans LA 70118 **800-774-7394** 504-581-4629

Florida Aquarium
701 Channelside Dr . . . . Tampa FL 33602 **800-353-4741** 813-273-4000

Key West Aquarium
One Whitehead St . . . . Key West FL 33040 **888-544-5927** 305-296-2051

Marineland of Florida
9600 Ocean Shore Blvd . . . . Saint Augustine FL 32080 **877-933-3402** 904-460-1275

Marinelife Ctr of Juno Beach
14200 US Hwy 1 Loggerhead Pk . . . . Juno Beach FL 33408 **800-843-5451** 561-627-8280

Maui Ocean Ctr
192 Maalaea Rd . . . . Wailuku HI 96793 **800-350-5634** 808-270-7000

Monterey Bay Aquarium
886 Cannery Row . . . . Monterey CA 93940 **866-963-9645** 831-648-4800

Newport Aquarium
One Aquarium Way . . . . Newport KY 41071 **800-406-3474** 859-261-7444

North Carolina Aquarium at Fort Fisher
900 Loggerhead Rd . . . . Kure Beach NC 28449 **800-832-3474** 910-458-8257

North Carolina Aquarium on Roanoke Island
374 Airport Rd PO Box 967 . . . . Manteo NC 27954 **866-332-3475** 252-473-3493

Oregon Coast Aquarium
2820 SE Ferry Slip Rd . . . . Newport OR 97365 **800-452-7888** 541-867-3474

Parc Aquarium du Quebec
1675 des Hotels Ave . . . . Quebec QC G1W4S3 **866-659-5264** 418-659-5264

Pittsburgh Zoo & PPG Aquarium
1 Wild Pl . . . . Pittsburgh PA 15206 **800-732-0999** 412-665-3640

Ripley's Aquarium
1110 Celebrity Cir . . . . Myrtle Beach SC 29577 **800-734-8888** 843-916-0888

Sea Life Park
41-202 Kalanianaole Hwy . . . . Waimanalo HI 96795 **866-365-7446** 808-259-2500

SeaWorld Orlando
7007 Sea World Dr . . . . Orlando FL 32821 **800-327-2424** 407-351-3600

South Carolina Aquarium
100 Aquarium Wharf . . . . Charleston SC 29401 **800-722-6455** 843-577-3474

Tennessee Aquarium
1 Broad St . . . . Chattanooga TN 37402 **800-262-0695** 423-802-6768

	Toll-Free	Phone
Texas State Aquarium		
2710 N Shoreline Blvd ....Corpus Christi TX 78402	**800-477-4853***	361-881-1200
*General		
Vancouver Aquarium Marine Science Ctr		
845 Avison Way ....Vancouver BC V6G3E2	**800-931-1186**	604-659-3474

40   ARBITRATION SERVICES - LEGAL

	Toll-Free	Phone
American Arbitration Assn Inc (AAA)		
1633 Broadway 10th Fl................New York NY 10019	**800-778-7879**	212-716-5800
Arbitration Forums Inc		
3350 Buschwood Pk Dr Ste 295.................Tampa FL 33618	**800-967-8889***	813-931-4004
*Cust Svc		
CIR Law Offices LLP		
8665 Gibbs Dr Ste 150................San Diego CA 92123	**800-496-8909**	
Council of Better Business Bureaus Inc		
Dispute Resolution Services & Mediation Training		
4200 Wilson Blvd Ste 800................Arlington VA 22203	**800-537-4600**	703-276-0100
CPR Institute for Dispute Resolution		
575 Lexington Ave 21st Fl................New York NY 10022	**866-723-1781**	212-949-6490
Family Credit Counseling Service		
111 N Wabash Ste 1408................Chicago IL 60602	**800-994-3328**	
Fasken Martineau DuMoulin LLP		
333 Bay St Bay Adelaide Centre		
Ste 2400 PO Box 20................Toronto ON M5H2T6	**800-268-8424**	416-366-8381
JAMS/Endispute		
500 N State College Blvd 14th Fl................Orange CA 92868	**800-352-5267**	714-939-1300
Jeffrey Byrne & Associates		
4042 Central St ....Kansas City MO 64111	**800-222-9233**	
Judicate West		
1851 E First St Ste 1450................Santa Ana CA 92705	**800-488-8805**	714-834-1340
July Business Services		
215 Mary Ave Ste 302 ....Waco TX 76701	**888-333-5859**	
National Arbitration & Mediation		
990 Stewart Ave ....Garden City NY 11530	**800-358-2550**	516-794-8950
Nines Hotel, The		
525 SW Morrison ....Portland OR 97204	**877-229-9995**	
Notus Career Management		
Five Centerpointe Dr Ste 400 ....Lake Oswego OR 97035	**800-431-1990**	
OneTouch Direct LLC		
4902 W Sligh Ave ....Tampa FL 33634	**866-948-4005**	
OTS 3924 Clock Pointe Trl ....Stow OH 44224	**877-445-2058**	
Parker Rose Design Inc		
10075 Mesa Rim Rd Ste A ....San Diego CA 92121	**800-403-2711**	
Quatred LLC		
532 Fourth Range Rd ....Pembroke NH 03275	**888-395-8534**	
Resolute Systems Inc		
1550 N Prospect Ave ....Milwaukee WI 53202	**800-776-6060**	414-276-4774
Valley Internet Inc		
102 Maple St East ....Fayetteville TN 37334	**888-433-1924**	931-433-1921

ARCHITECTS

SEE Engineering & Design

ART - COMMERCIAL

SEE Graphic Design

41   ART DEALERS & GALLERIES

	Toll-Free	Phone
Abbozzo Gallery		
401 Richmond Stt W Ste 128 ....Toronto ON M5V3A8	**866-844-4481**	416-260-2220
Feheley Fine Arts		
65 George St ....Toronto ON M5A4L8	**877-904-9114**	416-323-1373
Gallery 78 Inc		
796 Queen St ....Fredericton NB E3B1C6	**888-883-8322**	506-454-5192
Heffel Gallery Ltd		
2247 Granville St ....Vancouver BC V6H3G1	**800-528-9608**	604-732-6505
Inuit Gallery of Vancouver Ltd		
206 Cambie St Gastown ....Vancouver BC V6B2M9	**888-615-8399**	604-688-7323
Masters Gallery Ltd		
2115 Fourth St SW ....Calgary AB T2S1W8	**866-245-0616**	403-245-2064
Michael Gibson Gallery		
157 Carling St ....London ON N6A1H5	**866-644-2766**	519-439-0451
Odon Wagner Gallery		
196 Davenport Rd ....Toronto ON M5R1J2	**800-551-2465**	416-962-0438
Uno Langmann Ltd		
2117 Granville St ....Vancouver BC V6H3E9	**800-730-8825**	604-736-8825

42   ART MATERIALS & SUPPLIES - MFR

SEE ALSO Pens, Pencils, Parts

	Toll-Free	Phone
Alvin & Company Inc		
1335 Blue Hills Ave ....Bloomfield CT 06002	**800-444-2584**	860-243-8991
American Art Clay Co (AMACO)		
6060 Guion Rd ....Indianapolis IN 46254	**800-374-1600**	317-244-6871
American Metalcraft Inc		
2074 George St ....Melrose Park IL 60160	**800-333-9133**	708-345-1177
Ampersand Art Supply		
1235 S Loop 4 Ste 400................Buda TX 78610	**800-822-1939**	512-322-0278
ART Studio Clay Co		
9320 Michigan Ave ....Sturtevant WI 53177	**800-323-0212**	262-884-4278
Artist Brand Canvas		
2448 Loma Ave ....South El Monte CA 91733	**888-579-2704***	626-579-2740
*Orders		
Badger Air Brush Co		
9128 Belmont Ave ....Franklin Park IL 60131	**800-247-2787**	847-678-3104
Canson Inc		
21 Industrial Dr ....South Hadley MA 01075	**800-628-9283**	413-538-9250

	Toll-Free	Phone
Chartpak Inc 1 River Rd ....Leeds MA 01053	**800-628-1910**	413-584-5446
DecoArt Inc 49 Cotton Ave ....Stanford KY 40484	**800-367-3047**	606-365-3193
Duncan Enterprises		
5673 E Shields Ave ....Fresno CA 93727	**800-438-6226**	559-291-4444
Gare Inc 165 Rosemont St ....Haverhill MA 01832	**888-289-4273**	978-373-9131
Georgia's Ceramic & Clay Company Inc		
756 NE Lombard St ....Portland OR 97211	**800-999-2529**	503-283-1353
Golden Artists Colors Inc		
188 Bell Rd ....New Berlin NY 13411	**800-959-6543**	607-847-6154
Jack Richeson & Company Inc		
557 Marcella Dr ....Kimberly WI 54136	**800-233-2404**	920-738-0744
Martin/F Weber Co		
2727 Southampton Rd ....Philadelphia PA 19154	**800-876-8076**	215-677-5600
National Artcraft Supply Co		
300 Campus Dr ....Aurora OH 44202	**888-937-2723**	330-562-3500
Paasche Airbrush Co		
4311 N Normandy ....Chicago IL 60634	**800-621-1907***	773-867-9191
*Sales		
Plaid Enterprises Inc		
3225 Westech Dr ....Norcross GA 30092	**800-842-4197**	678-291-8100
Sargent Art Inc		
100 E Diamond Ave ....Hazleton PA 18201	**800-424-3596**	570-454-3596
Smooth-On Inc		
2000 St John St ....Easton PA 18042	**800-766-6841**	610-252-5800
Testor Corp		
440 Blackhawk Pk Ave ....Rockford IL 61104	**800-837-8677**	815-962-6654
Utrecht Art Supplies		
PO Box 1769 ....Galesburg IL 61402	**888-336-3114**	609-409-8001

43   ART MATERIALS & SUPPLIES - WHOL

	Toll-Free	Phone
Creative Hobbies Inc		
900 Creek Rd Ste A ....Bellmawr NJ 08031	**800-843-5456**	856-933-2540
CWI Gifts & Crafts		
77 Cypress St SW ....Reynoldsburg OH 43068	**800-666-5858**	740-964-6210
D&L Art Glass Supply		
1440 W 52nd Ave ....Denver CO 80221	**800-525-0940**	303-449-8737
Darice Inc		
13000 Darice Pkwy ....Strongsville OH 44149	**800-321-1494**	866-432-7433
Howell's Craftand Imports		
6030 NE 112th Ave ....Portland OR 97220	**800-547-0368**	
Pioneer Wholesale Co		
500 W Bagley Rd ....Berea OH 44017	**888-234-5400**	440-234-5400
Sbar's Inc 14 Sbar Blvd ....Moorestown NJ 08057	**800-989-7227**	856-234-8220
Sepp Leaf Products Inc		
381 Pk Ave S Ste 1301 ....New York NY 10016	**800-971-7377**	212-683-2840
Shop Hobby Lobby		
7717 SW 44th St ....Oklahoma City OK 73179	**800-888-0321**	405-745-1275

44   ART SUPPLY STORES

	Toll-Free	Phone
Al Friedman Company Inc		
44 W 18th St Fourth Fl ....New York NY 10011	**800-204-6352**	212-243-9000
Alabama Art Supply Inc		
1006 23rd St S ....Birmingham AL 35205	**800-749-4741***	205-322-4741
*Cust Svc		
Arizona Art Supply		
4025 N 16th St ....Phoenix AZ 85016	**877-264-9514**	602-264-9514
Art Supply Warehouse		
6672 Westminster Blvd ....Westminster CA 92683	**800-854-6467**	714-891-3626
Asel Art Supply		
2701 Cedar Springs ....Dallas TX 75201	**888-273-5278**	214-871-2425
Blaine's Art Supply		
1025 Photo Ave ....Anchorage AK 99503	**866-561-4278**	907-561-5344
Dick Blick Co PO Box 1267 ....Galesburg IL 61402	**800-447-8192***	309-343-6181
*Orders		
Douglas & Sturgess Inc		
1023 Factory St ....Richmond CA 94801	**800-762-0744**	510-235-8411
Fastframe USA Inc		
1200 Lawrence Dr Ste 300 ....Newbury Park CA 91320	**888-863-7263**	805-498-4463
Flax Art & Design		
1699 Market St ....San Francisco CA 94103	**844-352-9278**	415-552-2355
Georgie's Ceramic & Clay Company Inc		
756 NE Lombard St ....Portland OR 97211	**800-999-2529**	503-283-1353
Herweck's Art & Drafting Supplies		
300 Broadway St ....San Antonio TX 78205	**800-725-1349**	210-227-1349
Lantana Communications Corp		
1700 Tech Centre Pkwy Ste 100 ....Arlington TX 76014	**800-345-4211**	
Michaels Stores Inc		
8000 Bent Branch Dr ....Irving TX 75063	**800-642-4235***	972-409-1300
*Cust Svc		
National Art Shop		
509 S National Ave ....Springfield MO 65802	**800-949-3743**	417-866-3743
New York Central Art Supply		
62 Third Ave ....New York NY 10003	**800-950-6111**	
Pat Catan's Craft Centers		
21160 Drake Rd ....Strongsville OH 44149	**800-321-1494**	440-238-7318
Plaza Art		
633 Middleton St ....Nashville TN 37203	**866-668-6714**	615-254-3368
Plaza Artists Materials of the MidAtlantic Inc		
1990 K Str NW ....Washington DC 20006	**866-668-6714**	202-331-7090
Premier Pyrotechnics Inc		
25255 Hwy K ....Richland MO 65556	**888-647-6863**	
Rex Artist Supplies		
3160 SW 22 St ....Miami FL 33145	**800-739-2782**	305-445-1413
Spokane Art Supply Inc		
1303 N Monroe St ....Spokane WA 99201	**800-556-5568**	509-327-6622
Starvin' Art Supplies		
802 S Oak Pk ....Oak Park IL 60304	**800-427-8478**	708-358-3600
Texas Art Supply		
2001 Montrose Blvd ....Houston TX 77006	**800-888-9278**	713-526-5221
Thomsons Art Supply Inc		
184 Mamaroneck Ave ....White Plains NY 10601	**800-287-4885**	914-949-4885

			Toll-Free	Phone
Woodcraft Supply LLC				
1177 Rosemar Rd PO Box 1686	Parkersburg WV	26105	**800-535-4482**	

45 ASPHALT PAVING & ROOFING MATERIALS

			Toll-Free	Phone
Atlas Roofing Corp				
2322 Valley Rd	Meridian MS	39307	**800-478-0258***	601-483-7111
*Cust Svc				
Baker Rock Resources				
21880 SW Farmington Rd	Beaverton OR	97007	**800-340-7625**	503-642-2531
Brewer Co 1354 US Hwy 50	Milford OH	45150	**800-394-0017**	513-576-6300
Burkholder Paving				
621 Martindale Rd	Ephrata PA	17522	**866-839-3426**	717-354-1340
Capitol Aggregates Ltd				
12625 Wetmore Rd Ste 301	San Antonio TX	78247	**800-292-5315**	210-871-6100
CertainTeed Corp				
750 E Swedesford Rd	Valley Forge PA	19482	**800-782-8777***	610-341-7000
*Prod Info				
Community Asphalt Corp				
9675 NW 117 Ave Ste 108	Miami FL	33178	**800-741-0806***	305-884-9444
*General				
Crafco Inc				
420 N Roosevelt Ave	Chandler AZ	85226	**800-528-8242**	602-276-0406
Dalton Enterprises Inc				
131 Willow St	Cheshire CT	06410	**800-851-5606**	203-272-3221
Dewitt Products Co				
5860 Plumer Ave	Detroit MI	48209	**800-962-8599***	313-554-0575
*Cust Svc				
Fields Company LLC				
2240 Taylor Way	Tacoma WA	98421	**800-627-4098**	
GAF Materials Corp				
1361 Alps Rd	Wayne NJ	07470	**800-365-7353**	973-628-3000
Gardner-Gibson PO Box 5449	Tampa FL	33675	**800-237-1155**	813-248-2101
Garland Company Inc				
3800 E 91st St	Cleveland OH	44105	**800-321-9336**	216-641-7500
Glenn O Hawbaker Inc				
1952 Waddle Rd Ste 203	State College PA	16803	**800-221-1355**	814-237-1444
Heely-Brown Company Inc				
1280 Chattahoochee Ave	Atlanta GA	30318	**800-241-4628**	404-352-0022
Henry Co				
909 N Sepulveda Blvd Ste 650	El Segundo CA	90245	**800-598-7663**	310-955-9200
HRI Inc				
1750 W College Ave	State College PA	16801	**877-474-9999**	
Innovative Metals Company Inc (IMETCO)				
4648 S Old Peachtree Rd	Norcross GA	30084	**800-646-3826**	770-908-1030
Karnak Corp, The				
330 Central Ave	Clark NJ	07066	**800-526-4236**	732-388-0300
Koppers Inc				
436 Seventh Ave	Pittsburgh PA	15219	**800-321-9876**	412-227-2001
NYSE: KOP				
Lunday-Thagard Co				
9302 Garfield Ave	South Gate CA	90280	**800-266-6551**	562-928-7000
Malarkey Roofing Products				
PO Box 17217	Portland OR	97217	**800-545-1191**	503-283-1191
Martin Asphalt Co				
Three Riverway Ste 400	South Houston TX	77056	**800-662-0987**	713-350-6800
Neyra Industries				
10700 Evendale Dr	Cincinnati OH	45241	**800-543-7077**	513-733-1000
Pace Products Inc				
4510 W 89th St Ste 110	Prairie Village KS	66207	**888-389-8203**	
Package Pavement Company Inc				
PO Box 408	Stormville NY	12582	**800-724-8193**	845-221-2224
Palmer Asphalt Co				
196 W Fifth St PO Box 58	Bayonne NJ	07002	**800-352-9898**	201-339-0855
Pike Industries Inc				
3 Eastgate Pk Rd	Belmont NH	03220	**800-283-0803**	603-527-5100
Russell Standard Corp				
285 Kappa Dr Ste 300	Pittsburgh PA	15238	**800-323-3053***	
*General				
Seaboard Asphalt Products Co				
3601 Fairfield Rd	Baltimore MD	21226	**800-536-0332**	410-355-0330
Sika Sarnafil Inc 100 Dan Rd	Canton MA	02021	**800-451-2504**	781-828-5400
Simon Roofing & Sheet Metal Corp				
70 Karago Ave	Youngstown OH	44512	**800-523-7714**	330-629-7663
Suit-Kote Corp				
1911 Lorings Crossing Rd	Cortland NY	13045	**800-622-5636**	607-753-1100
Tilcon Connecticut Inc				
PO Box 1357	New Britain CT	06050	**888-845-2666**	860-224-6010
Vance Bros Inc				
5201 Brighton PO Box 300107	Kansas City MO	64130	**800-821-8549**	816-923-4325
Vulcan Materials Co				
1200 Urban Ctr Dr PO Box 385014	Birmingham AL	35238	**800-615-4331**	205-298-3000
NYSE: VMC				

46 ASSOCIATION MANAGEMENT COMPANIES

			Toll-Free	Phone
Allen Press Inc				
810 E Tenth St PO Box 1897	Lawrence KS	66044	**800-627-0932**	785-843-1235
Association Managers Inc				
12427 Hedges Run Dr Ste 104	Lake Ridge VA	22192	**800-403-3374**	703-426-8100
Bannister & Assoc Inc				
34 N High St	New Albany OH	43054	**800-995-3579**	614-895-1355
Center for Assn Growth				
1926 Waukegan Rd Ste 1	Glenview IL	60025	**800-492-6462**	847-657-6700
Center for Assn Resources Inc				
1901 N Roselle Rd Ste 920	Schaumburg IL	60195	**888-705-1434**	
CM Services Inc				
800 Roosevelt Rd Bldg C Ste 312	Glen Ellyn IL	60137	**800-613-6672**	630-858-7337
Grassley Group, The (FMCI)				
409 Washington St Ste A	Cedar Falls IA	50613	**866-619-5580**	
Hauck & Assoc Inc				
1255 23rd St NW Ste 200	Washington DC	20037	**800-767-7777**	202-452-8100

			Toll-Free	Phone
J Edgar Eubanks & Assoc				
One Windsor Cove Ste 305	Columbia SC	29223	**800-445-8629**	803-252-5646
LoBue & Majdalany Management Group				
572B Ruger St PO Box 29920	San Francisco CA	94129	**800-820-4690**	415-561-6110
NeuStar Inc				
21575 Ridgetop Cir	Sterling VA	20166	**855-638-2677**	571-434-5400
Prime Management Services				
3416 Primm Ln	Birmingham AL	35216	**866-609-1599**	205-823-6106
Raybourn Group International				
9100 PuRdue Rd Ste 200	Indianapolis IN	46268	**800-362-2546**	317-328-4636
Total Management Solutions Inc				
55 Harristown Rd	Glen Rock NJ	07452	**866-544-0707**	201-447-0707

47 ASSOCIATIONS & ORGANIZATIONS - GENERAL

SEE ALSO Performing Arts Organizations ; Political Action Committees ; Political Parties (Major)

47-1 Accreditation & Certification Organizations

			Toll-Free	Phone
Accreditation Commission for Acupuncture & Oriental Medicine (ACAOM)				
7501 Greenway Ctr Dr Ste 760	Greenbelt MD	20770	**800-735-2968**	301-313-0855
Accreditation Council for Accountancy & Taxation (ACAT)				
1010 N Fairfax St	Alexandria VA	22314	**888-289-7763**	703-549-2228
Accrediting Bureau of Health Education Schools (ABHES)				
7777 Leesburg Pike Ste 314 N	Falls Church VA	22043	**800-228-9290**	703-917-9503
Accrediting Council for Independent Colleges & Schools (ACICS)				
750 First St NE Ste 980	Washington DC	20002	**800-258-3826**	202-336-6780
American Assn for Accreditation of Ambulatory Surgery Facilities Inc (AAAASF)				
5101 Washington St 2F PO Box 9500	Gurnee IL	60031	**888-545-5222**	847-775-1985
American Assn for Laboratory Accreditation (A2LA)				
5301 Buckeystown Pike Ste 350	Frederick MD	21704	**888-627-8318**	301-644-3248
American Board of Internal Medicine (ABIM)				
510 Walnut St Ste 1700	Philadelphia PA	19106	**800-441-2246**	215-446-3500
American Culinary Federation Inc (ACF)				
180 Ctr Pl Way	Saint Augustine FL	32095	**800-624-9458**	904-824-4468
American Library Assn Committee on Accreditation				
50 E Huron St	Chicago IL	60611	**800-545-2433**	312-944-6780
American National Standards Institute (ANSI)				
25 W 43rd St 4th fl	New York NY	10036	**800-374-3818**	212-642-4900
American Osteopathic Assn (AOA)				
142 E Ontario St	Chicago IL	60611	**800-621-1773**	312-202-8000
American Veterinary Medical Assn Council on Education				
1931 N Meacham Rd Ste 100	Schaumburg IL	60173	**800-248-2862**	847-925-8070
Association for Assessment & Accreditation of Laboratory Animal Care International				
5283 Corporate Dr Ste 203	Frederick MD	21703	**800-926-0066**	301-696-9626
Canadian Assn of Occupational Therapists (CAOT)				
1125 Colonel By Dr	Ottawa ON	K1S5R1	**800-434-2268**	613-523-2268
Canadian Assn of Speech-Language Pathologists & Audiologists (CASLPA)				
One Nicholas St Ste 1000	Ottawa ON	K1N7B7	**800-259-8519**	613-567-9968
Canadian Information Processing Society (CIPS)				
5090 Explorer Dr Ste 801	Mississauga ON	L4W4T9	**877-275-2477**	905-602-1370
Certified Financial Planner Board of Standards Inc				
1425 K St NW Ste 500	Washington DC	20005	**800-487-1497**	202-379-2200
COLA				
9881 Broken Land Pkwy Ste 200	Columbia MD	21046	**800-981-9883**	410-381-6581
Commission on Accreditation for Dietetics Education (CADE)				
120 S Riverside Plz Ste 2000	Chicago IL	60606	**800-877-1600**	312-899-0040
Commission on Accreditation for Law Enforcement Agencies (CALEA)				
13575 Heathcote Blvd Ste 320	Gainesville VA	20155	**877-789-6904**	703-352-4225
Commission on Accreditation in Physical Therapy Education (CAPTE)				
1111 N Fairfax St	Alexandria VA	22314	**800-999-2782**	703-706-3245
Commission on Accreditation of Allied Health Education Programs (CAAHEP)				
1361 Pk St	Clearwater FL	33756	**800-228-2262**	727-210-2350
Commission on Accreditation of Rehabilitation Facilities International (CARF)				
6951 E Southpoint Rd	Tucson AZ	85756	**888-281-6531**	520-325-1044
Commission on Collegiate Nursing Education				
1 Dupont Cir NW Ste 530	Washington DC	20036	**800-441-1414**	202-887-6791
Commission on Dental Accreditation of Canada				
1815 Alta Vista Dr	Ottawa ON	K1G3Y6	**866-521-2322**	613-523-7114
Community Health Accreditation Program Inc (CHAP)				
1275 K St NW Ste 800	Washington DC	20005	**800-656-9656**	202-862-3413
Continuing Care Accreditation Commission (CARF-CCAC)				
1730 Rhode Island Ave NW Ste 209	Washington DC	20036	**866-888-1122**	202-587-5001
Council on Academic Accreditation in Audiology & Speech-Language Pathology				
2200 Research Blvd	Rockville MD	20850	**800-498-2071**	301-296-5700
Council on Accreditation (COA)				
45 Broadway 29th Fl	New York NY	10006	**866-262-8088**	212-797-3000
Council on Accreditation of Nurse Anesthesia Educational Programs				
222 S Prospect Ave	Park Ridge IL	60068	**855-526-2262**	847-692-7050
Council on Aviation Accreditation (CAA)				
Aviation Accreditation Board International				
3410 Skyway Dr	Auburn AL	36830	**800-767-4767**	334-844-2431
Council on Chiropractic Education Commission on Accreditation				
8049 N 85th Way	Scottsdale AZ	85258	**888-443-3506**	480-443-8877
Council on Occupational Education				
7840 Roswell Rd Bldg 300 Ste 325	Atlanta GA	30350	**800-917-2081**	770-396-3898
Engineers Canada				
180 Elgin St Ste 1100	Ottawa ON	K2P2K3	**877-408-9273**	613-232-2474
National Accrediting Commission of Cosmetology Arts & Sciences (NACCAS)				
4401 Ford Ave Ste 1300	Alexandria VA	22302	**877-212-5752**	703-600-7600
National Council for Accreditation of Teacher Education (NCATE)				
2010 Massachusetts Ave NW Ste 500	Washington DC	20036	**800-255-8664**	202-466-7496
National Recreation & Park Assn				
22377 Belmont Ridge Rd	Ashburn VA	20148	**800-626-6772**	703-858-0784
North Central Assn Commission on Accreditation & School Improvement (NCA CASI)				
9115 Westside Pkwy	Alpharetta GA	30009	**888-413-3669**	
North Central Assn Higher Learning Commission				
230 S LaSalle St	Chicago IL	60604	**800-621-7440**	312-263-0456
Society of Accredited Marine Surveyors Inc (SAMS)				
7855 Argyle Forest Blvd Ste 203	Jacksonville FL	32244	**800-344-9077**	904-384-1494
Southern Assn of Colleges & Schools				
1866 Southern Ln	Decatur GA	30033	**888-413-3669**	404-679-4500
TransNational Assn of Christian Colleges & Schools (TRACS)				
15935 Forest Rd PO Box 328	Forest VA	24551	**800-669-4000**	434-525-9539

47-2 Agricultural Organizations

			Toll-Free	Phone
American Angus Assn (AAA)				
3201 Frederick Ave	Saint Joseph MO	64506	800-821-5478	816-383-5100
American Assn of Bovine Practitioners (AABP)				
3320 Skyway Dr Ste 802 PO Box 3610	Auburn AL	36831	800-269-2227	334-821-0442
American Dairy Science Assn (ADSA)				
1111 N Dunlap Ave	Savoy IL	61874	888-670-2250	217-356-5146
American Egg Board (AEB)				
1460 Renaissance Dr Ste 301	Park Ridge IL	60068	888-549-2140	847-296-7043
American Farmland Trust (AFT)				
1200 18th St	Washington DC	20036	800-431-1499	202-331-7300
American Forest & Paper Assn (AF&PA)				
1111 19th St NW Ste 800	Washington DC	20036	800-878-8878	202-463-2700
American Gelbvieh Assn				
10900 Dover St	Westminster CO	80021	877-279-2195	303-465-2333
American Royal Assn				
1701 American Royal Ct	Kansas City MO	64102	800-767-8487	816-221-9800
American Seed Trade Assn (ASTA)				
225 Reinekers Ln Ste 650	Alexandria VA	22314	888-890-7333	703-837-8140
American Society for Horticultural Science (ASHS)				
1018 Duke St	Alexandria VA	22314	800-331-1600	703-836-4606
American Society of Agricultural Consultants (ASAC)				
N78W14573 Appleton Ave	Menomonee Falls WI	53051	800-327-6789	262-253-6902
American Society of Agronomy (ASA)				
5585 Guilford Rd	Madison WI	53711	866-359-9161	608-273-8080
American Society of Landscape Architects (ASLA)				
636 'I' St NW	Washington DC	20001	888-999-2752	202-898-2444
American Soybean Assn (ASA)				
12125 Woodcrest Executive Dr Ste 100	Saint Louis MO	63141	800-688-7692	314-576-1770
American-International Charolais Assn (AICA)				
11700 NW Plaza Cir	Kansas City MO	64153	800-270-7711	816-464-5977
Association of Consulting Foresters of America (ACF)				
312 Montgomery St Ste 208	Alexandria VA	22314	888-540-8733	703-548-0990
Association of Farmworker Opportunity Programs (AFOP)				
1726 M St NW Ste 602	Washington DC	20036	866-487-9243	202-828-6006
Association of Water Technologies (AWT)				
15245 Shady Grove Rd Ste 130	Rockville MD	20850	800-858-6683	301-740-1421
Breg Inc				
2611 Commerce Way Ste C	Vista CA	92081	800-897-2734	760-599-3000
Corn Refiners Assn Inc (CRA)				
1701 Pennsylvania Ave	Washington DC	20006	800-284-5779	202-331-1634
Cotton Inc 6399 Weston Pkwy	Cary NC	27513	800-334-5868	919-678-2220
CropLife America				
1156 15th St NW Ste 400	Washington DC	20005	800-266-9432	202-296-1585
Dairy Management Inc (DMI)				
10255 W Higgins Rd Ste 900	Rosemont IL	60018	800-853-2479	
Decatur Co-op Assn				
305 S York Ave PO Box 68	Oberlin KS	67749	800-886-2293	785-475-2234
Farmer's Co-op Assn				
110 S Keokuk Wash Rd	Keota IA	52248	877-843-4893	641-636-3748
Farmers Educational & Co-op Union of America				
20 F St NW Ste 300	Washington DC	20001	800-331-1212	202-554-1600
Golf Course Superintendents Assn of America (GCSAA)				
1421 Research Pk Dr	Lawrence KS	66049	800-472-7878	785-841-2240
Hohman Assoc Inc (HAI)				
6951 W Little York	Houston TX	77040	800-324-0978	713-896-0978
Holstein Assn USA Inc				
One Holstein Pl	Brattleboro VT	05302	800-952-5200*	802-254-4551
*Orders				
International Plant Nutrition Institute (IPNI)				
3500 PkwyLn Ste 550	Norcross GA	30092	800-521-3044	770-447-0335
International Society of Arboriculture (ISA)				
PO Box 3129	Champaign IL	61826	888-472-8733	217-355-9411
Livestock Marketing Assn (LMA)				
10510 N Ambassador Dr	Kansas City MO	64153	888-484-8477	816-891-0502
Mid-Kansas Co-op Assn (MKC)				
117 N Edwards Ave	Moundridge KS	67107	800-864-4428	620-345-6361
Milk Industry Foundation (MIF)				
1250 H St NW Ste 900	Washington DC	20005	866-225-4821	202-737-4332
Mohair Council of America				
233 W Twohig Rd	San Angelo TX	76903	800-583-3161	325-655-3161
National Agri-Marketing Assn (NAMA)				
11020 King St Ste 205	Overland Park KS	66210	800-530-5646	913-491-6500
National Association of Landscape Professionals Inc (PLANET)				
950 Herndon Pkwy Ste 450	Herndon VA	20170	800-395-2522	703-736-9666
National Cattlemen's Beef Assn (NCBA)				
9110 E Nichols Ave Ste 300	Centennial CO	80112	866-233-3872	303-694-0305
National Cotton Council of America				
7193 Goodlett Farms Pkwy	Memphis TN	38016	888-232-1738	901-274-9030
National Crop Insurance Services (NCIS)				
8900 Indian Creek Pkwy Ste 600	Overland Park KS	66210	800-951-6247	913-685-2767
National Farmers Organization (NFO)				
528 Billy Sunday Rd Ste 100 PO Box 2508	Ames IA	50010	800-247-2110	515-292-2000
National FFA Organization				
6060 FFA Dr	Indianapolis IN	46268	800-772-0939	317-802-6060
National Grange				
1616 H St NW	Washington DC	20006	888-447-2643	202-628-3507
National Turkey Federation (NTF)				
1225 New York Ave NW Ste 400	Washington DC	20005	866-536-7593	202-898-0100
National Woodland Owners Assn (NWOA)				
374 Maple Ave E Ste 310	Vienna VA	22180	800-476-8733	703-255-2700
Santa Gertrudis Breeders International				
PO Box 1257	Kingsville TX	78364	800-500-8242	361-592-9357
Shelburne Farms				
1611 Harbor Rd	Shelburne VT	05482	800-286-6022	802-985-8686
Southern Forest Products Assn (SFPA)				
2900 Indiana Ave	Kenner LA	70065	866-574-4155	504-443-4464
Tobacco Merchants Assn (TMA)				
PO Box 8019	Princeton NJ	08543	888-672-4991	609-275-4900
United Producers Inc				
8351 N High St Ste 250	Columbus OH	43235	800-456-3276	
United Soybean Board (USB)				
16305 Swingley Ridge Rd Ste 150	Chesterfield MO	63017	800-989-8721	636-530-1777

			Toll-Free	Phone
US Apple Assn				
8233 Old Courthouse Rd Ste 200	Vienna VA	22182	800-781-4443	703-442-8850
US Potato Board (USPB)				
7555 E Hampden Ave Ste 412	Denver CO	80231	866-632-9992	303-369-7783

47-3 Animals & Animal Welfare Organizations

			Toll-Free	Phone
African Wildlife Foundation (AWF)				
1400 16th St NW Ste 120	Washington DC	20036	888-494-5354	202-939-3333
American Animal Hospital Assn (AAHA)				
12575 W Bayaud Ave	Lakewood CO	80228	800-252-2242	303-986-2800
American Assn of Equine Practitioners (AAEP)				
4075 Iron Works Pkwy	Lexington KY	40511	800-443-0177	859-233-0147
American Donkey & Mule Society (ADMS)				
1346 Morningside Ave	Lewisville TX	75057	877-752-4068	972-219-0781
American Humane Assn (AHA)				
63 Inverness Dr E	Englewood CO	80112	800-227-4645	303-792-9900
American Morgan Horse Assn (AMHA)				
4066 Shelburne Rd Ste 5	Shelburne VT	05482	888-436-3700	802-985-4944
American Quarter Horse Assn (AQHA)				
1600 Quarter Horse Dr	Amarillo TX	79104	800-291-7323	806-376-4811
Appaloosa Horse Club (ApHC)				
2720 W Pullman Rd	Moscow ID	83843	888-304-7768	208-882-5578
ASPCA Animal Poison Control Ctr				
424 E 92nd St	New York NY	10128	888-426-4435	212-876-7700
Association of Zoos & Aquariums (AZA)				
8403 Colesville Rd Ste 710	Silver Spring MD	20910	800-821-4557	301-562-0777
Atlantic Salmon Federation (ASF)				
PO Box 5200	Saint Andrews NB	E5B3S8	800-565-5666	506-529-1033
Bat Conservation International (BCI)				
500 N Capital of Texas Hwy	Austin TX	78746	800-538-2287	512-327-9721
Bird Studies Canada				
115 Front St PO Box 160	Port Rowan ON	N0E1M0	888-448-2473	519-586-3531
Born Free USA United with Animal Protection Institute				
1122 S St	Sacramento CA	95814	800-348-7387	916-447-3085
Canadian Federation of Humane Societies (CFHS)				
30 Concourse Gate Ste 102	Ottawa ON	K2E7V7	888-678-2347	613-224-8072
Canadian Kennel Club (CKC)				
200 Ronson Dr Ste 400	Etobicoke ON	M9W5Z9	800-250-8040	416-675-5511
Canadian Peregrine Foundation				
1450 O'Connor Dr Bldg B Ste 214	Toronto ON	M4B2T8	888-709-3944	416-481-1233
Certified Horsemanship Assn (CHA)				
1795 Alysheba Way Ste 7102	Lexington KY	40509	800-399-0138	859-259-3399
Defenders of Wildlife				
1130 17th St NW	Washington DC	20036	800-385-9712	202-682-9400
Delta Waterfowl Foundation				
PO Box 3128	Bismarck ND	58502	888-987-3695	701-222-8857
Dian Fossey Gorilla Fund International				
800 Cherokee Ave SE	Atlanta GA	30315	800-851-0203	404-624-5881
Ducks Unlimited Inc				
One Waterfowl Way	Memphis TN	38120	800-453-8257	901-758-3825
Friends of Animals Inc (FOA)				
777 Post Rd Ste 205	Darien CT	06820	800-321-7387	203-656-1522
In Defense of Animals (IDA)				
3010 Kerner Blvd	San Rafael CA	94901	800-705-0425	415-448-0048
International Fund for Animal Welfare (IFAW)				
290 Summer St	Yarmouth Port MA	02675	800-932-4329	508-744-2000
International Society for Animal Rights (ISAR)				
PO Box F	Clarks Summit PA	18411	888-589-6397	570-586-2200
Jane Goodall Institute for Wildlife Research Education & Conservation (JGI)				
4245 N Fairfax Dr Ste 600	Arlington VA	22203	800-592-5263	703-682-9220
Missouri Fox Trotting Horse Breed Assn Inc				
PO Box 1027	Ava MO	65608	877-663-4203	417-683-2468
Mountain Lion Foundation				
PO Box 1896	Sacramento CA	95812	800-319-7621	916-442-2666
National Anti-Vivisection Society (NAVS)				
53 W Jackson Blvd Ste 1552	Chicago IL	60604	800-888-6287	312-427-6065
National Disaster Search Dog Foundation				
501 E Ojai Ave	Ojai CA	93023	888-459-4376	805-646-1015
National Wild Turkey Federation (NWTF)				
770 Augusta Rd PO Box 530	Edgefield SC	29824	800-843-6983*	803-637-3106
*Cust Svc				
National Wildlife Federation (NWF)				
11100 Wildlife Ctr Dr	Reston VA	20190	800-822-9919	703-438-6000
People for the Ethical Treatment of Animals (PETA)				
501 Front St	Norfolk VA	23510	800-248-7729	757-622-7382
Performing Animal Welfare Society (PAWS)				
11435 Simmerhorn Rd	Galt CA	95632	800-513-6560	209-745-2606
Pet Sitters International (PSI)				
201 E King St	King NC	27021	800-325-7353	336-983-9222
Ruffed Grouse Society (RGS)				
451 McCormick Rd	Coraopolis PA	15108	888-564-6747	412-262-4044
Save the Manatee Club (SMC)				
500 N Maitland Ave Ste 210	Maitland FL	32751	800-432-5646	407-539-0990
Thoroughbred Owners & Breeders Assn (TOBA)				
PO Box 910668	Lexington KY	40591	888-606-8622	859-276-2291
Trout Unlimited (TU)				
1300 N 17th St Ste 500	Arlington VA	22209	800-834-2419	703-522-0200
World Animal Protection (WSPA)				
450 Seventh Avenue 31st Floor	New York NY	10123	800-883-9772	
World Wildlife Fund (WWF)				
1250 24th St NW PO Box 97180	Washington DC	20090	800-225-5993	202-293-4800
World Wildlife Fund Canada (WWF)				
245 Eglinton Ave E Ste 410	Toronto ON	M4P3J1	800-267-2632	416-489-8800
Zoocheck Canada				
788 1/2 O'Connor Dr	Toronto ON	M4B2S6	888-801-3222	416-285-1744

47-4 Arts & Artists Organizations

			Toll-Free	Phone
American Academy of Arts & Sciences				
136 Irving St	Cambridge MA	02138	800-666-2211	617-576-5000
American Assn of Museums (AAM)				
1575 Eye St NW Ste 400	Washington DC	20005	866-226-2150	202-289-1818

			Toll-Free	Phone
American Choral Directors Assn (ACDA)				
545 Couch Dr	Oklahoma City OK	73102	**800-624-0166**	405-232-8161
American Craft Council				
72 Spring St Sixth Fl	New York NY	10012	**800-836-3470**	212-274-0630
American Federation of Musicians of the US & Canada (AFM)				
1501 Broadway Ste 600	New York NY	10036	**800-762-3444**	212-869-1330
American Guild of Musical Artists (AGMA)				
1430 Broadway 14th Fl	New York NY	10018	**800-543-2462**	212-265-3687
American Guild of Variety Artists (AGVA)				
363 Seventh Ave 17th Fl	New York NY	10001	**800-331-0890**	212-675-1003
American Institute of Architects (AIA)				
1735 New York Ave NW	Washington DC	20006	**800-242-3837***	202-626-7300
*Orders				
American Institute of Graphic Arts (AIGA)				
164 Fifth Ave	New York NY	10010	**800-548-1634**	212-807-1990
American Musicological Society (AMS)				
6010 College Stn	Brunswick ME	04011	**888-421-1442**	207-798-4243
American Society of Cinematographers (ASC)				
1782 N Orange Dr	Hollywood CA	90028	**800-448-0145**	323-969-4333
Americans for the Arts				
1000 Vermont Ave NW 6th Fl	Washington DC	20005	**866-471-2787**	202-371-2830
Arts & Business Council of Americans for the Arts				
1 E 53rd St 2nd Fl	New York NY	10022	**866-471-2787**	212-223-2787
Association of Film Commissioners International (AFCI)				
109 E 17th St	Cheyenne WY	82001	**888-765-5777**	307-637-4422
Association of Performing Arts Presenters				
1211 Connecticut Ave NW Ste 200	Washington DC	20036	**888-820-2787**	202-833-2787
Bix Beiderbecke Memorial Society				
PO Box 3688 Ste 201	Davenport IA	52808	**888-249-5487**	563-324-7170
Broadway League, The				
729 Seventh Ave 5th Fl	New York NY	10019	**866-442-9878**	212-764-1122
Chamber Music America (CMA)				
305 Seventh Ave 5th Fl	New York NY	10001	**888-221-9836**	212-242-2022
Choristers Guild				
2834 W Kingsley Rd	Garland TX	75041	**800-246-7478**	972-271-1521
Clowns of America International (COAI)				
PO Box 1171	Englewood FL	34295	**877-816-6941**	941-474-4351
Country Music Assn Inc (CMA)				
1 Music Cir S	Nashville TN	37203	**800-788-3045**	615-244-2840
Design Management Institute (DMI)				
38 Chauncy St Ste 800	Boston MA	02111	**800-200-5909**	617-338-6380
Drum Corps International (DCI)				
PO Box 3129	Indianapolis IN	46206	**800-495-7469***	317-275-1212
*Orders				
Glass Art Society (GAS)				
6512 23rd Ave NW Ste 329	Seattle WA	98121	**800-636-2377**	206-382-1305
International Interior Design Assn (IIDA)				
222 Merchandise Mart Plz Ste 567	Chicago IL	60654	**888-799-4432**	312-467-1950
National Academy of Recording Arts & Sciences				
3030 Olympic Blvd	Santa Monica CA	90404	**800-423-2017**	310-392-3777
National Association of Theatre Owners. (NATO)				
750 First St NE Ste 1130	Washington DC	20002	**800-365-5701***	202-962-0054
*General				
Percussive Arts Society (PAS)				
110 W Washington St	Indianapolis IN	46204	**888-990-6663**	317-974-4488
Professional Photographers of America Inc (PPA)				
229 Peachtree St NE Ste 2200	Atlanta GA	30303	**800-786-6277**	404-522-8600
Professional Picture Framers Assn (PPFA)				
2282 Springport Rd Ste F	Jackson MI	49202	**800-762-9287**	517-788-8100
Screen Actors Guild (SAG)				
5757 Wilshire Blvd	Los Angeles CA	90036	**800-724-0767**	323-954-1600
SESAC Inc 55 Music Sq E	Nashville TN	37203	**800-826-9996**	615-320-0055
Society for Ethnomusicology (SEM)				
Indiana University				
1165 E 3rd St Morrison Hall 005	Bloomington IN	47405	**800-933-9330**	812-855-6672
Society of American Archivists (SAA)				
17 N State St Ste 1425	Chicago IL	60602	**866-722-7858**	312-606-0722
World Monuments Fund (WMF)				
350 Fifth Ave Ste 2412	New York NY	10118	**800-547-9171**	646-424-9594

47-5 Charitable & Humanitarian Organizations

			Toll-Free	Phone
ACDI/VOCA				
50 F St NW Ste 1075	Washington DC	20001	**800-929-8622**	202-638-4661
Action Against Hunger				
247 W 37th St 10th Fl	New York NY	10018	**877-777-1420**	212-967-7800
Adventist Community Services				
12501 Old Columbia Pk	Silver Spring MD	20904	**877-227-2702**	301-680-6438
Adventist Development & Relief Agency International (ADRA)				
12501 Old Columbia Pk	Silver Spring MD	20904	**800-424-2372**	301-680-6380
Aga Khan Foundation USA (AKF)				
1825 K St NW Ste 901	Washington DC	20006	**800-267-2532**	202-293-2537
Alan Guttmacher Institute (AGI)				
125 Maiden Ln Seventh Fl	New York NY	10038	**800-355-0244**	212-248-1111
America's Second Harvest				
35 E Wacker Dr Ste 2000	Chicago IL	60601	**800-771-2303**	312-263-2303
American Anti-Slavery Group, The				
198 Tremont St	Boston MA	02116	**800-884-0719**	617-426-8161
American Jewish World Service (AJWS)				
45 W 36th St	New York NY	10018	**800-889-7146**	212-792-2900
American Lebanese Syrian Associated Charities (ALSAC)				
501 St Jude Pl	Memphis TN	38105	**800-822-6344**	901-578-2000
American Refugee Committee (ARC)				
430 Oak Grove St Ste 204	Minneapolis MN	55403	**800-875-7060**	612-872-7060
AmeriCares Foundation				
88 Hamilton Ave	Stamford CT	06902	**800-486-4357**	203-658-9500
Amigos de las Americas				
5618 Star Ln	Houston TX	77057	**800-231-7796**	713-782-5290
Amnesty International USA (AIUSA)				
5 Penn Plaza 16th Fl	New York NY	10001	**866-273-4466**	212-807-8400
Association of Fundraising Professionals (AFP)				
4300 Wilson Blvd Ste 300	Arlington VA	22203	**800-666-3863**	703-684-0410
Bread for the World				
50 F St NW Ste 500	Washington DC	20001	**800-822-7323***	202-639-9400
*Cust Svc				
CARE USA 151 Ellis St NE	Atlanta GA	30303	**800-521-2273**	404-681-2552

			Toll-Free	Phone
Catholic Medical Mission Board (CMMB)				
10 W 17th St	New York NY	10011	**800-678-5659**	212-242-7757
Catholic Relief Services (CRS)				
228 W Lexington St	Baltimore MD	21201	**800-235-2772**	410-625-2220
Children International				
2000 E Red Bridge Rd	Kansas City MO	64131	**800-888-3089**	816-942-2000
Christian Appalachian Project				
6550 S KY Rt 321 PO Box 459	Hagerhill KY	41222	**800-755-5322**	
Christian Blind Mission (CBM)				
450 E Pk Ave	Greenville SC	29601	**800-937-2264**	864-239-0065
Christian Reformed World Relief Committee (CRWRC)				
2850 Kalamazoo Ave SE	Grand Rapids MI	49560	**800-552-7972**	616-241-1691
Church World Service				
28606 Phillips St PO Box 968	Elkhart IN	46515	**800-297-1516**	574-264-3102
Church World Service Emergency Response Program				
475 Riverside Dr Ste 700	New York NY	10115	**888-297-2767**	212-870-3151
Coalition on Human Needs (CHN)				
1120 Connecticut Ave NW	Washington DC	20036	**800-822-7323**	202-223-2532
Community Food Bank of New Jersey Inc				
31 Evans Terminal	Hillside NJ	07205	**866-527-1087**	908-355-3663
Community Health Charities				
200 N Glebe Rd Ste 801	Arlington VA	22203	**800-654-0845**	703-528-1007
Compassion International				
12290 Voyager Pkwy	Colorado Springs CO	80921	**800-336-7676**	719-487-7000
Concern America				
2015 N Broadway	Santa Ana CA	92706	**800-266-2376**	714-953-8575
Council on Foundations				
2121 Crystal Dr Ste 700	Arlington VA	22202	**800-673-9036**	703-879-0600
CRISTA Ministries				
19303 Fremont Ave N	Seattle WA	98133	**800-346-9140***	206-546-7200
*Cust Svc				
Direct Relief International				
27 S La Patera Ln	Goleta CA	93117	**800-676-1638**	805-964-4767
Doctors Without Borders USA Inc				
333 Seventh Ave Second Fl	New York NY	10001	**888-392-0392**	212-679-6800
Enterprise Community Partners Inc				
10227 Wincopin Cir	Columbia MD	21044	**800-624-4298**	410-964-1230
Episcopal Migration Ministries (EMM)				
815 Second Ave	New York NY	10017	**800-334-7626**	212-716-6258
Episcopal Relief & Development				
815 Second Ave	New York NY	10017	**800-334-7626**	855-312-4325
Evangelical Council for Financial Accountability (ECFA)				
440 W Jubal Early Dr Ste 130	Winchester VA	22601	**800-323-9473**	540-535-0103
Feed the Children (FTC)				
PO Box 36	Oklahoma City OK	73101	**800-627-4556**	405-942-0228
Food for the Poor Inc (FFP)				
6401 Lyons Rd	Coconut Creek FL	33073	**800-427-9104**	954-427-2222
Freedom from Hunger				
1644 DaVinci Ct	Davis CA	95618	**800-708-2555**	530-758-6200
Goodwill Industries International Inc				
15810 Indianola Dr	Rockville MD	20855	**800-741-0197**	301-530-6500
Habitat for Humanity International Inc				
121 Habitat St	Americus GA	31709	**800-422-4828**	229-924-6935
Healing the Children (HTC)				
2624 W Beacon Ave	Spokane WA	99208	**888-233-9527**	509-327-4281
Hebrew Immigrant Aid Society (HIAS)				
333 Seventh Ave 16th Fl	New York NY	10001	**800-442-7714**	212-967-4100
Heifer International				
One World Ave	Little Rock AR	72202	**800-422-0474**	501-907-2600
Helen Keller International				
352 Pk Ave S Ste 1200	New York NY	10010	**877-535-5374**	212-532-0544
Housing Assistance Council (HAC)				
1025 Vermont Ave NW Ste 606	Washington DC	20005	**866-234-2689**	202-842-8600
Hunger Project, The				
Five Union Sq W	New York NY	10003	**800-228-6691**	212-251-9100
Independent Charities of America (ICA)				
1100 Larkspur Landing Cir Ste 340	Larkspur CA	94939	**800-477-0733**	415-925-2600
Independent Order of Foresters (IOF)				
789 Don Mills Rd	Toronto ON	M3C1T9	**800-828-1540**	416-429-3000
Independent Sector				
1602 L St NW Ste 900	Washington DC	20036	**888-737-9477**	202-467-6100
International Aid Inc				
17011 W Hickory St	Spring Lake MI	49456	**800-968-7490**	616-846-7490
International Medical Corps (IMC)				
1919 Santa Monica Blvd Ste 400	Santa Monica CA	90404	**800-481-4462**	310-826-7800
International Orthodox Christian Charities (IOCC)				
110 W Rd Ste 360	Towson MD	21204	**877-803-4622**	410-243-9820
International Planned Parenthood Federation - Western Hemisphere Region (IPPF/WHR)				
120 Wall St 9th Fl	New York NY	10005	**866-477-3947**	212-248-6400
International Rescue Committee (IRC)				
122 E 42nd St 12th Fl	New York NY	10168	**800-435-7352**	212-551-3000
Lutheran Disaster Response				
8765 W Higgins Rd	Chicago IL	60631	**800-638-3522**	
Make-A-Wish Foundation of America				
4742 N 24th St Ste 400	Phoenix AZ	85016	**800-722-9474**	602-279-9474
MAP International				
4700 Glynco Pkwy	Brunswick GA	31525	**800-225-8550**	912-265-6010
Medical Teams International (MTI)				
PO Box 10	Portland OR	97207	**800-959-4325**	503-624-1000
Mennonite Central Committee (MCC)				
21 S 12th St PO Box 500	Akron PA	17501	**888-563-4676**	717-859-1151
Mennonite Disaster Service (MDS)				
583 Airport Rd	Lititz PA	17543	**800-241-8111**	717-735-3536
MENTOR/National Mentoring Partnership				
1600 Duke St Ste 300	Alexandria VA	22314	**877-333-2464**	703-224-2200
Mercy Corps				
3015 SW First Ave	Portland OR	97201	**800-292-3355**	503-796-6800
Mercy-USA for Aid & Development Inc (M-USA)				
44450 Pinetree Dr Ste 201	Plymouth MI	48170	**800-556-3729**	734-454-0011
Michigan Municipal League				
1675 Green Rd PO Box 1487	Ann Arbor MI	48105	**800-653-2483**	734-662-3246
NA for the Exchange of Industrial Resources (NAEIR)				
560 McClure St	Galesburg IL	61401	**800-562-0955**	309-343-0704
National Alliance to End Homelessness				
1518 K St NW Ste 410	Washington DC	20005	**800-657-3769**	202-638-1526
National AMBUCS Inc (AMBUCS)				
4285 Regency Ct PO Box 5127	High Point NC	27265	**800-838-1845**	336-852-0052

	City	State	Zip	Toll-Free	Phone
National Coalition for the Homeless (NCH)					
2201 P St NW	Washington	DC	20037	**877-243-1576**	202-462-4822
National Peace Corps Assn (NPCA)					
1900 L St NW Ste 610	Washington	DC	20036	**800-424-8580**	202-293-7728
North American Mission Board SBC					
4200 N Pt Pkwy	Alpharetta	GA	30022	**800-634-2462**	770-410-6000
OIC International					
1500 Walnut St Ste 1304	Philadelphia	PA	19102	**800-653-6424**	215-842-0220
Operation USA					
3617 Hayden Ave Ste A	Culver City	CA	90232	**800-678-7255**	310-838-3455
ORBIS International Inc					
520 Eigth Ave 11th Fl	New York	NY	10018	**800-672-4787**	646-674-5500
Oregon Food Bank Inc					
PO Box 55370	Portland	OR	97238	**888-398-8702**	503-282-0555
ORT American Inc					
75 Maiden Ln 10th Fl	New York	NY	10038	**800-519-2678**	212-505-7700
Outreach International					
129 W Lexington PO Box 210	Independence	MO	64050	**888-833-1235**	816-833-0883
Oxfam America					
226 Cswy St Fifth Fl	Boston	MA	02114	**800-776-9326**	617-482-1211
Pan American Development Foundation (PADF)					
1889 F St NW 2nd Fl	Washington	DC	20006	**877-572-4484**	202-458-3969
Partners of the Americas					
1424 K St NW Ste 700	Washington	DC	20005	**800-322-7844**	202-628-3300
People-to-People Health Foundation					
255 Carter Hall Ln	Millwood	VA	22646	**800-544-4673**	540-837-2100
Physicians for Social Responsibility (PSR)					
1875 Connecticut Ave NW Ste 1012	Washington	DC	20009	**800-459-1887**	202-667-4260
Points of Light Foundation & Volunteer Ctr National Network					
1400 'I' St NW Ste 800	Washington	DC	20005	**866-269-0510**	202-729-8000
Population Connection					
2120 L St NW Ste 500	Washington	DC	20037	**800-767-1956**	202-332-2200
Presbyterian Disaster Assistance (PDA)					
100 Witherspoon St	Louisville	KY	40202	**800-728-7228**	
Project Concern International (PCI)					
5151 Murphy Canyon Rd Ste 320	San Diego	CA	92123	**877-724-4673**	858-279-9690
ProLiteracy Worldwide					
1320 Jamesville Ave	Syracuse	NY	13210	**800-448-8878**	315-422-9121
Rebuilding Together Inc					
1899 L St NW Ste 1000	Washington	DC	20036	**800-473-4229**	
Refugees International (RI)					
2001 S St NW Ste 700-K	Washington	DC	20009	**800-733-8433**	202-828-0110
Ronald McDonald House Charities (RMHC)					
1 Kroc Dr Dept 014	Oak Brook	IL	60523	**855-670-4787**	630-623-7048
Rotary Foundation, The					
1560 Sherman Ave	Evanston	IL	60201	**800-435-7352**	847-866-3000
Sertoma International					
1912 E Meyer Blvd	Kansas City	MO	64132	**800-593-5646**	816-333-8300
Share Our Strength					
1730 M St NW Ste 700	Washington	DC	20036	**800-969-4767**	202-393-2925
Smile Train Inc					
41 Madison Ave Ste 28	New York	NY	10010	**877-543-7645**	212-689-9199
Society of Saint Andrew (SoSA)					
3383 Sweet Hollow Rd	Big Island	VA	24526	**800-333-4597**	434-299-5956
Southeast Asia Resource Action Ctr (SEARAC)					
1628 16th St NW Third Fl	Washington	DC	20009	**888-907-1485**	202-667-4690
Special Wish Foundation Inc					
1250 Memory Ln N Ste B	Columbus	OH	43209	**800-486-9474**	614-258-3186
TechnoServe 49 Day St	Norwalk	CT	06854	**800-999-6757**	203-852-0377
Trickle Up Program Inc					
104 W 27th St 12th Fl	New York	NY	10001	**866-246-9980**	212-255-9980
Unitarian Universalist Service Committee (UUSC)					
689 Massachusetts Ave	Cambridge	MA	02139	**800-388-3920**	617-868-6600
United Way of America					
701 N Fairfax St	Alexandria	VA	22314	**800-892-2757**	703-836-7100
US Fund for UNICEF					
125 Maiden Ln	New York	NY	10038	**800-367-5437**	
USA for UNHCR					
1775 K St NW Ste 580	Washington	DC	20006	**800-770-1100**	202-296-1115
Veterans for Peace Inc (VFP)					
216 S Meramec Ave	Saint Louis	MO	63105	**877-429-0678**	314-725-6005
Voices of September 11th					
161 Cherry St	New Canaan	CT	06840	**866-505-3911**	203-966-3911
Volunteers of America					
1660 Duke St	Alexandria	VA	22314	**800-899-0089**	703-341-5000
War Resisters League					
339 Lafayette St	New York	NY	10012	**800-975-9688**	212-228-0450
World Concern					
19303 Fremont Ave N	Seattle	WA	98133	**800-755-5022**	206-546-7201
World Food Program USA (WFP)					
1725 Eye St NW Ste 510	Washington	DC	20036	**888-454-0555**	202-530-1694
World Hunger Year Inc (WHY)					
505 Eigth Ave Ste 2100	New York	NY	10018	**800-548-6479**	212-629-8850
World Learning					
1 Kipling Rd PO Box 676	Brattleboro	VT	05302	**800-257-7751**	802-257-7751
World Neighbors Inc (WN)					
4127 NW 122nd St	Oklahoma City	OK	73120	**800-242-6387**	405-752-9700
World Relief					
Seven E Baltimore St	Baltimore	MD	21202	**800-535-5433**	443-451-1900
World Vision Inc					
34834 Weyerhaeuser Way S					
PO Box 9716	Federal Way	WA	98001	**888-511-6548**	253-815-1000

47-6 Children & Family Advocacy Organizations

	City	State	Zip	Toll-Free	Phone
AARP 601 E St NW	Washington	DC	20049	**888-687-2277**	202-434-2277
AARP Grandparent Information Ctr					
601 E St NW	Washington	DC	20049	**888-687-2277**	202-434-3525
Adoption ARC Inc					
4701 Pine St Ste J-7	Philadelphia	PA	19143	**800-884-4004**	215-748-1441
Alliance for Aging Research (AAR)					
750 17th St NW Ste 1100	Washington	DC	20006	**866-840-6283**	202-293-2856
Alliance for Children & Families Inc					
11700 W Lk Pk Dr	Milwaukee	WI	53224	**800-221-3726**	414-359-1040
Alliance for Retired Americans					
815 16th St NW Fourth Fl	Washington	DC	20006	**888-373-6497**	202-637-5399
American Academy of Pediatrics (AAP)					
141 NW Pt Blvd	Elk Grove Village	IL	60007	**800-433-9016**	847-434-4000
American Coalition for Fathers & Children (ACFC)					
1718 M St NW Ste 1187	Washington	DC	20036	**800-978-3237**	
American Culinary Federation Chef & Child Foundation					
180 Ctr Pl Way	Saint Augustine	FL	32095	**800-624-9458**	904-824-4468
American Humane Assn (AHA)					
63 Inverness Dr E	Englewood	CO	80112	**800-227-4645**	303-792-9900
American Society on Aging (ASA)					
71 Stevenson St Ste 1450	San Francisco	CA	94105	**800-537-9728**	415-974-9600
Association for Couples in Marriage Enrichment (ACME)					
PO Box 21374	Winston-Salem	NC	27120	**800-634-8325**	336-724-1526
Believe In Tomorrow National Children's Foundation					
6601 Frederick Rd	Baltimore	MD	21228	**800-933-5470**	410-744-1032
Blue Grass Regional Mental Health-Mental Retardation Board Inc					
1351 Newtown Pike Bldg 1	Lexington	KY	40511	**800-928-8000**	859-253-1686
Boys Town					
14100 Crawford St	Boys Town	NE	68010	**800-448-3000**	402-498-1300
Buckner International					
600 N Pearl St Ste 2000 20th Fl	Dallas	TX	75201	**800-442-4800**	214-758-8000
Cal Farley's Boys Ranch					
600 W 11th St PO Box 1890	Amarillo	TX	79174	**800-687-3722**	806-372-2341
Camelot Community Care Inc					
4910 D Creekside Dr	Clearwater	FL	33760	**866-343-8606**	727-593-0003
Child Find Canada					
212-2211 McPhillips St	Winnipeg	MB	R2V3M5	**800-387-7962**	204-339-5584
Child Lures Prevention					
5166 Shelburne Rd	Shelburne	VT	05482	**800-552-2197**	802-985-8458
Childhelp USA					
4350 E Camelback Rd Bldg F250	Phoenix	AZ	85018	**800-422-4453**	480-922-8212
Children Awaiting Parents Inc (CAP)					
595 Blossom Rd Ste 306	Rochester	NY	14610	**888-835-8802**	585-232-5110
Children Inc 4205 Dover Rd	Richmond	VA	23221	**800-538-5381**	804-359-4562
Children of the Night					
14530 Sylvan St	Van Nuys	CA	91411	**800-551-1300**	818-908-4474
Children's Defense Fund (CDF)					
25 E St NW	Washington	DC	20001	**800-233-1200**	202-628-8787
Christian Foundation for Children & Aging (CFCA)					
One Elmwood Ave	Kansas City	KS	66103	**800-875-6564**	913-384-6500
Connecting Generations					
100 W Tenth St Ste 1115	Wilmington	DE	19801	**877-202-9050**	302-656-2122
Corps Network, The					
1100 G St NW Ste 1000	Washington	DC	20005	**800-245-5627**	202-737-6272
Covenant House					
Five Penn Plz Third Fl	New York	NY	10001	**800-999-9999**	212-727-4000
DePelchin Children's Ctr					
4950 Memorial Dr	Houston	TX	77007	**888-730-2335**	713-730-2335
Envision Inc 610 N Main St	Wichita	KS	67203	**888-425-7072**	316-440-1500
Evan B Donaldson Adoption Institute					
120 E 38th St	New York	NY	10016	**800-837-2655**	212-925-4089
Experience Works Inc					
2200 Clarendon Blvd Ste 1000	Arlington	VA	22203	**866-397-9757**	703-522-7272
Family Research Council (FRC)					
801 G St NW	Washington	DC	20001	**800-225-4008**	202-393-2100
Find the Children					
2656 29th St Ste 203	Santa Monica	CA	90405	**888-477-6721**	310-314-3213
First Candle					
1314 Bedford Ave Ste 210	Baltimore	MD	21208	**800-221-7437**	410-653-8226
Focus on the Family					
8605 Explorer Dr	Colorado Springs	CO	80920	**800-232-6459***	719-531-3400
*Sales					
Generations United (GU)					
1333 H St NW Ste 500-W	Washington	DC	20005	**800-677-1116**	202-289-3979
Girls Inc					
120 Wall St Third Fl	New York	NY	10005	**800-374-4475**	212-509-2000
Human Life International (HLI)					
Four Family Life Ln	Front Royal	VA	22630	**800-549-5433***	540-635-7884
*Orders					
Jewish Board of Family & Children Services (JBFCS)					
120 W 57th St	New York	NY	10019	**888-523-2769**	212-582-9100
Kansas Children's Service League (KCSL)					
3545 SW 5th	Topeka	KS	66606	**877-530-5275**	785-274-3100
Leading Age					
2519 Connecticut Ave NW	Washington	DC	20008	**866-702-3278**	202-783-2242
May Institute Inc					
41 Pacella Pk Dr	Randolph	MA	02368	**800-778-7601**	781-440-0400
MENTOR/National Mentoring Partnership					
1600 Duke St Ste 300	Alexandria	VA	22314	**877-333-2464**	703-224-2200
MOPS International					
2370 S Trenton Way	Denver	CO	80231	**888-910-6677***	303-733-5353
*General					
Mothers Against Drunk Driving (MADD)					
511 E John Carpenter Fwy Ste 700	Irving	TX	75062	**877-275-6233**	214-744-6233
National Caregiving Foundation					
801 N Pitt St	Alexandria	VA	22314	**800-930-1357**	703-299-9300
National Child Care Assn (NCCA)					
1325 G St NW Ste 500	Washington	DC	20005	**866-536-1945**	
National Coalition Against Domestic Violence (NCADV)					
One Broadway Ste B210	Denver	CO	80203	**800-799-7233**	303-839-1852
National Council on Family Relations (NCFR)					
1201 W River Pkwy Ste 200	Minneapolis	MN	55454	**888-781-9331**	
National Council on the Aging (NCOA)					
1901 L St NW Fourth Fl	Washington	DC	20036	**800-677-1116**	202-479-1200
National Court Appointed Special Advocate Assn (CASA)					
100 W Harrison St N Twr Ste 500	Seattle	WA	98119	**800-628-3233**	206-270-0072
National Ctr for Family Literacy (NCFL)					
325 W Main St Ste 300	Louisville	KY	40202	**877-326-5481**	502-584-1133
National Ctr for Missing & Exploited Children (NCMEC)					
699 Prince St	Alexandria	VA	22314	**800-843-5678**	703-274-3900
National Domestic Violence Hotline (NDVH)					
PO Box 161810	Austin	TX	78716	**800-799-7233**	512-794-1133
National Family Caregivers Assn (NFCA)					
10400 Connecticut Ave Ste 500	Kensington	MD	20895	**800-896-3650**	301-942-6430
National Hispanic Council on Aging (NHCOA)					
734 15th St NW Ste 1050	Washington	DC	20005	**800-633-4227**	202-347-9733
National Resource Ctr on Domestic Violence (NRCDV)					
6400 Flank Dr Ste 1300	Harrisburg	PA	17112	**800-799-7233**	

Classified Section

		Toll-Free	Phone
National Resource Ctr on Native American Aging (NRCNAA)			
501 N Columbia Rd Rm 4535 .... Grand Forks ND 58202		800-896-7628	701-777-6780
National Runaway Switchboard (NRS)			
3080 N Lincoln Ave .... Chicago IL 60657		800-786-2929	773-880-9860
National Urban Technology Ctr			
80 Maiden Ln Ste 606 .... New York NY 10038		800-998-3212	212-528-7350
National WIC Assn (NWA)			
2001 S St NW Ste 580 .... Washington DC 20009		866-782-6246	202-232-5492
North America Missing Children Assn Inc (NAMCA)			
201 Brownlow Ave .... Dartmouth NS B3B1W2		800-260-0753	902-494-2449
North American Council on Adoptable Children (NACAC)			
970 Raymond Ave Ste 106 .... Saint Paul MN 55114		877-823-2237	651-644-3036
Orphan Foundation of America (OFA)			
21351 Gentry Dr Ste 130 .... Sterling VA 20166		800-950-4673	571-203-0270
Parents Helping Parents (PHP)			
1400 Parkmoor Ave Ste 100 .... San Jose CA 95126		855-727-5775	408-727-5775
Parents of Murdered Children (POMC)			
4960 Ridge Ave Ste 2 .... Cincinnati OH 45209		888-818-7662	513-721-5683
Parsons Child & Family Ctr			
60 Academy Rd .... Albany NY 12208		800-342-3009	518-426-2600
Pension Rights Ctr			
1350 Connecticut Ave NW Ste 206 .... Washington DC 20036		866-735-7737	202-296-3776
Plan USA 155 Plan Way .... Warwick RI 02886		800-556-7918	401-738-5600
Planned Parenthood Federation of America			
434 W 33rd St .... New York NY 10001		800-230-7526	212-541-7800
Pressley Ridge			
5500 Corporate Dr Ste 400 .... Pittsburgh PA 15237		800-718-0356	412-872-9400
Promise Keepers (PK)			
PO Box 11798 .... Denver CO 80211		866-776-6473	
Rainbows 1360 Hamilton Pkwy .... Itasca IL 60143		800-266-3206	847-952-1770
Rape Abuse & Incest National Network (RAINN)			
2000 L St NW Ste 406 .... Washington DC 20036		800-656-4673	202-544-1034
SOS Children's Villages-USA			
1001 Connecticut Ave NW Ste 1250 .... Washington DC 20036		888-767-4543*	202-347-7920
*General			
Students Against Destructive Decisions (SADD)			
255 Main St .... Marlborough MA 01752		877-723-3462	508-481-3568
Well Spouse Assn			
63 W Main St Ste H .... Freehold NJ 07728		800-838-0879	732-577-8899
YMCA of the USA (YMCA)			
101 N Wacker Dr 14th Fl .... Chicago IL 60606		800-872-9622	312-977-0031
YWCA USA (YWCA)			
2025 M St NW Ste 550 .... Washington DC 20036		888-872-9259	202-467-0801

47-7　Civic & Political Organizations

		Toll-Free	Phone
Advocates for Self-Government			
1010 N Tennessee St Ste 215 .... Cartersville GA 30120		800-932-1776	770-386-8372
Americans for Democratic Action (ADA)			
1625 K St NW Ste 210 .... Washington DC 20006		855-712-8441	202-785-5980
Americans for Peace Now (APN)			
1101 14th St NW 6th Fl .... Washington DC 20005		877-429-0678	202-728-1893
Americans United for Separation of Church & State			
518 C St NE .... Washington DC 20002		800-875-3707	202-466-3234
Brady Campaign to Prevent Gun Violence			
1225 'I' St NW Ste 1100 .... Washington DC 20005		800-732-0999	202-898-0792
Campaign Legal Ctr			
Media Policy Program Campaign Legal Ctr			
.... Washington DC 20036		877-855-5007	202-736-2200
Center for Democracy & Technology (CDT)			
1634 'I' St NW 11th Fl .... Washington DC 20006		800-869-4499	202-637-9800
Christian Coalition of America			
PO Box 37030 .... Washington DC 20013		888-999-6778	202-479-6900
Citizens Against Government Waste (CAGW)			
1301 Pennsylvania Ave NW Ste 1075 .... Washington DC 20004		800-232-6479	202-467-5300
Citizens Committee for the Right to Keep & Bear Arms (CCRKBA)			
12500 NE Tenth Pl .... Bellevue WA 98005		800-426-4302	425-454-4911
Citizens for Tax Justice (CTJ)			
1616 P St NW Ste 200-B .... Washington DC 20036		888-626-2622	202-299-1066
Close Up Foundation			
1330 Braddock Pl Ste 400 .... Alexandria VA 22314		800-256-7387	703-706-3300
Community Assns Institute (CAI)			
6402 Arlington Blvd Ste 500 .... Falls Church VA 22042		888-224-4321	703-970-9220
Concord Coalition			
1011 Arlington Blvd Ste 300 .... Arlington VA 22209		888-333-4248	703-894-6222
Congress Watch			
215 Pennsylvania Ave SE .... Washington DC 20003		800-289-3787	202-546-4996
Constitutional Rights Foundation			
601 S Kingsley Dr .... Los Angeles CA 90005		800-488-4273	213-487-5590
EMILY's List			
1800 M St NW Ste 375N .... Washington DC 20036		800-683-6459	202-326-1400
Evangelicals for Social Action (ESA)			
PO Box 367 .... Wayne PA 19087		800-650-6600	484-384-2990
Families USA			
1201 New York Ave NW Ste 1100 .... Washington DC 20005		888-392-5132	202-628-3030
Federation for American Immigration Reform (FAIR)			
25 Massachusetts Ave NW Ste 330 .... Washington DC 20009		877-627-3247	202-328-7004
Foreign Policy Assn (FPA)			
470 Pk Ave S .... New York NY 10016		800-628-5754	212-481-8100
FreedomWorks			
601 Pennsylvania Ave NW Ste 700-N .... Washington DC 20004		888-564-6273	202-783-3870
Global Exchange			
2017 Mission St Ste 303 .... San Francisco CA 94110		800-497-1994	415-255-7296
Interfaith Alliance			
1212 New York Ave NW Ste 1250 .... Washington DC 20005		800-510-0969	202-238-3300
Judicial Watch Inc			
425 Third St SW Ste 800 .... Washington DC 20024		888-593-8442	202-646-5172
Junior Chamber International (JCI)			
15645 Olive Blvd .... Chesterfield MO 63017		800-905-5499	636-449-3100
National Committee to Preserve Social Security & Medicare (NCPSSM)			
10 G St NE Ste 600 .... Washington DC 20002		800-966-1935	202-216-0420
National Council on Public History (NCPH)			
425 University Blvd			
327 Cavanaugh Hall .... Indianapolis IN 46202		800-554-5542	317-274-2716
National Ctr for Neighborhood Enterprise (NCNE)			
1625 K St Ste 1200 .... Washington DC 20006		866-518-1263	202-518-6500

		Toll-Free	Phone
National Federation of Republican Women (NFRW)			
124 N Alfred St .... Alexandria VA 22314		800-373-9688	703-548-9688
National Taxpayers Union (NTU)			
108 N Alfred St .... Alexandria VA 22314		800-680-7289	703-683-5700
OMB Watch			
1742 Connecticut Ave NW .... Washington DC 20009		866-483-5137	202-234-8494
Organization of American States (OAS)			
1889 F St NW .... Washington DC 20006		888-442-4887	202-458-3000
People for the American Way (PFAW)			
2000 M St NW Ste 400 .... Washington DC 20036		800-326-7329	202-467-4999
Population Reference Bureau (PRB)			
1875 Connecticut Ave NW Ste 520 .... Washington DC 20009		800-877-9881	202-483-1100
Population-Environment Balance Inc			
2000 P St NW Ste 600 .... Washington DC 20036		800-866-6269	202-955-5700
Project Vote			
1350 I St NW Ste 1250 .... Washington DC 20005		888-546-4173	202-546-4173
US Junior Chamber of Commerce			
7447 S Lewis Ave .... Tulsa OK 74136		800-905-5499	636-681-1857
Young America's Foundation			
110 Elden St .... Herndon VA 20170		800-292-9231	800-872-1776

47-8　Civil & Human Rights Organizations

		Toll-Free	Phone
American Civil Liberties Union (ACLU)			
125 Broad St 18th Fl .... New York NY 10004		877-867-1025	212-549-2500
Americans for Effective Law Enforcement (AELE)			
841 W Touhy Ave .... Park Ridge IL 60068		800-763-2802	847-685-0700
Anti-Defamation League (ADL)			
605 Third Ave .... New York NY 10158		866-386-3235	212-885-7700
Asian American Legal Defense & Education Fund (AALDEF)			
99 Hudson St 12th Fl .... New York NY 10013		800-966-5946	212-966-5932
Becket Fund for Religious Liberty			
1350 Connecticut Ave NW Ste 605 .... Washington DC 20036		800-743-7734	202-955-0095
Center for Individual Rights (CIR)			
1233 20th St NW Ste 300 .... Washington DC 20036		877-426-2665	202-833-8400
Corporate Accountability International			
10 Milk St Ste 610 .... Boston MA 02108		800-688-8797	617-695-2525
Disability Rights Ctr Inc			
18 Low Ave .... Concord NH 03301		800-834-1721	603-228-0432
Families Against Mandatory Minimums (FAMM)			
1612 K St NW Ste 700 .... Washington DC 20006		800-435-7352	202-822-6700
Human Rights Campaign			
1640 Rhode Island Ave NW .... Washington DC 20036		800-777-4723	202-628-4160
Lambda Legal Defense & Education Fund			
120 Wall St Ste 1500 .... New York NY 10005		866-542-8336	212-809-8585
Leadership Conference on Civil Rights (LCCR)			
1629 K St NW Ste 1000 .... Washington DC 20006		888-460-0813	202-466-3311
Media Watch PO Box 618 .... Santa Cruz CA 95061		800-631-6355	831-423-6355
Medicare Rights Ctr (MRC)			
520 Eigth Ave N Wing Third Fl .... New York NY 10018		800-333-4114*	212-869-3850
*Hotline			
NA for the Advancement of Colored People (NAACP)			
4805 Mt Hope Dr .... Baltimore MD 21215		877-622-2798	410-580-5777
National Abortion Federation (NAF)			
1755 Massachusetts Ave NW .... Washington DC 20036		800-772-9100	202-667-5881
National Coalition Against Domestic Violence (NCADV)			
One Broadway Ste B210 .... Denver CO 80203		800-799-7233	303-839-1852
National Conference on Citizenship (NCOC)			
1875 K St NW 5th Fl .... Washington DC 20006		800-745-7275	202-729-8038
National Council on Crime & Delinquency (NCCD)			
1970 Broadway Ste 500 .... Oakland CA 94612		800-306-6223	510-208-0500
National Ctr for Victims of Crime, The			
2000 M St NW Ste 480 .... Washington DC 20036		800-394-2255	202-467-8700
National Freedom of Information Coalition			
Univ of Missouri .... Columbia MO 65211		866-682-6663	573-882-4856
National Organization for the Reform of Marijuana Laws (NORML)			
1600 K St NW Ste 501 .... Washington DC 20006		888-676-6765	202-483-5500
National Organization for Victim Assistance (NOVA)			
510 King St Ste 424 .... Alexandria VA 22314		800-879-6682	703-535-6682
Patients Rights Council (PRC)			
PO Box 760 .... Steubenville OH 43952		800-958-5678	740-282-3810
Rutherford Institute			
PO Box 7482 .... Charlottesville VA 22906		800-225-1791	434-978-3888
Second Amendment Foundation			
12500 NE Tenth Pl .... Bellevue WA 98005		800-426-4302	425-454-7012
Simon Wiesenthal Ctr			
1399 Roxbury Dr Ste 100 .... Los Angeles CA 90035		800-900-9036	310-553-9036
Urban Land Institute (ULI)			
1025 Thomas Jefferson St NW			
Ste 500W .... Washington DC 20007		800-321-5011*	202-624-7000
*Orders			
WeTip Inc			
PO Box 1296 .... Rancho Cucamonga CA 91729		800-782-7463	909-987-5005

47-9　Computer & Internet Organizations

		Toll-Free	Phone
Association for Computing Machinery (ACM)			
Two Penn Plz Ste 701 .... New York NY 10121		800-342-6626	212-626-0500
Computer Measurement Group (CMG)			
151 Fries Mill Rd Ste 104 .... Turnersville NJ 08012		800-436-7264	856-401-1700
Consortium for School Networking (CoSN)			
1025 Vermont Ave NW Ste 1010 .... Washington DC 20005		866-267-8747	202-861-2676
Data Interchange Standards Assn (DISA)			
7600 Leesburg Pike Ste 430 .... Falls Church VA 22043		866-205-5001	703-970-4480
Information Systems Audit & Control Assn (ISACA)			
3701 Algonquin Rd Ste 1010 .... Rolling Meadows IL 60008		888-491-8833	847-253-1545
Institute for Certification of Computing Professionals (ICCP)			
2400 E Devon Ave Ste 281 .... Des Plaines IL 60018		800-843-8227	847-299-4227
National Urban Technology Ctr			
80 Maiden Ln Ste 606 .... New York NY 10038		800-998-3212	212-528-7350
Network & Systems Professionals Assn Inc (NaSPA)			
7044 S 13th St .... Oak Creek WI 53154		877-777-3520	414-768-8000

				Toll-Free	Phone
Open Group					
44 Montgomery St Ste 960	San Francisco	CA	94104	800-433-6611	415-374-8280
Portable Computer & Communications Assn (PCCA)					
PO Box 680	Hood River	OR	97031	877-323-8888	541-490-5140
Print Services & Distribution Assn (PSDA)					
330 N. Wabash Ave Ste 2000	Chicago	IL	60611	800-336-4641	800-230-0175
Society for Information Management (SIM)					
401 N Michigan Ave Ste 2400	Chicago	IL	60611	800-387-9746	312-527-6734
TechServe Alliance					
1420 King St Ste 610	Alexandria	VA	22314	888-421-1442	703-838-2050

47-10 Consumer Interest Organizations

				Toll-Free	Phone
Accuracy in Media Inc (AIM)					
4455 Connecticut Ave NW Ste 330	Washington	DC	20008	800-787-4567	202-364-4401
Advocates for Highway & Auto Safety					
750 First St NE Ste 901	Washington	DC	20002	877-366-0711	202-408-1711
American Council on Science & Health (ACSH)					
1995 Broadway Second Fl	New York	NY	10023	866-905-2694	212-362-7044
Center for Auto Safety (CAS)					
1825 Connecticut Ave NW Ste 330	Washington	DC	20009	800-424-9393	202-328-7700
Consumer Federation of America (CFA)					
1620 I St NW Ste 200	Washington	DC	20006	877-382-4357	202-387-6121
Consumers' Research Council of America (CRCA)					
2020 Pennsylvania Ave NW Ste 300-A	Washington	DC	20006	800-675-5376	202-835-9698
Funeral Consumers Alliance					
33 Patchen Rd	South Burlington	VT	05403	800-765-0107	802-865-8300
Insurance Information Institute Inc (III)					
110 William St	New York	NY	10038	877-263-7995	212-346-5500
National Committee for Quality Assurance (NCQA)					
1100 13th St	Washington	DC	20005	888-275-7585	202-955-3500
National Consumers League (NCL)					
1701 K St NW Ste 1200	Washington	DC	20006	800-388-2227	202-835-3323
National Fraud Information Ctr (NFIC)					
1701 K St NW Ste 1200	Washington	DC	20006	800-333-4636	202-835-3323
Philanthropic Research Inc					
4801 Courthouse St Ste 220	Williamsburg	VA	23188	800-784-9378	757-229-4631
Private Citizen Inc					
PO Box 233	Naperville	IL	60566	888-382-1222	630-393-1555

47-11 Educational Associations & Organizations

				Toll-Free	Phone
A Better Chance Inc					
253 W 35th St 6th Fl.	New York	NY	10001	800-562-7865	646-346-1310
Alliance for Excellent Education					
1201 Connecticut Ave Ste 901	Washington	DC	20036	800-695-0285	202-828-0828
Alliance for International Educational & Cultural Exchange					
1776 Massachusetts Ave NW Ste 620	Washington	DC	20036	888-304-9023	202-293-6141
American Indian College Fund					
8333 Greenwood Blvd	Denver	CO	80221	800-776-3863	303-426-8900
Archaeological Institute of America (AIA)					
656 Beacon St 4th Fl	Boston	MA	02215	877-524-6300	617-353-9361
Braille Institute of America Inc					
741 N Vermont Ave	Los Angeles	CA	90029	800-272-4553	323-663-1111
Challenger Ctr for Space Science Education					
422 First St SE Third Fl	Washington	DC	20003	800-969-5747*	202-827-1580
*General					
Chickasaw Nation, The					
520 Arlington St PO Box 1548	Ada	OK	74821	866-466-1481	580-436-2603
College Board					
45 Columbus Ave	New York	NY	10023	800-927-4302	212-713-8000
College Parents of America (CPA)					
2200 Wilson Blvd Ste 102-396.	Arlington	VA	22201	888-761-6702	
Comstar Enterprises Inc					
PO Box 6698	Springdale	AR	72766	800-533-2343	479-361-2111
Council For Economic Opportunities In Greater Cleveland					
1228 Euclid Ave Ste 700.	Cleveland	OH	44115	888-262-3226	216-696-9077
Council for Opportunity in Education					
1025 Vermont Ave NW Ste 900.	Washington	DC	20005	800-633-7313	202-347-7430
Education Development Ctr Inc (EDC)					
55 Chapel St	Newton	MA	02458	800-225-4276	617-969-7100
Facing History & Ourselves					
16 HuRd Rd	Brookline	MA	02445	800-856-9039	617-232-1595
Family Career & Community Leaders of America (FCCLA)					
1910 Assn Dr	Reston	VA	20191	800-234-4425	703-476-4900
FIRST 200 Bedford St	Manchester	NH	03101	800-871-8326	603-666-3906
Foundation Ctr					
79 Fifth Ave Second Fl	New York	NY	10003	800-424-9836	212-620-4230
Future Business Leaders of America-Phi Beta Lambda Inc (FBLA-PBL)					
1912 Assn Dr	Reston	VA	20191	800-325-2946	
Graduate Management Admission Council (GMAC)					
11921 Freedom Dr Ste 300.	Reston	VA	20190	866-505-6559	703-668-9600
Great Books Foundation					
35 E Wacker Dr Ste 400	Chicago	IL	60601	800-222-5870	312-332-5870
Institute of General Semantics (IGS)					
72-11 Austin St	Forest Hills	NY	11375	800-346-1359	212-729-7973
Intercollegiate Studies Institute (ISI)					
3901 Centerville Rd	Wilmington	DE	19807	800-526-7022	302-652-4600
International Montessori Council & The Montessori Foundation					
2400 Miguel Bay Dr					
PO Box 130.	Terra Ceia Island	FL	34250	800-655-5843	941-729-9565
Junior Achievement of Canada (JACAN)					
1 Eva Rd Ste 218	Toronto	ON	M9C4Z5	800-265-0699	416-622-4602
Junior State of America (JSA)					
400 S El Camino Real Ste 300	San Mateo	CA	94402	800-334-5353	650-347-1600
Music for All					
39 W Jackson Pl Ste 150	Indianapolis	IN	46225	800-848-2263	317-636-2263
National Ctr for Family Literacy (NCFL)					
325 W Main St Ste 300.	Louisville	KY	40202	877-326-5481	502-584-1133
National Head Start Assn (NHSA)					
1651 Prince St	Alexandria	VA	22314	866-677-8724	703-739-0875
National Honor Society (NHS)					
1904 Assn Dr	Reston	VA	20191	800-253-7746	703-860-0200

				Toll-Free	Phone
Panhandle-Plains Higher Education Authority Inc (PPHEA)					
1303 23rd St PO Box 839	Canyon	TX	79015	877-629-3669	806-324-4100
Reading Is Fundamental Inc (RIF)					
1825 Connecticut Ave NW Ste 400	Washington	DC	20009	877-743-7323	202-536-3400
Scholarship America					
One Scholarship Way PO Box 297	Saint Peter	MN	56082	800-537-4180	507-931-1682
SkillsUSA					
14001 James Monroe Hwy	Leesburg	VA	20176	800-321-8422	703-777-8810
Woodrow Wilson National Fellowship Foundation					
5 Vaughn Dr # 300	Princeton	NJ	08540	800-899-9963	609-452-7007
World Learning International Development Programs					
1015 15th St NW Ste 750	Washington	DC	20005	800-345-2929	202-408-5420
Youth For Understanding USA					
6400 Goldsboro Rd Ste 100	Bethesda	MD	20817	800-424-3691	240-235-2100

47-12 Energy & Natural Resources Organizations

				Toll-Free	Phone
Air & Waste Management Assn (A&WMA)					
420 Fort Duquesne Blvd					
1 Gateway Ctr 3rd Fl	Pittsburgh	PA	15222	800-270-3444	412-232-3444
Alliance to Save Energy (ASE)					
1850 M St NW Ste 600	Washington	DC	20036	800-862-2086	202-857-0666
American Assn of Petroleum Geologists (AAPG)					
1444 S Boulder Ave PO Box 979	Tulsa	OK	74119	800-364-2274	918-584-2555
American Oil Chemists Society (AOCS)					
2710 S Boulder PO Box 17190	Urbana	IL	61802	866-535-2730	217-359-2344
American Public Gas Assn (APGA)					
201 Massachusetts Ave NE Ste C-4	Washington	DC	20002	800-927-4204	202-464-2742
American Public Power Assn (APPA)					
1875 Connecticut Ave Ste 1200	Washington	DC	20009	800-515-2772	202-467-2900
American Water Works Assn (AWWA)					
6666 W Quincy Ave	Denver	CO	80235	800-926-7337	303-794-7711
Association of Energy Engineers (AEE)					
4025 Pleasantdale Rd Ste 420	Atlanta	GA	30340	877-407-0784	770-447-5083
Association of Energy Service Cos (AESC)					
14531 Fm 529 Ste 250	Houston	TX	77095	800-692-0771	713-781-0758
Edison Electric Institute (EEI)					
701 Pennsylvania Ave NW	Washington	DC	20004	800-649-1202	202-508-5000
Environmental Industry Assn					
4301 Connecticut Ave NW Ste 300	Washington	DC	20008	800-424-2869	202-244-4700
Independent Petroleum Assn of America (IPAA)					
1201 15th St NW Ste 300	Washington	DC	20005	800-433-2851	202-857-4722
Institute of Clean Air Cos (ICAC)					
1730 M St NW Ste 206	Washington	DC	20036	888-383-5726	202-457-0911
Institute of Hazardous Materials Management (IHMM)					
11900 Parklawn Dr Ste 450	Rockville	MD	20852	800-437-0137	301-984-8969
Interstate Oil & Gas Compact Commission (IOGCC)					
900 NE 23rd St PO Box 53127	Oklahoma City	OK	73152	800-822-4015	405-525-3556
Methanol Institute (MI)					
4100 Fairfax Dr Ste 740	Arlington	VA	22203	888-275-0768	703-248-3636
National Ground Water Assn (NGWA)					
601 Dempsey Rd	Westerville	OH	43081	800-551-7379	614-898-7791
National Ocean Industries Assn (NOIA)					
1120 G St NW Ste 900	Washington	DC	20005	800-558-9994	202-347-6900
National Rural Electric Co-op Assn (NRECA)					
4301 Wilson Blvd	Arlington	VA	22203	866-759-2619	703-907-5939
National Water Resources Assn (NWRA)					
3800 Fairfax Dr # 4	Arlington	VA	22203	800-468-3533	703-524-1544
North American Electric Reliability Council (NERC)					
1325 G St NW Ste 600	Washington	DC	20005	877-668-4493	609-452-8060
Renewable Fuels Assn (RFA)					
425 Third St SW	Washington	DC	20024	800-433-8850	202-289-3835
Society of Petroleum Engineers (SPE)					
222 Palisades Creek Dr	Richardson	TX	75080	800-456-6863	972-952-9393
Western Forestry & Conservation Assn					
4033 SW Canyon Rd	Portland	OR	97221	888-722-9416	503-226-4562

47-13 Environmental Organizations

				Toll-Free	Phone
Adirondack Council					
103 Hand Ave Ste 3 PO Box 2	Elizabethtown	NY	12932	877-873-2240	518-873-2240
American Farmland Trust (AFT)					
1200 18th St	Washington	DC	20036	800-431-1499	202-331-7300
American Forests					
734 15th St NW	Washington	DC	20005	800-368-5748	202-737-1944
American Littoral Society (ALS)					
18 Hartshorne Dr Ste 1	Highlands	NJ	07732	800-424-8802	732-291-0055
American Rivers					
1101 14th St NW Ste 1400	Washington	DC	20005	877-347-7550	202-347-7550
American Shore & Beach Preservation Assn (ASBPA)					
5460 Beaujolais Ln	Fort Myers	FL	33919	800-331-1600	239-489-2616
Appalachian Mountain Club (AMC)					
Five Joy St	Boston	MA	02108	800-262-4455*	617-523-0655
*Orders					
Audubon Naturalist Society					
8940 Jones Mill Rd	Chevy Chase	MD	20815	888-744-4723	301-652-9188
Beyond Pesticides					
701 E St SE Ste 200	Washington	DC	20003	866-260-6653	202-543-5450
Canadian Parks & Wilderness Society (CPAWS)					
250 City Ctr Ave Ste 506	Ottawa	ON	K1R6K7	800-333-9453	613-569-7226
Canadian Wildlife Federation (CWF)					
350 Michael Cowpland Dr	Kanata	ON	K2M2W1	800-563-9453	613-599-9594
Civil War Preservation Trust (CWPT)					
1331 H St NW Ste 1001	Washington	DC	20005	888-606-1400	202-367-1861
Clean Water Action					
4455 Connecticut Ave NW	Washington	DC	20008	800-234-7284	202-895-0420
Co-op America					
1612 K St NW Ste 600	Washington	DC	20006	800-584-7336	202-872-5307
Coastal Conservation Assn (CCA)					
6919 Portwest Dr Ste 100	Houston	TX	77024	800-201-3474	713-626-4234
Conservation Fund					
1655 N Fort Myer Dr Ste 1300	Arlington	VA	22209	800-672-5839	703-525-6300

				Toll-Free	Phone
Conservation International (CI)					
2011 Crystal Dr Ste 500	Arlington	VA	22202	800-406-2306	703-341-2400
Earth Share					
7735 Old Georgetown Rd Ste 900	Bethesda	MD	20814	800-875-3863	240-333-0300
EarthRights International					
1612 K St NW Ste 401	Washington	DC	20006	888-224-9043	202-466-5188
Earthwatch Institute					
114 Western Ave	Boston	MA	02134	800-776-0188	978-461-0081
Ecojustice Canada					
131 Water St Ste 214	Vancouver	BC	V6B4M3	800-926-7744	604-685-5618
Environmental Defense					
257 Pk Ave S	New York	NY	10010	800-505-0703	212-505-2100
Environmental Information Assn (EIA)					
6935 Wisconsin Ave Ste 306	Chevy Chase	MD	20815	888-343-4342	301-961-4999
Environmental Law Institute (ELI)					
2000 L St NW Ste 620	Washington	DC	20036	800-433-5120	202-939-3800
Forest Landowners Assn (FLA)					
900 Cir 75 Pkwy Ste 205	Atlanta	GA	30339	800-325-2954	404-325-2954
Freshwater Society					
2500 Shadywood Rd	Excelsior	MN	55331	888-471-9773	952-471-9773
Friends of the Earth					
1717 Massachusetts Ave NW Ste 600	Washington	DC	20036	877-843-8687	202-783-7400
Friends of the River					
1418 20th St Ste 100	Sacramento	CA	95811	888-464-2477	916-442-3155
Greater Yellowstone Coalition (GYC)					
13 S Willson Ave Ste 2	Bozeman	MT	59715	800-775-1834	406-586-1593
Greenpeace Canada					
33 Cecil St	Toronto	ON	M5T1N1	800-320-7183	416-597-8408
Greenpeace USA					
702 H St NW Ste 300	Washington	DC	20001	800-326-0959	202-462-1177
Heritage Canada Foundation					
Five Blackburn Ave	Ottawa	ON	K1N8A2	866-964-1066	613-237-1066
Historic New England					
141 Cambridge St	Boston	MA	02114	800-722-2256	617-227-3956
International Society of Tropical Foresters (ISTF)					
5400 Grosvenor Ln	Bethesda	MD	20814	866-897-8720	301-530-4514
Izaak Walton League of America (IWLA)					
707 Conservation Ln	Gaithersburg	MD	20878	800-453-5463	301-548-0150
League to Save Lake Tahoe					
2608 Lake Tahoe Blvd	South Lake Tahoe	CA	96150	888-844-9904	530-541-5388
Montana Wilderness Assn (MWA)					
30 S Ewing St	Helena	MT	59601	855-406-4483	406-443-7350
National Arbor Day Foundation					
100 Arbor Ave	Nebraska City	NE	68410	888-448-7337	402-474-5655
National Audubon Society (NAS)					
225 Varick St	New York	NY	10014	800-274-4201	212-979-3000
National Council for Air & Stream Improvement Inc (NCASI)					
PO Box 13318	Research Triangle Park	NC	27709	888-448-2473	919-941-6400
National Parks Conservation Assn (NPCA)					
1300 19th St NW Ste 300	Washington	DC	20036	800-628-7275	202-223-6722
National Trust for Historic Preservation					
1785 Massachusetts Ave NW	Washington	DC	20036	800-944-6847	202-588-6000
Nature Conservancy					
4245 N Fairfax Dr Ste 100	Arlington	VA	22203	800-628-6860*	703-841-5300
*Cust Svc					
Nature Conservancy of Canada					
36 Eglinton Ave W Ste 400	Toronto	ON	M4R1A1	800-465-8005	416-932-3202
New England Wild Flower Society					
180 Hemenway Rd	Framingham	MA	01701	888-636-0033	508-877-7630
Ocean Conservancy					
1300 19th St NW Eighth Fl	Washington	DC	20036	800-519-1541	202-429-5609
Ocean Futures Society					
325 Chapala St	Santa Barbara	CA	93101	800-477-7500	805-899-8899
Public Lands Foundation (PLF)					
PO Box 7226	Arlington	VA	22207	866-985-9636	703-790-1988
Rainforest Action Network (RAN)					
221 Pine St Fifth Fl	San Francisco	CA	94104	800-368-1819	415-398-4404
Royal Oak Foundation, The					
35 W 35th St Ste 1200	New York	NY	10001	800-913-6565	212-480-2889
Save America's Forests					
4 Library Ct SE	Washington	DC	20003	800-729-1363	202-544-9219
Shelburne Farms					
1611 Harbor Rd	Shelburne	VT	05482	800-286-6022	802-985-8686
Sierra Club Canada					
412-1 Nicholas St	Ottawa	ON	K1N7B7	888-810-4204	613-241-4611
Society for Ecological Restoration International (SERI)					
1017 O St NW	Washington	DC	20001	866-895-4735	202-299-9518
Soil & Water Conservation Society (SWCS)					
945 SW Ankeny Rd	Ankeny	IA	50023	800-843-7645	515-289-2331
Student Conservation Assn (SCA)					
689 River Rd PO Box 550	Charlestown	NH	03603	888-722-9675	603-543-1700
Thornton W Burgess Society					
6 Discovery Hill Rd	East Sandwich	MA	02537	800-844-4542	508-888-6870
Tree Care Industry Assn (TCIA)					
136 Harvey Rd Ste 101	Londonderry	NH	03053	800-733-2622	603-314-5380
Trust for Public Land (TPL)					
116 New Montgomery St Fourth Fl	San Francisco	CA	94105	800-714-5263	415-495-4014
Union of Concerned Scientists (UCS)					
Two Brattle Sq Sixth Fl	Cambridge	MA	02238	800-666-8276	617-547-5552
Walden Woods Project, The					
44 Baker Farm Rd	Lincoln	MA	01773	800-554-3569	781-259-4700
Water Environment Federation (WEF)					
601 Wythe St	Alexandria	VA	22314	800-666-0206	703-684-2400
Western Canada Wilderness Committee (WCWC)					
227 Abbott St	Vancouver	BC	V6B2K7	800-661-9453	604-683-8220
Yosemite Assn					
Yosemite Conservancy					
5020 El Portal Rd PO Box 230	El Portal	CA	95318	800-469-7275	209-379-2317

47-14 Ethnic & Nationality Organizations

				Toll-Free	Phone
American Folklore Society (AFS)					
Ohio State Univ Mershon Ctr					
1501 Neil Ave	Columbus	OH	43201	866-311-1200	614-292-4715
American Hellenic Educational Progressive Assn (AHEPA)					
1909 Q St NW Ste 500	Washington	DC	20009	855-473-3512	202-232-6300

				Toll-Free	Phone
Armenian General Benevolent Union (AGBU)					
55 E St 7th Fl	New York	NY	10022	800-368-4262	212-319-6383
Assembly of Turkish American Assn (ATAA)					
1526 18th St NW	Washington	DC	20036	800-627-7692	202-483-9090
German-American National Congress (DANK)					
4740 N Western Ave Ste 206	Chicago	IL	60625	888-872-3265	773-275-1100
National Congress of American Indians (NCAI)					
1516 P St NW	Washington	DC	20005	800-503-3330	202-466-7767
National Council of La Raza (NCLR)					
1126 16th St NW 6th Fl	Washington	DC	20036	800-821-7060	202-785-1670
National Slovak Society of the USA (NSS)					
351 Vly Brook Rd	McMurray	PA	15317	800-488-1890	724-731-0094
Order Sons of Italy in America (OSIA)					
219 E St NE	Washington	DC	20002	800-552-6742	202-547-2900
Sons of Norway					
1455 W Lake St Second Fl	Minneapolis	MN	55408	800-945-8851	612-827-3611
Swedish Council of America					
2600 Pk Ave	Minneapolis	MN	55407	800-380-2711	612-871-0593
Ukrainian NA Inc (UNA)					
2200 Rt 10	Parsippany	NJ	07054	800-253-9862	
US Pan Asian American Chamber of Commerce (US PAACC)					
1329 18th St NW	Washington	DC	20036	800-696-7818	202-296-5221

47-15 Fraternal & Social Organizations

				Toll-Free	Phone
American Mensa Ltd					
1229 Corporate Dr W	Arlington	TX	76006	800-666-3672	817-607-0060
Association of Junior Leagues International Inc (AJLI)					
80 Maiden Ln Ste 305	New York	NY	10038	800-955-3248	212-951-8300
Boys & Girls Clubs of America					
1230 W Peachtree St NW	Atlanta	GA	30309	800-995-3579	404-487-5700
Civitan International					
PO Box 130744	Birmingham	AL	35213	800-248-4826	205-591-8910
Cosmopolitan International					
7341 W 80th St PO Box 4588	Shawnee Mission	KS	66204	800-648-4331	913-648-4330
DeMolay International					
10200 NW Ambassador Dr	Kansas City	MO	64153	800-336-6529*	816-891-8333
*Orders					
Fraternal Order of Police (FOP)					
701 Marriott Dr	Nashville	TN	37214	800-451-2711	615-399-0900
General Grand Chapter Order of the Eastern Star					
1618 New Hampshire Ave NW	Washington	DC	20009	800-648-1182	202-667-4737
Girl Scouts of the USA					
420 Fifth Ave	New York	NY	10018	800-223-0624	212-852-8000
Goodwill Industries of Central Texas					
1015 Norwood Pk Blvd	Austin	TX	78753	800-735-2989	512-637-7100
Grand Aerie Fraternal Order of Eagles					
1623 Gateway Cir S	Grove City	OH	43123	877-829-5500	614-883-2200
Independent Order of Odd Fellows					
422 N Trade St	Winston-Salem	NC	27101	800-235-8358	336-725-5955
Key Club International					
3636 Woodview Trace	Indianapolis	IN	46268	800-549-2647	317-875-8755
Klingberg Family Centers Inc					
370 Linwood St	New Britain	CT	06052	877-696-6775	860-224-9113
Knights of Columbus					
One Columbus Plz	New Haven	CT	06510	800-380-9995*	203-752-4000
*Cust Svc					
Lutheran Homes Society Inc					
2021 N McCord Rd	Toledo	OH	43615	877-646-4050	419-861-4990
Lutheran Social Services of Illinois					
1001 E Touhy Ave Ste 50	Des Plaines	IL	60018	888-671-0300	847-635-4600
Masonic Service Assn of North America (MSANA)					
8120 Fenton St Ste 203	Silver Spring	MD	20910	855-476-4010	301-588-4010
National Exchange Club					
3050 W Central Ave	Toledo	OH	43606	800-924-2643	419-535-3232
Optimist International					
4494 Lindell Blvd	Saint Louis	MO	63108	800-500-8130	314-371-6000
Oswego County Opportunities Inc					
239 Oneida St	Fulton	NY	13069	877-342-7618	315-598-4717
Partnerships In Community Living Inc					
480 Main St E PO Box 129	Monmouth	OR	97361	800-222-1222	503-838-2403
Presbyterian Homes Inc, The					
2109 Sandy Ridge Rd	Colfax	NC	27235	800-225-9573	336-886-6553
Professional Bull Riders Inc (PBR)					
101 W Riverwalk	Pueblo	CO	81003	800-366-8538	719-242-2800
Ruritan National					
5451 Lyons Rd PO Box 487	Dublin	VA	24084	877-787-8727	540-674-5431
Spectrum Health Systems Inc					
10 Mechanic St Ste 302	Worcester	MA	01608	800-464-9555	508-792-5400
Starr Commonwealth					
13725 Starr Commonwealth Rd	Albion	MI	49224	800-837-5591	517-629-5591
TelecomPioneers					
1801 California St 44th Fl	Denver	CO	80202	800-872-5995	303-571-1200
Toastmasters International					
23182 Arroyo Vista	Rancho Santa Margarita	CA	92688	877-738-8118	949-858-8255
Up With People 6830 Broadway	Denver	CO	80221	877-264-8856	303-460-7100
Way Station Inc					
230 W Patrick St PO Box 3826	Frederick	MD	21705	888-549-0629	301-662-0099

47-16 Greek Letter Societies

				Toll-Free	Phone
Alpha Chi Omega					
5939 Castle Creek Pkwy N Dr	Indianapolis	IN	46250	800-328-0522	317-579-5050
Alpha Chi Sigma					
2141 N Franklin Rd	Indianapolis	IN	46219	800-252-4369	317-357-5944
Alpha Epsilon Phi Sorority (AEPhi)					
11 Lake Ave Ext Ste 1-A	Danbury	CT	06811	888-668-4293	203-748-0029
Alpha Epsilon Pi Fraternity Inc					
8815 Wesleyan Rd	Indianapolis	IN	46268	800-684-3608	317-876-1913
Alpha Gamma Rho					
10101 NW Ambassador Dr	Kansas City	MO	64153	888-241-4546	816-891-9200
Alpha Omega International Dental Fraternity					
50 W Edmonston Dr	Rockville	MD	20852	877-368-6326	301-738-6400

					Toll-Free	Phone

Alpha Omicron Pi International
5390 Virginia Way . . . . Brentwood TN 37027 **855-230-1183** 615-370-0920

Alpha Sigma Phi National Fraternity
710 Adams St . . . . Carmel IN 46032 **866-515-4747** 317-843-1911

Alpha Tau Omega Fraternity (ATO)
One N Pennsylvania St 12th Fl . . . . Indianapolis IN 46204 **800-798-9286** 317-684-1865

Beta Gamma Sigma Inc (BGS)
125 Weldon Pkwy . . . . Maryland Heights MO 63043 **800-337-4677** 314-432-5650

Beta Theta Pi
5134 Bonham Rd PO Box 6277 . . . . Oxford OH 45056 **800-800-2382** 513-523-7591

Chi Phi Fraternity
1160 Satellite Blvd . . . . Suwanee GA 30024 **800-849-1824** 404-231-1824

Delta Chi Fraternity Inc
314 Church St . . . . Iowa City IA 52245 **888-827-9702** 319-337-4811

Delta Sigma Theta Sorority Inc
1707 New Hampshire Ave NW . . . . Washington DC 20009 **866-615-6464** 202-986-2400

Delta Tau Delta Fraternity
10000 Allisonville Rd . . . . Fishers IN 46038 **800-335-8795** 317-284-0203

Delta Theta Phi
225 Hillsborough St Ste 432 . . . . Raleigh NC 27603 **800-783-2600**

Eta Sigma Gamma
2000 University Ave . . . . Muncie IN 47306 **800-715-2559** 765-285-2258

Gamma Beta Phi Society
78 Mitchell Rd Ste A . . . . Oak Ridge TN 37830 **800-628-9920** 865-483-6212

International Fraternity of Phi Gamma Delta
1201 Red Mile Rd PO Box 4599 . . . . Lexington KY 40544 **888-668-4293** 859-255-1848

Kappa Alpha Order
115 Liberty Hall Rd . . . . Lexington VA 24450 **888-922-6335** 540-463-1865

Kappa Alpha Theta Fraternity
8740 Founders Rd . . . . Indianapolis IN 46268 **800-526-1870** 317-876-1870

Kappa Delta Pi
3707 Woodview Trace . . . . Indianapolis IN 46268 **800-284-3167** 317-871-4900

Kappa Delta Sorority
3205 Players Ln . . . . Memphis TN 38125 **800-536-1897** 901-748-1897

Kappa Kappa Gamma
PO Box 38 . . . . Columbus OH 43216 **866-554-1870** 614-228-6515

Lambda Chi Alpha International Fraternity
8741 Founders Rd . . . . Indianapolis IN 46268 **800-209-6837** 317-872-8000

Mu Phi Epsilon International Music Fraternity
4705 N Sonora Ave Ste 114 . . . . Fresno CA 93722 **888-259-1471** 559-277-1898

National Alpha Lambda Delta
328 Orange St . . . . Macon GA 31201 **800-925-7421** 478-744-9595

National Fraternity of Kappa Delta Rho (KDR)
331 S Main St . . . . Greensburg PA 15601 **800-536-5371** 724-838-7100

National Kappa Kappa Iota Inc
1875 E 15th St . . . . Tulsa OK 74104 **800-678-0389** 918-744-0389

Phi Alpha Theta
National History Honor Society
4202 E Fowler Ave SOC 107 . . . . Tampa FL 33620 **800-394-8195**

Phi Delta Kappa International (PDK)
408 N Union St . . . . Bloomington IN 47407 **800-766-1156** 812-339-1156

Phi Delta Phi International Legal Fraternity
1426 21st St NW . . . . Washington DC 20036 **800-368-5606** 202-223-6801

Phi Delta Theta
2 S Campus Ave . . . . Oxford OH 45056 **888-373-9855** 513-523-6345

Phi Kappa Psi
5395 Emerson Way . . . . Indianapolis IN 46226 **800-486-1852** 317-632-1852

Phi Kappa Tau
5221 Morning Sun Rd . . . . Oxford OH 45056 **800-758-1906** 513-523-4193

Phi Mu Alpha Sinfonia Fraternity of America Inc
10600 Old State Rd . . . . Evansville IN 47711 **800-473-2649** 812-867-2433

Phi Sigma Kappa International
2925 E 96th St . . . . Indianapolis IN 46240 **888-846-6851** 317-573-5420

Phi Sigma Pi National Honor Fraternity Inc
2119 Ambassador Cir . . . . Lancaster PA 17603 **800-366-1916** 717-299-4710

Phi Theta Kappa International Honor Society
1625 Eastover Dr . . . . Jackson MS 39211 **800-946-9995** 601-984-3504

Pi Lambda Phi Fraternity Inc
60 Newtown Rd Ste 118 . . . . Danbury CT 06810 **800-395-4724** 203-740-1044

PSI Upsilon Fraternity
3003 E 96th St . . . . Indianapolis IN 46240 **800-394-1833** 317-571-1833

Sigma Alpha Epsilon Fraternity (SAE)
1856 Sheridan Rd . . . . Evanston IL 60201 **800-233-1856** 847-475-1856

Sigma Chi Fraternity
1714 Hinman Ave . . . . Evanston IL 60201 **877-829-5500** 847-869-3655

Sigma Gamma Rho Sorority Inc
1000 Southhill Dr Ste 200 . . . . Cary NC 27513 **888-747-1922** 919-678-9720

Sigma Phi Epsilon Fraternity
310 S Blvd . . . . Richmond VA 23220 **800-767-1901** 804-353-1901

Sigma Pi Fraternity
106 N Castle Heights Ave . . . . Lebanon TN 37087 **800-332-1897** 615-373-5728

Sigma Theta Tau International
550 W N St . . . . Indianapolis IN 46202 **888-634-7575** 317-634-8171

Sigma Xi Scientific Research Society
3106 E NC Hwy 54
PO Box 13975 . . . . Research Triangle Park NC 27709 **800-243-6534** 919-549-4691

Tau Beta Pi Assn
1512 Middle Dr . . . . Knoxville TN 37996 **877-829-5500** 865-546-4578

Tau Beta Sigma National Honorary Band Sorority
PO Box 849 . . . . Stillwater OK 74076 **800-543-6505*** 405-372-2333
*Cust Svc

Theta Delta Chi Inc
214 Lewis Wharf . . . . Boston MA 02110 **800-999-1847** 617-742-8886

Theta Tau Professional Engineering Fraternity
1011 San Jacinto Ste 205 . . . . Austin TX 78701 **800-264-1904** 512-472-1904

Zeta Phi Beta Sorority Inc
1734 New Hampshire Ave NW . . . . Washington DC 20009 **800-393-2503** 202-387-3103

Zeta Psi Fraternity of North America
15 S Henry St . . . . Pearl River NY 10965 **800-477-1847** 845-735-1847

47-17 Health & Health-Related Organizations

					Toll-Free	Phone

Acoustic Neuroma Assn (ANA)
600 Peachtree Pkwy Ste 108 . . . . Cumming GA 30041 **877-200-8211** 770-205-8211

Alliance for Aging Research (AAR)
750 17th St NW Ste 1100 . . . . Washington DC 20006 **866-840-6283** 202-293-2856

Alliance for Lupus Research (ALA)
28 W 44th St Ste 501 . . . . New York NY 10036 **800-867-1743** 212-218-2840

Alzheimer's Assn
225 N Michigan Ave Ste 1700 . . . . Chicago IL 60601 **800-272-3900** 312-335-8700

American Assn of Acupuncture & Oriental Medicine (AAAOM)
PO Box 162340 . . . . Sacramento CA 95816 **866-455-7999** 916-443-4770

American Assn of Drugless Practitioners (AADP)
2200 Market St Ste 803 . . . . Galveston TX 77550 **888-764-2237** 409-621-2600

American Assn of Naturopathic Physicians (AANP)
4435 Wisconsin Ave NW Ste 403 . . . . Washington DC 20016 **866-538-2267** 202-237-8150

American Assn on Intellectual & Developmental Disabilities (AAIDD)
444 N Capitol St NW Ste 846 . . . . Washington DC 20001 **800-424-3688** 202-387-1968

American Autoimmune Related Disease Assn (AARDA)
22100 Gratiot Ave . . . . Eastpointe MI 48021 **800-598-4668** 586-776-3900

American Botanical Council
6200 Manor Rd PO Box 144345 . . . . Austin TX 78723 **800-373-7105** 512-926-4900

American Brain Tumor Assn (ABTA)
2720 River Rd . . . . Des Plaines IL 60018 **800-886-2282** 847-827-9910

American Cancer Society (ACS)
250 William St NW Ste 6001 . . . . Atlanta GA 30303 **800-227-2345** 404-320-3333

American Chronic Pain Assn (ACPA)
PO Box 850 . . . . Rocklin CA 95677 **800-533-3231** 916-632-0922

American Council of the Blind (ACB)
1155 15th St NW Ste 1004 . . . . Washington DC 20005 **800-424-8666** 202-467-5081

American Council on Alcoholism (ACA)
1000 E Indian School Rd . . . . Phoenix AZ 85014 **800-527-5344**

American Council on Exercise (ACE)
4851 Paramount Dr . . . . San Diego CA 92123 **800-825-3636** 858-576-6500

American Diabetes Assn (ADA)
1701 N Beauregard St . . . . Alexandria VA 22311 **800-232-3472** 703-549-1500

American Dietetic Assn (ADA)
120 S Riverside Plz Ste 2000 . . . . Chicago IL 60606 **800-877-1600** 312-899-0040

American Epilepsy Society (AES)
342 N Main St . . . . West Hartford CT 06117 **888-233-2334** 860-586-7505

American Foundation for Suicide Prevention (AFSP)
120 Wall St 22nd Fl . . . . New York NY 10005 **888-333-2377** 212-363-3500

American Foundation for the Blind (AFB)
2 Penn Plaza . . . . New York NY 10001 **800-232-5463** 212-502-7600

American Heart Assn (AHA)
7272 Greenville Ave . . . . Dallas TX 75231 **800-242-8721** 214-373-6300

American Holistic Nurses' Assn (AHNA)
323 N San Francisco St Ste 201 . . . . Flagstaff AZ 86001 **800-278-2462** 928-526-2196

American Kidney Fund (AKF)
6110 Executive Blvd Ste 1010 . . . . Rockville MD 20852 **800-638-8299**

American Liver Foundation (ALF)
39 Broadway . . . . New York NY 10006 **800-465-4837** 212-668-1000

American Lung Assn (ALA)
14 Wall St . . . . New York NY 10005 **800-586-4872** 212-315-8700

American Massage Therapy Assn (AMTA)
500 Davis St Ste 900 . . . . Evanston IL 60201 **877-905-2700** 847-864-0123

American Naturopathic Medical Assn (ANMA)
150 S Hwy 160 Ste 8-528 . . . . Pahrump NV 89048 **888-202-4440** 702-897-7053

American Pain Society (APS)
4700 W Lake Ave . . . . Glenview IL 60025 **877-752-4754** 847-375-4715

American Parkinson Disease Assn (APDA)
135 Parkinson Ave . . . . Staten Island NY 10305 **800-223-2732** 718-981-8001

American Sleep Apnea Assn (ASAA)
6856 Eastern Ave NW #203 . . . . Washington DC 20012 **888-292-6522** 202-293-3650

American Therapeutic Recreation Assn (ATRA)
629 N Main St . . . . Hattiesburg MS 39401 **800-433-5255** 601-450-2872

American Tinnitus Assn (ATA)
522 SW Fifth Ave Ste 825 . . . . Portland OR 97204 **800-634-8978** 503-248-9985

Arc of the US
1010 Wayne Ave Ste 650 . . . . Silver Spring MD 20910 **800-433-5255** 301-565-3842

Arthritis Foundation
1330 W Peachtree St Ste 100 . . . . Atlanta GA 30309 **800-283-7800** 404-872-7100

Associated Bodywork & Massage Professionals (ABMP)
25188 Genesee Trl Rd Ste 200 . . . . Golden CO 80401 **800-458-2267** 303-674-8478

Association for Applied & Therapeutic Humor (AATH)
65 Enterprise . . . . Aliso Viejo CA 92656 **888-747-2284** 815-708-6587

Association for Research & Enlightenment (ARE)
215 67th St . . . . Virginia Beach VA 23451 **800-333-4499** 757-428-3588

Asthma & Allergy Foundation of America (AAFA)
8201 Corporate Dr Ste 1000 . . . . Landover MD 20785 **800-727-8462** 202-466-7643

Autism Society of America (ASA)
7910 Woodmont Ave Ste 300 . . . . Bethesda MD 20814 **800-328-8476** 301-657-0881

BEGINNINGS for Parents of Children Who Are Deaf or Hard of Hearing Inc
302 Jefferson St Ste 110 . . . . Raleigh NC 27605 **800-541-4327** 919-715-4092

Better Vision Institute, The (BVI)
Vision Council, The
225 Reinekers Ln Ste 700 . . . . Alexandria VA 22314 **800-372-3937** 703-548-4560

Brain Injury Assn of America
1608 Spring Hill Rd Ste 110 . . . . Vienna VA 22182 **800-444-6443** 703-761-0750

Cancer Care Inc
275 Seventh Ave 22nd Fl . . . . New York NY 10001 **800-813-4673** 212-712-8400

Candlelighters Childhood Cancer Foundation
10920 Connecticut Ave Suuite A
PO Box 498 . . . . Kensington MD 20895 **800-366-2223** 301-962-3520

Canine Companions for Independence Inc (CCI)
2965 Dutton Ave PO Box 446 . . . . Santa Rosa CA 95402 **800-572-2275** 707-577-1700

Carcinoid Cancer Foundation Inc
333 Mamaroneck Ave Ste 492 . . . . White Plains NY 10605 **888-722-3132** 212-722-3132

Center for Practical Bioethics
1111 Main St Ste 500 . . . . Kansas City MO 64105 **800-344-3829** 816-221-1100

Children & Adults with Attention-Deficit/Hyperactivity Disorder (CHADD)
8181 Professional Pl Ste 150 . . . . Landover MD 20785 **800-233-4050** 301-306-7070

Children's Organ Transplant Assn (COTA)
2501 W Cota Dr . . . . Bloomington IN 47403 **800-366-2682** 812-336-8872

Children's Tumor Foundation
95 Pine St 16th Fl . . . . New York NY 10005 **800-323-7938** 212-344-6633

Children's Wish Foundation International
8615 Roswell Rd . . . . Atlanta GA 30350 **800-323-9474** 770-393-9474

Christopher Reeve Foundation
636 Morris Tpke Ste 3A . . . . Short Hills NJ 07078 **800-225-0292** 973-379-2690

Cleft Palate Foundation (CPF)
1504 E Franklin St Ste 102 . . . . Chapel Hill NC 27514 **800-242-5338** 919-933-9044

Compassion & Choices
PO Box 101810 . . . . Denver CO 80250 **800-247-7421** 303-639-1202

			Toll-Free	Phone

Cornelia de Lange Syndrome Foundation Inc (CdLS)
302 W Main St Ste 100...................Avon CT 06001 **800-753-2357** 860-676-8166

Creutzfeldt-Jakob Disease Foundation Inc
341 W 38th St Ste 501............New York NY 10018 **800-659-1991** 212-719-5900

Crohn's & Colitis Foundation of America (CCFA)
386 Pk Ave S 17th Fl.............New York NY 10016 **800-932-2423** 212-685-3440

Cystic Fibrosis Foundation
6931 Arlington Rd Ste 200..........Bethesda MD 20814 **800-344-4823** 301-951-4422

Dental Lifeline Network
1800 15th St Unit 100................Denver CO 80202 **888-471-6334** 303-534-5360

Depression & Bipolar Support Alliance (DBSA)
730 N Franklin St Ste 501.............Chicago IL 60610 **800-826-3632** 312-642-0049

Disability Rights Ctr Inc
18 Low Ave.......................Concord NH 03301 **800-834-1721** 603-228-0432

Disabled & Alone/Life Services for the Handicapped
1440 Broadway 23rd Floor..........New York NY 10018 **800-995-0066** 212-532-6740

Dystonia Medical Research Foundation
One E Wacker Dr Ste 2810............Chicago IL 60601 **800-377-3978*** 312-755-0198
*General

Easter Seals
230 W Monroe St Ste 1800............Chicago IL 60606 **800-221-6827** 312-726-6200

ECRI Institute
5200 Butler Pike............Plymouth Meeting PA 19462 **866-247-3004** 610-825-6000

El Paso First Health Plans Inc
1145 Westmoreland Dr................El Paso TX 79925 **877-532-3778** 915-532-3778

Elizabeth Glaser Pediatric AIDS Foundation
1140 Connecticut Ave NW Ste 200...Washington DC 20036 **888-499-4673** 202-296-9165

Endometriosis Assn
8585 N 76th Pl...................Milwaukee WI 53223 **800-992-3636** 414-355-2200

EngenderHealth
440 Ninth Ave 13th Fl.............New York NY 10001 **800-564-2872** 212-561-8000

Epilepsy Foundation
8301 Professional Pl E............Landover MD 20785 **800-332-1000** 301-459-3700

FaithTrust Institute
2400 N 45th St Ste 101..............Seattle WA 98103 **877-860-2255** 206-634-1903

Family Caregiver Alliance (FCA)
180 Montgomery St Ste 900.......San Francisco CA 94104 **800-445-8106** 415-434-3388

Family of the Americas Foundation
PO Box 1170....................Dunkirk MD 20754 **800-443-3395** 301-627-3346

Feingold Assn of the US
37 Shell Rd Second Fl............Rocky Point NY 11778 **800-321-3287** 631-369-9340

First Candle
1314 Bedford Ave Ste 210.........Baltimore MD 21208 **800-221-7437** 410-653-8226

Food Allergy & Anaphylaxis Network (FAAN)
11781 Lee Jackson Hwy Ste 160........Fairfax VA 22033 **800-929-4040** 703-691-3179

Foundation Fighting Blindness
11435 Cron Hill Dr..............Owings Mills MD 21117 **800-683-5555** 410-568-0150

Gay Men's Health Crisis (GMHC)
119 W 24th St...................New York NY 10011 **800-243-7692** 212-367-1000

Gift of Life Bone Marrow Foundation
800 Yamato Rd Ste 101............Boca Raton FL 33431 **800-962-7769** 561-982-2900

Glaucoma Research Foundation
251 Post St Ste 600............San Francisco CA 94108 **800-826-6693** 415-986-3162

Guide Dog Foundation for the Blind Inc
371 E Jericho Tkpe...............Smithtown NY 11787 **800-548-4337**

Guide Dogs for the Blind
350 Los Ranchitos Rd.............San Rafael CA 94903 **800-295-4050** 415-499-4000

Guide Dogs of America
13445 Glenoaks Blvd..................Sylmar CA 91342 **800-459-4843** 818-362-5834

Health Physics Society
1313 Dolley Madison Blvd Ste 402.......McLean VA 22101 **888-624-8373** 703-790-1745

Hearing Loss Assn of America
7910 Woodmont Ave Ste 1200........Bethesda MD 20814 **800-221-6827** 301-657-2248

Hepatitis Foundation International (HFI)
504 Blick Dr................Silver Spring MD 20904 **800-891-0707** 301-622-4200

Herb Research Foundation (HRF)
4140 15th St.....................Boulder CO 80304 **800-748-2617** 303-449-2265

Hospice Education Institute
Three Unity Sq PO Box 98.........Machiasport ME 04655 **800-331-1620** 207-255-8800

Human Factors & Ergonomics Society (HFES)
1124 Montana Ave Ste B
PO Box 1369...................Santa Monica CA 90406 **800-233-1234** 310-394-1811

Human Growth Foundation
997 Glen Cove Ave Ste 5...........Glen Head NY 11545 **800-451-6434** 516-671-4041

Huntington's Disease Society of America (HDSA)
505 Eigth Ave Ste 902............New York NY 10018 **800-345-4372** 212-242-1968

Hysterectomy Educational Resources & Services Foundation (HERS)
422 Bryn Mawr Ave............Bala Cynwyd PA 19004 **888-750-4377** 610-667-7757

Immune Deficiency Foundation (IDF)
40 W Chesapeake Ave Ste 308.........Towson MD 21204 **800-296-4433** 410-321-6647

International Assn for the Study of Pain (IASP)
111 Queen Anne Ave N Ste 501........Seattle WA 98109 **866-574-2654** 206-283-0311

International Dyslexia Assn, The (IDA)
40 York Rd Fourth Fl.................Towson MD 21204 **800-222-3123** 410-296-0232

International Hearing Society (IHS)
16880 Middlebelt Rd Ste 4............Livonia MI 48154 **800-521-5247** 734-522-7200

Juvenile Diabetes Research Foundation International (JDRF)
120 Wall St.....................New York NY 10005 **800-533-2873** 212-785-9500

Kristin Brooks Hope Ctr (KBHC)
1250 24th St NW...............Washington DC 20037 **800-784-2433** 202-536-3200

La Leche League International Inc (LLLI)
957 N Plum Grove Rd.............Schaumburg IL 60173 **800-525-3243** 847-519-7730

Lamaze International
2025 M St NW Ste 800...........Washington DC 20036 **800-368-4404** 202-367-1128

Laurent Clerc National Deaf Education Ctr
800 Florida Ave NE.............Washington DC 20002 **866-637-0102** 202-651-5050

Learning Disabilities Assn of America (LDA)
4156 Library Rd................Pittsburgh PA 15234 **888-300-6710** 412-341-1515

Lifespire
350 Fifth Ave Ste 301.............New York NY 10118 **800-221-5594** 212-741-0100

Light for Life Foundation International
PO Box 644...................Westminster CO 80036 **800-273-8255** 303-429-3530

Lighthouse International
111 E 59th St...................New York NY 10022 **800-829-0500** 212-821-9200

Living Bank PO Box 6725................Houston TX 77027 **800-528-2971** 713-961-9431

Lupus Foundation of America Inc (LFA)
2000 L St NW Ste 410...........Washington DC 20036 **800-558-0121** 202-349-1155

Lymphoma Research Foundation (LRF)
115 Broadway Ste 1301............New York NY 10006 **800-500-9976** 212-349-2910

Macula Foundation Inc
210 E 64th St 8th Fl..............New York NY 10065 **800-622-8524** 212-605-3777

Male Survivor
5505 Connecticut Ave NW PO Box 103....Washington DC 20015 **800-738-4181**

MedicAlert Foundation International
2323 Colorado Ave.................Turlock CA 95382 **800-432-5378*** 209-668-3333
*Cust Svc

Medicare Rights Ctr (MRC)
520 Eigth Ave N Wing Third Fl.......New York NY 10018 **800-333-4114*** 212-869-3850
*Hotline

Mended Hearts Inc, The
8150 N Central Expy M2075.............Dallas TX 75206 **888-432-7899** 214-296-9252

Mental Health America (MHA)
2000 N Beauregard St Sixth Fl......Alexandria VA 22311 **800-969-6642*** 703-684-7722
*Help Line

Multiple Sclerosis Foundation (MSF)
6350 N Andrews Ave.........Fort Lauderdale FL 33309 **800-225-6495** 954-776-6805

Muscular Dystrophy Assn (MDA)
3300 E Sunrise Dr..................Tucson AZ 85718 **800-572-1717** 520-529-2000

NA of People with AIDS (NAPWA)
8401 Colesville Rd Ste 505.........Silver Spring MD 20910 **866-846-9366** 240-247-0880

Narcolepsy Network Inc
129 Waterwheel Ln...........North Kingstown RI 02852 **888-292-6522** 401-667-2523

National Alliance on Mental Illness (NAMI)
3803 N Fairfax Dr Ste 100...........Arlington VA 22203 **800-950-6264** 703-524-7600

National Breast Cancer Coalition (NBCC)
1101 17th St NW Ste 1300........Washington DC 20036 **800-622-2838** 202-296-7477

National Cancer Registrars Assn (NCRA)
1340 Braddock Pl Ste 203.........Alexandria VA 22314 **800-621-4111** 703-299-6640

National Coalition for Cancer Survivorship (NCCS)
1010 Wayne Ave Ste 315..........Silver Spring MD 20910 **877-622-7937**

National Committee for Quality Assurance (NCQA)
1100 13th St...................Washington DC 20005 **888-275-7585** 202-955-3500

National Council on Alcoholism & Drug Dependence Inc (NCADD)
217 Broadway Ste 712............New York NY 10007 **800-622-2255** 212-269-7797

National Dissemination Ctr for Children with Disabilities
1825 Connecticut Ave............Washington DC 20009 **800-695-0285** 202-884-8200

National Down Syndrome Congress (NDSC)
1370 Ctr Dr Ste 102................Atlanta GA 30338 **800-232-6372** 770-604-9500

National Down Syndrome Society (NDSS)
666 Broadway 8th Fl..............New York NY 10012 **800-221-4602**

National Eating Disorders Assn
603 Stewart St Ste 803.............Seattle WA 98101 **800-931-2237**

National Federation of the Blind (NFB)
1800 Johnson St................Baltimore MD 21230 **800-392-5671** 410-659-9314

National Fibromyalgia Partnership Inc (NFP)
140 Zinn Way....................Linden VA 22642 **866-725-4404**

National Fire Protection Assn (NFPA)
One Batterymarch Pk................Quincy MA 02169 **800-344-3555** 617-770-3000

National Gaucher Foundation (NGF)
2227 Idlewood Rd Ste 6.............Tucker GA 30084 **800-504-3189** 770-934-2910

National Headache Foundation (NHF)
820 N Orleans St Ste 217.............Chicago IL 60610 **888-643-5552**

National Hearing Conservation Assn (NHCA)
3030 W 81st Ave................Westminster CO 80031 **800-445-8667** 303-224-9022

National Hemophilia Foundation (NHF)
116 W 32nd St 11th Fl............New York NY 10001 **800-424-2634** 212-328-3700

National Herpes Resource Ctr (HRC)
PO Box 13827............Research Triangle Park NC 27709 **877-478-5868** 919-361-8400

National Industries for the Blind (NIB)
1310 Braddock Pl...............Alexandria VA 22314 **800-433-2304*** 703-310-0500
*Cust Svc

National Inhalant Prevention Coalition (NIPC)
318 Lindsay St................Chattanooga TN 37403 **800-269-4237** 423-265-4662

National Kidney Foundation (NKF)
30 E 33rd St Eighth Fl.............New York NY 10016 **800-622-9010** 212-889-2210

National Marfan Foundation (NMF)
22 Manhasset Ave............Port Washington NY 11050 **800-862-7326** 516-883-8712

National Marrow Donor Program (NMDP)
3001 Broadway St NE Ste 100.......Minneapolis MN 55413 **800-526-7809** 612-627-5800

National Multiple Sclerosis Society
733 Third Ave Third Fl.............New York NY 10017 **800-344-4867** 212-986-3240

National Niemann-Pick Disease Foundation Inc (NNPDF)
401 Madison Ave Ste B PO Box 49.....Fort Atkinson WI 53538 **877-287-3672** 920-563-0930

National Oral Health Information Clearinghouse (NIDCR)
One NOHIC Way.................Bethesda MD 20892 **866-232-4528** 301-496-4261

National Organization for Albinism & Hypopigmentation (NOAH)
PO Box 959..............East Hampstead NH 03826 **800-648-2310** 603-887-2310

National Organization for Rare Disorders (NORD)
55 Kenosia Ave PO Box 1968...........Danbury CT 06813 **800-999-6673** 203-744-0100

National Organization of Circumcision Information Resource Centers (NOCIRC)
PO Box 2512.................San Anselmo CA 94979 **800-727-8622** 415-488-9883

National Osteoporosis Foundation (NOF)
1232 22nd St NW..............Washington DC 20037 **800-231-4222** 202-223-2226

National Ovarian Cancer Coalition (NOCC)
2501 Oak Lawn Ave Ste 435............Dallas TX 75219 **888-682-7426**

National Pesticide Information Ctr (NPIC)
333 Weniger Hall................Corvallis OR 97331 **800-858-7378**

National Psoriasis Foundation (NPF)
6600 SW 92nd Ave Ste 300..........Portland OR 97223 **800-723-9166** 503-244-7404

National Rehabilitation Assn (NRA)
633 S Washington St............Alexandria VA 22314 **888-258-4295** 703-836-0850

National Rehabilitation Information Ctr (NARIC)
8201 Corporate Dr Ste 600..........Landover MD 20785 **800-346-2742** 301-459-5900

National Reye's Syndrome Foundation (NRSF)
426 N Lewis St...................Bryan OH 43506 **800-233-7393** 419-924-9000

National Rosacea Society
800 S NW Hwy Ste 200..........Barrington IL 60010 **888-662-5874** 847-382-8971

National Safety Council (NSC)
1121 Spring Lk Dr.................Itasca IL 60143 **800-621-7615** 630-285-1121

National Spinal Cord Injury Assn (NSCIA)
75-20 Astoria Blvd Ste 120.......East Elmhurst NY 11370 **800-962-9629** 718-512-0010

National Stroke Assn (NSA)
9707 E Easter Ln................Centennial CO 80112 **800-787-6537***
*Cust Svc

	Toll-Free	Phone
National Stuttering Assn (NSA)		
119 W 40th St 14th Fl .... New York NY 10018	800-937-8888	212-944-4050
National Tay-Sachs & Allied Diseases Assn (NTSAD)		
2001 Beacon St Ste 204 .... Brighton MA 02135	800-906-8723	617-277-4463
National Wellness Institute (NWI)		
1300 College Ct PO Box 827 .... Stevens Point WI 54481	877-800-2729	715-342-2969
New West Health Services		
130 Neill Ave .... Helena MT 59601	888-500-3355	406-457-2200
Oley Foundation		
214 Hun Memorial MC-28		
Albany Medical Ctr .... Albany NY 12208	800-776-6539	518-262-5079
Oral Health America		
410 N Michigan Ave Ste 352 .... Chicago IL 60611	800-523-3438	312-836-9900
Parkinson's Disease Foundation (PDF)		
1359 Broadway .... New York NY 10018	800-457-6676	212-923-4700
Partnership for a Drug-Free America		
405 Lexington Ave Ste 1601 .... New York NY 10174	855-378-4373	212-922-1560
Pedorthic Footwear Assn (PFA)		
2025 M St NW Ste 800 .... Washington DC 20036	800-673-8447	202-367-1145
Phoenix Society for Burn Survivors Inc		
1835 RW Berends Dr SW .... Grand Rapids MI 49519	800-888-2876	616-458-2773
Postpartum Support International		
2200 Pacific Coast Hwy Ste 304A....... Hermosa Beach CA 90254	800-944-4773	
Prader-Willi Syndrome Assn (USA)		
8588 Potter Pk Dr Ste 500 .... Sarasota FL 34238	800-926-4797	941-312-0400
Prevent Blindness America		
211 W Wacker Dr Ste 1700 .... Chicago IL 60606	800-331-2020	
Prevent Cancer Foundation (PCF)		
1600 Duke St Ste 500 .... Alexandria VA 22314	800-227-2732	703-836-4412
Project Inform		
273 Ninth St .... San Francisco CA 94103	877-435-7443	415-558-8669
Public Health Institute		
555 12th St 10th Fl .... Oakland CA 94607	866-632-9992	510-285-5500
Recording for the Blind & Dyslexic (RFB&D)		
20 Roszel Rd .... Princeton NJ 08540	800-221-4792	
Research to Prevent Blindness Inc (RPB)		
645 Madison Ave 21st Fl .... New York NY 10022	800-621-0026	212-752-4333
RESOLVE: National Infertility Assn		
1760 Old Meadow Rd Ste 500 .... McLean VA 22102	888-592-4449	703-556-7172
Restless Legs Syndrome Foundation Inc		
1610 14th St NW Ste 300 .... Rochester MN 55901	877-463-6757	507-287-6465
Rocky Mountain Health Foundation		
2775 Crossroads Blvd .... Grand Junction CO 81506	800-843-0719	970-248-5027
Rolf Institute of Structural Integration		
5055 Chaparral Ct Ste 103 .... Boulder CO 80301	800-530-8875	303-449-5903
RP International		
PO Box 900 .... Woodland Hills CA 91365	877-999-8322	818-992-0500
Scleroderma Foundation		
300 Rosewood Dr Ste 105 .... Danvers MA 01923	800-722-4673	978-463-5843
Sickle Cell Disease Assn of America (SCDAA)		
3700 Koppers St Ste 570 .... Baltimore MD 21202	800-421-8453	410-528-1555
Spina Bifida Assn (SBAA)		
4590 MacArthur Blvd NW Ste 250 .... Washington DC 20007	866-546-8372	202-944-3285
Stuttering Foundation of America		
3100 Walnut Grove Rd Ste 603...... Memphis TN 38111	800-992-9392	901-452-7343
Susan G Komen for the Cure		
5005 LBJ Fwy Ste 250 .... Dallas TX 75244	800-227-2345	972-855-1600
TOPS Club Inc		
4575 S Fifth St .... Milwaukee WI 53207	800-932-8677	414-482-4620
Tourette Syndrome Assn Inc		
42-40 Bell Blvd Ste 205 .... Bayside NY 11361	888-486-8738	718-224-2999
UCare Minnesota		
500 Stinson Blvd NE PO Box 52 ..... Minneapolis MN 55413	866-457-7144	612-676-6500
Undersea & Hyperbaric Medical Society (UHMS)		
21 W Colony Pl Ste 280 .... Durham NC 27705	877-533-8467	919-490-5140
United Network for Organ Sharing (UNOS)		
700 N Fourth St .... Richmond VA 23219	888-894-6361	804-782-4800
Well Spouse Assn		
63 W Main St Ste H .... Freehold NJ 07728	800-838-0879	732-577-8899
Women Alive		
1566 Burnside Ave .... Los Angeles CA 90019	800-554-4876	323-965-1564

47-18 Hobby Organizations

	Toll-Free	Phone
Academy of Model Aeronautics (AMA)		
5161 E Memorial Dr .... Muncie IN 47302	800-435-9262	765-287-1256
American Contract Bridge League (ACBL)		
6575 Windchase Blvd .... Horn Lake MS 38637	800-264-2743*	662-253-3100
*Sales		
American Craft Council		
72 Spring St Sixth Fl .... New York NY 10012	800-836-3470	212-274-0630
American Federation of Astrologers (AFA)		
6535 S Rural Rd .... Tempe AZ 85283	888-301-7630	480-838-1751
American Horticultural Society (AHS)		
7931 E Blvd Dr .... Alexandria VA 22308	800-777-7931	703-768-5700
American Radio Relay League (ARRL)		
225 Main St .... Newington CT 06111	888-277-5289	860-594-0200
American Rose Society (ARS)		
8877 Jefferson Paige Rd .... Shreveport LA 71119	800-637-6534	318-938-5402
Barbershop Harmony Society		
110 Seventh Ave N .... Nashville TN 37203	800-876-7464	615-823-3993
Craft & Hobby Assn (CHA)		
319 E 54th St .... Elmwood Park NJ 07407	800-822-0494	201-835-1200
Experimental Aircraft Assn (EAA)		
3000 Poberezny Rd .... Oshkosh WI 54902	800-236-4800	920-426-4800
National Garden Clubs Inc (NGC)		
4401 Magnolia Ave .... Saint Louis MO 63110	800-550-6007	314-776-7574
National Gardening Assn (NGA)		
1100 Dorset St .... South Burlington VT 05403	800-538-7476	802-863-5251
National Genealogical Society (NGS)		
3108 Columbia Pk Ste 300........... Arlington VA 22204	800-473-0060	703-525-0050
National Model Railroad Assn (NMRA)		
4121 Cromwell Rd .... Chattanooga TN 37421	800-654-2256	423-892-2846
National NeedleArts Assn, The (TNNA)		
1100-H Brandywine Blvd .... Zanesville OH 43701	800-889-8662	740-455-6773

	Toll-Free	Phone
Sports Car Club of America (SCCA)		
6700 SW Topeka Blvd Ste 300 .... Topeka KS 66619	800-770-2055	785-357-7222
Sweet Adelines International		
9110 S Toledo Ave .... Tulsa OK 74137	800-992-7464	918-622-1444
US Chess Federation (USCF)		
PO Box 3967 .... Crossville TN 38557	800-903-8723	931-787-1234

47-19 Military, Veterans, Patriotic Organizations

	Toll-Free	Phone
Air Force Assn (AFA)		
1501 Lee Hwy Fourth Fl .... Arlington VA 22209	800-727-3337	703-247-5800
American Legion, The		
700 N Pennsylvania St .... Indianapolis IN 46204	800-433-3318*	317-630-1200
*Cust Svc		
American Logistics Assn (ALA)		
1133 15th St NW Ste 640........... Washington DC 20005	800-791-7146	202-466-2520
American Society of Military Comptrollers (ASMC)		
415 N Alfred St .... Alexandria VA 22314	800-462-5637	703-549-0360
AMVETS 4647 Forbes Blvd .... Lanham MD 20706	877-726-8387	301-459-9600
Armed Forces Communications & Electronics Assn (AFCEA)		
4400 Fair Lakes Ct .... Fairfax VA 22033	800-336-4583	703-631-6100
Armed Services Mutual Benefit Assn (ASMBA)		
PO Box 160384 .... Nashville TN 37216	800-251-8434	615-851-0800
Army Distaff Foundation		
6200 Oregon Ave NW .... Washington DC 20015	800-541-4255	202-541-0149
Association of Old Crows (AOC)		
1000 N Payne St Ste 300 .... Alexandria VA 22314	800-247-5626	703-549-1600
Association of the US Army (AUSA)		
2425 Wilson Blvd .... Arlington VA 22201	800-336-4570	703-841-4300
Disabled American Veterans (DAV)		
3725 Alexandria Pike .... Cold Spring KY 41076	877-426-2838	859-441-7300
Enlisted Assn of the National Guard of the US (EANGUS)		
3133 Mt Vernon Ave .... Alexandria VA 22305	800-234-3264	703-519-3846
Fleet Reserve Assn (FRA)		
125 NW St .... Alexandria VA 22314	800-372-1924	703-683-1400
Marine Corps Assn (MCA)		
PO Box 1775 .... Quantico VA 22134	800-336-0291	703-640-6161
Military Benefit Assn (MBA)		
14605 Avion Pkwy PO Box 221110 ..... Chantilly VA 20153	800-336-0100	703-968-6200
Military Officers Assn of America (MOAA)		
201 N Washington St .... Alexandria VA 22314	800-234-6622	703-549-2311
NA for Uniformed Services (NAUS)		
5535 Hempstead Way .... Springfield VA 22151	800-842-3451	703-750-1342
National Committee for Employer Support of the Guard & Reserve (ESGR)		
1555 Wilson Blvd Ste 319 .... Arlington VA 22209	800-336-4590	703-696-1386
National Fallen Firefighters Foundation		
PO Box 498 .... Emmitsburg MD 21727	888-744-6513	301-447-1365
National Guard Assn of the US (NGAUS)		
One Massachusetts Ave NW Ste 200 ... Washington DC 20001	888-226-4287	202-789-0031
Naval Enlisted Reserve Assn (NERA)		
6703 Farragut Ave .... Falls Church VA 22042	800-776-9020	703-534-1329
Navy League of the US		
2300 Wilson Blvd .... Arlington VA 22201	800-356-5760	703-528-1775
Navy-Marine Corps Relief Society (NMCRS)		
875 N Randolph St Ste 225 .... Arlington VA 22203	800-654-8364	703-696-4904
Non Commissioned Officers Assn (NCOA)		
9330 Corporate Dr Ste 701........... Selma TX 78154	800-662-2620	210-653-6161
Reserve Officers Assn of the US (ROA)		
One Constitution Ave NE .... Washington DC 20002	800-809-9448	202-479-2200
Society of American Military Engineers (SAME)		
607 Prince St .... Alexandria VA 22314	800-336-3097	703-549-3800
Tailhook Assn		
9696 Businesspark Ave .... San Diego CA 92131	800-322-4665	858-689-9223
US Naval Institute		
291 Wood Rd .... Annapolis MD 21402	800-233-8764	410-268-6110
Veterans for Peace Inc (VFP)		
216 S Meramec Ave .... Saint Louis MO 63105	877-429-0678	314-725-6005
Veterans of Foreign Wars of the US (VFW)		
406 W 34th St .... Kansas City MO 64111	800-963-3180	816-756-3390
Women in Military Service for America Memorial Foundation Inc		
Dept 560 .... Washington DC 20042	800-222-2294	703-533-1155

47-20 Religious Organizations

	Toll-Free	Phone
American Academy of Religion (AAR)		
825 Houston Mill Rd NE Ste 300 .... Atlanta GA 30329	800-282-6632	404-727-3049
American Baptist Assn (ABA)		
4605 N State Line Ave .... Texarkana TX 75503	800-264-2482	903-792-2783
American Baptist Churches USA		
PO Box 851 .... Valley Forge PA 19482	800-222-3872	610-768-2000
American Theological Library Assn (ATLA)		
300 S Wacker Dr Ste 2100 .... Chicago IL 60606	888-665-2852	312-454-5100
Antiochian Orthodox Christian Archdiocese of North America		
358 Mountain Rd .... Englewood NJ 07631	888-421-1442	201-871-1355
Archdiocese of Portland in Oregon		
2838 E Burnside St .... Portland OR 97214	800-235-8722	503-234-5334
Archdiocese of Saint Paul & Minneapolis		
226 Summit Ave .... Saint Paul MN 55102	877-290-1605	651-291-4411
Assemblies of God (A/G)		
1445 N Boonville Ave .... Springfield MO 65802	800-641-4310	417-862-2781
Avant Ministries		
10000 N Oak Trafficway .... Kansas City MO 64155	800-468-1892	816-734-8500
B'nai B'rith International		
2020 K St NW Seventh Fl .... Washington DC 20006	888-388-4224	202-857-6600
Baptist World Alliance		
405 N Washington St .... Falls Church VA 22046	866-291-7809	703-790-8980
Benny Hinn Ministries		
PO Box 162000 .... Irving TX 75016	800-433-1900	817-722-2000
Bible League PO Box 28000 .... Chicago IL 60628	866-825-4636	817-595-1664
Billy Graham Evangelistic Assn		
One Billy Graham Pkwy PO Box 1270 ..... Charlotte NC 28201	877-247-2426	704-401-2432
California Southern Baptist Convention		
678 E Shaw Ave .... Fresno CA 93710	888-462-7729	559-229-9533

			Toll-Free	Phone

Campus Crusade for Christ International
100 Lk Hart Dr .... Orlando FL 32832 **888-278-7233** 407-826-2500
Catholic Church Extension Society of the USA
150 S Wacker Dr 20th Fl .... Chicago IL 60606 **800-842-7804**
Catholic Supply of st Louis Inc
6759 Chippewa St .... Saint Louis MO 63109 **800-325-9026** 314-644-0643
Child Evangelism Fellowship Inc
17482 Hwy M .... Warrenton MO 63383 **800-748-7710** 636-456-4321
Christ in Youth Inc PO Box B .... Joplin MO 64801 **800-693-9653** 417-781-2273
Christian & Missionary Alliance
8595 Explorer Dr .... Colorado Springs CO 80920 **800-700-2651** 719-599-5999
Christian Reformed Church in North America (CRC)
2850 Kalamazoo Ave SE .... Grand Rapids MI 49560 **800-272-5125** 616-241-1691
Christophers, The
Five Hanover Sq 11th Fl .... New York NY 10004 **888-298-4050** 212-759-4050
Church of God in Christ Inc
930 Mason St .... Memphis TN 38126 **877-746-8578** 901-947-9300
Church of God Ministries
1201 E Fifth St .... Anderson IN 46012 **800-848-2464** 765-642-0256
Church of God World Missions (COGWM)
2490 Keith St PO Box 8016 .... Cleveland TN 37320 **800-345-7492** 423-478-7190
Church of the Brethren
1451 Dundee Ave .... Elgin IL 60120 **800-323-8039** 847-742-5100
Church Women United (CWU)
475 Riverside Dr Ste 243 .... New York NY 10115 **800-298-5551** 212-870-2347
Community of Christ
1001 W Walnut St .... Independence MO 64050 **800-825-2806** 816-833-1000
Connecting Businessmen to Christ (CBMC)
5746 Marlin Rd
Ste 602 Osborne Ctr .... Chattanooga TN 37411 **800-566-2262** 423-698-4444
Diocese of Greensburg
723 E Pittsburgh St .... Greensburg PA 15601 **866-409-6455** 724-837-0901
Diocese of St. Augustine Inc
11625 Old St Augustine .... Jacksonville FL 32258 **800-775-4659** 904-262-3200
Episcopal Church USA
815 Second Ave .... New York NY 10017 **800-334-7626** 212-716-6000
Evangelical Church Alliance (ECA)
205 W Broadway St PO Box 9 .... Bradley IL 60915 **888-855-6060** 815-937-0720
Evangelical Fellowship of Canada (EFC)
600 Alden Rd Ste 300 Markham Industrial Pk
.... Markham ON L3R0E7 **866-302-3362** 905-479-5885
Evangelical Lutheran Church in America (ELCA)
8765 W Higgins Rd .... Chicago IL 60631 **800-638-3522** 773-380-2700
Evangelical Training Assn (ETA)
PO Box 327 .... Wheaton IL 60187 **800-369-8291*** 630-384-6920
  *General
First Church of Christ Scientist
210 Massachusetts Ave P05-10 .... Boston MA 02115 **800-288-7155** 617-450-2000
Franciscan Sisters of Chicago Inc
1055 175th St Ste 202 .... Homewood IL 60430 **800-524-6126** 708-647-6500
General Assn of Regular Baptist Churches (GARBC)
1300 N Meacham Rd .... Schaumburg IL 60173 **888-588-1600** 847-585-0816
Greater Atlanta Christian
1575 Indian Trl Lilburn Rd .... Norcross GA 30093 **800-450-1327** 770-243-2000
Henderson Hills Baptist Church
1200 E I 35 Frontage Rd .... Edmond OK 73034 **877-901-4639** 405-341-4639
Holy Cross Family Ministries
518 Washington St .... North Easton MA 02356 **800-299-7729** 508-238-4095
IFCA International
3520 Fairlane Ave SW .... Grandville MI 49418 **800-347-1840** 616-531-1840
International Bible Society (IBS)
  Biblica
  1820 Jet Stream Dr .... Colorado Springs CO 80921 **800-524-1588*** 719-488-9200
  *Cust Svc
International Church of the Foursquare Gospel (ICFG)
1910 W Sunset Blvd PO Box 26902 .... Los Angeles CA 90026 **888-635-4234** 213-989-4234
Interserve USA
7000 Ludlow St .... Upper Darby PA 19082 **800-809-4440** 610-352-0581
InterVarsity Christian Fellowship/USA
6400 Schroeder Rd .... Madison WI 53711 **866-734-4823** 608-274-9001
Jewish National Fund (JNF)
42 E 69th St .... New York NY 10021 **800-542-8733** 212-879-9300
Jewish Reconstructionist Federation (JRF)
101 Greenwood Ave .... Jenkintown PA 19046 **877-226-7573** 215-885-5601
Jewish United Fund/Jewish Federation of Metropolitan Chicago (JUF)
30 S Wells St .... Chicago IL 60606 **855-275-5237** 312-346-6700
Jews for Jesus
60 Haight St .... San Francisco CA 94102 **800-366-5521** 415-864-2600
Jimmy Swaggart Ministries (JSM)
8919 World Ministry Blvd
PO Box 262550 .... Baton Rouge LA 70810 **800-288-8350*** 225-768-8300
  *Orders
Kingsway Charities
1119 Commonwealth Ave .... Bristol VA 24201 **800-321-9234** 276-466-3014
Lutheran Church Missouri Synod (LCMS)
1333 S Kirkwood Rd .... Saint Louis MO 63122 **888-843-5267** 314-965-9000
Lutheran Home at Hollidaysburg, The
916 Hickory St .... Hollidaysburg PA 16648 **800-400-2285** 814-696-4527
Lutheran Social Services of The South Inc (LSS)
8305 Cross Pk Dr PO Box 140767 .... Austin TX 78754 **800-938-5777** 512-459-1000
Mission Aviation Fellowship (MAF)
112 N Pilatus Ln .... Nampa ID 83687 **800-359-7623** 208-498-0800
NA of Congregational Christian Churches (NACCC)
8473 S Howell Ave .... Oak Creek WI 53154 **800-262-1620** 414-764-1620
NA of Free Will Baptists (NAFWB)
5233 Mt View Rd .... Antioch TN 37013 **877-767-7659** 615-731-6812
National Baptist Convention USA Inc
1700 Baptist World Ctr Dr .... Nashville TN 37207 **866-531-3054** 615-228-6292
Navigators of Canada
11 St John'S Dr .... Arva ON N0M1C0 **866-202-6287** 519-660-8300
Navigators, The
3820 N 30th St PO Box 6000 .... Colorado Springs CO 80934 **866-568-7827** 719-598-1212
New Hampshire Catholic Charities Inc
215 Myrtle St PO Box 686 .... Manchester NH 03104 **800-562-5249** 603-669-3030
New Tribes Mission (NTM)
1000 E First St .... Sanford FL 32771 **800-321-5375** 407-323-3430
Orthodox Union (OU)
11 Broadway .... New York NY 10004 **855-505-7500** 212-563-4000

Oshkosh Convention & Visitors Bureau
2401 W Waukau Ave .... Oshkosh WI 54904 **877-303-9200** 920-303-9200
Pentecostal Assemblies
3214 S Service Rd .... Burlington ON L7N3J2 **800-295-6368** 905-637-7558
Pioneers
10123 William Carey Dr .... Orlando FL 32832 **800-359-9297** 407-382-6000
Potomac Conference Corp of Seventh Day Adventists
606 Greenville Ave .... Staunton VA 24401 **800-732-1844** 540-886-0771
Presbyterian Childrens Services Inc
1220 N Lindbergh Blvd .... St. Louis MO 63132 **800-383-8147** 314-989-9727
Presbyterian Church (USA)
100 Witherspoon St .... Louisville KY 40202 **888-728-7228** 502-569-5000
Progressive National Baptist Convention Inc (PNBC)
601 50th St NE .... Washington DC 20019 **800-876-7622** 202-396-0558
Promise Keepers (PK)
PO Box 11798 .... Denver CO 80211 **866-776-6473**
Reformed Church in America
475 Riverside Dr 18th Fl .... New York NY 10115 **800-722-9977** 212-870-3071
Seat of the Soul Foundation
PO Box 3310 .... Ashland OR 97520 **877-733-4279** 541-482-1515
Seventh-day Adventist World Church
12501 Old Columbia Pike .... Silver Spring MD 20904 **800-226-1119** 301-680-6000
Sim USA Inc PO Box 7900 .... Charlotte NC 28241 **800-521-6449**
Society of Biblical Literature (SBL)
The Luce Ctr 825 Houston Mill Rd .... Atlanta GA 30329 **866-727-9955** 404-727-3100
Tennessee Baptist Convention
5001 Maryland Way .... Brentwood TN 37027 **800-558-2090** 615-371-2029
Texas Presbyterian Foundation
3500 Oak Lawn Ave Ste 300 .... Dallas TX 75219 **800-955-3155** 214-522-3155
United Church of Christ (UCC)
700 Prospect Ave .... Cleveland OH 44115 **866-822-8224** 216-736-2100
Urban Alternative
PO Box 4000 .... Dallas TX 75208 **800-800-3222** 214-943-3868
US Conference of Catholic Bishops (USCCB)
3211 Fourth St NE .... Washington DC 20017 **866-582-0943** 202-541-3000
Wheat Ridge Ministries
One Pierce Pl Ste 250E .... Itasca IL 60143 **800-762-6748** 630-766-9066
Wider Church Ministries
700 Prospect Ave Seventh Fl .... Cleveland OH 44115 **866-822-8224** 216-736-3200
Woman's Missionary Union (WMU)
100 Missionary Ridge .... Birmingham AL 35242 **800-968-7301** 205-991-8100
World Gospel Mission (WGM)
3783 E State Rd 18 PO Box 948 .... Marion IN 46952 **800-426-0846** 765-664-7331
WorldVenture
1501 W Mineral Ave .... Littleton CO 80120 **800-487-4224** 720-283-2000
Wycliffe Bible Translators
11221 John Wycliffe Blvd .... Orlando FL 32832 **800-992-5433** 407-852-3600
Young Israel of New Rochelle
1149 N Ave .... New Rochelle NY 10804 **888-942-3638** 914-636-2215

47-21 Self-Help Organizations

			Toll-Free	Phone

Al-Anon Family Group Inc
1600 Corporate Landing Pkwy .... Virginia Beach VA 23454 **888-425-2666** 757-563-1600
Calix Society, The
3881 Highland Ave Ste 201 .... St Paul MN 55110 **800-398-0524** 651-773-3117
Candlelighters Childhood Cancer Foundation
10920 Connecticut Ave Suuite A
PO Box 498 .... Kensington MD 20895 **800-366-2223** 301-962-3520
Chemically Dependent Anonymous (CDA)
PO Box 423 .... Severna Park MD 21146 **888-232-4673**
Children of Lesbians & Gays Everywhere (COLAGE)
1550 Bryant St Ste 830 .... San Francisco CA 94103 **855-426-5243** 415-861-5437
Co-Anon Family Groups
PO Box 12722 .... Tucson AZ 85732 **800-898-9985** 520-513-5028
Cocaine Anonymous World Services Inc (CA)
3740 Overland Ave Ste C .... Los Angeles CA 90034 **800-347-8998** 310-559-5833
Compassionate Friends
PO Box 3696 .... Oak Brook IL 60522 **877-969-0010** 630-990-0010
Concerned United Birthparents Inc (CUB)
PO Box 503475 .... San Diego CA 92150 **800-822-2777**
Concerns of Police Survivors Inc (COPS)
846 Old S 5 PO Box 3199 .... Camdenton MO 65020 **800-784-2677** 573-346-4911
Crystal Meth Anonymous General Service Organization (CMA)
4470 W Sunset Blvd
Ste 107 PO Box 555 .... Los Angeles CA 90027 **877-262-6691**
Debtors Anonymous (DA)
PO Box 920888 .... Needham MA 02492 **800-421-2383** 781-453-2743
DignityUSA Inc PO Box 376 .... Medford MA 02155 **800-877-8797** 202-861-0017
Gamblers Anonymous (GA)
PO Box 17173 .... Los Angeles CA 90017 **888-424-3577** 626-960-3500
LifeRing Secular Recovery
1440 Broadway Ste 312 .... Oakland CA 94612 **800-811-4142** 510-763-0779
Marijuana Anonymous World Services (MAWS)
PO Box 7807 .... Torrance CA 90504 **800-766-6779**
MISS Foundation PO Box 5333 .... Peoria AZ 85385 **888-455-6477** 623-979-1000
Overcomers in Christ
PO Box 34460 .... Omaha NE 68134 **866-573-0966** 402-573-0966
Overcomers Outreach
PO Box 92099 .... Sylmar CA 91392 **800-310-3001** 818-833-1803
Overeaters Anonymous Inc (OA)
PO Box 44020 .... Rio Rancho NM 87174 **866-505-4966** 505-891-2664
S-Anon International Family Groups Inc
PO Box 111242 .... Nashville TN 37222 **800-210-8141** 615-833-3152
Sex Addicts Anonymous (SAA)
PO Box 70949 .... Houston TX 77270 **800-477-8191** 713-869-4902
Sexaholics Anonymous (SA)
PO Box 3565 .... Brentwood TN 37024 **866-424-8777** 615-370-6062
SHARE Pregnancy & Infant Loss Support Inc
402 Jackson St .... Saint Charles MO 63301 **800-821-6819** 636-947-6164
Sisters Network Inc
2922 Rosedale St .... Houston TX 77004 **866-781-1808** 713-781-0255
SMART Recovery
7304 Mentor Ave Ste F .... Mentor OH 44060 **866-951-5357** 440-951-5357
Survivors Network of Those Abused by Priests (SNAP)
PO Box 6416 .... Chicago IL 60680 **877-762-7432** 312-455-1499

				Toll-Free	Phone
TOPS Club Inc					
4575 S Fifth St	Milwaukee	WI	53207	**800-932-8677**	414-482-4620
Twinless Twins Support Group International (TTSG)					
PO Box 980481	Ypsilanti	MI	48198	**888-205-8962**	
Valley of the Sun United Way					
1515 E Osborn Rd	Phoenix	AZ	85014	**877-322-8228**	602-631-4800
White Bison Inc					
701 N 20th St	Colorado Springs	CO	80904	**877-871-1495**	719-548-1000
Wings Foundation (WINGS)					
7550 W Yale Ave Ste B 201	Denver	CO	80227	**800-373-8671**	303-238-8660

47-22 Sports Organizations

				Toll-Free	Phone
Adventure Cycling Assn					
150 E Pine St PO Box 8308	Missoula	MT	59807	**800-755-2453**	406-721-1776
Aerobics & Fitness Assn of America (AFAA)					
15250 Ventura Blvd Ste 200	Sherman Oaks	CA	91403	**877-968-7263**	818-905-0040
Amateur Athletic Union of the US (AAU)					
1910 Hotel Plaza Blvd	Lake Buena Vista	FL	32830	**800-228-4872**	407-934-7200
Amateur Softball Assn of America Inc (ASA)					
2801 NE 50th St	Oklahoma City	OK	73111	**800-654-8337**	405-424-5266
Amateur Trapshooting Assn (ATA)					
601 W National Rd	Vandalia	OH	45377	**800-671-8042**	937-898-4638
American Alliance for Health Physical Education Recreation & Dance (AAH-PERD)					
1900 Assn Dr	Reston	VA	20191	**800-213-7193**	703-476-3400
American Amateur Baseball Congress (AABC)					
100 W Broadway	Farmington	NM	87401	**800-853-2414**	505-327-3120
American Bicycle Assn (ABA)					
1645 W Sunrise Blvd	Gilbert	AZ	85233	**866-650-4867**	480-961-1903
American Council on Exercise (ACE)					
4851 Paramount Dr	San Diego	CA	92123	**800-825-3636**	858-576-6500
American Football Coaches Assn (AFCA)					
100 Legends Ln	Waco	TX	76706	**877-557-5338**	254-754-9900
American Running Assn					
4405 E W Hwy Ste 405	Bethesda	MD	20814	**800-776-2732**	301-913-9517
American Volkssport Assn (AVA)					
1001 Pat Booker Rd Ste 101	Universal City	TX	78148	**855-999-5200**	210-659-2112
American Youth Soccer Organization (AYSO)					
19750 S Vermont Ave Ste 200	Torrance	CA	90502	**800-872-2976**	
AMOA-National Dart Assn (NDA)					
9100 PuRdue Rd Ste 200	Indianapolis	IN	46268	**800-808-9884**	317-387-1299
Babe Ruth League Inc					
1770 Brunswick Pk PO Box 5000	Trenton	NJ	08638	**800-880-3142**	609-695-1434
Boat Owners Assn of the US					
880 S Pickett St	Alexandria	VA	22304	**800-395-2628**	703-823-9550
Cross Country Ski Areas Assn (CCSAA)					
259 Bolton Rd	Winchester	NH	03470	**877-779-2754**	603-239-4341
Disabled Sports USA (DS/USA)					
451 Hungerford Dr Ste 100.	Rockville	MD	20850	**800-543-2754**	301-217-0960
Fellowship of Christian Athletes (FCA)					
8701 Leeds Rd	Kansas City	MO	64129	**800-289-0909**	816-921-0909
Hockey North America (HNA)					
45570 Shepard Dr	Sterling	VA	20164	**800-446-2539**	703-430-8100
IDEA Inc					
10455 Pacific Ctr Ct	San Diego	CA	92121	**800-999-4332**	858-535-8979
International Assn of Approved Basketball Officials (IAABO)					
PO Box 355	Carlisle	PA	17013	**800-526-1379**	717-713-8129
International Collegiate Licensing Assn (ICLA)					
24651 Detroit Rd	Westlake	OH	44145	**877-887-2261**	440-892-4000
International Health Racquet & Sportsclub Assn (IHRSA)					
70 Fargo St	Boston	MA	02210	**800-228-4772**	617-951-0055
Jockeys' Guild Inc					
103 Wind Haven Dr Ste 200	Nicholasville	KY	40356	**866-465-6257**	859-305-0606
NA of Collegiate Directors of Athletics (NACDA)					
24651 Detroit Rd	Westlake	OH	44145	**877-887-2261**	440-892-4000
National Aeronautic Assn					
Hanger 7 1 S Smith Blvd Ste 202	Arlington	VA	22202	**800-644-9777**	703-416-4888
National Alliance for Youth Sports					
2050 Vista Pkwy	West Palm Beach	FL	33411	**800-729-2057**	561-684-1141
National Athletic Trainers Assn (NATA)					
2952 N Stemmons Fwy Ste 200	Dallas	TX	75247	**800-879-6282**	214-637-6282
National Federation of State High School Assn (NFHS)					
PO Box 690	Indianapolis	IN	46206	**800-776-3462***	317-972-6900
*Cust Svc					
National Golf Foundation (NGF)					
1150 S US Hwy 1 Ste 401	Jupiter	FL	33477	**800-733-6006**	561-744-6006
National Little Britches Rodeo Assn (NLBRA)					
5050 Edison Ave Ste 105	Colorado Springs	CO	80915	**800-763-3694**	719-389-0333
National Senior Golf Assn (NSGA)					
200 Perrine Rd Ste 201.	Old Bridge	NJ	08857	**800-282-6772**	
National Soccer Coaches Assn of America (NSCAA)					
800 Ann Ave	Kansas City	KS	66101	**800-458-0678**	913-362-1747
National Strength & Conditioning Assn (NSCA)					
1885 Bob Johnson Dr	Colorado Springs	CO	80906	**800-815-6826**	719-632-6722
National Thoroughbred Racing Assn (NTRA)					
2525 Harrodsburg Rd Ste 500	Lexington	KY	40504	**800-792-6872**	859-223-5444
National Youth Sports Coaches Assn (NYSCA)					
2050 Vista Pkwy	West Palm Beach	FL	33411	**800-729-2057**	561-684-1141
PGA of America					
100 Ave of the Champions	Palm Beach Gardens	FL	33418	**800-477-6465**	561-624-8400
PONY Baseball/Softball Inc					
1951 Pony Pl PO Box 225	Washington	PA	15301	**800-321-4473**	724-225-1060
Pop Warner Little Scholars Inc					
586 Middletown Blvd Ste C-100.	Langhorne	PA	19047	**800-257-4268**	215-752-2691
Professional Assn of Diving Instructors International (PADI)					
30151 Tomas St	Rancho Santa Margarita	CA	92688	**800-729-7234***	949-858-7234
*Sales					
Professional Bowlers Assn (PBA)					
719 Second Ave Ste 701.	Seattle	WA	98104	**877-910-2695**	206-332-9688
Professional Tennis Registry					
PO Box 4739	Hilton Head Island	SC	29938	**800-421-6289**	843-785-7244
Senior Softball USA					
2701 K St Ste 101A	Sacramento	CA	95816	**888-244-9499**	916-326-5303
Special Olympics Inc					
1133 19th St NW 11th Fl	Washington	DC	20036	**800-700-8585**	202-628-3630

				Toll-Free	Phone
Sports Turf Managers Assn (STMA)					
805 New Hampshire Ste E	Lawrence	KS	66044	**800-323-3875**	785-843-2549
US Biathlon Assn					
49 Pineland Dr Ste 301-A.	New Gloucester	ME	04260	**800-242-8456***	207-688-6500
*General					
US Bobsled & Skeleton Federation (USBSF)					
196 Old Military Rd	Lake Placid	NY	12946	**888-431-3598**	518-523-1842
US Curling Assn (USCA)					
5525 Clem's Way	Stevens Point	WI	54482	**888-287-5377**	715-344-1199
US Fencing Assn (USFA)					
1 Olympic Plaza	Colorado Springs	CO	80909	**888-431-3598**	719-866-4511
US Golf Assn (USGA)					
77 Liberty Corner Rd	Far Hills	NJ	07931	**800-336-4446***	908-234-2300
*Orders					
US Parachute Assn (USPA)					
5401 Southpoint Ctr Blvd	Fredericksburg	VA	22407	**800-765-2336**	540-604-9740
US Professional Tennis Assn (USPTA)					
3535 Briarpark Dr Ste 1	Houston	TX	77042	**800-877-8248**	713-978-7782
US Rowing Assn					
Two Wall St	Princeton	NJ	08540	**800-314-4769**	609-924-1578
US Soccer Federation					
1801 S Prairie Ave	Chicago	IL	60616	**800-745-3000**	312-808-1300
US Synchronized Swimming					
132 E Washington St Ste 800	Indianapolis	IN	46204	**800-775-8762**	317-237-5700
US Trotting Assn (USTA)					
750 Michigan Ave	Columbus	OH	43215	**877-800-8782**	614-224-2291
USA Basketball					
5465 Mark Dabling Boulevard	Colorado Springs	CO	80918	**888-284-5383**	719-590-4800
USA Gymnastics					
201 S Capitol Ave Ste 300	Indianapolis	IN	46225	**800-345-4719**	317-237-5050
USA Hockey					
1775 Bob Johnson Dr	Colorado Springs	CO	80906	**800-566-3288**	719-576-8724
USA Judo Inc					
1 Olympic Plaza Ste 505.	Colorado Springs	CO	80909	**800-775-8762**	719-866-4730
USA Swimming					
1 Olympic Plaza	Colorado Springs	CO	80909	**800-333-3333**	719-866-4578
USA Table Tennis					
1 Olympic Plaza	Colorado Springs	CO	80909	**800-775-8762**	719-866-4583
USA Track & Field (USATF)					
132 E Washington St Ste 800	Indianapolis	IN	46204	**800-365-4663**	317-261-0500
USA Water Polo					
2124 Main St Ste 210.	Huntington Beach	CA	92648	**888-712-2166**	714-500-5445
USA Water Ski					
1251 Holy Cow Rd	Polk City	FL	33868	**800-533-2972**	863-324-4341
USA Weightlifting (USAW)					
1 Olympic Plaza	Colorado Springs	CO	80909	**800-775-8762**	719-866-4508
USA Wrestling					
6155 Lehman Dr	Colorado Springs	CO	80918	**888-431-3598**	719-598-8181
Women's Sports Foundation					
1899 Hempstead Tpke Ste 400 Eisenhower Pk	East Meadow	NY	11554	**800-227-3988**	516-542-4700

47-23 Travel & Recreation Organizations

				Toll-Free	Phone
Adirondack Mountain Club					
814 Goggins Rd	Lake George	NY	12845	**800-395-8080***	518-668-4447
*Orders					
Alberta Hotel & Lodging Assn (AHLA)					
2707 Ellwood Dr	Edmonton	AB	T6X0P7	**888-436-6112**	780-436-6112
America Outdoors					
5816 Kingston Pk	Knoxville	TN	37919	**800-524-4814**	865-558-3595
American Amusement Machine Assn (AAMA)					
450 E Higgins Rd Ste 201.	Elk Grove Village	IL	60007	**866-372-5190**	847-290-9088
American Assn for Physical Activity & Recreation (AAPAR)					
1900 Assn Dr	Reston	VA	20191	**800-213-7193**	703-476-3400
American Camp Assn (ACA)					
5000 State Rd 67 N	Martinsville	IN	46151	**800-428-2267**	765-342-8456
American Park & Recreation Society (APRS)					
22377 Belmont Ridge Rd	Ashburn	VA	20148	**800-765-3110**	703-858-0784
American Society of Travel Agents (ASTA)					
1101 King St Ste 200	Alexandria	VA	22314	**800-275-2782**	703-739-2782
American Trails					
PO Box 491797	Redding	CA	96049	**866-363-7226**	530-547-2060
American Whitewater (AW)					
PO Box 1540	Cullowhee	NC	28723	**866-262-8429**	828-586-1930
Amusement & Music Operators Assn (AMOA)					
600 Spring Hill Ring Rd Ste 111.	West Dundee	IL	60118	**800-937-2662**	847-428-7699
Appalachian Mountain Club (AMC)					
Five Joy St	Boston	MA	02108	**800-262-4455***	617-523-0655
*Orders					
Appalachian Trail Conservancy (ATC)					
799 Washington St PO Box 807	Harpers Ferry	WV	25425	**888-287-8673***	304-535-6331
*Sales					
Association of Corporate Travel Executives (ACTE)					
515 King St Ste 440	Alexandria	VA	22314	**800-375-2283**	703-683-5322
Back Country Horsemen of America (BCHA)					
PO Box 1367	Graham	WA	98338	**888-893-5161**	360-832-2461
Bowling Proprietors' Assn of America (BPAA)					
621 Six Flags Dr PO Box 5802	Arlington	TX	76011	**800-343-1329**	817-649-5105
Canadian Automobile Assn (CAA)					
2151 Thurston Dr Ste 200	Ottawa	ON	K1G6C9	**800-267-8713**	613-820-1890
Colorado Dude & Guest Ranch Assn (CDGRA)					
PO Box D	Shawnee	CO	80475	**866-942-3472**	
Cruise Lines International Assn (CLIA)					
910 SE 17th St Ste 400.	Fort Lauderdale	FL	33316	**877-486-9222**	754-224-2200
Dude Ranchers' Assn					
1122 12th St PO Box 2307	Cody	WY	82414	**866-399-2339**	307-587-2339
Elderhostel Inc					
11 Ave de Lafayette	Boston	MA	02111	**800-454-5768**	
Escapees RV Club					
100 Rainbow Dr	Livingston	TX	77399	**800-231-9896**	936-327-8873
Family Motor Coach Assn (FMCA)					
8291 Clough Pk	Cincinnati	OH	45244	**800-543-3622**	513-474-3622
Global Business Travel Assn, The (GBTA)					
123 N Pitt St	Alexandria	VA	22314	**888-574-6447**	703-684-0836
Good Sam Club PO Box 6888	Englewood	CO	80155	**800-234-3450**	

				Toll-Free	Phone
Hostelling International USA - American Youth Hostels (HI-AYH)					
8401 Colesville Rd Ste 600	Silver Spring	MD	20910	800-725-2331	301-495-1240
International Airline Passengers Assn (IAPA)					
PO Box 700188	Dallas	TX	75370	800-821-4272	972-404-9980
International Assn of Fairs & Expositions, The (IAFE)					
3043 E Cairo	Springfield	MO	65802	800-516-0313	417-862-5771
International Gay & Lesbian Travel Assn (IGLTA)					
1201 NE 26th St Ste 103	Fort Lauderdale	FL	33305	866-845-4472	954-630-1637
International Mountain Bicycling Assn (IMBA)					
207 Canyon Blvd Ste 301 PO Box 7578	Boulder	CO	80306	888-442-4622	303-545-9011
Leave No Trace Ctr for Outdoor Ethics Inc					
1830 17th St	Boulder	CO	80302	800-332-4100	303-442-8222
Lewis & Clark Trail Heritage Foundation					
4201 Giant Springs Rd	Great Falls	MT	59405	888-701-3434	406-454-1234
Mountaineers, The					
7700 Sand Pt Way NE	Seattle	WA	98115	800-573-8484	206-521-6000
National Club Assn (NCA)					
1201 15th St NW Ste 450	Washington	DC	20005	800-625-6221	202-822-9822
National Forest Recreation Assn (NFRA)					
PO Box 488	Woodlake	CA	93286	800-282-2444	559-564-2365
National Golf Course Owners Assn (NGCOA)					
291 Seven Farms Dr Second Fl	Charleston	SC	29492	800-933-4262	843-881-9956
National Indian Gaming Assn (NIGA)					
224 Second St SE	Washington	DC	20003	866-694-3937	202-546-7711
National Recreation and Park Association (NSPR)					
22377 Belmont Ridge Rd					
22377 Belmont Ridge Rd	Ashburn	VA	20148	800-626-6772	703-858-0784
National Tour Assn (NTA)					
546 E Main St	Lexington	KY	40508	800-682-8886	859-226-4444
North Country Trail Assn					
229 E Main St	Lowell	MI	49331	866-445-3628	616-897-5987
Oregon-California Trails Assn					
524 S Osage St PO Box 1019	Independence	MO	64051	888-811-6282	816-252-2276
Pacific Crest Trail Assn (PCTA)					
1331 Garden Hwy	Sacramento	CA	95833	888-728-7245	916-285-1846
Relais & Chateaux Assn					
10 E 53rd St	New York	NY	10022	800-735-2478	212-319-4880
Special Military Active Retired Travel Club (SMART)					
600 University Office Blvd Ste 1A	Pensacola	FL	32504	800-354-7681	850-478-1986
Travel Institute					
148 Linden St Ste 305	Wellesley	MA	02482	800-542-4282	781-237-0280
Wilderness Inquiry (WI)					
808 14th Ave SE	Minneapolis	MN	55414	800-728-0719	612-676-9400

47-24 Women's Organizations

				Toll-Free	Phone
Equal Rights Advocates (ERA)					
1170 Market St Ste 700	San Francisco	CA	94102	800-839-4372	415-621-0672
General Federation of Women's Clubs (GFWC)					
1734 N St NW	Washington	DC	20036	800-443-4392	202-347-3168
Girls Inc					
120 Wall St Third Fl	New York	NY	10005	800-374-4475	212-509-2000
International Alliance for Women (TIAW)					
1101 Pennsylvania Ave NW Fl 6	Washington	DC	20004	888-712-5200	
National Council of Jewish Women (NCJW)					
475 Riverside Dr Ste 1901	New York	NY	10115	800-829-6259	212-645-4048
National Council of Negro Women Inc (NCNW)					
633 Pennsylvania Ave NW	Washington	DC	20004	800-462-6420	202-737-0120
National Organization for Women (NOW)					
1100 H St NW 3rd Fl	Washington	DC	20005	855-212-0212	202-628-8669
Ninety-Nines Inc					
4300 Amelia Earhart Rd	Oklahoma City	OK	73159	800-994-1929	405-685-7969
Women's Sports Foundation					
1899 Hempstead Tpke					
Ste 400 Eisenhower Pk	East Meadow	NY	11554	800-227-3988	516-542-4700

48   ASSOCIATIONS & ORGANIZATIONS - PROFESSIONAL & TRADE

SEE ALSO Veterinary Medical Associations - State ; Labor Unions ; Library Associations - State & Province ; Medical Associations - State ; Nurses Associations - State ; Pharmacy Associations - State ; Realtor Associations - State ; Bar Associations - State ; Dental Associations - State

48-1 Accountants Associations

				Toll-Free	Phone
AACE International - Assn for the Advancement of Cost Engineering					
209 Prairie Ave Ste 100	Morgantown	WV	26501	800-858-2678	304-296-8444
AGN International-North America					
2851 S Parker Rd Ste 850	Aurora	CO	80014	800-782-2272	303-743-7880
American Institute of Certified Public Accountants (AICPA)					
1211 Ave of the Americas	New York	NY	10036	888-777-7077	212-596-6200
American Institute of Professional Bookkeepers (AIPB)					
6001 Montrose Rd Ste 500	Rockville	MD	20852	800-622-0121	
American Woman's Society of Certified Public Accountants (AWSCPA)					
136 S Keowee St	Dayton	OH	45402	800-297-2721	937-222-1872
Association of Certified Fraud Examiners (ACFE)					
716 W Ave	Austin	TX	78701	800-245-3321	512-478-9000
Association of Government Accountants (AGA)					
2208 Mt Vernon Ave	Alexandria	VA	22301	800-242-7211	703-684-6931
Association of Healthcare Internal Auditors (AHIA)					
10200 W 44th Ave Ste 304	Wheat Ridge	CO	80033	888-275-2442	303-327-7546
BKR International					
19 Fulton St Ste 401	New York	NY	10038	800-257-4685	212-964-2115
Construction Financial Management Assn (CFMA)					
100 Village Blvd Ste 200A	Princeton	NJ	08540	877-462-7827	609-452-8000
CPA Auto Dealer Consultants Assn (CADCA)					
624 Grassmere Pk Dr Ste 15	Nashville	TN	37211	800-231-2524	615-373-9880
CPAmerica International					
11801 Research Dr	Alachua	FL	32615	800-992-2324	386-418-4001
Financial Acctg Standards Board (FASB)					
401 Merritt 7 PO Box 5116	Norwalk	CT	06856	800-748-0659	203-847-0700

				Toll-Free	Phone
Hospitality Financial & Technology Professionals (HFTP)					
11709 Boulder Ln Ste 110	Austin	TX	78726	800-646-4387	512-249-5333
Institute of Management Accountants Inc (IMA)					
10 Paragon Dr Ste 1	Montvale	NJ	07645	800-638-4427	201-573-9000
International Federation of Accountants					
545 Fifth Ave 14th Fl	New York	NY	10017	888-272-2001	212-286-9344
National Association of Nonprofit Accountants & Consultants (NSA)					
624 Grassmere Park Dr Ste 15	Nashville	TN	37211	800-231-2524	615-373-9880
National CPA Health Care Advisors Assn (HCAA)					
624 Grassmere Pk Ste 15	Nashville	TN	37211	800-231-2524	615-373-9880
National Society of Accountants (NSA)					
1010 N Fairfax St	Alexandria	VA	22314	800-966-6679	703-549-6400
New York State Society of Certified Public Accountant (FAE)					
14 Wall St 19th Fl	New York	NY	10005	800-537-3635*	212-719-8300
*General					
Tax Executives Institute (TEI)					
1200 G St NW Ste 300	Washington	DC	20005	877-244-7711	202-638-5601

48-2 Banking & Finance Professionals Associations

				Toll-Free	Phone
ABA Marketing Network					
1120 Connecticut Ave NW	Washington	DC	20036	800-226-5377	202-663-5000
ACA International - Assn of Credit & Collection Professionals					
4040 W 70th St PO Box 390106	Minneapolis	MN	55439	800-844-5654	952-926-6547
Accuplan Benefits Services					
515 East 4500 South Ste G200	Salt Lake City	UT	84107	800-454-2649	801-266-9900
America's Community Bankers (ACB)					
1120 Connecticut Ave NW	Washington	DC	20036	800-226-5377	
American Assn of Daily Money Managers (AADMM)					
174 Crestview Dr	Bellefonte	PA	16823	877-326-5991	
American Assn of Individual Investors (AAII)					
625 N Michigan Ave Ste 1900	Chicago	IL	60611	800-428-2244	312-280-0170
American Bankers Assn (ABA)					
1120 Connecticut Ave NW	Washington	DC	20036	800-226-5377*	202-663-5000
*Cust Svc					
American Benefits Council					
1501 M St NW Ste 600	Washington	DC	20005	877-829-5500	202-289-6700
American Finance Assn (AFA)					
350 Main St	Malden	MA	02148	800-835-6770	781-388-8599
Bank Administration Institute (BAI)					
115 S LaSalle Ste 3300	Chicago	IL	60603	800-224-9889*	312-683-2464
*Cust Svc					
Better Investing					
PO Box 220	Royal Oak	MI	48068	877-275-6242	248-583-6242
Certified Financial Planner Board of Standards Inc					
1425 K St NW Ste 500	Washington	DC	20005	800-487-1497	202-379-2200
CFA Institute					
915 E High St PO Box 3668	Charlottesville	VA	22903	800-247-8132	434-951-5499
Community Banking Advisory Network (CBAN)					
624 Grassmere Pk Dr Ste 15	Nashville	TN	37211	800-231-2524	615-373-9880
Credit Research Foundation (CRF)					
8840 Columbia 100 Pkwy	Columbia	MD	21045	866-265-3298	410-740-5499
Credit Union Executives Society (CUES)					
5510 Research Pk Dr	Madison	WI	53711	800-252-2664	608-271-2664
Farm Credit Council					
50 F St NW Ste 900	Washington	DC	20001	866-632-9992	202-626-8710
Financial Managers Society (FMS)					
100 W Monroe St Ste 810	Chicago	IL	60603	800-275-4367*	312-578-1300
*Cust Svc					
Financial Planning Assn (FPA)					
7535 E Hampden Ave Ste 400	Denver	CO	80231	800-322-4237	303-759-4900
FINRA 1735 K St NW	Washington	DC	20006	800-289-9999	202-728-8000
Independent Community Bankers of America (ICBA)					
1615 L St NW Ste 900	Washington	DC	20036	800-422-8439	202-659-8111
Investment Management Consultants Assn (IMCA)					
5619 DTC Pkwy Ste 500	Greenwood Village	CO	80111	800-250-9083	303-770-3377
Mortgage Bankers Assn (MBA)					
1919 M St NW 5th Fl	Washington	DC	20036	800-793-6222	202-557-2700
Municipal Securities Rulemaking Board (MSRB)					
1900 Duke St Ste 600	Alexandria	VA	22314	888-475-8376	703-797-6600
NA of Cash Management (NACM)					
8840 Columbia 100 Pkwy	Columbia	MD	21045	800-955-8815	410-740-5560
NA of Federal Credit Unions (NAFCU)					
3138 Tenth St N	Arlington	VA	22201	800-336-4644	703-522-4770
NACHA - Electronic Payments Assn					
13665 Dulles Technology Dr Ste 300	Herndon	VA	20171	800-487-9180	703-561-1100
National Federation of Community Development Credit Unions (NFCDCU)					
39 Broadway Ste 2140	New York	NY	10006	800-437-8711	212-809-1850
National Futures Assn (NFA)					
300 S Riverside Plz Ste 1800	Chicago	IL	60606	800-621-3570	312-781-1300
National Investment Co Service Assn (NICSA)					
8400 Westpark Dr 2nd Fl	McLean	VA	22102	800-426-1122	508-485-1500
North American Securities Administrators Assn (NASAA)					
750 First St NE Ste 1140	Washington	DC	20002	800-222-1253	202-737-0900
Risk Management Assn (RMA)					
1801 Market St Ste 300	Philadelphia	PA	19103	800-677-7621*	215-446-4000
*Cust Svc					
Securities Industry & Financial Markets Assn (SIFMAA)					
120 Broadway 35th Fl	New York	NY	10271	888-367-7966	212-313-1200
Smart Card Alliance Inc					
191 Clarkville Rd	Princeton Junction	NJ	08550	800-556-6828	609-799-5654

48-3 Construction Industry Associations

				Toll-Free	Phone
American Fence Assn (AFA)					
800 Roosevelt Rd Bldg C-312	Glen Ellyn	IL	60137	800-822-4342	630-942-6598
American Road & Transportation Builders Assn (ARTBA)					
1219 28th St NW	Washington	DC	20007	800-636-2377	202-289-4434
American Society of Heating Refrigerating & Air-Conditioning Engineers Inc (ASHRAE)					
1791 Tullie Cir NE	Atlanta	GA	30329	800-527-4723*	404-636-8400
*Cust Svc					
American Society of Home Inspectors (ASHI)					
932 Lee St Ste 101	Des Plaines	IL	60016	800-743-2744	847-759-2820

				Toll-Free	Phone
American Society of Professional Estimators (ASPE)					
2525 Perimeter Pl Dr Ste 103	Nashville	TN	37214	**888-378-6283**	615-316-9200
American Subcontractors Assn Inc (ASA)					
1004 Duke St	Alexandria	VA	22314	**866-378-8866**	703-684-3450
American Welding Society (AWS)					
550 NW 42nd Ave	Miami	FL	33126	**800-443-9353**	305-443-9353
Architectural Woodwork Institute (AWI)					
46179 Westlake Dr Ste 120	Potomac Falls	VA	20165	**866-877-6933**	571-323-3636
Asphalt Roofing Manufacturers Assn (ARMA)					
529 14th St NW Ste 750	Washington	DC	20045	**800-247-6637**	202-207-0917
Associated Builders & Contractors Inc (ABC)					
4250 Fairfax Dr	Arlington	VA	22203	**866-262-0540**	703-812-2000
Associated General Contractors of America (AGC)					
2300 Wilson Blvd Ste 400	Arlington	VA	22201	**800-242-1766**	703-548-3118
Associated Locksmiths of America (ALOA)					
3500 Easy St	Dallas	TX	75247	**800-532-2562**	214-819-9733
Association for Retail Environment (ARE)					
4651 Sheridan St Ste 470	Hollywood	FL	33021	**800-421-3483**	954-893-7300
Brick Industry Assn (BIA)					
1850 Centennial Pk Dr Ste 301	Reston	VA	20191	**866-644-1293**	703-620-0010
Building & Construction Trades Dept AFL-CIO					
815 16th St NW Ste 600	Washington	DC	20006	**800-772-1213**	202-347-1461
Composite Panel Assn					
19465 Deerfield Ave Ste 306	Leesburg	VA	20176	**866-426-6767**	703-724-1128
Construction Financial Management Assn (CFMA)					
100 Village Blvd Ste 200A	Princeton	NJ	08540	**877-462-7827**	609-452-8000
Electronic Security Assn Inc (ESA)					
2300 Vly View Ln Ste 230	Irving	TX	75062	**888-447-1689**	214-260-5970
Interlocking Concrete Pavement Institute (ICPI)					
1444 'I' St NW Ste 700	Washington	DC	20005	**800-241-3652**	202-712-9036
International Assn of Electrical Inspectors (IAEI)					
901 Waterfall Way Ste 602	Richardson	TX	75080	**800-786-4234**	972-235-1455
International Code Council (ICC)					
500 New Jersey Ave NW 6th Fl	Washington	DC	20001	**888-422-7233**	202-370-1800
International Institute of Ammonia Refrigeration					
1001 N Fairfax St Ste 503	Alexandria	VA	22314	**800-937-8461**	703-312-4200
International Masonry Institute (IMI)					
42 E St	Annapolis	MD	21401	**800-803-0295**	410-280-1305
International Wood Products Assn (IWPA)					
4214 King St	Alexandria	VA	22302	**855-435-0005**	703-820-6696
Manufactured Housing Institute (MHI)					
2101 Wilson Blvd Ste 610	Arlington	VA	22201	**800-505-5500**	703-558-0400
Marble Institute of America (MIA)					
28901 Clemens Rd Ste 100	Westlake	OH	44145	**800-433-4903**	440-250-9222
Mason Contractors Assn of America (MCAA)					
33 S Roselle Rd	Schaumburg	IL	60193	**800-536-2225**	224-678-9709
Mechanical Contractors Assn of America (MCAA)					
1385 Piccard Dr	Rockville	MD	20850	**800-556-3653**	301-869-5800
Monument Builders of North America (MBNA)					
136 S Keowee St	Dayton	OH	45402	**800-233-4472**	
NA of Home Builders (NAHB)					
1201 15th St NW	Washington	DC	20005	**800-368-5242**	202-266-8200
NA of Women in Construction (NAWIC)					
327 S Adams St	Fort Worth	TX	76104	**800-552-3506**	817-877-5551
National Association of Tower Erectors (NATE)					
Eight Second St SE	Watertown	SD	57201	**888-882-5865**	605-882-5865
National Council of Examiners for Engineering & Surveying (NCEES)					
280 Seneca Creek Rd	Seneca	SC	29678	**800-250-3196**	864-654-6824
National Electrical Contractors Assn (NECA)					
3 Bethesda Metro Ctr Ste 1100	Bethesda	MD	20814	**800-214-0585**	301-657-3110
National Frame Builders Assn (NFBA)					
8735 W Higgins Rd Ste 300	Chicago	IL	60631	**800-557-6957**	
National Hardwood Lumber Assn (NHLA)					
6830 Raleigh-LaGrange Rd	Memphis	TN	38134	**800-933-0318**	901-377-1818
National Insulation Assn (NIA)					
99 Canal Ctr Plz Ste 222	Alexandria	VA	22314	**877-968-7642**	703-683-6422
National Kitchen & Bath Assn (NKBA)					
687 Willow Grove St	Hackettstown	NJ	07840	**800-843-6522**	
National Parking Assn (NPA)					
1112 16th St NW Ste 840	Washington	DC	20036	**800-647-7275**	202-296-4336
National Precast Concrete Assn (NPCA)					
10333 N Meridian St Ste 272	Indianapolis	IN	46290	**800-366-7731**	317-571-9500
National Ready Mixed Concrete Assn (NRMCA)					
900 Spring St	Silver Spring	MD	20910	**888-846-7622**	301-587-1400
National Roofing Contractors Assn (NRCA)					
10255 W Higgins Rd Ste 600	Rosemont	IL	60018	**800-323-9545***	847-299-9070
*Cust Svc					
National Stone Sand & Gravel Assn (NSSGA)					
1605 King St	Alexandria	VA	22314	**800-342-1415**	703-525-8788
National Wood Flooring Assn (NWFA)					
111 Chesterfield Industrial Blvd	Chesterfield	MO	63005	**800-422-4556**	636-519-9663
North American Bldg Material Distribution Assn (NBMDA)					
330 N Wabash Ave Ste 2000	Chicago	IL	60611	**888-747-7862**	312-321-6845
Operative Plasterers' & Cement Masons' International Assn of the US & Canada (OPCMIA)					
11720 Beltsville Dr Ste 700	Beltsville	MD	20705	**888-379-1558**	301-623-1000
Painting & Decorating Contractors of America (PDCA)					
2316 Millpark Dr Ste 220	Maryland Heights	MO	63043	**800-332-7322***	314-514-7322
*Cust Svc					
Plumbing-Heating-Cooling Contractors NA (PHCC)					
180 S Washington St	Falls Church	VA	22040	**800-533-7694**	703-237-8100
Refrigeration Service Engineers Society (RSES)					
1666 Rand Rd	Des Plaines	IL	60016	**800-297-5660**	847-297-6464
Sheet Metal Workers International Assn (SMWIA)					
1750 New York Ave NW Sixth Fl	Washington	DC	20006	**800-251-7045**	202-783-5880
Window & Door Manufacturers Assn (WDMA)					
330 N Wabash Ave Ste 2000	Chicago	IL	60611	**800-223-2301**	847-299-5200
Wood Moulding & Millwork Producers Assn (WMMPA)					
507 First St	Woodland	CA	95695	**800-550-7889**	530-661-9591

48-4 Consumer Sales & Service Professionals Associations

				Toll-Free	Phone
American Apparel & Footwear Assn (AAFA)					
1601 N Kent St Ste 1200	Arlington	VA	22209	**800-520-2262**	703-524-1864
American Gem Society (AGS)					
8881 W Sahara Ave	Las Vegas	NV	89117	**866-805-6500**	702-255-6500
American Gem Trade Assn (AGTA)					
3030 LBJ Fwy Ste 840	Dallas	TX	75234	**800-972-1162**	214-742-4367
American Institute of Floral Designers (AIFD)					
720 Light St	Baltimore	MD	21230	**877-865-5320**	410-752-3318
American Lighting Assn (ALA)					
2050 Stemmons Fwy Ste 10046	Dallas	TX	75207	**800-605-4448**	214-698-9898
American Pet Products Manufacturers Assn (APPMA)					
255 Glenville Rd	Greenwich	CT	06831	**800-452-1225**	203-532-0000
American Rental Assn (ARA)					
1900 19th St	Moline	IL	61265	**800-334-2177**	309-764-2475
American Watchmakers-Clockmakers Institute (AWI)					
701 Enterprise Dr	Harrison	OH	45030	**866-367-2924**	513-367-9800
Association for Linen Management					
2161 Lexington Rd Ste 2	Richmond	KY	40475	**800-669-0863**	859-624-0177
Association of Home Appliance Manufacturers (AHAM)					
1111 19th St NW Ste 402	Washington	DC	20036	**888-258-3247**	202-872-5955
Association of Pool & Spa Professionals (APSP)					
2111 Eisenhower Ave Ste 500	Alexandria	VA	22314	**800-323-3996**	703-838-0083
Automotive Recyclers Assn (ARA)					
3975 Fair Ridge Dr Ste 20N	Fairfax	VA	22033	**888-385-1005**	703-385-1001
Awards & Recognition Assn (ARA)					
4700 W Lake Ave	Glenview	IL	60025	**800-344-2148**	847-375-4800
Coin Laundry Assn (CLA)					
1s660 Midwest Rd Ste 205	Oakbrook Terrace	IL	60181	**800-570-5629**	630-953-7920
Contact Lens Manufacturers Assn					
PO Box 29398	Lincoln	NE	68529	**800-344-9060**	402-465-4122
Diamond Council of America (DCA)					
3212 W End Ave Ste 202	Nashville	TN	37203	**877-283-5669**	615-385-5301
Diving Equipment & Marketing Assn (DEMA)					
3750 Convoy St Ste 310	San Diego	CA	92111	**800-862-3483**	858-616-6408
Drycleaning & Laundry Institute					
14700 Sweitzer Ln	Laurel	MD	20707	**800-638-2627**	301-622-1900
Envelope Manufacturers Assn (EMA)					
500 Montgomery St Ste 550	Alexandria	VA	22314	**800-354-5892**	703-739-2200
Gemological Institute of America (GIA)					
5345 Armada Dr	Carlsbad	CA	92008	**800-421-7250**	760-603-4000
Home Furnishings Independents Assn (HFIA)					
2050 Stemmons World Fwy Ste 292	Dallas	TX	75207	**800-422-3778**	214-741-7632
Independent Jewelers Organization (IJO)					
136 Old Post Rd	Southport	CT	06890	**800-624-9252**	
International Cemetery Cremation & Funeral Assn (ICCFA)					
107 Carpenter Dr Ste 100	Sterling	VA	20164	**800-645-7700**	703-391-8400
International Engraved Graphics Assn					
305 Plus Pk Blvd	Nashville	TN	37217	**800-821-3138**	
International Executive Housekeepers Assn (IEHA)					
1001 Eastwind Dr Ste 301	Westerville	OH	43081	**800-200-6342**	614-895-7166
International Housewares Assn (IHA)					
6400 Shafer Ct Ste 650	Rosemont	IL	60018	**888-689-2838**	847-292-4200
International Order of the Golden Rule (OGR)					
3520 Executive Ctr Dr Ste 300	Austin	TX	78731	**800-637-8030**	512-334-5504
International Sign Assn (ISA)					
1001 N Fairfax St Ste 301	Alexandria	VA	22314	**866-949-7446**	703-836-4012
Jewelers of America (JA)					
52 Vanderbilt Ave 19th Fl	New York	NY	10017	**800-223-0673**	646-658-0246
Leather Industries of America (LIA)					
3050 K St NW Ste 400	Washington	DC	20007	**800-635-0617**	202-342-8497
Manufacturing Jewelers & Suppliers of America Inc (MJSA)					
57 John L Dietsch Sq	Attleboro Falls	MA	02763	**800-444-6572**	401-274-3840
National Cleaners Assn					
252 W 29th St Second Fl	New York	NY	10001	**800-888-1622***	212-967-3002
*General					
National Funeral Directors & Morticians Assn (NFDMA)					
6290 Shannon Pkwy	Union City	GA	30291	**800-434-0958**	770-969-0064
National Funeral Directors Assn (NFDA)					
13625 Bishop's Dr	Brookfield	WI	53005	**800-228-6332**	262-789-1880
National Home Furnishings Assn (NHFA)					
3910 Tinsley Dr Ste 101	High Point	NC	27265	**800-422-3778**	336-886-6100
National Shoe Retailers Assn (NSRA)					
7386 N La Cholla Blvd	Tucson	AZ	85741	**800-673-8446**	520-209-1710
National Sporting Goods Assn (NSGA)					
1601 Feehanville Dr Ste 300	Mount Prospect	IL	60056	**800-815-5422**	847-296-6742
National Volunteer Fire Council (NVFC)					
7852 Walker Dr Ste 450	Greenbelt	MD	20770	**888-275-6832**	202-887-5700
Pet Industry Joint Advisory Council (PIJAC)					
1220 19th St NW Ste 400	Washington	DC	20036	**800-553-7387**	202-452-1525
Professional Assn of Innkeepers International (PAII)					
207 White Horse Pk	Haddon Heights	NJ	08035	**800-468-7244**	856-310-1102
Recreation Vehicle Industry Assn (RVIA)					
1896 Preston White Dr	Reston	VA	20191	**800-336-0154**	703-620-6003
Security Industry Assn (SIA)					
635 Slaters Ln Ste 110	Alexandria	VA	22314	**866-817-8888**	703-683-2075
Selected Independent Funeral Homes					
500 Lake Cook Rd Ste 205	Deerfield	IL	60015	**800-323-4219**	847-236-9401
Society of American Florists (SAF)					
1601 Duke St	Alexandria	VA	22314	**800-336-4743**	703-836-8700
Textile Rental Services Assn (TRSA)					
1800 Diagonal Rd Ste 200	Alexandria	VA	22314	**877-770-9274**	703-519-0029
Tire Industry Assn (TIA)					
1532 Pointer Ridge Pl Ste G	Bowie	MD	20716	**800-876-8372**	301-430-7280
Toy Industry Assn					
1115 Broadway Ste 400	New York	NY	10010	**800-541-1345**	212-675-1141
Uniform & Textile Service Assn (UTSA)					
1300 N 17th St Ste 750	Arlington	VA	22209	**800-996-3426**	703-247-2600
Vision Council, The					
225 Reinekers Ln Ste 700	Alexandria	VA	22314	**866-826-0290**	703-548-4560
Wallcoverings Assn					
401 N Michigan Ave Ste 2200	Chicago	IL	60611	**800-575-8016**	312-644-6610
World Floor Covering Assn (WFCA)					
2211 Howell Ave	Anaheim	CA	92806	**800-624-6880**	714-978-6440

48-5 Education Professionals Associations

				Toll-Free	Phone
American Assn of Collegiate Registrars & Admissions Officers (AACRAO)					
1 Dupont Cir NW Ste 520	Washington	DC	20036	**800-222-4922**	202-293-9161
American Assn of Family & Consumer Sciences (AAFCS)					
400 N Columbus St Ste 202	Alexandria	VA	22314	**800-424-8080**	703-706-4600

			Toll-Free	Phone
American Assn of School Administrators (AASA)				
801 N Quincy St Ste 700	Arlington VA	22203	800-771-1162	703-528-0700
American Assn of State Colleges & Universities (AASCU)				
1307 New York Ave NW Fifth Fl	Washington DC	20005	800-558-3417	202-293-7070
American Assn of Teachers of German (AATG)				
112 Haddontowne Ct Ste 104	Cherry Hill NJ	08034	800-835-6770	856-795-5553
American Assn of Teachers of Spanish & Portuguese (AATSP)				
900 Ladd Rd	Walled Lake MI	48390	877-832-2457	248-960-2180
American Assn of University Professors (AAUP)				
1133 Nineteenth St Ste 200	Washington DC	20036	800-424-2973	202-737-5900
American Assn of University Women (AAUW)				
1111 16th St NW	Washington DC	20036	800-326-2289	202-785-7700
American Council on the Teaching of Foreign Languages (ACTFL)				
1001 N Fairfax St Ste 200	Alexandria VA	22314	844-685-4373	703-894-2900
American Dental Education Assn (ADEA)				
1400 K St NW Ste 1100	Washington DC	20005	800-353-2237	202-289-7201
American Educational Research Assn (AERA)				
1430 K St NW Ste 1200	Washington DC	20005	800-893-7950	202-238-3200
American Historical Assn (AHA)				
400 A St SE	Washington DC	20003	888-444-6664	202-544-2422
American Library Assn (ALA)				
50 E Huron St	Chicago IL	60611	800-545-2433	312-944-6780
American Medical Student Assn (AMSA)				
1902 Assn Dr	Reston VA	20191	800-767-2266	703-620-6600
American School Counselor Assn (ASCA)				
1101 King St Ste 625	Alexandria VA	22314	800-306-4722	703-683-2722
American Society for Training & Development (ASTD)				
1640 King St Third Fl PO Box 1443	Alexandria VA	22313	800-628-2783	703-683-8100
American Sociological Assn (ASA)				
1307 New York Ave	Washington DC	20005	800-524-9400	202-383-9005
American String Teachers Assn (ASTA)				
4155 Chain Bridge Rd	Fairfax VA	22030	800-821-7303	703-279-2113
American Studies Assn (ASA)				
1120 19th St NW Ste 301	Washington DC	20036	800-468-3571	202-467-4783
American Translators Assn (ATA)				
225 Reinekers Ln Ste 590	Alexandria VA	22314	800-253-2252	703-683-6100
Association for Advanced Training in the Behavioral Sciences (AATBS)				
5126 Ralston St	Ventura CA	93003	800-472-1931	805-676-3030
Association for Career & Technical Education (ACTE)				
1410 King St	Alexandria VA	22314	800-826-9972	703-683-3111
Association for Childhood Education International (ACEI)				
1101 16th St NW Ste 300	Washington DC	20036	800-423-3563	202-372-9986
Association for Continuing Higher Education (ACHE)				
1700 Asp Ave	Norman OK	73072	800-807-2243	
Association for Supervision & Curriculum Development (ASCD)				
1703 N Beauregard St	Alexandria VA	22311	800-933-2723	703-578-9600
Association for the Advancement of Computing in Education (AACE)				
PO Box 1545	Chesapeake VA	23327	800-352-5397	757-366-5606
Association of American Medical Colleges (AAMC)				
2450 N St NW	Washington DC	20037	800-273-8255	202-828-0400
Association of Christian Schools International (ACSI)				
731 Chapel Hills Dr	Colorado Springs CO	80920	800-367-0798*	719-528-6906
*Cust Svc				
Association of Collegiate Schools of Architecture (ACSA)				
1735 New York Ave NW 3rd Fl	Washington DC	20006	877-426-6323	202-785-2324
Association of Community College Trustees (ACCT)				
1233 20th St NW Ste 605	Washington DC	20036	866-895-2228	202-775-4667
Association of Governing Boards of Universities & Colleges (AGB)				
1133 20th St NW Ste 300	Washington DC	20036	800-356-6317	202-296-8400
Association of School Business Officials International (ASBO)				
11401 N Shore Dr	Reston VA	20190	866-682-2729	
Association of Test Publishers				
601 Pennsylvania Ave NW Ste 900	Washington DC	20004	866-240-7909	
Association of Universities for Research in Astronomy (AURA)				
1200 New York Ave NW Ste 350	Washington DC	20005	888-624-8373	202-483-2101
Association of University Centers on Disabilities (AUCD)				
1100 Wayne Avenue Suite 1000	Silver Spring MD	20910	888-572-2249	301-588-8252
Broadcast Education Assn (BEA)				
1771 N St NW	Washington DC	20036	888-326-1415	202-429-3935
Business Professionals of America				
5454 Cleveland Ave	Columbus OH	43231	800-334-2007	614-895-7277
Christian Schools International (CSI)				
3350 E Paris Ave SE	Grand Rapids MI	49512	800-635-8288	616-957-1070
College & University Professional Assn for Hum Res (CUPA-HR)				
1811 Commons Pt Dr	Knoxville TN	37932	877-287-2474	865-637-7673
College Music Society (CMS)				
312 E Pine St	Missoula MT	59802	800-729-0235	406-721-9616
Conference on College Composition & Communication (CCCC)				
1111 W Kenyon Rd	Urbana IL	61801	877-369-6283	217-328-3870
Council for Advancement & Support of Education (CASE)				
1307 New York Ave NW Ste 1000	Washington DC	20005	800-554-8536*	202-328-5900
*Orders				
Council for Professional Recognition				
2460 16th St NW	Washington DC	20009	800-424-4310	202-265-9090
Council of Administrators of Special Education (CASE)				
Osigian Office Centre 101 Katelyn Cir				
Ste E	Warner Robins GA	31088	800-585-1753	478-333-6892
Council of the Great City Schools				
1301 Pennsylvania Ave NW Ste 702	Washington DC	20004	888-280-7903	202-393-2427
Council on International Educational Exchange (CIEE)				
300 Fore St Second Fl	Portland ME	04101	888-268-6245*	207-553-4000
*Cust Svc				
Education Commission of the States (ECS)				
700 Broadway Ste 810	Denver CO	80203	877-584-8642	303-299-3600
Educational Housing Services Inc				
55 Clark St	Brooklyn NY	11201	800-385-1689	212-977-7622
Hispanic Assn of Colleges & Universities (HACU)				
8415 Datapoint Dr Ste 400	San Antonio TX	78229	800-780-4228	210-692-3805
International Reading Assn (IRA)				
800 Barksdale Rd PO Box 6021	Newark DE	19714	800-336-7323	302-731-1600
International Society for Technology in Education (ISTE)				
1710 Rhode Island Ave NW Ste 900	Washington DC	20036	800-336-5191*	202-861-7777
*General				
MENC: NA for Music Education				
1806 Robert Fulton Dr	Reston VA	20191	800-336-3768	703-860-4000
Modern Language Assn (MLA)				
26 Broadway 3rd Fl	New York NY	10004	800-323-4900	646-576-5000

			Toll-Free	Phone
Music Teachers NA (MTNA)				
441 Vine St Ste 3100	Cincinnati OH	45202	888-512-5278	513-421-1420
NA of Colleges & Employers (NACE)				
62 Highland Ave	Bethlehem PA	18017	800-544-5272	610-868-1421
NA of Elementary School Principals (NAESP)				
1615 Duke St	Alexandria VA	22314	800-386-2377	703-684-3345
National Art Education Assn (NAEA)				
1806 Robert Fulton Dr	Reston VA	20191	800-299-8321	703-860-8000
National Assn of Student Financial Aid Administrators (NASFAA)				
1101 Connecticut Ave Ste 1100	Washington DC	20036	800-877-8339	202-785-0453
National Catholic Educational Assn (NCEA)				
1077 30th St NW Ste 100	Washington DC	20007	800-711-6232	202-337-6232
National Council for the Social Studies (NCSS)				
8555 16th St Ste 500	Silver Spring MD	20910	800-683-0812*	301-588-1800
*Orders				
National Council of Teachers of English (NCTE)				
1111 W Kenyon Rd	Urbana IL	61801	877-369-6283	217-328-3870
National Council of Teachers of Mathematics (NCTM)				
1906 Assn Dr	Reston VA	20191	800-235-7566*	703-620-9840
*Orders				
National Council on Economic Education (NCEE)				
122 E 42nd St Ste 2600	New York NY	10168	800-338-1192	212-730-7007
National Education Assn (NEA)				
1201 16th St NW	Washington DC	20036	888-552-0624	202-833-4000
National Middle School Assn (NMSA)				
4151 Executive Pkwy Ste 300	Westerville OH	43081	800-528-6672	614-895-4730
National Science Teachers Assn (NSTA)				
1840 Wilson Blvd	Arlington VA	22201	800-722-6782*	703-243-7100
*Sales				
National Staff Development Council (NSDC)				
504 S Locust St	Oxford OH	45056	800-727-7288	513-523-6029
North Central Assn Higher Learning Commission				
230 S LaSalle St	Chicago IL	60604	800-621-7440	312-263-0456
Organization for Tropical Studies (OTS)				
410 Swift Ave PO Box 90630	Durham NC	27705	877-572-4484	919-684-5774
Organization of American Historians (OAH)				
112 N Bryan Ave	Bloomington IN	47408	888-737-7006	812-855-7311
Society for American Archaeology (SAA)				
900 Second St NE Ste 12	Washington DC	20002	800-759-5219	202-789-8200
Society for College & University Planning (SCUP)				
339 E Liberty St Ste 300	Ann Arbor MI	48104	800-257-2578	734-669-3270
Southern Assn of Colleges & Schools				
1866 Southern Ln	Decatur GA	30033	888-413-3669	404-679-4500
Teach For America				
315 W 36th St Seventh Fl	New York NY	10018	800-832-1230	212-279-2080
Teachers of English to Speakers of Other Languages (TESOL)				
700 S Washington St Ste 200	Alexandria VA	22314	888-547-3369	703-836-0774
Teaching & Mentoring Communities (TMC)				
PO Box 2579	Laredo TX	78044	888-836-5151	956-722-5174
Trees for Tomorrow (TFT)				
519 Sheridan St E PO Box 609	Eagle River WI	54521	800-838-9472	715-479-6456
Washington Education Assn Inc				
32032 Weyerhaeuser Way S				
PO Box 9100	Federal Way WA	98001	800-622-3393	253-941-6700

48-6 Food & Beverage Industries Professional Associations

			Toll-Free	Phone
American Beverage Licensees (ABL)				
5101 River Rd Ste 108	Bethesda MD	20816	800-656-3241	301-656-1494
American Culinary Federation Inc (ACF)				
180 Ctr Pl Way	Saint Augustine FL	32095	800-624-9458	904-824-4468
American Society for Nutrition (ASNS)				
9650 Rockville Pike Ste L3503A	Bethesda MD	20814	800-627-8723	301-634-7050
Beer Institute				
122 C St NW Ste 350	Washington DC	20001	800-379-2739	202-737-2337
Biscuit & Cracker Manufacturers Assn (B&CMA)				
6325 Woodside Ct Ste 125	Columbia MD	21046	877-701-8111	443-545-1645
Food Marketing Institute (FMI)				
2345 Crystal Dr Ste 800	Arlington VA	22202	800-732-2639	202-220-0600
Institute of Food Technologists (IFT)				
525 W Van Buren St Ste 1000	Chicago IL	60607	800-438-3663	312-782-8424
International Assn for Food Protection (IAFP)				
6200 Aurora Ave Ste 200W	Des Moines IA	50322	800-369-6337*	515-276-3344
*General				
International Assn of Culinary Professionals (IACP)				
1221 Ave of the Americas 42nd fl	New York NY	10020	800-928-4227	866-358-2524
International Bottled Water Assn (IBWA)				
1700 Diagonal Rd Ste 650	Alexandria VA	22314	800-928-3711	703-683-5213
International Dairy-Deli-Bakery Assn (IDDBA)				
636 Science Dr	Madison WI	53705	877-399-4925	608-238-7908
International Food Information Council Foundation (IFIC)				
1100 Connecticut Ave NW Ste 430	Washington DC	20036	888-723-3366	202-296-6540
Master Brewers Assn of the Americas (MBAA)				
3340 Pilot Knob Rd	Saint Paul MN	55121	800-328-7560	651-454-7250
National Beer Wholesalers Assn (NBWA)				
1101 King St Ste 600	Alexandria VA	22314	800-300-6417	703-683-4300
National Coffee Assn of USA Inc (NCA)				
45 Broadway Ste 1140	New York NY	10006	800-247-6755	212-766-4007
National Confectioners Assn (NCA)				
1101 30th St NW Ste 200	Washington DC	20007	800-433-1200	202-534-1440
National Milk Producers Federation (NMPF)				
2101 Wilson Blvd Ste 400	Arlington VA	22201	888-723-3366	703-243-6111
National Restaurant Assn (NRA)				
2055 L St NW Ste 700	Washington DC	20036	800-424-5156	202-331-5900
North American Meat Processors Assn (NAMP)				
1910 Assn Dr	Reston VA	20191	800-535-4555	703-758-1900
Produce Marketing Assn (PMA)				
1500 Casho Mill Rd	Newark DE	19711	800-872-7245	302-738-7100
Retail Confectioners International (RCI)				
2053 S Waverly St C	Springfield MO	65804	800-545-5381	417-883-2775
School Nutrition Assn (SNA)				
700 S Washington St Ste 300	Alexandria VA	22314	800-877-8822	703-739-3900
Snack Food Assn				
1600 Wilson Blvd Ste 650	Arlington VA	22209	800-628-1334	703-836-4500
Specialty Coffee Assn of America (SCAA)				
330 Golden Shore Ave Ste 50	Long Beach CA	90802	800-995-9019	562-624-4100

	Toll-Free	Phone

Tea Council of the USA Inc
362 Fifth Ave Ste 801 . . . . New York NY　10001　**877-212-5752**　212-986-9415
Wine & Spirits Shippers Assn Inc (WSSA)
11800 Sunrise Vly Dr . . . . Reston VA　20191　**800-368-3167***　703-860-2300
　*General
WineAmerica
1015 18th St NW Ste 500 . . . . Washington DC　20036　**800-824-5419**　202-783-2756

48-7 Government & Public Administration Professional Associations

	Toll-Free	Phone

American Assn of State Highway & Transportation Officials (AASHTO)
444 N Capitol St NW Ste 249 . . . . Washington DC　20001　**800-880-4117**　202-624-5800
American Correctional Assn (ACA)
206 N Washington St Ste 200 . . . . Alexandria VA　22314　**800-222-5646**　703-224-0000
American Federation of Police & Concerned Citizens
6350 Horizon Dr . . . . Titusville FL　32780　**800-435-7352**　321-264-0911
American Foreign Service Assn (AFSA)
2101 E St NW . . . . Washington DC　20037　**800-704-2372**　202-338-4045
American Public Works Assn (APWA)
2345 Grand Blvd Ste 700 . . . . Kansas City MO　64108　**800-848-2792**　816-472-6100
Association of Conservation Engineers (ACE)
Missouri Dept of Conservation
PO Box 180. . . . . Jefferson City MO　65102　**866-633-8110**　573-522-4115
Association of Public Health Laboratories (APHL)
8515 Georgia Ave Ste 700 . . . . Silver Spring MD　20910　**800-899-2278**　240-485-2745
Association of Public-Safety Communications Officials International Inc
351 N Williamson Blvd . . . . Daytona Beach FL　32114　**888-272-6911**　386-322-2500
Association of Social Work Boards (ASWB)
400 S Ridge Pkwy Ste B . . . . Culpeper VA　22701　**800-225-6880**　540-829-6880
Association of State Wetland Managers
32 Tandberg Trail Suite 2A . . . . Windham ME　04062　**800-451-6027**　207-892-3399
Commission on Accreditation for Law Enforcement Agencies (CALEA)
13575 Heathcote Blvd Ste 320 . . . . Gainesville VA　20155　**877-789-6904**　703-352-4225
Conference of State Bank Supervisors (CSBS)
1129 20th St NW Fifth Fl . . . . Washington DC　20036　**800-886-2727**　202-296-2840
Council of State & Territorial Epidemiologists (CSTE)
2872 Woodcock Blvd Ste 303 . . . . Atlanta GA　30341　**866-577-9956**　770-458-3811
Council of State Governments (CSG)
2760 Research Pk Dr . . . . Lexington KY　40511　**800-800-1910***　859-244-8000
　*Sales
Federation of State Medical Boards of the US Inc (FSMB)
400 Fuller Wiser Rd Ste 300. . . . . Euless TX　76039　**800-793-7939**　817-868-4000
Forest Service Employees for Environmental Ethics (FSEEE)
PO Box 11615 . . . . Eugene OR　97440　**800-270-7504**　541-484-2692
International Assn of Assessing Officers (IAAO)
314 W Tenth St . . . . Kansas City MO　64105　**800-616-4226**　816-701-8100
International Assn of Chiefs of Police (IACP)
515 N Washington St . . . . Alexandria VA　22314　**800-843-4227**　703-836-6767
International Assn of Fire Chiefs (IAFC)
4025 Fair Ridge Dr Ste 300 . . . . Fairfax VA　22033　**866-385-9110**　703-273-0911
International Assn of Plumbing & Mechanical Officials (IAPMO)
4755 E Philadelphia St . . . . Ontario CA　91761　**877-427-6601**　909-472-4100
International City/County Management Assn (ICMA)
777 N Capitol St NE Ste 500. . . . . Washington DC　20002　**800-745-8780**　202-289-4262
International Conference of Funeral Service Examining Boards Inc
1885 Shelby Ln . . . . Fayetteville AR　72704　**800-709-0180**　479-442-7076
International Institute of Municipal Clerks (IIMC)
8331 Utica Ave Ste 200 . . . . Rancho Cucamonga CA　91730　**800-251-1639**　909-944-4162
International Municipal Signal Assn (IMSA)
165 E Union St PO Box 539 . . . . Newark NY　14513　**800-723-4672**　315-331-2182
International Society of Fire Service Instructors (ISFSI)
14001C St Germain Dr . . . . Centreville VA　20121　**800-435-0005**
NA of Conservation Districts (NACD)
509 Capitol Ct NE . . . . Washington DC　20002　**888-695-2433**　202-547-6223
NA of Housing & Redevelopment Officials (NAHRO)
630 'I' St NW . . . . Washington DC　20001　**877-866-2476**　202-289-3500
National Academy of Public Administration
900 Seventh St NW Ste 600 . . . . Washington DC　20001　**800-883-3190**　202-347-3190
National American Indian Housing Council (NAIHC)
50 F St NW Ste 3300 . . . . Washington DC　20001　**800-284-9165**　202-789-1754
National Board of Boiler & Pressure Vessel Inspectors
1055 Crupper Ave . . . . Columbus OH　43229　**877-682-8772**　614-888-8320
National Conference of State Legislatures
7700 E First Pl . . . . Denver CO　80230　**866-229-2386**　303-364-7700
National Ctr for State Courts (NCSC)
300 Newport Ave . . . . Williamsburg VA　23185　**800-616-6164**　757-259-1525
National District Attorneys Assn (NDAA)
99 Canal Ctr Plaza Ste 510 . . . . Alexandria VA　22314　**888-325-9943**　703-549-9222
National Environmental Health Assn (NEHA)
720 S Colorado Blvd Ste 1000-N . . . . Denver CO　80246　**866-956-2258**　303-756-9090
National Fire Protection Assn (NFPA)
One Batterymarch Pk . . . . Quincy MA　02169　**800-344-3555**　617-770-3000
National Institute of Governmental Purchasing Inc (NIGP)
151 Spring St . . . . Herndon VA　20170　**800-367-6447**　703-736-8900
National Sheriffs' Assn (NSA)
1450 Duke St . . . . Alexandria VA　22314　**800-424-7827**　703-836-7827
National Volunteer Fire Council (NVFC)
7852 Walker Dr Ste 450 . . . . Greenbelt MD　20770　**888-275-6832**　202-887-5700
United Federations of Security
540 N State Rd . . . . Briarcliff Manor NY　10510　**800-227-4291**　914-941-4103
US Travel Assn
1100 New York Ave NW Ste 450 . . . . Washington DC　20005　**877-212-5752**　202-408-8422

48-8 Health & Medical Professionals Associations

	Toll-Free	Phone

Academy of General Dentistry (AGD)
211 E Chicago Ave Ste 900 . . . . Chicago IL　60611　**888-243-3368**　312-440-4300
Academy of Managed Care Pharmacy (AMCP)
100 N Pitt St Ste 400 . . . . Alexandria VA　22314　**800-827-2627**　703-683-8416
Academy of Osseointegration
85 W Algonquin Rd Ste 550 . . . . Arlington Heights IL　60005　**800-656-7736**　847-439-1919

	Toll-Free	Phone

Academy of Pharmacy Practice & Management
American Pharmacists Assn
1100 15th St NW Ste 400 . . . . Washington DC　20005　**800-237-2742**　202-628-4410
Academy of Students of Pharmacy
American Pharmacists Assn
1100 15th St NW Ste 400 . . . . Washington DC　20005　**800-237-2742**　202-628-4410
America's Blood Centers (ABC)
725 15th St NW Ste 700 . . . . Washington DC　20005　**888-872-5663**　202-393-5725
American Academy of Allergy Asthma & Immunology (AAAAI)
555 E Wells St Ste 1100 . . . . Milwaukee WI　53202　**800-654-2452**　414-272-6071
American Academy of Audiology (AAA)
11730 Plz America Dr Ste 300 . . . . Reston VA　20190　**800-222-2336**　703-790-8466
American Academy of Cosmetic Dentistry (AACD)
402 W Wilson St . . . . Madison WI　53703　**800-543-9220**　608-222-8583
American Academy of Dermatology (AAD)
930 E Woodfield Rd . . . . Schaumburg IL　60173　**800-868-2472**　847-330-0230
American Academy of Disability Evaluating Physicians (AADEP)
223 W Jackson Blvd Ste 1104 . . . . Chicago IL　60606　**800-456-6095**　312-663-1171
American Academy of Family Physicians (AAFP)
11400 Tomahawk Creek Pkwy . . . . Leawood KS　66211　**800-274-2237**　913-906-6000
American Academy of Neurology (AAN)
1080 Montreal Ave . . . . Saint Paul MN　55116　**800-879-1960**　651-695-1940
American Academy of Ophthalmology
655 Beach St . . . . San Francisco CA　94109　**866-561-8558**　415-561-8500
American Academy of Optometry (AAO)
6110 Executive Blvd Ste 506 . . . . Rockville MD　20852　**800-368-6263**　301-984-1441
American Academy of Orthopaedic Surgeons (AAOS)
6300 N River Rd . . . . Rosemont IL　60018　**800-346-2267**　847-823-7186
American Academy of Orthotists & Prosthetists (AAOP)
526 King St Ste 201 . . . . Alexandria VA　22314　**800-669-6024**　703-836-0788
American Academy of Otolaryngology-Head & Neck Surgery (AAO-HNS)
1650 Diagonal Rd . . . . Alexandria VA　22314　**877-722-6467**　703-836-4444
American Academy of Pain Management (AAPM)
13947 Mono Way Ste A . . . . Sonora CA　95370　**888-519-9901**　209-533-9744
American Academy of Pediatric Dentistry (AAPD)
211 E Chicago Ave Ste 1700 . . . . Chicago IL　60611　**800-974-3084**　312-337-2169
American Academy of Pediatrics (AAP)
141 NW Pt Blvd . . . . Elk Grove Village IL　60007　**800-433-9016**　847-434-4000
American Academy of Periodontology (AAP)
737 N Michigan Ave Ste 800 . . . . Chicago IL　60611　**800-282-4867**　312-787-5518
American Assn for Cancer Research (AACR)
615 Chestnut St 17th Fl . . . . Philadelphia PA　19106　**866-423-3965**　215-440-9300
American Assn for Thoracic Surgery (AATS)
900 Cummings Ctr Ste 221-U . . . . Beverly MA　01915　**800-424-5249**　978-927-8330
American Assn of Bioanalysts (AAB)
906 Olive St Ste 1200 . . . . Saint Louis MO　63101　**800-457-3332**　314-241-1445
American Assn of Clinical Endocrinologists (AACE)
245 Riverside Ave Ste 2000 . . . . Jacksonville FL　32202　**800-435-7352**　904-353-7878
American Assn of Colleges of Osteopathic Medicine (AACOM)
5550 Friendship Blvd Ste 310 . . . . Chevy Chase MD　20815　**800-356-7836**　301-968-4100
American Assn of Colleges of Podiatric Medicine (AACPM)
15850 Crabbs Branch Way Ste 320 . . . . Rockville MD　20855　**800-922-9266**　301-948-9760
American Assn of Critical-Care Nurses (AACN)
101 Columbia . . . . Aliso Viejo CA　92656　**800-809-2273**　949-362-2000
American Assn of Endodontists (AAE)
211 E Chicago Ave Ste 1100 . . . . Chicago IL　60611　**800-872-3636**　312-266-7255
American Assn of Gynecological Laparoscopists (AAGL)
6757 Katella Ave . . . . Cypress CA　90630　**800-554-2245**　714-503-6200
American Assn of Immunologists (AAI)
9650 Rockville Pike . . . . Bethesda MD　20814　**888-503-1050**　301-634-7178
American Assn of Medical Assistants (AAMA)
20 N Wacker Dr Ste 1575 . . . . Chicago IL　60606　**800-228-2262**　312-899-1500
American Assn of Medical Review Officers (AAMRO)
PO Box 12873 . . . . Research Triangle Park NC　27709　**800-489-1839**　919-489-5407
American Assn of Neurological Surgeons (AANS)
5550 Meadowbrook Dr . . . . Rolling Meadows IL　60008　**888-566-2267**　847-378-0500
American Assn of Neuromuscular & Electrodiagnostic Medicine (AANEM)
2621 Superior Dr NW . . . . Rochester MN　55901　**844-347-3277**　507-288-0100
American Assn of Neuroscience Nurses (AANN)
4700 W Lk Ave . . . . Glenview IL　60025　**888-557-2266**　847-375-4733
American Assn of Oral & Maxillofacial Surgeons (AAOMS)
9700 W Bryn Mawr Ave . . . . Rosemont IL　60018　**800-822-6637**　847-678-6200
American Assn of Orthodontists (AAO)
401 N Lindbergh Blvd . . . . Saint Louis MO　63141　**800-522-1899**　314-993-1700
American Assn of Poison Control Centers (AAPCC)
3201 New Mexico Ave Suite 310 . . . . Washington DC　20016　**800-222-1222**
American Assn of Tissue Banks (AATB)
1320 Old Chain Bridge Rd Ste 450 . . . . McLean VA　22101　**800-635-2282**　703-827-9582
American Autoimmune Related Disease Assn (AARDA)
22100 Gratiot Ave . . . . Eastpointe MI　48021　**800-598-4668**　586-776-3900
American Cancer Society (ACS)
250 William St NW Ste 6001 . . . . Atlanta GA　30303　**800-227-2345**　404-320-3333
American Chiropractic Assn (ACA)
1701 Clarendon Blvd Second Fl . . . . Arlington VA　22209　**800-986-4636**　703-276-8800
American College of Allergy Asthma & Immunology (ACAAI)
85 W Algonquin Rd Ste 550 . . . . Arlington Heights IL　60005　**800-466-3649**　847-427-1200
American College of Cardiology (ACC)
2400 N St NW . . . . Washington DC　20037　**800-253-4636***　202-375-6000
　*Cust Svc
American College of Chest Physicians (ACCP)
3300 Dundee Rd . . . . Northbrook IL　60062　**800-343-2227**　847-498-1400
American College of Emergency Physicians (ACEP)
1125 Executive Cir PO Box 619911 . . . . Dallas TX　75261　**800-798-1822**　972-550-0911
American College of Foot & Ankle Surgeons (ACFAS)
8725 W Higgins Rd Ste 555 . . . . Chicago IL　60631　**800-421-2237**　773-693-9300
American College of Forensic Examiners International (ACFEI)
2750 E Sunshine St . . . . Springfield MO　65804　**800-423-9737**　417-881-3818
American College of Osteopathic Family Physicians (ACOFP)
330 E Algonquin Rd Ste 1 . . . . Arlington Heights IL　60005　**800-323-0794**　847-952-5100
American College of Physician Executives (ACPE)
400 N Ashley Dr Ste 4001 . . . . Tampa FL　33602　**800-562-8088**　813-287-2000
American College of Physicians (ACP)
190 N Independence Mall W . . . . Philadelphia PA　19106　**800-523-1546**　215-351-2400
American College of Radiology (ACR)
1892 Preston White Dr . . . . Reston VA　20191　**800-227-5463**　703-648-8900
American College of Surgeons (ACS)
633 N St Clair St . . . . Chicago IL　60611　**800-621-4111**　312-202-5000

			Toll-Free	**Phone**

Classified Section

		Toll-Free	Phone

American Dental Assistants Assn (ADAA)
35 E Wacker Dr Ste 1730 .... Chicago IL 60601 — **877-874-3785** — 312-541-1550

American Dental Hygienists' Assn (ADHA)
444 N Michigan Ave Ste 3400 .... Chicago IL 60611 — **800-243-2342** — 312-440-8900

American Diabetes Assn (ADA)
1701 N Beauregard St .... Alexandria VA 22311 — **800-232-3472** — 703-549-1500

American Dietetic Assn (ADA)
120 S Riverside Plz Ste 2000 .... Chicago IL 60606 — **800-877-1600** — 312-899-0040

American Epilepsy Society (AES)
342 N Main St .... West Hartford CT 06117 — **888-233-2334** — 860-586-7505

American Federation for Aging Research (AFAR)
55 W 39th St 16th Fl. .... New York NY 10018 — **888-582-2327** — 212-703-9977

American Federation for Medical Research (AFMR)
900 Cummings Ctr Ste 221-U .... Beverly MA 01915 — **888-737-9477** — 978-927-8330

American Gastroenterological Assn (AGA)
4930 Del Ray Ave .... Bethesda MD 20814 — **800-228-9290** — 301-654-2055

American Health Care Assn (AHCA)
1201 L St NW .... Washington DC 20005 — **800-321-0343** — 202-842-4444

American Health Information Management Assn (AHIMA)
233 N Michigan Ave Ste 2100 .... Chicago IL 60601 — **800-335-5535** — 312-233-1100

American Healthcare Radiology Administrators (AHRA)
490-B Boston Post Rd Ste 200 .... Sudbury MA 01776 — **800-334-2472** — 978-443-7591

American Hospital Assn (AHA)
155 N Wacker Dr .... Chicago IL 60606 — **800-424-4301** — 312-422-3000

American Institute of Ultrasound in Medicine (AIUM)
14750 Sweitzer Ln Ste 100 .... Laurel MD 20707 — **800-638-5352** — 301-498-4100

American Lung Assn (ALA)
14 Wall St .... New York NY 10005 — **800-586-4872** — 212-315-8700

American Medical Assn (AMA)
515 N State St .... Chicago IL 60610 — **800-621-8335** — 312-464-5000

American Medical Directors Assn (AMDA)
11000 Broken Land Pkwy Ste 400 .... Columbia MD 21044 — **800-876-2632** — 410-740-9743

American Medical Rehabilitation Providers Assn (AMRPA)
1710 N St NW .... Washington DC 20036 — **888-346-4624** — 202-223-1920

American Medical Technologists (AMT)
10700 W Higgins Rd Ste 150 .... Rosemont IL 60018 — **800-275-1268** — 847-823-5169

American Nephrology Nurses Assn (ANNA)
200 E Holly Ave .... Sewell NJ 08080 — **888-600-2662** — 856-256-2320

American Nurses Assn (ANA)
8515 Georgia Ave Ste 400 .... Silver Spring MD 20910 — **800-274-4262** — 301-628-5000

American Occupational Therapy Assn Inc (AOTA)
4720 Montgomery Ln PO Box 31220 .... Bethesda MD 20824 — **800-877-1383** — 301-652-2682

American Orthopaedic Society for Sports Medicine (AOSSM)
6300 N River Rd Ste 500 .... Rosemont IL 60018 — **877-321-3500** — 847-292-4900

American Osteopathic Assn (AOA)
142 E Ontario St .... Chicago IL 60611 — **800-621-1773** — 312-202-8000

American Pain Society (APS)
4700 W Lake Ave .... Glenview IL 60025 — **877-752-4754** — 847-375-4715

American Physical Therapy Assn (APTA)
1111 N Fairfax St .... Alexandria VA 22314 — **800-999-2782** — 703-684-2782

American Podiatric Medical Assn (APMA)
9312 Old Georgetown Rd .... Bethesda MD 20814 — **800-275-2762** — 301-581-9200

American Psychiatric Nurses Assn (APNA)
1555 Wilson Blvd Ste 530 .... Arlington VA 22209 — **866-243-2443** — 703-243-2443

American Registry of Diagnostic Medical Sonographers (ARDMS)
51 Monroe St Plz E 1 .... Rockville MD 20850 — **800-541-9754** — 301-738-8401

American Roentgen Ray Society (ARRS)
44211 Slatestone Ct .... Leesburg VA 20176 — **800-438-2777** — 703-729-3353

American Society for Aesthetic Plastic Surgery, The (ASAPS)
11262 Monarch St .... Garden Grove CA 92841 — **800-364-2147** — 562-799-2356

American Society for Clinical Pathology (ASCP)
33 W Monroe St Ste 1600 .... Chicago IL 60603 — **800-621-4142*** — 312-541-4999
*Cust Svc

American Society for Colposcopy & Cervical Pathology (ASCCP)
152 W Washington St .... Hagerstown MD 21740 — **800-787-7227** — 301-733-3640

American Society for Gastrointestinal Endoscopy (ASGE)
1520 Kensington Rd Ste 202 .... Oak Brook IL 60523 — **866-353-2743** — 630-573-0600

American Society for Laser Medicine & Surgery Inc (ASLMS)
2100 Stewart Ave Ste 240 .... Wausau WI 54401 — **877-258-6028** — 715-845-9283

American Society for Parenteral & Enteral Nutrition (ASPEN)
8630 Fenton St Ste 412 .... Silver Spring MD 20910 — **800-727-4567** — 301-587-6315

American Society for Surgery of the Hand (ASSH)
822 W. Washington Blvd .... Chicago IL 60607 — **888-343-6337** — 312-880-1900

American Society for Therapeutic Radiology & Oncology (ASTRO)
8280 Willow Oaks Corporate Dr Ste 500 .... Fairfax VA 22031 — **800-962-7876** — 703-502-1550

American Society of Anesthesiologists (ASA)
520 N NW Hwy .... Park Ridge IL 60068 — **800-331-1600** — 847-825-5586

American Society of Cataract & Refractive Surgery (ASCRS)
4000 Legato Rd Ste 700 .... Fairfax VA 22033 — **800-451-1339** — 703-591-2220

American Society of Clinical Hypnosis (ASCH)
140 N Bloomingdale Rd .... Bloomingdale IL 60108 — **866-986-8779** — 630-980-4740

American Society of Clinical Oncology (ASCO)
2318 Mill Rd Ste 800 .... Alexandria VA 22314 — **888-282-2552** — 571-483-1300

American Society of Consultant Pharmacists (ASCP)
1321 Duke St .... Alexandria VA 22314 — **800-355-2727** — 703-739-1300

American Society of Dermatopathology, The
111 Deer Lake Rd Ste 100 .... Deerfield IL 60015 — **800-445-8667** — 847-400-5820

American Society of Health-System Pharmacists (ASHP)
7272 Wisconsin Ave .... Bethesda MD 20814 — **866-279-0681** — 301-664-8700

American Society of PeriAnesthesia Nurses (ASPAN)
90 Frontage Rd .... Cherry Hill NJ 08034 — **877-737-9696** — 856-616-9600

American Society of Plastic Surgeons (ASPS)
444 E Algonquin Rd .... Arlington Heights IL 60005 — **888-475-2784** — 847-228-9900

American Society of Radiologic Technologists (ASRT)
15000 Central Ave SE .... Albuquerque NM 87123 — **800-444-2778** — 505-298-4500

American Society of Regional Anesthesia & Pain Medicine (ASRA)
239 Fourth Ave Ste 1714 .... Pittsburgh PA 15222 — **855-795-2772** — 412-471-2718

American Speech-Language-Hearing Assn (ASHA)
2200 Research Blvd .... Rockville MD 20850 — **800-498-2071** — 301-296-5700

American Thoracic Society (ATS)
61 Broadway 4th Fl. .... New York NY 10006 — **866-316-2673** — 212-315-8600

American Urological Assn (AUA)
1000 Corporate Blvd .... Linthicum MD 21090 — **866-746-4282** — 410-689-3700

American Veterinary Medical Assn (AVMA)
1931 N Meacham Rd Ste 100 .... Schaumburg IL 60173 — **800-248-2862** — 847-925-8070

AORN Inc
2170 S Parker Rd Ste 300 .... Denver CO 80231 — **800-755-2676** — 303-755-6300

Arthroscopy Assn of North America (AANA)
6300 N River Rd Ste 104 .... Rosemont IL 60018 — **877-924-0305** — 847-292-2262

Association for Applied Psychophysiology & Biofeedback (AAPB)
10200 W 44th Ave Ste 304 .... Wheat Ridge CO 80033 — **800-477-8892** — 303-422-8436

Association for Healthcare Documentation Integrity (AHDI)
4230 Kiernan Ave Ste 130 .... Modesto CA 95356 — **800-982-2182** — 209-527-9620

Association for the Advancement of Medical Instrumentation (AAMI)
4301 N Fairfax Dr Ste 301 .... Arlington VA 22203 — **800-332-2264** — 703-525-4890

Association for Vascular Access (AVA)
5526 West 13400 South Ste 229 .... Herriman UT 84096 — **888-576-2826** — 801-792-9079

Association of Clinical Research Professionals (ACRP)
500 Montgomery St Ste 800 .... Alexandria VA 22314 — **888-508-5731** — 703-254-8100

Association of Military Surgeons of the United States (AMSUS)
9320 Old Georgetown Rd .... Bethesda MD 20814 — **800-761-9320** — 301-897-8800

Association of Nurses in AIDS Care (ANAC)
3538 Ridgewood Rd .... Akron OH 44333 — **800-260-6780** — 330-670-0101

Association of Osteopathic Directors & Medical Educators (AODME)
142 E Ontario St .... Chicago IL 60611 — **800-621-1773** — 312-202-8211

Association of Rehabilitation Nurses (ARN)
4700 W Lk Ave .... Glenview IL 60025 — **800-229-7530** — 847-375-4710

Association of Reproductive Health Professionals (ARHP)
1901 L St NW Ste 300 .... Washington DC 20036 — **877-311-8972** — 202-466-3825

Association of Schools & Colleges of Optometry (ASCO)
6110 Executive Blvd Ste 420 .... Rockville MD 20852 — **888- 26-8377** — 301-231-5944

Association of Staff Physician Recruiters (ASPR)
1000 Westgate Dr Ste 252 .... Saint Paul MN 55114 — **800-830-2777** —

Association of Surgical Technologists (AST)
Six W Dry Creek Cir Ste 200 .... Littleton CO 80120 — **800-637-7433** — 303-694-9130

Association of University Programs in Health Administration (AUPHA)
2000 N 14th St Ste 780 .... Arlington VA 22201 — **877-275-6462** — 703-894-0941

Association of Women's Health Obstetric & Neonatal Nurses (AWHONN)
2000 L St NW Ste 740 .... Washington DC 20036 — **800-673-8499** — 202-261-2400

Asthma & Allergy Foundation of America (AAFA)
8201 Corporate Dr Ste 1000 .... Landover MD 20785 — **800-727-8462** — 202-466-7643

Canada's Research-Based Pharmaceutical Cos (Rx&D)
55 Metcalfe St Ste 1220 .... Ottawa ON K1P6L5 — **800-363-0203** — 613-236-0455

Canadian Academy of Sport Medicine (CASM)
180 Elgin St Ste 1400 .... Ottawa ON K2P2K3 — **877-585-2394** — 613-748-5851

Canadian Assn of Emergency Physicians (CAEP)
1785 Alta Vista Dr Ste 104 .... Ottawa ON K1G3Y6 — **800-463-1158** — 613-523-3343

Canadian Medical Assn (CMA)
1867 Alta Vista Dr .... Ottawa ON K1G5W8 — **800-663-7336** — 613-731-9331

Case Management Society of America (CMSA)
6301 Ranch Dr .... Little Rock AR 72223 — **800-216-2672** — 501-225-2229

Christian Medical & Dental Assn (CMDA)
2604 Hwy 421 PO Box 7500 .... Bristol TN 37620 — **888-231-2637** — 423-844-1000

COLA
9881 Broken Land Pkwy Ste 200 .... Columbia MD 21046 — **800-981-9883** — 410-381-6581

College of American Pathologists (CAP)
325 Waukegan Rd .... Northfield IL 60093 — **800-323-4040** — 847-832-7000

Emergency Nurses Assn (ENA)
915 Lee St .... Des Plaines IL 60016 — **800-900-9659** — 847-460-4000

Endocrine Society
8401 Connecticut Ave Ste 900 .... Chevy Chase MD 20815 — **888-363-6274** — 301-941-0200

Eye Bank Assn of America (EBAA)
1015 18th St NW Ste 1010 .... Washington DC 20036 — **888-491-8833** — 202-775-4999

Federation of State Medical Boards of the US Inc (FSMB)
400 Fuller Wiser Rd Ste 300 .... Euless TX 76039 — **800-793-7939** — 817-868-4000

Gerontological Society of America, The
1220 L St NW Ste 901 .... Washington DC 20005 — **800-677-1116** — 202-842-1275

Gynecologic Oncology Group (GOG)
1600 JFK Blvd Ste 1020 .... Philadelphia PA 19103 — **800-225-3053** — 215-854-0770

Health Industry Business Communications Council (HIBCC)
2525 E Arizona Biltmore Cir Ste 127 .... Phoenix AZ 85016 — **800-755-5505** — 602-381-1091

Healthcare Financial Management Assn (HFMA)
Two Westbrook Corporate Ctr
Ste 700 .... Westchester IL 60154 — **800-252-4362** — 708-531-9600

Hospice Foundation of America (HFA)
1710 Rhode Island Ave NW Ste 400 .... Washington DC 20036 — **800-854-3402** — 202-457-5811

Infectious Diseases Society of America (IDSA)
1300 Wilson Blvd Ste 300 .... Arlington VA 22209 — **888-844-4372** — 703-299-0200

Infusion Nurses Society (INS)
315 Norwood Pk S .... Norwood MA 02062 — **800-694-0298** — 781-440-9408

Institute for Healthcare Improvement (IHI)
20 University Rd Seventh Fl .... Cambridge MA 02138 — **866-787-0831** — 617-301-4800

Institute for the Advancement of Human Behavior (IAHB)
PO BOX 5527 .... Santa Rosa CA 95402 — **800-258-8411** — 650-851-8411

International Academy of Compounding Pharmacists (IACP)
4638 Riverstone Blvd .... Missouri City TX 77459 — **800-927-4227** — 281-933-8400

International Chiropractors Assn (ICA)
6400 Arlington Blvd Ste 800 .... Falls Church VA 22042 — **800-423-4690** — 703-528-5000

International College of Dentists (ICD)
51 Monroe St Ste 1400 .... Rockville MD 20850 — **800-533-6825** — 301-251-8861

International Congress of Oral Implantologists (ICOI)
248 Lorraine Ave Third Fl .... Upper Montclair NJ 07043 — **800-442-0525** — 973-783-6300

International Society for Heart & Lung Transplantation (ISHLT)
14673 Midway Rd Ste 200 .... Addison TX 75001 — **888-722-2220** — 972-490-9495

International Society for Magnetic Resonance in Medicine (ISMRM)
2030 Addison St Ste 700 .... Berkeley CA 94704 — **877-837-4400** — 510-841-1899

International Society for Pharmacoeconomics & Outcomes Research (ISPOR)
3100 Princeton Pk Bldg 3 Ste E .... Lawrenceville NJ 08648 — **800-992-0643** — 609-219-0773

International Society for Pharmacoepidemiology (ISPE)
5272 River Rd Ste 630 .... Bethesda MD 20816 — **888-887-7955** — 301-718-6500

International Society of Refractive Surgery (ISRS)
655 Beach St PO Box 7424 .... San Francisco CA 94109 — **866-561-8558** — 415-561-8581

International Transplant Nurses Society (ITNS)
1739 E Carson St PO Box 351 .... Pittsburgh PA 15203 — **800-776-8636** — 412-343-4867

Lamaze International
2025 M St NW Ste 800 .... Washington DC 20036 — **800-368-4404** — 202-367-1128

Medical Group Management Assn (MGMA)
104 Inverness Terr E .... Englewood CO 80112 — **877-275-6462** — 303-799-1111

NA of Neonatal Nurses (NANN)
4700 W Lk Ave .... Glenview IL 60025 — **800-451-3795** — 847-375-3660

National Abortion Federation (NAF)
1755 Massachusetts Ave NW .... Washington DC 20036 — **800-772-9100** — 202-667-5881

National Community Pharmacists Assn (NCPA)
100 Daingerfield Rd .... Alexandria VA 22314 — **800-544-7447** — 703-683-8200

				Toll-Free	Phone
National Council of State Boards of Nursing (NCSBN)					
111 E Wacker Dr Ste 2900	Chicago	IL	60601	**866-293-9600**	312-525-3600
National Council on Problem Gambling Inc					
730 11th St NW Ste 601	Washington	DC	20001	**800-522-4700**	202-547-9204
National Hospice & Palliative Care Organization (NHPCO)					
1700 Diagonal Rd Ste 625	Alexandria	VA	22314	**800-658-8898***	703-837-1500
*Help Line					
National League for Nursing (NLN)					
61 Broadway 33rd Fl.	New York	NY	10006	**800-669-1656**	212-363-5555
National Medical Assn (NMA)					
8403 Colesville Rd Ste 920	Silver Spring	MD	20910	**800-662-0554**	202-347-1895
National Nursing Staff Development Organization (NNSDO)					
330 N Wabash Ave Ste 2000.	Chicago	IL	60611	**800-489-1995**	312-321-5135
National Organization for Rare Disorders (NORD)					
55 Kenosia Ave PO Box 1968.	Danbury	CT	06813	**800-999-6673**	203-744-0100
North American Spine Society (NASS)					
7075 Veterans Blvd	Burr Ridge	IL	60527	**877-774-6337**	630-230-3600
Oncology Nursing Society (ONS)					
125 Enterprise Dr	Pittsburgh	PA	15275	**866-257-4667**	412-859-6100
Optical Laboratories Assn (OLA)					
225 Reinekers Ln Ste 700.	Alexandria	VA	22314	**800-477-5652**	703-548-6619
Optical Society of America (OSA)					
2010 Massachusetts Ave NW	Washington	DC	20036	**800-843-6664**	202-223-8130
Physicians Committee for Responsible Medicine (PCRM)					
5100 Wisconsin Ave NW Ste 400.	Washington	DC	20016	**866-416-7276**	202-686-2210
Physicians for Social Responsibility (PSR)					
1875 Connecticut Ave NW Ste 1012.	Washington	DC	20009	**800-459-1887**	202-667-4260
Radiological Society of North America (RSNA)					
820 Jorie Blvd	Oak Brook	IL	60523	**800-381-6660**	630-571-2670
Radiology Business Management Assn (RBMA)					
10300 Eaton Pl Ste 460	Fairfax	VA	22030	**888-224-7262**	703-621-3355
Society for Healthcare Epidemiology of America					
1300 Wilson Blvd Ste 300	Arlington	VA	22209	**877-734-2726**	703-684-1006
Society for Healthcare Strategy & Market Development (SHSMD)					
155 N Wacker Dr Ste 400	Chicago	IL	60606	**800-242-2626**	312-422-3888
Society for Surgery of the Alimentary Tract (SSAT)					
900 Cummings Ctr Ste 221-U	Beverly	MA	01915	**866-849-5866**	978-927-8330
Society for Vascular Surgery (SVS)					
633 N St Clair St 22nd Fl.	Chicago	IL	60611	**800-258-7188**	312-334-2300
Society of Diagnostic Medical Sonography (SDMS)					
2745 Dallas Pkwy	Plano	TX	75093	**800-229-9506**	214-473-8057
Society of Gastroenterology Nurses & Assoc Inc (SGNA)					
401 N Michigan Ave	Chicago	IL	60611	**800-245-7462**	312-321-5165
Society of Interventional Radiology (SIR)					
3975 Fair Ridge Dr Ste 400 N.	Fairfax	VA	22033	**800-488-7284**	703-691-1805
Society of Nuclear Medicine (SNM)					
1850 Samuel Morse Dr	Reston	VA	20190	**888-633-5343**	703-708-9000
Society of Teachers of Family Medicine (STFM)					
11400 Tomahawk Creek Pkwy Ste 540	Leawood	KS	66211	**800-274-7928**	913-906-6000
Society of Thoracic Surgeons (STS)					
633 N St Clair St Ste 2320	Chicago	IL	60611	**877-865-5321**	312-202-5800
Society of Toxicology (SOT)					
1767 Business Ctr Dr	Reston	VA	20190	**800-826-6762**	703-438-3115
Southern Medical Assn (SMA)					
35 W Lakeshore Dr	Birmingham	AL	35209	**800-423-4992**	205-945-1840
Sports Cardiovascular & Wellness Nutritionists (SCAN)					
4500 Rockside Rd Ste 400	Cleveland	OH	44131	**800-249-2875***	216-503-0053
*General					
US Pharmacopeia (USP)					
12601 Twinbrook Pkwy	Rockville	MD	20852	**800-227-8772**	301-881-0666
Visiting Nurse Assns of America (VNAA)					
900 19th St NW Ste 200.	Washington	DC	20006	**888-866-8773**	202-384-1420
Wound Ostomy & Continence Nurses Society (WOCN)					
15000 Commerce Pkwy Ste C	Mount Laurel	NJ	08054	**888-224-9626**	

48-9 Insurance Industry Associations

				Toll-Free	Phone
America's Health Insurance Plans (AHIP)					
601 Pennsylvania Ave NW Ste 500.	Washington	DC	20004	**877-291-2247***	202-778-3200
*Cust Svc					
American Academy of Actuaries					
1100 17th St NW 7th Fl	Washington	DC	20036	**888-888-1778**	202-223-8196
American Assn of Insurance Services (AAIS)					
1745 S Naperville Rd.	Wheaton	IL	60189	**800-564-2247**	630-681-8347
American Assn of Managing General Agents (AAMGA)					
150 S Warner Rd Ste 156	King of Prussia	PA	19406	**800-467-8725**	610-225-1999
American Institute for CPCU & Insurance Institute of America (AICPCU/IIA)					
720 Providence Rd Ste 100	Malvern	PA	19355	**800-644-2101**	610-644-2100
American Nuclear Insurers (ANI)					
95 Glastonbury Blvd Ste 300	Glastonbury	CT	06033	**866-301-1301**	860-682-1301
Associated Risk Managers (ARM)					
2 Pierce Pl	Itasca	IL	60143	**800-735-5441**	630-285-4324
Association for Advanced Life Underwriting (AALU)					
11921 Freedom Dr Ste 1100.	Reston	VA	20190	**888-275-0092**	703-641-9400
Association for Co-op Operations Research & Development (ACORD)					
One Blue Hill Plz PO Box 1529.	Pearl River	NY	10965	**800-444-3341**	845-620-1700
Blue Cross & Blue Shield Assn					
225 N Michigan Ave	Chicago	IL	60601	**800-810-2583**	312-297-6000
Coalition Against Insurance Fraud					
1012 14th St NW Ste 200.	Washington	DC	20005	**800-835-6422**	202-393-7330
Council of Insurance Agents & Brokers					
701 Pennsylvania Ave NW Ste 750.	Washington	DC	20004	**877-267-9855**	202-783-4400
CPCU Society					
720 Providence Rd	Malvern	PA	19355	**800-932-2728**	
GAMA International					
2901 Telestar Ct	Falls Church	VA	22042	**800-345-2687***	
*Cust Svc					
Independent Insurance Agents & Brokers of America Inc (IIABA)					
127 S Peyton St	Alexandria	VA	22314	**800-221-7917**	703-683-4422
Institute for Business & Home Safety (IBHS)					
4775 E Fowler Ave	Tampa	FL	33617	**866-657-4247**	813-286-3400
Insurance Information Institute Inc (III)					
110 William St	New York	NY	10038	**877-263-7995**	212-346-5500
Insurance Institute for Highway Safety					
1005 N Glebe Rd Ste 800	Arlington	VA	22201	**888-327-4236**	703-247-1500

				Toll-Free	Phone
Insurance Research Council (IRC)					
720 Providence Rd	Malvern	PA	19355	**800-644-2101**	610-644-2212
LIMRA International Inc					
300 Day Hill Rd	Windsor	CT	06095	**866-540-4505**	860-688-3358
LOMA					
2300 Windy Ridge Pkwy Ste 600	Atlanta	GA	30339	**800-275-5662**	770-951-1770
Million Dollar Round Table (MDRT)					
325 W Touhy Ave	Park Ridge	IL	60068	**877-883-4865***	847-692-6378
*General					
NA of Insurance & Financial Advisors (NAIFA)					
2901 Telestar Ct	Falls Church	VA	22042	**877-866-2432***	703-770-8100
*Sales					
National Council for Prescription Drug Programs (NCPDP)					
9240 E Raintree Dr	Scottsdale	AZ	85260	**888-665-2600**	480-477-1000
National Crop Insurance Services (NCIS)					
8900 Indian Creek Pkwy Ste 600	Overland Park	KS	66210	**800-951-6247**	913-685-2767
National Insurance Crime Bureau (NICB)					
1111 E Touhy Ave Ste 400	Des Plaines	IL	60018	**800-447-6282**	847-544-7002
Professional Liability Underwriting Society					
5353 Wayzata Blvd Ste 600	Minneapolis	MN	55416	**800-845-0778**	952-746-2580
Property Loss Research Bureau (PLRB)					
3025 Highland Pkwy Ste 800	Downers Grove	IL	60515	**888-711-7572**	630-724-2200
Society of Financial Service Professionals (SFSP)					
19 Campus Blvd Ste 100	Newtown Square	PA	19073	**800-392-6900**	610-526-2500
Workmen's Circle/Arbeter Ring Inc					
247 W 37th St Fifth Fl.	New York	NY	10018	**800-922-2558**	212-889-6800

48-10 Legal Professionals Associations

				Toll-Free	Phone
ABA Commission on Domestic Violence					
321 N Clark St Ninth Fl.	Chicago	IL	60654	**800-799-7233**	312-988-5000
American Academy of Psychiatry & the Law (AAPL)					
One Regency Dr PO Box 30	Bloomfield	CT	06002	**800-331-1389**	860-242-5450
American Arbitration Assn Inc (AAA)					
1633 Broadway 10th Fl.	New York	NY	10019	**800-778-7879**	212-716-5800
American Assn for Justice (AAJ)					
777 Sixth St NW Ste 200	Washington	DC	20001	**800-424-2725**	202-965-3500
American Bar Assn (ABA)					
321 N Clark St	Chicago	IL	60610	**800-285-2221**	312-988-5000
American Judicature Society (AJS)					
2700 University Ave	Des Moines	IA	50311	**800-626-4089**	515-271-2281
American Land Title Assn (ALTA)					
1828 L St NW Ste 705	Washington	DC	20036	**800-787-2582**	202-296-3671
American Law Institute (ALI)					
4025 Chestnut St	Philadelphia	PA	19104	**800-253-6397**	215-243-1600
American Tort Reform Assn (ATRA)					
1101 Connecticut Ave NW Ste 400.	Washington	DC	20036	**877-333-2227**	202-682-1163
Association for Conflict Resolution (ACR)					
12100 Sunset Hills Rd Ste 130.	Reston	VA	20190	**800-880-7303**	703-234-4141
Association of Corporate Counsel (ACC)					
1025 Connecticut Ave NW Ste 200	Washington	DC	20036	**877-647-3411**	202-293-4103
Association of Legal Administrators (ALA)					
75 Tri-State International Ste 222	Lincolnshire	IL	60069	**877-675-5571**	847-267-1252
Battered Women's Justice Project					
1801 Nicollet Ave S Ste 102	Minneapolis	MN	55403	**800-903-0111**	612-824-8768
Commercial Law League of America (CLLA)					
70 E Lake St Ste 630.	Chicago	IL	60601	**800-978-2552**	312-781-2000
Defense Research Institute (DRI)					
55 W Monroe St Ste 20	Chicago	IL	60603	**866-525-6466**	312-795-1101
Environmental Law Institute (ELI)					
2000 L St NW Ste 620	Washington	DC	20036	**800-433-5120**	202-939-3800
Food & Drug Law Institute (FDLI)					
1155 15th St NW Ste 800.	Washington	DC	20005	**800-956-6293**	202-371-1420
International Municipal Lawyers Assn (IMLA)					
7910 Woodmont Ave Ste 1440	Bethesda	MD	20814	**800-942-7732**	202-466-5424
Lawyers' Committee for Civil Rights Under Law					
1401 New York Ave NW Ste 400.	Washington	DC	20005	**888-299-5227**	202-662-8600
National Council of Juvenile & Family Court Judges (NCJFCJ)					
Univ of Nevada PO Box 8970	Reno	NV	89507	**800-527-3223**	775-784-6012
National Court Reporters Assn (NCRA)					
8224 Old Courthouse Rd	Vienna	VA	22182	**800-272-6272**	703-556-6272
National Federation of Paralegal Assn (NFPA)					
23607 Hwy 99 Ste 2-C	Edmonds	WA	98020	**888-525-3675**	425-967-0045
National Legal Aid & Defender Assn (NLADA)					
1140 Connecticut Ave NW Ste 900.	Washington	DC	20036	**800-725-4513**	202-452-0620
Native American Rights Fund (NARF)					
1506 Broadway	Boulder	CO	80302	**888-280-0726**	303-447-8760
Pension Rights Ctr					
1350 Connecticut Ave NW Ste 206.	Washington	DC	20036	**866-735-7737**	202-296-3776
Practising Law Institute (PLI)					
810 Seventh Ave 26th Fl.	New York	NY	10019	**800-260-4754**	212-824-5700
Taxpayers Against Fraud Education Fund (TAF)					
1220 19th St NW Ste 501.	Washington	DC	20036	**800-873-2573***	202-296-4826
*General					

48-11 Library & Information Science Associations

				Toll-Free	Phone
American Assn of School Librarians (AASL)					
50 E Huron St	Chicago	IL	60611	**800-545-2433**	312-280-4386
American Library Assn (ALA)					
50 E Huron St	Chicago	IL	60611	**800-545-2433**	312-944-6780
American Theological Library Assn (ATLA)					
300 S Wacker Dr Ste 2100	Chicago	IL	60606	**888-665-2852**	312-454-5100
Association for Library & Information Science Education (ALISE)					
65 E Wacker Pl Ste 1900	Chicago	IL	60601	**800-522-0772**	312-795-0996
Association for Library Collections & Technical Services (ALCTS)					
50 E Huron St	Chicago	IL	60611	**800-545-2433**	312-280-5038
Association for Library Service to Children (ALSC)					
50 E Huron St	Chicago	IL	60611	**800-545-2433**	312-280-2163
Association for Library Trustees, Advocates, Friends & Foundations (ALTAFF)					
50 E Huron St	Chicago	IL	60611	**800-545-2433**	

				Toll-Free	Phone
Association of College & Research Libraries (ACRL)					
50 E Huron St	Chicago	IL	60611	**800-545-2433**	312-280-2519
Association of Specialized & Co-op Library Agencies (ASCLA)					
50 E Huron St	Chicago	IL	60611	**800-545-2433**	312-280-4395
Library & Information Technology Assn (LITA)					
50 E Huron St	Chicago	IL	60611	**800-545-2433**	312-280-4270
Library Leadership & Management Assn (LLAMA)					
50 E Huron St	Chicago	IL	60611	**800-545-2433**	
Medical Library Assn (MLA)					
65 E Wacker Pl Ste 1900	Chicago	IL	60601	**800-523-1850**	312-419-9094
Online Computer Library Ctr Inc (OCLC)					
6565 Kilgour Pl	Dublin	OH	43017	**800-848-5878**	
Public Library Assn (PLA)					
50 E Huron St	Chicago	IL	60611	**800-545-2433**	312-280-5752
Reference & User Services Assn (RUSA)					
50 E Huron St	Chicago	IL	60611	**800-545-2433**	312-280-4398
Special Libraries Assn (SLA)					
331 S Patrick St	Alexandria	VA	22314	**866-446-6069**	703-647-4900
Young Adult Library Services Assn (YALSA)					
50 E Huron St	Chicago	IL	60611	**800-545-2433**	312-280-4390

48-12 Management & Business Professional Associations

				Toll-Free	Phone
Academy of Management (AOM)					
235 Elm Rd PO Box 3020	Briarcliff Manor	NY	10510	**800-633-4931**	914-923-2607
American Business Women's Assn (ABWA)					
11050 Roe Ave Ste 200	Overland Park	KS	66211	**800-228-0007**	
American Businesspersons Assn (ABA)					
350 Fairway Dr Ste 200	Deerfield Beach	FL	33441	**800-221-2168**	954-571-1877
American Chamber of Commerce Executives (ACCE)					
4875 Eisenhower Ave Ste 250	Alexandria	VA	22304	**800-394-2223**	703-998-0072
American Seminar Leaders Assn (ASLA)					
2405 E Washington Blvd	Pasadena	CA	91104	**800-801-1886**	626-791-1211
American Society of Assn Executives (ASAE)					
1575 'I' St NW	Washington	DC	20005	**888-950-2723**	202-626-2723
American Staffing Assn (ASA)					
277 S Washington St Ste 200	Alexandria	VA	22314	**800-456-4324**	703-253-2020
APQC					
123 N Post Oak Ln Ste 300	Houston	TX	77024	**800-776-9676**	713-681-4020
ARMA International					
11880 College Blvd Ste 450	Overland Park	KS	66210	**800-422-2762**	913-341-3808
Association for Corporate Growth (ACG)					
71 S Wacker Dr Ste 2760	Chicago	IL	60606	**877-358-2220**	312-957-4260
Association for Mfg Technology (AMT)					
7901 Westpark Dr	McLean	VA	22102	**800-524-0475**	703-893-2900
Association of Fundraising Professionals (AFP)					
4300 Wilson Blvd Ste 300	Arlington	VA	22203	**800-666-3863**	703-684-0410
Business Forms Management Assn (BFMA)					
3800 Old Cheney Rd Ste 101-285	Lincoln	NE	68516	**888-367-3078**	402-216-0479
Christian Leadership Alliance (CLA)					
635 Camino De Los Mares Ste 216	San Clemente	CA	92673	**800-263-6317**	949-487-0900
Club Managers Assn of America (CMAA)					
1733 King St	Alexandria	VA	22314	**800-777-3529**	703-739-9500
ESOP Assn					
1726 M St NW Ste 501	Washington	DC	20036	**866-366-3832**	202-293-2971
Executive Women International (EWI)					
7414 S State St	Midvale	UT	84047	**877-439-4669**	801-355-2800
Institute for a Drug-Free Workplace (IDFW)					
10701 Parkridge Blvd Ste 300	Reston	VA	20191	**877-696-6775**	703-391-7222
Institute for Supply Management (ISM)					
2055 Centennial Cir	Tempe	AZ	85284	**800-888-6276***	480-752-6276
*Cust Svc					
Institute of Business Appraisers (IBA)					
1111 BrickyaRd Rd Ste 200	Salt Lake City	UT	84106	**800-299-4130**	
Institute of Certified Professional Managers (ICPM)					
James Madison University MSC 5504	Harrisonburg	VA	22807	**800-460-8013**	540-568-3247
Institute of Management Consultants USA Inc (IMC USA)					
2025 M St NW Ste 800	Washington	DC	20036	**800-221-2557**	202-367-1134
International Assn for Human Resource Information Management Inc (IHRIM)					
PO Box 1086	Burlington	MA	01803	**800-804-3983**	
International Assn of Business Communicators (IABC)					
601 Montgomery St Ste 1900	San Francisco	CA	94111	**800-766-4222**	415-544-4700
International Assn of Venue Managers Inc (IAVM)					
635 Fritz Dr Ste 100	Coppell	TX	75019	**800-935-4226**	972-906-7441
International Assn of Workforce Professionals (IAPES)					
1801 Louisville Rd	Frankfort	KY	40601	**888-898-9960**	502-223-4459
International Public Management Assn for Hum Res (IPMA-HR)					
1617 Duke St	Alexandria	VA	22314	**800-381-8378**	703-549-7100
International Society for Performance Improvement (ISPI)					
1400 Spring St Ste 260	Silver Spring	MD	20910	**800-825-7550**	301-587-8570
International Society of Certified Employee Benefit Specialists (ISCEBS)					
18700 W Bluemound Rd PO Box 209	Brookfield	WI	53008	**888-334-3327**	262-786-8771
International Trademark Assn (INTA)					
655 Third Ave 10th Fl	New York	NY	10017	**800-995-3579**	212-768-9887
Latin Business Assn (LBA)					
120 S San Pedro St Ste 530	Los Angeles	CA	90012	**877-551-7778**	213-628-8510
Meeting Professionals International (MPI)					
3030 LBJ Fwy Ste 1700	Dallas	TX	75234	**866-748-9561**	972-702-3000
NA of Parliamentarians (NAP)					
213 S Main St	Independence	MO	64050	**888-627-2929**	816-833-3892
National Business Assn (NBA)					
5151 Beltline Rd Ste 1150	Dallas	TX	75254	**800-456-0440**	972-458-0900
National Business Coalition on Health (NBCH)					
1015 18th St NW Ste 730	Washington	DC	20036	**800-223-4139**	202-775-9300
National Business Incubation Assn (NBIA)					
40 W St Ste 25	Athens	OH	45701	**800-766-3782**	740-593-4331
National Co-op Business Assn (NCBA)					
1401 New York Ave NW Ste 1100	Washington	DC	20005	**800-356-9655**	202-638-6222
National Coalition of Black Meeting Planners (NCBMP)					
700 N. Fairfax St Suite 510	Alexandria	VA	22314	**800-551-9369**	571-527-3110
National Contract Management Assn (NCMA)					
21740 Beaumeade Cir Ste 125	Ashburn	VA	20147	**800-344-8096**	571-382-0082
National Notary Assn (NNA)					
9350 DeSoto Ave	Chatsworth	CA	91313	**800-876-6827**	818-739-4000

				Toll-Free	Phone
National Right to Work Committee (NRTWC)					
8001 Braddock Rd Ste 500	Springfield	VA	22160	**800-325-7892**	703-321-8510
National Small Business Assn (NSBA)					
1156 15th St NW Ste 1100	Washington	DC	20005	**800-345-6728**	202-293-8830
Product Development & Management Assn (PDMA)					
330 N Wabash Ave Ste 2000	Chicago	IL	60611	**800-232-5241**	312-321-5145
Professional Convention Management Assn (PCMA)					
35 E Wacker Dr Ste 500	Chicago	IL	60601	**877-827-7262**	312-423-7262
Professional Services Council (PSC)					
4401 Wilson Blvd Ste 1110	Arlington	VA	22203	**800-353-9118**	703-875-8059
Profit Sharing/401(k) Council of America (PSCA)					
20 N Wacker Dr Ste 3700	Chicago	IL	60606	**866-614-8407**	312-419-1863
Project Management Institute (PMI)					
14 Campus Blvd	Newtown Square	PA	19073	**866-276-4764**	610-356-4600
Religious Conference Management Assn Inc (RCMA)					
7702 Woodland Dr Ste 120	Indianapolis	IN	46278	**800-221-8235**	317-632-1888
SCORE Assn					
1175 Herndon Pkwy Ste 900	Herndon	VA	20170	**800-634-0245**	
Society for Human Resource Management (SHRM)					
1800 Duke St	Alexandria	VA	22314	**800-283-7476**	703-548-3440
Society of Competitive Intelligence Professionals (SCIP)					
1700 Diagonal Rd Ste 600	Alexandria	VA	22314	**877-463-7678**	703-739-0696
US Council for International Business (USCIB)					
1212 Ave of the Americas 18th Fl	New York	NY	10036	**866-768-5925**	212-354-4480
WorldatWork					
14040 N Northsight Blvd	Scottsdale	AZ	85260	**877-951-9191**	202-315-5500
Young Presidents' Organization (YPO)					
600 E Las Colinas Blvd Ste 1000	Irving	TX	75039	**800-773-7976**	972-587-1500
YPO-WPO					
600 E Las Colinas Blvd Ste 1000	Irving	TX	75039	**800-773-7976**	972-587-1500

48-13 Manufacturing Industry Professional & Trade Associations

				Toll-Free	Phone
Aluminum Extruders Council (AEC)					
1000 N Rand Rd Ste 214	Wauconda	IL	60084	**800-354-5892**	847-526-2010
American Boiler Manufacturers Assn (ABMA)					
8221 Old Courthouse Rd Ste 207	Vienna	VA	22182	**800-227-1966**	703-356-7172
American Foundry Society (AFS)					
1695 N Penny Ln	Schaumburg	IL	60173	**800-537-4237**	847-824-0181
American Galvanizers Assn (AGA)					
6881 S Holly Cir Ste 108	Centennial	CO	80112	**800-468-7732**	720-554-0900
American Society for Quality (ASQ)					
600 N Plankinton Ave	Milwaukee	WI	53203	**800-248-1946**	414-272-8575
ASM International					
9639 Kinsman Rd	Materials Park	OH	44073	**800-336-5152**	440-338-5151
Association for Iron & Steel Technology (AIST)					
186 Thorn Hill Rd	Warrendale	PA	15086	**800-732-0999**	724-814-3000
Association of Equipment Manufacturers (AEM)					
6737 W Washington St Ste 2400	Milwaukee	WI	53214	**866-236-0442**	414-272-0943
Building Service Contractors Assn International (BSCAI)					
401 N Michigan Ave Ste 2200	Chicago	IL	60611	**800-368-3414**	312-321-5167
Can Manufacturers Institute (CMI)					
1730 Rhode Island Ave NW Ste 1000	Washington	DC	20036	**800-363-2726**	202-232-4677
Copper Development Assn Inc					
260 Madison Ave 16th Fl	New York	NY	10016	**800-232-3282**	212-251-7200
Council of Industrial Boiler Owners (CIBO)					
6035 Burke Ctr Pkwy Ste 360	Burke	VA	22015	**800-542-6096**	703-250-9042
Crane Manufacturers Assn of America (CMAA)					
8720 Red Oak Blvd Ste 201	Charlotte	NC	28217	**800-345-1815**	704-676-1190
Fabricators & Manufacturers Assn International (FMA)					
833 Featherstone Rd	Rockford	IL	61107	**888-394-4362**	815-399-8700
Food Processing Suppliers Assn (FPSA)					
1451 Dolley Madison Blvd Ste 101	McLean	VA	22101	**800-772-9247**	703-761-2600
Glass Assn of North America (GANA)					
800 SW Jackson St Ste 1500	Topeka	KS	66612	**877-275-2421**	785-271-0208
Industrial Fabrics Assn International (IFAI)					
1801 County Rd 'B' W	Roseville	MN	55113	**800-225-4324**	651-222-2508
Institute of Caster & Wheel Manufacturers (ICWM)					
8720 Red Oak Blvd Ste 201	Charlotte	NC	28217	**877-522-5431**	704-676-1190
Institute of Industrial Engineers (IIE)					
3577 PkwyLn Ste 200	Norcross	GA	30092	**800-494-0460***	770-449-0460
*Cust Svc					
Institute of Makers of Explosives (IME)					
1120 19th St NW Ste 310	Washington	DC	20036	**800-461-8841**	202-429-9280
Institute of Packaging Professionals (IoPP)					
1833 Centre Point Cir Ste 123	Naperville	IL	60563	**800-432-4085**	630-544-5050
Institute of Paper Science & Technology (IPST)					
500 Tenth St NW	Atlanta	GA	30332	**800-558-6611**	404-894-5700
International Ground Source Heat Pump Assn (IGSHPA)					
Oklahoma State University 374 Cordell S	Stillwater	OK	74078	**800-626-4747**	405-744-5175
Material Handling Industry of America (MHIA)					
8720 Red Oak Blvd Ste 201	Charlotte	NC	28217	**800-345-1815**	704-676-1190
Metal Powder Industries Federation (MPIF)					
105 College Rd E	Princeton	NJ	08540	**800-443-4862**	609-452-7700
Minerals Metals & Materials Society (TMS)					
184 Thorn Hill Rd	Warrendale	PA	15086	**800-759-4867**	724-776-9000
NACE International: Corrosion Society					
1440 S Creek Dr	Houston	TX	77084	**800-797-6223**	281-228-6200
National Coil Coating Assn (NCCA)					
1300 Sumner Ave	Cleveland	OH	44115	**800-532-0500**	216-241-7333
National Council of Textile Organizations (NCTO)					
910 17th St NW Ste 1020	Washington	DC	20006	**800-238-7192**	202-822-8028
National Electrical Manufacturers Assn (NEMA)					
1300 N 17th St Ste 1752	Rosslyn	VA	22209	**888-236-2427**	703-841-3200
National Glass Assn (NGA)					
8200 Greensboro Dr Ste 302	McLean	VA	22102	**866-342-5642**	703-442-4890
National Marine Electronics Assn (NMEA)					
Seven Riggs Ave	Severna Park	MD	21146	**800-808-6632**	410-975-9425
National Paint & Coatings Assn (NPCA)					
1500 Rhode Island Ave NW	Washington	DC	20005	**800-431-7900**	202-462-6272
National Tooling & Machining Assn (NTMA)					
6363 Oak Tree Blvd	Independence	OH	44131	**800-248-6862**	
North American Assn of Food Equipment Manufacturers (NAFEM)					
161 N Clark St Ste 2020	Chicago	IL	60601	**888-493-5961**	312-821-0201

					Toll-Free	Phone

North American Die Casting Assn (NADCA)
241 Holbrook Dr . . . . Wheeling IL 60090 **800-275-8373** 847-279-0001
Open Applications Group Inc (OAGI)
PO Box 4897 . . . . Marietta GA 30061 **800-236-4600** 404-402-1962
Packaging Machinery Manufacturers Institute (PMMI)
4350 N Fairfax Dr Ste 600 . . . . Arlington VA 22203 **888-275-7664** 703-243-8555
Precision Machined Products Assn (PMPA)
6700 W Snowville Rd . . . . Brecksville OH 44141 **800-233-1234** 440-526-0300
Reusable Industrial Packaging Assn (RIPA)
8401 Corporate Dr Ste 450 . . . . Landover MD 20785 **800-441-8780** 301-577-3786
Rubber Manufacturers Assn (RMA)
1400 K St NW Ste 900 . . . . Washington DC 20005 **800-220-7622** 202-682-4800
Society for Mining Metallurgy & Exploration Inc (SME)
8307 Shaffer Pkwy . . . . Littleton CO 80127 **800-763-3132** 303-973-9550
Society for Protective Coatings (SSPC)
40 24th St Sixth Fl . . . . Pittsburgh PA 15222 **877-281-7772** 412-281-2331
Society of Mfg Engineers (SME)
One SME Dr . . . . Dearborn MI 48128 **800-733-4763*** 313-425-3000
*Cust Svc
Society of Vacuum Coaters (SVC)
71 Pinon Hill Pl NE . . . . Albuquerque NM 87122 **800-777-4643** 505-856-7188
Spring Manufacturers Institute (SMI)
2001 Midwest Rd Ste 106 . . . . Oak Brook IL 60523 **866-482-5569** 630-495-8588
Technical Assn of the Pulp & Paper Industry (TAPPI)
15 Technology Pkwy S . . . . Norcross GA 30092 **800-332-8686*** 770-446-1400
*Sales
Valve Manufacturers Assn of America (VMA)
1050 17th St NW Ste 280 . . . . Washington DC 20036 **800-468-3571** 202-331-8105

48-14 Media Professionals Associations

					Toll-Free	Phone

Accuracy in Media Inc (AIM)
4455 Connecticut Ave NW Ste 330 . . . . Washington DC 20008 **800-787-4567** 202-364-4401
American Radio Relay League (ARRL)
225 Main St . . . . Newington CT 06111 **888-277-5289** 860-594-0200
Association of Alternative Newsweeklies (AAN)
115615th St NW . . . . Washington DC 20005 **866-415-0704** 202-289-8484
Association of Public Television Stations (APTS)
2100 Crystal Dr Ste 700 . . . . Arlington VA 22202 **855-948-5853** 202-654-4200
Catholic Press Assn (CPA)
205 W Monroe St Ste 470 . . . . Chicago IL 60606 **800-777-7432** 312-380-6789
Media Coalition Inc
275 Seventh Ave Ste 1504 . . . . New York NY 10001 **866-512-1600** 212-587-4025
National Cable Television Co-op Inc (NCTC)
11200 Corporate Ave . . . . Lenexa KS 66219 **800-720-5850** 913-599-5900
National Newspaper Assn (NNA)
PO Box 7540 . . . . Columbia MO 65205 **800-829-4662** 573-777-4980
Satellite Broadcasting & Communications Assn (SBCA)
1730 M St NW Ste 600 . . . . Washington DC 20036 **800-541-5981** 202-349-3620
Society of Broadcast Engineers Inc (SBE)
9102 N Meridian St Ste 150 . . . . Indianapolis IN 46260 **800-237-1776** 317-846-9000
Society of Environmental Journalists (SEJ)
115 W Ave . . . . Jenkintown PA 19046 **866-208-3372** 215-884-8174
Society of Professional Journalists (SPJ)
3909 N Meridian St . . . . Indianapolis IN 46208 **800-331-1212** 317-927-8000
Specialized Information Publishers Assn (SIPA)
8229 Boone Blvd Ste 260 . . . . Vienna VA 22182 **800-356-9302** 703-992-9339

48-15 Mental Health Professionals Associations

					Toll-Free	Phone

American Academy of Child & Adolescent Psychiatry (AACAP)
3615 Wisconsin Ave NW . . . . Washington DC 20016 **800-333-7636** 202-966-7300
American Academy of Psychiatry & the Law (AAPL)
One Regency Dr PO Box 30 . . . . Bloomfield CT 06002 **800-331-1389** 860-242-5450
American Counseling Assn (ACA)
5999 Stevenson Ave . . . . Alexandria VA 22304 **800-347-6647** 703-823-9800
American Group Psychotherapy Assn (AGPA)
25 E 21st St Sixth Fl . . . . New York NY 10010 **877-668-2472** 212-477-2677
American Mental Health Counselors Assn (AMHCA)
801 N Fairfax St Ste 304 . . . . Alexandria VA 22314 **800-326-2642** 703-548-6002
American Psychiatric Assn (APA)
1000 Wilson Blvd Ste 1825 . . . . Arlington VA 22209 **888-357-7924** 703-907-7300
American Psychiatric Nurses Assn (APNA)
1555 Wilson Blvd Ste 530 . . . . Arlington VA 22209 **866-243-2443** 703-243-2443
American Psychological Assn (APA)
750 First St NE . . . . Washington DC 20002 **800-374-2721** 202-336-5500
Association for Behavioral & Cognitive Therapies (ABCT)
305 Seventh Ave 16th Fl . . . . New York NY 10001 **800-685-2228** 212-647-1890
International Assn of Marriage & Family Counselors (IAMFC)
5999 Stevenson Ave . . . . Alexandria VA 22304 **800-347-6647**
Lifespring Inc
460 Spring St . . . . Jeffersonville IN 47130 **800-456-2117** 812-280-2080
National Psychological Assn for Psychoanalysis (NPAP)
40 W 13th St Ste 1 . . . . New York NY 10011 **800-365-7006** 212-924-7440
Northern Arizona Regional Behavioral Health Authority Inc (NARBHA)
1300 S Yale St . . . . Flagstaff AZ 86001 **877-923-1400** 928-774-7128
Northwestern Counseling Support & Services Inc
107 Fisher Pond Rd . . . . Saint Albans VT 05478 **800-834-7793** 802-524-6554
SAVE - Suicide Awareness Voices of Education
8120 Penn Ave S Ste 470 . . . . Bloomington MN 55431 **888-511-7283** 952-946-7998
Society for Social Work Leadership in Health Care
100 N 20th St Fourth Fl . . . . Philadelphia PA 19103 **866-237-9542** 215-599-6134
Society of Behavioral Medicine (SBM)
555 E Wells St Ste 1100 . . . . Milwaukee WI 53202 **800-784-8669** 414-918-3156

48-16 Publishing & Printing Professional Associations

					Toll-Free	Phone

Association of American Publishers Inc (AAP)
71 Fifth Ave . . . . New York NY 10003 **866-271-4968** 212-255-0200
Association of Directory Publishers (ADP)
116 Cass St . . . . Traverse City MI 49684 **800-267-9002** 231-486-2182

Canadian Newspaper Assn
890 Yonge St Ste 200 . . . . Toronto ON M4W3P4 **877-305-2262** 416-923-3567
Copyright Clearance Ctr Inc (CCC)
222 Rosewood Dr . . . . Danvers MA 01923 **855-239-3415** 978-750-8400
Editorial Freelancers Assn (EFA)
71 W 23rd St 4th Fl . . . . New York NY 10010 **866-929-5400** 212-929-5400
Epicomm (NAPL)
1 Meadowlands Plaza Ste 1511 . . . . East Rutherford NJ 07073 **800-642-6275** 201-634-9600
Greeting Card Assn (GCA)
1133 Westchester Ave Ste N136 . . . . White Plains NY 10604 **866-799-5384** 914-421-3331
Idealliance
7200 France Ave S Ste 223 . . . . Edina MN 55435 **800-255-8141** 952-896-1908
International Reprographic Assn (IRgA)
401 N Michigan Ave Ste 2200 . . . . Chicago IL 60611 **800-833-4742** 312-245-1026
Magazine Publishers of America (MPA)
810 Seventh Ave 24th Fl . . . . New York NY 10019 **800-234-3368** 212-872-3700
National Information Standards Organization (NISO)
3600 Clipper Mill Road Suite 302 . . . . Baltimore MD 21211 **877-375-2160** 301-654-2512
National Press Foundation (NPF)
1211 Connecticut Ave NW Ste 310 . . . . Washington DC 20036 **877-472-3779** 202-663-7280
NPES: Assn for Suppliers of Printing Publishing & Converting Technologies
1899 Preston White Dr . . . . Reston VA 20191 **866-381-9839** 703-264-7200
Printing Industries of America/Graphic Arts Technical Foundation (PIA/GATF)
200 Deer Run Rd . . . . Sewickley PA 15143 **800-910-4283** 412-741-6860
Specialty Graphic Imaging Assn (SGIA)
10015 Main St . . . . Fairfax VA 22031 **888-385-3588** 703-385-1335

48-17 Real Estate Professionals Associations

					Toll-Free	Phone

American Society of Appraisers (ASA)
555 Herndon Pkwy Ste 125 . . . . Herndon VA 20170 **800-272-8258** 703-478-2228
Appraisal Institute
550 W Van Buren St Ste 1000 . . . . Chicago IL 60607 **888-756-4624** 312-335-4100
Building Owners & Managers Assn International (BOMA)
1101 15th St NW Ste 800 . . . . Washington DC 20005 **800-426-6292** 202-408-2662
CCIM Institute
430 N Michigan Ave Ste 800 . . . . Chicago IL 60611 **800-621-7027** 312-321-4460
CoreNet Global Inc
260 Peachtree St NW Ste 1500 . . . . Atlanta GA 30303 **800-726-8111** 404-589-3200
Council of Real Estate Brokerage Managers (CRB)
430 N Michigan Ave Ste 300 . . . . Chicago IL 60611 **800-621-8738**
Council of Residential Specialists
430 N Michigan Ave Ste 300 . . . . Chicago IL 60611 **800-462-8841** 312-321-4400
Institute of Business Appraisers (IBA)
1111 BrickyaRd St Ste 200 . . . . Salt Lake City UT 84106 **800-299-4130**
Institute of Real Estate Management (IREM)
430 N Michigan Ave . . . . Chicago IL 60611 **800-837-0706** 312-329-6000
NA of REALTORS
430 N Michigan Ave . . . . Chicago IL 60611 **800-874-6500** 312-329-8200
National Apartment Assn (NAA)
4300 Wilson Blvd Ste 400 . . . . Arlington VA 22203 **800-632-3007** 703-518-6141
New Venture Communications
28 E Third Ave Ste 201 . . . . San Mateo CA 94401 **800-307-0762** 650-343-2735
Real Estate Buyer's Agent Council (REBAC)
430 N Michigan Ave . . . . Chicago IL 60611 **800-648-6224**
Women's Council of REALTORS (WCR)
430 N Michigan Ave . . . . Chicago IL 60611 **800-245-8512**

48-18 Sales & Marketing Professional Associations

					Toll-Free	Phone

Advertising Council Inc
815 Second Ave Fl 9 . . . . New York NY 10016 **888-200-4005** 212-922-1500
American Adv Federation (AAF)
1101 Vermont Ave NW Ste 500 . . . . Washington DC 20005 **800-999-2231** 202-898-0089
American Assn of Franchisees & Dealers (AAFD)
PO Box 10158 . . . . Palm Desert CA 92255 **800-733-9858** 619-209-3775
American Booksellers Assn (ABA)
200 White Plains Rd Ste 600 . . . . Tarrytown NY 10591 **800-637-0037** 914-591-2665
American International Automobile Dealers Assn (AIADA)
500 Montgomery St Ste 800 . . . . Alexandria VA 22314 **800-462-4232** 703-519-7800
American Marketing Assn (AMA)
311 S Wacker Dr Ste 5800 . . . . Chicago IL 60606 **800-262-1150** 312-542-9000
American Wholesale Marketers Assn (AWMA)
2750 Prosperity Ave Ste 530 . . . . Fairfax VA 22031 **800-482-2962** 703-208-3358
Associated Equipment Distributors (AED)
600 22nd St Ste 220 . . . . Oak Brook IL 60523 **800-388-0650** 630-574-0650
Association of Progressive Rental Organizations (APRO)
1504 Robin Hood Trl . . . . Austin TX 78703 **800-204-2776** 512-794-0095
Audit Bureau of Circulations (ABC)
48 W Seegers Road . . . . Arlington Heights IL 60005 **800-759-6397** 224-366-6939
Automotive Distribution Network
3085 Fountainside Dr Ste 210 . . . . Germantown TN 38138 **800-727-8112** 901-682-9090
Brick Industry Assn (BIA)
1850 Centennial Pk Dr Ste 301 . . . . Reston VA 20191 **866-644-1293** 703-620-0010
Business Marketing Assn (BMA)
708 Third Ave 33rd Fl . . . . New York NY 10017 **800-664-4262** 212-697-5950
Business Technology Assn (BTA)
12411 Wornall Rd Ste 200 . . . . Kansas City MO 64145 **800-325-7219** 816-941-3100
Chain Drug Marketing Assn (CDMA)
43157 W Nine-Mile Rd PO Box 995 . . . . Novi MI 48376 **800-935-2362** 248-449-9300
Dairyamerica Inc
7815 N Palm Ave Ste 250 . . . . Fresno CA 93711 **800-722-3110** 559-251-0992
Direct Marketing Assn Inc (DMA)
1120 Ave of the Americas . . . . New York NY 10036 **855-422-0749** 212-768-7277
Electronics Representatives Assn (ERA)
300 W Adams St Ste 617 . . . . Chicago IL 60606 **800-776-7377** 312-527-3050
Food Marketing Institute (FMI)
2345 Crystal Dr Ste 800 . . . . Arlington VA 22202 **800-732-2639** 202-220-0600
Global Offset & Countertrade Assn (GOCA)
818 Connecticut Ave NW 12th Fl . . . . Washington DC 20006 **800-343-6074** 202-887-9011
HARDI Hydronic Heating & Cooling Council
3455 Mill Run Dr Ste 820 . . . . Hilliard OH 43026 **888-253-2128** 614-345-4328

Organization	Address	City	State	ZIP	Toll-Free	Phone
Health Industry Distributors Assn (HIDA)	310 Montgomery St	Alexandria	VA	22314	**800-549-4432**	703-549-4432
Healthcare Convention & Exhibitors Assn (HCEA)	1100 Johnson Ferry Rd Ste 300	Atlanta	GA	30342	**800-236-1592**	404-252-3663
International Franchise Assn (IFA)	1501 K St NW Ste 350	Washington	DC	20005	**800-543-1038**	202-628-8000
International Home Furnishings Representatives Assn (IHFRA)	209 S Main St PO Box 670	High Point	NC	27261	**800-667-9506**	336-889-3920
International Sanitary Supply Assn (ISSA)	3300 Dundee Rd	Northbrook	IL	60062	**800-225-4772**	847-982-0800
Machinery Dealers NA (MDNA)	315 S Patrick St	Alexandria	VA	22314	**800-872-7807**	703-836-9300
NA of Chain Drug Stores (NACDS)	413 N Lee St	Alexandria	VA	22314	**800-678-6223**	703-549-3001
NA of College Stores (NACS)	500 E Lorain St	Oberlin	OH	44074	**800-622-7498**	440-775-7777
NA of Convenience Stores (NACS)	1600 Duke St *Cust Svc	Alexandria	VA	22314	**800-966-6227***	703-684-3600
NA of Electrical Distributors Inc (NAED)	1181 Corporate Lk Dr	Saint Louis	MO	63132	**888-791-2512**	314-991-9000
NAMM - International Music Products Assn	5790 Armada Dr	Carlsbad	CA	92008	**800-767-6266**	760-438-8001
National Agri-Marketing Assn (NAMA)	11020 King St Ste 205	Overland Park	KS	66210	**800-530-5646**	913-491-6500
National Art Materials Trade Assn	15806 Brookway Dr Ste 300	Huntersville	NC	28078	**877-970-0832**	704-892-6244
National Auctioneers Assn (NAA)	8880 Ballentine St	Overland Park	KS	66214	**877-657-1990**	913-541-8084
National Auto Auction Assn (NAAA)	5320 Spectrum Dr Ste D	Frederick	MD	21703	**800-232-5411**	301-696-0400
National Automobile Dealers Assn (NADA)	8400 Westpark Dr	McLean	VA	22102	**800-252-6232**	703-821-7000
National Cotton Council of America	7193 Goodlett Farms Pkwy	Memphis	TN	38016	**888-232-1738**	901-274-9030
National Electrical Manufacturers Representatives Assn (NEMRA)	28 Deer St Ste 302	Portsmouth	NH	03801	**800-446-3672**	914-524-8650
National Electronics Service Dealers Assn (NESDA)	3608 Pershing Ave	Fort Worth	TX	76107	**800-946-0201**	817-921-9061
National Independent Automobile Dealers Assn (NIADA)	2521 Brown Blvd	Arlington	TX	76006	**800-682-3837**	817-640-3838
National Mail Order Assn LLC (NMOA)	2807 Polk St NE	Minneapolis	MN	55418	**800-992-1377**	612-788-1673
National Marine Representatives Assn (NMRA)	PO Box 360	Gurnee	IL	60031	**800-890-3819**	847-662-3167
National Retail Federation (NRF)	325 Seventh St NW Ste 1100	Washington	DC	20004	**800-673-4692**	202-783-7971
National Retail Hardware Assn (NRHA)	5822 W 74th St *Cust Svc	Indianapolis	IN	46278	**800-772-4424***	317-290-0338
National School Supply & Equipment Assn (NSSEA)	8380 Colesville Rd Ste 250	Silver Spring	MD	20910	**800-395-5550**	301-495-0240
National Shoe Retailers Assn (NSRA)	7386 N La Cholla Blvd	Tucson	AZ	85741	**800-673-8446**	520-209-1710
North American Bldg Material Distribution Assn (NBMDA)	330 N Wabash Ave Ste 2000	Chicago	IL	60611	**888-747-7862**	312-321-6845
North American Equipment Dealers Assn (NAEDA)	1195 Smizer Mill Rd	Fenton	MO	63026	**866-532-7653**	636-349-5000
NPTA Alliance	330 N Wabash Ave Ste 2000	Chicago	IL	60611	**800-355-6782**	312-321-4092
Paint & Decorating Retailers Assn (PDRA)	1401 Triad Ctr Dr	Saint Peters	MO	63376	**800-737-0107**	636-326-2636
Photo Marketing Assn International (PMA)	3000 Picture Pl	Jackson	MI	49201	**800-762-9287**	517-788-8100
Professional Beauty Assn (PBA)	15825 N 71st St Ste 100	Scottsdale	AZ	85254	**800-468-2274**	480-281-0424
Promotional Products Assn International (PPAI)	3125 Skyway Cir N	Irving	TX	75038	**888-426-7724**	972-252-0404
Public Relations Society of America (PRSA)	33 Maiden Ln 11th Fl	New York	NY	10038	**800-350-0111**	212-460-1400
Radio Adv Bureau (RAB)	125 W 55th St 21st Fl	New York	NY	10019	**800-252-7234**	212-681-7200
Recreation Vehicle Dealers Assn (RVDA)	3930 University Dr Third Fl	Fairfax	VA	22030	**800-336-0355**	703-591-7130
Retail Adv & Marketing Assn (RAMA)	325 Seventh St NW Ste 1100	Washington	DC	20004	**800-673-4692**	202-783-7971
Retail Solutions Providers Assn (RSPA)	10130 Perimeter Pkwy Ste 420	Charlotte	NC	28216	**800-782-2693**	704-357-3124
Society for Marketing Professional Services (SMPS)	99 Canal Ctr Plz	Alexandria	VA	22314	**800-292-7677**	703-549-6117
Souvenirs Gifts & Novelties Trade Assn	588 Sutter St Ste 140	San Francisco	CA	19003	**800-284-5451**	610-645-6940
Specialty Tools & Fasteners Distributors Assn (STAFDA)	500 Elm Grove Rd Ste 210 PO Box 44	Elm Grove	WI	53122	**800-352-2981**	262-784-4774

48-19 Technology, Science, Engineering Professionals Associations

Organization	Address	City	State	ZIP	Toll-Free	Phone
AES Electrophoresis Society	1202 Ann St	Madison	WI	53713	**800-242-4363**	608-258-1565
American Assn for Clinical Chemistry Inc (AACC)	1850 K St NW Ste 625 *Cust Svc	Washington	DC	20006	**800-892-1400***	202-857-0717
American Assn for Laboratory Accreditation (A2LA)	5301 Buckeystown Pike Ste 350	Frederick	MD	21704	**888-627-8318**	301-644-3248
American Assn for the Advancement of Science (AAAS)	1200 New York Ave NW	Washington	DC	20005	**800-669-6820**	202-326-6400
American Assn of Engineering Societies (AAES)	1620 'I' St NW Ste 210 *Orders	Washington	DC	20006	**888-400-2237***	202-296-2237
American Assn of Pharmaceutical Scientists (AAPS)	2107 Wilson Blvd Ste 700	Arlington	VA	22201	**877-998-2277**	703-243-2800
American Assn of Variable Star Observers (AAVSO)	49 Bay State Rd	Cambridge	MA	02138	**888-802-7827**	617-354-0484
American Chemical Society (ACS)	1155 16th St NW	Washington	DC	20036	**800-227-5558**	202-872-4600

Organization	Address	City	State	ZIP	Toll-Free	Phone
American Council of Independent Laboratories (ACIL)	1875 I St NW Ste 500	Washington	DC	20006	**800-368-1131**	202-887-5872
American Council on Science & Health (ACSH)	1995 Broadway Second Fl	New York	NY	10023	**866-905-2694**	212-362-7044
American Geological Institute (AGI)	4220 King St	Alexandria	VA	22302	**800-334-2564**	703-379-2480
American Geophysical Union (AGU)	2000 Florida Ave NW	Washington	DC	20009	**800-966-2481**	202-462-6900
American Indian Science & Engineering Society (AISES)	2305 Renard SE Ste 200	Albuquerque	NM	87106	**800-759-5219**	505-765-1052
American Institute of Aeronautics & Astronautics Inc (AIAA)	1801 Alexander Bell Dr Ste 500	Reston	VA	20191	**800-639-2422**	703-264-7500
American Institute of Biological Sciences (AIBS)	1444 'I' St NW Ste 200	Washington	DC	20005	**800-992-2427**	202-628-1500
American Institute of Chemical Engineers (AIChE)	120 Wall St Fl 23 *Cust Svc	New York	NY	10005	**800-242-4363***	203-702-7660
American Institute of Chemists (AIC)	315 Chestnut St	Philadelphia	PA	19106	**800-829-0115**	215-873-8224
American Institute of Professional Geologists (AIPG)	1400 W 122nd Ave Ste 250	Westminster	CO	80234	**800-772-3773**	303-412-6205
American Mathematical Society (AMS)	201 Charles St *Cust Svc	Providence	RI	02904	**800-321-4267***	401-455-4000
American Meteorological Society (AMS)	45 Beacon St	Boston	MA	02108	**800-824-0405**	617-227-2425
American Nuclear Society (ANS)	555 N Kensington Ave	La Grange Park	IL	60526	**800-323-3044**	708-352-6611
American Physical Society (APS)	1 Physics Ellipse	College Park	MD	20740	**888-221-9425**	301-209-3200
American Society for Nondestructive Testing Inc (ASNT)	1711 Arlingate Ln PO Box 28518 *Orders	Columbus	OH	43228	**800-222-2768***	614-274-6003
American Society for Photobiology (ASP)	PO Box 1897	Lawrence	KS	66044	**800-627-0326**	785-843-1234
American Society of Human Genetics (ASHG)	9650 Rockville Pike	Bethesda	MD	20814	**866-486-4363**	301-634-7300
American Society of Limnology & Oceanography (ASLO)	5400 Bosque Blvd Ste 680	Waco	TX	76710	**800-929-2756**	254-399-9635
American Statistical Assn (ASA)	732 N Washington St	Alexandria	VA	22314	**888-231-3473**	703-684-1221
AOAC International	481 N Frederick Ave Ste 500	Gaithersburg	MD	20877	**800-379-2622**	301-924-7077
Association for Women in Science Inc (AWIS)	1321 Duke St Ste 210	Alexandria	VA	22314	**800-303-0129**	703-894-4490
Association of American Geographers (AAG)	1710 16th St NW	Washington	DC	20009	**800-696-7353**	202-234-1450
ASTM International	100 Barr Harbor Dr PO Box C700	West Conshohocken	PA	19428	**800-814-1017**	610-832-9500
Audio Engineering Society	60 E 42nd St Rm 2520	New York	NY	10165	**800-541-7299**	212-661-8528
AVS Science & Technology Society	120 Wall St 32nd Fl	New York	NY	10005	**800-547-1406**	212-248-0200
Biotechnology Industry Organization	1201 Maryland Ave SW Ste 900	Washington	DC	20024	**866-356-5155**	202-962-9200
Center for Chemical Process Safety (CCPS)	120 Wall St	New York	NY	10005	**800-242-4363**	646-495-1371
Coordinating Research Council Inc (CRC)	3650 Mansell Rd Ste 140	Alpharetta	GA	30022	**800-445-8667**	678-795-0506
Council for Responsible Genetics (CRG)	5 Upland Rd Ste 3	Cambridge	MA	02140	**888-591-3911**	617-868-0870
Custom Electronic Design & Installation Assn (CEDIA)	7150 Winton Dr Ste 300	Indianapolis	IN	46268	**800-669-5329**	317-328-4336
Drug Chemical & Associated Technologies Assn (DCAT)	One Washington Blvd Ste 7	Robbinsville	NJ	08691	**800-640-3228**	609-448-1000
Electronics Technicians Assn International (ETA)	Five Depot St	Greencastle	IN	46135	**800-288-3824**	765-653-8262
Entomological Society of America	10001 Derekwood Ln Ste 100	Lanham	MD	20706	**800-523-8635**	301-731-4535
Federation of American Societies for Experimental Biology (FASEB)	9650 Rockville Pk	Bethesda	MD	20814	**800-433-2732**	301-634-7000
Generic Pharmaceutical Assn (GPhA)	2300 Clarendon Blvd Ste 400	Arlington	VA	22201	**800-859-8003**	703-647-2480
Genetics Society of America (GSA)	9650 Rockville Pk	Bethesda	MD	20814	**866-486-4363**	301-634-7300
Geological Society of America, The (GSA)	3300 Penrose Pl PO Box 9140	Boulder	CO	80301	**800-472-1988**	303-357-1000
IEEE Broadcast Technology Society (BTS)	445 Hoes Ln	Piscataway	NJ	08854	**800-678-4333**	732-562-5407
IEEE Computer Society	2001 L St NW Ste 700	Washington	DC	20036	**800-272-6657**	202-371-0101
IEEE Consumer Electronics Society (CES)	445 Hoes Ln	Piscataway	NJ	08854	**800-678-4333**	732-981-0060
IEEE Education Society (ES)	IEEE Operations Ctr 445 Hoes Ln	Piscataway	NJ	08854	**800-678-4333**	732-981-0060
IEEE Electromagnetic Compatibility Society (EMC)	IEEE Operations Ctr 445 Hoes Ln	Piscataway	NJ	08854	**800-678-4333**	732-981-0060
IEEE Electron Devices Society (EDS)	IEEE Operations Ctr 445 Hoes Ln	Piscataway	NJ	08854	**800-678-4333**	732-981-0060
IEEE Engineering Management Society (EMS)	IEEE Operations Ctr 445 Hoes Ln	Piscataway	NJ	08854	**800-678-4333**	732-981-0060
IEEE Geoscience & Remote Sensing Society (GRSS)	IEEE Operations Ctr 445 Hoes Ln	Piscataway	NJ	08854	**800-678-4333**	732-562-5550
IEEE Industrial Electronics Society (IES)	IEEE Operations Ctr 445 Hoes Ln	Piscataway	NJ	08854	**800-678-4333**	732-981-0060
IEEE Instrumentation & Measurement Society (IM)	445 Hoes Ln	Piscataway	NJ	08854	**800-327-6677**	732-562-3844
IEEE Magnetics Society	445 Hoes Ln PO Box 459	Piscataway	NJ	08855	**800-678-4333**	908-981-0060
IEEE Microwave Theory & Techniques Society (MTT-S)	IEEE Operations Ctr 445 Hoes Ln	Piscataway	NJ	08555	**800-678-4333**	732-562-5400
IEEE Nuclear & Plasma Sciences Society (NPSS)	445 Hoes Ln	Piscataway	NJ	08854	**800-678-4333**	732-981-0060
IEEE Power Engineering Society (PES)	IEEE Operations Ctr 445 Hoes Ln	Piscataway	NJ	08854	**800-678-4333**	732-562-3883
IEEE Product Safety Engineering Society	IEEE Operations Ctr 445 Hoes Ln	Piscataway	NJ	08854	**800-678-4333**	732-981-0060

				Toll-Free	Phone
IEEE Reliability Society (RS)					
IEEE Operations Ctr 445 Hoes Ln	Piscataway	NJ	08854	800-678-4333	732-981-0060
IEEE Signal Processing Society					
IEEE Operations Ctr 445 Hoes Ln	Piscataway	NJ	08854	800-678-4333	732-981-0060
IEEE Society on Social Implications of Technology (SSIT)					
IEEE Operations Ctr 445 Hoes Ln	Piscataway	NJ	08854	800-678-4333	732-981-0060
IEEE Solid State Circuits Society (SSCS)					
445 Hoes Ln	Piscataway	NJ	08854	800-678-4333	732-981-3400
IEEE Ultrasonics Ferroelectrics & Frequency Control Society					
IEEE Operations Ctr 445 Hoes Ln	Piscataway	NJ	08854	800-678-4333	732-981-0060
Institute for Operations Research & the Management Sciences (INFORMS)					
7240 Pkwy Dr Ste 300	Hanover	MD	21076	800-446-3676	443-757-3500
International Biometric Society (IBS)					
1444 'I' St NW Ste 700	Washington	DC	20005	800-262-1171	202-712-9049
International Society of Certified Electronics Technicians (ISCET)					
3608 Pershing Ave	Fort Worth	TX	76107	800-946-0201	817-921-9101
Laser Institute of America (LIA)					
13501 Ingenuity Dr Ste 128	Orlando	FL	32826	800-345-2737	407-380-1553
Mathematical Assn of America (MAA)					
1529 18th St NW	Washington	DC	20036	800-331-1622	202-387-5200
National Academies					
500 Fifth St NW	Washington	DC	20001	800-624-6242	202-334-2138
National Council on Radiation Protection & Measurements (NCRP)					
7910 Woodmont Ave Ste 400	Bethesda	MD	20814	800-462-3683	301-657-2652
National Environmental Balancing Bureau (NEBB)					
8575 Grovemont Cir	Gaithersburg	MD	20877	866-497-4447	301-977-3698
National Geographic Society					
1145 17th St NW	Washington	DC	20036	800-647-5463	202-857-7000
National Society of Professional Engineers (NSPE)					
1420 King St	Alexandria	VA	22314	888-285-6773	703-684-2800
National Space Society (NSS)					
1620 'I' St NW Ste 615	Washington	DC	20006	888-624-8373	202-429-1600
New York Academy of Sciences					
250 Greenwich St 40th Fl	New York	NY	10007	800-843-6927	212-298-8600
Scientific Equipment & Furniture Assn (SEFA)					
65 Hilton Avenue	Garden City	NY	11530	877-294-5424	516-294-5424
Semiconductor Environmental Safety & Health Assn (SESHA)					
1313 Dolley Madison Blvd Ste 402	McLean	VA	22101	800-433-1790	703-790-1745
Semiconductor Equipment & Materials International					
3081 Zenker Rd	San Jose	CA	95134	877-746-7788	408-943-6900
Society for Biomaterials					
15000 Commerce Pkwy Ste C	Mount Laurel	NJ	08054	800-337-9255	856-439-0826
Society for Experimental Mechanics Inc (SEM)					
7 School St	Bethel	CT	06801	800-627-8258	203-790-6373
Society for Industrial & Applied Mathematics (SIAM)					
3600 Market St 6th Fl	Philadelphia	PA	19104	800-447-7426	215-382-9800
Society for Integrative & Comparative Biology (SICB)					
1313 Dolley Madison Blvd Ste 402	McLean	VA	22101	800-955-1236	703-790-1745
Society for Risk Analysis (SRA)					
1313 Dolley Madison Blvd Ste 402	McLean	VA	22101	800-364-5800	703-790-1745
Society for Sedimentary Geology (SEPM)					
4111 S Darlington Ste 100	Tulsa	OK	74135	800-865-9765	918-610-3361
Society for the Advancement of Material & Process Engineering (SAMPE)					
1161 Pk View Dr Ste 200	Covina	CA	91724	800-562-7360	626-331-0616
Society of Cable Telecommunications Engineers (SCTE)					
140 Philips Rd	Exton	PA	19341	800-542-5040	610-363-6888
Society of Women Engineers (SWE)					
120 S La Salle St Ste 1515	Chicago	IL	60603	877-793-4636	312-596-5223
Women in Technology International (WITI)					
13351-D Riverside Dr Ste 441	Sherman Oaks	CA	91423	800-334-9484	818-788-9484
World Future Society					
7910 Woodmont Ave Ste 450	Bethesda	MD	20814	800-989-8274	301-656-8274

48-20 Telecommunications Professionals Associations

				Toll-Free	Phone
Alliance for Telecommunications Industry Solutions (ATIS)					
1200 G St NW Ste 500	Washington	DC	20005	800-649-1202	202-628-6380
American Public Communications Council Inc (APCC)					
625 Slaters Ln Ste 104	Alexandria	VA	22314	800-868-2722	703-739-1322
Communications Supply Service Assn (CSSA)					
5700 Murray St	Little Rock	AR	72209	800-252-2772	501-562-7666
Enterprise Wireless Alliance (EWA)					
8484 Westpark Dr Ste 630	McLean	VA	22102	800-482-8282	703-528-5115
International Communications Industries Assn (ICIA)					
11242 Waples Mill Rd Ste 200	Fairfax	VA	22030	800-659-7469	703-273-7200
Society of Telecommunications Consultants (STC)					
13275 California 89	Old Station	CA	96071	800-782-7670	530-335-7313
US Telecom Assn (USTA)					
607-14th St NW Ste 400	Washington	DC	20005	877-869-6903	202-326-7300

48-21 Transportation Industry Associations

				Toll-Free	Phone
Aerospace Industries Assn of America (AIA)					
1000 Wilson Blvd Ste 1700	Arlington	VA	22209	866-923-7797	703-358-1000
Air Traffic Control Assn (ATCA)					
1101 King St Ste 300	Alexandria	VA	22314	866-953-2189	703-299-2430
Aircraft Owners & Pilots Assn (AOPA)					
421 Aviation Way	Frederick	MD	21701	800-872-2672	301-695-2000
American Ambulance Assn (AAA)					
8201 Greensboro Dr Ste 300	McLean	VA	22102	800-523-4447	703-610-9018
American Assn of Airport Executives (AAAE)					
601 Madison St Ste 400	Alexandria	VA	22314	800-609-7374	703-824-0500
American Assn of State Highway & Transportation Officials (AASHTO)					
444 N Capitol St NW Ste 249	Washington	DC	20001	800-880-4117	202-624-5800
American Helicopter Society International (AHS)					
217 N Washington St	Alexandria	VA	22314	855-247-4685	703-684-6777
American International Automobile Dealers Assn (AIADA)					
500 Montgomery St Ste 600	Alexandria	VA	22314	800-462-4232	703-519-7800
American Moving & Storage Assn (AMSA)					
1611 Duke St	Alexandria	VA	22314	888-849-2672	703-683-7410
American Society of Naval Engineers (ASNE)					
1452 Duke St	Alexandria	VA	22314	800-995-3579	703-836-6727

				Toll-Free	Phone
American Traffic Safety Services Assn (ATSSA)					
15 Riverside Pkwy Ste 100	Fredericksburg	VA	22406	800-272-8772	540-368-1701
American Trucking Assn (ATA)					
950 N Glebe Rd Ste 210	Arlington	VA	22203	800-282-5463	703-838-1700
Automatic Transmission Rebuilders Assn (ATRA)					
2400 Latigo Ave	Oxnard	CA	93030	866-464-2872	805-604-2000
Automotive Aftermarket Industry Assn (AAIA)					
7101 Wisconsin Ave	Bethesda	MD	20814	800-936-8906	301-654-6664
Automotive Engine Rebuilders Assn (AERA)					
500 Coventry Ln Ste 180	Crystal Lake	IL	60014	888-326-2372	847-541-6550
Automotive Industry Action Group (AIAG)					
26200 Lahser Rd Ste 200	Southfield	MI	48033	877-275-2424	248-358-3570
Automotive Oil Change Assn (AOCA)					
330 N. Wabash Ave Ste 2000	Chicago	IL	60611	800-230-0702	312-321-5132
Automotive Parts Remanufacturers Assn (APRA)					
4215 Lafayette Ctr Dr Ste 3	Chantilly	VA	20151	877-734-4827	703-968-2772
Automotive Recyclers Assn (ARA)					
3975 Fair Ridge Dr Ste 20N	Fairfax	VA	22033	888-385-1005	703-385-1001
Automotive Service Assn (ASA)					
1901 Airport Fwy	Bedford	TX	76021	800-272-7467*	
*Cust Svc					
Center for Auto Safety (CAS)					
1825 Connecticut Ave NW Ste 330	Washington	DC	20009	800-424-9393	202-328-7700
Coalition for Auto Repair Equality (CARE)					
105 Oronoco St Ste 115	Alexandria	VA	22314	800-229-5380	703-519-7555
Community Transportation Assn of America (CTAA)					
1341 G St NW 10th Fl	Washington	DC	20005	800-891-0590	202-628-1480
Dangerous Goods Advisory Council (DGAC)					
1100 H St NW Ste 740	Washington	DC	20005	800-923-9123	202-289-4550
General Aviation Manufacturers Assn (GAMA)					
1400 K St NW Ste 801	Washington	DC	20005	800-728-9607	202-393-1500
Helicopter Assn International (HAI)					
1635 Prince St	Alexandria	VA	22314	800-435-4976	703-683-4646
Institute of Navigation Inc (ION)					
8551 Rixlew Ln Ste 360	Manassas	VA	20109	800-696-7353	703-366-2723
Insurance Institute for Highway Safety					
1005 N Glebe Rd Ste 800	Arlington	VA	22201	888-327-4236	703-247-1500
Intelligent Transportation Society of America (ITS)					
1100 17th St NW Ste 1200	Washington	DC	20036	800-374-8472	202-484-4847
Intermodal Assn of North America (IANA)					
11785 Beltsville Rd Ste 1100	Calverton	MD	20705	877-438-8442	301-982-3400
International Airlines Travel Agent Network (IATAN)					
800 Pl Victoria P.O. Box 113	Montreal	QC	H4Z1A1	877-734-2826	514-868-8800
International Assn of Refrigerated Warehouses (IARW)					
1500 King St Ste 201	Alexandria	VA	22314	800-488-2900	703-373-4300
International Carwash Assn					
230 East Ohio Street	Chicago	IL	60611	888-422-8422	
International Motor Coach Group Inc (IMG)					
8695 College Blvd Ste 260	Overland Park	KS	66210	888-447-3466	913-906-0111
International Safe Transit Assn (ISTA)					
1400 Abbott Rd Ste 160	East Lansing	MI	48823	888-299-2208	517-333-3437
Jewelers Shipping Assn (JSA)					
125 Carlsbad St	Cranston	RI	02920	800-688-4572	401-943-6020
Mobile Air Conditioning Society Worldwide (MACS)					
225 S Broad St	Lansdale	PA	19446	800-641-1133	215-631-7020
National Air Transportation Assn (NATA)					
4226 King St	Alexandria	VA	22302	800-808-6282	703-845-9000
National Automobile Dealers Assn (NADA)					
8400 Westpark Dr	McLean	VA	22102	800-252-6232	703-821-7000
National Automotive Radiator Service Assn (NARSA)					
3000 Village Run Rd Ste 103 221	Wexford	PA	15090	800-551-3232	724-799-8415
National Business Aviation Assn (NBAA)					
1200 18th St NW Ste 400	Washington	DC	20036	800-394-6222	202-783-9000
National Motorists Assn (NMA)					
402 W Second St	Waunakee	WI	53597	800-882-2785	608-849-6000
National Truck Equipment Assn (NTEA)					
37400 Hills Tech Dr	Farmington Hills	MI	48331	800-441-6832	248-489-7090
National Waterways Conference Inc (NWC)					
4650 Washington Blvd Ste 608	Arlington	VA	22201	866-371-1390	703-243-4090
NATSO Inc					
1737 King St Ste 200	Alexandria	VA	22314	800-956-9160	703-549-2100
Owner-Operator Independent Drivers Assn Inc (OOIDA)					
One NW OOIDA Dr	Grain Valley	MO	64029	800-444-5791	816-229-5791
Passenger Vessel Assn (PVA)					
103 Oronoco St Ste 200	Alexandria	VA	22314	800-807-8360	703-518-5005
Railway Supply Institute Inc (RSI)					
425 Third St Ste 920	Washington	DC	20024	800-995-3579	202-347-4664
Recreation Vehicle Dealers Assn (RVDA)					
3930 University Dr Third Fl	Fairfax	VA	22030	800-336-0355	703-591-7130
Recreation Vehicle Industry Assn (RVIA)					
1896 Preston White Dr	Reston	VA	20191	800-336-0154	703-620-6003
Self Storage Assn (SSA)					
1900 N Beauregard St Ste 450	Alexandria	VA	22311	888-735-3784	703-575-8000
Shipowners Claims Bureau (SCB)					
1 Battery Pk Plaza 31st Fl	New York	NY	10004	800-774-8724	212-847-4500
Society of Automotive Engineers Inc (SAE)					
400 Commonwealth Dr	Warrendale	PA	15096	877-606-7323	724-776-4841
Specialty Vehicle Institute of America (SVIA)					
Two Jenner St Ste 150	Irvine	CA	92618	800-887-2887	949-727-3727
Transport Workers Union of America					
501 Third St NW 9th Fl	Washington	DC	20001	888-565-6898	202-719-3900
Transportation Intermediaries Assn (TIA)					
1625 Prince St Ste 200	Alexandria	VA	22314	800-435-1791	703-299-5700
Transportation Research Board (TRB)					
500 Fifth St NW	Washington	DC	20001	866-233-4642	202-334-2934
Truckload Carriers Assn (TCA)					
555 E Braddock Rd	Alexandria	VA	22314	800-666-2770	703-838-1950
United Motorcoach Assn (UMA)					
113 SW St Fourth Fl	Alexandria	VA	22314	800-424-8262	703-838-2929

Classified Section

49 ATTRACTIONS

				Toll-Free	Phone
Boardman Park 375 BoaRdman-Poland Rd	Boardman	OH	44512	888-795-2707	330-726-8107
Cathedral of Our Lady of the Angels 555 W Temple St	Los Angeles	CA	90012	800-838-1356	213-680-5200
Catholic Diocese of Peoria, The 607 NE Madison Ave	Peoria	IL	61603	800-340-5630	309-682-5823
Historic Trinity Lutheran Church 1345 Gratiot Ave	Detroit	MI	48207	800-268-3058	313-567-3100
Mesa Arizona Temple 101 S LeSueur	Mesa	AZ	85204	855-537-4357	480-833-1211
Mission of Nombre de Dios & Shrine of Our Lady of La Leche 27 Ocean Ave	Saint Augustine	FL	32084	800-342-6529	904-824-2809
National Shrine of Our Lady of the Snows 442 S De Mazenod Dr	Belleville	IL	62223	800-682-2879	618-397-6700
Salt Lake Temple 50 W N Temple St	Salt Lake City	UT	84150	800-453-3860	801-240-2640
Union Church of Pocantico Hills 555 Bedford Rd	Sleepy Hollow	NY	10591	800-638-7646	914-631-8200

49-1 Cultural & Arts Centers

				Toll-Free	Phone
Anderson Ranch Arts Ctr 5263 Owl Creek Rd PO Box 5598	Snowmass Village	CO	81615	800-525-6363	970-923-3181
Arkansas Arts Ctr 501 E Ninth St	Little Rock	AR	72202	800-264-2787	501-372-4000
Center for Puppetry Arts 1404 Spring St NW	Atlanta	GA	30309	800-642-3629	404-873-3089
Daybreak Star Ctr 3801 W Government Way PO Box 99100	Seattle	WA	98199	800-321-4321	206-285-4425
Dougherty Arts Ctr, The (DAC) 1110 Barton Springs Rd	Austin	TX	78704	855-787-2227	512-974-4000
Durango Arts Ctr 802 E Second Ave	Durango	CO	81301	800-838-3006	970-259-2606
Flint Cultural Ctr Corp 1310 E Kearsley St	Flint	MI	48503	888-823-6837	810-237-7333
Gerald R Ford Conservation Ctr 1326 S 32nd St	Omaha	NE	68105	800-634-6932	402-595-1180
Maitland Art Ctr 231 W Packwood Ave	Maitland	FL	32751	800-435-7352	407-539-2181
Mesa Arts Ctr 1 E Main St PO Box 1466	Mesa	AZ	85201	800-647-5463	480-644-6501
Oglebay Institute's Stifel Fine Arts Ctr 1330 National Rd	Wheeling	WV	26003	800-624-6988	304-242-7700
Peninsula Fine Arts Ctr 101 Museum Dr	Newport News	VA	23606	800-227-2788	757-596-8175
South Broadway Cultural Ctr 1025 Broadway Blvd SE	Albuquerque	NM	87102	866-441-6075	505-848-1320

49-2 Historic Homes & Buildings

				Toll-Free	Phone
Artillery Park Heritage Site Two D'Auteuil St PO Box 10 Stn B	Quebec	QC	G1K7A1	888-773-8888	418-648-7016
Ashland-The Henry Clay Estate 120 Sycamore Rd	Lexington	KY	40502	800-735-5251	859-266-8581
Barracks, The 43 Pinkney St	Annapolis	MD	21401	800-603-4020	410-267-7619
Corn Palace 604 N Main St	Mitchell	SD	57301	800-289-7469	605-996-5031
Cosanti Originals Inc 6433 Doubletree Ranch Rd	Paradise Valley	AZ	85253	800-752-3187	480-948-6145
Destrehan Plantation 13034 River Rd	Destrehan	LA	70047	877-453-2095	985-764-9315
Fort Meigs State Memorial 29100 W River Rd	Perrysburg	OH	43551	800-283-8916	419-874-4121
Frank Lloyd Wright's Martin House Complex 125 Jewett Pkwy	Buffalo	NY	14214	877-377-3858	716-856-3858
Fulton Mansion 317 N Fulton Beach Rd	Rockport	TX	78382	800-792-1112	361-729-0386
General Crook House Museum 5730 N 30th St Bldg 11B	Omaha	NE	68111	800-393-6198	402-455-9990
Glensheen Mansion 3300 London Rd	Duluth	MN	55804	888-454-4536	218-726-8910
Greenwood Plantation 6838 Highland Rd	Saint Francisville	LA	70775	800-259-4475	225-655-4475
Guenther House 205 E Guenther St	San Antonio	TX	78204	800-235-8186	210-227-1061
Historic Rock Ford Plantation 881 Rockford Rd	Lancaster	PA	17602	800-732-0999	717-392-7223
Houmas House Plantation & Gardens 40136 Hwy 942	Darrow	LA	70725	800-979-3370	225-473-7841
James J Hill House 240 Summit Ave	Saint Paul	MN	55102	888-727-8386	651-297-2555
Jane Addams Hull-House Museum 800 S Halsted St	Chicago	IL	60607	800-625-2013	312-413-5353
Loudoun House 209 Castlewood Dr	Lexington	KY	40505	866-945-7920	859-254-7024
Mathias Ham House Historic Site 2241 Lincoln Ave	Dubuque	IA	52001	800-226-3369	563-557-9545
Mission Mill Museum 1313 Mill St SE	Salem	OR	97301	800-782-6724	503-585-7012
Monticello 931 Thomas Jefferson Pkwy PO Box 316	Charlottesville	VA	22902	800-243-1743	434-984-9822
Old Alabama Town 301 Columbus St	Montgomery	AL	36104	888-240-1850	334-240-4500
Old Exchange & Provost Dungeon 122 E Bay St	Charleston	SC	29401	888-763-0448	843-727-2165
Old Idaho Penitentiary State Historic Site 2445 Old Penitentiary Rd	Boise	ID	83712	877-653-4367	208-334-2844
Paul Laurence Dunbar House 219 N Paul Laurence Dunbar St	Dayton	OH	45402	800-860-0148	937-224-7061
Ponce de Leon's Fountain of Youth 11 Magnolia Ave	Saint Augustine	FL	32084	800-356-8222	904-829-3168
Powel House 244 S Third St	Philadelphia	PA	19106	877-426-8056	215-627-0364
Reed Gold Mine State Historic Site 9621 Reed Mine Rd	Midland	NC	28107	877-628-6386	704-721-4653
Rosedown Plantation State Historic Site 12501 Hwy 10	Saint Francisville	LA	70775	888-376-1867	225-635-3332
Sears Tower 233 S Wacker Dr	Chicago	IL	60606	877-759-3325	312-875-9447
Shirley Plantation 501 Shirley Plantation Rd	Charles City	VA	23030	800-232-1613	804-829-5121
Vance Birthplace State Historic Site 911 Reems Creek Rd	Weaverville	NC	28787	800-767-1560	828-645-6706
Waterfront Warehouse Four Pinkney St	Annapolis	MD	21401	800-603-4020	410-267-7619

49-3 Monuments, Memorials, Landmarks

				Toll-Free	Phone
Chamizal National Memorial 800 S San Marcial St	El Paso	TX	79905	877-642-4743	915-532-7273
De Soto National Memorial 8300 Desoto Memorial Hwy	Bradenton	FL	34209	888-831-7526	941-792-0458
Empire State Bldg 350 Fifth Ave Ste 100	New York	NY	10118	877-692-8439	212-736-3100
George Washington Masonic National Memorial 101 Callahan Dr	Alexandria	VA	22301	800-435-7352	703-683-2007
Golden Gate Bridge Golden Gate Bridge Toll Plz Presidio Stn PO Box 9000	San Francisco	CA	94129	877-229-8655	415-921-5858
Littleton Coin Company LLC 1309 Mt Eustis Rd	Littleton	NH	03561	800-645-3122	603-444-5386
Space Needle LLC 203 Sixth Ave N	Seattle	WA	98109	800-937-9582	206-905-2200
Texas State Cemetery 909 Navasota St	Austin	TX	78702	877-673-6839	512-463-0605
USS Alabama Battleship Memorial Park 2703 Battleship Pkwy PO Box 65	Mobile	AL	36602	888-414-4448	251-433-2703
USS Kidd Veterans Memorial & Museum 305 S River Rd	Baton Rouge	LA	70802	800-638-0594	225-342-1942
USS Missouri Memorial Assn Inc 63 Cowpens St	Honolulu	HI	96818	877-644-4896	808-455-1600
Vietnam Women's Memorial Foundation Inc 1735 Connecticut Ave NW Third Fl	Washington	DC	20009	866-822-8963	

49-4 Nature Centers, Parks, Other Natural Areas

				Toll-Free	Phone
Black Hills Caverns 2600 Cavern Rd	Rapid City	SD	57702	800-837-9358	605-343-0542
Boyden Caverns 74101 E Kings Canyon Rd	Kings Canyon National Park	CA	93633	866-762-2837	209-736-2708
Butterfly House - Faust Park, The 15193 Olive Blvd	Chesterfield	MO	63017	800-642-8842	636-530-0076
Carson Hot Springs 1500 Hot Springs Rd	Carson City	NV	89706	888-917-3711	775-885-8844
DeGraaf Nature Ctr 600 Graafschap Rd	Holland	MI	49423	888-535-5792	616-355-1057
El Dorado Nature Ctr 7550 E Spring St	Long Beach	CA	90815	800-662-8887	562-570-1745
Genesee County Parks & Recreation 5045 Stanley Rd	Flint	MI	48506	800-648-7275	810-736-7100
Great Plains Nature Ctr 6232 E 29th St N	Wichita	KS	67220	800-222-1222	316-683-5499
Hanauma Bay Nature Preserve 100 Hanauma Bay Rd	Honolulu	HI	96825	800-690-6200	808-396-4229
Houston Arboretum & Nature Ctr 4501 Woodway Dr	Houston	TX	77024	866-510-7219	713-681-8433
Jefferson Barracks County Park 345 N Dr	Saint Louis	MO	63125	800-735-2966	314-544-5714
Katharine Ordway Preserve 4245 N Fairfax Dr Ste 100	Arlington	VA	22203	800-628-6860	203-226-4991
Lava Hot Springs State Foundation 430 E Main St PO Box 669	Lava Hot Springs	ID	83246	800-423-8597	208-776-5221
Linville Caverns Inc 19929 US 221 N	Marion	NC	28752	800-419-0540	
Lost River Caverns 726 Durham St PO Box M	Hellertown	PA	18055	888-529-1907	610-838-8767
New York State Office of Parks Recreation & Historic Preservation Empire State Plaza Agency Bldg 1	Albany	NY	12238	800-456-2267	716-354-9101
Oxbow Meadows Environmental Learning Ctr 3535 S Lumpkin Rd	Columbus	GA	31903	866-264-2035	706-507-8550
Raccoon Mountain Caverns 319 W Hills Dr	Chattanooga	TN	37419	800-823-2267	423-821-9403
Riveredge Nature Ctr 4458 W Hawthorne Dr PO Box 26	Newburg	WI	53060	800-287-8098	262-375-2715
Rock City Gardens 1400 Patten Rd	Lookout Mountain	GA	30750	800-854-0675	706-820-2531
Ruby Falls 1720 S Scenic Hwy	Chattanooga	TN	37409	800-755-7105	423-821-2544
Runge Conservation Nature Ctr 2901 W Truman Blvd	Jefferson City	MO	65109	800-392-1111	573-751-4115
Seven Falls Co 2850 S Cheyenne Canyon Rd	Colorado Springs	CO	80906	855-923-7272	719-632-0765
Springfield Conservation Nature Ctr 4600 S Chrisman Ave	Springfield	MO	65804	800-392-1111	417-888-4237

49-5 Shopping/Dining/Entertainment Districts

			Toll-Free	Phone
Bannister's Wharf				
1 Bannister's Wharf	Newport RI	02840	800-395-1343	401-846-4500
Barefoot Landing				
4898 Hwy 17 S	North Myrtle Beach SC	29582	800-217-1511	843-272-8349
Great Lakes Crossing Outlets				
4000 Baldwin Rd	Auburn Hills MI	48326	877-746-7452	248-454-5000
Harborplace & the Gallery				
201 E Pratt St	Baltimore MD	21202	800-722-8614	410-332-4191
John's Pass Village & Boardwalk				
150 John's Pass Boardwalk Pl	Madeira Beach FL	33708	800-755-0677	727-398-6577
Miracle Mile Shops at Planet Hollywood				
3663 Las Vegas Blvd S	Las Vegas NV	89109	888-800-8284	702-866-0703
Newport on the Levee				
One Levee Way Ste 1113	Newport KY	41071	866-538-3359	859-291-0550
River Walk				
110 Broadway Ste 500	San Antonio TX	78204	800-417-4139	210-227-4262

49-6 Wineries

The wineries listed in this category feature wine-tasting as an attraction.

			Toll-Free	Phone
Chateau Elan Winery				
100 Tour de France	Braselton GA	30517	800-233-9463	678-425-0900
Chateau Morrisette Winery				
287 Winery Rd SW	Floyd VA	24091	866-695-2001	540-593-2865
Chateau Ste Michelle Winery				
14111 NE 145th St	Woodinville WA	98072	800-267-6793	425-415-3300
Columbia Winery				
14030 NE 145th St PO Box 1248	Woodinville WA	98072	800-488-2347	425-488-2776
Eola Hills Wine Cellars				
501 S Pacific Hwy 99 W	Rickreall OR	97371	800-291-6730	503-623-2405
Forks of Cheat Winery				
2811 Stewart Town Rd	Morgantown WV	26508	877-989-4637	304-598-2019
Gruet Winery				
8400 Pan American Fwy NE	Albuquerque NM	87113	888-857-9463	505-821-0055
Honeywood Winery				
1350 Hines St SE	Salem OR	97302	800-726-4101	503-362-4111
King Estate Winery				
80854 Territorial Rd	Eugene OR	97405	800-884-4441	541-942-9874
Latah Creek Winery				
13030 E Indiana Ave	Spokane WA	99216	800-528-2427	509-926-0164
Llano Estacado Winery				
3426 E FM 1585 PO Box 3487	Lubbock TX	79404	800-634-3854	806-745-2258
Mazza Vineyards				
11815 E Lake Rd	North East PA	16428	800-796-9463	814-725-8695
Nassau Valley Vineyards				
32165 Winery Way	Lewes DE	19958	800-425-2355	302-645-9463
Oliver Winery				
8024 N SR-37	Bloomington IN	47404	800-258-2783	812-876-5800
Orfila Vineyards & Winery				
13455 San Pasqual Rd	Escondido CA	92025	800-868-9463	760-738-6500
Sakonnet Vineyards				
162 W Main Rd	Little Compton RI	02837	800-919-4637	401-635-8486
San Sebastian Winery				
157 King St	Saint Augustine FL	32084	888-352-9463	904-826-1594
Winery at Wolf Creek				
2637 Cleveland Massillon Rd	Norton OH	44203	800-436-0426	330-666-9285

50   AUCTIONS

			Toll-Free	Phone
ADESA Inc				
13085 Hamilton Crossing Blvd	Carmel IN	46032	800-923-3725	317-815-1100
Akron Auto Auction Inc				
2471 Ley Dr	Akron OH	44319	800-773-0033	330-773-8245
American Auction Co				
951 W Watkins	Phoenix AZ	85007	800-801-8880	602-252-4842
Bonhams & Butterfields				
220 San Bruno Ave	San Francisco CA	94103	800-223-2854	415-861-7500
Collectors Universe Inc				
PO Box 6280	Newport Beach CA	92658	800-325-1121	949-567-1234
NASDAQ: CLCT				
eBay Inc 2065 Hamilton Ave	San Jose CA	95125	800-322-9266	408-376-7400
NASDAQ: EBAY				
Fasig-Tipton Co Inc				
2400 Newtown Pike	Lexington KY	40511	877-945-2020	859-255-1555
Gallery of History Inc				
3601 W Sahara Ave Ste Promenade	Las Vegas NV	89102	800-425-5379	702-364-1000
Gordon Bros Group LLC				
101 Huntington Ave 10th Fl	Boston MA	02199	888-424-1903	
Greater Rockford Auto Auction Inc (GRAA)				
5937 Sandy Hollow Rd	Rockford IL	61109	800-830-4722	815-874-7800
Harry Davis & Co				
1725 Blvd of Allies	Pittsburgh PA	15219	800-775-2289	412-765-1170
Henderson Auctions				
13340 Florida Blvd PO Box 336	Livingston LA	70754	800-334-7443	225-686-2252
Heritage Place Inc				
2829 S MacArthur	Oklahoma City OK	73128	888-343-9831	405-682-4551
iCollector Technologies Inc				
1750 Coast Meridian Rd Ste 114	Port Coquitlam BC	V3C6R8	866-313-0123	604-941-2221
Insurance Auto Auctions Inc				
Two Westbrook Corporate Ctr				
Ste 500	Westchester IL	60154	800-872-1501	708-492-7000
Ironplanet Inc				
3825 Hopyard Rd Ste 250.	Pleasanton CA	94588	888-433-5426*	925-225-8600
*Cust Svc				
Kennedy-Wilson Inc				
9701 Wilshire Blvd Ste 700	Beverly Hills CA	90212	800-522-6664	310-887-6400

			Toll-Free	Phone
Liquidity Services Inc				
1920 L St NW Sixth Fl	Washington DC	20036	800-310-4604	202-467-6868
NASDAQ: LQDT				
Priceline.com LLC				
800 Connecticut Ave	Norwalk CT	06854	800-774-2354	
NASDAQ: PCLN				
Theriault's PO Box 151	Annapolis MD	21404	800-966-3655	410-224-3655
uBid Inc 740 Hilltop Dr	Itasca IL	60143	866-946-8243	

51   AUDIO & VIDEO EQUIPMENT

			Toll-Free	Phone
Alpine Electronics of America				
19145 Gramercy Pl	Torrance CA	90501	800-257-4631	310-326-8000
AmpliVox Sound Systems LLC				
3995 Commercial Ave	Northbrook IL	60062	800-267-5486	847-498-9000
Applied Research & Technology				
215 Tremont St	Rochester NY	14608	800-775-2427	585-436-2720
Atlas Sound				
1601 Jack McKay Blvd	Ennis TX	75119	800-876-3333	972-875-8413
Audio Command Systems				
694 Main St	Westbury NY	11590	800-382-2939	516-997-5800
Audiosears Corp Two S St	Stamford NY	12167	800-533-7863	607-652-7305
Audiovox Corp				
180 Marcus Blvd	Hauppauge NY	11788	800-645-4994	631-231-7750
NASDAQ: VOXX				
Biamp Systems Inc				
9300 SW Gemini Dr	Beaverton OR	97008	800-826-1457	
Bogen Communications International Inc				
50 Spring St	Ramsey NJ	07446	800-999-2809	201-934-8500
OTC: BOGN				
Bose Corp The Mountain	Framingham MA	01701	800-379-2073*	508-766-1099
*Sales				
Car Toys Inc 20 W Galer St	Seattle WA	98119	800-997-3644	206-443-0980
City of Chula Vista				
276 Fourth Ave	Chula Vista CA	91910	877-478-5478	619-691-5047
Clarion Corp of America				
6200 Gateway Dr	Cypress CA	90630	800-347-8667	310-327-9100
Community Professional Loudspeakers				
333 E Fifth St	Chester PA	19013	800-523-4934	610-876-3400
Creative Labs Inc				
1901 McCarthy Blvd	Milpitas CA	95035	800-998-1000*	408-428-6600
*Cust Svc				
Crest Electronics Inc				
3706 Alliance Dr	Greensboro NC	27407	888-502-7378	336-855-6422
Dana Innovations				
212 Avenida Fabricante	San Clemente CA	92672	800-582-7777	949-492-7777
DEI Holdings Inc				
One Viper Way	Vista CA	92081	800-876-0800	760-598-6200
OTC: DEIX				
Digital Innovations				
3436 N Kennicott Ste 200	Arlington Heights IL	60004	888-762-7858	847-463-9000
Dynamic Instruments Inc				
3860 Calle Fortunada	San Diego CA	92123	800-793-3358	858-278-4900
Educational Technology Inc				
300 Bedford Ave Ste 202	Bellmore NY	11710	800-942-2136*	516-221-8440
*Cust Svc				
Eminence Speaker LLC				
838 Mulberry Pike PO Box 360	Eminence KY	40019	800-897-8373	502-845-5622
Extron Electronics				
1230 S Lewis St	Anaheim CA	92805	800-633-9876*	714-491-1500
*Tech Supp				
Ford Audio-Video Systems Inc				
4800 W I-40	Oklahoma City OK	73128	800-654-6744	405-946-9966
Fujitsu Ten Corp of America				
19600 S Vermont Ave	Torrance CA	90502	800-233-2216	310-327-2151
Furman Sound LLC				
1690 Corporate Cir	Petaluma CA	94954	877-486-4738	707-763-1010
Harman International Industries Inc				
400 Atlantic St 15th Fl	Stamford CT	06901	800-473-0602	203-328-3500
NYSE: HAR				
JBL Professional				
8500 Balboa Blvd	Northridge CA	91329	800-852-5776	818-894-8850
JVC Professional Products Co				
1700 Valley Rd	Wayne NJ	07470	800-252-5722	973-317-5000
Kenwood USA Corp				
2201 E Dominguez St	Long Beach CA	90810	800-536-9663	310-639-9000
Klipsch LLC 137 Hempstead 278	Hope AR	71801	888-250-8561	
Koss Corp				
4129 N Port Washington Ave	Milwaukee WI	53212	800-872-5677	414-964-5000
NASDAQ: KOSS				
Law Enforcement Assoc Corp (LEA)				
120 Penmarc Dr Ste 125.	Raleigh NC	27616	800-354-9669	919-872-6210
OTC: LAWEQ				
Lectrosonics Inc				
PO Box 15900	Rio Rancho NM	87174	800-821-1121	505-892-4501
LifeSize Communications Inc				
1601 S Mopac Expwy Ste 100	Austin TX	78746	877-543-3749	512-347-9300
Logitech Inc 6505 Kaiser Dr	Fremont CA	94555	800-231-7717*	510-795-8500
*Sales				
LOUD Technologies Inc				
16220 Wood Red Rd NE	Woodinville WA	98072	866-858-5832	425-892-6500
OTC: LTEC				
Lowell Manufacturing Co				
100 Integram Dr	Pacific MO	63069	800-325-9660	636-257-3400
McIntosh Laboratory Inc				
Two Chambers St	Binghamton NY	13903	800-538-6576	607-723-3512
Metra Electronics Corp				
460 Walker St	Holly Hill FL	32117	800-221-0932*	386-257-1186
*Sales				
Mitsubishi Digital Electronics America Inc				
9351 Jeronimo Rd	Irvine CA	92618	800-332-2119	949-465-6000
Monster Cable Products Inc				
455 Valley Dr	Brisbane CA	94005	877-800-8989	415-840-2000
Mustek Inc				
15271 Barranca Pkwy	Irvine CA	92618	800-308-7226	949-790-3800

Classified Section

Audio & Video Equipment (Cont'd)

	Toll-Free	Phone
Omnitronics LLC 6573 Cochran Rd .... Solon OH 44139	800-762-9266	440-349-4900
Panasonic Avionics Corp 26200 Enterprise Way .... Lake Forest CA 92630	877-627-2300	949-672-2000
Panasonic Consumer Electronics Co 1 Panasonic Way .... Secaucus NJ 07094 *NYSE: PC*	800-103-1333	888-762-2097
Panasonic Corp of North America 1 Panasonic Way .... Secaucus NJ 07094 *Cust Svc	800-211-7262*	888-762-2097
Peavey Electronics Corp 5022 Hartley Peavey Dr .... Meridian MS 39305	877-732-8391	601-483-5365
Phase Technology 6400 Youngerman Cir .... Jacksonville FL 32244	888-742-7385	904-777-0700
Pioneer Electronics (USA) Inc 1925 E Dominguez St .... Long Beach CA 90810	800-421-1404	310-952-2000
Polk Audio Inc 5601 Metro Dr .... Baltimore MD 21215	800-377-7655	410-358-3600
Primo Microphones Inc 1805 Couch Dr .... McKinney TX 75069	800-767-7463	972-548-9807
QSC Audio Products LLC 1675 MacArthur Blvd .... Costa Mesa CA 92626	800-854-4079	714-754-6175
Quam-Nichols Company Inc 234 E Marquette Rd .... Chicago IL 60637	800-633-3669	773-488-5800
Rane Corp 10802 47th Ave W .... Mukilteo WA 98275	877-764-0093	425-355-6000
Record Play Tek Inc 110 E Vistula St .... Bristol IN 46507	800-809-5233	574-848-5233
Renkus-heinz Inc 19201 Cook St .... Foothill Ranch CA 92610	855-411-2364	949-588-9997
ReQuest Inc 100 Saratoga Village Blvd Ste 45 .. Ballston Spa NY 12020 *Sales	800-236-2812*	518-899-1254
Robert Bosch LLC 38000 Hills Tech Dr ...... Farmington Hills MI 48331 *Sales	800-893-6342*	248-876-1000
Rockford Corp 600 S Rockford Dr .... Tempe AZ 85281 *OTC: ROFO*	800-903-2897	480-967-3565
Sanyo Mfg Corp 3333 Sanyo Rd .... Forrest City AR 72335	800-100-3003	870-633-5030
SDI Technologies Inc 1299 Main St .... Rahway NJ 07065	800-333-3092	
Sharp Electronics Corp One Sharp Plz .... Mahwah NJ 07430	800-237-4277	201-529-8200
Shure Inc 5800 W Touhy Ave .... Niles IL 60714	800-257-4873	847-866-2200
Sima Products Corp 120 Pennsylvania Ave .... Oakmont PA 15139	800-345-7462	412-828-3700
Sony Corp of America 550 Madison Ave .... New York NY 10022	800-282-2848	212-833-6800
Sony Electronics Inc One Sony Dr .... Park Ridge NJ 07656 *Cust Svc	800-222-7669*	201-930-1000
Sound Com Corp 227 Depot St .... Berea OH 44017	800-628-8739	440-234-2604
Southern Audio Services 14763 Florida Blvd .... Baton Rouge LA 70819 *Cust Svc	800-843-8823*	225-272-7135
Stancil Corp 2644 S Croddy Way .... Santa Ana CA 92704	800-290-4103	714-546-2002
TDK USA Corp 525 RXR Plaza PO Box 9302 ...... Uniondale NY 11556 *General	800-285-2783*	516-535-2600
Telex Communications Inc 12000 Portland Ave S .... Burnsville MN 55337	877-863-4169	952-884-4051
Toshiba America Inc 1251 Ave of the Americas Ste 4100 .. New York NY 10020	800-457-7777	212-596-0600
Universal Audio Inc 1700 Green Hills Rd .... Scotts Valley CA 95066	877-698-2834	831-440-1176
Xantech Corp 1969 Kellogg Ave .... Carlsbad CA 92008 *Sales	800-843-5465*	818-362-0353
Yamaha Electronics Corp 6660 Orangethorpe Ave .... Buena Park CA 90620	800-292-2982	714-522-9888

52   AUTO CLUBS

	Toll-Free	Phone
AAA Allied Group Inc 15 W Central Pkwy .... Cincinnati OH 45202	800-543-2345	513-762-3100
AAA Carolinas 6600 AAA Dr .... Charlotte NC 28212	800-477-4222	704-569-3600
AAA Chicago Motor Club 975 Meridian Lake Dr .... Aurora IL 60504	866-968-7222	
AAA Colorado 4100 E Arkansas Ave .... Denver CO 80222	866-625-3601	303-753-8800
AAA East Penn 1020 W Hamilton St .... Allentown PA 18101	800-222-4357	
AAA Hawaii 1130 N Nimitz Hwy Ste A-170 ...... Honolulu HI 96817	800-736-2886	808-593-2221
AAA Massillon Auto Club 1972 Wales Rd NE .... Massillon OH 44646	800-222-4357	330-833-1084
AAA Michigan 1 Auto Vistula Dr .... Dearborn MI 48126	800-222-6424	313-336-1920
AAA Minnesota/Iowa 600 W Travelers Trl .... Burnsville MN 55337	800-222-1333	952-707-4500
AAA Missouri 12901 N Forty Dr .... Saint Louis MO 63141	800-222-4357	314-523-7350
AAA MountainWest 2100 11th Ave .... Helena MT 59601	800-332-6119	406-447-8100
AAA Nebraska 910 N 96th St .... Omaha NE 68114	800-222-6327	402-390-1000
AAA North Penn 1035 N Washington Ave .... Scranton PA 18509	800-222-4357	570-348-5211
AAA Northern New England 68 Marginal Way .... Portland ME 04104	800-222-4357	207-780-6800
AAA Northway 112 Railroad St .... Schenectady NY 12305	866-222-7283	518-374-4696
AAA Northwest Ohio 7150 W Central Ave .... Toledo OH 43617	800-428-0060	419-843-1200

	Toll-Free	Phone
AAA Ohio Auto Club 90 E Wilson Bridge Rd .... Worthington OH 43085	888-222-6446	614-431-7901
AAA Oklahoma 2121 E 15th St .... Tulsa OK 74104	800-222-2582	918-748-1000
AAA Southern New England 110 Royal Little Dr .... Providence RI 02904	800-222-7448	401-868-2000
AAA Southern Pennsylvania 2840 Eastern Blvd .... York PA 17402	800-222-1469	717-600-8700
AAA Washington-Inland 1745 114th Ave SE .... Bellevue WA 98004	800-222-4357	425-646-2058
AAA Western & Central New York 100 International Dr .... Williamsville NY 14221	800-836-2582	716-633-9860
AAA Wisconsin 8401 Excelsior Dr .... Madison WI 53717	800-236-1300	608-836-6555
AARP Motoring Plan 601 E Street N.W. .... Washington DC 20049	800-555-1121	
American Automobile Association, Inc. 435 E Broadway .... Louisville KY 40202	800-727-2552	502-582-3311
Auto Club Ltd PO Box 162526 .... Austin TX 78716	866-247-3728	
Auto Club of America Corp (ACA) 9411 N Georgia St ...... Oklahoma City OK 73120	800-411-2007	405-751-4430
Automobile Club of Southern California 2601 S Figueroa St .... Los Angeles CA 90007	800-400-4222	213-741-3686
BP MotorClub PO Box 4441 .... Carol Stream IL 60197	800-334-3300	
Brickell Financial Services Motor Club Inc 7300 Corporate Ctr Dr Ste 601 ...... Miami FL 33126	800-262-7262	305-392-4300
British Columbia Automobile Assn (BCAA) 4567 Canada Way .... Burnaby BC V5G4T1	800-222-4357	604-268-5000
CAA Central Ontario 60 Commerce Vly Dr E .... Thornhill ON L3T7P9	800-268-3750	905-771-3000
CAA Manitoba 870 Empress St .... Winnipeg MB R3C2Z3	800-222-4357	204-262-6166
CAA Maritimes Ltd 378 Westmorland Rd .... Saint John NB E2J2G4	800-471-1611	506-634-1400
CAA North & East Ontario PO Box 8350 .... Ottawa ON K1G3T2	800-267-8713	613-820-1890
CAA Quebec 444 Bouvier St .... Quebec QC G2J1E3	800-222-4357	418-624-8222
CAA Stoney Creek 163 Centennial Pkwy N .... Hamilton ON L8E1H8	800-992-8143	905-664-8000
California State Automobile Assn 150 Van Ness Ave ...... San Francisco CA 94102 *Cust Svc	800-922-8228*	
Canadian Automobile Assn (CAA) 2151 Thurston Dr Ste 200 .... Ottawa ON K1G6C9	800-267-8713	613-820-1890
Findlay Automobile Club 1550 Tiffin Ave .... Findlay OH 45840	800-222-4357	419-422-4961
National Motor Club of America Inc (NMC) 130 E John Carpenter Fwy .... Irving TX 75062	800-523-4582	972-999-1099
Pinnacle Motor Club 130 E John Carpenter Fwy .... Irving TX 75062	800-446-1289	
Travelers Motor Club 720 NW 50th St .... Oklahoma City OK 73154	800-654-9208	405-848-1711

53   AUTO SUPPLY STORES

	Toll-Free	Phone
A 1 Auto Recyclers 7804 S Hwy 79 .... Rapid City SD 57701	800-456-0715	605-348-8442
Advance Auto Parts Inc 5008 Airport Rd .... Roanoke VA 24012 *NYSE: AAP*	877-238-2623	540-561-8452
Ats All Tire Supply Co 6600 Long Point Rd Ste 101. .... Houston TX 77055	888-339-6665	
AutoZone Inc 123 S Front St .... Memphis TN 38103 *NYSE: AZO*	800-288-6966	901-495-6500
Bennett Auto Supply Inc 3141 SW Tenth St .... Pompano Beach FL 33069	800-766-5913	954-335-8700
Bond Auto Parts 45 Summer St .... Barre VT 05641	800-639-1982	802-476-3108
Carquest Corp 2635 E Millbrook Rd .... Raleigh NC 27604	800-876-1291	919-573-3000
Custom Truck Accessories Inc 13408 Hwy 65 Ne .... Ham Lake MN 55304	800-333-1282	763-757-5326
Hedahls Inc 100 East Broadway .... Bismarck ND 58502	800-433-2457	701-223-8393
KOI Warehouse Inc 2701 Spring Grove Ave .... Cincinnati OH 45225	800-354-0408	513-357-2400
Merle's Automotive Supply Inc 33 W University Blvd .... Tucson AZ 85705	800-546-6040	520-622-3526
NORD Drivesystems 800 Nord Dr .... Waunakee WI 53597	888-314-6673	
O'Reilly Automotive Inc 233 S Patterson .... Springfield MO 65802 *NASDAQ: ORLY*	888-327-7153	417-862-6708
Original Parts Group Inc (OPGI) 1770 Saturn Way .... Seal Beach CA 90740	800-243-8355	562-594-1000
Peerless Tire Co 5000 Kingston St .... Denver CO 80239	800-999-7810	303-371-4300
S & S Tire & Auto Service Center 1475 Jingle Bell Ln .... Lexington KY 40509	800-685-6794	
Specmo Auto Sound & Speed G3189 S Dort Hwy .... Burton MI 48529	800-545-7910	
Tire Warehouse 200 Holleder Pkwy .... Rochester NY 14615	800-876-6676	
Town Fair Tire Company Inc 460 Coe Ave .... East Haven CT 06512	800-972-2245	
Utilimaster Holding Co 603 Earthway Blvd .... Bristol IN 46507	800-237-7806	
Vanguard Trucks Centers 700 Ruskin Dr .... Forest Park GA 30297	866-216-7925	

54   AUTOMATIC MERCHANDISING EQUIPMENT & SYSTEMS

SEE ALSO Food Service

	Toll-Free	Phone
AIR-serv Group LLC 1370 Mendota Heights Rd .... Mendota Heights MN 55120	800-247-8363	651-454-0465

				Toll-Free	Phone

American Vending Sales Inc
750 Morse Ave . . . . Elk Grove Village IL 60007 **800-441-0009** 847-439-9400
Automatic Products International Ltd
165 Bridgepoint Dr . . . . Saint Paul MN 55075 **800-523-8363**
Bastian Material Handling LLC (BMH)
10585 N Meridian St Third Fl . . . . Indianapolis IN 46290 **800-772-0464** 317-575-9992
Betson Enterprises Inc
303 Patterson Plank Rd . . . . Carlstadt NJ 07072 **800-524-2343** 201-438-1300
Birmingham Vending Co
540 Second Ave N . . . . Birmingham AL 35204 **800-288-7635** 205-324-7526
Coin Acceptors Inc
300 Hunter Ave . . . . Saint Louis MO 63124 **800-325-2646** 314-725-0100
Coinstar Inc
1800 114th Ave SE . . . . Bellevue WA 98004 **800-928-2274** 425-943-8000
Dixie-Narco Inc
3330 Dixie-Narco Blvd . . . . Williston SC 29853 **800-688-9090** 803-266-5000
Glacier Water Services Inc
1385 Pk Ctr Dr . . . . Vista CA 92081 **800-452-2437** 760-560-1111
OTC: GWSV
Harcourt Outlines Inc
7765 S 175 W PO Box 128. . . . . Milroy IN 46156 **800-428-6584**
Northwestern Corp PO Box 490 . . . . Morris IL 60450 **800-942-1316** 815-942-1300

55 — AUTOMATIC TELLER MACHINES (ATMS)

				Toll-Free	Phone

Accu-time Systems Inc
420 Somers Rd . . . . Ellington CT 06029 **800-355-4648** 860-870-5000
Diebold Inc
5995 Mayfair Rd . . . . North Canton OH 44720 **800-999-3600** 330-490-4000
NYSE: DBD
Electronic Cash Systems Inc (ECS)
30352 Esperanza
Ste 110 . . . . Rancho Santa Margarita CA 92688 **888-327-2860** 949-888-8580
Everi Holdings Inc (GCA)
7250 S Tenaya Way Ste 100 . . . . Las Vegas NV 89113 **800-833-7110** 702-855-3000
NYSE: EVRI
Tidel Engineering Inc
2025 W Belt Line Rd Ste 114 . . . . Carrollton TX 75006 **800-678-7577** 972-484-3358

56 — AUTOMOBILE DEALERS & GROUPS

SEE ALSO Automobile Sales & Related Services - Online

				Toll-Free	Phone

A C Nelson Rv World
11818 L St . . . . Omaha NE 68137 **888-655-2332** 402-333-1122
Acura 101 West
24650 Calabasas Rd . . . . Calabasas CA 91302 **800-472-3173** 818-222-5555
Alberic Colon Auto Sales Inc
Ave John F Kennedy Carr Ste 2 KM 3.4 . . . . . San Juan PR 00920 **877-292-4610**
Allied Toyotalift
1640 Island Home Ave . . . . Knoxville TN 37920 **866-538-0667** 865-573-0995
American Augers Inc
135 US Rt 42 . . . . West Salem OH 44287 **800-324-4930** 419-869-7107
Ancira Winton Chevrolet
6111 Bandera Rd . . . . San Antonio TX 78238 **800-299-5286*** 210-390-6255
*General
Arrow Truck Sales Inc
3200 Manchester Trfy . . . . Kansas City MO 64129 **800-311-7144** 816-923-5000
Art Morrison Enterprises Inc
5301 Eighth St E . . . . Fife WA 98424 **888-640-0516** 253-922-7188
Asheville Chevrolet Inc
205 Smokey Pk Hwy . . . . Asheville NC 28806 **866-921-1073** 828-665-4444
Astoria Ford
710 W Marine Dr . . . . Astoria OR 97103 **888-760-9303** 503-325-6411
Atlantic British Ltd
Halfmoon Light Industrial Pk 6 Enterprise Ave
. . . . Clifton Park NY 12065 **800-533-2210** 518-664-6169
Autoland 170 Rt 22 E . . . . Springfield NJ 07081 **877-813-7239*** 973-467-2900
*Sales
Automobile Racing Club of America
8117 Lewis Ave . . . . Temperance MI 48182 **800-385-2503** 734-847-6726
AutoRevo LTD
7920 Belt Line Rd Ste 450 . . . . Dallas TX 75254 **888-311-7386** 972-715-8600
Barry Bunker Chevrolet Inc
1307 N Wabash Ave . . . . Marion IN 46952 **866-603-8625*** 765-664-1275
*Sales
Baskin Auto Truck & Tractor Inc
1844 Hwy 51 S . . . . Covington TN 38019 **877-476-2626** 901-476-2626
Bergstrom of Kaukauna
2929 Lawe St . . . . Kaukauna WI 54130 **866-939-0130**
Best Chevrolet Inc
128 Derby St . . . . Hingham MA 02043 **866-208-7873**
Biggers Chevrolet
1385 E Chicago St . . . . Elgin IL 60120 **866-431-1555** 847-742-9000
Bill Collins
4220 BaRdstown Rd . . . . Louisville KY 40218 **888-327-9095** 502-459-9550
Bill Snethkamp Lansing Dodge Inc
6131 S Pennsylvania Ave . . . . Lansing MI 48911 **800-863-6343** 517-394-1200
Blaise Alexander Chevrolet Inc
933 Broad St . . . . Montoursville PA 17754 **877-575-4256** 570-368-8677
Bob Allen Ford
9239 Metcalf Ave . . . . Overland Park KS 66212 **888-573-6364** 913-381-3000
Bob Davidson Ford Lincoln
1845 E Joppa Rd . . . . Baltimore MD 21234 **888-643-0263** 410-661-6400
Bob Stall Chevrolet
7601 Alvarado Rd . . . . La Mesa CA 91942 **800-295-2695** 619-460-1311
Bommarito Automotive Group
15736 Manchester Rd . . . . Ellisville MO 63011 **800-367-2289** 636-391-7200
Brasher Motor Company of Weimar Inc
1700 I- 10 . . . . Weimar TX 78962 **800-783-1746** 979-725-8515
Buchanan Automotive Group
50 Central Ave Ste 900 . . . . Sarasota FL 34236 **888-292-4883** 941-364-9500
Burr Truck & Trailer Sales Inc
2901 Vestal Rd . . . . Vestal NY 13850 **866-230-2383** 607-729-2211

Bus Andrews Truck Equipment Inc
2828 N E Ave . . . . Springfield MO 65803 **800-273-0733** 417-869-1541
Byerly Ford
4041 Dixie Hwy . . . . Louisville KY 40216 **888-436-0819** 502-448-1661
Cable-Dahmer Chevrolet Inc
1834 S Noland Rd . . . . Independence MO 64055 **888-738-5260** 816-521-7508
Capistrano Scion
33395 Camino Capistrano . . . . San Juan Capistrano CA 92675 **888-493-0040** 949-493-4100
Capital Ford Inc
4900 Capital Blvd . . . . Raleigh NC 27616 **877-659-2496** 919-790-4600
Capitol Chevrolet Montgomery
711 Eastern Blvd . . . . Montgomery AL 36117 **800-410-1137*** 334-272-8700
*Sales
Capitol Mitsubishi
750 Capitol Expy Automall . . . . San Jose CA 95136 **888-479-0842** 408-264-9999
Car City Motor Company Inc
3100 S US Hwy 169 . . . . Saint Joseph MO 64503 **800-525-7008** 816-233-9149
CarMax Inc
12800 Tuckahoe Creek Pkwy . . . . Richmond VA 23238 **888-722-7629** 804-747-0422
NYSE: KMX
Carolina International Trucks Inc
1619 Bluff Rd . . . . Columbia SC 29201 **800-868-4923** 803-799-4923
Charles Gabus Ford Inc
4545 Merle Hay Rd . . . . Des Moines IA 50310 **800-934-2287*** 515-270-0707
*Sales
Checkered Flag Motor Car Corp
5225 Virginia Beach Blvd . . . . Virginia Beach VA 23462 **866-414-7820** 757-687-3486
Cherry Creek Dodge
2727 S Havana St . . . . Denver CO 80014 **888-891-7522*** 303-751-1104
*Sales
Coffman Truck Sales
1149 W Lake S PO Box 151 . . . . Aurora IL 60507 **800-255-7641** 630-892-7093
College Station Ford
1351 Earl Rudder Fwy S . . . . College Station TX 77845 **888-508-0241** 979-694-2022
Conant Auto Retail Group
18900 Studebaker Rd . . . . Cerritos CA 90703 **888-318-5001**
Cooley Motors Corp
401 N Greenbush Rd . . . . Rensselaer NY 12144 **866-308-0724** 518-283-2902
Coral Springs Auto Mall
9400 W Atlantic Blvd . . . . Coral Springs FL 33071 **800-353-8660** 954-796-4525
Coulter Cadillac Inc
1188 E Camelback Rd . . . . Phoenix AZ 85014 **800-843-4237** 602-264-1188
Courtesy Chevrolet
1233 E Camelback Rd . . . . Phoenix AZ 85014 **877-295-4648** 602-235-0255
Crescent Ford Truck Sales
6121 Jefferson Hwy . . . . Harahan LA 70123 **800-575-8785** 504-818-1818
Crown Motors Ltd
196 Regent Blvd . . . . Holland MI 49423 **800-466-7000** 616-396-5268
Cumberland Chrysler Ctr
1550 Interstate Dr . . . . Cookeville TN 38501 **888-277-4902**
D-Patrick Inc
200 N Green River Rd . . . . Evansville IN 47716 **800-831-6870** 812-473-6500
Dan Wolf Chevrolet of Naperville
1515 W Ogden Ave . . . . Naperville IL 60540 **800-243-8872** 630-596-1189
DCH Honda of Nanuet
10 Rt 304 . . . . Nanuet NY 10954 **888-495-8660** 845-623-1200
Dearth Motors Inc
520 Eigth St . . . . Monroe WI 53566 **877-495-5321** 608-325-3181
Dellenbach Motors
3111 S College Ave . . . . Fort Collins CO 80525 **866-963-5689**
DeMontrond 888 I- 45 S . . . . Conroe TX 77304 **888-843-6583*** 281-443-2500
*Sales
Desert European Motorcars Ltd
71387 Hwy 111 . . . . Rancho Mirage CA 92270 **877-839-3035** 760-773-5000
Diehl Automotive Group Inc
258 Pittsburgh Rd . . . . Butler PA 16002 **866-543-4523** 724-282-8898
Don McGill Toyota Inc
11800 Katy Fwy . . . . Houston TX 77079 **877-259-6888** 281-496-2000
Dothan Chrysler-Dodge Inc
4074 Ross Clark Cir NW . . . . Dothan AL 36303 **877-674-9574**
DriveTime Corp
4020 E Indian School Rd . . . . Phoenix AZ 85018 **888-418-1212**
Dueck Auto Group
12100 Featherstone Way . . . . Richmond BC V6W1K9 **877-993-8325** 604-273-1311
Durocher Auto Sales Inc
4651 Rt 9 . . . . Plattsburgh NY 12901 **877-215-8954**
Earnhardt Auto Centers
7300 W Orchid Ln . . . . Chandler AZ 85226 **888-378-7711** 480-926-4000
East Bay Ford Truck Sales Inc
70 Hegenberger Loop . . . . Oakland CA 94621 **888-219-8551** 510-272-4400
Eastern Carolina Nissan
3315 Hwy 70 E . . . . New Bern NC 28564 **888-944-7822** 252-636-1000
El Camino Store, The
420 Athena Dr . . . . Athens GA 30601 **888-685-5987** 706-546-9217
Electro Enterprises Inc
3601 N I-35 Service Rd . . . . Oklahoma City OK 73111 **800-324-6591** 405-427-6591
Elm Chevrolet Co Inc
301 E Church St . . . . Elmira NY 14901 **877-265-6708** 607-734-4141
Erhard Bmw Of Bloomfield Hills
4065 W Maple Rd . . . . Bloomfield Hills MI 48301 **888-481-4058** 248-642-6565
F C Kerbeck & Sons
100 Rt 73 N . . . . Palmyra NJ 08065 **855-846-1500*** 856-829-8200
*General
Finish Line Ford Inc
2211 W Pioneer Pkwy . . . . Peoria IL 61615 **888-841-4002** 309-693-2525
First Truck Centre Inc
11313 170 St . . . . Edmonton AB T5M3P5 **888-882-8530** 780-413-8800
Five Star Dodge
3068 Riverside Dr . . . . Macon GA 31210 **877-748-9845** 478-474-3700
Fletch's Inc
825 Charlevoix Ave PO Box 265 . . . . Petoskey MI 49770 **877-238-0816** 231-347-9651
Fletcher Jones Imports
7300 W Sahara Ave . . . . Las Vegas NV 89117 **888-350-8850** 702-364-2700
Folsom Lake Ford
12755 Folsom Blvd . . . . Folsom CA 95630 **800-730-0457** 916-353-2000
Ford of Montebello Inc
2747 Via Campo . . . . Montebello CA 90640 **888-313-2305** 323-838-6920

			Toll-Free	Phone

FordDirect
1740 Us Hwy 60 PO Box 700 . . . . Republic MO 65738 **888-865-2576**

Fordham Auto Sales Inc
236 W Fordham Rd . . . . Bronx NY 10468 **800-407-1153**

Freightliner of Hartford Inc
222 Roberts St . . . . East Hartford CT 06108 **800-453-6967** 860-289-0201

Galpin Motors Inc
15505 Roscoe Blvd . . . . North Hills CA 91343 **800-256-7137** 818-787-3800

Gateway Industrial Power Inc
921 Fournie Ln . . . . Collinsville IL 62234 **888-865-8675** 618-345-0123

Gillman Cos
10595 W Sam Houston Pkwy S . . . . Houston TX 77099 **888-532-8956** 713-776-7000

Gilroy Chevrolet Cadillac Inc
6720 Bear Cat Ct . . . . Gilroy CA 95020 **800-201-7241** 408-842-9301

Gladstone Dodge
5610 N Oak Trafficway . . . . Gladstone MO 64118 **866-695-2043**

Glendale Infiniti
812 S Brand Blvd . . . . Glendale CA 91204 **800-449-9375** 818-543-5000

Global Filtration Inc
9207 Emmott St . . . . Houston TX 77040 **888-717-0888** 713-856-9800

Globe Motors Inc
2275 Stanley Ave . . . . Dayton OH 45404 **800-433-5700** 937-228-3171

Graff Truck Centers Inc
1401 S Saginaw St . . . . Flint MI 48503 **888-870-4203** 810-239-8300

Group 1 Automotive Inc
800 Gessner Ste 500 . . . . Houston TX 77024 **888-707-4094** 713-647-5700
NYSE: GPI

Grubbs Infiniti Ltd
1661 Airport Fwy . . . . Euless TX 76040 **800-685-1111** 817-318-1200

Hainen Ford Inc 800 Hwy 5 S . . . . Tipton MO 65081 **888-526-6979**

Hamilton Chevrolet
5800 E 14 Mile Rd . . . . Warren MI 48092 **888-466-7827** 586-264-1400

Harte Nissan Inc
165 W Service Rd . . . . Hartford CT 06120 **866-687-8971** 860-549-2800

Headquarter Toyota
5895 NW 167th St . . . . Miami FL 33015 **800-549-0947** 305-364-9800

Hendrick Buick GMC Cadillac
1151 W 104th St . . . . Kansas City MO 64114 **888-255-9362** 816-942-7100

Herb Chambers I 95 Inc
107 Andover St . . . . Danvers MA 01923 **877-907-1965**

Herb Easley Motors Inc
1125 Central Fwy . . . . Wichita Falls TX 76306 **866-232-8859** 940-723-6631

Herb Gordon Nissan
3131 Automobile Blvd . . . . Silver Spring MD 20904 **855-414-4810** 866-399-7502

Herson's Inc
15525 Frederick Rd . . . . Rockville MD 20855 **888-203-8318**

Holman Cadillac Co
1200 Rt 73 S . . . . Mount Laurel NJ 08054 **866-865-6973** 856-778-1000

Honda of Santa Monica
1726 Santa Monica Blvd . . . . Santa Monica CA 90404 **800-269-2031** 310-264-4900

Honda World
10645 Studebaker Rd . . . . Downey CA 90241 **888-458-9404** 562-929-7000

Hoover Toyota 2686 Hwy 150 . . . . Hoover AL 35244 **866-980-8082** 205-978-2600

Horwith Trucks Inc
PO Box 7 . . . . NortHampton PA 18067 **800-220-8807** 610-261-2220

Indy Honda
8455 US 31 S . . . . Indianapolis IN 46227 **888-752-4589** 317-887-0800

Island Lincoln-Mercury Inc
1850 E Merritt Island Cswy . . . . Merritt Island FL 32952 **800-392-3673** 321-452-9220

James Wood Motors Inc
2111 Us Hwy 287 S . . . . Decatur TX 76234 **888-833-7230** 940-627-2177

Joe Van Horn Chevrolet Inc
PO Box 238 . . . . Plymouth WI 53073 **800-236-1415** 920-893-6361

John Watson Chevrolet
3535 Wall Ave . . . . Ogden UT 84401 **866-647-9930** 801-394-2611

Johnson Motors Inc
1891 Blinker Pkwy . . . . Du Bois PA 15801 **800-537-1768** 814-371-4444

Joyce Motors Corp
3166 SR- 10 . . . . Denville NJ 07834 **844-332-5955** 973-361-3000

Keeler Motor Car Co
1111 Troy Schenectady Rd . . . . Latham NY 12110 **800-474-4197** 518-785-4197

Ken Fowler Motors
1265 Airport Pk Blvd . . . . Ukiah CA 95482 **800-287-0107** 707-468-0101

Ken Garff Automotive Group
405 S Main St . . . . Salt Lake City UT 84111 **888-630-6838** 801-257-3400

Kenworth Northwest Inc
20220 International Blvd S
PO Box 98967 . . . . SeaTac WA 98198 **800-562-0060** 206-433-5911

Kenworth of Indianapolis Inc
2929 S Holt Rd . . . . Indianapolis IN 46241 **800-827-8421** 317-247-8421

Kolosso Toyota
3000 W Wisconsin Ave . . . . Appleton WI 54914 **888-565-6776** 920-738-3666

Koons Ford of Annapolis Inc
2540 Riva Rd . . . . Annapolis MD 21401 **888-313-5524** 410-224-2100

L & S Truck Ctr of Appleton Inc
330 N Bluemound Dr PO Box 1255 . . . . Appleton WI 54914 **888-617-3140** 920-749-1700

La Beau Bros Inc
295 N Harrison Ave PO Box 246. . . . . Kankakee IL 60901 **800-747-9519** 815-933-5519

La Belle Dodge Chrysler Jeep Inc
501 S Main St . . . . Labelle FL 33935 **800-226-1193** 863-675-2701

La Mesa Rv Ctr Inc
7430 Copley Pk Pl . . . . San Diego CA 92111 **888-509-4199*** 858-874-8000
*Sales

Lafontaine Honda
2245 S Telegraph Rd . . . . Dearborn MI 48124 **866-567-5088**

Lakeside International LLC
11000 W Silver Spring Rd . . . . Milwaukee WI 53225 **800-236-0444** 414-353-4800

Lakeside Toyota
3701 N Cswy Blvd . . . . Metairie LA 70002 **877-512-8274*** 504-833-3311
*Sales

Lancaster Toyota Inc
5270 Manheim Pk . . . . East Petersburg PA 17520 **888-424-1295**

Landers Ford Inc
2082 W Poplar Ave . . . . Collierville TN 38017 **888-281-5266**

Landmark Lincoln-Mercury Inc
5000 S Broadway . . . . Englewood CO 80113 **866-971-7207** 303-761-1560

Lawrence Hall Chevrolet Inc
1385 S Danville Dr . . . . Abilene TX 79605 **800-568-7158** 325-695-8800

LEKTRO Inc
1190 SE Flightline Dr . . . . Warrenton OR 97146 **800-535-8767** 503-861-2288

Lemay Auto Group
8220-75th St . . . . Kenosha WI 53142 **866-689-1492** 262-694-2000

Les Stanford Chevrolet Inc
21730 Michigan Ave . . . . Dearborn MI 48124 **800-836-0972** 313-457-0364

Lexus of Memphis Inc
2600 Ridgeway Rd . . . . Memphis TN 38119 **877-876-9996*** 901-362-8833
*Sales

Lithia Motors Inc
360 E Jackson St . . . . Medford OR 97501 **866-318-9660**
NYSE: LAD

Loeber Motors Inc
4255 W Touhy Ave . . . . Lincolnwood IL 60712 **888-211-4485** 847-675-1000

Lordco Parts Ltd
22866 Dewdney Trunk Rd . . . . Maple Ridge BC V2X3K6 **877-591-1581** 604-467-1581

Lou Bachrodt Auto Group
7070 Cherryvale N Blvd . . . . Rockford IL 61112 **866-635-2349** 815-332-3000

Mac Haik Auto Group
11711 Katy Fwy . . . . Houston TX 77079 **888-877-1748** 281-596-6261

Markley Motors
3325 S College Ave . . . . Fort Collins CO 80525 **888-480-5167** 970-226-2214

McCloskey Motors Inc
6710 N Academy Blvd . . . . Colorado Springs CO 80918 **877-389-6671** 719-594-9400

McDevitt Trucks Inc
One Mack Way PO Box 4640. . . . . Manchester NH 03108 **800-370-6225** 603-668-1700

McGrath Auto Group
4610 Ctr Pt Rd NE . . . . Cedar Rapids IA 52402 **888-902-8414**

Mclean Implement Inc
793 Illinois Rte 130 . . . . Albion IL 62806 **888-720-4440** 618-445-3676

Mercedes-Benz of San Francisco
500 Eigth St . . . . San Francisco CA 94103 **877-554-6016** 415-673-2000

Metro Ford Inc
9000 NW Seventh Ave . . . . Miami FL 33150 **877-811-9402**

Mike Reed Chevrolet
1559 E Oglethorpe . . . . Hinesville GA 31313 **877-228-3943**

Mission Valley Ford Truck Sales Inc
780 E Brokaw Rd PO Box 611150. . . . . San Jose CA 95112 **888-284-7471** 408-933-2300

Modern Chevrolet of Winston-Salem
5955 University Pkwy . . . . Winston Salem NC 27105 **888-306-0825*** 336-722-4191
*General

Molle Toyota Inc
601 W 103rd St . . . . Kansas City MO 64114 **888-510-7705** 816-942-5200

Montesi Motors Inc
444 State St . . . . North Haven CT 06473 **866-598-2263** 203-281-0481

Motorcars International
3015 E Cairo St . . . . Springfield MO 65802 **866-970-6800** 417-831-9999

Nalley Lexus Smyrna
2750 Cobb Pkwy SE . . . . Smyrna GA 30080 **877-454-4206**

National Standard Parts Assoc Inc
4400 Mobile Hwy . . . . Pensacola FL 32506 **800-874-6813** 850-456-5771

National Tire & Wheel
Five Garden Ct . . . . Wheeling WV 26003 **800-847-3287** 304-233-7917

Nationwide Lift Trucks Inc
3900 N 28th Terr . . . . Hollywood FL 33020 **800-327-4431** 954-922-4645

New Country Volkswagen of Greenwich
200 W Putnam Ave . . . . Greenwich CT 06830 **866-584-6747**

Nextran Corp
1986 W Beaver St . . . . Jacksonville FL 32209 **800-347-6225** 904-354-3721

Nitrous Express Inc
5411 Seymour Hwy . . . . Wichita Falls TX 76310 **888-463-2781** 940-767-7694

Norman Frede Chevrolet Co
16801 Feather Craft Ln . . . . Houston TX 77058 **888-307-1703** 281-486-2200

Norris Ford
901 Merritt Blvd . . . . Baltimore MD 21222 **866-460-5275*** 410-285-0200
*Sales

North Bay Nissan Inc
1250 Auto Ctr Dr . . . . Petaluma CA 94952 **877-818-6866** 707-769-7700

North Park Lincoln
9207 San Pedro St . . . . San Antonio TX 78216 **888-696-5480** 210-341-8841

Northway Toyota
727 New Loudon Rd . . . . Latham NY 12110 **877-525-3488** 518-783-1951

O'Gara Coach Company LLC
8833 W Olympic Blvd . . . . Beverly Hills CA 90211 **888-291-5533**

Palm Automotive Group
1801 Tamiami Trail PO Box 512049 . . . . Punta Gorda FL 33950 **800-643-2112*** 941-639-1155
*General

Parsons Buick Co, The
151 E St . . . . Plainville CT 06062 **877-274-2613** 860-747-1693

Partschannel Inc
119 Regal Row Rd Ste B. . . . . Dallas TX 75247 **800-562-2126** 214-688-0018

Paul Heuring Motors Inc
720 N Hobart Rd . . . . Hobart IN 46342 **888-851-9702** 219-942-3673

Paul Moak Automotive Inc
740 Larson St . . . . Jackson MS 39202 **888-804-2108** 601-352-2700

Phil Long Dealerships
1212 Motor City Dr . . . . Colorado Springs CO 80905 **866-644-1378**

Phil Smart Inc
600 E Pike St . . . . Seattle WA 98122 **877-241-4528** 206-324-5959

Phillips Buick-Pontiac-Gmc Truck Inc
2160 US Hwy 441 . . . . Fruitland Park FL 34731 **888-664-7454** 352-728-1212

Piercey Automotive Group
16901 Millikan Ave . . . . Irvine CA 92606 **877-280-1044** 949-396-6000

Pitts Toyota Inc
210 N Jefferson St PO Box 4013 . . . . Dublin GA 31021 **888-561-8030** 478-272-3244

Porsche of Maplewood
2780 Maplewood Dr . . . . Maplewood MN 55109 **888-693-6579** 888-679-1698

Premier Subaru LLC
150 N Main St PO Box 3366. . . . . Branford CT 06405 **800-411-4551** 203-481-0687

Prestige Chrysler Dodge Inc
200 Alpine St . . . . Longmont CO 80501 **866-439-1926** 303-651-3000

Priority Chevrolet of Chesapeake
1495 S Military Hwy . . . . Chesapeake VA 23320 **855-315-0212** 757-424-1811

Prostrollo Motor Sales Inc
PO Box 1415 . . . . Huron SD 57350 **866-466-4515**

Rhoden Auto Ctr Inc
3400 S Expy St . . . . Council Bluffs IA 51501 **866-562-6248** 712-309-4000

			Toll-Free	Phone
Ricart Automotive Group				
4255 S Hamilton Rd	Columbus OH	43125	**888-225-6783**	888-631-9726
Riverside Ford				
1419 Ludington St	Escanaba MI	49829	**877-326-5326**	906-786-1130
Riverside Ford Inc				
2089 Riverside Dr PO Box 225	Macon GA	31204	**800-395-6210***	478-464-2900
*Sales				
RnR RV Ctr				
23203 E Knox Ave	Liberty Lake WA	99019	**866-386-4875**	
Roberson Motors Inc				
3100 Ryan Dr SE	Salem OR	97301	**888-281-6220**	503-363-4117
Roger Dean Chevrolet Inc				
2235 Okeechobee Blvd	West Palm Beach FL	33409	**877-827-4705**	561-683-8100
Romero Mazda				
1307 Kettering Dr	Ontario CA	91761	**888-317-2233**	909-390-8484
Ron Carter Automotive Group				
3205 FM 528	Alvin TX	77511	**800-531-8285**	281-331-3111
Rosner Auto Group				
3507 Jefferson Davis Hwy	Fredericksburg VA	22408	**855-271-7618***	855-265-5075
*Sales				
Rush Truck Center - Whittier				
2450 Kella Ave	Whittier CA	90601	**877-605-7623**	562-551-5000
Russell Karting Specialties Inc				
PO Box 1220	Raymore MO	64083	**800-821-3359**	816-322-3330
RV World Inc of Nokomis				
2110 Tamiami Trl N	Nokomis FL	34275	**800-262-2182**	941-966-2182
Sam Swope Volkswagen of Clarksville				
125 W Lewis & Clark Pkw	Clarksville IN	47129	**866-308-0592**	812-948-1541
Sandy Sansing Chevrolet				
6200 N Pensacola Blvd	Pensacola FL	32505	**888-885-1844***	850-476-2480
*Sales				
Schukei Chevrolet Inc				
721 S Monroe PO Box 1525	Mason City IA	50401	**866-918-6497**	641-423-5402
Scott Family of Dealerships				
3333 Lehigh St	Allentown PA	18103	**800-274-1039**	
Sears Imported Autos Inc				
13500 Wayzata Blvd	Minnetonka MN	55305	**800-493-1720***	952-546-5301
*Sales				
Seneca Tank Inc				
5585 NE 16th St	Des Moines IA	50313	**800-362-2910**	515-262-5900
Shelly Automotive Group				
Irvine BMW 9881 Research Dr	Irvine CA	92618	**888-853-7429**	
Sheppard Motors				
2300 W Seventh Ave	Eugene OR	97402	**877-362-1865***	541-343-8811
*Sales				
Showcase Honda				
1333 E Camelback Rd	Phoenix AZ	85014	**855-788-5798**	866-956-6481
Sierra Volkswagen Inc				
510 E Norris Dr PO Box 456	Ottawa IL	61350	**866-308-5670**	
Silver Star Automotive Group				
Lotus of Thousand Oaks				
3601 Auto Mall Dr	Thousand Oaks CA	91362	**800-472-5450**	
Sisbarro Dealerships				
425 W Boutz Rd	Las Cruces NM	88005	**888-241-1007**	575-524-7707
Sitton Buick GMC				
2640 Laurens Rd	Greenville SC	29607	**888-484-8009**	864-288-5600
Skybooks Inc				
1310 Tradeport Dr	Jacksonville FL	32218	**866-929-8700**	904-741-8700
Smith Motors Inc of Hammond				
6405 Indianapolis Blvd	Hammond IN	46320	**877-392-2689**	219-845-4000
Smoky Mountain Truck Ctr LLC				
841 Eastern Star Rd PO Box 5729	Kingsport TN	37663	**800-451-1508**	423-349-3000
Snyder Chevrolet				
524 N Perry St	Napoleon OH	43545	**800-569-3957**	419-599-1015
Sommer's Automotive				
7211 W Meq PO Box 37	Mequon WI	53092	**888-494-4193**	262-242-0100
South Charlotte Nissan				
9215 S Blvd	Charlotte NC	28273	**888-411-1423**	704-552-9191
South Tacoma Honda				
7802 S Tacoma Way	Tacoma WA	98409	**888-497-2416**	253-472-2300
Southfield Dodge Chrysler Jeep Ram				
28100 Telegraph Rd	Southfield MI	48034	**888-388-0451***	248-354-2950
*Sales				
Southwick Inc				
2400 Shattuck Ave	Berkeley CA	94704	**888-686-0046**	510-845-2530
Specialty Hearse & Ambulance Sale Corp				
60 Engineers Ln E	Farmingdale NY	11735	**800-349-6102***	516-349-7700
*General				
Standard Motors Ltd				
44 Second Ave NW	Swift Current SK	S9H3V6	**800-268-3131**	306-773-3131
Star Ford Lincoln				
1100 S Brand Blvd	Glendale CA	91204	**800-239-0755**	818-956-0977
Steele Truck Ctr Inc				
2150 Rockfill Rd	Fort Myers FL	33916	**888-806-4839**	239-334-7300
Steve Barry Buick Inc				
16000 Detroit Ave	Lakewood OH	44107	**866-327-5818**	216-920-0866
Steve Millen Sportparts Inc				
3176 Airway Ave	Costa Mesa CA	92626	**866-250-5542**	714-540-5566
Suburban Collection				
1810 Maplelawn Dr	Troy MI	48084	**877-471-7100**	
Susan Schein Automotive				
3171 Pelham Pkwy PO Box 215	Pelham AL	35124	**800-845-1578**	205-664-1491
Sutton Ford Inc				
21315 S Central Ave	Matteson IL	60443	**866-232-2966**	708-720-8115
T G H Aviation				
2389 Rickenbacker Way	Auburn CA	95602	**800-843-4976**	530-823-6204
Team Volkswagen of Hayward Corp				
25115 Mission Blvd	Hayward CA	94544	**866-308-2825**	
Tom Bensen Chevrolet Co Inc				
9400 San Pedro	San Antonio TX	78216	**866-635-6971**	210-341-3311
Toms Truck Ctr Inc				
1008 E Fourth St PO Box 88	Santa Ana CA	92701	**800-638-1015**	714-338-6060
Transwest				
20770 I-76 Frontage Rd	Brighton CO	80603	**800-289-3161**	303-289-3161
Tri County Ford Mercury Inc				
5101 W Hwy 146 PO Box 425	Buckner KY	40010	**800-945-2520**	502-241-7333
Tropical Ford				
9900 S Orange Blossom Trail	Orlando FL	32837	**800-790-7137***	407-851-3800
*Sales				

			Toll-Free	Phone
Truck Sales & Service Inc				
PO Box 262	Midvale OH	44653	**800-282-6100**	740-922-3412
Truck Works Inc				
3220 W Sherman St	Phoenix AZ	85009	**877-894-8757**	602-233-3713
Tustin Nissan 30 Auto Ctr Dr	Tustin CA	92782	**888-468-1391***	714-669-8282
*Sales				
Utility/Keystone Trailer Sales Inc				
1976 Auction Rd	Manheim PA	17545	**888-327-4236**	717-653-9444
V&H Inc				
1505 S Central Ave	Marshfield WI	54449	**800-826-2308**	715-486-8800
Valley Freightliner Inc				
277 Stewart Rd SW	Pacific WA	98047	**800-523-8014**	
Van Bortel Subaru				
6327 SR- 96	Victor NY	14564	**800-724-8872**	585-924-5230
Vin Devers Inc				
5570 Monroe St	Sylvania OH	43560	**888-847-9535**	419-885-5111
Vision Ford Lincoln				
1500 S White Sands Blvd	Alamogordo NM	88310	**888-811-2921**	888-285-7516
Visionaire Inc				
502 Jesse St	Grand Prairie TX	th St	**866-838-2810**	972-647-1056
Vista Auto				
21501 Ventura Blvd	Woodland Hills CA	91364	**888-887-6530**	888-313-4252
VT Inc				
8500 Shawnee Mission Pkwy	Shawnee Mission KS	66202	**800-747-4400**	913-895-0200
Wallingford Buick GMC				
1122 Old N Colony Rd	Wallingford CT	06492	**888-765-9107***	203-269-8741
*Cust Svc				
West-Herr Automotive Group Inc				
3448 McKinley Pkwy	Blasdell NY	14219	**800-643-2112**	716-649-5640
Westchester Toyota Service				
75 Vredenburgh Ave	Yonkers NY	10704	**866-232-7662**	914-968-6500
Western Bus Sales Inc				
30355 SE Hwy 212	Boring OR	97009	**800-258-2473**	503-905-0002
Western Slope Auto Co				
2264 Hwy 6 & 50	Grand Junction CO	81505	**888-461-3493**	970-243-0843
Westman Freightliner Inc				
2200 Fourth Ave Mankato PO Box 699	Mankato MN	56001	**866-576-6914**	507-625-4118
Whitaker Buick Co				
131 19th St SW	Forest Lake MN	55025	**877-324-8885**	651-674-3931
White Plains Honda				
344 Central Ave	White Plains NY	10606	**877-553-9292**	914-948-3305
Wilde Automotive Management of Wisc Onsin Inc				
1710 A Hwy 164	Waukesha WI	53186	**888-379-5817**	262-513-2770
Winslow BMW				
730 N Cir Dr	Colorado Springs CO	80909	**866-635-2349**	719-473-1373
Witt Lincoln				
588 Camino Del Rio N	San Diego CA	92108	**877-245-6856**	619-358-5000
WMK Inc 810 Moe Dr	Akron OH	44310	**877-275-4912**	330-633-1118
York Ford Inc 1481 Bwy	Saugus MA	01906	**888-874-0636**	781-231-1945
Zimmerman Auto Center				
4001 First Ave	Cedar Rapids IA	52402	**855-877-4223**	

AUTOMOBILE LEASING

SEE Credit & Financing - Consumer ; Credit & Financing - Commercial ; Fleet Leasing & Management

57   AUTOMOBILE SALES & RELATED SERVICES - ONLINE

SEE ALSO Automobile Dealers & Groups

			Toll-Free	Phone
Autobytel Inc				
18872 MacArthur Blvd	Irvine CA	92612	**888-422-8999**	949-225-4500
NASDAQ: ABTL				
Autofusion Corp				
6215 Ferris Sq Ste 200	San Diego CA	92121	**800-410-7354**	858-270-9444
Automobile Consumer Services Inc				
6249 Stewart Rd	Cincinnati OH	45227	**800-223-4882**	513-527-7700
Automotive Information Ctr				
18872 MacArthur Blvd	Irvine CA	92612	**888-422-8999**	
Carfax Inc				
10304 Eaton Pl Ste 500	Fairfax VA	10304	**800-274-2277**	703-934-2664
Cars.com				
175 W Jackson Blvd Ste 800	Chicago IL	60604	**888-246-6298**	312-601-5000
CarsDirect.com Inc				
909 N Sepulveda Blvd 11th Fl	El Segundo CA	90245	**888-227-7347***	
*Cust Svc				
Kelley Blue Book Company Inc				
195 Technology Dr	Irvine CA	92623	**800-258-3266**	949-770-7704
Williamson Cadillac Co				
7815 SW 104th St	Miami FL	33156	**877-228-6093**	305-670-7100

58   AUTOMOBILES - MFR

SEE ALSO Snowmobiles ; Motor Vehicles - Commercial & Special Purpose ; Motorcycles & Motorcycle Parts & Accessories ; All-Terrain Vehicles

			Toll-Free	Phone
American Honda Motor Company Inc				
1919 Torrance Blvd	Torrance CA	90501	**800-999-1009**	310-783-3170
Audi of America				
3800 Hamlin Rd	Auburn Hills MI	48326	**888-237-2834**	
BMW of North America LLC				
300 Chestnut Ridge Rd	Woodcliff Lake NJ	07677	**800-831-1117**	201-307-4000
Chrysler Group LLC				
1000 Chrysler Dr	Auburn Hills MI	48326	**800-423-6343***	
*Cust Svc				
Collins Bus Corp				
PO Box 2946	Hutchinson KS	67504	**800-533-1850**	620-662-9000
DaimlerChrysler Corp Jeep Div				
PO Box 21-8004	Auburn Hills MI	48321	**800-992-1997***	
*Cust Svc				
Eldorado National Inc				
9670 Galena St	Riverside CA	92509	**800-338-3211**	909-591-9557

				Toll-Free	Phone
Ferrara Fire Apparatus Inc PO Box 249	Holden	LA	70744	**800-443-9006**	225-567-7100
Ford Motor Co PO Box 6248	Dearborn	MI	48126	**800-392-3673**	313-845-8540
NYSE: F					
Freightliner Specialty Vehicles Inc 2300 S 13th St	Clinton	OK	73601	**800-358-7624**	580-323-4100
General Motors Corp Buick Motor Div 300 Renaissance Ctr PO Box 33136	Detroit	MI	48265	**800-521-7300***	
*Cust Svc					
Glaval Bus 914 County Rd 1	Elkhart	IN	46514	**800-445-2825**	574-262-2212
Hyundai Motor America 10550 Talbert Ave	Fountain Valley	CA	92708	**800-633-5151***	714-965-3000
*Cust Svc					
Land Rover North America Inc 555 MacArthur Blvd	Mahwah	NJ	07430	**800-637-6837**	
Lincoln-Mercury Co PO Box 6128	Dearborn	MI	48121	**800-521-4140**	
Lotus Cars USA Inc 2402 Tech Ctr Pkwy NE	Lawrenceville	GA	30043	**800-245-6887***	770-476-6540
*Cust Svc					
Mazda North American Operations 7755 Irvine Ctr Dr PO Box 19734	Irvine	CA	92618	**800-222-5500***	949-727-1990
*Cust Svc					
Mercedes-Benz USA LLC one Mercedes Dr	Montvale	NJ	07645	**800-367-6372***	201-573-0600
*Cust Svc					
Nissan Canada Inc (NCI) 5290 Orbitor Dr	Mississauga	ON	L4W4Z5	**800-387-0122**	
Nissan Motor Corp USA Infiniti Div One Nissan Way PO Box 685003	Franklin	TN	37067	**800-662-6200**	
Nissan North America Inc 25 Vantage way	Nashville	TN	37228	**800-647-7261**	
Peugeot Motors of America Inc 150 Clove Rd Ste 3	Little Falls	NJ	07424	**800-223-0587**	973-812-4444
Porsche Cars North America Inc 980 Hammond Dr Ste 1000	Atlanta	GA	30328	**800-505-1041**	770-290-3500
Saleen Automotive Inc 2735 Wardlow Rd	Corona	CA	92882	**800-888-8945**	
Subaru of America Inc 2235 Marlton Pike W	Cherry Hill	NJ	08002	**800-782-2783**	856-488-8500
Tesla Motors Inc 3500 Deer Creek Rd	Palo Alto	CA	94304	**888-518-3752**	650-681-5000
Toyota Canada Inc One Toyota Pl	Scarborough	ON	M1H1H9	**888-869-6828***	416-438-6320
*Cust Svc					
Toyota Motor Sales USA Inc 19001 S Western Ave	Torrance	CA	90501	**800-331-4331***	310-468-4000
Toyota Motor Sales USA Inc Lexus Div 19001 S Western Ave	Torrance	CA	90501	**800-255-3987***	
*Cust Svc					
Volkswagen Canada Inc 777 Bayly St W	Ajax	ON	L1S7G7	**800-822-8987**	905-428-6700
Volkswagen of America Inc 3800 Hamlin Rd	Auburn Hills	MI	48326	**800-822-8987**	
Volvo Cars of North America One Volvo Dr	Rockleigh	NJ	07647	**800-458-1552***	201-768-7300
*Cust Svc					

59   AUTOMOTIVE PARTS & SUPPLIES - MFR

SEE ALSO Gaskets, Packing, Sealing Devices ; Hose & Belting - Rubber or Plastics ; Motors (Electric) & Generators ; Carburetors, Pistons, Piston Rings, Valves ; Electrical Equipment for Internal Combustion Engines ; Engines & Turbines

				Toll-Free	Phone
Accuride Corp 7140 Office Cir	Evansville	IN	47715	**800-823-8332***	812-962-5000
*NYSE: ACW ▪ *Cust Svc					
Aer Mfg Inc PO Box 979	Carrollton	TX	75011	**800-753-5237**	972-417-2582
Airtex Products 407 W Main St	Fairfield	IL	62837	**800-880-3056**	618-842-2111
Alma Products Co 2000 Michigan Ave	Alma	MI	48801	**877-427-2624**	989-463-1151
AMBAC International Inc 910 Spears Creek Ct	Elgin	SC	29045	**800-628-6894**	803-735-1400
AP Exhaust Technologies Inc 300 Dixie Trial	Goldsboro	NC	27530	**800-277-2787**	919-580-2000
Atwood Mobile Products 1120 N Main St	Elkhart	IN	46514	**800-546-8759**	574-264-2131
Autocam Corp 4070 E Paris Ave	Kentwood	MI	49512	**800-747-6978**	616-698-0707
Baldwin Filters 4400 Hwy 30	Kearney	NE	68847	**800-822-5394**	
Beach Manufacturing Co PO Box 129	Donnelsville	OH	45319	**800-543-5942**	937-882-6372
Borla Performance Industries Inc 500 Borla Dr	Johnson City	TN	37604	**877-462-6752**	423-979-4000
Bushwacker Inc 6710 N Catlin Ave	Portland	OR	97203	**800-234-8920**	503-283-4335
Cardone Industries Inc 5501 Whitaker Ave	Philadelphia	PA	19124	**800-777-4780***	215-912-3000
*Cust Svc					
Carlisle Cos Inc 13925 Ballantyne Corporate Pl Ste 400	Charlotte	NC	28277	**800-248-5995**	704-501-1100
*NYSE: CSL					
Carlisle Industrial Brake 1031 E Hillside Dr	Bloomington	IN	47401	**800-873-6361**	812-336-3811
Clarcor Inc 840 Crescent Ctr Dr Ste 600	Franklin	TN	37067	**800-252-7267**	615-771-3100
*NYSE: CLC					
Competition Cams Inc 3406 Democrat Rd	Memphis	TN	38118	**800-999-0853**	901-795-2400
Consolidated Metco Inc 13940 N Rivergate Blvd	Portland	OR	97203	**800-547-9473***	
*Sales					

				Toll-Free	Phone
Cummins Filtration 2931 Elm Hill Pike	Nashville	TN	37214	**800-777-7064**	615-367-0040
Cummins Inc 500 Jackson St PO Box 3005	Columbus	IN	47201	**800-343-7357**	812-377-5000
*NYSE: CMI					
DACCO Transmission Parts 741 Dacco Dr PO Box 2789	Cookeville	TN	38502	**866-645-1452***	931-528-7581
*Cust Svc					
Danaher Corp 2200 Pennsylvania Ave NW Ste 800	Washington	DC	20037	**800-833-9200**	202-828-0850
*NYSE: DHR					
Davco Technology LLC 1600 Woodland Dr PO Box 487	Saline	MI	48176	**800-328-2611**	734-429-5665
Dayton Parts LLC 3500 Industrial Rd PO Box 5795	Harrisburg	PA	17110	**800-225-2159***	717-255-8500
*Cust Svc					
Decoma International Inc *Magna Exteriors & Interiors* 50 Casmir Ct	Concord	ON	L4K4J5	**888-348-2398**	905-669-2888
Denso International America Inc 24777 Denso Dr	Southfield	MI	48033	**800-321-6021**	248-350-7500
Dexter Axle 2900 Industrial Pkwy	Elkhart	IN	46516	**800-522-7291**	574-295-7888
Dorman Products Inc 3400 E Walnut St	Colmar	PA	18915	**800-523-2492**	215-997-1800
*NASDAQ: DORM					
Dura Automotive Systems Inc 1780 Pond Run	Auburn Hills	MI	48326	**800-362-3872**	248-299-7500
Edelbrock Corp 2700 California St	Torrance	CA	90503	**800-739-3737**	310-781-2222
EnPro Industries Inc 5605 Carnegie Blvd Ste 500	Charlotte	NC	28209	**800-356-6955**	704-731-1500
*NYSE: NPO					
Evercoat 6600 Cornell Rd	Cincinnati	OH	45242	**800-729-7600**	513-489-7600
Federal-Mogul Corp 27300 W 11 Mile Rd	Southfield	MI	48034	**800-325-8886***	248-354-7700
*NASDAQ: FDML ▪ *Cust Svc					
Firestone Industrial Products Co 250 W 96th St	Indianapolis	IN	46260	**800-888-0650**	317-818-8600
Flex-N-Gate Corp 1306 E University Ave	Urbana	IL	61802	**800-398-1496**	217-278-2600
Fontaine Fifth Wheel 7574 Commerce Cir	Trussville	AL	35173	**800-874-9780**	205-661-4900
Fontaine Truck Equipment Co 7574 Commerce Cir	Trussville	AL	35173	**800-874-9780**	205-661-4900
Griffin Thermal Products 100 Hurricane Creek Rd	Piedmont	SC	29673	**800-722-3723**	864-845-5000
Grote Industries Inc 2600 Lanier Dr	Madison	IN	47250	**800-628-0809**	812-273-2121
Gunite Corp 302 Peoples Ave	Rockford	IL	61104	**800-677-3786**	815-964-3301
Hastings Manufacturing Co 325 N Hanover St	Hastings	MI	49058	**800-776-1088**	269-945-2491
Hayden Automotive 1801 Waters Ridge Dr	Lewisville	TX	75057	**888-505-4567**	
Hendrickson International 800 S Frontage Rd	Woodridge	IL	60517	**855-743-3733**	630-910-2800
Hennessy Industries Inc 1601 JP Hennesey Dr	La Vergne	TN	37086	**800-688-6359**	615-641-7533
Holley Performance Products Inc 1801 Russellville Rd	Bowling Green	KY	42101	**800-638-0032***	270-782-2900
*Sales					
Hopkins Manufacturing Corp 428 Peyton St	Emporia	KS	66801	**800-524-1458**	620-342-7320
Hutchens Industries Inc 215 N Patterson Ave	Springfield	MO	65802	**800-654-8824**	417-862-5012
HWH Corp 2096 Moscow Rd	Moscow	IA	52760	**800-321-3494**	563-724-3396
Indian Head Industries Inc 8530 Cliff Cameron Dr	Charlotte	NC	28269	**800-527-1534**	704-547-7411
Indian Head Industries Inc MGM Brakes Div 8530 Cliff Cameron Dr	Charlotte	NC	28269	**800-527-1534**	704-547-7411
JASPER Engines & Transmissions 815 Wernsing Rd PO Box 650	Jasper	IN	47547	**800-827-7455**	812-482-1041
John Bean Co 309 Exchange Ave	Conway	AR	72032	**800-225-5786**	501-450-1500
Lund International Holdings Inc 4325 Hamilton Mill Rd Ste 400	Buford	GA	30518	**800-241-7219**	678-804-3912
MacLean-Fogg Co 1000 Allanson Rd	Mundelein	IL	60060	**800-323-4536**	847-566-0010
MAHLE Industries Inc 2020 Sanford St	Muskegon	MI	49444	**888-255-1942**	231-722-1300
Marmon-Herrington Co 13001 Magisterial Dr	Louisville	KY	40223	**800-227-0727**	502-253-0277
Neapco Inc 740 Queen St PO Box 399	Pottstown	PA	19464	**800-821-2374**	610-323-6000
P. T. M. Corp 6560 Bethuy Rd	Fair Haven	MI	48023	**800-486-2212**	586-725-2211
Penda Corp PO Box 449	Portage	WI	53901	**800-356-7704**	
Perfection Clutch Co 100 Perfection Way	Timmonsville	SC	29161	**800-258-8312**	843-326-5544
Phillips & Temro Industries 9700 W 74th St	Eden Prairie	MN	55344	**800-328-6108**	952-941-9700
Raybestos Powertrain LLC 711 Tech Dr	Crawfordsville	IN	47933	**800-729-7763**	
Remy International Inc 600 Corp Dr	Pendleton	IN	46064	**800-372-3555**	765-778-6499
*NYSE: REMY					
Ridewell Corp PO Box 4586	Springfield	MO	65808	**877-434-8088**	417-833-4565
Roush Manufacturing Inc 12068 Market St	Livonia	MI	48150	**800-215-9658**	734-779-7028
SmarTire Systems Inc 13151 Vanier Pl Ste 150	Richmond	BC	V5V2J1	**800-247-2725**	604-276-9884
Stanadyne Corp 92 Deerfield Rd	Windsor	CT	06095	**888-336-3473**	860-525-0821
Stemco LP 300 Industrial Blvd PO Box 1989	Longview	TX	75606	**800-527-8492**	903-758-9981

				Toll-Free	Phone
Strattec Security Corp					
3333 W Good Hope Rd	Milwaukee	WI	53209	**877-251-8799***	414-247-3333
NASDAQ: STRT ■ *General*					
Teleflex Medical					
2917 Weck Dr					
PO Box 12600	Research Triangle Park	NC	27709	**866-246-6990**	919-544-8000
TeleflexGFI Control Systems LP					
100 Hollinger Crescent	Kitchener	ON	N2K2Z3	**800-667-4275**	519-576-4270
Tenneco Inc					
500 N Field Dr	Lake Forest	IL	60045	**866-839-3259**	847-482-5000
NYSE: TEN					
Titan International Inc					
2701 Spruce St	Quincy	IL	62301	**800-872-2327**	217-228-6011
NYSE: TWI					
Titan Wheel Corp					
2701 Spruce St	Quincy	IL	62301	**800-872-2327**	217-228-6011
Trelleborg Automotive Americas					
400 Aylworth Ave	South Haven	MI	49090	**800-635-9331**	269-637-2116
Triangle Suspension Systems Inc					
47 E Maloney Rd	Du Bois	PA	15801	**800-458-6077**	814-375-7211
Universal Manufacturing Co					
405 Diagonal St PO Box 190	Algona	IA	50511	**800-651-7445**	515-295-3557
OTC: UFMG					
US Chemical & Plastics					
600 Nova Dr SE PO Box 709	Massillon	OH	44646	**800-321-0672**	330-830-6000
Velvac Inc					
2405 S Calhoun Rd	New Berlin	WI	53151	**800-783-8871**	262-786-0700
Visteon Corp					
1 Village Ctr Dr	Van Buren Township	MI	48111	**866-967-0260**	734-710-5000
NYSE: VC					
Webb Wheel Products Inc					
2310 Industrial Dr SW	Cullman	AL	35055	**800-633-3256**	256-739-6660
Wescast Industries Inc					
150 Savannah Oaks Dr	Brantford	ON	N3T5V7	**800-564-6253**	519-750-0000
TSE: WCS.A					

60   AUTOMOTIVE PARTS & SUPPLIES - WHOL

				Toll-Free	Phone
AA Wheel & Truck Supply Inc					
717 E 16th Ave	Kansas City	MO	64116	**800-486-4335**	816-221-9556
Ace Tool Co					
7337 Bryan Dairy Rd	Largo	FL	33777	**800-777-5910**	727-544-4331
Advantage Truck Accessories Inc					
5400 S State Rd PO Box 1747	Ann Arbor	MI	48108	**800-773-3110**	
Advantech International Inc					
PO Box 6739	Somerset	NJ	08875	**800-322-6150**	732-805-1900
Allomatic Products Co					
102 Jericho Tpke					
Ste 104 Floral Pk	Floral Park	NY	11001	**800-568-0330**	516-775-0330
Atsco ReMfg Inc					
4525 N 43rd Ave	Phoenix	AZ	85031	**800-470-2387**	623-842-4047
Automotive Distributors Company Inc					
2981 Morse Rd	Columbus	OH	43231	**800-421-5556**	
Automotive Parts Headquarters					
2959 Clearwater Rd	Saint Cloud	MN	56301	**800-247-0339**	320-252-5411
Barron Motor Inc					
1850 McCloud Pl NE PO Box 1327	Cedar Rapids	IA	52402	**800-332-7953**	
Bell Industries Inc Recreational Products Group					
580 Yankee Doodle Rd	Eagan	MN	55121	**800-866-5017**	651-450-9020
Bendix Commercial Vehicle Systems LLC					
901 Cleveland St	Elyria	OH	44035	**800-247-2725**	440-329-9000
Carolina Rim & Wheel Co					
1308 Upper Asbury Ave	Charlotte	NC	28206	**800-247-4337**	704-334-7276
Carolinas Auto Supply House Inc					
2135 Tipton Dr	Charlotte	NC	28206	**800-438-4070**	704-334-4646
Carquest Corp					
2635 E Millbrook Rd	Raleigh	NC	27604	**800-876-1291**	919-573-3000
Champion Power Equipment Inc					
10006 Santa Fe Springs Rd	Santa Fe Springs	CA	90670	**877-338-0999**	562-236-9422
Charleston Auto Parts Inc					
3108 Losee Rd	North Las Vegas	NV	89030	**800-879-7901**	
Coast Distribution System					
350 Woodview Ave	Morgan Hill	CA	95037	**800-495-5858**	408-782-6686
NYSE: CRV					
Custom Chrome Inc					
155 E Main Ave Ste 150	Morgan Hill	CA	95037	**800-729-3332**	408-778-0500
Dero Bike Racks Inc					
504 Malcolm Ave SE Ste 100	Minneapolis	MN	55414	**888-337-6729**	612-359-0689
Drive Train Industries Inc					
5555 Joliet St	Denver	CO	80239	**800-525-6177**	303-292-5176
Eagle Parts & Products Inc					
1411 Marvin Griffin Rd	Augusta	GA	30906	**888-972-9911**	706-790-6687
Enginetech Inc					
1205 W Crosby Rd	Carrollton	TX	75006	**800-869-8711**	972-245-0110
Flowers Auto Parts Co					
935 Hwy 70 SE	Hickory	NC	28602	**800-538-6272***	828-322-5414
Cust Svc					
Frank Edwards Co					
3626 Pkwy Blvd	West Valley City	UT	84120	**800-366-8851**	801-736-8000
General Truck Parts & Equipment Co					
3835 W 42nd St	Chicago	IL	60632	**800-621-3914**	773-247-6900
GK Industries Ltd					
50 Precidio Ct	Brampton	ON	L6S6E3	**800-463-8889**	905-799-1972
Harmonic Drive LLC					
247 Lynnfield St	Peabody	MA	01960	**800-921-3332**	978-532-1800
Hedahls Inc					
100 East Broadway	Bismarck	ND	58502	**800-433-2457**	701-223-8393
Henderson Wheel & Warehouse Supply					
1825 South 300 West	Salt Lake City	UT	84115	**800-748-5111**	801-486-2073
Instrument Sales & Service Inc					
16427 NE Airport Way	Portland	OR	97230	**800-333-7976**	503-239-0754
InterAmerican Motor Corp (IMC)					
8901 Canoga Ave	Canoga Park	CA	91304	**800-874-8925**	818-678-1200
Interstate Batteries					
12770 Merit Dr Ste 400	Dallas	TX	75251	**800-541-8419**	972-991-1444

				Toll-Free	Phone
JEGS Performance Auto Parts					
101 Jeg'S Pl	Delaware	OH	43015	**800-345-4545**	614-294-5050
Johnson Industries					
5944 Peachtree Corners E	Norcross	GA	30071	**800-922-8111***	770-441-1128
Orders					
Kansas City Peterbilt Inc					
8915 Woodend Rd	Kansas City	KS	66111	**800-489-1122**	913-441-2888
Keystone Automotive Operations Inc					
44 Tunkhannock Ave	Exeter	PA	18643	**800-521-9999**	570-655-4514
L & M Radiator Inc					
1414 E 37th St	Hibbing	MN	55746	**800-346-3500**	218-263-8993
Lakeshirts Inc					
750 Randolph Rd	Detroit Lakes	MN	56501	**800-627-2780**	218-847-2171
LKQ Corp					
120 N LaSalle St Ste 3300	Chicago	IL	60602	**877-557-2677**	312-621-1950
NASDAQ: LKQX					
McGard LLC					
3875 California Rd	Orchard Park	NY	14127	**800-444-5847**	716-662-8980
Mid America Motorworks					
17082 N Us Hwy 45 PO Box 1368	Effingham	IL	62401	**866-350-4543**	217-540-4200
Midwest Truck & Auto Parts Inc					
1001 W Exchange	Chicago	IL	60609	**800-934-2727**	773-247-3400
Mighty Distributing System of America Inc					
650 Engineering Dr	Norcross	GA	30092	**800-829-3900**	770-448-3900
Mile Marker International Inc					
2121 BLOUNT Rd	Pompano Beach	FL	33069	**800-886-8647**	
Mutual Wheel Co Inc					
2345 Fourth Ave	Moline	IL	61265	**800-798-6926**	309-757-1200
N.b.c. Truck Equipment Inc					
28130 Groesbeck Hwy	Roseville	MI	48066	**800-778-8207**	586-774-4900
National Automotive Parts Assn (NAPA)					
2999 Circle 75 Pkwy	Atlanta	GA	30339	**800-538-6272**	770-953-1700
Northeast Battery & Alternator Inc					
240 Washington St	Auburn	MA	01501	**800-441-8824**	508-832-2700
Northern Factory Sales Inc					
PO Box 660	Willmar	MN	56201	**800-328-8900**	320-235-2288
NTP Distribution Inc					
27150 SW Kinsman Rd	Wilsonville	OR	97070	**800-242-6987**	503-570-0171
Parts Central Inc					
3243 Whitfield St	Macon	GA	31204	**800-226-9396**	478-745-0878
Plaza Fleet Parts Inc					
1520 S Broadway	Saint Louis	MO	63104	**800-325-7618**	314-231-5047
Regional International Corp					
1007 Lehigh Stn Rd	Henrietta	NY	14467	**800-836-0409**	585-359-2011
Six Robblees' Inc					
11010 Tukwila International Blvd	Tukwila	WA	98168	**800-275-7499**	206-767-7970
Six States Distributors Inc					
247 West 1700 South	Salt Lake City	UT	84115	**800-453-5703***	801-488-4666
Cust Svc					
Stewart Title Insurance Co					
300 E 42nd St 10th Fl.	New York	NY	10017	**800-913-4170**	212-922-0050
Twinco Romax 4635 Willow Dr	Hamel	MN	55340	**800-682-3800***	763-478-2360
Cust Svc					
Vander Haag's Inc					
3809 Fourth Ave W	Spencer	IA	51301	**888-940-5030**	712-262-7000
WAIglobal					
411 Eagleview Blvd Ste 100	Exton	PA	19341	**800-877-3340**	484-875-6600
Western Truck Parts & Equip Co					
3801 Airport Way S	Seattle	WA	98108	**800-255-7383**	206-624-5099
Westin Automotive Products Inc					
5200 N Irwindale Ave Ste 220	Irwindale	CA	91706	**800-345-8476**	626-960-6762
WORLDPAC Inc					
37137 Hickory St	Newark	CA	94560	**800-888-9982**	510-742-8900
Wurth USA Inc 93 Grant St	Ramsey	NJ	07446	**800-987-8487**	201-825-2710

61   AUTOMOTIVE SERVICES

SEE ALSO Gas Stations

61-1 Appearance Care - Automotive

				Toll-Free	Phone
Autobell Car Wash Inc					
1521 E Third St	Charlotte	NC	28204	**800-582-8096**	704-527-9274
Color-Glo International					
7111 Ohms Ln	Minneapolis	MN	55439	**800-333-8523**	952-835-1338
Creative Colors International Inc					
19015 S Jodi Rd Ste E	Mokena	IL	60448	**800-933-2656**	708-478-1437
Dr Vinyl & Assoc Ltd					
1350 SE Hamblen Rd	Lees Summit	MO	64081	**800-531-6600***	816-525-6060
General					
Fleetwash Inc					
PO Box 1577	West Caldwell	NJ	07007	**800-847-3735**	
Mister Car Wash					
3561 E Sunrise Dr Ste 125	Tucson	AZ	85718	**866-254-3229***	520-615-4000
Cust Svc					
Precision Auto Care Inc					
748 Miller Dr SE	Leesburg	VA	20175	**800-438-8863**	703-777-9095
OTC: PACI					
Vizza Wash Services LLC					
2208 NW Loop 410	San Antonio	TX	78230	**866-493-8822***	210-493-8822
Cust Svc					
Wash Depot Holdings Inc					
14 Summer St	Malden	MA	02148	**800-339-3949**	781-324-2000
Ziebart International Corp					
1290 E Maple Rd	Troy	MI	48083	**800-877-1312**	248-588-4100

61-2 Glass Replacement - Automotive

				Toll-Free	Phone
All Star Glass Co Inc					
1845 Morena Blvd	San Diego	CA	92110	**800-225-4184**	619-275-3343
City Auto Glass Inc					
116 S Concord Exchange	South Saint Paul	MN	55075	**888-552-4272**	651-552-1000

	Toll-Free	Phone
Martin Glass Co		
25 Ctr Plz ....Belleville IL 62220	**800-325-1946**	618-277-1946
NOVUS Auto Glass		
12800 Hwy 13 S Ste 500 ....Savage MN 55378	**800-776-6887**	952-736-7843
Safelite Group Inc		
2400 Farmers Dr ....Columbus OH 43235	**877-664-8931**	
SuperGlass Windshield Repair Inc		
6101 Chancellor Dr Ste 200 ....Orlando FL 32809	**866-557-7497**	407-240-1920

61-3 Mufflers & Exhaust Systems Repair - Automotive

	Toll-Free	Phone
Car-X Assoc Corp		
1375 E Woodfield Rd Ste 500...........Schaumburg IL 60173	**800-359-2359**	847-273-8920
Midas International Corp		
1300 Arlington Heights Rd ....Itasca IL 60143	**800-621-8545**	630-438-3000
Monro Muffler Brake Inc		
200 Holleder Pkwy ....Rochester NY 14615	**800-876-6676**	585-647-6400
NASDAQ: MNRO		

61-4 Paint & Body Work - Automotive

	Toll-Free	Phone
CARSTAR Quality Collision Service		
8400 W 110th St Ste 200 ....Overland Park KS 66210	**800-227-7827***	913-451-1294
*Cust Svc		
Colors on Parade		
125 Daytona St PO Box 50940 ....Conway SC 29526	**866-756-4207***	843-347-8818
*Cust Svc		
Dent Clinic 711 48th Ave SE ....Calgary AB T2G2A7	**888-722-3368**	403-255-3111
Dent Wizard International		
4710 Earth City Expway ....Bridgeton MO 63044	**800-267-9369**	314-592-1800
Gerber Auto Collision & Glass Centers Inc		
8250 Skokie Blvd ....Skokie IL 60077	**877-743-7237**	847-679-0510
Gerber Collision & Glass		
44700 Enterprise Dr ....Clinton Township MI 48038	**877-743-7237***	586-954-3850
*General		
Maaco LLC		
440 S Church St Ste 700 ....Charlotte NC 28202	**800-523-1180**	704-377-8855
Mike Rose's Auto Body Inc		
2260 Via de Marcardos ....Concord CA 94520	**855-340-1739**	925-689-1739
Service King Collision Repair Centers		
808 S Central Expy ....Richardson TX 75080	**866-730-5464**	972-960-7595

61-5 Repair Service (General) - Automotive

	Toll-Free	Phone
All Tune & Lube Brakes & More Inc		
8334 Veteran's Hwy ....Millersville MD 21108	**877-978-1758**	410-987-1011
All Tune & Lube International Inc		
ATL International Inc		
8334 Veterans Hwy ....Millersville MD 21108	**877-978-1758***	410-987-1011
*Cust Svc		
Basin Tire & Auto Inc		
2700 E Main St ....Farmington NM 87402	**800-832-9832**	505-326-2231
Belle Tire Inc		
1000 Enterprise Dr ....Allen Park MI 48101	**888-462-3553**	313-271-9400
Bergey's Inc		
462 Harleysville Pike ....Souderton PA 18964	**800-237-4397**	215-723-6071
Bridgestone Americas Holding Inc		
535 Marriott Dr ....Nashville TN 37214	**877-201-2373***	615-937-1000
*Cust Svc		
Clark Tire & Auto Supply Co Inc		
220 S Ctr St ....Hickory NC 28602	**800-968-3092**	828-322-2303
Evans Tire & Service Centers Inc		
510 N Broadway ....Escondido CA 92025	**877-338-2678**	
Express Oil Change		
1880 S Pk Dr ....Hoover AL 35244	**888-945-1771**	205-945-1771
Fyda Freightliner Youngstown Inc		
5260 76th Dr ....Youngstown OH 44515	**800-837-3932**	330-797-0224
Grease Monkey International		
7450 E Progress Pl ....Greenwood Village CO 80111	**800-822-7706**	303-308-1660
Hunter Engineering Co		
11250 Hunter Dr ....Bridgeton MO 63044	**800-448-6848**	314-731-3020
Jack Williams Tire Co Inc		
PO Box 3655 ....Scranton PA 18505	**800-833-5051**	
Jiffy Lube PO Box 4427 ....Houston TX 77210	**800-344-6933**	
Jubitz Corp		
33 NE Middlefield Rd ....Portland OR 97211	**800-523-0600**	503-283-1111
Kansas City Peterbilt Inc		
8915 Woodend Rd ....Kansas City KS 66111	**800-489-1122**	913-441-2888
Merlin Corp		
3815 E Main St Ste D ....Saint Charles IL 60174	**800-652-9910**	630-513-8200
Mr Tire Auto Service Centers Inc		
200 Holleder Pkwy ....Rochester NY 14615	**800-876-6676**	
Parrish Tire Company Inc		
5130 Indiana Ave ....Winston-Salem NC 27106	**800-849-8473**	336-767-0202
Plaza Tire Service		
2075 Corporate Cr ....Cape Girardeau MO 63702	**877-787-1691**	
Precision Auto Care Inc		
748 Miller Dr SE ....Leesburg VA 20175	**800-438-8863**	703-777-9095
OTC: PACI		
Somerset Tire Services Inc		
PO Box 5936 ....Bridgewater NJ 08807	**800-445-1434**	732-356-8500
Sullivan Tire Co Inc		
PO Box 370 ....Rockland MA 02370	**877-855-4826**	781-871-2299
Techni-Car Inc		
450 Commerce Blvd ....Oldsmar FL 34677	**800-886-0022**	813-855-0022
Tire-Rama Inc		
1401 Industrial Ave PO Box 23509..........Billings MT 59104	**800-828-1642**	406-245-4006
Tires Plus Total Car Care		
2021 Sunnydale Blvd ....Clearwater FL 33765	**800-440-4167**	727-441-3727
Tuffy Assoc Corp		
7150 Granite Cir ....Toledo OH 43617	**800-228-8339**	419-865-6900

	Toll-Free	Phone
Wingfoot Commercial Tire Systems LLC		
1000 S 21st St ....Fort Smith AR 72901	**800-643-7330**	479-788-6400

61-6 Transmission Repair - Automotive

	Toll-Free	Phone
All Tune Transmissions		
8334 Veteran's Hwy ....Millersville MD 21108	**877-978-1758**	410-987-1011
Lee Myles Auto Group		
847 Fern Ave ....Reading PA 19607	**800-533-6953**	201-262-0555
Mr Transmission		
9675 Yonge St Second Fl ....Richmond Hill ON L4C1V7	**800-373-8432**	905-884-1511

61-7 Van Conversions

	Toll-Free	Phone
Clock Mobility		
6700 Clay Ave ....Grand Rapids MI 49548	**800-732-5625**	616-698-9400
Foley Inc		
855 Centennial Ave ....Piscataway NJ 08854	**888-417-6464**	732-885-5555
Marathon Coach		
91333 Coburg Industrial Way ....Coburg OR 97408	**800-234-9991**	541-343-9991
Monaco Coach Corp		
91320 Coburg Industrial Way ....Coburg OR 97408	**888-327-4236**	877-466-6226
Rollx Vans 6591 Hwy 13 W ....Savage MN 55378	**800-956-6668**	952-890-7851
Sherrod Vans Inc		
3151 Industrial Blvd ....Waycross GA 31503	**800-824-6333**	
Sidewinder Conversions		
44658 Yale Rd W ....Chilliwack BC V2R0G5	**888-266-2299**	604-792-2082
Van Conversions Inc		
925 S Trooper Rd ....Norristown PA 19403	**800-884-8267***	610-666-9100
*Cust Svc		
Vantage Mobility International (VMI)		
5202 S 28th Pl ....Phoenix AZ 85040	**800-348-8267**	602-243-2700
Waldoch Crafts Inc		
13821 Lake Dr NE ....Forest Lake MN 55025	**800-328-9259**	651-464-3215

62 AVIATION - FIXED-BASE OPERATIONS

SEE ALSO Air Cargo Carriers ; Air Charter Services ; Aircraft Rental ; Aircraft Service & Repair

	Toll-Free	Phone
Banyan Air Service		
5360 NW 20th Terr ....Fort Lauderdale FL 33309	**800-200-2031**	954-491-3170
BMG Aviation Inc		
984 S Kirby Rd ....Bloomington IN 47403	**888-457-3787**	812-825-7979
Central Flying Service Inc		
1501 Bond St ....Little Rock AR 72202	**800-888-5387**	501-375-3245
Columbia Air Services		
175 Tower Ave		
Groton-New London Airport ....Groton CT 06340	**800-787-5001**	860-449-1400
Cook Aviation Inc		
970 S Kirby Rd ....Bloomington IN 47403	**800-880-3499**	812-825-2392
Corporate Air LLC		
15 Allegheny County Airport ....West Mifflin PA 15122	**888-429-5377**	412-469-6800
Crow Executive Air Inc		
28331 Lemoyne Rd		
Toledo Metcalf Airport...............Millbury OH 43447	**800-972-2769**	419-838-6921
DB Aviation Inc		
3550 N McAree Rd ....Waukegan IL 60087	**888-362-6738**	847-336-9220
Dulles Aviation Inc		
10501 Observation Rd		
Manassas Regl Airport ....Manassas VA 20110	**888-835-9324**	703-361-2171
Eagle Aviation		
2861 Aviation Way		
Columbia Metropolitan Airport...........West Columbia SC 29170	**800-849-3245**	803-822-5555
Edwards Jet Ctr		
1691 Aviation Pl ....Billings MT 59105	**866-353-8245**	406-252-0508
Epps Aviation Inc		
One Aviation Way		
DeKalb Peachtree Airport ....Atlanta GA 30341	**800-241-6807**	770-458-9851
Felts Field Aviation Inc		
5829 E Rutter Ave ....Spokane WA 99212	**800-676-5538**	509-535-9011
Galvin Flying Services		
7149 Perimeter Rd ....Seattle WA 98108	**800-341-4102**	206-763-9706
Grand Aire Express Inc		
11777 W Airport Service Rd ....Swanton OH 43558	**800-704-7263**	
Hunt Pan Am Aviation Inc		
505 Amelia Earhart Dr ....Brownsville TX 78521	**800-888-7524**	956-542-9111
Interstate Aviation		
62 Johnson Ave ....Plainville CT 06062	**800-573-5519**	860-747-5519
Kansas City Aviation Ctr Inc		
15325 S Pflumm Rd ....Olathe KS 66062	**800-720-5222**	913-782-0530
Keystone Aviation Services Inc		
288 Christian St ....Oxford CT 06478	**866-436-2177**	203-264-6525
Landmark Aviation		
3501 Aviation Ave ....Sioux Falls SD 57104	**800-888-1646***	605-336-7791
*General		
Lane Aviation Corp		
4389 International Gateway ....Columbus OH 43219	**800-848-6263**	614-237-3747
Loyd's Aviation Services Inc		
1601 Skyway Dr Ste 100		
PO Box 80958...............Bakersfield CA 93308	**800-284-1334**	661-393-1334
Maine Instrument Flight Inc		
PO Box 2 ....Augusta ME 04332	**888-643-3597**	207-622-1211
McCall Aviation		
300 Deinhard Ln ....McCall ID 83638	**800-992-6559**	208-634-7137
Mid-Ohio Aviation		
6250 N Honeytown Rd ....Smithville OH 44677	**800-669-4243**	330-669-2671
Midwest Corporate Aviation		
3512 N Webb Rd ....Wichita KS 67226	**800-435-9622**	316-636-9700
Millenium Aviation		
2365 Bernville Rd		
Reading Regional Airport ....Reading PA 19605	**800-366-9419**	610-372-4728

				Toll-Free	Phone
Million Air					
4300 Westgrove Dr	Addison	TX	75001	**800-248-1602**	972-248-1600
Montgomery Aviation Corp					
4525 Selma Hwy	Montgomery	AL	36108	**800-392-8044**	334-288-7334
National Jets					
3495 SW Ninth Ave					
PO Box 22460	Fort Lauderdale	FL	33315	**800-327-3710**	954-359-9900
Northeast Airmotive Inc					
1011 Westbrook St	Portland	ME	04102	**877-354-7881**	207-774-6318
Pensacola Aviation Ctr Inc					
4145 Jerry L MayGarden Rd	Pensacola	FL	32504	**800-874-6580**	850-434-0636
Prior Aviation Service Inc					
50 N Airport Dr	Buffalo	NY	14225	**800-621-2923**	716-633-1000
Regional Jet Ctr					
12344 Tower Dr	Bentonville	AR	72712	**866-962-3835**	479-205-1100
Richmor Aviation Inc					
1142 Rt 9 H Columbia County Airport	Hudson	NY	12534	**800-331-6101**	518-828-9461
Sanford Aircraft Services Inc					
701 Rod Sullivan Rd	Sanford	NC	27330	**888-871-1947**	919-708-5549
SheltAir Aviation Services Fort Lauderdale					
4860 NE 12th Ave	Fort Lauderdale	FL	33334	**800-700-2210**	954-771-2210
Showalter Flying Service					
600 Herndon Ave PO Box 140753	Orlando	FL	32803	**800-894-7331**	407-326-6062
Sky Bright 65 Aviation Dr	Gilford	NH	03249	**800-639-6012**	603-528-6818
Skyservice Airlines Inc					
9785 Ryan Ave	Dorval	QC	H9P1A2	**888-985-1402**	514-636-3300
SkyTech Inc					
550 Airport Rd	Rock Hill	SC	29732	**888-386-3596**	803-366-5108
Snohomish Flying Service Inc					
9900 Airport Way	Snohomish	WA	98296	**800-827-1000**	360-568-1541
Southwest Airport Services Inc					
11811 N Brantly Ave Ste 500	Houston	TX	77034	**888-362-6738**	281-484-6551
Space Coast Jet Ctr					
7003 Challenger Ave	Titusville	FL	32780	**800-559-5473**	321-267-8355
St Paul Flight Ctr					
270 Airport Rd	Saint Paul	MN	55107	**800-368-0107**	651-227-8108
Stevens Aviation Inc					
600 Delaware St					
Donaldson Industrial Pk	Greenville	SC	29605	**800-359-7838**	864-678-6000
Stuart Jet Ctr LLC					
2501 Aviation Way	Stuart	FL	34996	**877-735-9538**	772-288-6700
TWC Aviation					
1162 Aviation Ave	San Jose	CA	95110	**800-359-7060**	408-286-3832
United States Aviation					
4141 N Memorial Dr	Tulsa	OK	74115	**800-897-5387**	918-836-7345
Vee Neal Aviation Inc					
148 Aviation Ln Ste 109	Latrobe	PA	15650	**800-278-2710**	724-539-4533
Western Aircraft Inc					
4300 S Kennedy St	Boise	ID	83705	**800-333-3442**	208-338-1800
Western Cardinal Inc					
205 Durley Ave	Camarillo	CA	93010	**800-882-3018**	805-482-2586
Wilson Air Ctr					
2930 Winchester Rd					
Memphis International Airport	Memphis	TN	38118	**800-464-2992**	901-345-2992
Wisconsin Aviation Inc					
1741 River Dr	Watertown	WI	53094	**800-657-0761**	920-261-4567
Woodland Aviation Inc					
25170 Aviation Ave	Davis	CA	95616	**800-442-1333**	530-759-6037

63 BABY PRODUCTS

SEE ALSO Toys, Games, Hobbies ; Household Furniture ; Paper Products - Sanitary ; Children's & Infants' Clothing

				Toll-Free	Phone
Baby Jogger Co					
8575 Magellan Pkwy Ste 1000	Richmond	VA	23227	**800-241-1848**	
Baby Trend Inc					
1567 S Campus Ave	Ontario	CA	91761	**800-328-7363***	
*Cust Svc					
Baby's Dream Furniture Inc					
411 Industrial Blvd PO Box 579	Buena Vista	GA	31803	**800-835-2742**	229-649-4404
Ball Bounce & Sport Inc/Hedstrom Plastics					
One Hedstrom Dr	Ashland	OH	44805	**800-765-9665**	419-289-9310
Britax Child Safety Inc					
13501 S Ridge Dr	Charlotte	NC	28273	**888-427-4829**	704-409-1700
Cardinal Gates					
79 Amlajack Way	Newnan	GA	30265	**800-318-3380**	770-252-4200
Central Specialties Ltd					
220 Exchange Dr	Crystal Lake	IL	60014	**800-873-4370**	815-459-6000
Crown Crafts Infant Products Inc					
711 W Walnut St	Compton	CA	90220	**800-421-0526**	310-763-8100
Delta Enterprises					
114 W 26th St Eighth Fl	New York	NY	10001	**800-377-3777**	212-736-7000
Dorel Juvenile Group USA					
2525 State St	Columbus	IN	47201	**800-544-1108**	812-372-0141
Evenflo Company Inc					
1801 Commerce Dr	Piqua	OH	45356	**800-233-5921**	
Fisher-Price Inc					
636 Girard Ave	East Aurora	NY	14052	**800-432-5437**	716-687-3000
Gerber Products Co					
445 State St	Fremont	MI	49413	**800-284-9488**	
Infantino LLC					
4920 Carroll Canyon Rd Ste 200	San Diego	CA	92121	**800-840-4916**	
Kelty 6235 Lookout Rd	Boulder	CO	80301	**800-423-2320**	800-535-3589
KidCo Inc					
1013 Technology Way	Libertyville	IL	60048	**800-553-5529**	847-549-8600
Kids II					
555 N Pt Ctr E Ste 600	Alpharetta	GA	30022	**877-325-7056**	770-751-0442
Kolcraft Enterprises Inc					
10832 NC Hwy 211 E	Aberdeen	NC	28315	**800-453-7673***	910-944-9345
*Cust Svc					
Little Tikes Co, The					
2180 Barlow Rd	Hudson	OH	44236	**800-321-0183***	
*Cust Svc					
Manhattan Toy					
300 First Ave N Suite 200	Minneapolis	MN	55401	**800-541-1345**	612-337-9600

				Toll-Free	Phone
Peg-Perego USA Inc					
3625 Independence Dr	Fort Wayne	IN	46808	**800-671-1701***	260-482-8191
*Cust Svc					
Prince Lionheart Inc					
2421 Westgate Rd	Santa Maria	CA	93455	**800-544-1132**	805-922-2250
REI 1700 45th St E	Sumner	WA	98352	**800-426-4840**	253-891-2500
Sassy Inc					
2305 Breton Industrial Pk Dr	Kentwood	MI	49508	**800-323-6336**	616-243-0767
Step2 Co					
10010 Aurora-Hudson Rd	Streetsboro	OH	44241	**800-347-8372***	330-656-0440
*Cust Svc					
Tough Traveler Ltd					
1012 State St	Schenectady	NY	12307	**800-468-6844***	518-377-8526
*Cust Svc					
Triboro Quilt Mfg Inc					
172 S Broadway	White Plains	NY	10605	**800-227-2077**	914-428-7551
Triple Play Products LLC					
904 Main St Ste 330	Hopkins	MN	55343	**800-829-1625**	952-938-0531

64 BAGS - PAPER

				Toll-Free	Phone
Bancroft Bag Inc					
425 Bancroft Blvd	West Monroe	LA	71292	**800-551-4950**	318-387-2550
Bemis Company Inc Paper Packaging Div					
2445 Deer Pk Blvd	Omaha	NE	68105	**800-541-4303**	
Bonita Pioneer Packaging Products Inc					
7333 SW Bonita Rd	Portland	OR	97224	**800-677-7725**	
Colonial Bag Co					
One Ocean Pond Ave PO Box 929	Lake Park	GA	31636	**800-392-4875**	229-559-8484
Hood Packaging Corp					
25 Woodgreen Pl	Madison	MS	39110	**800-321-8115**	601-853-7260
Pacific Bag Inc					
15300 Woodinville Redmond Rd NE					
Ste A	Woodinville	WA	98072	**800-562-2247**	425-455-1128
Ross & Wallace Paper Products Inc					
204 Old Covington Hwy	Hammond	LA	70403	**800-854-2300**	
Stewart Sutherland Inc					
5411 E 'V' Ave	Vicksburg	MI	49097	**800-253-1034**	269-649-0530
Werthan Packaging Inc					
605 HWY 76	White House	TN	37188	**800-467-0348**	615-672-3336
Weyerhaeuser Co					
33663 Weyerhaeuser Way S	Federal Way	WA	98003	**800-525-5440**	253-924-2345
NYSE: WY					
Zenith Specialty Bag Company Inc					
17625 E Railroad St					
PO Box 8445	City of Industry	CA	91748	**800-962-2247**	

65 BAGS - PLASTICS

				Toll-Free	Phone
Admiral Packaging Inc					
10 Admiral St	Providence	RI	02908	**800-556-6454**	401-274-7000
Ampac Packaging LLC					
12025 Tricon Rd	Cincinnati	OH	45246	**800-543-7030**	513-671-1777
Apco Extruders Inc					
180 National Rd	Edison	NJ	08817	**800-942-8725***	732-287-3000
*Orders					
Armand Manufacturing Inc					
2399 Silver Wolf Dr	Henderson	NV	89011	**800-669-9811**	702-565-7500
Associated Bag Co					
400 W Boden St	Milwaukee	WI	53207	**800-926-6100**	
Bag Makers Inc					
6606 S Union Rd	Union	IL	60180	**800-458-9031**	
Bema Incorporated					
744 N Oaklawn Ave	Elmhurst	IL	60126	**800-833-6657**	630-279-7800
Clear View Bag Co					
5 Burdick Dr	Albany	NY	12205	**800-458-7153**	518-458-7153
Clorox Co 1221 Broadway	Oakland	CA	94612	**800-424-9300***	510-271-7000
NYSE: CLX ▧ *Cust Svc					
Colonial Bag Corp					
205 E Fullerton Ave	Carol Stream	IL	60188	**800-445-7496**	630-690-3999
Enviro-Tote Inc 4 Cote Ln	Bedford	NH	03110	**800-868-3224**	603-647-7171
Fortune Plastics Inc					
One Williams Ln	Old Saybrook	CT	06475	**800-243-0306**	860-388-3426
Heritage Bags					
1648 Diplomat Dr	Carrollton	TX	75006	**800-527-2247**	
Home Care Industries Inc					
1 Lisbon St	Clifton	NJ	07013	**888-382-1222**	973-365-1600
International Poly Bag Inc					
990 Pk Ctr Dr Ste F	Vista	CA	92081	**800-976-5922**	760-598-2468
Mexico Plastics Company (Inc)					
2000 W Blvd	Mexico	MO	65265	**800-325-0216**	
Pacific Bag Inc					
15300 Woodinville Redmond Rd NE					
Ste A	Woodinville	WA	98072	**800-562-2247**	425-455-1128
Pactiv Corp					
1900 W Field Ct	Lake Forest	IL	60045	**888-828-2850**	847-482-2000
Pitt Plastics Inc					
1400 Atkinson Ave	Pittsburg	KS	66762	**800-835-0366**	
Plastic Packaging Inc					
1246 Main Ave SE	Hickory	NC	28602	**800-333-2466**	828-328-2466
Poly-America Inc					
2000 W Marshall Dr	Grand Prairie	TX	75051	**800-527-3322**	972-337-7100
Poly-Pak Industries Inc					
125 Spagnoli Rd	Melville	NY	11747	**800-969-1993**	
Presto Products Co					
670 N Perkins St PO Box 2399	Appleton	WI	54912	**800-558-3525**	920-739-9471
Roplast Industries Inc					
3155 S Fifth Ave	Oroville	CA	95965	**800-767-5278**	530-532-9500
Shields Bag & Printing Co					
1009 Rock Ave	Yakima	WA	98902	**800-541-8630**	509-248-7500
Superbag Corp					
9291 Baythrone Dr	Houston	TX	77041	**888-842-1177**	713-462-1173

Classified Section

				Toll-Free	Phone
Waverly Plastics Company Inc					
PO Box 801	Waverly	IA	50677	800-454-6377	319-352-3333
Webster Industries Inc					
95 Chestnut Ridge Rd,	Montvale	NJ	07645	800-955-2374	800-999-2374
White Bag Co Inc					
8027 Hwy 161 N PO Box 15357	North Little Rock	AR	72117	800-527-1733	501-835-1444
Wisconsin Film & Bag Inc					
3100 E Richmond St	Shawano	WI	54166	800-765-9224	715-524-2565

66 BAGS - TEXTILE

SEE ALSO Handbags, Totes, Backpacks ; Luggage, Bags, Cases

				Toll-Free	Phone
A Rifkin Co					
1400 Sans Souci Pkwy	Wilkes-Barre	PA	18706	800-458-7300*	570-825-9551
*Cust Svc					
Bulk Lift International Inc (BLI)					
1013 Tamarac Dr	Carpentersville	IL	60110	800-879-2247	847-428-6059
GEM Group					
Nine International Way	Lawrence	MA	01843	800-800-3200	978-691-2000
Halsted Corp					
78 Halladay St	Jersey City	NJ	07304	800-843-5184	201-433-3323
HBD Inc					
3901 Riverdale Rd	Greensboro	NC	27406	800-403-2247	336-275-4800
Indian Valley Industries Inc					
PO Box 810	Johnson City	NY	13790	800-659-5111	607-729-5111
J & M Industries Inc					
300 Ponchatoula Pkwy	Ponchatoula	LA	70454	800-989-1002	985-386-6000
LBU Inc 217 Brook Ave	Passaic	NJ	07055	800-678-4528	973-773-4800
Menardi One Maxwell Dr	Trenton	SC	29847	800-321-3218	803-663-6551
NYP Corp 805 E Grand St	Elizabeth	NJ	07201	800-524-1052	908-351-6550
Sacramento Bag Manufacturing Co					
440 N Pioneer Ave Ste 300	Woodland	CA	95776	800-287-2247	530-662-6130
Super Sack Manufacturing Corp					
11510 Data Dr	Dallas	TX	75218	800-331-9200	214-340-7060

67 BAKERIES

				Toll-Free	Phone
Atlanta Bread Co					
1200 Wilson Way Ste 100	Smyrna	GA	30082	800-398-3728	770-432-0933
Au Bon Pain					
19 Fid Kennedy Ave	Boston	MA	02210	800-825-5227	617-423-2100
Awrey Bakeries Inc					
12301 Farmington Rd	Livonia	MI	48150	800-950-2253	734-522-1100
Big Apple Bagels					
500 Lk Cook Rd Ste 475	Deerfield	IL	60015	800-251-6101	847-948-7520
Cheryl & Co					
646 McCorkle Blvd	Westerville	OH	43082	800-443-8124	
Collin Street Bakery Inc					
401 W Seventh Ave	Corsicana	TX	75151	800-504-1896*	903-872-8111
*Sales					
Cookies By Design Inc					
1865 Summit Ave Ste 605	Plano	TX	75074	800-945-2665	972-398-9536
Corner Bakery Cafe					
12700 Pk Central Dr Ste 1300	Dallas	TX	75251	800-309-4642*	972-619-4100
*General					
Damascus Bakery Inc					
56 Gold St	Brooklyn	NY	11201	800-367-7482	
Daylight Donut Flour Company LLC					
11707 E 11th St	Tulsa	OK	74128	800-331-2245	918-438-0800
Dunkin' Donuts 130 Royall St	Canton	MA	02021	800-859-5339*	781-737-3000
*Cust Svc					
East Balt Inc					
1801 W 31st Pl	Chicago	IL	60608	800-621-8555	773-376-4444
Eleni's 75 Ninth Ave	New York	NY	10011	888-435-3647	
Gold Medal Bakery Inc					
1397 Bay St	Fall River	MA	02724	800-642-7568	508-674-5766
Gonnella Baking Co					
1001 W Chicago Ave	Chicago	IL	60642	800-262-3442	312-733-2020
Great American Cookie Company Inc					
1346 Oakbrook Dr Ste 170	Norcross	GA	30093	877-639-2361	
Great Harvest Bread Co					
28 S Montana St	Dillon	MT	59725	800-442-0424	406-683-6842
Holsum Bakery Inc					
2322 W Lincoln St	Phoenix	AZ	85009	888-246-5786	602-252-2351
Honey Dew Assoc Inc					
Two Taunton St	Plainville	MA	02762	800-946-6393	508-699-3900
Hot Stuff Pizza					
2930 W Maple St	Sioux Falls	SD	57107	800-336-1320	605-336-6961
Krispy Kreme Doughnuts Corp					
370 Knollwood St Ste 500	Winston-Salem	NC	27103	800-457-4779	336-725-2981
NYSE: KKD					
Manhattan Bagel Co Inc					
555 Zang St Ste 300	Lakewood	CO	80228	800-224-3563	303-568-8000
Maple Donuts Inc					
3455 E Market St	York	PA	17402	800-627-5348	717-757-7826
Panera Bread Co					
3630 S Geyer Rd	Saint Louis	MO	63127	800-301-5566	314-984-1000
NASDAQ: PNRA					
PARTNERS A Tasteful Choice Co					
20232 72nd Ave	South Kent	WA	98032	800-632-7477	253-867-1580
Treats International Franchise Corp					
1550-A Laperriere Ave Ste 201	Ottawa	ON	K1Z7T2	800-461-4003	613-563-4073
Vie de France Yamazaki Inc					
2070 Chain Bridge Rd Ste 500	Vienna	VA	22182	800-446-4404*	703-442-9205
*General					

68 BANKING-RELATED SERVICES

				Toll-Free	Phone
Automatic Funds Transfer Services					
151 S Landers St Ste C.	Seattle	WA	98134	800-275-2033	206-254-0975

				Toll-Free	Phone
Blackhawk Bank PO Box 719	Beloit	WI	53511	888-769-2600	608-364-4534
Bremer Financial Corp					
2100 Bremer Tower 445 Minnesota St	Saint Paul	MN	55101	800-908-2265	651-227-7621
Capital Farm Credit Aca					
7000 Woodway Dr PO Box 20097	Waco	TX	76702	877-944-5500	254-776-7506
Citizens Federal Savings & Loan Assn					
110 N Main St PO Box 9.	Bellefontaine	OH	43311	800-436-5177	937-593-0015
Civista Bank					
100 E Water St	Sandusky	OH	44870	888-645-4121	419-625-4121
Comdata Corp					
5301 Maryland Way	Brentwood	TN	37027	800-266-3282	615-370-7000
Community Bank					
790 E Colorado Blvd	Pasadena	CA	91101	800-788-9999	
eCivis Inc					
418 N Fair Oaks Ave Ste 301	Pasadena	CA	91103	877-232-4847	
Emprise Financial Corp					
257 N Broadway St PO Box 2970	Wichita	KS	67202	800-201-7118*	316-383-4301
*Cust Svc					
Fiserv Inc					
255 Fiserv Dr PO Box 979	Brookfield	WI	53008	800-872-7882*	262-879-5000
NASDAQ: FISV ■ *Sales					
Hawaii National Bank					
45 N King St	Honolulu	HI	96817	800-528-2273	808-528-7711
Lockwood Advisors Inc					
760 Moore Rd	King Of Prussia	PA	19406	800-200-3033	
MoneyGram International Inc					
2828 N Harwood Fl 15	Dallas	TX	75201	800-666-3947	
NASDAQ: MGI					
Moneytree Inc					
6720 Ft Dent Way	Seattle	WA	98188	877-613-6669	206-246-3500
NYCE Corp 400 Plaza Dr	Secaucus	NJ	07094	888-323-0310	904-438-6000
Oak Ridge Financial					
701 Xenia Ave S Ste 100	Minneapolis	MN	55416	800-231-8364	763-923-2200
OANDA Corp					
140 Broadway 46th Fl.	New York	NY	10005	800-826-8164	416-593-9436
PULSE					
1301 McKinney St Ste 2500	Houston	TX	77010	800-420-2122	713-223-1400
Rock Springs National Bank					
200 Second St PO Box 880	Rock Springs	WY	82902	800-469-8801	307-362-8801
Western Union Holdings Inc					
12500 E Belford Ave	Englewood	CO	80112	800-325-6000*	720-332-1000
NYSE: WU ■ *Cust Svc					
Your Community Bank					
2323 Ring Rd	Elizabethtown	KY	42701	800-314-2265	270-765-2131

69 BANKS - COMMERCIAL & SAVINGS

SEE ALSO Bank Holding Companies ; Credit & Financing - Consumer ; Credit & Financing - Commercial ; Credit Unions

				Toll-Free	Phone
1st Colonial Bancorp Inc					
1040 Haddon Ave	Collingswood	NJ	08108	800-500-1044	856-858-1100
OTC: FCOB					
1st Community Bank					
2911 N Westwood Blvd	Poplar Bluff	MO	63901	888-785-1772	573-778-0101
1st Source Bank					
100 N Michigan St	South Bend	IN	46601	800-513-2360	574-235-2254
3rd Federal Bank					
3 Penns Trail	Newtown	PA	18940	800-822-3321	215-579-4600
Alliance Bank					
541 Lawrence Rd	Broomall	PA	19008	800-472-3272	610-353-2900
NASDAQ: ALLB					
Alostar Bank					
3680 Grandview Pkwy Ste 200	Birmingham	AL	35243	877-738-6391	205-298-6391
Amalgamated Bank of New York					
275 Seventh Ave	New York	NY	10001	800-662-0860	
Amarillo National Bank					
410 S Taylor St Plaza 1	Amarillo	TX	79101	800-253-1031	806-378-8000
Amboy National Bank					
3590 US Hwy 9 S	Old Bridge	NJ	08857	800-942-6269	732-591-8700
Amegy Bank of Texas					
4400 Post Oak Pkwy	Houston	TX	77027	800-287-0301	713-235-8800
American Bank of Texas NA					
200 N Austin St	Seguin	TX	78155	800-567-1817	830-379-5236
American Exchange Bank (AEB)					
510 W Main St PO Box 818	Henryetta	OK	74437	888-652-3321	918-652-3321
American Heritage Bank					
2 S Main PO Box 1408	Sapulpa	OK	74067	866-669-2427	918-224-3210
American National Bank					
PO Box 2139	Omaha	NE	68103	800-279-0007*	402-399-5000
*Cust Svc					
American Savings Bank FSB					
1001 Bishop St PO Box 2300	Honolulu	HI	96813	800-272-2566	808-539-7843
Ameriserv Financial					
216 Franklin St PO Box 520	Johnstown	PA	15907	800-837-2265	814-533-5300
NASDAQ: ASRV					
AmTrust Bank					
1801 E Ninth St	Cleveland	OH	44114	888-696-4444	216-736-3480
Anchor Bank					
1055 Wayzata Blvd E	Wayzata	MN	55391	800-425-5150	952-473-4606
AnchorBank					
25 W Main St PO Box 7933	Madison	WI	53703	800-252-6246	608-252-8827
Apple Bank for Savings					
122 E 42nd St Ninth Fl	New York	NY	10168	800-824-0710	914-902-2775
Arthur State Bank					
100 E Main St PO Box 769	Union	SC	29379	877-226-5246	864-427-1213
Artisan's Bank					
2961 Centerville Rd	Wilmington	DE	19808	800-282-8255	302-658-6881
Associated Bank					
2870 Holmgren Way	Green Bay	WI	54304	800-728-3501	262-879-0133
Associated Bank Green Bay NA					
200 N Adams St	Green Bay	WI	54301	800-728-3501	920-433-3200
Associated Bank Illinois NA					
612 N Main St	Rockford	IL	61103	800-236-8866	815-987-3500
Associated Bank Milwaukee					
401 E Kilbourn Ave	Milwaukee	WI	53202	800-236-8866	414-271-1786

Name / Address	City	ST	ZIP	Toll-Free	Phone
Associated Bank North 303 S First Ave	Wausau	WI	54401	800-236-8866	715-848-4793
Athens State Bank 6530 N State Rt 29	Springfield	IL	62707	800-367-7576	217-487-7766
Bancorp Bank 409 Silverside Rd Ste 105 *NASDAQ: TBBK *Cust Svc*	Wilmington	DE	19809	800-545-0289*	302-385-5000
Bangor Savings Bank Three State St	Bangor	ME	04401	877-226-4671	207-942-5211
Bank Financial 6415 W 95th St	Chicago Ridge	IL	60415	800-894-6900	
Bank Leumi USA 579 Fifth Ave	New York	NY	10017	800-892-5430	917-542-2343
Bank of Georgia, The 100 Westpark Dr	Peachtree City	GA	30269	866-645-1139	770-631-9488
Bank of Louisiana 300 St Charles Ave	New Orleans	LA	70130	866-392-9952	504-592-0600
Bank of Marin 504 Tamalpais Dr *NASDAQ: BMRC*	Corte Madera	CA	94925	800-654-5111	415-927-2265
Bank of McKenney 20718 First St *OTC: BOMK*	McKenney	VA	23872	800-528-2273	804-478-4434
Bank of Nevada 2700 W Sahara Ave	Las Vegas	NV	89102	877-750-0010	702-248-4200
Bank of North Dakota 1200 Memorial Hwy	Bismarck	ND	58504	800-472-2166	701-328-5600
Bank of Nova Scotia 1 Liberty Plaza 26th Fl *TSE: BNS*	New York	NY	10006	800-472-6842	212-225-5011
Bank of Oklahoma NA PO Box 2300	Tulsa	OK	74192	800-234-6181	918-588-6010
Bank of Stanly PO Box 338	Albemarle	NC	28002	800-438-6864	704-983-6181
Bank of Stockton PO Box 1110	Stockton	CA	95201	800-941-1494	209-929-1600
Bank of Sunset & Trust Co 863 Napoleon Ave	Sunset	LA	70584	800-264-5578	337-662-5222
Bank of the Carolinas 135 Boxwood Village Dr *OTC: BCAR*	Mocksville	NC	27028	877-751-5755	336-751-5755
Bank of the Ozarks 4328 Old Spanish Trail	Houston	TX	77021	800-274-4482	713-747-9000
Bank of the Sierra PO Box 1930 *Cust Svc*	Porterville	CA	93258	888-454-2265*	559-782-4900
Bank Of Utica 222 Genesee St *OTC: BKUT*	Utica	NY	13502	800-442-1028	315-797-2700
Bank of Virginia 11730 Hull St Rd *NASDAQ: BOVA*	Midlothian	VA	23112	800-500-1044	804-744-7576
BankAtlantic 200 W Second St	Winston-Salem	NC	27101	800-226-5228	888-628-3926
Bankers' Bank 7700 Mineral Point Rd	Madison	WI	53717	800-388-5550	608-833-5550
Bankwest Corporation 2050 N California Blvd	Walnut Creek	CA	94597	888-389-8668	925-933-7810
Bankwest Inc 420 S Pierre St PO Box 998	Pierre	SD	57501	800-253-0362	605-224-7391
Banner Bank 10 S First Ave PO Box 907	Walla Walla	WA	99362	800-272-9933	509-527-3636
Banterra Corp 1404 US Rt 45 S	Eldorado	IL	62930	877-541-2265	618-273-9346
Baylake Bank 217 N Fourth Ave	Sturgeon Bay	WI	54235	800-267-3610	920-743-5551
BB & T Corp 200 W Second St *NYSE: BBT*	Winston-Salem	NC	27101	800-226-5228	336-733-2500
Beneficial Mutual Savings Bank 530 Walnut St	Philadelphia	PA	19106	800-784-8490	215-864-6000
Berkshire Bank PO Box 1308	Pittsfield	MA	01202	800-773-5601	413-443-5601
Blue Ridge Bank & Trust Co 4240 Blue Ridge Blvd Ste 100	Kansas City	MO	64133	800-569-4287	816-358-5000
Blueharbor Bank 106 Corporate Park Dr	Mooresville	NC	28117	877-322-8228	704-662-7700
BMO Harris Bank 111 W Monroe St	Chicago	IL	60603	888-340-2265	847-238-2265
BNC National Bank 322 E Main Ave PO Box 4050	Bismarck	ND	58501	800-262-2265	701-250-3000
Boiling Springs Savings Bank (BSSB) 25 Orient Way	Rutherford	NJ	07070	888-388-7459	201-939-5000
Boone County National Bank 720 E Broadway PO Box 678	Columbia	MO	65201	800-842-2262	573-874-8535
Branch Banking & Trust Company of South Carolina 301 College St	Greenville	SC	29601	800-226-5228	
Burke & Herbert Bank & Trust Co 100 S Fairfax St	Alexandria	VA	22314	877-440-0800	703-751-7701
Byline Bank 3639 N Broadway St	Chicago	IL	60613	866-957-7700	773-244-7000
California Bank & Trust 11622 El Camino Real Ste 200	San Diego	CA	92130	800-400-6080	858-793-7400
Cambridge Savings Bank 1374 Massachusetts Ave	Cambridge	MA	02138	800-540-6322	617-441-4155
Canadian Imperial Bank of Commerce (CIBC) 199 Bay St Commerce Ct W *NYSE: CM*	Toronto	ON	M5L1A2	800-465-2422	
Canadian Western Bank 10303 Jasper Ave Ste 3000 *TSE: CWB*	Edmonton	AB	T5J3X6	866-317-0356	780-423-8888
Cape Cod Five Cents Savings Bank 19 W Rd PO Box 20	Orleans	MA	02653	800-678-1855	508-240-0555
Capital City Bank 2111 N Monroe St PO Box 900	Tallahassee	FL	32302	888-671-0400	850-402-7500
Capital One Auto Finance Inc PO Box 60511	City of Industry	CA	91716	800-946-0332	
Capitol FSB 700 S Kansas Ave	Topeka	KS	66603	800-432-2926	785-235-1341
Carolina Trust Bank 901 E Main St *NASDAQ: CART*	Lincolnton	NC	28092	877-983-5537	704-735-1104
Casey State Bank 305-307 N Central Ave	Casey	IL	62420	866-666-2754	217-932-2136
Central Pacific Bank PO Box 3590 *NYSE: CPF *Cust Svc*	Honolulu	HI	96811	800-342-8422*	808-544-0500
Central Valley Bank 537 W Second Ave *General*	Toppenish	WA	98948	800-422-1566*	509-865-2511
Century National Bank 14 S Fifth St *Cust Svc*	Zanesville	OH	43701	800-548-3557*	740-454-2521
CFG Community Bank 1422 Clarkview Rd	Baltimore	MD	21209	866-619-1417	410-823-0500
CharterBank 1233 OG Skinner Dr	West Point	GA	31833	800-763-4444	706-645-1391
Chase Bank One Chase Manhattan Plz	New York	NY	10081	800-935-9935	
Chinatrust Bank USA 801 S Figueroa St Ste 2300	Los Angeles	CA	90017	888-839-9000	310-791-2828
Citibank (Delaware) 4500 New Linden Hill Rd	Wilmington	DE	19808	800-374-9700	302-323-3600
Citibank NA 399 Pk Ave	New York	NY	10022	800-627-3999	
Citibank (South Dakota) NA 701 E 60th St N	Sioux Falls	SD	57104	800-627-3999	605-370-6261
Citizens Bank of Clovis 420 Wheeler	Texico	NM	88135	844-657-3553	575-482-3381
Citizens Bank of Massachusetts 28 State St	Boston	MA	02109	800-610-7300	
Citizens Bank of Mukwonago 301 N Rochester St PO Box 223	Mukwonago	WI	53149	877-546-5868	262-363-6500
Citizens Bank of Rhode Island One Citizens Plz *Cust Svc*	Providence	RI	02903	800-922-9999*	401-456-7000
Citizens Business Bank (CBB) 701 N Haven Ave *Cust Svc*	Ontario	CA	91764	888-222-5432*	909-980-4030
Citizens Financial Services 707 Ridge Rd	Munster	IN	46321	866-622-1370	219-836-5500
Citizens State Bank 1300 W Hildebrand Ave PO Box 5970	San Antonio	TX	78201	800-870-2472	210-785-2300
Citizens Trust Bank 1700 3rd Ave N	Birmingham	AL	35203	888-214-3099	205-328-2041
City National Bank 400 N Roxbury Dr *Cust Svc*	Beverly Hills	CA	90210	800-773-7100*	310-888-6000
City National Bank of Florida 450 E Las Olas Blvd Ste 160	Fort Lauderdale	FL	33301	800-762-2489	954-467-6667
City National Bank of New Jersey (CNB) 900 Broad St	Newark	NJ	07102	877-350-3524	973-624-0865
City National Bank of West Virginia 3601 McCorkle Ave	Charleston	WV	25304	888-816-8064	304-926-3324
Clearfield Bank & Trust Co 11 N Second St PO Box 171	Clearfield	PA	16830	888-765-7551	814-765-7551
Cnlbank 450 S Orange Ave Ste 400	Orlando	FL	32801	800-910-2187	407-244-3100
Coast Capital Savings 645 Tyee Rd Ste 400	Victoria	BC	V9A6X5	888-517-7000	250-483-7000
College Savings Bank Five Vaughn Dr Ste 100	Princeton	NJ	08540	800-888-2723	
Colorado Fsb 8400 E Prentice Ave Ste 545	Greenwood Village	CO	80111	877-484-2372	303-793-3555
Columbia Bank, The 7168 Columbia Gateway Dr	Columbia	MD	21046	888-822-2265	
Columbia Savings Bank 19-01 Rt 208 *Cust Svc*	Fair Lawn	NJ	07410	800-747-4428*	800-522-4167
Columbia State Bank PO Box 2156	Tacoma	WA	98401	800-305-1905	253-305-1900
Columbus Bank & Trust Co 1148 Broadway	Columbus	GA	31901	800-334-9007	706-649-4900
Comerica Bank 411 W Lafayette	Detroit	MI	48226	800-643-4418	313-222-3344
Comerica Bank-California 333 W Santa Clara St	San Jose	CA	95113	800-522-2265	408-556-5300
Comerica Bank-Texas 1717 Main St	Dallas	TX	75201	800-925-2160	
Comerica Inc 1717 Main St Comerica Bank Tower *NYSE: CMA*	Dallas	TX	75201	800-266-3742	
Commerce Bank & Trust Co 386 Main St	Worcester	MA	01608	800-698-2265	508-797-6842
Commercial Bank 301 N State St PO Box 638 *OTC: CEFC*	Alma	MI	48801	800-547-8531	989-463-2185
Community Bank of Florida 28801 SW 157th Ave	Homestead	FL	33033	866-820-1533	305-245-2211
Community Bank of Raymore PO Box 200	Raymore	MO	64083	800-322-6772	816-322-2100
Community Trust Bank NA 346 N Mayo Trl PO Box 2947	Pikeville	KY	41501	800-422-1090	606-432-1414
Conneaut Savings Bank 305 Main St PO Box 740	Conneaut	OH	44030	888-453-2311	440-599-8121
Country Bank for Savings 75 Main St	Ware	MA	01082	800-322-8233	413-967-6221
Credit Union of Denver 9305 W Alameda Ave	Lakewood	CO	80226	800-951-9014	303-234-1700
D L Evans Bank 397 N Overland PO Box 1188	Burley	ID	83318	888-873-9777	208-678-9076
DBS Bank Ltd 725 N Figueroa St	Los Angeles	CA	90017	800-232-5901	213-627-0222
Dedham Institution For Savings 55 Elm St PO Box 9107	Dedham	MA	02026	888-289-0342	781-329-6700
Devon Bank 6445 N Western Ave	Chicago	IL	60645	866-683-3866	
Dime Bank, The 820 Church St PO Box 509	Honesdale	PA	18431	888-469-3463	570-253-1902
Discover Bank PO Box 30416	Salt Lake City	UT	84130	800-347-7000	302-323-7810

Name / Address	City	State	ZIP	Toll-Free	Phone
Dollar Bank FSB 225 Forbes Ave	Pittsburgh	PA	15222	**800-828-5527**	412-261-2343
E*Trade Bank 671 N Glebe Rd	Arlington	VA	22203	**800-387-2331**	877-800-1208
East Boston Savings Bank 10 Meridian St	Boston	MA	02128	**800-657-3272**	617-567-1500
Eastern Bank One Eastern Pl	Lynn	MA	01901	**800-327-8376**	781-599-2100
El Dorado Savings Bank 4040 El Dorado Rd	Placerville	CA	95667	**800-874-9779**	530-622-1492
Elmira Savings Bank 333 E Water St *NASDAQ: ESBK*	Elmira	NY	14901	**888-372-9299**	607-734-3374
Empire Bank PO Box 3397	Springfield	MO	65808	**888-231-4637**	417-881-3100
Encore Bank 3003 Tamiami Trail N Ste 100	Naples	FL	34103	**800-472-3272**	239-919-5888
Enterprise Bank of SC 13497 Broxton Bridge Rd PO Box 8	Ehrhardt	SC	29081	**800-554-8969**	803-267-3191
Essex Savings Bank PO Box 950	Essex	CT	06426	**877-377-3922**	860-767-4414
Euro Pacific Capital Inc 88 Post Rd W Third Fl	Westport	CT	06880	**800-727-7922**	203-662-9700
Exchange State Bank 3992 Chandler St PO Box 68	Carsonville	MI	48419	**888-488-9300**	810-657-9333
F&M Bank PO Box 1130	Clarksville	TN	37041	**800-645-4199**	931-645-2400
Farm Bureau Bank 2165 Green Vista Dr Ste 204	Sparks	NV	89431	**800-492-3276**	775-673-4566
Farmers Bank, The 9 E Clinton St PO Box 129	Frankfort	IN	46041	**800-883-0131**	765-654-8731
Fauquier Bank, The (TFB) 10 Courthouse Sq PO Box 561	Warrenton	VA	20186	**800-638-3798**	540-347-2700
Fidelity Bancshares Nc Inc PO Box 8	Fuquay Varina	NC	27526	**800-816-9608**	919-552-2242
Fidelity Bank 100 E English St	Wichita	KS	67201	**800-658-1637**	
Fifth Third Bank Central Ohio 21 E State St	Columbus	OH	43215	**800-972-3030**	
First American Bank & Trust 2785 Hwy 20 W PO Box 550	Vacherie	LA	70090	**800-738-2265**	225-265-2265
First Bank Financial Centre (FBFC) 155 W Wisconsin Ave PO Box 1004	Oconomowoc	WI	53066	**888-569-9909**	262-569-9900
First Business Financial Services Inc 401 Charmany Dr *NASDAQ: FBIZ*	Madison	WI	53719	**888-455-2263**	608-238-8008
First Calgary Savings 510 16th Ave NE	Calgary	AB	T2E1K4	**866-923-4778**	
First Century Bank NA 500 Federal St	Bluefield	WV	24701	**877-214-9426**	304-325-8181
First Citizens Bank & Trust Co Inc 1230 Main St	Columbia	SC	29201	**888-612-4444**	803-733-2025
First Federal Lakewood 14806 Detroit Ave	Lakewood	OH	44107	**800-966-7300**	216-529-2700
First Financial Bank 300 High St *Cust Svc	Hamilton	OH	45011	**877-322-9530***	513-867-4744
First Foundation Bank 18101 Von Karman Ave Ste 750	Irvine	CA	92612	**800-224-7931**	949-202-4100
First Hawaiian Bank 999 Bishop St	Honolulu	HI	96813	**888-844-4444**	808-525-6340
First Interstate Bank 401 N 31st St PO Box 30918	Billings	MT	59101	**888-752-3341**	406-255-5000
First Mercantile Trust Co 57 Germantown Ct Fourth Fl	Cordova	TN	38018	**800-753-3682**	901-753-9080
First National Bank Alaska 101 W 36 Ave PO Box 100720 *OTC: FBAK*	Anchorage	AK	99510	**800-856-4362**	907-777-4362
First National Bank Creston PO Box 445	Creston	IA	50801	**877-782-2195**	641-782-2195
First National Bank of Muscatine 300 E Second St	Muscatine	IA	52761	**800-722-2678**	563-263-4221
First National Bank of Omaha 1620 Dodge St	Omaha	NE	68197	**800-228-4411**	402-341-0500
First National Bank of Oneida, The 18418 Alberta St PO Box 4699	Oneida	TN	37841	**866-546-8273**	423-569-8586
First National Bank of Santa Fe PO Box 609	Santa Fe	NM	87504	**888-912-2265**	505-992-2000
First National Bankers Bankshares Inc (FNBB) 7813 Office Pk Blvd	Baton Rouge	LA	70809	**800-421-6182**	225-924-8015
First NBC (CPB) 29092 Kretel Rd	Lacombe	LA	70445	**800-423-7503**	985-819-1200
First Niagara Financial Group 726 Exchange St Ste 618	Buffalo	NY	14210	**800-421-0004**	716-625-7500
First Palmetto Savings Bank Fsb PO Box 430	Camden	SC	29021	**800-922-7411**	803-432-2265
First Republic Bank 111 Pine St Third Fl *NYSE: FRC*	San Francisco	CA	94111	**800-392-1400**	415-392-1400
First Savings Bank 2804 N Telshor Blvd	Las Cruces	NM	88011	**800-555-6895**	575-521-7931
First State Bank & Trust Co 1005 E 23rd St	Fremont	NE	68025	**888-674-4344**	402-721-2500
First State Bank of Kansas City 650 Kansas Ave	Kansas City	KS	66105	**800-883-1242**	913-371-1242
First Tennessee Bank 165 Madison Ave	Memphis	TN	38103	**800-382-5465**	901-523-4883
First Texas Bank 501 E Third St PO Box 671	Lampasas	TX	76550	**866-220-1598**	512-556-3691
First Western Bank & Trust PO Box 1090	Minot	ND	58702	**800-688-2584**	701-852-3711
First-Knox National Bank One S Main St	Mount Vernon	OH	43050	**800-837-5266**	740-399-5500
Firstrust Savings Bank 15 E Ridge Pike 4th Fl	Conshohocken	PA	19428	**800-220-2265**	610-941-9898
Flagstar Bank FSB 5151 Corporate Dr	Troy	MI	48098	**800-945-7700**	248-312-2000
Four Oaks Bank & Trust Co PO Box 309	Four Oaks	NC	27524	**877-963-6257**	919-963-2177
Fowler State Bank 300 E Fifth St PO Box 511	Fowler	IN	47944	**800-439-3951**	765-884-1200
Fremont Bank PO Box 5101	Fremont	CA	94538	**800-359-2265**	510-792-2300

Name / Address	City	State	ZIP	Toll-Free	Phone
Frontenac Bank 3330 Rider Trl S	Earth City	MO	63045	**877-205-5777**	314-298-8200
Garden State Community Bank (GSCB) 36 Ferry St *NYSE: NYB*	Newark	NJ	07105	**877-786-6560**	973-589-8616
Genesis Capital LLC 3414 Peachtree Rd Ne Ste 700	Atlanta	GA	30326	**800-998-8479**	404-816-7540
Giantbank.com 6300 NE First Ave	Fort Lauderdale	FL	33334	**877-446-4200**	954-958-0001
Glenwood State Bank 5 E Minnesota Ave PO Box 197	Glenwood	MN	56334	**800-207-7333**	320-634-5111
Golden Valley Bank Community Foundation 190 Cohasset Rd Ste 170	Chico	CA	95926	**800-808-2070**	530-894-1000
Grants State Bank 824 W Santa Fe Ave PO Box 1088	Grants	NM	87020	**877-285-6611**	505-285-6611
Great Western Bank 6015 NW Radial Hwy	Omaha	NE	68104	**800-952-2043**	402-952-6000
Greenville First Bank 100 Verdae Blvd Ste 100	Greenville	SC	29072	**877-679-9646**	864-679-9000
Guaranty Bank 4000 W Brown Deer Rd	Brown Deer	WI	53209	**800-235-4636**	414-362-4000
Guaranty Bank & Trust Co PO Box 1807	Cedar Rapids	IA	52406	**888-777-4590**	319-286-6200
Guilford Savings Bank (GSB) PO Box 369	Guilford	CT	06437	**866-878-1480**	203-453-2015
Gulf Coast Bank 4310 Johnston St	Lafayette	LA	70503	**800-722-5363**	337-989-1133
Hamler State Bank 210 Randolph St PO Box 358	Hamler	OH	43524	**888-508-3955**	419-274-3955
Heritage Group Inc 1101 12th St	Aurora	NE	68818	**888-463-6611**	402-694-3136
Hickory Point Bank & Trust FSB PO Box 2548 *Cust Svc	Decatur	IL	62525	**800-872-0081***	217-875-3131
Hills Bank & Trust Co 131 Main St PO Box 70	Hills	IA	52235	**800-445-5725**	319-679-2291
Hingham Institution for Savings 55 Main St *NASDAQ: HIFS*	Hingham	MA	02043	**877-447-2265**	781-749-2200
Home Savings & Loan Company of Youngstown 275 W Federal St	Youngstown	OH	44503	**888-822-4751**	330-742-0500
HomeStreet Bank 601 Union St 2 Union Sq Ste 2000	Seattle	WA	98101	**800-654-1075**	206-623-3050
Hometown Bank 245 N Peters Ave	Fond du Lac	WI	54935	**877-261-2220**	920-907-2220
Homewood FSB 3228-30 Eastern Ave	Baltimore	MD	21224	**800-554-8969**	410-327-5220
Hudson City Savings Bank W 80 Century Rd	Paramus	NJ	07652	**800-222-0194**	201-967-1900
Huntington National Bank 41 S High St Huntington Ctr	Columbus	OH	43287	**800-480-2265**	614-480-8300
InsurBanc 10 Executive Dr	Farmington	CT	06032	**866-467-2262**	860-677-9701
Inter-County Bakers Inc 1095 Long Island Ave Ste 1	Deer Park	NY	11729	**800-696-1350**	631-957-1350
Investors Savings Bank 101 Wood Ave S *NASDAQ: ISBC*	Iselin	NJ	08830	**855-422-6548**	973-924-5100
Jeff Davis Bancshares Inc 507 N Main St PO Box 730 *OTC: JDVB*	Jennings	LA	70546	**866-889-8176**	337-824-3424
Jersey Shore State Bank 300 Market St PO Box 967	Williamsport	PA	17701	**888-412-5772**	570-322-1111
Kearny FSB 120 Passaic Ave	Fairfield	NJ	07004	**800-273-3406**	973-244-4500
Kennebec Savings Bank 150 State St PO Box 50	Augusta	ME	04332	**888-303-7788**	207-622-5801
Kentucky Bank PO Box 157	Paris	KY	40362	**877-322-8228**	859-987-1795
Key Bank 65 Dutch Hill Rd *Cust Svc	Orangeburg	NY	10962	**800-539-2968***	
Kingston National Bank Two N Main St PO Box 613	Kingston	OH	45644	**866-642-2191**	740-642-2191
Kish Bancorp Inc 4255 E Main St PO Box 917 *OTC: KISB*	Belleville	PA	17004	**888-554-4748**	717-935-2191
Labette Bank Fourth & Huston PO Box 497	Altamont	KS	67330	**800-711-5311**	620-784-5311
Lakeside Bank 55 W Wacker Dr	Chicago	IL	60601	**866-892-1572**	312-435-5100
LaPorte Savings Bank, The 710 Indiana Ave	LaPorte	IN	46350	**866-362-7511**	219-362-7511
Laurentian Bank of Canada 1981 McGill College Ave *TSE: LB*	Montreal	QC	H3A3K3	**800-252-1846**	514-284-4500
LCNB National Bank 3209 W Galbraith Rd	Cincinnati	OH	45239	**800-344-2265**	513-932-1414
Legacy Bank 1580 E Cheyenne Mtn Blvd	Colorado Springs	CO	80906	**866-627-0800**	719-579-9150
Liberty Bank 315 Main St	Middletown	CT	06457	**800-622-6732**	800-354-8950
Liberty Bank & Trust Co PO Box 60131	New Orleans	LA	70160	**800-883-3943**	504-240-5100
Liberty Savings Bank FSB 2251 Rombach Ave	Wilmington	OH	45177	**800-627-7890**	800-436-6300
Little Bank Inc, The 804 Carey Rd *OTC: LTLB*	Kinston	NC	28501	**855-449-0975**	252-939-9990
Luther Burbank Savings 804 Fourth St	Santa Rosa	CA	95404	**888-407-9904**	707-578-9216
M&T Bank One M & T Plz 13th Fl *NYSE: MTB*	Buffalo	NY	14203	**800-724-2440**	716-842-4470
Machias Savings Bank 4 Ctr St PO Box 318	Machias	ME	04654	**800-982-7179**	207-255-3347
Magyar Bank 400 Somerset St	New Brunswick	NJ	08901	**800-472-3272**	732-342-7600
Marquette Bank 10000 W 151st St	Orland Park	IL	60462	**888-254-9500**	708-226-8026

	City	State	ZIP	Toll-Free	Phone
Marquette Savings Bank					
920 Peach St	Erie	PA	16501	**866-672-3743**	814-455-4481
Maspeth Federal Savings					
56-18 69th St	Maspeth	NY	11378	**888-558-1300**	718-335-1300
Max Credit Union					
400 Eastdale Cir	Montgomery	AL	36117	**800-776-6776**	334-260-2600
Mc Kenzie Banking Co (MBC)					
676 N Main St	McKenzie	TN	38201	**866-321-7063**	731-352-2262
MCNB Bank & Trust Co					
PO Box 549	Welch	WV	24801	**800-532-9553**	304-436-4112
Mechanics Savings Bank					
100 Minot Ave PO Box 400	Auburn	ME	04210	**877-886-1020**	207-786-5700
Members Trust Co					
14025 Riveredge Dr Ste 280	Tampa	FL	33637	**888-727-9191**	813-631-9191
Mercantil Commercebank NA					
220 Alhambra Cir	Coral Gables	FL	33134	**888-629-0810**	305-460-8701
Meredith Village Savings Bank (MVSB)					
24 State Rt 25 PO Box 177	Meredith	NH	03253	**800-922-6872**	603-279-7986
Midamerica National Bancshares					
100 W Elm St	Canton	IL	61520	**877-647-5050**	309-647-5000
Middlesex Savings Bank					
120 Flanders Rd	Westborough	MA	01581	**877-463-6287**	508-653-0300
MidFirst Bank					
PO Box 76149	Oklahoma City	OK	73147	**888-643-3477**	405-943-8002
Midland National Bank					
527 N Main	Newton	KS	67114	**800-810-9457**	316-283-1700
Midwest Bank					
105 E Soo St PO Box 40	Parkers Prairie	MN	56361	**877-365-5155**	218-338-6054
Mifflinburg Bank & Trust Co (MBTC)					
250 E Chestnut St PO Box 186	Mifflinburg	PA	17844	**888-966-3131**	570-966-1041
Milford Bank 33 Broad St	Milford	CT	06460	**800-340-4862**	203-783-5700
Monroe Bank & Trust					
102 E Front St	Monroe	MI	48161	**800-321-0032**	734-241-3431
Mountain Valley Bank					
317 DAVIS Ave	Elkins	WV	26241	**800-555-3503**	304-637-2265
Mountain West Bank of Helena					
1225 Cedar St	Helena	MT	59604	**888-752-3341**	406-449-2265
MSB Financial Corp (MSBF)					
1902 Long Hill Rd	Millington	NJ	07946	**844-265-9680**	908-647-4000
NASDAQ: MSBF					
Murray Bank, The					
405 S 12th St	Murray	KY	42071	**877-965-1122**	270-753-5626
Mutual of Omaha Bank					
3333 Farnam St	Omaha	NE	68131	**866-351-5646**	877-471-7896
Nantucket Bank					
104 Pleasant St	Nantucket	MA	02554	**800-533-9313**	508-228-0580
National Australia Bank Americas					
245 Pk Ave Ste 2800	New York	NY	10167	**866-706-0509**	212-916-9500
National Bank of Arizona					
335 N Wilmot Rd Ste 100	Tucson	AZ	85711	**800-497-8168**	520-571-1500
National Bank of Blacksburg					
PO Box 90002	Blacksburg	VA	24062	**800-552-4123**	540-552-2011
National Bank of Kansas City (NBOFKC)					
3510 W 95th St	Leawood	KS	66206	**888-431-0097**	913-341-1144
National Bank, The					
852 Middle Rd	Bettendorf	IA	52722	**877-321-4347**	563-344-3935
Naugatuck Valley Financial Corp					
333 Church St	Naugatuck	CT	06770	**800-251-2161**	203-720-5000
NASDAQ: NVSL					
NBT Bank NA PO Box 351	Norwich	NY	13815	**800-628-2265**	607-337-2265
NCAL Bancorp					
12121 Wilshire Blvd	Los Angeles	CA	90025	**866-453-4042**	310-882-4800
OTC: NCAL					
Nevada State Bank					
PO Box 990	Las Vegas	NV	89125	**800-727-4743**	702-383-0009
New Washington State Bank					
402 E Main St PO Box 10	New Washington	IN	47162	**800-883-0131**	812-293-3321
Newburyport Five Cents Savings Bank Inc, The					
63 State St PO Box 350	Newburyport	MA	01950	**877-462-3136**	978-462-3136
Newtown Savings Bank Foundation Inc					
39 Main St PO Box 497	Newtown	CT	06470	**800-461-0672**	203-426-2563
North American Development Bank					
203 S St Mary'S Ste 300	San Antonio	TX	78205	**800-499-6232**	210-231-8000
North American Savings Bank (NASB)					
12520 S 71 Hwy	Grandview	MO	64030	**800-677-6272**	816-765-2200
North Middlesex Savings Bank Inc					
Seven Main St PO Box 469	Ayer	MA	01432	**800-762-3306**	978-772-3306
North Shore Bank FSB					
15700 W Bluemound Rd	Brookfield	WI	53005	**800-236-4672**	262-797-3858
Northern Trust Co					
50 S LaSalle St	Chicago	IL	60603	**888-289-6542**	312-630-6000
NASDAQ: NTRS					
Northfield Savings Bank (NSB)					
PO Box 347	Northfield	VT	05663	**800-672-2274**	802-485-5871
Northrim BanCorp Inc					
3111 C St	Anchorage	AK	99503	**800-478-3311**	907-562-0062
NASDAQ: NRIM					
Northwest Community Bank					
86 Main St PO Box 1019	Winsted	CT	06098	**800-455-6668**	860-379-7561
Northwest Georgia Bank					
5063 Alabama Hwy PO Box 789	Ringgold	GA	30736	**800-528-2273**	706-965-3000
Northwest Savings Bank					
100 Liberty St PO Box 128	Warren	PA	16365	**800-822-2009**	814-726-2140
Ocean Bank 780 NW 42nd Ave	Miami	FL	33126	**877-688-2265**	305-442-2660
OceanFirst Bank					
975 Hooper Ave PO Box 2009	Toms River	NJ	08753	**888-623-2633**	732-240-4500
Ocwen Federal Bank FSB					
1661 Worthington Rd Ste 100	West Palm Beach	FL	33409	**800-280-3863**	561-682-8000
Old Line Bank					
1525 Pointer Ridge Pl	Bowie	MD	20716	**800-416-6373**	301-430-2500
NASDAQ: WSB					
Old National Bank					
1 Main St PO Box 718	Evansville	IN	47705	**800-731-2265**	
Orange County Trust Co					
PO Box 790	Middletown	NY	10940	**888-341-5100**	845-341-5000
Oritani Financial Corp					
370 Pascack Rd					
PO Box 1329	Washington Township	NJ	07676	**888-674-8264**	201-664-5400
NASDAQ: ORIT					
Oxford Bank PO Box 129	Addison	IL	60101	**800-236-2442**	630-629-5000
Pacific Continental Corp					
111 W Seventh Ave PO Box 10727	Eugene	OR	97440	**877-231-2265**	541-686-8685
NASDAQ: PCBK					
People's United Bank					
850 Main St Bridgeport Ctr	Bridgeport	CT	06604	**800-772-1090**	203-338-7171
Peoples Financial Services Corp					
82 Franklin Ave	Hallstead	PA	18822	**888-868-3858**	570-879-2175
NASDAQ: PFIS					
Peoples National Bank					
5175 N Academy Blvd	Colorado Springs	CO	80918	**800-862-6696**	719-528-4000
Peoples Savings Bank (PSB)					
414 N Adams PO Box 248	Wellsburg	IA	50680	**877-493-3799**	641-869-3721
Pintoresco Advisors LLC					
466 Foothill Blvd					
Ste 333	La Canada Flintridge	CA	91011	**866-217-1140**	213-223-2070
Plaza Bank					
7460 W Irving Pk Rd	Norridge	IL	60706	**877-714-9599***	708-456-3440
*General					
PNC Bank 600 Grant St	Pittsburgh	PA	15219	**888-762-2265**	
NYSE: PNC-L					
PNC Bank Delaware					
300 Delaware Ave	Wilmington	DE	19899	**888-762-2265**	302-429-1361
PNC Bank NA					
249 Fifth Ave 1 PNC Plaza	Pittsburgh	PA	15222	**888-762-2265**	412-762-2000
Preferred Bank Los Angeles					
601 S Figueroa St 29th Fl	Los Angeles	CA	90017	**888-673-1808**	213-891-1188
NASDAQ: PFBC					
Premier Bank & Trust					
600 S Main St Ste C	North Canton	OH	44720	**855-728-6010**	330-499-1900
Premier Valley Bank					
255 E River Pk Cir Ste 180	Fresno	CA	93720	**877-438-2002**	559-438-2002
Presidential Online Bank					
4520 East-West Hwy	Bethesda	MD	20814	**800-383-6266**	301-652-0700
Profile Bank					
45 Wakefield St PO Box 1808	Rochester	NH	03866	**800-554-8969**	603-332-2610
Progressive Bank NA					
1090 E Bethlehem Blvd	Wheeling	WV	26003	**866-235-1923**	304-238-0040
Provident Savings Bank FSB					
3756 Central Ave	Riverside	CA	92506	**800-442-5201**	951-686-6060
Prudential Savings Bank					
1834 W Oregon Ave	Philadelphia	PA	19145	**800-554-8969**	215-755-1500
QNB Corp					
15 N Third St PO Box 9005	Quakertown	PA	18951	**800-491-9070**	215-538-5600
OTC: QNBC					
Queenstown Bank of Maryland					
7101 Main St PO Box 120	Queenstown	MD	21658	**888-827-4300**	410-827-8881
Rabo Bank					
1026 E Grand Ave	Arroyo Grande	CA	93420	**800-942-6222**	805-473-7710
Randolph Savings Bank					
129 N Main St PO Box 354	Randolph	MA	02368	**877-963-2100**	781-963-2100
RBC Royal Bank					
PO Box 6001 Ste A	Montreal	QC	H3C3A9	**800-769-2599**	
RBC Trust Company (Delaware) Ltd					
4550 New Linden Hill Rd Ste 200	Wilmington	DE	19808	**800-441-7698**	302-892-6976
Regents Bank NA					
PO Box 9137	La Jolla	CA	92038	**866-395-5800**	858-729-7700
Regions Bank					
1900 Fifth Ave N	Birmingham	AL	35203	**800-734-4667**	
Renasant Bank					
209 Troy St PO Box 709	Tupelo	MS	38802	**800-680-1601**	662-680-1001
Republic Bank & Trust Co					
601 W Market St	Louisville	KY	40202	**888-584-3600**	502-584-3600
Ridgewood Savings Bank					
71-02 Forest Ave	Ridgewood	NY	11385	**800-250-4832**	718-240-4800
River City Bank					
PO Box 15247	Sacramento	CA	95851	**800-564-7144***	916-567-2899
OTC: RCBC ■ *Cust Svc					
Riverview Community Bank					
900 Washington St Ste 100	Vancouver	WA	98660	**800-822-2076**	360-693-6650
Royal Bank of Canada					
200 Bay St Ninth Fl S Twr	Toronto	ON	M5J2J5	**800-769-2599**	416-955-7806
TSE: RY					
S&T Bank					
800 Philadelphia St PO Box 190	Indiana	PA	15701	**800-325-2265***	724-349-1800
*Cust Svc					
Salem Five & Savings Bank					
210 Essex St	Salem	MA	01970	**800-850-5000***	978-745-5555
*Cust Svc					
Sandy Spring National Bank of Maryland					
17801 Georgia Ave	Olney	MD	20832	**800-399-5919**	301-774-6400
SCB Bancorp Inc					
1501 E Eldorado St	Decatur	IL	62521	**888-769-2265**	217-428-7781
Seamen's Bank					
221 Commercial St PO Box 659	Provincetown	MA	02657	**855-227-5347**	508-487-0035
Security Bank of Pulaski County					
110 Lynn St PO Box S	Waynesville	MO	65583	**800-264-4274**	573-774-6417
Severn Bancorp Inc					
200 Westgate Cir Ste 200	Annapolis	MD	21401	**800-752-5854**	410-260-2000
NASDAQ: SVBI					
Signature Bank					
565 Fifth Ave 12th Fl	New York	NY	10017	**866-744-5463**	646-822-1500
NASDAQ: SBNY					
Silvergate Bank					
4275 Executive Sq Ste 800	La Jolla	CA	92037	**800-595-5856**	858-362-6300
Somerset Trust Co					
151 W Main St PO Box 777	Somerset	PA	15501	**800-972-1651**	814-443-9200
South Louisiana Bank (SLB)					
1362 W Tunnel Blvd PO Box 1718	Houma	LA	70361	**877-275-3342**	985-851-3434
Southbridge Savings Bank Inc					
253-257 Main St PO Box 370	Southbridge	MA	01550	**800-939-9103**	508-765-9103
Southern Michigan Bank & Trust					
51 W Pearl St PO Box 309	Coldwater	MI	49036	**800-379-7628**	517-279-5500
SouthWest Capital Bank					
622 Douglas Ave	Las Vegas	NM	87701	**800-748-2406**	505-425-7565

				Toll-Free	Phone
Southwest Missouri Bank					
2417 S Grand Ave	Carthage	MO	64836	**800-943-8488**	417-358-1770
Sovereign Bank FSB					
PO Box 12646	Reading	PA	19612	**877-768-2265***	
*Cust Svc					
Spencer Savings Bank					
PO Box 912	Spencer	MA	01562	**800-547-2885**	508-885-5313
Spencer Savings Bank SLA					
611 River Dr	Elmwood Park	NJ	07407	**800-363-8115**	973-772-6700
Standard Bank & Trust Co					
7800 W 95th St	Hickory Hills	IL	60457	**866-499-2265**	708-598-7400
State Bank 175 N Leroy St	Fenton	MI	48430	**800-535-0517**	810-629-2263
State Bank of Waterloo					
PO Box 148	Waterloo	IL	62298	**800-367-7576**	618-939-7194
State Farm Financial Services FSB					
PO Box 2316	Bloomington	IL	61702	**877-734-2265**	
Sterling Bank & Trust FSB					
1 Town Sq 19th Fl.	Southfield	MI	48076	**866-619-2265**	248-351-3442
Sterling Savings Bank					
105 W Simpson Ave	Mccleary	WA	98557	**800-650-7141**	
Stillman Banccorp NA					
PO Box 150	Stillman Valle	IL	61084	**877-275-3342**	815-645-2000
Summit Bank 2969 Broadway	Oakland	CA	94611	**800-380-9333**	510-839-8800
Sun National Bank					
350 Fellowship Road Ste. 101	Mount Laurel	NJ	08054	**800-786-9066**	
Suntrust Bank PO Box 4418	Atlanta	GA	30302	**800-786-8787**	
NYSE: STI					
Susquehanna Bank					
26 N Cedar St PO Box 100	Lititz	PA	17543	**800-311-3182**	717-626-4721
Swineford National Bank					
1255 N Susquehanna Trial					
PO Box 241	Hummels Wharf	PA	17831	**866-762-1903**	570-743-7786
TD Bank NA 1701 Rt 70 E	Cherry Hill	NJ	08034	**888-751-9000**	856-751-2739
TD Banknorth Massachusetts					
295 Pk Ave	Worcester	MA	01609	**800-747-7000***	508-752-2584
*Cust Svc					
Texas Capital Bank					
2000 McKinney Ave Ste 700.	Dallas	TX	75201	**877-839-2265**	214-932-6600
Texas Star Bank					
177 E Jefferson PO Box 608	Van Alstyne	TX	75495	**866-546-8273**	903-482-5234
Third Federal Savings & Loan Assn of Cleveland					
7007 Broadway Ave	Cleveland	OH	44105	**888-844-7333**	216-429-5228
Thomaston Savings Bank					
203 Main St PO Box 907	Thomaston	CT	06787	**855-344-1874***	860-283-1874
*General					
Tompkins Trust Co PO Box 460	Ithaca	NY	14851	**888-273-3210**	607-273-3210
NYSE: TMP					
Town Bank 850 W N Shore Dr	Hartland	WI	53029	**800-433-3076**	262-367-1900
TowneBank					
4501 Cox Rd PO Box 5310.	Glen Allen	VA	23060	**800-372-4445**	804-967-7000
Traditional Bank					
49 W Main St PO Box 326	Mount Sterling	KY	40353	**800-498-0414**	859-498-0414
Trust Bank					
600 E Main St PO Box 158.	Olney	IL	62450	**800-766-3451**	618-395-4311
Twin River National Bank					
1507 G St	Lewiston	ID	83501	**877-743-4948**	208-746-4848
UMB Bank NA					
1010 Grand Blvd	Kansas City	MO	64106	**800-821-2171**	816-860-7000
Umpqua Bank PO Box 1820	Roseburg	OR	97470	**866-486-7782**	503-973-5945
Unibank For Savings					
49 Church St	Whitinsville	MA	01588	**800-578-4270**	508-234-8112
Union Bank of California NA					
400 California St First Fl.	San Francisco	CA	94104	**800-238-4486**	415-765-3434
Union FSB					
1565 Mineral Spring Ave	North Providence	RI	02904	**888-226-0819**	401-353-8900
United American Bank					
101 S Ellsworth Ave	San Mateo	CA	94401	**877-275-3342**	650-579-1500
OTC: UABK					
United Bank					
11185 Fairfax Blvd	Fairfax	VA	22030	**800-327-9862**	703-219-4850
United Central Bank					
4555 W Walnut St	Garland	TX	75042	**855-773-8778**	972-487-1505
United Financial Bancorp Inc					
95 Elm St PO Box 9020	West Springfield	MA	01090	**866-959-2265**	413-787-1700
NASDAQ: UBNK					
United Security Bancshares					
2126 Inyo St Dept 98	Fresno	CA	93721	**888-683-6030**	559-248-4943
NASDAQ: UBFO					
UPS Capital Business Credit					
35 Glenlake Pkwy NE	Atlanta	GA	30328	**877-263-8772**	
US Bank NA					
800 Nicollet Mall	Minneapolis	MN	55402	**800-872-2657**	651-466-3000
USAA FSB (USAAFSB)					
10750 McDermott Fwy	San Antonio	TX	78288	**800-531-8722**	
Valley National Bank					
615 Main Ave	Passaic	NJ	07055	**800-522-4100**	973-777-6768
Vectra Bank Colorado NA					
2000 S Colorado Blvd Ste 2-1200	Denver	CO	80222	**800-232-8948**	720-947-7700
VirtualBank					
3801 PGA Blvd Ste 700					
PO Box 109638.	Palm Beach Gardens	FL	33410	**877-998-2265**	
Wachovia Bank					
11601 Wilshire Blvd	Los Angeles	CA	90025	**800-225-5935**	310-477-8004
Walpole Co-op Bank Inc					
982 Main St PO Box 350	Walpole	MA	02081	**877-322-8228**	508-668-1080
Weatherbank Inc					
1015 Waterwood Pkwy Ste J.	Edmond	OK	73034	**800-687-3562**	405-359-0773
Wells Fargo Bank 5622 Third St	Katy	TX	77493	**800-869-3557**	281-391-2101
Wells Fargo Bank Indiana NA					
111 E Wayne St	Fort Wayne	IN	46802	**800-869-3557**	260-461-6430
Wells Fargo Bank NA					
420 Montgomery St	San Francisco	CA	94104	**800-869-3557**	415-396-2619
Wells Fargo Bank Texas NA					
707 Castroville Rd	San Antonio	TX	78237	**800-869-3557**	210-856-6224
WesBanco Inc One Bank Plz	Wheeling	WV	26003	**800-328-3369**	304-234-9000
NASDAQ: WSBC					

				Toll-Free	Phone
West Coast Bank					
506 SW Coast Hwy	Newport	OR	97365	**800-895-3345***	877-272-3678
*Cust Svc					
West Suburban Bank					
711 Westmore Meyers Rd	Lombard	IL	60148	**800-258-4009**	630-652-2000
Westamerica Bancorp					
1108 Fifth Ave	San Rafael	CA	94901	**800-848-1088**	415-257-8000
NASDAQ: WABC					
Western Security Bank					
2812 First Ave N	Billings	MT	59101	**800-983-5537**	406-371-8200
Westpac Banking Corp Americas Div					
575 Fifth Ave 39th Fl	New York	NY	10017	**888-269-2377**	212-551-1800
White Sands Federal Credit Union					
2190 E Lohman Ave	Las Cruces	NM	88001	**800-658-9933**	575-647-4500
Whitney National Bank					
228 St Charles Ave	New Orleans	LA	70130	**800-844-4450**	504-586-7456
Wilmington Trust Co					
1100 N Market St	Wilmington	DE	19890	**800-441-7120**	302-651-1000
Wilshire State Bank					
3200 Wilshire Blvd Ste 1400	Los Angeles	CA	90010	**866-886-2265**	213-368-7700
Winter Hill Bank					
342 Broadway	Somerville	MA	02145	**800-444-4300**	617-666-8600
Woodforest Financial Group Inc					
PO Box 7889	Spring	TX	77387	**877-968-7962**	832-375-2000
Woodsville Guaranty Savings Bank					
10 Pleasant St PO Box 266.	Woodsville	NH	03785	**800-564-2735**	603-747-2735
WoodTrust Financial Corp					
181 Second St S	Wisconsin Rapids	WI	54494	**800-716-3742**	715-423-7600
Yadkin Bank 1318 N Bridge St	Elkin	NC	28621	**866-867-9979**	336-526-6371
NASDAQ: YDKN					
Yakima Federal Savings & Loan Assn					
118 E Yakima Ave	Yakima	WA	98901	**800-331-3225**	509-248-2634
York State Bank & Trust Co					
700 N Lincoln AvE	York	NE	68467	**888-295-5540**	402-362-4411
Zions First National Bank					
1 S Main St	Salt Lake City	UT	84111	**800-974-8800**	801-974-8800

70   BANKS - FEDERAL RESERVE

				Toll-Free	Phone
Eli Lilly Federal Credit Union					
225 SE St Ste 300.	Indianapolis	IN	46202	**800-621-2105**	317-276-2105
Federal Reserve Bank of Atlanta					
1000 Peachtree St NE	Atlanta	GA	30309	**888-500-7390**	404-498-8353
Birmingham Branch					
524 Liberty Pkwy	Birmingham	AL	35242	**800-257-7013**	205-968-6700
Federal Reserve Bank of Cleveland					
Cincinnati Branch					
150 E Fourth St	Cincinnati	OH	45202	**877-372-2457**	513-721-4787
Federal Reserve Bank of Dallas					
2200 N Pearl St PO Box 655906.	Dallas	TX	75201	**800-333-4460**	214-922-6000
San Antonio Branch					
402 Dwyer Ave	San Antonio	TX	78204	**800-333-4460**	210-978-1200
Federal Reserve Bank of Kansas City					
1 Memorial Dr PO Box 1200.	Kansas City	MO	64198	**800-333-1010**	816-881-2000
Denver Branch					
1 Memorial Dr	Kansas City	MO	64198	**888-851-1920**	
Oklahoma City Branch					
226 Dean A McGee Ave	Oklahoma City	OK	73102	**800-333-1030**	405-270-8400
Omaha Branch 2201 Farnam St	Omaha	NE	68102	**800-333-1040**	402-221-5500
Federal Reserve Bank of Minneapolis					
90 Hennepin Ave	Minneapolis	MN	55401	**800-553-9656**	612-204-5000
Federal Reserve Bank of Philadelphia					
10 Independence Mall	Philadelphia	PA	19106	**877-574-1776**	215-574-6000
Federal Reserve Bank of Saint Louis					
411 Locust St	Saint Louis	MO	63102	**800-333-0810**	314-444-8444
Little Rock Branch					
111 Ctr St Ste 1000 Stephens Bldg	Little Rock	AR	72201	**877-372-2457**	501-324-8300
Federal Reserve Bank of San Francisco (FRBSF)					
101 Market St	San Francisco	CA	94105	**800-227-4133**	415-974-2000
Portland Branch					
1500 SW First Ave Ste 100.	Portland	OR	97201	**800-227-4133**	503-276-3000
Salt Lake City Branch					
101 Market St	San Francisco	CA	94105	**800-227-4133**	415-974-2000
First Federal of Northern Michigan					
100 S Second Ave	Alpena	MI	49707	**800-916-8800**	989-356-9041
NASDAQ: FFNM					
First FSB 633 La Salle St	Ottawa	IL	61350	**800-443-8780**	815-434-3500
First Shore Federal					
106-108 S Div St PO Box 4248	Salisbury	MD	21803	**800-634-6309**	410-546-1101
Lincoln FSB					
1101 N St 68508 PO Box 80038.	Lincoln	NE	68501	**800-333-2158**	402-474-1400
Milford Federal Savings & Loan Assn					
PO Box 210	Milford	MA	01757	**800-478-6990**	508-634-2500
Naugatuck Savings Bank					
251 Church St PO Box 370.	Naugatuck	CT	06770	**877-729-4442**	203-729-5291
Pioneer Bank					
21 Second St PO Box 1048	Troy	NY	12181	**866-873-9573**	518-274-4800
Security Federal Bank (SFB)					
238 Richland Ave W	Aiken	SC	29801	**866-851-3000**	803-641-3000
Summit State Bank					
500 Bicentennial Way PO Box 6188	Santa Rosa	CA	95406	**800-428-5008**	707-568-6000
NASDAQ: SSBI					
Webster First Federal Credit Union					
271 Greenwood St	Worcester	MA	01607	**800-962-4452**	508-671-5000

71   BAR ASSOCIATIONS - STATE

SEE ALSO Legal Professionals Associations

				Toll-Free	Phone
Alabama State Bar					
415 Dexter Ave	Montgomery	AL	36104	**800-392-5660**	334-269-1515
Alaska Bar Assn					
550 W Seventh Ave Ste 1900					
PO Box 100279.	Anchorage	AK	99501	**800-478-4372**	907-272-7469

				Toll-Free	Phone

Delaware State Bar Assn
405 N King St ....Wilmington DE 19801 **855-872-5911** 302-658-5279

District of Columbia Bar, The
1101 K St NW Ste 200 ....Washington DC 20005 **877-333-2227** 202-737-4700

Florida Bar
651 E Jefferson St ....Tallahassee FL 32399 **800-342-8060** 850-561-5600

Idaho State Bar
525 W Jefferson St ....Boise ID 83702 **800-221-3295** 208-334-4500

Illinois State Bar Assn
424 S Second St ....Springfield IL 62701 **800-252-8908** 217-525-1760

Kansas Bar Assn
1200 SW Harrison St ....Topeka KS 66612 **800-928-3111** 785-234-5696

Louisiana State Bar Assn (LSBA)
601 St Charles Ave ....New Orleans LA 70130 **800-421-5722** 504-566-1600

Maine State Bar Assn
124 State St ....Augusta ME 04330 **800-475-7523** 207-622-7523

Maryland State Bar Assn Inc
520 W Fayette St ....Baltimore MD 21201 **800-492-1964** 410-685-7878

Minnesota State Bar Assn
600 Nicollet Mall Ste 380 ....Minneapolis MN 55402 **800-882-6722** 612-333-1183

Nebraska State Bar Assn
635 S 14th St Ste 200 ....Lincoln NE 68501 **800-927-0117** 402-475-7091

New York State Bar Assn
1 Elk St ....Albany NY 12207 **800-342-3661** 518-463-3200

North Carolina State Bar
217 E Edenton St PO Box 25996 ....Raleigh NC 27601 **800-662-7407** 919-828-4620

Ohio State Bar Assn (OSBA)
1700 Lk Shore Dr ....Columbus OH 43204 **800-282-6556** 614-487-2050

Oklahoma Bar Assn
1901 N Lincoln Blvd
PO Box 53036 ....Oklahoma City OK 73105 **800-522-8065** 405-416-7000

Oregon State Bar Assn
16037 SW Upper Boones Ferry Rd ....Tigard OR 97224 **800-452-8260** 503-620-0222

Pennsylvania Bar Assn
100 S St ....Harrisburg PA 17101 **800-932-0311** 717-238-6715

Rhode Island Bar Assn
115 Cedar St ....Providence RI 02903 **877-659-0801** 401-421-5740

South Carolina Bar
950 Taylor St ....Columbia SC 29201 **877-797-2227** 803-799-6653

State Bar Assn of North Dakota
504 N Washington St PO Box 2136 ....Bismarck ND 58502 **800-472-2685** 701-255-1404

State Bar of Arizona
4201 N 24th St Ste 200 ....Phoenix AZ 85016 **866-482-9227** 602-252-4804

State Bar of Georgia
104 Marietta St NW Ste 100 ....Atlanta GA 30303 **800-334-6865** 404-527-8700

State Bar of Michigan
306 Townsend St ....Lansing MI 48933 **800-968-1442** 517-346-6300

State Bar of Nevada
600 E Charleston Blvd ....Las Vegas NV 89104 **800-254-2797** 702-382-2200

State Bar of New Mexico
5121 Masthead St NE PO Box 92860 ....Albuquerque NM 87109 **800-876-6227** 505-797-6000

State Bar of Texas
1414 Colorado St ....Austin TX 78701 **800-204-2222** 512-427-1463

State Bar of Wisconsin
5302 Eastpark Blvd ....Madison WI 53718 **800-728-7788** 608-257-3838

Tennessee Bar Assn
221 Fourth Ave N Ste 400 ....Nashville TN 37219 **800-899-6993** 615-383-7421

Utah State Bar
645 S 200 E ....Salt Lake City UT 84111 **877-752-2611** 801-531-9077

Virginia State Bar
707 E Main St Ste 1500 ....Richmond VA 23219 **800-552-7977** 804-775-0500

Washington State Bar Assn
1325 Fourth Ave Ste 600 ....Seattle WA 98101 **800-945-9722** 206-727-8200

West Virginia State Bar
2000 Deitrick Blvd ....Charleston WV 25311 **866-989-8227** 304-553-7220

72	BASKETS, CAGES, RACKS, ETC - WIRE

SEE ALSO Pet Products

				Toll-Free	Phone

Bright Co-op Inc
803 W Seale St ....Nacogdoches TX 75964 **800-562-0730** 936-564-8378

Glamos Wire Products Company Inc
5561 N 152nd St ....Hugo MN 55038 **800-328-5062** 651-429-5386

InterMetro Industries Corp
651 N Washington St ....Wilkes-Barre PA 18705 **800-992-1776*** 570-825-2741
*Cust Svc

Kaspar Wire Works Inc
PO Box 667 ....Shiner TX 77984 **800-337-0610** 361-594-3327

Lab Products Inc
742 Sussex Ave PO Box 639 ....Seaford DE 19973 **800-526-0469** 302-628-4300

Midwest Wire Products Inc
800 Woodward Heights ....Ferndale MI 48220 **800-989-9881** 248-399-5100

Nashville Wire Products Manufacturing Co
199 Polk Ave ....Nashville TN 37210 **800-448-2125** 615-743-2500

Riverdale Mills Corp
130 Riverdale St PO Box 200 ....Northbridge MA 01534 **800-762-6374** 508-234-8715

73	BATTERIES

				Toll-Free	Phone

A123 Systems Inc 200 W St ....Waltham MA 02451 **800-224-7654** 617-778-5700

Applied Energy Solutions LLC
One Technology Pl ....Caledonia NY 14423 **800-836-2132** 585-538-4421

C & D Technologies Inc
1400 Union Meeting Rd PO Box 3053 ....Blue Bell PA 19422 **800-543-8630** 215-619-2700

Cell-con Inc
305 Commerce Dr Ste 300 ....Exton PA 19341 **800-771-7139** 610-280-7630

Continental Battery Corp
4919 Woodall St ....Dallas TX 75247 **800-442-0081** 214-631-5701

Crown Battery Manufacturing Co
1445 Majestic Dr ....Fremont OH 43420 **800-487-2879** 419-334-7181

Douglas Battery Manufacturing Co
500 Battery Dr ....Winston-Salem NC 27107 **800-368-4527**

Duracell 14 Research Dr ....Bethel CT 06801 **800-551-2355** 203-791-3014

				Toll-Free	Phone

EnerSys 2366 Bernville Rd ....Reading PA 19605 **800-538-3627** 610-208-1991
NYSE: ENS

Exide Technologies
13000 Deerfield Pkwy Bldg 200 ....Milton GA 30004 **800-782-7848** 678-566-9000
NASDAQ: XIDE

Hawker Powersource Inc
9404 Ooltewah Industrial Dr
PO Box 808 ....Ooltewah TN 37363 **800-238-8658** 423-238-5700

Industrial Battery & Charger Inc
5831 Orr Rd ....Charlotte NC 28213 **800-833-8412** 704-597-7330

Mathews Assoc Inc
220 Power Ct ....Sanford FL 32771 **800-871-5262** 407-323-3390

Micro Power Electronics Inc
13955 SW Millikan Way ....Beaverton OR 97005 **866-233-4553** 503-693-7600

Power Battery Co Inc
25 McLean Blvd ....Paterson NJ 07514 **800-455-0054** 973-523-8630

R & D Batteries Inc
3300 Corporate Ctr Dr PO Box 5007 ....Burnsville MN 55306 **800-950-1945** 952-890-0629

Surefire LLC
18300 Mt Baldy Cir ....Fountain Valley CA 92708 **800-828-8809** 714-545-9444

Tadiran Batteries
2001 Marcus Ave Ste 125E ....New Hyde Park NY 11042 **800-537-1368** 516-621-4980

TNR Technical Inc
301 Central Pk Dr ....Sanford FL 32771 **800-346-0601** 407-321-3011
OTC: TNRK

Trojan Battery Co
12380 Clark St ....Santa Fe Springs CA 90670 **800-423-6569*** 562-236-3000
*Cust Svc

Ultralife Batteries Inc
2000 Technology Pkwy ....Newark NY 14513 **800-332-5000** 315-332-7100
NASDAQ: ULBI

Valence Technology Inc
12303 Technology Blvd Ste 950 ....Austin TX 78727 **888-825-3623** 512-527-2900

74	BEARINGS - BALL & ROLLER

				Toll-Free	Phone

Accurate Bushing Company Inc
443 N Ave ....Garwood NJ 07027 **800-932-0076*** 908-789-1121
*Sales

AST Bearings 115 Main Rd ....Montville NJ 07045 **800-526-1250** 973-335-2230

Bearing Inspection Inc
4500 Mount Pleasant NW ....North Canton OH 44720 **800-416-8881*** 234-262-3000
*Cust Svc

Bearing Service Co of Pennsylvania
630 Alpha Dr RIDC Park ....Pittsburgh PA 15238 **800-783-2327** 412-963-7710

General Bearing Corp
44 High St ....West Nyack NY 10994 **800-431-1766*** 845-358-6000
*Sales

JTEKT Corporation
29570 Clemens Rd ....Westlake OH 44145 **800-263-5163*** 440-835-1000
*Cust Svc

Nachi America Inc
715 Pushville Rd ....Greenwood IN 46143 **888-340-2747** 317-530-1001

Peer Bearing Co
2200 Norman Dr S ....Waukegan IL 60085 **800-433-7337** 847-578-1000

Rotek Inc
1400 S Chillicothe Rd PO Box 312 ....Aurora OH 44202 **800-221-8043** 330-562-4000

Schaeffler Group USA Inc
308 Springhill Farm Rd ....Fort Mill SC 29715 **800-361-5841** 803-548-8500

Schatz Bearing Corp
10 Fairview Ave ....Poughkeepsie NY 12601 **800-554-1406** 845-452-6000

Timken Co 1835 Dueber Ave SW ....Canton OH 44706 **800-223-1954** 330-438-3000
NYSE: TKR

Winsted Precision Ball Corp
159 Colebrook River Rd ....Winsted CT 06098 **800-462-3075** 860-379-2788

75	BEAUTY SALON EQUIPMENT & SUPPLIES

				Toll-Free	Phone

Belvedere USA Corp
1 Belvedere Blvd ....Belvidere IL 61008 **800-435-5491** 815-544-3131

Betty Dain Creations Inc
9701 NW 112 Ave Ste 10 ....Miami FL 33178 **800-327-5256*** 305-769-3451
*General

Burmax Co
28 Barretts Ave ....Holtsville NY 11742 **800-645-5118**

Collins Manufacturing Co
2000 Bowser Rd ....Cookeville TN 38506 **800-292-6450** 931-528-5151

Dr Kern USA Inc
221 S Franklin Rd ....Indianapolis IN 46219 **800-908-9885** 317-472-0873

Jeunesse Global LLC
650 Douglas Ave ....Altamonte Springs FL 32714 **800-400-2676** 407-215-7414

Living Earth Crafts
3210 Executive Ridge Dr ....Vista CA 92081 **800-358-8292** 760-597-2155

National Salon Resources Inc
3109 Louisiana Ave N ....Minneapolis MN 55427 **800-622-0003** 763-541-1000

Pibbs Industries
133-15 32nd Ave ....Flushing NY 11354 **800-551-5020** 718-445-8046

Sally Beauty Company Inc
3001 Colorado Blvd ....Denton TX 76210 **800-777-5706** 940-898-7500

Takara Belmont USA Inc
101 Belmont Dr ....Somerset NJ 08873 **877-283-1289**

TouchAmerica
1403 S Third Street Ext ....Hillsborough NC 27278 **800-678-6824** 919-732-6968

William Marvy Company Inc
1540 St Clair Ave ....Saint Paul MN 55105 **800-874-2651** 651-698-0726

76	BEAUTY SALONS

				Toll-Free	Phone

Beauty Brands Inc
4600 Madison St Ste 400 ....Kansas City MO 64112 **877-640-2248** 816-531-2266

				Toll-Free	Phone
Gino Morena Enterprises LLC					
111 Starlite St	South San Francisco	CA	94080	800-227-6905	
Great Clips Inc					
7700 France Ave S Ste 425	Minneapolis	MN	55435	800-999-5959	952-893-9088
Holiday Hair					
7201 Metro Blvd	Minneapolis	MN	55439	800-345-7811	
Mohegan Tribal Gaming Authority					
One Mohegan Sun Blvd	Uncasville	CT	06382	888-226-7711	
Premier Salons Inc					
8341 Tenth Ave N Golden Vly	Golden Valley	MN	55427	800-542-4247	
Regis Corp					
7201 Metro Blvd	Minneapolis	MN	55439	888-888-7778	952-947-7777
NYSE: RGS					
Regis Corp MasterCuts Div					
7201 Metro Blvd	Minneapolis	MN	55439	877-857-2070	952-947-7777
Regis Corp Pro-Cuts Div					
7201 Metro Blvd	Minneapolis	MN	55439	877-857-2070	952-947-7777
Regis Corp Regis Hairstylists Div					
7201 Metro Blvd	Minneapolis	MN	55439	877-857-2070	952-947-7777
Regis Corp SmartStyle Div					
7201 Metro Blvd	Minneapolis	MN	55439	877-857-2070	952-947-7777
Regis Corp Trade Secret Div					
7201 Metro Blvd	Minneapolis	MN	55439	888-888-7778	952-947-7777
Sport Clips Inc					
110 Briarwood Dr	Georgetown	TX	78628	800-872-4247	512-869-1201
Stewart School of Cosmetology					
604 NW Ave	Sioux Falls	SD	57104	800-537-2625	605-336-2775
Supercuts					
7201 Metro Blvd	Minneapolis	MN	55439	877-857-2070	
Toni & Guy USA Inc					
2311 Midway Rd	Carrollton	TX	75006	800-256-9391	

77 BETTER BUSINESS BUREAUS - CANADA

				Toll-Free	Phone
Better Business Bureau of Vancouver Island					
220-1175 Cook St Ste 220	Victoria	BC	V8V4A1	877-826-4222	250-386-6348
Better Business Bureau Serving Mainland British Columbia					
788 Beatty St Ste 404	Vancouver	BC	V6B2M1	888-803-1222	604-682-2711
Better Business Bureau Serving Western Ontario					
200 Queens Ave Ste 308 PO Box 2153	London	ON	N6A3M8	877-283-9222	519-673-3222
Better Business Bureau Serving Winnipeg & Manitoba					
1030B Empress St	Winnipeg	MB	R3G3H4	800-385-3074	204-989-9010

78 BETTER BUSINESS BUREAUS - US

SEE ALSO Consumer Interest Organizations

				Toll-Free	Phone
Better Business Bureau Online					
Council of Better Business Bureaus, The					
4200 Wilson Blvd Ste 800	Arlington	VA	22203	800-459-8875	703-276-0100
Better Business Bureau Heartland					
11811 P St	Omaha	NE	68137	800-649-6814	402-391-7612
Better Business Bureau Inc					
1000 Broadway Ste 625	Oakland	CA	94607	866-411-2221	510-844-2000
Better Business Bureau of Ark-La-Tex					
401 Edwards St Ste 135	Shreveport	LA	71101	800-372-4222	318-222-7575
Better Business Bureau of Canton Region/West Virginia					
1434 Cleveland Ave NW	Canton	OH	44703	800-362-0494	330-454-9401
Better Business Bureau of Central & Eastern Kentucky					
1460 Newtown Pk	Lexington	KY	40511	800-866-6668	859-259-1008
Better Business Bureau of Central East Texas					
3600 Old BullaRd Rd Bldg 1	Tyler	TX	75701	800-443-0131	903-581-5704
Better Business Bureau of Central East Texas Longview Branch					
102 Commander Ste 7	Longview	TX	75605	800-443-0131	903-758-3222
Better Business Bureau of Central Illinois					
112 Harrison St	Peoria	IL	61602	800-763-4222	309-688-3741
Better Business Bureau of Central Indiana					
151 N Delaware St	Indianapolis	IN	46204	866-463-9222	317-488-2222
Better Business Bureau of Central Louisiana & Ark-La-Tex					
5220-C Rue Verdun	Alexandria	LA	71303	800-372-4222*	318-473-4494
*General					
Better Business Bureau of Central Northeast Northwest & Southwest Arizona					
4428 N 12th St	Phoenix	AZ	85014	877-291-6222	602-264-1721
Better Business Bureau of Central Ohio					
1169 Dublin Rd	Columbus	OH	43215	800-759-2400	614-486-6336
Better Business Bureau of Eastern Massachusetts Maine Rhode Island & Vermont					
290 Donald Lynch Blvd Ste 102	Marlborough	MA	01752	800-422-2811	508-652-4800
Better Business Bureau of Greater Kansas City					
8080 Ward Pkwy Ste 401	Kansas City	MO	64114	877-606-0695	816-421-7800
Better Business Bureau of Hawaii					
1132 Bishop St Ste 615	Honolulu	HI	96813	877-222-6551	808-536-6956
Better Business Bureau of Kansas Inc					
345 N Riverview St Ste 720	Wichita	KS	67203	800-856-2417	316-263-3146
Better Business Bureau of Louisville Southern Indiana & Western Kentucky					
844 S Fourth St	Louisville	KY	40203	800-388-2222	502-583-6546
Better Business Bureau of Maine					
290 Donald Lynch Blvd Ste 102	Marlborough	MA	01752	800-422-2811	508-652-4800
Better Business Bureau of New Jersey					
1700 Whitehorse-Hamilton Sq Rd Ste D-5	Trenton	NJ	08690	888-494-4009	609-588-0808
Better Business Bureau of Northeast Florida & The Southeast Atlantic					
4417 Beach Blvd Ste 202	Jacksonville	FL	32207	800-713-6661	904-721-2288
Better Business Bureau of Northeast Louisiana					
1900 N 18th St Ste 411	Monroe	LA	71201	800-960-7756	318-387-4600
Better Business Bureau of Northeast Ohio					
2800 Euclid Ave Fourth Fl	Cleveland	OH	44115	800-233-0361	216-241-7678
Better Business Bureau of Northern Colorado & East Central Wyoming					
8020 S County Rd 5 Ste 100	Fort Collins	CO	80528	800-564-0371	970-484-1348
Better Business Bureau of Northwest North Carolina					
500 W Fifth St Ste 202	Winston-Salem	NC	27101	800-777-8348	336-725-8348
Better Business Bureau of Northwest Ohio & Southeast Michigan					
7668 King's Pt Rd	Toledo	OH	43617	800-743-4222	419-531-3116
Better Business Bureau of Rockford					
330 North Wabash Ave Ste 3120	Chicago	IL	60611	800-955-5100	312-832-0500

				Toll-Free	Phone
Better Business Bureau of Southeast Florida & the Caribbean					
4411 Beacon Cir Ste 4	West Palm Beach	FL	33407	866-966-7226	561-842-1918
Better Business Bureau of Southeast Tennessee & Northwest Georgia					
508 N Market St	Chattanooga	TN	37405	800-548-4456	423-266-6144
Better Business Bureau of Southeast Texas					
550 Fannin St Ste 100	Beaumont	TX	77701	800-685-7650	409-835-5348
Better Business Bureau of Southwest Georgia					
PO Box 2587	Columbus	GA	31902	800-768-4222	706-324-0712
Better Business Bureau of Southwest Idaho & Eastern Oregon					
1200 N Curtis Rd PO Box 9817	Boise	ID	83706	800-218-1001	208-342-4649
Better Business Bureau of Southwest Louisiana Inc					
2309 E Prien Lk Rd	Lake Charles	LA	70601	800-542-7085	337-478-6253
Better Business Bureau of the Akron Inc					
222 W Market St	Akron	OH	44303	800-825-8887	330-253-4590
Better Business Bureau of the Bakersfield Area					
1601 H St Ste 101	Bakersfield	CA	93301	800-675-8118	661-322-2074
Better Business Bureau of the Denver-Boulder Metro Area					
1020 Cherokee St	Denver	CO	80204	800-356-6333	303-758-2100
Better Business Bureau of the Mid-South					
3693 Tyndale Dr	Memphis	TN	38125	800-222-8754	901-759-1300
Better Business Bureau of Utah					
5673 S Redwood Rd Ste 22	Salt Lake City	UT	84123	800-456-3907	801-892-6009
Better Business Bureau of West Florida					
2655 McCormick Dr	Clearwater	FL	33759	800-525-1447	727-535-5522
Better Business Bureau of West Georgia & East Alabama					
PO Box 2587	Columbus	GA	31902	800-768-4222	706-324-0712
Better Business Bureau of Western Massachusetts					
35 Ctr St Ste 203	Chicopee	MA	01013	866-566-9222	
Better Business Bureau Serving Central California					
4201 W Shaw Ave Ste 107	Fresno	CA	93722	800-675-8118	559-222-8111
Tri-State Better Business Bureau					
5401 Vogel Rd Ste 410	Evansville	IN	47715	800-359-0979	812-473-0202

79 BEVERAGES - MFR

SEE ALSO Water - Bottled ; Breweries

79-1 Liquor - Mfr

				Toll-Free	Phone
Anheuser-Busch Cos Inc					
1200 Lynch St	Saint Louis	MO	63118	800-379-2739	314-577-3559
Bacardi USA Inc					
2701 S Le Jeune Rd Ste 400	Coral Gables	FL	33134	800-222-2734	305-573-8511
Laird & Co One LaiRd Rd	Scobeyville	NJ	07724	877-438-5247	732-542-0312
Pernod Ricard USA					
100 Manhattanville Rd	Purchase	NY	10577	800-847-5949	914-848-4800
Sunrich LLC					
3824 SW 93rd St PO Box 128	Hope	MN	56046	800-297-5997	507-451-6030
Walker MS Inc					
20 Third Ave	Somerville	MA	02143	800-528-2787	617-776-6700

79-2 Soft Drinks - Mfr

				Toll-Free	Phone
Coca-Cola Co					
One Coca-Cola Plz PO Box 1734	Atlanta	GA	30313	800-438-2653	404-676-2121
NYSE: KO					
Cott Corp					
6525 Viscount Rd	Mississauga	ON	L4V1H6	888-378-4361	905-672-1900
NYSE: COT					
Crystal Rock Holdings Inc					
1050 Buckingham St	Watertown	CT	06795	800-525-0070	860-945-0661
NYSE: AMEX					
Dr Pepper/Seven-Up Inc					
5301 Legacy Dr	Plano	TX	75024	800-696-5891	972-673-7000
Fiji Water Company LLC					
11444 W Olympic Blvd Second Fl	Los Angeles	CA	90064	888-426-3454	310-312-2850
Great Plains Coca-Cola Bottling Company Inc					
600 N May Ave	Oklahoma City	OK	73107	800-753-2653	405-280-2000
Jones Soda Co					
234 Ninth Ave N	Seattle	WA	98109	800-690-6903	206-624-3357
OTC: JSDA					
Middlesboro Coca-Cola Bottling Works Inc					
1324 Cumberland Ave PO Box 1485	Middlesboro	KY	40965	800-442-0102	877-692-4679
Monarch Beverage Co					
1123 Zonolite Rd NE Ste 10	Atlanta	GA	30306	800-408-3590	404-262-4040
Polar Beverages Inc					
1001 Southbridge St	Worcester	MA	01610	800-734-9800*	508-753-4300
*Cust Svc					
Shasta Beverages Inc					
26901 Industrial Blvd	Hayward	CA	94545	800-834-9980	510-783-3200
Wallingford Coffee Mills Inc					
11401 Rockfield Ct	Cincinnati	OH	45241	800-533-3690	513-771-4570
White Rock Products Corp					
141-07 20th Ave Ste 403	Whitestone	NY	11357	800-969-7625	718-746-3400

79-3 Wines - Mfr

				Toll-Free	Phone
Beaulieu Vineyard					
1960 St Helena Hwy	Rutherford	CA	94573	800-373-5896	707-967-5233
Bronco Wine Co					
6342 Bystrum Rd	Ceres	CA	95307	855-874-2394	209-538-3131
Canandaigua Wine Company Inc					
235 N Bloomfield Rd	Canandaigua	NY	14424	888-659-7900	585-396-7600
Clos du Bois					
19410 Geyserville Ave	Geyserville	CA	95441	800-222-3189*	707-857-1651
*Sales					
Columbia Crest Winery					
Hwy 221 Columbia Crest Dr PO Box 231	Paterson	WA	99345	888-309-9463	509-875-4227
Domaine Chandon Inc					
One California Dr	Yountville	CA	94599	888-242-6366	

	Toll-Free	Phone
Franciscan Estates		
1178 Galleron Rd .... Saint Helena CA 94574	800-529-9463	707-967-3830
Hogue Cellars 2800 Lee Rd .... Prosser WA 99350	800-565-9779	
Kendall-Jackson Wine Estates Ltd		
425 Aviation Blvd .... Santa Rosa CA 95403	800-769-3649	707-544-4000
Kysela Pere Et Fils Ltd		
331 Victory Rd .... Winchester VA 22602	877-492-7917	540-722-9228
Laetitia Vineyards & Winery Inc		
453 Laetitia Vineyard Dr .... Arroyo Grande CA 93420	888-809-8463	805-481-1772
Louis M Martini Winery		
254 S St Helena Hwy .... Saint Helena CA 94574	866-549-2582	
Magnotta Winery Corp		
271 Chrislea Rd .... Vaughan ON L4L8N6	800-461-9463	905-738-9463
Mendocino Wine Co		
501 PaRducci Rd .... Ukiah CA 95482	800-362-9463	707-463-5350
Michel-schlumberger Partners LP		
4155 Wine Creek Rd .... Healdsburg CA 95448	800-447-3060	707-433-7427
Old Mill Winery		
403 S Broadway .... Geneva OH 44041	800-227-6972	
Pine Ridge Winery LLC		
5901 Silverado Trail .... Napa CA 94558	800-575-9777	
Ravenswood Winery Inc		
18701 Gehricke Rd .... Sonoma CA 95476	888-669-4679	
Raymond Vineyard		
849 Zinfandel Ln .... Saint Helena CA 94574	800-525-2659	707-963-6941
Robert Mondavi Co		
7801 St Helena Hwy .... Oakville CA 94562	888-766-6328	707-226-1395
Rodney Strong Vineyards		
11455 Old Redwood Hwy .... Healdsburg CA 95448	800-678-4763	707-431-1533
Sebastiani Vineyards Inc		
389 Fourth St E .... Sonoma CA 95476	855-232-2338	707-933-3230
Trefethen Vineyards Winery Inc		
1160 Oak Knoll Ave .... Napa CA 94558	866-895-7696	707-255-7700
Warner Vineyards Inc		
706 S Kalamazoo St .... Paw Paw MI 49079	800-756-5357	269-657-3165
Weibel Vineyards		
One Winemaster Way .... Lodi CA 95240	800-932-9463	209-365-9463
Willamette Valley Vineyards Inc		
8800 Enchanted Way SE .... Turner OR 97392	800-344-9463*	503-588-9463
NASDAQ: WVVI ■ *Sales*		

80   BEVERAGES - WHOL

80-1   Beer & Ale - Whol

	Toll-Free	Phone
Arkansas Distributing Company LLC		
800 E Barton Ave .... West Memphis AR 72301	877-735-3506	870-735-3506
Associated Distributors LLC		
401 Woodlake Dr .... Chesapeake VA 23320	800-308-2600	757-424-6300
Atlas Distributing Corp		
44 Southbridge St .... Auburn MA 01501	800-649-6221	508-791-6221
Banko Beverage Co		
5001 Crackersport Rd .... Allentown PA 18104	800-322-9295*	610-434-0147
General		
Beauchamp Distributing Co		
1911 S Santa Fe Ave .... Compton CA 90221	800-734-5102	310-639-5320
Blach Distributing Co		
131 W Main St .... Elko NV 89801	800-310-5099	775-738-7111
Bonanza Beverage Co		
6333 Ensworth St .... Las Vegas NV 89119	800-677-4166*	702-361-4166
Cust Svc		
Buck Distributing Company Inc		
15827 Commerce Ct .... Upper Marlboro MD 20774	800-750-2825*	301-952-0400
Cust Svc		
Central Distributors Inc		
15 Foss Rd .... Lewiston ME 04240	800-427-5757*	207-784-4026
Cust Svc		
Columbia Distributing Co		
6840 N Cutter Cir .... Portland OR 97217	888-417-5001	503-289-9600
Commercial Distributing Co Inc		
46 S Broad St .... Westfield MA 01085	800-332-8999*	413-562-9691
Cust Svc		
Consolidated Beverages Inc		
12 St Mark St .... Auburn MA 01501	800-922-8128	508-832-5311
Dutchess Beer Distributors Inc		
5 Laurel St .... Poughkeepsie NY 12601	800-427-6308*	845-452-0940
Cust Svc		
Frank B Fuhrer Wholesale Co		
3100 E Carson St .... Pittsburgh PA 15203	800-837-2212	412-488-8844
Gambrinus Co, The		
14800 San Pedro Ave Third Fl .... San Antonio TX 78232	800-596-6486	210-490-9128
Georgia Crown Distributing Co		
100 Georgia Crown Dr .... McDonough GA 30253	800-342-2350	770-302-3000
Gretz Beer Co		
710 E Main St .... Norristown PA 19401	800-310-5099*	610-275-0285
General		
Iron City Distributing Co		
2670 Commercial Ave .... Mingo Junction OH 43938	800-759-2671*	740-598-4171
Cust Svc		
Labatt Breweries of Canada		
207 Queen's Quay W Ste 299 .... Toronto ON M5J1A7	800-268-2337*	416-361-5050
Cust Svc		
Lion Brewery Inc		
700 N Pennsylvania Ave .... Wilkes-Barre PA 18705	888-295-2337	570-823-8801
Maple City Ice Co Inc		
371 Cleveland Rd .... Norwalk OH 44857	877-762-9119*	419-668-2531
Cust Svc		
Mautino Distributing Co		
500 N Richards St .... Spring Valley IL 61362	800-851-2756*	815-664-4311
Cust Svc		
McLaughlin & Moran Inc		
40 Slater Rd .... Cranston RI 02920	800-423-0156	401-463-5454
Merrimack Valley Distributing Co		
50 Prince St .... Danvers MA 01923	800-698-0250	978-777-2213

	Toll-Free	Phone
New Hampshire Distributors Inc		
65 Regional Dr .... Concord NH 03301	800-852-3781	603-224-9991
NKS Distributors Inc		
399 Churchmans Rd .... New Castle DE 19720	800-310-5099	302-322-1811
Pine State Trading Co		
8 Ellis Ave .... Augusta ME 04330	800-873-3825	207-622-3741
Premium Distributors		
3500 Fort Lincoln Dr NE .... Washington DC 20018	800-827-4020	202-526-3900
Saratoga Eagle Sales & Service Inc		
45 Duplainville Rd .... Saratoga Springs NY 12866	800-310-5099	518-581-7377
Savannah Distributing Co Inc		
2425 W Gwinnett St PO Box 1388 .... Savannah GA 31415	800-551-0777*	912-233-1167
General		
Silver Eagle Distributors LP		
7777 Washington Ave .... Houston TX 77007	855-332-2110	713-869-4361
Southern Wine & Spirits of Colorado		
5270 Fox St PO Box 5603 .... Denver CO 80216	800-332-9956	303-292-1711
Standard Sales Co Inc		
4800 E 42nd St Ste 400 .... Odessa TX 79762	800-331-5453	432-367-7662
Star Distributors Inc		
460 Frontage Rd .... West Haven CT 06516	877-922-3501	203-932-3636
Western Wyoming Beverages Inc		
100 Reliance Rd .... Rock Springs WY 82901	800-551-8244	307-362-6332
Williams Distributing Corp		
880 Burnett Rd .... Chicopee MA 01020	800-332-9634	413-594-4900

80-2   Soft Drinks - Whol

	Toll-Free	Phone
Atlas Distributing Corp		
44 Southbridge St .... Auburn MA 01501	800-649-6221	508-791-6221
Buffalo Rock Co		
111 Oxmoor Rd .... Birmingham AL 35209	800-822-9799	205-942-3435
Coca-Cola Bottling Co Consolidated		
4100 Coca-Cola Plaza .... Charlotte NC 28211	800-777-2653	704-557-4000
NASDAQ: COKE		
Swire Coca-Cola USA		
12634 S 265 W .... Draper UT 84020	800-497-2653	801-816-5300
Vital Pharmaceuticals Inc		
1600 N Pk Dr .... Weston FL 33326	800-954-7904	954-641-0570
Western Wyoming Beverages Inc		
100 Reliance Rd .... Rock Springs WY 82901	800-551-8244	307-362-6332

80-3   Wine & Liquor - Whol

	Toll-Free	Phone
Alabama Crown Distributing		
421 Industrial Ln .... Birmingham AL 35211	800-548-1869	205-941-1155
Badger Liquor Company Inc		
850 S Morris St .... Fond du Lac WI 54936	800-242-9708	920-923-8160
Badger West Wine & Spirits LLC		
5400 Old Town Hall Rd PO Box 869 ..... Eau Claire WI 54701	800-472-6674	715-836-8600
Ben Arnold Beverage Company LP		
101 Beverage Blvd .... Ridgeway SC 29130	888-262-9787*	803-337-3500
Acctg		
Beverage Distributors Co		
14200 E Moncrieff Pl .... Aurora CO 80011	800-772-2096*	303-371-3421
General		
Castle Brands Inc		
122 E 42nd St Ste 4700 .... New York NY 10168	800-882-8140	646-356-0200
NYSE: ROX		
Central Distributors Inc		
15 Foss Rd .... Lewiston ME 04240	800-427-5757*	207-784-4026
Cust Svc		
Charmer Sunbelt Group, The		
60 E 42nd St Ste 1915 .... New York NY 10165	800-772-2096	212-699-7000
Columbia Distributing Co		
6840 N Cutter Cir .... Portland OR 97217	888-417-5001	503-289-9600
Constellation Brands Inc		
207 High Pt Dr Bldg 100 .... Victor NY 14564	888-724-2169	
NYSE: STZ		
Fedway Assoc Inc		
505 Westgate Dr .... Basking Ridge NJ 07920	800-447-4736	973-624-6444
Frederick Wildman & Sons Ltd		
307 E 53rd St .... New York NY 10022	800-733-9463*	212-355-0700
General		
Georgia Crown Distributing Co		
100 Georgia Crown Dr .... McDonough GA 30253	800-342-2350	770-302-3000
Glazer's Wholesale Drug Company Inc		
14911 Quorum Dr Ste 400 .... Dallas TX 75254	800-275-2854	972-392-8200
Johnson Bros Wholesale Liquor Co		
1999 ShepaRd Rd .... Saint Paul MN 55116	800-723-2424	651-649-5800
Merrimack Valley Distributing Co		
50 Prince St .... Danvers MA 01923	800-698-0250	978-777-2213
NKS Distributors Inc		
399 Churchmans Rd .... New Castle DE 19720	800-310-5099	302-322-1811
Pernod Ricard USA		
100 Manhattanville Rd .... Purchase NY 10577	800-847-5949	914-848-4800
Phillips Distributing Corp		
3010 Nob Hill Rd .... Madison WI 53713	800-236-7269	608-222-9177
Premier Beverage Company of Florida		
9801 Premier Pkwy .... Miramar FL 33025	800-432-2002	954-436-9200
R & R Marketing LLC		
10 Patton Dr .... West Caldwell NJ 07006	800-772-2096	973-228-5100
Remy Cointreau USA Inc		
1290 Ave of the Americas .... New York NY 10104	800-858-9898*	212-399-4200
General		
Savannah Distributing Co Inc		
2425 W Gwinnett St PO Box 1388 .... Savannah GA 31415	800-551-0777*	912-233-1167
General		
Southern Wine & Spirits of America Inc		
1600 NW 163rd St .... Miami FL 33169	800-776-0180	305-625-4171
Southern Wine & Spirits of Colorado		
5270 Fox St PO Box 5603 .... Denver CO 80216	800-332-9956	303-292-1711

	Toll-Free	Phone
Southern Wine & Spirits of Illinois		
300 E Crossroads Pkwy		
Bolingbrook Corp Ctr ....Bolingbrook IL 60440	800-776-0180	630-685-3000
Terlato Wine Group, The (TWG)		
900 Armour Dr ....Lake Bluff IL 60044	800-950-7676	847-604-8900
Winebow Inc		
75 Chestnut Ridge Rd ....Montvale NJ 07645	800-859-0689	201-445-0620
Wirtz Beverage Illinois LLC (WBI)		
3333 S Laramie Ave 11th Fl ....Cicero IL 60804	800-344-2838	708-298-3333
Young's Market Company LLC		
500 S Central Ave ....Los Angeles CA 90013	800-627-2777	213-612-1248

81   BICYCLES & BICYCLE PARTS & ACCESSORIES

SEE ALSO Sporting Goods ; Toys, Games, Hobbies

	Toll-Free	Phone
Cane Creek Cycling Components		
355 Cane Creek Rd ....Fletcher NC 28732	800-234-2725	828-684-3551
Huffy Bicycle Co		
6551 Centerville Business Pkwy ....Centerville OH 45459	800-872-2453	937-865-2800
Raleigh America Inc		
6004 S 190th St Ste 101.....................Kent WA 98032	800-222-5527	
Raleigh USA		
6004 S 190th St Ste 101.....................Kent WA 98032	800-222-5527	253-395-1100
SMITH Mfg Company Inc		
1610 S Dixie Hwy ....Pompano Beach FL 33060	800-653-9311	954-941-9744
Specialized Bicycle Components		
15130 Concord Cir ....Morgan Hill CA 95037	877-808-8154	408-779-6229
SRAM Corp		
1333 N Kingsbury St 4th Fl ....Chicago IL 60622	800-346-2928	312-664-8800
Terry Precision Bicycles for Women Inc		
47 Maple St ....Burlington VT 05401	800-289-8379	
Worksman Trading Corp		
94-15 100th St ....Ozone Park NY 11416	800-962-2453	718-322-2000

82   BIOMETRIC IDENTIFICATION EQUIPMENT & SOFTWARE

	Toll-Free	Phone
Bio Medic Data Systems Inc		
One Silas Rd ....Seaford DE 19973	800-526-2637	302-628-4100
Count Me In LLC		
1530 E Dundee Ste 150 ....Palatine IL 60074	866-514-5888	
Crossmatch		
720 Bay Rd Ste 100 ....Redwood City CA 94063	866-463-7792	650-474-4000
MorphoTrak Inc		
113 S Columbus St 4th Fl ....Alexandria VA 22314	800-601-6790	703-797-2600
NEC Corp of America		
10850 Gold Ctr Dr Ste 200 ....Rancho Cordova CA 95670	800-632-4636	916-463-7000
SIRCHIE Finger Print Laboratories Inc		
100 Hunter Pl ....Youngsville NC 27596	800-356-7311	919-554-2244

83   BIO-RECOVERY SERVICES

Companies listed here provide services for managing and eliminating biohazard dangers that may be present after a death or injury. These services include cleaning, disinfecting, and deodorizing biohazard scenes resulting from accidents, homicides, suicides, natural deaths, and similar events.

	Toll-Free	Phone
Bio-Recovery Corp		
1863 Pond Rd Ste 4 ....Ronkonkoma NY 11779	800-556-0621	631-676-2600
Bio-Scene Recovery		
13191 Meadow St NE ....Alliance OH 44601	877-380-5500	330-823-5500
Grangeville Environmental Services (GES)		
GES Property Pros LLC		
585 McAllister St ....Hanover PA 17331	866-437-5151	717-637-6152
JP Maguire Assoc Inc		
266 Brookside Rd ....Waterbury CT 06708	877-576-2484	203-755-2297
Peerless Cleaners Inc		
519 N Monroe St ....Decatur IL 62522	800-879-7056	217-423-7703

84   BIOTECHNOLOGY COMPANIES

SEE ALSO Medicinal Chemicals & Botanical Products ; Pharmaceutical Companies ; Pharmaceutical Companies - Generic Drugs ; Diagnostic Products

	Toll-Free	Phone
Alkermes Inc 852 Winter St ....Waltham MA 02451	800-848-4876	781-609-6000
NASDAQ: ALKS		
Alnylam Pharmaceuticals Inc		
300 Third St 3rd Fl ....Cambridge MA 02142	866-330-0326	617-551-8200
NASDAQ: ALNY		
American Bio Medica Corp (ABMC)		
122 Smith Rd ....Kinderhook NY 12106	800-227-1243*	518-758-8158
OTC: ABMC ■ *General		
Amgen Canada Inc		
6775 Financial Dr Ste 100 ....Mississauga ON L5N0A4	800-665-4273	905-285-3000
Amgen Inc		
One Amgen Ctr Dr ....Thousand Oaks CA 91320	800-563-9798	805-447-1000
AmpliPhi Biosciences Corp		
4870 Sadler Rd Ste 300 ....Glen Allen VA 23060	877-795-3647	804-205-5069
OTC: APHB		
Antibodies Inc PO Box 1560 ....Davis CA 95617	800-824-8540	
ArQule Inc		
19 Presidential Way ....Woburn MA 01801	800-373-7827	781-994-0300
NASDAQ: ARQL		
Array BioPharma Inc		
3200 Walnut St ....Boulder CO 80301	877-633-2436	303-381-6600
NASDAQ: ARRY		
Astellas Pharma US Inc		
One Astellas Way ....Northbrook IL 60062	800-695-4321	
Astex Pharmaceuticals		
4140 Dublin Blvd Ste 200............Dublin CA 94568	877-534-2590	925-560-0100

			Toll-Free	Phone
AtriCure Inc				
6217 Centre Pk Dr ....West Chester OH		45069	888-347-6403	513-755-4100
NASDAQ: ATRC				
BD Biosciences PharMingen				
10975 Torreyana Rd ....San Diego CA		92121	800-848-6227	858-812-8800
Bellus Health Inc				
275 Armand Frappier Blvd ....Laval QC		H7V4A7	877-680-4500	450-680-4500
TSE: BLU				
Biogen Idec Inc				
133 Boston Post Rd ....Weston MA		02493	877-750-8536	781-464-2000
NASDAQ: BIIB				
BioReliance Corp				
14920 Broschart Rd ....Rockville MD		20850	800-553-5372	301-738-1000
Cangene Corp				
155 Innovation Dr ....Winnipeg MB		R3T5Y3	800-768-2304	204-275-4200
TSE: CNJ				
Cardiome Pharma Corp				
6190 Agronomy Rd 6th Fl......Vancouver BC		V6T1Z3	800-330-9928	604-677-6905
NASDAQ: CRME				
CEL-SCI Corp				
8229 Boone Blvd Ste 802 ....Vienna VA		22182	800-422-6237	703-506-9460
NYSE: CVM				
Celgene Corp 86 Morris Ave ....Summit NJ		07901	888-771-0141	908-673-9000
NASDAQ: CELG				
Cell Therapeutics Inc (CTI)				
501 Elliott Ave W Ste 400 ....Seattle WA		98119	800-215-2355	206-282-7100
NASDAQ: CTIC				
Cerus Corp 2550 Stanwell Dr ......Concord CA		94520	800-401-1957	925-288-6000
NASDAQ: CERS				
Colorado Serum Co				
4950 York St PO Box 16428 ....Denver CO		80216	800-525-2065*	303-295-7527
*Orders				
CombiMatrix Corp				
300 Goddard Ste 100 ....Irvine CA		92618	800-710-0624	949-753-0624
NASDAQ: CBMX				
Cook Biotech Inc				
1425 Innovation Pl ......West Lafayette IN		47906	888-299-4224	765-497-3355
Covance Inc				
210 Carnegie Ctr ....Princeton NJ		08540	888-268-2623	609-419-2240
NYSE: CVD				
Cryolife Inc				
1655 Roberts Blvd NW ....Kennesaw GA		30144	800-438-8285	770-419-3355
NYSE: CRY				
Cubist Pharmaceuticals Inc				
65 Hayden Ave ....Lexington MA		02421	877-282-4786	781-860-8660
NASDAQ: CBST				
Cytokinetics Inc				
280 E Grand Ave .....South San Francisco CA		94080	800-546-5141	650-624-3000
NASDAQ: CYTK				
Dendreon Corp				
3005 First Ave ....Seattle WA		98121	877-256-4545	206-256-4545
OTC: DNDNQ				
DexCom Inc				
6340 Sequence Dr ....San Diego CA		92121	888-738-3646	858-200-0200
NASDAQ: DXCM				
Dow AgroSciences LLC				
9330 Zionsville Rd ....Indianapolis IN		46268	800-258-1470	317-337-3000
DUSA Pharmaceuticals Inc				
25 Upton Dr ....Wilmington MA		01887	877-533-3872	978-657-7500
NASDAQ: DUSA				
EMD Serono Inc				
1 Technology Pl ....Rockland MA		02370	800-283-8088	781-982-9000
Encore Medical Corp				
9800 Metric Blvd ....Austin TX		78758	800-456-8696	512-832-9500
Enzo Biochem Inc				
527 Madison Ave ....New York NY		10022	800-522-5052	212-583-0100
NYSE: ENZ				
Galectin Therapeutics				
Seven Wells Ave Ste 34 ....Newton MA		02459	888-286-8010	617-559-0033
Genaera Corp				
5110 Campus Dr ......Plymouth Meeting PA		19462	800-299-9156	610-941-4020
Generex Biotechnology Corp				
555 Richmond St W Ste 202.......Toronto ON		M5J2G2	800-391-6755	416-364-2551
OTC: GNBT				
Genomic Health Inc				
101 Galveston Dr ....Redwood City CA		94063	866-662-6897	650-556-9300
NASDAQ: GHDX				
Genzyme Corp				
500 Kendall St ....Cambridge MA		02142	800-745-4447	617-252-7500
Gilead Sciences Inc				
333 Lakeside Dr ....Foster City CA		94404	800-445-3235	650-574-3000
NASDAQ: GILD				
Grifols USA LLC				
2410 Lillyvale Ave ....Los Angeles CA		90032	888-474-3657	
Idenix Pharmaceuticals Inc				
One Merck Dr P.O. Box 100 .Whitehouse Station NJ		08889	800-770-4674	908-423-1000
NYSE: MRK				
Illumina Inc				
9885 Towne Centre Dr ....San Diego CA		92121	800-809-4566	858-202-4500
NASDAQ: ILMN				
Immunomedics Inc				
300 American Rd ....Morris Plains NJ		07950	800-327-7211	973-605-8200
NASDAQ: IMMU				
Integra LifeSciences Holdings Corp				
311 Enterprise Dr ....Plainsboro NJ		08536	800-654-2873	609-275-0500
NASDAQ: IART				
Irvine Scientific				
2511 Daimler St ....Santa Ana CA		92705	800-577-6097	949-261-7800
Isis Pharmaceuticals Inc				
2855 Gazelle Ct ....Carlsbad CA		92008	800-679-4747	760-931-9200
NASDAQ: ISIS				
Ivers-Lee Inc 31 Hansen S ....Brampton ON		L6W3H7	800-265-1009	905-451-5535
Leo Pharma Inc				
123 Commerce Vly Dr E Ste 400 ...Thornhill ON		L3T7W8	800-668-7234*	905-886-9822
*General				
Lexicon Pharmaceuticals Inc				
8800 Technology Forest Pl .....The Woodlands TX		77381	855-828-4651	281-863-3000
NASDAQ: LXRX				

				Toll-Free	Phone

LifeCore Biomedical LLC
3515 Lyman Blvd . . . . Chaska MN 55318 · **800-752-2663*** · 952-368-4300
*Cust Svc

LiphaTech Inc
3600 W Elm St . . . . Milwaukee WI 53209 · **888-331-7900**

Medicines Co
Eight Sylvan Way . . . . Parsippany NJ 07054 · **800-388-1183** · 973-290-6000
NASDAQ: MDCO

Mera Pharmaceuticals Inc
73-4460 Queen Kaahumanu Hwy
Ste 110 . . . . Kailua-Kona HI 96740 · **800-480-6515** · 808-326-9301

Myriad Genetics Inc
320 Wakara Way . . . . Salt Lake City UT 84108 · **800-469-7423** · 801-584-3600
NASDAQ: MYGN

N.E.T. Inc
5651 Palmer Way Ste C . . . . Carlsbad CA 92010 · **800-888-4638** · 760-929-5980
Nordion 447 March Rd . . . . Ottawa ON K2K1X8 · **800-465-3666** · 613-592-2790
NYSE: NDZ

Novartis Vaccines & Diagnostics
One Health Plz Bldg 122 . . . . East Hanover NJ 07936 · **888-644-8585** · 862-778-8300
NYSE: NVS

Novavax Inc
9920 Belward Campus Dr . . . . Rockville MD 20850 · **800-642-1687** · 240-268-2000
NASDAQ: NVAX

Nuo Therapeutics Inc
207A Perry Pkwy Ste 1 . . . . Gaithersburg MD 20877 · **866-298-6633**
OTC: NUOT

Nuvo Research Inc
7560 Airport Rd Unit 10 . . . . Mississauga ON L4T4H4 · **888-398-3463** · 905-673-6980
TSE: NRI

Oakwood Laboratories LLC
7670 First Pl Ste A . . . . Oakwood Village OH 44146 · **888-625-9352** · 440-359-0000

Oncolytics Biotech Inc
1167 Kensington Crescent NW Ste 210 . . . . Calgary AB T2N1X7 · **800-731-5319** · 403-670-7377
TSE: ONC

Onyx Pharmaceuticals Inc
249 E Grand Av . . . . South San Francisco CA 94080 · **877-669-9121** · 650-266-0000
NASDAQ: ONXX

Osteotech Inc
710 Medtronic Pkwy . . . . Minneapolis MN 55432 · **800-633-8766** · 763-514-4000

Paladin Labs Inc
100 Blvd Alexis Nihon Ste 600 . . . . St-Laurent QC H4M2P2 · **888-376-7830** · 514-340-1112
TSE: PLB

Peregrine Pharmaceuticals Inc
14282 Franklin Ave Ste 100 . . . . Tustin CA 92780 · **800-987-8256** · 714-508-6000
NASDAQ: PPHM

Pharmacyclics Inc
995 E Arques Ave . . . . Sunnyvale CA 94085 · **800-458-0330** · 408-774-0330
NASDAQ: PCYC

Primorigen Biosciences Inc
510 Charmany Dr . . . . Madison WI 53719 · **866-372-7442** · 608-441-8332

Progenics Pharmaceuticals Inc
777 Old Saw Mill River Rd . . . . Tarrytown NY 10591 · **866-644-7188** · 914-789-2800
NASDAQ: PGNX

Protein Sciences Corp
1000 Research Pkwy . . . . Meriden CT 06450 · **800-488-7099** · 203-686-0800

Psychemedics Corp
125 Nagog Pk Ste 200 . . . . Acton MA 01720 · **800-628-8073** · 978-206-8220
NASDAQ: PMD

QLT Inc
887 Great Northern Way Ste 101 . . . . Vancouver BC V5T4T5 · **800-663-5486** · 604-707-7000
NASDAQ: QLT

Questcor Pharmaceuticals Inc
1300 N Kellogg Ste D . . . . Anaheim Hills CA 92807 · **888-435-2284** · 714-786-4200
NASDAQ: QCOR

Regeneron Pharmaceuticals Inc
777 Old Saw Mill River Rd . . . . Tarrytown NY 10591 · **800-637-8322** · 914-847-7000
NASDAQ: REGN

Repligen Corp 41 Seyon St . . . . Waltham MA 02453 · **800-622-2259*** · 781-250-0111
NASDAQ: RGEN ■ *Sales

Roche Palo Alto LLC
4300 Hacienda Dr . . . . Pleasanton CA 94588 · **866-796-1569** · 925-730-8000

RTI Biologics Inc
11621 Research Cir . . . . Alachua FL 32615 · **877-343-6832** · 386-418-8888
NASDAQ: RTIX

Sanofi Pasteur Inc
Discovery Dr . . . . Swiftwater PA 18370 · **800-822-2463*** · 570-839-7187
*Orders

Sanofi-Aventis Canada
2150 St Elzear Blvd W . . . . Laval QC H7L4A8 · **800-363-6364** · 514-331-9220

Santarus Inc
3721 Vly Centre Dr
Ste 400 Fourth Fl . . . . San Diego CA 92130 · **888-778-0887*** · 858-314-5700
NASDAQ: SNTS ■ *Cust Svc

Sequenom Inc
3595 John Hopkins Ct . . . . San Diego CA 92121 · **877-821-7266** · 858-202-9000
NASDAQ: SQNM

Soligenix Inc
29 Emmons Dr Ste C-10 . . . . Princeton NJ 08540 · **877-407-3974** · 609-538-8200
OTC: SNGX

Spectrum Pharmaceuticals Inc
11500 S Eastern Ave Ste 240 . . . . Henderson NV 89052 · **800-332-1088** · 702-835-6300
NASDAQ: SPPI

Takeda Canada Inc
435 N Service Rd W Ste 101 . . . . Oakville ON L6M4X8 · **888-367-3331** · 905-469-9333

Telesta Therapeutics Inc
275 Labrosse Ave . . . . Pointe-Claire QC H9R1A3 · **800-387-0825** · 514-697-6636
TSE: TST

Threshold Pharmaceuticals Inc
170 Harbor Way Suite 300 . . . . South San Francisco CA 94080 · **866-276-9886** · 650-474-8200
NASDAQ: THLD

Titan Pharmaceuticals Inc
400 Oyster Pt Blvd
Ste 505 . . . . South San Francisco CA 94080 · **888-417-8516** · 650-244-4990
OTC: TTNP

ViroPharma Inc
730 Stockton Dr . . . . Exton PA 19341 · **877-841-4559** · 610-458-7300
NASDAQ: VPHM

XOMA (US) LLC
2910 Seventh St . . . . Berkeley CA 94710 · **800-468-9716** · 510-204-7200
NASDAQ: XOMA

ZymoGenetics Inc
1201 Eastlake Ave E . . . . Seattle WA 98102 · **800-332-2056** · 206-442-6600

85   BLANKBOOKS & BINDERS

SEE ALSO Checks - Personal & Business

				Toll-Free	Phone

Abco Inc 1621 Wall St . . . . Dallas TX 75215 · **800-969-2226** · 214-565-1191
Advanced Looseleaf Technologies Inc
1424 Somerset Ave . . . . Dighton MA 02715 · **800-339-6354** · 508-669-6354
Allison Payment Systems LLC
2200 Production Dr . . . . Indianapolis IN 46241 · **800-755-2440**
American Thermoplastic Co (ATC)
106 Gamma Dr . . . . Pittsburgh PA 15238 · **800-245-6600**
Avery Dennison Corp
207 Goode Ave . . . . Glendale CA 91203 · **888-567-4387*** · 626-304-2000
NYSE: AVY ■ *Cust Svc
Blackbourn
200 Fourth Ave N . . . . Edgerton MN 56128 · **800-842-7550**
Blair Packaging Inc
1515 Independence St . . . . Cape Girardeau MO 63703 · **800-624-3150** · 573-334-2146
Colad Group 801 Exchange St . . . . Buffalo NY 14210 · **800-950-1755** · 716-961-1776
Continental Binder & Specialty Corp
407 W Compton Blvd . . . . Gardena CA 90248 · **800-872-2897** · 310-324-8227
Continental Loose Leaf Inc
1122 16th Ave . . . . Minneapolis MN 55414 · **888-719-5013** · 612-378-4800
Data Management Inc
537 New Britain Ave . . . . Farmington CT 06034 · **800-243-1969*** · 860-677-8586
*Orders
Dilley Manufacturing Co
215 E Third St . . . . Des Moines IA 50309 · **800-247-5087** · 515-288-7289
EBSCO Industries Inc Vulcan Information Packaging Div
PO Box 29 . . . . Vincent AL 35178 · **800-633-4526**
Eckhart & Company Inc
4011 W 54th St . . . . Indianapolis IN 46254 · **800-443-3791** · 317-347-2665
Federal Business Products Inc
95 Main Ave . . . . Clifton NJ 07014 · **800-927-5123** · 973-667-9800
Fey Industries Inc
200 Fourth Ave N . . . . Edgerton MN 56128 · **800-533-5340** · 507-442-4311
Formflex Inc
PO Box 218 . . . . Bloomingdale IN 47832 · **800-255-7659**
General Loose Leaf Bindery Co
3811 Hawthorn Ct . . . . Waukegan IL 60087 · **800-621-0493** · 847-244-9700
Holum & Sons Company Inc
740 Burr Oak Dr . . . . Westmont IL 60559 · **800-447-4479** · 630-654-8222
Kurtz Bros Company Inc
400 Reed St PO Box 392 . . . . Clearfield PA 16830 · **800-252-3811** · 814-765-6561
Michael Lewis Co
8900 W 50th St . . . . McCook IL 60525 · **800-323-8808** · 708-688-2200
NAPCO Inc 120 Trojan Ave . . . . Sparta NC 28675 · **800-854-8621** · 336-372-5228
Northeast Data Services
1316 College Ave . . . . Elmira NY 14901 · **800-699-5636*** · 607-733-5541
*Cust Svc
Roaring Spring Blank Book Co
740 Spang St . . . . Roaring Spring PA 16673 · **800-441-1653** · 814-224-5141
Samsill Corp
5740 Hartman Rd . . . . Fort Worth TX 76119 · **800-255-1100** · 817-536-1906
Southwest Plastic Binding Co
109 Millwell Ct . . . . Maryland Heights MO 63043 · **800-325-3628** · 314-739-4400
Spiral Binding Company Inc
One Maltese Dr . . . . Totowa NJ 07511 · **800-631-3572** · 973-256-0666
Superior Press Inc
11930 Hamden Pl . . . . Santa Fe Springs CA 90670 · **888-590-7998*** · 562-948-1866
*Cust Svc
Trendex Inc
240 E Maryland Ave . . . . Saint Paul MN 55117 · **800-328-9200** · 651-489-4655
Union Group 649 Alden St . . . . Fall River MA 02722 · **800-289-3523** · 508-675-4545
US Ring Binder
6800 Arsenal St . . . . Saint Louis MO 63139 · **800-888-8772** · 314-645-7880
ViaTech Publishing Solutions
1440 Fifth Ave . . . . Bay Shore NY 11706 · **800-645-8558** · 631-968-8500

86   BLINDS & SHADES

				Toll-Free	Phone

Aeroshade Inc
433 Oakland Ave . . . . Waukesha WI 53186 · **800-331-7179** · 262-547-2101
Beauti-Vue Products Inc
8555 194th Ave Bristol Industrial Pk . . . . Bristol WI 53104 · **800-558-9431** · 262-857-2306
Budget Blinds Inc
1927 N Glassell St . . . . Orange CA 92865 · **800-800-9250** · 714-637-2100
Comfortex Window Fashions Inc
21 Elm St . . . . Maplewood NY 12189 · **800-843-4151*** · 518-273-3333
*Cust Svc
Delaine James Inc
10508C Boyer Blvd Ste 400 . . . . Austin TX 78758 · **800-999-5333*** · 512-835-5333
*Claims
Hunter Douglas Inc
1 Hunter Douglas Dr . . . . Cumberland MD 21502 · **800-365-3399** · 301-722-7700
Kenney Mfg Co
1000 Jefferson Blvd . . . . Warwick RI 02886 · **800-753-6639*** · 401-739-2200
*Cust Svc
Lafayette Venetian Blind Inc
3000 Klondike Rd.
P.O. Box 2838 . . . . West Lafayette IN 47996 · **800-342-5523**
Levolor Kirsch Window Fashions
4110 Premier Dr . . . . High Point NC 27265 · **800-752-9677** · 336-812-8181
Mill Supply Div 266 Morse St . . . . Hamden CT 06517 · **888-585-9354*** · 203-777-7668
*General
Sun Control Products Window Shades
1908 Second St SW . . . . Rochester MN 55902 · **800-533-0010** · 507-282-2620
Warm Co 5529 186th Pl SW . . . . Lynnwood WA 98037 · **800-234-9276** · 425-248-2424

87 — BLISTER PACKAGING

				Toll-Free	Phone
Andex Industries Inc					
1911 Fourth Ave N	Escanaba	MI	49829	800-338-9882	
Card Pak Inc 29601 Solon Rd	Solon	OH	44139	800-824-3342	440-542-3100
Placon Corp 6096 McKee Rd	Madison	WI	53719	800-541-1535	608-271-5634
Primary Packaging Inc					
10810 Industrial Pkwy NW	Bolivar	OH	44612	800-774-2247	330-874-3131
Wynalda Packaging					
8221 Graphic Dr NE	Belmont	MI	49306	800-952-8668*	616-866-1561
*General					

88 — BLOOD CENTERS

SEE ALSO Laboratories - Drug-Testing ; Laboratories - Genetic Testing ; Laboratories - Medical
The centers listed here are members of America's Blood Centers (ABC), the national network of non-profit, independent community blood centers. ABC members are licensed and regulated by the US Food & Drug Administration.

				Toll-Free	Phone
Belle Bonfils Memorial Blood Ctr					
717 Yosemite St	Denver	CO	80230	800-365-0006	303-341-4000
Blood Assurance Inc					
705 E Fourth St	Chattanooga	TN	37403	800-962-0628	423-756-0966
Blood Bank of Delmarva					
100 Hygeia Dr	Newark	DE	19713	800-548-4009	302-737-8405
Blood Bank of Hawaii					
2043 Dillingham Blvd	Honolulu	HI	96819	800-372-9966	808-845-9966
Blood Bank of the Redwoods					
2324 Bethards Dr	Santa Rosa	CA	95405	888-393-4483	707-545-1222
Blood Centers of the Pacific					
250 Bush St	San Francisco	CA	94104	888-393-4483	415-567-6400
Blood Ctr of New Jersey					
45 S Grove St	East Orange	NJ	07018	866-228-1500	973-676-4700
Blood Ctr, The					
2609 Canal St	New Orleans	LA	70112	800-862-5663	504-524-1322
BloodCenter of Wisconsin					
638 N 18th St	Milwaukee	WI	53233	877-232-4376	414-933-5000
BloodSource 1608 Q St	Sacramento	CA	95811	800-995-4420	916-456-1500
Carter BloodCare					
2205 Hwy 121	Bedford	TX	76021	800-366-2834	817-412-5000
Cascade Regional Blood Services					
220 S 'I' St	Tacoma	WA	98405	877-242-5663	253-383-2553
Central Illinois Community Blood Ctr					
1134 S Seventh St	Springfield	IL	62703	800-448-3253*	217-753-1530
*Help Line					
Central Jersey Blood Ctr					
494 Sycamore Ave	Shrewsbury	NJ	07702	888-712-5663	732-842-5750
Central Kentucky Blood Ctr					
3121 Beaumont Centre Cir	Lexington	KY	40513	800-775-2522	859-276-2534
Central Pennsylvania Blood Bank					
8167 Adams Dr	Hummelstown	PA	17036	800-771-0059	717-566-6161
Coastal Bend Blood Ctr					
209 N Padre Island Dr	Corpus Christi	TX	78406	800-299-4943	361-855-4943
Community Blood Bank of Northwest Pennsylvania					
2646 Peach St	Erie	PA	16508	877-842-0631	814-456-4206
Community Blood Ctr					
349 S Main St	Dayton	OH	45402	800-388-4483	937-461-3450
Blue Springs Ctr					
4040 Main St	Kansas City	MO	64111	888-647-4040	816-753-4040
Community Blood Ctr Inc					
4406 W Spencer St	Appleton	WI	54914	800-280-4102	920-738-3131
Community Blood Ctr of the Ozarks					
220 W Plainview Rd	Springfield	MO	65810	800-280-5337	417-227-5000
Community Blood Services of Illinois					
1408 W University Ave	Urbana	IL	61801	800-217-4483	217-367-2202
Delta Blood Bank					
65 N Commerce St	Stockton	CA	95201	888-942-5663	209-943-3830
Gulf Coast Regional Blood Ctr					
1400 La Concha Ln	Houston	TX	77054	888-482-5663	713-790-1200
Heartland Blood Centers					
1200 N Highland Ave	Aurora	IL	60506	800-786-4483	630-892-7055
Hemacare Corp					
15350 Sherman Way Ste 350	Van Nuys	CA	91406	877-310-0717	818-226-1968
Hoxworth Blood Ctr University of Cincinnati Medical Ctr					
3130 Highland Ave ML0055	Cincinnati	OH	45267	800-265-1515	513-558-1200
Inland Northwest Blood Ctr					
210 W Cataldo Ave	Spokane	WA	99201	800-423-0151	509-624-0151
Lifeblood Mid-South Regional Blood Ctr					
1040 Madison Ave	Memphis	TN	38104	888-543-3256	901-522-8585
LifeServe Blood Ctr					
431 E Locust St	Des Moines	IA	50309	800-287-4903	
LifeShare Blood Centers					
8910 Linwood Ave	Shreveport	LA	71106	800-256-4483	318-222-7770
LifeShare Community Blood Services					
105 Cleveland St	Elyria	OH	44035	800-317-5412	440-322-5700
LifeSource Blood Services					
2764 Aurora Ave	Naperville	IL	60540	877-543-3768	
LifeSouth Community Blood Centers					
4039 Newberry Rd	Gainesville	FL	32607	888-795-2707	
LifeSouth Community Blood Centers Atlanta					
4891 Ashford Dunwoody Rd	Atlanta	GA	30338	888-795-2707	404-329-1994
Memorial Blood Centers (MBC)					
737 Pelham Blvd	Saint Paul	MN	55114	888-448-3253*	651-332-7000
*Cust Svc					
Michigan Community Blood Centers					
1036 Fuller Ave NE	Grand Rapids	MI	49503	866-642-5663	616-774-2300
Michigan Community Blood Centers Northwest					
2575 Aero Pk Dr	Traverse City	MI	49686	866-642-5663*	231-935-3030
*General					
Mississippi Blood Services					
115 Tree St	Flowood	MS	39232	888-902-5663	601-981-3232

				Toll-Free	Phone
Mississippi Valley Regional Blood Ctr					
5500 Lakeview Pkwy	Davenport	IA	52807	800-747-5401	563-359-5401
MVRBC 5500 Lakeview Pkwy	Davenport	IA	52501	800-747-5401	641-682-8149
Nebraska Community Blood Bank					
100 N 84th St	Lincoln	NE	68505	877-486-9414	402-486-9414
Oklahoma Blood Institute (OBI)					
1001 N Lincoln Blvd	Oklahoma City	OK	73104	866-708-4995	405-278-3100
Puget Sound Blood Ctr					
921 Terry Ave	Seattle	WA	98104	800-366-2831	206-292-6500
Rhode Island Blood Ctr					
405 Promenade St	Providence	RI	02908	800-283-8385	401-453-8360
Rock River Valley Blood Ctr					
3065 N Perryville Rd Ste 105	Rockford	IL	61114	877-778-2299*	815-965-8751
*General					
San Diego Blood Bank					
440 Upas St	San Diego	CA	92103	800-479-3902	619-296-6393
SeraCare Life Sciences Inc					
37 Birch St	Milford	MA	01757	800-676-1881	508-244-6400
NASDAQ: SRLS					
South Texas Blood & Tissue Ctr					
6211 IH-10 W	San Antonio	TX	78201	800-292-5534	210-731-5555
United Blood Services					
6210 E Oak St PO Box 1867	Scottsdale	AZ	85257	800-288-2199	480-946-4201
United Blood Services of Arizona					
Chandler					
6220 E Oak St Ste 33	Scottsdale	AZ	85252	877-827-4376	
San Luis Obispo					
4119 Broad St Ste 100	San Luis Obispo	CA	93401	877-827-4376	805-543-4290
United Blood Services of Colorado					
146 Sawyer Dr	Durango	CO	81303	800-288-2199	970-385-4601
United Blood Services of Mississippi					
Meridian 1115 25th Ave	Meridian	MS	39301	877-827-4376	601-482-2482
United Blood Services of Montana					
Billings 1444 Grand Ave	Billings	MT	59102	800-365-4450	406-248-9168
Albuquerque					
1515 University Blvd NE	Albuquerque	NM	87102	800-333-8037	
United Blood Services of New Mexico					
Farmington 475 E 20th St	Farmington	NM	87401	888-804-9913	
Las Cruces					
1200 Commerce Dr	Las Cruces	NM	88011	800-582-3146*	575-527-1322
*General					
United Blood Services of North Dakota					
Bismarck 517 S Seventh St	Bismarck	ND	58504	800-456-6159	
Fargo 3231 S 11th St	Fargo	ND	58104	800-288-2199*	701-293-9453
*General					
United Blood Services of Texas					
El Paso 424 S Mesa Hills	El Paso	TX	79912	877-827-4376	915-544-5422
McAllen 1400 S Sixth St	McAllen	TX	78501	888-827-4376*	956-213-7500
*General					
San Angelo					
2020 W Beauregard Ave	San Angelo	TX	76901	800-756-0024*	325-223-7500
*General					

89 — BOATS - RECREATIONAL

				Toll-Free	Phone
Alumaweld Boats Inc					
1601 Ave F	White City	OR	97503	800-401-2628	541-826-7171
Bertram Yacht Inc					
3663 NW 21st St	Miami	FL	33142	800-256-4646	305-633-8011
Boston Whaler Inc					
100 Whaler Way	Edgewater	FL	32141	877-294-5645	
Carolina Skiff Inc					
3231 Fulford Rd	Waycross	GA	31503	800-422-7282	912-287-0547
Chris-Craft Boats					
8161 15th St E	Sarasota	FL	34243	800-845-5255	941-351-4900
Cobalt Boats LLC					
1715 N Eigth St	Neodesha	KS	66757	800-468-5764	620-325-2653
Concept Boats Corp					
2410 NW 147th St	Opa Locka	FL	33054	888-635-8712	305-635-8712
Correct Craft Inc					
14700 Aerospace Pkwy	Orlando	FL	32809	800-346-2092	407-855-4141
Donzi Marine					
1653 WhichaRds Beach Rd PO Box 457	Washington	NC	27889	800-624-3304	
Ebbtide Corp					
2545 Jones Creek Rd	White Bluff	TN	37187	866-467-4010	615-797-3193
Egg Harbor Yachts Inc					
801 Philadelphia Ave					
PO Box 702	Egg Harbor City	NJ	08215	800-960-6764	609-965-2300
Everglades Boats					
544 Air Pk Rd	Edgewater	FL	32132	800-368-5647	386-409-2202
Glacier Bay Catamarans					
1090 W Saint James St	Tarboro	NC	27886	855-662-4855	
Glastron Boats					
710 Co Rd 75	St Joseph	MN	56374	855-272-2709	320-433-2141
Hinckley Co, The					
One Little Harbor Landing	Portsmouth	RI	02871	866-446-2553	401-683-7005
Hobie Cat Co					
4925 Oceanside Blvd	Oceanside	CA	92056	800-462-4349	760-758-9100
Island Runner Boats					
PO Box 530098	Lake Park	FL	33403	800-749-4322	954-829-3252
Johnson Outdoors Inc					
555 Main St	Racine	WI	53403	800-468-9716	262-631-6600
NASDAQ: JOUT					
Larson Boats					
700 Paul Larson Memorial Dr	Little Falls	MN	56345	800-336-2628*	320-632-5481
*General					
Lowe Boats					
2900 Industrial Dr	Lebanon	MO	65536	800-641-4372	417-532-9101
Mainship Corp					
255 Diesel Rd	St Augustine	FL	32084	800-771-5556	904-827-2007
MasterCraft Boat Co					
100 Cherokee Cove Dr	Vonore	TN	37885	800-443-8774	423-884-2221
Porta-Bote International					
1074 Independence Ave	Mountain View	CA	94043	800-227-8882	650-961-5334
Porter Inc 2200 W Monroe St	Decatur	IN	46733	800-736-7685	260-724-9111

				Toll-Free	Phone

Pursuit Boats
3901 St Lucie Blvd . . . . Fort Pierce FL 34946 **800-947-8778** 772-465-6006

Regal Marine Industries Inc
2300 Jetport Dr . . . . Orlando FL 32809 **800-877-3425** 407-851-4360

Riverside Marine Inc
11051 Pulaski Hwy . . . . White Marsh MD 21162 **800-448-6872** 410-335-1500

Silverton Marine Corp
301 Riverside Dr . . . . Millville NJ 08332 **800-524-2804** 856-825-4117

Smoker Craft PO Box 65 . . . . New Paris IN 46553 **866-719-7873**

Stamas Yacht Inc
300 Pampas Ave . . . . Tarpon Springs FL 34689 **800-782-6271*** 727-937-4118
*Sales

Starcraft Marine LLC
68143 Clunette St PO Box 65 . . . . New Paris IN 46553 **800-535-5722** 574-831-2103

Stevens Marine Inc
9180 SW Burnham St . . . . Tigard OR 97223 **800-225-7023** 503-620-7023

World Cat
1090 W St James St . . . . Tarboro NC 27886 **866-485-8899** 252-641-8000

90 BOILER SHOPS

				Toll-Free	Phone

Adamson Global Technology Corp
13101 N Eron Church Rd . . . . Chester VA 23836 **800-525-7703**

Aerofin Corp
4621 Murray Pl PO Box 10819 . . . . Lynchburg VA 24506 **800-237-6346** 434-845-7081

American Welding & Tank Co
4718 Old Gettysburg Rd Ste 300 . . . . Mechanicsburg PA 17055 **800-345-2495** 717-763-5080

API Heat Transfer Inc
2777 Walden Ave . . . . Buffalo NY 14225 **877-274-4328** 716-684-6700

Arrow Tank & Engineering Co
650 N Emerson St . . . . Cambridge MN 55008 **888-892-7769** 763-689-3360

AustinMohawk & Company Inc
2175 Beechgrove Pl . . . . Utica NY 13501 **800-765-3110** 315-793-3000

Babcock & Wilcox Co
20 S Van Buren Ave . . . . Barberton OH 44203 **800-222-2625** 330-753-4511

Babcock Power Inc
One Corporate Place
55 Ferncroft Road Ste 210 . . . . Danvers MA 01923 **800-523-0480** 978-646-3300

Chicago Boiler Co
1300 NW Ave . . . . Gurnee IL 60031 **800-522-7343*** 847-662-4000
*Cust Svc

Chicago Boiler Co CB Mills Div
1300 NW Ave . . . . Gurnee IL 60031 **800-522-7343** 847-662-4000

Clawson Tank Co
4545 Clawson Tank Dr . . . . Clarkston MI 48346 **800-272-1367** 248-625-8700

Columbian Tectank
2101 S 21st St PO Box 996 . . . . Parsons KS 67357 **800-555-8265** 620-421-0200

Eaton Metal Products Co
4803 York St . . . . Denver CO 80216 **800-208-2657** 303-296-4800

Enerfab Inc
4955 Spring Grove Ave . . . . Cincinnati OH 45232 **800-772-5066** 513-641-0500

Energy Exchanger Co
1844 N Garnett Rd . . . . Tulsa OK 74116 **800-760-6700** 918-437-3000

Engineered Storage Products Co
345 Harvestore Dr . . . . DeKalb IL 60115 **800-880-3663** 815-756-1551

Essick Air Products Inc
5800 Murray St . . . . Little Rock AR 72209 **800-643-8341** 501-562-1094

Fafco Inc 435 Otterson Dr . . . . Chico CA 95928 **800-994-7652** 530-332-2100

Hammersmith Mfg & Sales Inc
401 Central Ave . . . . Horton KS 66439 **800-375-8245** 785-486-2121

Harsco Industrial Air-X-Changers
5215 Arkansas Rd PO Box 1804 . . . . Catoosa OK 74015 **800-404-3904** 918-619-8000

Hurst Boiler & Welding Company Inc
PO Box 530 . . . . Coolidge GA 31738 **877-994-8778** 229-346-3545

ITT Standard
175 Standard Pkwy . . . . Cheektowaga NY 14227 **800-447-7700** 800-281-4111

Mgs Inc
178 Muddy Creek Church Rd . . . . Denver PA 17517 **800-952-4228** 717-336-7528

MiTek Industries Inc
14515 N Outer 40 Rd Ste 300 . . . . Chesterfield MO 63017 **800-325-8075** 314-434-1200

Modern Welding Company Inc
2880 New Hartford Rd . . . . Owensboro KY 42303 **800-922-1932** 270-685-4400

Ohmstede 895 N Main St . . . . Beaumont TX 77704 **800-568-2328** 409-833-6375

Pentair Residential Filtration LLC
20580 Enterprise Ave . . . . Brookfield WI 53008 **888-784-9065** 262-784-4490

Plant Maintenance Service Corp
3000 Fite Rd . . . . Memphis TN 38168 **800-459-9131** 901-353-9880

PVI Industries LLC
3209 Galvez Ave PO Box 7124 . . . . Fort Worth TX 76111 **800-784-8326** 817-335-9531

Redman Equipment & Mfg Co
19800 Normandie Ave . . . . Torrance CA 90502 **888-733-2602** 310-329-1134

Rocky Mountain Fabrication Inc
PO Box 16409 . . . . Salt Lake City UT 84116 **888-763-5307** 801-596-2400

Ross Technology Corp
104 N Maple Ave . . . . Leola PA 17540 **800-345-8170** 717-656-2200

Roy E Hanson Jr Mfg
1600 E Washington Blvd . . . . Los Angeles CA 90021 **800-421-9395** 213-747-7514

Sen-Dure Products Inc
6785 NW 17th Ave . . . . Fort Lauderdale FL 33309 **800-394-5112** 954-973-1260

Snap-Tite Autoclave Engineers Div
8325 Hessinger Dr . . . . Erie PA 16509 **800-458-0409** 814-838-5700

SPX Cooling Technologies
7401 W 129th St . . . . Overland Park KS 66213 **800-462-7539** 913-664-7400

Superior Boiler Works Inc
3524 E Fourth St PO Box 1527 . . . . Hutchinson KS 67504 **800-444-6693** 620-662-6693

Superior Die Set Corp
900 W Drexel Ave . . . . Oak Creek WI 53154 **800-558-6040** 414-764-4900

Sussman Automatic Corp
43-20 34th St . . . . Long Island City NY 11101 **800-727-8326** 718-937-4500

ThermaSys Corp
2776 Gunter Pk Dr E Ste RS . . . . Montgomery AL 36109 **877-274-4328** 334-244-9240

Thermodynetics Inc
651 Day Hill Rd . . . . Windsor CT 06095 **800-394-1633** 860-683-2005
OTC: TDYT

Tranter Inc
1900 Old Burk Hwy . . . . Wichita Falls TX 76306 **800-414-6908** 940-723-7125

				Toll-Free	Phone

Winbco Tank Co
1200 E Main St PO Box 618 . . . . Ottumwa IA 52501 **800-822-1855**

Worthington Industries
200 Old E Wilson Bridge Rd . . . . Columbus OH 43085 **866-928-2657** 614-438-3013

91 BOOK BINDING & RELATED WORK

SEE ALSO Printing Companies - Book Printers

				Toll-Free	Phone

Bindagraphics Inc
2701 Wilmarco Ave . . . . Baltimore MD 21223 **800-326-0300** 410-362-7200

Booksource Inc
1230 Macklind Ave . . . . Saint Louis MO 63110 **800-444-0435** 314-647-0600

Bound to Stay Bound Books Inc (BTSB)
1880 W Morton Ave . . . . Jacksonville IL 62650 **800-637-6586** 217-245-5191

Library Binding Service (LBS)
1801 Thompson Ave . . . . Des Moines IA 50316 **800-247-5323** 515-262-3191

Parker Powis Inc
775 Heinz Ave . . . . Berkeley CA 94710 **800-321-2463** 510-848-2463

Perma-Bound
617 E Vandalia Rd . . . . Jacksonville IL 62650 **800-637-6581** 217-243-5451

Reindl Bindery Company Inc
W194 N11381 McCormick Dr . . . . Germantown WI 53022 **800-878-1121** 262-293-1444

Rickard Circular Folding Co
325 N Ashland Ave . . . . Chicago IL 60607 **800-747-1389** 312-243-6300

Riverside Group
655 Driving Pk Ave . . . . Rochester NY 14613 **800-777-2463** 585-458-2090

Roswell Bookbinding Co
2614 N 29th Ave . . . . Phoenix AZ 85009 **888-803-8883** 602-272-9338

Wert Bookbinding Inc
9975 Allentown Blvd . . . . Grantville PA 17028 **800-344-9378*** 717-469-0629
*Cust Svc

92 BOOK, MUSIC, VIDEO CLUBS

				Toll-Free	Phone

NetFlix Inc
100 Winchester Cir . . . . Los Gatos CA 95032 **800-290-8191** 408-540-3700
NASDAQ: NFLX

Scholastic Arrow Book Club
555 Broadway . . . . New York NY 10012 **800-724-6527*** 212-343-6100
*Orders

Writer's Digest Book Club
4700 E Galbraith Rd . . . . Cincinnati OH 45236 **800-759-0963*** 513-531-2690
*Cust Svc

93 BOOK PRODUCERS

Book producers, or book packagers, work with authors, editors, printers, publishers, and others to provide all publication services except sales and order fulfillment. These publication services include editing of manuscripts, formatting of computer disks, producing books as a finished product, and helping the book publisher to develop marketing plans. Book producers listed here are members of the American Book Producers Association.

				Toll-Free	Phone

Focus Strategic Communications Inc
2474 Waterford St . . . . Oakville ON L6L5E6 **866-263-6287** 905-825-8757

Schlager Group Inc
325 N Saint Paul Ste 3425 . . . . Dallas TX 75201 **888-416-5727**

94 BOOKS, PERIODICALS, NEWSPAPERS - WHOL

				Toll-Free	Phone

21st Century Christian Inc
PO Box 40526 . . . . Nashville TN 37204 **800-251-2477** 615-383-3842

Advantage Mktg Inc
14 W Main St . . . . Ashland OH 44805 **800-670-7479** 419-281-4762

Baker & Taylor Inc
2550 W Tyvola Rd Ste 300 . . . . Charlotte NC 28217 **800-775-1800**

BMI Educational Services
PO Box 800 . . . . Dayton NJ 08810 **800-222-8100** 732-329-6991

Bookazine Company Inc
75 Hook Rd . . . . Bayonne NJ 07002 **800-221-8112** 201-339-7777

Booksource Inc
1230 Macklind Ave . . . . Saint Louis MO 63110 **800-444-0435** 314-647-0600

Brodart Company Book Services Div
500 Arch St . . . . Williamsport PA 17701 **800-474-9816** 570-326-2461

C2F Inc 6600 SW 111th Ave . . . . Beaverton OR 97008 **800-544-8825** 503-643-9050

Canadian Industrial Distributors Inc
175 Sun Pac Blvd Ste 2A . . . . Brampton ON L6S5Z6 **877-280-0243** 905-595-0411

Choice Books LLC
2387 Grace Chapel Rd . . . . Harrisonburg VA 22801 **800-224-5006** 540-434-1827

Comag Marketing Group LLC
155 Village Blvd 3rd Fl . . . . Princeton NJ 08540 **866-790-9353** 609-524-1800

Directory Distributing Assoc (DDA)
1602 Pk 370 Ct . . . . Hazelwood MO 63042 **800-325-1964*** 314-592-8600
*General

EBSCO Subscription Services
110 Olmsted St Ste 100 . . . . Birmingham AL 35242 **800-653-2726** 205-995-1596

Educational Development Corp
10302 E 55th Pl . . . . Tulsa OK 74146 **800-475-4522** 918-622-4522
NASDAQ: EDUC

ePromos Promotional Products Inc
120 Broadway Ste 1360 . . . . New York NY 10271 **877-377-6667** 212-286-8008

Follett Corp
3 Westbrook Corporate Center
Ste 200 . . . . Westchester IL 60154 **800-365-5388**

Follett Educational Services
1433 Internationale Blvd . . . . Woodridge IL 60517 **800-621-4272** 630-972-5600

General Pet Supply Inc
7711 N 81st St . . . . Milwaukee WI 53223 **800-433-9786** 414-365-3400

				Toll-Free	Phone
Harlequin Enterprises Ltd Distribution Ctr 3010 Walden Ave	Depew	NY	14043	**888-432-4879**	716-684-1800
Independent Publishers Group 814 N Franklin St *Orders	Chicago	IL	60610	**800-888-4741***	312-337-0747
Ingram Book Group 1 Ingram Blvd	La Vergne	TN	37086	**800-937-8000**	615-793-5000
MBS Textbook Exchange Inc 2711 W Ash St *Cust Svc	Columbia	MO	65203	**800-325-0530***	573-445-2243
Midwest Library Service Inc 11443 St Charles Rock Rd	Bridgeton	MO	63044	**800-325-8833**	314-739-3100
Nebraska Book Co 4700 S 19th St	Lincoln	NE	68512	**800-869-0366**	402-421-7300
Publishers' Warehouse 2700 Crestwood Blvd	Irondale	AL	35210	**800-653-2726**	205-956-2078
Quality Books Inc 1003 W Pines Rd *Cust Svc	Oregon	IL	61061	**800-323-4241***	815-732-4450
Readerlink Distribution Services LLC 1420 Kensington Rd Ste 300	Oak Brook	IL	60523	**800-549-5389**	708-547-4400
Rittenhouse Book Distributors Inc 511 Feheley Dr *Cust Svc	King of Prussia	PA	19406	**800-345-6425***	
Scholastic Book Fairs Inc 1080 Greenwood Blvd	Lake Mary	FL	32746	**800-874-4809**	407-829-7300
Seda France Inc 8301 Springdale Rd Ste 800	Austin	TX	78724	**800-474-0854**	512-206-0105
Southwestern/Great American 2451 Atrium Way *Cust Svc	Nashville	TN	37214	**888-602-7867***	
Spring Arbor Distributors One Ingram Blvd	La Vergne	TN	37086	**800-395-4340**	615-793-5000
Vulcan Service 5724 Hwy 280 E	Birmingham	AL	35242	**800-841-9600**	
YBP Library Services 999 Maple St	Contoocook	NH	03229	**800-258-3774**	603-746-3102

95 BOOK STORES

				Toll-Free	Phone
Amazon.com Inc 1200 12th Ave S Ste 1200 *NASDAQ: AMZN* ■ *Cust Svc	Seattle	WA	98144	**800-201-7575***	206-266-1000
barnesandnoble.com Inc 76 Ninth Ave Fl 9	New York	NY	10011	**800-843-2665**	212-414-6000
Book House Inc, The 208 W Chicago St	Jonesville	MI	49250	**800-248-1146**	
Book Passage 51 Tamal Vista Blvd	Corte Madera	CA	94925	**800-999-7909**	415-927-0960
Book Soup 8818 Sunset Blvd	West Hollywood	CA	90069	**888-527-8238**	310-659-3110
BookPal LLC 18101 Von Karman Ave Ste 1240	Irvine	CA	92612	**866-522-6657**	
BookPeople 603 N Lamar	Austin	TX	78703	**800-853-9757**	512-472-5050
Books on the Square 471 Angell St	Providence	RI	02906	**888-669-9660**	401-331-9097
Books-A-Million Inc 402 Industrial Ln *NASDAQ: BAMM*	Birmingham	AL	35211	**800-201-3550**	205-942-3737
BookSense.com 200 White Plains Rd	Tarrytown	NY	10591	**800-637-0037**	914-631-2415
Boulder Book Store 1107 Pearl St	Boulder	CO	80302	**800-244-4651**	303-447-2074
Childrens Plus Inc 1387 Dutch American Way	Beecher	IL	60401	**800-230-1279**	
Deseret Book Co 57 W S Temple	Salt Lake City	UT	84111	**800-453-4532**	801-534-1515
Dickens Books Ltd 219 N Milwaukee St Third Fl	Milwaukee	WI	53202	**800-236-7323**	
Drama Book Shop Inc 250 E 40th St Frnt 2	New York	NY	10018	**800-322-0595**	212-944-0595
Elliott Bay Book Co 101 S Main St	Seattle	WA	98104	**800-962-5311**	206-624-6600
Follett Corp 3 Westbrook Corporate Center Ste 200	Westchester	IL	60154	**800-365-5388**	
Follett Higher Education Group Three Westbrook Corporate Ctr Ste 200	Westchester	IL	60154	**800-323-4506**	
Full Cir Bookstore 1900 NW Expy	Oklahoma City	OK	73118	**800-683-7323**	405-842-2900
Hastings Entertainment Inc 3601 Plains Blvd *NASDAQ: HAST* ■ *Cust Svc	Amarillo	TX	79102	**877-427-8464***	
Indigo Books & Music Inc 468 King St W Ste 500 *NYSE: IDG* ■ *Cust Svc	Toronto	ON	M5V1L8	**800-832-7569***	416-364-4499
LibertyTree 100 Swan Way	Oakland	CA	94621	**800-927-8733**	510-632-1366
Matthews Book Co 11559 Rock Island Ct	Maryland Heights	MO	63043	**800-633-2665**	314-432-1400
Merchant One Payment Systems Inc 524 Arthur Godfrey Rd 3rd Fl	Miami Beach	FL	33140	**888-854-0347**	305-534-1666
Northshire Information Inc 4869 Main St	Manchester Center	VT	05255	**800-437-3700**	802-362-2200
Page One Bookstore 11018 Montgomery Blvd NE	Albuquerque	NM	87111	**800-521-4122**	505-294-2026
Poisoned Pen Bookstore 4014 N Goldwater Blvd	Scottsdale	AZ	85251	**888-560-9919**	480-947-2974
Politics & Prose Bookstore 5015 Connecticut Ave NW	Washington	DC	20008	**800-722-0790**	202-364-1919
Powell's Books Inc Seven NW Ninth Ave	Portland	OR	97209	**800-878-7323**	503-228-0540
Powell's City of Books 40 NW Tenth Ave	Portland	OR	97209	**800-878-7323**	503-228-4651
Seagull Book & Tape Inc 1720 S Redwood Rd	Salt Lake City	UT	84104	**800-999-6257**	
Social Studies School Service 10200 Jefferson Blvd PO Box 802	Culver City	CA	90232	**800-421-4246**	310-839-2436
Square Books 160 Courthouse Sq	Oxford	MS	38655	**800-648-4001**	662-236-2262
Tattered Cover Book Store Inc 1628 16th St	Denver	CO	80202	**800-833-9327**	303-436-1070
Unicor Medical Inc 4160 Carmichael Rd	Montgomery	AL	36106	**800-825-7421**	
University of Oregon Bookstore Inc PO Box 3176	Eugene	OR	97403	**800-352-1733**	541-346-4331
University Press Books (UPB) 2430 Bancroft Way	Berkeley	CA	94704	**800-676-8722**	510-548-0585

96 BOTANICAL GARDENS & ARBORETA

SEE ALSO Zoos & Wildlife Parks

				Toll-Free	Phone
Bellagio Conservatory & Botanical Gardens 3600 S Las Vegas Blvd	Las Vegas	NV	89109	**888-987-6667**	702-693-7111
Bellingrath Gardens & Home 12401 Bellingrath Garden Rd	Theodore	AL	36582	**800-247-8420**	251-973-2217
Better Homes & Gardens Test Garden 1716 Locust St	Des Moines	IA	50309	**800-374-4244**	515-284-3994
Botanical Gardens at Asheville 151 WT Weaver Blvd	Asheville	NC	28804	**888-823-4622**	828-252-5190
Boyce Thompson Arboretum 37615 US Hwy 60	Superior	AZ	85273	**877-763-5315**	520-689-2723
Brookgreen Gardens 1931 Brookgreen Dr	Murrells Inlet	SC	29576	**800-849-1931**	843-235-6000
Brookside Gardens 1800 Glenallan Ave	Wheaton	MD	20902	**800-366-2012**	301-962-1400
Butchart Gardens, The 800 Benvenuto Ave	Brentwood Bay	BC	V8M1J8	**866-652-4422**	250-652-4422
Calgary Zoo Botanical Garden & Prehistoric Park 1300 Zoo Rd NE	Calgary	AB	T2E7V6	**800-588-9993**	403-232-9300
Callaway Gardens 17800 Hwy 27	Pine Mountain	GA	31822	**800-225-5292**	706-663-2281
Cathedral Church of Saint Peter & Saint Paul 3101 Wisconsin Ave NW	Washington	DC	20016	**800-622-6304**	202-537-6200
Cedar Crest College 100 College Dr *Admissions	Allentown	PA	18104	**800-360-1222***	610-437-4471
Cheekwood Museum of Art & Botanical Garden 1200 Forrest Pk Dr	Nashville	TN	37205	**877-356-8150**	615-356-8000
Chicago Botanic Garden 1000 Lake Cook Rd	Glencoe	IL	60022	**877-829-5500**	847-835-5440
Chimney Rock Park 431 Main St	Chimney Rock	NC	28720	**800-277-9611**	828-625-9611
Cincinnati Zoo & Botanical Garden 3400 Vine St	Cincinnati	OH	45220	**800-944-4776**	513-281-4700
Cornell Plantations 1 Plantations Rd	Ithaca	NY	14850	**800-269-8368**	607-255-2400
Cox Arboretum MetroPark 6733 Springboro Pike	Dayton	OH	45449	**877-359-3291**	937-434-9005
Dawes Arboretum 7770 Jacksontown Rd SE	Newark	OH	43056	**800-443-2937**	740-323-2355
Earl Burns Miller Japanese Garden 1250 Bellflower Blvd	Long Beach	CA	90840	**800-985-8880**	562-985-8885
Edith J Carrier Arboretum & Botanical Gardens at James Madison University 780 University Blvd MSC 3705	Harrisonburg	VA	22807	**888-568-2586**	540-568-3194
Erie Zoo 423 W 38th St	Erie	PA	16508	**877-371-5422**	814-864-4091
Filoli 86 Canada Rd	Woodside	CA	94062	**866-691-9080**	650-364-8300
Flamingo Gardens 3750 S Flamingo Rd	Davie	FL	33330	**800-435-7352**	954-473-2955
Foellinger-Freimann Botanical Conservatory 1100 S Calhoun St	Fort Wayne	IN	46802	**866-220-8842**	260-427-6440
Franklin Park Conservatory & Botanical Gardens 1777 E Broad St	Columbus	OH	43203	**800-241-7275**	614-715-8000
Frederik Meijer Gardens & Sculpture Park 1000 E Beltline Ave NE	Grand Rapids	MI	49525	**877-975-3171**	616-957-1580
Gardens of the American Rose Ctr 8877 Jefferson-Paige Rd	Shreveport	LA	71119	**800-637-6534**	318-938-5402
Garvan Woodland Gardens 550 Arkridge Rd PO Box 22240	Hot Springs	AR	71903	**800-366-4664**	501-262-9300
Green Bay Botanical Garden 2600 Larsen Rd	Green Bay	WI	54303	**877-355-4224**	920-490-9457
Huntsville Botanical Garden 4747 Bob Wallace Ave	Huntsville	AL	35805	**800-300-4916**	256-830-4447
Idaho Botanical Garden 2355 N Penitentiary Rd	Boise	ID	83712	**877-527-8233**	208-343-8649
JC Raulston Arboretum North Carolina State University PO Box 7522	Raleigh	NC	27695	**888-842-2442**	919-513-7457
Journey Museum 222 New York St	Rapid City	SD	57701	**877-343-8220**	605-394-6923
Kenilworth Aquatic Gardens 1550 Anacostia Ave NE	Washington	DC	20019	**877-642-4743**	202-426-6905
Lady Bird Johnson Wildflower Ctr 4801 LaCrosse Ave	Austin	TX	78739	**877-945-3357**	512-292-4200
Lakewold Gardens 12317 Gravelly Lk Dr SW	Lakewood	WA	98499	**888-858-4106**	253-584-4106
Lincoln Botanical Garden & Arboretum (BGA) University of Nebraska 1309 N 17th St	Lincoln	NE	68588	**800-742-8800**	402-472-2679
Longwood Gardens PO Box 501	Kennett Square	PA	19348	**800-737-5500**	610-388-1000
Magnolia Plantation & Gardens 3550 Ashley River Rd	Charleston	SC	29414	**800-367-3517**	843-571-1266
Matthaei Botanical Gardens 1800 N Dixboro Rd	Ann Arbor	MI	48105	**800-666-8693**	734-647-7600
Memphis Botanic Garden 750 Cherry Rd	Memphis	TN	38117	**877-829-5500**	901-576-4100
Mercer Arboretum & Botanic Gardens 22306 Aldine Westfield Rd	Humble	TX	77338	**877-321-2652**	281-443-8731
Missouri Botanical Garden 4344 Shaw Blvd	Saint Louis	MO	63110	**800-642-8842**	314-577-5100

			Toll-Free	Phone
Montgomery Botanical Ctr				
11901 Old Cutler Rd	Miami FL	33156	800-435-7352	305-667-3800
Monticello				
931 Thomas Jefferson Pkwy				
PO Box 316	Charlottesville VA	22902	800-243-1743	434-984-9822
Mynelle Gardens				
4736 Clinton Blvd	Jackson MS	39209	800-354-7695	601-960-1894
New England Wild Flower Society				
180 Hemenway Rd	Framingham MA	01701	888-636-0033	508-877-7630
Niagara Parks Botanical Gardens				
2565 Niagara Pkwy N PO Box 150	Niagara Falls ON	L2E6T2	877-642-7275	905-356-8554
Oregon Garden, The				
879 W Main St PO Box 155	Silverton OR	97381	877-674-2733	503-874-8100
Polynesian Cultural Ctr				
55-370 Kamehameha Hwy	Laie HI	96762	800-367-7060	808-293-3005
Rhododendron Species Botanical Garden				
2525 S 336th St PO Box 3798	Federal Way WA	98063	877-242-2528	253-838-4646
Royal Botanical Gardens (RBG)				
680 Plains Rd W	Burlington ON	L7T4H4	800-694-4769	905-527-1158
Royal Roads University Botanical Garden				
2005 Sooke Rd	Victoria BC	V9B5Y2	800-788-8028	250-391-2511
Schoepfle Garden				
12882 Diagonal Rd	La Grange OH	44050	800-526-7275	440-458-5121
Schreiner's Iris Gardens				
3625 Quinaby Rd NE	Salem OR	97303	800-525-2367	503-393-3232
Shambhala Mountain Ctr				
151 Shambhala Wy	Red Feather Lakes CO	80545	888-788-7221	970-881-2184
Stan Hywet Hall & Gardens				
714 N Portage Path	Akron OH	44303	888-836-5533	330-836-5533
University of Missouri Botanic Garden				
General Services Bldg	Columbia MO	65211	800-856-2181	573-882-4240
University of Southern Maine Arboretum				
PO Box 9300	Portland ME	04104	800-800-4876	
Vanderbilt University				
2201 W End Ave	Nashville TN	37240	800-288-0432	615-322-7311
Vermont Garden Park				
1100 Dorset St	South Burlington VT	05403	800-538-7476	802-863-5251
Winterthur Museum & Country Estate				
5105 Kennett Pk	Winterthur DE	19735	800-448-3883	302-888-4600

BOTTLES - GLASS

97   BOTTLES - PLASTICS

			Toll-Free	Phone
Alpha Packaging				
1555 Page Industrial Blvd	Saint Louis MO	63132	800-421-4772	314-427-4300
Colt's Plastics Co				
969 N Main St PO Box 429	Dayville CT	06241	800-222-2658	860-774-2301
Comar LLC				
141 N Fifth St	Saddle Brook NJ	07663	800-962-6627	201-909-3400
NEW Plastics Corp				
112 Fourth St	Luxemburg WI	54217	800-666-5207	920-845-2326
Nutrifaster Inc				
209 S Bennett St	Seattle WA	98108	800-800-2641	206-767-5054
Ozarks Coca-Cola Dr Pepper Bottling Co				
1777 N Packer Rd	Springfield MO	65803	866-223-4498	417-865-9900
Progressive Plastics Inc				
14801 Emery Ave	Cleveland OH	44135	800-252-0053	216-252-5595
Quality Containers of New England				
247 Portland St Ste 300	Yarmouth ME	04096	800-639-1550	207-846-5420
Silgan Plastics Corp				
14515 N Outer Forty Ste 210	Chesterfield MO	63017	800-274-5426	

98   BOWLING CENTERS

			Toll-Free	Phone
AMF Bowling Worldwide Inc				
7313 Bell Creek Rd	Mechanicsville VA	23111	800-342-5263	

99   BOXES - CORRUGATED & SOLID FIBER

			Toll-Free	Phone
Artistic Carton Co				
1975 Big Timber Rd	Elgin IL	60123	800-735-7225	847-741-0247
Arvco Container Corp				
845 Gibson St	Kalamazoo MI	49001	800-968-9127	269-381-0900
Atlas Container Corp				
8140 Telegraph Rd	Severn MD	21144	800-394-4894	410-551-6300
Bates Container				
6433 Davis Blvd	North Richland Hills TX	76182	800-792-8736	817-498-3200
Beacon Container Corp				
700 W First St	Birdsboro PA	19508	800-422-8383	610-582-2222
Buckeye Container Inc				
3350 Long Rd	Wooster OH	44691	800-968-6894	330-264-6336
Bulk-pack Inc				
1025 N Ninth St	Monroe LA	71201	800-498-4215	318-387-3260
Carolina Container Co				
909 Prospect St	High Point NC	27260	800-627-0825	336-883-7146
Ferguson Supply & Box Manufacturing Co				
10820 Quality Dr	Charlotte NC	28278	800-821-1023	704-597-0310
Great Lakes Packaging Corp				
W 190 N 11393 Carnegie Dr	Germantown WI	53022	800-261-4572	262-255-2100
Great Northern Corp				
395 Stroebe Rd	Appleton WI	54914	800-236-3671	920-739-3671
Green Bay Packaging Inc				
1700 Webster Ct	Green Bay WI	54302	800-236-8400	920-433-5111
Key Container Corp				
21 Campbell St	Pawtucket RI	02861	800-343-8811	401-723-2000
Lawrence Paper Co				
2801 Lakeview Rd	Lawrence KS	66049	800-535-4553	785-843-8111

			Toll-Free	Phone
Lone Star Container Corp				
700 N Wildwood Dr	Irving TX	75061	800-552-6937	
Menasha Corp				
1645 Bergstrom Rd	Neenah WI	54956	800-558-5073	920-751-1000
Menasha Packaging Co				
1645 Bergstrom Rd	Neenah WI	54956	800-558-5073	920-751-1000
New England Wooden Ware Corp				
205 School St Ste 201	Gardner MA	01440	800-252-9214	978-632-3600
North American Container Corp				
1811 W Oak Pkwy Ste D	Marietta GA	30062	800-929-0610	770-431-4858
Packaging Corp of America				
1955 W Field Ct	Lake Forest IL	60045	800-456-4725	
NYSE: PKG				
Pactiv Corp				
1900 W Field Ct	Lake Forest IL	60045	888-828-2850	847-482-2000
Rock TENN 1415 W 44th St	Chicago IL	60609	877-643-5414	773-254-1030
Rock-Tenn Co				
504 Thrasher St	Norcross GA	30071	877-643-5414	770-448-2193
NYSE: RKT				
Shoreline Container Inc				
4450 N 136th Ave PO Box 1993	Holland MI	49422	800-968-2088	616-399-2088
Stephen Gould Corp				
35 S Jefferson Rd	Whippany NJ	07981	800-456-7896	973-428-1500
Stronghaven Inc				
5090 McDougall Dr SW	Atlanta GA	30336	866-374-9148	404-699-1952
Tharco Inc				
2222 Grant Ave	San Lorenzo CA	94580	800-772-2332	
TimBar Packaging & Display				
148 N Penn St PO Box 449	Hanover PA	17331	800-572-6061	717-632-4727
Welch Packaging Group				
1020 Herman St	Elkhart IN	46516	800-246-2475	574-295-2460

100   BOXES - PAPERBOARD

Products made by these companies include setup, folding, and nonfolding boxes.

			Toll-Free	Phone
Apex Paper Box Co				
5601 Walworth Ave	Cleveland OH	44102	800-438-2269*	216-416-9475
*Cust Svc				
Burd & Fletcher				
3000 W Geospace Dr	Independence MO	64056	800-821-2776	816-257-0291
Caraustar Industries Inc				
5000 Austell-Powder Springs Rd				
Ste 300	Austell GA	30106	800-223-1373	770-948-3100
Carton Service Inc				
First Quality Dr PO Box 702	Shelby OH	44875	800-533-7744*	419-342-5010
*General				
Climax Packaging Inc				
4515 Easton Rd	Saint Joseph MO	64503	800-225-4629	816-233-3181
Complemar Partners				
500 Lee Rd Ste 200	Rochester NY	14606	800-388-7254	585-647-5800
Dee Paper Box Company Inc				
100 Broomall St	Chester PA	19013	800-359-0041	610-876-9285
Diamond Packaging Company Inc				
111 Commerce Dr PO Box 23620	Rochester NY	14692	800-333-4079	585-334-8030
Graphic Packaging International				
1500 Riveredge Parkway NW	Atlanta GA	30328	888-548-8395	770-240-7200
NYSE: GPK				
Hub Folding Box Co Inc				
774 Norfolk St	Mansfield MA	02048	800-334-1113	508-339-0005
Mafcote Industries Inc				
108 Main St	Norwalk CT	06851	800-221-3056*	203-847-8500
*Cust Svc				
Malnove Inc 13434 F St	Omaha NE	68137	800-228-9877	402-330-1100
Menasha Corp				
1645 Bergstrom Rd	Neenah WI	54956	800-558-5073	920-751-1000
MOD-PAC Corp				
1801 Elmwood Ave	Buffalo NY	14207	866-216-6193*	716-873-0640
NASDAQ: MPAC ■ *Cust Svc				
Pactiv Corp				
1900 W Field Ct	Lake Forest IL	60045	888-828-2850	847-482-2000
Panoramic Inc				
1500 N Parker Dr	Janesville WI	53545	800-333-1394	608-754-8850
Paragon Packaging Inc				
7700 Centerville Rd	Ferndale CA	95536	888-615-0065	707-786-4004
Rice Packaging Inc				
356 Somers Rd	Ellington CT	06029	800-367-6725	860-872-8341
Rose City Printing & Packaging Inc				
900 SE Tech Crt Dr	Vancouver WA	98683	800-704-8693	
RTS Packaging LLC				
504 Thrasher St	Norcross GA	30071	800-558-6984	
Rusken Packaging Inc				
PO Box 2000	Cullman AL	35056	800-232-8108	256-734-0092
Seaboard Folding Box Co Inc				
35 Daniels St	Fitchburg MA	01420	800-225-6313	978-342-8921
Stephen Gould Corp				
35 S Jefferson Rd	Whippany NJ	07981	800-456-7896	973-428-1500
Sterling Paper Co				
2155 E Castor Ave	Philadelphia PA	19134	800-745-5350	215-744-5350

101   BREWERIES

SEE ALSO Malting Products

			Toll-Free	Phone
Abita Brewing Co				
21084 Hwy 36	Covington LA	70433	800-737-2311	985-893-3143
Anchor Brewing Co				
1705 Mariposa St	San Francisco CA	94107	800-478-2227	415-863-8350
Boston Beer Co				
One Design Ctr Pl Ste 850	Boston MA	02210	888-661-2337	617-368-5000
NYSE: SAM				
BridgePort Brewing Co				
1318 NW Northrup St	Portland OR	97209	888-834-7546	503-241-7179

				Toll-Free	Phone
Jacob Leinenkugel Brewing Co					
124 E Elm St	Chippewa Falls	WI	54729	**888-534-6437***	715-723-5558
*General					
Keurig Inc					
55 Walkers Brook Dr	Reading	MA	01867	**866-901-2739**	
Labatt Breweries of Canada					
207 Queen's Quay W Ste 299	Toronto	ON	M5J1A7	**800-268-2337***	416-361-5050
*Cust Svc					
Lion Brewery Inc					
700 N Pennsylvania Ave	Wilkes-Barre	PA	18705	**888-295-2337**	570-823-8801
Malt Products Corp					
88 Market St	Saddle Brook	NJ	07663	**800-526-0180**	201-845-4420
McMenamins					
430 N Killingsworth	Portland	OR	97217	**800-669-8610**	503-223-0109
Molson Coors Brewing Co					
1225 17th St Ste 3200	Denver	CO	80202	**800-645-5376**	303-927-2337
NYSE: TAP					
North Coast Brewing Company Inc					
455 N Main St	Fort Bragg	CA	95437	**866-955-4190**	707-964-2739
Odell Brewing Co					
800 E Lincoln Ave	Fort Collins	CO	80524	**888-887-2797**	970-498-9070
Pabst Brewing Co, The					
10635 Santa Monica Blvd Ste 350	Los Angeles	CA	90025	**800-947-2278**	

BROKERS

SEE Securities Brokers & Dealers ; Insurance Agents, Brokers, Servic-es ; Mortgage Lenders & Loan Brokers ; Real Estate Agents & Brokers ; Commodity Contracts Brokers & Dealers ; Electronic Communications Networks (ECNs)

102   BRUSHES & BROOMS

SEE ALSO Art Materials & Supplies - Mfr

				Toll-Free	Phone
Abco Cleaning Products					
6800 NW 36th Ave	Miami	FL	33147	**888-694-2226**	305-694-2226
Carlisle Sanitary Maintenance Products					
402 S Black River St	Sparta	WI	54656	**800-654-8210**	608-269-2151
Corona Brushes Inc					
5065 Savarese Cir	Tampa	FL	33634	**800-458-3483**	813-885-2525
Crystal Lake Manufacturing Inc					
2225 Alabama 14 PO Box 159	Autaugaville	AL	36003	**800-633-8720**	334-365-3342
Detroit Quality Brush Mfg					
32165 Schoolcraft Rd	Livonia	MI	48150	**800-722-3037**	734-525-5660
Felton Brush Inc					
Seven Burton Dr	Londonderry	NH	03053	**800-258-9702**	603-425-0200
Fuller Brush Co, The					
P.O. Box 729 1 Fuller Way	Great Bend	KS	67530	**800-522-0499***	620-792-1711
*Cust Svc					
Gordon Brush Mfg Company Inc					
6247 Randolph St	Commerce	CA	90040	**800-950-7950**	323-724-7777
Greenwood Mop & Broom Inc					
312 Palmer St	Greenwood	SC	29646	**800-635-6849**	864-227-8411
Harper Brush Works Inc					
400 N Second St	Fairfield	IA	52556	**800-223-7894**	641-472-5186
Industrial Brush Company Inc					
105 Clinton Rd	Fairfield	NJ	07004	**800-241-9860**	973-575-0455
Industries for the Blind					
445 S Curtis Rd	West Allis	WI	53214	**800-642-8778**	414-778-3040
Laitner Brush Co					
1561 Laitner Dr	Traverse City	MI	49686	**800-423-6805***	231-929-3300
*Cust Svc					
Libman Co 220 N Sheldon St	Arcola	IL	61910	**800-646-6262**	
Magnolia Brush Mfg Ltd					
1000 N Cedar PO Box 932	Clarksville	TX	75426	**800-248-2261**	903-427-2261
Mill-Rose Co 7995 Tyler Blvd	Mentor	OH	44060	**800-321-3533**	440-255-9171
Osborn International					
5401 Hamilton Ave	Cleveland	OH	44114	**800-720-3358***	216-361-1900
*Cust Svc					
Padco Inc					
2220 Elm St SE	Minneapolis	MN	55414	**800-328-5513**	612-378-7270
PFERD Milwaukee Brush Company Inc					
30 Jytek Dr	Leominster	MA	01453	**800-342-9015**	978-840-6420
Rubberset Co					
101 W Prospect Ave	Cleveland	OH	44115	**800-345-4939**	
Sanderson-MacLeod Inc					
1199 S Main St PO Box 50	Palmer	MA	01069	**866-522-3481**	413-283-3481
SM Arnold Inc					
7901 Michigan Ave	Saint Louis	MO	63111	**800-325-7865***	314-544-4103
*Cust Svc					
Sweepster Inc 2800 N Zeeb Rd	Dexter	MI	48130	**800-456-7100**	734-996-9116
Universal Brush Manufacturing Co					
16200 Dixie Hwy	Markham	IL	60428	**800-323-3474**	708-331-1700
Weiler Corp 1 Wildwood Dr	Cresco	PA	18326	**800-835-9999***	570-595-7495
*Cust Svc					
Wooster Brush Co					
604 Madison Ave	Wooster	OH	44691	**800-392-7246**	330-264-4440

103   BUILDING MAINTENANCE SERVICES

SEE ALSO Cleaning Services

				Toll-Free	Phone
DMS Facility Services Inc					
417 East Huntington Dr	Monrovia	CA	91016	**800-443-8677**	626-305-8500
Drayton Group					
2295 N Opdyke Rd Ste D	Auburn Hills	MI	48326	**888-655-4442**	
FBG Service Corp					
407 S 27th Ave	Omaha	NE	68131	**800-777-8326**	402-346-4422
Shannon Diversified Inc					
1190 N Del Rio Pl	Ontario	CA	91764	**800-794-2345**	
Style Crest Inc					
2450 Enterprise St	Fremont	OH	43420	**800-925-4440**	419-332-7369

104   BUILDINGS - PREFABRICATED - METAL

				Toll-Free	Phone
American Buildings Co					
1150 State Docks Rd	Eufaula	AL	36027	**888-307-4338**	334-687-2032
Behlen Manufacturing Co					
4025 E 23rd St	Columbus	NE	68601	**800-553-5520**	402-564-3111
CEMCO					
263 N Covina Ln	City Of Industry	CA	91744	**800-775-2362**	
Erect-A-Tube Inc					
701 W Pk St PO Box 100	Harvard	IL	60033	**800-624-9219**	815-943-4091
Four Seasons Solar Products LLC					
5005 Veterans Memorial Hwy	Holbrook	NY	11741	**800-368-7732**	631-563-4000
Garco Bldg Systems					
2714 S Garfield Rd	Airway Heights	WA	99001	**800-941-2291**	509-244-5611
Imperial Industries Inc					
505 Industrial Pk Ave	Rothschild	WI	54474	**800-558-2945**	715-359-0200
Kirby Bldg Systems Inc					
124 Kirby Dr	Portland	TN	37148	**800-348-7799**	615-325-4165
Mesco Bldg Solutions					
5244 Bear Creek Ct	Irving	TX	75061	**800-556-3726**	214-687-9999
Metl-Span LLC					
1720 Lakepointe Dr Ste 101	Lewisville	TX	75057	**877-585-9969**	972-221-6656
Mid-West Steel Bldg Co					
7301 Fairview	Houston	TX	77041	**800-777-9378**	713-466-7788
Morton Buildings Inc					
252 W Adams St PO Box 399	Morton	IL	61550	**800-447-7436**	309-263-7474
Mueller Inc					
1913 Hutchins Ave	Ballinger	TX	76821	**877-268-3553**	325-365-3555
Pacific Building Systems (PBS)					
2100 N Pacific Hwy	Woodburn	OR	97071	**800-727-7844***	503-981-9581
*General					
Package Industries Inc					
15 Harback Rd	Sutton	MA	01590	**800-225-7242**	508-865-5871
Parkline Inc PO Box 65	Winfield	WV	25213	**800-786-4855**	304-586-2113
Porta-Fab Corp					
18080 Chesterfield Airport Rd	Chesterfield	MO	63005	**800-325-3781**	636-537-5555
PorterCorp 4240 136th Ave	Holland	MI	49424	**800-354-7721**	616-399-1963
Red Dot Corp					
1209 W Corsicana St	Athens	TX	75751	**800-657-2234***	
*Cust Svc					
Rigid Bldg Systems Ltd					
18933 Aldine Westfield Rd	Houston	TX	77073	**888-467-4443**	281-443-9065
Ruffin Bldg Systems Inc					
6914 Louisiana 2	Oak Grove	LA	71263	**800-421-4232**	318-428-2305
ShelterLogic Corp					
150 Callendar Rd	Watertown	CT	06795	**800-932-9344**	860-945-6442
Star Bldg Systems					
8600 S I-35	Oklahoma City	OK	73149	**800-879-7827**	
Temo Sunrooms Inc					
20400 Hall Rd	Clinton Township	MI	48038	**800-344-8366**	
Trachte Bldg Systems Inc					
314 Wilburn Rd	Sun Prairie	WI	53590	**800-356-5824**	
Whirlwind Steel					
8234 Hansen Rd	Houston	TX	77075	**800-324-9992**	713-946-7140
Worldwide Steel Buildings					
PO Box 588	Peculiar	MO	64078	**800-825-0316**	
XS Smith Inc 932 Page Rd	Washington	NC	27889	**800-631-2226**	252-940-5060

105   BUILDINGS - PREFABRICATED - WOOD

				Toll-Free	Phone
Acorn Deck House Co					
852 Main St	Acton	MA	01720	**800-727-3325**	978-263-6800
Barden & Robeson Corp					
103 Kelly Ave	Middleport	NY	14105	**800-724-0141**	716-735-3732
Blazer Industries Inc					
PO Box 489	Aumsville	OR	97325	**877-211-3437**	503-749-1900
Deluxe Bldg Systems Inc					
499 W Third St	Berwick	PA	18603	**800-843-7372**	570-752-5914
Demtec Inc					
50, Blvd Industriel	Princeville	QC	G6L4P2	**800-560-2043**	819-364-2043
Design Homes Inc					
600 N Marquette Rd	Prairie du Chien	WI	53821	**800-627-9443**	608-326-6041
Dickinson Homes Inc					
404 N Stephenson Ave Hwy US-2					
PO Box 2245	Iron Mountain	MI	49801	**800-438-4687**	906-774-2186
Dynamic Homes LLC					
525 Roosevelt Ave	Detroit Lakes	MN	56501	**800-492-4833**	218-847-2611
Flexospan Steel Buildings Inc					
253 Railroad St	Sandy Lake	PA	16145	**800-245-0396**	724-376-7221
Foremost Industries Inc					
2375 Buchanan Trl W	Greencastle	PA	17225	**877-284-5334**	717-597-7166
Homes by Keystone Inc					
13338 Midvale Rd PO Box 69	Waynesboro	PA	17268	**800-890-7926**	
Indaco Metal					
Three American Way	Shawnee	OK	74804	**877-300-7334**	
International Homes of Cedar Inc (IHC)					
PO Box 886	Woodinville	WA	98072	**800-767-7674**	360-668-8511
Keiser Homes					
56 Mechanic Falls Rd PO Box 9000	Oxford	ME	04270	**888-333-1748**	
KIT HomeBuilders West LLC					
1124 Garber St	Caldwell	ID	83605	**800-859-0347**	208-454-5000
Lester Bldg Systems LLC					
1111 Second Ave S	Lester Prairie	MN	55354	**800-826-4439**	320-395-2531
Lindal Cedar Homes Inc					
4300 S 104th Pl	Seattle	WA	98178	**800-426-0536***	206-725-0900
*Prod Info					
Manufactured Structures Corp (MSC)					
3089 E Fort Wayne Rd PO Box 350	Rochester	IN	46975	**800-662-5344**	574-223-4794
Mod-U-Kraf Homes LLC					
260 Weaver St PO Box 573	Rocky Mount	VA	24151	**888-663-5723**	540-483-0291
Morgan Bldg Systems Inc					
2800 McCree Rd	Garland	TX	75041	**800-935-0321**	972-864-7300

			Toll-Free	Phone
Nationwide Custom Homes				
1100 Rives Rd	Martinsville VA	24115	800-216-7001	
New Acton Mobile Industries LLC				
809 Gleneagles Ct	Baltimore MD	21286	800-251-1600	
New England Homes				
270 Ocean Rd	Greenland NH	03840	800-800-8831	603-436-8830
Nexus Corp				
10983 Leroy Dr	Northglenn CO	80233	800-228-9639	303-457-9199
Northeastern Log Homes Inc				
10 Ames Rd	Kenduskeag ME	04450	800-624-2797	207-884-7000
Original Lincoln Logs Ltd				
Five Riverside Dr PO Box 135	Chestertown NY	12817	800-833-2461	
Pacific Modern Homes Inc (PMHI)				
9723 Railroad St	Elk Grove CA	95624	800-395-1011	916-685-9514
Pan Abode Cedar Homes Inc				
1100 Maple Ave SW	Renton WA	98057	800-782-2633	425-255-8260
Schulte Building Systems Inc				
17600 Badtke Rd	Hockley TX	77447	877-257-2534	281-304-6111
Simplex Homes 1 Simplex Dr	Scranton PA	18504	800-233-4233	570-346-5113
Stratford Homes LP				
402 S Weber Ave	Stratford WI	54484	800-448-1524	715-687-3133
Timberland Homes Inc				
1201 37th St NW	Auburn WA	98001	800-488-5036	253-735-3435
Unibilt Industries Inc				
8005 Johnson Stn Rd PO Box 373	Vandalia OH	45377	800-777-9942	
Ward Cedar Log Homes				
37 Bangor St PO Box 72	Houlton ME	04730	800-341-1566*	
*Cust Svc				

106   BUS SERVICES - CHARTER

			Toll-Free	Phone
A Yankee Line 370 W First St	Boston MA	02127	800-942-8890	617-268-8890
All West Coach Lines				
7701 Wilbur Way	Sacramento CA	95828	800-843-2121	916-423-4000
Anderson Coach & Travel				
One Anderson Plz	Greenville PA	16125	800-345-3435	724-588-8310
Arrow Stage Lines				
720 E Norfolk Ave	Norfolk NE	68701	800-672-8302	402-371-3850
B & C Transportation Inc				
427 Continental Dr	Maryville TN	37804	877-812-2287	865-983-4653
Badger Bus 5501 Femrite Dr	Madison WI	53718	800-442-8259	608-255-1511
Blue Lakes Charters & Tours				
12154 N Saginaw Rd	Clio MI	48420	800-282-4287	810-686-4287
Boise-Winnemucca Stage Lines Inc				
1105 S La Pt St	Boise ID	83706	800-448-5692	208-336-3300
Brown Coach Inc				
50 Venner Rd	Amsterdam NY	12010	800-424-4700	518-843-4700
Carl R Bieber Tourways Inc				
320 Fair St PO Box 180	Kutztown PA	19530	800-243-2374	610-683-7333
Central States Coach Repairs				
3426 Gilbert Rd	Grand Prairie TX	75050	800-533-1939	972-399-1059
Chippewa Trails				
510 E S Ave	Chippewa Falls WI	54729	866-777-1399	715-726-2457
Citizen Auto Stage Co				
67 E Baffert Dr	Nogales AZ	85621	800-276-1528	520-281-0400
Coach Tours Ltd				
475 Federal Rd	Brookfield CT	06804	800-822-6224	203-740-1118
Colorado Charter Lines				
4960 Locust St	Commerce City CO	80022	800-821-7491	303-287-0239
Croswell Bus Lines Inc				
975 W Main St	Williamsburg OH	45176	800-782-8747	513-724-2206
CYR Bus Lines				
153 Gilman Falls Ave	Old Town ME	04468	800-244-2335	207-827-2335
DATTCO Inc 583 S St	New Britain CT	06051	800-229-4879	860-229-4878
Elite Coach 1685 W Main St	Ephrata PA	17522	800-722-6206	717-733-7710
Eyre Bus Service Inc				
13600 Triadelphia Rd PO Box 239	Glenelg MD	21737	800-321-3973	410-442-1330
Good Time Tours				
455 Corday St	Pensacola FL	32503	800-446-0886	850-476-0046
Greyhound Canada Transportation Corp				
1111 International Blvd Ste 700	Burlington ON	L7L6W1	800-661-8747	
Harms Charters				
532 N Vly View Rd	Sioux Falls SD	57106	800-678-6543	605-336-3339
Hawkeye Stages Inc				
703 Dudley St	Decorah IA	52101	877-464-2954	563-382-3639
Indian Trails Inc				
109 E Comstock St	Owosso MI	48867	800-292-3831	989-725-5105
Kerrville Bus Co				
One S Main St	Del Rio TX	78840	800-474-3352	830-775-7515
Lamers Bus Lines Inc				
2407 S Pt Rd	Green Bay WI	54313	800-236-1240	920-496-3600
Martz First Class Coach Company Inc				
4783 37th St N	Saint Petersburg FL	33714	800-282-8020	727-526-9086
Mid-America Charter Lines				
2513 E Higgins Rd	Elk Grove Village IL	60007	800-323-0312	847-437-3779
Northfield Lines Inc				
32611 Northfield Blvd	Northfield MN	55057	888-670-8068	507-645-5267
Onondaga Coach Corp				
PO Box 277	Auburn NY	13021	800-451-1570	315-255-2216
Pacific Western Transportation Ltd				
6999 ordan Dr	Mississauga ON	L5T1K6	800-387-6787	905-564-3232
Peter Pan Bus Lines				
PO Box 1776	Springfield MA	01102	800-343-9999	
Peter Pan Bus Lines Inc				
1776 Main St	Springfield MA	01103	800-237-8747	413-786-9300
Premier Coach Company Inc				
946 Rte 7 S	Milton VT	05468	800-532-1811	802-655-4456
Punchbowl Inc				
50 Speen St Ste 202	Framingham MA	01701	877-570-4340	508-589-4486
Red Carpet Charters				
4820 SW 20th	Oklahoma City OK	73128	888-878-5100	405-672-5100
Rimrock Stages Inc				
1660 W Broadway St	Missoula MT	59808	800-255-7655	406-549-2339
Riteway Bus Service Inc Motorcoach Div				
W201 N13900 Fond du Lac Ave	Richfield WI	53076	800-776-7026	262-677-3282

			Toll-Free	Phone
Salter Bus Lines Inc				
212 Hudson Ave	Jonesboro LA	71251	800-223-8056	318-259-2522
Shafer's Tour & Charter				
500 N St	Endicott NY	13760	800-287-8986	607-797-2006
Silver Fox Tours & Motorcoaches				
Three Silver Fox Dr	Millbury MA	01527	800-342-5998	508-865-6000
Starr Bus Charter & Tours				
2531 E State St	Trenton NJ	08619	800-782-7703	609-587-0626
Storer Coachways				
3519 McDonald Ave	Modesto CA	95358	800-621-3383	209-521-8250
Swarthout Coaches Inc				
115 Graham Rd	Ithaca NY	14850	800-772-7267	607-257-2277
Trailways Transportation System Inc				
3554 Chain Bridge Rd Ste 301	Fairfax VA	22030	877-467-3346	703-691-3052
Van Galder Bus Co				
715 S Pearl St	Janesville WI	53548	800-747-0994	608-752-5407
VIP Tour & Charter Bus Co				
129-137 Fox St	Portland ME	04101	800-231-2222*	207-772-4457
*General				
Wilson Bus Lines Inc				
203 Patriots Rd PO Box 415	East Templeton MA	01438	800-253-5235	978-632-3894
Winn Transportation				
1831 Westwood Ave	Richmond VA	23227	800-296-9466	804-358-9466
Wisconsin Coach Lines Inc				
1520 Arcadian Ave	Waukesha WI	53186	877-324-7767	262-542-8861
Young Transportation & Tours				
843 Riverside Dr	Asheville NC	28804	800-622-5444	828-258-0084

107   BUS SERVICES - INTERCITY & RURAL

SEE ALSO Mass Transportation (Local & Suburban) ; Bus Services - School

			Toll-Free	Phone
Adirondack Trailways				
499 Hurley Ave	Hurley NY	12443	800-858-8555	845-339-4230
Colorado Valley Transit Inc				
108 Cardinal Ln PO Box 940	Columbus TX	78934	800-548-1068	979-732-6281
Geauga County Transit				
12555 Merritt Rd	Chardon OH	44024	888-287-7190*	440-279-2150
*Cust Svc				
Greyhound Canada Transportation Corp				
1111 International Blvd Ste 700	Burlington ON	L7L6W1	800-661-8747	
Jefferson Lines				
2100 E 26th St	Minneapolis MN	55404	800-767-5333*	612-359-3400
*Cust Svc				
Jefferson Partners LP				
2100 E 26th St	Minneapolis MN	55404	800-767-5333*	612-359-3400
*Cust Svc				
Ozark Regional Transit				
2423 E Robinson Ave	Springdale AR	72764	800-865-5901	479-756-5901
Pacific Transit System				
216 N Second St	Raymond WA	98577	800-833-6388	360-875-9418
Pelivan Transit				
333 S Oak St PO Box B.	Big Cabin OK	74332	800-482-4594	918-783-5793
Peter Pan Bus Lines Inc				
1776 Main St	Springfield MA	01103	800-237-8747	413-786-9300
Powder River Transportation				
1700 U S 14	Gillette WY	82716	888-970-7233	307-682-0960
Rimrock Stages Inc				
1660 W Broadway St	Missoula MT	59808	800-255-7655	406-549-2339
Rural Transit Enterprises Coordinated Inc (RTEC)				
100 E Main St	Mount Vernon KY	40456	800-321-7832	606-256-9835
Suburban Transit Corp				
750 Somerset St	New Brunswick NJ	08901	800-222-0492	732-249-1100
Thunderbird Rural Public Transportation System				
2801 W Loop 306 Ste A PO Box 60050	San Angelo TX	76904	877-947-8729	325-944-9666
Trans-Bridge Lines Inc				
2012 Industrial Dr	Bethlehem PA	18017	800-962-9135	610-868-6001
Viking Trailways				
201 Glendale Rd	Joplin MO	64804	800-400-2779	417-781-2779

108   BUS SERVICES - SCHOOL

			Toll-Free	Phone
Birnie Bus Service Inc				
248 Otis St	Rome NY	13441	800-734-3950	315-336-3950
Davidsmeyer Bus Service Inc				
2513 E Higgins Rd	Elk Grove Village IL	60007	800-323-0312	847-437-3767
Dean Transportation Inc				
4812 Aurelius Rd	Lansing MI	48910	800-282-3326	517-319-8300
Hastings Bus Co				
425 31st St E	Hastings MN	55033	800-210-6362	651-437-1888
John T Cyr & Sons Inc				
153 Gilman Falls Ave	Old Town ME	04468	800-244-2335	207-827-2335
Kobussen Buses Ltd				
W914 County Rd CE	Kaukauna WI	54130	800-447-0116	920-766-0606
Michael's Transportation Service Inc				
140 Yolano Dr	Vallejo CA	94589	800-295-2448*	707-643-2099
*Cust Svc				
Riteway Bus Service Inc Motorcoach Div				
W201 N13900 Fond du Lac Ave	Richfield WI	53076	800-776-7026	262-677-3282
Stock Transportation Ltd				
128 Wellington St W Ste 201	Barrie ON	L4N1K9	888-952-0878	
Student Transportation of America Inc (STA)				
3349 Hwy 138 Bldg B Ste D	Wall NJ	07719	888-942-2250	732-280-4200

109   BUSINESS FORMS

SEE ALSO Printing Companies - Commercial Printers

			Toll-Free	Phone
Ace Forms of Kansas Inc				
2900 N Rotary Terr	Pittsburg KS	66762	800-223-9287	
Allison Payment Systems LLC				
2200 Production Dr	Indianapolis IN	46241	800-755-2440	

				Toll-Free	Phone
Amsterdam Printing & Litho Corp					
166 Wallins Corners Rd	Amsterdam	NY	12010	**800-833-6231***	518-842-6000
*Cust Svc					
Apex Color					
200 N Lee St	Jacksonville	FL	32204	**800-367-6790**	
Bestforms Inc					
1135 Avenida Acaso	Camarillo	CA	93012	**800-350-0618**	805-383-6993
Central States Business Forms Inc					
2500 Industrial Pkwy	Dewey	OK	74029	**800-331-0920**	
Champion Industries Inc					
PO Box 2968 PO Box 2968	Huntington	WV	25728	**800-624-3431**	304-528-2791
OTC: CHMP					
Curtis 1000 Inc					
1725 Breckinridge Pkwy Ste 500	Duluth	GA	30096	**877-287-8715**	678-380-9095
Custom Business Forms Inc					
210 Edge Pl	Minneapolis	MN	55418	**800-234-1221***	612-789-0002
*General					
Data Papers Inc					
468 Industrial Pk Rd	Muncy	PA	17756	**800-233-3032**	
Data Source Inc					
1400 Universal Ave	Kansas City	MO	64120	**877-846-9120**	816-483-3282
Datatel Resources Corp					
1729 Pennsylvania Ave	Monaca	PA	15061	**800-245-2688**	724-775-5300
DFS Group 500 Main St	Groton	MA	01471	**800-225-9528***	
*General					
Dupli-Systems Inc					
8260 Dow Cir	Strongsville	OH	44136	**800-321-1610**	440-234-9415
Eastern Business Forms Inc					
PO Box 10	Mauldin	SC	29662	**800-387-2648**	
Federal Business Products Inc					
95 Main Ave	Clifton	NJ	07014	**800-927-5123**	973-667-9800
FedEx 450 W First Ave	Roselle	NJ	07203	**800-463-3339**	908-245-4400
Flesh Co 2118 59th St	Saint Louis	MO	63110	**800-869-3330**	314-781-4400
Forms Manufacturers Inc					
312 E Forest Ave	Girard	KS	66743	**800-835-0614**	620-724-8225
Freedom Graphic Systems Inc (FGS)					
1101 S Janesville St	Milton	WI	53563	**800-334-3540**	
General Credit Forms Inc (GCF)					
3595 Rider Trl S	Earth City	MO	63045	**888-423-6397**	314-216-8600
Genoa Business Forms Inc					
445 Pk Ave	Sycamore	IL	60178	**800-383-2801**	
Gulf Business Forms Inc					
2460 S IH-35 PO Box 1073	San Marcos	TX	78667	**800-433-4853**	512-353-8313
Highland Computer Forms Inc					
1025 W Main St	Hillsboro	OH	45133	**800-669-5213**	937-393-4215
Hospital Forms & Systems Corp					
8900 Ambassador Row	Dallas	TX	75247	**800-527-5081**	214-634-8900
IBS Direct					
431 Yerkes Rd	King of Prussia	PA	19406	**800-220-1255**	610-265-8210
Imperial Graphics Inc					
3100 Walkent Dr NW	Grand Rapids	MI	49544	**800-777-2591**	
Kaye-Smith					
4101 Oakesdale Ave SW	Renton	WA	98057	**800-822-9987**	425-228-8600
New Jersey Business Forms Manufacturing Co					
55 W Sheffield Ave	Englewood	NJ	07631	**800-466-6523**	201-569-4500
Paris Business Products					
800 Highland Dr	Westampton	NJ	08060	**800-523-6454***	609-265-9200
*Cust Svc					
Patterson Office Supplies					
3310 N Duncan Rd	Champaign	IL	61822	**800-637-1140**	217-351-5400
Performance Office Papers					
21565 Hamburg Ave	Lakeville	MN	55044	**800-458-7189**	
PrintEdd Products of North America					
2641 N Forum Dr	Grand Prairie	TX	75052	**800-367-6728**	972-660-3800
Rotary Forms Press Inc					
835 S High St	Hillsboro	OH	45133	**800-654-2876**	937-393-3426
Royal Business Forms Inc					
3301 Ave E E	Arlington	TX	76011	**800-255-9303**	817-640-5248
Socrates Media LLC					
111 S Wacker Dr	Chicago	IL	60606	**877-860-4649**	
Specialized Printed Forms Inc					
352 Ctr St	Caledonia	NY	14423	**800-688-2381**	585-538-2381
Standard Register Co					
600 Albany St	Dayton	OH	45417	**800-755-6405**	937-221-1825
OTC: SRCTQ					
Sterling Business Forms					
PO Box 2486	White City	OR	97503	**800-759-3676***	
*Cust Svc					
Stry-Lenkoff Co Inc					
1100 W Broadway	Louisville	KY	40232	**800-626-8247**	502-587-6804
Victor Printing Inc					
One Victor Way	Sharon	PA	16146	**800-443-2845**	724-342-2106
Ward-Kraft Inc					
2401 Cooper St	Fort Scott	KS	66701	**800-821-4021**	620-223-5500
Wilmer Service Line					
515 W Sycamore St	Coldwater	OH	45828	**800-494-5637**	
Wise Business Forms Inc					
555 McFarland 400 Dr	Alpharetta	GA	30004	**888-815-9473**	770-442-1060
Witt Printing Company Inc					
301 Oak St	El Dorado Springs	MO	64744	**800-641-4342**	417-876-4721
Wright Business Graphics (WBG)					
18440 NE San Rafael St PO Box 20489	Portland	OR	97230	**800-547-8397**	

110 — BUSINESS MACHINES - MFR

SEE ALSO Photocopying Equipment & Supplies ; Business Machines - Whol ; Calculators - Electronic ; Computer Equipment

				Toll-Free	Phone
Abbott Vascular					
26531 Ynez Rd	Temecula	CA	92591	**800-227-9902**	
Agissar Corp					
526 Benton St	Stratford	CT	06615	**800-627-8256**	203-375-8662
Amano Cincinnati Inc					
140 Harrison Ave	Roseland	NJ	07068	**800-526-2559**	973-403-1900
Better Packages Inc					
255 Canal St PO Box 711	Shelton	CT	06484	**800-237-9151**	203-926-3722

				Toll-Free	Phone
Brother International Corp					
100 Somerset Corporate Blvd	Bridgewater	NJ	08807	**877-552-6255***	908-704-1700
*Cust Svc					
Cummins-Allison Corp					
852 Feehanville Dr	Mount Prospect	IL	60056	**800-786-5528**	847-299-9550
Dynetics Engineering Corp					
515 Bond St	Lincolnshire	IL	60069	**800-888-8110**	847-541-7300
Ecco Business Systems Inc					
60 W 38th St 4th Fl	New York	NY	10018	**800-558-6777**	212-921-4545
ECRM Inc 554 Clark Rd	Tewksbury	MA	01876	**800-537-3276**	978-851-0207
Fellowes Inc					
1789 Norwood Ave	Itasca	IL	60143	**800-945-4545**	630-893-1600
Fireside Hearth & Home					
7571 215th St W	Lakeville	MN	55044	**800-669-4328**	
Imaging Business Machines LLC					
2750 Crestwood Blvd	Birmingham	AL	35210	**800-627-2269**	205-439-7100
International Business Machines Corp (IBM)					
One New OrchaRd Rd	Armonk	NY	10504	**800-426-4968**	914-499-1900
NYSE: IBM					
Lathem Time Corp					
200 Selig Dr SW	Atlanta	GA	30336	**800-241-4990**	404-691-0400
Lynde-Ordway Company Inc					
3308 W Warner Ave	Santa Ana	CA	92704	**800-762-7057**	714-957-1311
Martin Yale Industries Inc					
251 Wedcor Ave	Wabash	IN	46992	**800-225-5644**	260-563-0641
MBM Corp (MBM)					
3134 Industry Dr	North Charleston	SC	29418	**800-223-2508***	843-552-2700
*Cust Svc					
Neopost Inc Canada					
150 Steelcase Rd W	Markham	ON	L3R3J9	**800-636-7678**	905-475-3722
Newbold Corp					
450 Weaver St	Rocky Mount	VA	24151	**800-552-3282**	540-489-4400
Ossur					
27412 Aliso Viejo Pkwy	Aliso Viejo	CA	92656	**800-233-6263**	
Pitney Bowes Inc					
One Elmcroft Rd	Stamford	CT	06926	**800-672-6937**	203-356-5000
NYSE: PBI					
Pubco Corp					
3830 Kelley Ave	Cleveland	OH	44114	**800-878-3399**	216-881-5300
Royal Consumer Information Products Inc					
379 Campus Dr 2nd Fl	Somerset	NJ	08873	**888-261-4555***	732-627-9977
*Sales					
Schaumburg Specialties Co					
550 Albion Ave Unit 30	Schaumburg	IL	60193	**800-834-8125**	
Security Engineered Machinery Company Inc					
Five Walkup Dr PO Box 1045	Westborough	MA	01581	**800-225-9293***	508-366-1488
*Sales					
Sharp Electronics Corp					
One Sharp Plz	Mahwah	NJ	07430	**800-237-4277**	201-529-8200
Staplex Co 777 Fifth Ave	Brooklyn	NY	11232	**800-221-0822***	718-768-3333
*Cust Svc					
Swintec Corp					
320 W Commercial Ave	Moonachie	NJ	07074	**800-225-0867**	201-935-0115

111 — BUSINESS MACHINES - WHOL

SEE ALSO Photocopying Equipment & Supplies ; Business Machines - Mfr ; Computer Equipment & Software - Whol

				Toll-Free	Phone
Adams Remco Inc					
PO Box 3968	South Bend	IN	46619	**800-627-2113**	574-288-2113
Canon Business Solutions-Central					
425 N Martingale Rd Ste 100	Schaumburg	IL	60173	**800-706-3303**	847-706-3400
Canon Business Solutions-Southeast Inc					
300 Commerce Sq Blvd	Burlington	NJ	08016	**844-443-4636**	609-387-8700
Canon Business Solutions-West					
One Canon Park	Melville	CA	11747	**844-443-4636**	
Carr Business Systems Inc					
130 Spagnoli Rd	Melville	NY	11747	**800-244-1880**	631-249-9880
Copiers Northwest Inc					
601 Dexter Ave N	Seattle	WA	98109	**866-692-0700**	206-282-1200
CRS Inc					
4851 White Bear Pkwy	Saint Paul	MN	55110	**800-333-4949**	651-294-2700
Daisy IT Supplies Sales & Service					
8575 Red Oak Ave	Rancho Cucamonga	CA	91730	**800-266-5585**	909-989-5585
Datamax Office Systems Inc					
6717 Waldemar Ave	Saint Louis	MO	63139	**800-325-9299**	314-633-1400
Dieterich-Post Co					
616 Monterey Pass Rd	Monterey Park	CA	91754	**800-955-3729**	626-289-5021
El Dorado Trading Group Inc					
760 San Antonio Rd	Palo Alto	CA	94303	**800-227-8292**	
FP Mailing Solutions					
140 N Mitchell Ct	Addison	IL	60101	**800-341-6052**	630-827-5500
Global Imaging Systems Inc					
3820 Northdale Blvd Ste 200A	Tampa	FL	33624	**888-628-7834**	813-960-5508
Illinois Wholesale Cash Register Inc					
2790 Pinnacle Dr	Elgin	IL	60124	**800-544-5493**	847-310-4200
Merchants Solutions Co					
4422 Roosevelt Rd	Hillside	IL	60162	**800-486-3214**	708-449-6650
Metro - Sales Inc					
1640 E 78th St	Minneapolis	MN	55423	**800-862-7414**	612-861-4000
Numeridex Inc					
632 S Wheeling Rd	Wheeling	IL	60090	**800-323-7737**	
Pitney Bowes Inc					
One Elmcroft Rd	Stamford	CT	06926	**800-672-6937**	203-356-5000
NYSE: PBI					
Ricoh Americas Corp					
Five Dedrick Pl	West Caldwell	NJ	07006	**800-727-1885**	973-882-2000
Secap USA Inc					
10 Clipper Rd	Conshohocken	PA	19428	**800-523-0320**	610-825-6205
Standard Duplicating Machines Corp					
10 Connector Rd	Andover	MA	01810	**800-526-4774**	978-470-1920
Stewart Engineering Supply Inc					
3221 E Pioneer Pkwy	Arlington	TX	76010	**800-533-1265**	817-640-1767
Systel Business Equipment Company Inc					
3756 Sycamore Dairy Rd	Fayetteville	NC	28303	**800-849-5900**	910-483-7114

	Toll-Free	Phone

Transco Business Technologies (TBT)
34 Leighton Rd .... Augusta ME 04330   **800-322-0003**   207-622-6251

BUSINESS ORGANIZATIONS

SEE Management & Business Professional Associations ; Chambers of Commerce - Canadian ; Chambers of Commerce - US - Local ; Chambers of Commerce - US - State

112   BUSINESS SERVICE CENTERS

	Toll-Free	Phone

Allegra Network LLC
47585 Galleon Dr .... Plymouth MI 48170   **800-726-9050***   248-596-8600
*General

Aloha Petroleum Ltd
1132 Bishop St Ste 1700 .... Honolulu HI 96813   **800-621-4654**   808-522-9700

Alphanumeric Systems Inc
3801 Wake Forest Rd .... Raleigh NC 27609   **800-638-6556**   919-781-7575

Annex Brands Inc
7580 Metropolitan Dr Ste 200 .... San Diego CA 92108   **877-722-5236**   619-563-4800

Asi System Integration Inc
48 W 37th St .... New York NY 10018   **866-308-3920**

Concentrix Corp
3750 Monroe Ave .... Pittsford NY 14534   **800-747-0583**   585-218-5300

Corporation Service Co
2711 Centerville Rd Ste 400 .... Wilmington DE 19808   **866-403-5272**   302-636-5400

Craters & Freighters
331 Corporate Cir Ste J .... Golden CO 80401   **800-736-3335**

Duncan-Parnell Inc
900 S McDowell St .... Charlotte NC 28204   **800-849-7708**   704-372-7766

Group O Inc 4905 77th Ave .... Milan IL 61264   **800-752-0730***   309-736-8300
*Cust Svc

Mail Boxes Etc
6060 Cornerstone Ct W .... San Diego CA 92121   **800-789-4623**   858-455-8800

Navis Logistics Network
6551 S Revere Pkwy Ste 250 .... Centennial CO 80111   **800-344-3528**

Navis Pack & Ship Centers
6551 S Revere Pkwy Ste 250 .... Centennial CO 80111   **800-344-3528**

Office Depot Inc
2200 Old Germantown Rd .... Delray Beach FL 33445   **800-937-3600**   561-438-4800
NASDAQ: ODP

Pak Mail Centers of America Inc
7173 S Havana St Ste 600 .... Centennial CO 80112   **800-778-6665***   303-957-1000
*Cust Svc

Parcel Plus Inc
13121 Louetta Rd .... Cypress TX 77429   **888-280-2053**   281-376-0054

Peachtree Planning Corp
5040 Roswell Rd NE .... Atlanta GA 30342   **800-366-0839**   404-260-1600

Postal Connections of America
6136 Frisco Sq Blvd Ste 400 .... Frisco TX 75034   **800-767-8257**

PostalAnnex+ Inc
7580 Metropolitan Dr Ste 200 .... San Diego CA 92108   **800-456-1525**   619-563-4800

PostNet International Franchise Corp
1819 Wazee St .... Denver CO 80202   **800-841-7171**   303-771-7100

Sharp Decisions Inc
1040 Ave of the A .... New York NY 10018   **800-742-7792**   212-481-5533

Shee Atika Inc
315 Lincoln St Ste 300 .... Sitka AK 99835   **800-478-3534**   907-747-3534

Sir Speedy Inc
26722 Plaza Dr .... Mission Viejo CA 92691   **800-854-8297**   949-348-5000

Total Energy Solutions LLC (TES)
100 International Dr Ste 260 .... Portsmouth NH 03801   **877-436-9812**

Ubics Inc
333 Technology Dr Ste 210 .... Canonsburg PA 15317   **800-441-0077**   724-746-6001
OTC: UBIX

UPS Store, The
6060 Cornerstone Ct W .... San Diego CA 92121   **800-789-4623**   858-455-8800

Zoom Information Inc
307 Waverley Oaks Rd .... Waltham MA 02452   **800-949-7040**   781-693-7500

113   BUYER'S GUIDES - ONLINE

SEE ALSO Investment Guides - Online

	Toll-Free	Phone

Ace Mart - Downtown San Antonio
1220 S St Mary's .... San Antonio TX 78210   **888-898-8079**   210-224-0082

InsWeb Inc
11290 Pyrites Way Ste 200 .... Gold River CA 95670   **866-697-9085**   916-853-3300

Market America Inc
1302 Pleasant Ridge Rd .... Greensboro NC 27409   **866-420-1709**   336-605-0040

Parke-Bell Ltd Inc
709 W 12th St .... Huntingburg IN 47542   **800-457-7456**   812-683-3707

114   CABINETS - WOOD

SEE ALSO Household Furniture ; Carpentry & Flooring Contractors

	Toll-Free	Phone

Bloch Industries
140 Commerce Dr .... Rochester NY 14623   **800-992-5624**   585-334-9600

Brandom Cabinets Co
404 Hawkins St .... Hillsboro TX 76645   **800-366-8001***   512-805-0280
*Cust Svc

Cabinetry By Karman Inc
6000 Stratler St .... Salt Lake City UT 84107   **800-255-3581**   801-281-6400

California Kitchen Cabinet Door Corp
400 Cochrane Cir .... Morgan Hill CA 95037   **888-225-3667**   408-782-5700

Canyon Creek Cabinet Co
16726 Tye St SE .... Monroe WA 98272   **800-228-1830**   360-348-4973

Chandlers Plywood Products Inc
3716 Waverly Rd .... Huntington WV 25704   **800-414-1311**   304-429-1311

Conestoga Wood Specialties Inc
245 Reading Rd .... East Earl PA 17519   **800-964-3667**

	Toll-Free	Phone

Crystal Cabinet Works Inc
1100 Crystal Dr .... Princeton MN 55371   **800-347-5045**

Decore-ative Specialties Inc
2772 S Peck Rd .... Monrovia CA 91016   **800-729-7277**   626-254-9191

Grabill Cabinet Company Inc
13844 Sawmill Dr .... Grabill IN 46741   **877-472-2782**

Grandview Products Co
1601 Superior Dr .... Parsons KS 67357   **800-247-9105**   620-421-6950

Haas Cabinet Company Inc
625 W Utica St .... Sellersburg IN 47172   **800-457-6458**   812-246-4431

HomeCrest Cabinetry
1002 Eisenhower Dr N .... Goshen IN 46526   **800-960-3660**   574-535-9300

Huntwood Industries
23800 E Apple Way .... Liberty Lake WA 99019   **800-873-7350**   509-924-5858

Jim Bishop Cabinets Inc
5640 Bell Rd .... Montgomery AL 36116   **800-410-2444**

Kraftmaid Cabinetry Inc
15535 S State Ave PO Box 1055 .... Middlefield OH 44062   **888-562-7744**

Marsh Furniture Co
PO Box 870 .... High Point NC 27261   **800-696-2774**   336-884-7363

Masco Cabinetry LLC
5353 W US 223 PO Box 1946 .... Adrian MI 49221   **866-850-8557**   517-263-0771

Masco Corp 21001 Van Born Rd .... Taylor MI 48180   **888-627-6397**   313-274-7400
NYSE: MAS

Mastercraft Industries Inc
777 S St .... Newburgh NY 12550   **800-835-7812**   845-565-8850

Medallion Cabinetry
1 Medallion Way .... Waconia MN 55387   **800-543-4074**   952-442-5171

Mouser Custom Cabinetry
2112 N Hwy 31 W .... Elizabethtown KY 42701   **800-345-7537**   270-737-7477

Norcraft cabinetry
3020 Denmark Ave .... Eagan MN 55121   **877-888-0002**   651-234-3300

Northern Contours Inc
1355 Mendota Heights Rd
Ste 100 .... Mendota Heights MN 55120   **866-344-8132**   651-695-1698

Patrick Industries Inc
107 W Franklin St PO Box 638 .... Elkhart IN 46515   **800-331-2151**   574-294-7511
NASDAQ: PATK

Plato Woodwork Inc
200 Third St SW .... Plato MN 55370   **800-328-5924**   320-238-2193

Republic Industries Inc
1400 Warren Dr .... Marshall TX 75672   **866-284-0941**   903-935-3680

Rosebud Mfg Co Inc
701 SE 12th St .... Madison SD 57042   **800-256-4561**   605-256-4561

RSI Home Products Inc
400 E Orangethorpe Ave .... Anaheim CA 92801   **888-774-8062**   714-449-2200

Rynone Mfg Corp PO Box 128 .... Sayre PA 18840   **800-839-1654**   570-888-5272

Starmark Cabinetry
600 E 48th St N .... Sioux Falls SD 57104   **800-755-7789**   800-594-9444

Ultracraft Co
6163 Old 421 Rd .... Liberty NC 27298   **800-262-4046**

Valley Cabinet Inc
845 Prosper Rd .... De Pere WI 54115   **800-236-8981**   920-336-3174

Wellborn Forest Products Inc
2212 Airport Blvd .... Alexander City AL 35010   **800-846-2562**   256-234-7900

115   CABLE & OTHER PAY TELEVISION SERVICES

	Toll-Free	Phone

Big Bend Telephone Company Inc
808 N Fifth St .... Alpine TX 79830   **800-520-0092**   432-364-1000

Cable Connection, The
52 Heppner Dr .... Carson City NV 89706   **800-851-2961**   775-885-1443

Cable One Inc
210 E Earll Drive .... Phoenix AZ 85012   **877-692-2253**   602-364-6000

CableAmerica Corp
350 E 10th Dr .... Mesa AZ 85210   **866-871-4492**

Campus Televideo Inc
100 First Stamford Pl .... Stamford CT 06902   **866-615-8674**   203-983-5400

Cass Cable Tv Inc
100 Redbud Rd .... Virginia IL 62691   **800-252-1799**   217-452-7725

Charter Communications Inc
12405 Powerscourt Dr Ste 100 .... Saint Louis MO 63131   **888-438-2427**   314-965-0555
NASDAQ: CHTR

Cogeco Cable Inc
5 Pl Ville-Marie Ste 915 .... Montreal QC H3B2G2   **800-855-0511**   514-874-2600

Cox Communications Inc
1400 Lake Hearn Dr .... Atlanta GA 30319   **866-961-0027**   404-843-5000

DIRECTV Inc
2230 E Imperial Hwy .... El Segundo CA 90245   **800-531-5000***   310-535-5000
*Cust Svc

DISH Network LLC
9601 S Meridian Blvd .... Englewood CO 80112   **800-823-4929**
NASDAQ: DISH

Hamilton Telephone Co
1001 12th St .... Aurora NE 68818   **800-821-1831**   402-694-5101

High Power Technical Services Inc (HPTS)
2230 Ampere Dr .... Louisville KY 40299   **866-398-3474**

Kincardine Cable TV Ltd
223 Bruce Ave .... Kincardine ON N2Z2P2   **800-265-3064**   519-396-8880

Kmtelecom 18 Second Ave NW .... Kasson MN 55944   **888-232-3796**   507-634-2511

Ksbj 1722 Treble Dr .... Humble TX 77338   **877-644-5725**   281-446-5725

Ksby-Tv
1772 Calle Joaquin .... San Luis Obispo CA 93405   **800-583-4135**   805-541-6666

Link Electronics Inc
2137 Rust Ave .... Cape Girardeau MO 63703   **800-776-4411**   573-334-4433

Mediacom Communications Corp
100 Crystal Run Rd .... Middletown NY 10941   **800-479-2082***   845-695-2600
*General

Midcontinent Communications
PO Box 5010 .... Sioux Falls SD 57117   **800-888-1300**   605-274-9810

National Cable Television Co-op Inc (NCTC)
11200 Corporate Ave .... Lenexa KS 66219   **800-720-5850**   913-599-5900

Otter Tail Telcom
230 W Lincoln Ave .... Fergus Falls MN 56537   **800-247-2706**   218-826-6161

Paragould Light Water & Cable (PLWC)
1901 Jones Rd .... Paragould AR 72450   **800-482-8998**   870-239-7700

			Toll-Free	Phone
Rooftop Media Inc				
530 Howard St Ste 400	San Francisco CA	94105	800-860-0293	
Service Electric Cable TV & Communications				
2260 Ave A	Bethlehem PA	18017	800-232-9100	610-865-9100
Shaw Communications Inc				
630 Third Ave SW	Calgary AB	T2P4L4	888-472-2222	403-750-4500
TSE: SJR/B				
Southern Vermont Cable Co				
PO Box 166	Bondville VT	05340	800-544-5931	
Suddenlink Communications				
6151 Paluxy Dr	Tyler TX	75703	877-694-9474	
Tele-Media Corp				
804 Jacksonville Rd P.O. Box 39	Bellefonte PA	16823	800-704-4254	814-353-2025
TiVo Inc 2160 Gold St	Alviso CA	95002	877-367-8486	408-519-9100
NASDAQ: TIVO				

116 CABLE REELS

			Toll-Free	Phone
American Reeling Devices Inc				
15 Airpark Vista Blvd	Dayton NV	89403	800-354-7335*	
*Sales				
Conductix 10102 F St	Omaha NE	68127	800-521-4888	402-339-9300
Gleason Reel Corp				
600 S Clark St	Mayville WI	53050	888-504-5151	920-387-4120
Hannay Reels Inc				
553 SR 143	Westerlo NY	12193	877-467-3357	518-797-3791

117 CALCULATORS - ELECTRONIC

			Toll-Free	Phone
Calculated Industries Inc				
4840 Hytech Dr	Carson City NV	89706	800-854-8075	775-885-4900
Sharp Electronics Corp				
One Sharp Plz	Mahwah NJ	07430	800-237-4277	201-529-8200
Texas Instruments Inc				
12500 TI Blvd	Dallas TX	75243	800-336-5236*	972-995-3773
NASDAQ: TXN ▓ *Cust Svc				
Victor Technology LLC				
175 E Crossroads Pkwy	Boling Brook IL	60440	800-628-2420	630-754-4400

118 CAMERAS & RELATED SUPPLIES - RETAIL

			Toll-Free	Phone
Abe's of Maine Cameras & Electronics				
Five Fernwood Ave	Edison NJ	08837	800-992-2237	732-225-1777
Adorama Camera Inc				
42 W 18th St	New York NY	10011	800-223-2500	212-741-0052
B & H Photo-Video-Pro Audio Corp				
420 Ninth Ave	New York NY	10001	800-947-9954	212-444-6600
Beach Camera				
203 Rt 22 E	Green Brook NJ	08812	800-572-3224	732-968-6400
Black Photo Corp				
200 Consilium Pl Ste 1600	Toronto ON	M1H3J3	800-668-3826	416-279-0007
CambridgeWorld				
34 Franklin Ave	Brooklyn NY	11205	800-221-2253	718-858-5002
Camera Corner Inc				
PO Box 1899	Burlington NC	27216	800-868-2462	336-228-0251
Dodd Camera				
2077 E 30th St	Cleveland OH	44115	800-507-1676	216-361-6800
Dury's 701 Ewing Ave	Nashville TN	37203	800-824-2379	615-255-3456
F-11 Photographic Supplies				
16 E Main St	Bozeman MT	59715	888-548-0203	406-586-3281
Focus Camera Inc				
905 McDonald Ave	Brooklyn NY	11218	800-221-0828	718-437-8810
Kenmore Camera Inc				
18031 67th Ave NE PO Box 82467	Kenmore WA	98028	888-485-7447	425-485-7447
Ritz Camera & Image				
2 Bergen Turnpike	Ridgefield Park NJ	07660	855-622-7489*	201-881-1900
*Cust Svc				
Samy's Camera Inc				
431 S Fairfax Ave	Los Angeles CA	90036	800-321-4726	323-938-2420

119 CAMPERS, TRAVEL TRAILERS, MOTOR HOMES

			Toll-Free	Phone
Coach House Inc				
3480 Technology Dr	Nokomis FL	34275	800-235-0984	941-485-0984
Cool Amphibious Manufacturers International LLC				
714 Okeetee Rd	Ridgeland SC	29936	888-926-6553	843-717-2444
Cruise America				
11 W Hampton Ave	Mesa AZ	85210	800-671-8042	480-464-7300
Custom Fiberglass Mfg Corp				
Snugtop				
1711 Harbor Ave PO Box 121	Long Beach CA	90813	800-768-4867	562-432-5454
Dutchmen Mfg Inc				
2164 Caragana Ct PO Box 2164	Goshen IN	46527	866-425-4369	574-537-0600
Foretravel Motorcoach Inc				
1221 NW Stallings Dr	Nacogdoches TX	75964	800-955-6226	936-564-8367
Four Wheel Campers				
1460 Churchill Downs Ave	Woodland CA	95776	800-242-1442	530-666-1442
Gulf Stream Coach Inc				
503 S Oakland Ave PO Box 1005	Nappanee IN	46550	800-289-8787	574-773-7761
Jayco Inc 903 S Main St	Middlebury IN	46540	800-283-8267*	574-825-5861
*Cust Svc				
Keystone RV Co				
2642 Hackberry Dr PO Box 2000	Goshen IN	46527	866-425-4369	574-535-2100
Lance Camper Mfg Corp				
43120 Venture St	Lancaster CA	93535	800-423-7996	661-949-3322
Monaco Coach Corp				
91320 Coburg Industrial Way	Coburg OR	97408	888-327-4236	877-466-6226

			Toll-Free	Phone
New Horizons RV Corp				
2401 Lacy Dr	Junction City KS	66441	800-235-3140	785-238-7575
Newell Coach Corp				
6411 S Hwy 69 PO Box 511	Miami OK	74354	888-363-9355	918-542-3344
Newmar Corp				
355 Delaware St	Nappanee IN	46550	800-731-8300	574-773-7791
Nu-Wa Industries Inc				
3701 Johnson Rd	Chanute KS	66720	800-835-0676	620-431-2088
pace-edwards				
2400 Commercial Rd	Centralia WA	98531	800-338-3697	360-736-9991
Peterson Industries Inc				
616 E Hwy 36	Smith Center KS	66967	800-368-3759	785-282-6825
Renegade/Kibbi LLC				
52216 State Rd 15	Bristol IN	46507	888-522-1126	574-848-1126
Rexhall Industries Inc				
46147 Seventh St W	Lancaster CA	93534	800-765-7500	661-726-0565
OTC: REXLQ				
Skyline Corp				
2520 By-Pass Rd	Elkhart IN	46514	800-348-7469	574-294-6521
NYSE: SKY				
Winnebago Industries Inc				
605 W Crystal Lk Rd PO Box 152	Forest City IA	50436	800-643-4892	641-585-3535
NYSE: WGO				

120 CAMPGROUND OPERATORS

			Toll-Free	Phone
Holiday Trails Resorts (Western) Inc				
53730 Bridal Falls Rd	Rosedale BC	V0X1X1	800-663-2265	604-794-7876
Kampgrounds of America Inc (KOA)				
PO Box 30558	Billings MT	59114	888-562-0000	
Leisure Systems Inc				
50 W Techne Ctr Dr Ste G	Milford OH	45150	866-928-9644	513-831-2100
Western Horizon Resorts (WHR)				
103 W Tomichi Ave Ste 201A	Gunnison CO	81230	800-378-3709	970-641-5387

121 CANDLES

SEE ALSO Gift Shops

			Toll-Free	Phone
Dadant & Sons Inc				
51 S Second St	Hamilton IL	62341	888-922-1293	217-847-3324
General Wax & Candle Co				
6863 Beck Ave PO Box 9398	North Hollywood CA	91605	800-929-7867	818-765-5800
Knorr Beeswax Products Inc				
14906 Via De La Valle	Del Mar CA	92014	800-807-2337	760-431-2007
Original Cake Candle Co, The				
102 Sundale Rd PO Box 97	Norwich OH	43767	800-288-2340	740-872-3248
Root Candles Co				
623 W Liberty St	Medina OH	44256	800-289-7668	330-725-6677
Swans Candles				
8933 Gravelly Lk Dr SW	Lakewood WA	98499	888-848-7926	253-584-4666

122 CANDY STORES

			Toll-Free	Phone
Candy Bouquet International Inc				
510 Mclean St	Little Rock AR	72202	877-226-3901	501-375-9990
Gardners Candies Inc				
2600 Adams Ave PO Box E	Tyrone PA	16686	800-242-2639	814-684-3925
Gertrude Hawk Chocolates Inc				
9 Keystone Pk	Dunmore PA	18512	866-932-4295	800-822-2032
Kilwins Quality Confections Inc (KQC)				
1050 Bay View Rd	Petoskey MI	49770	888-454-5946	
Lammes Candies Since 1885 Inc				
PO Box 1885	Austin TX	78767	800-252-1885	512-310-2223
Provide Commerce Inc				
4840 Eastgate Mall	San Diego CA	92121	800-776-3569*	858-638-4900
*Cust Svc				
Rocky Mountain Chocolate Factory Inc (RMCF)				
265 Turner Dr	Durango CO	81303	888-525-2462*	970-259-0554
NASDAQ: RMCF ▓ *Cust Svc				
See's Candies Inc				
210 El Camino Real	South San Francisco CA	94080	800-877-7337*	650-761-2490
*Cust Svc				

123 CANS - METAL

SEE ALSO Containers - Metal (Barrels, Drums, Kegs)

			Toll-Free	Phone
BWAY Corp				
8607 Roberts Dr Ste 250	Atlanta GA	30350	800-527-2267	770-645-4800
Crown Holdings Inc				
One Crown Way	Philadelphia PA	19154	800-523-3644	215-698-5100
NYSE: CCK				
JL Clark Mfg Co				
923 23rd Ave	Rockford IL	61104	877-482-5275	815-962-8861
KOR Water Inc				
95 Enterprise Ste 310	Aliso Viejo CA	92656	877-708-7567	714-708-7567
Protectoseal Co				
225 W Foster Ave	Bensenville IL	60106	800-323-2268	630-595-0800
Rexam Inc				
4201 Congress St Ste 340	Charlotte NC	28209	800-944-2217	704-551-1500
Ring Container Technology				
65 Industrial Park Rd	Oakland TN	38060	800-280-6333	

124 CANS, TUBES, DRUMS - PAPER (FIBER)

			Toll-Free	Phone
Acme Spirally Wound Paper Products Inc				
4810 W 139th St PO Box 35320	Cleveland OH	44135	800-274-2797	216-267-2950

			Toll-Free	Phone
Callenor Company Inc				
N 60 W 15725 Kohler Ln	Menomonee Falls WI	53051	800-813-7429	262-252-3343
Caraustar Industries Inc				
5000 Austell-Powder Springs Rd				
Ste 300	Austell GA	30106	800-223-1373	770-948-3100
Custom Paper Tubes Inc				
15900 Industrial Pkwy	Cleveland OH	44135	800-343-8823	216-362-2964
Greif Inc 425 Winter Rd	Delaware OH	43015	877-781-9797	740-549-6000
NYSE: GEF				
Industrial Paper Tube Inc				
1335 E Bay Ave	Bronx NY	10474	800-345-0960	
LCH Paper Tube & Core Co				
11930 Larc Industrial Blvd	Burnsville MN	55337	800-472-3477	952-358-3587
Master Package Corp				
200 Madson St	Owen WI	54460	800-396-8425	715-229-2156
OX Paper Tube & Core Inc				
331 Maple Ave	Hanover PA	17331	800-414-2476	
Pacific Paper Tube Inc				
1025 98th Ave	Oakland CA	94603	888-377-8823	510-562-8823
Self-Seal Container Corp				
401 E Fourth St	Bridgeport PA	19405	800-334-1428	610-275-2300
TEKPAK Inc				
1410 Washington St	Marion AL	36756	866-901-8073	334-683-6121
Yazoo Mills Inc				
PO Box 369	New Oxford PA	17350	800-242-5216*	717-624-8993
*Cust Svc				

125   CAR RENTAL AGENCIES

SEE ALSO Truck Rental & Leasing ; Fleet Leasing & Management

			Toll-Free	Phone
A Betterway Rent-a-car Inc				
1110 Northchase Pkwy SE	Marietta GA	30067	800-527-0700	770-240-3305
ACE Rent A Car				
5773 W Washington St	Indianapolis IN	46241	800-242-7368	317-248-5686
Advantage Rent-A-Car				
1288 Old Bayshore Hwy Ste 116	Burlingame CA	94010	800-777-5500*	650-343-3052
*Cust Svc				
Affiliated Car Rental				
105 Hwy 36	Eatontown NJ	07724	800-367-5159	
Affordable Car Rental LC				
105 Hwy 36	Eatontown NJ	07724	800-367-5159	732-272-8736
Auto Europe				
39 Commercial St	Portland ME	04101	800-223-5555	207-842-2000
Avis Rent A Car System Inc				
6 Sylvan Way	Parsippany NJ	07054	800-331-1212	973-496-3500
Budget Rent A Car System Inc				
Six Sylvan Way	Parsippany NJ	07054	800-527-0700	800-283-4382
Dewey Ford Inc				
3055 SE Delaware Ave	Ankeny IA	50021	888-378-8516	515-289-4949
Discount Car & Truck Rentals Ltd				
720 Arrow Rd	North York ON	M9M2M1	866-742-5968	
Dollar Rent A Car Inc				
5330 E 31st St	Tulsa OK	74135	800-800-4000	918-669-3000
Dollar Thrifty Automotive Group Inc				
5330 E 31st St PO Box 35985	Tulsa OK	74135	800-334-1705	918-660-7700
Enterprise Rent-A-Car				
600 Corporate Pk Dr	Saint Louis MO	63105	800-325-8007	314-512-5000
Europe by Car				
40 Exchange Pl Ste 1720	New York NY	10005	800-223-1516	212-581-3040
Hale Trailer Brake & Wheel Inc				
Rt 73 & Cooper Rd	Voorhees NJ	08043	800-232-6535	856-768-1330
Hertz Global Holdings Inc				
225 Brae Blvd	Park Ridge NJ	07656	800-654-3131	201-307-2000
NYSE: HTZ				
Kemwel Inc				
39 Commercial St	Portland ME	04112	800-678-0678	207-842-2285
Omaha Truck Center Inc				
10710 I St PO Box 27379	Omaha NE	68127	800-866-2204	402-592-2440
Thrifty Car Rental				
5330 E 31st St	Tulsa OK	74135	888-400-8877	918-665-3930
U-Save Auto Rental of America Inc				
1052 Highland Colony Pkwy Ste 204	Ridgeland MS	39157	800-438-2300*	601-713-4333
*General				

126   CARBON & GRAPHITE PRODUCTS

			Toll-Free	Phone
Advance Carbon Products Inc				
2036 National Ave	Hayward CA	94545	800-283-1249	510-293-5930
Helwig Carbon Products Inc				
8900 W Tower Ave	Milwaukee WI	53224	800-365-3113	414-354-2411
Mersen USA BN Corp				
400 Myrtle Ave	Boonton NJ	07005	800-526-0877*	
*General				
National Electrical Carbon				
251 Forrester Dr	Greenville SC	29607	800-471-7842	864-284-9728
Saturn Industries Inc				
157 Union Tpke	Hudson NY	12534	800-775-1651	518-828-9956
SGL Carbon LLC				
307 Jamestown Rd	Morganton NC	28655	800-828-6601	828-437-3221
Superior Graphite				
10 S Riverside Plaza Ste 1470	Chicago IL	60606	800-327-0337*	312-559-2999
*Cust Svc				

127   CARBURETORS, PISTONS, PISTON RINGS, VALVES

SEE ALSO Aircraft Engines & Engine Parts ; Automotive Parts & Supplies - Mfr

			Toll-Free	Phone
Compressor Products International				
4410 Greenbriar Dr	Stafford TX	77477	800-675-6646	281-207-4600

			Toll-Free	Phone
Grant Piston Rings				
1360 Jefferson St	Anaheim CA	92807	800-854-3540	714-996-0050
Grover Corp				
2759 S 28th St	Milwaukee WI	53234	800-776-3602	414-384-9472
Hastings Manufacturing Co				
325 N Hanover St	Hastings MI	49058	800-776-1088	269-945-2491
Holley Performance Products Inc				
1801 Russellville Rd	Bowling Green KY	42101	800-638-0032*	270-782-2900
*Sales				
MAHLE Industries Inc				
2020 Sanford St	Muskegon MI	49444	888-255-1942	231-722-1300
Martin Wells Industries				
PO Box 01406	Los Angeles CA	90001	800-421-6000	323-581-6266
Safety Seal Piston Ring Co				
4000 Airport Rd	Marshall TX	75672	800-962-3631*	903-938-9241
*Sales				
Total Seal Inc				
22642 N 15th Ave	Phoenix AZ	85027	800-874-2753	623-587-7400
United Engine & Machine Company Inc				
1040 Corbett St	Carson City NV	89706	800-648-7970	775-882-7790
Wiseco Piston Inc				
7201 Industrial Pk Blvd	Mentor OH	44060	800-321-1364	440-951-6600

128   CARD SHOPS

SEE ALSO Gift Shops

			Toll-Free	Phone
American Greetings Corp Carlton Cards Div				
1 American Rd	Cleveland OH	44144	800-777-4891	216-252-7300
Hallmark Cards Inc				
2501 McGee St	Kansas City MO	64108	800-425-5627	816-274-5111
Papyrus Franchise Corp				
500 Chadbourne Rd	Fairfield CA	94533	800-789-1649	
Recycled Paper Greetings Inc				
111 N Canal St Ste 700	Chicago IL	60606	800-777-3331	

129   CARDS - GREETING - MFR

			Toll-Free	Phone
Amber Lotus Publishing				
PO Box 11329	Portland OR	97211	800-326-2375	503-284-6400
American Greetings Corp				
1 American Rd	Cleveland OH	44144	800-777-4891*	216-252-7300
NYSE: AM ■ *Sales				
AtticSalt Greetings Inc				
PO Box 5773	Topeka KS	66605	888-345-6005	
Avanti Press Inc				
155 W Congress St Ste 200	Detroit MI	48226	800-228-2684	313-961-0022
Bayview Press				
30 Knox St PO Box 153	Thomaston ME	04861	800-903-2346	207-354-9919
Birchcraft Studios Inc				
10 Railroad St	Abington MA	02351	800-333-0405	781-878-5152
Blue Mountain Arts Inc				
PO Box 4549	Boulder CO	80306	800-545-8573*	303-449-0536
*Sales				
Bonair Daydreams				
PO Box 1522	Wrightsville Beach NC	28480	888-226-6247	910-617-3887
Carole Joy Creations Inc				
1087 Federal Rd Unit 8	Brookfield CT	06804	800-223-6945*	203-740-4490
Colors By Design				
7723 Densmore Ave	Van Nuys CA	91406	800-832-8436	
DaySpring Cards Inc				
21154 Hwy 16 E	Siloam Springs AR	72761	800-944-8000	479-524-9301
Design Design Inc				
19 La Grave SE	Grand Rapids MI	49503	800-334-3348	616-774-2448
Eclectik 1332 W Lake St	Chicago IL	60607	866-308-1231	312-676-2442
Fantus Paper Products P.S. Greetings Inc				
5730 N Tripp Ave	Chicago IL	60646	800-621-8823*	773-267-6069
*Sales				
Freedom Greeting Card Company Inc				
774 American Dr	Bensalem PA	19020	800-359-3301*	215-604-0300
*Sales				
Galison Publishing LLC				
28 W 44th St Ste 1411	New York NY	10036	800-670-7441	212-354-8840
Gallant Greetings Corp				
4300 United Pkwy	Schiller Park IL	60176	800-621-4279	847-671-6500
Gina B Designs Inc				
12700 Industrial Pk Blvd Ste 40	Plymouth MN	55441	800-228-4856	763-559-7595
Graphique De France				
Nine State St	Woburn MA	01801	800-444-1464*	781-935-3405
*Sales				
Great Arrow Graphics				
2495 Main St Ste 457	Buffalo NY	14214	800-835-0490	716-836-0408
Hallmark Cards Inc				
2501 McGee St	Kansas City MO	64108	800-425-5627	816-274-5111
Hallmark International				
PO Box 419034	Kansas City MO	64141	800-425-5627	816-274-5111
Laughing Elephant				
3645 Interlake Ave N	Seattle WA	98103	800-354-0400	
Laurel Ink 911 N 145th St	Seattle WA	98133	800-850-0081*	
*Cust Svc				
Marian Heath Greeting Cards Inc				
Nine Kendrick Rd	Wareham MA	02571	800-688-9998*	508-291-0766
*Sales				
Meri Meri 63 Leonard St	Belmont MA	02478	800-638-2881	617-484-5571
Museum Facsimiles				
117 Fourth St	Pittsfield MA	01201	877-499-0020	413-499-0020
New England Art Publisher				
10 Railroad St	North Abington MA	02351	800-333-0405	781-616-2508
NobleWorks Inc				
500 Paterson Plank Rd	Union City NJ	07087	800-346-6253	201-420-0095
Northern Exposure Greeting Cards				
2301 Circadian Way Ste 300	Santa Rosa CA	95407	800-237-3524	707-546-2153

				Toll-Free	Phone

Nouvelles Images Inc
68 Morgan Ave . . . . Danbury CT 06810 **800-345-1383** 203-730-1004

Palm Press Inc
1442A Walnut St PO Box 120 . . . . Berkeley CA 94709 **800-322-7256** 510-486-0502

Paperdoll Co 4944 Encino Ave . . . . Encino CA 91316 **866-223-1145** 818-906-8411

Peaceable Kingdom Press
950 Gilman St Ste 200 . . . . Berkeley CA 94710 **877-444-5195** 510-558-2051

Penny Laine Papers
2211 Century Ctr Blvd Ste 110 . . . . Irving TX 75062 **800-456-6484** 972-812-3000

Persimmon Press PO Box 297 . . . . Belmont CA 94002 **800-910-5080** 650-802-8325

Posty Cards
1600 Olive St . . . . Kansas City MO 64127 **800-821-7968** 816-231-2323

Recycled Paper Greetings Inc
111 N Canal St Ste 700 . . . . Chicago IL 60606 **800-777-3331**

Schurman Fine Papers
500 Chadbourne Rd PO Box 6030 . . . . Fairfield CA 94533 **800-789-1649***
*Sales

StellArt 2012 Waltzer Rd . . . . Santa Rosa CA 95403 **866-621-1987** 707-569-1378

Sunshine Business Class
150 Kingswood Rd PO Box 8465 . . . . Mankato MN 56001 **800-873-7681**

Up With Paper 6049 Hi-Tek Ct . . . . Mason OH 45040 **800-852-7677** 513-759-7473

Victorian Trading Co
15600 W 99th St . . . . Lenexa KS 66219 **800-700-2035*** 913-438-3995
*Cust Svc

Willow Creek Press Inc
9931 Hwy 70 W PO Box 147 . . . . Minocqua WI 54548 **800-850-9453*** 715-358-7010
*Cust Svc

130 CARPETS & RUGS

SEE ALSO Tile - Ceramic (Wall & Floor) ; Flooring - Resilient
The companies listed here include carpet finishers and makers of mats and padding.

				Toll-Free	Phone

Architectural Floor Systems Inc
595 Supreme Dr . . . . Bensenville IL 60106 **877-437-3567**

Artisans Inc
W4146 Second St PO Box 278 . . . . Glen Flora WI 54526 **800-311-8756** 715-322-5285

Atlas Carpet Mills Inc
2200 Saybrook Ave . . . . City of Commerce CA 90040 **800-272-8527** 323-724-9000

Beaulieu of America Inc
1502 Coronet Dr PO Box 1248 . . . . Dalton GA 30722 **800-227-7211**

Bentley Prince Street
14641 E Don Julian Rd . . . . City of Industry CA 91746 **800-423-4709**

Bloomsburg Carpet Industries Inc
4999 Columbia Blvd . . . . Bloomsburg PA 17815 **800-233-8773** 570-784-9188

Camelot Carpet Mills Inc
17111 Red Hill Ave . . . . Irvine CA 92614 **800-854-8331** 949-474-4000

Capel Inc 831 N Main St . . . . Troy NC 27371 **800-334-3711** 800-382-6574

Dixie Group Inc
104 Nowlin Ln Ste 101 . . . . Chattanooga TN 37421 **800-289-4811** 423-510-7000
NASDAQ: DXYN

Dorsett Industries Inc
1304 May St PO Box 805 . . . . Dalton GA 30721 **800-241-4035** 706-278-1961

Durkan Patterned Carpet Inc
405 Virgil Dr . . . . Dalton GA 30721 **800-981-2009**

Flex Foam 617 N 21st Ave . . . . Phoenix AZ 85009 **800-266-3626** 602-252-5819

Garland Sales Inc
PO Box 1870 . . . . Dalton GA 30720 **800-524-0361** 706-278-7880

Home Dynamix LLC
One Carol Pl . . . . Moonachie NJ 07074 **800-726-9290** 201-807-0111

Indian Summer Carpet Mills Inc
601 Callahan Rd PO Box 3577 . . . . Dalton GA 30719 **800-824-4010** 706-277-6277

J & J Industries Inc
818 J & J Dr PO Box 1287 . . . . Dalton GA 30721 **800-241-4586** 706-529-2100

Jaipur Rugs Inc
2775 Pacific Dr . . . . Norcross GA 30071 **888-676-7330** 404-351-2360

Johnsonite Inc
16910 Munn Rd . . . . Chagrin Falls OH 44023 **800-899-8916** 440-543-8916

Lexmark Carpet Mills Inc
285 Kraft Dr . . . . Dalton GA 30721 **800-871-3211**

Maples Industries Inc
2210 Moody Ridge Rd . . . . Scottsboro AL 35768 **800-537-5447***
*Hum Res

Masland Carpets Inc
716 Bill Myles Dr . . . . Saraland AL 36571 **800-633-0468**

Milliken & Co KEX Div
201 Lukken Industrial Dr W MS 801 . . . . LaGrange GA 30240 **800-241-4826** 706-880-5511

Mohawk Industries Inc
160 S Industrial Blvd . . . . Calhoun GA 30703 **800-241-4494** 706-629-7721
NYSE: MHK

Mohawk Industries Inc Karastan Div
508 E Morris St . . . . Dalton GA 30721 **800-234-1120**

Mohawk Industries Inc Lees Carpets Div
160 S Industrial Blvd Ste 300 . . . . Calhoun GA 30701 **800-241-4494** 706-629-7721

Netchannel Inc
8310 Rio Grande Blvd NW . . . . Albuquerque NM 87114 **888-843-8282** 505-843-8282

Oriental Weavers of America
3252 Lower Dug Gap Rd SW . . . . Dalton GA 30720 **800-832-8020** 706-277-9666

Packerland Rent-a-mat Inc
12580 W Rohr Ave . . . . Butler WI 53007 **800-472-9339** 262-781-5321

Royalty Carpet Mills Inc
17111 Red Hill Ave . . . . Irvine CA 92614 **800-854-8331** 949-474-4000

S & S Mills Inc
414 C N Pk Dr . . . . Dalton GA 30720 **800-241-4013** 706-277-3677

Scottdel Inc 400 Church St . . . . Swanton OH 43558 **800-446-2341** 419-825-2341

Shaw Industries Inc
616 E Walnut Ave . . . . Dalton GA 30722 **800-441-7429**

Tandus Centiva
311 Smith Industrial Blvd PO Box 1447 . . . . Dalton GA 30722 **800-248-2878** 706-259-9711

Unique Carpets Ltd
7360 Jurupa Ave . . . . Riverside CA 92504 **800-547-8266** 951-352-8125

131 CASINO COMPANIES

SEE ALSO Games & Gaming

				Toll-Free	Phone

Ameristar Casinos Inc
3773 Howard Hughes Pkwy Ste 490-S . . . . Las Vegas NV 89169 **888-203-1112** 702-567-7000
NASDAQ: ASCA

Boomtown Inc 2100 Garson Rd . . . . Verdi NV 89439 **800-648-3790** 775-345-6000

Boyd Gaming Corp
3883 Howard Hughes Pkwy 9th Fl . . . . Las Vegas NV 89169 **800-522-4700** 702-792-7200
NYSE: BYD

Century Casinos Inc
2860 S Cir Dr Ste 350 . . . . Colorado Springs CO 80906 **888-966-2257** 719-527-8300
NASDAQ: CNTY

Delaware North Cos Gaming & Entertainment
40 Fountain Plz . . . . Buffalo NY 14202 **800-828-7240** 716-858-5000

Fond du Lac Band of Lake Superior Chippewa
1720 Big Lake Rd . . . . Cloquet MN 55720 **888-888-6007** 218-879-4593

Four Winds Casino Resort
11111 Wilson Rd . . . . New Buffalo MI 49117 **866-494-6371**

Full House Resorts Inc
4670 S Fort Apache Rd Ste 190 . . . . Las Vegas NV 89147 **800-240-6709** 702-221-7800
NASDAQ: FLL

Harrah's Las Vegas
3475 Las Vegas Blvd S . . . . Las Vegas NV 89109 **800-214-9110**

Kerzner International Ltd
1000 S Pine Island Rd Ste 800 . . . . Plantation FL 33324 **800-321-3000** 954-809-2000

Lakes Entertainment Inc
130 Cheshire Ln Ste 101 . . . . Minnetonka MN 55305 **800-946-9464** 952-449-9092

Majestic Investor Holdings LLC
One Buffington Harbor Dr . . . . Gary IN 46406 **800-522-4700**

Mille Lacs Band of Ojibwe
43408 Oodena Dr . . . . Onamia MN 56359 **800-709-6445** 320-532-4181

Palace Casino 158 Howard Ave . . . . Biloxi MS 39530 **800-725-2239** 228-432-8888

Pinnacle Entertainment Inc
3980 Howard Hughes Pkwy . . . . Las Vegas NV 89169 **877-764-8750** 702-541-7777
NYSE: PNK

Red Lake Gaming Enterprises Inc
PO Box 543 . . . . Red Lake MN 56671 **888-679-2501** 218-679-2111

Station Casinos Inc
1505 S Pavilion Ctr Dr . . . . Las Vegas NV 89135 **800-634-3101*** 702-495-3000
*Resv

132 CASINOS

SEE ALSO Games & Gaming
Listings for casinos are alphabetized by states.

				Toll-Free	Phone

Birmingham Race Course
1000 John Rogers Dr . . . . Birmingham AL 35210 **800-998-8238** 205-838-7500

Deerfoot Inn & Casino
1000 11500 35th St SE . . . . Calgary AB T2Z3W4 **877-236-5225** 403-236-7529

Casino Arizona at Salt River
524 N 92nd St . . . . Scottsdale AZ 85256 **866-877-9897*** 480-850-7777
*General

Fort McDowell Casino
10424 N Ft McDowell Rd . . . . Fort Mcdowell AZ 85264 **800-843-3678** 480-837-1424

River Rock Casino Resort
8811 River Rd . . . . Richmond BC V6X3P8 **866-748-3718** 604-247-8900

Agua Caliente Casino Resort Spa
32-250 Bob Hope Dr . . . . Rancho Mirage CA 92270 **888-999-1995** 760-321-2000

Augustine Casino
84-001 Ave 54 . . . . Coachella CA 92236 **888-752-9294** 760-391-9500

Barona Resort & Casino
1932 Wildcat Canyon Rd . . . . Lakeside CA 92040 **888-722-7662** 619-443-2300

Eagle Mountain Casino
681 S Tule Resv Rd . . . . Porterville CA 93257 **800-903-3353** 559-788-6220

Fantasy Springs Resort Casino
84-245 Indio Springs Pkwy . . . . Indio CA 92203 **800-827-2946*** 760-342-5000
*Cust Svc

Golden West Casino
1001 S Union Ave . . . . Bakersfield CA 93307 **800-267-3983** 661-324-6936

Pala Casino Resort & Spa
35008 Pala-Temecula Rd . . . . Pala CA 92059 **877-946-7252** 760-510-5100

Pechanga Resort & Casino
45000 Pechanga Pkwy . . . . Temecula CA 92592 **877-711-2946** 951-693-1819

San Manuel Indian Bingo & Casino
777 San Manuel Blvd . . . . Highland CA 92346 **800-359-2464**

Spa Resort Casino
401 E Amado Rd . . . . Palm Springs CA 92262 **888-999-1995**

Spotlight 29 Casino
46-200 Harrison Pl . . . . Coachella CA 92236 **800-655-1330** 760-775-5566

Sycuan Casino & Resort
5469 Casino Way . . . . El Cajon CA 92019 **800-279-2826*** 619-445-6002
*General

Table Mountain Casino
8184 Table Mountain Rd . . . . Friant CA 93626 **800-541-3637** 559-822-7777

Thunder Valley Casino
1200 Athens Ave . . . . Lincoln CA 95648 **877-468-8777** 916-408-7777

Viejas Casino
5000 Willows Rd . . . . Alpine CA 91901 **800-847-6537** 619-445-5400

Bronco Billy's Casino
233 E Bennett Ave PO Box 590 . . . . Cripple Creek CO 80813 **877-989-2142** 719-689-2142

Dostal Alley Casino
1 Dostal Alley . . . . Central City CO 80427 **888-949-2757** 303-582-1610

Double Eagle Hotel & Casino
442 E Bennett Ave . . . . Cripple Creek CO 80813 **800-711-7234** 719-689-5000

Isle of Capri Casino
401 Main St . . . . Black Hawk CO 80422 **800-843-4753*** 303-998-7777
*resv

Midnight Rose Hotel & Casino
256 E Bennett Ave . . . . Cripple Creek CO 80813 **800-635-5825** 719-689-2446

Reserve Casino Hotel
321 Gregory St . . . . Central City CO 80427 **800-924-6646** 303-582-0800

Name / Address	City	ST	Zip	Toll-Free	Phone
Sky Ute Casino 14324 US Hwy 172 N	Ignacio	CO	81137	**888-842-4180**	970-563-7777
Ute Mountain Casino Three Weeminuche Dr	Towaoc	CO	81334	**800-258-8007**	970-565-8800
Mohegan Sun Resort & Casino One Mohegan Sun Blvd	Uncasville	CT	06382	**888-226-7711**	860-862-8150
Winners Sports Haven 600 Long Wharf Dr	New Haven	CT	06511	**800-468-2260**	
Gulfstream Park 901 S Federal Hwy	Hallandale	FL	33009	**866-840-8069**	954-454-7000
Seminole Casino Hollywood 4150 N State Rd 7	Hollywood	FL	33021	**866-222-7466**	954-961-3220
Seminole Casino Immokalee 506 S First St	Immokalee	FL	34142	**800-218-0007**	
Seminole Coconut Creek Casino 5550 NW 40th St	Coconut Creek	FL	33073	**866-222-7466**	954-977-6700
Seminole Hard Rock Hotel & Casino Tampa (SHRH & C) 5223 N Orient Rd *General	Tampa	FL	33610	**866-222-7466***	813-627-7625
Argosy's Alton Belle Casino One Piasa St	Alton	IL	62002	**800-711-4263**	
Casino Queen 200 S Front St	East Saint Louis	IL	62201	**800-777-0777**	618-874-5000
Harrah's Joliet 151 N Joliet St	Joliet	IL	60432	**800-522-4700**	815-740-7800
Hollywood Casino Joliet 777 Hollywood Blvd	Joliet	IL	60436	**800-426-2537**	
Belterra Casino Resort 777 Belterra Dr	Florence	IN	47020	**888-235-8377**	812-427-7777
Blue Chip Casino Inc 777 Blue Chip Dr	Michigan City	IN	46360	**888-879-7711**	219-879-7711
Casino Aztar 421 NW Riverside Dr	Evansville	IN	47708	**800-342-5386**	812-433-4000
Horseshoe Casino 777 Casino Ctr Dr	Hammond	IN	46320	**800-522-4700**	219-473-7000
Majestic Star Casino & Hotel One Buffington Harbor Dr	Gary	IN	46406	**800-522-4700**	219-977-7777
Rising Star Casino Resort 777 Rising Star Dr	Rising Sun	IN	47040	**800-472-6311**	812-438-1234
Ameristar Casino Hotel Council Bluffs 2200 River Rd	Council Bluffs	IA	51501	**866-667-3386**	712-328-8888
Harrah's Council Bluffs 1 Harrahs Blvd	Council Bluffs	IA	51501	**800-342-7724**	712-329-6000
Meskwaki Bingo Hotel Casino 1504 305th St	Tama	IA	52339	**800-728-4263**	
Prairie Meadows Racetrack & Casino 1 Prairie Meadows Dr PO Box 1000	Altoona	IA	50009	**800-325-9015**	515-967-1000
Rhythm City Casino 101 W River Dr	Davenport	IA	52801	**844-852-4386**	563-328-8000
Prairie Band Casino & Resort 12305 150th Rd	Mayetta	KS	66509	**888-727-4946**	785-966-7777
Belle of Baton Rouge Casino 103 France St	Baton Rouge	LA	70802	**800-676-4847**	
Boomtown Casino New Orleans 4132 Peters Rd	Harvey	LA	70058	**800-366-7711**	504-366-7711
Coushatta Casino Resort 777 Coushatta Dr PO Box 1510	Kinder	LA	70648	**800-584-7263**	
DiamondJacks Casino Resort 711 Diamond Jacks Blvd	Bossier City	LA	71111	**866-552-9629**	318-678-7777
Eldorado Resort Casino Shreveport 451 Clyde Fant Pkwy	Shreveport	LA	71101	**877-602-0711**	318-220-0711
Harrah's New Orleans 8 Canal St	New Orleans	LA	70130	**800-427-7247**	504-533-6000
Hollywood Casino Baton Rouge 1717 River Rd N	Baton Rouge	LA	70802	**800-447-6843**	877-770-7867
Horseshoe Southern Indiana Hotel & Casino 711 Horseshoe Blvd	Bossier City	LA	71111	**800-895-0711**	
Isle of Capri Casino Hotel Lake Charles 100 W Lake Ave	Westlake	LA	70669	**800-843-4753**	
Paragon Casino Resort 711 Paragon Pl	Marksville	LA	71351	**800-946-1946**	
Sam's Town Hotel & Casino Shreveport 315 Clyde Fant Pkwy	Shreveport	LA	71101	**877-770-7867**	
Treasure Chest Casino 5050 Williams Blvd	Kenner	LA	70065	**800-298-0711**	504-443-8000
Rosecroft Raceway 6336 Rosecroft Dr	Fort Washington	MD	20744	**877-818-9467**	301-567-4500
Suffolk Downs 111 Waldemar Ave	East Boston	MA	02128	**800-225-3460**	617-567-3900
MGM Grand Detroit 1777 Third St	Detroit	MI	48226	**877-888-2121**	313-465-1400
MotorCity Casino Hotel 2901 Grand River Ave	Detroit	MI	48201	**866-752-9622**	313-237-7711
Soaring Eagle Casino & Resort 6800 E Soaring Eagle Blvd	Mount Pleasant	MI	48858	**888-732-4537**	
Black Bear Casino Resort 1785 Hwy 210 PO Box 777	Carlton	MN	55718	**888-771-0777**	218-878-2327
Grand Casino Hinckley 777 Lady Luck Dr	Hinckley	MN	55037	**800-472-6321**	
Grand Casino Mille Lacs 777 Grand Ave PO Box 343	Onamia	MN	56359	**800-626-5825**	
Jackpot Junction Casino Hotel 39375 County Hwy 24 PO Box 420	Morton	MN	56270	**800-946-2274**	507-697-8000
Mystic Lake Casino Hotel 2400 Mystic Lk Blvd	Prior Lake	MN	55372	**800-262-7799**	952-445-9000
Bally's Casino Tunica 1450 Bally's Blvd	Robinsonville	MS	38664	**866-422-5597**	
Boomtown Casino Biloxi 676 Bayview Ave	Biloxi	MS	39530	**800-627-0777**	228-435-7000
Fitzgeralds Casino & Hotel Tunica 711 Lucky Ln	Robinsonville	MS	38664	**888-766-5825**	662-363-5825
Gold Strike Casino Resort 1010 Casino Ctr Dr *Resv	Tunica Resorts	MS	38664	**888-245-7829***	662-357-1111
Golden Nugget Hotels & Casinos 151 Beach Blvd	Biloxi	MS	39530	**800-777-7568**	228-435-5400
Hard Rock Hotel & Casino Biloxi 777 Beach Blvd	Biloxi	MS	39530	**877-877-6256**	228-374-7625
Harrah's Tunica 1021 Casino Ctr Dr	Robinsonville	MS	38664	**800-946-4946**	800-303-7463
Hollywood Casino Bay Saint Louis 711 Hollywood Blvd	Bay Saint Louis	MS	39520	**866-758-2591**	
IP Casino Resort & Spa 850 Bayview Ave *Resv	Biloxi	MS	39530	**888-946-2847***	228-436-3000
Island View Casino Resort 3300 W Beach Blvd PO Box 1600 *General	Gulfport	MS	39502	**888-777-9696***	228-314-2100
Casino New Brunswick LP 21 Casino Dr	Moncton	NB	E1G0R7	**877-859-7775**	506-859-7770
Aquarius Casino Resort 1900 S Casino Dr	Laughlin	NV	89029	**888-662-5825**	702-298-5111
Arizona Charlie's Boulder Casino & Hotel 4575 Boulder Hwy	Las Vegas	NV	89121	**888-236-9066**	702-951-5800
Arizona Charlie's Decatur Casino & Hotel 740 S Decatur Blvd	Las Vegas	NV	89107	**888-236-8645**	702-258-5200
Atlantis Casino Resort 3800 S Virginia St	Reno	NV	89502	**800-723-6500**	775-825-4700
Bally's Las Vegas 3645 Las Vegas Blvd S *Resv	Las Vegas	NV	89109	**800-522-4700***	702-967-4111
Best Western Carson Station Hotel & Casino 900 S Carson St	Carson City	NV	89701	**800-501-2929**	775-883-0900
Boomtown Casino & Hotel Reno 2100 Garson Rd *Resv	Verdi	NV	89439	**800-648-3790***	775-345-6000
Boulder Station Hotel & Casino 4111 Boulder Hwy	Las Vegas	NV	89121	**800-683-7777**	702-432-7777
Buffalo Bill's Resort & Casino 31900 Las Vegas Blvd S	Primm	NV	89019	**888-386-7867**	702-386-7867
California Hotel & Casino 12 E Ogden Ave	Las Vegas	NV	89101	**800-634-6505**	702-385-1222
Carson City Nugget 507 N Carson St	Carson City	NV	89701	**800-426-5239**	775-882-1626
Casino Royale Hotel 3411 Las Vegas Blvd S	Las Vegas	NV	89109	**800-854-7666**	702-737-3500
Circus Circus Hotel & Casino Reno 500 N Sierra St	Reno	NV	89503	**800-648-5010**	775-329-0711
Circus Circus Hotel Casino & Theme Park Las Vegas 2880 Las Vegas Blvd S *Resv	Las Vegas	NV	89109	**800-634-3450***	702-734-0410
Colorado Belle Hotel & Casino 2100 S Casino Dr *Resv	Laughlin	NV	89029	**877-460-0777***	702-298-4000
Don Laughlin's Riverside Resort & Casino 1650 Casino Dr	Laughlin	NV	89029	**800-227-3849**	702-298-2535
Edgewater Hotel & Casino 2020 S Casino Dr *Resv	Laughlin	NV	89029	**800-677-4837***	702-298-2453
El Cortez Hotel & Casino 600 E Fremont St	Las Vegas	NV	89101	**800-634-6703**	702-385-5200
Eldorado Casino Hotel 345 N Virginia St *Resv	Reno	NV	89501	**800-879-8879***	775-786-5700
Excalibur Hotel & Casino 3850 Las Vegas Blvd S PO Box 96776	Las Vegas	NV	89109	**877-750-5464**	702-597-7777
Fiesta Rancho Casino Hotel 2400 N Rancho Dr *Resv	Las Vegas	NV	89130	**800-731-7333***	702-631-7000
Fremont Hotel & Casino 200 Fremont St	Las Vegas	NV	89101	**800-634-6460**	702-385-3232
Gold Coast Hotel & Casino 4000 W Flamingo Rd	Las Vegas	NV	89103	**800-331-5334**	702-367-7111
Gold Dust West Carson City 2171 E William St	Carson City	NV	89701	**877-519-5567**	775-885-9000
Gold Ranch Casino & RV Resort 350 Gold Ranch Rd PO Box 160	Verdi	NV	89439	**877-914-6789**	775-345-6789
Gold Strike Hotel & Gambling Hall One Main St PO Box 19278	Jean	NV	89019	**800-634-1359**	702-477-5000
Golden Nugget Laughlin 2300 S Casino Dr	Laughlin	NV	89029	**800-950-7700**	702-298-7111
Grand Sierra Resort & Casino 2500 E Second St	Reno	NV	89595	**800-501-2651**	775-789-2000
Green Valley Ranch Resort Casino & Spa 2300 Paseo Verde Pkwy *Resv	Henderson	NV	89052	**866-782-9487***	702-617-7777
Harrah's Laughlin 2900 S Casino Dr	Laughlin	NV	89029	**800-427-7247**	702-298-4600
Harveys Lake Tahoe Hwy 50 at Stateline Ave PO Box 128	Lake Tahoe	NV	89449	**800-522-4700**	775-588-6611
Hooters Casino Hotel 115 E Tropicana Ave	Las Vegas	NV	89109	**866-584-6687**	702-739-9000
Hyatt Regency Lake Tahoe Resort & Casino 111 Country Club Dr	Incline Village	NV	89451	**800-233-1234**	775-832-1234
John Ascuaga's Nugget Hotel Casino 1100 Nugget Ave	Sparks	NV	89431	**800-648-1177**	775-356-3300
Las Vegas Club Hotel & Casino (LVC) 18 E Fremont St	Las Vegas	NV	89101	**800-634-6532**	702-385-1664
Laughlin River Lodge. 2700 S Casino Dr	Laughlin	NV	89029	**800-835-7903**	702-298-2242
Luxor Hotel & Casino 3900 Las Vegas Blvd S *Resv	Las Vegas	NV	89119	**800-288-1000***	702-262-4000
Mandalay Bay Resort & Casino 3950 Las Vegas Blvd S	Las Vegas	NV	89119	**877-632-7800**	702-632-7777
MGM Grand Hotel & Casino 3799 Las Vegas Blvd S	Las Vegas	NV	89109	**877-880-0880**	702-891-1111
Monte Carlo Resort & Casino 3770 Las Vegas Blvd S	Las Vegas	NV	89109	**800-311-8999**	702-730-7777
New York New York Hotel & Casino 3790 Las Vegas Blvd S	Las Vegas	NV	89109	**800-689-1797**	702-740-6969
Orleans Las Vegas Hotel & Casino 4500 W Tropicana Ave	Las Vegas	NV	89103	**800-675-3267**	702-365-7111
Palace Station Hotel & Casino 2411 W Sahara Ave *Resv	Las Vegas	NV	89102	**800-634-3101***	702-367-2411

Casinos (Cont'd)

Name / Address	City	State	Zip	Toll-Free	Phone
Palms Casino Resort 4321 W Flamingo Rd	Las Vegas	NV	89103	866-942-7777	702-942-7777
Peppermill Hotel & Casino 2707 S Virginia St	Reno	NV	89502	800-648-6992	775-826-2121
Railroad Pass Hotel & Casino 2800 S Boulder Hwy	Henderson	NV	89002	800-654-0877	702-294-5000
Red Rock Resort Spa & Casino 11011 W Charleston Blvd	Las Vegas	NV	89135	866-767-7773	702-797-7777
Riviera Hotel & Casino 2901 Las Vegas Blvd S *Resv	Las Vegas	NV	89109	866-275-6030*	702-734-5110
Sam's Town Hotel & Gambling Hall 5111 Boulder Hwy	Las Vegas	NV	89122	800-897-8696	702-456-7777
Santa Fe Station 4949 N Rancho Dr *Resv	Las Vegas	NV	89130	888-786-7389*	702-658-4900
Silver Legacy Resort & Casino 407 N Virginia St	Reno	NV	89501	800-687-8733	775-325-7401
Silverton Hotel & Casino 3333 Blue Diamond Rd	Las Vegas	NV	89139	866-722-4608	702-263-7777
South Point Hotel & Casino 9777 Las Vegas Blvd S	Las Vegas	NV	89183	866-796-7111	702-796-7111
Stratosphere Tower Hotel & Casino 2000 S Las Vegas Blvd	Las Vegas	NV	89104	800-998-6937	702-380-7777
Suncoast Hotel & Casino 9090 Alta Dr	Las Vegas	NV	89145	877-677-7111	702-636-7111
Sunset Station Hotel & Casino 1301 W Sunset Rd	Henderson	NV	89014	888-786-7389	702-547-7777
Texas Station Gambling Hall & Hotel 2101 Texas Star Ln *Resv	North Las Vegas	NV	89032	800-654-8888*	702-631-1000
Treasure Island Hotel & Casino 3300 Las Vegas Blvd S	Las Vegas	NV	89109	800-288-7206	702-894-7111
Tropicana Express 2121 S Casino Dr	Laughlin	NV	89029	800-243-6846	702-298-4200
Tuscany Suites & Casino 255 E Flamingo Rd *Resv	Las Vegas	NV	89169	877-887-2261*	702-893-8933
Western Village Inn & Casino 815 Nichols Blvd	Sparks	NV	89434	800-648-1170	
Wynn Las Vegas 3131 Las Vegas Blvd S	Las Vegas	NV	89109	877-321-9966	702-770-7000
Harrah's Resort Atlantic City 777 Harrah's Blvd	Atlantic City	NJ	08401	800-342-7724	609-441-5000
Resorts Casino Hotel 1133 Boardwalk	Atlantic City	NJ	08401	800-334-6378	
Tropicana Entertainment 2831 Boardwalk OTC: TPCA	Atlantic City	NJ	08401	800-843-8767	
Trump Taj Mahal Casino Resort 1000 Boardwalk & Virginia Ave	Atlantic City	NJ	08401	800-426-2537	609-449-1000
Camel Rock Casino 17486A Hwy 84/285	Santa Fe	NM	87506	800-483-1040	505-983-2667
Cities of Gold Casino 10-B Cities of Gold Rd	Santa Fe	NM	87506	800-455-3313	505-455-3313
Route 66 Casino Hotel 14500 Central Ave	Albuquerque	NM	87121	866-352-7866	505-352-7866
Sandia Resort & Casino 30 Rainbow Rd NE	Albuquerque	NM	87113	800-526-9366	505-796-7500
Seneca Niagara Casino 310 Fourth St	Niagara Falls	NY	14303	877-873-6322	716-299-1100
Turning Stone Resort Casino LLC 5218 Patrick Rd	Verona	NY	13478	800-771-7711	315-361-7711
Harrah's Cherokee Casino & Hotel 777 Casino Dr *General	Cherokee	NC	28719	877-811-0777*	828-497-7777
Prairie Knights Casino & Resort 7932 Hwy 24	Fort Yates	ND	58538	800-425-8277	701-854-7777
Casino Nova Scotia 1983 Upper Water St	Halifax	NS	B3J3Y5	888-642-6376	902-425-7777
Caesars License Company LLC 377 Riverside Dr E	Windsor	ON	N9A7H7	800-991-7777	519-258-7878
Casino Niagara 5705 Falls Ave	Niagara Falls	ON	L2E6T3	888-325-5788	905-374-3598
Fallsview Casino Resort 6380 Fallsview Blvd	Niagara Falls	ON	L2G7X5	888-325-5788	
Newport Grand Jai Alai 150 Admiral Kalbfus Rd	Newport	RI	02840	800-451-2500	401-849-5000
Saskatchewan Indian Gaming Authority 250 - 103 C Packham Ave	Saskatoon	SK	S7N4K4	800-306-6789	306-477-7777
Emerald Downs 2300 Emerald Downs Dr PO Box 617	Auburn	WA	98001	888-931-8400	253-288-7000
Emerald Queen Casino (EQC) 2024 E 29th St	Tacoma	WA	98404	888-831-7655	253-594-7777
Lucky Eagle Casino 12888 188th Ave SW	Rochester	WA	98579	800-720-1788	360-273-2000
Northern Quest Casino 100 N Hayford Rd	Airway Heights	WA	99001	877-871-6772	509-242-7000
Red Wind Casino 12819 Yelm Hwy	Olympia	WA	98513	866-946-2444	360-412-5000
Skagit Valley Casino Resort 5984 N Darrk Ln	Bow	WA	98232	877-275-2448	360-724-7777
Wheeling Island Gaming Inc One S Stone St	Wheeling	WV	26003	877-943-3546	304-232-5050
Dairyland Greyhound Park 5522 104th Ave	Kenosha	WI	53144	800-233-3357	262-657-8200
Ho-Chunk Casino S 3214 County Rd BD	Baraboo	WI	53913	800-746-2486	
Lake of the Torches Resort Casino 510 Old Abe Rd	Lac du Flambeau	WI	54538	800-258-6724	715-588-7070
Potawatomi Bingo Casino 1721 W Canal St	Milwaukee	WI	53233	800-729-7244	414-645-6888

---

133   CASKETS & VAULTS

SEE ALSO Mortuary, Crematory, Cemetery Products & Services

Name / Address	City	State	Zip	Toll-Free	Phone
Batesville Casket Co 1 Batesville Blvd *Cust Svc	Batesville	IN	47006	800-622-8373*	812-934-7500
Paul Casket Co 505 S Green St	Cambridge City	IN	47327	800-521-8202	765-478-3991
York Group Inc 2 Northshore Ctr Ste 100	Pittsburgh	PA	15212	800-223-4964	412-995-1600

134   CEMENT

Name / Address	City	State	Zip	Toll-Free	Phone
Ash Grove Cement Co 8900 Indian Creek Pkwy OTC: ASHG	Overland Park	KS	66210	800-545-1882	913-451-8900
California Portland Cement Co 2025 E Financial Way Ste 200 *Cust Svc	Glendora	CA	91741	800-272-1891*	626-852-6200
Cemex USA 840 Gessner Ste 1400 NYSE: CX	Houston	TX	77024	888-292-0070	713-650-6200
CGM Inc 1445 Ford Rd	Bensalem	PA	19020	800-523-6570	215-638-4400
Coastal Cement Corp 36 Drydock Ave	Boston	MA	02210	800-828-8352	617-350-0183
Continental Cement Company LLC 14755 N Outer 40 Ste 514	Chesterfield	MO	63017	800-625-1144	636-532-7440
Dragon Products Co 960 Ocean Ave	Portland	ME	04103	800-828-8352	207-774-6355
ESSROC Materials Inc 3251 Bath Pike	Nazareth	PA	18064	800-437-7762	610-837-6725
Federal White Cement Ltd PO Box 1609 *Sales	Woodstock	ON	N4S0A8	800-265-1806*	519-485-5410
Lehigh Inland Cement Ltd 12640 Inland Way *Orders	Edmonton	AB	T5V1K2	800-252-9304*	780-420-2500
Prairie Group Inc 7601 W 79th St *Sales	Bridgeview	IL	60455	800-649-3690*	708-458-0400
Titan America Inc 1151 Azalea Garden Rd	Norfolk	VA	23502	800-468-7622	757-858-6500

135   CEMETERIES - NATIONAL

SEE ALSO Parks - National - US ; Historic Homes & Buildings

Name / Address	City	State	Zip	Toll-Free	Phone
Alexandria National Cemetery 209 E Shamrock St	Pineville	LA	71360	800-827-1000	318-449-1793
Alton National Cemetery 600 Pearl St	Alton	IL	62003	800-535-1117	314-845-8320
Baltimore National Cemetery 5501 Frederick Ave	Baltimore	MD	21228	800-535-1117	410-644-9696
Beaufort National Cemetery 1601 Boundary St	Beaufort	SC	29902	800-273-8255	843-524-3925
Calverton National Cemetery 210 Princeton Blvd	Calverton	NY	11933	800-829-1040	631-727-5410
Camp Butler National Cemetery 5063 Camp Butler Rd	Springfield	IL	62707	877-907-8585	217-492-4070
Camp Nelson National Cemetery 6980 Danville Rd	Nicholasville	KY	40356	800-827-1000	859-885-5727
Chattanooga National Cemetery 1200 Bailey Ave	Chattanooga	TN	37404	877-907-8585	423-855-6590
Corinth National Cemetery 1551 Horton St	Corinth	MS	38834	800-273-8255	901-386-8311
Culpeper National Cemetery 305 US Ave	Culpeper	VA	22701	800-827-1000	540-825-0027
Cypress Hills National Cemetery 625 Jamaica Ave	Brooklyn	NY	11208	800-535-1117	631-454-4949
Danville National Cemetery 1900 E Main St	Danville	IL	61832	800-827-1000	217-554-4550
Dayton National Cemetery 4100 W Third St	Dayton	OH	45428	800-273-8255	937-262-2115
Eagle Point National Cemetery 2763 Riley Rd	Eagle Point	OR	97524	800-535-1117	541-826-2511
Finn's Point National Cemetery 454 Ft. Mott Rd	Pennsville	NJ	08070	800-827-1000	215-504-5610
Florence National Cemetery 803 E National Cemetery Rd	Florence	SC	29506	877-907-8585	843-669-8783
Florida National Cemetery 6502 SW 102nd Ave	Bushnell	FL	33513	877-907-8585	352-793-7740
Fort Bliss National Cemetery PO Box 6342	El Paso	TX	79906	800-273-8255	915-564-0201
Fort Custer National Cemetery 15501 Dickman Rd	Augusta	MI	49012	800-273-8255	269-731-4164
Fort Smith National Cemetery 522 Garland Ave	Fort Smith	AR	72901	800-535-1117	479-783-5345
Grafton National Cemetery 431 Walnut St	Grafton	WV	26354	800-535-1117	304-265-2044
Jefferson Barracks National Cemetery 2900 Sheridan Rd	Saint Louis	MO	63125	800-827-1000	314-845-8320
Jefferson City National Cemetery 1024 E McCarty St	Jefferson City	MO	65101	877-907-8585	314-845-8320
Keokuk National Cemetery 1701 J St	Keokuk	IA	52632	800-273-8255	309-782-2094
Kerrville National Cemetery 3600 Memorial Blvd	Kerrville	TX	78028	800-273-8255	210-820-3891
Marietta National Cemetery 500 Washington Ave	Marietta	GA	30060	866-236-8159	

	Toll-Free	Phone
Massachusetts National Cemetery		
Conery Rd .... Bourne MA 02532	**800-827-1000**	508-563-7113
Mobile National Cemetery		
1202 Virginia St .... Mobile AL 36604	**800-827-1000**	850-453-4108
Mountain Home National Cemetery		
PO Box 8 .... Mountain Home TN 37684	**800-827-1000**	423-979-3535
New Bern National Cemetery		
1711 National Ave .... New Bern NC 28560	**800-827-1000**	252-637-2912
Prescott National Cemetery		
500 Hwy 89 N .... Prescott AZ 86301	**800-827-1000**	928-717-7569
Roseburg National Cemetery		
1770 Harvard Blvd .... Roseburg OR 97470	**800-535-1117**	541-826-2511
Saint Augustine National Cemetery		
104 Marine St .... Saint Augustine FL 32084	**800-273-8255**	352-793-7740
Seven Pines National Cemetery		
400 E Williamsburg Rd .... Sandston VA 23150	**800-535-1117**	804-795-2031
Sitka National Cemetery		
803 Sawmill Creek Rd .... Sitka AK 99835	**800-273-8255**	907-384-7075
Staunton National Cemetery		
901 Richmond Ave .... Staunton VA 24401	**800-273-8255**	540-825-0027
Tahoma National Cemetery		
18600 SE 240th St .... Kent WA 98042	**800-827-1000**	425-413-9614
Togus National Cemetery		
VA Regional Office Ctr .... Togus ME 04330	**800-273-8255**	508-563-7113
West Virginia National Cemetery		
42 Veterans Memorial Lane .... Grafton WV 26354	**800-273-8255**	304-265-2044
Wilmington National Cemetery		
2011 Market St .... Wilmington NC 28403	**800-535-1117**	910-815-4877
Wood National Cemetery		
5000 W National Ave Bldg 1301 .... Milwaukee WI 53295	**888-878-3256**	414-382-5300
Woodlawn National Cemetery		
1825 Davis St .... Elmira NY 14901	**877-907-8585**	607-732-5411

136   CHAMBERS OF COMMERCE

	Toll-Free	Phone
Association of American Chambers of Commerce in Latin America		
1615 H St NW 3rd Fl .... Washington DC 20062	**800-638-6582**	202-463-5485
Chinese Chamber of Commerce of Los Angeles		
977 N Broadway Ground Fl Ste E ...... Los Angeles CA 90012	**800-400-7115**	213-617-0396
French-American Chamber of Commerce in New York		
1350 Broadway Ste 2101 .... New York NY 10018	**800-821-2241**	212-867-0123
Italy-America Chamber of Commerce Southeast Inc		
2 S Biscayne Blvd Ste 1880 .... Miami FL 33131	**800-428-3003**	305-577-9868
Labor Law Center Inc		
12534 Vly view st .... Garden Grove CA 92845	**800-745-9970**	
Meclabs LLC		
1300 Marsh Landing Pkwy		
Ste 106 .... Jacksonville Beach FL 32250	**800-517-5531**	
US-Mexico Chamber of Commerce California Pacific Chapter		
2450 Colorado Ave Ste 400E .... Santa Monica CA 90404	**800-997-9148**	310-586-7901

137   CHAMBERS OF COMMERCE - CANADIAN

Listings are organized by provinces and then are alphabetized within each province grouping according to the name of the city in which each chamber is located.

	Toll-Free	Phone
Alberta Chambers of Commerce		
10025 - 102A Ave Edmonton Ctr		
Ste 1808 .... Edmonton AB T5J2Z2	**800-272-8854**	780-425-4180
Belleville & District Chamber of Commerce		
Five Moira St E .... Belleville ON K8N5B3	**888-852-9992**	613-962-4597
Cambridge Chamber of Commerce		
750 Hespeler Rd .... Cambridge ON N3H5L8	**800-749-7560***	519-622-2221
*General		
Comox Valley Chamber of Commerce		
2040 Cliffe Ave .... Courtenay BC V9N2L3	**888-357-4471**	250-334-3234
Dryden District Chamber of Commerce		
284 Government St Hwy 17 .... Dryden ON P8N2P3	**877-934-6922**	807-223-2622
Enterprise Fredericton		
10 Knowledge Pk Dr Ste 110 ...... Fredericton NB E3C2M7	**866-534-9270**	506-444-4686
Greater Peterborough Chamber of Commerce		
175 George St N .... Peterborough ON K9J3G6	**877-640-4037**	705-748-9771
Leamington District Chamber of Commerce		
318 Erie St S .... Leamington ON N8H3C5	**800-393-3769**	519-326-2721
North Bay & District Chamber of Commerce		
1375 Seymour St PO Box 747 .... North Bay ON P1B8J8	**888-249-8998**	705-472-8480
Penticton & Wine Country Chamber of Commerce		
553 Railway St .... Penticton BC V2A8S3	**800-663-5052**	250-492-4103
Vaughan Chamber of Commerce		
25 Edilcan Dr Ste 2. .... Vaughan ON L4K3S4	**888-943-8937**	905-761-1366
West Shore Chamber of Commerce		
2830 Aldwynd Rd .... Victoria BC V9B3S7	**888-234-3566**	250-478-1130
West Vancouver Chamber of Commerce		
1846 Marine Dr .... West Vancouver BC V7V1J6	**888-471-9996**	604-926-6614

138   CHAMBERS OF COMMERCE - US - LOCAL

SEE ALSO Civic & Political Organizations
Chambers listed here represent areas with a population of 25,000 or more. Listings are organized by states and then are alphabetized within each state grouping according to the name of the city in which each chamber is located.

Alabama

	Toll-Free	Phone
Greater Limestone County Chamber of Commerce		
101 S Beaty St .... Athens AL 35611	**866-953-6565**	256-232-2600
Bessemer Area Chamber of Commerce		
321 N 18th St .... Bessemer AL 35020	**888-423-7736**	205-425-3253
Cullman Area Chamber of Commerce		
301 Second Ave SW .... Cullman AL 35055	**800-313-5114**	256-734-0454
Dothan Area Chamber of Commerce		
102 Jamestown Blvd .... Dothan AL 36301	**800-221-1027**	334-792-5138

	Toll-Free	Phone
Shoals Chamber of Commerce		
20 Hightower Pl PO Box 1331 .... Florence AL 35630	**877-764-4661**	256-764-4661
South Baldwin Chamber of Commerce (SBCC)		
112 W Laurel Ave PO Box 1117 .... Foley AL 36535	**877-461-3712**	251-943-3291
Gadsden & Etowah County Chamber		
One Commerce Sq .... Gadsden AL 35901	**800-659-2955**	256-543-3472
Greenville Area Chamber of Commerce		
1 Depot Sq .... Greenville AL 36037	**800-959-0717**	334-382-3251
Walker County Chamber of Commerce		
204 19th St E Ste 101. .... Jasper AL 35501	**800-384-4571***	205-384-4571
*General		
Mobile Area Chamber of Commerce		
451 Government St .... Mobile AL 36602	**800-422-6951**	251-433-6951
Ozark Area Chamber of Commerce		
294 Painter Ave .... Ozark AL 36360	**800-582-8497**	334-774-9321
Phenix City-Russell County Chamber of Commerce		
1107 Broad St .... Phenix City AL 36867	**800-892-2248**	334-298-3639
Greater Jackson County Chamber of Commerce		
PO Box 973 .... Scottsboro AL 35768	**800-259-5508**	256-259-5500
Selma-Dallas County Chamber of Commerce		
912 Selma Ave .... Selma AL 36701	**800-457-3562**	334-875-7241
Fairbanks Chamber of Commerce		
100 Cushman St Ste 102 .... Fairbanks AK 99701	**800-770-8255**	907-452-1105
Juneau Chamber of Commerce		
9301 Glacier Hwy Suite 110 .... Juneau AK 99801	**888-581-2201**	907-463-3488

Arizona

	Toll-Free	Phone
Bullhead Area Chamber of Commerce		
1251 Hwy 95 .... Bullhead City AZ 86429	**800-987-7457**	928-754-4121
Chandler Chamber of Commerce		
25 S Arizona Pl Ste 201 .... Chandler AZ 85225	**800-963-4571**	480-963-4571
Lake Havasu Area Chamber of Commerce		
314 London Bridge Rd .... Lake Havasu City AZ 86403	**800-307-3610**	928-855-4115
Rim Country Regional Chamber of Commerce		
100 W Main St .... Payson AZ 85547	**800-249-2678**	928-474-4515
Prescott Chamber of Commerce		
117 W Goodwin St .... Prescott AZ 86303	**800-266-7534**	928-445-2000
Prescott Valley Chamber of Commerce		
3001 N Main St Ste 2A .... Prescott Valley AZ 86314	**800-355-0843**	928-772-8857
Graham County Chamber of Commerce		
1111 Thatcher Blvd .... Safford AZ 85546	**888-837-1841**	928-428-2511
Greater Sierra Vista Area Chamber of Commerce		
21 E Wilcox Dr .... Sierra Vista AZ 85635	**800-288-3861**	520-458-6940
Yuma County Chamber of Commerce		
180 W First St Ste A .... Yuma AZ 85364	**877-782-0438**	928-782-2567

Arkansas

	Toll-Free	Phone
Fayetteville Chamber of Commerce		
123 W Mountain St .... Fayetteville AR 72702	**866-893-5007**	479-521-1710
Jacksonville Chamber of Commerce		
200 Dupree Dr .... Jacksonville AR 72076	**888-857-3019**	501-982-1511
Mountain Home Area Chamber of Commerce		
1023 Hwy 62 .... Mountain Home AR 72653	**800-822-3536**	870-425-5111
Rogers-Lowell Area Chamber of Commerce		
317 W Walnut St .... Rogers AR 72756	**800-364-1240**	479-636-1240
Russellville Area Chamber of Commerce		
708 W Main St .... Russellville AR 72801	**855-678-2447**	479-968-2530

California

	Toll-Free	Phone
Atascadero Chamber of Commerce		
6904 El Camino Real .... Atascadero CA 93422	**877-204-9830**	805-466-2044
Auburn Area Chamber of Commerce		
601 Lincoln Way .... Auburn CA 95603	**800-310-2355**	530-885-5616
Kern County Board of Trade		
2101 Oak St .... Bakersfield CA 93301	**800-787-9920***	661-868-5376
*General		
Berkeley Chamber of Commerce		
1834 University Ave .... Berkeley CA 94703	**800-847-4823**	510-549-7000
Beverly Hills Chamber of Commerce		
239 S Beverly Dr .... Beverly Hills CA 90212	**800-345-2210**	310-248-1000
Chico Chamber of Commerce		
441 Main St .... Chico CA 95928	**800-852-8570**	530-891-5556
Greater Concord Chamber of Commerce		
2280 Diamond Blvd Ste 200. .... Concord CA 94520	**800-427-8686**	925-685-1181
Downey Chamber of Commerce		
11131 Brookshire Ave .... Downey CA 90241	**877-345-4633**	562-923-2191
Encinitas Chamber of Commerce		
527 Encinitas Blvd .... Encinitas CA 92024	**800-953-6041**	760-753-6041
Greater Eureka Chamber of Commerce, The		
2112 Broadway .... Eureka CA 95501	**866-267-4255**	707-442-3738
Mendocino Coast Chamber of Commerce		
217 S Main St PO Box 1141 .... Fort Bragg CA 95437	**800-382-7244**	707-961-6300
Garden Grove Chamber of Commerce		
12866 Main St Ste 102. .... Garden Grove CA 92840	**800-959-5560**	714-638-7950
Glendora Chamber of Commerce		
131 E Foothill Blvd .... Glendora CA 91741	**866-987-1611**	626-963-4128
Goleta Valley Chamber of Commerce		
271 N Fairview Ave Ste 104 .... Goleta CA 93117	**800-646-5382**	805-967-2500
Hawthorne Chamber of Commerce		
12629 Crenshaw Blvd .... Hawthorne CA 90250	**800-977-4770**	310-676-1163
Hesperia Chamber of Commerce		
16816 Main St Ste D .... Hesperia CA 92345	**855-574-7337**	760-244-2135
Indio Chamber of Commerce		
82921 Indio Blvd .... Indio CA 92201	**800-464-7928**	760-347-0676
Irvine Chamber of Commerce		
2485 McCabe Way Ste 150 .... Irvine CA 92614	**800-321-2211***	949-660-9112
*General		
Amador County Chamber of Commerce		
115 Main St PO Box 596 .... Jackson CA 95642	**800-822-9466***	209-223-0350
*General		
Lakeport Regional Chamber of Commerce		
875 Lakeport Blvd PO Box 295. .... Lakeport CA 95453	**866-525-3767**	707-263-5092

				Toll-Free	Phone
Lompoc Valley Chamber of Commerce & Visitors Bureau					
PO Box 626	Lompoc CA	93438		800-240-0999	805-736-4567
Century City Chamber of Commerce					
2029 Century Pk E Concourse Level	Los Angeles CA	90067		800-462-7899	310-553-2222
Madera District Chamber of Commerce					
120 NE St	Madera CA	93638		866-382-7822	559-673-3563
Malibu Chamber of Commerce					
23805 Stuart Ranch Rd Ste 210	Malibu CA	90265		800-442-4988	310-456-9025
Martinez Area Chamber of Commerce					
603 Marina Vista	Martinez CA	94553		877-855-5506	925-228-2345
Greater Merced Chamber of Commerce					
1640 N St Ste 120	Merced CA	95340		800-877-2345	209-384-7092
Chamber of Commerce Mountain View					
580 Castro St	Mountain View CA	94041		800-229-7728	650-968-8378
Napa Chamber of Commerce					
1556 First St	Napa CA	94559		877-807-2249	707-226-7455
Norwalk Chamber of Commerce					
12040 Foster Rd	Norwalk CA	90650		800-427-2200	562-864-7785
Novato Chamber of Commerce					
807 DeLong Ave	Novato CA	94945		800-897-1164	415-897-1164
Orange Chamber of Commerce					
439 E Chapman Ave	Orange CA	92866		866-273-9817	714-538-3581
Oroville Area Chamber of Commerce					
1789 Montgomery St	Oroville CA	95965		800-655-4653	530-538-2542
Palm Springs Chamber of Commerce					
190 W Amado Rd	Palm Springs CA	92262		888-947-6667	760-325-1577
Paradise Chamber of Commerce					
5550 Sky Way Ste 1	Paradise CA	95969		800-838-3006	530-877-9356
Placentia Chamber of Commerce					
201 E Yorba Linda Blvd Ste C	Placentia CA	92870		844-730-0418	714-528-1873
El Dorado County Chamber of Commerce					
542 Main St	Placerville CA	95667		800-457-6279	530-621-5885
Pleasanton Chamber of Commerce					
777 Peters Ave	Pleasanton CA	94566		877-807-2249	925-846-5858
Ramona Chamber of Commerce					
960 Main St	Ramona CA	92065		800-411-7343	760-789-1311
Rancho Cucamonga Chamber of Commerce					
9047 Arrow Route Suite 180	Rancho Cucamonga CA	91730		800-677-5434	909-987-1012
Redlands Chamber of Commerce					
1 E Redlands Blvd	Redlands CA	92373		800-966-6428	909-793-2546
Rialto Chamber of Commerce					
120 N Riverside Ave	Rialto CA	92376		800-597-4955	909-875-5364
Richmond Chamber of Commerce					
3925 Macdonald Ave	Richmond CA	94805		800-921-1117	510-234-3512
Rocklin Area Chamber of Commerce					
3700 Rocklin Rd	Rocklin CA	95677		800-228-3380	916-624-2548
Rohnert Park Chamber of Commerce					
101 Golf Course Dr Ste C-7	Rohnert Park CA	94928		888-364-7379	707-584-1415
Salinas Valley Chamber of Commerce					
119 E Alisal St	Salinas CA	93901		888-678-2871	831-751-7725
San Bernardino Area Chamber of Commerce					
PO Box 658	San Bernardino CA	92402		800-928-5091	909-885-7515
San Clemente Chamber of Commerce					
1100 N El Camino Real	San Clemente CA	92672		877-411-3662	949-492-1131
San Francisco Chamber of Commerce					
235 Montgomery St 12th Fl	San Francisco CA	94104		888-834-3040	415-392-4520
San Marcos Chamber of Commerce					
939 Grand Ave	San Marcos CA	92078		800-814-7241	760-744-1270
San Rafael Chamber of Commerce					
817 Mission Ave	San Rafael CA	94901		888-378-0777	415-454-4163
Santa Cruz Chamber of Commerce					
611 Ocean St Ste 1	Santa Cruz CA	95060		866-282-5900	831-457-3713
Santa Maria Valley Chamber of Commerce					
614 S Broadway	Santa Maria CA	93454		800-331-3779	805-925-2403
Tuolumne County Chamber of Commerce					
222 S Shepherd St	Sonora CA	95370		877-532-4212	209-532-4212
Studio City Chamber of Commerce					
4024 Radford Ave Edit 2 Ste F	Studio City CA	91604		877-227-0088	818-655-5916
Sun Valley Area Chamber of Commerce					
11501 Strathern St PO Box 308	Sun Valley CA	91352		877-834-7064	818-768-2014
Lassen County Chamber of Commerce					
75 N Weatherlow St	Susanville CA	96130		877-686-7878	530-257-4323
Temecula Valley Chamber of Commerce (TVCC)					
26790 Ynez Ct Ste A	Temecula CA	92591		866-676-5090	951-676-5090
Turlock Chamber of Commerce					
115 S Golden State Blvd	Turlock CA	95380		800-834-0401	209-632-2221
Vallejo Chamber of Commerce					
427 York St	Vallejo CA	94590		877-397-7936	707-644-5551
Westminster Chamber of Commerce					
1025 Westminster Mall	Westminster CA	92683		800-929-3556	714-898-2559
Willows Chamber of Commerce					
118 W Sycamore	Willows CA	95988		855-233-6362	530-934-8150
Woodland Chamber of Commerce					
307 First St	Woodland CA	95695		888-843-2636	530-662-7327
Woodland Hills Chamber of Commerce					
20121 Ventura Blvd Ste 309	Woodland Hills CA	91364		877-527-3247	818-347-4737
Yucca Valley Chamber of Commerce					
56711 29 Palms Hwy	Yucca Valley CA	92284		855-568-5348	760-365-6323

Colorado

				Toll-Free	Phone
Aspen Chamber Resort Assn					
425 Rio Grande Pl	Aspen CO	81611		800-670-0792	970-925-1940
Aurora Chamber of Commerce					
14305 E Alameda Ave Ste 300	Aurora CO	80012		877-770-4438	303-344-1500
Vail Valley Chamber of Commerce					
101 Fawcett Rd Ste 240	Avon CO	81620		800-525-3875	970-476-1000
Canon City Chamber of Commerce					
403 Royal Gorge Blvd	Canon City CO	81212		800-876-7922	719-275-2331
Durango Area Chamber of Commerce					
111 S Camino del Rio	Durango CO	81303		888-414-0835	970-247-0312
Fort Collins Area Chamber of Commerce					
225 S Meldrum St	Fort Collins CO	80521		877-652-8607	970-482-3746
Fort Morgan Area Chamber of Commerce					
300 Main St	Fort Morgan CO	80701		800-354-8660	970-867-6702
Grand Junction Area Chamber of Commerce					
360 Grand Ave	Grand Junction CO	81501		800-352-5286	970-242-3214
Greeley-Weld Chamber of Commerce					
902 Seventh Ave	Greeley CO	80631		800-449-3866	970-352-3566
La Veta/Cuchara Chamber of Commerce					
132 W Ryus Ave	La Veta CO	81055		866-277-5550	719-742-3676
Montrose Chamber of Commerce					
1519 E Main St	Montrose CO	81401		800-923-5515	970-249-5000
Greater Pueblo Chamber of Commerce					
302 N Santa Fe Ave	Pueblo CO	81003		800-233-3446	719-542-1704
Metro North Chamber of Commerce					
14583 Orchard Pkwy Ste 300	Westminster CO	80023		877-888-8811	303-288-1000

Connecticut

				Toll-Free	Phone
Greater Bristol Chamber of Commerce					
200 Main St	Bristol CT	06010		855-344-1874	860-584-4718
Greater Meriden Chamber of Commerce					
3 Colony St Ste 301	Meriden CT	06451		877-283-8158	203-235-7901
Mystic Chamber of Commerce					
12 Roosevelt Ave,2nd Fl PO Box 143	Mystic CT	06355		866-572-9578	860-572-9578
Stamford Chamber of Commerce					
733 Summer St Ste 104	Stamford CT	06901		866-262-4548	203-359-4761
Tolland County Chamber of Commerce					
30 Lafayette Sq	Vernon CT	06066		800-243-3174	860-872-0587
Windham Region Chamber of Commerce					
1010 Main St	Willimantic CT	06226		800-635-9161	860-423-6389

Delaware

				Toll-Free	Phone
Rehoboth Beach-Dewey Beach Chamber of Commerce					
501 Rehoboth Ave	Rehoboth Beach DE	19971		800-441-1329	302-227-2233

Florida

				Toll-Free	Phone
Apalachicola Bay Chamber of Commerce					
122 Commerce St	Apalachicola FL	32320		866-269-3022	850-653-9419
Lower Keys Chamber of Commerce					
31020 Overseas Hwy	Big Pine Key FL	33043		800-872-3722	305-872-2411
Greater Boca Raton Chamber of Commerce					
1800 N Dixie Hwy	Boca Raton FL	33432		800-435-7352	561-395-4433
Bonita Springs Area Chamber of Commerce					
25071 Chamber of Commerce Dr	Bonita Springs FL	34135		800-226-2943	239-992-2943
Clearwater Regional Chamber of Commerce					
401 Cleveland St	Clearwater FL	33755		877-447-7356	727-461-0011
DeLand Area Chamber of Commerce					
336 N Woodland Blvd	DeLand FL	32720		800-611-5207	386-734-4331
Destin Area Chamber of Commerce					
4484 Legendary Dr Ste A	Destin FL	32541		877-487-2671	850-837-6241
Englewood-Cape Haze Area Chamber of Commerce					
601 S Indiana Ave	Englewood FL	34223		800-603-7198	941-474-5511
Greater Fort Lauderdale Chamber of Commerce					
512 NE Third Ave	Fort Lauderdale FL	33301		800-683-8338	954-462-6000
Greater Fort Myers Chamber of Commerce					
2310 Edwards Dr	Fort Myers FL	33901		800-366-3622	239-332-3624
Fort Myers Beach Chamber of Commerce					
17200 San Carlos Blvd	Fort Myers Beach FL	33931		866-998-9250	239-454-7500
Gainesville Area Chamber of Commerce					
300 E University Ave Ste 100	Gainesville FL	32601		888-795-2707	352-334-7100
Greater Homestead/Florida City Chamber of Commerce					
455 N Flagler Ave	Homestead FL	33030		888-247-5012	305-247-2332
Islamorada Chamber of Commerce					
PO Box 915	Islamorada FL	33036		800-322-5397	305-664-4503
Northern Palm Beach County Chamber of Commerce					
800 N US Hwy 1	Jupiter FL	33477		800-482-8293	561-746-7111
Key Largo Chamber of Commerce					
106000 Overseas Hwy	Key Largo FL	33037		866-820-1533	305-451-1414
Palms West Chamber of Commerce					
13901 Southern Blvd	Loxahatchee FL	33470		800-790-2364	561-790-6200
Greater Marathon Chamber of Commerce					
12222 Overseas Hwy	Marathon FL	33050		800-262-7284	305-743-5417
Marco Island Chamber of Commerce					
1102 N Collier Blvd	Marco Island FL	34145		800-788-6272	239-394-7549
Cocoa Beach Area Chamber of Commerce					
400 Fortenberry Rd	Merritt Island FL	32952		888-874-2674	321-459-2200
Greater Miami Chamber of Commerce					
1601 Biscayne Blvd	Miami FL	33132		888-660-5955	305-350-7700
Miami Beach Chamber of Commerce					
1920 Meridian Ave 3rd Fl	Miami Beach FL	33139		800-501-0401	305-672-1270
Santa Rosa County Chamber of Commerce					
5247 Stewart St	Milton FL	32570		800-239-8732	850-623-2339
Ocala-Marion County Chamber of Commerce					
310 SE Third St	Ocala FL	34471		800-466-5055	352-629-8051
Clay County Chamber of Commerce					
1734 Kingsley Ave	Orange Park FL	32073		800-435-7352	904-264-2651
Greater Plant City Chamber of Commerce					
106 N Evers St	Plant City FL	33563		800-760-2315	813-754-3707
Gadsden County Chamber of Commerce					
208 N Adams St	Quincy FL	32351		800-627-9231	850-627-9231
Tampa Bay Beaches Chamber of Commerce					
6990 Gulf Blvd	Saint Pete Beach FL	33706		855-344-5999	727-360-6957
Chamber South					
6410 SW 80th St	South Miami FL	33143		800-206-3715	305-661-1621
Stuart-Martin County Chamber of Commerce					
1650 S Kanner Hwy	Stuart FL	34994		800-962-2873	772-287-1088
Greater Tallahassee Chamber of Commerce					
115 N Calhoun St	Tallahassee FL	32301		866-566-6106	850-224-8116
Greater Tampa Chamber of Commerce					
201 N Franklin St Ste 201	Tampa FL	33602		877-693-5236	813-228-7777
Titusville Area Chamber of Commerce					
2000 S Washington Ave	Titusville FL	32780		800-435-7352	321-267-3036
Indian River County Chamber of Commerce					
1216 21st St	Vero Beach FL	32960		888-703-8130	772-567-3491
West Orange Chamber of Commerce					
12184 W Colonial Dr	Winter Garden FL	34787		877-999-9981	407-656-1304

	Toll-Free	Phone
Winter Park Chamber of Commerce 151 W Lyman Ave ... Winter Park FL 32789	**877-972-4262***	407-644-8281
*Help Line		
Zephyrhills Chamber of Commerce 38550 Fifth Ave ... Zephyrhills FL 33542	**800-851-8754**	813-782-1913

Georgia

	Toll-Free	Phone
Albany Area Chamber of Commerce 225 W Broad Ave ... Albany GA 31701	**800-475-8700**	229-434-8700
Greater North Fulton Chamber of Commerce (GNFCC) 11605 Haynes Bridge Rd Ste 100 ... Alpharetta GA 30009	**866-840-5770**	770-993-8806
Cobb Chamber of Commerce 240 I- N Pkwy ... Atlanta GA 30339	**800-228-2545**	770-980-2000
Gordon County Chamber of Commerce 300 S Wall St ... Calhoun GA 30701	**800-887-3811**	706-625-3200
Chatsworth-Murray County Chamber of Commerce PO Box 516 ... Chatsworth GA 30705	**800-969-9490**	706-695-2834
White County Chamber of Commerce 122 N Main St ... Cleveland GA 30528	**800-392-8279**	706-865-5356
Greater Columbus Chamber of Commerce 1200 Sixth Ave PO Box 1200 ... Columbus GA 31902	**800-360-8552**	706-327-1566
Habersham County Chamber of Commerce 668 Clarkesville St ... Cornelia GA 30531	**800-835-2559**	706-778-4654
Newton County Chamber of Commerce 2101 Clark St ... Covington GA 30014	**866-462-6873**	770-786-7510
Douglas-Coffee County Chamber of Commerce 211 S Gaskin Ave ... Douglas GA 31533	**888-426-3334**	912-384-1873
Dublin-Laurens County Chamber of Commerce 1200 Bellvue ... Dublin GA 31021	**800-829-4933**	478-272-5546
Fayette County Chamber of Commerce 200 Courthouse Sq ... Fayetteville GA 30214	**877-527-3712**	770-461-9983
Liberty County Chamber of Commerce 425 W Oglethorpe Hwy ... Hinesville GA 31313	**855-766-2466**	912-368-4445
Jackson County Area Chamber of Commerce 270 Athens St PO Box 629 ... Jefferson GA 30549	**800-243-6921**	706-387-0300
Clayton County Chamber of Commerce 2270 Mt Zion Rd ... Jonesboro GA 30236	**877-790-1831**	678-610-4021
Moultrie-Colquitt County Chamber of Commerce 116 First Ave SE ... Moultrie GA 31768	**888-408-4748**	229-985-2131
Greater Rome Chamber of Commerce One Riverside Pkwy ... Rome GA 30161	**800-234-3154**	706-291-7663
Camden County Chamber of Commerce 2603 Osborne Rd Ste R ... Saint Marys GA 31558	**888-837-4002**	912-729-5840
Savannah Area Chamber of Commerce 101 E Bay St ... Savannah GA 31401	**877-728-2662**	912-644-6400
Effingham County Chamber of Commerce 520 W Third St PO Box 1078 ... Springfield GA 31329	**800-241-3333**	912-754-3301
Statesboro-Bulloch Chamber of Commerce 102 S Main St ... Statesboro GA 30458	**855-478-5551**	912-764-6111
Tifton-Tift County Chamber of Commerce 100 Central Ave ... Tifton GA 31794	**800-550-8438**	229-382-6200
DeKalb Chamber of Commerce 125 Clairemont Ave Ste 235 ... Tucker GA 30084	**800-428-7337**	404-378-8000

Hawaii

	Toll-Free	Phone
Hawaii Island Chamber of Commerce 117 Keawe St ... Hilo HI 96720	**877-482-4411**	808-935-7178
Kailua Chamber of Commerce 600 Kailua Rd Ste 107 ... Kailua HI 96734	**888-261-7997**	808-261-2727

Idaho

	Toll-Free	Phone
Caldwell Chamber of Commerce 704 Blaine St ... Caldwell ID 83605	**877-375-7382**	208-459-7493
Coeur d'Alene Area Chamber of Commerce 105 N First St Ste 100 ... Coeur d'Alene ID 83814	**877-782-9232**	208-664-3194
Sun Valley/Ketchum Chamber & Visitors Bureau 491 Sun Vly Rd ... Ketchum ID 83340	**800-634-3347**	208-726-3423
Meridian Chamber of Commerce 215 E Franklin Rd ... Meridian ID 83642	**866-833-3330**	208-888-2817
Moscow Chamber of Commerce 411 S Main St ... Moscow ID 83843	**855-202-0973**	208-882-1800
Twin Falls Area Chamber of Commerce 858 Blue Lakes Blvd N ... Twin Falls ID 83301	**866-734-3838**	208-733-3974

Illinois

	Toll-Free	Phone
Berwyn Development Corp 3322 S Oak Pk Ave 2nd Fl ... Berwyn IL 60402	**877-247-7792**	708-788-8100
Crystal Lake Chamber of Commerce 427 W Virginia St ... Crystal Lake IL 60014	**800-946-2248**	815-459-1300
Downers Grove Area Chamber of Commerce & Industry 2001 Butterfield Rd Ste 105 ... Downers Grove IL 60515	**800-922-3565**	630-968-4050
Elgin Area Chamber of Commerce 31 S Grove Ave ... Elgin IL 60120	**800-621-3362**	847-741-5660
Greater O'Hare Assn of Industry & Commerce PO Box 1516 ... Elk Grove Village IL 60009	**877-355-4768**	630-773-2944
Freeport Area Chamber of Commerce 27 W Stephenson St ... Freeport IL 61032	**877-881-7339**	815-233-1350
Glen Ellyn Chamber of Commerce 800 Roosevelt Rd Bldg D Ste 108 ... Glen Ellyn IL 60137	**800-622-9000**	630-469-0907
Growth Assn of Southwestern Illinois 5800 Godfrey Rd Alden Hall ... Godfrey IL 62035	**855-852-9460**	618-467-2280
West Suburban Chamber of Commerce 9440 Joliet Rd Ste B ... Hodgkins IL 60525	**800-796-9696**	708-387-7550
Joliet Region Chamber of Commerce & Industry 63 N Chicago St ... Joliet IL 60432	**877-499-9669**	815-727-5371
Macomb Area Chamber of Commerce & Downtown Development Corp 214 N Lafayette St ... Macomb IL 61455	**800-232-0270**	309-837-4855
Greater Marion Area Chamber of Commerce 2305 W Main St ... Marion IL 62959	**800-699-1760**	618-997-6311
Grundy County Chamber of Commerce & Industry 909 Liberty St ... Morris IL 60450	**800-825-1785**	815-942-0113
Mount Prospect Chamber of Commerce 107 S Main St ... Mount Prospect IL 60056	**800-584-4452**	847-398-6616
Northbrook Chamber of Commerce & Industry 2002 Walters Ave ... Northbrook IL 60062	**855-354-3337**	847-498-5555
Oak Forest - Crestwood Area Chamber of Commerce 15440 S Central Ave ... Oak Forest IL 60452	**800-526-7879**	708-687-4600
Rockford Chamber of Commerce 308 W State St Ste 190 ... Rockford IL 61101	**888-375-3000**	815-987-8100
Round Lake Area Chamber of Commerce & Industry 2007 Civic Ctr Way ... Round Lake Beach IL 60073	**800-334-7661**	847-546-2002

Indiana

	Toll-Free	Phone
Chamber of Commerce of Harrison County 111 W Walnut St ... Corydon IN 47112	**800-666-0255**	812-738-0120
Greater Fort Wayne Chamber of Commerce 826 Ewing St ... Fort Wayne IN 46802	**888-259-9175**	260-424-1435
Goshen Chamber of Commerce 232 S Main St ... Goshen IN 46526	**800-307-4204**	574-533-2102
Greater Greenwood Chamber of Commerce 65 Airport Pkwy ... Greenwood IN 46143	**800-462-7585**	317-888-4856
Lakeshore Chamber of Commerce 5246 Hohman Ave Ste 100 ... Hammond IN 46320	**855-464-6368**	219-931-1000
Greater Lawrence Township Chamber of Commerce 9120 Otis Ave Ste 100 ... Indianapolis IN 46216	**800-473-2328**	317-541-9876
LaGrange County Chamber of Commerce 901 S Detroit St Ste A ... LaGrange IN 46761	**877-735-0340**	260-463-2443
Dearborn County Chamber of Commerce 320 Walnut St ... Lawrenceburg IN 47025	**800-322-8198**	812-537-0814
Greater Monticello Chamber of Commerce 116 N Main St ... Monticello IN 47960	**800-541-7906**	574-583-7220
Muncie-Delaware County Chamber of Commerce 401 S High St ... Muncie IN 47305	**800-336-1373**	765-288-6681
One Southern Indiana 4100 Charlestown Rd ... New Albany IN 47150	**800-521-2232**	812-945-0266
Miami County Chamber of Commerce 13 E Main St ... Peru IN 46970	**800-521-9945**	765-472-1923
Shelby County Chamber of Commerce 501 N Harrison St ... Shelbyville IN 46176	**800-318-4083**	317-398-6647

Iowa

	Toll-Free	Phone
Burlington/West Burlington Area Chamber of Commerce 610 N Fourth St Ste 200 ... Burlington IA 52601	**800-827-4837**	319-752-6365
Council Bluffs Area Chamber of Commerce 149 W Bdwy ... Council Bluffs IA 51503	**800-228-6878**	712-325-1000
Greater Des Moines Partnership 700 Locust St Ste 100 ... Des Moines IA 50309	**800-376-9059**	515-286-4950
Dubuque Area Chamber of Commerce 300 Main St Ste 200 ... Dubuque IA 52001	**800-798-4748**	563-557-9200
Iowa City Area Chamber of Commerce 325 E Washington St Ste 100 ... Iowa City IA 52240	**800-283-6592**	319-337-9637
Marshalltown Area Chamber of Commerce 709 S Ctr St PO Box 1000 ... Marshalltown IA 50158	**800-725-5301**	641-753-6645
Greater Cedar Valley Chamber of Commerce 10 W 4th St Ste 310 ... Waterloo IA 50703	**800-288-1047**	319-232-1156

Kansas

	Toll-Free	Phone
Emporia Area Chamber of Commerce 719 Commercial St ... Emporia KS 66801	**800-279-3730**	620-342-1600
Hutchinson/Reno County Chamber of Commerce 117 N Walnut St ... Hutchinson KS 67501	**800-691-4262**	620-662-3391
Lenexa Chamber of Commerce 11180 Lackman Rd ... Lenexa KS 66219	**800-679-0177**	913-888-1414
Manhattan Area Chamber of Commerce 501 Poyntz Ave ... Manhattan KS 66502	**800-759-0134**	785-776-8829
Pittsburg Area Chamber of Commerce 117 W Fourth St ... Pittsburg KS 66762	**800-794-4780**	620-231-1000

Kentucky

	Toll-Free	Phone
Ashland Alliance Chamber of Commerce 1733 Winchester Ave ... Ashland KY 41101	**800-233-3826**	606-324-5111
Bowling Green Area Chamber of Commerce 710 College St ... Bowling Green KY 42101	**866-330-2422**	270-781-3200
Glasgow-Barren County Chamber of Commerce 118 E Public Sq ... Glasgow KY 42141	**800-264-3161**	270-651-3161
Greenville-Muhlenberg Chamber of Commerce 100 E Main Cross PO Box 313 ... Greenville KY 42345	**866-227-4812**	270-338-5422
Hopkinsville-Christian County Chamber of Commerce 2800 Port Campbell Blvd ... Hopkinsville KY 42240	**800-842-9959**	270-885-9096
Somerset-Pulaski County Chamber of Commerce 445 S Hwy 27 Ste 101 ... Somerset KY 42501	**877-629-9722**	606-679-7323

Louisiana

	Toll-Free	Phone
Bossier Chamber of Commerce 710 Benton Rd ... Bossier City LA 71111	**888-414-2695**	318-746-0252
Monroe Chamber of Commerce 212 Walnut St Ste 100 ... Monroe LA 71201	**888-677-5200**	318-323-3461
Natchitoches Area Chamber of Commerce 550 Second St ... Natchitoches LA 71457	**877-646-6689**	318-352-6894
Iberville Parish Chamber of Commerce 23675 Church St ... Plaquemine LA 70764	**800-266-2692**	225-687-3560
Ruston/Lincoln Chamber of Commerce 211 N Trenton ... Ruston LA 71270	**800-392-9032**	318-255-2031
Greater Shreveport Chamber of Commerce 400 Edwards St ... Shreveport LA 71101	**800-448-5432**	318-677-2500

East St Tammany Chamber of Commerce
118 W Hall Ave ....Slidell LA 70460 **800-870-3673** 985-643-5678

Maine

					Toll-Free	Phone

Bar Harbor Chamber of Commerce
Two Cottage St ....Bar Harbor ME 04609 **888-540-9990** 207-288-5103
Belfast Area Chamber of Commerce
14 Main St ....Belfast ME 04915 **877-338-9015** 207-338-5900
Ellsworth Area Chamber of Commerce
163 High St ....Ellsworth ME 04605 **855-635-6278** 207-667-5584
Southern Midcoast Maine Chamber
Two Main St Border Trust Business Ctr. ....Topsham ME 04086 **877-725-8797** 207-725-8797

Maryland

					Toll-Free	Phone

Harford County Chamber of Commerce
108 S Bond St ....Bel Air MD 21014 **800-682-8536** 410-838-2020
Greater Bethesda-Chevy Chase Chamber of Commerce
7910 Woodmont Ave Ste 1204 ....Bethesda MD 20814 **800-333-6778** 301-652-4900
Greater Crofton Chamber of Commerce
PO Box 4146 ....Crofton MD 21114 **866-852-4237** 410-721-9131
Charles County Chamber of Commerce
101 Centennial St Ste A ....La Plata MD 20646 **800-992-3194** 301-932-6500
Garrett County Chamber of Commerce
15 Visitors Ctr Dr ....McHenry MD 21541 **888-387-5237** 301-387-4386
Greater Ocean City Chamber of Commerce
12320 Ocean Gateway ....Ocean City MD 21842 **888-626-3386** 410-213-0144
Eastern Baltimore Area Chamber of Commerce
102 W Pennsylvania Ave Ste 101 ....Towson MD 21204 **888-224-9740** 410-825-6200
Wheaton-Kensington Chamber of Commerce
2401 Blueridge Ave Ste 101 ....Wheaton MD 20902 **800-927-9061** 301-949-0080

Massachusetts

					Toll-Free	Phone

Middlesex West Chamber of Commerce
179 Great Road Suite 104B. ....Acton MA 01720 **800-439-0183** 978-263-0010
United Regional Chamber of Commerce
42 Union St ....Attleboro MA 02703 **800-333-6624** 508-222-0801
Metro South Chamber of Commerce
60 School St ....Brockton MA 02301 **877-777-4414** 508-586-0500
Cape Cod Canal Regional Chamber of Commerce
70 Main St ....Buzzards Bay MA 02532 **888-332-2732** 508-759-6000
Cape Cod Chamber of Commerce
Five Shoot Flying Hill Rd ....Centerville MA 02632 **888-332-2732** 508-362-3225
Nashoba Valley Chamber of Commerce
100 Sherman Ave ....Devens MA 01434 **877-322-8228** 978-772-6976
Fall River Area Chamber of Commerce & Industry
200 Pocasset St ....Fall River MA 02721 **800-647-2824** 508-676-8226
Falmouth Chamber of Commerce
20 Academy Ln ....Falmouth MA 02540 **800-526-8532** 508-548-8500
Metro West Chamber of Commerce
1671 Worcester Rd Ste 201 ....Framingham MA 01701 **866-709-9401** 508-879-5600
Merrimack Valley Chamber of Commerce
264 Essex St ....Lawrence MA 01840 **800-966-3375** 978-686-0900
Greater Lowell Chamber of Commerce
131 Merrimack St ....Lowell MA 01852 **800-338-0221** 978-459-8154
Greater Northampton Chamber of Commerce
99 Pleasant St ....NorthHampton MA 01060 **800-392-6090** 413-584-1900
Affiliated Chamber of Commerce of Greater Springfield
1441 Main St ....Springfield MA 01103 **888-283-3757** 413-787-1555
Taunton Area Chamber of Commerce
12 Taunton Green Ste 201 ....Taunton MA 02780 **800-225-0394** 508-824-4068
Blackstone Valley Chamber of Commerce
110 Church St ....Whitinsville MA 01588 **800-841-0919** 508-234-9090

Michigan

					Toll-Free	Phone

Alpena Area Chamber of Commerce
235 W Chisholm St ....Alpena MI 49707 **800-425-7362** 989-354-4181
Dearborn Chamber of Commerce
22100 Michigan Ave ....Dearborn MI 48124 **800-844-5440** 313-584-6100
Delta County Area Chamber of Commerce
230 Ludington St ....Escanaba MI 49829 **888-335-8264** 906-786-2192
Genesee Regional Chamber of Commerce
519 S Saginaw St Ste 200 ....Flint MI 48502 **888-823-6837** 810-600-1404
Holland Area Chamber of Commerce
272 E Eigth St ....Holland MI 49423 **800-421-3512** 616-392-2389
Keweenaw Peninsula Chamber of Commerce
902 College Ave PO Box 336 ....Houghton MI 49931 **800-796-0004** 906-482-5240
Dickinson Area Partnership
600 S Stephenson Ave ....Iron Mountain MI 49801 **888-543-2139** 906-774-2002
Greater Jackson Chamber of Commerce
141 S Jackson St ....Jackson MI 49201 **800-366-3699** 517-782-8221
Midland Area Chamber of Commerce
300 Rodd St Ste 101. ....Midland MI 48640 **800-715-0074** 989-839-9901
Monroe County Chamber of Commerce
1645 N Dixie Hwy Ste 20 ....Monroe MI 48162 **855-386-1280** 734-384-3366
Macomb County Chamber
28 First St Ste B ....Mount Clemens MI 48043 **800-564-3136** 586-493-7600
Muskegon Area Chamber of Commerce
380 W Western Ste 202 ....Muskegon MI 49440 **800-659-2955** 231-722-3751
Novi Chamber of Commerce, The
41875 W 11 Mile Rd Ste 201 ....Novi MI 48375 **888-440-7325** 248-349-3743
Blue Water Area Chamber of Commerce
512 McMorran Blvd ....Port Huron MI 48060 **800-361-0526** 810-985-7101
Saginaw County Chamber of Commerce
515 N Washington Ave 2nd Fl ....Saginaw MI 48607 **888-609-8342** 989-752-7161
Traverse City Area Chamber of Commerce
202 E Grandview Pkwy ....Traverse City MI 49684 **800-942-5322** 231-947-5075
Westland Chamber of Commerce
36900 Ford Rd ....Westland MI 48185 **800-737-4859** 734-326-7222

Minnesota

					Toll-Free	Phone

Alexandria Lakes Area Chamber of Commerce
206 Broadway ....Alexandria MN 56308 **800-235-9441** 320-763-3161
Apple Valley Chamber of Commerce
14800 Galaxie Ave Ste 101. ....Apple Valley MN 55124 **800-301-9435** 952-432-8422
Bemidji Area Chamber of Commerce
300 Bemidji Ave ....Bemidji MN 56601 **800-458-2223** 218-444-3541
Brainerd Lakes Area Chamber of Commerce
124 N Sixth St PO Box 356. ....Brainerd MN 56401 **800-450-2838** 218-829-2838
Cloquet Area Chamber of Commerce
225 Sunnyside Dr ....Cloquet MN 55720 **800-554-4350** 218-879-1551
Detroit Lakes Regional Chamber of Commerce
700 Summit Ave ....Detroit Lakes MN 56501 **800-542-3992** 218-847-9202
Duluth Area Chamber of Commerce
5 W First St Ste 101 ....Duluth MN 55802 **800-385-8842** 218-722-5501
Grand Rapids Area Chamber of Commerce
One NW Third St ....Grand Rapids MN 55744 **800-472-6366** 218-326-6619
Hastings Area Chamber of Commerce & Tourism Bureau
111 E Third St ....Hastings MN 55033 **888-612-6122** 651-437-6775
Lakeville Area Chamber of Commerce & Convention & Visitors Bureau
19950 Dodd Blvd Ste 101. ....Lakeville MN 55044 **888-525-3845** 952-469-2020
Owatonna Area Chamber of Commerce & Tourism
320 Hoffman Dr ....Owatonna MN 55060 **800-423-6466** 507-451-7970
Leech Lake Area Chamber of Commerce
205 Minnesota Ave E ....Walker MN 56484 **800-833-1118** 218-547-1313

Mississippi

					Toll-Free	Phone

Panola Partnership Inc
150-A Public Sq ....Batesville MS 38606 **888-872-6652** 662-563-3126
Rankin County Chamber of Commerce
101 Service Dr ....Brandon MS 39043 **800-987-8280** 601-825-2268
Brookhaven-Lincoln County Chamber of Commerce
230 S Whitworth Ave ....Brookhaven MS 39601 **800-613-4667** 601-833-1411
Clarksdale-Coahoma County Chamber of Commerce & Industrial Foundation
1540 DeSoto Ave ....Clarksdale MS 38614 **800-626-3764** 662-627-7337
Alliance, The 810 Tate St ....Corinth MS 38834 **877-347-0545** 662-287-5269
Area Development Partnership
One Convention Ctr Plz ....Hattiesburg MS 39401 **800-238-4288** 601-296-7500
Jones County Chamber of Commerce
PO Box 527 ....Laurel MS 39441 **800-392-9629*** 601-649-3031
*General
Pike County Chamber of Commerce & Economic Development District
112 N Railroad Blvd ....McComb MS 39648 **800-844-2653** 601-684-2291
Oxford-Lafayette County Chamber of Commerce
299 W Jackson Ave ....Oxford MS 38655 **800-880-6967** 662-234-4651
Community Development Partnership
410 Poplar Ave 256 W Beacon ....Philadelphia MS 39350 **877-752-2643** 601-656-1000
Greater Starkville Development Partnership
200 E Main St ....Starkville MS 39759 **800-649-8687** 662-323-3322
Yazoo County Chamber of Commerce
212 E Broadway Ste 7. ....Yazoo City MS 39194 **800-638-6582** 662-746-1273

Missouri

					Toll-Free	Phone

Branson/Lakes Area Chamber of Commerce
PO Box 1897 ....Branson MO 65615 **800-214-3661** 417-334-4084
Chesterfield Chamber of Commerce
101 Chesterfield Business Pkwy ....Chesterfield MO 63005 **888-242-4262** 636-532-3399
Kingdom of Callaway Chamber of Commerce
409 Ct St ....Fulton MO 65251 **800-257-3554** 573-642-3055
Jefferson City Area Chamber of Commerce
213 Adams St ....Jefferson City MO 65101 **866-223-6535** 573-634-3616
Greater Kansas City Chamber of Commerce
911 Main St Ste 2600. ....Kansas City MO 64105 **800-767-7700** 816-221-2424
Lebanon Area Chamber of Commerce
186 N Adams St ....Lebanon MO 65536 **888-588-5710** 417-588-3256
Lee's Summit Chamber of Commerce
220 SE Main St ....Lee's Summit MO 64063 **888-816-5757** 816-524-2424
Rolla Area Chamber of Commerce
1311 KingsHwy ....Rolla MO 65401 **888-809-3817** 573-364-3577
Saint Joseph Area Chamber of Commerce
3003 Frederick Ave ....Saint Joseph MO 64506 **800-748-7856** 816-232-4461

Montana

					Toll-Free	Phone

Billings Area Chamber of Commerce
815 S 27th St ....Billings MT 59101 **855-328-9116** 406-245-4111
Butte-Silver Bow Chamber of Commerce
1000 George St ....Butte MT 59701 **800-735-6814** 406-723-3177
Great Falls Area Chamber of Commerce
100 First Ave N ....Great Falls MT 59401 **800-735-8535** 406-761-4434
Helena Area Chamber of Commerce
225 Cruse Ave ....Helena MT 59601 **800-743-5362** 406-442-4120
Missoula Area Chamber of Commerce
825 E Front St ....Missoula MT 59802 **800-814-2342** 406-543-6623

Nebraska

					Toll-Free	Phone

Kearney Area Chamber of Commerce
1007 Second Ave PO Box 607 ....Kearney NE 68848 **800-227-8340** 308-237-3101

Nevada

					Toll-Free	Phone

Carson Valley Chamber of Commerce & Visitors Authority
1477 Hwy 395 N Ste A ....Gardnerville NV 89410 **800-727-7677** 775-782-8144
Las Vegas Chamber of Commerce
575 Symphony Park Ave Ste 100 ....Las Vegas NV 89105 **888-635-7272** 702-641-5822

New Jersey

				Toll-Free	Phone
Greater Atlantic City Chamber 12 S Virginia Ave	Atlantic City	NJ	08401	**800-123-4567**	609-345-4524
Brick Township Chamber of Commerce 270 Chambers Bridge Rd	Brick	NJ	08723	**877-539-2020**	732-477-4949
Cherry Hill Regional Chamber of Commerce 1060 Kings Hwy N Ste 200	Cherry Hill	NJ	08034	**800-669-6801**	856-667-1600
Greater Monmouth Chamber of Commerce 57 Schanck Rd Ste C-3	Freehold	NJ	07728	**800-700-6400**	732-462-3030
Newark Regional Business Partnership 744 Broad St 26th Fl	Newark	NJ	07102	**800-662-6878**	973-522-0099
Sussex County Chamber of Commerce 120 Hampton House Rd	Newton	NJ	07860	**844-256-7328**	973-579-1811
Greater Paterson Chamber of Commerce 100 Hamilton Plaza Ste 1201	Paterson	NJ	07505	**800-220-2892**	973-881-7300
Southern Ocean County Chamber of Commerce 265 W Ninth St	Ship Bottom	NJ	08008	**800-292-6372**	609-494-7211
Greater Vineland Chamber of Commerce 2115 S Delsea Dr	Vineland	NJ	08360	**800-922-1766**	856-691-7400

New Mexico

				Toll-Free	Phone
Alamogordo Chamber of Commerce 1301 N White Sands Blvd	Alamogordo	NM	88310	**800-826-0294**	575-437-6120
Carlsbad Chamber of Commerce 302 S Canal St PO Box 910	Carlsbad	NM	88220	**866-822-9226**	575-887-6516
Clovis/Curry County Chamber of Commerce 105 E Third St	Clovis	NM	88101	**800-261-7656**	575-763-3435
Grants/Cibola County Chamber of Commerce 100 N Iron Ave	Grants	NM	87020	**866-270-5110**	505-287-4802
Hobbs Chamber of Commerce 400 N Marland Blvd	Hobbs	NM	88240	**800-658-6291**	575-397-3202
Roswell Chamber of Commerce 131 W Second St	Roswell	NM	88202	**877-849-7679**	575-623-5695
Silver City-Grant County Chamber of Commerce 201 N Hudson St	Silver City	NM	88061	**800-548-9378**	575-538-3785

New York

				Toll-Free	Phone
Genesee County Chamber of Commerce 210 E Main St	Batavia	NY	14020	**800-622-2686**	585-343-7440
Buffalo Niagara Partnership 665 Main St Ste 200	Buffalo	NY	14203	**800-241-0474**	716-852-7100
St Lawrence County Chamber of Commerce 101 Main St	Canton	NY	13617	**877-228-7810**	315-386-4000
Corning Area Chamber of Commerce One W Market St Ste 302	Corning	NY	14830	**866-463-6264**	607-936-4686
Chemung County Chamber of Commerce 400 E Church St *General	Elmira	NY	14901	**800-627-5892***	607-734-5137
Livingston County Chamber of Commerce 4635 Millennium Dr	Geneseo	NY	14454	**800-538-7365**	585-243-2222
Adirondack Regional Chambers of Commerce 136 Glen St Ste 3	Glens Falls	NY	12801	**888-516-7247**	518-798-1761
Huntington Township Chamber of Commerce 164 Main St	Huntington	NY	11743	**888-962-9932**	631-423-6100
Queens Chamber of Commerce 75-20 Astoria Blvd Ste 140	Jackson Heights	NY	11370	**877-256-5556**	718-898-8500
Kenmore-Town of Tonawanda Chamber of Commerce 3411 Delaware Ave	Kenmore	NY	14217	**888-710-6626**	716-874-1202
Lake Placid/Essex County Visitors Bureau 49 Parkside Dr	Lake Placid	NY	12946	**800-447-5224**	518-523-2445
Lewis County Chamber of Commerce 7576 S State St	Lowville	NY	13367	**800-724-0242**	315-376-2213
Herkimer County Chamber of Commerce 28 W Main St	Mohawk	NY	13407	**877-984-4636**	315-866-7820
Manhattan Chamber of Commerce 1375 Broadway 3rd F	New York	NY	10018	**855-868-7692**	212-479-7772
Tri-State Chamber of Commerce 5 S Broome St	Port Jervis	NY	12771	**800-707-6925**	845-856-6694
Dutchess County Regional Chamber of Commerce 1 Civic Ctr Plaza Ste 400	Poughkeepsie	NY	12601	**800-817-2918**	845-454-1700
Saratoga County Chamber of Commerce 28 Clinton St	Saratoga Springs	NY	12866	**855-765-7873**	518-584-3255
Chamber of Schenectady County 306 State St	Schenectady	NY	12305	**800-962-8007**	518-372-5656
Rensselaer County Regional Chamber of Commerce 255 River St	Troy	NY	12180	**800-822-2400**	518-274-7020
Greater Watertown-North Country Chamber of Commerce 1241 Coffeen St	Watertown	NY	13601	**800-642-4272**	315-788-4400

North Carolina

				Toll-Free	Phone
Asheville Area Chamber of Commerce 36 Montford Ave	Asheville	NC	28802	**888-314-1041**	828-258-6101
Black Mountain-Swannanoa Chamber of Commerce 201 E State St	Black Mountain	NC	28711	**800-669-2301**	828-669-2300
Blowing Rock Chamber of Commerce 7738 Vly Blvd	Blowing Rock	NC	28605	**800-295-7851**	828-295-7851
Brevard-Transylvania Chamber of Commerce 175 E Main St	Brevard	NC	28712	**800-648-4523**	828-883-3700
Lake Norman Chamber of Commerce 19900 W Catawba Ave Ste 101	Cornelius	NC	28031	**800-305-2508**	704-892-1922
Gaston Chamber of Commerce 601 W Franklin Blvd	Gastonia	NC	28052	**800-933-3909**	704-864-2621
High Point Chamber of Commerce 1634 N Main St	High Point	NC	27262	**877-852-9462**	336-882-5000
Jacksonville/Onslow Chamber of Commerce 1099 Gum Branch Rd	Jacksonville	NC	28541	**800-877-8339**	910-347-3141
Carteret County Chamber of Commerce 801 Arendell St Ste 1	Morehead City	NC	28557	**800-622-6278**	252-726-6350
Greater Mount Airy Chamber of Commerce 200 N Main St	Mount Airy	NC	27030	**800-948-0949**	336-786-6116
New Bern Area Chamber of Commerce 316 S Front St	New Bern	NC	28560	**877-811-1776**	252-637-3111
Greater Raleigh Chamber of Commerce PO Box 2978	Raleigh	NC	27602	**866-291-0854**	919-664-7000
Rocky Mount Area Chamber of Commerce 100 Coastline St Ste 200	Rocky Mount	NC	27804	**800-682-6746**	252-446-0323
Brunswick County Chamber of Commerce 4948 Main St	Shallotte	NC	28459	**800-426-6644**	910-754-6644
Jackson County Chamber of Commerce 773 W Main St	Sylva	NC	28779	**800-962-1911**	828-586-2155
Tarboro Edgecombe Chamber of Commerce 509 Trade St	Tarboro	NC	27886	**888-404-3424**	252-823-7241
Haywood County Chamber of Commerce 28 Walnut Street	Waynesville	NC	28786	**877-456-3073**	828-456-3021
Greater Wilmington Chamber of Commerce 1 Estell Lee Pl	Wilmington	NC	28401	**800-829-4477**	910-762-2611
Wilson Chamber of Commerce 200 Nash St NE	Wilson	NC	27893	**855-905-0604**	252-237-0165
Windsor-Bertie Area Chamber of Commerce 121 Granville St PO Box 572	Windsor	NC	27983	**800-334-5010**	252-794-4277

North Dakota

				Toll-Free	Phone
Grand Forks Chamber of Commerce 202 N Third St	Grand Forks	ND	58203	**855-233-6362**	701-772-7271

Ohio

				Toll-Free	Phone
Athens Area Chamber of Commerce 449 E State St Ste 1	Athens	OH	45701	**877-360-3608**	740-594-2251
Logan County Chamber of Commerce 100 S Main St	Bellefontaine	OH	43311	**877-360-3608**	937-599-5121
Canton Regional Chamber of Commerce 222 Market Ave N	Canton	OH	44702	**800-533-4302**	330-456-7253
Carroll County Chamber of Commerce & Economic Development 61 N Lisbon St PO Box 277	Carrollton	OH	44615	**800-956-4684**	330-627-4811
Greater Cleveland Partnership 50 Public Sq Ste 200	Cleveland	OH	44113	**888-304-4769**	216-621-3300
Columbus Chamber of Commerce 150 S Front St Ste 200	Columbus	OH	43215	**888-382-1574**	614-221-1321
Dayton Area Chamber of Commerce 1 Chamber Plaza Ste 200	Dayton	OH	45402	**800-621-9131**	937-226-1444
Hardin County Chamber of Commerce (HCCBA) 225 S Detroit St	Kenton	OH	43326	**888-642-7346**	419-673-4131
Mentor Chamber of Commerce 6972 Spinach Dr	Mentor	OH	44060	**800-825-6755**	440-255-1616
Chamber of Commerce serving Middletown Monroe & Trenton 1500 Central Ave	Middletown	OH	45044	**800-837-3200**	513-422-4551
Milford-Miami Township Chamber of Commerce 983 Lila Ave	Milford	OH	45150	**877-723-0513**	513-831-2411
Napoleon/Henry County Chamber of Commerce 611 N Perry St	Napoleon	OH	43545	**800-322-6849**	419-592-1786
North Canton Area Chamber of Commerce 121 S Main St	North Canton	OH	44720	**888-263-3423**	330-499-5100
Portsmouth Area Chamber of Commerce 342 Second St PO Box 509	Portsmouth	OH	45662	**800-648-2574**	740-353-7647
Greater Lawrence County Area Chamber of Commerce 216 Collins Ave	South Point	OH	45680	**800-408-1334**	740-377-4550
Champaign County Chamber of Commerce 113 Miami St	Urbana	OH	43078	**877-873-5764**	937-653-5764
Adams County Travel & Visitors Bureau 509 E Main St	West Union	OH	45693	**877-232-6764**	937-544-5639
Willoughby Area Chamber of Commerce 28 Public Sq	Willoughby	OH	44094	**877-229-4361**	440-942-1632
Youngstown Warren Regional Chamber 11 Central Sq Ste 1600	Youngstown	OH	44503	**877-807-2249**	330-744-2131
Zanesville-Muskingum County Chamber of Commerce 205 N Fifth St	Zanesville	OH	43701	**800-743-2303**	740-455-8282

Oklahoma

				Toll-Free	Phone
Greater Enid Chamber of Commerce PO Box 907	Enid	OK	73702	**877-233-4232**	580-237-2494
South Oklahoma City Chamber of Commerce 701 SW 74 St	Oklahoma City	OK	73139	**877-309-2070**	405-634-1436
Greater Shawnee Area Chamber of Commerce 131 N Bell Ave	Shawnee	OK	74801	**800-762-7695**	405-273-6092
Stillwater Chamber of Commerce 409 S Main St	Stillwater	OK	74075	**800-593-5573**	405-372-5573
Tulsa Metro Chamber One West Third St Ste 100	Tulsa	OK	74103	**888-424-9411**	918-585-1201

Oregon

				Toll-Free	Phone
Bend Chamber of Commerce 777 NW Wall St Ste 200	Bend	OR	97701	**800-905-2363**	541-382-3221
Florence Area Chamber of Commerce 290 Hwy 101	Florence	OR	97439	**800-585-3737**	541-997-3128
Grants Pass Chamber of Commerce 1995 NW Vine St PO Box 970	Grants Pass	OR	97526	**800-547-5927**	541-476-7717
La Grande-Union County Chamber of Commerce 102 Elm St	La Grande	OR	97850	**800-848-9969**	541-963-8588
Greater Newport Chamber of Commerce 555 SW Coast Hwy	Newport	OR	97365	**800-262-7844**	541-265-8801
Portland Business Alliance 200 SW Market St Ste 150	Portland	OR	97201	**800-224-1180**	503-224-8684
Springfield Chamber of Commerce 101 S 'A' St	Springfield	OR	97477	**866-346-1651**	541-746-1651

Pennsylvania

				Toll-Free	Phone
Greater Lehigh Valley Chamber of Commerce 840 Hamilton St Ste 205	Allentown	PA	18101	800-845-7941	610-841-5800
Bedford County Chamber of Commerce 137 E Pitt St	Bedford	PA	15522	800-732-0999	814-623-2233
Perkiomen Valley Chamber of Commerce 351 E Main St	Collegeville	PA	19426	800-349-7623	610-489-6660
Erie Regional Chamber & Growth Partnership 208 E Bayfront Pkwy	Erie	PA	16507	888-300-3743	814-454-7191
Lower Bucks County Chamber of Commerce 409 Hood Blvd	Fairless Hills	PA	19030	800-786-2234	215-943-7400
Franklin Area Chamber of Commerce (FACC) 1259 Liberty St	Franklin	PA	16323	888-547-2377	814-432-5823
Gettysburg-Adams County Area Chamber of Commerce 18 Carlisle St Ste 203	Gettysburg	PA	17325	800-699-1176	717-334-8151
Westmoreland Chamber of Commerce 241 Tollgate Hill Rd	Greensburg	PA	15601	866-468-1231	724-834-2900
Harrisburg Regional Chamber 3211 N Front St Ste 201	Harrisburg	PA	17110	877-883-8339	717-232-4099
Norwin Chamber of Commerce 321 Main St	Irwin	PA	15642	800-480-2265	724-863-0888
Greater Johnstown/Cambria County Chamber of Commerce 245 Market St Ste 100	Johnstown	PA	15901	800-790-4522	814-536-5107
Southern Chester County Chamber of Commerce 217 W State St	Kennett Square	PA	19348	800-343-6583	610-444-0774
PennSuburban Chamber of Commerce 34 Susquehanna Ave	Lansdale	PA	19446	800-847-9772	215-362-9200
Juniata Valley Area Chamber of Commerce 1 W Market St	Lewistown	PA	17044	866-377-1234	717-248-6713
Clinton County Economic Partnership 212 N Jay St	Lock Haven	PA	17745	888-388-6991	570-748-5782
Meadville-Western Crawford County Chamber of Commerce 908 Diamond Pk	Meadville	PA	16335	800-332-2338	814-337-8030
Monroeville Area Chamber of Commerce 4268 Northern Pike	Monroeville	PA	15146	800-527-8941	412-856-0622
Nazareth Area Chamber of Commerce 201 N Main St PO Box 173	Nazareth	PA	18064	866-776-8240	610-759-9188
Tri County Area Chamber of Commerce 152 E High St Ste 360	Pottstown	PA	19464	800-869-5566	610-326-2900
Schuylkill Chamber of Commerce 91 S Progress Ave	Pottsville	PA	17901	800-755-1942	570-622-1942
Upper Bucks Chamber of Commerce 2170 Portzer Rd	Quakertown	PA	18951	888-942-8257	215-536-3211
Greater Reading Chamber of Commerce & Industry 201 Penn St	Reading	PA	19601	877-438-4338	610-376-6766
Greater Susquehanna Valley Chamber of Commerce 2859 N Susquehanna Trl PO Box 10	Shamokin Dam	PA	17876	800-410-2880	570-743-4100
Shenango Valley Chamber of Commerce 41 Chestnut St	Sharon	PA	16146	800-732-0993	724-981-5880
Chamber of Business & Industry of Centre County 200 Innovation Blvd Ste 150	State College	PA	16803	877-234-5050	814-234-1829
Fayette Chamber of Commerce 65 W Main St	Uniontown	PA	15401	800-916-9365	724-437-4571
Greater Wilkes-Barre Chamber of Business & Industry 2 Public Sq PO Box 5340	Wilkes-Barre	PA	18710	800-701-8449	570-823-2101
Williamsport/Lycoming Chamber of Commerce 100 W Third St	Williamsport	PA	17701	800-732-2258	570-326-1971

Rhode Island

				Toll-Free	Phone
East Bay Chamber of Commerce 16 Cutler St Ste 102	Warren	RI	02885	877-797-9790	401-245-0750

South Carolina

				Toll-Free	Phone
Anderson Area Chamber of Commerce 907 N Main St Ste 200	Anderson	SC	29621	800-922-1150	864-226-3454
Kershaw County Chamber of Commerce 607 S Broad St	Camden	SC	29020	800-968-4037	803-432-2525
West Metro Chamber of Commerce 1006 12th St	Cayce	SC	29033	866-720-5400	803-794-6504
Laurens County Chamber of Commerce 291 Professional Pk Rd	Clinton	SC	29325	866-548-9674	864-833-2716
Conway Area Chamber of Commerce 203 Main St	Conway	SC	29526	888-272-8700	843-248-2273
Georgetown County Chamber of Commerce 531 Front St	Georgetown	SC	29440	800-777-7705	843-546-8436
Greater Greenville Chamber of Commerce 24 Cleveland St	Greenville	SC	29601	866-485-5262	864-242-1050
Greater Hartsville Chamber of Commerce PO Box 578	Hartsville	SC	29551	866-747-0060	843-332-6401
Hilton Head Island-Bluffton Chamber of Commerce One Chamber Dr	Hilton Head Island	SC	29928	800-523-3373	843-785-3673
Lexington Chamber of Commerce 321 S Lake Dr	Lexington	SC	29072	866-851-3000	803-359-6113
Clarendon County Chamber of Commerce 19 N Brooks St	Manning	SC	29102	800-731-5253	803-435-4405
Berkeley County Chamber of Commerce PO Box 968	Moncks Corner	SC	29461	800-882-0337	843-761-8238
Myrtle Beach Area Chamber of Commerce 1200 N Oak St	Myrtle Beach	SC	29577	800-356-3016	843-626-7444
Orangeburg County Chamber of Commerce 155 Riverside Dr SW PO Box 328	Orangeburg	SC	29116	800-545-6153	803-534-6821
Greater Sumter Chamber of Commerce 32 E Calhoun St	Sumter	SC	29150	888-868-0737	803-775-1231
Union County Chamber of Commerce 135 Main St	Union	SC	29379	877-202-8755	864-427-9039

South Dakota

				Toll-Free	Phone
Aberdeen Area Chamber of Commerce 516 S Main St	Aberdeen	SD	57401	800-874-9038	605-225-2860

				Toll-Free	Phone
Pierre Area Chamber of Commerce 800 W Dakota Ave	Pierre	SD	57501	800-962-2034	605-224-7361

Tennessee

				Toll-Free	Phone
Chattanooga Area Chamber of Commerce 811 Broad St	Chattanooga	TN	37402	877-756-7684	423-756-2121
Clarksville Area Chamber of Commerce 25 Jefferson St Ste 300	Clarksville	TN	37040	800-530-2487	931-647-2331
Cleveland/Bradley Chamber of Commerce 225 Keith St	Cleveland	TN	37311	800-533-9930	423-472-6587
Cookeville Area-Putnam County Chamber of Commerce One W First St	Cookeville	TN	38501	800-264-5541	931-526-2211
Crossville Cumberland County Chamber of Commerce 34 S Main St	Crossville	TN	38555	877-465-3861	931-484-8444
Jefferson County Chamber of Commerce 532 Patriot Dr	Dandridge	TN	37725	877-237-3847	865-397-9642
Dickson County Chamber of Commerce 119 Hwy 70 E	Dickson	TN	37055	877-718-4967	615-446-2349
Fayetteville-Lincoln County Chamber of Commerce 208 S Elk Ave	Fayetteville	TN	37334	888-433-1238	931-433-1234
Williamson County-Franklin Chamber of Commerce 5005 Meridian Blvd Ste 150	Franklin	TN	37067	800-356-3445	615-771-1912
Jackson Area Chamber of Commerce 197 Auditorium St	Jackson	TN	38301	866-262-8867	731-423-2200
Johnson City/Jonesborough/Washington County Chamber of Commerce 603 E Market St	Johnson City	TN	37601	800-852-3392	423-461-8000
Lawrence County Chamber of Commerce 1609 N Locust Ave PO Box 86	Lawrenceburg	TN	38464	877-388-4911	931-762-4911
Rutherford County Chamber of Commerce 501 Memorial Blvd	Murfreesboro	TN	37129	800-716-7560	615-893-6565
Donelson-Hermitage Chamber of Commerce 125 Donelson Pike PO Box 140200	Nashville	TN	37214	800-688-9889	615-883-7896
Paris-Henry County Chamber of Commerce 2508 Eastwood St	Paris	TN	38242	800-345-1103	731-642-3431
Shelbyville-Bedford County Chamber of Commerce 100 N Cannon Blvd	Shelbyville	TN	37160	888-662-2525	931-684-3482
Claiborne County Chamber of Commerce 1732 Main St PO Box 649	Tazewell	TN	37879	800-332-8164	423-626-4149
Franklin County Chamber of Commerce 44 Chamber Way PO Box 280	Winchester	TN	37398	866-462-5991	931-967-6788

Texas

				Toll-Free	Phone
Alvin-Manvel Area Chamber of Commerce 105 W Willis St	Alvin	TX	77511	888-755-6864	281-331-3944
Greater Austin Chamber of Commerce 535 E 5th St	Austin	TX	78701	888-409-5380	512-478-9383
Washington County Chamber of Commerce 314 S Austin St	Brenham	TX	77833	888-273-6426	979-836-3695
Bryan-College Station Chamber of Commerce 4001 E 29th St Ste 175	Bryan	TX	77802	800-777-8292	979-260-5200
Canyon Chamber of Commerce 1518 Fifth Ave	Canyon	TX	79015	800-999-9481	806-655-7815
Cleburne Chamber of Commerce 1511 W Henderson St	Cleburne	TX	76033	888-253-2876	817-645-2455
Corsicana Area Chamber of Commerce 120 N 12th St	Corsicana	TX	75110	866-222-7100	903-874-4731
Del Rio Chamber of Commerce (DRCoC) 1915 Veterans Blvd *General	Del Rio	TX	78840	800-889-8149*	830-775-3551
Denton Chamber of Commerce 414 W Pkwy St	Denton	TX	76201	800-747-2316	940-382-9693
Eagle Pass Chamber of Commerce 400 E Garrison St	Eagle Pass	TX	78852	888-355-3224	830-773-3224
Edinburg Chamber of Commerce 602 W University Dr	Edinburg	TX	78540	800-800-7214	956-383-4974
Grapevine Chamber of Commerce 200 Vine St	Grapevine	TX	76051	866-322-8667	817-481-1522
Clear Lake Area Chamber of Commerce 1201 NASA Pkwy	Houston	TX	77058	800-877-8339	281-488-7676
Huntsville-Walker County Chamber of Commerce 1327 11th St	Huntsville	TX	77340	800-289-0389	936-295-8113
Greater Killeen Chamber of Commerce One Santa Fe Plz	Killeen	TX	76540	866-790-4769	254-526-9551
Laredo-Webb County Chamber of Commerce 2310 San Bernardo Ave	Laredo	TX	78042	800-292-2122	956-722-9895
Longview Partnership 410 N Ctr St	Longview	TX	75601	800-338-7232	903-237-4000
Lufkin/Angelina County Chamber of Commerce 1615 S Chestnut St	Lufkin	TX	75901	800-409-5659	936-634-6644
Greater Cedar Creek Lake Area Chamber of Commerce 604 S Third St Ste E	Mabank	TX	75147	800-331-6844	903-887-3152
Greater Marshall Chamber of Commerce 213 W Austin St	Marshall	TX	75670	800-953-7868	903-935-7868
Mesquite Chamber of Commerce 617 N Ebrite St	Mesquite	TX	75149	800-541-2355	972-285-0211
Midland Chamber of Commerce 109 N Main St	Midland	TX	79701	800-624-6435	432-683-3381
Mineral Wells Area Chamber of Commerce 511 E Hubbard St	Mineral Wells	TX	76067	800-252-6989	940-325-2557
New Braunfels Chamber of Commerce 390 S Seguin St	New Braunfels	TX	78130	800-572-2626	830-625-2385
Odessa Chamber of Commerce 700 N Grant St Ste 200	Odessa	TX	79761	800-780-4678	432-332-9111
Lamar County Chamber of Commerce 1125 Bonham St	Paris	TX	75460	800-727-4789	903-784-2501
Pearland Area Chamber of Commerce 6117 Broadway St	Pearland	TX	77581	888-604-5888	281-485-3634
Rosenberg-Richmond Area Chamber of Commerce 4120 Ave H	Rosenberg	TX	77471	877-382-7414	281-342-5464
Round Rock Chamber of Commerce 212 E Main St	Round Rock	TX	78664	800-227-7776	512-255-5805

	Toll-Free	Phone
Greater San Antonio Chamber of Commerce		
602 E Commerce St ....San Antonio TX 78205	888-828-8680	210-229-2100
North San Antonio Chamber of Commerce		
12930 Country Pkwy ....San Antonio TX 78216	877-495-5888	210-344-4848
San Marcos Area Chamber of Commerce		
202 N CM Allen Pkwy ....San Marcos TX 78666	888-200-5620	512-393-5900
Seguin Area Chamber of Commerce		
116 N Camp St ....Seguin TX 78155	888-674-7224	830-379-6382
Texas City-La Marque Chamber of Commerce		
9702 Emmett F Lowry Expy ....Texas City TX 77591	877-986-8719*	409-935-1408
*General		
Tyler Area Chamber of Commerce		
315 N Broadway Ave ....Tyler TX 75702	800-235-5712	903-592-1661
Weatherford Chamber of Commerce		
401 Ft Worth St ....Weatherford TX 76086	888-594-3801	817-596-3801
Rio Grande Valley Chamber of Commerce		
322 S Missouri St ....Weslaco TX 78596	800-628-5115	956-968-3141
Weslaco Area Chamber of Commerce		
301 W Railroad ....Weslaco TX 78596	800-700-2443	956-968-2102

Utah

	Toll-Free	Phone
Murray Area Chamber of Commerce (MACC)		
5250 S Commerce Dr Ste 180 ....Murray UT 84107	877-209-0068	801-263-2632
Tooele County Chamber of Commerce		
154 S Main ....Tooele UT 84074	800-378-0690	435-882-0690

Vermont

	Toll-Free	Phone
Bennington Area Chamber of Commerce		
100 Veterans Memorial Dr ....Bennington VT 05201	800-229-0252	802-447-3311
Central Vermont Chamber of Commerce		
33 Stewart Rd ....Berlin VT 05602	877-887-3678	802-229-5711
Brattleboro Area Chamber of Commerce		
180 Main St ....Brattleboro VT 05301	877-254-4565	802-254-4565
Lake Champlain Regional Chamber of Commerce		
60 Main St Ste 100......................Burlington VT 05401	877-686-5253	802-863-3489
Vermont's North Country Chamber of Commerce		
246 Cswy St ....Newport VT 05855	800-635-4643	802-334-7782

Virginia

	Toll-Free	Phone
Fredericksburg Regional Chamber of Commerce		
2300 Fall Hill Ave Ste 240 ....Fredericksburg VA 22401	888-338-0252	540-373-9400
Virginia Peninsula Chamber of Commerce		
21 Enterprise Pkwy Ste 100 ....Hampton VA 23666	800-462-3204	757-262-2000
Prince William County-Greater Manassas Chamber of Commerce		
9720 Capital Ct Ste 203 ....Manassas VA 20110	877-867-3853	703-368-6600
Prince William Regional Chamber of Commerce		
9720 Capital Ct Suite 203................Manassas VA 20110	877-867-3853	703-368-6600
Martinsville-Henry County Chamber of Commerce		
115 Broad St ....Martinsville VA 24112	800-811-6302	276-632-6401
Greater Reston Chamber of Commerce		
1763 Fountain Dr ....Reston VA 20190	844-430-7073	703-707-9045
Roanoke Regional Chamber of Commerce		
210 S Jefferson St ....Roanoke VA 24011	800-506-0489	540-983-0700
Tazewell Area Chamber of Commerce		
Tazewell Mall PO Box 6 ....Tazewell VA 24651	855-233-6362	276-988-5091
Williamsburg Area Chamber of Commerce		
421 N Boundary St PO Box 3495 ......Williamsburg VA 23187	800-368-6511	757-229-6511

Washington

	Toll-Free	Phone
Grays Harbor Chamber of Commerce		
506 Duffy St ....Aberdeen WA 98520	800-321-1924	360-532-1924
Camas-Washougal Chamber of Commerce		
422 NE Fourth Ave ....Camas WA 98607	800-468-5865	360-834-2472
Centralia-Chehalis Chamber of Commerce		
500 NW Chamber of Commerce Way ....Chehalis WA 98532	800-525-3323	360-748-8885
Greater Issaquah Chamber of Commerce		
155 NW Gilman Blvd ....Issaquah WA 98027	800-668-3030	425-392-7024
Kent Chamber of Commerce		
524 W Meeker St Ste 1 ....Kent WA 98032	800-321-2808	253-854-1770
Moses Lake Area Chamber of Commerce		
324 S Pioneer Way ....Moses Lake WA 98837	800-992-6234	509-765-7888
Pullman Chamber of Commerce		
415 N Grand Ave ....Pullman WA 99163	800-365-6948	509-334-3565
Greater Renton Chamber of Commerce		
625 S Fourth St ....Renton WA 98057	877-467-3686	425-226-4560
Greater Seattle Chamber of Commerce		
1301 Fifth Ave Ste 1500 ....Seattle WA 98101	866-978-2997	206-389-7200
Shelton-Mason County Chamber of Commerce		
215 W Railroad Ave PO Box 2389 ....Shelton WA 98584	800-576-2021	360-426-2021
Greater Spokane Inc		
801 W Riverside Ave Ste 100 ....Spokane WA 99201	800-776-5263	509-624-1393
Southwest King County Chamber of Commerce		
14220 Interurban Ave S Ste 134...........Tukwila WA 98168	800-638-8613	206-575-1633
Walla Walla Valley Chamber of Commerce		
29 E Sumach St ....Walla Walla WA 99362	866-826-9422	509-525-0850
Wenatchee Valley Chamber of Commerce		
2 S Mission St ....Wenatchee WA 98801	800-572-7753	509-662-2116

West Virginia

	Toll-Free	Phone
Beckley-Raleigh County Chamber of Commerce		
245 N Kanawha St ....Beckley WV 25801	877-987-3847	304-252-7328
Charleston Regional Chamber of Commerce		
1116 Smith St ....Charleston WV 25301	800-792-4326	304-340-4253
Marion County Chamber of Commerce		
110 Adams St ....Fairmont WV 26554	800-975-8379	304-363-0442
Greater Greenbrier Chamber of Commerce		
200 W Washington St Ste C ....Lewisburg WV 24901	800-833-2068	304-645-2818

	Toll-Free	Phone
Martinsburg-Berkeley County Chamber of Commerce		
198 Viking Way ....Martinsburg WV 25401	800-332-9007	304-267-4841
Morgantown Area Chamber of Commerce		
1029 University Ave Ste 101...........Morgantown WV 26505	800-618-2525*	304-292-3311
*General		
Frontier Communications		
1522 N Walker St ....Princeton WV 24740	877-378-9289	304-487-1502

Wisconsin

	Toll-Free	Phone
Fox Cities Chamber of Commerce & Industry		
125 N Superior St ....Appleton WI 54911	800-456-0152	920-734-7101
Greater Beloit Chamber of Commerce		
500 Public Ave ....Beloit WI 53511	866-981-5969	608-365-8835
Chippewa Falls Area Chamber of Commerce		
10 S Bridge St ....Chippewa Falls WI 54729	888-723-0024	715-723-0331
Fond du Lac Area Assn of Commerce		
207 N Main St ....Fond du Lac WI 54935	800-279-8811	920-921-9500
Manitowoc-Two Rivers Area Chamber of Commerce		
1515 Memorial Dr ....Manitowoc WI 54220	866-727-5575	920-684-5575
Greater Menomonie Area Chamber of Commerce		
342 E Main St ....Menomonie WI 54751	800-283-1862	715-235-9087
Merrill Area Chamber of Commerce		
705 N Ctr Ave ....Merrill WI 54452	877-907-2757	715-536-9474
Metropolitan Milwaukee Assn of Commerce		
756 N Milwaukee St ....Milwaukee WI 53202	800-362-9472	414-287-4100
Shawano Country Chamber of Commerce		
1263 S Main St ....Shawano WI 54166	800-235-8528	715-524-2139
Sheboygan County Chamber of Commerce		
621 S Eigth St ....Sheboygan WI 53081	800-457-9497	920-457-9491
Superior-Douglas County Chamber of Commerce		
205 Belknap St ....Superior WI 54880	800-942-5313	715-394-7716
Waukesha County Chamber of Commerce		
2717 N Grandview Blvd Ste 204 ....Waukesha WI 53188	800-937-2965	262-542-4249
West Allis-West Milwaukee Chamber of Commerce		
6737 W Washington St Ste 2141 ....West Allis WI 53214	800-554-1448	414-302-9901
West Bend Area Chamber of Commerce		
304 S Main St ....West Bend WI 53095	888-338-8666	262-338-2666

Wyoming

	Toll-Free	Phone
Casper Area Chamber of Commerce		
500 N Ctr St ....Casper WY 82601	866-234-5311	307-234-5311
Campbell County Chamber of Commerce		
314 S Gillette Ave ....Gillette WY 82716	877-682-3481	307-682-3673
Laramie Area Chamber of Commerce		
800 S Third St ....Laramie WY 82070	866-876-1012	307-745-7339
Rock Springs Chamber of Commerce		
1897 Dewar Dr ....Rock Springs WY 82901	800-463-8637	307-362-3771
Sheridan County Chamber of Commerce		
1517 E Fifth St ....Sheridan WY 82801	800-453-3650	307-672-2485

139   CHAMBERS OF COMMERCE - US - STATE

	Toll-Free	Phone
US Chamber of Commerce		
1615 H St NW ....Washington DC 20062	800-638-6582	202-659-6000
Arizona Chamber of Commerce & Industry		
3200 N Central Ave Ste 1125 ....Phoenix AZ 85012	800-498-6973	602-248-9172
Arkansas State Chamber of Commerce		
1200 W Capitol Ave PO Box 3645 ....Little Rock AR 72203	800-482-1127	501-372-2222
Association of Washington Business		
PO Box 658 ....Olympia WA 98507	800-521-9325	360-943-1600
Business Council of Alabama		
Two N Jackson St PO Box 76 ....Montgomery AL 36101	800-665-9647	334-834-6000
Business Council of New York State Inc		
152 Washington Ave ....Albany NY 12210	800-358-1202	518-465-7511
Delaware State Chamber of Commerce		
1201 N Orange St Ste 200		
PO Box 671...........................Wilmington DE 19899	800-292-9507	302-655-7221
Florida Chamber of Commerce		
136 S Bronough St PO Box 11309 .....Tallahassee FL 32302	877-521-1230	850-521-1200
Georgia Chamber of Commerce		
233 Peachtree St NE Ste 2000 ....Atlanta GA 30303	800-241-2286	404-223-2264
Iowa Assn of Business & Industry		
400 E Ct Ave Ste 100 ....Des Moines IA 50309	800-383-4224	515-280-8000
Kentucky Chamber of Commerce		
464 Chenault Rd ....Frankfort KY 40601	800-533-0127	502-695-4700
Louisiana Assn of Business & Industry		
3113 Vly Creek Dr PO Box 80258.......Baton Rouge LA 70898	888-816-5224	225-928-5388
Michigan Chamber of Commerce		
600 S Walnut St ....Lansing MI 48933	800-748-0266	517-371-2100
Minnesota Chamber of Commerce		
400 Robert St N Ste 1500 ....Saint Paul MN 55101	800-821-2230	651-292-4650
Mississippi Economic Council		
PO Box 23276 ....Jackson MS 39225	800-748-7626	601-969-0022
Montana Chamber of Commerce		
900 Gibbon St PO 1730 ....Helena MT 59624	888-442-6668	406-442-2405
North Dakota Chamber of Commerce		
2000 Schafer St PO Box 2639 ....Bismarck ND 58502	800-382-1405	701-222-0929
Ohio Chamber of Commerce		
230 E Town St PO Box 15159...........Columbus OH 43215	800-622-1893	614-228-4201
Pennsylvania Chamber of Business & Industry		
417 Walnut St ....Harrisburg PA 17101	800-225-7224	717-255-3252
South Carolina Chamber of Commerce		
1201 Main St Ste1100 ....Columbia SC 29201	800-799-4601	803-799-4601
South Dakota Chamber of Commerce & Industry		
108 N Euclid Ave ....Pierre SD 57501	800-742-8112	605-224-6161
Vermont Chamber of Commerce		
PO Box 37 ....Montpelier VT 05601	800-451-4279	802-223-3443
Virginia Chamber of Commerce		
919 E Main St ....Richmond VA 23219	800-847-4882	804-644-1607

	Toll-Free	Phone

140   CHECK CASHING SERVICES

		Toll-Free	Phone
ACE Cash Express 1231 Greenway Dr Ste 600 . . . . .Irving TX 75038		800-817-5106	972-550-5000
Advance America Cash Advance Centers Inc 135 N Church St . . . . Spartanburg SC 29306 *NYSE: AEA*		800-538-1579	864-342-5600
Cash Plus Inc 3002 Dow Ave Ste 120 . . . . .Tustin CA 92780		888-707-2274	714-731-2274
Mister Money Investment 2057 Vermont Dr . . . . Fort Collins CO 80525		888-336-0403	970-493-0574
Pay-O-Matic Corp 160 Oak Dr . . . . .Syosset NY 11791		888-545-6311	516-496-4900
QC Holdings Inc 9401 Indian Creek Pkwy Ste 1500 . . . . .Overland Park KS 66210 *NASDAQ: QCCO*		866-660-2243	

141   CHECKS - PERSONAL & BUSINESS

		Toll-Free	Phone
4checks.com 8245 N Union Blvd . . . . .Colorado Springs CO 80920		866-923-0451	
Artistic Checks Inc PO Box 40003 PO Box 1000. . . . . .Colorado Springs CO 80935		800-243-2577	
Check Printers Inc 1530 Antioch Pike . . . . .Antioch TN 37013		800-766-1217	
Checks In The Mail Inc 2435 Goodwin Ln . . . . New Braunfels TX 78135		800-733-4443	830-609-5500
Checks Unlimited 8245 N Union Blvd PO Box 35630. . . . . .Colorado Springs CO 80920		800-634-2563	
Deluxe Business Forms 3680 Victoria St N . . . . .Shoreview MN 55126 *Cust Svc		800-328-7205*	651-483-7111
Safeguard Business Systems Inc 8585 N Stemmons Fwy Ste 600 N . . . . .Dallas TX 75247		800-523-2422	

CHEMICALS - AGRICULTURAL

SEE Fertilizers & Pesticides

142   CHEMICALS - INDUSTRIAL (INORGANIC)

		Toll-Free	Phone
Air Liquide America LP 2700 Post Oak Blvd Ste 1800 . . . . .Houston TX 77056		877-855-9533	
Air Products & Chemicals Inc 7201 Hamilton Blvd . . . . .Allentown PA 18195 *NYSE: APD ■ *Prod Info		800-345-3148*	610-481-4911
AkzoNobel Surface Chemistry LLC 525 W Van Buren St .Chicago IL 60607 *Cust Svc		877-565-8432*	312-544-7000
Almatis Inc 501 W Pk Rd . . . . .Leetsdale PA 15056		800-643-8771	412-630-2800
Americhem Inc 2000 Americhem Way . . . . .Cuyahoga Falls OH 44221		800-228-3476	330-929-4213
Ampacet Corp 660 White Plains Rd .Tarrytown NY 10591 *Cust Svc		800-888-4267*	914-631-6600
Ashta Chemicals Inc 3509 Middle Rd . . . . .Ashtabula OH 44004 *Cust Svc		800-492-5082*	440-997-5221
BASF Canada 100 Milverton Dr Fifth Fl . . . . .Mississauga ON L5R4H1 *Cust Svc		866-485-2273*	289-360-1300
BASF Corp 100 Campus Dr . . . . .Florham Park NJ 07932		800-526-1072	973-245-6000
Bio-Lab Inc 1725 N Brown Rd PO Box 30000 . . . . .Lawrenceville GA 30043		800-859-7946	678-502-4000
Cabot Corp 2 Seaport Ln Ste 1300 . . . . .Boston MA 02210 *NYSE: CBT*		800-322-1236	617-345-0100
Calgon Carbon Corp 500 Calgon Carbon Dr . . . . .Pittsburgh PA 15205 *NYSE: CCC ■ *Cust Svc		800-422-7266*	412-787-6700
Carus Corp 315 Fifth St . . . . .Peru IL 61354		800-435-6856	815-223-1500
Centrus Energy Corp 6903 Rockledge Dr Ste 400 . . . . .Bethesda MD 20817 *NYSE: USU*		800-273-7754	301-564-3200
Chemical Products Corp 102 Old Mill Rd .Cartersville GA 30120 *Cust Svc		877-210-9814*	770-382-2144
Dow Chemical Co 2030 Dow Ctr . . . . .Midland MI 48674 *NYSE: DOW ■ *Cust Svc		800-422-8193*	989-636-1463
DuPont Titanium Technologies 1007 Market St . . . . .Wilmington DE 19898		800-441-7515	302-774-1000
Elementis Specialties Inc 469 Old Trenton Rd . . . . .East Windsor NJ 08512		800-866-6800	
FMC Corp 1735 Market St .Philadelphia PA 19103 *NYSE: FMC*		888-548-4486	215-299-6000
FMC Corp Industrial Chemicals Group 1735 Market St .Philadelphia PA 19103		800-323-7107	215-299-6000
General Chemical Group Inc 90 E Halsey Rd . . . . .Parsippany NJ 07054		800-244-6224	973-515-0900
Green Plains Renewable Energy Inc 450 Regency Pkwy Ste 400. . . . . .Omaha NE 68114 *NASDAQ: GPRE*		877-886-2288	402-884-8700
Hawkins Inc 3100 E Hennepin Ave . . . . .Minneapolis MN 55413 *NASDAQ: HWKN*		800-328-5460	612-331-6910
Heucotech Ltd 99 Newbold Rd .Fairless Hills PA 19030		800-483-2224	

		Toll-Free	Phone
Horsehead Corp 4955 Steubenville Pk Ste 405. . . . . .Pittsburgh PA 15205		800-648-8897	724-774-1020
Interstate Chemical Co Inc 2797 Freedland Rd . . . . .Hermitage PA 16148		800-422-2436	724-981-3771
Jones Hamilton Co 30354 Tracy Rd .Walbridge OH 43465		888-858-4425	419-666-9838
Kanto Corp 13424 N Woodrush Way . . . . .Portland OR 97203		866-609-5571	503-283-0405
Keystone Aniline Corp 2501 W Fulton St . . . . .Chicago IL 60612		800-522-4393	312-666-2015
Martin Marietta Magnesia Specialties Inc 8140 Corporate Dr Ste 220. . . . . .Nottingham MD 21236		800-648-7400	410-780-5500
NL Industries 16801 Greenspoint Pk Dr . . . . .Houston TX 77060 *NYSE: NL*		800-866-5600	281-423-3300
Old Bridge Chemicals Inc PO Box 175 . . . . .Old Bridge NJ 08857		800-275-3924	732-727-2225
OMYA Inc 39 Main St . . . . .Proctor VT 05765		800-451-4468	802-459-3311
Phibro Animal Health Corp 300 Frank W Burr Blvd Ste 21 . . . . .Teaneck NJ 07660		800-223-0434	201-329-7300
Plasticolors Inc 2600 Michigan Ave PO Box 816. . . . . .Ashtabula OH 44005		888-661-7675	440-997-5137
Potash Corp 1101 Skokie Blvd . . . . .Northbrook IL 60062		800-667-0403	847-849-4200
Praxair Inc 39 Old Ridgebury Rd . . . . .Danbury CT 06810 *NYSE: PX*		800-772-9247	203-837-2000
Rutgers Organics Corp (ROC) 201 Struble Rd . . . . .State College PA 16801		888-469-2188	814-238-2424
Silberline Mfg Company Inc 130 Lincoln Dr PO Box B . . . . .Tamaqua PA 18252		800-348-4824	570-668-6050
Solvay America Inc 3333 Richmond Ave . . . . .Houston TX 77098 *General		800-365-6565*	713-525-6000
Southern Ionics Inc 201 Commerce St . . . . .West Point MS 39773		800-953-3585	662-494-3055
Synalloy Corp 775 Spartan Blvd Ste 102 PO Box 5627. . . . . .Spartanburg SC 29304 *NASDAQ: SYNL ■ *Orders		800-937-5449*	864-585-3605
Tanner Systems Inc 625 19th Ave NE . . . . .Saint Joseph MN 56374		800-461-6454	320-363-1800
TETRA Technologies Inc 25025 I-45 N . . . . .The Woodlands TX 77380 *NYSE: TTI*		800-327-7817	281-367-1983
Texas United Corp 4800 San Felipe . . . . .Houston TX 77056		800-554-8658	713-877-2600
Tronox Inc 3301 NW 150th St . . . . .Oklahoma City OK 73134		866-775-5009	405-775-5000
UOP LLC 25 E Algonquin Rd . . . . .Des Plaines IL 60017		800-877-6184	847-391-2000
Vulcan Materials Co 1200 Urban Ctr Dr PO Box 385014 . . . . .Birmingham AL 35238 *NYSE: VMC*		800-615-4331	205-298-3000
Westlake Chemical Corp 2801 Post Oak Blvd Ste 600 . . . . .Houston TX 77056 *NYSE: WLK*		888-953-3623	713-960-9111

143   CHEMICALS - INDUSTRIAL (ORGANIC)

		Toll-Free	Phone
Ampacet Corp 660 White Plains Rd . . . . .Tarrytown NY 10591 *Cust Svc		800-888-4267*	914-631-6600
Bayer Corp 100 Bayer Rd . . . . .Pittsburgh PA 15205		800-422-9374	412-777-2000
Bayer Inc 77 Belfield Rd . . . . .Toronto ON M9W1G6		800-622-2937	416-248-0771
BP PLC 28100 Torch Pkwy . . . . .Warrenville IL 60555 *NYSE: BP*		877-638-5672	630-420-5111
Cambrex Corp 1 Meadowlands Plaza 15th Fl. . . . . .East Rutherford NJ 07073 *NYSE: CBM*		866-286-9133	201-804-3000
Cardolite Corp 500 Doremus Ave .Newark NJ 07105		800-322-7365	
Chemstar Products Co 3915 Hiawatha Ave . . . . .Minneapolis MN 55406		800-328-5037	612-722-0079
Chevron Phillips Chemical Company LP 10001 Six Pines Dr . . . . .The Woodlands TX 77380		800-231-1212	832-813-4100
Dow Chemical Canada Inc (DCCI) 450 First St SW Ste 2100 . . . . .Calgary AB T2P5H1		800-447-4369	403-267-3500
Dow Chemical Co 2030 Dow Ctr . . . . .Midland MI 48674 *NYSE: DOW ■ *Cust Svc		800-422-8193*	989-636-1463
Dow Corning Corp PO Box 994 . . . . .Midland MI 48686 *Cust Svc		800-248-2481*	989-496-4000
DSM Chemicals North America Inc 1 Columbia Nitrogen Rd . . . . .Augusta GA 30901		800-526-0189	706-849-6600
Eastman Chemical Co 200 S Wilcox Dr .Kingsport TN 37660 *NYSE: EMN ■ *Cust Svc		800-327-8626*	423-229-2000
First Chemical Corp 1001 Industrial Rd . . . . .Pascagoula MS 39581		877-243-6178	228-762-0870
Heucotech Ltd 99 Newbold Rd .Fairless Hills PA 19030		800-483-2224	
Huntsman Corp 500 Huntsman Way . . . . .Salt Lake City UT 84108 *NYSE: HUN*		888-490-8484	801-584-5700
ICC Industries Inc 460 Pk Ave .New York NY 10022		800-422-1720	212-521-1700
Inolex Chemical Co 2101 S Swanson St . . . . .Philadelphia PA 19148 *Cust Svc		800-521-9891*	215-271-0800
International Specialty Products Inc (ISP) 1361 Alps Rd . . . . .Wayne NJ 07470		800-622-4423	973-628-4000
Light Fabrications Inc 40 Hytec Cir . . . . .Rochester NY 14606		800-836-6920	585-426-5330

				Toll-Free	Phone

Methanex Corp
1800 Waterfront Centre 200 Burrard St
..... Vancouver BC V6C3M1 **800-661-8851** 604-661-2600
TSE: MX

Mitsui Chemicals America Inc
800 Westchester Ave ..... Rye Brook NY 10573 **800-972-7252** 914-701-5245

National Enzyme Co Inc
15366 US Hwy 160 ..... Forsyth MO 65653 **800-825-8545** 417-546-4796

Niacet Corp
400 47th St ..... Niagara Falls NY 14304 **800-828-1207** 716-285-1474

Oakwood Products Inc
1741 Old Dunbar Rd ..... West Columbia SC 29172 **800-467-3386** 803-739-8800

Pencco Inc
831 Bartlett Rd PO Box 600 ..... San Felipe TX 77473 **800-864-1742** 979-885-0005

Perstorp Polyols Inc
600 Matzinger Rd ..... Toledo OH 43612 **800-537-0280*** 419-729-5448
*Cust Svc

PMC Specialties Group Inc
501 Murray Rd ..... Cincinnati OH 45217 **800-543-2466** 513-242-3300

RT Vanderbilt Company Inc
30 Winfield St ..... Norwalk CT 06855 **800-243-6064*** 203-853-1400
*Cust Svc

Selee Corp
700 Shepherd St ..... Hendersonville NC 28792 **800-842-3818** 828-697-2411

Shin-Etsu Silicones of America
1150 Damar Dr ..... Akron OH 44305 **800-544-1745** 330-630-9860

Struktol Company of America Inc
PO Box 1649 ..... Stow OH 44224 **800-327-8649** 330-928-5188

Sun Chemical Corp
35 Waterview Blvd ..... Parsippany NJ 07054 **800-543-2323** 973-404-6000

Sunoco Chemicals
1735 Market St Ste LL ..... Philadelphia PA 19103 **800-786-6261** 215-977-3000

Sunoco Inc
1735 Market St Ste LL ..... Philadelphia PA 19103 **800-786-6261** 215-977-3000
NYSE: SUN

Synalloy Corp
775 Spartan Blvd Ste 102
PO Box 5627 ..... Spartanburg SC 29304 **800-937-5449*** 864-585-3605
NASDAQ: SYNL ■ *Orders

Tedia Company Inc
1000 Tedia Way ..... Fairfield OH 45014 **800-787-4891** 513-874-5340

Velsicol Chemical Corp
10400 W Higgins Rd Ste 700 ..... Rosemont IL 60018 **877-847-8351*** 847-813-7888
*Cust Svc

Vulcan Materials Co
1200 Urban Ctr Dr PO Box 385014 ..... Birmingham AL 35238 **800-615-4331** 205-298-3000
NYSE: VMC

Wacker Chemical Corp
3301 Sutton Rd ..... Adrian MI 49221 **888-922-5374** 517-264-8500

Wausau Chemical Corp
2001 N River Dr ..... Wausau WI 54403 **800-950-6656** 715-842-2285

CHEMICALS - MEDICINAL

144 CHEMICALS - SPECIALTY

				Toll-Free	Phone

ADA-ES Inc
8100 Southpark Way Ste B ..... Littleton CO 80120 **888-822-8617** 303-734-1727
NASDAQ: ADES

Airosol Company Inc
1206 Illinois St ..... Neodesha KS 66757 **800-633-9576** 620-325-2666

Akzo Nobel Chemicals Inc
10 Finderne Ave ..... Bridgewater NJ 08807 **888-331-6212**

Alex C Fergusson LLC (AFCO)
5000 Letterkenny Rd ..... Chambersburg PA 17201 **800-345-1329**

Alfa Aesar Co
26 Parkridge Rd Second Fl ..... Ward Hill MA 01835 **800-343-0660** 978-521-6300

American Polywater Corp
11222 60th St N ..... Stillwater MN 55082 **800-328-9384** 651-430-2270

American Radiolabeled Chemicals Inc (ARC)
101 ARC Dr ..... Saint Louis MO 63146 **800-331-6661** 314-991-4545

AMPAC Fine Chemicals (AFC)
MS 1007 PO Box 1718 ..... Rancho Cordova CA 95741 **800-311-9668** 916-357-6880

AMREP Inc
990 Industrial Pk Dr ..... Marietta GA 30062 **800-241-7766*** 770-422-2071
*Cust Svc

Anderson Chemical Co
325 S Davis ..... Litchfield MN 55355 **800-366-2477** 320-693-2477

Angstrom Technologies Inc
7880 Foundation Dr ..... Florence KY 41042 **800-543-7358*** 859-282-0020
*Cust Svc

Arch Chemicals Inc
1200 Old Lower River Rd PO Box 800 ..... Charleston TN 37310 **800-638-8174** 423-780-2724
NYSE: ARJ

Athea Laboratories Inc
1900 W Cornell St ..... Milwaukee WI 53209 **800-743-6417**

Baker Hughes Inc Baker Petrolite Div
12645 W Airport Blvd ..... Sugar Land TX 77478 **800-231-3606** 281-276-5400

Birchwood Laboratories Inc
7900 Fuller Rd ..... Eden Prairie MN 55344 **800-328-6156** 952-937-7900

Brulin & Company Inc
2920 Dr AJ Brown Ave ..... Indianapolis IN 46205 **800-776-7149** 317-923-3211

Buckman Laboratories Inc
1256 N McLean Blvd ..... Memphis TN 38108 **800-282-5626** 901-278-0330

Bullen Midwest
900 E 103rd St ..... Chicago IL 60628 **800-621-8553** 773-785-2300

Cabot Corp
2 Seaport Ln Ste 1300 ..... Boston MA 02210 **800-322-1236** 617-345-0100
NYSE: CBT

Cabot Microelectronics Corp
870 N Commons Dr ..... Aurora IL 60504 **800-811-2756** 630-375-6631
NASDAQ: CCMP

Cabot Specialty Fluids Co
Waterway Plaza Two 10001 Woodlock Forest Dr
Ste 275 ..... The Woodlands TX 77380 **800-322-1236** 281-298-9955

Cambridge Isotope Laboratories Inc
50 Frontage Rd ..... Andover MA 01810 **800-322-1174** 978-749-8000

Chemtronics Inc
8125 Cobb Centre Dr ..... Kennesaw GA 30152 **800-645-5244** 770-424-4888

Claire Manufacturing Co
1005 S Westgate Ave ..... Addison IL 60101 **800-252-4731*** 630-543-7600
*Sales

Columbian Chemicals Co
1800 W Oak Commons Ct ..... Marietta GA 30062 **800-235-4003** 770-792-9400

Coral Chemical Co
1915 Industrial Ave ..... Zion IL 60099 **800-228-4646** 847-246-6666

Cortec Corp
4119 White Bear Pkwy ..... Saint Paul MN 55110 **800-426-7832** 651-429-1100

CPC Aeroscience Inc
2700 SW 14th St ..... Pompano Beach FL 33069 **800-327-1835***
*Cust Svc

CRC Industries Inc
885 Louis Dr ..... Warminster PA 18974 **800-556-5074*** 215-674-4300
*Cust Svc

Croda Inc
300 Columbus Cir Ste A ..... Edison NJ 08837 **888-842-7632** 732-417-0800

Cytec Industries Inc
Five Garret Mtn Plz ..... West Paterson NJ 07424 **800-652-6013** 973-357-3100
NYSE: CYT

Delta Chemical Corp
2601 Cannery Ave ..... Baltimore MD 21226 **800-282-5322** 410-354-0100

Diversified Chemical Technologies Inc (DCT)
15477 Woodrow Wilson St ..... Detroit MI 48238 **800-243-1424** 313-867-5444

Dober Chemical Group
11230 Katherine Crossing Ste 100 ..... Woodridge IL 60517 **800-323-4983** 630-410-7300

Dover Chemical Corp
3676 Davis Rd NW ..... Dover OH 44622 **800-321-8805*** 330-343-7711
*General

DSM Desotech Inc
1122 St Charles St ..... Elgin IL 60120 **800-222-7189** 847-697-0400

DuPont Chemical Solutions
1007 Market St ..... Wilmington DE 19898 **800-441-7515** 302-774-1000

Dynaloy LLC
6445 Olivia Ln ..... Indianapolis IN 46226 **800-669-5709** 317-788-5694

Elantas PDG Inc
5200 N Second St ..... Saint Louis MO 63147 **800-325-7492** 314-621-5700

Enthone Inc
350 Frontage Rd ..... West Haven CT 06516 **800-431-2200** 203-934-8611

Excelda Manufacturing Co
12785 Emerson Dr ..... Brighton MI 48116 **877-486-3801** 248-486-3800

Foseco Metallurgical Inc
20200 Sheldon Rd ..... Cleveland OH 44142 **800-321-3132** 440-826-4548

Frac Tech Services LLC
301 E 18th St ..... Cisco TX 76437 **866-877-1008** 817-850-1008

Fremont Industries Inc
4400 Vly Industrial Blvd N PO Box 67 ..... Shakopee MN 55379 **800-436-1238** 952-445-4121

GE Betz 4636 Somerton Rd ..... Trevose PA 19053 **866-439-2837*** 215-355-3300
*Cust Svc

Genieco Inc 200 N Laflin St ..... Chicago IL 60607 **800-223-8217** 312-421-2383

Gold Eagle Co
4400 S Kildare Ave ..... Chicago IL 60632 **800-367-3245**

Grace Davison
7500 Grace Dr ..... Columbia MD 21044 **800-638-6014** 410-531-4000

Harcros Chemicals Inc
5200 Speaker Rd ..... Kansas City KS 66106 **800-504-8071** 913-321-3131

Honeywell
101 Columbia Rd ..... Morristown NJ 07960 **800-822-7673** 973-455-2000

Honeywell Fluorine Products
101 Columbia Rd ..... Morristown NJ 07962 **800-951-1527** 973-455-2000

Houghton Chemical Corp
52 Cambridge St ..... Allston MA 02134 **800-777-2466** 617-254-1010

International Chemical Co
2628 N Mascher St ..... Philadelphia PA 19133 **888-225-5422** 215-739-2313

JM Huber Corp
499 Thornall St 8th Fl ..... Edison NJ 08837 **877-418-0038** 732-549-8600

Kao Specialties Americas LLC
243 Woodbine St PO Box 2316 ..... High Point NC 27261 **800-727-2214** 336-884-2214

Kester Inc
800 W Thorndale Ave ..... Itasca IL 60143 **800-253-7837** 630-616-4000

KIK Custom Products
2730 Middlebury St ..... Elkhart IN 46516 **800-479-6603** 574-295-0000

KIK Pool Additives Inc
5160 E Airport Dr ..... Ontario CA 91761 **800-745-4536** 909-390-9912

King Industries Inc
One Science Rd ..... Norwalk CT 06852 **800-431-7900** 203-866-5551

Kolene Corp
12890 Westwood Ave ..... Detroit MI 48223 **800-521-4182** 313-273-9220

Koppers Inc
436 Seventh Ave ..... Pittsburgh PA 15219 **800-321-9876** 412-227-2001
NYSE: KOP

Kronos Worldwide Inc
14950 Heathrow Forest Prkwy Ste 230 ..... Houston TX 77060 **800-866-5600** 281-423-3300
NYSE: KRO

Leadership Performance Sustainability Laboratories
4647 Hugh Howell Rd ..... Tucker GA 30084 **800-241-8334**

Lloyd Laboratories Inc
24 Fitch Ct ..... Wakefield MA 01880 **800-361-6766** 781-224-0083

Lubrizol Corp
29400 Lakeland Blvd ..... Wickliffe OH 44092 **800-380-5397** 440-943-4200
NYSE: LZ

Master Builders Solutions by BASF
23700 Chagrin Blvd ..... Cleveland OH 44122 **800-628-9990** 216-839-7500

McGean-Rohco Inc
2910 Harvard Ave ..... Cleveland OH 44105 **800-932-7006*** 216-441-4900
*Orders

Miller-Stephenson Chemical Co
55 Backus Ave ..... Danbury CT 06810 **800-992-2424*** 203-743-4447
*Tech Supp

Momar Inc
1830 Ellsworth Industrial Dr ..... Atlanta GA 30318 **800-556-3967** 404-355-4580

Monroe Fluid Technology Inc
36 Draffin Rd PO Box 810 ..... Hilton NY 14468 **800-828-6351** 585-392-3434

Montello Inc
6106 E 32nd Pl Ste 100 ..... Tulsa OK 74135 **800-331-4628**

					Toll-Free	Phone

Nalco Co 1601 W Diehl Rd ....Naperville IL 60563 **800-288-0879** 630-305-1000
National Starch & Chemical Co
10 Finderne Ave ....Bridgewater NJ 08807 **866-961-6285**
Nox-Crete Inc 1444 S 20th St ....Omaha NE 68108 **800-669-2738** 402-341-2080
OM Group Inc 811 Sharon Dr ....Westlake OH 44145 **800-519-0083** 440-899-2950
NYSE: OMG
OMNOVA Solutions Inc Performance Chemicals Div
165 S Cleveland Ave ....Mogadore OH 44260 **888-253-5454** 330-628-6536
Pacific Ethanol Corp
400 Capitol Mall Ste 2060 ....Sacramento CA 95814 **866-508-4969** 916-403-2123
NASDAQ: PEIX
Pavco Inc
1935 John Crosland Jr Dr ....Charlotte NC 28208 **800-321-7735*** 704-496-6800
*Orders
Peach State Labs Inc (PSL)
180 Burlington Rd PO Box 1087 ....Rome GA 30162 **800-634-1653** 706-291-8743
Penray Cos Inc
440 Denniston Ct ....Wheeling IL 60090 **800-373-6729** 847-459-5000
Precision Laboratories Inc
1429 S Shields Dr ....Waukegan IL 60085 **800-323-6280** 847-596-3001
Premier Colors Inc
100 Industrial Dr ....Union SC 29379 **800-245-6944** 864-427-0338
PVS Chemicals Inc
10900 Harper Ave ....Detroit MI 48213 **800-932-8860** 313-921-1200
Quaker Chemical Corp
901 Hector St ....Conshohocken PA 19428 **800-523-7010** 610-832-4000
NYSE: KWR
Radiator Specialty Co
1900 Wilkinson Blvd ....Charlotte NC 28208 **877-464-4865** 704-688-2405
Rochester Midland Corp
333 Hollenbeck St ....Rochester NY 14621 **800-836-1627** 585-336-2200
Royal Chemical Co
1755 Enterprise Pkwy Ste 600 ....Twinsburg OH 44087 **800-468-2975** 330-467-1300
SA Day Mfg Co Inc
1489 Niagara St ....Buffalo NY 14213 **800-747-0030** 716-881-3030
Sigma-Aldrich Corp
3050 Spruce St ....Saint Louis MO 63103 **800-325-3010** 314-771-5765
NASDAQ: SIAL
Sika Corp 201 Polito Ave ....Lyndhurst NJ 07071 **800-933-7452** 201-933-8800
Solutek Corp 94 Shirley St ....Boston MA 02119 **800-403-0770** 617-445-5335
Spartan Chemical Company Inc
1110 Spartan Dr ....Maumee OH 43537 **800-537-8990** 419-531-5551
Specco Industries Inc
13087 Main St ....Lemont IL 60439 **800-441-6646** 630-257-5060
Sprayway Inc
500 S Vista Ave ....Addison IL 60101 **800-332-9000** 630-628-3000
Stapleton Technologies Inc
1350 W 12th St ....Long Beach CA 90813 **800-266-0541** 562-437-0541
Stepan Co
22 W Frontage Rd ....Northfield IL 60093 **800-745-7837*** 847-446-7500
*Cust Svc
Symrise Inc 300 N St ....Teterboro NJ 07608 **800-422-1559*** 201-288-3200
*General
Technical Chemical Co
3327 Pipeline Rd ....Cleburne TX 76033 **800-527-0885** 817-645-6088
United Color Manufacturing Inc (UCM)
PO Box 480 ....Newtown PA 18940 **800-852-5942** 215-860-2165
United Laboratories Inc
320 37th Ave ....Saint Charles IL 60174 **800-323-2594**
United Salt Corp
4800 San Felipe St ....Houston TX 77056 **800-554-8658** 713-877-2600
WR Grace & Co
7500 Grace Dr ....Columbia MD 21044 **800-638-6014** 410-531-4000
NYSE: GRA
XL Brands 198 Nexus Dr ....Dalton GA 30721 **800-367-4583** 706-272-5800
Zinkan Enterprises Inc
1919 Case Pkwy N ....Twinsburg OH 44087 **800-229-6801**

145   CHEMICALS & RELATED PRODUCTS - WHOL

					Toll-Free	Phone

Airgas Inc
259 N Radnor-Chester Rd Ste 100 ....Radnor PA 19087 **800-255-2165** 610-687-5253
NYSE: ARG
Aramsco Inc
1480 Grandview Ave ....Paulsboro NJ 08086 **800-767-6933** 856-686-7700
Astro Chemicals Inc
126 Memorial Dr ....Springfield MA 01104 **800-223-0776** 413-781-7240
Barton Solvents Inc
1920 NE Broadway Ave ....Des Moines IA 50313 **800-728-6488** 515-265-7998
Berryman Products Inc
3800 E Randol Mill Rd ....Arlington TX 76011 **800-433-1704** 817-640-2376
Brenntag Canada Inc
35 Vulcan St ....Rexdale ON M9W1L3 **866-516-9707** 416-243-9615
Brenntag Great Lakes LLC
PO Box 444 ....Butler WI 53007 **800-558-8501** 262-252-3550
Brenntag Mid-South Inc
1405 Hwy 136 W ....Henderson KY 42419 **800-950-1727** 270-830-1200
Brenntag Pacific
4545 Ardine St ....South Gate CA 90280 **800-732-0562** 323-832-5000
Brenntag Southeast Inc
2000 E Pedigree St ....Durham NC 27703 **800-849-7000** 919-596-0681
Brenntag Southwest Inc
610 Fisher Rd ....Longview TX 75604 **800-945-4528** 903-759-7151
Brown Machine LLC
330 N Ross St ....Beaverton MI 48612 **877-702-4142** 989-435-7741
Callahan Chemical Co
200 Industrial Ave ....Ridgefield Park NJ 07660 **800-526-7000** 201-440-9000
Chemsolv Inc
1140 Industry Ave SE ....Roanoke VA 24013 **800-523-3099** 540-427-4000
Connell Bros Co Ltd
345 California St 27th Fl ....San Francisco CA 94104 **800-210-9839** 415-772-4000
Coolant Control Inc
5353 Spring Grove Ave ....Cincinnati OH 45217 **800-535-3885** 513-471-8770
Dar-tech Inc
16485 Rockside Rd ....Cleveland OH 44137 **800-228-7347** 216-663-7600

					Toll-Free	Phone

DB Becker Company Inc
46 Leigh St ....Clinton NJ 08809 **800-394-3991** 908-730-6010
Denso North America Inc
9747 Whithorn Dr ....Houston TX 77095 **888-821-2300** 281-821-3355
DM Figley Company Inc
10 Kelly Ct ....Menlo Park CA 94025 **800-292-9919** 650-329-8700
Dorsett & Jackson Inc
3800 Noakes St ....Los Angeles CA 90023 **800-871-8365** 323-268-1815
Durr Marketing Assoc Inc
PO Box 17600 ....Pittsburgh PA 15235 **800-937-3877**
Ellsworth Corp
PO Box 1002 ....Germantown WI 53022 **877-454-9224** 262-253-8600
ET Horn Co
16050 Canary Ave ....La Mirada CA 90638 **800-442-4676** 714-523-8050
EW Kaufmann Co
140 Wharton Rd ....Bristol PA 19007 **800-635-5358** 215-364-0240
Gallade Chemical Inc
1230 E St Gertrude Pl ....Santa Ana CA 92707 **888-830-9092** 714-546-9901
General Air Service & Supply Company Inc
1105 Zuni St ....Denver CO 80204 **877-782-8434** 303-892-7003
George S Coyne Chemical Co
3015 State Rd ....Croydon PA 19021 **800-523-1230** 215-785-3000
Harcros Chemicals Inc
5200 Speaker Rd ....Kansas City KS 66106 **800-504-8071** 913-321-3131
Haviland Enterprises Inc
421 Ann St NW ....Grand Rapids MI 49504 **800-456-1134** 616-361-6691
Hill Bros Chemical Co
1675 N Main St ....Orange CA 92867 **800-994-8801** 714-998-8800
HM Royal Inc
689 Pennington Ave ....Trenton NJ 08618 **800-257-9452** 609-396-9176
Hubbard-Hall Inc
563 S Leonard St ....Waterbury CT 06708 **800-331-6871** 203-756-5521
Hydrite Chemical Co
300 N Patrick Blvd ....Brookfield WI 53045 **800-543-4560** 262-792-1450
ICC Chemical Corp
460 Pk Ave ....New York NY 10022 **800-422-1720** 212-521-1700
Ideal Chemical & Supply Co
4025 Air Pk St ....Memphis TN 38118 **800-232-6776** 901-363-7720
Independent Chemical Corp
79-51 Cooper Ave ....Glendale NY 11385 **800-892-2578** 718-894-0700
Industrial Chemicals Inc
2042 Montreat Dr ....Vestavia AL 35216 **800-476-2042*** 205-823-7330
*Cust Svc
John R Hess & Company Inc
400 Stn St PO Box 3615 ....Cranston RI 02910 **800-828-4377** 401-785-9300
John R White Company Inc
PO Box 10043 ....Birmingham AL 35202 **800-245-1183** 205-595-8381
KA Steel Chemicals Inc
15185 Main St PO Box 729 ....Lemont IL 60439 **800-677-8335** 630-257-3900
Kraft Chemical Co
1975 N Hawthorne Ave ....Melrose Park IL 60160 **800-345-5200** 708-345-5200
LV Lomas Ltd
99 Summerlea Rd ....Brampton ON L6T4V2 **800-575-3382** 905-458-1555
Maroon Inc 1390 Jaycox Rd ....Avon OH 44011 **877-627-6661*** 440-937-1000
*General
McCullough & Assoc
1746 NE Expy PO Box 29803 ....Atlanta GA 30329 **800-969-1606** 404-325-1606
MF Cachat Co
14725 Detroit Ave Ste 300 ....Lakewood OH 44107 **800-729-8900** 216-228-8900
NuCo2 Inc
2800 SE Marketplace ....Stuart FL 34997 **800-472-2855** 772-221-1754
Palmer Holland Inc
25000 Country Club Blvd Ste 444 ....North Olmsted OH 44070 **800-635-4822**
Pidilite USA Inc
902 South US Highway 1 Ste 18 ....Jupiter FL 33477 **800-843-7813** 561-775-9600
Plaza Group Inc
10375 Richmond Ave Ste 1620 ....Houston TX 77042 **800-876-3738** 713-266-0707
Pride Solvents & Chemical Co of New York Inc
6 Long Island Ave ....Holtsville NY 11742 **800-424-8802** 631-758-0200
Quadra Chemicals Ltd
3901 Fixtessier ....Vaudreuil-Dorion QC J7V5V5 **800-665-6553** 450-424-0161
Reagent Chemical & Research Inc
115 Rt 202 ....Ringoes NJ 08551 **800-231-1807** 908-284-2800
Ribelin Sales Inc
3857 Miller Pk Dr ....Garland TX 75042 **800-374-1594** 972-272-1594
Rowell Chemical Corp
15 Salt Creek Ln Ste 205 ....Hinsdale IL 60521 **888-261-7963** 630-920-8833
SARCOM Inc AEP Colloids Div
6299 Rt 9N ....Hadley NY 12835 **800-848-0658** 518-696-9900
Shamrock Technologies Inc
Foot Of Pacific St ....Newark NJ 07114 **800-349-1822** 973-242-2999
Solvents & Chemicals Inc
4704 Shank Rd PO Box 490 ....Pearland TX 77581 **800-622-3990** 281-485-5377
Specified Technologies Inc
200 Evans Way Ste 2 ....Somerville NJ 08876 **800-992-1180** 908-526-8000
Spectra Colors Corp
25 Rizzolo Rd ....Kearny NJ 07032 **800-527-8588** 201-997-0606
Strem Chemicals Inc
Seven Mulliken Way ....Newburyport MA 01950 **800-647-8736** 978-499-1600
Tanner Industries Inc
735 Davisville Rd Third Fl ....SouthHampton PA 18966 **800-643-6226** 215-322-1238
Tarr LLC
2429 N Borthwick St ....Portland OR 97227 **800-422-5069**
Tilley Chemical Company Inc
501 Chesapeake Pk Plz ....Baltimore MD 21220 **800-638-6968** 410-574-4500
Tm Deer Park Services LP
2525 Battleground Rd PO Box 1914 ....Deer Park TX 77536 **800-488-0648** 281-930-2525
TransChemical Inc
419 De Soto Ave ....Saint Louis MO 63147 **888-873-6481** 314-231-6905
Univar USA Inc
17425 NE Union Hill Rd ....Redmond WA 98052 **855-888-8648** 425-889-3400
Whitaker Oil Co
1557 Marietta Rd NW ....Atlanta GA 30318 **888-895-3506** 404-355-8220
Wilson Industrial Sales Company Inc
201 S Wilson ....Brook IN 47922 **800-633-5427** 219-275-7333

146 CHILD CARE MONITORING SYSTEMS - INTERNET

		Toll-Free	Phone
Mississippi Action For Progress Inc (MAP)			
1751 Morson Rd ....Jackson MS 39209		800-924-4615	601-923-4100

147 CHILDREN'S LEARNING CENTERS

		Toll-Free	Phone
Bright Horizons Family Solutions LLC			
200 Talcott Ave S ....Watertown MA 02472		800-324-4386	617-673-8000
Child Development Assoc Inc			
678 Third Ave Ste 201 ....Chula Vista CA 91910		888-755-2445	619-427-4411
Childcare Network Inc			
1501 13th St Ste D........................Columbus GA 31901		866-521-5437	706-562-8600
Computer Explorers			
12715 Telge Rd ....Cypress TX 77429		800-531-5053	
DePelchin Children's Ctr			
4950 Memorial Dr ....Houston TX 77007		888-730-2335	713-730-2335
FasTracKids International Ltd			
6900 E Belleview Ave			
Ste 100 ....Greenwood Village CO 80111		888-576-6888	303-224-0200
Goddard Systems Inc			
1016 W Ninth Ave ....King of Prussia PA 19406		800-463-3273	610-265-8510
Golflogix Inc			
15685 N Greenway-Hayden Loop			
Ste 100A.................................Scottsdale AZ 85260		877-977-0162	
Gymboree Corp Play & Music Program			
500 Howard St ....San Francisco CA 94105		877-449-6932*	415-278-7000
*Cust Svc			
Huntington Learning Centers Inc			
496 Kinderkamack Rd ....Oradell NJ 07649		800-653-8400	201-261-8400
KinderCare Learning Centers Inc			
650 NE Holladay St Ste 1400			
PO Box 6760..................................Portland OR 97232		800-633-1488	
Kumon North America Inc			
300 Frank W Burr Blvd Glenpointe Ctr E			
Ste 6..Teaneck NJ 07666		800-222-6284	201-928-0444
Learning Care Group Inc			
21333 Haggerty Rd Ste 300 ....Novi MI 48375		877-817-3883	248-697-9000
New Horizon Kids Quest Inc			
3405 Annapolis Ln N Ste 100..............Plymouth MN 55447		800-941-1007	
Primrose School Franchising Co			
3660 Cedarcrest Rd ....Acworth GA 30101		800-745-0677	770-529-4100
Rural Resources Community Action			
956 S Main St Ste A............................Colville WA 99114		800-538-7659	509-684-8421

148 CIRCUS, CARNIVAL, FESTIVAL OPERATORS

		Toll-Free	Phone
Big Apple Circus			
One Metrotech Ctr Third Fl.....................Brooklyn NY 11201		800-922-3772	212-268-2500
Cirque du Soleil Inc			
8400 Second Ave ....Montreal QC H1Z4M6		800-678-2119	514-722-2324
Maryland Renaissance Festival			
PO Box 315 ....Crownsville MD 21032		800-296-7304	410-266-7304

149 CLAY PRODUCTS - STRUCTURAL

SEE ALSO Brick, Stone, Related Materials

		Toll-Free	Phone
Acme Brick Co			
3024 Acme Brick Plaza ....Fort Worth TX 76109		866-430-2263	817-332-4101
Boral Bricks Inc			
9143 Bob Williams Pkwy ....Covington GA 30014		800-526-7255	678-625-4051
Cherokee Brick & Tile Co Inc			
3250 Waterville Rd ....Macon GA 31206		800-277-2745	478-781-6800
Colloid Environmental Technologies Co (CETCO)			
2870 Forbs Ave ....Hoffman Estates IL 60192		800-527-9948	847-851-1899
Cunningham Brick Co Inc			
701 N Main St ....Lexington NC 27292		800-672-6181	336-248-8541
General Shale Products LLC			
3015 Bristol Hwy ....Johnson City TN 37601		800-414-4661	423-282-4661
Henry Brick Co Inc			
3409 Water Ave ....Selma AL 36703		800-218-3906	334-875-2600
International Chimney Corp			
55 S Long St ....Williamsville NY 14221		800-828-1446	
Kinney Brick Co			
100 Prosperity Rd PO Box 1804 ....Albuquerque NM 87103		800-464-4605	505-877-4550
Lee Brick & Tile Co			
3704 Hawkins Ave PO Box 1027 ....Sanford NC 27330		800-672-7559	919-774-4800
Logan Clay Products Co			
201 S Walnut St ....Logan OH 43138		800-848-2141	
Ludowici Roof Tile Inc			
4757 Tile Plant Rd PO Box 69 ....New Lexington OH 43764		800-945-8453*	740-342-1995
*Cust Svc			
Marion Ceramics Inc			
PO Box 1134 ....Marion SC 29571		800-845-4010	843-423-1311
McNear Brick & Block			
One McNear BrickyaRd Rd			
PO Box 151380.............................San Rafael CA 94901		888-442-6811	415-453-7702
Mutual Materials Co			
605 119th Ave NE ....Bellevue WA 98005		800-477-3008	425-452-2300
Old Virginia Brick Co			
2500 W Main St ....Salem VA 24153		800-879-8227	540-389-2357
Palmetto Brick Co			
3501 BrickyaRd Rd ....Wallace SC 29596		800-922-4423	843-537-7861
Pine Hall Brick Co			
2701 Shorefair Dr ....Winston-Salem NC 27116		800-334-8689	
Redland Brick Inc			
15718 Clear Spring Rd ....Williamsport MD 21795		800-366-2742	301-223-7700

		Toll-Free	Phone
Statesville Brick Co			
391 BrickyaRd Rd ....Statesville NC 28677		800-522-4716	704-872-4123
Superior Clay Corp			
6566 Superior Rd SE ....Uhrichsville OH 44683		800-848-6166	740-922-4122
Triangle Brick Co			
6523 NC Hwy 55 ....Durham NC 27713		800-672-8547	919-544-1796
Whitacre Greer Fireproofing Inc			
1400 S Mahoning Ave ....Alliance OH 44601		800-947-2837*	330-823-1610
*Cust Svc			

150 CLEANING PRODUCTS

SEE ALSO Mops, Sponges, Wiping Cloths ; Brushes & Brooms

		Toll-Free	Phone
ABC Compounding Company Inc & Acme Wholesale			
6970 Jonesboro Rd ....Morrow GA 30260		800-795-9222	770-968-9222
Adco Inc 1909 W Oakridge ....Albany GA 31707		800-821-7556	
American Cleaning Solutions			
39-30 Review Ave ....Long Island City NY 11101		888-929-7587	718-392-8080
Arrow-Magnolia International			
2646 Rodney Ln ....Dallas TX 75229		800-527-2101	972-247-7111
Aztec International Inc			
3010 Henson Rd ....Knoxville TN 37921		800-369-5357	865-588-5357
BAF Industries Inc			
1451 Edinger Ave ....Tustin CA 92780		800-437-9893	714-258-8055
Buckeye International Inc			
2700 Wagner Pl ....Maryland Heights MO 63043		800-321-2583	314-291-1900
Bullen Cos			
1640 Delmar Dr PO Box 37 ....Folcroft PA 19032		800-444-8900	610-534-8900
C & H Chemical Inc			
13505 Industrial Park Blvd ....Plymouth MN 55441		800-966-2909	763-582-1140
Camco Chemical Co			
8145 Holton Dr ....Florence KY 41042		800-354-1001*	859-727-3200
*Cust Svc			
Canberra Corp			
3610 Holland Sylvania Rd ....Toledo OH 43615		800-832-8992	419-841-6616
Car-Freshner Corp			
21225 Little Tree Dr PO Box 719 ....Watertown NY 13601		800-545-5454	315-788-6250
Carroll Co			
2900 W Kingsley Rd ....Garland TX 75041		800-527-5722	972-278-1304
Cello Professional Products			
1354 Old Post Rd ....Havre de Grace MD 21078		800-638-4850	410-939-1234
Champion Chemical Co			
8319 S Greenleaf Ave ....Whittier CA 90602		800-424-9300	
Chemical Specialties Manufacturing Corp			
901 N Newkirk St ....Baltimore MD 21205		800-638-7370*	410-675-4800
*Sales			
Clorox Co 1221 Broadway ....Oakland CA 94612		800-424-9300*	510-271-7000
NYSE: CLX ▦ *Cust Svc*			
Correlated Products Inc			
5616 Progress Rd ....Indianapolis IN 46242		800-428-3266	317-243-3248
Damon Industries Inc			
12435 Rockhill Ave NE ....Alliance OH 44601		800-362-9850	330-821-5310
Delta Carbona LP			
376 Hollywood Ave Ste 208 ....Fairfield NJ 07004		888-746-5599	973-808-6260
Diamond Chemical Company Inc			
Union Ave & Dubois St ....East Rutherford NJ 07073		800-654-7627	201-935-4300
Dreumex USA 3445 BoaRd Rd ....York PA 17406		800-233-9382	717-767-6881
Dubois Chemicals			
3630 E Kemper Rd ....Cincinnati OH 45241		800-438-2647	
Dura Wax Co			
4101 W Albany St ....McHenry IL 60050		800-435-5705	815-385-5000
Empire Cleaning Supply			
12821 S Figueroa St ....Los Angeles CA 90061		888-868-7336	310-527-0132
Falcon Safety Products Inc			
25 Chubb Way ....Somerville NJ 08876		800-332-5266	908-707-4900
Fine Organics Corp			
420 Kuller Rd PO Box 2277 ....Clifton NJ 07015		800-526-7480	973-478-1000
Heritage-Crystal Clean Inc			
2175 Pt Blvd Ste 375 ....Elgin IL 60123		877-938-7948	847-836-5670
Hill Mfg Company Inc			
1500 Jonesboro Rd SE ....Atlanta GA 30315		800-445-5123	404-522-8364
Hillyard Chemical Company Inc			
302 N Fourth St ....Saint Joseph MO 64501		800-365-1555	816-233-1321
Impact Products LLC			
2840 Centennial Rd ....Toledo OH 43617		800-333-1541*	419-841-2891
*Cust Svc			
ITW Dymon 805 E Old 56 Hwy ....Olathe KS 66061		800-443-9536	913-829-6296
James Austin Co			
115 Downieville Rd PO Box 827....................Mars PA 16046		800-245-1942	724-625-1535
Kay Chemical Co			
8300 Capital Dr ....Greensboro NC 27409		877-315-1115	336-668-7290
Koger/Air Corp			
PO Box 2098 ....Martinsville VA 24113		800-368-2096	276-638-8821
Leadership Performance Sustainability Laboratories			
4647 Hugh Howell Rd ....Tucker GA 30084		800-241-8334	
Madison Chemical Company Inc			
3141 Clifty Dr ....Madison IN 47250		800-345-1915	812-273-6000
Magic American Corp			
26901 Cannon Rd Ste 190 ....Bedford Heights OH 44146		800-729-9029*	
*Cust Svc			
Maxim Technologies Inc			
1607 Derwent Way ....Delta BC V3M6K8		800-663-9925	
Meguiar's Inc			
17991 Mitchell S ....Irvine CA 92614		800-347-5700*	949-752-8000
*Cust Svc			
Micro Care Corp			
595 John Downey Dr ....New Britain CT 06051		800-638-0125	860-827-0626
Mother's Polishes Waxes & Cleaners			
5456 Industrial Dr ....Huntington Beach CA 92649		800-221-8257	714-891-3364
National Chemical Laboratories Inc			
401 N Tenth St ....Philadelphia PA 19123		800-628-2436	215-922-1200
National Chemicals Inc			
105 Liberty St PO Box 32 ....Winona MN 55987		800-533-0027*	507-454-5640
*Cust Svc			
NCH Corp			
2727 Chemsearch Blvd ....Irving TX 75062		800-527-9919	972-438-0211

				Toll-Free	Phone
Ocean Bio-Chem Inc (OBCI)					
4041 SW 47th Ave	Fort Lauderdale	FL	33314	**800-327-8583**	954-587-6280
NASDAQ: OBCI					
Paramount Chemical Specialties Inc					
14750 NE 95th St	Redmond	WA	98052	**877-846-7826**	425-882-2673
Prosoco Inc					
3741 Greenway Cir	Lawrence	KS	66046	**800-255-4255**	
Reckitt Benckiser Inc					
399 Interpace Pkwy PO Box 225	Parsippany	NJ	07054	**800-333-3899***	973-404-2600
*Cust Svc					
Safeguard Chemical Corp					
411 Wales Ave	Bronx	NY	10454	**800-536-3170**	718-585-3170
Safetec of America Inc					
887 Kensington Ave	Buffalo	NY	14215	**800-456-7077**	716-895-1822
SC Johnson & Son Inc					
1525 Howe St	Racine	WI	53403	**800-494-4855**	262-260-2154
Scott Fetzer Company Scot Laboratories Div					
16841 Pk Cir Dr	Chagrin Falls	OH	44023	**800-486-7268**	440-543-3033
Scott's Liquid Gold Inc					
4880 Havana St	Denver	CO	80239	**800-447-1919**	303-373-4860
OTC: SLGD					
Seventh Generation Inc					
60 Lake St	Burlington	VT	05401	**800-456-1191**	802-658-3773
Share Corp					
7821 N Faulkner Rd	Milwaukee	WI	53224	**800-776-7192**	414-355-4000
Simoniz USA 201 Boston Tpke	Bolton	CT	06043	**800-227-5536**	860-646-0172
State Industrial Products					
3100 Hamilton Ave	Cleveland	OH	44114	**877-747-6986**	216-861-7114
Stearns Packaging Corp					
4200 Sycamore Ave	Madison	WI	53714	**800-655-5008**	608-246-5150
Summit Industries Inc					
PO Box 7329	Marietta	GA	30065	**800-241-6996**	
Sunshine Makers Inc					
15922 Pacific Coast Hwy	Huntington Harbour	CA	92649	**800-228-0709**	562-795-6000
Unit Chemical Corp					
7360 Commercial Way	Henderson	NV	89015	**800-879-8648**	702-564-6454
Warsaw Chemical Company Inc					
Argonne Rd PO Box 858	Warsaw	IN	46580	**800-548-3396**	574-267-3251
WD-40 Co 1061 Cudahy Pl	San Diego	CA	92110	**800-448-9340**	619-275-1400
NASDAQ: WDFC					
West Penetone Corp					
700 Gotham Pkwy	Carlstadt	NJ	07072	**800-631-1652**	201-567-3000
Willert Home Products Inc					
4044 Pk Ave	Saint Louis	MO	63110	**877-373-4858**	314-772-2822
ZEP Inc					
1310 Seaboard Industrial Blvd NW	Atlanta	GA	30318	**877-428-9937**	404-352-1680
NYSE: ZEP					

151   CLEANING SERVICES

SEE ALSO Bio-Recovery Services ; Building Maintenance Services

				Toll-Free	Phone
1-800-Water Damage					
1167 Mercer St	Seattle	WA	98109	**800-928-3732**	206-381-3041
Boston's Best Chimney Sweep					
76 Bacon St	Waltham	MA	02451	**800-660-6708***	781-893-6611
*Cust Svc					
Clean Power LLC					
124 N 121st St	Milwaukee	WI	53226	**888-566-1717**	414-302-3000
Cleaning Authority					
7230 Lee DeForest Dr Ste 200	Columbia	MD	21046	**888-658-0659**	410-740-1900
CleanNet USA					
9861 Brokenland Pkwy Ste 208	Columbia	MD	21046	**800-735-8838**	410-720-6444
Coverall Cleaning Concepts					
5201 Congress Ave Ste 275	Boca Raton	FL	33487	**800-537-3371**	866-296-8944
Diversified Maintenance Systems Inc					
5110 Eisenhower Blvd Ste250	Tampa	FL	33634	**800-351-1557**	813-383-0238
Duraclean International Inc					
220 W Campus Dr	Arlington Heights	IL	60004	**800-862-5326**	847-704-7100
Federal Bldg Services Inc					
1641 Barclay Blvd	Buffalo Grove	IL	60089	**800-982-9234**	847-279-7360
Fish Window Cleaning Services Inc					
200 Enchanted Pkwy	Manchester	MO	63021	**877-707-3474**	636-779-1500
GCA Services Group					
1350 Euclid Ave Ste 1500	Cleveland	OH	44115	**800-422-8760**	
Healthcare Services Group Inc (HCSG)					
3220 Tillman Dr Ste 300	Bensalem	PA	19020	**800-486-3289**	215-639-4274
Heaven's Best Carpet & Upholstery Cleaning					
PO Box 607	Rexburg	ID	83440	**800-359-2095**	208-359-1106
Ih Services Inc					
PO Box 5033	Greenville	SC	29606	**800-340-9088**	864-297-3748
Jan-Pro International Inc (JPI)					
2520 Northwinds Pkwy Ste 375	Alpharetta	GA	30009	**866-355-1064**	678-336-1780
Jani-King International Inc					
16885 Dallas Pkwy	Addison	TX	75001	**800-526-4546**	972-991-0900
Maid Brigade USA/Minimaid Canada					
Four Concourse Pkwy Ste 200	Atlanta	GA	30328	**800-722-6243**	770-551-9630
MaidPro Corp 180 Canal St	Boston	MA	02114	**888-624-3776**	617-742-8787
Maids International					
9394 W Dodge Rd Ste 140	Omaha	NE	68114	**800-843-6243**	402-558-8600
Merry Maids					
3839 Forrest Hill-Irene Rd	Memphis	TN	38125	**866-212-5846**	800-776-4663
MPW Industrial Services Group Inc					
9711 Lancaster Rd SE PO Box 10	Hebron	OH	43025	**800-827-8790**	740-927-8790
Rainbow International					
1010 N University Pk Dr	Waco	TX	76707	**855-724-6269**	254-756-5463
ServiceMaster Clean					
3839 Forrest Hill Irene Rd	Memphis	TN	38125	**800-255-9687***	800-245-4622
*General					
Servpro Industries Inc					
801 Industrial Blvd	Gallatin	TN	37066	**800-826-9586**	615-451-0600
Steam Bros Inc					
2400 Vermont Ave	Bismarck	ND	58504	**800-767-5064**	701-222-1263
Steamatic Inc					
3333 Quorum Dr Ste 280	Fort Worth	TX	76137	**888-783-2628***	817-332-1575
*General					

				Toll-Free	Phone
Support Services of America Inc					
12440 Firestone Blvd Ste 312	Norwalk	CA	90650	**888-564-0005**	562-868-3550
Swisher Hygiene Co					
4725 Piedmont Row Dr	Charlotte	NC	28210	**800-444-4138**	704-364-7707
T.u.c.s. Cleaning Service Inc					
166 Central Ave	Orange	NJ	07050	**800-992-5998**	973-673-0700
Vanguard Cleaning Systems Inc					
655 Mariners Island Blvd Ste 303	San Mateo	CA	94404	**800-564-6422**	650-287-2400
Venoco Inc					
370 17th St Ste 3900	Denver	CO	80202	**877-777-4778**	303-626-8300
NYSE: VQ					
Window Gang					
405 Arendell St	Morehead City	NC	28557	**877-946-4264**	252-726-1463

152   CLOCKS, WATCHES, RELATED DEVICES, PARTS

				Toll-Free	Phone
Bulova Corp 1 Bulova Ave	Woodside	NY	11377	**800-228-5682**	718-204-3300
Canterbury International					
5632 W Washington Blvd	Los Angeles	CA	90016	**800-935-7111**	323-936-7111
Citizen Watch Co of America Inc					
1000 W 190th St	Torrance	CA	90502	**800-321-1023**	
E Gluck Corp					
60-15 Little Neck Pkwy	Little Neck	NY	11362	**800-840-2933**	718-784-0700
Movado Group Inc					
650 From Rd Ste 375	Paramus	NJ	07652	**800-810-2311***	201-267-8000
NYSE: MOV ■ *Cust Svc					
Pyramid Technologies Inc					
45 Gracey Ave	Meriden	CT	06451	**888-479-7264**	203-238-0550
Seiko Corp of America					
1111 MacArthur Blvd	Mahwah	NJ	07430	**800-545-2783***	201-529-5730
*Cust Svc					
Seiko Instruments USA Inc					
21221 S Western Ave Ste 250	Torrance	CA	90501	**800-688-0817***	310-517-7700
*Sales					
Swatch Group					
1200 Harbor Blvd 7th Fl	Weehawken	NJ	07086	**800-456-5354**	201-271-1400
Timex Group USA Inc					
555 Christian Rd PO Box 310	Middlebury	CT	06762	**800-448-4639**	203-346-5000
Verdin Co, The					
444 Reading Rd	Cincinnati	OH	45202	**800-543-0488**	
Vulcan Inc 410 E Berry Ave	Foley	AL	36535	**888-846-2728**	
World of Watches					
101 S State Rd 7 Ste 201	Hollywood	FL	33023	**866-961-8463**	954-983-2181

153   CLOSURES - METAL OR PLASTICS

				Toll-Free	Phone
Caplugs LLC					
2150 Elmwood Ave	Buffalo	NY	14207	**888-227-5847***	716-876-9855
*Cust Svc					
Essentra PLC 3123 Stn Rd	Erie	PA	16510	**800-847-0486**	814-899-9263
StockCap					
123 Manufacturers Dr	Arnold	MO	63010	**800-827-2277**	636-282-6800
Tipper Tie Inc 2000 Lufkin Rd	Apex	NC	27502	**800-331-2905**	919-362-8811
Weatherchem Corp					
2222 Highland Rd	Twinsburg	OH	44087	**800-316-0072**	330-425-4206

154   CLOTHING & ACCESSORIES - MFR

SEE ALSO Footwear ; Leather Goods - Personal ; Personal Protective Equipment & Clothing ; Baby Products ; Clothing & Accessories - Whol ; Fashion Design Houses

154-1   Athletic Apparel

				Toll-Free	Phone
Bristol Products Corp					
700 Shelby St	Bristol	TN	37620	**800-336-8775***	423-968-4140
*Orders					
Champion Athletic Wear					
1000 E Hanes Mill Rd	Winston-Salem	NC	27105	**800-315-0563**	
Choi Bros Inc 3401 W Div St	Chicago	IL	60651	**800-524-2464**	773-489-2800
Columbia Sportswear Co					
14375 NW Science Pk Dr	Portland	OR	97229	**800-622-6953**	503-985-4000
NASDAQ: COLM					
Cutter & Buck Inc					
701 N 34th St Ste 400	Seattle	WA	98103	**800-713-7810**	888-338-9944
Dodger Industries					
2075 Stultz Rd PO Box 711	Martinsville	VA	24112	**800-247-7879***	
*Cust Svc					
Elite Sportswear LP					
2136 N 13th St	Reading	PA	19604	**800-345-4087***	610-921-1469
*Cust Svc					
Gear for Sports Inc					
9700 Commerce Pkwy	Lenexa	KS	66219	**800-255-1065**	913-693-3200
MJ Soffe Co 1 Soffe Dr	Fayetteville	NC	28312	**888-257-8673**	
Race Face Components Inc					
100 Braid St Unit 100	New Westminster	BC	V3L3P4	**800-527-9244**	604-527-9996
Royal Textile Mills Inc					
929 Firetower Rd	Yanceyville	NC	27379	**800-334-9361**	

154-2   Belts (Leather, Plastics, Fabric)

				Toll-Free	Phone
Gem Dandy Inc					
200 W Academy St	Madison	NC	27025	**800-334-5101**	336-548-9624

154-3   Casual Wear (Men's & Women's)

				Toll-Free	Phone
Attraction Inc					
672 Rue du Parc	Lac-Drolet	QC	G0Y1C0	**800-567-6095**	819-549-2477

				Toll-Free	Phone
Badger Sportswear Inc					
111 Badger Ln	Statesville	NC	28625	**888-871-0990**	704-871-0990
Big Dogs					
519 Lincoln County Pkwy	Lincolnton	NC	28092	**800-244-3647**	
Bobby Jones Retail Corp					
2093 Old Route 15 PO Box 214	New Columbia	PA	17856	**855-437-5537***	855-785-1930
*Cust Svc					
Columbia Sportswear Co					
14375 NW Science Pk Dr	Portland	OR	97229	**800-622-6953**	503-985-4000
NASDAQ: COLM					
Crazy Shirts Inc					
99-969 Iwaena St	Aiea	HI	96701	**800-771-2720**	808-487-9919
Deckers Outdoor Corp					
495-A S Fairview Ave	Goleta	CA	93117	**877-337-8333**	805-967-7611
NYSE: DECK					
Delta Apparel Inc					
2750 Premier Pkwy Ste 100	Duluth	GA	30097	**800-285-4456**	678-775-6900
NYSE: DLA					
Fruit of the Loom Inc					
One Fruit of the Loom Dr					
PO Box 90015	Bowling Green	KY	42102	**888-378-4829**	270-781-6400
Hamrick Inc 742 Peachoid Rd	Gaffney	SC	29341	**800-487-5411**	864-489-6095
Sherry Mfg Co 3287 NW 65th St	Miami	FL	33147	**800-741-4750**	305-693-7000
Sport-Haley Inc					
200 Union Blvd Ste 400	Denver	CO	80228	**800-627-9211**	303-320-8800
Tonix Corp					
40910 Encyclopedia Cir	Fremont	CA	94538	**800-227-2072**	510-651-8050
Wolf Manufacturing Co					
1801 W Waco Dr PO Box 3100	Waco	TX	76707	**800-437-0940**	254-753-7301

154-4 Children's & Infants' Clothing

				Toll-Free	Phone
Byer California					
66 Potrero Ave	San Francisco	CA	94103	**844-628-4498**	415-626-7844
Florence Eiseman company LLC					
1966 S Fourth St	Milwaukee	WI	53204	**800-558-9013**	
Gerber Childrenswear Inc					
7005 Pelham Rd Ste D	Greenville	SC	29602	**800-642-4452**	864-987-5200
New ICM LP PO Box 1060	El Campo	TX	77437	**800-987-9008**	979-578-0543
S Schwab Co Inc					
12101 Upper Potomac Industrial Pk St					
	Cumberland	MD	21502	**800-638-2937**	301-729-4488

154-5 Coats (Overcoats, Jackets, Raincoats, etc)

				Toll-Free	Phone
Alpha Industries Inc					
14200 Pk Meadow Dr Ste 110S	Chantilly	VA	20151	**866-631-0719***	703-378-1420
*General					
Essex Mfg Inc					
350 Fifth Ave Ste 501	New York	NY	10118	**800-648-6010**	212-239-0080
Helly Hansen US Inc					
4104 C St NE Ste 200	Auburn	WA	98002	**800-435-5901**	
Holloway Sportswear Inc					
2633 Campbell Rd	Sidney	OH	45365	**800-331-5156**	
London Fog 1615 Kellogg Dr	Douglas	GA	31535	**877-588-8189**	912-384-8189
MECA Sportswear					
1120 Townline Rd	Tomah	WI	54660	**800-729-6322**	608-374-6450
Pendleton Woolen Mills Inc					
220 NW Broadway	Portland	OR	97209	**800-760-4844**	503-226-4801
RefrigiWear Inc					
54 Breakstone Dr	Dahlonega	GA	30533	**800-645-3744***	706-864-5757
*Cust Svc					
Rennoc Corp 645 Pine St	Greenville	OH	45331	**800-372-7100**	
Sport Obermeyer Ltd USA Inc					
115 AABC	Aspen	CO	81611	**800-525-4203**	970-925-5060
Sport-Haley Inc					
200 Union Blvd Ste 400	Denver	CO	80228	**800-627-9211**	303-320-8800
Standard Mfg Company Inc					
750 Second Ave	Troy	NY	12182	**800-227-1056***	518-235-2200
*Cust Svc					
Woolrich Inc 2 Mill St	Woolrich	PA	17779	**800-995-1299**	570-769-6464

154-6 Costumes

				Toll-Free	Phone
Costume Gallery					
4451 Rt 130	Burlington	NJ	08016	**800-222-8125**	609-386-6501
Costume Specialists Inc					
211 N Fifth St	Columbus	OH	43215	**800-596-9357**	614-464-2115
Curtain Call Costumes					
333 E Seventh Ave	York	PA	17404	**888-808-0801**	717-852-6910
Disguise 12120 Kear Pl	Poway	CA	92064	**877-875-2557**	858-391-3600

154-7 Furs Goods

				Toll-Free	Phone
American Legend Co-op					
PO Box 58308	Seattle	WA	98138	**800-266-3314**	425-251-3200

154-8 Gloves & Mittens

				Toll-Free	Phone
Carolina Glove Co					
116 Mclin Creek Rd PO Box 999	Conover	NC	28613	**800-335-1918**	828-464-1132
Fownes Bros & Company Inc					
16 E 34th St	New York	NY	10016	**800-345-6837***	212-683-0150
*All					
Gloves Inc					
1950 Collins Boulevard	Austell	MA	30106	**800-476-4568**	770-944-9186

				Toll-Free	Phone
Guard-Line Inc					
215 S Louise St PO Box 1030	Atlanta	TX	75551	**800-527-8822**	903-796-4111
Illinois Glove Co					
3701 Commercial Ave	Northbrook	IL	60062	**800-342-5458**	847-291-1700
Kinco International					
4286 NE 185th Dr	Portland	OR	97230	**800-547-8410***	
*General					
Magid Glove & Safety Manufacturing Co					
2060 N Kolmar Ave	Chicago	IL	60639	**800-444-8010**	773-384-2070
MCR Safety 5321 E Shelby Dr	Memphis	TN	38118	**800-955-6887**	901-795-5810
Midwest Quality Gloves Inc					
835 Industrial Rd	Chillicothe	MO	64601	**800-821-3028**	660-646-2165
Montpelier Glove Co Inc					
129 N Main St	Montpelier	IN	47359	**800-645-3931**	765-728-2481
North Star Glove Co					
2916 S Steele St	Tacoma	WA	98409	**800-423-1616**	253-627-7107
Saranac Glove Co					
999 LOmbardi Ave	Green Bay	WI	54304	**800-727-2622**	920-435-3737
Southern Glove Mfg Company Inc					
749 AC Little Dr	Newton	NC	28658	**800-222-1113***	828-464-4884
*Cust Svc					
Swany America Corp					
115 Corp Dr	Johnstown	NY	12095	**800-237-9269**	518-725-3333
Totes Isotoner Corp					
9655 International Blvd	Cincinnati	OH	45246	**800-762-8712**	513-682-8200
Wells Lamont Corp					
6640 W Touhy Ave	Niles	IL	60714	**800-323-2830**	847-647-8200
Wells Lamont Industry Group					
6640 W Touhy Ave	Niles	IL	60714	**800-247-3295**	

154-9 Hats & Caps

				Toll-Free	Phone
180s Inc					
700 S Caroline St	Baltimore	MD	21231	**877-725-4386**	410-534-6320
Ahead LLC					
270 Samuel Barnet Blvd	New Bedford	MA	02745	**800-282-2246**	508-985-9898
Bollman Hat Co					
110 E Main St PO Box 517	Adamstown	PA	19501	**800-959-4287**	717-484-4361
F & M Hat Co Inc					
103 Walnut St PO Box 40	Denver	PA	17517	**800-953-4287**	717-336-5505
Korber Hats Inc					
394 Kilburn St	Fall River	MA	02724	**800-428-9911***	508-672-7033
*Cust Svc					
MPC Promotions					
4300 Produce Rd PO Box 34336	Louisville	KY	40232	**800-331-0989**	502-451-4900
New Era Cap Company Inc					
160 Delaware Ave	Buffalo	NY	14202	**877-632-5950***	716-604-9000
*General					
Paramount Apparel International Inc					
One Paramount Dr	Bourbon	MO	65441	**800-255-4287**	573-732-4411
Stratton Hats Inc					
3200 Randolph St	Bellwood	IL	60104	**877-453-3777**	708-544-5220
Town Talk Inc					
6310 Cane Run Rd PO Box 58157	Louisville	KY	40258	**800-626-2220**	502-933-7575

154-10 Hosiery & Socks

				Toll-Free	Phone
Fox River Mills Inc					
227 Poplar Stq PO Box 298	Osage	IA	50461	**800-247-1815**	641-732-3798
Jefferies Socks					
2203 Tucker St	Burlington	NC	27215	**800-334-6831**	336-226-7315
Jockey International Inc					
2300 60th St PO Box 1417	Kenosha	WI	53140	**800-562-5391**	
Keepers International Inc					
9420 Eton Ave	Chatsworth	CA	91311	**800-797-6257**	
Moretz Inc 514 W 21st St	Newton	NC	28658	**866-714-8486**	828-464-0751
Renfro Corp					
661 Linville Rd	Mount Airy	NC	27030	**800-334-9091**	336-719-8000
Thor-Lo Inc					
2210 Newton Dr	Statesville	NC	28677	**888-846-7567**	704-872-6522
Trimfit Inc					
1900 Frost Rd Ste 111	Bristol	PA	19007	**800-347-7697**	215-781-0600
Twin City Knitting Company Inc (TCK)					
104 Rock Barn Rd NE	Conover	NC	28613	**800-438-6884**	828-464-4830
Wigwam Mills Inc					
3402 Crocker Ave	Sheboygan	WI	53082	**800-558-7760**	920-457-5551

154-11 Jeans

				Toll-Free	Phone
Aalfs Mfg Co					
1005 Fourth St	Sioux City	IA	51101	**888-412-2537**	712-252-1877
Jordache Enterprises					
1400 Broadway	New York	NY	10018	**888-295-3267**	212-944-1330
Lee Jeans 9001 W 67th St	Merriam	KS	66202	**800-453-3348***	913-384-4000
*Cust Svc					
Levi Strauss & Co					
1155 Battery St	San Francisco	CA	94111	**866-290-6064**	415-501-6000
Reed Mfg Co Inc					
1321 S Veterans Blvd	Tupelo	MS	38804	**800-466-1154**	662-842-4472

154-12 Men's Clothing

				Toll-Free	Phone
After Six 118 W 20th St	New York	NY	10011	**800-444-8304**	646-638-9600
American Apparel LLC					
747 Warehouse St	Los Angeles	CA	90021	**888-747-0070**	213-488-0226
Anniston Sportswear Corp					
P.O. Box 189	Anniston	AL	36201	**866-814-9253**	256-236-1551

				Toll-Free	Phone
Antigua Sportswear Inc					
16651 N 84 Ave	Peoria	AZ	85382	**800-528-3133**	623-523-6000
Gitman & Co					
2309 Chestnut St	Ashland	PA	17921	**800-526-3929**	570-875-3100
Gitman Bros Shirt Company Inc					
641 Lexington Ave 19th Fl	New York	NY	10019	**800-526-3929**★	212-581-6968
*General					
Granite Knitwear Inc					
805 S Salberry Ave Hwy 52S	Granite Quarry	NC	28072	**800-476-9944**★	704-279-5526
*Cust Svc					
H Freeman & Son Inc					
411 N Cranberry Rd	Westminster	MD	21157	**800-876-7700**	410-857-5774
Haggar Clothing Co					
11511 Luna Rd 2 Colinas Crossing	Dallas	TX	75234	**877-841-2219**	214-352-8481
Hardwick Clothes Inc					
3800 Old Tasso Rd	Cleveland	TN	37312	**800-251-6392**	
Hart Schaffner Marx (HSM)					
1680 E Touhy Ave	Des Plaines	IL	60018	**800-327-4466**	
Hickey Freeman					
1155 N Clinton Ave	Rochester	NY	14621	**844-755-7344**★	585-467-7021
*Cust Svc					
Jos A Bank Clothiers					
500 Hanover Pk	Hampstead	MD	21074	**800-999-7472**★	410-239-2700
*Cust Svc					
Phillips-Van Heusen Corp					
200 Madison Ave	New York	NY	10016	**866-214-6694**	212-381-3500
NYSE: PVH					
Tom James Co					
263 Seaboard Ln	Franklin	TN	37067	**800-236-9023**	615-771-0795
Weatherproof Garment Co					
1071 Ave of the Americas	New York	NY	10018	**800-645-7788**	212-695-7716

154-13 Neckwear

				Toll-Free	Phone
Carolina Mfg					
7025 Augusta Rd	Greenville	SC	29605	**800-845-2744**	864-299-0600
Carter & Holmes					
N1510 Geneva Ave	Lake Geneva	WI	53147	**800-621-4646**	262-215-5494
Echo Design Group					
10 E 40th St 16th Fl	New York	NY	10016	**800-331-3246**★	212-686-8771
*General					

154-14 Robes (Ceremonial)

				Toll-Free	Phone
Academic Apparel					
20644 Superior St	Chatsworth	CA	91311	**800-626-5000**	818-886-8697
CM Almy Inc One Ruth Rd	Pittsfield	ME	04967	**800-225-2569**	207-487-3232
Gaspard Inc					
200 N Janacek Rd	Brookfield	WI	53045	**800-784-6868**	262-784-6800
Jostens Inc					
3601 Minnesota Ave Ste 400	Minneapolis	MN	55435	**800-235-4774**	952-830-3300
Oak Hall Industries					
840 Union St	Salem	VA	24153	**800-223-0429**	540-387-0000
Thomas Creative Apparel Inc					
One Harmony Pl	New London	OH	44851	**800-537-2575**	419-929-1506
Willsie Cap & Gown Co					
1220 S 13th St	Omaha	NE	68108	**800-234-4696**	402-341-6536

154-15 Sleepwear

				Toll-Free	Phone
Miss Elaine Inc					
8430 Valcour Ave	Saint Louis	MO	63123	**800-458-1422**	314-631-1900
Wormser Corp					
150 Coolidge Ave	Englewood	NJ	07631	**800-546-4040**	

154-16 Sweaters (Knit)

				Toll-Free	Phone
Binghamton Knitting Co Inc					
11 Alice St	Binghamton	NY	13904	**877-746-3368**	607-722-6941

154-17 Swimwear

				Toll-Free	Phone
Blue Sky Swimwear					
729 E International Speedway Blvd	Daytona Beach	FL	32118	**800-799-6445**★	386-255-2590
*Orders					
TYR Sport 1790 Apollo Ct	Seal Beach	CA	90740	**800-252-7878**	714-897-0799
Venus Swimwear					
11711 Marco Beach Dr 1 Venus Plz	Jacksonville	FL	32224	**800-366-7946**	904-645-6000

154-18 Undergarments

				Toll-Free	Phone
Champion Athletic Wear					
1000 E Hanes Mill Rd	Winston-Salem	NC	27105	**800-315-0563**	
Gelmart Industries Inc					
136 Madison Ave 4th Fl	New York	NY	10016	**800-746-0014**★	212-743-6900
*General					
Indera Mills Co					
350 W Maple St PO Box 309	Yadkinville	NC	27055	**800-334-8605**	336-679-4440
Jockey International Inc					
2300 60th St PO Box 1417	Kenosha	WI	53140	**800-562-5391**	

				Toll-Free	Phone
Leading Lady					
24050 Commerce Pk	Beachwood	OH	44122	**800-321-4804**★	216-464-5490
*Cust Svc					
Reliable of Milwaukee Inc					
6737 W Washington Ste 3200	Milwaukee	WI	53214	**800-336-6876**	414-272-5084
Robinson Mfg Company Inc					
798 Market St PO Box 338	Dayton	TN	37321	**800-251-7286**	423-775-2212
Spirite Industries Inc					
150 S Dean St	Englewood	NJ	07631	**800-272-6897**	201-871-4910
Wacoal America					
50 Polito Ave	Lyndhurst	NJ	07071	**800-922-6250**	212-743-9600
Wacoal Europe					
65 Sprague St	Hyde Park	MA	02136	**800-733-8964**	617-361-7559

154-19 Uniforms & Work Clothes

				Toll-Free	Phone
A+ School Apparel					
401 Knoss Ave	Star City	AR	71667	**800-227-3215**	
Action Sports Systems Inc					
617 Carbon City Rd PO Box 1442	Morganton	NC	28655	**800-631-1091**	828-584-8000
Algy Team Collection					
440 NE First Ave	Hallandale	FL	33009	**800-458-2549**	954-457-8100
Barco Uniforms Inc					
350 W Rosecrans Ave	Gardena	CA	90248	**800-421-1874**	310-323-7315
Berne Apparel Co					
2210 Summit St	New Haven	IN	46774	**800-843-7657**	260-469-3136
Blauer Mfg Co Inc					
20 Aberdeen St	Boston	MA	02215	**800-225-6715**	617-536-6606
Blue Generation Div of M Rubin & Sons Inc					
34-01 38th Ave	Long Island City	NY	11101	**888-336-4687**	718-361-2800
Carhartt Inc					
5750 Mercury Dr	Dearborn	MI	48126	**800-833-3118**	313-271-8460
Choi Bros Inc 3401 W Div St	Chicago	IL	60651	**800-524-2464**	773-489-2800
DeMoulin Bros & Company Inc					
1025 S Fourth St	Greenville	IL	62246	**800-228-8134**	618-664-2000
Dennis Uniform Mfg Company Inc					
135 SE Hawthorne Blvd	Portland	OR	97214	**800-544-7123**	503-234-7431
Earl's Apparel Inc					
908 S Fourth St PO Box 939	Crockett	TX	75835	**800-527-3148**	936-544-5521
Elbeco Inc					
4418 Pottsville Pk	Reading	PA	19605	**800-468-4654**	610-921-0651
Encompass Group LLC					
615 Macon Rd	McDonough	GA	30253	**800-284-4540**	770-957-1211
Fechheimer Bros Company Inc					
4545 Malsbary Rd	Cincinnati	OH	45242	**800-543-1939**	513-793-5400
Gibson & Barnes					
1900 Weld Blvd Ste 140	El Cajon	CA	92020	**800-748-6693**★	619-440-6977
*Sales					
Howard Uniform Co					
1915 Annapolis Rd	Baltimore	MD	21230	**800-628-8299**	410-727-3086
I Spiewak & Sons Inc					
463 Seventh Ave	New York	NY	10018	**800-223-6850**	212-695-1620
Key Industries Inc					
400 Marble Rd	Fort Scott	KS	66701	**800-835-0365**	620-223-2000
Landau Uniforms Inc					
8410 W Sandidge Rd	Olive Branch	MS	38654	**800-387-0641**★	662-895-7200
*General					
LC King Mfg Company Inc					
24 Seventh St PO Box 367	Bristol	TN	37620	**800-826-2510**	423-764-5188
Leventhal Ltd					
PO Box 564	Fayetteville	NC	28302	**800-847-4095**★	
*General					
Lion Apparel Inc					
7200 Poe Ave Ste 400	Dayton	OH	45414	**800-548-6614**	937-898-1949
Riverside Manufacturing Co					
301 Riverside Dr	Moultrie	GA	31768	**800-841-8677**	229-985-5210
SCORE American Soccer Company Inc					
726 E Anaheim St	Wilmington	CA	90744	**800-626-7774**	
Stanbury Uniforms Inc					
108 Stanbury Industrial Dr					
PO Box 100	Brookfield	MO	64628	**800-826-2246**	660-258-2246
Standard Textile Company Inc					
One Knollcrest Dr	Cincinnati	OH	45237	**800-999-0400**	513-761-9255
Superior Uniform Group Inc					
10055Seminole Blvd	Seminole	FL	33772	**800-727-8643**★	727-397-9611
NASDAQ: SGC ■ *Cust Svc					
Topps Safety Apparel Inc					
2516 E State Rd 14	Rochester	IN	46975	**800-348-2990**	574-223-4311
Universal Overall Co					
1060 W Van Buren St	Chicago	IL	60607	**800-621-3344**★	312-226-3336
*Cust Svc					
Wenaas AGS Inc					
12211 Parc Crest Dr Bldg Ste 100	Stafford	TX	77477	**888-576-2668**	281-931-4300
Williamson-Dickie Mfg Co					
509 W Vickery Blvd	Fort Worth	TX	76104	**866-411-1501**	

154-20 Western Wear (Except Hats & Boots)

				Toll-Free	Phone
Niver Western Wear Inc					
PO Box 101224	Fort Worth	TX	76185	**800-433-5752**★	817-924-4299
*Orders					
Rockmount Ranch Wear Manufacturing Co					
1626 Wazee St	Denver	CO	80202	**800-776-2566**	303-629-7777
Sidran Inc					
1050 Venture Ct Ste 100	Carrollton	TX	75006	**800-969-5015**	214-352-7979

154-21 Women's Clothing

				Toll-Free	Phone
Alfred Angelo Inc					
1301 Virginia Dr	Fort Washington	PA	19034	**888-218-0044**	215-659-5300

				Toll-Free	Phone
bebe stores Inc					
400 Valley Dr	Brisbane	CA	94005	**877-232-3777**	415-715-3900
NASDAQ: BEBE					
Byer California					
66 Potrero Ave	San Francisco	CA	94103	**844-628-4498**	415-626-7844
Christine Alexander Inc					
34210 Ninth Ave S Ste 101	Federal Way	WA	98003	**800-554-2539***	253-874-5570
*General					
Darue of California Inc					
14102 S Broadway	Los Angeles	CA	90061	**877-693-2783**	310-323-1350
Donna Karan International Inc					
550 Seventh Ave 15th Fl	New York	NY	10018	**888-737-5743***	212-789-1500
*General					
JLM Couture Inc					
525 Seventh Ave Ste 1703	New York	NY	10018	**800-924-6475**	212-221-8203
Jones Apparel Group Inc Jones New York Collection Div					
1411 Broadway	New York	NY	10018	**800-999-1877**	212-355-4449
Leon Max Inc					
3100 New York Dr	Pasadena	CA	91107	**888-334-4629**	626-797-9991
Tanner Cos LLC					
581Rock Rd	Rutherfordton	NC	28139	**877-872-4578**	828-287-4205
Ursula of Switzerland Inc					
31 Mohawk Ave	Waterford	NY	12188	**800-826-4041**	

155   CLOTHING & ACCESSORIES - WHOL

				Toll-Free	Phone
Crew Outfitters Inc					
1001 Virginia Ave	Atlanta	GA	30354	**888-345-5353**	
Herman's Inc					
2820 Blackhawk Rd	Rock Island	IL	61201	**800-447-1295**	309-788-9568
Jacob Ash Company Inc					
301 Munson Ave	McKees Rocks	PA	15136	**800-245-6111**	412-331-6660
TSC Apparel LLC					
12080 Mosteller Rd	Cincinnati	OH	45241	**800-543-7230**	513-771-1138
WS Emerson Co Inc 15 Acme Rd	Brewer	ME	04412	**800-789-6120**	

156   CLOTHING STORES

SEE ALSO Department Stores

156-1 Children's Clothing Stores

				Toll-Free	Phone
Children's Place Retail Stores Inc					
500 Plz Dr	Secaucus	NJ	07094	**877-752-2387**	201-558-2400
NASDAQ: PLCE					
Gymboree Corp					
500 Howard St	San Francisco	CA	94105	**877-449-6932**	415-278-7000
NASDAQ: GYMB					
Valor Brands LLC					
3159 Royal Dr Ste 360	Alpharetta	GA	30022	**866-949-9098**	770-346-9250
Winmark Corp					
605Hwy 169 N Ste 400	Minneapolis	MN	55441	**800-433-2540**	763-520-8500
NASDAQ: WINA					

156-2 Family Clothing Stores

				Toll-Free	Phone
Bob's Stores Inc					
160 Corporate Ct	Meriden	CT	06450	**866-333-2627**	203-235-5775
Citi Trends Inc					
104 Coleman Blvd	Savannah	GA	31408	**800-605-8174**	912-236-1561
NASDAQ: CTRN					
Dawahares Inc					
1845 Alexandria Dr	Lexington	KY	40504	**800-677-9108**	859-278-0422
Foursome Inc					
3570 Vicksveurg Ln N Ste 100	Plymouth	MN	55447	**888-368-7766**	763-473-4667
Kittery Trading Post					
301 US 1	Kittery	ME	03904	**888-587-6246**	603-334-1157
Palais Royal					
10201 S Main St	Houston	TX	77025	**800-743-8730**	713-346-2430
Puritan of Cape Cod					
408 Main St	Hyannis	MA	02601	**800-924-0606**	508-775-2400
TJ Maxx					
770 Cochituate Rd	Framingham	MA	01701	**800-926-6299***	508-390-1000
*Cust Svc					
Wakefield's Inc					
1212 Quintard Ave PO Box 400	Anniston	AL	36201	**800-333-1552**	256-237-9521
Zumiez Inc					
6300 Merrill Creek Pkwy Ste B	Everett	WA	98203	**877-828-6929**	425-551-1500
NASDAQ: ZUMZ					

156-3 Men's Clothing Stores

				Toll-Free	Phone
Carroll & Co					
425 N Canon Dr	Beverly Hills	CA	90210	**800-238-9400**	310-273-9060
Dr. Denim Inc					
1136 Market St	Philadelphia	PA	19107	**888-761-6520**	215-564-2767
Jos A Bank Clothiers					
500 Hanover Pk	Hampstead	MD	21074	**800-999-7472***	410-239-2700
*Cust Svc					
Louis Boston 60 Northern Ave	Boston	MA	02210	**800-225-5135**	617-262-6100
Men's Wearhouse Inc					
6380 Rogerdale Rd	Houston	TX	77072	**877-986-9669**	281-776-7000
NYSE: MW					
Miltons Inc					
250 Granite St	Braintree	MA	02184	**800-645-8673**	781-848-1880
Patrick James Inc					
780 W Shaw Ave	Fresno	CA	93704	**888-427-6003**	559-224-5500

				Toll-Free	Phone
Paul Fredrick Menstyle					
223 W Poplar St	Fleetwood	PA	19522	**800-247-1417**	610-944-0909
Rubenstein Bros Inc					
102 St Charles Ave	New Orleans	LA	70130	**800-102-7862**	504-581-6666

156-4 Men's & Women's Clothing Stores

				Toll-Free	Phone
American Eagle Outfitters Inc					
77 Hot Metal St	Pittsburgh	PA	15203	**888-232-4535***	412-432-3300
NYSE: AEO ■ *Cust Svc					
Bergdorf Goodman Inc					
754 Fifth Ave	New York	NY	10019	**800-558-1855***	212-753-7300
*Cust Svc					
Buckle Inc 2407 W 24th St	Kearney	NE	68845	**800-626-1255**	308-236-8491
NYSE: BKE					
Eddie Bauer LLC					
PO Box 7001	Groveport	OH	43125	**800-426-8020***	
*Orders					
Gap Inc Two Folsom St	San Francisco	CA	94105	**800-333-7899**	650-952-4400
NYSE: GPS					
J Crew Group Inc					
770 Broadway	New York	NY	10003	**800-562-0258**	212-209-2500
Joe's Jeans Inc					
2340 S Eastern Ave	Commerce	CA	90040	**877-528-5637**	323-837-3700
NASDAQ: JOEZ					
Maurices Inc					
105 W Superior St	Duluth	MN	55802	**866-977-1542**	218-727-8431
Pacific Sunwear of California Inc					
3450 E Miraloma Ave	Anaheim	CA	92806	**800-444-6770**	714-414-4000
NASDAQ: PSUN					
Patagonia Inc					
259 W Santa Clara St PO Box 150	Ventura	CA	93001	**800-638-6464***	805-643-8616
*Cust Svc					
Paul Stuart Inc					
Madison Ave & 45th St	New York	NY	10017	**800-678-8278***	212-682-0320
*Orders					
Plato's Closet					
23021 Outer Dr	Allen Park	MI	48101	**800-592-8049**	313-278-2300
Specialty Retailers Inc					
10201 S Main St	Houston	TX	77025	**800-579-2302**	
Stanley Korshak					
500 Crescent Ct Ste 100	Dallas	TX	75201	**855-749-9539**	214-871-3600
TJX Cos Inc					
770 Cochituate Rd	Framingham	MA	01701	**800-926-6299**	508-390-1000
NYSE: TJX					
Urban Outfitters Inc					
30 Industrial Pk Blvd	Trenton	SC	29847	**800-282-2200**	

156-5 Specialty Clothing Stores

Specialty clothing stores are those which sell a specific type of clothing, such as Western wear, uniforms, etc.

				Toll-Free	Phone
5.11 Inc 4300 Spyres Way	Modesto	CA	95356	**866-451-1726**	209-527-4511
Country Curtains					
PO Box 955	Stockbridge	MA	01262	**800-937-1237**	413-243-1474
Hat World Corp					
7555 Woodland Dr	Indianapolis	IN	46278	**888-564-4287**	
Hilo Hattie					
700 N Nimitz Hwy	Honolulu	HI	96817	**800-233-8912**	
HorseLoverZ com					
254 N Cedar St	Hazleton	PA	18201	**877-804-7810**	570-579-0054
Mark's Work Warehouse					
30-1035 64th Ave SE	Calgary	AB	T2H2J7	**800-663-6275**	403-255-9220
Mobile Nations					
3151 E Thomas St	Inverness	FL	34453	**888-599-8998**	352-400-4400
Modell's Sporting Goods					
498 Seventh Ave 20th Fl	New York	NY	10018	**888-645-8667**	800-275-6633
Niver Western Wear Inc					
PO Box 101224	Fort Worth	TX	76185	**800-433-5752***	817-924-4299
*Orders					
Northwest Designs Ink Inc					
13456 SE 27th Pl Ste 200	Bellevue	WA	98005	**800-925-9327**	
Overland Sheepskin Company Inc					
2096 Nutmeg Ave	Fairfield	IA	52556	**800-683-7526**	641-472-8434
Sheplers Inc					
6501 W Kellogg Dr	Wichita	KS	67209	**888-835-4004**	
U S Cavalry Inc					
2855 Centennial Ave	Radcliff	KY	40160	**800-777-7172**	270-351-1164
Wilsons Leather Inc					
7401 Boone Ave N	Brooklyn Park	MN	55428	**800-967-6270**	763-391-4000
Work 'n Gear Stores					
2300 Crown Colony Dr Ste 300	Quincy	MA	02169	**800-987-0218**	

156-6 Women's Clothing Stores

				Toll-Free	Phone
A'Gaci LLC					
12460 Network Blvd Ste 106	San Antonio	TX	78249	**866-265-3036**	210-377-3393
Ann Inc Seven Times Sq	New York	NY	10036	**800-677-6788**	212-541-3300
NYSE: ANN					
AnnTaylor Inc					
Seven Times Sq	New York	NY	10036	**800-677-6788**	212-541-3300
Avenue Stores Inc					
365 W Passaic St	Rochelle Park	NJ	07662	**888-843-2836**	201-845-0880
Bluefly Inc					
42 W 39th St Ninth Fl	New York	NY	10018	**877-258-3359***	212-944-8000
NASDAQ: BFLY ■ *Cust Svc					
Born Into It Inc					
185 New Boston St	Woburn	MA	01801	**800-560-2840**	781-491-0707
Capsmith Inc					
2240 Old Lk Mary Rd	Sanford	FL	32771	**800-228-3889**	407-328-7660

				Toll-Free	Phone
Cato Corp, The					
8100 Denmark Rd	Charlotte	NC	28273	800-526-9169	704-554-8510
Charlotte Russe Inc					
5910 Pacific Center Blvd	San Diego	CA	92121	888-211-7271	
Chico's FAS Inc					
11215 Metro Pkwy	Fort Myers	FL	33966	800-690-6903	888-855-4986
NYSE: CHS					
Claire's Accessories					
2400 W Central Rd	Hoffman Estates	IL	60192	800-252-4737	847-765-1100
David's Bridal Inc					
1001 Washington St	Conshohocken	PA	19428	800-823-2403	610-943-5000
Destination Maternity Corp					
456 N Fifth St	Philadelphia	PA	19123	800-466-6223	215-873-2200
NASDAQ: DEST					
Drapers & Damons					
Nine Pasteur Ste 200	Irvine	CA	92618	800-843-1174	
Express One Limited Pkwy	Columbus	OH	43230	888-397-1980	
NYSE: EXPR					
Forever 21 Inc					
2001 S Alameda St	Los Angeles	CA	90058	800-966-1355*	213-741-5100
*Cust Svc					
Frederick's of Hollywood Inc					
PO Box 2949	Phoenix	AZ	85062	800-323-9525	
Henri Bendel Inc					
712 Fifth Ave	New York	NY	10019	866-875-7975	212-247-1100
Irresistibles					
Seven Hawkes St	Marblehead	MA	01945	800-555-9865	781-631-1248
Lady Grace Stores Inc					
Five Commonwealth Ave Ste 1	Woburn	MA	01801	800-922-0504	781-569-0727
Lane Bryant Inc					
3344 Morse Crossing	Columbus	OH	43215	866-886-4731*	954-970-2205
*Cust Svc					
Louis Vuitton NA Inc					
One E 57th St	New York	NY	10022	866-884-8866*	212-758-8877
*Cust Svc					
Mandee Shop 12 Vreeland Ave	Totowa	NJ	07512	877-756-1958*	973-890-0021
*Cust Svc					
Motherhood Maternity					
456 N Fifth St	Philadelphia	PA	19123	800-291-7800	215-873-2200
New York & Co					
330 W 34th St 5th Fl.	New York	NY	10001	800-961-9906	
NYDJ Apparel LLC					
5401 S Soto St	Vernon	CA	90058	800-407-6001	323-581-9040
rue21 Inc					
800 Commonwealth Dr Ste 100	Warrendale	PA	15086	888-871-2744	724-776-9780
NASDAQ: RUE					
Swim 'n Sport Retail Inc					
2396 NW 96th Ave	Miami	FL	33172	800-497-2111	
Sydneys Closet					
11840 Dorsett Rd	Maryland Heights	MO	63043	888-479-3639	314-344-5066
Vanity Shop of Grand Forks Inc					
2410 Great Northern Dr	Fargo	ND	58102	866-247-7920	701-237-3330
Victoria's Secret Stores					
4 Limited Pkwy	Reynoldsburg	OH	43068	800-411-5116	
Wedding Shoppe Inc, The					
1196 Grand Ave	Saint Paul	MN	55105	877-294-4991	651-298-1144
Wet Seal Inc					
26972 Burbank Ave	Foothill Ranch	CA	92610	866-746-7938	949-699-3900
NASDAQ: WTSLA					
White House/Black Market (WHBM)					
11215 Metro Pkwy	Fort Myers	FL	33966	877-948-2525	239-277-6200
Windsor Inc					
4533 Pacific Blvd	Vernon	CA	90058	888-494-6376	323-282-9000

157 COAST GUARD INSTALLATIONS

				Toll-Free	Phone
Cape Cod Coast Guard Air Station					
2300 Wilson Blvd Ste 500	Arlington	VA	20598	877-669-8724	202-372-4620
Integrated Support Command Miami Beach					
100 MacArthur Cswy	Miami Beach	FL	33139	866-772-8724	305-535-4300
Milwaukee Coast Guard Base					
2420 S Lincoln Memorial Dr	Milwaukee	WI	53207	866-772-8724	414-747-7100
US Coast Guard Air Station Detroit					
1461 N Perimeter Rd Selfridge ANGB	Selfridge	MI	48045	800-424-8802	

158 COFFEE & TEA STORES

				Toll-Free	Phone
Caribou Coffee Company Inc					
3900 Lakebreeze Ave N	Minneapolis	MN	55429	888-227-4268*	763-592-2200
NASDAQ: CBOU ▪ *Cust Svc					
Coffee Beanery Ltd, The					
3429 Pierson Pl	Flushing	MI	48433	800-441-2255	
Coffee People Inc					
33 Coffee Ln	Waterbury	VT	05676	888-879-4627	
Dunkin' Donuts 130 Royall St	Canton	MA	02021	800-859-5339*	781-737-3000
*Cust Svc					
Hawaii Coffee Company Inc					
1555 Kalani St	Honolulu	HI	96817	800-338-8353	808-847-3600
International Coffee & Tea Inc					
1945 S La Cienega Blvd	Los Angeles	CA	90034	877-653-1963	310-237-2326
McNulty's Tea & Coffee Company Inc					
109 Christopher St	New York	NY	10014	800-356-5200	212-242-5351
Montana Coffee Traders Inc					
5810 Hwy 93 S	Whitefish	MT	59937	800-345-5282	406-862-7633
Peet's Coffee & Tea Inc					
1400 Pk Ave	Emeryville	CA	94608	800-999-2132*	510-594-2100
NASDAQ: GMCR ▪ *Orders					
Seattle's Best Coffee Co					
PO Box 3717	Seattle	WA	98124	800-611-7793	
Second Cup Ltd					
6303 Airport Rd	Mississauga	ON	L4V1R8	877-212-1818	
Starbucks Coffee Co					
2401 Utah Ave S	Seattle	WA	98134	800-782-7282	206-447-1575

159 COLLECTION AGENCIES

				Toll-Free	Phone
A.R.M. Solutions Inc					
PO Box 2929	Camarillo	CA	93011	888-772-6468	
AllianceOne Inc					
4850 E St Rd Ste 300	Trevose	PA	19053	866-405-7241	215-354-5511
Allied International Credit Corp					
16635 Young St Unit 26	Newmarket	ON	L3X1V6	877-451-2594	
American Accounts & Advisors					
PO Box 250	Cottage Grove	MN	55016	866-714-0489	651-287-6100
Asset Acceptance Capital Corp (AACC)					
28405 Van Dyke Ave	Warren	MI	48093	800-545-9931	586-939-9600
NASDAQ: AACC					
Atlantic Credit & Finance Inc					
2727 Franklin Rd	Roanoke	VA	24014	800-888-9419	540-772-7800
Bonneville Billing & Collection Inc					
1186 East 4600 South Ste 100	Ogden	UT	84403	888-621-7880	801-621-7880
Computer Credit Inc					
640 W Fourth St	Winston-Salem	NC	27101	800-942-2995	336-761-1524
Continental Service Group Inc					
200 Cross Keys Office Pk	Fairport	NY	14450	800-724-7500	585-421-1000
Credit Control Services Inc (CCS)					
2 Wells Ave Ste 1	Newton	MA	02459	800-526-0532	617-965-2000
Credit Management LP					
4200 International Pkwy	Carrollton	TX	75007	800-377-7713	
Creditors Adjustment Bureau-LC Financial (CABLCF)					
14226 Ventura Blvd	Sherman Oaks	CA	91423	800-800-4523	818-990-4800
Dynamic Recovery Services Inc					
4101 McEwen Rd Ste 150.	Farmers Branch	TX	75244	800-886-8088	972-241-5611
Encore Capital Group Inc					
8875 Aero Dr Ste 200	San Diego	CA	92123	877-445-4581	858-560-2600
NASDAQ: ECPG					
Expert Global Solutions, Inc					
507 Prudential Rd	Horsham	PA	19044	800-220-2274	215-441-3000
Focus Receivables Management LLC					
1130 Northchase Pkwy Ste 150	Marietta	GA	30067	877-362-8766	678-305-9606
GC Services LP					
6330 Gulfton St	Houston	TX	77081	800-756-6524	713-777-4441
General Revenue Corp					
4660 Duke Dr Ste 300	Mason	OH	45040	800-234-6258	
Gulf Coast Collection Bureau Inc					
5630 Marquesas Cir	Sarasota	FL	34233	877-827-4820	941-927-6999
Hill Top Collections Inc					
38 W 32nd St Ste 1510.	New York	NY	10001	800-361-6871	212-564-2322
Hospital Billing & Collection Service Ltd					
118 Lukens Dr	New Castle	DE	19720	877-254-9580	302-552-8000
Nationwide Credit Inc (NCI)					
2002 Summit Blvd Ste 600.	Atlanta	GA	30319	800-456-4729	
Nationwide Recovery Systems Inc (NRS)					
4635 McEwen Rd	Dallas	TX	75244	800-458-6357	972-798-1000
Pentagroup Financial LLC					
5959 Corp Dr Ste 1400.	Houston	TX	77036	800-385-9060	832-615-2100
Portfolio Recovery Assoc LLC					
120 Corporate Blvd					
Ste 100 Reverside Commerce Ctr	Norfolk	VA	23502	888-772-7326	
NASDAQ: PRAA					
Transworld Systems Inc					
2235 Mercury Way Ste 275	Santa Rosa	CA	95407	888-446-4733	707-236-3800
Twenty-First Century Assoc					
266 Summit Ave	Hackensack	NJ	07601	888-760-5052	201-678-1144
United Recovery Systems LP					
5800 N Course Dr	Houston	TX	77072	800-568-0399	713-977-1234
Van Ru Credit Corp					
1350 E Touhy Ave Ste 300E	Des Plaines	IL	60018	800-468-2678	
Vengroff Williams & Assoc Inc (VWA)					
2099 S State College Bvld	Anaheim	CA	92806	800-238-9655	866-737-4344

160 COLLEGES - BIBLE

SEE ALSO Colleges & Universities - Christian

				Toll-Free	Phone
Alaska Bible College					
248 E Elmwood Ave	Palmer	AK	99645	800-478-7884	907-822-3201
Allegheny Wesleyan College					
2161 Woodsdale Rd	Salem	OH	44460	800-292-3153	330-337-6403
Baptist Bible College					
538 VenaRd Rd	Clarks Summit	PA	18411	800-451-7664*	570-586-2400
*General					
Baptist University of the Americas					
8019 S Pan Am Expy	San Antonio	TX	78224	800-721-1396	210-924-4338
Barclay College					
607 N Kingman St	Haviland	KS	67059	800-862-0226	620-862-5252
Beulah Heights Bible College					
892 Berne St SE PO Box 18145	Atlanta	GA	30316	888-777-2422	404-627-2681
Boise Bible College					
8695 W Marigold St	Boise	ID	83714	800-893-7755	208-376-7731
Calvary Bible College & Theological Seminary					
15800 Calvary Rd	Kansas City	MO	64147	800-326-3960	816-322-3960
Central Christian College of the Bible					
911 E Urbandale Dr	Moberly	MO	65270	888-263-3900	660-263-3900
Cincinnati Christian University					
2700 Glenway Ave	Cincinnati	OH	45204	800-949-4228	513-244-8100
Columbia International University					
7435 Monticello Rd	Columbia	SC	29203	800-777-2227	803-754-4100
Crossroads Bible College					
601 N Shortridge Rd	Indianapolis	IN	46219	800-822-3119	317-352-8736
Crossroads College					
920 Mayowood Rd SW	Rochester	MN	55902	800-456-7651	507-288-4563
Crown College					
8700 College View Dr	Saint Bonifacius	MN	55375	800-682-7696	952-446-4100
Dallas Christian College					
2700 Christian Pkwy	Dallas	TX	75234	800-688-1029	972-241-3371

			Toll-Free	Phone

Ecclesia College
9653 Nations Dr .... Springdale AR 72762 **800-735-9926** 479-248-7236

Emmaus Bible College
2570 Asbury Rd .... Dubuque IA 52001 **800-397-2425** 563-588-8000

Faith Baptist Bible College
1900 NW Fourth St .... Ankeny IA 50023 **800-409-3305** 515-964-0601

Florida Christian College
1011 Bill Beck Blvd .... Kissimmee FL 34744 **888-468-6322** 407-847-8966

Free Will Baptist Bible College
3606 W End Ave .... Nashville TN 37205 **800-763-9222** 615-844-5000

God's Bible School & College
1810 Young St .... Cincinnati OH 45202 **800-486-4637** 513-721-7944

Grace Bible College
1011 Aldon St SW PO Box 910 .... Grand Rapids MI 49509 **800-968-1887** 616-538-2330

Grace University
1311 S Ninth St .... Omaha NE 68108 **800-383-1422** 402-449-2800

Great Lakes Christian College
6211 W Willow Hwy .... Lansing MI 48917 **800-937-4522*** 517-321-0242
*Admissions

Heritage Christian University
3625 Helton Dr PO Box HCU .... Florence AL 35630 **800-367-3565** 256-766-6610

Hobe Sound Bible College
PO Box 1065 .... Hobe Sound FL 33475 **800-881-5534** 772-546-5534

Johnson University
7900 Johnson Dr .... Knoxville TN 37998 **800-827-2122** 865-573-4517

Kentucky Mountain Bible College
855 Hwy 541 PO Box 10 .... Vancleve KY 41385 **800-879-5622** 606-693-5000

Kuyper College
3333 E Beltline Ave NE .... Grand Rapids MI 49525 **800-511-3749** 616-222-3000

Lancaster Bible College
901 Eden Rd PO Box 83403 .... Lancaster PA 17608 **800-544-7335** 717-569-7071

Laurel University
1215 Eastchester Dr .... High Point NC 27265 **855-528-7358** 336-887-3000

Life Pacific College
1100 W Covina Blvd .... San Dimas CA 91773 **877-886-5433** 909-599-5433

Lincoln Christian College Seminary
100 Campus View Dr .... Lincoln IL 62656 **888-522-5228** 217-732-3168

Manhattan Christian College
1415 Anderson Ave .... Manhattan KS 66502 **877-246-4622** 785-539-3571

Mid-Atlantic Christian Universit
715 N Poindexter St .... Elizabeth City NC 27909 **866-996-6228** 252-334-2070

Moody Bible Institute
820 N La Salle St .... Chicago IL 60610 **800-967-4624** 312-329-4400

Multnomah Bible College & Biblical Seminary
8435 NE Glisan St .... Portland OR 97220 **800-275-4672** 503-255-0332

Oak Hills Christian College
1600 Oak Hills Rd SW .... Bemidji MN 56601 **888-751-8670** 218-751-8670

Ozark Christian College
1111 N Main St .... Joplin MO 64801 **800-299-4622** 417-624-2518

Saint Louis Christian College
1360 Grandview Dr .... Florissant MO 63033 **800-887-7522*** 314-837-6777
*Admissions

Toccoa Falls College
107 Kincaid Dr .... Toccoa Falls GA 30598 **800-868-3257*** 706-886-6831
*General

Tri-State Bible College
506 Margaret St .... South Point OH 45680 **800-333-3243** 740-377-2520

Trinity Bible College
50 Sixth Ave N .... Ellendale ND 58436 **800-523-1603** 701-349-3621

Trinity College of Florida
2430 Welbilt Blvd .... Trinity FL 34655 **800-388-0869** 727-376-6911

Washington Bible College/Capital Bible Seminary
6511 Princess Garden Pkwy .... Lanham MD 20706 **877-793-7227** 301-552-1400

Zion Bible College
27 Middle Hwy .... Barrington RI 02806 **800-356-4014** 401-246-0900

161	COLLEGES - COMMUNITY & JUNIOR

SEE ALSO Vocational & Technical Schools ; Colleges - Fine Arts ; Colleges - Tribal ; Colleges & Universities - Four-Year
Institutions that offer academic degrees that can be transferred to a four-year college or university.

			Toll-Free	Phone

Us Health Connect Inc
500 Office Ctr Dr .... Fort Washington PA 19034 **800-889-4944**

Alabama

			Toll-Free	Phone

Alabama Southern Community College
30755 Hwy 43 .... Thomasville AL 36784 **866-901-1117** 334-636-9642

Bevill State Community College
Jasper 1411 Indiana Ave .... Jasper AL 35501 **800-648-3271** 205-387-0511
Huntsville 102B Wynn Dr .... Huntsville AL 35805 **800-626-3628** 256-890-4701

Calhoun Community College
Redstone Arsenal
6250 Hwy 31 N .... Tanner AL 35671 **800-626-3628** 256-306-2500

Central Alabama Community College
1675 Cherokee Rd .... Alexander City AL 35010 **800-643-2657** 256-234-6346

Faulkner State Community College
Bay Minette
1900 Hwy 31 S .... Bay Minette AL 36507 **800-381-3722** 251-580-2111
Fairhope 440 Fairhope Ave .... Fairhope AL 36532 **800-231-3752** 251-990-0420
Gulf Shores
3301 Gulf Shores Pkwy .... Gulf Shores AL 36542 **800-231-3752** 251-968-3101

Gadsden State Community College
1001 George Wallace Dr PO Box 227 .... Gadsden AL 35902 **800-226-5563** 256-549-8200

Jefferson State Community College
2601 Carson Rd .... Birmingham AL 35215 **800-239-5900** 205-853-1200

Lurleen B Wallace Community College
Andalusia
1000 Dannelly Blvd PO Box 1418 .... Andalusia AL 36420 **877-382-4357** 334-222-6591

Marion Military Institute
1101 Washington St .... Marion AL 36756 **800-664-1842** 334-683-2306

Northeast Alabama Community College
PO Box 159 .... Rainsville AL 35986 **866-572-5433** 256-228-6001

Northwest-Shoals Community College
Phil Campbell
2080 College Rd .... Phil Campbell AL 35581 **800-645-8967** 256-331-6200

Southern Union State Community College
Opelika 1701 Lafayette Pkwy .... Opelika AL 36801 **800-707-0057** 334-745-6437
Valley 321 Fob James Dr .... Valley AL 36854 **800-707-0057** 334-756-4151

Wallace Community College
1141 Wallace Dr .... Dothan AL 36303 **800-543-2426** 334-983-3521

Wallace State Community College
801 Main St .... Hanceville AL 35077 **866-350-9722** 256-352-8000

Alaska

			Toll-Free	Phone

University of Alaska Anchorage Kenai Peninsula College
156 College Rd .... Soldotna AK 99669 **877-262-0330**

University of Alaska Anchorage Kodiak College
117 Benny Benson Dr .... Kodiak AK 99615 **800-486-7660** 907-486-4161
Northwest
400 E Front St PO Box 400 .... Nome AK 99762 **800-478-2202** 907-443-2201

University of Alaska Southeast Ketchikan
2600 Seventh Ave .... Ketchikan AK 99901 **877-465-6400** 907-225-6177

University of Alaska Southeast Sitka
1332 Seward Ave .... Sitka AK 99835 **800-478-6653** 907-747-6653

Arizona

			Toll-Free	Phone

Arizona Western College
2020 S Ave 8 E .... Yuma AZ 85366 **888-293-0392** 928-317-6000

Central Arizona College
8470 N Overfield Rd .... Coolidge AZ 85228 **800-237-9814** 520-494-5444

Cochise College
4190 W Hwy 80 .... Douglas AZ 85607 **800-966-7943** 520-364-7943
Sierra Vista
901 N Colombo Ave .... Sierra Vista AZ 85635 **800-966-7943** 520-515-0500

Coconino Community College
Lonetree
2800 S Lone Tree Rd .... Flagstaff AZ 86001 **800-350-7122** 928-527-1222

Eastern Arizona College
615 N Stadium Ave .... Thatcher AZ 85552 **800-678-3808** 928-428-8472

GateWay Community College
108 N 40th St .... Phoenix AZ 85034 **888-994-4433** 602-286-8000

Mesa Community College
1833 W Southern Ave .... Mesa AZ 85202 **866-532-4983** 480-461-7000
Bullhead City
3400 Hwy 95 .... Bullhead City AZ 86442 **866-664-2832** 928-758-3926
Lake Havasu
1977 W Acoma Blvd .... Lake Havasu City AZ 86403 **866-664-2832** 928-855-7812

Mohave Community College
North Mohave
PO Box 980 .... Colorado City AZ 86021 **800-678-3992** 928-875-2799

Northland Pioneer College
PO Box 610 .... Holbrook AZ 86025 **800-266-7845** 928-532-6111

Pima Community College
West 2202 W Anklam Rd .... Tucson AZ 85709 **800-860-7462** 520-206-6600

Scottsdale Community College
9000 E Chaparral Rd .... Scottsdale AZ 85256 **800-784-2433** 480-423-6000

South Mountain Community College
7050 S 24th St .... Phoenix AZ 85042 **855-622-2332** 602-243-8000

Yavapai College
1100 E Sheldon St .... Prescott AZ 86301 **800-922-6787** 928-445-7300
Verde Valley
601 Black Hills Dr .... Clarkdale AZ 86324 **800-922-6787** 928-634-7501

Arkansas

			Toll-Free	Phone

Arkansas State University Newport
7648 Victory Blvd .... Newport AR 72112 **800-976-1676** 870-512-7800

Black River Technical College
1410 Hwy 304 E .... Pocahontas AR 72455 **866-890-6933** 870-248-4000

Crowley's Ridge College
100 College Dr .... Paragould AR 72450 **800-264-1096** 870-236-6901

National Park Community College
101 College Dr .... Hot Springs AR 71913 **800-760-1825** 501-760-4222

North Arkansas College
1515 Pioneer Dr .... Harrison AR 72601 **800-679-6622** 870-743-3000

NorthWest Arkansas Community College
One College Dr .... Bentonville AR 72712 **800-995-6922** 479-636-9222

Ozarka College
218 College Dr .... Melbourne AR 72556 **800-821-4335** 870-368-7371

South Arkansas Community College
PO Box 7010 .... El Dorado AR 71731 **800-955-2289** 870-862-8131

Southeast Arkansas College
1900 Hazel St .... Pine Bluff AR 71603 **888-732-7582** 870-543-5915

California

			Toll-Free	Phone

Barstow College
2700 Barstow Rd .... Barstow CA 92311 **877-823-2378** 760-252-2411

Butte College
3536 Butte Campus Dr .... Oroville CA 95965 **800-933-8322*** 530-895-2511
*Hum Res

Cabrillo College
6500 Soquel Dr .... Aptos CA 95003 **800-218-0013** 831-479-6100

Cerro Coso Community College
Bishop 4090 W Line St .... Bishop CA 93514 **888-537-6932** 760-872-1565
Indian Wells Valley
3000 College Heights Blvd .... Ridgecrest CA 93555 **888-537-6932** 760-384-6100
Kern River Valley
5520 Lk Isabella Blvd .... Lake Isabella CA 93240 **888-537-6932** 760-379-5501
Mammoth
101 College Pkwy PO Box 1865 .... Mammoth Lakes CA 93546 **888-537-6932** 760-934-2875

City College of San Francisco
50 Phelan Ave .... San Francisco CA 94112 **800-433-3243** 415-239-3000

				Toll-Free	Phone

Coastline Community College
11460 Warner Ave ....Fountain Valley CA 92708 — 866-422-2645 — 714-546-7600
College of the Redwoods
7351 Tompkins Hill Rd ....Eureka CA 95501 — 800-641-0400 — 707-476-4100
Del Norte
883 W Washington Blvd ....Crescent City CA 95531 — 800-641-0400 — 707-465-2300
Mendocino Coast
440 Alger St ....Fort Bragg CA 95437 — 800-641-0400 — 707-962-2600
College of the Siskiyous
800 College Ave ....Weed CA 96094 — 888-397-4339 — 530-938-4461
Cuesta College
PO Box 8106 ....San Luis Obispo CA 93403 — 800-675-2526 — 805-546-3100
Cuyamaca College
900 Rancho San Diego Pkwy ....El Cajon CA 92019 — 800-234-1597 — 619-660-4000
Diablo Valley College
312 Golf Club Rd ....Pleasant Hill CA 94523 — 800-227-1060 — 925-685-1230
Feather River College
570 Golden Eagle Ave ....Quincy CA 95971 — 800-442-9799 — 530-283-0202
Foothill College
12345 El Monte Rd ....Los Altos Hills CA 94022 — 800-234-1597 — 650-949-7777
Fresno City College
1101 E University Ave ....Fresno CA 93741 — 866-245-3276 — 559-442-4600
Hartnell College
156 Homestead Ave ....Salinas CA 93901 — 888-678-2871 — 831-755-6700
Long Beach City College
4901 E Carson St ....Long Beach CA 90808 — 888-442-4551 — 562-938-4111
Los Angeles City College
855 N Vermont Ave ....Los Angeles CA 90029 — 800-266-6883 — 323-953-4000
Los Medanos College
2700 E Leland Rd ....Pittsburg CA 94565 — 800-677-6337 — 925-439-2181
Merced College 3600 M St ....Merced CA 95348 — 800-784-2433 — 209-384-6000
Oceanside
One Barnard Dr Ste 7 ....Oceanside CA 92056 — 888-201-8480 — 760-757-2121
MiraCosta College
San Elijo
3333 Manchester Ave ....Cardiff CA 92007 — 888-201-8480 — 760-944-4449
Monterey Peninsula College
980 Fremont St ....Monterey CA 93940 — 877-663-5433 — 831-646-4000
Mount Saint Mary's University Doheny
10 Chester Pl ....Los Angeles CA 90007 — 800-999-9893* — 213-477-2500
*Admissions
Mount San Jacinto College
1499 N State St ....San Jacinto CA 92583 — 800-624-5561 — 951-487-6752
Napa Valley College
2277 Napa-Vallejo Hwy ....Napa CA 94558 — 800-826-1077 — 707-256-7000
Reedley College
995 N Reed Ave ....Reedley CA 93654 — 866-245-3276 — 559-638-3641
Santa Rosa Junior College
1501 Mendocino Ave ....Santa Rosa CA 95401 — 800-564-7752 — 707-527-4011
Sierra College
Nevada County
250 Sierra College Dr ....Grass Valley CA 95945 — 800-242-4004 — 530-274-5300
Southwestern College
900 Otay Lakes Rd ....Chula Vista CA 91910 — 866-262-9881 — 619-421-6700
Taft College 29 Emmons Pk Dr ....Taft CA 93268 — 800-379-6784 — 661-763-7700
Victor Valley Community College
18422 Bear Valley Rd ....Victorville CA 92392 — 877-741-8532 — 760-245-4271
West Hills College
Coalinga 300 Cherry Ln ....Coalinga CA 93210 — 800-266-1114 — 559-934-2000

Colorado

				Toll-Free	Phone

Aims Community College
5401 W 20th St ....Greeley CO 80634 — 800-301-5388 — 970-330-8008
Arapahoe Community College
5900 S Santa Fe Dr ....Littleton CO 80160 — 888-800-9198 — 303-797-0100
Alpine
1330 Bob Adams Dr ....Steamboat Springs CO 80487 — 800-621-8559 — 970-870-4444
Aspen 0255 Sage Way ....Aspen CO 81611 — 800-621-8559 — 970-925-7740
Colorado Mountain College
Roaring Fork-Spring Valley
3000 County Rd 114 ....Glenwood Springs CO 81601 — 800-621-8559 — 970-945-7481
Colorado Northwestern Community College
500 Kennedy Dr ....Rangely CO 81648 — 800-562-1105 — 970-675-3335
Craig 50 College Dr ....Craig CO 81625 — 800-562-1105
Community College of Aurora
16000 E Centretech Pkwy ....Aurora CO 80011 — 844-493-8255 — 303-360-4700
Front Range Community College (FRCC)
Boulder County
2190 Miller Dr ....Longmont CO 80501 — 888-800-9198 — 303-678-3722
Larimer
4616 S Shields St ....Fort Collins CO 80526 — 888-800-9198 — 970-226-2500
Lamar Community College
2401 S Main St ....Lamar CO 81052 — 800-968-6920 — 719-336-2248
Morgan Community College
920 Barlow Rd ....Fort Morgan CO 80701 — 800-622-0216 — 970-542-3100
Northeastern Junior College
100 College Ave ....Sterling CO 80751 — 800-626-4637 — 970-521-6600
Pikes Peak Community College
Centennial
5675 S Academy Blvd ....Colorado Springs CO 80906 — 800-456-6847 — 719-502-2000
Downtown Studio
100 W Pikes Peak Ave ....Colorado Springs CO 80903 — 800-456-6847 — 719-502-2000
Rampart Range
11195 Hwy 83 ....Colorado Springs CO 80921 — 800-456-6847 — 719-502-2000
Pueblo Community College
900 W Orman Ave ....Pueblo CO 81004 — 888-642-6017 — 719-549-3200
Trinidad State Junior College
600 Prospect St ....Trinidad CO 81082 — 800-621-8752 — 719-846-5011

Connecticut

				Toll-Free	Phone

Asnuntuck Community College
170 Elm St ....Enfield CT 06082 — 800-501-3967 — 860-253-3000
Capital Community College
950 Main St ....Hartford CT 06103 — 800-894-6126 — 860-906-5000

Housatonic Community College
900 Lafayette Blvd ....Bridgeport CT 06604 — 866-733-2463 — 203-332-5000
Manchester Community College
PO Box 1046 ....Manchester CT 06045 — 888-999-5545 — 860-512-2800
Norwalk Community College
188 Richards Ave ....Norwalk CT 06854 — 800-565-3036 — 203-857-7060
Avery Point
1084 Shennecossett Rd ....Groton CT 06340 — 888-247-5556 — 860-405-9019

Florida

				Toll-Free	Phone

Brevard Community College (BCC)
Cocoa 1519 Clearlake Rd ....Cocoa FL 32922 — 888-747-2802 — 321-632-1111
Melbourne
3865 N Wickham Rd ....Melbourne FL 32935 — 888-747-2802 — 321-632-1111
Palm Bay
250 Community College Pkwy ....Palm Bay FL 32909 — 888-747-2802 — 321-632-1111
Titusville 1311 N US 1 ....Titusville FL 32796 — 888-747-2802 — 321-632-1111
Broward Community College
Downtown Ctr
111 E Las Olas Blvd ....Fort Lauderdale FL 33301 — 888-654-6482 — 954-201-7350
North
1000 Coconut Creek Blvd ....Coconut Creek FL 33066 — 888-654-6482 — 954-201-2240
Daytona Beach Community College
1200 W International Speedway Blvd
.........................Daytona Beach FL 32114 — 800-352-2583 — 386-506-3000
Charlotte
26300 Airport Rd ....Punta Gorda FL 33950 — 800-749-2322 — 941-637-5629
Collier County
7007 Lely Cultural Pkwy ....Naples FL 34113 — 800-749-2322 — 239-732-3701
Edison College
Lee County
8099 College Pkwy SW ....Fort Myers FL 33919 — 800-749-2322 — 239-489-9054
Florida Community College at Jacksonville
Downtown
101 State St W ....Jacksonville FL 32202 — 877-633-5950 — 904-633-8100
Florida Keys Community College
5901 College Rd ....Key West FL 33040 — 866-567-2665 — 305-296-9081
Gulf Coast Community College
5230 W Hwy 98 ....Panama City FL 32401 — 800-311-3685 — 850-769-1551
Indian River State College (IRSC)
3209 Virginia Ave ....Fort Pierce FL 34981 — 866-792-4772 — 772-462-4772
North Florida Community College
325 NW Turner Davis Dr ....Madison FL 32340 — 877-501-0956 — 850-973-2288
Lake Worth
4200 Congress Ave ....Lake Worth FL 33461 — 866-576-7222 — 561-868-3350
Palm Beach Community College
Palm Beach Gardens
3160 PGA Blvd ....Palm Beach Gardens FL 33410 — 866-576-7222 — 561-207-5340
Pasco-Hernando Community College
North
11415 Ponce de Leon Blvd ....Brooksville FL 34601 — 877-879-7422 — 352-796-6726
Pensacola Junior College
Warrington 5555 W Hwy 98 ....Pensacola FL 32507 — 888-897-3605 — 850-484-2200
Saint Johns River Community College
5001 St Johns Ave ....Palatka FL 32177 — 888-757-2293 — 386-312-4200
Seminole State College
2701 Boren Blvd PO Box 351 ....Sanford FL 32773 — 877-738-6365 — 405-382-9950

Georgia

				Toll-Free	Phone

Abraham Baldwin Agricultural College
2802 Moore Hwy ABAC 3 ....Tifton GA 31793 — 800-733-3653 — 229-391-5001
Andrew College
501 College St ....Cuthbert GA 39840 — 800-664-9250
Darton College
2400 Gillionville Rd ....Albany GA 31707 — 866-775-1214 — 229-430-6742
East Georgia College
131 College Cir ....Swainsboro GA 30401 — 800-715-4255 — 478-289-2000
Emory University Oxford College
201 Dowman Dr PO Box 1418 ....Atlanta GA 30322 — 800-723-8328 — 404-727-6069
Cartersville
5441 Hwy 20 NE ....Cartersville GA 30121 — 800-332-2406 — 678-872-8000
Georgia Highlands College
Floyd 3175 Cedartown Hwy ....Rome GA 30161 — 800-332-2406 — 706-802-5000
Georgia Military College
201 E Green St ....Milledgeville GA 31061 — 800-342-0413 — 478-387-4900
Young Harris College
PO Box 116 ....Young Harris GA 30582 — 800-241-3754 — 706-379-3111

Hawaii

				Toll-Free	Phone

Kauai Community College
3-1901 Kaumualii Hwy ....Lihue HI 96766 — 800-776-4816 — 808-245-8311
Leeward Community College
96-045 Ala Ike ....Pearl City HI 96782 — 888-442-4551 — 808-455-0011
Maui Community College
310 W Kaahumanu Ave ....Kahului HI 96732 — 800-479-6692 — 808-984-3267

Idaho

				Toll-Free	Phone

North Idaho College
1000 W Garden Ave ....Coeur d'Alene ID 83814 — 877-404-4536 — 208-769-3300

Illinois

				Toll-Free	Phone

Black Hawk College
East 1501 State Hwy 78 ....Kewanee IL 61443 — 800-233-5671 — 309-852-5671
Quad Cities 6600 34th Ave ....Moline IL 61265 — 800-334-1311 — 309-796-5000
Carl Sandburg College
2400 Tom L Wilson Blvd ....Galesburg IL 61401 — 877-236-1862 — 309-344-2518
City Colleges of Chicago
226 W Jackson ....Chicago IL 60606 — 866-908-7582 — 312-553-2500

			Toll-Free	Phone

Danville Area Community College
2000 E Main St .... Danville IL 61832   **877-342-3042**   217-443-3222

Elgin Community College
1700 Spartan Dr .... Elgin IL 60123   **855-850-2525**   847-697-1000

Harry S Truman College
1145 W Wilson Ave .... Chicago IL 60640   **877-863-6339**   773-878-1700

Joliet Junior College
North 1215 Houbolt Rd .... Joliet IL 60431   **800-899-4722**   815-729-9020

Kankakee Community College
100 College Dr .... Kankakee IL 60901   **800-526-0844**   815-802-8100

Kishwaukee College
21193 Malta Rd .... Malta IL 60150   **888-656-7329**   815-825-2086

Lincoln College
300 Keokuk St .... Lincoln IL 62656   **800-569-0556**   217-732-3155

Lincoln Land Community College
5250 Shepherd Rd PO Box 19256 .... Springfield IL 62794   **800-727-4161**   217-786-2200

Lincoln Trail College
11220 State Hwy 1 .... Robinson IL 62454   **866-582-4322**   618-544-8657

Malcolm X College
1900 W Van Buren St .... Chicago IL 60612   **877-542-0285**   312-850-7000

McHenry County College
8900 US Hwy 14 .... Crystal Lake IL 60012   **888-977-4847**   815-455-3700

Oakton Community College
Skokie Campus
7701 N Lincoln Ave .... Skokie IL 60077   **877-823-2378**   847-635-1600

Olney Central College
305 NW St .... Olney IL 62450   **866-622-4322**   618-395-7777

Parkland College
2400 W Bradley Ave .... Champaign IL 61821   **888-467-6065**   217-351-2200

Prairie State College
202 S Halsted St .... Chicago Heights IL 60411   **866-255-5437**   708-709-3500

Rend Lake College
468 N Ken Gray Pkwy .... Ina IL 62846   **800-369-5321**   618-437-5321

Rock Valley College
3301 N Mulford Rd .... Rockford IL 61114   **800-973-7821**   815-921-7821

Southeastern Illinois College
3575 College Rd .... Harrisburg IL 62946   **866-338-2742**   618-252-6376

Southwestern Illinois College
2500 Carlyle Ave .... Belleville IL 62221   **800-222-5131**   618-235-2700

Spoon River College (SRC)
23235 N County Hwy 22 .... Canton IL 61520   **800-334-7337**   309-647-4645

Springfield College in Illinois - Benedictine University
1500 N Fifth St .... Springfield IL 62702   **800-635-7289**   217-525-1420

Indiana

			Toll-Free	Phone

Vincennes University
1002 N First St .... Vincennes IN 47591   **800-742-9198**   812-888-4313
Jasper 850 College Ave .... Jasper IN 47546   **800-809-8852**   812-482-3030

Iowa

			Toll-Free	Phone

Clinton Community College
1000 Lincoln Blvd .... Clinton IA 52732   **877-495-3320**   563-244-7001

Des Moines Area Community College
Ankeny 2006 S Ankeny Blvd .... Ankeny IA 50021   **800-362-2127**   515-964-6200
Boone 1125 Hancock Dr .... Boone IA 50036   **800-362-2127**   515-432-7203
Carroll 906 N Grant Rd .... Carroll IA 51401   **800-622-3334**   712-792-1755
Urban/Des Moines
1100 Seventh St .... Des Moines IA 50314   **800-622-3334**   515-244-4226

Ellsworth Community College
1100 College Ave .... Iowa Falls IA 50126   **800-322-9235**   641-648-4611

Hawkeye Community College
1501 E Orange Rd .... Waterloo IA 50704   **800-670-4769**   319-296-2320

Indian Hills Community College
525 Grandview Ave .... Ottumwa IA 52501   **800-726-2585**   641-683-5111

Iowa Central Community College
2031 Quail Ave .... Fort Dodge IA 50501   **800-362-2793**   515-576-7201

Iowa Lakes Community College
300 S 18th St .... Estherville IA 51334   **800-242-5106**   712-362-2604

Iowa Western Community College
Clarinda
923 E Washington St .... Clarinda IA 51632   **800-521-2073**   712-542-5117

Kirkwood Community College
6301 Kirkwood Blvd SW .... Cedar Rapids IA 52404   **800-332-2055**   319-398-5411

Marshalltown Community College
3700 S Ctr St .... Marshalltown IA 50158   **866-622-4748**   641-752-7106

Muscatine Community College
152 Colorado St .... Muscatine IA 52761   **888-336-3907**   563-288-6001

North Iowa Area Community College
500 College Dr .... Mason City IA 50401   **888-466-4222**   641-423-1264

Northeast Iowa Community College
Calmar
1625 Hwy 150 S PO Box 400 .... Calmar IA 52132   **800-728-2256**   563-562-3263
Peosta 10250 Sundown Rd .... Peosta IA 52068   **800-728-7367**   563-556-5110

Northwest Iowa Community College
603 W Pk St .... Sheldon IA 51201   **800-352-4907**   712-324-5061

Scott Community College
500 Belmont Rd .... Bettendorf IA 52722   **888-336-3907**   563-441-4001

Southeastern Community College North
1500 W Agency Rd .... West Burlington IA 52655   **866-722-4692**   319-752-2731

Southeastern Community College South
335 Messenger Rd .... Keokuk IA 52632   **866-722-4692**   319-524-3221

Southwestern Community College
1501 W Townline St .... Creston IA 50801   **800-247-4023**   641-782-7081

Kansas

			Toll-Free	Phone

Allen County Community College
1801 N Cottonwood St .... Iola KS 66749   **800-444-0535**   620-365-5116

Barton County Community College
245 NE 30th Rd .... Great Bend KS 67530   **800-722-6842**   620-792-2701

Cloud County Community College
2221 Campus Dr .... Concordia KS 66901   **800-729-5101**   785-243-1435

Coffeyville Community College
400 W 11th St .... Coffeyville KS 67337   **877-517-2836**   620-251-7700

Colby Community College
1255 S Range Ave .... Colby KS 67701   **888-634-9350**   785-462-3984

Cowley County Community College & Area Vocational-Technical School
PO Box 1147 .... Arkansas City KS 67005   **800-593-2222**   620-442-0430

Dodge City Community College
2501 N 14th Ave .... Dodge City KS 67801   **800-367-3222**   620-225-1321

Donnelly College
608 N 18th St .... Kansas City KS 66102   **800-908-9946**   913-621-6070

Fort Scott Community College
2108 S Horton St .... Fort Scott KS 66701   **800-874-3722**   620-223-2700

Garden City Community College
801 N Campus Dr .... Garden City KS 67846   **800-658-1696**   620-276-7611

Hesston College
325 S College Dr PO Box 3000 .... Hesston KS 67062   **800-995-2757**   620-327-4221

Hutchinson Community College & Area Vocational School
1300 N Plum St .... Hutchinson KS 67501   **800-289-3501**   620-665-3500

Independence Community College
1057 W College Ave PO Box 708 .... Independence KS 67301   **800-842-6063**   620-331-4100

Johnson County Community College
12345 College Blvd .... Overland Park KS 66210   **866-896-5893**   913-469-8500

Labette Community College
200 S 14th St .... Parsons KS 67357   **888-522-3883**   620-421-6700

Seward County Community College
1801 N Campus Ave PO Box 1137 .... Liberal KS 67905   **800-373-9951**   620-624-1951

Kentucky

			Toll-Free	Phone

Ashland Community & Technical College
1400 College Dr .... Ashland KY 41101   **800-928-4256**   606-326-2000

Big Sandy Community & Technical College
One Bert T Combs Dr .... Prestonsburg KY 41653   **888-641-4132**   606-886-3863

Bluegrass Community & Technical College
Cooper Campus
470 Cooper Dr .... Lexington KY 40506   **866-774-4872**   859-246-6200

Elizabethtown Community & Technical College
600 College St Rd .... Elizabethtown KY 42701   **877-246-2322**   270-769-2371

Hazard Community & Technical College
One Community College Dr .... Hazard KY 41701   **800-246-7521**   606-436-5721
Hazard Campus 101 Vo Tech Dr .... Hazard KY 41701   **800-246-7521**   606-435-6101
Lees Campus
601 Jefferson Ave .... Jackson KY 41339   **800-246-7521**   606-666-7521

Henderson Community College
2660 S Green St .... Henderson KY 42420   **800-696-9958**   270-827-1867

Hopkinsville Community College
720 N Dr .... Hopkinsville KY 42240   **866-534-2224**   270-886-3921

Jefferson Community & Technical College
109 E Broadway .... Louisville KY 40202   **855-246-5282**   502-584-0181

Madisonville Community College
2000 College Dr .... Madisonville KY 42431   **866-227-4812**   270-821-2250

Maysville Community & Technical College
1755 US 68 .... Maysville KY 41056   **888-452-7322**   606-759-7141

Somerset Community College
808 Monticello St .... Somerset KY 42501   **877-629-9722**   606-679-8501

Southeast Kentucky Community & Technical College
Cumberland
700 College Rd .... Cumberland KY 40823   **888-274-7322**   606-589-2145
Middlesboro
1300 Chichester Ave .... Middlesboro KY 40965   **888-274-7322**   606-242-2145
Whitesburg Two Long Ave .... Whitesburg KY 41858   **888-274-7322**   606-633-0279

West Kentucky Community & Technical College
4810 Alben Barkley Dr PO Box 7380 .... Paducah KY 42001   **855-469-5282**   270-554-9200

Louisiana

			Toll-Free	Phone

Baton Rouge Community College (BRCC)
201 Community College Dr .... Baton Rouge LA 70806   **866-217-9823**   225-216-8000

Elaine P Nunez Community College
3710 Paris Rd .... Chalmette LA 70043   **866-825-1954**   504-278-7497

Louisiana Delta Community College
7500 Millhaven Rd .... Monroe LA 71203   **866-500-5322**   318-345-9000
Eunice PO Box 1129 .... Eunice LA 70535   **888-367-5783**   337-457-7311

Maine

			Toll-Free	Phone

Kennebec Valley Community College
92 Western Ave .... Fairfield ME 04937   **800-528-5882**   207-453-5000

York County Community College
112 College Dr .... Wells ME 04090   **800-580-3820**   207-646-9282

Maryland

			Toll-Free	Phone

Allegany College of Maryland
12401 Willowbrook Rd SE .... Cumberland MD 21502   **800-974-0203**   301-784-5000

Baltimore City Community College
2901 Liberty Heights Ave .... Baltimore MD 21215   **888-203-1261**   410-462-8000

College of Southern Maryland
Leonardtown
22950 Hollywood Rd .... Leonardtown MD 20650   **800-933-9177**   240-725-5300
Prince Frederick
115 J W Williams Rd .... Prince Frederick MD 20678   **800-933-9177**   443-550-6000

Community College of Baltimore County
Essex 7201 Rossville Blvd .... Baltimore MD 21237   **877-557-2575**   410-682-6000
Owings Mills
110 Painters Mill Rd .... Owings Mills MD 21117   **877-557-2575**   410-363-4111

Garrett College
687 Mosser Rd .... McHenry MD 21541   **866-554-2773**   301-387-3000

Howard Community College
10901 Little Patuxent Pkwy .... Columbia MD 21044   **888-442-4551**   410-772-4800

Wor-Wic Community College
32000 Campus Dr .... Salisbury MD 21804   **800-735-2258**   410-334-2800

Massachusetts

				Toll-Free	Phone
Bunker Hill Community College					
Charlestown					
250 New Rutherford Ave	Boston	MA	02129	877-218-8829	617-228-2000
Cape Cod Community College					
2240 Iyanough Rd	West Barnstable	MA	02668	877-846-3672	508-362-2131
Dean College 99 Main St	Franklin	MA	02038	877-879-3326	508-541-1508
Fisher College 118 Beacon St	Boston	MA	02116	866-266-6007	617-236-8800
Holyoke Community College					
303 Homestead Ave	Holyoke	MA	01040	877-442-6222	413-538-7000
Massachusetts Bay Community College					
Wellesley Hills					
50 Oakland St	Wellesley Hills	MA	02481	800-233-3182	781-239-3000
Northern Essex Community College					
100 Elliott St	Haverhill	MA	01830	800-422-4453	978-556-3000
Quincy College					
150 Newport Ave Ext Ste 1	Quincy	MA	02171	800-698-1700	617-984-1700
Springfield Technical Community College					
1 Armory Sq PO Box 900	Springfield	MA	01102	800-326-6142	413-781-7822

Michigan

				Toll-Free	Phone
Alpena Community College (ACC)					
665 Johnson St	Alpena	MI	49707	888-468-6222	989-356-9021
Bay de Noc Community College					
2001 N Lincoln Rd	Escanaba	MI	49829	800-221-2001	906-786-5802
Bay Mills Community College					
12214 W Lakeshore Dr	Brimley	MI	49715	800-844-2622	906-248-3354
Delta College					
1961 Delta Rd	University Center	MI	48710	888-636-4211	989-686-9000
Glen Oaks Community College					
62249 Shimmel Rd	Centreville	MI	49032	888-994-7818	269-467-9945
Gogebic Community College					
E 4946 Jackson Rd	Ironwood	MI	49938	800-682-5910	906-932-4231
Henry Ford Community College					
5101 Evergreen Rd	Dearborn	MI	48128	800-585-4322	313-845-9600
Jackson Community College					
2111 Emmons Rd	Jackson	MI	49201	888-522-7344	517-787-0800
Hillsdale					
3120 W Carleton Rd PO Box 712	Hillsdale	MI	49242	888-522-7344	517-437-3343
Kirtland Community College					
10775 N St Helen Rd	Roscommon	MI	48653	866-632-9992	989-275-5000
Bertrand Crossing					
1905 Foundation Dr	Niles	MI	49120	800-252-1562	269-695-1391
Lake Michigan College					
South Haven					
125 Veterans Blvd	South Haven	MI	49090	800-252-1562	269-639-8442
Lansing Community College					
419 N Washington Sq	Lansing	MI	48933	800-644-4522	517-483-1957
Macomb Community College					
Center					
44575 Garfield Rd	Clinton Township	MI	48038	866-622-6621	586-445-7999
South 14500 E 12-Mile Rd	Warren	MI	48088	866-622-6621	586-445-7000
Monroe County Community College					
1555 S Raisinville Rd	Monroe	MI	48161	877-937-6222	734-242-7300
Muskegon Community College					
221 S Quarterline Rd	Muskegon	MI	49442	866-711-4622	231-773-9131
North Central Michigan College					
1515 Howard St	Petoskey	MI	49770	888-298-6605	231-348-6605
Northwestern Michigan College					
1701 E Front St	Traverse City	MI	49686	800-748-0566	231-995-1000
Oakland Community College					
2480 Opdyke Rd	Bloomfield Hills	MI	48304	800-829-1040	248-341-2000
Highland Lakes					
7350 Cooley Lake Rd	Waterford	MI	48327	800-829-1040	248-942-3100
Southfield					
2480 Opdyke Rd	Bloomfield Hills	MI	48304	800-829-1040	248-341-2000
Saginaw Chippewa Tribal College					
2274 Enterprise Dr	Mount Pleasant	MI	48858	800-225-8172	989-775-4123
Schoolcraft College					
18600 Haggerty Rd	Livonia	MI	48152	844-727-6763	734-462-4400
Southwestern Michigan College (SMC)					
58900 Cherry Grove Rd	Dowagiac	MI	49047	800-456-8675	269-782-1000
Niles Area 2229 US 12	Niles	MI	49120	800-456-8675	269-782-1233
West Shore Community College					
PO Box 277	Scottville	MI	49454	800-848-9722	231-845-6211

Minnesota

				Toll-Free	Phone
Brainerd 501 W College Dr	Brainerd	MN	56401	800-933-0346	218-855-8199
Central Lakes College					
Staples 1830 Airport Rd	Staples	MN	56479	800-247-6836	218-894-5100
Century College					
3300 Century Ave N	White Bear Lake	MN	55115	800-228-1978	651-779-3300
Fond du Lac Tribal & Community College					
2101 14th St	Cloquet	MN	55720	800-657-3712	218-879-0800
Hibbing Community College					
1515 E 25th St	Hibbing	MN	55746	800-224-4422	218-262-6700
Inver Hills Community College					
2500 80th St E	Inver Grove Heights	MN	55076	866-576-0689	651-450-8500
Itasca Community College					
1851 E Us Hwy 169	Grand Rapids	MN	55744	800-996-6422	218-327-4460
Lake Superior College					
2101 Trinity Rd	Duluth	MN	55811	800-432-2884	218-733-7600
Leech Lake Tribal College					
6945 Little Wolf Rd PO Box 180	Cass Lake	MN	56633	800-627-3529	218-335-4200
Mesabi Range Community & Technical College					
1100 Industrial Pk Dr PO Box 648	Eveleth	MN	55734	800-657-3860	218-741-3095
Minneapolis Community & Technical College					
1501 Hennepin Ave	Minneapolis	MN	55403	800-247-0911	612-659-6200
Detroit Lakes					
900 Hwy 34E	Detroit Lakes	MN	56501	800-492-4836	218-846-3700
Minnesota State Community & Technical College					
Fergus Falls					
1414 College Way	Fergus Falls	MN	56537	877-450-3322	218-736-1500
Moorhead 1900 28th Ave S	Moorhead	MN	56560	800-426-5603	218-299-6500
Minnesota West Community & Technical College					
1450 Collegeway	Worthington	MN	56187	800-657-3966	507-372-3400
Normandale Community College					
9700 France Ave S	Bloomington	MN	55431	866-880-8740	952-487-8200
North Hennepin Community College					
7411 85th Ave N	Brooklyn Park	MN	55445	800-818-0395	763-424-0702
Northland Community & Technical College					
1101 US Hwy 1 E	Thief River Falls	MN	56701	800-959-6282	218-681-0701
East Grand Forks					
2022 Central Ave NE	East Grand Forks	MN	56721	800-451-3441	218-773-3441
Rainy River Community College					
1501 Hwy 71	International Falls	MN	56649	800-456-3996	218-285-7722
Riverland Community College					
1900 Eigth Ave NW	Austin	MN	55912	800-247-5039	507-433-0600
Rochester Community & Technical College					
851 30th Ave SE	Rochester	MN	55904	800-247-1296	507-285-7210
Faribault 1225 Third St	Faribault	MN	55021	800-422-0391	507-332-5800
South Central College					
Mankato 1920 Lee Blvd	North Mankato	MN	56003	800-722-9359	507-389-7200
Vermilion Community College					
1900 E Camp St	Ely	MN	55731	800-657-3608	218-365-7200

Mississippi

				Toll-Free	Phone
Copiah-Lincoln Community College					
PO Box 649	Wesson	MS	39191	866-296-6522	601-643-8488
Natchez 11 Co-Lin Cir	Natchez	MS	39120	866-296-6522	601-442-9111
East Central Community College					
PO Box 129	Decatur	MS	39327	877-462-3222	601-635-2111
Hinds Community College					
501 E Main St PO Box 1100	Raymond	MS	39154	800-446-3722	601-857-5261
Holmes Community College					
PO Box 399	Goodman	MS	39079	800-465-6374	662-472-2312
Itawamba Community College					
Fulton 602 W Hill St	Fulton	MS	38843	800-433-3243	662-862-8000
Meridian Community College					
910 Hwy 19 N	Meridian	MS	39307	800-622-8431	601-483-8241
Jackson County					
2300 Hwy 90 PO Box 100	Gautier	MS	39553	866-735-1122	228-497-9602
Mississippi Gulf Coast Community College					
Jefferson Davis					
2226 Switzer Rd	Gulfport	MS	39507	866-735-1122	228-896-3355
Northeast Mississippi Community College					
101 Cunningham Blvd	Booneville	MS	38829	800-555-2154	662-728-7751
Pearl River Community College					
101 Hwy 11 N	Poplarville	MS	39470	877-772-2338	601-403-1000

Missouri

				Toll-Free	Phone
Cottey College					
1000 W Austin Blvd	Nevada	MO	64772	888-526-8839	417-667-8181
Crowder College					
601 Laclede Ave	Neosho	MO	64850	866-238-7788	417-451-3223
East Central College					
1964 Prairie Dell Rd	Union	MO	63084	800-273-8255	636-583-5193
Metropolitan Community College Penn Valley					
3201 SW Trafficway	Kansas City	MO	64111	866-676-6224	816-759-4000
Moberly Area Community College					
101 College Ave	Moberly	MO	65270	800-622-2070	660-263-4110
North Central Missouri College					
1301 Main St	Trenton	MO	64683	800-880-6180	660-359-3948
State Fair Community College					
3201 W 16th St	Sedalia	MO	65301	877-311-7322	660-530-5800
Three Rivers Community College					
2080 Three Rivers Blvd	Poplar Bluff	MO	63901	877-879-8722	573-840-9600

Montana

				Toll-Free	Phone
Dawson Community College					
300 College Dr	Glendive	MT	59330	800-821-8320	
Flathead Valley Community College					
777 Grandview Dr	Kalispell	MT	59901	800-313-3822	406-756-3822
Miles Community College					
2715 Dickinson St	Miles City	MT	59301	800-541-9281	406-874-6100
Salish Kootenai College					
PO Box 70	Pablo	MT	59855	877-752-6553	406-275-4800

Nebraska

				Toll-Free	Phone
McCook Community College					
1205 E Third St	McCook	NE	69001	800-658-4348	308-345-8100
Metropolitan Community College					
PO Box 3777	Omaha	NE	68103	800-228-9553	402-457-2400
Nebraska Indian Community College					
PO Box 428	Macy	NE	68039	844-440-6422	402-837-5078
North Platte Community College					
North 1101 Halligan Dr	North Platte	NE	69101	800-658-4308	308-535-3601
South					
601 W State Farm Rd	North Platte	NE	69101	800-658-4348	
Beatrice 4771 W Scott Rd	Beatrice	NE	68310	800-233-5027	402-228-3468
Southeast Community College					
Lincoln 8800 'O' St	Lincoln	NE	68520	800-642-4075	402-471-3333
Western Nebraska Community College					
1601 E 27th St	Scottsbluff	NE	69361	800-348-4435	308-635-3606

Nevada

				Toll-Free	Phone
Western Nevada Community College (WNC)					
Douglas 1680 Bently Pkwy S	Minden	NV	89423	877-838-2778	775-782-2413

New Hampshire

			Toll-Free	Phone
Lakes Region Community College (LRCC)				
379 Belmont Rd	Laconia NH	03246	800-357-2992	603-524-3207
NHTI Concord's Community College				
31 College Dr	Concord NH	03301	800-247-0179	603-271-6484
White Mountains Community College (WMCC)				
2020 Riverside Dr	Berlin NH	03570	800-445-4525	603-752-1113

New Jersey

			Toll-Free	Phone
Bergen Community College				
400 Paramus Rd	Paramus NJ	07652	877-612-5381	201-447-7200
Brookdale Community College				
765 Newman Springs Rd	Lincroft NJ	07738	866-767-9512	732-842-1900
Camden County College				
200 College Dr	Blackwood NJ	08012	888-228-2466	856-227-7200
County College of Morris				
214 Ctr Grove Rd	Randolph NJ	07869	888-726-3260	973-328-5000
Cumberland County College				
3322 College Dr	Vineland NJ	08360	800-433-3243	856-691-8600
Mercer County Community College				
PO Box B	Trenton NJ	08690	800-982-9491	609-586-4800
Kerney Ctr				
N Broad & Academy St	Trenton NJ	08608	800-982-9491	609-586-4800
West Windsor				
1200 Old Trenton Rd	West Windsor NJ	08550	800-982-9491	609-586-4800
Middlesex County College				
2600 Woodbridge Ave PO Box 3050.	Edison NJ	08818	888-442-4551	732-548-6000
Raritan Valley Community College				
PO Box 3300	Somerville NJ	08876	888-326-4058	908-526-1200
Union County College				
1033 Springfield Ave	Cranford NJ	07016	877-468-3229	908-709-7000

New Mexico

			Toll-Free	Phone
Clovis Community College (CCC)				
417 Schepps Blvd	Clovis NM	88101	800-769-1409	575-769-2811
Dona Ana Branch Community College (DACC)				
2800 N Sonoma Ranch Blvd				
PO Box 30001.	Las Cruces NM	88011	800-903-7503	575-528-7000
Eastern New Mexico University Roswell				
52 University Blvd PO Box 6000.	Roswell NM	88202	800-243-6687	
Luna Community College				
366 Luna Dr	Las Vegas NM	87701	800-588-7232	505-454-2500
New Mexico Junior College				
One Thunderbird Cir	Hobbs NM	88240	800-657-6260	505-392-4510
Carlsbad				
1500 University Dr	Carlsbad NM	88220	888-888-2199	505-234-9200
Northern New Mexico College				
921 Paseo de Onate	Espanola NM	87532	800-477-3632	505-747-2100
San Juan College				
4601 College Blvd	Farmington NM	87402	866-426-1233	505-326-3311
Valencia 280 La Entrada	Los Lunas NM	87031	800-225-5866	505-925-8580

New York

			Toll-Free	Phone
Borough of Manhattan Community College				
199 Chambers St Rm S-300.	New York NY	10007	877-222-8387	212-220-1265
Bronx Community College				
2155 University Ave	Bronx NY	10453	866-888-8777	718-289-5100
Broome Community College				
901 Front St	Binghamton NY	13905	800-836-0689	607-778-5000
Cayuga Community College				
197 Franklin St	Auburn NY	13021	866-598-8883	315-255-1743
Columbia-Greene Community College				
4400 Rt 23	Hudson NY	12534	888-668-4293	518-828-4181
Genesee Community College				
1 College Rd	Batavia NY	14020	866-225-5422	585-343-0068
Herkimer County Community College				
100 Reservoir Rd	Herkimer NY	13350	844-464-4375	315-866-0300
Hostos Community College				
500 Grand Concourse	Bronx NY	10451	888-993-7650	718-518-4444
Hudson Valley Community College				
80 Vandenburgh Ave	Troy NY	12180	877-325-4822	518-629-4822
Jamestown Community College				
525 Faulkner St PO Box 20.	Jamestown NY	14702	800-388-8557	716-338-1000
Cattaraugus County				
260 N Union St PO Box 5901.	Olean NY	14760	800-388-9776	716-376-7500
Jefferson Community College				
1220 Coffeen St	Watertown NY	13601	888-435-6522	315-786-2200
Niagara County Community College				
3111 Saunders Settlement Rd	Sanborn NY	14132	800-875-6269	716-614-6222
North Country Community College				
23 Santanoni Ave	Saranac Lake NY	12983	888-879-6222	518-891-2915
Onondaga Community College				
4941 Onondaga Rd	Syracuse NY	13215	800-827-1000	315-498-2622
Queensborough Community College				
222-05 56th Ave	Bayside NY	11364	877-253-7122	718-631-6262
Rockland Community College				
145 College Rd	Suffern NY	10901	800-722-7666	845-574-4000
Canton 34 Cornell Dr	Canton NY	13617	800-388-7123	315-386-7011
College of Technology at Alfred				
10 Upper College Dr	Alfred NY	14802	800-425-3733	607-587-4215
Delhi Two Main St	Delhi NY	13753	800-963-3544	607-746-4000
Suffolk County Community College				
Grant				
1001 Crooked Hill Rd	Brentwood NY	11717	800-621-3362	631-851-6700
Tompkins Cortland Community College				
170 N St	Dryden NY	13053	888-567-8211	607-844-8211
Ulster County Community College				
Cottekill Rd	Stone Ridge NY	12484	800-724-0833	845-687-5000

			Toll-Free	Phone
Westchester Community College				
75 Grasslands Rd	Valhalla NY	10595	800-235-7267	914-606-6600

North Carolina

			Toll-Free	Phone
Alamance Community College				
PO Box 8000	Graham NC	27253	877-667-7533	336-578-2002
Brunswick Community College				
50 College Rd	Bolivia NC	28422	800-754-1050	910-755-7300
Cape Fear Community College				
411 N Front St	Wilmington NC	28401	877-498-8868	910-362-7000
Catawba Valley Community College				
2550 US Hwy 70 SE	Hickory NC	28602	800-433-3243	828-327-7000
Central Piedmont Community College				
1201 Elizabeth Ave	Charlotte NC	28204	877-530-8815	704-330-2722
Davidson County Community College				
PO Box 1287	Lexington NC	27293	800-233-4050	336-249-8186
Edgecombe Community College				
2009 W Wilson St	Tarboro NC	27886	877-823-2378	252-823-5166
Fayetteville Technical Community College				
2201 Hull Rd	Fayetteville NC	28303	877-245-5520	910-678-8400
Gaston College 201 Hwy 321-S	Dallas NC	28034	800-634-7854	704-922-6200
Haywood Community College				
185 Freedlander Dr	Clyde NC	28721	866-468-6422	828-627-2821
Lenoir Community College				
PO Box 188	Kinston NC	28502	800-848-5497	252-527-6223
Louisburg College				
501 N Main St	Louisburg NC	27549	800-775-0208	919-496-2521
Mayland Community College				
200 Mayland Dr PO Box 547	Spruce Pine NC	28777	800-462-9526	828-765-7351
Randolph Community College				
629 Industrial Pk Ave	Asheboro NC	27205	800-433-3243	336-633-0200
Richmond Community College				
PO Box 1189	Hamlet NC	28345	800-908-9946	910-410-1700
Sandhills Community College				
3395 Airport Rd	Pinehurst NC	28374	800-338-3944	910-692-6185
South Piedmont Community College				
680 Hwy 74	Polkton NC	28135	800-766-0319	704-272-5300
Vance-Granville Community College				
South PO Box 39	Creedmoor NC	27522	877-823-2378	919-528-4737
Warren County PO Box 207	Warrenton NC	27536	877-823-2378	252-257-1900
Wayne Community College				
3000 Wayne Memorial Dr PO Box 8002	Goldsboro NC	27533	866-414-5064	919-735-5151

North Dakota

			Toll-Free	Phone
Bismarck State College				
1500 Edwards Ave	Bismarck ND	58501	800-445-5073	701-224-5400
Cankdeska Cikana Community College				
PO Box 269	Fort Totten ND	58335	888-783-1463	701-766-4415
Lake Region State College				
1801 College Dr N	Devils Lake ND	58301	800-443-1313	701-662-1514
Minot State University Bottineau				
105 Simrall Blvd	Bottineau ND	58318	800-542-6866	701-228-5451
North Dakota State College of Science				
800 Sixth St N	Wahpeton ND	58076	800-342-4325	701-671-2401
Turtle Mountain Community College				
10145 BIA Rd 7	Belcourt ND	58316	800-827-1100	701-477-7862
Williston State College				
1410 University Ave PO Box 1326	Williston ND	58802	888-863-9455	701-774-4200

Ohio

			Toll-Free	Phone
Cincinnati State Technical & Community College				
3520 Central Pkwy	Cincinnati OH	45223	877-569-0115	513-569-1500
Columbus State Community College				
550 E Spring St	Columbus OH	43215	800-621-6407	614-287-2400
Eastern				
4250 Richmond Rd	Highland Hills OH	44122	800-954-8742	216-987-2024
Cuyahoga Community College				
Metropolitan				
2900 Community College Ave	Cleveland OH	44115	800-954-8742	216-987-4200
Western				
11000 Pleasant Valley Rd	Parma OH	44130	800-954-8742	216-987-2800
Edison Community College				
1973 Edison Dr	Piqua OH	45356	800-922-3722	937-778-8600
Ashtabula 3300 Lake Rd W	Ashtabula OH	44004	800-988-5368	440-964-3322
Lakeland Community College				
7700 Clocktower Dr	Kirtland OH	44094	800-589-8520	440-525-7000
Lorain County Community College				
1005 N Abbe Rd	Elyria OH	44035	800-995-5222	440-365-5222
Findlay 3200 Bright Rd	Findlay OH	45840	800-466-9367	
Owens Community College				
Toledo 30335 Oregon Rd	Perrysburg OH	43551	800-466-9367	419-661-7000
Southern State Community College				
North 1850 Davids Dr	Wilmington OH	45177	877-644-6562	937-382-6645
South 12681 US Rt 62	Sardinia OH	45171	877-644-6562	937-695-0307
Terra Community College				
2830 Napoleon Rd	Fremont OH	43420	800-334-3886	419-334-8400
University of Akron Wayne College				
1901 Smucker Rd	Orrville OH	44667	800-221-8308	330-683-2010
University of Cincinnati Clermont College				
4200 Clermont College Dr	Batavia OH	45103	866-446-2822	513-732-5200
University of Rio Grande Rio Grande Community College				
218 N College Ave	Rio Grande OH	45674	800-282-7201	740-245-5353
Wright State University Lake				
7600 Lk Campus Dr	Celina OH	45822	800-237-1477	419-586-0300

Oklahoma

			Toll-Free	Phone
Comanche Nation College				
1608 SW Ninth St	Lawton OK	73501	877-591-0203	580-591-0203

					Toll-Free	Phone

Connors State College
1000 College Rd .... Warner OK 74469 **888-594-5171** 918-463-2931
Murray State College
One Murray Campus .... Tishomingo OK 73460 **800-342-0698** 580-371-2371
Northern Oklahoma College
1220 E Grand St PO Box 310 .... Tonkawa OK 74653 **866-278-7134** 580-628-6200
Oklahoma City
900 N Portland Ave .... Oklahoma City OK 73107 **800-560-4099** 405-947-4421
Redlands Community College
1300 S Country Club Rd .... El Reno OK 73036 **866-415-6367** 405-262-2552
Rogers State University Bartlesville
1701 W Will Rogers Blvd .... Claremore OK 74107 **800-256-7511** 918-343-7777
Rogers State University Pryor
421 S Elliott St .... Pryor OK 74361 **800-256-7511** 918-825-6117
Tulsa Community College
Metro 909 S Boston Ave .... Tulsa OK 74119 **866-970-0233** 918-595-7000
Western Oklahoma State College
2801 N Main St .... Altus OK 73521 **800-662-1113** 580-477-2000

Oregon

					Toll-Free	Phone

Clatsop Community College
1653 Jerome Ave .... Astoria OR 97103 **855-252-8767** 503-325-0910
Lane Community College
4000 E 30th Ave .... Eugene OR 97405 **800-321-2211** 541-463-3000
Florence 3149 Oak St .... Florence OR 97439 **800-222-3290** 541-997-8444
Rogue Community College
3345 Redwood Hwy .... Grants Pass OR 97527 **800-411-6508** 541-956-7500
Southwestern Oregon Community College
1988 Newmark Ave .... Coos Bay OR 97420 **800-962-2838** 541-888-2525
Tillamook Bay Community College
4301 Third St .... Tillamook OR 97141 **888-306-8222** 503-842-8222
Treasure Valley Community College
650 College Blvd .... Ontario OR 97914 **888-292-5247** 541-881-8822
Umpqua Community College
1140 Umpqva College Rd PO Box 967 .... Roseburg OR 97470 **800-820-5161** 541-440-4600

Pennsylvania

					Toll-Free	Phone

Butler County Community College
107 College Dr .... Butler PA 16002 **888-826-2829** 724-287-8711
Community College of Beaver County
One Campus Dr .... Monaca PA 15061 **800-335-0222** 724-775-8561
Delaware County Community College
901 Media Line Rd .... Media PA 19063 **800-908-9946** 610-359-5000
Harcum College
750 Montgomery Ave .... Bryn Mawr PA 19010 **800-650-0035** 610-525-4100
Harrisburg Area Community College
Gettysburg
731 Old Harrisburg Rd .... Gettysburg PA 17325 **800-222-4222** 717-337-3855
Lebanon 735 Cumberland St .... Lebanon PA 17042 **800-222-4222** 717-270-4222
Lackawanna College
501 Vine St .... Scranton PA 18509 **877-346-3552** 570-961-7810
Lehigh Carbon Community College
4525 Education Pk Dr .... Schnecksville PA 18078 **800-414-3975*** 610-799-2121
General
Morgan Ctr 234 High St .... Tamaqua PA 18252 **800-424-2460** 570-668-6880
Luzerne County Community College
1333 S Prospect St .... Nanticoke PA 18634 **800-377-5222**
NanoHorizons Inc
270 Rolling Ridge Dr Ste 100 .... Bellefonte PA 16823 **866-584-6235** 814-355-4700
Northampton Community College
3835 Green Pond Rd .... Bethlehem PA 18020 **877-543-0998** 610-861-5300
Monroe
Three Old Mill Rd PO Box 530 .... Tannersville PA 18372 **877-543-0998** 570-620-9221
Beaver 100 University Dr .... Monaca PA 15061 **877-564-6778** 724-773-3500
DuBois One College Pl .... Du Bois PA 15801 **800-346-7627** 814-375-4700
Fayette
2201 University Dr .... Lemont Furnace PA 15456 **877-568-4130** 724-430-4100
Hazleton 76 University Dr .... Hazleton PA 18202 **800-279-8495** 570-450-3000
Mont Alto One Campus Dr .... Mont Alto PA 17237 **800-392-6173** 717-749-6000
Schuylkill
200 University Dr .... Schuylkill Haven PA 17972 **800-243-2374** 570-385-6000
Shenango 147 Shenango Ave .... Sharon PA 16146 **888-275-7009** 724-983-2803
York 1031 Edgecomb Ave .... York PA 17403 **800-778-6227** 717-771-4000
Reading Area Community College
10 S Second St PO Box 1706 .... Reading PA 19603 **800-626-1665** 610-372-4721
University of Pittsburgh
Titusville 504 E Main St .... Titusville PA 16354 **888-878-0462**
Valley Forge Military Academy & College
1001 Eagle Rd .... Wayne PA 19087 **800-234-8362** 610-989-1300
Westmoreland County Community College
145 Pavilion Ln .... Youngwood PA 15697 **800-262-2103** 724-925-4000

Quebec

					Toll-Free	Phone

College Merici
755 Ch St-Louis .... Quebec City QC G1S1C1 **800-208-1463** 418-683-1591

South Carolina

					Toll-Free	Phone

Clinton Junior College
1029 Crawford Rd .... Rock Hill SC 29730 **877-837-9645** 803-327-7402
Greenville Technical College
Barton
506 S Pleasantburg Dr .... Greenville SC 29607 **800-723-0673*** 864-250-8111
All
Greer 2522 Locust Hill Rd .... Taylors SC 29687 **800-723-0673**
Midlands Technical College
PO Box 2408 .... Columbia SC 29202 **800-922-8038** 803-738-1400
North Greenville University
7801 N Tigerville Rd PO Box 1892 .... Tigerville SC 29688 **800-468-6642** 864-977-7000

Northeastern Technical College
1201 Chesterfield Hwy .... Cheraw SC 29520 **800-921-7399** 843-921-6900
Spartanburg Methodist College
1000 Powell Mill Rd .... Spartanburg SC 29301 **800-772-7286** 864-587-4000
Union 401 E Main St .... Union SC 29379 **800-768-5566** 864-429-8728
Williamsburg Technical College
601 MLK Jr Ave .... Kingstree SC 29556 **800-768-2021** 843-355-4110
York Technical College
452 S Anderson Rd .... Rock Hill SC 29730 **800-922-8324** 803-327-8000

South Dakota

					Toll-Free	Phone

Kilian Community College
300 E Sixth St .... Sioux Falls SD 57103 **800-888-1147** 605-221-3100
Lake Area Technical Institute
230 11th St NE PO Box 730 .... Watertown SD 57201 **800-657-4344** 605-882-5284
Mitchell Technical Institute
821 N Capital St .... Mitchell SD 57301 **800-952-0042** 800-675-1969

Tennessee

					Toll-Free	Phone

Chattanooga State Technical Community College
4501 Amnicola Hwy .... Chattanooga TN 37406 **866-547-3733** 423-697-4400
Hiwassee College
225 Hiwassee College Dr .... Madisonville TN 37354 **800-356-2187** 423-442-2001
Motlow State Community College
PO Box 8500 .... Lynchburg TN 37352 **800-654-4877** 931-393-1500
Roane State Community College
276 Patton Ln .... Harriman TN 37748 **800-343-9104** 865-354-3000
Southwest Tennessee Community College
PO Box 780 .... Memphis TN 38101 **877-717-7822** 901-333-5000
Volunteer State Community College
1480 Nashville Pk .... Gallatin TN 37066 **888-335-8722** 615-452-8600
Walters State Community College
500 S Davy Crockett Pkwy .... Morristown TN 37813 **800-225-4770** 423-585-2600

Texas

					Toll-Free	Phone

Austin Community College (ACC)
5930 Middle Fiskville Rd .... Austin TX 78752 **877-442-3522** 512-223-7000
Eastview 3401 Webberville Rd .... Austin TX 78702 **888-626-1697** 512-223-5100
Northridge
11928 Stonehollow Dr .... Austin TX 78758 **877-990-0462** 512-223-4000
Pinnacle 7748 Hwy 290 W .... Austin TX 78736 **888-626-1697** 512-223-8001
Rio Grande
1212 Rio Grande St .... Austin TX 78701 **877-990-0462** 512-223-3000
Riverside 1020 Grove Blvd .... Austin TX 78741 **877-990-0462** 512-223-6000
Brazosport College
500 College Dr .... Lake Jackson TX 77566 **877-717-7873** 979-230-3000
Central Texas College
PO Box 1800 .... Killeen TX 76540 **800-792-3348** 254-526-7161
Clarendon College
1122 College Dr PO Box 968 .... Clarendon TX 79226 **800-687-9737** 806-874-3571
Coastal Bend College
Beeville 3800 Charco Rd .... Beeville TX 78102 **866-722-2838** 361-358-2838
Del Mar College
East
101 Baldwin Blvd .... Corpus Christi TX 78404 **800-652-3357** 361-698-1200
Eastfield College
3737 Motley Dr .... Mesquite TX 75150 **800-260-8000** 972-860-7100
El Paso Community College
Valle Verde 919 Hunter Dr .... El Paso TX 79915 **800-531-8292** 915-831-2000
Galveston College
4015 Ave Q .... Galveston TX 77550 **866-483-4242** 409-763-6551
Howard College
1001 Birdwell Ln .... Big Spring TX 79720 **877-898-3833** 432-264-5000
Kingwood College
20000 Kingwood Dr .... Kingwood TX 77339 **800-883-7939** 281-312-1600
Lamar State College
Port Arthur PO Box 310 .... Port Arthur TX 77641 **800-477-5872** 409-983-4921
McLennan Community College
1400 College Dr .... Waco TX 76708 **866-339-5555** 254-299-8000
Navarro College
3200 W Seventh Ave .... Corsicana TX 75110 **800-628-2776** 903-874-6501
Northeast Texas Community College
1735 Chapel Hill Rd .... Mount Pleasant TX 75455 **800-870-0142** 903-572-1911
Odessa College
201 W University Blvd .... Odessa TX 79764 **866-968-2862** 432-335-6400
Paris Junior College
2400 Clarksville St .... Paris TX 75460 **800-232-5804** 903-785-7661
Ranger College
1100 College Cir .... Ranger TX 76470 **800-772-1213** 254-647-3234
Smith System Driver Improvement Institute Inc
2201 Brookhollow Plz Dr Ste 200 .... Arlington TX 76006 **800-777-7648** 817-652-6969
Southwest Texas Junior College
2401 Garner Field Rd .... Uvalde TX 78801 **888-886-8490** 830-278-4401
Northeast 828 W Harwood Rd .... Hurst TX 76054 **800-799-7233** 817-515-8223
Tarrant County College
Northwest
4801 Marine Creek Pkwy .... Fort Worth TX 76179 **800-799-7233** 817-515-7100
Temple College
2600 S First St .... Temple TX 76504 **800-460-4636*** 254-298-8300
Admissions
Texarkana College
2500 N Robison Rd .... Texarkana TX 75599 **877-275-4377** 903-838-4541
Texas Southmost College
80 Fort Brown St .... Brownsville TX 78520 **800-850-0160** 956-882-8200
Abilene 650 E Hwy 80 .... Abilene TX 79601 **800-852-8784** 325-672-7091
Harlingen 1902 N Loop 499 .... Harlingen TX 78550 **800-852-8784** 956-364-4000
Texas State Technical College
Sweetwater
300 Homer K Taylor Dr .... Sweetwater TX 79556 **877-450-3595** 325-235-7300
Waco 3801 Campus Dr .... Waco TX 76705 **800-792-8784** 254-799-3611

	City	State	ZIP	Toll-Free	Phone
Trinity Valley Community College					
Athens 100 Cardinal Dr	Athens	TX	75751	**866-882-2937**	903-675-6200
Tyler Junior College					
PO Box 9020	Tyler	TX	75711	**800-687-5680**	903-510-2523
Vernon College					
4400 College Dr	Vernon	TX	76384	**866-336-9371**	940-552-6291
Weatherford College					
225 College Pk Dr	Weatherford	TX	76086	**800-287-5471**	817-594-5471
Western Texas College					
6200 College Ave	Snyder	TX	79549	**888-468-6982**	325-573-8511
Wharton County Junior College					
911 Boling Hwy	Wharton	TX	77488	**800-561-9252**	979-532-4560
Sugar Land					
14004 University Blvd	Sugar Land	TX	77479	**800-561-9252**	281-243-8447

Utah

	City	State	ZIP	Toll-Free	Phone
College of Eastern Utah					
451 E 400 N	Price	UT	84501	**800-336-2381**	435-797-1000
San Juan					
639 West 100 South	Blanding	UT	84511	**800-395-2969**	435-678-2201
Snow College					
150 College Ave PO Box 1028	Ephraim	UT	84627	**800-848-3399**	435-283-7000
Stevens Henager College					
1890 South 1350 West	Ogden	UT	84401	**800-622-2640**	
Utah Valley State College					
800 W University Pkwy	Orem	UT	84058	**800-952-8220**	801-863-4636

Vermont

	City	State	ZIP	Toll-Free	Phone
Community College of Vermont					
Bennington 324 Main St	Bennington	VT	05201	**800-431-0025**	802-447-2361
Brattleboro					
70 Landmark Hill Ste 101	Brattleboro	VT	05301	**800-431-0025**	802-254-6370
Middlebury					
10 Merchants Row Ste 223	Middlebury	VT	05753	**800-431-0025**	802-388-3032
Montpelier PO Box 489	Montpelier	VT	05602	**800-228-6686**	802-828-4060
Morrisville					
197 Harrell St Ste 2	Morrisville	VT	05661	**800-431-0025**	802-888-4258
Newport 100 Main St Ste 150	Newport	VT	05855	**800-431-0025**	802-334-3387
Rutland 60 W St	Rutland	VT	05701	**800-228-6686**	802-786-6996
Upper Valley					
145 Billings Farm Rd	White River Junction	VT	05001	**800-431-0025**	802-295-8822

Virginia

	City	State	ZIP	Toll-Free	Phone
Blue Ridge Community College					
1 College Ln PO Box 80	Weyers Cave	VA	24486	**888-750-2722**	540-234-9261
Danville Community College					
1008 S Main St	Danville	VA	24541	**800-560-4291**	434-797-2222
Lord Fairfax Community College					
Middletown					
173 Skirmisher Ln	Middletown	VA	22645	**800-906-5322**	540-868-7000
New River Community College					
5251 College PO Box 1127	Dublin	VA	24084	**866-462-6722**	540-674-3600
Alexandria					
3001 N Beauregard St	Alexandria	VA	22311	**855-259-1019**	703-845-6200
Northern Virginia Community College					
Annandale					
8333 Little River Tpke	Annandale	VA	22003	**877-408-2028**	703-323-3000
Manassas 6901 Sudley Rd	Manassas	VA	20109	**855-259-1019**	703-257-6600
Patrick Henry Community College					
645 Patriot Ave PO Box 5311	Martinsville	VA	24112	**855-874-6692**	276-638-8777
Paul D Camp Community College					
100 N College Dr PO Box 737	Franklin	VA	23851	**866-933-0508**	757-569-6700
Hobbs Suffolk 271 Kenyon Rd	Suffolk	VA	23434	**855-877-3918**	757-925-6300
Rappahannock Community College					
Glenns 12745 College Dr	Glenns	VA	23149	**800-836-9381**	804-758-6700
Warsaw 52 Campus Dr	Warsaw	VA	22572	**800-836-9381**	804-333-6700
Southside Virginia Community College					
109 Campus Dr	Alberta	VA	23821	**888-220-7822**	434-949-1000
Southwest Virginia Community College					
724 Community College Rd	Cedar Bluff	VA	24609	**855-877-3944**	276-964-2555
Chesapeake 1428 Cedar Rd	Chesapeake	VA	23322	**800-371-0898**	757-822-5100
Norfolk 315 Granby St	Norfolk	VA	23510	**800-371-0898**	757-822-1110
Tidewater Community College					
Portsmouth					
7000 College Dr	Portsmouth	VA	23703	**800-371-0898**	757-822-2124
Virginia Beach					
1700 College Crescent	Virginia Beach	VA	23453	**800-371-0898**	757-822-7100
Virginia Western Community College					
3094 Colonial Ave PO Box 14007	Roanoke	VA	24038	**855-874-6690**	540-857-8922

Washington

	City	State	ZIP	Toll-Free	Phone
Edmonds Community College					
20000 68th Ave W	Lynnwood	WA	98036	**866-886-4854**	425-640-1500
Everett Community College					
2000 Tower St	Everett	WA	98201	**866-575-9027**	425-388-9100
Grays Harbor College					
1620 Edward P Smith Dr	Aberdeen	WA	98520	**800-562-4830**	360-532-9020
Lower Columbia College					
1600 Maple St PO Box 3010	Longview	WA	98632	**866-900-2311**	360-442-2301
North Seattle Community College					
9600 College Way N	Seattle	WA	98103	**877-299-3593**	206-527-3600
Northwest Indian College					
2522 Kwina Rd	Bellingham	WA	98226	**866-676-2772**	360-676-2772
Olympic College					
1600 Chester Ave	Bremerton	WA	98337	**800-259-6718**	360-792-6050
Shelton 937 W Alpine Way	Shelton	WA	98584	**800-259-6718**	360-427-2119
Pierce College					
Puyallup 1601 39th Ave SE	Puyallup	WA	98374	**877-353-6763**	253-840-8400
Shoreline Community College					
16101 Greenwood Ave N	Shoreline	WA	98133	**866-427-4747**	206-546-4101
Skagit Valley College					
2405 E College Way	Mount Vernon	WA	98273	**877-385-5360**	360-416-7600
Spokane Community College					
1810 N Greene St	Spokane	WA	99217	**800-248-5644**	509-533-7000
Spokane Falls Community College					
3410 W Ft George Wright Dr	Spokane	WA	99224	**888-509-7944**	509-533-3500
Walla Walla Community College					
500 Tausick Way	Walla Walla	WA	99362	**877-992-9922**	509-522-2500
Wenatchee Valley College					
1300 Fifth St	Wenatchee	WA	98801	**877-982-4968**	509-682-6800
Whatcom Community College					
237 W Kellogg Rd	Bellingham	WA	98226	**855-767-9003**	360-676-2170

West Virginia

	City	State	ZIP	Toll-Free	Phone
Eastern West Virginia Community & Technical College					
316 Eastern Dr	Moorefield	WV	26836	**877-982-2322**	304-434-8000
Potomac State College					
101 Ft Ave	Keyser	WV	26726	**800-262-7332**	304-788-6800
Parkersburg					
300 Campus Dr	Parkersburg	WV	26104	**800-982-9887**	304-424-8000

Wisconsin

	City	State	ZIP	Toll-Free	Phone
College of Menominee Nation					
PO Box 1179	Keshena	WI	54135	**800-567-2344**	715-799-5600
Lac Courte Oreilles Ojibwa Community College					
13466 W Trepania Rd	Hayward	WI	54843	**888-526-6221**	715-634-4790
Baraboo/Sauk County					
1006 Connie Rd	Baraboo	WI	53913	**800-621-7440**	608-355-5200
Barron County					
1800 College Dr	Rice Lake	WI	54868	**800-608-4578**	715-234-8176
Fox Valley 1478 Midway Rd	Menasha	WI	54952	**800-273-8255**	920-832-2600
Manitowoc 705 Viebahn St	Manitowoc	WI	54220	**800-657-3866**	920-683-4700
Marathon County					
518 S Seventh Ave	Wausau	WI	54401	**888-367-8962**	715-261-6100
Marshfield/Wood County					
2000 W Fifth St	Marshfield	WI	54449	**800-273-8255**	715-389-6530
Richland					
1200 Hwy 14 W	Richland Center	WI	53581	**800-947-3529**	608-647-6186
Washington County					
400 S University Dr	West Bend	WI	53095	**800-240-0276**	262-335-5200

Wyoming

	City	State	ZIP	Toll-Free	Phone
Casper College					
125 College Dr	Casper	WY	82601	**800-442-2963**	307-268-2110
Central Wyoming College					
2660 Peck Ave	Riverton	WY	82501	**800-735-8418**	307-855-2000
Eastern Wyoming College					
3200 W 'C' St	Torrington	WY	82240	**800-658-3195**	307-532-8200
Laramie County Community College					
1400 E College Dr	Cheyenne	WY	82007	**800-522-2993**	307-778-5222
Albany County					
1125 Boulder Dr	Laramie	WY	82070	**800-522-2993**	307-721-5138
Northwest College					
231 W Sixth St	Powell	WY	82435	**800-560-4692**	307-754-6000
Sheridan College					
Gillette 300 W Sinclair St	Gillette	WY	82718	**800-913-9139**	307-686-0254
Western Wyoming Community College					
2500 College Dr	Rock Springs	WY	82901	**800-226-1181**	307-382-1600

162 COLLEGES - CULINARY ARTS

	City	State	ZIP	Toll-Free	Phone
Arizona Culinary Institute					
10585 N 114th St Ste 401	Scottsdale	AZ	85259	**866-294-2433**	480-603-1066
Baltimore International College					
17 Commerce St	Baltimore	MD	21202	**800-624-9926**	410-752-4710
Capital Culinary Institute of Keiser College					
Melbourne					
900 S Babcock St	Melbourne	FL	32901	**877-636-3618**	321-409-4800
Cooking & Hospitality Institute of Chicago					
361 W Chestnut St	Chicago	IL	60610	**877-828-7772***	312-944-0882
*Admissions					
Culinary Institute Alain & Marie LeNotre					
7070 Allensby	Houston	TX	77022	**888-536-6873**	713-692-0077
Culinary Institute of America					
1946 Campus Dr	Hyde Park	NY	12538	**800-285-4627***	845-452-9430
*Admissions					
Culinary Institute of Charleston					
7000 Rivers Ave	Charleston	SC	29406	**877-349-7184**	843-574-6111
Florida Culinary Institute					
2410 Metro Centre Blvd	West Palm Beach	FL	33407	**800-254-0547**	561-842-8324
French Culinary Institute					
462 Broadway	New York	NY	10013	**888-324-2433**	
Institute of Culinary Education					
50 W 23rd St	New York	NY	10010	**800-522-4610**	212-847-0700
Kendall College					
900 N North Branch St	Chicago	IL	60622	**866-667-3344**	312-752-2000
Kitchen Academy					
6370 W Sunset Blvd	Hollywood	CA	90028	**866-548-2223**	
L'Academie de Cuisine Inc					
16006 Industrial Dr	Gaithersburg	MD	20877	**800-664-2433**	301-670-8670
Le Cordon Bleu College of Culinary Arts					
Atlanta 1927 Lakeside Pkwy	Tucker	GA	30084	**888-549-8222**	770-938-4711
LINCOLN EDUCATIONAL SERVICES					
85 Sigourney St	Hartford	CT	06105	**800-762-4337**	800-254-0547
Suffield 8 PROGRESS DR	Shelton	CT	06484	**800-254-0547**	203-929-0592
Louisiana Culinary Institute					
10550 Airline Hwy	Baton Rouge	LA	70816	**877-533-3198**	

		Toll-Free	Phone
New England Culinary Institute			
56 College St	Montpelier VT 05602	**877-223-6324**	802-223-6324
Robert Morris University Institute of Culinary Arts			
401 S State St	Chicago IL 60605	**800-762-5960**	312-935-4100
Dupage 905 Meridian Lk Dr	Aurora IL 60504	**800-762-5960**	
Sclafani's Cooking School Inc			
107 Gennaro Pl	Metairie LA 70001	**800-583-1282**	504-833-7861
Scottsdale Culinary Institute			
8100 E Camelback Rd Ste 1001	Scottsdale AZ 85251	**888-557-4222**	480-990-3773
Stratford University School of Culinary Arts			
7777 Leesburg Pk	Falls Church VA 22043	**800-444-0804**	703-821-8570

163   COLLEGES - FINE ARTS

SEE ALSO Vocational & Technical Schools ; Colleges & Universities - Four-Year

		Toll-Free	Phone
American Academy of Art			
332 S Michigan Ave 3rd Fl	Chicago IL 60604	**888-461-0600**	312-461-0600
American Academy of Dramatic Arts			
120 Madison Ave	New York NY 10016	**800-463-8990**	212-686-9244
Antonelli Institute			
300 Montgomery Ave	Erdenheim PA 19038	**800-722-7871**	215-836-2222
Art Academy of Cincinnati			
1212 Jackson St	Cincinnati OH 45202	**800-323-5692**	513-562-6262
Art Institute of Atlanta			
6600 Peachtree Dunwoody Rd NE 100 Embassy Row.	Atlanta GA 30328	**800-275-4242**	770-394-8300
Art Institute of Boston at Lesley (AIB)			
700 Beacon St Ste 202	Boston MA 02215	**800-773-0494**	617-585-6600
Inland Empire			
674 E Brier Dr	San Bernardino CA 92408	**800-353-0812**	909-915-2100
Los Angeles			
2900 31st St	Santa Monica CA 90405	**888-646-4610**	310-752-4700
Art Institute of California			
San Diego			
7650 Mission Valley Rd	San Diego CA 92108	**888-624-0300**	858-598-1200
San Francisco			
1170 Market St	San Francisco CA 94102	**888-493-3261**	415-865-0198
Art Institute of Charlotte			
2110 Water Ridge Pkwy 3 LakePointe Plz	Charlotte NC 28217	**800-872-4417**	704-357-8020
Art Institute of Colorado			
1200 Lincoln St	Denver CO 80203	**800-275-2420**	303-837-0825
Art Institute of Dallas			
8080 Pk Ln Ste 100	Dallas TX 75231	**800-275-4243**	214-692-8080
Art Institute of Fort Lauderdale			
1799 SE 17th St	Fort Lauderdale FL 33316	**800-275-7603**	954-463-3000
Art Institute of Houston			
1900 Yorktown St	Houston TX 77056	**800-275-4244**	713-623-2040
Art Institute of Indianapolis			
3500 Depauw Blvd	Indianapolis IN 46268	**866-441-9031**	317-613-4800
Art Institute of Las Vegas			
2350 Corporate Cir	Henderson NV 89074	**800-833-2678**	702-369-9944
Art Institute of Ohio			
Cincinnati			
8845 Covernor's Hill Dr Ste 100	Cincinnati OH 45249	**866-613-5184**	513-833-2400
Art Institute of Philadelphia			
1622 Chestnut St	Philadelphia PA 19103	**800-275-2474**	215-567-7080
Art Institute of Pittsburgh			
420 Blvd of the Allies	Pittsburgh PA 15219	**800-275-2470**	412-263-6600
Art Institute of Portland			
1122 NW Davis St	Portland OR 97209	**888-228-6528**	503-228-6528
Art Institute of Seattle			
2323 Elliott Ave	Seattle WA 98121	**800-275-2471**	206-448-0900
Art Institute of Tampa			
4401 N Himes Ave Ste 150	Tampa FL 33614	**866-703-3277**	813-873-2112
Art Institute of Washington			
1820 N Ft Myer Dr	Arlington VA 22209	**877-303-3771**	703-358-9550
Art Institutes International Minnesota			
15 S Ninth St	Minneapolis MN 55402	**800-777-3643**	612-332-3361
Bradley Academy for the Visual Arts			
1409 Williams Rd	York PA 17402	**800-864-7725**	717-755-2300
California College of the Arts			
Oakland 5212 Broadway	Oakland CA 94618	**800-447-1278**	510-594-3600
San Francisco			
1111 Eigth St	San Francisco CA 94107	**800-447-1278**	415-703-9500
California Design College			
3440 Wilshire Blvd 10th Fl	Los Angeles CA 90010	**877-468-6232**	213-251-3636
California Institute of the Arts			
24700 McBean Pkwy	Valencia CA 91355	**800-545-2787**	661-255-1050
Cleveland Institute of Art			
11141 E Blvd	Cleveland OH 44106	**800-223-4700**	
Columbus College of Art & Design			
60 Cleveland Ave	Columbus OH 43215	**877-997-2223**	614-224-9101
Cornish College of the Arts			
710 E Roy St	Seattle WA 98121	**800-726-2787**	206-323-1400
Fashion Institute of Design & Merchandising			
Los Angeles			
919 S Grand Ave	Los Angeles CA 90015	**800-624-1200***	213-624-1200
Admissions			
Orange County			
17590 Gillette Ave	Irvine CA 92614	**888-974-3436**	949-851-6200
San Diego 350 Tenth Ave	San Diego CA 92101	**800-243-3436**	619-235-2049
San Francisco			
55 Stockton St	San Francisco CA 94108	**800-422-3436**	415-675-5200
Chicago			
350 N Orleans St Ste 136-L	Chicago IL 60654	**800-351-3450**	312-280-3500
Illinois Institute of Art			
Schaumburg 1000 N Plz Dr	Schaumburg IL 60173	**800-314-3450**	847-619-3450
Institute of American Indian Arts (IAIA)			
83 Avan Nu Po Rd	Santa Fe NM 87508	**800-804-6422**	505-424-2300
Chicago			
One N State St Ste 500	Chicago IL 60602	**888-318-6111**	312-386-7681
Las Vegas			
2495 Village View Dr	Henderson NV 89074	**866-400-4238**	702-990-0150

		Toll-Free	Phone
International Academy of Design & Technology			
Tampa 5104 Eisenhower Blvd	Tampa FL 33634	**866-302-4238***	813-881-0007
General			
Kansas City Art Institute			
4415 Warwick Blvd	Kansas City MO 64111	**800-522-5224**	816-474-5224
Maine College of Art			
97 Spring St	Portland ME 04101	**800-639-4808**	207-775-3052
Memphis College of Art			
1930 Poplar Ave	Memphis TN 38104	**800-727-1088**	901-272-5100
Miami International University of Art & Design			
1501 Biscayne Blvd	Miami FL 33132	**800-225-9023**	305-428-5700
Minneapolis College of Art & Design			
2501 Stevens Ave	Minneapolis MN 55404	**800-874-6223**	612-874-3760
Moore College of Art & Design			
20th St & the Pkwy	Philadelphia PA 19103	**800-523-2025**	215-965-4000
New England Institute of Art			
10 Brookline Pl W	Brookline MA 02445	**800-903-4425**	617-739-1700
New Hampshire Institute of Art			
148 Concord St	Manchester NH 03104	**866-241-4918**	603-623-0313
Otis College of Art & Design			
9045 Lincoln Blvd	Los Angeles CA 90045	**800-527-6847**	310-665-6820
Pennsylvania Academy of the Fine Arts			
School of Fine Arts			
118 N Broad St	Philadelphia PA 19102	**800-799-7233**	215-972-7600
Rhode Island School of Design			
Two College St	Providence RI 02903	**800-364-7473**	401-454-6100
Ringling College of Art & Design			
2700 N Tamiami Trl	Sarasota FL 34234	**800-255-7695**	941-351-5100
San Francisco Art Institute			
800 Chestnut St	San Francisco CA 94133	**800-345-7324**	415-771-7020
Savannah College of Art & Design			
Atlanta			
1600 Peachtree St PO Box 77300	Atlanta GA 30357	**877-722-3285**	404-253-2700
School of Visual Arts			
209 E 23rd St	New York NY 10010	**800-436-4204**	212-592-2000
University of the Arts			
320 S Broad St	Philadelphia PA 19102	**800-616-2787**	215-717-6049
Virginia Marti College of Art & Design			
11724 Detroit Ave	Lakewood OH 44107	**800-473-4350**	216-221-8584
Watkins College of Art & Design			
2298 Rose Parks Blvd	Nashville TN 37228	**866-877-6395**	615-383-4848

164   COLLEGES - TRIBAL

SEE ALSO Colleges - Community & Junior
Tribal Colleges generally serve geographically isolated American Indian populations that have no other means of accessing education beyond the high school level. They are unique institutions that combine personal attention with cultural relevance.

		Toll-Free	Phone
Bay Mills Community College			
12214 W Lakeshore Dr	Brimley MI 49715	**800-844-2622**	906-248-3354
Cankdeska Cikana Community College			
PO Box 269	Fort Totten ND 58335	**888-783-1463**	701-766-4415
College of Menominee Nation			
PO Box 1179	Keshena WI 54135	**800-567-2344**	715-799-5600
Comanche Nation College			
1608 SW Ninth St	Lawton OK 73501	**877-591-0203**	580-591-0203
Fond du Lac Tribal & Community College			
2101 14th St	Cloquet MN 55720	**800-657-3712**	218-879-0800
Institute of American Indian Arts (IAIA)			
83 Avan Nu Po Rd	Santa Fe NM 87508	**800-804-6422**	505-424-2300
Lac Courte Oreilles Ojibwa Community College			
13466 W Trepania Rd	Hayward WI 54843	**888-526-6221**	715-634-4790
Leech Lake Tribal College			
6945 Little Wolf Rd PO Box 180	Cass Lake MN 56633	**800-627-3529**	218-335-4200
Nebraska Indian Community College			
PO Box 428	Macy NE 68039	**844-440-6422**	402-837-5078
Northwest Indian College			
2522 Kwina Rd	Bellingham WA 98226	**866-676-2772**	360-676-2772
Saginaw Chippewa Tribal College			
2274 Enterprise Dr	Mount Pleasant MI 48858	**800-225-8172**	989-775-4123
Salish Kootenai College			
PO Box 70	Pablo MT 59855	**877-752-6553**	406-275-4800
Southwestern Indian Polytechnic Institute			
9169 Coors Blvd NW PO Box 10146	Albuquerque NM 87120	**800-586-7474**	505-346-2306
Turtle Mountain Community College			
10145 BIA Rd 7	Belcourt ND 58316	**800-827-1100**	701-477-7862

165   COLLEGES - WOMEN'S (FOUR-YEAR)

		Toll-Free	Phone
Agnes Scott College			
141 E College Ave	Decatur GA 30030	**800-868-8602**	404-471-6000
Alverno College			
PO Box 343922	Milwaukee WI 53234	**800-933-3401**	414-382-6100
Bay Path College			
588 Longmeadow St	Longmeadow MA 01106	**800-782-7284**	
Bennett College			
900 E Washington St	Greensboro NC 27401	**800-413-5323***	336-370-8624
Admissions			
Blue Mountain College			
PO Box 160	Blue Mountain MS 38610	**800-235-0136**	662-685-4771
Brenau University			
500 Washington St	Gainesville GA 30501	**800-252-5119**	770-534-6299
Bryn Mawr College			
101 N Merion Ave	Bryn Mawr PA 19010	**800-262-2586***	610-526-5000
Admissions			
Carlow University			
3333 Fifth Ave	Pittsburgh PA 15213	**800-333-2275**	412-578-6000
Cedar Crest College			
100 College Dr	Allentown PA 18104	**800-360-1222***	610-437-4471
Admissions			
Chatham University			
1 Woodland Rd	Pittsburgh PA 15232	**800-837-1290**	412-365-1100

			Toll-Free	Phone

College of New Rochelle
29 Castle Pl . . . . New Rochelle NY 10805 **800-933-5923** 914-654-5000

College of Notre Dame of Maryland
4701 N Charles St . . . . Baltimore MD 21210 **800-753-3757*** 410-435-0100
*Admissions

College of Saint Catherine
2004 Randolph Ave . . . . Saint Paul MN 55105 **800-945-4599** 651-690-6000
Minneapolis
601 25th Ave S . . . . Minneapolis MN 55454 **800-945-4599** 651-690-7700

College of Saint Elizabeth
2 Convent Rd . . . . Morristown NJ 07960 **800-210-7900*** 973-290-4700
*Admissions

College of Saint Mary
7000 Mercy Rd . . . . Omaha NE 68106 **800-926-5534** 402-399-2400

Converse College
580 E Main St . . . . Spartanburg SC 29302 **800-766-1125*** 864-596-9000
*Admissions

Fordham University
Westchester
400 Westchester Ave . . . . West Harrison NY 10604 **800-606-6090** 914-332-8295

Georgian Court University
900 Lakewood Ave . . . . Lakewood NJ 08701 **800-458-8422**

Hollins University
PO BOX 9707 . . . . Roanoke VA 24020 **800-456-9595*** 540-362-6401
*Admissions

Judson College 302 Bibb St . . . . Marion AL 36756 **800-447-9472*** 334-683-5110
*Admissions

Mary Baldwin College
318 Prospect St . . . . Staunton VA 24401 **800-468-2262*** 540-887-7019
*Admissions

Meredith College
3800 Hillsborough St . . . . Raleigh NC 27607 **800-637-3348*** 919-760-8581
*All

Midway College
512 E Stephens St . . . . Midway KY 40347 **800-755-0031** 859-846-5346

Mills College
5000 MacArthur Blvd . . . . Oakland CA 94613 **877-746-4557*** 510-430-2135
*Admissions

Moore College of Art & Design
20th St & the Pkwy . . . . Philadelphia PA 19103 **800-523-2025** 215-965-4000

Mount Holyoke College
50 College St . . . . South Hadley MA 01075 **800-642-4483** 413-538-2000

Mount Mary College
2900 N Menomonee River Pkwy . . . . Milwaukee WI 53222 **800-321-6265*** 414-256-1219
*Admissions

Mount Saint Mary's University
12001 Chalon Rd . . . . Los Angeles CA 90049 **800-999-9893*** 310-954-4250
*Admissions

Newcomb College Institute for Women
43 Newcomb Pl . . . . New Orleans LA 70118 **888-327-0009** 504-865-5422

Pine Manor College
400 Heath St . . . . Chestnut Hill MA 02467 **800-762-1357** 617-731-7104

Randolph College
2500 Rivermont Ave . . . . Lynchburg VA 24503 **800-745-7692*** 434-947-8000
*Admissions

Regis College
235 Wellesley St . . . . Weston MA 02493 **866-438-7344** 781-768-7000

Rosemont College
1400 Montgomery Ave . . . . Rosemont PA 19010 **800-331-0708*** 610-527-0200
*Admissions

Russell Sage College
45 Ferry St . . . . Troy NY 12180 **888-837-9724*** 518-244-2217
*Admissions

Saint Mary's College
Le Mans Hall Rm 122 . . . . Notre Dame IN 46556 **800-551-7621*** 574-284-4587
*Admissions

Saint Mary-of-the-Woods College
3301 St Mary Rd . . . . Saint Mary Of The Woods IN 47876 **800-926-7692** 812-535-5106

Salem College
601 S Church St . . . . Winston-Salem NC 27101 **800-327-2536*** 336-721-2600
*Admissions

Scripps College
1030 Columbia Ave . . . . Claremont CA 91711 **800-770-1333** 909-621-8149

Simmons College
300 The Fenway . . . . Boston MA 02115 **800-345-8468** 617-521-2000

Smith College
Seven College Ln . . . . NorthHampton MA 01063 **800-383-3232** 413-584-2700

Spelman College
350 Spelman Ln SW . . . . Atlanta GA 30314 **800-982-2411*** 404-681-3643
*Admissions

Sweet Briar College
134 Chappel Rd . . . . Sweet Briar VA 24595 **800-381-6142*** 434-381-6100
*Admissions

Texas Woman's University
304 Admin Dr PO Box 425589 . . . . Denton TX 76204 **866-809-6130** 940-898-3188

University of Richmond
Westhampton College
28 Westhampton Way . . . . University Of Richmond VA 23173 **800-700-1662** 804-289-8000

Ursuline College
2550 Lander Rd . . . . Pepper Pike OH 44124 **888-778-5463** 440-449-4200

Wesleyan College
4760 Forsyth Rd . . . . Macon GA 31210 **800-447-6610** 478-477-1110

William Peace University
15 E Peace St . . . . Raleigh NC 27604 **800-732-2347** 919-508-2000

Wilson College
1015 Philadelphia Ave . . . . Chambersburg PA 17201 **800-421-8402*** 717-264-4141
*Admissions

---

166   COLLEGES & UNIVERSITIES - CHRISTIAN

SEE ALSO Colleges - Bible ; Colleges & Universities - Jesuit
The institutions listed here are members of the Council for Christian Colleges & Universities (CCCU). Although many other colleges and universities describe themselves as "religiously affiliated," members of CCCU are intentionally Christ-centered. Among the criteria for membership in CCCU, schools must have curricular and extra-curricular programs that reflect the integration of scholarship, biblical faith, and service.

			Toll-Free	Phone

Anderson University
1100 E Fifth St . . . . Anderson IN 46012 **800-428-6414*** 765-649-9071
*Admissions

Asbury College
One Macklem Dr . . . . Wilmore KY 40390 **800-888-1818*** 859-858-3511
*Admissions

Azusa Pacific University
901 E Alosta Ave PO Box 7000 . . . . Azusa CA 91702 **800-825-5278** 626-969-3434

Belhaven College
1500 Peachtree St PO Box 153 . . . . Jackson MS 39202 **800-960-5940** 601-968-5940

Bethel College
1001 W McKinley Ave . . . . Mishawaka IN 46545 **800-422-4101*** 574-807-7000
*Admissions

Biola University
13800 Biola Ave . . . . La Mirada CA 90639 **800-652-4652*** 562-903-6000
*Admissions

Bluffton University
1 University Dr . . . . Bluffton OH 45817 **800-488-3257** 419-358-3000

Bryan College
721 Bryan Dr PO Box 7000 . . . . Dayton TN 37321 **800-277-9522** 423-775-2041

California Baptist University
8432 Magnolia Ave . . . . Riverside CA 92504 **877-228-8866** 951-689-5771

Calvin College
3201 Burton St SE . . . . Grand Rapids MI 49546 **800-688-0122** 616-526-6000

Campbellsville University
One University Dr . . . . Campbellsville KY 42718 **800-264-6014*** 270-789-5000
*Admissions

Carson-Newman College
1646 Russell Ave . . . . Jefferson City TN 37760 **800-678-9061** 865-471-2000

Cedarville University
251 N Main St . . . . Cedarville OH 45314 **800-233-2784** 937-766-7700

College of the Ozarks
1 Industrial Dr PO Box 17 . . . . Point Lookout MO 65726 **800-222-0525*** 417-334-6411
*Admissions

Colorado Christian University
8787 W Alameda Ave . . . . Lakewood CO 80226 **800-443-2484** 303-963-3200

Corban College
5000 Deer Pk Dr SE . . . . Salem OR 97317 **800-845-3005** 503-581-8600

Cornerstone University
1001 E Beltline Ave NE . . . . Grand Rapids MI 49525 **800-787-9778*** 616-222-1426
*Admissions

Covenant College
14049 Scenic Hwy . . . . Lookout Mountain GA 30750 **888-451-2683** 706-820-1560

Crown College
8700 College View Dr . . . . Saint Bonifacius MN 55375 **800-682-7696** 952-446-4100

Dallas Baptist University
3000 Mtn Creek Pkwy . . . . Dallas TX 75211 **800-460-1328** 214-333-7100

Dordt College
498 Fourth Ave NE . . . . Sioux Center IA 51250 **800-343-6738** 712-722-6080

East Texas Baptist University
1209 N Grove St . . . . Marshall TX 75670 **800-804-3828** 903-935-7963

Eastern Mennonite University
1200 Pk Rd . . . . Harrisonburg VA 22802 **800-368-2665*** 540-432-4118
*Admissions

Eastern Nazarene College
23 E Elm Ave . . . . Quincy MA 02170 **800-883-6288** 617-745-3000

Eastern University
1300 Eagle Rd . . . . Wayne PA 19087 **800-452-0996*** 610-341-5800
*Admissions

Erskine College
Two Washington St . . . . Due West SC 29639 **800-241-8721*** 864-379-2131
*Admissions

Evangel University
1111 N Glenstone Ave . . . . Springfield MO 65802 **800-382-6435** 417-865-2815

Fresno Pacific University
1717 S Chestnut Ave PO Box 2005 . . . . Fresno CA 93702 **800-660-6089** 559-453-2039

Geneva College
3200 College Ave . . . . Beaver Falls PA 15010 **800-847-8255** 724-847-6500

George Fox University
414 N Meridian St . . . . Newberg OR 97132 **800-765-4369** 503-538-8383

Gordon College
255 Grapevine Rd . . . . Wenham MA 01984 **800-343-1379** 978-927-2300

Goshen College
1700 S Main St . . . . Goshen IN 46526 **800-348-7422** 574-535-7000

Grace College
200 Seminary Dr . . . . Winona Lake IN 46590 **800-544-7223** 574-372-5100

Greenville College
315 E College Ave . . . . Greenville IL 62246 **800-345-4440** 618-664-7100

Hardin-Simmons University
2200 Hickory St . . . . Abilene TX 79698 **877-464-7889** 325-670-1206

Hope International University
2500 E Nutwood Ave . . . . Fullerton CA 92831 **866-722-4673** 714-879-3901

Houghton College
One Willard Ave PO Box 128 . . . . Houghton NY 14744 **800-777-2556** 585-567-9200

Houston Baptist University
7502 Fondren Rd . . . . Houston TX 77074 **800-969-3210*** 281-649-3000
*Admissions

Howard Payne University
1000 Fisk Ave . . . . Brownwood TX 76801 **800-950-8465** 325-646-2502

Huntington University
2303 College Ave . . . . Huntington IN 46750 **800-642-6493*** 260-356-6000

Indiana Wesleyan University
4201 S Washington St . . . . Marion IN 46953 **800-332-6901** 765-677-2138

				Toll-Free	Phone
John Brown University					
2000 W University St	Siloam Springs	AR	72761	**877-528-4636***	479-524-9500
*Admissions					
Judson College 302 Bibb St	Marion	AL	36756	**800-447-9472***	334-683-5110
*Admissions					
Judson University					
1151 N State St	Elgin	IL	60123	**800-879-5376***	847-628-2500
*Admissions					
Kentucky Christian University					
100 Academic Pkwy	Grayson	KY	41143	**800-522-3181***	606-474-3000
*Admissions					
King College					
1350 King College Rd	Bristol	TN	37620	**800-362-0014***	423-652-4861
*Admissions					
King's University College					
9125 50th St	Edmonton	AB	T6B2H3	**800-661-8582**	780-465-3500
Lee University					
1120 N Ocoee St	Cleveland	TN	37311	**800-533-9930**	423-614-8000
LeTourneau University					
2100 S Mobberly Ave	Longview	TX	75602	**800-759-8811**	903-233-3000
Lipscomb University					
3901 Granny White Pk	Nashville	TN	37204	**800-333-4358**	615-966-1000
Louisiana College					
1140 College Dr	Pineville	LA	71359	**800-487-1906**	318-487-7011
Malone College					
515 25th St NW	Canton	OH	44709	**800-521-1146**	330-471-8100
Master's College					
21726 Placerita Canyon Rd	Santa Clarita	CA	91321	**800-568-6248**	661-259-3540
Messiah College					
PO Box 3005	Grantham	PA	17027	**800-233-4220**	717-691-6000
MidAmerica Nazarene University					
2030 E College Way	Olathe	KS	66062	**800-800-8887**	913-782-3750
Milligan College					
PO Box 500	Milligan College	TN	37682	**800-262-8337**	423-461-8730
Mississippi College					
200 S Capitol St PO Box 4026	Clinton	MS	39058	**800-738-1236**	601-925-3000
Missouri Baptist University					
One College Pk Dr	Saint Louis	MO	63141	**877-434-1115**	314-434-1115
Montreat College					
310 Gaither Cir PO Box 1267	Montreat	NC	28757	**800-622-6968**	828-669-8011
Mount Vernon Nazarene University					
800 Martinsburg Rd	Mount Vernon	OH	43050	**800-766-8206***	740-392-6868
*Admissions					
North Greenville University					
7801 N Tigerville Rd PO Box 1892	Tigerville	SC	29688	**800-468-6642**	864-977-7000
North Park University					
3225 W Foster Ave	Chicago	IL	60625	**800-888-6728**	773-244-5500
Northwest Christian College					
828 E 11th Ave	Eugene	OR	97401	**877-463-6622**	541-343-1641
Northwest Nazarene University					
623 Holly St	Nampa	ID	83686	**877-668-4968***	208-467-8000
*Admissions					
Northwest University					
5520 108th Ave NE	Kirkland	WA	98033	**800-669-3781***	425-822-8266
*Admissions					
Northwestern College					
101 Seventh St SW	Orange City	IA	51041	**800-747-4757**	712-707-7000
Nyack College One S Blvd	Nyack	NY	10960	**800-336-9225***	845-358-1710
*Admissions					
Oklahoma Baptist University					
500 W University St	Shawnee	OK	74804	**800-654-3285**	405-275-2850
Oklahoma Christian University					
PO Box 11000	Oklahoma City	OK	73136	**800-877-5010**	405-425-5000
Olivet Nazarene University					
One University Ave	Bourbonnais	IL	60914	**800-648-1463**	815-939-5011
Oral Roberts University					
7777 S Lewis Ave	Tulsa	OK	74171	**800-678-8876**	918-495-6161
Palm Beach Atlantic University					
PO Box 24708	West Palm Beach	FL	33416	**888-468-6722**	561-803-2000
Point Loma Nazarene University					
3900 Lomaland Dr	San Diego	CA	92106	**800-733-7770***	619-849-2200
*Admissions					
Redeemer University College					
777 Garner Rd E	Ancaster	ON	L9K1J4	**877-779-0913**	905-648-2131
Roberts Wesleyan College					
2301 Westside Dr	Rochester	NY	14624	**800-777-4792***	585-594-6000
*Admissions					
Seattle Pacific University					
3307 Third Ave W	Seattle	WA	98119	**800-366-3344**	206-281-2000
Simpson University					
2211 College View Dr	Redding	CA	96003	**888-974-6776**	530-226-4606
Southeastern University					
1000 Longfellow Blvd	Lakeland	FL	33801	**800-500-8760**	863-667-5000
Southern Nazarene University					
6729 NW 39th Expy	Bethany	OK	73008	**800-648-9899**	405-789-6400
Southern Wesleyan University					
907 Wesleyan Dr	Central	SC	29630	**800-282-8798**	864-644-5000
Southwest Baptist University					
1600 University Ave	Bolivar	MO	65613	**800-526-5859**	
Spring Arbor University					
106 E Main St	Spring Arbor	MI	49283	**800-968-9103***	517-750-1200
*Admissions					
Tabor College					
400 S Jefferson St	Hillsboro	KS	67063	**800-822-6799***	620-947-3121
*Admissions					
Taylor University					
236 W Reade Ave	Upland	IN	46989	**800-882-3456**	765-998-2751
Trevecca Nazarene University					
333 Murfreesboro Rd	Nashville	TN	37210	**888-210-4868**	615-248-1200
Trinity International University					
2065 Half Day Rd	Deerfield	IL	60015	**800-822-3225**	847-945-8800
Trinity Western University					
7600 Glover Rd	Langley	BC	V2Y1Y1	**888-468-6898**	604-888-7511
Union University					
1050 Union University Dr	Jackson	TN	38305	**800-338-6466**	731-661-5210
University of Sioux Falls					
1101 W 22nd St	Sioux Falls	SD	57105	**800-888-1047**	605-331-6600
Vanguard University of Southern California					
55 Fair Dr	Costa Mesa	CA	92626	**800-722-6279***	714-556-3610
*Admissions					
Warner Pacific College					
2219 SE 68th Ave	Portland	OR	97215	**800-804-1510**	503-517-1020
Warner Southern College					
13895 Hwy 27	Lake Wales	FL	33859	**800-309-9563**	
Wayland Baptist University					
1900 W Seventh St	Plainview	TX	79072	**800-588-1928**	806-291-1000
Waynesburg College					
51 W College St	Waynesburg	PA	15370	**800-225-7393***	724-627-8191
*Admissions					
Westmont College					
955 La Paz Rd	Santa Barbara	CA	93108	**800-777-9011***	805-565-6000
*Admissions					
Whitworth College					
300 W Hawthorne Rd	Spokane	WA	99251	**800-533-4668***	509-777-1000
*Admissions					
Williams Baptist College					
60 W Fulbright St	Walnut Ridge	AR	72476	**800-722-4434**	870-886-6741

167 COLLEGES & UNIVERSITIES - FOUR-YEAR

SEE ALSO Universities - Canadian ; Vocational & Technical Schools ; Military Service Academies ; Colleges - Community & Junior ; Colleges - Fine Arts ; Colleges - Women's (Four-Year) ; Colleges & Universities - Christian ; Colleges & Universities - Graduate & Professional Schools ; Colleges & Universities - Historically Black ; Colleges & Universities - Jesuit

Alabama

				Toll-Free	Phone
Alabama Agricultural & Mechanical University					
4900 Meridian St PO Box 1087	Huntsville	AL	35810	**800-553-0816**	256-372-5000
Alabama State University					
915 S Jackson St	Montgomery	AL	36104	**800-253-5037***	334-229-4100
*Admissions					
Amridge University					
1200 Taylor Rd	Montgomery	AL	36117	**888-790-8080**	334-387-3877
Auburn University					
202 Mary Martin Hall	Auburn University	AL	36849	**866-389-6770***	334-844-6425
*Admissions					
Montgomery 7440 E Dr	Montgomery	AL	36117	**800-227-2649**	334-244-3000
Birmingham-Southern College					
900 Arkadelphia Rd	Birmingham	AL	35254	**800-523-5793**	205-226-4600
Faulkner University					
5345 Atlanta Hwy	Montgomery	AL	36109	**800-879-9816**	334-272-5820
Huntingdon College					
1500 E Fairview Ave	Montgomery	AL	36106	**800-763-0313***	334-833-4497
*Admissions					
Jacksonville State University					
700 Pelham Rd N	Jacksonville	AL	36265	**800-231-5291**	256-782-5781
Judson College 302 Bibb St	Marion	AL	36756	**800-447-9472***	334-683-5110
*Admissions					
Miles College					
5500 Myron Massey Blvd	Fairfield	AL	35064	**800-445-0708***	205-929-1000
*Admissions					
Oakwood College					
7000 Adventist Blvd	Huntsville	AL	35896	**800-824-5312**	256-726-7356
Samford University					
800 Lakeshore Dr	Birmingham	AL	35229	**800-888-7218***	205-726-3673
*Admissions					
South University					
Montgomery					
5355 Vaughn Rd	Montgomery	AL	36116	**866-629-2962**	334-395-8800
Spring Hill College					
4000 Dauphin St	Mobile	AL	36608	**800-742-6704***	251-380-4000
*Admissions					
Stillman College					
3601 Stillman Blvd	Tuscaloosa	AL	35401	**800-841-5722**	205-349-4240
Talladega College					
627 W Battle St	Talladega	AL	35160	**866-540-3956**	256-362-0206
Troy University					
600 University Ave	Troy	AL	36082	**800-551-9716**	334-670-3100
Montgomery					
231 Montgomery St PO Box 4419	Montgomery	AL	36104	**888-357-8843**	
Tuskegee University					
1200 W Montgomery Rd	Tuskegee	AL	36088	**800-622-6531***	334-727-8011
*Admissions					
University of Alabama					
PO Box 870132	Tuscaloosa	AL	35487	**800-933-2262***	205-348-6010
*Admissions					
Birmingham					
1530 Third Ave S THT 647	Birmingham	AL	35294	**800-421-8743**	205-996-6670
Huntsville					
301 Sparkman Dr	Huntsville	AL	35899	**800-824-2255**	256-824-1000
University of Mobile					
5735 College Pkwy	Mobile	AL	36613	**800-946-7267**	251-675-5990
University of North Alabama					
1 Harrison Plaza	Florence	AL	35632	**800-825-5862**	256-765-4608
University of South Alabama					
2500 Meisler Hall	Mobile	AL	36688	**800-872-5247**	251-460-6141
University of West Alabama					
Stn 200 UWA	Livingston	AL	35470	**800-621-8044***	205-652-3400
*Admissions					

Alaska

				Toll-Free	Phone
Alaska Pacific University					
4101 University Dr	Anchorage	AK	99508	**800-252-7528**	907-564-8248
University of Alaska Anchorage					
3211 Providence Dr	Anchorage	AK	99508	**888-822-8973**	907-786-1800
University of Alaska Fairbanks					
Bristol Bay					
527 Seward St PO Box 1070	Dillingham	AK	99576	**800-478-5109**	907-842-5109

					Toll-Free	Phone

University of Alaska Southeast
11120 Glacier Hwy . . . . Juneau AK　99801　877-465-4827　907-296-6000

Arizona

	Toll-Free	Phone

American Indian College of the Assemblies of God
10020 N 15th Ave . . . . Phoenix AZ　85021　800-621-7440　602-944-3335
West PO Box 37100 . . . . Phoenix AZ　85069　855-278-5080　602-543-5500
Embry-Riddle Aeronautical University Prescott
3700 Willow Creek Rd . . . . Prescott AZ　86301　800-888-3728　928-777-3728
Grand Canyon University
3300 W Camelback Rd . . . . Phoenix AZ　85017　800-800-9776　602-639-7500
Indian Bible College
2918 N Aris Ave . . . . Flagstaff AZ　86004　866-503-7789　928-774-3890
Northern Arizona University
PO Box 4084 . . . . Flagstaff AZ　86011　888-628-2968*　928-523-5511
*Admissions
Ottawa University Phoenix
10020 N 25th Ave . . . . Phoenix AZ　85021　800-235-9586　602-371-1188
Prescott College
220 Grove Ave . . . . Prescott AZ　86301　877-350-2100
Western International University
9215 N Black Canyon Hwy . . . . Phoenix AZ　85021　866-948-4636　602-943-2311

Arkansas

	Toll-Free	Phone

Arkansas State University
PO Box 1630 . . . . State University AR　72467　800-382-3030　870-972-3024
Harding University
900 E Ctr Ave . . . . Searcy AR　72149　800-477-4407　501-279-4000
Henderson State University
1100 Henderson St . . . . Arkadelphia AR　71999　800-228-7333　870-230-5000
Hendrix College
1600 Washington Ave . . . . Conway AR　72032　800-277-9017　501-329-6811
John Brown University
2000 W University St . . . . Siloam Springs AR　72761　877-528-4636*　479-524-9500
*Admissions
Ouachita Baptist University
410 Ouachita St . . . . Arkadelphia AR　71998　800-342-5628*　870-245-5000
*Admissions
Philander Smith College
900 Daisy Bates Dr . . . . Little Rock AR　72202　800-446-6772　501-370-5221
Southern Arkansas University
100 E University St . . . . Magnolia AR　71753　800-332-7286　870-235-4000
University of Arkansas
232 Silas Hunt Hall . . . . Fayetteville AR　72701　800-377-8632*　479-575-5346
*Admissions
Monticello PO Box 3600 . . . . Monticello AR　71656　800-844-1826　870-460-1026
Pine Bluff
1200 N University Dr . . . . Pine Bluff AR　71601　800-264-6585*　870-575-8000
*Admissions
University of Central Arkansas
201 Donaghey Ave . . . . Conway AR　72035　888-407-4747*　501-450-5000
*Admissions
University of the Ozarks
415 N College Ave . . . . Clarksville AR　72830　800-264-8636*　479-979-1227
*Admissions
Williams Baptist College
60 W Fulbright St . . . . Walnut Ridge AR　72476　800-722-4434　870-886-6741

California

	Toll-Free	Phone

Academy of Art University
79 New Montgomery St . . . . San Francisco CA　94105　800-544-2787　415-274-2200
Alliant International University
10455 Pomerado Rd . . . . San Diego CA　92131　866-825-5426　858-635-4772
Azusa Pacific University
901 E Alosta Ave PO Box 7000 . . . . Azusa CA　91702　800-825-5278　626-969-3434
Biola University
13800 Biola Ave . . . . La Mirada CA　90639　800-652-4652*　562-903-6000
*Admissions
California Baptist University
8432 Magnolia Ave . . . . Riverside CA　92504　877-228-8866　951-689-5771
California Institute of Technology
1200 E California Blvd . . . . Pasadena CA　91125　800-568-8324　626-395-6811
California Lutheran University
60 W Olsen Rd . . . . Thousand Oaks CA　91360　877-258-3678　805-493-3135
California Maritime Academy
200 Maritime Academy Dr . . . . Vallejo CA　94590　800-561-1945　707-654-1330
California Polytechnic State University
1 Grand Ave . . . . San Luis Obispo CA　93407　800-424-6723　805-756-1111
Chico CSU Chico . . . . Chico CA　95929　800-542-4426*　530-898-6321
*Admissions
Dominguez Hills
1000 E Victoria St . . . . Carson CA　90747　888-545-6512　310-243-3300
East Bay
25800 Carlos Bee Blvd . . . . Hayward CA　94542　877-829-5500　510-885-3000
Fresno 5241 N Maple Ave . . . . Fresno CA　93740　800-700-2320　559-278-4240
Fullerton
800 N State College Blvd . . . . Fullerton CA　92834　888-433-9406　714-278-2011
Long Beach
1250 Bellflower Blvd . . . . Long Beach CA　90840　800-663-1144　562-985-4111
Northridge
18111 Nordhoff St . . . . Northridge CA　91330　800-399-4529　818-677-1200
San Bernardino
5500 University Pkwy . . . . San Bernardino CA　92407　866-275-3772　909-537-5188
San Marcos
333 S Twin Oaks Valley Rd . . . . San Marcos CA　92096　888-225-5427　760-750-4000
Stanislaus 1 University Cir . . . . Turlock CA　95382　800-235-9292　209-667-3152
Chapman University
One University Dr . . . . Orange CA　92866　888-282-7759　714-997-6815
Cogswell Polytechnical College
1175 Bordeaux Dr . . . . Sunnyvale CA　94089　800-264-7955　408-541-0100
Columbia College Hollywood
18618 Oxnard St . . . . Tarzana CA　91356　800-785-0585　818-345-8414

					Toll-Free	Phone

Concordia University Irvine
1530 Concordia W . . . . Irvine CA　92612　800-229-1200　949-854-8002
Dominican University of California
50 Acacia Ave . . . . San Rafael CA　94901　888-323-6763*　415-457-4440
*Admissions
Fresno Pacific University
1717 S Chestnut Ave PO Box 2005 . . . . Fresno CA　93702　800-660-6089　559-453-2039
Harvey Mudd College
301 Platt Blvd Kingston Hall . . . . Claremont CA　91711　877-827-5462　909-621-8011
Hebrew Union College Los Angeles
3077 University Ave . . . . Los Angeles CA　90007　800-899-0925　213-749-3424
Holy Names University
3500 Mountain Blvd . . . . Oakland CA　94619　800-430-1321　510-436-1000
Hope International University
2500 E Nutwood Ave . . . . Fullerton CA　92831　866-722-4673　714-879-3901
Humboldt State University
One Harpst St . . . . Arcata CA　95521　866-850-9556　707-826-3011
Humphreys College
6650 Inglewood Ave . . . . Stockton CA　95207　800-433-3243　209-478-0800
John F Kennedy University
100 Ellinwood Way . . . . Pleasant Hill CA　94523　800-696-5358　925-969-3300
La Sierra University
4500 Riverwalk Pkwy . . . . Riverside CA　92515　800-874-5587　951-785-2000
Laguna College of Art & Design
2222 Laguna Canyon Rd . . . . Laguna Beach CA　92651　800-255-0762　949-376-6000
Loyola Marymount University
One LMU Dr . . . . Los Angeles CA　90045　800-568-4636　310-338-2700
Master's College
21726 Placerita Canyon Rd . . . . Santa Clarita CA　91321　800-568-6248　661-259-3540
Menlo College
1000 El Camino Real . . . . Atherton CA　94027　800-556-3656　650-543-3753
Mills College
5000 MacArthur Blvd . . . . Oakland CA　94613　877-746-4557*　510-430-2135
*Admissions
Mount Saint Mary's University
12001 Chalon Rd . . . . Los Angeles CA　90049　800-999-9893*　310-954-4250
*Admissions
National Hispanic University
14271 Story Rd . . . . San Jose CA　95127　877-762-9801　408-254-6900
National University
11255 N Torrey Pines Rd . . . . La Jolla CA　92037　800-628-8648　858-642-8000
Northwestern Polytechnic University
47671 Westinghouse Dr . . . . Fremont CA　94539　877-878-8883　510-657-5913
Notre Dame de Namur University
1500 Ralston Ave . . . . Belmont CA　94002　800-263-0545　650-508-3600
Occidental College
1600 Campus Rd . . . . Los Angeles CA　90041　800-825-5262*　323-259-2700
*Admissions
Pacific Union College
One Angwin Ave . . . . Angwin CA　94508　800-862-7080　707-965-6336
Patten University
2433 Coolidge Ave . . . . Oakland CA　94601　877-472-8836　510-261-8500
Pitzer College
1050 N Mills Ave . . . . Claremont CA　91711　800-748-9371　909-621-8129
Point Loma Nazarene University
3900 Lomaland Dr . . . . San Diego CA　92106　800-733-7770*　619-849-2200
*Admissions
Ryokan College
11965 Venice Blvd Ste 304 . . . . Los Angeles CA　90066　866-796-5261　310-390-7560
Saint Mary's College of California
1928 St Mary's Rd . . . . Moraga CA　94556　800-800-4762*　925-631-4000
*Admissions
Samuel Merritt College
370 Hawthorne Ave . . . . Oakland CA　94609　800-607-6377*　510-869-6576
*Admissions
San Diego Christian College
2100 Greenfield Dr . . . . El Cajon CA　92019　800-676-2242　619-441-2200
San Francisco Conservatory of Music
50 Oak St . . . . San Francisco CA　94102　800-999-8219　415-864-7326
San Jose State University
1 Washington Sq . . . . San Jose CA　95192　800-273-8255　408-924-1000
Scripps College
1030 Columbia Ave . . . . Claremont CA　91711　800-770-1333　909-621-8149
Simpson University
2211 College View Dr . . . . Redding CA　96003　888-974-6776　530-226-4606
South Baylo University
1126 N Brookhurst St . . . . Anaheim CA　92801　888-642-2956　714-533-1495
Stanford University
450 Serra Mall . . . . Stanford CA　94305　877-407-9529　650-723-2091
Thomas Aquinas College
10000 Ojai Rd . . . . Santa Paula CA　93060　800-634-9797　805-525-4417
University of California (UCLA)
Berkeley
110 Sproul Hall MC Ste 5800 . . . . Berkeley CA　94720　866-740-1260　510-642-6000
Merced PO Box 2039 . . . . Merced CA　95344　866-270-7301　209-724-4400
Riverside
900 University Ave
1120 Hinderaker Hall . . . . Riverside CA　92521　800-426-2586　951-827-3411
Santa Barbara
1210 Cheadle Hall . . . . Santa Barbara CA　93106　888-488-8272　805-893-8000
Santa Cruz
1156 High St Hahn Bldg Rm 150 . . . . Santa Cruz CA　95064　800-933-7584　831-459-2131
University of Judaism
15600 Mulholland Dr . . . . Los Angeles CA　90077　888-853-6763　310-476-9777
University of La Verne
1950 Third St . . . . La Verne CA　91750　800-876-4858*　909-593-3511
*Admissions
University of Redlands
1200 E Colton Ave PO Box 3080 . . . . Redlands CA　92373　800-455-5064　909-793-2121
University of San Diego
5998 Alcala Pk . . . . San Diego CA　92110　800-248-4873　619-260-4506
University of San Francisco
2130 Fulton St . . . . San Francisco CA　94117　800-225-5873*　415-422-5555
*Admissions
University of the Pacific
3601 Pacific Ave . . . . Stockton CA　95211　800-959-2867　209-946-2211
Vanguard University of Southern California
55 Fair Dr . . . . Costa Mesa CA　92626　800-722-6279*　714-556-3610
*Admissions

				Toll-Free	Phone
Westmont College 955 La Paz Rd	Santa Barbara	CA	93108	800-777-9011*	805-565-6000
*Admissions					
William Jessup University 333 Sunset Blvd	Rocklin	CA	95765	800-355-7522	916-577-2200
Woodbury University 7500 Glenoaks Blvd	Burbank	CA	91510	800-784-9663	818-767-0888
World University 107 N Ventura St PO Box 1567	Ojai	CA	93024	888-370-7589	805-646-1444

Colorado

				Toll-Free	Phone
Adams State College 208 Edgemont Blvd	Alamosa	CO	81102	800-824-6494	719-587-7712
Beth-El College of Nursing & Health Sciences 1420 Austin Bluffs Pkwy	Colorado Springs	CO	80918	800-990-8227	719-255-8227
Colorado Christian University 8787 W Alameda Ave	Lakewood	CO	80226	800-443-2484	303-963-3200
Loveland 3553 Clydesdale Pkwy Ste 300	Loveland	CO	80538	800-443-2484	970-669-8700
Colorado College 14 E Cache La Poudre St	Colorado Springs	CO	80903	800-542-7214	719-389-6344
Colorado School of Mines 1600 Maple St	Golden	CO	80401	800-446-9488	303-273-3000
Colorado State University *Pueblo* 2200 Bonforte Blvd	Pueblo	CO	81001	877-307-5678	719-549-2100
Colorado Technical University 4435 N Chestnut St	Colorado Springs	CO	80907	855-230-0555	719-598-0200
Fort Lewis College 1000 Rim Dr	Durango	CO	81301	877-352-2656	970-247-7010
Johnson & Wales University Denver 7150 E Montview Blvd	Denver	CO	80220	877-598-3368	303-256-9300
Mesa State College 1100 N Ave	Grand Junction	CO	81501	800-982-6372	970-248-1020
Naropa University 2130 Arapahoe Ave	Boulder	CO	80302	800-772-6951	303-444-0202
National American University Colorado Springs 1915 Jamboree Dr Ste 185	Colorado Springs	CO	80920	855-448-2318	316-448-5400
Regis University *Colorado Springs* 7450 Campus Dr Ste 100	Colorado Springs	CO	80920	800-568-8932	
University of Colorado *Colorado Springs* PO Box 7150	Colorado Springs	CO	80933	800-990-8227	719-262-3000
University of Denver 2199 S University Blvd	Denver	CO	80210	800-525-9495	303-871-2036
University of Northern Colorado 501 20th St CB 92	Greeley	CO	80639	888-700-4862*	970-351-2881
*Admissions					
US Air Force Academy (USAFA) 2304 Cadet Dr Ste 2300	Air Force Academy	CO	80840	800-443-9266	719-333-1110
Western State College of Colorado 600 N Adams St	Gunnison	CO	81231	800-876-5309*	970-943-2119
*Admissions					

Connecticut

				Toll-Free	Phone
Albertus Magnus College 700 Prospect St	New Haven	CT	06511	800-578-9160*	203-773-8550
*Admissions					
Briarwood College 2279 Mt Vernon Rd	Southington	CT	06489	800-952-2444	860-628-4751
Connecticut College 270 Mohegan Ave	New London	CT	06320	800-892-3363	860-439-2000
Eastern Connecticut State University 83 Windham St	Willimantic	CT	06226	877-353-3278*	860-465-5000
*Admissions					
Hartford Seminary 77 Sherman St	Hartford	CT	06105	877-860-2255	860-509-9500
Mitchell College 437 Pequot Ave	New London	CT	06320	800-443-2811*	860-701-5000
*Admitting					
Post University 800 Country Club Rd	Waterbury	CT	06723	800-345-2562	203-596-4500
Quinnipiac University 275 Mt Carmel Ave	Hamden	CT	06518	800-462-1944*	203-582-8600
*Admissions					
Southern Connecticut State University 501 Crescent St	New Haven	CT	06515	888-500-7278	203-392-5200
University of Bridgeport 126 Pk Ave	Bridgeport	CT	06604	800-392-3582	203-576-4000
University of Hartford 200 Bloomfield Ave	West Hartford	CT	06117	800-947-4303	860-768-4296
University of New Haven 300 Boston Post Rd	West Haven	CT	06516	800-342-5864	203-932-7319
US Coast Guard Academy 15 Mohegan Ave	New London	CT	06320	800-883-8724	860-444-8500

Delaware

				Toll-Free	Phone
Delaware State University 1200 N DuPont Hwy	Dover	DE	19901	800-845-2544*	302-857-6351
*Admissions					
Goldey Beacom College 4701 Limestone Rd	Wilmington	DE	19808	800-833-4877	302-998-8814
Wilmington University 320 N DuPont Hwy	New Castle	DE	19720	877-967-5464*	302-356-6739
*Admissions					

District of Columbia

				Toll-Free	Phone
American University 4400 Massachusetts Ave NW	Washington	DC	20016	800-829-1040	202-885-1000
Gallaudet University 800 Florida Ave NE	Washington	DC	20002	800-995-0550	202-651-5000
George Washington University *Mount Vernon College* 2100 Foxhall Rd NW	Washington	DC	20007	800-447-3765	202-994-1000
Howard University 2400 Sixth St NW	Washington	DC	20059	800-822-6363	202-806-6100
Strayer University *Takoma Park* 6830 Laurel St NW	Washington	DC	20012	888-311-0355	202-722-8100

Florida

				Toll-Free	Phone
American Intercontinental University South Florida 2250 N Commerce Pkwy	Weston	FL	33326	855-377-1888	954-446-6100
Ave Maria University 5050 Ave Maria Blvd	Naples	FL	34119	877-283-8648	239-280-2500
Baptist College of Florida 5400 College Dr	Graceville	FL	32440	800-328-2660	850-263-3261
Orlando 1650 Sandlake Rd Ste 390	Orlando	FL	32809	800-756-6000	407-438-4150
Tallahassee 325 John Knox Rd Bldg A	Tallahassee	FL	32303	800-756-6000	850-385-2279
Bethune-Cookman College 640 Dr Mary McLeod Bethune Blvd	Daytona Beach	FL	32114	800-448-0228*	386-481-2900
*Admissions					
Clearwater Christian College 3400 Gulf to Bay Blvd	Clearwater	FL	33759	800-348-4463*	727-726-1153
*Admissions					
Columbia College Orlando 2600 Technology Dr Ste 100	Orlando	FL	32804	800-231-2391	407-293-9911
Eckerd College 4200 54th Ave S	Saint Petersburg	FL	33711	800-456-9009*	727-867-1166
*Admissions					
Embry-Riddle Aeronautical University *Daytona Beach* 600 S Clyde Morris Blvd	Daytona Beach	FL	32114	800-862-2416	386-226-6000
Flagler College 74 King St	Saint Augustine	FL	32084	800-304-4208*	904-829-6481
*Admissions					
Florida Atlantic University (FAU) 777 Glades Rd	Boca Raton	FL	33431	800-299-4328*	561-297-3000
*Admissions					
Davie 3200 College Ave	Davie	FL	33314	800-764-2222	954-236-1000
Fort Lauderdale 111 E Las Olas Blvd	Fort Lauderdale	FL	33301	800-764-2222	954-236-1000
MacArthur 5353 Parkside Dr	Jupiter	FL	33458	888-328-2586	561-799-8500
Florida College 119 N Glen Arven Ave	Temple Terrace	FL	33617	800-326-7655	813-988-5131
Florida Institute of Technology 150 W University Blvd	Melbourne	FL	32901	800-888-4348	321-674-8000
Florida International University 11200 SW Eigth St	Miami	FL	33199	800-677-6337	305-348-2000
Florida Memorial University 15800 NW 42nd Ave	Miami Gardens	FL	33054	800-822-1362	305-626-3600
Florida Southern College 111 Lk Hollingsworth Dr	Lakeland	FL	33801	800-274-4131*	863-680-4131
*Admissions					
Hodges University 2655 Northbrooke Dr	Naples	FL	34119	800-466-8017	239-513-1122
Fort Myers 4501 Colonial Blvd	Fort Myers	FL	33966	800-466-0019	239-482-0019
Jacksonville University 2800 University Blvd N	Jacksonville	FL	32211	800-225-2027	904-256-8000
Johnson & Wales University North Miami 1701 NE 127th St	North Miami	FL	33181	866-598-3567	305-892-7551
Jones College 5353 Arlington Expy	Jacksonville	FL	32211	800-331-0176	904-743-1122
Logos Christian College 9000 Regency Sq Blvd	Jacksonville	FL	32211	800-252-4253	904-745-3311
Lynn University 3601 N Military Trl	Boca Raton	FL	33431	800-888-5966*	561-237-7900
*Admissions					
New College of Florida 5800 Bay Shore Rd	Sarasota	FL	34243	800-435-7352	941-487-5000
Northwood University Florida 2600 N Military Trl	West Palm Beach	FL	33409	800-458-8325*	561-478-5500
*Admissions					
Nova Southeastern University 3301 College Ave	Fort Lauderdale	FL	33314	800-541-6682	954-262-8000
Palm Beach Atlantic University PO Box 24708	West Palm Beach	FL	33416	888-468-6722	561-803-2000
Pensacola Christian College 250 Brent Ln	Pensacola	FL	32503	800-722-4636	850-478-8496
Rollins College 1000 Holt Ave	Winter Park	FL	32789	800-799-2586	407-646-2000
Saint Leo University 33701 State Rd 52	Saint Leo	FL	33574	800-334-5532	352-588-8200
Palatka Ctr 33701 State Rd 52 PO Box 6665	Saint Leo	FL	33574	800-334-5532	352-588-8200
Saint Thomas University 16401 NW 37th Ave	Miami Gardens	FL	33054	800-367-9010	305-628-6546
South University West Palm Beach 9801 Belvedere Rd University Ctr	West Palm Beach	FL	33411	800-688-0932	561-273-6500
Southeastern University 1000 Longfellow Blvd	Lakeland	FL	33801	800-500-8760	863-667-5000
Stetson University 421 N Woodland Blvd Unit 8378	DeLand	FL	32723	800-688-0101*	386-822-7100
*Admissions					
Trinity International University South Florida 8190 W SR 84	Davie	FL	33324	800-822-3225	954-382-6400
University of Florida 219 Grinter Hall PO Box 115500	Gainesville	FL	32611	866-876-4472	352-392-3261
University of North Florida 4567 St Johns Bluff Rd S	Jacksonville	FL	32224	866-697-7150	904-620-1000

Classified Section

Name / Address	City	ST	ZIP	Toll-Free	Phone
Sarasota-Manatee 8350 N Tamiami Trail	Sarasota	FL	34243	866-974-1222	941-359-4200
University of South Florida *Tampa* 4202 E Fowler Ave	Tampa	FL	33620	877-873-2855	813-974-2011
University of South Florida Polytechnic *Lakeland* 3433 Winter Lake Rd	Lakeland	FL	33803	800-873-5636	863-667-7017
Warner Southern College 13895 Hwy 27	Lake Wales	FL	33859	800-309-9563	
Webber International University 1201 N Scenic Hwy	Babson Park	FL	33827	800-741-1844	863-638-2910

Georgia

Name / Address	City	ST	ZIP	Toll-Free	Phone
Agnes Scott College 141 E College Ave	Decatur	GA	30030	800-868-8602	404-471-6000
American InterContinental University *Atlanta* 6600 Peachtree Dunwoody Rd 500 Embassy Row NE	Atlanta	GA	30328	800-491-0182	404-965-6500
Dunwoody 6600 Peachtree-Dunwoody Rd 500 Embassy Row	Atlanta	GA	30328	855-377-1888	404-965-6500
Armstrong Atlantic State University 11935 Abercorn St	Savannah	GA	31419	800-633-2349	
Atlanta Christian College 2605 Ben Hill Rd	East Point	GA	30344	855-377-6468	404-761-8861
Augusta State University 2500 Walton Way	Augusta	GA	30904	800-341-4373	706-737-1632
Berry College 2277 Martha Berry Hwy PO Box 490159	Mount Berry	GA	30149	800-237-7942	706-232-5374
Brenau University 500 Washington St	Gainesville	GA	30501	800-252-5119	770-534-6299
Brewton-Parker College 201 David-Eliza Fountain Cir Hwy 280 PO Box 197	Mount Vernon	GA	30445	800-342-1087	912-583-2241
Clark Atlanta University 223 James P Brawley Dr SW *Admissions	Atlanta	GA	30314	800-688-3228*	404-880-8000
Columbus State University 4225 University Ave	Columbus	GA	31907	866-264-2035	706-507-8800
Covenant College 14049 Scenic Hwy	Lookout Mountain	GA	30750	888-451-2683	706-820-1560
Dalton State College 650 N College Dr	Dalton	GA	30720	800-829-4436	706-272-4436
Emmanuel College 181 Spring St	Franklin Springs	GA	30639	800-860-8800	706-245-7226
Emory University 201 Dowman Dr *Admissions	Atlanta	GA	30322	800-727-6036*	404-727-6036
Fort Valley State University 1005 State University Dr	Fort Valley	GA	31030	877-462-3878	478-825-6211
Georgia College & State University *Macon* 433 Cherry St	Macon	GA	31206	800-342-0471	478-752-4278
Georgia Southwestern State University 800 Gsw State University Dr *Admissions	Americus	GA	31709	800-338-0082*	229-928-1273
Kennesaw State University 1000 Chastain Rd	Kennesaw	GA	30144	800-542-2233	770-423-6000
LaGrange College 601 Broad St *Admissions	LaGrange	GA	30240	800-593-2885*	706-880-8005
Macon State College 100 College Stn Dr	Macon	GA	31206	800-272-7619	478-471-2700
Medical College of Georgia 1120 15th St	Augusta	GA	30912	800-736-2273	706-721-0211
Mercer University 1400 Coleman Ave	Macon	GA	31207	800-637-2378	478-301-2650
Cecil B Day 3001 Mercer University Dr	Atlanta	GA	30341	800-840-8577	678-547-6089
Oglethorpe University 3000 Woodrow Way NE	Atlanta	GA	30319	800-428-4484	404-364-8307
Paine College 1235 15th St	Augusta	GA	30901	800-476-7703	706-821-8200
Piedmont College 165 Central Ave	Demorest	GA	30535	800-277-7020	706-776-0103
Reinhardt College 7300 Reinhardt College Cir	Waleska	GA	30183	877-346-4273	770-720-5526
Shorter University 315 Shorter Ave	Rome	GA	30165	800-868-6980	706-233-7319
South University Savannah 709 Mall Blvd	Savannah	GA	31406	800-688-0932	912-201-8000
Southern Polytechnic State University 1100 S Marietta Pkwy *Admissions	Marietta	GA	30060	800-635-3204*	678-915-4188
Spelman College 350 Spelman Ln SW *Admissions	Atlanta	GA	30314	800-982-2411*	404-681-3643
Thomas University 1501 Millpond Rd	Thomasville	GA	31792	800-538-9784	229-226-1621
Truett-McConnell College 100 Alumni Dr	Cleveland	GA	30528	800-226-8621	706-865-2134
Valdosta State University 1500 N Patterson St	Valdosta	GA	31698	800-618-1878	229-333-5800
Wesleyan College 4760 Forsyth Rd	Macon	GA	31210	800-447-6610	478-477-1110

Hawaii

Name / Address	City	ST	ZIP	Toll-Free	Phone
Chaminade University 3140 Waialae Ave	Honolulu	HI	96816	800-735-3733	808-735-4711
Hawaii Pacific University *Windward Hawaii Loa* 1164 Bishop St *Admissions	Honolulu	HI	96813	866-225-5478*	808-544-0200
University of Hawaii *Hilo* 200 W Kawili St *Admissions	Hilo	HI	96720	800-897-4456*	808-974-7414
Manoa 2600 Campus Rd Rm 001 *Admissions	Honolulu	HI	96822	800-823-9771*	808-956-8975
West Oahu 96-129 Ala Ike	Pearl City	HI	96782	866-299-8656	808-454-4700

Idaho

Name / Address	City	ST	ZIP	Toll-Free	Phone
Boise State University 1910 University Dr	Boise	ID	83725	800-824-7017	208-426-1156
College of Idaho 2112 Cleveland Blvd *Admissions	Caldwell	ID	83605	800-224-3246*	208-459-5011
Lewis-Clark State College 500 Eigth Ave	Lewiston	ID	83501	800-933-5272	208-792-5272
Northwest Nazarene University 623 Holly St	Nampa	ID	83686	877-668-4968*	208-467-8000
University of Idaho *Boise* 322 E Front St Ste 190	Boise	ID	83702	866-264-7384	208-334-2999

Illinois

Name / Address	City	ST	ZIP	Toll-Free	Phone
American InterContinental University Los Angeles 231 N Martingale Rd Sixth Fl	Schaumburg	IL	60173	877-701-3800	
Augustana College 639 38th St	Rock Island	IL	61201	800-798-8100	309-794-7000
Aurora University 347 S Gladstone Ave	Aurora	IL	60506	800-742-5281	630-844-5533
Benedictine University 5700 College Rd	Lisle	IL	60532	888-829-6363	630-829-6300
Blackburn College 700 College Ave	Carlinville	IL	62626	800-233-3550	217-854-3231
Bradley University 1501 W Bradley Ave	Peoria	IL	61625	800-447-6460*	309-676-7611
Columbia College 600 S Michigan Ave 3rd Fl	Chicago	IL	60605	866-705-0200	312-663-1600
Concordia University Chicago 7400 Augusta St	River Forest	IL	60305	888-258-6773	708-771-8300
Dominican University 7900 W Div St	River Forest	IL	60305	800-828-8475	708-366-2490
East-West University 816 S Michigan Ave Ste 800	Chicago	IL	60605	877-398-9376	312-939-0111
Eastern Illinois University 600 Lincoln Ave *Admissions	Charleston	IL	61920	800-252-5711*	217-581-2223
Elmhurst College 190 Prospect Ave	Elmhurst	IL	60126	800-697-1871	630-617-3400
Eureka College 300 E College Ave	Eureka	IL	61530	888-438-7352*	309-467-6350
Governors State University 1 University Pkwy	University Park	IL	6048	800-478-8478	708-534-5000
Greenville College 315 E College Ave	Greenville	IL	62246	800-345-4440	618-664-7100
Harrington College of Design 200 W Madison St	Chicago	IL	60606	866-590-4423	
Illinois College 1101 W College Ave *Admissions	Jacksonville	IL	62650	866-464-5265*	217-245-3030
Illinois Institute of Technology 10 W 33rd St	Chicago	IL	60616	800-448-2329	312-567-3025
Illinois State University North and School Streets Hovey Hall 201 *Admissions	Normal	IL	61790	800-366-2478*	309-438-2111
Illinois Wesleyan University 1312 Pk St *Admissions	Bloomington	IL	61701	800-332-2498*	309-556-3031
Judson University 1151 N State St *Admissions	Elgin	IL	60123	800-879-5376*	847-628-2500
Knox College 2 E S St *Admissions	Galesburg	IL	61401	800-678-5669*	309-341-7000
Lake Forest College 555 N Sheridan Rd	Lake Forest	IL	60045	800-828-4751	847-234-3100
Lewis University One University Pkwy Unit 297	Romeoville	IL	60446	800-897-9000	815-836-5250
Loyola University Chicago *Water Tower* 820 N Michigan Ave *Admissions	Chicago	IL	60611	800-262-2373*	312-915-6500
MacMurray College 447 E College Ave	Jacksonville	IL	62650	800-252-7485	217-479-7056
McKendree University 701 College Rd	Lebanon	IL	62254	800-232-7228	618-537-4481
Millikin University 1184 W Main St	Decatur	IL	62522	800-373-7733	217-424-6211
Monmouth College 700 E Broadway Ave	Monmouth	IL	61462	888-827-8268	309-457-2311
National University of Health Sciences 200 E Roosevelt Rd	Lombard	IL	60148	800-826-6285	630-629-2000
National-Louis University 1000 Capitol Dr	Wheeling	IL	60090	800-443-5522	847-947-5718
Chicago 122 S Michigan Ave	Chicago	IL	60603	800-443-5522	888-658-8632
North Central College 30 N Brainard St	Naperville	IL	60540	800-411-1861	630-637-5800
North Park University 3225 W Foster Ave	Chicago	IL	60625	800-888-6728	773-244-5500
Northeastern Illinois University 5500 N St Louis Ave	Chicago	IL	60625	800-393-0865	773-442-4050
Northern Illinois University 1425 W Lincoln Hwy	DeKalb	IL	60115	800-892-3050	815-753-1000

			Toll-Free	Phone

Northwestern University
1801 Hinman Ave ....Evanston IL 60208 **800-227-7368** 847-491-7271

Olivet Nazarene University
One University Ave ....Bourbonnais IL 60914 **800-648-1463** 815-939-5011

Principia College
One Maybeck Pl ....Elsah IL 62028 **800-277-4648** 618-374-2131

Quincy University
1800 College Ave ....Quincy IL 62301 **866-703-4004** 217-222-8020
Chicago 401 S State St ....Chicago IL 60605 **800-762-5960** 312-935-6800
DuPage 905 Meridian Lk Dr ....Aurora IL 60504 **800-762-5960*** 630-375-8100
*Admissions

Robert Morris College
Orland Park
43 Orland Sq Dr ....Orland Park IL 60462 **800-225-1520** 708-226-3800
Springfield
3101 Montvale Dr ....Springfield IL 62704 **800-762-5960** 217-793-2500

Rockford College
5050 E State St ....Rockford IL 61108 **800-892-2984** 815-226-4000

Roosevelt University
430 S Michigan Ave ....Chicago IL 60605 **877-277-5978*** 312-341-3500
*Admissions
Albert A Robin
1400 N Roosevelt Blvd ....Schaumburg IL 60173 **877-277-5978*** 847-619-8600
*Admissions

Saint Xavier University
3700 W 103rd St ....Chicago IL 60655 **800-462-9288** 773-298-3000

School of the Art Institute of Chicago
36 S Wabash Ave ....Chicago IL 60603 **800-232-7242*** 312-629-6100
*Admissions

Shimer College
3424 S State St ....Chicago IL 60616 **800-215-7173** 312-235-3506

Southern Illinois University
Edwardsville SR 157 ....Edwardsville IL 62026 **888-328-5168** 618-650-2000

Trinity International University
2065 Half Day Rd ....Deerfield IL 60015 **800-822-3225** 847-945-8800

University of Illinois
Springfield
One University Plz MS UHB 1080 ....Springfield IL 62703 **888-977-4847** 217-206-4847

University of St Francis
500 Wilcox St ....Joliet IL 60435 **800-735-7500**

Western Illinois University
1 University Cir ....Macomb IL 61455 **877-742-5948*** 309-298-1414
*Admissions
Quad Cities 3561 60th St ....Moline IL 61265 **877-742-5948** 309-762-9481

Indiana

			Toll-Free	Phone

Anderson University
1100 E Fifth St ....Anderson IN 46012 **800-428-6414*** 765-649-9071
*Admissions

Ball State University
2000 W University Ave ....Muncie IN 47306 **800-382-8540** 765-289-1241

Bethel College
1001 W McKinley Ave ....Mishawaka IN 46545 **800-422-4101*** 574-807-7000
*Admissions

Butler University
4600 Sunset Ave ....Indianapolis IN 46208 **800-368-6852** 317-940-8100

Calumet College of Saint Joseph
2400 New York Ave ....Whiting IN 46394 **877-700-9100** 219-473-4215

DePauw University
101 E Seminary St ....Greencastle IN 46135 **800-447-2495** 765-658-4006

Earlham College
801 National Rd W ....Richmond IN 47374 **800-327-5426** 765-983-1600

Franklin College
101 Branigin Blvd ....Franklin IN 46131 **800-852-0232** 317-738-8000

Goshen College
1700 S Main St ....Goshen IN 46526 **800-348-7422** 574-535-7000

Grace College
200 Seminary Dr ....Winona Lake IN 46590 **800-544-7223** 574-372-5100

Hanover College 484 Ball Dr ....Hanover IN 47243 **800-213-2178** 812-866-7000

Huntington University
2303 College Ave ....Huntington IN 46750 **800-642-6493*** 260-356-6000
*Admissions

Indiana State University
200 N Seventh St ....Terre Haute IN 47809 **800-468-6478**

Indiana Tech
1600 E Washington Blvd ....Fort Wayne IN 46803 **800-937-2448** 260-422-5561

Indiana University
East 2325 Chester Blvd ....Richmond IN 47374 **800-959-3278** 765-973-8208
Kokomo
2300 S Washington St PO Box 9003 ....Kokomo IN 46904 **888-875-4485** 765-455-9217
Northwest 3400 Broadway ....Gary IN 46408 **888-968-7486** 219-980-6500
South Bend
1700 Mishawaka Ave PO Box 7111 ....South Bend IN 46634 **877-462-4872** 574-520-4870

Indiana University-Purdue University
Fort Wayne
2101 E Coliseum Blvd ....Fort Wayne IN 46805 **800-324-4739** 260-481-6100

Indiana Wesleyan University
4201 S Washington St ....Marion IN 46953 **800-332-6901** 765-677-2138

Manchester University
604 E College Ave ....North Manchester IN 46962 **800-852-3648*** 260-982-5000
*Admissions

Marian University
3200 Cold Spring Rd ....Indianapolis IN 46222 **800-772-7264*** 317-955-6038
*Admissions

Oakland City University
138 N Lucretia St ....Oakland City IN 47660 **800-737-5125** 812-749-4781

Purdue University
Calumet 2200 169th St ....Hammond IN 46323 **800-447-8738** 219-989-2400

Rose-Hulman Institute of Technology
5500 Wabash Ave ....Terre Haute IN 47803 **800-248-7448*** 812-877-1511
*Admissions

Saint Mary's College
Le Mans Hall Rm 122 ....Notre Dame IN 46556 **800-551-7621*** 574-284-4587

Saint Mary-of-the-Woods College
3301 St Mary Rd ....Saint Mary Of The Woods IN 47876 **800-926-7692** 812-535-5106

			Toll-Free	Phone

Taylor University
236 W Reade Ave ....Upland IN 46989 **800-882-3456** 765-998-2751
Fort Wayne
915 W Rudisill Blvd ....Fort Wayne IN 46807 **800-882-3456*** 260-744-8790
*General

University of Evansville
1800 Lincoln Ave ....Evansville IN 47722 **800-423-8633** 812-488-2000

University of Indianapolis
1400 E Hanna Ave ....Indianapolis IN 46227 **800-232-8634** 317-788-3368

University of Southern Indiana
8600 University Blvd ....Evansville IN 47712 **800-467-1965** 812-464-1765

Valparaiso University
1700 Chapel Dr ....Valparaiso IN 46383 **888-468-2576** 219-464-5011

Wabash College
410 W Wabash Ave PO Box 352 ....Crawfordsville IN 47933 **800-345-5385** 765-361-6225

Iowa

			Toll-Free	Phone

Ashford University
400 N Bluff Blvd ....Clinton IA 52732 **800-242-4153** 563-242-4023

Briar Cliff University
3303 Rebecca St ....Sioux City IA 51104 **800-662-3303** 712-279-5321

Buena Vista University
610 W Fourth St ....Storm Lake IA 50588 **800-383-9600** 712-749-2253

Central College
812 University St ....Pella IA 50219 **877-462-3687** 641-628-5285

Clarke College
1550 Clarke Dr ....Dubuque IA 52001 **888-825-2753** 563-588-6300

Coe College
1220 First Ave NE ....Cedar Rapids IA 52402 **877-225-5263** 319-399-8500

Cornell College
600 First St SW ....Mount Vernon IA 52314 **800-747-1112*** 319-895-4215
*Admissions

Divine Word College
102 Jacoby Dr SW ....Epworth IA 52045 **800-553-3321** 563-876-3353

Dordt College
498 Fourth Ave NE ....Sioux Center IA 51250 **800-343-6738** 712-722-6080

Drake University
2507 University Ave ....Des Moines IA 50311 **800-443-7253** 515-271-3181

Graceland University
1 University Pl ....Lamoni IA 50140 **800-859-1215** 641-784-5000

Grand View College
1200 Grandview Ave ....Des Moines IA 50316 **800-444-6083** 515-263-2800

Grinnell College
1115 8th Ave ....Grinnell IA 50112 **800-247-0113** 641-269-3600

Iowa State University
100 Alumni Hall ....Ames IA 50011 **800-262-3810*** 515-294-4111
*Admissions

Iowa Wesleyan College
601 N Main St ....Mount Pleasant IA 52641 **800-582-2383**

Loras College
1450 Alta Vista St ....Dubuque IA 52001 **800-245-6727** 563-588-7100

Luther College
700 College Dr ....Decorah IA 52101 **800-458-8437** 563-387-2000

Maharishi University of Management
1000 N Fourth St ....Fairfield IA 52557 **800-369-6480** 641-472-1110

Morningside College
1501 Morningside Ave ....Sioux City IA 51106 **800-831-0806** 712-274-5000

Mount Mercy College
1330 Elmhurst Dr NE ....Cedar Rapids IA 52402 **800-248-4504** 319-368-6460

Northwestern College
101 Seventh St SW ....Orange City IA 51041 **800-747-4757** 712-707-7000

Saint Ambrose University
518 W Locust St ....Davenport IA 52803 **800-383-2627*** 563-333-6000
*Admissions

Simpson College
701 N 'C' St ....Indianola IA 50125 **800-362-2454** 515-961-6251

University of Dubuque
2000 University Ave ....Dubuque IA 52001 **800-722-5583** 563-589-3000

University of Iowa
107 Calvin Hall ....Iowa City IA 52242 **800-553-4692** 319-335-3847

University of Northern Iowa
1222 W 27th St ....Cedar Falls IA 50614 **800-772-2037*** 319-273-2281
*Admissions

Upper Iowa University
605 Washington St PO Box 1857 ....Fayette IA 52142 **800-553-4150*** 563-425-5200
*Admissions

Waldorf College
106 S Sixth St ....Forest City IA 50436 **800-292-1903** 641-585-2450

Wartburg College
100 Wartburg Blvd ....Waverly IA 50677 **800-772-2085** 319-352-8264

William Penn University
201 Trueblood Ave ....Oskaloosa IA 52577 **800-779-7366**

Kansas

			Toll-Free	Phone

Benedictine College
1020 N Second St ....Atchison KS 66002 **800-467-5340** 913-367-5340

Central Christian College
PO Box 1403 ....McPherson KS 67460 **800-835-0078** 620-241-0723

Emporia State University
1200 Commercial St CB 4023 ....Emporia KS 66801 **877-468-6378** 620-341-1200

Fort Hays State University
600 Pk St ....Hays KS 67601 **800-628-3478*** 785-628-4000
*Admissions

Friends University
2100 University St ....Wichita KS 67213 **800-794-6945** 316-295-5000

Kansas State University
119 Anderson Hall ....Manhattan KS 66506 **800-432-8270*** 785-532-6250
*Admissions

Kansas Wesleyan University
100 E Claflin Ave ....Salina KS 67401 **800-874-1154** 785-827-5541

McPherson College
PO Box 1402 ....McPherson KS 67460 **800-365-7402** 620-241-0731

MidAmerica Nazarene University
2030 E College Way ....Olathe KS 66062 **800-800-8887** 913-782-3750

				Toll-Free	Phone
Newman University 3100 McCormick Ave	Wichita	KS	67213	**877-639-6268**	316-942-4291
Ottawa University 1001 S Cedar St *Admissions	Ottawa	KS	66067	**800-755-5200***	785-242-5200
Pittsburg State University 1701 S Broadway St	Pittsburg	KS	66762	**800-854-7488**	620-235-4251
Tabor College 400 S Jefferson St *Admissions	Hillsboro	KS	67063	**800-822-6799***	620-947-3121
University of Saint Mary 4100 S Fourth St	Leavenworth	KS	66048	**800-752-7043**	913-682-5151
Washburn University 1700 SW College Ave	Topeka	KS	66621	**800-736-9060**	785-670-1010
Wichita State University 1845 Fairmount St *Admissions	Wichita	KS	67260	**800-362-2594***	316-978-3456

Kentucky

				Toll-Free	Phone
Alice Lloyd College 100 Purpose Rd *Admissions	Pippa Passes	KY	41844	**888-280-4252***	606-368-6000
Asbury College One Macklem Dr *Admissions	Wilmore	KY	40390	**800-888-1818***	859-858-3511
Bellarmine University 2001 Newburg Rd	Louisville	KY	40205	**800-274-4723**	502-272-8000
Berea College 101 Chestnut St	Berea	KY	40403	**800-326-5948**	859-985-3500
Brescia University 717 Frederica St *Admissions	Owensboro	KY	42301	**877-273-7242***	270-685-3131
Campbellsville University One University Dr *Admissions	Campbellsville	KY	42718	**800-264-6014***	270-789-5000
Centre College 600 W Walnut St	Danville	KY	40422	**800-423-6236**	859-238-5350
Eastern Kentucky University 521 Lancaster Ave	Richmond	KY	40475	**800-465-9191**	859-622-2106
Georgetown College 400 E College St *Admissions	Georgetown	KY	40324	**800-788-9985***	502-863-8000
Kentucky Christian University 100 Academic Pkwy *Admissions	Grayson	KY	41143	**800-522-3181***	606-474-3000
Kentucky State University 400 E Main St *Admissions	Frankfort	KY	40601	**800-325-1716***	502-597-6000
Kentucky Wesleyan College 3000 Frederica St *Admissions	Owensboro	KY	42301	**800-999-0592***	270-852-3120
Lindsey Wilson College 210 Lindsey Wilson St	Columbia	KY	42728	**800-264-0138**	270-384-2126
Louisville Bible College PO Box 91046	Louisville	KY	40291	**888-676-7458**	502-231-5221
Mid-Continent University 99 Powell Rd E	Mayfield	KY	42066	**888-628-4723**	270-247-8521
Midway College 512 E Stephens St	Midway	KY	40347	**800-755-0031**	859-846-5346
Morehead State University 100 Admissions Ctr	Morehead	KY	40351	**800-585-6781**	606-783-2000
Murray State University 102 Curris Ctr	Murray	KY	42071	**800-272-4678**	270-809-3741
Northern Kentucky University Nunn Dr *Admissions	Highland Heights	KY	41099	**800-637-9948***	859-572-5220
Pikeville College 147 Sycamore St	Pikeville	KY	41501	**866-232-7700**	606-218-5250
Spalding University 851 S Fourth St	Louisville	KY	40203	**800-896-8941**	502-585-9911
Sullivan University 3101 Bardstown Rd	Louisville	KY	40205	**800-844-1354**	502-456-6505
Thomas More College 333 Thomas More Pkwy	Crestview Hills	KY	41017	**800-825-4557**	859-344-3332
Transylvania University 300 N Broadway	Lexington	KY	40508	**800-872-6798**	859-233-8242
University of Kentucky 800 Rose St	Lexington	KY	40536	**866-900-4685**	859-257-9000
University of Louisville 2301 S Third St	Louisville	KY	40292	**800-334-8635**	502-852-5555
University of the Cumberlands 6191 College Stn Dr	Williamsburg	KY	40769	**800-343-1609**	606-539-4201
Western Kentucky University 1906 College Heights Blvd *Admissions	Bowling Green	KY	42101	**800-495-8463***	270-745-0111

Louisiana

				Toll-Free	Phone
Centenary College of Louisiana 2911 Centenary Blvd *Admissions	Shreveport	LA	71104	**800-234-4448***	318-869-5131
Grambling State University 403 Main St	Grambling	LA	71245	**800-569-4714**	318-247-3811
Louisiana College 1140 College Dr	Pineville	LA	71359	**800-487-1906**	318-487-7011
Louisiana State University *Alexandria* 8100 US Hwy 71 S *Admissions	Alexandria	LA	71302	**888-473-6417***	318-445-3672
Baton Rouge 110 Thomas Boyd Hall	Baton Rouge	LA	70803	**888-846-6810**	225-578-3202
Louisiana Tech University 305 Wisteria St	Ruston	LA	71272	**800-528-3241***	318-257-2000

				Toll-Free	Phone
Loyola University *New Orleans* 6363 St Charles Ave CB 18 *Admissions	New Orleans	LA	70118	**800-456-9652***	504-865-3240
McNeese State University 4205 Ryan St	Lake Charles	LA	70609	**800-622-3352**	337-475-5000
Newcomb College Institute for Women 43 Newcomb Pl	New Orleans	LA	70118	**888-327-0009**	504-865-5422
Nicholls State University 906 E First St *Admissions	Thibodaux	LA	70310	**877-446-0561***	985-448-4507
Northwestern State University 200 Central Ave	Natchitoches	LA	71497	**800-767-8115**	318-357-6361
Our Lady of Holy Cross College 4123 Woodland Dr	New Orleans	LA	70131	**800-259-7744**	504-394-7744
Our Lady of the Lake College 7434 Perkins Rd *Admissions	Baton Rouge	LA	70808	**877-242-3509***	225-768-1700
Southeastern Louisiana University 500 Western Ave	Hammond	LA	70402	**800-222-7358**	985-549-2062
Southern University & A & M College 156 Elton C Harrison Dr PO Box 9757 *Admissions	Baton Rouge	LA	70813	**800-256-1531***	225-771-5180
Tulane University 6823 St Charles Ave *Admissions	New Orleans	LA	70118	**800-873-9283***	504-865-5000
Lafayette 611 McKinley St	Lafayette	LA	70504	**800-752-6553**	337-482-1000
University of Louisiana *Monroe* 700 University Ave *Admissions	Monroe	LA	71209	**800-372-5127***	318-342-5430
University of New Orleans Administrative Bldg Rm 103 Lakefront	New Orleans	LA	70148	**800-256-5866***	504-280-6000
Xavier University of Louisiana 1 Drexel Dr	New Orleans	LA	70125	**877-520-7388**	504-486-7411

Maine

				Toll-Free	Phone
Bates College 2 Andrews Rd Ln Hall	Lewiston	ME	04240	**888-522-8371**	207-786-6255
Bowdoin College 5000 College Stn	Brunswick	ME	04011	**800-829-1040**	207-725-3000
Colby College 4800 Mayflower Hill *Admissions	Waterville	ME	04901	**800-723-3032***	207-859-4800
College of the Atlantic 105 Eden St *Admissions	Bar Harbor	ME	04609	**800-528-0025***	207-288-5015
Husson College One College Cir	Bangor	ME	04401	**800-448-7766**	207-941-7000
Maine Maritime Academy 66 Pleasant St *Admissions	Castine	ME	04420	**800-227-8465***	207-326-4311
New England Bible College 879 Sawyer St PO Box 2886	South Portland	ME	04116	**800-286-1859**	207-799-5979
Saint Joseph's College of Maine 278 Whites Bridge Rd *Admissions	Standish	ME	04084	**800-338-7057***	207-893-7746
Thomas College 180 W River Rd *Admissions	Waterville	ME	04901	**800-339-7001***	207-859-1111
Unity College 90 Quaker Hill Rd	Unity	ME	04988	**800-624-1024**	207-948-3131
University of Maine 5713 Chadbourne Hall *Admissions	Orono	ME	04469	**877-486-2364***	207-581-1110
Fort Kent 23 University Dr *Admissions	Fort Kent	ME	04743	**888-879-8635***	207-834-7500
Machias Nine O'Brien Ave *Admissions	Machias	ME	04654	**888-468-6866***	207-255-1200
University of New England 11 Hills Beach Rd *Admissions	Biddeford	ME	04005	**800-477-4863***	207-283-0171
Westbrook College 716 Stevens Ave *Admissions	Portland	ME	04103	**800-477-4863***	207-797-7261
University of Southern Maine 96 Falmouth St	Portland	ME	04103	**800-800-4876**	207-780-4141
Gorham 37 College Ave	Gorham	ME	04038	**800-800-4876**	207-780-5670
Lewiston-Auburn College 51 Westminster St	Lewiston	ME	04240	**800-800-4876**	207-753-6500

Maryland

				Toll-Free	Phone
Bowie State University 14000 Jericho Pk Rd	Bowie	MD	20715	**877-772-6943**	301-860-4000
Capitol Technology University 11301 Springfield Rd	Laurel	MD	20708	**800-950-1992**	301-369-2800
College of Notre Dame of Maryland 4701 N Charles St *Admissions	Baltimore	MD	21210	**800-753-3757***	410-435-0100
Coppin State University 2500 W N Ave	Baltimore	MD	21216	**800-635-3674***	410-951-3600
Goucher College 1021 Dulaney Vly Rd	Towson	MD	21204	**800-468-2437**	410-337-6000
Hood College 401 Rosemont Ave	Frederick	MD	21701	**800-922-1599**	301-696-3400
Loyola College 4501 N Charles St	Baltimore	MD	21210	**800-221-9107**	410-617-5012
McDaniel College 2 College Hill *Admissions	Westminster	MD	21157	**800-638-5005***	410-857-2230

				Toll-Free	Phone
Morgan State University					
1700 E Cold Spring Ln	Baltimore	MD	21251	**800-319-4678**	443-885-3333
Mount Saint Mary's University					
16300 Old Emmitsburg Rd	Emmitsburg	MD	21727	**800-448-4347***	301-447-5214
*Admissions					
Peabody Institute of the Johns Hopkins University					
Peabody Conservatory of Music					
One E Mt Vernon Pl	Baltimore	MD	21202	**800-368-2521**	410-659-8110
Saint Mary's College of Maryland					
18952 E Fisher Rd	Saint Marys City	MD	20686	**800-492-7181***	240-895-2000
*Admissions					
Salisbury University					
1200 Camden Ave	Salisbury	MD	21801	**888-543-0148**	410-543-6000
Sojourner-Douglass College					
200 N Central Ave	Baltimore	MD	21202	**800-732-2630**	410-276-0306
Strayer University Prince George's					
4710 Auth Pl Ste 100	Suitland	MD	20746	**866-344-3297**	888-311-0355
Towson University					
8000 York Rd	Towson	MD	21252	**866-301-3375**	410-704-2113
University of Baltimore					
1420 N Charles St	Baltimore	MD	21201	**877-277-5982***	410-837-4200
*Admitting					
University of Maryland					
Baltimore County					
1000 Hilltop Cir	Baltimore	MD	21250	**800-810-0271**	410-455-1000
US Naval Academy					
121 Blake Rd	Annapolis	MD	21402	**888-249-7707***	410-293-1000
*Admissions					
Villa Julie College					
1525 Green Spring Valley Rd	Stevenson	MD	21153	**877-468-6852**	410-486-7001
Washington Adventist University					
7600 Flower Ave	Takoma Park	MD	20912	**800-835-4212**	301-891-4000
Washington College					
300 Washington Ave	Chestertown	MD	21620	**800-422-1782**	410-778-2800

Massachusetts

				Toll-Free	Phone
American International College					
1000 State St	Springfield	MA	01109	**800-242-3142***	413-205-3201
*Admissions					
Amherst College					
220 S Pleasant St	Amherst	MA	01002	**866-542-4438**	413-542-2000
Anna Maria College					
50 Sunset Ln	Paxton	MA	01612	**800-344-4586**	
Assumption College					
500 Salisbury St	Worcester	MA	01609	**888-882-7786**	508-767-7000
Atlantic Union College					
338 Main St	South Lancaster	MA	01561	**800-282-2030**	978-368-2000
Babson College					
231 Forest St	Babson Park	MA	02457	**800-488-3696***	781-235-1200
*Admissions					
Bay Path College					
588 Longmeadow St	Longmeadow	MA	01106	**800-782-7284**	
Becker College					
61 Sever St	Worcester	MA	01609	**877-523-2537**	508-791-9241
Bentley College					
175 Forest St	Waltham	MA	02452	**800-642-7131***	781-891-2244
*Admissions					
Berklee College of Music					
1140 Boylston St	Boston	MA	02215	**800-421-0084**	617-747-2221
Boston College					
140 Commonwealth Ave	Chestnut Hill	MA	02467	**800-360-2522**	617-552-3100
Brandeis University					
415 S St	Waltham	MA	02454	**800-622-0622**	781-736-3500
Clark University					
950 Main St	Worcester	MA	01610	**800-462-5275**	508-793-7711
College of the Holy Cross					
1 College St	Worcester	MA	01610	**800-442-2421**	508-793-2011
Curry College					
1071 Blue Hill Ave	Milton	MA	02186	**800-669-0686**	617-333-2210
Eastern Nazarene College					
23 E Elm Ave	Quincy	MA	02170	**800-883-6288**	617-745-3000
ELMS College					
291 Springfield St	Chicopee	MA	01013	**800-255-3567***	413-592-3189
*Admissions					
Emerson College					
10 Boylston Pl	Boston	MA	02116	**888-627-7115**	617-824-8500
Endicott College					
376 Hale St	Beverly	MA	01915	**800-325-1114***	978-232-2021
*Admissions					
Framingham State College					
100 State St PO Box 9101	Framingham	MA	01701	**866-361-8970**	508-620-1220
Gordon College					
255 Grapevine Rd	Wenham	MA	01984	**800-343-1379**	978-927-2300
Lasell College					
1844 Commonwealth Ave	Newton	MA	02466	**888-527-3554***	617-243-2225
*Admissions					
Lesley University					
29 Everett St	Cambridge	MA	02138	**800-999-1959**	617-868-9600
Massachusetts College of Art					
621 Huntington Ave	Boston	MA	02115	**800-834-3242**	617-879-7222
Massachusetts College of Pharmacy & Health Sciences					
179 Longwood Ave	Boston	MA	02115	**800-225-5506**	617-732-2850
Massachusetts Maritime Academy					
101 Academy Dr	Buzzards Bay	MA	02532	**800-544-3411***	508-830-5000
*Admissions					
Montserrat College of Art					
23 Essex St PO Box 26	Beverly	MA	01915	**800-836-0487**	978-921-4242
Mount Holyoke College					
50 College St	South Hadley	MA	01075	**800-642-4483**	413-538-2000
Newbury College					
129 Fisher Ave	Brookline	MA	02445	**800-755-7071**	617-730-7000
Nichols College 124 Ctr Rd	Dudley	MA	01571	**800-470-3379**	508-213-1560
Northeastern University					
360 Huntington Ave	Boston	MA	02115	**855-476-3391**	617-373-2000
Pine Manor College					
400 Heath St	Chestnut Hill	MA	02467	**800-762-1357**	617-731-7104
Regis College					
235 Wellesley St	Weston	MA	02493	**866-438-7344**	781-768-7000
School of the Museum of Fine Arts					
230 The Fenway	Boston	MA	02115	**800-643-6078***	617-369-3626
*Admissions					
Simmons College					
300 The Fenway	Boston	MA	02115	**800-345-8468**	617-521-2000
Smith College					
Seven College Ln	NorthHampton	MA	01063	**800-383-3232**	413-584-2700
Springfield College					
263 Alden St	Springfield	MA	01109	**800-343-1257***	413-748-3136
*Admissions					
Suffolk University					
Eight Ashburton Pl	Boston	MA	02108	**800-678-3365**	617-573-8460
Tufts University 4 Colby St	Medford	MA	02155	**800-326-4001**	617-628-5000
Wentworth Institute of Technology					
550 Huntington Ave	Boston	MA	02115	**800-556-0610**	617-989-4590
Wheaton College 26 E Main St	Norton	MA	02766	**800-394-6003***	508-286-8200
*Admissions					
Wheelock College					
200 The Riverway	Boston	MA	02215	**800-734-5212**	617-879-2206
Williams College					
880 Main St	Williamstown	MA	01267	**877-374-7526**	413-597-3131

Michigan

				Toll-Free	Phone
Adrian College					
110 S Madison St	Adrian	MI	49221	**800-877-2246***	517-265-5161
*Admissions					
Albion College					
611 E Porter St	Albion	MI	49224	**800-858-6770**	517-629-1000
Alma College 614 W Superior St	Alma	MI	48801	**800-321-2562**	989-463-7139
Andrews University					
3976 Rose Dr	Berrien Springs	MI	49103	**800-253-2874**	269-471-7771
Auburn Hills					
1500 University Dr	Auburn Hills	MI	48326	**888-429-0410**	248-340-0600
Cadillac 9600 E 13th St	Cadillac	MI	49601	**888-313-3463**	231-876-3100
Clinton Township					
34950 Little Mack Ave	Clinton Township	MI	48035	**888-272-2842**	586-791-6610
Flint 1050 W Bristol Rd	Flint	MI	48507	**800-964-4299**	810-767-7600
Baker College					
Jackson 2800 Springport Rd	Jackson	MI	49202	**888-343-3683**	517-788-7800
Owosso 1020 S Washington St	Owosso	MI	48867	**800-879-3797**	989-729-3350
Port Huron					
3403 Lapeer Rd	Port Huron	MI	48060	**888-262-2442**	810-985-7000
Calvin College					
3201 Burton St SE	Grand Rapids	MI	49546	**800-688-0122**	616-526-6000
Central Michigan University					
102 Warriner Hall	Mount Pleasant	MI	48859	**888-292-5366***	989-774-4000
*Admissions					
Concordia University Ann Arbor					
4090 Geddes Rd	Ann Arbor	MI	48105	**888-282-2338**	734-995-7322
Cornerstone University					
1001 E Beltline Ave NE	Grand Rapids	MI	49525	**800-787-9778***	616-222-1426
*Admissions					
Dearborn 4801 Oakman Blvd	Dearborn	MI	48126	**800-585-1479**	313-581-4400
Flint 4318 Miller Rd Ste A	Flint	MI	48507	**800-727-1443**	810-732-9977
Lansing 220 E Kalamazoo St	Lansing	MI	48933	**800-686-1600**	517-484-2600
Davenport University					
Lettinga Campus					
6191 Kraft Ave SE	Grand Rapids	MI	49512	**866-925-3884**	616-698-7111
Saginaw 5300 Bay Rd	Saginaw	MI	48604	**800-968-8133**	989-799-7800
Warren 27650 Dequindre Rd	Warren	MI	48092	**800-724-7708**	586-558-8700
Eastern Michigan University					
1000 College Pl	Ypsilanti	MI	48197	**800-468-6368**	734-487-1849
Traverse City					
2200 Dendrinos Dr Ste 200H	Traverse City	MI	49684	**866-857-1954**	231-995-1734
Finlandia University					
601 Quincy St	Hancock	MI	49930	**800-682-7604**	906-482-5300
Grand Valley State University					
1 Campus Dr	Allendale	MI	49401	**800-748-0246**	616-331-5000
Hillsdale College					
33 E College St	Hillsdale	MI	49242	**888-886-1174**	517-437-7341
Hope College					
69 E Tenth St PO Box 9000	Holland	MI	49422	**800-968-7850***	616-395-7850
*Admissions					
Kalamazoo College					
1200 Academy St	Kalamazoo	MI	49006	**800-253-3602***	269-337-7166
*Admissions					
Kendall College of Art & Design of Ferris State University					
17 Fountain St NW	Grand Rapids	MI	49503	**800-676-2787**	616-451-2787
Kettering University					
1700 University Ave	Flint	MI	48504	**800-955-4464**	810-762-9500
Lake Superior State University					
650 W Easterday Ave	Sault Sainte Marie	MI	49783	**888-800-5778***	906-632-6841
*Admissions					
Lawrence Technological University					
21000 W 10-Mile Rd	Southfield	MI	48075	**800-225-5588**	248-204-3160
Madonna University					
36600 Schoolcraft Rd	Livonia	MI	48150	**800-852-4951**	734-432-5339
Marygrove College					
8425 W McNichols Rd	Detroit	MI	48221	**866-313-1927***	313-927-1200
*Admissions					
Michigan Technological University					
1400 Townsend Dr	Houghton	MI	49931	**888-688-1885**	906-487-2335
Northern Michigan University					
1401 Presque Isle Ave	Marquette	MI	49855	**800-682-9797**	906-227-2650
Northwood University Michigan					
4000 Whiting Dr	Midland	MI	48640	**800-622-9000**	989-837-4200
Oakland University					
2200 Squirrel Rd	Rochester	MI	48309	**800-625-8648***	248-370-2100
*Admissions					
Olivet College 320 S Main St	Olivet	MI	49076	**800-456-7189**	269-749-7000
Rochester College					
800 W Avon Rd	Rochester Hills	MI	48307	**800-521-6010**	248-218-2011
Saginaw Valley State University					
7400 Bay Rd	University Center	MI	48710	**800-968-9500**	989-964-4200

	Toll-Free	Phone
Siena Heights University		
1247 E Siena Heights Dr ....Adrian MI 49221	800-521-0009	517-263-0731
Spring Arbor University		
106 E Main St ....Spring Arbor MI 49283	800-968-9103*	517-750-1200
*Admissions		
University of Detroit Mercy		
4001 W McNichols Rd ....Detroit MI 48221	800-635-5020*	313-993-1000
*Admissions		
University of Michigan		
Flint 303 E Kearsley St ....Flint MI 48502	800-942-5636	810-762-3000
Wayne State University		
42 W Warren ....Detroit MI 48202	877-978-4636	313-577-3577

Minnesota

	Toll-Free	Phone
Argosy University		
1515 Central Pkwy ....Eagan MN 55121	888-844-2004	651-846-2882
Augsburg College		
2211 Riverside Ave ....Minneapolis MN 55454	800-788-5678	612-330-1000
Bemidji State University		
1500 Birchmont Dr NE ....Bemidji MN 56601	800-475-2001*	218-755-2001
*Admissions		
Bethany Lutheran College		
700 Luther Dr ....Mankato MN 56001	800-944-3066	507-344-7000
Bethel University		
3900 Bethel Dr ....Saint Paul MN 55112	800-255-8706	651-638-6400
Carleton College		
100 S College St ....Northfield MN 55057	800-995-2275*	507-646-4000
*Admissions		
College of Saint Catherine		
2004 Randolph Ave ....Saint Paul MN 55105	800-945-4599	651-690-6000
Minneapolis		
601 25th Ave S ....Minneapolis MN 55454	800-945-4599	651-690-7700
College of Saint Scholastica		
1200 Kenwood Ave ....Duluth MN 55811	800-447-5444	218-723-6046
Concordia College		
901 Eigth St S ....Moorhead MN 56562	800-699-9897	218-299-4000
Gustavus Adolphus College		
800 W College Ave ....Saint Peter MN 56082	800-487-8288	507-933-8000
Hamline University		
1536 Hewitt Ave ....Saint Paul MN 55104	800-753-9753	651-523-2207
Macalester College		
1600 Grand Ave ....Saint Paul MN 55105	800-231-7974*	651-696-6357
*Admissions		
Martin Luther College		
1995 Luther Ct ....New Ulm MN 56073	877-652-1995	507-354-8221
Metropolitan State University		
700 E Seventh St ....Saint Paul MN 55106	888-234-2690	651-793-1300
Mankato 122 Taylor Ctr ....Mankato MN 56001	800-722-0544*	507-389-1822
*Admissions		
Minnesota State University		
Moorhead		
1104 Seventh Ave S ....Moorhead MN 56563	800-593-7246	218-477-2161
North Central University		
910 Elliot Ave S ....Minneapolis MN 55404	800-289-6222*	612-343-4460
*Admissions		
Saint John's University		
PO Box 2000 ....Collegeville MN 56321	800-544-1489*	320-363-2196
*Admissions		
Saint Mary's University of Minnesota		
700 Terr Heights ....Winona MN 55987	800-635-5987	507-452-4430
Southwest Minnesota State University		
1501 State St ....Marshall MN 56258	800-642-0684	
Crookston		
2900 University Ave 170 Owen Hall ....Crookston MN 56716	800-862-6466	218-281-8569
Duluth 1049 University Dr ....Duluth MN 55812	800-232-1339	218-726-8000
Morris 600 E Fourth St ....Morris MN 56267	800-992-8863	320-589-6035
University of Minnesota		
Twin Cities		
240 Williamson Hall		
231 Pillsbury Dr SE ....Minneapolis MN 55455	800-752-1000	612-625-2008
Winona State University		
175 W Mark St ....Winona MN 55987	800-342-5978	507-457-5000

Mississippi

	Toll-Free	Phone
Belhaven College		
1500 Peachtree St PO Box 153 ....Jackson MS 39202	800-960-5940	601-968-5940
Blue Mountain College		
PO Box 160 ....Blue Mountain MS 38610	800-235-0136	662-685-4771
Delta State University		
1003 W Sunflower Rd ....Cleveland MS 38733	800-468-6378	662-846-4020
Jackson State University		
1400 John R Lynch St ....Jackson MS 39217	800-848-6817	601-979-2121
Millsaps College		
1701 N State St ....Jackson MS 39210	800-352-1050*	601-974-1000
*Admissions		
Mississippi College		
200 S Capitol St PO Box 4026 ....Clinton MS 39058	800-738-1236	601-925-3000
Mississippi University for Women		
1100 College St MUW-1613 ....Columbus MS 39701	877-462-8439	662-329-4750
Mississippi Valley State University		
14000 Hwy 82 ....Itta Bena MS 38941	800-844-6885	662-254-9041
Rust College		
150 Rust Ave ....Holly Springs MS 38635	888-886-8492	662-252-8000
Tougaloo College		
500 W County Line Rd ....Tougaloo MS 39174	888-424-2566*	601-977-7700
*Admissions		
University of Mississippi		
Tupelo 1918 Briar Ridge Rd ....Tupelo MS 38804	888-846-5622	662-844-5622
University of Southern Mississippi		
118 College Dr ....Hattiesburg MS 39406	800-446-0892	601-266-1000
William Carey University		
498 Tuscan Ave ....Hattiesburg MS 39401	800-962-5991	601-318-6051

Missouri

	Toll-Free	Phone
Avila University		
11901 Wornall Rd ....Kansas City MO 64145	800-862-3678	816-501-2400
Central Methodist University		
411 Central Methodist Sq ....Fayette MO 65248	877-268-1854	660-248-3391
Chamberlain College of Nursing		
11830 Westline Industrial Ste 106 ....Saint Louis MO 63146	888-556-8226	314-991-6200
College of the Ozarks		
1 Industrial Dr PO Box 17 ....Point Lookout MO 65726	800-222-0525*	417-334-6411
*Admissions		
Columbia College Jefferson City		
3314 Emerald Ln ....Jefferson City MO 65109	800-231-2391	573-634-3250
Columbia College Lake of the Ozarks		
900 College Blvd ....Osage Beach MO 65065	800-231-2391	573-348-6463
Drury University		
900 N Benton Ave ....Springfield MO 65802	800-922-2274	417-873-7879
Evangel University		
1111 N Glenstone Ave ....Springfield MO 65802	800-382-6435	417-865-2815
Graceland University Independence		
1401 W Truman Rd ....Independence MO 64050	800-833-0524	816-833-0524
Hannibal-LaGrange College		
2800 Palmyra Rd ....Hannibal MO 63401	800-454-1119*	573-221-3675
*Admissions		
Lincoln University		
820 Chestnut St B-7 Young Hall ....Jefferson City MO 65102	800-521-5052*	573-681-5599
*Admissions		
Lindenwood University		
209 S Kingshighway ....Saint Charles MO 63301	877-615-8212	636-949-2000
Missouri Baptist University		
One College Pk Dr ....Saint Louis MO 63141	877-434-1115	314-434-1115
Missouri Southern State University		
3950 Newman Rd ....Joplin MO 64801	866-818-6778	417-625-9300
Missouri State University (MSU)		
901 S National Ave ....Springfield MO 65897	800-492-7900	417-836-5000
Missouri University of Science & Technology		
Rolla		
1870 Miner Cir G2 Parker Hall ....Rolla MO 65409	800-522-0938	573-341-4111
Missouri Valley College		
500 E College St ....Marshall MO 65340	800-999-8219	660-831-4000
Missouri Western State University		
4525 Downs Dr ....Saint Joseph MO 64507	800-662-7041	816-271-4266
National American University Independence		
3620 Arrowhead Ave ....Independence MO 64057	866-628-1288	816-412-7700
Northwest Missouri State University		
800 University Dr ....Maryville MO 64468	800-633-1175	660-562-1148
Park University		
8700 NW River Pk Dr ....Parkville MO 64152	800-745-7275	816-741-2000
Rockhurst University		
1100 Rockhurst Rd ....Kansas City MO 64110	800-842-6776	816-501-4000
Saint Louis College of Pharmacy		
4588 Parkview Pl ....Saint Louis MO 63110	800-278-5267	314-367-8700
Saint Louis University		
221 N Grand Blvd ....Saint Louis MO 63103	800-758-3678	314-977-7288
Southeast Missouri State University		
1 University Plaza ....Cape Girardeau MO 63701	866-562-6801	573-651-2000
Southwest Baptist University		
1600 University Ave ....Bolivar MO 65613	800-526-5859	
Truman State University		
100 E Normal St ....Kirksville MO 63501	800-892-7792	660-785-4000
University of Missouri (UMSL)		
Columbia 104 Jesse Hall ....Columbia MO 65211	800-856-2181	573-882-6333
Kansas City		
5100 Rockhill Rd ....Kansas City MO 64110	800-775-8652	816-235-1000
Saint Louis		
One University Blvd ....Saint Louis MO 63121	888-462-8675*	314-516-5000
*Admissions		
Washington University in Saint Louis		
One Brookings Dr ....Saint Louis MO 63130	800-638-0700	314-935-5000
Westminster College		
501 Westminster Ave ....Fulton MO 65251	800-475-3361*	573-592-5251
*Admissions		
William Jewell College		
500 College Hill WJC PO Box 1002 ....Liberty MO 64068	888-253-9355	816-781-7700
William Woods University		
One University Ave ....Fulton MO 65251	800-995-3159*	573-592-4221
*Admissions		

Montana

	Toll-Free	Phone
Carroll College		
1601 N Benton Ave ....Helena MT 59625	800-992-3648	406-447-4300
Montana State University		
Bozeman PO Box 172190 ....Bozeman MT 59717	888-678-2287*	406-994-2452
*Admissions		
Northern PO Box 7751 ....Havre MT 59501	800-662-6132	406-265-3700
Montana Tech of the University of Montana		
1300 W Pk St ....Butte MT 59701	800-445-8324*	406-496-4101
*Admissions		
Rocky Mountain College		
1511 Poly Dr ....Billings MT 59102	800-877-6259	406-657-1000
University of Great Falls		
1301 20th St S ....Great Falls MT 59405	800-856-9544*	
*Admissions		
Western 710 S Atlantic St ....Dillon MT 59725	877-683-7331*	406-683-7011
*Admissions		
Yellowstone Baptist College		
1515 S Shiloh Rd ....Billings MT 59106	800-487-9950	406-656-9950

Nebraska

	Toll-Free	Phone
Bellevue University		
1000 Galvin Rd S ....Bellevue NE 68005	800-756-7920	402-293-2000

Classified Section

				Toll-Free	Phone
Chadron State College					
1000 Main St	Chadron	NE	69337	800-242-3766	308-432-6263
Clarkson College					
101 S 42nd St	Omaha	NE	68131	800-647-5500	402-552-3100
College of Saint Mary					
7000 Mercy Rd	Omaha	NE	68106	800-926-5534	402-399-2400
Concordia University Nebraska					
800 N Columbia Ave	Seward	NE	68434	800-535-5494	402-643-3651
Creighton University					
2500 California Plz	Omaha	NE	68178	800-282-5835	402-280-2700
Doane College					
1014 Boswell Ave	Crete	NE	68333	800-333-6263	402-826-2161
Grand Island					
3180 W US Hwy 34	Grand Island	NE	68801	800-333-6263	308-398-0800
Lincoln 303 N 52nd St	Lincoln	NE	68504	888-803-6263	402-466-4774
Hastings College					
710 N Turner Ave	Hastings	NE	68901	800-532-7642	402-463-2402
Midland University					
900 N Clarkson St	Fremont	NE	68025	800-642-8382	402-941-6270
Nebraska Wesleyan University					
5000 St Paul Ave	Lincoln	NE	68504	800-541-3818	402-466-2371
Peru State College					
600 Hoyt St PO Box 10	Peru	NE	68421	800-742-4412	402-872-3815
Summit Christian College					
2025 21st St	Gering	NE	69341	888-305-8083	308-632-6933
Union College					
3800 S 48th St	Lincoln	NE	68506	800-228-4600*	402-486-2504
*Admissions					
University of Nebraska					
Kearney 905 W 25th St	Kearney	NE	68849	800-532-7639	308-865-8441
Lincoln 1410 Q St	Lincoln	NE	68588	800-742-8800	402-472-2023
Omaha 6001 Dodge St	Omaha	NE	68182	800-858-8648	402-554-2800
Wayne State College					
1111 Main St	Wayne	NE	68787	800-228-9972	402-375-7000
York College 1125 E Eigth St	York	NE	68467	800-950-9675	402-363-5600

Nevada

				Toll-Free	Phone
Great Basin College					
1500 College Pkwy	Elko	NV	89801	888-590-6726	775-738-8493
Sierra Nevada College					
999 Tahoe Blvd	Incline Village	NV	89451	866-412-4636	775-831-1314
University of Nevada					
Reno 1664 N Virginia St	Reno	NV	89557	866-263-8232	775-784-1110

New Hampshire

				Toll-Free	Phone
Colby-Sawyer College					
541 Main St	New London	NH	03257	800-272-1015*	603-526-3700
*Admissions					
Daniel Webster College					
20 University Dr	Nashua	NH	03063	800-325-6876	603-577-6000
Concord Five Chenell Dr	Concord	NH	03301	800-437-0048	603-228-1155
Franklin Pierce University					
Keene 17 Bradco St	Keene	NH	03431	800-325-1090	603-357-0079
Lebanon					
24 Airport Rd Ste 19	West Lebanon	NH	03784	800-325-1090	603-298-5549
Manchester					
670 N Commercial St	Manchester	NH	03101	800-437-0048*	603-626-4972
*Admissions					
Portsmouth					
73 Corporate Dr	Portsmouth	NH	03801	800-325-1090	603-433-2000
Rindge 40 University Dr	Rindge	NH	03461	800-437-0048*	603-899-4000
*Admissions					
Granite State College					
Eight Old Suncook Rd	Concord	NH	03301	888-228-3000	603-228-3000
Hesser College					
3 Sundial Ave	Manchester	NH	03103	888-971-2190	603-668-6660
Keene State College					
229 Main St	Keene	NH	03435	800-572-1909	603-352-1909
New England College					
98 Bridge St	Henniker	NH	03242	800-521-7642*	603-428-2223
*Admissions					
Plymouth State University					
17 High St	Plymouth	NH	03264	800-842-6900	603-535-2237
Rivier College 420 S Main St	Nashua	NH	03060	800-447-4843	603-888-1311
Saint Anselm College					
100 St Anselm Dr	Manchester	NH	03102	888-426-7356	603-641-7500
Southern New Hampshire University					
2500 N River Rd	Manchester	NH	03106	800-668-1249	603-668-2211
University of New Hampshire					
Manchester					
400 Commercial St	Manchester	NH	03101	800-287-9793	603-641-4321

New Jersey

				Toll-Free	Phone
Bloomfield College					
467 Franklin St	Bloomfield	NJ	07003	800-848-4555	973-748-9000
Caldwell College					
Nine Ryerson Ave	Caldwell	NJ	07006	888-864-9516*	973-618-3500
*Admissions					
Centenary College					
400 Jefferson St	Hackettstown	NJ	07840	800-236-8679*	908-852-1400
*Admissions					
College of New Jersey					
2000 Pennington Rd PO Box 7718	Ewing	NJ	08628	800-644-3562	609-771-1855
College of Saint Elizabeth					
2 Convent Rd	Morristown	NJ	07960	800-210-7900*	973-290-4700
*Admissions					
Fairleigh Dickinson University					
285 Madison Ave	Madison	NJ	07940	800-338-8803	973-443-8500
Metropolitan 1000 River Rd	Teaneck	NJ	07666	800-338-8803	201-692-2000
Felician College					
Rutherford					
223 Montross Ave	Rutherford	NJ	07070	888-442-4551	201-559-6000

				Toll-Free	Phone
Georgian Court University					
900 Lakewood Ave	Lakewood	NJ	08701	800-458-8422	
Kean University					
1000 Morris Ave Kean Hall	Union	NJ	07083	800-882-1037	908-737-7100
Monmouth University					
400 Cedar Ave	West Long Branch	NJ	07764	800-543-9671	732-571-3456
Montclair State University					
1 Normal Ave	Montclair	NJ	07043	800-331-9205*	973-655-4000
*Admissions					
New Jersey City University					
2039 JFK Blvd	Jersey City	NJ	07305	888-441-6528	201-200-2000
New Jersey Institute of Technology					
University Heights	Newark	NJ	07102	800-925-6548	973-596-3000
Princeton University					
33 Washington Rd	Princeton	NJ	08544	877-609-2273	609-258-3000
Rider University					
Westminster Choir College					
101 Walnut Ln	Princeton	NJ	08540	800-962-4647	609-921-7100
Rowan University					
201 Mullica Hill Rd	Glassboro	NJ	08028	877-787-6926*	856-256-4200
Seton Hall University					
400 S Orange Ave	South Orange	NJ	07079	800-992-4723	973-761-9332
Stevens Institute of Technology					
Castle Pt on the Hudson	Hoboken	NJ	07030	800-458-5323	201-216-5194
Thomas Edison State College					
101 W State St	Trenton	NJ	08608	888-442-8372	
William Paterson University					
300 Pompton Rd	Wayne	NJ	07470	877-978-3923	973-720-2000

New Mexico

				Toll-Free	Phone
College of Santa Fe					
1600 St Michaels Dr	Santa Fe	NM	87505	800-862-7759	505-473-6011
College of the Southwest					
6610 N Lovington Hwy	Hobbs	NM	88240	800-530-4400	575-392-6561
Eastern New Mexico University					
1500 S Ave K Stn 7	Portales	NM	88130	800-367-3668	575-562-1011
New Mexico Highlands University					
901 University Ave	Las Vegas	NM	87701	877-850-9064	505-425-7511
New Mexico Institute of Mining & Technology (NMT)					
801 Leroy Pl	Socorro	NM	87801	800-428-8324*	505-835-5434
*Admissions					
New Mexico State University (NMSU)					
MSC-3A PO Box 30001	Las Cruces	NM	88003	800-662-6678*	575-646-3121
*Admissions					
Santa Fe University of Art & Design					
1600 St Michaels Dr	Santa Fe	NM	87505	800-456-2673	
University of New Mexico (UNM)					
One University of New Mexico	Albuquerque	NM	87131	800-225-5866	505-277-0111
Gallup 200 College Rd	Gallup	NM	87301	800-225-5866	505-863-7500
Western New Mexico University					
1000 W College St PO Box 680	Silver City	NM	88061	800-872-9668*	505-538-6011
*Admissions					

New York

				Toll-Free	Phone
Adelphi University					
PO Box 701	Garden City	NY	11530	800-233-5744	516-877-3050
Manhattan Ctr					
75 Varick St Second Fl	New York	NY	10013	800-233-5744	212-965-8340
Albany College of Pharmacy (ACPHS)					
106 New Scotland Ave	Albany	NY	12208	888-203-8010*	518-694-7221
*General					
Bard College					
PO Box 5000	Annandale-on-Hudson	NY	12504	800-872-7423	845-758-7472
Baruch College					
55 Lexington Ave at 24th St	New York	NY	10010	800-273-8255	646-312-1000
Binghamton University					
4400 Vestal Pkwy E	Binghamton	NY	13902	800-782-0289	607-777-2000
Canisius College					
2001 Main St	Buffalo	NY	14208	800-843-1517	716-888-2200
Cazenovia College					
Eight Sullivan St	Cazenovia	NY	13035	800-654-3210	315-655-7208
City College of New York					
138th St & Convent Ave	New York	NY	10031	800-286-9937*	212-650-6448
*Admissions					
Clarkson University					
10 Clarkson Ave	Potsdam	NY	13699	800-527-6577*	315-268-6480
*Admissions					
College of Mount Saint Vincent					
6301 Riverdale Ave	Riverdale	NY	10471	877-392-6844	718-405-3304
College of New Rochelle					
29 Castle Pl	New Rochelle	NY	10805	800-933-5923	914-654-5000
College of Saint Rose					
432 Western Ave	Albany	NY	12203	800-637-8556	518-454-5150
College of Staten Island					
2800 Victory Blvd	Staten Island	NY	10314	888-442-4551	718-982-2000
Concordia College New York					
171 White Plains Rd	Bronxville	NY	10708	800-937-2655*	914-337-9300
*Admissions					
Cooper Union for the Advancement of Science & Art					
30 Cooper Sq	New York	NY	10003	800-872-2777	212-353-4100
D'Youville College					
320 Porter Ave	Buffalo	NY	14201	800-777-3921	716-829-7600
Daemen College 4380 Main St	Amherst	NY	14226	800-462-7652	716-839-8225
Dominican College					
470 Western Hwy	Orangeburg	NY	10962	866-432-4636	845-359-7800
Dowling College					
150 Idle Hour Blvd	Oakdale	NY	11769	800-369-5464	631-244-3000
Elmira College 1 Pk Pl	Elmira	NY	14901	800-935-6472*	607-735-1724
*Admissions					
Excelsior College					
Seven Columbia Cir	Albany	NY	12203	888-647-2388	518-464-8500
College at Lincoln Ctr					
113 W 60th St	New York	NY	10023	800-367-3426	212-636-6710

				Toll-Free	Phone

Fordham University
Westchester
400 Westchester Ave ....West Harrison NY 10604 **800-606-6090** 914-332-8295

Hamilton College
198 College Hill Rd ....Clinton NY 13323 **800-843-2655*** 315-859-4421
*Admissions

Hartwick College
One Hartwick Dr ....Oneonta NY 13820 **888-427-8942** 607-431-4150

Hilbert College
5200 S Pk Ave ....Hamburg NY 14075 **800-649-8003** 716-649-7900

Hobart & William Smith Colleges
300 Pulteney St ....Geneva NY 14456 **800-852-2256*** 315-781-3000
*Admissions

Hofstra University
1000 Fulton Ave ....Hempstead NY 11549 **800-463-7872** 516-463-6600

Houghton College
One Willard Ave PO Box 128 ....Houghton NY 14744 **800-777-2556** 585-567-9200

Iona College 715 N Ave ....New Rochelle NY 10801 **800-264-6350** 914-633-2502

Ithaca College 953 Danby Rd ....Ithaca NY 14850 **800-429-4274*** 607-274-3124
*Admissions

Keuka College
141 Central Ave ....Keuka Park NY 14478 **800-335-3852*** 315-279-5254
*Admissions

Laboratory Institute of Merchandising
12 E 53rd St ....New York NY 10022 **800-677-1323** 212-752-1530

Le Moyne College
1419 Salt Springs Rd ....Syracuse NY 13214 **800-333-4733*** 315-445-4100
*Admissions

Lehman College
250 Bedford Pk Blvd W ....Bronx NY 10468 **800-311-5656** 718-960-8000

Long Island University
Brooklyn
One University Plz ....Brooklyn NY 11201 **800-548-7526** 718-488-1011

Manhattan College
4513 Manhattan College Pkwy ....Bronx NY 10471 **800-622-9235** 718-862-8000

Manhattanville College
2900 Purchase St ....Purchase NY 10577 **800-328-4553** 914-323-5464

Marist College
3399 N Rd ....Poughkeepsie NY 12601 **800-436-5483** 845-575-3000

Marymount Manhattan College
221 E 71st St ....New York NY 10021 **866-667-6572** 212-517-0400

Medaille College
18 Agassiz Cir ....Buffalo NY 14214 **800-292-1582** 716-880-2200

Medgar Evers College
1650 Bedford Ave ....Brooklyn NY 11225 **866-277-5719** 718-270-4900

Mercy College
555 Broadway ....Dobbs Ferry NY 10522 **800-637-2969** 914-693-4500
Manhattan 66 W 35th St ....New York NY 10001 **800-637-2969** 212-615-3313
White Plains
277 Martine Ave ....White Plains NY 10601 **888-464-6737** 914-948-3666
Yorktown Heights
2651 Strang Blvd ....Yorktown Heights NY 10598 **877-637-2946** 914-245-6100

Metropolitan College of New York
431 Canal St ....New York NY 10013 **800-338-4465** 212-343-1234

Molloy College
1000 Hempstead Ave
PO Box 5002. ....Rockville Centre NY 11571 **888-466-5569*** 516-678-5000
*Admissions

Morrisville State College
80 Eaton St PO Box 901 ....Morrisville NY 13408 **800-258-0111*** 315-684-6000
*Admissions

Mount Saint Mary College
330 Powell Ave ....Newburgh NY 12550 **888-937-6762** 845-569-3248

Nazareth College of Rochester
4245 E Ave ....Rochester NY 14618 **800-860-6942** 585-389-2525

New York City College of Technology
300 Jay St ....Brooklyn NY 11201 **855-492-3633** 718-260-5000

New York Institute of Technology
New York Institute of Technology Northern Blvd
PO Box 8000. ....Old Westbury NY 11568 **800-345-6948** 516-686-1000
Islip PO Box 9029 ....Central Islip NY 11722 **800-345-6948** 516-686-1000
Manhattan 1855 Broadway ....New York NY 10023 **800-345-6948** 212-261-1500

New York School of Interior Design
170 E 70th St ....New York NY 10021 **800-336-9743** 212-472-1500

New York University
22 Washington Sq N ....New York NY 10011 **888-243-2358** 212-998-4500

Niagara University
5795 Lewiston Rd
PO Box 2011. ....Niagara University NY 14109 **800-462-2111** 716-286-8700

Nyack College One S Blvd ....Nyack NY 10960 **800-336-9225*** 845-358-1710
*Admissions

Pace University
One Pace Plz ....New York NY 10038 **866-722-3338** 212-346-1200
Pleasantville/Briarcliff
861 Bedford Rd ....Pleasantville NY 10570 **866-722-3338** 914-773-3200

Parsons New School for Design
65 Fifth Ave Rm 103 ....New York NY 10003 **800-252-0852*** 212-229-8989
*Admissions

Paul Smith's College
Rt 30 & 86 PO Box 265 ....Paul Smiths NY 12970 **800-421-2605*** 518-327-6227
*Admissions

Polytechnic University
Long Island 105 Maxess Rd ....Melville NY 11747 **877-503-7659*** 631-755-4300
*Admissions

Pratt Institute
200 Willoughby Ave ....Brooklyn NY 11205 **800-331-0834** 718-636-3669

Purchase College
735 Anderson Hill Rd ....Purchase NY 10577 **800-553-8118** 914-251-6000

Queens College
65-30 Kissena Blvd ....Flushing NY 11367 **888-888-0606** 718-997-5000

Roberts Wesleyan College
2301 Westside Dr ....Rochester NY 14624 **800-777-4792*** 585-594-6000
*Admissions

Russell Sage College
45 Ferry St ....Troy NY 12180 **888-837-9724*** 518-244-2217
*Admissions

Sage College of Albany
140 New Scotland Ave ....Albany NY 12208 **888-837-9724*** 518-292-1730
*Admissions

Saint Lawrence University
23 Romoda Dr ....Canton NY 13617 **800-285-1856*** 315-229-5261
*Admissions

Sarah Lawrence College
One Meadway ....Bronxville NY 10708 **800-888-2858**

Siena College
515 Loudon Rd ....Loudonville NY 12211 **888-287-4362*** 518-783-2300
*Admissions

Skidmore College
815 N Broadway ....Saratoga Springs NY 12866 **800-867-6007** 518-580-5000

State University of New York
Brockport
350 New Campus Dr ....Brockport NY 14420 **888-800-0029** 585-395-2751
College of Agriculture & Technology at Cobleskill
Rt 7 ....Cobleskill NY 12043 **800-295-8988** 518-255-5525
College of Environmental Science & Forestry
One Forestry Dr ....Syracuse NY 13210 **800-777-7373*** 315-470-6500
*Admissions
Empire State College
One Union Ave ....Saratoga Springs NY 12866 **800-847-3000** 518-587-2100
Geneseo 1 College Cir ....Geneseo NY 14454 **866-245-5211*** 585-245-5571
*Admitting
Institute of Technology
PO Box 3050 ....Utica NY 13504 **866-278-6948** 315-792-7500
Maritime College
6 Pennyfield Ave Fort Schuyler. ....Bronx NY 10465 **888-800-0029** 718-409-7200
New Paltz One Hawk Dr ....New Paltz NY 12561 **877-696-7411** 845-257-3212
Plattsburgh
101 Broad St ....Plattsburgh NY 12901 **888-673-0012*** 518-564-2040
*Admissions
Potsdam 44 Pierrpont Ave ....Potsdam NY 13676 **877-768-7326*** 315-267-2180
*Admissions
University at Buffalo
12 Capen Hall ....Buffalo NY 14260 **888-822-3648** 716-645-2450

Syracuse University
900 S Crouse Ave ....Syracuse NY 13244 **800-782-5867** 315-443-3611

Touro College
27-33 W 23rd St ....New York NY 10010 **888-247-1387** 212-463-0400

University at Albany
1400 Washington Ave ....Albany NY 12222 **800-293-7869** 518-442-3300

University of Rochester
Wallace Hall PO Box 270251 ....Rochester NY 14627 **888-822-2256*** 585-275-2121
*Admissions

University of Saint Francis
180 Remsen St ....Brooklyn Heights NY 11201 **800-356-8329** 718-522-2300

US Merchant Marine Academy
300 Steamboat Rd ....Kings Point NY 11024 **866-546-4778** 516-726-5800

Utica College
1600 Burrstone Rd ....Utica NY 13502 **800-782-8884*** 315-792-3111
*Admissions

Vassar College
124 Raymond Ave ....Poughkeepsie NY 12604 **800-827-7270** 845-437-7000

Vaughn College of Aeronautics & Technology
86-01 23rd Ave ....East Elmhurst NY 11369 **800-695-3317** 718-429-6600

Wagner College
1 Campus Rd ....Staten Island NY 10301 **800-221-1010*** 718-390-3400
*Admissions

Webb Institute
298 Crescent Beach Rd ....Glen Cove NY 11542 **866-708-9322** 516-671-2213

Wells College
170 Main St PO Box 500 ....Aurora NY 13026 **800-952-9355*** 315-364-3266
*Admissions

North Carolina

				Toll-Free	Phone

Barton College PO Box 5000 ....Wilson NC 27893 **800-345-4973** 252-399-6300

Belmont Abbey College
100 Belmont-Mt Holly Rd ....Belmont NC 28012 **888-222-0110** 704-461-6748

Bennett College
900 E Washington St ....Greensboro NC 27401 **800-413-5323*** 336-370-8624

Brevard College
One Brevard College Dr ....Brevard NC 28712 **800-527-9090*** 828-883-8292
*Admissions

Campbell University
450 Leslie Campbell Ave
PO Box 546. ....Buies Creek NC 27506 **800-334-4111** 910-893-1290

Catawba College
2300 W Innes St ....Salisbury NC 28144 **800-228-2922** 704-637-4111

Chowan University
1 University Pl ....Murfreesboro NC 27855 **888-424-6926*** 252-398-6439
*Admissions

Davidson College
PO Box 7156 ....Davidson NC 28035 **800-768-0380** 704-894-2000

Elizabeth City State University
1704 Weeksville Rd ....Elizabeth City NC 27909 **800-347-3278*** 252-335-3400
*Admissions

Elon University
314 E Haggard Ave ....Elon NC 27244 **800-334-8448** 336-278-2000

Fayetteville State University
1200 Murchison Rd ....Fayetteville NC 28301 **800-222-2594*** 910-672-1371
*Admissions

Gardner-Webb University
PO Box 817 ....Boiling Springs NC 28017 **800-253-6472** 704-406-4498

Greensboro College
815 W Market St ....Greensboro NC 27401 **800-346-8226** 336-272-7102

Guilford College
5800 W Friendly Ave ....Greensboro NC 27410 **800-992-7759*** 336-316-2000
*Admissions

Heritage Bible College
1747 Bud Hawkins Rd PO Box 1628. ....Dunn NC 28334 **800-297-6351** 910-892-3178

High Point University
833 Montlieu Ave ....High Point NC 27262 **800-345-6993** 336-841-9216

Johnson & Wales University Charlotte
801 W Trade St ....Charlotte NC 28202 **866-598-2427** 980-598-1100

Johnson C Smith University
100 Beatties Ford Rd ....Charlotte NC 28216 **800-782-7303*** 704-378-1000
*Admissions

				Toll-Free	Phone

Lees-McRae College
191 Main St W .... Banner Elk NC 28604 **800-280-4562** 828-898-5241
Lenoir-Rhyne University
625 Seventh Ave NE ....Hickory NC 28601 **800-277-5721** 828-328-7300
Livingstone College
701 W Monroe St ....Salisbury NC 28144 **800-835-3435** 704-216-6963
Meredith College
3800 Hillsborough St ....Raleigh NC 27607 **800-637-3348*** 919-760-8581
*All
Methodist University
5400 Ramsey St ....Fayetteville NC 28311 **800-488-7110** 910-630-7000
Montreat College
310 Gaither Cir PO Box 1267 ....Montreat NC 28757 **800-622-6968** 828-669-8011
Mount Olive College
634 Henderson St ....Mount Olive NC 28365 **800-653-0854** 919-658-2502
North Carolina A & T State University
1601 E Market St ....Greensboro NC 27411 **800-443-8964*** 336-334-7946
*Admissions
North Carolina Central University
1801 Fayetteville St ....Durham NC 27707 **877-667-7533*** 919-530-6100
*Admissions
North Carolina State University
2200 Hillsborough St ....Raleigh NC 27695 **800-662-7301** 919-515-2011
North Carolina Wesleyan College
3400 N Wesleyan Blvd ....Rocky Mount NC 27804 **800-488-6292*** 252-985-5100
*Admissions
Pfeiffer University
48380 Hwy 52 N ....Misenheimer NC 28109 **800-338-2060** 704-463-1360
Piedmont Baptist College
420 S Broad St ....Winston-Salem NC 27101 **800-937-5097*** 336-725-8344
*Admissions
Queens University of Charlotte
1900 Selwyn Ave ....Charlotte NC 28274 **800-849-0202** 704-337-2212
Saint Andrews Presbyterian College
1700 Dogwood Mile ....Laurinburg NC 28352 **800-763-0198** 910-277-5555
Saint Augustine's College
1315 Oakwood Ave ....Raleigh NC 27610 **800-948-1126*** 919-516-4016
*Admissions
Salem College
601 S Church St ....Winston-Salem NC 27101 **800-327-2536*** 336-721-2600
*Admissions
Shaw University 118 E S St ....Raleigh NC 27601 **800-214-6683*** 919-546-8275
*Admissions
University of North Carolina
Asheville
One University Heights CPO 1320 ....Asheville NC 28804 **800-531-9842** 828-251-6481
Greensboro
1400 Spring Garden St ....Greensboro NC 27412 **877-862-4123** 336-334-5000
Pembroke PO Box 1510 ....Pembroke NC 28372 **800-949-8627** 910-521-6000
Wilmington
601 S College Rd ....Wilmington NC 28403 **800-596-2880** 910-962-3000
Warren Wilson College
701 Warren Wilson Rd ....Swannanoa NC 28778 **800-934-3536*** 828-298-3325
*Admissions
Western Carolina University (WCU)
One University Dr ....Cullowhee NC 28723 **877-928-4968** 828-227-7211
William Peace University
15 E Peace St ....Raleigh NC 27604 **800-732-2347** 919-508-2000
Wingate University
315 E Wilson St ....Wingate NC 28174 **800-755-5550** 704-233-8000
Winston-Salem State University
601 S ML King Jr Dr
206 Thompson Ctr ....Winston-Salem NC 27110 **800-257-4052*** 336-750-2000
*Admissions

North Dakota

				Toll-Free	Phone

Dickinson State University
291 Campus Dr ....Dickinson ND 58601 **800-279-4295** 701-483-2507
Jamestown College
6000 College Ln ....Jamestown ND 58405 **800-336-2554** 701-252-3467
Mayville State University
330 Third St NE ....Mayville ND 58257 **800-437-4104**
Minot State University
500 University Ave W ....Minot ND 58707 **800-777-0750** 701-858-3000
North Dakota State University
1301 12th Ave N ....Fargo ND 58105 **800-488-6378** 701-231-8643
University of Mary
7500 University Dr ....Bismarck ND 58504 **800-288-6279*** 701-255-7500
*Admissions
University of North Dakota
PO Box 8357 ....Grand Forks ND 58202 **800-225-5863** 701-777-3000
Valley City State University
101 College St SW ....Valley City ND 58072 **800-532-8641** 701-845-7990

Ohio

				Toll-Free	Phone

Ashland University
401 College Ave ....Ashland OH 44805 **800-882-1548** 419-289-4142
Baldwin-Wallace College
275 Eastland Rd ....Berea OH 44017 **877-292-7759** 440-826-2222
Bluffton University
1 University Dr ....Bluffton OH 45817 **800-488-3257** 419-358-3000
Bowling Green State University
1001 E Wooster St ....Bowling Green OH 43403 **866-246-6732** 419-372-2531
Capital University
College & Main St ....Columbus OH 43209 **866-544-6175** 614-236-6101
Case Western Reserve University
2061 Cornell Rd ....Cleveland OH 44106 **800-967-8898** 216-368-2000
Cedarville University
251 N Main St ....Cedarville OH 45314 **800-233-2784** 937-766-7700
Central State University
1400 Brush Row Rd PO Box 1004 ....Wilberforce OH 45384 **800-388-2781** 937-376-6011
Cleveland State University
2121 Euclid Ave ....Cleveland OH 44115 **888-278-6446** 216-687-2000

				Toll-Free	Phone

College of Mount Saint Joseph
5701 Delhi Rd ....Cincinnati OH 45233 **800-654-9314** 513-244-4200
College of Wooster
1189 Beall Ave ....Wooster OH 44691 **800-877-9905** 330-263-2000
Defiance College
701 N Clinton St ....Defiance OH 43512 **800-520-4632** 419-784-4010
Denison University
100 W College St ....Granville OH 43023 **800-336-4766** 740-587-6394
Franklin University
201 S Grant Ave ....Columbus OH 43215 **877-341-6300** 614-797-4700
Heidelberg University
310 E Market St ....Tiffin OH 44883 **800-434-3352** 419-448-2000
Hiram College PO Box 67 ....Hiram OH 44234 **800-362-5280*** 330-569-5169
*Admissions
Hondros College
4140 Executive Pkwy ....Westerville OH 43081 **888-466-3767**
John Carroll University
20700 N Pk Blvd ....Cleveland OH 44118 **888-335-6800** 216-397-1886
Kent State University
800 E. Summit St PO Box 5190 ....Kent OH 44242 **800-988-5368** 330-672-2121
Ashtabula 3300 Lake Rd W ....Ashtabula OH 44004 **800-988-5368** 440-964-3322
Stark
6000 Frank Ave NW ....North Canton OH 44720 **800-988-5368** 330-499-9600
Trumbull Campus
4314 Mahoning Ave NW ....Warren OH 44483 **800-988-5368** 330-847-0571
Tuscarawas
330 University Dr NE ....New Philadelphia OH 44663 **800-988-5368** 330-339-3391
Kenyon College
103 College Dr ....Gambier OH 43022 **800-848-2468** 740-427-5000
Lake Erie College
391 W Washington St ....Painesville OH 44077 **800-533-4996** 440-375-7050
Lourdes College
6832 Convent Blvd ....Sylvania OH 43560 **800-878-3210** 419-885-5291
Malone College
515 25th St NW ....Canton OH 44709 **800-521-1146** 330-471-8100
Marietta College
215 Fifth St ....Marietta OH 45750 **800-331-7896*** 740-376-4000
*Admissions
Miami University
501 E High St ....Oxford OH 45056 **866-426-4643** 513-529-1809
Middletown
4200 E University Blvd ....Middletown OH 45042 **877-898-4656** 513-727-3200
Mount Union College
1972 Clark Ave ....Alliance OH 44601 **800-334-6682*** 330-823-2590
Mount Vernon Nazarene University
800 Martinsburg Rd ....Mount Vernon OH 43050 **800-766-8206*** 740-392-6868
*Admissions
Muskingum College
163 Stormont St ....New Concord OH 43762 **800-752-6082*** 740-826-8211
*Admissions
Ohio Dominican University
1216 Sunbury Rd ....Columbus OH 43219 **800-955-6446** 614-251-4500
Ohio Northern University
525 S Main St ....Ada OH 45810 **888-408-4668*** 419-772-2000
*Admissions
Ohio State University
154 W 12th Ave ....Columbus OH 43210 **800-426-5046** 614-292-3980
Lima 4240 Campus Dr ....Lima OH 45804 **800-228-1102** 419-995-8391
Newark 1179 University Dr ....Newark OH 43055 **800-963-9275** 740-366-3321
Ohio University
Chillicothe
101 University Dr ....Chillicothe OH 45601 **877-462-6824** 740-774-7200
Eastern
45425 National Rd ....Saint Clairsville OH 43950 **800-648-3331** 740-695-1720
Lancaster
1570 Granville Pike ....Lancaster OH 43130 **800-444-2910** 740-654-6711
Southern 1804 Liberty Ave ....Ironton OH 45638 **800-626-0513** 740-533-4600
Otterbein College
One S Grove St ....Westerville OH 43081 **800-488-8144*** 614-823-1500
*Admissions
Shawnee State University
940 Second St ....Portsmouth OH 45662 **800-959-2778** 740-351-3221
Tiffin University
155 Miami St ....Tiffin OH 44883 **800-968-6446** 419-447-6442
Union Institute & University
440 E McMillan St ....Cincinnati OH 45206 **800-486-3116** 513-861-6400
University of Akron
277 E Buchtel Ave ....Akron OH 44325 **800-655-4884*** 330-972-7100
*Admissions
University of Cincinnati
2600 Clifton Ave PO Box 210091 ....Cincinnati OH 45221 **866-397-3382** 513-556-1100
University of Dayton
300 College Pk ....Dayton OH 45469 **800-837-7433** 937-229-4411
University of Findlay
1000 N Main St ....Findlay OH 45840 **800-472-9502** 419-422-8313
University of Rio Grande
218 N College Ave ....Rio Grande OH 45674 **800-282-7201** 740-245-5353
University of Toledo
2801 W Bancroft St ....Toledo OH 43606 **800-586-5336** 419-530-4636
Ursuline College
2550 Lander Rd ....Pepper Pike OH 44124 **888-778-5463** 440-449-4200
Walsh University
2020 E Maple St ....North Canton OH 44720 **800-362-9846*** 330-499-7090
*Admissions
Wilberforce University
1055 N Bickett Rd PO Box 1001 ....Wilberforce OH 45384 **800-367-8568*** 937-376-2911
*Admissions
Wilmington College of Ohio
1870 Quaker Way ....Wilmington OH 45177 **800-341-9318** 937-382-6661
Wittenberg University
200 W Ward St PO Box 720 ....Springfield OH 45501 **800-677-7558** 937-327-6314
Wright State University
3640 Colonel Glenn Hwy ....Dayton OH 45435 **800-247-1770*** 937-775-5740
*Admissions
Xavier University
3800 Victory Pkwy ....Cincinnati OH 45207 **800-344-4698** 513-745-3000

				Toll-Free	Phone
Youngstown State University					
One University Plz	Youngstown	OH	44555	**877-468-6978***	330-941-3000
*Admissions					

Oklahoma

				Toll-Free	Phone
Bacone College					
2299 Old Bacone Rd	Muskogee	OK	74403	**888-682-5514***	918-683-4581
*Admissions					
Cameron University					
2800 W Gore Blvd	Lawton	OK	73505	**888-454-7600***	580-581-2289
*Admissions					
Hillsdale Free Will Baptist College					
PO Box 7208	Moore	OK	73153	**800-460-6328**	405-912-9000
Muskogee 2400 W Shawnee	Muskogee	OK	74401	**800-722-9614**	918-683-0040
Northeastern State University					
Tahlequah 600 N Grand Ave	Tahlequah	OK	74464	**800-722-9614**	918-456-5511
Oklahoma Baptist University					
500 W University St	Shawnee	OK	74804	**800-654-3285**	405-275-2850
Oklahoma Christian University					
PO Box 11000	Oklahoma City	OK	73136	**800-877-5010**	405-425-5000
Oklahoma City University					
2501 N Blackwelder Ave	Oklahoma City	OK	73106	**800-633-7242***	405-208-5050
*Admissions					
Oklahoma Panhandle State University					
323 Eagle Blvd	Goodwell	OK	73939	**800-664-6778**	580-349-2611
Oklahoma State University					
219 Student Union Bldg	Stillwater	OK	74078	**800-852-1255**	405-744-5000
Tulsa 700 N Greenwood Ave	Tulsa	OK	74106	**800-522-4002**	918-594-8000
Oral Roberts University					
7777 S Lewis Ave	Tulsa	OK	74171	**800-678-8876**	918-495-6161
Rogers State University					
1701 W Will Rogers Blvd	Claremore	OK	74017	**800-256-7511**	918-343-7546
Saint Gregory's University					
1900 W MacArthur St	Shawnee	OK	74804	**888-784-7347***	405-878-5100
*Admissions					
Southeastern Oklahoma State University					
1405 N Fourth St	Durant	OK	74701	**800-435-1327**	580-745-2000
Southern Nazarene University					
6729 NW 39th Expy	Bethany	OK	73008	**800-648-9899**	405-789-6400
Southwestern Christian University					
7210 NW 39th Expy PO Box 340	Bethany	OK	73008	**888-418-9272**	405-789-7661
University of Oklahoma					
1000 Asp Ave	Norman	OK	73019	**800-234-6868**	405-325-0311
University of Sciences & Arts of Oklahoma					
1727 W Alabama Ave	Chickasha	OK	73018	**800-933-8726**	405-224-3140
University of Tulsa					
800 S Tucker Rd	Tulsa	OK	74104	**800-331-3050**	918-631-2307

Oregon

				Toll-Free	Phone
Concordia University Portland					
2811 NE Holman St	Portland	OR	97211	**800-321-9371**	503-288-9371
Corban College					
5000 Deer Pk Dr SE	Salem	OR	97317	**800-845-3005**	503-581-8600
Eastern Oregon University					
One University Blvd	La Grande	OR	97850	**800-452-8639**	541-962-3393
George Fox University					
414 N Meridian St	Newberg	OR	97132	**800-765-4369**	503-538-8383
Lewis & Clark College					
0615 SW Palatine Hill Rd	Portland	OR	97219	**800-444-4111***	503-768-7040
*Admissions					
Linfield College					
900 SE Baker St	McMinnville	OR	97128	**800-640-2287***	503-883-2213
*Admissions					
Marylhurst University					
17600 Pacific Hwy 43 PO Box 261	Marylhurst	OR	97036	**800-634-9982**	503-636-8141
Northwest Christian College					
828 E 11th Ave	Eugene	OR	97401	**877-463-6622**	541-343-1641
Oregon Health & Science University Hospital					
3181 SW Sam Jackson Pk Rd	Portland	OR	97239	**800-292-4466**	503-494-8311
Oregon Institute of Technology					
3201 Campus Dr	Klamath Falls	OR	97601	**800-422-2017**	541-885-1150
Oregon State University					
104 Kerr Admin Bldg	Corvallis	OR	97331	**800-291-4192**	541-737-4411
Pacific Northwest College of Art					
1241 NW Johnson St	Portland	OR	97209	**888-390-7499**	503-226-4391
Pacific University					
2043 College Way	Forest Grove	OR	97116	**800-677-6712***	503-352-2007
*Admissions					
Portland State University					
1825 SW Broadway	Portland	OR	97201	**800-547-8887**	503-725-3000
Reed College					
3203 SE Woodstock Blvd	Portland	OR	97202	**800-547-4750***	503-777-7511
*Admissions					
Southern Oregon University					
1250 Siskiyou Blvd Britt Hall	Ashland	OR	97520	**800-482-7672**	541-552-6411
University of Oregon					
1585 E 13th Ave	Eugene	OR	97403	**800-232-3825***	541-346-1000
*Admissions					
University of Portland					
5000 N Willamette Blvd	Portland	OR	97203	**888-627-5601**	503-943-7147
Warner Pacific College					
2219 SE 68th Ave	Portland	OR	97215	**800-804-1510**	503-517-1020
Western Oregon University					
345 Monmouth Ave N	Monmouth	OR	97361	**877-877-1593***	503-838-8000
*Admissions					
Willamette University					
900 State St	Salem	OR	97301	**877-542-2787**	503-370-6303

Pennsylvania

				Toll-Free	Phone
Albright College					
1621 N 13th St	Reading	PA	19604	**800-252-1856**	610-921-2381
Allegheny College					
520 N Main St	Meadville	PA	16335	**800-521-5293**	814-332-4351
Alvernia College					
540 Upland Ave	Reading	PA	19611	**888-258-3764**	610-796-8200
Arcadia University					
450 S Easton Rd	Glenside	PA	19038	**888-232-8373**	215-572-2900
Bloomsburg University					
400 E Second St	Bloomsburg	PA	17815	**888-651-6117**	570-389-3900
Bryn Mawr College					
101 N Merion Ave	Bryn Mawr	PA	19010	**800-262-2586***	610-526-5000
*Admissions					
Cabrini College					
610 King of Prussia Rd	Radnor	PA	19087	**800-848-1003**	610-902-8552
California University of Pennsylvania					
250 University Ave	California	PA	15419	**888-412-0479**	724-938-4000
Carlow University					
3333 Fifth Ave	Pittsburgh	PA	15213	**800-333-2275**	412-578-6000
Carnegie Mellon University					
5000 Forbes Ave	Pittsburgh	PA	15213	**844-625-4600**	412-268-2000
Cedar Crest College					
100 College Dr	Allentown	PA	18104	**800-360-1222***	610-437-4471
*Admissions					
Chatham University					
1 Woodland Rd	Pittsburgh	PA	15232	**800-837-1290**	412-365-1100
Chestnut Hill College					
9601 Germantown Ave	Philadelphia	PA	19118	**800-248-0052**	215-248-7001
Cheyney University of Pennsylvania					
1837 University Cir PO Box 200	Cheyney	PA	19319	**800-243-9639**	610-399-2275
Clarion University of Pennsylvania					
840 Wood St	Clarion	PA	16214	**800-672-7171**	814-393-2306
Venango 1801 W First St	Oil City	PA	16301	**800-672-7171**	814-676-6591
Curtis Institute of Music					
1726 Locust St	Philadelphia	PA	19103	**800-640-4155**	215-893-5252
Delaware Valley College					
700 E Butler Ave	Doylestown	PA	18901	**800-233-5825**	215-489-2211
DeSales University					
2755 Stn Ave	Center Valley	PA	18034	**877-433-7253**	610-282-1100
Dickinson College					
PO Box 1773	Carlisle	PA	17013	**800-644-1773**	717-243-5121
Drexel University					
3141 Chestnut St	Philadelphia	PA	19104	**866-358-1010***	215-895-2000
*Admissions					
Duquesne University					
600 Forbes Ave	Pittsburgh	PA	15282	**800-456-0590**	412-396-6000
East Stroudsburg University					
200 Prospect St	East Stroudsburg	PA	18301	**877-230-5547***	570-422-3542
*Admissions					
Eastern University					
1300 Eagle Rd	Wayne	PA	19087	**800-452-0996***	610-341-5800
*Admissions					
Edinboro University of Pennsylvania					
200 E Normal St	Edinboro	PA	16444	**888-846-2676**	814-732-2761
Franklin & Marshall College					
PO Box 3003	Lancaster	PA	17604	**877-678-9111**	717-291-3951
Gannon University					
109 University Sq	Erie	PA	16541	**800-426-6668***	814-871-7000
*Admissions					
Geneva College					
3200 College Ave	Beaver Falls	PA	15010	**800-847-8255**	724-847-6500
Gettysburg College					
300 N Washington St	Gettysburg	PA	17325	**800-431-0803**	717-337-6000
Gratz College					
7605 Old York Rd	Melrose Park	PA	19027	**800-475-4635**	215-635-7300
Gwynedd-Mercy College					
1325 Sunneytown Pk PO Box 901	Gwynedd Valley	PA	19437	**800-342-5462***	215-646-7300
*Admissions					
Holy Family University					
9801 Frankford Ave	Philadelphia	PA	19114	**800-422-0010**	215-637-7700
Immaculata University					
1145 King Rd	Immaculata	PA	19345	**877-428-6329**	610-647-4400
Indiana University of Pennsylvania					
1011 S Dr Sutton Hall Ste 117	Indiana	PA	15705	**800-442-6830**	724-357-2230
Juniata College					
1700 Moore St	Huntingdon	PA	16652	**877-586-4282**	814-641-3000
Keystone College					
One College Green	La Plume	PA	18440	**800-824-2764**	570-945-5141
King's College					
133 N River St	Wilkes-Barre	PA	18711	**800-955-5777**	570-208-5858
Kutztown University					
15200 Kutztown Rd	Kutztown	PA	19530	**877-628-1915**	610-683-4000
La Roche College					
9000 Babcock Blvd	Pittsburgh	PA	15237	**800-838-4572***	412-367-9300
*Admissions					
La Salle University					
1900 W Olney Ave	Philadelphia	PA	19141	**800-328-1910**	215-951-1500
Lebanon Valley College					
101 N College Ave	Annville	PA	17003	**866-582-4236**	717-867-6181
Lock Haven University					
401 N Fairview St	Lock Haven	PA	17745	**800-233-8978**	570-484-2011
Lycoming College					
700 College Pl	Williamsport	PA	17701	**800-345-3920**	570-321-4000
Mansfield University					
Alumni Hall	Mansfield	PA	16933	**800-577-6826***	570-662-4000
*Admissions					
Marywood University					
2300 Adams Ave	Scranton	PA	18509	**866-279-9663**	570-348-6234
Mercyhurst College					
501 E 38th St	Erie	PA	16546	**800-825-1926**	814-824-2202
Messiah College					
PO Box 3005	Grantham	PA	17027	**800-233-4220**	717-691-6000
Millersville University of Pennsylvania					
One S George St PO Box 1002	Millersville	PA	17551	**800-682-3648**	717-872-3011
Misericordia University					
301 Lake St	Dallas	PA	18612	**866-262-6363**	570-674-6400
Mount Aloysius College					
7373 Admiral Perry Hwy	Cresson	PA	16630	**888-823-2220**	814-886-6383
Neumann College 1 Neumann Dr	Aston	PA	19014	**855-563-8626**	610-459-0905
Peirce College					
1420 Pine St	Philadelphia	PA	19102	**888-467-3472**	215-545-6400

				Toll-Free	Phone
Pennsylvania State University					
Altoona 3000 Ivyside Pk	Altoona	PA	16601	**800-848-9843**	814-949-5466
Harrisburg					
777 W Harrisburg Pk	Middletown	PA	17057	**800-222-2056**	717-948-6250
Pennsylvania State University at Erie					
Behrend College					
4701 College Dr	Erie	PA	16563	**866-374-3378**	814-898-6000
Philadelphia University					
4201 Henry Ave	Philadelphia	PA	19144	**800-951-7287***	215-951-2800
*Admissions					
Point Park University					
201 Wood St	Pittsburgh	PA	15222	**800-321-0129***	412-391-4100
*Admissions					
Robert Morris University					
6001 University Blvd	Moon Township	PA	15108	**800-762-0097**	412-262-8200
Rosemont College					
1400 Montgomery Ave	Rosemont	PA	19010	**800-331-0708***	610-527-0200
*Admissions					
Saint Joseph's University					
5600 City Ave	Philadelphia	PA	19131	**888-232-4295**	610-660-1000
Saint Vincent College					
300 Fraser Purchase Rd	Latrobe	PA	15650	**800-782-5549**	724-532-6600
Seton Hill University					
One Seton Hill Dr	Greensburg	PA	15601	**800-826-6234**	724-838-4255
Shippensburg University					
1871 Old Main Dr	Shippensburg	PA	17257	**800-822-8028**	717-477-1231
Slippery Rock University					
One Morrow Way	Slippery Rock	PA	16057	**800-929-4778**	724-738-9000
Susquehanna University					
514 University Ave	Selinsgrove	PA	17870	**800-326-9672**	570-374-0101
Swarthmore College					
500 College Ave	Swarthmore	PA	19081	**800-667-3110***	610-328-8300
*Admissions					
Thiel College					
75 College Ave	Greenville	PA	16125	**800-248-4435**	724-589-2000
Thomas Jefferson University					
1020 Walnut St	Philadelphia	PA	19107	**866-594-4722**	215-955-6000
University of Pennsylvania					
3451 Walnut St	Philadelphia	PA	19104	**800-537-5487**	215-898-5000
Bradford 300 Campus Dr	Bradford	PA	16701	**800-872-1787**	814-362-7555
Greensburg 150 Finoli Dr	Greensburg	PA	15601	**888-843-4563**	724-837-7040
Johnstown					
157 Blackington Hall	Johnstown	PA	15904	**800-765-4875**	814-269-7050
University of Scranton					
800 Linden St St Thomas Hall	Scranton	PA	18510	**888-727-2686**	570-941-7400
University of the Sciences in Philadelphia					
600 S 43rd St	Philadelphia	PA	19104	**888-857-6264**	215-596-8800
Ursinus College					
601 E Main St PO Box 1000	Collegeville	PA	19426	**877-448-3282**	610-409-3200
Valley Forge Christian College					
1401 Charlestown Rd	Phoenixville	PA	19460	**800-432-8322**	610-935-0450
Washington & Jefferson College					
60 S Lincoln St	Washington	PA	15301	**888-926-3529**	724-222-4400
Waynesburg College					
51 W College St	Waynesburg	PA	15370	**800-225-7393***	724-627-8191
*Admissions					
West Chester University					
700 S High St	West Chester	PA	19383	**877-315-2165**	610-436-1000
Widener University					
One University Pl	Chester	PA	19013	**888-943-3637***	610-499-4000
*Admissions					
Wilkes University					
84 W S St	Wilkes-Barre	PA	18766	**800-945-5378**	
Wilson College					
1015 Philadelphia Ave	Chambersburg	PA	17201	**800-421-8402***	717-264-4141
*Admissions					

Rhode Island

				Toll-Free	Phone
Bryant University					
1150 Douglas Pk	Smithfield	RI	02917	**800-622-7001***	401-232-6000
*Admissions					
Johnson & Wales University					
Providence					
Eight Abbott Pk Pl	Providence	RI	02903	**800-342-5598**	401-598-1000
Providence College					
One Cunningham Sq	Providence	RI	02918	**800-721-6444***	401-865-1000
*Admissions					
Rhode Island College					
600 Mt Pleasant Ave	Providence	RI	02908	**800-669-5760**	401-456-8000
Roger Williams University					
One Old Ferry Rd	Bristol	RI	02809	**800-458-7144**	401-254-3500
Salve Regina University					
100 Ochre Pt Ave	Newport	RI	02840	**888-467-2583**	401-847-6650

South Carolina

				Toll-Free	Phone
Allen University					
1530 Harden St	Columbia	SC	29204	**877-625-5368**	803-376-5700
Benedict College					
1600 Harden St	Columbia	SC	29204	**800-868-6598**	803-253-5000
Bob Jones University					
1700 Wade Hampton Blvd	Greenville	SC	29614	**800-252-6363***	864-242-5100
*Admissions					
Charleston Southern University					
9200 University Blvd	Charleston	SC	29423	**800-947-7474**	843-863-7050
Citadel, The					
171 Moultrie St	Charleston	SC	29409	**800-868-1842**	843-953-5230
Claflin University					
400 Magnolia St	Orangeburg	SC	29115	**800-922-1276**	803-535-5000
Clemson University					
105 Sikes Hall	Clemson	SC	29634	**800-640-2657**	864-656-3311
Coastal Carolina University					
PO Box 261954	Conway	SC	29528	**800-277-7000**	843-349-2170
Coker College					
300 E College Ave	Hartsville	SC	29550	**800-950-1908**	843-383-8000

				Toll-Free	Phone
College of Charleston					
66 George St	Charleston	SC	29424	**800-355-9983**	843-805-5507
Converse College					
580 E Main St	Spartanburg	SC	29302	**800-766-1125***	864-596-9000
*Admissions					
Erskine College					
Two Washington St	Due West	SC	29639	**800-241-8721***	864-379-2131
*Admissions					
Francis Marion University					
PO Box 100547	Florence	SC	29501	**800-368-7551**	843-661-1231
Lander University					
320 Stanley Ave	Greenwood	SC	29649	**800-922-1117***	864-388-8307
*Admissions					
Limestone College					
1115 College Dr	Gaffney	SC	29340	**800-795-7151**	864-489-7151
Medical University of South Carolina					
41 Bee St MSC 203	Charleston	SC	29425	**800-424-6872**	843-792-3281
Morris College					
100 W College St	Sumter	SC	29150	**866-853-1345***	803-934-3200
*Admissions					
Newberry College					
2100 College St	Newberry	SC	29108	**800-845-4955**	803-276-5010
Presbyterian College					
503 S Broad St	Clinton	SC	29325	**800-476-7272**	864-833-2820
South Carolina State University					
300 College St NE PO Box 7127	Orangeburg	SC	29117	**800-260-5956***	803-536-7000
*Admissions					
South University Columbia					
Nine Science Ct	Columbia	SC	29203	**800-688-0932**	803-799-9082
Southern Wesleyan University					
907 Wesleyan Dr	Central	SC	29630	**800-282-8798**	864-644-5000
University of South Carolina					
1600 Hampton St	Columbia	SC	29208	**800-868-5872**	803-777-7000
Aiken 471 University Pkwy	Aiken	SC	29801	**800-937-0762**	803-648-6851
Beaufort 801 Carteret St	Beaufort	SC	29902	**866-455-4753**	843-521-4100
Sumter 200 Miller Rd	Sumter	SC	29150	**888-872-7868**	803-775-8727
Upstate					
800 University Way	Spartanburg	SC	29303	**800-277-8727**	864-503-5246
Voorhees College					
213 Wiggins Dr PO Box 678	Denmark	SC	29042	**800-446-6250***	803-780-1234
*Admissions					

South Dakota

				Toll-Free	Phone
Black Hills State University					
1200 University St Unit 9502	Spearfish	SD	57799	**800-255-2478**	605-642-6343
Dakota State University					
820 N Washington Ave	Madison	SD	57042	**888-378-9988**	605-256-5139
Dakota Wesleyan University					
1200 W University Ave	Mitchell	SD	57301	**800-333-8506**	605-995-2600
Mount Marty College					
1105 W Eigth St	Yankton	SD	57078	**800-658-4552***	605-668-1545
*Admissions					
National American University					
321 Kansas City St	Rapid City	SD	57701	**800-843-8892**	605-394-4800
Sioux Falls					
5801 S Kiwanis Ave	Sioux Falls	SD	57108	**800-388-5430**	605-336-4600
Northern State University					
1200 S Jay St	Aberdeen	SD	57401	**800-678-5330**	605-626-3011
Presentation College					
1500 N Main St	Aberdeen	SD	57401	**800-437-6060**	605-225-1634
South Dakota School of Mines & Technology					
501 E St Joseph St	Rapid City	SD	57701	**800-544-8162**	605-394-2414
South Dakota State University					
PO Box 2201	Brookings	SD	57007	**800-952-3541**	605-688-4121
University of Sioux Falls					
1101 W 22nd St	Sioux Falls	SD	57105	**800-888-1047**	605-331-6600
University of South Dakota					
414 E Clark St	Vermillion	SD	57069	**877-269-6837**	605-677-5341

Tennessee

				Toll-Free	Phone
Aquinas College					
4210 HaRding Rd	Nashville	TN	37205	**800-649-9956***	615-297-7545
*Admissions					
Austin Peay State University					
601 College St	Clarksville	TN	37044	**800-844-2778***	931-221-7661
*Admissions					
Belmont University					
1900 Belmont Blvd	Nashville	TN	37212	**800-563-6765**	615-460-6000
Bryan College					
721 Bryan Dr PO Box 7000	Dayton	TN	37321	**800-277-9522**	423-775-2041
Carson-Newman College					
1646 Russell Ave	Jefferson City	TN	37760	**800-678-9061**	865-471-2000
Christian Bros University					
650 E Pkwy S	Memphis	TN	38104	**800-288-7576***	901-321-3000
*Admissions					
Cumberland University					
One Cumberland Sq	Lebanon	TN	37087	**800-467-0562**	615-444-2562
East Tennessee State University					
PO Box 70731	Johnson City	TN	37614	**800-462-3878**	423-439-4213
Fisk University					
1000 17th Ave N	Nashville	TN	37208	**888-702-0022**	615-329-8500
Freed-Hardeman University					
158 E Main St	Henderson	TN	38340	**800-348-3481**	731-989-6651
King College					
1350 King College Rd	Bristol	TN	37620	**800-362-0014***	423-652-4861
*Admissions					
Lambuth University					
705 Lambuth Blvd	Jackson	TN	38301	**800-526-2305**	731-427-4725
Lane College 545 Ln Ave	Jackson	TN	38301	**800-960-7533***	731-426-7500
*Admissions					
Lee University					
1120 N Ocoee St	Cleveland	TN	37311	**800-533-9930**	423-614-8000
Lincoln Memorial University					
6965 Cumberland Gap Pkwy	Harrogate	TN	37752	**800-325-0900**	423-869-3611

	Toll-Free	Phone
Lipscomb University		
3901 Granny White Pk .... Nashville TN 37204	800-333-4358	615-966-1000
Martin Methodist College		
433 W Madison St .... Pulaski TN 38478	800-467-1273	931-363-9804
Maryville College		
502 E Lamar Alexander Pkwy .... Maryville TN 37804	800-597-2687	865-981-8000
Middle Tennessee State University		
1301 E Main St .... Murfreesboro TN 37132	800-433-6878*	615-898-2111
*Admissions		
Milligan College		
PO Box 500 .... Milligan College TN 37682	800-262-8337	423-461-8730
O'More College of Design		
423 S Margin St .... Franklin TN 37064	888-662-1970	615-794-4254
Rhodes College 2000 N Pkwy .... Memphis TN 38112	800-844-5969	901-843-3700
Southern Adventist University		
4881 Taylor Cir .... Collegedale TN 37315	800-768-8437	423-236-2000
Tennessee State University		
3500 John A Merritt Blvd		
PO Box 9609 .... Nashville TN 37209	888-463-6878*	615-963-5000
*Admissions		
Tennessee Technological University		
One William L Jones Dr .... Cookeville TN 38505	800-255-8881	931-372-3888
Tennessee Temple University		
1815 Union Ave .... Chattanooga TN 37404	800-553-4050	423-493-4100
Tennessee Wesleyan College		
204 E College St PO Box 40 .... Athens TN 37371	800-742-5892	423-745-7504
Trevecca Nazarene University		
333 Murfreesboro Rd .... Nashville TN 37210	888-210-4868	615-248-1200
Tusculum College		
60 Shiloh Rd Hwy 107 .... Greeneville TN 37743	800-729-0256	423-636-7300
Union University		
1050 Union University Dr .... Jackson TN 38305	800-338-6466	731-661-5210
University of Tennessee		
Chattanooga		
615 McCallie Ave .... Chattanooga TN 37403	800-882-6627	423-425-4111
Martin 544 University St .... Martin TN 38238	800-829-8861	731-881-7020
University of the South		
735 University Ave .... Sewanee TN 37383	800-522-2234	931-598-1238
Vanderbilt University		
2201 W End Ave .... Nashville TN 37240	800-288-0432	615-322-7311

Texas

	Toll-Free	Phone
Angelo State University		
2601 W Ave N ASU Stn 11014 .... San Angelo TX 76909	800-946-8627	325-942-2041
Austin College		
900 N Grand Ave .... Sherman TX 75090	866-776-0056	903-813-3000
Austin Graduate School of Theology		
7640 Guadalupe St .... Austin TX 78752	866-287-4723	512-476-2772
Baylor University		
1311 S Fifth St 1 Bear Pl 98013 .... Waco TX 76798	800-229-5678	254-710-3718
Concordia University Austin		
3400 IH-35 N .... Austin TX 78705	800-865-4282	512-486-2000
Criswell College		
4010 Gaston Ave .... Dallas TX 75246	800-899-0012	214-821-5433
Dallas Baptist University		
3000 Mtn Creek Pkwy .... Dallas TX 75211	800-460-1328	214-333-7100
East Texas Baptist University		
1209 N Grove St .... Marshall TX 75670	800-804-3828	903-935-7963
Hardin-Simmons University		
2200 Hickory St .... Abilene TX 79698	877-464-7889	325-670-1206
Houston Baptist University		
7502 Fondren Rd .... Houston TX 77074	800-969-3210*	281-649-3000
*Admissions		
Howard Payne University		
1000 Fisk Ave .... Brownwood TX 76801	800-950-8465	325-646-2502
Huston-Tillotson University		
900 Chicon St .... Austin TX 78702	877-487-8702	512-505-3000
LeTourneau University		
2100 S Mobberly Ave .... Longview TX 75602	800-759-8811	903-233-3000
Lubbock Christian University		
5601 19th St .... Lubbock TX 79407	800-933-7601	806-720-7151
McMurry University		
1 McMurry University 1400 Sayles Blvd. .... Abilene TX 79697	800-460-2392	325-793-4700
Midwestern State University		
3410 Taft Blvd .... Wichita Falls TX 76308	800-842-1922*	940-397-4000
*Admissions		
Northwood University		
Texas 1114 W FM 1382 .... Cedar Hill TX 75104	800-927-9663	972-291-1541
Our Lady of the Lake University		
411 SW 24th St .... San Antonio TX 78207	800-436-6558	210-434-6711
Paul Quinn College		
3837 Simpson Stuart Rd .... Dallas TX 75241	800-433-3243	214-376-1000
Prairie View A & M University		
PO Box 519 .... Prairie View TX 77446	800-787-7826	936-857-2626
Rice University		
6100 Main St .... Houston TX 77005	800-527-6957	713-348-0000
Saint Mary's University		
One Camino Santa Maria .... San Antonio TX 78228	800-367-7868*	210-436-3126
*Admissions		
Sam Houston State University		
1903 University Ave .... Huntsville TX 77340	866-232-7528	936-294-1111
Schreiner University		
2100 Memorial Blvd .... Kerrville TX 78028	800-343-4919	830-792-7217
Southern Methodist University		
6425 Boaz Ln .... Dallas TX 75205	800-323-0672	214-768-2000
Southwestern Adventist University		
100 W Hillcrest Dr PO Box 567 .... Keene TX 76059	888-732-7928*	817-645-3921
*Admissions		
Southwestern Assemblies of God University		
1200 Sycamore St .... Waxahachie TX 75165	888-937-7248	972-937-4010
Southwestern Christian College		
PO Box 10 .... Terrell TX 75160	800-925-9357	972-524-3341
Southwestern University		
PO Box 770 .... Georgetown TX 78627	800-252-3166	512-863-1200
Sul Ross State University		
E Hwy 90 .... Alpine TX 79832	888-722-7778	432-837-8011

	Toll-Free	Phone
Tarleton State University		
1333 W Washington PO Box T-0030 .... Stephenville TX 76402	800-687-8236	254-968-9000
Texas A & M International University		
5201 University Blvd .... Laredo TX 78041	888-489-2648	956-326-2001
Texas A & M University		
Rudder Tower Ste 205 .... College Station TX 77843	888-890-5667	979-845-8901
Galveston		
200 Seawolf Pkwy Bldg 3026 .... Galveston TX 77553	877-322-4443	409-740-4428
Kingsville		
700 University Blvd MSC 128 .... Kingsville TX 78363	800-726-8192	361-593-2111
Texarkana		
7101 University Ave .... Texarkana TX 75503	866-791-9120	903-223-3000
Texas Christian University		
TCU PO Box 297043 .... Fort Worth TX 76129	800-828-3764	817-257-7490
Texas College		
2404 N Grand Ave .... Tyler TX 75702	800-306-6299	903-593-8311
Texas Lutheran University		
1000 W Ct St .... Seguin TX 78155	800-771-8521	830-372-8000
Texas Southern University		
3100 Cleburne St .... Houston TX 77004	800-252-5400	713-313-7011
Texas State University		
San Marcos		
601 University Dr .... San Marcos TX 78666	866-294-0987*	512-245-2340
*Admissions		
Texas Tech University		
PO Box 45005 .... Lubbock TX 79409	888-270-3369	806-742-1480
Texas Wesleyan University		
1201 Wesleyan St .... Fort Worth TX 76105	800-580-8980	817-531-4444
Texas Woman's University		
304 Admin Dr PO Box 425589 .... Denton TX 76204	866-809-6130	940-898-3188
Trinity University		
One Trinity Pl .... San Antonio TX 78212	800-874-6489	210-999-7011
University of Dallas		
1845 E Northgate Dr .... Irving TX 75062	800-628-6999*	972-721-5266
*Admissions		
University of Houston		
Victoria		
3007 N Ben Wilson St .... Victoria TX 77901	877-970-4848	361-570-4848
University of Mary Hardin-Baylor		
900 College St PO Box 8004 .... Belton TX 76513	800-727-8642	254-295-8642
University of North Texas		
PO Box 311277 .... Denton TX 76203	800-868-8211	940-565-2681
University of Saint Thomas		
3800 Montrose Blvd .... Houston TX 77006	800-856-8565	713-522-7911
Brownsville		
80 Fort Brown St .... Brownsville TX 78520	800-892-3348	956-882-8200
Dallas		
800 W Campbell Rd Ste Be3204 .... Richardson TX 75080	800-889-2443	972-883-2111
El Paso		
500 W University Ave .... El Paso TX 79968	800-551-0294*	915-747-5000
*Admissions		
Pan American		
1201 W University Dr .... Edinburg TX 78539	866-441-8872	956-381-8872
Permian Basin		
4901 E University Blvd .... Odessa TX 79762	866-552-8872*	432-552-2020
*Admissions		
University of Texas		
San Antonio		
6900 N Loop 1604 W .... San Antonio TX 78249	800-669-0919	210-458-4011
Tyler 3900 University Blvd .... Tyler TX 75799	800-888-9537	903-566-7000
University of the Incarnate Word		
4301 Broadway St .... San Antonio TX 78209	800-749-9673*	210-829-6000
*Admissions		
Wayland Baptist University		
1900 W Seventh St .... Plainview TX 79072	800-588-1928	806-291-1000
West Texas A & M University		
2501 Fourth Ave .... Canyon TX 79016	877-656-2065	806-651-2020
Wiley College		
711 Wiley Ave .... Marshall TX 75670	800-658-6889*	903-927-3300
*Admissions		

Utah

	Toll-Free	Phone
Dixie State College of Utah		
225 S 700 E .... Saint George UT 84770	855-628-8140	435-652-7500
Utah State University		
1600 Old Main Hill .... Logan UT 84322	800-488-8108	435-797-1116
Davis		
2750 N University Pk Blvd .... Layton UT 84041	800-848-7770	801-395-3473

Vermont

	Toll-Free	Phone
Bennington College		
One College Dr .... Bennington VT 05201	800-833-6845	802-442-5401
Burlington College		
351 N Ave .... Burlington VT 05401	800-862-9616	
Castleton State College		
86 Seminary St .... Castleton VT 05735	800-639-8521	802-468-5611
Champlain College		
163 S Willard St .... Burlington VT 05401	800-570-5858	802-860-2700
College of Saint Joseph in Vermont		
71 Clement Rd .... Rutland VT 05701	877-270-9998*	802-773-5900
*Admissions		
Goddard College		
123 Pitkin Rd .... Plainfield VT 05667	800-468-4888	802-454-8311
Green Mountain College		
One Brennan Cir .... Poultney VT 05764	800-776-6675*	802-287-8000
*Admissions		
Johnson State College		
337 College Hill .... Johnson VT 05656	800-635-2356	802-635-2356
Lyndon State College		
1001 College Rd PO Box 919 .... Lyndonville VT 05851	800-225-1998	802-626-6413
Marlboro College		
2582 S Rd PO Box A .... Marlboro VT 05344	800-343-0049	802-257-4333
Middlebury College		
131 S Main St .... Middlebury VT 05753	877-214-3330	802-443-3000

				Toll-Free	Phone
Norwich University 158 Harmon St	Northfield	VT	05663	800-468-6679	802-485-2001
Saint Michael's College One Winooski Pk	Colchester	VT	05439	800-762-8000	802-654-2000
Southern Vermont College 982 Manison Dr	Bennington	VT	05201	800-378-2782	802-442-5427
University of Vermont 85 S Prospect St	Burlington	VT	05405	800-499-0113	802-656-3131

Virginia

				Toll-Free	Phone
Bluefield College 3000 College Dr	Bluefield	VA	24605	800-872-0175	276-326-3682
Bridgewater College 402 E College St	Bridgewater	VA	22812	800-759-8328	540-828-5375
Christendom College 134 Christendom Dr	Front Royal	VA	22630	800-877-5456	540-636-2900
Christopher Newport University One University Pl *Admissions	Newport News	VA	23606	800-333-4268*	757-594-7015
Eastern Mennonite University 1200 Pk Rd *Admissions	Harrisonburg	VA	22802	800-368-2665*	540-432-4118
Emory & Henry College PO Box 10 *Admissions	Emory	VA	24327	800-848-5493*	276-944-4121
Ferrum College 215 Ferrum Mtn Rd	Ferrum	VA	24088	800-868-9797	540-365-2121
George Mason University 4400 University Dr	Fairfax	VA	22030	888-627-6612	703-993-1000
Hampden-Sydney College PO Box 667 *Admissions	Hampden Sydney	VA	23943	800-755-0733*	434-223-6120
Hampton University 100 E Queen St	Hampton	VA	23668	800-624-3341	757-727-5000
Hollins University PO BOX 9707 *Admissions	Roanoke	VA	24020	800-456-9595*	540-362-6401
Liberty University 1971 University Blvd	Lynchburg	VA	24502	800-543-5317	434-582-2000
Longwood University 201 High St	Farmville	VA	23909	800-281-4677	434-395-2060
Lynchburg College 1501 Lakeside Dr	Lynchburg	VA	24501	800-426-8101	434-544-8100
Mary Baldwin College 318 Prospect St *Admissions	Staunton	VA	24401	800-468-2262*	540-887-7019
Marymount University 2807 N Glebe Rd	Arlington	VA	22207	800-548-7638	703-522-5600
Norfolk State University 700 Pk Ave	Norfolk	VA	23504	800-274-1821	757-823-8600
Old Dominion University Rollins Hall	Norfolk	VA	23529	800-348-7926	757-683-3685
Radford University 801 E Main St *Admissions	Radford	VA	24142	800-890-4265*	540-831-5371
Randolph College 2500 Rivermont Ave *Admissions	Lynchburg	VA	24503	800-745-7692*	434-947-8000
Randolph-Macon College PO Box 5005	Ashland	VA	23005	800-888-1762	804-752-7200
Roanoke College 221 College Ln *Admissions	Salem	VA	24153	800-388-2276*	540-375-2270
Shenandoah University 1460 University Dr	Winchester	VA	22601	800-432-2266	540-665-4581
Southern Virginia University One University Hill Dr	Buena Vista	VA	24416	800-229-8420	540-261-8400
Strayer University Alexandria 2730 Eisenhower Ave	Alexandria	VA	22314	888-311-0355	
Strayer University Arlington 2121 15th St N	Arlington	VA	22201	888-478-7293	703-892-5100
Strayer University Fredericksburg 150 Riverside Pkwy Ste 100	Fredericksburg	VA	22406	888-311-0355	540-374-4300
Sweet Briar College 134 Chappel Rd *Admissions	Sweet Briar	VA	24595	800-381-6142*	434-381-6100
University of Mary Washington 1301 College Ave *Admissions	Fredericksburg	VA	22401	800-468-5614*	540-654-2000
University of Richmond Westhampton College 28 Westhampton Way	University Of Richmond	VA	23173	800-700-1662	804-289-8000
University of Virginia's College at Wise One College Ave *Admissions	Wise	VA	24293	888-282-9324*	276-328-0102
Virginia Commonwealth University 910 W Franklin St	Richmond	VA	23284	800-841-3638	804-828-0100
Virginia Military Institute 319 Letcher Ave	Lexington	VA	24450	800-767-4207	540-464-7211
Virginia Polytechnic Institute & State University 112 Burruss Hall	Blacksburg	VA	24061	800-555-9292	540-231-6000
Virginia State University One Hayden Dr *Admissions	Petersburg	VA	23806	800-871-7611*	804-524-5000
Virginia Union University 1500 N Lombardy St	Richmond	VA	23220	800-368-3227	804-342-3570
Virginia Wesleyan College 1584 Wesleyan Dr	Norfolk	VA	23502	800-737-8684	757-455-3200
Washington & Lee University 204 W Washington St	Lexington	VA	24450	800-221-3943	540-458-8710

Washington

				Toll-Free	Phone
Antioch University 2326 Sixth Ave	Seattle	WA	98121	888-268-4477	206-441-5352
Central Washington University 400 E University Way *Admissions	Ellensburg	WA	98926	866-298-4968*	509-963-1111
City University 11900 NE First St *Admissions	Bellevue	WA	98005	800-426-5596*	425-637-1010
Evergreen State College 2700 Evergreen Pkwy	Olympia	WA	98505	888-492-9480	360-867-6000
Gonzaga University 502 E Boone Ave	Spokane	WA	99258	800-986-9585	509-323-6572
Heritage University 3240 Ft Rd	Toppenish	WA	98948	888-272-6190	509-865-8500
Northwest University 5520 108th Ave NE *Admissions	Kirkland	WA	98033	800-669-3781*	425-822-8266
Pacific Lutheran University 1010 122nd St S	Tacoma	WA	98444	800-274-6758	253-531-6900
Saint Martin's University 5300 Pacific Ave SE *Admissions	Lacey	WA	98503	800-368-8803*	360-438-4311
Seattle Pacific University 3307 Third Ave W	Seattle	WA	98119	800-366-3344	206-281-2000
Seattle University 901 12th Ave	Seattle	WA	98122	800-426-7123	206-296-6000
University of Puget Sound 1500 N Warner St	Tacoma	WA	98416	800-396-7191	253-879-3100
Walla Walla University 204 S College Ave	College Place	WA	99324	800-541-8900	509-527-2327
Washington State University PO Box 641040	Pullman	WA	99164	888-468-6978	509-335-3564
Spokane 310 N Riverpoint Blvd PO Box 1495	Spokane	WA	99210	800-233-3247	509-358-7978
Whitman College 345 Boyer Ave *Admissions	Walla Walla	WA	99362	877-462-9448*	509-527-5111
Whitworth College 300 W Hawthorne Rd *Admissions	Spokane	WA	99251	800-533-4668*	509-777-1000

West Virginia

				Toll-Free	Phone
Alderson-Broaddus College 101 College Hill Rd CB 2003 *Admissions	Philippi	WV	26416	800-263-1549*	304-457-1700
Bethany College One Main St	Bethany	WV	26032	800-922-7611	304-829-7000
Bluefield State College 219 Rock St	Bluefield	WV	24701	800-654-7798	304-327-4000
Concord University PO Box 1000	Athens	WV	24712	800-344-6679	304-384-3115
Davis & Elkins College 100 Campus Dr	Elkins	WV	26241	800-624-3157	304-637-1900
Fairmont State University 1201 Locust Ave *Admissions	Fairmont	WV	26554	800-641-5678*	304-367-4892
Glenville State College 200 High St *Admissions	Glenville	WV	26351	800-924-2010*	304-462-7361
Marshall University One John Marshall Dr	Huntington	WV	25755	800-642-3463	304-696-3170
Ohio Valley University One Campus View Dr *Admissions	Vienna	WV	26105	877-446-8668*	304-865-6000
Salem International University 223 W Main St	Salem	WV	26426	800-283-4562	304-326-1109
Shepherd University 301 N King St	Shepherdstown	WV	25443	800-344-5231	304-876-5000
University of Charleston 2300 MacCorkle Ave SE *Admissions	Charleston	WV	25304	800-995-4682*	304-357-4800
West Virginia State University Barron Dr Rt 25 E PO Box 1000	Institute	WV	25112	800-987-2112	304-766-3000
West Virginia University PO Box 6009	Morgantown	WV	26506	800-344-9881	304-293-2121
Institute of Technology 405 Fayette Pk	Montgomery	WV	25136	888-554-8324	304-442-1000
West Virginia Wesleyan College 59 College Ave *Admitting	Buckhannon	WV	26201	800-722-9933*	304-473-8000
Wheeling Jesuit University 316 Washington Ave	Wheeling	WV	26003	800-624-6992	304-243-2000

Wisconsin

				Toll-Free	Phone
Alverno College PO Box 343922	Milwaukee	WI	53234	800-933-3401	414-382-6100
Bellin College of Nursing 3201 Eaton Rd	Green Bay	WI	54311	800-236-8707	920-433-6699
Beloit College 700 College St *Admissions	Beloit	WI	53511	800-331-4943*	608-363-2500
Cardinal Stritch University 6801 N Yates Rd	Milwaukee	WI	53217	800-347-8822	414-410-4000
Carroll University 100 NE Ave	Waukesha	WI	53186	800-227-7655	262-547-1211
Carthage College 2001 Alford Pk Dr *Admissions	Kenosha	WI	53140	800-351-4058*	262-551-8500
Columbia College of Nursing (CCON) 4425 N Port Washington Rd	Glendale	WI	53212	800-221-5573	414-326-2330
Concordia University Wisconsin 12800 N Lake Shore Dr *Admissions	Mequon	WI	53097	888-628-9472*	262-243-5700
Edgewood College 1000 Edgewood College Dr	Madison	WI	53711	800-444-4861	608-663-2294
Lakeland College PO Box 359	Sheboygan	WI	53082	800-569-2166	920-565-2111

				Toll-Free	Phone

Lawrence University
115 S Drew St . . . . Appleton WI 54911 **888-959-2016** 920-832-7000

Maranatha Baptist Bible College
745 W Main St . . . . Watertown WI 53094 **800-622-2947** 920-206-2330

Marquette University
1217 W Wisconsin Ave . . . . Milwaukee WI 53233 **800-222-6544*** 414-288-7302
*Admissions

Milwaukee Institute of Art & Design
273 E Erie St . . . . Milwaukee WI 53202 **888-749-6423** 414-276-7889

Milwaukee School of Engineering
1025 N Broadway St . . . . Milwaukee WI 53202 **800-332-6763** 414-277-6763

Mount Mary College
2900 N Menomonee River Pkwy . . . . Milwaukee WI 53222 **800-321-6265*** 414-256-1219
*Admissions

Northland Baptist Bible College (NBBC)
W10085 Pike Plains Rd . . . . Dunbar WI 54119 **800-425-9385** 715-324-6900

Northland College
1411 Ellis Ave . . . . Ashland WI 54806 **800-753-1840** 715-682-1224

Ripon College
300 Seward St PO Box 248 . . . . Ripon WI 54971 **800-947-4766***
*Admissions

Saint Norbert College
100 Grant St . . . . De Pere WI 54115 **800-236-4878*** 920-403-3005
*Admissions

Silver Lake College
2406 S Alverno Rd . . . . Manitowoc WI 54220 **800-236-4752** 920-686-6175

University of Wisconsin
Eau Claire
105 Garfield Ave PO Box 4004 . . . . Eau Claire WI 54701 **800-473-2255** 715-836-2637
Green Bay 2420 Nicolet Dr . . . . Green Bay WI 54311 **800-465-4329** 920-465-2000
La Crosse
1725 State St 115 Graff Main Hall . . . . La Crosse WI 54601 **800-382-2150** 608-785-8000
Platteville
One University Plz . . . . Platteville WI 53818 **800-362-5515** 608-342-1125
River Falls
410 S Third St B3 E Hathorn Hall . . . . River Falls WI 54022 **800-852-5711** 715-425-3911
Stout 802 S Broadway . . . . Menomonie WI 54751 **800-447-8688*** 715-232-1232
*Admissions
Superior
Belknap & Catlin PO Box 2000 . . . . Superior WI 54880 **877-345-3494** 715-394-8101

Viterbo University
900 Viterbo Dr . . . . La Crosse WI 54601 **800-848-3726** 608-796-3000

Wisconsin Lutheran College
8800 W Bluemound Rd . . . . Milwaukee WI 53226 **800-765-4977** 414-443-8800

Wyoming

				Toll-Free	Phone

University of Wyoming
1000 E University Ave Dept 3435 . . . . Laramie WY 82071 **800-342-5996*** 307-766-5160
*Admissions

168 COLLEGES & UNIVERSITIES - GRADUATE & PROFESSIONAL SCHOOLS

				Toll-Free	Phone

American Public University System (AMU)
111 W Congress St . . . . Charles Town WV 25414 **877-777-9081** 304-724-3700

168-1 Law Schools

Law schools listed here are approved by the American Bar Association.

				Toll-Free	Phone

Albany Law School of Union University (ALS)
80 New Scotland Ave . . . . Albany NY 12208 **800-448-3500** 518-445-2311

American University Washington College of Law
4801 Massachusetts Ave NW . . . . Washington DC 20016 **800-995-6423** 202-274-4101

Appalachian School of Law
1169 Edgewater Dr . . . . Grundy VA 24614 **800-895-7411** 276-935-4349

Arizona State University
Sandra Day O'Connor College of Law
PO Box 877906 . . . . Tempe AZ 85287 **855-278-5080** 480-965-6181

Baylor University School of Law
1114 S University Parks Dr
1 Bear Pl 97288 . . . . Waco TX 76798 **800-229-5678** 254-710-1911

Benjamin N Cardozo School of Law Yeshiva University
55 Fifth Ave Brookdale Ctr . . . . New York NY 10003 **800-232-5463** 212-790-0200

Boston College Law School
885 Centre St . . . . Newton MA 02459 **800-321-2211** 617-552-8550

Boston University School of Law
765 Commonwealth Ave . . . . Boston MA 02215 **800-321-2211** 617-353-3100

California Western School of Law
225 Cedar St . . . . San Diego CA 92101 **800-255-4252** 619-525-1401

Campbell University Norman Adrian Wiggins School of Law
113 Main St . . . . Buies Creek NC 27506 **800-334-4111** 919-865-5991

Capital University Law School
303 E Broad St . . . . Columbus OH 43215 **800-362-2779** 614-236-6500

Case Western Reserve University School of Law
11075 E Blvd . . . . Cleveland OH 44106 **800-756-0036** 216-368-3600

Cleveland State University Cleveland-Marshall College of Law
1801 Euclid Ave LB 138 . . . . Cleveland OH 44115 **866-687-2304** 216-687-2344

DePaul University College of Law
25 E Jackson Blvd . . . . Chicago IL 60604 **800-445-8667** 312-362-8701

Drake University School of Law
2507 University Ave . . . . Des Moines IA 50311 **800-443-7253** 515-271-2824

Duke University School of Law
201 Science Dr PO Box 90362 . . . . Durham NC 27708 **888-529-2586** 919-613-7006

Duquesne University School of Law
600 Forbes Ave . . . . Pittsburgh PA 15282 **800-732-8353** 412-396-6300

Florida Coastal School of Law
8787 Bay Pine Rd . . . . Jacksonville FL 32256 **877-210-2591** 904-680-7700

Golden Gate University School of Law
536 Mission St . . . . San Francisco CA 94105 **800-448-4968** 415-442-6600

				Toll-Free	Phone

Gonzaga University School of Law
721 N Cincinnati St PO Box 3528 . . . . Spokane WA 99220 **800-793-1710*** 509-313-3700
*Admissions

Hamline University School of Law
1536 Hewitt Ave . . . . Saint Paul MN 55104 **800-388-3688** 651-523-2800

Hofstra University School of Law
121 Hofstra University . . . . Hempstead NY 11549 **800-463-7872** 516-463-5916

Howard University School of Law
2900 Van Ness St NW . . . . Washington DC 20008 **800-829-9019** 202-806-8000

John Marshall Law School
315 S Plymouth Ct . . . . Chicago IL 60604 **800-285-2221** 312-427-2737
School of Law
25 E Pearson St . . . . Chicago IL 60611 **866-596-7890** 312-915-7120

Michigan State University College of Law
368 Law College Bldg . . . . East Lansing MI 48824 **800-844-9352** 517-432-6810

New York University School of Law
110 W Third St . . . . New York NY 10012 **800-522-0925** 212-998-6100

Northeastern University School of Law
400 Huntington Ave . . . . Boston MA 02115 **800-732-3400** 617-373-2395

Northern Illinois University College of Law
Swen Parson Hall . . . . DeKalb IL 60115 **800-892-3050** 815-753-9655

Northwestern University School of Law
357 E Chicago Ave . . . . Chicago IL 60611 **800-229-2032** 312-503-3100

Nova Southeastern University Shepard Broad Law Ctr
3305 College Ave . . . . Fort Lauderdale FL 33314 **800-986-6529** 954-262-6100

Ohio Northern University Claude W Pettit College of Law
525 S Main St . . . . Ada OH 45810 **877-452-9668** 419-772-2211

Oklahoma City University School of Law
2501 N Blackwelder Ave . . . . Oklahoma City OK 73106 **800-230-3012** 405-208-5000

Pennsylvania State University Dickinson School of Law
150 S College St . . . . Carlisle PA 17013 **800-840-1122** 717-240-5000

Quinnipiac University School of Law
275 Mt Carmel Ave . . . . Hamden CT 06518 **800-462-1944** 203-582-3400

Roger Williams University Ralph R Papitto School of Law
10 Metacom Ave . . . . Bristol RI 02809 **800-633-2727** 401-254-4500

Rutgers the State University of New Jersey
School of Law Camden
217 N Fifth St . . . . Camden NJ 08102 **800-466-7561** 856-225-6375

Saint Louis University School of Law
3700 Lindell Blvd . . . . Saint Louis MO 63108 **800-758-3678** 314-977-2766

Saint Thomas University School of Law
16401 NW 37th Ave . . . . Miami Gardens FL 33054 **800-245-4569** 305-623-2310

Southern Illinois University School of Law
1209 W Chautauqua Rd . . . . Carbondale IL 62901 **800-739-9187** 618-453-8858

Southern Methodist University Dedman School of Law
3300 University Blvd . . . . Dallas TX 75205 **888-768-5291** 214-768-2550

Southern University Law Ctr
Two Roosevelt Steptoe Dr
PO Box 9294 . . . . Baton Rouge LA 70813 **800-537-1135** 225-771-6297

Temple University James E Beasley School of Law
1719 N Broad St . . . . Philadelphia PA 19122 **800-560-1428** 215-204-7861

Texas Wesleyan University School of Law
1515 Commerce St . . . . Fort Worth TX 76102 **800-733-9529** 817-212-4000

Thomas Jefferson School of Law
1155 Island Ave . . . . San Diego CA 92101 **877-318-6901** 619-297-9700

Tulane University Law School
6329 Freret St Weinmann Hall . . . . New Orleans LA 70118 **800-328-6819** 504-865-5930

University of Akron School of Law
150 University Ave . . . . Akron OH 44325 **800-655-4884** 330-972-7331

University of Arkansas School of Law
1045 W Maple St . . . . Fayetteville AR 72701 **800-295-9118** 479-575-5601

University of Connecticut School of Law
45 Elizabeth St . . . . Hartford CT 06105 **800-633-7867** 860-570-5100

University of Dayton School of Law
300 College Pk . . . . Dayton OH 45469 **800-837-7433** 937-229-3211

University of Detroit Mercy School of Law
651 E Jefferson Ave . . . . Detroit MI 48226 **888-726-6921** 313-596-0264

University of Florida Fredric G Levin College of Law
2500 SW Second Ave . . . . Gainesville FL 32611 **877-429-1297** 352-273-0890

University of Houston Law Ctr
100 Law Ctr . . . . Houston TX 77204 **800-252-9690** 713-743-2100

University of Idaho College of Law
Sixth & Rayburn St PO Box 442321 . . . . Moscow ID 83844 **888-884-3246** 208-885-4977

University of Illinois College of Law
504 E Pennsylvania Ave . . . . Champaign IL 61820 **800-369-6151** 217-333-0930

University of Iowa College of Law
130 Byington Rd . . . . Iowa City IA 52242 **800-553-4692** 319-335-9034

University of Kansas School of Law
1535 W 15th St . . . . Lawrence KS 66045 **877-404-5823** 785-864-4550

University of Kentucky College of Law
620 S Limestone St . . . . Lexington KY 40506 **800-888-8189** 859-257-1678

University of Memphis Cecil C Humphreys School of Law
3715 Central Ave . . . . Memphis TN 38152 **800-872-3728** 901-678-2421

University of Saint Thomas School of Law
1000 LaSalle Ave . . . . Minneapolis MN 55403 **800-328-6819** 651-962-4892

University of San Diego School of Law
5998 Alcala Pk . . . . San Diego CA 92110 **800-248-4873** 619-260-4528

University of South Dakota School of Law
414 E Clark St . . . . Vermillion SD 57069 **877-269-6837** 605-677-5443

University of Virginia School of Law
580 Massie Rd . . . . Charlottesville VA 22903 **877-307-0158** 434-924-7354

University of Washington School of Law
William H Gates Hall PO Box 353020 . . . . Seattle WA 98195 **866-866-0158** 206-543-4078

University of Wisconsin Law School
975 Bascom Mall . . . . Madison WI 53706 **866-301-1753** 608-262-2240

University of Wyoming College of Law
1000 E University Ave Dept 3035 . . . . Laramie WY 82071 **800-442-6757** 307-766-6416

Valparaiso University School of Law
651 College Ave . . . . Valparaiso IN 46383 **888-825-7652** 219-465-7829

Vermont Law School
168 Chelsea St PO Box 96 . . . . South Royalton VT 05068 **800-227-1395** 802-831-1239

Western New England College School of Law
1215 Wilbraham Rd . . . . Springfield MA 01119 **800-325-1122** 413-782-3111

Western State University College of Law
1111 N State College Blvd . . . . Fullerton CA 92831 **800-978-4529** 714-459-1101

Widener University Commonwealth Law School
3800 Vartan Way . . . . Harrisburg PA 17110 **888-943-3637** 717-541-3900

Classified Section

				Toll-Free	Phone
Widener University School of Law Wilmington					
4601 Concord Pk	Wilmington	DE	19803	**888-943-3637***	302-477-2100
*General					
Willamette University College of Law					
245 Winter St SE	Salem	OR	97301	**844-232-7228**	503-370-6282
William Mitchell College of Law					
875 Summit Ave	Saint Paul	MN	55105	**888-962-5529**	651-227-9171

168-2 Medical Schools

Medical schools listed here are accredited, MD-granting members of the Association of American Medical Colleges. Accredited Canadian schools that do not offer classes in English are not included among these listings.

				Toll-Free	Phone
Brody School of Medicine at East Carolina University					
600 Moye Blvd	Greenville	NC	27834	**800-722-3281**	252-744-1020
Cincinnati Children's Hospital Medical Ctr					
3333 Burnet Ave	Cincinnati	OH	45229	**800-344-2462**	513-636-4200
Creighton University School of Medicine					
2500 California Plz	Omaha	NE	68178	**800-325-4405**	402-280-2799
Duke University School of Medicine					
Office of Admissions DUMC 3710	Durham	NC	27710	**888-275-3853**	919-684-2985
George Washington University School of Medicine & Health Sciences					
2300 'I' St NW Ross Hall 716	Washington	DC	20037	**866-846-1107**	202-994-3506
Harvard Medical School					
25 Shattuck St	Boston	MA	02115	**866-606-0573**	617-432-1550
Jefferson Medical College of Thomas Jefferson University					
1015 Walnut St	Philadelphia	PA	19107	**800-533-3669**	215-955-6983
Joan & Sanford Weill Medical College of Cornell University					
445 E 69th St	New York	NY	10021	**800-422-0711**	212-746-5454
Joan C Edwards School of Medicine at Marshall University					
1600 Medical Ctr Dr	Huntington	WV	25701	**877-691-1600**	304-691-1700
Loma Linda University School of Medicine					
11175 Campus St	Loma Linda	CA	92350	**800-422-4558**	909-558-4467
Louisiana State University School of Medicine in New Orleans					
433 Bolivar St	New Orleans	LA	70112	**844-503-7283**	504-568-6262
Louisiana State University School of Medicine in Shreveport					
1501 Kings Hwy PO Box 33932	Shreveport	LA	71130	**800-337-3627**	318-675-5069
Medical College of Georgia School of Medicine					
1120 15th St	Augusta	GA	30912	**800-736-2273**	706-721-0211
New York University School of Medicine					
560 First Ave	New York	NY	10016	**855-698-2220**	212-263-7300
Northeast Ohio Medical University					
4209 State Rt 44 PO Box 95	Rootstown	OH	44272	**800-686-2511**	330-325-2511
School of Medicine					
3181 SW Sam Jackson Pk Rd L-109	Portland	OR	97239	**800-775-5460**	503-494-7800
Rosalind Franklin University of Medicine & Science					
3333 Green Bay Rd	North Chicago	IL	60064	**800-254-0460**	847-578-3205
Saint Louis University School of Medicine					
One North Grand Rm17	Saint Louis	MO	63103	**800-758-3678**	
Southern Illinois University School of Medicine					
520 N Fourth St PO Box 19670	Springfield	IL	62702	**800-342-5748**	217-545-8000
State University of New York Upstate Medical University					
766 Irving Ave	Syracuse	NY	13210	**800-736-2171**	315-464-4570
University of California Davis School of Medicine					
4610 X St	Sacramento	CA	95817	**855-221-4673**	916-734-4800
University of California Irvine School of Medicine					
1001 Health Sciences Rd					
252 Irvine Hall	Irvine	CA	92697	**800-824-5388**	949-824-6119
University of Iowa Roy J & Lucille A Carver College of Medicine					
200 CMAB	Iowa City	IA	52242	**800-725-8460**	319-335-6707
University of Kentucky College of Medicine					
Office of Medical Education					
MN 104 UKMC	Lexington	KY	40536	**800-273-8255**	859-323-6161
University of Louisville School of Medicine					
323 E Chestnut St					
Abell Bldg Rm 413	Louisville	KY	40202	**800-334-8635**	502-852-5193
University of Minnesota Medical School Twin Cities					
420 Delaware St SE Mayo MC 293	Minneapolis	MN	55455	**800-752-1000**	612-624-5100
University of Mississippi School of Medicine					
2500 N State St	Jackson	MS	39216	**888-815-2005**	601-984-1080
University of Missouri-Kansas City School of Medicine					
2411 Holmes St	Kansas City	MO	64108	**800-735-2466**	816-235-1111
University of Nebraska School of Medicine					
985527 Nebraska Medical Ctr	Omaha	NE	68198	**800-626-8431**	402-559-2259
University of New Mexico School of Medicine					
1 University of New Mexico	Albuquerque	NM	87131	**877-977-2263**	505-272-4766
University of North Dakota School of Medicine & Health Sciences					
501 N Columbia Rd	Grand Forks	ND	58203	**800-225-5863**	701-777-5046
University of Ottawa Faculty of Medicine					
451 Smyth Rd	Ottawa	ON	K1H8M5	**877-868-8292**	613-562-5700
University of Rochester School of Medicine & Dentistry					
601 Elmwood Ave	Rochester	NY	14642	**888-661-6162**	585-275-0017
University of South Florida College of Medicine (USF)					
12901 Bruce B Downs Blvd	Tampa	FL	33612	**877-338-2577**	813-974-2229
University of Texas Medical Branch					
301 University Blvd	Galveston	TX	77555	**800-228-1841**	409-772-2618
University of Texas Southwestern Medical Ctr Dallas					
Southwestern Medical School					
5323 Harry Hines Blvd	Dallas	TX	75390	**866-648-2455**	214-648-3111
University of Toledo College of Medicine					
2801 W Bancroft	Toledo	OH	43606	**800-586-5336**	419-530-4636
University of Utah School of Medicine					
30 N 1900 E	Salt Lake City	UT	84132	**844-988-7284**	801-581-7201
University of Vermont College of Medicine					
89 Beaumont Ave E-126 Given Bldg	Burlington	VT	05405	**800-571-0668**	802-656-2156
Vanderbilt University School of Medicine					
215 Light Hall	Nashville	TN	37232	**866-263-8263**	615-322-2145
Virginia Commonwealth University School of Medicine					
1101 E Marshall St PO Box 980565	Richmond	VA	23298	**800-332-8813**	804-828-9629
Wake Forest University School of Medicine					
Medical Ctr Blvd	Winston-Salem	NC	27157	**800-445-2255**	336-716-4264
West Virginia University School of Medicine					
Medical Ctr Dr					
Health Sciences Ctr N Rm 1146	Morgantown	WV	26506	**800-543-5650**	304-293-2408

				Toll-Free	Phone
Wright State University Boonshoft School of Medicine					
3640 Col Glenn Hwy	Dayton	OH	45435	**800-338-4057**	937-775-2934
Yale University School of Medicine					
333 Cedar St	New Haven	CT	06510	**877-925-3637**	203-785-2643

168-3 Theological Schools

Theological schools listed here are members of the Association of Theological Schools (ATS), an organization of graduate schools in the U.S. and Canada that conduct post-baccalaureate professional and academic degree programs to educate persons for the practice of ministry and for teaching and research in the theological disciplines. Listings include ATS accredited member schools, candidates for accredited membership, and associate member schools.

				Toll-Free	Phone
Acadia Divinity College					
38 Highland Ave	Wolfville	NS	B4P2R6	**866-875-8975**	902-585-2210
American Baptist Seminary of the West					
2606 Dwight Way	Berkeley	CA	94704	**800-799-7233**	510-841-1905
Anderson University					
1100 E Fifth St	Anderson	IN	46012	**800-428-6414***	765-649-9071
*Admissions					
Andover Newton Theological School					
210 Herrick Rd	Newton Centre	MA	02459	**800-964-2687**	617-964-1100
Andrews University Seventh-day Adventist Theological Seminary					
4145 E Campus Cir Dr					
Andrews University	Berrien Springs	MI	49104	**800-253-2874**	269-471-3537
Aquinas Institute of Theology					
23 S Spring Ave	Saint Louis	MO	63108	**800-977-3869**	314-256-8800
Asbury Theological Seminary					
204 N Lexington Ave	Wilmore	KY	40390	**800-227-2879**	859-858-3581
Assemblies of God Theological Seminary					
1435 N Glenstone Ave	Springfield	MO	65802	**800-467-2487**	417-268-1000
Associated Mennonite Biblical Seminary					
3003 Benham Ave	Elkhart	IN	46517	**800-964-2627**	574-295-3726
Azusa Pacific University					
901 E Alosta Ave PO Box 7000	Azusa	CA	91702	**800-825-5278**	626-969-3434
Bangor Theological Seminary					
159 State St	Portland	ME	04101	**800-287-6781**	207-942-6781
Baptist Missionary Assn Theological Seminary					
1530 E Pine St	Jacksonville	TX	75766	**800-259-5673**	903-586-2501
Baptist Theological Seminary at Richmond					
8040 Villa Park Dr Ste 250	Richmond	VA	23227	**888-345-2877**	804-355-8135
Bethany Theological Seminary					
615 National Rd W	Richmond	IN	47374	**800-287-8822**	765-983-1800
Bethel Seminary					
3949 Bethel Dr	Saint Paul	MN	55112	**800-255-8706**	651-638-6400
Biblical Theological Seminary					
200 N Main St	Hatfield	PA	19440	**800-235-4021**	215-368-5000
Biola University					
13800 Biola Ave	La Mirada	CA	90639	**800-652-4652***	562-903-6000
*Admissions					
Calvin Theological Seminary					
3233 Burton St SE	Grand Rapids	MI	49546	**800-388-6034**	616-957-6036
Campbell University					
450 Leslie Campbell Ave					
PO Box 546	Buies Creek	NC	27506	**800-334-4111**	910-893-1290
Canadian Southern Baptist Seminary					
200 Seminary View	Cochrane	AB	T4C2G1	**877-922-2727**	403-932-6622
Central Baptist Theological Seminary					
6601 Monticello Rd	Shawnee	KS	66226	**800-677-2287**	913-667-5700
Christian Theological Seminary					
1000 W 42nd St	Indianapolis	IN	46208	**800-585-0108**	317-924-1331
Cincinnati Christian University					
2700 Glenway Ave	Cincinnati	OH	45204	**800-949-4228**	513-244-8100
Claremont School of Theology					
1325 N College Ave	Claremont	CA	91711	**800-733-5181**	909-447-2500
Colgate Rochester Crozer Divinity School					
1100 S Goodman St	Rochester	NY	14620	**888-937-3732**	585-271-1320
Columbia International University					
7435 Monticello Rd	Columbia	SC	29203	**800-777-2227**	803-754-4100
Concordia Seminary					
801 Seminary Pl	Saint Louis	MO	63105	**800-822-9545**	314-505-7000
Concordia Theological Seminary					
6600 N Clinton St	Fort Wayne	IN	46825	**800-481-2155**	260-452-2100
Cornerstone University					
1001 E Beltline Ave NE	Grand Rapids	MI	49525	**800-787-9778***	616-222-1426
*Admissions					
Dallas Theological Seminary					
3909 Swiss Ave	Dallas	TX	75204	**800-992-0998**	800-387-9673
Denver Seminary					
6399 S Santa Fe Dr	Littleton	CO	80120	**800-922-3040**	303-761-2482
Dominican School of Philosophy & Theology					
2301 Vine St	Berkeley	CA	94708	**888-450-3778**	510-849-2030
Duke University Divinity School					
407 Chapel Drive PO Box 90968	Durham	NC	27708	**800-367-3853**	919-660-3400
Earlham School of Religion					
228 College Ave	Richmond	IN	47374	**800-432-1377**	765-983-1423
Eastern Mennonite University					
1200 Pk Rd	Harrisonburg	VA	22802	**800-368-2665***	540-432-4118
*Admissions					
Eden Theological Seminary					
475 E Lockwood Ave	Saint Louis	MO	63119	**800-969-3627**	314-961-3627
Episcopal Divinity School					
99 Brattle St	Cambridge	MA	02138	**866-333-8742**	617-868-3450
Episcopal Theological Seminary of the Southwest (SSW)					
501 E 32nd PO Box 2247	Austin	TX	78705	**800-252-5400**	512-472-4133
Erskine Theological Seminary					
2 Washington St PO Box 338	Due West	SC	29639	**888-359-4358**	864-379-8885
Evangelical School of Theology					
121 S College St	Myerstown	PA	17067	**800-532-5775**	717-866-5775
Franciscan School of Theology					
1712 Euclid Ave	Berkeley	CA	94709	**855-355-1550**	760-547-1800
Fuller Theological Seminary					
135 N Oakland Ave	Pasadena	CA	91182	**800-235-2222**	626-584-5200

	City	State	ZIP	Toll-Free	Phone
General Theological Seminary 440 W 21st St	New York	NY	10011	**888-487-5649**	212-243-5150
George Fox Evangelical Seminary 12753 SW 68th Ave	Portland	OR	97223	**800-493-4937**	503-554-6150
Golden Gate Baptist Theological Seminary 201 Seminary Dr	Mill Valley	CA	94941	**888-442-8701**	415-380-1300
Gordon-Conwell Theological Seminary 130 Essex St	South Hamilton	MA	01982	**800-428-7329**	978-468-7111
Grace Theological Seminary 200 Seminary Dr	Winona Lake	IN	46590	**800-544-7223**	574-372-5100
Graduate Theological Union 2400 Ridge Rd	Berkeley	CA	94709	**800-826-4488**	510-649-2400
Harding University Graduate School of Religion 915 E Market Ave	Searcy	AR	72143	**800-477-4407**	501-279-4407
Hartford Seminary 77 Sherman St	Hartford	CT	06105	**877-860-2255**	860-509-9500
Howard University School of Divinity 1400 Shepherd St NE	Washington	DC	20017	**800-822-6363**	202-806-0500
Iliff School of Theology 2201 S University Blvd	Denver	CO	80210	**800-678-3360**	303-744-1287
Interdenominational Theological Ctr 700 Martin Luther King Jr Dr	Atlanta	GA	30314	**800-908-9946**	404-527-7700
Jesuit School of Theology at Berkeley 1735 LeRoy Ave	Berkeley	CA	94709	**800-824-0122**	510-549-5000
La Sierra University 4500 Riverwalk Pkwy	Riverside	CA	92515	**800-874-5587**	951-785-2000
Lancaster Theological Seminary 555 W James St	Lancaster	PA	17603	**800-393-0654**	717-393-0654
Lexington Theological Seminary 631 S Limestone St	Lexington	KY	40508	**866-296-6087**	859-252-0361
Lincoln Christian College Seminary 100 Campus View Dr	Lincoln	IL	62656	**888-522-5228**	217-732-3168
Lipscomb University 3901 Granny White Pk	Nashville	TN	37204	**800-333-4358**	615-966-1000
Louisville Presbyterian Theological Seminary 1044 Alta Vista Rd	Louisville	KY	40205	**800-264-1839**	502-895-3411
Luther Seminary 2481 Como Ave	Saint Paul	MN	55108	**800-588-4373**	651-641-3456
Lutheran School of Theology at Chicago 1100 E 55th St	Chicago	IL	60615	**800-635-1116**	773-256-0700
Lutheran Theological Seminary at Gettysburg 61 Seminary Ridge	Gettysburg	PA	17325	**800-658-8437**	717-334-6286
Lutheran Theological Seminary at Philadelphia 7301 Germantown Ave	Philadelphia	PA	19119	**800-286-4616**	215-248-4616
McCormick Theological Seminary 5460 S University Ave	Chicago	IL	60615	**800-228-4687**	773-947-6300
Meadville Lombard Theological School 5701 S Woodlawn Ave	Chicago	IL	60637	**800-848-0979**	773-256-3000
Mennonite Brethren Biblical Seminary 4824 E Butler Ave	Fresno	CA	93727	**800-251-6227**	559-453-2000
Methodist Theological School in Ohio 3081 Columbus Pk	Delaware	OH	43015	**800-333-6876**	740-363-1146
Michigan Theological Seminary 41550 E Ann Arbor Trail	Plymouth	MI	48170	**800-356-6639**	734-207-9581
Mid-America Reformed Seminary 229 Seminary Dr	Dyer	IN	46311	**888-440-6277**	219-864-2400
Midwestern Baptist Theological Seminary 5001 N Oak Trafficway	Kansas City	MO	64118	**877-414-3720**	816-414-3700
Moravian Theological Seminary 1200 Main St	Bethlehem	PA	18018	**800-843-6541**	610-861-1516
Mount Saint Mary's University 16300 Old Emmitsburg Rd *Admissions	Emmitsburg	MD	21727	**800-448-4347***	301-447-5214
Multnomah Bible College & Biblical Seminary 8435 NE Glisan St	Portland	OR	97220	**800-275-4672**	503-255-0332
Nashotah House 2777 Mission Rd	Nashotah	WI	53058	**800-627-4682**	262-646-6500
Nazarene Theological Seminary 1700 E Meyer Blvd	Kansas City	MO	64131	**800-831-3011**	816-333-6254
New Brunswick Theological Seminary 17 Seminary Pl	New Brunswick	NJ	08901	**800-445-6287**	732-247-5241
New Orleans Baptist Theological Seminary 3939 Gentilly Blvd	New Orleans	LA	70126	**800-662-8701**	504-282-4455
North Park Theological Seminary 3225 W Foster Ave	Chicago	IL	60625	**800-964-0101**	773-244-6210
Northern Seminary 660 E Butterfield Rd	Lombard	IL	60148	**800-937-6287**	630-620-2180
NYACK 350 N Highland Ave	Nyack	NY	10960	**800-541-6891**	845-353-2020
Oakland City University 138 N Lucretia St	Oakland City	IN	47660	**800-737-5125**	812-749-4781
Oral Roberts University 7777 S Lewis Ave	Tulsa	OK	74171	**800-678-8876**	918-495-6161
Pacific Lutheran Theological Seminary 2770 Marin Ave	Berkeley	CA	94708	**800-235-7587**	510-524-5264
Pacific School of Religion 1798 Scenic Ave	Berkeley	CA	94709	**800-999-0528**	510-848-0528
Palmer Theological Seminary 588 N Gulph Rd	King Of Prussia	PA	19406	**800-220-3287**	610-896-5000
Payne Theological Seminary 1230 Wilberforce Clifton Rd	Wilberforce	OH	45384	**888-816-8933**	937-376-2946
Pentecostal Theological Seminary 900 Walker St NE	Cleveland	TN	37311	**800-228-9126**	423-478-1131
Phillips Theological Seminary 901 N Mingo Rd	Tulsa	OK	74116	**800-843-4675**	918-610-8303
Phoenix Seminary 4222 E Thomas Rd Ste 400	Phoenix	AZ	85018	**888-443-1020**	602-850-8000
Pittsburgh Theological Seminary 616 N Highland Ave	Pittsburgh	PA	15206	**800-451-4194**	412-362-5610
Pontifical College Josephinum 7625 N High St	Columbus	OH	43235	**888-252-5812**	614-885-5585
Princeton Theological Seminary 64 Mercer St	Princeton	NJ	08540	**800-622-6767**	609-921-8300
Protestant Episcopal Theological Seminary in Virginia 3737 Seminary Rd	Alexandria	VA	22304	**800-941-0083**	703-370-6600
Providence College & Seminary 10 College Crescent	Otterburne	MB	R0A1G0	**800-668-7768**	204-433-7488
Queen's College Faculty of Theology 210 Prince Philip Dr Ste 3000	Saint John's	NL	A1B3R6	**877-753-0116**	709-753-0116
Reformed Theological Seminary 5422 Clinton Blvd	Jackson	MS	39209	**800-543-2703**	601-923-1600
Regent College 5800 University Blvd	Vancouver	BC	V6T2E4	**800-663-8664**	604-224-3245
Roberts Wesleyan College 2301 Westside Dr *Admissions	Rochester	NY	14624	**800-777-4792***	585-594-6000
Saint Paul School of Theology 5123 Truman Rd	Kansas City	MO	64127	**800-825-0378**	
Samford University 800 Lakeshore Dr *Admissions	Birmingham	AL	35229	**800-888-7218***	205-726-3673
San Francisco Theological Seminary 105 Seminary Rd	San Anselmo	CA	94960	**800-447-8820**	415-451-2800
Shaw University 118 E S St *Admissions	Raleigh	NC	27601	**800-214-6683***	919-546-8275
Sioux Falls Seminary 2100 S Summit	Sioux Falls	SD	57105	**800-440-6227**	605-336-6588
Southeastern Baptist Theological Seminary 120 S Wingate St	Wake Forest	NC	27587	**800-284-6317**	919-556-3101
Southern Baptist Theological Seminary 2825 Lexington Rd	Louisville	KY	40280	**800-626-5525**	502-897-4011
Southwestern Baptist Theological Seminary PO Box 22740	Fort Worth	TX	76122	**877-467-9287**	817-923-1921
Starr King School for the Ministry 2441 LeConte Ave	Berkeley	CA	94709	**866-727-4894**	510-845-6232
Taylor University College & Seminary 11525 23rd Ave	Edmonton	AB	T6J4T3	**800-567-4988**	780-431-5200
Trinity Episcopal School for Ministry 311 11th St	Ambridge	PA	15003	**800-874-8754**	724-266-3838
Trinity International University 2065 Half Day Rd	Deerfield	IL	60015	**800-822-3225**	847-945-8800
Trinity Lutheran Seminary 2199 E Main St	Columbus	OH	43209	**866-610-8571**	614-235-4136
Trinity Western University 7600 Glover Rd	Langley	BC	V2Y1Y1	**888-468-6898**	604-888-7511
Tyndale University College & Seminary 25 Ballyconnor Ct	Toronto	ON	M2M4B3	**877-896-3253**	416-226-6380
Union Theological Seminary 3041 Broadway	New York	NY	10027	**800-251-9489**	212-662-7100
Union Theological Seminary & Presbyterian School of Christian Education 3401 Brook Rd	Richmond	VA	23227	**800-229-2990**	804-355-0671
United Theological Seminary of the Twin Cities 3000 Fifth St NW	New Brighton	MN	55112	**800-937-1316**	651-633-4311
University of Dubuque Theological Seminary 2000 University Ave	Dubuque	IA	52001	**800-369-8387**	563-589-3122
University of Saskatchewan 1121 College Dr	Saskatoon	SK	S7N0W3	**877-653-8501**	306-966-8970
University of the South 735 University Ave	Sewanee	TN	37383	**800-522-2234**	931-598-1238
Vancouver School of Theology 6040 Iona Dr	Vancouver	BC	V6T2E8	**866-822-9031**	604-822-9031
Virginia Union University 1500 N Lombardy St	Richmond	VA	23220	**800-368-3227**	804-342-3570
Wartburg Theological Seminary 333 Wartburg Pl	Dubuque	IA	52003	**800-225-5987**	563-589-0200
Washington Bible College/Capital Bible Seminary 6511 Princess Garden Pkwy	Lanham	MD	20706	**877-793-7227**	301-552-1400
Wesley Theological Seminary 4500 Massachusetts Ave NW	Washington	DC	20016	**800-882-4987**	202-885-8600
Western Seminary 5511 SE Hawthorne Blvd	Portland	OR	97215	**877-517-1800**	503-517-1800
Western Theological Seminary 101 E 13th St	Holland	MI	49423	**800-392-8554**	616-392-8555
Westminster Theological Seminary 2960 Church Rd	Glenside	PA	19038	**800-373-0119**	215-887-5511
Winebrenner Theological Seminary 950 N Main St	Findlay	OH	45840	**800-992-4987**	419-434-4200
Yale Divinity School Admissions Office 409 Prospect St	New Haven	CT	06511	**866-358-3806**	203-432-5360

169 COLLEGES & UNIVERSITIES - HISTORICALLY BLACK

Historically Black Colleges & Universities (HBCUs) are colleges or universities that were established before 1964 with the intention of serving the African-American community. (Prior to 1964, African-Americans were almost always excluded from higher education opportunities at the predominantly white colleges and universities.)

	City	State	ZIP	Toll-Free	Phone
Allen University 1530 Harden St	Columbia	SC	29204	**877-625-5368**	803-376-5700
Benedict College 1600 Harden St	Columbia	SC	29204	**800-868-6598**	803-253-5000
Bennett College 900 E Washington St *Admissions	Greensboro	NC	27401	**800-413-5323***	336-370-8624
Bethune-Cookman College 640 Dr Mary McLeod Bethune Blvd *Admissions	Daytona Beach	FL	32114	**800-448-0228***	386-481-2900
Bluefield State College 219 Rock St	Bluefield	WV	24701	**800-654-7798**	304-327-4000
Bowie State University 14000 Jericho Pk Rd	Bowie	MD	20715	**877-772-6943**	301-860-4000
Central State University 1400 Brush Row Rd PO Box 1004	Wilberforce	OH	45384	**800-388-2781**	937-376-6011
Cheyney University of Pennsylvania 1837 University Cir PO Box 200	Cheyney	PA	19319	**800-243-9639**	610-399-2275
Claflin University 400 Magnolia St	Orangeburg	SC	29115	**800-922-1276**	803-535-5000
Clark Atlanta University 223 James P Brawley Dr SW *Admissions	Atlanta	GA	30314	**800-688-3228***	404-880-8000
Clinton Junior College 1029 Crawford Rd	Rock Hill	SC	29730	**877-837-9645**	803-327-7402

Classified Section

		Toll-Free	Phone
Coppin State University			
2500 W N Ave ....Baltimore MD 21216		800-635-3674*	410-951-3600
*Admissions			
Delaware State University			
1200 N DuPont Hwy ....Dover DE 19901		800-845-2544*	302-857-6351
*Admissions			
Elizabeth City State University			
1704 Weeksville Rd ....Elizabeth City NC 27909		800-347-3278*	252-335-3400
*Admissions			
Fayetteville State University			
1200 Murchison Rd ....Fayetteville NC 28301		800-222-2594*	910-672-1371
*Admissions			
Fisk University			
1000 17th Ave N ....Nashville TN 37208		888-702-0022	615-329-8500
Florida Memorial University			
15800 NW 42nd Ave ....Miami Gardens FL 33054		800-822-1362	305-626-3600
Fort Valley State University			
1005 State University Dr ....Fort Valley GA 31030		877-462-3878	478-825-6211
Grambling State University			
403 Main St ....Grambling LA 71245		800-569-4714	318-247-3811
Hampton University			
100 E Queen St ....Hampton VA 23668		800-624-3341	757-727-5000
Hinds Community College			
501 E Main St PO Box 1100 ....Raymond MS 39154		800-446-3722	601-857-5261
Howard University			
2400 Sixth St NW ....Washington DC 20059		800-822-6363	202-806-6100
Huston-Tillotson University			
900 Chicon St ....Austin TX 78702		877-487-8702	512-505-3000
Interdenominational Theological Ctr			
700 Martin Luther King Jr Dr ....Atlanta GA 30314		800-908-9946	404-527-7700
Jackson State University			
1400 John R Lynch St ....Jackson MS 39217		800-848-6817	601-979-2121
Johnson C Smith University			
100 Beatties Ford Rd ....Charlotte NC 28216		800-782-7303*	704-378-1000
*Admissions			
Kentucky State University			
400 E Main St ....Frankfort KY 40601		800-325-1716*	502-597-6000
*Admissions			
Lane College 545 Ln Ave ....Jackson TN 38301		800-960-7533*	731-426-7500
*Admissions			
Lincoln University			
820 Chestnut St B-7 Young Hall......Jefferson City MO 65102		800-521-5052*	573-681-5599
*Admissions			
Livingstone College			
701 W Monroe St ....Salisbury NC 28144		800-835-3435	704-216-6963
Miles College			
5500 Myron Massey Blvd ....Fairfield AL 35064		800-445-0708*	205-929-1000
*Admissions			
Mississippi Valley State University			
14000 Hwy 82 ....Itta Bena MS 38941		800-844-6885	662-254-9041
Morgan State University			
1700 E Cold Spring Ln ....Baltimore MD 21251		800-319-4678	443-885-3333
Morris College			
100 W College St ....Sumter SC 29150		866-853-1345*	803-934-3200
*Admissions			
Norfolk State University			
700 Pk Ave ....Norfolk VA 23504		800-274-1821	757-823-8600
North Carolina A & T State University			
1601 E Market St ....Greensboro NC 27411		800-443-8964*	336-334-7946
*Admissions			
North Carolina Central University			
1801 Fayetteville St ....Durham NC 27707		877-667-7533*	919-530-6100
*Admissions			
Oakwood College			
7000 Adventist Blvd ....Huntsville AL 35896		800-824-5312	256-726-7356
Paine College 1235 15th St ......Augusta GA 30901		800-476-7703	706-821-8200
Paul Quinn College			
3837 Simpson Stuart Rd ....Dallas TX 75241		800-433-3243	214-376-1000
Prairie View A & M University			
PO Box 519 ....Prairie View TX 77446		800-787-7826	936-857-2626
Rust College			
150 Rust Ave ....Holly Springs MS 38635		888-886-8492	662-252-8000
Saint Augustine's College			
1315 Oakwood Ave ....Raleigh NC 27610		800-948-1126*	919-516-4016
*Admissions			
Shaw University 118 E S St ......Raleigh NC 27601		800-214-6683*	919-546-8275
*Admissions			
South Carolina State University			
300 College St NE PO Box 7127.....Orangeburg SC 29117		800-260-5956*	803-536-7000
*Admissions			
Southern University & A & M College			
156 Elton C Harrison Dr			
PO Box 9757...............Baton Rouge LA 70813		800-256-1531*	225-771-5180
*Admissions			
Southwestern Christian College			
PO Box 10 ....Terrell TX 75160		800-925-9357	972-524-3341
Spelman College			
350 Spelman Ln SW ....Atlanta GA 30314		800-982-2411*	404-681-3643
*Admissions			
Stillman College			
3601 Stillman Blvd ....Tuscaloosa AL 35401		800-841-5722	205-349-4240
Tennessee State University			
3500 John A Merritt Blvd			
PO Box 9609................Nashville TN 37209		888-463-6878*	615-963-5000
*Admissions			
Texas College			
2404 N Grand Ave ....Tyler TX 75702		800-306-6299	903-593-8311
Texas Southern University			
3100 Cleburne St ....Houston TX 77004		800-252-5400	713-313-7011
Tougaloo College			
500 W County Line Rd ....Tougaloo MS 39174		888-424-2566*	601-977-7700
*Admissions			
Trenholm State Technical College			
1225 Air Base Blvd ....Montgomery AL 36108		800-917-2081	334-420-4200
Tuskegee University			
1200 W Montgomery Rd ....Tuskegee AL 36088		800-622-6531*	334-727-8011
*Admissions			

		Toll-Free	Phone
Pine Bluff			
1200 N University Dr ....Pine Bluff AR 71601		800-264-6585*	870-575-8000
*Admissions			
El Paso			
500 W University Ave ....El Paso TX 79968		800-551-0294*	915-747-5000
Virginia State University			
One Hayden Dr ....Petersburg VA 23806		800-871-7611*	804-524-5000
Virginia Union University			
1500 N Lombardy St ....Richmond VA 23220		800-368-3227	804-342-3570
Voorhees College			
213 Wiggins Dr PO Box 678.......Denmark SC 29042		800-446-6250*	803-780-1234
*Admissions			
West Virginia State University			
Barron Dr Rt 25 E PO Box 1000 .....Institute WV 25112		800-987-2112	304-766-3000
Wilberforce University			
1055 N Bickett Rd PO Box 1001.....Wilberforce OH 45384		800-367-8568*	937-376-2911
*Admissions			
Wiley College			
711 Wiley Ave ....Marshall TX 75670		800-658-6889*	903-927-3300
*Admissions			
Winston-Salem State University			
601 S ML King Jr Dr			
206 Thompson Ctr ....Winston-Salem NC 27110		800-257-4052*	336-750-2000
*Admissions			
Xavier University of Louisiana			
1 Drexel Dr ....New Orleans LA 70125		877-520-7388	504-486-7411

170 COLLEGES & UNIVERSITIES - JESUIT

The institutions listed here are members of the Association of Jesuit Colleges & Universities.

		Toll-Free	Phone
Boston College			
140 Commonwealth Ave ....Chestnut Hill MA 02467		800-360-2522	617-552-3100
Canisius College			
2001 Main St ....Buffalo NY 14208		800-843-1517	716-888-2200
College of the Holy Cross			
1 College St ....Worcester MA 01610		800-442-2421	508-793-2011
Creighton University			
2500 California Plz ....Omaha NE 68178		800-282-5835	402-280-2700
College at Lincoln Ctr			
113 W 60th St ....New York NY 10023		800-367-3426	212-636-6710
Gonzaga University			
502 E Boone Ave ....Spokane WA 99258		800-986-9585	509-323-6572
John Carroll University			
20700 N Pk Blvd ....Cleveland OH 44118		888-335-6800	216-397-1886
Le Moyne College			
1419 Salt Springs Rd ....Syracuse NY 13214		800-333-4733*	315-445-4100
*Admissions			
Loyola College			
4501 N Charles St ....Baltimore MD 21210		800-221-9107	410-617-5012
Loyola Marymount University			
One LMU Dr ....Los Angeles CA 90045		800-568-4636	310-338-2700
Loyola University			
New Orleans			
6363 St Charles Ave CB 18 ....New Orleans LA 70118		800-456-9652*	504-865-3240
*Admissions			
Loyola University Chicago			
Water Tower			
820 N Michigan Ave ....Chicago IL 60611		800-262-2373*	312-915-6500
Marquette University			
1217 W Wisconsin Ave ....Milwaukee WI 53233		800-222-6544*	414-288-7302
*Admissions			
Rockhurst University			
1100 Rockhurst Rd ....Kansas City MO 64110		800-842-6776	816-501-4000
Saint Joseph's University			
5600 City Ave ....Philadelphia PA 19131		888-232-4295	610-660-1000
Saint Louis University			
221 N Grand Blvd ....Saint Louis MO 63103		800-758-3678	314-977-7288
Seattle University			
901 12th Ave ....Seattle WA 98122		800-426-7123	206-296-6000
Spring Hill College			
4000 Dauphin St ....Mobile AL 36608		800-742-6704*	251-380-4000
*Admissions			
University of Detroit Mercy			
4001 W McNichols Rd ....Detroit MI 48221		800-635-5020*	313-993-1000
*Admissions			
University of San Francisco			
2130 Fulton St ....San Francisco CA 94117		800-225-5873*	415-422-5555
*Admissions			
University of Scranton			
800 Linden St St Thomas Hall ....Scranton PA 18510		888-727-2686	570-941-7400
Wheeling Jesuit University			
316 Washington Ave ....Wheeling WV 26003		800-624-6992	304-243-2000
Xavier University			
3800 Victory Pkwy ....Cincinnati OH 45207		800-344-4698	513-745-3000

171 COMMODITY CONTRACTS BROKERS & DEALERS

SEE ALSO Securities Brokers & Dealers ; Investment Advice & Management

		Toll-Free	Phone
Basic Commodities Inc			
863 S Orlando Ave ....Winter Park FL 32789		800-338-7006	407-629-2000
GFI Group Inc 55 Water St ....New York NY 10041		888-750-5884	212-968-4100
NYSE: GFIG			
Keeley Investment Corp			
401 S La Salle St Ste 1201 ....Chicago IL 60605		800-533-5344	312-786-5000
Koch Mineral Services LLC			
4111 E 37th St N ....Wichita KS 67220		800-750-5834	316-828-5500
Koch Supply & Trading LP			
4111 E 37th St N ....Wichita KS 67220		800-245-2243	713-544-4123
OptionsXpress Inc			
311 W Monroe Ste 1000............Chicago IL 60606		888-280-8020	312-630-3300

				Toll-Free	Phone
RJ O'Brien & Assoc					
222 S Riverside Plz Ste 900	Chicago	IL	60606	**866-438-7564**	312-373-5000
Zaner Group LLC					
150 S Wacker Dr Ste 2350	Chicago	IL	60606	**800-621-1414**	312-277-0050

172   COMMUNICATIONS TOWER OPERATORS

SEE ALSO Communications Lines & Towers Construction

Listed here are companies that own, operate, lease, maintain, and/or manage towers used by telecommunications services and radio broadcast companies, including free-standing towers as well as antenna systems mounted on monopoles or rooftops. Many of these companies also build their communications towers, but companies that only do the building are classified as heavy construction contractors.

				Toll-Free	Phone
American Tower Corp					
116 Huntington Ave 11th Fl	Boston	MA	02116	**877-282-7483**	617-375-7500
NYSE: AMT					
Crown Castle International Corp					
1220 Augusta Dr Ste 500	Houston	TX	77057	**877-486-9377**	713-570-3000
NYSE: CCI					
Crown Castle USA Inc					
2000 Corporate Dr	Canonsburg	PA	15317	**877-486-9377**	724-746-3600
SBA Communications Corp					
5900 Broken Sound Pkwy NW	Boca Raton	FL	33487	**800-487-7483**	561-995-7670
NASDAQ: SBAC					
Tower Innovations					
3266 Tower Dr	Newburgh	IN	47630	**800-664-8222**	812-853-0595

173   COMMUNITIES - ONLINE

SEE ALSO Internet Service Providers (ISPs)

				Toll-Free	Phone
Knot Inc, The					
462 Broadway 6th Fl	New York	NY	10013	**800-390-9784**	212-219-8555
lawyers.com					
Martindale-Hubbell					
121 Chanlon Rd	New Providence	NJ	07974	**800-526-4902**	908-464-6800
Sensitech Inc					
800 Cummings Ctr Ste 258x	Beverly	MA	01915	**800-843-8367**	978-927-7033
SHRM Global Forum					
1800 Duke St	Alexandria	VA	22314	**800-283-7476**	703-548-3440

COMPRESSORS - AIR CONDITIONING & REFRIGERATION

SEE Air Conditioning & Heating Equipment - Commercial/Industrial

174   COMPRESSORS - AIR & GAS

				Toll-Free	Phone
Airtek Inc PO Box 466	Irwin	PA	15642	**800-424-7835**	724-863-1350
Cameron Compression Systems					
16250 Port NW Dr	Houston	TX	77041	**800-323-9160**	713-354-1900
Cameron Turbocompressor					
3101 Broadway	Buffalo	NY	14225	**877-805-7911**	716-896-6600
Compressed Air Systems Inc					
9303 Stannum St	Tampa	FL	33619	**800-626-8177**	813-626-8177
Compressor Engineering Corp (CECO)					
5440 Alder Dr	Houston	TX	77081	**800-879-2326**	713-664-7333
Corken Inc					
3805 NW 36th St	Oklahoma City	OK	73112	**800-631-4929**	405-946-5576
CSI Compressor Systems Inc					
3809 W FM 1788 PO Box 60760	Midland	TX	79711	**800-676-0654**	432-563-1170
Curtis Dyna-Fog Ltd					
17335 US Hwy 31 N	Westfield	IN	46074	**800-544-8990**	317-896-2561
Curtis-Toledo Inc					
1905 Kienlen Ave	Saint Louis	MO	63133	**800-925-5431**	314-383-1300
Dresser-Rand Co Reciprocating Products Div					
100 Chemung St	Painted Post	NY	14870	**877-590-7858**	619-656-4740
Elliott Group					
901 N Fourth St	Jeannette	PA	15644	**800-635-2208**	724-527-2811
Federal Equipment Co					
5298 River Rd	Cincinnati	OH	45233	**877-435-4723**	513-621-5260
Fountainhead Group Inc					
23 Garden St	New York Mills	NY	13417	**800-311-9903**	315-736-0037
Gardner Denver Compressor Div					
1800 Gardner Expwy	Quincy	IL	62305	**800-682-9868**	217-222-5400
Gardner Denver Inc					
1800 Gardner Expy	Quincy	IL	62305	**800-682-9868**	217-222-5400
NYSE: GDI					
Gardner Denver Nash					
1800 Gardner Expy	Quincy	IL	62305	**800-637-5729**	217-222-5400
Gardner Denver Water Jetting Systems Inc					
12300 N Houston Rosslyn	Houston	TX	77086	**800-682-9868***	281-448-5800
*General					
Gas Technology Energy Concepts LLC					
401 William L Gaiter Pkwy Ste 4	Buffalo	NY	14215	**800-451-8294**	
Gast Mfg Inc					
2300 M-139 Hwy PO Box 97	Benton Harbor	MI	49023	**800-665-1196**	269-926-6171
Guardair Corp					
54 Second Ave	Chicopee	MA	01020	**800-482-7324**	413-594-4400
ITW Ransburg					
320 Phillips Ave	Toledo	OH	43612	**800-233-3366***	419-470-2000
*Cust Svc					
Manchester Tank					
1000 Corp Centre Dr Ste 300	Franklin	TN	37067	**800-399-5628**	615-370-6300
Master Mfg Co					
747 N Yale Ave	Villa Park	IL	60181	**800-864-1649**	630-833-7060
Mattson Spray Equipment					
230 W Coleman St	Rice Lake	WI	54868	**800-877-4857**	715-234-1617
Norwalk Compressor Co					
1650 Stratford Ave	Stratford	CT	06615	**800-556-5001**	203-386-1234

				Toll-Free	Phone
Saylor Beall Mfg Company Inc					
400 N Kibbee St	Saint Johns	MI	48879	**800-248-9001**	989-224-2371
Scales Air Compressor Corp					
110 Voice Rd	Carle Place	NY	11514	**877-798-0454**	516-248-9096
Spencer Turbine Co					
600 Day Hill Rd	Windsor	CT	06095	**800-232-4321**	860-688-8361
Sullair Corp					
3700 E Michigan Blvd	Michigan City	IN	46360	**800-785-5247**	219-879-5451
Sullivan-Palatek Inc					
1201 W US Hwy 20	Michigan City	IN	46360	**800-438-6203**	219-874-2497
Sulzer Metco US Inc					
1101 Prospect Ave	Westbury	NY	11590	**877-280-2342**	516-334-1300
Thermionics Laboratory					
1842 Sabre St	Hayward	CA	94545	**800-962-2310**	510-538-3304
Tuthill Vacuum Systems					
4840 W Kearney St	Springfield	MO	65803	**800-634-2695**	417-865-8715
Wagner Spray Tech Corp					
1770 Fernbrook Ln	Plymouth	MN	55447	**800-328-8251**	763-553-7000
Zeks Compressed Air Solutions					
1302 Goshen Pkwy	West Chester	PA	19380	**800-888-2323**	610-692-9100

175   COMPUTER EQUIPMENT

SEE ALSO Point-of-Sale (POS) & Point-of-Information (POI) Systems ; Automatic Teller Machines (ATMs) ; Business Machines - Mfr ; Calculators - Electronic ; Modems ; Computer Networking Products & Systems ; Flash Memory Devices

COMPUTER & INTERNET TRAINING PROGRAMS

SEE Training & Certification Programs - Computer & Internet

175-1   Computers

				Toll-Free	Phone
Aberdeen LLC					
9130 Norwalk Blvd	Santa Fe Springs	CA	90670	**800-500-9526**	562-699-6998
Acer America Corp					
333 W San Carlos St Ste 1500	San Jose	CA	95110	**800-253-2687**	408-533-7700
ACMA Computers Inc					
1565 Reliance Way	Fremont	CA	94539	**800-800-6328***	510-651-8886
*Sales					
Amax Engineering Corp					
1565 Reliance Way	Fremont	CA	94539	**800-889-2629***	510-651-8886
*Cust Svc					
Apple Inc					
One Infinite Loop	Cupertino	CA	95014	**800-275-2273***	408-996-1010
NASDAQ: AAPL ▥ *Cust Svc					
Azul Systems Inc					
1600 Plymouth St	Mountain View	CA	94043	**800-258-4199**	650-230-6500
Bytespeed LLC					
3131 24th Ave S	Moorhead	MN	56560	**877-553-0777**	218-227-0445
Chem USA Corp					
38507 Cherry St	Newark	CA	94560	**800-866-2436**	510-608-8818
Comark Corp 93 W St	Medfield	MA	02052	**800-280-8522**	508-359-8161
CSP Inc 43 Manning Rd	Billerica	MA	01821	**800-325-3110**	978-663-7598
NASDAQ: CSPI					
CSS Laboratories Inc					
1641 McGaw Ave	Irvine	CA	92614	**800-852-2680**	949-852-8161
Datalux Corp					
155 Aviation Dr	Winchester	VA	22602	**800-328-2589**	540-662-1500
Dedicated Computing					
N26 W23880 Commerce Cir	Waukesha	WI	53188	**877-523-3301**	262-951-7200
Dell Inc One Dell Way	Round Rock	TX	78682	**800-879-3355**	512-338-4400
NASDAQ: DELL					
Drive Thru Technology Inc					
1755 N Main St	Los Angeles	CA	90031	**800-933-8388**	323-576-1400
Ectaco Inc					
31-21 31st St	Long Island City	NY	11106	**800-710-7920**	718-728-6110
Electrovaya Inc					
2645 Royal Windsor Dr	Mississauga	ON	L5J1K9	**800-388-2865**	905-855-4610
TSE: EFL					
Equus Computer Systems Inc					
5801 Clearwater Dr	Minnetonka	MN	55343	**866-378-8727**	612-617-6200
Franklin Electronic Publishers Inc					
One Franklin Plz	Burlington	NJ	08016	**800-266-5626**	609-386-2500
Fujitsu America Inc					
1250 E Arques Ave	Sunnyvale	CA	94085	**800-538-8460**	408-746-6200
Gateway Inc					
7565 Irvine Ctr Dr	Irvine	CA	92618	**800-846-2000**	949-471-7040
Hewlett-Packard (Canada) Ltd (HP)					
5150 Spectrum Way	Mississauga	ON	L4W5G1	**888-447-4636**	905-206-4725
Hewlett-Packard Co					
3000 Hanover St	Palo Alto	CA	94304	**800-752-0900***	650-857-1501
NYSE: HPQ ▥ *Sales					
International Business Machines Corp (IBM)					
One New OrchaRd Rd	Armonk	NY	10504	**800-426-4968**	914-499-1900
NYSE: IBM					
Kontron Mobile Computing Inc					
7631 Anagram Dr	Eden Prairie	MN	55344	**888-343-5396**	952-974-7000
LXE Inc					
125 Technology Pkwy	Norcross	GA	30092	**800-664-4593**	770-447-4224
MaxVision Corp					
495 Production Ave	Madison	AL	35758	**800-533-5805**	256-772-3058
Mercury Computer Systems Inc					
201 Riverneck Rd	Chelmsford	MA	01824	**866-627-6951**	978-967-1401
NASDAQ: MRCY					
Micro Electronics, Inc.					
2701 Charter St Ste A	Columbus	OH	43228	**877-636-9793**	614-326-8500
Micro Express Inc					
Eight Hammond Dr Ste 105	Irvine	CA	92618	**800-989-9900**	949-460-9911

				Toll-Free	Phone
Microtech Computers Inc					
4921 Legends Dr	Lawrence	KS	66049	800-828-9533*	785-841-9513
*Tech Supp					
Panasonic Corporation of North America					
Two Riverfront Plaza	Newark	NJ	07102	888-223-1012	
Pinnacle Data Systems Inc					
6600 Port Rd Ste 100	Groveport	OH	43125	800-882-8282	614-748-1150
Quantum3D Inc					
6330 San Ignacio Ave	San Jose	CA	95119	888-747-1020	408-361-9999
Sharp Electronics Corp					
One Sharp Plz	Mahwah	NJ	07430	800-237-4277	201-529-8200
Sony Electronics Inc					
One Sony Dr	Park Ridge	NJ	07656	800-222-7669*	201-930-1000
*Cust Svc					
Stealth Computer Corp					
530 Rowntree Dairy Rd Bldg 4	Woodbridge	ON	L4L8H2	888-783-2584	905-264-9000
Superchips Inc					
1790 E Airport Blvd	Sanford	FL	32773	888-227-2447	407-585-7000
Systemax Inc					
11 Harbor Pk Dr	Port Washington	NY	11050	888-645-0878	516-608-7000
NYSE: SYX					
Tangent Inc					
191 Airport Blvd	Burlingame	CA	94010	800-342-9388	650-342-9388
Technology Advancement Group Inc					
22355 Tag Way	Sterling	VA	20166	800-824-7693	703-406-3000
Toshiba America Inc					
1251 Ave of the Americas Ste 4100	New York	NY	10020	800-457-7777	212-596-0600
Toshiba America Information Systems Inc					
9740 Irvine Blvd	Irvine	CA	92618	800-457-7777*	949-583-3000
*Cust Svc					
Transource Computers Corp					
2405 W Utopia Rd	Phoenix	AZ	85027	800-486-3715	623-879-8882
Twinhead Corp					
48303 Fremont Blvd	Fremont	CA	94538	800-995-8946*	
*Sales					
Versalogic Corp					
4211 W 11th Ave	Eugene	OR	97402	800-824-3163	541-485-8575
WYSE Technology Inc					
3471 N First St	San Jose	CA	95134	800-800-9973	408-473-1200

175-2 Computer Input Devices

				Toll-Free	Phone
3M Touch Systems					
501 Griffin Brook Dr	Methuen	MA	01844	866-407-6666	978-659-9000
Aten Technology Inc					
23 Hubble	Irvine	CA	92618	888-999-2836	949-428-1111
Cirque Corp					
2463 South 3850 West Ste A	Salt Lake City	UT	84120	800-454-3375	801-467-1100
Elo TouchSystems Inc					
301 Constitution Dr	Menlo Park	CA	94025	800-557-1458	650-361-4700
Esterline Interface Technologies					
600 W Wilbur Ave	Coeur d'Alene	ID	83815	800-444-5923	208-765-8000
Gyration Inc					
3601-B Calle Tecate	Camarillo	CA	93012	888-340-0033	
Immersion Corp					
30 Rio Robles	San Jose	CA	95134	877-223-6273	408-467-1900
NASDAQ: IMMR					
Kensington Computer Products Group					
333 Twin Dolphin Dr Sixth Fl	Redwood Shores	CA	94065	800-535-4242	650-572-2700
Kinesis Corp					
22030 20th Ave SE Ste 102	Bothell	WA	98021	800-454-6374	425-402-8100
KYE Systems Corp					
1301 NW 84th Ave Ste 127	Doral	FL	33126	800-488-3111	305-468-9250
Logitech Inc 6505 Kaiser Dr	Fremont	CA	94555	800-231-7717*	510-795-8500
*Sales					
Macally USA Mace Group Inc					
4601 E Airport Dr	Ontario	CA	91761	800-644-1132	909-230-6888
Mad Catz Interactive Inc					
7480 Mission Vly Rd Ste 101	San Diego	CA	92108	800-659-2287	619-683-9830
NYSE: MCZ					
Numonics Corp					
101 Commerce Dr PO Box 1005	Montgomeryville	PA	18936	800-523-6716	215-362-2766
PolyVision Corp					
3970 Johns Creek Ct Ste 325	Suwanee	GA	30024	800-620-7659	678-542-3100
SMART Modular Technologies Inc					
39870 Eureka Dr	Newark	CA	94560	800-956-7627	510-623-1231
NASDAQ: SMOD					
SMART Technologies Inc					
3636 Research Road NW	Calgary	AB	T2L1Y1	888-427-6278	403-245-0333
TSE: SMA					
TouchSystems Corp					
220 Tradesmen Dr	Hutto	TX	78634	800-320-5944	512-846-2424
Wacom Technology Corp					
1311 SE Cardinal Ct	Vancouver	WA	98683	800-922-6613	360-896-9833

175-3 Modems

				Toll-Free	Phone
ActionTec Electronics Inc					
760 N Mary Ave	Sunnyvale	CA	94085	888-436-0657*	408-752-7700
*Tech Supp					
Avocent Corp					
4991 Corporate Dr	Huntsville	AL	35805	866-286-2368	256-430-4000
Biscom Inc					
321 Billerica Rd	Chelmsford	MA	01824	800-477-2472	978-250-1800
Canoga Perkins Corp					
20600 Prairie St	Chatsworth	CA	91311	800-360-6642*	818-718-6300
*Tech Supp					
Cermetek Microelectronics Inc					
374 Turquoise St	Milpitas	CA	95035	800-882-6271	408-752-5000
Copia International Ltd					
1220 Iroquois Dr Ste 180	Naperville	IL	60563	800-689-8898*	630-778-8898
*Sales					
CXR Larus Corp					
894 Faulstich Ct	San Jose	CA	95112	800-999-9946	408-573-2700

				Toll-Free	Phone
Dataforth Corp					
3331 E Hemisphere Loop	Tucson	AZ	85706	800-444-7644	520-741-1404
FreeWave Technologies Inc					
1880 S Flatiron Ct Ste F	Boulder	CO	80301	866-923-6168*	303-444-3862
*Cust Svc					
GRE America Inc					
425 Harbor Blvd	Belmont	CA	94002	800-233-5973	650-591-1400
Multi-Tech Systems					
2205 Woodale Dr	Mounds View	MN	55112	800-328-9717*	763-785-3500
*Cust Svc					
Novatel Wireless Inc					
9645 Scranton Rd Ste 205	San Diego	CA	92121	888-888-9231	
NASDAQ: NVTL					
Unlimited Systems Corp Inc					
9530 Padgett St	San Diego	CA	92126	800-275-6354	858-537-5010
US Robotics Corp					
1300 E Woodfield Dr Ste 506	Schaumburg	IL	60173	877-710-0884	847-874-2000
Western Telematic Inc					
5 Sterling	Irvine	CA	92618	800-854-7226	949-586-9950
Works Computing Inc					
1801 American Blvd E Ste 12	Bloomington	MN	55425	866-222-4077	952-746-1580
ZyXEL Communications Inc					
1130 N Miller St	Anaheim	CA	92806	800-255-4101	714-632-0882

175-4 Monitors & Displays

				Toll-Free	Phone
Aydin Displays Inc					
One Riga Ln	Birdsboro	PA	19508	866-367-2934	610-404-7400
Barco Electronic Systems Pvt Ltd					
11101 Trade Ctr Dr	Rancho Cordova	CA	95670	888-414-7226	916-859-2500
Conrac Inc					
5124 Commerce Dr	Baldwin Park	CA	91706	800-451-5288	626-480-0095
Daktronics Inc					
201 Daktronics Dr	Brookings	SD	57006	800-325-8766	605-692-0200
NASDAQ: DAKT					
Dotronix Inc					
160 First St SE	New Brighton	MN	55112	800-720-7218	651-633-1742
Eizo Nanao Technologies Inc					
5710 Warland Dr	Cypress	CA	90630	800-800-5202	562-431-5011
Envision Peripherals Inc (EPI)					
47490 Seabridge Dr	Fremont	CA	94538	888-838-6388*	510-770-9988
*Tech Supp					
General Digital Corp					
Eight Nutmeg Rd S	South Windsor	CT	06074	800-952-2535	860-282-2900
LG Electronics USA Inc					
1000 Sylvan Ave	Englewood Cliffs	NJ	07632	800-180-9999*	201-816-2000
*Tech Supp					
NEC Corp of America					
10850 Gold Ctr Dr Ste 200	Rancho Cordova	CA	95670	800-632-4636	916-463-7000
NEC Display Solutions of America Inc					
500 Pk Blvd Ste 1100	Itasca	IL	60143	800-632-4662*	630-467-3000
*Cust Svc					
Pioneer Electronics (USA) Inc					
1925 E Dominguez St	Long Beach	CA	90810	800-421-1404	310-952-2000
Planar Systems Inc					
1195 NW Compton Dr	Beaverton	OR	97006	866-475-2627	503-748-1100
NASDAQ: PLNR					
Sharp Electronics Corp					
One Sharp Plz	Mahwah	NJ	07430	800-237-4277	201-529-8200
Sony Electronics Inc					
One Sony Dr	Park Ridge	NJ	07656	800-222-7669*	201-930-1000
*Cust Svc					
Tatung Company of America Inc					
2850 El Presidio St	Long Beach	CA	90810	800-827-2850	310-637-2105
Trans-Lux Corp 26 Pearl St	Norwalk	CT	06850	800-243-5544	203-853-4321
OTC: TNLX					
Trans-Lux Fair-Play Inc					
1700 Delaware Ave	Des Moines	IA	50317	800-247-0265	515-265-5305
Video Display Corp					
1868 Tucker Industrial Rd	Tucker	GA	30084	800-241-5005*	770-938-2080
NASDAQ: VIDE ■ *Cust Svc					
ViewSonic Corp					
381 Brea Canyon Rd	Walnut	CA	91789	800-888-8583	909-444-8888
Wells-Gardner Electronics Corp					
9500 W 55th St Ste A	McCook	IL	60525	800-336-6630	708-290-2100
NYSE: WGA					

175-5 Multimedia Equipment & Supplies

				Toll-Free	Phone
Corsair Memory Inc					
46221 Landing Pkwy	Fremont	CA	94538	888-222-4346	510-657-8747
Creative Labs Inc					
1901 McCarthy Blvd	Milpitas	CA	95035	800-998-1000*	408-428-6600
*Cust Svc					
Kinyo Company Inc					
14235 Lomitas Ave	La Puente	CA	91746	800-735-4696	626-333-3711
SpeakerCraft Inc					
940 Columbia Ave	Riverside	CA	92507	800-448-0976	951-787-0543

175-6 Printers

				Toll-Free	Phone
AMT Datasouth Corp					
803 Camarillo Springs Rd Ste D	Camarillo	CA	93012	800-215-9192	805-388-5799
Astro-Med Inc					
600 E Greenwich Ave	West Warwick	RI	02893	800-343-4039	401-828-4000
NASDAQ: ALOT					
Citizen Systems America Corp					
363 Van Ness Way Ste 404	Torrance	CA	90501	800-421-6516	310-781-1460
Datamax Corp					
4501 Pkwy Commerce Blvd	Orlando	FL	32808	800-656-2062	407-578-8007

	City	State	ZIP	Toll-Free	Phone
Digital Design Inc 67 Sand Pk Rd	Cedar Grove	NJ	07009	800-967-7746	973-857-0900
Epson America Inc 3840 Kilroy Airport Way	Long Beach	CA	90806	800-463-7766	562-981-3840
GCC Printers USA 209 Burlington Rd *Sales	Bedford	MA	01730	800-422-7777*	781-275-1115
Hewlett-Packard (Canada) Ltd (HP) 5150 Spectrum Way	Mississauga	ON	L4W5G1	888-447-4636	905-206-4725
Hewlett-Packard Co 3000 Hanover St *NYSE: HPQ* ■ *Sales	Palo Alto	CA	94304	800-752-0900*	650-857-1501
International Business Machines Corp (IBM) One New OrchaRd Rd *NYSE: IBM*	Armonk	NY	10504	800-426-4968	914-499-1900
Kroy LLC 3830 Kelley Ave *Cust Svc	Cleveland	OH	44114	888-888-5769*	216-426-5600
Lexmark International Inc 740 W New Cir Rd *NYSE: LXK* ■ *Cust Svc	Lexington	KY	40550	800-539-6275*	859-232-2000
Mutoh America Inc 2602 S 47th St Ste 102	Phoenix	AZ	85034	800-996-8864	480-968-7772
NEC Corp of America 10850 Gold Ctr Dr Ste 200	Rancho Cordova	CA	95670	800-632-4636	916-463-7000
Oce-USA Inc 5450 N Cumberland Ave Sixth Fl	Chicago	IL	60656	800-877-6232	773-714-8500
Oki Data Americas Inc 2000 Bishops Gate Blvd *Cust Svc	Mount Laurel	NJ	08054	800-654-3282*	856-235-2600
Pentax Imaging Co 633 17th St Ste 2600	Denver	CO	80202	800-877-0155	303-799-8000
Plastic Card Systems Inc 31 Pierce St	Northborough	MA	01532	800-742-2273	508-351-6210
Primera Technology Inc Two Carlson Pkwy N Ste 375	Plymouth	MN	55447	800-797-2772	763-475-6676
Printek Inc 1517 Townline Rd	Benton Harbor	MI	49022	800-368-4636	269-925-3200
Printronix Inc 14600 Myford Rd	Irvine	CA	92606	800-665-6210	714-368-2300
RISO Inc Eight New England Executive Park Ste 390 *General	Burlington	MA	01803	800-942-7476*	978-777-7377
Roland DGA Corp 15363 Barranca Pkwy	Irvine	CA	92618	800-542-2307	949-727-2100
Sato America Inc 10350A Nations Ford Rd	Charlotte	NC	28273	888-871-8741	704-644-1650
Seiko Instruments USA Inc 21221 S Western Ave Ste 250 *Sales	Torrance	CA	90501	800-688-0817*	310-517-7700
Seiko Instruments USA Inc Micro Printer Div 2990 Lomita Blvd	Torrance	CA	90505	800-688-0817	310-517-7778
Sharp Electronics Corp One Sharp Plz	Mahwah	NJ	07430	800-237-4277	201-529-8200
Star Micronics America Inc 1150 King George's Post Rd	Edison	NJ	08837	800-782-7636	732-623-5500
Stratix 4920 Avalon Ridge Pkwy	Norcross	GA	30071	800-883-8300	770-326-7580
TallyGenicom 15345 Barranca Pkwy Ste 100	Irvine	CA	92618	800-436-4266	714-368-2300
Telpar Inc 187 Crosby Rd Ste 100	Dover	NH	03820	800-872-4886	603-750-7237
Toshiba America Inc 1251 Ave of the Americas Ste 4100	New York	NY	10020	800-457-7777	212-596-0600
TransAct Technologies Inc one Hamden Ctr 2319 Whitney Ave Ste 3B *NASDAQ: TACT*	Hamden	CT	06518	800-243-8941	203-859-6800
Unimark Products 9818 Pflumm Rd *Cust Svc	Lenexa	KS	66215	800-255-6356*	913-649-2424
Xante Corp 2800 Dauphin St Ste 100	Mobile	AL	36606	800-926-8839	251-473-6502
Xerox Corp 45 Glover Ave PO Box 4505 *NYSE: XRX*	Norwalk	CT	06856	800-327-9753	203-968-3000
Zebra Technologies Corp 475 Half Day Rd Ste 500 *NASDAQ: ZBRA*	Lincolnshire	IL	60069	800-423-0422	847-634-6700

175-7 Scanning Equipment

	City	State	ZIP	Toll-Free	Phone
Accu-Sort Systems Inc 511 School House Rd	Telford	PA	18969	800-227-2633	215-723-0981
AirClic Inc 900 Northbrook Dr Ste 100	Trevose	PA	19053	800-419-8495	215-504-0560
BenQ America Corp 15375 Barranca Ste A205	Irvine	CA	92618	866-600-2367	949-255-9500
BOWE Bell + Howell 760 S Wolf Rd	Wheeling	IL	60090	800-220-3030	847-675-7600
CardScan Inc 25 First St Ste 107	Cambridge	MA	02141	800-942-6739	617-492-4200
Computerwise Inc 302 N Winchester Ln	Olathe	KS	66062	800-255-3739	913-829-0600
Datalogic Scanning 959 Terry St	Eugene	OR	97402	800-695-5700	541-683-5700
Hewlett-Packard Co 3000 Hanover St *NYSE: HPQ* ■ *Sales	Palo Alto	CA	94304	800-752-0900*	650-857-1501
Hitachi Canada Ltd 5450 Explore Dr Suite 501	Mississauga	ON	L4W5N1	866-797-4332	905-629-9300
iCAD Inc Four Townsend W Ste 17 *NASDAQ: ICAD*	Nashua	NH	03063	866-280-2239	603-882-5200
InPath Devices 3610 Dodge St Ste 200	Omaha	NE	68131	800-988-1914	402-345-9200
Mustek Inc 15271 Barranca Pkwy	Irvine	CA	92618	800-308-7226	949-790-3800
Oce-USA Inc 5450 N Cumberland Ave Sixth Fl	Chicago	IL	60656	800-877-6232	773-714-8500
Order-Matic Corp 340 S Eckroat St PO Box 25463	Oklahoma City	OK	73129	800-767-6733	405-672-1487
Peripheral Dynamics Inc 5150 Campus Dr Whitemarsh Industrial Pk	Plymouth Meeting	PA	19462	800-523-0253	610-825-7090
Roland DGA Corp 15363 Barranca Pkwy	Irvine	CA	92618	800-542-2307	949-727-2100
Scan-Optics Inc 169 Progress Dr	Manchester	CT	06042	800-543-8681	860-645-7878
Scantron Corp 34 Parker	Irvine	CA	92618	800-722-6876	949-639-7500
Stratix 4920 Avalon Ridge Pkwy	Norcross	GA	30071	800-883-8300	770-326-7580
Wizcom Technologies Inc Boston Post Rd W 33 Ste 320	Marlborough	MA	01752	888-777-0552	508-251-5388
ZBA Inc 94 Old Camplain Rd	Hillsborough	NJ	08844	800-750-4239	908-359-2070

175-8 Storage Devices

	City	State	ZIP	Toll-Free	Phone
Appro International Inc 901 Fifth Ave Ste 1000	Seattle	WA	98164	800-950-2729	206-701-2000
Apricorn Inc 12191 Kirkham Rd	Poway	CA	92064	800-458-5448	858-513-2000
Avere Systems Inc 5000 Mcknight Rd Ste 404	Pittsburgh	PA	15237	888-882-8373	412-894-2570
BridgeSTOR LLC 18060 Old Coach Dr	Poway	CA	92064	800-280-8204	858-375-7076
Cirrascale Corp 12140 Community Rd	Poway	CA	92064	888-942-3800	858-874-3800
CMS Peripherals Inc 12 Mauchly Unit E	Irvine	CA	92618	800-327-5773	714-424-5520
Creative Labs Inc 1901 McCarthy Blvd *Cust Svc	Milpitas	CA	95035	800-998-1000*	408-428-6600
CRU Acquisitions Group LLC 1000 SE Tech Ctr Dr Ste 160	Vancouver	WA	98683	800-260-9800	360-816-1800
DataDirect Networks 9320 Lurline Ave	Chatsworth	CA	91311	800-837-2298	818-700-7600
Datalink Corp 8170 Upland Cir *NASDAQ: DTLK*	Chanhassen	MN	55317	800-448-6314	952-944-3462
Digital Peripheral Solutions Inc 8015 E Crystal Dr	Anaheim	CA	92807	877-998-3440	
Disc Makers 7905 N Rt 130	Pennsauken	NJ	08110	800-468-9353	856-663-9030
Dynamic Network Factory Inc 21353 Cabot Blvd	Hayward	CA	94545	800-947-4742	510-265-1122
Edge Electronics Inc 75 Orville Dr	Bohemia	NY	11716	800-647-3343	631-471-3343
Fujitsu Computer Products of America Inc 1255 E Arques Ave	Sunnyvale	CA	94085	800-626-4686	408-746-7000
Gridstore Inc 1975 W El Camino Real Ste 306	Mountain View	CA	94040	855-786-7065	650-316-5515
H Company Computer Products Inc 16812 Hale Ave	Irvine	CA	92606	800-726-2477	949-833-3222
Hewlett-Packard (Canada) Ltd (HP) 5150 Spectrum Way	Mississauga	ON	L4W5G1	888-447-4636	905-206-4725
Hewlett-Packard Co 3000 Hanover St *NYSE: HPQ* ■ *Sales	Palo Alto	CA	94304	800-752-0900*	650-857-1501
Hie Electronics Inc 321 N Central Expy Ste 260	Mckinney	TX	75070	888-782-7937	972-542-2327
Hitachi America Ltd Computer Div 2000 Sierra Pt Pkwy	Brisbane	CA	94005	800-448-2244	
Hitachi Data Systems Corp 750 Central Expy	Santa Clara	CA	95050	877-437-3849	408-970-1000
Idealstor LLC 1100 Lakeway Dr Ste100	Lakeway	TX	78734	888-864-3257	512-279-4321
Imation Corp One Imation Pl *NYSE: IMN*	Oakdale	MN	55128	888-466-3456	651-704-4000
International Business Machines Corp (IBM) One New OrchaRd Rd *NYSE: IBM*	Armonk	NY	10504	800-426-4968	914-499-1900
Kanguru Solutions 1360 Main St *Sales	Millis	MA	02054	888-526-4878*	508-376-4245
LG Electronics USA Inc 1000 Sylvan Ave *Tech Supp	Englewood Cliffs	NJ	07632	800-180-9999*	201-816-2000
Luminex Software Inc 871 Marlborough Ave *Sales	Riverside	CA	92507	888-586-4639*	951-781-4100
Microboards Technology LLC 8150 Mallory Ct PO Box 846	Chanhassen	MN	55317	800-646-8881	952-556-1600
NEC Corp of America 10850 Gold Ctr Dr Ste 200	Rancho Cordova	CA	95670	800-632-4636	916-463-7000
Pioneer Electronics (USA) Inc 1925 E Dominguez St	Long Beach	CA	90810	800-421-1404	310-952-2000
Qualstar Corp 3990-B Heritage Oak Ct *NASDAQ: QBAK*	Simi Valley	CA	93063	800-468-0680	805-583-7744
Quantum Corp 224 Airport Pkwy Ste 300 *NYSE: QTM* ■ *Tech Supp	San Jose	CA	95110	800-677-6268*	408-944-4000
Quantum/ATL 141 Innovation Dr	Irvine	CA	92617	800-677-6268	949-856-7800
Rimage Corp 7725 Washington Ave S	Minneapolis	MN	55439	800-553-8312	952-944-8144
Shaffstall Corp 8531 Bash St	Indianapolis	IN	46250	800-357-6250	317-842-2077
Sony Electronics Inc One Sony Dr *Cust Svc	Park Ridge	NJ	07656	800-222-7669*	201-930-1000

Company / Address	City	State	ZIP	Toll-Free	Phone
Tandberg Data					
10225 Westmoor Dr Ste 125	Westminster	CO	80021	**800-392-2983**	303-442-4333
TDK USA Corp					
525 RXR Plaza PO Box 9302	Uniondale	NY	11556	**800-285-2783***	516-535-2600
*General					
Toshiba America Inc					
1251 Ave of the Americas Ste 4100	New York	NY	10020	**800-457-7777**	212-596-0600
VeriStor Systems Inc					
3308 Peachtree Industrial Blvd	Duluth	GA	30096	**866-956-2948**	678-990-1593
Western Digital Corp					
3355 Michelson Dr Ste 100	Irvine	CA	92612	**800-832-4778**	949-672-7000
NASDAQ: WDC					

176 COMPUTER EQUIPMENT & SOFTWARE - WHOL

SEE ALSO Business Machines - Whol ; Electrical & Electronic Equipment & Parts - Whol

Company / Address	City	State	ZIP	Toll-Free	Phone
Access Specialties International LLC					
15230 Carrousel Way	Rosemount	MN	55068	**800-332-1013**	651-453-1283
Ahearn & Soper Inc					
100 Woodbine Downs Blvd	Rexdale	ON	M9W5S6	**800-263-4258**	416-675-3999
Alexander Open Systems Inc					
12851 Foster St	Overland Park	KS	66213	**800-473-1110**	913-307-2300
Allied Group Inc, The					
25 Amflex Dr	Cranston	RI	02921	**800-556-6310**	401-946-6100
Altametrics Inc					
3191 Red Hill Ave Ste 100	Costa Mesa	CA	92626	**800-676-1281**	
American Portwell Technology Inc					
44200 Christy St	Fremont	CA	94538	**877-278-8899**	510-403-3399
APCON Inc					
9255 SW Pioneer Ct	Wilsonville	OR	97070	**800-624-6808**	503-682-4050
ASA Tire Systems Inc					
651 S Stratford Dr	Meridian	ID	83642	**800-241-8472**	208-855-0781
ASI Corp 48289 Fremont Blvd	Fremont	CA	94538	**800-200-0274**	510-226-8000
Atlantix Global Systems					
One Sun Ct	Norcross	GA	30092	**877-552-8526**	770-248-7700
Autostar Solutions Inc					
1300 Summit Ave Ste 800	Fort Worth	TX	76102	**800-682-2215**	
AVAD Canada Ltd					
205 Courtneypark Dr W	Mississauga	ON	L5W0A5	**866-523-2823**	
Avnet Inc 2211 S 47th St	Phoenix	AZ	85034	**888-822-8638**	480-643-2000
NYSE: AVT					
Avnet Technology Solutions					
8700 S Price Rd	Tempe	AZ	85284	**800-409-1483**	480-794-6500
Axiom Memory Solutions LLC					
19651 Descartes	Foothill Ranch	CA	92610	**888-658-3326**	949-581-1450
Bay Technical Assoc Inc					
5239 Ave A	Long Beach Industrial Park	MS	39560	**800-523-2702**	228-563-7334
Butler Technologies Inc					
231 W Wayne St	Butler	PA	16001	**800-494-6656**	724-283-6656
CAD/CAM Consulting Services Inc (CCCS)					
996 Lawrence Dr Ste 101	Newbury Park	CA	91320	**888-375-7676**	805-375-7676
Cadec Corp 645 Harvey Rd	Manchester	NH	03103	**800-252-2332**	603-668-1010
Champion Solutions Group					
791 Pk of Commerce Blvd Ste 200	Boca Raton	FL	33487	**800-771-7000**	561-997-2900
Columbia Ultimate Business Systems Inc					
4400 NE 77th Ave Ste 100	Vancouver	WA	98662	**800-488-4420**	360-256-7358
Comprehensive Traffic Systems Inc					
4860 Robb St Ste 205	Wheat Ridge	CO	80033	**888-353-9002**	303-432-3777
Computer Aided Technology Inc					
165 N Arlington Heights Rd					
Ste 101	Buffalo Grove	IL	60089	**888-308-2284**	
Computer Connection of Central New York Inc					
11206 Cosby Manor Rd	Utica	NY	13502	**800-566-4786**	315-724-2209
Computer Dynamics Inc					
3030 Whitehall Pk Dr	Charlotte	NC	28273	**866-599-6512**	
Comstor Inc					
14850 Conference Ctr Dr Ste 200	Chantilly	VA	20151	**800-955-9590**	703-345-5100
Cranel Inc					
8999 Gemini Pkwy	Columbus	OH	43240	**800-288-3475***	614-431-8000
*General					
Crown Micro Inc					
48351 Fremont Blvd	Fremont	CA	94538	**800-963-7070**	510-490-8187
D & H Distributing Company Inc					
2525 N Seventh St	Harrisburg	PA	17110	**800-340-1001**	
Data Impressions					
17418 Studebaker Rd	Cerritos	CA	90703	**800-777-6488**	562-207-9050
Data Sales Company Inc					
3450 W Burnsville Pkwy	Burnsville	MN	55337	**800-328-2730**	952-890-8838
De Marque inc					
400 Boul Jean-Lesage Bureau 540	Quebec	QC	G1K8W1	**888-458-9143**	418-658-9143
Desire2Learn Inc					
151 Charles SW Ste 400	Kitchener	ON	N2G1H6	**888-772-0325**	519-772-0325
DigiLink Inc					
840 S Pickett St	Alexandria	VA	22304	**877-806-3453**	703-340-1800
Digital Storage Inc					
7611 Green Meadows Dr	Lewis Center	OH	43035	**800-232-3475**	740-548-7179
Dlt Solutions					
13861 Sunrise Valley Dr Ste 400	Herndon	VA	20171	**800-262-4358**	703-709-7172
DPC DATA Inc					
103 Eisenhower Pkwy Ste 300	Roseland	NJ	07068	**800-996-4747**	201-346-0701
Dynamic Computer Corp					
23400 Industrial Pk Ct	Farmington Hills	MI	48335	**866-257-2111**	248-473-2200
Electronic Environments Corp					
410 Forest St	Marlborough	MA	01752	**800-342-5332**	508-229-1400
Elk River Systems Inc					
777 E Main Ste 108	Bozeman	MT	59715	**888-771-0809**	406-632-4763
Enseo Inc					
1680 Prospect Dr Ste 100	Richardson	TX	75081	**800-270-8747**	972-234-2513
General Data Co Inc					
4354 Ferguson Dr	Cincinnati	OH	45245	**800-733-5252**	513-752-7978
Global Computer Supplies Inc					
11 Harbor Pk Dr	Port Washington	NY	11050	**800-446-9662**	
Good Printers Inc					
213 Dry River Rd	Bridgewater	VA	22812	**800-296-3731**	540-828-4663
Graphic Products Inc					
PO Box 4030	Beaverton	OR	97076	**888-326-9244**	503-644-5572
GTSI Corp					
2553 Dulles View Dr Ste 100	Herndon	VA	20171	**800-999-4874**	703-502-2000
NASDAQ: GTSI					
Helmel Engineering Products Inc					
6520 Lockport Rd	Niagara Falls	NY	14305	**800-237-8266**	716-297-8644
Home Automated Living Inc					
14401 Sweitzer Ln Sixth Fl	Laurel	MD	20707	**800-935-5313**	301-498-6000
Iceptstechnology Group Inc					
1301 Fulling Mill Rd	Middletown	PA	17057	**888-477-7989**	717-704-1000
Infotel Distributors					
6450 Poe Ave Ste 200	Dayton	OH	45414	**888-528-4504**	
Ingram Micro Inc					
1600 E St Andrew Pl	Santa Ana	CA	92705	**800-456-8000***	714-566-1000
NYSE: IM ■ *Sales					
Intelligent Computer Solutions Inc					
9350 Eton Ave	Chatsworth	CA	91311	**888-994-4678**	818-998-5805
Journey Education Marketing Inc					
13755 Hutton Dr Ste 500	Dallas	TX	75234	**800-874-9001**	972-481-2000
Laser Pros International					
One International Ln	Rhinelander	WI	54501	**888-558-5277**	715-369-5995
Leadman Electronic USA Inc					
382 Laurelwood Dr	Santa Clara	CA	95054	**877-532-3626**	408-738-1751
Lindsey & Company Inc					
2302 Llama Dr	Searcy	AR	72143	**800-890-7058**	501-268-5324
Long View Systems Corp					
3100 255 Fifth Ave SW	Calgary	AB	T2P3G6	**866-515-6900**	403-515-6900
M & A Technology Inc					
2045 Chenault Dr	Carrollton	TX	75006	**800-225-1452**	972-490-5803
Max Group Corp					
17011 Green Dr	City of Industry	CA	91745	**800-256-9040**	626-935-0050
MontaVista Software Inc					
2929 Patrick Henry Dr	Santa Clara	CA	95054	**888-624-4846**	408-572-8000
Onix Networking Corp					
18519 Detroit Ave	Lakewood	OH	44107	**800-664-9638**	
Open Storage Solutions Inc					
2 Castleview Dr	Toronto	ON	L6T5S9	**800-387-3419**	905-790-0660
Open Systems of Cleveland Inc					
22999 Forbes Rd Ste A	Cleveland	OH	44146	**888-881-6660**	440-439-2332
Pact-One Solutions Inc					
8215 S Eastern Ave Ste 101	Las Vegas	NV	89123	**866-722-8663**	
Paragon Development Systems Inc					
1823 Executive Dr	Oconomowoc	WI	53066	**800-966-6090**	
Peak Technologies Inc					
10330 Old Columbia Rd	Columbia	MD	21046	**800-926-9212**	
Programmer's Paradise Inc					
1157 Shrewsbury Ave Ste C	Shrewsbury	NJ	07702	**800-441-1511**	732-389-8950
Promark Technology Inc					
10900 Pump House Rd Ste B	Annapolis Junction	MD	20701	**800-634-0255**	240-280-8030
Prostar Computer Inc					
837 Lawson St	City of Industry	CA	91748	**888-576-4742**	626-839-6472
Provantage Corp					
7249 Whipple Ave NW	North Canton	OH	44720	**800-336-1166**	330-494-8715
Rave Computer Assn Inc					
7171 Sterling Ponds Ct	Sterling Heights	MI	48312	**800-966-7283**	586-939-8230
Rorke Data Inc					
7626 Golden Triangle Dr	Eden Prairie	MN	55344	**800-328-8147**	952-829-0300
Rpl Supplies Inc					
141 Lanza Ave Bldg 3A	Garfield	NJ	07026	**800-524-0914**	973-767-0880
ScanSource Inc					
Six Logue Ct	Greenville	SC	29615	**800-944-2432**	864-288-2432
NASDAQ: SCSC					
Scivantage Inc					
10 Exchange Pl Unit 13	Jersey City	NJ	07302	**866-724-8268**	646-452-0050
SED International Inc					
4916 N Royal Atlanta Dr	Tucker	GA	30084	**800-444-8962***	770-491-8962
*Sales					
Softmart Inc					
450 Acorn Ln	Downingtown	PA	19335	**800-328-1319***	610-518-4000
*Cust Svc					
Software House International (SHI)					
290 Davidson Ave	Somerset	NJ	08873	**888-764-8888**	
Stardock Systems Inc					
15090 N Beck Rd Ste 300	Plymouth	MI	48170	**888-782-7362**	734-927-0677
Static Control Components Inc					
3010 Lee Ave PO Box 152	Sanford	NC	27331	**800-488-2426**	919-774-3808
Synnex Corp 44201 Nobel Dr	Fremont	CA	94538	**800-756-1888***	510-656-3333
NYSE: SNX ■ *Cust Svc					
Tanner Research Inc					
825 S Myrtle Ave	Monrovia	CA	91016	**877-325-2223**	626-471-9700
Tech Data Corp					
5350 Tech Data Dr	Clearwater	FL	33760	**800-237-8931**	727-539-7429
NASDAQ: TECD					
Think Computer Corp					
3260 Hillview Ave	Palo Alto	CA	94304	**888-815-8599**	415-670-9350
TigerDirect Inc					
7795 W Flagler St Ste 35	Miami	FL	33144	**800-800-8300**	
Us Micro Corp					
7000 Highlnds Pkwy SE	Smyrna	GA	30082	**888-876-4276**	770-437-0706
WDL Systems					
220 Chatham Business Dr	Pittsboro	NC	27312	**800-548-2319***	919-545-2500
*Sales					
West-Com Nurse Call Systems Inc					
2200 Cordelia Rd	Fairfield	CA	94534	**800-761-1180**	707-428-5900
Westcon Group Inc					
520 White Plains Rd 2nd Fl	Tarrytown	NY	10591	**800-527-9516**	914-829-7000
Westcon Group, Inc					
Westcon Convergence					
520 White Plains Rd Ste 100	Omaha	NE	68154	**877-642-7750**	
Westham Trade Co Ltd					
3620 NW 114th Ave	Doral	FL	33178	**888-852-5000**	305-717-5400
Wintec Industries Inc					
675 Sycamore Dr	Milpitas	CA	95035	**866-989-4683**	408-856-0500
Woot Inc					
4121 International Pkwy	Carrollton	TX	75007	**866-551-6881**	972-417-3959

		Toll-Free	Phone

177 COMPUTER MAINTENANCE & REPAIR

			Toll-Free	Phone
Accram Inc				
2901 W Clarendon Ave	Phoenix AZ	85017	**800-786-0288**	
Computer Troubleshooters USA				
755 Commerce Dr Ste 605	Decatur GA	30030	**877-704-1702**	404-477-1302
ComputerPlus Sales & Service Inc				
Five Northway Ct	Greer SC	29651	**800-849-4426**	
Data Exchange Corp				
3600 Via Pescador	Camarillo CA	93012	**800-237-7911**	805-388-1711
DBK Concepts Inc				
12905 SW 129 Ave	Miami FL	33186	**800-725-7226**	305-596-7226
DecisionOne Corp				
426 W Lancaster Ave	Devon PA	19333	**800-767-2876**	610-296-6000
Desktop Consulting Services				
43311 Joy Rd	Canton MI	48187	**888-600-2731**	
Essential Technologies Inc				
1107 Hazeltine Blvd Ste 477	Chaska MN	55318	**800-818-1125**	952-368-9001
Everprint International Inc				
18021 Cortney Ct	City of Industry CA	91748	**800-984-5777**	
IIS Group LLC				
1015 Virginia Dr Ste 1 W	Fort Washington PA	19034	**855-443-5777**	
Integration Technologies Group Inc				
2745 Hartland Rd Ste 200	Falls Church VA	22043	**800-835-7823**	703-698-8282
Interactive Services Group Inc				
600 Delran Pkwy Ste C	Delran NJ	08075	**800-566-3310**	
Intratek Computer Inc				
5431 Industrial Dr	Huntington Beach CA	92649	**800-892-8282**	
Matthijssen Inc				
14 Rt 10	East Hanover NJ	07936	**800-845-2200**	973-887-1100
NCE Computer Group				
1866 Friendship Dr	El Cajon CA	92020	**800-767-2587***	619-212-3000
*Cust Svc				
Precision Computer Services Inc (PCS)				
175 Constitution Blvd S	Shelton CT	06484	**800-340-9890**	203-929-0000
Rescuecom Corp				
2560 Burnet Ave	Syracuse NY	13206	**800-737-2837**	
Systems Maintenance Services Inc (SMS)				
10420 Harris Oaks Blvd Suite C	Charlotte NC	28269	**877-405-0330**	

178 COMPUTER NETWORKING PRODUCTS & SYSTEMS

SEE ALSO Telecommunications Equipment & Systems ; Modems ; Systems & Utilities Software

			Toll-Free	Phone
Allied Telesyn International Corp				
19800 N Creek Pkwy Ste 100	Bothell WA	98011	**800-424-4284**	425-481-3895
American Megatrends Inc (AMI)				
5555 Oakbrook Pkwy Bldg 200	Norcross GA	30093	**800-828-9264**	770-246-8600
ASA Computers Inc				
645 National Ave	Mountain View CA	94043	**800-732-5727**	650-230-8000
Asante Technologies Inc				
673 S Milpitas Blvd Ste 100	Milpitas CA	95035	**800-303-9121**	408-435-8388
OTC: ASNL				
Avaya Inc				
211 Mt Airy Rd	Basking Ridge NJ	07920	**800-237-3239**	908-953-6000
Axis Communications Inc (ACI)				
100 Apollo Dr	Chelmsford MA	01824	**800-444-2947**	978-614-2000
Black Box Corp 1000 Pk Dr	Lawrence PA	15055	**877-877-2269**	724-746-5500
NASDAQ: BBOX				
Blue Coat Systems Inc				
420 N Mary Ave	Sunnyvale CA	94085	**866-302-2628**	408-220-2200
NASDAQ: BCSI				
Brocade Communications Systems Inc				
130 Holger Way	San Jose CA	95134	**800-752-8061**	408-333-8000
NASDAQ: BRCD				
Cambex Corp				
337 Tpke Rd	Southborough MA	01772	**800-325-5565**	508-281-0209
OTC: CBEX				
Chatsworth Products Inc				
31425 Agoura Rd	Westlake Village CA	91361	**800-834-4969**	818-735-6100
Cisco Systems Inc				
170 W Tasman Dr	San Jose CA	95134	**800-553-6387**	408-526-4000
NASDAQ: CSCO				
Compex Inc				
7918 Jones Branch Dr	Mclean VA	22102	**800-279-8891**	703-642-5910
CompuCom Systems Inc				
7171 Forest Ln	Dallas TX	75230	**800-597-0555***	972-856-3600
*Cust Svc				
Comtrol Corp				
6655 Wedgewood Rd Ste 120	Maple Grove MN	55311	**800-926-6876**	763-494-4100
Continental Resources Inc				
175 Middlesex Tpke	Bedford MA	01730	**800-937-4688**	781-275-0850
Crossroads Systems Inc				
8300 N MoPac Expy	Austin TX	78759	**800-643-7148**	512-349-0300
NASDAQ: CRDS				
Crystal Group Inc				
850 Kacena Rd	Hiawatha IA	52233	**877-279-7863**	319-378-1636
Cubix Corp				
2800 Lockheed Way	Carson City NV	89706	**800-829-0550***	775-888-1000
*Sales				
Cyberdata Corp				
Three Justin Ct	Monterey CA	93940	**800-363-8010**	831-373-2601
D-Link Systems Inc				
17595 Mt Herrmann St	Fountain Valley CA	92708	**800-326-1688**	714-885-6000
Daly Computers Inc				
22521 Gateway Ctr Dr	Clarksburg MD	20871	**800-955-3259**	301-670-0381
Dell Inc One Dell Way	Round Rock TX	78682	**800-879-3355**	512-338-4400
NASDAQ: DELL				
Digi International Inc				
11001 Bren Rd E	Minnetonka MN	55343	**877-912-3444**	952-912-3444
NASDAQ: DGII				

			Toll-Free	Phone
Dot Hill Systems Corp				
1351 S Sunset St	Longmont CO	80501	**800-872-2783**	303-845-3200
NASDAQ: HILL				
Echelon Corp				
550 Meridian Ave	San Jose CA	95126	**888-324-3566**	408-938-5200
NASDAQ: ELON				
Egenera Inc				
80 Central St	Boxborough MA	01719	**866-301-3117**	978-206-6300
Electronics for Imaging Inc				
303 Velocity Way	Foster City CA	94404	**888-334-8650**	650-357-3500
NASDAQ: EFII				
Emulex Corp				
3333 Susan St	Costa Mesa CA	92626	**800-854-7112**	714-662-5600
NYSE: ELX				
eSoft Inc				
295 Interlocken Blvd Ste 500	Broomfield CO	80021	**888-903-7638**	303-444-1600
Extreme Networks Inc				
3585 Monroe St	Santa Clara CA	95051	**888-257-3000**	408-579-2800
NASDAQ: EXTR				
Ezenia! Inc				
14 Celina Ave Unit 17	Nashua NH	03063	**800-966-2301**	781-505-2100
F5 Networks Inc				
401 Elliott Ave W	Seattle WA	98119	**888-882-4447**	206-272-5555
NASDAQ: FFIV				
Fujitsu Computer Systems Corp				
1250 E Arques Ave	Sunnyvale CA	94085	**800-538-8460**	408-746-6000
Futurex Inc				
864 Old Boerne Rd	Bulverde TX	78163	**800-251-5112**	830-980-9782
iGo Inc				
17800 N Perimeter Dr Ste 200	Scottsdale AZ	85255	**888-205-0093**	480-596-0061
NASDAQ: IGOI				
iLinc Communications Inc				
2999 N 44th St Ste 650	Phoenix AZ	85018	**800-767-9054**	602-952-1200
IMC Networks Corp				
19772 Pauling	Foothill Ranch CA	92610	**800-624-1070**	949-465-3000
Interphase Corp				
2901 N Dallas Pkwy Ste 200	Plano TX	75093	**800-327-8638**	214-654-5000
NASDAQ: INPH				
Juniper Networks Inc				
1194 N Mathilda Ave	Sunnyvale CA	94089	**888-586-4737**	408-745-2000
NYSE: JNPR				
Marvell Semiconductor Inc				
5488 Marvell Ln	Santa Clara CA	95054	**855-627-8355***	408-222-2500
*Cust Svc				
NEC Corp of America				
10850 Gold Ctr Dr Ste 200	Rancho Cordova CA	95670	**800-632-4636**	916-463-7000
Netplanner Systems Inc				
3145 Northwoods Pkwy Ste 800	Norcross GA	30071	**800-795-1975**	770-662-5482
Network Appliance Inc				
495 E Java Dr	Sunnyvale CA	94089	**800-443-4537***	408-822-6000
NASDAQ: NTAP ■ *Sales				
Network Dynamics Inc				
640 Brooker Creek Blvd Ste 410	Oldsmar FL	34677	**877-818-8597**	813-818-8597
Overland Storage Inc				
4820 Overland Ave	San Diego CA	92123	**800-729-8725**	858-571-5555
NASDAQ: OVRL				
Peak 10 752 Barret Ave	Louisville KY	40204	**866-732-5836**	502-315-6015
Polycom Inc				
4750 Willow Rd	Pleasanton CA	94588	**800-765-9266**	
PrimeArray Systems Inc				
127 Riverneck Rd	Chelmsford MA	01824	**800-433-5133**	978-654-6250
Ringdale Inc				
101 Halmar Cove	Georgetown TX	78628	**888-288-9080**	512-288-9080
Safari Circuits Inc				
411 Washington St	Otsego MI	49078	**888-694-7230**	269-694-9471
SafeNet Inc				
4690 Millennium Dr	Belcamp MD	21017	**800-533-3958***	410-931-7500
*Sales				
SARCOM Inc				
8337 Green Meadows Dr N Ste A	Lewis Center OH	43035	**800-700-1000**	614-854-1300
Server Technology Inc				
1040 Sandhill Dr	Reno NV	89521	**800-835-1515**	775-284-2000
SOHOware Inc				
1250 Oakmead Pkwy Ste 210	Sunnyvale CA	94085	**800-632-1118**	408-565-9888
Solectek Corp				
6370 Nancy Ridge Dr Ste 109	San Diego CA	92121	**888-299-8057**	858-450-1220
SonicWALL Inc				
2001 Logic Dr	San Jose CA	95124	**888-557-6642**	408-745-9600
SteelCloud Inc				
20110 Ashbrook Pl Ste 270	Ashburn VA	20147	**800-296-3866**	703-674-5500
OTC: SCLD				
StoneFly Inc				
21353 Cabot Blvd	Hayward CA	94545	**888-786-6335**	510-265-1616
Storage Engine Inc				
One Sheila Dr Bldg 6A	Tinton Falls NJ	07724	**866-734-8899**	732-747-6995
Strictly Business Computer Systems Inc				
848 Fourth Ave Ste 200	Huntington WV	25701	**888-529-0401**	
Symon Communications Inc				
500 N Central Expy Ste 175	Plano TX	75074	**800-827-9666**	972-578-8484
Systech Corp				
16510 Via Esprillo	San Diego CA	92127	**800-800-8970**	858-674-6500
Systemax Inc				
11 Harbor Pk Dr	Port Washington NY	11050	**888-645-0878**	516-608-7000
NYSE: SYX				
TalkPoint Communications Inc				
100 William St	New York NY	10038	**866-323-8660**	212-909-2900
Technology Integration Group (TIG)				
7810 Trade St	San Diego CA	92121	**800-858-0549**	858-566-1900
Tekworks Inc				
13000 Gregg St Ste B	Poway CA	92064	**877-835-9675**	
Telebyte Inc				
355 Marcus Blvd	Hauppauge NY	11788	**800-835-3298**	631-423-3232
Telkonet Inc				
10200 W Innovation Dr Ste 300	Milwaukee WI	53226	**888-703-9398***	414-223-0473
OTC: TKOI ■ *Sales				
Transition Networks Inc				
10900 Red Cir Dr	Minnetonka MN	55343	**800-526-9267**	952-941-7600
Transource Computers Corp				
2405 W Utopia Rd	Phoenix AZ	85027	**800-486-3715**	623-879-8882

				Toll-Free	Phone

Trendware International Inc
20675 Manhattan Pl . . . . Torrance CA 90501 **888-326-6061** 310-961-5500

Ultera Systems Inc
26081 Merit Cir Ste 125 . . . . Laguna Hills CA 92653 **877-462-7362** 949-367-8800

UNICOM
565 Brea Canyon Rd Ste A . . . . Walnut CA 91789 **800-346-6668** 626-964-7873

Unimark Products
9818 Pflumm Rd . . . . Lenexa KS 66215 **800-255-6356*** 913-649-2424
*Cust Svc

US Robotics Corp
1300 E Woodfield Dr Ste 506 . . . . Schaumburg IL 60173 **877-710-0884** 847-874-2000

ViewCast Corp
3701 W Plano Pkwy Ste 300 . . . . Plano TX 75075 **800-540-4119** 972-488-7200

Virtela Technology Services Inc
5680 Greenwood Plz Blvd
Ste 200 . . . . Greenwood Village CO 80111 **877-803-9629** 720-475-4000

Visara International Inc
2700 Gateway Centre Blvd Ste 600 . . . . Morrisville NC 27560 **888-334-4380** 919-882-0200

WatchGuard Technologies Inc
505 Fifth Ave S Ste 500 . . . . Seattle WA 98104 **800-734-9905*** 206-613-6600
*Sales

WAV Inc 2380 Prospect Dr . . . . Aurora IL 60504 **800-678-2419** 630-818-1000

WideBand Corp
401 W Grand St . . . . Gallatin MO 64640 **888-663-3050** 660-663-3000

Winchester Systems Inc
101 Billerica Ave Bldg 5 . . . . North Billerica MA 01862 **800-325-3700*** 781-265-0200
*Cust Svc

Works Computing Inc
1801 American Blvd E Ste 12 . . . . Bloomington MN 55425 **866-222-4077** 952-746-1580

World Data Products Inc
121 Cheshire Ln . . . . Minnetonka MN 55305 **888-210-7636** 952-476-9000

ZT Group International Inc
350 Meadowlands Pkwy . . . . Secaucus NJ 07094 **888-984-8899** 201-559-1000

179   COMPUTER PROGRAMMING SERVICES - CUSTOM

SEE ALSO Computer Software ; Computer Systems Design Services

				Toll-Free	Phone

4th Source Inc
2400 Veterans Blvd Ste 480 . . . . Kenner LA 70062 **855-875-4700**

Access Innovations Inc
4725 Indian School Rd NE Ste 100 . . . . Albuquerque NM 87110 **800-926-8328** 505-265-3591

AccuCode Inc
6886 S Yosemite St Ste 100 . . . . Centennial CO 80112 **866-705-9879** 303-639-6111

Actsoft Inc
8910 N Dale Mabry Hwy . . . . Tampa FL 33614 **888-732-6638** 813-936-2331

Advanced Digital Data Inc
Six Laurel Dr . . . . Flanders NJ 07836 **800-922-0972** 973-584-4026

Alta Via Consulting LLC
127 ConKinnon Dr . . . . Lenoir City TN 37772 **877-258-2842**

Altech Services Inc
1160 Parsippany Blvd Ste 202 . . . . Parsippany NJ 07054 **888-725-8324**

Analytical Graphics Inc
220 Vly Creek Blvd . . . . Exton PA 19341 **800-220-4785** 610-981-8000

Aparaa Corp
14900 Landmark Blvd Ste 630 . . . . Dallas TX 75254 **888-441-2535**

Applied Software Inc
3919 National Dr Ste 200 . . . . Burtonsville MD 20866 **888-624-8439**

Aruba Networks Inc
1344 Crossman Ave . . . . Sunnyvale CA 94089 **800-943-4526** 408-227-4500
NASDAQ: ARUN

Assist Cornerstone Technologies Inc
150 West Civic Ctr Dr Ste 601 . . . . Sandy UT 84070 **800-732-0136**

Axcient Inc
1161 San Antonio Rd . . . . Mountain View CA 94043 **800-715-2339**

Boingo Wireless Inc
10960 Wilshire Blvd Ste 800 . . . . Los Angeles CA 90024 **800-880-4117** 310-586-5180

Carnegie Learning Inc
437 Grant St . . . . Pittsburgh PA 15219 **888-851-7094** 412-690-6284

Channelnet
Three Harbor Dr Ste 206 . . . . Sausalito CA 94965 **800-667-6858** 415-332-4704

Charles River Analytics Inc
625 Mt Auburn St Ste 3 . . . . Cambridge MA 02138 **877-547-4600** 617-491-3474

Cherryroad Technologies Inc
301 Gibraltar Dr Ste 2C . . . . Morris Plains NJ 07950 **877-402-7804** 973-402-7802

Claricent Inc
22 Preserve way . . . . Sturbridge MA 01566 **888-325-6496**

Clients First Business Solutions LLC
670 N Beers St Bldg 4 . . . . Holmdel NJ 07733 **866-677-6290**

CMA Consulting Services Inc
700 Troy Schenectady Rd . . . . Latham NY 12110 **800-276-6101** 518-783-9003

CollabNet Inc
8000 Marina Blvd Ste 600 . . . . Brisbane CA 94005 **888-532-6823** 650-228-2500

College Health Services LLC
144 Turnpike Rd Ste 240 . . . . Southboro MA 01772 **866-636-8336**

Commercial Programming Systems Inc
4400 Coldwater Canyon Ave . . . . Studio City CA 91604 **888-277-4562** 323-851-2681

Companion Professional Services LLC
1301 Gervais St Ste 1700 . . . . Columbia SC 29201 **800-780-1170** 803-765-1310

Compusearch Software Systems Inc
21251 Ridgetop Cir . . . . Dulles VA 20166 **855-817-2720** 703-481-3699

Computer Aid Inc (CAI)
1390 Ridgeview Dr . . . . Allentown PA 18104 **877-432-7228** 610-530-5000

Computer Guidance Corp
15035 N 75th St . . . . Scottsdale AZ 85260 **888-361-4551** 480-444-7000

Computrition Inc
19808 Nordhoff Pl . . . . Chatsworth CA 91311 **800-222-4488**

CONIX Systems Inc
7252 Main St . . . . Manchester Center VT 05255 **800-332-1899**

Construx Software
11820 Northup Way Ste E-200 . . . . Bellevue WA 98005 **866-296-6300** 425-636-0100

Corptax LLC
1751 Lk Cook Rd Ste 100 . . . . Deerfield IL 60015 **800-966-1639**

Credant Technologies Inc
15303 Dallas Pkwy Ste 1420 . . . . Addison TX 75001 **800-929-8331** 972-458-5400

Customer Service Delivery Platform Corp
15615 Alton Pkwy Ste 310 . . . . Irvine CA 92618 **888-741-2737**

Cyber-Ark Software Inc
60 Wells Ave Ste 20A . . . . Newton MA 02459 **888-808-9005** 617-965-1544

Dataflux Corp
940 NW Cary Pkwy Ste 201 . . . . Cary NC 27513 **800-727-0025** 919-447-3000

DecisionPoint Systems Inc
19655 Descartes . . . . Foothill Ranch CA 92610 **800-336-3670** 949-465-0065
OTC: DPSI

Denim Group Ltd
1354 N Loop 1604 E Ste 110 . . . . San Antonio TX 78232 **844-572-4400**

Edge Systems LLC
3S721 W Ave Ste 200 . . . . Warrenville IL 60555 **800-352-3343*** 630-810-9669
*Tech Supp

Edgenet Inc
3445 Peachtree Rd NE . . . . Atlanta GA 30326 **866-865-6602** 615-371-3848

Experts Inc, The
2400 E Commercial Blvd
Ste 614 . . . . Fort Lauderdale FL 33308 **888-748-3526** 954-493-8040

Extensis
1800 SW First Ave Ste 500 . . . . Portland OR 97201 **800-796-9798** 503-274-2020

Eyefinity Inc
10875 International Dr Ste 200 . . . . . Rancho Cordova CA 95670 **877-448-0707**

FusionStorm
Two Bryant St Ste 150 . . . . San Francisco CA 94105 **800-228-8324** 415-623-2626

GDI Infotech Inc
3775 Varsity Dr . . . . Ann Arbor MI 48108 **800-608-7682** 734-477-6900

Genesisfour Corp
7747 Ten Acre Rd . . . . Andrews SC 29510 **800-937-4364** 843-461-4117

Gnuco LLC
20 N Wacker Dr Ste 1870 . . . . Chicago IL 60606 **800-800-8805** 312-669-9600

Gst Information Technology Solutions
13043 166th St . . . . Cerritos CA 90703 **800-833-0128** 562-345-8700

H & W Computer Systems Inc
PO Box 46019 . . . . Boise ID 83711 **800-338-6692** 208-377-0336

Harvey Software Inc
7050 Winkler Rd Ste 104 . . . . Fort Myers FL 33919 **800-231-0296**

Health Care Software Inc
PO Box 2430 . . . . Farmingdale NJ 07727 **800-524-1038**

Healthcare Automation Inc
41 Sharpe Dr . . . . Cranston RI 02920 **800-738-8850** 401-572-3040

Human Factors International Inc
410 W Lowe Ave . . . . Fairfield IA 52556 **800-242-4480** 641-472-4480

Infosource Inc
1300 City View Ctr . . . . Oviedo FL 32765 **800-393-4636** 407-796-5200

Inmedius Inc
2247 Babcock Blvd Ste 200 . . . . Pittsburgh PA 15237 **800-697-7110**

Innovasystems International LLC
2385 Northside Dr Ste 300 . . . . San Diego CA 92108 **866-566-7778** 619-955-5800

Innovative Systems Group Inc
799 Roosevelt Rd . . . . Glen Ellyn IL 60137 **800-739-2400** 630-858-8500

IV Most Consulting Inc
25 Meadow Ln . . . . Chappaqua NY 10514 **800-448-6678**

Ivenuecom
9925 Painter Ave Ste A . . . . Whittier CA 90605 **800-683-8314**

KEYW Corp
7740 Milestone Pkwy Ste 400 . . . . Hanover MD 21076 **800-340-1001** 443-733-1600

Knowles - Mcniff
12862 Garden Grove Blvd Ste C . . . . Garden Grove CA 92843 **800-820-5254**

Krillion Inc 607A W Dana St . . . . Irvine CA 92618 **877-784-0805** 949-784-0800

Lynx Medical Systems Inc
15325 SE 30th Pl Ste 200 . . . . Bellevue WA 98007 **800-767-5969** 425-641-4451

MaxPoint Interactive Inc
3020 Carrington Mill Blvd Ste 300 . . . . Morrisville NC 27560 **800-916-9960**

Medivo Inc
55 Broad St 16th Fl. . . . . New York NY 10004 **888-362-4321**

Meridian Technology Group Inc
12909 SW 68th Pkwy Ste 340 . . . . Portland OR 97223 **800-755-1038** 503-697-1600

Mil Corp
4000 Mitchellville Rd . . . . Bowie MD 20716 **800-875-0867** 301-805-8500

Money Tree Software Ltd
2430 NW Professional Wy . . . . Corvallis OR 97330 **877-421-9815** 541-754-3701

Mortgageflex Systems Inc
1200 Riverplace Blvd Ste 650 . . . . Jacksonville FL 32207 **800-326-3539*** 904-356-2490
*General

Mysql Inc
20400 Stevens Creek Blvd . . . . Cupertino CA 95014 **866-221-0634** 408-213-6600

nCircle Network Security Inc
101 Second St Ste 400 . . . . Portland OR 94105 **866-897-8776** 503-276-7500

Network Dynamics Inc
640 Brooker Creek Blvd Ste 410 . . . . Oldsmar FL 34677 **877-818-8597** 813-818-8597

Neudesic LLC
8105 Irvine Ctr Dr . . . . Irvine CA 92618 **800-805-1805** 949-754-4500

Nexlan 28 W N St . . . . Danville IL 61832 **877-263-9526** 217-431-7236

nextPoint Inc
4043 N Ravenswood Ave . . . . Chicago IL 60613 **888-929-6398**

Noetix Corp
5010 148th Ave NE Ste 100 . . . . Redmond WA 98052 **866-466-3849** 425-372-2699

NowDocs International Inc
1985 Lookout Dr . . . . North Mankato MN 56003 **888-669-3627**

Oeconnection LLC
4205 Highlander Pkwy . . . . Richfield OH 44286 **888-776-5792** 330-523-1830

Orchard Software Corp
701 Congressional Blvd Ste 360 . . . . Carmel IN 46032 **800-856-1948** 317-573-2633

Paladin Data Systems Corp
19362 Powder Hill Pl NE . . . . Poulsbo WA 98370 **800-532-8448** 360-779-2400

Panasas Inc
969 W Maude Ave . . . . Sunnyvale CA 94085 **800-726-2727** 408-215-6800

Park Place Technologies Inc
5910 Landerbrook Dr . . . . Cleveland OH 44124 **877-778-8707**

Patni Americas Inc
116 Pine St Ste 320 . . . . Harrisburg PA 17101 **877-209-0463** 617-914-8000

Patriot Technologies Inc
5108 Pegasus Ct Ste F . . . . Frederick MD 21704 **888-417-9899** 301-695-7500

Pattern Insight Inc
465 Fairchild Dr Ste 209 . . . . Mountain View CA 94043 **866-582-2655**

Phunware Inc
7800 Shoal Creek Blvd . . . . Austin TX 78757 **855-521-8485**

Portable Technology Solutions LLC
221 David Ct . . . . Calverton NY 11933 **877-640-4152**

			Toll-Free	Phone

Providge Consulting LLC
2207 Concord Pike Ste 537 . . . . Wilimington DE 19803 **888-927-6583**

Proximo Consulting Services Inc
2500 Plz Five . . . . Jersey City NJ 07311 **800-236-9250**

Rapid Insight Inc
53 Technology Ln Ste 112 . . . . Conway NH 03818 **888-585-6511**

RDA Corp
303 International Cir Ste 340 . . . . Hunt Valley MD 21030 **888-441-1278** 410-308-9300

Rediker Software Inc
2 Wilbraham Rd . . . . Hampden MA 01036 **800-213-9860** 413-566-3463

Resource & Financial Management Systems Inc
3073 Palisades Ct . . . . Tuscaloosa AL 35405 **800-701-7367**

SAP America Inc
1721 Moon Lake Blvd Ste 300 . . . . Hoffman Estates IL 60169 **800-872-1727** 847-230-3800

Satmetrix Systems Inc
1100 Pk Pl . . . . San Mateo CA 94403 **888-800-2313** 650-227-8300

Sirsi Corp
3300 N Ashton Blvd Ste 500 . . . . Lehi UT 84043 **800-288-8020**

Smartronix Inc
44150 Smartronix Way . . . . Hollywood MD 20636 **866-442-7767** 301-373-6000

Softchalk LLC
22 S Auburn Ave . . . . Richmond VA 23221 **877-638-2425**

Softerware Inc
132 Welsh Rd Ste 140 . . . . Horsham PA 19044 **800-220-8111** 215-628-0400

Sparta Systems Inc
Holmdel Corporate Plz 2137 Hwy 35 . . . . Holmdel NJ 07733 **888-261-5948** 732-203-0400

Steadmantech
1153 Powderhouse Rd . . . . Vestal NY 13850 **866-772-0882**

Stenograph LLC
1500 Bishop Ct . . . . Mount Prospect IL 60056 **800-323-4247** 847-803-1400

Tallan Inc
175 Capital Blvd Ste 401 . . . . Rocky Hill CT 06067 **800-677-3693** 860-633-3693

Tangoe Inc 35 Executive Blvd . . . . Orange CT 06477 **877-571-4737** 203-859-9300
NASDAQ: TNGO

Terra Dotta LLC
501 W Franklin St Ste 105 . . . . Chapel Hill NC 27516 **877-368-8277**

Titan Lenders Corp
5353 W Dartmouth Ave Ste 50 . . . . Denver CO 80227 **866-412-9180**

Tizbi Inc
800 Saint Mary's St Ste 402 . . . . Raleigh NC 27605 **888-729-0951**

TopCoder Inc
95 Glastonbury Blvd . . . . Glastonbury CT 06033 **866-867-2633** 860-633-5540

TriZetto Corporation
501 N Broadway 3rd Fl . . . . Sacramento CA 95814 **800-969-3666**

United Systems & Software Inc
300 Colonial Ctr Pkwy Ste 150
PO Box 958444 . . . . Lake Mary FL 32746 **800-522-8774** 407-875-2120

Verecloud Inc
555 Eldorado Blvd Ste 200 . . . . Broomfield CO 80021 **877-300-2158**

Vertical Management Systems Inc
Seven N Fair Oaks Ave Second Fl . . . . Pasadena CA 91103 **800-867-4357**

VideoMining Corp
403 S Allen St Ste 101 . . . . State College PA 16801 **800-898-9950**

Vision Technologies Inc
530 McCormick Dr Ste G . . . . Glen Burnie MD 21061 **866-746-1122** 410-424-2183

Visual Learning Systems Inc
PO Box 8226 . . . . Missoula MT 59807 **866-968-7857**

WebNet Services Inc
247 Rt 100 . . . . Somers NY 10589 **866-923-4811** 914-232-6900

Weidenhammer Systems Corp
935 Berkshire Blvd . . . . Reading PA 19610 **866-497-2227** 610-378-1149

Welligent Inc
5205 Colley Ave . . . . Norfolk VA 23508 **888-317-5960**

Winware Inc 1955 W Oak Cir . . . . Marietta GA 30062 **888-419-1399** 770-419-1399

Wolfram Research Inc
100 Trade Ctr Dr . . . . Champaign IL 61820 **800-965-3726** 217-398-0700

Youngsoft Inc
49197 Wixom Tech Dr . . . . Wixom MI 48393 **888-470-4553** 248-675-1200

Z-Law Software Inc
80 Upton Ave PO Box 40602 . . . . Providence RI 02940 **800-526-5588** 401-331-3002

Zasio Enterprises Inc
12601 W Explorer Dr Ste 250 . . . . Boise ID 83713 **800-513-1000**

COMPUTER RESELLERS

SEE Computer Equipment & Software - Whol

180   COMPUTER SOFTWARE

SEE ALSO Application Service Providers (ASPs) ; Computer Equipment & Software - Whol ; Computer Networking Products & Systems ; Computer Programming Services - Custom ; Computer Stores ; Computer Systems Design Services ; Educational Materials & Supplies

			Toll-Free	Phone

Williamson Law Book Co
790 Canning Pkwy . . . . Victor NY 14564 **800-733-9522** 585-924-3400

180-1   Business Software (General)

Companies listed here make general-purpose software products that are designed for use by all types of businesses, professionals, and, to some extent, personal users.

			Toll-Free	Phone

1MAGE Software Inc
384 Inverness Pkwy Ste 206 . . . . Englewood CO 80112 **800-844-1468**

4D Inc
3031 Tisch Way Ste 900 . . . . San Jose CA 95128 **800-785-3303** 408-557-4600

ACI Worldwide
4965 Preston Pk Blvd Ste 800 . . . . Plano TX 75093 **877-238-3095** 972-599-5600

ACOM Solutions Inc
2850 E 29th St . . . . Long Beach CA 90806 **800-347-3638** 562-424-7899

Action Technologies Inc
10970 International Blvd Second Fl . . . . Oakland CA 94603 **800-967-5356** 510-638-8300

Actuate Corp
2207 Bridgepointe Pkwy Ste 500 . . . . San Mateo CA 94404 **800-914-2259*** 650-645-3000
NASDAQ: OTEX ▪ *Sales

Adexa Inc
5933 W Century Blvd 12th Fl . . . . Los Angeles CA 90045 **888-300-7692** 310-642-2100

Adobe Systems Inc
345 Pk Ave . . . . San Jose CA 95110 **800-833-6687** 408-536-6000
NASDAQ: ADBE

Advent Software Inc
600 Townsend St Ste 500 5th Fl . . . . San Francisco CA 94103 **800-727-0605** 415-543-7696
NASDAQ: ADVS

AgilQuest Corp
9407 Hull St Rd . . . . Richmond VA 23236 **888-745-7455** 804-745-0467

American Business Systems Inc
315 Littleton Rd . . . . Chelmsford MA 01824 **800-356-4034**

American Software Inc
470 E Paces Ferry Rd . . . . Atlanta GA 30305 **800-726-2946** 404-261-4381
NASDAQ: AMSWA

APPX Software Inc
11363 San Jose Blvd Ste 301 . . . . Jacksonville FL 32223 **800-879-2779** 904-880-5560

Astea International Inc
240 Gibraltar Rd Ste 300 . . . . Horsham PA 19044 **800-878-4657** 215-682-2500
NASDAQ: ATEA

athenahealth Inc
311 Arsenal St . . . . Watertown MA 02472 **800-981-5084** 617-402-1000
NASDAQ: ATHN

Atos Origin
2500 Westchester Ave Ste 300 . . . . Purchase NY 10577 **866-875-8902** 914-881-3000

AttachmateWRQ
1500 Dexter Ave N . . . . Seattle WA 98109 **800-872-2829*** 206-217-7500
*Sales

Attunity Inc
70 Blanchard Rd . . . . Burlington MA 01803 **866-288-8648** 781-730-4070

Baudville Inc
5380 52nd St SE . . . . Grand Rapids MI 49512 **800-728-0888*** 616-698-0889
*Orders

Blackbaud Inc
2000 Daniel Island Dr . . . . Charleston SC 29492 **800-468-8996** 843-216-6200
NASDAQ: BLKB

BMC Software Inc
2101 City W Blvd . . . . Houston TX 77042 **800-841-2031** 713-918-8800
NASDAQ: BMC

Bottomline Technologies
325 Corporate Dr . . . . Portsmouth NH 03801 **800-243-2528** 603-436-0700
NASDAQ: EPAY

Bradmark Technologies Inc
4265 San Felipe St Ste 700 . . . . Houston TX 77027 **800-621-2808** 713-621-2808

Brady Identification Solutions
6555 W Good Hope Rd . . . . Milwaukee WI 53223 **800-537-8791*** 414-358-6600
*Cust Svc

Brainworks Software Inc
100 S Main St . . . . Sayville NY 11782 **800-755-1111** 631-563-5000

CA Inc One CA Plz . . . . Islandia NY 11749 **800-225-5224** 631-342-6000
NASDAQ: CA

CDC Trade Beam Inc
Two Waters Pk Dr Ste 100 . . . . San Mateo CA 94403 **888-311-1415** 650-653-4800

Cicero Inc
8000 Regency Pkwy Ste 542 . . . . Cary NC 27518 **866-538-3588** 919-380-5000

Cincom Systems Inc
55 Merchant St . . . . Cincinnati OH 45246 **800-224-6266** 513-612-2300

Computershare Plans Software
Two Enterprise Dr . . . . Shelton CT 06484 **888-340-4267** 203-944-7300

Compuware Corp
One Campus Martius St . . . . Detroit MI 48226 **800-292-7432** 313-227-7300
NASDAQ: CPWR

Current Analysis Inc
21335 Signal Hill Plz Ste 200 . . . . Sterling VA 20164 **877-787-8947** 703-404-9200

Cyma Systems Inc
2330 W University Dr Ste 4 . . . . Tempe AZ 85281 **800-292-2962**

D&B Sales & Marketing Solutions
460 Totten Pond Rd . . . . Waltham MA 02451 **866-473-3932** 781-672-9200

Data Pro Acctg Software Inc
111 Second Ave NE Ste 1200 . . . . Saint Petersburg FL 33701 **800-237-6377** 727-803-1500

Datamatics Management Services Inc
330 New Brunswick Ave . . . . Fords NJ 08863 **800-673-0366** 732-738-9600

Deltek Inc
13880 Dulles Corner Ln . . . . Herndon VA 20171 **800-456-2009** 703-734-8606
NASDAQ: PROJ

Drake Software
235 E Palmer St . . . . Franklin NC 28734 **800-890-9500**

E*Trade Financial Corp Corporate Services
4500 Bohannon Dr . . . . Menlo Park CA 94025 **800-786-2575** 650-331-6000

eCredit
777 Yamato Rd Ste 500 . . . . Boca Raton FL 33431 **800-276-2321** 561-226-9000

Edge Technologies Inc
3702 Pender Dr Ste 250 . . . . Fairfax VA 22030 **888-771-3343** 703-691-7900

eSignal 3955 Pt Eden Way . . . . Hayward CA 94545 **800-815-8256** 510-266-6000

FileMaker Inc
5201 Patrick Henry Dr . . . . Santa Clara CA 95054 **800-325-2747*** 408-987-7000
*Cust Svc

Fischer International Systems Corp
5801 Pelican Bay Blvd Ste 300 . . . . Naples FL 34108 **800-776-7258*** 239-643-1500
*Tech Supp

FlexiInternational Software Inc
Two Enterprise Dr . . . . Shelton CT 06484 **800-353-9492** 203-925-3040
OTC: FLXI

FrontRange Solutions USA Inc
5675 Gibraltar Dr . . . . Pleasanton CA 94588 **800-776-7889** 925-398-1800

Gemstone Systems Inc
1260 NW Waterhouse Ave Ste 200 . . . . Beaverton OR 97006 **800-243-4772** 503-533-3000

Global Shop Solutions Inc
975 Evergreen Cir . . . . The Woodlands TX 77380 **800-364-5958*** 281-681-1959
*Sales

Global Software Inc
3201 Beechleaf Ct Ste 170 . . . . Raleigh NC 27604 **800-326-3444** 919-872-7800

Glovia International Inc
2250 E Imperial Hwy Ste 200 . . . . El Segundo CA 90245 **888-245-6842** 310-563-7000

Grandite Inc PO Box 47133 . . . . Quebec QC G1S4X1 **866-808-3932** 581-318-2018

Classified Section

Company / Address	City	ST	ZIP	Toll-Free	Phone
GSE Systems Inc 1332 Londontown Blvd Ste 200 *NYSE: GVP ■ *Cust Svc*	Sykesville	MD	21784	800-638-7912*	410-970-7800
Halogen Software 495 March Rd	Kanata	ON	K2K3G1	866-566-7778	613-270-1011
HarrisData 13555 Bishops Ct Ste 300	Brookfield	WI	53005	800-225-0585	262-784-9099
HighJump Software 5600 W 83rd St Ste 600	Minneapolis	MN	55437	800-328-3271	952-947-4088
HK Systems Inc 2855 S James Dr	New Berlin	WI	53151	800-424-7365	262-860-7000
I-many Inc 1735 Market St 37th Fl	Philadelphia	PA	19103	877-774-2451	215-344-1900
iCIMS Inc 90 Matawan Rd Pkwy 120 Fifth Fl	Matawan	NJ	07747	800-889-4422	732-847-1941
Iconixx Software 3420 Executive Ctr Dr Ste 250	Austin	TX	78731	877-426-6499	
IFS North America Inc 300 Pk Blvd Ste 555	Chicago	IL	60143	888-437-4968	
Informatica Corp 100 Cardinal Way *NASDAQ: INFA*	Redwood City	CA	94063	800-653-3871	650-385-5000
Information & Computing Services Inc (ICS) 1650 Prudential Dr Ste 300	Jacksonville	FL	32207	800-676-4427	904-399-8500
InfoVista Corp 12950 Worldgate Dr Ste 250	Herndon	VA	20170	866-921-9219	703-435-2435
Innovative Systems Inc 790 Holiday Dr Bldg 11	Pittsburgh	PA	15220	800-622-6390	412-937-9300
Inova Solutions Inc 110 Avon St	Charlottesville	VA	22902	800-637-1077	434-817-8000
Inspiration Software Inc 5125 SW Macadam Ave Ste 145	Beaverton	OR	97239	800-877-4292	503-297-3004
International Business Machines Corp (IBM) One New OrchaRd Rd *NYSE: IBM*	Armonk	NY	10504	800-426-4968	914-499-1900
InterraTech Corp PO Box 4	Mount Ephraim	NJ	08059	888-589-4889	856-854-5100
ISG Novasoft (ISGN) 600 A N John Rodes Blvd	Melbourne	FL	32934	800-939-8258	
K-Systems Inc 2104 Aspen Dr	Mechanicsburg	PA	17055	800-221-0204	717-795-7711
Kalido 1 Wall St Ste 3	Burlington	MA	01803	866-466-3849	781-202-3200
Logility Inc 470 E Paces Ferry Rd	Atlanta	GA	30305	800-762-5207	404-261-9777
Longview Solutions 100 Matsonford Rd Ste 230	Radnor	PA	19087	888-456-6484	610-977-0995
M2 Technology Inc 21702 Hardy Oak Ste 100	San Antonio	TX	78258	800-267-1760	210-566-3773
Malvern Systems Inc 81 Lancaster Ave Ste 219	Malvern	PA	19355	800-296-9642	
Maverick Technologies 265 Admiral Trost Rd PO Box 470	Columbia	IL	62236	888-917-9109	618-281-9100
Mediagrif Interactive Technologies Inc 1111 St-Charles St W E Tower Ste 255 *TSE: MDF*	Longueuil	QC	J4K5G4	877-677-9088	450-449-0102
Meridian Systems 1720 Prairie City Rd Ste 120	Folsom	CA	95630	800-850-2660	916-294-2000
MicroBiz Corp 655 Oak Grove Ave Ste 493 Ste 493	Menlo Park	CA	94025	800-937-2289	702-749-5353
Microlink Enterprise Inc 20955 Pathfinder Rd Ste 100	Diamond Bar	CA	91765	800-829-3688	562-205-1888
Microsoft Great Plains Business Solutions 3900 Great Plains Dr S	Fargo	ND	58104	888-477-7877	701-281-6500
Milner Technologies Inc 5125 Peachtree Industrial Blvd	Norcross	GA	30092	800-592-3766	770-734-5300
Multi-Ad Inc 1720 W Detweiller Dr	Peoria	IL	61615	800-348-6485	309-692-1530
NetMotion Wireless Inc 701 N 34th St Ste 250	Seattle	WA	98103	877-818-7626	206-691-5500
New Century Education Foundation PO Box 43052	Upper Montclair	NJ	07043	866-326-1133	
NewlineNoosh Inc 625 Ellis St Ste 300	Mountain View	CA	94043	888-286-6674	650-637-6000
Newport Wave Inc 15 McLean	Irvine	CA	92620	800-999-2611	949-651-1099
Novell Inc 1800 S Novell Pl	Provo	UT	84606	800-529-3400	801-861-4272
Objectivity Inc 640 W California Ave Ste 210	Sunnyvale	CA	94086	800-767-6259	408-992-7100
OMD Corp 3705 Missouri Blvd	Jefferson City	MO	65109	866-440-8664	573-893-8930
OneSCM 6805 Capital of Texas Hwy Ste 370	Austin	TX	78731	800-324-5143	512-231-8191
Open Systems Inc 4301 Dean Lakes Blvd *Sales	Shakopee	MN	55379	800-328-2276*	
OpenText Corp 8600 W Bryn Mawr Ave Ste 710 N	Chicago	IL	60631	800-499-6544	773-632-1400
Oracle Corp 500 Oracle Pkwy *NYSE: ORCL ■ *Sales*	Redwood Shores	CA	94065	800-392-2999*	650-506-7000
Oracle USA 500 Oracle Pkwy	Redwood Shores	CA	94065	800-392-2999	650-506-7000
Palisade Corp 798 Cascadilla St	Ithaca	NY	14850	800-432-7475	607-277-8000
Paperclip Software Inc One University Plz	Hackensack	NJ	07601	800-929-3503	201-525-1221
Passport Corp 85 Chestnut Ridge Rd	Montvale	NJ	07645	800-926-6736	201-573-0038
Payspan Inc 7751 Belfort Pkwy Ste 200	Jacksonville	FL	32256	877-331-7154	
Pentagon 2000 Software Inc 15 W 34th St Fifth Fl	New York	NY	10001	800-643-1806	212-629-7521
PeopleStrategy Inc 5883 Glenridge Dr Ste 200	Atlanta	GA	30328	855-488-4100	
Percussion Software Inc 600 Unicorn Pk Dr	Woburn	MA	01801	800-283-0800	781-438-9900
Personnel Data Systems Inc (PDS) 470 Norritown Rd Ste 202	Blue Bell	PA	19422	800-243-8737	610-238-4600
Pitney Bowes Group 1 Software 4200 Parliament Pl Ste 600	Lanham	MD	20706	800-367-6950	301-731-2300
Planview Inc 8300 N Mopac Ste 300	Austin	TX	78759	800-856-8600	512-346-8600
Platform Computing Inc 3760 14th Ave	Markham	ON	L3R3T7	877-528-3676	905-948-8448
Portrait Software Inc 125 Summer St 16th Fl	Boston	MA	02110	800-327-8627	617-457-5200
Print-O-Stat Inc 1011 W Market St	York	PA	17404	800-711-8014	717-854-7821
Progress Software Corp 14 Oak Pk *NASDAQ: PRGS*	Bedford	MA	01730	800-477-6473	781-280-4000
QAD Inc 100 Innovation Pl *NASDAQ: QADB*	Santa Barbara	CA	93108	888-641-4141	805-684-6614
Quest Software Inc Five Polaris Way *NASDAQ: QSFT*	Aliso Viejo	CA	92656	800-306-9329	949-754-8000
Realtime Software Corp 24 Deane Rd	Bernardston	MA	01337	800-323-1143	847-803-1100
Red Wing Software Inc 491 Hwy 19	Red Wing	MN	55066	800-732-9464	651-388-1106
Redemtech Inc 4115 Leap Rd	Hilliard	OH	43026	800-393-7627	614-850-3366
Rentrak Corp 7700 NE Ambassador Pl Third Fl *NASDAQ: RENT*	Portland	OR	97220	800-929-0070	503-284-7581
Sage Fixed Assets 2325 Dulles Corner Blvd Ste 700	Herndon	VA	20171	800-368-2405	8.0-036-8e+009
Sand Technology Inc 4115 Rue Sherbrooke Ouest *NYSE: SNDTF*	Westmount	QC	H3Z1B1	877-468-2538	514-939-3477
SAP 100 Consilium Pl	Scarborough	ON	M1H3E3	888-777-1727	416-791-7100
SAS Institute Inc 100 SAS Campus Dr	Cary	NC	27513	800-727-0025	919-677-8000
Satori Software Inc 1301 5th Ave Ste 2200	Seattle	WA	98101	800-553-6477	206-357-2900
Sciforma Corp 985 University Ave Ste 5 *Sales	Los Gatos	CA	95032	800-533-9876*	408-354-0144
Selectica Inc 2121 S. El Camino Rl 10th Fl *NASDAQ: SLTC*	San Mateo	CA	94403	877-712-9560	650-532-1500
SERENA Software Inc 1900 Seaport Blvd Second Fl	Redwood City	CA	94063	800-457-3736	650-481-3400
Silvon Software Inc 900 Oakmont Ln Ste 400	Westmont	IL	60559	800-874-5866	630-655-3313
Soffront Software Inc 45437 Warm Springs Blvd	Fremont	CA	94539	800-763-3766	510-413-9000
Software AG USA 11700 Plz America Dr Ste 700	Reston	VA	20190	877-724-4965	703-860-5050
Sophos Inc 3 Van de Graaff Dr 2nd Fl	Burlington	MA	01803	866-866-2802	
Source Technologies 2910 Whitehall Pk Dr	Charlotte	NC	28273	800-922-8501	704-969-7500
SP Systems Inc 7500 Greenway Ctr Dr Ste 850	Greenbelt	MD	20770	877-327-8732	301-614-1322
Stamps.com Inc 1990 E Grand Ave *NASDAQ: STMP*	El Segundo	CA	90245	855-889-7867	
StrataCare Inc 17838 Gillette Ave	Irvine	CA	92614	800-277-6512	
Superior Software Inc 16055 Ventura Blvd Ste 650	Encino	CA	91436	800-421-3264	818-990-1135
Sybase Inc 1 Sybase Dr	Dublin	CA	94568	800-792-2735	925-236-5000
SYSPRO 959 S Coast Dr Ste 100	Costa Mesa	CA	92626	800-369-8649	714-437-1000
Taleo Corp 4140 Dublin Blvd Ste 400 *NYSE: ORCL*	Dublin	CA	94568	800-672-2531	925-452-3000
TECSYS Inc 1 Pl Alexis Nihon Ste 800	Montreal	QC	H3Z3B8	800-922-8649	514-866-0001
Tenrox 401 Congress Avenue	Austin	TX	78701	855-944-7526	626-796-6640
Thomson Tax & Acctg 7322 Newman Blvd *Cust Svc	Dexter	MI	48130	800-968-8900*	
Tribridge 4830 W Kennedy Blvd Ste 890	Tampa	FL	33609	877-744-1360	
Trintech Inc 15851 Dallas Pkwy Ste 900	Addison	TX	75001	800-416-0075	972-701-9802
Ultimate Software Group Inc 2000 Ultimate Way *NASDAQ: ULTI*	Weston	FL	33326	800-432-1729	954-331-7000
Validar Inc 800 Maynard Ave S Ste 401	Seattle	WA	98134	888-784-2929	206-264-9151
Versant Corp 255 Shoreline Dr Ste 450 *NASDAQ: VSNT*	Redwood City	CA	94065	888-446-4737	650-232-2400
Vertex Inc 1041 Old Cassatt Rd	Berwyn	PA	19312	800-355-3500	610-640-4200
VFA Inc 99 Bedford St	Boston	MA	02111	800-693-3132	617-451-5100
Vignette Corp 1301 S Mopac Expy Ste 100	Austin	TX	78746	800-540-7292	512-741-4300
Visible Systems Corp 201 Spring St *Sales	Lexington	MA	02421	888-850-9911*	781-778-0200
Vitria Technology Inc 945 Stewart Dr Ste 200	Sunnyvale	CA	94085	877-365-5935	
Wave Systems Corp 480 Pleasant St *NASDAQ: WAVX*	Lee	MA	01238	800-928-3638	413-243-1600
Worden Bros Inc 4905 Pine Cone Dr	Durham	NC	27707	800-776-4940	919-408-0542

180-2 Computer Languages & Development Tools

				Toll-Free	Phone
Applied Dynamics International Inc					
3800 Stone School Rd	Ann Arbor	MI	48108	**888-465-4329**	734-973-1300
BSQUARE Corp					
110 110th Ave NE Ste 200	Bellevue	WA	98004	**888-820-4500**	425-519-5900
NASDAQ: BSQR					
Data Access Corp					
14000 SW 119th Ave	Miami	FL	33186	**800-451-3539**	305-238-0012
Empress Software Inc					
11785 Beltsville Dr	Beltsville	MD	20705	**866-626-8888**	301-220-1919
FMS Inc					
8150 Leesburg Pk Ste 600	Vienna	VA	22182	**866-367-7801**	703-356-4700
Forth Inc					
5959 W Century Blvd Ste 700	Los Angeles	CA	90045	**800-553-6784**	310-999-6784
Green Hills Software Inc					
30 W Sola St	Santa Barbara	CA	93101	**800-765-4733**	805-965-6044
Instantiations Inc					
Officers Row Ste 1325B	Vancouver	WA	98661	**855-476-2558**	503-649-3836
Lattice Inc					
1751 S Naperville Rd Ste 100	Wheaton	IL	60189	**800-444-4309***	630-949-3250
*Sales					
Mix Software Inc					
1203 Berkeley Dr	Richardson	TX	75081	**800-333-0330**	972-231-0949
Numara Software Inc					
2202 NW Shore Blvd Ste 650	Tampa	FL	33607	**800-557-3031***	813-227-4500
*Sales					
Prolifics					
114 W 47th St 20th Fl.	New York	NY	10036	**800-458-3313**	212-267-7722
Revelation Software					
99 Kinderkamack Rd	Westwood	NJ	07675	**800-262-4747**	201-594-1422
Rogue Wave Software Inc					
5500 Flatiron Pkwy	Boulder	CO	80301	**800-487-3217**	303-473-9118
SlickEdit Inc					
3000 Aerial Ctr Pkwy Ste 120	Morrisville	NC	27560	**800-934-3348**	919-473-0070
Thoroughbred Software International Inc					
285 Davidson Ave Ste 302	Somerset	NJ	08873	**800-524-0430**	732-560-1377
Zortec International					
25 Century Blvd Ste 103.	Nashville	TN	37214	**800-361-7005**	615-361-7000

180-3 Educational & Reference Software

				Toll-Free	Phone
Allen Communication Learning Services					
55 West 900 South Ste 100	Salt Lake City	UT	84101	**866-310-7800**	801-537-7800
Blackboard Inc					
1899 L St NW Fifth Fl.	Washington	DC	20036	**800-424-9299**	202-463-4860
CompassLearning Inc					
203 Colorado St	Austin	TX	78701	**800-232-9556**	512-478-9600
Fuel Education LLC					
7506 Broadway Ext	Oklahoma City	OK	73116	**800-222-2811**	
Individual Software Inc					
4255 HopyaRd Rd Ste 2	Pleasanton	CA	94588	**800-822-3522**	925-734-6767
Inscape Publishing Inc					
6465 Wayzata Blvd Ste 800	Minneapolis	MN	55426	**877-735-8383**	763-765-2222
Inspiration Software Inc					
5125 SW Macadam Ave Ste 145.	Beaverton	OR	97239	**800-877-4292**	503-297-3004
LDP Inc					
75 Kiwanis Blvd PO Box O	West Hazleton	PA	18201	**800-522-8413**	
MindPlay Educational Software					
440 S Williams Blvd Ste 206	Tucson	AZ	85711	**800-221-7911**	520-888-1800
Optimum Resource Inc					
18 Hunter Rd	Hilton Head Island	SC	29926	**888-784-2592**	843-689-8000
Queue Inc 80 Hathaway Dr	Stratford	CT	06615	**800-232-2224**	
Renaissance Learning Inc					
2911 Peach St	Wisconsin Rapids	WI	54494	**800-338-4204**	715-424-3636
Saba Software Inc					
2400 Bridge Pkwy	Redwood Shores	CA	94065	**877-722-2101**	650-581-2500
OTC: SABA					
Scientific Learning Corp					
300 Frank H Ogawa Plz Ste 600	Oakland	CA	94612	**888-665-9707**	510-444-3500
OTC: SCIL					
TIBCO Software Inc					
1700 Westlake Ave N Ste 500.	Seattle	WA	98109	**866-247-8182**	206-283-8802
Tom Snyder Productions Inc					
100 Talcott Ave	Watertown	MA	02472	**800-342-0236**	617-926-6000
Transparent Language Inc					
12 Murphy Dr	Nashua	NH	03062	**800-538-8867**	
Wordsmart Corp					
10025 Mesa Rim Rd	San Diego	CA	92121	**800-858-9673**	858-565-8068

180-4 Electronic Purchasing & Procurement Software

				Toll-Free	Phone
Apptis Inc					
4800 Westfields Blvd	Chantilly	VA	20151	**888-277-8478**	703-579-0471
Ariba Inc 807 11th Ave	Sunnyvale	CA	94089	**866-772-7422**	650-390-1000
NASDAQ: ARBA					
CA Inc One CA Plz	Islandia	NY	11749	**800-225-5224**	631-342-6000
NASDAQ: CA					
Covisint					
1 Campus Martius Suite 700	Detroit	MI	48226	**800-229-4125**	
Elavon					
Two Concourse Pkwy Ste 300.	Atlanta	GA	30328	**800-725-1243**	678-731-5000
GXS Inc					
9711 Washingtonian Blvd	Gaithersburg	MD	20878	**800-560-4347**	301-340-4000
International Business Machines Corp (IBM)					
One New OrchaRd Rd	Armonk	NY	10504	**800-426-4968**	914-499-1900
NYSE: IBM					
SciQuest Inc					
6501 Weston Pkwy Ste 200	Cary	NC	27513	**888-638-7322**	919-659-2100

180-5 Engineering Software

				Toll-Free	Phone
Accelrys Inc					
10188 Telesis Ct Ste 100	San Diego	CA	92121	**888-249-2284**	858-799-5000
NASDAQ: ACCL					
Altium Inc					
3207 Grey Hawk Ct Ste 100	Carlsbad	CA	92010	**800-544-4186***	760-231-0760
*Sales					
ANSYS Inc					
275 Technology Dr	Canonsburg	PA	15317	**800-937-3321**	724-746-3304
NASDAQ: ANSS					
Ashlar Inc					
9600 Great Hills Trl Ste 150W-1625.	Austin	TX	78759	**800-877-2745**	512-250-2186
Aspen Technology Inc					
200 Wheeler Rd	Burlington	MA	01803	**888-996-7100**	781-221-6400
NASDAQ: AZPN					
Autodesk Inc					
111 McInnis Pkwy	San Rafael	CA	94903	**800-964-6432***	415-507-5000
*NASDAQ: ADSK ■ *Tech Supp*					
Bentley Systems Inc					
685 Stockton Dr	Exton	PA	19341	**800-236-8539**	610-458-5000
Bohannan Huston Inc					
7500 Jefferson St NE Courtyard 1.	Albuquerque	NM	87109	**800-877-5332**	505-823-1000
Cadence Design Systems Inc					
2655 Seely Ave	San Jose	CA	95134	**800-746-6223***	408-943-1234
*NASDAQ: CDNS ■ *Cust Svc*					
CambridgeSoft Corp					
100 CambridgePark Dr	Cambridge	MA	02140	**800-315-7300**	617-588-9100
Comarco Inc					
25541 Commerce Ctr Dr	Lake Forest	CA	92630	**800-792-0250**	949-599-7400
OTC: CMRO					
CSA Inc					
280 I- N Cir SE Ste 250	Atlanta	GA	30339	**800-844-6584**	770-955-3518
Direct Source Inc					
8176 Mallory Ct	Chanhassen	MN	55317	**800-934-8055**	952-934-8000
DP Technology Corp					
1150 Avenida Acaso	Camarillo	CA	93012	**800-627-8479**	805-388-6000
Evolution Computing					
7000 N 16th St Ste 120 514	Phoenix	AZ	85020	**800-874-4028**	
Geocomp Corp					
1145 Massachusetts Ave	Boxborough	MA	01719	**800-822-2669***	978-635-0012
*Cust Svc					
Gibbs & Assoc					
323 Science Dr	Moorpark	CA	93021	**800-654-9399***	805-523-0004
*Cust Svc					
Infinite Graphics Inc					
4611 E Lake St	Minneapolis	MN	55406	**800-679-0676**	612-721-6283
OTC: INFG					
Intergraph Corp					
19 Interpro Rd	Madison	AL	35758	**800-345-4856**	256-730-2000
Kubotek USA					
Two Mt Royal Ave Ste 500	Marlborough	MA	01752	**800-372-3872**	508-229-2020
LINDO Systems Inc					
1415 N Dayton St	Chicago	IL	60622	**800-441-2378***	312-988-7422
*Sales					
Mentor Graphics Corp					
8005 SW Boeckman Rd	Wilsonville	OR	97070	**800-592-2210**	503-685-7000
NASDAQ: MENT					
MSC.Software Corp					
Two MacArthur Pl	Santa Ana	CA	92707	**800-345-2078**	714-540-8900
National Instruments Corp					
11500 N Mopac Expy	Austin	TX	78759	**800-433-3488***	512-794-0100
*NASDAQ: NATI ■ *Cust Svc*					
Parametric Technology Corp (PTC)					
140 Kendrick St	Needham	MA	02494	**800-613-7535**	781-370-5000
NASDAQ: PTC					
Planit Solutions Inc					
3800 Palisades Dr	Tuscaloosa	AL	35405	**800-280-6932**	205-556-9199
PMS Systems Corp					
2800 28th St Ste 109	Santa Monica	CA	90405	**800-755-3968**	310-450-2566
Science Application International Corp Inc (SAIC Inc)					
1710 SAIC Dr	McLean	VA	22102	**866-400-7242**	703-676-4300
Tripos Inc					
1699 S Hanley Rd	Saint Louis	MO	63144	**800-323-2960**	314-647-1099
Zuken USA					
238 Littleton Rd Ste 100	Westford	MA	01886	**800-447-7332**	978-692-4900

180-6 Games & Entertainment Software

				Toll-Free	Phone
Disney Consumer Products					
500 S Buena Vista St	Burbank	CA	91521	**877-282-8322***	818-560-1000
*PR					
Her Interactive Inc					
1150 114th Ave SE Ste 200	Bellevue	WA	98004	**800-461-8787***	425-460-8787
*Orders					
iEntertainment Network Inc					
124 Quade Dr P.O. Box 3897	Cary	NC	27519	**800-395-8425**	919-238-4090
OTC: IENT					
MakeMusic! Inc					
7615 Golden Triangle Dr Ste M	Eden Prairie	MN	55344	**800-843-2066**	952-937-9611
NASDAQ: MMUS					
Nintendo of America Inc					
4820 150th Ave NE	Redmond	WA	98052	**800-255-3700***	425-882-2040
*Cust Svc					

180-7 Internet & Communications Software

				Toll-Free	Phone
@Comm Corp 150 Dow St	Manchester	NH	03101	**800-641-5400**	650-375-8188
Adaptive Micro Systems Inc					
7840 N 86th St	Milwaukee	WI	53224	**800-558-4187**	414-357-2020

				Toll-Free	Phone
Akamai Technologies Inc					
Eight Cambridge Ctr	Cambridge	MA	02142	**877-425-2624**	617-444-3000
NASDAQ: AKAM					
Amcom Software Inc					
10400 Yellow Cir Dr	Eden Prairie	MN	55343	**800-852-8935**	952-230-5200
Answers Corp					
237 W 35th St Ste 1101	New York	NY	10001	**888-885-5008**	646-502-4778
AnyDoc Software Inc					
28500 Clemens Road Ste 800	Westlake	OH	44145	**888-495-2638**	
Apex Voice Communications Inc					
21031 Ventura Blvd Second Fl	Woodland Hills	CA	91364	**800-727-3970**	818-379-8400
Ariba Inc 807 11th Ave	Sunnyvale	CA	94089	**866-772-7422**	650-390-1000
NASDAQ: ARBA					
Asure Softwar					
110 Wild Basin Rd	Austin	TX	78746	**888-323-8835**	512-437-2700
NASDAQ: ASUR					
AttachmateWRQ					
1500 Dexter Ave N	Seattle	WA	98109	**800-872-2829***	206-217-7500
*Sales					
Authorize.Net Corp					
PO Box 8999	San Francisco	CA	94128	**877-447-3938**	801-492-6450
Avistar Communications Corp					
1875 S Grant St 10th Fl	San Mateo	CA	94402	**800-803-0153**	650-525-3300
OTC: AVSR					
Axeda Systems Inc					
25 Forbes Blvd	Foxboro	MA	02035	**800-613-7535**	508-337-9200
Big Sky Technologies					
9325 Sky Pk Ct Ste 120	San Diego	CA	92123	**800-736-2751**	858-715-5000
Blast Inc					
220 Chatham Business Dr PO Box 818	Pittsboro	NC	27312	**800-242-5278**	919-533-0143
Callware Technologies Inc					
9100 S 500 W	Sandy	UT	84070	**800-888-4226**	801-988-6800
ClickSoftware Inc					
35 Corporate Dr Ste 400	Burlington	MA	01803	**888-438-3308**	781-272-5903
NASDAQ: CKSW					
Cothern Computer Systems Inc					
1640 Lelia Dr Ste 200	Jackson	MS	39216	**800-844-1155**	601-969-1155
DataMotion Inc					
35 Airport Rd Ste 120	Morristown	NJ	07960	**800-672-7233**	973-455-1245
DealerTrack Holdings Inc					
1111 Marcus Ave Ste M04	New Hyde Park	NY	11042	**877-357-8725**	516-734-3600
NASDAQ: TRAK					
Deerfield Communications Co					
4241 Old US 27 S PO Box 851	Gaylord	MI	49735	**800-599-8856**	989-732-8856
Dynamic Instruments Inc					
3860 Calle Fortunada	San Diego	CA	92123	**800-793-3358**	858-278-4900
eAcceleration Corp					
1050 NE Hostmark St Ste 100-B	Poulsbo	WA	98370	**800-803-4588***	360-779-6301
*Sales					
Education Management Solutions Inc					
436 Creamery Way Ste 300	Exton	PA	19341	**877-367-5050**	610-701-7002
Elance Inc					
441 Logue Ave Ste 150	Mountain View	CA	94043	**877-435-2623**	650-316-7500
EXTOL International Inc					
529 Terry Reiley Way	Pottsville	PA	17901	**800-542-7284**	570-628-5500
FutureSoft Inc					
1660 Townhurst Dr Ste E	Houston	TX	77043	**800-989-8908**	281-496-9400
GeoTrust Inc					
350 Ellis St Bldg J	Mountain View	CA	94043	**866-511-4141**	650-426-5010
Hilgraeve Inc 115 E Elm Ave	Monroe	MI	48162	**800-826-2760***	734-243-0576
*Sales					
Hyland Software Inc					
28500 Clemens Rd	Westlake	OH	44145	**888-495-2638**	440-788-5000
Imecom Group					
Eight Governor Wentworth Hwy	Wolfeboro	NH	03894	**800-329-9099**	603-569-0600
InfoNow Corp					
1875 Lawrence St Ste 1200	Denver	CO	80202	**855-524-3282**	303-293-0212
Information Builders Inc					
Two Penn Plz	New York	NY	10121	**800-969-4636**	212-736-4433
IntelliNet Technologies Inc					
1990 W New Haven Ave Ste 303	Melbourne	FL	32904	**888-726-0686**	321-726-0686
Interactive Intelligence Inc					
7601 Interactive Way	Indianapolis	IN	46278	**800-267-1364**	317-872-3000
NASDAQ: ININ					
InternetSafety.com Inc					
3979 S Main St Ste 230	Acworth	GA	30101	**877-944-8080**	
Ion Networks Inc					
120 Corporate Blvd Ste A	South Plainfield	NJ	07080	**800-722-8986**	908-546-3900
Keynote Systems Inc					
777 Mariners Island Blvd	San Mateo	CA	94404	**888-539-7978**	650-403-2400
NASDAQ: KEYN					
LassoSoft LLC PO Box 33	Manchester	WA	98353	**888-286-7753**	954-302-3526
Mark/Space Softworks					
1999 S Bascom Ave Ste 325	Campbell	CA	95008	**800-799-1718**	408-293-7299
Mirror Image Internet Inc					
2 Highwood Dr	Tewksbury	MA	01876	**800-353-2923**	781-376-1100
Moai Technologies Inc					
100 First Ave 9th Fl	Pittsburgh	PA	15222	**800-814-1548**	412-454-5550
MODCOMP Inc					
1500 S Powerline Rd	Deerfield Beach	FL	33442	**800-940-1111**	954-571-4600
Momentum Systems Ltd					
41 Twosome Dr Ste 9	Moorestown	NJ	08057	**800-279-1384**	856-727-0777
NetScout Systems Inc					
310 Littleton Rd	Westford	MA	01886	**800-357-7666**	978-614-4000
NASDAQ: NTCT					
NetVillage.com LLC					
342 Main St	Laurel	MD	20707	**888-638-8455**	301-498-7797
NICE Systems Inc					
301 Rt 17 N 10th Fl	Rutherford	NJ	07070	**800-994-4498**	201-964-2600
Nuance Communications Inc					
One Wayside Rd	Burlington	MA	01803	**800-654-1187**	781-565-5000
NASDAQ: NUAN					
OmTool Ltd Six Riverside Dr	Andover	MA	01810	**800-886-7845**	978-327-5700
OTC: OMTL					
One Touch Systems Inc					
2346 Bering Dr	San Jose	CA	95131	**800-721-8682**	408-436-4600
Open Text Corp					
275 Frank Tompa Dr	Waterloo	ON	N2L0A1	**800-499-6544***	519-888-7111
*TSE: OTC ■ *General*					
Open Text Corp (USA)					
100 Tri-State International Pkwy					
3rd Fl	Lincolnshire	IL	60069	**800-507-5777***	847-267-9330
*TSE: OTC ■ *Sales*					
OpenConnect Systems Inc					
2711 LBJ Fwy Ste 700	Dallas	TX	75234	**800-551-5881**	972-484-5200
Paloma Systems Inc					
11250 Waples Mill Rd	Fairfax	VA	22030	**855-300-2686**	703-626-5024
PartsRiver Inc					
3155 Kearney St Ste 210	Fremont	CA	94538	**855-700-7278**	
Powersteering Software Inc					
25 First St	Cambridge	MA	02141	**866-390-9088**	617-492-0707
Propel Software Corp					
1010 Rincon Cir	San Jose	CA	95131	**866-799-4767**	408-571-6300
QSA ToolWorks LLC					
3100 47th Ave	Long Island City	NY	11101	**800-784-7018**	516-935-9151
Selectica Inc					
2121 S. El Camino Rl 10th Fl	San Mateo	CA	94403	**877-712-9560**	650-532-1500
NASDAQ: SLTC					
Sendmail Inc					
6475 Christie Ave Ste 350	Emeryville	CA	94608	**888-594-3150**	510-594-5400
Support.com Inc					
900 Chesapeake Dr 2nd Fl	Redwood City	CA	94063	**877-493-2778**	650-556-9440
NASDAQ: SPRT					
Surety LLC					
12020 Sunrise Vly Dr Ste 250	Reston	VA	20191	**800-298-3115**	571-748-5800
Sybase Inc 1 Sybase Dr	Dublin	CA	94568	**800-792-2735**	925-236-5000
Symantec Corp					
350 Ellis St	Mountain View	CA	94043	**800-441-7234**	650-527-8000
NASDAQ: SYMC					
UmeVoice Inc					
20C Pimentel Ct Ste 1	Novato	CA	94949	**888-230-3300**	415-883-1500
Vertical Communications Inc					
3940 Freedom Cr Ste 110	Santa Clara	CA	95054	**800-914-9985***	408-404-1600
*OTC: VRCC ■ *Sales*					
WaveLink Corp					
1011 Western Ave Ste 601	Seattle	WA	98104	**888-697-9283***	206-274-4280
*Tech Supp					
Websense Inc					
10240 Sorrento Vly Rd	San Diego	CA	92121	**800-723-1166**	858-320-8000
NASDAQ: WBSN					
YellowBrix Inc					
200 North Glebe Rd Ste 1025	Arlington	VA	22203	**888-325-9366**	703-548-3300
Zone Alarm					
800 Bridge Pkwy	Redwood City	CA	94065	**877-966-5221**	415-633-4500

180-8 Multimedia & Design Software

				Toll-Free	Phone
3D Systems Inc					
333 Three D Systems Cir	Rock Hill	SC	29730	**800-793-3669**	803-326-3900
ACD Systems International Inc					
129-1335 Bear Mtn Pkwy	Victoria	BC	V9B6T9	**800-579-5309**	250-419-6700
Adobe Systems Inc					
345 Pk Ave	San Jose	CA	95110	**800-833-6687**	408-536-6000
NASDAQ: ADBE					
Apple Inc					
One Infinite Loop	Cupertino	CA	95014	**800-275-2273***	408-996-1010
*NASDAQ: AAPL ■ *Cust Svc*					
Auto FX Software					
141 Village St Ste 2	Birmingham	AL	35242	**800-839-2008**	205-980-0056
Avid Technology Inc					
65-75 Network Dri	Burlington	MA	01803	**800-949-2843**	978-640-6789
NASDAQ: AVID					
Chyron Corp 5 Hub Dr	Melville	NY	11747	**800-642-1687**	631-845-2000
NASDAQ: CHYR					
Concurrent					
4375 River Green Pkwy Ste 100	Duluth	GA	30096	**877-978-7363**	678-258-4000
NASDAQ: CCUR					
Corel Corp 1600 Carling Ave	Ottawa	ON	K1Z8R7	**800-772-6735***	613-728-8200
*Orders					
DeLorme					
Two DeLorme Dr PO Box 298	Yarmouth	ME	04096	**800-452-5931***	207-846-7000
*Sales					
Equilibrium Inc					
3 Harbor Dr	Sausalito	CA	94965	**855-378-4542**	415-332-4343
eWorkplace Solutions Inc					
24461 Ridge Rt Dr Ste 210	Laguna Hills	CA	92653	**888-477-7989**	949-583-1646
HydroCAD Software Solutions LLC					
PO Box 477	Chocorua	NH	03817	**800-927-7246**	603-323-8666
Image Labs International					
PO Box 1545	Belgrade	MT	59714	**800-785-5995**	406-585-7225
International Microcomputer Software Inc					
25 Leveroni Ct	Novato	CA	94949	**800-833-8082**	415-483-8000
Media 100 Inc					
450 Donald Lynch Blvd	Marlborough	MA	02210	**888-772-6747**	508-460-1600
MicroVision Development Inc					
5541 Fermi Ct Ste 120	Carlsbad	CA	92008	**800-998-4555**	760-438-7781
Nemetschek North America					
7150 Riverwood Dr	Columbia	MD	21046	**888-646-4223**	410-290-5114
NewTek Inc					
5131 Beckwith Blvd	San Antonio	TX	78249	**800-862-7837***	210-370-8000
*Cust Svc					
PC/Nametag					
124 Horizon Dr PO Box 8604	Verona	WI	53593	**877-626-3824**	
Presagis					
1301 W George Bush Fwy Ste 120	Richardson	TX	75080	**800-361-6424**	
Quark Inc 1800 Grant St	Denver	CO	80203	**800-676-4575***	
*Cust Svc					
RealNetworks Inc					
2601 Elliott Ave Ste 1000	Seattle	WA	98121	**888-484-8256***	206-674-2700
*NASDAQ: RNWK ■ *Cust Svc*					
Scan-Optics Inc					
169 Progress Dr	Manchester	CT	06042	**800-543-8681**	860-645-7878
Sigma Design					
5521 Jackson St	Alexandria	LA	71303	**888-990-0900***	318-449-9900
*Sales					

				Toll-Free	Phone

SoftPress Systems Inc
3020 Bridgeway Ste 408 . . . . Sausalito CA 94965 **800-853-6454** 415-331-4820

TechSmith Corp
2405 Woodlake Dr . . . . Okemos MI 48864 **800-517-3001** 517-381-2300

Telestream Inc
848 Gold Flat Rd Ste 1 . . . . Nevada City CA 95959 **877-681-2088** 530-470-1300

Three D Graphics Inc
11340 W Olympic Blvd Ste 352 . . . . Los Angeles CA 90064 **800-913-0008** 310-231-3330

Videotex Systems Inc
10255 Miller Rd . . . . Dallas TX 75238 **800-888-4336** 972-231-9200

Worlds.com Inc
11 Royal Rd . . . . Brookline MA 02445 **800-315-2580** 617-725-8900

180-9 Personal Software

				Toll-Free	Phone

APEX Analytix Inc
1501 Highwoods Blvd Ste 200-A . . . . Greensboro NC 27410 **866-577-8183** 336-272-4669

Avery Dennison Corp
207 Goode Ave . . . . Glendale CA 91203 **888-567-4387*** 626-304-2000
NYSE: AVY ▩ *Cust Svc

Corel Corp 1600 Carling Ave . . . . Ottawa ON K1Z8R7 **800-772-6735*** 613-728-8200
*Orders

Equis International
90 South 400 West Ste 620 . . . . Salt Lake City UT 84101 **800-882-3040*** 801-265-9996
*Sales

Intuit Inc
2632 Marine Way . . . . Mountain View CA 94043 **800-446-8848*** 650-944-6000
NASDAQ: INTU ▩ *Cust Svc

Nolo.com 950 Parker St . . . . Berkeley CA 94710 **800-728-3555**

Radialpoint
2050 Bleury St Ste 300 . . . . Montreal QC H3A2J5 **866-286-2636** 514-286-2636

Sony Creative Software
1617 Sherman Ave . . . . Madison WI 53704 **800-577-6642** 608-256-3133

Stevens Creek Software
PO Box 2126 . . . . Cupertino CA 95015 **800-823-4279** 408-725-0424

Symantec Corp
350 Ellis St . . . . Mountain View CA 94043 **800-441-7234** 650-527-8000
NASDAQ: SYMC

180-10 Professional Software (Industry-Specific)

Companies listed here manufacture software designed for specific professions or business sectors (i.e., architecture, banking, investment, physical sciences, real estate, etc.).

				Toll-Free	Phone

AGFA HealthCare Corp
10 S Academy St . . . . Greenville SC 29601 **877-777-2432** 864-421-1600

AIMS Inc 235 Desiard St . . . . Monroe LA 71201 **800-729-2467** 318-323-2467

Allot Communications
300 Tradecenter Ste 4680 . . . . Woburn MA 01801 **877-255-6826** 781-939-9300

Allscripts Healthcare Solutions
222 Merchandise Mart Plz Ste 2024 . . . . Chicago IL 60654 **800-654-0889**
NASDAQ: MDRX

Amdocs Ltd
1390 Timberlake Manor Pkwy . . . . Chesterfield MO 63017 **866-426-8003** 314-212-7000
NYSE: DOX

Anchor Computer Inc
1900 New Hwy . . . . Farmingdale NY 11735 **800-728-6262** 631-293-6100

ARI Network Services Inc
10850 W Pk Pl Ste 1200 . . . . Milwaukee WI 53224 **877-805-0803** 414-973-4300

ASI DataMyte Inc
2800 Campus Dr Ste 60 . . . . Plymouth MN 55441 **800-207-5631** 763-553-1040

Aspyra Inc
4360 Pk Terr Dr Ste 100 . . . . Westlake Village CA 91361 **800-437-9000** 818-449-8671
OTC: APYI

Avantus
15 W Strong St Ste 20A . . . . Pensacola FL 32501 **800-600-2510** 850-470-9336

Avaya Government Solutions Inc
12730 Fair Lakes Cir . . . . Fairfax VA 22033 **800-492-6769** 703-653-8000

BatchMaster Software Inc
24461 Ridge Rt Dr Ste 210 . . . . Laguna Hills CA 92653 **800-359-0920** 949-583-1646

BenefitMall Inc
4851 LBJ Fwy Ste 1100 . . . . Dallas TX 75244 **888-338-6293** 469-791-3300

Brodart Co 500 Arch St . . . . Williamsport PA 17701 **800-233-8467** 570-326-2461

CAM Commerce Solutions Inc
17075 Newhope St Ste A . . . . Fountain Valley CA 92708 **800-726-3282** 714-241-9241

CareCentric Inc
20 Church Street 12th Fl . . . . Hartford CT 06103 **866-467-8263** 800-808-1902

Carousel Industries of North America Inc
659 S County Trl . . . . Exeter RI 02822 **800-401-0760**

CCH Small Firm Services
225 Chastain Meadows Ct NW Ste 200 . . . . . . Kennesaw GA 30144 **866-345-4171***
*Sales

Cedara Software Corp
6303 Airport Rd Ste 500 . . . . Mississauga ON L4V1R8 **800-724-5970** 905-364-8000

CliniComp International
9655 Towne Ctr Dr . . . . San Diego CA 92121 **800-350-8202** 858-546-8202

Cobalt Group Inc
2200 First Ave S Ste 400 . . . . Seattle WA 98134 **800-909-8244**

Command Alkon Inc
1800 International Pk Dr Ste 400 . . . . Birmingham AL 35243 **800-624-1872** 205-879-3282

Computers Unlimited
2407 Montana Ave . . . . Billings MT 59101 **800-763-0308** 406-255-9500

Construction Software Technologies Inc
4500 W Lake Forest Ste 502 . . . . Cincinnati OH 45242 **800-364-2059** 513-645-8004

Construction Systems Software Inc
494 Covered Bridge . . . . Schertz TX 78154 **800-531-1035** 210-979-6494

CoStar Group Inc
Two Bethesda Metro Ctr 10th Fl . . . . Bethesda MD 20814 **800-613-1303** 301-215-8300
NASDAQ: CSGP

Datatel Inc
4375 Fair Lakes Ct . . . . Fairfax VA 22033 **800-223-7036**

DealerTrack Holdings Inc
1111 Marcus Ave Ste M04 . . . . New Hyde Park NY 11042 **877-357-8725** 516-734-3600
NASDAQ: TRAK

DIS Corp
1315 Cornwall Ave . . . . Bellingham WA 98225 **800-426-8870*** 360-733-7610
*Cust Svc

Document Security Systems Inc
28 E Main St Ste 1525 . . . . Rochester NY 14614 **877-407-8031** 585-325-3610
NYSE: DSS

Eagle Point Software Corp
4131 Westmark Dr . . . . Dubuque IA 52002 **800-678-6565** 563-556-8392

Ellucian 4375 Fair Lakes Ct . . . . Fairfax VA 22033 **800-223-7036** 610-647-5930

Enghouse Systems Ltd
80 Tiverton Ct Ste 800 . . . . Markham ON L3R0G4 **866-206-0240** 905-946-3200
TSE: ESL

Environmental Systems Research Institute Inc
380 New York St . . . . Redlands CA 92373 **800-447-9778*** 909-793-2853
*Sales

Equis International
90 South 400 West Ste 620 . . . . Salt Lake City UT 84101 **800-882-3040*** 801-265-9996
*Sales

eResearch Technology Inc
1818 Market St Ste 1000 . . . . Philadelphia PA 19103 **800-704-9698** 215-972-0420
NASDAQ: ERT

Ericsson 1 Telcordia Dr . . . . Piscataway NJ 08854 **800-521-2673** 732-699-2000

Final Draft Inc
26707 W Agoura Rd Ste 205 . . . . Calabasas CA 91302 **800-231-4055** 818-995-8995

Financial Engines Inc
1804 Embarcadero Rd . . . . Palo Alto CA 94303 **888-443-8577** 650-565-4900
NASDAQ: FNGN

First DataBank Inc (FDB)
701 Gateway Blvd Ste 600 . . . . South San Francisco CA 94080 **800-633-3453***
*General

FishNet Security
2575 E Camelback Rd . . . . Phoenix AZ 85016 **888-732-9406** 602-343-2300

Follett Software Co
1391 Corporate Dr . . . . McHenry IL 60050 **800-323-3397** 815-344-8700

FXCM Inc 32 Old Slip . . . . New York NY 10005 **888-503-6739** 212-897-7660
NYSE: FXCM

General Dynamics C4 Systems
400 John Quincy Adams Rd Bldg 80 . . . . Taunton MA 02780 **877-449-0600**

GHG Corp
960 Clear Lk City Blvd . . . . Webster TX 77598 **866-380-4146** 281-488-8806

Glimmerglass Networks Inc
26142 Eden Landing Rd . . . . Hayward CA 94545 **877-723-1900** 510-723-1900

Global Turnkey Systems Inc
2001 US 46 . . . . Parsippany NJ 07054 **800-221-1746** 973-331-1010

gomembers Inc
1155 Perimeter Center West Bldg 700 . . . . Atlanta GA 30338 **888-288-4634** 855-411-2783

Guidance Software Inc
215 N Marengo Ave 2nd Fl . . . . Pasadena CA 91101 **866-229-9199** 626-229-9191

IHS Energy Group
15 Inverness Way E . . . . Englewood CO 80112 **800-447-2273** 303-736-3000

ImageWare Systems Inc
10815 Rancho BernaRdo Rd Ste 310 . . . . San Diego CA 92127 **800-842-4199** 858-673-8600

Info Tech Inc
5700 SW 34th St Ste 1235 . . . . Gainesville FL 32608 **888-352-2439** 352-381-4400

Infor Global Solutions
13560 Morris Rd Ste 4100 . . . . Alpharetta GA 30004 **866-244-5479** 678-319-8000

Inmagic Inc
600 Unicorn Pk Dr . . . . Woburn MA 01801 **800-229-8398** 781-938-4444

Innovative Technologies Corp (ITC)
1020 Woodman Dr Ste 100 . . . . Dayton OH 45432 **800-745-8050** 937-252-2145

Input 1 LLC
6200 Canoga Ave Ste 400 . . . . Woodland Hills CA 91367 **888-882-2554** 818-713-2303

Intradiem
3650 Mansell Rd Ste 500 . . . . Alpharetta GA 30022 **888-566-9457** 678-356-3500

Island Pacific Inc
17310 Red Hill Ave Ste 320 . . . . Irvine CA 92614 **800-994-3847**

iWay Software Two Penn Plz . . . . New York NY 10121 **800-736-6130** 212-736-4433

Jenzabar Inc
101 Huntington Ave Ste 2200 . . . . Boston MA 02199 **800-593-0028** 617-492-9099

Kinaxis 700 Silver Seven Rd . . . . Ottawa ON K2V1C3 **877-546-2947*** 613-592-5780
*General

Land & Legal Solutions Inc
300 S Hamilton Ave . . . . Greensburg PA 15601 **800-245-7900** 724-853-8992

Landacorp Inc
500 Orient St Ste 110 . . . . Chico CA 95928 **866-828-8263** 530-891-0853

Lumedx Corp
555 12th St Ste 2060 . . . . Oakland CA 94607 **800-966-0699** 510-419-1000

LynxWorks Inc
855 Embedded Way . . . . San Jose CA 95138 **800-255-5969** 408-979-3900

Management Information Control Systems Inc (MICS)
2025 Ninth St . . . . Los Osos CA 93402 **800-838-6427** 805-543-7000

Manhattan Assoc Inc
2300 Windy Ridge Pkwy 10th Fl . . . . Atlanta GA 30339 **877-756-7435** 770-955-7070
NASDAQ: MANH

Market Scan Information Systems Inc
811 Camarillo Springs Ste B . . . . Camarillo CA 93012 **800-658-7226**

Marshall & Swift
777 S Figueroa St 12th Fl . . . . Los Angeles CA 90017 **800-544-2678** 213-683-9000

McKesson Information Solutions
5995 Windward Pkwy . . . . Alpharetta GA 30005 **800-981-8601** 404-338-6000

MDI Achieve
10900 Hampshire Ave South Ste 100 . . . . Bloomington MN 55438 **800-869-1322** 952-995-9800

Media Cybernetics Inc
4340 E W Hwy Ste 400 . . . . Bethesda MD 20814 **800-263-2088*** 301-495-3305
*Sales

MedPlus Inc 4690 Pkwy Dr . . . . Mason OH 45040 **800-444-6235** 513-229-5500

Merrick Systems Inc
55 Waugh Dr Ste 400 . . . . Houston TX 77007 **800-842-8389** 713-579-3400

MicroBilt Corp
1640 Airport Rd Ste 115 . . . . Kennesaw GA 30144 **800-884-4747**

Midrange Software Inc
11770 Riverside Dr . . . . Studio City CA 91607 **800-737-6766** 818-762-8539

Mortgage Builders Software
24370 NW Hwy Ste 200 . . . . Southfield MI 48075 **800-850-8060**

Mzinga Inc 230 Third Ave . . . . Waltham MA 02451 **888-694-6428** 781-930-5430

New England Computer Services Inc
168 Boston Post Rd Stes 6 & 7 . . . . Madison CT 06443 **800-766-6327*** 203-245-3999
*Sales

				Toll-Free	Phone

NIC Inc
25501 W Valley Pkwy Ste 300 . . . . .Olathe KS 66061 **877-234-3468**
NASDAQ: EGOV

OATSystems Inc
309 Waverley Oaks Rd Ste 306 . . . . .Waltham MA 02452 **877-628-7877** 781-907-6100

Olson Research Assoc Inc
10290 Old Columbia Rd . . . . .Columbia MD 21046 **888-657-6680** 410-290-6999

OpenTable Inc
One Montgomery St Fourth Fl . . . . .San Francisco CA 94103 **800-673-6822** 415-344-4200
NASDAQ: OPEN

Opex Corp
305 Commerce Dr . . . . .Moorestown NJ 08057 **800-835-2362** 856-727-1100

Pason Systems Inc
6130 Third St SE . . . . .Calgary AB T2H1K4 **877-255-3158** 403-301-3400
TSE: PSI

Passport Health Communications Inc
720 Cool Springs Blvd Ste 200 . . . . .Franklin TN 37067 **888-661-5657** 615-661-5657

PKC Corp
One Mill St C13 Ste 355 . . . . .Burlington VT 05401 **800-752-5351** 802-658-5351

ProCard Inc
1819 Denver W Dr Bldg 26 Ste 300 . . . . .Lakewood CO 80401 **800-469-6578** 303-279-2255

Promodel Corp
3400 Bath Pike Ste 200 . . . . .Bethlehem PA 18017 **888-900-3090** 801-223-4600

QlikTech International AB
150 N Radnor Chester Rd Ste E220 . . . . .Radnor PA 19087 **888-828-9768**
NASDAQ: QLIK

Quality Systems Inc (QSI)
18111 Von Karman Ave Ste 600 . . . . .Irvine CA 92612 **800-888-7955*** 949-255-2600
NASDAQ: QSII ■ *Cust Svc*

QUMAS 66 York St . . . . .Jersey City NJ 07302 **800-577-1545***
*Sales

Qvidian Corp
175 Cabot St Ste 210 . . . . .Lowell MA 01854 **800-272-0047** 513-631-1155

RainMaker Software Inc
1777 Sentry Pkwy W . . . . .Blue Bell PA 19422 **800-336-0339** 610-567-3409

Raytheon Company
10 Moulton St . . . . .Cambridge MA 02138 **866-230-1307** 617-873-8000

Red Wing Software Inc
491 Hwy 19 .Red Wing MN 55066 **800-732-9464** 651-388-1106

RESUMate Inc
2500 Packard St Ste 200 . . . . .Ann Arbor MI 48104 **800-530-9310*** 734-477-9402
*Cust Svc

Retail Pro International LLC
400 Plz Dr Ste 200 . . . . .Folsom CA 95630 **800-738-2457** 916-605-7200
OTC: RTPRQ

Reynolds & Reynolds Co
One Reynolds Way . . . . .Dayton OH 45430 **800-767-0080** 937-485-2000

RiskWatch (RWI)
1237 N Gulfstream Ave . . . . .Sarasota Fl 34236 **800-360-1898**

Sapiens International Corp
4000 CentreGreen Way Ste 150 . . . . .Cary NC 27513 **888-281-1167** 919-405-1500
NASDAQ: SPNS

Scantron Corp 34 Parker . . . . .Irvine CA 92618 **800-722-6876** 949-639-7500

Siemens Product Lifecycle Management Software Inc
5800 Granite Pkwy Ste 600 . . . . .Plano TX 75024 **800-498-5351** 972-987-3000

Simulations Plus Inc
42505 Tenth St W . . . . .Lancaster CA 93534 **888-266-9294** 661-723-7723
NASDAQ: SLP

Snap-on Diagnostics
420 Barclay Blvd . . . . .Lincolnshire IL 60069 **800-424-7226** 847-478-0700

SolidWorks Corp
300 Baker Ave .Concord MA 01742 **800-693-9000** 978-371-5011

Spillman Technologies Inc
4625 Lake Pk Blvd . . . . .Salt Lake City UT 84120 **800-860-8026*** 801-902-1200
*General

SQN Banking Systems
65 Indel Ave Second Fl . . . . .Rancocas NJ 08073 **888-744-7226** 609-261-5500

Synergex International Corp
2330 Gold Meadow Way . . . . .Rancho Cordova CA 95670 **800-366-3472** 916-635-7300

Synopsys Inc
700 E Middlefield Rd . . . . .Mountain View CA 94043 **800-541-7737** 650-584-5000
NASDAQ: SNPS

System Automation
7110 Samuel Morse Dr Ste 100 . . . . .Columbia MD 21046 **800-839-4729** 301-837-8000

System Innovators Inc
10550 Deerwood Pk Blvd Ste 700 . . . . .Jacksonville FL 32256 **800-963-5000**

Thomson Elite
800 Corporate Pointe Ste 150 . . . . .Los Angeles CA 90230 **800-354-8337*** 424-243-2100
*Cust Svc

TMW Systems Inc
21111 Chagrin Blvd . . . . .Beachwood OH 44122 **800-401-6682** 216-831-6606

TradeStation Group Inc
8050 SW Tenth St Ste 2000 . . . . .Plantation FL 33324 **800-871-3577** 954-652-7000

Transentric
1400 Douglas St Ste 0840 . . . . .Omaha NE 68179 **800-877-0328** 402-544-6000

TransWorks
9910 Dupont Cir Dr E Ste 200 . . . . .Fort Wayne IN 46825 **800-435-4691** 260-487-4400

Tyler Technologies Inc
5949 Sherry Ln Ste 1400 . . . . .Dallas TX 75225 **800-431-5776**
NYSE: TYL

US Dataworks Inc
1 Sugar Creek Ctr Blvd 5th Fl . . . . .Sugar Land TX 77478 **888-254-8821** 281-504-8000
OTC: UDWK

US Digital Corp
1400 NE 136th Ave . . . . .Vancouver WA 98684 **800-736-0194** 360-260-2468

Vermont Systems Inc
12 Market Pl . . . . .Essex Junction VT 05452 **877-883-8757** 802-879-6993

ViPS Inc
1 W Pennsylvania Ave Ste 700 . . . . .Towson MD 21204 **800-242-0230** 410-832-8300

Vital Images Inc
5850 Opus Pkwy Ste 300 . . . . .Minnetonka MN 55343 **800-208-3005** 952-487-9500

Wausau Financial Systems Inc
875 Indianhead Dr PO Box 37 . . . . .Mosinee WI 54455 **800-937-0017** 715-359-0427

Weather Services International
400 Minuteman Rd . . . . .Andover MA 01810 **800-872-2359** 978-983-6300

Wolters Kluwer Financial Services Inc
100 S Fifth St Ste 700 . . . . .Minneapolis MN 55402 **800-552-9408** 612-656-7700

Worksoft Inc
15851 Dallas Pkwy Ste 855 . . . . .Addison TX 75001 **866-836-1773** 214-239-0400

				Toll-Free	Phone

Xybernet Inc
10640 Scripps Ranch Blvd . . . . .San Diego CA 92131 **800-228-9026*** 858-530-1900
*Cust Svc

180-11 Service Software

				Toll-Free	Phone

Applied Systems Inc
200 Applied Pkwy . . . . .University Park IL 60466 **800-999-5368*** 708-534-5575
*Sales

Aptech Computer Systems Inc
135 Delta Dr .Pittsburgh PA 15238 **800-245-0720** 412-963-7440

ARINC 2551 Riva Rd . . . . .Annapolis MD 21401 **866-321-6060** 410-266-4000

Aristotle Inc
205 Pennsylvania Ave SE . . . . .Washington DC 20003 **800-296-2747*** 202-543-8345
*Sales

Cerner Corp
2800 Rockcreek Pkwy . . . . .North Kansas City MO 64117 **888-827-7220** 816-221-1024
NASDAQ: CERN

Datamann Inc
1994 Hartford Ave .Wilder VT 05088 **800-451-4263** 802-295-6600

DHI Computing Service Inc
1525 West 820 North PO Box 51427 . . . . .Provo UT 84601 **800-992-1344** 801-373-8518

Digital Solutions Inc
955 SE Olson Dr . . . . .Waukee IA 50263 **888-464-8770*** 515-987-6227
*Cust Svc

DPSI Inc
1801 Stanley Rd Ste 301 . . . . .Greensboro NC 27407 **800-897-7233** 336-854-7700

Ebix Inc
5 Concourse Pkwy Ste 3200 . . . . .Atlanta GA 30328 **800-755-2326** 678-281-2020
NASDAQ: EBIX

Firstwave Technologies Inc
6263 N Scottsdale Rd Ste 180 . . . . .Scottsdale AZ 85250 **800-540-6061** 678-672-3112

Galaxy Hotel Systems LLC
15621 Red Hill Ave Ste 100 . . . . .Tustin CA 92780 **800-434-9990** 714-258-5800

IHS Inc
321 Inverness Dr S . . . . .Englewood CO 80112 **800-525-7052** 303-790-0600
NYSE: IHS

Incontact Inc
7730 S Union Pk Ave Ste 500 . . . . .Salt Lake City UT 84047 **800-363-6177** 801-320-3200
NASDAQ: SAAS

Insurance Data Processing Inc (IDP)
8101 Washington Ln . . . . .Wyncote PA 19095 **800-523-6745** 215-885-2150

Jack Henry & Assoc Inc
663 W Hwy 60 PO Box 807 . . . . .Monett MO 65708 **800-299-4222** 417-235-6652
NASDAQ: JKHY

Jobscope Corp
355 Woodruff Rd . . . . .Greenville SC 29607 **800-443-5794** 864-458-3100

Kalibrate Technologies PLC
25B Hanover Rd . . . . .Florham Park NJ 07932 **800-727-6774*** 973-549-1850
*Cust Svc

Keane Care Inc
8383 158th Ave NE Ste 100 . . . . .Redmond WA 98052 **800-426-2675**

Key Information Systems Inc
21700 Oxnard St Ste 250 . . . . .Woodland Hills CA 91367 **877-442-3249** 818-992-8950

Kronos Inc
297 Billerica Rd . . . . .Chelmsford MA 01824 **888-293-5549** 978-250-9800

Manatron Inc
510 E Milham Ave . . . . .Portage MI 49002 **866-471-2900*** 269-567-2900
*Cust Svc

Mediware Information Systems Inc
11711 W 79th St .Lenexa KS 66214 **800-255-0026** 913-307-1000
NASDAQ: MEDW

Meta Health Technology Inc
330 Seventh Ave 14th Fl . . . . .New York NY 10001 **800-334-6840** 212-695-5870

Metafile Information Systems Inc
2900 43rd St NW . . . . .Rochester MN 55901 **800-638-2445*** 507-286-9232
*Sales

MicroStrategy
1850 Towers Crescent Plz . . . . .Tysons Corner VA 22182 **888-266-0321** 703-848-8600
NASDAQ: MSTR

Netsmart Technologies Inc
3500 Sunrise Hwy Ste D-122 . . . . .Great River NY 11739 **800-421-7503** 631-968-2000

Radware Inc
575 Corporate Dr Lobby 2 . . . . .Mahwah NJ 07430 **888-234-5763** 201-512-9771

Sandata Technologies Inc
26 Harbor Pk Dr . . . . .Port Washington NY 11050 **800-544-7263*** 516-484-4400
*Sales

SS & C Technologies Inc
80 Lamberton Rd . . . . .Windsor CT 06095 **800-234-0556** 860-298-4500

Strictly Business Computer Systems Inc
848 Fourth Ave Ste 200 . . . . .Huntington WV 25701 **888-529-0401**

Successfactors Inc
1500 Fashion Island Blvd Ste 300 . . . . .San Mateo CA 94404 **800-809-9920** 650-645-2000
NYSE: SFSF

SunGard Pentamation Inc
1000 Business Ctr Dr Ste 1 . . . . .Lake mary FL 32746 **866-965-7732*** 610-691-3616
*Cust Svc

Synergistics Inc 16 Tech Cir . . . . .Natick MA 01760 **866-455-5222** 508-655-1340

TimeValue Software
22 Mauchly . . . . .Irvine CA 92618 **800-426-4741*** 949-727-1800
*Sales

TMA Systems LLC
5100 E Skelly Dr Ste 900 . . . . .Tulsa OK 74135 **800-862-1130** 918-858-6600

Xactware Solutions Inc
One Xactware Plz . . . . .Orem UT 84097 **800-424-9228*** 801-764-5900
*Sales

Xora Inc
850 N Shoreline Blvd . . . . .Mountain View CA 94043 **877-477-9672** 650-314-6460

180-12 Systems & Utilities Software

				Toll-Free	Phone

activePDF Inc
27405 Puerta Real Ste 100 . . . . .Mission Viejo CA 92691 **866-468-6733** 949-582-9002

			Toll-Free	Phone
Allen Systems Group Inc (ASG)				
1333 Third Ave S	Naples FL	34102	**800-932-5536**	239-435-2200
Avatier Corp				
2603 Camino Ramon Ste 110	San Ramon CA	94583	**800-609-8610**	925-217-5170
Basis International Ltd				
5901 Jefferson St NE	Albuquerque NM	87109	**800-423-1394***	505-345-5232
*Orders				
BenchmarkQA Inc				
7301 Ohms Ln Ste 590	Edina MN	55439	**877-425-2581**	952-392-2400
Blue Lance Inc				
410 Pierce St Ste 950	Houston TX	77002	**800-856-2583**	713-255-4800
CA Inc One CA Plz	Islandia NY	11749	**800-225-5224**	631-342-6000
NASDAQ: CA				
CardLogix 16 Hughes Ste 100	Irvine CA	92618	**866-392-8326**	949-380-1312
Certicom Corp				
4701 Tahoe Blvd Bldg A	Mississauga ON	L4W0B5	**800-561-6100**	905-507-4220
Check Point Software Technologies Ltd				
800 Bridge Pkwy	Redwood City CA	94065	**800-429-4391**	650-628-2000
NASDAQ: CHKP				
Cincom Systems Inc				
55 Merchant St	Cincinnati OH	45246	**800-224-6266**	513-612-2300
Citrix Systems Inc				
851 W Cypress Creek Rd	Fort Lauderdale FL	33309	**800-393-1888**	954-267-3000
NASDAQ: CTXS				
Columbia Data Products Inc				
925 Sunshine Ln Ste 1080	Altamonte Springs FL	32714	**800-613-6288***	407-869-6700
*Sales				
CommuniGate Systems Inc				
655 Redwood Hwy 275	Mill Valley CA	94941	**800-262-4722**	415-383-7164
ComponentOne LLC				
201 S Highland Ave Third Fl 3rd Fl	Pittsburgh PA	15206	**800-858-2739**	412-681-4343
Condusiv Technologies				
7590 N Glenoaks Blvd	Burbank CA	91504	**800-829-6468***	818-771-1600
*Sales				
Crossmatch				
720 Bay Rd Ste 100	Redwood City CA	94063	**866-463-7792**	650-474-4000
CSI International Inc				
8120 State Rt 138	Williamsport OH	43164	**800-795-4914**	740-420-5400
CSP Inc 43 Manning Rd	Billerica MA	01821	**800-325-3110**	978-663-7598
NASDAQ: CSPI				
DataViz Inc				
612 Wheelers Farms Rd	Milford CT	06460	**800-733-0030**	203-874-0085
Datawatch Corp				
271 Mill Rd	Chelmsford MA	01824	**800-445-3311**	978-441-2200
NASDAQ: DWCH				
Descartes Systems Group Inc				
120 Randall Dr	Waterloo ON	N2V1C6	**800-419-8495**	519-746-8110
TSE: DSG				
Digimarc Corp				
9405 SW Gemini Dr	Beaverton OR	97008	**800-344-4627**	503-469-4800
NASDAQ: DMRC				
EasyLink Services Corp				
6025 The Corners Pwy Ste 100	Norcross GA	30092	**800-209-6245**	678-823-4600
eMag Solutions LLC				
3495 Piedmont Rd				
11 Piedmont Ctr Ste 500	Atlanta GA	30305	**800-364-9838**	404-995-6060
EMC Corp				
2831 Mission College Blvd	Santa Clara CA	95054	**877-534-2867***	408-566-2000
*Tech Supp				
Entrust Inc				
5400 LBJ Fwy Ste 1340	Dallas TX	75240	**888-690-2424***	972-728-0447
*Sales				
Esker Inc				
1212 Deming Way Ste 350	Madison WI	53717	**800-368-5283**	608-828-6000
Expert Choice Inc				
1501 Lee Hwy Ste 302	Arlington VA	22209	**888-259-6400**	703-243-5595
Heroix Corp				
165 Bay State Dr	Braintree MA	02184	**800-229-6500**	781-848-1701
HID Global Corp				
611 Center Ridge Dr	Austin TX	78753	**800-237-7769**	512-776-9000
Hitachi Data Systems Corp				
750 Central Expy	Santa Clara CA	95050	**877-437-3849**	408-970-1000
Innodata-Isogen Inc				
Three University Plz Dr	Hackensack NJ	07601	**877-454-8400**	201-371-8000
NASDAQ: INOD				
International Business Machines Corp (IBM)				
One New Orchard Rd	Armonk NY	10504	**800-426-4968**	914-499-1900
NYSE: IBM				
InterTrust Technologies Corp				
920 Stewart Dr Ste 100	Sunnyvale CA	94085	**800-393-2272**	408-616-1600
Intrusion Inc				
1101 E Arapaho Rd	Richardson TX	75081	**888-637-7770**	972-234-6400
Ipswitch Inc				
83 Hartwell Ave	Lexington MA	02421	**800-793-4825**	781-676-5700
Kroll Ontrack Inc				
9023 Columbine Rd	Eden Prairie MN	55347	**800-872-2599**	952-937-5161
LapLink Software Inc				
600 108th Ave NE Ste 610	Bellevue WA	98004	**800-343-8080**	425-952-6000
Lattice Inc				
1751 S Naperville Rd Ste 100	Wheaton IL	60189	**800-444-4309***	630-949-3250
*Sales				
Luminex Software Inc				
871 Marlborough Ave	Riverside CA	92507	**888-586-4639***	951-781-4100
*Sales				
Mainstay				
1320 Flynn Rd Ste 401	Camarillo CA	93012	**800-362-2605***	805-484-9400
*Orders				
Management Science Assoc Inc				
6565 Penn Ave	Pittsburgh PA	15206	**800-672-4636**	412-362-2000
MARX Software Security Inc				
2900 Chamblee-Tucker Rd				
Bldg 9 Ste 100	Atlanta GA	30341	**800-627-9468**	770-986-8887
McAfee Inc				
2821 Mission College Blvd	Santa Clara CA	95054	**888-847-8766***	408-988-3832
*Cust Svc				
McCabe Software Inc				
3300 N Ridge Rd	Ellicott City MD	21043	**800-638-6316**	410-381-3710
Mitem Corp 640 Menlo Ave	Menlo Park CA	94025	**800-826-4836***	650-323-1500
*Sales				

			Toll-Free	Phone
MTI Systems Inc				
59 Interstate D	West Springfield MA	01089	**800-644-4318**	413-733-1972
NetIQ Corp 1233 W Loop S	Houston TX	77027	**888-323-6768***	713-548-1700
*Sales				
Network Appliance Inc				
495 E Java Dr	Sunnyvale CA	94089	**800-443-4537***	408-822-6000
NASDAQ: NTAP ▪ *Sales				
New Year Tech Inc				
12330 Pinecrest Rd Ste 100	Reston VA	20191	**800-525-7767**	703-564-0290
Norman Data Defense Systems Inc				
9302 Lee Hwy	Fairfax VA	22031	**888-466-6762**	703-267-6109
NTP Software				
20A NW Blvd Ste 136	Nashua NH	03063	**800-226-2755**	603-622-4400
Numara Software Inc				
2202 NW Shore Blvd Ste 650	Tampa FL	33607	**800-557-3031***	813-227-4500
*Sales				
Oracle Corp				
500 Oracle Pkwy	Redwood Shores CA	94065	**800-392-2999***	650-506-7000
NYSE: ORCL ▪ *Sales				
Perceptics Corp				
9737 Cogdill Rd Ste 200	Knoxville TN	37932	**800-448-8544**	
Pervasive Software Inc				
12365 Riata Trace Pkwy Bldg B	Austin TX	78727	**800-287-4383**	512-231-6000
NASDAQ: PVSW				
Phoenix Technologies Ltd				
915 Murphy Ranch Rd	Milpitas CA	95035	**800-677-7305**	408-570-1000
Pragma Systems Inc				
13809 Research Blvd Ste 675	Austin TX	78750	**800-224-1675**	512-219-7270
Process Software Corp				
959 Concord St	Framingham MA	01701	**800-722-7770**	508-879-6994
RadView Software Inc				
111 Deerwood Rd Ste 200	San Ramon CA	94583	**888-723-8439**	908-526-7756
Raxco Software Inc				
Six Montgomery Village Ave				
Ste 200	Gaithersburg MD	20879	**800-546-9728***	301-527-0803
*Tech Supp				
Red Hat Inc 1801 Varsity Dr	Raleigh NC	27606	**888-733-4281**	919-754-3700
NYSE: RHT				
Relais International				
1690 Woodward Dr Ste 215	Ottawa ON	K2C3R8	**888-294-5244**	613-226-5571
RSA Security Inc				
174 Middlesex Tpke	Bedford MA	01730	**800-995-5095**	781-515-5000
ScriptLogic Corp				
6000 Broken Sound Pkwy NW	Boca Raton FL	33487	**800-306-9329**	561-886-2400
Serengeti Systems Inc				
812 W 11th St Third Fl	Austin TX	78701	**800-634-3122**	512-345-2211
Simtrol Inc				
520 Guthridge Ct	Norcross GA	30092	**800-423-0769**	678-533-1200
Skyward Inc				
5233 Coye Dr	Stevens Point WI	54481	**800-236-0001**	715-341-9406
SNMP Research International Inc				
3001 Kimberlin Heights Rd	Knoxville TN	37920	**877-644-5866**	865-579-3311
Software Engineering of America Inc (SEA)				
1230 Hempstead Tpke	Franklin Square NY	11010	**800-272-7322**	516-328-7000
Software Pursuits Inc				
1900 S Norfolk St	San Mateo CA	94403	**800-367-4823**	650-372-0900
Stratus Technologies				
111 Powdermill Rd	Maynard MA	01754	**800-787-2887**	978-461-7000
Symantec Corp				
350 Ellis St	Mountain View CA	94043	**800-441-7234**	650-527-8000
NASDAQ: SYMC				
TeamQuest Corp				
One TeamQuest Way	Clear Lake IA	50428	**800-551-8326**	641-357-2700
TechSmith Corp				
2405 Woodlake Dr	Okemos MI	48864	**800-517-3001**	517-381-2300
Thales e-Security Inc				
2200 N Commerce Pkwy Ste 200	Weston FL	33326	**888-744-4976**	954-888-6200
TigerLogic Corp				
25-A Technology Dr	Irvine CA	92618	**800-367-7425**	949-442-4400
NASDAQ: TIGR				
TrendMicro Inc				
10101 N De Anza Blvd	Cupertino CA	95014	**800-228-5651**	408-257-1500
Tripwire Inc				
101 SW Main St Ste 1500	Portland OR	97204	**800-874-7947***	503-276-7500
*General				
UltraBac Software				
15015 Main St Ste 200	Bellevue WA	98007	**866-554-8562**	425-644-6000
VanDyke Software Inc				
4848 Tramway Ridge Dr NE Ste 101	Albuquerque NM	87111	**800-952-5210**	505-332-5700
VCG LLC 1805 Old Alabama Rd	Roswell GA	30076	**800-318-4983**	770-246-2300
Vendant Inc				
26 Parker St	Newburyport MA	01950	**800-714-4900**	978-462-0737
Vision Solutions Inc				
15300 Barranca Pkwy	Irvine CA	92618	**800-683-4667**	949-253-6500
VisionAIR Inc				
5601 Barbados Blvd	Castle Hayne NC	28429	**800-882-2108**	910-675-9117
Webroot Software Inc				
2560 55th St	Boulder CO	80301	**800-772-9383**	303-442-3813
WildPackets Inc				
1340 Treat Blvd Ste 500	Walnut Creek CA	94597	**800-466-2447**	925-937-3200
Wilson WindowWare Inc				
5421 California Ave SW	Seattle WA	98136	**800-762-8383**	206-938-1740
Wind River Systems Inc				
500 Wind River Way	Alameda CA	94501	**800-545-9463**	510-748-4100
XIOtech Corp				
9950 Federal Dr Ste 100	Colorado Springs CO	80921	**866-472-6764**	719-388-5500
Yrrid Software Inc				
507 Monroe St	Chapel Hill NC	27516	**800-443-0065**	919-968-7858
Zix Corp				
2711 N Haskell Ave Ste 2300-LB	Dallas TX	75204	**888-771-4049**	214-370-2000
NASDAQ: ZIXI				
Zone Alarm				
800 Bridge Pkwy	Redwood City CA	94065	**877-966-5221**	415-633-4500

Classified Section

				Toll-Free	Phone

181   COMPUTER STORES

SEE ALSO Appliance & Home Electronics Stores

				Toll-Free	Phone
A Matter of Fax					
105 Harrison Ave	Harrison	NJ	07029	800-433-3329	973-482-3700
Aberdeen LLC					
9130 Norwalk Blvd	Santa Fe Springs	CA	90670	800-500-9526	562-699-6998
Automated Medical Systems Inc					
2310 N Patterson St Bldg H	Valdosta	GA	31602	800-256-3240	
Balihoo Inc					
404 S Eighth St Ste 300	Boise	ID	83702	866-446-9914	
Barcoding Inc					
2220 Boston St	Baltimore	MD	21231	888-412-7226	410-385-8532
Carrillo Business Technologies Inc					
750 The City Dr S Ste 225	Orange	CA	92868	888-241-7585	
CDW Corp					
200 N Milwaukee Ave	Vernon Hills	IL	60061	800-800-4239	847-465-6000
Concepts In Data Management Inc					
205 Oxford St E	London	ON	N6A5G6	800-668-8768	
ConnectWise Inc					
4110 George Rd Ste 200.	Tampa	FL	33634	800-671-6898	813-463-4700
GameStop Corp					
625 Westport Pkwy	Grapevine	TX	76051	800-883-8895	817-424-2000
NYSE: GME					
Gateway Inc					
7565 Irvine Ctr Dr	Irvine	CA	92618	800-846-2000	949-471-7040
Govconnection Inc					
7503 Standish Pl	Rockville	MD	20855	800-998-0009	
Innovative Information Solutions Inc					
61 I- Ln	Waterbury	CT	06705	800-343-8121	203-756-4243
Insight Enterprises Inc					
6820 S Harl Ave	Tempe	AZ	85283	800-467-4448	480-333-3000
NASDAQ: NSIT					
Jive Communications Inc					
1275 West 1600 North Ste 100.	Orem	UT	84057	866-768-5429	
KLJ Computer Solutions Inc					
115 Joseph Zatzman Dr	Dartmouth	NS	B3B1N3	888-455-5669	
Knowledge Information Solutions Inc					
2877 Guardian Ln Ste 201	Virginia Beach	VA	23452	877-547-7248	757-463-0033
Launch Pad 18130 Jorene Rd	Odessa	FL	33556	888-920-3450	
Newegg Inc					
16839 E Gale Ave	City of Industry	CA	91745	800-390-1119	626-271-9700
PC Connection Inc					
730 Milford Rd Rt 101A	Merrimack	NH	03054	888-213-0607	603-683-2000
NASDAQ: PCCC					
PC Connection Inc MacConnection Div					
730 Milford Rd Rt 101A	Merrimack	NH	03054	888-213-0260	
PC Mall Inc					
2555 W 190th St	Torrance	CA	90504	800-555-6255	310-354-5600
NASDAQ: PCMI					
Physmark Inc					
101 E Pk Blvd Ste 600	Plano	TX	75074	800-922-7060	972-231-8000
Questica Inc					
980 Fraser Dr Ste 105.	Burlington	ON	L7L5P5	877-707-7755	
Recursion Software Inc					
2591 Dallas Pkwy Ste 200	Frisco	TX	75034	800-727-8674	972-731-8800
Service Communications Inc					
10675 Willows Rd NE Ste 100	Redmond	WA	98052	800-488-0468	
Top Producer Systems Inc					
10651 Shellbridge Way Ste 155	Richmond	BC	V6X2W8	888-821-3657	
Translations.com Inc					
Three Pk Ave 39th Fl.	New York	NY	10016	800-688-7205	212-689-1616

182   COMPUTER SYSTEMS DESIGN SERVICES

SEE ALSO Web Site Design Services
Companies that plan and design computer systems that integrate hardware, software, and communication technologies.

				Toll-Free	Phone
Abacus Technology Corp					
5454 Wisconsin Ave Ste 1100	Chevy Chase	MD	20815	800-225-2135	301-907-8500
Achilles Guard Inc					
4201 Spring Vly Rd Ste 1400	Dallas	TX	75244	866-525-8680	
Advanced Information Systems Group Inc					
11315 Corporate Blvd Ste 210	Orlando	FL	32817	800-593-8359	407-581-2929
AETEA Information Technology Inc					
1445 Research Blvd Ste 300.	Rockville	MD	20850	888-772-3832	301-721-4200
AGSI					
3343 Peachtree Rd NE Ste 510.	Atlanta	GA	30326	800-768-2474	404-816-7577
Allied Technology Inc					
1803 Research Blvd Ste 601.	Rockville	MD	20850	888-294-8560	301-309-1234
American Systems Corp					
14151 Pk Meadow Dr Ste 500	Chantilly	VA	20151	800-733-2721	703-968-6300
Analysts International Corp					
7700 France Ave S Ste 200.	Minneapolis	MN	55435	800-800-5044	952-838-3000
NASDAQ: ANLY					
Arlington Computer Products Inc					
851 Commerce Ct	Buffalo Grove	IL	60089	800-548-5105*	847-541-6333
*Orders					
AVT Inc					
341 Bonnie Cir Ste 102	Corona	CA	92880	877-424-3663	
B Green Innovations Inc					
750 Hwy 34	Matawan	NJ	07747	877-996-9333	732-441-7700
Bell Techlogix					
5777 Decatur Blvd	Indianapolis	IN	46241	866-782-2355	317-333-7777
Bluelock LLC					
6325 Morenci Trl	Indianapolis	IN	46268	888-402-2583	
Blytheco LLC					
23161 Mill Creek Dr	Laguna Hills	CA	92653	800-425-9843	949-583-9500
Bridgeline Digital					
80 BlanchaRd Rd	Burlington	MA	01803	800-603-9936	781-376-5555
CACI International Inc					
1100 N Glebe Rd	Arlington	VA	22201	866-606-3471	703-841-7800
NYSE: CACI					
Cadre Computer Resources Co					
201 East Fifth Street Suite 1800	Cincinnati	OH	45202	866-762-6700	513-762-7350
Calibre Systems Inc					
6354 Walker Ln Ste 300 Metro Pk	Alexandria	VA	22310	888-225-4273	703-797-8500
Camber Corp					
635 Discovery Dr NW	Huntsville	AL	35806	800-998-7988	256-922-0200
Catapult Systems Inc					
1221 S MoPac Expwy Ste 350	Austin	TX	78746	800-528-6248	512-328-8181
Cdo Technologies Inc					
5200 Sprngfld St Ste 320	Dayton	OH	45431	866-307-6616	937-258-0022
CGI Group Inc					
1130 Sherbrooke St W Seventh Fl	Montreal	QC	H3A2M8	800-828-8377	514-841-3200
TSE: GIB/A					
CIBER Inc					
6363 S Fiddler's Green Cir Ste 1400	Greenwood Village	CO	80111	800-242-3799	303-220-0100
NYSE: CBR					
Clarkston Consulting					
1007 Slater Rd Ste 400.	Durham	NC	27703	800-652-4274	919-484-4400
Clever Devices Ltd					
300 Crossways Pk Dr	Woodbury	NY	11797	800-872-6129	516-433-6100
Cognizant Technology Solutions Corp					
500 Frank W Burr Blvd	Teaneck	NJ	07666	888-937-3277	201-801-0233
NASDAQ: CTSH					
Computer Analytical Systems Inc (CASI)					
1418 S Third St	Louisville	KY	40208	800-977-3475	502-635-2019
Computer Sciences Corp					
2100 E Grand Ave	El Segundo	CA	90245	866-310-0950	310-615-0311
NYSE: CSC					
Computer Task Group Inc (CTG)					
800 Delaware Ave	Buffalo	NY	14209	800-992-5350	716-882-8000
OTC: CTG					
Covansys Corp					
32605 W 12 Mile Rd Ste 250	Farmington Hills	MI	48334	866-310-0950	248-488-2088
Custom Computer Specialists Inc (CCS)					
70 Suffolk Ct	Hauppauge	NY	11788	800-598-8989	631-864-6699
CWPS Inc					
14120 A Sullyfield Cir	Chantilly	VA	20151	877-297-7472	
Delta Corporate Services Inc					
129 Littleton Rd	Parsippany	NJ	07054	800-335-8220	973-334-6260
Denali Advance Integration (DAI)					
17735 NE 65th St Ste 130	Redmond	WA	98052	877-467-8008	425-885-4000
Design Strategy Corp					
805 Third Ave 11th Fl.	New York	NY	10016	800-331-8726	212-370-0000
Dialogic Inc					
1504 Mccarthy Blvd.	Milpitas	CA	95035	800-755-4444	408-750-9400
DPE Systems Inc					
425 Pontius Ave N Ste 430.	Seattle	WA	98109	800-541-6566	206-223-3737
Dyonyx LP 1235 N Loop W	Houston	TX	77008	855-749-6758*	713-485-7000
*General					
Electronic Warfare Assoc Inc (EWA Inc)					
13873 Pk Ctr Rd Ste 500	Herndon	VA	20171	888-392-0002*	703-904-5700
*General					
eVerge Group Inc					
4965 Preston Pk Blvd Ste 700	Plano	TX	75093	888-548-1973	972-608-1803
Force 3 Inc					
2151 Priest Bridge Dr Ste 7	Crofton	MD	21114	800-391-0204	301-261-0204
Frontier Computer Corp					
1275 Business Pk Dr	Traverse City	MI	49686	866-226-6344	231-929-1386
Fujitsu Consulting					
1250 E Arques Ave	Sunnyvale	CA	94085	800-831-3183	
General Dynamics Information Technology					
3211 Jermantown Rd	Fairfax	VA	22030	800-242-0230	703-246-0200
Genesis Corp					
950 Third Ave Fl 26	New York	NY	10022	800-261-1776	212-688-5522
GeoLogics Corp					
5285 Shawnee Rd Ste 300	Alexandria	VA	22312	800-684-3455	703-750-4000
Global Consultants Inc					
25 Airport Rd	Morristown	NJ	07960	877-264-6424	973-889-5200
Global Help Desk Services Inc					
2080 Silas Deane Hwy	Rocky Hill	CT	06067	800-770-1075	
Global Technology Resources Inc					
990 S Broadway Ste 400.	Denver	CO	80209	877-603-1984	303-455-8800
Globalspec Inc 350 Jordan Rd	Troy	NY	12180	800-261-2052	518-880-0200
GP Strategies Corp					
11000 Broken Land Parkway Suite 200	Columbia	MD	21044	888-843-4784	443-367-9600
Greenpages Inc					
33 Badgers Island W	Kittery	ME	03904	888-687-4876	207-439-7310
Hartford Computer Group Inc					
10440 Little Patuxent Pkwy 3rd Fl	Columbia	MD	21044	800-370-5849	410-740-3020
Hexaware Technologies Inc					
1095 Cranbury Rd	Jamesburg	NJ	08831	866-746-2133	609-409-6950
Howard Systems International					
2777 Summer St	Stamford	CT	06905	800-326-4860	
Ibaset					
27442 Portola Pkwy	Foothill Ranch	CA	92610	877-422-7381	949-598-5200
Iconixx Software					
3420 Executive Ctr Dr Ste 250	Austin	TX	78731	877-426-6499	
iMakeNews Inc 200 Fifth Ave	Waltham	MA	02451	866-964-6397	781-890-4700
Information Analysis Inc					
11240 Waples Mill Rd Ste 201	Fairfax	VA	22030	800-829-7614	703-383-3000
Integrated Systems Analysts Inc					
2001 N Beauregard St Ste 600	Alexandria	VA	22311	800-929-1024	703-824-0700
Intelligent Decisions Inc					
21445 Beaumeade Cir	Ashburn	VA	20147	800-929-8331	703-554-1600
IntelliSoft Group LLC					
61 Spit Brook Rd	Nashua	NH	03060	888-634-4464	
Interactive Business Systems Inc					
2625 Butterfield Rd	Oak Brook	IL	60523	800-555-5427	630-571-9100
Kemtah Group Inc					
7601 Jefferson St NE Ste 120	Albuquerque	NM	87109	877-753-6824	505-346-4900
KForce Government Soultions					
2750 Prosperity Ave Ste 300	Fairfax	VA	22031	800-200-7465	703-245-7350
Lighthouse Computer Services Inc					
6 Blackstone Valley Pl Ste 205	Lincoln	RI	02865	888-542-8030	401-334-0799

				Toll-Free	Phone
Logicease Solutions Inc 1 Bay Plaza Ste 520	Burlingame	CA	94010	**866-212-3273**	650-373-1111
Mainline Information Systems Inc 1700 Summit Lk Dr	Tallahassee	FL	32317	**866-490-6246**	850-219-5000
Mercom Inc 313 Commerce Dr	Pawleys Island	SC	29585	**877-223-8330**	843-979-9957
Network America Inc 118 107th Ave	Treasure Island	FL	33706	**877-624-8311**	
NewAgeSys Inc 231 Clarksville Rd Ste 200	Princeton Junction	NJ	08550	**888-863-9243**	609-919-9800
Novacoast Inc 1505 Chapala St	Santa Barbara	CA	93101	**800-949-9933**	
nQueue Inc 7890 S Hardy Dr Ste 105	Tempe	AZ	85284	**800-299-5933**	
NTT DATA, Inc 100 City Sq	Boston	MA	02129	**800-745-3263**	
Official Payments Corp 3550 Engineering Dr	Norcross	GA	30092	**877-754-4413**	770-325-3100
ONESPRING LLC 980 Birmingham Rd Ste 501-165	Alpharetta	GA	30004	**888-472-1840**	
Planned Systems International Inc 10632 Lttle Patuxent Pkwy	Columbia	MD	21044	**800-275-7749**	410-964-8000
Pointe Technology Group Inc 7272 Pk Cir Dr Ste 200	Hanover	MD	21076	**800-730-6171**	410-712-9425
Pomeroy IT Solutions Inc 1020 Petersburg Rd	Hebron	KY	41048	**800-846-8727**	859-586-0600
Presidio Networked Solutions Inc 7601 Ora Glen Dr Ste 100	Greenbelt	MD	20770	**800-452-6926**	301-313-2000
Professional Software Engineering Inc 780 Lynnhaven Pkwy Ste 350	Virginia Beach	VA	23452	**800-924-1091**	757-431-2400
Protocol Networks Inc 15 Shore Dr	Johnston	RI	02919	**877-676-0146**	
RiverPoint Group LLC 2200 E Devon Ave Ste 385	Des Plaines	IL	60018	**800-297-5601**	847-233-9600
Rolta Tusc Inc 333 E Butterfield Rd Ste 900	Lombard	IL	60148	**800-755-8872**	630-960-2909
Sayers Group LLC 825 Corporate Woods Pkwy	Vernon Hills	IL	60061	**800-323-5357**	
SCC Soft Computer Inc 5400 Tech Data Dr	Clearwater	FL	33760	**800-763-8352**	727-789-0100
Securance LLC 6922 W Linebaugh Ave Ste 101	Tampa	FL	33625	**877-578-0215**	
SecureInfo Corp 211 N Loop 1604 E Ste 200	San Antonio	TX	78232	**888-677-9351**	210-403-5600
SMS Data Products Group Inc 1751 Pinnacle Dr 12th Fl	McLean	VA	22102	**800-331-1767**	
Software Information Systems Inc (SIS) 165 Barr St	Lexington	KY	40507	**800-337-6914**	859-977-4747
Software Technology Group 555 S 300 E	Salt Lake City	UT	84111	**888-595-1001**	801-595-1000
SRA International Inc 4300 Fair Lakes Ct	Fairfax	VA	22033	**800-511-6398**	703-803-1500
Stefanini TechTeam Inc 27335 W Eleven-Mile Rd	Southfield	MI	48034	**800-522-4451**	248-357-2866
Stg International Inc 4900 Seminary Rd Ste 1100	Alexandria	VA	22311	**855-507-0660**	703-578-6030
Svam International Inc 233 E Shore Rd Ste 201	Great Neck	NY	11023	**800-903-6716**	516-466-6655
Sykes Enterprises Inc 400 N Ashley Dr Ste 2800 *NASDAQ: SYKE*	Tampa	FL	33602	**800-867-9537**	813-274-1000
Synergy Associates LLC 550 Clydesdale Trl	Medina	MN	55340	**888-763-9920**	
Tribridge 4830 W Kennedy Blvd Ste 890	Tampa	FL	33609	**877-744-1360**	
US-Analytics Solutions Group LLC 600 E Las Colinas Blvd Ste 2222 *General	Irving	TX	75039	**877-828-8727***	214-630-0081
Visionary Integration Professionals Inc 80 Iron Pt Cir Ste 100	Folsom	CA	95630	**800-434-2673**	916-985-9625
Vistronix Inc 11091 Sunset Hills Rd Ste 700	Reston	VA	20190	**800-483-2434**	703-463-2059
YouMail Inc 43 Corporate Park Ste 200	Irvine	CA	92606	**800-374-0013**	
ZyQuest Inc 1385 W Main Ave Ste 101	De Pere	WI	54115	**800-992-0533**	920-499-0533

183 CONCERT, SPORTS, OTHER LIVE EVENT PRODUCERS & PROMOTERS

				Toll-Free	Phone
Gilmore Entertainment Group 8901-A Business 17 N	Myrtle Beach	SC	29572	**800-843-6779**	843-913-4000
Harlem Globetrotters International Inc 400 E Van Buren St Ste 300	Phoenix	AZ	85004	**800-641-4667**	602-258-0000
House of Blues Entertainment Inc 7060 Hollywood Blvd	Hollywood	CA	90028	**877-632-7600**	323-769-4600
Speedway Motorsports Inc (SMI) 5555 Concord Pkwy S *NYSE: TRK*	Concord	NC	28027	**800-461-9330**	704-455-3239
World Wrestling Entertainment Inc 1241 E Main St *NYSE: WWE*	Stamford	CT	06902	**866-993-7467**	203-352-8600

184 CONCRETE - READY-MIXED

				Toll-Free	Phone
Baccala Concrete Corp 100 Armento St	Johnston	RI	02919	**866-705-2382**	401-231-8300
Bonded Concrete Inc 303 Rt 155	Watervliet	NY	12189	**800-252-8589**	518-273-5800
Boston Sand & Gravel Company Inc 100 N Washington St PO Box 9187 *OTC: BSND*	Boston	MA	02114	**800-624-2724**	617-227-9000
Builders Redi-Mix Inc 30701 W 10 Mile Rd Ste 500 PO Box 2900	Farmington Hills	MI	48333	**888-988-4400**	
Building Products Corp 950 Freeburg Ave	Belleville	IL	62220	**800-233-1996**	618-233-4427
CalPortland Co 5975 E Marginal Way S PO Box 1730	Seattle	WA	98134	**800-750-0123**	206-764-3000
Cemex USA 840 Gessner Ste 1400 *NYSE: CX*	Houston	TX	77024	**888-292-0070**	713-650-6200
Cemstone Products Co 2025 Centre Pt Blvd Ste 300	Mendota Heights	MN	55120	**800-236-7866**	651-688-9292
Central Builders Supply Company Inc 125 Bridge Ave PO Box 152	Sunbury	PA	17801	**800-326-9361**	570-286-6461
Central Concrete Supply Company Inc 755 Stockton Ave	San Jose	CA	95126	**866-404-1000**	408-293-6272
Century Ready-Mix Corp 3250 Armand St PO Box 4420	Monroe	LA	71211	**800-732-3969**	318-322-4444
Champion Inc 180 Traders Mine Rd PO Box 490 *Sales	Iron Mountain	MI	49801	**800-568-8881***	906-779-2300
Clayton Cos, The PO Box 3015	Lakewood	NJ	08701	**800-662-3044**	
Dolese Bros Co 20 NW 13th St	Oklahoma City	OK	73103	**800-375-2311**	405-235-2311
Dragon Products Co 960 Ocean Ave	Portland	ME	04103	**800-828-8352**	207-774-6355
Eastern Concrete Materials Inc 475 Market St	Elmwood Park	NJ	07407	**800-822-7242**	201-797-7979
Ernst Enterprises Inc 3361 Successful Way	Dayton	OH	45414	**800-353-1555**	937-233-5555
Geneva Rock Products Inc 302 W 5400 S Ste 200	Murray	UT	84107	**855-614-6497**	801-281-7900
Janesville Sand & Gravel Co (JSG) 1110 Harding St	Janesville	WI	53547	**800-955-7702**	608-754-7701
King's Material Inc 650 12th Ave SW	Cedar Rapids	IA	52404	**800-332-5298**	319-363-0233
Kirkpatrick Concrete Co 2000-A Southbridge Pkwy Ste 610	Birmingham	AL	35209	**800-489-0205**	205-423-2600
Krehling Industries Inc 1399 Hagy Way	Harrisburg	PA	17110	**800-839-1654**	717-232-7936
Kuhlman Corp 1845 Indian Woods Cir	Maumee	OH	43537	**800-669-3309**	419-897-6000
L Suzio Concrete Company Inc 975 Westfield Rd	Meriden	CT	06450	**888-789-4626**	203-237-8421
Lycon Inc 1110 Harding St PO Box 427	Janesville	WI	53547	**800-955-8758**	608-754-7701
Mid-Continent Concrete Co PO Box 3878	Tulsa	OK	74102	**800-225-5422**	918-582-8111
Prairie Group Inc 7601 W 79th St *Sales	Bridgeview	IL	60455	**800-649-3690***	708-458-0400
RiverStone Group Inc 1701 Fifth Ave	Moline	IL	61265	**800-906-2489**	309-757-8250
Sequatchie Concrete Service Inc 406 Cedar Ave	South Pittsburg	TN	37380	**800-824-0824**	423-837-7913
Shelby Materials PO Box 280	Shelbyville	IN	46176	**800-548-9516**	
Silvi Concrete Products Inc 355 Newbold Rd	Fairless Hills	PA	19030	**800-426-6273**	215-295-0777
Smith Ready Mix Inc 251 W Lincolnway	Valparaiso	IN	46383	**888-632-5656**	219-462-3191
Speedway Redi Mix Inc 1201 N Taylor Rd	Garrett	IN	46738	**800-227-5649**	260-357-6885
Tilcon Connecticut Inc PO Box 1357	New Britain	CT	06050	**888-845-2666**	860-224-6010
Titan America Inc 1151 Azalea Garden Rd	Norfolk	VA	23502	**800-468-7622**	757-858-6500
United Materials LLC The Woodlands Corporate Ctr E 3949 Forest Pkwy Ste 400	North Tonawanda	NY	14120	**888-918-6483**	716-213-5832

185 CONCRETE PRODUCTS - MFR

				Toll-Free	Phone
A Duchini Inc 2550 McKinley Ave	Erie	PA	16514	**800-937-7317**	814-456-7027
Abresist Corp PO Box 38	Urbana	IN	46990	**800-348-0717**	260-774-3327
AC Miller Concrete Products Inc 31 E Bridge St PO Box 199	Spring City	PA	19475	**800-229-2922**	610-948-4600
Accord Industries 4001 Forsyth Rd *General	Winter Park	FL	32792	**800-876-6989***	407-671-6989
Adams Products Co 5701 McCrimmon Pkwy PO Box 189	Morrisville	NC	27560	**800-672-3131**	919-467-2218
Atlantic Concrete Products Inc 8900 Old Rt 13	Tullytown	PA	19007	**888-318-9473**	215-945-5600
Basalite Concrete Products LLC 605 Industrial Way	Dixon	CA	95620	**800-776-6690**	707-678-1901
Binkley & Ober Inc 2742 Lancaster Rd	Manheim	PA	17545	**800-682-5625**	717-569-0441
Blakeslee Arpaia Chapman Inc 200 N Branford Rd	Branford	CT	06405	**800-922-6203**	203-488-2500
BNZ Materials Inc 6901 S Pierce St Ste 260	Littleton	CO	80128	**800-999-0890**	303-978-1199
Buehner Block Co 2800 SW Temple	Salt Lake City	UT	84115	**800-999-2565**	801-467-5456
Cement Industries Inc 2925 Hanson St PO Box 823	Fort Myers	FL	33902	**800-332-1440**	239-332-1440
Cement Products & Supply Co Inc 516 W Main St	Lakeland	FL	33815	**800-248-2385**	863-686-5141
Century Group Inc, The 1106 W Napoleon St PO Box 228	Sulphur	LA	70664	**800-527-5232**	337-527-5266
Chaney Enterprises 12480 Mattawoman Dr PO Box 548	Waldorf	MD	20604	**888-244-0411**	301-932-5000
Clayton Block Co PO Box 3015	Lakewood	NJ	08701	**800-662-3044**	

			Toll-Free	Phone
Clayton Cos, The				
PO Box 3015	Lakewood NJ	08701	**800-662-3044**	
Con Cast Pipe LP				
299 Brock Rd S RR#3	Guelph ON	N1H6H9	**800-668-7473**	
Con Forms				
777 Maritime Dr	Port Washington WI	53074	**800-223-3676**	262-284-7800
Construction Products Inc				
1631 Ashport Rd	Jackson TN	38305	**800-238-8226**	731-668-7305
DN Tanks 351 Cypress Ln	El Cajon CA	92020	**800-227-8181**	619-440-8181
Dolese Bros Co				
20 NW 13th St	Oklahoma City OK	73103	**800-375-2311**	405-235-2311
Dura-Stress Inc				
11325 County Rd 44	Leesburg FL	34788	**800-342-9239***	352-787-1422
*General				
E Dillon & Co				
2522 Swords Creek Rd PO Box 160	Swords Creek VA	24649	**800-234-8970**	276-873-6816
EP Henry Corp 201 Pk Ave	Woodbury NJ	08096	**800-444-3679**	856-845-6200
Ernest Maier Inc				
4700 Annapolis Rd	Bladensburg MD	20710	**888-927-8303**	301-927-8300
Fabcon Inc 6111 Hwy 13 W	Savage MN	55378	**800-727-4444**	952-890-4444
Federal Block Corp				
247 Walsh Ave	New Windsor NY	12553	**800-724-1999**	845-561-4108
Flexicore of Texas				
PO Box 450049	Houston TX	77245	**888-359-4267**	281-437-5700
Fritz Industries Inc				
180 Gordon Dr Ste 113	Exton PA	19341	**800-345-6202**	
General Shale Products LLC				
3015 Bristol Hwy	Johnson City TN	37601	**800-414-4661**	423-282-4661
Goria Enterprises				
PO Box 14489	Greensboro NC	27415	**800-446-7421**	
Grand Blanc Cement Products				
10709 Ctr Rd	Grand Blanc MI	48439	**800-875-7500**	810-694-7500
Hancock Concrete Products Inc				
17 Atlantic Ave	Hancock MN	56244	**800-321-1558**	320-392-5207
High Concrete Structures Inc				
125 Denver Rd	Denver PA	17517	**800-773-2278**	717-336-9300
Isabel Bloom LLC				
736 Federal St Ste 2100	Davenport IA	52803	**800-273-5436**	
Jensen Precast				
625 Bergin Way	Sparks NV	89431	**800-648-1134**	775-359-6200
JW Peters Inc				
500 W Market St	Burlington WI	53105	**866-265-7888**	262-806-9009
King's Material Inc				
650 12th Ave SW	Cedar Rapids IA	52404	**800-332-5298**	319-363-0233
Kistner Concrete Products Inc				
8713 Read Rd	East Pembroke NY	14056	**800-809-2801**	585-762-8216
L M Scofield Co				
6533 Bandini Blvd	Los Angeles CA	90040	**800-800-9900**	323-720-8810
MantelsDirect				
217 N Seminary St	Florence AL	35630	**888-493-8898**	
Metromont Corp				
PO Box 2486	Greenville SC	29602	**888-295-0383**	864-295-0295
Midwest Tile & Concrete Products Inc				
4309 Webster Rd	Woodburn IN	46797	**800-359-4701**	260-749-5173
Modern Inc/Environmental & Wastewater				
210 Durham Rd	Ottsville PA	18942	**888-965-3227**	610-847-5112
Molin Concrete Products Co				
415 Lilac St	Lino Lakes MN	55014	**800-336-6546**	651-786-7722
Montfort Bros Inc				
44 Elm St	Fishkill NY	12524	**800-724-1777**	845-896-6225
Montfort Group, The				
44 Elm St	Fishkill NY	12524	**800-724-1777**	845-896-6225
Mutual Materials Co				
605 119th Ave NE	Bellevue WA	98005	**800-477-3008**	425-452-2300
National Oilwell Varco (NOV)				
7909 Parkwood Cir Dr	Houston TX	77036	**888-262-8645**	713-375-3700
NYSE: NOV				
NC Products Corp				
920 Withers Rd PO Box 27077	Raleigh NC	27603	**888-965-3227**	919-772-6301
New Milford Block & Supply				
574 Danbury Rd	New Milford CT	06776	**800-724-1888**	860-355-1101
Northfield an Oldcastle Co				
2200 S Main St	West Bend WI	53095	**800-227-6512**	262-338-5700
Oldcastle Inc				
900 Ashwood Pkwy Ste 600	Atlanta GA	30338	**800-899-8455**	770-804-3363
Olson Precast Co (OPC)				
2750 Marion Dr	Las Vegas NV	89115	**800-876-8374**	702-643-4371
Orco Block Co Inc				
11100 Beach Blvd	Stanton CA	90680	**800-473-6726**	714-527-2239
Pre-Cast Specialties Inc				
1380 NE 48th St	Pompano Beach FL	33064	**800-749-4041**	954-781-4040
Preload Inc				
49 Wireless Blvd STE 200	Hauppauge NY	11788	**888-773-5623**	631-231-8100
QUIKRETE Cos				
3490 Piedmont Rd Ste 1300	Atlanta GA	30305	**800-282-5828**	404-634-9100
RCP Block & Brick Inc				
8240 Broadway	Lemon Grove CA	91945	**800-794-4727**	619-460-7250
Reading Precast Inc				
5494 Pottsville Pike	Leesport PA	19533	**800-724-4881**	610-926-5000
Reading Rock Inc				
4600 Devitt Dr	Cincinnati OH	45246	**800-482-6466**	513-874-2345
RI Lampus Co				
816 RI Lampus Ave PO Box 167	Springdale PA	15144	**800-872-7310**	412-362-3800
Rinker Materials Corp Concrete Pipe Div				
8311 W Carder Ct	Littleton CO	80125	**800-909-7763**	303-791-1600
Rockwood Retaining Walls Inc				
7200 Hwy 63 N	Rochester MN	55906	**800-535-2375**	888-288-4045
Royal Concrete Pipe Inc				
PO Box 430	Stacy MN	55079	**800-817-3240**	651-462-2130
SD Ireland Co				
193 Industrial Ave	Williston VT	05495	**800-339-4565**	802-863-6222
Sequatchie Concrete Service Inc				
406 Cedar Ave	South Pittsburg TN	37380	**800-824-0824**	423-837-7913
Stubbe's Precast				
30 Muir Line	Harley ON	N0E1E0	**866-355-2183**	519-424-2183
Superlite Block Co Inc				
4150 W Turney Ave	Phoenix AZ	85019	**800-366-7877**	602-352-3500

			Toll-Free	Phone
Terre Hill Silo Company Inc				
PO Box 10	Terre Hill PA	17581	**800-242-1509**	717-445-3100
Tindall Corp				
3076 N Blackstock Rd PO Box 1778	Spartanburg SC	29301	**800-849-4521**	864-576-3230
Trenwyth Industries Inc				
One Connely Rd PO Box 438	Emigsville PA	17318	**800-233-1924***	717-767-6868
*Cust Svc				
Unistress Corp				
550 Cheshire Rd	Pittsfield MA	01201	**800-927-9468**	413-499-1441
Valley Blox Inc				
210 Stone Spring Rd	Harrisonburg VA	22801	**800-648-6725**	540-434-6725
Wausau Tile Inc PO Box 1520	Wausau WI	54402	**800-388-8728**	715-359-3121
Wells Concrete Products Inc				
835 Hwy 109 NE PO Box 308	Wells MN	56097	**800-658-7049**	507-553-3138
Wieser Concrete Products Inc				
W3716 US Hwy 10	Maiden Rock WI	54750	**800-325-8456**	715-647-2311
Wingra Stone Co				
2975 Kapec Rd PO Box 44284	Madison WI	53744	**800-249-6908**	608-271-5555
York Bldg Products Co				
950 Smile Way	York PA	17404	**800-673-2408**	717-848-2831

186   CONFERENCE & EVENTS COORDINATORS

			Toll-Free	Phone
ASD				
6255 Sunset Blvd 19th Fl	Los Angeles CA	90028	**888-441-7575**	323-817-2200
Conference & Travel				
5655 Coventry Ln	Fort Wayne IN	46804	**800-346-9807**	260-434-6600
Courtesy Assoc				
2025 M St NW Ste 800	Washington DC	20036	**800-647-4689**	
Creative Impact Group Inc				
801 Skokie Blvd Ste 108	Northbrook IL	60062	**800-445-2171**	847-945-7401
Destination Resources				
5435 Balboa Blvd Ste 106	Encino CA	91316	**800-422-6524**	818-995-7915
Destination Services of Colorado Inc (DSC)				
PO Box 3660	Avon CO	81620	**800-372-7686**	970-476-6565
Event Planning International Corp				
10900 Granite St	Charlotte NC	28273	**800-940-2164**	980-233-3777
Expo Group, The				
5931 W Campus Cir Dr	Irving TX	75063	**800-736-7775**	972-580-9000
Gavel International Corp				
300 Tri State International				
Ste 320	Lincolnshire IL	60069	**800-544-2835**	847-945-8150
GES Exposition Services				
7000 Lindell Rd	Las Vegas NV	89118	**800-443-9767**	702-515-5500
Great Events & TEAMS Inc				
2170 S Parker Rd Ste 290	Denver CO	80231	**866-706-7814**	303-394-2022
International Meeting Managers Inc				
4550 Post Oak Pl Ste 342	Houston TX	77027	**800-423-7175**	713-965-0566
Meeting Connection Inc, The				
893 High St	Worthington OH	43085	**800-398-2568**	614-888-2568
National Trade Productions Inc				
313 S Patrick St	Alexandria VA	22314	**800-687-7469**	703-683-8500
Prestige Accommodations International				
1231 E Dyer Rd Ste 240	Santa Ana CA	92705	**800-321-6338**	714-957-9100
Resource Connection Inc				
161 S Main St	Middleton MA	01949	**800-649-5228**	978-777-9333
RX Worldwide Meetings Inc				
3060 Communications Pkwy Ste 200	Plano TX	75093	**800-562-1713**	214-291-2920
T3 Expo LLC				
Eight Lakeville Business Park Unit 1				
	Lakeville MA	02347	**888-698-3397**	
Travizon Meeting Management				
275 Mishawum Rd Ste 300	Woburn MA	01801	**800-423-2500**	888-781-5200
Vega Group				
7220 Washington Ave	New Orleans LA	70125	**800-771-2979**	504-488-5222

187   CONGLOMERATES

SEE ALSO Holding Companies

A business conglomerate is defined here as a corporation that consists of many business units in different industries.

			Toll-Free	Phone
3M Co				
3M Ctr Bldg 225-3S-06	Saint Paul MN	55144	**800-364-3577**	651-733-1110
NYSE: MMM				
Alexander & Baldwin Inc				
822 Bishop St	Honolulu HI	96813	**800-454-0477**	808-525-6611
NYSE: ALEX				
Andersons Inc				
480 W Dussel Dr	Maumee OH	43537	**800-537-3370**	419-893-5050
NASDAQ: ANDE				
API Group Inc				
1100 Old Hwy 8 NW	New Brighton MN	55112	**800-223-4922**	
ARAMARK Corp				
1101 Market St	Philadelphia PA	19107	**800-388-3300**	937-660-4708
Archer Daniels Midland Co (ADM)				
4666 E Faries Pkwy	Decatur IL	62526	**800-637-5843**	217-424-5200
NYSE: ADM				
Ashland Inc				
50 E River Ctr Blvd PO Box 391	Covington KY	41012	**877-546-2782**	859-815-3333
NYSE: ASH				
Berkshire Hathaway Inc				
3555 Farnam St Ste 1440	Omaha NE	68131	**800-223-2064**	402-346-1400
NYSE: BRK/A				
Brown-Forman Corp				
850 Dixie Hwy PO Box 1080	Louisville KY	40210	**800-831-9146**	502-585-1100
NYSE: BFB				
Canadian Tire Corp Ltd				
2180 Yonge St PO Box 770 Stn K	Toronto ON	M4P2V8	**800-387-8803**	416-480-3000
TSE: CTC				
Chemed Corp				
255 E Fifth St Ste 2600	Cincinnati OH	45202	**800-982-7650***	513-762-6900
NYSE: CHE ■ *General				

					Toll-Free	Phone

Clorox Co 1221 Broadway .... Oakland CA 94612 **800-424-9300*** 510-271-7000
　NYSE: CLX ■ *Cust Svc*
Delaware North Cos Inc
　40 Fountain Plz .... Buffalo NY 14202 **800-828-7240** 716-858-5000
EBSCO Industries Inc
　5724 Hwy 280 .... Birmingham AL 35242 **800-527-5901** 205-991-6600
Fortune Brands Inc
　520 Lk Cook Rd .... Deerfield IL 60015 **800-225-2719** 847-484-4400
　NYSE: FBHS
Harsco Corp
　350 Poplar Church Rd .... Camp Hill PA 17011 **866-470-3900** 717-763-7064
　NYSE: HSC
Hitachi America Ltd
　50 Prospect Ave .... Tarrytown NY 10591 **800-448-2244** 914-332-5800
Holiday Cos
　4567 American Blvd W PO Box 1224 .... Bloomington MN 55437 **800-745-7411** 952-830-8700
HT Hackney Co
　502 S Gay St PO Box 238 .... Knoxville TN 37901 **800-406-1291** 865-546-1291
iHeartMedia, Inc
　200 E Basse Rd .... San Antonio TX 78209 **888-283-6901** 210-822-2828
Intermec Inc
　6001 36th Ave W .... Everett WA 98203 **800-755-5505** 425-348-2600
　NYSE: IN
Johnson & Johnson
　One Johnson & Johnson Plz .... New Brunswick NJ 08933 **800-565-0122** 732-524-0400
　NYSE: JNJ
Kimball International Inc
　1600 Royal St .... Jasper IN 47549 **800-482-1616** 812-482-1600
　NASDAQ: KBAL
Kohler Co Inc
　444 Highland Dr .... Kohler WI 53044 **800-456-4537** 920-457-4441
Kraus-Anderson Co (KA)
　523 S Eigth St .... Minneapolis MN 55404 **888-547-3983** 612-305-2934
Loews Corp 667 Madison Ave .... New York NY 10065 **800-235-6397** 212-521-2000
MDU Resources Group Inc
　1200 W Century Ave PO Box 5650 .... Bismarck ND 58506 **866-760-4852** 701-530-1000
　NYSE: MDU
NACCO Industries Inc
　5875 Landerbrook Dr Ste 300. .... Cleveland OH 44124 **877-756-5118** 440-449-9600
　NYSE: NC
Newell Rubbermaid Inc
　Three Glenlake Pkwy .... Atlanta GA 30328 **800-752-9677** 770-418-7000
　NYSE: NWL
PepsiCo Inc
　700 Anderson Hill Rd .... Purchase NY 10577 **800-433-2652*** 914-253-2000
　NYSE: PEP ■ *PR*
Seaboard Corp
　9000 W 67th St .... Shawnee Mission KS 66202 **866-676-8886** 913-676-8800
　NYSE: SEB
Siemens Corp
　527 Madison Ave Ste 8. .... New York NY 10022 **800-743-6367** 212-258-4000
SPX Corp
　13515 Ballantyne Corporate Pl .... Charlotte NC 28277 **877-247-3797** 704-752-4400
　NYSE: SPW
Standex International Corp
　11 Keewaydin Dr .... Salem NH 03079 **800-514-5275** 603-893-9701
　NYSE: SXI
Sten Corp
　13828 Lincoln St NE .... Ham Lake MN 55304 **800-328-7958** 952-545-2776
Teleflex Inc
　155 S Limerick Rd .... Limerick PA 19468 **866-246-6990** 610-948-5100
　NYSE: TFX
Trinity Industries Inc
　2525 Stemmons Fwy .... Dallas TX 75207 **800-631-4420** 214-631-4420
　NYSE: TRN
United Services Automobile Assn (USAA)
　10750 McDermott Fwy .... San Antonio TX 78288 **800-531-8722**
Weyerhaeuser Co
　33663 Weyerhaeuser Way S .... Federal Way WA 98003 **800-525-5440** 253-924-2345
　NYSE: WY

188　CONSTRUCTION - BUILDING CONTRACTORS - NON-RESIDENTIAL

					Toll-Free	Phone

1st Choice Facilities Services Corp
　1941 Whitfield Park Loop .... Sarasota FL 34243 **866-241-0070**
Abrams Construction Inc
　Seven Kent St Ste 2 .... Brookline MA 02445 **800-935-9350** 617-566-9090
Advanced Industrial Services Inc
　3250 Susquehanna Trial .... York PA 17406 **800-544-5080** 717-764-9811
Ameris Bank
　24 Second Ave SE PO Box 3668 .... Moultrie GA 31768 **866-616-6020**
Apex Homes Inc
　7172 Rt 522 .... Middleburg PA 17842 **800-326-9524** 570-837-2333
Bank of the Orient
　233 Sansome St .... San Francisco CA 94104 **877-275-3342** 415-338-0843
Barlovento LLC
　431 Technology Dr .... Dothan AL 36303 **877-498-6039** 334-983-9979
Baywood Homes
　1140 Sheppard Ave W Ste 13 .... Toronto ON M3K2A2 **888-751-2223** 416-633-7333
Brannan Paving Coltd
　111 Elk Dr PO Box 3403 .... Victoria TX 77903 **800-626-7064** 361-573-3130
Brasfield & Gorrie LLC
　3021 Seventh Ave S .... Birmingham AL 35233 **800-239-8017** 205-328-4000
BT Mancini Co Inc
　876 S Milpitas Blvd .... Milpitas CA 95035 **800-787-6381** 408-942-7900
BT Mancini Co Inc Brookman Div
　876 S Milpitas Blvd .... Milpitas CA 95035 **800-787-6381** 408-942-7900
Budreck Truck Lines Inc
　8040 S Roberts Rd .... Bridgeview IL 60455 **800-621-0013** 708-496-0522
C.a. Murren & Sons Co Inc
　2275 Loganville Hwy .... Grayson GA 30017 **800-523-2200** 770-682-2940
Ca Lindman Inc
　10401 Guilford Rd .... Jessup MD 20794 **877-737-8675** 301-470-4700
Cedar Grove Composting Inc
　7343 E Marginal Way S .... Seattle WA 98108 **888-832-3008** 206-832-3000

CG Schmidt Inc
　11777 W Lake Pk Dr .... Milwaukee WI 53224 **800-248-1254** 414-577-1177
Clark Construction Group LLC
　7500 Old Georgetown Rd .... Bethesda MD 20814 **800-655-1330** 301-272-8100
Clark Transfer Inc
　800A Paxton St .... Harrisburg PA 17104 **800-488-7585** 717-238-0801
Clarksdale Municipal School District
　101 McGuire St PO Box 1088. .... Clarksdale MS 38614 **877-820-7831** 662-627-8500
Daryl Flood Inc
　450 Airline Dr Ste 100 .... Coppell TX 75019 **888-454-9481** 972-471-1496
Daw Construction Group LLC
　12552 South 125 West .... Draper UT 84020 **800-748-4778** 801-553-9111
Deltec Homes Inc
　69 Bingham Rd .... Asheville NC 28806 **800-642-2508** 828-253-0483
Diffenbaugh Inc
　6865 Airport Dr .... Riverside CA 92504 **800-394-5334** 951-351-6865
Duffield Assoc Inc
　5400 Limestone Rd .... Wilmington DE 19808 **877-732-9633** 302-239-6634
Dyad Constructors Inc
　8505 Holt St .... Houston TX 77054 **800-803-9202** 713-799-9380
Flintco LLC 1624 W 21st St .... Tulsa OK 74107 **800-947-2828** 918-587-8451
G & D Transportation Inc
　50 Commerce Dr .... Morton IL 61550 **800-451-6680** 309-266-1472
Gaines Motor Lines Inc
　2349 13th Ave SW PO Box 1549 .... Hickory NC 28603 **800-438-7311** 828-322-2000
GE Johnson Construction Co
　25 N Cascade Ave Ste 400 .... Colorado Springs CO 80903 **800-640-9501** 719-473-5321
Gerald H Phipps
　5995 Greenwood Florida Plaza Blvd
　Ste 100 .... Greenwood Village CO 80111 **866-487-2365** 303-571-5377
Gerloff Company Inc
　14955 Bulverde Rd .... San Antonio TX 78247 **800-486-3621** 210-490-2777
Gilbane Bldg Co New England Regional Office
　7 Jackson Walkway .... Providence RI 02903 **800-445-2263** 401-456-5800
Gilbane Bldg Company Mid-Atlantic Regional Office
　7901 Sandy Spring Rd Ste 500. .... Laurel MD 20707 **800-445-2263** 301-317-6100
Gilbane Bldg Company Southwest Regional Office
　1331 Lamar St Ste 1170 .... Houston TX 77010 **800-445-2263** 713-209-1873
Grant Parish School Board (GPSB)
　512 Main St PO Box 208 .... Colfax LA 71417 **877-277-3812** 318-627-3274
Gray Construction
　10 Quality St .... Lexington KY 40507 **800-814-8468** 859-281-5000
Hardy Bros Inc
　6406 Siloam Rd .... Siloam NC 27047 **800-525-5354** 336-374-5050
Harkins Builders Inc
　2201 Warwick Way .... Marriottsville MD 21104 **800-227-2345** 410-750-2600
Haskell Co
　111 Riverside Ave .... Jacksonville FL 32202 **800-622-4326** 904-791-4500
Hensel Phelps Construction Co
　420 Sixth Ave PO Box 0 .... Greeley CO 80632 **800-826-6309** 970-352-6565
Horst Group Inc
　320 Granite Run Dr PO Box 3330 .... Lancaster PA 17604 **800-732-0330** 717-581-9800
Housley Communications Inc
　3550 S Bryant Blvd .... San Angelo TX 76903 **800-880-9905** 325-944-9905
Jaynes Corp
　2906 Broadway NE .... Albuquerque NM 87107 **800-393-6343** 505-345-8591
John E Jones Oil Co Inc
　1016 S Cedar PO Box 546 .... Stockton KS 67669 **800-323-9821** 785-425-6746
Kustom FI LLC
　265 Hunt Park Cv .... Longwood FL 32750 **866-679-0699**
Lewis & Michael Inc
　1827 Woodman Dr .... Dayton OH 45420 **800-543-3524** 937-252-6683
Logan Trucking Inc
　3224 Navarre Rd SW .... Canton OH 44706 **800-683-0142** 330-478-1404
Market Contractors Ltd of Oregon
　10250 NE Marx St .... Portland OR 97220 **800-793-1448** 503-255-0977
McGough Construction Co Inc
　2737 Fairview Ave N .... Saint Paul MN 55113 **800-552-7670** 651-633-5050
Merced Irrigation District
　PO Box 2288 .... Merced CA 95344 **855-800-2267** 209-722-5761
Meyer & Najem Inc
　13099 Parkside Dr .... Fishers IN 46038 **888-578-5131** 317-577-0007
MGM Mirage Design Group Inc
　3260 Industrial Rd .... Las Vegas NV 89109 **800-929-1111** 702-650-7400
Mine & Mill Industrial Supply Company Inc
　2500 S Combee Rd .... Lakeland FL 33801 **800-282-8489** 863-665-5601
Mosser Construction
　122 S Wilson Ave .... Fremont OH 43420 **800-589-3801** 419-334-3801
Motor Service Inc
　130 Byassee Dr .... Hazelwood MO 63042 **800-966-5080** 314-731-4111
Nor-Son Inc 7900 Hastings Rd .... Baxter MN 56425 **800-858-1722** 218-828-1722
Odebrecht Construction Inc
　201 Alhambra Cir Ste 1400 .... Coral Gables FL 33134 **800-771-0001** 305-341-8800
Orcutt/Winslow
　3003 N Central Ave .... Phoenix AZ 85012 **800-331-5842** 602-257-1764
P A Landers Inc
　351 Winter St .... Hanover MA 02339 **800-660-6404** 781-826-8818
Parkway Construction & Assoc LP
　1000 Civic Cir .... Lewisville TX 75067 **800-869-4567** 972-221-1979
PDC Facilities Inc
　700 Walnut Ridge Dr .... Hartland WI 53029 **800-545-5998** 262-367-7700
Pence Kelly Construction LLC
　2747 Pence Loop SE .... Salem OR 97302 **800-434-6654** 503-399-7223
PM Construction Co Inc
　PO Box 728 .... Saco ME 04072 **800-646-0068** 207-282-7697
Port Jervis City School District
　PO Box 1104 .... Port Jervis NY 12771 **877-544-6664** 845-858-3100
Porta-King Building Systems
　4133 Shoreline Dr .... Earth City MO 63045 **800-284-5346**
Prime Contractors Inc
　525 N Sam Houston Pkwy E .... Houston TX 77060 **800-692-8378** 281-999-0875
R W Mercer Co
　2322 Brooklyn Rd PO Box 180 .... Jackson MI 49204 **877-763-7237** 517-787-2960
Ramtech Bldg Systems Inc
　1400 Hwy 287 S .... Mansfield TX 76063 **855-887-1888**
Renfrow Bros Inc
　855 Gossett Rd PO Box 4786 .... Spartanburg SC 29307 **888-522-5958** 864-579-0558

	Toll-Free	Phone
Ricks Barbecue Inc		
2367 Hwy 43 S ....Leoma TN 38468	800-544-5864	931-852-2324
Roy Anderson Corp		
11400 Reichold Rd ....Gulfport MS 39503	800-688-4003	228-896-4000
Rycon Construction Inc		
2525 Liberty Ave ....Pittsburgh PA 15222	800-883-1901	412-392-2525
Schneider Electric Buildings LLC		
1354 Clifford Ave ....Loves Park IL 61111	888-444-1311	
Septagon Construction		
113 E Third St ....Sedalia MO 65301	800-733-5999	660-827-2115
Snyder Langston Inc		
17962 Cowan St ....Irvine CA 92614	800-899-4122	949-863-9200
Stellar Group		
2900 Hartley Rd ....Jacksonville FL 32257	800-488-2900	904-260-2900
Stidham Trucking Inc		
PO Box 308 ....Yreka CA 96097	800-827-9500	530-842-4161
Streeter Assoc Inc		
101 E Woodlawn Ave PO Box 118 ....Elmira NY 14902	866-493-1640	607-734-4151
Sundt Construction Inc		
2015 W River Rd Ste 101 ....Tucson AZ 85704	800-467-5544	520-750-4600
Trehel Corp PO Box 1707 ....Clemson SC 29633	800-319-7006	864-654-6582
University Moving & Storage Co		
23305 Commerce Dr ....Farmington Hills MI 48335	800-448-6683	248-615-7000
USM Inc 1880 Markley St ....Norristown PA 19401	800-355-4000	610-278-9000
Virtexco Corp		
977 Norfolk Sq ....Norfolk VA 23502	800-766-1082	757-466-1114
Walsh Group Inc		
929 W Adams St ....Chicago IL 60607	800-957-1842	312-563-5400
Wanzek Construction Inc		
2028 2nd Ave NW ....West Fargo ND 58078	877-492-6935	701-282-6171
Ware County Board of Education		
1301 Bailey St PO Box 1789. ....Waycross GA 31502	800-419-3191	912-283-8656
Washington Local Schools		
3505 W Lincolnshire Blvd ....Toledo OH 43606	800-462-3589	419-473-8251
Whiting-Turner Contracting Co		
300 E Joppa Rd Eighth Fl ....Towson MD 21286	800-638-4279	410-821-1100
Windstar Lines Inc		
1903 US Hwy 71 N ....Carroll IA 51401	888-494-6378	712-792-4221
Woodfield Inc 3161 Hwy 376 S ....Camden AR 71701	800-501-6020	870-231-6020

189 CONSTRUCTION - BUILDING CONTRACTORS - RESIDENTIAL

	Toll-Free	Phone
Air Contact Transport Inc		
PO Box 570 ....Budd Lake NJ 07828	800-765-2769	
Arthur Rutenberg Homes Inc		
13922 58th St N ....Clearwater FL 33760	800-274-6637	727-536-5900
Ball Homes LLC		
3609 Walden Dr ....Lexington KY 40517	888-268-1101	859-268-1191
Bar None Auction Inc		
4751 Power Inn Rd ....Sacramento CA 95826	866-372-1700	
Bozzuto Group		
7850 Walker Dr Ste 400 ....Greenbelt MD 20770	866-698-7513*	301-220-0100
*General		
Breeden Homes Inc		
366 E 40th Ave ....Eugene OR 97405	800-870-1367*	541-686-9431
*Sales		
Dot-Line Transportation		
PO Box 8739 ....Fountain Valley CA 92728	800-423-3780	323-780-9010
Drees Co		
211 Grandview Dr ....Fort Mitchell KY 41017	866-265-2980	859-578-4200
Excel Homes Inc		
10642 S Susquehanna Trail ....Liverpool PA 17045	800-521-8599*	717-444-3395
*Sales		
Eyde Co		
4660 S Hagadorn Ste 660. ....East Lansing MI 48823	800-422-3933	517-351-2480
Harkins Builders Inc		
2201 Warwick Way ....Marriottsville MD 21104	800-227-2345	410-750-2600
JB Sandlin Cos		
5137 Davis Blvd ....Fort Worth TX 76180	800-821-4663	817-281-3509
Jim Walter Homes LLC		
3000 Riverchase Galleria Ste 1700. ....Birmingham AL 35244	800-643-0202	205-745-2615
LAS Enterprises Inc		
2413 L & A Rd ....Metairie LA 70001	800-264-1527	504-887-1515
Mercy Housing Inc		
1999 Broadway Ste 1000 ....Denver CO 80202	866-338-0557	303-830-3300
Nordaas American Homes Company Inc		
10091 State Hwy 22 ....Minnesota Lake MN 56068	800-658-7076	507-462-3331
Norris School District		
6940 Calloway Dr ....Bakersfield CA 93312	800-877-8339	661-387-7000
Olgoonik Development LLC		
3201 C St Ste 700 ....Anchorage AK 99503	855-763-2613	907-562-8728
Perry Homes PO Box 34306 ....Houston TX 77234	800-247-3779	713-947-1750
Providence Homes Inc		
4901 Belfort Rd Ste 140 ....Jacksonville FL 32256	866-836-0981	904-262-9898
Rio Verde Development Inc		
25609 N Danny Ln ....Rio Verde AZ 85263	800-233-7103	480-471-1962
Selmer Co		
2200 Woodale Ave ....Green Bay WI 54313	800-992-6538	920-434-0230
Southern California Boiler Inc		
5331 Business Dr ....Huntington Beach CA 92649	800-775-2645	714-891-0701
Staples Construction Company Inc		
1501 Eastman Ave ....Ventura CA 93003	800-881-4650	805-658-8786
Structural Component Systems Inc (SCS)		
1255 Front St ....Fremont NE 68026	800-844-5622	402-721-5622
TH Properties		
345 Main St ....Harleysville PA 19438	800-225-5847*	215-513-4270
*Sales		
Triple Crown Corp		
5351 Jaycee Ave ....Harrisburg PA 17112	877-822-4663	717-657-5729
United-Bilt Homes Inc		
8500 Line Ave ....Shreveport LA 71106	800-551-8955	318-861-4572
Village Green Cos		
30833 NW Hwy ....Farmington Hills MI 48334	800-521-2220	248-851-9600
Walsh Group Inc		
929 W Adams St ....Chicago IL 60607	800-957-1842	312-563-5400

Weavertown Environmental Group

		Toll-Free	Phone
Two Dorrington Rd ....Carnegie PA	15106	800-746-4850	724-746-4850

190 CONSTRUCTION - HEAVY CONSTRUCTION CONTRACTORS

	Toll-Free	Phone

190-1 Communications Lines & Towers Construction

		Toll-Free	Phone
MasTec Inc			
800 Douglas Rd 12th Fl ....Coral Gables FL	33134	800-531-5000	305-599-1800
NYSE: MTZ			
NAT-COM Inc			
2622 Audubon Rd ....Eagleville PA	19403	800-486-7947	610-666-7947
Seacomm Erectors Inc			
32527 SR 2 PO Box 1740. ....Sultan WA	98294	800-497-8320	360-793-6564
Utility Services Inc			
400 N Fourth St ....Bismarck ND	58501	800-638-3278	701-222-7900

190-2 Foundation Drilling & Pile Driving

		Toll-Free	Phone
LG Barcus & Sons Inc			
1430 State Ave ....Kansas City KS	66102	800-255-0180	913-621-1100
Malcolm Drilling Co Inc			
3503 Breakwater Ct ....Hayward CA	94545	800-523-2200	510-780-9181

190-3 Golf Course Construction

		Toll-Free	Phone
Harris Miniature Golf			
141 W Burk Ave ....Wildwood NJ	08260	888-294-6530	609-522-4200

190-4 Highway, Street, Bridge, Tunnel Construction

		Toll-Free	Phone
Adams Construction Co			
523 Rutherford Ave NE ....Roanoke VA	24016	800-237-6060	540-982-2366
Ajax Paving Industries Inc			
PO Box 7058 ....Troy MI	48007	888-468-5489	248-244-3300
Allan A Myers Inc			
1805 Berks Rd PO Box 1340 ....Worcester PA	19490	800-596-6118	610-222-8800
Allen Company Inc			
525 Burbank St PO Box 445. ....Broomfield CO	80020	800-876-8600	303-469-1857
Barriere Construction Co LLC			
1 Galleria Blvd Ste 1650. ....Metairie LA	70001	866-645-3060	504-581-7283
Boh Bros Construction Co LLC			
730 S Tonti St ....New Orleans LA	70119	800-284-3377	504-821-2400
Clark Construction Group LLC			
7500 Old Georgetown Rd ....Bethesda MD	20814	800-655-1330	301-272-8100
Crowder Construction Company Inc			
PO Box 30007 ....Charlotte NC	28230	800-849-2966	704-372-3541
Cummins Construction Company Inc			
1420 W Chestnut Ave ....Enid OK	73702	800-375-6001	580-233-6000
Dean Word Company Ltd			
1245 River Rd PO Box 310330. ....New Braunfels TX	78131	800-683-3926	830-625-2365
DH Blattner & Sons Inc			
392 County Rd 50 ....Avon MN	56310	800-877-2866	320-356-7351
Duininck Inc			
408 Sixth St PO Box 208 ....Prinsburg MN	56281	800-328-8949*	
*General			
Elam Construction Inc			
556 Struthers Ave ....Grand Junction CO	81501	800-675-4598	970-242-5370
Fred Weber Inc			
2320 Creve Coeur Mill Rd ....Maryland Heights MO	63043	866-739-8855	314-344-0070
Gallagher Asphalt Corp			
18100 S Indiana Ave ....Thornton IL	60476	800-536-7160	708-877-7160
Glasgow Inc			
104 Willow Grove Ave ....Glenside PA	19038	877-222-5514	215-884-8800
Gray & Sons Inc			
430 W Padonia Rd ....Timonium MD	21093	800-254-0752	410-771-4311
Harper Industries Inc			
616 Northview St ....Paducah KY	42001	866-487-9243	270-442-2753
Herzog Contracting Corp			
600 S Riverside Rd ....Saint Joseph MO	64507	800-541-7846	816-233-9001
Hoover Construction Co Inc			
PO Box 1007 ....Virginia MN	55792	800-741-0970	218-741-3280
HRI Inc			
1750 W College Ave ....State College PA	16801	877-474-9999	
Hubbard Construction Co			
1936 Lee Rd 3rd Fl ....Winter Park FL	32789	800-476-1228	407-645-5500
Hunter Contracting Co			
701 N Cooper Rd ....Gilbert AZ	85233	877-992-0521	480-892-0521
Hutchens Construction Co			
1007 Main St ....Cassville MO	65625	888-728-3482	417-847-2489
Jack B Parson Cos			
2350 South 1900 West ....Ogden UT	84401	888-672-7766	801-731-1111
James H Drew Corp			
8701 Zionsville Rd ....Indianapolis IN	46268	800-772-7342	317-876-3739
JF Shea Construction Inc			
655 Brea Canyon Rd ....Walnut CA	91789	888-779-7333	909-594-9500
JF White Contracting Co			
10 Burr St ....Framingham MA	01701	866-539-4400	508-879-4700
Kokosing Construction Company Inc			
17531 Waterford Rd PO Box 226 ....Fredericktown OH	43019	800-800-6315	740-694-6315
Lehigh Asphalt Paving & Construction Co Inc			
PO Box 549 ....Tamaqua PA	18252	877-222-5514	570-668-4303
Manatt's Inc 1775 Old 6 Rd ....Brooklyn IA	52211	800-532-1121	641-522-9206

Company	Address	City	State	ZIP	Toll-Free	Phone
Mathy Construction Co Inc	920 Tenth Ave N	Onalaska	WI	54650	**800-822-5246**	608-783-6411
Matich Corp	1596 Harry Sheppard Blvd	San Bernardino	CA	92408	**800-404-4975**	909-382-7400
Michael Baker Corp	100 Airsite Dr Airsite Business Pk	Moon Township	PA	15108	**800-553-1153**	412-269-6300
NYSE: BKR						
Oakgrove Construction Inc	6900 Seneca St	Elma	NY	14059	**866-435-1499**	716-652-2200
Odebrecht Construction Inc	201 Alhambra Cir Ste 1400	Coral Gables	FL	33134	**800-771-0001**	305-341-8800
Palmer Paving Corp	25 Blanchard St	Palmer	MA	01069	**800-244-8354**	413-283-8354
Parsons Corp	100 W Walnut St	Pasadena	CA	91124	**800-883-7300***	626-440-2000
*All						
Pike Industries Inc	3 Eastgate Pk Rd	Belmont	NH	03220	**800-283-0803**	603-527-5100
PJ Keating Co	998 Reservoir Rd	Lunenburg	MA	01462	**800-441-4119**	978-582-5200
Ranger Construction Industries Inc	101 Sansbury's Way	West Palm Beach	FL	33411	**800-969-9402**	561-793-9400
Reeves Construction Co Inc	101 Sheraton Ct	Macon	GA	31210	**800-743-0593**	478-474-9092
Reliable Contracting Co Inc	1 Church View Rd	Millersville	MD	21108	**800-492-4357**	410-987-0313
Sargent Corp	378 Bennoch Rd	Stillwater	ME	04489	**800-533-1812**	207-827-4435
Scott Construction Inc	560 Munroe Ave	Lake Delton	WI	53940	**800-843-1556**	608-254-2555
Scruggs Company Inc	PO Box 2065	Valdosta	GA	31604	**800-230-7263**	229-242-2388
Staker Parson Cos	2350 South 1900 West	Ogden	UT	84401	**888-672-7766**	801-731-1111
Sukut Construction Inc	4010 W Chandler Ave	Santa Ana	CA	92704	**888-785-8801**	714-540-5351
Sundt Construction Inc	2015 W River Rd Ste 101	Tucson	AZ	85704	**800-467-5544**	520-750-4600
Traylor Bros Inc	835 N Congress Ave	Evansville	IN	47715	**866-895-1491**	812-477-1542
Vecellio & Grogan Inc	2251 Robert C Byrd Dr	Beckley	WV	25802	**800-255-6575**	304-252-6575
Walsh Group Inc	929 W Adams St	Chicago	IL	60607	**800-957-1842**	312-563-5400
Washington Corp	PO Box 16630	Missoula	MT	59808	**800-832-7329**	406-523-1300

190-5 Marine Construction

Company	Address	City	State	ZIP	Toll-Free	Phone
Andrie Inc	561 E Western Ave	Muskegon	MI	49442	**800-722-2421**	231-728-2226
Bellingham Marine Industries Inc	1001 C St	Bellingham	WA	98225	**800-733-5679**	360-676-2800
Corey Delta Inc	4931 Park Rd PO Box 637	Benicia	CA	94510	**800-727-2260**	707-747-7500
Dot-Line Transportation	PO Box 8739	Fountain Valley	CA	92728	**800-423-3780**	323-780-9010
Frontier-Kemper Constructors Inc	1695 Allen Rd	Evansville	IN	47710	**877-554-8600**	812-426-2741
JR Filanc Construction Company Inc	740 N Andreasen Dr	Escondido	CA	92029	**877-225-5428**	760-941-7130
Manson Construction Co	5209 E Marginal Way S	Seattle	WA	98134	**800-262-6766***	206-762-0850
*General						
Norris School District	6940 Calloway Dr	Bakersfield	CA	93312	**800-877-8339**	661-387-7000
Washington Corp	PO Box 16630	Missoula	MT	59808	**800-832-7329**	406-523-1300

190-6 Mining Construction

Company	Address	City	State	ZIP	Toll-Free	Phone
AME Inc	2467 Coltharp Rd	Fort Mill	SC	29715	**800-849-7766**	803-548-7766
Frontier-Kemper Constructors Inc	1695 Allen Rd	Evansville	IN	47710	**877-554-8600**	812-426-2741
Sundt Construction Inc	2015 W River Rd Ste 101	Tucson	AZ	85704	**800-467-5544**	520-750-4600

190-7 Plant Construction

Company	Address	City	State	ZIP	Toll-Free	Phone
Brasfield & Gorrie LLC	3021 Seventh Ave S	Birmingham	AL	35233	**800-239-8017**	205-328-4000
Cajun Constructors Inc	15635 Airline Hwy	Baton Rouge	LA	70817	**877-401-5911**	225-753-5857
Clark Construction Group LLC	7500 Old Georgetown Rd	Bethesda	MD	20814	**800-655-1330**	301-272-8100
Day & Zimmermann Group Inc	1818 Market St	Philadelphia	PA	19130	**877-319-0270**	215-299-8000
Gilbane Bldg Co	Seven Jackson Walkway	Providence	RI	02903	**800-445-2263**	401-456-5800
Gray Construction	10 Quality St	Lexington	KY	40507	**800-814-8468**	859-281-5000
Haskell Co	111 Riverside Ave	Jacksonville	FL	32202	**800-622-4326**	904-791-4500
Hunter Contracting Co	701 N Cooper Rd	Gilbert	AZ	85233	**877-992-0521**	480-892-0521
JF White Contracting Co	10 Burr St	Framingham	MA	01701	**866-539-4400**	508-879-4700
Koch Specialty Plant Services	12221 E Sam Houston Pkwy N	Houston	TX	77044	**800-765-9177**	713-427-7700
Northeast Remsco Construction Inc	1433 Hwy 34 S Bldg B1	Farmingdale	NJ	07727	**800-879-8204**	732-557-6100
Parsons Corp	100 W Walnut St	Pasadena	CA	91124	**800-883-7300***	626-440-2000
*All						
Sargent Corp	378 Bennoch Rd	Stillwater	ME	04489	**800-533-1812**	207-827-4435
Shook Construction	4977 Northcutt Pl	Dayton	OH	45414	**800-664-1844**	937-276-6666
Turner Industries Group LLC	8687 United Plaza Blvd Ste 500	Baton Rouge	LA	70809	**800-288-6503**	225-922-5050
Walsh Group Inc	929 W Adams St	Chicago	IL	60607	**800-957-1842**	312-563-5400
Whiting-Turner Contracting Co	300 E Joppa Rd Eighth Fl	Towson	MD	21286	**800-638-4279**	410-821-1100

190-8 Railroad Construction

Company	Address	City	State	ZIP	Toll-Free	Phone
Atlas Railroad Construction LLC	1370 Washington Pike Ste 202	Bridgeville	PA	15017	**800-829-4059**	412-677-2020
Parsons Corp	100 W Walnut St	Pasadena	CA	91124	**800-883-7300***	626-440-2000
*All						
Swanson Contracting Co	11701 S Mayfield Ave	Alsip	IL	60803	**800-622-6850**	708-388-0623
WE Yoder Inc	41 S Maple St	Kutztown	PA	19530	**800-889-5149**	610-683-7383

190-9 Refinery (Petroleum or Oil) Construction

Company	Address	City	State	ZIP	Toll-Free	Phone
ARB Inc	26000 Commercentre Dr	Lake Forest	CA	92630	**800-622-2699**	949-598-9242
Austin Industrial Inc	2801 E 13th S PO Box 87888	La Porte	TX	77571	**866-308-2592**	713-641-3400
Parsons Corp	100 W Walnut St	Pasadena	CA	91124	**800-883-7300***	626-440-2000
*All						
Turner Industries Group LLC	8687 United Plaza Blvd Ste 500	Baton Rouge	LA	70809	**800-288-6503**	225-922-5050
Underground Construction Company Inc	5145 Industrial Way	Benicia	CA	94510	**800-424-6521**	707-746-8800

190-10 Water & Sewer Lines, Pipelines, Power Lines Construction

Company	Address	City	State	ZIP	Toll-Free	Phone
B Frank Joy LLC	5355 Kilmer Pl	Hyattsville	MD	20781	**800-992-3569**	301-779-9400
BRB Contractors Inc	3805 NW 25th St	Topeka	KS	66618	**800-833-6747**	785-232-1245
Cajun Constructors Inc	15635 Airline Hwy	Baton Rouge	LA	70817	**877-401-5911**	225-753-5857
Elkins Constructors Inc	701 W Adams St	Jacksonville	FL	32204	**800-772-1213**	904-353-6500
Frontier-Kemper Constructors Inc	1695 Allen Rd	Evansville	IN	47710	**877-554-8600**	812-426-2741
Global Industries Ltd	8000 Global Dr	Sulphur	LA	70665	**800-525-3483**	337-583-5000
Henkels & McCoy Inc	985 Jolly Rd	Blue Bell	PA	19422	**800-523-2568**	215-283-7600
Hubbard Construction Co	1936 Lee Rd 3rd Fl	Winter Park	FL	32789	**800-476-1228**	407-645-5500
Insituform Technologies Inc	17988 Edison Ave	Chesterfield	MO	63005	**800-234-2992***	636-530-8000
*Cust Svc						
JF Shea Construction Inc	655 Brea Canyon Rd	Walnut	CA	91789	**888-779-7333**	909-594-9500
JF White Contracting Co	10 Burr St	Framingham	MA	01701	**866-539-4400**	508-879-4700
JR Filanc Construction Company Inc	740 N Andreasen Dr	Escondido	CA	92029	**877-225-5428**	760-941-7130
Koch Specialty Plant Services	12221 E Sam Houston Pkwy N	Houston	TX	77044	**800-765-9177**	713-427-7700
Landmark Structures LP	1665 Harmon Rd	Fort Worth	TX	76177	**800-888-6816**	817-439-8888
Layne	4520 N State Rd 37	Orleans	IN	47452	**855-529-6301***	812-865-3232
*All						
MasTec Inc	800 Douglas Rd 12th Fl	Coral Gables	FL	33134	**800-531-5000**	305-599-1800
NYSE: MTZ						
Mears Group Inc	4500 N Mission Rd	Rosebush	MI	48878	**800-632-7727**	989-433-2929
Michels Corp	817 W Main St	Brownsville	WI	53006	**877-297-8663**	920-583-3132
Miller Pipeline Corp	8850 Crawfordsville Rd	Indianapolis	IN	46234	**800-428-3742**	317-293-0278
Northeast Remsco Construction Inc	1433 Hwy 34 S Bldg B1	Farmingdale	NJ	07727	**800-879-8204**	732-557-6100
Penn Line Service Inc	300 Scottdale Ave	Scottdale	PA	15683	**800-448-9110***	724-887-9110
*All						
Satellite Store	7412 Preston Hwy	Louisville	KY	40219	**800-693-9393**	502-966-0045
Stuart C Irby Co	815 S President St	Jackson	MS	39201	**866-687-4729**	601-960-7346
Underground Construction Company Inc	5145 Industrial Way	Benicia	CA	94510	**800-424-6521**	707-746-8800
URS	7633 E 63rd Pl Ste 500	Tulsa	OK	74133	**800-564-6253**	918-294-3030
Utility Services Inc	400 N Fourth St	Bismarck	ND	58501	**800-638-3278**	701-222-7900
West Valley Construction Company Inc	580 McGlincey Ln	Campbell	CA	95008	**800-588-5510**	

					Toll-Free	Phone

Wharton-Smith Inc
PO Box 471028 . . . . Lake Monroe FL 32747 **888-393-0068*** 407-321-8410
*Help Line

191 CONSTRUCTION - SPECIAL TRADE CONTRACTORS

SEE ALSO Swimming Pools

	Toll-Free	Phone

191-1 Building Equipment Installation or Erection

	Toll-Free	Phone

APi Group Inc Specialty Construction Services Group
1100 Old Hwy 8 NW . . . . New Brighton MN 55112 **800-223-4922**
AWC Commercial Window Coverings Inc
825 Williamson Ave . . . . Fullerton CA 92832 **800-252-2280** 714-879-3880
Aycock LLC
8261 Derry St . . . . Hummelstown PA 17036 **800-772-5066** 717-566-5066
Baltimore Rigging Company Inc, The
8149 Norris Ln PO Box 18401 . . . . Dundalk MD 21222 **800-626-2150** 443-696-4001
Bigge Crane & Rigging Company Inc
10700 Bigge St PO Box 1657 . . . . San Leandro CA 94577 **888-337-2444** 510-638-8100
Columbia Elevator Products Company Inc
380 Horace St . . . . Bridgeport NY 06610 **888-858-1558**
Elward Construction Co
680 Harlan St . . . . Lakewood CO 80214 **800-933-5339** 303-239-6303
James Machine Works LLC
1521 Adams St . . . . Monroe LA 71201 **800-259-6104** 318-322-6104
Schindler Elevator Corp
20 Whippany Rd . . . . Morristown NJ 07960 **800-225-3123** 973-397-6500
W & H Systems Inc
120 Asia Pl . . . . Carlstadt NJ 07072 **800-966-6993** 201-933-7840

191-2 Carpentry & Flooring Contractors

	Toll-Free	Phone

Archadeck
2924 Emerywood Pkwy Ste 101 . . . . Richmond VA 23294 **800-722-4668** 804-353-6999
Associated Floors
32 Morris Ave . . . . Springfield NJ 07081 **800-800-4320**
Carpenter Contractors of America Inc
3900 Ave D NW . . . . Winter Haven FL 33880 **800-959-8806** 863-294-6449
Cincinnati Floor Company Inc
5162 Broerman Ave . . . . Cincinnati OH 45217 **800-886-4501** 513-641-4500
E&K Companies 343 Carol Ln . . . . Elmhurst IL 60126 **800-365-5760** 630-530-9001
Kalman Floor Company Inc
1202 Bergen Pkwy Ste 110 . . . . Evergreen CO 80439 **800-525-7840** 303-674-2290
Meyer & Lundahl
2345 W Lincoln St . . . . Phoenix AZ 85009 **800-264-9286** 602-254-9286
Overhead Door Company of Sacramento Inc
6756 Franklin Blvd . . . . Sacramento CA 95823 **800-929-3667** 916-421-3747
Sundt Construction
2620 S 55th St . . . . Tempe AZ 85282 **800-280-3000** 480-293-3000

191-3 Concrete Contractors

	Toll-Free	Phone

Baker Concrete Construction Inc
900 N Garver Rd . . . . Monroe OH 45050 **800-359-3935** 513-539-4000
Blair Concrete Services
1410-B Diggs Dr . . . . Raleigh NC 27603 **800-815-7395** 919-833-9088
Ceco Concrete Construction LLC
9135 Barton . . . . Overland Park KS 66214 **800-285-1131** 913-362-1855
Culbertson Enterprises Inc (CEI)
600A Snyder Ave . . . . West Chester PA 19382 **800-382-2685** 610-436-6400
Damon G Douglas Co
245 Birchwood Ave . . . . Cranford NJ 07016 **800-724-1759** 908-272-0100
Dywidag Systems International
320 Marmon Dr . . . . Bolingbrook IL 60440 **800-457-7633** 630-739-1100
Hubbard Construction Co
1936 Lee Rd 3rd Fl . . . . Winter Park FL 32789 **800-476-1228** 407-645-5500
Kalman Floor Company Inc
1202 Bergen Pkwy Ste 110 . . . . Evergreen CO 80439 **800-525-7840** 303-674-2290
Larson Contracting Inc
508 West Main St . . . . Lake Mills IA 50450 **800-765-1426** 641-592-5800
Manafort Bros Inc
414 New Britain Ave . . . . Plainville CT 06062 **888-626-2367** 860-229-4853
Musselman & Hall Contractors LLC
4922 E Blue Banks PO Box 300858 . . . . Kansas City MO 64130 **800-257-4255** 816-861-1234
Oldcastle Precast Bldg Systems Div
1401 Trimble Rd . . . . Edgewood MD 21040 **800-523-9144**
Proshot Concrete Inc
4158 Musgrove Dr . . . . Florence AL 35630 **800-633-3141** 256-764-5941
Suncoast Post-Tension LP
509 N Sam Houston Pkwy Ste 400 E . . . . Houston TX 77060 **800-847-8886** 281-668-1840
Weaver-Bailey Contractors Inc
PO Box 60 . . . . El Paso AR 72045 **800-253-3385** 501-796-2301

191-4 Electrical Contractors

	Toll-Free	Phone

A. M. Ortega Construction Inc
10125 Ch Rd . . . . Lakeside CA 92040 **800-909-1988** 619-390-1988
AC Corp
301 Creek Ridge Rd . . . . Greensboro NC 27406 **800-422-7378** 336-273-4472
Althoff Industries Inc
8001 S Rt 31 . . . . Crystal Lake IL 60014 **800-225-2443** 815-455-7000
Anixter Inc
2301 Patriot Blvd . . . . Glenview IL 60026 **800-264-9837** 224-521-8000

Arrow Electric Company Inc
317 Wabasso Ave . . . . Louisville KY 40209 **888-999-5591** 502-367-0141
Aschinger Electric Co
877 Horan Dr PO Box 26322 . . . . Fenton MO 63026 **800-280-4061** 636-343-1211
Athena Engineering Inc
456 E Foothill Blvd . . . . San Dimas CA 91773 **877-777-4778** 909-599-0947
Barth Electric Company Inc
1934 N Illinois St . . . . Indianapolis IN 46202 **800-666-6226** 317-924-6226
Bell Electrical Contractors Inc
128 Millwell Dr . . . . Maryland Heights MO 63043 **800-717-2355** 314-739-7744
Bergelectric Corp
5650 W Centinela Ave . . . . Los Angeles CA 90045 **800-734-2374** 310-337-1377
Brothers Inc
1000 Sussex Blvd . . . . Broomall PA 19008 **866-276-7462** 610-328-0670
Bruce & Merrilees Electric Co
930 Cass St . . . . New Castle PA 16101 **800-652-5560** 724-652-5566
Cache Valley Electric Inc
875 N 1000 W . . . . Logan UT 84321 **888-558-0600** 435-752-6405
Campbell Alliance Group Inc
8045 Arco Corporate Dr Ste 500 . . . . Raleigh NC 27617 **888-297-2001** 919-844-7100
Cleveland Electric Company Inc
1281 Fulton Industrial Blvd NW . . . . Atlanta GA 30336 **800-282-7150** 404-696-4550
Cleveland Group Inc
1281 Fulton Industrial Blvd . . . . Atlanta GA 30336 **800-282-7150** 404-696-4550
Collins Electric Co Inc
53 Second Ave . . . . Chicopee MA 01020 **877-553-2810** 413-592-9221
Custom Cable Industries Inc
3221 Cherry Palm Dr . . . . Tampa FL 33619 **800-552-2232** 813-623-2232
Dynalectric Corp
4462 Corporate Ctr Dr . . . . Los Alamitos CA 90720 **866-890-7794** 714-828-7000
EC Co PO Box 10286 . . . . Portland OR 97296 **800-462-3370** 800-659-3511
EC Ernst Inc
132 Log Canoe Cir . . . . Stevensville MD 21666 **800-683-7770** 301-350-7770
Edwin L Heim Co
1918 Greenwood St . . . . Harrisburg PA 17104 **800-692-7316** 717-233-8711
Electronic Contracting Co
PO Box 29195 . . . . Lincoln NE 68529 **800-366-5320** 402-466-8274
EMCOR Group Inc
301 Merritt 7 Sixth Fl . . . . Norwalk CT 06851 **866-890-7794** 203-849-7800
NYSE: EME
Engineered Protection Systems Inc
750 Front Ave NW Ste 300 . . . . . . Grand Rapids MI 49504 **800-966-9199** 616-459-0281
Gaylor Electric
5770 Castle Creek Pkwy N Dr
Ste 400 . . . . Indianapolis IN 46250 **800-878-0577** 317-843-0577
GEM Inc 6842 Commodore Dr . . . . Walbridge OH 43465 **866-720-2700*** 419-666-6554
*General
Guarantee Electrical Co
3405 Bent Ave . . . . Saint Louis MO 63116 **800-854-4326*** 314-772-5400
*General
Hooper Corp
2030 Pennsylvania Ave . . . . Madison WI 53704 **800-242-8511** 608-249-0451
Industrial Contractors Inc
701 Ch Dr . . . . Bismarck ND 58501 **800-467-3089** 701-258-9908
Industrial Power & Lighting Corp
701 Seneca St Ste 500 . . . . Buffalo NY 14210 **800-639-3702** 716-854-1811
Interstates Construction Services Inc
1520 N Main Ave . . . . Sioux Center IA 51250 **800-827-1662** 712-722-1662
Koontz-Wagner Electric Company Inc
3801 Voorde Dr . . . . South Bend IN 46628 **800-345-2051** 574-232-2051
Merit Electric Company Inc
6520 125th Ave N . . . . Largo FL 33773 **800-330-5945** 727-536-5945
Miller Electric Co
2251 Rosselle St . . . . Jacksonville FL 32204 **877-540-2160*** 904-513-2818
*Sales
MMR Group Inc
15961 Airline Hwy . . . . Baton Rouge LA 70817 **800-880-5090** 225-756-5090
Msf Electric Inc
10455 Fountaingate Dr . . . . Stafford TX 77477 **866-366-7943** 281-494-4700
Muth Electric Inc
1717 N Sanborn PO Box 1400 . . . . Mitchell SD 57301 **800-888-1597** 605-996-3983
Mutual Telecom Services Inc
250 First Ave Ste 301 . . . . Needham MA 02494 **800-687-2884**
Netsville Inc
72 Cascade Dr . . . . Rochester NY 14614 **888-638-7845** 585-232-5670
Network Infrastructure Corp
8945 S Harl Ave Ste 102 . . . . Tempe AZ 85284 **866-456-4422** 480-850-5050
Parsons Electric LLC
5960 Main St NE . . . . Minneapolis MN 55432 **800-403-4832** 763-571-8000
Perreca Electric Co
520 Broadway . . . . Newburgh NY 12550 **800-973-7732** 845-562-4080
Phillips Bros Electrical Contractors Inc
235 Sweet Spring Rd . . . . Glenmoore PA 19343 **800-220-5051** 610-458-8578
Pieper Electric Inc
5070 N 35th St . . . . Milwaukee WI 53209 **800-424-8802** 414-462-7700
Pike Electric Corp
100 Pike Way PO Box 868 . . . . Mount Airy NC 27030 **800-424-7453** 336-789-2171
NYSE: PIKE
R K Electric Inc
42021 Osgood Rd . . . . Fremont CA 94539 **800-400-4418** 510-770-5660
Rex Moore Electrical Contractors & Engineers
6001 Outfall Cir . . . . Sacramento CA 95828 **800-266-1922** 916-372-1300
RFI Communications & Security Systems
360 Turtle Creek Ct . . . . San Jose CA 95125 **800-341-9292** 408-298-5400
Rosendin Electric Inc
880 N Mabury Rd . . . . San Jose CA 95133 **800-540-4734*** 408-286-2800
*General
Shambaugh & Son LP
7614 Opportunity Dr . . . . Fort Wayne IN 46825 **866-890-7794** 260-487-7777
Shawver & Son Inc
144 NE 44th St . . . . Oklahoma City OK 73105 **800-320-5121** 405-525-9451
Southern Air Inc
2655 Lakeside Dr . . . . Lynchburg VA 24501 **800-743-1214** 434-385-6200
Staley Inc
8101 Fourche Rd . . . . Little Rock AR 72209 **877-616-0661** 501-565-3006
Teknon Corp
15443 NE 95th St . . . . Redmond WA 98052 **800-338-6142** 425-895-8535

				Toll-Free	Phone

Tri-City Electrical Contractors Inc
430 W Dr . . . . Altamonte Springs FL 32714 800-768-2489 407-788-3500
Wayne J Griffin Electric Inc
116 Hopping Brook Rd . . . . Holliston MA 01746 800-421-0151
Wellington Power Corp
40th & Butler Sts . . . . Pittsburgh PA 15201 800-540-0017 412-681-0103
Welsbach Electric Corp
111-01 14th Ave . . . . College Point NY 11356 866-890-7794 718-670-7900
White Electrical Construction Co
1730 Chattahoochee Ave . . . . Atlanta GA 30318 888-519-4483 404-351-5740

191-5 Excavation Contractors

				Toll-Free	Phone

BR Kreider & Son Inc
63 Kreider Ln . . . . Manheim PA 17545 800-689-7651 717-898-7651
Dywidag Systems International
320 Marmon Dr . . . . Bolingbrook IL 60440 800-457-7633 630-739-1100
Foundation Constructors Inc
81 Big Break Rd PO Box 97 . . . . Oakley CA 94561 800-841-8740 925-754-6633
Hayward Baker Inc
1130 Annapolis Rd Ste 202 . . . . Odenton MD 21113 800-456-6548 410-551-8200
Independence Excavating Inc
5720 Schaaf Rd . . . . Independence OH 44131 800-524-3478 216-524-1700
J Fletcher Creamer & Son Inc
101 E Broadway . . . . Hackensack NJ 07601 800-835-9801 201-488-9800
Manafort Bros Inc
414 New Britain Ave . . . . Plainville CT 06062 888-626-2367 860-229-4853
Moretrench American Corp
100 Stickle Ave PO Box 316 . . . . Rockaway NJ 07866 800-394-6673 973-627-2100
Nicholson Construction Co
12 McClane St . . . . Cuddy PA 15031 800-388-2340 412-221-4500
Phillips & Jordan Inc
6621 Wilbanks Rd . . . . Knoxville TN 37912 800-955-0876 865-688-8342
Pleasant Excavating Co Inc
24024 Frederick Rd Ste 200 . . . . Clarksburg MD 20871 800-842-1180 301-428-0800
Raymond Excavating Co Inc
800 Gratiot Blvd . . . . Marysville MI 48040 800-837-6770 810-364-6881
Urban Foundation/Engineering LLC
32-33 111th St . . . . East Elmhurst NY 11369 800-843-6664 718-478-3021

191-6 Glass & Glazing Contractors

				Toll-Free	Phone

Benson Industries LLC
1650 NW Naito Pkwy Ste 250 . . . . Portland OR 97209 800-999-5113 503-226-7611
Culbertson Enterprises Inc (CEI)
600A Snyder Ave . . . . West Chester PA 19382 800-382-2685 610-436-6400
Enclos Corp
2770 Blue Water Rd . . . . Eagan MN 55121 888-234-2966 651-796-6100
Giroux Glass Inc
850 W Washington Blvd . . . . Los Angeles CA 90015 800-684-5277 213-747-7406
Karas & Karas Glass Company Inc
455 Dorchester Ave . . . . Boston MA 02127 800-888-1235 617-268-8800
Lee & Cates Glass Inc
5355 Shawland Rd . . . . Jacksonville FL 32254 888-844-1989 904-358-8555
Sashco Inc
720 S Rochester Ave Ste D . . . . Ontario CA 91761 800-600-3232 909-937-8222
Sound Glass Sales Inc
5501 75th St W . . . . Tacoma WA 98499 800-468-9949 253-473-7477

191-7 Masonry & Stone Contractors

				Toll-Free	Phone

Brisk Waterproofing Company Inc
720 Grand Ave . . . . Ridgefield NJ 07657 800-325-2801 201-945-0210
Culbertson Enterprises Inc (CEI)
600A Snyder Ave . . . . West Chester PA 19382 800-382-2685 610-436-6400
Gallegos Corp PO Box 821 . . . . Vail CO 81658 800-425-5346 970-926-3737
International Chimney Corp
55 S Long St . . . . Williamsville NY 14221 800-828-1446
Mid-Continental Restoration Company Inc
401 E Hudson Rd PO Box 429 . . . . Fort Scott KS 66701 800-835-3700 620-223-3700
Ron Kendall Masonry Inc
101 Benoist Farms Rd . . . . West Palm Beach FL 33411 866-844-1404 561-793-5924

191-8 Painting & Paperhanging Contractors

				Toll-Free	Phone

Brock Services LLC
1675 Spindletop Rd . . . . Beaumont TX 77705 800-600-9675 409-833-7571
CertaPro Painters Ltd
150 Green Tree Rd Ste 1003 . . . . Oaks PA 19456 800-689-7271
Hess Sweitzer Inc
2805 S 160th St . . . . New Berlin WI 53151 800-491-4377 262-641-9100
K2 Industrial Services
5233 Hohman Ave . . . . Hammond IN 46320 866-524-6387 219-933-5300
Long Painting Co
21414 68th Ave S . . . . Kent WA 98032 800-678-5664 253-234-8050
Midwest Pro Painting Inc
12845 Farmington Rd . . . . Livonia MI 48150 800-860-6757 734-427-1040
ML McDonald LLC
50 Oakland St PO Box 315 . . . . Watertown MA 02471 800-733-6243 617-923-0900
National Services Group Inc
1682 Langley Ave . . . . Irvine CA 92614 800-394-6000 714-564-7900
TMI Coatings Inc
3291 Terminal Dr . . . . Saint Paul MN 55121 800-328-0229 651-452-6100

191-9 Plastering, Drywall, Acoustical, Insulation Contractors

				Toll-Free	Phone

Acousti Engineering Co of Florida Inc
4656 34th St SW . . . . Orlando FL 32811 800-434-3467 407-425-3467
Allied Construction Services & Color Inc
2122 Fleur Dr PO Box 937 . . . . Des Moines IA 50304 800-365-4855 515-288-4855
APi Construction Co
1100 Old Hwy 8 NW . . . . New Brighton MN 55112 800-223-4922 651-636-4320
Baker Triangle
415 Highway 80 East PO Box 850227 . . . . Mesquite TX 75150 800-458-3480 972-289-5534
BHN Corp 435 Madison Ave . . . . Memphis TN 38103 800-238-9046 901-521-9500
CE Thurston & Sons Inc
3335 Croft St . . . . Norfolk VA 23513 800-444-7713 757-855-7700
Davenport Insulation Inc
7400 Gateway Ct . . . . Manassas VA 20109 855-626-6459 703-631-7744
E&K Companies 343 Carol Ln . . . . Elmhurst IL 60126 800-365-5760 630-530-9001
FL Crane & Sons Inc
508 S Spring St PO Box 428 . . . . Fulton MS 38843 800-748-9523 662-862-2172
Irex Contracting Group
120 N Lime St . . . . Lancaster PA 17608 800-487-7255
KHS & S Contractors Inc
5422 Bay Ctr Dr Ste 200. . . . . Tampa FL 33609 866-991-7277 813-628-9330
Kramig Insulation
323 S Wayne Ave . . . . Cincinnati OH 45215 888-579-0079 513-761-4010
Land Coast Insulation Inc
4017 Second St . . . . New Iberia LA 70560 800-333-9424 337-367-7741
ML McDonald LLC
50 Oakland St PO Box 315 . . . . Watertown MA 02471 800-733-6243 617-923-0900
Precision Walls Inc
1230 NE MaynaRd Rd . . . . Cary NC 27513 800-849-9255 919-832-0380
Western Partitions Inc
8300 SW Hunziker Rd . . . . Tigard OR 97223 800-783-0315 503-620-1600

191-10 Plumbing, Heating, Air Conditioning Contractors

				Toll-Free	Phone

AC Corp
301 Creek Ridge Rd . . . . Greensboro NC 27406 800-422-7378 336-273-4472
ACCO Engineered Systems
6265 San Fernando Rd . . . . Glendale CA 91201 800-998-2226* 818-243-1727
*Cust Svc
Air Comfort Corp
2550 Braga Dr . . . . Broadview IL 60155 800-466-3779 708-345-1900
Aire Serv Heating & Air Conditioning Inc
5387 Texas 6 Fwy Ste 101 . . . . Woodway TX 76712 855-983-0630 254-523-3600
Alaka'i Mechanical Corp
2655 Waiwai Loop . . . . Honolulu HI 96819 800-600-1085 808-834-1085
Allied Fire Protection LP
PO Box 2842 . . . . Pearland TX 77588 800-604-2600 281-485-6803
Allied Mechanical Services Inc
5688 E MI Ave Ste A . . . . Kalamazoo MI 49048 888-237-3017 269-344-0191
Althoff Industries Inc
8001 S Rt 31 . . . . Crystal Lake IL 60014 800-225-2443 815-455-7000
American Residential Services LLC
9010 Maier Rd Ste 105. Laurel MD 20723 866-399-2885 901-271-9700
Armistead Mechanical Inc
168 Hopper Ave . . . . Waldwick NJ 07463 800-587-5267 201-447-6740
B-G Mechanical Service Inc
12 Second Ave . . . . Chicopee MA 01020 800-992-7386 413-888-1500
Baker Group
4224 Hubbell Ave . . . . Des Moines IA 50317 855-262-4000 515-262-4000
Bay Mechanical Inc
2696 Reliance Dr Ste 200 . . . . Virginia Beach VA 23452 888-229-6324 757-468-6700
Beutler Air Conditioning Service
855 National Dr Ste 109 . . . . Sacramento CA 95834 866-559-0108
C & R Mechanical
12825 Pennridge Dr . . . . Bridgeton MO 63044 800-524-3828 314-739-1800
Coastal Mechanical Services LLC
394 E Dr . . . . Melbourne FL 32904 866-584-9528 321-725-3061
Cobb Mechanical Contractors
2906 W Morrison . . . . Colorado Springs CO 80904 800-808-2622* 719-471-8958
*General
ColonialWebb Contractors Co
2820 Ackley Ave . . . . Richmond VA 23228 877-208-3894 804-916-1400
Comfort Systems USA Inc
675 Bering Ste 400. Houston TX 77057 800-723-8431 713-830-9600
NYSE: FIX
DeBra-Kuempel
3976 Southern Ave . . . . Cincinnati OH 45227 800-395-5741 513-271-6500
Dunbar Mechanical Inc
2806 N Reynolds Rd . . . . Toledo OH 43615 800-719-2201 419-537-1900
EMCOR Group Inc
301 Merritt 7 Sixth Fl . . . . Norwalk CT 06851 866-890-7794 203-849-7800
NYSE: EME
Fisher Container Corp
1111 Busch Pkwy . . . . Buffalo Grove IL 60089 800-837-2247 847-541-0000
Fitzgerald Contractors Inc
7103 St Vincent Ave . . . . Shreveport LA 71106 800-259-3264 318-869-3262
Fox Service Co PO Box 19047 . . . . Austin TX 78760 866-668-4749 512-442-6782
Frank Lill & Son Inc
785 Old Dutch Road . . . . Victoriaville NY 14564 800-756-0490 585-265-0490
GEM Inc 6842 Commodore Dr . . . . Walbridge OH 43465 866-720-2700* 419-666-6554
*General
Goyette Mechanical Co
3842 Gorey Ave . . . . Flint MI 48501 877-469-3883 810-743-6883
Grunau Company Inc
1100 W Anderson Ct . . . . Oak Creek WI 53154 800-365-1920 414-216-6900
Harder Mechanical Contractors Inc
2148 NE M L King Blvd . . . . Portland OR 97212 800-392-3729 503-281-1112
Hardy Corp
350 Industrial Dr . . . . Birmingham AL 35211 800-289-4822 205-252-7191
Harold G Butzer Inc
730 Wicker Ln . . . . Jefferson City MO 65109 800-769-1065 573-636-4115

				Toll-Free	Phone

HE Neumann Inc
100 Middle Creek Rd . . . . Triadelphia WV 26059 **800-627-5312** 304-232-3040

Herman Goldner Co Inc
7777 Brewster Ave . . . . Philadelphia PA 19153 **800-355-5997** 215-365-5400

Hooper Corp
2030 Pennsylvania Ave . . . . Madison WI 53704 **800-242-8511** 608-249-0451

Hubbard & Drake General Mechanical Contractors Inc
PO Box 1867 . . . . Decatur AL 35602 **800-353-9245** 256-353-9244

IMCOR-Interstate Mechanical Corp
1841 E Washington St . . . . Phoenix AZ 85034 **800-628-0211** 602-257-1319

Industrial Contractors Inc
701 Ch Dr . . . . Bismarck ND 58501 **800-467-3089** 701-258-9908

Industrial Piping Inc
800 Culp Rd . . . . Pineville NC 28134 **800-951-0988** 704-588-1100

Janazzo Services Corp
140 Norton St Rt 10 PO Box 469 . . . . Milldale CT 06467 **800-297-3931** 860-621-7381

JF Ahern Co
855 Morris St . . . . Fond du Lac WI 54935 **800-532-0155** 920-921-9020

John W Danforth Co
300 Colvin Woods Pkwy . . . . Tonawanda NY 14150 **800-888-6119** 716-832-1940

Kuhlman Inc
N 56 W 16865 Ridgewood Dr . . . . Menomonee Falls WI 53051 **800-781-9229** 262-252-9400

Lee Co Inc
331 Mallory Stn Rd . . . . Franklin TN 37067 **888-567-7747** 615-567-1000

Lutz Frey Corp
1195 Ivy Dr . . . . Lancaster PA 17601 **800-280-6794** 717-898-6808

MacDonald-Miller Facility Solutions Inc
7717 Detroit Ave SE . . . . Seattle WA 98106 **800-962-5979** 206-763-9400

McClure Co
4101 N Sixth St . . . . Harrisburg PA 17110 **800-382-1319** 717-232-9743

McCrea Equipment Company Inc
4463 Beech Rd . . . . Temple Hills MD 20748 **800-597-0091** 301-423-4585

McKenney's Inc
1056 Moreland Industrial Blvd SE . . . . Atlanta GA 30316 **877-440-4204** 404-622-5000

McKinstry Co
5005 Third Ave S . . . . Seattle WA 98134 **800-669-6223** 206-762-3311

Mechanical Inc
2283 US Rt 20 E . . . . Freeport IL 61032 **877-426-6628** 815-235-2200

Midwest Mechanical Group
801 Parkview Blvd . . . . Lombard IL 60148 **800-214-3680** 630-850-2300

Mr Rooter Corp
1010 N University Parks Dr . . . . Waco TX 76707 **877-766-8305** 800-583-8003

Murphy Co Mechanical Contractors & Engineers
1233 N Price Rd . . . . Saint Louis MO 63132 **888-838-4038** 314-997-6600

National HVAC Service Ltd
101 Bradford Rd Ste 340 . . . . Wexford PA 15090 **800-281-3608** 724-935-9390

P1 Group Inc
2151 Haskell Ave Bldg 1 . . . . Lawrence KS 66046 **800-376-2911** 785-843-2910

Pace Mechanical Services Inc
301 Merritt Seven . . . . Norwalk CT 06851 **866-890-7794** 203-849-7800

Performance Contracting Group Inc
16400 College Blvd . . . . Lenexa KS 66219 **800-255-6886** 913-888-8600

Piedmont Mechanical Inc
116 John Dodd Rd . . . . Spartanburg SC 29303 **800-849-5725** 864-578-9114

Postler & Jaeckle Corp
615 S Ave . . . . Rochester NY 14620 **800-724-4252** 585-546-7450

PSF Industries Inc
65 S Horton St . . . . Seattle WA 98134 **800-426-1204*** 206-622-1252
*General

RK Mechanical Inc
3800 Xanthia St . . . . Denver CO 80238 **877-576-9696** 303-355-9696

Roth Bros Inc
PO Box 4209 . . . . Youngstown OH 44515 **800-872-7684** 330-793-5571

Roto-Rooter Inc
255 E Fifth St 2500 Chemed Ctr . . . . Cincinnati OH 45202 **800-768-6911** 513-762-6690

RW Warner Inc
217 Monroe Ave . . . . Frederick MD 21701 **800-854-5387** 301-662-5387

Shambaugh & Son LP
7614 Opportunity Dr . . . . Fort Wayne IN 46825 **866-890-7794** 260-487-7777

Southern Air Inc
2655 Lakeside Dr . . . . Lynchburg VA 24501 **800-743-1214** 434-385-6200

Southern Industrial Constructors Inc
6101 Triangle Dr . . . . Raleigh NC 27617 **866-890-7794** 919-782-4600

Wellington Power Corp
40th & Butler Sts . . . . Pittsburgh PA 15201 **800-540-0017** 412-681-0103

William E Walter Inc
1917 Howard Ave . . . . Flint MI 48503 **800-681-3320** 810-232-7459

Worth & Company Inc
6263 Kellers Church Rd . . . . Pipersville PA 18947 **800-220-5130** 267-362-1100

191-11 Remodeling, Refinishing, Resurfacing Contractors

				Toll-Free	Phone

Bathcrest Inc
5195 W 4700 S . . . . Salt Lake City UT 84118 **800-826-6790** 801-957-1400

California Closet Co
610A DuBois St . . . . San Rafael CA 94901 **888-336-9707*** 415-256-8500
*General

Closet Factory
12800 S Broadway . . . . Los Angeles CA 90061 **800-838-7995** 310-516-7000

DreamMaker Bath & Kitchen by Worldwide
510 N Valley Mills Dr Ste 304 . . . . Waco TX 76710 **800-583-2133**

Handyman Connection Inc
11115 Kenwood Rd . . . . Cincinnati OH 45242 **800-884-2639** 513-771-3003

Kitchen Tune-Up Inc
813 Cir Dr . . . . Aberdeen SD 57401 **800-333-6385** 605-225-4049

Miracle Method US Corp
4239 N Nevada Ave Ste 115 . . . . Colorado Springs CO 80907 **800-444-8827** 719-594-9091

Perma-Glaze Inc
1638 Research Loop Rd Ste 160 . . . . Tucson AZ 85710 **800-332-7397** 520-722-9718

Re-Bath LLC
16879 N 75th Ave Ste 101 . . . . Peoria AZ 85382 **800-426-4573**

191-12 Roofing, Siding, Sheet Metal Contractors

				Toll-Free	Phone

All-South Subcontractors Inc
2678 Queenstown Rd . . . . Birmingham AL 35210 **800-873-8110** 205-836-8111

Baker Roofing Co
517 Mercury St . . . . Raleigh NC 27603 **800-849-4096** 919-828-2975

Beldon Enterprises Inc
PO Box 13380 . . . . San Antonio TX 78213 **800-688-7663** 210-341-3100

Birdair Inc
65 Lawrence Bell Dr . . . . Amherst NY 14221 **800-622-2246** 716-633-9500

Bonland Industries Inc
50 Newark-Pompton Tpke . . . . Wayne NJ 07470 **800-232-6600** 973-694-3211

Brazos Urethane Inc
1031 Sixth St N . . . . Texas City TX 77590 **866-527-2967** 409-965-0011

BT Mancini Co Inc
876 S Milpitas Blvd . . . . Milpitas CA 95035 **800-787-6381** 408-942-7900

Centimark Corp
12 Grandview Cir . . . . Canonsburg PA 15317 **800-558-4100**

Commercial Siding & Maintenance Co, The
8059 Crile Rd . . . . Painesville OH 44077 **800-229-4276** 440-352-7800

DC Taylor Co
312 29th St NE . . . . Cedar Rapids IA 52402 **800-876-6346** 319-363-2073

Dee Cramer Inc
4221 E Baldwin Rd . . . . Holly MI 48442 **888-342-6995** 810-579-5000

Flynn Canada Ltd
1390 Spruce St . . . . Winnipeg MB R3E2V7 **877-856-8566*** 204-786-6951
*General

Heidler Roofing Services Inc
2120 Alpha Dr . . . . York PA 17408 **866-792-3549** 717-792-3549

IG Inc 720 S Sara Rd . . . . Mustang OK 73137 **800-654-8433** 405-376-9393

Jottan Inc PO Box 166 . . . . Florence NJ 08518 **800-364-4234** 609-447-6200

National International Roofing Corp
11317 Smith Dr . . . . Huntley IL 60142 **800-221-7663** 847-669-3444

North American Roofing Services Inc
41 Dogwood Rd . . . . Asheville NC 28806 **800-876-5602** 828-687-7767

Schreiber Corp 29945 Beck Rd . . . . Wixom MI 48393 **800-558-2706** 248-926-1500

Schust Engineering Inc
701 North St . . . . Auburn IN 46706 **800-686-9297**

Standard Roofing Co
516 N McDonough St PO Box 1309 . . . . Montgomery AL 36102 **800-239-5705** 334-265-1262

US Industries Inc
1701 First Ave . . . . Evansville IN 47710 **800-456-8721** 812-425-2428

191-13 Sprinkler System Installation (Fire Sprinklers)

				Toll-Free	Phone

All-South Subcontractors Inc
2678 Queenstown Rd . . . . Birmingham AL 35210 **800-873-8110** 205-836-8111

APi Group Inc Fire Protection Group
1100 Old Hwy 8 NW . . . . New Brighton MN 55112 **800-223-4922**

August Winter & Sons Inc
2323 N Roemer Rd . . . . Appleton WI 54911 **800-236-8882** 920-739-8881

Brendle Sprinkler Co Inc
3635 S Montgomery St . . . . Tacoma WA 98409 **800-392-8021** 334-270-8571

Cosco Fire Protection Inc
1075 W Lambert Rd Bldg D . . . . Brea CA 92821 **800-485-3795** 714-989-1800

JF Ahern Co
855 Morris St . . . . Fond du Lac WI 54935 **800-532-0155** 920-921-9020

National Automatic Sprinkler Industries
8000 Corporate Dr . . . . Landover MD 20785 **800-638-2603** 301-577-1700

SA Comunale Company Inc
2900 Newpark Dr . . . . Barberton OH 44203 **800-776-7181** 330-706-3040

Security Fire Protection Co Inc
4495 Mendenhall Rd S . . . . Memphis TN 38141 **888-274-8595** 901-362-6250

191-14 Structural Steel Erection

				Toll-Free	Phone

Albany Steel Inc
566 Broadway . . . . Albany NY 12204 **800-342-9317** 518-436-4851

CBI Services Inc
24 Read's Way . . . . New Castle DE 19720 **800-642-8675** 302-325-8400

Central Maintenance & Welding Inc (CMW)
2620 E Keysville Rd . . . . Lithia FL 33547 **877-704-7411** 813-737-1402

Century Steel Erectors Co
210 Washington Ave PO Box 490 . . . . Dravosburg PA 15034 **888-601-8801** 412-469-8800

Chicago Bridge & Iron Co
6001 Rogerdale Rd . . . . Houston TX 77072 **866-235-5687*** 713-485-1000
NYSE: CBI ■ *General

Lafayette Steel Erector Inc
313 Westgate Rd . . . . Lafayette LA 70506 **877-234-9435** 337-234-9435

Pittsburg Tank & Tower Co Inc
1 Watertank Pl . . . . Henderson KY 42420 **800-222-5555** 270-826-9000

Schuff Steel Co
420 S 19th Ave . . . . Phoenix AZ 85009 **800-435-8528** 602-252-7787

Waldinger Corp
2601 Bell Ave . . . . Des Moines IA 50321 **800-473-4934** 515-284-1911

WO Grubb Steel Erection Inc
5120 Jefferson Davis Hwy . . . . Richmond VA 23234 **866-964-7822** 804-271-9471

191-15 Water Well Drilling

				Toll-Free	Phone

Alsay Inc 6615 Gant St . . . . Houston TX 77066 **800-833-5969** 281-444-6960

Raba-Kistner Consultants Inc
12821 W Golden Ln . . . . San Antonio TX 78249 **866-722-2547** 210-699-9090

Rosencrantz-Bemis Water Well Co
1105 Hwy 281 Bypass . . . . Great Bend KS 67530 **800-466-2467** 620-793-5512

Tri-State Drilling Inc
16940 Hwy 55 W . . . . Plymouth MN 55446 **800-383-1033** 763-553-1234

191-16 Wrecking & Demolition Contractors

			Toll-Free	Phone
Allied Erecting & Dismantling Company Inc				
2100 Poland Ave	Youngstown OH	44502	800-624-2867	330-744-0808
Bierlein Cos Inc				
2000 Bay City Rd	Midland MI	48642	800-336-6626	989-496-0066
Cherry Demolition				
6131 Selinsky Rd	Houston TX	77048	800-444-1123	713-987-0000
Ferma Corp				
1265 Montecito Ave	Mountain View CA	94043	877-337-6211	650-961-2742
Kipin Industries Inc				
4194 Green Garden Rd	Aliquippa PA	15001	800-782-8050	724-495-6200
Manafort Bros Inc				
414 New Britain Ave	Plainville CT	06062	888-626-2367	860-229-4853
NCM 404 N Berry St	Brea CA	92821	800-283-2933	714-672-3500
O'Rourke Wrecking Co				
660 Lunken Pk Dr	Cincinnati OH	45226	800-354-9850	513-871-1400
Patuxent Cos				
2124 Priest Bridge Dr Ste 18	Crofton MD	21114	800-628-4942	410-793-0181

192 CONSTRUCTION MACHINERY & EQUIPMENT

SEE ALSO Industrial Machinery, Equipment, & Supplies ; Material Handling Equipment

			Toll-Free	Phone
Allied Construction Products LLC				
3900 Kelley Ave	Cleveland OH	44114	800-321-1046*	216-431-2600
*Cust Svc				
Atlantic Construction Fabrics Inc				
2831 CaRdwell Rd	Richmond VA	23234	800-448-3636	804-271-2363
Bandit Industries Inc				
6750 W Millbrook Rd	Remus MI	49340	800-952-0178	989-561-2270
Barnhart Crane & Rigging Co				
1701 Dunn Ave	Memphis TN	38106	800-727-0149	901-775-3000
Bay Shore Systems Inc				
14206 N Ohio St	Rathdrum ID	83858	888-569-3745	208-687-3311
Bid-Well Corp PO Box 97	Canton SD	57013	800-843-9824	
Boart Longyear Co				
2640 W 1700 S	Salt Lake City UT	84104	800-453-8740	801-972-6430
Bomag Americas Inc				
2000 Kentville Rd	Kewanee IL	61443	800-782-6624	309-853-3571
Caron Compactor Co				
1204 Ullrey Ave	Escalon CA	95320	800-542-2766	209-838-2062
Cemen Tech Inc				
1700 N 14th St	Indianola IA	50125	800-247-2464	515-961-7407
Central Mine Equipment Company Inc				
4215 Rider Trl N	Earth City MO	63045	800-325-8827	314-291-7700
Centurion Industries Inc				
1107 N Taylor Rd	Garrett IN	46738	888-832-4466	260-357-6665
Charles Machine Works Inc				
PO Box 66	Perry OK	73077	800-654-6481*	580-336-4402
*Cust Svc				
CRC Evans Pipeline International Inc				
10700 E Independence St	Tulsa OK	74116	800-664-9224	918-438-2100
Demag Cranes & Components				
29201 Aurora Rd	Solon OH	44139	866-920-3000	440-248-2400
ED Etnyre & Co				
1333 S Daysville Rd	Oregon IL	61061	800-995-2116	815-732-2116
Esco Corp 2141 NW 25th Ave	Portland OR	97210	800-523-3795	503-228-2141
F&M Mafco Inc				
PO Box 11013	Cincinnati OH	45211	800-333-2151	513-367-2151
Gencor Industries Inc				
5201 N Orange Blossom Trail	Orlando FL	32810	888-887-1266*	407-290-6000
NASDAQ: GENC *General				
H & E Equipment Services Inc				
11100 Mead Rd	Baton Rouge LA	70809	866-467-3682	225-298-5200
NASDAQ: HEES				
Hensley Industries Inc				
2108 Joe Field Rd PO Box 29779	Dallas TX	75229	888-406-6262	972-241-2321
Hunter Heavy Equipment Inc				
2829 Texas Ave	Texas City TX	77590	800-562-7368	409-945-2382
Inquipco				
2730 N Nellis Blvd	Las Vegas NV	89115	800-598-3465	702-644-1700
JH Fletcher & Co Inc				
402 High St	Huntington WV	25705	800-327-6203	304-525-7811
Kor-it Inc				
2442 Rice Ave	West Sacramento CA	95691	888-727-4560	
Liebherr-America Inc				
4100 Chestnut Ave	Newport News VA	23607	866-879-6312	757-245-5251
McLellan Equipment Inc				
251 Shaw Rd	South San Francisco CA	94080	800-848-8449	650-873-8100
Midwestern Industries Inc				
915 Oberlin Rd SW	Massillon OH	44647	877-474-9464*	330-837-4203
*Cust Svc				
Mr Crane Inc				
647 N Hariton St	Orange CA	92868	800-672-7263	714-633-2100
Pengo Corp 500 E Hwy 10	Laurens IA	50554	800-599-0211*	712-845-2540
*Cust Svc				
Pierce Pacific Manufacturing Inc				
4424 NE 158th Pl PO Box 30509	Portland OR	97294	800-760-3270	503-808-9110
Putzmeister America				
1733 90th St	Sturtevant WI	53177	800-553-3414	
Ramsey Winch Company Inc				
1600 N Garnett Rd	Tulsa OK	74116	800-777-2760	918-438-2760
Reco Equipment Inc				
41245 Reco Rd	Belmont OH	41245	800-686-7326	740-782-1314
RKI Inc 2301 Central Pkwy	Houston TX	77092	800-346-8988	713-688-4414
Roadtec Inc				
800 Manufacturers Rd				
PO Box 180515	Chattanooga TN	37405	800-272-7100	423-265-0600
Robertson Transformer Co				
13611 Thornton Rd	Blue Island IL	60406	800-323-5633	708-388-2315

			Toll-Free	Phone
Simco Drilling Equipment Inc				
PO Box 448	Osceola IA	50213	855-222-8570	641-342-2166
Superwinch Inc 359 Lake Rd	Dayville CT	06241	800-323-2031	860-928-7787
Swenson Spreader Co				
127 Walnut St	Lindenwood IL	61049	888-825-7323	815-393-4455
Varel International				
1625 W Crosby Dr Ste 124	Carrollton TX	75006	800-827-3526	972-242-1160
Wacker Neuson				
N 92 W 15000 Anthony Ave	Menomonee Falls WI	53051	800-770-0957	262-255-0500
Web Equipment				
464 Central Rd	Fredericksburg VA	22401	800-225-3858	540-657-5855
Xcaliber LP 5051 Fm 2920	Spring TX	77388	866-620-8586	281-219-8100
Young Corp 3231 Utah Ave S	Seattle WA	98134	800-321-9090	206-624-1071

193 CONSTRUCTION MATERIALS

SEE ALSO Home Improvement Centers

193-1 Brick, Stone, Related Materials

			Toll-Free	Phone
AHI Supply Inc				
PO Box 884	Friendswood TX	77549	800-873-5794	281-331-0088
All Tile Inc				
1201 Chase Ave	Elk Grove Village IL	60007	877-255-8453	847-979-2500
Atlas Construction Supply Inc				
4640 Brinnell St	San Diego CA	92111	877-588-2100	858-277-2100
Bierschbach Equipment & Supply Co				
PO Box 1444	Sioux Falls SD	57101	800-843-3707	605-332-4466
Century Roof Tile				
23135 Saklan Rd	Hayward CA	94545	888-233-7548	510-780-9489
FAYBLOCK Materials Inc				
130 Builders Blvd	Fayetteville NC	28302	800-326-9198	910-323-9198
Foundation Technologies Inc				
1400 Progress Industrial Blvd	Lawrenceville GA	30043	800-773-2368	678-407-4640
Fullen Dock & Warehouse Inc				
382 Klinke Rd	Memphis TN	38127	800-467-7104	901-358-9544
Graniterock Co				
350 Technology Dr PO Box 50001	Watsonville CA	95077	888-762-5100	831-768-2000
Henry Products Inc				
302 S 23rd Ave	Phoenix AZ	85009	800-525-5533	602-253-3191
In-O-Vate Technologies Inc				
810 Saturn St Ste 21	Jupiter FL	33477	888-443-7937	561-743-8696
Jaeckle Wholesale Inc				
4101 Owl Creek Dr	Madison WI	53718	800-236-7225	608-838-5400
Kobrin Builders Supply Inc				
1924 W Princeton St	Orlando FL	32804	800-273-5511	407-843-1000
L Thorn Co Inc				
6000 Grant Line Rd PO Box 198	New Albany IN	47150	800-662-4594	812-246-4461
Lyman-Richey Corp				
4315 Cuming St	Omaha NE	68131	800-727-8432	402-558-2727
Vimco Inc				
300 Hansen Access Rd	King Of Prussia PA	19406	888-468-4626*	610-768-0500
*Cust Svc				

193-2 Construction Materials (Misc)

			Toll-Free	Phone
Acoustical Material Services Inc				
1620 S Maple Ave	Montebello CA	90640	888-531-1416	323-721-9011
Alliance Wood Group Engineering LP				
330 Barker Cypress Rd	Houston TX	77094	866-313-0052	281-828-6000
American Fence Inc				
2502 N 27th Ave	Phoenix AZ	85009	888-691-4565	602-272-2333
APi Group Inc Materials Distribution Group				
1100 Old Hwy 8 NW	New Brighton MN	55112	800-223-4922	
Arabel Inc				
16301 NW 49th Ave	Hialeah FL	33014	800-759-5959*	305-623-8302
*Sales				
Basic Components Inc				
1201 S Second Ave	Mansfield TX	76063	800-452-1780	817-473-7224
Chemung Supply Corp				
PO Box 527	Elmira NY	14903	800-733-5508	607-733-5506
CR Laurence Company Inc				
2503 E Vernon Ave PO Box 58923	Los Angeles CA	90058	800-421-6144	323-588-1281
DS Brown Co				
300 E Cherry St	North Baltimore OH	45872	800-848-1730	419-257-3561
Empire Bldg Materials Inc				
PO Box 220	Bozeman MT	59771	800-332-4577	800-548-8201
Gossen /Corp				
2030 W Bender Rd	Milwaukee WI	53209	800-558-8984	414-228-9800
J O Galloup Co				
135 Manufacturers Dr	Holland MI	49424	888-755-3110	269-965-4005
Kuriyama of America Inc				
360 E State Pkwy	Schaumburg IL	60173	800-800-0320	847-755-0360
Penrod Co				
2809 S Lynnhaven Rd Ste 350	Virginia Beach VA	23452	800-537-3497	757-498-0186
Robert N Karpp Company Inc				
480 E First St	Boston MA	02127	800-244-5886	617-269-5880
Star Sales & Distributing Corp				
29 Commerce Way	Woburn MA	01801	800-222-8118	781-933-8830

193-3 Lumber & Building Supplies

			Toll-Free	Phone
84 Lumber Co				
1019 Rt 519	Eighty Four PA	15330	800-664-1984	724-228-8820
Alamo Lumber Co				
10800 Sentinel Dr	San Antonio TX	78217	855-828-9792	210-352-1300
Allied Bldg Products Corp				
15 E Union Ave	East Rutherford NJ	07073	800-541-2198	201-507-8400

Company / Address	City	State	Zip	Toll-Free	Phone
Alpine Lumber Co 1120 W 122nd Ave Ste 301	Denver	CO	80234	**800-499-1634**	303-451-8001
American International Forest Products LLC (AIFP) 5560 SW 107th Ave	Beaverton	OR	97005	**800-366-1611**	503-641-1611
Arnold Lumber Co 251 Fairgrounds Rd	West Kingston	RI	02892	**800-339-0116**	401-783-2266
Auburn Corp 10490 164th Pl	Orland Park	IL	60467	**800-393-1826**	
Babcock Lumber Company Inc 2220 Palmer St PO Box 8348	Pittsburgh	PA	15218	**800-553-4441**	412-351-3515
Baille Lumber Co 4002 Legion Dr PO Box 6	Hamburg	NY	14075	**800-950-2850**	716-649-2850
Banner Supply Co 7195 NW 30th St	Miami	FL	33122	**888-511-4004**	305-593-2946
Beavertooth Oak Inc 401 S Fir St	Medford	OR	97501	**800-306-1942**	541-779-1942
Big C Lumber Inc 50860 Princess Way PO Box 176	Granger	IN	46530	**888-297-0010**	574-277-4550
Birmingham International Forest Products LLC 300 Riverhills Business Pk	Birmingham	AL	35242	**800-767-2437**	205-972-1500
Boise Cascade Bldg Materials Distribution Div 1111 W Jefferson Ste 300 PO Box 50	Boise	ID	83728	**800-367-4611**	208-384-7700
Britton Lumber Company Inc Seven Ely Rd PO Box 389	Fairlee	VT	05045	**800-343-5300**	802-333-4388
Buckeye Pacific LLC 4386 SW Macadam Ave Ste 200	Portland	OR	97207	**800-767-9191**	503-274-2284
Builders General Supply Co 15 Sycamore Ave	Little Silver	NJ	07739	**800-570-7227**	
Causeway Lumber Co 3318 SW Second Ave	Fort Lauderdale	FL	33315	**800-375-5050**	954-763-1224
Chelsea Lumber Co One Old Barn Cir	Chelsea	MI	48118	**800-875-9126**	734-475-9126
Chicago Lumber Company of Omaha, The 1324 Pierce St PO Box 3487	Omaha	NE	68103	**800-642-8210**	402-342-0840
Cleary Millwork Company Inc 235 Dividend Rd	Rocky Hill	CT	06067	**800-486-7600**	860-721-0520
Counter Pro Inc 210 Lincoln St	Manchester	NH	03103	**800-899-2444**	603-647-2444
Coventry Lumber Inc 2030 Nooseneck Hill Rd	Coventry	RI	02816	**800-390-0919**	401-821-2800
Creative Pultrusions Inc 214 Industrial Ln	Alum Bank	PA	15521	**888-274-7855**	814-839-4186
Doka USA Ltd 214 Gates Rd	Little Ferry	NJ	07643	**877-365-2872**	201-329-7839
Door Systems Inc PO Box 511	Framingham	MA	01704	**800-545-3667**	508-875-3508
Forest City Trading Group LLC 10250 SW Greenburg Rd Ste 200 PO Box 4209	Portland	OR	97223	**800-767-3284**	503-246-8500
Foxworth-Galbraith Lumber Co 4965 Preston Pk Blvd Ste 400	Plano	TX	75093	**800-688-8082**	972-665-2400
Frank Paxton Lumber Co 7455 Dawson Rd	Cincinnati	OH	45243	**800-325-9800**	513-984-8200
Guardian Building Products (GBPD) 979 Batesville Rd	Greer	SC	29651	**800-569-4262**	864-297-6101
Hawaii Planing Mill Ltd (HPM) 16-166 Melekahiwa St	Keaau	HI	96749	**877-841-7633**	808-966-5693
Holt & Bugbee Co 1600 Shawsheen St	Tewksbury	MA	01876	**800-325-6010**	978-851-7201
Howard Lumber Co 475 Columbia Industrial Blvd PO Box 1039	Evans	GA	30809	**800-868-3227**	706-868-8400
Hutchison Inc 7460 Hwy 85 PO Box 1158	Adams City	CO	80022	**800-525-0121**	303-287-2826
Huttig Bldg Products Inc (HBP) 555 Maryville University Dr Ste 400 *OTC: HBPI*	Saint Louis	MO	63141	**800-325-4466**	314-216-2600
Idaho Pacific Lumber Co (IdaPac) 7255 Franklin Rd	Boise	ID	83709	**800-231-2310**	208-375-8052
Jb Wholesale Roofing & Bldg Supplies Inc 21524 Nordhoff St PO Box 5289 *General	Chatsworth	CA	91311	**800-464-2461***	818-998-0440
Jewett-Cameron Trading Company Ltd 32275 NW Hillcrest PO Box 1010 *NASDAQ: JCTCF*	North Plains	OR	97133	**800-547-5877**	503-647-0110
Kleet Lumber Company Inc 777 Pk Ave	Huntington	NY	11743	**800-696-5533**	631-427-7060
Magnolia Forest Products Inc 13252 I- 55 S PO Box 99	Terry	MS	39170	**800-366-6374**	
Matheus Lumber Company Inc 15800 Woodinville-Redmond Rd NE PO Box 2260	Woodinville	WA	98072	**800-284-7501**	425-489-3000
Mead Clark Lumber Co Hearn Ave & Dowd Dr PO Box 529	Santa Rosa	CA	95402	**800-585-9663**	707-576-3333
MID-AM Bldg Supply Inc 1615 Omar Bradley Dr PO Box 645	Moberly	MO	65270	**800-892-5850**	660-263-2140
Millard Lumber Inc 12900 I St PO Box 45445	Omaha	NE	68145	**800-228-9260**	402-896-2800
National Industrial Lumber Co 1 Chicago Ave	Elizabeth	PA	15037	**800-289-9352**	
Ohio Valley Supply Co 3512 Spring Grove Ave	Cincinnati	OH	45223	**800-696-5608**	513-681-8300
Omega Products International 1681 California Ave	Corona	CA	92881	**800-600-6634**	951-737-7447
Pacific Source Inc PO Box 2323	Woodinville	WA	98072	**888-343-1515**	
Palmer-Donavin Manufacturing Co 1200 Steelwood Rd	Columbus	OH	43212	**800-589-4412**	614-486-9657
Parker Lumber Co of Port Arthur Inc 2948 Gulfway Dr	Port Arthur	TX	77642	**855-828-9792**	409-983-2745
Parksite Inc 1563 Hubbard Ave	Batavia	IL	60510	**800-338-3355**	630-761-9490
Pyramid Interiors Distributors Inc PO Box 181058	Memphis	TN	38181	**800-456-0592**	901-375-4197
Quality Plywood Specialties Inc 4500 110th Ave N	Clearwater	FL	33762	**888-722-1181**	727-572-0500
Raymond Bldg Supply Corp 7751 Bayshore Rd	North Fort Myers	FL	33917	**877-731-7272**	239-731-8300
Reliable Wholesale Lumber Inc 7600 Redondo Cir	Huntington Beach	CA	92648	**877-795-4638**	714-848-8222
Richmond International Forest Products Inc 4050 Innslake Dr Ste 100	Glen Allen	VA	23060	**800-767-0111**	804-747-0111
Riverhead Bldg Supply Corp 1093 Pulaski St	Riverhead	NY	11901	**800-378-3650**	631-727-3650
Riverside Forest Products Inc 2912 Professional Pkwy	Augusta	GA	30907	**888-855-8733**	706-855-5500
Russin Lumber Corp 21 Leonards Dr	Montgomery	NY	12549	**800-724-0010**	845-457-4000
Seaboard International Forest Products LLC 22F Cotton Rd Ste F	Nashua	NH	03063	**800-669-6800**	603-881-3700
Service Construction Supply Inc PO Box 13405	Birmingham	AL	35202	**866-729-4968**	205-252-3158
Solar Industries Inc PO Box 27337	Tucson	AZ	85726	**800-449-2323**	520-519-8258
Spellman Hardwoods Inc 4645 N 43rd Ave	Phoenix	AZ	85031	**800-624-5401**	602-272-2313
Stan's Lumber Inc 226 E Main St	Twin Lakes	WI	53181	**800-535-2890**	262-877-2181
Stock Bldg Supply 8020 Arco Corporate Dr	Raleigh	NC	27617	**877-734-6365**	919-431-1000
Timber Products Co 305 S Fourth St PO Box 269	Springfield	OR	97477	**800-547-9520**	541-747-4577
Tri-state Forest Products Inc 2105 Sheridan Ave	Springfield	OH	45505	**800-949-6325**	937-323-6325
Verhalen Inc 500 Pilgrim Way PO Box 11968	Green Bay	WI	54304	**800-895-0071**	920-431-8900
Viking Forest Products LLC 7615 Smetana Ln	Eden Prairie	MN	55344	**800-733-3801**	952-941-6512
Western Lumber Cy LLC 2240 Tower E Ste 200	Medford	OR	97504	**800-633-5554**	541-779-5121
Wheeler Lumber LLC 9330 James Ave S	Bloomington	MN	55431	**800-328-3986**	952-929-7854
White Cap Industries Inc 1723 S Ritchie St	Santa Ana	CA	92705	**800-944-8322**	714-258-3300
Window Rama Enterprises Inc 71 Heartland Blvd	Edgewood	NY	11717	**800-897-7262**	800-695-7262

193-4 Roofing, Siding, Insulation Materials

Company / Address	City	State	Zip	Toll-Free	Phone
ABC Seamless 3001 Fiechtner Dr	Fargo	ND	58103	**800-732-6577**	701-293-5952
ABC Supply Company Inc One ABC Pkwy	Beloit	WI	53511	**888-492-1047**	608-362-7777
Beacon Roofing Supply Inc One Lakeland Pk Dr *NASDAQ: BECN*	Peabody	MA	01960	**877-645-7663**	978-535-7668
Carlisle Cos Inc 13925 Ballantyne Corporate Pl Ste 400 *NYSE: CSL*	Charlotte	NC	28277	**800-248-5995**	704-501-1100
Carlisle SynTec 1285 Ritner Hwy PO Box 7000	Carlisle	PA	17013	**800-479-6832**	717-245-7000
Crane Composites Inc 23525 W Eames St	Channahon	IL	60410	**800-435-0080**	815-467-8600
EJ Bartells Co 700 Powell Ave SW PO Box 4160	Renton	WA	98057	**800-468-9528**	425-228-4111
Frank Roberts & Sons Inc 1130 Robertsville Rd	Punxsutawney	PA	15767	**800-262-8955**	814-938-5000
General Insulation Company Inc 278 Mystic Ave Ste 209	Medford	MA	02155	**800-442-6662**	781-391-2070
Harvey Industries Inc 1400 Main St	Waltham	MA	02451	**800-598-5400**	
Howred Corp 7887 San Felipe St Ste 122	Houston	TX	77063	**800-535-5053**	713-781-3980
James Hardie Bldg Products 26300 La Alameda Ave Ste 400	Mission Viejo	CA	92691	**888-542-7343**	949-348-1800
Lansing Bldg Products 8501 Sanford Dr	Richmond	VA	23228	**800-768-5762**	804-266-8771
MacArthur Co 2400 Wycliff St	Saint Paul	MN	55114	**800-777-7507**	651-646-2773
McClure-Johnston Co 201 Corey Ave	Braddock	PA	15104	**800-232-0018**	412-351-4300
Norandex Bldg Materials Distribution Inc 300 Executive Pkwy W Ste 100	Hudson	OH	44236	**800-528-0942**	
North Carolina Foam Industries Inc 1515 Carter St	Mount Airy	NC	27030	**800-346-8229**	336-789-9161
Oberfields LLC 1165 Alum Creek Dr	Columbus	OH	43209	**800-845-7644**	614-252-0955
Olympia Tile International Inc 1000 Lawrence Ave W	Toronto	ON	M6A1C6	**800-268-1613**	416-785-6666
Onduline North America Inc 4900 Ondura Dr	Fredericksburg	VA	22407	**800-777-7663**	540-898-7000
Philadelphia Reserve Supply Co 200 Mack Dr	Croydon	PA	19021	**800-347-7726**	215-785-3141
Plastatech Engineering Ltd 725 Morley Dr	Saginaw	MI	48601	**800-892-9358**	989-754-6500
Roofing Wholesale Co Inc 1918 W Grant St *Cust Svc	Phoenix	AZ	85009	**800-528-4532***	602-258-3794
SG Wholesale Roofing Supplies Inc 1101 E Sixth St *Cust Svc	Santa Ana	CA	92701	**888-747-8500***	714-568-1906
Shook & Fletcher Insulation Co 4625 Valleydale Rd	Birmingham	AL	35242	**888-829-2575**	205-991-7606
Spec Bldg Materials Inc 4300 W Ave	San Antonio	TX	78213	**800-588-3892**	210-342-2727
Specialty Products & Insulation Co (SPI) 1650 Manheim Pk Ste 202	Lancaster	PA	17601	**800-788-7764**	717-569-3900
Variform Inc 5020 Weston Pkwy Ste 400	Cary	NC	27513	**800-800-2244**	888-975-9436
Wesco Cedar Inc PO Box 520	Creswell	OR	97426	**800-547-2511**	541-688-5020

194   CONSULTING SERVICES - ENVIRONMENTAL

SEE ALSO Remediation Services ; Waste Management ; Recyclable Materials Recovery

				Toll-Free	Phone
Ameresco Inc 111 Speen St Ste 410	Framingham	MA	01701	866-263-7372	508-661-2200
ATC Assoc Inc 104 E 25th St 10th Fl	New York	NY	10010	800-476-5886	212-353-8280
Badger Express LLC 181 Quality Ct	Fall River	WI	53932	800-972-0084	920-484-5808
Blade Energy Partners Ltd 2600 Network Blvd Ste 550	Frisco	TX	75034	800-849-1545	972-712-8407
Blue Pillar Inc 9025 N River Rd Ste 150	Indianapolis	IN	46240	888-234-3212	
Caravan Facilities Management LLC 1400 Weiss St	Saginaw	MI	48602	855-211-7450	
Clark Pest Control Inc 555 N Guild Ave	Lodi	CA	95240	877-918-9988	
Climate Registry, The 523 W Sixth St Ste 445	Los Angeles	CA	90014	866-523-0764	
Compaction Technologies Inc 1171 Northland Dr Ste 121	Mendota Heights	MN	55120	877-860-6900	
Earth Systems Services Inc 895 Aerovista Pl Ste 102	San Luis Obispo	CA	93401	866-781-0112	805-781-0112
Environmental & Safety Designs Inc 5724 Summer Trees Dr	Memphis	TN	38134	800-588-7962	901-372-7962
Fauske & Assoc LLC 16w070 83rd St	Burr Ridge	IL	60527	877-328-7531	630-323-8750
First Environment Inc 91 Fulton St	Boonton	NJ	07005	800-486-5869	973-334-0003
Gilman & Pastor LLP 63 Atlantic Ave Third Fl	Boston	MA	02110	877-428-7374	617-742-9700
Glacial Energy 2701 N Dallas Pkwy Ste 120	Plano	TX	75093	877-569-2841	
Heath Consultants Inc 9030 Monroe Rd	Houston	TX	77061	800-432-8487	713-844-1300
Karbone Inc 130 W 42nd St 9th Fl	New York	NY	10036	800-728-2056	646-291-2900
Kemron Environmental Services Inc 8521 Leesburg Pike Ste 175	Vienna	VA	22182	888-429-3516	703-893-4106
Los Alamos Technical Assoc Inc 999 Central Ave Ste 300	Los Alamos	NM	87544	800-888-1745	505-662-9080
Medallion Laboratories 9000 Plymouth Ave N	Minneapolis	MN	55427	800-245-5615	763-764-4453
Micah Group 389 Waller Ave Ste 210	Lexington	KY	40504	877-260-7760	859-260-7760
MPS Group Inc 2920 Scotten St	Detroit	MI	48210	800-741-8779	313-841-7588
Mwh Global Inc 380 Interlocken Crescent Ste 200	Broomfield	CO	80021	866-257-5984	303-533-1900
Navarro Research & Engineering Inc 669 Emory Valley Rd	Oak Ridge	TN	37830	866-681-5265	865-220-9650
Neo Corp 289 Silkwood Dr	Canton	NC	28716	800-822-1247	
Next Step Living Inc 21 Drydock Ave Second Fl	Boston	MA	02210	866-867-8729	
Ontario Clean Water Agency 1 Yonge St	Toronto	ON	M5E1E5	800-515-2759	416-314-5600
P E La Moreaux & Assoc Inc PO Box 2310	Tuscaloosa	AL	35403	800-682-6338	205-752-5543
Parsons Infrastructure & Technology 100 W Walnut St	Pasadena	CA	91124	800-300-0287	626-440-4000
Partner Assessment Corp 2154 Torrance Blvd Ste 200	Torrance	CA	90501	800-419-4923	
Perma-Fix Environmental Services Inc 8302 Dunwoody Pl Ste 250	Atlanta	GA	30350	800-365-6066	770-587-9898
NASDAQ: PESI					
PSC 5151 San Felipe Ste 1100	Houston	TX	77056	800-726-1300	
R E I Consultants Inc PO Box 286	Beaver	WV	25813	800-999-0105	304-255-2500
Regreen Inc 2928 N Main St	Los Angeles	CA	90031	855-573-4733	
RJN Group Inc 200 W Front St	Wheaton	IL	60187	800-227-7838	630-682-4700
S & ME Inc 3201 Spring Forest Rd	Raleigh	NC	27616	800-849-2517*	919-872-2660
*Cust Svc					
Source Intelligence LLC 1921 Palomar Oaks Way Ste 205	Carlsbad	CA	92008	877-916-6337	
Spherix Inc 6430 Rockledge Dr Ste 503	Bethesda	MD	20817	855-816-0624	301-897-2540
NASDAQ: SPEX					
Sullivan International Group Inc 2750 Womble Rd	San Diego	CA	92106	888-744-1432	619-260-1432
SWCA Inc 3033 N Central Ave Ste 145	Phoenix	AZ	85012	800-828-8517	602-274-3831
Tetra Tech EC Inc 1000 the American Rd	Morris Plains	NJ	07950	800-580-3765	973-630-8000
TRC Cos Inc 21 Griffin Rd N	Windsor	CT	06095	800-365-8254	860-298-9692
U.S. Facilities Inc 30 N 41 St Ste 400	Philadelphia	PA	19104	800-236-6241	
Utility Service Company Inc 535 Courtney Hodges Blvd	Perry	GA	31069	855-526-4413	478-987-0303
Vertex Engineering Services Inc 400 Libbey Pkwy	Weymouth	MA	02189	888-298-5162	781-952-6000
Vivint Solar Inc 4931 North 300 West	Provo	UT	84604	877-404-4129	
Western Technologies Inc 3737 E Broadway Rd	Phoenix	AZ	85040	800-580-3737	602-437-3737
Zerowait Corp 707 Kirkwood Hwy	Wilmington	DE	19805	888-811-0808	302-996-9408

195   CONSULTING SERVICES - HUMAN RESOURCES

SEE ALSO Professional Employer Organizations (PEOs)

				Toll-Free	Phone
ACRT Inc 1333 Home Ave	Akron	OH	44310	800-622-2562	330-945-7500
Alliance For Employee Growth & Development Inc, The 80 Cottontail Ln Ste 320	Somerset	NJ	08873	800-323-3436	
Alpine Access Inc 1120 Lincoln St Ste 1400	Denver	CO	80203	866-279-0585*	303-279-0585
*General					
Arthur J Gallagher & Co 2 Pierce Pl	Itasca	IL	60143	888-285-5106	630-773-3800
NYSE: AJG					
Ashtead Technology Inc 19407 Pk Row Ste 170	Houston	TX	77084	800-242-3910	281-398-9533
B. E. Smith Inc 9777 Ridge Dr	Lenexa	KS	66219	800-467-9117	
Benz Communications LLC 209 Mississippi St	San Francisco	CA	94107	888-550-5251	
Carnow Conibear & Assoc Ltd 600 W Van Buren Ste 500	Chicago	IL	60607	800-860-4486	312-782-4486
Clark Consulting 2100 Ross Ave	Dallas	TX	75201	800-999-3125	214-871-8717
Collaborative Consulting LLC 70 BlanchaRd Rd Ste 500	Burlington	MA	01803	877-376-9900	781-565-2600
Development Dimensions International 1225 Washington Pike	Bridgeville	PA	15017	800-933-4463*	412-257-0600
*Mktg					
Floyd Browne Group 3875 Embassy Parkway	Akron	OH	44333	800-325-7647*	330-375-0800
*General					
FPMI Solutions Inc 1033 N Fairfax St Ste 200	Alexandria	VA	22314	888-644-3764	
Gabriel Roeder Smith & Co 1 Towne Sq Ste 800	Southfield	MI	48076	800-521-0498	248-799-9000
Geomet Technologies LLC 20251 Century Blvd	Germantown	MD	20874	877-407-8033	301-428-9898
Globe Consultants Inc 3112 Porter St Ste D	Soquel	CA	95073	800-208-0663	
Goodwill Industries of Akron Ohio Inc, The 570 E Waterloo Rd	Akron	OH	44319	800-989-8428	330-724-6995
Hanley Wood Market Intelligence 555 Anton Blvd Ste 950	Costa Mesa	CA	92626	800-938-8839	714-540-8500
Hay Group Inc 1650 Arch St Ste 2300	Philadelphia	PA	19107	800-716-4429	215-861-2000
Huthwaite Inc 901 N Glebe Rd Ste 200	Arlington	VA	22203	800-851-3842	703-467-3800
Insight 444 Scott Dr	Bloomingdale	IL	60108	800-467-4448	
Insight Global Inc (IGI) 4170 Ashford Dunwoody Rd Ste 580	Atlanta	GA	30319	888-336-7463	404-257-7900
ITR Group Inc 2520 Lexington Ave S Ste 500	Saint Paul	MN	55120	866-290-3423	
Lee Hecht Harrison LLC 50 Tice Blvd	Woodcliff Lake	NJ	07677	800-611-4544	
LifeCourse Associates Inc 9080 Eaton Park Rd	Great Falls	VA	22066	866-537-4999	
Mercer LLC 400 W Market St	Louisville	KY	40202	800-333-3070	502-561-4500
Michael C. Fina Corporate Sales 3301 Hunters Point Ave	Long Island City	NY	11101	800-999-3462	
Modern Management Inc 253 Commerce Dr Ste 105	Grayslake	IL	60030	800-323-1331	847-945-7400
National Ctr for Retirement Benefits Inc 666 Dundee Rd Ste 1200	Northbrook	IL	60062	800-666-1000	
Pembrooke Occupational Health Inc 2307 N Parham Rd	Richmond	VA	23229	888-378-4832	804-346-1010
Personnel Decisions International Corp 33 S Sixth St Ste 4900	Minneapolis	MN	55402	800-344-2415	612-339-0927
Quantus Software 32-62 Scurfield Blvd	Winnipeg	MB	R3Y1M5	866-478-1308	
Ricklin-Echikson Assoc 374 Millburn Ave	Millburn	NJ	07041	800-544-2317	973-376-2020
Right Management Consultants Inc 1818 Market St 33rd Fl	Philadelphia	PA	19103	800-237-4448	215-988-1588
Roux Assoc Inc 209 Shafter St	Islandia	NY	11749	800-322-7689	631-232-2600
Runzheimer International Runzheimer Pk	Rochester	WI	53167	800-558-1702	262-971-2200
Stanley Hunt DuPree & Rhine Inc (SHDR) 7701 Airport Ctr Dr	Greensboro	NC	27409	888-999-4701	800-768-4873
Superior Environmental Corp 1128 Franklin Ct	Marne	MI	49435	877-667-4142	616-667-4000
Total Resource Management Inc 510 King St Ste 300	Alexandria	VA	22314	877-548-5100	703-548-4285

196   CONSULTING SERVICES - MANAGEMENT

SEE ALSO Management Services ; Association Management Companies

				Toll-Free	Phone
1secureaudit LLC 1600 Tysons Blvd Fl 8	Mc Lean	VA	22102	800-321-0706	703-245-3020
360 Solutions LLC 2114 Austin Ave	Waco	TX	76701	877-755-7888	254-755-7000
A C e International Company Inc 85 Independence Dr	Taunton	MA	02780	800-223-4685	508-884-9600
Abba Technologies Inc 1501 San Pedro Dr NE	Albuquerque	NM	87110	888-222-2832	505-889-3337
Advancement LLC 32200 Solon Rd	Solon	OH	44139	866-364-3370	440-248-8550
Advantage Performance Group Inc 700 Larkspur Landing Cir	Larkspur	CA	94939	800-494-6646	415-925-6832
Advisory Board Co, The 2445 M St NW	Washington	DC	20037	800-784-8669	202-266-5600
NASDAQ: ABCO					

	Toll-Free	Phone
AFC Industries Inc		
13-16 133rd Pl ....College Point NY 11356	800-663-3412	718-747-0237
Affiliated Power Purchasers International LLC		
224 Phillip Morris Dr Ste 402.............Salisbury MD 21804	800-520-6685	
Affinitas Corp		
1015 N 98th St Ste 100 ....Omaha NE 68114	800-369-6495	402-505-5000
Airbus North America Holdings		
198 Van Buren St Ste 300.............Herndon VA 20170	888-340-2375	703-834-3400
Allant Group Inc, The		
2056 Westings Ave Ste 500.............Naperville IL 60563	800-367-7311	
Allsup Inc 300 Allsup Pl ....Belleville IL 62223	800-854-1418	
Alpha & Omega Financial Management Consultants Inc		
8580 La Mesa Blvd Ste 100 ....La Mesa CA 91942	800-755-5060	
Alpine Innovations		
275 North 950 East ....Lehi UT 84043	866-489-6788	801-766-4994
Altair Customer Intelligence		
341 Cool Springs Blvd Ste 450 ....Franklin TN 37067	800-241-6631	615-468-6938
Altair Engineering Inc		
1820 E Big Beaver Rd ....Troy MI 48083	888-222-7822	248-614-2400
Altman Weil Inc		
PO Box 625 ....Newtown Square PA 19073	866-886-3600	610-359-9900
Altoros Systems		
830 Stewart Dr Ste 119.............Sunnyvale CA 94085	855-258-6767	650-395-7002
Ami Adini & Assoc Inc		
4609 Russell Ave ....Los Angeles CA 90027	888-400-4260	323-913-4073
Amino Transport Inc		
223 NE Loop 820 Ste 101.............Hurst TX 76053	800-304-3360	
Anchor QEA LLC		
720 Olive Way Ste 1900 ....Seattle WA 98101	800-887-8681	206-287-9130
Artifex Technology Consulting Inc		
614 George Washington Hwy ....Lincoln RI 02865	888-278-4339	401-723-6644
Asset Based Lending Consultant		
1641 NW 71st Ter ....Hollywood FL 33024	800-861-5711	954-962-0099
Audio Advisor		
3427 Kraft Ave SE ....Grand Rapids MI 49512	800-942-0220	616-254-8870
Austin Ribbon & Computer Supplies Inc (ARC)		
9211 Waterford Centre Blvd Ste 202.............Austin TX 78758	800-783-7459	512-452-0651
Axiom Resource Management Inc		
5203 Leesburg Pk Ste 300 ....Falls Church VA 22041	800-566-9305	703-208-3000
Beacon Assoc Inc		
900-A S Main St Ste 102 ....Bel Air MD 21014	877-846-5046	410-638-7279
Becker''s ASC Review		
77 Wacker ....Chicago IL 60611	800-417-2035	312-750-6016
Behavioral Science Technology Inc		
417 Bryant Cir ....Ojai CA 93023	800-548-5781	805-646-0166
Benemax Inc		
Seven W Mill St ....Medfield MA 02052	800-528-1530	
Berkeley Communications Corp		
1321 67th St ....Emeryville CA 94608	877-237-5266	510-644-1599
BIA Financial Network Inc		
15120 Enterprise Ct ....Chantilly VA 20151	800-331-5086	703-818-2425
Blaine Tech Services Inc		
1680 Rogers Ave ....San Jose CA 95112	800-545-7558	408-573-0555
Blanton & Assoc Inc		
5 Lakeway Centre Ct Ste 200 ....Austin TX 78734	888-863-5881	512-264-1095
Bonanza Trade & Supply		
6853 Lankershim Blvd ....North Hollywood CA 91605	888-965-6577	818-765-6577
Boomer Consulting		
610 Humboldt St ....Manhattan KS 66502	800-739-9998	785-537-2358
Booz Allen Hamilton Inc		
8283 Greensboro Dr ....McLean VA 22102	866-390-3908	703-902-5000
Brakke Consulting Inc		
2735 Villa Creek Ste 140 ....Dallas TX 75234	877-399-6354	972-243-4033
BTS USA Inc		
300 Stamford Pl Ste 425...............Stamford CT 06902	800-445-7089	203-316-2740
Bucher & Christian Consulting Inc		
10 W Market St Ste 1300 ....Indianapolis IN 46204	866-363-1132	317-423-8980
Building Performance Institute Inc		
107 Hermes Rd Ste 110 ....Malta NY 12020	877-274-1274	518-899-2727
Burchfield Group Inc, The		
1295 Northland Dr Ste 350...............St Paul MN 55120	800-778-1359	651-389-5640
Business Resource Group (BRG)		
10440 N Central Expy Ste 1150 ....Dallas TX 75231	888-391-9166	214-777-5100
Callisto Integration		
635 Fourth Line Ste 16...............Oakville ON L6L5B3	800-387-0467	905-339-0059
Calnet Inc		
12359 Sunrise Vly Dr Ste 270...............Reston VA 20191	877-322-5638*	703-547-6800
*General		
CartwrightDownes Inc		
950 Lee St Ste 110 ....Des Plaines IL 60016	800-323-2049	847-685-2700
Cascade Financial Management Inc		
950 17th St Ste 950 ....Denver CO 80202	800-353-0008	
Ceeva Inc		
643 First Ave Ste 300 ....Pittsburgh PA 15219	866-233-8248	412-690-2300
Cenergistic Inc		
5950 Sherry Ln Ste 900 ....Dallas TX 75225	888-782-7937	214-346-5950
Century Health Solutions Inc		
2951 SW Woodside Dr ....Topeka KS 66614	800-227-0089	785-233-1816
Cgn & Assoc Inc		
415 SW Washington St ....Peoria IL 61602	888-746-4246	309-495-2100
ChaCha Search Inc		
14550 Clay Terr Blvd Ste 130...............Carmel IN 46032	800-224-2242	317-660-6680
Champion College Services Inc		
4600 S Mill Ave Ste 180...............Tempe AZ 85282	800-761-7376	480-947-7375
Cipher Systems LLC		
2661 Riva Rd Ste 1000...............Annapolis MD 21401	888-899-1523	410-412-3326
Circadian Technologies Inc		
Two Main St Ste 310...............Stoneham MA 02180	800-284-5001	781-439-6300
Communispond Inc		
12 Barns Ln ....East Hampton NY 11937	800-529-5925	631-907-8010
Compensation Resources Inc		
310 Rt 17 N ....Upper Saddle River NJ 07458	877-934-0505	201-934-0505
Comprehensive Pharmacy Services Inc (CPS)		
6409 N Quail Hollow Rd ....Memphis TN 38120	800-968-6962	901-748-0470
Condor Earth Technologies Inc		
PO Box 3905 ....Sonora CA 95370	800-800-0490	209-532-0361
Contract Land Staff LLC		
2245 Texas Dr Ste 200 ....Sugar Land TX 77479	800-874-4519	281-240-3370

	Toll-Free	Phone
CoreTech		
660 American Ave ....King of Prussia PA 19406	800-220-3337	
Cornerstone Systems Inc		
3250 Players Club Pkwy ....Memphis TN 38125	855-288-7720	901-842-0660
Corporate Executive Board Co		
1919 N Lynn St ....Arlington VA 22209	866-913-2632	571-303-3000
NYSE: CEB		
D Hilton Assoc Inc		
9450 Grogans Mill Rd ....Spring TX 77380	800-367-0433	281-292-5088
Davies Consulting Inc		
6935 Wisconsin Ave Ste 600 ....Chevy Chase MD 20815	800-811-8336	301-652-4535
Dell		
8270 Willow Oaks Corporate Dr Ste 300 ....Fairfax VA 22031	877-219-6982	703-289-8000
Diversified Lenders Inc		
5607 S Ave Q ....Lubbock TX 79412	800-288-3024	
DM Transportation Management Services Inc		
PO Box 621 ....Boyertown PA 19512	888-399-0162	610-367-0162
DME-Direct Inc		
28486 Westinghouse Pl Ste 120.............Valencia CA 91355	877-721-7701	
ECG Management Consultants Inc		
1111 Third Ave Ste 2700 ....Seattle WA 98101	800-729-7635	206-689-2200
Echo Global Logistics Inc		
600 W Chicago Ave Ste 725 ....Chicago IL 60654	800-354-7993	
Ehlers & Assoc Inc		
3060 Centre Pointe Dr ....Roseville MN 55113	800-552-1171	651-697-8500
EnerVision Inc		
4170 Ashford Dunwoody Rd Ste 550 ....Atlanta GA 30319	888-999-8840	678-510-2900
England Logistics Inc		
1325 South 4700 West ....Salt Lake City UT 84104	800-848-7810	801-656-4500
ExaDigm Inc		
2871 Pullman St ....Santa Ana CA 92705	800-933-0064	949-486-0320
Faulk & Winkler LLC		
6811 Jefferson Hwy ....Baton Rouge LA 70806	800-927-6811	225-927-6811
First Niagara RISK Management		
1215 Manor Dr ....Mechanicsburg PA 17055	800-421-0004	717-795-8666
Fisher & Arnold Inc		
9180 Crestwyn Hills Dr ....Memphis TN 38125	888-583-9724	901-748-1811
Flex-Pay Business Services Inc		
723 Coliseum Dr Ste 200 ....Winston-Salem NC 27106	800-457-2143	336-773-0128
Fluor Corp		
6700 Las Colinas Blvd ....Irving TX 75039	800-405-6637	469-398-7000
FMI Corp		
5171 Glenwood Ave Ste 200.............Raleigh NC 27612	800-669-1364*	919-787-8400
*General		
Franchoice Inc		
7500 Flying Cloud Dr ....Eden Prairie MN 55344	877-396-4238	952-345-8400
Front Runner Consulting LLC		
6850 O'Bannon Bluff ....Loveland OH 45140	877-328-3360	513-697-6850
Fusion Solutions Inc		
16901 N Dallas Pkwy Ste 114.............Dallas TX 75001	888-817-1951	972-764-1708
Geneva Capital LLC		
522 Broadway St Ste 4 ....Alexandria MN 56308	800-408-9352	
Genex Services Inc		
440 E Swedesford Rd Ste 1000.............Wayne PA 19087	888-464-3639	610-964-5100
Greenwich Assoc LLC		
6 High Ridge Pk ....Stamford CT 06905	800-704-1027	203-629-1200
Hay Group Inc		
1650 Arch St Ste 2300 ....Philadelphia PA 19107	800-716-4429	215-861-2000
Healthforce Partners Inc		
18323 Bothell Everett Hwy ....Bothell WA 98012	877-437-2497	425-806-5700
Human Resource Development Press Inc		
22 Amherst Rd ....Amherst MA 01002	800-822-2801	413-253-3488
IBT Enterprises LLC		
1770 Indian Trail Rd Ste 300 ....Norcross GA 30093	877-242-8428	770-381-2023
Inca Engineers Inc		
400 112th Ave NE Ste 400 ....Bellevue WA 98004	800-825-4622	425-635-1000
Irvine Technology Corp		
201 E Sandpointe Ave Ste 300 ....Santa Ana CA 92707	866-322-4482	
iWay Software Two Penn Plz ....New York NY 10121	800-736-6130	212-736-4433
Kepner-Tregoe Inc		
PO Box 704 ....Princeton NJ 08542	800-537-6378	609-921-2806
Keystone Equities Group, The		
1003 B Egypt Rd ....Oaks PA 19456	800-715-9905	610-415-6300
Keystone Fruit Marketing Inc		
11 N Carlisle St Ste 102		
PO Box 189...............Greencastle PA 17225	800-779-1156	717-597-2112
Kipp Foundation		
135 Main St Ste 1700...............San Francisco CA 94105	866-345-5477	415-399-1556
Kline & Company Inc		
150 Clove Rd Seventh Fl ....Little Falls NJ 07424	800-290-5214	973-435-6262
Knight Electronics Inc		
10557 Metric Dr ....Dallas TX 75243	800-323-2439	214-340-0265
Lamont Engineers		
548 Main St ....Cobleskill NY 12043	800-882-9721	518-234-4028
LEK Consulting		
28 State St 16th Fl ....Boston MA 02109	800-929-4535	617-951-9500
Lewin Group		
3130 Fairview Pk Dr Ste 800 ....Falls Church VA 22042	877-227-5042	703-269-5500
Lynda.com Inc		
6410 Via Real ....Carpinteria CA 93013	888-335-9632	805-477-3900
M Floyd John & Assoc Inc (JMFA)		
125 N Burnett Dr ....Baytown TX 77520	800-809-2307	
Marsh Berry & Company Inc		
4420 Sherwin Rd ....Willoughby OH 44094	800-426-2774	440-354-3230
Marshall & Stevens Inc		
355 S Grand Ave Ste 1750 ....Los Angeles CA 90071	800-950-9588	213-612-8000
MAXIMUS Inc		
11419 Sunset Hills Rd ....Reston VA 20190	800-629-4687	703-251-8500
NYSE: MMS		
MBL International Corp		
Four H Constitution Way ....Woburn MA 01801	800-200-5459	781-939-6964
McBee Assoc Inc		
997 Old Eagle School Rd Ste 205.............Wayne PA 19087	800-767-6203	610-964-9680
Medical Doctor Assoc Inc		
145 Technology Pkwy NW ....Norcross GA 30092	800-780-3500	770-246-9191
Medifit Corporate Services Inc		
25 Hanover Rd ....Florham Park NJ 07932	888-723-6334	973-593-9000

				Toll-Free	Phone

MilesTek Corp
1506 Interstate 35 W .... Denton TX 76207 **800-958-5173** 940-484-9400

Mitsubishi Power Systems Inc
100 Colonial Ctr Pkwy .... Lake Mary FL 32746 **800-445-9723** 407-688-6201

Monroe Financial Partners Inc
100 N Riverside Plz Ste 1620 .... Chicago IL 60606 **800-766-5560** 312-327-2530

Morley Company Inc
2717 Schust .... Saginaw MI 48603 **800-323-1492** 989-791-2565

Motivano Inc
5810 W Cypress St Ste H .... Tampa FL 33607 **866-664-4621**

Muzea Insider Consulting Services LLC
1575 Delucchi Ln Ste 204 .... Reno NV 89502 **866-642-6427** 775-850-9480

Mx Group, The
7020 High Grove Blvd .... Burr Ridge IL 60527 **800-827-0170**

Mzinga
10 Burlington Mall Rd Ste 111 .... Burlington MA 01803 **888-694-6428**

Navigant Consulting Inc
30 S Wacker Dr Ste 3100 .... Chicago IL 60606 **888-461-9425** 312-583-5700
NYSE: NCI

Navitaire Inc
333 S Seventh St Ste 500 .... Minneapolis MN 55402 **877-216-6787** 612-317-7000

Neace Lukens Inc
2305 River Rd .... Louisville KY 40206 **888-499-8092** 502-894-2100

Network Innovations Inc
4424 Manilla Rd SE ....Calgary AB T2G4B7 **888-466-2772** 403-287-5000

North Central Pennsylvania Regional Planning & Development Commission
651 Montmorenci Rd .... Ridgway PA 15853 **800-942-9467** 814-773-3162

Novotus LLC
5508 Parkcrest Dr Ste 100 ....Austin TX 78731 **800-856-0143** 512-733-2244

Organizational Dynamics Inc
790 Boston Rd Ste 201 .... Billerica MA 01821 **800-634-4636** 978-671-5454

Orion Mobility LLC
4 Mountainview Terrace Ste 101 .... Danbury CT 06810 **800-476-7787** 203-762-0365

Pacrim Hospitality Services Inc
30 Damascus Rd ....Bedford NS B4A0C1 **877-680-7666** 902-404-7474

Palladium Group Inc
55 Old Bedford Rd Ste 100 .... Lincoln MA 01773 **800-773-2399** 781-259-3737

Penske Vehicle Services Inc
1225 E Maple Rd .... Troy MI 48083 **877-210-5290** 248-729-5400

Philip Crosby Assoc
306 Dartmouth St .... Boston MA 02116 **877-276-7295**

Pinnacle Management Systems Inc
8500 North Stemmons Freeway Ste 6010.....Dallas TX 75247 **888-975-1119** 703-382-9161

Pinnacle Performance Improvement Worldwide (PPIW)
101 Main St .... Pepperell MA 01463 **800-368-3408** 978-925-9797

Pragmatek Consulting Group
8500 Normandale Lake Blvd
Ste 1060 ....Bloomington MN 55437 **800-833-3164** 612-333-3164

Presidio Group Inc, The
5295 South 300 West Ste 550 .... Salt Lake City UT 84107 **800-924-1404** 801-924-1400

Press Ganey Associates Inc
404 Columbia Pl ....South Bend IN 46601 **800-232-8032**

Pritchett LLC
13355 Noel Rd Ste 1650......................Dallas TX 75240 **800-992-5922** 214-239-9600

Professional Bank Services Inc
6200 Dutchmans Ln Ste 305 .... Louisville KY 40205 **800-523-4778** 502-451-6633

Professional Research Consultants Inc
11326 P St .... Omaha NE 68137 **800-428-7455** 402-592-5656

Program Planning Professionals
1340 Eisenhower Pl ....Ann Arbor MI 48108 **877-728-2331** 734-741-7770

Progressive Mktg Products Inc
3130 E Miraloma Ave .... Anaheim CA 92806 **800-368-9700** 714-632-7100

Protected Investors of America Inc
235 Montgomery St Ste 1050.......San Francisco CA 94104 **800-786-2559**

Public Consulting Group Inc
148 State St .... Boston MA 02109 **800-210-6113**

Quadel Consulting
1200 G St NW Ste 700 .... Washington DC 20005 **866-640-1019** 202-789-2500

Rath & Strong Inc
1666 Massachusetts Ave PO Box 170 ...... Lexington MA 02420 **800-622-2025** 781-861-1700

Revere Group, The
325 N LaSalle Ste 325 .... Chicago IL 60654 **800-745-3263** 312-873-3400

RHR International LLP
233 S Wacker Dr 95th Fl..................... Chicago IL 60606 **800-892-4496** 312-924-0800

Robert E Nolan Company Inc
92 Hopmeadow St .... Weatogue CT 06089 **800-653-1941** 860-658-1941

Robert Half Management Resources (RHIMR)
2884 Sand Hill Rd Ste 200 .... Menlo Park CA 94025 **888-400-7474** 650-234-6000

Robson Forensic Inc
354 N Prince St .... Lancaster PA 17603 **800-813-6736** 717-293-9050

Rose Displays Ltd
35 Congress St .... Salem MA 01970 **800-631-9707** 978-219-8100

Sandy Corp
300 E Big Beaver Rd Ste 500 .... Troy MI 48083 **866-876-0606** 248-729-4628

Sapient Corp
131 Dartmouth St 3rd Fl................... Boston MA 02116 **866-796-6860** 617-621-0200
NASDAQ: SAPE

Scott Madden & Assoc Inc
2626 Glenwood Ave Ste 480.................Raleigh NC 27608 **800-321-9774** 919-781-4191

Secova Inc
5000 Birch St W Tower Ste 1400 .... Newport Beach CA 92660 **800-257-0011** 714-384-0530

Selling Source LLC
325 E Warm Springs Rd Ste 200 .... Las Vegas NV 89119 **800-251-6147** 702-407-0707

Sirius Solution LLC
1233 W Loop S .... Houston TX 77027 **800-585-1085** 713-888-0488

Spectrum Financial System Inc
163 McKenzie Rd .... Mooresville NC 28115 **800-525-0555** 704-663-4466

Ssci 3065 Kent Ave .... West Lafayette IN 47906 **800-375-2179** 765-463-0112

Stewart Environmental Consultants LLC
3801 Automation Way Ste 200 .... Fort Collins CO 80525 **800-373-1348** 970-226-5500

Stratosphere Multimedia LLC
551 Madison Ave Seventh Fl .... New York NY 10022 **888-212-0700** 212-702-0700

Tbm Consulting Group Inc
4400 Ben Franklin Blvd .... Durham NC 27704 **866-532-6826** 919-471-5535

Tech Usa Inc
8334 Veterans Hwy .... Millersville MD 21108 **888-584-8181** 410-729-4328

Tele-Measurements Inc
145 Main Ave .... Clifton NJ 07014 **800-223-0052** 973-473-8822

				Toll-Free	Phone

Termnet Merchant Services Inc
1601 Dodge St Ste 1600...................... Omaha NE 68102 **800-228-2443**

Thomson ISI ResearchSoft
2141 Palomar Airport Rd Ste 350.........Carlsbad CA 92009 **800-722-1227** 760-438-5526

Thyssen Krupp Hearn
59 I- Dr ....Wentzville MO 63385 **877-854-7178** 636-332-1772

Tom McCall & Assoc Inc
20180 Governors Hwy Ste 100........... Olympia Fields IL 60461 **800-715-5474** 708-747-5707

Tompkins International
6870 Perry Creek Rd .... Raleigh NC 27616 **800-789-1257** 919-876-3667

Travelclick
Seven Times Sq 38th Fl .... New York NY 10036 **866-674-4549** 212-817-4800

Urban Science
400 Renaissance Ctr Ste 2900 .... Detroit MI 48243 **800-321-6900** 313-259-9900

Verity International Ltd
200 King St W Ste 1301 ....Toronto ON M5H3T4 **877-623-2396** 416-862-8422

Washington Group Consultants LLC
PO Box A .... Fairfax VA 22031 **800-236-7323** 703-591-6600

Watermark Learning Inc
7300 Metro Blvd Ste 207 .... Minneapolis MN 55439 **800-646-9362** 952-921-0900

Welocalize Inc
241 E Fourth St Ste 207 .... Frederick MD 21701 **800-370-9515** 301-668-0330

West Monroe Partners LLC
222 W Adams St .... Chicago IL 60606 **800-828-6708** 312-602-4000

Westcare Management Inc
3155 River Rd S Ste 100................... Salem OR 97302 **800-541-3732**

WorkCare.com
300 S Harbor Blvd Ste 600 .... Anaheim CA 92805 **800-455-6155**

197   CONSULTING SERVICES - MARKETING

				Toll-Free	Phone

220 Marketing
3405 Kenyon St Ste 501 ....San Diego CA 92110 **877-220-6584**

7Summits LLC
1110 Old World Third St Ste 500 .... Milwaukee WI 53203 **866-705-6372**

Acosta Sales & Marketing Co
665 W N Ave Ste 300 ....Lombard IL 60148 **888-281-9810*** 630-620-7600
*General

Advisors Excel LLC
1300 SW Arrowhead Rd Ste 200............ Topeka KS 66604 **866-363-9595**

AIS RealTime
4440 Bowen Blvd SE .... Grand Rapids MI 49508 **877-314-1100**

Bellomy Research Inc
175 Sunnynoll Ct .... Winston Salem NC 27106 **800-443-7344**

Beverage Marketing Corp
850 Third Ave 18th Fl .... New York NY 10022 **800-275-4630** 212-688-7640

Boomers & Beyond Inc
1998 Ruffin Mill Rd ....Colonial Heights VA 23834 **800-958-8324** 804-524-9888

Campus Special LLC, The
3575 Koger Blvd Ste 300 .... Duluth GA 30096 **800-365-8520**

ComNet Marketing Group Inc
1214 Stowe Ave .... Medford OR 97501 **877-581-2565**

ComStar Networks LLC
1820 NE Jensen Beach Blvd
Ste 564.....................Jensen Beach FL 34957 **800-516-1595**

Crossmark Inc 5100 Legacy Dr .... Plano TX 75024 **877-699-6275** 469-814-1000

Dane Media LLC
385 Sylvan Ave Ste 24 .... Englewood Cliffs NJ 07632 **888-233-2863**

DCI Marketing Inc
2727 W Good Hope Rd .... Milwaukee WI 53209 **800-778-4805** 414-228-7000

Eclipse Marketing Services Inc
490 Headquarters Plz
N Tower 10th Fl...............Morristown NJ 07960 **800-837-4648**

eGumBall Inc
8687 Research Dr Ste 200 .... Irvine CA 92618 **800-890-8940**

Eze Castle Integration Inc
260 Franklin St 12th Fl...................... Boston MA 02110 **800-752-1382** 617-217-3000

Faith Popcorn's BrainReserve
885 Second Ave
16th Fl 1 Dad Hammarskjold Plz...... New York NY 10017 **800-873-6337** 212-772-7778

Fulcrum Analytics Inc
70 W 40th St 10th Fl .... New York NY 10018 **888-245-9450** 212-651-7000

Gannett Offset
7950 Jones Branch Dr .... McLean VA 22107 **800-255-1457** 703-750-8673

Great Falls Marketing LLC
121 Mill St .... Auburn ME 04210 **800-221-8895**

Harte-Hanks Market Intelligence
9980 Huennekens St ....San Diego CA 92121 **800-854-8409**

Hcpro Inc
75 Sylvan St Ste A-10. .... Danvers MA 01923 **800-650-6787**

Hunter Business Group LLC
4650 N Port Washington Rd .... Milwaukee WI 53212 **800-423-4010** 414-203-8060

Innotrac Corp
6465 E Johns Crossing ....Johns Creek GA 30097 **800-322-2885** 678-584-4000
NASDAQ: INOC

Khong Guan Corp
30068 Eigenbrodt Way .... Union City CA 94587 **877-889-8968** 510-487-7800

Landor Assoc Ltd
1001 Front St ....San Francisco CA 94111 **888-252-6367** 415-365-1700

LocBox
400 Second St Ste 400 ....San Francisco CA 94107 **855-256-2269**

MarketBridge Inc
4350 East-West Hwy Sixth Fl...........Bethesda MD 20814 **888-468-6658** 240-752-1800

MarketingProfs LLC
419 N Larchmont Blvd #295 .... Los Angeles CA 90004 **866-557-9625**

Missouri Enterprise
1706 E 10th St ....Rolla MO 65401 **800-956-2682**

Netmark.com
1930 N Woodruff Ave .... Idaho Falls ID 83401 **800-935-5133**

Netsertive Inc
2400 Perimeter Park Dr
Ste 100.........Research Triangle Region NC 27560 **800-940-4351**

Omgeo LLC 55 Thomson Pl .... Boston MA 02210 **866-496-6436**

			Toll-Free	Phone
PDI Inc				
300 Interpace Pkwy				
Morris Corp Ctr 1 Bldg A	Parsippany NJ	07054	**800-242-7494**	
NASDAQ: PDII				
Pedowitz Group, The				
810 Mayfield Rd	Milton GA	30009	**855-738-6584**	
Printfection LLC				
3700 Quebec St Unit 100-136	Denver CO	80207	**866-459-7990**	
Sales Readiness Group Inc				
8015 SE 28th St Ste 206	Mercer Island WA	98040	**800-490-0715**	
Sound Impressions Music Marketing L.L.C				
14290 Gillis Rd Ste A	Dallas TX	75244	**888-512-9119**	
Suarez Corp Industries				
7800 Whipple Ave NW	North Canton OH	44720	**800-764-0008**	330-494-5504
Suss Consulting				
801 Old York Rd Noble Plz Ste 305	Jenkintown PA	19046	**888-984-5900**	215-884-5900
Symbolist 1090 Texan Trl	Grapevine TX	76051	**800-498-6885**	
TASC Technical Services LLC				
73 Newton Rd	Plaistow NH	03865	**877-304-8272**	
Technical Communities Inc				
1000 Cherry Ave Ste 100	San Bruno CA	94066	**888-665-2765**	650-624-0525
Thobe Group Inc				
2727 Raintree Dr	Carrollton TX	75006	**888-462-3477**	972-245-9444
United Marketing Group LLC				
929 N Plum Grove Rd	Schaumburg IL	60173	**800-513-7000**	847-240-2005
VeraData.com LLC				
7680 Cambridge Manor Pl Ste 200	Fort Myers FL	33907	**800-561-9927**	
ViewCentral				
900 E Hamilton Ave	Campbell CA	95008	**800-631-1545**	408-626-3800
OTC: RMKR				
WSI Internet				
5580 Explorer Dr Ste 600	Mississauga ON	L4W4Y1	**888-678-7588**	905-678-7588

198   CONSULTING SERVICES - TELECOMMUNICATIONS

			Toll-Free	Phone
Ajilon Communications				
970 Peachtree Industrial Blvd Ste 200	Suwanee GA	30024	**800-843-6910**	678-482-5103
Atrion Networking Corp				
30 Service Ave	Warwick RI	02886	**800-890-4526**	401-736-6400
Benefitvision Inc				
4522 RFD	Long Grove IL	60047	**800-810-2200**	
Bluemetal Architects Inc				
44 Pleasant St	Watertown MA	02472	**866-252-0111**	
BrightMove Inc				
320 High Tide Dr # 201	Saint Augustine FL	32080	**877-482-8840**	
Channel Solutions LLC				
3145 E Chandler Blvd Ste 110	Phoenix AZ	85048	**866-501-9690**	
Conde Group Inc				
4141 Jutland Dr Ste 130	San Diego CA	92117	**800-838-0819**	
Core Vision IT Solutions				
600 Dakota Ste D	Crystal Lake IL	60012	**855-788-5835**	
Corporate It Solutions Inc				
661 Pleasant St	Norwood MA	02062	**888-521-2487**	
CRM Dynamics Inc				
245 Glenforest Rd	Toronto ON	M4N2A5	**866-740-2424**	
DelaGet LLC				
6608 Flying Cloud Dr	Eden Prairie MN	55344	**866-264-5050**	
Document Access Systems				
9019 Forest Hill Ave Ste 9C	Richmond VA	23235	**866-544-9876**	
Dynamics Edge Inc				
2635 N First St Ste #148	San Jose CA	95134	**800-453-5961**	
Ericsson 1 Telcordia Dr	Piscataway NJ	08854	**800-521-2673**	732-699-2000
Evogi Group Inc, The				
20645 N Pima Rd Bldg N Ste 130	Scottsdale AZ	85255	**888-277-5573**	
I.T. Blueprint Solutions Consulting Inc				
170-422 Richards St	Vancouver BC	V6B2Z4	**866-261-8981**	
iMethods LLC				
10748 Deerwood Park Blvd Ste 150	Jacksonville FL	32256	**888-306-2261**	
iMomentous				
20 Gibraltar Rd Ste 109	Horsham PA	19044	**888-985-7755**	
Infogrow Corp				
2140 Front St	Cuyahoga Falls OH	44221	**800-897-9807**	
Kaseya Corp				
400 Totten Pond Rd Ste 200	Waltham MA	02451	**877-926-0001**	
KDC Technologies				
27201 Tourney Rd Ste 201	Valencia CA	91355	**877-532-1112**	
Lawrence Behr Assoc Inc				
3400 Tupper Dr PO Box 8026	Greenville NC	27834	**800-522-4464**	252-757-0279
LED Supply Co				
747 Sheridan Blvd Unit 8E	Lakewood CO	80214	**877-595-4769**	
MCM Services Group				
1300 Corporate Ctr Curve	Eagan MN	55121	**888-507-6262**	
MediRevv Inc				
2600 University Pkwy	Coralville IA	52241	**888-665-6310**	
Mercury Z				
1150 Se Maynard Rd Ste 140	Cary NC	27511	**877-548-4052**	
MOBI Wireless Management LLC				
6100 W 96th St Ste 150	Indianapolis IN	46278	**855-259-6624**	
Netlink Software Group America Inc				
999 Tech Row	Madison Heights MI	48071	**800-485-4462**	
Oceanus Partners				
16540 Pointe Village Dr Ste 208	Lutz FL	33558	**888-496-1117**	
OPTIO LLC 390 Spaulding Ave SE	Ada MI	49301	**888-981-3282**	
Pollution Control Corp				
500 W Country Club Rd	Chickasha OK	73018	**800-966-1265**	
ProSource Solutions LLC				
4199 Kinross Lakes Pkwy Ste 150	Richfield OH	44286	**866-549-0279**	
Quality Management Solutions LLC				
146 Lowell St Ste 300B	Wakefield MA	01889	**800-645-6430**	
RedLegg				
902 S Randall Rd Ste C 319	St. Charles IL	60174	**877-811-5040**	
Revention Inc				
1315 W Sam Houston Pkwy North Ste 100	Houston TX	77043	**877-738-7444**	
Root Inc 5470 Main St	Sylvania OH	43560	**800-852-1315**	

			Toll-Free	Phone
SatisfYd				
47 E Chicago Ave Ste 310	Naperville IL	60540	**800-562-9557**	
Sererra Consulting Group LLC				
5430 Trabuco Rd Ste 150	Irvine CA	92620	**877-276-3774**	
Simplicity Consulting Inc				
11250 Kirkland Way Ste 203	Kirkland WA	98033	**888-252-0385**	
Sonoma Technical Support Services				
8840 210th St Ste 342	Langley BC	V1M2Y2	**866-898-3123**	
Technology Futures Inc (TFI)				
13740 Research Blvd (N Hwy 183)				
Ste C-1	Austin TX	78750	**800-835-3887**	512-258-8898
thinkASG				
15265 Alton Pkwy Ste 300	Irvine CA	92618	**800-991-9274**	
Tradescape Inc				
520 S El Camino Real Ste 640	San Mateo CA	94402	**800-697-6068**	
Tri-basin Natural Resources District				
1723 Burlington St	Holdrege NE	68949	**877-995-6688**	
Trinity Systems Technologies Inc				
5885 Cumming Hwy Ste 108-273	Sugar Hill GA	30518	**888-828-5655**	
TrueCloud 2147 E Baseline Rd	Tempe AZ	85283	**866-990-8783**	
Verologix LLC				
Ste 700 6 Centerpointe Dr	La Palma CA	90623	**800-403-8041**	
ViWo Inc				
10801 National blvd 410	Los Angeles CA	90064	**877-958-5174**	
Wireless Facilities Inc (WFI)				
4800 Westfields Blvd Ste 200	Chantilly VA	20151	**877-566-7277**	703-563-7100
NASDAQ: WFII				

199   CONSUMER INFORMATION RESOURCES - GOVERNMENT

			Toll-Free	Phone
Alzheimer's Disease Education & Referral Ctr				
PO Box 8250	Silver Spring MD	20907	**800-438-4380**	301-495-1080
National Center for Immunization & Respiratory Diseases				
1600 Clifton Rd NE MS E-05	Atlanta GA	30333	**800-232-4636**	
Centers for Disease Control & Prevention				
Travelers Health				
1600 Clifton Rd NE	Atlanta GA	30333	**800-232-4636**	
Consumer Product Safety Commission (CPSC)				
4340 E W Hwy Ste 502	Bethesda MD	20814	**800-638-2772**	301-504-7923
Corp for National & Community Service				
AmeriCorps USA				
1201 New York Ave NW	Washington DC	20525	**800-833-3722**	202-606-5000
Learn & Serve America				
1201 New York Ave NW	Washington DC	20525	**800-833-3722**	202-606-5000
Education Resource Information Ctr (ERIC)				
c/o CSC 655 15th St NW Ste 500	Washington DC	20005	**800-538-3742**	
Eldercare Locator				
1730 Rhode Island Ave NW Ste 1200	Washington DC	20036	**800-677-1116**	
Energy Efficiency & Renewable Energy Information Ctr				
1000 Independence Ave SW	Washington DC	20585	**877-337-3463**	202-586-4849
FedWorld.gov				
National Technical Information Service				
5285 Port Royal Rd	Alexandria VA	22312	**800-553-6847**	703-605-6000
Foster Grandparent Program c/o Senior Corps				
1201 New York Ave NW	Washington DC	20525	**800-424-8867**	202-606-5000
Grants.gov				
Dept of Health & Human Services				
200 Independence Ave SW HHH Bldg	Washington DC	20201	**800-518-4726**	
Taxpayer Advocate Service				
77 K St NE Ste 1500	Washington DC	20002	**877-777-4778**	202-803-9000
National Clearinghouse for Alcohol & Drug Information				
11426 Rockville Pk PO Box 2345	Rockville MD	20847	**800-729-6686**	
National Institute for Literacy (NIFL)				
1775 'I' St NW Ste 730	Washington DC	20006	**800-228-8813**	202-233-2025
National Mental Health Information Ctr				
PO Box 42557	Washington DC	20015	**800-487-4889**	
National Women's Health Information Ctr				
200 Independence Ave S.W	Washington DC	20201	**800-994-9662**	
Project Safe Neighborhoods				
Office of Justice Programs				
810 Seventh St NW	Washington DC	20531	**888-744-6513**	202-616-6500
PubMed				
US National Library of Medicine				
8600 Rockville Pike	Bethesda MD	20894	**888-346-3656**	
Recreation.gov				
1849 C St NW	Washington DC	20240	**877-444-6777**	202-208-4743
Retired & Senior Volunteer Program (RSVP)				
1201 New York Ave NW	Washington DC	20525	**800-833-3722**	202-606-5000
Senior Corps				
1201 New York Ave NW	Washington DC	20525	**800-833-3722**	202-606-5000
Center for Substance Abuse Treatment				
1 Choke Cherry Rd PO Box 2345	Rockville MD	20857	**877-726-4727**	240-276-2130
US Dept of Labor Women's Bureau				
200 Constitution Ave NW Rm S-3002	Washington DC	20210	**800-827-5335**	202-693-6710
US General Services Administration				
1800 F St NW	Washington DC	20405	**800-488-3111**	
US Geological Survey				
Ask USGS				
12201 Sunrise Valley Dr	Reston VA	20192	**888-275-8747**	703-648-5953
USA Freedom Corps				
1201 New York Ave NW	Washington DC	20005	**800-833-3722**	202-606-5000

200   CONTAINERS - METAL (BARRELS, DRUMS, KEGS)

			Toll-Free	Phone
Champion Co				
400 Harrison St	Springfield OH	45505	**800-328-0115***	937-324-5681
*Sales				
Container Research Corp (CRC)				
1 Hollow Hill Rd	Glen Riddle PA	19037	**844-220-9574**	610-459-2160
Csi Industries Inc				
6910 W Ridge Rd	Fairview PA	16415	**800-937-9033**	814-474-9353
Greif Inc 425 Winter Rd	Delaware OH	43015	**877-781-9797**	740-549-6000
NYSE: GEF				

					Toll-Free	Phone
Imperial Industries Inc	505 Industrial Pk Ave	Rothschild	WI	54474	**800-558-2945**	715-359-0200
Industrial Container Services	7152 First Ave S	Seattle	WA	98108	**800-273-3786**	206-763-2345
Innovative Fluid Handling Systems	3300 E Rock Falls Rd	Rock Falls	IL	61071	**800-435-7003**	815-626-1018
Justrite Manufacturing Co	2454 E Dempster St Ste 300	Des Plaines	IL	60016	**800-798-9250**	847-298-9250
Myers Container Corp	8435 NE Killingsworth	Portland	OR	97220	**800-406-9377**	503-501-5830
Packaging Specialties Inc	300 Lake Rd	Medina	OH	44256	**800-344-9271**	330-723-6000
Stackbin Corp	29 Powderhill Rd	Lincoln	RI	02865	**800-333-1603***	401-333-1600
	*Sales					
USA Container Company Inc	1776 S Second St	Piscataway	NJ	08854	**888-752-7722**	732-752-7722
Von Duprin Inc	2720 Tobey Dr	Indianapolis	IN	46219	**800-999-0408**	

201 CONTAINERS - PLASTICS (DRUMS, CANS, CRATES, BOXES)

					Toll-Free	Phone
Akro-Mils Inc	1293 S Main St	Akron	OH	44301	**800-253-2467**	
Beden-Baugh Products Inc	105 Lisbon Rd	Laurens	SC	29360	**866-598-5794**	864-682-3136
Belco Mfg Company Inc	2303 Taylors Vly Rd	Belton	TX	76513	**800-251-8265**	254-933-9000
Berry Plastics Corp	101 Oakley St	Evansville	IN	47710	**877-662-3779**	812-424-2904
Buckhorn Inc	55 W Techne Ctr Dr	Milford	OH	45150	**800-543-4454**	513-831-4402
Case Design Corp	333 School Ln	Telford	PA	18969	**800-847-4176**	215-703-0130
Chem-Tainer Industries Inc	361 Neptune Ave	West Babylon	NY	11704	**800-275-2436**	631-661-8300
Gatekeeper Systems Inc	8 Studebaker	Irvine	CA	92618	**888-808-9433**	949-453-1940
Handley Industries Inc	2101 Brooklyn Rd	Jackson	MI	49203	**800-870-5088**	517-787-8821
Hedwin Corp	1600 Roland Heights Ave	Baltimore	MD	21211	**800-638-1012**	410-467-8209
HGI Skydyne	100 River Rd	Port Jervis	NY	12771	**800-428-2273**	
Iroquois Products of Chicago	2220 W 56th St	Chicago	IL	60636	**800-453-3355**	
Jewel Case Corp	110 Dupont Dr	Providence	RI	02907	**800-441-4447**	401-943-1400
McConkey Co	1615 Puyallup St PO Box 1690	Sumner	WA	98390	**800-426-8124**	253-863-8111
Menasha Corp	1645 Bergstrom Rd	Neenah	WI	54956	**800-558-5073**	920-751-1000
Molded Fiber Glass Tray Co	6175 US Hwy 6	Linesville	PA	16424	**800-458-6050***	814-683-4500
	*Sales					
ORBIS Corp	1055 Corporate Ctr Dr	Oconomowoc	WI	53066	**800-999-8683**	262-560-5000
Pelican Products Inc	147 N Main St	South Deerfield	MA	01373	**800-542-7344**	413-665-2163
Plano Molding Co	431 E S St	Plano	IL	60545	**800-226-9868**	630-552-3111
Plas-Tanks Industries Inc	39 Standen Dr	Hamilton	OH	45015	**800-247-6709**	513-942-3800
Plastic Forming Company Inc	20 S Bradley Rd	Woodbridge	CT	06525	**800-732-2060**	203-397-1338
Rehrig Pacific Co	4010 E 26th St	Los Angeles	CA	90023	**800-421-6244**	323-262-5145
River Bend Industries	2421 16th Ave S	Moorhead	MN	56560	**800-365-3070**	218-236-1818
Rocket Box Inc	125 E 144th St	Bronx	NY	10451	**800-762-5521**	718-292-5370
RPM Industries Inc	26 Aurelius Ave	Auburn	NY	13021	**800-669-3676**	315-255-1105
Schaefer Systems International Inc	10021 Westlake Dr	Charlotte	NC	28241	**800-876-6000**	704-944-4500
Specialty Plastic Fabricators Inc	9658 196th St	Mokena	IL	60448	**800-747-9509**	708-479-5501
Stack-On Products Co	1360 N Old Rand Rd	Wauconda	IL	60084	**800-323-9601**	847-526-1611
Toter Inc	PO Box 5338	Statesville	NC	28677	**800-424-0422**	704-872-8171
US Plastic Corp	1390 Newbrecht Rd	Lima	OH	45801	**800-537-9724**	419-228-2242

202 CONTAINERS - WOOD

SEE ALSO Pallets & Skids

					Toll-Free	Phone
Abbot & Abbot Box Corp	37-11 Tenth St	Long Island City	NY	11101	**888-525-7186**	
Greif Inc	425 Winter Rd	Delaware	OH	43015	**877-781-9797**	740-549-6000
	NYSE: GEF					
Mele & Co	2007 Beechgrove Pl	Utica	NY	13501	**800-635-6353**	315-733-4600
Monte Package Company Inc	3752 Riverside Rd	Riverside	MI	49084	**800-653-2807**	269-849-1722
Pallet Services Inc	12926 Farm to Market Rd	Mount Vernon	WA	98273	**800-769-2245**	
Texas Basket Co	100 Myrtle Dr	Jacksonville	TX	75766	**800-657-2200**	903-586-8014
Wisconsin Box Company Inc	929 Townline Rd	Wausau	WI	54402	**800-876-6658**	715-842-2248

203 CONTROLS - INDUSTRIAL PROCESS

					Toll-Free	Phone
ADA-ES Inc	8100 Southpark Way Ste B	Littleton	CO	80120	**888-822-8617**	303-734-1727
	NASDAQ: ADES					
ADS Environmental Services	4940 Research Dr	Huntsville	AL	35805	**800-633-7246**	256-430-3366
ALL-TEST Pro LLC	123 Spencer Plain Rd	Old Saybrook	CT	06475	**800-952-8776**	860-399-4222
Alpha Technologies Services LLC	3030 Gilchrist Rd	Akron	OH	44305	**800-356-9886**	330-745-1641
AMETEK Automation & Process Technologies	1080 N Crooks	Clawson	MI	48017	**800-635-0289**	248-435-0700
Anderson Instrument Co	156 Auriesville Rd	Fultonville	NY	12072	**800-833-0081**	518-922-5315
Applied Microstructures Inc	1020 Rincon Cir	San Jose	CA	95131	**877-683-2678**	408-907-2885
Arcet Equipment Company Inc	1700 Chamberlayne Ave	Richmond	VA	23222	**800-388-0302**	
ARi Industries Inc	381 Ari Ct	Addison	IL	60101	**800-237-6725**	630-953-9100
Arzel Zoning Technology Inc	4801 Commerce Pkwy	Cleveland	OH	44128	**800-611-8312**	216-831-6068
Athena Controls Inc	5145 Campus Dr	Plymouth Meeting	PA	19462	**800-782-6776**	610-828-2490
Automation Products Group Inc (APG)	1025 West 1700 North	Logan	UT	84321	**888-525-7300**	435-753-7300
Automation Service	13871 Parks Steed Dr	Earth City	MO	63045	**800-325-4808**	314-785-6600
Azonix Corp	900 Middlesex Tpke Bldg 6	Billerica	MA	01821	**800-967-5558**	978-670-6300
Bacharach Inc	621 Hunt Vly Cir	New Kensington	PA	15068	**800-736-4666**	724-334-5000
Barksdale Inc	3211 Fruitland Ave	Los Angeles	CA	90058	**800-835-1060**	323-589-6181
Brookfield Engineering Lab Inc	11 Commerce Blvd	Middleboro	MA	02346	**800-628-8139**	508-946-6200
Buhler Inc	13105 12th Ave N	Plymouth	MN	55441	**800-722-7483**	763-847-9900
Canfield Connector Div	8510 Foxwood Ct	Youngstown	OH	44514	**800-554-5071**	
Cec Controls Co Inc	14555 Barber Ave	Warren	MI	48088	**877-924-0303**	586-779-0222
Celesco Transducer Products Inc	20630 Plummer St	Chatsworth	CA	91311	**800-423-5483**	818-701-2750
Cincinnati Test Systems Inc	5555 Dry Fork Rd	Cleves	OH	45002	**800-850-3189**	513-367-6699
Conax Buffalo Technologies LLC	2300 Walden Ave	Buffalo	NY	14225	**800-223-2389**	716-684-4500
Cooper Atkins Corp	33 Reeds Gap Rd	Middlefield	CT	06455	**800-835-5011***	860-349-3473
	*Sales					
Crane Company Dynalco Controls Div	3690 NW 53rd St	Fort Lauderdale	FL	33309	**800-368-6666**	954-739-4300
Daniel Measurement & Control Inc	5650 Brittmoore Rd	Houston	TX	77041	**800-518-1623**	713-467-6000
Dickson Co	930 S Westwood Ave	Addison	IL	60101	**800-757-3747**	630-543-3747
Eldridge Products Inc	2700 Garden Rd Bldg A	Monterey	CA	93940	**800-321-3569**	831-648-7777
Emulation Technology Inc	759 Flynn Rd	Camarillo	CA	93012	**800-232-7837**	805-383-8480
Encoder Products Co	464276 Hwy 95 S PO Box 249	Sagle	ID	83860	**800-366-5412**	208-263-8541
Endress+Hauser Inc	2350 Endress Pl	Greenwood	IN	46143	**888-363-7377**	317-535-7138
Fairchild Industrial Products Co	3920 Westpoint Blvd	Winston-Salem	NC	27103	**800-334-8422**	336-659-3400
Fast Heat Inc	776 Oaklawn Ave	Elmhurst	IL	60126	**877-747-8575**	630-833-5400
Fluid Components International	1755 La Costa Meadows Dr	San Marcos	CA	92078	**800-863-8703**	760-744-6950
Forney Corp	3405 Wiley Post Rd	Carrollton	TX	75006	**800-356-7740***	972-458-6100
	*Cust Svc					
GE Infrastructure Sensing	1100 Technology Pk Dr	Billerica	MA	01821	**800-833-9438**	978-437-1000
Gefran ISI Inc	Eight Lowell Ave	Winchester	MA	01890	**888-888-4474**	781-729-5249
Gems Sensors Inc	One Cowles Rd	Plainville	CT	06062	**800-378-1600**	860-747-3000
General Devices Company Inc	1410 S Post Rd	Indianapolis	IN	46239	**800-821-3520**	317-897-7000
Geotech Environmental Equipment Inc	2650 E 40th Ave	Denver	CO	80205	**800-833-7958**	303-320-4764
GfG Instrumentation Inc	1194 Oak Vly Dr Ste 20	Ann Arbor	MI	48108	**800-959-0329**	734-769-0573
Hart Scientific Inc	799 E Utah Vly Dr	American Fork	UT	84003	**800-438-4278**	801-763-1600
HO Trerice Co	12950 W Eight-Mile Rd	Oak Park	MI	48237	**888-873-7423**	248-399-8000
HSQ Technology	26227 Research Rd	Hayward	CA	94545	**800-486-6684**	510-259-1334
Industrial Scientific Corp	7848 Steubenville Pk	Oakdale	PA	15071	**800-338-3287**	412-788-4353
Intelligent Instrumentation Inc	419 NE 10th Ave	Portland	OR	97232	**800-685-9911**	503-928-3188
ISCO Inc	4700 Superior St PO Box 82531	Lincoln	NE	68501	**800-228-4250**	402-464-0231
ITT Industries Inc	1133 Westchester Ave	White Plains	NY	10604	**800-254-2823**	914-641-2000
	NYSE: ITT					
Kistler-Morse Corp	150 Venture Blvd	Spartanburg	SC	29306	**800-426-9010**	864-574-2763
Lake Monitors Inc	8809 Industrial Dr	Franksville	WI	53126	**800-850-6110**	262-884-9800
Lake Shore Cryotronics	575 McCorkle Blvd	Westerville	OH	43082	**877-969-0010**	614-891-2243
LaMotte Co	802 Washington Ave	Chestertown	MD	21620	**800-344-3100**	410-778-3100
Linear Laboratories	42025 Osgood Rd	Fremont	CA	94539	**800-536-0262**	510-226-0488

				Toll-Free	Phone
Magnetrol International Inc					
5300 Belmont Rd ....Downers Grove	IL	60515		800-624-8765	630-969-4000
Mahr Federal Inc					
1144 Eddy St ....Providence	RI	02905		800-343-2050*	401-784-3100
*Orders					
Malema Engineering Corp					
1060 S Rogers Cir ....Boca Raton	FL	33487		800-637-6418	561-995-0595
MAMAC Systems Inc					
8189 Century Blvd ....Minneapolis	MN	55317		800-843-5116	952-556-4900
Marsh Bellofram Corp					
8019 Ohio River Blvd ....Newell	WV	26050		800-727-5646	304-387-1200
McCrometer Inc					
3255 W Stetson Ave ....Hemet	CA	92545		800-220-2279	951-652-6811
Micro Motion Inc					
7070 Winchester Cir ....Boulder	CO	80301		800-522-6277	303-530-8400
MicroMod Automation Inc					
75 Town Centre Dr ....Rochester	NY	14623		800-480-1975	585-321-9200
MKS Instruments Inc					
2 Tech Dr Ste 201 ....Andover	MA	01810		800-428-9401	978-645-5500
Moore Industries International Inc					
16650 Schoenborn St ....North Hills	CA	91343		800-999-2900	818-894-7111
Nearfield Systems Inc					
19730 Magellan Dr ....Torrance	CA	90502		800-334-7384	310-525-7000
NRD LLC					
2937 Alt Blvd PO Box 310 ....Grand Island	NY	14072		800-525-8076	716-773-7634
Omega Engineering Inc					
One Omega Dr PO Box 4047 ....Stamford	CT	06907		800-826-6342	203-359-1660
Onset Computer Corp					
PO Box 3450 ....Pocasset	MA	02559		800-564-4377	508-759-9500
OPW Fuel Management Systems					
6900 Santa Fe Dr ....Hodgkins	IL	60525		800-547-9393	708-485-4200
Orange Research Inc					
140 Cascade Blvd ....Milford	CT	06460		800-989-5657	203-877-5657
Orion Instruments LLC					
2105 Oak Villa Blvd ....Baton Rouge	LA	70815		866-556-7466	225-906-2343
PakSense Inc					
6223 N Discovery Pl ....Boise	ID	83713		877-832-0720	208-489-9010
Parker Hannifin Corp Veriflo Div					
250 Canal Blvd ....Richmond	CA	94804		800-272-7537	510-235-9590
PdMA Corp					
5909-C Hampton Oaks Pkwy ....Tampa	FL	33610		800-476-6463	813-621-6463
Pearpoint Inc					
72055 Corporate Way ....Thousand Palms	CA	92276		800-688-8094	760-343-7350
Pentair 7433 Harwin Dr ....Houston	TX	77036		800-545-6258	
Portage Electric Products Inc					
7700 Freedom Ave NW ....North Canton	OH	44720		888-464-7374	330-499-2727
Porter Instrument Company Inc					
245 Township Line Rd PO Box 907 ....Hatfield	PA	19440		888-723-4001	215-723-4000
Potter Electric Signal Company Inc					
5757 Phantom Dr Ste 125 ....Hazelwood	MO	63042		800-325-3936	314-878-4321
Pressure Profile Systems Inc					
5757 Century Blvd Ste 600 ....Los Angeles	CA	90045		888-249-2464	310-641-8100
RAE Systems					
3775 N First St ....San Jose	CA	95134		877-723-2878	408-952-8200
Raven Industries Inc					
205 E Sixth St ....Sioux Falls	SD	57104		800-243-5435	605-336-2750
NASDAQ: RAVN					
Robertshaw Industrial Products					
1602 Mustang Dr ....Maryville	TN	37801		800-228-7429	865-981-3100
Rochester Gauges Inc of Texas					
11616 Harry Hines Blvd ....Dallas	TX	75229		800-821-1829	972-241-2161
Ronan Engineering Co					
21200 Oxnard St ....Woodland Hills	CA	91367		800-327-6626	
Roper Industries Inc					
6901 Professional Pkwy Ste 200 ....Sarasota	FL	34240		888-227-3565	941-556-2601
NYSE: ROP					
Rosemount Analytical Inc Process Analytical Div					
6565 P Davis Industrial Pkwy ....Solon	OH	44139		800-433-6076	440-914-1261
Scully Signal Co					
70 Industrial Way ....Wilmington	MA	01887		800-272-8559	617-692-8600
See Water Inc					
121 N Dillon St ....San Jacinto	CA	92583		888-733-9283	951-487-8073
Sensidyne Inc					
16333 Bay Vista Dr ....Clearwater	FL	33760		800-451-9444	727-530-3602
Sierra Instruments Inc					
Five Harris Ct Bldg L ....Monterey	CA	93940		800-866-0200	831-373-0200
SJE-Rhombus					
22650 County Hwy 6 PO Box 1708 ....Detroit Lakes	MN	56502		800-746-6287	218-847-1317
SOR Inc 14685 W 105th St ....Lenexa	KS	66215		800-676-6794	913-888-2630
Spectronics Corp					
956 Brush Hollow Rd ....Westbury	NY	11590		800-274-8888	
Spirax Sarco Inc					
1150 Northpoint Blvd ....Blythewood	SC	29016		800-883-4411	803-714-2000
Sterling Inc					
2900 S 160th St ....New Berlin	WI	53151		800-783-7835*	262-641-8600
*Cust Svc					
Taylor Precision Products LLC					
2311 W 22nd St ....Oak Brook	IL	60523		866-843-3905	
Teledyne Advanced Pollution Instrumentation					
9480 Carroll Pk Dr ....San Diego	CA	92121		800-324-5190	858-657-9800
Teledyne Monitor Labs Inc (TML)					
35 Inverness Dr E ....Englewood	CO	80112		800-422-1499	303-792-3300
Thermo Fisher Scientific Inc					
81 Wyman St PO Box 9046 ....Waltham	MA	02454		800-678-5599	781-622-1000
NYSE: TMO					
Transcat Inc					
35 Vantage Pt Dr ....Rochester	NY	14624		800-800-5001	585-352-9460
NASDAQ: TRNS					
Troxler Electronic Laboratories Inc					
3008 E Cornwallis Rd					
PO Box 12057 ....Research Triangle Park	NC	27709		877-876-9537	919-549-8661
TSI Inc 500 CaRdigan Rd ....Shoreview	MN	55126		800-874-2811	651-483-0900
Veeder-Root					
125 Powder Forest Dr ....Simsbury	CT	06070		888-262-7539	860-651-2700
Wika Instrument Corp					
1000 Wiegand Blvd ....Lawrenceville	GA	30043		888-945-2872	770-513-8200

				Toll-Free	Phone
Winland Electronics Inc					
1950 Excel Dr ....Mankato	MN	56001		800-635-4269	507-625-7231
NYSE: WEX					
World Energy Alternatives LLC					
2 Constitution Ctr ....Boston	MA	02129		800-829-3676	617-889-7300
Yokogawa Corp of America					
12530 W Airport Blvd ....Sugar Land	TX	77478		800-888-6400	281-340-3800
YSI Inc					
1700-1725 Brannum Ln ....Yellow Springs	OH	45387		800-765-4974*	937-767-7241
*Cust Svc					
ZK Celltest Inc					
256 Gibraltar Dr Ste 109 ....Sunnyvale	CA	94089		800-837-8235	408-752-0449

204 CONTROLS - TEMPERATURE - RESIDENTIAL & COMMERCIAL

				Toll-Free	Phone
Azonix Corp					
900 Middlesex Tpke Bldg 6 ....Billerica	MA	01821		800-967-5558	978-670-6300
CAPP/USA					
201 Marple Ave ....Clifton Heights	PA	19018		800-356-8000	610-394-1100
Cooper Atkins Corp					
33 Reeds Gap Rd ....Middlefield	CT	06455		800-835-5011*	860-349-3473
*Sales					
DeltaTRAK Inc PO Box 398 ....Pleasanton	CA	94566		800-962-6776	925-249-2250
Emerson Climate Technologies - Retail Solutions					
1065 Big Shanty Rd NW Ste 100 ....Kennesaw	GA	30144		800-829-2724	770-425-2724
Hallcrest Inc					
1820 Pickwick Ln ....Glenview	IL	60026		800-527-1419*	847-998-8580
*General					
Hansen Technologies Corp					
6827 High Grove Blvd ....Burr Ridge	IL	60527		800-426-7368	630-325-1565
HSQ Technology					
26227 Research Rd ....Hayward	CA	94545		800-486-6684	510-259-1334
Johnson Controls Systems					
9410 Bunsen Pkwy Ste 100-B ....Louisville	KY	40220		800-765-7773	502-671-7300
Kidde-Fenwal Inc					
400 Main St ....Ashland	MA	01721		800-872-6527*	508-881-2000
*Hum Res					
KMC Controls Inc					
19476 Industrial Dr ....New Paris	IN	46553		877-444-5622	574-831-5250
Novar Controls Corp					
6060 Rockside Woods Blvd Ste 400 ....Cleveland	OH	44131		800-348-1235	
Portage Electric Products Inc					
7700 Freedom Ave NW ....North Canton	OH	44720		888-464-7374	330-499-2727
Prentke Romich Co					
1022 Heyl Rd ....Wooster	OH	44691		800-848-8008	330-262-1984
Residential Control Systems					
11481 Sunrise Gold Cir Ste 1 ....Rancho Cordova	CA	95742		888-727-4822	916-635-6784
Siemens Bldg Technologies Inc					
1000 Deerfield Pkwy ....Buffalo Grove	IL	60089		800-877-7545*	847-215-1000
*General					
SPX Corp Robinair Div					
655 Eisenhower Dr ....Owatonna	MN	55060		800-628-6496	507-455-7000
Taylor Precision Products LLC					
2311 W 22nd St ....Oak Brook	IL	60523		866-843-3905	
Watlow Winona					
1241 Bundy Blvd ....Winona	MN	55987		800-928-5692	507-454-5300

205 CONTROLS & RELAYS - ELECTRICAL

				Toll-Free	Phone
ABB SSAC 8242 Loop Rd ....Baldwinsville	NY	13027		800-377-7722*	315-638-1300
*Tech Supp					
Allied Controls Inc					
150 E Aurora St ....Waterbury	CT	06708		800-788-0955	203-757-4200
AMETEK National Controls Corp					
1725 Western Dr ....West Chicago	IL	60185		800-323-2593	630-231-5900
AMX Corp					
3000 Research Dr ....Richardson	TX	75082		855-269-8585	469-624-8585
Anaheim Automation					
910 E Orangefair Ln ....Anaheim	CA	92801		800-345-9401*	714-992-6990
*Sales					
Bright Image Corp					
2830 S18th Ave ....Broadview	IL	60155		888-449-5656	
Cleveland Motion Controls Inc					
7550 Hub Pkwy ....Cleveland	OH	44125		800-321-8072	216-524-8800
Contrex Inc					
8900 Zachary Ln N ....Maple Grove	MN	55369		800-342-4411	763-424-7800
DST Controls 651 Stone Rd ....Benicia	CA	94510		800-251-0773	707-745-5117
Ducommun Inc					
23301 Wilmington Ave ....Carson	CA	90745		800-667-6589	310-513-7280
NYSE: DCO					
Duct-O-Wire Co 345 Adams Cir ....Corona	CA	92882		800-752-6001	951-735-8220
Electric Regulator Corp					
6189 El Camino Real ....Carlsbad	CA	92009		800-458-6566	760-438-7873
Electronic Theatre Controls Inc					
3031 Pleasantview Rd ....Middleton	WI	53562		800-688-4116	608-831-4116
Enercon Engineering Inc					
One Altorfer Ln ....East Peoria	IL	61611		800-218-8831	309-694-1418
FSI Technologies Inc					
668 E Western Ave ....Lombard	IL	60148		800-468-6009	630-932-9380
GE Digital Energy					
650 Markland St ....Markham	ON	L6C0M1		877-605-6777	905-294-6222
GET Engineering Corp					
9350 Bond Ave ....El Cajon	CA	92021		877-494-1820	619-443-8295
Glendinning Marine Products					
740 Century Cir ....Conway	SC	29526		800-500-2380	843-399-6146
Globe Electronic Hardware Inc					
34-24 56th St ....Woodside	NY	11377		800-221-1505	718-457-0303
Guardian Electric Mfg Company Inc					
1425 Lake Ave ....Woodstock	IL	60098		800-762-0369	815-334-3600
Honeywell Sensing & Control					
11 W Spring St ....Freeport	IL	61032		800-537-6945*	815-235-5500
*Cust Svc					

				Toll-Free	Phone
Icm Controls Corp					
7313 William Barry Blvd	North Syracuse	NY	13212	**800-365-5525**	315-233-5266
IDEC Corp 1175 Elko Dr	Sunnyvale	CA	94089	**800-262-4332**	408-747-0550
Imperial Irrigation District (IID)					
PO Box 937	Imperial	CA	92251	**800-303-7756**	760-482-9600
Inertia Dynamics Inc					
31 Industrial Pk Rd	New Hartford	CT	06057	**800-800-6445**	860-482-4444
Joslyn Clark Corp					
2100 W Broad St	Elizabethtown	NC	28337	**800-476-6952**	
KB Electronics Inc					
12095 NW 39th St	Coral Springs	FL	33065	**800-221-6570**	954-346-4900
Leach International Corp					
6900 Orangethorpe Ave	Buena Park	CA	90622	**800-232-7700**	714-736-7598
Lutron Electronics Company Inc					
7200 Suter Rd	Coopersburg	PA	18036	**800-523-9466***	610-282-6280
*Tech Supp					
MagneTek Inc					
N49 W13650 Campbell Dr	Menomonee Falls	WI	53051	**800-288-8178**	
NASDAQ: MAG					
Maxcess International, Inc.					
222 W Memorial Rd PO Box 26508	Oklahoma City	OK	73114	**800-333-3433**	405-755-1600
Moog Inc Jamison Rd	East Aurora	NY	14052	**800-336-2112**	716-652-2000
NYSE: MOG/A					
OMRON Corp					
One Commerce Dr	Schaumburg	IL	60173	**800-556-6766**	847-843-7900
OMRON Scientific Technologies Inc					
6550 Dumbarton Cir	Fremont	CA	94555	**888-510-4357**	510-608-3400
Ormec Systems Corp					
19 Linden Pk	Rochester	NY	14625	**800-656-7632**	585-385-3520
Panasonic Electric Works Corp of America					
629 Central Ave	New Providence	NJ	07974	**800-276-6289**	908-464-3550
Parker Hannifin Corp Electromechanical Automation Div					
5500 Business Pk Dr	Rohnert Park	CA	94928	**800-358-9068**	707-584-7558
Parker McCrory Manufacturing Co					
2000 Forest Ave	Kansas City	MO	64108	**800-662-1038**	816-221-2000
Payne Engineering Co					
Rt 29 PO Box 70	Scott Depot	WV	25560	**800-331-1345***	304-757-7353
*Orders					
Polytron Corp					
4400 Wyland Dr	Elkhart	IN	46516	**888-228-0246**	574-522-0246
PVA Tepla America Inc					
251 Corporate Terr	Corona	CA	92879	**800-527-5667***	951-371-2500
*Sales					
RCI Custom Products					
801 NE St Ste 2A	Frederick	MD	21701	**800-546-4724**	301-620-9130
Rockford Systems Inc					
4620 Hydraulic Rd	Rockford	IL	61109	**800-922-7533***	815-874-7891
*Cust Svc					
Sendec Corp					
72 Perinton Pkwy	Fairport	NY	14450	**800-295-8000**	585-425-3390
SOR Inc 14685 W 105th St	Lenexa	KS	66215	**800-676-6794**	913-888-2630
Sparton 27 Hale Spring Rd	Plaistow	NH	03865	**800-443-4132**	603-382-3840
Sprecher + Schuh					
15910 International Plaza Dr	Houston	TX	77032	**877-721-5913**	281-442-9000
Sturdy Corp					
1822 Carolina Beach Rd	Wilmington	NC	28401	**800-721-3282**	910-763-2500
Time Mark Corp					
11440 E Pine St	Tulsa	OK	74116	**800-862-2875**	918-438-1220
Time-O-Matic Inc					
1015 Maple St	Danville	IL	61832	**800-637-2645**	217-442-0611
Triumph Controls Inc					
205 Church Rd	North Wales	PA	19454	**800-322-2885**	215-699-4861
Wago Corp					
N120 W19129 Freistadt Rd	Germantown	WI	53022	**800-346-7245**	
X-COM Systems LLC					
12345-B Sunrise Vly Dr	Reston	VA	20191	**800-342-8408**	703-390-1087
Yaskawa America Inc					
2121 Norman Dr S	Waukegan	IL	60085	**800-927-5292**	847-887-7000

206   CONVENIENCE STORES

SEE ALSO Gas Stations ; Grocery Stores

				Toll-Free	Phone
7-Eleven Inc					
1722 Routh Ste 100	Dallas	TX	75221	**800-255-0711**	972-828-7011
E-Z Mart Stores					
602 W Falvey Ave PO Box 1426	Texarkana	TX	75501	**800-234-6502**	903-832-6502
Fkg Oil Co 721 W Main	Belleville	IL	62220	**800-873-3546**	618-233-6754
Holiday Stationstores					
4567 American Blvd W	Bloomington	MN	55437	**800-745-7411**	952-830-8700
Lassus BROS Handy Dandy					
1800 Magnavox Way	Fort Wayne	IN	46804	**800-686-2836***	260-436-1415
*General					
Loaf N' Jug Mini Mart					
442 Keeler Pkwy	Pueblo	CO	81001	**866-562-3658**	719-948-3071
Love's Travel Stops & Country Stores Inc					
10601 N Pennsylvania Ave	Oklahoma City	OK	73120	**800-388-0983**	
Mac's Convenience Stores Inc					
305 Milner Ave Ste 400 4th Fl	Toronto	ON	M1B3V4	**800-268-5574**	
Maverik Inc					
880 W Center St	North Salt Lake	UT	84054	**800-789-4455***	877-936-5557
*Cust Svc					
Open Pantry Food Marts					
10505 Corporate Dr Ste 101	Pleasant Prairie	WI	53158	**800-242-3358**	262-857-1156
Pantry Inc 305 Gregson Dr	Cary	NC	27511	**877-798-4792**	919-774-6700
NASDAQ: PTRY					
Plaid Pantries Inc					
10025 SW Allen Blvd	Beaverton	OR	97005	**800-677-5243**	503-646-4246
QuikTrip Corp					
4705 S 129th E Ave	Tulsa	OK	74134	**800-441-0253**	918-615-7700
Sheetz Inc 5700 Sixth Ave	Altoona	PA	16602	**800-487-5444**	814-941-5106
Speedway LLC 500 Speedway Dr	Enon	OH	45323	**800-643-1948***	937-864-3001
*Cust Svc					
Stripes Convenience Stores					
4525 Ayers St	Corpus Christi	TX	78415	**800-569-3585**	361-884-2464
NYSE: SUSS					
Wawa Inc 260 W Baltimore Pike	Media	PA	19063	**800-444-9292**	610-358-8000

				Toll-Free	Phone
Xtramart					
221 Quinebaug Rd	North Grosvenordale	CT	06255	**800-243-6366**	

207   CONVENTION CENTERS

SEE ALSO Stadiums & Arenas ; Performing Arts Facilities
Listings are alphabetized by city names within state groupings.

				Toll-Free	Phone
AmericasMart					
240 Peachtree St NW Ste 2200	Atlanta	GA	30303	**800-285-6278**	404-220-3000
Asheville Civic Ctr					
87 Haywood St	Asheville	NC	28801	**888-464-4218**	828-259-5743
Beaumont Civic Ctr Complex					
701 Main St	Beaumont	TX	77701	**800-782-3081**	409-838-3435
Bell Harbor International Conference Ctr					
2211 Alaskan Way Pier 66	Seattle	WA	98121	**888-772-4422**	206-441-6666
Bossier Civic Ctr					
620 Benton Rd	Bossier City	LA	71111	**800-522-4842**	318-741-8900
Buffalo Niagara Convention Ctr					
153 Franklin St Convention Ctr Plz	Buffalo	NY	14202	**800-995-7570**	716-855-5555
California Market Ctr					
110 E Ninth St	Los Angeles	CA	90079	**800-225-6278**	213-630-3600
Casper Events Ctr					
1 Events Dr	Casper	WY	82601	**800-442-2256**	307-235-8441
Centennial Hall Convention Ctr					
101 Egan Dr	Juneau	AK	99801	**800-478-4176**	907-586-5283
Chattanooga Convention Ctr					
1150 Carter St PO Box 6008	Chattanooga	TN	37402	**800-962-5213**	423-756-0001
City of Pendleton					
500 SW Dorion Ave	Pendleton	OR	97801	**800-238-5355**	541-966-0201
Colorado Springs City Auditorium					
221 E Kiowa St	Colorado Springs	CO	80903	**800-888-4748**	719-385-5969
Dallas Convention Ctr					
650 S Griffin St	Dallas	TX	75202	**877-850-2100**	214-939-2750
Dallas Market Ctr					
2100 Stemmons Fwy Ste 113	Dallas	TX	75207	**800-325-6587**	214-655-6100
Duluth Entertainment Convention Ctr					
350 Harbor Dr	Duluth	MN	55802	**800-628-8385**	218-722-5573
El Paso Convention & Performing Arts Ctr					
One Civic Ctr Plz	El Paso	TX	79901	**800-351-6024**	915-534-0600
Elko Convention & Visitors Authority					
700 Moren Way	Elko	NV	89801	**800-248-3556**	775-738-4091
Evansville Auditorium & Convention Ctr					
715 Locust St	Evansville	IN	47708	**844-381-4751**	812-435-5770
Expo Square 4145 E 21st St	Tulsa	OK	74114	**877-781-2660**	918-744-1113
Festival Plaza					
101 Crockett St Ste A	Shreveport	LA	71101	**888-458-4748**	318-673-5100
Florence Events Ctr					
715 Quince St	Florence	OR	97439	**888-968-4086**	541-997-1994
Fort Worth Convention Ctr					
1201 Houston St	Fort Worth	TX	76102	**866-630-2588**	817-392-6338
Frankfort Convention Ctr					
405 Mero St	Frankfort	KY	40601	**800-426-7866**	502-564-5335
Frontier Airlines Ctr					
400 W Wisconsin Ave	Milwaukee	WI	53203	**800-745-3000**	414-908-6000
Gateway Ctr					
One Gateway Dr	Collinsville	IL	62234	**800-289-2388**	618-345-8998
George R Brown Convention Ctr					
1001 Avenida de las Americas	Houston	TX	77010	**800-427-4697**	713-853-8000
Georgia International Convention Ctr					
2000 Convention Ctr Concourse	College Park	GA	30337	**888-331-4422**	770-997-3566
Grapevine Convention Ctr, The					
1209 S Main St	Grapevine	TX	76051	**866-782-7897**	817-410-3459
Greater Columbus Convention Ctr					
400 N High St	Columbus	OH	43215	**800-626-0241**	614-827-2500
Greater Tacoma Convention & Trade Ctr					
1500 Broadway	Tacoma	WA	98402	**800-745-3000**	253-830-6601
Hampton Inn Philadelphia Ctr City-Convention Ctr					
1301 Race St	Philadelphia	PA	19107	**800-426-7866**	215-665-9100
Harborside Event Ctr					
1375 Monroe St	Fort Myers	FL	33901	**800-294-9516**	239-321-8110
Hawaii Convention Ctr					
1801 Kalakaua Ave	Honolulu	HI	96815	**800-295-6603**	808-943-3500
Henderson Convention Ctr					
200 S Water St	Henderson	NV	89015	**877-775-5252**	702-267-2171
Henry B Gonzalez Convention Ctr					
200 E Market St	San Antonio	TX	78205	**877-504-8895**	210-207-8500
Horizon Convention Ctr					
401 S High St	Muncie	IN	47305	**888-288-8860**	765-288-8860
Hot Springs Convention Ctr (HSCVB)					
134 Convention Blvd PO Box 6000	Hot Springs	AR	71902	**800-625-7576**	501-321-2277
International Exposition Ctr					
1-X Ctr Dr	Cleveland	OH	44135	**855-436-8683**	216-676-6000
Jekyll Island Convention Ctr					
1 N Beachview Dr	Jekyll Island	GA	31527	**877-453-5955**	912-635-5203
John B Hynes Veterans Memorial Convention Ctr					
900 Boylston St	Boston	MA	02115	**800-392-6089**	617-954-2000
John S Knight Ctr					
77 E Mill St	Akron	OH	44308	**800-245-4254**	330-374-8900
Kansas City Convention & Entertainment Centers					
301 W 13th St	Kansas City	MO	64105	**800-821-7060**	816-513-5000
Kansas Expocentre					
One Expocentre Dr	Topeka	KS	66612	**800-745-3000**	785-235-1986
Kentucky International Convention Ctr					
221 S Fourth St	Louisville	KY	40202	**800-701-5831**	502-595-4381
Las Vegas Convention Ctr					
3150 Paradise Rd	Las Vegas	NV	89109	**877-847-4858**	702-892-0711
Manatee Convention Ctr					
1 Haben Blvd	Palmetto	FL	34221	**800-822-2017**	941-722-3244
Mayo Civic Ctr					
30 Civic Ctr Dr SE	Rochester	MN	55904	**800-422-2199**	507-328-2220
Meadowlands Exposition Ctr					
355 Plaza Dr	Secaucus	NJ	07094	**888-560-3976**	201-330-7773
Merchandise Mart					
222 Merchandise Mart Plz Ste 470	Chicago	IL	60654	**800-677-6278**	312-527-4141
MetraPark PO Box 2514	Billings	MT	59103	**800-366-8538**	406-256-2400

Name / Address	City	State	ZIP	Toll-Free	Phone
Mississippi Coast Coliseum & Convention Ctr 2350 Beach Blvd	Biloxi	MS	39531	**800-726-2781**	228-594-3700
Monterey Conference Ctr One Portola Plz	Monterey	CA	93940	**800-742-8091***	831-646-3770
*Sales					
Moody Gardens Convention Ctr Seven Hope Blvd	Galveston	TX	77554	**888-388-8484**	409-741-8484
Myrtle Beach Convention Ctr 2101 N Oak St	Myrtle Beach	SC	29577	**800-537-1690**	843-918-1225
Natchez Convention Ctr 211 Main St	Natchez	MS	39120	**888-475-9144**	601-442-5880
Navy Pier 600 E Grand Ave	Chicago	IL	60611	**800-595-7437**	312-595-5400
New Jersey Convention & Exposition Ctr 97 Sunfield Ave	Edison	NJ	08837	**800-367-0070**	732-417-1400
Northwest Georgia Trade & Convention Ctr 2211 Dug Gap Battle Rd	Dalton	GA	30720	**800-824-7469**	706-272-7676
Oakland Convention Ctr 1001 Broadway	Oakland	CA	94607	**800-228-9290**	510-451-4000
Ocean Ctr 101 N Atlantic Ave	Daytona Beach	FL	32118	**800-858-6444**	386-254-4500
Ocean Shores Convention Ctr 120 W Chance a La Mer Ave	Ocean Shores	WA	98569	**800-874-6737**	360-289-4411
Office of General Services Corning Tower 41st Fl Empire State Plz	Albany	NY	12242	**877-426-6006**	518-474-3899
Ogden Eccles Conference Ctr 2415 Washington Blvd	Ogden	UT	84401	**866-472-4627**	801-689-8600
Oncenter Complex 800 S State St	Syracuse	NY	13202	**800-776-7548**	315-435-8000
Ontario Convention Ctr 2000 E Convention Ctr Way	Ontario	CA	91764	**800-455-5755**	909-937-3000
Orange County Convention Ctr (OCCC) 9800 International Dr	Orlando	FL	32819	**800-345-9845**	407-685-9800
Oregon Convention Ctr 777 NE Martin Luther King Jr Blvd	Portland	OR	97232	**800-791-2250**	503-235-7575
Palm Springs Convention Ctr 277 N Avenida Caballeros	Palm Springs	CA	92262	**800-898-7256**	760-325-6611
Pennsylvania Convention Ctr 1101 Arch St	Philadelphia	PA	19107	**800-428-9000**	215-418-4700
Phoenix Convention Ctr 100 N Third St	Phoenix	AZ	85004	**800-282-4842**	602-262-6225
Pontchartrain Ctr 4545 Williams Blvd	Kenner	LA	70065	**800-745-3000**	504-465-9985
Quad City Conservation Alliance Expo Ctr 2621 Fourth Ave	Rock Island	IL	61201	**877-734-1565**	309-788-5912
Reno-Sparks Convention Ctr 4590 S Virginia St	Reno	NV	89502	**800-367-7366**	775-827-7600
Rushmore Plaza Civic Ctr 444 Mt Rushmore Rd N	Rapid City	SD	57701	**800-468-6463**	605-394-4115
Saint Louis Executive Conference Ctr 701 Convention Plz	Saint Louis	MO	63101	**800-325-7962**	314-342-5050
Salem Conference Ctr 200 Commercial St SE	Salem	OR	97301	**877-589-1700***	503-589-1700
*Sales					
San Diego Convention Ctr 111 W Harbor Dr	San Diego	CA	92101	**800-525-7322**	619-525-5000
San Jose Convention Center (SJC) 150 W San Carlos St	San Jose	CA	95110	**800-726-5673**	408-792-4194
Santa Monica Civic Auditorium 1855 Main St	Santa Monica	CA	90401	**866-728-3229**	310-458-8551
Savannah International Trade & Convention Ctr One International Dr	Savannah	GA	31421	**888-644-6822**	912-447-4000
Seaside Civic & Convention Ctr 415 First Ave	Seaside	OR	97138	**800-394-3303**	503-738-8585
Sharonville Convention Ctr 11355 Chester Rd	Sharonville	OH	45246	**800-294-3179**	513-771-7744
Sioux City Convention Ctr 801 Fourth St	Sioux City	IA	51101	**800-593-2228**	712-279-4800
South Padre Island Convention Centre 7355 Padre Blvd	South Padre Island	TX	78597	**800-657-2373**	956-761-3000
Statehouse Convention Ctr 426 W Markham PO Box 3232	Little Rock	AR	72203	**800-844-4781**	501-376-4781
Tampa Convention Ctr 333 S Franklin St	Tampa	FL	33602	**866-790-4111**	813-274-8511
Tulsa Convention Ctr 100 Civic Ctr	Tulsa	OK	74103	**800-678-7177**	918-894-4350
Tyson Events Ctr 401 Gordon Dr	Sioux City	IA	51101	**800-593-2228**	712-279-4850
US Cellular Ctr 370 First Ave E	Cedar Rapids	IA	52401	**800-745-3000**	319-398-5211
Vancouver Convention & Exposition Centre (VCEC) 1055 Canada Pl	Vancouver	BC	V6C0C3	**866-785-8232**	604-689-8232
Visalia Convention Ctr 303 E Acequia Ave	Visalia	CA	93291	**800-640-4888**	559-713-4000
Washington Convention Ctr Authority 801 Mt Vernon Pl NW	Washington	DC	20001	**800-368-9000**	202-249-3000
Wildwoods Convention Ctr 4501 Boardwalk	Wildwood	NJ	08260	**800-992-9732**	609-729-9000
Yakima Convention Ctr 10 N Eigth St	Yakima	WA	98901	**800-221-0751**	509-575-6062
Yuma Civic Ctr 1440 W Desert Hills Dr	Yuma	AZ	85365	**800-410-2554**	928-373-5040

208 CONVENTION & VISITORS BUREAUS

SEE ALSO Travel & Tourism Information - Canadian ; Travel & Tourism Information - Foreign Travel
Listings are alphabetized by city names.

Name / Address	City	State	ZIP	Toll-Free	Phone
Aberdeen Convention & Visitors Bureau 10 Railroad Ave SW PO Box 78	Aberdeen	SD	57401	**800-645-3851**	605-225-2414
Abilene Convention & Visitors Bureau 1101 N First St	Abilene	TX	79601	**800-727-7704**	325-676-2556
Abingdon Convention & Visitors Bureau 335 Cummings St	Abingdon	VA	24210	**800-435-3440**	276-676-2282
Akron/Summit County Convention & Visitors Bureau 77 E Mill St	Akron	OH	44308	**800-245-4254**	330-374-8900
Albany County Convention & Visitors Bureau 25 Quackenbush Sq	Albany	NY	12207	**800-258-3582**	518-434-1217
Albany Visitors Assn 300 Second Ave SW	Albany	OR	97321	**800-526-2256**	541-928-0911
Albuquerque Convention & Visitors Bureau 20 First Plz Ste 601	Albuquerque	NM	87102	**800-733-9918**	505-842-9918
Alexandria Convention & Visitors Assn 221 King St	Alexandria	VA	22314	**800-388-9119**	703-746-3301
Alexandria/Pineville Area Convention & Visitors Bureau (APACVB) 707 Main St PO Box 1070	Alexandria	LA	71301	**800-551-9546**	318-442-9546
Allegan County Tourist & Recreational Council 3255 122nd Ave Ste 103	Allegan	MI	49010	**888-425-5342**	269-686-9088
Lehigh Valley Visitor Ctr 840 Hamilton St Ste 200	Allentown	PA	18101	**800-747-0561**	610-882-9200
Alpena Area Convention & Visitors Bureau 235 W Chisholm St	Alpena	MI	49707	**800-425-7362**	989-354-4181
Alton Regional Convention & Visitors Bureau (ARCVB) 200 Piasa St	Alton	IL	62002	**800-258-6645**	618-465-6676
Amana Colonies Convention & Visitors Bureau 622 46th Ave	Amana	IA	52203	**800-579-2294**	319-622-7622
Amarillo Convention & Visitor Council 1000 S Polk St PO Box 9480	Amarillo	TX	79105	**800-692-1338**	806-374-1497
Lorain County Visitors Bureau 8025 Leavitt Rd	Amherst	OH	44001	**800-334-1673**	440-984-5282
Anaheim/Orange County Visitor & Convention Bureau 800 W Katella Ave PO Box 4270	Anaheim	CA	92802	**855-405-5020**	714-765-8888
Anchorage Convention & Visitors Bureau 524 W Fourth Ave	Anchorage	AK	99501	**800-445-8667**	907-276-4118
Anderson/Madison County Visitors & Convention Bureau 6335 S Scatterfield Rd	Anderson	IN	46013	**800-533-6569**	765-643-5633
Steuben County Tourism Bureau 430 N Wayne St Ste 1B	Angola	IN	46703	**888-665-5668**	260-665-5386
Ann Arbor Area Convention & Visitors Bureau 120 W Huron St	Ann Arbor	MI	48104	**800-888-9487**	734-995-7281
Southernmost Illinois Tourism Bureau PO Box 378	Anna	IL	62906	**800-248-4373**	618-833-9928
Annapolis & Anne Arundel County Conference & Visitors Bureau (AAACCVB) 26 W St	Annapolis	MD	21401	**888-302-2852**	410-280-0445
Fox Cities Convention & Visitors Bureau 3433 W College Ave	Appleton	WI	54914	**800-236-6673**	920-734-3358
Arlington Convention & Visitors Bureau 1905 E Randol Mill Rd	Arlington	TX	76011	**800-433-5374**	817-265-7721
Asheville Area Convention & Visitors Bureau 36 Montford Ave	Asheville	NC	28801	**800-257-5583**	828-258-6101
Aspen Chamber Resort Assn 425 Rio Grande Pl	Aspen	CO	81611	**800-670-0792**	970-925-1940
Athens Convention & Visitors Bureau 300 N Thomas St	Athens	GA	30601	**800-653-0603**	706-357-4430
Athens County Convention & Visitors Bureau 667 E State St	Athens	OH	45701	**800-878-9767**	740-592-1819
Atlanta Convention & Visitors Bureau 233 Peachtree St NE Ste 1400	Atlanta	GA	30303	**800-285-2682**	404-521-6600
Cobb Travel & Tourism One Galleria Pkwy	Atlanta	GA	30339	**800-451-3480**	678-303-2622
Atlantic City Convention & Visitors Authority 2314 Pacific Ave	Atlantic City	NJ	08401	**888-228-4748**	609-348-7100
Auburn-Opelika Tourism Bureau 714 E Glenn Ave	Auburn	AL	36830	**866-880-8747**	334-887-8747
Augusta Metropolitan Convention & Visitors Bureau 1450 Greene St Ste 110	Augusta	GA	30901	**800-726-0243**	706-823-6600
Aurora Area Convention & Visitors Bureau 43 W Galena Blvd	Aurora	IL	60506	**800-477-4369**	630-897-5581
Austin Convention & Visitors Bureau 301 Congress Ave Ste 200	Austin	TX	78701	**800-926-2282**	512-474-5171
Baker County Visitors & Convention Bureau 490 Campbell St	Baker City	OR	97814	**800-523-1235**	541-523-3356
Greater Bakersfield Convention & Visitors Bureau 515 Truxtun Ave	Bakersfield	CA	93301	**866-425-7353**	661-852-7282
Baltimore Area Convention & Visitors Assn (BACVA) 100 Light St 12th Fl	Baltimore	MD	21202	**877-225-8466**	410-659-7300
Bandera County Convention & Visitors Bureau 126 State Hwy 16 S PO Box 171	Bandera	TX	78003	**800-364-3833**	830-796-3045
Greater Bangor Convention & Visitors Bureau 40 Harlow St	Bangor	ME	04401	**800-916-6673**	207-947-5205
Clermont County Convention & Visitors Bureau (CCCVB) 410 E Main St PO Box 100	Batavia	OH	45103	**800-796-4282**	513-732-3600
Baton Rouge Convention & Visitors Bureau 359 Third St	Baton Rouge	LA	70801	**800-527-6843**	225-383-1825
Battle Creek/Calhoun County Convention & Visitors Bureau 77 E Michigan Ave Ste 100	Battle Creek	MI	49017	**800-397-2240**	269-962-2240
Beaumont Convention & Visitors Bureau 505 Willow St	Beaumont	TX	77701	**800-392-4401**	409-880-3749
Greene County Convention & Visitors Bureau 1221 Meadowbridge Dr	Beavercreek	OH	45434	**800-733-9109**	937-429-9100
Washington County Visitors Assn 11000 SW Stratus St Ste 170	Beaverton	OR	97008	**800-537-3149**	503-644-5555
Southern West Virginia Convention & Visitors Bureau 1406 Harper Rd	Beckley	WV	25801	**800-847-4898**	304-252-2244
Bedford County Visitors Bureau 131 S Juliana St	Bedford	PA	15522	**800-765-3331**	814-623-1771
Gaston County Travel & Tourism 620 N Main St	Belmont	NC	28012	**800-849-9994**	704-825-4044
Beloit Convention & Visitors Bureau 500 Public Ave	Beloit	WI	53511	**800-423-5648**	608-365-4838
Bucks County Conference & Visitors Bureau (BCCVB) 3207 St Rd	Bensalem	PA	19020	**800-836-2825**	215-639-0300
Beverly Hills Conference & Visitors Bureau 239 S Beverly Dr	Beverly Hills	CA	90212	**800-345-2210**	310-248-1000
Greater Big Rapids Convention & Visitors Bureau 246 N State St	Big Rapids	MI	49307	**800-999-9069**	231-796-7640
Big Spring Convention & Visitor Bureau 215 W Third St PO Box 3359	Big Spring	TX	79720	**866-222-7100**	432-264-6032
Billings Convention & Visitors Bureau 815 S 27th St PO Box 31177	Billings	MT	59107	**800-735-2635**	406-245-4111
Mississippi Gulf Coast Convention & Visitors Bureau 2350 Beach Blvd Ste A	Biloxi	MS	39531	**888-467-4853**	228-896-6699
Greater Birmingham Convention & Visitors Bureau 2200 Ninth Ave N	Birmingham	AL	35203	**800-458-8085**	205-458-8000

	Toll-Free	Phone
Bismarck-Mandan Convention & Visitors Bureau		
1600 Burnt Boat Dr ....Bismarck ND 58503	800-767-3555	701-222-4308
Bloomington Convention & Visitors Bureau (BCVB)		
7900 International Dr Ste 990........Bloomington MN 55425	800-346-4289	952-858-8500
Bloomington-Normal Area Convention & Visitors Bureau		
3201 CIRA Dr Ste 201 ....Bloomington IL 61704	800-433-8226	309-665-0033
Bloomington/Monroe County Convention & Visitors Bureau		
2855 N Walnut St ....Bloomington IN 47404	800-800-0037	812-334-8900
Columbia-Montour Visitors Bureau		
121 Papermill Rd ....Bloomsburg PA 17815	800-847-4810	570-784-8279
Mercer County Convention & Visitors Bureau		
704 Bland St PO Box 4088........Bluefield WV 24701	800-221-3206	304-325-8438
Boise Convention & Visitors Bureau		
1199 Main St ....Boise ID 83702	800-635-5240	208-344-7777
North Carolina High Country Host		
1700 Blowing Rock Rd ....Boone NC 28607	800-438-7500	828-264-1299
Greater Boston Convention & Visitors Bureau (GBCVB)		
Two Copley Pl Ste 105 ....Boston MA 02116	888-733-2678	617-536-4100
Boulder Convention & Visitors Bureau		
2440 Pearl St ....Boulder CO 80302	800-444-0447	303-442-2911
Brenham/Washington County Convention & Visitor Bureau		
314 S Austin St ....Brenham TX 77833	888-273-6426	979-836-3695
Greater Bridgeport Conference & Visitors Ctr		
164 W Main St ....Bridgeport WV 26330	800-368-4324	304-842-7272
Minneapolis Northwest		
6200 Shingle Creek Pkwy Ste 130........Brooklyn Center MN 55430	800-541-4364	763-852-7500
Northwest Pennsylvania's Great Outdoors Visitors Bureau		
2801 Maplevale Rd ....Brookville PA 15825	800-348-9393	814-849-5197
Brownsville Convention & Visitors Bureau		
650 Ruben M Torres Sr Blvd ....Brownsville TX 78521	800-626-2639	956-546-3721
Brunswick & The Golden Isles of Georgia Visitors Bureau		
Four Glynn Ave ....Brunswick GA 31520	800-933-2627	912-265-0620
Buena Park Convention & Visitors Office		
6601 Beach Blvd ....Buena Park CA 90621	800-541-3953	
Buffalo Niagara Convention & Visitors Bureau		
617 Main St Ste 200........Buffalo NY 14203	800-283-3256	716-852-2356
San Mateo County Convention & Visitors Bureau		
111 Anza Blvd Ste 410........Burlingame CA 94010	800-288-4748	650-348-7600
Burlington/Alamance County Convention & Visitors Bureau		
610 S Lexington Ave PO Box 519........Burlington NC 27216	800-637-3804	336-570-1444
Vermont Convention Bureau		
60 Main St Ste 100........Burlington VT 05401	877-264-3503	802-860-0606
Cadillac Area Visitors Bureau		
201 N Mitchell St ....Cadillac MI 49601	800-225-2537	231-775-0657
Tourism Calgary		
200 238 11th Ave SE ....Calgary AB T2G0X8	800-661-1678	403-263-8510
Finger Lakes Visitors Connection		
25 Gorham St ....Canandaigua NY 14424	877-386-4669	585-394-3915
Canton/Stark County Convention & Visitors Bureau		
222 Market Ave N ....Canton OH 44702	800-552-6051	330-454-1439
Cape Girardeau Convention & Visitors Bureau		
400 Broadway Ste 100 ....Cape Girardeau MO 63701	800-777-0068	573-335-1631
Carlsbad Convention & Visitors Bureau		
400 Carlsbad Village Dr ....Carlsbad CA 92008	800-227-5722	760-434-6093
Hamilton County Convention & Visitors Bureau Inc		
37 E Main St ....Carmel IN 46032	800-776-8687	317-848-3181
Carrington Convention & Visitors Bureau		
871 Main St PO Box 439 ....Carrington ND 58421	800-641-9668	701-652-2524
Casper Area Convention & Visitors Bureau		
992 N Poplar St ....Casper WY 82601	800-852-1889	307-234-5362
Cedar City-Brian Head Tourism & Convention Bureau		
581 N Main St Ste A........Cedar City UT 84721	800-354-4849	435-586-5124
Cedar Rapids Area Convention & Visitors Bureau		
119 First Ave SE PO Box 5339........Cedar Rapids IA 52401	800-735-5557	319-398-5009
Champaign County Convention & Visitors Bureau		
108 S Neil St ....Champaign IL 61820	800-369-6151	217-351-4133
Chapel Hill/Orange County Visitors Bureau		
501 W Franklin St ....Chapel Hill NC 27516	888-968-2060	
Charleston Area Convention & Visitors Bureau		
423 King St ....Charleston SC 29403	800-868-8118	843-853-8000
Charlotte Convention & Visitors Bureau		
500 S College St Ste 300........Charlotte NC 28202	800-722-1994	704-334-2282
Chattanooga Area Convention & Visitors Bureau		
215 Broad St ....Chattanooga TN 37402	800-322-3344	423-756-8687
Chautauqua County Visitors Bureau		
Chautauqua Main Gate Rt 394 PO Box 1441........Chautauqua NY 14722	800-242-4569	716-357-4569
Cherokee Tribal Travel & Promotions		
498 Tsali Blvd PO Box 460........Cherokee NC 28719	877-440-9990	828-359-6492
Chesapeake Conventions & Tourism Bureau (CCT)		
860 Greenbrier Cir Ste 101........Chesapeake VA 23320	888-889-5551	757-502-4898
Cheyenne Area Convention & Visitors Bureau		
121 W 15th St Ste 202........Cheyenne WY 82001	800-426-5009	307-778-3133
Chicago Office of Tourism & Culture		
78 E Washington St 4th Fl ....Chicago IL 60602	866-966-5335	312-744-2400
Greater Cincinnati Convention & Visitors Bureau		
525 Vine St Ste 1500........Cincinnati OH 45202	800-543-2613	513-621-2142
Pickaway County Visitors Bureau		
325 W Main St ....Circleville OH 43113	800-283-4678	740-474-3636
Clarksville/Montgomery County Tourist Commission		
25 Jefferson St Ste 300........Clarksville TN 37040	800-530-2487	931-647-2331
Clear Lake Convention & Visitors Bureau		
205 Main Ave PO Box 188........Clear Lake IA 50428	800-285-5338	641-357-2159
Visit St Petersburg Clearwater		
13805 58th St N Ste 2-200........Clearwater FL 33760	877-352-3224	727-464-7200
Positively Cleveland Visitors Ctr		
100 Public Sq Ste 100 ....Cleveland OH 44113	800-321-1001	216-875-6680
Brevard County Tourism Development		
430 Brevard Ave Ste 150 ....Cocoa Village FL 32922	877-572-3224	321-433-4470
Park County Travel Council (PCTC)		
836 Sheridan Ave PO Box 2454 ....Cody WY 82414	800-393-2639	307-587-2297
Colby Convention & Visitors Bureau		
350 S Range Ste 10 ....Colby KS 67701	800-611-8835	785-460-7643
Bryan/College Station Convention & Visitors Bureau (BCSCVB)		
715 University Dr E ....College Station TX 77840	800-777-8292	979-260-9898
Colorado Springs Convention & Visitors Bureau		
515 S Cascade Ave ....Colorado Springs CO 80903	800-888-4748	719-635-7506
Columbia Convention & Visitors Bureau		
300 S Providence Rd ....Columbia MO 65203	800-652-0987	573-875-1231
Columbia Metropolitan Convention & Visitors Bureau		
1101 Lincoln St PO Box 15 ....Columbia SC 29202	800-264-4884	803-545-0000
Columbus Area Visitors Ctr		
506 Fifth St ....Columbus IN 47201	800-468-6564	812-378-2622
Columbus Convention & Visitors Bureau		
318 7th St N ....Columbus MS 39701	800-327-2686	662-329-1191
Greater Columbus Convention & Visitors Bureau		
277 W Nationwide Blvd Ste 125........Columbus OH 43215	866-397-2657	614-221-6623
Polk County Travel & Tourism		
20 E Mills St PO Box 308........Columbus NC 28722	800-440-7848	828-894-2324
New Hampshire Div of Travel & Tourism Development		
172 Pembroke Rd PO Box 1856 ....Concord NH 03302	800-262-6660	603-271-2665
Coos Bay-North Bend Visitor & Convention Bureau		
50 Central Ave ....Coos Bay OR 97420	800-824-8486	541-269-0215
Iowa City/Coralville Area Convention & Visitors Bureau		
900 First Ave Hayden Fry Way ....Coralville IA 52241	800-283-6592	319-337-6592
Corinth Area Convention & Visitors Bureau		
215 N Fillmore St ....Corinth MS 38834	800-748-9048	662-287-8300
Corpus Christi Convention & Visitors Bureau		
101 N Shoreline Blvd Ste 430........Corpus Christi TX 78401	800-678-6232	361-881-1888
Corvallis Tourism		
420 NW Second St ....Corvallis OR 97330	800-334-8118	541-757-1544
Northern Kentucky Convention & Visitors Bureau (NKYCVB)		
50 E RiverCenter Blvd Ste 200 ....Covington KY 41011	877-659-8474	859-261-4677
Montgomery County Visitors & Convention Bureau		
218 E Pike St ....Crawfordsville IN 47933	800-866-3973	765-362-5200
Crescent City-Del Norte County Chamber of Commerce (CCDNCVB)		
1001 Front St ....Crescent City CA 95531	800-343-8300	707-464-3174
Dallas Convention & Visitors Bureau		
325 N St Paul St Ste 700 ....Dallas TX 75201	800-232-5527	214-571-1000
Central Florida Visitors & Convention Bureau		
101 Adventure Ct ....Davenport FL 33837	800-828-7655	863-420-2586
Tucker County Convention & Visitors Bureau		
410 William Ave ....Davis WV 26260	800-782-2775	304-259-5315
Dayton/Montgomery County Convention & Visitors Bureau		
One Chamber Plz Ste A........Dayton OH 45402	800-221-8235	937-226-8211
Decatur Area Convention & Visitors Bureau		
202 E N St ....Decatur IL 62523	800-331-4479	217-423-7000
Decatur/Morgan County Convention & Visitors Bureau (DMCCVB)		
719 Sixth Ave SE PO Box 2349 ....Decatur AL 35602	800-232-5449	256-350-2028
Wicomico County Convention & Visitors Bureau		
8480 Ocean Hwy ....Delmar MD 21875	800-332-8687	410-548-4914
Denver Metro Convention & Visitors Bureau		
1555 California St Ste 300 ....Denver CO 80202	800-480-2010	303-892-1112
Greater Des Moines Convention & Visitors Bureau		
400 Locust St Ste 265 ....Des Moines IA 50309	800-451-2625	515-286-4960
Detroit Metropolitan Convention & Visitors Bureau		
211 W Fort St Ste 1000 ....Detroit MI 48226	877-424-5554	313-202-1800
Dickinson Convention & Visitors Bureau		
72 E Museum Dr ....Dickinson ND 58601	800-279-7391	701-483-4988
Dothan Area Convention & Visitors Bureau		
3311 Ross Clark Cir PO Box 8765 ....Dothan AL 36301	888-449-0212	334-794-6622
Kent County & Greater Dover Delaware Convention & Visitors Bureau		
435 N DuPont Hwy ....Dover DE 19901	800-233-5368	302-734-1736
DuQuoin Tourism Commission		
20 N Chestnut St PO Box 1037........Du Quoin IL 62832	800-455-9570	618-542-8338
Dublin Convention & Visitors Bureau		
Nine S High St ....Dublin OH 43017	800-245-8387	614-792-7666
Atlanta's Gwinnett Convention & Visitors Bureau (GCVB)		
6500 Sugarloaf Pkwy Ste 200........Duluth GA 30097	888-494-6638	770-623-3600
Duluth Convention & Visitors Bureau		
21 W Superior St Ste 100 ....Duluth MN 55802	800-438-5884	218-722-4011
Durango Area Tourism Office		
111 S Camino del Rio ....Durango CO 81301	800-525-8855	970-247-3500
Durham Convention & Visitors Bureau		
101 E Morgan St ....Durham NC 27701	800-446-8604	919-687-0288
Eagan Convention & Visitors Bureau		
1501 Central Pkwy ....Eagan MN 55121	866-324-2620	651-675-5546
Visit Eau Claire		
4319 Jeffers Rd Ste 201........Eau Claire WI 54703	888-523-3866	715-831-2345
Effingham Convention & Visitors Bureau		
201 E Jefferson Ave ....Effingham IL 62401	800-772-0750	217-342-5305
El Paso Convention & Visitors Bureau		
One Civic Ctr Plz ....El Paso TX 79901	800-351-6024	915-534-0600
Elgin Area Convention & Visitors Bureau		
77 S Riverside Dr Ste 1........Elgin IL 60120	800-217-5362	847-695-7540
Elkhart County Convention & Visitors Bureau		
219 Caravan Dr ....Elkhart IN 46514	800-250-4827	574-262-8161
Howard County Tourism Council		
8267 Main St Side Entrance ....Ellicott City MD 21043	800-243-3425	410-313-1900
Grays Harbor Tourism		
PO Box 1229 ....Elma WA 98541	800-621-9625	360-482-2651
VisitErie		
208 E Bayfront Pkwy Ste 103 ....Erie PA 16507	800-524-3743	814-454-1000
Travel Lane County		
PO Box 10286 ....Eugene OR 97440	800-547-5445	541-484-5307
Humboldt County Convention & Visitors Bureau		
1034 Second St ....Eureka CA 95501	800-346-3482	707-443-5097
Evansville Convention & Visitors Bureau		
401 SE Riverside Dr ....Evansville IN 47713	800-433-3025	812-421-2200
Fairbanks Convention & Visitors Bureau		
101 Dunkel St Ste 111 ....Fairbanks AK 99701	800-327-5774	907-456-5774
Fairfax County Convention & Visitors Bureau (FXVA)		
3702 Pender Dr Ste 420 ....Fairfax VA 22030	800-732-4732	703-790-0643
Convention & Visitors Bureau of Marion County		
1000 Cole St Ste A ....Fairmont WV 26554	800-834-7365	304-368-1123
Fairmont Convention & Visitors Bureau		
323 E Blue Earth Ave ....Fairmont MN 56031	800-657-3280	507-235-8585
Tourism Bureau Southwestern Illinois		
10950 Lincoln Trail ....Fairview Heights IL 62208	800-442-1488	618-397-1488
Fargo-Moorhead Convention & Visitors Bureau		
2001 44th St ....Fargo ND 58103	800-235-7654	701-282-3653
Farmington Convention & Visitors Bureau		
3041 E Main St ....Farmington NM 87402	800-448-1240	505-326-7602
Fayetteville Area Convention & Visitors Bureau (FACVB)		
245 Person St ....Fayetteville NC 28301	800-255-8217	910-483-5311

Name / Address	City	State	ZIP	Toll-Free	Phone
Flagstaff Convention & Visitors Bureau 323 W Aspen Ave	Flagstaff	AZ	86001	**800-217-2367**	928-779-7611
Florence Convention & Visitors Bureau 3290 W Radio Dr *General	Florence	SC	29501	**800-325-9005***	843-664-0330
Tropical Everglades Visitor Assn 160 US Hwy Ste 1	Florida City	FL	33034	**800-272-6232**	305-245-9180
Fond du Lac Convention & Visitors Bureau 171 S Pioneer Rd	Fond du Lac	WI	54935	**800-937-9123**	920-923-3010
Fort Collins Convention & Visitors Bureau 19 Old Town Sq Ste 137	Fort Collins	CO	80524	**800-274-3678**	970-232-3840
Greater Fort Lauderdale Convention & Visitors Bureau 100 E Broward Blvd Ste 200	Fort Lauderdale	FL	33301	**800-227-8669**	954-765-4466
Fort Madison 614 Ninth St	Fort Madison	IA	52627	**800-210-8687**	319-372-5471
Lee County Visitors & Convention Bureau 12800 University Dr Ste 550	Fort Myers	FL	33907	**800-237-6444**	239-338-3500
Fort Smith Convention & Visitors Bureau 2 N 'B'	Fort Smith	AR	72901	**800-637-1477**	479-783-8888
Fort Wayne/Allen County Convention & Visitors Bureau 927 S Harrison St	Fort Wayne	IN	46802	**800-767-7752**	260-424-3700
Fort Worth Convention & Visitors Bureau 111 W Fourth St Ste 200	Fort Worth	TX	76102	**800-433-5747**	817-336-8791
Frankenmuth Convention & Visitors Bureau 635 S Main St	Frankenmuth	MI	48734	**800-386-8696**	989-652-6106
Frankfort/Franklin County Tourist & Convention Commission 100 Capitol Ave	Frankfort	KY	40601	**800-960-7200**	502-875-8687
Fredericksburg Chamber of Commerce 302 E Austin St	Fredericksburg	TX	78624	**888-997-3600**	830-997-6523
Fremont/Sandusky County Convention & Visitors Bureau 712 N St Ste 102	Fremont	OH	43420	**800-255-8070**	419-332-4470
Fresno & Clovis Convention & Visitors Bureau 1550 E Shaw Ave Ste 101	Fresno	CA	93710	**800-788-0836**	559-981-5500
Alachua County Visitors & Convention Bureau 30 E University Ave	Gainesville	FL	32601	**866-778-5002**	352-374-5260
Galesburg Area Convention & Visitors Bureau 2163 E Main St	Galesburg	IL	61401	**800-916-3330**	309-343-2485
Finney County Convention & Visitors Bureau 1511 E Fulton Terr	Garden City	KS	67846	**866-267-4638**	620-275-1900
Georgetown Convention & Visitors Bureau 1101 N College St	Georgetown	TX	78626	**800-436-8696**	512-930-3545
Gettysburg Convention & Visitors Bureau 571 W Middle St PO Box 4117	Gettysburg	PA	17325	**800-337-5015**	717-334-6274
Greater Grand Forks Convention & Visitors Bureau 4251 Gateway Dr	Grand Forks	ND	58203	**800-866-4566**	701-746-0444
Grand Junction Visitors & Convention Bureau 740 Horizon Dr	Grand Junction	CO	81506	**800-962-2547**	970-244-1480
Grand Rapids/Kent County Convention & Visitors Bureau 171 Monroe Ave NW Ste 700	Grand Rapids	MI	49503	**800-678-9859**	616-459-8287
Grants Pass Visitors & Convention Bureau 1995 NW Vine St	Grants Pass	OR	97526	**800-547-5927**	541-476-5510
Houma Area Convention & Visitors Bureau 114 Tourist Dr	Gray	LA	70359	**800-688-2732**	985-868-2732
Greeley Convention & Visitors Bureau 902 Seventh Ave	Greeley	CO	80631	**800-449-3866**	970-352-3567
Packer Country Visitor & Convention Bureau 1901 S Oneida St	Green Bay	WI	54304	**888-867-3342**	920-494-9507
Putnam County Convention & Visitors Bureau 12 W Washington St	Greencastle	IN	46135	**800-829-4639**	765-653-8743
Greensboro Area Convention & Visitors Bureau 2200 Pinecroft Rd Ste 200	Greensboro	NC	27407	**800-344-2282**	336-274-2282
Greater Greenville Convention & Visitors Bureau 148 River St Ste 222	Greenville	SC	29601	**800-351-7180**	864-421-0000
Greenville-Pitt County Convention & Visitors Bureau (GPCCVB) 303 SW Greenville Blvd PO Box 8027	Greenville	NC	27835	**800-537-5564**	252-329-4200
Greenwood Convention & Visitors Bureau 111 E Market St	Greenwood	MS	38930	**800-748-9064**	662-453-9197
Alabama Gulf Coast Convention & Visitors Bureau 3150 Gulf Shores Pkwy PO Box 457	Gulf Shores	AL	36547	**800-745-7263**	251-968-7511
Lake County Convention & Visitors Bureau 5465 W Grand Ave Ste 100	Gurnee	IL	60031	**800-525-3669**	847-662-2700
Hagerstown/Washington County Convention & Visitors Bureau 16 Public Sq	Hagerstown	MD	21740	**888-257-2600**	301-791-3246
Hampton Conventions & Visitors Bureau 1919 Commerce Dr Ste 290	Hampton	VA	23666	**800-487-8778**	757-722-1222
Hannibal Convention & Visitors Bureau 505 N Third St	Hannibal	MO	63401	**866-263-4825**	573-221-2477
Jefferson County Convention & Visitors Bureau 37 Washington Ct	Harpers Ferry	WV	25425	**866-435-5698**	304-535-2627
Hershey Harrisburg Region Visitors Bureau 17 S Second St	Harrisburg	PA	17101	**877-727-8573**	717-231-7788
Long Island Convention & Visitors Bureau & Sports Commission 330 Motor Pkwy Ste 203	Hauppauge	NY	11788	**877-386-6654**	
Hays Convention & Visitors Bureau 2700 Vine St PO Box 490	Hays	KS	67601	**800-569-4505**	785-628-8202
Alpine Helen/White County Convention & Visitors Bureau 726 Bruckenstrasse PO Box 730	Helen	GA	30545	**800-858-8027**	706-878-2181
Henderson County Tourist Commission 101 N Water St Ste B	Henderson	KY	42420	**800-648-3128**	270-826-3128
Henderson County Travel & Tourism 201 S Main St	Hendersonville	NC	28792	**800-828-4244**	828-693-9708
Huntingdon County Visitors Bureau 6993 Seven Pt Rd Ste 2	Hesston	PA	16647	**888-729-7869**	814-658-0060
Hickory Metro Convention & Visitors Bureau 1960 13th Ave Dr SE	Hickory	NC	28602	**800-509-2444**	828-322-1335
High Point Convention & Visitors Bureau 300 S Main St	High Point	NC	27260	**800-720-5255**	336-884-5255
Hilton Head Island Visitors & Convention Bureau 1 Chamber Dr PO Box 5647	Hilton Head Island	SC	29938	**800-523-3373**	843-785-3673
Holland Area Convention & Visitors Bureau 76 E Eigth St	Holland	MI	49423	**800-506-1299**	616-394-0000
Hawaii Visitors & Convention Bureau 2270 Kalakaua Ave Ste 801	Honolulu	HI	96815	**800-464-2924**	
Hot Springs Convention & Visitors Bureau 134 Convention Blvd	Hot Springs	AR	71901	**800-543-2284**	501-321-2277
Greater Houston Convention & Visitors Bureau 901 Bagby St Ste 100	Houston	TX	77002	**800-446-8786**	713-437-5200
Cabell-Huntington Convention & Visitors Bureau PO Box 347	Huntington	WV	25708	**800-635-6329**	304-525-7333
Huntington County Visitors & Convention Bureau 407 N Jefferson St	Huntington	IN	46750	**800-848-4282**	260-359-8687
Huntington Beach Marketing & Visitors Bureau 301 Main St Ste 208	Huntington Beach	CA	92648	**800-729-6232**	714-969-3492
Huntsville/Madison County Convention & Visitor's Bureau 500 Church St Ste 1	Huntsville	AL	35801	**800-843-0468**	256-551-2230
Huron Chamber & Visitors Bureau 1725 Dakota Ave S	Huron	SD	57350	**800-487-6673**	605-352-0000
Hurricane Convention & Visitors Bureau 3255 Teays Vly Rd PO Box 1086	Hurricane	WV	25526	**877-487-7982**	304-562-5896
Greater Hutchinson Convention & Visitors Bureau 117 N Walnut St PO Box 519	Hutchinson	KS	67504	**800-691-4262**	620-662-3391
Incline Village/Crystal Bay Visitors Bureau 969 Tahoe Blvd	Incline Village	NV	89451	**800-468-2463**	775-832-1606
Indiana County Tourist Bureau 2334 Oakland Ave Ste 68	Indiana	PA	15701	**877-746-3426**	724-463-7505
Indianapolis Convention & Visitors Assn 200 S Capitol Ave Ste 300	Indianapolis	IN	46225	**800-862-6912**	317-262-3000
Western Upper Peninsula Convention & Visitor Bureau 405 N Lake St PO Box 706	Ironwood	MI	49938	**800-522-5657**	906-932-4850
Irving Convention & Visitors Bureau 222 W Las Colinas Blvd Ste 1550	Irving	TX	75039	**800-247-8464**	972-252-7476
Ithaca/Tompkins County Convention & Visitors Bureau 904 E Shore Dr	Ithaca	NY	14850	**800-284-8422**	607-272-1313
Jackson County Convention & Visitors Bureau 141 S Jackson St	Jackson	MI	49201	**800-245-5282**	517-764-4440
Metro Jackson Convention & Visitors Bureau 111 E Capitol St Ste 102	Jackson	MS	39202	**800-354-7695**	601-960-1891
Jacksonville Convention & Visitors Bureau 310 E State St	Jacksonville	IL	62650	**800-593-5678**	217-243-5678
Onslow County Tourism 1099 Gum Branch Rd	Jacksonville	NC	28540	**800-932-2144**	
Visit Jacksonville 208 N Laura St Ste 1	Jacksonville	FL	32202	**800-733-2668**	904-798-9111
Jamestown Promotions & Tourism Ctr 404 Louis L'Amour Ln	Jamestown	ND	58401	**800-222-4766**	701-251-9145
Jefferson City Convention & Visitors Bureau 100 E High St PO Box 2227	Jefferson City	MO	65101	**800-769-4183**	573-632-2820
Clark-Floyd Counties Convention & Tourism Bureau 315 Southern Indiana Ave	Jeffersonville	IN	47130	**800-552-3842**	812-282-6654
Greater Johnstown/Cambria County Convention & Visitors Bureau 416 Main St Ste 100	Johnstown	PA	15901	**800-237-8590**	814-536-7993
Heritage Corridor Convention & Visitors Bureau 339 W Jefferson St	Joliet	IL	60435	**800-926-2262**	815-727-2323
Juneau Convention & Visitors Bureau 101 Egan Dr	Juneau	AK	99801	**888-581-2201**	907-586-1737
Kalamazoo County Convention & Visitors Bureau 141 E Michigan Ave Ste 100	Kalamazoo	MI	49007	**800-888-0509**	269-488-9000
Flathead Convention & Visitors Bureau 15 Depot Pk	Kalispell	MT	59901	**800-543-3105**	406-756-9091
Cabarrus County Convention & Visitors Bureau 3003 Dale Earnhardt Blvd	Kannapolis	NC	28083	**800-848-3740**	704-782-4340
Kansas City Convention & Visitors Assn 1100 Main St Ste 2200	Kansas City	MO	64105	**800-767-7700**	816-221-5242
Kansas City Kansas Convention & Visitors Bureau Inc 901 N Eigth St PO Box 171517	Kansas City	KS	66117	**800-264-1563**	913-321-5800
Tri-Cities Visitor & Convention Bureau 7130 W Grandridge Blvd Ste B	Kennewick	WA	99336	**800-254-5824**	509-735-8486
Kenosha Area Convention & Visitors Bureau 812 56th St	Kenosha	WI	53140	**800-654-7309**	262-654-7307
Kerrville Convention & Visitors Bureau 2108 Sidney Baker St	Kerrville	TX	78028	**800-221-7958**	830-792-3535
Ketchikan Visitors Bureau 131 Front St	Ketchikan	AK	99901	**800-770-3300**	907-225-6166
Key West Visitors Ctr 510 Greene St 1st Fl *General	Key West	FL	33040	**800-533-5397***	305-294-2587
Monroe County Tourist Development Council 1201 White St Ste 102	Key West	FL	33040	**800-242-5229**	305-296-1552
Valley Forge Convention & Visitors Bureau 1000 First Ave Ste 101 *General	King of Prussia	PA	19406	**888-847-4883***	610-834-1550
Kingsport Convention & Visitors Bureau (KCVB) 400 Clinchfield St Ste 100	Kingsport	TN	37660	**800-743-5282**	423-392-8820
Kinston Convention & Visitors Bureau 301 N Queen St	Kinston	NC	28501	**800-869-0032**	252-523-2500
Armstrong County Tourist Bureau 125 Market St Ste 2	Kittanning	PA	16201	**888-265-9954**	724-543-4003
Discover Klamath 205 Riverside Dr Ste B	Klamath Falls	OR	97601	**800-445-6728**	541-882-1501
Knoxville Tourism & Sports Corp 301 S Gay St	Knoxville	TN	37902	**800-727-8045**	865-523-7263
Lake Barkley Tourist Commission 82 Days Inn Dr	Kuttawa	KY	42055	**800-355-3885**	270-388-5300
La Crosse Area Convention & Visitors Bureau 410 Veterans Memorial Dr	La Crosse	WI	54601	**800-658-9424**	608-782-2366
Lafayette Convention & Visitors Commission 1400 NW Evangeline Thwy	Lafayette	LA	70501	**800-346-1958**	337-232-3737
Lafayette-West Lafayette Convention & Visitors Bureau 301 Frontage Rd	Lafayette	IN	47905	**800-872-6648**	765-447-9999
Laguna Beach Visitors & Conference Bureau 381 Forest Ave	Laguna Beach	CA	92651	**800-877-1115**	949-497-9229
Southwest Louisiana Convention & Visitors Bureau 1205 N Lakeshore Dr	Lake Charles	LA	70601	**800-456-7952**	337-436-9588
Seminole County Convention & Visitors Bureau 1515 International Pkwy Suite 1013	Lake Mary	FL	32746	**800-800-7832**	407-665-2900
Lake Placid Convention & Visitors Bureau 49 Parkside Dr	Lake Placid	NY	12946	**800-447-5224**	518-523-2445
Chicago Southland Convention & Visitors Bureau 2304 173rd St	Lansing	IL	60438	**888-895-8233**	708-895-8200
Greater Lansing Convention & Visitors Bureau 500 E Michigan Ave Ste 180	Lansing	MI	48912	**888-252-6746**	517-487-0077
Las Cruces Convention & Visitors Bureau 211 N Water St	Las Cruces	NM	88001	**800-429-9488**	575-541-2444
Las Vegas Convention & Visitors Authority 3150 Paradise Rd	Las Vegas	NV	89109	**877-847-4858**	702-892-0711

	Toll-Free	Phone
Leavenworth Convention & Visitors Bureau 518 Shawnee St PO Box 44 .... Leavenworth KS 66048	800-844-4114	913-682-4113
Greenbrier County Convention & Visitors Bureau 540 N Jefferson St Ste N. .... Lewisburg WV 24901	800-833-2068	304-645-1000
Lexington Convention & Visitors Bureau 301 E Vine St .... Lexington KY 40507	800-845-3959	859-233-7299
Laurel Highlands Visitors Bureau 120 E Main St .... Ligonier PA 15658	800-333-5661	724-238-5661
Lima/Allen County Convention & Visitors Bureau 144 S Main St Ste 101 .... Lima OH 45801	888-222-6075	419-222-6075
Lincoln Convention & Visitors Bureau 1135 M St Ste 300 .... Lincoln NE 68508	800-423-8212	402-434-5335
Lincoln City Visitor & Convention Bureau 801 SW Hwy 101 Ste 401 .... Lincoln City OR 97367	800-452-2151	541-996-1274
Lisle Convention & Visitors Bureau 925 Burlington Ave .... Lisle IL 60532	800-733-9811	630-769-1000
Little Rock Convention & Visitors Bureau 426 W Markham St PO Box 3232 .... Little Rock AR 72203	800-844-4781	501-376-4781
Lodi Conference & Visitors Bureau 115 S School St Ste 5. .... Lodi CA 95240	800-798-1810	209-365-1195
London/Laurel County Tourist Commission 140 Faith Assembly Church Rd .... London KY 40741	800-348-0095	606-878-6900
Long Beach Convention & Visitors Bureau 301 E Ocean Blvd .... Long Beach CA 90802	800-452-7829	562-436-3645
Louisville & Jefferson County Convention & Visitors Bureau 401 W Main St Ste 2300. .... Louisville KY 40202	800-626-5646	502-584-2121
Greater Merrimack Valley Convention & Visitors Bureau 40 French St Second Fl .... Lowell MA 01852	800-443-3332	978-459-6150
Lubbock Convention & Visitors Bureau 1500 Broadway St Sixth Fl .... Lubbock TX 79401	800-692-4035	806-747-5232
Lumberton Area Visitors Bureau 3431 Lackey St .... Lumberton NC 28360	800-359-6971	910-739-9999
Mackinaw Area Visitors Bureau 10800 US 23 .... Mackinaw City MI 49701	800-666-0160	231-436-5664
Macon-Bibb County Convention/Visitors Bureau 450 Martin Luther King Jr Blvd .... Macon GA 31201	800-768-3401	478-743-1074
Greater Madison Convention & Visitors Bureau 615 E Washington Ave .... Madison WI 53703	800-373-6376	608-255-2537
Madison Convention & Visitors Bureau 115 E Jefferson St .... Madison GA 30650	800-709-7406	706-342-4454
Saint Tammany Parish Tourist & Convention Commission 68099 Hwy 59 .... Mandeville LA 70471	800-634-9443	985-892-0520
Manhattan Convention & Visitors Bureau 501 Poyntz Ave .... Manhattan KS 66502	800-759-0134	785-776-8829
Manitowoc Area Visitor & Convention Bureau PO Box 966 .... Manitowoc WI 54221	800-627-4896	
Greater Mankato Growth 1961 Premier Dr .... Mankato MN 56001	800-697-0652	507-385-6640
Mansfield/Richland County Convention & Visitors Bureau 124 N Main St .... Mansfield OH 44902	800-642-8282	419-525-1300
Outer Banks Visitors Bureau One Visitor Ctr Cir .... Manteo NC 27954	877-629-4386	252-473-2138
Marion-Grant County Convention & Visitors Bureau 428 S Washington St Ste 261 .... Marion IN 46953	800-662-9474	765-668-5435
Williamson County Tourism Bureau 1602 Sioux Dr .... Marion IL 62959 *General	800-433-7399*	618-997-3690
Marquette Country Convention & Visitors Bureau 337 W Washington St .... Marquette MI 49855	800-544-4321	906-228-7749
Marshfield Convention & Visitors Bureau 700 S Central Ave PO Box 868 .... Marshfield WI 54449	800-422-4541	715-384-3454
Mason City Convention & Visitors Bureau 2021 Fourth St SW Hwy 122 W .... Mason City IA 50401	800-423-5724	641-422-1663
Brandywine Conference & Visitors Bureau 1501 N Providence Rd .... Media PA 19063	800-343-3983	610-565-3679
Melbourne Regional Chamber of East Central Florida 1005 E Strawbridge Ave .... Melbourne FL 32901	855-894-4673	321-724-5400
Memphis Convention & Visitors Bureau 47 Union Ave .... Memphis TN 38103	888-633-9099	901-543-5300
Merced Conference & Visitors Bureau (MCVB) 710 W 16th St .... Merced CA 95340	800-446-5353	209-384-2791
Meridian/Lauderdale County Tourism Bureau 212 Constitution Ave PO Box 5313 .... Meridian MS 39301	888-868-7720	601-482-8001
Greater Miami Convention & Visitors Bureau 701 Brickell Ave Ste 2700. .... Miami FL 33131	800-933-8448	305-539-3000
LaPorte County Convention & Visitors Bureau 4073 S Franklin St .... Michigan City IN 46360	800-634-2650	219-872-5055
Midland County Convention & Visitors Bureau 300 Rodd St Ste 101. .... Midland MI 48640	800-444-9979	989-839-0340
Visit Milledgeville 200 W Hancock St .... Milledgeville GA 31061	800-653-1804	478-452-4687
Greater Milwaukee Convention & Visitors Bureau 648 N Plankinton Ave Ste 425 .... Milwaukee WI 53203	800-554-1448	414-273-7222
Meet Minneapolis 250 Marquette Ave Ste 1300. .... Minneapolis MN 55401	800-445-7412	612-767-8000
Minot Convention & Visitors Bureau 1020 S Broadway .... Minot ND 58701	800-264-2626	701-857-8206
Modesto Convention & Visitors Bureau 1150 Ninth St Ste C .... Modesto CA 95354	888-640-8467	209-526-5588
Quad Cities Convention & Visitors Bureau 1601 River Dr Ste 110 .... Moline IL 61265	800-747-7800	309-277-0937
Monterey County Convention & Visitors Bureau PO Box 1770 .... Monterey CA 93942	888-221-1010	831-657-6400
Montgomery Area Chamber of Commerce Convention & Visitor Bureau 300 Water St .... Montgomery AL 36104	800-240-9452	334-261-1100
Montrose Visitor & Convention Bureau 1519 E Main St .... Montrose CO 81401	888-212-8294	970-249-5000
Greater Morgantown Convention & Visitors Bureau 68 Donley St .... Morgantown WV 26501	800-458-7373	304-292-5081
Knox County Convention & Visitors Bureau 107 S Main St .... Mount Vernon OH 43050	800-837-5282	740-392-6102
Mount Vernon Convention & Visitors Bureau 200 Potomac Blvd .... Mount Vernon IL 62864	800-252-5464	618-242-3151
Muncie Visitors Bureau 3700 S Madison St .... Muncie IN 47302	800-568-6862	765-284-2700
Muskegon County Convention & Visitors Bureau 610 W Western Ave .... Muskegon MI 49440	800-250-9283	231-724-3100
Myrtle Beach Area Convention Bureau 1200 N Oak St .... Myrtle Beach SC 29577	800-356-3016	843-626-7444
Nacogdoches Convention & Visitors Bureau 200 E Main St .... Nacogdoches TX 75961	888-653-3788	936-564-7351
Greater Naples Marco Island Everglades Convention & Visitors Bureau 2800 Horseshoe Dr .... Naples FL 34104	800-688-3600	239-252-2384
Brown County Convention & Visitors Bureau 10 N Van Buren St PO Box 840 .... Nashville IN 47448	800-753-3255	812-988-7303
Nashville Convention & Visitors Bureau (NCVB) 150 Fourth Ave N Ste G250 .... Nashville TN 37219	800-657-6910	615-259-4730
Natchez Convention & Visitors Bureau 640 S Canal St .... Natchez MS 39120	800-647-6724	601-446-6345
Craven County Convention & Visitors Bureau 203 S Front St .... New Bern NC 28560	800-437-5767	252-637-9400
Greater New Braunfels Chamber of Commerce Inc, The 390 S Seguin Ave PO Box 311417 .... New Braunfels TX 78130	800-572-2626	830-625-2385
Lawrence County Tourist Promotion Agency 229 S Jefferson St .... New Castle PA 16101	888-284-7599	724-654-8408
Jefferson Convention & Visitors Bureau 1221 Elmwood Pk Blvd Ste 411 .... New Orleans LA 70123	877-572-7474	504-731-7083
New Orleans Metropolitan Convention & Visitors Bureau 2020 St Charles Ave .... New Orleans LA 70130	800-672-6124	504-566-5011
Newberry Area Tourism Assn, The PO Box 308 .... Newberry MI 49868	800-831-7292	906-293-5562
Newport County Convention & Visitors Bureau 23 America's Cup Ave .... Newport RI 02840	800-976-5122	401-849-8048
Newport Beach Conference & Visitors Bureau 1200 Newport Ctr Dr Ste 120 .... Newport Beach CA 92660	800-942-6278	949-719-6100
Newport News Tourism Development Office 700 Town Ctr Dr Ste 320 .... Newport News VA 23606	888-493-7386	757-926-1400
Newton Convention & Visitor Bureau 300 E 17th St S Ste 400 .... Newton IA 50208	800-798-0299	641-792-0299
Niagara Tourism & Convention Corp 10 Rainbow Blvd .... Niagara Falls NY 14303	877-325-5787	716-282-8992
Norfolk Convention & Visitors Bureau 232 E Main St .... Norfolk VA 23510	800-368-3097	757-664-6620
Norman Convention & Visitors Bureau 309 E Main St .... Norman OK 73069	800-767-7260	405-366-8095
DuPage Convention & Visitors Bureau 915 Harger Rd Ste 240 .... Oak Brook IL 60523	800-232-0502	630-575-8070
Oak Park Area Convention & Visitors Bureau 1118 Westgate .... Oak Park IL 60301	888-625-7275	708-524-7800
Oak Ridge Convention & Visitors Bureau 102 Robertsville Rd Ste C .... Oak Ridge TN 37830	800-887-3429	865-482-7821
Ocean City Convention & Visitors Bureau 4001 Coastal Hwy .... Ocean City MD 21842	800-626-2326	410-289-8181
Oconomowoc Convention & Visitors Bureau 174 E Wisconsin Ave .... Oconomowoc WI 53066	888-936-7463	262-569-2186
Odessa Convention & Visitors Bureau 700 N Grant Ave Ste 200 .... Odessa TX 79761	800-780-4678	432-333-7871
Ogden/Weber Convention & Visitors Bureau 2438 Washington Blvd .... Ogden UT 84401	800-255-8824	801-778-6250
Oklahoma City Convention & Visitors Bureau 123 Pk Ave .... Oklahoma City OK 73102	800-225-5652	405-297-8912
McDowell County Tourism Development Authority 25 W Main St .... Old Fort NC 28762	888-233-6111	828-668-4282
Olympia Lacey Tumwater Visitor & Convention Bureau 103 Sid Snyder Ave SW .... Olympia WA 98501	877-704-7500	360-704-7544
Greater Omaha Convention & Visitors Bureau 1001 Farnam St Ste 200 .... Omaha NE 68102	866-937-6624	402-444-4660
Onalaska Ctr for Commerce & Tourism 1101 Main St .... Onalaska WI 54650	800-873-1901	608-781-9570
Ontario Convention & Visitors Bureau 2000 E Convention Ctr Way .... Ontario CA 91764	800-455-5755	909-937-3000
Orlando/Orange County Convention & Visitors Bureau Inc 6700 Forum Dr Ste 100 .... Orlando FL 32821	800-972-3304	407-363-5872
Lake of the Ozarks Convention & Visitors Bureau 5815 Hwy 54 PO Box 1498. .... Osage Beach MO 65065	800-386-5253	573-348-1599
Ottawa Tourism & Convention Authority 130 Albert St Ste 1800 .... Ottawa ON K1P5G4	800-363-4465	613-237-5150
Ottawa Visitors Ctr 106 W Lafayette St .... Ottawa IL 61350	888-688-2924	815-434-2737
Overland Park Convention & Visitors Bureau 9001 W 110th St Ste 100 .... Overland Park KS 66210	800-262-7275	913-491-0123
Owensboro-Daviess County Tourist Commission 215 E Second St .... Owensboro KY 42303	800-489-1131	270-926-1100
Oxford Convention & Visitors Bureau 102 Ed Perry Blvd .... Oxford MS 38655	800-758-9177	662-232-2367
Oxnard Convention & Visitors Bureau 1000 Town Ctr Dr Ste 130 .... Oxnard CA 93036	800-269-6273	805-385-7545
Panama City Beach Convention & Visitors Bureau 17001 Panama City Beach Pkwy .... Panama City Beach FL 32413	800-722-3224	850-233-5070
Park City Chamber of Commerce/Convention & Visitors Bureau 1910 Prospector Ave PO Box 1630. .... Park City UT 84060	800-453-1360	435-649-6100
Greater Parkersburg Convention & Visitors Bureau 350 Seventh St .... Parkersburg WV 26101	800-752-4982	304-428-1130
Pasadena Convention & Visitors Bureau 300 E Green St .... Pasadena CA 91101	800-307-7977	626-795-9311
Pensacola Convention & Visitors Bureau 1401 E Gregory St .... Pensacola FL 32502	800-874-1234	850-434-1234
Peoria Area Convention & Visitors Bureau 456 Fulton St Ste 300. .... Peoria IL 61602	800-747-0302	309-676-0303
Petoskey Area Visitors Bureau 401 E Mitchell St .... Petoskey MI 49770	800-845-2828	231-348-2755
Greater Phoenix Convention & Visitors Bureau 400 E Van Buren St Ste 600 .... Phoenix AZ 85004	877-225-5749	602-254-6500
Pigeon Forge Dept of Tourism P.O. Box 1390 .... Pigeon Forge TN 37868	800-251-9100	865-453-8574
Pine Bluff Convention & Visitors Bureau (PBCVB) One Convention Ctr Plz .... Pine Bluff AR 71601	800-536-7660	870-536-7600
Greater Pittsburgh Convention & Visitors Bureau 120 Fifth Ave Fifth Ave Pl, 1st Level .... Pittsburgh PA 15222	800-359-0758	412-281-7711
Plano Convention & Visitors Bureau 2000 E Spring Creek Pkwy .... Plano TX 75074	800-817-5266	972-941-5840
Ponca City Tourism 420 E Grand Ave PO Box 1109 .... Ponca City OK 74602	866-763-8092	580-765-4400

				Toll-Free	Phone
North Olympic Peninsula Visitor & Convention Bureau					
338 W First St Ste 104 PO Box 670	Port Angeles	WA	98362	**800-942-4042**	360-452-8552
Port Arthur Convention & Visitors Bureau					
3401 Cultural Ctr Dr	Port Arthur	TX	77642	**800-235-7822**	409-985-7822
Lake Erie Shores & Islands Welcome Ctr					
770 SE Catawba Rd	Port Clinton	OH	43452	**800-441-1271**	419-734-4386
Indiana Dunes the Casual Coast					
1215 N State Rd 49	Porter	IN	46304	**800-283-8687**	219-926-2255
Travel Portland					
1000 SW Broadway Ste 2300	Portland	OR	97205	**800-962-3700**	503-275-9750
Providence Warwick Convention & Visitors Bureau					
10 Memorial Blvd	Providence	RI	02903	**800-233-1636**	401-456-0200
Utah Valley Convention & Visitors Bureau					
111 S University Ave	Provo	UT	84601	**800-222-8824**	801-851-2100
Plumas County Visitors Bureau					
550 Crescent St	Quincy	CA	95971	**800-326-2247**	530-283-6345
Quincy Area Convention & Visitors Bureau (QACVB)					
532 Gardner Expy	Quincy	IL	62301	**800-978-4748**	217-214-3700
Greater Raleigh Convention & Visitors Bureau					
421 Fayetteville St Mall Ste 1505	Raleigh	NC	27602	**800-849-8499**	919-834-5900
Palm Springs Desert Resorts Convention & Visitors Authority					
70-100 Hwy 111	Rancho Mirage	CA	92270	**800-967-3767**	760-770-9000
Rapid City Convention & Visitors Bureau					
444 Mt Rushmore Rd N	Rapid City	SD	57701	**800-487-3223**	605-718-8484
Reading & Berks County Visitors Bureau					
2525 N 12th St Ste 101	Reading	PA	19605	**800-443-6610**	610-375-4085
Rehoboth Beach Convention Ctr					
229 Rehoboth Ave	Rehoboth Beach	DE	19971	**888-743-3628**	302-227-4641
Reno-Sparks Convention & Visitors Authority					
PO Box 837	Reno	NV	89504	**800-443-1482**	775-827-7600
Richardson Convention & Visitors Bureau					
411 W Arapaho Rd Ste 105	Richardson	TX	75080	**888-690-7287**	972-744-4034
Richmond Metropolitan Convention & Visitors Bureau					
401 N Third St	Richmond	VA	23219	**800-370-9004**	804-782-2777
Richmond/Wayne County Convention & Tourism Bureau					
5701 National Rd E	Richmond	IN	47374	**800-828-8414**	765-935-8687
Ridgecrest Area Convention & Visitors Bureau (RACVB)					
139 Balsam St Ste 1700	Ridgecrest	CA	93555	**800-847-4830**	760-375-8202
Riverside Convention & Visitors Bureau					
3750 University Ave Ste 175	Riverside	CA	92501	**888-748-7733**	951-222-4700
Roanoke Valley Convention & Visitors Bureau					
101 Shenandoah Ave NE	Roanoke	VA	24016	**800-635-5535**	540-342-6025
Tunica County Convention & Visitors Bureau					
13625 Hwy 61 N	Robinsonville	MS	38664	**888-488-6422**	
Rochester Convention & Visitors Bureau					
30 Civic Ctr Dr SE Ste 200	Rochester	MN	55904	**800-634-8277**	507-288-4331
Visit Rochester					
45 E Ave Ste 400	Rochester	NY	14604	**800-677-7282**	585-279-8300
Rockhill-York County Convention & Visitors Bureau					
452 S Anderson Rd	Rock Hill	SC	29730	**888-702-1320**	803-329-5200
Rockford Area Convention & Visitors Bureau					
102 N Main St	Rockford	IL	61101	**800-521-0849**	815-963-8111
Conference & Visitors Bureau of Montgomery County MD Inc					
111 Rockville Pk Ste 800	Rockville	MD	20850	**877-789-6904**	240-777-2060
Greater Rome Convention & Visitors Bureau					
402 Civics Ctr Dr	Rome	GA	30161	**800-444-1834**	706-295-5576
Historic Roswell Convention & Visitors Bureau					
617 Atlanta St	Roswell	GA	30075	**800-776-7935**	770-640-3253
Wausau Central Wisconsin Convention & Visitors Bureau (CWCVB)					
10204 Pk Plz Ste B	Rothschild	WI	54474	**888-948-4748**	715-355-8788
Sacramento Convention & Visitors Bureau					
1608 'I' St	Sacramento	CA	95814	**800-292-2334**	916-808-7777
Greater Saint Charles Convention & Visitors Bureau					
230 S Main St	Saint Charles	MO	63301	**800-366-2427**	636-946-7776
Saint Cloud Area Convention & Visitors Bureau					
525 Hwy 10 S Ste 1	Saint Cloud	MN	56304	**800-264-2940**	320-251-4170
Saint Joseph Convention & Visitors Bureau					
109 S Fourth St	Saint Joseph	MO	64501	**800-785-0360**	816-233-6688
Auglaize & Mercer Counties Convention & Visitors Bureau					
900 Edgewater Dr	Saint Marys	OH	45885	**800-860-4726**	419-394-1294
Salem Convention & Visitors Assn					
181 High St NE	Salem	OR	97301	**800-874-7012**	503-581-4325
Rowan County Convention & Visitors Bureau					
204 E Innes St Ste 120	Salisbury	NC	28144	**800-332-2343**	704-638-3100
Salt Lake Convention & Visitors Bureau					
90 SW Temple	Salt Lake City	UT	84101	**800-541-4955**	801-534-4900
San Angelo Chamber of Commerce					
418 W Ave B	San Angelo	TX	76903	**800-252-1381**	325-655-4136
San Antonio Convention & Visitors Bureau					
203 S St Marys St Ste 200	San Antonio	TX	78205	**800-447-3372**	210-207-6700
San Bernardino Convention & Visitors Bureau					
1955 Hunts Ln Ste 102	San Bernardino	CA	92408	**800-867-8366**	909-891-1151
San Francisco Convention & Visitors Bureau					
201 Third St Ste 900	San Francisco	CA	94103	**855-847-6272**	415-974-6900
San Jose Convention & Visitors Bureau					
408 Almaden Blvd	San Jose	CA	95110	**800-726-5673**	408-295-9600
Puerto Rico Convention Bureau					
100 Convention Blvd	San Juan	PR	00907	**800-214-0420**	787-725-2110
Marin Convention & Visitors Bureau					
1 Mitchell Blvd Ste B	San Rafael	CA	94903	**866-925-2060**	415-925-2060
Santa Barbara Visitors Bureau & Film Commission					
1601 Anacapa St	Santa Barbara	CA	93101	**800-676-1266**	805-966-9222
Santa Clara Convention/Visitors Bureau					
1850 Warburton Ave	Santa Clara	CA	95050	**800-272-6822**	408-244-9660
Santa Cruz County Conference & Visitors Council					
303 Water St Ste 100	Santa Cruz	CA	95060	**800-833-3494**	831-425-1234
Santa Fe Convention Ctr					
201 W Marcy St	Santa Fe	NM	87501	**800-777-2489**	505-955-6200
Santa Monica Convention & Visitors Bureau					
1920 Main St Ste B	Santa Monica	CA	90405	**800-544-5319**	310-319-6263
Visit Sarasota County					
1777 Main St Ste 302	Sarasota	FL	34236	**800-522-9799**	941-955-0991
Sault Sainte Marie Convention & Visitors Bureau					
1808 Ashmun St	Sault Sainte Marie	MI	49783	**800-647-2858**	906-632-3366
Savannah Area Convention & Visitors Bureau					
101 E Bay St	Savannah	GA	31401	**877-728-2662**	912-644-6400

Classified Section

				Toll-Free	Phone
Greater Woodfield Convention & Visitors Bureau					
1375 E Woodfield Rd Ste 120	Schaumburg	IL	60173	**800-847-4849**	847-490-1010
Scottsdale Convention & Visitors Bureau					
4343 N Scottsdale Rd Ste 170	Scottsdale	AZ	85251	**800-782-1117**	480-421-1004
Lackawanna County Convention & Visitors Bureau					
99 Glenmaura National Blvd	Scranton	PA	18507	**800-229-3526**	570-496-1701
Seattle's Convention & Visitors Bureau					
701 Pike St Ste 800	Seattle	WA	98101	**866-732-2695**	206-461-5800
Visit MercerCounty PA					
50 N Water Ave	Sharon	PA	16146	**800-637-2370**	724-346-3771
Shelby County Office of Tourism					
315 E Main St	Shelbyville	IL	62565	**800-874-3529**	217-774-2244
Shepherdsville-Bullitt County Tourist & Convention Commission					
395 Paroquet Springs Dr	Shepherdsville	KY	40165	**800-526-2068**	502-543-8687
Shipshewana/LaGrange County Convention & Visitors Bureau					
350 S Van Buren St Ste H	Shipshewana	IN	46565	**800-254-8090**	260-768-4008
Shreveport-Bossier Convention & Tourist Bureau					
629 Spring St	Shreveport	LA	71101	**800-551-8682**	318-222-9391
Sioux City Tourism Bureau					
801 Fourth St	Sioux City	IA	51101	**800-593-2228**	712-279-4800
Sioux Falls Convention & Visitors Bureau					
200 N Phillips Ave Ste 102	Sioux Falls	SD	57104	**800-333-2072**	605-336-1620
Sitka Convention & Visitors Bureau					
303 Lincoln St Ste 4	Sitka	AK	99835	**800-557-4852**	907-747-5940
Skagway Visitor Information					
245 Broadway PO Box 1029	Skagway	AK	99840	**888-762-1898**	907-983-2855
Johnston County Convention & Visitors Bureau					
235 E Market St	Smithfield	NC	27577	**800-441-7829**	919-989-8687
South Bend/Mishawaka Convention & Visitors Bureau					
401 E Colfax Ave Ste 310	South Bend	IN	46617	**800-519-0577**	574-234-0051
Lake Tahoe Visitors Authority					
3066 Lk Tahoe Blvd	South Lake Tahoe	CA	96150	**800-288-2463**	530-544-5050
South Padre Island Convention & Visitors Bureau					
7355 Padre Blvd	South Padre Island	TX	78597	**800-767-2373**	956-761-6433
South Sioux City Convention & Visitors Bureau					
3900 Dakota Ave Ste 11	South Sioux City	NE	68776	**866-494-1307**	402-494-1307
Convention & Visitors Bureau-Village of Pinehurst Southern Pines Aberdeen Area					
10677 Hwy 15-501	Southern Pines	NC	28387	**800-346-5362**	910-692-3330
Spokane Convention & Visitors Bureau					
801 W Riverside Ste 301	Spokane	WA	99201	**800-662-0084**	509-624-1341
Greater Springfield Convention & Visitors Bureau					
1441 Main St	Springfield	MA	01103	**800-723-1548**	413-787-1548
Springfield Convention & Visitors Bureau					
109 N Seventh St	Springfield	IL	62701	**800-545-7300**	217-789-2360
Springfield Missouri Convention & Visitors Bureau					
815 E St Louis St Ste 100	Springfield	MO	65806	**800-678-8767**	417-881-5300
Centre County Convention & Visitors Bureau					
800 E Pk Ave	State College	PA	16803	**800-358-5466**	814-231-1400
Pocono Mountains Vacation Bureau					
1004 Main St	Stroudsburg	PA	18360	**800-722-9199**	570-421-5791
Racine County Convention & Visitors Bureau					
14015 Washington Ave	Sturtevant	WI	53177	**800-272-2463**	262-884-6400
Superior/Douglas County Convention & Visitors Bureau					
305 Harborview Pkwy	Superior	WI	54880	**800-942-5313**	715-392-7151
Tacoma Regional Convention & Visitor Bureau					
1516 Pacific Ave Ste 500	Tacoma	WA	98402	**800-272-2662**	253-627-2836
North Lake Tahoe Resort Assn					
100 N Lake Blvd	Tahoe City	CA	96145	**800-824-6348**	530-581-6900
North Lake Tahoe Visitors & Convention Bureau					
PO Box 1757	Tahoe City	CA	96145	**800-462-5196**	530-581-8700
Chambers of Commerce / Tourism					
106 E Jefferson St	Tallahassee	FL	32301	**800-628-2866**	850-606-2305
Tampa Bay & Co					
401 E Jackson St Ste 2100	Tampa	FL	33602	**877-230-0078**	813-223-1111
Tempe Convention & Visitors Bureau					
51 W Third St Ste 105	Tempe	AZ	85281	**866-914-1052**	480-894-8158
Terre Haute Convention & Visitors Bureau					
5353 E Margaret Dr	Terre Haute	IN	47803	**800-366-3043**	
Thief River Falls Convention & Visitors Bureau (TRFCVB)					
102 Main Ave N	Thief River	MN	56701	**800-657-3700**	218-686-9785
City of Thomasville Tourism Authority					
144 E Jackson St	Thomasville	GA	31792	**800-533-4587**	229-226-3424
Three Lakes Information Bureau					
1704 Superior St PO Box 268	Three Lakes	WI	54562	**800-972-6103**	715-546-3344
River Country Tourism Bureau					
PO Box 214	Three Rivers	MI	49093	**800-447-2821**	
Greater Toledo Convention & Visitors Bureau					
401 Jefferson Ave	Toledo	OH	43604	**800-243-4667**	419-321-6404
Tomah Convention & Visitors Bureau					
901 Kilbourn Ave PO Box 625	Tomah	WI	54660	**800-948-6624**	608-372-2166
Visit Topeka Inc					
618 S Kansas Ave	Topeka	KS	66603	**800-235-1030**	785-234-1030
Toronto Convention & Visitors Assn					
207 Queen's Quay W Ste 405 PO Box 126	Toronto	ON	M5J1A7	**800-499-2514**	416-203-2600
Smoky Mountain Visitors Bureau					
7906 E Lamar Alexander Pkwy	Townsend	TN	37882	**800-525-6834**	865-448-6134
Traverse City Convention & Visitors Bureau					
101 W Grandview Pkwy	Traverse City	MI	49684	**800-940-1120**	231-947-1120
Atlanta's DeKalb Convention & Visitors Bureau					
1957 Lakeside Pkwy Ste 510	Tucker	GA	30084	**800-999-6055**	770-492-5000
Metropolitan Tucson Convention & Visitors Bureau					
100 S Church Ave	Tucson	AZ	85701	**800-638-8350**	520-624-1817
Tulsa Convention & Visitors Bureau					
One W Third St Ste 100	Tulsa	OK	74103	**800-558-3311**	
Colbert County Tourism & Convention Bureau					
719 Hwy 72 W PO Box 740425	Tuscumbia	AL	35674	**800-344-0783**	256-383-0783
Tyler Convention & Visitors Bureau (TCVB)					
315 N Broadway	Tyler	TX	75702	**800-235-5712**	903-592-1661
Oneida County Convention & Visitors Bureau					
PO Box 551	Utica	NY	13503	**800-426-3132**	315-724-7221
Vail Valley Tourism Bureau					
PO Box 1130	Vail	CO	81658	**800-525-3875**	970-476-1000
Vallejo Convention & Visitors Bureau					
289 Mare Island Way	Vallejo	CA	94590	**866-921-9277***	707-642-3653
*General					
Southwest Washington Convention & Visitors Bureau					
1220 Main S Ste 220	Vancouver	WA	98660	**877-600-0800**	360-750-1553

				Toll-Free	Phone

Ventura Visitors & Convention Bureau
101 S California St .... Ventura CA 93001 — **800-333-2989** — 805-648-2075

Iron Range Tourism Bureau
403 N First St .... Virginia MN 55792 — **800-777-8497** — 218-749-8161

Virginia Beach Convention & Visitor Bureau (VBCVB)
2101 Parks Ave Ste 500 .... Virginia Beach VA 23451 — **800-700-7702** — 757-385-4700

Visalia Convention & Visitors Bureau
PO Box 2734 .... Visalia CA 93279 — **800-524-0303** — 559-334-0141

Waco Convention & Visitors Bureau
100 Washington Ave .... Waco TX 76701 — **800-321-9226** — 254-750-5810

Warren County Visitors Bureau
22045 Rt 6 .... Warren PA 16365 — **800-624-7802** — 814-726-1222

Kosciusko County Convention & Visitors Bureau (KOSCVB)
111 Capital Dr .... Warsaw IN 46582 — **800-800-6090** — 574-269-6090

Washington DC Convention & Tourism Corp
901 Seventh St NW 4th Fl. .... Washington DC 20001 — **800-422-8644** — 202-789-7000

Waterloo Convention & Visitor Bureau
500 Jefferson St .... Waterloo IA 50701 — **800-728-8431** — 319-233-8350

Tioga County Visitors Bureau
2053 Rt 660 PO Box 139 .... Wellsboro PA 16901 — **888-846-4228** — 570-724-0635

West Hollywood Convention & Visitors Bureau
8687 Melrose Ave Ste M38 .... West Hollywood CA 90069 — **800-368-6020** — 310-289-2525

Monroe-West Monroe Convention & Visitors Bureau
601 Constitution Dr PO Box 1436 .... West Monroe LA 71292 — **800-843-1872** — 318-387-5691

Palm Beach County Convention & Visitors Bureau
1555 Palm Beach Lakes Blvd
Ste 800 .... West Palm Beach FL 33401 — **800-554-7256** — 561-233-3000

Wheeling Convention & Visitors Bureau
1401 Main St .... Wheeling WV 26003 — **800-828-3097** — 304-233-7709

Wichita Convention & Visitors Bureau
515 Main St Ste 115 .... Wichita KS 67202 — **800-288-9424** — 316-265-2800

Williamsburg Destination Marketing Committee
421 N Boundary St PO Box 3495 .... Williamsburg VA 23187 — **800-368-6511** — 757-229-6511

Martin County Travel & Tourism Authority
100 E Church St PO Box 382 .... Williamston NC 27892 — **800-776-8566** — 252-792-6605

Cape Fear Coast Convention & Visitors Bureau
505 Nutt St Unit A. .... Wilmington NC 28401 — **877-406-2356** — 910-341-4030

Greater Wilmington Convention & Visitors Bureau
100 W Tenth St Ste 20 .... Wilmington DE 19801 — **800-489-6664**

Wilson Visitors Bureau
209 Broad St .... Wilson NC 27893 — **800-497-7398** — 252-243-8440

Winnemucca Convention & Visitors Authority
50 W Winnemucca Blvd .... Winnemucca NV 89445 — **800-962-2638** — 775-623-5071

Winona Convention & Visitors Bureau
160 Johnson St .... Winona MN 55987 — **800-657-4972** — 507-452-0735

Winston-Salem Convention & Visitors Bureau
200 Brookstown Ave .... Winston-Salem NC 27101 — **866-728-4200** — 336-728-4200

Wisconsin Dells Visitors & Convention Bureau
701 Superior St PO Box 390. .... Wisconsin Dells WI 53965 — **800-223-3557** — 608-254-8088

Wayne County Convention & Visitors Bureau
428 W Liberty St .... Wooster OH 44691 — **800-362-6474** — 330-264-1800

Worcester County Convention & Visitors Bureau
30 Elm St Second Fl. .... Worcester MA 01609 — **866-755-7439** — 508-755-7400

Mahoning County Convention & Visitors Bureau
21 W Boardman St .... Youngstown OH 44503 — **800-447-8201** — 330-740-2130

Ypsilanti Area Convention & Visitors Bureau
106 W Michigan Ave .... Ypsilanti MI 48197 — **800-265-9045** — 734-483-4444

Yuma Convention & Visitors Bureau
201 N Fourth Ave .... Yuma AZ 85364 — **800-293-0071** — 928-783-0071

Zanesville-Muskingum County Convention & Visitors Bureau
205 N Fifth St .... Zanesville OH 43701 — **800-743-2303** — 740-455-8282

209   CONVEYORS & CONVEYING EQUIPMENT

SEE ALSO Material Handling Equipment

				Toll-Free	Phone

Airfloat LLC
2230 Brush College Rd .... Decatur IL 62526 — **800-888-0018** — 217-423-6001

Allor Manufacturing Inc
12534 Emerson Dr .... Brighton MI 48116 — **888-244-4028** — 248-486-4500

AMF Bakery Systems
2115 W Laburnum Ave .... Richmond VA 23227 — **800-225-3771** — 804-355-7961

Automatic Systems Inc
9230 E 47th St .... Kansas City MO 64133 — **800-366-3488** — 816-356-0660

Beltservice Corp
4143 Rider Trl N .... Earth City MO 63045 — **800-727-2358** — 314-344-8500

Bilt-Rite Conveyors
735 Industrial Loop Rd .... New London WI 54961 — **800-558-3616** — 920-982-6600

BW Container Systems
1305 Lakeview Ave .... Romeoville IL 60446 — **800-527-0494** — 630-759-6800

C & M Conveyor 4598 SR 37 .... Mitchell IN 47446 — **800-551-3195** — 812-849-5647

Cambelt International Corp
2820 West 1100 South .... Salt Lake City UT 84104 — **855-226-2358** — 801-972-5511

Cambridge Inc
105 Goodwill Rd PO Box 399. .... Cambridge MD 21613 — **800-638-9560** — 410-228-3000

Can Lines Engineering
9839 Downey Norwalk Rd PO Box 7039. .... Downey CA 90241 — **800-233-4597** — 562-861-2996

Carrier Vibrating Equipment Inc
3400 Fern Vly Rd .... Louisville KY 40213 — **800-547-7278** — 502-969-3171

Christianson Systems Inc
20421 15th St SE PO Box 138 .... Blomkest MN 56216 — **800-328-8896** — 320-995-6141

Conveyor Components Co
130 Seltzer Rd .... Croswell MI 48422 — **800-233-3233*** — 810-679-4211
*Cust Svc

Cyclonaire Corp PO Box 366 .... York NE 68467 — **800-445-0730** — 402-362-2000

Dematic
507 Plymouth Ave NE .... Grand Rapids MI 49505 — **877-725-7500***
*Cust Svc

Engineered Products Inc
500 Furman Hall Rd .... Greenville SC 29609 — **888-301-1421** — 864-234-4888

Essmueller Co
334 Ave A PO Box 1966 .... Laurel MS 39440 — **800-325-7175** — 601-649-2400

Evana Automation
5825 Old Boonville Hwy .... Evansville IN 47715 — **800-468-6774** — 812-479-8246

Feeco International Inc
3913 Algoma Rd .... Green Bay WI 54311 — **800-373-9347** — 920-468-1000

Flexible Steel Lacing Co
2525 Wisconsin Ave .... Downers Grove IL 60515 — **800-323-3444** — 630-971-0150

Garvey Corp 208 S Rt 73 .... Blue Anchor NJ 08037 — **800-257-8581** — 609-561-2450

Hansen Manufacturing Corp
5100 W 12th St .... Sioux Falls SD 57107 — **800-328-1785** — 605-332-3200

Hapman 6002 E N Ave .... Kalamazoo MI 49048 — **800-427-6260** — 269-343-1675

Intelligrated Products
475 E High St PO Box 899 .... London OH 43140 — **866-936-7300** — 513-701-7300

Interroll Corp
3000 Corporate Dr .... Wilmington NC 28405 — **800-830-9680*** — 910-799-1100
*Sales

Jorgensen Conveyors Inc
10303 N Baehr Rd .... Mequon WI 53092 — **800-325-7705** — 262-242-3089

Kice Industries Inc
5500 N Mill Heights Dr .... Wichita KS 67219 — **877-289-5423** — 316-744-7151

KWS Mfg Company Ltd
3041 Conveyor Dr .... Burleson TX 76028 — **800-543-6558** — 817-295-2247

Laitram LLC 200 Laitram Ln .... Harahan LA 70123 — **800-535-7631** — 504-733-6000

Martin Engineering
One Martin Pl .... Neponset IL 61345 — **800-544-2947** — 309-594-2384

Metzgar Conveyor Co Inc
901 Metzgar Dr NW .... Comstock Park MI 49321 — **888-266-8390** — 616-784-0930

NKC of America Inc
1584 E Brooks Rd .... Memphis TN 38116 — **800-532-6727** — 901-396-5353

Prab Inc
5944 E Kilgore Rd .... Kalamazoo MI 49048 — **800-968-7722** — 269-382-8200

Rapat Corp 919 Odonnel St .... Hawley MN 56549 — **800-325-6377** — 218-483-3344

Rapid Industries
4003 Oaklawn Dr .... Louisville KY 40219 — **800-727-4381** — 502-968-3645

Renold Jeffrey
2307 Maden Dr .... Morristown TN 37813 — **800-251-9012** — 423-586-1951

Richards-Wilcox Inc
600 S Lake St .... Aurora IL 60506 — **800-253-5668**

Schroeder Industries LLC
580 W Pk Rd .... Leetsdale PA 15056 — **800-722-4810** — 724-318-1100

Shick Tube Veyor Corp
4346 Clary Blvd .... Kansas City MO 64130 — **877-744-2587** — 816-861-7224

Shuttleworth Inc
10 Commercial Rd .... Huntington IN 46750 — **800-444-7412** — 260-356-8500

Stewart Systems
808 Stewart Ave .... Plano TX 75074 — **800-966-5808** — 972-422-5808

Sweet Mfg Company Inc
2000 E Leffel Ln .... Springfield OH 45505 — **800-334-7254*** — 937-325-1511
*Cust Svc

Swisslog 10825 E 47th St .... Denver CO 80239 — **800-525-1841** — 303-371-7770

Thomas Conveyor Co
555 N Burleson Blvd .... Burleson TX 76028 — **800-433-2217** — 817-295-7151

Transco Industries Inc
5534 NE 122nd Ave PO Box 20429 .... Portland OR 97230 — **800-545-9991** — 503-256-1955

Universal Industries Inc
5800 Nordic Dr .... Cedar Falls IA 50613 — **800-553-4446** — 319-277-7501

W & H Systems Inc
120 Asia Pl .... Carlstadt NJ 07072 — **800-966-6993** — 201-933-7840

Westfalia Technologies Inc
3655 Sandhurst Dr .... York PA 17406 — **800-673-2522** — 717-764-1115

Whirl Air Flow Corp
20055 177th St .... Big Lake MN 55309 — **800-373-3461** — 763-262-1200

Wire Belt Company of America
154 Harvey Rd .... Londonderry NH 03053 — **800-922-2637*** — 603-644-2500
*Cust Svc

Young Industries Inc
16 Painter St .... Muncy PA 17756 — **800-546-3165** — 570-546-3165

210   CORD & TWINE

				Toll-Free	Phone

All Line Inc
16851 E Parkview Ave Unit 2 .... Fountain Hills AZ 85268 — **800-843-5733** — 480-306-6001

Ashaway Line & Twine Manufacturing Co
24 Laurel St .... Ashaway RI 02804 — **800-556-7260** — 401-377-2221

Atkins & Pearce Inc
1 Braid Way .... Covington KY 41017 — **800-837-7477** — 859-356-2001

Bridon Cordage LLC
909 E 16th St .... Albert Lea MN 56007 — **800-533-6002** — 507-377-1601

Carron Net Company Inc
1623 17th St PO Box 177 .... Two Rivers WI 54241 — **800-558-7768** — 920-793-2217

I & I Sling Inc PO Box 2423 .... Aston PA 19014 — **800-874-3539** — 610-485-8500

New England Ropes Inc
848 Airport Rd .... Fall River MA 02720 — **800-333-6679** — 508-678-8200

Pacific Fibre & Rope Company Inc
903 Flint St PO Box 187. .... Wilmington CA 90744 — **800-825-7673** — 310-834-4567

Pelican Rope Works Inc
4001 W Carriage Dr .... Santa Ana CA 92704 — **800-464-7673** — 714-545-0116

PlymKraft Inc
479 Export Cir .... Newport News VA 23601 — **800-992-0854** — 757-595-0364

Puget Sound Rope Corp
1012 Second St .... Anacortes WA 98221 — **888-525-8488** — 360-293-8488

Rocky Mount Cord Co
381 N Grace St .... Rocky Mount NC 27804 — **800-342-9130*** — 252-977-9130
*Orders

Samson Rope Technologies Inc
2090 Thornton Rd .... Ferndale WA 98248 — **800-227-7673*** — 360-384-4669
*Cust Svc

211   CORK & CORK PRODUCTS

SEE ALSO Office & School Supplies

				Toll-Free	Phone

Expanko Inc
180 Gordon Dr Ste 113. .... Exton PA 19341 — **800-345-6202**

Manton Industrial Cork Products Inc
415 Oser Ave Unit U .... Hauppauge NY 11788 — **800-663-1921** — 631-273-0700

Maryland Cork Co Inc
505 Blue Ball Rd PO Box 126 .... Elkton MD 21922 — **800-662-2675** — 410-398-2955

212   CORPORATE HOUSING

				Toll-Free	Phone
Alikar Gardens Resort, The					
1123 Verde Dr	Colorado Springs	CO	80910	800-456-1123	719-475-2564
Churchill Corporate Services					
56 Utter Ave	Hawthorne	NJ	07506	800-941-7458	973-636-9400
Coast to Coast Corporate Housing					
10773 Los Alamitos Blvd	Los Alamitos	CA	90720	800-451-9466	562-795-0250
ExecSuite					
Third Ave SW Ste 702	Calgary	AB	T2P3B4	800-667-4980	403-294-5800
Klein & Company Corporate Housing Services Inc					
914 Washington Ave	Golden	CO	80401	800-208-9826	303-796-2100
ExecuStay Corp					
2222 Corinth Ave	Los Angeles	CA	90064	800-990-9292	
Oakwood Crystal City					
400 15th St S	Arlington	VA	22202	877-969-5142	703-920-9550
Oakwood Worldwide					
2222 Corinth Ave	Los Angeles	CA	90064	800-888-0808	310-478-1021
SuiteAmerica					
4970 Windplay Dr Ste C-1	El Dorado Hills	CA	95762	800-410-4305	916-941-7970

213   CORRECTIONAL & DETENTION MANAGEMENT (PRIVATIZED)

SEE ALSO Juvenile Detention Facilities ; Correctional Facilities - State

				Toll-Free	Phone
Colorado Correctional Industries					
2862 S Cir Dr	Colorado Springs	CO	80906	800-685-7891*	719-226-4206
*Cust Svc					
Corrections Corp of America					
10 Burton Hills Blvd	Nashville	TN	37215	800-624-2931	615-263-3000
NYSE: CXW					

214   CORRECTIONAL FACILITIES

				Toll-Free	Phone
Administrative-Maximum US Penitentiary					
Florence PO Box 8500	Florence	CO	81226	877-623-8426	719-784-9464
Federal Correctional Complex					
Coleman 846 NE 54th Terr	ÿColeman	FL	33521	877-623-8426	352-689-5000
Butner					
Old NC Hwy 75 PO Box 1000	Butner	NC	27509	877-623-8426	919-575-4541
Danbury Rt 37	Danbury	CT	06811	877-623-8426	203-743-6471
Englewood					
9595 W Quincy Ave	Littleton	CO	80123	877-623-8426	303-985-1566
Fairton					
655 Fairton-Millville Rd PO Box 280	Fairton	NJ	08320	877-623-8426	856-453-1177
Federal Correctional Institution					
Forrest City					
1400 Dale Bumpers Rd PO Box 8000	Forrest City	AR	72335	877-623-8426	870-630-6000
Loretto PO Box 1000	Loretto	PA	15940	877-623-8426	814-472-4140
Manchester					
805 Fox Hollow Rd PO Box 4000	Manchester	KY	40962	877-623-8426	606-598-1900
McKean					
6975 Rt 59 PO Box 8000	Lewis Run	PA	16738	877-623-8426	814-362-8900
Yazoo City					
2225 Haley Barbour Pkwy					
PO Box 5050	Yazoo City	MS	39194	877-623-8426	662-751-4800
Federal Detention Ctr					
SeaTac PO Box 13901	Seattle	WA	98198	877-623-8426	206-870-5700
Federal Prison Camp					
Duluth					
6902 Airport Rd PO Box 1400	Duluth	MN	55814	877-623-8426	218-722-8634
Montgomery Maxwell AFB	Montgomery	AL	36112	877-623-8426	334-293-2100
Medical Ctr for Federal Prisoners Springfield					
1900 W Sunshine St	Springfield	MO	65807	877-623-8426	417-862-7041
Metropolitan Correctional Ctr					
Chicago 71 W Van Buren St	Chicago	IL	60605	877-623-8426	312-322-0567
US Penitentiary					
Atwater					
1 Federal Way PO Box 019001	Atwater	CA	95301	877-623-8426	209-386-0257

215   CORRECTIONAL FACILITIES - STATE

SEE ALSO Juvenile Detention Facilities ; Correctional & Detention Management (Privatized)

				Toll-Free	Phone
Algoa Correctional Ctr					
8501 No More Victims Rd	Jefferson City	MO	65102	800-392-1111	573-751-3911
Arizona State Prison Complex-Eyman					
4374 E Butte Ave PO Box 3500	Florence	AZ	85132	866-333-2039	520-868-0201
Arkansas Dept of Corrections Maximum Security Unit					
2501 State Farm Rd	Tucker	AR	72168	866-801-3435	501-842-3800
Arkansas Dept of Corrections Tucker Unit					
2400 State Farm Rd PO Box 240	Tucker	AR	72168	800-682-7377	501-842-2519
Boonville Correctional Ctr					
1216 E Morgan St	Boonville	MO	65233	800-392-8486	660-882-6521
C Paul Phelps Correctional Ctr					
14925 Hwy 27 N PO Box 1056	Dequincy	LA	70633	888-524-3578	337-786-7963
Charles E Egeler Correctional Facility					
3855 Cooper St	Jackson	MI	49201	855-444-3911	517-780-5600
Chillicothe Correctional Ctr					
3151 Litton Rd	Chillicothe	MO	64601	800-392-8486	660-646-4032
Deerfield Correctional Ctr					
21360 Deerfield Dr	Capron	VA	23829	800-560-4292	434-658-4368
Fairbanks Correctional Ctr					
1931 Eagan Ave	Fairbanks	AK	99701	877-741-0741	907-458-6700
G Robert Cotton Correctional Facility					
3500 N Elm Rd	Jackson	MI	49201	855-444-3911	517-780-5000
Goodman Correctional Institution					
4556 Broad River Rd	Columbia	SC	29210	866-230-7761	803-896-8565

				Toll-Free	Phone
Huron Valley Correctional Facility					
3201 Bemis Rd	Ypsilanti	MI	48197	855-444-3911	734-572-9900
Kentucky Correctional Institution for Women					
3000 Ash Ave	Pewee Valley	KY	40056	877-687-6818	502-241-8454
Lee Correctional Institution					
990 Wisacky Hwy	Bishopville	SC	29010	877-846-3472	803-428-2800
Lorain Correctional Institution					
2075 Avon Belden Rd	Grafton	OH	44044	888-988-4768	440-748-1049
Luther Luckett Correctional Complex					
Dawkins Rd PO Box 6	LaGrange	KY	40031	800-511-1670	502-222-0363
Mike Durfee State Prison					
1412 Wood St	Springfield	SD	57062	800-537-0025	605-369-2201
Minnesota Correctional Facility-Faribault					
1101 Linden Ln	Faribault	MN	55021	800-657-3830	507-334-0700
Mississippi State Penitentiary					
Hwy 49 W PO Box 1057	Parchman	MS	38738	800-844-0898	662-745-6611
Montana State Prison					
400 Conley Lk Rd	Deer Lodge	MT	59722	888-739-9122	406-846-1320
Mule Creek State Prison					
4001 Hwy 104	Ione	CA	95640	877-256-6877	209-274-4911
Nebraska Correctional Ctr for Women					
1107 Recharge Rd	York	NE	68467	877-634-8463	402-362-3317
Nebraska State Penitentiary					
4201 S 14th St	Lincoln	NE	68502	877-634-8463	402-471-3161
New Hampshire State Prison for Women					
317 Mast Rd	Goffstown	NH	03045	800-639-1122	603-668-6137
Northern Regional Correctional Facility					
112 Northern Regional Correctional Dr					
	Moundsville	WV	26041	866-984-8463	304-843-4067
Okeechobee Correctional Institution					
3420 NE 168th St	Okeechobee	FL	34972	800-574-5729	863-462-5400
Palmer Correctional Ctr					
PO Box 919	Palmer	AK	99645	877-741-0741	907-745-5054
Pelican Bay State Prison (PBSP)					
5905 Lake Earl Dr PO Box 7000	Crescent City	CA	95531	877-256-6877	707-465-1000
Pleasant Valley State Prison					
24863 W Jayne Ave PO Box 8500	Coalinga	CA	93210	877-256-6877	559-935-4900
Riverbend Maximum Security Institution					
7475 Cockrill Bend Blvd	Nashville	TN	37243	800-770-8277	615-350-3100
RJ Donovan Correctional Facility at Rock Mountain					
480 Alta Rd	San Diego	CA	92179	877-256-6877	619-661-6500
SCI-Coal Township					
1 Kelley Dr	Coal Township	PA	17866	800-322-4472	570-644-7890
South Bay Correctional Facility					
600 US Hwy 27 S	South Bay	FL	33493	800-574-5729	561-992-9505
South Central Correctional Facility					
555 Forest Ave PO Box 279	Clifton	TN	38425	800-251-3589	931-676-5372
Thumb Correctional Facility					
3225 John Conley Dr	Lapeer	MI	48446	855-444-3911	810-667-2045
Topeka Correctional Facility					
815 SE Rice Rd	Topeka	KS	66603	888-317-8204	785-296-3317
Wake Correctional Ctr					
1000 Rock Quarry Rd	Raleigh	NC	27610	866-719-0108	919-733-7988
Warren Correctional Institution					
379 Collins Rd PO Box 728	Manson	NC	27553	866-719-0108	252-456-3400
Wayne County Boot Camp					
PO Box 182	Clifton	TN	38425	855-876-7283	931-676-3345

216   CREDIT & FINANCING - CONSUMER

SEE ALSO Banks - Commercial & Savings ; Credit & Financing - Commercial ; Credit Unions

				Toll-Free	Phone
Atlantic Bay Mortgage Group					
596 Lynnhaven Pkwy Ste 102	Virginia Beach	VA	23452	866-877-3143	757-213-1660
Budget Finance Co					
1849 Sawtelle Blvd	Los Angeles	CA	90025	800-225-6267	310-696-4050
Credit Acceptance Corp					
25505 W 12 Mile Rd	Southfield	MI	48034	800-634-1506	248-353-2700
DHI Mortgage Co Ltd					
10700 Pecan Park Blvd Suite 450	Austin	TX	78750	800-315-8434	512-502-0545
Dollar Loan Ctr LLC					
6122 W Sahara Ave	Las Vegas	NV	89146	866-550-4352	702-693-5626
Farm Credit of The Virginias Aca					
106 Sangers Ln	Staunton	VA	24401	800-559-1016	540-886-3435
Finance Factors Ltd					
1164 Bishop St	Honolulu	HI	96813	800-648-7136	808-548-4940
First Insurance Funding Corp					
450 Skokie Blvd Ste 1000	Northbrook	IL	60062	800-837-3707	
Ford Motor Credit Co					
One American Rd PO Box 1732	Dearborn	MI	48121	800-727-7000	313-322-3000
Franklin Credit Management Corp					
101 Hudson St	Jersey City	NJ	07302	800-255-5897	201-604-1800
Gateway Mortgage Group LLC					
6910 E 14th St	Tulsa	OK	74112	877-406-8109	918-712-9000
General Motors Acceptance Corp (GMAC)					
200 Renaissance Ctr	Detroit	MI	48265	800-200-4622	877-320-2559
Green Tree Servicing LLC					
345 St Peter St	Saint Paul	MN	55102	800-643-0202	800-423-9527
Guaranteed Rate Inc					
3940 N Ravenswood	Chicago	IL	60613	866-934-7283	773-290-0505
Harley-Davidson Financial Services Inc					
PO Box 21489	Carson City	NV	89721	888-691-4337	
Imperial Finance & Trading					
701 Pk of Commerce Blvd Ste 301	Boca Raton	FL	33487	888-364-6775	
Mercedes-Benz Financial Services USA LLC					
PO Box 685	Roanoke	TX	76262	800-654-6222	
Nelnet Inc					
121 S 13th St Ste 201	Lincoln	NE	68501	888-486-4722	402-458-2370
NYSE: NNI					
Nicholas Financial Inc					
2454 McMullen Booth Rd Bldg C	Clearwater	FL	33759	800-237-2721	727-726-0763
NASDAQ: NICK					
Ontario Centres of Excellence Inc					
156 Front St W Ste 200	Toronto	ON	M5J2L6	866-759-6014	416-861-1092

				Toll-Free	Phone

PreCash Inc
1800 W Loop S Ste 1400 .... Houston TX 77027 **800-773-2274** 713-600-2200

Prestige Financial Services Inc
1420 S 500 W .... Salt Lake City UT 84115 **888-822-7422** 801-844-2100

Prime Rate Premium Finance Corp
2141 Enterprise Dr PO Box 100507 .... Florence SC 29501 **800-777-7458*** 843-669-0937
*Cust Svc

Redwood Credit Union
PO Box 6104 .... Santa Rosa CA 95406 **800-479-7928** 707-545-4000

Regional Acceptance Corp
1424 E Fire Tower Rd .... Greenville NC 27858 **877-722-7299** 252-321-7700

Sallie Mae
12061 Bluemont Way .... Reston VA 20190 **888-272-5543*** 703-810-3000
*Cust Svc

Security Finance Corp
PO Box 811 .... Spartanburg SC 29304 **800-395-8195*** 864-582-8193
*All

Select Portfolio Servicing Inc
3815 SW Temple .... Salt Lake City UT 84115 **800-258-8602**

SLM Corp 12061 Bluemont Way .... Reston VA 20190 **888-272-5543*** 703-810-3000
NASDAQ: SLM ■ *Cust Svc

Toyota Financial Services
19001 S Western Ave .... Torrance CA 90501 **800-874-8822*** 212-715-7386
*Cust Svc

Wallick & Volk Mortgage
222 E 18th St .... Cheyenne WY 82001 **800-280-8655** 307-634-5941

Wells Fargo Education Financial Services
PO Box 5185 .... Sioux Falls SD 57117 **800-658-3567**

217   COSMETICS, SKIN CARE, AND OTHER PERSONAL

SEE ALSO Perfumes

				Toll-Free	Phone

AHAVA North America
330 7th Avenue .... New York NY 10001 **800-366-7254**

Aire-Master of America Inc
1821 N State Hwy Cc .... Nixa MO 65714 **800-525-0957** 417-725-2691

Apothecary Products
11750 12th Ave S Burnsville .... Burnsville MN 55337 **800-328-2742**

At Last Naturals Inc
401 Columbus Ave .... Valhalla NY 10595 **800-527-8123**

Aveda Corp
4000 Pheasant Ridge Dr .... Blaine MN 55449 **800-644-4831** 763-951-4000

Avon Products Inc
1345 Ave of the Americas .... New York NY 10017 **800-367-2866*** 212-282-7000
NYSE: AVP ■ *Cust Svc

Bath & Body Works
Seven Limited Pkwy E .... Reynoldsburg OH 43068 **800-395-1001**

BeautiControl Inc
2121 Midway Rd PO Box 815189 .... Carrollton TX 75006 **800-232-8841** 972-458-0601

Belcam Inc Delagar Div
27 Montgomery St .... Rouses Point NY 12979 **800-328-3006** 518-297-3366

BeneFit Cosmetics
225 Bush St .... San Francisco CA 94104 **800-781-2336*** 415-781-8153
*Cust Svc

Bronner Bros Inc
2141 Powers Ferry Rd .... Marietta GA 30067 **800-241-6151** 770-988-0015

CBI Laboratories
4201 Diplomacy Rd .... Fort Worth TX 76155 **800-822-7546** 972-241-7546

CCA Industries Inc
200 Murray Hill Pkwy .... East Rutherford NJ 07073 **800-524-2720*** 201-935-3232
NYSE: CAW ■ *Cust Svc

Clinique Laboratories Inc
767 Fifth Ave 37th Fl .... New York NY 10153 **800-419-4041** 212-572-3983

Combe Inc
1101 Westchester Ave .... White Plains NY 10604 **800-431-2610** 914-694-5454

Crabtree & Evelyn Ltd
102 Peake Brook Rd .... Woodstock CT 06281 **800-272-2873** 860-928-2761

DEB Inc
2815 Coliseum Centre Dr Ste 600 .... Charlotte NC 28217 **800-248-7190** 704-263-4240

Farouk Systems Inc
250 Pennbright Dr .... Houston TX 77090 **800-237-9175** 281-876-2000

Forever Living Products International Inc
7501 E McCormick Pkwy .... Scottsdale AZ 85258 **888-440-2563** 480-998-8888

Fruit of The Earth Inc
3101 High Rver Rd Ste 175 .... Fort Worth TX 76155 **800-527-7731** 972-790-0808

GOJO Industries Inc
One GOJO Plz Ste 500 .... Akron OH 44311 **800-321-9647** 330-255-6000

Guest Supply Inc
4301 US Hwy 1 PO Box 902 .... Monmouth Junction NJ 08852 **800-446-7819*** 609-514-9696
*Cust Svc

Gurwitch Products LLC
8 Greenway Plz .... Stafford TX 77046 **888-637-2437** 281-275-7000

H2O Plus Inc
845 W Madison St .... Chicago IL 60607 **800-242-2284*** 312-850-9283
*Cust Svc

Hillshire Brands PO Box 3901 .... Peoria IL 61612 **800-323-7117**

Jafra Cosmetics International
2451 Townsgate Rd .... Westlake Village CA 91361 **800-551-2345** 805-449-3000

Jan Marini Skin Research Inc
6951 Via Del Oro .... San Jose CA 95119 **800-347-2223** 408-362-0130

John Amico Haircare Products
4731 W 136th St .... Crestwood IL 60445 **800-676-5264** 708-824-4000

John Paul Mitchell Systems
1888 Century Park E ste 1600 .... Los Angeles CA 90067 **800-793-8790***
*Cust Svc

Johnson & Johnson Consumer Products Co
199 Grandview Rd .... Skillman NJ 08558 **866-565-2229** 908-874-1000

Johnson & Johnson Inc
7101 Notre-Dame E .... Montreal QC H1N2G4 **800-361-8990** 514-251-5100

Kao Brands Co
2535 Spring Grove Ave .... Cincinnati OH 45214 **800-742-8798** 513-421-1400

Key West Aloe
13095 N Telecom Pkwy .... Tampa FL 33637 **800-445-2563** 305-293-1885

L'Oreal USA 575 Fifth Ave .... New York NY 10017 **800-322-2036** 212-818-1500

				Toll-Free	Phone

Luster Products Inc
1104 W 43rd St .... Chicago IL 60609 **800-621-4255** 773-579-1800

Mana Products Inc
32-02 Queens Blvd .... Long Island City NY 11101 **800-221-3071*** 718-361-2550
*Cust Svc

Mary Kay Inc PO Box 799045 .... Dallas TX 75379 **800-627-9529*** 972-687-6300
*Cust Svc

Maybelline New York
575 Fifth Ave PO Box 1010 .... New York NY 10017 **800-944-0730**

Merle Norman Cosmetics Inc
9130 Bellanca Ave .... Los Angeles CA 90045 **800-421-6648** 310-641-3000

Neutrogena Corp
5760 W 96th St .... Los Angeles CA 90045 **800-582-4048** 310-642-1150

Nutramax Laboratories Inc
2208 Lakeside Blvd .... Edgewood MD 21040 **800-925-5187** 410-776-4000

Obagi Medical Products Inc
3760 Kilroy Airport Way Ste 500 .... Long Beach CA 90806 **800-636-7546** 562-628-1007

Origins Natural Resources Inc
767 Fifth Ave .... New York NY 10153 **800-674-4467***
*Cust Svc

Paramount Cosmetics Inc
93 Entin Rd Ste 4 .... Clifton NJ 07014 **800-522-9880** 973-472-2323

Person & Covey Inc
616 Allen Ave .... Glendale CA 91201 **800-423-2341**

Pfizer Inc 235 E 42nd St .... New York NY 10017 **800-879-3477** 212-733-2323
NYSE: PFE

Philosophy Inc
3809 E Watkins .... Phoenix AZ 85034 **800-568-3151**

Prescriptives Inc
767 Fifth Ave .... New York NY 10153 **866-290-6471**

Prestige Cosmetics Corp
1601 Green Rd .... Pompano Beach FL 33064 **800-722-7488*** 954-480-9202
*General

Revlon Consumer Products Corp
1501 Williamsboro St .... Oxford NC 27565 **800-473-8566** 212-527-4000

Rozelle Cosmetics
4260 Loop Rd .... Westfield VT 05874 **800-451-4216** 802-744-2270

Scolding Locks Corp
1520 W Rogers Ave .... Appleton WI 54914 **800-537-9707** 920-733-5561

sephora.com Inc
525 Market St
First Market Twr 32nd Fl .... San Francisco CA 94105 **877-737-4672*** 415-284-3300
*Cust Svc

SkinMedica Inc
5770 Armada Dr .... Carlsbad CA 92008 **866-577-3072** 760-448-3600

Sothys USA Inc
1500 NW 94th Ave .... Miami FL 33172 **800-325-0503** 305-594-4222

Star Nail Products Inc
29120 Ave Paine .... Valencia CA 91355 **800-762-6245** 661-257-7827

Tom's of Maine Inc
302 Lafayette Ctr .... Kennebunk ME 04043 **800-367-8667** 800-985-3874

ULTA Beauty
1000 Remington Blvd Ste 120 .... Bolingbrook IL 60440 **866-983-8582** 630-410-4800

Urban Decay
833 W 16th St .... Newport Beach CA 92663 **800-784-8722** 949-631-4504

Vi-Jon Labs Inc
8515 Page Ave .... Saint Louis MO 63114 **800-424-9300** 314-427-1000

Wahl Clipper Corp
2900 Locust St .... Sterling IL 61081 **800-767-9245** 815-625-6528

WE Bassett Co
100 Trap Falls Rd Ext .... Shelton CT 06484 **800-394-8746** 203-929-8483

Wella Corp
6109 DeSoto Ave .... Woodland Hills CA 91367 **800-829-4422** 818-999-5112

Zotos International Inc
100 Tokeneke Rd .... Darien CT 06820 **888-242-4247** 203-655-8911

218   CREDIT & FINANCING - COMMERCIAL

SEE ALSO Banks - Commercial & Savings ; Credit & Financing - Consumer

				Toll-Free	Phone

AFCO Credit Corp
14 Wall St .... New York NY 10005 **800-288-6901** 212-401-4400

Agricredit Acceptance LLC
8001 Birchwood Ct Ste C PO Box 2000 .... Johnston IA 50131 **800-577-8504** 515-314-9203

American AgCredit (ACA)
PO Box 1120 .... Santa Rosa CA 95402 **800-800-4865** 707-545-1200

Arkansas Capital Corp Group
200 S Commerce St Ste 400 .... Little Rock AR 72201 **800-216-7237** 501-374-9247

ATEL Capital Group
600 California St Sixth Fl .... San Francisco CA 94108 **800-543-2835** 415-989-8800

Automotive Finance Corp (AFC)
13085 Hamilton Crossing Blvd .... Carmel IN 46032 **888-335-6675** 865-384-8250

AutoStar
114 Ave of the Americas Ste 39 .... New York NY 10036 **800-288-6782** 212-930-9400

BMO Financial Corp
1 First Canadian Place 11th Fl .... Toronto ON M5X1A1 **800-553-0332** 416-359-4440

Bombardier Capital Group
261 Mountain View Dr 4th Fl .... Colchester VT 05446 **800-949-5568** 802-764-5232

Cascade Federal Credit Union
18020 80th Ave S .... Kent WA 98032 **800-562-2853** 425-251-8888

CDC Small Business Finance Corp
2448 Historic Decatur Rd Ste 200 ..... San Diego CA 92106 **800-611-5170** 619-291-3594

Co-op Finance Assn Inc, The
10100 N Ambassador Dr Ste 315
PO Box 901532 .... Kansas City MO 64153 **877-835-5232** 816-214-4200

Colonial Farm Credit Aca
7104 Mechanicsville Tpke
PO Box 790 .... Mechanicsville VA 23111 **800-777-8908** 804-746-4581

Equity Funding
12505 Bel-Red Rd Ste 200 .... Bellevue WA 98005 **866-332-3863** 425-283-1040

Farm Credit Leasing (FCL)
600 Hwy 169 S Ste 300 .... Minneapolis MN 55426 **800-444-2929** 952-417-7800

Farm Credit Of Central Florida Aca
115 S Missouri Ave Ste 400 .... Lakeland FL 33815 **800-533-2773** 863-682-4117

Farm Credit Of Northwest Florida Aca
5052 Hwy 90 .... Marianna FL 32446 **800-527-0647** 850-526-4910

	Toll-Free	Phone
Financial Pacific Co		
3455 S 344th Way Ste 300 . . . . Federal Way WA 98001	800-447-7107	
First Carolina Corporate Credit Union		
7900 Triad Ctr Dr Ste 410 . . . . Greensboro NC 27409	800-585-4317	
First Community Financial Corp (FCFC)		
4000 N Central Ave Ste 100 . . . . Phoenix AZ 85012	877-777-4778	602-265-7715
OTC: FMFP		
First South FarmCredit		
713 S Pear OrchaRd Ste 300 . . . . Ridgeland MS 39158	800-955-1722	601-977-8381
Ford Motor Credit Co		
One American Rd PO Box 1732 . . . . Dearborn MI 48121	800-727-7000	313-322-3000
GE Vendor Financial Services		
10 Riverview Dr . . . . Danbury CT 06810	800-626-2000	203-373-2039
Green Tree Servicing LLC		
345 St Peter St . . . . Saint Paul MN 55102	800-643-0202	800-423-9527
Greenstone Farm Credit Services Aca		
3515 West Road . . . . East Lansing MI 48823	800-444-3276	800-968-0061
Imh Financial Corp		
4900 N Scottsdale Rd Ste 5000 . . . . Scottsdale AZ 85251	800-510-6445	480-840-8400
Imperial PFS (UPAC)		
8245 Nieman Rd . . . . Lenexa KS 66214	800-877-7848	913-894-6150
iStar Financial Inc		
1114 Ave of the Americas 39th Fl . . . . New York NY 10036	888-603-5847	212-930-9400
NYSE: STAR		
John Deere Credit Co		
6400 NW 86th St . . . . Johnston IA 50131	800-275-5322	515-267-3000
Key Equipment Finance		
1000 S McCaslin Blvd . . . . Superior CO 80027	888-301-6238	
Kraus-Anderson Capital Inc		
523 S Eigth St Ste 523 . . . . Minneapolis MN 55404	888-547-3983	612-305-2934
Lawfinance Group Inc		
1401 Los Gamos Dr Ste 140. . . . . San Rafael CA 94903	800-572-1986	415-446-2300
Medallion Financial Corp		
437 Madison Ave 38th Fl . . . . New York NY 10022	877-633-2554	212-328-2100
NASDAQ: TAXI		
MicroFinancial Inc		
16 New England Executive Pk		
Ste 200 . . . . Burlington MA 01803	877-868-3800	781-994-4800
NASDAQ: MFI		
New York Business Development Corp (NYBDC)		
50 Beaver St Sixth Fl . . . . Albany NY 12207	800-923-2504	518-463-2268
Park Community Federal Credit Union		
PO Box 18630 . . . . Louisville KY 40261	800-626-2870	502-968-3681
PDS Gaming Corp		
6280 Annie Oakley Dr . . . . Las Vegas NV 89120	800-479-3612	702-736-0700
Phoenix American Inc		
2401 Kerner Blvd . . . . San Rafael CA 94901	866-895-5050	
Phoenix Growth Capital Corp		
2401 Kerner Blvd . . . . San Rafael CA 94901	866-895-5050	
Phoenix Leasing Inc		
2401 Kerner Blvd . . . . San Rafael CA 94901	866-895-5050	
Pinnacle Business Finance Inc		
615 Commerce St Ste 101 . . . . Tacoma WA 98402	800-566-1993	253-284-5600
PMC Commercial Trust		
17950 Preston Rd Ste 600 . . . . Dallas TX 75252	800-486-3223	972-349-3200
NASDAQ: CMCT		
Priority Capital Inc		
174 Green St . . . . Melrose MA 02176	800-761-2118	781-321-8778
Puerto Rico Farm Credit Aca		
PO Box 363649 . . . . San Juan PR 00936	800-981-3323	787-753-0579
Republic Financial Corp		
3300 S Parker Rd Ste 500. . . . . Aurora CO 80014	888-822-8766	303-751-3501
Schroder Investment Management North America Inc (SIMNA)		
875 Third Ave 22nd Fl . . . . New York NY 10022	800-730-2932	
Siemens Financial Services Inc		
170 Wood Ave S . . . . Iselin NJ 08830	800-327-4443	732-590-6500
Snap-on Credit LLC		
950 Technology Way Ste 301 . . . . Libertyville IL 60048	877-777-8455	
Sta International		
1400 Old Country Rd Ste 411. . . . . Westbury NY 11590	866-970-9882	516-997-2400
Taycor LLC		
6065 Bristol Pkwy . . . . Culver City CA 90230	800-322-9738	310-895-7704
Tyndall Federal Credit Union Inc		
PO Box 59760 . . . . Panama City FL 32412	888-896-3255	850-769-9999
Verizon Credit Inc		
201 N Tampa St . . . . Tampa FL 33602	800-483-7988	813-229-6000
Watson Group Financial Corp		
6501 Highland Rd . . . . Waterford MI 48327	800-666-1572	248-666-2700
Wells Fargo		
420 Montgomery St . . . . San Francisco CA 94104	800-877-4833	
NYSE: WFC		
Wells Fargo Equipment Finance Inc		
733 Marquette Ave Ste 700. . . . . Minneapolis MN 55402	877-322-8228	612-667-9876
Western Agcredit		
PO Box 95850 . . . . South Jordan UT 84095	800-824-9198	801-571-9200
Xerox Financial Services Inc		
800 Long Ridge Rd . . . . Stamford CT 06904	800-275-9376	203-968-3000

219   CREDIT CARD PROVIDERS & RELATED SERVICES

Companies listed here include those that issue credit cards as well as companies that provide services to these companies (i.e., rewards programs, theft prevention, etc.).

	Toll-Free	Phone
American Express Company Inc		
World Financial Ctr 200 Vesey St . . . . New York NY 10285	800-528-4800	212-640-2000
NYSE: AXP		
Applied Card Systems		
50 Applied Card Way . . . . Glen Mills PA 19342	866-227-5627	
Bank of America Card Services		
One Commercial Pl Second Fl . . . . Norfolk VA 23510	800-732-9194	757-441-4770
Capital One Financial Corp		
1680 Capital One Dr . . . . McLean VA 22102	800-655-2265	800-926-1000
NYSE: COF		
Chevron Texaco Credit Card Ctr		
PO Box P . . . . Concord CA 94524	800-243-8766	
Diners Club International		
111 W Monroe . . . . Chicago IL 60603	800-234-6377	

	Toll-Free	Phone
Intersections Inc		
3901 Stonecroft Blvd PO Box 222455 . . . . Chantilly VA 20151	800-695-7536	703-488-6100
NASDAQ: INTX		
MasterCard Inc		
2000 Purchase St . . . . Purchase NY 10577	800-100-1087	914-249-2000
NYSE: MA		
Rewards Network		
2 N Riverside Plaza Suite 200. . . . . Chicago IL 60606	877-392-7313	866-559-3463
Transaction Network Services Inc.		
10740 Parkridge Blvd Ste 100 . . . . Reston VA 20191	800-240-2824	703-453-8300
Visa Inc PO Box 8999 . . . . San Francisco CA 94128	866-765-9644	650-432-3200
NYSE: V		
Wright Express Corp		
97 Darling Ave . . . . South Portland ME 04106	800-761-7181	207-773-8171
NYSE: WEX		

220   CREDIT REPORTING SERVICES

SEE ALSO

	Toll-Free	Phone
Coface Services North America Inc		
50 Millstone Rd . . . . East Windsor NJ 08520	877-626-3223	609-469-0400
Constellation Technology Corp		
7887 Bryan Dairy Rd Ste 100 . . . . Largo FL 33777	800-335-7355	727-547-0600
Equifax Credit Marketing Services		
1550 Peachtree St NW . . . . Atlanta GA 30309	800-660-5125*	404-885-8000
NYSE: EFX ■ *Sales		
Equifax Inc		
1550 Peachtree St NW . . . . Atlanta GA 30309	888-202-4025*	404-885-8000
NYSE: EFX ■ *Sales		
Experian Information Solutions Inc		
475 Anton Blvd . . . . Costa Mesa CA 92626	888-397-3742*	714-830-7000
*Cust Svc		
Fitch Ratings Inc		
One State St Plz . . . . New York NY 10004	800-753-4824	212-908-0500
Kroll Factual Data Inc		
5200 Hahns Peak Dr . . . . Loveland CO 80538	800-929-3400	970-663-5700
Merchants Credit Bureau		
955 Green St . . . . Augusta GA 30901	800-426-5265	706-823-6246
Screeningone Inc		
2233 W 190th St . . . . Torrance CA 90504	888-327-6511	
Tele-Track		
5550 Peach Tree Pkwy Ste 600 . . . . Norcross GA 30092	800-729-6981	770-449-8809
TransUnion LLC		
555 W Adams St . . . . Chicago IL 60661	866-922-2100	

221   CREDIT UNIONS

	Toll-Free	Phone
66 Federal Credit Union		
PO Box 1358 . . . . Bartlesville OK 74005	800-897-6991	918-336-7662
Affinity Federal Credit Union		
73 Mountain View Blvd		
PO Box 621. . . . . Basking Ridge NJ 07920	800-325-0808	
Air Force Federal Credit Union		
1560 Cable Ranch Rd Ste 200 . . . . San Antonio TX 78245	800-227-5328	210-673-5610
Alaska USA Federal Credit Union		
4000 Credit Union Dr PO Box 196613 . . . . Anchorage AK 99503	800-525-9094	907-563-4567
Allegacy Federal Credit Union		
1691 Westbrook Plaza Dr . . . . Winston-Salem NC 27103	800-782-4670	336-774-3400
America First Credit Union		
1344 West 4675 South . . . . Ogden UT 84405	800-999-3961	801-627-0900
American Airlines Employees Federal Credit Union		
4151 Amon Carter Blvd		
PO Box 155489. . . . . Fort Worth TX 76155	800-533-0035	817-952-4500
American Eagle Federal Credit Union		
417 Main St . . . . East Hartford CT 06118	800-842-0145	860-568-2020
Amoco Federal Credit Union		
PO Box 889 . . . . Texas City TX 77592	800-231-6053	409-948-8541
Andrews Federal Credit Union (AFCU)		
5711 Allentown Rd . . . . Suitland MD 20746	800-487-5500	301-702-5500
ANG Federal Credit Union		
PO Box 170204 . . . . Birmingham AL 35217	800-237-6211	205-841-4525
APCO Employees Credit Union		
750 17th St N . . . . Birmingham AL 35203	800-249-2726	205-257-3601
Arizona Federal Credit Union		
PO Box 60070 . . . . Phoenix AZ 85082	800-523-4603	602-683-1000
Ascend Federal Credit Union		
520 Airpark Dr PO Box 1210 . . . . Tullahoma TN 37388	800-342-3086	931-455-5441
Atlanta Postal Credit Union		
501 Pulliam St SW Ste 350 . . . . Atlanta GA 30312	800-849-8431	404-768-4126
Autotruck Federal Credit Union		
3611 Newburg Rd PO Box 18890 . . . . Louisville KY 40218	800-459-2328	502-459-8981
Bank-Fund Staff Federal Credit Union		
PO Box 27755 . . . . Washington DC 20038	800-923-7328	202-458-4300
BayPort Credit Union Inc		
3711 Huntington Ave . . . . Newport News VA 23607	800-928-8801	757-928-8850
Beacon Credit Union		
PO Box 627 . . . . Wabash IN 46992	800-762-3136	260-563-7443
Bellco First Federal Credit Union		
7600 E OrchaRd Rd Ste 400N. . . . . . Greenwood Village CO 80111	800-235-5261	303-689-7800
Bethpage Federal Credit Union		
899 S Oyster Bay Rd . . . . Bethpage NY 11714	800-628-7070	
Boulder Valley Credit Union Inc		
5505 Arapahoe Ave . . . . Boulder CO 80303	800-783-8850	303-442-8850
Campus Federal Credit Union		
PO Box 98036 . . . . Baton Rouge LA 70898	888-769-8841	225-769-8841
Campus USA Credit Union		
PO Box 147029 . . . . Gainesville FL 32614	800-367-6440	352-335-9090
Chartway Federal Credit Union		
160 Newtown Rd . . . . Virginia Beach VA 23462	800-678-8765	757-552-1000
Citadel Federal Credit Union		
520 Eagleview Blvd . . . . Exton PA 19341	800-666-0191	610-380-6000

Name / Address	City	State	Zip	Toll-Free	Phone
Citizens Equity First Credit Union					
5401 W Dirksen Pkwy	Peoria	IL	61607	**800-633-7077***	309-633-7000
*Cust Svc					
Class Act Federal Credit Union					
3620 Fern Vly Rd	Louisville	KY	40219	**800-292-2960**	502-964-7575
Coast Central Credit Union Inc					
2650 Harrison Ave	Eureka	CA	95501	**800-974-9727**	707-445-8801
Coastal Federal Credit Union					
1000 St Albans Dr	Raleigh	NC	27609	**800-868-4262**	919-420-8000
Commonwealth Credit Union					
PO Box 978	Frankfort	KY	40602	**800-228-6420**	502-564-4775
Community America Credit Union (CACU)					
9777 Ridge Dr	Lenexa	KS	66219	**800-892-7957**	913-905-7000
Community Resource Federal Credit Union					
20 Wade Rd	Latham	NY	12110	**888-783-2211**	518-783-2211
Contra Costa Federal Credit Union					
PO Box 509	Martinez	CA	94553	**888-387-8632**	925-228-7550
Coors Credit Union					
816 Washington Ave	Golden	CO	80401	**800-770-6414**	303-279-6414
Coosa Pines Federal Credit Union					
17591 Plant Rd	Childersburg	AL	35044	**800-237-9789**	256-378-5559
Credit Union of Southern California					
PO Box 200	Whittier	CA	90608	**866-287-6225**	562-698-8326
Credit Union of Texas					
PO Box 517028	Dallas	TX	75251	**800-314-3828**	972-263-9497
Dearborn Federal Credit Union					
400 Town Ctr Dr	Dearborn	MI	48126	**888-336-2700**	313-336-2700
Deer Valley Federal Credit Union					
16215 N 28th Ave	Phoenix	AZ	85053	**800-579-5051**	602-375-7300
Delta Employees Credit Union					
1025 Virginia Ave	Atlanta	GA	30354	**800-544-3328**	404-715-4725
Denver Fire Dept Federal Credit Union (DFDFCU)					
2201 Federal Blvd	Denver	CO	80211	**866-880-7770**	303-228-5300
Desert Schools Federal Credit Union					
148 N 48th St	Phoenix	AZ	85034	**800-456-9171**	602-433-7000
Digital Employees' Federal Credit Union					
220 Donald Lynch Blvd	Marlborough	MA	01752	**800-328-8797**	508-263-6700
Direct Federal Credit Union					
PO Box 9123	Needham	MA	02494	**800-449-7728**	781-455-6500
Dow Chemical Employees' Credit Union					
600 E Lyon Rd	Midland	MI	48640	**800-835-7794**	989-835-7794
Educational Employees Credit Union					
PO Box 5242	Fresno	CA	93755	**800-538-3328**	559-437-7700
Educators Credit Union (ECU)					
1400 N Newman Rd PO Box 81040	Racine	WI	53406	**800-236-5898**	262-260-9393
Eglin Federal Credit Union					
838 Eglin Pkwy NE	Fort Walton Beach	FL	32547	**800-367-6159**	850-862-0111
Ent Federal Credit Union					
7250 Campus Dr	Colorado Springs	CO	80920	**800-525-9623**	719-574-1100
Evansville Teachers Federal Credit Union					
PO Box 5129	Evansville	IN	47716	**800-800-9271**	812-477-9271
FAA Credit Union					
PO Box 26406	Oklahoma City	OK	73126	**800-448-1990**	405-682-1990
Fairwinds Federal Credit Union					
3087 N Alafaya Trl	Orlando	FL	32826	**800-443-6887**	407-277-5045
Finance Ctr Federal Credit Union					
PO Box 26501	Indianapolis	IN	46226	**800-473-2328**	317-916-7700
Financial Partners Credit Union					
PO Box 7005	Downey	CA	90241	**800-950-7328**	562-923-0311
Firefighters Community Credit Union Inc					
2300 St Clair Ave NE	Cleveland	OH	44114	**800-621-4644**	216-621-4644
First Community Credit Union (FCCU)					
PO Box 1030	Chesterfield	MO	63006	**800-767-8880**	636-728-3333
Fort Knox Federal Credit Union					
PO Box 900	Radcliff	KY	40159	**800-756-3678**	502-942-0254
Fort Worth City Credit Union					
PO Box 100099	Fort Worth	TX	76185	**888-732-3085**	817-732-2803
Fort Worth Community Credit Union					
1905 Forest Ridge Dr PO Box 210848	Bedford	TX	76021	**800-817-8234**	817-835-5000
Forum Credit Union					
PO Box 50738	Indianapolis	IN	46250	**800-382-5414**	317-558-6000
Founders Federal Credit Union					
607 N Main St	Lancaster	SC	29720	**888-918-7403***	803-289-5927
*Tech Supp					
Georgia's Own Credit Union					
1155 Peachtree St NE Ste 400					
PO Box 105205	Atlanta	GA	30309	**800-533-2062**	404-874-1166
Gesa Credit Union					
51 Gage Blvd PO Box 500	Richland	WA	99352	**888-946-4372**	509-946-1611
Greylock Federal Credit Union					
150 W St	Pittsfield	MA	01201	**800-207-5555**	413-236-4000
GTE Federal Credit Union					
PO Box 172599	Tampa	FL	33672	**888-871-2690**	813-871-2690
Guadalupe Credit Union					
3601 Mimbres Ln	Santa Fe	NM	87507	**800-540-5382**	505-982-8942
Hamilton City Employees Federal Credit Union					
309 Ct St	Hamilton	OH	45011	**800-264-5578**	513-868-5881
HarborOne Credit Union					
770 Oak St PO Box 720	Brockton	MA	02301	**800-244-7592**	508-895-1000
Hudson Valley Federal Credit Union					
159 Barnegat Rd	Poughkeepsie	NY	12601	**800-468-3011**	845-463-3011
Hughes Federal Credit Union Inc					
PO Box 11900	Tucson	AZ	85734	**866-760-3156**	520-794-8341
I B M Southeast Employees Federal Credit Union					
PO Box 5090	Boca Raton	FL	33431	**888-567-8688**	561-982-4700
Indiana Credit Union League					
5975 Castle Creek Parkway N					
Ste 300	Indianapolis	IN	46250	**800-285-5300**	317-594-5300
Indiana Members Credit Union (IMCU)					
7110 W Tenth St	Indianapolis	IN	46214	**800-556-9268**	317-248-8556
Island Federal Credit Union					
120 Motor Pkwy	Hauppauge	NY	11788	**800-475-5263**	631-851-1100
Keesler Federal Credit Union					
PO Box 7001	Biloxi	MS	39534	**888-533-7537**	228-385-5500
Kern Schools Federal Credit Union					
PO Box 9506	Bakersfield	CA	93389	**800-221-3311**	661-833-7900
KeyPoint Credit Union					
2805 Bowers Ave	Santa Clara	CA	95051	**888-255-3637**	408-731-4100
Kinecta Federal Credit Union					
1440 Rosecrans Ave					
PO Box 10003	Manhattan Beach	CA	90266	**800-854-9846**	310-643-5400
L & N Federal Credit Union					
9265 Smyrna Pkwy	Louisville	KY	40229	**800-443-2479**	502-368-5858
La Capitol Federal Credit Union					
PO Box 3398	Baton Rouge	LA	70821	**800-522-2748**	225-342-5055
Lafayette Federal Credit Union (Inc)					
3535 University Blvd W	Kensington	MD	20895	**800-888-6560**	301-929-7990
Landmark Credit Union					
5445 S Westridge Dr PO Box 510910	New Berlin	WI	53151	**800-801-1449**	262-796-4500
Langley Federal Credit Union					
1055 W Mercury Blvd	Hampton	VA	23666	**800-826-7490**	757-827-7200
Leominster Credit Union					
20 Adams St	Leominster	MA	01453	**800-649-4646**	978-537-8021
Local Government Federal Credit Union					
323 W Jones St Ste 600	Raleigh	NC	27603	**888-732-8562**	919-857-2150
Lockheed Federal Credit Union (LFCU)					
2340 Hollywood Way	Burbank	CA	91505	**800-328-5328**	818-565-2020
Los Angeles Federal Credit Union					
PO Box 53032	Los Angeles	CA	90053	**877-695-2328**	818-242-8640
Los Angeles Police Federal Credit Union					
PO Box 10188	Van Nuys	CA	91410	**877-695-2732**	818-787-6520
Meriwest Credit Union					
PO Box 530953	San Jose	CA	95153	**877-637-4937**	
Midwest America Federal Credit Union					
1104 Medical Pk Dr	Fort Wayne	IN	46825	**800-348-4738**	260-482-3334
Miramar Federal Credit Union					
PO Box 261370	San Diego	CA	92196	**800-640-1228**	858-695-9494
Mission Federal Credit Union					
PO Box 919023	San Diego	CA	92121	**800-500-6328**	858-524-2850
Mountain America Credit Union					
PO Box 9001	West Jordan	UT	84084	**800-748-4302**	801-325-6228
Municipal Credit Union					
PO Box 3205	New York	NY	10007	**866-512-6109**	212-693-4900
Nassau Financial Federal Credit Union					
1325 Franklin Ave Ste 500	Garden City	NY	11530	**800-216-2328**	516-742-4900
Neighbors Federal Credit Union					
PO Box 2831	Baton Rouge	LA	70821	**866-819-2178**	225-819-2178
New England Federal Credit Union					
PO Box 527	Williston	VT	05495	**800-400-8790**	802-879-8790
New Orleans Firemens Federal Credit Union					
PO Box 689	Metairie	LA	70004	**800-647-1689**	504-889-9090
North Country Federal Credit Union Inc					
69 Swift St Ste 100	South Burlington	VT	05403	**800-660-3258**	802-657-6847
North Island Credit Union					
5898 Copley Dr	San Diego	CA	92111	**800-848-5654***	619-656-6525
*Cust Svc					
NuUnion Credit Union					
501 S Capitol Ave	Lansing	MI	48933	**888-267-7200**	517-267-7200
Oklahoma Federal Credit Union					
517 NE 36th St	Oklahoma City	OK	73105	**800-522-8510**	405-524-6467
Orange County's Credit Union					
PO Box 11777	Santa Ana	CA	92711	**888-354-6228**	714-755-5900
Owensboro Federal Credit Union					
717 Harvard Dr PO Box 1189	Owensboro	KY	42302	**800-264-1054**	270-683-1054
Pacific Marine Credit Union					
M C X Complex	Camp Pendleton	CA	92055	**800-736-4500**	760-430-7511
Pacific NW Federal Credit Union (PNWFCU)					
12106 NE Marx St	Portland	OR	97220	**866-692-8669**	503-256-5858
Pacific Service Federal Credit Union					
PO Box 8191	Walnut Creek	CA	94596	**888-858-6878**	925-296-6200
Pearl Harbor Federal Credit Union (PHFCU)					
94-449 Ukee St	Waipahu	HI	96797	**800-987-5583**	
Pennsylvania State Employees Credit Union					
One Credit Union Pl	Harrisburg	PA	17110	**800-237-7328**	717-234-8484
Pentagon Federal Credit Union					
2930 Eisenhower Ave	Alexandria	VA	22314	**800-247-5626**	
Pine Bluff Cotton Belt Federal Credit Union					
1703 River Pines Blvd	Pine Bluff	AR	71601	**888-249-1904**	870-535-6365
Police & Fire Federal Credit Union					
901 Arch St	Philadelphia	PA	19107	**800-228-8801**	215-931-0300
Portland Teachers Credit Union					
PO Box 3750	Portland	OR	97208	**800-527-3932**	503-228-7077
Premier America Credit Union					
19867 Prairie St PO Box 2178	Chatsworth	CA	91313	**800-772-4000**	818-772-4000
Premier Members Federal Credit Union					
5495 Arapahoe Ave	Boulder	CO	80303	**800-468-0634**	303-657-7000
Provident Central Credit Union					
303 Twin Dolphin Dr	Redwood City	CA	94065	**800-632-4600**	650-508-0300
Randolph-Brooks Federal Credit Union					
PO Box 2097	Universal City	TX	78148	**800-580-3300**	210-945-3300
Redstone Federal Credit Union					
220 Wynn Dr NW	Huntsville	AL	35893	**800-234-1234**	256-837-6110
Rhode Island State Employees Credit Union					
160 Francis St	Providence	RI	02903	**855-322-7428**	401-751-7440
Rockland Federal Credit Union					
241 Union St	Rockland	MA	02370	**800-562-7328**	781-878-0232
RTN Federal Credit Union					
600 Main St Ste 3	Waltham	MA	02452	**800-338-0221**	781-736-9900
SAC Federal Credit Union (SAFCU)					
11515 S 39th St PO Box 1149	Bellevue	NE	68123	**800-228-0392**	402-292-8000
Safe 1 Credit Union					
PO Box 2203	Bakersfield	CA	93303	**800-322-4529**	661-327-3818
SAFE Credit Union					
3720 Madison Ave	North Highlands	CA	95660	**800-733-7233**	916-979-7233
Safeamerica Credit Union					
6001 Gibraltar Dr	Pleasanton	CA	94588	**800-972-0999**	925-734-4111
San Antonio Federal Credit Union					
PO Box 1356	San Antonio	TX	78295	**800-234-7228**	210-258-1234
San Diego County Credit Union					
6545 Sequence Dr	San Diego	CA	92121	**877-732-2848**	
San Francisco Federal Credit Union					
770 Golden Gate Ave	San Francisco	CA	94102	**800-852-7598**	415-775-5377
Sb1 Federal Credit Union					
PO Box 7480	Philadelphia	PA	19101	**800-806-9465**	215-569-3700
Schools Financial Credit Union					
1485 Response Rd Ste 126	Sacramento	CA	95815	**800-962-0990**	916-569-5400

				Toll-Free	Phone
Secure First Credit Union					
PO Box 170070	Birmingham	AL	35217	877-520-2115	205-520-2115
Security Service Federal Credit Union					
16211 La Cantera Pkwy	San Antonio	TX	78256	800-527-7328	210-476-4000
South Carolina Federal Credit Union					
PO Box 190012	North Charleston	SC	29419	800-845-0432	843-797-8300
Space Coast Credit Union					
8045 N Wickham Rd PO Box 419001	Melbourne	FL	32941	800-447-7228	321-752-2222
Stanford Federal Credit Union					
1860 Embarcadero Rd	Palo Alto	CA	94303	888-723-7328	650-723-2509
Star One Federal Credit Union					
PO Box 3643	Sunnyvale	CA	94088	866-543-5202	408-543-5202
State Employees Credit Union of Maryland Inc					
971 Corporate Blvd	Linthicum	MD	21090	800-879-7328	410-487-7328
State Employees Federal Credit Union					
700 Patroon Creek Blvd					
Patroon Creek Corporate Ctr.	Albany	NY	12206	800-727-3328	518-452-8234
State Employees' Credit Union (SECU)					
PO Box 29606	Raleigh	NC	27626	888-732-8562	919-857-2150
Teachers Credit Union (TCU)					
PO Box 1395	South Bend	IN	46624	800-552-4745	574-284-6247
Teachers Federal Credit Union (TFCU)					
2410 N Ocean Ave PO Box 9029	Farmingville	NY	11738	800-341-4333	631-698-7000
Tech Credit Union					
10951 Broadway	Crown Point	IN	46307	800-276-8324	219-663-5120
Telcoe Federal Credit Union					
820 Lousiana St	Little Rock	AR	72201	800-482-9009	501-375-5321
Texans Credit Union					
777 E Campbell Rd	Richardson	TX	75081	800-843-5295	972-348-2000
Texas Dow Employees Credit Union (TDECU)					
1001 FM 2004	Lake Jackson	TX	77566	800-839-1154	979-297-1154
Tower Federal Credit Union					
7901 Sandy Spring Rd	Laurel	MD	20707	800-787-8328	301-497-7000
Travis Federal Credit Union					
One Travis Way	Vacaville	CA	95687	800-877-8328	707-449-4000
Truliant Federal Credit Union					
3200 Truliant Way	Winston-Salem	NC	27103	800-822-0382	336-659-1955
Tyco Electronics Federal Credit Union					
PO Box 3449	Redwood City	CA	94064	888-673-3288	
U S Employees O C Federal Credit Union					
PO Box 44000	Oklahoma City	OK	73144	800-227-6366	405-685-6200
Ukrainian National Federal Credit Union					
215 Second Ave PO Box 160	New York	NY	10003	866-859-5848	212-533-2980
United Nations Federal Credit Union (UNFCU)					
24-01 44th Rd Ct Sq Pl	Long Island City	NY	11101	800-891-2471	347-686-6000
Unitus Community Credit Union					
PO Box 1937	Portland	OR	97207	800-452-0900	503-227-5571
University & State Employees Credit Union					
10120 Pacific Heights Blvd Ste 100	San Diego	CA	92121	866-873-2448	858-795-6100
University of Hawaii Federal Credit Union					
PO Box 22070	Honolulu	HI	96823	800-927-3397	808-983-5500
University of Hawaii Foundation, The					
2444 Dole St Bachman Hall 105	Honolulu	HI	96822	866-846-4262	808-956-8849
US Alliance Federal Credit Union					
600 Midland Ave	Rye	NY	10580	800-431-2754	
US New Mexico Federal Credit Union (USNMFCU)					
3939 Osuna Rd NE PO Box 129	Albuquerque	NM	87109	888-342-8766	505-342-8888
Valley First Credit Union					
PO Box 1411	Modesto	CA	95353	877-549-4567	209-549-8500
Vantage Credit Union (VCU)					
PO Box 4433	Bridgeton	MO	63044	800-522-6009	314-298-0055
Verity Credit Union					
PO Box 75974	Seattle	WA	98175	800-444-4589	206-440-9000
Virginia Credit Union					
7500 Boulders View Dr	Richmond	VA	23225	800-285-5051	804-323-6000
Visions Federal Credit Union (VFUC)					
24 McKinley Ave	Endicott	NY	13760	800-242-2120	607-754-7900
Vystar Credit Union					
1802 Kernan Blvd S	Jacksonville	FL	32246	800-445-6289	904-777-6000
Washington State Employees Credit Union					
400 E Union Ave	Olympia	WA	98501	800-562-0999	360-943-7911
Wescom Credit Union					
123 S Marengo Ave PO Box 7058	Pasadena	CA	91101	888-493-7266	626-535-1000
Wings Financial Credit Union					
14985 Glazier Ave Ste 100	Apple Valley	MN	55124	800-692-2274	952-997-8000
Workers' Credit Union					
815 Main St PO Box 900	Fitchburg	MA	01420	800-221-4020	978-345-1021
Wright-Patt Credit Union Inc					
2455 Executive Pk Blvd PO Box 286.	Fairborn	OH	45324	800-762-0047	937-912-7000
Y-12 Federal Credit Union					
501 Lafayette Dr PO Box 2512	Oak Ridge	TN	37830	800-482-1043	865-482-1043

222   CRUISE LINES

SEE ALSO Travel Agencies ; Ports & Port Authorities ; Casinos ; Cruises - Riverboat

				Toll-Free	Phone
Baja Expeditions Inc					
3096 Palm St	San Diego	CA	92104	800-843-6967	858-581-3311
Blount Small Ship Adventures					
461 Water St	Warren	RI	02885	800-556-7450	401-247-0955
Bluewater Adventures Ltd					
252 E First St Ste 3.	North Vancouver	BC	V7L1B3	888-877-1770	604-980-3800
Carnival Cruise Lines					
3655 NW 87th Ave	Miami	FL	33178	800-764-7419	305-599-2600
China Ocean Shipping Co Americas Inc (COSCO)					
100 Lighting Way	Secaucus	NJ	07094	800-242-7354	201-422-0500
Costa Cruise Lines					
200 S Pk Rd Ste 200.	Hollywood	FL	33021	800-462-6782	954-266-5600
Cruise West					
3826 18th Ave W Suite 401	Seattle	WA	98119	888-862-8881	206-283-9322
Cunard Line Ltd					
24303 Town Ctr Dr Ste 200	Valencia	CA	91355	800-728-6273	661-753-1000
Discovery Cruises Inc					
1775 NW 70th Ave	Miami	FL	33126	800-866-8687	305-597-0336

				Toll-Free	Phone
Great Lakes Cruise Co					
3270 Washtenaw Ave	Ann Arbor	MI	48104	888-891-0203	
Holland America Line					
300 Elliott Ave W	Seattle	WA	98119	800-426-0327	206-281-3535
Hurtigruten 405 Pk Ave	New York	NY	10022	866-552-0371	212-319-1300
Lindblad Expeditions					
96 Morton St Ninth Fl.	New York	NY	10014	800-397-3348	212-765-7740
Maine Windjammer Cruises					
PO Box 617	Camden	ME	04843	800-736-7981	207-236-2938
Oceania Cruises Inc					
8300 NW 33rd St Ste 308.	Miami	FL	33122	800-531-5619	305-514-2300
Princess Cruises					
24844 Rockefeller Ave	Santa Clarita	CA	91355	800-774-6237	661-753-0000
Rockport Schooner Cruises					
PO Box 272	Belfast	ME	04915	866-732-2473	207-338-3088
Royal Caribbean International					
1050 Caribbean Way	Miami	FL	33132	800-327-6700	305-539-6000
Sea Cloud Cruises Inc					
282 Grand Ave Ste 3.	Englewood	NJ	07631	888-732-2568	201-227-9404
SeaDream Yacht Club					
601 Brickell Key Dr Ste 1050	Miami	FL	33131	800-707-4911	305-631-6110
Silversea Cruises					
110 E Broward Blvd	Fort Lauderdale	FL	33301	800-722-9955	954-522-4477
Star Clippers Inc					
760 NW 107th Ave	Miami	FL	33172	800-442-0556*	305-442-0550
*Resv					
Travel Dynamics International					
132 E 70th St	New York	NY	10021	800-257-5767	212-517-7555
Windstar Cruises					
2101 Fourth Ave Ste 210	Seattle	WA	98121	800-258-7245*	206-292-9606
*Resv					

223   CRUISES - RIVERBOAT

SEE ALSO Casinos ; Cruise Lines

				Toll-Free	Phone
American Cruise Lines					
741 Boston Post Rd Ste 200.	Guilford	CT	06437	800-814-6880	203-453-6800
Englund Marine & Industrial Supply Company Inc					
95 Hamburg Ave PO Box 296.	Astoria	OR	97103	800-228-7051	503-325-4341
French Country Waterways Ltd					
PO Box 2195	Duxbury	MA	02331	800-222-1236	781-934-2454
Uniworld 17323 Ventura Blvd	Encino	CA	91316	800-733-7820	818-382-7820
Victoria Cruises Inc					
57-08 39th Ave	Woodside	NY	11377	800-348-8084*	212-818-1680
*Cust Svc					
Viking River Cruises					
5700 Canoga Ave Ste 200	Woodland Hills	CA	91367	877-668-4546*	818-227-1234
*Cust Svc					

224   CUTLERY

SEE ALSO Silverware

				Toll-Free	Phone
Atlanta Cutlery Corp					
2147 Gees Mill Rd	Conyers	GA	30013	800-883-0300	770-922-3700
Buck Knives Inc					
660 S Lochsa St	Post Falls	ID	83854	800-326-2825	208-262-0500
Crescent Manufacturing Co					
1310 Majestic Dr	Fremont	OH	43420	800-537-1330	419-332-6484
Cutco Corp 1116 E State St	Olean	NY	14760	800-828-0448	716-372-3111
Dexter-Russell Inc					
44 River St	Southbridge	MA	01550	800-343-6042	508-765-0201
Douglas/Quikut Co					
118 E Douglas Rd	Walnut Ridge	AR	72476	800-982-5233	
Fiskars Brands Inc					
2537 Daniels St	Madison	WI	53718	866-348-5661	
KA-BAR Knives Inc					
200 Homer St	Olean	NY	14760	800-282-0130	716-372-5952
Lamson & Goodnow Mfg Co					
45 Conway St	Shelburne Falls	MA	01370	800-872-6564	413-625-0201
Master Cutlery Inc					
700 Penhorn Ave	Secaucus	NJ	07094	888-271-7229	201-271-7600
Midwest Tool & Cutlery Co Inc					
1210 Progress St PO Box 160	Sturgis	MI	49091	800-782-4659	269-651-7964
Ontario Knife Co					
26 Empire St	Franklinville	NY	14737	800-222-5233	716-676-5527
Pacific Handy Cutter Inc					
17819 Gillette Ave	Irvine	CA	92614	800-229-2233*	714-662-1033
*Cust Svc					
Professional Cutlery Direct LLC					
242 Branford St	North Branford	CT	06471	800-792-6650	
Queen Cutlery Co					
507 Chestnut St	Titusville	PA	16354	800-222-5233*	814-827-3673
*Sales					
Rada Manufacturing Co					
PO Box 838	Waverly	IA	50677	800-311-9691	319-352-5454
Swiss Army Brands Inc					
7 Victoria Dr PO Box 874	Monroe	CT	06468	800-442-2706*	203-929-6391
*Cust Svc					
Wenger North America Inc					
15 Corporate Dr	Orangeburg	NY	10962	800-431-2996*	845-365-3500
*Cust Svc					
WR Case & Sons Cutlery Co					
50 Owens Way PO Box 4000	Bradford	PA	16701	800-523-6350	

225   CYLINDERS & ACTUATORS - FLUID POWER

SEE ALSO Automotive Parts & Supplies - Mfr

				Toll-Free	Phone
Bosch Rexroth Corp					
5150 Prairie Stone Pkwy	Hoffman Estates	IL	60192	800-860-1055	847-645-3600

				Toll-Free	Phone

Clippard Instrument Lab
7390 Colerain Ave .... Cincinnati OH 45239 **877-245-6247** 513-521-4261

Cunningham Manufacturing Co
318 S Webster St .... Seattle WA 98108 **800-767-0038** 206-767-3713

Eckel Mfg Company Inc
8035 N County Rd W .... Odessa TX 79764 **800-654-4779** 432-362-4336

Hader/Seitz Inc
15600 W Lincoln Ave PO Box 510260 .... New Berlin WI 53151 **877-388-2101**

Hannon Hydraulics LLC
625 N Loop 12 .... Irving TX 75061 **800-333-4266** 972-438-2870

Helac Corp
225 Battersby Ave .... Enumclaw WA 98022 **800-327-2589** 360-825-1601

Hol-Mac Corp
2730-A Hwy 15 PO Box 349 .... Bay Springs MS 39422 **800-844-3019** 601-764-4121

Humphrey Products Co
5070 E N Ave PO Box 2008 .... Kalamazoo MI 49048 **800-477-8707** 269-381-5500

ITT Industries Inc Engineered Valves Div
33 Centerville Rd .... Lancaster PA 17603 **800-366-1111** 717-509-2200

Luxfer Gas Cylinders
3016 Kansas Ave .... Riverside CA 92507 **800-764-0366** 951-684-5110

Micromatic LLC 525 Berne St .... Berne IN 46711 **800-333-5752** 260-589-2136

Norris Cylinder Co
4818 W Loop 281 .... Longview TX 75603 **800-527-8418** 903-757-7633

Parker Hannifin Corp
6035 Parkland Blvd .... Cleveland OH 44124 **800-272-7537*** 216-896-3000
NYSE: PH ▧ *Cust Svc*

Parker Hannifin Corp Automation Actuator Div
135 Quadral Dr .... Wadsworth OH 44281 **800-272-7537** 330-336-3511

Parker Hannifin Corp Cylinder Div
500 S Wolf Rd .... Des Plaines IL 60016 **800-272-7537** 847-298-2400

Parker Instrumentation Group
6035 Parkland Blvd .... Cleveland OH 44124 **800-272-7537** 216-896-3000

PHD Inc
9009 Clubridge Dr .... Fort Wayne IN 46809 **800-624-8511** 260-747-6151

Sargent Controls & Aerospace
5675 W Burlingame Rd .... Tucson AZ 85743 **800-230-0359** 520-744-1000

Standex International Corp Custom Hoists Div
771 County Rd 30A W PO Box 98 .... Hayesville OH 44838 **800-837-4668** 419-368-4721

Tol-O-Matic Inc
3800 County Rd 116 .... Hamel MN 55340 **800-328-2174** 763-478-8000

Wabash Technologies
1375 Swan St PO Box 829 .... Huntington IN 46750 **800-487-6865** 260-355-4100

226 DATA COMMUNICATIONS SERVICES FOR WIRELESS DEVICES

Companies listed here deliver data such as customized news or stock information, other personalized content, and/or multimedia, audio, and video from the Internet to wireless devices (cellular phones, Personal Digital Assistants, pagers, laptop computers).

				Toll-Free	Phone

Accel Networks LLC
4905 34th StS #227 .... St. Petersburg FL 33711 **877-406-8585**

BlackBerry 295 Phillip St .... Waterloo ON N2L3W8 **877-255-2377** 519-888-7465

Broadcast Microwave Services Inc (BMS)
12367 Crosthwaite Cir .... Poway CA 92064 **800-669-9667** 858-391-3050

Buyatab Online Inc
204 - 576 Seymour St .... Vancouver BC V6B3K1 **888-267-0447**

Carousel Industries of North America Inc
659 S County Trl .... Exeter RI 02822 **800-401-0760**

chatr wireless
333 Bloor St E Eighth Fl .... Toronto ON M4W1G9 **800-485-9745**

Condo Control Central
First Canadian Pl 100 King St W
Ste 5700 .... Toronto ON M5X1C7 **888-762-6636**

Dial800 LLC
9911 Pico Blvd Ste 1200 .... Los Angeles CA 90035 **800-342-5800**

DriverDO LLC
734 Massachusetts St .... Lawrence KS 66044 **844-366-6837**

Dtreds LLC
1329 Shepard Dr Ste 2 .... Sterling VA 20164 **877-694-7766**

FreshGrade Inc
301-1447 Ellis St .... Kelowna BC V1Y2A3 **877-957-7757**

FundThrough Inc
260 Spadina Ave Ste 400 .... Toronto ON M5T2E4 **800-766-0460**

GreenSky Trade Credit LLC
1797 Northeast Expy Ste 100 .... Atlanta GA 30329 **866-936-0602**

Hotwire Communications LLC
One Belmont Ave Ste 1100 .... Bala Cynwyd PA 19004 **800-409-4733**

iLeads.com LLC
567 San Nicolas Dr Ste 180 .... Newport Beach CA 92660 **877-245-3237**

Immediatek Inc(NDA)
Ste 200 3301 Airport Fwy .... Bedford TX 76021 **888-661-6565**

Intermec Technologies Corp
6001 36th Ave W .... Everett WA 98203 **800-934-3163*** 425-348-2600
*Sales

Masergy Communications Inc
2740 N Dallas Pkwy Ste 260 .... Plano TX 75093 **866-588-5885** 214-442-5700

Network Earth Inc
14 Cambridge Ct .... Wappingers Falls NY 12590 **888-201-5160**

Nitel Inc
1101 W Lk St Sixth Fl .... Chicago IL 60607 **888-450-2100**

Parago Inc
700 State Hwy 121 Bypass Ste 200 ...... Lewisville TX 75067 **866-219-7533**

Roam Mobility Inc
400 - 311 Water St .... Vancouver BC V6B1B8 **888-762-6487**

SoundConnect LLC
One Batterymarch Park Ste 104 .... Quincy MA 02169 **888-827-4462**

SPROUT Wellness Solutions Inc
366 Adelaide St W Ste 301 .... Toronto ON M5V1R9 **866-535-5027**

Superheat Fgh Services Inc
680 Industrial Pk Dr .... Evans GA 30809 **888-508-3226**

Synchronoss Technologies Inc
200 Crossing Blvd .... Bridgewater NJ 08807 **866-620-3940**
NASDAQ: SNCR

TeleCommunication Systems Inc
275 W St Ste 400 .... Annapolis MD 21401 **800-810-0827** 410-263-7616
NASDAQ: TSYS

				Toll-Free	Phone

Trade Service Company LLC
15092 Ave of Science .... San Diego CA 92128 **800-854-1527**

TrouveMoiUnPro Inc
736 Wellington Ste 100 .... Montreal QC H3C1T4 **855-360-1390**

Trulioo Inc
300 - 420 W Hastings St .... Vancouver BC V6B1L1 **888-773-0179**

Wireless Analytics LLC
230 N St Ste 4 .... Danvers MA 01923 **888-588-5550**

Zingle Inc
5235 Avenida Encinas Ste A .... Carlsbad CA 92008 **877-946-4536**

Zyme Solutions Inc
240 Twin Dolphin Dr Ste E .... Redwood Shores CA 94065 **888-200-6629**

227 DATA PROCESSING & RELATED SERVICES

SEE ALSO Payroll Services ; Electronic Transaction Processing

				Toll-Free	Phone

Assessment Technology Inc
6700 E Speedway Blvd .... Tucson AZ 85710 **800-367-4762** 520-323-9033

Automatic Data Processing Inc (ADP)
One ADP Blvd .... Roseland NJ 07068 **800-225-5237** 973-994-5000
NASDAQ: ADP

AutoVision Wireless Inc
360 Deerhide Crescent .... Toronto ON M9M2Y6 **866-514-8030** 416-747-4444

Beanstalk Data
656 michael wylie dr .... Charlotte NC 28217 **800-892-3997**

BlueTie Inc
2480 Browncroft Blvd Ste 2b .... Rochester NY 14625 **800-258-3843** 585-586-2000

Carahsoft Technology Corp
12369 Sunrise Vly Dr Ste D2 .... Reston VA 20191 **888-662-2724** 703-871-8500

CCC Information Services Inc
222 Merchandise Mart Plz .... Chicago IL 60654 **800-621-8070**

Central Service Assn
93 S Coley Rd .... Tupelo MS 38801 **877-842-5962** 662-842-5962

CitiusTech Inc
Two Research Way Second Fl .... Princeton NJ 08540 **877-248-4871**

Claimsnet.com Inc
14860 Montfort Dr Ste 250 .... Dallas TX 75254 **800-356-1511** 972-458-1701

Collective Technologies LLC
9433 Bee Caves Rd .... Austin TX 78733 **800-994-1640** 512-263-5500

Communication Data Services
1901 Bell Ave .... Des Moines IA 50315 **866-897-7987** 515-246-6837

Computer Consultants Inc (CCI)
43252 Woodward Ave Ste 240 .... Bloomfield Hills MI 48302 **800-693-1066** 248-858-7701

Computer Services Inc
3901 Technology Dr .... Paducah KY 42001 **800-545-4274** 270-442-7361
OTC: CSVI

Continental Graphics Corp
4060 N Lakewood Blvd
Bldg 801 5th Fl .... Long Beach CA 90808 **800-862-5691** 714-503-4200

Crosscom National LLC
900 Deerfield Pkwy .... Buffalo Grove IL 60089 **888-471-6050** 847-520-9200

Dantom Systems Inc
29241 Beck Rd .... Wixom MI 48393 **866-536-2376** 248-567-7300

DataBank
12000 Baltimore Ave .... Beltsville MD 20705 **800-873-9426** 301-837-0197

Desert Dog Marketing LLC
4641 N 12th St Ste 200 .... Phoenix AZ 85014 **800-506-0398**

Discovery Research Group
6975 Union Pk Ctr Ste 150 .... Midvale UT 84047 **800-678-3748**

Docufree Corp
1175 Northmeadow Pkwy Ste 140 ...... Roswell GA 30076 **877-220-4350** 770-643-2900

DoxTek Inc 264 W Center St .... Orem UT 84057 **877-705-7226**

DPF Data Services Group Inc
1990 Swarthmore Ave .... Lakewood NJ 08701 **800-431-4416** 732-370-8840

E Ink Holdings Inc
733 Concord Ave .... Cambridge MA 02138 **866-311-1999** 617-499-6000

Equifax Inc
1550 Peachtree St NW .... Atlanta GA 30309 **888-202-4025*** 404-885-8000
NYSE: EFX ▧ *Sales*

Fair Isaac Corp
2665 Long Lake Rd Bldg C .... Roseville MN 55113 **888-342-6336*** 612-758-5200
NYSE: FICO ▧ *Cust Svc*

Genetec Inc
2280 Alfred-Nobel Blvd Ste 400 .... Montreal QC H4S2A4 **866-684-8006** 514-332-4000

GEOSPAN Corp
10990 73rd Ave N Ste 136 .... Minneapolis MN 55369 **800-436-7726** 763-493-9320

Glance Networks Inc
1167 Massachusetts Ave .... Arlington MA 02476 **877-452-6236** 781-646-8505

Global Health Care Exchange LLC (GHX)
1315 W Century Dr .... Louisville CO 80027 **800-968-7449** 720-887-7000

Goold Health Systems Inc
PO Box 1090 .... Augusta ME 04332 **800-832-9672** 207-622-7153

Health Management Systems Inc
401 Pk Ave S .... New York NY 10016 **877-467-0184** 212-857-5000

Inspired eLearning Inc
613 NW Loop 410 Ste 530 .... San Antonio TX 78216 **800-631-2078** 210-579-0224

Kelser Corp
111 Roberts St Ste D .... East Hartford CT 06108 **800-647-5316** 860-528-9819

Learning Enhancement Corp
200 S Wacker Dr Ste 3100 .... Chicago IL 60606 **877-272-4610** 312-455-1758

Lumension Security Inc
8660 E Hartford Dr Ste 300 .... Scottsdale AZ 85255 **888-725-7828**

Mid America Computer Corp
PO Box 700 .... Blair NE 68008 **800-622-2502** 402-426-6222

Nexcess.net LLC
21700 Melrose Ave .... Southfield MI 48075 **866-639-2377**

PenTeleData
540 Delaware Ave PO Box 197 .... Palmerton PA 18071 **800-281-3564**

Pinnacle Business Systems Inc
3824 S Blvd St Ste 200 .... Edmond OK 73013 **800-311-0757**

Printmail Systems Inc
23 Friends Ln .... Newtown PA 18940 **800-910-4844** 215-860-4250

PRISMHR
50 Resnik Rd Ste 200 .... Plymouth MA 02360 **877-837-4311** 508-747-7261

Ramco Systems Corp
3150 Brunswick Pk Ste 130 .... Lawrenceville NJ 08648 **800-472-6261** 609-620-4800

	City	State	Zip	Toll-Free	Phone
Rangam Consultants Inc 370 Campus Dr Ste 103	Somerset	NJ	08873	**877-583-7054**	908-704-8843
Renew Data Corp 9500 Arboretum Blvd	Austin	TX	78759	**888-811-3789**	512-276-5500
Right Systems Inc 2600 Willamette Dr NE Ste C	Lacey	WA	98516	**800-571-1717**	360-956-0414
Scicom Data Services Ltd 10101 Bren Rd E	Minnetonka	MN	55343	**800-488-9087**	952-933-4200
Skybank Financial Services Corp 1444 Biscayne Blvd Ste 309	Miami	FL	33132	**800-617-9980**	
Sof Tec Solutions Inc 384 Inverness Pkwy # 211	Englewood	CO	80112	**888-376-3832**	303-662-1010
Softlayer Technologies Inc 4849 Alpha Rd *Sales	Dallas	TX	75244	**866-398-7638***	214-442-0600
SourceMedical Solutions Inc 100 Grandview Pl Ste 400	Birmingham	AL	35243	**866-245-8093**	
SunGard Data Systems Inc 680 E Swedesford Rd	Wayne	PA	19087	**866-264-4829**	800-468-7483
Taskstream LLC 71 W 23rd St	New York	NY	10010	**800-311-5656**	212-868-2700
Techware Distribution Inc 7720 W 78th St	Minneapolis	MN	55439	**800-295-0083**	952-944-0083
Tecnicard Inc 3191 Coral Way Ste 800	Miami	FL	33145	**800-317-6020**	305-442-0018
Teradata Corp 10000 Innovation Dr *NYSE: TDC*	Dayton	OH	45342	**866-548-8348**	
Triton-Tek Inc 445 W Erie St Ste 208	Chicago	IL	60654	**866-387-4866**	312-467-9201
Vam USA LLC 19210 Hardy Rd	Houston	TX	77041	**800-634-6612**	713-479-3200
Vertafore Inc 11724 NE 195th St	Bothell	WA	98011	**800-444-4813**	425-402-1000
Web Age Solutions Inc 439 University Ave Ste 820	Toronto	ON	M5G1Y8	**866-206-4644**	
Williams Records Management 1925 E Vernon Ave *Cust Svc	Los Angeles	CA	90058	**800-207-3267***	323-234-3453
Wrightsoft Corp 131 Hartwell Ave	Lexington	MA	02421	**800-225-8697**	
Z57 Internet Solutions 10045 Mesa Rim Rd	San Diego	CA	92121	**800-899-8148**	

228 DATING SERVICES

	City	State	Zip	Toll-Free	Phone
Digiscribe International LLC 150 Clearbrook Rd Ste 125	Elmsford	NY	10523	**800-686-7577**	
Friendfinder Network Inc 6800 Broken Sound Pkwy Ste 200 *TSE: FFN*	Boca Raton	FL	33487	**800-388-0760**	561-912-7000
Omni Cubed Inc 1390 Broadway Ste B155	Placerville	CA	95667	**877-311-1976**	

229 DENTAL ASSOCIATIONS - STATE

SEE ALSO Health & Medical Professionals Associations

	City	State	Zip	Toll-Free	Phone
Arizona Dental Assn 3193 N Drinkwater Blvd	Scottsdale	AZ	85251	**800-866-2732**	480-344-5777
California Dental Assn 1201 K St	Sacramento	CA	95853	**800-736-7071**	916-443-0505
Colorado Dental Assn 3690 S Yosemite St Ste 400	Denver	CO	80237	**866-777-4771**	303-740-6900
Florida Dental Assn 1111 E Tennessee St	Tallahassee	FL	32308	**800-877-9922**	850-681-3629
Georgia Dental Assn 7000 Peachtree Dnwdy Rd NE Ste 200 Bldg 17	Atlanta	GA	30328	**800-432-4357**	404-636-7553
Hawaii Dental Assn 1345 S Beretania St Ste 301	Honolulu	HI	96814	**800-359-6725**	808-593-7956
Illinois State Dental Society 1010 S Second St	Springfield	IL	62704	**888-286-2447**	217-525-1406
Indiana Dental Assn 401 W Michigan St	Indianapolis	IN	46202	**800-562-5646**	317-634-2610
Iowa Dental Assn 8797 NW 54th Ave Ste 100	Johnston	IA	50131	**800-828-2181**	515-331-2298
Louisiana Dental Assn 7833 Office Pk Blvd	Baton Rouge	LA	70809	**800-388-6642**	225-926-1986
Massachusetts Dental Society Two Willow St Ste 200	Southborough	MA	01745	**800-342-8747**	508-480-9797
Michigan Dental Assn 3657 Okemos Rd Ste 200	Okemos	MI	48864	**800-589-2632**	517-372-9070
Minnesota Dental Assn 1335 Industrial Blvd Ste 200	Minneapolis	MN	55413	**800-950-3368**	612-767-8400
Mississippi Dental Assn 2630 Ridgewood Rd Ste C	Jackson	MS	39216	**866-982-0442**	601-982-0442
Missouri Dental Assn 3340 American Ave	Jefferson City	MO	65109	**800-688-1907**	573-634-3436
Montana Dental Assn 17 1/2 S Last Chance Gulch PO Box 1154	Helena	MT	59624	**800-257-4988**	406-443-2061
Nebraska Dental Assn 7160 S 29th St Ste 1	Lincoln	NE	68516	**888-789-2614**	402-476-1704
Nevada Dental Assn 8863 W Flamingo Rd Ste 102	Las Vegas	NV	89147	**800-962-6710**	702-255-4211
New Mexico Dental Assn 9201 Montgomery Blvd NE Ste 601	Albuquerque	NM	87111	**888-997-2583**	505-294-1368
New York State Dental Assn 20 Corporate Woods Blvd #602	Albany	NY	12211	**800-255-2100**	518-465-0044
North Carolina Dental Society 1600 Evans Rd	Cary	NC	27513	**800-662-8754**	919-677-1396
North Dakota Dental Assn PO Box 1332	Bismarck	ND	58502	**800-444-1330**	701-223-8870
Ohio Dental Assn 1370 Dublin Rd	Columbus	OH	43215	**800-497-6076**	614-486-2700
Oklahoma Dental Assn 317 NE 13th St	Oklahoma City	OK	73104	**800-876-8890**	405-848-8873
Oregon Dental Assn PO Box 3710	Wilsonville	OR	97070	**800-452-5628**	503-620-3230
South Carolina Dental Assn 120 Stonemark Ln	Columbia	SC	29210	**800-327-2598**	803-750-2277
South Dakota Dental Assn 804 N Euclid Ave Ste 103	Pierre	SD	57501	**866-551-8023**	605-224-9133
Texas Dental Assn 1946 S IH-35 Ste 400	Austin	TX	78704	**800-832-1145**	512-443-3675
Vermont State Dental Society 100 Dorset St Ste 18	South Burlington	VT	05403	**800-300-3046**	802-864-0115
Virginia Dental Assn (VDA) 3460 Mayland Ct Ste 110	Richmond	VA	23233	**877-726-0850**	804-288-5750
Wisconsin Dental Assn 6737 W Washington St Ste 2360	West Allis	WI	53214	**800-364-7646**	414-276-4520

230 DENTAL EQUIPMENT & SUPPLIES - MFR

	City	State	Zip	Toll-Free	Phone
3M ESPE Dental Products Div 3M Ctr Bldg 0275-02-SE-03	Saint Paul	MN	55144	**800-634-2249**	651-575-5144
3M Unitek 2724 Peck Rd	Monrovia	CA	91016	**800-634-5300**	
A-dec Inc 2601 Crestview Dr *Cust Svc	Newberg	OR	97132	**800-547-1883***	503-538-7478
Accutron Inc 1733 Parkside Ln	Phoenix	AZ	85027	**800-531-2221**	623-780-2020
Air Techniques Inc 1295 Walt Whitman Rd	Melville	NY	11747	**888-247-8481**	516-433-7676
Alpha Pro Tech Ltd 60 Centurian Dr Ste 112	Markham	ON	L3R9R2	**800-749-1363**	905-479-0654
American Medical Technologies Inc 5655 Bear Ln *OTC: ADLI*	Corpus Christi	TX	78405	**800-359-1959**	361-289-1145
American Orthodontics Corp 1714 Cambridge Ave	Sheboygan	WI	53081	**800-558-7687**	920-457-5051
Barnhardt Mfg Co 1100 Hawthorne Ln	Charlotte	NC	28205	**800-277-0377**	
Bicon LLC 501 Arborway	Boston	MA	02130	**800-882-4266**	617-524-4443
Brasseler USA One Brasseler Blvd	Savannah	GA	31419	**800-841-4522**	
Centrix Inc 770 River Rd	Shelton	CT	06484	**800-235-5862**	203-929-5582
Coltene/Whaledent Inc 235 Ascot Pkwy	Cuyahoga Falls	OH	44223	**800-221-3046**	330-916-8800
Darby Group Cos Inc 300 Jericho Quad	Jericho	NY	11753	**888-683-5001**	516-683-1800
Den-Mat Corp 2727 Skyway Dr	Santa Maria	CA	93455	**800-433-6628**	805-922-8491
DEN-TAL-EZ Group Inc Two W Liberty Blvd Ste 160	Malvern	PA	19355	**866-383-4636**	610-725-8004
DEN-TAL-EZ Inc Equipment Div 2500 Hwy 31 S	Bay Minette	AL	36507	**800-383-4636**	251-937-6781
Dentsply Caulk 38 W Clarke Ave	Milford	DE	19963	**800-532-2855**	302-422-4511
DENTSPLY International 221 W Philadelphia St P.O. Box 872	York	PA	17405	**800-800-2888**	717-845-7511
Dentsply International Inc 221 W Philadelphia St PO Box 872 *NASDAQ: XRAY*	York	PA	17405	**800-877-0020**	717-845-7511
Dentsply International Inc Rinn Div 1212 Abbott Dr	Elgin	IL	60123	**800-323-0970**	847-742-1115
Dentsply International Inc Tulsa Dental Div 5100 E Skelly Dr Ste 300	Tulsa	OK	74135	**800-662-1202**	918-493-6598
G & H Wire Company Inc 2165 Earlywood Dr	Franklin	IN	46131	**800-526-1026**	317-346-6655
GC America Inc 3737 W 127th St *Cust Svc	Alsip	IL	60803	**800-323-7063***	708-597-0900
Great Lakes Orthodontic Laboratories Div 200 Cooper Ave	Tonawanda	NY	14150	**800-828-7626**	
Heraeus 300 Heraeus Way *General	South Bend	IN	46614	**800-431-1785***	
Hu-Friedy Mfg Company Inc 3232 N Rockwell St	Chicago	IL	60618	**800-483-7433**	773-975-6100
Hygenic Corp 1245 Home Ave	Akron	OH	44310	**800-321-2135**	330-633-8460
Isolite Systems 111 Castilian Dr	Santa Barbara	CA	93117	**800-560-6066**	805-560-9888
Keystone Dental Inc 144 Middlesex Tpke	Burlington	MA	01803	**866-902-9272**	781-328-3490
Lancer Orthodontics Inc 1493 Poinsettia Bldg 143 *NYSE: LANZ* ■ *Cust Svc	Vista	CA	92081	**800-854-2896***	760-744-5585
LifeCore Biomedical LLC 3515 Lyman Blvd *Cust Svc	Chaska	MN	55318	**800-752-2663***	952-368-4300
M & M Innovations 7424 Blythe Island Hwy	Brunswick	GA	31523	**800-688-3384**	912-265-7110
Midwest Dental Equipment Services & Supplies 2700 Commerce St	Wichita Falls	TX	76301	**800-766-2025**	
Myotronics-noromed Inc 5870 S 194th St	Kent	WA	98032	**800-426-0316**	206-243-4214
Net32 Inc 250 Towne Village Dr	Cary	NC	27513	**800-517-1997**	919-468-1177
Nobel Biocare USA Inc 22715 Savi Ranch Pkwy	Yorba Linda	CA	92887	**800-993-8100**	714-282-4800
ORMCO Corp 1717 W Collins Ave *Cust Svc	Orange	CA	92867	**800-854-1741***	714-516-7400
Pentron Clinical Technologies LLC 53 N Plains Industrial Rd	Wallingford	CT	06492	**800-243-3969**	
Premier Dental Products Co 1710 Romano Dr PO Box 4500	Plymouth Meeting	PA	19462	**888-773-6872**	610-239-6000
Quantum Dental Technologies Inc 748 Briar Hill Ave	Toronto	ON	M6B1L3	**866-993-9910**	
Rocky Mountain Orthodontics Inc (RMO Inc) 650 W Colfax Ave	Denver	CO	80204	**800-525-6375**	303-592-8200
Sunstar Americas Inc 4635 W Foster Ave	Chicago	IL	60630	**888-777-3101**	

			Toll-Free	Phone

TP Orthodontics Inc
100 Ctr Plz . . . . La Porte IN 46350 **800-348-8856** 219-785-2591
Water Pik Inc
1730 E Prospect Rd . . . . Fort Collins CO 80553 **800-525-2774**

231	DEPARTMENT STORES

			Toll-Free	Phone

Bloomingdale's
1000 Third Ave . . . . New York NY 10022 **800-950-0047** 212-705-2000
Bob's Sporting Goods
1111 Hudson St . . . . Longview WA 98632 **800-292-5551** 360-425-3870
Bon-Ton Stores Inc
2801 E Market St . . . . York PA 17402 **800-945-4438** 717-757-7660
NASDAQ: BONT
Fred's Inc
4300 New Getwell Rd . . . . Memphis TN 38118 **800-374-7417** 901-365-8880
NASDAQ: FRED
Gordman 12100 W Ctr Rd . . . . Omaha NE 68144 **800-456-7463** 402-691-4000
Kohl's Corp
N 56 W 17000 Ridgewood Dr . . . . Menomonee Falls WI 53051 **855-564-5705** 262-703-7000
NYSE: KSS
Langstons Co
2034 NW Seventh St . . . . Oklahoma City OK 73106 **800-658-2831** 405-235-9536
Lord & Taylor
424 Fifth Ave . . . . New York NY 10018 **800-223-7440** 212-391-3344
Macy's Inc
Seven W Seventh St . . . . Cincinnati OH 45202 **800-261-5385** 513-579-7000
NYSE: M
Marine Corps Community Services
3044 Catlin Ave . . . . Quantico VA 22134 **866-400-8753** 703-784-3809
Masters Inc
5741 NW Cornelius Pass Road . . . . Hillsboro OR 97124 **877-652-5656** 503-531-3308
Peebles Inc 1 Peebles St . . . . South Hill VA 23970 **800-723-4548** 434-447-5200
Sears Canada Inc
290 Yonge St Ste 700 . . . . Toronto ON M5B2C3 **877-987-3277** 416-362-1711
TSE: SCC
SmartBargains Inc
101 S State Rd 7 Ste 201 . . . . Hollywood FL 33023 **877-222-6660**
Target Corp
1000 Nicollet Mall . . . . Minneapolis MN 55403 **800-440-0680*** 612-304-6073
*NYSE: TGT ■ *Cust Svc*
Tongass Trading Co
201 Dock St . . . . Ketchikan AK 99901 **800-235-5102** 907-225-5101
Wal-Mart Stores Inc
702 SW Eigth St . . . . Bentonville AR 72716 **800-925-6278*** 479-273-4000
*NYSE: WMT ■ *Cust Svc*
Wal-Mart Stores Inc Supercenter Div
702 SW Eigth St . . . . Bentonville AR 72716 **800-925-6278** 479-273-4000
Walmart.com
7000 Marina Blvd . . . . Brisbane CA 94005 **800-925-6278**

232	DEVELOPMENTAL CENTERS

Residential facilities for the developmentally disabled.

			Toll-Free	Phone

Productive Alternatives Inc
1205 N Tower Rd . . . . Fergus Falls MN 56537 **800-627-3529** 218-998-5630
Sonoma Developmental Ctr
15000 Arnold Dr . . . . Eldridge CA 95431 **800-862-0007** 707-938-6000
Woodward Resource Ctr
1251 334th St . . . . Woodward IA 50276 **888-229-9223** 515-438-2600

233	DIAGNOSTIC PRODUCTS

SEE ALSO Medicinal Chemicals & Botanical Products ; Pharmaceutical Companies ; Pharmaceutical Companies - Generic Drugs ; Biotechnology Companies

			Toll-Free	Phone

A & Z Pharmaceutical Inc
180 Oser Ave . . . . Hauppauge NY 11788 **800-810-9819** 631-952-3802
Abaxis Inc
3240 Whipple Rd . . . . Union City CA 94587 **800-822-2947** 510-675-6500
NASDAQ: ABAX
Abbott Laboratories Abbott Diagnostics Div
100 Abbott Pk Rd . . . . Abbott Park IL 60064 **800-387-8378** 847-937-6100
Accurate Chemical & Scientific Corp
300 Shames Dr . . . . Westbury NY 11590 **800-645-6264** 516-333-2221
Advanced Biotechnologies Inc (ABI)
9108 Guilford Rd . . . . Columbia MD 21046 **800-426-0764** 410-792-9779
Akorn Inc
1925 W Field Ct . . . . Lake Forest IL 60045 **800-932-5676** 847-279-6100
NASDAQ: AKRX
ALerCHEK Inc
15 Oak St Ste 302 . . . . Springvale ME 04083 **877-282-9542** 207-490-2266
Alere Inc
51 Sawyer Rd Ste 200 . . . . Waltham MA 02453 **877-441-7440** 781-647-3900
Alere San Diego Inc
9975 Summers Ridge Rd . . . . San Diego CA 92121 **800-286-2111** 781-647-3900
Allermed Laboratories Inc
7203 Convoy Ct . . . . San Diego CA 92111 **800-221-2748**
Aloha Medicinals Inc
2300 Arrowhead Dr . . . . Carson City NV 89706 **877-835-6091** 775-886-6300
Ambion Inc 2130 Woodward St . . . . Austin TX 78744 **866-952-3559** 512-651-0200
Amresco Inc 6681 Cochran Rd . . . . Solon OH 44139 **800-448-4442** 440-349-1313
AnaSpec Inc 34801 Campus Dr . . . . Fremont CA 94555 **800-452-5530** 510-791-9560
AntiCancer Inc
7917 Ostrow St . . . . San Diego CA 92111 **800-511-2555** 858-654-2555
Ascend Therapeutics Inc
607 Herndon Pkwy Ste 110 . . . . Herndon VA 20170 **888-412-5751** 703-471-4744
Athena Diagnostics Inc
377 Plantation St 2nd Fl . . . . Worcester MA 01605 **800-394-4493** 508-756-2886

Bachem-Peninsula Laboratories Inc
305 Old County Rd . . . . San Carlos CA 94070 **800-922-1516** 650-801-6090
Baker Cummins
4400 Biscayne Blvd . . . . Miami FL 33173 **800-226-8629**
Baxter Corp
7125 Mississauga Rd . . . . Mississauga ON L5N0C2 **866-234-2345** 905-369-6000
BD Diagnostics
Seven Loveton Cir . . . . Sparks MD 21152 **800-666-6433** 410-316-4000
Beckman Coulter Genomics
36 Cherry Hill Dr . . . . Danvers MA 01923 **800-361-7780** 978-867-2600
Becton Dickinson & Co
One Becton Dr . . . . Franklin Lakes NJ 07417 **888-237-2762*** 201-847-6800
*NYSE: BDX ■ *Cust Svc*
Berlex Laboratories Inc
Six W Belt . . . . Wayne NJ 07470 **888-842-2937** 973-694-4100
Bio-Rad Laboratories
1000 Alfred Nobel Dr . . . . Hercules CA 94547 **800-424-6723** 510-724-7000
NYSE: BIO
Biocell Laboratories Inc
2001 University Dr . . . . Rancho Dominguez CA 90220 **800-222-8382** 310-537-3300
BioGenex Laboratories Inc
4600 Norris Canyon Rd . . . . San Ramon CA 94583 **800-421-4149** 925-275-0550
Biohelix Corp
500 Cummings Ste 5550 . . . . Beverly MA 01915 **866-800-5458** 978-927-5056
Biomerica Inc
1533 Monrovia Ave . . . . Newport Beach CA 92663 **800-854-3002*** 949-645-2111
*OTC: BMRA ■ *Cust Svc*
BioMerieux Inc
595 Anglum Rd . . . . Hazelwood MO 63042 **800-634-7656** 314-731-8500
Bionostics Inc
Seven Jackson Rd . . . . Devens MA 01434 **800-776-3856*** 978-772-7070
**General*
BioSource International Inc
542 Flynn Rd . . . . Camarillo CA 93012 **800-242-0607** 805-987-0086
BiosPacific Inc
5980 Horton St Ste 225 . . . . Emeryville CA 94608 **800-344-6686** 510-652-6155
Boreal Genomics Inc
5150 El Camino Real . . . . Los Altos CA 94022 **800-681-5644** 604-822-8268
Burlington Drug Co Inc
91 Catamount Dr . . . . Milton VT 05468 **800-338-8703** 802-893-5105
Cancap Pharmaceutical Ltd
13111 Vanier Pl Ste 180 . . . . Richmond BC V6V2J1 **877-998-2378** 604-278-2188
Cancer Genetics Inc
Meadows Office Complex 201 Rt 17 N
Second Fl . . . . Rutherford NJ 07070 **888-334-4988** 201-528-9200
Cangene bioPharma Inc
1111 S Paca St . . . . Baltimore MD 21230 **800-441-4225** 410-843-5000
Cedarlane Laboratories Inc
4410 Paletta Ct . . . . Burlington ON L7L5R2 **800-268-5058** 905-878-8891
Chematics Inc
PO Box 293 . . . . North Webster IN 46555 **800-348-5174** 574-834-2406
Cholestech Corp
9975 Summers Ridge Rd . . . . San Diego CA 92121 **800-733-0404** 510-732-7200
Chromaprobe Inc
378 Fee Fee Rd . . . . Maryland Heights MO 63043 **888-964-1400** 314-738-0001
CST Technologies Inc
55 Northern Blvd Ste 200 . . . . Great Neck NY 11021 **800-448-4407** 516-482-9001
DakoCytomation
6392 Via Real . . . . Carpinteria CA 93013 **800-400-3256*** 805-566-6655
**Cust Svc*
Diamond Drugs Inc
645 Kolter Dr . . . . Indiana PA 15701 **800-882-6337** 724-349-1111
DiaSorin Inc 1951 NW Ave . . . . Stillwater MN 55082 **855-677-0600** 651-439-9710
Digestive Care Inc
1120 Win Dr . . . . Bethlehem PA 18017 **877-882-5950** 610-882-0349
DMS Pharmaceutical Group Inc
810 Busse Hwy . . . . Park Ridge IL 60068 **877-788-1100** 847-518-1100
DuPont Qualicon
Henry Clay Rd Bldg 400 Rt 141
PO Box 80357. . . . . Wilmington DE 19880 **800-863-6842** 302-695-5300
Edgemont Pharmaceuticals LLC
1250 Capital of Texas Hwy S Bldg 3
Ste 400 . . . . Austin TX 78746 **888-594-4332** 512-550-8555
Enzo Biochem Inc
527 Madison Ave . . . . New York NY 10022 **800-522-5052** 212-583-0100
NYSE: ENZ
Enzo Life Sciences Inc
10 Executive Blvd . . . . Farmingdale NY 11735 **800-942-0430** 631-694-7070
Exalpha Biologicals Inc
Five Clock Tower Pl Ste 255 . . . . Maynard MA 01754 **800-395-1137**
Face Stockholm Ltd
324 Joslen Blvd . . . . Hudson NY 12534 **888-334-3223** 518-828-6600
Gen-Probe Inc
10210 Genetic Ctr Dr . . . . San Diego CA 92121 **800-523-5001** 858-410-8000
GenBio
15222 Ave of Science Ste A . . . . San Diego CA 92128 **800-288-4368*** 858-592-9300
**Tech Supp*
Gibson Laboratories Inc
1040 Manchester St . . . . Lexington KY 40508 **800-477-4763** 859-254-9500
Golden State Medical Supply Inc
5187 Camino Ruiz . . . . Camarillo CA 93012 **800-284-8633** 805-477-9866
Goodwin Biotechnology Inc
1850 NW 69th Ave . . . . Plantation FL 33313 **800-814-8600** 954-327-9656
Guerbet LLC
1185 W Second St . . . . Bloomington IN 47403 **877-729-6679** 812-333-0059
Harlan Bioproducts for Science Inc (HBPS)
298 S Carroll Rd . . . . Indianapolis IN 46229 **800-793-7287**
Helena Laboratories Inc
1530 Lindbergh Dr . . . . Beaumont TX 77704 **800-231-5663** 409-842-3714
Hemagen Diagnostics Inc
9033 Red Branch Rd . . . . Columbia MD 21045 **800-436-2436** 443-367-5500
OTC: HMGN
hermo Fisher Scientific Inc
8365 Valley Pike PO Box 307 . . . . Middletown VA 22645 **800-528-0494** 800-556-2323
Hitachi Chemical Diagnostics
630 Clyde Ct . . . . Mountain View CA 94043 **800-233-6278** 650-961-5501
Honeys Place Inc
640 Glenoaks Blvd . . . . San Fernando CA 91340 **800-910-3246** 818-256-1101

Classified Section

Company / Address	City	ST	Zip	Toll-Free	Phone
Hycor Biomedical Inc 7272 Chapman Ave *Cust Svc	Garden Grove	CA	92841	800-382-2527*	
IDEXX Laboratories Inc One IDEXX Dr *NASDAQ: IDXX*	Westbrook	ME	04092	800-548-6733	207-556-0300
ImmucorGamma Inc 3130 Gateway Dr PO Box 5625 *NASDAQ: BLUD ■ *Cust Svc*	Norcross	GA	30091	800-829-2553*	770-441-2051
Immuno-Mycologics Inc (IMMY) 2700 Technology Pl	Norman	OK	73071	800-654-3639	
ImmunoDiagnostics Inc One Presidential Way Ste 104	Woburn	MA	01801	800-573-1700	781-938-6300
Immunovision Inc 1820 Ford Ave	Springdale	AR	72764	800-541-0960	479-751-7005
Inova Diagnostics Inc 9900 Old Grove Rd	San Diego	CA	92131	800-545-9495	858-586-9900
Interleukin Genetics Inc 135 Beaver St 3rd Fl *OTC: ILIU ■ *Cust Svc*	Waltham	MA	02452	800-826-6762*	781-398-0700
International Immunology Corp 25549 Adams Ave	Murrieta	CA	92562	800-843-2853	951-677-5629
International Isotopes Inc 4137 Commerce Cir *OTC: INIS*	Idaho Falls	ID	83401	800-699-3108	208-524-5300
InVitro International 17751 Sky Pk Cir Ste G	Irvine	CA	92614	800-246-8487	949-851-8356
Invivoscribe Technologies Inc 6330 Nancy Ridge Dr Ste 106	San Diego	CA	92121	866-623-8105	858-224-6600
Iso-Tex Diagnostics Inc PO Box 909	Friendswood	TX	77549	800-477-4839	
Jackson ImmunoResearch Laboratories Inc 872 W Baltimore Pk PO Box 9	West Grove	PA	19390	800-367-5296	610-869-4024
Kern Health Systems 9700 Stockdale Hwy	Bakersfield	CA	93311	888-466-2219	661-664-5000
Kibow Biotech Inc 4781 W Chester Pike Newtown Business Ctr	Newtown Square	PA	19073	888-271-2560	610-353-5130
Kirkegaard & Perry Laboratories Inc 910 Clopper Rd	Gaithersburg	MD	20878	800-638-3167	301-948-7755
KMI Diagnostics Inc 8201 Central Ave NE Ste P	Minneapolis	MN	55432	888-564-3424	763-231-3313
Kohl & Frisch Ltd 7622 Keele St	Concord	ON	L4K2R5	800-265-2520	
Lawton's Drug Stores Ltd 236 Brownlow Ave Ste 270	Dartmouth	NS	B3B1V5	866-990-1599	902-468-1000
LifeScan Inc 1000 Gibraltar Dr	Milpitas	CA	95035	800-227-8862	408-263-9789
LipoScience Inc 2500 Sumner Blvd	Raleigh	NC	27616	877-547-6837	919-212-1999
Maine Biotechnology Services Inc 1037 R Forest Ave	Portland	ME	04103	800-925-9476	207-797-5454
Mallinckrodt Inc 675 McDonnell Blvd	Hazelwood	MO	63042	800-778-7898	314-654-2000
Marianna Industries Inc 11222 "I" St	Omaha	NE	68137	800-228-9060	402-593-0211
Medical Analysis Systems Inc 46360 Fremont Blvd	Fremont	CA	94538	800-232-3342	510-979-5000
MEDTOX Diagnostics Inc 1238 Anthony Rd	Burlington	NC	27215	800-334-1116	336-226-6311
Meridian Bioscience Inc 3471 River Hills Dr *NASDAQ: VIVO ■ *Cust Svc*	Cincinnati	OH	45244	800-543-1980*	513-271-3700
Monobind Inc 100 N Pt Dr	Lake Forest	CA	92630	800-854-6265	949-951-2665
Moss Inc PO Box 189	Pasadena	MD	21123	800-932-6677	410-768-3442
National Diagnostics Inc 305 Patton Dr	Atlanta	GA	30336	800-526-3867	404-699-2121
Neci 334 Hecla St	Lake Linden	MI	49945	888-648-7283	906-296-1000
Neogen Corp 620 Lesher Pl *NASDAQ: NEOG*	Lansing	MI	48912	800-234-5333	517-372-9200
New Horizons Diagnostics Corp 9110 Red Branch Rd	Columbia	MD	21045	800-888-5015	410-992-9357
Novartis Vaccines & Diagnostics One Health Plz Bldg 122 *NYSE: NVS*	East Hanover	NJ	07936	888-644-8585	862-778-8300
Odan Laboratories Ltd 325 Stillview Ave	Pointe-Claire	QC	H9R2Y6	800-387-9342	514-428-1628
Ondine Biomedical Inc 1100 Melville St Ste 910	Vancouver	BC	V6E4A6	800-564-6253	604-669-0555
OraSure Technologies Inc 220 E First St *NASDAQ: OSUR*	Bethlehem	PA	18015	800-869-3538	610-882-1820
Ortho-Clinical Diagnostics Inc 1001 US Rt 202 N PO Box 350	Raritan	NJ	08869	800-828-6316	
Oxford Biomedical Research Inc 2165 Avon Industrial Dr	Rochester Hills	MI	48309	800-692-4633	248-852-8815
Pacific Biometrics Inc 645 Elliott Ave W Ste 300	Seattle	WA	98119	800-767-9151	206-298-0068
Parchem Trading Ltd 415 Huguenot St	New Rochelle	NY	10801	800-282-3982	914-654-6800
Peptides International Inc 11621 Electron Dr	Louisville	KY	40299	800-777-4779	502-266-8787
Phadia US Inc 4169 Commercial Ave	Portage	MI	49002	800-346-4364	269-492-1940
Pharmaceutical Assoc Inc 1700 Perimeter Rd	Greenville	SC	29605	888-233-2334	864-277-7282
Pharmalucence Inc 29 Dunham Rd	Billerica	MA	01821	800-221-7554	781-275-7120
Pharmascience Inc 6111 Royalmount Ave Ste 100	Montreal	QC	H4P2T4	866-853-1178	514-340-9800
Pharmetics Inc 3695 AutoRt Des Laurentides	Laval	QC	H7L3H7	877-472-4433	450-682-8580
Phoenix Pharmaceuticals Inc 330 Beach Rd	Burlingame	CA	94010	800-988-1205	650-558-8898
Pointe Scientific Inc 5449 Research Dr PO Box 87188	Canton	MI	48188	800-445-9853	734-487-8300
Polymedco Inc 510 Furnace Dock Rd	Cortlandt Manor	NY	10567	800-431-2123	914-739-5400
PolyPeptide Laboratories Inc 365 Maple Ave	Torrance	CA	90503	800-338-4965	310-782-3569
Polysciences Inc 400 Valley Rd *Cust Svc*	Warrington	PA	18976	800-523-2575*	215-343-6484
Prasco LLC 6125 Commerce Ct	Mason	OH	45040	866-469-1414	513-618-3333
Promega Corp 2800 Woods Hollow Rd	Madison	WI	53711	800-356-9526	608-274-4330
Prozyme Inc 3832 Bay Ctr Pl	Hayward	CA	94545	800-457-9444	510-638-6900
Quality Biological Inc 7581 Lindbergh Dr	Gaithersburg	MD	20879	800-443-9331	301-840-9331
Quantimetrix Corp 2005 Manhattan Beach Blvd	Redondo Beach	CA	90278	800-624-8380	310-536-0006
Quidel Corp 10165 McKellar Ct *NASDAQ: QDEL*	San Diego	CA	92121	800-874-1517	858-552-1100
R & D Systems Inc 614 McKinley Pl NE	Minneapolis	MN	55413	800-343-7475	612-379-2956
Research & Diagnostic Antibodies 2645 W Cheyenne Ave	North Las Vegas	NV	89032	800-858-7322	702-638-7800
Roche Diagnostics Corp (RDC) 9115 Hague Rd PO Box 50457 *Cust Svc*	Indianapolis	IN	46250	800-428-5076*	317-521-2000
Rockland Immunochemicals Inc PO Box 326	Gilbertsville	PA	19525	800-656-7625	610-369-1008
Sammann Co Inc 9935 N Us Hwy 12 E	Michigan City	IN	46360	800-348-2508	219-872-4413
SCIMEDX Corp 100 Ford Rd	Denville	NJ	07834	800-221-5598	973-625-8822
Sigma-Aldrich Corp 3050 Spruce St *NASDAQ: SIAL*	Saint Louis	MO	63103	800-325-3010	314-771-5765
Southern Biotechnology Assoc Inc 160A Oxmoor Blvd	Birmingham	AL	35209	800-722-2255	205-945-1774
St Renatus LLC 1000 Centre Ave	Fort Collins	CO	80526	888-686-2314	970-282-0156
Stanbio Laboratory LP 1261 N Main St	Boerne	TX	78006	800-531-5535	830-249-0772
Straight Arrow Products Inc 2020 Highland Ave	Bethlehem	PA	18020	800-827-9815	610-882-9606
Strategic Diagnostics Inc 111 Pencader Dr *NASDAQ: SDIX*	Newark	DE	19702	800-544-8881	302-456-6789
Streck Inc 7002 S 109th St	Omaha	NE	68128	800-228-6090	402-333-1982
Sunovion Pharmaceuticals Inc 84 Waterford Dr	Marlborough	MA	01752	888-394-7377	508-481-6700
SurModics Inc 9924 W 74th St *NASDAQ: SRDX*	Eden Prairie	MN	55344	866-787-6639	952-829-2700
Tec Laboratories Inc 7100 Tec Labs Way SW	Albany	OR	97321	800-482-4464	541-926-4577
Techne Corp 614 McKinley Pl NE *NASDAQ: TECH*	Minneapolis	MN	55413	800-343-7475	612-379-8854
Teco Diagnostics 1268 N Lakeview Ave	Anaheim	CA	92807	800-222-9880	714-463-1111
Theragenics Corp 5203 Bristol Industrial Way *NYSE: TGX*	Buford	GA	30518	800-458-4372	770-271-0233
Thermo Scientific 12076 Santa Fe Dr PO Box 14428	Lenexa	KS	66215	800-255-6730	913-888-0939
Trana Discovery Inc 2054-260 Kildare Farm Rd	Cary	NC	27518	866-390-3452	
Triad Isotopes Inc 4205 Vineland Rd Ste L1	Orlando	FL	32811	866-310-0086	407-455-6700
Trinity Biotech PLC 5919 Farnsworth Ct *NASDAQ: TRIB*	Carlsbad	CA	92008	800-331-2291	760-929-0500
Tyger Scientific Inc 324 Stokes Ave	Ewing	NJ	08638	888-329-8990	609-434-0143
Uman Pharma Inc 100 De L'Industrie Blvd	Candiac	QC	J5R1J1	877-444-9989	450-444-9989
Utak Laboratories Inc 25020 Ave Tibbitts	Valencia	CA	91355	800-235-3442	661-294-3935
Valeo Pharma Inc 16667 Hymus Blvd Kirkland	Montreal	QC	H9H4R9	888-694-0865	514-694-0150
Wako Chemicals USA Inc 1600 Bellwood Rd	Richmond	VA	23237	800-992-9256	804-271-7677
World Wide Packaging LLC 15 Vreeland Rd Ste 4	Florham Park	NJ	07932	800-950-0390	973-805-6500
Worthington Biochemical Corp 730 Vassar Ave	Lakewood	NJ	08701	800-445-9603	732-942-1660
Xeris Pharmaceuticals Inc 3208 Red River St Ste 300	Austin	TX	78705	888-570-4781	
Zepto Metrix Corp 872 Main St *Cust Svc*	Buffalo	NY	14202	800-274-5487*	716-882-0920

234   DISPLAYS - EXHIBIT & TRADE SHOW

Company / Address	City	ST	Zip	Toll-Free	Phone
3D Exhibits Inc 2900 Lively Blvd	Elk Grove Village	IL	60007	800-471-9617	847-250-9000
Derse Exhibits Inc 3800 W Canal St	Milwaukee	WI	53208	800-562-2300	414-257-2000
Downing Displays Inc 550 Techne Ctr Dr	Milford	OH	45150	800-883-1800	513-248-9800
Expon Exhibits 909 Fee Dr	Sacramento	CA	95815	800-783-9766	916-924-1600
Gilbert Displays Inc 110 Spagnoli Rd	Melville	NY	11747	855-577-1100	631-577-1100
Siegel Display Products 300 Sixth Ave N	Minneapolis	MN	55401	800-626-0322	612-340-1493

235 — DISPLAYS - POINT-OF-PURCHASE

SEE ALSO Signs

				Toll-Free	Phone
Acrylic Design Assoc					
6050 Nathan Ln N	Plymouth	MN	55442	800-445-2167	763-559-8395
AMD Industries Inc					
4620 W 19th St	Cicero	IL	60804	800-367-9999	708-863-8900
Archbold Container Corp					
800 W Barre Rd PO Box 10	Archbold	OH	43502	800-446-2520	419-445-8865
Array Marketing					
45 Progress Ave	Toronto	ON	M1P2Y6	800-295-4120	416-299-4865
Art-Phyl Creations					
16250 NW 48th Ave	Hialeah	FL	33014	800-327-8318	305-624-2333
Chicago Display Marketing Corp					
2021 W St	River Grove	IL	60171	800-681-4340	708-842-0001
Colony Inc 2500 Galvin Dr	Elgin	IL	60123	800-735-1300	847-426-5300
Display Smart LLC					
801 W 27th Terr	Lawrence	KS	66046	888-843-1870	785-843-1869
Display Technologies LLC					
1111 Marcus Ave Ste M68	Lake Success	NY	11042	800-424-4220	
Felbro Inc					
3666 E Olympic Blvd	Los Angeles	CA	90023	800-733-5276	323-263-8686
Frank Mayer & Assoc Inc					
1975 Wisconsin Ave	Grafton	WI	53024	855-294-2875	
Harbor Industries Inc					
14130 172nd Ave	Grand Haven	MI	49417	800-968-6993	616-842-5330
Hunter Display					
14 Hewlett Ave	East Patchogue	NY	11772	800-767-2110	631-475-5900
Lingo Manufacturing Co					
7400 Industrial Rd	Florence	KY	41042	800-354-9771*	859-371-2662
*Cust Svc					
MDI Worldwide					
38271 W 12-Mile Rd	Farmington Hills	MI	48331	800-228-8925*	248-553-1900
*Sales					
Nashville Display					
306 Hartmann Dr	Lebanon	TN	37087	800-251-1150	615-743-2900
New Dimensions Research Corp					
260 Spagnoli Rd	Melville	NY	11747	800-637-8870	631-694-1356
Ovation Instore					
57-13 49th Pl	Maspeth	NY	11378	800-553-2202	718-628-2600
Rapid Displays					
4300 W 47th St	Chicago	IL	60632	800-356-5775	773-927-1091
Thorco Industries Inc					
1300 E 12th St	Lamar	MO	64759	800-445-3375	417-682-3375
United Displaycraft					
333 E Touhy Ave	Des Plaines	IL	60018	877-632-8767*	847-375-3800
*General					
Universal Display & Fixtures Co					
726 E Hwy 121	Lewisville	TX	75057	800-235-0701	972-221-5022
Visual Marketing Inc					
154 W Erie St	Chicago	IL	60654	800-662-8640	312-664-9177
Vulcan Industries Inc					
300 Display Dr	Moody	AL	35004	888-444-4417	205-640-2400

DOOR & WINDOW GLASS

SEE Glass - Flat, Plate, Tempered

236 — DOORS & WINDOWS - METAL

SEE ALSO Shutters - Window (All Types)

				Toll-Free	Phone
Amsco Windows Inc					
1880 S 1045 W	Salt Lake City	UT	84104	800-748-4661	801-978-5000
Anemostat					
1220 Watsoncenter Rd PO Box 4938	Carson	CA	90745	877-423-7426	310-835-7500
Asi Technologies Inc					
5848 N 95th Ct	Milwaukee	WI	53225	800-558-7068	414-464-6200
ASSA ABLOY 110 Sargent Dr	New Haven	CT	06511	800-377-3948	
Babcock-Davis					
9300 73rd Ave N	Brooklyn Park	MN	55428	888-412-3726	763-488-9247
Clopay Bldg Products Inc					
8585 Duke Blvd	Mason	OH	45040	800-225-6729	
Columbia Mfg Corp					
14400 S San Pedro St	Gardena	CA	90248	800-729-3667	310-327-9300
Cookson Co 2417 S 50th Ave	Phoenix	AZ	85043	800-294-4358	602-272-4244
Cornell Iron Works Inc					
24 Elmwood Rd	Mountain Top	PA	18707	800-233-8366	570-474-6773
Dominion Bldg Products					
6949 Fairbanks N Houston Rd	Houston	TX	77040	800-826-2617	
Door Components Inc					
7980 Redwood Ave	Fontana	CA	92336	866-989-3667	909-770-5700
Dunbarton Corp PO Box 8577	Dothan	AL	36304	800-633-7553	
EFCO Corp 1000 County Rd	Monett	MO	65708	800-221-4169	417-235-3193
Elixir Industries Inc					
24800 Chrisanta Dr Ste 210	Mission Viejo	CA	92691	800-421-1942	949-860-5000
Fleming Door Products Ltd					
101 Ashbridge Cir	Woodbridge	ON	L4L3R5	800-263-7515	
General Aluminum Company of Texas LLP					
1001 W Crosby Rd	Carrollton	TX	75006	800-727-0835	972-242-5271
GlassCraft Door Co					
2002 Brittmoore Rd	Houston	TX	77043	800-766-2196	713-690-8282
Graham Architectural Products Corp					
1551 Mt Rose Ave	York	PA	17403	800-755-6274	717-849-8100
Hufcor Inc					
2101 Kennedy Rd	Janesville	WI	53545	800-356-6968	608-756-1241
Hygrade Metal Moulding Manufacturing Corp					
1990 Highland Ave	Bethlehem	PA	18020	800-645-9475	610-866-2441
International Revolving Door Co					
2138 N Sixth Ave	Evansville	IN	47710	800-745-4726	812-425-3311
International Window Corp					
5625 E Firestone Blvd	South Gate	CA	90280	800-477-4032	562-928-6411

				Toll-Free	Phone
Jamison Door Co					
55 JV Jamison Dr PO Box 70	Hagerstown	MD	21740	800-532-3667	301-733-3100
Jantek Industries 230 Rt 70	Medford	NJ	08055	888-782-7937	609-654-1030
Joyce Windows					
1125 Berea Industrial Pkwy	Berea	OH	44017	800-824-7988	440-239-9100
Kane Manufacturing Corp					
515 N Fraley St	Kane	PA	16735	800-952-6399	814-837-6464
Krieger Specialty Products Co					
4880 Gregg Rd	Pico Rivera	CA	90660	866-203-5060	562-695-0645
LaForce Inc					
1060 W Mason St	Green Bay	WI	54303	800-236-8858	920-497-7100
Lockheed Window Corp					
Rt 100 PO Box 166	Pascoag	RI	02859	800-537-3061	401-568-3061
Loxcreen Co Inc, The					
1630 Old Dunbar Rd PO Box 4004	West Columbia	SC	29172	800-330-5699	803-822-8200
M-D Bldg Products Inc					
4041 N Santa Fe Ave	Oklahoma City	OK	73118	800-654-8454*	405-528-4411
*Cust Svc					
McKeon Door Co					
44 Sawgrass Dr	Bellport	NY	11713	800-266-9392	631-803-3000
MI Windows & Doors Inc					
650 W Market St	Gratz	PA	17030	800-727-0835	717-365-3300
MM Systems Corp					
50 MM Way	Pendergrass	GA	30567	800-241-3460	706-824-7500
Moss Supply Company Inc					
5001 N Graham St	Charlotte	NC	28269	800-438-0770	704-596-8717
National Guard Products Inc					
4985 E Raines Rd	Memphis	TN	38118	800-647-7874	
Nystrom Inc					
9300 73rd Ave N	Minneapolis	MN	55428	800-547-2635	763-488-9200
O'Keeffe's Inc					
325 Newhall St	San Francisco	CA	94124	888-653-3333	415-822-4222
Overhead Door Corp					
2501 S State Hwy 121 Bus Ste 200	Lewisville	TX	75067	800-275-3290	469-549-7100
Overly Manufacturing Co					
574 W Otterman St	Greensburg	PA	15601	800-979-7300	724-834-7300
Peelle Co					
373 Nesconset Hwy Ste 311	Hauppauge	NY	11788	800-787-5020	905-846-4545
Peerless Products Inc					
2403 S Main St	Fort Scott	KS	66701	800-279-9999	620-223-4610
PGT Industries					
1070 Technology Dr	Nokomis	FL	34275	800-282-6019	941-480-1600
Quaker Window Products Inc					
504 S Hwy 63 PO Box 128	Freeburg	MO	65035	800-347-0438	
Raynor Garage Doors					
1101 E River Rd	Dixon	IL	61021	800-472-9667	815-288-1431
Rebco Inc					
1171-1225 Madison Ave	Paterson	NJ	07509	800-777-0787	973-684-0200
Reese Enterprises Inc					
16350 Asher Ave	Rosemount	MN	55068	800-328-0953	651-423-1126
Richards-Wilcox Inc					
600 S Lake St	Aurora	IL	60506	800-253-5668	
Silver Line Bldg Products					
1 Silver Line Dr	North Brunswick	NJ	08902	800-234-4228*	732-247-2030
*Sales					
Southeastern Aluminum Products Inc					
6701 Suemac Pl	Jacksonville	FL	32254	800-243-8200*	904-781-8200
*Sales					
Southeastern Metals Mfg Company Inc					
11801 Industry Dr	Jacksonville	FL	32218	800-874-0335	904-757-4200
Special-Lite Inc PO Box 6	Decatur	MI	49045	800-821-6531	269-423-7068
Stanley Access Technologies					
65 Scott Swamp Rd	Farmington	CT	06032	800-722-2377	860-677-2861
Steelcraft Mfg Co					
9017 Blue Ash Rd	Cincinnati	OH	45242	877-613-8766*	513-745-6400
*Cust Svc					
Steves & Sons Inc					
203 Humble Ave	San Antonio	TX	78225	800-617-8586*	210-924-5111
*Sales					
Super Sky Products Inc					
10301 N Enterprise Dr	Mequon	WI	53092	800-558-0467	262-242-2000
Taylor Bldg Products					
631 N First St	West Branch	MI	48661	800-248-3600	989-345-5110
Therma-Tru Corp					
1750 Indian Wood Cir	Maumee	OH	43537	800-537-8827	419-891-7400
Thermo-Twin Industries Inc					
1155 Allegheny Ave	Oakmont	PA	15139	800-641-2211	412-826-1000
TRACO					
71 Progress Ave	Cranberry Township	PA	16066	800-992-4444	724-776-7000
Tubelite Inc					
4878 Mackinaw Trl	Reed City	MI	49677	800-866-2227	
Wayne-Dalton Corp					
One Door Dr PO Box 67	Mount Hope	OH	44660	800-827-3667	330-674-7015
West Window Corp					
226 Industrial Pk Dr	Martinsville	VA	24112	800-446-4167	276-638-2394
Won-Door Corp					
1865 South 3480 West	Salt Lake City	UT	84104	800-453-8494	801-973-7500

237 — DOORS & WINDOWS - VINYL

				Toll-Free	Phone
American Exteriors LLC					
1169 W Littleton Blvd	Littleton	CO	80120	800-794-6369	303-794-6369
Amerimax Bldg Products Inc					
5208 Tennyson Pkwy	Plano	TX	75024	800-448-4033	469-366-3200
Associated Materials Inc Alside Div					
PO Box 2010	Akron	OH	44309	800-922-6009*	
*Cust Svc					
CertainTeed Corp					
750 E Swedesford Rd	Valley Forge	PA	19482	800-782-8777*	610-341-7000
*Prod Info					
Champion Window Mfg Inc					
12121 Champion Way	Cincinnati	OH	45241	877-424-2674	513-346-4600
Chelsea Bldg Products					
565 Cedar Way	Oakmont	PA	15139	800-424-3573	
Harry G Barr Co					
6500 S Zero St	Fort Smith	AR	72903	800-829-2277	479-646-7891

					Toll-Free	Phone
Larson Manufacturing Co						
2333 Eastbrook Dr	Brookings	SD	57006		800-352-3360*	605-692-6115
*Cust Svc						
Moss Supply Company Inc						
5001 N Graham St	Charlotte	NC	28269		800-438-0770	704-596-8717
PGT Industries						
1070 Technology Dr	Nokomis	FL	34275		800-282-6019	941-480-1600
Provia Door Inc						
2150 SR- 39	Sugarcreek	OH	44681		800-669-4711*	330-852-4711
*General						
Quanex Building Products Corp						
1900 W Loop S Ste 1500	Houston	TX	77027		888-475-0633*	713-961-4600
*Cust Svc						
Rehau Inc						
1501 EdwaRds Ferry Rd NE	Leesburg	VA	20176		800-247-9445	703-777-5255
Royal Group, The						
30 Royal Group Crescent	Woodbridge	ON	L4H1X9		800-263-2353	905-264-0701
RubbAir Door Div Eckel Industries Inc						
100 Groton Shirley Rd	Ayer	MA	01432		800-966-7822	978-772-0480
Soft-Lite LLC						
10250 Philipp Pkwy	Streetsboro	OH	44241		800-551-1953	330-528-3400
Statewide Remodeling Inc						
2940 N Hwy 360 Ste 300	Grand Prairie	TX	75050		800-317-8283	214-677-9000
Superseal Mfg Co Inc						
PO Box 795	South Plainfie	NJ	07080		800-433-4873	908-561-5910
Thermal Industries Inc						
3700 Haney C	Murrysville	PA	15668		800-245-1540	724-733-3880
Veka Inc 100 Veka Dr	Fombell	PA	16123		800-654-5589	724-452-1000
Weather Shield Manufacturing Inc						
One Weather Shield Plz PO Box 309.	Medford	WI	54451		800-222-2995	715-748-2100
West Window Corp						
226 Industrial Pk Dr	Martinsville	VA	24112		800-446-4167	276-638-2394
Windsor Windows & Doors						
900 S 19th St	West Des Moines	IA	50265		800-218-6186	515-223-6660

238 — DOORS & WINDOWS - WOOD

SEE ALSO Shutters - Window (All Types) ; Millwork

					Toll-Free	Phone
Algoma Hardwoods Inc						
1001 Perry St	Algoma	WI	54201		800-678-8910	920-487-5221
Allmar Inc						
287 Riverton Ave	Winnipeg	MB	R2L0N2		800-230-5516	204-668-1000
Andersen Corp						
100 Fourth Ave N	Bayport	MN	55003		888-888-7020	651-264-5150
Endura Products Inc						
8817 W Market St	Colfax	NC	27235		800-334-2006	336-668-2472
Great Day Improvements LLC						
700 E Highland Rd	Macedonia	OH	44056		800-230-8301	330-468-0700
Haley Bros Inc						
6291 Orangethorpe Ave	Buena Park	CA	90620		800-854-5951	714-670-2112
Industrial Door Company Inc						
360 Coon Rapids Blvd	Minneapolis	MN	55433		888-798-0199	763-786-4730
Jenkins Mfg Company Inc						
1608 Frank Akers Rd	Anniston	AL	36207		800-633-2323	256-831-7000
Larson Manufacturing Co						
2333 Eastbrook Dr	Brookings	SD	57006		800-352-3360*	605-692-6115
*Cust Svc						
Lincoln Wood Products Inc						
1400 W Taylor St PO Box 375	Merrill	WI	54452		800-967-2461	
Marvin Windows & Doors						
PO Box 100	Warroad	MN	56763		888-537-7828	218-386-1430
Masonite International Corp						
201 N Franklin St Ste 300.	Tampa	FL	33602		800-895-2723	813-877-2726
Mathews Bros Co						
22 Perkins Rd	Belfast	ME	04915		800-615-2004	207-338-6490
National Vinyl LLC						
Seven Coburn St	Chicopee	MA	01013		800-424-5300	413-420-0548
Pella Corp 102 Main St	Pella	IA	50219		877-473-5527*	641-621-1000
*Cust Svc						
Quaker Window Products Inc						
504 S Hwy 63 PO Box 128	Freeburg	MO	65035		800-347-0438	
Semling-Menke Company Inc						
PO Box 378	Merrill	WI	54452		800-333-2206	715-536-9411
SNE Enterprises Inc						
880 Southview Dr	Mosinee	WI	54455		800-826-5509	715-693-7000
Steves & Sons Inc						
203 Humble Ave	San Antonio	TX	78225		800-617-8586*	210-924-5111
*Sales						
Trustile Doors LLC						
1780 E 66th Ave	Denver	CO	80229		866-442-5302	303-286-3931
Vancouver Door Company Inc						
203 Fifth St NW	Puyallup	WA	98371		800-999-3667	253-845-9581
Weather Shield Manufacturing Inc						
One Weather Shield Plz PO Box 309.	Medford	WI	54451		800-222-2995	715-748-2100
Windsor Windows & Doors						
900 S 19th St	West Des Moines	IA	50265		800-218-6186	515-223-6660

DRUGS - MFR

SEE Vitamins & Nutritional Supplements ; Medicinal Chemicals & Botanical Products ; Pharmaceutical Companies ; Pharmaceutical Companies - Generic Drugs ; Biotechnology Companies ; Diagnostic Products

239 — DRUG STORES

SEE ALSO Health Food Stores

					Toll-Free	Phone
Arbor Centers for Eyecare						
2640 183rd St Ste 2	Homewood	IL	60430		866-798-6633	708-798-6633
Community Pharmacies LP						
16 Commerce Dr Ste 1	Augusta	ME	04332		800-730-4840	
CVS Corp One CVS Dr	Woonsocket	RI	02895		888-607-4287*	401-765-1500
*Cust Svc						

					Toll-Free	Phone
Discount Drug Mart Inc						
211 Commerce Dr	Medina	OH	44256		800-833-6278	330-725-2340
Drugstore.com Inc						
411 108th Ave NE Ste 1400	Bellevue	WA	98004		800-378-4786	
Fruth Pharmacy Inc						
4016 Ohio River Rd	Point Pleasant	WV	25550		800-438-5390	304-675-1612
Harmon Stores Inc						
650 Liberty Ave	Union	NJ	07083		866-427-6661	
Jean Coutu Group (PJC) Inc						
530 Rue Beriault	Longueuil	QC	J4G1S8		877-695-6175	450-646-9760
TSE: PJC.A						
Katz Group						
10104 103rd Ave 1702 Bell Tower	Edmonton	AB	T5J0H8		866-323-9695	780-990-0505
Lee Silsby Compounding Pharmacy						
3216 Silsby Rd	Cleveland Heights	OH	44118		800-918-8831	216-321-4300
Liberty Drug & Surgical Inc						
195 Main St	Chatham	NJ	07928		877-816-0111	973-635-6200
Medicap Pharmacies Inc						
1 Rider Trail Plaza Dr	Earth City	MO	63045		800-407-8055	314-993-6000
Mission Pharmacy Services LLC						
201 N Jefferson St Ste 300	Kittanning	PA	16201		877-758-2039	
Oncology Plus Inc						
1070 E Brandon Blvd	Brandon	FL	33511		877-410-0779	
Rite Aid Corp						
30 Hunter Ln	Camp Hill	PA	17011		800-748-3243	717-761-2633
NYSE: RAD						
Rxusa Inc						
81 Seaview Blvd	Port Washington	NY	11050		800-764-3648	516-467-2500
Thrifty White Stores						
6055 Nathan Lane N Ste 200	Plymouth	MN	55442		800-642-3275	763-513-4300
Vitacost.com Inc						
5400 Broken Sound Blvd NW Ste 500	Boca Raton	FL	33487		800-381-0759	
Vitamin Shoppe Inc						
2101 91st St	North Bergen	NJ	07047		800-223-1216	201-868-5959
NYSE: VSI						
Walgreen Co 200 Wilmot Rd	Deerfield	IL	60015		800-925-4733*	847-940-2500
*Cust Svc						

240 — DRUGS & PERSONAL CARE PRODUCTS - WHOL

Companies listed here distribute pharmaceuticals, over-the-counter (OTC) drugs, and/or personal care products typically found in drug stores.

					Toll-Free	Phone
AmerisourceBergen Corp						
1300 Morris Dr Ste 100						
PO Box 959.	Chesterbrook	PA	19087		800-829-3132	610-727-7000
NYSE: ABC						
Auspex Pharmaceuticals Inc						
3366 N Torrey Pines Ct Ste 225	La Jolla	CA	92037		800-487-7671	858-558-2400
Bedford Road Pharmacy Inc						
11306 Bedford Rd Ne	Cumberland	MD	21502		800-788-6693	301-777-1771
BioMotiv LLC						
3605 Warrensville Ctr Rd	Cleveland	OH	44122		800-477-6307	216-455-3200
Buffalo Supply Inc						
1650A Coal Creek Dr	Lafayette	CO	80026		800-366-1812	
Cadeau Express Inc						
3494 E Sunset Rd	Las Vegas	NV	89120		800-240-0301	702-433-1333
Cardinal Health Nuclear Pharmacy Services						
7000 Cardinal Pl	Dublin	OH	43017		800-326-6457	614-757-5000
Dakota Drug Inc 28 Main St N	Minot	ND	58703		800-437-2018	701-852-2141
DRAXIMAGE Inc						
16751 Transcanada Hwy	Kirkland	QC	H9H4J4		888-633-5343	514-630-7080
Ferring Pharmaceuticals Inc						
100 Interpace Pkwy Third Fl	Parsippany	NJ	07054		888-337-7464	973-796-1600
Forever Spring						
2629 E Craig Rd Ste E	Las Vegas	NV	89030		800-523-4334	702-633-4283
Gavis Pharmaceuticals LLC						
400 Campus Dr	Somerset	NJ	08873		866-403-7592	908-603-6080
Iredale Mineral Cosmetics Ltd						
28 Church St	Great Barrington	MA	01230		877-869-9420	413-528-1078
J&B Medical Supply Co Inc						
50496 W Pontiac Trail	Wixom	MI	48393		800-980-0047	248-896-6210
Kinray Inc						
152-35 Tenth Ave	Whitestone	NY	11357		800-854-6729	718-767-1234
Lil' Drug Store Products Inc						
1201 Continental Pl Ne	Cedar Rapids	IA	52402		800-553-5022	
London Drugs Ltd						
12251 Horseshoe Way	Richmond	BC	V7A4X5		888-991-2299	604-272-7400
Mechanical Servants Inc						
2755 Thomas St	Melrose Park	IL	60160		800-351-2000	708-615-9439
Methapharm Inc						
11772 W Sample Rd	Coral Springs	FL	33065		800-287-7686	954-341-0795
Morris & Dickson Co Ltd						
410 Kay Ln	Shreveport	LA	71115		800-388-3833	318-797-7900
Neil Medical Group Inc						
2545 Jetport Rd	Kinston	NC	28504		800-735-9111	
North Carolina Mutual Wholesale Drug Co						
816 Ellis Rd	Durham	NC	27703		800-800-8551	919-596-2151
Pamlab LLC						
4099 Hwy 190 E Service Rd	Covington	LA	70433		844-639-9725	985-893-4097
Parmed Pharmaceuticals Inc						
4220 Hyde Pk Blvd	Niagara Falls	NY	14305		800-727-6331	716-284-5666
Reese Pharmaceutical Co						
10617 Frank Ave	Cleveland	OH	44106		800-321-7178	
Sothys USA Inc						
1500 NW 94th Ave	Miami	FL	33172		800-325-0503	305-594-4222
UNFI Specialty Distribution Services						
88 Huntoon Memorial Hwy	Leicester	MA	01524		877-476-8749	508-892-8171
US WorldMeds LLC						
4010 Dupont Cir Ste L-07	Louisville	KY	40207		888-900-8796	502-815-8000
Value Drug Mart Assoc Ltd						
16504 - 121A Ave	Edmonton	AB	T5V1J9		888-554-8258	780-453-1701
Victory Pharma Inc						
11682 El Camino Real	San Diego	CA	92130		866-427-6819	858-720-4500

241   DUDE RANCHES

SEE ALSO Resorts & Resort Companies

	Toll-Free	Phone
63 Ranch PO Box 979 .... Livingston MT 59047	**888-395-5151**	
7 D Ranch 7D Ranch PO Box 100 .... Cody WY 82414	**888-587-9885**	307-587-9885
Bar Lazy J Guest Ranch 447 County Rd 3 PO Box N .... Parshall CO 80468	**800-396-6279**	970-725-3437
Black Mountain Ranch 4000 Conger Mesa Rd .... McCoy CO 80463	**800-967-2401**	970-653-4226
Bonanza Creek Country Guest Ranch 523 Bonanza Creek Rd .... Martinsdale MT 59053	**800-476-6045**	406-572-3366
Brooks Lake Lodge & Guest Ranch 458 Brooks Lk Rd .... Dubois WY 82513	**866-213-4022**	
Cherokee Park Ranch 436 Cherokee Hills Dr .... Livermore CO 80536	**800-628-0949**	970-493-6522
Circle Z Ranch PO Box 194 .... Patagonia AZ 85624	**888-854-2525**	
CM Ranch 167 Fish Hatchery Rd PO Box 217 .... Dubois WY 82513	**800-455-0721**	307-455-2331
Colorado Trails Ranch 12161 County Rd 240 .... Durango CO 81301	**800-323-3833**	970-247-5055
Coulter Lake Guest Ranch 80 County Rd 273 .... Rifle CO 81650	**800-858-3046**	970-625-1473
Drowsy Water Ranch PO Box 147 .... Granby CO 80446	**800-845-2292**	970-725-3456
Dryhead Schively Ranch 1062 Rd 15 .... Lovell WY 82431	**800-628-9081**	307-548-6688
Eatons' Ranch 270 Eatons' Ranch Rd .... Wolf WY 82844	**800-210-1049**	307-655-9285
Elk Mountain Ranch PO Box 910 .... Buena Vista CO 81211	**800-432-8812**	
Flying E Ranch 2801 W Wickenburg Way .... Wickenburg AZ 85390	**888-684-2650**	928-684-2690
Fresh Air Fund 633 Third Ave 14th Fl .... New York NY 10017	**800-367-0003**	
Grapevine Canyon Ranch Inc PO Box 302 .... Pearce AZ 85625	**800-245-9202**	520-826-3185
Greenhorn Creek Guest Ranch 2116 Greenhorn Ranch Rd .... Quincy CA 95971	**800-334-6939**	530-283-0930
Hawley Mountain Guest Ranch PO Box 4 .... McLeod MT 59052	**877-496-7848**	406-932-5791
Heart Six Ranch 16985 Buffalo Vly Rd PO Box 70 .... Moran WY 83013	**888-543-2477**	
Hideout at Flitner Ranch Resort PO Box 206 .... Shell WY 82441	**800-354-8637**	307-765-2080
Home Ranch PO Box 822 .... Clark CO 80428	**800-688-2982**	970-879-1780
Homeplace Ranch RR 1 Site 2 .... Priddis AB T0L1W0	**877-931-3245**	403-969-4444
Horse Prairie Ranch 3300 Bachelor Mountain Rd .... Dillon MT 59725	**888-726-2454**	406-681-3166
Kay El Bar Guest Ranch PO Box 2480 .... Wickenburg AZ 85358	**800-684-7583**	928-684-7593
Laramie River Dude Ranch 25777 County Rd 103 .... Jelm WY 82063	**800-551-5731**	970-435-5716
Latigo Ranch PO Box 237 .... Kremmling CO 80459	**800-227-9655**	970-724-9008
Lazy L & B Ranch 1072 E Fork Rd .... Dubois WY 82513 *Cust Svc	**800-453-9488***	307-455-2839
Lone Mountain Ranch 750 Lone Mtn Ranch Rd PO Box 160069 .... Big Sky MT 59716	**800-514-4644**	406-995-4644
Long Hollow Ranch 71105 Holmes Rd .... Sisters OR 97759	**877-923-1901**	541-923-1901
Lozier's Box R Ranch 552 Willow Creek Rd PO Box 100 .... Cora WY 82925	**800-822-8466**	307-367-4868
Mountain Sky Guest Ranch PO Box 1219 .... Emigrant MT 59027	**800-548-3392**	406-333-4911
North Fork Ranch (NFR) 55395 Hwy 285 PO Box B .... Shawnee CO 80475	**800-843-7895**	303-838-9873
Peaceful Valley Ranch 475 Peaceful Vly Rd .... Lyons CO 80540	**800-955-6343**	303-747-2881
Pine Butte Guest Ranch 351 S Fork Rd .... Choteau MT 59422	**877-812-3698**	406-466-2158
Price Canyon Ranch PO Box 39 .... Rodeo NM 88056	**800-727-0065**	520-558-2383
Rainbow Trout Ranch (RTR) 1484 FDR 250 PO Box 458 .... Antonito CO 81120	**800-633-3397**	719-376-5659
Rancho de la Osa Guest Ranch PO Box 1 .... Sasabe AZ 85633	**800-872-6240**	520-823-4257
Rawah Ranch 11447 N County Rd 103 .... Glendevey CO 82063	**800-820-3152**	
Rich Ranch 939 Cottonwood Lakes Rd .... Seeley Lake MT 59868	**800-532-4350**	406-677-2317
Sundance Trail Guest Ranch 17931 Red Feather Lakes Rd .... Red Feather Lakes CO 80545	**800-357-4930**	970-224-1222
Sylvan Dale Guest Ranch 2939 N County Rd 31 D .... Loveland CO 80538	**877-667-3999**	970-667-3915
T Cross Ranch LLC 82 Parque Creek Rd PO Box 638 .... Dubois WY 82513	**877-827-6770**	307-455-2206
Tanque Verde Ranch 14301 E Speedway .... Tucson AZ 85748	**800-234-3833**	520-296-6275
Tarryall River Ranch 270015 County Rd 77 .... Lake George CO 80827	**800-408-8407**	719-748-1214
Three Bars Cattle & Guest Ranch 9500 Wycliffe Perry Creek Rd .... Cranbrook BC V1C7C7	**877-426-5230**	250-426-5230
Triangle C Dude Ranch 3737 Hwy 26 .... Dubois WY 82513	**800-661-4928**	307-455-2225
Triple J Wilderness Ranch 91 Mortimer Rd PO Box 310 .... Augusta MT 59410	**800-826-1300**	406-562-3653
Tumbling River Ranch 3715 Pk County Rd 62 PO Box 30 .... Grant CO 80448	**800-654-8770**	303-838-5981
Vee Bar Guest Ranch 38 Vee Bar Ranch Rd .... Laramie WY 82070	**800-483-3227**	307-745-7036
Vista Verde Guest & Ski Ranch PO Box 770465 .... Steamboat Springs CO 80477	**800-526-7433**	970-879-3858
White Stallion Ranch 9251 W Twin Peaks Rd .... Tucson AZ 85743	**888-977-2624**	520-297-0252

	Toll-Free	Phone
Wilderness Trails Ranch 1766 County Rd 302 .... Durango CO 81303	**800-527-2624**	970-247-0722
Wind River Ranch PO Box 3410 .... Estes Park CO 80517	**800-523-4212**	970-586-4212

242   DUPLICATION & REPLICATION SERVICES

	Toll-Free	Phone
Corporate Disk Co 4610 Crime Pkwy .... McHenry IL 60050	**800-634-3475**	815-331-6000
Digital Video Services 4592 40th St SE .... Grand Rapids MI 49512	**800-747-8273**	616-975-9911
Online Copy Corp 48815 Kato Rd .... Fremont CA 94539	**800-833-4460**	510-226-6810
Standard Digital Imaging 4426 S 108th St .... Omaha NE 68137	**800-642-8062**	402-592-1292
Thomas Reprographics 600 N Central Expy .... Richardson TX 75080	**800-877-3776**	972-231-7227

243   DUTY-FREE SHOPS

SEE ALSO Gift Shops

	Toll-Free	Phone
Baja Duty Free (BDF) 4590 Border Village Rd .... San Ysidro CA 92173	**877-438-8937**	619-428-6671
Niagara Duty Free Shop 5726 Falls Ave .... Niagara Falls ON L2G7T5	**877-642-4337**	905-374-3700
Peace Bridge Duty Free Inc One Peace Bridge Plz PO Box 339 .... Fort Erie ON L2A5N1	**800-361-1302**	
Starboard Cruise Services Inc 8400 NW 36th St .... Miami FL 33166	**800-540-4785**	786-845-7300
Tunnel Duty Free Shop Inc 465 Goyeau St .... Windsor ON N9A1H1	**800-669-2105**	519-252-2713

EDUCATIONAL INSTITUTIONS

SEE Preparatory Schools - Boarding ; Children's Learning Centers ; Colleges - Tribal ; Colleges & Universities - Historically Black ; Colleges & Universities - Jesuit

244   EDUCATIONAL INSTITUTION OPERATORS & MANAGERS

	Toll-Free	Phone
Apollo Group Inc 4025 E Elwood St .... Phoenix AZ 85040 *NASDAQ: APOL*	**800-990-2765**	
Bridgepoint Education Inc 13500 Evening Creek Dr N Ste 600 .... San Diego CA 92128 *NYSE: BPI*	**866-475-0317**	858-668-2586
Capella Education Co 225 S Sixth St Ninth Fl .... Minneapolis MN 55402 *NASDAQ: CPLA ▪ *Cust Svc*	**888-227-3552***	612-339-8650
Career Education Corp (CEC) 2895 Greenspoint Pkwy Ste 600 .... Hoffman Estates IL 60196 *NASDAQ: CECO*	**877-559-9222**	847-781-3600
Corinthian Colleges Inc 6 Hutton Centre Dr Ste 400 .... Santa Ana CA 92707 *NASDAQ: COCO*	**888-370-7589**	916-431-6959
Education Management Corp (EDMC) 210 Sixth Ave 33rd Fl .... Pittsburgh PA 15222 *NASDAQ: EDMC*	**800-275-2440**	412-562-0900
ITT Educational Services Inc 13000 N Meridian St .... Carmel IN 46032 *NYSE: ESI*	**800-388-3368**	317-706-9200
Laureate Education Inc 650 S Exeter Street .... Baltimore MD 21202	**866-452-8732**	410-843-6100
Leona Group LLC 4660 S Hagadorn Rd Ste 500 .... East Lansing MI 48823	**800-656-6763**	517-333-9030
National Heritage Academies 3850 Broadmoor Ave SE Ste 201 .... Grand Rapids MI 49512 *General	**877-223-6402***	
Schoolwires Inc 330 Innovation Blvd Ste 301 .... State College PA 16803	**877-427-9413**	
Sylvan Learning Centers 1001 Fleet St .... Baltimore MD 21202	**888-338-2283**	

245   EDUCATIONAL MATERIALS & SUPPLIES

SEE ALSO Office & School Supplies ; Educational & Reference Software

	Toll-Free	Phone
American Educational Products Inc 401 Hickory St PO Box 2121 .... Fort Collins CO 80522	**800-289-9299**	970-484-7445
Carolina Biological Supply Co 2700 York Rd .... Burlington NC 27215	**800-334-5551**	336-584-0381
Carson-Dellosa Publishing Company Inc 7027 Albert Pick Rd .... Greensboro NC 27409	**800-321-0943**	336-632-0084
Center Enterprises Inc 30 Shield St .... West Hartford CT 06110 *Orders	**800-542-2214***	860-953-4423
Chenille Kraft Co 65 Ambrogio Dr PO Box 269 .... Gurnee IL 60031	**800-621-1261**	
Claridge Products & Equipment Inc 601 Hwy 62 65 .... Harrison AR 72601	**800-434-4610**	870-743-2200
Creative Teaching Press Inc 6262 Katella Ave .... Cypress CA 92649	**800-444-4287**	714-895-5047
Delta Education LLC 80 NW Blvd .... Nashua NH 03063	**800-258-1302**	603-889-8899
Didax Inc 395 Main St .... Rowley MA 01969	**800-458-0024**	978-948-2340
Education Ctr Inc 3515 W Market St Ste 200 .... Greensboro NC 27403	**800-714-7991**	336-854-0309

			Toll-Free	Phone
Educational Insights Inc				
380 N Fairway Dr	Vernon Hills IL	60061	800-995-4436	
Educators Resource Inc				
2575 Schillingers Rd	Semmes AL	36575	800-868-2368*	
*Cust Svc				
Evan-Moor Educational Publishers Inc				
18 Lower Ragsdale Dr	Monterey CA	93940	800-777-4362	831-649-5901
Excelligence Learning Corp				
2 Lower Ragsdale Dr Ste 125	Monterey CA	93940	800-627-2829	831-333-5572
Fisher Science Education				
4500 Turnberry Dr	Hanover Park IL	60133	800-955-1177	800-766-7000
Frog Street Press Inc				
800 Industrial Blvd Ste 100	Grapevine TX	76051	800-884-3764	
Ghent Manufacturing Inc				
2999 Henkle Dr	Lebanon OH	45036	800-543-0550	513-932-3445
Great Source Education Group				
181 Ballardvale St	Wilmington MA	01887	800-289-4490	
Guidecraft USA				
55508 Hwy 19 W PO Box U	Winthrop MN	55396	800-524-3555	507-647-5030
Hayes School Publishing Co Inc				
321 Pennwood Ave	Pittsburgh PA	15221	800-926-0704	412-371-2373
Incentive Publications Inc				
2400 Crestmoor Dr	Nashville TN	37215	800-967-5325*	615-385-2934
*Mktg				
Kaplan Early Learning Co				
1310 Lewisville-Clemmons Rd	Lewisville NC	27023	800-334-2014	336-766-7374
Learning Resources				
380 N Fairway Dr	Vernon Hills IL	60061	800-222-3909	847-573-8400
Learning Wrap-Ups Inc				
1660 W Gordon Ave Ste 4	Layton UT	84041	800-992-4966	801-497-0050
McDonald Publishing				
567 Hanley Industrial Ct	Saint Louis MO	63144	800-722-8080	314-781-7400
McGraw-Hill Cos Inc SRA/McGraw-Hill Div				
8787 Orion Pl	Columbus OH	43240	800-334-7344	
National School Products				
1523 Old Niles Ferry Rd	Maryville TN	37803	800-627-9393	865-984-3960
Questar Assessment Inc				
5550 Upper 147th St W PO Box 382	Apple Valley MN	55124	800-800-2598*	800-471-5448
OTC: QUSA ▓ *Cust Svc				
Rock 'N Learn Inc				
105 Commercial Cir	Conroe TX	77304	800-348-8445	936-539-2731
Roylco Inc				
3251 Abbeville Hwy PO Box 13409	Anderson SC	29624	800-362-8656	864-296-0043
Scholastic News				
557 Broadway	New York NY	10012	800-724-6527*	212-343-6100
*Orders				
School Specialty Inc				
PO Box 1579	Appleton WI	54912	888-388-3224	920-734-5712
NASDAQ: SCHS				
Teacher Created Resources				
6421 Industry Way	Westminster CA	92683	888-343-4335	
TREND Enterprises Inc				
300 Ninth Ave SW	New Brighton MN	55112	800-860-6762*	651-631-2850
*Cust Svc				
World*Class Learning Materials				
PO Box 639	Candler NC	28715	800-638-6470	

246 EDUCATIONAL TESTING SERVICES - ASSESSMENT & PREPARATION

			Toll-Free	Phone
Barron's Educational Series Inc				
250 Wireless Blvd	Hauppauge NY	11788	800-645-3476	631-434-3311
Castle Worldwide Inc				
900 Perimeter Pk Rd Ste G	Morrisville NC	27560	800-655-4845	919-572-6880
College Board				
45 Columbus Ave	New York NY	10023	800-927-4302	212-713-8000
H & H Publishing Company Inc				
1231 Kapp Dr	Clearwater FL	33765	800-366-4079	727-442-7760
Kaplan Inc				
6301 Kaplan University Ave	Fort Lauderdale FL	33309	800-258-2432*	954-515-3993
*Cust Svc				
McGraw-Hill Cos Inc CTB/McGraw-Hill Div				
20 Ryan Ranch Rd	Monterey CA	93940	800-538-9547	831-393-0700
Praxis Series Online Educational Testing Service Teaching & Learning Div (ETS)				
PO Box 6051	Princeton NJ	08541	800-772-9476	609-771-7395
Prometric				
1501 S Clinton St	Baltimore MD	21224	866-776-6387	443-455-8000
Riverside Publishing Co				
3800 Golf Rd Ste 200	Rolling Meadows IL	60008	800-323-9540*	630-467-7000
*Cust Svc				

247 ELECTRIC COMPANIES - COOPERATIVES (RURAL)

SEE ALSO Utility Companies

Companies listed here are members of the National Rural Electric Cooperative Association; most are consumer-owned, but some are public power districts. In addition, the companies listed are electricity distribution cooperatives. Companies that generate and/or transmit electricity, but do not distribute it, are not included.

Alabama

			Toll-Free	Phone
Baldwin County Electric Membership Corp				
19600 Hwy 59	Summerdale AL	36580	800-837-3374	251-989-6247
Central Alabama Electric Co-op				
1802 Hwy 31 N	Prattville AL	36067	800-545-5735	334-365-6762
Cherokee Electric Co-op				
1550 Clarence Chestnut Bypass PO Box O	Centre AL	35960	800-952-2667	256-927-5524
Coosa Valley Electric Co-op				
69220 Alabama Hwy 77 PO Box 837	Talladega AL	35160	800-273-7210	256-362-4180
Covington Electric Co-op Inc				
18836 US Hwy 84	Andalusia AL	36421	800-239-4121	334-222-4121

			Toll-Free	Phone
Cullman Electric Co-op				
1749 Eva Rd NE PO Box 1168	Cullman AL	35055	800-242-1806	256-737-3201
Dixie Electric Co-op				
9100 Atlanta Hwy	Montgomery AL	36117	888-349-4332	334-288-1163
Franklin Electric Co-op Inc				
225 Franklin St NW	Russellville AL	35653	800-410-2732	256-332-2730
Joe Wheeler Electric Membership Corp				
PO Box 460	Trinity AL	35673	800-239-6518	256-552-2300
North Alabama Electric Co-op				
41103 US Hwy 72	Stevenson AL	35772	800-572-2900	256-437-2281
Pea River Electric Co-op				
1311 W Roy Parker Rd PO Box 969	Ozark AL	36360	800-264-7732	334-774-2545
Sand Mountain Electric Co-op				
402 Main St W	Rainsville AL	35986	877-843-2512	256-638-2153
South Alabama Electric Co-op (SAEC)				
PO Box 449	Troy AL	36081	800-556-2060	334-566-2060
Tallapoosa River Electric Co-op				
15163 US Hwy 431 S PO Box 675	Lafayette AL	36862	800-332-8732	334-864-9331
Tombigbee Electric Co-op Inc				
7686 US Hwy PO Box 610	Guin AL	35563	800-621-8069	205-468-3325

Alaska

			Toll-Free	Phone
Chugach Electric Assn Inc				
5601 Electron Dr	Anchorage AK	99518	800-478-7494	907-563-7494
Copper Valley Electric Assn Inc (CVEA)				
Mile 187 Glenn Hwy PO Box 45	Glennallen AK	99588	866-835-2832	907-822-3211
Golden Valley Electrical Assn Inc				
758 Illinois St	Fairbanks AK	99701	800-770-4832	907-452-1151
Homer Electric Assn Inc				
3977 Lake St	Homer AK	99603	800-478-8551	907-235-8551
Nushagak Electric & Telephone Assn Inc				
557 Kenny Wren Rd	Dillingham AK	99576	800-478-5296	907-842-5251

Arizona

			Toll-Free	Phone
Duncan Valley Electric Co-op Inc				
PO Box 440	Duncan AZ	85534	800-669-2503	928-359-2503
Graham County Electric Co-op Inc				
9 W Center St	Pima AZ	85543	800-577-9266	928-485-2451
Navopache Electric Co-op Inc				
1878 W White Mtn Blvd	Lakeside AZ	85929	800-543-6324	928-368-5118
Sulphur Springs Valley Electric Co-op Inc				
PO Box 820	Willcox AZ	85644	877-877-6861	520-384-2221

Arkansas

			Toll-Free	Phone
Arkansas Valley Electric Co-op Corp				
1811 W Commercial St PO Box 47	Ozark AR	72949	800-468-2176	479-667-2176
Ashley-Chicot Electric Co-op Inc				
307 E Jefferson St	Hamburg AR	71646	800-281-5212	870-853-5212
Carroll Electric Co-op Corp				
920 Hwy 62 Spur	Berryville AR	72616	800-432-9720	870-423-2161
Clay County Electric Co-op Corp				
300 N Missouri Ave	Corning AR	72422	800-521-2450	870-857-3521
Craighead Electric Co-op Corp				
4314 Stadium Blvd PO Box 7503	Jonesboro AR	72403	800-794-5012	870-932-8301
First Electric Co-op Corp				
1000 S JP Wright Loop Rd	Jacksonville AR	72076	800-489-7405	501-982-4545
Mississippi County Electric Co-op				
510 N Broadway St	Blytheville AR	72315	800-439-4563	870-763-4563
Ozarks Electric Co-op Corp				
3641 W Wedington Dr	Fayetteville AR	72704	800-521-6144	479-521-2900
Petit Jean Electric Co-op				
270 Quality Dr PO Box 37	Clinton AR	72031	800-786-7618	501-745-2493
Rich Mountain Electric Co-op				
515 Janssen PO Box 897	Mena AR	71953	877-828-4074	479-394-4140
South Central Arkansas Electric Co-op				
1140 Main St	Arkadelphia AR	71923	800-814-2931	870-246-6701
Woodruff Electric Co-op				
PO Box 1619	Forrest City AR	72336	888-559-6400	870-633-2262

California

			Toll-Free	Phone
Plumas-Sierra Rural Electric Co-op				
73233 SR 70 Ste A	Portola CA	96122	800-555-2207	530-832-4261
Surprise Valley Electric Co-op				
22595 US 395	Alturas CA	96101	866-843-2667	530-233-3511

Colorado

			Toll-Free	Phone
Empire Electric Assn Inc				
801 N Broadway	Cortez CO	81321	800-709-3726	970-565-4444
Grand Valley Rural Power Lines Inc				
845 22 Rd PO Box 190	Grand Junction CO	81505	877-760-7435	970-242-0040
Gunnison County Electric Assn Inc				
37250 W Hwy 50 PO Box 180	Gunnison CO	81230	800-726-3523	970-641-3520
Highline Electric Assn				
1300 S Interocean Ave	Holyoke CO	80734	800-816-2236	970-854-2236
Holy Cross Energy				
PO Box 2150	Glenwood Springs CO	81602	877-833-2555	970-945-5491
Intermountain Rural Electric Assn				
5496 Hwy 85	Sedalia CO	80135	800-332-9540	303-688-3100
KC Electric Assn 422 Third Ave	Hugo CO	80821	800-700-3123	719-743-2431
La Plata Electric Assn Inc				
45 Stewart St	Durango CO	81303	888-839-5732	970-247-5786
Morgan County Rural Electric Assn				
20169 US Hwy 34	Fort Morgan CO	80701	877-495-6487	970-867-5688
Mountain Parks Electric Inc				
321 W Agate Ave	Granby CO	80446	877-887-3378	970-887-3378
Mountain View Electric Assn Inc				
1655 Fifth St	Limon CO	80828	800-388-9881	719-775-2861

Name	Address	City	State	ZIP	Toll-Free	Phone
Poudre Valley Rural Electric Assn Inc	7649 Rea Pkwy	Fort Collins	CO	80528	**800-432-1012**	970-226-1234
San Isabel Electric	893 E Enterprise Dr	Pueblo West	CO	81007	**800-279-7432**	719-547-2160
San Luis Valley Rural Electric Co-op	3625 US Hwy 160 W	Monte Vista	CO	81144	**800-332-7634**	719-852-3538
San Miguel Power Assn Inc	170 W Tenth Ave	Nucla	CO	81424	**800-864-7256**	970-864-7311
Sangre de Cristo Electric Assn	29780 US Hwy 24	Buena Vista	CO	81211	**800-933-3823**	719-395-2412
Southeast Colorado Power Assn (SECPA)	901 W 3rd	La Junta	CO	81050	**800-332-8634**	719-384-2551
United Power Inc	500 Co-op Way	Brighton	CO	80603	**800-468-8809**	303-659-0551
White River Electric Assn (WREA)	PO Box 958	Meeker	CO	81641	**800-922-1987**	970-878-5041
Y-W Electric Assn Inc	250 Main Ave PO Box Y	Akron	CO	80720	**800-660-2291**	970-345-2291
Yampa Valley Electric Assn Inc	32 Tenth St	Steamboat Springs	CO	80487	**888-873-9832**	970-879-1160

Delaware

Name	Address	City	State	ZIP	Toll-Free	Phone
Delaware Electric Co-op Inc	PO Box 600	Greenwood	DE	19950	**800-282-8595**	302-349-3147

Florida

Name	Address	City	State	ZIP	Toll-Free	Phone
Central Florida Electric Co-op Inc	1124 N Young Blvd	Chiefland	FL	32644	**800-227-1302**	352-493-2511
Choctawhatchee Electric Co-op Inc	1350 W Baldwin Ave	DeFuniak Springs	FL	32435	**800-342-0990**	850-892-2111
Clay Electric Co-op Inc	7450 State Rd 100	Keystone Heights	FL	32656	**800-224-4917**	352-473-8000
Escambia River Electric Co-op Inc	3425 Florida 4	Jay	FL	32565	**800-235-3848**	850-675-4521
Florida Keys Electric Co-op Assn	91630 Overseas Hwy	Tavernier	FL	33070	**800-858-8845**	305-852-2431
Gulf Coast Electric Co-op Inc	722 Florida 22	Wewahitchka	FL	32465	**800-333-9392**	850-639-2216
Lee County Electric Co-op Inc	4980 Bayline Dr PO Box 3455	North Fort Myers	FL	33917	**800-282-1643**	239-995-2121
Peace River Electric Co-op Inc	210 Metheny Rd PO Box 1310	Wauchula	FL	33873	**800-282-3824**	
Sumter Electric Co-op Inc	PO Box 301	Sumterville	FL	33585	**800-732-6141**	352-793-3801
Suwannee Valley Electric Co-op	PO Box 160	Live Oak	FL	32064	**800-752-0025**	386-362-2226
Talquin Electric Co-op Inc	1640 W Jefferson St	Quincy	FL	32351	**888-271-8778**	850-627-7651
West Florida Electric Co-op	5282 Peanut Rd	Graceville	FL	32440	**800-342-7400**	850-263-3231

Georgia

Name	Address	City	State	ZIP	Toll-Free	Phone
Altamaha Electric Membership Corp	611 W Liberty Ave PO Box 346	Lyons	GA	30436	**800-822-4563**	912-526-8181
Amicalola Electric Membership Corp	544 Hwy 515 S	Jasper	GA	30143	**800-282-7411**	706-253-5200
Canoochee Electric Membership Corp	342 E Brazell St	Reidsville	GA	30453	**800-342-0134**	
Central Georgia Electric Membership Corp	923 S Mulberry St	Jackson	GA	30233	**800-222-4877**	770-775-7857
Coastal Electric Co-op	1265 S Coastal Hwy PO Box 109	Midway	GA	31320	**800-421-2343**	912-884-3311
Coweta-Fayette Electric Membership Corp	807 Collinsworth Rd	Palmetto	GA	30268	**877-746-4362**	770-502-0226
Diverse Power Inc	1400 S Davis Rd	LaGrange	GA	30241	**800-845-8362**	706-845-2000
Flint Energies	103 Macon Rd	Reynolds	GA	31076	**800-342-3616**	478-847-3415
Grady Electric Membership Corp (EMC)	1499 US Hwy 84 W PO Box 270	Cairo	GA	39828	**800-942-4362**	229-377-4182
Habersham Electric Membership Corp	6135 Georgia 115	Clarkesville	GA	30523	**800-640-6812**	706-754-2114
Hart Electric Membership Corp	1071 Elberton Hwy	Hartwell	GA	30643	**800-241-4109**	706-376-4714
Irwin Electric Membership Corp	915 W Fourth St	Ocilla	GA	31774	**800-237-3745**	229-468-7415
Jackson Electric Membership Corp	850 Commerce Rd	Jefferson	GA	30549	**800-462-3691**	706-367-5281
Jefferson Energy Co-op	3077 Hwy 17 PO Box 457	North Wrens	GA	30833	**888-634-7336**	706-547-2167
Middle Georgia Electric Membership Corp	600 Tippettville Rd	Vienna	GA	31092	**800-342-0144**	229-268-2671
Mitchell Electric Membership Corp	475 Cairo Rd	Camilla	GA	31730	**800-479-6034**	229-336-5221
Ocmulgee Electric Membership Corp	5722 Eastman St	Eastman	GA	31023	**800-342-5509**	478-374-7001
Oconee Electric Membership Corp	3445 US Hwy 80 W	Dudley	GA	31022	**800-522-2930**	478-676-3191
Okefenoke Rural Electric Membership Corp (REMC)	14384 Cleveland St PO Box 602	Nahunta	GA	31553	**800-262-5131**	912-462-5131
Planters Electric Membership Corp	1740 Hwy 25 N PO Box 979	Millen	GA	30442	**888-397-3742**	478-982-4722
Snapping Shoals Electric Membership Corp	14750 Brown Bridge Rd	Covington	GA	30016	**888-999-1416**	770-786-3484
Sumter Electric Membership Corp	1120 Felder St	Americus	GA	31709	**800-342-6978**	229-924-8041
Three Notch Electric Membership Corp	PO Box 295	Donalsonville	GA	39845	**800-239-5377**	229-524-5377
Tri-County Electric Membership Corp	PO Box 487	Gray	GA	31032	**866-254-8100**	478-986-8100
Tri-State Electric Membership Corp (TSEMC)	2310 Blue Ridge Dr	Blue Ridge	GA	30513	**800-351-1111**	706-492-3251
Washington Electric Membership Corp	258 N Harris St	Sandersville	GA	31082	**800-552-2577**	478-552-2577

Idaho

Name	Address	City	State	ZIP	Toll-Free	Phone
Clearwater Power Co	4230 Hatwai Rd PO Box 997	Lewiston	ID	83501	**888-743-1501**	208-743-1501
Fall River Rural Electric Co-op Inc	1150 N 3400 E	Ashton	ID	83420	**800-632-5726**	208-652-7431
Idaho County Light & Power Co-op	1065 Hwy 13 PO Box 300	Grangeville	ID	83530	**877-212-0424**	208-983-1610
Kootenai Electric Co-op Inc	2451 W Dakota Ave	Hayden	ID	83835	**800-240-0459**	208-765-1200
Raft River Rural Electric Co-op Inc	155 N Main St PO Box 617	Malta	ID	83342	**800-342-7732**	208-645-2211
Salmon River Electric Co-op Inc	1130 Main St PO Box 384	Challis	ID	83226	**877-806-2283**	208-879-2283
United Electric Co-op Inc	1330 21st St	Heyburn	ID	83336	**800-342-1585**	208-679-2222

Illinois

Name	Address	City	State	ZIP	Toll-Free	Phone
Adams Electric Co-op	700 Eastwood St PO Box 247	Camp Point	IL	62320	**800-232-4797**	217-593-7701
Clinton County Electric Co-op Inc	475 N Main St PO Box 40	Breese	IL	62230	**800-526-7282**	618-526-7282
Coles-Moultrie Electric Co-op	104 DeWitt Ave E PO Box 709	Mattoon	IL	61938	**888-661-2632**	217-235-0341
Corn Belt Energy Corp	One Energy Way	Bloomington	IL	61705	**800-879-0339**	309-662-5330
Eastern Illini Electric Co-op	330 W Ottawa PO Box 96	Paxton	IL	60957	**800-824-5102**	217-379-2131
Egyptian Electric Co-op Assn	PO Box 38	Steeleville	IL	62288	**800-606-1505**	618-965-3434
Jo-Carroll Energy	793 US Hwy 20 W	Elizabeth	IL	61028	**800-858-5522**	815-858-2207
Menard Electric Co-op	14300 State Hwy 97 PO Box 200	Petersburg	IL	62675	**800-872-1203**	217-632-7746
MJM Electric Co-op Inc (MJMEC)	264 NE St PO Box 80	Carlinville	IL	62626	**800-648-4729**	217-854-3137
Norris Electric Co-op	8543 N State Hwy 130 PO Box 6000	Newton	IL	62448	**877-783-8765**	618-783-8765
Rural Electric Convenience Co-op Co	3973 W SR 104 PO Box 19	Auburn	IL	62615	**800-245-7322**	217-438-6197
Shelby Electric Co-op (SEC)	Rt 128 N Sixth St PO Box 560	Shelbyville	IL	62565	**800-677-2612**	217-774-3986
SouthEastern Illinois Electric Co-op	585 Hwy 142 S PO Box 251	Eldorado	IL	62930	**800-833-2611**	618-273-2611
Southern Illinois Electric Co-op	7420 US Hwy 51 S	Dongola	IL	62926	**800-762-1400**	618-827-3555
Southwestern Electric Co-op Inc	525 US Rt 40 PO Box 549	Greenville	IL	62246	**800-637-8667**	
Spoon River Electric Co-op Inc (SREC)	930 S Fifth Ave PO Box 340	Canton	IL	61520	**877-404-2572**	309-647-2700
Wayne-White Counties Electric Co-op	1501 W Main St	Fairfield	IL	62837	**888-871-7695**	618-842-2196
Western Illinois Electrical Co-op	524 N Madison St PO Box 338	Carthage	IL	62321	**800-576-3125**	217-357-3125

Indiana

Name	Address	City	State	ZIP	Toll-Free	Phone
Bartholomew County Rural Electric Membership Corp	1697 W. Deaver Rd	Columbus	IN	47201	**800-927-5672**	812-372-2546
Boone County Rural Electric Membership Corp	1207 Indianapolis Ave	Lebanon	IN	46052	**800-897-7362**	765-482-2390
Clark County REMC	7810 State Rd 60 PO Box 411	Sellersburg	IN	47172	**800-462-6988**	812-246-3316
Daviess-Martin County REMC	12628 E 75 N PO Box 430	Loogootee	IN	47553	**800-762-7362**	812-295-4200
Decatur County Rural Electric Membership Corp	1430 W Main St PO Box 46	Greensburg	IN	47240	**800-844-7362**	812-663-3391
Fulton County Rural Electric Membership Corp	1448 W State Rd 14 PO Box 230	Rochester	IN	46975	**800-286-2265**	574-223-3156
Hendricks Power Co-op	86 N County Rd 500 E	Avon	IN	46123	**800-876-5473**	317-745-5473
Jackson County Rural Electric Membership Corp	274 E Base Rd	Brownstown	IN	47220	**800-288-4458**	812-358-4458
Jasper County Rural Electric Membership Corp	280 E 400 S	Rensselaer	IN	47978	**888-866-7362**	219-866-4601
Jay County Rural Electric Membership Corp	484 S 200 W PO Box 904	Portland	IN	47371	**800-835-7362**	260-726-7121
Johnson County Rural Electric Membership Corp	750 International Dr	Franklin	IN	46131	**800-382-5544**	317-736-6174
LaGrange County Rural Electric Membership Corp	1995 E US Hwy 20	LaGrange	IN	46761	**877-463-7165**	260-463-7165
Miami-Cass County Rural Electric Membership Corp	3086 W 100 N PO Box 168 *General	Peru	IN	46970	**800-844-6668***	765-473-6668
Noble REMC	300 Weber Rd PO Box 137	Albion	IN	46701	**800-933-7362**	260-636-2113
Orange County Rural Electric Membership Corp	7133 N State Rd 337 PO Box 208	Orleans	IN	47452	**888-337-5900**	812-865-2229
Parke County Rural Electric Membership Corp	119 W High St	Rockville	IN	47872	**800-537-3913**	765-569-3133
Rush Shelby Energy Inc	2777 S 840 W PO Box 55 *General	Manilla	IN	46150	**800-706-7362***	765-544-2600
South Central Indiana Rural Electric Membership Corp	300 Morton Ave PO Box 3100	Martinsville	IN	46151	**800-264-7362**	765-342-3344
Southeastern Indiana Rural Electric Membership Corp	712 S Buckeye St	Osgood	IN	47037	**800-737-4111**	812-689-4111
Southern Indiana Rural Electric Co-op Inc	1776 Tenth St PO Box 219	Tell City	IN	47586	**800-323-2316**	812-547-2316
Steuben County Rural Electric Membership Corp	1212 S Wayne St	Angola	IN	46703	**888-233-9088**	260-665-3563

			Toll-Free	Phone
Tipmont Rural Electric Membership Corp 403 S Main St	Linden IN	47955	800-726-3953	
United Rural Electric Membership Corp 4563 E Markle Rd	Markle IN	46770	800-542-6339	260-758-3155
Wabash County Rural Electric Membership Corp 350 Wedcor Ave	Wabash IN	46992	800-563-2146	260-563-2146
Warren County Rural Electric Membership Corp 15 Midway St PO Box 37	Williamsport IN	47993	800-872-7319	765-762-6114
White County Rural Electric Membership Corp 302 N Sixth St	Monticello IN	47960	800-844-7161	574-583-7161
Whitewater Valley Rural Electric Membership Corp 101 Brownsville Ave	Liberty IN	47353	800-529-5557	765-458-5171
WIN Energy Rural Electric Membership Corp 3981 S US Hwy 41	Vincennes IN	47591	800-882-5140	812-882-5140

Iowa

			Toll-Free	Phone
Access Energy Co-op 1800 W Washington St	Mount Pleasant IA	52641	866-242-4232	319-385-1577
Allamakee-Clayton Electric Co-op (ACEC) 229 Hwy 51 PO Box 715	Postville IA	52162	888-788-1551	563-864-7611
Butler County Rural Electric Co-op 521 N Main PO Box 98	Allison IA	50602	888-267-2726	319-267-2726
Calhoun County Electric Co-op Assn 1015 Tonawanda St PO Box 312	Rockwell City IA	50579	800-821-4879	712-297-7112
Chariton Valley Electric Co-op 2090 Hwy 5 PO Box 486	Albia IA	52531	800-475-1702	641-932-7126
Consumers Energy 2074 242nd St	Marshalltown IA	50158	800-696-6552	641-752-1593
East-Central Iowa Rural Electric Co-op 2400 Bing Miller Ln	Urbana IA	52345	877-850-4343	319-443-4343
Eastern Iowa Light & Power Co-op 600 E Fifth St PO Box 3003	Wilton IA	52778	800-728-1242	563-732-2211
Franklin Rural Electric Co-op 1560 Hwy 65 PO Box 437	Hampton IA	50441	800-750-3557	641-456-2557
Grundy County Rural Electric Co-op 102 E 'G' Ave	Grundy Center IA	50638	800-390-7605	319-824-5251
Hawkeye REC 24049 Iowa 9	Cresco IA	52136	800-658-2243	563-547-3801
Heartland Power Co-op 216 Jackson St PO Box 65	Thompson IA	50478	888-584-9732	641-584-2251
Humboldt County Rural Electric Co-op (HCREC) 1210 13th St N	Humboldt IA	50548	800-452-1111	515-332-1616
Iowa Lakes Electric Co-op 702 S First St	Estherville IA	51334	800-225-4532	712-362-7870
Lyon Rural Electric Co-op 116 S Marshall St	Rock Rapids IA	51246	800-658-3976	712-472-2506
Maquoketa Valley Rural Electric Co-op 109 N Huber St	Anamosa IA	52205	800-927-6068	319-462-3542
Midland Power Co-op 1005 E Lincolnway PO Box 420	Jefferson IA	50129	800-833-8876	515-386-4111
Nishnabotna Valley Rural Electric Co-op 1317 Chatburn Ave	Harlan IA	51537	800-234-5122	712-755-2166
North West REC 1505 Albany Pl SE PO Box 435	Orange City IA	51041	800-383-0476	712-707-4935
Osceola Electric Co-op Inc 1102 Egret Dr PO Box 127	Sibley IA	51249	888-754-2519	712-754-2519
Pella Co-op Electric Assn 2615 Washington St	Pella IA	50219	800-619-1040	641-628-1040
Raccoon Valley Electric Co-op 28725 Hwy 30 PO Box 486	Glidden IA	51443	800-253-6211	712-659-3649
Southern Iowa Electric Co-op Inc 22458 Hwy 2 PO Box 70	Bloomfield IA	52537	800-607-2027	641-664-2277
Southwest Iowa Rural Electric Co-op 1801 Grove Ave	Corning IA	50841	888-591-1261	641-322-3165
TIP Rural Electric Co-op 612 W Des Moines St PO Box 534	Brooklyn IA	52211	800-934-7976	641-522-9221
Western Iowa Power Co-op 809 Iowa 39	Denison IA	51442	800-253-5189	712-263-2943
Woodbury County Rural Electric Co-op Assn 1495 Humboldt Ave	Moville IA	51039	800-469-3125	712-873-3125

Kansas

			Toll-Free	Phone
Ark Valley Electric Co-op Assn 10 E Tenth St	South Hutchinson KS	67504	888-297-9212	620-662-6661
Bluestem Electric Co-op Inc 614 E Hwy 24 PO Box 5	Wamego KS	66547	800-558-1580	785-456-2212
Butler Rural Electric Co-op Assn Inc 216 S Vine St PO Box 1242	El Dorado KS	67042	800-464-0060	316-321-9600
Caney Valley Electric Co-op Assn Inc, The 401 Lawrence St PO Box 308	Cedar Vale KS	67024	800-310-8911	620-758-2262
CMS Electric Co-op Inc 509 E Carthage St	Meade KS	67864	800-794-2353	620-873-2184
DS&O Electric Cooperative Inc 129 W Main St PO Box 286	Solomon KS	67480	800-376-3533	785-655-2011
Heartland Rural Electric Co-op 110 Enterprise St	Girard KS	66743	888-835-9585	620-724-8251
Kaw Valley Electric Co-op Inc 1100 SW Auburn Rd	Topeka KS	66615	800-794-2011	785-478-3444
Lane-Scott Electric Co-op Inc 410 S High	Dighton KS	67839	800-407-2217	620-397-5327
Leavenworth-Jefferson Electric Co-op Inc 507 N Union St	McLouth KS	66054	888-796-6111	
Lyon-Coffey Electric Co-op Inc 1013 N 4th PO Box 229	Burlington KS	66839	800-748-7395	620-364-2116
Midwest Energy Inc 1330 Canterbury Dr	Hays KS	67601	800-222-3121	785-625-3437
Nemaha-Marshall Electric Co-op 402 Prairie St PO Box O *Cust Svc	Axtell KS	66403	866-736-2347*	785-736-2345
Pioneer Electric Co-op Inc 1850 W Oklahoma St PO Box 368	Ulysses KS	67880	800-794-9302	620-356-1211
Prairie Land Electric Co-op Inc 14935 US Hwy 36	Norton KS	67654	800-577-3323	785-877-3323
Radiant Electric Co-op Inc 100 N 15th St	Fredonia KS	66736	800-821-0956	620-378-2161
Rolling Hills Electric Co-op Inc 122 W Main St PO Box 307	Mankato KS	66956	877-906-5903	785-378-3151
Sedgwick County Electric Co-op 1355 S 383rd St W PO Box 220	Cheney KS	67025	866-542-4732	316-542-3131
Sumner-Cowley Electric Co-op Inc 2223 N A St PO Box 220	Wellington KS	67152	888-326-3356	620-326-3356
Twin Valley Electric Co-op Inc 501 S Huston Ave PO Box 385	Altamont KS	67330	866-784-5500	620-784-5500
Victory Electric Co-op Assn Inc 3230 N 14th Ave	Dodge City KS	67801	800-279-7915	620-227-2139
Western Co-op Electric Assn Inc 635 S 13th St	WaKeeney KS	67672	800-330-1025	785-743-5561
Wheatland Electric Co-op Inc 101 S Main St	Scott City KS	67871	800-762-0436	620-872-5885

Kentucky

			Toll-Free	Phone
Big Sandy Rural Electric Co-op Corp 504 11th St	Paintsville KY	41240	888-789-7322	606-789-4095
Blue Grass Energy Co-op Corp 1201 Lexington Rd	Nicholasville KY	40356	888-546-4243	859-885-4191
Clark Energy Co-op Inc 2640 Ironworks Rd	Winchester KY	40391	800-992-3269	859-744-4251
Cumberland Valley Electric Inc 6219 N US Hwy 25 E	Gray KY	40734	800-513-2677	
Farmers Rural Electric Co-op Corp 504 S Broadway St	Glasgow KY	42141	800-253-2191	270-651-2191
Fleming Mason Energy Co-op 1449 Elizaville Rd	Flemingsburg KY	41041	800-464-3144	606-845-2661
Grayson Rural Electric Co-op Corp 109 Bagby Pk	Grayson KY	41143	800-562-3532	606-474-5136
Hickman-Fulton Counties Rural Electric Co-op Corp 1702 Moscow Ave PO Box 190	Hickman KY	42050	800-633-1391	270-236-2521
Inter-County Energy Co-op 1009 Hustonville Rd	Danville KY	40422	888-266-7322	859-236-4561
Jackson Energy Co-op 115 Jackson Energy Ln	McKee KY	40447	800-262-7480	606-364-1000
Jackson Purchase Energy Corp 2900 Irvin Cobb Dr	Paducah KY	42002	800-633-4044	270-442-7321
Kenergy Corp 6402 Old Corydon Rd	Henderson KY	42419	800-844-4832	270-826-3991
Owen Electric Co-op Inc 8205 Hwy 127 N PO Box 400	Owenton KY	40359	800-372-7612	502-484-3471
Pennyrile Rural Electric Co-op Corp 2000 Harrison St PO Box 2900 *Cust Svc	Hopkinsville KY	42241	800-297-4710*	270-886-2555
Salt River Electric Co-op Corp 111 W Brashear Ave	Bardstown KY	40004	800-221-7465	502-348-3931
Shelby Energy Co-op Inc 620 Old Finchville Rd	Shelbyville KY	40065	800-292-6585	502-633-4420
South Kentucky Rural Electrical Co-op 925 N Main St PO Box 910	Somerset KY	42502	800-264-5112	606-678-4121
Taylor County RECC 625 W Main St PO Box 100	Campbellsville KY	42719	800-931-4551	270-465-4101
Warren Rural Electric Co-op Corp 951 Fairview Ave	Bowling Green KY	42101	866-319-3234	270-842-6541
West Kentucky Rural Electric Co-op Corp PO Box 589	Mayfield KY	42066	877-495-7322	270-247-1321

Louisiana

			Toll-Free	Phone
Beauregard Electric Co-op Inc 1010 E First St	DeRidder LA	70634	800-367-0275	337-463-6221
Concordia Electric Co-op Inc 1865 Hwy 84 W PO Box 98	Jonesville LA	71343	800-617-6282	318-339-7969
Dixie Electric Membership Corp (DEMCO) PO Box 15659	Baton Rouge LA	70895	800-262-0221	225-261-1221
Jefferson Davis Electric Co-op 906 N Lk Arthur Ave PO Drawer 1229	Jennings LA	70546	800-256-5332	337-824-4330
Pointe Coupee Electric Membership Corp 2506 False River Dr PO Box 160	New Roads LA	70760	800-738-7232	225-638-3751
Southwest Louisiana Electric Membership Corp 3420 NE Evangeline Thruway	Lafayette LA	70509	888-275-3626	337-896-5384
Washington-Saint Tammany Electric Co-op 950 Pearl St PO Box N	Franklinton LA	70438	866-672-9773	985-839-3562

Maine

			Toll-Free	Phone
Eastern Maine Electric Co-op Inc 21 Union St	Calais ME	04619	800-696-7444	207-454-7555

Maryland

			Toll-Free	Phone
Choptank Electric Co-op Inc 24820 Meeting House Rd PO Box 430	Denton MD	21629	877-892-0001	

Michigan

			Toll-Free	Phone
Cherryland Electric Co-op 5930 US 31 S PO Box 298	Grawn MI	49637	800-442-8616	231-486-9200
Great Lakes Energy Co-op 1323 Boyne Ave	Boyne City MI	49712	888-485-2537	
HomeWorks Tri-County Electric Co-op 7973 E Grand River Ave PO Box 350	Portland MI	48875	800-848-9333	517-647-7554
Midwest Energy Co-op 901 E State St	Cassopolis MI	49031	800-492-5989	
Presque Isle Electric & Gas Co-op PO Box 308	Onaway MI	49765	800-423-6634	989-733-8515

Minnesota

			Toll-Free	Phone
Agralite Electric Co-op 320 Hwy 12 SE	Benson MN	56215	800-950-8375	320-843-4150

				Toll-Free	Phone
Arrowhead Electric Co-op Inc					
5401 W Hwy 61 PO Box 39	Lutsen	MN	55612	800-864-3744	218-663-7239
Beltrami Electric Co-op Inc					
4111 Technology Dr NW	Bemidji	MN	56601	800-955-6083	218-444-2540
Benco Electric Co-op					
20946 549 Ave PO Box 8	Mankato	MN	56002	888-792-3626	507-387-7963
Brown County Rural Electric Assn					
24386 State Hwy 4 PO Box 529	Sleepy Eye	MN	56085	800-658-2368	507-794-3331
Clearwater-Polk Electric Co-op					
315 Main Ave N	Bagley	MN	56621	888-694-3833	218-694-6241
Connexus Energy Co-op					
14601 Ramsey Blvd	Ramsey	MN	55303	877-382-4357	763-323-2650
Crow Wing Co-op Power & Light Co					
Hwy 371 N PO Box 507	Brainerd	MN	56401	800-648-9401	218-829-2827
Dakota Electric Assn					
4300 220th St W	Farmington	MN	55024	800-874-3409	651-463-6144
East Central Energy					
PO Box 39	Braham	MN	55006	800-254-7944	
Federated Rural Electric Assn					
77100 US Hwy 71 PO Box 69	Jackson	MN	56143	800-321-3520	507-847-3520
Freeborn-Mower Co-op Services					
2501 E Main St	Albert Lea	MN	56007	800-734-6421	507-373-6421
Goodhue County Co-op Electric Assn					
1410 Northstar Dr	Zumbrota	MN	55992	800-927-6864	507-732-5117
Great River Energy					
12300 Elm Creek Blvd	Maple Grove	MN	55369	888-521-0130	763-445-5000
Lake Country Power					
2810 Elida Dr	Grand Rapids	MN	55744	800-421-9959	
Lake Region Co-op Electrical Assn					
1401 S Broadway PO Box 643	Pelican Rapids	MN	56572	800-552-7658	218-863-1171
Lyon-Lincoln Electric Co-op Inc (LLEC)					
205 N Hwy 14 PO Box 639	Tyler	MN	56178	800-927-6276	507-247-5505
McLeod Co-op Power Assn					
1231 Ford Ave N	Glencoe	MN	55336	800-494-6272	320-864-3148
Meeker Co-op Light & Power Assn					
1725 E US Hwy 12 PO Box 68	Litchfield	MN	55355	800-232-6257	320-693-3231
Mille Lacs Electric Co-op					
PO Box 230	Aitkin	MN	56431	800-450-2191	218-927-2191
Minnesota Valley Co-op Light & Power Assn					
501 S First St	Montevideo	MN	56265	800-247-5051	320-269-2163
Minnesota Valley Electric Co-op					
125 Minnesota Vly Electric Dr					
PO Box 77024	Jordan	MN	55352	800-282-6832	952-492-2313
Nobles Co-op Electric					
22636 US Hwy 59 PO Box 788	Worthington	MN	56187	800-776-0517	507-372-7331
North Itasca Electric Co-op Inc					
301 Main Ave PO Box 227	Bigfork	MN	56628	800-762-4048	218-743-3131
North Star Electric Co-op					
441 State Hwy 172 NW PO Box 719	Baudette	MN	56623	888-634-2202	218-634-2202
People's Energy Co-op					
1775 Lk Shady Ave S	Oronoco	MN	55960	800-214-2694	507-367-7000
PKM Electric Co-op Inc					
406 N Minnesota St	Warren	MN	56762	800-552-7366	218-745-4711
Red Lake Electric Co-op Inc					
412 International Dr					
PO Box 430	Red Lake Falls	MN	56750	800-245-6068	218-253-2168
Red River Valley Co-op Power Assn					
109 Second Ave E	Halstad	MN	56548	800-788-7784	218-456-2139
Renville-Sibley Co-op Power Assn					
103 Oak St PO Box 68	Danube	MN	56230	800-826-2593	320-826-2593
Roseau Electric Co-op Inc					
1107 Third St NE	Roseau	MN	56751	888-847-8840	218-463-1543
South Central Electric Assn					
71176 Tiell Dr PO Box 150	Saint James	MN	56081	888-805-7232	507-375-3164
Stearns ElectricAssn					
900 E Kraft Dr	Melrose	MN	56352	800-962-0655	320-256-4241
Steele-Waseca Co-op Electric (SWCE)					
2411 W Bridge St PO Box 485	Owatonna	MN	55060	800-526-3514	507-451-7340
Todd-Wadena Electric Co-op					
550 Ash Ave NE PO Box 431	Wadena	MN	56482	800-321-8932	218-631-3120
Traverse Electric Co-op Inc					
1618 Broadway PO Box 66	Wheaton	MN	56296	800-927-5443	320-563-8616
Wild Rice Electric Co-op Inc					
502 N Main PO Box 438	Mahnomen	MN	56557	800-244-5709	218-935-2517
Wright-Hennepin Co-op Electric Assn					
6800 Electric Dr PO Box 330	Rockford	MN	55373	800-943-2667	763-477-3000

Mississippi

				Toll-Free	Phone
Alcorn County Electric Power Assn					
1909 S Tate St	Corinth	MS	38834	866-448-3046	662-287-4402
Coast Electric Power Assn					
18020 Hwy Ste 603	Kiln	MS	39556	800-624-3348*	228-363-7000
*Cust Svc					
Dixie Electric Power Assn					
PO Box 88	Laurel	MS	39441	888-465-9209	601-425-2535
Monroe County Electric Power Assn					
601 N Main St	Amory	MS	38821	866-656-2962	662-256-7196
North East MS EPA					
10 PR 2050 PO Box 1037	Oxford	MS	38655	877-234-6331	662-234-6331
Pearl River Valley Electric Power Assn					
1422 Hwy 13 N PO Box 1217	Columbia	MS	39429	855-277-8372	601-736-2666
Southern Pine Electric Power Assn					
110 Risher St PO Box 60	Taylorsville	MS	39168	800-231-5240	601-785-6511
Southwest Mississippi Electric Power Assn					
18671 Hwy 61 PO Box 5	Lorman	MS	39096	800-287-8564	
Yazoo Valley Electric Power Assn					
PO Box 8	Yazoo City	MS	39194	800-281-5098	662-746-4251

Missouri

				Toll-Free	Phone
Atchison-Holt Electric Co-op					
18585 Industrial Rd PO Box 160	Rock Port	MO	64482	888-744-5366	660-744-5344
Barry Electric Co-op					
4015 Main St PO Box 307	Cassville	MO	65625	866-847-2333	417-847-2131
Barton County Electric Co-op					
91 W Hwy 160 PO Box 459	Lamar	MO	64759	800-286-5636	417-682-5636
Black River Electric Co-op					
2600 Hwy 67 PO Box 31	Fredericktown	MO	63645	800-392-4711	573-783-3381
Boone Electric Co-op					
1413 Rangeline St	Columbia	MO	65201	800-225-8143	573-449-4181
Callaway Electric Co-op					
1313 Co-op Dr PO Box 250	Fulton	MO	65251	888-642-4840	573-642-3326
Co-Mo Electric Co-op Inc					
29868 Hwy 5 PO Box 220	Tipton	MO	65081	800-781-0157	660-433-5521
Consolidated Electric Co-op					
3940 E Liberty St	Mexico	MO	65265	800-621-0091	573-581-3630
Crawford Electric Co-op Inc					
10301 N Service Rd PO Box 10	Bourbon	MO	65441	800-677-2667	573-732-4415
Cuivre River Electric Co-op					
1112 E Cherry St	Troy	MO	63379	800-392-3709	636-528-8261
Farmers' Electric Co-op					
201 W Business 36 PO Box 680	Chillicothe	MO	64601	800-279-0496	660-646-4281
Gascosage Electric Co-op					
803 S Hwy 28 PO Box G	Dixon	MO	65459	866-568-8243	573-759-7146
Grundy Electric Co-op Inc					
4100 Oklahoma Ave	Trenton	MO	64683	800-279-2249	660-359-3941
Howard Electric Co-op					
205 Hwy 5 & 240 N PO Box 391	Fayette	MO	65248	877-352-0122	660-248-3311
Howell-Oregon Electric Co-op Inc					
6327 N US Hwy 63 PO Box 649	West Plains	MO	65775	855-385-9903	417-256-2131
Laclede Electric Co-op					
1400 E Rt 66	Lebanon	MO	65536	800-299-3164	417-532-3164
Lewis County Rural Electric Co-op					
18256 Hwy 16 PO Box 68	Lewistown	MO	63452	888-454-4485	573-215-4000
Macon Electric Co-op					
31571 Bus Hwy 36 E PO Box 157	Macon	MO	63552	800-553-6901	660-385-3157
Osage Valley Electric Co-op Assn					
1321 N Orange St	Butler	MO	64730	800-889-6832	660-679-3131
Ozark Border Electric Co-op					
3281 S Westwood	Poplar Bluff	MO	63901	800-392-0567	573-785-4631
Pemiscot-Dunklin Electric Co-op					
Hwy 412 W PO Box 509	Hayti	MO	63851	800-558-6641	573-757-6641
Platte-Clay Electric Co-op Inc					
1000 W Hwy 92 PO Box 100	Kearney	MO	64060	800-431-2131	816-628-3121
Ralls County Electric Co-op					
17594 Hwy 19 PO Box 157	New London	MO	63459	877-985-8711	573-985-8711
Sac Osage Electric Co-op Inc					
4815 E Hwy 54 PO Box 111	El Dorado Springs	MO	64744	800-876-2701	417-876-2721
Webster Electric Co-op					
1240 Spur Dr	Marshfield	MO	65706	800-643-4305	417-859-2216
White River Valley Electric Co-op Inc					
2449 State Hwy 76 E	Branson	MO	65616	800-879-4056	417-335-9335

Montana

				Toll-Free	Phone
Beartooth Electric Co-op Inc					
1306 N Broadway St PO Box 1110	Red Lodge	MT	59068	800-472-9821	406-446-2310
Big Flat Electric Co-op Inc					
333 S Seventh St	Malta	MT	59538	800-242-2040	406-654-2040
Flathead Electric Co-op Inc					
2510 Hwy 2 E	Kalispell	MT	59901	800-735-8489	406-751-4483
Glacier Electric Co-op Inc					
410 E Main St	Cut Bank	MT	59427	800-347-6795	406-873-5566
Hill County Electric Co-op Inc					
PO Box 2330	Havre	MT	59501	877-394-7804	
Lincoln Electric Co-op Inc (LEC)					
500 Osloski Rd PO Box 628	Eureka	MT	59917	800-442-2994	406-889-3301
McCone Electric Co-op Inc					
110 Main St	Circle	MT	59215	800-684-3605	406-485-3430
Missoula Electric Co-op Inc					
1700 W Broadway	Missoula	MT	59808	800-352-5200	406-541-4433
Park Electric Co-op Inc					
5706 US Hwy 89 S PO Box 1119	Livingston	MT	59047	888-298-0657	406-222-3100
Sheridan Electric Co-op Inc					
PO Box 227	Medicine Lake	MT	59247	800-553-4344	406-789-2231
Southeast Electric Co-op Inc (SECO)					
110 S Main St	Ekalaka	MT	59324	888-485-8762	406-775-8762
Sun River Electric Co-op Inc					
310 First Ave S PO Box 309	Fairfield	MT	59436	800-452-7516	406-467-2527
Yellowstone Valley Electric Co-op					
150 Co-op Way	Huntley	MT	59037	800-736-5323	406-348-3411

Nebraska

				Toll-Free	Phone
Burt County Public Power District					
613 N 13th St PO Box 209	Tekamah	NE	68061	888-835-1620	402-374-2631
Butler County Rural Public Power District					
1331 N Fourth St	David City	NE	68632	800-230-0569	402-367-3081
Chimney Rock Public Power District					
805 W Eigth St PO Box 608	Bayard	NE	69334	877-773-6300	308-586-1824
Cuming County Public Power District					
500 S Main St	West Point	NE	68788	877-572-2463	402-372-2463
Custer Public Power District					
625 E SE St PO Box 10	Broken Bow	NE	68822	888-749-2453	308-872-2451
Dawson Public Power District					
75191 Rd 433	Lexington	NE	68850	800-752-8305	308-324-2386
Elkhorn Rural Public Power District					
206 N Fourth St	Battle Creek	NE	68715	800-675-2185	402-675-2185
Howard Greeley Rural Power					
422 Howard Ave PO Box 105	Saint Paul	NE	68873	800-280-4962	308-754-4457
KBR Rural Public Power District					
374 N Pine St PO Box 187	Ainsworth	NE	69210	800-672-0009	402-387-1120
Loup Public Power District (LPPD)					
2404 15th St PO Box 988	Columbus	NE	68602	866-869-2087	402-564-3171
McCook Public Power District					
1510 N Hwy 83	McCook	NE	69001	800-658-4285	308-345-2500
Midwest Electric Co-op Corp					
104 Washington Ave	Grant	NE	69140	800-451-3691	308-352-4356
Nebraska Public Power District					
1414 15th St PO Box 499	Columbus	NE	68602	877-275-6773	402-564-8561

	Toll-Free	Phone
Norris Public Power District		
606 Irving St PO Box 399 ....Beatrice NE 68310	800-858-4707	402-223-4038
North Central Public Power District		
1409 Main St PO Box 90 ....Creighton NE 68729	800-578-1060	402-358-5112
Northeast Nebraska Public Power District		
1410 W Seventh St PO Box 350 ....Wayne NE 68787	800-750-9277	402-375-1360
Northwest Rural Public Power District		
5613 State Hwy 87 PO Box 249 .....Hay Springs NE 69347	800-847-0492	308-638-4445
Perennial Public Power District		
2122 S Lincoln Ave ....York NE 68467	800-289-0288	402-362-3355
Polk County Rural Public Power District		
115 W 3rd St PO Box 465 ....Stromsburg NE 68666	888-242-5265	402-764-4381
South Central Public Power District (SCPPD)		
275 S Main St PO Box 406 ....Nelson NE 68961	800-557-5254	402-225-2351
Southern Public Power District (SPPD)		
4550 W Husker Hwy PO Box 1687 ....Grand Island NE 68803	800-652-2013	308-384-2350
Southwest Public Power District		
221 S Main St PO Box 289 ....Palisade NE 69040	800-379-7977	308-285-3295
Stanton County Public Power District		
807 Douglas St ....Stanton NE 68779	877-439-2300	402-439-2228
Twin Valleys Public Power District		
1145 Nasby St ....Cambridge NE 69022	800-658-4266	308-697-3315
Wheat Belt Public Power District		
2104 Illinois St ....Sidney NE 69162	800-261-7114	308-254-5871

Nevada

	Toll-Free	Phone
Overton Power District # 5		
615 N Moapa Vly Blvd PO Box 395 ......Overton NV 89040	888-409-6735	702-397-2512
Valley Electric Assn Inc		
800 E Hwy 372 PO Box 237 ....Pahrump NV 89048	800-742-3330	775-727-5312

New Hampshire

	Toll-Free	Phone
New Hampshire Electric Co-op		
579 Tenney Mtn Hwy ....Plymouth NH 03264	800-698-2007	603-536-1800

New Jersey

	Toll-Free	Phone
Sussex Rural Electric Co-op		
64 County Rt 639 PO Box 346 ....Sussex NJ 07461	877-504-6463	973-875-5101

New Mexico

	Toll-Free	Phone
Columbus Electric Co-op Inc		
900 N Gold St PO Box 631 ....Deming NM 88031	800-950-2667	505-546-8838
Jemez Mountains Electric Co-op		
PO Box 128 ....Espanola NM 87532	888-755-2105	505-753-2105
Mora-San Miguel Electric Co-op		
PO Box 240 ....Mora NM 87732	800-421-6773	575-387-2205
Otero County Electric Co-op Inc		
202 Burro Ave PO Box 227 ....Cloudcroft NM 88317	800-548-4660	575-682-2521
Socorro Electric Co-op Inc		
215 Manzanares Ave PO Box H ......Socorro NM 87801	800-351-7575	575-835-0560
Springer Electric Co-op		
408 Maxwell Ave PO Box 698 ....Springer NM 87747	800-288-1353	505-483-2421

New York

	Toll-Free	Phone
Oneida-Madison Electric Co-op Inc		
6630 State Rt 20 ....Bouckville NY 13310	866-632-9992	315-893-1851
Steuben Rural Electric Co-op Inc		
Nine Wilson Ave ....Bath NY 14810	800-843-3414	607-776-4161

North Carolina

	Toll-Free	Phone
Albemarle Electric Membership Corp		
P.O. Box 69 ....Hertford NC 27944	800-215-9915	252-426-5735
Blue Ridge Electric Membership Corp		
1216 Blowing Rock Blvd ....Lenoir NC 28645	800-451-5474	828-758-2383
Brunswick Electric Membership Corp		
795 Ocean Hwy PO Box 226 ....Shallotte NC 28459	800-842-5871	910-754-4391
Cape Hatteras Electric Co-op		
47109 Light Plant Rd PO Box 9 ....Buxton NC 27920	800-454-5616	252-995-5616
Carteret-Craven Electric Co-op (CCEC)		
1300 Hwy 24 W PO Box 1490 ....Newport NC 28570	800-682-2217	252-247-3107
Central Electric Membership Corp		
128 Wilson Rd ....Sanford NC 27331	800-446-7752	919-774-4900
Edgecombe-Martin County Electric Membership Corp		
NC Hwy 33 E ....Tarboro NC 27886	800-445-6486	252-823-2171
EnergyUnited Electric Membership Corp		
PO Box 1831 ....Statesville NC 28687	800-522-3793	704-873-5241
Four County Electric Membership Corp		
1822 NC Hwy 53 W PO Box 667 ....Burgaw NC 28425	888-368-7289	910-259-2171
Haywood Electric Membership Corp		
376 Grindstone Rd ....Waynesville NC 28785	800-951-6088	828-452-2281
Jones-Onslow Electric Membership Corp		
259 Western Blvd ....Jacksonville NC 28546	800-682-1515	910-353-1940
Lumbee River Electric Membership Corp		
PO Box 830 ....Red Springs NC 28377	800-683-5571	910-843-4131
Pee Dee Electric Membership Corp (PDEMC)		
575 US Hwy 52 S ....Wadesboro NC 28170	800-992-1626	704-694-2114
Randolph Electric Membership Corp		
879 McDowell Rd PO Box 40 ....Asheboro NC 27204	800-672-8212	336-625-5177
Roanoke Electric Co-op		
518 NC 561 W ....Aulander NC 27805	800-433-2236	252-539-4600
Rutherford Electric Membership Corp		
186 Hudlow Rd PO Box 1569 ....Forest City NC 28043	800-521-0920	828-245-1621
South River Electric Membership Corp		
17494 US 421 S PO Box 931 ....Dunn NC 28335	800-338-5530	910-892-8071

	Toll-Free	Phone
Surry-Yadkin Electric Membership Corp		
510 S Main St ....Dobson NC 27017	800-682-5903	336-356-8241
Tideland Electric Membership Corp		
25831 Hwy 264 E ....Pantego Nc 27860	800-637-1079	252-943-3046
Union Power Co-op		
1525 N Rocky River Rd ....Monroe NC 28110	800-922-6840	704-289-3145
Wake Electric		
100 S Franklin St PO Box 1229 ...Wake Forest NC 27588	800-474-6300	919-863-6300

North Dakota

	Toll-Free	Phone
Cass County Electric Co-op Inc		
4100 32nd Ave SW ....Fargo ND 58104	800-248-3292	701-356-4400
Dakota Valley Electric Co-op		
7296 Hwy 281 ....Edgeley ND 58433	800-342-4671	701-493-2281
KEM Electric Co-op Inc		
107 S Broadway ....Linton ND 58552	800-472-2673	701-254-4666
McLean Electric Co-op Inc		
4031 Hwy 37 Bypass NW ....Garrison ND 58540	800-263-4922	701-463-2291
Mor-Gran-Sou Electric Co-op Inc		
202 Sixth Ave W ....Flasher ND 58535	800-750-8212	701-597-3301
Mountrail-Williams Electric Co-op		
218 58th St W PO Box 1346 ....Williston ND 58802	800-279-2667	701-577-3765
Nodak Electric Co-op Inc		
4000 32nd Ave S ....Grand Forks ND 58201	800-732-4373	701-746-4461
North Central Electric Co-op Inc		
538 11th St W ....Bottineau ND 58318	800-247-1197	701-228-2202
Northern Plains Electric Co-op		
1515 W Main St ....Carrington ND 58421	800-882-2500	701-652-3156
Slope Electric Co-op Inc		
116 E 12th St PO Box 338 ....New England ND 58647	800-559-4191	701-579-4191
Verendrye Electric Co-op Inc		
615 Hwy 52 ....Velva ND 58790	800-472-2141	701-338-2855

Ohio

	Toll-Free	Phone
Adams Rural Electric Co-op Inc		
4800 SR 125 ....West Union OH 45693	800-283-1846	937-544-2305
Buckeye Rural Electric Co-op		
PO Box 200 ....Rio Grande OH 45674	800-231-2732	740-379-2025
Butler Rural Electric Co-op Inc (BREC)		
3888 Still-Beckett Rd ....Oxford OH 45056	800-255-2732	513-867-4400
Carroll Electric Co-op Inc		
350 Canton Rd NW ....Carrollton OH 44615	800-232-7697	330-627-2116
Darke Rural Electric Co-op Inc		
1120 Fort Jefferson Rd ....Greenville OH 45331	866-692-6330	937-548-4114
Denier Electric Co Inc		
10891 SR- 128 ....Harrison OH 45030	800-676-3282	513-738-2641
Firelands Electric Co-op Inc		
One Energy Pl PO Box 32 ....New London OH 44851	800-533-8658	419-929-1571
Frontier Power Co		
770 S 2nd St PO Box 280 ....Coshocton OH 43812	800-624-8050	740-622-6755
Hancock-Wood Electric Co-op Inc (HWEC)		
1399 Business Pk Dr S		
PO Box 190 ....North Baltimore OH 45872	800-445-4840	419-257-3241
Holmes-Wayne Electric Co-op Inc		
6060 Ohio 83 ....Millersburg OH 44654	866-674-1055	330-674-1055
Lorain-Medina Rural Electric Co-op Inc		
22898 W Rd ....Wellington OH 44090	800-222-5673	440-647-2133
Mid Ohio Energy Co-op Inc		
555 W Franklin St ....Kenton OH 43326	888-382-6732	419-673-7289
North Western Electric Co-op Inc		
04125 State Rt 576 PO Box 391 ......Bryan OH 43506	800-647-6932	419-636-5051
Paulding-Putnam Electric Co-op		
910 N Williams St ....Paulding OH 45879	800-686-2357	419-399-5015
Pioneer Electric Co-op		
344 W US Rt 36 PO Box 1307 ....Piqua OH 45356	800-762-0997	937-773-2523
South Central Power Company Inc		
2780 Coon Path Rd ....Lancaster OH 43130	800-282-5064	740-653-4422
Union Rural Electric Co-op Inc		
15461 US 36E ....Marysville OH 43040	800-642-1826	937-642-1826
Washington Electric Co-op Inc		
406 Colegate Dr ....Marietta OH 45750	877-594-9324	740-373-2141

Oklahoma

	Toll-Free	Phone
Alfalfa Electric Co-op Inc		
121 E Main St ....Cherokee OK 73728	888-736-3837	580-596-3333
Caddo Electric Co-op		
PO Box 70 ....Binger OK 73009	800-522-6543	405-656-2322
Canadian Valley Electric Co-op		
11277 S 356 PO Box 751 ....Seminole OK 74868	877-382-3680	405-382-3680
Central Rural Electric Co-op		
3304 S Boomer Rd PO Box 1809 ......Stillwater OK 74076	800-375-2884	405-372-2884
Choctaw Electric Co-op Inc		
1033 N 4250 Rd ....Hugo OK 74743	800-780-6486	580-326-6486
Cimarron Electric Co-op		
PO Box 299 ....Kingfisher OK 73750	800-375-4121	405-375-4121
Cookson Hills Electric Co-op Inc		
1002 E Main St ....Stigler OK 74462	800-328-2368	918-967-4614
Cotton Electric Co-op Inc		
226 N Broadway ....Walters OK 73572	800-522-3520	580-875-3351
East Central Oklahoma Electric Co-op Inc		
2001 S Wood Dr PO Box 1178 ......Okmulgee OK 74447	800-783-9317	918-756-0833
Harmon Electric Assn Inc (HEA)		
114 N First St PO Box 393 ....Hollis OK 73550	800-643-7769	580-688-3342
Indian Electric Co-op Inc		
2506 E Hwy 64 ....Cleveland OK 74020	800-482-2750	918-358-2514
Kay Electric Co-op (KEC)		
300 W Doolin Ave ....Blackwell OK 74631	800-535-1079	580-363-1260
Kiamichi Electric Co-op Inc (KEC)		
966 SW Hwy 2 PO Box 340 ....Wilburton OK 74578	800-888-2731	918-465-2338
Kiwash Electric Co-op Inc		
120 W First St ....Cordell OK 73632	888-832-3362	580-832-3361

Company / Address	City	State	Zip	Toll-Free	Phone
Lake Region Electric Co-op Inc 516 S Lake Region Rd	Hulbert	OK	74441	**800-364-5732**	918-772-2526
Northeast Oklahoma Electric Co-op Inc 443857 E Hwy 60 PO Box 948	Vinita	OK	74301	**800-256-6405**	918-256-6405
Northwestern Electric Co-op Inc 2925 William Ave	Woodward	OK	73802	**800-375-7423**	580-256-7425
Rural Electric Co-op Inc (REC) 801 N Industrial Heights PO Box 609	Lindsay	OK	73052	**800-259-3504**	405-756-3104
Southeastern Electric Co-op Inc 1514 E Hwy 70 PO Box 1370	Durant	OK	74702	**866-924-1315**	580-924-2170
Southwest Rural Electric Assn 700 N Broadway PO Box 310	Tipton	OK	73570	**800-256-7973**	580-667-5281
Tri-County Electric 302 E Glaydas St PO Box 880	Hooker	OK	73945	**800-522-3315**	580-652-2418
Verdigris Valley Electric Co-op 8901 E 146th St N	Collinsville	OK	74021	**800-870-5948**	918-371-2584

Oregon

Company / Address	City	State	Zip	Toll-Free	Phone
Blachly-Lane Inc PO Box 70	Junction City	OR	97448	**800-446-8418**	541-688-8711
Consumers Power Inc (CPI) 6990 W Hills Rd PO Box 1180	Philomath	OR	97370	**800-872-9036**	541-929-3124
Midstate Electric Co-op Inc 16755 Finley Butte Rd	La Pine	OR	97739	**800-722-7219**	541-536-2126
Tillamook People's Utility District 1115 Pacific Ave	Tillamook	OR	97141	**800-422-2535**	503-842-2535
West Oregon Electric Co-op Inc 652 Rose Ave PO Box 69	Vernonia	OR	97064	**800-777-1276**	503-429-3021

Pennsylvania

Company / Address	City	State	Zip	Toll-Free	Phone
Adams Electric Co-op Inc 1338 Biglerville Rd PO Box 1055	Gettysburg	PA	17325	**888-232-6732**	717-334-2171
Bedford Rural Electric Co-op Inc 8846 Lincoln Hwy	Bedford	PA	15522	**800-808-2732**	814-623-5101
Citizens' Electric Co 1775 Industrial Blvd PO Box 551	Lewisburg	PA	17837	**877-487-9384**	570-524-2231
Claverack Rural Electric Co-op Inc 32750 W US 6	Wysox	PA	18854	**800-326-9799**	570-265-2167
New Enterprise Rural Electric Co-op Inc 3596 Brumbaugh Rd	New Enterprise	PA	16664	**800-270-3177**	814-766-3221
Northwestern Rural Electric Co-op Assn Inc 22534 State Rte Ste 86	Cambridge Springs	PA	16403	**800-352-0014**	800-472-7910
REA Energy Co-op Inc 75 Airport Rd	Indiana	PA	15701	**800-211-5667**	724-349-4800
Somerset Rural Electric Co-op 223 Industrial Pk Rd PO Box 270	Somerset	PA	15501	**800-443-4255**	814-445-4106
Sullivan County Rural Electric Co-op Inc (SCREC) 5675 Rt 87 PO Box 65	Forksville	PA	18616	**800-570-5081**	570-924-3381
Tri-County Rural Electric Co-op Inc 22 N Main St PO Box 526	Mansfield	PA	16933	**800-343-2559**	570-662-2175
Valley Rural Electric Co-op Inc 10700 Fairgrounds Rd PO Box 477	Huntingdon	PA	16652	**800-432-0680**	814-643-2650
Warren Electric Co-op Inc (WEC) 320 E Main St PO Box 208	Youngsville	PA	16371	**800-364-8640**	814-563-7548

South Carolina

Company / Address	City	State	Zip	Toll-Free	Phone
Aiken Electric Co-op Inc 2790 Wagener Rd *Tech Supp	Aiken	SC	29802	**877-264-5368***	803-649-6245
Broad River Electric Co-op Inc 811 Hamrick St	Gaffney	SC	29342	**866-687-2667**	864-489-5737
Coastal Electric Co-op Inc 2269 Jefferies Hwy	Walterboro	SC	29488	**866-708-0913**	843-538-5700
Edisto Electric Co-op Inc 896 Calhoun St	Bamberg	SC	29003	**800-433-3292**	803-245-5141
Laurens Electric Co-op Inc 2254 S Carolina 14	Laurens	SC	29360	**800-942-3141**	
Little River Electric Co-op Inc (LRECI) PO Box 220	Abbeville	SC	29620	**800-459-2141**	864-366-2141
Lynches River Electric Co-op Inc 1104 W McGregor St	Pageland	SC	29728	**800-922-3486**	843-672-6111
Mid-Carolina Electric Co-op Inc PO Box 669 *Cust Svc	Lexington	SC	29071	**888-813-8000***	803-749-6555
Newberry Electric Co-op Inc 882 Wilson Rd	Newberry	SC	29108	**800-479-8838**	803-276-1121
Santee Electric Co-op Inc 424 Sumter Hwy	Kingstree	SC	29556	**800-922-1604**	843-355-6187
Tri-County Electric Co-op 6473 Old State Rd PO Box 217	Saint Matthews	SC	29135	**877-874-1215**	803-874-1215
York Electric Co-op Inc PO Box 150	York	SC	29745	**800-582-8810**	803-684-4247

South Dakota

Company / Address	City	State	Zip	Toll-Free	Phone
Black Hills Electric Co-op 25191 Co-op Way PO Box 792	Custer	SD	57730	**800-742-0085**	605-673-4461
Bon Homme Yankton Electric Assn 134 S Lidice St	Tabor	SD	57063	**800-925-2929**	605-463-2507
Butte Electric Co-op PO Box 137	Newell	SD	57760	**800-928-8839**	605-456-2494
Cam-Wal Electric Co-op Inc 404 W Scranton St PO Box 135	Selby	SD	57472	**800-269-7676**	
Charles Mix Electric Assn Inc 440 Lake St	Lake Andes	SD	57356	**800-208-8587**	605-487-7321
Clay-Union Electric Corp 1410 E Cherry St PO Box 317	Vermillion	SD	57069	**800-696-2832**	605-624-2673
Codington-Clark Electric Co-op 3520 Ninth Ave SW PO Box 880	Watertown	SD	57201	**800-463-8938**	605-886-5848
Dakota Energy Co-op Inc PO Box 830	Huron	SD	57350	**800-353-8591**	605-352-8591
FEM Electric Assn Inc PO Box 468	Ipswich	SD	57451	**800-587-5880**	605-426-6891
Grand Electric Co-op Inc 801 Coleman Ave PO Box 39	Bison	SD	57620	**800-592-1803**	605-244-5211
H-D Electric Co-op Inc 423 Third Ave S	Clear Lake	SD	57226	**800-781-7474**	605-874-2171
Lake Region Electric Assn Inc 1212 Main St	Webster	SD	57274	**800-657-5869**	605-345-3379
Moreau-Grand Electric Co-op Inc 405 Ninth St	Timber Lake	SD	57656	**800-952-3158**	605-865-3511
Northern Electric Co-op Inc 39456 133nd St	Bath	SD	57427	**800-529-0310**	605-225-0310
Oahe Electric Co-op Inc 102 S Cranford St PO Box 216	Blunt	SD	57522	**800-640-6243**	605-962-6243
Sioux Valley-Southwestern Electric Co-op Inc 47092 SD Hwy 34 PO Box 216	Colman	SD	57017	**800-234-1960**	605-534-3535
West Central Electric Co-op Inc 204 Main St PO Box 17	Murdo	SD	57559	**800-242-9232**	605-669-2472
West River Electric Assn Inc 1200 W Fourth Ave PO Box 412	Wall	SD	57790	**888-279-2135**	
Whetstone Valley Electric Co-op 1101 E Fourth Ave	Milbank	SD	57252	**800-568-6631**	605-432-5331

Tennessee

Company / Address	City	State	Zip	Toll-Free	Phone
Caney Fork Electric Co-op Inc 920 Smithville Hwy PO Box 272	McMinnville	TN	37110	**888-505-3030**	931-473-3116
Chickasaw Electric Co-op 17970 US Hwy 64 E PO Box 459	Somerville	TN	38068	**866-465-3591**	901-465-3591
Fayetteville Public Utilities 408 W College St	Fayetteville	TN	37334	**800-379-2534**	931-433-1522
Greeneville Light & Power System PO Box 1690	Greeneville	TN	37744	**866-466-1438**	423-636-6200
La Follette Utilities Board 302 N Tennessee Ave PO Box 1411	La Follette	TN	37766	**800-352-1340**	423-562-3316
Mountain Electric Co-op Inc PO Box 180 *Cust Svc	Mountain City	TN	37683	**800-638-3788***	423-727-1800
Pickwick Electric Co-op 530 Mulberry Ave	Selmer	TN	38375	**800-372-8258**	731-645-3411
Sequachee Valley Electric Co-op 512 Cedar Ave PO Box 31	South Pittsburg	TN	37380	**800-923-2203**	423-837-8605
Southwest Tennessee Electric Membership Corp 1009 E Main St	Brownsville	TN	38012	**800-772-0472**	731-772-1322
Tennessee Valley Electric Co-op 590 Florence Rd	Savannah	TN	38372	**866-925-4916**	731-925-4916
Upper Cumberland Electric Membership Corp 138 Gordonsville Hwy	South Carthage	TN	37030	**800-261-2940**	615-735-2940

Texas

Company / Address	City	State	Zip	Toll-Free	Phone
Bandera Electric Co-op Inc 3172 State Hwy 16 N	Bandera	TX	78003	**866-226-3372**	
Big Country Electric Co-op 1010 W S First St PO Box 518	Roby	TX	79543	**888-662-2232**	325-776-2244
Bowie-Cass Electric Co-op Inc 117 N St	Douglassville	TX	75560	**800-794-2919**	903-846-2311
Central Texas Electric Co-op Inc (CTEC) 386 Friendship Ln PO Box 553 *General	Fredericksburg	TX	78624	**800-900-2832***	830-997-2126
Coleman County Electric Co-op Inc 3300 N Hwy 84 PO Box 860	Coleman	TX	76834	**800-560-2128**	325-625-2128
Comanche Electric Co-op Assn 201 W Wrights Ave	Comanche	TX	76442	**800-915-2533**	325-356-2533
Cooke County Electric Co-op 11799 W US Hwy 82 PO Box 530	Muenster	TX	76252	**800-962-0296**	940-759-2211
CoServ Electric 7701 S Stemmons Fwy	Corinth	TX	76210	**800-274-4014**	940-321-7800
Deaf Smith Electric Co-op Inc 1501 E First St	Hereford	TX	79045	**800-687-8189**	806-364-1166
Deep East Texas Electric Co-op Inc 880 Texas Hwy 21 E PO Box 736	San Augustine	TX	75972	**800-392-5986**	936-275-2314
Farmers Electric Co-op Inc 2000 E I-30	Greenville	TX	75402	**800-541-2662**	903-455-1715
Fayette Electric Co-op Inc 357 N Washington St	La Grange	TX	78945	**800-874-8290**	979-968-3181
Grayson-Collin Electric Co-op (GCEC) PO Box 548	Van Alstyne	TX	75495	**800-967-5235**	903-482-7100
Greenbelt Electric Co-op Inc PO Box 948	Wellington	TX	79095	**800-527-3082**	806-447-2536
Guadalupe Valley Electric Co-op Inc 825 E Sarah Dewitt Dr	Gonzales	TX	78629	**800-223-4832**	830-857-1200
Hamilton County Electric Co-op Assn 420 N Rice St PO Box 753	Hamilton	TX	76531	**800-595-3401**	254-386-3123
Hilco Electric Co-op Inc 115 E Main PO Box 127	Itasca	TX	76055	**800-338-6425**	254-687-2331
Karnes Electric Co-op Inc 1007 N Hwy 123	Karnes City	TX	78118	**888-807-3952**	830-780-3952
Lamar County Electric Co-op Assn 1485 N Main St	Paris	TX	75460	**800-252-8080**	903-784-4303
Lamb County Electric Co-op Inc 2415 S Phelps Ave	Littlefield	TX	79339	**800-365-9000**	806-385-5191
Lighthouse Electric Co-op Inc PO Box 600	Floydada	TX	79235	**800-657-7192**	806-983-2814
Magic Valley Electric Co-op Inc 1 3/4 Mile W Hwy 83 PO Box 267	Mercedes	TX	78570	**866-225-5683**	956-903-3048
McLennan County Electric Co-op 1111 Johnson Dr PO Box 357	McGregor	TX	76657	**800-840-2957**	254-840-2871
Medina Electric Co-op Inc PO Box 370	Hondo	TX	78861	**866-632-3532**	830-741-3334
Navarro County Electric Co-op Inc 3800 Texas 22 PO Box 616	Corsicana	TX	75110	**800-771-9095**	903-874-7411
Navasota Valley Electric Co-op Inc 2281 E US Hwy 79 PO Box 848	Franklin	TX	77856	**800-443-9462**	979-828-3232
North Plains Electric Co-op Inc 14585 Hwy 83 N PO Box 1008	Perryton	TX	79070	**800-272-5482**	806-435-5482

Name / Address	City	ST	ZIP	Toll-Free	Phone
Nueces Electric Co-op (NEC) 709 E Main St PO Box 260970	Robstown	TX	78380	800-632-9288	361-387-2581
Panola-Harrison Electric Co-op 410 E Houston St PO Box 1058	Marshall	TX	75670	800-972-1093	903-935-7936
Pedernales Electric Co-op Inc PO Box 1	Johnson City	TX	78636	888-554-4732	830-868-7155
Rio Grande Electric Co-op Inc Hwy 90 & State Hwy 131 PO Box 1509	Brackettville	TX	78832	800-749-1509	830-563-2444
Sam Houston Electric Co-op Inc 1157 E Church St	Livingston	TX	77351	800-458-0381	936-327-5711
San Bernard Electric Co-op Inc 309 W Main St	Bellville	TX	77418	800-364-3171	979-865-3171
San Patricio Electric Co-op Inc 402 E Sinton St	Sinton	TX	78387	888-740-2220	361-364-2220
South Plains Electric Co-op Inc PO Box 1830	Lubbock	TX	79408	800-658-2655	806-775-7766
Southwest Texas Electric Co-op Inc 101 E Gillis St PO Box 677	Eldorado	TX	76936	800-643-3980	325-853-2544
Swisher Electric Co-op Inc 401 SW Second St PO Box 67	Tulia	TX	79088	800-530-4344	806-995-3567
Texas Electric Co-ops Inc 1122 Colorado St 24th Fl	Austin	TX	78701	800-301-2860	512-454-0311
Tri-County Electric Co-op Inc 600 NW Pkwy	Azle	TX	76020	800-367-8232	817-444-3201
Trinity Valley Electric Co-op Inc (TVEC) 1800 Hwy 243 E PO Box 888	Kaufman	TX	75142	800-766-9576	972-932-2214
Victoria Electric Co-op Inc (VEC) 102 S Ben Jordan St	Victoria	TX	77901	800-344-8377	361-573-2428
Wharton County Electric Co-op Inc (WCEC) 1815 E Jackson St	El Campo	TX	77437	800-460-6271	979-543-6271
Wise Electric Co-op Inc 1900 N Trinity St	Decatur	TX	76234	888-627-9326	940-627-2167
Wood County Electric Co-op Inc 501 S Main St	Quitman	TX	75783	800-762-2203	903-763-2203
Dixie-Escalante Rural Electric Assn 71 E Hwy 56	Beryl	UT	84714	800-874-0904	435-439-5311
Garkane Energy Co-op Inc 120 West 300 South PO Box 465	Loa	UT	84747	800-747-5403	435-836-2795
Vermont Electric Co-op Inc 42 Wescom Rd	Johnson	VT	05656	800-832-2667	802-635-2331
Washington Electric Co-op 40 Church Street	East Montpelier	VT	05602	800-932-5245	802-223-5245
BARC Electric Co-op 84 High St PO Box 264	Millboro	VA	24460	800-846-2272	
Central Virginia Electric Co-op 800 Co-op Way PO Box 247	Lovingston	VA	22949	800-367-2832	434-263-8336
Community Electric Co-op 52 W Windsor Blvd	Windsor	VA	23487	855-700-2667	757-242-6181
Mecklenburg Electric Co-op 11633 Hwy Ninety Two	Chase City	VA	23924	800-989-4161	434-372-6100
Northern Neck Electric Co-op Inc 85 St Johns St PO Box 288	Warsaw	VA	22572	800-243-2860	804-333-3621
Northern Virginia Electric Co-op PO Box 2710	Manassas	VA	20108	888-335-0500	703-335-0500
Southside Electric Co-op Inc 2000 W Virgina Ave	Crewe	VA	23930	800-552-2118	434-645-7721
Benton Rural Electric Assn (BREA) 402 Seventh St PO Box 1150	Prosser	WA	99350	800-221-6987	509-786-2913
Big Bend Electric Co-op 1373 N Hwy 261 PO Box 348	Ritzville	WA	99169	866-844-2363	509-659-1700
Columbia Rural Electric Assn Inc 115 E Main St	Dayton	WA	99328	800-642-1231	509-382-2578
Energy Northwest 76 N Power Plant Loop	Richland	WA	99354	800-468-6883	509-372-5000
Inland Power & Light Company Inc 10110 W Hallett Rd	Spokane	WA	99224	800-747-7151	509-747-7151
Nespelem Valley Electric Co-op Inc 1009 F St	Nespelem	WA	99155	866-377-8642	509-634-4571
Peninsula Light Co 13315 Goodnough Dr NW	Gig Harbor	WA	98332	888-809-8021	253-857-5950
Tanner Electric Co 45710 SE North Bend Way	North Bend	WA	98045	800-472-0208	425-888-0623
Adams-Columbia Electric Co-op 401 E Lake St	Friendship	WI	53934	800-831-8629	608-339-3346
Barron Electric Co-op 1434 State Hwy 25 N	Barron	WI	54812	800-322-1008	715-537-3171
Bayfield Electric Co-op Inc 7400 Iron River Dam Rd	Iron River	WI	54847	800-278-0166	715-372-4287
Chippewa Valley Electric Co-op 317 S Eigth St	Cornell	WI	54732	800-300-6800	715-239-6800
Clark Electric Co-op 124 N Main St PO Box 190	Greenwood	WI	54437	800-272-6188	715-267-6188
Dunn Energy Co-op PO Box 220	Menomonie	WI	54751	800-924-0630	715-232-6240
Jackson Electric Co-op N6868 County Rd F PO Box 546	Black River Falls	WI	54615	800-370-4607	715-284-5385
Jump River Electric Co-op PO Box 99	Ladysmith	WI	54848	866-273-5111	715-532-5524
Oakdale Electric Co-op PO Box 128	Oakdale	WI	54649	800-241-2468	608-372-4131
Oconto Electric Co-op 7478 Rea Rd PO Box 168	Oconto Falls	WI	54154	800-472-8410	920-846-2816
Pierce Pepin Co-op Services W7725 US Hwy 10 PO Box 420	Ellsworth	WI	54011	800-924-2133	715-273-4355
Polk-Burnett Electric Co-op (PBEC) 1001 State Rd 35	Centuria	WI	54824	800-421-0283	715-646-2191
Price Electric Co-op 508 N Lake Ave PO Box 110	Phillips	WI	54555	800-884-0881	715-339-2155
Richland Electric Co-op 1027 N Jefferson St	Richland Center	WI	53581	800-242-8511	608-647-3173
Riverland Energy Co-op N28988 State Rd 93 PO Box 277	Arcadia	WI	54612	800-411-9115	608-323-3381
Saint Croix Electric Co-op 1925 Ridgeway St	Hammond	WI	54015	800-924-3407	715-796-7000
Scenic Rivers Energy Co-op 231 N Sheridan St	Lancaster	WI	53813	800-236-2141	608-723-2121
Taylor Electric Co-op N1831 State Hwy 13	Medford	WI	54451	800-862-2407	715-678-2411
Vernon Electric Co-op 110 Saugstad Rd	Westby	WI	54667	800-447-5051	608-634-3121
Big Horn Rural Electric Co-op 208 S Fifth St PO Box 270	Basin	WY	82410	800-564-2419	307-568-2419
Bridger Valley Extreme Access 40014 Business Loop 1-80 PO Box 399	Mountain View	WY	82939	800-276-3481	307-786-2800
Carbon Power & Light Inc 100 E Willow Ave PO Box 579	Saratoga	WY	82331	800-359-0249	307-326-5206
High Plains Power Inc 1775 E Monroe PO Box 713	Riverton	WY	82501	800-445-0613	307-856-9426
High West Energy Inc (HWE) 6270 County Rd 212	Pine Bluffs	WY	82082	888-834-1657	307-245-3261
Lower Valley Energy 236 N Washington PO Box 188	Afton	WY	83110	800-882-5875	307-885-3175
Powder River Energy Corp (PRE) 221 Main St PO Box 930	Sundance	WY	82729	800-442-3630	
Wheatland Rural Electric Assn 2154 S St PO Box 1209	Wheatland	WY	82201	800-344-3351	307-322-2125
Wyrulec Co 3978 US Hwy 26/85	Torrington	WY	82240	800-628-5266	307-837-2225

248 ELECTRICAL & ELECTRONIC EQUIPMENT & PARTS - WHOL

Name / Address	City	ST	ZIP	Toll-Free	Phone
ACF Components & Fasteners Inc 31012 Huntwood Ave *Cust Svc	Hayward	CA	94544	800-227-2901*	510-487-2100
Adi American Distributors Inc Two Emery Ave Ste 1	Randolph	NJ	07869	800-877-0510	973-328-1181
Advanced MP Technology 1010 Calle Sombra	San Clemente	CA	92673	800-492-3113	949-492-3113
Aesco Electronics Inc 2230 Picton Pkwy	Akron	OH	44312	877-442-6987	330-245-2630
Allied Electronics Inc 7151 Jack Newell Blvd S	Fort Worth	TX	76118	866-433-5722	817-595-3500
Allstar Magnetics LLC 6205 NE 63rd St	Vancouver	WA	98661	800-356-5977	360-693-0213
America II Electronics Inc 2600 118th Ave N	Saint Petersburg	FL	33716	800-767-2637	727-573-0900
Amerinet Inc Two City Pl Dr Ste 400	St. Louis	MO	63141	877-711-5700	
Anixter International Inc 2301 Patriot Blvd *NYSE: AXE*	Glenview	IL	60025	800-492-1212	224-521-8000
Area 51 Esg Inc 51 Post	Irvine	CA	92618	877-476-8751	949-387-0051
Argo International Corp 160 Chubb Ave	Lyndhurst	NJ	07071	877-274-6468	201-561-7010
Astrex Inc 205 Express St	Plainview	NY	11803	800-633-6360	516-433-1700
Audio-technica Us Inc 1221 Commerce Dr	Stow	OH	44224	800-667-3745	330-686-2600
Avnet Inc 2211 S 47th St *NYSE: AVT*	Phoenix	AZ	85034	888-822-8638	480-643-2000
Barbey Electronics Corp 210 Corporate Dr PO Box 2	Reading	PA	19605	800-822-2251	610-916-7955
Barnett Inc 801 W Bay St	Jacksonville	FL	32204	888-803-4467	904-384-6530
Bearcom Inc 4009 Distribution Dr Ste 200 *Sales	Garland	TX	75041	800-527-1670*	
Becker Electric Supply Inc 1341 E Fourth St	Dayton	OH	45402	800-762-9515	937-226-1341
Beyond Components 5 Carl Thompson Rd	Westford	MA	01886	800-971-4242	
Billows Electric Supply Co 9100 State Rd	Philadelphia	PA	19136	877-519-7302	215-332-9700
Bisco Industries Inc 1500 N Lakeview Ave	Anaheim	CA	92807	800-323-1232	
Border States Electric Supply 105 25th St N	Fargo	ND	58102	800-800-0199	701-293-5834
Broadfield Distributing Inc 67A Glen Cove Ave	Glen Cove	NY	11542	800-634-5178	516-676-2378
Buckles-Smith 801 Savaker Ave	San Jose	CA	95126	800-833-7362	408-280-7777
Burst Communication Inc 8200 S Akron St Ste 108	Centennial	CO	80112	800-891-8593	303-649-9600
Butler Supply Inc 965 Horan Dr	Fenton	MO	63026	800-850-9949	636-349-9000
Byram Laboratories Inc One Columbia Rd	Branchburg	NJ	08876	800-766-1212	
Carlton Bates Co 3600 W 69th St	Little Rock	AR	72209	800-482-9313	501-562-9100
Cell-Tel Government Systems Inc 8226-B Phillips Hwy Ste 290	Jacksonville	FL	32256	800-737-7545	904-363-1111
Century Fasteners Corp 50-20 Ireland St	Elmhurst	NY	11373	800-221-0769	718-446-5000
Cms Communications Inc 722 Goddard Ave	Chesterfield	MO	63005	800-755-9169	
Codale Electric Supply Inc 5225 West 2400 South PO Box 702070	Salt Lake City	UT	84120	800-300-6634	801-975-7300
Commodity Components International Inc 100 Summit St	Peabody	MA	01960	800-424-7364	978-538-0020
Communications Supply Corp (CSC) 200 E Lies Rd	Carol Stream	IL	60188	800-468-2121	630-221-6400
Comtel Corp 39810 Grand River Ave Ste 180	Novi	MI	48375	800-335-2505	248-888-4730
Corporate Telephone Services 184 W Second St	Boston	MA	02127	800-274-1211	617-625-1200
Cortelco Inc 1703 Sawyer Rd	Corinth	MS	38834	800-288-3132	662-287-5281
Cross Automation Inc 2001 Oak Pkwy PO Box 1026 *General	Belmont	NC	28012	800-272-7537*	704-523-2222
Crum Electric Supply Co 1165 W English Ave	Casper	WY	82601	800-726-2239	307-266-1278

					Toll-Free	Phone

Dakota Supply Group (DSG)
2601 Third Ave N . . . . Fargo ND 58102   **800-437-4702**   701-237-9440

Dee Electronics Inc
2500 16th Ave SW . . . . Cedar Rapids IA 52404   **800-747-3331**   319-365-7551

Dependable Component Supply Corp
1003 E Newport Ctr Dr . . . . Deerfield Beach FL 33442   **800-336-7100**   954-283-5800

Digi-Key Corp
701 Brooks Ave S . . . . Thief River Falls MN 56701   **800-344-4539**   218-681-6674

Diversified Electronics Co Inc
PO Box 566 . . . . Forest Park GA 30298   **800-646-7278**   404-361-4840

Dominion Electric Supply Company Inc
5053 Lee Hwy . . . . Arlington VA 22207   **800-525-5006**   703-536-4400

Dow Electronics Inc
8603 E Adamo Dr . . . . Tampa FL 33619   **800-627-2900**   813-626-5195

E Sam Jones Distributor Inc
4898 S Atlanta Rd . . . . Smyrna GA 30080   **800-624-9849**   404-351-3250

Electric Supply & Equipment Co
1812 E Wendover Ave . . . . Greensboro NC 27405   **800-632-0268**   336-272-4123

Electric Supply Inc
4407 N Manhattan Ave . . . . Tampa FL 33614   **800-678-1894**   813-872-1894

Electro Brand Inc
1127 S Mannheim Rd Ste 305 . . . . Westchester IL 60154   **800-982-3954**   708-338-4400

Electro-Matic Products Inc
23409 Industrial Pk Ct . . . . Farmington Hills MI 48335   **888-879-1088**   248-478-1182

ElectroTech Inc
7101 Madison Ave W . . . . Minneapolis MN 55427   **800-544-4288**   763-544-4288

Elliott Electric Supply Co
2526 N Stallings Dr PO Box 630610 . . . . Nacogdoches TX 75963   **877-777-0242**   936-569-1184

Englewood Electrical Supply
716 Belvedere Dr . . . . Kokomo IN 46901   **800-417-7543**   765-452-4087

Eric Electronics
2220 Lundy Ave . . . . San Jose CA 95131   **800-495-3742***   408-432-1111
*General

Evans Enterprises Inc
1536 S Western Ave . . . . Oklahoma City OK 73109   **800-423-8267**   405-631-1344

Facility Solutions Group (FSG)
4401 Westgate Blvd Ste 310. . . . . Austin TX 78745   **800-854-6465**   512-440-7985

FD Lawrence Electric Company Inc
3450 Beekman St . . . . Cincinnati OH 45223   **800-582-4490***   513-542-1100
*Cust Svc

Fiber Instruments Sales Inc
161 Clear Rd . . . . Oriskany NY 13424   **800-500-0347***   315-736-2206
*Sales

Flame Enterprises Inc
21500 Gledhill St . . . . Chatsworth CA 91311   **800-854-2255**   818-700-2905

Foxcom Inc
136 Main St Ste 300b . . . . Princeton NJ 08540   **866-663-7284**   609-514-1800

Friedman Electric
1321 Wyoming Ave . . . . Exeter PA 18643   **800-545-5517**   570-654-3371

Fromm Electric Supply Corp
2101 Centre Ave PO Box 15147 . . . . Reading PA 19605   **800-360-4441**   610-374-4441

FSG Lighting
4401 Westgate Blvd Ste 310. . . . . Austin TX 78745   **800-854-6465**   512-440-7985

FTG Inc
725 Marshall Phelps Rd . . . . Windsor CT 06095   **888-610-6020**   860-610-6000

Future Electronics
237 Hymus Blvd . . . . Pointe-Claire QC H9R5C7   **800-675-1619***   514-694-7710
*Cust Svc

Galco Industrial Electronics Inc
26010 Pinehurst Dr . . . . Madison Heights MI 48071   **888-783-4611**   248-542-9090

GBH Communications Inc
1309 S Myrtle Ave . . . . Monrovia CA 91016   **800-222-5424**

George R Peters Assoc Inc
PO Box 850 . . . . Troy MI 48099   **800-929-5972**   248-524-2211

Graybar Electric Co Inc
34 N Meramec Ave . . . . Saint Louis MO 63105   **800-472-9227**   314-573-9200

Gross Electric Inc
2807 N Reynolds Rd . . . . Toledo OH 43615   **800-824-7268**   419-537-1818

Hammond Electronics Inc
1230 W Central Blvd . . . . Orlando FL 32805   **800-929-3672***   407-849-6060
*Sales

Hartford Electric Supply Co (HESCO)
30 Inwood Rd Ste 1 . . . . Rocky Hill CT 06067   **800-969-5444**   860-236-6363

Heartland Label Printers Inc
1700 Stephen St . . . . Little Chute WI 54140   **800-236-7914***
*General

Heilind Electronics Inc
58 Jonspin Rd . . . . Wilmington MA 01887   **800-400-7041**   978-657-4870

Hite Co 3101 Beale Ave . . . . Altoona PA 16601   **800-252-3598**   814-944-6121

HITEC Group Ltd
1743 Quincy Ave Unit 155 . . . . Naperville IL 60540   **800-288-8303**

HL Dalis Inc
35-35 24th St . . . . Long Island City NY 11106   **800-453-2547**   718-361-1100

Houston Wire & Cable Co (HWC)
10201 N Loop E . . . . Houston TX 77029   **800-468-9473**   713-609-2100

IBS Electronics Inc
3506 W Lk Ctr Dr Ste D . . . . Santa Ana CA 92704   **800-527-2888**   714-751-6633

IMS Inc 340 Progress Dr . . . . Manchester CT 06040   **800-264-9837***   860-649-4415
*General

Independent Electric Supply Inc
1370 Bayport Ave . . . . San Carlos CA 94070   **855-437-4968**   650-594-9440

Industrial Electric Wire & Cable Inc (IEWC)
5001 S Towne Dr . . . . New Berlin WI 53151   **800-344-2323**   262-782-2323

Interstate Connecting Components Inc
120 Mt Holly By Pass . . . . Lumberton NJ 08048   **888-899-1990**

Interstate Electrical Supply Inc
2300 Second Ave . . . . Columbus GA 31901   **800-903-4409**   706-324-1000

Jaco Electronics Inc
415 Oser Ave . . . . Hauppauge NY 11788   **877-373-5226**
OTC: JACO

Janesway Electronic Corp
404 N Terr Ave . . . . Mount Vernon NY 10552   **800-431-1348**   914-699-6710

Jasco Products Inc
10 E Memorial Rd . . . . Oklahoma City OK 73114   **800-654-8483**   405-752-0710

JH Larson Co
10200 51st Ave N . . . . Plymouth MN 55442   **800-292-7970**   763-545-1717

Kansas City Electrical Supply Co (KCES)
10900 MidAmerica Ave . . . . Lenexa KS 66219   **866-271-6456**   913-563-7002

Kehoe Component Sales Inc
34 Foley Dr . . . . Sodus NY 14551   **800-228-7223**

Kendall Electric Inc
131 Grand Trunk Ave . . . . Battle Creek MI 49037   **800-632-5422**   269-963-5585

Leff Electric
4700 Spring Rd . . . . Cleveland OH 44131   **800-686-5333**   216-432-3000

Lester Sales Co Inc
4312 W Minnesota St . . . . Indianapolis IN 46241   **800-544-6183**   317-244-7811

Lewis Electric Supply Company Inc
1306 Second St PO Box 2237 . . . . Muscle Shoals AL 35662   **800-239-0681**   256-383-0681

Lowe Electric Supply Co
1525 Forsyth St PO Box 4767 . . . . Macon GA 31208   **800-868-8661**   478-743-8661

Loyd's Electric Supply Inc (LES)
838 Stonetree Dr . . . . Branson MO 65616   **800-492-4030**   417-334-2171

Maltby Electric Supply Company Inc
336 Seventh St . . . . San Francisco CA 94103   **800-339-0668**   415-863-5000

Mars Electric Co
38868 Mentor Ave . . . . Willoughby OH 44094   **800-288-6277**   440-946-2250

Marsh Electronics Inc
1563 S 101st St . . . . Milwaukee WI 53214   **800-236-8327***   414-475-6000
*Cust Svc

Mayer Electric Supply Co
3405 Fourth Ave S PO Box 1328 . . . . Birmingham AL 35222   **866-637-1255**   205-583-3500

McNaughton-McKay Electric Company Inc
1357 E Lincoln Ave . . . . Madison Heights MI 48071   **888-626-2785**   248-399-7500

Metro Wire & Cable Co
6636 Metropolitan Pkwy . . . . Sterling Heights MI 48312   **800-633-1432**   586-264-3050

Mid-Island Electrical Supply
59 Mall Dr . . . . Commack NY 11725   **877-324-2636**   631-864-4242

Minnesota Electric Supply Co
1209 E Hwy 12 . . . . Willmar MN 56201   **800-992-8830**   320-235-2255

Mouser Electronics Corp
1000 N Main St . . . . Mansfield TX 76063   **800-346-6873**   817-804-3888

Murdock Industrial Supply
1111 E 1st . . . . Wichita KS 67202   **800-362-2422**   316-262-4476

Music People Inc
154 Woodlawn Rd Ste C . . . . Berlin CT 06037   **800-289-8889**

NACB Group Inc
10 Starwood Dr . . . . Hampstead NH 03841   **800-370-2737**   603-329-4551

Nedco Electronics
594 American Way . . . . Payson UT 84651   **800-605-2323**   801-465-1790

Nelson Electric Supply Co Inc
926 State St . . . . Racine WI 53404   **800-806-3576**   262-635-5050

NEP Electronics Inc
805 Mittel Dr . . . . Wood Dale IL 60191   **800-284-7470**   630-595-8500

NF Smith & Assoc LP
5306 Hollister Rd . . . . Houston TX 77040   **800-468-7866**   713-430-3000

Nora Lighting Inc
6505 Gayhart St . . . . Commerce CA 90040   **800-686-6672**   323-767-2600

North American Communications Resource Inc
3344 Hwy 149 . . . . Eagan MN 55121   **888-321-6227**   651-994-6800

Northern Video Systems Inc
3625 Cincinnati Ave . . . . Rocklin CA 95765   **800-366-4472**   916-543-4000

Norvell Electronics Inc
PO Box 701027 . . . . Dallas TX 75370   **800-893-0593**   972-858-3713

Nsync Services Inc
850 Greenview Dr . . . . Grand Prairie TX 75050   **866-706-7962**   972-641-7426

Nu Horizons Electronics Corp
70 Maxess Rd . . . . Melville NY 11747   **800-432-5742**   631-396-5000

Nu-Lite Electrical Wholesalers
850 Edwards Ave . . . . Harahan LA 70123   **800-256-1603**   504-733-3300

Paige Electric Company LP
1160 Springfield Rd . . . . Union NJ 07083   **800-327-2443**   908-687-7810

Path Master Inc
1960 Midway Dr . . . . Twinsburg OH 44087   **855-738-2722**   330-425-4994

Peerless Electronics Inc
700 Hicksville Rd . . . . Bethpage NY 11714   **800-285-2121**   516-594-3500

PEI-Genesis
2180 Hornig Rd . . . . Philadelphia PA 19116   **800-675-1214**   215-673-0400

Platt Electric Supply
10605 SW Allen Blvd . . . . Beaverton OR 97005   **800-257-5288**   503-641-6121

Powell Electronics Inc
200 Commodore Dr . . . . Swedesboro NJ 08085   **800-235-7880**   856-241-8000

Power & Telephone Supply Company Inc
2673 Yale Ave . . . . Memphis TN 38112   **800-238-7514***   901-866-3300
*Cust Svc

Priority Wire & Cable Inc
PO Box 398 . . . . North Little Rock AR 72115   **800-945-5542***   501-372-5444
*General

Professional Electric Products Co (PEPCO)
33210 Lakeland Blvd . . . . Eastlake OH 44095   **800-872-7000**   440-946-3790

Projections Unlimited Inc
15311 Varrenca Pkwy . . . . Irvine CA 92618   **800-551-4405***   714-544-2700
*Cust Svc

QED Inc 1661 W Third Ave . . . . Denver CO 80223   **800-700-5011**   303-825-5011

Ralph Pill Electrical Supply Co
50 Von Hillern Street . . . . Boston MA 02125   **800-897-1769**   617-265-8800

Reagan Wireless Corp
720 S Powerline Rd Ste D . . . . Deerfield Beach FL 33442   **877-724-3266**   954-596-2355

Regency Lighting Co
9261 Jordan Ave . . . . Chatsworth CA 91311   **800-284-2024**

Renco Electronics Inc
595 International Pl . . . . Rockledge FL 32955   **800-645-5828**   321-637-1000

Rexel Ryall Electrical Supplies
11775 E 45th Ave . . . . Denver CO 80239   **888-739-3577**   303-629-7721

Richardson Electronics Ltd
40 W 267 Keslinger Rd PO Box 393 . . . . LaFox IL 60147   **800-348-5580***   630-208-2200
NASDAQ: RELL ▦ *Sales

RS Electronics Inc
34443 Schoolcraft Rd . . . . Livonia MI 48150   **866-600-6040**   734-525-1155

Rumsey Electric Co
15 Colwell Ln . . . . Conshohocken PA 19428   **800-462-2402**   610-832-9000

S K C Communication Products Inc
8320 Hedge Ln Terr . . . . Shawnee Mission KS 66227   **800-882-7779**   913-422-4222

Sager Electronics Inc
19 Lorena Dr . . . . Middleboro MA 02346   **800-724-3780**   508-947-8888

Sandusky Electric Inc
1513 Sycamore Line PO Box 2353 . . . . Sandusky OH 44870   **800-356-1243**   419-625-4915

Company / Address	City	State	ZIP	Toll-Free	Phone
Schuster Electronics Inc 2057-D E Aurora Rd	Twinsburg	OH	44087	800-521-1358	
Scott Electric 1000 S Main St PO Box S	Greensburg	PA	15601	800-442-8045	724-834-4321
SED International Inc 4916 N Royal Atlanta Dr *Sales	Tucker	GA	30084	800-444-8962*	770-491-8962
Sennheiser Electronics Corp One Enterprise Dr	Old Lyme	CT	06371	877-736-6434	860-434-9190
Shepherd Electric Supply 7401 Pulaski Hwy *Sales	Baltimore	MD	21237	800-253-1777*	410-866-6000
Singing Machine Company Inc, The 6601 Lyons Rd Bldg A-7 *OTC: SMDM*	Coconut Creek	FL	33073	866-670-6888	954-596-1000
Skywalker Communications Inc 9390 Veterans Memorial Pkwy	O'Fallon	MO	63366	800-844-9555	636-272-8025
Sommer Electric Corp 818 Third St NE	Canton	OH	44704	800-766-6373	330-455-9454
Southern Controls Inc 3511 Wetumpka Hwy	Montgomery	AL	36110	800-392-5770	
Spectra Integrated Systems Inc 8100 Arrowridge Blvd	Charlotte	NC	28273	800-443-7561	704-525-7099
Spectra Merchandising International Inc 4230 N Normandy Ave	Chicago	IL	60634	800-777-5331	773-202-8408
Springfield Electric Supply Co 700 N Ninth St	Springfield	IL	62702	800-747-2101	217-788-2100
Standard Electric Co 2650 Trautner Dr PO Box 5289	Saginaw	MI	48603	800-322-0215	989-497-2100
Standard Electric Supply Co 222 N Emmber Ln PO Box 651	Milwaukee	WI	53233	800-776-8222	414-272-8100
Stanion Wholesale Electric Co 812 S Main St PO Box F	Pratt	KS	67124	866-782-6466	620-672-5678
State Electric Supply Company Inc 2010 Second Ave *Cust Svc	Huntington	WV	25703	800-624-3417*	304-523-7491
Steiner Electric Co 1250 Touhy Ave	Elk Grove Village	IL	60007	800-783-4637	847-228-0400
Steven Engineering Inc 230 Ryan Way	South San Francisco	CA	94080	800-258-9200	650-588-9200
Stokes Electric Company Inc 1701 McCalla Ave	Knoxville	TN	37915	800-999-0351	865-525-0351
Stoneway Electric Supply Co 402 N Perry St	Spokane	WA	99202	800-841-1408	509-535-2933
Storage Battery Systems Inc (SBS) N56 W16665 Ridgewood Dr	Menomonee Falls	WI	53051	800-554-2243	262-703-5800
Summit Electric Supply Co 2900 Stanford NE	Albuquerque	NM	87107	800-824-4400	505-346-9000
Surface Mount Distribution Inc (SMD) 1 Oldfield	Irvine	CA	92618	800-820-7634	949-470-7700
Syn-Tech Inc 3100 Ridgelake Dr Ste 101	Metairie	LA	70002	800-535-7619	504-835-7825
Tacoma Electric Supply Inc 1311 S Tacoma Way	Tacoma	WA	98409	800-422-0540	253-475-0540
Taitron Components Inc 28040 W Harrison Pkwy *NASDAQ: TAIT*	Valencia	CA	91355	800-247-2232	661-257-6060
TeL Systems 7235 Jackson Rd	Ann Arbor	MI	48103	800-686-7235	734-761-4506
Tele-Communications Inc 5125 W 140th St	Brookpark	OH	44142	877-841-8914	216-267-0800
Teleco Inc 430 Woodruff Rd Ste 300	Greenville	SC	29607	800-800-6159	864-297-4400
Telesource Services LLC 1450 Highwood E	Pontiac	MI	48340	800-525-4300	248-335-3000
Telmar Technology 901 Jupiter Rd	Plano	TX	75074	866-835-6276	972-836-0400
Terry-Durin Co 409 Seventh Ave SE	Cedar Rapids	IA	52401	800-332-8114	319-364-4106
TESSCO Technologies Inc 11126 McCormick Rd *NASDAQ: TESS*	Hunt Valley	MD	21031	800-472-7373	410-229-1000
Tri-Ed Distribution Inc 135 Crossways Pk Dr W	Woodbury	NY	11797	888-874-3336	516-941-2800
Tri-State Armature & Electrical Works Inc 330 GE Patterson PO Box 466	Memphis	TN	38126	800-238-7654	901-527-8412
Tri-State Utility Products Inc 1030 Atlanta Industrial Dr	Marietta	GA	30066	800-282-7985	770-427-3119
TTI Inc 2441 NE Pkwy *Sales	Fort Worth	TX	76106	800-225-5884*	817-740-9000
Unique Communications Inc 3650 Coral Ridge Dr	Coral Springs	FL	33065	800-881-8182	954-735-4002
United Electrical Sales Ltd 4496 36th St	Orlando	FL	32811	800-432-5126	407-246-1992
United Utility Supply Co-op Inc 4515 Bishop Ln	Louisville	KY	40218	800-366-4887	502-957-2568
Valley Electric Supply Corp 1361 N State Rd PO Box 724	Vincennes	IN	47591	800-825-7877	812-882-7860
Van Meter Industrial Inc 850 32nd Ave SW	Cedar Rapids	IA	52404	800-247-1410	319-366-5301
Venkel Ltd 5900 Shepherd Mtn Cove	Austin	TX	78730	800-950-8365	512-794-0081
Viking Electric Supply Inc 451 Industrial Blvd W	Minneapolis	MN	55413	800-435-3345	612-627-1300
Virginia West Electric Supply Co (WVES) 250 12-th St W	Huntington	WV	25704	800-624-3433	304-525-0361
Voss Lighting PO Box 22159	Lincoln	NE	68542	866-292-0529	402-328-2281
Vsa Inc 6929 Seward Ave	Lincoln	NE	68507	800-888-2140	402-467-3668
Wabash Electric Supply Inc 1400 S Wabash St	Wabash	IN	46992	800-552-7777	260-563-4146
Walters Wholesale Electric Co 2825 Temple Ave	Signal Hill	CA	90755	800-700-5483	562-988-3100
Werner Electric Supply Co 2341 Industrial Dr	Neenah	WI	54956	800-236-5026	920-729-4500
Wes-Garde Components Group Inc 190 Elliott St	Hartford	CT	06114	800-554-8866	860-525-6907
West-Lite Supply Company Inc 12951 166th St	Cerritos	CA	90703	800-660-6678	
Western Extralite Co 1470 Liberty St	Kansas City	MO	64102	800-279-8833	816-421-8404
Whitlock Group 12820 W Creekk Pkwy Ste M	Richmond	VA	23238	800-726-9843	804-273-9100
Wieland Electric Inc (WEI) 49 International Rd	Burgaw	NC	28425	800-943-5263	910-259-5050
Williams Supply Inc 210 Seventh St	Roanoke	VA	24016	800-533-6969	540-343-9333
Wiremasters Inc 1788 N Pt Rd	Columbia	TN	38401	800-635-5342	615-791-0281
WW Grainger Inc 100 Grainger Pkwy *NYSE: GWW*	Lake Forest	IL	60045	888-361-8649	847-535-1000
XP Power 990 Benicia Ave	Sunnyvale	CA	94085	800-253-0490	408-732-7777
Zack Electronics Inc 1070 Hamilton Rd	Duarte	CA	91010	800-466-0449	626-303-0655

249 ELECTRICAL EQUIPMENT FOR INTERNAL COMBUSTION ENGINES

SEE ALSO Motors (Electric) & Generators ; Automotive Parts & Supplies - Mfr

Company / Address	City	State	ZIP	Toll-Free	Phone
American Electronic Components 1101 Lafayette St	Elkhart	IN	46516	888-847-6552	574-295-6330
Autotronic Controls Corp 1490 Henry Brennan Dr	El Paso	TX	79936	800-213-3083	915-857-5200
CE Niehoff & Co 2021 Lee St *Tech Supp	Evanston	IL	60202	800-643-4633*	847-866-6030
Edge Products 1080 S Depot Dr	Ogden	UT	84404	888-360-3343	801-476-3343
ETCO Inc Automotive Products Div 3004 62nd Ave E	Bradenton	FL	34203	800-689-3826	941-756-8426
Flight Systems Inc 505 Fishing Creek Rd	Lewisberry	PA	17339	800-403-3728	717-932-9900
Goodall Manufacturing Co 7558 Washington Ave S	Eden Prairie	MN	55344	800-328-7730	952-941-6666
Ignition Systems & Controls LP 6300 W Hwy 80	Midland	TX	79706	800-777-5559	432-697-6472
Motorcar Parts & Accessories 2929 California St	Torrance	CA	90503	800-890-9988	310-212-7910
NGK Spark Plugs Inc 46929 Magellan	Wixom	MI	48393	877-473-6767	248-926-6900
Precision Parts & Remanufacturing Co 4411 SW 19th St	Oklahoma City	OK	73108	800-654-3846	405-681-2592
Prestolite Wire Corp 200 Galleria Officentre Ste 212	Southfield	MI	48034	800-498-3132	248-355-4422
Remy International Inc 600 Corp Dr *NYSE: REMY*	Pendleton	IN	46064	800-372-3555	765-778-6499
Transpo Electronics Inc 2150 Brengle Ave	Orlando	FL	32808	800-327-6903	
Van Bergen & Greener Inc 1818 Madison St	Maywood	IL	60153	800-621-3889	708-343-4700

250 ELECTRICAL SIGNALS MEASURING & TESTING INSTRUMENTS

Company / Address	City	State	ZIP	Toll-Free	Phone
3M Telecommunications Div 6801 River Pl Blvd	Austin	TX	78726	800-426-8688	
Aeroflex 400 New Century Pkwy	New Century	KS	66031	800-843-1553	913-764-2452
Allied Motion Technologies Inc 495 Commerce Dr Ste 3 *NASDAQ: AMOT*	Amherst	NY	14228	888-392-5543	716-242-8634
Analog Devices Inc Three Technology Way *NASDAQ: ADI*	Norwood	MA	02062	800-262-5643	781-329-4700
Anritsu Co 490 Jarvis Dr	Morgan Hill	CA	95037	800-267-4878	408-778-2000
Associated Equipment Corp 5043 Farlan Ave	Saint Louis	MO	63115	800-949-1472	314-385-5178
Bird Electronic Corp 30303 Aurora Rd	Solon	OH	44139	866-695-4569	440-248-1200
Bird Technologies Group Inc 30303 Aurora Rd	Solon	OH	44139	866-695-4569	440-248-1200
Bruel & Kjaer Instruments Inc 2815 Colonnades Ct Ste A	Norcross	GA	30071	800-332-2040	770-209-6907
Cascade Microtech Inc 2430 NW 206th Ave *NASDAQ: CSCD*	Beaverton	OR	97006	800-854-8400	503-601-1000
Chatsworth Data Corp 9735 Lurline Ave	Chatsworth	CA	91311	877-380-6855	818-350-5072
Cohu Inc 12367 Crosthwaite Cir *NASDAQ: COHU*	Poway	CA	92064	800-685-5050	858-848-8100
Communications Manufacturing Co (CMC) 2234 Colby Ave *Orders	Los Angeles	CA	90064	800-462-5532*	310-828-3200
Curtis Instruments Inc 200 Kisco Ave	Mount Kisco	NY	10549	800-777-3433	914-666-2971
CXR Larus Corp 894 Faulstich Ct	San Jose	CA	95112	800-999-9946	408-573-2700
CyberOptics Corp 5900 Golden Hills Dr *NASDAQ: CYBE* ■ *Cust Svc	Minneapolis	MN	55416	800-746-6315*	763-542-5000
Delta Design Inc 12367 Crosthwaite Cir	Poway	CA	92064	877-660-6853	858-848-8000
DIT-MCO International Corp 5612 Brighton Terr	Kansas City	MO	64130	800-821-3487	816-444-9700
Doble Engineering Co Inc 85 Walnut St	Watertown	MA	02472	800-759-5219	617-926-4900
Dranetz-BMI 1000 New Durham Rd	Edison	NJ	08818	800-372-6832	732-287-3680
EADS North American Defense Test & Services Inc 4 Goodyear *Cust Svc	Irvine	CA	92618	800-722-2528*	949-859-8999

Classified Section

	Toll-Free	Phone
EXFO Inc 400 Godin Ave ....Quebec QC G1M2K2 *NASDAQ: EXFO*	800-663-3936	418-683-0211
Fluke Biomedical 6920 Seaway Blvd ....Everett WA 98203	800-443-5853	425-446-6945
Fluke Corp 6920 Seaway Blvd ....Everett WA 98203	877-355-3225	425-446-6100
Fluke Networks Inc 6920 Seaway Blvd ....Everett WA 98203	800-283-5853	425-446-4519
Giga-Tronics Inc 4650 Norris Canyon Rd ....San Ramon CA 94583 *NASDAQ: GIGA*	800-726-4442	925-328-4650
Gleason M & M Precision Systems Corp 300 Progress Rd ....Dayton OH 45449	800-727-6333	937-859-8273
Greenlee Textron 1390 Aspen Way ....Vista CA 92081	800-642-2155	760-598-8900
Hickok Inc 10514 Dupont Ave ....Cleveland OH 44108 *OTC: HICKA*	800-342-5080	216-541-8060
Hughes Corp Weschler Instruments Div 16900 Foltz Pkwy ....Cleveland OH 44149	800-557-0064	440-238-2550
ILX Lightwave Corp 31950 E Frontage Rd ....Bozeman MT 59715	800-459-9459	406-586-1244
Itron Inc 2111 N Molter Rd ....Liberty Lake WA 99019 *NASDAQ: ITRI*	800-635-5461	509-924-9900
Ixia 26601 W Agoura Rd ....Calabasas CA 91302 *NASDAQ: XXIA*	877-367-4942	818-871-1800
Keithley Instruments Inc 28775 Aurora Rd ....Cleveland OH 44139	800-552-1115	440-248-0400
KLA-Tencor Corp One Technology Dr ....Milpitas CA 95035 *NASDAQ: KLAC*	800-600-2829	408-875-3000
Knopp Inc 1307 66th St ....Emeryville CA 94608	800-227-1848	510-653-1661
Landis Gyr Inc 2800 Duncan Rd ....Lafayette IN 47904	888-390-5733	765-742-1001
LeCroy Corp 700 Chestnut Ridge Rd ....Chestnut Ridge NY 10977 *NASDAQ: LCRY*	800-553-2769	845-425-2000
Megger 4271 Bronze Way ....Dallas TX 75237	800-723-2861	214-333-3201
Micro Control Co 7956 Main St NE ....Minneapolis MN 55432	800-328-9923	763-786-8750
Monroe Electronics Inc 100 Housel Ave ....Lyndonville NY 14098	800-821-6001	585-765-2254
National Instruments Corp 11500 N Mopac Expy ....Austin TX 78759 *NASDAQ: NATI* ■ *Cust Svc*	800-433-3488*	512-794-0100
Newport Electronics Inc 2229 S Yale St ....Santa Ana CA 92704 *Cust Svc*	800-639-7678*	714-540-4914
Phase Matrix Inc 109 Bonaventura Dr ....San Jose CA 95134	877-447-2736	408-428-1000
Radiodetection Corp 154 Portland Rd ....Bridgton ME 04009	877-247-3797	207-647-9495
Schweitzer E O Mfg Company Inc 450 Enterprise Pkwy ....Lake Zurich IL 60047	888-870-7350	847-362-8304
Snap-on Diagnostics 420 Barclay Blvd ....Lincolnshire IL 60069	800-424-7226	847-478-0700
TEGAM Inc 10 Tegam Way ....Geneva OH 44041	800-666-1010	440-466-6100
Trek Inc 11601 Maple Ridge Rd ....Medina NY 14103	800-367-8735	585-798-3140
Trilithic Inc 9710 Pk Davis Dr ....Indianapolis IN 46235	800-344-2412	317-895-3600
Xcerra Corporation 1355 California Cir ....Milpitas CA 95035 *NASDAQ: XCRA*	800-451-2400	408-635-4300
Yokogawa Corp of America 12530 W Airport Blvd ....Sugar Land TX 77478	800-888-6400	281-340-3800
Zetec Inc 8226 Bracken Pl SE Ste 100 ....Snoqualmie WA 98065	800-643-1771	425-974-2700

251 ELECTRICAL SUPPLIES - PORCELAIN

	Toll-Free	Phone
Ceradyne Inc 3169 Redhill Ave ....Costa Mesa CA 92626 *NYSE: MMM*	877-992-7749	714-549-0421
CoorsTek Inc 600 Ninth St ....Golden CO 80401	800-821-6110	303-278-4000
Fair-Rite Products Corp One Commerical Row PO Box J ....Wallkill NY 12589	888-324-7748	845-895-2055
International Ceramic Engineering 235 Brooks St ....Worcester MA 01606	800-779-3321	508-853-4700
Kyocera Industrial Ceramics Corp 5713 E Fourth Plain Rd ....Vancouver WA 98661	800-826-0527	360-696-8950
Medler Eelectric Company Inc 2155 Menard Dr ....Alma MI 48801	800-229-5740	
Saint-Gobain Advanced Ceramics Latrobe 4702 Rt 982 ....Latrobe PA 15650	800-438-7237	724-539-6000
Sunbelt Transfomer Ltd 1922 S Martin Luther King Jr Dr ....Temple TX 76504	800-433-3128	254-771-3777

252 ELECTROMEDICAL & ELECTROTHERAPEUTIC EQUIPMENT

SEE ALSO Medical Instruments & Apparatus - Mfr

	Toll-Free	Phone
ABIOMED Inc 22 Cherry Hill Dr ....Danvers MA 01923 *NASDAQ: ABMD*	800-422-8666	978-777-5410
Affymetrix Inc 3420 Central Expy ....Santa Clara CA 95051 *NASDAQ: AFFX*	888-362-2447	408-731-5000
Astro-Med Inc 600 E Greenwich Ave ....West Warwick RI 02893 *NASDAQ: ALOT*	800-343-4039	401-828-4000
Avancen MOD Corp 1156 Bowman Rd Ste 200 ....Mount Pleasant SC 29464	800-607-1230	

	Toll-Free	Phone
Bio Medical Innovations 814 Airport Way ....Sandpoint ID 83864	800-201-3958	
Bovie Medical Corp 734 Walt Whitman Rd Ste 207 ....Melville NY 11747 *NYSE: BVX*	800-888-4999	631-421-5452
Cardiac Science Corp 3303 Monte Villa Pkwy ....Bothell WA 98021 *Cust Svc*	800-426-0337*	425-402-2000
CAS Medical Systems Inc 44 E Industrial Rd ....Branford CT 06405 *NASDAQ: CASM*	800-227-4414	203-488-6056
Conmed Corp 525 French Rd ....Utica NY 13502 *NASDAQ: CNMD*	800-448-6506	315-797-8375
Cook Medical Inc 1186 Montgomery Ln ....Vandergrift PA 15690 *General*	800-245-4715*	724-845-8621
Criticare Systems Inc N7W22025 Johnson Dr ....Waukesha WI 53186	800-458-4615	262-798-8282
Draeger Medical Inc 3135 Quarry Rd ....Telford PA 18969	800-437-2437	
Dynatronics Corp 7030 Pk Centre Dr ....Salt Lake City UT 84121 *NASDAQ: DYNT*	800-874-6251	801-568-7000
Fisher & Paykel Healthcare Inc 15365 Barranca Pkwy ....Irvine CA 92618	800-446-3908	949-453-4000
Gambro Renal Products 14143 Denver W Pkwy ....Lakewood CO 80401	800-525-2623	303-232-6800
GE Healthcare Information Technologies 8200 W Tower Ave ....Milwaukee WI 53223	800-558-5102	414-355-5000
GN ReSound North America 8001 E Bloomington Fwy ....Bloomington MN 55420	888-735-4327	
HealthTronics Inc 9825 Spectrum Dr Bldg 3 ....Austin TX 78717	888-252-6575	512-328-2892
Inovio Pharmaceuticals Inc 1787 Sentry PkwyW Bldg 18 ....Blue Bell PA 19422 *NASDAQ: INOVIO*	877-446-6846	267-440-4200
IVY Biomedical Systems Inc 11 Business Pk Dr ....Branford CT 06405	800-247-4614	203-481-4183
Kelyniam Global Inc 97 River Rd ....Canton CT 06019	800-280-8192	
MAQUET Cardiac Assist 15 Law Dr ....Fairfield NJ 07004	800-777-4222	973-244-6100
Masimo Corp 40 Parker ....Irvine CA 92618	800-326-4890	949-297-7000
Medical Education Technologies Inc (METI) 6300 Edgelake Dr ....Sarasota FL 34240	866-462-7920	941-377-5562
Medical Graphics Corp 350 Oak Grove Pkwy ....Saint Paul MN 55127 *NASDAQ: ANGN*	800-950-5597	651-484-4874
Medtronic Inc 710 Medtronic Pkwy NE ....Minneapolis MN 55432 *NYSE: MDT* ■ *Cust Svc*	800-328-2518*	763-514-4000
Medtronic of Canada Ltd 6733 Kitimat Rd ....Mississauga ON L5N1W3	800-268-5346	905-826-6020
Medtronic Perfusion Systems 7611 Northland Dr ....Brooklyn Park MN 55428	800-328-3320	763-391-9000
Meridian Medical Technologies Inc 6350 Stevens Forest Rd Ste 301 ....Columbia MD 21046	800-638-8093	443-259-7800
Mortara Instrument Inc 7865 N 86th St ....Milwaukee WI 53224	800-231-7437	414-354-1600
Natus Medical Inc 1501 Industrial Rd ....San Carlos CA 94070 *NASDAQ: BABY*	800-255-3901	650-802-0400
NeuroMetrix 62 Fourth Ave ....Waltham MA 02451 *NASDAQ: NURO*	888-786-7287	781-890-9989
Neuromonics Inc 2810 Emrick Blvd ....Bethlehem PA 18020	866-606-3876	
Oscor Inc 3816 DeSoto Blvd ....Palm Harbor FL 34683 *Cust Svc*	800-726-7267*	727-937-2511
Paradigm Medical Industries Inc 4273 South 590 West ....Salt Lake City UT 84123 *OTC: PDMI*	800-742-0671	801-977-8970
Physio-Control Inc 11811 Willows Rd NE ....Redmond WA 98052	800-442-1142	425-867-4000
Respironics Novametrix LLC Five Technology Dr ....Wallingford CT 06492	800-345-6443	724-387-4000
Richard Wolf Medical Instruments Corp 353 Corporate Woods Pkwy ....Vernon Hills IL 60061	800-323-9653	847-913-1113
Rockwell Medical Inc 30142 Wixom Rd ....Wixom MI 48393 *NASDAQ: RMTI*	800-449-3353	248-960-9009
SensorMedics Corp 22745 Savi Ranch Pkwy ....Yorba Linda CA 92887	800-231-2466	714-283-2228
Siemens Medical Solutions Inc 51 Valley Stream Pkwy ....Malvern PA 19355	800-888-7436	800-225-5336
Solta Medical Inc 25881 Industrial Blvd ....Hayward CA 94545	877-782-2286	
Spacelabs Health Care 35301 SE Center St ....Snoqualmie WA 98065	800-522-7025	425-396-3300
Thoratec Corp 6035 Stoneridge Dr ....Pleasanton CA 94588 *NASDAQ: THOR*	800-528-2577	925-847-8600
Vasomedical Inc 180 Linden Ave ....Westbury NY 11590 *OTC: VASO*	800-455-3327	516-997-4600
Watermark Medical LLC 1641 Worthington Rd Ste 320 ....West Palm Beach FL 33409	877-710-6999	
Welch Allyn Medical Products 4341 State St Rd ....Skaneateles Falls NY 13152	800-289-2500	315-685-4100
Welch Allyn Monitoring Inc 8500 SW Creekside Pl ....Beaverton OR 97008 *Cust Svc*	800-289-2500*	503-530-7500
ZOLL Medical Corp 269 Mill Rd ....Chelmsford MA 01824	800-348-9011	978-421-9655

			Toll-Free	Phone

253　ELECTRONIC BILL PRESENTMENT & PAYMENT SERVICES

SEE ALSO Application Service Providers (ASPs)

			Toll-Free	Phone
Alpha Card Services Inc				
475 Veit Rd	Huntingdon Valley PA	19006	**866-253-2227**	
FIX Flyer LLC				
225 Broadway Ste 1600	New York NY	10007	**888-349-3593**	
Heartland Payment Systems Inc				
90 Nassau St Second Fl	Princeton NJ	08542	**888-798-3131**	609-683-3831
NYSE: HPY				
Lear Capital Inc				
1990 S Bundy Dr Ste 600	Los Angeles CA	90025	**800-576-9355**	
U.S. Bankcard Services Inc				
17171 E Gale Ave Ste 110	City Of Industry CA	91745	**888-888-8872**	
USA Technologies Inc				
Ste 140 100 Deerfield Ln Chester	Malvern PA	19355	**800-633-0340**	

254　ELECTRONIC COMMUNICATIONS NETWORKS (ECNS)

SEE ALSO Securities Brokers & Dealers ; Securities & Commodities Exchanges
ECNs are computerized trade-matching systems that unite best bid and offer prices and provide anonymity to investors.

			Toll-Free	Phone
Comm-Works Holdings LLC				
1405 Xenium Ln N Ste 120	Minneapolis MN	55441	**800-853-8090**	763-258-5800
Entropic Communications Inc				
6290 Sequence Dr	San Diego CA	92121	**888-510-1765**	858-768-3600
NASDAQ: ENTR				
Layer 3 Communications LLC				
1555 Oakbrook Dr Ste 100	Norcross GA	30093	**866-535-3924**	770-225-5300
Network Telephone Services Inc				
21135 Erwin St	Woodland Hills CA	91367	**800-742-5687**	818-992-4300

255　ELECTRONIC COMPONENTS & ACCESSORIES - MFR

SEE ALSO Semiconductors & Related Devices ; Printed Circuit Boards

			Toll-Free	Phone
3M Electronic Handling & Protection Div				
6801 River Pl Blvd	Austin TX	78726	**800-328-1368**	
3M Interconnect Solutions Div				
6801 River Pl Blvd	Austin TX	78726	**800-225-5373**	512-984-1800
Aavid Thermalloy LLC				
70 Commercial St Ste 200	Concord NH	03301	**855-322-2843**	603-224-9988
Advanced Bionics LLC				
28515 Westinghouse Pl	Valencia CA	91355	**877-829-0026**	661-362-1400
Aeroflex Inc				
35 S Service Rd PO Box 6022	Plainview NY	11803	**800-843-1553**	516-694-6700
TSE: ARX				
AESP Inc 16295 NW 13th Ave	Miami FL	33169	**800-446-2377**	305-944-7710
Aldelo LP				
4641 Spyres Way Ste 4	Modesto CA	95356	**800-801-6036**	209-338-5488
Alpha Group, The				
3767 Alpha Way	Bellingham WA	98226	**800-322-5742**	360-647-2360
American International Inc				
1040 Avendia Acaso	Camarillo CA	93012	**800-336-6500**	805-388-6800
American Power Conversion Corp (APC)				
132 Fairgrounds Rd	West Kingston RI	02892	**800-788-2208***	401-789-5735
Cust Svc				
AMETEK Automation & Process Technologies				
1080 N Crooks	Clawson MI	48017	**800-635-0289**	248-435-0700
Ametek HDR Power Systems Inc				
3563 Interchange Rd	Columbus OH	43204	**888-797-2685**	614-308-5500
AMETEK Solidstate Controls				
875 Dearborn Dr	Columbus OH	43085	**800-635-7300**	614-846-7500
Amphenol Aerospace				
40-60 Delaware Ave	Sidney NY	13838	**800-678-0141**	607-563-5011
Amphenol Interconnect Products Corp (AIPC)				
20 Valley St	Endicott NY	13760	**888-275-2472**	607-754-4444
Amphenol RF				
Four Old Newtown Rd	Danbury CT	06810	**800-627-7100**	203-743-9272
Amphenol Spectra-Strip				
720 Sherman Ave	Hamden CT	06514	**800-846-6400**	203-281-3200
Amphenol-Tuchel Electronics				
6900 Haggerty Rd Ste 200	Canton MI	48187	**800-380-8052**	734-451-6400
AmRad Engineering Inc				
32 Hargrove Grade	Palm Coast FL	32137	**800-445-6033**	386-445-6000
Anaren Microwave Inc				
6635 Kirkville Rd	East Syracuse NY	13057	**800-544-2414**	315-432-8909
NASDAQ: ANEN				
Antec Inc				
47900 Fremont Blvd	Fremont CA	94538	**800-222-6832**	510-770-1200
AudioQuest Inc 2621 White Rd	Irvine CA	92614	**800-747-2770**	949-585-0111
AVG Automation				
4140 Utica St	Bettendorf IA	52722	**877-774-3279**	
Avionic Instruments Inc				
1414 Randolph Ave	Avenel NJ	07001	**800-468-3571**	732-388-3500
Avnet Electronics Marketing Inc				
2211 S 47th St	Phoenix AZ	85034	**888-822-8638**	480-643-2000
Banner Engineering Corp				
9714 Tenth Ave N	Minneapolis MN	55441	**888-373-6767**	763-544-3164
Beacon Power Corp				
65 Middlesex Rd	Tyngsboro MA	01879	**888-938-9112**	978-694-9121
BEI Technologies Inc Industrial Encoder Div				
7230 Hollister Ave	Goleta CA	93117	**800-350-2727***	805-968-0782
Sales				
Bergquist Co				
18930 W 78th St	Chanhassen MN	55317	**800-347-4572**	952-835-2322
C & D Technologies Inc				
1400 Union Meeting Rd PO Box 3053	Blue Bell PA	19422	**800-543-8630**	215-619-2700

			Toll-Free	Phone
C&D Technologies				
11 Cabot Blvd	Mansfield MA	02048	**800-233-2765**	508-339-3000
Califone International Inc				
1145 Arroyo St Ste A	San Fernando CA	91340	**800-722-0500**	818-407-2400
Camesa Inc 1615 Spur 529	Rosenberg TX	77471	**800-866-0001**	281-342-4494
Celestica Inc				
844 Don Mills Rd	Toronto ON	M3C1V7	**888-899-9998**	416-448-5800
NYSE: CLS				
Clary Corp				
150 E Huntington Dr	Monrovia CA	91016	**800-551-6111**	626-359-4486
Coilcraft Inc				
1102 Silver Lk Rd	Cary IL	60013	**800-322-2645**	847-639-2361
Comdel Inc				
11 Kondelin Rd	Gloucester MA	01930	**800-468-3144**	978-282-0620
Communications & Power Industries Inc EIMAC Div (CPI)				
607 Hansen Way	Palo Alto CA	94304	**800-414-8823**	
Communications & Power Industries LLC				
607 Hansen Way	Palo Alto CA	94303	**800-231-4818**	650-846-2900
Cooper Industries				
600 Travis St Ste 5400	Houston TX	77002	**866-853-4293**	713-209-8400
NYSE: ETN				
Corning Gilbert Inc				
5310 W Camelback Rd	Glendale AZ	85301	**800-528-0199***	623-245-1050
Cust Svc				
Cornucopia Tool & Plastics Inc				
448 Sherwood Rd PO Box 1915	Paso Robles CA	93447	**800-235-4144**	805-369-0030
Crystek Crystals Corp				
12730 Commonwealth Dr	Fort Myers FL	33913	**800-237-3061**	239-561-3311
CTS Corp 905 W Blvd N	Elkhart IN	46514	**800-757-6686**	574-293-7511
NYSE: CTS				
Cyber Power Systems Inc				
4241 12th Ave E Ste 400	Shakopee MN	55379	**877-297-6937**	952-403-9500
Cyberex 5900 Eastport Blvd	Richmond VA	23231	**800-238-5000**	804-236-3300
Data Device Corp				
105 Wilbur Pl	Bohemia NY	11716	**800-332-5757***	631-567-5600
Cust Svc				
Dielectric Laboratories Inc				
2777 US Rt 20	Cazenovia NY	13035	**800-656-9499**	315-655-8710
Digital Power Corp				
41324 Christy St	Fremont CA	94538	**866-344-7697**	510-353-4023
Dow-Key Microwave Corp				
4822 McGrath St	Ventura CA	93003	**800-266-3695**	805-650-0260
Eby Co 4300 H St	Philadelphia PA	19124	**800-329-3430**	215-537-4700
Electrex Inc PO Box 948	Hutchinson KS	67504	**800-319-3676**	
Electrocube Inc				
3366 Pomona Blvd	Pomona CA	91768	**800-515-1112**	909-595-4037
Emerson Network Power Connectivity Solutions				
1050 Dearborn Dr	Columbus OH	43085	**800-275-3500**	614-888-0246
Forbes Snyder Tristate Cash				
54 Northampton St	Easthampton MA	01027	**800-222-4064**	413-529-2950
Franklin Empire Inc				
8421 Darnley Rd	Montreal QC	H4T2B2	**800-361-5044**	514-341-9720
Greenlee Textron				
1390 Aspen Way	Vista CA	92081	**800-642-2155**	760-598-8900
Heliene Inc				
520 Allen'S Side Rd	Sault Ste Marie ON	P6A6K4	**855-363-2797**	705-575-6556
Herley-CTI Inc				
9 Whippany Rd	Whippany NJ	07981	**866-606-5867**	973-884-2580
HiRel Systems				
11100 Wayzata Blvd Ste 501	Minnetonka MN	55305	**888-604-5888**	952-544-1344
Hitachi Canada Ltd				
5450 Explore Dr Suite 501	Mississauga ON	L4W5N1	**866-797-4332**	905-629-9300
Hubbell Power Systems Inc				
210 N Allen St	Centralia MO	65240	**800-346-3062**	573-682-5521
Illinois Capacitor Inc				
3757 W Touhy Ave	Lincolnwood IL	60712	**800-263-9275**	847-675-1760
Integrated Magnetics Inc				
11248 Playa Ct	Culver City CA	90230	**800-421-6692**	310-391-7213
Interconnect Devices Inc (IDI)				
5101 Richland Ave	Kansas City KS	66106	**866-433-5722**	913-342-5544
Interpoint Corp				
PO Box 97005	Redmond WA	98073	**800-822-8782**	425-882-3100
ipDataTel LLC				
13110 SW Fwy	Sugar Land TX	77478	**866-896-1818**	713-452-2700
ITT Industries Inc				
1133 Westchester Ave	White Plains NY	10604	**800-254-2823**	914-641-2000
NYSE: ITT				
JAE Electronics Inc				
142 Technology Dr Ste 100	Irvine CA	92618	**800-523-7278**	949-753-2600
Jenkins Electric Inc				
5933 Brookshire Blvd	Charlotte NC	28216	**800-438-3003**	
Jewell Instruments LLC				
850 Perimeter Rd	Manchester NH	03103	**800-227-5955**	603-669-6400
Johanson Mfg Corp				
301 Rockaway Valley Rd	Boonton NJ	07005	**800-477-1272**	973-334-2676
Kepco Inc				
131-38 Sanford Ave	Flushing NY	11355	**800-526-2324**	718-461-7000
La Marche Mfg Co				
106 Bradrock Dr	Des Plaines IL	60018	**888-232-9562**	847-299-1188
Larco				
210 NE Tenth Ave PO Box 547	Brainerd MN	56401	**800-523-6996***	218-829-9797
Cust Svc				
Lenexpo Inc				
1293 Mtn View Alviso Rd Ste A	Sunnyvale CA	94089	**877-536-3976**	408-962-0515
Lexel Imaging Systems Inc				
1501 Newtown Pike	Lexington KY	40511	**800-397-8121**	859-243-5500
Lumex Inc 290 E Helen Rd	Palatine IL	60067	**800-278-5666**	847-359-2790
MagneTek Inc				
N49 W13650 Campbell Dr	Menomonee Falls WI	53051	**800-288-8178**	
NASDAQ: MAG				
Marlow Industries Inc				
10451 Vista Pk Rd	Dallas TX	75238	**877-627-5691**	214-340-4900
Maxwell Technologies Inc				
5271 Viewridge Ct Ste 100	San Diego CA	92123	**877-511-4324**	858-503-3300
NASDAQ: MXWL				
Methode Electronics Inc				
7401 W Wilson Ave	Chicago IL	60706	**877-316-7700**	708-867-6777
NYSE: MEI				

					Toll-Free	Phone
Micro-coax Inc	206 Jones Blvd	Pottstown	PA	19464	**800-223-2629**	610-495-0110
Molex Inc	2222 Wellington Ct; *NASDAQ: MOLX* ■ *Cust Svc	Lisle	IL	60532	**800-786-6539***	630-969-4550
MtronPTI	1703 E Hwy 50	Yankton	SD	57078	**800-762-8800**	605-665-9321
Murata Electronics North America Inc	2200 Lake Pk Dr	Smyrna	GA	30080	**800-704-6079**	770-436-1300
Namco Controls Corp	2100 W Broad St	Elizabethtown	NC	28337	**800-390-6405**	910-862-2511
Newport Corp	1791 Deere Ave; *NASDAQ: NEWP* ■ *Sales	Irvine	CA	92606	**800-222-6440***	949-863-3144
Niles Audio Corp	1969 Kellog Ave	Carlsbad	CA	92008	**800-289-4434**	760-710-0992
Nortech Systems Inc	1120 Wayzata Blvd E Ste 201; *NASDAQ: NSYS*	Wayzata	MN	55391	**800-237-9576**	952-345-2244
Nortek Security & Control LLC	1950 Camino Vida Roble Ste 150; *Cust Svc	Carlsbad	CA	92008	**800-421-1587***	760-438-7000
NWL Transformers Inc	312 Rising Sun Rd	Bordentown	NJ	08505	**800-742-5695**	609-298-7300
Ohmite Manufacturing Co	1600 Golf Rd Ste 850	Rolling Meadows	IL	60008	**866-964-6483**	847-258-0300
OK International	12151 Monarch St	Garden Grove	CA	92841	**800-495-1775**	714-799-9910
Onyx EMS LLC	2920 Kelly Ave	Watertown	SD	57201	**800-258-7989**	605-886-2519
Panamax Inc	1690 Corporate Cir	Petaluma	CA	94954	**800-472-5555**	707-283-5900
Para Systems Inc	*Minuteman UPS*; 1455 LeMay Dr	Carrollton	TX	75007	**800-238-7272**	972-446-7363
PCB Group Inc	3425 Walden Ave	Depew	NY	14043	**800-828-8840**	716-684-0001
PG Life Link Inc	167 Gap Way	Erlanger	KY	41018	**800-287-4123**	859-283-5900
Piller Inc	45 Turner Rd	Middletown	NY	10941	**800-597-6937**	
Plastronics Socket Co Inc	2601 Texas Dr; *Cust Svc	Irving	TX	75062	**800-582-5822***	972-258-2580
Plug Power Inc	968 Albany-Shaker Rd; *NASDAQ: PLUG*	Latham	NY	12110	**877-474-1993**	518-782-7700
Positronic Industries Inc	423 N Campbell Ave PO Box 8247	Springfield	MO	65801	**800-641-4054**	417-866-2322
Post Glover Resistors Inc	4750 Olympic Blvd Bldg B; *Cust Svc	Erlanger	KY	41018	**800-537-6144***	859-283-0778
Precision Devices Inc	8840 N Greenview Dr	Middleton	WI	53562	**800-274-9825**	608-831-4445
Precision Interconnect Corp	10025 SW Freeman Ct	Wilsonville	OR	97070	**800-522-6752**	503-685-9300
Qualitel Corp	11831 Beverly Pk Rd	Everett	WA	98204	**800-647-7706**	425-423-8388
Raritan Computer Inc	400 Cottontail Ln	Somerset	NJ	08873	**800-724-8090**	732-764-8886
Record USA	4324 Phil Hargett Ct; *Sales	Monroe	NC	28105	**800-438-1937***	704-289-9212
RF Industries	7610 Miramar Rd Bldg 6000; *NASDAQ: RFIL*	San Diego	CA	92126	**800-233-1728**	858-549-6340
Samtec Inc	520 Parkeast Blvd	New Albany	IN	47150	**800-726-8329**	812-944-6733
Schumacher Electric Corp	801 E Business Ctr Dr	Mount Prospect	IL	60056	**800-621-5485**	
Seiko Instruments USA Inc	21221 S Western Ave Ste 250; *Sales	Torrance	CA	90501	**800-688-0817***	310-517-7700
Sendec Corp	72 Perinton Pkwy	Fairport	NY	14450	**800-295-8000**	585-425-3390
Sigma Electronics Inc	1027 Commercial Ave	East Petersburg	PA	17520	**866-569-2681**	717-569-2926
Signal Transformer Company Inc	500 Bayview Ave	Inwood	NY	11096	**866-239-5777**	516-239-5777
Simplex Inc	5300 Rising Moon Rd	Springfield	IL	62711	**800-637-8603**	217-483-1600
SL Power Electronics Inc	6050 King Dr Bldg A	Ventura	CA	93003	**800-235-5929**	805-486-4565
Smart Power Systems Inc	1760 Stebbins Dr	Houston	TX	77043	**800-241-6880**	713-464-8000
SNC Mfg Company Inc	101 W Waukau Ave	Oshkosh	WI	54902	**800-558-3325**	920-231-7370
Standex Electronics Inc	4538 Camberwell Rd	Cincinnati	OH	45209	**866-782-6339**	513-871-3777
Stevens Water Monitoring Systems	12067 NE Glenn Widing Dr Ste 106	Portland	OR	97220	**800-452-5272**	503-469-8000
Superconductor Technologies Inc (STI)	460 Ward Dr; *NASDAQ: SCON*	Santa Barbara	CA	93111	**800-727-3648**	805-690-4500
Sypris Electronics LLC	10901 N McKinley Dr	Tampa	FL	33612	**800-937-9220**	813-972-6000
Sypris Solutions Inc	101 Bullitt Ln Ste 450; *NASDAQ: SYPR*	Louisville	KY	40222	**800-588-9119**	502-329-2000
System Sensor	3825 Ohio Ave; *Tech Supp	Saint Charles	IL	60174	**800-736-7672***	630-377-6580
Taiyo Yuden (USA) Inc	1930 N Thoreau Dr Ste 190	Schaumburg	IL	60173	**800-348-2496**	847-925-0888
TDI-Transistor Devices Inc	85 Horsehill Rd	Cedar Knolls	NJ	07927	**800-488-6724**	973-267-1900
Telonic Berkeley Inc	1080 La Mirada Ct; *Sales	Vista	CA	92081	**800-311-8805***	760-744-8350
Threshold Financial Technologies Inc	3269 American Dr	Mississauga	ON	L4V1X5	**888-414-3733**	905-678-7373
Times Microwave Systems Inc	PO Box 5039	Wallingford	CT	06492	**800-867-2629**	203-949-8400
Toshiba America Inc	1251 Ave of the Americas Ste 4100	New York	NY	10020	**800-457-7777**	212-596-0600
Total Technologies Ltd	Nine Studebaker	Irvine	CA	92618	**800-669-4885**	949-465-0200
TRAK Microwave Corp	4726 Eisenhower Blvd	Tampa	FL	33634	**888-283-8444**	813-901-7200
Triton Systems Inc	21405 B St	Long Beach	MS	39560	**866-787-4866**	228-575-3100
TSI Power Corp	1103 W Pierce Ave	Antigo	WI	54409	**800-874-3160**	715-623-0636
United Chemi-Con Inc	9801 W Higgins Rd	Rosemont	IL	60018	**800-344-4539**	847-696-2000
Usi Electronics Inc	2775 W Cypress Creek Rd	Fort Lauderdale	FL	33309	**800-874-8111**	954-493-8111
Valpey Fisher Corp	75 S St	Hopkinton	MA	01748	**800-982-5737**	508-435-6831
Viatran Corp	3829 Forest Pkwy Ste 500	Wheatfield	NY	14120	**800-688-0030**	716-629-3800
Vicor Corp	25 Frontage Rd; *NASDAQ: VICR*	Andover	MA	01810	**800-869-5300**	978-470-2900
Vishay Intertechnology Inc	63 Lancaster Ave; *NYSE: VSH*	Malvern	PA	19355	**800-567-6098**	610-644-1300
Western Electronics LLC	1550 S Tech Ln	Meridian	ID	83642	**888-857-5775**	208-955-9700
Wireless Xcessories Group Inc	1840 County Line Rd Ste 301; *OTC: WIRX*	Huntingdon Valley	PA	19006	**800-233-0013**	215-322-4600
World Electronics Sales & Service Inc	3000 Kutztown Rd	Reading	PA	19605	**800-523-0427**	610-939-9800
Xantrex Technology Inc	3700 Gilmore Way	Burnaby	BC	V5G4M1	**800-670-0707**	604-422-8595
Z Communications Inc	14118 Stowe Dr Ste B	Poway	CA	92064	**877-808-1226**	858-621-2700

256 ELECTRONIC ENCLOSURES

					Toll-Free	Phone
Buckeye ShapeForm	555 Marion Rd	Columbus	OH	43207	**800-728-0776**	614-445-8433
Equipto Electronics Corp	351 Woodlawn Ave	Aurora	IL	60506	**800-204-7225**	630-897-4691
TRI MAP International Inc	111 Val Dervin Pkwy	Stockton	CA	95206	**888-687-4627**	209-234-0100
Zero Manufacturing Inc	500 West 200 North	North Salt Lake	UT	84054	**800-959-5050**	801-298-5900

257 ELECTRONIC TRANSACTION PROCESSING

					Toll-Free	Phone
Avid Payment Solutions	950 S Old Woodward Ste 220	Birmingham	MI	48009	**888-855-8644**	
Chase Paymentech Solutions LLC	14221 Dallas Pkwy; *Cust Svc	Dallas	TX	75254	**800-708-3740***	
Covera Solutions Inc	1021 Watervliet-Shaker Rd PO Box 13539	Albany	NY	12205	**866-526-8372**	
Elavon	Two Concourse Pkwy Ste 300	Atlanta	GA	30328	**800-725-1243**	678-731-5000
Global Payments Inc	10 Glenlake Pkwy N Twr; *NYSE: GPN*	Atlanta	GA	30328	**800-560-2960**	770-829-8000
National Processing Co	5100 Interchange Way; *General	Louisville	KY	40229	**877-300-7757***	800-683-2289

258 ELEVATORS, ESCALATORS, MOVING WALKWAYS

					Toll-Free	Phone
Able Services	868 Folsom St	San Francisco	CA	94107	**800-461-9577**	415-546-6534
Abx Engineering	880 Hinckley Rd	Burlingame	CA	94010	**800-366-4588**	650-552-2322
Allied Corrosion Industries Inc	1550 Cobb Industrial Dr	Marietta	GA	30066	**800-241-0809**	770-425-1355
American Aerospace Controls Inc	570 Smith St	Farmingdale	NY	11735	**888-873-8559**	631-694-5100
Apex Geoscience Inc	2120 Brandon Dr	Tyler	TX	75703	**800-755-8461**	903-581-8080
Astrodyne Corp	375 Forbes Blvd	Mansfield	MA	02048	**800-823-8082**	508-964-6300
B M Ross & Assoc Ltd	62 N St	Goderich	ON	N7A2T4	**888-524-2641**	519-524-2641
Benesyst Inc	800 Washington Ave N 8th Fl	Minneapolis	MN	55401	**866-786-3366**	800-422-4661
BRIC Engineered Systems Ltd	1101 Wentworth St W Ste D1	Oshawa	ON	L1J8P7	**800-937-5135**	905-436-8867
Burns Engineering Inc	10201 Bren Rd E	Minnetonka	MN	55343	**800-328-3871**	952-935-4400
Chisholm Fleming & Assoc	317 Renfrew Dr Ste 301	Markham	ON	L3R9S8	**888-241-4149**	905-474-1458
City of Clarksville	199 10th St	Clarksville	TN	37040	**800-342-1003**	931-645-7464
Clean Ones Corp	PO Box 40008	Portland	OR	97204	**800-367-4587**	503-224-5211
Controlled Contamination Services LLC	4182 Sorrento Valley Blvd	San Diego	CA	92121	**888-263-9886**	858-457-7598
Corradino Group	200 s Fifth st	Louisville	KY	40202	**800-880-8241**	502-587-7221
Corrpro Canada Inc	10848 - 214 St	Edmonton	AB	T5S2A7	**800-661-8390**	780-447-4565
Degree Controls Inc	18 Meadowbrook Dr	Milford	NH	03055	**877-334-7332**	603-672-8900

Classified Section

				Toll-Free	Phone
Dirt Pros of Fort Lauderdale					
PO Box 16453	Plantation	FL	33318	**877-750-7767**	954-318-2477
DJ & A PC					
3203 S Russell St	Missoula	MT	59801	**800-398-3522**	406-721-4320
Dynamic Design Solutions Inc					
3565 Centre Cir	Fort Mill	SC	29715	**866-337-2010**	803-548-3609
Elevator Equipment Corp					
4035 Goodwin Ave	Los Angeles	CA	90039	**888-577-3326**	323-245-0147
Environmental Health & Engineering Inc					
117 Fourth Ave	Needham	MA	02494	**800-825-5343**	781-247-4300
ESE Inc PO Box 1107	Marshfield	WI	54449	**800-236-4778**	715-387-4778
Falcon Crest Aviation Supply Inc					
8318 Braniff	Houston	TX	77061	**800-833-8229**	713-644-2290
FUTEK Advanced Sensor Technology Inc					
10 Thomas	Irvine	CA	92618	**800-233-8835**	949-465-0900
Geotek Engineering & Testing Services Inc					
909 E 50th St N	Sioux Falls	SD	57104	**800-354-5512**	605-335-5512
Giffin Koerth Inc					
40 University Ave Ste 800	Toronto	ON	M5J1T1	**800-564-5313**	416-368-1700
Giles Engineering Assoc Inc					
N8 W22350 Johnson Rd Ste A1	Waukesha	WI	53186	**800-782-0610**	262-544-0118
Globex Corp 3620 Stutz Dr	Canfield	OH	44406	**800-533-8610**	330-533-0030
GMI Building Services Inc					
8001 Vickers St	San Diego	CA	92111	**866-803-4464**	
HESS Construction + Engineering Services Inc					
804 W Diamond Ave Ste 300	Gaithersburg	MD	20878	**800-544-6056**	301-670-9000
HH Angus & Assoc Ltd					
1127 Leslie St	Toronto	ON	M3C2J6	**866-955-8201**	416-443-8200
Hunt Guillot & Assoc LLC					
603 Reynolds Dr	Ruston	LA	71270	**866-255-6825**	318-255-6825
InfoTech Enterprises America Inc					
330 Roberts St Ste 102	East Hartford	CT	06108	**866-746-2133**	860-528-5430
JM Turner Engineering Inc					
1325 College Ave	Santa Rosa	CA	95404	**800-514-4220**	707-528-4503
Johnson Engineering Inc					
2122 Johnson St	Fort Myers	FL	33901	**866-367-4400**	239-334-0046
Kelly's Janitorial Service Inc					
228 Hazel Ave	Ewing	NJ	08638	**800-227-0366**	609-771-0365
Kussmaul Electronics Company Inc					
170 Cherry Ave	West Sayville	NY	11796	**800-346-0857**	631-567-0314
LARON Inc 4255 Santa Fe Dr	Kingman	AZ	86401	**800-248-3430**	928-757-8424
Lochmueller Group					
6200 Vogel Rd	Evansville	IN	47715	**800-423-7411**	812-479-6200
Matot Inc					
2501 Van Buren St	Bellwood	IL	60104	**800-369-1070**	708-547-1888
Matrix Energy Services Inc					
3221 Ramos Cir	Sacramento	CA	95827	**800-556-2123**	916-363-9283
Matrix LLC 19 Ave D	Johnson City	NY	13790	**800-338-5603**	607-766-0700
Moffitt Corp Inc					
1351 13th Ave S Ste 130	Jacksonville Beach	FL	32250	**800-474-3267**	904-241-9944
Motion Control Engineering Inc					
11380 White Rock Rd	Rancho Cordova	CA	95742	**800-444-7442**	916-463-9200
Ricon Corp					
7900 Nelson Rd	Panorama City	CA	91402	**800-322-2884**	818-267-3000
Schindler Elevator Corp					
20 Whippany Rd	Morristown	NJ	07960	**800-225-3123**	973-397-6500
Schumacher Elevator Co					
One Schumacher Way PO Box 393	Denver	IA	50622	**800-779-5438**	319-984-5676
Technical Systems Integration Inc					
816 Greenbrier Cir Ste 208	Chesapeake	VA	23320	**800-566-8744**	757-424-5793
ThyssenKrupp Access Inc					
4001 E 138th St	Grandview	MO	64030	**800-669-9047**	816-763-3100
Waupaca Elevator Co Inc					
1726 N BallaRd Rd	Appleton	WI	54911	**800-238-8739**	920-991-9082
York Building Services Inc					
99 Grand St Ste 3	Moonachie	NJ	07074	**855-443-9675**	

259 EMBASSIES & CONSULATES - FOREIGN, IN THE US

SEE ALSO Travel & Tourism Information - Foreign Travel
Foreign embassies in the U.S. generally include consular services among their functions. These embassy-based consulates are listed here only if their address differs from the embassy's.

				Toll-Free	Phone
Afghanistan Embassy					
2341 Wyoming Ave NW	Washington	DC	20008	**866-323-8609**	202-483-6410
Antigua & Barbuda					
Embassy					
3216 New Mexico Ave NW	Washington	DC	20016	**866-978-7299**	202-362-5122
Australia					
Consulate General					
1000 Bishop St PH	Honolulu	HI	96813	**866-343-3086**	808-529-8100
Embassy					
2005 Massachusetts Ave NW	Washington	DC	20036	**800-345-6541**	202-558-2216
Austria					
Consulate General					
11859 Wilshire Blvd Ste 501	Los Angeles	CA	90025	**800-255-2414**	310-444-9310
Embassy					
3524 International Ct NW	Washington	DC	20008	**800-255-2414**	202-895-6700
Bahamas					
Embassy					
2220 Massachusetts Ave NW	Washington	DC	20008	**800-883-7421**	202-319-2660
Brazil					
Consulate General					
1233 W Loop S Ste 1150	Houston	TX	77027	**800-326-2289**	713-961-3063
Consulate General					
8484 Wilshire Blvd Ste 711	Beverly Hills	CA	90211	**877-782-5477**	323-651-2664
Bulgaria					
Embassy 1621 22nd St NW	Washington	DC	20008	**800-961-6836**	202-387-0174
Burkina Faso Embassy					
2005 Massachusetts Ave NW	Washington	DC	20008	**800-345-6541**	202-332-5577
Consulate General					
500 N Akard St Ste 2900	Dallas	TX	75201	**800-267-8376**	214-922-9806
Consulate General					
1251 Ave of the Americas					
Concourse Level	New York	NY	10020	**800-267-8376**	212-596-1628

				Toll-Free	Phone
Embassy					
501 Pennsylvania Ave NW	Washington	DC	20001	**800-567-6868**	202-682-1740
Cape Verde					
Embassy					
3415 Massachusetts Ave NW	Washington	DC	20007	**800-343-2347**	202-965-6820
Denmark					
Consulate General					
875 N Michigan Ave Ste 3950	Chicago	IL	60611	**800-345-6541**	
Fiji Embassy					
2000 M St NW Ste 710	Washington	DC	20036	**800-932-3454**	202-337-8320
France					
Consulate General					
205 N Michigan Ave Ste 3700	Chicago	IL	60601	**888-642-2787**	312-327-5200
Consulate General					
1395 Brickell Ave Ste 1050	Miami	FL	33131	**877-624-8737**	305-403-4185
Consulate General					
777 Post Oak Blvd Ste 600	Houston	TX	77056	**888-902-5322**	713-572-2799
Consulate General					
934 Fifth Ave	New York	NY	10021	**800-772-1213**	212-606-3600
Consulate General					
540 Bush St	San Francisco	CA	94108	**800-843-3779**	415-397-4330
Consulate General					
3475 Piedmont Rd NE Ste 1840	Atlanta	GA	30305	**866-347-2523**	404-495-1660
Embassy					
4101 Reservoir Rd NW	Washington	DC	20007	**800-622-6232**	202-944-6000
Germany					
Consulate General					
285 Peachtree Ctr Ave NE Ste 901	Atlanta	GA	30303	**866-687-8561**	404-659-4760
Honduras					
Embassy					
3007 Tilden St NW	Washington	DC	20008	**800-375-5283**	202-966-7702
India					
Consulate General					
540 Arguello Blvd	San Francisco	CA	94118	**866-978-0055**	415-668-0662
Ireland					
Embassy					
2234 Massachusetts Ave NW	Washington	DC	20008	**866-560-1050**	202-462-3939
Italy					
Consulate General					
600 Atlantic Ave 17th Fl	Boston	MA	02210	**888-225-5427**	617-722-9201
Consulate General					
150 S Independence Mall W					
Public Ledger Bldg Ste 1026	Philadelphia	PA	19106	**800-531-0840**	215-592-7329
Consulate General					
1300 Post Oak Blvd Ste 660	Houston	TX	77056	**800-637-9314**	713-850-7520
Consulate General					
12400 Wilshire Blvd Ste 300	Los Angeles	CA	90025	**800-313-7133**	310-820-0622
Embassy					
3000 Whitehaven St NW	Washington	DC	20008	**800-222-1222**	202-612-4400
Kenya Embassy					
2249 R St NW	Washington	DC	20008	**888-502-2642**	202-387-6101
Korea Republic of					
Consulate General					
2033 Sixth Ave Ste 1125	Seattle	WA	98121	**800-375-5283**	206-441-1011
Kuwait Embassy					
2940 Tilden St NW	Washington	DC	20008	**800-688-9889**	202-966-0702
Consulate General					
4506 Carolinas St	Houston	TX	77004	**877-639-4835**	713-271-6800
Micronesia					
Consulate					
1725 N St NW Ste 910	Washington	DC	20036	**877-730-9753**	202-223-4383
Netherlands					
Consulate General					
666 Third Ave 19th Fl	New York	NY	10017	**877-388-2443**	
Consulate General					
303 E Wacker Dr Ste 2600	Chicago	IL	60601	**877-388-2443**	312-856-0110
Embassy					
4200 Linnean Ave NW	Washington	DC	20008	**877-388-2443**	
New Zealand					
Embassy					
37 Observatory Cir NW	Washington	DC	20008	**855-844-2835**	202-328-4800
Peru					
Consulate General					
5177 Richmond Ave 695	Houston	TX	77056	**800-444-1027**	713-355-9517
Consulate General					
870 Market St Ste 1067	San Francisco	CA	94102	**877-714-7378**	415-362-7136
Consulate General					
100 Hamilton Plaza	Paterson	NJ	07505	**877-714-7378**	973-278-3324
Consulate General					
3450 Wilshire Blvd Ste 800	Los Angeles	CA	90010	**800-444-1027**	213-252-5910
Consulate General					
444 Brickell Ave Ste M135	Miami	FL	33131	**877-714-7378**	
Consulate General					
180 N Michigan Ave Ste 1830	Chicago	IL	60601	**877-714-7378**	312-782-1599
Philippines					
Consulate General					
447 Sutter St					
6th Fl Philippine Ctr Bldg	San Francisco	CA	94108	**877-700-0669**	415-433-6666
Consulate General					
30 N Michigan Ave Ste 2100	Chicago	IL	60602	**888-259-7838**	312-332-6458
Consulate General					
3600 Wilshire Blvd Ste 500	Los Angeles	CA	90010	**800-527-2820**	213-639-0980
Consulate General					
556 Fifth Ave	New York	NY	10036	**866-589-1878**	212-764-1330
Embassy					
1600 Massachusetts Ave NW	Washington	DC	20036	**888-373-7888**	202-467-9300
Saint Lucia					
Embassy					
3216 New Mexico Ave NW	Washington	DC	20016	**800-456-3984**	202-364-6792
Consulate General					
1990 Post Oak Blvd Ste 1300	Houston	TX	77056	**888-566-7656**	713-622-5849
Consulate General					
6300 Wilshire Blvd Ste 2010	Los Angeles	CA	90048	**800-874-8875**	323-655-8832
Turkey					
Embassy					
2525 Massachusetts Ave NW	Washington	DC	20008	**877-367-8875**	202-612-6700

260 EMBROIDERY & OTHER DECORATIVE STITCHING

Company	Address	City	State	Zip	Toll-Free	Phone
Branded Emblem Co Inc	7920 Foster St	Overland Park	KS	66204	**800-448-2267**	913-648-0573
CR Daniels Inc	3451 Ellicott Ctr Dr	Ellicott City	MD	21043	**800-933-2638**	410-461-2100
EmbroidMe Inc	2121 Vista Pkwy	West Palm Beach	FL	33411	**877-877-0234**	561-640-7367
Fabri-Quilt Inc	901 E 14th Ave	North Kansas City	MO	64116	**800-279-0622**	816-421-2000
FlagZone LLC	105A Industrial Dr	Gilbertsville	PA	19525	**800-976-4201**	
Herrschners Inc	2800 Hoover Rd	Stevens Point	WI	54481	**800-713-1239**	715-341-8686
Lion Bros Company Inc	10246 Reisterstown Rd	Owings Mills	MD	21117	**800-365-6543***	410-363-1000
	*Cust Svc					
Luv N' Care Ltd	3030 Aurora Ave	Monroe	LA	71201	**800-588-6227**	
Moritz Embroidery Works Inc	1455 Industrial Pk PO Box 187	Mount Pocono	PA	18344	**800-533-4183**	570-839-9600
National Emblem Inc	17036 S Avalon Blvd	Carson	CA	90746	**800-877-6185**	310-515-5055
Penn Emblem Co	10909 Dutton Rd	Philadelphia	PA	19154	**800-793-7366**	
Saint Louis Embroidery	1759 Scherer Pkwy	Saint Charles	MO	63303	**800-457-6676**	636-724-2200
Schweizer Emblem Co	1022 Busse Hwy	Park Ridge	IL	60068	**800-942-5215***	847-292-1022
	*Cust Svc					

261 EMPLOYMENT OFFICES - GOVERNMENT

Company	Address	City	State	Zip	Toll-Free	Phone
Colorado						
Labor & Employment Dept	633 17th St Ste 201	Denver	CO	80203	**800-390-7936**	303-318-8000
Indiana						
Workforce Development Dept	10 N Senate Ave	Indianapolis	IN	46204	**800-891-6499**	317-232-7670
Iowa						
Workforce Development	1000 E Grand Ave	Des Moines	IA	50319	**800-562-4692**	515-281-5387
Louisiana						
Workforce Commission	1001 N 23rd St	Baton Rouge	LA	70802	**877-529-6757**	225-342-3111
Michigan						
Career Education & Workforce Programs	201 N Washington Sq Victor Office Center	Lansing	MI	48913	**888-253-6855**	517-335-5858
Mississippi						
Employment Security Commission	1235 Echelon Pkwy PO Box 1699	Jackson	MS	39215	**888-844-3577**	601-321-6000
New Hampshire (NHES)						
Employment Security	32 S Main St	Concord	NH	03301	**800-852-3400**	603-224-3311
New York						
Labor Dept	WA Harriman Campus Bldg 12	Albany	NY	12240	**888-469-7365**	518-457-9000
Ohio						
Workforce Development Office	4020 E Fifth Ave PO Box 1618	Columbus	OH	43219	**888-296-7541**	

262 EMPLOYMENT SERVICES - ONLINE

Company	Address	City	State	Zip	Toll-Free	Phone
agriCAREERS Inc	613 Main St PO Box 140	Massena	IA	50853	**800-633-8387**	
All-Star Recruiting LLC	4400 W Sample Rd Ste 250	Coconut Creek	FL	33073	**800-928-0229**	
Beyond	1060 First Ave Ste 100	King of Prussia	PA	19406	**800-227-7469**	610-878-2800
Catalyst Awareness Inc	355 Elmira Rd N Ste 127	Guelph	ON	N1K1S5	**866-749-3697**	
ComputerJobs.com Inc	1995 N Pk Pl SE	Atlanta	GA	30339	**800-850-0045**	770-850-0045
Dice Inc	4101 NW Urbandale Dr	Urbandale	IA	50322	**877-386-3323**	515-280-1144
Emerge Financial Wellness Inc	530 Church St Ste 301	Nashville	TN	37219	**800-791-1725**	
EmplawyerNet	2331 Westwood Blvd	Los Angeles	CA	90064	**800-270-2688**	
EmploymentGuide.com	150 Granby St	Norfolk	VA	23510	**877-876-4039**	
ExecUNet Inc	295 Westport Ave	Norwalk	CT	06851	**800-637-3126**	203-750-1030
HealthCareSource Inc	100 Sylvan Rd Ste 100	Woburn	MA	01801	**800-869-5200**	
Industry Specific Solutions LLC	24901 Northwestern Hwy Ste 502	Southfield	MI	48075	**877-356-3450**	
Intellect Resources Inc	3824 N Elm St Ste 102	Greensboro	NC	27455	**877-554-8911**	
International Foundation of Employee Benefit Plans (IFEBP)	18700 W Bluemound Rd	Brookfield	WI	53045	**888-334-3327**	262-786-6700
JobMonkey Inc	PO Box 3956	Seattle	WA	98124	**800-230-1095**	
Jobpostings.ca	100-25 Imperial St	Toronto	ON	M5P1B9	**877-900-5627**	
Kendall & Davis Company Inc	3668 S Geyer Rd Ste 100	St. Louis	MO	63127	**866-675-3755**	
Kovasys Inc	3575 St Laurent Blvd Ste 511	Montreal	QC	H2X2T7	**888-568-2747**	
KWCG Inc	12255 Pkwy Centre Dr	San Diego	CA	92064	**877-464-5924**	
MDT Labor LLC	2325 Paxton Church Rd Ste B	Harrisburg	PA	17110	**888-454-9202**	
National Diversity Newspaper Job Bank *c/o Morris Communications*	725 Broad St	Augusta	GA	30901	**800-622-6358**	706-724-0851
NationJob Inc	920 Morgan St Ste T	Des Moines	IA	50309	**800-292-7731**	
Net-Temps Inc	55 Middlesex St Ste 220	North Chelmsford	MA	01863	**800-307-0062**	978-251-7272
NSTAR Global Services Inc	120 Partlo St	Garner	NC	27529	**877-678-2766**	
Peterson's Nelnet LLC	121 S 13th St Ste 201	Lincoln	NE	68508	**877-338-7772**	609-896-8669
PRN Health Services Inc	4321 W College Ave Ste 200	Appleton	WI	54914	**888-830-8811**	
Run Consultants LLC	925 N Point Pkwy Ste 160	Alpharetta	GA	30005	**866-457-2193**	
Salus Group Benefits Inc	37525 Mound Rd	Sterling Heights	MI	48310	**866-991-9907**	
Skillforce Inc	405 Williams Court Ste 100	Baltimore	MD	21220	**866-581-8989**	
Sprocket Staffing Services	35 Colby Ave	Manasquan	NJ	08736	**800-269-1441**	
Staffworks Group	20505 W 12 Mile Rd	Southfield	MI	48076	**877-304-9690**	
TalentLens Inc	19500 Bulverde Rd	San Antonio	TX	78259	**888-298-6227**	
Targeted Job Fairs Inc	4441 Glenway Ave	Cincinnati	OH	45205	**800-695-1939**	

263 ENGINEERING & DESIGN

SEE ALSO Surveying, Mapping, Related Services

Company	Address	City	State	Zip	Toll-Free	Phone
AKRF Inc	440 Pk Ave S	New York	NY	10016	**800-899-2573**	212-696-0670
Alion Science & Technology	1750 Tysons Blvd Ste 1300	McLean	VA	22102	**877-439-9227**	703-918-4480
AM Kinney	150 E Fourth St Ste 6	Cincinnati	OH	45202	**800-265-3682**	513-421-2265
American Engineering Testing Inc	550 Cleveland Ave N	Saint Paul	MN	55114	**800-972-6364**	651-659-9001
Ams Mechanical Systems Inc	140 E Tower Dr	Burr Ridge	IL	60527	**800-794-5033**	630-887-7700
Anvil Corp	1675 W Bakerview Rd	Bellingham	WA	98226	**877-412-6845**	360-671-1450
Apollo Professional Svc	29 Stiles Rd Ste 302	Salem	NH	03079	**866-277-3343**	
Applied Technology & Management Inc	5550 NW 111th Blvd	Gainesville	FL	32653	**800-275-6488**	
ASG Renaissance	22226 Garrison St	Dearborn	MI	48124	**800-238-0890**	313-565-4700
Astorino	227 Fort Pitt Blvd	Pittsburgh	PA	15222	**800-518-0464**	412-765-1700
Barr Engineering Co	4700 W 77th St	Minneapolis	MN	55435	**800-632-2277**	952-832-2600
Bartlett & West Engineers Inc	1200 SW Executive Dr	Topeka	KS	66615	**888-200-6464**	785-272-2252
Belcan Corp	10200 Anderson Way	Cincinnati	OH	45242	**800-423-5226**	513-891-0972
Bergmann Assoc Inc	28 E Main St 200 1st Federal Plaza	Rochester	NY	14614	**800-724-1168**	585-232-5135
Berryman & Henigar	11590 W Bernardo Ct Ste 100	San Diego	CA	92127	**800-272-9829**	858-451-6100
Bionetics Corp, The	101 Production Dr Ste 100	Yorktown	VA	23693	**800-868-0330**	757-873-0900
BL Cos	355 Research Pkwy	Meriden	CT	06450	**800-301-3077**	203-630-1406
Braun Intertec Corp	11001 Hampshire Ave S	Bloomington	MN	55438	**800-279-6100**	952-995-2000
Bricmont Inc	500 Technology Dr Southpointe Industrial Pk	Canonsburg	PA	15317	**888-274-2462**	724-746-2300
Brinjac Engineering Inc	114 N Second St Ste 1	Harrisburg	PA	17101	**877-274-6526**	717-233-4502
Brock Solutions Inc	86 Ardelt Ave	Kitchener	ON	N2C2C9	**877-702-7625**	519-571-1522
Burgess & Niple Inc	5085 Reed Rd	Columbus	OH	43220	**800-282-1761**	614-459-2050
C & S Companies (CSCOS)	499 Col Eileen Collins Blvd	Syracuse	NY	13212	**877-277-6583**	315-455-2000
Cannon Design	2170 Whitehaven Rd	Grand Island	NY	14072	**800-340-9511**	716-773-6800
Carollo Engineers	2700 Ygnacio Vly Rd Ste 300	Walnut Creek	CA	94598	**800-523-5826**	925-932-1710
CAS Inc	PO Box 11190	Huntsville	AL	35814	**800-729-8686**	256-971-6126
CDI Corporation	1717 Arch St 35th Fl	Philadelphia	PA	19103	**866-472-2203**	215-569-2200
Chemtex International Inc	1979 Eastwood Rd	Wilmington	NC	28403	**877-243-6839**	910-509-4400
Chevron Energy Solutions	345 California St 18th Fl	San Francisco	CA	94104	**800-368-8357**	415-733-4500
Civil & Environmental Consultants Inc	333 Baldwin Rd	Pittsburgh	PA	15205	**800-365-2324**	412-429-2324
Clough Harbour & Assoc (CHA)	Three Winners Cir PO Box 5269	Albany	NY	12205	**800-836-0817**	518-453-4500
Concepts NREC	217 Billings Farm Rd	White River Junction	VT	05001	**888-299-8057**	802-296-2321
Corrpro Cos Inc	1055 W Smith Rd	Medina	OH	44256	**800-443-3516**	330-723-5082
CPH Engineers	500 W Fulton St PO Box 2808	Sanford	FL	32771	**866-609-0688**	
CSS-Dynamac Corp	10301 Democracy Ln Ste 300	Fairfax	VA	22030	**800-888-4612**	703-691-4612
CT Consultants Inc	8150 Sterling Ct	Mentor	OH	44060	**800-925-0988**	440-951-9000

			Toll-Free	Phone
Ctl Engineering Inc PO Box 44548	Columbus OH	43204	**866-366-3832**	614-276-8123
D3 Technologies Inc 4838 Ronson Ct	San Diego CA	92111	**866-487-2365**	858-571-1685
Dataline LLC 7918 Jones Branch Dr Ste 650	McLean VA	22102	**800-666-9858**	703-847-7412
David Evans & Assoc Inc (DEA) 2100 SW River Pkwy	Portland OR	97201	**800-721-1916**	503-223-6663
Dayton T Brown Inc 1175 Church St	Bohemia NY	11716	**800-232-6300**	631-589-6300
Defense Group Inc 307 Annandale Rd Ste 110	Falls Church VA	22042	**877-233-5789**	703-532-0802
DLZ Corp 6121 Huntley Rd	Columbus OH	43229	**800-336-5352**	614-888-0040
Doerfer Engineering Corp PO Box 816	Waverly IA	50677	**877-483-4700**	
Dyer Riddle Mills & Precourt Inc (DRMP) 941 Lk Baldwin Ln	Orlando FL	32814	**800-375-3767**	407-896-0594
E2 Consulting Engineers Inc 450 E 17th Ave Ste 200	Denver CO	80203	**888-772-9773**	303-232-9800
EADS Group 1126 Eigth Ave	Altoona PA	16602	**800-626-0904**	814-944-5035
ENSCO Inc 3110 Fairview Pk Dr Ste 300	Falls Church VA	22042	**800-367-2682**	703-321-9000
Fanning/Howey Assoc Inc 1200 Irmscher Blvd	Celina OH	45822	**888-499-2292**	419-586-2292
Farwest Corrosion Control Co 1480 W Artesia Blvd	Gardena CA	90248	**888-532-7937**	310-532-9524
FATA Hunter Inc 1040 Iowa Ave Ste 100	Riverside CA	92507	**800-248-6837**	951-328-0200
Fay Spofford & Thorndike LLC 5 Burlington Woods	Burlington MA	01803	**800-835-8666**	781-221-1000
Foster Wheeler AG 53 Frontage Rd PO Box 9000	Hampton NJ	08827	**888-288-1464**	908-730-4000
NYSE: LSE				
Fuss & O'Neill Consulting Engineers Inc 146 Hartford Rd	Manchester CT	06040	**800-286-2469**	860-646-2469
Gannett Fleming Inc 207 Senate Ave	Camp Hill PA	17011	**800-233-1055**	717-763-7211
Garver Engineers 4701 Northshore Dr	North Little Rock AR	72118	**800-264-3633**	501-376-3633
GEI Consultants Inc 400 Unicorn Pk Dr	Woburn MA	01801	**888-434-9679**	781-721-4000
GeoEngineers Inc 8410 154th Ave NE	Redmond WA	98052	**888-624-8373**	425-861-6000
GeoSyntec Consultants Inc 5901 Broken Sound Pkwy NW Ste 300	Boca Raton FL	33487	**866-676-1101**	561-995-0900
Ghafari Assoc Inc 17101 Michigan Ave	Dearborn MI	48126	**800-289-7822**	313-441-3000
Greeley & Hansen 100 S Wacker Dr Ste 1400	Chicago IL	60606	**800-837-9779**	312-558-9000
GRW Engineers Inc 801 Corporate Dr	Lexington KY	40503	**800-432-9537**	859-223-3999
Hammel Green & Abrahamson Inc 701 Washington Ave N	Minneapolis MN	55401	**888-442-8255**	612-758-4000
Harris Group Inc 300 Elliott Ave W	Seattle WA	98119	**800-488-7410**	206-494-9400
Hazen & Sawyer PC 498 Seventh Ave 11th Fl.	New York NY	10018	**800-858-9876**	212-777-8400
HDR Engineering Inc 8404 Indian Hills Dr	Omaha NE	68114	**800-366-4411**	402-399-1000
Heery International Inc 999 Peachtree St NE	Atlanta GA	30309	**866-840-3940**	404-881-9880
HMC Archtiect 3546 Councours St	Ontario CA	91764	**800-350-9979**	909-989-9979
Howard R Green Co 8710 Earhart Ln SW	Cedar Rapids IA	52404	**800-728-7805**	319-841-4000
HPD, LLC 23563 W Main St	Plainfield IL	60544	**866-362-0993**	815-609-2000
HRP Associates Inc 197 Scott Swamp Rd	Farmington CT	06032	**800-246-9021**	
Huitt-Zollars Inc 1717 McKinney Ave Ste 1400.	Dallas TX	75202	**866-667-6572**	214-871-3311
IDEO 100 Forest Ave	Palo Alto CA	94301	**866-369-9888**	650-289-3400
Intertek Group PLC 801 Travis St Ste 1500	Houston TX	77002	**800-967-5352**	713-407-3500
Intrinsix Corp 100 Campus Dr	Marlborough MA	01752	**800-783-0330**	508-658-7600
James Machine Works LLC 1521 Adams St	Monroe LA	71201	**800-259-6104**	318-322-6104
John M. Campbell & Co 1215 Crossroads Blvd	Norman OK	73072	**800-821-5933**	405-321-1383
Johnson Mirmiran & Thompson (JMT) 72 Loveton Cir	Sparks MD	21152	**800-472-2310**	410-329-3100
KBR Inc 601 Jefferson St	Houston TX	77002	**866-313-3046**	713-753-2000
KCI Technologies Inc 936 Ridgebrook Rd	Sparks MD	21152	**800-572-7496**	410-316-7800
King Engineering Assoc Inc 4921 Memorial Hwy Ste 300	Tampa FL	33634	**800-723-1403**	813-880-8881
Kratos Defense & Security Solutions Inc 4820 Eastgate Mall Ste 200	San Diego CA	92121	**877-548-7911**	858-332-3700
KSA Engineers Inc 140 E Tyler St Ste 600 Ste 600	Longview TX	75601	**877-572-3647**	903-236-7700
Kta-Tator Inc 115 Technology Dr	Pittsburgh PA	15275	**800-582-4243**	412-788-1300
Larson Design Group Inc 1000 Commerce Pk Dr Ste 201 PO Box 487.	Williamsport PA	17701	**877-323-6603**	570-323-6603
Lauren Engineers & Constructors Inc PO Box 1761	Abilene TX	79604	**800-433-7300**	325-670-9660
LBA Group Inc 3400 Tupper Dr	Greenville NC	27834	**800-522-4464**	252-757-0279
LJB Inc 2500 Newmark Dr PO Box 20246.	Miamisburg OH	45342	**866-552-3536**	937-259-5000
Lumos & Assoc Inc 800 E College Pkwy	Carson City NV	89706	**800-621-7155**	775-883-7077
Macaulay-Brown Inc 4021 Executive Dr	Dayton OH	45430	**800-669-4000**	937-426-3421
Management Consulting Inc 1961 Diamond Springs Rd	Virginia Beach VA	23455	**877-624-8090**	757-460-0879
Marine Systems Corp 70 Fargo St Seaport Ctr	Boston MA	02210	**800-559-9293**	617-542-3345
MBS Assoc Inc 10148 Commerce Pk Dr	Cincinnati OH	45246	**888-469-9301**	513-645-1600
McDonough Bolyard Peck Inc (MBP) 3040 Williams Dr Williams Plz 1 Ste 300	Fairfax VA	22031	**800-898-9088**	703-641-9088
McLaughlin Research Corp 132 Johnnycake Hill Rd	Middletown RI	02842	**800-556-7154**	401-849-4010
MDA Information Systems Inc 6011 Executive Blvd	Rockville MD	20852	**800-642-1687**	240-833-8200
Merrick & Co 2450 S Peoria St	Aurora CO	80014	**800-544-1714**	303-751-0741
Michael Baker Corp 100 Airside Dr Airsite Business Pk.	Moon Township PA	15108	**800-553-1153**	412-269-6300
NYSE: BKR				
Missman Inc 1011 27th Ave PO Box 6040.	Rock Island IL	61201	**800-969-3029**	309-788-7644
Moffatt & Nichol Engineers 3780 Kilroy Airport Way # 750	Long Beach CA	90806	**888-399-6609**	562-590-6500
Moody Nolan Inc 300 Spruce St Ste 300	Columbus OH	43215	**877-530-4984**	614-461-4664
Multax Systems Inc 505 N Sepulveda Blvd Ste 7	Manhattan Beach CA	90266	**800-888-0199**	310-379-8398
Mustang Engineering LP 16001 Pk Ten Pl	Houston TX	77084	**866-313-0052**	713-215-8000
Neel-Schaffer Inc 125 S Congress St Ste 1100.	Jackson MS	39201	**800-264-6335**	601-948-3178
Ninyo & Moore 5710 Ruffin Rd	San Diego CA	92123	**800-427-0401**	858-576-1000
NV5 2525 Natomas Pk Dr Ste 300	Sacramento CA	95833	**877-941-2068**	916-641-9100
Olsson Assoc 1111 Lincoln Mall Ste 111	Lincoln NE	68508	**877-831-6389**	402-474-6311
Operational Technologies Corp 4100 NW Loop 410 Ste 230	San Antonio TX	78229	**855-276-6136**	210-731-0000
Orchard Hiltz & McCliment Inc (OHM) 34000 Plymouth Rd	Livonia MI	48150	**888-522-6711**	734-522-6711
Parkhill Smith & Cooper Inc 4222 85th St	Lubbock TX	79423	**800-400-6646**	806-473-2200
Parsons Corp 100 W Walnut St	Pasadena CA	91124	**800-883-7300***	626-440-2000
*All				
Parsons Infrastructure & Technology 100 W Walnut St	Pasadena CA	91124	**800-300-0287**	626-440-4000
Patrick Engineering Inc 4970 Varsity Dr	Lisle IL	60532	**800-799-7050**	630-795-7200
PCA Engineering Inc 57 Cannonball Rd PO Box 196.	Pompton Lakes NJ	07442	**800-666-7221**	973-616-4501
Perteet Inc 2707 Colby Ave Ste 900 Ste900	Everett WA	98201	**800-615-9900**	425-252-7700
Power Engineering Corp PO Box 766	Wilkes-Barre PA	18703	**800-626-0903**	570-823-8822
PPM Consultants Inc 2508 Ticheli Rd	Monroe LA	71202	**800-761-8675**	318-323-7270
Professional Service Industries Inc (PSI) 1901 S Meyers Rd Ste 400	Oakbrook Terrace IL	60181	**800-548-7901**	630-691-1490
RBF Consulting 14725 Alton Pkwy	Irvine CA	92618	**800-479-3808**	949-472-3505
RCM Technologies Inc 2500 McClellan Ave Ste 350	Pennsauken NJ	08109	**800-322-2885**	856-356-4500
NASDAQ: RCMT				
Rentenbach Engineering Co 2400 Sutherland Ave	Knoxville TN	37919	**877-546-2440**	865-546-2440
Respec Inc 3824 Jet Dr	Rapid City SD	57703	**877-737-7321**	605-394-6400
Rettew Assoc Inc 3020 Columbia Ave	Lancaster PA	17603	**800-738-8395**	717-394-3721
Reynolds Smith & Hills Inc 10748 Deerwood Pk Blvd	Jacksonville FL	32256	**800-741-2014**	904-256-2500
RMF Engineering Inc 5520 Research Pk Dr Third Fl.	Baltimore MD	21228	**800-938-5760**	410-576-0505
S E A Consultants Inc 215 First St Ste 320	Cambridge MA	02142	**855-746-4849**	617-497-7800
SA Healy Co 1910 S Highland Ave Ste 300	Lombard IL	60148	**888-724-3259**	630-678-3110
Sabre Industries Inc 8653 E Hwy 67	Alvarado TX	76009	**866-254-3707**	817-852-1700
Schneider Corp 8901 Otis Ave	Indianapolis IN	46216	**866-973-7100**	317-826-7100
SCS Engineers 3900 Kilroy Airport Way Ste 100	Long Beach CA	90806	**800-326-9544**	562-426-9544
Sebesta Blomberg & Assoc Inc 1450 Energy Park Dr Ste 300	St Paul MN	55108	**877-706-6858**	651-634-0775
Shive-Hattery Inc (SH) 316 Second St SE Ste 500 PO Box 1599.	Cedar Rapids IA	52406	**800-798-0227**	319-362-0313
Short-Elliott-Hendrickson Inc 3535 Vadnais Ctr Dr	Saint Paul MN	55110	**800-325-2055**	651-490-2000
Simpson Gumpertz & Heger Inc 41 Seyon St Bldg 1 Ste 500	Waltham MA	02453	**800-729-7429**	781-907-9000
Snyder & Assoc Inc PO Box 1159	Ankeny IA	50023	**888-964-2020***	515-964-2020
*General				
Sonalysts Inc 215 Waterford Pkwy N	Waterford CT	06385	**800-526-8091**	860-442-4355
SPACECO Inc 9575 W Higgins Rd Ste 700	Rosemont IL	60018	**888-772-2326**	847-696-4060
SPI/Mobile Pulley Works Inc 905 S Ann St	Mobile AL	36605	**866-334-6325**	251-653-0606
Stanley Consultants Inc 225 Iowa Ave	Muscatine IA	52761	**800-553-9694**	563-264-6600
Stantec Inc 400 E Vine St Ste 300.	Lexington KY	40507	**866-782-6832**	859-233-2100
NYSE: STN				
Stratasys Inc 7665 Commerce Way	Eden Prairie MN	55344	**800-937-3010**	952-937-3000
NASDAQ: SSYS				

	City	State	Zip	Toll-Free	Phone
Sullivan International Group Inc 2750 Womble Rd	San Diego	CA	92106	**888-744-1432**	619-260-1432
Sunland Group Inc 1033 La Posada Dr Ste 370	Austin	TX	78752	**866-732-8500**	512-494-0208
Support Systems Assoc Inc (SSAI) 709 S Harbor City Blvd Ste 350	Melbourne	FL	32901	**877-234-7724**	321-724-5566
Syska & Hennessy Group 11 W 42nd St	New York	NY	10036	**800-328-1600**	212-921-2300
Teledyne Brown Engineering Inc 300 Sparkman Dr PO Box 070007	Huntsville	AL	35807	**800-933-2091**	256-726-1000
Terracon 18001 W 106th St	Olathe	KS	66061	**800-593-7777**	913-599-6886
Tetra Tech EC Inc 1000 the American Rd	Morris Plains	NJ	07950	**800-580-3765**	973-630-8000
Tetra Tech/KCM 3475 E Foothill Blvd *NASDAQ: TTEK*	Pasadena	CA	91107	**888-288-8288**	626-351-4664
TLC Engineering for Architecture 255 S Orange Ave # 1600	Orlando	FL	32801	**800-835-9926**	407-841-9050
TransCore Holdings Inc 8158 Adams Dr	Hummelstown	PA	17036	**800-923-4824**	717-561-2400
Truevance Management Inc 7666 Blanding Blvd PO Box 440879	Jacksonville	FL	32244	**800-285-2028**	904-777-9052
Ulteig Engineers Inc 3350 38th Ave S PO Box 9615	Fargo	ND	58104	**888-858-3441**	701-280-8500
Unified Industries Inc 6551 Loisdale Ct Ste 400	Springfield	VA	22150	**800-666-1642**	703-922-9800
United States Steel Corp 600 Grant St *NYSE: X*	Pittsburgh	PA	15219	**866-433-4801**	412-433-1121
UniversalPegasus International Inc 4848 Loop Central Dr *General	Houston	TX	77081	**800-966-1811***	713-977-7770
URS Corp 600 Montgomery St 26th Fl *NYSE: URS*	San Francisco	CA	94111	**877-877-8970**	415-774-2700
Vanadium Group Corp 134 Three Degree Rd	Pittsburgh	PA	15237	**800-685-0354**	412-367-6060
Vanteon Corp 250 Cross Keys Office Pk Bldg 250	Fairport	NY	14450	**888-506-5677**	585-419-9555
Vectech Pharmaceutical Consultants Inc 12501 E Grand River Ave	Brighton	MI	48116	**800-966-8832**	248-478-5820
Veenstra & Kimm Inc 3000 Westown Pkwy	West Des Moines	IA	50266	**800-241-8000**	515-225-8000
Versar Inc 6850 Versar Ctr *NYSE: VSR* ■ *Cust Svc	Springfield	VA	22151	**800-283-7727***	703-750-3000
VSE Corp 2550 Huntington Ave *NASDAQ: VSEC*	Alexandria	VA	22303	**800-455-4873**	703-960-4600
Wade-Trim Group Inc 500 Griswold Ave Ste 2500	Detroit	MI	48226	**800-482-2864**	313-961-3650
Wallace Roberts & Todd LLC 1700 Market St 28th Fl	Philadelphia	PA	19103	**800-978-4450**	215-732-5215
Walter P Moore 1301 Mckinney St Ste 1100	Houston	TX	77010	**800-364-7300**	713-630-7300
Washington Corp PO Box 16630	Missoula	MT	59808	**800-832-7329**	406-523-1300
Weston & Sampson Inc Five Centennial Dr	Peabody	MA	01960	**800-726-7766**	978-532-1900
Willdan 2401 E Katella Ave Ste 300	Anaheim	CA	92806	**800-424-9144**	714-940-6300
Wiss Janney Elstner Assoc Inc 330 Pfingsten Rd	Northbrook	IL	60062	**800-345-3199**	847-272-7400
Woodard & Curran 41 Hutchins Dr	Portland	ME	04102	**800-426-4262**	207-774-2112
Yoder 4899 Commerce Pkwy	Cleveland	OH	44128	**800-631-0520**	216-292-4460
Zephyr Environmental Corp 2600 Via Fortuna Ste 450	Austin	TX	78746	**800-452-5558**	512-329-5544

264 ENGINES & TURBINES

SEE ALSO Motors (Electric) & Generators ; Aircraft Engines & Engine Parts ; Automotive Parts & Supplies - Mfr

	City	State	Zip	Toll-Free	Phone
Arrow Engine Co 2301 E Independence St	Tulsa	OK	74110	**800-331-3662**	918-583-5711
Briggs & Stratton Corp 12301 W Wirth St *NYSE: BGG*	Milwaukee	WI	53222	**800-444-7774**	414-259-5333
Capstone Turbine Corp 21211 Nordhoff St *NASDAQ: CPST*	Chatsworth	CA	91311	**866-422-7786**	818-734-5300
Clayton Industries 17477 Hurley St	City of Industry	CA	91744	**800-423-4585**	626-435-1200
Cummins Inc 500 Jackson St PO Box 3005 *NYSE: CMI*	Columbus	IN	47201	**800-343-7357**	812-377-5000
Delaware Mfg Industries Corp 3776 Commerce Ct	Wheatfield	NY	14120	**800-248-3642**	716-743-4360
Electro Steam Generator Corp 50 Indel Ave PO Box 438	Rancocas	NJ	08073	**866-617-0764**	609-288-9071
EnPro Industries Inc 5605 Carnegie Blvd Ste 500 *NYSE: NPO*	Charlotte	NC	28209	**800-356-6955**	704-731-1500
EnPro Industries Inc Fairbanks Morse Engine 701 White Ave	Beloit	WI	53511	**800-356-6955**	
GE Energy 4200 Wildwood Pkwy	Atlanta	GA	30339	**800-368-1316**	203-373-2211
Hatch & Kirk Inc 5111 Leary Ave NW	Seattle	WA	98107	**800-426-2818**	206-783-2766
Hercules Engine Components Co 2770 S Erie St	Massillon	OH	44646	**800-345-0662**	330-830-2498
JASPER Engines & Transmissions 815 Wernsing Rd PO Box 650	Jasper	IN	47547	**800-827-7455**	812-482-1041
John Deere Power Systems 3801 W Ridgeway Ave PO Box 5100	Waterloo	IA	50704	**800-533-6446**	
KMS Ventures Inc 1301 W 25th St Ste 300	Austin	TX	78705	**844-282-7433**	512-474-6312
Kohler Engines 444 Highland Dr	Kohler	WI	53044	**800-544-2444**	920-457-4441
Northern Lights Inc 4420 14th Ave NW	Seattle	WA	98107	**800-762-0165**	206-789-3880
NREC Power Systems 5222 Hwy 311	Houma	LA	70360	**800-851-6732**	985-872-5480
Pratt & Whitney Canada Inc 1000 Marie-Victorin Blvd	Longueuil	QC	J4G1A1	**800-268-8000**	450-677-9411
Springfield ReManufacturing Corp 650 N Broadview Pl	Springfield	MO	65802	**800-772-7733**	417-862-3501
Volvo Penta of the Americas Inc 1300 Volvo Penta Dr	Chesapeake	VA	23320	**800-522-1959**	757-436-2800
Wartsila North America Inc 16330 Air Ctr Blvd	Houston	TX	77032	**877-927-8745**	281-233-6200
Westerbeke Corp 150 John Hancock Rd Miles Standish Industrial Pk	Taunton	MA	02780	**800-582-7846**	508-823-7677
Western Diesel Services Inc 1100 Research Blvd	Saint Louis	MO	63132	**855-257-6937**	314-868-8620

265 ENVELOPES

	City	State	Zip	Toll-Free	Phone
ADM Corp 100 Lincoln Blvd	Middlesex	NJ	08846	**800-327-0718**	732-469-0900
Alvah Bushnell Co 519 E Chelten Ave	Philadelphia	PA	19144	**800-255-7434**	215-842-9520
AmericanChurch Inc 525 McClurg Rd PO Box 3120	Youngstown	OH	44513	**800-446-3035**	330-758-4545
B & W Press Inc 401 E Main St	Georgetown	MA	01833	**877-246-3467**	978-352-6100
Curtis 1000 Inc 1725 Breckinridge Pkwy Ste 500	Duluth	GA	30096	**877-287-8715**	678-380-9095
Heinrich Envelope Corp 925 Zane Ave N	Minneapolis	MN	55422	**800-346-7957**	763-544-3571
Love Envelopes Inc 10733 E Ute St	Tulsa	OK	74116	**800-532-9747**	918-836-3535
Mackay Envelope Corp 2100 Elm St SE	Minneapolis	MN	55414	**800-622-5299**	
National Church Supply Co, The PO Box 269	Chester	WV	26034	**800-627-9900**	304-387-5200
Papercone Corp 3200 Fern Vly Rd	Louisville	KY	40213	**800-626-5308**	502-961-9493
Poly-Pak Industries Inc 125 Spagnoli Rd	Melville	NY	11747	**800-969-1993**	
Response Envelope Inc 1340 S Baker Ave	Ontario	CA	91761	**800-750-0046**	909-923-5855
Tension Envelope Corp 819 E 19th St	Kansas City	MO	64108	**800-388-5122**	
Top Flight Inc 1300 Central Ave	Chattanooga	TN	37408	**800-777-3740**	423-266-8171
Western States Envelope & Label Co 4480 N 132nd St	Butler	WI	53007	**800-558-0514**	262-781-5540
Worcester Envelope Co 22 Millbury St PO Box 406	Auburn	MA	01501	**800-343-1398**	508-832-5394

266 EQUIPMENT RENTAL & LEASING

SEE ALSO Credit & Financing - Consumer ; Credit & Financing - Commercial ; Fleet Leasing & Management

266-1 Computer Equipment Leasing

	City	State	Zip	Toll-Free	Phone
Data Sales Company Inc 3450 W Burnsville Pkwy	Burnsville	MN	55337	**800-328-2730**	952-890-8838
Electro Rent Corp 6060 Sepulveda Blvd *NASDAQ: ELRC* ■ *Sales	Van Nuys	CA	91411	**800-688-1111***	818-787-2100
First Equipment Co PO Box 2129	Addison	TX	75001	**888-780-8631**	972-380-2300
Newport Leasing Inc 4750 Von Karman Ave *Cust Svc	Newport Beach	CA	92660	**800-274-0042***	949-476-8476
Rent-A-PC Inc 265 Oser Ave	Hauppauge	NY	11788	**800-800-8686**	631-273-8888

266-2 Home & Office Equipment Rental (General)

	City	State	Zip	Toll-Free	Phone
Bestway Inc 12400 Coit Rd Ste 950	Dallas	TX	75251	**800-316-4567**	214-630-6655
Brook Furniture Rental Inc 100 N Field Dr Ste 220	Lake Forest	IL	60045	**877-285-7368**	847-810-4000
Buddy's Home Furnishings 6608 E Adamo Dr	Tampa	FL	33619	**866-779-5085**	
Classic Party Rentals 11766 Wilshire Blvd Ste 350	Los Angeles	CA	90025	**800-678-3854**	310-535-3660
GFC Leasing Co 2675 Research Pk Dr	Madison	WI	53711	**800-333-5905**	800-677-7877
LMG Inc PO Box 770429	Orlando	FL	32877	**888-226-3100**	407-850-0505
Marlin Business Services Inc 300 Fellowship Rd Ste 170 *NASDAQ: MRLN*	Mount Laurel	NJ	08054	**888-479-9111**	
Projection Presentation Technology 5803 Rolling Rd	Springfield	VA	22152	**800-377-7650**	703-912-1334
Rent-A-Center Inc 5501 Headquarters Dr *NASDAQ: RCII*	Plano	TX	75024	**800-422-8186**	

			Toll-Free	Phone
Rug Doctor LP				
4701 Old Shepard Pl	Plano TX	75093	**800-784-3628**	972-673-1400
Somerset Capital Group Ltd				
612 Wheelers Farms Rd	Milford CT	06461	**877-282-9922**	203-701-5100

266-3 Industrial & Heavy Equipment Rental

			Toll-Free	Phone
AH Harris & Son Inc				
367 Alumni Rd	Newington CT	06111	**800-382-6555**	860-665-9494
Ahern Rentals Inc				
4241 Arville St	Las Vegas NV	89103	**800-589-6797**	702-362-0623
Allied Steel Construction Co Inc				
2211 NW First Terr PO Box 1111	Oklahoma City OK	73107	**800-522-4658**	405-232-7531
Broussard Bros Inc				
25817 Louisiana Hwy 333	Abbeville LA	70510	**800-299-5303**	337-893-5303
Buck & Knobby Equipment Co				
6220 Sterns Rd	Ottawa Lake MI	49267	**855-213-2825**	734-856-2811
Cloverdale Equipment Co				
13133 Cloverdale St	Oak Park MI	48237	**888-388-9182**	248-399-6600
Equipment Technology LLC				
341 NW 122nd St	Oklahoma City OK	73114	**888-748-3841**	
Ervin Leasing Co				
3893 Research Pk Dr	Ann Arbor MI	48108	**800-748-0015**	
H & E Equipment Services Inc				
11100 Mead Rd	Baton Rouge LA	70809	**866-467-3682**	225-298-5200
NASDAQ: HEES				
Hawthorne Machinery Co				
16945 Camino San Bernardo	San Diego CA	92127	**800-437-4228**	858-674-7000
HB Rentals LC				
5813 Hwy 90 E	Broussard LA	70518	**800-262-6790**	337-839-1641
Hertz Equipment Rental Corp				
225 Brae Blvd	Park Ridge NJ	07656	**800-654-3131**	201-307-2000
Klochko Equipment Rental Company Inc				
2782 Corbin Ave	Melvindale MI	48122	**800-783-7368**	313-386-7220
Leppo Inc PO Box 154	Tallmadge OH	44278	**800-453-7762**	330-633-3999
Marco Crane & Rigging Co				
221 S 35th Ave	Phoenix AZ	85009	**800-668-2671**	602-272-2671
Maxim Crane Works				
1225 Washington Pk	Bridgeville PA	15017	**877-629-5438**	412-504-0200
Medico Industries Inc				
1500 Hwy 315	Wilkes-Barre PA	18711	**800-633-0027**	570-825-7711
Modern Group 2501 Durham Rd	Bristol PA	19007	**877-879-4188**	
National Construction Rentals Inc				
15319 Chatsworth St	Mission Hills CA	91345	**800-352-5675**	818-221-6000
Norcal Rental Group LLC				
318 Stealth Ct	Livermore CA	94551	**800-649-6629**	925-961-0130
Quantum Analytics				
3400 East Third Ave	Foster City CA	94404	**800-992-4199**	650-312-0900
Raymond Handling Concepts Corp				
41400 Boyce Rd	Fremont CA	94538	**800-675-2500**	510-745-7500
Rush Enterprises Inc				
555 IH 35 S Ste 500	New Braunfels TX	78130	**800-973-7874**	830-626-5200
NASDAQ: RUSHA				
Safway Services Inc				
N 19 W 24200 Riverwood Dr	Waukesha WI	53188	**800-558-4772**	262-523-6500
Skyworks LLC				
100 Thielman Dr	Buffalo NY	14206	**866-983-1184**	716-822-5438
Star Rentals Inc				
1919 Fourth Ave S	Seattle WA	98134	**800-825-7880**	206-622-7880
Stephenson Equipment Inc (SEI)				
7201 Paxton St	Harrisburg PA	17111	**800-325-6455**	717-564-3434
Sunbelt Rentals Inc				
2341 Deerfield Dr	Fort Mill SC	29715	**800-667-9328***	704-348-2676
*General				
Tetra Corporate Services LLC				
6995 Union Park Ctr Suite 360	Salt Lake City UT	84047	**800-417-0548**	801-566-2600
Timco Services Inc				
1724 E Milton Rd	Lafayette LA	70508	**800-749-2054**	337-233-5185
Traffic Control Service Inc				
2435 Lemon Ave	Signal Hill CA	90755	**800-763-3999**	
United Rentals				
3266 E Washington St	Phoenix AZ	85233	**800-624-1808**	602-267-3898
United Rentals Inc				
224 Selleck St	Stamford CT	06902	**800-877-3687**	203-622-3131
NYSE: URI				
Western Oilfields Supply Co				
3404 State Rd	Bakersfield CA	93308	**800-350-7246**	661-399-9124

266-4 Medical Equipment Rental

			Toll-Free	Phone
American Shared Hospital Services				
Four Embarcadero Ctr Ste 3700	San Francisco CA	94111	**800-735-0641**	415-788-5300
NYSE: AMS				
Dynasplint Systems Inc				
770 Ritchie Hwy Ste W21	Severna Park MD	21146	**800-638-6771**	410-544-9530
First Lease Inc				
1300 Virginia Dr Ste 450	Fort Washington PA	19034	**866-493-4778**	
Freedom Medical Inc				
219 Welsh Pool Rd	Exton PA	19341	**800-784-8849**	610-903-0200
Universal Hospital Services Inc				
7700 France Ave S Ste 275	Minneapolis MN	55435	**800-847-7368**	952-893-3200

266-5 Transport Equipment Rental

			Toll-Free	Phone
Andersons Inc Rail Group				
480 W Dussel Dr PO Box 119	Maumee OH	43537	**800-537-3370***	419-893-5050
*General				
Cronos Containers Inc				
1 Front St Ste 925	San Francisco CA	94111	**866-275-3711**	415-677-8990
Flexi-Van Leasing Inc				
251 Monroe Ave	Kenilworth NJ	07033	**866-965-9288**	908-276-8000

			Toll-Free	Phone
GE Rail Car Services				
161 N Clark St 7th Fl	Chicago IL	60601	**800-626-2000**	312-853-5000
Greenbrier Co				
One Centerpointe Dr Ste 200	Lake Oswego OR	97035	**800-343-7188**	503-684-7000
NYSE: GBX				
Railserve Inc				
1691 Phoenix Blvd Ste 110	Atlanta GA	30349	**800-345-7245**	770-996-6838
TTX Co 101 N Wacker Dr	Chicago IL	60606	**800-889-4357**	312-853-3223

267 ETHICS COMMISSIONS

			Toll-Free	Phone
Federal Election Commission				
999 E St NW	Washington DC	20463	**800-424-9530**	202-694-1100
Arkansas				
Ethics Commission				
PO Box 1917	Little Rock AR	72203	**800-422-7773**	501-324-9600
California				
Fair Political Practices Commission				
428 J St Ste 620	Sacramento CA	95814	**866-275-3772**	916-322-5660
Georgia				
Transparency & Campaign Finance Commission				
200 Piedmont Ave SE Ste 1402	Atlanta GA	30334	**866-589-7327**	404-463-1980
Louisiana				
Ethics Board				
617 N Third St				
LaSalle Bldg Ste 10-36	Baton Rouge LA	70802	**800-842-6630**	225-219-5600
Maryland				
Ethics Commission				
45 Calvert St 3rd Fl	Annapolis MD	21401	**877-669-6085**	410-260-7770
Minnesota				
Campaign Finance & Public Disclosure Board				
658 Cedar St Ste 190	Saint Paul MN	55155	**800-657-3889**	651-296-5148
New Mexico				
Ethics Administration				
325 Don Gaspar St Ste 300	Santa Fe NM	87501	**800-477-3632**	505-827-3600
Pennsylvania				
State Ethics Commission				
309 Finance Bldg PO Box 11470	Harrisburg PA	17108	**800-932-0936**	717-783-1610
West Virginia				
Ethics Commission				
210 Brooks St Ste 300	Charleston WV	25301	**866-558-0664**	304-558-0664

268 EXECUTIVE RECRUITING FIRMS

			Toll-Free	Phone
Boyden World Corp				
50 Broadway	Hawthorne NY	10532	**877-226-9336**	914-747-0093
Christian & Timbers				
25825 Science Pk Dr	Cleveland OH	44122	**800-299-9630**	216-464-8710
Cole Warren & Long Inc				
Two Penn Ctr Ste 312	Philadelphia PA	19102	**800-394-8517**	215-563-0701
Daniel & Yeager (D&Y)				
6767 Old Madison Pk Ste 690	Huntsville AL	35806	**800-955-1919**	
Diversified Search Cos				
2005 Market St 33rd Fl	Philadelphia PA	19103	**800-423-3932**	215-732-6666
Egon Zehnder International Inc				
1 N Wacker Dr Ste 2300	Chicago IL	60606	**800-367-3989**	312-260-8800
Korn/Ferry International				
1900 Ave of the Stars Ste 2600	Los Angeles CA	90067	**877-345-3610**	310-552-1834
NYSE: KFY				
Management Recruiters International Worldwide Inc				
1717 Arch St 36th Fl	Philadelphia PA	19103	**800-875-4000**	
Russell Reynolds Assoc Inc				
200 Pk Ave 23rd Fl	New York NY	10166	**800-259-0470**	212-351-2000
Spencer Reed Group Inc				
6900 College Blvd Ste 1	Overland Park KS	66211	**800-477-5035**	913-663-4400
Tyler & Co				
400 Northridge Rd Ste 1250	Atlanta GA	30350	**800-989-6789**	770-396-3939
Witt/Kieffer Ford Hadelman & Lloyd				
2015 Spring Rd Ste 510	Oak Brook IL	60523	**888-281-1370**	630-990-1370

269 EXERCISE & FITNESS EQUIPMENT

SEE ALSO Sporting Goods

			Toll-Free	Phone
Body-Solid Inc				
1900 Des Plaines Ave	Forest Park IL	60130	**800-833-1227**	708-427-3500
Cybex International Inc				
10 Trotter Dr	Medway MA	02053	**888-462-9239**	508-533-4300
NASDAQ: CYBI				
Heartline Fitness Products Inc				
8041 Cessna Ave Ste 200	Gaithersburg MD	20879	**800-262-3348**	301-921-0661
Hoggan Health Industries Inc				
8020 South 1300 West	West Jordan UT	84088	**800-678-7888**	801-572-6500
Hoist Fitness Systems Inc				
9990 Empire St Ste 130	San Diego CA	92126	**800-548-5438**	858-578-7676
HYDRO-FIT Inc 160 Madison St	Eugene OR	97402	**800-346-7295***	541-484-4361
*Cust Svc				
ICON Health & Fitness Inc				
1500 South 1000 West	Logan UT	84321	**800-999-3756**	435-750-5000
IronMaster LLC				
14562 167th Ave SE Ste E	Monroe WA	98272	**800-533-3339**	360-217-7780
Nautilus Inc				
16400 SE Nautilus Dr	Vancouver WA	98684	**800-628-8458**	360-694-7722
NYSE: NLS				
New York Barbells				
160 Home St	Elmira NY	14904	**800-446-1833**	607-733-8038
Paramount Fitness Corp				
6450 E Bandini Blvd	Los Angeles CA	90040	**800-721-2121**	323-721-2121
Precor Inc				
20031 142nd Ave NE	Woodinville WA	98072	**800-786-8404**	425-486-9292
Pro Star Sports Inc				
1133 Winchester Ave	Kansas City MO	64126	**800-821-8482**	816-241-9737

			Toll-Free	Phone
Soloflex Inc				
22590 NW Badertscher Rd	Hillsboro OR	97124	**800-547-8802**	
Spirit Manufacturing Inc				
2601 Commerce Dr	Jonesboro AR	72402	**800-258-4555**	870-935-1107
Star Trac by Unisen Inc				
14410 Myford Rd	Irvine CA	92606	**800-228-6635**	714-669-1660
True Fitness Technology Inc				
865 Hoff Rd	O'Fallon MO	63366	**800-426-6570**	636-272-7100
Vectra Fitness Inc				
7901 S 190th St	Kent WA	98032	**800-283-2872**	425-291-9550
Woodway USA				
W229 N591 Foster Ct	Waukesha WI	53186	**800-966-3929**	262-548-6235
York Barbell Co Inc				
3300 BoaRd Rd	York PA	17406	**800-358-9675***	717-767-6481
*Cust Svc				

270 EXPLOSIVES

			Toll-Free	Phone
Alliant Powder				
2299 Snake River Ave PO Box 6	Lewiston ID	83501	**800-276-9337**	800-379-1732
Austin Powder Co				
25800 Science Pk Dr Ste 300	Cleveland OH	44122	**800-321-0752**	216-464-2400
Buckley Powder Co				
42 Inverness Dr E	Englewood CO	80112	**800-333-2266**	303-790-7007
Dyno Nobel Inc				
2795 E Cottonwood Pkwy Ste 500	Salt Lake City UT	84121	**800-473-2675**	801-364-4800
Schaefer Pyrotechnics Inc				
376 Hartman Bridge Rd	Ronks PA	17572	**877-598-2264**	717-687-0647
Special Devices Inc				
14370 White Sage Rd	Moorpark CA	93021	**888-782-0082**	805-553-1200

271 EYE BANKS

SEE ALSO Transplant Centers - Blood Stem Cell ; Organ & Tissue Banks
Eye banks listed here are members of the Eye Bank Association of America (EBAA), an accrediting body for eye banks. The EBAA medical standards for member eye banks are endorsed by the American Academy of Ophthalmology.

			Toll-Free	Phone
Alabama Eye Bank				
500 Robert Jemison Rd	Birmingham AL	35209	**800-423-7811**	
Alcon Laboratories Inc				
6201 S Fwy	Fort Worth TX	76134	**800-862-5266**	817-293-0450
Center for Organ Recovery & Education (CORE)				
204 Sigma Dr RIDC Pk	Pittsburgh PA	15238	**800-366-6777**	412-963-3550
Donor Network of Arizona				
201 W Coolidge St	Phoenix AZ	85013	**800-447-9477**	602-222-2200
Eye Bank Assn of America (EBAA)				
1015 18th St NW Ste 1010	Washington DC	20036	**888-491-8833**	202-775-4999
Eye Bank for Sight Restoration Inc				
120 Wall St 3rd Fl	New York NY	10005	**866-287-3937**	212-742-9000
Heartland Lions Eye Bank				
10100 N Ambassador Dr Ste 200	Kansas City MO	64153	**800-756-4824**	816-454-5454
Idaho Lions Eye Bank				
1090 N Cole Rd	Boise ID	83704	**800-546-6889**	208-338-5466
International Cornea Project				
9246 Lightwave Ave Ste 120	San Diego CA	92123	**800-393-2265**	858-694-0400
International Sight Restoration Inc				
3808 Gunn Hwy Ste B	Tampa FL	33618	**877-477-3210**	813-264-6003
LABS Inc				
6933 S Revere Pkwy	Centennial CO	80112	**866-393-2244**	720-528-4750
LifePoint Inc				
3950 Faber Pl Dr	Charleston SC	29405	**800-462-0755**	843-763-7755
LifeShare of the Carolinas				
1200 Ridgefield Blvd Ste 150	Asheville NC	28806	**800-932-4483**	828-665-0107
Lions Eye Bank of Manitoba & Northwest Ontario Inc				
691 Wolseley Ave	Winnipeg MB	R3G1C3	**800-552-6820**	204-788-8507
Lions Eye Bank of Nebraska Inc				
University of Nebraska Medical Ctr				
UNMC 985541	Omaha NE	68198	**800-225-7244**	402-559-4039
Lions Eye Bank of North Dakota				
410 E Thayer Ave Ste 201	Bismarck ND	58501	**800-372-3751**	701-250-9390
Lions Eye Bank of Wisconsin				
2401 American Ln	Madison WI	53704	**877-233-2354**	608-233-2354
Lions Medical Eye Bank & Research Ctr of Eastern Virginia Inc				
600 Gresham Dr	Norfolk VA	23507	**800-453-6059**	
Lone Star Lions Eye Bank				
102 E Wheeler St PO Box 347	Manor TX	78653	**800-977-3937**	512-457-0638
Medical Eye Bank of Maryland				
815 Pk Ave	Baltimore MD	21201	**800-756-4824**	410-752-2020
Midwest Eye Banks				
4889 Venture Dr	Ann Arbor MI	48108	**800-247-7250**	734-780-2100
Minnesota Lions Eye Bank				
1000 Westgate Dr Ste 260	Saint paul MN	55114	**866-887-4448***	612-625-5159
*Cust Svc				
National Disease Research Interchange (NDRI)				
1628 John F Kennedy Blvd				
8 Penn Ctr 8th Fl	Philadelphia PA	19103	**800-222-6374**	215-557-7361
New Mexico Lions Eye Bank				
2501 Yale Blvd SE Ste 100	Albuquerque NM	87106	**888-616-3937**	505-266-3937
North Carolina Eye Bank Inc				
3900 Westpoint Blvd Ste F	Winston-Salem NC	27103	**800-552-9956**	336-765-0932
Oregon Lions Sight & Hearing Foundation				
1010 NW 22nd Ave Ste 144	Portland OR	97210	**800-635-4667**	503-413-7399
Regional Tissue Bank QEII Health Sciences Centre				
5788 University Ave				
Rm 431 MacKenzie Bldg	Halifax NS	B3H1V7	**800-314-6515**	902-473-4171
Rochester Eye & Tissue Bank				
524 White Spruce Blvd	Rochester NY	14623	**800-568-4321**	585-272-7890
Rocky Mountain Lions Eye Bank (RMLEB)				
1675 Aurora Crt Ste EI2049 PO Box 6026	Aurora CO	80045	**800-444-7479**	720-848-3937
San Diego Eye Bank (SDEB)				
9246 Lightwave Ave Ste 120	San Diego CA	92123	**800-393-2265**	858-694-0400

			Toll-Free	Phone
Sight Society of Northeastern New York Inc				
Lions Eye Bank at Albany				
6 Executive Pk Dr	Albany NY	12203	**888-615-3937**	518-489-7606
SightLife				
221 Yale Ave N Ste 450	Seattle WA	98109	**800-847-5786**	206-682-8500
South Dakota Lions Eye Bank				
4501 W 61st St N	Sioux Falls SD	57107	**800-245-7846**	605-373-1008
Upstate New York Transplant Services Inc				
110 Broadway	Buffalo NY	14203	**800-227-4771**	716-853-6667
Western Texas Lions Eye Bank Alliance				
2030 Pullman St Ste 4	San Angelo TX	76902	**866-226-7632**	325-653-8666

272 FABRIC STORES

SEE ALSO Patterns - Sewing

			Toll-Free	Phone
Everfast Inc				
203 Gale Ln	Kennett Square PA	19348	**800-213-6366***	610-444-9700
*Cust Svc				
Jo-Ann Fabrics & Crafts				
5555 Darrow Rd	Hudson OH	44236	**888-739-4120**	330-656-2600
Jo-Ann Stores Inc (JAS)				
5555 Darrow Rd	Hudson OH	44236	**888-739-4120**	330-656-2600
Mary Maxim Inc				
2001 Holland Ave PO Box 5019	Port Huron MI	48061	**800-962-9504**	810-987-2000

273 FACILITIES MANAGEMENT SERVICES

SEE ALSO Correctional & Detention Management (Privatized)

			Toll-Free	Phone
ARAMARK Uniform & Career Apparel LLC				
1101 Market St	Philadelphia PA	19107	**800-272-6275**	
Delaware North Cos Gaming & Entertainment				
40 Fountain Plz	Buffalo NY	14202	**800-828-7240**	716-858-5000
Delaware North Cos Parks & Resorts				
40 Fountain Plz	Buffalo NY	14202	**800-828-7240**	716-858-5000
IAP Worldwide Services Inc				
7315 N Atlantic Ave	Cape Canaveral FL	32920	**877-296-8010**	321-784-7100
New York State Bridge Authority				
PO Box 1010	Highland NY	12528	**800-333-8655**	845-691-7245
OMNIPLEX World Services Corp				
14151 Pk Meadow Dr Ste 300	Chantilly VA	20151	**800-356-3406**	703-652-3100
Philotechnics Ltd				
201 Renovare Blvd	Oak Ridge TN	37830	**888-723-9278**	865-483-1551
Phoenix Park 'n Swap				
3801 E Washington St	Phoenix AZ	85034	**800-772-0852**	602-273-1250
United Space Alliance (USA)				
600 Gemini Ave	Houston TX	77058	**800-367-5690**	281-212-6200
Viox Services Inc				
15 W Voorhees St	Cincinnati OH	45215	**888-846-9462**	513-948-8469
Xanterra Parks & Resorts				
6312 S Fiddlers Green Cir				
Ste 600-N	Greenwood Village CO	80111	**800-236-7916**	303-600-3400

274 FACTORS

Factors are companies that buy accounts receivable (invoices) from other businesses at a discount.

			Toll-Free	Phone
Accounts Receivable Funding Corp (ARFC)				
PO Box 35750	Houston TX	77235	**800-992-1717**	
Action Capital Corp				
230 Peachtree St Ste 910	Atlanta GA	30343	**800-525-7767**	404-524-3181
Advantage Funding Corp				
1000 Parkwood Cir SE	Atlanta GA	30339	**800-241-2274**	770-955-2274
AmeriFactors				
215 Celebration Pl Ste 340	Celebration FL	34747	**800-884-3863**	407-566-1150
Asta Funding Inc				
210 Sylvan Ave	Englewood Cliffs NJ	07632	**866-389-7627**	201-567-5648
NASDAQ: ASFI				
Bibby Financial Services				
1901 South Congress ave				
Ste 150	Boynton Beach, FL	33426	**877-882-4229**	
Crestmark Bank				
5480 Corporate Dr Ste 350	Troy MI	48098	**888-999-8050**	
Diversified Funding Services Inc				
255 N Main St Ste 873	Jonesboro GA	30237	**888-603-0055**	770-603-0055
Goodman Factors				
3010 LBJ Fwy Ste 140	Dallas TX	75234	**877-446-6362**	972-241-3297
Hamilton Group				
100 Elwood Davis Rd	North Syracuse NY	13212	**800-351-3066**	315-413-0086
LSQ Funding Group LC				
2600 Lucien Way Ste 100	Maitland FL	32751	**800-474-7606**	
Magnolia Financial Inc				
187 W Broad St	Spartanburg SC	29306	**866-573-0611**	864-573-9900
Mazon Assoc Inc				
800 W Airport Fwy Ste 900	Irving TX	75062	**800-442-2740**	972-554-6967
Merchant Factors Corp				
1441 Broadway 22nd Fl	New York NY	10018	**800-929-3293***	212-840-7575
*All				
Porter Capital Corp				
2112 First Ave N	Birmingham AL	35203	**800-737-7344**	205-322-5442
Quantum Corporate Funding Ltd				
1140 Ave of the Americas 16th Fl	New York NY	10036	**800-352-2535**	212-768-1200
Riviera Finance				
220 Ave I	Redondo Beach CA	90277	**800-872-7484**	
Rosenthal & Rosenthal Inc				
1370 Broadway	New York NY	10018	**800-999-4800**	212-356-1400
RTS Financial Service				
8601 Monrovia	Lenexa KS	66215	**877-242-4390**	
Seven Oaks Capital Assoc LLC				
7854 Anselmo Ln PO Box 82360	Baton Rouge LA	70810	**800-511-4588**	225-757-1919

Company	City	State	ZIP	Toll-Free	Phone
TCE Capital Corp 505 Consumers Rd Ste 707	Toronto	ON	M2J4V8	**800-465-0400**	416-497-7400

275 FARM MACHINERY & EQUIPMENT - MFR

SEE ALSO Lawn & Garden Equipment

Company	City	State	ZIP	Toll-Free	Phone
ADM Alliance Nutrition Inc 1000 N 30th St	Quincy	IL	62301	**800-292-3333**	217-222-7100
AGCO Corp (AGCO) 4205 River Green Pkwy *NYSE: AGCO*	Duluth	GA	30096	**877-525-4384**	770-813-9200
Alamo Group Inc 1627 E Walnut *NYSE: ALG ■ *Cust Svc*	Seguin	TX	78155	**800-788-6066***	830-379-1480
All-American Co-op PO Box 125	Stewartville	MN	55976	**888-354-4058**	507-533-4222
Allied Systems Co 21433 SW Oregon St	Sherwood	OR	97140	**800-285-7000**	503-625-2560
Amarillo Wind Machine Co 20513 Ave 256	Exeter	CA	93221	**800-311-4498**	559-592-4256
Arts-Way Mfg Co Inc 5556 Hwy 9 PO Box 288 *NASDAQ: ARTW*	Armstrong	IA	50514	**800-535-4517**	712-864-3131
Automatic Equipment Manufacturing Co One Mill Rd Industrial Pk	Pender	NE	68047	**800-228-9289**	402-385-3051
B & H Manufacturing Inc 141 County Rd 34 E	Jackson	MN	56143	**800-240-3288**	507-847-2802
Berg Equipment Co 2700 W Veterans Pkwy	Marshfield	WI	54449	**800-494-1738**	715-384-2151
Bowie Industries Inc 1004 E Wise St	Bowie	TX	76230	**800-433-0934**	940-872-1106
Brillion Iron Works Inc 200 Pk Ave PO Box 127	Brillion	WI	54110	**855-320-0373**	920-756-2121
Brock Grain Systems 611 N Higbee St P.O. Box 2000	Milford	IN	46542	**800-541-7900**	574-658-4191
Brown Mfg Corp 6001 E Hwy 27	Ozark	AL	36360	**800-633-8909**	
Broyhill Co One N Market Sq	Dakota City	NE	68731	**800-228-1003**	402-987-3412
Bucklin Tractor & Implement Co 115 W Railroad PO Box 127	Bucklin	KS	67834	**800-334-4823**	620-826-3271
Buhler Versatile Inc 1260 Clarence Ave	Winnipeg	MB	R3T1T2	**888-524-1003**	204-661-8711
Cal-Coast Dairy Systems Inc 424 S Tegner Rd *Cust Svc	Turlock	CA	95380	**800-732-6826***	209-634-9026
Chick Master Incubator Co 945 Lafayette Rd PO Box 704	Medina	OH	44258	**800-727-8726**	330-722-5591
Conrad-American Inc PO Box 2000 *General	Houghton	IA	52631	**800-553-1791***	
CTB Inc 611 N Higbee St PO Box 2000	Milford	IN	46542	**800-261-8651**	574-658-4191
Custom Products of Litchfield Inc 1715 S Sibley Ave	Litchfield	MN	55355	**800-222-5463**	320-693-3221
Dig Corp 1210 Activity Dr	Vista	CA	92081	**800-322-9146**	760-727-0914
DuraTech Industries International Inc PO Box 1940	Jamestown	ND	58401	**800-243-4601**	701-252-4601
EVH Mfg Company LLC 4895 Red Bluff Rd	Loris	SC	29569	**888-990-2555**	843-756-2555
EZ Trail Inc 1050 E Columbia St PO Box 168	Arthur	IL	61911	**800-677-2802**	217-543-3471
Fabrication JR Tardif Inc 62 Blvd Cartier	Rivi Re-Du-Loup	QC	G5R6B2	**877-962-7273**	418-862-7273
Finn Corp 9281 Le St Dr	Fairfield	OH	45014	**800-543-7166**	513-874-2818
Forsbergs Inc 1210 Pennington Ave PO Box 510 *Cust Svc	Thief River Falls	MN	56701	**800-654-1927***	218-681-1927
Gandy Co 528 Gandrud Rd	Owatonna	MN	55060	**800-443-2476**	507-451-5430
GMP Metal Products Inc 3883 Delor St	Saint Louis	MO	63116	**800-325-9808**	314-481-0300
Hagie Manufacturing Co PO Box 273	Clarion	IA	50525	**800-247-4885**	515-532-2861
Hardi Inc 1500 W 76th St	Davenport	IA	52806	**866-770-7063**	563-386-1730
Hastings Equity Grain Bin Mfg Co 1900 Summit Ave	Hastings	NE	68901	**888-883-2189**	402-462-2189
HCC Inc 1501 First Ave	Mendota	IL	61342	**800-548-6633**	815-539-9371
HD Hudson Manufacturing Co 500 N Michigan Ave Ste 2300	Chicago	IL	60611	**800-977-7293**	312-644-2830
Heartland Equipment Inc 2100 N Falls Blvd	Wynne	AR	72396	**800-530-7617**	
Henderson Manufacturing Inc 1085 S Third St	Manchester	IA	52057	**800-359-4970**	563-927-2828
Herschel-Adams Inc 1301 N 14th St	Indianola	IA	50125	**800-247-2167**	
Hiniker Co 58766 240th St	Mankato	MN	56002	**800-433-5620**	507-625-6621
Hutchinson/Mayrath/TerraTrack Industries 514 W Crawford PO Box 629	Clay Center	KS	67432	**800-523-6993**	785-632-2161
Jamesway Incubator Co Inc 30 High Ridge Ct	Cambridge	ON	N1R7L3	**800-438-8077**	519-624-4646
KBH Corp, The 395 Anderson Blvd	Clarksdale	MS	38614	**800-843-5241**	662-624-5471
Kelley Manufacturing Co 80 Vernon Dr PO Box 1467	Tifton	GA	31793	**800-444-5449**	229-382-9393
Kelly Ryan Equipment Co 900 Kelly Ryan Dr	Blair	NE	68008	**800-640-6967**	402-426-2151
KMW Ltd PO Box 327	Sterling	KS	67579	**800-445-7388**	620-278-3641
Kubota Tractor Corp 3401 Del Amo Blvd	Torrance	CA	90503	**888-458-2682**	310-370-3370
Lindsay Corp 2222 N 111th St *NYSE: LNN*	Omaha	NE	68164	**866-404-5049**	402-829-6800
Loftness Specialized Farm Equipment Inc 650 S Main St PO Box 337	Hector	MN	55342	**800-828-7624**	320-848-6266
Mathews Co 500 Industrial Ave	Crystal Lake	IL	60012	**800-323-7045**	815-459-2210
Mertz Mfg LLC 1701 N Waverly St	Ponca City	OK	74601	**800-654-6433**	580-762-5646
Miller Saint Nazianz Inc 511 E Main St	Saint Nazianz	WI	54232	**800-247-5557**	920-773-2121
Orthman Manufacturing Inc 75765 Rd 435 PO Box 638	Lexington	NE	68850	**800-658-3270**	308-324-4654
Osborne Industries Inc 120 N Industrial Ave	Osborne	KS	67473	**800-255-0316**	785-346-2192
Precision Tank & Equipment Company Inc 3503 Conover Rd	Virginia	IL	62691	**800-258-4197**	217-452-7228
Reinke Mfg Co Inc 5325 Reinke Rd	Deshler	NE	68340	**866-365-7381**	402-365-7251
Root-Lowell Manufacturing Co 1000 Foreman Rd PO Box 289	Lowell	MI	49331	**800-748-0098**	616-897-9211
Scranton Mfg Company Inc 101 State St PO Box 336	Scranton	IA	51462	**800-831-1858**	712-652-3396
Shivvers Inc 614 W English St	Corydon	IA	50060	**800-245-9093**	641-872-1005
Simonsen Industries Inc 500 Iowa 31	Quimby	IA	51049	**800-831-4860**	712-445-2211
Sioux Steel Co 196 1/2 E Sixth St	Sioux Falls	SD	57104	**800-557-4689**	605-336-1750
Stock Equipment Co 16490 Chillicothe Rd	Chagrin Falls	OH	44023	**888-742-1249**	440-543-6000
Sudenga Industries Inc 2002 Kingbird Ave	George	IA	51237	**888-783-3642**	712-475-3301
Sun Circle Inc 286 S G St	Arcata	CA	95521	**800-458-6543**	707-822-5777
T-l Irrigation Co 151 E Hwy 6 AB Rd PO Box 1047	Hastings	NE	68902	**800-330-4264**	402-462-4128
Top Air Sprayers 601 S Broad St	Kalida	OH	45853	**800-322-6301**	419-532-3121
Toro Co Irrigation Div 5825 Jasmine St	Riverside	CA	92504	**800-654-1882**	
Unverferth Mfg Company Inc 601 S Broad St	Kalida	OH	45853	**800-322-6301**	419-532-3121
Valmont Industries Inc One Valmont Plz *NYSE: VMI*	Omaha	NE	68154	**800-825-6668**	402-963-1000
Wiese Industries Inc 1501 Fifth St PO Box 39	Perry	IA	50220	**800-568-4391**	515-465-9854
Woods Equipment Co 2606 S Illinois Rt 2 PO Box 1000	Oregon	IL	61061	**800-319-6637**	815-732-2141
Wylie Spray Center 702 E 40th St	Lubbock	TX	79404	**888-249-5162**	806-763-1335
Yetter Manufacturing Inc 109 S McDonough St PO Box 358	Colchester	IL	62326	**800-447-5777**	309-776-4111

276 FARM MACHINERY & EQUIPMENT - WHOL

Company	City	State	ZIP	Toll-Free	Phone
Abilene Machine Inc PO Box 129	Abilene	KS	67410	**800-255-0337**	785-655-9455
Ag West Supply Inc 9055 Rickreall Rd	Rickreall	OR	97371	**800-842-2224**	503-363-2332
Agri-Service 3204 Kimberly Rd E	Twin Falls	ID	83301	**800-388-3599**	208-734-7772
Arends & Sons Inc 715 S Sangamon Ave	Gibson City	IL	60936	**800-637-6052**	217-784-4241
Arends Bros Inc 1190 E 1200N Rd	Melvin	IL	60952	**800-356-6811**	217-388-7717
Barnett Implement Co Inc 4220 Old Hwy 99 S	Snohomish	WA	98273	**800-453-9274**	425-334-4048
BE Implement Co 1645 FM 403 PO Box 752	Brownfield	TX	79316	**800-725-5435**	806-637-3594
Belarus Tractor International Inc 7842 N Faulkner Rd	Milwaukee	WI	53224	**800-356-2336**	
Bell Equipment Inc 511 Fourth St	Nezperce	ID	83543	**800-343-2355**	208-937-2402
Berchtold Equipment Co Inc 330 E 19th St	Bakersfield	CA	93305	**800-691-7817**	661-323-7817
Blanchard Compact Equipment 1410 Ashville Hwy	Spartanburg	SC	29303	**888-799-3606**	864-582-1245
Burks Tractor Co Inc 3140 Kimberly Rd	Twin Falls	ID	83301	**800-247-7419**	208-733-5543
Carco International Inc 2721 Midland Blvd	Fort Smith	AR	72904	**800-824-3215**	479-441-3270
Carrico Implement Company Inc 3160 US 24 Hwy	Beloit	KS	67420	**877-542-4099**	785-738-5744
Delta Implement Co Inc 3180 U.S. 82	Greenville	MS	38703	**800-264-2741**	662-332-2683
Farm Implement & Supply Company Inc 1200 S Washington Hwy 183	Plainville	KS	67663	**888-589-6029**	785-434-4824
Farmer Boy Ag Systems Inc PO Box 435	Myerstown	PA	17067	**800-845-3374**	
Farmers Supply Sales Inc 1409 E Ave	Kalona	IA	52247	**800-493-4917**	319-656-2291
Gardner Inc 3641 Interchange Rd	Columbus	OH	43204	**800-848-8946**	614-456-4000
Garton Tractor Inc 2400 N Golden State Blvd	Turlock	CA	95382	**877-872-2767**	209-632-3931
Giles & Ransome Inc Ransome Engine Power Div 2975 Galloway Rd	Bensalem	PA	19020	**877-726-7663**	215-639-4300
Golden Spike Equipment Co 1352 W Main St PO Box 70	Tremonton	UT	84337	**800-821-4474**	435-257-5346
Greenline Equipment 14750 S Pony Express Rd	Bluffdale	UT	84065	**888-201-5500**	801-966-4231
Grossenburg Implement Inc 31341 US Hwy 18	Winner	SD	57580	**800-658-3440**	605-842-2040
Harcourt Equipment 313 Hwy 169 & 175 E	Harcourt	IA	50544	**800-445-5646**	515-354-5332
HB Duvall Inc 901 E Patrick St PO Box 70	Frederick	MD	21701	**800-325-2252**	301-662-1125
Hillsboro Equipment Inc E18898 Hwy 33	Hillsboro	WI	54634	**800-521-5133**	608-489-2275
Hollingsworth Inc 1775 SW 30th St	Ontario	OR	97914	**800-541-1612**	541-889-7254

Classified Section

	Toll-Free	Phone
HOLT Texas Ltd 3302 S WW White Rd . . . . San Antonio TX 78222	800-275-4658	210-648-1111
Hoober Inc 3452 Old Philadelphia Pk PO Box 518. . . . . Intercourse PA 17534	800-732-0017	717-768-8231
Hultgren Implements Inc 5698 State Hwy 175 . . . . Ida Grove IA 51445	800-827-1650	712-364-3105
Hurst Farm Supply Inc 105 Ave D . . . . Abernathy TX 79311	800-535-8903	806-298-2541
JD Equipment Inc 1660 US 42 NE . . . . London OH 43140	800-659-5646	614-879-6620
Jerry Pate Turf & Irrigation Inc 301 Schubert Dr . . . . Pensacola FL 32504	800-700-7004	850-479-4653
John Day Co 6263 Abbott Dr . . . . Omaha NE 68110	800-767-2273	402-455-8000
Larchmont Engineering & Irrigation Co 11 Larchmont Ln PO Box 66. . . . . Lexington MA 02420	877-862-2550	781-862-2550
Liechty Farm Equipment Inc 1701 S Defiance St . . . . Archbold OH 43502	800-272-5898	419-445-1565
Littau Harvester Inc 855 Rogue Ave . . . . Stayton OR 97383	866-262-2495	503-769-5953
Mid-State Equipment Inc W 1115 Bristol Rd . . . . Columbus WI 53925	877-677-4020	920-623-4020
Peterson Tractor Co 955 Marina Blvd . . . . San Leandro CA 94577	800-590-5945	510-357-6200
Premier Equipment LLC 2025 US Hwy 14 W . . . . Huron SD 57350	800-627-5469	605-352-7100
RDO Equipment Co 3401 38th St S . . . . Fargo ND 58104	800-342-4643	701-282-5400
Revels Tractor Company Inc 2217 N Main St . . . . Fuquay-Varina NC 27526	800-849-5469	919-552-5697
Rockingham New Holland Inc 600 W Market St . . . . Harrisonburg VA 22802	888-864-5503	540-434-6791
Roeder Implement Inc 2550 Rockdale Rd . . . . Dubuque IA 52003	800-557-1184	563-557-1184
SEMA Equipment Inc 11555 Hwy 60 Blvd . . . . Wanamingo MN 55983	800-569-1377	507-824-2256
Simpson Norton Corp 4144 S Bullard Ave . . . . Goodyear AZ 85338	877-859-8676	623-932-5116
Sioux Automation Ctr Inc 877 First Ave NW . . . . Sioux Center IA 51250	866-722-1488	712-722-1488
Sloan Implement Co 120 N Business 51 . . . . Assumption IL 62510	800-745-4020	217-226-4411
Spartan Distributors Inc 487 W Div St . . . . Sparta MI 49345	800-822-2216	616-887-7301
Straub International Inc 214 SW 40th Ave PO Box 1606 . . . . Great Bend KS 67530	800-658-1706	620-792-5256
Teeter Irrigation Inc 2729 W Oklahoma . . . . Ulysses KS 67880	800-524-5497	620-353-1111
Tom Hassenfritz Equipment Co 1300 W Washington St . . . . Mount Pleasant IA 52641	800-634-4885	319-385-3114
Tractor Supply Co 200 Powell Pl . . . . Brentwood TN 37027 *NASDAQ: TSCO*	877-718-6750	
Van-Wall Equipment Inc 22728 141st Dr PO Box 575 . . . . Perry IA 50220	800-568-2381	515-465-5681
Washington County Tractor Inc PO Box 1619 . . . . Brenham TX 77834	800-256-5655	979-836-4591
White's Inc 4614 Navigation Blvd PO Box 2344 . . . . Houston TX 77011	800-231-9559	713-928-2632
Witmer's Inc 39821 SR 14 . . . . Salem OH 44460	888-427-6025	330-427-2147
Wyatt-Quarles Seed Co 730 US Hwy 70 W . . . . Garner NC 27529	800-662-7591	919-772-4243

277 FARM PRODUCT RAW MATERIALS

	Toll-Free	Phone
Alliance Grain Co 1306 W Eigth St . . . . Gibson City IL 60936	800-222-2451	217-784-4284
Aurora Co-op Elevator Co 605 12th St PO Box 209 . . . . Aurora NE 68818	800-642-6795	402-694-2106
Cargill Inc 15407 McGinty Rd W . . . . Wayzata MN 55391	800-227-4455	952-742-7575
Central Connecticut Co-op Farmers Assn 10 Apel Pl PO Box 8500 . . . . Manchester CT 06042	800-640-4523	860-649-4523
Central Iowa Co-op 2829 Westown Pkwy Ste 350 . . . . West Des Moines IA 50266	800-513-3938	515-225-1334
Ceres Solutions LLP 2112 Indianapolis Rd PO Box 432 . . . . Crawfordsville IN 47933 *General	800-878-0952*	765-362-6700
Co-Alliance LLP 5250 E US Hwy 36 Bldg 1000 . . . . Avon IN 46123	800-525-0272	317-745-4491
Co-op Elevator Co 7211 E Michigan Ave . . . . Pigeon MI 48755	800-968-0601	989-453-4500
Effingham Equity Inc 201 W Roadway Ave . . . . Effingham IL 62401	800-223-1337	217-342-4101
Farmers Co-op 208 W Depot . . . . Dorchester NE 68343	800-642-6439	402-946-2211
Frontier Co-op 211 S Lincoln PO Box 37 . . . . Brainard NE 68626	800-869-0379	402-545-2811
Heartland Co-op 2829 Westown Pkwy Ste 350 . . . . West Des Moines IA 50266	800-513-3938	515-225-1334
Italgrani USA Inc 7900 Van Buren St . . . . Saint Louis MO 63111	800-274-1274	314-638-1447
Joy Dog Food PO Box 305 . . . . Pinckneyville IL 62274	800-245-4125	
MaxYield Co-op 313 Third Ave NE PO Box 49 . . . . West Bend IA 50597	800-383-0003	515-887-7211
NEW Co-op Inc 2626 First Ave S . . . . Fort Dodge IA 50501	800-362-2233	515-955-2040
Northwest Grain Growers Inc 850 N Fourth Ave . . . . Walla Walla WA 99362	800-994-4290	509-525-6510
Parrish & Heimbecker Ltd (P&H) 201 Portage Ave Ste 1400 . . . . Winnipeg MB R3B3K6	800-665-8937	204-956-2030
Pendleton Grain Growers Inc 1000 SW Dorian St PO Box 1248 . . . . Pendleton OR 97801	800-422-7611	541-276-7611

	Toll-Free	Phone
Plains Cotton Co-op Assn 3301 E 50th St PO Box 2827 . . . . Lubbock TX 79408	800-333-8011	806-763-8011
Scoular Co 2027 Dodge St . . . . Omaha NE 68102	800-488-3500	402-342-3500
South Dakota Wheat Growers Assn 908 Lamont St SE . . . . Aberdeen SD 57401	888-429-4902	605-225-5500
Staplcotn Co-op Assn Inc 214 W Market St . . . . Greenwood MS 38930	800-293-6231	662-453-6231
Stratton Equity Co-op Co Inc 98 Colorado Ave PO Box 25 . . . . Stratton CO 80836	800-438-7070	719-348-5326
Watonwan Farm Service 233 W Ciro St . . . . Truman MN 56088	800-657-3282	507-776-2831
Western Iowa Co-op 3330 Moville St PO Box 106 . . . . Hornick IA 51026	800-488-3201	712-874-3211

278 FARM SUPPLIES

	Toll-Free	Phone
Agfinity 260 Factory Rd . . . . Eaton CO 80615	800-433-4688	970-454-4000
AgVantage FS Inc 1600 Eigth St SW . . . . Waverly IA 50677	800-346-0058	319-483-4900
Alforex Seeds 38001 County Rd 27 . . . . Woodland CA 95695	877-560-5181	530-666-3331
American Pride Co-Op 55 W Bromley Ln . . . . Brighton CO 80601	800-332-6478	303-659-1230
Bleyhl Farm Service Inc 940 E Wine Country Rd . . . . Grandview WA 98930 *Cust Svc	800-862-6806*	509-882-2248
Bradley Caldwell Inc 200 Kiwanis Blvd . . . . Hazleton PA 18202 *Cust Svc	800-257-9100*	570-455-7511
Central Valley Co-op 900 30th Pl NW . . . . Owatonna MN 55060	800-270-2339	507-451-1230
Co-op Feed Dealers Inc 380 Broome Corporate Pkwy PO Box 670 . . . . . Conklin NY 13748 *Cust Svc	800-333-0895*	607-651-9078
Countryside Co-op 514 E Main St . . . . Durand WI 54736	800-236-7585	715-672-8947
CropKing Inc 134 W Dr . . . . Lodi OH 44254	800-321-5656	330-302-4203
Crystal Valley Coop 721 W Humphrey PO 210. . . . . Lake Crystal MN 56055	800-622-2910	507-726-6455
Dragon Claw USA Inc 16033 Arrow Hwy . . . . Irwindale CA 91706	800-238-5296	626-480-0068
Edon Farmers Co-op Assn Inc 205 S Michigan PO Box 308 . . . . Edon OH 43518	800-878-4093	419-272-2121
Evergreen FS Inc 402 N Hershey Rd . . . . Bloomington IL 61704	877-963-2392	309-663-2392
Farm Service Co-op 2308 Pine St . . . . Harlan IA 51537	800-452-4372	712-755-3185
Farmers Co-op Assn 105 Jackson St . . . . Jackson MN 56143	800-864-3847	507-847-4160
Federation Co-op 108 N Water St . . . . Black River Falls WI 54615	800-944-1784	715-284-5354
Fifield Land Co 4307 Fifield Rd . . . . Brawley CA 92227	800-536-6395	760-344-6391
Frenchman Valley Farmers Co-op Exchange 202 Broadway . . . . Imperial NE 69033	800-538-2667	308-882-3200
Gold Star FS Inc 101 NE St PO Box 79 . . . . Cambridge IL 61238	800-443-8497	309-937-3369
Gowan Company LLC PO Box 5569 . . . . Yuma AZ 85366	800-883-1844	928-783-8844
Grangetto's Farm & Garden Supply Co 1105 W Mission Ave . . . . Escondido CA 92025	800-536-4671	760-745-4671
Growth Products Ltd 80 Lafayette Ave . . . . White Plains NY 10603	800-648-7626	914-428-1316
Hummert International Inc 4500 Earth City Expy . . . . Earth City MO 63045	800-325-3055	314-506-4500
Hutchinson Co-Op PO Box 158 . . . . Hutchinson MN 55350	800-795-1299	320-587-4647
Kreamer Feed Inc PO Box 38 . . . . Kreamer PA 17833	800-767-4537	570-374-8148
Kugler Co 209 W Third St PO Box 1748 . . . . McCook NE 69001	800-445-9116	308-345-2280
Martrex Inc 1107 Hazeltine Blvd Ste 535 . . . . Minnetonka MN 55345	800-328-3627	952-933-5000
McFarlane Mfg Company Inc 1259 Water St PO Box 100 . . . . Sauk City WI 53583	800-627-8569	608-643-3321
Meherrin Agricultural & Chemical Co Inc 413 Main St . . . . Severn NC 27877	800-775-0333	252-585-1744
NEW Co-op Inc 2626 First Ave S . . . . Fort Dodge IA 50501	800-362-2233	515-955-2040
Northwest Wholesale Inc 1567 N Wenatchee Ave . . . . Wenatchee WA 98801	800-874-6607	509-662-2141
Nu Way Co-op Inc PO Box Q . . . . Trimont MN 56176	800-445-4118	507-639-2311
Orangeburg Pecan Company Inc 761 Russell St . . . . Orangeburg SC 29115	800-845-6970	803-534-4277
Orscheln Farm & Home LLC 1800 Overcenter Dr PO Box 698 . . . . Moberly MO 65270	800-498-5090	660-263-4377
Panhandle Co-op Assn 401 S Beltline Hwy W . . . . Scottsbluff NE 69361 *Cust Svc	800-732-4546*	308-632-5301
Paris Farmers' Union PO Box D . . . . South Paris ME 04281	800-639-3603	207-743-8976
Quality Liquid Feeds Inc PO Box 240 . . . . Dodgeville WI 53533	800-236-2345	608-935-2345
Red River Specialties Inc PO Box 7241 . . . . Shreveport LA 71137	800-256-3344	318-425-5944
Reedsville Co-op Assn Inc PO Box 460 . . . . Reedsville WI 54230	800-236-4047	920-754-4321
S R C Corp PO Box 30676 . . . . Salt Lake City UT 84130	800-888-4545	801-268-4500
Siegers Seed Co 13031 Reflections Dr . . . . Holland MI 49424	800-962-4999	616-786-4999
Silver Edge Co-op 39999 Hilton Rd . . . . Edgewood IA 52042	800-632-5953	563-928-6419
Southern FS Inc 2002 E Main St PO Box 728 . . . . Marion IL 62959	800-492-7684	618-993-2833
Southern States Co-op Inc 6606 W Broad St . . . . Richmond VA 23230	866-372-8272	804-281-1000

Classified Section

				Toll-Free	Phone
Southern States Frederick Co-op Inc					
500 E South St	Frederick	MD	21705	866-633-5747	301-663-6164
Stanislaus Farm Supply Co					
624 E Service Rd	Modesto	CA	95358	800-323-0725	209-538-7070
Tennessee Farmers Co-op					
180 Old Nashville Hwy	La Vergne	TN	37086	800-366-2667	615-793-8011
United Suppliers Inc					
30473 260th St PO Box 538	Eldora	IA	50627	800-782-5123	641-858-2341
Van Horn Inc PO Box 380	Cerro Gordo	IL	61818	800-252-1615	217-677-2131
Wabash Valley Service Company Inc					
909 N Ct St	Grayville	IL	62844	888-869-8127	618-375-2311
Western Consolidated Co-op					
520 Co Rd 9 PO Box 78	Holloway	MN	56249	800-368-3310	320-394-2171
Western Reserve Farm Co-op Inc					
14961 S State Ave PO Box 339	Middlefield	OH	44062	888-427-6672	440-632-1192
Wilco Farmers					
200 Industrial Way	Mount Angel	OR	97362	800-382-5339	503-845-6122

279　FASHION DESIGN HOUSES

SEE ALSO Clothing & Accessories - Mfr

				Toll-Free	Phone
Armani Exchange					
568 Broadway	New York	NY	10012	800-717-2929	212-431-6000
Christian Dior					
712 Fifth Ave 37th Fl	New York	NY	10019	800-929-3467	212-582-0500
Diane Von Furstenberg					
440 W 14th St	New York	NY	10014	888-472-2383	212-741-6607
Donna Karan International Inc					
550 Seventh Ave 15th Fl	New York	NY	10018	888-737-5743*	212-789-1500
*General					
Kay Green Design Inc					
859 Outer Rd	Orlando	FL	32814	800-226-5186	407-246-7155

280　FASTENERS & FASTENING SYSTEMS

SEE ALSO Hardware - Mfr ; Precision Machined Products

				Toll-Free	Phone
Atlas Bolt & Screw Co					
1628 Troy Rd	Ashland	OH	44805	800-321-6977	419-289-6171
B & G Mfg Company Inc					
3067 Unionville Pk	Hatfield	PA	19440	800-366-3067	215-822-1925
Captive Fastener Corp					
19 Thornton Rd	Oakland	NJ	07436	800-526-4430	201-337-6800
ELF Fastening Systems Inc					
29019 Solon Rd	Solon	OH	44139	800-248-2376	440-248-8655
Ford Fasteners Inc					
110 S Newman St	Hackensack	NJ	07601	800-272-3673	201-487-3151
Hohmann & Barnard Inc					
30 Rasons Ct	Hauppauge	NY	11788	800-645-0616	631-234-0600
ITW Brands					
955 National Pkwy Ste 95500	Schaumburg	IL	60173	877-489-2726	847-944-2260
ITW Buildex 1349 W Bryn Mawr	Itasca	IL	60143	800-284-5339	630-595-3500
Mid-States Bolt & Screw Co					
4126 Somers Dr	Burton	MI	48529	800-482-0867	810-744-0123
Ms Aerospace Inc					
13928 Balboa Blvd	Sylmar	CA	91342	866-487-2365	818-833-9095
National Rivet & Manufacturing Co					
21 E Jefferson St	Waupun	WI	53963	888-324-5511	920-324-5511
Ohio Nut & Bolt Co					
5250 W 164th St	Brook Park	OH	44142	800-362-0291	216-267-2240
Pan American Screw Inc					
630 Reese Dr SW	Conover	NC	28613	800-951-2222*	828-466-0060
*Cust Svc					
PennEngineering & Manufacturing Corp					
5190 Old Easton Rd	Danboro	PA	18916	800-237-4736	215-766-8853
Robertson Inc 97 Bronte St N	Milton	ON	L9T2N8	800-268-5090	905-878-2861
Scovill Fasteners Inc					
1802 Scovill Dr	Clarkesville	GA	30523	888-726-8455*	706-754-1000
*Cust Svc					
Stafast Products Inc					
505 Lk Shore Blvd	Painesville	OH	44077	800-782-3278	440-357-5546

281　FENCES - MFR

SEE ALSO Recycled Plastics Products

				Toll-Free	Phone
Accu-Systems Inc					
1810 West 5000 South	Salt Lake City	UT	84118	800-369-5746	
Acorn Wire & Iron Works Inc					
2035 S Racine Ave	Chicago	IL	60608	800-552-2676	773-585-0600
Dare Products Inc					
860 Betterly Rd PO Box 157	Battle Creek	MI	49015	800-922-3273	269-965-2307
Master Halco Inc					
1321 Greenway Dr	Irving	TX	75038	800-883-8384	972-714-7300
Merchants Metals Inc					
900 Ashwood Pkwy Ste 600	Atlanta	GA	30338	866-888-5611	678-731-8077
Riverdale Mills Corp					
130 Riverdale St PO Box 200	Northbridge	MA	01534	800-762-6374	508-234-8715
Tru-Link Fence Co					
5440 Touhy Ave	Skokie	IL	60077	800-568-9300	847-568-9300

282　FERTILIZERS & PESTICIDES

SEE ALSO Farm Supplies

				Toll-Free	Phone
Abell Corp					
2500 Sterlington Rd	Monroe	LA	71203	800-325-7204	
Agrium Inc					
13131 Lk Fraser Dr SE	Calgary	AB	T2J7E8	877-247-4861	403-225-7000
NYSE: AGU					

				Toll-Free	Phone
Airgas Specialty Products					
2530 Sever Rd Ste 300	Lawrenceville	GA	30043	800-295-2225	
Alabama Farmers Co-op Inc					
PO Box 2227	Decatur	AL	35601	888-255-2667	256-353-6843
Amvac Chemical Corp					
4100 E Washington Blvd	Los Angeles	CA	90023	800-424-9300	323-264-3910
California Ammonia Co (CALAMCO)					
1776 W March Ln Ste 420	Stockton	CA	95207	800-624-4200	209-982-1000
Certis USA LLC					
9145 Guilford Rd Ste 175	Columbia	MD	21046	800-250-5024	
CFC Farm & Home Ctr					
15172 Brandy Rd PO Box 2002	Culpeper	VA	22701	800-284-2667	540-825-2200
Coastal Agrobusiness Inc					
3702 Evans St PO Box 856	Greenville	NC	27835	800-758-1828	252-756-1126
Degesch America Inc					
PO Box 116	Weyers Cave	VA	24486	800-330-2525	540-234-9281
Dow AgroSciences LLC					
9330 Zionsville Rd	Indianapolis	IN	46268	800-258-1470	317-337-3000
DuPont Crop Protection					
PO Box 80705	Wilmington	DE	19880	888-638-7668	302-774-1000
Enforcer Products Inc					
PO Box 1060	Cartersville	GA	30120	888-805-4357	
FMC Corp					
1735 Market St	Philadelphia	PA	19103	888-548-4486	215-299-6000
NYSE: FMC					
Frit Industries Inc					
1792 Jodie Parker Rd	Ozark	AL	36360	800-633-7685	334-774-2515
Hillshire Brands PO Box 3901	Peoria	IL	61612	800-323-7117	
Intrepid Potash Inc					
700 17th St Ste 1700	Denver	CO	80202	800-451-2888	303-296-3006
NYSE: IPI					
JR Simplot Co					
999 W Main St Ste 1300	Boise	ID	83702	800-832-8893	208-336-2110
Kirby Agri Inc					
500 Running Pump Rd PO Box 6277	Lancaster	PA	17607	800-745-7524	717-299-2541
Kronos Micronutrients					
213 W Moxee Ave PO Box 1167	Moxee	WA	98936	800-541-4086	509-248-4911
Landec Ag LLC					
201 N Michigan St	Oxford	IN	47971	800-241-7252	765-385-1000
Lebanon Seaboard Corp					
1600 E Cumberland St	Lebanon	PA	17042	800-233-0628	717-273-1685
Miller Chemical & Fertilizer Corp					
120 Radio Rd PO Box 333	Hanover	PA	17331	800-233-2040	717-632-8921
Na-Churs/Alpine Solutions					
421 Leader St	Marion	OH	43302	800-622-4877	740-382-5701
PBI/Gordon Corp					
1217 W 12th St PO Box 014090	Kansas City	MO	64101	800-821-7925	816-421-4070
Potash Corp					
1101 Skokie Blvd	Northbrook	IL	60062	800-667-0403	847-849-4200
Potash Corp of Saskatchewan Inc					
122 First Ave S Ste 500	Saskatoon	SK	S7K7G3	800-667-3930	306-933-8500
NYSE: POT					
Safeguard Chemical Corp					
411 Wales Ave	Bronx	NY	10454	800-536-3170	718-585-3170
SC Johnson & Son Inc					
1525 Howe St	Racine	WI	53403	800-494-4855	262-260-2154
Scotts Miracle Gro Products Inc					
14111 Scottslawn Rd	Marysville	OH	43041	888-270-3714	937-644-0011
Scotts Miracle-Gro Co					
14111 Scottslawn Rd	Marysville	OH	43041	800-543-8873*	937-644-0011
NYSE: SMG ■ *Cust Svc					
Share Corp					
7821 N Faulkner Rd	Milwaukee	WI	53224	800-776-7192	414-355-4000
Southern States Chemical Co					
1600 E President St	Savannah	GA	31404	888-337-8922	912-232-1101
Spectrum Brands					
3001 Deming Way	Middleton	WI	53711	800-566-7899	608-275-3340
Stoller USA					
4001 W Sam Houston Pkwy N Ste 100	Houston	TX	77043	800-539-5283	713-461-1493
Summit Chemical Co					
235 S Kresson St	Baltimore	MD	21224	800-227-8664	410-522-0661
Syngenta Corp					
3411 Silverside Rd Ste 100	Wilmington	DE	19810	800-555-2470	302-425-2000
Syngenta Crop Protection Inc					
410 Swing Rd PO Box 18300	Greensboro	NC	27409	800-797-5040	336-632-6000
Tender Corp 106 Burndy Rd	Littleton	NH	03561	800-258-4696	603-444-5464
Van Diest Supply Co					
1434 220th St PO Box 610	Webster City	IA	50595	800-779-2424	515-832-2366
Woodstream Corp					
69 N Locust St	Lititz	PA	17543	800-800-1819*	717-626-2125
*All					
Y-Tex Corp					
1825 Big Horn Ave PO Box 1450	Cody	WY	82414	800-443-6401	307-587-5515

283　FESTIVALS - BOOK

				Toll-Free	Phone
Great Salt Lake Book Festival					
Utah Humanities Council					
202 W 300 N	Salt Lake City	UT	84103	877-786-7598	801-359-9670
Los Angeles Times Festival of Books					
Los Angeles Times 202 W First St	Los Angeles	CA	90012	800-528-4637	213-237-2335
National Book Festival					
Library of Congress					
101 Independence Ave SE	Washington	DC	20540	888-714-4696	202-707-2777
Texas Book Festival					
610 Brazos St Ste 200	Austin	TX	78701	800-222-8733	512-477-4055

284　FESTIVALS - FILM

				Toll-Free	Phone
Austin Film Festival					
1801 Salina St Ste 210	Austin	TX	78702	800-310-3378	512-478-4795
Chicago International Film Festival					
Cinema Chicago 30 E Adams St Ste 800	Chicago	IL	60603	800-982-2787	312-683-0121

				Toll-Free	Phone
Denver International Film Festival 1510 York 3rd Fl	Denver	CO	80206	800-228-5838	303-595-3456
Sarasota Film Festival 332 Cocoanut Ave	Sarasota	FL	34236	866-575-3456	941-364-9514
Toronto International Film Festival Inc Reitman Sq 350 King St W	Toronto	ON	M5V3X5	888-599-8433	
Worldfest Houston International Film Festival PO Box 56566	Houston	TX	77256	866-965-9955	713-629-3700

285 FIRE PROTECTION SYSTEMS

SEE ALSO Safety Equipment - Mfr ; Security Products & Services ; Personal Protective Equipment & Clothing

				Toll-Free	Phone
BRK Brands Inc 3901 Liberty St Rd	Aurora	IL	60504	800-323-9005	630-851-7330
Chemetron Fire Systems 16 W 361 S Frontage Rd Ste 125 *Cust Svc	Burr Ridge	IL	60527	800-878-5631*	708-748-1503
Fike Corp 704 SW Tenth St	Blue Springs	MO	64015	877-342-3453	816-229-3405
Fire & Life Safety America 3017 Vernon Rd Ste 100	Richmond	VA	23228	800-252-5069	804-222-1381
Firecom Inc 39-27 59th St	Woodside	NY	11377	888-347-3269	718-899-6100
First Alert Inc 3901 Liberty St Rd	Aurora	IL	60504	800-323-9005	630-851-7330
Gamewell FCI 12 Clintonville Rd	Northford	CT	06472	800-606-1983	203-484-7161
General Monitors Inc 26776 Simpatica Cir	Lake Forest	CA	92630	866-686-0741	949-581-4464
Honeywell Fire Solutions One Fire-Lite Pl	Northford	CT	06472	800-627-3473	203-484-7161
Potter Electric Signal Company Inc 5757 Phantom Dr Ste 125	Hazelwood	MO	63042	800-325-3936	314-878-4321
Siemens Bldg Technologies Inc Fire Safety Div 8 Fernwood Rd	Florham Park	NJ	07932	888-303-3353	973-593-2600
Silent Knight 7550 Meridian Cir Ste 100	Maple Grove	MN	55369	800-328-0103	763-493-6400
Task Force Tips Inc 3701 Innovation Way	Valparaiso	IN	46383	800-348-2686	219-462-6161
Tyco SimplexGrinnell 50 Technology Dr	Westminster	MA	01441	800-746-7539	978-731-2500
Viking Corp 210 N Industrial Pk Dr	Hastings	MI	49058	800-968-9501	269-945-9501

286 FIREARMS & AMMUNITION (NON-MILITARY)

SEE ALSO Sporting Goods

				Toll-Free	Phone
Beretta USA Corp 17601 Beretta Dr	Accokeek	MD	20607	800-237-3882	301-283-2191
Connecticut Valley Arms (CVA) 1685 Boggs Rd Ste 300	Duluth	GA	30096	800-320-8767	770-449-4687
Crosman Corp 7629 Rt 5 & 20	Bloomfield	NY	14469	800-724-7486	585-657-6161
Defense Technology/Federal Laboratories 1855 S Loop PO Box 248	Casper	WY	82601	877-248-3835	307-235-2136
Federal Cartridge Co 900 Ehlen Dr	Anoka	MN	55303	800-379-1732	
Gun Parts Corp 226 Williams Ln	Kingston	NY	12401	866-686-7424	845-679-4867
H & R 1871 60 Industrial Rowe	Gardner	MA	01440	866-776-9292	
Hornady Manufacturing Co 3625 W Old Potash Hwy	Grand Island	NE	68803	800-338-3220	308-382-1390
Knight Rifles 213 Dennis st Athens	Athens	TN	37303	866-518-4181	
Lyman Products Corp 475 Smith St	Middletown	CT	06457	800-225-9626	860-632-2020
Marlin Firearms Co PO Box 1871 *Cust Svc	Madison	NC	27025	800-544-8892*	
OF Mossberg & Sons Inc Seven Grasso Ave	North Haven	CT	06473	800-363-3555	203-230-5300
Olin Corp Winchester Div 427 N Shamrock St	East Alton	IL	62024	800-356-2666	618-258-2000
Remington Arms Company Inc 870 Remington Dr PO Box 700	Madison	NC	27025	800-243-9700	336-548-8700
Savage Arms Inc 100 Springdale Rd	Westfield	MA	01085	800-243-3220	413-568-7001
SIG SAUER Inc 18 Industrial Dr	Exeter	NH	03833	866-345-6744	603-772-2302
Smith & Wesson Corp 2100 Roosevelt Ave *Cust Svc	Springfield	MA	01104	800-331-0852*	413-781-8300
Smith & Wesson Holding Corp 2100 Roosevelt Ave *NASDAQ: SWHC*	Springfield	MA	01104	800-372-6454	413-781-8300
Springfield Armory 420 W Main St	Geneseo	IL	61254	800-680-6866	309-944-5631
Taurus International Mfg Inc 16175 NW 49th Ave	Miami	FL	33014	800-327-3776	305-624-1115
Weatherby Inc 1605 Commerce Way	Paso Robles	CA	93446	800-227-2016	805-227-2600
Williams Gun Sight Co 7389 Lapeer Rd	Davison	MI	48423	800-530-9028	810-653-2131

287 FISHING - COMMERCIAL

				Toll-Free	Phone
Arctic Storm Management Group LLC 2727 Alaskan Way Pier 69	Seattle	WA	98121	800-929-0908	206-547-6557
Blue North Fisheries Inc 2930 Westlake Ave N Ste 300	Seattle	WA	98109	877-878-3263	206-352-9252
Bon Secour Fisheries Inc 17449 County Rd 49 S	Bon Secour	AL	36511	800-633-6854	251-949-7411
Canadian Fishing Co Foot of Gore Ave	Vancouver	BC	V6A2Y7	877-506-1294	604-681-0211
Nova Fisheries 2532 Yale Ave E	Seattle	WA	98102	888-458-6682	206-781-2000
Ocean Beauty Seafoods Inc 1100 W Ewing St	Seattle	WA	98119	800-365-8950	206-285-6800
Trident Seafood Corp 5303 Shilshole Ave NW	Seattle	WA	98107	800-426-5490	206-783-3818

288 FIXTURES - OFFICE & STORE

SEE ALSO Commercial & Industrial Furniture

				Toll-Free	Phone
Able Steel Equipment Co Inc 50-02 23rd St	Long Island City	NY	11101	800-428-8722	718-361-9240
Angola Wire Products Inc 803 Wohlert St	Angola	IN	46703	800-800-7225	260-665-9447
Architectural Bronze Aluminum Corp 655 Deerfield Rd Ste 100	Deerfield	IL	60015	800-339-6581	
Benner-Nawman Inc 3450 Sabin Brown Rd	Wickenburg	AZ	85390	800-992-3833	928-684-2813
Best-Rite Mfg 2885 Lorraine Ave PO Box D	Temple	TX	76501	800-749-2258	
Borroughs Corp 3002 N Burdick St	Kalamazoo	MI	49004	800-748-0227	269-342-0161
Boston Group 400 Riverside Ave	Medford	MA	02155	800-225-1633	
Churchill Cabinet Co 4616 W 19th St *Sales	Cicero	IL	60804	800-379-9776*	708-780-0070
Consolidated Storage Cos 225 Main St *Cust Svc	Tatamy	PA	18085	800-323-0801*	610-253-2775
Cres-Cor 5925 Heisley Rd	Mentor	OH	44060	877-273-7267	440-350-1100
Datum Filing Systems Inc 89 Church Rd	Emigsville	PA	17318	800-828-8018	717-764-6350
DeBourgh Manufacturing Co 27505 Otero Ave PO Box 981	La Junta	CO	81050	800-328-8829	
Dixie Store Fixtures & Sales Company Inc 2425 First Ave N	Birmingham	AL	35203	800-323-4943	205-322-2442
Durham Manufacturing Co 201 Main St	Durham	CT	06422	800-243-3774	860-349-3427
Econoco Corp 300 Karin Ln	Hicksville	NY	11801	800-645-7032	516-935-7700
EQUIPTO 225 Main St	Tatamy	PA	18085	800-323-0801	610-253-2775
Ex-Cell Metal Products Inc 11240 Melrose St	Franklin Park	IL	60131	800-392-3557	847-451-0451
Frazier Industrial Co 91 Fairview Ave	Long Valley	NJ	07853	800-859-1342	908-876-3001
Goebel Fixture Co 528 Dale St	Hutchinson	MN	55350	800-727-4646	320-587-2112
Hamilton Sorter Co Inc 3158 Production Dr	Fairfield	OH	45014	800-503-9966	513-870-4400
Handy Store Fixtures Inc 337 Sherman Ave	Newark	NJ	07114	800-631-4280	973-242-1600
Harbor Industries Inc 14130 172nd Ave	Grand Haven	MI	49417	800-968-6993	616-842-5330
Hoosier Co 5421 W 86th St PO Box 681064	Indianapolis	IN	46268	800-521-4184	317-872-8125
Hufcor Inc 2101 Kennedy Rd	Janesville	WI	53545	800-356-6968	608-756-1241
InterMetro Industries Corp 651 N Washington St *Cust Svc	Wilkes-Barre	PA	18705	800-992-1776*	570-825-2741
International Visual Corp (IVC) 11839 Rodolphe Forget	Montreal	QC	H1E7J8	866-643-0570	514-643-0570
Jesco-Wipco Industries Inc 950 Anderson Rd PO Box 388	Litchfield	MI	49252	800-455-0019	517-542-2903
JL Industries Inc 4450 W 78th St Cir	Bloomington	MN	55435	800-554-6077	952-835-6850
John Boos & Co 3601 S Banker St PO Box 609	Effingham	IL	62401	888-431-2667	217-347-7701
Kardex Systems Inc 114 Westview Ave PO Box 171	Marietta	OH	45750	800-639-5805	740-374-9300
Karges Furniture Company Inc 1501 W Maryland St	Evansville	IN	47710	800-252-7437	812-425-2291
Kent Corp 4446 Pinson Valley Pkwy	Birmingham	AL	35215	800-252-5368	205-853-3420
Killion Industries Inc 1380 Poinsettia Ave	Vista	CA	92081	800-421-5352	760-727-5102
Kwik-Wall Co 1010 E Edwards St	Springfield	IL	62703	800-280-5945	217-522-5553
LA Darling Co 1401 Hwy 49B	Paragould	AR	72450	800-643-3499	870-239-9564
Lista International Corp 106 Lowland St *Cust Svc	Holliston	MA	01746	800-722-3020*	508-429-1350
Lozier Corp 6336 John J Pershing Dr	Omaha	NE	68110	800-228-9882	402-457-8000
Lyon Work Space Products 420 N Main St	Montgomery	IL	60538	800-433-8488	630-892-8941
M.E.G. LLC 502 S Green St PO Box 240 *Cust Svc	Cambridge City	IN	47327	800-645-3315*	
Modernfold Inc 215 W New Rd	Greenfield	IN	46140	800-869-9685	
National Partitions 10300 Goldenfern Ln	Knoxville	TN	37931	888-818-5749	865-670-2100
NNM Peterson Manufacturing Co 24133 W 143rd St	Plainfield	IL	60544	800-826-9086	815-436-9201
Pacific Fixture Company Inc 12860 San Fernando Rd Unit B	Sylmar	CA	91342	800-272-2349	818-362-2130

				Toll-Free	Phone
Packard Industries Inc					
1515 US 31 N	Niles	MI	49120	800-253-0866	269-684-2550
Pan-Osten Co					
6944 Louisville Rd	Bowling Green	KY	42101	800-472-6678	270-783-3900
Panelfold Inc					
10700 NW 36th Ave	Miami	FL	33167	800-433-3222	305-688-3501
Pentwater Wire Products Inc (PWP)					
474 Carroll St PO Box 947	Pentwater	MI	49449	877-869-6911	231-869-6911
Plasticrest Products Inc					
4519 W Harrison St	Chicago	IL	60624	800-828-2163	773-826-2163
Racks Inc PO Box 530840	San Diego	CA	92153	877-920-7225	619-661-0987
RC Smith Co					
14200 Southcross Dr W	Burnsville	MN	55306	800-747-7648	952-854-0711
Reeve Store Equipment Co					
9131 Bermudez St PO Box 276	Pico Rivera	CA	90660	800-927-3383	562-949-2535
Republic Storage Systems LLC					
1038 Belden Ave NE	Canton	OH	44705	800-477-1255*	330-438-5800
*Sales					
Ridg-U-Rak Inc					
120 S Lake St PO Box 150	North East	PA	16428	866-479-7225	814-725-8751
Russ Bassett Co					
8189 Byron Rd	Whittier	CA	90606	800-350-2445	562-945-2445
Salsbury Industries Inc					
1010 E 62nd St	Los Angeles	CA	90001	800-624-5299	323-846-6700
Sandusky Cabinets Inc					
16125 Widmere Rd PO Box 517	Arvin	CA	93203	800-886-8688*	661-854-5551
*Cust Svc					
Semasys Inc 702 Ashland St	Houston	TX	77007	800-231-1425*	713-869-8331
*Cust Svc					
Southern Imperial Inc					
1400 Eddy Ave	Rockford	IL	61103	800-747-4665*	815-877-7041
*Cust Svc					
SpaceGuard Products Inc					
711 S Commerce Dr	Seymour	IN	47274	800-841-0680	812-523-3044
Spacesaver Corp					
1450 Janesville Ave	Fort Atkinson	WI	53538	800-492-3434	800-255-8170
Sparks Marketing Group Inc					
2828 Charter Rd	Philadelphia	PA	19154	800-925-7727	215-676-1100
Spectrum Industries Inc					
925 First Ave	Chippewa Falls	WI	54729	800-235-1262	715-723-6750
SPG International					
11230 Harland Dr	Covington	GA	30014	877-503-4774	
Stanley Vidmar Storage Technologies					
11 Grammes Rd	Allentown	PA	18103	800-523-9462	
Streater Inc					
411 S First Ave	Albert Lea	MN	56007	800-527-4197	
Structural Concepts Corp					
888 Porter Rd	Muskegon	MI	49441	800-433-9489	231-798-8888
Stylmark Inc					
PO Box 32008	Minneapolis	MN	55432	800-328-2495	763-574-7474
Tesko Welding & Manufacturing Co					
7350 W Montrose Ave	Norridge	IL	60706	800-621-4514	708-452-0045
Timely Inc 10241 Norris Ave	Pacoima	CA	91331	800-247-6242	818-492-3500
TJ Hale Co					
W 139 N 9499 Hwy 145					
PO Box 250	Menomonee Falls	WI	53051	800-236-4253	262-255-5555
Trendway Corp					
13467 Quincy St PO Box 9016	Holland	MI	49422	800-968-5344	616-399-3900
Trion Industries Inc					
297 Laird St	Wilkes-Barre	PA	18702	800-444-4665	570-824-1000
Unarco Material Handling Inc					
701 16th Ave E	Springfield	TN	37172	800-862-7261	
Viking Metal Cabinet Co					
24047 W Lockport St Ste 209	Plainfield	IL	60544	800-776-7767	
W/M Display Group					
1040 W 40th St	Chicago	IL	60609	800-443-2000	773-254-3700
Western Pacific Storage Systems Inc					
300 E Arrow Hwy	San Dimas	CA	91773	800-732-9777	

289 FLAGS, BANNERS, PENNANTS

				Toll-Free	Phone
Aaa Flag & Banner Manufacturing Co					
8955 National Blvd	Los Angeles	CA	90034	800-266-4222	
Annin & Co					
105 Eisenhower Pkwy	Roseland	NJ	07068	800-534-5611	973-228-9400
Eder Flag Mfg Company Inc					
1000 W Rawson Ave	Oak Creek	WI	53154	800-558-6044	414-764-3522
National Banner Co					
11938 Harry Hines Blvd	Dallas	TX	75234	800-527-0860	972-241-2131
Olympus Flag & Banner					
9000 W Heather Ave	Milwaukee	WI	53224	800-558-9620	414-355-2010

290 FLASH MEMORY DEVICES

				Toll-Free	Phone
Advanced Micro Devices Inc (AMD)					
One AMD Pl PO Box 3453	Sunnyvale	CA	94088	800-538-8450	408-749-4000
NYSE: AMD					
Kingston Technology Co					
17600 Newhope St	Fountain Valley	CA	92708	800-835-6575	714-435-2600
Lexar Media Inc					
47300 Bayside Pkwy	Fremont	CA	94538	877-747-4031	510-413-1200
Micron Technology Inc					
8000 S Federal Way	Boise	ID	83707	888-363-2589	208-368-4000
NASDAQ: MU					
PNY Technologies Inc					
299 Webro Rd	Parsippany	NJ	07054	800-769-7079	973-515-9700
Sony Electronics Inc					
One Sony Dr	Park Ridge	NJ	07656	800-222-7669*	201-930-1000
*Cust Svc					
Spansion Inc					
915 DeGuigne Dr	Sunnyvale	CA	94085	866-772-6746	408-962-2500
NYSE: CODE					

FLOOR COVERINGS - MFR

SEE Tile - Ceramic (Wall & Floor) ; Carpets & Rugs ; Flooring - Resilient

291 FLEET LEASING & MANAGEMENT

				Toll-Free	Phone
Allstate Leasing Inc					
One Olympic Pl	Towson	MD	21204	800-223-4885	410-363-6500
Donlen Corp					
2315 Sanders Rd	Northbrook	IL	60062	800-323-1483	847-714-1400
Emkay Inc					
805 W Thorndale Ave	Itasca	IL	60143	800-621-2001	630-250-7400
Executive Car Leasing Inc					
7807 Santa Monica Blvd	Los Angeles	CA	90046	800-994-2277	323-654-5000
GE Capital Fleet Services					
Three Capital Dr	Eden Prairie	MN	55344	800-469-0044	
Lease Plan USA					
1165 Sanctuary Pkwy	Alpharetta	GA	30004	800-457-8721	770-933-9090
Leasing Assoc Inc					
12600 N Featherwood Dr Ste 400	Houston	TX	77034	800-449-4807	832-300-1300
Motorlease Corp					
1506 New Britain Ave	Farmington	CT	06032	800-243-0182	860-677-9711
Park Avenue Auto Group					
250 W Passaic St	Maywood	NJ	07607	800-269-2891*	201-843-7900
*General					
RUAN Transportation Management Systems					
666 Grand Ave 3200 Ruan Ctr	Des Moines	IA	50309	866-782-6669	515-245-2500

292 FLOOR COVERINGS STORES

				Toll-Free	Phone
Century Tile Supply Co					
747 E Roosevelt Rd	Lombard	IL	60148	888-845-3968	630-495-2300
Dolphin Carpet & Tile					
3550 NW 77th Ct	Miami	FL	33122	800-639-3566	305-591-4141
Floor Coverings International					
5250 Triangle Pkwy Ste 100	Norcross	GA	30092	800-955-4324*	770-874-7600
*Sales					
Flooring Sales Group					
1251 First Ave S	Seattle	WA	98134	877-478-3577	206-624-7800
Furniture Outlets USA Inc					
140 E Hinks Ln	Sioux Falls	SD	57104	877-395-8998	605-336-5000
Lumber Liquidators Inc					
1455 VFW Pkwy	West Roxbury	MA	02132	800-227-0332	617-327-1222
Roysons Corp					
40 Vanderhoof Ave	Rockaway	NJ	07866	888-769-7667	973-625-7923
Tom Duffy Co					
5200 Watt Ct Ste B	Fairfield	CA	94534	800-479-5671	

293 FLOORING - RESILIENT

SEE ALSO Recycled Plastics Products

				Toll-Free	Phone
American Floor Products Company Inc					
7977 Cessna Ave	Gaithersburg	MD	20879	800-342-0424	
Armstrong World Industries Inc					
2500 Columbia Ave	Lancaster	PA	17603	800-233-3823*	717-397-0611
NYSE: AWI ■ *Cust Svc					
Columbia Forest Products Inc					
7900 Triad Ctr Dr Ste 200	Greensboro	NC	27409	800-637-1609	336-291-5905
Congoleum Corp					
3500 Quakerridge Rd PO Box 3127	Mercerville	NJ	08619	800-274-3266	609-584-3000
Expanko Inc					
180 Gordon Dr Ste 113	Exton	PA	19341	800-345-6202	
Forbo Flooring Systems					
Eight Maplewood Dr					
Humboldt Industrial Pk	Hazleton	PA	18202	800-842-7839*	
*Cust Svc					
Formica Corp					
10155 Reading Rd	Cincinnati	OH	45241	800-367-6422	513-786-3400
Mannington Mills Inc					
75 Mannington Mills Rd	Salem	NJ	08079	800-356-6787*	856-935-3000
*Cust Svc					
Pergo Inc					
3128 Highwoods Blvd Ste 100	Raleigh	NC	27604	800-337-3746	919-773-6000
RCA Rubber Co					
1833 E Market St	Akron	OH	44305	800-321-2340	330-784-1291
Regupol America					
33 Keystone Dr	Lebanon	PA	17042	800-537-8737	
Roppe Corp 1602 N Union St	Fostoria	OH	44830	800-537-9527	419-435-8546
Stonhard Inc					
1000 E Pk Ave	Maple Shade	NJ	08052	800-854-0310*	856-779-7500
*Cust Svc					
Superior Mfg Group					
5655 W 73rd St	Chicago	IL	60638	800-621-2802	708-458-4600
Surface Shields Inc					
10457 163rd Pl	Orland Park	IL	60467	800-913-5667	708-226-9810
Tarkett Inc					
1001 Yamaska St E	Farnham	QC	J2N1J7	800-363-9276	450-293-3173

294 FLORISTS

SEE ALSO Garden Centers

				Toll-Free	Phone
1-800-Flowers.com Inc					
One Old Country Rd Ste 500	Carle Place	NY	11514	800-356-9377	516-237-6000
NASDAQ: FLWS					
Arrow Florist & Park Avenue Greenhouses Inc					
757 Pk Ave	Cranston	RI	02910	800-556-7097	401-785-1900

		Toll-Free	Phone

Astoria-Pacific Inc
15130 SE 82nd Dr . . . . Clackamas OR 97015   **800-536-3111**   503-657-3010

Bachman's Inc
6010 Lyndale Ave S . . . . Minneapolis MN 55419   **888-222-4626**   612-861-7311

Baisch & Skinner Inc
2721 Lasalle St . . . . Saint Louis MO 63104   **800-523-0013**   314-664-1212

Barry-owen Co Inc
5625 Smithway St . . . . Los Angeles CA 90040   **800-682-6682**   323-724-4800

BloomNation LLC
8889 W Olympic Blvd . . . . Beverly Hills CA 90211   **877-702-5666**

Boesen the Florist
3422 Beaver Ave . . . . Des Moines IA 50310   **800-274-4761**   515-274-4761

Burchell Nursery Inc, The
12000 Hwy 120 . . . . Oakdale CA 95361   **800-828-8733**   209-845-8733

Cactus Flower Florists
10822 N Scottsdale Rd . . . . Scottsdale AZ 85254   **800-922-2887**   480-483-9200

Canada Flowers
4073 Longhurst Ave . . . . Niagara Falls ON L2E6G5   **888-705-9999**   905-354-2713

Connell's Map Lee Flowers & Gifts
2408 E Main St . . . . Bexley OH 43209   **800-790-8980**   614-237-8653

Country Lane Flower Shop
729 S Michigan Ave . . . . Howell MI 48843   **800-764-7673**   517-546-1111

Dr Delphinium Designs & Events
5806 W Lovers Ln & Tollway . . . . Dallas TX 75225   **800-783-8790**   214-522-9911

Eastern Floral & Gift Shop
818 Butterworth St SW . . . . Grand Rapids MI 49504   **800-494-2202**   616-949-2200

Felly's Flowers Inc
PO Box 6620 . . . . Madison WI 53716   **800-993-7673**

Flower Patch Inc
4370 S 300 W . . . . Murray UT 84107   **888-865-6858***   801-747-2824
*General

Flower Pot Florists
2314 N Broadway St . . . . Knoxville TN 37917   **800-824-7792**   865-523-5121

FlowerClub PO Box 60910 . . . . Los Angeles CA 90060   **800-493-5610**   310-966-8644

Foster City Flowers & Gifts
1160 Chess Dr Ste 1 . . . . Foster City CA 94404   **800-970-7673**   650-573-6607

Fruit Co, The
2900 Van Horn Dr . . . . Hood River OR 97031   **800-387-3100**   541-387-3100

FTD Inc
3113 Woodcreek Dr . . . . Downers Grove IL 60515   **800-736-3383***
*Cust Svc

Greeters of Hawaii Ltd
300 Rodgers Blvd Ste 266 . . . . Honolulu HI 96819   **800-366-8559**   808-836-0161

Grower Direct Fresh Cut Flowers
9613 41 Ave Ste 201 . . . . Edmonton AB T6E5X7   **877-277-4787**   780-436-7774

Higdon Florist 201 E 32nd St . . . . Joplin MO 64804   **800-641-4726**   417-624-7171

Howard Bros Florists
8700 S Pennsylvania Ave . . . . Oklahoma City OK 73159   **800-648-0524**   405-632-4747

John Wolf Florist
6228 Waters Ave . . . . Savannah GA 31406   **800-944-6435**   912-352-9843

Johnston the Florist Inc
14179 Lincoln Way . . . . North Huntingdon PA 15642   **800-356-9371**   412-751-2821

Joyce Florist
2729 S Hampton Rd . . . . Dallas TX 75224   **800-527-1520**   214-942-1776

Ken's Flower Shop
140 W S Boundary St . . . . Perrysburg OH 43551   **800-253-0100**   419-874-1333

Kuhn Flowers Inc
3802 Beach Blvd . . . . Jacksonville FL 32207   **800-458-5846**   904-398-8601

Lester's Florist Inc
2100 Bull St . . . . Savannah GA 31401   **800-841-1103**   912-233-6066

Lloyd's Florist
9216 Preston Hwy . . . . Louisville KY 40229   **800-264-1825**   502-968-5428

Martina's Flowers & Gifts
3830 Washington Ave . . . . Martinez GA 30907   **800-927-1204**   706-863-7172

Mayesh Wholesale Florist Inc
5401 W 104th St . . . . Los Angeles CA 90045   **888-462-9374**   310-348-4921

Mellano & Co
766 Wall St . . . . Los Angeles CA 90014   **888-635-5266**   213-622-0796

Metropolitan Plant & Flower Exchange
2125 Fletcher Ave . . . . Fort Lee NJ 07024   **800-638-7613**   201-944-1050

Nakase Bros Wholesale Nursery
9441 Krepp Dr . . . . Huntington Beach CA 92646   **800-747-4388**   714-962-6604

Nanz & Kraft Florists Inc
141 Breckenridge Ln . . . . Louisville KY 40207   **800-897-6551**   502-897-6551

National Floral Supply Inc
3825 LeonaRdtown Rd Ste 4 . . . . Waldorf MD 20601   **800-932-2772**   301-932-7600

Norton's Flowers & Gifts
2900 Washtenaw Ave . . . . Ypsilanti MI 48197   **800-682-8667**   734-434-2700

Phillip's Flower Shops Inc
524 N Cass Ave . . . . Westmont IL 60559   **800-356-7257**   630-719-5200

Phoenix Flower Shops
5733 E Thomas Rd Ste 4 . . . . Scottsdale AZ 85251   **888-311-0404**   480-289-4000

Proflowers.com
4840 Eastgate Mall . . . . San Diego CA 92121   **800-580-2913**

Provide Commerce Inc
4840 Eastgate Mall . . . . San Diego CA 92121   **800-776-3569***   858-638-4900
*Cust Svc

Russell Florist Inc
5001 Gravois Ave . . . . Saint Louis MO 63116   **800-351-9003**   314-351-4676

Schroeder's Flowerland Inc
1530 S Webster Ave . . . . Green Bay WI 54301   **800-236-4769**   920-436-6363

Strange's Florist Inc
3313 Mechanicsville Pk . . . . Richmond VA 23223   **800-421-4070**   804-321-2200

Sunwest Silver Company Inc
324 Lomas Blvd NW . . . . Albuquerque NM 87102   **800-771-3781**   505-243-3781

Thirstystone Resources Inc
1304 Corporate Dr . . . . Gainesville TX 76240   **800-829-6888**   940-668-6793

Veldkamp's Flowers
9501 W Colfax Ave . . . . Lakewood CO 80215   **800-247-3730**   303-232-2673

Villere's Florist
750 Martin Behrman Ave . . . . Metairie LA 70005   **800-845-5373**   504-833-3716

Winston Bros Inc
131 Newbury St . . . . Boston MA 02116   **800-457-4901**   617-541-1100

Winward International Inc
3089 Whipple Rd . . . . Union City CA 94587   **800-888-8898**   510-487-8686

---

295   FLOWERS & NURSERY STOCK - WHOL

SEE ALSO Horticultural Products Growers

		Toll-Free	Phone

Allstate Floral & Craft Inc
14038 Park Pl . . . . Cerritos CA 90703   **800-433-4056**   562-926-2302

Ball Horticultural Co
622 Town Rd . . . . West Chicago IL 60185   **800-879-2255**   630-231-3600

Claymore C Sieck Wholesale Florist
311 E Chase St . . . . Baltimore MD 21202   **800-624-7134**   410-685-4660

Cleveland Plant & Flower Co
12920 Corporate Dr . . . . Cleveland OH 44130   **800-688-8012**   216-898-3500

Cut Flower Wholesale Inc
2122 Faulkner Rd NE . . . . Atlanta GA 30324   **888-997-8367**   404-320-1619

Delaware Valley Wholesale Florist Inc (DVWF)
520 Mantua Blvd N . . . . Sewell NJ 08080   **800-676-1212**   856-468-7000

Denver Wholesale Florists Co
4800 Dahlia St . . . . Denver CO 80216   **800-829-8280**   303-399-0970

Distinctive Designs International Inc
120 Sibley Dr . . . . Russellville AL 35654   **800-243-4787**   256-332-7390

Esprit Miami
3043 NW 107th Ave . . . . Miami FL 33172   **800-327-2320**   305-591-2244

Florist Distributing Inc
2403 Bell Ave . . . . Des Moines IA 50321   **800-373-3741**   515-243-5228

Holmberg Farms Inc
13430 Hobson Simmons Rd . . . . Lithia FL 33547   **800-282-3562**

Karthauser & Sons Inc
W 147 N 11100 Fond du Lac Ave . . . . Germantown WI 53022   **800-338-8620**   262-255-7815

Kennicott Bros
452 N Ashland Ave . . . . Chicago IL 60622   **866-346-2826**   312-492-8200

L & L Nursery Supply Co Inc
2552 Shenandoah Way . . . . San Bernardino CA 92407   **800-624-2517**   909-591-0461

Norben Import Corp
99 S Newman St . . . . Hackensack NJ 07601   **800-526-4652***   201-487-0855
*General

Pittsburgh Cut Flower Co
1901 Liberty Ave . . . . Pittsburgh PA 15222   **800-837-2837**   412-355-7000

Tapscott's 1403 E 18th St . . . . Owensboro KY 42303   **800-626-1922**   270-684-2308

Teters Floral Products Inc
1425 S Lillian Ave . . . . Bolivar MO 65613   **800-999-5996**   417-326-7654

Teufel Nursery Inc
3431 NW John Olsen Pl . . . . Hillsboro OR 97124   **800-483-8335**   503-646-1111

Van Well Nursery
2821 Grant Rd . . . . East Wenatchee WA 98802   **800-572-1553**   509-886-8189

Van Zyverden Inc
8079 Van Zyverden Rd . . . . Meridian MS 39305   **800-332-2852**   601-679-8274

Zieger & Sons Inc
6215 Ardleigh St . . . . Philadelphia PA 19138   **800-752-2003**   215-438-7060

---

296   FOIL & LEAF - METAL

		Toll-Free	Phone

Air Cycle Corp
2200 Ogden Ave Ste 100 . . . . Lisle IL 60532   **800-909-9709**

Alamo Industrial Inc
1502 East Walnut St . . . . Seguin TX 78155   **800-356-6286**

Chemetal 39 O'Neil St . . . . EastHampton MA 01027   **800-807-7341**   413-529-0718

Crown Roll Leaf Inc
91 Illinois Ave . . . . Paterson NJ 07503   **800-631-3831**   973-742-4000

Hodge Products Inc
1410 Hill St . . . . El Cajon CA 92020   **800-778-2217**

Ideal Shield LLC
2525 Clark St . . . . Detroit MI 48209   **866-825-8659**   313-842-7290

Oak-Mitsui Inc
80 First St . . . . Hoosick Falls NY 12090   **800-424-8802**   518-686-4961

October Company Inc
51 Ferry St . . . . EastHampton MA 01027   **800-628-9346**   413-527-9380

Warren Co, The
2201 Loveland Ave . . . . Erie PA 16506   **800-562-0357**

---

297   FOOD PRODUCTS - MFR

SEE ALSO Salt ; Ice - Manufactured ; Livestock & Poultry Feeds - Prepared ; Meat Packing Plants ; Pet Products ; Poultry Processing ; Agricultural Products ; Bakeries ; Beverages - Mfr

		Toll-Free	Phone

Flatout Inc 1422 Woodland Dr . . . . Saline MI 48176   **866-944-5445**   734-944-4262

Thomsen Group LLC
1303 43rd St . . . . Kenosha WI 53140   **800-558-4018**

Wixon Inc
1390 E Bolivar Ave . . . . Saint Francis WI 53235   **800-841-5304**   414-769-3000

297-1 Bakery Products - Fresh

		Toll-Free	Phone

Alfred Nickles Bakery Inc
26 N Main St . . . . Navarre OH 44662   **800-635-1110**   330-879-5635

Amoroso's Baking Co
845 S 55th St . . . . Philadelphia PA 19143   **800-377-6557**   215-471-4740

Bimbo Bakeries USA
PO Box 976 . . . . Horsham PA 19044   **800-984-0989**

Calise & Sons Bakery Inc
Two Quality Dr . . . . Lincoln RI 02865   **800-225-4737**   401-334-3444

De Wafelbakkers LLC
10000 Crystal Hill Rd. . . . . North Little Rock AR 72113   **800-924-3391**   501-791-3320

Delight Grecian Foods Inc
1201 Tonne Rd . . . . Elk Grove Village IL 60007   **800-621-4387**   847-364-1010

Dinkel's Bakery
3329 N Lincoln Ave . . . . Chicago IL 60657   **800-822-8817***   773-281-7300
*Orders

				Toll-Free	Phone
Fantini Baking Company Inc					
375 Washington St	Haverhill	MA	01832	**800-223-9037**	978-373-1273
Greyston Bakery Inc					
104 Alexander St	Yonkers	NY	10701	**800-289-2253**	914-375-1510
H & S Bakery Inc					
601 S Caroline St	Baltimore	MD	21231	**800-959-7655**	410-276-7254
Heiners Bakery Inc					
1300 Adams Ave	Huntington	WV	25704	**800-776-8411**	304-523-8411
Klosterman Baking Company Inc					
4760 Paddock Rd	Cincinnati	OH	45229	**877-301-1004**	513-242-1004
Lawler Foods Ltd Inc					
PO Box 2558	Humble	TX	77347	**800-541-8285**	281-446-0059
Leidenheimer Baking Co					
1501 Simon Bolivar Ave	New Orleans	LA	70113	**800-259-9099**	504-525-1575
Lewis Bakeries Inc					
500 N Fulton Ave	Evansville	IN	47710	**800-365-2812**	812-425-4642
Martin's Famous Pastry Shoppe Inc					
1000 Potato Roll Ln	Chambersburg	PA	17201	**800-548-1200***	717-263-9580
*Cust Svc					
McKee Foods Corp					
PO Box 750	Collegedale	TN	37315	**800-522-4499***	423-238-7111
*Cust Svc					
Morabito Baking Company Inc					
757 Kohn St	Norristown	PA	19401	**800-525-7747**	610-275-5419
Orlando Baking Company Inc					
7777 Grand Ave	Cleveland	OH	44104	**800-362-5504**	216-361-1872
Pan-O-Gold Baking Co					
444 E St Germain	Saint Cloud	MN	56304	**800-444-7005**	320-251-9361
Pepperidge Farm Inc					
595 Westport Ave	Norwalk	CT	06851	**888-737-7374***	203-846-7000
*PR					
Piantedosi Baking Company Inc					
240 Commercial St	Malden	MA	02148	**800-339-0080**	781-321-3400
Rothbury Farms					
PO Box 202	Grand Rapids	MI	49501	**877-684-2879**	
Schmidt Baking Company Inc					
7801 Fitch Ln	Baltimore	MD	21236	**800-456-2253**	410-668-8200
Schwebel Baking Co					
PO Box 6018	Youngstown	OH	44501	**800-860-2867**	330-783-2860
Signature Breads Inc					
100 Justin Dr	Chelsea	MA	02150	**888-602-6533**	
Sokol & Co					
5315 Dansher Rd	Countryside	IL	60525	**800-328-7656***	708-482-8250
*Cust Svc					
Svenhard's Swedish Bakery Inc					
335 Adeline St	Oakland	CA	94607	**800-705-3379**	510-834-5035
Tasty Baking Co					
4300 S 26th St Ste 200	Philadelphia	PA	19112	**800-248-2789**	215-221-8500
Wenner Bread Products Inc					
33 Rajon Rd	Bayport	NY	11705	**800-869-6262**	631-563-6262
Wolferman's					
2500 S Pacific Hwy PO Box 9100	Medford	OR	97501	**800-999-0169**	

297-2 Bakery Products - Frozen

				Toll-Free	Phone
Athens Pastries & Frozen Foods Inc					
13600 Snow Rd	Brookpark	OH	44142	**800-837-5683**	216-676-8500
Bridgford Foods Corp					
1308 N Patt St	Anaheim	CA	92801	**800-854-3255**	714-526-5533
NASDAQ: BRID					
Dessert Innovations Inc					
25-B Enterprise Blvd	Atlanta	GA	30336	**800-359-7351**	404-691-5000
Eli's Cheesecake Co					
6701 W Forest Preserve Dr	Chicago	IL	60634	**800-999-8300**	773-736-3417
Guttenplans Frozen Dough					
100 Hwy 36	Middletown	NJ	07748	**888-422-4357***	732-495-9480
*General					
James Skinner Baking Co					
4657 G St	Omaha	NE	68117	**800-358-7428**	402-734-1672
Main Street Gourmet Inc					
170 Muffin Ln	Cuyahoga Falls	OH	44223	**800-678-6246**	330-929-0000
Maplehurst Inc					
50 Maplehurst Dr	Brownsburg	IN	46112	**800-344-4235**	317-858-9000
Rhino Foods Inc					
79 Industrial Pkwy	Burlington	VT	05401	**800-542-3463**	802-862-0252
Vie de France Yamazaki Inc					
2070 Chain Bridge Rd Ste 500	Vienna	VA	22182	**800-446-4404***	703-442-9205
*General					

297-3 Butter (Creamery)

				Toll-Free	Phone
AMPI 315 N Broadway	New Ulm	MN	56073	**800-533-3580**	507-354-8295
Cabot Creamery					
One Home Farm Way	Montpelier	VT	05602	**888-792-2268**	802-229-9361
Grassland Dairy Products Company Inc					
N 8790 Fairgrounds Ave PO Box 160	Greenwood	WI	54437	**800-428-8837**	715-267-6182
Land O'Lakes Inc					
4001 Lexington Ave N	Arden Hills	MN	55126	**800-328-9680**	651-481-2222
O-AT-KA Milk Products Co-op Inc					
700 Ellicott St	Batavia	NY	14020	**800-828-8152**	585-343-0536
Plainview Milk Products Co-Op					
130 Second St SW	Plainview	MN	55964	**800-356-5606**	507-534-3872

297-4 Cereals (Breakfast)

				Toll-Free	Phone
Big G Cereals					
PO Box 9452 PO Box 9452	Minneapolis	MN	55440	**800-248-7310**	
Bob's Red Mill Natural Foods Inc					
13521 SE Pheasant Ct	Milwaukie	OR	97222	**800-553-2258**	503-654-3215
Homestead Mills					
221 N River St PO Box 1115	Cook	MN	55723	**800-652-5233**	218-666-5233

				Toll-Free	Phone
Honeyville Grain Inc					
11600 Dayton Dr	Rancho Cucamonga	CA	91730	**888-810-3212**	909-980-9500
Kellogg Co					
One Kellogg Sq PO Box 3599	Battle Creek	MI	49016	**800-962-1413***	269-961-2000
NYSE: K ■ *Cust Svc					
New England Natural Bakers					
74 Fairview St E	Greenfield	MA	01301	**800-910-2884**	413-772-2239
Organic Milling Co					
505 W Allen Ave	San Dimas	CA	91773	**800-638-8686**	909-599-0961
Quaker Oats Co					
555 W Monroe St	Chicago	IL	60661	**800-367-6287**	312-821-1000
Weetabix Co Inc					
300 Nickerson Rd	Marlborough	MA	01752	**800-343-0590**	978-368-0991

297-5 Cheeses - Natural, Processed, Imitation

				Toll-Free	Phone
AMPI 315 N Broadway	New Ulm	MN	56073	**800-533-3580**	507-354-8295
Berner Foods Inc					
2034 E Factory Rrd	Dakota	IL	61018	**800-819-8199**	815-563-4222
Biery Cheese Co					
6544 Paris Ave	Louisville	OH	44641	**800-243-3731**	330-875-3381
Burnett Dairy Co-op					
11631 SR- 70	Grantsburg	WI	54840	**800-854-2716**	715-689-2468
Cabot Creamery					
One Home Farm Way	Montpelier	VT	05602	**888-792-2268**	802-229-9361
Cacique Inc					
14923 Procter Ave	La Puente	CA	91746	**800-521-6987**	626-961-3399
Calabro Cheese Corp					
580 Coe Ave PO Box 120186	East Haven	CT	06512	**800-969-1311**	203-469-1311
ConAgra Foods Retail Products Co Deli Foods Group					
215 W Field Rd	Naperville	IL	60563	**877-266-2472**	630-857-1000
Dairiconcepts LP					
3253 E Chestnut Expy	Springfield	MO	65802	**877-596-4374**	417-829-3400
Dairy Farmers of America Inc					
10220 N Ambassador Dr					
Northpointe Tower	Kansas City	MO	64153	**888-332-6455**	816-801-6455
Galaxy Nutritional Foods Inc					
66 Whitecap Dr	North Kingstown	RI	02852	**800-441-9419**	401-667-5000
Gossner Foods Inc					
1051 N 1000 W	Logan	UT	84321	**800-944-0454**	435-713-6100
Grande Cheese Co					
301 E Main St	Lomira	WI	53048	**800-772-3210**	
Hilmar Cheese Company Inc					
PO Box 910	Hilmar	CA	95324	**888-300-4465**	209-667-6076
Jerome Cheese Co					
547 W Nez Perce	Jerome	ID	83338	**800-757-7611**	208-324-8806
Land O'Lakes Inc					
4001 Lexington Ave N	Arden Hills	MN	55126	**800-328-9680**	651-481-2222
Le Sueur Cheese Company Inc					
719 N Main St	Le Sueur	MN	56058	**800-247-0871**	507-665-3353
Leprino Foods Co					
1830 W 38th Ave	Denver	CO	80211	**800-537-7466**	303-480-2600
Sargento Foods Inc					
1 Persnickety Pl	Plymouth	WI	53073	**800-243-3737**	920-893-8484
Sartori Food Corp					
107 Pleasant View Rd	Plymouth	WI	53073	**800-558-5888***	920-893-6061
*Cust Svc					
Swiss Valley Farms					
247 Research Pkwy PO Box 4493	Davenport	IA	52808	**800-747-6113**	563-468-6600
Tropical Cheese Industries Inc					
450 Fayette St PO Box 1357	Perth Amboy	NJ	08861	**888-874-4928**	732-442-4898

297-6 Chewing Gum

				Toll-Free	Phone
Concord Confections Ltd					
345 Courtland Ave	Concord	ON	L4K5A6	**800-267-0037**	905-660-8989
Topps Company Inc					
One Whitehall St	New York	NY	10004	**800-489-9149**	212-376-0300
Wrigley Co, The					
410 N Michigan Ave	Chicago	IL	60611	**888-985-2064**	312-644-2121

297-7 Coffee - Roasted (Ground, Instant, Freeze-Dried)

				Toll-Free	Phone
Allegro Coffee Co					
12799 Claude Ct	Thornton	CO	80241	**800-530-3995**	303-444-4844
ARCO Coffee Company					
2206 Winter St	Superior	WI	54880	**800-283-2726**	715-392-4771
Autocrat Coffee Inc					
10 Blackstone Vly Pl	Lincoln	RI	02865	**800-288-6272**	401-333-3300
Boyd Coffee Co					
19730 NE Sandy Blvd	Portland	OR	97230	**800-545-4077***	503-666-4545
*Cust Svc					
Cadillac Coffee Co					
194 E Maple Rd	Troy	MI	48083	**800-438-6900**	248-545-2266
Coffee Holding Company Inc					
3475 Victory Blvd	Staten Island	NY	10314	**800-458-2233**	718-832-0800
NASDAQ: JVA					
Community Coffee Co					
PO Box 2311	Baton Rouge	LA	70821	**800-688-0990**	800-884-5282
DeCoty Coffee Company Inc					
1920 Austin St	San Angelo	TX	76903	**800-588-8001**	
Farmer Bros Co					
20333 S Normandie Ave	Torrance	CA	90502	**800-735-2878**	310-787-5200
NASDAQ: FARM					
Frontier Natural Products Co-op					
3021 78th St PO Box 299	Norway	IA	52318	**800-669-3275**	319-227-7996
Hawaiian Isles Kona Coffee Company					
2839 Mokumoa St	Honolulu	HI	96819	**800-657-7716***	808-839-3255
*Orders					

	Toll-Free	Phone
Keurig Green Mountain Inc		
33 Coffee Ln ....Waterbury VT 05676	**888-879-4627***	
NASDAQ: GMCR ▩ *Cust Svc		
McCullagh Coffee		
245 Swan St ....Buffalo NY 14204	**800-753-3473**	
Melitta Canada Inc		
10-6201 Hwy Ste 7............Vaughan ON L4H0K7	**800-565-4882**	905-851-9375
New England Coffee Co		
100 Charles St ....Malden MA 02148	**800-225-3537**	
Old Mansion Foods		
3811 Corporate Rd PO Box 1838 ....Petersburg VA 23805	**800-476-1877**	804-862-9889
Paul deLima Co Inc		
7546 Morgan Rd ....Liverpool NY 13090	**800-962-8864**	315-457-3725
Red Diamond Inc 400 Park Ave ....Moody AL 35004	**800-292-4651**	205-577-4000
Reily Foods Co		
640 Magazine St ....New Orleans LA 70130	**800-535-1961**	504-524-6131
Royal Cup Coffee		
160 Cleage Dr ....Birmingham AL 35217	**800-366-5836***	
S & D Coffee Inc		
300 Concord Pkwy PO Box 1628 ....Concord NC 28026	**800-933-2210***	704-782-3121
*Cust Svc		
Texas Coffee Co Inc		
3297 S M L King Jr Pkwy ....Beaumont TX 77705	**800-259-3400**	409-835-3434
Torke Coffee Roasting Company Inc		
3455 Paine Ave PO Box 694............Sheboygan WI 53081	**800-242-7671**	920-458-4114
Van Roy Coffee Co, The		
4569 Spring Rd ....Cleveland OH 44131	**877-826-7669**	216-749-7069
White Coffee Corp		
18-35 Steinway Pl ....Astoria NY 11105	**800-221-0140**	718-204-7900

297-8 Confectionery Products

	Toll-Free	Phone
Adams & Brooks Inc		
1915 S Hoover St PO Box 7303 ....Los Angeles CA 90007	**800-999-9808***	213-749-3226
*Orders		
ADM Cocoa Div		
12500 W Carmen Ave ....Milwaukee WI 53225	**800-637-5843**	217-424-5200
Anthony-Thomas Candy Co		
1777 Arlingate Ln ....Columbus OH 43228	**877-226-3921**	614-274-8405
Asher's Chocolates		
80 Wambold Rd ....Souderton PA 18964	**800-223-4420**	215-721-3000
Atkinson Candy Co		
1608 W Frank Ave ....Lufkin TX 75904	**800-231-1203**	936-639-2333
Barry Callebaut USA LLC		
400 Industrial Pk Rd ....Saint Albans VT 05478	**800-556-8845**	802-524-9711
Best Sweet Inc		
288 Mazeppa Rd ....Mooresville NC 28115	**888-211-5530**	704-664-4300
Blommer Chocolate Co		
600 W Kinzie St ....Chicago IL 60654	**800-621-1606**	312-226-7700
Brown & Haley PO Box 1596 ....Tacoma WA 98401	**800-426-8400**	253-620-3085
Cherrydale Farms Fundraising		
707 N Vly Forge Rd ....Lansdale PA 19446	**877-619-4822**	
Chocolates a la Carte Inc		
28455 Livingston Ave ....Valencia CA 91355	**800-818-2462***	
*Cust Svc		
Decko Products Inc		
2105 Superior St ....Sandusky OH 44870	**800-537-4487***	419-626-5757
*General		
Eaton Farm Confectioners Inc		
30 Burbank Rd ....Sutton MA 01590	**800-343-9300**	508-865-5235
Esther Price Candies Inc		
1709 Wayne Ave ....Dayton OH 45410	**800-782-0326**	937-253-2121
Ferrara Cafe 195 Grand St ....New York NY 10013	**800-871-6068**	212-226-6150
Fowler's Chocolate Co		
100 River Rock Dr Ste 102............Buffalo NY 14207	**800-824-2263**	716-877-9983
Gertrude Hawk Chocolates Inc		
9 Keystone Pk ....Dunmore PA 18512	**866-932-4295**	800-822-2032
Ghirardelli Chocolate Co		
1111 139th Ave ....San Leandro CA 94578	**800-877-9338**	
Goetze's Candy Company Inc		
3900 E Monument St ....Baltimore MD 21205	**800-295-8058***	410-342-2010
*Orders		
Guittard Chocolate Co		
10 GuittaRd Rd ....Burlingame CA 94010	**800-468-2462**	650-697-4427
Harry London Candies Inc		
5353 Lauby Rd ....North Canton OH 44720	**800-333-3629***	330-494-0833
*Cust Svc		
Hershey Co 100 Crystal A Dr ....Hershey PA 17033	**800-468-1714***	
NYSE: HSY ▩ *Cust Svc		
Hillside Candy Co		
35 Hillside Ave ....Hillside NJ 07205	**800-524-1304**	973-926-2300
James Candy Co		
1519 Boardwalk ....Atlantic City NJ 08401	**800-441-1404***	609-344-1519
*Orders		
Jelly Belly Candy Co		
1 Jelly Belly Ln ....Fairfield CA 94533	**800-323-9380**	707-428-2800
Just Born Inc		
1300 Stefko Blvd ....Bethlehem PA 18017	**800-445-5787**	610-867-7568
Katharine Beecher Candies		
1250 Slate Hill Rd ....Camp Hill PA 17011	**800-233-7082**	717-761-5440
Koeze Co PO Box 9470 ....Grand Rapids MI 49509	**800-555-9688**	
Lammes Candies Since 1885 Inc		
PO Box 1885 ....Austin TX 78767	**800-252-1885**	512-310-2223
Lindt & Sprungli USA		
1 Fine Chocolate Pl ....Stratham NH 03885	**877-695-4638**	603-778-8100
Lucks Co, The 3003 S Pine St ....Tacoma WA 98409	**800-426-9778**	253-383-4815
Madelaine Chocolate Novelties Inc		
9603 Beach Ch Dr ....Rockaway Beach NY 11693	**800-322-1505**	718-945-1500
Malleys Chocolates		
13400 Brookpark Rd ....Cleveland OH 44135	**800-835-5684**	216-362-8700
Mars Snack Food		
800 High St ....Hackettstown NJ 07840	**800-551-0895**	908-852-1000
Moonstruck Chocolate Co		
6600 N Baltimore Ave ....Portland OR 97203	**800-557-6666**	503-247-3448

	Toll-Free	Phone
Morley Candy Makers Inc		
23770 Hall Rd ....Clinton Township MI 48036	**800-651-7263**	586-468-4300
Munson's Candy Kitchen Inc		
174 Hop River Rd ....Bolton CT 06043	**888-686-7667**	860-649-4332
Paradise Inc		
1200 W MLK Blvd PO Box Y ....Plant City FL 33563	**800-330-8952**	
OTC: PARF		
Pearson's Candy Co		
2140 W Seventh St ....Saint Paul MN 55116	**800-328-6507***	651-698-0356
*Cust Svc		
Pennsylvania Dutch Candies		
1250 Slate Hill Rd ....Camp Hill PA 17011	**800-233-7082**	717-761-5440
PLB Sports Inc		
Penn Ctr W Bldg 3 Ste 411............Pittsburgh PA 15276	**877-752-7778**	412-787-8800
Russell Stover Candies Inc		
4900 Oak St ....Kansas City MO 64112	**800-477-8683**	816-842-9240
See's Candies Inc		
210 El Camino Real ....South San Francisco CA 94080	**800-877-7337***	650-761-2490
*Cust Svc		
Sorbee International Ltd		
9990 Global Rd ....Philadelphia PA 19115	**800-654-3997**	215-645-1111
Spangler Candy Co		
400 N Portland St PO Box 71 ....Bryan OH 43506	**888-636-4221***	419-636-4221
*Sales		
Storck USA LP		
325 N LaSalle St Ste 400 ....Chicago IL 60654	**800-852-5542**	312-467-5700
Sweet Candy Co Inc		
3780 W Directors Row ....Salt Lake City UT 84104	**800-669-8669**	801-886-1444
T R Toppers Inc		
320 Fairchild ....Pueblo CO 81001	**800-748-4635**	719-948-4902
Tootsie Roll Industries Inc		
7401 S Cicero Ave ....Chicago IL 60629	**866-972-6879**	773-838-3400
NYSE: TR		
Vitasoy USA Inc		
1 New England Way ....Ayer MA 01432	**800-848-2769**	800-462-7692
Waymouth Farms Inc		
5300 Boone Ave ....New Hope MN 55428	**800-527-0094**	763-533-5300
Wolfgang Candy Co		
50 E Fourth Ave ....York PA 17404	**800-248-4273**	717-843-5536
World's Finest Chocolate Inc		
4801 S Lawndale ....Chicago IL 60632	**888-821-8452**	
Zachary Confections Inc		
2130 IN-28 ....Frankfort IN 46041	**800-445-4222***	
*Cust Svc		

297-9 Cookies & Crackers

	Toll-Free	Phone
Benzel's Pretzel Bakery Inc		
5200 Sixth Ave ....Altoona PA 16602	**800-344-4438**	814-942-5062
Bremner Biscuit Co		
4600 Joliet St ....Denver CO 80239	**866-972-6879**	303-371-8180
Christie Cookie Co		
1205 Third Ave N ....Nashville TN 37208	**800-458-2447**	615-242-3817
Delyse Inc 505 Reactor Way ....Reno NV 89502	**800-441-6887**	775-857-1811
Ferrara Cafe 195 Grand St ....New York NY 10013	**800-871-6068**	212-226-6150
J & J Snack Foods Corp		
6000 Central Hwy ....Pennsauken NJ 08109	**800-486-9533**	856-665-9533
NASDAQ: JJSF		
Joy Cone Co 3435 Lamor Rd ....Hermitage PA 16148	**800-242-2663**	724-962-5747
Keystone Pretzels		
124 W Airport Rd ....Lititz PA 17543	**888-572-4500**	
Norse Dairy Systems		
1740 Joyce Ave ....Columbus OH 43219	**800-637-2663**	614-294-4931
Pretzels Inc		
123 Harvest Rd PO Box 503 ....Bluffton IN 46714	**800-456-4838**	260-824-4838
Rudolph Foods Company Inc		
6575 Bellefontaine Rd ....Lima OH 45804	**800-241-7675**	419-648-3611
Silver Lake Cookie Company Inc		
141 Freeman Ave ....Islip NY 11751	**800-645-9048**	631-581-4000
Snyder's of Hanover		
1250 York St PO Box 6917 ....Hanover PA 17331	**800-233-7125**	717-632-4477
T. Marzetti Company.		
P.O. Box 29163 ....Columbus OH 43229	**800-999-1835**	
Tom Sturgis Pretzels Inc		
2267 Lancaster Pk ....Reading PA 19607	**800-817-3834**	610-775-0335
Venus Wafers Inc		
100 Research Rd ....Hingham MA 02043	**800-545-4538**	781-740-1002
Wege Pretzel Co PO Box 334 ....Hanover PA 17331	**800-888-4646**	717-843-0738

297-10 Dairy Products - Dry, Condensed, Evaporated

	Toll-Free	Phone
Abbott Laboratories Ross Products Div		
625 Cleveland Ave ....Columbus OH 43215	**800-227-5767***	614-624-7485
*PR		
AMPI 315 N Broadway ....New Ulm MN 56073	**800-533-3580**	507-354-8295
Dairy Farmers of America Inc		
10220 N Ambassador Dr		
Northpointe Tower............Kansas City MO 64153	**888-332-6455**	816-801-6455
Davisco International Inc		
719 N Main St ....Le Sueur MN 56058	**800-757-7611**	507-665-8811
Erie Foods International Inc		
401 Seventh Ave PO Box 648 ....Erie IL 61250	**800-447-1887**	309-659-2233
Foremost Farms USA		
E10889A Penny Ln ....Baraboo WI 53913	**800-362-9196**	608-355-8700
Gehl's Guernsey Farms Inc		
N116 W15970 Main St ....Germantown WI 53022	**800-521-2873**	262-251-8572
Instantwhip Foods Inc		
2200 Cardigan Ave ....Columbus OH 43215	**800-544-9447***	614-488-2536
*Cust Svc		
John Volpi & Company Inc		
5263 Northrup Ave ....St Louis MO 63110	**800-288-3439**	314-772-8550
Land O'Lakes Inc		
4001 Lexington Ave N ....Arden Hills MN 55126	**800-328-9680**	651-481-2222

	Toll-Free	Phone
Maple Island Inc		
2497 Seventh Ave E Ste 105 . . . . North Saint Paul MN 55109	800-369-1022	651-773-1000
Milk Products LLC		
PO Box 150 . . . . Chilton WI 53014	800-657-0793	920-849-2348
O-AT-KA Milk Products Co-op Inc		
700 Ellicott St . . . . Batavia NY 14020	800-828-8152	585-343-0536
Sinton Dairy Foods Co LLC		
3801 Sinton Rd . . . . Colorado Springs CO 80907	800-388-4970	719-633-3821

297-11 Diet & Health Foods

	Toll-Free	Phone
AMS Health Sciences Inc		
4000 N Lindsay . . . . Oklahoma City OK 73105	800-426-4267	405-842-0131
Eden Foods Inc		
701 Tecumseh Rd . . . . Clinton MI 49236	800-248-0320*	517-456-7424
*Cust Svc		
Isagenix International LLC		
2225 S Price Rd . . . . Chandler AZ 85286	877-877-8111	480-889-5747
Medifast Inc		
11445 Cronhill Dr . . . . Owings Mills MD 21117	800-209-0878	
NYSE: MED		
RC Fine Foods PO Box 236 . . . . Belle Mead NJ 08502	800-526-3953	908-359-5500
Tahitian Noni International		
333 W Riverpark Dr . . . . Provo UT 84604	800-445-2969*	801-234-1000
*Cust Svc		
Vitaminerals Inc		
1815 Flower St . . . . Glendale CA 91201	800-432-1856	

297-12 Fats & Oils - Animal or Marine

	Toll-Free	Phone
Darling International Inc		
251 O'Connor Ridge Blvd Ste 300 . . . . Irving TX 75038	855-327-7761	972-717-0300
NYSE: DAR		
GA Wintzer & Son Co		
204 W Auglaize St . . . . Wapakoneta OH 45895	800-331-1801	419-739-4900
Jacob Stern & Sons Inc		
1464 E Valley Rd . . . . Santa Barbara CA 93108	800-223-7054*	805-565-1411
*Cust Svc		
Werner G Smith Inc		
1730 Train Ave . . . . Cleveland OH 44113	800-535-8343*	216-861-3676
*General		

297-13 Fish & Seafood - Canned

	Toll-Free	Phone
Beaver Street Fisheries Inc		
1741 W Beaver St . . . . Jacksonville FL 32209	800-874-6426	904-354-8533
Bumble Bee Seafoods Inc		
9655 Granite Ridge Dr Ste 100 . . . . San Diego CA 92123	800-800-8572	858-715-4000
Nelson Crab Inc		
3088 Kindred Ave . . . . Tokeland WA 98590	800-262-0069	360-267-2911
Noon Hour Food Products Inc		
215 N Des Plaines . . . . Chicago IL 60661	888-463-6332*	312-596-4225
*Cust Svc		
Overwaitea Food Group		
19855 92A Ave . . . . Langley BC V1M3B6	800-242-9229	604-888-1213
Peter Pan Seafoods Inc		
2200 Sixth Ave Ste 1000 . . . . Seattle WA 98121	800-331-3522	206-728-6000
Petersburg Fisheries		
PO Box 1147 . . . . Petersburg AK 99833	877-772-4294	907-772-4294
Vita Food Products Inc		
2222 W Lake St . . . . Chicago IL 60612	800-989-8482	312-738-4500

297-14 Fish & Seafood - Fresh or Frozen

	Toll-Free	Phone
Blount Seafood Corp		
630 Currant Rd . . . . Fall River MA 02720	800-274-2526*	774-888-1300
*Hotline		
Bon Secour Fisheries Inc		
17449 County Rd 49 S . . . . Bon Secour AL 36511	800-633-6854	251-949-7411
Camanchaca Inc		
7200 NW 19th St Ste 410 . . . . Miami FL 33126	800-335-7553	305-406-9560
Consolidated Catfish Cos LLC		
299 S St PO Box 271 . . . . Isola MS 38754	800-228-3474	662-962-3101
Crocker & Winsor Seafoods Inc		
PO Box 51905 . . . . Boston MA 02205	800-225-1597	617-269-3100
Freshwater Farm Products LLC		
4554 State Hwy 12 E PO Box 850 . . . . Belzoni MS 39038	800-748-9338	662-247-4205
Gorton's Inc		
128 Rogers St . . . . Gloucester MA 01930	800-222-6846	978-283-3000
King & Prince Seafood Corp		
One King & Prince Blvd . . . . Brunswick GA 31520	800-841-0205	912-265-5155
Luther L Smith & Son Inc		
PO Box 67 . . . . Atlantic NC 28511	800-328-8313	252-225-3341
Morey's Seafood International LLC		
1218 Hwy 10 S . . . . Motley MN 56466	800-808-3474	218-352-6345
Ocean Beauty Seafoods Inc		
1100 W Ewing St . . . . Seattle WA 98119	800-365-8950	206-285-6800
Overwaitea Food Group		
19855 92A Ave . . . . Langley BC V1M3B6	800-242-9229	604-888-1213
Pinnacle Foods Corp		
399 Jefferson Rd . . . . Parsippany NJ 07054	866-266-7596	973-541-6620
Riverside Foods Inc		
2520 Wilson St . . . . Two Rivers WI 54241	800-678-4511	920-793-4511
Sea Harvest Packing Co		
PO Box 818 . . . . Brunswick GA 31521	800-627-4300	912-264-3212
Stoller Fisheries		
1301 18th St PO Box B . . . . Spirit Lake IA 51360	800-831-5174	712-336-1750

	Toll-Free	Phone
Tampa Bay Fisheries Inc		
3060 Gallagher Rd . . . . Dover FL 33527	800-732-3663	813-752-8883
Trident Seafood Corp		
5303 Shilshole Ave NW . . . . Seattle WA 98107	800-426-5490	206-783-3818
UniSea Inc		
15400 NE 90th St PO Box 97019 . . . . Redmond WA 98073	800-535-8509	425-881-8181

297-15 Flavoring Extracts & Syrups

	Toll-Free	Phone
Brady Enterprises Inc		
167 Moore Rd . . . . East Weymouth MA 02189	800-225-5126	781-337-5000
David Michael & Co Inc		
10801 Decatur Rd . . . . Philadelphia PA 19154	800-363-5286	215-632-3100
DD Williamson & Company Inc		
100 S Spring St . . . . Louisville KY 40206	800-227-2635	502-895-2438
Dr Pepper Snapple Group Inc		
5301 Legacy Dr . . . . Plano TX 75024	800-686-7398	972-673-7000
NYSE: DPS		
Emerald Kalama Chemical LLC		
1296 Third St NW . . . . Kalama WA 98625	877-300-9545	360-673-2550
Frutarom Corp		
9500 Railroad Ave . . . . North Bergen NJ 07047	866-229-7198	201-861-9500
I Rice & Company Inc		
11500 Roosevelt Blvd Bldg D . . . . Philadelphia PA 19116	800-232-6022	215-673-7423
Jel Sert Co		
Rt 59 & Conde St . . . . West Chicago IL 60185	800-323-2592	630-876-4838
Kalsec Inc 3713 W Main St . . . . Kalamazoo MI 49006	800-323-9320	269-349-9711
Limpert Bros Inc		
202 NW Blvd PO Box 1480 . . . . Vineland NJ 08362	800-691-1353	856-691-1353
Lyons Magnus Inc		
3158 E Hamilton Ave . . . . Fresno CA 93702	800-344-7130	
Mother Murphy's Labs Inc		
2826 S Elm St PO Box 16846 . . . . Greensboro NC 27416	800-849-1277	336-273-1737
Nielsen-Massey Vanillas Inc		
1550 S Shields Dr . . . . Waukegan IL 60085	800-525-7873	847-578-1550
Ottens Flavors		
7800 Holstein Ave . . . . Philadelphia PA 19153	800-523-0767	215-365-7800
Sea Breeze Inc 441 Rt 202 . . . . Towaco NJ 07082	800-732-2733	973-334-7777
Sensient Technologies Corp		
777 E Wisconsin Ave 11th Fl . . . . Milwaukee WI 53202	800-558-9892	414-271-6755
NYSE: SXT		
Sethness Products Co		
3422 W Touhy Ave . . . . Lincolnwood IL 60712	888-772-1880	847-329-2080
Symrise Inc 300 N St . . . . Teterboro NJ 07608	800-422-1559*	201-288-3200
*General		
Western Syrup Co		
13766 Milroy Pl . . . . Santa Fe Springs CA 90670	800-521-3888	562-921-4485
Wild Flavors Inc		
1261 Pacific Ave . . . . Erlanger KY 41018	800-263-5286	859-342-3600

297-16 Flour Mixes & Doughs

	Toll-Free	Phone
Abitec Corp Inc PO Box 569 . . . . Columbus OH 43215	800-555-1255*	614-429-6464
*Sales		
Bake'n Joy Foods Inc		
351 Willow St . . . . North Andover MA 01845	800-666-4937	978-683-1414
Caravan Products Company Inc		
100 Adams Dr . . . . Totowa NJ 07512	800-526-5261	973-256-8886
Dawn Food Products Inc		
3333 Sargent Rd . . . . Jackson MI 49201	800-292-1362*	517-789-4400
*Cust Svc		
Langlois Co		
10810 San Sevaine Way . . . . Mira Loma CA 91752	800-962-5993	951-360-3900
Pinnacle Foods Corp		
399 Jefferson Rd . . . . Parsippany NJ 07054	866-266-7596	973-541-6620
Puratos Corp		
1941 Old Cuthbert Rd . . . . Cherry Hill NJ 08034	800-654-0036*	856-428-4300
*All		
Rhodes International Inc		
PO Box 25487 . . . . Salt Lake City UT 84125	800-876-7333*	801-972-0122
*Cust Svc		
Subco Foods Inc		
4350 S Taylor Dr . . . . Sheboygan WI 53081	800-473-0757	920-457-7761
Watson Foods Company Inc		
301 Heffernan Dr . . . . West Haven CT 06516	800-388-3481	203-932-3000

297-17 Food Emulsifiers

	Toll-Free	Phone
ADM Specialty Food Ingredients Div		
4666 E Faries Pkwy . . . . Decatur IL 62526	800-637-5843	217-424-5200
American Lecithin Company Inc		
115 Hurley Rd Unit 2B . . . . Oxford CT 06478	800-364-4416	203-262-7100
Frutarom Corp		
9500 Railroad Ave . . . . North Bergen NJ 07047	866-229-7198	201-861-9500

297-18 Fruits & Vegetables - Dried or Dehydrated

	Toll-Free	Phone
Basic American Foods		
2185 N California Blvd Ste 215 . . . . Walnut Creek CA 94596	800-227-4050	925-472-4000
Bernard Food Industries Inc		
1125 Hartrey Ave . . . . Evanston IL 60204	800-323-3663	847-869-5222
Custom Culinary		
2505 S Finley Rd . . . . Lombard IL 60148	800-621-8827*	630-928-4898
*Cust Svc		
Del Monte Foods Co		
1 Maritime Plaza . . . . San Francisco CA 94111	800-543-3090*	415-247-3000
*Cust Svc		

				Toll-Free	Phone
Freskeeto Frozen Foods Inc					
8019 Rt 209	Ellenville	NY	12428	800-356-3663	845-647-5111
Garry Packing Co					
11272 E Central Ave PO Box 249	Del Rey	CA	93616	800-248-2126	559-888-2126
Graceland Fruit Inc					
1123 Main St	Frankfort	MI	49635	800-352-7181	231-352-7181
Idaho-Pacific Corp					
4723 E 100 N PO Box 478	Ririe	ID	83443	800-238-5503*	208-538-6971
*Sales					
Larsen Farms 2650 N 2375 E	Hamer	ID	83425	800-767-6104*	208-662-5501
*Sales					
Nonpareil Corp 40 N 400 W	Blackfoot	ID	83221	800-522-2223	208-785-5880
Oregon Freeze Dry Inc					
PO Box 1048	Albany	OR	97321	800-547-4060	541-926-6001
Oregon Potato Co PO Box 3110	Pasco	WA	99302	800-336-6311	509-545-4545
Small Planet Foods Inc					
106 Woodworth St	Sedro Woolley	WA	98284	800-624-4123	360-855-0100
Stapleton-Spence Packing Co					
1530 The Alameda Ste 320	San Jose	CA	95126	800-297-8815	408-297-8815
Sunsweet Growers Inc					
901 N Walton Ave	Yuba City	CA	95993	800-417-2253	530-674-5010
Tree Top Inc 220 E Second Ave	Selah	WA	98942	800-237-0515	509-697-7251

297-19 Fruits & Vegetables - Pickled

				Toll-Free	Phone
Beaverton Foods Inc					
7100 NW Century Blvd	Hillsboro	OR	97124	800-223-8076	503-646-8138
Best Maid Products Inc					
PO Box 1809	Fort Worth	TX	76101	800-447-3581	817-335-5494
Cain's Foods Inc 114 E Main St	Ayer	MA	01432	800-225-0601	978-772-0300
Clorox Co 1221 Broadway	Oakland	CA	94612	800-424-9300*	510-271-7000
NYSE: CLX ■ *Cust Svc					
Conway Import Co Inc					
11051 W Addison St	Franklin Park	IL	60131	800-323-8801	847-455-5600
Eastern Foods Inc					
1000 Naturally Fresh Blvd	Atlanta	GA	30349	800-765-1950	
Kaplan & Zubrin Inc					
146 Kaighns Ave	Camden	NJ	08103	800-248-1736	856-964-1083
Ken's Foods Inc					
1 D'Angelo Dr	Marlborough	MA	01752	800-633-5800*	508-229-1100
*General					
Langlois Co					
10810 San Sevaine Way	Mira Loma	CA	91752	800-962-5993	951-360-3900
Lee Kum Kee Inc					
14841 Don Julian Rd	City of Industry	CA	91746	800-654-5082*	626-709-1888
*Orders					
Litehouse Inc					
1109 N Ella Ave	Sandpoint	ID	83864	800-669-3169	208-263-7569
MA Gedney Co					
2100 Stoughton Ave	Chaska	MN	55318	888-244-0653	952-448-2612
Maurice's Gourmet Barbeque					
PO Box 6847	West Columbia	SC	29171	800-628-7423	803-791-5887
McIlhenny Co Hwy 329	Avery Island	LA	70513	800-634-9599*	337-365-8173
*Orders					
Moody Dunbar Inc					
2000 Waters Edge Dr Ste 21	Johnson City	TN	37604	800-251-8202	423-952-0100
NewStar Fresh Foods LLC					
900 Work St	Salinas	CA	93901	888-782-7220	831-758-7800
Olds Products Co					
10700 88th Ave	Pleasant Prairie	WI	53158	800-233-8064	262-947-3500
Spring Glen Fresh Foods Inc					
314 Spring Glen Dr PO Box 518	Ephrata	PA	17522	800-641-2853	717-733-2201
T Marzetti Co					
1105 Schrock Rd	Columbus	OH	43229	800-999-1835	614-846-2232
Walden Farms					
1209 W St Georges Ave	Linden	NJ	07036	800-229-1706	

297-20 Fruits, Vegetables, Juices - Canned or Preserved

				Toll-Free	Phone
American Spoon Foods Inc					
1668 Clarion Ave	Petoskey	MI	49770	800-222-5886	231-347-9030
Apple & Eve Inc					
2 Seaview Blvd	Port Washington	NY	11050	800-969-8018	516-621-1122
Braswell Foods Inc					
226 N Zetterower Ave	Statesboro	GA	30458	800-673-9388	912-764-6191
Bruce Foods Corp					
PO Drawer 1030	New Iberia	LA	70561	800-299-9082	337-365-8101
Campbell Soup Co					
One Campbell Pl	Camden	NJ	08103	800-257-8443	856-342-4800
NYSE: CPB					
Carriage House Cos Inc, The					
196 Newton St	Fredonia	NY	14063	800-828-8915	716-673-1000
Cincinnati Preserving Company Inc					
3015 E Kemper Rd	Cincinnati	OH	45241	800-222-9966*	513-771-2000
*Cust Svc					
Clement Pappas & Company Inc					
One Colons Dr Ste 200	Carneyspoint	NJ	08069	800-257-7019	856-455-1000
Cornelius Seed Corn Co					
14760 317th Ave	Bellevue	IA	52031	800-218-1862	563-672-3463
Del Monte Foods Co					
1 Maritime Plaza	San Francisco	CA	94111	800-543-3090*	415-247-3000
*Cust Svc					
Del Monte Fresh Produce Co					
241 Sevilla Ave	Coral Gables	FL	33134	800-950-3683*	305-520-8400
*Cust Svc					
Don Pepino Sales Co					
123 Railroad Ave	Williamstown	NJ	08094	888-281-6400	856-629-7429
Escalon Premier Brands					
1905 McHenry Ave	Escalon	CA	95320	800-255-5790	209-838-7341
Furmano Foods Inc					
770 Cannery Rd PO Box 500	Northumberland	PA	17857	877-877-6032	570-473-3516
Giorgio Foods Inc PO Box 96	Temple	PA	19560	800-220-2139	610-926-2139
Hanover Foods Corp					
1550 York St PO Box 334	Hanover	PA	17331	800-888-4646	717-632-6000
OTC: HNFSA					

				Toll-Free	Phone
Hirzel Canning Company & Farms					
411 Lemoyne Rd	Northwood	OH	43619	800-837-1631	419-693-0531
HJ Heinz Co					
One PPG Pl Ste 3100	Pittsburgh	PA	15230	800-255-5750	412-456-5700
House Foods America Corp					
7351 Orangewood Ave	Garden Grove	CA	92841	877-333-7077	714-901-4350
Jasper Wyman & Son					
PO Box 100	Milbridge	ME	04658	800-341-1758*	
*Sales					
JM Smucker Co					
One Strawberry Ln	Orrville	OH	44667	888-550-9555	330-682-3000
NYSE: SJM					
Johanna Foods Inc					
20 Johanna Farm Rd PO Box 272	Flemington	NJ	08822	800-727-6700	908-788-2200
Lakeside Foods Inc					
808 Hamilton St	Manitowoc	WI	54220	800-466-3834	920-684-3356
Leelanau Fruit Co					
2900 SW Bay Shore Dr	Suttons Bay	MI	49682	800-431-0718	231-271-3514
Lyons Magnus Inc					
3158 E Hamilton Ave	Fresno	CA	93702	800-344-7130	
Moody Dunbar Inc					
2000 Waters Edge Dr Ste 21	Johnson City	TN	37604	800-251-8202	423-952-0100
Morgan Foods Inc					
90 W Morgan St	Austin	IN	47102	888-430-1780	812-794-1170
Mott's LLP PO Box 869077	Plano	TX	75086	800-426-4891*	
*Consumer Info					
Muir Glen Organic Tomato Products					
PO Box 18932	Denver	CO	80218	800-832-6345	800-248-7310
National Fruit Product Co Inc					
701 Fairmont Ave PO Box 2040	Winchester	VA	22601	800-655-4022	540-723-9614
Ocean Spray Cranberries Inc					
1 Ocean Spray Dr	Lakeville-Middleboro	MA	02349	800-662-3263	508-946-1000
Pacific Coast Producers					
631 N Cluff Ave	Lodi	CA	95240	877-618-4776	209-367-8800
Pastorelli Food Products Inc					
162 N Sangamon St	Chicago	IL	60607	800-767-2829	312-666-2041
Simply Orange Juice Co					
2659 Orange Ave	Apopka	FL	32703	800-871-2653	
Stanislaus Food Products Co					
1202 D St	Modesto	CA	95354	800-327-7201	
Stapleton-Spence Packing Co					
1530 The Alameda Ste 320	San Jose	CA	95126	800-297-8815	408-297-8815
Sun Orchard Inc					
1198 W Fairmont Dr	Tempe	AZ	85282	800-505-8423	
Talk O'Texas Brands Inc					
1610 Roosevelt St	San Angelo	TX	76905	800-749-6572	325-655-6077
Tip Top Canning Co					
505 S Second St PO Box 126	Tipp City	OH	45371	800-352-2635	937-667-3713
Tree Top Inc 220 E Second Ave	Selah	WA	98942	800-237-0515	509-697-7251
Truitt Bros Inc					
1105 Front St NE	Salem	OR	97301	800-547-8712	503-362-3674
Vegetable Juices Inc					
7400 S Narragansett Ave	Chicago	IL	60638	888-776-9752*	708-924-9500
*General					
Whitlock Packaging Corp					
1701 S Lee St	Fort Gibson	OK	74434	800-833-9382	918-478-4300
Zeigler Beverage Co					
1513 N Broad St	Lansdale	PA	19446	800-854-6123*	215-855-5161
*Sales					

297-21 Fruits, Vegetables, Juices - Frozen

				Toll-Free	Phone
Apio Inc PO Box 727	Guadalupe	CA	93434	800-454-1355*	805-343-2835
*Sales					
Bernatello's PO Box 729	Maple Lake	MN	55358	800-622-6935	952-831-6622
Capitol City Produce					
16550 Commercial Ave	Baton Rouge	LA	70816	800-349-1583	225-272-8153
Coloma Frozen Foods Inc					
4145 Coloma Rd	Coloma	MI	49038	800-642-2723	269-849-0500
Dole Food Company Inc					
One Dole Dr	Westlake Village	CA	91362	800-232-8888	818-879-6600
NYSE: DOLE					
Fresh Frozen Foods LLC					
1814 Washington St PO Box 215	Jefferson	GA	30549	800-277-9851	706-367-9851
Giorgio Foods Inc PO Box 96	Temple	PA	19560	800-220-2139	610-926-2139
Graceland Fruit Inc					
1123 Main St	Frankfort	MI	49635	800-352-7181	231-352-7181
HJ Heinz Co					
One PPG Pl Ste 3100	Pittsburgh	PA	15230	800-255-5750	412-456-5700
HPC Foods Ltd 288 Libby St	Honolulu	HI	96819	877-370-0919	808-848-2431
JR Simplot Co					
999 W Main St Ste 1300	Boise	ID	83702	800-832-8893	208-336-2110
Lakeside Foods Inc					
808 Hamilton St	Manitowoc	WI	54220	800-466-3834	920-684-3356
Leelanau Fruit Co					
2900 SW Bay Shore Dr	Suttons Bay	MI	49682	800-431-0718	231-271-3514
McCain Foods Ltd					
181 Bay St Ste 3600	Toronto	ON	M5J2T3	800-938-7799	416-955-1700
McCain Foods USA Inc					
2275 Cabot Dr	Lisle	IL	60532	800-938-7799	
NORPAC Foods Inc					
930 W Washington St	Stayton	OR	97383	800-733-9311	503-769-2101
Penobscot McCrum LLC					
28 Pierce St	Belfast	ME	04915	800-435-4456	207-338-4360
Sweet Ovations					
1741 Tomlinson Rd	Philadelphia	PA	19116	800-280-9387	215-676-3900
Tree Top Inc 220 E Second Ave	Selah	WA	98942	800-237-0515	509-697-7251

297-22 Gelatin

				Toll-Free	Phone
Langlois Co					
10810 San Sevaine Way	Mira Loma	CA	91752	800-962-5993	951-360-3900
Nitta Gelatin Inc					
598 Airport Blvd Ste 900	Morrisville	NC	27560	888-648-8287	919-238-3300

					Toll-Free	Phone

Subco Foods Inc
4350 S Taylor Dr .... Sheboygan WI 53081 **800-473-0757** 920-457-7761

297-23 Grain Mill Products

					Toll-Free	Phone

ACH Food Cos Inc
7171 Goodlet Farms Pkwy .... Cordova TN 38016 **800-691-1106** 901-381-3000
ADM Corn Processing Div
4666 E Faries Pkwy .... Decatur IL 62526 **800-637-5843** 217-424-5200
ADM Milling Co (ADM)
8000 W 110th St .... Overland Park KS 66210 **800-422-1688** 913-491-9400
Ag Processing Inc
12700 W Dodge Rd PO Box 2047 .... Omaha NE 68103 **800-247-1345** 402-496-7809
Bay State Milling Co
100 Congress St .... Quincy MA 02169 **800-553-5687**
Blendex Company Inc
11208 Electron Dr .... Louisville KY 40299 **800-626-6325** 502-267-1003
Chelsea Milling Co
201 W N St PO Box 460 .... Chelsea MI 48118 **800-727-2460** 734-475-1361
Farmers Rice Co-op
PO Box 15223 .... Sacramento CA 95851 **800-326-2799** 916-923-5100
Gold Medal PO Box 9452 .... Minneapolis MN 55440 **800-248-7310**
Hodgson Mill Inc
1100 Stevens Ave .... Effingham IL 62401 **800-347-0105** 217-347-0105
House-Autry Mills Inc
7000 US Hwy 301 S .... Four Oaks NC 27524 **800-849-0802**
Indian Harvest Specialtifoods Inc
1012 Paul Bunyan Dr SE .... Bemidji MN 56601 **800-346-7032***
*Orders
Knappen Milling Co
110 S Water St .... Augusta MI 49012 **800-562-7736** 269-731-4141
Mallet & Company Inc
51 Arch St Ext .... Carnegie PA 15106 **800-245-2757** 412-276-9000
Manildra Group USA
4210 Shawnee Mission Pkwy
Ste 312A.................... Shawnee Mission KS 66205 **800-323-8435** 913-362-0777
Mars Snack Food
800 High St .... Hackettstown NJ 07840 **800-551-0895** 908-852-1000
McShares Inc PO Box 1460 .... Salina KS 67402 **800-234-7174** 785-825-2181
Mennel Milling Co
128 W Crocker St .... Fostoria OH 44830 **800-688-8151** 419-435-8151
MGP Ingredients Inc
100 Commercial St PO Box 130 .... Atchison KS 66002 **800-255-0302** 913-367-1480
NASDAQ: MGPI
Morrison Milling Co
319 E Prairie St .... Denton TX 76201 **800-531-7912** 940-387-6111
North Dakota Mill & Elevator
1823 Mill Rd .... Grand Forks ND 58203 **800-538-7721** 701-795-7000
Pacific Grain Products International Inc
351 Hanson Way PO Box 2060......... Woodland CA 95776 **800-333-0110*** 530-662-5056
*Cust Svc
Pacific International Rice Mills Inc
845 Kentucky Ave .... Woodland CA 95695 **800-747-4764** 530-661-6028
Producers Rice Mill Inc
PO Box 1248 .... Stuttgart AR 72160 **800-369-7675** 870-673-4444
RiceTec Inc
1925 FM 2917 PO Box 1305 .... Alvin TX 77511 **877-580-7423** 281-393-3502
Rock River Lumber & Grain Co
5502 Lyndon Rd PO Box 68 .... Prophetstown IL 61277 **800-605-4333** 815-537-5131
Shawnee Milling Company Inc
201 S Broadway PO Box 1567 .... Shawnee OK 74802 **800-654-2600** 405-273-7000
Siemer Milling Co
111 W Main St PO Box 670 .... Teutopolis IL 62467 **800-826-1065** 217-857-3131
Wilkins-Rogers Inc
27 Frederick Rd .... Ellicott City MD 21043 **877-438-4338*** 410-465-5800
*Cust Svc

297-24 Honey

					Toll-Free	Phone

Dutch Gold Honey Inc
2220 Dutch Gold Dr .... Lancaster PA 17601 **800-846-2753** 717-393-1716
Glorybee Foods Inc
120 N Seneca Rd .... Eugene OR 97402 **800-456-7923** 541-689-0913
Honey Acres 1557 Hwy 67 N .... Ashippun WI 53003 **800-558-7745**
Honeytree Inc 8570 M 50 .... Onsted MI 49265 **800-968-1889** 517-467-2482
Sioux Honey Assn Co-op
301 Lewis Blvd .... Sioux City IA 51101 **888-270-6956** 712-258-0638

297-25 Ice Cream & Frozen Desserts

					Toll-Free	Phone

Anderson Erickson Dairy Co
2420 E University Ave .... Des Moines IA 50317 **800-234-7257** 515-265-2521
Baldwin Richardson Foods Company Inc
20201 S La Grange Rd Ste 200.......... Frankfort IL 60423 **866-644-2732*** 815-464-9994
*Cust Svc
Broughton Foods Co
1701 Green St .... Marietta OH 45750 **800-283-2479** 740-373-4121
Cedar Crest Specialties Inc
7269 Hwy 60 PO Box 260............. Cedarburg WI 53012 **800-877-8341*** 262-377-7252
*Hotline
Coleman Dairy Inc
6901 I-30 .... Little Rock AR 72209 **800-365-1551** 501-748-1700
Creamland Dairies Inc
10 Indian School Rd NW .... Albuquerque NM 87105 **800-334-3865** 505-247-0721
Farrs Better Foods
2575 South 300 West .... South Salt lake City UT 84115 **877-553-2777** 801-484-8724
Galliker Dairy Company Inc
143 Donald Ln .... Johnstown PA 15907 **800-477-6455** 814-266-8702
Gandy's Dairies Inc
201 University Blvd .... Lubbock TX 79415 **877-382-4357** 806-765-8833

Graeter's Inc
2145 Reading Rd .... Cincinnati OH 45202 **800-721-3323** 513-721-3323
Green Foods Corp
2220 Camino Del Sol .... Oxnard CA 93030 **800-777-4430** 805-983-7470
Hershey Creamery Co
301 S Cameron St .... Harrisburg PA 17101 **888-240-1905** 717-238-8134
Hiland Dairy Co
PO Box 2270 .... Springfield MO 65801 **800-641-4022** 417-862-9311
Ice Cream Specialties
8419 Hanley Industrial Ct .... Saint Louis MO 63144 **800-662-7550** 314-962-2550
J & J Snack Foods Corp
6000 Central Hwy .... Pennsauken NJ 08109 **800-486-9533** 856-665-9533
NASDAQ: JJSF
Perry's Ice Cream Company Inc
One Ice Cream Plz .... Akron NY 14001 **800-873-7797** 716-542-5492
Royal Ice Cream Co
6200 Euclid Ave .... Cleveland OH 44103 **888-645-6606** 216-432-1144
Schwan Food Co
115 W College Dr .... Marshall MN 56258 **800-533-5290** 507-532-3274
Stonyfield Farm Inc
10 Burton Dr .... Londonderry NH 03053 **800-776-2697** 603-437-4040
Sugar Creek Foods International
301 N El Paso St .... Russellville AR 72801 **800-445-2715**
Turkey Hill Dairy Inc
2601 River Rd .... Conestoga PA 17516 **800-693-2479** 717-872-5461
Turner Dairy Farms Inc
1049 Jefferson Rd .... Pittsburgh PA 15235 **800-892-1039** 412-372-2211
Umpqua Dairy Products Co
333 SE Sykes Ave PO Box 1306 .... Roseburg OR 97470 **888-672-6455** 541-672-2638
Wells Enterprises Inc
1 Blue Bunny Dr .... Le Mars IA 51031 **888-309-1742*** 712-546-4000
*All
YoCream International Inc
5858 NE 87th Ave .... Portland OR 97220 **800-962-7326** 503-256-3754

297-26 Meat Products - Prepared

					Toll-Free	Phone

Aidells Sausage Co
1625 Alvarado St .... San Leandro CA 94577 **877-243-3557** 510-614-5450
Albertville Quality Foods Inc
130 Quality Dr PO Box 756. .... Albertville AL 35950 **800-353-2806** 256-840-9923
Alderfer Inc
382 Main St PO Box 2 .... Harleysville PA 19438 **800-341-1121*** 215-256-8818
*Sales
Aliments Asta Inc
511 Ave De La Gare
.... St Alexandre-De-Kamouraska QC G0L2G0 **800-463-1355** 418-495-2728
American Foods Group Inc
544 Acme St .... Green Bay WI 54302 **800-345-0293** 920-437-6330
Ballard's Farm Sausage Inc
2131 Right Fork Wilson Creek Rd
PO Box 699. .... Wayne WV 25570 **800-346-7675*** 304-272-5147
*General
Bar-S Foods Co PO Box 29049 .... Phoenix AZ 85038 **800-699-4115**
Berks Packing Company Inc
307-323 Bingaman St PO Box 5919 ..... Reading PA 19610 **800-882-3757** 610-376-7291
Best Provision Company Inc
144 Avon Ave .... Newark NJ 07108 **800-631-4466** 973-242-5000
Bridgford Foods Corp
1308 N Patt St .... Anaheim CA 92801 **800-854-3255** 714-526-5533
NASDAQ: BRID
Burger's Ozark Country Cured Hams Inc
32819 hwy 87 .... California MO 65018 **800-203-4424** 573-796-3134
Caribbean Products Ltd
3624 Falls Rd .... Baltimore MD 21211 **888-689-5068** 410-235-7700
Carl Buddig & Co
950 175th St .... Homewood IL 60430 **888-633-5684** 708-798-0900
Carlton Foods Corp
880 Texas 46 .... New Braunfels TX 78130 **800-628-9849** 830-625-7583
Cattaneo Bros Inc
769 Caudill St .... San Luis Obispo CA 93401 **800-243-8537** 805-543-7188
Cher-Make Sausage Co
2915 Calumet Ave .... Manitowoc WI 54220 **800-242-7679** 920-683-5980
Chicago Meat Authority Inc (CMA)
1120 W 47th Pl .... Chicaog IL 60609 **800-383-3811** 773-254-3811
Chicopee Provision Co Inc
19 Sitarz St .... Chicopee MA 01013 **800-924-6328** 413-594-4765
Citterio USA Corp
2008 SR 940 .... Freeland PA 18224 **800-435-8888** 570-636-3171
Cloverdale Foods Co
3015 34th St NW .... Mandan ND 58554 **800-669-9511**
Cook's Ham Inc
200 S Second St .... Lincoln NE 68508 **800-332-8400** 402-475-6700
Daniele Inc PO Box 106 .... Pascoag RI 02859 **800-451-2535** 401-568-6228
Dewied International Inc
5010 IH- 10 E .... San Antonio TX 78219 **800-992-5600** 210-661-6161
Dietz & Watson Inc
5701 Tacony St .... Philadelphia PA 19135 **800-333-1974** 215-831-9000
Family Brands International LLC
1001 Elm Hill Rd PO Box 429. .... Lenoir City TN 37771 **800-356-4455**
Fred Usinger Inc
1030 N Old World Third St .... Milwaukee WI 53203 **800-558-9998** 414-276-9100
Gaytan Foods
15430 Proctor Ave .... City Of Industry CA 91745 **800-242-9826** 626-330-4553
Green Tree Packing Co
65 Central Ave .... Passaic NJ 07055 **800-562-6934** 973-473-1305
Grote & Weigel Inc
76 Granby St .... Bloomfield CT 06002 **800-943-6376** 860-242-8528
Habbersett Scrapple Inc
103 S Railroad Ave .... Bridgeville DE 19933 **800-338-4727**
Hatfield Quality Meats Inc
2700 Clemens Rd .... Hatfield PA 19440 **800-743-1191** 215-368-2500
Hazle Park Packing Co
260 Washington Ave Hazle Pk ..... Hazletownship PA 18202 **800-238-4331** 570-455-7571

	Toll-Free	Phone

Hormel Foods Corp
1 Hormel Pl ....Austin MN 55912 — **800-523-4635** — 507-437-5611
NYSE: HRL

John Morrell & Co
805 E Kemper Rd ....Cincinnati OH 45246 — **800-722-1127** — 513-346-3540

Johnsonville Sausage LLC
PO Box 906 ....Sheboygan Falls WI 53085 — **888-556-2728**

Jones Dairy Farm
800 Jones Ave ....Fort Atkinson WI 53538 — **800-635-6637** — 920-563-2431

Karl Ehmer Inc
48 S Ocean Ave ....Patchogue NY 11772 — **800-487-5275** — 631-289-3448

Kayem Foods Inc
75 Arlington St ....Chelsea MA 02150 — **800-426-6100** — 617-889-1600

Kent Quality Foods Inc
703 Leonard St NW ....Grand Rapids MI 49504 — **800-748-0141**

Kessler's Inc
1201 Hummel Ave ....Lemoyne PA 17043 — **800-382-1328** — 717-763-7162

Klement Sausage Co Inc
207 E Lincoln Ave ....Milwaukee WI 53207 — **800-553-6368** — 414-744-2330

Kronos Products Inc
One Kronos Dr ....Glendale Heights IL 60139 — **800-621-0099**

Land O'Frost Inc
16850 Chicago Ave ....Lansing IL 60438 — **800-323-3308** — 708-474-7100

Les Trois Petits Cochons Inc
4223 First Ave Second Fl ....Brooklyn NY 11232 — **800-537-7283*** — 212-219-1230
*General

Louie's Finer Meats Inc
PO Box 774 ....Cumberland WI 54829 — **800-270-4297** — 715-822-4728

Maid-Rite Steak Company Inc
105 Keystone Industrial Pk ....Dunmore PA 18512 — **800-233-4259** — 570-343-4748

Marathon Enterprises Inc
Nine Smith St ....Englewood NJ 07631 — **800-722-7388** — 201-935-3330

Miller Packing Co
1122 Industrial Way PO Box 1390 ......Lodi CA 95241 — **800-624-2328** — 209-339-2310

Mongolia Casing Corp
4706 Grand Ave ....Maspeth NY 11378 — **800-472-2197** — 718-628-3800

Natural Casing Co
410 E Railroad St PO Box A ....Peshtigo WI 54157 — **877-515-0270**

Neto Sausage Co Inc
1313 Franklin St ....Santa Clara CA 95050 — **888-482-6386** — 408-296-0818

Oberto Sausage Co
7060 S 238th St ....Kent WA 98032 — **877-453-7591** — 253-854-7056

Odom's Tennessee Pride Sausage Inc
1201 Neelys Bend Rd ....Madison TN 37115 — **866-484-8641** — 615-868-1360

Old Wisconsin Sausage Co
5030 PlaybiRd Rd ....Sheboygan WI 53083 — **877-451-7988**

Palmyra Bologna Company Inc
230 N College St ....Palmyra PA 17078 — **800-282-6336** — 717-838-6336

Park 100 Foods Inc
326 E Adams St ....Tipton IN 46072 — **800-854-6504** — 765-675-3480

Peer Foods Group Inc
1200 W 35th St Ste 5E ....Chicago IL 60609 — **800-365-5644** — 773-927-1440

Plumrose USA Inc
1901 Butterfield Rd Ste 305 .....Downers Grove IL 60515 — **800-526-4909** — 732-624-4040

Pocino Foods Co
14250 Lomitas Ave ....City of Industry CA 91746 — **800-345-0150** — 626-968-8000

Premio Foods Inc
50 Utter Ave ....Hawthorne NJ 07506 — **800-864-7622** — 973-427-1106

Randolph Packing Co
275 Roma Jean Pkwy ....Streamwood IL 60107 — **800-451-1607** — 630-830-3100

Reser's Fine Foods Inc
15570 SW Jenkins Rd ....Beaverton OR 97006 — **800-333-6431** — 503-643-6431

Saags Products Inc
1799 Factor Ave ....San Leandro CA 94577 — **800-352-7224** — 510-352-8000

Sadler's Smokehouse Ltd
PO Box 1088 ....Henderson TX 75653 — **800-777-5581** — 903-655-7262

Sahlen Packing Company Inc
318 Howard St ....Buffalo NY 14206 — **800-466-8165** — 716-852-8677

Schaller & Weber Inc
22-35 46th St ....Astoria NY 11105 — **800-847-4115*** — 718-721-5480
*Orders

Silver Star Meats Inc
1720 Middletown Rd PO Box 393.......McKees Rocks PA 15136 — **800-548-1321** — 412-771-5539

Smithfield Foods Inc
200 Commerce St ....Smithfield VA 23430 — **800-276-6158** — 757-365-3000
NYSE: SFD

Stampede Meat Inc
7351 S 78th Ave ....Bridgeview IL 60455 — **800-353-0933**

Standard Meat Company LP
5105 Investment Dr ....Dallas TX 75236 — **866-859-6313** — 214-561-0561

Stock Yards Packing Co Inc
2457 W North Ave ....Melrose Park IL 60160 — **877-785-9273**

Sugar Creek Packing Co
2101 Kenskill Ave ...Washington Court House OH 43160 — **800-848-8205** — 740-335-7440

Sysco Kansas City Inc
1915 E Kansas City Rd ....Olathe KS 66061 — **800-735-3341** — 913-829-5555

TF Kinnealey & Company Inc
1100 Pearl St ....Brockton MA 02301 — **800-225-4950** — 508-638-7700

Tyson Prepared Foods Inc
5701 McNutt Rd ....Santa Teresa NM 88008 — **888-301-7304** — 575-589-0100

US Premium Beef LLC (USPB)
12200 N Ambassador Dr
PO Box 20103.................Kansas City MO 64163 — **866-877-2525** — 816-713-8800

Vienna Sausage Manufacturing Co
2501 N Damen Ave ....Chicago IL 60647 — **800-366-3647** — 773-278-7800

Vollwerth & Co
200 Hancock St PO Box 239............Hancock MI 49930 — **800-562-7620** — 906-482-1550

Wimmer's Meat Products Inc
126 W Grant St ....West Point NE 68788 — **800-762-9865*** — 402-372-2437
*Cust Svc

Wolfson Casing Corp
700 S Fulton Ave ....Mount Vernon NY 10550 — **800-221-8042** — 914-668-9000

297-27 Milk & Cream Products

	Toll-Free	Phone

Alta Dena Dairy
17851 E Railrd ....City of Industry CA 91748 — **800-535-1369***
*Orders

AMPI 315 N Broadway ....New Ulm MN 56073 — **800-533-3580** — 507-354-8295

Anderson Erickson Dairy Co
2420 E University Ave ....Des Moines IA 50317 — **800-234-7257** — 515-265-2521

Broughton Foods Co
1701 Green St ....Marietta OH 45750 — **800-283-2479** — 740-373-4121

Clover Farms Dairy
PO Box 14627 ....Reading PA 19612 — **800-323-0123** — 610-921-9111

Cloverland Green Spring Dairy Inc
2701 Loch Raven Rd ....Baltimore MD 21218 — **800-492-0094*** — 410-235-4477
*Orders

Coleman Dairy Inc
6901 I-30 ....Little Rock AR 72209 — **800-365-1551** — 501-748-1700

Dean Foods Co
2711 N Haskell Ave Ste 3400 ....Dallas TX 75204 — **800-395-7004** — 214-303-3400
NYSE: DF

Eagle Family Foods Inc
One Strawberry Ln ....Orrville OH 44667 — **888-656-3245**

Galliker Dairy Company Inc
143 Donald Ln ....Johnstown PA 15907 — **800-477-6455** — 814-266-8702

Guida-Seibert Dairy Co
433 Pk St ....New Britain CT 06051 — **800-832-8929** — 860-224-2404

Harrisburg Dairies Inc
2001 Herr St ....Harrisburg PA 17105 — **800-692-7429** — 717-233-8701

Heritage Foods LLC
4002 Westminster Ave ....Santa Ana CA 92703 — **800-321-5960*** — 714-775-5000
*Orders

Hiland Dairy Co
PO Box 2270 ....Springfield MO 65801 — **800-641-4022** — 417-862-9311

Kemps LLC 1270 Energy Ln ....Saint Paul MN 55108 — **800-322-9566** — 651-379-6500

Land O'Lakes Inc
4001 Lexington Ave N ....Arden Hills MN 55126 — **800-328-9680** — 651-481-2222

Land O'Lakes Inc Dairyman's Div
400 S 'M' St ....Tulare CA 93274 — **800-328-4155** — 559-687-8287

Lifeway Foods Inc
6431 W Oakton St ....Morton Grove IL 60053 — **877-281-3874** — 847-967-1010
NASDAQ: LWAY

Marcus Dairy Inc
Four Eagle Rd ....Danbury CT 06810 — **800-243-2511** — 203-748-5611

McArthur Dairy
456 Flamingo Dr ....West Palm Beach FL 33401 — **800-432-4872** — 561-659-4811

Meadow Brook Dairy
2365 Buffalo Rd ....Erie PA 16510 — **800-352-4010** — 814-899-3191

Milkco Inc
220 Deaverview Rd ....Asheville NC 28806 — **800-842-8021** — 828-254-9560

Oakhurst Dairy
364 Forest Ave ....Portland ME 04101 — **800-482-0718** — 207-772-7468

Parmalat Canada Ltd
405 the W Mall 10th Fl ....Toronto ON M9C5J1 — **800-563-1515**

Prairie Farms Dairy Inc
1100 N Broadway St ....Carlinville IL 62626 — **800-654-2547** — 217-854-2547

Producers Dairy Foods Inc
250 E Belmont Ave ....Fresno CA 93701 — **800-660-1171** — 559-264-6583

Royal Crest Dairy Inc
350 S Pearl St ....Denver CO 80209 — **888-226-6455** — 303-777-2227

Schneider Valley Farms Dairy
1860 E Third St ....State College PA 17701 — **800-516-1750** — 814-237-3426

Shamrock Foods
3900 E Camelback Rd Ste 300 ....Phoenix AZ 85018 — **800-289-3663** — 602-477-2500

Smith Dairy 1381 Dairy Ln ....Orrville OH 44667 — **800-776-7076** — 330-683-8710

Southeast Milk Inc
1950 SE Hwy 484 PO Box 3790 ....Belleview FL 34420 — **800-598-7866**

Stonyfield Farm Inc
10 Burton Dr ....Londonderry NH 03053 — **800-776-2697** — 603-437-4040

Superior Dairy Inc
4719 Navarre Rd SW ....Canton OH 44706 — **800-597-5460** — 330-477-4515

Umpqua Dairy Products Co
333 SE Sykes Ave PO Box 1306 ......Roseburg OR 97470 — **888-672-6455** — 541-672-2638

United Dairy Farmers
3955 Montgomery Rd ....Cincinnati OH 45212 — **800-654-2809*** — 513-396-8700
*General

United Dairy Inc
300 N Fifth St ....Martins Ferry OH 43935 — **800-252-1542** — 740-633-1451

297-28 Nuts - Edible

	Toll-Free	Phone

Azar Nut Co 1800 NW Dr ....El Paso TX 79912 — **800-351-8178** — 915-877-4079

Dahlgren & Co Inc
1220 Sunflower St ....Crookston MN 56716 — **877-312-9198** — 218-281-2985

Hines Nut Co Inc
990 S St Paul St ....Dallas TX 75201 — **800-561-6374** — 214-939-0253

John B Sanfilippo & Son Inc
1703 N Randall Rd ....Elgin IL 60123 — **800-874-8734** — 847-289-1800
NASDAQ: JBSS

Kar's Nuts
1200 E 14 Mile Rd ....Madison Heights MI 48071 — **800-527-6887** — 248-588-1903

King Nut Co 31900 Solon Rd ....Solon OH 44139 — **800-860-5464** — 440-248-8484

Koinonia Partners
1324 Georgia Hwy 49 S ....Americus GA 31719 — **877-738-1741** — 229-924-0391

Priester Pecan Company Inc
PO Box 381 ....Fort Deposit AL 36032 — **800-277-3226** — 334-227-4301

South Georgia Pecan Co
309 S Lee St ....Valdosta GA 31601 — **800-627-6630** — 229-244-1321

Trophy Nut Company Inc
320 N Second St ....Tipp City OH 45371 — **800-729-6887** — 937-667-8478

Young Pecan Co
1831 W Evans St Ste 200 ....Florence SC 29501 — **800-829-6864*** — 843-662-8591
*All

297-29 Oil Mills - Cottonseed, Soybean, Other Vegetable Oils

	Toll-Free	Phone
Abitec Corp Inc PO Box 569 .... Columbus OH 43215	800-555-1255*	614-429-6464
*Sales		
Ag Processing Inc		
12700 W Dodge Rd PO Box 2047.................... Omaha NE 68103	800-247-1345	402-496-7809
American Lecithin Company Inc		
115 Hurley Rd Unit 2B .... Oxford CT 06478	800-364-4416	203-262-7100
Cargill Inc		
15407 McGinty Rd W .... Wayzata MN 55391	800-227-4455	952-742-7575
Owensboro Grain Co		
822 E Second St .... Owensboro KY 42303	800-874-0305	270-926-2032
Planters Cotton Oil Mill Inc		
2901 Planters Dr .... Pine Bluff AR 71601	800-264-7070	870-534-3631

297-30 Oils - Edible (Margarine, Shortening, Table Oils, etc)

	Toll-Free	Phone
ACH Food Cos Inc		
7171 Goodlet Farms Pkwy .... Cordova TN 38016	800-691-1106	901-381-3000
Golden Foods/Golden Brands LLC		
2520 Seventh St Rd .... Louisville KY 40208	800-622-3055	502-636-3712
Kagome Creative Foods LLC		
710 N Pearl St .... Osceola AR 72370	800-643-0006	870-563-2601
Par-Way Tryson Co		
107 Bolte Ln .... Saint Clair MO 63077	800-844-4554	636-629-4545
Ventura Foods LLC 40 Pt Dr .... Brea CA 92821	800-421-6257	714-257-3700
Veronica Foods Co		
1991 Dennison St .... Oakland CA 94606	800-370-5554	510-535-6833

297-31 Pasta

	Toll-Free	Phone
Dakota Growers Pasta Company Inc		
One Pasta Ave .... Carrington ND 58421	800-543-5561	701-652-2855
Monterey Pasta Co		
2315 Moore Ave .... Fullerton CA 92833	800-588-7782	
New World Pasta Co		
85 Shannon Rd .... Harrisburg PA 17112	800-730-5957*	717-526-2200
*Sales		
OB Macaroni Co PO Box 53 .... Fort Worth TX 76101	800-553-4336*	817-335-4629
*Orders		
Peking Noodle Co Inc		
1514 N San Fernando Rd .... Los Angeles CA 90065	877-735-4648	323-223-2023

297-32 Peanut Butter

	Toll-Free	Phone
Carriage House Cos Inc, The		
196 Newton St .... Fredonia NY 14063	800-828-8915	716-673-1000
Edwards-Freeman		
441 E Hector St .... Conshohocken PA 19428	877-448-6887	
Jimbo's Jumbos Inc		
185 Peanut Dr PO Box 465 .... Edenton NC 27932	800-334-4771*	
*General		
JM Smucker Co		
One Strawberry Ln .... Orrville OH 44667	888-550-9555	330-682-3000
NYSE: SJM		
John B Sanfilippo & Son Inc		
1703 N Randall Rd .... Elgin IL 60123	800-874-8734	847-289-1800
NASDAQ: JBSS		
Producers Peanut Company Inc		
PO Box 250 .... Suffolk VA 23434	800-847-5491	757-539-7496

297-33 Salads - Prepared

	Toll-Free	Phone
D'Arrigo Bros Company of California Inc		
PO Box 850 .... Salinas CA 93902	800-995-5939*	831-455-4500
*Cust Svc		
Herold's Salads Inc		
17512 Miles Ave .... Cleveland OH 44128	800-427-2523	216-991-7500
Kayem Foods Inc		
75 Arlington St .... Chelsea MA 02150	800-426-6100	617-889-1600
Ready Pac Produce Inc		
4401 Foxdale Ave .... Irwindale CA 91706	800-800-7822	
Reser's Fine Foods Inc		
15570 SW Jenkins Rd .... Beaverton OR 97006	800-333-6431	503-643-6431
Sandridge Food Group (SFC)		
133 Commerce Dr .... Medina OH 44256	800-672-2523	330-725-2348
Suter Company Inc		
258 May St .... Sycamore IL 60178	800-435-6942	815-895-9186

297-34 Sandwiches - Prepared

	Toll-Free	Phone
Bridgford Foods Corp		
1308 N Patt St .... Anaheim CA 92801	800-854-3255	714-526-5533
NASDAQ: BRID		
Cloverdale Foods Co		
3015 34th St NW .... Mandan ND 58554	800-669-9511	
Hormel Foods Corp		
1 Hormel Pl .... Austin MN 55912	800-523-4635	507-437-5611
NYSE: HRL		
Konop Cos		
1725 Industrial Dr .... Green Bay WI 54302	800-770-0477	920-468-8517

	Toll-Free	Phone
Landshire Inc		
12 Tucker Dr .... Caseyville IL 62232	800-468-3354	618-293-6525

297-35 Snack Foods

	Toll-Free	Phone
Better Made Snack Foods Inc		
10148 Gratiot Ave .... Detroit MI 48213	800-332-2394	313-925-4774
Bickel's Snack Foods		
1120 Zinns Quarry Rd .... York PA 17404	800-233-1933	717-843-0738
Cape Cod Potato Chip Co		
100 Breed's Hill Rd .... Hyannis MA 02601	888-881-2447	508-775-3358
Chester Inc		
555 Eastport Ctr Dr .... Valparaiso IN 46383	800-778-1131	219-465-7555
CJ Vitner & Co		
4202 W 45th St .... Chicago IL 60632	800-523-7900*	773-523-7900
*General		
Evans Food Group Ltd		
4118 S Halsted St .... Chicago IL 60609	866-254-7400	773-254-7400
Frito-Lay North America		
7701 Legacy Dr .... Plano TX 75024	800-352-4477	972-334-7000
Golden Flake Snack Foods Inc		
One Golden Flake Dr .... Birmingham AL 35205	800-239-2447	205-323-6161
Herr Foods Inc		
20 Herr Dr PO Box 300 .... Nottingham PA 19362	800-344-3777	610-932-9330
Martin's Potato Chips Inc		
5847 Lincoln Hwy W PO Box 28 .... Thomasville PA 17364	800-272-4477	717-792-3565
Mike-Sell's Potato Chip Co		
333 Leo St PO Box 115 .... Dayton OH 45404	800-257-4742	937-228-9400
Mission Foods		
1159 Cottonwood Ln Ste 200 .... Irving TX 75038	800-443-7994	972-232-5200
Old Dutch Foods Inc		
2375 Terminal Rd .... Roseville MN 55113	800-989-2447	651-633-8810
Smith Bros Co		
3501 W 48th Pl .... Chicago IL 60632	800-621-0225	773-927-3737
Snacks Unlimited		
One General Mills Blvd .... Minneapolis MN 55426	800-248-7310	763-764-7600
Snyder of Berlin		
1313 Stadium Dr .... Berlin PA 15530	800-374-7949	814-267-4641
Tim's Cascade Snacks		
1150 Industry Dr N .... Algona WA 98001	800-533-8467	253-833-0255
Uncle Ray's LLC		
14245 Birwood St .... Detroit MI 48238	800-800-3286	313-834-0800
UTZ Quality Foods Co		
900 High St .... Hanover PA 17331	800-367-7629	717-637-6644
Wise Foods Inc		
245 Townpark Dr Ste 75 .... Kennesaw GA 30144	888-759-4401	770-426-5821
Wyandot Inc 135 Wyandot Ave .... Marion OH 43302	800-992-6368	740-383-4031

297-36 Specialty Foods

	Toll-Free	Phone
Alphin Bros Inc 2302 US 301 S .... Dunn NC 28334	800-672-4502	910-892-8751
Armanino Foods of Distinction Inc		
30588 San Antonio St .... Hayward CA 94544	800-255-5855	510-441-9300
OTC: AMNF		
Ateeco Inc		
600 E Ctr St PO Box 606 .... Shenandoah PA 17976	800-233-3170	570-462-2745
Avanti Foods 109 Depot St .... Walnut IL 61376	800-243-3739	815-379-2155
Beech-Nut Nutrition Corp		
One Nutritious Pl .... Amsterdam NY 12010	800-233-2468	
Bellisio Foods Inc		
1201 Harman Pl Ste 302 .... Minneapolis MN 55403	800-368-7337	612-371-8222
Bruce Foods Corp		
PO Drawer 1030 .... New Iberia LA 70561	800-299-9082	337-365-8101
Camino Real Foods Inc		
2638 E Vernon Ave .... Vernon CA 90058	800-421-6201	323-585-6599
Campbell Soup Co		
One Campbell Pl .... Camden NJ 08103	800-257-8443	856-342-4800
NYSE: CPB		
Chungs Gourmet Foods		
3907 Dennis St .... Houston TX 77004	800-824-8640	713-741-2118
Cromers Inc 1700 Huger St .... Columbia SC 29201	800-322-7688	
Cuisine Solutions Inc		
4106 Wheeler Ave Ste 450 .... Alexandria VA 22304	888-285-4679	703-270-2900
OTC: CUSI		
D & D Foods Inc		
9425 N 48th St .... Omaha NE 68152	800-208-0364	402-571-4113
Del Monte Foods Co		
1 Maritime Plaza .... San Francisco CA 94111	800-543-3090*	415-247-3000
*Cust Svc		
Deli Express		
16101 W 78th St .... Eden Prairie MN 55344	800-328-8184	
Don Miguel Mexican Foods Inc		
One Hormel Pl .... Austin MN 55912	800-725-7212	
Durrset Amigos Ltd		
4669 Hwy 90 W .... San Antonio TX 78237	800-580-3477	210-798-5360
Eden Foods Inc		
701 Tecumseh Rd .... Clinton MI 49236	800-248-0320*	517-456-7424
*Cust Svc		
El Encanto Inc		
2001 Fourth St SW PO Box 293 .... Albuquerque NM 87103	800-888-7336	505-243-2722
Ener-G Foods Inc		
5960 First Ave S PO Box 84487 .... Seattle WA 98124	800-331-5222	206-767-3928
Gerber Products Co		
445 State St .... Fremont MI 49413	800-284-9488	
Hain Celestial Group Inc		
4600 Sleepytime Dr Ste 250 .... Boulder CO 80301	800-434-4246	
NASDAQ: HAIN		
Hanover Foods Corp		
1550 York St PO Box 334 .... Hanover PA 17331	800-888-4646	717-632-6000
OTC: HNFSA		
HJ Heinz Co		
One PPG Pl Ste 3100 .... Pittsburgh PA 15230	800-255-5750	412-456-5700

				Toll-Free	Phone
Home Market Foods Inc					
140 Morgan Dr	Norwood	MA	02062	**800-367-8325**	781-948-1500
Hormel Foods Corp					
1 Hormel Pl	Austin	MN	55912	**800-523-4635**	507-437-5611
NYSE: HRL					
JM Smucker Co					
One Strawberry Ln	Orrville	OH	44667	**888-550-9555**	330-682-3000
NYSE: SJM					
Juanita's Foods Inc					
P.O. Box 847 PO Box 847	Wilmington	CA	90748	**800-303-2965**	
Kahiki Foods Inc					
1100 Morrison Rd	Columbus	OH	43230	**855-524-4540**	614-322-3180
La Reina Inc					
316 N Ford Blvd	Los Angeles	CA	90022	**800-367-7522**	323-268-2791
Little Lady Foods Inc					
2323 Pratt Blvd	Elk Grove Village	IL	60007	**800-439-1440**	847-631-3500
McCain Foods Ltd					
181 Bay St Ste 3600	Toronto	ON	M5J2T3	**800-938-7799**	416-955-1700
McCain Foods USA Inc					
2275 Cabot Dr	Lisle	IL	60532	**800-938-7799**	
Michael Angelo's Gourmet Foods Inc					
200 Michael Angelo Way	Austin	TX	78728	**877-482-5426**	512-218-3500
Morgan Foods Inc					
90 W Morgan St	Austin	IN	47102	**888-430-1780**	812-794-1170
Mott's LLP PO Box 869077	Plano	TX	75086	**800-426-4891***	
*Consumer Info					
Nardone Bros Baking Company Inc					
420 New Commerce Blvd	Wilkes-Barre	PA	18706	**800-822-5320**	570-823-0141
Overhill Farms Inc					
2727 E Vernon Ave	Vernon	CA	90058	**800-859-6406**	323-582-9977
NYSE: OFI					
Papa John's International Inc					
PO Box 99900	Louisville	KY	40269	**877-547-7272**	
NASDAQ: PZZA					
Pastorelli Food Products Inc					
162 N Sangamon St	Chicago	IL	60607	**800-767-2829**	312-666-2041
Pinnacle Foods Corp					
399 Jefferson Rd	Parsippany	NJ	07054	**866-266-7596**	973-541-6620
Preferred Meal Systems Inc					
5240 St Charles Rd	Berkeley	IL	60163	**800-886-6325***	708-318-2500
*Cust Svc					
Quaker Oats Co					
555 W Monroe St	Chicago	IL	60661	**800-367-6287**	312-821-1000
Request Foods Inc					
PO Box 2577	Holland	MI	49422	**800-748-0378***	616-786-0900
*Sales					
Ruiz Foods Inc PO Box 37	Dinuba	CA	93618	**800-477-6474**	559-591-5510
Schwan Food Co					
115 W College Dr	Marshall	MN	56258	**800-533-5290**	507-532-3274
Small Planet Foods Inc					
106 Woodworth St	Sedro Woolley	WA	98284	**800-624-4123**	360-855-0100
Suter Company Inc					
258 May St	Sycamore	IL	60178	**800-435-6942**	815-895-9186
Vanee Foods Company Inc					
5418 McDermott Dr	Berkeley	IL	60163	**800-654-6647***	708-449-7300
*Cust Svc					
Windsor Foods					
3355 W Alabama St Ste 730	Houston	TX	77098	**800-458-4054**	713-843-5200
Winter Gardens Quality Foods Inc					
304 Commerce St PO Box 339	New Oxford	PA	17350	**800-242-7637**	717-624-4911

297-37 Spices, Seasonings, Herbs

				Toll-Free	Phone
Abco Laboratories Inc					
2450 S Watney Way	Fairfield	CA	94533	**800-678-2226**	707-432-2200
American Outdoor Products Inc					
6350 Gunpark Dr	Boulder	CO	80301	**800-641-0500**	303-581-0518
Basic American Foods					
2185 N California Blvd Ste 215	Walnut Creek	CA	94596	**800-227-4050**	925-472-4000
Benson's Gourmet Seasonings					
PO Box 638	Azusa	CA	91702	**800-325-5619**	626-969-4443
Blendex Company Inc					
11208 Electron Dr	Louisville	KY	40299	**800-626-6325**	502-267-1003
Frontier Natural Products Co-op					
3021 78th St PO Box 299	Norway	IA	52318	**800-669-3275**	319-227-7996
Fuchs North America					
9740 Reisterstown Rd	Owings Mills	MD	21117	**800-365-3229**	410-363-1700
Griffith Laboratories Worldwide Inc					
1 Griffith Ctr	Alsip	IL	60803	**800-346-9494***	708-371-0900
*Cust Svc					
Johnny's Fine Foods Inc					
319 E 25th St	Tacoma	WA	98421	**855-654-9590***	253-383-4597
*General					
McCormick & Co Inc					
18 Loveton Cir	Sparks	MD	21152	**800-632-5847**	410-771-7244
NYSE: MKC					
McCormick & Company Inc Food Service Div					
226 Schilling Cir	Hunt Valley	MD	21031	**800-322-7742**	410-771-7500
McCormick & Company Inc McCormick Flavor Div					
226 Schilling Cir	Hunt Valley	MD	21031	**800-322-7742**	410-771-7500
McCormick Ingredients					
18 Loveton Cir	Sparks	MD	21152	**800-632-5847**	410-771-7301
Newly Weds Foods Inc					
4140 W Fullerton Ave	Chicago	IL	60639	**800-621-7521**	773-489-7000
Pepsi Bottling Ventures LLC					
4141 Parklake Ave Ste 600	Raleigh	NC	27612	**800-662-8792**	919-865-2300
Precision Foods Inc					
11457 Olde Cabin Rd Ste 100	Saint Louis	MO	63141	**800-442-5242**	314-567-7400
SensoryEffects Flavor Co					
231 Rock Industrial Park Dr	Bridgeton	MO	63044	**800-422-5444**	314-291-5444
Spice Hunter Inc					
184 Suburban Rd PO Box 8110	San Luis Obispo	CA	93403	**800-444-3061**	
Spice World Inc					
8101 Presidents Dr	Orlando	FL	32809	**800-433-4979**	
World Spice Inc					
223 E Highland Pkwy	Roselle	NJ	07203	**800-234-1060**	908-245-0600

297-38 Sugar & Sweeteners

				Toll-Free	Phone
C & H Sugar Co Inc					
850 Loring Ave	Crockett	CA	94525	**800-773-1803**	
Western Sugar Co-op					
7555 E Hampden Ave Ste 600	Denver	CO	80231	**800-523-7497**	303-830-3939

297-39 Syrup - Maple

				Toll-Free	Phone
Carriage House Cos Inc, The					
196 Newton St	Fredonia	NY	14063	**800-828-8915**	716-673-1000
Maple Grove Farms of Vermont					
1052 Portland St	Saint Johnsbury	VT	05819	**800-525-2540**	802-748-5141
Pinnacle Foods Corp					
399 Jefferson Rd	Parsippany	NJ	07054	**866-266-7596**	973-541-6620
Richards Maple Products Inc					
545 Water St	Chardon	OH	44024	**800-352-4052**	
Sea Breeze Inc 441 Rt 202	Towaco	NJ	07082	**800-732-2733**	973-334-7777

297-40 Tea

				Toll-Free	Phone
Bigelow Tea					
201 Black Rock Tpke	Fairfield	CT	06825	**888-244-3569**	
Celestial Seasonings Inc					
4600 Sleepytime Dr	Boulder	CO	80301	**800-351-8175**	303-530-5300
Redco Foods Inc					
One Hansen Island	Little Falls	NY	13365	**800-556-6674**	315-823-1300
S & D Coffee Inc					
300 Concord Pkwy PO Box 1628	Concord	NC	28026	**800-933-2210***	704-782-3121
*Cust Svc					

297-41 Vinegar & Cider

				Toll-Free	Phone
Boyajian Inc 144 Will Dr	Canton	MA	02021	**800-965-0665***	781-828-9966
*General					
Heintz & Weber Co Inc					
150 Reading Ave	Buffalo	NY	14220	**800-438-6878**	716-852-7171
MA Gedney Co					
2100 Stoughton Ave	Chaska	MN	55318	**888-244-0653**	952-448-2612
Mizkan Americas Inc					
1661 Feehanville Dr Ste 300	Mount Prospect	IL	60056	**800-323-4358**	847-590-0059
National Fruit Product Co Inc					
701 Fairmont Ave PO Box 2040	Winchester	VA	22601	**800-655-4022**	540-723-9614
Pastorelli Food Products Inc					
162 N Sangamon St	Chicago	IL	60607	**800-767-2829**	312-666-2041

297-42 Yeast

				Toll-Free	Phone
Brolite Products Inc					
1900 S Pk Ave	Streamwood	IL	60107	**888-276-5483**	630-830-0340
DSM Food Specialties Inc					
45 Waterview Blvd	Parsippany	NJ	07054	**800-526-0189**	973-257-1063
Lesaffre Yeast Corp					
7475 W Main St	Milwaukee	WI	53214	**877-677-7000***	
*Cust Svc					
Minn-Dak Yeast Company Inc					
18175 Red River Rd W	Wahpeton	ND	58075	**800-348-0991**	701-642-3300
Ohly Americas					
3388 Bacon St	Rhinelander	WI	54501	**800-321-2689**	320-587-2481

---

298   FOOD PRODUCTS - WHOL

SEE ALSO Beverages - Whol

298-1 Baked Goods - Whol

				Toll-Free	Phone
Wheat Montana Farms Inc					
10778 US Hwy 287	Three Forks	MT	59752	**800-535-2798**	406-285-3614

298-2 Coffee & Tea - Whol

				Toll-Free	Phone
Barrie House Coffee Company Inc					
Four Warehouse Ln	Elmsford	NY	10523	**800-876-2233**	
Becharas Bros Coffee Co Inc					
14501 Hamilton Ave	Highland Park	MI	48203	**800-944-9675**	313-869-4700
Capricorn Coffees Inc					
353 Tenth St	San Francisco	CA	94103	**800-541-0758**	415-621-8500
Coffee Bean International					
9120 NE Alderwood Rd	Portland	OR	97220	**800-877-0474**	503-227-4490
Coffee Masters Inc					
7606 Industrial Ct	Spring Grove	IL	60081	**800-334-6485**	815-675-0088
Red Diamond Inc 400 Park Ave	Moody	AL	35004	**800-292-4651**	205-577-4000
Royal Cup Coffee					
160 Cleage Dr	Birmingham	AL	35217	**800-366-5836***	
*Cust Svc					

298-3 Confectionery & Snack Foods - Whol

	Toll-Free	Phone
AMCON Distributing Co		
7405 Irvington Rd .... Omaha NE 68122	888-201-5997	402-331-3727
NYSE: DIT		
Brown & Haley PO Box 1596 .... Tacoma WA 98401	800-426-8400	253-620-3085
Burklund Distributors Inc		
2500 N Main St Ste 3 .... East Peoria IL 61611	800-322-2876	309-694-1900
Continental Concession Supplies Inc		
575 Jericho Turnpike Ste 300 .... Jericho NY 11753	800-516-0090	516-739-8777
Eby-Brown Co		
280 W Shuman Blvd Ste 280 .... Naperville IL 60563	800-553-8249	630-778-2800
Foreign Candy Company Inc		
One Foreign Candy Dr .... Hull IA 51239	800-831-8541	712-439-1496
Frito-Lay North America		
7701 Legacy Dr .... Plano TX 75024	800-352-4477	972-334-7000
Hammons Products Co		
105 Hammons Dr PO Box 140 .... Stockton MO 65785	888-429-6887	
Harold Levinson Assoc (HLA)		
21 Banfi Plz .... Farmingdale NY 11735	800-325-2512	631-962-2400
Hines Nut Co Inc		
990 S St Paul St .... Dallas TX 75201	800-561-6374	214-939-0253
Keilson-Dayton Co		
107 Commerce Pk Dr .... Dayton OH 45404	800-759-3174	937-236-1070
Kennedy Wholesale Inc		
16014 Adelante St .... Irwindale CA 91706	877-292-2639	818-241-9977
McDonald Wholesale Co		
2350 W Broadway St .... Eugene OR 97402	877-722-5503	541-345-8421
Old Dutch Foods Inc		
2375 Terminal Rd .... Roseville MN 55113	800-989-2447	651-633-8810
Sultana Distribution Services Inc		
600 Food Ctr Dr .... Bronx NY 10474	877-617-5500	718-617-5500
Trophy Nut Company Inc		
320 N Second St .... Tipp City OH 45371	800-729-6887	937-667-8478

298-4 Dairy Products - Whol

	Toll-Free	Phone
Ambriola Company Inc		
Seven Patton Dr .... West Caldwell NJ 07006	800-962-8224	
AMPI 315 N Broadway .... New Ulm MN 56073	800-533-3580	507-354-8295
Broughton Foods Co		
1701 Green St .... Marietta OH 45750	800-283-2479	740-373-4121
Clofine Dairy Products Inc		
1407 New Rd .... Linwood NJ 08221	800-441-1001	609-653-1000
Clover-Stornetta Farms Inc		
PO Box 750369 .... Petaluma CA 94975	800-237-3315	707-769-3235
Cream-O-Land Dairy Inc		
529 Cedar Ln PO Box 146 .... Florence NJ 08518	800-220-6455	609-499-3601
Erie Foods International Inc		
401 Seventh Ave PO Box 648 .... Erie IL 61250	800-447-1887	309-659-2233
Hillcrest Foods		
2695 E 40th St .... Cleveland OH 44115	800-952-4344	216-361-4625
Luberski Inc		
310 N Harbor Blvd Ste 205 .... Fullerton CA 92832	800-326-3220	714-680-3447
Maryland & Virginia Milk Producers Co-op Assn Inc		
1985 Isaac Newton Sq W .... Reston VA 20190	800-552-1976	703-742-6800
Masters Gallery Foods Inc		
328 County Hwy PP PO Box 170 ...... Plymouth WI 53073	800-236-8431*	920-893-8431
General		
Plains Dairy Products		
300 N Taylor St .... Amarillo TX 79107	800-365-5608	806-374-0385
Prairie Farms Dairy Inc		
1100 N Broadway St .... Carlinville IL 62626	800-654-2547	217-854-2547
Roberts Dairy Co		
2901 Cuming St .... Omaha NE 68131	800-779-4321	402-344-4321
Rockview Dairies Inc		
7011 Stewart & Gray Rd .... Downey CA 90241	800-423-2479	562-927-5511
Sunshine Dairy Foods Inc		
801 NE 21st Ave .... Portland OR 97232	800-544-0554	503-234-7526
Sure Winner Foods Inc		
Two Lehner Rd .... Saco ME 04072	800-640-6447	207-282-1258
Umpqua Dairy Products Co		
333 SE Sykes Ave PO Box 1306 ...... Roseburg OR 97470	888-672-6455	541-672-2638

298-5 Fish & Seafood - Whol

	Toll-Free	Phone
Beaver Street Fisheries Inc		
1741 W Beaver St .... Jacksonville FL 32209	800-874-6426	904-354-8533
Blount Seafood Corp		
630 Currant Rd .... Fall River MA 02720	800-274-2526*	774-888-1300
Hotline		
Bon Secour Fisheries Inc		
17449 County Rd 49 S .... Bon Secour AL 36511	800-633-6854	251-949-7411
Golden-Tech International Inc		
2461 152nd Ave NE .... Redmond WA 98052	800-311-8090	425-869-1461
Inland Seafood Corp		
1651 Montreal Cir .... Tucker GA 30084	800-883-3474	404-350-5850
Ipswich Shellfish Co Inc		
8 Hayward St .... Ipswich MA 01938	800-477-9424	978-356-6800
LD Amory & Co Inc		
101 S King St .... Hampton VA 23669	800-552-9963	757-722-1915
Maine Lobster Direct		
48 Union Wharf .... Portland ME 04101	800-556-2783	
Metropolitan Poultry & Seafood Co		
1920 Stanford Ct .... Landover MD 20785	800-522-0060	301-772-0060
Morey's Seafood International LLC		
1218 Hwy 10 S .... Motley MN 56466	800-808-3474	218-352-6345
Quirch Foods Co		
7600 NW 82nd Pl .... Miami FL 33166	800-458-5252	305-691-3535

	Toll-Free	Phone
Slade Gorton Company Inc		
225 Southampton St .... Boston MA 02118	800-225-1573	617-442-5800
Stavis Seafoods Inc		
212 Northern Ave Ste 305 .... Boston MA 02210	800-390-5103	617-482-6349
Troyer Foods Inc		
17141 State Rd 4 .... Goshen IN 46528	800-876-9377	574-533-0302

298-6 Frozen Foods (Packaged) - Whol

	Toll-Free	Phone
Dot Foods Inc		
One Dot Way PO Box 192 .... Mount Sterling IL 62353	800-366-3687	217-773-4411

298-7 Fruits & Vegetables - Fresh - Whol

	Toll-Free	Phone
Albert's Organics Inc		
3268 E Vernon Ave .... Vernon CA 90058	800-899-5944	
Alpine Fresh Inc		
9300 NW 58th St Ste 201 .... Miami FL 33178	800-292-8777	305-594-9117
Banacol Marketing Corp		
355 Alhambra Cir Ste 1510 .... Coral Gables FL 33134	877-324-7619	305-441-9036
Belair Produce Company Inc		
7226 Pkwy Dr .... Hanover MD 21076	888-782-8008	410-782-8000
Bix Produce Co		
1415 L'Orient St .... Saint Paul MN 55117	800-642-9514	651-487-8000
Calavo Growers Inc		
1141-A Cummings Rd .... Santa Paula CA 93060	800-654-8758	805-525-1245
NASDAQ: CVGW		
Caro Foods Inc		
2324 Bayou Blue Rd .... Houma LA 70364	800-395-2276	985-872-1483
Community Suffolk Inc		
304 Second St .... Everett MA 02149	800-225-4470	617-389-5200
Costa Fruit & Produce		
18 Bunker Hill Industrial Pk		
PO Box 290754 .... Boston MA 02129	800-322-1374	617-241-8007
Crosset Company Inc		
10295 Toebben Dr .... Independence KY 41051	800-347-4902	859-283-5830
Del Monte Fresh Produce Co		
241 Sevilla Ave .... Coral Gables FL 33134	800-950-3683*	305-520-8400
Cust Svc		
DiMare Fresh Inc		
1049 Ave H E .... Arlington TX 76011	800-322-2184*	817-385-3000
General		
Dole Food Company Hawaii		
802 Mapunapuna St .... Honolulu HI 96819	800-697-9100	808-861-8015
Egan Bernard & Co		
1900 Old Dixie Hwy .... Fort Pierce FL 34946	800-327-6676	
Frieda's Inc		
4465 Corporate Ctr Dr .... Los Alamitos CA 90720	800-241-1771	714-826-6100
General Produce Co		
1330 N 'B' St .... Sacramento CA 95814	800-366-4991	916-441-6431
Hearn Kirkwood		
7251 Standard Dr .... Hanover MD 21076	800-777-9489*	410-712-6000
General		
Heeren Bros Inc		
1060 Hall St SW .... Grand Rapids MI 49503	800-733-5466	616-452-8641
Hollar & Greene Produce Co Inc		
230 Cabbage Rd PO Box 3500 .... Boone NC 28607	800-222-1077	828-264-2177
Indianapolis Fruit Company Inc		
4501 Massachusetts Ave .... Indianapolis IN 46218	800-377-2425	317-546-2425
Kegel's Produce Inc		
2851 Old Tree Dr .... Lancaster PA 17603	800-535-3435	717-392-6612
Melissa's/World Variety Produce Inc		
5325 S Soto St .... Vernon CA 90058	800-588-0151	
Mission Produce Inc		
2500 Vineyard Ave Ste 300 .... Oxnard CA 93036	800-549-3420	805-981-3650
Moore Food Distributors Co		
9910 Page Ave .... Saint Louis MO 63132	800-467-7878	314-426-1300
Muir Enterprises Inc		
3575 West 900 South		
PO Box 26775 .... Salt Lake City UT 84104	877-268-2002	801-363-7695
North Bay Produce Inc		
PO Box 988 .... Traverse City MI 49685	800-678-1941	
Oneonta Trading Corp		
1 Oneonta Way .... Wenatchee WA 98801	800-688-2191	509-663-2191
Organic Valley Family of Farms		
One Organic Way .... LaFarge WI 54639	888-444-6455	
Pacific Coast Fruit Co		
201 NE Second Ave Ste 100 .... Portland OR 97232	800-423-4945	503-234-6411
Peak of the Market		
1200 King Edward St .... Winnipeg MB R3H0R5	888-289-7325	204-632-7325
Produce Source Partners		
13167 Telcourt Rd .... Ashland VA 23005	800-344-4728	804-262-8300
Progressive Produce Co		
5790 Peachtree St .... Los Angeles CA 90040	800-900-0757	323-890-8100
ProPacificfresh		
70 Pepsi Way PO Box 1069 .... Durham CA 95938	888-232-0908	530-893-0596
Sambazon Inc		
1160 Calle Cordillera .... San Clemente CA 92673	877-726-2296	949-498-8618
Sandridge Food Corp (SFC)		
133 Commerce Dr .... Medina OH 44256	800-672-2523	330-725-2348
Taylor Farms Inc		
PO Box 1649 .... Salinas CA 93902	866-675-6120	831-676-9765
W. R. Vernon Produce Co		
PO Box 4054 .... Winston Salem NC 27101	800-222-6406	336-725-9741

298-8 Groceries - General Line

	Toll-Free	Phone
Acme Food Sales Inc		
5940 1st Ave S .... Seattle WA 98108	800-777-2263	206-762-5150
Active Organics Inc		
1097 Yates St .... Lewisville TX 75057	800-541-1478	972-221-7500

					Toll-Free	Phone

Affiliated Foods Inc
1401 W Farmers Ave .... Amarillo TX 79118 **800-234-3661** 806-372-3851

Albert Guarnieri Co
1133 E Market St .... Warren OH 44483 **800-686-2639** 330-394-5636

AMCON Distributing Co
7405 Irvington Rd .... Omaha NE 68122 **888-201-5997** 402-331-3727
NYSE: DIT

Amster-Kirtz Co
2830 Cleveland Ave NW .... Canton OH 44709 **800-257-9338** 330-535-6021

Anderson-DuBose Co
5300 Tod Ave SW .... Lordstown OH 44481 **800-248-1080** 440-248-8800

Animal Supply Company LLC
32001 32nd Ave S Ste 420 .... Federal Way WA 98001 **800-323-2963** 253-237-0400

Associated Food Stores Inc
1850 West 2100 South .... Salt Lake City UT 84119 **888-574-7100*** 801-973-4400
*Cust Svc

Associated Grocers Inc
8600 Anselmo Ln .... Baton Rouge LA 70810 **800-637-2021** 225-444-1000

Associated Grocers of New England Inc
11 Co-op Way .... Pembroke NH 03275 **800-242-2248** 603-223-6710

Associated Grocers of the South
3600 Vanderbilt Rd .... Birmingham AL 35217 **800-695-6051** 205-841-6781

Associated Wholesalers Inc
PO Box 67 .... Robesonia PA 19551 **800-927-7771** 610-693-3161

Brenham Wholesale Grocery Co
602 W First St .... Brenham TX 77833 **800-392-4869** 979-836-7925

Cambrooke Foods Inc
Four Copeland Dr .... Ayer MA 01432 **866-456-9776** 508-782-2300

Camp Olympia 723 Olympia Dr .... Trinity TX 75862 **800-735-6190** 936-594-2541

Cash-Wa Distributing Co
401 W Fourth St .... Kearney NE 68845 **800-652-0010** 308-237-3151

CB Ragland Co
2720 Eugenia Ave .... Nashville TN 37211 **866-770-5263** 615-254-2841

Coastal Pacific Food Distributors Inc (CPFD)
1015 Performance Dr .... Stockton CA 95206 **800-500-2611** 209-983-2454

Core-Mark International
395 Oyster Pt Blvd
Ste 415 .... South San Francisco CA 94080 **800-622-1713** 650-589-9445

Deb-El Food Products LLC
2 Papetti Plaza .... Elizabeth NJ 07206 **800-421-0330** 908-351-0330

DiCarlo Distributors Inc
1630 N Ocean Ave .... Holtsville NY 11742 **800-342-2756** 631-758-6000

Dutch Valley Bulk Food Distributors Inc
7615 Lancaster Ave .... Myerstown PA 17067 **800-733-4191** 717-933-4191

F Mcconnell & Sons Inc
11102 Lincoln Hwy E .... New Haven IN 46774 **800-552-0835** 260-493-6607

Farner-Bocken Co
1751 US Hwy 30 E PO Box 368 .... Carroll IA 51401 **800-274-8692** 712-792-3503

Feesers Inc
5561 Grayson Rd .... Harrisburg PA 17111 **800-326-2828** 717-564-4636

Flavor Dynamics Inc
640 Montrose Ave .... South Plainfield NJ 07080 **888-271-8424** 908-822-8855

Food Services of America Inc
16100 N 71st St Ste 400 .... Scottsdale AZ 85254 **800-528-9346** 480-927-4000

Fuji Health Science Inc
Three Terri Ln Ste 12 .... Burlington NJ 08016 **877-385-4777** 609-386-3030

G r Manufacturing Inc
4800 Commerce Dr .... Trussville AL 35173 **800-841-8001** 205-655-8001

George E DeLallo Co Inc
6390 Rt 30 .... Jeannette PA 15644 **877-335-2556** 724-523-6577

Glazier Foods Co
11303 Antoine Dr .... Houston TX 77066 **800-989-6411*** 832-375-6300
*General

Gold Coast Ingredients Inc
2429 Yates Ave .... Commerce CA 90040 **800-352-8673** 323-724-8935

Granite Falls Energy LLC
15045 Hwy 23 SE .... Granite Falls MN 56241 **877-485-8595** 320-564-3100

Grocers Supply Company Inc
3131 E Holcombe Blvd PO Box 14200 .... Houston TX 77021 **800-352-8003** 713-747-5000

Grocery Supply Co
130 Hillcrest Dr .... Sulphur Springs TX 75482 **800-231-1938** 903-885-7621

Hansen Beverage Co
One Monster Way .... Corona CA 92879 **800-426-7367**

Harris Soup Co, The
17711 NE Riverside Pkwy .... Portland OR 97230 **800-307-7687** 503-257-7687

Imperial Trading Co Inc
701 Edwards Ave PO Box 23508 .... Elmwood LA 70123 **800-775-4504*** 504-733-1400
*Cust Svc

Institution Food House Inc (IFH)
543 12th St Dr NW .... Hickory NC 28601 **800-800-0434**

Jace Holdings Ltd
6649 Butler Crescent .... Saanichton BC V8M1Z7 **800-667-8280** 250-483-1715

JM Swank Co
395 Herky St .... North Liberty IA 52317 **800-593-6333** 319-626-3683

Johnson Bros Bakery Supply
10731 N Interstate 35 .... San Antonio TX 78233 **877-446-2767** 800-590-2575

Jordano's Inc
550 S Patterson Ave .... Santa Barbara CA 93111 **800-325-2278** 805-964-0611

La Petite Bretonne Inc
1210 Boul Mich Le-Bohec .... Blainville QC J7C5S4 **800-361-3381** 450-435-3381

Larue Coffee 2631 S 156th Cir .... Omaha NE 68130 **800-658-4498** 402-333-9099

Laurel Grocery Co Inc
129 Barbourville Rd .... London KY 40744 **800-467-6601**

Maines Paper & Food Service Co
101 Broome Corporate Pkwy .... Conklin NY 13748 **800-366-3669** 607-779-1200

Marquez Bros International Inc
5801 Rue Ferrari .... San Jose CA 95138 **800-858-1119** 408-960-2700

McLane Company Inc
4747 McLane Pkwy .... Temple TX 76504 **800-299-1401** 254-771-7500

McLane Foodservice Inc
2085 Midway Rd .... Carrollton TX 75006 **800-299-1401** 972-364-2000

Merchants Co
1100 Edwards St .... Hattiesburg MS 39401 **800-451-8346** 601-583-4351

Mineral Resources International
1990 W 3300 S .... Ogden UT 84401 **800-731-7866** 801-731-7040

nuherbs co
3820 Penniman Ave .... Oakland CA 94619 **800-233-4307** 510-534-4372

					Toll-Free	Phone

Olean Wholesale Grocery Co-op Inc
1587 Haskell Rd PO Box 1070 .... Olean NY 14760 **866-774-9751** 716-372-2020

Oppenheimer Cos Inc
877 W Main Ste 700 .... Boise ID 83702 **800-727-9939** 208-343-4883

P J Noyes Company Inc
89 Bridge St .... Lancaster NH 03584 **800-522-2469** 603-788-4952

Paris Gourmet of New York Inc
145 Grand St .... Carlstadt NJ 07072 **800-727-8791**

Peter Gillhams Natural Vitality
4879 Fountain Ave .... Los Angeles CA 90029 **888-324-9904**

Piggly Wiggly Carolina Company Inc
PO Box 118047 .... Charleston SC 29423 **800-243-9880** 843-554-9880

Purity Wholesale Grocers Inc
5400 Broken Sound Blvd NW .... Boca Raton FL 33487 **800-323-6838** 561-994-9360

S Abraham & Sons Inc
PO Box 1768 .... Grand Rapids MI 49501 **866-248-3163*** 616-453-6358
*General

Shamrock Foods
3900 E Camelback Rd Ste 300 .... Phoenix AZ 85018 **800-289-3663** 602-477-2500

Shanks Extracts Inc
350 Richardson Dr .... Lancaster PA 17603 **800-346-3135** 717-393-4441

Southco Distributing Co
2201 S John St .... Goldsboro NC 27530 **800-969-3172** 919-735-8012

Specialty Brands Of America Inc
1400 Old Country Rd .... Westbury NY 11590 **877-795-3599** 516-997-6969

Super Store Industries
16888 McKinley Ave PO Box 549 .... Lathrop CA 95330 **888-292-8004** 209-858-2010

SUPERVALU Inc
7075 Flying Cloud Dr .... Eden Prairie MN 55344 **877-322-8228*** 952-828-4000
NYSE: SVU ■ *Cust Svc

SYGMA Network Inc
5550 Blazer Pkwy Ste 300 .... Dublin OH 43017 **877-441-1144**

Sysco Central Ohio Inc
2400 Harrison Rd .... Columbus OH 43204 **800-735-3341** 614-272-0655

Sysco Denver Inc
5000 Beeler St .... Denver CO 80238 **800-366-6696** 303-585-2000

Sysco Food Services of Idaho Inc
5710 Pan Am Ave .... Boise ID 83716 **800-747-9726** 208-345-9500

Sysco Grand Rapids
3700 Sysco Ct SE .... Grand Rapids MI 49512 **800-669-6967** 616-949-3700

Sysco Hampton Roads Inc
7000 Harbour View Blvd .... Suffolk VA 23435 **800-234-2451** 757-673-4000

Thoms Proestler Co
8001 TPC Rd .... Rock Island IL 61204 **800-747-1234** 309-787-1234

Thor Inc 1280 W 2550 S St .... Ogden UT 84401 **888-846-7462** 801-393-3312

Topco Assoc LLC
7711 Gross Pt Rd .... Skokie IL 60077 **888-423-0139** 847-676-3030

UNFI Specialty Distribution Services
88 Huntoon Memorial Hwy .... Leicester MA 01524 **877-476-8749** 508-892-8171

Unified Grocers Inc
5200 Sheila St .... Commerce CA 90040 **800-724-7762** 323-264-5200

Vistar/VSA Corp
12650 E Arapahoe Rd Bldg D .... Centennial CO 80112 **800-880-9900** 303-662-7100

W L Halsey Grocery Company Inc
PO Box 6485 .... Huntsville AL 35824 **800-621-0240** 256-772-9691

Wakefern Food Corp
600 York St .... Elizabeth NJ 07207 **800-746-7748** 908-527-3300

Winkler Inc 535 E Medcalf St .... Dale IN 47523 **800-621-3843** 812-937-4421

Wood-Fruitticher Grocery Company Inc
2900 Alton Rd .... Birmingham AL 35210 **800-328-0026** 205-836-9663

298-9 Meats & Meat Products - Whol

					Toll-Free	Phone

Agar Supply Company Inc
225 John Hancock Rd .... Taunton MA 02780 **800-669-6040** 508-821-2060

Bruss Co 3548 N Kostner Ave .... Chicago IL 60641 **800-621-3882** 773-282-2900

Calumet Diversified Meats Inc
10000 80th Ave .... Pleasant Prairie WI 53158 **800-752-7427** 262-947-7200

Cambridge Packing Co Inc
41-43 Foodmart Rd .... Boston MA 02118 **800-722-6726** 617-269-6700

Cardinal Meat Specialists Ltd
155 Hedgedale Rd .... Brampton ON L6T5P3 **800-363-1439** 905-459-4436

Cell Response Formulation LLC
4115 S Pub Pl .... Jackson WY 83002 **888-364-7839** 307-734-7839

Cusack Wholesale Meat Inc
301 SW 12th St .... Oklahoma City OK 73109 **800-241-6328** 405-232-2114

Deen Meats
PO Box 4155 PO Box 4155 .... Fort Worth TX 76164 **800-333-3953** 817-335-2257

Green Tree Packing Co
65 Central Ave .... Passaic NJ 07055 **800-562-6934** 973-473-1305

Heartland Meat Company Inc
3461 Main St .... Chula Vista CA 91911 **888-407-3668** 619-407-3668

Holten Meat Inc
1682 Sauget Business Blvd .... Sauget IL 62206 **800-851-4684** 618-337-8400

Manda Fine Meats
2445 Sorrel Ave .... Baton Rouge LA 70802 **800-343-2642** 225-344-7636

Michael's Finer Meats & Seafoods
3775 Zane Trace Dr .... Columbus OH 43228 **800-282-0518** 614-527-4900

Midamar Corp
PO Box 218 .... Cedar Rapids IA 52406 **800-362-3711** 319-362-3711

Paper Pak Industries (PPI)
1941 N White Ave .... La Verne CA 91750 **888-293-6529** 909-392-1750

Porky Products Corp
400 Port Carteret Dr .... Carteret NJ 07008 **800-952-0265*** 732-541-0200
*General

Quality Meats & Seafoods
700 Ctr St .... West Fargo ND 58078 **800-342-4250** 701-282-0202

Quirch Foods Co
7600 NW 82nd Pl .... Miami FL 33166 **800-458-5252** 305-691-3535

Sampco Inc
651 W Washington Blvd Ste 300 .... Chicago IL 60661 **800-767-0689** 312-346-1506

Tri-City Meats Inc
1346 N Hickory Ave .... Meridian ID 83642 **800-747-9726** 208-884-2600

Trim-Rite Food Corp
801 Commerce Pkwy .... Carpentersville IL 60110 **800-626-9442** 847-649-3400

			Toll-Free	Phone

Troyer Foods Inc
17141 State Rd 4 . . . . Goshen IN   46528   **800-876-9377**   574-533-0302

U W Provision Company Inc
PO Box 620038 . . . . Middleton WI   53562   **800-832-0517**   608-836-7421

Williams Sausage Company Inc
5132 Old Troy Hickman Rd . . . . Union City TN   38261   **800-844-4242**   731-885-5841

298-10 Poultry, Eggs, Poultry Products - Whol

			Toll-Free	Phone

Agar Supply Company Inc
225 John Hancock Rd . . . . Taunton MA   02780   **800-669-6040**   508-821-2060

Butts Foods Inc
432 N Royal St PO Box 2466 . . . . Jackson TN   38301   **800-962-8570**   731-423-3456

Chino Valley Ranchers
5611 Peck Rd . . . . Arcadia CA   91006   **800-354-4503**

Dutt & Wagner of Virginia Inc
1142 W Main St . . . . Abingdon VA   24210   **800-688-2116**   276-628-2116

House of Raeford Farms Inc
520 E Central Ave . . . . Raeford NC   28376   **800-888-7539**   910-875-5161

Metropolitan Poultry & Seafood Co
1920 Stanford Ct . . . . Landover MD   20785   **800-522-0060**   301-772-0060

Norbest Inc PO Box 890 . . . . Moroni UT   84646   **800-453-5327**

Quirch Foods Co
7600 NW 82nd Pl . . . . Miami FL   33166   **800-458-5252**   305-691-3535

Troyer Foods Inc
17141 State Rd 4 . . . . Goshen IN   46528   **800-876-9377**   574-533-0302

Zacky Farms
13200 Crossroads Pkwy N
Ste 250 . . . . City of Industry CA   91746   **800-888-0235**   562-641-2020

298-11 Specialty Foods - Whol

			Toll-Free	Phone

Charles C. Parks Co
500 Belvedere Dr . . . . Gallatin TN   37066   **800-873-2406**   615-452-2406

Conway Import Co Inc
11051 W Addison St . . . . Franklin Park IL   60131   **800-323-8801**   847-455-5600

CRS Onesource
2803 Tamarack Rd PO Box 1984 . . . . Owensboro KY   42302   **800-264-0710**   270-684-1469

Diaz Wholesale & Mfg Co Inc
5501 Fulton Industrial Blvd . . . . Atlanta GA   30336   **800-394-4639**   404-344-5421

Ellis Coffee Co
2835 Bridge St . . . . Philadelphia PA   19137   **800-822-3984**   215-537-9500

Essex Grain Products
Nine Lee Blvd . . . . Frazer PA   19355   **800-441-1017**   610-647-3800

Hain Celestial Group Inc
4600 Sleepytime Dr Ste 250 . . . . Boulder CO   80301   **800-434-4246**
NASDAQ: HAIN

J Sosnick & Sons Inc
258 Littlefield Ave . . . . South San Francisco CA   94080   **800-443-6737**   650-952-2226

JFC International Inc
7101 E Slauson Ave . . . . Los Angeles CA   90040   **800-633-1004**   323-721-6100

Joffrey's Coffee & Tea Co
3803 Corporex Pk Dr . . . . Tampa FL   33619   **800-458-5282**   813-250-0404

John E Koerner & Company Inc
4820 Jefferson Hwy . . . . New Orleans LA   70121   **800-333-1913**

Love & Quiches Desserts
178 Hanse Ave . . . . Freeport NY   11520   **800-525-5251**   516-623-8800

Nantze Springs Inc
156 W Carroll St . . . . Dothan AL   36301   **800-239-7873**   334-794-4218

O S F Flavors Inc
40 Baker Hollow Rd . . . . Windsor CT   06095   **800-466-6015**   860-298-8350

Otto Brehm Inc PO Box 249 . . . . Yonkers NY   10710   **800-272-6886**   914-968-6100

Producers Rice Mill Inc
PO Box 1248 . . . . Stuttgart AR   72160   **800-369-7675**   870-673-4444

Rain Creek Baking Co, The
2401 W Almond Ave . . . . Madera CA   93637   **800-530-0505**   559-674-4445

ReNew Life Formulas Inc
2076 Sunnydale Blvd . . . . Clearwater FL   33765   **800-830-1800**   727-450-1061

Schreiber Foods International Inc
600 E Crescent Ave Ste 103 . . . . Upper Saddle River NJ   07458   **800-631-7070**   201-327-3535

Silver Springs Bottled Water Company Inc
PO Box 926 . . . . Silver Springs FL   34489   **800-556-0334**

Sturm Foods Inc PO Box 287 . . . . Manawa WI   54949   **800-347-8876**   920-596-2511

Sugar Foods Corp
950 Third Ave 21st Fl . . . . New York NY   10022   **800-732-8963**   212-753-6900

Sunsweet Growers Inc
901 N Walton Ave . . . . Yuba City CA   95993   **800-417-2253**   530-674-5010

Sysco Indianapolis LLC
4000 W 62nd St . . . . Indianapolis IN   46268   **800-347-3920**   317-291-2020

United Sugars Corp
7803 Glenroy Rd Ste 300 . . . . Bloomington MN   55439   **800-984-3585**   952-896-0131

299   FOOD PRODUCTS MACHINERY

SEE ALSO Food Service Equipment & Supplies

			Toll-Free	Phone

Acme Pizza & Bakery Equipment Inc
7039 E Slauson Blvd . . . . Commerce CA   90040   **800-428-2263**   323-722-7900

Adamatic Equipment Corp
607 Industrial Way W . . . . Eatontown NJ   07724   **800-526-2807**   732-544-8400

Alto-Shaam Inc
W 164 N 9221 Water St
PO Box 450 . . . . Menomonee Falls WI   53052   **800-329-8744**   262-251-3800

American Permanent Ware Inc
729 Third Ave . . . . Dallas TX   75226   **800-527-2100**   214-421-7366

Anderson International Corp
6200 Harvard Ave . . . . Cleveland OH   44105   **800-336-4730**   216-641-1112

APV 1415 California Ave . . . . Brockville ON   K6V7H7   **800-263-3958**   613-345-2280

Atlas Metal Industries
1135 NW 159th Dr . . . . Miami FL   33169   **800-762-7565***   305-625-2451
*Cust Svc

			Toll-Free	Phone

Atlas Pacific Engineering Co
1 Atlas Ave . . . . Pueblo CO   81001   **800-588-5438**   719-948-3040

Belshaw Bros Inc
1750 22nd Ave S . . . . Seattle WA   98144   **800-578-2547**   206-322-5474

Bettcher Industries Inc
PO Box 336 . . . . Vermilion OH   44089   **800-321-8763**   440-965-4422

Brewmatic Co
20333 S Normandie Ave PO Box 2959 . . . . Torrance CA   90509   **800-421-6860**   310-787-5444

C Cretors & Co
3243 N California Ave . . . . Chicago IL   60618   **800-228-1885**   773-588-1690

Carlisle Cos Inc
13925 Ballantyne Corporate Pl
Ste 400 . . . . Charlotte NC   28277   **800-248-5995**   704-501-1100
NYSE: CSL

Casa Herrerra Inc
2655 N Pine St . . . . Pomona CA   91767   **800-624-3916**   909-392-3930

CE Rogers Co 1895 Frontage Rd . . . . Mora MN   55051   **800-279-8081**   320-679-2172

Chester-Jensen Company Inc
PO Box 908 . . . . Chester PA   19016   **800-685-3750**   610-876-6276

Cleveland Range Co
1333 E 179th St . . . . Cleveland OH   44110   **800-338-2204**   216-481-4900

CPM Wolverine Proctor LLC
251 Gibraltar Rd . . . . Horsham PA   19044   **800-428-0846**   215-443-5200

Delfield Co
980 S Isabella Rd . . . . Mount Pleasant MI   48858   **800-733-8821**   989-773-7981

Duke Manufacturing Co
2305 N Broadway . . . . Saint Louis MO   63102   **800-735-3853**   314-231-1130

Dunkley International Inc
1910 Lake St . . . . Kalamazoo MI   49001   **800-666-1264**   269-343-5583

Edlund Company Inc
159 Industrial Pkwy . . . . Burlington VT   05401   **800-772-2126**   802-862-9661

Feldmeier Equipment Inc
6800 Townline Rd . . . . Syracuse NY   13211   **800-258-0118**   315-454-8608

Fish Oven & Equipment Corp
120 W Kent Ave . . . . Wauconda IL   60084   **877-526-8720**   847-526-8686

Food Warming Equipment Company Inc
7900 S Rt 31 . . . . Crystal Lake IL   60014   **800-222-4393***   815-459-7500
*Sales

Frymaster LLC
8700 Line Ave . . . . Shreveport LA   71106   **800-221-4583***   318-865-1711
*Cust Svc

Garland Commercial Industries
185 S St . . . . Freeland PA   18224   **800-424-2411**   570-636-1000

Globe Food Equipment Co
2153 Dryden Rd . . . . Dayton OH   45439   **800-347-5423**   937-299-5493

Great Western Mfg Co Inc
2017 S Fourth St PO Box 149 . . . . Leavenworth KS   66048   **800-682-3121**   913-682-2291

Grindmaster Crathco Systems Inc
4003 Collins Ln . . . . Louisville KY   40245   **800-695-4500**   502-425-4776

GS Blodgett Corp
44 Lakeside Ave . . . . Burlington VT   05401   **800-331-5842**   802-658-6600

Hayes & Stolz Industrial Manufacturing Co
3521 Hemphill St PO Box 11217 . . . . Fort Worth TX   76110   **800-725-7272**   817-926-3391

Heat & Control Inc
21121 Cabot Blvd . . . . Hayward CA   94545   **800-227-5980**   510-259-0500

Henny Penny Corp
1219 US 35 W PO Box 60 . . . . Eaton OH   45320   **800-417-8417**   937-456-8400

Hobart Corp 701 S Ridge Ave . . . . Troy OH   45374   **800-333-7447***   937-332-3000
*Cust Svc

Key Technology Inc
150 Avery St . . . . Walla Walla WA   99362   **877-341-5668**   509-529-2161
NASDAQ: KTEC

Kwik Lok Corp
2712 S 16th Ave PO Box 9548 . . . . Yakima WA   98909   **800-688-5945**   509-248-4770

Lawrence Equipment Inc
2034 Peck Rd . . . . El Monte CA   91733   **800-423-4500**   626-442-2894

Lewis M Carter Mfg Co
PO Box 428 . . . . Donalsonville GA   39845   **800-332-8232**   229-524-2197

LK Industries
1357 W Beaver St . . . . Jacksonville FL   32209   **800-531-4975**   904-354-8882

Lucks Co, The 3003 S Pine St . . . . Tacoma WA   98409   **800-426-9778**   253-383-4815

Luthi Machinery Co Inc
1 Magnuson Ave . . . . Pueblo CO   81003   **800-227-0682**   719-948-1110

Manitowoc Beverage Equipment
2100 Future Dr . . . . Sellersburg IN   47172   **800-367-4233**   812-246-7000

Market Forge Industries Inc
35 Garvey St . . . . Everett MA   02149   **866-698-3188**   617-387-4100

Marlen International Inc
9202 Barton St . . . . Overland Park KS   66214   **800-862-7536**

Merco-Savory Inc
1111 N Hadley Rd . . . . Fort Wayne IN   46804   **888-417-5462***   260-459-8200
*Cust Svc

Microfluidics International Corp
30 Ossipee Rd PO Box 9101 . . . . Newton MA   02464   **800-370-5452**   617-969-5452

Middleby Corp
1400 Toastmaster Dr . . . . Elgin IL   60120   **800-331-5842**   847-741-3300
NASDAQ: MIDD

Nitta Casings Inc
141 Southside Ave PO Box 858 . . . . Bridgewater NJ   08807   **800-526-3970***   908-218-4400
*Cust Svc

Oliver Products Co
445 Sixth St NW . . . . Grand Rapids MI   49504   **800-253-3893**   616-456-7711

Peerless Food Equipment
500 S Vandemark Rd . . . . Sidney OH   45365   **800-999-3327**   937-492-4158

Peerless Machinery Corp
500 S Vandemark Rd PO Box 769 . . . . Sidney OH   45365   **877-795-7377**   937-492-4158

Philadelphia Mixing Solutions, Ltd
1221 E Main St . . . . Palmyra PA   17078   **800-956-4937**   717-832-2800

Piper Products Inc
300 S 84th Ave . . . . Wausau WI   54401   **800-544-3057**   715-842-2724

Pitco Frialator Inc
PO Box 501 . . . . Concord NH   03302   **800-258-3708**   603-225-6684

Prince Castle Inc
355 E Kehoe Blvd . . . . Carol Stream IL   60188   **800-722-7853**   630-462-8800

Ross Industries Inc
5321 Midland Rd . . . . Midland VA   22728   **800-336-6010**   540-439-3271

S Howes Company Inc
25 Howard St . . . . Silver Creek NY   14136   **888-255-2611**   716-934-2611

	Toll-Free	Phone
SaniServ Inc		
451 E County Line Rd .... Mooresville IN 46158	**800-733-8073**	317-831-7030
Schlueter Co		
310 N Main St .... Janesville WI 53545	**800-359-1700**	608-755-5444
Server Products Inc		
3601 Pleasant Hill Rd PO Box 98 .... Richfield WI 53076	**800-558-8722**	262-628-5600
Southbend Inc		
1100 Old Honeycutt Rd .... Fuquay-Varina NC 27526	**800-755-4777**	919-762-1000
Stoelting LLC 502 Hwy 67 .... Kiel WI 53042	**800-558-5807**	920-894-2293
Stolle Machinery Co LLC		
6949 S Potomac St .... Centennial CO 80112	**800-433-8333**	303-708-9044
Taylor 750 N Blackhawk Blvd .... Rockton IL 61072	**800-255-0626**	815-624-8333
Tomlinson Industries		
13700 Broadway Ave .... Cleveland OH 44125	**800-945-4589**	216-587-3400
Town Food Service Equipment Co		
72 Beadel St .... Brooklyn NY 11222	**800-221-5032**	718-388-5650
Union Standard Equipment Co		
801 E 141st St .... Bronx NY 10454	**877-282-7333**	718-585-0200
United Bakery Equipment Co Inc		
15815 W 110th St .... Lenexa KS 66219	**888-823-2253**	913-541-8700
Univex Corp		
Three Old Rockingham Rd .... Salem NH 03079	**800-258-6358**	603-893-6191
Urschel Laboratories Inc		
2503 Calumet Ave PO Box 2200 .... Valparaiso IN 46384	**844-877-2435**	219-464-4811
Van Doren Sales Inc		
10 NE Cascade Ave .... East Wenatchee WA 98802	**866-886-1837**	509-886-1837
Viking Range Corp		
111 Front St .... Greenwood MS 38930	**888-845-4641**	662-455-1200
Walker Stainless Equipment Co LLC		
625 W State St .... New Lisbon WI 53950	**800-356-5734**	608-562-7500
Wells Bloomfield Industries		
10 Sunnen Dr .... Saint Louis MO 63143	**888-356-5362**	
Wilbur Curtis Company Inc		
6913 Acco St .... Montebello CA 90640	**800-421-6150**	323-837-2300
Winston Industries LLC		
2345 Carton Dr .... Louisville KY 40299	**800-234-5286**	502-495-5400

300   FOOD SERVICE

SEE ALSO Restaurant Companies

	Toll-Free	Phone
Advance Food Company Inc		
9987 Carver Rd Ste 500 .... Cincinnati OH 45242	**800-969-2747**	
American Food & Vending Corp		
124 Metropolitan Pk Dr .... Syracuse NY 13088	**800-466-9261**	315-457-9950
ARAMARK Food & Support Services		
1101 Market St .... Philadelphia PA 19107	**800-388-3300**	215-238-3000
Atlas Food Systems & Services Inc		
205 Woods Lk Rd .... Greenville SC 29607	**800-476-1123**	864-232-1885
Blue Line Foodservice Distribution		
24120 Haggerty Rd .... Farmington Hills MI 48335	**800-892-8272***	
*General		
Bran-Zan Holdings Inc		
1548 Barclay Blvd .... Buffalo Grove IL 60089	**866-266-9670**	
Canteen Service Co		
712 Industrial Dr .... Owensboro KY 42301	**800-467-2471**	270-683-2471
Canteen Vending Services		
Compass Group		
2400 Yorkmont Rd .... Charlotte NC 28217	**800-357-0012**	704-328-4000
Cara Operations Ltd		
199 Four Valley Dr .... Vaughan ON L4K0B8	**800-860-4082**	905-760-2244
Centerplate		
2187 Atlantic St .... Stamford CT 06902	**800-698-6992**	203-975-5900
Compass Group North American Div (CGNAD)		
2400 Yorkmont Rd .... Charlotte NC 28217	**800-357-0012**	704-328-4000
Excelsior Grand		
2380 Hylan Blvd .... Staten Island NY 10306	**888-233-6743**	718-987-4800
Five Star Food Service Inc		
6005 Century Oaks Dr Ste 100 .... Chattanooga TN 37416	**800-327-0043**	423-643-2600
Food Bank For New York City		
39 Broadway 10th Fl .... New York NY 10006	**866-692-3663**	212-566-7855
General Mills Inc		
One General Mills Blvd .... Minneapolis MN 55426	**800-248-7310**	
NYSE: GIS		
Guest Services Inc		
3055 Prosperity Ave .... Fairfax VA 22031	**800-345-7534**	703-849-9300
Institution Food House Inc (IFH)		
543 12th St Dr NW .... Hickory NC 28601	**800-800-0434**	
Institutional Wholesale Co		
535 Dry Vly Rd .... Cookeville TN 38506	**800-239-9588**	931-537-4000
Island Oasis		
141 Norfolk St PO Box 769 .... Walpole MA 02081	**800-777-4752**	508-660-1176
Love & Quiches Desserts		
178 Hanse Ave .... Freeport NY 11520	**800-525-5251**	516-623-8800
Morrison Management Specialists Inc		
5801 Peachtree Dunwoody Rd .... Atlanta GA 30342	**800-367-5690***	800-225-4368
*General		
Nantze Springs Inc		
156 W Carroll St .... Dothan AL 36301	**800-239-7873**	334-794-4218
Open Kitchen Inc		
1161 W 21st St .... Chicago IL 60608	**800-339-5334**	312-666-5335
Signature Services Corp		
2705 Hawes Ave PO Box 35885 .... Dallas TX 75235	**800-929-5519**	214-353-2661
Sodexo Inc		
9801 Washingtonian Blvd .... Gaithersburg MD 20878	**800-763-3946**	
Sportservice Corp		
40 Fountain Plz .... Buffalo NY 14202	**800-828-7240**	716-858-5000
Summit Food Service Distributors Inc		
580 Industrial Rd .... London ON N5V1V1	**800-265-9267**	519-453-3410
Sysco Jacksonville Inc		
1501 Lewis Industrial Dr		
PO Box 37045 .... Jacksonville FL 32254	**800-786-2611***	904-786-2600
*General		
Universal Sodexho		
5749 Susitna Dr .... Harahan LA 70123	**888-763-3967**	301-987-4000

301   FOOD SERVICE EQUIPMENT & SUPPLIES

SEE ALSO Food Products Machinery

	Toll-Free	Phone
Adams-Burch Inc		
1901 Stanford Ct .... Landover MD 20785	**800-347-8093***	301-276-2000
*Cust Svc		
Advance Tabco		
200 Heartland Blvd .... Edgewood NY 11717	**800-645-3166**	631-242-4800
Anderson-DuBose Co		
5300 Tod Ave SW .... Lordstown OH 44481	**800-248-1080**	440-248-8800
Atlanta Fixture & Sales Co		
3185 NE Expy .... Atlanta GA 30341	**800-282-1977**	770-455-8844
Bargreen Ellingson Inc		
2925 70th Ave E .... Fife WA 98424	**866-722-2665**	253-722-2600
Boelter Cos Inc		
N22W23685 Ridgeview Pkwy W .... West Waukesha WI 53188	**800-263-5837**	262-523-6200
Bolton & Hay Inc		
2701 Delaware Ave .... Des Moines IA 50317	**800-362-1861**	515-265-2554
Browne & Co 100 Esna Pk Dr .... Markham ON L3R1E3	**866-306-3672**	905-475-6104
Browne-Halco Inc		
2840 Morris Ave .... Union NJ 07083	**888-289-1005**	973-232-1065
Buffalo Hotel Supply Company Inc		
375 Commerce Dr .... Amherst NY 14228	**800-333-1678**	716-691-8080
Cambro Manufacturing Co		
5801 Skylab Rd .... Huntington Beach CA 92647	**800-833-3003**	714-848-1555
Carlisle FoodService Products Inc		
4711 E Hefner Rd .... Oklahoma City OK 73131	**800-654-8210**	405-475-5600
Curtis Restaurant Supply & Equipment Co		
6577 E 40th St .... Tulsa OK 74145	**800-766-2878**	918-622-7390
Eagle Group Inc		
100 Industrial Blvd .... Clayton DE 19938	**800-441-8440**	302-653-3000
Edward Don & Co		
2500 S Harlem Ave .... North Riverside IL 60546	**800-777-4366***	
*Cust Svc		
Genpak Carthage		
505 E Cotton St .... Carthage TX 75633	**800-626-6695**	903-693-7151
Hotel & Restaurant Supply Inc		
5020 Arundel Rd PO Box 6 .... Meridian MS 39302	**800-782-6651**	601-482-7127
Intedge Mfg		
1875 Chumley Rd .... Woodruff SC 29388	**866-969-9605**	864-969-9601
InterMetro Industries Corp		
651 N Washington St .... Wilkes-Barre PA 18705	**800-992-1776***	570-825-2741
*Cust Svc		
Kittredge Equipment Co Inc		
100 Bowles Rd .... Agawam MA 01001	**800-423-7082**	413-304-4100
Lakeside Manufacturing Inc		
4900 W Electric Ave .... West Milwaukee WI 53219	**800-558-8565**	414-902-6400
Lancaster Colony Commercial Products Inc		
3902 Indianola Ave .... Columbus OH 43214	**800-292-7260**	614-263-2850
Maines Paper & Food Service Co		
101 Broome Corporate Pkwy .... Conklin NY 13748	**800-366-3669**	607-779-1200
McLane Foodservice Inc		
2085 Midway Rd .... Carrollton TX 75006	**800-299-1401**	972-364-2000
N Wasserstrom & Sons Inc		
2300 Lockbourne Rd .... Columbus OH 43207	**800-444-4697**	614-228-5550
PBI Market Equipment Inc		
2667 Gundry Ave .... Signal Hill CA 90755	**800-421-3753**	562-595-4785
Perkins Equipment Div		
630 John Hancock Rd .... Taunton MA 02780	**800-733-5708**	508-824-2800
RAPIDS Wholesale Equipment Co		
6201 S Gateway Dr .... Marion IA 52302	**800-472-7431**	319-447-1670
Reinhart Food Service		
7735 Westside Industrial Dr .... Jacksonville FL 32219	**888-781-5464**	904-781-9888
Restaurant & Stores Equipment Co		
230 West 700 South .... Salt Lake City UT 84101	**800-877-0087**	801-364-1981
Restaurant Technologies Inc		
2250 Pilot Knob Rd Ste 100 .... Mendota Heights MN 55120	**888-796-4997**	651-796-1600
Service Ideas Inc		
2354 Ventura Dr .... Woodbury MN 55125	**800-328-4493**	651-730-8800
Smith & Greene Co		
19015 66th Ave S .... Kent WA 98032	**800-232-8050**	425-656-8000
Standex International Corp Food Service Equipment Group		
11 Keewaydin Dr .... Salem NH 03079	**800-647-1284**	603-893-9701
NYSE: SXI		
TriMark USA Inc		
505 Collins St .... South Attleboro MA 02703	**800-755-5580**	508-399-2400
US Foods Culinary Equipment & Supplies		
2621 Fairview Ave N Ste 2 .... Roseville MN 55113	**866-636-2338**	651-638-8993
Vollrath Co LLC, The		
1236 N 18th St .... Sheboygan WI 53081	**800-624-2051**	920-457-4851
Wasserstrom Co		
477 S Front St .... Columbus OH 43215	**866-634-8927**	614-228-6525

302   FOOTWEAR

			Toll-Free	Phone
Acor Orthopaedic Inc				
18530 S Miles Pkwy .... Cleveland OH	44128		**800-237-2267**	216-662-4500
Acushnet Co 333 Bridge St .... Fairhaven MA	02719		**800-225-8500**	508-979-2000
Aerosoles Inc 201 Meadow Rd .... Edison NJ	08817		**800-798-9478**	732-985-6900
Aldo Shoes				
2300 Emile Belanger .... Montreal QC	H4R3J4		**888-818-2536**	514-747-2536
Allen-Edmonds Shoe Corp				
201 E Seven Hills Rd .... Port Washington WI	53074		**800-235-2348***	262-235-6512
*Cust Svc				
Asics America Corp				
29 Parker Ste 100 .... Irvine CA	92618		**800-333-8404**	949-453-8888
Badorf Shoe Co Inc				
1958 Auction Road PO Box 367 .... Manheim PA	17545		**800-325-1545**	717-653-0155
Barbour Welting Company Div Barbour Corp				
1001 N Montello St .... Brockton MA	02301		**800-955-9649**	508-583-8200
Brooks Sports Inc				
19910 N Creek Pkwy Ste 200 .... Bothell WA	98011		**800-227-6657**	

Classified Section

				Toll-Free	Phone
Capezio/Ballet Makers Inc					
One Campus Rd	Totowa	NJ	07512	**800-533-1887***	973-595-9000
*Acctg					
Chinese Laundry Shoes					
3485 S La Cienega Blvd	Los Angeles	CA	90016	**888-935-8825**	310-838-2103
Clark Cos NA					
156 Oak St	Newton Upper Falls	MA	02464	**800-211-5461***	617-964-1222
*Cust Svc					
Cole-Haan					
8701 Keystone Crossing	Indianapolis	IN	46240	**800-695-8945**	317-810-0160
Consolidated Shoe Company Inc					
22290 Timberlake Rd	Lynchburg	VA	24502	**800-368-7463**	434-239-0391
Cowtown Boots					
11401 Gateway Blvd W	El Paso	TX	79936	**800-580-2698**	915-593-2709
Crocs Inc 6328 Monarch Pk Pl	Niwot	CO	80503	**866-306-3179**	303-848-7000
NASDAQ: CROX					
Danner Shoe Manufacturing Co					
17634 NE Airport	Portland	OR	97230	**800-345-0430***	503-251-1100
*Cust Svc					
Deckers Outdoor Corp					
495-A S Fairview Ave	Goleta	CA	93117	**877-337-8333**	805-967-7611
NYSE: DECK					
Drew Shoe Corp					
252 Quarry Rd	Lancaster	OH	43130	**800-837-3739**	740-653-4271
East Lion Corp					
318 Brea Canyon Rd	City of Industry	CA	91789	**877-939-1818**	626-912-1818
Eastland Shoe Mfg Corp					
4 Meeting House Rd	Freeport	ME	04032	**888-988-1998**	207-865-6314
ES Originals Inc					
440 9th Ave 7th Fl	New York	NY	10001	**800-677-6577***	212-736-8124
*General					
Famous Footwear					
7010 Mineral Pt Rd	Madison	WI	53717	**800-888-7198***	608-833-3340
*Cust Svc					
Finish Line Inc, The					
3308 N Mitthoeffer Rd	Indianapolis	IN	46235	**888-777-3949**	317-899-1022
NASDAQ: FINL					
Florsheim Inc					
333 W Estabrook Blvd	Glendale	WI	53212	**866-454-0449**	
Foot Locker Inc					
112 W 34th St	New York	NY	10120	**800-952-5210**	212-720-3700
NYSE: FL					
Foot Solutions Inc					
2359 Windy Hill Rd Ste 400	Marietta	GA	30067	**888-358-3668***	770-984-0844
*General					
Footaction Inc					
112 W 34th St	New York	NY	10120	**800-863-8932**	715-261-9588
Footstar Inc					
933 MacArthur Blvd	Mahwah	NJ	07430	**800-322-2885**	201-934-2000
Gateway Shoe Co					
910 Kehro Mill Rd Ste 112	Ballwin	MO	63011	**800-539-6063**	636-256-7050
Georgia Boot Inc					
39 E Canal St	Nelsonville	OH	45764	**877-795-2410**	740-753-1951
HH Brown Shoe Company Inc					
124 W Putnam Ave	Greenwich	CT	06830	**888-444-2769**	203-661-2424
Hush Puppies Co					
9341 Courtland Dr NE	Rockford	MI	49351	**866-699-7365**	616-866-5500
Impo International Inc					
PO Box 639	Santa Maria	CA	93456	**800-367-4676**	805-922-7753
Inter-Pacific Corp					
2257 Colby Ave	Los Angeles	CA	90064	**877-605-8414**	310-473-7591
John Reyer Shoe Store					
40 S Water Ave	Sharon	PA	16146	**800-245-1550***	
*Cust Svc					
Johnston & Murphy Inc					
1415 Murfreesboro Rd	Nashville	TN	37217	**800-424-2854**	615-367-7168
Justin Boot Co Inc					
610 W Daggett St	Fort Worth	TX	76104	**866-240-8853***	817-332-7797
*Cust Svc					
K-Swiss Inc					
31248 Oak Crest Dr	Westlake Village	CA	91361	**800-938-8000**	818-706-5100
NASDAQ: KSWS					
Keds Corp					
1400 Industries Rd	Richmond	IN	47374	**800-680-0966**	
Kenneth Cole Productions Inc					
603 W 50th St	New York	NY	10019	**800-536-2653**	212-265-1500
NYSE: KCP					
LaCrosse Footwear Inc					
17634 NE Airport	Portland	OR	97230	**800-323-2668***	
*Cust Svc					
Lady Foot Locker (LFL)					
112 W 34th St	New York	NY	10120	**800-991-6686**	
Lamey-Wellehan Inc					
940 Turner St	Auburn	ME	04210	**800-370-6900**	207-784-6595
Lucchese Boot Co					
20 ZANE GREY	El Paso	TX	79906	**800-637-6888**	888-582-1883
Marty's Shoe Outlet Inc					
121 Carver Ave	Westwood	NJ	07675	**888-662-7897***	201-497-6637
*General					
Merrell Footwear					
9341 Courtland Dr NE	Rockford	MI	49351	**800-288-3124***	616-866-5500
*Cust Svc					
Mizuno USA					
4925 Avalon Ridge Pkwy	Norcross	GA	30071	**800-966-1211**	770-441-5553
Munro & Co Inc					
3770 Malvern Rd 71901 PO Box 6048	Hot Springs	AR	71902	**800-819-1901**	501-262-6000
New Balance Athletic Shoe Inc					
20 Guest St Brighton Landing	Brighton	MA	02135	**800-595-9138**	617-783-4000
Nike Inc One Bowerman Dr	Beaverton	OR	97005	**800-344-6453***	503-671-6453
NYSE: NKE ■ *Cust Svc					
Novus Inc					
655 Calle Cubitas	Guaynabo	PR	00969	**888-530-4546**	787-272-4546
ONGUARD Industries					
1850 Clark Rd	Havre de Grace	MD	21078	**800-365-2282**	410-272-2000
Otomix Inc					
747 Glasgow Ave	Inglewood	CA	90301	**800-701-7867**	310-215-6100
Payless ShoeSource Inc					
3231 SE Sixth Ave	Topeka	KS	66607	**877-452-7500**	785-233-5171

				Toll-Free	Phone
Phoenix Footwear Group Inc					
5937 Darwin Ct Ste 109	Carlsbad	CA	92008	**888-218-7275**	760-602-9688
OTC: PXFG					
Propet USA Inc					
2415 W Valley Hwy N	Auburn	WA	98001	**800-877-6738**	253-854-7600
Puma North America Inc					
10 Lyberty Way	Westford	MA	01886	**888-565-7862***	978-698-1000
*General					
PW Minor & Son Inc					
3 Tread Easy Ave PO Box 678	Batavia	NY	14020	**800-333-4067**	585-343-1500
Red Wing Shoe Company Inc					
314 Main St	Red Wing	MN	55066	**800-733-9464***	651-388-8211
*Cust Svc					
Reebok International Ltd					
1895 JW Foster Blvd	Canton	MA	02021	**866-870-1743**	781-401-5000
RG Barry Corp					
13405 Yarmouth Dr NW	Pickerington	OH	43147	**800-848-7560**	614-864-6400
NASDAQ: DFZ					
Rockport Company Inc					
1895 JW Foster Blvd	Canton	MA	02021	**800-828-0545**	781-401-5000
Rocky Shoes & Boots Inc					
39 E Canal St	Nelsonville	OH	45764	**877-795-2410**	740-753-3130
NASDAQ: RCKY					
Romika USA LLC					
3405 Del Webb Ave NE	Salem	OR	97301	**888-777-4174**	503-485-1848
SAS Shoemakers					
1717 SAS Dr	San Antonio	TX	78224	**877-782-7463**	
Saucony Inc 191 Spring St	Lexington	MA	02420	**800-282-6575**	
Saxon Shoes Inc					
11800 W Broad St Ste 2750	Richmond	VA	23233	**800-686-5616***	804-285-3473
*General					
Sebago Inc					
9341 Courtland Dr	Rockford	MI	49351	**866-699-7367**	616-866-5500
Shoe Carnival Inc					
7500 E Columbia St	Evansville	IN	47715	**800-430-7463***	812-867-6471
NASDAQ: SCVL ■ *Cust Svc					
Shoe Show of Rocky Mountain Inc					
2201 Trinity Church Rd	Concord	NC	28027	**888-557-4637***	704-782-4143
*Cust Svc					
Skechers USA Inc					
228 Manhattan Beach Blvd					
Ste 200	Manhattan Beach	CA	90266	**800-746-3411***	310-318-3100
NYSE: SKX ■ *Cust Svc					
Spalding PO Box 90015	Bowling Green	KY	42103	**855-253-4533**	
Stride Rite Corp					
191 Spring St	Lexington	MA	02420	**800-299-6575***	617-824-6000
*Cust Svc					
Teva Sport Sandals					
123 N Leroux St	Flagstaff	AZ	86001	**800-367-8382***	928-779-5938
*General					
Timberland Co, The					
200 Domain Dr	Stratham	NH	03885	**800-258-0855**	603-772-9500
NYSE: VFC					
Trimfoot Co LLC					
115 Trimfoot Terr	Farmington	MO	63640	**800-325-6116**	
TT Group Inc					
702 Carnation Dr	Aurora	MO	65605	**800-445-0886***	417-678-2181
*General					
Vans Inc					
15700 Shoemaker Ave	Santa Fe Springs	CA	90670	**855-909-8267**	562-565-8267
Weinbrenner Shoe Co Inc					
108 S Polk St	Merrill	WI	54452	**800-569-6817***	715-536-5521
*General					
West Coast Shoe Co					
52828 NW Shoe Factory Ln PO Box 607	Scappoose	OR	97056	**800-326-2711**	503-543-7114

303 FORESTRY SERVICES

SEE ALSO Timber Tracts

				Toll-Free	Phone
Hal Hays Construction Inc					
4181 Latham St	Riverside	CA	92501	**888-425-4297**	951-788-0703
Resource Management Service LLC					
31 Inverness Ctr Pkwy Ste 360	Birmingham	AL	35242	**800-995-9516**	
Vestra Resources Inc					
5300 Aviation Dr	Redding	CA	96002	**877-983-7872**	530-223-2585

304 FOUNDATIONS - COMMUNITY

SEE ALSO Charitable & Humanitarian Organizations

				Toll-Free	Phone
Arizona Community Foundation					
2201 E Camelback Rd Ste 405B	Phoenix	AZ	85016	**800-222-8221**	602-381-1400
Colorado Trust					
1600 Sherman St	Denver	CO	80203	**888-847-9140**	303-837-1200
Community Foundation for Greater New Haven					
70 Audubon St	New Haven	CT	06510	**877-829-5500**	203-777-2386
Dayton Foundation					
40 N Main St Ste 500	Dayton	OH	45423	**877-222-0410**	937-222-0410
Foundation for the Carolinas					
217 S Tryon St	Charlotte	NC	28202	**800-973-7244**	704-973-4500
Hawaii Community Foundation					
65-1279 Kawaihae Rd Ste 203	Kamuela	HI	96743	**888-731-3863**	808-537-6333
Minneapolis Foundation					
80 S Eigth St 800 IDS Ctr	Minneapolis	MN	55402	**866-305-0543**	612-672-3878
New York Community Trust					
909 Third Ave 22nd Fl	New York	NY	10022	**877-829-5500**	212-686-0010
Omaha Community Foundation (OCF)					
302 S 36th St Ste 100	Omaha	NE	68131	**800-794-3458**	402-342-3458
Saint Paul Foundation					
55 E Fifth St Ste 600	Saint Paul	MN	55101	**800-875-6167**	651-224-5463

305 FOUNDATIONS - CORPORATE

SEE ALSO Charitable & Humanitarian Organizations

	Toll-Free	Phone
Cargill Foundation		
15407 McGinty Rd W Ste 46 .... Wayzata MN 55391	800-227-4455	877-765-8867
CIGNA Foundation		
900 Cottage Grove Rd .... Bloomfield CT 06002	866-438-2446	
NYSE: CI		
Cisco Systems Foundation		
170 W Tasman Dr .... San Jose CA 95134	800-553-6387	408-527-3040
Coca-Cola Foundation Inc		
PO Box 1734 .... Atlanta GA 30301	800-438-2653	800-306-2653
Dow Chemical Company Foundation		
2030 Dow Ctr .... Midland MI 48674	800-331-6451	989-636-1000
Eli Lilly & Co Foundation		
Lilly Corporate Ctr .... Indianapolis IN 46285	800-545-5979	317-276-2000
Freddie Mac Foundation		
8250 Jones Branch Dr .... McLean VA 22102	800-424-5401	703-918-5000
General Mills Foundation		
PO Box 9452 .... Minneapolis MN 55440	800-248-7310	
General Motors Foundation Inc		
PO Box 33170 .... Detroit MI 48232	800-222-1020	
Humana Foundation Inc		
500 W Main St Ste 208. .... Louisville KY 40202	888-431-4748	502-580-4140
Levi Strauss Foundation		
1155 Battery St .... San Francisco CA 94111	866-290-6064	415-501-6000
Lutheran Community Foundation		
625 Fourth Ave S Ste 200. .... Minneapolis MN 55415	800-365-4172	612-340-4110
Principal Financial Group Foundation Inc		
711 High St .... Des Moines IA 50392	800-986-3343	515-247-7227
Revlon Foundation Inc		
237 Pk Ave .... New York NY 10017	800-473-8566*	
*Cust Svc		
SBC Foundation		
130 E Travis St Ste 350. .... San Antonio TX 78205	800-591-9663	
Scripps Howard Foundation		
312 Walnut St PO Box 5380 .... Cincinnati OH 45201	800-888-3000	513-977-3035
Siemens Foundation		
170 Wood Ave S .... Iselin NJ 08830	877-822-5233	
Wal-Mart Foundation		
702 SW Eigth St .... Bentonville AR 72716	800-438-6278	479-273-4000
NYSE: WMT		
Whirlpool Foundation		
2000 N M-63 .... Benton Harbor MI 49022	800-952-9245	269-923-5000
Xerox Foundation		
45 Glover Ave .... Norwalk CT 06856	800-275-9376	

306 FOUNDATIONS - PRIVATE

SEE ALSO Charitable & Humanitarian Organizations

	Toll-Free	Phone
Annie E Casey Foundation		
701 St Paul St .... Baltimore MD 21202	800-222-1099	410-547-6600
Arthur Vining Davis Foundations		
225 Water St .... Jacksonville FL 32202	800-222-3448	904-359-0670
Bill & Melinda Gates Foundation		
PO Box 23350 .... Seattle WA 98102	800-728-3843	206-709-3100
Carnegie Corp of New York		
437 Madison Ave 26th Fl .... New York NY 10022	800-336-7323	212-371-3200
Colonial Williamsburg Foundation		
PO Box 1776 .... Williamsburg VA 23187	800-447-8679	757-229-1000
Corporation for Public Broadcasting (CPB)		
401 Ninth St NW .... Washington DC 20004	800-272-2190	202-879-9600
Dave Thomas Foundation for Adoption		
716 Mt Airyshire Blvd Ste 100 .... Columbus OH 43235	800-275-3832	
Ewing Marion Kauffman Foundation (EMKF)		
4801 Rockhill Rd .... Kansas City MO 64110	800-385-1607	816-932-1000
Gates Family Foundation		
1390 Lawrence Street .... Denver CO 80204	866-590-4377	303-722-1881
Hearst Foundation, The		
300 W 57th St 26th Fl. .... New York NY 10019	800-841-7048	212-649-3750
Herbert H & Grace A Dow Foundation		
1018 W Main St .... Midland MI 48640	800-362-4874	989-631-3699
Kiwanis International Foundation		
3636 Woodview Trace .... Indianapolis IN 46268	800-549-2647	317-875-8755
Liberty Fund Inc		
8335 Allison Pt Trial Ste 300 .... Indianapolis IN 46250	800-955-8335	317-842-0880
Lumina Foundation for Education		
30 S Meridian St Ste 700. .... Indianapolis IN 46204	800-834-5756	317-951-5300
Meadows Foundation Inc		
3003 Swiss Ave .... Dallas TX 75204	800-826-9431	214-826-9431
Michael J Fox Foundation for Parkinson's Research		
Grand Central Stn PO Box 4777 .... New York NY 10163	800-708-7644	
National Foundation for Cancer Research (NFCR)		
4600 E W Hwy Ste 525. .... Bethesda MD 20814	800-321-2873	301-654-1250
Nellie Mae Education Foundation		
1250 Hancock St Ste 205N. .... Quincy MA 02169	877-635-5436	781-348-4200
Patient Advocate Foundation Inc		
700 Thimble Shoals Blvd Ste 200. .... Newport News VA 23606	800-532-5274	
Pew Charitable Trusts		
2005 Market St		
1 Commerce Sq Ste 1700. .... Philadelphia PA 19103	800-595-4889	215-575-9050
Public Welfare Foundation		
1200 U St NW .... Washington DC 20009	800-275-7934	202-965-1800
Richard King Mellon Foundation		
500 Grant St Ste 4106 .... Pittsburgh PA 15219	800-424-9836	412-392-2800
Robert R McCormick Tribune Foundation		
205 N Michigan Ave Ste 4300 .... Chicago IL 60611	800-435-7352	312-445-5000
Salesforce.Com Foundation		
The Landmark @ One Market		
Ste 300 .... San Francisco CA 94105	800-667-6389	
Women's Independence Scholarship Program Inc (WISP)		
4900 Randall Pkwy Ste H .... Wilmington NC 28403	866-255-7742	910-397-7742

307 FOUNDRIES - INVESTMENT

	Toll-Free	Phone
Consolidated Casting Corp		
1501 S I-45 .... Hutchins TX 75141	800-649-5289	972-225-7305
Northern Precision Casting Co		
300 Interchange N PO Box 580. .... Lake Geneva WI 53147	800-934-4903	262-248-4461
Remet Corp 210 Commons Rd .... Utica NY 13502	877-939-0171	315-797-8700
Waltek Inc		
14310 Sunfish Lk Blvd .... Ramsey MN 55303	800-937-9496	763-427-3181

308 FOUNDRIES - IRON & STEEL

SEE ALSO Foundries - Nonferrous (Castings)

	Toll-Free	Phone
Allegheny Technologies Inc		
1000 Six PPG Pl .... Pittsburgh PA 15222	800-258-3586*	412-394-2800
*NYSE: ATI ■ *Sales		
Alloy Engineering & Casting Co		
1700 W Washington St .... Champaign IL 61821	866-352-8001	217-398-3200
American Cast Iron Pipe Co (ACIPCO)		
1501 31st Ave N .... Birmingham AL 35207	800-442-2347	205-325-7701
Atlantic States Cast Iron Pipe Co		
183 Sitgreaves St .... Phillipsburg NJ 08865	800-634-4746	908-454-1161
Bremen Castings Inc		
500 N Baltimore St .... Bremen IN 46506	800-837-2411	
Castalloy Inc		
1701 Industrial Ln PO Box 827. .... Waukesha WI 53189	800-211-0900	262-547-0070
Charter Dura-Bar		
2100 W Lake Shore Dr .... Woodstock IL 60098	800-227-6455	815-338-3900
Columbia Steel Casting Co Inc		
10425 N Bloss Ave .... Portland OR 97203	800-547-9471	503-286-0685
Complex Steel & Wire Corp		
36254 Annapolis Rd .... Wayne MI 48184	800-521-0666	734-326-1600
Delta Centrifugal Corp		
PO Box 1043 .... Temple TX 76503	888-433-3100*	254-773-9055
*Sales		
EJ Group Inc		
301 Spring St .... East Jordan MI 49727	800-874-4100	231-536-2261
Frog Switch & Mfg Co		
600 E High St .... Carlisle PA 17013	800-233-7194	717-243-2454
Harrison Steel Castings Co Inc		
900 S Mound St .... Attica IN 47918	888-782-7937	765-762-2481
Hensley Industries Inc		
2108 Joe Field Rd PO Box 29779. .... Dallas TX 75229	888-406-6262	972-241-2321
Hitachi Metals America Ltd		
2 Manhattanville Rd Ste 301. .... Purchase NY 10577	800-777-5757	914-694-9200
Howco Metals Management		
9611 Telge Rd .... Houston TX 77095	800-392-7720	281-649-8800
Jencast PO Box 1509 .... Coffeyville KS 67337	800-331-2662	620-251-5700
McWane Inc		
2900 Hwy 280 Ste 300 .... Birmingham AL 35223	877-231-0904	205-414-3100
Neenah Foundry Co		
2121 Brooks Ave .... Neenah WI 54956	800-558-5075	920-725-7000
Rodney Hunt Co 46 Mill St .... Orange MA 01364	800-448-8860	978-544-2511
Sharon Coating LLC		
277 Sharpsville Ave .... Sharon PA 16146	800-456-1794	724-981-3545
Sioux City Foundry Co		
801 Div St .... Sioux City IA 51102	800-831-0874	712-252-4181
Standard Alloys & Mfg		
PO Box 969 .... Port Arthur TX 77640	800-231-8240	409-983-3201
Steel Service Corp		
2260 Flowood Dr PO Box 321425 .... Jackson MS 39232	800-844-9222	601-939-9222
Talladega Castings & Machine Co Inc		
228 N Ct St .... Talladega AL 35160	800-766-6708	256-362-5550
Talladega Machinery & Supply Co Inc		
301 N Johnson Ave PO Box 736. .... Talladega AL 35161	800-289-8672*	256-362-4124
*Cust Svc		
Tyler Pipe Co 11910 CR 492 .... Tyler TX 75706	800-527-8478	903-882-5511
US Pipe & Foundry Co		
Two Chase Corporate Drive		
Suite 200 .... Birmingham AL 35244	866-347-7473	
Waukesha Foundry Company Inc		
1300 Lincoln Ave .... Waukesha WI 53186	800-727-0741	262-542-0741
Waupaca Foundry		
1955 Brunner Dr PO Box 249 .... Waupaca WI 54981	800-669-6820	715-258-6611

309 FOUNDRIES - NONFERROUS (CASTINGS)

SEE ALSO Foundries - Iron & Steel

	Toll-Free	Phone
Bunting Bearings Corp		
1001 Holland Pk Blvd .... Holland OH 43528	888-286-8464	419-866-7000
Consolidated Metco Inc		
13940 N Rivergate Blvd .... Portland OR 97203	800-547-9473*	
*Sales		
Deco Products Co		
506 Sanford St .... Decorah IA 52101	800-327-9751	563-382-4264
Del Mar Die Casting Co		
12901 S Western Ave .... Gardena CA 90249	800-624-7468	323-321-0600
Dynacast Inc		
14045 Ballantyne Corporate Pl .... Charlotte NC 28277	866-662-2750	704-927-2790
Electric Materials Co		
50 S Washington St .... North East PA 16428	800-356-2211	814-725-9621
Falcon Foundry Co		
96 Sixth St .... Lowellville OH 44436	800-253-8624	330-536-6221
General Die Casters Inc		
2150 Highland Rd .... Twinsburg OH 44087	800-332-2278	330-657-2300
Halex Co		
23901 Aurora Rd .... Bedford Heights OH 44146	800-749-3261	440-439-1616

				Toll-Free	Phone
Lee Brass Co					
1800 Golden Springs Rd	Anniston	AL	36207	**800-876-1811***	
*General					
Littlestown Foundry Inc					
150 Charles St PO Box 69	Littlestown	PA	17340	**800-471-0844**	717-359-4141
Madison-Kipp Corp					
201 Waubesa St	Madison	WI	53704	**800-356-6148**	
Magnolia Metal Corp					
10675 Bedford Ave Ste 200	Omaha	NE	68134	**800-228-4043**	402-455-8760
NGK Metals Corp					
917 Hwy 11 S	Sweetwater	TN	37874	**800-523-8268**	423-337-5500
Piad Precision Casting Corp					
112 Industrial Pk Rd	Greensburg	PA	15601	**800-441-9858**	724-838-5500
Premier Die Casting Co					
1177 Rahway Ave	Avenel	NJ	07001	**800-394-3006**	732-634-3000
Premier Tool & Die Cast Corp					
9886 N Tudor Rd	Berrien Springs	MI	49103	**800-417-8717**	269-471-7715
Reliable Castings Corp					
3530 Spring Grove Ave	Cincinnati	OH	45223	**866-722-2278**	513-541-2627
Southern Centrifugal Inc					
4180 S Creek Rd	Chattanooga	TN	37406	**800-634-8176**	423-622-4131
Stahl Specialty Co					
11 E Pacific PO Box 6	Kingsville	MO	64061	**800-821-7852**	816-597-3322
Talladega Castings & Machine Co Inc					
228 N Ct St	Talladega	AL	35160	**800-766-6708**	256-362-5550
Techni-Cast Corp					
11220 Garfield Ave	South Gate	CA	90280	**800-923-4585**	562-923-4585
United Titanium Inc					
3450 Old Airport Rd	Wooster	OH	44691	**800-321-4938**	330-264-2111

310   FRAMES & MOULDINGS

				Toll-Free	Phone
Alexandria Moulding					
20352 Powerdam Rd	Alexandria	ON	K0C1A0	**866-377-2539**	613-525-2784
Groovfold Inc					
1050 W State St	Newcomerstown	OH	43832	**800-367-1133**	740-498-8363
Larson-Juhl					
3900 Steve Reynolds Blvd	Norcross	GA	30093	**800-221-4123**	
North American Enclosures Inc					
65 Jetson Ln	Central Islip	NY	11722	**800-645-9209**	631-234-9500
PB & H Moulding Corp					
124 Pickard Dr E	Syracuse	NY	13211	**800-746-9724**	315-455-5602
Quanex Building Products					
2270 Woodale Dr	Mounds View	MN	55112	**800-233-4383**	763-231-4000
Royal Mouldings Ltd					
135 Bearcreek Rd PO Box 610	Marion	VA	24354	**800-368-3117**	276-783-8161
Uniek Inc 805 Uniek Dr	Waunakee	WI	53597	**800-248-6435**	608-849-9999
Woodgrain Distribution					
80 Shelby St	Montevallo	AL	35115	**800-756-0199**	205-665-2546

FRAMES & MOULDINGS - METAL

SEE Doors & Windows - Metal

311   FRANCHISES

SEE ALSO Restaurant Companies ; Staffing Services ; Travel Agency Networks ; Weight Loss Centers & Services ; Health Food Stores ; Home Inspection Services ; Hotels & Hotel Companies ; Ice Cream & Dairy Stores ; Laundry & Drycleaning Services ; Optical Goods Stores ; Pest Control Services ; Printing Companies - Commercial Printers ; Real Estate Agents & Brokers ; Auto Supply Stores ; Automotive Services ; Bakeries ; Beauty Salons ; Business Service Centers ; Candles ; Car Rental Agencies ; Children's Learning Centers ; Cleaning Services ; Remodeling, Refinishing, Resurfacing Contractors ; Convenience Stores

Please see the category on Hotel & Resort Operation & Management for listings of hotel franchises.

				Toll-Free	Phone
1-800-Got-Junk					
301 - 887 Great Northern Way 3rd Fl	Vancouver	BC	V5T4T5	**800-468-5865**	
1-800-Water Damage					
1167 Mercer St	Seattle	WA	98109	**800-928-3732**	206-381-3041
ABC Seamless					
3001 Fiechtner Dr	Fargo	ND	58103	**800-732-6577**	701-293-5952
ActionCOACH					
5781 S Ft Apache Rd	Las Vegas	NV	89148	**888-483-2828**	702-795-3188
Aire Serv Heating & Air Conditioning Inc					
5387 Texas 6 Fwy Ste 101	Woodway	TX	76712	**855-983-0630**	254-523-3600
Aire-Master of America Inc					
1821 N State Hwy Cc	Nixa	MO	65714	**800-525-0957**	417-725-2691
All Tune & Lube Brakes & More Inc					
8334 Veteran's Hwy	Millersville	MD	21108	**877-978-1758**	410-987-1011
AmeriSpec Inc					
889 Ridge Lk Blvd	Memphis	TN	38120	**800-426-2270**	901-820-8500
Archadeck					
2924 Emerywood Pkwy Ste 101	Richmond	VA	23294	**800-722-4668**	804-353-6999
Baskin-Robbins Inc					
130 Royall St	Canton	MA	02021	**800-859-5339**	781-737-3000
Beef O'Bradys Inc					
5660 W Cypress St Ste A	Tampa	FL	33607	**800-728-8878**	813-226-2333
Bellacino's Corp					
10096 Shaver Rd	Portage	MI	49024	**877-379-0700**	269-329-0782
Benjamin Franklin Plumbing					
50 Central Ave Ste 920	Sarasota	FL	34236	**800-471-0809**	941-366-9692
Big Apple Bagels					
500 Lk Cook Rd Ste 475	Deerfield	IL	60015	**800-251-6101**	847-948-7520
Bojangles' Restaurants Inc					
9432 Southern Pine Blvd	Charlotte	NC	28273	**800-366-9921**	704-335-1804
Boston Pizza Restaurants LP					
1501 LBJ Fwy Ste 450	Dallas	TX	75234	**866-277-8721**	972-484-9022

				Toll-Free	Phone
BrickKicker Inc					
849 N Ellsworth St	Naperville	IL	60563	**800-821-1820**	630-420-9900
Candy Bouquet International Inc					
510 Mclean St	Little Rock	AR	72202	**877-226-3901**	501-375-9990
Captain D's LLC					
624 Grassmere Park Dr Ste 30	Nashville	TN	37211	**800-314-4819**	615-391-5461
Car-X Assoc Corp					
1375 E Woodfield Rd Ste 500	Schaumburg	IL	60173	**800-359-2359**	847-273-8920
CardSmart Retail Corp					
11 Executive Ave	Edison	NJ	08817	**888-782-7050**	
Carlson Wagonlit Travel Inc					
701 Carlson Pkwy	Minnetonka	MN	55305	**800-213-7295**	
Carvel Express					
200 Glenridge Pt Pkwy Ste 200	Atlanta	GA	30342	**800-322-4848**	
CertaPro Painters Ltd					
150 Green Tree Rd Ste 1003	Oaks	PA	19456	**800-689-7271**	
Certified Restoration DryCleaning Network LLC					
2060 Coolidge Hwy	Berkley	MI	48072	**800-963-2736**	
Charley's Grilled Subs					
2500 Farmers Dr Ste 140	Columbus	OH	43235	**800-437-8325**	614-923-4700
Checkers Drive-In Restaurants Inc					
4300 W Cypress St Ste 600	Tampa	FL	33607	**800-800-8072**	813-283-7000
Chester's International LLC					
3500 Colonnade Pkwy Ste 325	Birmingham	AL	35243	**800-554-4537**	205-949-4690
Cleaning Authority					
7230 Lee DeForest Dr Ste 200	Columbia	MD	21046	**888-658-0659**	410-740-1900
Closet Factory					
12800 S Broadway	Los Angeles	CA	90061	**800-838-7995**	310-516-7000
Coffee Beanery Ltd, The					
3429 Pierson Pl	Flushing	MI	48433	**800-441-2255**	
Cold Stone Creamery Inc					
9311 E Via De Ventura	Scottsdale	AZ	85258	**866-452-4252***	480-362-4800
*Cust Svc					
Color Me Mine Enterprises Inc					
3722 San Fernando Rd	Glendale	CA	91204	**888-265-6764**	818-291-5900
Color-Glo International					
7111 Ohms Ln	Minneapolis	MN	55439	**800-333-8523**	952-835-1338
ComForcare Senior Services Inc					
2520 Telegraph Rd Ste 100	Bloomfield Hills	MI	48302	**800-886-4044**	248-745-9700
Computer Explorers					
12715 Telge Rd	Cypress	TX	77429	**800-531-5053**	
Computer Troubleshooters USA					
755 Commerce Dr Ste 605	Decatur	GA	30030	**877-704-1702**	404-477-1302
Contours Express Inc					
156 Imperial Way	Nicholasville	KY	40356	**855-589-9662**	
Cookies By Design Inc					
1865 Summit Ave Ste 605	Plano	TX	75074	**800-945-2665**	972-398-9536
Coverall Cleaning Concepts					
5201 Congress Ave Ste 275	Boca Raton	FL	33487	**800-537-3371**	866-296-8944
Craters & Freighters					
331 Corporate Cir Ste J	Golden	CO	80401	**800-736-3335**	
Creative Colors International Inc					
19015 S Jodi Rd Ste E	Mokena	IL	60448	**800-933-2656**	708-478-1437
Critter Control Inc					
9435 E Cherry Bend Rd	Traverse City	MI	49684	**800-451-6544**	231-947-2400
CruiseOne Inc					
1201 W Cypress Creek Rd Ste 100	Fort Lauderdale	FL	33309	**800-278-4731**	
D'Angelo Sandwich Shops					
600 Providence Hwy	Dedham	MA	02026	**800-727-2446**	781-461-1200
Dairy Queen					
7505 Metro Blvd	Minneapolis	MN	55439	**800-883-4279**	952-830-0200
Decor & You Inc					
900 Main St S	Southbury	CT	06488	**800-477-3326**	203-264-3500
Decorating Den Systems Inc					
8659 Commerce Dr	Easton	MD	21601	**800-332-3367**	410-822-9001
DirectBuy Inc					
8450 Broadway	Merrillville	IN	46410	**800-320-3462**	219-736-1100
Dr Vinyl & Assoc Ltd					
1350 SE Hamblen Rd	Lees Summit	MO	64081	**800-531-6600***	816-525-6060
*General					
DreamMaker Bath & Kitchen by Worldwide					
510 N Valley Mills Dr Ste 304	Waco	TX	76710	**800-583-2133**	
Dunkin' Donuts 130 Royall St	Canton	MA	02021	**800-859-5339***	781-737-3000
*Cust Svc					
Duraclean International Inc					
220 W Campus Dr	Arlington Heights	IL	60004	**800-862-5326**	847-704-7100
Edible Arrangements LLC					
95 Barnes Rd	Wallingford	CT	06492	**877-363-7848***	304-894-8901
*Cust Svc					
EmbroidMe Inc					
2121 Vista Pkwy	West Palm Beach	FL	33411	**877-877-0234**	561-640-7367
Express Employment Professionals					
8516 NW Expy	Oklahoma City	OK	73162	**800-222-4057**	405-840-5000
Express Oil Change					
1880 S Pk Dr	Hoover	AL	35244	**888-945-1771**	205-945-1771
Extreme Pita					
2187 Dunwin Dr	Mississauga	ON	L5L1X2	**888-729-7482**	905-820-7887
Famous Dave's of America Inc					
12701 Whitewater Dr Ste 200	Minnetonka	MN	55343	**800-929-4040**	952-294-1300
NASDAQ: DAVE					
Fast-Fix Jewelry & Watch Repairs					
451 Altamonte Ave	Altamonte Springs	FL	32701	**800-359-0407**	407-261-1595
FasTracKids International Ltd					
6900 E Belleview Ave Ste 100	Greenwood Village	CO	80111	**888-576-6888**	303-224-0200
Figaro's Italian Pizza Inc					
1500 Liberty St SE Ste 160	Salem	OR	97302	**888-344-2767**	503-371-9318
Firehouse Restaurant Group Inc					
3400 Kori Rd Ste 8	Jacksonville	FL	32257	**877-309-7332**	904-886-8300
Fish Window Cleaning Services Inc					
200 Enchanted Pkwy	Manchester	MO	63021	**877-707-3474**	636-779-1500
Floor Coverings International					
5250 Triangle Pkwy Ste 100	Norcross	GA	30092	**800-955-4324***	770-874-7600
*Sales					
Foot Solutions Inc					
2359 Windy Hill Rd Ste 400	Marietta	GA	30067	**888-358-3668***	770-984-0844
*General					

				Toll-Free	Phone

Fox's Pizza Den Inc
4425 Willaim Penn Hwy ....Murrysville PA 15668 **800-899-3697** 724-733-7888

Furniture Medic
3839 S Forest Hill Irene Rd ....Memphis TN 38125 **800-877-9933**

GNC Inc
300 Sixth Ave 14th Fl ....Pittsburgh PA 15222 **877-462-4700**
NYSE: GNC

Goddard Systems Inc
1016 W Ninth Ave ....King of Prussia PA 19406 **800-463-3273** 610-265-8510

Grease Monkey International
7450 E Progress Pl ....Greenwood Village CO 80111 **800-822-7706** 303-308-1660

Great American Cookie Company Inc
1346 Oakbrook Dr Ste 170 ....Norcross GA 30093 **877-639-2361**

Great Clips Inc
7700 France Ave S Ste 425. ....Minneapolis MN 55435 **800-999-5959** 952-893-9088

Great Harvest Bread Co
28 S Montana St ....Dillon MT 59725 **800-442-0424** 406-683-6842

Great Steak & Potato Co
9311 E Via de Ventura ....Scottsdale AZ 85258 **866-452-4252** 480-362-4800

Griswold Special Care Inc
717 Bethlehem Pike Ste 300. ....Erdenheim PA 19038 **855-303-9470** 215-402-0200

Growth Coach, The
10700 Montgomery Rd Ste 300 ....Cincinnati OH 45242 **888-292-7992**

Gymboree Corp
500 Howard St ....San Francisco CA 94105 **877-449-6932** 415-278-7000
NASDAQ: GYMB

Gymboree Corp Play & Music Program
500 Howard St ....San Francisco CA 94105 **877-449-6932*** 415-278-7000
*Cust Svc

Handyman Matters Inc
12567 W Cedar Dr Ste 250. ....Lakewood CO 80228 **866-349-6946** 303-984-0177

Hayes Handpiece Franchises Inc
5375 Avenida Encinas Ste C ....Carlsbad CA 92008 **800-228-0521** 760-602-0521

Homes & Land Magazine Affiliates LLC
1830 E Pk Ave ....Tallahassee FL 32301 **800-277-7800** 850-575-0189

HomeTeam Inspection Service Inc
575 Chamber Dr ....Milford OH 45150 **800-598-5297**

HomeVestors of America Inc
6500 Greenville Ave Ste 400. ....Dallas TX 75206 **800-442-8937** 972-761-0046

HouseMaster
850 Bear Tavern RD Ste 303. ....Ewing NJ 08628 **800-526-3939** 732-469-6565

Ident-A-Kid Services of America
1780 102nd Ave N Ste 100. ....Saint Petersburg FL 33716 **800-890-1000** 727-577-4646

IHOP Corp 450 N Brand Blvd ....Glendale CA 91203 **800-901-5248** 818-240-6055

Instant Imprints
5897 Oberlin Dr Ste 200. ....San Diego CA 92121 **800-542-3437** 858-642-4848

Interim HealthCare Inc
1601 Sawgrass Corporate Pkwy ....Sunrise FL 33323 **800-338-7786** 954-858-6000

Jackson Hewitt Inc
Three Sylvan Way Ste 301 ....Parsippany NJ 07054 **800-234-1040**
OTC: JHTXQ

Jazzercise Inc
2460 Impala Dr ....Carlsbad CA 92010 **800-348-4748*** 760-476-1750
*Cust Svc

Jenny Craig International Inc
5770 Fleet St ....Carlsbad CA 92008 **800-443-2331** 760-696-4000

KFC Corp
1441 Gardiner Ln ....Louisville KY 40213 **800-225-5532** 818-780-6990

Kinderdance International Inc
1333 Gateway Dr Ste 1033 ....Melbourne FL 32901 **800-554-2334** 321-984-4448

Kitchen Tune-Up Inc
813 Cir Dr ....Aberdeen SD 57401 **800-333-6385** 605-225-4049

Lady of America Franchise Corp
159 Weston RD Ste 1650 ....Weston FL 33326 **800-833-5239** 954-217-8660

Lawn Doctor Inc 142 SR 34 ....Holmdel NJ 07733 **800-631-5660**

Learning Express Inc
29 Buena Vista St ....Devens MA 01434 **800-924-2296** 978-889-1000

Liberty Tax Service Inc
1716 Corporate Landing Pkwy ....Virginia Beach VA 23454 **800-790-3863*** 757-493-8855
*Cust Svc

Little Caesars Inc
2211 Woodward Ave ....Detroit MI 48201 **800-722-3727** 313-983-6409

Little Gym International Inc
7001 N Scottsdale Rd ....Paradise Valley AZ 85253 **888-228-2878***
*General

Living Assistance Services Inc
937 Haverford Rd Ste 200. ....Bryn Mawr PA 19010 **800-365-4189** 610-924-0630

Mad Science Group
8360 Bougainville St Ste 201 ....Montreal QC H4P2G1 **800-586-5231** 514-344-4181

MaggieMoo's International LLC
1346 Oakbrook Dr Ste 170 ....Norcross GA 30093 **877-639-2361**

Magnetsigns Adv Inc
4225 38th St ....Camrose AB T4V3Z3 **800-219-8977** 780-672-8720

Maid Brigade USA/Minimaid Canada
Four Concourse Pkwy Ste 200 ....Atlanta GA 30328 **800-722-6243** 770-551-9630

MaidPro Corp 180 Canal St ....Boston MA 02114 **888-624-3776** 617-742-8787

Mail Boxes Etc
6060 Cornerstone Ct W ....San Diego CA 92121 **800-789-4623** 858-455-8800

Manhattan Bagel Co Inc
555 Zang St Ste 300 ....Lakewood CO 80228 **800-224-3563** 303-568-8000

Martinizing Dry Cleaning
8944 Columbia Rd Ste J. ....Loveland OH 45140 **800-827-0207**

Mathnasium LLC
5120 W Goldleaf Cir Ste 300 ....Los Angeles CA 90056 **877-601-6284** 323-421-8000

McDonald's Corp
One McDonald's Plz ....Oak Brook IL 60523 **800-244-6227** 630-623-3000
NYSE: MCD

Medicap Pharmacies Inc
1 Rider Trail Plaza Dr ....Earth City MO 63045 **800-407-8055** 314-993-6000

Merle Norman Cosmetics Inc
9130 Bellanca Ave ....Los Angeles CA 90045 **800-421-6648** 310-641-3000

Merlin Corp
3815 E Main St Ste D ....Saint Charles IL 60174 **800-652-9910** 630-513-8200

Midas International Corp
1300 Arlington Heights Rd ....Itasca IL 60143 **800-621-8545** 630-438-3000

Minuteman Press International Inc
61 Executive Blvd ....Farmingdale NY 11735 **800-645-3006** 631-249-1370

Money Mailer LLC
12131 Western Ave ....Garden Grove CA 92841 **800-468-5865** 714-889-3800

Mr Appliance Corp
1020 N University Parks Dr ....Waco TX 76707 **888-998-2011** 256-415-5069

Mr Handyman International LLC
3796 Plz Dr Ste 1C...........................Ann Arbor MI 48108 **800-289-4600***
*Cust Svc

Mr Hero Restaurants
7010 Engle Rd Ste 100. ....Middleburg Heights OH 44130 **888-860-5082** 440-625-3080

My Favorite Muffin
500 Lk Cook Rd Ste 475. ....Deerfield IL 60015 **800-251-6101** 847-948-7520

Nathan's Famous Inc
One Jericho Plz Second Fl ....Jericho NY 11753 **800-628-4267** 516-338-8500
NASDAQ: NATH

National Property Inspections Inc (NPI)
9375 Burt St Ste 201 ....Omaha NE 68114 **800-333-9807** 402-333-9807

Navis Pack & Ship Centers
6551 S Revere Pkwy Ste 250 ....Centennial CO 80111 **800-344-3528**

NOVUS Auto Glass
12800 Hwy 13 S Ste 500 ....Savage MN 55378 **800-776-6887** 952-736-7843

OpenWorks
4742 N 24th St Ste 450 ....Phoenix AZ 85016 **800-777-6736** 602-224-0440

Orange Julius of America
7505 Metro Blvd ....Minneapolis MN 55439 **866-793-7582** 952-830-0200

Padgett Business Services
160 Hawthorne Pk ....Athens GA 30606 **800-723-4388**

Pak Mail Centers of America Inc
7173 S Havana St Ste 600 ....Centennial CO 80112 **800-778-6665*** 303-957-1000
*Cust Svc

Papa Murphy's International Inc
8000 NE Pkwy Dr Ste 350. ....Vancouver WA 98662 **800-778-7879** 360-260-7272

Party City Corp
25 Green Pond Rd Ste 1 ....Rockaway NJ 07866 **800-727-8924** 973-453-8600

Perkins Restaurant & Bakery
6075 Poplar Ave Ste 800 ....Memphis TN 38119 **800-877-7375** 901-766-6400

Perma-Glaze Inc
1638 Research Loop Rd Ste 160. ....Tucson AZ 85710 **800-332-7397** 520-722-9718

Petland Inc
250 Riverside St ....Chillicothe OH 45601 **800-221-5935** 740-775-2464

Physicians Weight Loss Centers of America Inc
395 Springside Dr ....Akron OH 44333 **800-205-7887** 330-666-7952

Pizza Inn Inc
3551 Plano Pkwy ....The Colony TX 75056 **800-880-9955** 469-384-5000
NASDAQ: RAVE

Pizza Ranch Inc
204 19th St SE ....Orange City IA 51041 **800-321-3401**

Plato's Closet
23021 Outer Dr ....Allen Park MI 48101 **800-592-8049** 313-278-2300

Postal Connections of America
6136 Frisco Sq Blvd Ste 400 ....Frisco TX 75034 **800-767-8257**

PostalAnnex+ Inc
7580 Metropolitan Dr Ste 200 ....San Diego CA 92108 **800-456-1525** 619-563-4800

PostNet International Franchise Corp
1819 Wazee St ....Denver CO 80202 **800-841-7171** 303-771-7100

Precision Auto Care Inc
748 Miller Dr SE ....Leesburg VA 20175 **800-438-8863** 703-777-9095
OTC: PACI

PremierGarage Systems LLC
21405 N 15th Ln ....Phoenix AZ 85027 **866-590-9411** 480-483-3030

Pressed4Time Inc
Eight Clock Tower Pl Ste 110 ....Maynard MA 01754 **800-423-8711**

Primrose School Franchising Co
3660 Cedarcrest Rd ....Acworth GA 30101 **800-745-0677** 770-529-4100

ProForma
8800 E Pleasant Vly Rd ....Independence OH 44131 **800-825-1525** 216-520-8400

Property Damage Appraisers Inc (PDA)
6100 SW Blvd Ste 200 ....Fort Worth TX 76109 **800-749-7324**

RadioShack Corp
300 RadioShack Cir ....Fort Worth TX 76102 **800-843-7422** 800-442-7221
NYSE: RSH

Rainbow International
1010 N University Pk Dr ....Waco TX 76707 **855-724-6269** 254-756-5463

Re-Bath LLC
16879 N 75th Ave Ste 101 ....Peoria AZ 85382 **800-426-4573**

RE/MAX International Inc
5075 S Syracuse St ....Denver CO 80237 **800-525-7452*** 303-770-5531
*Cust Svc

Real Living Inc
77 E Nationwide Blvd ....Columbus OH 43215 **800-848-7400** 614-459-7400

Realty Executives International Inc
7600 N 16th St Ste 100 ....Phoenix AZ 85020 **800-252-3366** 602-957-0747

Red Robin Gourmet Burgers Inc
6312 S Fiddlers Green Cir
Ste 200-N. ....Greenwood Village CO 80111 **877-733-6543** 303-846-6000
NASDAQ: RRGB

Rescuecom Corp
2560 Burnet Ave ....Syracuse NY 13206 **800-737-2837**

Results Travel
701 Carlson Pkwy ....Minnetonka MN 55305 **800-456-4000** 763-212-5000

Right at Home Inc
6464 Crt St Ste 150 ....Omaha NE 68106 **877-697-7537** 402-697-7537

RSVP Publications
6730 W Linebaugh Ave Ste 201 ....Tampa FL 33625 **800-360-7787** 813-960-7787

Ruby Tuesday Inc
150 W Church Ave ....Maryville TN 37801 **800-325-0755** 865-379-5700
NYSE: RT

Sandler Sales Institute
10411 Stevenson Rd ....Stevenson MD 21153 **800-669-3537** 410-653-1993

Sea Tow Services International Inc
1560 Youngs Ave PO Box 1178 ....Southold NY 11971 **800-473-2869** 631-765-3660

Second Cup Ltd
6303 Airport Rd ....Mississauga ON L4V1R8 **877-212-1818**

Signs by Tomorrow USA Inc
8681 Robert Fulton Dr ....Columbia MD 21046 **800-765-7446** 410-312-3600

Sir Speedy Inc
26722 Plaza Dr ....Mission Viejo CA 92691 **800-854-8297** 949-348-5000

Snap-on Inc 2801 80th St ....Kenosha WI 53143 **877-762-7664** 262-656-5200
NYSE: SNA

				Toll-Free	Phone
Sport Clips Inc					
110 Briarwood Dr	Georgetown	TX	78628	**800-872-4247**	512-869-1201
Spring-Green Lawn Care Corp					
11909 Spaulding School Dr	Plainfield	IL	60585	**800-435-4051**	815-436-8777
Stork News of America Inc					
1305 Hope Mills Rd Ste A	Fayetteville	NC	28304	**800-633-6395**	910-429-2229
Stretch-N-Grow International Inc					
PO Box 7599	Seminole	FL	33775	**800-348-0166**	
Successories Inc					
1040 Holland Dr	Boca Raton	FL	33487	**800-535-2773**	
SuperCoups					
350 Revolutionary Dr	East Taunton	MA	02718	**800-626-2620**	508-977-2000
Supercuts					
7201 Metro Blvd	Minneapolis	MN	55439	**877-857-2070**	
Terminix International Company LP					
860 Ridge Lk Blvd	Memphis	TN	38120	**866-399-0453**	
Treats International Franchise Corp					
1550-A Laperriere Ave Ste 201	Ottawa	ON	K1Z7T2	**800-461-4003**	613-563-4073
Truly Nolen of America Inc					
3636 E Speedway Blvd	Tucson	AZ	85716	**800-468-7859**	800-528-3442
Tuffy Assoc Corp					
7150 Granite Cir	Toledo	OH	43617	**800-228-8339**	419-865-6900
UPS Store, The					
6060 Cornerstone Ct W	San Diego	CA	92121	**800-789-4623**	858-455-8800
Valpak Direct Marketing Systems Inc					
8605 Largo Lakes Dr	Largo	FL	33773	**800-237-6266**	
Wild Birds Unlimited Inc					
11711 N College Ave Ste 146	Carmel	IN	46032	**800-326-4928**	317-571-7100
WineStyles Inc					
5515 Mills Civic Pkwy Ste 110	West Des Moines	IA	50266	**866-424-9463**	
Wing Zone Franchise Corp					
900 Cir 75 Pkwy Ste 930	Atlanta	GA	30339	**877-946-4966**	404-875-5045
Wireless Toyz Ltd					
29155 NW Hwy	Southfield	MI	48034	**866-237-2624**	248-426-8200
Wireless Zone					
34 Industrial Pk Pl	Middletown	CT	06457	**888-881-2622**	860-632-9494
Woodcraft Supply LLC					
1177 Rosemar Rd PO Box 1686	Parkersburg	WV	26105	**800-535-4482**	
World Inspection Network International Inc					
12345 Lk City Way NE Ste 365	Seattle	WA	98125	**800-309-6753**	
Worldwide Express					
2828 Routh St Ste 400	Dallas	TX	75201	**800-758-7447**	214-720-2400
WSI Internet					
5580 Explorer Dr Ste 600	Mississauga	ON	L4W4Y1	**888-678-7588**	905-678-7588
Ziebart International Corp					
1290 E Maple Rd	Troy	MI	48083	**800-877-1312**	248-588-4100

312   FREIGHT FORWARDERS

SEE ALSO Logistics Services (Transportation & Warehousing)

				Toll-Free	Phone
A & S Services Group LLC					
310 N Zarfoss Dr	York	PA	17404	**800-227-6782**	717-759-3017
Airways Freight Corp					
3849 W Wedington Dr	Fayetteville	AR	72704	**800-643-3525**	479-442-6301
Alba Wheels Up International Inc					
525 Washington Blvd	Jersey City	NJ	07310	**888-720-9917**	201-435-7050
Arrow Freight Management Inc					
PO Box 371974	El Paso	TX	79937	**888-598-9891**	915-778-3999
Barthco International Inc					
5101 S Broad St	Philadelphia	PA	19112	**877-401-6400***	215-238-8600
*General					
Blue-Grace Logistics LLC					
2846 S Falkenburg Rd	Riverview	FL	33578	**800-697-4477**	813-641-0357
CDS Logistics Management Inc					
1225 Bengies Rd Ste A	Baltimore	MD	21220	**866-649-9559**	410-314-8000
ContainerWorld Forwarding Services Inc					
16133 Blundell Rd	Richmond	BC	V6W0A3	**877-838-8880**	604-276-1300
Continental Traffic Service Inc (CTSI)					
5100 Poplar Ave 15th Fl	Memphis	TN	38137	**888-836-5135**	901-766-1500
Evans Delivery Company Inc					
PO Box 268	Pottsville	PA	17901	**800-666-7885**	570-385-9048
FESCO Agencies NA Inc					
1000 Second Ave Ste 1310	Seattle	WA	98104	**800-275-3372**	206-583-0860
Fetch Logistics Inc					
25 Northpointe Pkwy Ste 200	Amherst	NY	14228	**800-964-4940**	716-689-4556
Freight Logistics Inc					
PO Box 1712	Medford	OR	97501	**800-866-7882**	541-734-5617
Frontier Logistics LP					
1806 S 16th St	La Porte	TX	77571	**800-610-6808**	
Gold Coast Freightways Inc					
12250 NW 28th Ave	Miami	FL	33167	**877-465-3585**	305-687-3560
HA Logistics Inc					
5175 Johnson Dr	Pleasanton	CA	94588	**800-449-5778**	925-251-9300
Hassett Air Express					
877 S Rt 83	Elmhurst	IL	60126	**800-323-9422**	630-530-6524
Interdom LLC					
11800 S 75th Ave Ste 2N	Palos Heights	IL	60463	**800-935-0851**	
J & A Freight Systems Inc					
4704 Irving Park Rd Ste 8	Chicago	IL	60641	**877-668-3378**	
Knitney Lines Inc					
PO Box 350	Scranton	PA	18501	**800-266-7883***	570-457-5060
*General					
L E Coppersmith Inc					
525 S Douglas St	El Segundo	CA	90245	**888-827-4388**	310-607-8000
LeanLogistics Inc					
1351 S Waverly Rd	Holland	MI	49423	**866-584-7280**	616-738-6400
Logistics Plus Inc					
1406 Peach St	Erie	PA	16501	**866-564-7587**	814-461-7600
Lynden Inc					
18000 International Blvd Ste 800	Seattle	WA	98188	**888-596-3361**	206-241-8778
MSM Transportation Inc					
124 Commercial Rd	Bolton	ON	L7E1K4	**800-667-4175**	905-951-6800
Pacific Alaska Freightways Inc					
2812 70th Ave E	Fife	WA	98424	**800-426-9940**	253-926-3292
Phoenix International Freight Services Ltd					
14701 Charlson Road	Eden Prairie	MN	55347	**855-229-6128**	952-937-6761

				Toll-Free	Phone
Pioneer Transfer LLC					
2034 S St Aubin St PO Box 2567	Sioux City	IA	51106	**800-325-4650**	
Quality Customs Broker Inc					
4464 S Whitnall Ave	Saint Francis	WI	53235	**888-813-4647**	414-482-9447
Quality Transportation					
36-40 37th St Ste 201	Long Island City	NY	11101	**800-677-2838**	212-308-6333
Rmx Global Logistics					
35715 US Hwy 40 Bldg B	Evergreen	CO	80439	**888-824-7365**	
Rock-It Cargo USA Inc					
5438 W 104th St PO Box 90519	Los Angeles	CA	90045	**800-973-1727**	310-410-0935
Romar Transportation Systems Inc					
3500 S Kedzie Ave	Chicago	IL	60632	**800-621-5416**	773-376-8800
Satellite Logistics Group Inc					
12621 Featherwood Ste 390	Houston	TX	77034	**877-795-7540**	281-902-5500
Scott Logistics Corp					
PO Box 391	Rome	GA	30162	**800-893-6689**	706-234-1184
Senderex Cargo Inc					
5451 104th St	Los Angeles	CA	90045	**800-421-5846**	310-342-2900
Sho-Air International					
5401 Argosy Ave	Huntington Beach	CA	92649	**800-227-9111**	949-476-9111
Sunset Transportation Inc					
11325 Concord Village Ave	St Louis	MO	63123	**800-849-6540**	
Terminal Corp, The					
1657 S Highland Ave Ste A	Baltimore	MD	21224	**800-560-7207**	
Time Definite Services Inc					
1360 Madeline Ln Ste 300	Elgin	IL	60124	**800-466-8040**	
Total Quality Logistics Inc (TQL)					
4289 Ivy Pointe Blvd	Cincinnati	OH	45245	**800-580-3101**	513-831-2600
Towne Air Freight					
24805 US 20 W	South Bend	IN	46628	**800-468-6963**	574-233-3183
Trans-Border Global Freight Systems Inc					
2103 Route 9	Round Lake	NY	12151	**800-493-9444**	518-785-6000
TRANSInternational System Inc					
130 E Wilson Bridge Rd Ste 150					
Ste 150	Worthington	OH	43085	**800-340-7540**	614-891-4942
Transportation Management Assoc Inc					
344 Oak Grove Church Rd	Mocksville	NC	27028	**800-745-8292**	
Tricor America Inc					
717 Airport Blvd	South San Francisco	CA	94080	**800-669-7874**	650-877-3650

313   FREIGHT TRANSPORT - DEEP SEA (DOMESTIC PORTS)

				Toll-Free	Phone
Alaska Marine Lines Inc					
5615 W Marginal Way SW	Seattle	WA	98106	**800-326-8346***	206-763-4244
*Cust Svc					
Coastal Transportation Inc					
4025 13th Ave W	Seattle	WA	98119	**800-544-2580**	206-282-9979
Crowley Maritime Corp					
9487 Regency Square Blvd					
Ste 2130	Jacksonville	FL	32225	**800-276-9539**	904-727-2200
Freightquote.com Inc					
16025 W 113th St	Lenexa	KS	66219	**800-323-5441**	913-642-4700
Hapag-Lloyd America Inc					
401 E Jackson St	Tampa	FL	33602	**800-282-8977**	813-276-4600
Horizon Lines Inc					
4064 Colony Rd Ste 200	Charlotte	NC	28211	**877-678-7447***	704-973-7000
*Cust Svc					
International Shipholding Corp					
11 N Water Ste 18290	Mobile	AL	36602	**800-826-3513**	251-243-9100
NYSE: ISH					
Matson Navigation Co					
555 12th St	Oakland	CA	94607	**800-462-8766***	510-628-4000
*Cust Svc					
Northland Services Inc					
6700 W Marginal Way SW	Seattle	WA	98106	**800-426-3113**	206-763-3000
Overseas Shipholding Group Inc					
666 Third Ave	New York	NY	10017	**800-851-9677**	212-953-4100
Sea Star Line LLC					
10550 Deerwood Pk Blvd Ste 509	Jacksonville	FL	32256	**877-775-7447**	904-855-1260
Seaboard Marine					
8001 NW 79th Ave	Miami	FL	33166	**866-676-8886**	305-863-4444
Totem Ocean Trailer Express Inc					
32001 32nd Ave S Ste 200	Federal Way	WA	98001	**800-426-0074**	253-449-8100
Trailer Bridge Inc					
10405 New Berlin Rd E	Jacksonville	FL	32226	**800-554-1589**	904-751-7100
OTC: TRBRQ					
US Shipping Corp					
399 Thornall St 8th Fl	Edison	NJ	08837	**866-942-6592**	732-635-1500
Western Pioneer Inc					
4601 Shilshole Ave NW	Seattle	WA	98107	**800-426-6783**	206-789-1930
Young Bros Ltd PO Box 3288	Honolulu	HI	96801	**800-572-2743**	808-543-9311

314   FREIGHT TRANSPORT - DEEP SEA (FOREIGN PORTS)

				Toll-Free	Phone
Atlantic Container Line (ACL)					
50 Cardinal Dr	Westfield	NJ	07090	**800-225-1235**	908-518-5300
Fednav Ltd					
1000 Rue de la GauchetiFre O					
Bureau 3500	Montreal	QC	H3B4W5	**800-678-4842***	514-878-6500
*General					
Hamburg Sud North America Inc					
465 S St	Morristown	NJ	07960	**888-228-8241**	973-775-5300
Hapag-Lloyd America Inc					
401 E Jackson St	Tampa	FL	33602	**800-282-8977**	813-276-4600
Interlog USA Inc					
2818A Anthony Ln S	Minneapolis	MN	55418	**800-603-6030**	612-789-3456
International Shipholding Corp					
11 N Water Ste 18290	Mobile	AL	36602	**800-826-3513**	251-243-9100
NYSE: ISH					
K Line America Inc					
8730 Stony Pt Pkwy Ste 400	Richmond	VA	23235	**800-609-3221**	804-560-3600
Northern Transportation Co Ltd					
42003 Mackenzie Hwy	Hay River	NT	X0E0R9	**866-935-6825**	867-587-2442

		Toll-Free	Phone
Overseas Shipholding Group Inc			
666 Third Ave .... New York NY 10017		800-851-9677	212-953-4100
Seaboard Marine			
8001 NW 79th Ave .... Miami FL 33166		866-676-8886	305-863-4444
Tidewater Inc			
601 Poydras St Ste 1900 .... New Orleans LA 70130		800-678-8433	504-568-1010
NYSE: TDW			
Tropical Shipping			
Five E 11th St .... Riviera Beach FL 33404		800-367-6200	561-881-3900

315 FREIGHT TRANSPORT - INLAND WATERWAYS

		Toll-Free	Phone
American Commercial Barge Lines Inc			
1701 E Market St .... Jeffersonville IN 47130		800-457-6377	812-288-0100
American Commercial Lines Inc			
1701 E Market St .... Jeffersonville IN 47130		800-899-7195	812-288-0100
Andrie Inc			
561 E Western Ave .... Muskegon MI 49442		800-722-2421	231-728-2226
Crowley Maritime Corp			
9487 Regency Square Blvd			
Ste 2130 .... Jacksonville FL 32225		800-276-9539	904-727-2200
Custom Global Logistics LLC			
317 W Lk St .... Northlake IL 60164		800-446-8336	
Fednav Ltd			
1000 Rue de la GauchetiFre O			
Bureau 3500 .... Montreal QC H3B4W5		800-678-4842*	514-878-6500
*General			
Hackbarth Delivery Service Inc			
3504 Brookdale Dr N .... Mobile AL 36618		800-277-3322	251-478-1401
J s Logistics			
4550 Gustine Ave .... Saint Louis MO 63116		800-814-2634	314-832-6008
LTI Trucking Services Inc			
411 N 10th St Ste 500 .... St. Louis MO 63101		800-642-7222	
Tidewater Barge Lines Inc			
6305 NW Old Lower River Rd .... Vancouver WA 98660		800-562-1607	360-693-1491
Tri-line Carriers L.p			
235185 Ryan Rd .... Rocky View AB T1X0K1		800-661-9191	

316 FRUIT GROWERS

SEE ALSO Crop Preparation Services ; Wines - Mfr

316-1 Berry Growers

		Toll-Free	Phone
Driscoll Strawberry Assoc Inc			
345 Westridge Dr .... Watsonville CA 95077		800-871-3333	
Jasper Wyman & Son			
PO Box 100 .... Milbridge ME 04658		800-341-1758*	
*Sales			

316-2 Citrus Growers

		Toll-Free	Phone
Egan Bernard & Co			
1900 Old Dixie Hwy .... Fort Pierce FL 34946		800-327-6676	
Limoneira Co			
1141 Cummings Rd .... Santa Paula CA 93060		866-321-8953	805-525-5541
NASDAQ: LMNR			
Silver Springs Citrus Inc			
25411 N Mare Ave .... Howey in the Hills FL 34737		800-940-2277	352-324-2101

316-3 Deciduous Tree Fruit Growers

		Toll-Free	Phone
Capital Agricultural Property Services Inc			
801 Warrenville Rd Ste 150 .... Lisle IL 60532		800-243-2060	630-434-9150
National Fruit Product Co Inc			
701 Fairmont Ave PO Box 2040 .... Winchester VA 22601		800-655-4022	540-723-9614
Oregon Cherry Growers Inc			
1520 Woodrow NE .... Salem OR 97301		800-367-2536	503-364-8421
Rice Fruit Co			
2760 Carlisle Rd PO Box 66 .... Gardners PA 17324		800-627-3359	717-677-8131

316-4 Fruit Growers (Misc)

		Toll-Free	Phone
Brooks Tropicals Inc			
18400 SW 256th St PO Box 900160 .... Homestead FL 33090		800-327-4833	305-247-3544
Calavo Growers Inc			
1141-A Cummings Rd .... Santa Paula CA 93060		800-654-8758	805-525-1245
NASDAQ: CVGW			
Del Monte Fresh Produce Co			
241 Sevilla Ave .... Coral Gables FL 33134		800-950-3683*	305-520-8400
*Cust Svc			
Dole Food Company Inc			
One Dole Dr .... Westlake Village CA 91362		800-232-8888	818-879-6600
NYSE: DOLE			
Mission Produce Inc			
2500 Vineyard Ave Ste 300 .... Oxnard CA 93036		800-549-3420	805-981-3650

316-5 Grape Vineyards

		Toll-Free	Phone
Spring Mountain Vineyards			
2805 Spring Mtn Rd .... Saint Helena CA 94574		877-769-4637	707-967-4188
Windsor Vineyards			
205 Concourse Blvd .... Santa Rosa CA 95403		800-289-9463	

317 FUEL DEALERS

		Toll-Free	Phone
AC & T Company Inc			
11535 Hopewell Rd .... Hagerstown MD 21740		800-458-3835	301-582-2700
Alvin Hollis & Co			
One Hollis St .... South Weymouth MA 02190		800-649-5090	781-335-2100
AmeriGas Partners LP			
460 N Gulph Rd .... King of Prussia PA 19406		800-427-4968	610-337-7000
NYSE: APU			
Apollo Oil LLC			
1175 Early Dr .... Winchester KY 40391		800-473-5823	859-744-5444
Automotive Service Inc			
910 Mtn Home Rd PO Box 2157 .... Sinking Spring PA 19608		800-383-3421	610-678-3421
Blossman Gas Inc			
809 Washington Ave .... Ocean Springs MS 39564		800-256-7762	888-256-7762
Bowden Oil Company Inc			
PO Box 145 .... Sylacauga AL 35150		800-280-0393	256-245-5611
Carroll Independent Fuel Co			
2700 Loch Raven Rd .... Baltimore MD 21218		800-834-8590	410-235-1070
Ed Staub & Sons Petroleum Inc			
1301 Esplanade Ave .... Klamath Falls OR 97601		800-435-3835	
FC Haab Company Inc			
2314 Market St .... Philadelphia PA 19103		800-486-5663	215-563-0800
Ferrellgas Partners LP			
1 Liberty Plaza .... Liberty MO 64068		888-337-7355	816-792-1600
NYSE: FGP			
First Corporate Sedans Inc			
60 E 42nd St Ste 2424 .... New York NY 10165		800-473-8876	212-972-2282
Fred M Schildwachter & Sons Inc			
1400 Ferris Pl .... Bronx NY 10461		800-642-3646	718-828-2500
Glassmere Fuel Service Inc			
1967 Saxonburg Blvd .... Tarentum PA 15084		800-235-9054	724-265-4646
Kingston Oil Supply Corp			
2926 Rt 32 N .... Saugerties NY 12477		800-755-6726	845-247-2200
Kolkhorst Petroleum Co			
1685 E Washington PO Box 410 .... Navasota TX 77868		800-548-6671	936-825-6868
Lincoln Land Oil Co			
PO Box 4307 .... Springfield IL 62708		800-238-4912	217-523-5050
Martin Resource Management Corp (MRMC)			
PO Box 191 .... Kilgore TX 75663		888-334-7473	903-983-6200
Metro Energy Group			
1011 Hudson Ave .... Ridgefield NJ 07657		800-951-2941	201-941-3470
Mirabito Fuel Group Inc			
49 Ct St PO Box 5306 .... Binghamton NY 13902		800-934-9480	607-352-2800
Mitchell Supreme Fuel Co			
532 Freeman St .... Orange NJ 07050		800-832-7090	973-678-1800
Mutual Liquid Gas & Equipment Co Inc			
17117 S Broadway St .... Gardena CA 90248		800-633-3574	323-321-3771
Polsinello Fuels Inc			
41 Riverside Ave .... Rensselaer NY 12144		800-334-5823	518-463-0084
Shipley Energy 415 Norway St .... York PA 17403		800-839-1849	717-848-4100
Star Gas Partners LP			
2187 Atlantic St .... Stamford CT 06902		877-237-3063	203-328-7310
NYSE: SGU			
Stripes Convenience Stores			
4525 Ayers St .... Corpus Christi TX 78415		800-569-3585	361-884-2464
NYSE: SUSS			
Suburban Propane LP			
One Suburban Plz 240 Rt 10 W			
PO Box 206 .... Whippany NJ 07981		800-776-7263	973-887-5300
Wilson of Wallingford Inc			
221 Rogers Ln PO Box 185 .... Wallingford PA 19086		888-607-2621	610-566-7600
Woodruff Energy			
73 Water St PO Box 777 .... Bridgeton NJ 08302		800-557-1121	856-455-1111
Worley & Obetz Inc			
85 White Oak Rd PO Box 429 .... Manheim PA 17545		800-697-6891	717-665-6891

318 FUND-RAISING SERVICES

		Toll-Free	Phone
APC Integrated Services Inc			
770 SPIRIT OF SAINT LOUIS Blvd ...... CHESTERFIELD MO 63005		888-294-7886	
Barnet Associates LLC			
Two Round Lk Rd .... Ridgefield CT 06877		888-827-7070	
Barton Cotton Inc			
3030 Waterview Ave .... Baltimore MD 21230		800-638-4652	800-348-1102
BeenVerified Inc			
307 Fifth Ave 16th Fl .... New York NY 10016		888-579-5910	
Bentz Whaley Flessner			
7251 Ohms Ln .... Minneapolis MN 55439		800-921-0111	952-921-0111
Brakeley Briscoe Inc			
322 W Bellevue Ave Ste 204 .... San Mateo CA 94402		800-416-3086	650-344-8883
Cargill Assoc Inc			
4701 Altamesa Blvd .... Fort Worth TX 76133		800-433-2233	817-292-9374
eLawMarketing			
25 Robert Pitt Dr Ste 209G .... Monsey NY 10952		866-833-6245	
Fam Funds			
384 N Grand St PO Box 310 .... Cobleskill NY 12043		800-721-5391	518-234-4393
Field Nation LLC			
310 Fourth Ave S Ste 8100 .... Minneapolis MN 55415		877-573-4353	
Gale Force Petroleum Inc			
Ste 5700 100 King St W .... Toronto ON M5X1C7		888-440-3411	
Gilligan & Ferneman LLC			
1754 Business Ctr Ln .... Kissimmee FL 34758		800-720-4152	
Global Pacific Financial Services Ltd			
10430 144 St .... Surrey BC V3T4V5		800-561-1177	
GroveWare Technologies Ltd			
Ste 411 90 Eglinton Ave E .... Toronto ON M4P2Y3		877-701-9378	
LW Robbins Assoc			
201 Summer St .... Holliston MA 01746		800-229-5972	
MyUSACorporation.com Inc			
One Radisson Plz Ste 800 .... New Rochelle NY 10801		877-330-2677	

			Toll-Free	Phone
NorAm Capital Holdings Inc				
15303 N Dallas Pkwy Ste 1030	Addison TX	75001	888-886-6726	
oberoSPM				
7560 Airport Rd Unit 12	Mississauga ON	L4T4H4	888-815-2996	
Payment Services Corp Inc				
360 Albert St Ste 1220	Ottawa ON	K1R7X7	866-972-0616	
Ruotolo Assoc Inc (RA)				
29 Broadway Ste 210	Cresskill NJ	07626	800-786-8656	201-568-3898
Skystone Ryan				
Skystone Partners LLC				
635 W Seventh St Ste 107	Cincinnati OH	45203	800-883-0801	513-241-6778

319 FURNACES & OVENS - INDUSTRIAL PROCESS

			Toll-Free	Phone
Ajax Tocco Magnethermic Corp				
1745 Overland Ave NE	Warren OH	44483	800-547-1527	330-372-8511
Alabama Specialty Products Inc				
152 Metal Samples Rd PO Box 8	Munford AL	36268	888-388-1006	256-358-5200
Alpha 1 Induction Service Ctr Inc				
1525 Old Alum Creek Dr	Columbus OH	43209	800-991-2599	614-253-8900
Armor Group Inc, The				
4600 N Mason-Montgomery Rd	Mason OH	45040	800-255-0393	
AVS Inc 60 Fitchburg Rd	Ayer MA	01432	800-772-0710	978-772-0710
Bloom Engineering Co Inc				
5460 Curry Rd	Pittsburgh PA	15236	800-451-5491	412-653-3500
BriskHeat Corp				
1055 Gibbard Ave	Columbus OH	43201	800-848-7673	614-294-3376
Cambridge Engineering Inc				
PO Box 1010	Chesterfield MO	63006	800-899-1989	636-532-2233
CCI Thermal Technologies Inc				
5918 Roper Rd	Edmonton AB	T6B3E1	800-661-8529*	780-466-3178
*Cust Svc				
CMI EFCO Inc 435 W Wilson St	Salem OH	44460	877-225-2674	330-332-4661
Despatch Industries Inc				
8860 207th St W	Lakeville MN	55044	800-726-0110	952-469-5424
Detroit Radiant Product Co				
21400 Hoover Rd	Warren MI	48089	800-222-1100	586-756-0950
Detroit Stoker Co				
1510 E First St	Monroe MI	48161	800-786-5374	734-241-9500
Eclipse Inc				
1665 Elmwood Rd	Rockford IL	61103	888-826-3473	815-877-3031
Fast Heat Inc				
776 Oaklawn Ave	Elmhurst IL	60126	877-747-8575	630-833-5400
Gas-Fired Products Inc				
305 Doggett St	Charlotte NC	28203	800-830-3983	704-372-3485
Glenro Inc 39 McBride Ave	Paterson NJ	07501	888-453-6761	973-279-5900
Glo-Quartz Electric Heater Company Inc				
7084 Maple St	Mentor OH	44060	800-321-3574*	440-255-9701
*Sales				
Heatrex Inc PO Box 515	Meadville PA	16335	800-394-6589	814-724-1800
Inductoheat Inc				
32251 N Avis Dr	Madison Heights MI	48071	800-624-6297	248-585-9393
Inductotherm Group				
10 Indel Ave PO Box 157	Rancocas NJ	08073	800-257-9527	609-267-9000
Industronics Service Co				
489 Sullivan Ave PO Box 649	South Windsor CT	06074	800-878-1551	860-289-1551
Ipsen Inc PO Box 6266	Rockford IL	61125	800-727-7625	815-332-4941
John Zink Company LLC				
11920 E Apache St	Tulsa OK	74116	800-421-9242	918-234-1800
Johnson Gas Appliance Co				
520 E Ave NW	Cedar Rapids IA	52405	800-553-5422	319-365-5267
Lanly Co, The				
26201 Tungsten Rd	Cleveland OH	44132	800-327-8064	216-731-1115
Novatec Inc				
222 Thomas Ave	Baltimore MD	21225	800-237-8379	410-789-4811
Paragon Industries Inc				
2011 S Town E Blvd	Mesquite TX	75149	800-876-4328	972-288-7557
Pillar Induction Co				
21905 Gateway Rd	Brookfield WI	53045	800-558-7733	262-317-5300
Radyne Corp				
211 W Boden St	Milwaukee WI	53207	800-236-8360	414-481-8360
Rapid Engineering Inc				
1100 7-Mile Rd NW	Comstock Park MI	49321	800-536-3461	616-784-0500
Red-Ray Mfg Co Inc				
10-22 County Line Rd	Branchburg NJ	08876	800-883-9218	908-722-0040
Selas Heat Technology Company LLC				
130 Keystone Dr	Montgomeryville PA	18936	800-523-6500	215-646-6600
ST Johnson Co				
925 Stanford Ave	Oakland CA	94608	800-225-1348	510-652-6000
Steelman Industries Inc				
2800 Hwy 135 N PO Box 1461	Kilgore TX	75662	800-287-6633	903-984-3061
StrikoDynarad				
501 E Roosevelt Ave	Zeeland MI	49464	855-787-4561	616-772-3705
Surface Combustion Inc				
1700 Indian Wood Cir	Maumee OH	43537	800-537-8980	419-891-7150
Tempco Electric Heater Corp				
607 N Central Ave	Wood Dale IL	60191	888-268-6396	630-350-2252
Thermal Circuits Inc				
One Technology Way	Salem MA	01970	800-808-4328	978-745-1162
Thermal Engineering Corp				
2741 The Blvd	Columbia SC	29209	800-331-0097	803-783-0750
Thermal Product Solutions				
3827 Riverside Rd	Riverside MI	49084	800-873-4468	269-849-2700
Trent Inc				
201 Leverington Ave	Philadelphia PA	19127	800-544-8736	215-482-5000
Truheat Inc 700 Grand St	Allegan MI	49010	800-879-6199	269-673-2145

320 FURNITURE - MFR

SEE ALSO Recycled Plastics Products ; Mattresses & Adjustable Beds ; Baby Products ; Cabinets - Wood ; Fixtures - Office & Store

			Toll-Free	Phone

320-1 Commercial & Industrial Furniture

			Toll-Free	Phone
Abco Office Furniture				
4121 Rushton St	Florence AL	35630	800-336-0070	256-767-4100
Adelphia Steel Equipment Co				
7372 State Rd	Philadelphia PA	19136	800-865-8211	215-333-6300
Allied Plastics Company Inc				
2001 Walnut St	Jacksonville FL	32206	800-999-0386*	904-359-0386
*Cust Svc				
Allsteel Inc				
2210 Second Ave	Muscatine IA	52761	888-255-7833*	563-272-4800
*Cust Svc				
Anthro Corp				
10450 SW Manhasset Dr	Tualatin OR	97062	800-325-3841	503-691-2556
Bestar Inc				
4220 Villeneuve St	Lac-Megantic QC	G6B2C3	888-823-7827	819-583-1017
Bevco Precision Manufacturing Co				
21320 Doral Rd	Waukesha WI	53186	800-864-2991	262-798-9200
BGD Cos Inc				
5323 Lakeland Ave N	Minneapolis MN	55429	800-699-3537	612-338-6804
Biofit Engineered Products				
15500 Biofit Way	Bowling Green OH	43402	800-597-0246	419-823-1089
Borroughs Corp				
3002 N Burdick St	Kalamazoo MI	49004	800-748-0227	269-342-0161
Bright Chair Co				
51 Railroad Ave PO Box 269	Middletown NY	10940	888-524-5997	845-343-2196
Carolina Business Furniture LLC				
535 Archdale Blvd	Archdale NC	27263	800-763-0212	336-431-9400
Cramer Inc				
1222 Quebec St	North Kansas City MO	64116	800-366-6700	
Danver One Grand St	Wallingford CT	06492	888-441-0537	203-269-2300
Dar-Ran Furniture Industries				
2402 Shore St	High Point NC	27263	800-334-7891	336-861-2400
Dauphin North America				
300 Myrtle Ave	Boonton NJ	07005	800-631-1186*	973-263-1100
*Cust Svc				
Emeco				
805 W Elm Ave PO Box 179	Hanover PA	17331	800-366-5951	717-637-5951
Ergotron Inc				
1181 Trapp Rd	Saint Paul MN	55121	800-888-8458*	651-681-7600
*Sales				
Executive Office Concepts Inc				
1705 S Anderson Ave	Compton CA	90220	800-421-5927	310-537-1657
Fillip Metal Cabinet Co				
4500 W 47th St	Chicago IL	60632	800-535-0733	773-733-7527
First Office				
1204 E Sixth St	Huntingburg IN	47542	800-983-4415	
Flex-Y-Plan Industries Inc				
6960 W Ridge Rd	Fairview PA	16415	800-458-0552*	814-474-1565
*Cust Svc				
Flexible-Montisa				
323 Acorn St	Plainwell MI	49080	800-875-6836*	269-924-0730
*Cust Svc				
Foldcraft Co				
615 Centennial Dr	Kenyon MN	55946	800-759-6653	507-789-5111
Geiger International Inc				
6095 Fulton Industrial Blvd SW	Atlanta GA	30336	800-456-6452	404-344-1100
Global Industries Inc				
17 W Stow Rd	Marlton NJ	08053	800-220-1900	856-596-3390
Groupe Lacasse LLC				
99 St-Pierre St	Sainte-Pie QC	J0H1W0	888-522-2773	450-772-2495
Gunlocke Company LLC				
One Gunlocke Dr	Wayland NY	14572	800-828-6300*	585-728-5111
*Cust Svc				
H Wilson Co 2245 Delany Rd	Waukegan IL	60087	800-245-7224	
Hausmann Industries Inc				
130 Union St	Northvale NJ	07647	888-428-7626	201-767-0255
Haworth Inc One Haworth Ctr	Holland MI	49423	800-344-2600	616-393-3000
Herman Miller Inc				
855 E Main Ave	Zeeland MI	49464	888-443-4357	616-654-3000
NASDAQ: MLHR				
High Point Furniture Industries Inc				
1104 Bedford St PO Box 2063	High Point NC	27261	800-447-3462	336-431-7101
Hirsh Industries Inc				
3636 Westown Pkwy Ste 100	West Des Moines IA	50266	800-383-7414	515-299-3200
HON Co 200 Oak St	Muscatine IA	52761	800-553-8230	563-272-7100
Huot Manufacturing Co				
550 Wheeler St N	Saint Paul MN	55104	800-832-3838	651-646-1869
IAC Industries 895 Beacon St	Brea CA	92821	800-989-1422	714-990-8997
Indiana Furniture				
1224 Mill St	Jasper IN	47546	800-422-5727	812-482-5727
Invincible Office Furniture Co				
842 S 26th St PO Box 1117	Manitowoc WI	54220	877-682-4601	920-682-4601
Jasper Desk Co				
415 E Sixth St	Jasper IN	47546	800-365-7994*	812-482-4132
*Cust Svc				
Jasper Seating Company Inc				
Jasper Group 225 Clay St	Jasper IN	47546	800-622-5661	812-482-3204
JOFCO PO Box 71	Jasper IN	47547	800-235-6326	812-482-5154
Khoury Inc				
1129 Webster Ave PO Box 1746	Waco TX	76703	800-725-6765	254-754-5481
KI 1330 Bellevue St	Green Bay WI	54302	800-424-2432	920-468-8100
Kimball Hospitality				
1180 E 16th St	Jasper IN	47549	800-634-9510	276-666-8933
Kimball Office Furniture Co				
1600 Royal St	Jasper IN	47549	800-482-1818	
Knoll Inc				
1235 Water St	East Greenville PA	18041	800-343-5665*	215-679-7991
*NYSE: KNL ■ *Cust Svc*				
Lakeside Manufacturing Inc				
4900 W Electric Ave	West Milwaukee WI	53219	800-558-8565	414-902-6400
LB Furniture Industries LLC				
99 S Third St	Hudson NY	12534	800-221-8752	518-828-1501
Luxor Div EBSCO Industries Inc				
2245 Delany Rd	Waukegan IL	60087	800-323-4656	847-244-1800

			Toll-Free	Phone
Magna Design Inc				
26246 Twelve Trees Ln NW	Poulsbo WA	98370	**800-426-1202**	360-394-1300
Martin Furniture				
2345 Britannia Blvd	San Diego CA	92154	**800-268-5669***	
*Cust Svc				
Marvel Group Inc				
3843 W 43rd St	Chicago IL	60632	**800-621-8846***	
*Cust Svc				
Maxon Furniture Inc				
660 SW 39th St Ste 150	Renton WA	98057	**800-876-4274***	
*Cust Svc				
Mayline Group				
619 N Commerce St PO Box 728	Sheboygan WI	53082	**800-822-8037**	920-457-5537
McDowell-Craig Office Furniture				
13146 Firestone Blvd	Norwalk CA	90650	**877-921-2100**	562-921-4441
MLP Seating Corp				
2125 Lively Blvd	Elk Grove Village IL	60007	**800-723-3030**	847-956-1700
National Business Services				
1601 Magoffin Ave	El Paso TX	79901	**800-777-7807***	915-544-1271
*Sales				
National Office Furniture				
1205 Kimball Blvd	Jasper IN	47549	**800-482-1717**	
NER Data Products Inc				
307 S Delsea Dr	Glassboro NJ	08028	**888-637-3282**	
Neutral Posture Inc				
3904 N Texas Ave	Bryan TX	77803	**800-446-3746**	979-778-0502
Nomanco Inc 501 Nmc Dr	Zebulon NC	27597	**800-345-7279**	919-269-6500
Nova Solutions Inc				
421 Industrial Ave	Effingham IL	62401	**800-730-6682**	217-342-7070
Office Chairs Inc				
14815 Radburn Ave	Santa Fe Springs CA	90670	**866-624-4968**	562-802-0464
Omni International Inc				
435 12th St SW PO Box 1409.	Vernon AL	35592	**800-844-6664**	205-695-9173
Open Plan Systems Inc				
4700 Deepwater Terminal Rd	Richmond VA	23234	**888-869-4681**	804-275-2468
Paoli Inc 201 E Martin St	Orleans IN	47452	**800-472-8669**	
Penco Products Inc				
99 Brower Ave	Oaks PA	19456	**800-562-1000**	610-666-0500
Reconditioned Systems Inc (RSI)				
2636 S Wilson St Ste 105.	Tempe AZ	85282	**800-280-5000**	480-968-1772
Robertson Furniture Company Inc				
890 Elberton St	Toccoa GA	30577	**800-241-0713**	706-886-1494
Rush Industries Inc				
118 N Wrenn St	High Point NC	27260	**800-524-0258**	336-886-7700
Safco Products Co				
9300 W Research Ctr Rd	New Hope MN	55428	**800-328-3020***	763-536-6700
*Cust Svc				
Shure Manufacturing Corp				
1901 W Main St	Washington MO	63090	**800-227-4873**	636-390-7100
Spectrum Industries Inc				
925 First Ave	Chippewa Falls WI	54729	**800-235-1262**	715-723-6750
Steelcase Inc				
801 44th St SE PO Box 1967	Grand Rapids MI	49501	**888-783-3522**	616-247-2710
NYSE: SCS				
Stylex PO Box 5038	Delanco NJ	08075	**800-257-5742**	
TAB Products Co				
605 Fourth St	Mayville WI	53050	**888-466-8228**	
Techline USA LLC				
500 S Div St	Waunakee WI	53597	**800-356-8400**	
Tennsco Corp				
201 Tennsco Dr PO Box 1888.	Dickson TN	37056	**866-446-8686***	615-446-8000
*Cust Svc				
Trendway Corp				
13467 Quincy St PO Box 9016.	Holland MI	49422	**800-968-5344**	616-399-3900
Tuohy Furniture Corp				
42 St Albans Pl	Chatfield MN	55923	**800-533-1696***	507-867-4280
*Cust Svc				
Viking Acoustical Corp				
21480 Heath Ave	Lakeville MN	55044	**800-328-8385**	952-469-3405
Vitro Seating Products Inc				
201 Madison St	Saint Louis MO	63102	**800-325-7093***	314-241-2265
*Cust Svc				
Watson Furniture Group Inc				
26246 Twelve Trees Ln NW	Poulsbo WA	98370	**800-426-1202**	360-394-1300
West Coast Industries Inc				
10 Jackson St	San Francisco CA	94111	**800-243-3150**	415-621-6656
Workplace Systems Inc				
562 Mammoth Rd	Londonderry NH	03053	**800-258-9700**	603-622-3727
Wright Line LLC				
160 Gold Star Blvd	Worcester MA	01606	**800-225-7348**	508-852-4300

320-2 Household Furniture

			Toll-Free	Phone
Albany Industries Inc				
504 N Glenfield Rd	New Albany MS	38652	**877-534-9804**	662-534-9800
Ameriwood Industries Inc				
410 E S First St	Wright City MO	63390	**800-489-3351***	636-745-3351
*General				
Ashley Furniture Industries Inc				
One Ashley Way	Arcadia WI	54612	**800-477-2222**	608-323-6225
Baby's Dream Furniture Inc				
411 Industrial Blvd PO Box 579	Buena Vista GA	31803	**800-835-2742**	229-649-4404
Bassett Furniture Industries Inc				
3525 Fairystone Pk Hwy PO Box 626	Bassett VA	24055	**877-525-7070**	714-222-1010
NASDAQ: BSET				
Broyhill Furniture Industries Inc				
3483 Hickory Blvd	Hudson NC	28638	**800-327-6944***	828-396-2361
*Cust Svc				
Brueton Industries Inc				
146 Hanse Ave	Freeport NY	11520	**800-221-6783***	516-379-3400
*Cust Svc				
Bush Industries Inc				
1 Mason Dr	Jamestown NY	14701	**800-950-4782**	716-665-2000
Carrom 218 E Dowland St	Ludington MI	49431	**800-223-6047**	231-845-1263
Century Furniture LLC				
401 11th St NW	Hickory NC	28601	**800-852-5552**	828-328-1851

			Toll-Free	Phone
DeFehr Furniture Ltd				
125 Furniture Pk	Winnipeg MB	R2G1B9	**877-333-3471**	204-988-5630
DMI Furniture Inc				
9780 Ormsby Stn Rd Ste 2000	Louisville KY	40223	**888-750-5834**	502-426-4351
Dutailier Group Inc				
299 Rue Chaput	Sainte-Pie QC	J0H1W0	**800-363-9817**	450-772-2403
El Ran Furniture Ltd				
2751 Transcanada Hwy	Pointe-Claire QC	H9R1B4	**800-361-6546**	514-630-5656
Evenflo Company Inc				
1801 Commerce Dr	Piqua OH	45356	**800-233-5921**	
Finnleo Sauna				
575 Cokato St E	Cokato MN	55321	**800-346-6536**	
Hooker Furniture Corp				
440 E Commonwealth Blvd	Martinsville VA	24112	**800-422-1511***	276-632-0459
NASDAQ: HOFT ▦ *Cust Svc				
Human Touch				
3030 Walnut Ave	Long Beach CA	90807	**800-742-5493**	562-426-8700
Klaussner Home Furnishings				
405 Lewallen Rd	Asheboro NC	27205	**888-732-5948**	336-625-6174
La-Z-Boy Inc				
1284 N Telegraph Rd	Monroe MI	48162	**800-375-6890**	734-242-1444
NYSE: LZB				
Lamont Ltd 1530 Bluff Rd	Burlington IA	52601	**800-553-5621**	319-753-5131
Leathercraft				
102 Section House Rd	Hickory NC	28601	**800-627-1561**	
Lexington Home Brands				
1300 National Hwy	Thomasville NC	27360	**800-952-5210**	336-474-5300
Little Tikes Co, The				
2180 Barlow Rd	Hudson OH	44236	**800-321-0183***	
*Cust Svc				
Mantua Mfg Co				
7900 Northfield Rd	Walton Hills OH	44146	**800-333-8333***	
*Orders				
McGuire Furniture Co				
1201 Bryant St	San Francisco CA	94103	**800-662-4847**	415-626-1414
Mitchell Gold & Bob Williams Co (MGBW)				
135 One Comfortable Pl	Taylorsville NC	28681	**800-789-5401**	828-632-9200
Norwalk Furniture Corp				
100 Furniture Pkwy	Norwalk OH	44857	**800-837-2565***	419-744-3200
*Orders				
Pearson Co				
1420 Progress Ave	High Point NC	27260	**800-225-0265**	336-882-8135
Robern Inc 701 N Wilson Ave	Bristol PA	19007	**800-877-2376**	215-826-9800
Room & Board Inc				
4600 Olson Memorial Hwy	Golden Valley MN	55422	**800-301-9720**	763-521-4411
Rumble Tuff Inc				
865 North 1430 West	Orem UT	84057	**855-228-8388**	801-609-8168
Rush Industries Inc				
118 N Wrenn St	High Point NC	27260	**800-524-0258**	336-886-7700
Sauder Woodworking Co				
502 Middle St PO Box 156	Archbold OH	43502	**800-523-3987***	419-446-2711
*Cust Svc				
Schnadig International Corp				
4200 Tudor Ln	Greensboro NC	27410	**800-468-8730**	
Sico North America Inc				
7525 Cahill Rd	Minneapolis MN	55439	**800-328-6138**	952-941-1700
Standard Furniture Mfg Company Inc				
801 Hwy 31 S	Bay Minette AL	36507	**877-788-1899***	251-937-6741
*General				
Storkcraft Baby				
7433 Nelson Rd	Richmond BC	V6W1G3	**877-274-0277**	604-274-5121
Suncast Corp 701 N Kirk Rd	Batavia IL	60510	**800-444-3310**	630-879-2050
Techline USA LLC				
500 S Div St	Waunakee WI	53597	**800-356-8400**	
Walter E Smithe Furniture Inc				
1251 W Thorndale Ave	Itasca IL	60143	**800-948-4263**	630-285-8000
Whittier Wood Products				
3787 W First Ave PO Box 2827	Eugene OR	97402	**800-653-3336**	541-687-0213
Zenith Products Corp				
400 Lukens Dr	New Castle DE	19720	**800-892-3986**	

320-3 Institutional & Other Public Buildings Furniture

			Toll-Free	Phone
Achieva Inc				
197 Funder Dr PO Box 729.	Mocksville NC	27028	**800-788-7213**	336-751-7104
Adden Furniture Inc				
710 Chelmsford St	Lowell MA	01851	**800-625-3876**	978-454-7848
American Desk				
1302 Industrial Blvd	Temple TX	76504	**800-433-3142**	
American Seating Co				
401 American Seating Ctr NW	Grand Rapids MI	49504	**800-748-0268***	616-732-6600
*Cust Svc				
Artco-Bell Corp				
1302 Industrial Blvd	Temple TX	76504	**877-778-1811**	254-778-1811
Bretford Manufacturing Inc				
11000 Seymour Ave	Franklin Park IL	60131	**800-521-9614**	847-678-2545
Brodart Co 500 Arch St	Williamsport PA	17701	**800-233-8467**	570-326-2461
ENOCHS Examining Room Furniture				
PO Box 50559	Indianapolis IN	46250	**800-428-2305***	
*Cust Svc				
ErgoGenesis LLC				
One BodyBilt Pl	Navasota TX	77868	**800-364-5299**	936-825-1700
Fleetwood Group Inc				
11832 James St	Holland MI	49424	**800-257-6390**	616-396-1142
Fordham Equipment Co				
1204 Village Market Place				
Suite 262	Morrisville NC	27560	**866-467-0708**	919-467-0708
Gaylord Bros				
7282 William Barry Blvd	Syracuse NY	13212	**800-345-5330**	315-457-5070
Gunlocke Company LLC				
One Gunlocke Dr	Wayland NY	14572	**800-828-6300***	585-728-5111
*Cust Svc				
Hard Mfg Company Inc				
230 Grider St	Buffalo NY	14215	**800-873-4273**	
Herman Miller for Health Care				
855 E Main Ave PO Box 302.	Zeeland MI	49464	**888-443-4357**	616-654-3000

Company / Address	City	State	ZIP	Toll-Free	Phone
Hill-Rom Services Inc 1069 SR 46 E	Batesville	IN	47006	800-267-2337	812-934-7777
Hussey Seating Co 38 Dyer St Ext	North Berwick	ME	03906	800-341-0401	207-676-2271
Imperial Woodworks Inc 7201 Mars Dr PO Box 7835	Waco	TX	76714	800-234-6624	
Irwin Seating Company Inc 3251 Fruit Ridge NW	Grand Rapids	MI	49544	866-464-7946	616-574-7400
Joerns Healthcare 5001 Joerns Dr	Stevens Point	WI	54481	800-826-0270	715-341-3600
Kimball Hospitality 1180 E 16th St	Jasper	IN	47549	800-634-9510	276-666-8933
KLN Steel Products Co Two Winnco Dr	San Antonio	TX	78218	800-624-9101	210-227-4747
LB Furniture Industries LLC 99 S Third St	Hudson	NY	12534	800-221-8752	518-828-1501
List Industries Inc 401 Jim Moran Blvd	Deerfield Beach	FL	33442	800-776-1342	954-429-9155
Luxor Div EBSCO Industries Inc 2245 Delany Rd	Waukegan	IL	60087	800-323-4656	847-244-1800
Meco Corp 1500 Industrial Rd	Greeneville	TN	37745	800-251-7558	
Midwest Folding Products Inc 1414 S Western Ave	Chicago	IL	60608	800-621-4716	312-666-3366
Mitchell Furniture Systems Inc 1700 W St Paul Ave	Milwaukee	WI	53201	800-290-5960	414-342-3111
Mity-Lite Inc 1301 West 400 North	Orem	UT	84057	800-909-8034	801-224-0589
MLP Seating Corp 2125 Lively Blvd	Elk Grove Village	IL	60007	800-723-3030	847-956-1700
Nemschoff Healthcare Furniture and Clinic Furniture 909 N Eigth St *Cust Svc	Sheboygan	WI	53081	800-203-8916*	
New Holland Church Furniture 313 Prospect St PO Box 217	New Holland	PA	17557	800-648-9663	
Omni International Inc 435 12th St SW PO Box 1409	Vernon	AL	35592	800-844-6664	205-695-9173
Royal Seating Ltd 1110 Industrial Blvd *Cust Svc	Cameron	TX	76520	888-388-3224*	254-605-5500
Shelby Williams Industries Inc 810 W Hwy 25/70 *General	Newport	TN	37821	800-873-3252*	423-623-0031
Sico North America Inc 7525 Cahill Rd	Minneapolis	MN	55439	800-328-6138	952-941-1700
Spectrum Industries Inc 925 First Ave	Chippewa Falls	WI	54729	800-235-1262	715-723-6750
Sturdisteel Co PO Box 2655	Waco	TX	76702	800-433-3116	
Tesco Industries LP 1035 E Hacienda	Bellville	TX	77418	800-699-5824	
TMI Systems Design Corp 50 S Third Ave W	Dickinson	ND	58601	800-456-6716	701-456-6716
UMF Medical 1316 Eisenhower Blvd	Johnstown	PA	15904	800-638-5322	814-266-8726
Valley City Mfg Co Ltd, The 64 Hatt St	Dundas	ON	L9H2G3	800-306-3319	905-628-2253
Virco Manufacturing Corp 2027 Harpers Way NASDAQ: VIRC ■ *Cust Svc	Torrance	CA	90501	800-448-4726*	310-533-0474
Wieland 13737 Main St PO Box 1000	Grabill	IN	46741	888-943-5263	260-627-3686
Winco Inc 5516 SW First Ln	Ocala	FL	34474	800-237-3377	352-854-2929
Worden Company Inc 199 E 17th St	Holland	MI	49423	800-748-0561	616-392-1848

320-4 Outdoor Furniture

Company / Address	City	State	ZIP	Toll-Free	Phone
A Homecrest Outdoor Living LLC 1250 Homecrest Ave	Wadena	MN	56482	888-346-4852	218-631-1000
Belson Outdoors Inc 111 N River Rd	North Aurora	IL	60542	800-323-5664	630-897-8489
Bemis Manufacturing Co 300 Mill St	Sheboygan Falls	WI	53085	800-558-7651	920-467-4621
Brown Jordan Co 9860 Gidley St	El Monte	CA	91731	800-743-4252	
Cox Industries Inc 860 Cannon Bridge Rd PO Box 1124	Orangeburg	SC	29116	800-476-4401	803-534-7467
DuMor Inc PO Box 142	Mifflintown	PA	17059	800-598-4018	717-436-2106
Gardenside Ltd 808 Anthony St Ste 140	Berkeley	CA	94710	888-999-8325	415-455-4500
Hatteras Hammocks Inc 305 Industrial Blvd	Greenville	NC	27834	800-643-3522	252-758-0641
J Robert Scott Inc 500 N Oak St	Inglewood	CA	90302	877-207-5130	310-680-4300
Kay Park Recreation Corp 1301 Pine St *Cust Svc	Janesville	IA	50647	800-553-2476*	
Mallin Casual Furniture One Minson Way	Montebello	CA	90640	800-251-6537	
Minson Corp 1 Minson Way	Montebello	CA	90640	800-251-6537	323-513-1041
OW Lee Company Inc 1822 E Francis St	Ontario	CA	91761	800-776-9533	909-947-3771
Tropitone Furniture Co Inc 5 Marconi *All	Irvine	CA	92618	800-654-7000*	949-951-2010
Twin Oaks Hammocks 138 Twin Oaks Rd	Louisa	VA	23093	800-688-8946	540-894-5125
Wabash Valley Manufacturing Inc 505 E Main St	Silver Lake	IN	46982	800-253-8619	260-352-2102
Walpole Woodworkers Inc 767 E St Rt 7 *Cust Svc	Walpole	MA	02081	800-343-6948*	508-668-2800

321   FURNITURE - WHOL

Company / Address	City	State	ZIP	Toll-Free	Phone
Adirondack Direct 3040 48th Ave	Long Island City	NY	11101	800-221-2444	718-204-4500
ATD-American Co 135 Greenwood Ave	Wyncote	PA	19095	866-283-9327	215-576-1380
Brown & Saenger 711 W Russell St PO Box 84040	Sioux Falls	SD	57118	800-952-3509	605-336-1960
Business Furniture Corp 6102 Victory Way	Indianapolis	IN	46278	800-774-5544	317-216-1600
California Office Furniture 1724 Tenth St	Sacramento	CA	95811	877-442-6959	916-442-6959
Carithers Wallace Courtenay Co 4343 NE Expy	Atlanta	GA	30340	800-292-8220	770-493-8200
Carroll Seating Company Inc 10 Lincoln St	Kansas City	KS	66103	800-972-3779	816-471-2929
Champion Industries Inc PO Box 2968 PO Box 2968 OTC: CHMP	Huntington	WV	25728	800-624-3431	304-528-2791
COECO Office Systems Co 2521 N Church St PO Box 2088	Rocky Mount	NC	27804	800-682-6844	252-977-1121
Dancker Sellew & Douglas 291 Evans Way	Somerville	NJ	08876	800-326-2537	908-231-1600
Empire Office Inc 105 Madison Ave Ste 15	New York	NY	10016	877-533-6747	212-607-5500
Evergreen Enterprises Inc 5915 Midlothian Trnpk	Richmond	VA	23225	877-558-1511	804-231-1800
Glover Sales Group LLC 221 Cockeysville Rd	Cockeysville	MD	21030	800-966-9016	410-771-8000
Haldeman-Homme Inc 430 Industrial Blvd NE	Minneapolis	MN	55413	800-795-0696	612-331-4880
Hudson Seating & Mobility 151 Rockwell Rd	Newington	CT	06111	800-321-4442	860-666-7500
J L Business Interiors Inc 515 Schoenhaar Dr PO Box 303	West Bend	WI	53090	866-338-5524	262-338-2221
Kentwood Office Furniture Inc 3063 Breton Rd SE	Grand Rapids	MI	49512	877-698-6250	616-957-2320
Najarian Furniture Company Inc 17560 Rowland St	City of Industry	CA	91748	888-781-3088	626-839-8700
National Business Furniture Inc 735 N Water St Ste 440 *Sales	Milwaukee	WI	53202	800-558-1010*	414-276-8511
North Country Business Products Inc 1112 S Railroad St SE	Bemidji	MN	56619	800-937-4140	218-751-4140
Office Environments Inc 11407 Granite St	Charlotte	NC	28273	888-861-2525	704-714-7200
Office Star Products 1901 S Archibald PO Box 3520	Ontario	CA	91761	800-950-7262	909-930-2000
Ohio Desk Co 1122 Prospect Ave E	Cleveland	OH	44115	800-334-4922	216-623-0600
R & M Office Furniture 9615 Oates Dr	Sacramento	CA	95827	800-660-1756	916-362-1756
Red Thread 300 E River Dr	East Hartford	CT	06108	800-334-4922	860-528-9981
Superior Medical Supply Inc 11005 Dover St Unit 1100	Broomfield	CO	80021	877-460-1411	
Trade Products Corp 12124 Popes Head Rd	Fairfax	VA	22030	888-352-3580	703-502-9000
Trinity Hardwood Distributors Inc 110 East Oregon	Dallas	TX	75203	800-492-9856	214-948-3001
Wasserstrom Co 477 S Front St	Columbus	OH	43215	866-634-8927	614-228-6525

322   FURNITURE STORES

SEE ALSO Department Stores

Company / Address	City	State	ZIP	Toll-Free	Phone
Activeforevercom 10799 N 90th St	Scottsdale	AZ	85260	800-377-8033	480-459-3202
Afinety Inc 1956 Cotner Ave	Los Angeles	CA	90025	877-423-4638	310-996-2700
All Makes Office Equipment Co 2558 Farnam St	Omaha	NE	68131	800-341-2413	402-341-2413
American Furniture Warehouse Co 8501 Grant St	Thornton	CO	80229	888-615-9415	303-289-3300
American Home Furnishings 3535 Menaul Blvd NE	Albuquerque	NM	87107	800-854-6755	505-883-2211
Arizona Leather Company Inc 4235 Schaefer Ave	Chino	CA	91710	888-669-5328	909-993-5101
Bar Productscom Inc 1990 Lake Ave SE	Largo	FL	33771	800-256-6396	727-584-2093
Barn Furniture Mart Inc 6206 N Sepulveda Blvd	Van Nuys	CA	91411	888-302-2276	818-780-4070
Beaufurn LLC 5269 US Hwy 158	Advance	NC	27006	888-766-7706	
Best Material Handling Inc 4754 N Chestnut St	Colorado Springs	CO	80907	800-933-5270	719-599-9191
Boss Chair Inc 5353 Jillson St	Commerce	CA	90040	800-593-1888	323-262-1919
City Furniture Inc 6701 N Hiatus Rd	Tamarac	FL	33321	866-930-4233	954-597-2200
Darvin Furniture 15400 S La Grange Rd	Orland Park	IL	60462	800-232-7846	708-460-4100
El Dorado Furniture Corp 4200 NW 167th St	Miami	FL	33054	888-451-7800	305-624-2400
Fastfurnishings.com 340 S Lemon Ave Ste 6043	Walnut	CA	91789	877-404-6072	443-371-3278
Gardner Mattress Corp 254 Canal St	Salem	MA	01970	800-564-2736	978-744-1810
Great American Home Store 5295 Pepper Chase Dr	Southaven	MS	38671	877-303-1964	662-996-1000

				Toll-Free	Phone
Haverty Furniture Cos Inc					
780 Johnson Ferry Rd NE Ste 800	Atlanta	GA	30342	**888-428-3789**	404-443-2900
NYSE: HVT					
IKEA 420 Alan Wood Rd	Conshohocken	PA	19428	**800-434-4532**	610-834-0180
Interior Design Services Inc					
209 Powell Pl	Brentwood	TN	37027	**800-433-7446**	615-376-1200
International Contract Furnishings Inc (ICF)					
19 Ohio Ave	Norwich	CT	06360	**800-237-1625**	860-886-1700
Inviting Home.com					
4700 SW 51st St Unit 219	Davie	FL	33314	**866-751-6606**	781-444-8001
Jerome's Furniture Warehouse					
16960 Mesamint St	San Diego	CA	92127	**866-633-4094**	
Lack's Valley Stores Ltd					
1300 San Patricia St	Pharr	TX	78577	**800-870-6999**	956-702-3361
Living Spaces Furniture LLC					
14501 Artesia Blvd	La Mirada	CA	90638	**877-266-7300**	
MacKenzie-Childs LLC					
3260 SR- 90	Aurora	NY	13152	**888-665-1999**	315-364-7123
Mathis Bros Furniture Inc					
6611 S 101 St E Ave	Tulsa	OK	74133	**800-329-3434***	918-461-7785
*Cust Svc					
Moser Corp 601 N 13th St	Rogers	AR	72756	**800-632-4564**	479-636-3481
N Tepperman Ltd					
2595 Ouellette Ave	Windsor	ON	N8X4V8	**800-265-5062**	519-969-9700
Nashville Office Interiors					
1621 Church St	Nashville	TN	37203	**877-342-0294**	615-329-1811
Nebraska Furniture Mart Inc					
700 S 72nd St	Omaha	NE	68114	**800-336-9136**	402-397-6100
Nucraft Furniture Co					
5151 W River Dr	Comstock Park	MI	49321	**877-682-7238**	616-784-6016
Olum's of Binghamton Inc					
3701 Vestal Pkwy E	Vestal	NY	13850	**855-264-8674***	607-729-5775
*Cust Svc					
Otterbine Barebo Inc					
3840 Main Rd E	Emmaus	PA	18049	**800-237-8837**	610-965-6018
Parker Furniture					
10375 SW Beaverton-Hillsdale Hwy	Beaverton	OR	97005	**866-515-9673**	503-644-0155
Patioshoppers Inc					
41188 Sandalwood Cir	Murrieta	CA	92562	**800-940-6123**	951-696-1700
Pier 1 Kids					
100 Pier 1 Pl	Fort Worth	TX	76102	**800-433-4035**	817-252-8000
Porters of Racine					
301 Sixth St	Racine	WI	53403	**800-558-3245**	262-633-6363
Rotmans Furniture & Carpet					
725 Southbridge St	Worcester	MA	01610	**800-768-6267**	508-755-5276
Sam Clar Office Furniture Inc					
1221 Diamond Way	Concord	CA	94520	**800-726-2527**	925-602-3900
Schmidt-Goodman Office Products					
1920 N Broadway	Rochester	MN	55906	**800-247-0663**	507-282-3870
Sedlak Interiors Inc					
34300 Solon Rd	Solon	OH	44139	**800-260-2949**	440-248-2424
Selden's Home Furnishings					
1802 62nd Ave E	Tacoma	WA	98424	**800-870-7880**	253-922-5700
Shops at Carolina Furniture of Williamsburg					
5425 Richmond Rd	Williamsburg	VA	23188	**800-582-8916**	757-565-3000
Smart Furniture Inc					
430 Market St	Chattanooga	TN	37402	**888-467-6278**	423-267-7007
Smulekoff's Fine Home Furnishings					
PO Box 74090	Cedar Rapids	IA	52407	**888-384-6995**	319-362-2181
Star Furniture Company Inc					
16666 Barker Springs Rd	Houston	TX	77084	**800-364-6661**	281-492-6661
Steinhafels					
W 231 N 1013 County Hwy F	Waukesha	WI	53186	**866-351-4600***	262-436-4600
*Cust Svc					
USA Baby 793 Springer Dr	Lombard	IL	60148	**800-767-9464**	630-652-0600
Value City Furniture					
4300 E Fifth Ave	Columbus	OH	43219	**888-751-8552**	888-672-2411
Walker's Furniture Inc					
2611 N Woodruff Rd	Spokane	WA	99206	**866-667-6655**	509-535-1995
Warehouse Home Furnishings Distributors Inc					
1851 Telfair St PO Box 1140	Dublin	GA	31021	**800-456-0424**	
Wayside Furniture Inc					
1367 Canton Rd	Akron	OH	44312	**877-499-3968**	330-733-6221
WG&R Furniture Co					
900 Challenger Dr	Green Bay	WI	54311	**888-947-7782**	920-469-4880
Wieser & Cawley Furniture					
1301 Colegate Dr	Marietta	OH	45750	**800-339-0094**	740-373-1676
Workplace Resource LLC					
4400 NE Loop 410 Ste 130	San Antonio	TX	78218	**800-580-3000**	512-472-7300
WS Badcock Corp (WSBC)					
PO Box 497	Mulberry	FL	33860	**800-223-2625**	

323   GAMES & GAMING

SEE ALSO Toys, Games, Hobbies ; Lotteries, Games, Sweepstakes ; Casino Companies ; Casinos

				Toll-Free	Phone
Ac Coin & Slot					
201 W Decatur Ave	Pleasantville	NJ	08232	**800-284-7568**	609-641-7811
American Gaming & Electronics					
9500 W 55th St Ste A	Countryside	IL	60525	**800-336-6630**	708-290-2100
Amtote International Inc					
11200 Pepper Rd	Hunt Valley	MD	21031	**800-345-1566**	410-771-8700
Arachnid Inc					
6212 Material Ave	Loves Park	IL	61111	**800-435-8319**	815-654-0212
Aristocrat Technologies					
7230 Amigo St	Las Vegas	NV	89119	**800-748-4156**	702-270-1000
Douglas Press Inc					
2810 Madison St	Bellwood	IL	60104	**800-323-0705**	708-547-8400
Gaming Partners International Corp					
1700 Industrial Rd	Las Vegas	NV	89102	**800-728-5766**	702-384-2425
NASDAQ: GPIC					
International Game Technology (IGT)					
9295 Prototype Dr	Reno	NV	89521	**800-522-4700**	775-448-7777
NYSE: IGT					

				Toll-Free	Phone
Konami Gaming Inc					
585 Trade Ctr Dr	Las Vegas	NV	89119	**866-544-7568**	702-616-1400
Multimedia Games Inc					
206 Wild Basin Rd Bldg B 4th Fl	Austin	TX	78746	**800-833-7110**	512-334-7500
NASDAQ: MGAM					
Scientific Games Corp					
750 Lexington Ave 25th Fl	New York	NY	10022	**800-827-2946**	212-754-2233
NASDAQ: SGMS					
Smart Industries Corp					
1626 Delaware Ave	Des Moines	IA	50317	**800-553-2442**	515-265-9900
Valley-Dynamo					
7224 Burns Rd	Richland Hills	TX	76118	**800-826-7856**	972-595-5365
Video King Gaming Systems (VKGS LLC)					
2717 N 118 Cir Ste 210	Omaha	NE	68164	**800-635-9912**	402-951-2970
WMS Gaming Inc					
800 S Northpoint Blvd	Waukegan	IL	60085	**800-522-4700**	847-785-3000

324   GARDEN CENTERS

SEE ALSO Seed Companies ; Horticultural Products Growers

				Toll-Free	Phone
Earl May Seed & Nursery					
208 N Elm St	Shenandoah	IA	51603	**877-800-5556**	712-246-1020
Gardener's Supply Co					
128 Intervale Rd	Burlington	VT	05401	**800-863-1700**	802-660-3500
Greenbrier Farms Inc					
225 Sign Pine Rd	Chesapeake	VA	23322	**800-829-2141**	757-421-2141
Home & Garden Showplace					
8600 W Bryn Mawr	Chicago	IL	60631	**877-502-4641**	773-695-5000
Home Depot Inc					
2455 Paces Ferry Rd NW	Atlanta	GA	30339	**800-553-3199***	770-433-8211
*NYSE: HD ▣ *Cust Svc					
Johnson's Garden Centers					
2707 W 13th St	Wichita	KS	67203	**888-542-8463**	316-942-1443
JW Jung Seed Co					
335 S High St	Randolph	WI	53956	**800-297-3123**	
Lowe's Cos Inc					
1000 Lowe's Blvd	Mooresville	NC	28117	**800-445-6937**	704-758-1000
NYSE: LOW					
McKay Nursery Company Inc					
750 S Monroe St PO Box 185	Waterloo	WI	53594	**800-236-4242**	920-478-2121
Milaeger's Inc					
4838 Douglas Ave	Racine	WI	53402	**800-669-1229**	262-639-2040
Panhandle Co-op Assn					
401 S Beltline Hwy W	Scottsbluff	NE	69361	**800-732-4546***	308-632-5301
*Cust Svc					
Plants of the Southwest					
3095 Agua Fria Rd	Santa Fe	NM	87507	**800-788-7333**	505-438-8888
Pleasant View Gardens Inc					
7316 Pleasant St	Loudon	NH	03307	**866-862-2974**	603-435-8361
Ritchie Tractor					
1746 W Lmar Alxander Pkwy	Maryville	TN	37801	**888-319-0282**	865-981-3199
Round Butte Seed Growers Inc					
505 C St	Culver	OR	97734	**866-385-7001**	541-546-5222
Village Nurseries					
1589 N Main St	Orange	CA	92867	**800-542-0209**	
Wal-Mart Stores Inc					
702 SW Eigth St	Bentonville	AR	72716	**800-925-6278***	479-273-4000
*NYSE: WMT ▣ *Cust Svc					
Weingartz Supply Co					
46061 Van Dyke Ave	Utica	MI	48317	**855-669-7278**	586-731-7240
White Flower Farm Inc					
30 Irene St	Torrington	CT	06790	**800-411-6159***	860-496-9624
*Cust Svc					

325   GAS STATIONS

SEE ALSO Convenience Stores

				Toll-Free	Phone
Alpena Oil Co Inc					
235 Water St	Alpena	MI	49707	**800-968-1098**	989-356-1098
AMBEST Inc					
5115 Maryland Way	Brentwood	TN	37027	**800-910-7220**	615-371-5187
BP PLC 28100 Torch Pkwy	Warrenville	IL	60555	**877-638-5672**	630-420-5111
NYSE: BP					
Busler Enterprises Inc					
2601 N St Joseph Ave	Evansville	IN	47720	**800-457-3232**	812-424-7511
Chevron Corp					
6001 Bollinger Canyon Rd	San Ramon	CA	94583	**800-243-8766***	925-842-1000
*NYSE: CVX ▣ *Cust Svc					
Dakota Plains Co-op					
151 Ninth Ave NW	Valley City	ND	58072	**800-288-7922**	701-845-0812
Dunlap Oil Company Inc					
759 S Haskell Ave	Willcox	AZ	85643	**800-854-1646**	520-384-2248
Englefield Oil Co					
447 James Pkwy	Heath	OH	43056	**800-837-4458***	740-928-8215
*Cust Svc					
Erickson Oil Products Inc					
1231 Industrial St	Hudson	WI	54016	**800-521-0104**	715-386-8241
Exxon Mobil Corp					
5959 Las Colinas Blvd	Irving	TX	75039	**800-252-1800**	972-444-1000
NYSE: XOM					
Forward Corp					
219 N Front St	Standish	MI	48658	**800-664-4501**	989-846-4501
GasAmerica Services Inc					
2700 W Main St	Greenfield	IN	46140	**800-643-1948**	317-468-2515
Gate Petroleum Co					
9540 San Jose Blvd PO Box 23627	Jacksonville	FL	32241	**866-571-1982**	904-737-7220
Getty Realty Corp					
125 Jericho Tpke Ste 103	Jericho	NY	11753	**866-399-4335**	516-478-5400
NYSE: GTY					
Houston Food Bank, The					
535 Portwall St	Houston	TX	77029	**866-384-4277**	713-223-3700
Hunt & Sons Inc					
5750 S Watt Ave	Sacramento	CA	95829	**800-734-2999**	916-383-4868

				Toll-Free	Phone

Imperial Oil Resources Ltd
237 Fourth Ave SW PO Box 2480 Stn M . . . . Calgary AB T2P3M9 **800-567-3776**

Iowa 80 Group Inc
515 Sterling Dr PO Box 639 . . . . Walcott IA 52773 **800-336-9889** 563-284-6965

J & H Oil Co
2696 Chicago Dr SW . . . . Wyoming MI 49519 **800-442-9110** 616-534-2181

Jubitz Corp
33 NE Middlefield Rd . . . . Portland OR 97211 **800-523-0600** 503-283-1111

Lassus Bros Oil Inc
1800 Magnavox Way . . . . Fort Wayne IN 46804 **800-686-2836** 260-436-1415

Mid-Atlantic Convenience Stores LLC
1011 Boulder Springs Dr Ste 100 . . . . Richmond VA 23225 **877-468-7797** 804-706-4702

Monroe Oil Co
519 E Franklin St PO Box 1109 . . . . Monroe NC 28111 **800-452-2717*** 704-289-5438
*General

NELLA Oil Co
2360 Lindbergh St . . . . Auburn CA 95602 **800-995-0401** 530-885-0401

Ney Oil Company Inc
145 S Water St PO Box 155 . . . . Ney OH 43549 **800-962-9839** 419-658-2324

O'Connell Oil Assoc Inc
545 Merrill Rd . . . . Pittsfield MA 01201 **800-464-4894** 413-499-4800

Pilot Travel Centers LLC
PO Box 10146 . . . . Knoxville TN 37939 **800-562-6210** 865-938-1439

RaceTrac Petroleum Inc
3225 Cumberland Blvd Ste 100 . . . . Atlanta GA 30339 **888-636-5589** 770-431-7600

Rip Griffin Truck Travel Ctr Inc
4710 Fourth St . . . . Lubbock TX 79416 **800-333-9330** 806-795-8785

Sampson-Bladen Oil Co Inc
510 Commerce St PO Box 469 . . . . Clinton NC 28329 **800-849-4177** 910-592-4177

Scott-Gross Company Inc
664 Magnolia Ave . . . . Lexington KY 40505 **800-967-6874**

Shirtcliff Oil Co
PO Box 6003 . . . . Myrtle Creek OR 97457 **800-422-0536** 541-863-5268

Speedway LLC 500 Speedway Dr . . . . Enon OH 45323 **800-643-1948*** 937-864-3001
*Cust Svc

Spencer Cos Inc
120 Woodson St PO Box 18128 . . . . Huntsville AL 35801 **800-633-2910** 256-533-1150

Thornton Oil Corp
10101 Linn Stn Rd Ste 200 . . . . Louisville KY 40223 **800-928-8022** 502-425-8022

Town Pump Inc 600 S Main St . . . . Butte MT 59701 **800-823-4931** 406-497-6700

TravelCenters of America
24601 Ctr Ridge Rd Ste 200 . . . . Westlake OH 44145 **800-632-9240** 440-808-9100

Vermont Gas Systems Inc
85 Swift St . . . . South Burlington VT 05403 **800-639-8081** 802-863-4511

W & H Co-op Oil Co
407 13th St N . . . . Humboldt IA 50548 **800-392-3816** 515-332-2782

Wallis Oil Co
106 E Washington St . . . . Cuba MO 65453 **800-467-6652** 573-885-2277

Wesco Inc
1460 Whitehall Rd . . . . Muskegon MI 49445 **800-968-0200**

326 GAS TRANSMISSION - NATURAL GAS

Companies that transmit or store natural gas but do not distribute it.

				Toll-Free	Phone

ANR Pipeline Co
717 Texas St . . . . Houston TX 77002 **800-827-5267** 832-320-5230

Atlas Pipeline Partners LP
110 W 7th Ste 2300 . . . . Tulsa OK 74119 **877-950-7473** 918-574-3500

Boardwalk Pipeline Partners LP
3800 Frederica St . . . . Owensboro KY 42301 **866-913-2122** 270-686-3620
NYSE: BWP

Cheniere Energy Inc
700 Milam St Ste 800 . . . . Houston TX 77002 **877-375-5002** 713-375-5000
NYSE: LNG

Duke Energy Corp
5400 Westheimer C Mail Drop WP 890 . . . . Houston TX 77056 **800-521-2232** 713-627-5400

Iroquois Gas Transmission System LP
1 Corporate Dr Ste 600 . . . . Shelton CT 06484 **800-888-3982** 203-925-7200

Kern River Gas Transmission Co
2755 E Cottonwood Pkwy Ste 300 . . . . Salt Lake City UT 84121 **800-420-7500** 801-937-6000

Kinder Morgan
1001 Louisiana St Ste 1000 . . . . Houston TX 77002 **800-247-4122** 713-369-9000
NYSE: KMI

Kinder Morgan Energy Partners LP
500 Dallas St Ste 1000 . . . . Houston TX 77002 **866-208-3372** 713-369-9000
NYSE: KMI

Kinder Morgan Management LLC
500 Dallas St 1 Allen Ctr Ste 1000 . . . . Houston TX 77002 **800-781-4152** 713-369-9000
NYSE: KMI

Kinder Morgan Texas Pipeline LLC
500 Dallas St Ste 1000 . . . . Houston TX 77002 **800-324-2900** 713-369-9000

Northern Natural Gas Co
1111 S 103rd St . . . . Omaha NE 68124 **877-654-0646** 402-398-7000

Questar Gas Management Co
PO Box 45360 . . . . Salt Lake City UT 84145 **800-323-5517** 801-324-5111

Spark Energy Gas LP
2105 Citywest Blvd . . . . Houston TX 77042 **877-547-7275**

TransCanada Pipelines Ltd
450 First St SW . . . . Calgary AB T2P5H1 **800-661-3805** 403-920-2000

Tri-Gas & Oil Company Inc
3941 Federalsburg Hwy PO Box 465 . . . . Federalsburg MD 21632 **800-638-7802** 410-754-8184

WBI Energy
1250 W Century Ave . . . . Bismarck ND 58503 **877-924-4677** 701-530-1064

WBI Holdings Inc
1250 W Century Ave . . . . Bismarck ND 58503 **877-924-4677***
*General

Williams Gas Pipeline Gulfstream
1905 Intermodal Cir Ste 310 . . . . Palmetto FL 34221 **800-440-8475**

Williams Partners LP
One Williams Ctr . . . . Tulsa OK 74172 **800-600-3782** 918-573-2000
NYSE: WPZ

327 GASKETS, PACKING, SEALING DEVICES

SEE ALSO Automotive Parts & Supplies - Mfr

				Toll-Free	Phone

Abric (North America) Inc
220 Barren Springs Dr Ste 1 . . . . Houston TX 77090 **888-922-7429** 281-569-7100

Akron Gasket & Packing Enterprises Inc
445 NE Ave . . . . Tallmadge OH 44278 **800-888-2088** 330-633-3742

American Casting & Manufacturing Corp
51 Commercial St . . . . Plainview NY 11803 **800-342-0333** 516-349-7010

American Packing & Gasket Co (APG)
6039 Armour Dr PO Box 213 . . . . Houston TX 77020 **800-888-5223** 713-675-5271

APM Hexseal Corp
44 Honeck St . . . . Englewood NJ 07631 **800-498-9034** 201-569-5700

Apple Rubber Products Inc
310 Erie St . . . . Lancaster NY 14086 **800-828-7745*** 716-684-6560
*Cust Svc

AR Thomson Group
7930 130th St . . . . Surrey BC V3W0H7 **800-410-9116** 604-507-6050

Atlantic Gasket Corp
3908 Frankford Ave . . . . Philadelphia PA 19124 **800-229-8881** 215-533-6400

Auburn Manufacturing Co
29 Stack St . . . . Middletown CT 06457 **800-427-5387** 860-346-6677

Bal Seal Engineering Company Inc
19650 Pauling . . . . Foothill Ranch CA 92610 **800-366-1006** 949-460-2100

California Gasket & Rubber Corp
533 W Collins Ave . . . . Orange CA 92867 **800-635-7084** 310-323-4250

Calpico Inc
1387 San Mateo Ave . . . . South San Francisco CA 94080 **800-998-9115** 650-588-2241

CE Conover & Company Inc
4106 Blanche Rd . . . . Bensalem PA 19020 **800-266-6837** 215-639-6666

CGR Products Inc
4655 US Hwy 29 N . . . . Greensboro NC 27405 **877-313-6785** 336-621-4568

Chicago Gasket Co
1285 W N Ave . . . . Chicago IL 60622 **800-833-5666** 773-486-3060

Chicago-Wilcox Mfg Co
16928 State St PO Box 126 . . . . South Holland IL 60473 **800-323-5282**

Cometic Gasket Inc
8090 Auburn Rd . . . . Concord OH 44077 **800-752-9850** 440-354-0777

Corpus Christi Gasket & Fastener Inc
PO Box 4074 . . . . Corpus Christi TX 78469 **800-460-6366** 361-884-6366

Ct Gasket & Polymer Company Inc
12308 Cutten Rd . . . . Houston TX 77066 **800-299-1685**

Eagle Burgmann Industries LP
10035 Brookriver Dr . . . . Houston TX 77040 **800-303-7735***
*General

EnPro Industries Inc
5605 Carnegie Blvd Ste 500 . . . . Charlotte NC 28209 **800-356-6955** 704-731-1500
NYSE: NPO

Flow Dry Technology Inc
379 Albert Rd PO Box 190 . . . . Brookville OH 45309 **800-533-0077** 937-833-2161

Flowserve Corp
5215 N O'Connor Blvd Ste 2300 . . . . Irving TX 75039 **800-350-1082** 972-443-6500
NYSE: FLS

Gasket Manufacturing Co
18001 Main St . . . . Gardena CA 90248 **800-442-7538** 310-217-5600

Gaskets Inc 301 W Hwy 16 . . . . Rio WI 53960 **800-558-1833** 920-992-3137

Gunite Supply & Equipment Company - West
1726 S Magnolia Ave . . . . Monrovia CA 91016 **888-393-8635** 626-358-0143

Houston Mfg Specialty Company Inc
9909 Wallisville Rd . . . . Houston TX 77013 **800-231-6030** 713-675-7400

IG Inc 720 S Sara Rd . . . . Mustang OK 73137 **800-654-8433** 405-376-9393

Ilene Industries Inc
301 Stanley Blvd . . . . Shelbyville TN 37160 **800-251-1602** 931-684-8731

Industrial Custom Products Inc
2801 37th Ave NE . . . . Minneapolis MN 55421 **800-654-0886** 612-781-2255

Industrial Gasket & Shim Company Inc (IGS)
200 Country Club Rd . . . . Meadow Lands PA 15347 **800-229-1447** 724-222-5800

Intek Plastic Inc
1000 Spiral Blvd . . . . Hastings MN 55033 **888-468-3531**

Interface Solutions Inc
216 Wohlsen Way . . . . Lancaster PA 17603 **800-942-7538** 717-207-6000

Jade Engineered Plastic Inc
121 Broadcommon Rd . . . . Bristol RI 02809 **800-557-9155** 401-253-4440

John Crane Inc
6400 W Oakton St . . . . Morton Grove IL 60053 **800-732-5464** 847-967-2400

Lamons Gasket Co
7300 Airport Blvd . . . . Houston TX 77061 **800-231-6906** 713-222-0284

Marco Rubber
35 Woodworkers Way . . . . Seabrook NH 03874 **800-775-6525** 603-468-3600

Netherland Rubber Co
2931 Exon Ave . . . . Cincinnati OH 45241 **800-582-1877** 513-733-0883

Novagard Solutions Inc
5109 Hamilton Ave . . . . Cleveland OH 44114 **800-380-0138** 216-881-8111

Ohio Gasket & Shim Company Inc
976 Evans Ave . . . . Akron OH 44305 **800-321-2438** 330-630-2030

Omega Shielding Products Inc
1384 Pompton Ave . . . . Cedar Grove NJ 07009 **800-828-5784** 973-890-7455

Pacific States Felt & Mfg Company Inc
23850 Clawiter Rd . . . . Hayward CA 94545 **800-566-8866** 510-783-0277

Pemko Mfg Company Inc
4226 Transport St . . . . Ventura CA 93003 **800-283-9988** 805-642-2600

PPC Mechanical Seals
2769 Mission Dr . . . . Baton Rouge LA 70805 **800-731-7325** 225-356-4333

Press-Seal Gasket Corp
2424 W State Blvd . . . . Fort Wayne IN 46808 **800-348-7325** 260-436-0521

Presscut Industries Inc
1730 Briercroft Ct . . . . Carrollton TX 75006 **800-442-4924** 972-389-0615

Rotor Clip Company Inc
187 Davidson Ave . . . . Somerset NJ 08873 **800-557-6867*** 732-469-7333
*Cust Svc

Schlegel Systems Inc
1555 Jefferson Rd . . . . Rochester NY 14623 **888-924-7694** 585-427-7200

Seal Methods Inc
11915 Shoemaker Ave . . . . Santa Fe Springs CA 90670 **800-423-4777** 562-944-0291

				Toll-Free	Phone

Sealing Devices Inc
4400 Walden Ave . . . . Lancaster NY 14086 **800-727-3257*** 716-684-7600
*Cust Svc

Sealing Equipment Products Co Inc
123 Airpark Industrial Rd . . . . Alabaster AL 35007 **800-633-4770***
*Cust Svc

Specification Rubber Products Inc
1568 First St N . . . . Alabaster AL 35007 **800-633-3415** 205-663-2521

Sur-Seal Gasket & Packing Inc
6156 Wesselman Rd . . . . Cincinnati OH 45248 **800-345-8966**

T & E Industries Inc
215 Watchung Ave . . . . Orange NJ 07050 **800-245-7080*** 973-672-5454
*Sales

UTEX Industries Inc
10810 Katy Fwy Ste 100 . . . . Houston TX 77043 **800-359-9230** 713-467-1000

Vellumoid Inc
54 Rockdale St . . . . Worcester MA 01606 **800-609-5558** 508-853-2500

William H Harvey
4334 S 67th St . . . . Omaha NE 68117 **800-321-9532** 402-331-1175

Zero International Inc
415 Concord Ave . . . . Bronx NY 10455 **800-635-5335** 718-585-3230

---

328   GIFT SHOPS

SEE ALSO Home Furnishings Stores ; Card Shops ; Duty-Free Shops

				Toll-Free	Phone

Brookstone Inc
1 Innovation Way . . . . Merrimack NH 03054 **800-846-3000*** 603-880-9500
*Cust Svc

CM Paula Co 6049 Hi-Tek Ct . . . . Mason OH 45040 **800-543-4464**

Disney Consumer Products
500 S Buena Vista St . . . . Burbank CA 91521 **877-282-8322*** 818-560-1000
*PR

GiftCertificates.com
11510 Blondo St . . . . Omaha NE 68164 **800-773-7368**

Historical Research Ctr Inc
2107 Corporate Dr . . . . Boynton Beach FL 33426 **800-985-9956** 561-732-5263

Mole Hollow Candles Ltd
208 Charlton Rd Rt 20 PO Box 223 . . . . Sturbridge MA 01566 **800-445-6653***
*Cust Svc

Oregon Connection
1125 S First St . . . . Coos Bay OR 97420 **800-255-5318** 541-267-7804

San Francisco Music Box Co
5370 W 95th St . . . . Prairie Village KS 66207 **800-227-2190**

Sanrio Inc
570 Eccles Ave . . . . South San Francisco CA 94080 **800-759-6454** 650-952-2880

Silver Towne LP
120 E Union City Pike PO Box 424 . . . . Winchester IN 47394 **800-788-7481** 765-584-7481

Tuesday Morning Corp
6250 LBJ Fwy . . . . Dallas TX 75240 **800-457-0099** 972-387-3562
NASDAQ: TUES

Wendell August Forge Inc
2074 Leesburg-Grove City Rd . . . . Mercer PA 16137 **866-354-5192** 724-748-9501

Yankee Candle Company Inc
PO Box 110 . . . . South Deerfield MA 01373 **877-803-6890** 413-665-8306

---

329   GIFTS & NOVELTIES - WHOL

				Toll-Free	Phone

Accoutrements
10915 47th Ave W . . . . Mukilteo WA 98275 **800-886-2221** 425-349-3838

Blair Cedar & Novelty Works Inc
680 W US Hwy 54 . . . . Camdenton MO 65020 **800-325-3943** 573-346-2235

Boyds Collection Ltd
300 Frederick St . . . . Hanover PA 17331 **800-436-3726** 717-633-9898

Drysdales Inc
3220 S Memorial Dr . . . . Tulsa OK 74145 **800-444-6481** 918-664-6481

Fridgedoor.com 65 School St . . . . Quincy MA 02169 **800-955-3741** 617-770-7913

Hayes Specialties Corp
1761 E Genesee . . . . Saginaw MI 48601 **800-248-3603** 989-755-6541

Hollywood Ribbon Industries Inc
9000 Rochester Ave . . . . Rancho Cucamonga CA 91730 **800-457-7652** 323-266-0670

Hornung's Golf Products Inc
815 Morris St . . . . Fond du Lac WI 54935 **800-323-3569** 920-922-2640

Kurt S Adler Inc
Seven W 34th St . . . . New York NY 10001 **866-919-9757** 212-924-0900

Sanrio Inc
570 Eccles Ave . . . . South San Francisco CA 94080 **800-759-6454** 650-952-2880

Star Sales Company Inc
1803 N Central St . . . . Knoxville TN 37917 **800-347-9494** 865-524-0771

Trends International LLC
5188 W 74th St . . . . Indianapolis IN 46268 **866-406-7771** 317-388-1212

Unique Industries Inc
4750 League Island Blvd . . . . Philadelphia PA 19112 **800-888-0559** 215-336-4300

US Balloon Mfg Company Inc
140 58th St . . . . Brooklyn NY 11220 **800-285-4000**

Variety Distributors Inc
609 Seventh St . . . . Harlan IA 51537 **800-274-1095** 712-755-2184

WinCraft Inc 1124 W Fifth St . . . . Winona MN 55987 **800-533-8006** 507-454-5510

---

330   GLASS - FLAT, PLATE, TEMPERED

				Toll-Free	Phone

AGC Flat Galss North America Inc
11175 Cicero Dr Ste 400 . . . . Alpharetta GA 30022 **800-251-0441** 404-446-4200

Anthony International
12391 Montera Ave . . . . Sylmar CA 91342 **800-772-0900** 818-365-9451

Apogee Enterprises Inc
4400 W 78th St Ste 520 . . . . Minneapolis MN 55435 **877-752-3432** 952-835-1874
NASDAQ: APOG

Basco Shower Enclosures
7201 Snider Rd . . . . Mason OH 45040 **800-543-1938** 513-573-1900

Binswanger Glass
965 Ridge Lk Blvd Ste 305 . . . . Memphis TN 38120 **800-365-9922**

Bullseye Glass Co
3722 SE 21st Ave . . . . Portland OR 97202 **888-220-3002** 503-232-8887

D & W Inc 941 Oak St . . . . Elkhart IN 46514 **800-255-0829** 574-264-9674

Glaz-Tech Industries Inc
2207 E Elvira Rd . . . . Tucson AZ 85756 **800-755-8062** 520-629-0268

Gray Glass Co
217-44 98th Ave . . . . Queens Village NY 11429 **800-523-3320** 718-217-2943

Guardian Industries Corp
2300 Harmon Rd . . . . Auburn Hills MI 48326 **800-822-5599** 248-340-1800

Hartung Agalite Glass Co
17830 W Valley Hwy . . . . Seattle WA 98188 **800-552-2227** 425-656-2626

Hartung Glass Industries
10450 SW Ridder Rd . . . . Wilsonville OR 97070 **800-552-2227** 503-682-3846

Kokomo Opalescent Glass Co
1310 S Market St . . . . Kokomo IN 46902 **877-475-6329** 765-457-8136

Northwestern Industries Inc
2500 W Jameson St . . . . Seattle WA 98199 **800-426-2771** 206-285-3140

ODL Inc 215 E Roosevelt Ave . . . . Zeeland MI 49464 **800-253-3900** 616-772-9111

Oldcastle BuildingEnvelope
4161 S Morgan St . . . . Chicago IL 60609 **866-653-2278** 773-523-8400

Rainbow Art Glass Inc
1761 Rt 34 S . . . . Farmingdale NJ 07727 **800-526-2356** 732-681-6003

Saint-Gobain Corp
750 E Swedesford Rd . . . . Valley Forge PA 19482 **800-506-7427** 610-341-7000

Schott North America Inc
555 Taxter Rd . . . . Elmsford NY 10523 **877-261-2100** 914-831-2200

Spectrum Glass Co
PO Box 646 . . . . Woodinville WA 98072 **800-426-3120** 425-483-6699

Tru Vue Inc 9400 W 55th St . . . . McCook IL 60525 **800-621-8339** 708-485-5080

Viracon Inc 800 Pk Dr . . . . Owatonna MN 55060 **800-533-2080** 507-451-9555

Virginia Mirror Co Inc
300 Moss St S . . . . Martinsville VA 24112 **800-368-3011** 276-632-9816

Wasco Products Inc
22 Pioneer Ave PO Box 351 . . . . Sanford ME 04073 **800-388-0293** 207-324-8060

---

331   GLASS FIBERS

				Toll-Free	Phone

Fiberoptics Technology Inc
One Quassett Rd . . . . Pomfret CT 06258 **800-433-5248*** 860-928-0443
*Cust Svc

Sentinel Process
3265 Sunset Ln . . . . Hatboro PA 19040 **800-345-3569** 919-462-7108

---

332   GLASS PRODUCTS - INDUSTRIAL (CUSTOM)

				Toll-Free	Phone

Abrisa Technologies
200 S Hallock Dr . . . . Santa Paula CA 93060 **877-622-7472**

Flex-O-Lite Inc
50 Crestwood Executive Ctr
Ste 522 . . . . Saint Louis MO 63126 **800-325-9525**

Henderson Glass Inc
715 S Blvd E . . . . Rochester Hills MI 48307 **800-694-0672** 855-543-8663

King Precision Glass Inc
177 S Indian Hill Blvd . . . . Claremont CA 91711 **866-554-2773** 909-626-3526

Lenoir Mirror Company Inc
401 Kincaid St . . . . Lenoir NC 28645 **800-438-8204** 828-728-3271

North American Specialty Glass
2175 Kumry Rd PO Box 70 . . . . Trumbauersville PA 18970 **888-785-5962** 215-536-0333

Precision Electronic Glass Inc
1013 Hendee Rd . . . . Vineland NJ 08360 **800-982-4734** 856-691-2234

Richland Glass Company Inc
1640 SW Blvd . . . . Vineland NJ 08360 **800-959-0312** 856-691-1697

Swift Glass Company Inc
131 W 22nd St . . . . Elmira Heights NY 14903 **800-537-9438** 607-733-7166

---

333   GLASSWARE - LABORATORY & SCIENTIFIC

				Toll-Free	Phone

Ace Glass Inc
1430 NW Blvd PO Box 688 . . . . Vineland NJ 08360 **800-223-4524** 856-692-3333

Bellco Glass Inc
340 Edrudo Rd . . . . Vineland NJ 08360 **800-257-7043** 856-691-1075

Quadrex Corp PO Box 3881 . . . . Woodbridge CT 06525 **800-275-7033*** 203-393-3112
*Sales

Schott North America Inc
555 Taxter Rd . . . . Elmsford NY 10523 **877-261-2100** 914-831-2200

Wale Apparatus Co Inc
400 Front St . . . . Hellertown PA 18055 **800-334-9253** 610-838-7047

---

334   GLASSWARE & POTTERY - HOUSEHOLD

SEE ALSO Table & Kitchen Supplies - China & Earthenware

				Toll-Free	Phone

Berney-Karp Inc
3350 E 26th St . . . . Los Angeles CA 90058 **800-237-6395** 323-260-7122

Blenko Glass Co PO Box 67 . . . . Milton WV 25541 **877-425-3656** 304-743-9081

Ceramo Company Inc
681 Kasten Dr . . . . Jackson MO 63755 **800-325-8303** 573-243-3138

Enesco LLC 225 Windsor Dr . . . . Itasca IL 60143 **800-436-3726** 630-875-5300

Fenton Art Glass Co
700 Elizabeth St . . . . Williamstown WV 26187 **800-933-6766*** 304-375-6122
*Cust Svc

Friedman Bros Decorative Arts
9015 NW 105th Way . . . . Medley FL 33178 **800-327-1065** 305-887-3170

Gainey Ceramics Inc
1200 Arrow Hwy . . . . La Verne CA 91750 **800-451-8155*** 909-593-3533
*Cust Svc

				Toll-Free	Phone
Gardner Glass Products Inc 301 Elkin Hwy PO Box 1570	North Wilkesboro	NC	28659	**800-334-7267**	
Haeger Industries Inc Seven Maiden Ln *Cust Svc	Dundee	IL	60118	**800-288-2529***	847-426-3441
Haggerty Enterprises Inc 370 Kimberly Dr	Carol Stream	IL	60188	**800-336-5282**	630-315-3300
Libbey Inc 300 Madison Ave PO Box 10060 *NYSE: LBY*	Toledo	OH	43699	**888-794-8469**	419-325-2100
Marshall Pottery 4901 Elysian Fields Rd	Marshall	TX	75672	**888-768-8721**	903-927-5400
Pfaltzgraff Co PO Box 21769	York	PA	17402	**800-999-2811**	
Swarovski North America Ltd One Kenney Dr	Cranston	RI	02920	**800-289-4900**	401-463-6400

335 GLOBAL DISTRIBUTION SYSTEMS (GDSS)

A global distribution system (GDS) is a computer reservations system that includes reservations databases of air travel suppliers in many countries. GDSs typically are owned jointly by airlines operating in different countries.

				Toll-Free	Phone
Amadeus North America Inc 3470 NW 82nd Ave Ste 1000	Miami	FL	33122	**888-262-3387**	305-499-6000
Pegasus Solutions Inc 5430 LBJ Fwy Ste 1100	Dallas	TX	75240	**800-843-4343**	214-234-4000

336 GOURMET SPECIALTY SHOPS

				Toll-Free	Phone
Graber Olive House Inc 315 E Fourth St	Ontario	CA	91764	**800-996-5483**	
Harry & David Holdings Inc 2500 S Pacific Hwy *Cust Svc	Medford	OR	97501	**877-322-1200***	
Hickory Farms Inc 811 Madison Ave	Toledo	OH	43604	**800-753-8558**	
Logan Farms Honey Glazed Hams 10560 Westheimer Rd	Houston	TX	77042	**800-833-4267**	713-781-4335

337 GOVERNMENT - CITY

				Toll-Free	Phone
Greenville City Hall 206 S Main St	Greenville	SC	29601	**800-829-4477**	864-232-2273
Ocean City City Hall 301 Baltimore Ave	Ocean City	MD	21842	**800-626-2326**	410-289-8931
Ottawa City Hall 110 Laurier Ave W	Ottawa	ON	K1P1J1	**866-261-9799**	613-580-2400

338 GOVERNMENT - COUNTY

				Toll-Free	Phone
Aiken County 828 Richland Ave W	Aiken	SC	29801	**866-876-7074**	803-642-2012
Aleutians East Borough 3380 C St Ste 205	Anchorage	AK	99503	**888-383-2699**	907-274-7555
Allen Parish PO Box 1280	Oberlin	LA	70655	**888-639-4868**	337-639-4868
Ashe County Chamber of Commerce 1 N Jefferson Ave Ste C	West Jefferson	NC	28694	**888-343-2743**	336-846-9550
Atchison County 405 S Main St PO Box 243	Rock Port	MO	64482	**800-989-4115**	660-744-6562
Bell County 101 E Central Ave PO Box 480	Belton	TX	76513	**800-460-2355**	254-933-5160
Bennington County 100 Veterans Memorial Dr	Bennington	VT	05201	**800-229-0252**	802-447-3311
Blaine County 420 Ohio St	Chinook	MT	59523	**800-666-6124**	406-442-9830
Butler County 205 W Central Ave	El Dorado	KS	67042	**800-822-6104**	316-322-4300
Carbon County PO Box 1017	Rawlins	WY	82301	**800-228-3547**	
Caribou County 159 S Main	Soda Springs	ID	83276	**800-972-7660**	208-547-4324
Carroll County 8215 Black Oak Road	Mount Carroll	IL	61053	**800-485-0145**	815-244-2035
Carter County 101 1St Ave SW	Ardmore	OK	73401	**800-231-8668**	580-223-8162
Cherokee County 165 E Sixth St Ste 203 PO Box 259	Rusk	TX	75785	**800-541-2524**	903-683-6540
Chester County 313 W Market St Ste 6202 PO Box 2748	West Chester	PA	19380	**800-692-1100**	610-344-6100
Chisago County 313 N Main St	Center City	MN	55012	**888-234-1246**	651-257-1300
Coconino County 219 E Cherry Ave	Flagstaff	AZ	86001	**800-559-9289**	928-774-5011
Collin County 200 S McDonald St Ste 120	McKinney	TX	75069	**800-336-5996**	
Comal County 199 Main Plaza	New Braunfels	TX	78130	**877-724-9475**	830-221-1100
County of Greene 93 E High St	Waynesburg	PA	15370	**888-852-5399**	724-852-5210
Crow Wing County 326 Laurel St	Brainerd	MN	56401	**888-829-6680**	218-824-1067
Dauphin County 2 S Second St 3rd Fl	Harrisburg	PA	17101	**800-328-0058**	717-780-6636
Esmeralda County PO Box 547	Goldfield	NV	89013	**800-884-4072**	775-485-6309
Floyd County 100 S Main St	Floydada	TX	79235	**800-521-8565**	806-983-2197
Franklin County 355 W Main St	Malone	NY	12953	**800-397-8686**	518-483-6770
Fremont County 450 N Second St	Lander	WY	82520	**800-967-2297**	307-332-2405
Garfield County 375 North 700 West	Panguitch	UT	84759	**800-636-8826**	435-676-2678
Gates County 200 Ct St	Gatesville	NC	27938	**800-272-9829**	252-357-2411
Gila County 1400 E Ash St	Globe	AZ	85501	**800-304-4452**	928-425-3231
Graham County 34 Wall St Suite 407	Asheville	NC	28801	**866-962-6246**	828-255-0182
Grant County 301 W Main St	John Day	OR	97845	**800-769-5664**	541-575-0547
Greeley County 510 Broadway PO Box 656	Tribune	KS	67879	**888-204-1781**	620-376-2548
Green County 1016 16th Ave	Monroe	WI	53566	**800-947-3529**	608-328-9430
Greenbrier County 200 W Washington St	Lewisburg	WV	24901	**800-833-2068**	304-647-6602
Hancock County 12630 Broad St	Sparta	GA	31087	**800-255-0135**	706-444-5746
Hardy County 204 Washington St Rm 111	Moorefield	WV	26836	**800-222-1222**	304-530-0250
Harlan County 311 Main St	Alma	NE	68920	**800-762-5498**	
Harper County 201 N Jennings Ave	Anthony	KS	67003	**877-537-2110**	620-842-5555
Harris County 112 S College St PO Box 426	Hamilton	GA	31811	**888-478-0010**	706-628-0010
Hidalgo County PO Box 58	Edinburg	TX	78540	**888-318-2811**	956-318-2100
Hoke County 227 N Main St	Raeford	NC	28376	**888-302-9793**	910-875-8751
Hudspeth County 109 Brown St	Sierra Blanca	TX	79851	**888-368-4689**	915-369-2331
Indiana County 350 N Fourth St	Indiana	PA	15701	**888-559-6355**	724-465-3805
Jefferson County PO Box 890	Dandridge	TN	37725	**877-237-3847**	865-397-9642
Kane County 78 S 100 E	Kanab	UT	84741	**800-733-5263**	435-644-5033
King County 401 5th Ave Ste 800	Seattle	WA	98104	**800-325-6165**	206-296-1586
Klamath County 305 Main St	Klamath Falls	OR	97601	**800-377-6094**	541-883-5134
Lafourche Parish 402 Green St PO Box 5548	Thibodaux	LA	70302	**800-834-8832**	985-446-8427
Lake County 895 Michigan Ave PO Box 130	Baldwin	MI	49304	**800-245-3240**	231-745-4331
LaSalle County 707 E Etna Rd	Ottawa	IL	61350	**800-247-5243**	815-433-3366
Lawrence County County Courthouse 430 Court St	New Castle	PA	16101	**855-564-6116**	724-658-2541
Leelanau County 8527 E Government Ctr Dr	Suttons Bay	MI	49682	**866-256-9711**	231-256-9824
Lewis County 499 US Hwy 33 E Ste 102	Weston	WV	26452	**800-296-7329**	304-269-7328
Lincoln County 300 Central Ave	Carrizozo	NM	88301	**800-687-2705**	575-648-2385
Madison County 248 SW Range Ave PO Box 237	Madison	FL	32340	**877-272-3642**	850-973-2788
Marion County 200 S Third St Ste 104	Marion	KS	66861	**800-305-8851**	620-382-2185
McKean County 500 W Main St	Smethport	PA	16749	**800-482-1280**	814-887-5571
McKenzie County PO Box 699	Watford City	ND	58854	**800-701-2804**	701-444-2804
Mercer County 704 Bland St PO Box 4088	Bluefield	WV	24701	**800-221-3206**	304-325-8438
Morgan County 1226 Knoxville Hwy	Wartburg	TN	37887	**888-205-5017**	
Morrison County 213 SE First Ave	Little Falls	MN	56345	**866-401-1111**	320-632-2941
Nassau County PO Box 870	Fernandina Beach	FL	32035	**888-615-4398**	904-491-7300
Newton County 201 N 3rd St	Kentland	IN	47951	**888-663-9866**	219-474-6081
Northumberland County 201 Market St 2nd Fl	Sunbury	PA	17801	**800-692-7208**	570-988-4167
Noxubee County 503 S Washington St PO Box 308	Macon	MS	39341	**800-487-0165**	
Park County 1002 Sheridan Ave	Cody	WY	82414	**800-786-2844**	307-527-8510
Perry County 333 7th St	Tell City	IN	47586	**888-343-6262**	812-547-7933
Pickett County 1 Courthouse Sq Ste 200	Byrdstown	TN	38549	**888-406-4704**	931-864-3798
Pine County 635 Northridge Dr NW	Pine City	MN	55063	**800-450-7463**	320-591-1400
Pocahontas County PO Box 275	Marlinton	WV	24954	**800-336-7009**	
Portage County 449 S Meridian St 7th Fl	Ravenna	OH	44266	**800-772-3799**	330-297-3600
Putnam County 130 Orie Griffin Blvd PO Box 1578	Palatka	FL	32178	**800-426-9975**	386-329-0800
Ramsey County 15 W Kellogg Blvd Rm 250	Saint Paul	MN	55102	**866-520-7225**	651-266-8000
Randolph County 1302 N Randolph Ave	Elkins	WV	26241	**800-422-3304**	304-636-2780
Rutland Region Chamber of Commerce 50 Merchants Row	Rutland	VT	05701	**800-756-8880**	802-773-2747
San Bernardino County 385 N Arrowhead Ave Fl 5	San Bernardino	CA	92415	**888-818-8988**	909-387-8306
Santa Fe County 102 Grant Ave	Santa Fe	NM	87504	**877-607-0741**	505-986-6200
Sawyer County 10610 Main St Ste 10	Hayward	WI	54843	**877-699-4110**	715-634-4866
Shelby County 612 Ct St	Harlan	IA	51537	**800-735-3942**	712-755-3831
Towns County 1411 Jack Dayton Cir	Young Harris	GA	30582	**800-984-1543**	706-896-4966
Trego County 18001 283 Hwy	WaKeeney	KS	67672	**877-962-7248**	785-743-6385
Turner County PO Box 191	Ashburn	GA	31714	**800-436-7442**	229-567-2011
Uintah County 147 E Main St	Vernal	UT	84078	**800-966-4680**	435-781-0770
Union County 1103 S First St	Clayton	NM	88415	**800-390-7858**	575-374-9253
Vermillion County 255 S Main St	Newport	IN	47966	**800-340-8155**	765-492-5345
Wood County 1 Courthouse Sq	Bowling Green	OH	43402	**866-860-4140**	419-354-9000

Classified Section

339   GOVERNMENT - STATE

SEE ALSO Sports Commissions & Regulatory Agencies - State ; Student Assistance Programs ; Veterans Nursing Homes - State ; Legislation Hotlines ; Lotteries, Games, Sweepstakes ; Parks - State ; Correctional Facilities - State ; Employment Offices - Government ; Ethics Commissions

339-1 Alabama

			Toll-Free	Phone
Administrative Office of Alabama Courts				
300 Dexter Ave	Montgomery AL	36104	866-954-9411	334-954-5000
Conservation & Natural Resources Dept				
64 N Union St PO Box 301450	Montgomery AL	36130	800-262-3151	334-242-3486
Crime Victims Compensation Commission				
5845 Carmichael Rd	Montgomery AL	36117	800-541-9388	334-290-4420
Emergency Management Agency				
5898 County Rd 41 PO Box 2160	Clanton AL	35046	800-843-0699	205-280-2200
Mental Health & Mental Retardation Dept				
100 N Union St PO Box 301410	Montgomery AL	36130	800-367-0955	334-242-3454
Prepaid Affordable College Tuition (PACT) Program				
100 N Union St Ste 660	Montgomery AL	36130	800-252-7228	334-242-7514
Public Health Dept				
201 Monroe St	Montgomery AL	36104	800-252-1818	334-206-5300
Public Service Commission				
100 N Union St RSA Union				
PO Box 304260	Montgomery AL	36130	800-392-8050	334-242-5218
Rehabilitation Services Dept				
602 S Lawrence St	Montgomery AL	36104	800-441-7607	334-293-7500
Securities Commission				
770 Washington Ave Ste 570	Montgomery AL	36130	800-222-1253	334-242-2984
State Legislature				
State House 11 S Union St	Montgomery AL	36130	800-499-3051	334-242-7600
State Parks Div				
64 N Union St	Montgomery AL	36130	800-252-7275	
Tourism Department				
401 Adams Ave PO Box 4927	Montgomery AL	36104	800-252-2262	334-242-4169

339-2 Alaska

			Toll-Free	Phone
Banking Securities & Corporations Div				
333 Willoughby Ave Fl 9 PO Box 110807	Juneau AK	99801	888-925-2521	907-465-2521
Commission on Postsecondary Education				
PO Box 110510	Juneau AK	99811	800-441-2962	907-465-2962
Enterprise Technology Services Div				
PO Box 110206	Juneau AK	99811	888-565-8680	
Housing Finance Corp				
4300 Boniface Pkwy 99504				
PO Box 101020	Anchorage AK	99504	800-478-2432	907-338-6100
Military & Veterans Affairs Dept (DMVA)				
PO Box 5800	Fort Richardson AK	99505	888-248-3682	907-428-6896
Postsecondary Education Commission				
3030 Vintage Blvd PO Box 110510	Juneau AK	99801	800-441-2962	907-465-2962
Vocational Rehabilitation Div				
801 W Tenth St Ste 200	Juneau AK	99801	800-478-2815	907-465-2814

339-3 Arizona

			Toll-Free	Phone
Attorney General				
1275 W Washington St	Phoenix AZ	85007	888-377-6108	602-542-5025
Children Youth & Families Div				
1789 W Jefferson St	Phoenix AZ	85007	866-229-5553	602-542-0419
Historic Preservation Office				
1300 W Washington St	Phoenix AZ	85007	800-285-3703	602-542-4174
Legislature				
Capitol Complex 1700 W Washington St	Phoenix AZ	85007	800-352-8404	602-926-3559
Motor Vehicle Div				
PO Box 2100	Phoenix AZ	85001	800-251-5866	602-255-0072
Rehabilitation Services Admin				
1789 W Jefferson St 2nd Fl NW	Phoenix AZ	85007	800-563-1221	602-542-3332
Tourism Office				
1110 W Washington St Ste 155	Phoenix AZ	85007	888-520-3434	602-364-3700
Treasurer				
1700 W Washington St 1st Fl	Phoenix AZ	85007	877-365-8310	602-542-7800
Weights & Measures Dept				
4425 W Olive Ave Ste 134	Glendale AZ	85302	800-277-6675	602-771-4920

339-4 Arkansas

			Toll-Free	Phone
Attorney General				
323 Ctr St Ste 200	Little Rock AR	72201	800-482-8982*	501-682-2007
*Consumer Info				
Child Support Enforcement Office				
1509 W Seventh St	Little Rock AR	72201	800-264-2445	501-682-8398
Crime Victims Reparations Board				
323 Ctr St Ste 200	Little Rock AR	72201	800-448-3014	501-682-1020
Ethics Commission				
PO Box 1917	Little Rock AR	72203	800-422-7773	501-324-9600
Financial Aid Office				
114 Silas Hunt Hall	Fayetteville AR	72701	800-547-8839	479-575-3806
Game & Fish Commission				
2 Natural Resource Dr	Little Rock AR	72205	800-364-4263	501-223-6300
Highway & Transportation Dept				
10324 I- 30	Little Rock AR	72209	800-245-1672	501-569-2000

			Toll-Free	Phone
Insurance Dept				
1200 W Third St	Little Rock AR	72201	800-282-9134	501-371-2600
Parks & Tourism Dept				
1 Capitol Mall	Little Rock AR	72201	800-628-8725	501-682-7777
Rehabilitation Services				
525 W Capitol Ave	Little Rock AR	72201	800-330-0632	501-296-1600
Securities Dept				
201 E Markham St Rm 300	Little Rock AR	72201	800-981-4429	501-324-9260
Vital Records Div				
4815 W Markham St Slot 44	Little Rock AR	72205	800-637-9314	501-661-2000
Worker's Compensation Commission				
PO Box 950	Little Rock AR	72203	800-622-4472	501-682-3930

339-5 California

			Toll-Free	Phone
Arts Council				
1300 'I' St Ste 930	Sacramento CA	95814	800-201-6201	916-322-6555
Child Support Services Dept				
PO Box 419064	Sacramento CA	95741	866-901-3212	916-464-5000
Corporations Dept				
1515 K St Ste 200	Sacramento CA	95814	866-275-2677	916-445-7205
Corrections Dept				
PO Box 942883	Sacramento CA	94283	877-256-6877	
Fair Political Practices Commission				
428 J St Ste 620	Sacramento CA	95814	866-275-3772	916-322-5660
Fish & Game Dept				
1416 Ninth St 12th Fl	Sacramento CA	95814	888-334-2258	916-445-0411
Health Care Services Dept				
PO Box 997413 MS 8502	Sacramento CA	95899	800-735-2929	
Housing Finance Agency				
500 Capitol Mall Ste 1400	Sacramento CA	95814	877-922-5432	916-322-3991
Parks & Recreation Dept				
PO Box 942896	Sacramento CA	94296	800-777-0369	916-653-6995
Public Utilities Commission				
505 Van Ness Ave	San Francisco CA	94102	800-848-5580	415-703-2782
Student Aid Commission				
PO Box 419027	Rancho Cordova CA	95741	888-224-7268	916-526-8999
Teacher Credentialing Commission				
1900 Capitol Ave	Sacramento CA	95814	888-921-2682	916-445-7254
Veterans Affairs Dept				
1227 'O' St	Sacramento CA	95814	800-221-8998	916-653-2158
Victim Compensation Program				
PO Box 3036	Sacramento CA	95812	800-777-9229	

339-6 Colorado

			Toll-Free	Phone
Aging & Adult Services Div				
1575 Sherman St Ground Fl	Denver CO	80203	800-773-1366	303-866-2636
CollegeInvest				
1560 Broadway Ste 1700	Denver CO	80202	800-448-2424	303-376-8800
Housing & Finance Authority				
1981 Blake St	Denver CO	80202	800-877-2432	303-297-2432
Labor & Employment Dept				
633 17th St Ste 201	Denver CO	80203	800-390-7936	303-318-8000
Lottery				
212 W Third St Ste 210	Pueblo CO	81003	800-999-2959	719-546-2400
Natural Resources Dept				
1313 Sherman St Rm 718	Denver CO	80203	800-536-5308	303-866-3311
Parks & Outdoor Recreation Div				
1313 Sherman St Rm 618	Denver CO	80203	800-678-2267*	303-866-3437
*Campground Resv				
Public Health & Environment Dept (CDPHE)				
4300 Cherry Creek Dr S	Denver CO	80246	800-886-7689	303-692-2000
Public Utilities Commission				
1560 Broadway Ste 250	Denver CO	80203	800-888-0170	303-894-2000
Regulatory Agencies Dept				
1560 Broadway Ste 1550	Denver CO	80202	800-886-7675	303-894-7855
State Court Administrator				
1301 Pennsylvania St Ste 300	Denver CO	80203	800-888-0001	303-837-3668
Supreme Court				
1560 Broadway Ste 1800	Denver CO	80202	877-888-1370	303-866-6400
Victims Programs Office				
700 Kipling St Ste 1000	Lakewood CO	80215	888-282-1080	303-239-5719
Vocational Rehabilitation Div				
1575 Sherman St 4th Fl	Denver CO	80203	866-870-4595	303-866-4150
Workers Compensation Div				
633 17th St Ste 400	Denver CO	80202	888-390-7936	303-318-8700

339-7 Connecticut

			Toll-Free	Phone
Banking Dept				
260 Constitution Plaza	Hartford CT	06103	800-831-7225	860-240-8299
Chief Medical Examiner				
11 Shuttle Rd	Farmington CT	06032	800-842-1508	860-679-3980
Consumer Protection Dept				
165 Capitol Ave	Hartford CT	06106	800-842-2649	860-713-6100
Emergency Management & Homeland Security Div				
25 Sigourney St 6th Fl	Hartford CT	06106	800-397-8876	860-256-0800
Higher Education Dept				
61 Woodland St	Hartford CT	06105	800-842-0229	860-947-1800
Public Utility Control Dept				
10 Franklin Sq	New Britain CT	06051	800-382-4586	860-827-2935
Real Estate & Professional Trades Div				
165 Capitol Ave	Hartford CT	06106	800-842-2649	860-713-6100
Rehabilitation Services Bureau				
25 Sigourney St 11th Fl	Hartford CT	06106	800-537-2549	860-424-4844
State Parks Div 79 Elm St	Hartford CT	06106	866-287-2757	860-424-3000
Veterans Affairs Dept				
287 W St	Rocky Hill CT	06067	800-447-0961	860-721-5891

				Toll-Free	Phone
Victim Services Office					
225 Spring St 4th Fl	Wethersfield	CT	06109	**800-822-8428**	
Weights & Measures Div					
165 Capitol Ave	Hartford	CT	06106	**800-842-2649**	860-713-6100
Workers Compensation Commission					
21 Oak St 4th Fl	Hartford	CT	06106	**800-223-9675**	860-493-1500

339-8 Delaware

				Toll-Free	Phone
Agriculture Dept					
2320 S DuPont Hwy	Dover	DE	19901	**800-282-8685**	302-739-4811
Child Support Enforcement Div (DCSE)					
84A Christiana Rd	New Castle	DE	19720	**800-464-4357**	302-577-7171
Emergency Management Agency					
165 Brick Store Landing Rd	Smyrna	DE	19977	**877-729-3362**	302-659-3362
Parks & Recreation Div					
89 Kings Hwy	Dover	DE	19901	**877-987-2757***	302-739-9200
*Campground Resv					
Tourism Office 99 Kings Hwy	Dover	DE	19901	**866-284-7483**	302-739-4271
Weights & Measures Office					
2320 S DuPont Hwy	Dover	DE	19901	**800-282-8685**	302-739-4811

339-9 District of Columbia

				Toll-Free	Phone
Convention & Tourism Corp					
901 7th St NW 4th Fl	Washington	DC	20001	**800-422-8644**	202-789-7000
Tuition Assistance Grant Program					
810 First St NE	Washington	DC	20001	**877-485-6751**	202-727-2824

339-10 Florida

				Toll-Free	Phone
Attorney General					
State Capitol PL-01	Tallahassee	FL	32399	**866-966-7226**	850-487-1963
Bill Status					
111 W Madison St Rm 704	Tallahassee	FL	32399	**800-342-1827**	850-488-4371
Business & Professional Regulation Dept					
1940 N Monroe St	Tallahassee	FL	32399	**866-532-1440**	850-487-1395
Consumer Services Div					
2005 Apalachee Pkwy	Tallahassee	FL	32399	**800-435-7352**	
Education Dept					
325 W Gaines St Ste 1514	Tallahassee	FL	32399	**800-445-6739**	850-245-0505
Financial Services Dept					
200 E Gaines St	Tallahassee	FL	32399	**800-342-2762**	850-413-3100
Insurance Regulation Office					
200 E Gaines St	Tallahassee	FL	32301	**800-342-2762**	850-413-3140
Recreation & Parks Div					
3900 Commonwealth Blvd MS 500	Tallahassee	FL	32399	**800-326-3521***	850-245-2157
*Campground Resv					
Secretary of State					
RA Gray Bldg 500 S Bronough St	Tallahassee	FL	32399	**800-955-8771**	850-245-6500
Student Financial Assistance Office					
1940 N Monroe St Ste 70	Tallahassee	FL	32303	**888-827-2004**	850-410-5200
Vocational Rehabilitation Services Div					
2002 Old St Augustine Rd Bldg A	Tallahassee	FL	32301	**800-451-4327**	850-245-3399

339-11 Georgia

				Toll-Free	Phone
State Government Information					
7 Martin Luther King JrDr Ste 643	Atlanta	GA	30303	**800-436-7442**	678-436-7442
Arts Council					
260 14th St NW Ste 401	Atlanta	GA	30318	**800-222-6006**	404-685-2400
Corrections Dept					
300 Patrol Rd Forsyth	Atlanta	GA	31029	**888-343-5627**	404-656-4661
Emergency Management Agency (GEMA)					
935 E Confederate Ave SE PO Box 18055	Atlanta	GA	30316	**800-879-4362**	404-635-7000
Environmental Protection Div					
2 Martin Luther King Jr Dr					
Ste 1152 E Tower	Atlanta	GA	30334	**888-373-5947**	404-657-5947
Governor's Office of Consumer Protection					
2 ML King Jr Dr Ste 356	Atlanta	GA	30334	**800-869-1123**	
Ports Authority					
PO Box 2406	Savannah	GA	31402	**800-342-8012**	912-964-3811
Securities & Business Regulation Div					
2 Martin Luther King Jr Dr					
W Tower Ste 802	Atlanta	GA	30334	**844-753-7825**	478-207-2440
Student Finance Commission					
2082 E Exchange Pl Ste 200	Tucker	GA	30084	**800-505-4732**	770-724-9000
Tourism Div					
75 Fifth St NW Ste 1200	Atlanta	GA	30308	**800-255-0056***	404-962-4000
*Resv					
Transparency & Campaign Finance Commission					
200 Piedmont Ave SE Ste 1402	Atlanta	GA	30334	**866-589-7327**	404-463-1980

339-12 Hawaii

				Toll-Free	Phone
Child Support Enforcement Agency					
601 Kamokila Blvd Ste 251	Kapolei	HI	96707	**888-317-9081**	
Postsecondary Education Commission					
2444 Dole St Bachman Hall Rm 209	Honolulu	HI	96822	**877-531-2333**	808-956-8213
Taxation Dept					
830 Punchbowl St Rm 221	Honolulu	HI	96813	**800-222-3229**	808-587-4242
Vocational Rehabilitation Div					
1901 Bachelot St	Honolulu	HI	96817	**800-316-8005**	808-586-9744

339-13 Idaho

				Toll-Free	Phone
Aging Commission (ICOA)					
341 W Washington Fl 3 PO Box 83720	Boise	ID	83702	**800-926-2588**	208-334-3833
Arts Commission					
2410 Old Penitentiary Rd	Boise	ID	83712	**800-278-3863**	208-334-2119
Board of Medicine					
1755 N Westgate Dr Ste 140 PO Box 83720	Boise	ID	83704	**800-333-0073**	208-327-7000
Commerce Dept					
700 W State St PO Box 83720	Boise	ID	83720	**800-842-5858**	208-334-2470
Crime Victims Compensation Program					
PO Box 83720	Boise	ID	83720	**800-950-2110**	208-334-6000
Homeland Security Bureau					
4040 W Guard St Bldg 600	Boise	ID	83705	**800-344-0984**	208-422-3040
Housing & Finance Assn					
565 W Myrtle Ave	Boise	ID	83702	**800-526-7145**	208-331-4882
Lottery					
1199 Shoreline Ln Ste 100	Boise	ID	83702	**800-432-5688**	208-334-2600
Parks & Recreation Dept					
5657 Warm Springs Ave	Boise	ID	83716	**855-514-2429**	
Public Utilities Commission					
PO Box 83720	Boise	ID	83720	**800-432-0369**	208-334-0300
Real Estate Commission					
575 E Parkcenter Blvd Ste 180	Boise	ID	83706	**866-447-5411**	208-334-3285
Tax Commission 800 E Pk Blvd	Boise	ID	83712	**800-972-7660**	208-334-7660
Tourism Development Div					
700 W State St PO Box 83720	Boise	ID	83720	**800-847-4843***	208-334-2470
*General					

339-14 Illinois

				Toll-Free	Phone
Child Support Enforcement Div					
509 S Sixth St	Springfield	IL	62701	**800-447-4278**	
Crime Victims Services Div					
100 W Randolf Rd 13th Fl	Chicago	IL	60601	**800-228-3368**	312-814-2581
Human Services Dept					
100 S Grand Ave E 3rd Fl	Springfield	IL	62762	**800-843-6154**	217-557-1601
Lottery					
101 W Jefferson St	Springfield	IL	62702	**800-252-1775**	217-524-6435
Mental Health Div					
100 W Randolf St Ste 3-400	Chicago	IL	60601	**800-252-2923**	312-814-2811
Revenue Dept					
101 W Jefferson St	Springfield	IL	62702	**800-732-8866**	217-782-3336
Secretary of State					
213 State Capitol	Springfield	IL	62756	**800-252-8980**	217-782-2201
Student Assistance Commission					
1755 Lake Cook Rd	Deerfield	IL	60015	**800-899-4722**	847-948-8500
Tourism Bureau					
100 W Randolph St Ste 3-400	Chicago	IL	60601	**800-226-6632**	312-814-4732
Veterans Affairs Dept					
James R. Thompson Ctr 100 W Randolph					
Ste 5-570	Chicago	IL	60601	**800-437-9824**	312-814-5391
Workers Compensation Commission					
100 W Randolph St 8th Fl	Chicago	IL	60601	**866-352-3033**	312-814-6611

339-15 Indiana

				Toll-Free	Phone
State Government Information					
402 W Washington St Rm W160A	Indianapolis	IN	46204	**800-457-8283**	317-233-0800
Child Support Bureau					
402 W Washington St	Indianapolis	IN	46204	**800-840-8757**	317-232-2350
Consumer Protection Div					
402 W Washington St 5th Fl	Indianapolis	IN	46204	**800-382-5516**	317-232-6330
Disability Aging & Rehabilitative Services Div					
402 W Washington St Rm W451	Indianapolis	IN	46204	**800-545-7763**	317-232-1147
Environmental Management Dept					
100 N Senate Ave Rm 1301	Indianapolis	IN	46204	**800-451-6027**	317-232-8611
General Assembly					
State House 200 W Washington St	Indianapolis	IN	46204	**800-382-9842**	317-232-9600
Insurance Dept					
311 W Washington St Ste 300	Indianapolis	IN	46204	**800-622-4461***	317-232-2385
*Cust Svc					
Lottery					
201 S Capitol Ave Ste 1100	Indianapolis	IN	46225	**800-955-6886**	317-264-4800
Port Commission					
150 W Market St Ste 100	Indianapolis	IN	46204	**800-232-7678**	317-232-9200
State Parks & Reservoirs Div					
402 W Washington St Rm W298	Indianapolis	IN	46204	**800-622-4931**	317-232-4124
Students Assistance Commission					
150 W Market St Ste 500	Indianapolis	IN	46204	**888-528-4719**	317-232-2350
Tourism Development Office					
1 N Capitol Ave Ste 100	Indianapolis	IN	46204	**800-457-8283**	317-232-8860
Victims Services Div					
101 West Washington Street					
Suite 1170	East Tower Indianapolis	IN	46204	**800-353-1484**	317-232-1233
Workforce Development Dept					
10 N Senate Ave	Indianapolis	IN	46204	**800-891-6499**	317-232-7670

339-16 Iowa

				Toll-Free	Phone
Adult Children & Family Services Div					
1305 E Walnut St	Des Moines	IA	50319	**800-735-2942**	15--281--3094
Child Support Recovery Unit					
PO Box 9125	Des Moines	IA	50306	**888-229-9223**	
Consumer Protection Div					
1305 E Walnut St 2nd Fl	Des Moines	IA	50319	**888-777-4590**	515-281-5926

				Toll-Free	Phone
Elder Affairs Dept					
510 E 12th Street Ste 2	Des Moines	IA	50309	800-532-3213	515-242-3333
Motor Vehicle Div					
100 Euclid Ave PO Box 9204	Des Moines	IA	50306	800-532-1121	515-244-9124
Revenue & Finance Dept					
1305 E Walnut	Des Moines	IA	50319	800-367-3388	515-281-3204
Utilities Board					
1375 E Ct Ave Rm 69	Des Moines	IA	50319	877-565-4450	515-725-7300
Workforce Development					
1000 E Grand Ave	Des Moines	IA	50319	800-562-4692	515-281-5387

339-17 Kansas

				Toll-Free	Phone
Consumer Protection Div					
534 S Kansas Ave Ste 1210	Topeka	KS	66603	800-452-6727	785-296-5059
Healing Arts Board					
800 SW Jackson Lower Level Ste A	Topeka	KS	66612	888-886-7205	785-296-7413
Insurance Dept					
420 SW Ninth St	Topeka	KS	66612	800-432-2484	785-296-3071
Lottery 128 N Kansas Ave	Topeka	KS	66603	800-544-9467	785-296-5700
Travel & Tourism Development Div					
1020 S Kansas Ave Ste 200	Topeka	KS	66612	800-252-6727	785-296-2009
Treasurer					
900 SW Jackson St Ste 201	Topeka	KS	66612	800-432-0386	785-296-3171
Workers Compensation Div					
401 SW Topeka Blvd Ste 2	Topeka	KS	66603	800-332-0353	785-296-4000

339-18 Kentucky

				Toll-Free	Phone
State Government Information					
229 W Main St Ste 400	Frankfort	KY	40601	877-855-3573	502-875-3733
Arts Council					
500 Mero St 21st Fl Capital Plaza Tower	Frankfort	KY	40601	888-833-2787	502-564-3757
Child Support Div					
730 Schenkel Ln	Frankfort	KY	40601	800-248-1163	502-564-2285
Consumer Protection Div					
1024 Capital Ctr Dr Ste 200	Frankfort	KY	40601	888-432-9257	502-696-5389
Crime Victims Compensation Board					
130 Brighton Pk Blvd	Frankfort	KY	40601	800-469-2120	502-573-2290
Education Professional Standards Board					
100 Airport Dr 3rd Fl	Frankfort	KY	40601	888-598-7667	502-564-4606
Financial Institutions Dept					
1025 Capital Ctr Dr Ste 200	Frankfort	KY	40601	800-223-2579	502-573-3390
Fish & Wildlife Resources Dept					
1 Game Farm Rd	Frankfort	KY	40601	800-858-1549	502-564-3400
General Assembly					
700 Capitol Ave State Capitol Bldg	Frankfort	KY	40601	800-372-7181	502-564-8100
Higher Education Assistance Authority					
100 Airport Rd	Frankfort	KY	40602	800-928-8926	
Historical Society					
100 W Broadway	Frankfort	KY	40601	877-444-7867	502-564-1792
Housing Corp					
1231 Louisville Rd	Frankfort	KY	40601	800-633-8896	502-564-7630
Insurance Dept					
215 W Main St	Frankfort	KY	40602	800-595-6053	502-564-3630
Lottery Corp					
1011 W Main St	Louisville	KY	40202	800-937-8946	502-560-1500
Public Service Commission					
PO Box 615	Frankfort	KY	40602	800-772-4636	502-564-3940
Real Estate Commission (KREC)					
10200 Linn Stn Rd Ste 201	Louisville	KY	40223	888-373-3300*	502-429-7250
*General					
Travel & Tourism Dept					
500 Mero St Ste 2200	Frankfort	KY	40601	800-225-8747	502-564-4930
Veterans Affairs Dept (KDVA)					
1111B Louisville Rd	Frankfort	KY	40601	800-572-6245	502-564-9203
Vocational Rehabilitation Dept					
275 E Main St MS 2E-K	Frankfort	KY	40601	800-372-7172	502-564-4440
Workers Claims Dept (DWC)					
657 Chamberlin Ave	Frankfort	KY	40601	800-554-8601	502-564-5550

339-19 Louisiana

				Toll-Free	Phone
Community Services Office					
627 N 4th St	Baton Rouge	LA	70802	888-524-3578	
Consumer Protection Office					
PO Box 94095	Baton Rouge	LA	70804	800-351-4889	
Department of Education					
1201 N Third St PO Box 94064	Baton Rouge	LA	70802	877-453-2721	
Education Dept					
PO Box 94064	Baton Rouge	LA	70804	877-453-2721	
Environmental Quality Dept					
602 N Fifth St	Baton Rouge	LA	70802	866-896-5337	225-219-5337
Ethics Board					
617 N Third St LaSalle Bldg Ste 10-36	Baton Rouge	LA	70802	800-842-6630	225-219-5600
Housing Finance Agency					
2415 Quail Dr	Baton Rouge	LA	70808	888-454-2001	225-763-8700
Insurance Dept					
PO Box 94214	Baton Rouge	LA	70804	800-259-5300	225-342-5900
Legislature					
PO Box 94062	Baton Rouge	LA	70804	800-256-3793	225-342-2456
Office of Student Financial Assistance					
602 N Fifth St PO Box 91202	Baton Rouge	LA	70802	800-259-5626	225-219-1012
Office of the Governor					
PO Box 94004	Baton Rouge	LA	70804	866-366-1121	225-342-7015
Public Service Commission					
PO Box 91154	Baton Rouge	LA	70821	800-256-2397	225-342-4404

				Toll-Free	Phone
Real Estate Commission					
PO Box 14785	Baton Rouge	LA	70898	800-821-4529	225-765-0191
State Parks Office					
PO Box 44426	Baton Rouge	LA	70804	888-677-1400	225-342-8111
Veterans Affairs Dept					
PO Box 94095	Baton Rouge	LA	70804	877-432-8982	225-219-5000
Wildlife & Fisheries Dept					
PO Box 98000	Baton Rouge	LA	70898	800-442-2511	225-765-2800
Workforce Commission					
1001 N 23rd St	Baton Rouge	LA	70802	877-529-6757	225-342-3111

339-20 Maine

				Toll-Free	Phone
State Government Information					
26 Edison Dr	Augusta	ME	04330	888-577-6690	207-624-9494
Consumer Protection Unit					
6 State House Stn	Augusta	ME	04333	800-436-2131	207-626-8849
Economic & Community Development Dept					
59 State House Stn	Augusta	ME	04333	800-541-5872	207-624-9800
Elder Services Office					
11 Statehouse Stn	Augusta	ME	04333	800-624-8404	
Environmental Protection Dept					
17 State House Stn	Augusta	ME	04333	800-452-1942	207-287-7688
Finance Authority					
5 Community Dr PO Box 949	Augusta	ME	04332	800-228-3734	207-623-3263
Financial Institutions Bureau					
35 Anthony Ave 11 State House Stn	Augusta	ME	04333	800-452-1926	207-624-8090
Governor 1 State House Stn	Augusta	ME	04333	888-577-6690	207-287-3531
Insurance Bureau					
34 State House Stn	Augusta	ME	04333	800-300-5000	207-624-8475
Rehabilitation Services Bureau					
150 State House Stn	Augusta	ME	04333	800-698-4440	

339-21 Maryland

				Toll-Free	Phone
State Government Information					
State House	Annapolis	MD	21401	800-811-8336	410-974-3901
Assessments & Taxation Dept					
301 W Preston St 8th Fl	Baltimore	MD	21201	888-246-5941	410-767-1184
Budget & Management Dept					
45 Calvert St	Annapolis	MD	21401	800-705-3493	
Court of Appeals					
361 Rowe Blvd 4th Fl	Annapolis	MD	21401	800-926-2583	410-260-1500
Criminal Injuries Compensation Board					
6776 Reisterstown Rd Ste 206	Baltimore	MD	21215	888-679-9347	410-585-3010
Education Dept					
200 W Baltimore St	Baltimore	MD	21201	888-246-0016	410-767-0100
Emergency Management Agency					
5401 Rue St Lo Dr	Reisterstown	MD	21136	877-636-2872	410-517-3600
Environment Dept					
1800 Washington Blvd	Baltimore	MD	21230	800-633-6101	410-537-3000
Ethics Commission					
45 Calvert St 3rd Fl	Annapolis	MD	21401	877-669-6085	410-260-7770
Higher Education Commission					
839 Bestgate Rd Ste 400	Annapolis	MD	21401	800-974-0203	410-260-4500
Housing & Community Development Dept					
100 Community Pl	Crownsville	MD	21032	800-756-0119	
Insurance Administration					
525 St Paul Pl	Baltimore	MD	21202	800-492-6116	410-468-2000
Legislative Services Dept					
90 State Cir	Annapolis	MD	21401	800-492-7122	410-946-5400
Natural Resources Dept					
580 Taylor Ave	Annapolis	MD	21401	877-620-8367	410-260-8021
Parole & Probation Div					
6776 Reisterstown Rd	Baltimore	MD	21215	877-227-8031	410-585-3500
Physician Quality Assurance Board					
4201 Patterson Ave	Baltimore	MD	21215	800-492-6836	410-764-4777
Public Service Commission					
6 St Paul St 16th Fl	Baltimore	MD	21202	800-492-0474	410-767-8000
State Forest & Park Service					
580 Taylor Ave Rm E-3	Annapolis	MD	21401	877-620-8367*	410-260-8186
*Campground Resv					
State Police					
1201 Reisterstown Rd	Pikesville	MD	21208	800-525-5555	410-653-4200
Teacher Certification & Accreditation Div					
200 W Baltimore St	Baltimore	MD	21201	866-772-8922	410-767-0412
Tourism Development Office					
217 E Redwood St 9th Fl	Baltimore	MD	21202	800-543-1036	410-767-3400
Treasurer					
80 Calvert St Rm 109	Annapolis	MD	21401	800-974-0468	410-260-7533
Veterans Affairs Dept					
31 Hopkins Plaza Rm 1231	Baltimore	MD	21201	800-446-4926	410-230-4444
Vital Records Div					
6550 Reisterstown Rd	Baltimore	MD	21215	800-832-3277	410-764-3038

339-22 Massachusetts

				Toll-Free	Phone
Banks Div					
1000 Washington St Ste 710	Boston	MA	02118	800-495-2265	617-956-1501
Bill Status					
1 Ashburton Pl Rm 1611	Boston	MA	02108	800-392-6090	617-727-7030
Child Support Enforcement Div					
51 Sleeper St 4th Fl	Boston	MA	02205	800-332-2733	617-660-1234
Executive Office of Transportation					
10 Pk Plaza Ste 3170	Boston	MA	02116	800-219-9936	617-973-7000
Insurance Div					
1000 Washington St Ste 810	Boston	MA	02118	877-563-4467	617-521-7794
Parole Board 12 Mercer Rd	Natick	MA	01760	888-298-6272	508-650-4500
Revenue Dept PO Box 7010	Boston	MA	02204	800-392-6089	617-626-2201

					Toll-Free	Phone
Travel & Tourism Office						
10 Pk Plaza Ste 4510	Boston	MA	02116		800-227-6277	617-973-8500

339-23 Michigan

					Toll-Free	Phone
Attorney General						
525 W Ottawa St	Lansing	MI	48933		877-765-8388	517-373-1110
Career Education & Workforce Programs						
201 N Washington Sq						
Victor Office Center	Lansing	MI	48913		888-253-6855	517-335-5858
Child Support Office						
235 S Grand Ave PO Box 30037	Lansing	MI	48933		866-661-0005	
Civil Service Dept						
Capitol Commons Ctr 400 S Pine St	Lansing	MI	48913		800-788-1766	517-373-3030
Community Health Dept						
Capitol View Bldg 201 Townsend St	Lansing	MI	48913		800-649-3777	517-373-3740
Crime Victims Services Commission						
320 S Walnut St Garden Level						
Lewis Cass Bldg	Lansing	MI	48913		877-251-7373	
Economic Development Corp (MEDC)						
300 N Washington Sq	Lansing	MI	48913		888-522-0103	517-373-9808
Education Trust						
PO Box 30198	Lansing	MI	48909		800-638-4543*	517-335-4767
*General						
eLibrary Information						
702 W Kalamazoo St PO Box 30007	Lansing	MI	48909		877-479-0021	517-373-4331
Financial & Insurance Regulation						
PO Box 30220	Lansing	MI	48909		877-999-6442	517-373-0220
Parks & Recreation Div						
PO Box 30257	Lansing	MI	48909		800-447-2757*	517-373-9900
*Campground Resv						
Student Financial Services Bureau						
Austin Bldg 430 W Allegan	Lansing	MI	48922		800-642-5626*	888-447-2687
*General						
Travel Michigan						
300 N Washington Sq	Lansing	MI	48913		888-784-7328	517-373-0670

339-24 Minnesota

					Toll-Free	Phone
Aging Board 540 Cedar St	Saint Paul	MN	55155		800-882-6262	651-431-2500
Arts Board						
400 Sibley St Ste 200	Saint Paul	MN	55101		800-866-2787	651-215-1600
Attorney General						
1400 Bremer Tower 445 Minnesota St	Saint Paul	MN	55101		800-657-3787	651-296-3353
Attorney General's Office						
445 Minnesota St Ste 1400	Saint Paul	MN	55101		800-657-3787	651-296-3353
Campaign Finance & Public Disclosure Board						
658 Cedar St Ste 190	Saint Paul	MN	55155		800-657-3889	651-296-5148
Employment & Economic Development Dept (DEED)						
1st National Bank Bldg 332 Minnesota St						
Ste E200	Saint Paul	MN	55101		800-657-3858	651-259-7114
Finance Dept						
658 Cedar St Ste 400	Saint Paul	MN	55155		800-627-3529	651-201-8000
Governor						
130 State Capitol						
75 Rev Dr Martin Luther King Jr Blvd	Saint Paul	MN	55155		800-657-3717	651-201-3400
Health Dept PO Box 64975	Saint Paul	MN	55164		888-345-0823	651-201-5000
Historical Society						
345 Kellogg Blvd W	Saint Paul	MN	55102		800-657-3773	651-259-3000
Housing Finance Authority						
400 Sibley St Ste 300	Saint Paul	MN	55101		800-657-3769	651-296-7608
Labor & Industry Dept						
443 Lafayette Rd N	Saint Paul	MN	55155		800-342-5354	651-284-5005
Legislature						
75 Constitution Ave State Capitol	Saint Paul	MN	55155		800-657-3550	651-296-2146
Medical Practice Board						
2829 University Ave SE Ste 500	Minneapolis	MN	55414		800-657-3709	612-617-2130
Natural Resources Dept						
500 Lafayette Rd	Saint Paul	MN	55155		888-646-6367	651-296-6157
Office of Higher Education						
1450 Energy Pk Dr Ste 350	Saint Paul	MN	55108		800-657-3866	651-642-0567
Parks & Recreation Div						
500 Lafayette Rd	Saint Paul	MN	55155		888-646-6367	651-296-6157
Public Utilities Commission						
121 Seventh Pl E Ste 350	Saint Paul	MN	55101		800-657-3782	651-296-7124
Revenue Dept						
600 N Roberts St	Saint Paul	MN	55101		800-652-9094	651-296-3403
Transportation Dept						
395 John Ireland Blvd	Saint Paul	MN	55155		800-657-3774	651-296-3000
Workers Compensation Div						
443 Lafayette Rd	Saint Paul	MN	55155		800-342-5354	651-284-5005

339-25 Mississippi

					Toll-Free	Phone
State Government Information						
200 S Lamar Ste 800	Jackson	MS	39201		877-290-9487	601-351-5023
Banking & Consumer Finance Dept						
PO Box 23729	Jackson	MS	39225		800-844-2499	601-359-1031
Child Support Enforcement Div						
750 N State St	Jackson	MS	39202		800-345-6347	601-359-4929
Consumer Protection Div						
PO Box 22947	Jackson	MS	39225		800-281-4418	601-359-4230
Contractors Board						
215 Woodline Dr Ste B	Jackson	MS	39232		800-880-6161	601-354-6161
Emergency Management Agency						
PO Box 5644	Pearl	MS	39288		800-222-6362	601-933-6362
Employment Security Commission						
1235 Echelon Pkwy PO Box 1699	Jackson	MS	39215		888-844-3577	601-321-6000
Family & Children Services Div						
750 N State St	Jackson	MS	39202		800-345-6347	601-359-4570
Higher Learning Institutions Board of Trustees						
3825 Ridgewood Rd Ste 915	Jackson	MS	39211		800-327-2980	601-432-6198
Insurance Dept						
1001 Woolfolk State Office Bldg 501 NW St						
PO Box 79	Jackson	MS	39201		800-562-2957	601-359-3569
Rehabilitation Services Dept						
1281 Highway 51 PO Box 1698	Madison	MS	39110		800-443-1000	
Student Financial Aid Office						
3825 Ridgewood Rd	Jackson	MS	39211		800-327-2980	601-432-6997

339-26 Missouri

					Toll-Free	Phone
Child Support Enforcement Div						
PO Box 109002	Jefferson City	MO	65102		800-859-7999	
Consumer Protection Div						
207 W High St PO Box 899	Jefferson City	MO	65102		800-392-8222	573-751-3321
Elementary & Secondary Education Dept						
205 Jefferson St PO Box 480	Jefferson City	MO	65101		800-735-2966	573-751-4212
Finance Div						
PO Box 716	Jefferson City	MO	65102		888-246-7225	573-751-3242
Higher Education Dept						
3515 Amazonas Dr	Jefferson City	MO	65109		800-473-6757	573-751-2361
Natural Resources Dept						
PO Box 176	Jefferson City	MO	65102		800-361-4827*	573-751-3443
*Cust Svc						
Professional Registration Div						
3605 Missouri Blvd PO Box 1335	Jefferson City	MO	65102		800-735-2966	573-751-0293
Public Service Commission						
200 Madison St PO Box 360	Jefferson City	MO	65102		800-819-3180	573-751-3234
Securities Div						
600 W Main St PO Box 1276	Jefferson City	MO	65102		800-721-7996	573-751-4704
State Courts Administrator						
PO Box 104480	Jefferson City	MO	65110		888-541-4894	
State Parks Div						
PO Box 176	Jefferson City	MO	65102		800-334-6946	573-751-2479
Supreme Court						
207 W High St	Jefferson City	MO	65101		888-541-4894	573-751-4144
Tourism Div						
PO Box 1055	Jefferson City	MO	65102		800-519-2100	573-751-4133
Transportation Dept						
105 W Capitol Ave	Jefferson City	MO	65102		888-275-6636	573-751-2551
Vocational & Adult Education Div						
3024 Dupont Cir PO Box 480	Jefferson City	MO	65109		877-222-8963	573-751-3251
Workers Compensation Div						
PO Box 58	Jefferson City	MO	65102		800-775-2667	573-751-4231

339-27 Montana

					Toll-Free	Phone
Arts Council PO Box 202201	Helena	MT	59620		800-282-3092	406-444-6430
Banking & Financial Institutions Div						
Rm 155 Mitchell Bldg 125 N Roberts St						
PO Box 200101	Helena	MT	59620		800-914-8423	406-841-2920
Child & Family Services Div						
PO Box 8005	Helena	MT	59604		866-820-5437	406-841-2400
Consumer Protection Office						
POBox 200151	Helena	MT	59620		800-481-6896	406-444-4500
Higher Education Board of Regents						
2500 Broadway St PO Box 203201	Helena	MT	59620		877-501-1722	406-444-6570
Information Technology Services Div						
125 N Roberts St	Helena	MT	59601		800-628-4917	406-444-2700
Revenue Dept PO Box 5805	Helena	MT	59604		866-859-2254	406-444-6900
Securities Div						
840 Helena Ave	Helena	MT	59601		800-332-6148	406-444-2040
Victim Services Office						
2225 11th Ave PO Box 201410	Helena	MT	59620		800-498-6455	406-444-1907
Vital Records Bureau						
111 N Sanders St	Helena	MT	59604		888-877-1946	406-444-4228

339-28 Nebraska

					Toll-Free	Phone
Arts Council 1004 Farnam St	Omaha	NE	68131		800-341-4067	402-595-2122
Child Support Enforcement Div						
PO Box 95026	Lincoln	NE	68509		877-631-9973	402-471-3121
Economic Development Dept						
301 Centennial Mall S PO Box 94666	Lincoln	NE	68509		800-426-6505	402-471-3747
Emergency Management Agency						
1300 Military Rd	Lincoln	NE	68508		877-297-2368	402-471-7421
Environmental Quality Dept						
1200 N St Ste 400	Lincoln	NE	68508		877-253-2603	402-471-2186
Health & Human Services Dept						
301 Centennial Mall S	Lincoln	NE	68508		800-430-3244	402-471-3121
Historical Society						
1500 R St	Lincoln	NE	68501		800-833-6747	402-471-3270
Insurance Dept						
941 O St Ste 400	Lincoln	NE	68508		877-564-7323	402-471-2201
Investment Finance Authority						
1230 'O' St Ste 200	Lincoln	NE	68508		800-204-6432	402-434-3900
Public Service Commission						
1200 N St Ste 300	Lincoln	NE	68508		800-526-0017	402-471-3101
Travel & Tourism Div						
PO Box 98907	Lincoln	NE	68509		877-632-7275	402-471-3796
Vocational Rehabilitation Services Div						
3901 N 27th St Ste 6	Lincoln	NE	68521		800-472-3382	402-471-3231
Workers Compensation Court						
1010 Lincoln Mall Ste 100	Lincoln	NE	68508		800-599-5155	402-471-6468

339-29 Nevada

	Toll-Free	Phone
Bill Status		
401 S Carson St .... Carson City NV 89701	800-978-2878	775-684-3360
Child Support Enforcement Office		
1470 College Pkwy .... Carson City NV 89706	800-992-0900	775-684-0500
Economic Development Commission		
808 W Nye Ln .... Carson City NV 89703	800-336-1600	775-687-9900
Motor Vehicles Dept		
555 Wright Way .... Carson City NV 89711	877-368-7828	775-684-4368
Secretary of State		
101 N Carson St Ste 3 .... Carson City NV 89701	800-450-8594	775-684-5708
Tourism Commission		
401 N Carson St .... Carson City NV 89701	800-237-0774	775-687-4322
Welfare Div		
1470 College Pkwy .... Carson City NV 89706	800-992-0900	775-684-0500

339-30 New Hampshire

	Toll-Free	Phone
Banking Dept		
53 Regional Dr Ste 200............ Concord NH 03301	800-437-5991	603-271-3561
Child Support Services		
129 Pleasant St .... Concord NH 03301	800-852-3345	603-271-4427
Employment Security		
32 S Main St .... Concord NH 03301	800-852-3400	603-224-3311
Environmental Services Dept		
29 Hazen Dr PO Box 95 .... Concord NH 03301	800-735-2964	603-271-3503
Housing Finance Authority		
PO Box 5087 .... Manchester NH 03108	800-439-7247	603-472-8623
Lottery Commission		
14 Integra Dr .... Concord NH 03301	800-852-3324	603-271-3391
Postsecondary Education Commission		
64 South Street Ste 300 .... Concord NH 03301	800-735-2964	603-271-2555
Public Utilities Commission		
21 S Fruit St Ste 10 .... Concord NH 03301	800-852-3793*	603-271-2431
*Consumer Assistance		
Travel & Tourism Development Office		
PO Box 1856 .... Concord NH 03302	800-262-6660	603-271-2665
Victims Assistance Commission		
33 Capitol St .... Concord NH 03301	800-300-4500	603-271-1284
Vital Records Administration Div		
71 S Fruit St .... Concord NH 03301	800-735-2964	603-271-4650
Vocational Rehabilitation Office		
21 S Fruit St Ste 20 .... Concord NH 03301	800-299-1647	603-271-3471

339-31 New Jersey

	Toll-Free	Phone
Banking & Insurance Dept		
20 W State St PO Box 325 .... Trenton NJ 08625	800-446-7467	609-292-7272
Bill Status		
State House Annex PO Box 068 ...... Trenton NJ 08625	800-792-8630	609-292-4840
Child Support Office		
175 S Broad St PO Box 8068 .... Trenton NJ 08650	877-655-4371	
Higher Education Student Assistance Authority		
4 Quakerbridge Plaza PO Box 540 ... Trenton NJ 08625	800-792-8670	609-584-4480
Mental Health Services Div		
PO Box 272 .... Trenton NJ 08625	800-382-6717	609-777-0700
Military & Veterans Affairs Dept		
101 Eggert Crossing Rd .... Lawrenceville NJ 08648	800-624-0508	609-530-4600
Motor Vehicle Commission		
225 E State St PO Box 160 .... Trenton NJ 08666	888-486-3339	609-292-6500
Securities Bureau		
153 Halsey St Sixth Fl PO Box 47029.. Newark NJ 07101	866-446-8378	973-504-3600
Travel & Tourism Div		
225 W State St PO Box 460 .... Trenton NJ 08625	800-847-4865	609-599-6540
Victims of Crime Compensation Board		
50 Pk Pl .... Newark NJ 07102	877-658-2221	973-648-2107

339-32 New Mexico

	Toll-Free	Phone
Children Youth & Families Dept		
PO Drawer 5160 .... Santa Fe NM 87502	800-610-7610	800-432-2075
Crime Victims Reparation Commission		
8100 Mountain Rd NE Ste 106 ... Albuquerque NM 87110	800-306-6262	505-841-9432
Economic Development Dept		
PO Box 20003 .... Santa Fe NM 87504	800-374-3061	505-827-0300
Environment Dept		
1190 St Francis Dr Ste 4050. ...... Santa Fe NM 87502	800-219-6157	505-827-2855
Ethics Administration		
325 Don Gaspar St Ste 300 .... Santa Fe NM 87501	800-477-3632	505-827-3600
Financial Aid & Student Services Unit		
2048 Galisteo St .... Santa Fe NM 87505	800-279-9777	505-476-8400
Higher Education Dept		
2048 Galisteo St .... Santa Fe NM 87505	800-279-9777	505-476-8400
Highway & Transportation Dept (NMDOT)		
1120 Cerrillos Rd PO Box 1149 ..... Santa Fe NM 87504	800-432-4269*	505-827-5100
*General		
Lieutenant Governor		
490 Old Santa Fe Trail Rm 417 ..... Santa Fe NM 87501	800-432-4406	505-476-2250
Mortgage Finance Authority		
344 Fourth St SW .... Albuquerque NM 87102	800-444-6880	505-843-6880
Secretary of State		
325 Don Gaspar Ave Ste 300 .... Santa Fe NM 87503	800-477-3632	505-827-3600
Tourism Dept		
491 Old Santa Fe Trail .... Santa Fe NM 87503	800-545-2070	
Veterans Services Dept		
490 Old SF Trail .... Santa Fe NM 87504	866-433-8387	505-827-6300

339-33 New York

	Toll-Free	Phone
Vital Records & Health Statistics Bureau		
1105 S St Francis Dr .... Santa Fe NM 87502	866-534-0051	505-827-0121
Vocational Rehabilitation Div		
435 St Michaels Dr Bldg D .... Santa Fe NM 87505	800-224-7005	505-954-8500
Workers Compensation Admin		
2410 Ctr Ave SE PO Box 27198 .... Albuquerque NM 87125	800-255-7965	505-841-6000

(New York listings)

	Toll-Free	Phone
Aging Office		
2 Empire State Plaza .... Albany NY 12223	800-342-9871	
Athletic Commission		
123 William St 20th Fl .... New York NY 10038	866-269-3769	212-417-5700
Banking Dept 1 State St .... New York NY 10004	877-226-5697	800-342-3736
Bill Status		
202 Legislative Office Bldg .... Albany NY 12248	800-342-9860	518-455-4218
Consumer Protection Div		
5 Empire State Plaza Ste 2101 ...... Albany NY 12223	800-697-1220	518-474-3514
Empire State Development		
30 S Pearl St .... Albany NY 12245	800-782-8369	518-292-5100
Health Dept		
Empire State Plaza Corning II Tower ... Albany NY 12237	866-881-2809	
Higher Education Services Corp		
99 Washington Ave .... Albany NY 12255	888-697-4372	518-473-1574
Historic Preservation Div		
PO Box 189 .... Waterford NY 12188	800-456-2267	518-237-8643
Labor Dept		
WA Harriman Campus Bldg 12 ...... Albany NY 12240	888-469-7365	518-457-9000
Mental Health Office		
44 Holland Ave .... Albany NY 12229	800-597-8481	518-474-4403
Motor Vehicles Dept		
6 Empire State Plaza .... Albany NY 12228	800-368-1186	518-473-5595
Office of Court Admin		
25 Beaver St Rm 852 .... New York NY 10004	800-268-7869	212-428-2100
Parks Recreation & Historic Preservation Office		
1 Empire State Plaza .... Albany NY 12238	800-456-2267*	518-474-0456
*Campground Resv		
Taxation & Finance Dept		
WA Harriman Campus Bldg 9. ...... Albany NY 12227	800-225-5829	518-457-5149
Temporary & Disability Assistance Office		
40 N Pearl St 16th Fl .... Albany NY 12243	800-342-3009	518-473-1090
Tourism Div PO Box 2603 .... Albany NY 12223	800-225-5697	518-473-1064
Veterans' Affairs Dept		
333 E Washington St Ste 430 .... Albany NY 12223	888-838-7697	315-428-4046
Vital Records Office		
PO Box 2602 .... Albany NY 12220	877-854-4481	518-474-3077
Workers Compensation Board		
328 State St .... Schenectady NY 12305	877-632-4996	518-462-8880

339-34 North Carolina

	Toll-Free	Phone
Marine Fisheries Div		
PO Box 769 .... Morehead City NC 28557	800-682-2632	252-726-7021
Parks & Recreation Div		
217 W Jones St 1615 MSC .... Raleigh NC 27604	877-722-6762	919-707-9300
State Ports Authority		
2202 Burnett Blvd PO Box 9002...... Wilmington NC 28402	800-334-0682	910-763-1621
Tourism Div		
301 N Wilmington St .... Raleigh NC 27601	800-847-4862	919-733-4171
Transportation Dept		
1 S Wilmington St .... Raleigh NC 27611	877-368-4968	
Utilities Commission		
4325 Mail Service Ctr .... Raleigh NC 27699	866-380-9816	919-733-7328
Victims Compensation Services Div		
4232 Mail Service Ctr .... Raleigh NC 27699	800-826-6200	919-733-7974

339-35 North Dakota

	Toll-Free	Phone
Accountancy Board		
2701 S Columbia Rd .... Grand Forks ND 58201	800-532-5904	701-775-7100
Agriculture Dept		
600 E Blvd Ave Dept 602 .... Bismarck ND 58505	800-242-7535	701-328-2231
Attorney General		
600 E Blvd Ave Dept 125 .... Bismarck ND 58505	800-366-6888	701-328-2210
Child Support Enforcement Div		
1600 E Century Ave Ste 7.......... Bismarck ND 58501	800-231-4255	701-328-3582
Consumer Protection Div		
1050 E Interstate Ave Ste 200 ...... Bismarck ND 58503	800-472-2600	701-328-3404
Crime Victims Compensation Program		
PO Box 5521 .... Bismarck ND 58506	800-445-2322	701-328-6195
Economic Development & Finance Div		
1600 E Century Ave Ste 200-B ...... Bismarck ND 58503	866-432-5682	701-328-5300
Financial Institutions Dept		
2000 Schafer St Ste G. .... Bismarck ND 58501	800-366-6888	701-328-9933
Housing Finance Agency		
PO Box 1535 .... Bismarck ND 58502	800-292-8621	701-328-8080
Insurance Dept		
600 E Blvd Ave Dept 401 .... Bismarck ND 58505	800-247-0560	701-328-2440
Parks & Recreation Dept		
1600 E Century Ave Ste 3.......... Bismarck ND 58503	800-807-4723	701-328-5357
Secretary of State		
600 E Blvd Ave Dept 108 .... Bismarck ND 58505	800-352-0867	701-328-2900
Tourism Div		
1600 E Century Ave Ste 200S ...... Bismarck ND 58502	800-435-5663	701-328-2525
Veterans Affairs Dept		
4201 38th St S Ste 104............ Fargo ND 58104	866-634-8387	701-239-7165
Vocational Rehabilitation Div		
1237 W Divide Ave Ste 2 .... Bismarck ND 58501	800-755-2745	701-328-8800
Workers Compensation		
1600 E Century Ave Ste 1000 ...... Bismarck ND 58503	800-777-5033	701-328-3800

339-36 Ohio

	Toll-Free	Phone
Agriculture Dept		
8995 E Main St ....Reynoldsburg OH 43068	800-282-1955	614-728-6201
Consumer Protection Section		
30 E Broad St 14th Fl ....Columbus OH 43215	800-282-0515	614-466-8831
Education Dept		
25 S Front St ....Columbus OH 43215	877-644-6338	614-995-1545
Financial Institutions Div		
77 S High St 21st Fl ....Columbus OH 43266	866-278-0003	614-728-8400
Highway Patrol (OSHP)		
1970 W Broad St PO Box 182074..........Columbus OH 43223	877-772-8765	614-466-2660
Insurance Dept		
50 W Town St Third Fl Ste 300...........Columbus OH 43215	800-686-1526	614-644-2658
Mental Health Dept		
30 E Broad St 8th Fl ....Columbus OH 43215	888-636-4889	614-466-2596
Parks & Recreation Div		
2045 Morse Rd Bldg C-3 ....Columbus OH 43229	800-282-7275	614-265-6561
Taxation Dept		
30 E Broad St 22nd Fl PO Box 530........Columbus OH 43215	888-405-4089	614-466-2166
Travel & Tourism Div		
PO Box 1001 ....Columbus OH 43216	800-282-5393	614-466-8844
Tuition Trust Authority		
580 S High St Ste 208 ....Columbus OH 43215	800-233-6734*	614-752-9400
*Cust Svc		
Wildlife Div		
2045 Morse Rd Bldg G....................Columbus OH 43229	800-945-3543	614-265-6300
Workers Compensation Bureau		
30 W Spring St ....Columbus OH 43215	800-644-6292	614-644-6292
Workforce Development Office		
4020 E Fifth Ave PO Box 1618............Columbus OH 43219	888-296-7541	

339-37 Oklahoma

	Toll-Free	Phone
Child Support Enforcement Div		
PO Box 248822 ....Oklahoma City OK 73124	800-522-2922	405-522-2273
Commerce Dept		
900 N Stiles Ave ....Oklahoma City OK 73104	800-879-6552	405-815-6552
Environmental Quality Dept		
707 N Robinson Ave PO Box 1677........Oklahoma City OK 73101	800-869-1400	405-702-1000
Housing Finance Agency		
100 NW 63rd St Ste 200..............Oklahoma City OK 73116	800-256-1489	405-848-1144
Insurance Dept (OID)		
3625 NW 56th Ste 100 ....Oklahoma City OK 73152	800-522-0071	405-521-2828
Parks Div		
PO Box 52002 ....Oklahoma City OK 73152	800-654-8240	405-230-8300
Rehabilitative Services Dept		
5501 N Portland Ave ....Oklahoma City OK 73112	800-845-8476	405-951-3400
Wildlife Conservation Dept (ODWC)		
PO Box 53465 ....Oklahoma City OK 73152	800-522-8039	405-521-4660

339-38 Oregon

	Toll-Free	Phone
Business Development Dept		
775 Summer St NE Ste 200 ....Salem OR 97301	800-735-2900*	503-986-0123
*General		
Crime Victims Service Div		
1162 Ct St NE ....Salem OR 97301	877-877-9392	503-378-4400
Financial Fraud/Consumer Protection Section		
1162 Ct St NE ....Salem OR 97301	877-877-9392	503-378-4400
Fish & Wildlife Dept (ODFW)		
3406 Cherry Ave NE ....Salem OR 97303	800-720-6339	503-947-6000
Legislative Assembly		
900 Ct St NE ....Salem OR 97301	800-332-2313	
Parks & Recreation Dept (OPRD)		
725 Summer St NE Ste C ....Salem OR 97301	800-551-6949	503-986-0707
Transportation Dept		
355 Capitol St NE Ste 135 Rm 222.........Salem OR 97301	888-275-6368	503-986-4000
Vocational Rehabilitation Services Office (OVRS)		
700 Summer St NE E-87....................Salem OR 97301	877-277-0513	800-692-9666

339-39 Pennsylvania

	Toll-Free	Phone
Banking Dept		
17 N Second St Market Square Plz..........Harrisburg PA 17101	800-722-2657	717-783-4721
Higher Education Assistance Agency		
1200 N Seventh St ....Harrisburg PA 17102	800-233-0557	
Insurance Dept		
1326 Strawberry Sq ....Harrisburg PA 17120	877-881-6388	
Public Utility Commission		
400 N St Keystone Bldg PO Box 3265 ......Harrisburg PA 17120	800-692-7380	717-783-1740
State Ethics Commission		
309 Finance Bldg PO Box 11470 ....Harrisburg PA 17108	800-932-0936	717-783-1610
State Parks Bureau		
PO Box 8551 ....Harrisburg PA 17105	888-727-2757	717-787-6640
State System of Higher Education		
2986 N Second St ....Harrisburg PA 17110	800-732-0999	717-720-4000
Transportation Dept		
400 N St ....Harrisburg PA 17120	800-932-4600	717-787-2838
Vocational Rehabilitation Office (OVR)		
1521 N Sixth St ....Harrisburg PA 17102	800-442-6351	717-787-5244
Workers Compensation Bureau		
1171 S Cameron St Rm 324 ....Harrisburg PA 17104	800-482-2383	717-783-5421

339-40 Rhode Island

	Toll-Free	Phone
Higher Education Assistance Authority (RIHEAA)		
560 Jefferson Blvd ....Warwick RI 02886	800-922-9855	401-736-1100
Tourism Div		
315 Iron Horse Way Ste 101................Providence RI 02908	800-556-2484	

339-41 South Carolina

	Toll-Free	Phone
State Government Information		
1301 Gervais St Ste 710 ....Columbia SC 29201	866-340-7105	803-771-0131
Child Support Enforcement Office		
3150 Harden St Ext ....Columbia SC 29203	800-768-5858	803-898-9210
Commerce Dept		
1201 Main St Ste 1600.....................Columbia SC 29201	800-868-7232	803-737-0400
Higher Education Tuition Grants Commission		
115 Atrium Wy Ste 102....................Columbia SC 29203	877-382-4357	803-896-1120
State Ports Authority		
176 Concord St ....Charleston SC 29401	800-845-7106	843-723-8651
Veterans Affairs Div		
1205 Pendleton St Ste 463 ....Columbia SC 29201	800-827-1000	803-734-0200
Vocational Rehabilitation Dept		
1410 Boston Ave PO Box 15.............West Columbia SC 29171	800-832-7526	803-896-6500

339-42 South Dakota

	Toll-Free	Phone
Child Support Div		
700 Governors Dr ....Pierre SD 57501	800-286-9145	605-773-3641
Crime Victims' Compensation Program		
700 Governors Dr ....Pierre SD 57501	800-696-9476	605-773-6317
Economic Development Office		
711 E Wells Ave ....Pierre SD 57501	800-872-6190	605-773-3301
Health Dept		
600 E Capitol Ave ....Pierre SD 57501	800-738-2301	605-773-4961
Parks & Recreation Div		
523 E Capitol Ave ....Pierre SD 57501	800-710-2267*	605-773-3391
*Campground Resv		
Rehabilitation Services Div		
500 E Capitol Ave ....Pierre SD 57501	800-265-9684	605-773-3195
Tourism Office		
711 E Wells Ave ....Pierre SD 57501	800-952-3625	605-773-3301

339-43 Tennessee

	Toll-Free	Phone
Child Support Services Div		
400 Deaderick St 12th Fl ....Nashville TN 37248	800-838-6911	615-313-4880
Economic & Community Development Dept (ECD)		
312 Eigth Ave N 11th Fl ....Nashville TN 37243	877-768-6374	615-741-1888
Mental Health & Developmental Disabilities Dept		
425 Fifth Ave N 3rd Fl.....................Nashville TN 37243	800-669-1851	615-532-6500
Real Estate Commission		
500 James Robertson Pkwy Ste 180.........Nashville TN 37243	800-342-4031	615-741-2273
Securities Div		
500 James Robertson Pkwy Ste 680.........Nashville TN 37243	800-863-9117	615-741-2947
State Parks Div		
401 Church St 7th Fl ....Nashville TN 37243	888-867-2757	615-532-0001
Supreme Court		
511 Union St		
Nashville City Ctr Ste 600..................Nashville TN 37219	800-448-7970	615-741-2687

339-44 Texas

	Toll-Free	Phone
State Government Information		
1501 N Congress Ste 4224..................Austin TX 78711	877-452-9060	512-936-9500
Aging & Disability Services		
701 W 51st St Ste W253....................Austin TX 78751	888-388-6332	512-438-3011
Agriculture Dept		
PO Box 12847 ....Austin TX 78711	800-835-5832*	512-463-7476
*Cust Svc		
Arts Commission		
920 Colorado Ste 501 PO Box 13406........Austin TX 78701	800-252-9415	512-463-5535
Banking Dept		
2601 N Lamar Blvd ....Austin TX 78705	877-276-5554	512-475-1300
Child Support Div		
300 W 15th St ....Austin TX 78701	800-252-8014	512-460-6000
Comptroller of Public Accounts		
111 E 17th St ....Austin TX 78774	800-531-5441	512-463-4600
Consumer Protection Div		
PO Box 12548 ....Austin TX 78711	800-621-0508*	
*General		
Crime Victims Services Div		
PO Box 12198 ....Austin TX 78711	800-983-9933	512-936-1200
Environmental Quality Commission (TCEQ)		
12100 Pk 35 Cir PO Box 13087.............Austin TX 78711	800-735-2989	512-239-1000
General Land Office		
1700 N Congress Ave Ste 935 ....Austin TX 78701	800-998-4456	512-463-5001
Governor PO Box 12428 ....Austin TX 78711	800-843-5789	512-463-2000
Insurance Dept		
333 Guadalupe St PO Box 149104..........Austin TX 78714	800-252-3439	512-463-6169
Medical Board PO Box 2018 ....Austin TX 78768	800-248-4062*	512-305-7010
*Cust Svc		
Motor Vehicle Div		
4000 Jackson Ave PO Box 2293............Austin TX 78731	888-368-4689	

				Toll-Free	Phone

Parks & Wildlife Dept
4200 Smith School Rd . . . . Austin TX 78744   **800-792-1112**   512-389-4800

Public Utility Commission
PO Box 13326 . . . . Austin TX 78711   **888-782-8477**   512-936-7000

Railroad Commission
PO Box 12967 . . . . Austin TX 78711   **877-228-5740**   512-463-7131

Veterans Commission
PO Box 12277 . . . . Austin TX 78711   **800-252-8387**   512-463-5538

Vital Statistics Bureau
1100 W 49th St PO Box 12040 . . . . . . Austin TX 78756   **888-963-7111**

Workers Compensation Commission
7551 Metro Ctr Dr . . . . Austin TX 78744   **800-252-7031***   512-804-4000
*Cust Svc

339-45 Utah

				Toll-Free	Phone

Aging & Adult Services Div
195 N 1950 W Rm 325 . . . . Salt Lake City UT 84116   **877-424-4640**   801-538-3910

Child & Family Services Div
195 N 1950 W Rm 225 . . . . Salt Lake City UT 84116   **855-323-3237**   801-538-4100

Community & Economic Development Dept
60 E S Temple 3rd Fl . . . . Salt Lake City UT 84111   **855-204-9046**   801-538-8680

Environmental Quality Dept
195 N 1950 W . . . . Salt Lake City UT 84116   **800-458-0145**   801-536-4400

Governor
350 N State St Ste 200
PO Box 142220 . . . . Salt Lake City UT 84114   **800-705-2464**   801-538-1000

Higher Education Assistance Authority
PO Box 145112 . . . . Salt Lake City UT 84114   **877-336-7378**   801-321-7294

Labor Commission
PO Box 146600 . . . . Salt Lake City UT 84114   **800-530-5090**   801-530-6800

Lieutenant Governor
PO Box 142325 . . . . Salt Lake City UT 84114   **800-705-2464**

Motor Vehicle Div
PO Box 30412 . . . . Salt Lake City UT 84130   **800-368-8824**   801-297-7780

Occupational & Professional Licensing Div
PO Box 146741 . . . . Salt Lake City UT 84111   **866-275-3675**   801-530-6628

Office of Tourism
300 N State St . . . . Salt Lake City UT 84114   **800-200-1160**   801-538-1900

Parks & Recreation Div
1594 W N Temple Ste 116 . . . . Salt Lake City UT 84116   **800-322-3770**   801-538-7220

Rehabilitation Office
250 E 500 S . . . . Salt Lake City UT 84111   **800-473-7530**   801-538-7530

Workers Compensation Fund
100 W Towne Ridge Pkwy . . . . Sandy UT 84070   **800-446-2667**   385-351-8000

339-46 Vermont

				Toll-Free	Phone

Children & Families Dept
103 S Main St 2nd Fl 5 N . . . . Waterbury VT 05671   **800-786-3214**   802-241-2100

Consumer Assistance Program
146 University Pl . . . . Burlington VT 05405   **800-649-2424**   802-656-3183

Emergency Management Office
103 S Main St . . . . Waterbury VT 05671   **800-347-0488**   802-241-5000

Historic Preservation Div
National Life Bldg 6th Fl . . . . Montpelier VT 05620   **800-639-1522**   802-828-3213

Veterans Affairs Office
118 State St . . . . Montpelier VT 05602   **888-666-9844**   802-828-3379

Vocational Rehabilitation Div
103 S Main St . . . . Waterbury VT 05671   **866-879-6757**   802-241-2186

339-47 Virginia

				Toll-Free	Phone

Aging & Rehabilitative Services Dept
8004 Franklin Farms Dr . . . . Richmond VA 23229   **800-552-5019**   804-662-7000

Child Support Enforcement Div
730 E Broad St . . . . Richmond VA 23219   **800-468-8894**

Criminal Injuries Compensation Fund (CICF)
PO Box 26927 . . . . Richmond VA 23261   **800-552-4007**

Governor
1111 E Broad St PO Box 1475 . . . . . Richmond VA 23219   **800-828-1120**   804-786-2211

Health Professions Dept
9960 Mayland Dr Ste 300 . . . . Henrico VA 23233   **800-533-1560**   804-367-4400

Housing Development Authority
601 S Belvidere St . . . . Richmond VA 23220   **800-968-7837**   804-782-1986

Information Technologies Agency (VITA)
11751 Meadowville Ln . . . . Chester VA 23836   **866-637-8482**

State Parks Div
203 Governor St Ste 306 . . . . Richmond VA 23219   **800-933-7275***
*Resv

Vital Records Div
2001 Maywill St PO Box 1000 . . . . . Richmond VA 23230   **877-572-6333**   804-662-6200

339-48 Washington

				Toll-Free	Phone

Bill Status PO Box 40600 . . . . Olympia WA 98504   **800-562-6000**   360-786-7573

Financial Institutions Dept
PO Box 41200 . . . . Olympia WA 98504   **877-746-4334**   360-902-8703

Health Dept PO Box 47890 . . . . Olympia WA 98504   **800-525-0127**   360-236-4501

Historical Society
1911 Pacific Ave . . . . Tacoma WA 98402   **888-238-4373**   253-272-3500

Housing Finance Commission
1000 Second Ave Ste 2700 . . . . Seattle WA 98104   **800-767-4663**   206-464-7139

Natural Resources Dept
1111 Washington St SE PO Box 47000 . Olympia WA 98504   **800-258-5990**   360-902-1000

Revenue Dept PO Box 47478 . . . . Olympia WA 98504   **800-647-7706**   360-705-6714

Social & Health Services Dept
PO Box 45130 . . . . Olympia WA 98504   **800-737-0617**   360-902-8400

				Toll-Free	Phone

State Lottery PO Box 43000 . . . . Olympia WA 98504   **800-732-5101**   360-664-4720

State Parks & Recreation Commission
1111 Israel Rd SW . . . . Olympia WA 98504   **888-226-7688***   360-902-8500
*Campground Resv

Utilities & Transportation Commission
1300 S Evergreen Pk Dr SW
PO Box 47250 . . . . Olympia WA 98504   **888-333-9882**   360-664-1160

Veterans Affairs Dept
PO Box 41150 . . . . Olympia WA 98504   **800-562-2308**   360-753-5586

Vocational Rehabilitation Div
PO Box 45340 . . . . Olympia WA 98504   **800-637-5627**   360-438-8000

339-49 West Virginia

				Toll-Free	Phone

Bill Status
State Capitol Complex
Rm MB27 Bldg 1 . . . . Charleston WV 25305   **877-565-3447**   304-347-4836

Child Support Enforcement Bureau
231 Capitol St Ste 111 . . . . Charleston WV 25301   **800-571-4864**   304-347-8688

Children & Families Bureau
350 Capitol St Rm R-730 . . . . Charleston WV 25301   **800-642-8589**   304-558-0628

Community Development Div
1900 Kanawha Blvd E . . . . Charleston WV 25311   **800-982-3386**   304-558-2234

Consumer Protection Div
812 Quarrier St 1st Fl . . . . Charleston WV 25301   **800-368-8808**   304-558-8986

Crime Victims Compensation Fund
1900 Kanawha Blvd E Rm W-334 . . . Charleston WV 25305   **877-562-6878**   304-347-4850

Development Office
1900 Kanawha Blvd E Bldg 6 Rm 525B . Charleston WV 25305   **800-982-3386**   304-558-2234

Ethics Commission
210 Brooks St Ste 300 . . . . Charleston WV 25301   **866-558-0664**   304-558-0664

Higher Education Policy Commission
1018 Kanawha Blvd E Ste 700 . . . . . Charleston WV 25301   **888-825-5707**   304-558-2101

Housing Development Fund
814 Virginia St E . . . . Charleston WV 25301   **800-933-9843**   304-345-6475

Insurance Commission
PO Box 50540 . . . . Charleston WV 25305   **888-879-9842**   304-558-3354

Motor Vehicles Div
5707 MacCorkle Ave SE Ste 400 . . . . Charleston WV 25304   **800-642-9066**   304-558-3900

Public Service Commission
208 Brooke St PO Box 812 . . . . Charleston WV 25301   **800-344-5113**   304-340-0300

Rehabilitation Services Div
107 Capitol St . . . . Charleston WV 25301   **800-642-8207**

Secretary of State
1900 Kanawha Blvd E
Bldg 1 Ste 157K . . . . Charleston WV 25305   **866-767-8683**   304-558-6000

Securities Div
1900 Kanawha Blvd E
Bldg 1 Rm W-100 . . . . Charleston WV 25305   **877-982-9148**   304-558-2257

State Parks & Forests
324 4th Ave . . . . Charleston WV 25305   **800-225-5982**   304-558-2764

Tourism Div
90 MacCorkle Ave SW . . . . Charleston WV 25303   **800-225-5982**

Treasurer
1900 Kanawha Blvd E
Bldg 1 Ste E-145 . . . . Charleston WV 25305   **800-422-7498**   304-558-5000

Veterans Affairs Div
1321 Plaza E Ste 101 . . . . Charleston WV 25301   **888-838-2332**   304-558-3661

339-50 Wisconsin

				Toll-Free	Phone

Bill Status 1 E Main St . . . . Madison WI 53708   **800-362-9472**   608-266-9960

Crime Victims Services Office
PO Box 7951 . . . . Madison WI 53707   **800-446-6564**   608-264-9497

Housing & Economic Development Authority
201 W Washington Ave Ste 700 . . . . . Madison WI 53703   **800-334-6873**   608-266-7884

Insurance Commission
PO Box 7873 . . . . Madison WI 53707   **800-236-8517**   608-266-3585

Legislature State Capitol . . . . Madison WI 53702   **800-362-9472**   608-266-9960

Parks & Recreation Bureau
101 S Webster St PO Box 7921 . . . . . Madison WI 53707   **888-936-7463**   608-266-2621

Public Instruction Dept
125 S Webster St PO Box 7841 . . . . . Madison WI 53707   **800-441-4563**   608-266-3390

Teacher Education & Licensing Bureau
125 S Webster St . . . . Madison WI 53703   **800-441-4563**   608-266-3390

Treasurer PO Box 2114 . . . . Madison WI 53707   **855-375-2274**

Veterans Affairs Dept
201 W Washington Ave PO Box 7843 . . Madison WI 53703   **800-947-8387**   608-266-1311

Vocational Rehabilitation Div
201 East Washington Avenue
PO Box 7852 . . . . Madison WI 53707   **800-442-3477**   608-261-0050

339-51 Wyoming

				Toll-Free	Phone

Aging Div
6101 Yellowstone Rd N Rm 259B . . . . Cheyenne WY 82002   **800-442-2766**   307-777-7986

Highway Patrol (WHP)
5300 Bishop Blvd . . . . Cheyenne WY 82009   **800-442-9090**   307-777-4301

Legislative Service Office
3001 E Pershing Blvd . . . . Cheyenne WY 82002   **800-342-9570**   307-777-7881

State Parks & Historical Sites Div
2301 Central Ave . . . . Cheyenne WY 82002   **877-996-7275**   307-777-6323

Tourism Div
1520 Etchepare Cir . . . . Cheyenne WY 82007   **800-225-5996**   307-777-7777

340	GOVERNMENT - US - EXECUTIVE BRANCH

SEE ALSO Military Bases ; Parks - National - US ; Cemeteries - National ; Coast Guard Installations

	Toll-Free	Phone
Office of National Drug Control Policy		
PO Box 6000 ....Rockville MD 20849	800-666-3332	
USA Freedom Corps		
1201 New York Ave NW ....Washington DC 20005	800-833-3722	202-606-5000

340-1 US Department of Agriculture

	Toll-Free	Phone
Center for Nutrition Policy & Promotion (CNPP)		
3101 Pk Ctr Dr 10th Fl ....Alexandria VA 22302	888-779-7264	703-305-7600
Food & Nutrition Service		
Food Stamp Program		
3101 Pk Ctr Dr ....Alexandria VA 22302	800-221-5689	703-305-2022
Forest Service (USFS)		
1400 Independence Ave SW ....Washington DC 20050	800-832-1355	202-205-8333
Forest Service Regional Offices		
Region 8 (Southern Region)		
1720 Peachtree St Ste 760S ....Atlanta GA 30309	877-372-7248	404-347-4177
National Agricultural Statistics Service (NASS)		
1400 Independence Ave SW ....Washington DC 20250	800-727-9540	202-720-2707
Rural Housing Service		
1400 Independence Ave SW Rm 5014 ....Washington DC 20250	800-414-1226	202-690-1533

340-2 US Department of Commerce

	Toll-Free	Phone
Minority Business Development Agency Regional Offices		
Chicago Region		
105 W Adams St Ste 2300 ....Chicago IL 60603	888-324-1551	312-353-0182
National Environmental Satellite Data & Information Service		
National Coastal Data Development Ctr		
Bldg 1100 Ste 101 ....Stennis Space Center MS 39529	866-732-2382	228-688-2936
National Institute of Standards & Technology (NIST)		
100 Bureau Dr Sp 1070 ....Gaithersburg MD 20899	800-877-8339	301-975-6478
National Marine Fisheries Service Regional Offices		
Pacific Islands Region		
1601 Kapiolani Blvd Rm 1110 ....Honolulu HI 96814	888-674-7411	808-944-2200
National Technical Information Service (NTIS)		
5285 Port Royal Rd ....Springfield VA 22161	800-553-6847*	703-605-6000
*Orders		
North American Industry Classification System (NAICS)		
US Census Bureau		
4600 Silver Hill Rd ....Washington DC 20233	800-923-8282	301-763-4636
US Census Bureau Regional Offices		
Atlanta		
101 Marietta St NW Ste 3200 ....Atlanta GA 30303	800-424-6974	404-730-3832
Boston 4 Copley Pl Ste 301 ....Boston MA 02117	800-562-5721	617-424-4501
Chicago		
1111 W 22nd St Ste 400 ....Oak Brook IL 60523	800-865-6384	630-288-9200
Denver		
6900 W Jefferson Ave Ste 100 ....Denver CO 80235	800-852-6159	303-264-0202
Los Angeles		
15350 Sherman Way Ste 300 ....Van Nuys CA 91406	800-992-3530	818-267-1700
New York		
395 Hudson St Ste 800 ....New York NY 10014	800-991-2520	212-584-3400
Philadelphia		
833 Chestnut St Ste 504 ....Philadelphia PA 19107	800-262-4236	215-717-1800
US Patent & Trademark Office		
PO Box 1450 ....Alexandria VA 22313	800-786-9199	571-272-1000

340-3 US Department of Defense

	Toll-Free	Phone
Defense Hotline for Fraud Waste & Abuse		
The Pentagon ....Washington DC 20301	800-424-9098	703-604-8799
Defense Technical Information Ctr (DTIC)		
8725 John J Kingman Rd Ste 0944 ....Fort Belvoir VA 22060	800-225-3842	703-767-9100
Defense Threat Reduction Agency		
8725 John T Kingman Rd MS 6201 ....Fort Belvoir VA 22060	800-701-5096	703-767-5870

340-4 US Department of Defense - Department of the Army

	Toll-Free	Phone
Army National Guard		
Army National Guard Readiness Ctr		
111 S George Mason Dr ....Arlington VA 22204	800-404-8273	703-607-2584
US Army War College		
122 Forbes Ave ....Carlisle PA 17013	800-453-0992	717-245-3131

340-5 US Department of Defense - Department of the Navy

	Toll-Free	Phone
Navy Personnel Command (NPC)		
5720 Integrity Dr ....Millington TN 38055	866-827-5672	901-874-3165

340-6 US Department of Education

	Toll-Free	Phone
Department of Education		
400 Maryland Ave SW ....Washington DC 20202	800-872-5327	202-401-2000

	Toll-Free	Phone
Inspector General's Fraud & Abuse Hotline		
400 Maryland Ave SW ....Washington DC 20202	800-647-8733	
Office of Elementary & Secondary Education		
400 Maryland Ave SW ....Washington DC 20202	800-872-5327	
Office of Vocational & Adult Education		
400 Maryland Ave SW Room 4W116 ....Washington DC 20202	800-872-5327	
US Dept of Education		
Region 6		
1999 Bryan St Ste 1620 ....Dallas TX 75201	877-521-2172	214-661-9600
National Institute for Literacy (NIFL)		
1775 'I' St NW Ste 730 ....Washington DC 20006	800-228-8813	202-233-2025
Secretary of Education		
400 Maryland Ave SW ....Washington DC 20202	800-872-5327	202-401-3000

340-7 US Department of Energy

	Toll-Free	Phone
Department of Energy (DOE)		
1000 Independence Ave SW ....Washington DC 20585	800-342-5363	202-586-5450
Office of Civilian Radioactive Waste Management		
1000 Independence Ave SW ....Washington DC 20585	888-363-7289	202-586-4940
Office of Energy Efficiency & Renewable Energy		
1000 Independence Ave SW ....Washington DC 20585	877-337-3463	202-586-9171
Office of Nuclear Energy		
1000 Independence Ave SW ....Washington DC 20585	800-342-5363	
Federal Energy Regulatory Commission		
888 First St NE ....Washington DC 20426	866-208-3372	202-502-8004

340-8 US Department of Health & Human Services

	Toll-Free	Phone
Department of Health & Human Services (HHS)		
330 Independence Ave SW ....Washington DC 20201	877-696-6775	202-619-0150
US Health & Human Services Department		
Region 9		
90 7th St Ste 4-100 ....San Francisco CA 94103	800-368-1019	
Agency for Healthcare Research & Quality		
540 Gaither Rd ....Rockville MD 20850	800-358-9295	301-427-1200
Agency for Toxic Substances & Disease Registry		
4770 Buford Hwy NE ....Atlanta GA 30341	800-232-4636	
AIDSinfo PO Box 6303 ....Rockville MD 20849	800-448-0440	301-519-0459
National Center for Chronic Disease Prevention & Health Promotion (NCCDPHP)		
4770 Buford Hwy NE ....Atlanta GA 30341	800-232-4636	
National Center for Emerging & Zoonotic Infectious Diseases		
1600 Clifton Rd ....Atlanta GA 30333	800-232-4636	404-639-3311
National Center for Environmental Health		
4770 Buford Hwy Bldg 101 ....Atlanta GA 30341	800-232-4636	404-639-3311
National Center for Health Marketing		
1600 Clifton Rd ....Atlanta GA 30333	800-311-3435	404-498-1515
National Center for HIV/AIDS Viral Hepatitis STD & TB Prevention		
1600 Clifton Rd ....Atlanta GA 30333	800-232-4636	
National Center for Immunization & Respiratory Diseases		
1600 Clifton Rd NE MS E-05 ....Atlanta GA 30333	800-232-4636	
National Center for Injury Prevention & Control (NCIPC)		
4770 Buford Hwy NE ....Atlanta GA 30341	800-232-4636	
National Center for Public Health Informatics		
1600 Clifton Rd NE MS E-78 ....Atlanta GA 30333	800-232-4636	
National Center on Birth Defects & Developmental Disabilities		
1600 Clifton Rd ....Atlanta GA 30329	800-232-4636	770-498-3800
National Institute for Occupational Safety & Health		
200 Independence Ave SW ....Washington DC 20201	800-356-4674	404-639-3286
Centers for Disease Control & Prevention		
Travelers Health		
1600 Clifton Rd NE ....Atlanta GA 30333	800-232-4636	
Centers for Medicare & Medicaid Services (CMS)		
7500 Security Blvd ....Baltimore MD 21244	800-633-4227	
Medicare Hotline		
7500 Security Blvd ....Baltimore MD 21244	800-633-4227	
Child Welfare Information Gateway		
1250 Maryland Ave SW 8th Fl ....Washington DC 20024	800-394-3366	703-385-7565
Center for Devices & Radiological Health (CDRH)		
10903 New Hampshire Ave		
W066-5429 ....Silver Spring MD 20993	800-638-2041	301-796-7100
Center for Drug Evaluation & Research		
10001 New Hampshire Ave		
Hillandale Bldg 4th Fl ....Silver Spring MD 20993	855-543-3784	301-796-3400
Center for Food Safety & Applied Nutrition		
5100 Paint Branch Pkwy ....College Park MD 20740	888-723-3366	
Food & Drug Administration		
National Center for Toxicological Research		
3900 N Ctr Rd ....Jefferson AR 72079	800-638-3321	870-543-7000
Health Resources & Services Administration (HRSA)		
5600 Fishers Ln ....Rockville MD 20857	888-275-4772	301-443-2216
National Child Care Information & Technical Assistance Ctr (NCCIC)		
9300 Lee Hwy ....Fairfax VA 22031	877-296-2250	
National Clearinghouse for Alcohol & Drug Information		
11426 Rockville Pk PO Box 2345 ....Rockville MD 20847	800-729-6686	
National Hansen's Disease Program (NHDP)		
1770 Physicians Pk Dr ....Baton Rouge LA 70816	800-642-2477	225-756-3700
National Institutes of Health		
National Cancer Institute		
Public Inquiries Office 6116 Executive Blvd		
Rm 3036A ....*...........Bethesda MD 20892	800-422-6237	301-435-3848
National Center for Complementary & Alternative Medicine		
National Institutes of Health		
31 Ctr Dr Bldg 31 ....Bethesda MD 20892	888-644-6226	301-594-7103
National Institute of Mental Health		
6001 Executive Blvd Rm 8184 MSC 9663 ...Bethesda MD 20892	866-615-6464	301-443-4513
National Institute of Neurological Disorders & Stroke		
PO Box 5801 ....Bethesda MD 20824	800-352-9424	301-496-5751
National Institute on Deafness & Other Communication Disorders		
31 Ctr Dr Bldg 31 Rm 3C35 ....Bethesda MD 20892	800-241-1044	301-496-7243
National Library of Medicine		
National Institutes of Health		
8600 Rockville Pike Bldg 38 ....Bethesda MD 20894	888-346-3656	301-594-5983

		Toll-Free	Phone

National Mental Health Information Ctr
PO Box 42557 .... Washington DC 20015 **800-487-4889**
National Women's Health Information Ctr
200 Independence Ave S.W .... Washington DC 20201 **800-994-9662**
NIH Osteoporosis & Related Bone Diseases-National Resource Ctr
2 AMS Cir ....Bethesda MD 20892 **800-624-2663** 202-223-0344
Substance Abuse & Mental Health Services Administration (SAMHSA)
1 Choke Cherry Rd ....Rockville MD 20857 **877-726-4727** 240-276-2000
Center for Mental Health Services
1 Choke Cherry Ln ....Rockville MD 20857 **877-726-4727**
Center for Substance Abuse Prevention
1 Choke Cherry Rd ....Rockville MD 20857 **877-726-4727** 240-276-2420
Center for Substance Abuse Treatment
1 Choke Cherry Rd PO Box 2345..............Rockville MD 20857 **877-726-4727** 240-276-2130

340-9 US Department of Homeland Security

		Toll-Free	Phone

Federal Emergency Management Agency
FEMA for Kids
500 C St SW Ste 714 .... Washington DC 20472 **800-621-3362**
National Flood Insurance Program
500 C St SW .... Washington DC 20472 **888-379-9531**
Region 1 99 High St .... Boston MA 02110 **877-336-2734** 617-956-7551
Region 10
Federal Regional Ctr 130 228th St SW.......... Bothell WA 98021 **800-772-1252*** 425-487-4600
*General
Region 3
1 Independence Mall
615 Chestnut St 6th Fl .... Philadelphia PA 19106 **800-621-3362** 215-931-5500
Region 5
536 S Clark St 6th Fl .... Chicago IL 60605 **877-336-2627** 312-408-5500
Region 6 800 N Loop 288 .... Denton TX 76209 **800-426-5460** 940-898-5399
Federal Emergency Management Agency Regional Offices
Region 9
1111 Broadway Ste 1200 .... Oakland CA 94607 **877-336-2627** 510-627-7100
Transportation Security Administration (TSA)
601 S 12th St .... Arlington VA 22202 **866-289-9673** 202-282-8000
Federal Air Marshal Service
601 S 12th St .... Arlington VA 22202 **866-289-9673**
US Citizenship & Immigration Services Regional Offices
Eastern Region
70 Kimball Ave .... South Burlington VT 05403 **800-767-1833**
US Coast Guard
National Maritime Ctr
100 Forbes Dr .... Martinsburg WV 25404 **888-427-5662** 304-433-3400
US Coast Guard Academy
15 Mohegan Ave ....New London CT 06320 **800-883-8724** 860-444-8500
US Customs & Border Protection
1300 Pennsylvania Ave NW .... Washington DC 20229 **877-227-5511** 703-526-4200
US Immigration & Customs Enforcement (ICE)
425 'I' St NW .... Washington DC 20536 **866-347-2423** 202-514-1900

340-10 US Department of Housing & Urban Development

		Toll-Free	Phone

Department of Housing & Urban Development (HUD)
451 Seventh St SW ....Washington DC 20410 **800-569-4287** 202-708-0685
Public Affairs Office
451 Seventh St SW ....Washington DC 20410 **800-333-4636** 202-708-0980
Department of Housing & Urban Development Regional Offices
Boston 10 Cswy St 3rd Fl..................... Boston MA 02222 **800-225-5342** 617-994-8200
Mid-Atlantic Region
100 Penn Sq E ....Philadelphia PA 19107 **800-225-5342** 215-656-0500
New York City Regional Office
26 Federal Plaza Ste 3541 .... New York NY 10278 **800-496-4294** 212-264-8000
Pacific/Hawaii Region
600 Harrison St 3rd Fl ....San Francisco CA 94107 **800-347-3739** 415-489-6572
Rocky Mountain Region
1670 Bdwy 25th Fl .... Denver CO 80202 **800-955-2232** 303-672-5440
HUD Office of Fair Housing & Equal Opportunity
Housing Discrimination Hotline
451 Seventh St SW .... Washington DC 20410 **800-333-4636** 202-708-1112
HUD Office of Housing and Urban Development (FHA)
451 Seventh St SW Ste 9100 .... Washington DC 20410 **800-767-7468** 202-708-1112
HUD Office of Public & Indian Housing
451 Seventh St SW Rm 4100 .... Washington DC 20410 **800-955-2232** 202-708-0950
Real Estate Assessment Ctr
550 12th St SW Ste 100.................. Washington DC 20410 **888-245-4860** 202-708-1112

340-11 US Department of the Interior

		Toll-Free	Phone

Bureau of Indian Affairs Regional Offices (BIA)
Alaska Region
3601 C St Ste 1100 .... Anchorage AK 99503 **800-645-8397** 907-271-1536
Bureau of Land Management
National Wild Horse & Burro Program
1849 C Street NW Rm. 5665 .... Washington DC 20240 **866-468-7826** 202-208-3801
US Fish & Wildlife Service (USFWS)
1849 C St NW .... Washington DC 20240 **800-344-9453** 202-208-4717
US Fish & Wildlife Service Regional Offices
Great Lakes/Big Rivers Region
5600 American Blvd W Ste 900 ....Bloomington MN 55437 **800-877-8339** 612-713-5360
US Geological Survey
Ask USGS
12201 Sunrise Valley Dr .... Reston VA 20192 **888-275-8747** 703-648-5953

340-12 US Department of Justice

		Toll-Free	Phone

Community Oriented Policing Services (COPS)
1100 Vermont Ave NW 10th Fl .... Washington DC 20530 **800-421-6770** 202-616-2888
Federal Bureau of Prisons
National Institute of Corrections
320 First St NW .... Washington DC 20534 **800-995-6423** 202-307-3106
National Institute of Corrections Information Cent
11900 E Cornell Ave Unit C .... Aurora CO 80014 **800-877-1461**
Office of Justice Programs
Bureau of Justice Statistics
810 Seventh St NW .... Washington DC 20531 **800-851-3420** 202-307-0765
Office of Special Counsel for Immigration-Related Unfair Employment Practices
950 Pennsylvania Ave NW .... Washington DC 20038 **800-255-7688** 202-616-5594
US Marshals Service
401 Courthouse Square .... Alexandria VA 22314 **800-336-0102*** 202-307-9100
*General
US Parole Commission
5550 Friendship Blvd Rm 420 .... Chevy Chase MD 20815 **888-585-9103** 301-492-5990

340-13 US Department of Labor

		Toll-Free	Phone

Job Corps
200 Constitution Ave NW Ste N4463 .... Washington DC 20210 **800-733-5627** 202-693-3000
Office of Administrative Law Judges
200 Constitution Ave NW Ste 400 N........... Washington DC 20210 **877-889-5627** 202-693-7300
Department of Labor
Public Affairs Office
200 Constitution Ave NW .... Washington DC 20210 **866-487-2365** 202-693-4650
Employment & Training Administration Regional Offices
Region III - Atlanta
Federal Ctr 61 Forsyth St SW Rm 6M12.......... Atlanta GA 20210 **877-872-5627**
Employment Standards Administration
200 Constitution Ave NW Rm S2321 .... Washington DC 20210 **866-487-2365** 202-693-0200
Mine Safety & Health Administration (MSHA)
1100 Wilson Blvd .... Arlington VA 22209 **800-746-1553** 202-693-9400
Occupational Safety & Health Administration (OSHA)
200 Constitution Ave NW .... Washington DC 20210 **800-321-6742** 202-693-1999
Occupational Safety & Health Administration Regional Offices
Region 1
JFK Federal Bldg Rm E-340 .... Boston MA 02203 **800-321-6742** 617-565-9860
Region 10
300 Fifth Ave Ste 1280 .... Seattle WA 98104 **800-321-6742*** 206-757-6700
*Help Line
Region 2
201 Varick St Ste 670................ New York NY 10014 **800-321-6742** 212-337-2378
Region 3
Curtis Ctr 170 S Independence Mall W
Ste 740W .... Philadelphia PA 19106 **800-321-6742** 215-861-4900
Office of Disability Employment Policy
200 Constitution Ave NW Ste S1303 .... Washington DC 20210 **866-633-7365** 202-693-7880
Secretary of Labor
200 Constitution Ave NW Rm S2018 .... Washington DC 20210 **866-487-2365** 202-693-6000
Women's Bureau
200 Constitution Ave NW Rm S3002 .... Washington DC 20210 **800-827-5335** 202-693-6710
Region 10
1111 Third Ave Rm 925 .... Seattle WA 98101 **800-827-5335** 206-553-1534
Women's Bureau Regional Offices
Region 2
201 Varick St Rm 602................. New York NY 10014 **800-827-5335** 212-337-2389
Region 3
200 Constitution Ave NW Ste 631E .... Washington DC 20210 **800-827-5335** 866-487-2365
Region 4
Sam Nunn Federal Ctr
61 Forsyth St SW Ste 6B75 .... Atlanta GA 30303 **800-827-5335** 404-562-2336
Region 5
Federal Bldg
230 S Dearborn St Rm 1022................ Chicago IL 60604 **800-827-5335** 312-353-6985
Region 6
Federal Bldg 525 Griffin St Ste 735 ....Dallas TX 75202 **800-827-5335** 972-850-4700
Region 7
2300 Main St Ste 1050............... Kansas City MO 64108 **800-827-5335** 816-285-7233
Region 8
1999 Broadway Ste 1620 PO Box 46550 .... Denver CO 80201 **800-827-5335** 303-844-1286
Region 9
90 Seventh St Ste 2650 ....San Francisco CA 94103 **800-827-5335** 415-625-2638

340-14 US Department of State

		Toll-Free	Phone

Bureau of Consular Affairs
2201 C St NW SA-29 .... Washington DC 20520 **888-407-4747** 202-501-4444
Office of Children's Issues
SA-17 9th Fl .... Washington DC 20522 **888-407-4747** 202-501-4444
Passport Services
1111 19th St NW Ste 500.................. Washington DC 20524 **888-874-7793** 877-487-2778
Colorado Passport Agency
Colorado Agency
3151 S Vaughn Way Ste 600 .... Aurora CO 80014 **888-874-7793** 877-487-2778
International Boundary & Water Commission - US & Mexico
4171 N Mesa Ste C-100.................El Paso TX 79902 **800-262-8857** 915-832-4101
Boston Agency
10 Cswy St Rm 247
Tip O'Neill Federal Bldg .... Boston MA 02222 **877-487-2778**
Connecticut Agency
850 Canal Street .... Stamford CT 06902 **877-487-2778**
Honolulu Agency
300 Ala Moana Bldg Ste 1-330 .... Honolulu HI 96850 **877-487-2778**
Passport Services Regional Offices
Los Angeles Agency
11000 Wilshire Blvd Ste 1000 ....Los Angeles CA 90024 **877-487-2778**
New Orleans Agency
365 Canal St Ste 1300 ....New Orleans LA 70130 **877-487-2778**
New York Agency
376 Hudson St 10th Fl .... New York NY 10014 **877-487-2778**

			Toll-Free	Phone
Philadelphia Agency				
US Custom House				
200 Chesnut St Rm 103	Philadelphia PA	19106	**877-487-2778**	
San Francisco Agency				
95 Hawthorne St 5th Fl	San Francisco CA	94105	**877-487-2778**	
Washington (DC) Agency				
600 19th St NW				
First Floor Sidewalk Level	Washington DC	20006	**877-487-2778**	
Under Secretary for Political Affairs				
Bureau of South & Central Asian Affairs				
2201 C St NW	Washington DC	20520	**800-877-8339**	202-647-4000

340-15 US Department of Transportation

			Toll-Free	Phone
Federal Aviation Administration (FAA)				
800 Independence Ave SW	Washington DC	20591	**866-835-5322**	
Safety Hotline				
800 Independence Ave SW	Washington DC	20591	**800-255-1111**	
Federal Aviation Administration Northwest Mountain Region				
1601 Lind Ave SW	Renton WA	98057	**800-220-5715**	425-227-2001
Federal Highway Administration				
National Highway Institute				
4600 Fairfax Dr Ste 800	Arlington VA	22203	**877-558-6873**	703-235-0500
Federal Motor Carrier Safety Administration (FMCSA)				
1200 New Jersey Ave SE	Washington DC	20590	**800-832-5660**	
Federal Railroad Administration Regional Offices (FRA)				
Region 1				
55 Broadway Room 1077	Cambridge MA	02142	**800-724-5991**	617-494-2302
Region 2				
Baldwin Tower Ste 660				
1510 Chester Pike	Crum Lynne PA	19022	**800-724-5992**	610-521-8200
Region 3				
61 Forsyth St SW Ste 16T20	Atlanta GA	30303	**800-724-5993**	404-562-3800
Region 4 200 W Adams St	Chicago IL	60606	**800-724-5040**	312-353-6203
Region 6				
901 Locust St Ste 464	Kansas City MO	64106	**800-724-5996**	816-329-3840
Region 8				
703 Broadway Ste 650	Vancouver WA	98660	**800-724-5998**	360-696-7536
Maritime Administration (MARAD)				
1200 New Jersey Ave SE	Washington DC	20590	**800-996-2723***	202-366-5807
*Hotline				
National Center for Statistics & Analysis				
1200 New Jersey Ave SE	Washington DC	20590	**800-934-8517**	202-366-1503
National Highway Traffic Safety Administration				
Vehicle Research & Test Ctr				
10820 SR 347 PO Box B37	East Liberty OH	43319	**800-262-8309**	937-666-4511
National Highway Traffic Safety Administration Regional Offices				
NHTSA Region 3				
1200 New Jersey Ave Ste 6700	Washington DC	20590	**888-327-4236**	
Pipeline & Hazardous Materials Safety Administration				
Office of Hazardous Materials Safety				
1200 New Jersey Ave SE	Washington DC	20590	**800-467-4922**	202-366-4433
Research & Innovative Technology Administration				
Bureau of Transportation Statistics				
1200 New Jersey Ave SE	Washington DC	20590	**800-853-1351**	202-366-1270
Office of Research Development & Technology				
1200 New Jersey Ave SE	Washington DC	20590	**800-853-1351**	
Saint Lawrence Seaway Development Corp				
1200 New Jersey Ave SE	Washington DC	20590	**800-785-2779**	202-366-0091

340-16 US Department of the Treasury

			Toll-Free	Phone
Alcohol & Tobacco Tax & Trade Bureau				
1310 G St NW Ste 300	Washington DC	20220	**877-882-3277**	202-453-2000
Bureau of Engraving & Printing				
14th & C Sts SW	Washington DC	20228	**877-874-4114**	
Bureau of the Public Debt				
TreasuryDirect				
PO Box 7015	Parkersburg WV	26106	**800-722-2678**	304-480-7711
Comptroller of the Currency				
250 E St SW	Washington DC	20219	**800-613-6743***	202-874-5000
*Cust Svc				
Internal Revenue Service (IRS)				
1111 Constitution Ave NW	Washington DC	20224	**800-829-1040**	202-622-9511
Taxpayer Advocate Service				
77 K St NE Ste 1500	Washington DC	20002	**877-777-4778**	202-803-9000
US Mint 801 Ninth St NW	Washington DC	20220	**800-872-6468***	202-756-6468
*Cust Svc				
San Francisco				
155 Hermann St	San Francisco CA	94102	**800-872-6468**	415-575-8000

340-17 US Department of Veterans Affairs

			Toll-Free	Phone
Department of Veterans Affairs (VA)				
810 Vermont Ave NW	Washington DC	20420	**800-827-1000***	202-461-7600
*Cust Svc				
Public & Intergovernmental Affairs Office				
810 Vermont Ave NW	Washington DC	20420	**800-273-8255**	
Board of Veterans' Appeals				
810 Vermont Ave NW	Washington DC	20420	**800-923-8387**	
Center for Veterans Enterprise				
810 Vermont Ave	Washington DC	20420	**800-273-8255**	800-827-1000
Secretary of Veterans Affairs				
Center for Women Veterans				
810 Vermont Ave NW	Washington DC	20420	**800-827-1000**	
Veterans Benefits Administration				
810 Vermont Ave NW	Washington DC	20420	**800-827-1000**	
Veterans Health Administration				
Office of Research & Development				
810 Vermont Ave NW MC 12	Washington DC	20420	**800-827-1000**	

340-18 US Independent Agencies Government Corporations & Quasi-Official Agencies

Included also among these listings are selected Federal Boards, Committees, and Commissions.

			Toll-Free	Phone
Federal Election Commission				
999 E St NW	Washington DC	20463	**800-424-9530**	202-694-1100
Architectural & Transportation Barriers Compliance Board				
1331 F St NW Ste 1000	Washington DC	20004	**800-872-2253**	202-272-0080
Commodity Futures Trading Commission				
3 Lafayette Ctr 1155 21 St NW	Washington DC	20581	**866-366-2382**	202-418-5000
Consumer Product Safety Commission (CPSC)				
4340 E W Hwy Ste 502	Bethesda MD	20814	**800-638-2772**	301-504-7923
Corp for National & Community Service				
AmeriCorps USA				
1201 New York Ave NW	Washington DC	20525	**800-833-3722**	202-606-5000
Learn & Serve America				
1201 New York Ave NW	Washington DC	20525	**800-833-3722**	202-606-5000
Senior Corps				
1201 New York Ave NW	Washington DC	20525	**800-833-3722**	202-606-5000
Defense Nuclear Facilities Safety Board				
625 Indiana Ave NW Ste 700	Washington DC	20004	**800-788-4016**	202-694-7000
Denali Commission				
510 L St Ste 410	Anchorage AK	99501	**888-480-4321**	907-271-1414
Environmental Protection Agency (EPA)				
1200 Pennsylvania Ave NW	Washington DC	20460	**888-372-8255**	202-564-4700
US National Response Team				
1200 Pennsylvania Ave NW	Washington DC	20593	**800-424-9346**	202-267-2675
Region 1				
1 Congress St Ste 1100	Boston MA	02114	**888-372-7341**	617-918-1111
Region 10				
1200 Sixth Ave Ste 900	Seattle WA	98101	**800-424-4372**	206-553-1200
Region 3 1650 Arch St	Philadelphia PA	19103	**800-438-2474**	215-814-5000
Environmental Protection Agency Regional Offices				
Region 4				
Federal Ctr 61 Forsyth St SW	Atlanta GA	30303	**800-241-1754**	404-562-9900
Region 6				
1445 Ross Ave Ste 1200	Dallas TX	75202	**800-887-6063**	214-665-2200
Region 8 1595 Wynkoop St	Denver CO	80202	**800-227-8917**	303-312-6312
Region 9				
75 Hawthorne St	San Francisco CA	94105	**866-372-9378**	415-947-8000
Equal Employment Opportunity Commission (EEOC)				
1801 L St NW	Washington DC	20507	**800-669-4000**	202-663-4191
Equal Employment Opportunity Commission Regional Offices				
Atlanta District				
100 Alabama St SW Ste 4R30	Atlanta GA	30303	**800-669-6820**	
Birmingham District				
1130 22nd St S Ste 2000	Birmingham AL	35205	**800-669-4000**	205-212-2100
Charlotte District				
129 W Trade St Ste 400	Charlotte NC	28202	**800-669-4000**	704-344-6682
Dallas District				
207 S Houston St 3rd Fl	Dallas TX	75202	**800-669-4000**	214-253-2700
Houston District				
1201 Louisiana St 6th Fl	Houston TX	77002	**800-669-4000**	
Los Angeles District				
255 E Temple St 4th Fl	Los Angeles CA	90012	**800-669-4000**	
New York District				
33 Whitehall St 5th Fl	New York NY	10004	**866-408-8075**	212-336-3620
Saint Louis District				
1222 Spruce St Rm 8.100	Saint Louis MO	63103	**800-669-4000**	314-539-7800
San Francisco District				
450 Golden Gate Ave 5 W				
PO Box 36025	San Francisco CA	94102	**800-669-4000**	
Export-Import Bank of the US				
811 Vermont Ave NW	Washington DC	20571	**800-565-3946**	202-565-3946
Federal Communications Commission (FCC)				
445 12th St SW	Washington DC	20554	**888-225-5322**	
Federal Deposit Insurance Corp				
550 17th St NW	Washington DC	20429	**877-275-3342**	202-898-7192
Federal Deposit Insurance Corp Regional Offices				
Atlanta Area Office				
10 Tenth St NW Ste 800	Atlanta GA	30309	**800-765-3342**	678-916-2200
Boston Area Office				
15 Braintree Hill Office Pk Ste 300	Braintree MA	02184	**866-728-9953**	781-794-5500
Chicago Area Office				
300 S Riverside Plaza Ste 1700	Chicago IL	60606	**800-944-5343**	312-382-6000
Dallas Area Office				
1601 Bryan St	Dallas TX	75201	**800-568-9161**	214-754-0098
Kansas City Area Office				
2345 Grand Blvd Ste 1200	Kansas City MO	64108	**800-209-7459**	816-234-8000
Memphis Area Office				
5100 Poplar Ave Ste 1900	Memphis TN	38137	**800-210-6354**	901-685-1603
New York Area Office				
350 5th Ave Ste 1200	New York NY	11215	**800-334-9593**	917-320-2500
San Francisco Area Office				
25 Jessie St at Ecker Sq				
Ste 2300	San Francisco CA	94105	**800-756-3558**	415-546-0160
Federal Trade Commission (FTC)				
600 Pennsylvania Ave NW	Washington DC	20580	**877-382-4357**	202-326-2222
National Do Not Call Registry				
600 Pennsylvania Ave NW	Washington DC	20580	**888-382-1222**	
East Central Region				
1111 Superior Ave Ste 200	Cleveland OH	44114	**877-382-4357**	216-263-3455
Midwest Region				
55 W Monroe St Ste 1825	Chicago IL	60603	**877-382-4357**	312-960-5634
Northwest Region				
915 Second Ave Rm 2896	Seattle WA	98174	**877-382-4357**	
Federal Trade Commission Regional Offices				
Southeast Region				
60 Forsyth St SW	Atlanta GA	30303	**877-282-4357**	404-656-1390
Southwest Region				
1999 Bryan St Ste 2150	Dallas TX	75201	**877-382-4357**	
Western Region				
901 Market Street Ste 570	San Francisco CA	94103	**877-382-4357**	

				Toll-Free	Phone

General Services Administration
FCIC National Contact Ctr

				Toll-Free	Phone
PO Box 100	Pueblo	CO	81009	**888-878-3256**	

Region 1 - New England
10 Cswy St Rm 1010
| Thomas P O'Neill Federal Bldg | Boston | MA | 02222 | **866-734-1727** | 617-565-5860 |

Region 3 - Mid-Atlantic
Strawbridge Bldg 20 N 8th St
| | Philadelphia | PA | 19107 | **800-333-4636** | 215-446-5100 |

Region 4 - Southeast Sunbelt
| 1800 F St NW Ste 600 | Washington | DC | 20405 | **800-333-4636** | |

General Services Administration Regional Offices
Region 8 - Rocky Mountain
| Denver Federal Ctr Bldg 41 | Denver | CO | 80225 | **888-999-4777** | 303-236-7329 |

Indian Arts & Crafts Board
Dept of the Interior 1849 C St NW
| MS 2528-MIB | Washington | DC | 20240 | **888-278-3253** | 202-208-3773 |

Merit Systems Protection Board (MSPB)
| 1615 M St NW | Washington | DC | 20419 | **800-209-8960** | 202-653-7200 |

Merit Systems Protection Board Regional Offices (MSPB)
Atlanta Region
| 401 W Peachtree St NW 10th Fl | Atlanta | GA | 30308 | **800-209-8960** | 404-730-2755 |

National Archives & Records Administration (NARA)
| 8601 Adelphi Rd | College Park | MD | 20740 | **866-272-6272** | |

Archival Research Catalog
| 8601 Adelphi Rd | College Park | MD | 20740 | **866-272-6272** | |

National Archives & Records Administration Regional Offices
Northeast Region
| 380 Trapelo Rd | Waltham | MA | 02452 | **866-406-2379** | 781-663-0130 |

Pacific Alaska Region
| 6125 Sand Pt Way NE | Seattle | WA | 98115 | **866-325-7208** | 206-336-5115 |

National Credit Union Administration
| 1775 Duke St | Alexandria | VA | 22314 | **800-827-9650*** | 703-518-6300 |
*Fraud Hotline

National Endowment for the Humanities (NEH)
| 400 7th St SW | Washington | DC | 20506 | **800-634-1121** | 202-606-8400 |

National Labor Relations Board (NLRB)
| 1099 14th St NW | Washington | DC | 20570 | **866-667-6572** | 202-273-1991 |

National Labor Relations Board Regional Offices
| Region 1 10 Cswy St 6th Fl | Boston | MA | 02222 | **866-667-6572** | 617-565-6700 |

Region 11
| 4035 University Pkwy Ste 200 | Winston-Salem | NC | 27106 | **866-667-6572** | 336-631-5201 |

Region 14
| 1222 Spruce St Rm 8.302 | Saint Louis | MO | 63103 | **866-667-6572** | 314-539-7770 |

Region 16
| Federal Bldg 819 Taylor St Rm 8A24 | Fort Worth | TX | 76102 | **866-667-6572** | 817-978-2921 |

Region 18
| 330 Second Ave S Ste 790 | Minneapolis | MN | 55401 | **866-667-6572** | 612-348-1757 |

Region 20
| 901 Market St Ste 400 | San Francisco | CA | 94103 | **866-667-6572** | 415-356-5130 |

Region 25
| 575 N Pennsylvania St Ste 238 | Indianapolis | IN | 46204 | **866-667-6572** | 317-226-7381 |

Region 3
Niagara Ctr Bldg
| 130 S Elmwood Ave Ste 630 | Buffalo | NY | 14202 | **866-667-6572** | 716-551-4931 |

Region 31
| 11150 W Olympic Blvd Ste 700 | Los Angeles | CA | 90064 | **866-667-6572** | 310-235-7352 |

Region 8
| 1240 E Ninth St Rm 1695 | Cleveland | OH | 44199 | **866-667-6572** | 216-522-3715 |

Region 9
| 550 Main St Rm 3003 | Cincinnati | OH | 45202 | **866-667-6572** | 513-684-3686 |

National Railroad Passenger Corp
| 60 Massachusetts Ave NE | Washington | DC | 20002 | **800-872-7245** | 202-906-3741 |

National Science Foundation (NSF)
| 4201 Wilson Blvd | Arlington | VA | 22230 | **800-877-8339** | 703-292-5111 |

Nuclear Regulatory Commission Regional Offices
Region 1
| 2100 Renaissance Blvd | King of Prussia | PA | 19406 | **800-432-1156** | 610-337-5000 |

Region 2
| 61 Forsyth St SW Ste 23T85 | Atlanta | GA | 30303 | **800-577-8510** | 404-562-4400 |

Region 3
| 2443 Warrenville Rd Ste 210 | Lisle | IL | 60532 | **800-522-3025** | 630-829-9500 |

Region 4
| 1600 E Lamar Blvd | Arlington | TX | 76011 | **800-952-9677** | 817-860-8100 |

Occupational Safety & Health Review Commission Regional Offices
Atlanta Region
| 100 Alabama St SW Rm 2R90 | Atlanta | GA | 30303 | **800-321-6742** | 404-562-1640 |

Office of Special Counsel
| 1730 M St NW Ste 218 | Washington | DC | 20036 | **800-872-9855** | 202-254-3600 |

Office of Special Counsel Regional Offices
Dallas Field Office
| 525 Griffin St Rm 824 PO Box 103 | Dallas | TX | 75202 | **800-872-9855** | 214-747-1519 |

San Francisco Bay Area Field Office
| Federal Bldg 1301 Clay St Ste 1220-N | Oakland | CA | 94612 | **800-872-9855** | 510-637-3460 |

Peace Corps
| 1111 20th St NW | Washington | DC | 20526 | **800-424-8580** | 202-692-1040 |

Peace Corps Regional Offices
Atlanta Regional Office
| 1111 20th Street NW | Washington | DC | 20526 | **855-855-1961** | 404-562-3456 |

Chicago Regional Office
| 55 W Monroe St Ste 450 | Chicago | IL | 60603 | **800-424-8580** | 312-353-4990 |

Dallas Regional Office
| 1100 Commerce St Ste 427 | Dallas | TX | 75242 | **855-855-1961** | |

Los Angeles Regional Office
| 2361 Rosecrans Ave Ste 155 | El Segundo | CA | 90245 | **800-424-8580** | 310-356-1100 |

Mid-Atlantic Regional Office
| 1525 Wilson Blvd Ste 100 | Arlington | VA | 22209 | **800-424-8580** | 202-692-1040 |

New York Regional Office
| 201 Varick St Ste 1025 | New York | NY | 10014 | **800-424-8580** | 212-352-5440 |

Northwest Regional Office
| 1601 Fifth Ave Ste 605 | Seattle | WA | 98101 | **800-424-8580** | 206-553-5490 |

San Francisco Regional Office
| 1301 Clay St Ste 620-N | Oakland | CA | 94610 | **800-424-8580** | 510-452-8444 |

Pension Benefit Guaranty Corp
| 1200 K St NW | Washington | DC | 20005 | **800-400-7242*** | 202-326-4000 |
*Cust Svc

Railroad Retirement Board
| 844 N Rush St | Chicago | IL | 60611 | **877-772-5772** | 312-751-4300 |

Securities & Exchange Commission (SEC)
| 100 F St NE | Washington | DC | 20549 | **800-732-0330** | 202-942-8088 |

				Toll-Free	Phone
Region 1 PO Box 94638	Palatine	IL	60094	**888-655-1825**	847-688-6888

Selective Service System Regional Offices
| Region 2 PO Box 94638 | Palatine | IL | 60094 | **888-655-1825** | 847-688-6888 |

Small Business Administration (SBA)
| 409 Third St SW | Washington | DC | 20416 | **800-827-5722** | 202-205-6600 |

Region 10
| 701 Fifth Ave Ste 2900 | Seattle | WA | 98104 | **800-772-1213** | 206-615-2236 |

Small Business Administration Regional Offices
| Region 6 1301 Young St | Dallas | TX | 75202 | **800-772-1213** | 214-767-9401 |

Social Security Administration (SSA)
| 6401 Security Blvd | Baltimore | MD | 21235 | **800-772-1213** | 410-965-8904 |

Social Security Administration Regional Offices
Region 2
| 26 Federal Plaza Rm 40-102 | New York | NY | 10278 | **800-772-1213** | 212-264-4036 |

Region 4
| 61 Forsyth St SW Ste 23T30 | Atlanta | GA | 30303 | **800-772-1213** | |

Region 5
| 600 W Madison St PO Box 8280 | Chicago | IL | 60680 | **800-772-1213** | 312-575-4050 |

US Commission on Civil Rights Regional Offices
Midwestern Regional Office
| 55 W Monroe St Ste 410 | Chicago | IL | 60603 | **800-552-6843** | 312-353-8311 |

US Election Assistance Commission
| 1201 New York Ave NW Ste 300 | Washington | DC | 20005 | **866-747-1471** | 202-566-3100 |

US General Services Administration
| 1800 F St NW | Washington | DC | 20405 | **800-488-3111** | |

US Postal Service (USPS)
| 475 L'Enfant Plaza W SW | Washington | DC | 20260 | **800-275-8777*** | 202-268-2000 |
*Cust Svc

341	**GOVERNMENT - US - JUDICIAL BRANCH**

341-1 US Bankruptcy Courts

				Toll-Free	Phone

US Bankruptcy Court
Alaska
| 605 W Fourth Ave Ste 138 | Anchorage | AK | 99501 | **800-859-8059** | 907-271-2655 |

Minnesota
| 300 S Fourth St 7W US Courthouse | Minneapolis | MN | 55415 | **866-260-7337** | 612-664-5260 |

Missouri Eastern
| 111 S Tenth St 4th Fl | Saint Louis | MO | 63102 | **866-803-9517** | 314-244-4500 |

Pennsylvania Middle
| 197 S Main St | Wilkes-Barre | PA | 18701 | **877-298-2053** | 570-831-2500 |

Texas Northern
| 1100 Commerce St Rm 1254 | Dallas | TX | 75242 | **800-442-6850** | 214-753-2000 |

Washington Eastern
| 904 W Riverside Ave Ste 304 | Spokane | WA | 99201 | **800-519-2549** | 509-353-2404 |

Wisconsin Eastern
US Courthouse
| 517 E Wisconsin Ave Rm 126 | Milwaukee | WI | 53202 | **877-781-7277** | 414-297-3291 |

341-2 US District Courts

				Toll-Free	Phone

US District Court Colorado
| 901 19th St | Denver | CO | 80294 | **800-359-8699** | 303-844-3433 |

US District Court for the District of Alaska
| 222 W Seventh Ave St 4 | Anchorage | AK | 99513 | **866-243-3814** | 907-677-6100 |

US District Court Mississippi Southern
| PO Box 23552 | Jackson | MS | 39225 | **866-517-7682** | 601-965-4439 |

US District Court Nebraska
| 111 S 18th Plaza Ste 1152 | Omaha | NE | 68102 | **866-220-4381** | 402-661-7350 |

US District Court North Carolina Western
| 401 W Trade St | Charlotte | NC | 28202 | **866-851-1605** | 704-350-7400 |

US District Court Oklahoma Northern
| 333 W Fourth St | Tulsa | OK | 74103 | **866-213-1957** | 918-699-4700 |

US District Court Texas Western
| 655 E Durango Blvd Rm G65 | San Antonio | TX | 78206 | **800-659-2497** | 210-472-6550 |

US District Court Vermont
| 11 Elmwood Ave Rm 506 PO Box 945 | Burlington | VT | 05402 | **800-837-8718** | 802-951-6301 |

342	**GOVERNMENT - US - LEGISLATIVE BRANCH**

SEE ALSO Legislation Hotlines

				Toll-Free	Phone

Library of Congress
National Library Service for the Blind & Physically Handicapped
| 1291 Taylor St NW | Washington | DC | 20011 | **888-657-7323** | 202-707-5100 |

US Government Printing Office Bookstore (GPO)
| 732 N Capitol St NW | Washington | DC | 20401 | **866-512-1800** | 202-512-1800 |

342-1 US Congressional Committees

				Toll-Free	Phone

US House of Representatives
Permanent Select Committee on Intelligence
Capitol Visitor Ctr HVC-304
| US Capitol Bldg | Washington | DC | 20515 | **877-858-9040** | 202-225-4121 |

343	**GRAPHIC DESIGN**

SEE ALSO Typesetting & Related Services

				Toll-Free	Phone

Armada Group Inc, The
| 325 Soquel Ave Ste A | Santa Cruz | CA | 95062 | **800-408-2120** | |

B&B Image Group
| 1712 Marshall St NE | Minneapolis | MN | 55413 | **888-788-9461** | 612-788-9461 |

BrandEquity International
| 2330 Washington St | Newton | MA | 02462 | **800-969-3150** | |

			Toll-Free	Phone
Graphic Reproduction 1381 Franquette Ave Bldg B1	Concord CA	94520	800-498-9939	925-674-0900
Imprimis Group Inc 4835 Lyndon B Johnson Fwy	Dallas TX	75244	888-772-9682	972-419-1700
Kane Graphical Corp 2255 W Logan Blvd	Chicago IL	60647	800-992-2921	773-384-1200
Lansmont Corp Ryan Ranch Research Pk 17 Mandeville Ct	Monterey CA	93940	800-526-7666	831-655-6600
Metro Creative Graphics Inc 519 Eigth Ave	New York NY	10018	800-223-1600	212-947-5100
Printing House Ltd, The 1403 Bathurst St	Toronto ON	M5R3H8	800-874-0870	416-536-6113
Signature Graphics Inc 1000 Signature Dr	Porter IN	46304	800-356-3235	219-926-4994
Spire Inc 65 Bay St	Boston MA	02125	877-350-8837	617-350-8837
Subia Corp 6612 Gulton Ct NE	Albuquerque NM	87109	800-275-2636	505-345-2636
Vista Color Lab Inc 2048 Fulton Rd	Cleveland OH	44113	800-890-0062	216-651-2830
West Canadian Digital Imaging Inc 200 - 1601 Ninth Ave SE	Calgary AB	T2G0H4	800-267-2555	403-245-2555

344 GROCERY STORES

SEE ALSO Wholesale Clubs ; Gourmet Specialty Shops ; Health Food Stores ; Ice Cream & Dairy Stores ; Bakeries ; Convenience Stores

			Toll-Free	Phone
A.g. Ferrari Foods 14234 Catalina St	San Leandro CA	94577	877-878-2783	510-346-2100
Acme Markets Inc 75 Valley Stream Pkwy	Malvern PA	19355	877-932-7948	610-889-4000
Alaska Commercial Co 550 W 64th Ave Ste 200	Anchorage AK	99518	800-563-0002	907-273-4600
ALDI Inc 1200 N Kirk Rd	Batavia IL	60510	800-388-2534	630-879-8100
Alliance Foods Inc 605 W Chicago Rd	Coldwater MI	49036	800-388-4158	517-278-2396
Amax Nutrasource Inc 14291 E Don Julian Rd	City Of Industry CA	91746	800-893-5306	626-961-6600
Autry Greer & Sons Inc 2850 W Main St	Mobile AL	36612	800-999-7750	251-457-8655
Bashas Inc 22402 S Bashas Rd	Chandler AZ	85248	800-755-7292	480-895-9350
BI-LO LLC PO Box 99	Mauldin SC	29662	800-862-9293	
Big Y Foods Inc 2145 Roosevelt Ave *Cust Svc	Springfield MA	01102	800-828-2688*	413-784-0600
Brookshire Bros Ltd 1201 Ellen Trout Dr	Lufkin TX	75904	855-467-7837	936-634-8155
Byrd Cookie Company Inc 6700 Waters Ave	Savannah GA	31406	800-291-2973	912-355-1716
Capitol Distributing Inc 3500 E Commercial Ct	Meridian ID	83642	800-769-5659	208-888-5112
Econo Foods 1600 Stephenson PO Box 1107	Iron Mountain MI	49801	877-295-4558	906-774-1911
EuroPharma Inc 955 Challenger Dr	Green Bay WI	54311	866-598-5487	920-406-6500
Federated Group Inc 3025 W Salt Creek Ln	Arlington Heights IL	60005	800-234-0011	847-577-1200
Food City 1005 N Arizona Ave	Chandler AZ	85224	800-755-7292	480-857-2198
FreshDirect Inc 23-30 Borden Ave	Long Island City NY	11101	866-511-1240	718-928-1000
Frontera Foods Inc 449 N Clark St Ste 205	Chicago IL	60654	800-509-4441	312-595-1624
Fry's Food Stores of Arizona Inc 500 S 99th Ave	Tolleson AZ	85353	866-221-4141	
Giant Eagle Inc 101 Kappa Dr *Cust Svc	Pittsburgh PA	15238	800-553-2324*	412-963-6200
Giant Food Inc 8301 Professional Pl Ste 115	Landover MD	20785	888-469-4426	
Giant Food Stores Inc 1149 Harrisburg Pike	Carlisle PA	17013	888-814-4268	717-249-4000
Golub Corp 461 Nott St	Schenectady NY	12308	800-666-7667	
Gs Foods Inc 5925 S Alcoa Ave	Vernon CA	90058	800-273-6637	323-581-6161
Hancock County Co-op Oil Assn 245 State St	Garner IA	50438	800-924-2667	641-923-2635
Harps Food Stores Inc 918 S Gutensohn Rd	Springdale AR	72762	877-772-8193	479-751-7601
Harris Teeter Inc 701 Crestdale Rd PO Box 10100 *Cust Svc	Matthews NC	28105	800-432-6111*	704-844-3100
Holly Poultry Inc 2221 Berlin St	Baltimore MD	21230	800-342-9464	410-727-6210
IGA Inc 8725 W Higgins Rd Ste 350	Chicago IL	60631	800-321-5442	773-693-4520
Ingles Markets Inc 2913 US Hwy 70 W *NASDAQ: IMKTA*	Black Mountain NC	28711	800-635-5066	828-669-2941
InVite Health Inc One Garden State Plz	Paramus NJ	07652	800-349-0929	201-587-2222
JSB Industries Inc 130 Crescent Ave	Chelsea MA	02150	800-554-2887	617-846-1565
K-VA-T Food Stores Inc PO Box 1158	Abingdon VA	24212	800-826-8451	276-623-5100
Kroger Co 1014 Vine St *NYSE: KR*	Cincinnati OH	45202	800-576-4377	513-762-4000
Kuukpik Corp PO Box 89187	Nuiqsut AK	99789	866-480-6220	907-480-6220
Life Force International Corp 495 Raleigh Ave	El Cajon CA	92064	800-531-4877	858-218-3200
Loblaw Cos Ltd One President's Choice Cir	Brampton ON	L6Y5S5	888-495-5111	905-459-2500
Lowes Food Stores Inc 1381 Old Mill Cir Ste 200	Winston-Salem NC	27103	800-669-5693	336-659-0180

			Toll-Free	Phone
Market Day Corp 555 W Pierce Rd Ste 200	Itasca IL	60143	877-632-7753	630-285-1470
Martin & Bayley Inc 1311 A W Main	Carmi IL	62821	800-876-2511	618-382-2334
McClancy Seasoning Co One Spice Rd	Fort Mill SC	29707	800-843-1968	803-548-2366
Meijer Inc 2929 Walker Ave NW	Grand Rapids MI	49544	800-543-3704	616-453-6711
Meijer Stores Inc 2929 Walker Ave NW	Grand Rapids MI	49544	800-543-3704	616-453-6711
Merchants Grocery Co 800 Maddox Dr PO Box 1268	Culpeper VA	22701	877-897-9893	540-825-0786
Nature's Best 6 Pt Dr Ste 300	Brea CA	92821	800-800-7799	714-255-4600
Overwaitea Food Group 19855 92A Ave	Langley BC	V1M3B6	800-242-9229	604-888-1213
Peapod LLC 9933 Woods Dr	Skokie IL	60077	800-573-2763	847-583-9400
Piggly Wiggly Carolina Company Inc PO Box 118047	Charleston SC	29423	800-243-9880	843-554-9880
Publix Super Markets Inc 3300 Publix Corporate Pkwy *PR	Lakeland FL	33811	800-242-1227*	863-688-1188
Raley's 500 W Capitol Ave PO Box 15618	Sacramento CA	95852	800-925-9989	916-373-3333
Ralphs Grocery Co 1014 Vine Street *Cust Svc	Cincinnati, OH	45202	800-576-4377*	
Redner's Markets Inc 3 Quarry Rd	Reading PA	19605	888-673-4663	610-926-3700
Resource Plus 9636 Heckscher Dr	Jacksonville FL	32226	888-678-8966	
Roasterie Inc, The 1204 W 27th St	Kansas City MO	64108	800-376-0245	816-931-4000
Save-A-Lot Ltd 100 Corporate Office Dr *General	Earth City MO	63045	800-346-3808*	314-592-9100
Schnuck Markets Inc 11420 Lackland Rd	Saint Louis MO	63146	800-264-4400	314-994-9900
Scolari's Food & Drug Co 950 Holman Way	Sparks NV	89431	800-219-7401	775-575-1381
Shop 'n Save 10461 Manchester Rd	Kirkwood MO	63122	800-428-6974	314-984-0900
Shoppers Food & Pharmacy 10501 Martin Luther King Jr Hwy	Bowie MD	20720	800-866-0514	240-544-0180
ShopRite PO Box 7812	Edison NJ	08818	800-746-7748	
ShopRite Supermarkets Inc 600 York St	Elizabeth NJ	07207	800-746-7748	908-527-3300
Smart & Final Inc 600 Citadel Dr	Commerce CA	90040	800-894-0511	323-869-7500
Starco Impex Inc 2710 S 11th St	Beaumont TX	77701	866-740-9601	
Super H Mart Inc 2550 Pleasant Hill Rd	Duluth GA	30096	877-427-7386	678-543-4000
SUPERVALU Inc 7075 Flying Cloud Dr *NYSE: SVU ▬ *Cust Svc*	Eden Prairie MN	55344	877-322-8228*	952-828-4000
Supreme Mfg Company Inc Five Connerty Ct	East Brunswick NJ	08816	800-772-7632	732-254-0087
Village Super Market Inc 733 Mountain Ave *NASDAQ: VLGEA*	Springfield NJ	07081	800-746-7748	973-467-2200
VitaDigest Inc 20687-2 Amar Rd Ste 258	Walnut CA	91789	877-848-2168	
Waldbaums Two Paragon Dr	Montvale NJ	07645	866-443-7374	
Wedge Community Co-Op Inc 2105 Lyndale Ave S	Minneapolis MN	55405	800-535-4555	612-871-3993
Wegmans Food Markets Inc 1500 Brooks Ave PO Box 30844	Rochester NY	14603	800-934-6267	585-328-2550
Weis Markets 1000 S Second St PO Box 471 *NYSE: WMK*	Sunbury PA	17801	866-999-9347	
Western Bagel Baking Corp 7814 Sepulveda Blvd	Van Nuys CA	91405	800-555-0882	818-786-5847
WinCo Foods Inc PO Box 5756	Boise ID	83705	888-674-6854	208-377-0110
Wing Hing Foods Inc 2539 E Philadelphia St	Ontario CA	91761	855-734-2742	
ZeaVision LLC Spirit Business Ctr Ii 680F Crown Industrial Ct	Chesterfield MO	63005	866-833-2800	314-628-1000

345 GYM & PLAYGROUND EQUIPMENT

			Toll-Free	Phone
American Athletic Inc (AAI) 200 American Ave	Jefferson IA	50129	800-247-3978	515-386-3125
American Playground Corp 505 E 31st St Ste X	Anderson IN	46016	800-541-1602	765-642-0288
BCI Burke Company Inc 660 Van Dyne Rd	Fond du Lac WI	54937	800-356-2070	920-921-9220
Columbia Cascade Co 1300 SW Sixth Ave Ste 310	Portland OR	97201	800-547-1940	503-223-1157
Grounds For Play Inc 1401 N Dallas St	Mansfield TX	76063	800-552-7529	817-453-5703
Jaypro Sports Inc 976 Hartford Tpke *Cust Svc	Waterford CT	06385	800-243-0533*	860-447-3001
Landscape Structures Inc 601 Seventh St S	Delano MN	55328	800-328-0035	763-972-3391
Miracle Recreation Equipment Co 878 Hwy 60	Monett MO	65708	800-523-4202	417-235-6917
PlayCore Inc 401 Chestnut St Ste 410	Chattanooga TN	37402	877-762-7563	
Playworld Systems Inc 1000 Buffalo Rd	Lewisburg PA	17837	800-233-8404	570-522-9800
School-Tech Inc 745 State Cir PO Box 1941	Ann Arbor MI	48106	800-521-2832	
SportsPlay Equipment Inc 5642 Natural Bridge Ave	Saint Louis MO	63120	800-727-8180	314-389-4140

346 GYPSUM PRODUCTS

			Toll-Free	Phone

American Gypsum Co
3811 Turtle Creek Blvd Ste 1200 . . . . Dallas TX 75219 **866-439-5800** 214-530-5500
Canadian Gypsum Company Inc
350 Burnhamthorpe Rd W Fifth Fl . . . . . . Mississauga ON L5B3J1 **800-565-6607** 905-803-5600
CertainTeed Gypsum
2424 Lakeshore Rd W . . . . Mississauga ON L5J1K4 **800-233-8990** 905-823-9881
National Gypsum Co
2001 Rexford Rd . . . . Charlotte NC 28211 **800-628-4662** 704-365-7300
PABCO Gypsum 37851 Cherry St . . . . Newark CA 94560 **877-449-7786** 510-792-9555
USG Corp 550 W Adams St . . . . Chicago IL 60661 **800-874-4968** 312-436-4000
NYSE: USG

347 HAIRPIECES, WIGS, TOUPEES

			Toll-Free	Phone

Aderans Hair Goods Inc
Simplicity Hair Extensions
5130 N State Rd Seven ft Ninth Fl . . . . Lauderdale FL 33319 **877-413-5225***
*Sales
Alkinco PO Box 278 . . . . New York NY 10116 **800-424-7118** 212-719-3070
Headstart Hair For Men Inc
3395 Cypress Gardens Rd . . . . Winter Haven FL 33884 **800-645-6525** 863-324-5559
Henry Margu Inc
540 Commerce Dr . . . . Yeadon PA 19050 **800-345-8284** 610-622-0515
HPH Corp
1529 SE 47th Terr . . . . Cape Coral FL 33904 **800-654-9884** 239-540-0085
Jacquelyn Wigs
15 W 37th St Fourth Fl . . . . New York NY 10018 **800-272-2424** 212-302-2266
Jean Paree Weegs Inc
4041 South 700 East Ste 2 . . . . Salt Lake City UT 84107 **800-422-9447***
*Orders
Jon Renau Collection
2510 Island View Way . . . . Vista CA 92081 **800-462-9447** 760-598-0067
Louis Ferre Inc
302 Fifth Ave Ste 10 . . . . New York NY 10001 **800-695-1061** 212-239-1600
National Fiber Technology LLC
300 Canal St . . . . Lawrence MA 01840 **800-842-2751*** 978-686-2964
*Cust Svc
Peggy Knight Solutions Inc
1750 Bridgeway . . . . Sausalito CA 94965 **800-997-7753** 415-289-1777
Wig America Co
27317 Industrial Blvd . . . . Hayward CA 94545 **800-338-7600** 510-887-9579
World of Wigs
2305 E 17th St . . . . Santa Ana CA 92705 **800-794-5572** 714-547-4461
YK International Co
3246 W Montrose Ave . . . . Chicago IL 60618 **800-266-5254** 773-583-5270

348 HANDBAGS, TOTES, BACKPACKS

SEE ALSO Sporting Goods ; Tarps, Tents, Covers ; Leather Goods - Personal ; Luggage, Bags, Cases

			Toll-Free	Phone

Dow Cover Co Inc
373 Lexington Ave . . . . New Haven CT 06513 **800-735-8877** 203-469-5394
Kate Spade
135 5th Ave Set 7 . . . . New York NY 10010 **866-999-5283** 212-358-0420
LBU Inc 217 Brook Ave . . . . Passaic NJ 07055 **800-678-4528** 973-773-4800
Vera Bradley Designs
2208 Production Rd . . . . Fort Wayne IN 46808 **800-975-8372** 260-482-4673

349 HARDWARE - MFR

			Toll-Free	Phone

Aceco 4419 Federal Way . . . . Boise ID 83716 **800-359-7012** 208-343-7712
Acorn Manufacturing Company Inc
457 School St . . . . Mansfield MA 02048 **800-835-0121**
Acryline USA Inc
2015 Becancour . . . . Lyster QC G0S1V0 **800-567-0920**
Adams Rite Manufacturing Co
260 W Santa Fe St . . . . Pomona CA 91767 **800-872-3267** 909-632-2300
AGM Container Controls Inc
PO Box 40020 . . . . Tucson AZ 85717 **800-995-5590** 520-881-2130
American Bolt & Screw Manufacturing Corp
601 Kettering Dr . . . . Ontario CA 91761 **800-325-0844** 909-390-0522
Anderson Electrical Products Inc
1615 Moores St PO Box 455 . . . . Leeds AL 35094 **800-423-0730** 573-682-5521
Arrow Lock Co
100 Arrow Dr . . . . New Haven CT 06511 **800-839-3157**
ASSA Inc 110 Sargent Dr . . . . New Haven CT 06511 **800-235-7482** 203-624-5225
Attwood Corp
1016 N Monroe St . . . . Lowell MI 49331 **844-808-5704** 616-897-9241
Automotive Racing Products Inc
1863 Eastman Ave . . . . Ventura CA 93003 **800-826-3045** 805-339-2200
Baier Marine Company Inc
2920 Airway Ave . . . . Costa Mesa CA 92626 **800-455-3917**
Baldwin Hardware Corp
841 E Wyomissing Blvd . . . . Reading PA 19611 **800-566-1986** 610-777-7811
Band-It-IDEX Inc
4799 Dahlia St . . . . Denver CO 80216 **800-525-0758** 303-320-4555
Barnhill Bolt Company Inc
2500 Princeton Dr Ne . . . . Albuquerque NM 87107 **800-472-3900** 505-884-1808
Baron Mfg Company LLC
1200 Capitol Dr . . . . Addison IL 60101 **800-368-8585** 630-628-9110
Belwith International Ltd
3100 Broadway Ave . . . . Grandville MI 49418 **800-235-9484**
Best Access Systems
6161 E 75th St . . . . Indianapolis IN 46250 **855-365-2407** 317-849-2250

			Toll-Free	Phone

Bete Fog Nozzle Inc
50 Greenfield St . . . . Greenfield MA 01301 **800-235-0049** 413-772-0846
Blum Inc 7733 Old Plank Rd . . . . Stanley NC 28164 **800-438-6788** 704-827-1345
Bommer Industries Inc
PO Box 187 . . . . Landrum SC 29356 **800-334-1654** 864-457-3301
Brainerd Mfg Company Inc
140 Business Pk Dr . . . . Winston-Salem NC 27107 **800-652-7277** 336-769-4077
Bronze Craft Corp 37 Will St . . . . Nashua NH 03060 **800-488-7747** 603-883-7747
Cal-Royal Products Inc
6605 Flotilla St . . . . City Of Commerce CA 90040 **800-876-9258** 323-888-6601
Chamberlain Group
845 Larch Ave . . . . Elmhurst IL 60126 **800-528-9131** 630-279-3600
Charles Leonard Inc
145 Kennedy Dr . . . . Hauppauge NY 11788 **800-999-7202** 631-273-6700
Classic Brass Inc
2051 Stoneman Cir . . . . Lakewood NY 14750 **800-869-3173** 716-763-1400
Colonial Bronze Co
511 Winsted Rd . . . . Torrington CT 06790 **800-355-7903*** 860-489-9233
*All
Component Hardware Group Inc
1890 Swarthmore Ave . . . . Lakewood NJ 08701 **800-526-3694** 732-363-4700
Corbin Russwin Inc
225 Episcopal Rd . . . . Berlin CT 06037 **800-438-1951** 860-225-7411
Craft Inc
1929 County St PO Box 3049 . . . . South Attleboro MA 02703 **800-827-2388** 508-761-7917
Dayton Superior Corp
1125 Byers Rd . . . . Miamisburg OH 45342 **800-745-3700** 937-866-0711
DE-STA-CO
1025 Doris Rd . . . . Auburn Hills MI 48326 **888-337-8226** 248-836-6700
Dixie Industries
3510 N Orchard Knob Ave . . . . Chattanooga TN 37406 **800-933-4943** 423-698-3323
Door Engineering & Mfg LLC
400 Cherry St . . . . Kasota MN 56050 **800-959-1352** 507-931-6910
DORMA Group North America
Dorma Dr . . . . Reamstown PA 17567 **800-523-8483** 717-336-3881
Doug Mockett & Company Inc
1915 Abalone Ave . . . . Torrance CA 90501 **800-523-1269** 310-318-2491
Duo Fast Northeast
22 Tolland St . . . . East Hartford CT 06108 **888-399-5712** 860-289-6861
East Teak Trading Group Inc
1106 Drake Rd . . . . Donalds SC 29638 **800-338-5636** 864-379-2111
Eberhard Mfg Co
PO Box 368012 . . . . Cleveland OH 44149 **800-334-6706** 440-238-9720
Emtek Products Inc
15250 Stafford St . . . . City of Industry CA 91744 **800-356-2741** 626-961-0413
Engineered Products Co (EPCO)
601 Kelso St PO Box 108 . . . . Flint MI 48506 **888-414-3726** 810-767-2050
ER Wagner Mfg Company Inc
4611 N 32nd St . . . . Milwaukee WI 53209 **800-558-5596** 414-871-5080
ESPE Mfg Company Inc
9220 Ivanhoe St . . . . Schiller Park IL 60176 **800-367-3773*** 847-678-8950
*Cust Svc
Fastbolt Corp
200 Louis St . . . . South Hackensack NJ 07606 **800-631-1980** 201-440-9100
Faultless Caster
3438 Briley Pk Blvd N . . . . Nashville TN 37207 **800-322-7359***
*Cust Svc
Folger Adam Security Inc
4634 S Presa St . . . . San Antonio TX 78223 **888-745-0530** 210-533-1231
Freud America Inc
218 Feld Ave . . . . High Point NC 27263 **800-334-4107** 336-434-3171
Fulton Corp 303 Eigth Ave . . . . Fulton IL 61252 **800-252-0002**
G G Schmitt & Sons Inc
2821 Old Tree Dr . . . . Lancaster PA 17603 **866-724-6488** 717-394-3701
Genie Co
One Door Dr PO Box 67 . . . . Mount Hope OH 44660 **800-354-3643**
Grass America Inc
1202 Hwy 66 S . . . . Kernersville NC 27284 **800-334-3512**
HA Guden Company Inc
99 Raynor Ave . . . . Ronkonkoma NY 11779 **800-344-6437** 631-737-2900
Hager Co 139 Victor St . . . . Saint Louis MO 63104 **800-325-9995** 314-772-4400
Halex Corp
750 S Reservoir St . . . . Pomona CA 91766 **800-576-1636** 909-622-3537
Hampton Products International Corp
50 Icon . . . . Foothill Ranch CA 92610 **800-562-5625** 949-472-4256
Helton Industries Ltd
30840 Peardonville Rd . . . . Abbotsford BC V2T6K2 **877-300-7412** 604-854-3660
Hindley Mfg Company Inc
Nine Havens St . . . . Cumberland RI 02864 **800-323-9031** 401-722-2550
Hudson Lock Inc 81 Apsley St . . . . Hudson MA 01749 **800-434-8960**
Ideal Clamp 8100 Tridon Dr . . . . Smyrna TN 37167 **800-251-3220** 615-459-5800
Inventory Sales Inc
9777 Reavis Rd . . . . St Louis MO 63123 **866-417-3801** 314-776-6200
Jacknob Corp
290 Oser Ave PO Box 18032 . . . . Hauppauge NY 11788 **800-424-7495** 631-546-6560
Jacob Holtz Co
10 Industrial Hwy MS-6
Airport Business Complex B . . . . Lester PA 19029 **800-445-4337** 215-423-2800
Jarvis Caster Co
881 Lower Brownsville Rd . . . . Jackson TN 38301 **800-995-9876**
Kaba Ilco Corp
400 Jeffreys Rd . . . . Rocky Mount NC 27804 **800-334-1381** 252-446-3321
Kanebridge Corp
153 Bauer Dr . . . . Oakland NJ 07436 **888-222-9221** 201-337-2300
Kason Industries Inc
57 Amlajack Blvd . . . . Newnan GA 30265 **800-935-3550** 770-304-3000
Keystone Electronics Corp
31-07 20th Rd . . . . Astoria NY 11105 **800-221-5510** 718-956-8900
Knape & Vogt Manufacturing Co
2700 Oak Industrial Dr NE . . . . Grand Rapids MI 49505 **800-253-1561** 616-459-3311
LE Johnson Products Inc
2100 Sterling Ave . . . . Elkhart IN 46516 **800-837-5664** 574-293-5664
Le Smith Co 1030 E Wilson St . . . . Bryan OH 43506 **888-537-6484** 419-636-4555
Liberty Hardware Mfg Corp
140 Business Pk Dr . . . . Winston-Salem NC 27107 **800-542-3789**
Lockmasters Security Institute
2101 John C Watts Dr . . . . Nicholasville KY 40356 **800-654-0637** 859-885-6041

				Toll-Free	Phone
Master Lock Company LLC					
137 W Forest Hill Ave PO Box 927	Oak Creek	WI	53154	800-464-2088	
Medeco Security Locks Inc					
3625 Alleghany Dr	Salem	VA	24153	800-839-3157	540-380-5000
Mountz Inc 1080 N 11th St	San Jose	CA	95112	888-925-2763	408-292-2214
Nagel Chase Inc					
2323 Delaney Rd	Gurnee	IL	60031	800-323-4552	
Newell Rubbermaid Inc Tools & Hardware Group					
8935 NorthPointe Executive Dr	Huntersville	NC	28078	800-464-7946	704-987-4555
Nik-O-Lok Co					
3130 N Mitthoeffer Rd	Indianapolis	IN	46235	800-428-4348	317-899-6955
Paneloc Corp					
PO Drawer 547	Farmington	CT	06034	800-394-6711	860-677-6711
Payson Casters Inc					
2323 N Delaney Rd	Gurnee	IL	60031	800-323-4552	847-336-6200
Premiere Lock Co					
8301 E 81st St	Tulsa	OK	74133	800-575-2658	918-294-8179
Purdy Corp					
101 Prospect Ave	Cleveland	OH	44115	800-547-0780	
Qual-Craft Industries					
PO Box 559	Stoughton	MA	02072	800-231-5647	781-344-1000
Renovator's Supply Inc					
Renovators Old ML	Millers Falls	MA	01349	800-659-2211	413-423-3300
Rockford Process Control Inc					
2020 Seventh St	Rockford	IL	61104	800-228-3779	815-966-2000
Rocky Mountain Hardware Inc					
1020 Airport Way PO Box 4108	Hailey	ID	83333	888-788-2013	208-788-2013
Rousseau Metal Inc					
105 Ave De Gasp Ouest	St Jean-Port-Joli	QC	G0R3G0	866-463-4270	418-598-3381
RWM Casters Co PO Box 668	Gastonia	NC	28053	800-634-7704	
S Parker Hardware Manufacturing Corp					
PO Box 9882	Englewood	NJ	07631	800-772-7537	201-569-1600
Salice America Inc					
2123 Crown Centre Dr	Charlotte	NC	28227	800-222-9652	704-841-7810
Sargent & Greenleaf Inc					
One Security Dr	Nicholasville	KY	40356	800-826-7652	859-885-9411
Sargent Manufacturing Co					
100 Sargent Dr	New Haven	CT	06511	800-727-5477	
Saturn Fasteners Inc					
425 S Varney St	Burbank	CA	91502	800-947-9414	818-846-7145
Savant Manufacturing Inc					
2930 Hwy 383 PO Box 520	Kinder	LA	70648	800-326-6880	337-738-5896
Seastrom Mfg Company Inc					
456 Seastrom St	Twin Falls	ID	83301	800-634-2356	208-737-4300
Securitron Magnalock Corp					
10027 S 51st St Ste 102	Phoenix	AZ	85044	800-624-5625*	623-582-4626
*Sales					
Selby Furniture Hardware Company Inc					
321 Rider Ave	Bronx	NY	10451	800-224-0058	718-993-3700
Signature Hardware					
2700 Crescent Springs Pike	Erlanger	KY	41017	866-855-2284	859-647-7564
Simpson Strong-Tie Company Inc					
5956 W Las Positas Blvd	Pleasanton	CA	94588	800-925-5099	925-560-9000
Spokane Hardware Supply Inc					
2001 E Trent Ave	Spokane	WA	99202	800-888-1663	509-535-1663
Sunex International Inc					
100 Roe Rd	Travelers Rest	SC	29690	800-833-7869	864-834-8759
Trimark Corp PO Box 350	New Hampton	IA	50659	800-447-0343	641-394-3188
Trimco/Builders Brass Works					
3528 Emery St	Los Angeles	CA	90023	800-637-8746	323-262-4191
Truth Hardware Inc					
700 W Bridge St	Owatonna	MN	55060	800-866-7884*	507-451-5620
*Cust Svc					
Unicorp 291 Cleveland St	Orange	NJ	07050	800-526-1389	973-674-1700
Weber-Knapp Co					
441 Chandler St	Jamestown	NY	14701	800-828-9254	716-484-9135
Weiser Lock A Masco Co					
19701 Da Vinci	Lake Forest	CA	92610	800-677-5625	
Yale Residential Security Products Inc					
100 Yale Ave	Lenoir City	TN	37771	800-438-1951*	
*Cust Svc					
Yale Security Inc.ÿ					
1902 Airport Rd	Monroe	NC	28110	800-438-1951	
Yardley Products Corp					
10 W College Ave	Yardley	PA	19067	800-457-0154	215-493-2723

350 HARDWARE - WHOL

				Toll-Free	Phone
Action Bolt & Tool Co (WURTH)					
2051 E Blue Heron Blvd	Riviera Beach	FL	33404	800-423-0700	
Aero-Space Southwest Inc					
21450 N Third Ave	Phoenix	AZ	85027	800-289-2779	623-582-2779
All-Pro Fasteners Inc					
1916 Peyco Dr N	Arlington	TX	76001	800-361-6627	817-467-5700
Allied International					
13207 Bradley Ave	Sylmar	CA	91342	800-533-8333*	818-364-2333
*General					
Associated Steel Corp					
18200 Miles Rd	Cleveland	OH	44128	800-321-9300	
Baer Supply Co					
909 Forest Edge Dr	Vernon Hills	IL	60061	800-944-2237	847-913-2237
Bargain Supply Co					
844 E Jefferson St	Louisville	KY	40206	800-322-5226	502-562-5000
Barnett Inc					
801 W Bay St	Jacksonville	FL	32204	888-803-4467	904-384-6530
Blish-Mize Co					
223 S Fifth St	Atchison	KS	66002	800-995-0525	913-367-1250
Bostwick-Braun Co PO Box 912	Toledo	OH	43697	800-777-9640	419-259-3600
Builders Hardware & Supply Company Inc					
1516 15th Ave W PO Box C-79005	Seattle	WA	98119	800-828-1437	206-281-3700
Cascade Wholesale Hardware Inc					
5650 NW	Hillsboro	OR	97124	800-877-9987*	503-614-2600
*General					
Desoto Sales Inc					
20945 E Osborne St	Canoga Park	CA	91304	800-826-9779	818-998-0853

				Toll-Free	Phone
Dixie Construction Products Inc					
970 Huff Rd NW	Atlanta	GA	30318	800-992-1180	404-351-1100
Earnest Machine Products Co					
12502 Plz Dr	Cleveland	OH	44130	800-327-6378	216-362-1100
EB Bradley Co					
5080 S Alameda St	Los Angeles	CA	90058	800-533-3030	323-585-9201
Fastec Industrial					
2219 Eddie Williams Rd	Johnson City	TN	37601	800-837-2505	
Fastenal Co					
2001 Theurer Blvd	Winona	MN	55987	877-507-7555	507-454-5374
NASDAQ: FAST					
General Fasteners Co					
37584 Amrhein Rd Ste 150	Livonia	MI	48150	800-945-2658	734-452-2400
Handy Hardware Wholesale Inc					
8300 Tewantin Dr	Houston	TX	77061	800-364-3835	713-644-1495
Hans Johnsen Co					
8901 Chancellor Row	Dallas	TX	75247	800-879-1515*	214-879-1550
*Sales					
Hardware Distribution Warehouses Inc (HDW)					
6900 Woolworth Rd	Shreveport	LA	71129	800-256-8527*	318-686-8527
*Cust Svc					
Hardware Suppliers of America Inc (HSI)					
1400 E Fire Tower Rd	Greenville	NC	27858	800-334-5625	
Hillman Group Inc					
10590 Hamilton Ave	Cincinnati	OH	45231	800-800-4900	513-851-4900
Hodell-natco Industries Inc					
7825 Hub Pkwy	Cleveland	OH	44125	800-321-4862	216-447-0165
Home Depot Supply					
3100 Cumberland Blvd Ste 1480	Atlanta	GA	30339	855-615-8372	770-852-9000
House-Hasson Hardware Inc					
3125 Water Plant Rd	Knoxville	TN	37914	800-333-0520	865-525-0471
Jensen Distribution Services					
PO Box 3708	Spokane	WA	99220	800-234-1321*	
*General					
JSJ Corp Dake Div					
724 Robbins Rd	Grand Haven	MI	49417	800-846-3253	616-842-7110
Kentec Inc					
3250 Centerville Hwy	Snellville	GA	30039	800-241-0148	770-985-1907
Long-Lewis Hardware Co					
430 Ninth St N	Birmingham	AL	35203	800-322-0492	205-322-2561
Max Tool Inc					
119b Citation Ct	Birmingham	AL	35209	800-783-6298	205-942-2466
Monroe Hardware Co					
101 N Sutherland Ave	Monroe	NC	28110	800-222-1974	704-289-3121
Omaha Wholesale Hardware Co					
PO Box 3628	Omaha	NE	68102	800-238-4566	402-444-1673
Onity Inc					
2232 Northmont Pkwy Ste 100	Duluth	GA	30096	800-424-1433	
Orgill Inc 3742 Tyndale Dr	Memphis	TN	38125	800-347-2860	901-754-8850
Parts Assoc Inc 12420 Plz Dr	Parma	OH	44130	800-321-1128	216-433-7700
Regitar USA Inc					
2575 Container Dr	Montgomery	AL	36109	877-734-4827	334-244-1885
Repairclinic.com Inc					
48600 Michigan Ave	Canton	MI	48188	800-269-2609	734-495-3079
Ryobi Technologies Inc					
1428 Pearman Dairy Rd	Anderson	SC	29625	800-525-2579	
Serv-a-lite Products Inc					
3451 Morton Dr	East Moline	IL	61244	800-800-4900	
Specialty Bolt & Screw Inc					
235 Bowles Rd	Agawam	MA	01001	800-322-7878	413-789-6700
Supply Technologies LLC					
6065 Parkland Blvd	Cleveland	OH	44124	800-695-8650	440-947-2100
Techni-Tool Inc					
1547 N Trooper Rd PO Box 1117	Worcester	PA	19490	800-832-4866*	610-941-2400
*Cust Svc					
Triangle Fastener Corp					
1925 Preble Ave	Pittsburgh	PA	15233	800-486-1832*	412-321-5000
*General					
Wallace Hardware Company Inc					
5050 S Davy Crockett Pkwy					
PO Box 6004	Morristown	TN	37815	800-776-0976	423-586-5650
Wurth Service Supply Inc					
4935 W 86th St	Indianapolis	IN	46268	877-999-8784	317-704-1000
WW Grainger Inc					
100 Grainger Pkwy	Lake Forest	IL	60045	888-361-8649	847-535-1000
NYSE: GWW					

351 HEALTH CARE PROVIDERS - ANCILLARY

SEE ALSO Vision Correction Centers ; Home Health Services ; Hospices

				Toll-Free	Phone
Amedisys Inc					
5959 S Sherwood Forest Blvd					
Ste 300	Baton Rouge	LA	70816	800-464-0020	225-292-2031
NASDAQ: AMED					
American Family Care					
2147 Riverchase Office Rd	Birmingham	AL	35244	800-258-7535	205-403-8902
American Red Cross In Greater New York (Inc)					
520 W 49th St	New York	NY	10019	877-733-2767	
AmeriHealth Mercy Health Plan					
8040 Carlson Rd Ste 500	Harrisburg	PA	17112	888-991-7200	717-651-3540
AmSurg Corp					
1A Burton Hills Blvd 5th Fl	Nashville	TN	37215	800-945-2301	615-665-1283
NASDAQ: AMSG					
CareSource 230 N Main St	Dayton	OH	45402	800-488-0134	937-224-3300
Children's Bureau of Southern California					
1910 Magnolia Ave	Los Angeles	CA	90004	800-730-3933	213-342-0100
DaVita Inc 1551 Wewatta St	Denver	CO	80202	800-310-4872	303-405-2100
NYSE: DVA					
Fresenius Medical Care North America					
920 Winter St	Waltham	MA	02451	800-662-1237	781-699-9000
Hanger Orthopedic Group Inc					
10910 Domain Dr Ste 300	Austin	TX	78758	877-442-6437	512-777-3800
HealthDrive Corp					
888 Worcester St	Wellesley	MA	02482	888-964-6681	

					Toll-Free	Phone

HealthSouth Corp
3660 Grandview Pkwy Ste 200 . . . . Birmingham AL 35243 **800-765-4772** 205-967-7116
NYSE: HLS

Healthways Inc
701 Cool Springs Blvd Ste 300 . . . . Franklin TN 37067 **800-327-3822**
NASDAQ: HWAY

MedCath Inc
10720 Sikes Pl Ste 300 . . . . Charlotte NC 28277 **800-461-9330** 704-708-6600
NASDAQ: MDTH

Miracle-Ear Inc
5000 Cheshire Pkwy N Ste 1 . . . . Minneapolis MN 55446 **800-464-8002**

Radiation Therapy Services Inc
2270 Colonial Blvd . . . . Fort Myers FL 33907 **800-437-1619** 239-931-7275

SCAN Health Plan
3800 Kilroy Airport Way Ste 100 . . . . Long Beach CA 90806 **800-247-5091** 562-989-5100

US Physical Therapy
1300 W Sam Houston Pkwy S Ste 300 . . . . Houston TX 77042 **800-580-6285** 713-297-7000
NYSE: USPH

352   HEALTH CARE SYSTEMS

SEE ALSO General Hospitals - US
Health Care Systems are one or more hospitals owned, leased, sponsored, or managed by a central organization. Single-hospital systems are not included here; however, some large hospital networks or alliances may be listed.

					Toll-Free	Phone

Addus HealthCare Inc
2401 S Plum Grove Rd . . . . Palatine IL 60067 **888-233-8746** 847-303-5300
NASDAQ: ADUS

Adventist Health
2100 Douglas Blvd . . . . Roseville CA 95661 **877-336-3566** 916-781-2000

Albert Einstein Healthcare Network
5501 Old York Rd . . . . Philadelphia PA 19141 **800-346-7834** 215-456-7890

American Kidney Stone Management Ltd (AKSM)
797 Thomas Ln . . . . Columbus OH 43214 **800-637-5188** 614-447-0281

American Renal Assoc Inc
66 Cherry Hill Dr . . . . Beverly MA 01915 **877-997-3625** 978-922-3080

Amery Regional Medical Ctr
265 Griffin St E . . . . Amery WI 54001 **800-424-5273** 715-268-8000

Appalachian Regional Healthcare Service (ARH)
2285 Executive Dr PO Box 8086 . . . . Lexington KY 40505 **877-243-4782** 859-226-2440

Baptist Health South Florida Inc
6855 Red Rd Ste 600 . . . . Coral Gables FL 33143 **800-622-2838** 786-662-7000

Baptist Memorial Health Care Corp
350 N Humphreys Blvd . . . . Memphis TN 38120 **800-422-7847** 901-227-5920

Benedictine Health System
503 E Third St Ste 400 . . . . Duluth MN 55805 **800-833-7208** 218-786-2370

Catholic Healthcare Partners
615 Elsinore Pl . . . . Cincinnati OH 45202 **800-367-9212** 513-639-2800

Centra Health Inc
1920 Atherholt Rd . . . . Lynchburg VA 24501 **877-635-4651** 434-947-3000

Childhaven 316 Broadway . . . . Seattle WA 98122 **877-300-9164** 206-624-6477

CHRISTUS Schumpert Health System
1 St Mary Pl . . . . Shreveport LA 71101 **844-444-8440** 318-681-4500

CHRISTUS Spohn Health System
1702 Santa Fe St . . . . Corpus Christi TX 78404 **800-247-6574** 361-881-3000

Community Health Systems Inc
4000 Meridian Blvd . . . . Franklin TN 37067 **888-373-9600** 615-465-7000
NYSE: CYH

Community Services Group (CSG)
320 Highland Dr PO Box 597 . . . . Mountville PA 17554 **877-907-7970** 717-285-7121

Crozer-Keystone Health System (CKHS)
190 W Sproul Rd . . . . Springfield PA 19064 **800-254-3258** 610-328-8700

Fairview Health Services
2450 Riverside Ave . . . . Minneapolis MN 55454 **800-824-1953** 612-672-6000

Geisinger Health System
100 N Academy Ave . . . . Danville PA 17822 **800-275-6401** 570-271-6211

Great Plains Health Alliance Inc
625 Third St . . . . Phillipsburg KS 67661 **800-432-2779** 785-543-2111

Greenville Hospital System (GHS)
701 Grove Rd . . . . Greenville SC 29605 **877-447-4636** 864-455-8976

Guthrie Healthcare System
1 Guthrie Sq . . . . Sayre PA 18840 **888-448-8474** 570-887-4401

HCA Midwest Health System
903 E 104th St Ste 500 . . . . Kansas City MO 64131 **800-386-9355** 816-508-4000

Health Net Of Arizona Inc
1230 W Washington St . . . . Tempe AZ 85281 **800-291-6911** 602-794-1400

Henry Ford Health System
One Ford Pl . . . . Detroit MI 48202 **800-436-7936**

IASIS Healthcare Corp
117 Seaboard Ln Bldg E . . . . Franklin TN 37067 **877-898-6080** 615-844-2747

Inova Health System
8110 Gatehouse Rd . . . . Falls Church VA 22042 **855-694-6682**

Intermountain HealthCare
36 S State St . . . . Salt Lake City UT 84111 **800-843-7820*** 801-442-2000
*Hum Res

Kindred Healthcare Inc
680 S Fourth Ave . . . . Louisville KY 40202 **800-545-0749** 502-596-7300
NYSE: KND

LifePoint Health
330 Seven Springs Way . . . . Brentwood TN 37027 **888-982-9144** 615-920-7000
NASDAQ: LPNT

Lifespring Inc
460 Spring St . . . . Jeffersonville IN 47130 **800-456-2117** 812-280-2080

MedCath Inc
10720 Sikes Pl Ste 300 . . . . Charlotte NC 28277 **800-461-9330** 704-708-6600
NASDAQ: MDTH

MedStar Health
5565 Sterrett Pl 5th Fl . . . . Columbia MD 21044 **877-772-6505** 410-772-6500

Methodist Healthcare Ministries of South Texas Inc
4507 Medical Dr . . . . San Antonio TX 78229 **800-959-6673** 210-692-0234

Methodist Hospitals of Dallas
1441 N Beckley Ave . . . . Dallas TX 75203 **800-725-9664** 214-947-8181

Northwestern Counseling Support & Services Inc
107 Fisher Pond Rd . . . . Saint Albans VT 05478 **800-834-7793** 802-524-6554

Oakwood Healthcare Inc
18101 Oakwood Blvd PO Box 2500 . . . . Dearborn MI 48124 **800-543-9355** 313-593-7000

Palomar Pomerado Health
15615 Pomerado Rd . . . . Poway CA 92064 **800-628-2880** 858-613-4000

Premier Inc
12255 El Camino Real . . . . San Diego CA 92130 **877-777-1552** 858-481-2727

Schumacher Group
200 Corporate Blvd Ste 201 . . . . Lafayette LA 70508 **800-893-9698** 337-354-1332

Scripps Health
4275 Campus Pt Ct . . . . San Diego CA 92121 **800-727-4777**

Sea Mar Community Health Ctr
1040 S Henderson St . . . . Seattle WA 98108 **855-289-4503** 206-763-5277

Senior Whole Health LLC (SWH)
58 Charles St 2nd Fl . . . . Cambridge MA 02141 **888-794-7268** 617-494-5353

Shriners Hospitals for Children
2900 N Rocky Pt Dr . . . . Tampa FL 33607 **800-237-5055** 813-281-0300

Southern Illinois Healthcare
1239 E Main St . . . . Carbondale IL 62902 **866-744-2468** 618-457-5200

SSM Healthy
1000 N. Lee St . . . . Oklahoma City OK 73102 **866-203-5846** 618-242-4600

Sutter Health
2200 River Plaza . . . . Sacramento CA 95833 **888-888-6044** 916-733-8800

Terros Inc
3003 N Central Ave Ste 200 . . . . Phoenix AZ 85012 **800-631-1314** 602-222-9444

TheraCare
116 W 32nd St 8th Fl . . . . New York NY 10001 **800-505-7000** 212-564-2350

Universal Health Services Inc
367 S Gulph Rd . . . . King of Prussia PA 19406 **800-347-7750** 610-768-3300
NYSE: UHS

University of Maryland Medical System
22 S Greene St . . . . Baltimore MD 21201 **800-492-5538** 410-328-8667

University of Pittsburgh Medical Ctr Health System
200 Lothrop St . . . . Pittsburgh PA 15213 **800-533-8762** 412-647-2345

Washington County Mental Health Services Inc (WCMHS)
PO Box 647 . . . . Montpelier VT 05601 **800-649-2642** 802-229-0591

West Penn Allegheny Health System
4800 Friendship Ave . . . . Pittsburgh PA 15224 **800-994-6610**

353   HEALTH & FITNESS CENTERS

SEE ALSO Spas - Health & Fitness ; Weight Loss Centers & Services

					Toll-Free	Phone

Auberge et spa Le Nordik Inc
16 ch Nordik . . . . Old Chelsea QC J9B2P7 **866-575-3700** 819-827-1111

Big Fitness
190 Frenchtown Rd . . . . North Kingstown RI 02852 **800-383-2008** 401-885-5200

Brick Bodies Fitness Services Inc
201 Old Padonia Rd . . . . Cockeysville MD 21030 **866-952-7425** 410-252-8058

Contours Express Inc
156 Imperial Way . . . . Nicholasville KY 40356 **855-589-9662**

Corporate Fitness Works Inc
1200 16th St N . . . . St Petersburg FL 33705 **855-417-9697** 301-417-9697

Crunch Fitness International
220 W 19th St . . . . New York NY 10011 **888-227-8624** 212-370-0998

Dumbell Man Fitness Equipment, The
655 Hawaii Ave . . . . Torrance CA 90503 **800-432-6266** 310-381-2900

Equinox Fitness Holdings Inc
895 Broadway . . . . New York NY 10003 **866-332-6549** 212-677-0180

Fitness Depot
1808 Lower Roswell Rd . . . . Marietta GA 30068 **800-974-6828** 770-971-6828

Flex Hr
10700 Medlock Bridge Rd Ste 206 . . . . Johns Creek GA 30097 **877-735-3947** 770-814-4225

Healthtrax Fitness & Wellness
2345 Main St . . . . Glastonbury CT 06033 **800-998-0880** 860-652-7066

Iron Tribe Franchise LLC
300 27th St S . . . . Birmingham AL 35233 **855-226-8699** 205-226-8669

Jonas Fitness Inc
16969 n texas ave . . . . Webster TX 77598 **800-324-9800**

Kinderdance International Inc
1333 Gateway Dr Ste 1033 . . . . Melbourne FL 32901 **800-554-2334** 321-984-4448

Lady of America Franchise Corp
159 Weston RD Ste 1650 . . . . Weston FL 33326 **800-833-5239** 954-217-8660

Little Gym International Inc
7001 N Scottsdale Rd . . . . Paradise Valley AZ 85253 **888-228-2878***
*General

Premier & Curzons Fitness Clubs
5100 Dixie Rd . . . . Mississauga ON L4W1C9 **866-371-7307** 905-602-9912

TuffStuff Fitness Equipment Inc
13971 Norton Ave . . . . Chino CA 91710 **888-884-8275** 909-629-1600

Wellbridge Co
6140 Greenwood Plaza Blvd
Ste 200 . . . . Greenwood Village CO 80111 **888-458-0489*** 303-866-0800
*Acctg

Work Out World 762 SR- 18 . . . . Brunswick NJ 08816 **888-564-6969** 732-390-7390

World Health
7222 Edgemont Blvd NW . . . . Calgary AB T3A2X7 **866-278-4131** 403-239-4048

354   HEALTH FOOD STORES

					Toll-Free	Phone

Christopher Enterprises
155 West 2050 North . . . . Spanish Fork UT 84660 **800-453-1406**

Ginsberg's Foods Inc
29 Ginsberg Ln PO Box 17 . . . . Hudson NY 12534 **800-999-6006** 518-828-4004

GNC Inc
300 Sixth Ave 14th Fl . . . . Pittsburgh PA 15222 **877-462-4700**
NYSE: GNC

Netrition Inc
25 Corporate Cir Ste 118 . . . . Albany NY 12203 **888-817-2411** 518-464-0765

Whole Foods Market Inc
550 Bowie St . . . . Austin TX 78703 **888-992-6227** 512-477-4455
NASDAQ: WFM

HEATING EQUIPMENT - ELECTRIC

SEE Air Conditioning & Heating Equipment - Residential

355 HEALTH & MEDICAL INFORMATION - ONLINE

				Toll-Free	Phone
At Health Inc					
7829 Center Blvd SE	Snoqualmie	WA	98065	**888-284-3258**	425-292-0329
BabyCenter LLC					
163 Freelon St	San Francisco	CA	94107	**866-241-2229**	415-537-0900
eMedicine.com Inc					
8420 W Dodge Rd Ste 402	Omaha	NE	68114	**866-241-9601**	402-341-3222
MedlinePlus					
National Library of Medicine					
8600 Rockville Pk	Bethesda	MD	20894	**888-346-3656**	301-594-5983
Pain.com					
Dannemiller Memorial Educational Foundation					
5711 NW Pkwy Ste 100	San Antonio	TX	78246	**800-328-2308**	210-572-2512
PubMed					
US National Library of Medicine					
8600 Rockville Pike	Bethesda	MD	20894	**888-346-3656**	

356 HEATING EQUIPMENT - GAS, OIL, COAL

SEE ALSO Furnaces & Ovens - Industrial Process ; Air Conditioning & Heating Equipment - Commercial/Industrial ; Air Conditioning & Heating Equipment - Residential ; Boiler Shops

				Toll-Free	Phone
Aerco International Inc					
159 Paris Ave	Northvale	NJ	07647	**800-526-0288**	201-768-2400
Aquatherm Industries Inc					
1940 Rutgers University Blvd	Lakewood	NJ	08701	**800-535-6307**	
Burner Systems International Inc (BSI)					
3600 Cummings Rd	Chattanooga	TN	37419	**800-251-6318**	423-822-3600
Electro-Flex Heat Inc					
Five Northwood Rd	Bloomfield	CT	06002	**800-585-4213**	860-242-6287
Empire Comfort Systems Inc					
918 Freeburg Ave	Belleville	IL	62222	**800-851-3153**	618-233-7420
Freeman Gas Inc					
1186 Asheville Hwy PO Box 4366	Spartanburg	SC	29303	**800-277-5730**	864-582-5475
John Zink Company LLC					
11920 E Apache St	Tulsa	OK	74116	**800-421-9242**	918-234-1800
Johnston Boiler Co					
300 Pine St	Ferrysburg	MI	49409	**800-748-0295***	616-842-5050
*General					
LB White Company Inc					
W 6636 LB White Rd	Onalaska	WI	54650	**800-345-7200**	608-783-5691
Meeder Equipment Co					
12323 Sixth St	Rancho Cucamonga	CA	91739	**800-423-3711**	909-463-0600
New Yorker Boiler Company Inc					
PO Box 10	Hatfield	PA	19440	**800-535-4679**	215-855-8055
Powrmatic Inc					
2906 Baltimore Blvd PO Box 439	Finksburg	MD	21048	**800-966-9100**	410-833-9100
Rasmussen Iron Works Inc					
12028 E Philadelphia St	Whittier	CA	90601	**888-301-0440**	562-696-8718
Raypak Inc 2151 Eastman Ave	Oxnard	CA	93030	**800-438-4328**	805-278-5300
Reimers Electra Steam Inc					
4407 Martinsburg Pk PO Box 37	Clear Brook	VA	22624	**800-872-7562**	540-662-3811
Roberts-Gordon Inc					
1250 William St PO Box 44	Buffalo	NY	14240	**800-828-7450**	716-852-4400
RW Beckett Corp PO Box 1289	Elyria	OH	44036	**800-645-2876**	440-327-1060
Schwank Inc					
Two Schwank Way at Hwy 56N	Waynesboro	GA	30830	**877-446-3727**	
Spectrolab Inc					
12500 Gladstone Ave	Sylmar	CA	91342	**800-936-4888**	818-365-4611
Taco Inc 1160 Cranston St	Cranston	RI	02920	**888-778-2733**	401-942-8000
Thermal Solutions LLC					
PO Box 3244	Lancaster	PA	17604	**800-860-5726**	717-239-7642
Utica Boilers Inc PO Box 4729	Utica	NY	13504	**800-325-5479**	866-847-6656
Water Furnace International Inc					
9000 Conservation Way	Fort Wayne	IN	46809	**800-222-5667**	260-478-5667
Wayne Combustion Systems					
801 Glasgow Ave	Fort Wayne	IN	46803	**855-929-6327**	260-425-9200

357 HEAVY EQUIPMENT DISTRIBUTORS

SEE ALSO Industrial Equipment & Supplies (Misc) - Whol ; Farm Machinery & Equipment - Whol

				Toll-Free	Phone
Admar Supply Co Inc					
1950 Brighton Henriett	Rochester	NY	14623	**800-836-2367**	585-272-9390
Alban Tractor Co					
8531 Pulaski Hwy	Baltimore	MD	21237	**800-492-6994**	410-686-7777
Anderson Equipment Co					
1000 Washington Pk	Bridgeville	PA	15017	**800-414-4554**	412-343-2300
Arnold Machinery Co					
2975 West 2100 South	Salt Lake City	UT	84119	**800-821-0548***	801-972-4000
*Cust Svc					
Bacon-Universal Company Inc					
918 Ahua St	Honolulu	HI	96819	**800-352-3508**	808-839-7202
Balzer Pacific Equipment Co					
2136 SE Eigth Ave	Portland	OR	97214	**800-442-0966**	503-232-5141
Bane Machinery Inc					
PO Box 541355	Dallas	TX	75354	**800-594-2263**	214-352-2468
Chadwick-BaRoss Inc					
160 Warren Ave	Westbrook	ME	04092	**800-804-0775**	207-854-8411
Cherry's Industrial Equipment					
600 Morse Ave	Elk Grove Village	IL	60007	**800-350-0011**	
Cleveland Bros Equipment Company Inc					
5300 Paxton St	Harrisburg	PA	17111	**866-551-4602**	717-564-2121

				Toll-Free	Phone
Diamond Equipment Inc					
1060 E Diamond Ave	Evansville	IN	47711	**800-258-4428**	812-425-4428
Ecoa Industrial Products					
7700 Nw 74th Ave	Medley	FL	33166	**800-433-3833**	
Elliott & Frantz Inc					
450 E Church Rd	King Of Prussia	PA	19406	**800-220-3025**	610-279-5200
Empire Southwest Co					
1725 S Country Club Dr	Mesa	AZ	85210	**800-367-4731**	480-633-4000
Erb Equipment Co Inc					
200 Erb Industrial Dr	Fenton	MO	63026	**800-634-9661**	636-349-0200
Franks Supply Company Inc					
3311 Stanford Dr NE	Albuquerque	NM	87107	**800-432-5254**	505-884-0000
Garden State Engine & Equipment Co					
3509 US Hwy 22	Somerville	NJ	08876	**800-479-3857**	908-534-5444
General Equipment & Supplies Inc					
4300 Main Ave	Fargo	ND	58103	**800-437-2924**	701-282-2662
Global Equipment Marketing Inc					
PO Box 810483	Boca Raton	FL	33481	**866-750-8662**	561-750-8662
Golden Equipment Co					
721 Candelaria NE	Albuquerque	NM	87107	**800-880-8580**	505-345-7811
Heavy Machines Inc					
3926 E Rains Rd	Memphis	TN	38118	**888-366-9028**	901-260-2200
Improved Construction Methods					
1040 N Redmond Rd	Jacksonville	AR	72076	**877-494-5793**	
Janell Inc					
6130 Cornell Rd	Cincinnati	OH	45242	**888-489-9111**	513-489-9111
John Fabick Tractor Co					
1 Fabick Dr	Fenton	MO	63026	**800-845-9188***	636-343-5900
*Cust Svc					
Kibble Equipment					
1150 S Victory Dr	Mankato	MN	56001	**800-624-8983**	507-387-8201
M R L Equipment Company Inc					
PO Box 31154	Billings	MT	59107	**877-788-2907**	406-869-9900
MacAllister Machinery Company Inc					
7515 E 30th St	Indianapolis	IN	46219	**800-227-3228**	317-545-2151
Markem-Imaje Inc					
5448 Timberlea Blvd	Mississauga	ON	L4W2T7	**800-267-5108**	
Mississippi Valley Equipment Company Inc					
1198 Pershall Rd	Saint Louis	MO	63137	**800-325-8001**	314-869-8600
Mister Safety Shoes Inc					
6-2300 Finch Ave W	Toronto	ON	M9M2Y3	**800-707-0051**	416-746-3000
Mobile Parts Inc					
2472 Evans Rd	Val Caron	ON	P3N1P5	**800-461-4055**	705-897-4955
Moodie Implement Co					
80335 US Hwy 87 W	Lewistown	MT	59457	**800-823-3373**	406-538-5433
Mustang Tractor & Equipment Co					
12800 NW Hwy	Houston	TX	77040	**800-256-1001**	713-460-2000
Ohio Machinery Co					
3993 E Royalton Rd	Broadview Heights	OH	44147	**800-837-6200**	440-526-6200
Patten Industries Inc					
635 W Lake St	Elmhurst	IL	60126	**877-688-2228**	630-279-4400
Petersen Inc					
1527 North 2000 West	Ogden	UT	84404	**800-410-6789**	801-732-2000
Power Motive Corp					
5000 Vasquez Blvd	Denver	CO	80216	**800-627-0087**	303-355-5900
Rasmussen Equipment Co					
3333 West 2100 South	Salt Lake City	UT	84119	**800-453-8032**	801-972-5588
RBI Corp					
10201 Cedar Ridge Dr	Ashland	VA	23005	**800-444-7370**	
RDO Equipment Co					
3401 38th St S	Fargo	ND	58104	**800-342-4643**	701-282-5400
Roland Machinery Co					
816 N Dirksen Pkwy	Springfield	IL	62702	**800-252-2926**	217-789-7711
Rudd Equipment Co					
4344 Poplar Level Rd	Louisville	KY	40213	**800-527-2282**	502-456-4050
Southeastern Equipment Company Inc					
10874 E Pike Rd	Cambridge	OH	43725	**800-798-5438**	740-432-6303
Stan Houston Equipment Co					
501 S Marion Rd	Sioux Falls	SD	57106	**800-952-3033**	605-336-3727
Tyler Equipment Corp					
251 Shaker Rd PO Box 544	East Longmeadow	MA	01028	**800-292-6351**	413-525-6351
US Equipment Company Inc					
8311 Sorensen Ave	Santa Fe Springs	CA	90670	**800-255-4731**	
Valin Corp					
555 E California Ave	Sunnyvale	CA	94086	**800-774-5630**	408-730-9850
Victor L Phillips Co					
4100 Gardner Ave	Kansas City	MO	64120	**800-878-9290**	816-241-9290
Western States Equipment Co					
500 E Overland Rd PO Box 38	Meridian	ID	83642	**800-836-4308**	208-888-2287
White's Farm Supply Inc					
4154 State Rt 31	Canastota	NY	13032	**800-633-4443**	315-697-2214
Winchester Equipment Co					
121 Indian Hollow Rd	Winchester	VA	22603	**800-323-3581**	
Wyoming Machinery Co					
5300 Old W Yellowstone Hwy	Casper	WY	82604	**800-244-0527**	307-472-1000

358 HELICOPTER TRANSPORT SERVICES

SEE ALSO Air Charter Services ; Ambulance Services

				Toll-Free	Phone
Air Logistics Inc					
4605 Industrial Dr	New Iberia	LA	70560	**800-365-6771**	337-365-6771
Bristow Alaska Inc					
1915 Donald Ave	Fairbanks	AK	99701	**800-686-4080**	907-452-1197
Carson Helicopters					
952 Blooming Glen Rd	Perkasie	PA	18944	**800-523-2335**	215-249-3535
Coastal Helicopters Inc					
8995 Yandukin Dr	Juneau	AK	99801	**800-789-5610**	907-789-5600
Corporate Helicopters of San Diego					
3753 John J Montgomery Dr Ste 2	San Diego	CA	92123	**800-345-6737**	858-505-5650
Island Express Helicopter Service					
1175 Queens Hwy S	Long Beach	CA	90802	**800-228-2566***	310-510-2525
*Cust Svc					
Midwest Helicopter Airways Inc					
525 Executive Dr	Willowbrook	IL	60527	**800-323-7609**	630-325-7860

			Toll-Free	Phone

PHI Inc
2001 SE Evangeline Thwy ....Lafayette LA 70508 **866-815-7101** 337-235-2452
NASDAQ: PHII

Victoria International Airport
1962 Canso Rd ....North Saanich BC V8L5V5 **866-844-4354** 250-656-3987

Yellowhead Helicopters Ltd
3010 Selwyn Rd ....Valemount BC V0E2Z0 **888-566-4401** 250-566-4401

359 HOLDING COMPANIES

SEE ALSO Conglomerates

A holding company is a company that owns enough voting stock in another firm to control management and operations by influencing or electing its board of directors.

	Toll-Free	Phone

359-1 Airlines Holding Companies

			Toll-Free	Phone

Frontier Airlines Inc
7001 Tower Rd ....Denver CO 80249 **800-432-1359** 720-374-4200

JetBlue Airways Corp
118-29 Queens Blvd ....Forest Hills NY 11375 **800-538-2583** 718-286-7900
NASDAQ: JBLU

Republic Airways Holdings Inc
8909 PuRdue Rd Ste 300 ....Indianapolis IN 46268 **800-433-7300** 317-484-6000
NASDAQ: RJET

US Airways Group Inc
111 W Rio Salado Pkwy ....Tempe AZ 85281 **800-428-4322** 480-693-0800
NYSE: LCC

359-2 Bank Holding Companies

			Toll-Free	Phone

Access National Corp
1800 Robert Fulton Dr Ste 310 ....Reston VA 20191 **800-931-0370** 703-871-2100
NASDAQ: ANCX

Accuristix
2844 Bristol Cir ....Oakville ON L6H6G4 **866-356-6830** 905-829-9927

Allegheny Valley Bank
5137 Butler St ....Pittsburgh PA 15201 **800-889-6440** 412-781-1464
OTC: AVLY

Alpine Bank of Colorado
2200 Grand Ave ....Glenwood Springs CO 81601 **888-425-7463** 970-945-2424

AMB Financial Corp
8230 Hohman Ave ....Munster IN 46321 **800-436-5113** 219-836-5870
OTC: AMFC

Amboy Bancorp
3590 US Hwy 9 S ....Old Bridge NJ 08857 **800-942-6269** 732-591-8700

Ameriana Bancorp
2118 Bundy Ave PO Box H ....New Castle IN 47362 **866-844-7584** 765-529-2230
NASDAQ: ASBI

American River Bankshares
3100 Zinfandel Dr Ste 450 ....Rancho Cordova CA 95670 **800-544-0545**
NASDAQ: AMRB

American State Bank
1401 Ave Q ....Lubbock TX 79401 **800-531-1401** 806-767-7000

AmericanWest Bancorp
41 W Riverside Ave Ste 100 ....Spokane WA 99201 **800-772-5479** 509-927-3028

Ameris Bancorp
24 Second Ave SE ....Moultrie GA 31768 **800-347-9680** 229-890-1111
NASDAQ: ABCB

Anchor BanCorp Wisconsin Inc
25 W Main St ....Madison WI 53707 **800-252-6246** 608-252-8700
NYSE: ABCW

Andrus Transportation Services LLC
3185 East Deseret Dr North
PO Box 880 ....Saint George UT 84790 **800-888-5838** 435-673-1566

Annapolis Bancorp Inc
1000 Bestgate Rd ....Annapolis MD 21401 **800-555-5455** 410-224-4483
NASDAQ: ANNB

Arrow Financial Corp
250 Glen St ....Glens Falls NY 12801 **800-937-5449** 518-745-1000
NASDAQ: AROW

Associated Banc-Corp
1200 Hansen Rd ....Green Bay WI 54304 **800-236-2722*** 920-491-7000
*NYSE: ASB ▪ *PR*

Atlantic Coast Bank (ACFC)
505 Haines Ave ....Waycross GA 31501 **800-342-2824** 912-283-4711
NASDAQ: ACFC

BancorpSouth Inc
2910 W Jackson St ....Tupelo MS 38801 **888-797-7711** 662-680-2000
NYSE: BXS

Bank Independent
710 S Montgomery Ave ....Sheffield AL 35660 **877-865-5050** 256-386-5000

Bank Mutual Corp
4949 W Brown Deer Rd ....Milwaukee WI 53223 **844-256-8684** 414-354-1500
NASDAQ: BKMU

Bank of Commerce Holdings
1901 Churn Creek Rd ....Redding CA 96002 **800-421-2575** 530-224-3333
NASDAQ: BOCH

Bank of Hawaii Corp
130 Merchant St 20th Fl ....Honolulu HI 96813 **888-643-3888**
NYSE: BOH

Bank of South Carolina Corp
256 Meeting St ....Charleston SC 29401 **800-523-4175** 843-724-1500
NASDAQ: BKSC

Bank of the Ozarks Inc
12615 Chenal Pkwy PO Box 8811 ....Little Rock AR 72211 **800-628-3552** 501-978-2265
NASDAQ: OZRK

Bar Harbor Bankshares
82 Main St PO Box 400 ....Bar Harbor ME 04609 **888-853-7100** 207-288-3314
NYSE: BHB

Barnes Transportation Services Inc
2309 Whitley Rd ....Wilson NC 27895 **800-898-5897**

Bay Bank
2328 W Joppa Rd ....Lutherville MD 21093 **800-222-6566** 410-494-2580
NASDAQ: BYBK

BB & T Corp
200 W Second St ....Winston-Salem NC 27101 **800-226-5228** 336-733-2500
NYSE: BBT

BBCN Bank
3731 Wilshire Blvd Ste 1000 ....Los Angeles CA 90010 **888-811-6272** 213-639-1700
NASDAQ: NARA

Benny Whitehead Inc
3265 S Eufaula Ave ....Eufaula AL 36027 **800-633-7617** 334-687-8055

Berkshire Hills Bancorp Inc
24 N St ....Pittsfield MA 01201 **800-773-5601** 413-443-5601
NYSE: BHLB

Bmo Bankcorp Inc
111 W Monroe St ....Chicago IL 60603 **888-340-2265**

Boston Private Financial Holdings Inc
10 Post Office Sq ....Boston MA 02109 **855-738-8916** 617-912-1900
NASDAQ: BPFH

Brannen Banks Of Florida Inc
PO Box 1929 ....Inverness FL 34451 **866-546-8273** 352-726-1221

Bridge Capital Holdings
55 Almaden Blvd Ste 200 ....San Jose CA 95113 **866-273-4265*** 408-423-8500
*NASDAQ: BBNK ▪ *General*

Broadway Financial Corp
4800 Wilshire Blvd ....Los Angeles CA 90010 **800-227-0845** 323-634-1700
NASDAQ: BYFC

Brookline Bank
PO Box 470469 ....Brookline MA 02445 **877-668-2265*** 617-730-3520
*NASDAQ: BRKL ▪ *Cust Svc*

Bryn Mawr Bank Corp
801 Lancaster Ave ....Bryn Mawr PA 19010 **855-381-2631** 610-525-1700
NASDAQ: BMTC

C & F Financial Corp
802 Main St PO Box 391 ....West Point VA 23181 **800-583-3863** 804-843-4584
NASDAQ: CFFI

Camden National Corp
Two Elm St ....Camden ME 04843 **800-860-8821** 207-236-8821
NYSE: CAC

Capital City Bank Group Inc
PO Box 900 ....Tallahassee FL 32302 **888-671-0400** 850-402-7500
NASDAQ: CCBG

Capitol City Bancshares Inc
562 Lee St ....Atlanta GA 30310 **866-758-6395** 404-752-6067

Capitol Federal Financial
700 Kansas Ave ....Topeka KS 66603 **888-822-7333** 785-235-1341
NASDAQ: CFFN

Cardinal Financial Corp
8270 Greensboro Dr Ste 500 ....McLean VA 22102 **800-473-3247** 703-584-3400
NASDAQ: CFNL

Carolina Bank Holdings Inc
101 N Spring St ....Greensboro NC 27401 **800-472-3272** 336-288-1898
NASDAQ: CLBH

Cascade Bancorp
1100 NW Wall St ....Bend OR 97701 **877-617-3400*** 541-385-6205
*NASDAQ: CACB ▪ *Cust Svc*

Cathay General Bancorp Inc
777 N Broadway ....Los Angeles CA 90012 **800-922-8429** 213-625-4700
NASDAQ: CATY

Central Federal Corp
2923 Smith Rd ....Fairlawn OH 44333 **866-668-4606** 330-666-7979
NASDAQ: CFBK

Central Pacific Financial Corp
PO Box 3590 ....Honolulu HI 96811 **800-342-8422** 808-544-0500
NYSE: CPF

Central Valley Community Bancorp
7100 N Financial Dr Ste 101 ....Fresno CA 93720 **866-294-9588** 559-298-1775
NASDAQ: CVCY

Century Bancorp Inc
400 Mystic Ave ....Medford MA 02155 **866-823-6887** 781-393-4160
NASDAQ: CNBKA

CFS Bancorp Inc
707 Ridge Rd ....Munster IN 46321 **866-622-1370** 219-513-5123
NASDAQ: CITZ

Chemical Financial Corp
333 E Main St ....Midland MI 48640 **800-867-9757** 989-839-5350
NASDAQ: CHFC

Citizens Financial Group Inc
One Citizens Dr ....Riverside RI 02915 **800-922-9999** 401-456-7000

Citizens South Banking Corp
519 S New Hope Rd PO Box 2249 ....Gastonia NC 28054 **877-311-2265** 704-868-5200
NASDAQ: CSBC

Clifton Savings Bancorp Inc
1433 Van Houten Ave 3rd Fl ....Clifton NJ 07015 **888-562-6727** 973-473-2200
NASDAQ: CSBK

CNB Financial Corp
One S Second St PO Box 42 ....Clearfield PA 16830 **800-492-3221** 814-765-9621
NASDAQ: CCNE

Colorado Business Bank
821 17th St ....Denver CO 80202 **800-574-4714** 303-293-2265

Columbia Bank
1301 A St Ste 800 ....Tacoma WA 98402 **800-305-1905** 253-305-1900
NASDAQ: COLB

Commercial National Financial Corp
900 Ligonier St ....Latrobe PA 15650 **800-803-2265** 724-539-3501
OTC: CNAF

Community Bank Shares of Indiana Inc
101 W Spring St ....New Albany IN 47150 **866-944-2004** 812-944-2224
NASDAQ: YCB

Community Bank System Inc
5790 Widewaters Pkwy ....Syracuse NY 13214 **800-847-2911** 315-445-2282
NYSE: CBU

Community Investors Bancorp Inc
119 S Sandusky Ave ....Bucyrus OH 44820 **800-222-4955** 419-562-7055
OTC: CIBN

Community Shores Bank Corp
1030 W Norton Ave ....Muskegon MI 49441 **888-853-6633** 231-780-1800
OTC: CSHB

			Toll-Free	Phone

Community State Bank
208 N Ctr . . . . Shelbina MO 63468 **877-588-4121*** 573-588-4101
*General

Community Trust Bancorp Inc
346 N Mayo Trl . . . . Pikeville KY 41501 **800-422-1090** 606-432-1414
NASDAQ: CTBI

Compass Bancshares Inc
15 S 20th St . . . . Birmingham AL 35233 **800-266-7277** 205-297-3584

Crazy Woman Creek Bancorp Inc
PO Box 1020 . . . . Buffalo WY 82834 **877-684-2766** 307-684-5591

Cullen/Frost Bankers Inc
100 W Houston St . . . . San Antonio TX 78205 **800-562-6732** 210-220-4011
NYSE: CFR

CVB Financial Corp
701 N Haven Ave PO Box 51000 . . . . Ontario CA 91764 **888-222-5432** 909-980-4030
NASDAQ: CVBF

Dime Community Bancshares Inc
209 Havemeyer St . . . . Brooklyn NY 11211 **800-321-3463** 718-782-6200
NASDAQ: DCOM

Doral Financial Corp
1441 F D Roosevelt Ave . . . . San Juan PR 00920 **866-296-3743** 787-749-4949
NYSE: DRL

Eagle Bancorp Inc
7815 Woodmont Ave . . . . Bethesda MD 20814 **800-364-8313** 240-497-2044
NASDAQ: EGBN

East West Bancorp Inc
1881 W Main St . . . . Alhambra CA 91801 **888-895-5650** 626-308-2012
NASDAQ: EWBC

Eastern Bank Corp
265 Franklin St . . . . Boston MA 02110 **800-327-8376*** 617-897-1008
*Cust Svc

Eastern Virginia Bankshares Inc
330 Hospital Rd . . . . Tappahannock VA 22560 **866-296-3743*** 804-443-8400
NASDAQ: EVBS ■ *General

Enterprise Financial Services Corp
150 N Meramec Ave . . . . Clayton MO 63105 **800-396-8141** 314-725-5500
NASDAQ: EFSG

Evans Bancorp Inc
One Grimsby Dr . . . . Hamburg NY 14075 **866-310-0763** 716-926-2000
NYSE: EVBN

Farmer State Bank of Sublette
303 S Pennsylvania Ave PO Box 20 . . . . Sublette IL 61367 **866-269-1722** 815-849-5242

Farmers Capital Bank Corp
PO Box 309 . . . . Frankfort KY 40602 **800-776-9437** 502-227-1668
NASDAQ: FFKT

Fauquier Bankshares Inc
10 Courthouse Sq . . . . Warrenton VA 20186 **800-638-3798** 540-347-2700
NASDAQ: FBSS

FFD Financial Corp
321 N Wooster Ave . . . . Dover OH 44622 **800-558-3424** 330-364-7777
OTC: FFDF

FFW Corp 1205 N Cass St . . . . Wabash IN 46992 **800-377-4984** 260-563-3185
OTC: FFWC

Financial Institutions Inc
220 Liberty St . . . . Warsaw NY 14569 **866-296-3743** 585-786-1100
NASDAQ: FISI

First BanCorp PO Box 9146 . . . . San Juan PR 00908 **866-695-2511** 787-725-2511
NYSE: FBP

First Banctrust Corp
101 S Central Ave . . . . Paris IL 61944 **800-228-6381** 217-465-6381
OTC: FIRT

First Banks Inc
135 N Meramec Ave . . . . Clayton MO 63105 **800-760-2265** 314-854-4600

First Busey Corp
100 W University Ave . . . . Champaign IL 61820 **800-672-8739** 217-365-4516
NASDAQ: BUSE

First Citizens Bancorp Inc
PO Box 29 . . . . Columbia SC 29202 **888-612-4444**
OTC: FCBN

First Citizens Bank
1801 Century Pk E Ste 800 . . . . Los Angeles CA 90067 **888-323-4732**

First Citizens National Bank Charitable Foundation
PO Box 1708 . . . . Mason City IA 50402 **800-423-1602** 641-423-1600

First Commonwealth Financial Corp
601 Philadelphia St . . . . Indiana PA 15701 **800-711-2265** 724-349-7220
NYSE: FCF

First Community Corp (FCC)
5455 Sunset Blvd . . . . Lexington SC 29072 **800-829-6372** 803-951-0555
NASDAQ: FCCO

First Defiance Financial Corp
601 Clinton St . . . . Defiance OH 43512 **800-472-6292** 419-782-5015
NASDAQ: FDEF

First Federal Bancshares of Arkansas Inc
1401 Hwy 62-65 N . . . . Harrison AR 72601 **866-242-3324** 870-741-7641
NASDAQ: FFBH

First Financial Bancorp (FFB)
255 E Fifth St Ste 700 . . . . Cincinnati OH 45202 **877-322-9530** 513-979-5837
NASDAQ: FFBC

First Financial Bankshares Inc
PO Box 701 . . . . Abilene TX 79604 **888-588-2623** 325-627-7155
NASDAQ: FFIN

First Financial Corp
One First Financial Plz . . . . Terre Haute IN 47807 **800-511-0045** 812-238-6000
NASDAQ: THFF

First FSB of Frankfort
216 W Main St PO Box 535 . . . . Frankfort KY 40602 **888-818-3372** 502-223-1638

First Horizon National Corp
165 Madison . . . . Memphis TN 38103 **800-489-4040** 901-523-4444
NYSE: FHN

First Independence Corp
112 E Myrtle St PO Box 947 . . . . Independence KS 67301 **800-455-0744** 620-331-1660
NYSE: FFSL

First Interstate Bancsystem Inc
401 N 31st St . . . . Billings MT 59101 **888-752-3341** 406-255-5000
NASDAQ: FIBK

First Merchants Corp
200 E Jackson St . . . . Muncie IN 47305 **800-205-3464** 765-747-1500
NASDAQ: FRME

			Toll-Free	Phone

First Midwest Bancorp Inc
One Pierce Pl Ste 1500 . . . . Itasca IL 60143 **800-322-3623** 630-875-7200
NASDAQ: FMBI

First Mutual Bancshares Inc
400 108th Ave NE PO Box 1647 . . . . Bellevue WA 98009 **800-735-7303** 425-455-7300

First National Bank
4220 William Penn Hwy . . . . Monroeville PA 15146 **800-555-5455**

First National Lincoln Corp
223 Main St PO Box 940 . . . . Damariscotta ME 04543 **800-564-3195** 207-563-3195

First National of Nebraska Inc
PO BOX 2490 . . . . Omaha NE 68197 **800-688-7070** 402-341-0500

First of Long Island Corp
10 Glen Head Ave . . . . Glen Head NY 11545 **800-554-8969** 516-671-4900
NASDAQ: FLIC

First South Bancorp Inc
1311 Carolina Ave . . . . Washington NC 27889 **800-946-4178** 252-946-4178
NASDAQ: FSBK

First Southern Bank
301 S Ct St . . . . Florence AL 35630 **800-625-7131*** 256-718-4200
*General

First State Bank
730 Harry Sauner Rd . . . . Hillsboro OH 45133 **800-987-2566*** 937-393-9170
*General

First United Corp
19 S Second St . . . . Oakland MD 21550 **888-692-2654**
NASDAQ: FUNC

FirstFed Bancorp Inc
1630 Fourth Ave N PO Box 340 . . . . Bessemer AL 35020 **800-436-5112** 205-428-8472

Flushing Financial Corp
1979 Marcus Ave . . . . New Hyde Park NY 11042 **800-581-2889** 718-961-5400
NASDAQ: FFIC

German American Bancorp
711 Main St . . . . Jasper IN 47546 **800-482-1314** 812-482-1314
NASDAQ: GABC

Glacier Bancorp Inc
PO Box 27 . . . . Kalispell MT 59903 **800-735-4371** 406-756-4200
NASDAQ: GBCI

Great American Bancorp Inc
1311 S Neil St . . . . Champaign IL 61820 **800-962-4284** 217-356-2265
OTC: GTPS

Greene County Bancorp Inc
302 Main St . . . . Catskill NY 12414 **888-439-4272** 518-943-2600
NASDAQ: GCBC

Greenwood Racing Inc
3001 St Rd . . . . Bensalem PA 19020 **888-238-2946** 215-639-9000

Guaranty Bancshares Inc
100 W Arkansas St PO Box 1158 . . . . Mount Pleasant TX 75455 **888-572-9881** 903-572-9881

Hancock Holding Co
2510 14th St . . . . Gulfport MS 39501 **800-522-6542** 228-822-4371

Hanmi Bank
3660 Wilshire Blvd Ste PH-A . . . . Los Angeles CA 90010 **877-808-4266** 213-382-2200

Harleysville Savings Financial Corp
271 Main St . . . . Harleysville PA 19438 **888-256-8828** 215-256-8828
NASDAQ: HARL

Hawthorn Bancshares Inc
300 SW Longview Blvd . . . . Lee's Summit MO 64081 **800-761-8362** 816-347-8100
NASDAQ: HWBK

Heartland Financial USA Inc
1398 Central Ave . . . . Dubuque IA 52001 **888-739-2100** 563-589-2100
NASDAQ: HTLF

Heritage Bank
201 Fifth Ave SW . . . . Olympia WA 98501 **800-455-6126** 360-943-1500

Heritage Commerce Corp
150 Almaden Blvd . . . . San Jose CA 95113 **800-468-9716** 408-947-6900
NASDAQ: HTBK

Heritage Financial Corp
201 Fifth Ave SW . . . . Olympia WA 98501 **800-962-4284** 360-943-1500
NASDAQ: HFWA

HF Financial Corp
225 S Main Ave . . . . Sioux Falls SD 57104 **800-244-2149** 605-333-7556
NASDAQ: HFFC

High Country Bancorp Inc
7360 W Hwy 50 PO Box 309 . . . . Salida CO 81201 **800-201-0557** 719-539-2516
OTC: HCBC

HMN Financial Inc
1016 Civic Ctr Dr NW . . . . Rochester MN 55901 **888-257-2000** 507-535-1309
NASDAQ: HMNF

Home City Financial Corp
2454 N Limestone St PO Box 1288 . . . . Springfield OH 45503 **866-421-2331** 937-390-0470
OTC: HCFL

Home Federal Bank
1602 Cumberland Ave . . . . Middlesboro KY 40965 **800-354-0182** 606-248-1095
OTC: HFBA

Honat Bancorp Inc
733 Main St PO Box 350 . . . . Honesdale PA 18431 **800-462-9515** 570-253-3355
OTC: HONT

HSBC North America Holdings Inc
2700 Sanders Rd . . . . Prospect Heights IL 60070 **800-975-4722** 847-564-5000

Huntington Bancshares Inc
7 Easton Oval . . . . Columbus OH 43219 **800-480-2265**
NASDAQ: HBAN

IBERIABANK Corp
200 W Congress St . . . . Lafayette LA 70501 **800-968-0801**
NASDAQ: IBKC

Independent Bank Corp
230 W Main St PO Box 491 . . . . Ionia MI 48846 **888-300-3193** 616-527-2400
NASDAQ: IBCP

Intervest Bancshares Corp
1 Rockefeller Plaza Ste 400 . . . . New York NY 10020 **877-226-5462** 212-218-8383
NASDAQ: IBCA

Jacksonville Bancorp Inc
100 N Laura St . . . . Jacksonville FL 32202 **888-699-5292** 904-421-3040
NASDAQ: JAXB

Keweenaw Financial Corp
235 Quincy St . . . . Hancock MI 49930 **866-482-0404** 906-482-0404

KeyCorp 127 Public Sq . . . . Cleveland OH 44114 **800-539-9055** 216-689-8481
NYSE: KEY

Lake Sunapee Bank
9 Main St PO Box 29 . . . . Newport NH 03773 **800-281-5772** 603-863-5772

					Toll-Free	Phone

Lakeland Bancorp Inc
250 Oak Ridge Rd . . . . Oak Ridge NJ 07438 **866-224-1379** 973-697-2000
NASDAQ: LBAI

Lakeland Financial Corp
202 E Ctr St . . . . Warsaw IN 46580 **800-827-4522** 574-267-6144
NASDAQ: LKFN

LNB Bancorp Inc 457 Broadway . . . . Lorain OH 44052 **800-860-1007** 440-989-3348
NASDAQ: LNBB

Logansport Financial Corp
723 E Broadway PO Box 569 . . . . Logansport IN 46947 **800-541-9154** 574-722-3855
OTC: LOGN

Macatawa Bank Corp
10753 Macatawa Dr PO Box 3119 . . . . Holland MI 49424 **877-820-2265** 616-820-1444
NASDAQ: MCBC

Malaga Financial Corp
2514 Via Tejon . . . . Palos Verdes Estates CA 90274 **888-562-5242** 310-375-9000
OTC: MLGF

MB Financial Inc
6111 N River Rd . . . . Rosemont IL 60018 **888-422-6562**
NASDAQ: MBFI

MBT Financial Corp
102 E Front St . . . . Monroe MI 48161 **800-321-0032** 734-241-3431
NASDAQ: MBTF

Mercantile Bank
200 N 33rd St PO Box 3455 . . . . Quincy IL 62305 **800-405-6372** 217-223-7300
NYSE: MBCR

Mercantile Bank Corp
310 Leonard St NW . . . . Grand Rapids MI 49504 **888-345-6296** 616-406-3000
NASDAQ: MBWM

Merchants Bancshares Inc
PO Box 1009 . . . . Burlington VT 05402 **800-322-5222** 802-658-3400
NASDAQ: MBVT

Mesa Systems Inc
681 Railroad Blvd . . . . Grand Junction CO 81505 **800-654-3225** 888-229-1409

Mid Penn Bancorp Inc
349 Union St . . . . Millersburg PA 17061 **866-642-7736** 717-692-2133
NASDAQ: MPB

MidSouth Bancorp Inc
102 Versailles Blvd . . . . Lafayette LA 70501 **800-213-2265** 337-237-8343
NYSE: MSL

MidWestOne Financial Group Inc
102 S Clinton St PO Box 1700 . . . . Iowa City IA 52240 **800-247-4418*** 319-356-5800
NASDAQ: MOFG ▣ **Cust Svc*

MutualFirst Financial Inc
110 E Charles St . . . . Muncie IN 47305 **800-382-8031** 765-747-2800
NASDAQ: MFSF

NASB Financial Inc
12500 S 71 Hwy . . . . Grandview MO 64030 **800-677-6272** 816-765-2200
NASDAQ: NASB

National Bankshares Inc
101 Hubbard St . . . . Blacksburg VA 24060 **800-552-4123** 540-951-6300
NASDAQ: NKSH

National Penn Bancshares Inc
PO Box 547 . . . . Boyertown PA 19512 **800-822-3321**
NASDAQ: NPBC

NBT Bancorp Inc
52 S Broad St . . . . Norwich NY 13815 **800-628-2265** 607-337-2265
NASDAQ: NBTB

New York Community Bancorp Inc
615 Merrick Ave . . . . Westbury NY 11590 **877-786-6560** 516-683-4100
NYSE: NYCB

North State Bank Inc
6204 Falls of Neuse Rd . . . . Raleigh NC 27609 **877-357-2265** 919-787-9696

Northbridge Financial Corp
105 Adelaide St W Ste 700 . . . . Toronto ON M5H1P9 **855-620-6262** 416-350-4400

Northeast Bancorp
500 Canal St . . . . Lewiston ME 04240 **800-284-5989** 207-786-3245
NASDAQ: NBN

Northeast Indiana Bancorp Inc
648 N Jefferson St . . . . Huntington IN 46750 **800-550-3372** 260-356-3311
OTC: NIDB

Northern States Financial Corp
1601 N Lewis Ave . . . . Waukegan IL 60085 **800-339-4432** 847-244-6000
OTC: NSFC

Northwest Bancorp Inc
PO Box 128 . . . . Warren PA 16365 **800-859-1000** 814-728-7263

OceanFirst Financial Corp
975 Hooper Ave . . . . Toms River NJ 08753 **888-623-2633** 732-240-4500
NASDAQ: OCFC

Ocwen Financial Corp
1661 Worthington Rd Ste 100
PO Box 24737. . . . . West Palm Beach FL 33409 **800-746-2936** 561-681-8000
NYSE: OCN

Ohio Valley Banc Corp
420 Third Ave . . . . Gallipolis OH 45631 **800-468-6682** 740-446-2631
NASDAQ: OVBC

Old Point Financial Corp
One W Mellen St PO Box 3392 . . . . Hampton VA 23663 **800-952-0051** 757-728-1200
NASDAQ: OPOF

Old Second Bancorp Inc
37 S River St . . . . Aurora IL 60506 **888-892-6565** 630-892-0202
NASDAQ: OSBC

Oneida Financial Corp
182 Main St . . . . Oneida NY 13421 **800-211-0564** 315-363-2000
NASDAQ: ONFC

Opus Bank
19900 MacArthur Blvd 12th Fl . . . . Irvine CA 92612 **855-678-7226** 949-250-9800

Owen Community Bank
279 E Morgan St PO Box 187 . . . . Spencer IN 47460 **800-690-2095** 812-829-2095

Pacific & Western Credit Corp
140 Fullarton St Ste 2002 . . . . London ON N6A5P2 **866-979-1919** 519-645-1919
TSE: PWC

Pacific Mercantile Bancorp
949 S Coast Dr Ste 105 . . . . Costa Mesa CA 92626 **877-450-2265*** 714-438-2600
NASDAQ: PMBC ▣ **General*

Pacific Premier Bancorp Inc
1600 Sunflower Ave . . . . Costa Mesa CA 92626 **888-388-5433** 714-431-4000
NASDAQ: PPBI

Park Bancorp Inc
5400 S Pulaski Rd . . . . Chicago IL 60632 **888-727-5333** 773-582-8616
OTC: PFED

Park National Bank
50 N Third St PO Box 3500 . . . . Newark OH 43058 **888-791-8633** 740-349-8451
NASDAQ: PRK

Pathfinder Bancorp Inc
214 W First St . . . . Oswego NY 13126 **800-811-5620** 315-343-0057
NASDAQ: PBHC

Patriot National Bancorp Inc
900 Bedford St . . . . Stamford CT 06901 **888-728-7468** 203-251-7200
NASDAQ: PNBK

Peapack-Gladstone Bank
500 Hills Dr Ste 300 PO Box 700 . . . . Bedminster NJ 07921 **800-742-7595** 908-234-0700
NASDAQ: PGC

People's Mutual Holdings
850 Main St . . . . Bridgeport CT 06604 **800-392-3009** 203-338-7171

Peoples Bancorp Inc
138 Putnam St . . . . Marietta OH 45750 **800-374-6123** 740-373-3155
NASDAQ: PEBO

Peoples Bancorp of North Carolina Inc
518 W 'C' St . . . . Newton NC 28658 **800-948-7195** 828-464-5620
NASDAQ: PEBK

PlainsCapital Corp
2323 Victory Ave Ste 1400 . . . . Dallas TX 75219 **866-762-8392** 214-252-4100

PNC Financial Services Group Inc
249 Fifth Ave 1 PNC Plz . . . . Pittsburgh PA 15222 **877-762-2000** 412-762-2000
NYSE: PNC

Princeton National Bancorp Inc
606 S Main St . . . . Princeton IL 61356 **888-897-2276** 309-662-4444
OTC: PNBC

PrivateBancorp Inc
120 S LaSalle St . . . . Chicago IL 60603 **800-662-7748**
NASDAQ: PVTB

Prosperity Bancshares Inc
1301 N Mechanic . . . . El Campo TX 77437 **800-862-9098** 979-578-8181
NYSE: PB

Provident Bank
3756 Central Ave . . . . Riverside CA 92506 **800-442-5201** 951-686-6060
NASDAQ: PROV

Provident Community Bancshares Inc
2700 Celanese Rd . . . . Rock Hill SC 29732 **800-933-3030** 803-325-9400
OTC: PCBS

Pulaski Financial Corp
12300 Olive Blvd . . . . Saint Louis MO 63141 **888-649-3320** 314-878-2210
NASDAQ: PULB

Quad City Bank & Trust
3551 Seventh St . . . . Moline IL 61265 **866-676-0551** 309-736-3580
NASDAQ: QCRH

RBC Centura Banks Inc
PO Box 1220 . . . . Rocky Mount NC 27802 **800-769-2553**

Regions Financial Corp
1900 Fifth Ave N . . . . Birmingham AL 35203 **866-688-0658**
NYSE: RF

Renasant Corp
209 Troy St PO Box 709 . . . . Tupelo MS 38802 **800-680-1601*** 662-680-1001
NASDAQ: RNST ▣ **Cust Svc*

Republic Bancorp Inc
601 W Market St . . . . Louisville KY 40202 **888-540-5363** 502-584-3600
NASDAQ: RBCAA

Republic First Bancorp Inc
50 S 16th St Ste 2400. . . . . Philadelphia PA 19102 **888-875-2265** 215-735-4422
NASDAQ: FRBK

River Valley Bancorp
430 Clifty Dr . . . . Madison IN 47250 **800-994-4849** 812-273-4949
NASDAQ: RIVR

S&T Bancorp Inc
800 Philadelphia St . . . . Indiana PA 15701 **800-325-2265** 724-349-1800
NASDAQ: STBA

Salisbury Bancorp Inc
Five Bissell St PO Box 1868 . . . . Lakeville CT 06039 **800-222-9801** 860-435-9801
NASDAQ: SAL

Sandy Spring Bancorp Inc
17801 Georgia Ave . . . . Olney MD 20832 **800-399-5919** 301-774-6400
NASDAQ: SASR

SCBT Financial Corp
950 John C Calhoun Dr . . . . Orangeburg SC 29115 **800-277-2175** 803-534-2175
NASDAQ: SCBT

Seacoast Banking Corp of Florida
815 Colorado Ave PO Box 9012 . . . . Stuart FL 34994 **800-706-9991*** 772-287-4000
NASDAQ: SBCF ▣ **All*

Simmons First National Corp
501 Main St . . . . Pine Bluff AR 71601 **866-246-2400** 870-541-1000
NASDAQ: SFNC

SouthFirst Bancshares Inc
126 N Norton Ave PO Box 167 . . . . Sylacauga AL 35150 **800-239-1492** 256-245-4365
OTC: SZBI

Southside Bancshares Inc
1201 S Beckham Ave . . . . Tyler TX 75701 **877-639-3511** 903-531-7111
NASDAQ: SBSI

Southwest Bancorp Inc
608 S Main St PO Box 1988 . . . . Stillwater OK 74076 **888-762-4762**
NASDAQ: OKSB

Southwest Georgia Financial Corp
201 First St SE . . . . Moultrie GA 31768 **888-683-2265** 229-985-1120
NYSE: SGB

Sun Bancorp Inc (SNBC)
226 Landis Ave . . . . Vineland NJ 08360 **800-786-9066**
NASDAQ: SNBC

SunTrust Banks Inc
303 Peachtree St NE . . . . Atlanta GA 30308 **800-786-8787** 404-588-7711
NYSE: STI

Susquehanna Bancshares Inc
26 N Cedar St PO Box 1000 . . . . Lititz PA 17543 **800-311-3182** 717-626-4721
NASDAQ: SUSQ

Sussex Bank
200 Munsonhurst Rd . . . . Franklin NJ 07416 **800-511-9900** 973-827-2914
NASDAQ: SBBX

Company / Address	City	ST	Zip	Toll-Free	Phone
SVB Financial Group 3005 Tasman Dr *NASDAQ: SIVB*	Santa Clara	CA	95054	800-760-9644	408-654-7400
SY Bancorp Inc 1040 E Main St *NASDAQ: SYBT*	Louisville	KY	40206	800-625-9066	502-582-2571
Synovus Financial Corp 1111 Bay Ave Ste 500 PO Box 120 *NYSE: SNV*	Columbus	GA	31902	888-796-6887	706-649-2311
Taylor Capital Group Inc 9550 W Higgins Rd *NASDAQ: TAYC*	Rosemont	IL	60018	866-750-9107	847-653-7978
TF Financial Corp 3 Penns Trail *NASDAQ: THRD*	Newtown	PA	18940	800-822-3321	215-579-4000
TIB Financial Corp 121 Alhambra Plz Ste 1601 *NASDAQ: TIBB*	Coral Gables	FL	33134	800-639-5111	
Timberland Bancorp Inc 624 Simpson Ave *NASDAQ: TSBK*	Hoquiam	WA	98550	800-562-8761	360-533-4747
Titonka Bancshares Inc PO Box 309	Titonka	IA	50480	866-985-3247	515-928-2142
Tower Financial Corp 116 E Berry St *NASDAQ: TOFC*	Fort Wayne	IN	46802	800-731-2265	317-706-9500
TriCo Bancshares 63 Constitution Dr *NASDAQ: TCBK*	Chico	CA	95973	800-922-8742	530-898-0300
Trustco Bank Corp NY PO Box 1082 *NASDAQ: TRST*	Schenectady	NY	12301	800-670-3110	518-377-3311
Trustmark National Bank 248 E Capitol St PO Box 291 *NASDAQ: TRMK ■ *Cust Svc*	Jackson	MS	39201	800-243-2524*	601-208-5111
UMB Financial Corp 1010 Grand Blvd *NASDAQ: UMBF*	Kansas City	MO	64106	800-821-2171	816-860-7000
Umpqua Holdings Corp One SW Columbia St Ste 1200 *NASDAQ: UMPQ*	Portland	OR	97258	866-486-7782	503-727-4100
Union Bankshares Inc 20 Lower Main St *NASDAQ: UNB*	Morrisville	VT	05661	866-862-1891	802-888-6600
United Bancorp Inc 201 S Fourth St *NASDAQ: UBCP*	Martins Ferry	OH	43935	888-275-5566	740-633-0445
United Bancshares Inc 100 S High St PO Box 67 *NASDAQ: UBOH*	Columbus Grove	OH	45830	800-837-8111	419-659-2141
United Bankshares Inc 514 Market St *NASDAQ: UBSI*	Parkersburg	WV	26101	800-327-9862	304-424-8800
United Community Banks Inc PO Box 398 *NASDAQ: UCBI*	Blairsville	GA	30514	866-270-7200	706-781-2265
United Community Financial Corp PO Box 1111 *NASDAQ: UCFC*	Youngstown	OH	44501	877-272-7661	330-742-0500
United Security Bancshares Inc PO Box 249 *NASDAQ: USBI*	Thomasville	AL	36784	866-546-8273	334-636-5424
Unity Bancorp Inc 64 Old Hwy 22 *NASDAQ: UNTY*	Clinton	NJ	08809	800-618-2265	908-730-7630
Universal Enterprises Inc 8030 SW Nimbus	Beaverton	OR	97008	800-547-5740	503-644-8723
Univest Corp of Pennsylvania 14 N Main St PO Box 64197 *NASDAQ: UVSP*	Souderton	PA	18964	877-723-5571	
US Bancorp 800 Nicollet Mall *NYSE: USB ■ *Cust Svc*	Minneapolis	MN	55402	800-872-2657*	651-466-3000
Valley National Bancorp 1455 Valley Rd *NYSE: VLY*	Wayne	NJ	07470	800-522-4100	973-305-8800
Veteran's Truck Line Inc 800 Black Hawk Dr	Burlington	WI	53105	800-456-9476	262-539-3400
VIST Financial Corp PO Box 6219 PO Box 6219 *NASDAQ: VIST*	Wyomissing	PA	19610	888-238-3330	610-926-7632
Washington Federal Inc 425 Pike St *NASDAQ: WAFD*	Seattle	WA	98101	800-324-9375	206-624-7930
Washington Trust Bancorp Inc 23 Broad St *NASDAQ: WASH*	Westerly	RI	02891	800-475-2265	401-348-1200
Wayne Bank 717 Main St	Honesdale	PA	18431	800-598-5002	570-253-1455
Wayne Savings Bancshares Inc 151 N Market St *NASDAQ: WAYN*	Wooster	OH	44691	800-414-1103	330-264-5767
Webster City Federal Bancorp 820 Des Moines St *NYSE: WCFB*	Webster City	IA	50595	866-519-4004	515-832-3071
Webster Financial Corp PO Box 10305 *NYSE: WBS*	Waterbury	CT	06726	800-325-2424	
West Bancorp Inc PO Box 65020 *NASDAQ: WTBA*	West Des Moines	IA	50265	800-810-2301	515-222-2300
West Side Unlimited Corp 4201 16th Ave SW	Cedar Rapids	IA	52404	800-373-2957	319-390-4466
Westfield Financial Inc 141 Elm St *NASDAQ: WFD*	Westfield	MA	01085	800-995-5734	413-568-1911
Westwood Holdings Group Inc 200 Crescent Ct Ste 1200 *NYSE: WHG*	Dallas	TX	75201	800-687-0372	214-756-6900
Winona National Bankÿÿÿ PO Box 499	Winona	MN	55987	800-546-4392	507-454-4320

Company / Address	City	ST	Zip	Toll-Free	Phone
WSFS Financial Corp 500 Delaware Ave *NASDAQ: WSFS*	Wilmington	DE	19801	888-973-7226	302-792-6000

359-3 Holding Companies (General)

Company / Address	City	ST	Zip	Toll-Free	Phone
Alutiiq LLC 3909 Arctic Blvd Ste 400	Anchorage	AK	99503	800-829-8547	907-222-9500
American Standard Cos Inc 1 Centennial Ave	Piscataway	NJ	08855	800-442-1902	
AMETEK Inc 1100 Cassatt Rd PO Box 1764 *NYSE: AME*	Berwyn	PA	19312	800-473-1286	610-647-2121
Atlas Copco North America LLC 7 Campus Dr Ste 200	Parsippany	NJ	07054	877-342-8527	973-397-3432
Atlas World Group Inc 1212 St George Rd	Evansville	IN	47711	800-252-8885	812-424-2222
Boca Resorts 501 E Camino Real	Boca Raton	FL	33432	888-543-1277	561-447-3000
BT Conferencing Inc 150 Newport Ave. Ext, Ste 300	North Quincy	MA	02171	866-770-8777	
Carnival Corp 3655 NW 87th Ave *NYSE: CCL*	Miami	FL	33178	800-438-6744	305-599-2600
CBRL Group Inc PO Box 787	Lebanon	TN	37088	800-333-9566	
CenturyTel Inc 100 Centurylink Dr PO Box 4065 *NYSE: CTL*	Monroe	LA	71211	877-290-5458	318-388-9000
Clayton Holdings LLC 100 BeaRd Sawmill Rd Ste 200	Shelton	CT	06484	877-291-5301	203-926-5600
Comcast Corp 1701 JFK Blvd *NASDAQ: CMCSA*	Philadelphia	PA	19103	800-266-2278	215-665-1700
ConAgra Foods Inc One ConAgra Dr *NYSE: CAG*	Omaha	NE	68102	877-266-2472	402-240-4000
CONSOL Energy Inc 1000 Consol Energy Dr *NYSE: CNX*	Canonsburg	PA	15317	800-544-8024	724-485-4000
Dash Multi-Corp Inc 2500 Adie Rd	Maryland Heights	MO	63043	888-889-9655	314-432-3200
Dectron International Inc 4300 Poirier Blvd	Montreal	QC	H4R2C5	888-332-8766	514-334-9609
Deluxe Corp 3680 N Victoria St *NYSE: DLX*	Shoreview	MN	55126	800-328-7205	651-483-7111
Elvis Presley Enterprises Inc 3734 Elvis Presley Blvd	Memphis	TN	38116	800-238-2000	901-332-3322
ESCO Technologies Inc 9900A Clayton Rd *NYSE: ESE*	Saint Louis	MO	63124	800-368-5948	314-213-7200
Esmark Steel Group 2500 Euclid Ave	Chicago Heights	IL	60411	800-323-0340	708-756-0400
FedEx Corp 3610 Hacks Cross Rd *NYSE: FDX*	Memphis	TN	38125	800-463-3339	901-369-3600
Fresh Del Monte Produce Co 241 Sevilla Ave PO Box 149222 *NYSE: FDP ■ *Cust Svc*	Coral Gables	FL	33134	800-950-3683*	305-520-8400
George Weston Ltd 22 St Clair Ave E *TSE: WN*	Toronto	ON	M4T2S7	800-564-6253	416-922-2500
Hickory Tech Corp 221 E Hickory St PO Box 3248 *NASDAQ: ENVE*	Mankato	MN	56002	866-442-5679	507-387-1151
Hitch Enterprises Inc 309 Northridge Cir PO Box 1308	Guymon	OK	73942	800-951-2533	580-338-8575
Home Capital Group Inc 145 King St W Ste 2300 *TSE: HCG*	Toronto	ON	M5H1J8	800-990-7881	416-360-4663
Hunt Consolidated Inc 1900 N Akard St Ste 1500	Dallas	TX	75201	800-424-9300	214-978-8000
Icahn Enterprises LP 767 Fifth Ave 47th Fl *NASDAQ: IEP*	New York	NY	10153	800-255-2737	212-702-4300
IsoRay Medical Inc 350 Hills St Ste 106	Richland	WA	99354	877-447-6729	509-375-1202
Kyocera International Inc 8611 Balboa Ave	San Diego	CA	92123	877-248-4237	858-576-2600
Liberty Diversified International Inc 5600 Hwy 169 N	New Hope	MN	55428	800-421-1270	763-536-6600
Lincoln Electric Holdings Inc 22801 St Clair Ave *NASDAQ: LECO*	Cleveland	OH	44117	800-833-9353	216-481-8100
Marsh & McLennan Cos Inc 1166 Ave of the Americas *NYSE: MMC*	New York	NY	10036	866-374-2662	212-345-5000
McKesson Corp One Post St *NYSE: MCK*	San Francisco	CA	94104	800-482-3784	415-983-8300
MDC Holdings Inc 4350 S Monaco St Ste 500 *NYSE: MDC*	Denver	CO	80237	888-500-7060	303-773-1100
NewMarket Corp 330 S Fourth St *NYSE: NEU*	Richmond	VA	23219	800-625-5191	804-788-5000
NextWave Wireless Inc 10350 Science Ctr Dr Ste 210 *OTC: WAVE*	San Diego	CA	92121	800-461-9330	858-731-5300
North American Stainless Inc 6870 Hwy 42 East	Ghent	KY	41045	800-499-7833	502-347-6000
Nustar GP Holdings LLC PO Box 781609 *NYSE: NSH*	San Antonio	TX	78248	800-866-9060	210-918-2000
OKI Developments Inc 1416 112th Ave NE	Bellevue	WA	98004	877-465-3654	425-454-2800

	Toll-Free	Phone

Otter Tail Corp
4334 18th Ave SW PO Box 9156 .... Fargo ND 58106 — **866-410-8780** — 218-739-8479
NASDAQ: OTTR

Pacer International Inc
2300 Clayton Rd Ste 1200 .... Concord CA 94520 — **877-917-2237** — 925-887-1400
NYSE: XPO

Pro-Dex Inc 2361 McGaw Ave .... Irvine CA 92614 — **800-562-6204**
NASDAQ: PDEX

Revlon Inc 237 Pk Ave .... New York NY 10017 — **800-473-8566** — 212-527-4000
NYSE: REV

Sandvik Inc
1702 Nevins Rd .... Fair Lawn NJ 07410 — **800-726-3845** — 201-794-5000

Schott North America Inc
555 Taxter Rd .... Elmsford NY 10523 — **877-261-2100** — 914-831-2200

SGS North America Inc
201 State Rt 17 N .... Rutherford NJ 07070 — **800-645-5227** — 201-508-3000

Shenandoah Telecommunications Co
500 Shentel Way .... Edinburg VA 22824 — **800-743-6835** — 540-984-5224
NASDAQ: SHEN

Siebert Financial Corp
885 Third Ave .... New York NY 10022 — **877-327-8379** — 212-644-2400
NASDAQ: SIEB

Sumitomo Corp of America
600 Third Ave 42nd Fl .... New York NY 10016 — **877-980-3283** — 212-207-0700

T Rowe Price Group Inc
100 E Pratt St .... Baltimore MD 21202 — **800-638-7890** — 410-345-2000
NASDAQ: TROW

Taylor Corp
1725 Roe Crest Dr ...... North Mankato MN 56003 — **800-545-6620** — 507-625-2828

Telephone & Data Systems Inc
30 N La Salle St Ste 4000 .... Chicago IL 60602 — **877-337-1575** — 312-630-1900
NYSE: TDS

ThyssenKrupp Elevator
9280 Crestwyn Hills Dr .... Memphis TN 38125 — **877-230-0303**

Toyota Motor North America Inc
601 Lexington Ave 49th Fl ...... New York NY 10022 — **800-331-4331**

Tredegar Corp
1100 Boulders Pkwy Ste 200 ...... Richmond VA 23225 — **800-411-7441** — 804-330-1000
NYSE: TG

Union Pacific Corp
1400 Douglas St .... Omaha NE 68179 — **888-870-8777** — 402-544-5000
NYSE: UNP

VENSURE Employer Services Inc
4140 E Baseline Rd Ste 201 .... Mesa AZ 85206 — **800-409-8958**

Warren Equities Inc
27 Warren Way .... Providence RI 02905 — **877-623-6765** — 401-781-9900

Williams Cos Inc
1 Williams Ctr .... Tulsa OK 74103 — **800-945-5426** — 918-573-2000
NYSE: WMB

Worthington Direct Holdings LLC
6301 Gaston Ave Ste 670 .... Dallas TX 75214 — **800-599-6636**

YRC Worldwide Inc
10990 Roe Ave .... Overland Park KS 66211 — **800-846-4300** — 913-696-6100
NASDAQ: YRCW

359-4 Insurance Holding Companies

	Toll-Free	Phone

Affirmative Insurance Holdings Inc
150 Harvester Dr Ste 250 .... Burr Ridge IL 60527 — **800-877-0226** — 972-728-6300
OTC: AFFM

AFLAC Inc 1932 Wynnton Rd ...... Columbus GA 31999 — **800-992-3522** — 706-323-3431
NYSE: AFL

AIG SunAmerica Inc
21650 Oxnard St .... Woodland Hills CA 91367 — **800-445-7862**

Allstate Corp
2775 Sanders Rd Allstate Plz .... Northbrook IL 60062 — **800-255-7828** — 847-402-5000
NYSE: ALL

AMBAC Financial Group Inc
One State Plz 15th Fl .... New York NY 10004 — **800-221-1854** — 212-668-0340
OTC: ABKFQ

American Equity Investment Life Holding Co
6000 Westown Pkwy Ste 440
PO Box 71216 .... West Des Moines IA 50266 — **888-221-1234** — 515-221-0002
NYSE: AEL

American Fidelity Assurance Co
2000 N Classen Blvd .... Oklahoma City OK 73106 — **800-654-8489** — 405-523-2000

American Medical Security (AMS)
3100 AMS Blvd PO Box 19032 ...... Green Bay WI 54307 — **800-232-5432** — 800-657-8205

Americo Life Inc
300 W 11th St .... Kansas City MO 64105 — **800-231-0801*** — 816-391-2000
*General

Ameritas Holding Co
5900 O St .... Lincoln NE 68510 — **800-311-7871** — 402-467-1122

Anthem Insurance Cos Inc
120 Monument Cir Ste 200 ...... Indianapolis IN 46204 — **800-331-1476** — 317-488-6000

Aon Corp 200 E Randolph St .... Chicago IL 60601 — **877-384-4276** — 312-381-1000

Assurant Group
11222 Quail Roost Dr .... Miami FL 33157 — **800-852-2244** — 305-253-2244

Capitol Transamerica Corp
1600 Aspen Commons .... Middleton WI 53562 — **800-475-4450** — 608-829-4200

Chubb Corp
15 Mountain View Rd .... Warren NJ 07059 — **800-252-4670** — 908-903-2000
NYSE: CB

Citizens Financial Corp
12910 Shelbyville Rd Ste 300 .... Louisville KY 40243 — **800-843-7752** — 502-244-2420
OTC: CFIN

Citizens Inc
400 E Anderson Ln .... Austin TX 78752 — **877-785-9659*** — 512-837-7100
*NYSE: CIA ■ *General*

CNA Financial Corp
333 S Wabash Ave .... Chicago IL 60604 — **800-262-4357** — 312-822-5000
NYSE: CNA

Conseco Inc
11825 N Pennsylvania St .... Carmel IN 46032 — **866-595-2255** — 317-817-3012
NYSE: CNO

CUNA Mutual Group
5910 Mineral Pt Dr .... Madison WI 53705 — **800-937-2644** — 608-238-5851

	Toll-Free	Phone

Donegal Group Inc
1195 River Rd .... Marietta PA 17547 — **800-877-0600** — 717-426-1931
NASDAQ: DGICA

EMC Insurance Group Inc
717 Mulberry St .... Des Moines IA 50309 — **800-447-2295** — 515-280-2511
NASDAQ: EMCI

Everest Re Group Ltd
477 Martinsville Rd PO Box 830 ...... Liberty Corner NJ 07938 — **800-269-6660** — 908-604-3000

Farmers Insurance Group
4680 Wilshire Blvd .... Los Angeles CA 90010 — **800-327-6377** — 323-932-3200

Federated Insurance Cos
121 E Pk Sq PO Box 328 .... Owatonna MN 55060 — **800-533-0472** — 507-455-5200

First Investors Corp
110 Wall St .... New York NY 10005 — **800-832-7783***
*General

GMAC Insurance Holdings Inc
PO Box 3199 .... Winston-Salem NC 27102 — **888-293-5108**

Hanover Insurance Group Inc
440 Lincoln St .... Worcester MA 01653 — **800-628-0250** — 508-855-1000
NYSE: THG

Harleysville Group Inc
355 Maple Ave .... Harleysville PA 19438 — **800-523-6344** — 215-256-5000
NASDAQ: HGIC

Horace Mann Educators Corp
One Horace Mann Plz .... Springfield IL 62715 — **800-999-1030** — 217-789-2500
NYSE: HMN

Investors Title Co
121 N Columbia St .... Chapel Hill NC 27514 — **800-326-4842** — 919-968-2200
NASDAQ: ITIC

Kansas City Life Insurance Co
3520 Broadway .... Kansas City MO 64111 — **800-821-6164** — 816-753-7000
NASDAQ: KCLI

Kingsway America Inc (KAI)
150 NW Pt Blvd .... Elk Grove Village IL 60007 — **800-232-0631** — 847-700-9100

Legal & General America Inc
1701 Research Blvd .... Rockville MD 20850 — **800-638-8428** — 301-279-4800

Lifetime Healthcare Cos, The
165 Ct St .... Rochester NY 14647 — **800-847-1200** — 585-454-1700

Lincoln National Corp (LNC)
150 N Radnor-Chester Rd .... Radnor PA 19087 — **877-275-5462** — 484-583-1400
NYSE: LNC

Manulife Financial Corp
200 Bloor St E .... Toronto ON M4W1E5 — **800-795-9767** — 416-926-3000
NYSE: MFC

Markel Corp
4521 Highwoods Pkwy .... Glen Allen VA 23060 — **877-566-6323** — 800-431-1270
NYSE: MKL

Meadowbrook Insurance Group Inc
26255 American Dr .... Southfield MI 48034 — **800-482-2726** — 248-358-1100
NYSE: MIG

Midland Co 7000 Midland Blvd ...... Amelia OH 45102 — **800-759-9008** — 800-543-2644

Mutual of Omaha Inc
Mutual of Omaha Plz .... Omaha NE 68175 — **800-775-6000** — 402-342-7600

Navigators Group Inc
One Penn Plz 32nd Fl .... New York NY 10119 — **800-942-6906** — 212-244-2333
NASDAQ: NAVG

Pacific Mutual Holding Co
700 Newport Ctr Dr .... Newport Beach CA 92660 — **800-347-7787** — 949-219-3011

Penn Treaty American Corp
3440 Lehigh St .... Allentown PA 18103 — **800-362-0700**

Phoenix Cos Inc, The
One American Row PO Box 5056 ...... Hartford CT 06102 — **800-628-1936** — 860-403-5000
NYSE: PNX

PICO Holdings Inc
7979 Ivanhoe Ave Ste 301 .... La Jolla CA 92037 — **888-389-3222** — 858-456-6022
NASDAQ: PICO

PMI Group Inc
3003 Oak Rd .... Walnut Creek CA 94597 — **800-288-1970**
OTC: PMI

Principal Financial Group Inc
711 High St .... Des Moines IA 50392 — **800-986-3343** — 515-247-5111
NYSE: PFG

ProAssurance Corp
100 Brookwood Pl Ste 300 ...... Birmingham AL 35209 — **800-282-6242** — 205-877-4400
NYSE: PRA

Protective Life Corp
2801 Hwy 280 S .... Birmingham AL 35223 — **800-333-3418** — 205-268-1000
NYSE: PL

Reinsurance Group of America Inc
1370 Timberlake Manor Pkwy ...... Chesterfield MO 63017 — **800-985-4326** — 636-736-7000
NYSE: RGA

RLI Corp 9025 N Lindbergh Dr .... Peoria IL 61615 — **800-331-4929*** — 309-692-1000
*NYSE: RLI ■ *Cust Svc*

Security Benefit Group of Cos
One Security Benefit Pl .... Topeka KS 66636 — **800-888-2461** — 785-438-3000

Selective Insurance Group Inc
40 Wantage Ave .... Branchville NJ 07890 — **800-777-9656** — 973-948-3000
NASDAQ: SIGI

Sentry Insurance Group
1800 N Pt Dr .... Stevens Point WI 54481 — **800-373-6879** — 715-346-6000

Summit Holding Southeast Inc
PO Box 600 .... Gainesville GA 30503 — **800-971-2667** — 678-450-5825

Sun Life Financial Inc
150 King St W .... Toronto ON M5H1J9 — **877-786-5433** — 416-979-9966
TSE: SLF

Swiss Re Life & Health America Inc
175 King St .... Armonk NY 10504 — **800-937-5449** — 914-828-8000

Torchmark Corp
3700 S Stonebridge Dr .... McKinney TX 75070 — **877-577-3899** — 972-569-4000
NYSE: TMK

Travelers Cos Inc
385 Washington St .... Saint Paul MN 55102 — **800-328-2189** — 651-310-7911
NYSE: TRV

ULLICO Inc
1625 Eye St NW .... Washington DC 20006 — **800-431-5425**

United Fire Group
118 Second Ave SE PO Box 73909 ...... Cedar Rapids IA 52407 — **800-332-7977** — 319-399-5700

United Trust Group Inc (UTGI)
5250 S Sixth St .... Springfield IL 62705 — **800-323-0050** — 217-241-6410
OTC: UTGN

	Toll-Free	Phone
Universal American Corp (UAFC)		
44 S Broadway Ste 1200..............White Plains NY 10601	**866-249-8668**	914-934-5200
NYSE: UAM		
UnumProvident Corp		
1 Fountain Sq................Chattanooga TN 37402	**800-262-0018**	423-294-1011
Western & Southern Financial Group		
400 Broadway..............Cincinnati OH 45202	**800-333-5222**	513-629-1800
White Mountains Insurance Group Ltd		
80 S Main St..............Hanover NH 03755	**866-295-3762**	603-640-2200
NYSE: WTM		

359-5 Utilities Holding Companies

	Toll-Free	Phone
ALLETE Inc 30 W Superior St...............Duluth MN 55802	**800-228-4966**	218-279-5000
NYSE: ALE		
Ameren Corp		
1901 Chouteau Ave...........Saint Louis MO 63103	**800-552-7583**	314-621-3222
NYSE: AEE		
American Electric Power Company Inc		
One Riverside Plz............Columbus OH 43215	**800-277-2177***	614-716-1000
NYSE: AEP ■ *Cust Svc*		
American States Water Co		
630 E Foothill Blvd..........San Dimas CA 91773	**800-999-4033**	909-394-3600
NYSE: AWR		
American Water Works Co Inc		
1025 Laurel Oak Rd...........Voorhees NJ 08043	**888-282-6816**	856-346-8200
NYSE: AWK		
Artesian Resources Corp		
664 Churchmans Rd............Newark DE 19702	**800-332-5114**	302-453-6900
NASDAQ: ARTNA		
Atmos Energy Corp		
5430 LBJ Fwy Ste 1800...........Dallas TX 75240	**888-954-4321**	972-934-9227
NYSE: ATO		
Black Hills Corp		
625 Ninth St.............Rapid City SD 57701	**866-264-8003**	605-721-1700
NYSE: BKH		
CenterPoint Energy Inc		
1111 Louisiana St............Houston TX 77002	**800-495-9880***	713-207-1111
NYSE: CNP ■ *Cust Svc*		
CH Energy Group Inc		
284 S Ave.............Poughkeepsie NY 12601	**800-527-2714**	845-452-2000
NYSE: CHG		
CMS Energy Corp		
One Energy Plz..............Jackson MI 49201	**800-477-5050**	517-788-0550
NYSE: CMS		
Connecticut Water Service Inc		
93 W Main St..............Clinton CT 06413	**800-286-5700**	860-669-8636
NASDAQ: CTWS		
Consolidated Edison Inc		
Four Irving Pl..............New York NY 10003	**800-752-6633**	212-460-4600
NYSE: ED		
Dominion Resources Inc		
120 Tredegar St.............Richmond VA 23219	**800-552-4034**	804-819-2000
NYSE: D		
DPL Inc 1065 Woodman Dr............Dayton OH 45432	**800-433-8500**	800-736-3001
NYSE: DPL		
DTE Energy Co		
One Energy Plz..............Detroit MI 48226	**800-477-4747**	313-235-4000
NYSE: DTE		
Duquesne Light Holdings Inc		
411 Seventh Ave.............Pittsburgh PA 15219	**888-393-7000**	412-393-7000
Dynegy Inc		
601 Travis St Ste 1400.........Houston TX 77002	**800-633-4704**	713-507-6400
NYSE: DYN		
Edison International		
2244 Walnut Grove Ave..........Rosemead CA 91770	**800-655-4555***	626-302-1212
NYSE: EIX ■ *Cust Svc*		
Enbridge Energy Management LLC		
1100 Louisiana St Ste 3300........Houston TX 77002	**866-337-4636**	713-821-2000
NYSE: EEQ		
Energen Corp		
605 Richard Arrington Blvd N......Birmingham AL 35203	**800-654-3206**	205-326-2700
NYSE: EGN		
Entergy Corp		
639 Loyola Ave.............New Orleans LA 70113	**800-368-3749**	504-576-4000
NYSE: ETR		
FirstEnergy Corp 76 S Main St..........Akron OH 44308	**800-633-4766**	
NYSE: FE		
FPL Group Inc		
NextEra Energy Inc		
700 Universe Blvd..........Juno Beach FL 33408	**800-979-3967**	561-694-4000
NYSE: NEE		
Holly Energy Partners LP		
100 Crescent Ct Ste 1600.........Dallas TX 75201	**800-642-1687**	214-871-3555
Integrys Energy Group Inc		
130 E Randolph Dr............Chicago IL 60601	**800-699-1269**	312-228-5400
Laclede Group Inc		
720 Olive St Rm 1517.........Saint Louis MO 63101	**800-884-4225**	314-342-0500
NYSE: LG		
National Fuel Gas Co		
6363 Main St.............Williamsville NY 14221	**800-365-3234***	716-857-7000
NYSE: NFG ■ *Cust Svc*		
National Grid USA Service Company Inc		
25 Research Dr...........Westborough MA 01582	**800-548-8000**	508-389-2000
NSTAR 800 Boylston St..........Boston MA 02199	**800-592-2000**	617-424-2000
NYSE: NST		
OGE Energy Corp		
321 N Harvey St..........Oklahoma City OK 73102	**800-272-9741**	405-553-3000
NYSE: OGE		
PG & E Corp		
77 Beale St 24th Fl...........San Francisco CA 94105	**800-743-5000**	415-267-7000
NYSE: PCG		
Pinnacle West Capital Corp		
400 N Fifth St..............Phoenix AZ 85004	**800-457-2983**	602-250-1000

	Toll-Free	Phone
PNM Resources Inc		
Alvarado Sq..............Albuquerque NM 87158	**888-342-5766**	505-241-2700
NYSE: PNM		
PPL Corp Two N Ninth St...........Allentown PA 18101	**800-342-5775**	610-774-5151
NYSE: PPL		
Progress Energy Inc		
410 S Wilmington St PO Box 2041......Raleigh NC 27601	**800-452-2777**	919-546-6111
NYSE: PGN		
Public Service Enterprise Group Inc		
80 Pk Plz..............Newark NJ 07102	**800-436-7734***	973-430-7000
NYSE: PEG ■ *Cust Svc*		
Questar Corp		
333 S State St PO Box 45433......Salt Lake City UT 84145	**800-323-5517**	801-324-5000
NYSE: STR		
SCANA Corp 220 Operation Way..........Cayce SC 29033	**800-251-7234**	803-217-9000
NYSE: SCG		
Sempra Energy Corp		
101 Ash St..............San Diego CA 92101	**800-411-7343**	619-696-2000
NYSE: SRE		
UIL Holdings Corp		
157 Church St..............New Haven CT 06506	**800-722-5584**	203-499-2000
NYSE: UIL		
Unitil Corp		
Six Liberty Ln W...........Hampton NH 03842	**800-852-3339**	603-772-0775
NYSE: UTL		
Vectren Corp		
211 NW Riverside Dr PO Box 209......Evansville IN 47708	**800-227-1376**	812-491-4000
NYSE: VVC		
Westar Energy Inc		
818 S Kansas Ave...........Topeka KS 66612	**800-383-1183**	785-575-6300
NYSE: WR		
WGL Holdings Inc		
101 Constitution Ave NW........Washington DC 20080	**800-645-3751**	703-750-2000
NYSE: WGL		
Wisconsin Energy Corp		
231 W Michigan St.........Milwaukee WI 53203	**800-242-9137***	414-221-2345
NYSE: WEC ■ *General*		

360   HOME FURNISHINGS - WHOL

	Toll-Free	Phone
AA Importing Co Inc		
7700 Hall St.............Saint Louis MO 63147	**800-325-0602***	314-383-8800
Cust Svc		
Adleta Co		
1645 Diplomat Dr Ste 200.........Carrollton TX 75006	**800-423-5382**	972-620-5600
Architex International		
3333 Commercial Ave..........Northbrook IL 60062	**800-621-0827**	847-205-1333
Atlantic Scale Co Inc		
136 Washington Ave............Nutley NJ 07110	**888-627-5836**	973-661-7090
B & F System Inc		
3920 S Walton Walker..........Dallas TX 75236	**877-586-2926**	214-333-2111
Bettendorf-stanford		
1370 W Main St..............Salem IL 62881	**800-548-2253**	618-548-3555
Bishop Distributing Co		
5200 36th St SE...........Grand Rapids MI 49512	**800-748-0363***	
Cust Svc		
Bisque Imports		
406 E Catawba St............Belmont NC 28012	**888-568-5991**	704-829-9290
Boston Warehouse Trading Corp		
59 Davis Ave..............Norwood MA 02062	**888-923-2982**	781-769-8550
BR Funsten & Co		
5200 Watt Ct Ste B...........Fairfield CA 94534	**888-261-2871**	209-825-5375
Caber Sure Fit Inc		
35 Valleywood Dr Ste 1.........Markham ON L3R5L9	**800-520-3152**	905-479-5803
Cambridge Silversmith Ltd		
116 Lehigh Dr..............Fairfield NJ 07004	**800-890-3366**	973-227-4400
Carlton Group Inc		
120 Landmark Dr...........Greensboro NC 27409	**800-722-7824**	336-668-7677
CCA Global Partners		
4301 Earth City Expy..........Earth City MO 63045	**800-466-6984**	314-506-0000
Cool Gear International LLC		
10 Cordage Park Cir..........Plymouth MA 02360	**855-393-2665**	508-830-3440
Decorative Crafts Inc		
50 Chestnut St.............Greenwich CT 06830	**800-431-4455**	203-531-1500
Derr Flooring Company Inc		
525 Davisville Rd PO Box 912......Willow Grove PA 19090	**800-523-3457**	215-657-6300
Fabricut Inc 9303 E 46th St...........Tulsa OK 74145	**800-999-8200**	918-622-7700
Farrey's Wholesale Hardware Company Inc		
1850 NE 146th St...........North Miami FL 33181	**888-854-5483**	305-947-5451
Georgian Plantation Shutter Co		
455 Wilbanks Dr...........Ball Ground GA 30107	**888-684-0382**	678-454-1100
Home Essentials & Beyond Inc		
200 Theodore Conrad Dr.........Jersey City NJ 07305	**800-417-6218**	732-590-3600
Horizons Window Fashions Inc		
1705 Waukegan Rd............Waukegan IL 60085	**800-858-2352**	
Innovative Hearth Products		
2701 S Harbor Blvd..........Santa Ana CA 92704	**866-328-4537**	
JJ Haines & Company Inc		
6950 Aviation Blvd..........Glen Burnie MD 21061	**800-922-9248**	
Kanawha Scales & Systems Inc		
Rock Branch Industrial Pk 303 Jacobson Dr		
..............Poca WV 25159	**800-955-8321**	304-755-8321
Kiefer Specialty Flooring Inc		
2910 Falling Waters Blvd........Lindenhurst IL 60046	**800-322-5448**	847-245-8450
L Bornstein & Co Inc		
321 Washington St...........Somerville MA 02143	**800-842-1111**	617-776-3555
Lanz Cabinet Shop Inc		
3025 W Seventh Pl............Eugene OR 97402	**800-788-6332**	541-485-4050
Larson Distributing Co Inc		
5925 Broadway.............Denver CO 80216	**800-999-8115**	303-296-7253
Legends of England		
3520 Roberts Cut Off Rd.........Fort Worth TX 76114	**800-578-1065**	817-236-3141
Longust Distributing Inc		
2432 W Birchwood Ave...........Mesa AZ 85202	**800-352-0521**	480-820-6244
Lonseal Inc 928 E 238th St...........Carson CA 90745	**800-832-7111**	310-830-7111

				Toll-Free	Phone

M Block & Sons Inc
5020 W 73rd St . . . . Bedford Park IL 60638 **800-621-8845** 708-728-8400

Maxtex Inc
3620 Francis Cir . . . . Alpharetta GA 30004 **800-241-1836** 770-772-6757
MDS N30 W22377 Green Rd . . . . Waukesha WI 53186 **888-523-2611**

National Glass Ltd
5744 198th St . . . . Langley BC V3A7J2 **800-663-8168** 604-530-2311

OneCoast Network LLC
230 Spring St Ste 1800 . . . . Atlanta GA 30303 **866-592-5514**

Peking Handicraft Inc
1388 San Mateo Ave . . . . South San Francisco CA 94080 **800-872-6888** 650-871-3788

Revere Mills Inc
2860 S River Rd Ste 250 . . . . Des Plaines IL 60018 **800-367-8258** 847-759-6800

Selective Enterprises Inc
10701 Texland Blvd . . . . Charlotte NC 28273 **800-334-1207** 704-588-3310

Sewing Source Inc, The
PO Box 639 . . . . Spring Hope NC 27882 **800-849-6945** 252-478-3900

Shelving Inc
32 S Squirrel Rd . . . . Auburn Hills MI 48326 **800-637-9508** 248-852-8600

Sobel Westex Inc
2670 Western Ave . . . . Las Vegas NV 89109 **888-887-6235**

SOG Specialty Knives & Tools LLC
6521 212th St SW . . . . Lynnwood WA 98036 **888-405-6433** 425-771-6230

Southern Tile Distributors Inc
4590 Village Ave . . . . Norfolk VA 23502 **800-333-8970** 757-855-8041

Springs Window Fashions LP
7549 Graber Rd . . . . Middleton WI 53562 **877-792-0002** 608-836-1011

Sterling Cut Glass Company Inc
3233 Mineola Pk . . . . Erlanger KY 41018 **800-368-1158** 859-283-2333

T & A Supply Company Inc
6821 S 216th St Bldg A PO Box 927 . . . . Kent WA 98032 **800-562-2857** 253-872-3682

Tailored Living LLC
1927 N Glassell St . . . . Orange CA 92865 **866-675-8819**

Thompson Olde Inc
3250 Camino Del Sol . . . . Oxnard CA 93030 **800-827-1565** 805-983-0388

Three Hands Corp
13259 Ralston Ave . . . . Sylmar CA 91342 **800-443-5443** 818-833-1200

Virginia Tile Co
28320 Plymouth Rd . . . . Livonia MI 48150 **877-356-7461** 734-762-2400

Wanke Cascade Co
6330 N Cutter Cir . . . . Portland OR 97217 **800-365-5053** 503-289-8609

Weightech
1649 Country Elite Dr . . . . Waldron AR 72958 **800-457-3720** 479-637-4182

WMF Americas Inc
3512 Faith Church Rd . . . . Indian Trail NC 28079 **800-966-3009** 704-882-3898

---

361   **HOME FURNISHINGS STORES**

SEE ALSO Furniture Stores ; Department Stores

				Toll-Free	Phone

Altmeyer Home Stores Inc
6515 Rt 22 . . . . Delmont PA 15626 **800-394-6628** 724-468-3434

Anna's Linens Inc
3550 Hyland Ave . . . . Costa Mesa CA 92626 **866-266-2728** 714-850-0504

Beacon Products LLC
2041 58th Ave Cir E . . . . Bradenton FL 34203 **800-345-4928**

Bed Bath & Beyond Inc
650 Liberty Ave . . . . Union NJ 07083 **800-462-3966** 908-688-0888
NASDAQ: BBBY

Besco Electric Supply Co
711 S 14th St . . . . Leesburg FL 34748 **800-541-6618**

Blanco America Inc
110 Mount Holly By-Pass . . . . Lumberton NJ 08048 **800-451-5782**

Burlington Coat Factory
1830 Rt 130 N . . . . Burlington NJ 08016 **855-355-2875** 609-387-7800

Chef's Catalog
5070 Centennial Blvd . . . . Colorado Springs CO 80919 **800-541-6390***
*Cust Svc

Container Store, The
500 Freeport Pkwy . . . . Coppell TX 75019 **800-733-3532** 972-538-6000

Cooking.com
2850 Ocean Pk Blvd Ste 310 . . . . Santa Monica CA 90405 **800-663-8810** 310-450-3270

Cost Plus Inc 200 Fourth St . . . . Oakland CA 94607 **877-967-5362** 510-893-7300
NASDAQ: CPWM

Cutlery & More LLC
135 Prairie Lk Rd . . . . East Dundee IL 60118 **800-650-9866**

Design Within Reach Inc
711 Canal St 3rd fl 3rd Fl . . . . Stamford CT 06902 **800-944-2233** 203-614-0600
OTC: DWRI

DirectBuy Inc
8450 Broadway . . . . Merrillville IN 46410 **800-320-3462** 219-736-1100

Force Flow Inc
2430 Stanwell Dr . . . . Concord CA 94520 **800-893-6723**

GEARYS Beverly Hills
351 N Beverly Dr . . . . Beverly Hills CA 90210 **800-793-6670** 310-273-4741

Gracious Home
1220 Third Ave . . . . New York NY 10021 **800-338-7809** 212-517-6300

Granite City Electric Supply Co
19 Quincy Ave . . . . Quincy MA 02169 **800-850-9400** 617-472-6500
Gump's 135 Post St . . . . San Francisco CA 94108 **800-766-7628** 415-982-1616

Hammacher Schlemmer & Co
9307 N Milwaukee Ave . . . . Niles IL 60714 **800-321-1484**
Kirkland's Inc 431 Smith Ln . . . . Jackson TN 38301 **877-541-4855**
NASDAQ: KIRK

Kitchen Collection Inc
71 E Water St . . . . Chillicothe OH 45601 **888-548-2651*** 740-773-9150
*General

Mason Structural Steel Inc
7500 Northfield Rd . . . . Walton Hills OH 44146 **800-686-1223** 440-439-1040

Mattress Firm Inc
5815 Gulf Fwy . . . . Houston TX 77023 **800-821-6621** 713-923-1090

Michael C Fina Inc
545 Fifth Ave . . . . New York NY 10022 **800-289-3462** 212-557-2500

Pier 1 Imports Inc
100 Pier 1 Pl . . . . Fort Worth TX 76102 **800-245-4595** 817-252-8000
NYSE: PIR

Restoration Hardware Inc
2900 N MacArthur Dr Ste 100 . . . . Tracy CA 95376 **800-910-9836**

Seattle Lighting Fixture Co
222 Second Ave Ext S . . . . Seattle WA 98104 **800-689-1000*** 206-622-4736
*Cust Svc

Southern Wholesale Flooring Company Inc
955B Cobb Pl Blvd PO Box 440069 . . . . Kennesaw GA 30144 **800-282-7590** 770-514-7110

Sur La Table
5701 Sixth Ave S Ste 486 . . . . Seattle WA 98108 **800-243-0852**

TJX Cos Inc
770 Cochituate Rd . . . . Framingham MA 01701 **800-926-6299** 508-390-1000
NYSE: TJX

Villeroy & Boch Tableware Ltd
Five Vaughn Dr . . . . Princeton NJ 08540 **800-536-2284**

Williams-Sonoma Inc
3250 Van Ness Ave . . . . San Francisco CA 94109 **800-838-2589** 415-421-7900
NYSE: WSM

Z Gallerie Inc
1855 W 139th St . . . . Gardena CA 90249 **800-358-8288** 310-630-1200

---

362   **HOME HEALTH SERVICES**

SEE ALSO Hospices

				Toll-Free	Phone

Alacare Home Health & Hospice
2400 John Hawkins Pkwy . . . . Birmingham AL 35244 **800-852-4724** 205-981-8000

Allcare Medical Inc
125 Newtown Rd Ste 300 . . . . Plainview NY 11803 **800-244-4660**

Almost Family Inc
9510 Ormsby Stn Rd Ste 300 . . . . Louisville KY 40223 **800-828-9769** 502-891-1000
NASDAQ: AFAM

Altamed Health Services Corp
500 Citadel Dr Ste 490 . . . . Los Angeles CA 90040 **877-462-2582** 323-725-8751

Amedisys Inc
5959 S Sherwood Forest Blvd
Ste 300 . . . . Baton Rouge LA 70816 **800-464-0020** 225-292-2031
NASDAQ: AMED

American HomePatient Inc
5200 Maryland Way Ste 400 . . . . Brentwood TN 37027 **800-890-7271** 615-221-8884

Androscoggin Home Health Services Inc
PO Box 819 . . . . Lewiston ME 04243 **800-482-7412** 207-777-7740

Apria Healthcare Group Inc
26220 Enterprise Ct . . . . Lake Forest CA 92630 **800-277-4288** 949-639-2000

ARK Diagnostics Inc
48089 Fremont Blvd . . . . Fremont CA 94538 **877-869-2320** 510-270-6270

Aroostook Home Health Services
658 Main St Ste 2 . . . . Caribou ME 04736 **877-688-9977** 207-492-8290

Care Partners
68 Sweeten Creek Rd . . . . Asheville NC 28803 **800-627-1533** 828-252-2255

Caresource Health Plan
740 SE Seventh St . . . . Grants Pass OR 97526 **888-460-0185** 541-471-4106

Carter Healthcare
3105 S Meridian Ave . . . . Oklahoma City OK 73119 **888-951-1112** 405-947-7700

Christian Homes Inc
200 N Postville Dr . . . . Lincoln IL 62656 **800-535-8717** 217-732-9651

ComForcare Senior Services Inc
2520 Telegraph Rd Ste 100 . . . . Bloomfield Hills MI 48302 **800-886-4044** 248-745-9700

Confident Care Corp
Three University Plz Dr . . . . Hackensack NJ 07601 **866-839-2273** 201-498-9400

Continucare Corp
7200 Corporate Ctr Dr Ste 600 . . . . Miami FL 33126 **866-312-7154** 305-500-2000

Coram Healthcare Corp
555 17th St Ste 1500 . . . . Denver CO 80202 **800-267-2642**

Delaware Hospice Inc
3515 Silverside Rd . . . . Wilmington DE 19810 **800-838-9800** 302-478-5707

Fletcher'S Medical Supplies Inc
6851 S Distribution Ave . . . . Jacksonville FL 32256 **855-541-7809** 904-387-4481

General Healthcare Resources Inc
2250 Hickory Rd Ste 240 . . . . Plymouth Meeting PA 19462 **800-879-4471** 610-834-1122

Griswold Special Care Inc
717 Bethlehem Pike Ste 300 . . . . Erdenheim PA 19038 **855-303-9470** 215-402-0200

Halt Medical Inc
131 Sand Creek Rd Ste B . . . . Brentwood CA 94513 **877-412-3828** 925-634-7943

Help At Home Inc
One N State St Ste 800 . . . . Chicago IL 60602 **800-404-3191** 312-762-0900

Home Bound Healthcare Inc
1615 Vollmer Rd . . . . Flossmoor IL 60422 **800-444-7028** 708-798-0800

Home Instead Inc
13330 California St Ste 200 . . . . Omaha NE 68154 **888-484-5759** 402-498-4466

Home IV Care & Nutritional Service
PO Box 700 . . . . Stuarts Draft VA 24477 **800-552-6576**

Hospice Atlanta-Visiting Nurse Health System
1244 Pk Vista Dr . . . . Atlanta GA 30319 **866-374-4776** 404-869-3000

Interim HealthCare Inc
1601 Sawgrass Corporate Pkwy . . . . Sunrise FL 33323 **800-338-7786** 954-858-6000

Kelly Home Care Services Inc
999 W Big Beaver Rd . . . . Troy MI 48084 **800-755-8636** 248-362-4444

LHC Group LLC
420 W Pinhook Rd . . . . Lafayette LA 70503 **866-542-4768** 337-289-8188
NASDAQ: LHCG

Lifelink Foundation Inc
409 Bayshore Blvd . . . . Tampa FL 33606 **800-262-5775** 813-253-2640

Living Assistance Services Inc
937 Haverford Rd Ste 200 . . . . Bryn Mawr PA 19010 **800-365-4189** 610-924-0630

Medical Ctr at Princeton Home Care
905 Herrontown Rd . . . . Princeton NJ 08540 **877-932-8395** 609-497-4900

Medical Services of America Inc (MSA)
171 Monroe Ln . . . . Lexington SC 29072 **800-845-5850** 803-957-0500

Metro Pavia Health System Inc
MaraMar Plz Bldg Avenida San Patricio
Ste 950-960 . . . . Guaynabo PR 00968 **888-882-0882**

National Home Health Care Corp
700 White Plains Rd Ste 275 . . . . Scarsdale NY 10583 **800-422-4661** 914-722-9000

New York Health Care Inc
20 E Sunrise Hwy Ste 201 . . . . Valley Stream NY 11581 **888-978-6942** 718-375-6700
OTC: BBAL

				Toll-Free	Phone

North Los Angel County Regional Ctr
15400 Sherman Way Ste 170 . . . . Van Nuys CA 91406 **800-430-4263** 818-778-1900

Ohel Children's Home & Family Services Inc
4510 16th Ave . . . . Brooklyn NY 11204 **800-603-6435** 718-851-6300

Ontario Medical Supply Ltd
1100 Algoma Rd . . . . Ottawa ON K1B0A3 **800-804-1112** 613-244-8620

Pediatric Services of America Inc
310 Technology Pkwy . . . . Norcross GA 30092 **800-408-4442** 770-441-1580

Personal-Touch Home Care Inc
186-18 Hillside Ave . . . . Jamaica NY 11432 **888-275-4147** 718-468-2500

Promera Health
61 accord park dr . . . . Norwell MA 02061 **888-878-9058**

Right at Home Inc
6464 Crt St Ste 150 . . . . Omaha NE 68106 **877-697-7537** 402-697-7537

Selfhelp Community Services Inc
520 Eigth Ave Fifth Fl . . . . New York NY 10018 **866-735-1234**

Sta-Home Hospice
406 Briarwood Dr Bldg 200 . . . . Jackson MS 39206 **800-782-4663** 601-956-5100

Star Multi Care Services Inc
115 Broad Hollow Rd Ste 275 . . . . Melville NY 11747 **877-920-0600** 631-424-7827

Visiting Nurse Assn of Morris County (Inc)
175 South St . . . . Morristown NJ 07960 **800-938-4748** 973-539-1216

VITAS Healthcare Corp
100 S Biscayne Ste 400 . . . . Miami FL 33131 **866-418-4827** 305-374-4143

Vna of Rhode Island
475 Kilvert St . . . . Warwick RI 02886 **800-638-6274** 401-574-4900

We Care Health Services Inc
151 Bloor St W Ste 602 . . . . Toronto ON M5S1S4 **888-429-3227** 416-922-7601

WorldMed Assist
1230 Mtn Side Ct . . . . Concord CA 94521 **866-999-3848**

---

363   HOME IMPROVEMENT CENTERS

SEE ALSO Construction Materials

				Toll-Free	Phone

Alaska Industrial Hardware Inc
2192 Viking Dr . . . . Anchorage AK 99501 **800-478-7201** 907-276-7201

Arlington Coal & Lumber Company Inc
41 Pk Ave . . . . Arlington MA 02476 **800-649-8101** 781-643-8100

Atlanta Hardwood Corp
5596 Riverview Rd SE . . . . Mableton GA 30126 **800-476-5393** 404-792-2290

Busy Beaver Bldg Centers
2940 Library Rd . . . . Pittsburgh PA 15234 **800-732-0999** 412-882-6633

Cape Cod Lumber Co Inc
225 Groveland St . . . . Abington MA 02351 **800-368-3117** 781-878-0715

Carter Lumber Co Inc
601 Tallmadge Rd . . . . Kent OH 44240 **877-586-2374** 330-673-6100

Herrman Lumber Co
1917 S State Hwy N . . . . Springfield MO 65802 **888-238-9778** 417-862-3737

Home Depot Inc
2455 Paces Ferry Rd NW . . . . Atlanta GA 30339 **800-553-3199*** 770-433-8211
NYSE: HD *Cust Svc

Len-Co Lumber Corp
1445 Seneca St . . . . Buffalo NY 14210 **800-258-4585** 716-822-0243

Linen Chest Inc
4455 AutoRt Des Laurentides . . . . Laval QC H7L5X8 **800-363-3832** 514-341-7077

Lowe's Cos Inc
1000 Lowe's Blvd . . . . Mooresville NC 28117 **800-445-6937** 704-758-1000
NYSE: LOW

Lowe's Home Centers Inc
PO Box 1111 . . . . North Wilkesboro NC 28656 **800-445-6937**

MarJam Supply Co Inc
20 Rewe St . . . . Brooklyn NY 11211 **800-848-8407*** 718-388-6465
*All

Martin Door Manufacturing Inc
2828 South 900 West . . . . Salt Lake City UT 84119 **800-388-9310** 801-973-9310

National Lumber
71 Maple St . . . . Mansfield MA 02048 **800-370-9663** 508-339-8020

Northern Tool & Equipment Co
2800 Southcross Dr W . . . . Burnsville MN 55306 **800-222-5381*** 952-894-9510
*Cust Svc

Pandel Inc 21 River Dr . . . . Cartersville GA 30120 **800-537-3868** 770-382-1034

Paramount Builders Inc
501 Central Dr . . . . Virginia Beach VA 23454 **888-340-9002** 757-340-9000

Reisterstown Lumber Co, The
PO Box 337 . . . . Reisterstown MD 21136 **800-289-8739** 410-833-1300

RONA Inc
220 Ch du Tremblay . . . . Boucherville QC J4B8H7 **877-599-5900** 514-599-5100
TSE: RON

Stanton Carpet Corp
211 Robbins Ln . . . . Syosset NY 11791 **888-809-2989** 516-822-5878

WE Aubuchon Company Inc
95 Aubuchon Dr . . . . Westminster MA 01473 **800-431-2712** 978-874-0521

---

364   HOME INSPECTION SERVICES

				Toll-Free	Phone

AmeriSpec Inc
889 Ridge Lk Blvd . . . . Memphis TN 38120 **800-426-2270** 901-820-8500

BrickKicker Inc
849 N Ellsworth St . . . . Naperville IL 60563 **800-821-1820** 630-420-9900

HomeTeam Inspection Service Inc
575 Chamber Dr . . . . Milford OH 45150 **800-598-5297**

HouseMaster
850 Bear Tavern RD Ste 303 . . . . Ewing NJ 08628 **800-526-3939** 732-469-6565

iv3 Solutions Inc
50 Minthorn Blvd Ste 301 . . . . Markham ON L3T7X8 **877-995-2651**

National Property Inspections Inc (NPI)
9375 Burt St Ste 201 . . . . Omaha NE 68114 **800-333-9807** 402-333-9807

World Inspection Network International Inc
12345 Lk City Way NE Ste 365 . . . . Seattle WA 98125 **800-309-6753**

---

365   HOME SALES & OTHER DIRECT SELLING

				Toll-Free	Phone

4Life Research
9850 South 300 West . . . . Sandy UT 84070 **888-454-3374*** 801-256-3102
*Sales

Advocare International Lp
2801 Summit Ave . . . . Plano TX 75074 **800-542-4800** 972-665-5800

Amway Corp 7575 Fulton St E . . . . Ada MI 49355 **800-253-6500** 616-787-4000

Avon Products Inc
1345 Ave of the Americas . . . . New York NY 10017 **800-367-2866*** 212-282-7000
NYSE: AVP   *Cust Svc

Color Me Beautiful
7000 Infantry Ridge Rd Ste 200 . . . . Manassas VA 20109 **800-265-6763**

Colorado Prime Foods
500 Bi-County Blvd Ste 400 . . . . Farmingdale NY 11735 **800-365-2404** 631-694-1111

Conklin Company Inc
551 Valley Pk Dr . . . . Shakopee MN 55379 **800-888-8838** 952-445-6010

Dew-El Corp
10841 Paw Paw Dr . . . . Holland MI 49424 **800-443-3935** 616-396-6554

Email Co, The
15 Kainona Ave . . . . Toronto ON M3H3H4 **877-933-6245**

Getconnect
14114 Dallas Pkwy Ste 430 . . . . Dallas TX 75254 **888-200-1831**

Golden Neo-Life Diamite International
3500 Gateway Blvd . . . . Fremont CA 94538 **800-432-5842**

Goldshield Elite
1501 Northpoint Pkwy . . . . West Palm Beach FL 33407 **866-218-8142** 561-615-4701

JR Watkins Inc
150 Liberty St PO Box 5570 . . . . Winona MN 55987 **800-243-9423** 507-457-3300

Magnets.com
51 Pacific Ave Ste 4 . . . . Jersey City NJ 07304 **866-229-8237**

Mail Shark
4125 New Holland Rd . . . . Mohnton PA 19540 **888-457-4275**

Mary Kay Inc PO Box 799045 . . . . Dallas TX 75379 **800-627-9529*** 972-687-6300
*Cust Svc

Melaleuca Inc
3910 S Yellowstone Hwy . . . . Idaho Falls ID 83402 **800-282-3000*** 208-522-0700
*Sales

Noevir USA Inc 1095 Main St . . . . Irvine CA 92614 **800-872-8817** 949-660-1111

Pampered Chef Ltd
1 Pampered Chef Ln . . . . Addison IL 60101 **888-687-2433**

Partylite Gifts Inc
59 Armstrong Rd . . . . Plymouth MA 02360 **888-999-5706** 508-830-3100

Princess House Inc
470 Miles Standish Blvd . . . . Taunton MA 02780 **800-622-0039*** 508-823-0711
*Sales

Reliv International Inc
136 Chesterfield Industrial Blvd
. . . . Chesterfield MO 63005 **800-735-4887** 636-537-9715
NASDAQ: RELV

Saladmaster Inc
230 Westway Pl Ste 101 . . . . Arlington TX 76018 **800-765-5795** 817-633-3555

Shaklee Corp
4747 Willow Rd . . . . Pleasanton CA 94588 **800-742-5533** 925-924-2000

SK Food Group Inc
4600 37th Ave SW . . . . Seattle WA 98126 **800-722-6290** 206-935-8100

Smartpak Equine LLC
40 Grissom Rd Ste 500 . . . . Plymouth MA 02360 **888-752-5171** 774-773-1000

Specialty Merchandise Corp
996 Flower Glen St . . . . Simi Valley CA 93065 **800-345-4762*** 805-578-5500
*Orders

Success Motivation International Inc
4567 Lakeshore Dr . . . . Waco TX 76710 **888-391-0050*** 254-776-9966
*Sales

Sunrider International
1625 Abalone Ave . . . . Torrance CA 90501 **888-278-6743*** 310-781-3808
*Orders

TouchPoint Technologies LLC
2319 Oak Myrtle Ln Ste 104 . . . . Wesley Chapel FL 33544 **877-898-6824**

Vector Marketing Co
322 Houghton Ave . . . . Olean NY 14760 **800-828-0448**

Verndale Corp, The
28 Damrell St Ste 300 . . . . Boston MA 02127 **866-942-8376**

Viking Magazine Service Inc
PO Box 201059 . . . . Bloomington MN 55420 **800-339-9492**

Vorwerk USA Company LP
1964 Corporate Sq . . . . Longwood FL 32750 **800-562-6726** 407-830-9988

WEBCARGO Inc
800 Pl Victoria
Ste 2603 Tour de la bourse CP 329 . . . . . . Montreal QC H4Z1G8 **866-905-0123**

WebEyeCare Inc
10 Canal St Ste 302 . . . . Bristol PA 19007 **888-536-7480**

---

366   HOME WARRANTY SERVICES

				Toll-Free	Phone

American Home Shield
889 Ridge Lake Blvd PO Box 851 . . . . Memphis TN 38120 **800-776-4663** 901-537-8000

Asset Marketing Systems Insurance Services LLC
15050 Ave of Science . . . . San Diego CA 92128 **888-303-8755**

Blue Ribbon Home Warranty Inc
95 S Wadsworth Blvd . . . . Lakewood CO 80226 **800-571-0475** 303-986-3900

Cross Country Home Services
1625 NW 136th Ave Ste 200 . . . . Fort Lauderdale FL 33323 **800-778-8000*** 954-845-2468
*Cust Svc

Cypress Care Inc
2736 Meadow Church Rd Ste 300 . . . . Duluth GA 30097 **800-419-7191**

First American Home Buyers Protection Corp
7833 Haskell Ave PO Box 10180 . . . . Van Nuys CA 91410 **800-444-9030** 818-781-5050

Home Security of America Inc
310 N Midvale Blvd . . . . Madison WI 53705 **800-367-1448**

Warrantech Corp Inc
2200 Hwy 121 . . . . Bedford TX 76021 **800-833-8801** 817-785-6601

367 HORSE BREEDERS

SEE ALSO Livestock Improvement Services

				Toll-Free	Phone

Glencrest Farm
1576 Moores Mill Rd PO Box 4468 . . . . .Midway KY 40347 **800-903-0136** 859-233-7032

Lane's End Farm
1500 Midway Rd PO Box 626. . . . . Versailles KY 40383 **800-456-3412** 859-873-7300

Mill Ridge Farm
2800 Bowman Mill Rd . . . . .Lexington KY 40513 **800-950-6397** 859-231-0606

368 HORTICULTURAL PRODUCTS GROWERS

SEE ALSO Seed Companies ; Garden Centers

				Toll-Free	Phone

Alex R Masson Inc
12819 198th St . . . . .Linwood KS 66052 **800-879-2539*** 913-301-3281
*General

Altman Specialty Plants Inc
3742 Blue BiRd Canyon Rd . . . . .Vista CA 92084 **800-773-7667** 760-744-8191

Aris Horticulture Inc
115 Third St SE . . . . .Barberton OH 44203 **800-232-9557**

Battlefield Farms Inc
23190 Clarks Mtn Rd . . . . .Rapidan VA 22733 **800-722-0744**

Bay City Flower Company Inc
2265 Cabrillo Hwy S . . . . .Half Moon Bay CA 94019 **800-399-5858*** 650-726-5535
*Sales

Bettinger Farms Inc
11602 Frankfort Rd . . . . .Swanton OH 43558 **855-629-7661** 419-829-2771

Burgett Floral Inc
868 Fuller NE . . . . .Grand Rapids MI 49503 **800-404-2999** 616-456-1999

CD Ford & Sons Inc
PO Box 300 . . . . .Geneseo IL 61254 **800-383-4661** 309-944-4661

Color Spot Nurseries Inc
2575 Olive Hill Rd . . . . .Fallbrook CA 92028 **800-554-4065** 760-695-1480

Costa Nursery Farms Inc
21800 SW 162nd Ave . . . . .Miami FL 33170 **800-327-7074**

Cuthbert Greenhouses Inc
4900 Hendron Rd . . . . .Groveport OH 43125 **800-321-1939** 614-836-3866

Dallas Johnson Greenhouse Inc
2802 Twin City Dr . . . . .Council Bluffs IA 51501 **800-445-4794** 712-366-0407

Dan Schantz Farm & Greenhouses LLC
8025 Spinnerstown Rd . . . . .Zionsville PA 18092 **800-451-3064** 610-967-2181

DeLeon's Bromeliads Co
13745 SW 216th St . . . . .Miami FL 33170 **800-448-8649** 305-238-6028

Dramm & Echter Inc
1150 Quail Gardens Dr . . . . .Encinitas CA 92024 **800-854-7021** 760-436-0188

Farmers West
5300 Foothill Rd . . . . .Carpinteria CA 93013 **800-549-0085** 805-684-5531

Garden State Growers
99 Locust Grove Rd . . . . .Pittstown NJ 08867 **800-288-8484** 908-730-8888

Green Valley Floral Co
24999 Potter Rd . . . . .Salinas CA 93908 **800-228-1255** 831-424-7691

Greenleaf Nursery Co
28406 Hwy 82 . . . . .Park Hill OK 74451 **800-331-2982** 918-457-5172

Harts Nursery of Jefferson Inc
4049 Jefferson-Scio Rd . . . . .Jefferson OR 97352 **800-356-9335** 541-327-3366

Johannes Flowers Inc
4990 Foothill Rd . . . . .Carpinteria CA 93013 **800-365-9476** 805-684-5686

Kerry's Nursery Inc
21840 SW 258th St . . . . .Homestead FL 33031 **800-331-9127**

Knox Nursery Inc
940 Avalon Rd . . . . .Winter Garden FL 34787 **800-441-5669**

Kurt Weiss Greenhouses Inc
95 Main St . . . . .Center Moriches NY 11934 **800-344-7805** 631-878-2500

Matsui Nursery Inc
1645 Old Stage Rd . . . . .Salinas CA 93908 **800-793-6433** 831-422-6433

McLellan Botanicals
2352 San Juan Rd . . . . .Aromas CA 95004 **800-467-2443**

Metrolina Greenhouses Inc
16400 Huntersville-Concord Rd . . . . .Huntersville NC 28078 **800-543-3915** 704-875-1371

Nurserymen's Exchange
2651 N Cabrillo Hwy . . . . .Half Moon Bay CA 94019 **800-227-5229*** 650-712-4195
*General

Ocean Breeze International (OBI)
3910 Via Real . . . . .Carpinteria CA 93013 **888-715-8888** 805-684-1747

Panzer Nursery Inc
17980 W Baseline Rd . . . . .Beaverton OR 97006 **888-212-5327** 503-645-1185

Parks Bros Farm Inc
6733 Parks Rd . . . . .Van Buren AR 72956 **800-334-5770** 479-474-1125

Post Gardens Inc
21189 Huron River Dr . . . . .Rockwood MI 48173 **800-834-4630** 734-379-9688

Rockwell Farms Inc
332 Rockwell Farms Rd . . . . .Rockwell NC 28138 **800-635-6576**

Smith Gardens Inc
4164 Meridian St Ste 400. . . . . .Bellingham WA 98226 **800-755-6256** 360-733-4671

Speedling Inc
4447 Old 41 Hwy S . . . . .Ruskin FL 33570 **800-881-4769***
*Cust Svc

Sun Valley Floral Farms Inc
3160 Upper Bay Rd . . . . .Arcata CA 95521 **800-747-0396**

Van Wingerden International Inc
4112 Haywood Rd . . . . .Mills River NC 28759 **800-226-3597** 828-891-4116

White's Nursery & Greenhouses Inc
3133 Old Mill Rd . . . . .Chesapeake VA 23323 **800-966-9969** 757-487-2300

Woodburn Nursery & Azaleas
13009 McKee School Rd NE . . . . .Woodburn OR 97071 **888-634-2232*** 503-634-2231
*Sales

Young's Plant Farm
PO Box 3410 . . . . .Auburn AL 36830 **800-304-8609**

369 HOSE & BELTING - RUBBER OR PLASTICS

SEE ALSO Automotive Parts & Supplies - Mfr

				Toll-Free	Phone

ABC Industrie PO Box 77 . . . . .Warsaw IN 46581 **800-426-0921** 574-267-5166

Aero Rubber Company Inc
8100 W 185th St . . . . .Tinley Park IL 60487 **800-662-1009** 708-430-4900

American Hose & Rubber Co
3645 E 44th St . . . . .Tucson AZ 85713 **800-272-7537** 520-514-1666

Ammeraal Beltech USA
7501 N St Louis Ave . . . . .Skokie IL 60076 **800-323-4170*** 847-673-6720
*Cust Svc

Apache Hose & Belting Co Inc
4805 Bowling St SW PO Box 1719. . . . . .Cedar Rapids IA 52404 **800-553-5455*** 319-365-0471
*Sales

Atco Rubber Products Inc
7101 Atco Dr . . . . .Fort Worth TX 76118 **800-877-3828** 817-595-2894

Belting Industries Company Inc
20 Boright Ave . . . . .Kenilworth NJ 07033 **800-843-2358** 908-272-8591

Carlstar Group LLC, The
725 Cool Springs Blvd Ste 500 . . . . .Franklin TN 37067 **866-773-2926** 615-503-0220

Chemprene Inc
483 Fishkill Ave PO Box 471 . . . . .Beacon NY 12508 **800-431-9981** 845-831-2800

Coilhose Pneumatics Inc
19 Kimberly Rd .East Brunswick NJ 08816 **800-424-9300** 732-390-8480

Cooper Tire & Rubber Co
701 Lima Ave . . . . .Findlay OH 45840 **800-854-6288** 419-423-1321
NYSE: CTB

Dormont Manufacturing Co
6015 Enterprise Dr . . . . .Export PA 15632 **800-367-6668**

Fenner Drives
311 W Stiegel St . . . . .Manheim PA 17545 **800-243-3374*** 717-665-2421
*Sales

Flexaust Co
1510 Armstrong Rd . . . . .Warsaw IN 46580 **800-343-0428** 574-267-7909

Freelin-Wade Co
1730 NE Miller St . . . . .McMinnville OR 97128 **888-373-9233** 503-434-5561

Gates Corp 1551 Wewatta St . . . . .Denver CO 80202 **800-709-6001** 303-744-1911

Habasit ABT Inc
150 Industrial Pk Rd . . . . .Middletown CT 06457 **800-522-2358** 860-632-2211

Habasit Belting Inc
1400 Clinton St . . . . .Buffalo NY 14206 **800-325-1585** 716-824-8484

HBD/Thermoid Inc
1301 W Sandusky Ave . . . . .Bellefontaine OH 43311 **800-543-8070** 937-593-5010

Key Fire Hose Corp (KFH)
PO Box 7107 . . . . .Dothan AL 36302 **800-447-5666** 334-671-5532

Legg Company Inc
325 E Tenth St . . . . .Halstead KS 67056 **800-835-1003***
*Sales

Lockwood Products Inc
5615 Willow Ln . . . . .Lake Oswego OR 97035 **800-423-1625** 503-635-8113

Mulhern Belting Inc
148 Bauer Dr . . . . .Oakland NJ 07436 **800-253-6300** 201-337-5700

NewAge Industries Inc
145 James Way . . . . .SouthHampton PA 18966 **800-506-3924** 215-526-2300

Parker Fluid Connectors Group
6035 Parkland Blvd . . . . .Cleveland OH 44124 **800-272-7537*** 216-896-3000
*General

Ro-Lab American Rubber Co Inc
8830 W Linne Rd . . . . .Tracy CA 95304 **800-678-0726** 209-836-0965

Salem-Republic Rubber Co
475 W California Ave . . . . .Sebring OH 44672 **800-686-4199** 330-938-9801

Sparks Belting Co
3800 Stahl Dr SE . . . . .Grand Rapids MI 49546 **800-451-4537** 616-949-2750

Titeflex Corp
603 Hendee St . . . . .Springfield MA 01139 **800-765-2525** 413-739-5631

Unaflex LLC
1350 S Dixie Hwy E . . . . .Pompano Beach FL 33064 **800-327-1286** 954-943-5002

Voss Belting & Specialty Co
6965 N Hamlin Ave . . . . .Lincolnwood IL 60712 **800-323-3935** 847-673-8900

370 HOSPICES

SEE ALSO Specialty Hospitals

				Toll-Free	Phone

HomeCare of East Alabama Medical Ctr
665 Opelika Rd . . . . .Auburn AL 36830 **866-542-4768** 334-826-3131

Hospice of Marshall County
408 Martling Rd . . . . .Albertville AL 35951 **888-334-9336** 256-891-7724

Hospice of the Valley
240 Johnston St SE . . . . .Decatur AL 35601 **877-260-3657** 256-350-5585

Hospice of West Alabama
3851 Loop Rd . . . . .Tuscaloosa AL 35404 **877-362-7522** 205-523-0101

Hospice of Arizona
19820 N Seventh Ave Ste 130 . . . . .Phoenix AZ 85027 **888-330-8560** 602-678-1313

Arkansas Hospice
14 Parkstone Cir . . . . .North Little Rock AR 72116 **877-257-3400** 501-748-3333

Hospice Home Care
2200 S Bowman . . . . .Little Rock AR 72211 **800-479-1219** 501-296-9043

Community Hospice Inc
4368 Spyres Way . . . . .Modesto CA 95356 **866-645-4567** 209-578-6300

Elizabeth Hospice
150 W Crest St . . . . .Escondido CA 92025 **800-797-2050** 760-737-2050

Hinds Hospice
1616 W Shaw Ste C-1 . . . . .Fresno CA 93711 **800-400-4677** 559-248-8591

Hoffmann Hospice of the Valley
8501 Brimhall Rd Bldg 100 . . . . .Bakersfield CA 93312 **888-833-3900** 661-410-1010

Hospice Caring Project of Santa Cruz County
940 Disc Dr . . . . .Scotts Valley CA 95066 **877-688-6144** 831-430-3000

Livingston Memorial Visiting Nurse Assn Hospice
1996 Eastman Ave Ste 101 . . . . .Ventura CA 93003 **800-830-8881** 805-642-1608

Seasons Hospice & Palliative Care of California-Orange
750 The City Dr . . . . .Orange CA 92868 **877-508-0644** 714-980-0900

				Toll-Free	Phone
VITAS Healthcare Corp of California 16830 Ventura Blvd Ste 315	Encino	CA	91436	**800-582-9533**	818-385-0273
VITAS Healthcare Corp of San Gabriel Cities 1343 N Grand Ave	Covina	CA	91724	**800-582-9533**	626-918-2273
VNA & Hospice of Northern California 1900 Powell St Ste 300	Emeryville	CA	94608	**800-698-1273**	510-450-8596
VNA & Hospice of Southern California 150 W First St Ste 270	Claremont	CA	91711	**888-357-3574**	909-624-3574
Hospice & Palliative Care of Northern Colorado 2726 W 11th St Rd	Greeley	CO	80634	**800-564-5563**	970-352-8487
Hospice & Palliative Care of Western Colorado 2754 Compass Dr Ste 377	Grand Junction	CO	81506	**866-310-8900**	970-241-2212
Hospice of Southeastern Connecticut Inc 227 Dunham St	Norwich	CT	06360	**877-654-4035**	860-848-5699
Compassionate Care Hospice of Delaware 702 Wilmington Ave *General	Wilmington	DE	19805	**800-219-0092***	302-993-9090
Bigbend Hospice 1723 Mahan Ctr Blvd	Tallahassee	FL	32308	**800-772-5862**	850-878-5310
Chapters Health System 12973 Telecom Pkwy Ste 100	Temple Terrace	FL	33637	**866-204-8611**	813-871-8111
Covenant Hospice 5041 N 12th Ave	Pensacola	FL	32504	**800-541-3072**	850-433-2155
Gulfside Hospice Inc 6224 Lafayette St	New Port Richey	FL	34652	**800-561-4883**	727-845-5707
Hospice by the Sea 1531 W Palmetto Pk Rd	Boca Raton	FL	33486	**800-633-2577**	561-395-5031
Hospice of Lake & Sumter Inc 2445 Ln Pk Rd	Tavares	FL	32778	**888-728-6234**	352-343-1341
Hospice of Marion County 3231 SW 34th Ave	Ocala	FL	34474	**888-482-5018**	352-873-7400
Hospice of Northeast Florida 4266 Sunbeam Rd	Jacksonville	FL	32257	**866-253-6681**	904-268-5200
Hospice of Palm Beach County 5300 E Ave	West Palm Beach	FL	33407	**800-287-4722**	561-848-5200
Hospice of Saint Francis Inc 1250 Grumman Pl Ste B	Titusville	FL	32780	**866-269-4240**	321-269-4240
Hospice of the Comforter 480 W Central Pkwy	Altamonte Springs	FL	32714	**877-696-6775**	407-682-0808
Hospice of the Treasure Coast 5090 Dunn Rd	Fort Pierce	FL	34981	**800-299-4677**	772-462-8900
HospiceCare of Southeast Florida Inc 309 SE 18th St Ste 200	Fort Lauderdale	FL	33316	**866-231-5695**	954-467-7423
Lifepath Hospice 3010 W Azeele St	Tampa	FL	33609	**800-209-2200**	813-877-2200
Tidewell Hospice 5955 Rand Blvd	Sarasota	FL	34238	**800-959-4291**	941-552-7500
Treasure Coast Hospice 1201 SE Indian St	Stuart	FL	34997	**800-299-4677**	772-403-4500
Visiting Nurse Assn of the Treasure Coast 1110 35th Ln	Vero Beach	FL	32960	**800-749-5760**	772-567-5551
VITAS Hospice Care 100 S Biscayne Blvd Ste 1300 *General	Miami	FL	33131	**800-582-9533***	305-374-4143
Heyman HospiceCare 420 E Second Ave	Rome	GA	30161	**800-324-1078**	706-509-3200
Hospice Atlanta-Visiting Nurse Health System 1244 Pk Vista Dr	Atlanta	GA	30319	**866-374-4776**	404-869-3000
Hospice of Southwest Georgia 114 A Mimosa Dr	Thomasville	GA	31792	**800-290-6567**	229-584-5500
Hospice Savannah Inc PO Box 13190	Savannah	GA	31416	**888-355-4911**	912-355-2289
Pine Pointe Hospice & Palliative Care 6261 Peak Rd	Macon	GA	31210	**800-211-1084**	478-633-5660
Trinity Hospital of Augusta 2803 Wrightsboro Rd Ste 38	Augusta	GA	30909	**800-999-6673**	706-729-6000
United Hospice of Atlanta 1626 Jeurgens Ct	Norcross	GA	30093	**800-222-0321**	770-279-6200
Carle Hospice 611 W Park St	Urbana	IL	61801	**800-239-3620**	217-383-3311
Harbor Light Hospice 800 Roosevelt Rd Bldg C Ste 206	Glen Ellyn	IL	60137	**800-419-0542**	630-942-0100
Horizon Hospice 833 W Chicago Ave	Chicago	IL	60642	**866-733-6028**	312-733-8900
Hospice of Lincolnland 1000 Health Ctr Dr	Mattoon	IL	61938	**800-454-4055**	
Hospice of Southern Illinois 305 S Illinois St	Belleville	IL	62220	**800-233-1708**	618-235-1703
Joliet Area Community Hospice 250 Water Stone Cir	Joliet	IL	60431	**800-360-1817**	815-740-4104
OSF Hospice 2265 W Altorfer Dr	Peoria	IL	61615	**800-673-5288**	
Center for Hospice Care Inc 111 Sunnybrook Ct	South Bend	IN	46637	**800-413-9083**	574-243-3100
Hosparus Inc 624 E Market St	New Albany	IN	47150	**800-895-5633**	812-945-4596
Hospice of the Calumet Area 600 Superior Ave	Munster	IN	46321	**855-225-5344**	219-922-2732
Cedar Valley Hospice 2101 Kimball Ave Ste 401	Waterloo	IA	50702	**800-617-1972**	319-272-2002
Hospice of Central Iowa (HCI) 401 Railroad Pl	West Des Moines	IA	50265	**800-806-9934**	515-333-5810
Hospice of North Iowa 232 Second St SE	Mason City	IA	50401	**800-297-4719**	641-428-6208
Hospice of Siouxland 4300 Hamilton Blvd	Sioux City	IA	51104	**800-383-4545**	712-233-4100
Harry Hynes Memorial Hospice 313 S Market St	Wichita	KS	67202	**800-767-4965**	316-265-9441
Hospice of Reno County 1600 N Lorraine	Hutchinson	KS	67502	**800-267-6891**	620-665-2473
Midland Hospice Care 200 SW Frazier Cir	Topeka	KS	66606	**800-491-3691**	785-232-2044
Community Hospice 1480 Carter Ave	Ashland	KY	41101	**800-926-6184**	606-329-1890
Heritage Hospice 120 Enterprise Dr PO Box 1213	Danville	KY	40423	**800-203-6633**	859-236-2425
Hospice of Lake Cumberland 100 Pkwy Dr	Somerset	KY	42503	**800-937-9596**	606-679-4389

				Toll-Free	Phone
Hospice of Southern Kentucky 5872 Scottsville Rd	Bowling Green	KY	42104	**800-344-9479**	270-782-3402
Hospice of the Bluegrass 2312 Alexandria Dr	Lexington	KY	40504	**800-876-6005**	859-276-5344
Lourdes Homecare & Hospice 2855 Jackson St	Paducah	KY	42003	**800-870-7460**	270-444-2262
Saint Anthony's Hospice 2410 S Green St	Henderson	KY	42420	**866-380-2326**	270-826-2326
Hospice of Acadiana 2600 Johnston St Ste 200	Lafayette	LA	70503	**800-738-2226**	337-232-1234
Hospice of Baton Rouge 9063 Siegen Ln	Baton Rouge	LA	70810	**888-447-0433**	225-767-4673
Carroll Hospice 292 Stoner Ave	Westminster	MD	21157	**844-211-5403**	410-871-8000
Coastal Hospice & Palliative Care 2604 Old Ocean City Rd PO Box 1733	Salisbury	MD	21804	**800-780-7886**	410-742-8732
Gilchrist Hospice Care 11311 McCormick Rd	Hunt Valley	MD	21031	**800-735-2258**	443-849-8200
Hospice of the Chesapeake 445 Defense Hwy *General	Annapolis	MD	21401	**877-462-1101***	410-987-2003
Montgomery Hospice 1355 Piccard Dr Ste 100	Rockville	MD	20850	**800-994-6610**	301-921-4400
Baystate Visiting Nurse Assn & Hospice 50 Maple St	Springfield	MA	01103	**800-249-8298**	413-794-6411
Community VNA 10 Emory St	Attleboro	MA	02703	**800-220-0110**	508-222-0118
Hospice & Palliative Care of Cape Cod Inc 765 Attucks Ln	Hyannis	MA	02601	**800-642-2423**	508-957-0200
Hospice Care 100 Sylvan Rd	Woburn	MA	01801	**866-279-7103**	781-569-2888
Hospice of the North Shore 75 Sylvan St Ste B102	Danvers	MA	01923	**888-283-1722**	978-774-7566
Merrimack Valley Hospice 360 Merrimack St Bldg 9	Lawrence	MA	01843	**800-933-5593**	
Old Colony Hospice 1 Credit Union Way	Randolph	MA	02368	**800-370-1322**	781-341-4145
Angela Hospice Home Care 14100 Newburgh Rd *General	Livonia	MI	48154	**866-464-7810***	734-464-7810
Arbor Hospice & Home Care 2366 Oak Vly Dr	Ann Arbor	MI	48103	**888-992-2273**	734-662-5999
Hospice at Home 4025 Health Pk Ln	Saint Joseph	MI	49085	**800-717-3811**	269-429-7100
Hospice of Henry Ford Health System 655 W 13 Mile Rd 1st Fl	Madison Heights	MI	48071	**800-436-7936**	248-585-5270
Hospice of Holland Inc 270 Hoover Blvd	Holland	MI	49423	**800-255-3522**	616-396-2972
Hospice of Lansing 4052 Legacy Pkwy Ste 200	Lansing	MI	48911	**877-882-4500**	517-882-4500
Hospice of Michigan 400 Mack Ave	Detroit	MI	48201	**888-247-5701**	313-578-5000
MidMichigan Home Care 3007 N Saginaw Rd	Midland	MI	48640	**800-852-9350**	989-633-1400
Munson Healthcare 1105 Sixth St	Traverse City	MI	49684	**800-468-6766**	231-935-5000
Saint Joseph Mercy Home Care & Hospice 5301 McAuley Dr	Ypsilanti	MI	48197	**888-884-6569**	734-712-3456
Fairview Hospice 2450 26th Ave S	Minneapolis	MN	55406	**800-285-5647**	612-728-2455
Mayo Foundation for Medical Education and Research 200 First St SW	Rochester	MN	55902	**800-679-9084**	507-284-4002
Hospice Ministries 450 Towne Ctr Blvd	Ridgeland	MS	39157	**800-273-7724**	601-898-1053
North Mississippi Medical Ctr Hospice (NMHC) 830 S Gloster St	Tupelo	MS	38801	**800-882-6274**	662-377-3000
Hands of Hope Hospice 137 N Belt Hwy	Saint Joseph	MO	64506	**800-443-1143**	816-271-7190
Odyssey Healthcare of Kansas City 4911 S Arrowhead Dr	Independence	MO	64055	**800-944-4357**	816-795-1333
SSM Hospice 2 Harbor Bend Ct	Lake Saint Louis	MO	63367	**800-835-1212**	636-695-2050
VNA Hospice Care (VNA) 11440 Olive Blvd Ste 200	Creve Coeur	MO	63141	**800-392-4740**	314-918-7171
VNA of Greater St Louis *Hospice Care* 11440 Olive Blvd Ste 200	Creve Coeur	MO	63141	**800-392-4740**	314-918-7171
Visiting Nurse Assn 12565 W Ctr Rd Ste 100	Omaha	NE	68144	**800-456-8869**	402-342-5566
Family Home Hospice 2724 N Tenaya Way Ste 201	Las Vegas	NV	89128	**800-748-6773**	702-242-7000
Home Health & Hospice Care Seven Executive Park Dr	Merrimack	NH	03054	**800-887-5973**	603-882-2941
Hospice of New Jersey 400 Broadacres Dr 1St Fl	Bloomfield	NJ	07003	**800-501-0451**	973-893-0818
Karen Ann Quinlan Hospice 99 Sparta Ave	Newton	NJ	07860	**800-882-1117**	973-383-0115
Lighthouse Hospice 1040 Kings Hwy N Ste 100 *General	Cherry Hill	NJ	08034	**888-467-7423***	856-414-1155
Samaritan Hospice Five Eves Dr Ste 300	Marlton	NJ	08053	**800-229-8183**	856-596-1600
South Jersey Healthcare HospiceCare 2848 S Delsea Dr Bldg 1	Vineland	NJ	08360	**800-770-7547**	
VNA of Central Jersey (VNACJ) 176 Riverside Ave	Red Bank	NJ	07701	**800-862-3330**	
Catskill Area Hospice & Palliative Care Inc One Birchwood Dr	Oneonta	NY	13820	**800-306-3870**	607-432-6773
East End Hospice 481 Westhampton-Riverhead Rd PO Box 1048	WestHampton Beach	NY	11978	**877-513-0099**	631-288-8400
HomeCare & Hospice 1225 W State St	Olean	NY	14760	**800-339-7011**	716-372-5735
Hospice Care Inc 4277 Middle Settlement Rd	New Hartford	NY	13413	**800-317-5661**	315-735-6484
Hospice Care Network 99 Sunnyside Blvd	Woodbury	NY	11797	**800-405-6731**	516-832-7100
Hospice Family Care 550 E Main St	Batavia	NY	14020	**800-719-7129**	585-343-7596

		Toll-Free	Phone
Hospice of Orange & Sullivan Counties 800 Stony Brook Ct	Newburgh NY 12550	800-924-0157	845-561-6111
Niagara Hospice 4675 Sunset Dr	Lockport NY 14094	800-662-1220	716-439-4417
CarePartners Mountain Area Hospice PO Box 5779	Asheville NC 28813	800-627-1533	828-255-0231
Four Seasons Hospice & Palliative Care 571 S Allen Rd	Flat Rock NC 28731	866-466-9734	828-692-6178
Hospice & Palliative CareCenter 101 Hospice Ln	Winston-Salem NC 27103	888-876-3663	336-768-3972
Hospice of Alamance Caswell 914 Chapel Hill Rd	Burlington NC 27215	800-588-8879	336-532-0100
Hospice of Rutherford County 374 Hudlow Rd PO Box 336	Forest City NC 28043	800-218-2273	828-245-0095
Hospice of Stanly County 960 N First St	Albemarle NC 28001	800-230-4236	704-983-4216
Hospice of Wake County Inc 250 Hospice Cir 4th Fl	Raleigh NC 27607	888-900-3959	919-828-0890
Kitty Askins Hospice Ctr 107 Handley Pk Ct	Goldsboro NC 27534	800-692-4442	919-735-5887
Lower Cape Fear Hospice & Life Care 1414 Physicians Dr	Wilmington NC 28401	800-733-1476	910-796-7900
Richmond County Hospice 1119 N US Hwy 1	Rockingham NC 28379	800-322-2997	910-997-4464
Hospice of the Red River Valley 1701 38th St S Ste 101	Fargo ND 58103	800-237-4629	701-356-1500
Bridge Home Health & Hospice 15100 Birchaven Ln	Findlay OH 45840	800-982-3306	419-423-5351
FairHope Hospice & Palliative Care Inc 282 Sells Rd	Lancaster OH 43130	800-994-7077	740-654-7077
Homereach Hospice 800 McConnell Dr	Columbus OH 43214	800-837-2455	614-566-5377
Hospice of Central Ohio 2269 Cherry Vly Rd	Newark OH 43055	800-804-2505	740-344-0311
Hospice of Cincinnati 4360 Cooper Rd	Cincinnati OH 45242	800-691-7255	513-891-7700
Hospice of Dayton 324 Wilmington Ave	Dayton OH 45420	800-653-4490	937-256-4490
Hospice of Medina County 5075 Windfall Rd	Medina OH 44256	800-700-4771	330-722-4771
Hospice of Miami County 550 Summit Ave Ste 101	Troy OH 45373	800-372-0009	937-335-5191
Hospice of North Central Ohio 1050 Dauch Dr	Ashland OH 44805	800-952-2207	419-281-7107
Hospice of Northwest Ohio 30000 E River Rd	Perrysburg OH 43551	866-661-4001	419-661-4001
Hospice of the Cleveland Clinic 6801 Brecksville Rd Ste 10	Independence OH 44131	800-263-0403	216-444-9819
Hospice of Visiting Nurse Service 3358 Ridgewood Rd	Akron OH 44333	800-335-1455	330-665-1455
State of the Heart Home Health & Hospice 1350 N Broadway	Greenville OH 45331	800-417-7535	937-548-2999
Stein Hospice Service 1912 Hayes Ave Ste 3	Sandusky OH 44870	800-625-5269	419-625-5269
Valley Hospice Inc 380 Summit Ave	Steubenville OH 43952	877-467-7423	740-284-4440
Visiting Nurse Assn of Ohio 2500 E 22nd St	Cleveland OH 44115	877-698-6264	216-931-1400
Good Shepherd Hospice 4350 Will Rogers Pkwy Ste 400	Oklahoma City OK 73108	800-687-9808	405-943-0903
Lovejoy Hospice 939 SE Eigth St	Grants Pass OR 97526	888-758-8569	541-474-1193
Willamette Valley Hospice 1015 Third St NW	Salem OR 97304	800-555-2431	503-588-3600
Berks VNA 1170 Berkshire Blvd	Wyomissing PA 19610	855-843-8627	
Celtic Healthcare 150 Scharberry Ln	Mars PA 16046	800-355-8894	
Chandler Hall Hospice 99 Barclay St	Newtown PA 18940	888-603-1973	215-860-4000
Compassionate Care Hospice 3331 St Rd Ste 410	Bensalem PA 19020	800-584-8165	215-245-3525
Family Hospice & Palliative Care 50 Moffett St	Pittsburgh PA 15243	800-513-2148	412-572-8800
Forbes Hospice 4800 Friendship Ave	Pittsburgh PA 15224	800-381-8080	412-578-5000
Heartland Hospice Services 333 N Summit St	Toledo OH 43604	800-366-1232	419-252-5500
Hospice of Central Pennsylvania 1320 Linglestown Rd	Harrisburg PA 17110	866-779-7374	717-732-1000
Hospice of Lancaster County 685 Good Dr PO Box 4125	Lancaster PA 17604	888-236-9563	717-295-3900
Lehigh Valley Hospice 2166 S 12th St Ste 401	Allentown PA 18103	888-584-2273	610-969-0300
SUN Home Health Services Inc 61 Duke St PO Box 232	Northumberland PA 17857	888-478-6227	570-473-8320
VITAS Healthcare Corp of Pennsylvania 1787 Sentry Pk W Bldg 16 Ste 400	Blue Bell PA 19422	800-582-9533	215-542-3000
VNA 154 Hindman Rd	Butler PA 16001	877-862-6659	724-282-6806
VNA Hospice & Home Health of Lackawanna County 301 Delaware Ave	Olyphant PA 18447	800-936-7671	570-383-5180
Home Hospice Care of Rhode Island 1085 N Main St	Providence RI 02904	800-338-6555	401-415-4200
Hospice Community Care PO Box 993	Rock Hill SC 29731	800-895-2273	803-329-1500
Hospice of the Upstate 1835 Rogers Rd	Anderson SC 29621	800-261-8636	864-224-3358
McLeod Hospice 1203 E Cheves St	Florence SC 29506	800-768-4556	843-777-2564
Open Arms Hospice 1836 W Georgia Rd	Simpsonville SC 29680	866-473-6276	864-688-1700
Palmetto Health Home Care & Hospice 1400 Pickens St	Columbia SC 29202	800-238-1884	803-296-3100
Alive Hospice Inc 1718 Patterson St	Nashville TN 37203	800-327-1085	615-327-1085
Amedisys Hospice 1423 W Morris Blvd Ste C	Morristown TN 37813	800-659-2633	423-587-9484

		Toll-Free	Phone
Baptist Trinity Home Care & Hospice 6019 Walnut Grove Rd	Memphis TN 38120	800-422-7847	901-226-5000
Hospice of Chattanooga 4411 Oakwood Dr	Chattanooga TN 37416	800-267-6828	423-892-4289
Methodist Alliance Hospice 6400 Shelby View Dr Ste 101	Memphis TN 38134	800-541-8277	901-516-1999
AseraCare Hospice of Austin 14205 Burnet Rd	Austin TX 78728	800-332-3982	512-218-9890
CHRISTUS Spohn Hospice 6200 Saratoga Blvd Bldg B Ste 104	Corpus Christi TX 78414	844-444-8440	361-994-3400
Community Hospice of Texas 6100 Western Pl Ste 500	Fort Worth TX 76107	800-226-0373	817-870-2795
Hendrick Hospice Care 1682 Hickory St	Abilene TX 79601	800-622-8516	325-677-8516
Hope Hospice 611 N Walnut Ave	New Braunfels TX 78130	800-499-7501	830-625-7500
Hospice at the Texas Medical Ctr 1905 Holcombe Blvd	Houston TX 77030	800-630-7894	713-467-7423
Hospice Austin 4107 Spicewood Springs Rd Ste 100	Austin TX 78759	800-445-3261	512-342-4700
Hospice Brazos Valley 502 W 26th St	Bryan TX 77803	800-824-2326	979-821-2266
Hospice Care Team 1708 N Amburn Rd Ste C	Texas City TX 77591	800-545-8738	409-938-0070
Hospice of East Texas 4111 University Blvd	Tyler TX 75701	800-777-9860	903-266-3400
Hospice of San Angelo 36 E Twohig St PO Box 471	San Angelo TX 76903	800-499-6524	325-658-6524
Hospice of South Texas 605 E Locust Ave	Victoria TX 77901	800-874-6908	361-572-4300
Good Samaritan Hospice 2408 Electric Rd	Roanoke VA 24018	888-466-7809	540-776-0198
Hospice of the Piedmont 675 Peter Jefferson Pkwy Ste 300	Charlottesville VA 22911	800-975-5501	434-817-6900
Hospice of the Rapidan 1200 Sunset Ln Ste 2320	Culpeper VA 22701	800-676-2012	540-825-4840
Mary Washington Hospice 5012 Southpoint Pkwy	Fredericksburg VA 22407	800-257-1667	540-741-1667
Evergreen Hospice Services 12822 124th Ln NE	Kirkland WA 98034	877-980-7500	425-899-1070
Hospice of Spokane 121 S Arthur St	Spokane WA 99202	888-459-0438	509-456-0438
Providence Hospice of Seattle 425 Pontius Ave N Ste 300	Seattle WA 98109	888-782-4445	206-320-4000
Providence Sound Home Care & Hospice 3432 S Bay Rd NE	Olympia WA 98506	800-869-7062	360-459-8311
Tri-Cities Chaplaincy 2108 W Entiat Ave	Kennewick WA 99336	800-783-0544	509-783-7416
Hospice of Huntington 1101 Sixth Ave	Huntington WV 25701	800-788-5480	304-529-4217
Hospice of the Panhandle 330 Hospice Ln	Kearneysville WV 25430	800-345-6538	304-264-0406
Kanawha Hospice Care 1606 Kanawha Blvd W	Charleston WV 25387	800-560-8523	304-768-8523
AseraCare Hospice of Milwaukee 7160 Dallas Pkwy Ste 400	Plano TX 75024	800-598-5132	262-785-1356
Aurora VNA Zilber Family Hospice 1155 N Honey Creek Pkwy	Wauwatosa WI 53213	888-206-6955	414-615-5900
Beloit Regional Hospice 655 Third St Ste 200	Beloit WI 53511	877-363-7421	608-363-7421
Gundersen Lutheran at Home HomeCare & Hospice 914 Green Bay St	La Crosse WI 54601	800-362-9567*	608-775-8400
*General			
Horizon Home Care & Hospice 11400 W Lake Park Dr	Milwaukee WI 53224	800-468-4660	414-365-8300
Hospice Alliance 10220 Prairie Ridge Blvd	Pleasant Prairie WI 53158	800-830-8344	262-652-4400
HospiceCare 5395 E Cheryl Pkwy	Madison WI 53711	800-553-4289	608-276-4660
Theda Care at Home 3000 E College Ave	Appleton WI 54915	800-984-5554	920-969-0919
Unity Hospice 2366 Oak Ridge Cir	De Pere WI 54115	800-990-9249	920-338-1111

371 HOSPITAL HOSPITALITY HOUSES

		Toll-Free	Phone
American Cancer Society Hope Lodge of Baltimore 636 W Lexington St	Baltimore MD 21201	888-227-6333	410-547-2522
American Cancer Society Hope Lodge of Charleston 269 Calhoun St	Charleston SC 29401	800-227-2345	843-958-0930
American Cancer Society Joe Lee Griffin Hope Lodge 1104 Ireland Way	Birmingham AL 35205	888-513-9933	205-558-7860
Bannister Family House 406 Dickinson St	San Diego CA 92103	800-926-8273	619-543-7977
Barnes Lodge 4520 Clayton Ave	Saint Louis MO 63110	800-551-3492	314-652-4319
Baylor Plaza Hotel 3600 Gaston Ave	Dallas TX 75246	800-422-9567	
Beacon House 1301 N Third St	Marquette MI 49855	800-562-9753	906-225-7100
Brent's Place 11980 E 16th Ave	Aurora CO 80010	800-895-1999	303-831-4545
Casa Esperanza 1005 Yale NE	Albuquerque NM 87106	866-654-1338	505-277-9880
Children's Hope House 7922 W Jefferson Blvd	Fort Wayne IN 46804	800-706-9941	260-459-8550
Children's House at Johns Hopkins 1915 McElderry St	Baltimore MD 21205	800-933-5470	410-614-2560
Cynthia C. & William E. Perry Pavilion 9400 Turkey Lake Rd	Orlando FL 32819	800-447-1435	321-842-8844
Gift of Life Transplant House 705 Second St SW	Rochester MN 55902	800-479-7824	507-288-7470
Hubbard House, The 29 W Miller St	Orlando FL 32806	800-648-3818	407-649-6886

				Toll-Free	Phone
Inn at Virginia Mason					
1006 Spring St	Seattle	WA	98104	800-283-6453	206-583-6453
Kohl's House at Children's Memorial Hospital					
225 E Chicago Ave	Chicago	IL	60611	800-543-7362	312-227-4000
Mario Pastega Guest House					
3505 NW Samaritan Dr	Corvallis	OR	97330	888-872-0760	541-768-4650
Nebraska House					
983285 Nebraska Medical Ctr	Omaha	NE	68198	800-401-4444	402-559-5000
Pete Gross House					
525 Minor Ave N	Seattle	WA	98109	800-331-3131	206-262-1000
Rosenbaum Family House					
1 Medical Ctr Dr PO Box 8228	Morgantown	WV	26506	855-988-2273	304-598-6094
Steven's Hope for Children Inc					
1014 W Foothill Blvd Ste B	Upland	CA	91786	866-378-3836	909-373-0678
Travis & Beverly Cross Guest Housing Ctr					
9320 SW Barnes Rd	Portland	OR	97225	888-550-1575	503-216-1575
Zachary & Elizabeth Fisher House					
111 Rockville Pk Ste 420	Rockville	MD	20850	888-294-8560	

372 HOSPITAL HOSPITALITY HOUSES - RONALD MCDONALD HOUSE

				Toll-Free	Phone
Akron 245 Locust St	Akron	OH	44302	800-262-0333	330-253-5400
Albany 139 S Lake Ave	Albany	NY	12208	866-244-8464	518-438-2655
Ronald McDonald House					
Albuquerque					
1011 Yale Ave NE	Albuquerque	NM	87106	877-842-8960	505-842-8960
Ann Arbor					
1600 Washington Heights	Ann Arbor	MI	48104	800-544-8684	734-994-4442
Camden 550 Mickle Blvd	Camden	NJ	08103	877-858-3539	856-966-4663
Chapel Hill					
101 Old Mason Farm Rd	Chapel Hill	NC	27517	800-835-5479	919-913-2040
Chattanooga					
200 Central Ave	Chattanooga	TN	37403	855-670-4787	423-778-4300
Cleveland					
10415 Euclid Ave	Cleveland	OH	44106	800-223-2273	216-229-5758
Detroit 3911 Beaubien	Detroit	MI	48201	800-426-7667	313-745-5909
Durham 506 Alexander Ave	Durham	NC	27705	866-244-8464	919-286-9305
Falls Church					
3312 Gallows Rd	Falls Church	VA	22042	855-227-7435	703-698-7080
Fort Myers					
16100 Roserush Ct	Fort Myers	FL	33908	800-435-7352	239-437-0202
Galveston 301 14th St	Galveston	TX	77550	800-275-2946	409-762-8770
Hershey 745 W Governor Rd	Hershey	PA	17033	800-732-0999	717-533-4001
Huntington 1500 17th St	Huntington	WV	25701	855-227-7435	304-529-1122
Kansas City					
2502 Cherry St	Kansas City	MO	64108	888-353-4537	816-842-8321
Las Vegas 2323 Potosi St	Las Vegas	NV	89146	888-248-1561	702-252-4663
Philadelphia					
3925 Chestnut St	Philadelphia	PA	19104	800-723-0999	215-387-8406
Providence 45 Gay St	Providence	RI	02905	888-353-4537	401-274-4447
Richmond 2330 Monument Ave	Richmond	VA	23220	800-368-3472	804-355-6517
Scranton 332 Wheeler Ave	Scranton	PA	18510	800-775-9610	570-969-8998
Seattle 5130 40th Ave NE	Seattle	WA	98105	866-987-9330	206-838-0600
Wilmington					
1901 Rockland Rd	Wilmington	DE	19803	888-656-4847	302-656-4847
Winston-Salem					
419 S Hawthorne Rd	Winston-Salem	NC	27103	855-227-7435	336-723-0228
Gainesville					
1600 SW 14th St	Gainesville	FL	32608	800-435-7352	352-374-4404

373 HOSPITALS

SEE ALSO Veterans Nursing Homes - State ; Health Care Providers - Ancillary ; Health Care Systems ; Hospices

	Toll-Free	Phone

HOSPITALS - DEVELOPMENTAL DISABILITIES

331-4 Military Hospitals

				Toll-Free	Phone
Brooke Army Medical Ctr (BAMC)					
3551 Roger Brooke Dr	Fort Sam Houston	TX	78234	800-443-2262	210-916-4141
Darnall Army Medical Ctr					
36000 Darnall Loop	Fort Hood	TX	76544	800-305-6421	254-288-8000
David Grant US Air Force Medical Ctr					
101 Bodin Cir	Travis AFB	CA	94535	800-264-3462	707-423-3735
Keller Army Community Hospital					
900 Washington Rd	West Point	NY	10996	800-552-2907	845-938-7992
Naval Hospital Bremerton					
One Boone Rd	Bremerton	WA	98312	800-422-1383	360-475-4000
Tripler Army Medical Ctr					
1 Jarrett White Rd Tripler AMC	Honolulu	HI	96859	877-880-2184	808-433-6661
US Air Force 375th Medical Group					
310 W Losey St	Scott AFB	IL	62225	866-683-2778	

373-1 Children's Hospitals

				Toll-Free	Phone
Arnold Palmer Hospital for Children & Women					
92 W Miller St	Orlando	FL	32806	800-648-3818	407-649-9111
Children's Healthcare of Atlanta at Egleston					
1405 Clifton Rd NE	Atlanta	GA	30322	888-785-7778	404-785-6000
Children's Healthcare of Atlanta at Scottish Rite					
1001 Johnson Ferry Rd NE	Atlanta	GA	30342	888-785-7778	404-785-5252
Children's Hospital					
200 Henry Clay Ave	New Orleans	LA	70118	800-299-9511	504-899-9511
Children's Hospital Central California					
9300 Valley Children's Pl	Madera	CA	93638	800-548-5435	559-353-3000

				Toll-Free	Phone
Children's Hospital Medical Ctr of Akron					
one Perkins Sq	Akron	OH	44308	800-262-0333	330-543-1000
Children's Hospitals & Clinics Minneapolis					
2525 Chicago Ave	Minneapolis	MN	55404	866-225-3251	612-813-6000
Children's Institute of Pittsburgh					
1405 Shady Ave	Pittsburgh	PA	15217	877-433-1109	412-420-2400
Children's Medical Ctr					
one Children's Plaza	Dayton	OH	45404	800-228-4055	937-641-3000
Children's Mercy Hospital & Clinics					
2401 Gillham Rd	Kansas City	MO	64108	866-512-2168	816-234-3000
Children's National Medical Ctr (CNMC)					
111 Michigan Ave NW	Washington	DC	20010	800-884-5433	202-476-5000
Cincinnati Children's Hospital Medical Ctr					
3333 Burnet Ave	Cincinnati	OH	45229	800-344-2462	513-636-4200
Copper Hills Youth Ctr					
5899 Rivendell Dr	West Jordan	UT	84081	800-776-7116	
Covenant Children's Hospital (CCH)					
4015 22nd Pl	Lubbock	TX	79410	800-378-4189	806-725-0000
CS Mott Children's Hospital					
1500 E Medical Ctr Dr	Ann Arbor	MI	48109	800-211-8181	734-936-4000
Devereux					
1291 Stanley Rd NW PO Box 1688	Kennesaw	GA	30156	800-342-3357	678-303-5233
Devereux Cleo Wallace					
8405 Church Ranch Blvd	Westminster	CO	80021	800-456-2536	303-466-7391
Driscoll Children's Hospital					
3533 S Alameda St	Corpus Christi	TX	78411	800-324-5683	361-694-5000
Gillette Children's Specialty Healthcare					
200 E University Ave	Saint Paul	MN	55101	800-719-4040	651-291-2848
Gulf Coast Treatment Ctr					
1015 Mar-Walt Dr	Fort Walton Beach	FL	32547	800-537-5433	850-863-4160
Hawthorn Ctr					
18471 Haggerty Rd	Northville	MI	48167	855-444-3911	248-349-3000
Helen DeVos Children's Hospital					
100 Michigan St NE	Grand Rapids	MI	49503	800-222-1222	616-391-9000
HSC Pediatric Ctr					
1731 Bunker Hill Rd NE	Washington	DC	20017	800-226-4444	202-832-4400
JD McCarty Ctr for Children with Developmental Disabilities					
2002 E Robinson St	Norman	OK	73071	800-777-1272	405-307-2800
Kennedy Krieger Institute					
707 N Broadway	Baltimore	MD	21205	800-873-3377	443-923-9200
KidsPeace Orchard Hills Campus					
5300 Kids Peace Dr	Orefield	PA	18069	800-257-3223	
Lucile Packard Children's Hospital (LPCH)					
725 Welch Rd	Palo Alto	CA	94304	800-995-5724	650-497-8000
Mary Bridge Children's Hospital & Health Ctr					
317 Martin Luther King Jr Way	Tacoma	WA	98405	800-552-1419	253-403-1400
Miami Children's Hospital					
3100 SW 62nd Ave	Miami	FL	33155	800-432-6837	305-666-6511
New York City Children's Ctr-Queens Campus (NYCCC)					
74-03 Commonwealth Blvd	Bellerose	NY	11426	800-597-8481	718-264-4500
Phoenix Children's Hospital					
1919 E Thomas Rd	Phoenix	AZ	85016	888-908-5437	602-546-1000
Rady Children's Hospital (RCH)					
3020 Children's Way MC 5101	San Diego	CA	92123	800-788-9029	858-576-1700
Saint Louis Children's Hospital					
One Children's Pl	Saint Louis	MO	63110	800-427-4626	314-454-6000
Seattle Children's Hospital					
4800 Sand Pt Way NE	Seattle	WA	98105	866-987-2000	206-987-2000
Shriners Hospitals for Children Boston					
51 Blossom St	Boston	MA	02114	800-255-1916	617-722-3000
Shriners Hospitals for Children Cincinnati					
3229 Burnet Ave	Cincinnati	OH	45229	800-875-8580	513-872-6000
Shriners Hospitals for Children Erie					
1645 W Eigth St	Erie	PA	16505	800-873-5437	814-875-8700
Shriners Hospitals for Children Greenville					
950 W Faris Rd	Greenville	SC	29605	800-361-7256	864-271-3444
Shriners Hospitals for Children Honolulu					
1310 Punahou St	Honolulu	HI	96826	888-888-6314	808-941-4466
Shriners Hospitals for Children Lexington					
1900 Richmond Rd	Lexington	KY	40502	800-668-4634	859-266-2101
Shriners Hospitals for Children Los Angeles					
3160 Geneva St	Los Angeles	CA	90020	888-486-5437	213-388-3151
Shriners Hospitals for Children Salt Lake City					
Fairfax Rd & Virginia St	Salt Lake City	UT	84103	800-313-3745	801-536-3500
Shriners Hospitals for Children Tampa					
12502 N Pine Dr	Tampa	FL	33612	800-237-5055	813-972-2250
Streamwood Behavioral Health Ctr					
1400 E Irving Pk Rd	Streamwood	IL	60107	800-272-7790	630-837-9000
Texas Children's Hospital					
6621 Fannin St	Houston	TX	77030	800-364-5437	832-824-1000
Texas Scottish Rite Hospital for Children					
2222 Welborn St	Dallas	TX	75219	800-421-1121	214-559-5000
Women's & Children's Hospital of Buffalo					
219 Bryant St	Buffalo	NY	14222	800-462-7653	716-878-7000
Youth Villages Inner Harbour					
4685 Dorsett Shoals Rd	Douglasville	GA	30135	800-255-8657	770-852-6333

373-2 General Hospitals - Canada

				Toll-Free	Phone
Belleville General Hospital					
265 Dundas St E	Belleville	ON	K8N5A9	800-483-2811	613-969-7400
British Columbia's Women's Hospital & Health Centre					
4500 Oak St	Vancouver	BC	V6H3N1	888-300-3088	604-875-2424
Centre Hospitalier Le Gardeur					
911 Montee des Pionniers	Terrebonne	QC	J6V2H2	888-654-7525	450-654-7525
Centre Hospitalier Pierre Boucher					
1333 Boul Jacques-Cartier E	Longueuil	QC	J4M2A5	866-277-3553	450-468-8111
Children's Hospital of Eastern Ontario					
401 Smyth Rd	Ottawa	ON	K1H8L1	866-797-0007	613-737-7600
CHU Sainte-Justine					
3175 Ch de la Cote-Sainte-Catherine	Montreal	QC	H3T1C5	888-235-3667	514-345-4931
Colchester Regional Hospital					
207 Willow St	Truro	NS	B2N5A1	800-460-2110	902-893-4321
Concordia Hospital					
1095 Concordia Ave	Winnipeg	MB	R2K3S8	888-315-9257	204-667-1560

				Toll-Free	Phone
Credit Valley Hospital 2200 Eglinton Ave W	Mississauga	ON	L5M2N1	**877-292-4284**	905-813-2200
Jeffrey Hale - St Brigid's Hospital 1250 ch Sainte-Foy	Quebec	QC	G1S2M6	**888-984-5333**	418-684-5333
Joseph Brant Memorial Hospital (JBMH) 1230 N Shore Blvd	Burlington	ON	L7S1W7	**800-810-0000**	905-632-3730
Kelowna General Hospital (KGH) 2268 Pandosy St	Kelowna	BC	V1Y1T2	**888-877-4442**	250-862-4000
Lakeridge Health Oshawa One Hospital Ct	Oshawa	ON	L1G2B9	**866-338-1778**	905-576-8711
Lions Gate Hospital 231 E 15th St	North Vancouver	BC	V7L2L7	**800-984-1131**	604-988-3131
Ross Memorial Hospital (RMH) 10 Angeline St N	Lindsay	ON	K9V4M8	**800-510-7365**	705-324-6111
Saint Michael's Hospital 30 Bond St	Toronto	ON	M5B1W8	**866-797-0000**	416-360-4000

373-3 General Hospitals - US

				Toll-Free	Phone
Advocate Sherman Hospital 1425 N Randall Rd	Elgin	IL	60123	**800-397-9000**	847-742-9800
Affiliated Community Medical Centers (ACMC) 101 Willmar Ave SW	Willmar	MN	56201	**888-225-6580**	320-231-5000
Affinity Medical Ctr 875 Eigth St NE	Massillon	OH	44646	**800-999-6673**	330-832-8761
Aiken Regional Medical Centers 302 University Pkwy	Aiken	SC	29801	**800-245-3679**	803-641-5000
Akron General Medical Ctr 400 Wabash Ave	Akron	OH	44307	**800-221-4601**	330-344-6000
Alaska Native Medical Ctr (ANMC) 4315 Diplomacy Dr *Admitting	Anchorage	AK	99508	**800-478-6661***	907-563-2662
Albert Einstein Medical Ctr 5501 Old York Rd	Philadelphia	PA	19141	**800-346-7834**	
Alexian Bros Medical Ctr 800 Biesterfield Rd	Elk Grove Village	IL	60007	**800-432-5005**	847-437-5500
Allegiance Health 205 NE Ave	Jackson	MI	49201	**800-872-6480**	517-788-4800
Allen Memorial Hospital 1825 Logan Ave	Waterloo	IA	50703	**888-343-4165**	319-235-3941
Alpena Regional Medical Ctr 1501 W Chisholm St	Alpena	MI	49707	**800-556-8842**	989-356-7000
Altoona Regional Health System Altoona Hospital 620 Howard Ave	Altoona	PA	16601	**877-855-8152**	814-889-2011
Altru Hospital 1200 S Columbia Rd	Grand Forks	ND	58201	**800-732-4277**	701-780-5000
Appleton Medical Ctr 1818 N Meade St	Appleton	WI	54911	**800-236-4101**	920-731-4101
Arkansas Valley Regional Medical Ctr (AVRMC) 1100 Carson Ave	La Junta	CO	81050	**877-696-6775**	719-384-5412
Arrowhead Regional Medical Ctr 400 N Pepper Ave	Colton	CA	92324	**855-422-8029**	909-580-1000
Aspirus Wausau Hospital 333 Pine Ridge Blvd	Wausau	WI	54401	**800-283-2881**	715-847-2121
Atrium Medical Ctr One Medical Ctr Dr	Middletown	OH	45005	**800-338-4057**	513-424-2111
Auburn Regional Medical Ctr 202 N Div St Plaza 1	Auburn	WA	98001	**866-268-7223**	253-833-7711
Augusta Medical Ctr (AMC) 78 Medical Ctr Dr PO Box 1000	Fishersville	VA	22939	**800-932-0262**	540-932-4000
Aurora Sinai Medical Ctr 945 N 12th St	Milwaukee	WI	53201	**888-863-5502**	414-219-2000
Aventura Hospital 20900 Biscayne Blvd	Aventura	FL	33180	**800-523-5772**	305-682-7000
Avera Queen of Peace Hospital 525 N Foster St	Mitchell	SD	57301	**888-531-1685**	605-995-2000
Avera Saint Luke's Hospital 305 S State St	Aberdeen	SD	57401	**800-658-3535**	605-622-5000
Baltimore Washington Medical Ctr 301 Hospital Dr	Glen Burnie	MD	21061	**800-994-6610**	410-787-4000
Banner Del E Webb Memorial Hospital 14502 W Meeker Blvd	Sun City West	AZ	85375	**800-254-4357**	623-214-4000
Baptist Health 1 Trillium Way	Corbin	KY	40701	**800-395-4435**	606-528-1212
Baptist Health Louisville 4000 Kresge Way	Louisville	KY	40207	**800-489-3002**	502-897-8100
Baptist Health Paducah (WBH) 2501 Kentucky Ave	Paducah	KY	42003	**877-271-4176**	270-575-2100
Baptist Hospital of Miami 8900 SW 88th St	Miami	FL	33176	**800-994-6610**	786-596-1960
Baptist Medical Ctr 800 Prudential Dr	Jacksonville	FL	32207	**800-874-8567**	904-202-2000
Baptist Memorial Hospital Golden Triangle 2520 Fifth St N	Columbus	MS	39703	**800-422-7847**	662-244-1000
Bassett Healthcare Network 1 Atwell Rd	Cooperstown	NY	13326	**800-227-7388**	607-547-3456
Bay Area Medical Ctr (BAMC) 3100 Shore Dr	Marinette	WI	54143	**888-788-2070**	715-735-4200
Bay Medical Ctr 615 N Bonita Ave	Panama City	FL	32401	**800-222-1222**	850-769-1511
Bay Regional Medical Ctr (BRMC) 1900 Columbus Ave	Bay City	MI	48708	**800-656-3950**	989-894-3000
Bayhealth Medical Ctr 21 W Clarke Ave	Milford	DE	19963	**877-453-7107**	302-430-5738
Baylor Regional Medical Ctr at Grapevine 1650 W College St	Grapevine	TX	76051	**800-422-9567**	817-481-1588
Bayshore Medical Ctr 4000 Spencer Hwy	Pasadena	TX	77504	**866-503-7546**	713-359-2000
Beaufort Memorial Hospital 955 Ribaut Rd	Beaufort	SC	29902	**877-532-6472**	843-522-5200
Beloit Health System 1969 W Hart Rd	Beloit	WI	53511	**800-637-2641**	608-363-5724
Benefis Healthcare *East Campus* 1101 26th St S	Great Falls	MT	59405	**800-648-6632**	406-455-5000
Beth Israel Deaconess Medical Ctr (BIDMC) 330 Brookline Ave	Boston	MA	02215	**800-667-5356**	617-667-7000
Bethesda Hospital 2951 Maple Ave	Zanesville	OH	43701	**800-322-4762**	740-454-4000
Billings Clinic 2800 Tenth Ave N	Billings	MT	59101	**800-332-7156**	406-657-4000
Bluefield Regional Medical Ctr (BRMC) 500 Cherry St	Bluefield	WV	24701	**800-994-6610**	304-327-1100
Bon Secours Memorial Regional Medical Ctr 8260 Atlee Rd	Mechanicsville	VA	23116	**888-455-3766**	804-764-6000
Bon Secours Saint Mary's Hospital 5801 Bremo Rd	Richmond	VA	23226	**877-342-1500**	804-285-2011
Brattleboro Memorial Hospital Inc 17 Belmont Ave Ste 1	Brattleboro	VT	05301	**866-972-5266**	802-257-0341
Broadlawns Medical Ctr 1801 Hickman Rd	Des Moines	IA	50314	**866-904-5755**	515-282-2200
Bronson Methodist Hospital 601 John St	Kalamazoo	MI	49007	**800-276-6766**	269-341-7654
BronxCare Family Wellness Center 1276 Fulton Ave	Bronx	NY	10456	**877-451-9361**	718-590-1800
Brooksville Regional Hospital 17240 Cortez Blvd	Brooksville	FL	34601	**844-455-8708**	352-796-5111
Bryan LGH Medical Ctr East 1600 S 48th St	Lincoln	NE	68506	**800-742-7844**	402-481-7333
Buena Vista Regional Medical Ctr PO Box 309	Storm Lake	IA	50588	**877-401-8030**	712-732-4030
Buffalo General Hospital 100 High St	Buffalo	NY	14203	**800-506-6480**	716-859-5600
Cambridge Medical Ctr (CMC) 701 S Dellwood St	Cambridge	MN	55008	**800-252-4133**	763-689-7700
Camden-Clark Memorial Hospital (CCMH) 800 Garfield Ave	Parkersburg	WV	26101	**800-541-3160**	304-424-2111
Capital Medical Ctr 3900 Capital Mall Dr SW	Olympia	WA	98502	**888-677-9757**	360-754-5858
Capital Regional Medical Ctr (CRMC) 2626 Capital Medical Blvd	Tallahassee	FL	32308	**800-994-6610**	850-325-5000
Carilion New River Valley Medical Ctr 2900 Lamb Cir	Christiansburg	VA	24073	**800-432-7874**	540-731-2000
Carolinas Medical Center-NorthEast 920 Church St N	Concord	NC	28025	**800-575-1275**	704-403-1275
Carolinas Medical Center-University 8800 N Tryon St	Charlotte	NC	28262	**800-821-1535**	704-863-6000
Carolinas Medical Ctr Mercy 2001 Vail Ave	Charlotte	NC	28207	**800-821-1535**	
Catholic Medical Ctr (CMC) 100 McGregor St	Manchester	NH	03102	**800-437-9666**	603-668-3545
Catskill Regional Medical Ctr 68 Harris-Bushville Rd PO Box 800	Harris	NY	12742	**888-846-5945**	845-794-3300
Cedars-Sinai Medical Ctr (CSMC) 8700 Beverly Blvd	Los Angeles	CA	90048	**800-233-2771**	310-423-3277
Centegra Memorial Medical Ctr 3701 Doty Rd	Woodstock	IL	60098	**877-236-8347**	815-338-2500
Central Carolina Hospital 1135 Carthage St	Sanford	NC	27330	**800-292-2262**	919-774-2100
Central DuPage Hospital 25 N Winfield Rd	Winfield	IL	60190	**800-223-9776**	630-933-1600
Central Texas Medical Ctr (CTMC) 1301 Wonder World Dr	San Marcos	TX	78666	**800-927-9004**	512-353-8979
CGH Medical Ctr (CGHMC) 100 E LeFevre Rd	Sterling	IL	61081	**800-625-4790**	815-625-0400
Chandler Regional Hospital 475 S Dobson Rd	Chandler	AZ	85224	**877-728-5414**	480-728-3000
Chesapeake Regional Medical Ctr 736 Battlefield Blvd N	Chesapeake	VA	23320	**800-582-8350**	757-312-8121
CHI St. Joseph's Health 2500 Fairway St *General	Dickinson	ND	58601	**800-446-6215***	701-456-4000
Christ Hospital 2139 Auburn Ave	Cincinnati	OH	45219	**800-527-8919**	513-585-2000
CHRISTUS Hospital - St Elizabeth 2830 Calder St	Beaumont	TX	77702	**866-683-3627**	409-892-7171
CHRISTUS Saint Mary Hospital 3600 Gates Blvd Ste 3	Port Arthur	TX	77642	**866-683-3627**	409-985-7431
City Hospital 2500 Hospital Dr	Martinsburg	WV	25401	**888-988-1362**	304-264-1000
City of Hope National Medical Ctr 1500 E Duarte Rd *Admissions	Duarte	CA	91010	**800-826-4673***	626-256-4673
CJW Medical Ctr 7101 Jahnke Rd	Richmond	VA	23225	**800-468-6620**	804-320-3911
Clarion Hospital (CH) One Hospital Dr	Clarion	PA	16214	**800-522-0505**	814-226-9500
Clearfield Hospital 809 Tpke Ave PO Box 992	Clearfield	PA	16830	**800-281-8000**	814-765-5341
Cleveland Clinic 9500 Euclid Ave	Cleveland	OH	44195	**800-223-2273**	216-444-2200
Cleveland Clinic Hospital 2950 Cleveland Clinic Blvd	Weston	FL	33331	**866-293-7866**	954-689-5000
Clifton Springs Hospital & Clinic 2 Coulter Rd	Clifton Springs	NY	14432	**888-786-4347**	315-462-9561
Clinton Memorial Hospital (CMH) 610 W Main St PO Box 600	Wilmington	OH	45177	**800-803-9648**	937-382-6611
Coffeyville Regional Medical Ctr 1400 W Fourth St	Coffeyville	KS	67337	**800-540-2762**	620-251-1200
Colquitt Regional Medical Ctr (CRMC) 3131 S Main St PO Box 40	Moultrie	GA	31768	**888-262-2762**	229-985-3420
Columbia Memorial Hospital 71 Prospect Ave	Hudson	NY	12534	**866-539-1370**	518-828-7601
Columbus Regional Hospital 2400 E 17th St	Columbus	IN	47201	**800-841-4938**	812-379-4441
Community Health Ctr of Branch County (CHCBC) 274 E Chicago St	Coldwater	MI	49036	**800-994-6610**	517-279-5400
Community Hospital Anderson (CHA) 1515 N Madison Ave	Anderson	IN	46011	**800-777-7775**	765-298-4242
Community Hospital of Long Beach 1720 Termino Ave	Long Beach	CA	90804	**800-994-6610**	562-498-1000
Community Hospital of the Monterey Peninsula (CHOMP) 23625 Holman Hwy	Monterey	CA	93940	**888-452-4667**	831-624-5311

Hospital / Address	City	ST	ZIP	Toll-Free	Phone
Community Medical Ctr (CMC) 99 Hwy 37 W	Toms River	NJ	08755	888-724-7123	732-557-8000
Conroe Regional Medical Ctr 504 Medical Ctr Blvd	Conroe	TX	77304	888-633-2687	936-539-1111
Contra Costa Health Services 2500 Alhambra Ave	Martinez	CA	94553	877-661-6230	925-370-5000
Cooper University Hospital Three Cooper Plz	Camden	NJ	08103	800-826-6737	856-342-2000
Coral Gables Hospital Inc (CGH) 3100 Douglas Rd	Coral Gables	FL	33134	866-728-3677	305-445-8461
Corning Hospital 176 Denison Pkwy E	Corning	NY	14830	877-750-2042	607-937-7200
Dallas County Hospital 610 10th St	Perry	IA	50220	800-877-7541	515-465-3547
Danbury Hospital (DH) 24 Hospital Ave	Danbury	CT	06810	800-516-3658	203-739-6398
Danville Regional Medical Ctr 142 S Main St	Danville	VA	24541	800-688-3762	434-799-2100
Davis Hospital & Medical Ctr (DHMC) 1600 W Antelope Dr	Layton	UT	84041	877-898-6080	801-807-1000
Deaconess Hospital 311 Straight St	Cincinnati	OH	45219	800-398-5699	513-559-2100
Decatur Memorial Hospital 2300 N Edward St	Decatur	IL	62526	866-364-3600	217-876-8121
Delnor-Community Hospital (DCH) 300 Randall Rd	Geneva	IL	60134	800-223-9776	630-208-3000
Desert Regional Medical Ctr 1150 N Indian Canyon Dr	Palm Springs	CA	92262	800-491-4990	760-323-6511
DesPeres Hospital 2345 Dougherty Ferry Rd	Saint Louis	MO	63122	888-457-5203	314-966-9100
Doctors Hospital at White Rock Lake 9440 Poppy Dr	Dallas	TX	75218	866-893-8446	214-324-6100
Doctors Hospital of Laredo 10700 McPherson Rd	Laredo	TX	78045	844-244-4874	956-523-2000
Doctors Medical Ctr 1441 Florida Ave	Modesto	CA	95350	800-994-6610	209-578-1211
East Georgia Regional Medical Ctr (EGRMC) 1499 Fair Rd	Statesboro	GA	30458	844-455-8708	912-486-1000
East Jefferson General Hospital (EJGH) 4200 Houma Blvd	Metairie	LA	70006	866-280-7737	504-454-4000
Eastern New Mexico Medical Ctr 405 W Country Club Rd	Roswell	NM	88201	800-222-1222	575-622-8170
Edinburg Regional Medical Ctr (ERMC) 1102 W Trenton Rd	Edinburg	TX	78539	800-465-5585	956-388-6000
Elliot Hospital 1 Elliot Way Ste 100	Manchester	NH	03103	800-922-4999	603-627-1669
Enloe Medical Ctr 1531 Esplanade	Chico	CA	95926	800-822-8102	530-332-7300
Ephraim McDowell Regional Medical Ctr 217 S Third St	Danville	KY	40422	800-686-4121	859-239-1000
Erlanger Medical Ctr 975 E Third St	Chattanooga	TN	37403	877-849-8338	423-778-7000
Evanston Hospital 2650 Ridge Ave	Evanston	IL	60201	888-364-6400	847-570-2000
Fairfield Medical Ctr (FMC) 401 N Ewing St	Lancaster	OH	43130	800-548-2627	740-687-8000
Fairview Hospital 18101 Lorain Ave	Cleveland	OH	44111	800-801-2273	216-476-7000
Fairview University Medical Ctr Mesabi 750 E 34th St	Hibbing	MN	55746	888-870-8626	218-262-4881
FHN Memorial Hospital 1045 W Stephenson St	Freeport	IL	61032	800-747-4131	815-599-6000
Finley Hospital 350 N Grandview Ave	Dubuque	IA	52001	800-582-1891	563-582-1881
Firelands Regional Medical Ctr 1111 Hayes Ave	Sandusky	OH	44870	800-342-1177	419-557-7400
Fisher-Titus Medical Ctr (FTMC) 272 Benedict Ave	Norwalk	OH	44857	800-589-3862	419-668-8101
Florida Hospital Heartland Medical Ctr 4200 Sun 'n Lake Blvd PO Box 9400	Sebring	FL	33871	800-756-4447	863-314-4466
Flowers Hospital 4370 W Main St	Dothan	AL	36305	877-456-9617	334-793-5000
Floyd Medical Ctr 304 Turner McCall Blvd	Rome	GA	30165	866-874-2772	706-509-5000
Floyd Memorial Hospital 1850 State St	New Albany	IN	47150	800-423-1513	812-944-7701
Forrest General Hospital 6051 US Hwy 49	Hattiesburg	MS	39402	800-503-5980	601-288-7000
Fountain Valley Regional Hospital & Medical Ctr 17100 Euclid St	Fountain Valley	CA	92708	866-904-6871	714-966-7200
Franciscan St. Elizabeth Health 1501 Hartford St	Lafayette	IN	47904	800-371-6011	765-423-6011
Frankfort Regional Medical Ctr 299 King's Daughters Dr	Frankfort	KY	40601	888-696-4505	502-875-5240
Franklin Community Health Network 111 Franklin Health Commons	Farmington	ME	04938	800-398-6031	207-778-6031
Franklin Square Hospital Ctr 9000 Franklin Sq Dr	Baltimore	MD	21237	855-633-8880	443-777-7000
Frick Hospital 508 S Church St	Mount Pleasant	PA	15666	877-771-1234	724-547-1500
Gateway Regional Medical Ctr (GRMC) 2100 Madison Ave	Granite City	IL	62040	800-422-6237*	618-798-3000
*General					
Genesis Medical Ctr Illini Campus 801 Illini Dr	Silvis	IL	61282	800-250-6020	309-792-9363
George Washington University Hospital 900 23rd St NW	Washington	DC	20037	888-449-3627	202-715-4000
Glacial Ridge Hospital Foundation Inc 10 Fourth Ave SE	Glenwood	MN	56334	866-667-4747	320-634-4521
GlenOaks Hospital 701 Winthrop Ave	Glendale Heights	IL	60139	866-751-7127	630-545-8000
Glens Falls Hospital 100 Pk St	Glens Falls	NY	12801	800-994-6610	518-926-1000
Golden Valley Memorial Hospital 1600 N Second St	Clinton	MO	64735	888-225-6903	660-885-5511
Good Samaritan Hospital 10 E 31st St	Kearney	NE	68847	800-277-4306	308-865-7100
Good Samaritan Regional Medical Ctr 3600 NW Samaritan Dr	Corvallis	OR	97330	888-872-0760	541-768-5111
Grady Memorial Hospital 2220 Iowa Ave	Chickasha	OK	73018	800-299-9665	405-224-2300
Grand Strand Regional Medical Ctr 809 82nd Pkwy	Myrtle Beach	SC	29572	800-342-2383	843-692-1000
Great Plains Regional Medical Ctr (GPRMC) 601 W Leota St PO Box 1167	North Platte	NE	69101	800-662-0011	308-696-8000
Greenwich Hospital 5 Perryridge Rd	Greenwich	CT	06830	800-657-8355	203-863-3000
Gulf Coast Medical Ctr 13681 Doctors Way	Fort Myers	FL	33912	800-809-9906	239-343-1000
Gundersen Lutheran Medical Ctr 1836 S Ave	La Crosse	WI	54601	800-362-9567	608-782-7300
Hanover Hospital 300 Highland Ave	Hanover	PA	17331	800-673-2426	717-637-3711
Harbor Hospital Ctr 3001 S Hanover St	Baltimore	MD	21225	800-280-9006	410-350-3200
Harlan ARH Hospital 81 Ballpark Rd	Harlan	KY	40831	800-274-9375	606-573-8100
Harrington Memorial Hospital (HMH) 100 S St	Southbridge	MA	01550	800-416-6072	508-765-9771
Harrisburg Hospital 111 S Front St	Harrisburg	PA	17101	888-782-5678	717-782-3131
Hartford Hospital 80 Seymour St	Hartford	CT	06102	800-545-7664	860-545-5000
Harton Regional Medical Ctr 1801 N Jackson St	Tullahoma	TN	37388	800-999-6673*	931-393-3000
*General					
Hays Medical Ctr (HMC) 2220 Canterbury Dr	Hays	KS	67601	800-248-0073	785-650-2759
Heart of Lancaster Regional Medical Ctr 1500 Highland Dr	Lititz	PA	17543	800-999-6673	717-625-5000
Henry Ford Hospital 2799 W Grand Blvd	Detroit	MI	48202	800-999-4340	313-916-2600
High Point Regional Health System (HPRHS) 601 N Elm St PO Box HP-5	High Point	NC	27262	877-878-7644	336-878-6000
Highlands Regional Medical Ctr 5000 KY Rt 321	Prestonsburg	KY	41653	800-533-4762	606-886-8511
Hilton Head Regional Medical Ctr 25 Hospital Ctr Blvd	Hilton Head Island	SC	29926	888-689-8207	843-681-6122
Holmes Regional Medical Ctr 1350 Hickory St	Melbourne	FL	32901	800-716-7737	321-434-7000
Holy Cross Hospital 1500 Forest Glen Rd	Silver Spring	MD	20910	800-358-9001	301-754-7000
Holy Family Memorial Medical Ctr 2300 Western Ave PO Box 1450	Manitowoc	WI	54220	800-994-3662	920-320-2011
Holy Redeemer Hospital & Medical Ctr 1648 Huntingdon Pk	Meadowbrook	PA	19046	800-818-4747	215-947-3000
Holy Rosary Healthcare 2600 Wilson St	Miles City	MT	59301	800-843-3820	406-233-2600
Hospital of Saint Raphael 1450 Chapel St	New Haven	CT	06511	888-700-6543	203-789-3000
Howard County General Hospital 5755 Cedar Ln	Columbia	MD	21044	866-323-4615	410-740-7890
Hunt Regional Healthcare 4215 Joe Ramsey Blvd	Greenville	TX	75401	800-984-9223	903-408-5000
Hurley Medical Ctr One Hurley Plz	Flint	MI	48503	800-336-8999	810-262-9000
Indiana University Hospital 550 N University Blvd	Indianapolis	IN	46202	800-248-1199	317-274-5000
INTEGRIS Baptist Regional Health Ctr 200 Second Ave SW	Miami	OK	74355	888-951-2277	918-542-6611
INTEGRIS Bass Baptist Health Ctr 600 S Monroe	Enid	OK	73701	888-951-2277	580-233-2300
INTEGRIS Southwest Medical Ctr 4401 S Western St	Oklahoma City	OK	73109	888-949-3816	405-636-7000
Intermountain Healthcare Logan Regional Hospital 500 E 1400 N	Logan	UT	84341	800-442-4845	435-716-1000
Irvington General Hospital 95 Old Short Hills Rd	West Orange	NJ	07052	888-724-7123	
Ivinson Memorial Hospital 255 N 30th St	Laramie	WY	82072	877-858-0990	307-742-2141
Jackson County Memorial Hospital 1200 E Pecan St	Altus	OK	73521	800-595-0455	580-379-5000
Jackson Purchase Medical Ctr 1099 Medical Ctr Cir	Mayfield	KY	42066	800-994-6610	270-251-4100
Jennie Stuart Medical Ctr 320 W 18th St PO Box 2400	Hopkinsville	KY	42241	800-887-5762	270-887-0100
Jersey Shore University Medical Ctr 1945 Rt 33	Neptune	NJ	07753	800-560-9990	732-775-5500
John D Archbold Memorial Hospital 915 Gordon Ave	Thomasville	GA	31792	800-341-1009	229-228-2000
John Muir Medical Ctr (JMMC) 1601 Ygnacio Valley Rd	Walnut Creek	CA	94598	844-398-5376	925-939-3000
Jordan Hospital 275 Sandwich St	Plymouth	MA	02360	800-256-7326	508-746-2000
Kadlec Regional Medical Ctr 888 Swift Blvd	Richland	WA	99352	800-780-6067	509-946-4611
Kaiser Permanente Foundation Hospital 9400 E Rosecrans Ave	Bellflower	CA	90706	866-279-8954	562-461-3000
Kaiser Permanente Harbor City Medical Ctr 25825 S Vermont Ave	Harbor City	CA	90710	800-464-4000	310-325-5111
Kaiser Permanente Hospital 441 N Lakeview Ave	Anaheim	CA	92807	800-464-4000	714-279-4000
Kaiser Permanente Medical Center-South Sacramento 6600 Bruceville Rd	Sacramento	CA	95823	800-464-4000	916-688-2000
Kaiser Permanente Medical Ctr 710 Lawrence Expy	Santa Clara	CA	95051	800-464-4000	408-851-1717
Kaiser Permanente Parma Medical Ctr 12301 Snow Rd	Cleveland	OH	44130	800-524-7372	216-362-2000
Kaiser Permanente Riverside Medical Ctr 10800 Magnolia Ave	Riverside	CA	92505	800-464-4000*	951-353-2000
*Cust Svc					
Kaiser Permanente Walnut Creek Medical Ctr 1425 S Main St	Walnut Creek	CA	94596	800-464-4000	925-295-4000
Kalispell Regional Medical Ctr 310 Sunnyview Ln	Kalispell	MT	59901	800-228-1574	406-752-5111

				Toll-Free	Phone

Katherine Shaw Bethea Hospital
403 E First St .... Dixon IL 61021 · 800-582-9731 · 815-288-5531

Kaweah Delta Hospital
400 W Mineral King Ave .... Visalia CA 93291 · 800-717-5670 · 559-624-2000

Kennedy Health System-Cherry Hill
2201 Chapel Ave W .... Cherry Hill NJ 08002 · 866-224-0264 · 856-488-6500

Kenosha Medical Ctr
6308 Eigth Ave .... Kenosha WI 53143 · 800-994-6610 · 262-656-2011

Kent General Hospital
640 S State St .... Dover DE 19901 · 888-761-8300 · 302-674-4700

Kingman Regional Medical Ctr (KRMC)
3269 Stockton Hill Rd .... Kingman AZ 86409 · 877-757-2101 · 928-757-2101

Kishwaukee Community Hospital
1 Kish Hospital Dr .... DeKalb IL 60115 · 800-397-1521 · 815-756-1521

La Porte Hospital (LPH)
1007 Lincolnway PO Box 250 .... La Porte IN 46350 · 800-235-6204 · 219-326-1234

Lahey Clinic Foundation Inc
41 Mall Rd .... Burlington MA 01805 · 800-524-3955 · 781-744-8000

Lake Pointe Medical Ctr (LPMC)
6800 Scenic Dr .... Rowlett TX 75088 · 866-525-5762 · 972-412-2273

Lake Region Hospital
712 S Cascade St .... Fergus Falls MN 56537 · 800-439-6424 · 218-736-8000

Lakeland Medical Center-Niles
31 N St Joseph Ave .... Niles MI 49120 · 800-968-0115 · 269-683-5510

Lakewood Hospital
14519 Detroit Ave .... Lakewood OH 44107 · 866-588-2264 · 216-521-4200

Lancaster Regional Medical Ctr
250 College Ave .... Lancaster PA 17603 · 800-999-6673 · 717-291-8211

Lankenau Medical Ctr
100 E Lancaster Ave .... Wynnewood PA 19096 · 866-225-5654 · 484-476-2000

Lapeer Regional Hospital
1375 N Main St .... Lapeer MI 48446 · 888-327-0671 · 810-667-5500

Laughlin Memorial Hospital
1420 Tuscolum Blvd .... Greeneville TN 37745 · 800-852-7157 · 423-787-5000

Lawrence Memorial Hospital (LMH)
325 Maine St .... Lawrence KS 66044 · 800-749-4144 · 785-505-5000

LDS Hospital
8th Ave & C St .... Salt Lake City UT 84143 · 888-301-3880 · 801-408-1100

Lea Regional Medical Ctr
5419 N Lovington Hwy .... Hobbs NM 88240 · 877-492-8001 · 575-492-5000

Legacy Emanuel Hospital & Health Ctr
2801 N Gantenbein Ave .... Portland OR 97227 · 888-598-4232 · 503-413-2200

Legacy Good Samaritan Hospital
1015 NW 22nd Ave .... Portland OR 97210 · 800-733-9959 · 503-335-3500

Legacy Salmon Creek Hospital
2211 NE 139th St .... Vancouver WA 98686 · 877-270-5566 · 360-487-1000

Lehigh Valley Health Network
700 E Broad St .... Hazleton PA 18201 · 800-528-1234 · 570-501-4000

Lewis-Gale Medical Ctr
1900 Electric Rd .... Salem VA 24153 · 800-722-4673 · 540-776-4000

Lewistown Hospital
400 Highland Ave .... Lewistown PA 17044 · 800-248-0505 · 717-248-5411

Liberty Hospital
2525 Glenn Hendren Dr .... Liberty MO 64068 · 800-344-3829 · 816-781-7200

Lifeline Medical Assoc LLC
99 Cherry Hill Rd Ste 220 .... Parsippany NJ 07054 · 800-845-2785 · 973-316-0307

Lima Memorial Hospital
1001 Bellefontaine Ave .... Lima OH 45804 · 800-252-3337 · 419-228-3335

Lodi Memorial Hospital
975 S Fairmont Ave .... Lodi CA 95240 · 800-323-3360 · 209-334-3411

Logan Regional Medical Ctr
20 Hospital Dr .... Logan WV 25601 · 888-982-9144 · 304-831-1101

Loma Linda University Medical Ctr
11234 Anderson St .... Loma Linda CA 92354 · 877-558-6248 · 909-558-4000

Long Island College Hospital (LICH)
339 Hicks St .... Brooklyn NY 11201 · 800-227-8922 · 718-780-1000

Los Alamitos Medical Ctr
3751 Katella Ave .... Los Alamitos CA 90720 · 800-540-4000 · 562-598-1311

Lovelace Medical Ctr
5400 Gibson Blvd SE .... Albuquerque NM 87108 · 888-281-6531 · 505-262-7000

Lower Keys Medical Ctr
5900 College Rd .... Key West FL 33040 · 800-355-2470 · 305-294-5531

Loyola University Medical Ctr
2160 S First Ave .... Maywood IL 60153 · 888-584-7888

Lutheran Hospital of Indiana
7950 W Jefferson Blvd .... Fort Wayne IN 46804 · 800-444-2001 · 260-435-7001

MacNeal Hospital
3249 S Oak Pk Ave .... Berwyn IL 60402 · 888-622-6325 · 708-783-9100

Maine Medical Ctr (MMC)
22 Bramhall St .... Portland ME 04102 · 877-339-3107 · 207-662-0111

Manatee Memorial Hospital
206 Second St E .... Bradenton FL 34208 · 844-854-9613 · 941-746-5111

Maricopa Medical Ctr
2601 E Roosevelt St .... Phoenix AZ 85008 · 866-749-2876 · 602-344-5011

Marietta Memorial Hospital
401 Matthew St .... Marietta OH 45750 · 800-523-3977 · 740-374-1400

Marin General Hospital
250 Bon Air Rd .... Greenbrae CA 94904 · 888-996-9644 · 415-925-7000

Martha Jefferson Hospital (MJH)
500 Martha Jefferson Dr .... Charlottesville VA 22902 · 888-652-6663 · 434-982-7000

Martin Memorial Health Systems (MMHS)
200 SE Hospital Ave PO Box 9010 .... Stuart FL 34994 · 800-368-3375 · 772-287-5200

Mary Washington Hospital
1001 Sam Perry Blvd .... Fredericksburg VA 22401 · 800-395-2455 · 540-741-1100

Marymount Hospital
12300 McCracken Rd .... Garfield Heights OH 44125 · 800-801-2273 · 216-581-0500

Maui Memorial Hospital
221 Mahalani St .... Wailuku HI 96793 · 800-427-5940 · 808-244-9056

Mayo Clinic Health System Austin
1000 First Dr NW .... Austin MN 55912 · 888-609-4065 · 507-433-7351

Mayo Clinic Health System Southwest Minnesota
1025 Marsh St .... Mankato MN 56001 · 800-327-3721 · 507-625-4031

McLaren Regional Medical Ctr
401 S Ballenger Hwy .... Flint MI 48532 · 800-821-6517 · 810-342-2000

Meadville Medical Ctr (MMC)
751 Liberty St .... Meadville PA 16335 · 800-254-5164 · 814-333-5000

Medcenter One Hospital
300 N Seventh St .... Bismarck ND 58501 · 800-932-8758 · 701-323-6000

Medical College of Georgia Hospital & Clinics
1120 15th St .... Augusta GA 30912 · 800-736-2273 · 706-721-0211

Medical Ctr Enterprise (MCE)
400 N Edwards St .... Enterprise AL 36330 · 800-994-6610 · 334-347-0584

Medical Ctr of Southeastern Oklahoma
1800 University Blvd .... Durant OK 74701 · 888-280-6276 · 580-924-3080

Medical University of South Carolina Medical Ctr
171 Ashley Ave .... Charleston SC 29425 · 800-424-6872 · 843-792-2300

Memorial Health System (MHS)
Central
1400 E Boulder St .... Colorado Springs CO 80909 · 877-422-3648 · 719-365-5000

Memorial Healthcare Ctr
826 W King St .... Owosso MI 48867 · 800-206-8706 · 989-723-5211

Memorial Hermann Memorial City Hospital
921 Gessner Rd .... Houston TX 77024 · 800-526-2121 · 713-242-3000

Memorial Hospital
715 S Taft Ave .... Fremont OH 43420 · 800-971-8203 · 419-332-7321

Memorial Hospital of Rhode Island (MHRI)
111 Brewster St .... Pawtucket RI 02860 · 800-647-4362 · 401-729-2000

Memorial Hospital of South Bend
615 N Michigan St .... South Bend IN 46601 · 800-850-7913 · 574-647-1000

Memorial Hospital of Sweetwater County
1200 College Dr .... Rock Springs WY 82901 · 866-571-0944* · 307-362-3711
*General

Memorial Medical Ctr
1615 Maple Ln .... Ashland WI 54806 · 877-611-1988 · 715-685-5500

Mendocino Coast District Hospital
700 River Dr .... Fort Bragg CA 95437 · 866-767-3224 · 707-961-1234

Mercer County Joint Township Community Hospital
800 W Main St .... Coldwater OH 45828 · 888-844-2341 · 419-678-2341

Mercy 1235 E Cherokee .... Springfield MO 65804 · 800-909-8326 · 417-820-2000

Mercy Hospital
144 State St .... Portland ME 04101 · 800-293-6583 · 207-879-3000

Mercy Hospital & Trauma Ctr
1000 Mineral Pt Ave .... Janesville WI 53548 · 800-756-4147 · 608-756-6000

Mercy Iowa City
500 E Market St .... Iowa City IA 52245 · 800-637-2942 · 319-339-0300

Mercy Medical Ctr
1111 Sixth Ave .... Des Moines IA 50314 · 800-637-2993 · 515-247-3121

Mercy Medical Ctr North Iowa
1000 Fourth St SW .... Mason City IA 50401 · 800-433-3883 · 641-428-7000

Mercy Medical Ctr Redding
2175 Rosaline Ave .... Redding CA 96001 · 800-521-6377 · 530-225-6000

Mercy Memorial Health Ctr (MMHC)
1011 14th Ave NW .... Ardmore OK 73401 · 888-637-2937 · 580-223-5400

Meritus Health
11116 Medical Campus Rd .... Hagerstown MD 21742 · 800-735-2258 · 301-790-8000

Methodist Hospital
1305 N Elm St .... Henderson KY 42420 · 888-318-1498 · 270-827-7700

Methodist Hospital of Southern California
300 W Huntington Dr .... Arcadia CA 91007 · 888-388-2838 · 626-898-8000

Metro Health Hospital
5900 Byron Ctr Ave .... Wyoming MI 49519 · 800-968-0051 · 616-252-7200

MetroHealth Medical Ctr
2500 MetroHealth Dr .... Cleveland OH 44109 · 800-554-5251 · 216-778-7800

Metroplex Hospital
2201 S Clear Creek Rd .... Killeen TX 76549 · 800-926-7664 · 254-526-7523

MetroWest Medical Ctr
115 Lincoln St .... Framingham MA 01702 · 800-357-6060 · 508-383-1000

Miami Valley Hospital
One Wyoming St .... Dayton OH 45409 · 800-544-0630* · 937-208-8000
*All

Mid Coast Hospital
123 Medical Ctr Dr .... Brunswick ME 04011 · 800-994-6610 · 207-729-0181

Middle Tennessee Medical Ctr
1700 Medical Center Pkwy .... Murfreesboro TN 37129 · 800-400-5800* · 615-396-4100
*General

Middlesex Hospital
28 Crescent St .... Middletown CT 06457 · 800-548-2394 · 860-358-6000

Midland Memorial Hospital
2200 W Illinois Ave .... Midland TX 79701 · 800-833-2916 · 432-685-1111

Midwest Regional Medical Ctr
2825 Parklawn Dr .... Midwest City OK 73110 · 877-456-9617 · 405-610-4411

Mille Lacs Health System
200 Elm St N .... Onamia MN 56359 · 877-535-3154 · 320-532-3154

Missouri Baptist Hospital of Sullivan
751 Sappington Bridge Rd .... Sullivan MO 63080 · 866-888-8918 · 573-468-4186

Missouri Baptist Medical Ctr
3015 N Ballas Rd .... Saint Louis MO 63131 · 800-392-0936 · 314-996-5000

Monmouth Medical Ctr
300 Second Ave .... Long Branch NJ 07740 · 888-724-7123 · 732-222-5200

Monongalia General Hospital
1200 JD Anderson Dr .... Morgantown WV 26505 · 800-992-7600 · 304-598-1200

Monroe Clinic Hospital
515 22nd Ave .... Monroe WI 53566 · 800-338-0568 · 608-324-2000

Moore Regional Hospital
155 Memorial Dr PO Box 3000 .... Pinehurst NC 28374 · 866-415-2778 · 910-715-1000

Morris Hospital
150 W High St .... Morris IL 60450 · 877-743-3123 · 815-942-2932

Moses H Cone Memorial Hospital
1200 N Elm St .... Greensboro NC 27401 · 866-391-2734 · 336-832-7000

Mount Carmel West Hospital
793 W State St .... Columbus OH 43222 · 800-346-1009 · 614-234-5000

Mount Nittany Medical Ctr
1800 E Pk Ave .... State College PA 16803 · 866-686-6171 · 814-231-7000

Mount Sinai Hospital Medical Ctr of Chicago
California Ave 15th St .... Chicago IL 60608 · 877-448-7848 · 773-542-2000

Mount Sinai Medical Ctr, The
1 Gustave L Levy Pl .... New York NY 10029 · 800-637-4627 · 212-241-6500

Nacogdoches Medical Ctr
4920 NE Stallings Dr .... Nacogdoches TX 75965 · 866-898-8446 · 936-569-9481

Nashville General Hospital
1818 Albion St .... Nashville TN 37208 · 800-318-2596 · 615-341-4000

New England Baptist Hospital
125 Parker Hill Ave .... Boston MA 02120 · 800-370-6324 · 617-754-5000

New Hanover Regional Medical Ctr
2131 S 17th St .... Wilmington NC 28401 · 877-228-8135 · 910-343-7000

				Toll-Free	Phone
North Central Bronx Hospital 3424 Kossuth Ave	Bronx	NY	10467	**877-207-2134**	718-519-5000
North Fulton Hospital 3000 Hospital Blvd	Roswell	GA	30076	**877-228-3638**	770-751-2500
North Shore Medical Ctr 1100 NW 95th St	Miami	FL	33150	**800-984-3434**	305-835-6000
North Shore University Hospital 300 Community Dr	Manhasset	NY	11030	**888-214-4065**	516-562-0100
North Suburban Medical Ctr (NSMC) 9191 Grant St	Thornton	CO	80229	**877-647-7440**	303-451-7800
Northport Medical Ctr 2700 Hospital Dr	Northport	AL	35476	**866-840-0750**	205-333-4500
Northwest Hospital & Medical Ctr 1550 N 115th St	Seattle	WA	98133	**877-694-4677**	206-364-0500
Northwest Hospital Ctr 5401 Old Ct Rd	Randallstown	MD	21133	**800-876-1175**	410-521-2200
Northwest Texas Hospital 1501 S Coulter	Amarillo	TX	79106	**800-887-1114**	806-354-1000
Norwalk Hospital 34 Maple St	Norwalk	CT	06856	**800-789-4584**	203-852-2000
Norwegian-American Hospital 1044 N Francisco St	Chicago	IL	60622	**877-624-9333**	773-292-8200
Oakwood Annapolis Hospital 33155 Annapolis Rd	Wayne	MI	48184	**800-543-9355**	734-467-4000
Oakwood Heritage Hospital 10000 Telegraph Rd	Taylor	MI	48180	**800-543-9355**	313-295-5000
Oakwood Hospital & Medical Ctr 18101 Oakwood Blvd	Dearborn	MI	48124	**800-543-9355**	313-593-7000
Oakwood Southshore Medical Ctr 5450 Fort St	Trenton	MI	48183	**800-543-9355**	734-671-3800
Ocean Medical Ctr (OMC) 425 Jack Martin Blvd	Brick	NJ	08724	**800-560-9990**	732-840-2200
Ochsner Clinic Foundation Hospital 1514 Jefferson Hwy	New Orleans	LA	70121	**800-343-0269**	504-842-3000
Ochsner Medical Ctr West Bank 2500 Belle Chasse Hwy	Gretna	LA	70056	**800-231-5257**	504-391-5454
Oconomowoc Memorial Hospital 791 Summit Ave	Oconomowoc	WI	53066	**800-242-0313**	262-569-9400
Ogden Regional Medical Ctr 5475 Adams Ave Pkwy	Ogden	UT	84405	**877-870-3745**	801-479-2111
Olympia Medical Ctr 5900 W Olympic Blvd	Los Angeles	CA	90036	**800-874-4325**	310-657-5900
Olympic Medical Ctr 939 Caroline St	Port Angeles	WA	98362	**888-362-6260**	360-417-7000
Orange City Area Health System 1000 Lincoln Cir SE	Orange City	IA	51041	**800-808-6264**	712-737-4984
Orange Coast Memorial Medical Ctr (OCMMC) 9920 Talbert Ave	Fountain Valley	CA	92708	**877-597-4777**	714-378-7000
Orange Regional Medical Ctr 60 Prospect Ave	Middletown	NY	10940	**888-321-6762**	845-343-2424
Oregon Health & Science University Hospital 3181 SW Sam Jackson Pk Rd	Portland	OR	97239	**800-292-4466**	503-494-8311
Orlando Regional Medical Ctr (ORMC) 1414 Kuhl Ave	Orlando	FL	32806	**800-424-6998**	321-841-5111
OSF HealthCare 1100 E Norris Dr	Ottawa	IL	61350	**800-635-1440**	815-433-3100
OSF Saint Anthony Medical Ctr 5666 E State St	Rockford	IL	61108	**800-343-3185**	815-226-2000
OSF Saint Francis Medical Ctr 530 NE Glen Oak Ave	Peoria	IL	61637	**888-627-5673**	309-655-2000
OSF Saint Mary Medical Ctr 3333 N Seminary St	Galesburg	IL	61401	**877-795-0416**	309-344-3161
Ouachita County Medical Ctr (OCMC) PO Box 797	Camden	AR	71711	**877-836-2472**	870-836-1000
Our Lady of Lourdes Medical Ctr 1600 Haddon Ave	Camden	NJ	08103	**888-568-7337**	856-757-3500
Owensboro Medical Health Systems (OMHS) 811 E Parish Ave PO Box 20007	Owensboro	KY	42303	**877-888-6647**	270-688-2000
Palestine Regional Medical Ctr 2900 S Loop 256	Palestine	TX	75801	**800-222-1222**	903-731-1000
Palms West Hospital (PWH) 13001 Southern Blvd	Loxahatchee	FL	33470	**877-549-9337**	561-798-3300
Parkridge East Hospital 941 Spring Creek Rd	Chattanooga	TN	37412	**800-605-1527**	423-894-7870
Parkview Hospital 2200 Randallia Dr	Fort Wayne	IN	46805	**888-737-9311**	260-373-4000
Parkview Medical Ctr 400 W 16th St	Pueblo	CO	81003	**800-543-4046**	719-584-4000
Peace River Regional Medical Ctr 2500 Harbor Blvd	Port Charlotte	FL	33952	**888-941-2495**	941-766-4122
PeaceHealth St Joseph Medical Ctr 2901 Squalicum Pkwy	Bellingham	WA	98225	**800-541-7209**	360-734-5400
Pender Memorial Hospital 507 E Fremont St	Burgaw	NC	28425	**888-468-5474**	910-259-5451
Peninsula Regional Medical Ctr 100 E Carroll St	Salisbury	MD	21801	**800-543-7780**	410-546-6400
Penn Presbyterian Medical Ctr (PPMC) 39th & Market Sts	Philadelphia	PA	19104	**800-789-7366**	215-662-8000
Pennsylvania Hospital 800 Spruce St	Philadelphia	PA	19107	**800-789-7366**	215-829-3000
Phoebe Putney Memorial Hospital 417 W Third Ave	Albany	GA	31702	**877-312-1167**	229-312-1000
Piedmont Medical Ctr 222 S Herlong Ave	Rock Hill	SC	29732	**800-222-4218**	803-329-1234
Pinnacle Health Hospital at Community General 4300 Londonderry Rd	Harrisburg	PA	17109	**888-782-5678**	717-652-3000
Placentia-Linda Hospital 1301 N Rose Dr	Placentia	CA	92870	**888-754-9729**	714-993-2000
Plains Regional Medical Ctr 2100 N ML King Blvd	Clovis	NM	88101	**800-923-6980**	505-769-2141
POH Regional Medical Ctr 50 N Perry St	Pontiac	MI	48342	**888-327-0671**	248-338-5000
Ponca City Medical Ctr 1900 N 14th St	Ponca City	OK	74601	**800-222-1222**	580-765-3321
Poplar Bluff Regional Medical Ctr 2620 N Westwood Blvd	Poplar Bluff	MO	63901	**800-327-0275**	573-785-7721
Poplar Bluff Regional Medical Ctr South Campus 621 WPine Blvd	Poplar Bluff	MO	63901	**800-327-0275**	573-686-4111
Port Huron Hospital (PHH) 1221 Pine Grove Ave	Port Huron	MI	48060	**888-327-0671**	810-987-5000
Portsmouth Regional Hospital 333 Borthwick Ave	Portsmouth	NH	03801	**800-685-8282**	603-436-5110
Poudre Valley Hospital 1024 S Lemay Ave	Fort Collins	CO	80524	**800-994-6610**	970-495-7000
Prairie Lakes Hospital & Care Ctr 401 Ninth Ave NW	Watertown	SD	57201	**877-917-7547**	605-882-7000
Pratt Regional Medical Ctr Corp 200 Commodore St	Pratt	KS	67124	**877-572-2787**	620-672-7451
Presbyterian Hospital 1100 Central Ave SE	Albuquerque	NM	87106	**888-977-2333**	505-841-1234
Presbyterian Kaseman Hospital 8300 Constitution Ave NE	Albuquerque	NM	87110	**800-432-4600**	505-291-2000
Promise Regional Medical Ctr-Hutchinson 1701 E 23rd Ave	Hutchinson	KS	67502	**800-267-6891**	620-665-2000
Provena Covenant Medical Ctr 1400 W Pk St	Urbana	IL	61801	**800-245-6697**	217-337-2000
Provena Saint Mary's Hospital 500 W Ct St	Kankakee	IL	60901	**888-740-4111**	815-937-2400
Providence Centralia Hospital 914 S Scheuber Rd *Help Line	Centralia	WA	98531	**877-736-2803***	360-736-2803
Providence Hospitals 2435 Forest Dr	Columbia	SC	29204	**877-256-5381**	803-256-5300
Providence Medford Medical Ctr 1111 Crater Lk Ave	Medford	OR	97504	**877-541-0588**	541-732-5000
Providence Medical Ctr 8929 Parallel Pkwy	Kansas City	KS	66112	**800-281-7777**	913-596-4000
Providence Portland Medical Ctr 4805 NE Glisan St	Portland	OR	97213	**800-833-8899**	503-215-1111
Providence Sacred Heart Medical Ctr 101 W Eigth Ave	Spokane	WA	99204	**800-442-8534**	509-474-3170
Providence Saint Peter Hospital (PSPH) 413 Lilly Rd NE	Olympia	WA	98506	**888-492-9480**	360-491-9480
Providence Saint Vincent Medical Ctr 9205 SW Barnes Rd Ste 20	Portland	OR	97225	**800-677-6752**	503-216-2401
Providence St Mary Medical Ctr 401 W Poplar St PO Box 1477	Walla Walla	WA	99362	**877-215-7833**	509-525-3320
Qualis Health PO Box 33400	Seattle	WA	98133	**800-949-7536**	206-364-9700
Queens Hospital Ctr 82-68 164th St	Jamaica	NY	11432	**888-692-6116**	718-883-3000
Raulerson Hospital 1796 Hwy 441 N	Okeechobee	FL	34972	**800-449-8642**	863-763-2151
Redlands Community Hospital Foundation PO Box 3391	Redlands	CA	92373	**888-397-4999**	909-335-5500
Regional Hospital of Jackson 367 Hospital Blvd	Jackson	TN	38305	**800-454-9970**	731-661-2000
Regional Medical Ctr, The 3000 St Matthews Rd	Orangeburg	SC	29118	**800-476-3377**	803-395-2200
Reston Hospital Ctr 1850 Town Ctr Pkwy *General	Reston	VA	20190	**888-327-8882***	703-689-9000
Retreat Hospital 2621 Grove Ave	Richmond	VA	23220	**800-888-3627**	804-254-5100
Richland Hospital Inc, The 333 E Second St	Richland Center	WI	53581	**888-467-7485**	608-647-6321
Riddle Memorial Hospital 1068 W Baltimore Pike	Media	PA	19063	**866-225-5654**	484-227-9400
Rideout Memorial Hospital 726 Fourth St	Marysville	CA	95901	**888-923-3800**	530-749-4300
Ridgeview Medical Ctr (RMC) 500 S Maple St	Waconia	MN	55387	**800-967-4620**	952-442-2191
River Oaks Hospital 1525 River Oaks Rd W	New Orleans	LA	70123	**800-366-1740**	504-734-1740
River Parishes Hospital 500 Rue De Sante	Laplace	LA	70068	**800-231-5275**	985-652-7000
River Region West Campus 2100 Highway 61 North/1111 N Frontage Road	Vicksburg	MS	39183	**800-843-2131**	601-883-5000
Riverside Methodist Hospital 3535 Olentangy River Rd	Columbus	OH	43214	**800-837-7555**	614-566-5000
Riverton Memorial Hospital LLC 2100 W Sunset Dr	Riverton	WY	82501	**888-982-9144**	307-856-4161
Riverview Hospital 395 Westfield Rd	Noblesville	IN	46060	**800-523-6001**	317-773-0760
Robert J Dole VA Medical Center 5500 E Kellogg St	Wichita	KS	67218	**888-878-6881**	316-685-2221
Robert Packer Hospital One Guthrie Sq	Sayre	PA	18840	**888-448-8474**	570-888-6666
Robert Wood Johnson University Hospital 1 Robert Wood Johnson Pl	New Brunswick	NJ	08901	**888-637-9584**	732-828-3000
Rochester General Health System (RGHS) 1425 Portland Ave	Rochester	NY	14621	**877-922-5465**	585-922-4000
Rockingham Memorial Hospital (RMH) 2010 Health Campus Dr	Harrisonburg	VA	22801	**800-736-8272**	540-689-1000
Rose Medical Ctr 4567 E Ninth Ave	Denver	CO	80220	**866-746-4282**	303-320-2121
Rowan Regional Medical Ctr (RRMC) 612 Mocksville Ave	Salisbury	NC	28144	**888-844-0080**	704-210-5000
Rush-Copley Medical Ctr (RCMC) 2000 Ogden Ave	Aurora	IL	60504	**866-426-7539**	630-978-6200
Sacred Heart HealthCare System 421 Chew St	Allentown	PA	18102	**800-994-6610**	610-776-4500
Sacred Heart Hospital 900 W Clairemont Ave	Eau Claire	WI	54701	**888-445-4554**	715-717-4121
Sacred Heart Hospital of Pensacola 5151 N Ninth Ave	Pensacola	FL	32504	**800-874-1026**	850-416-7000
Sacred Heart Medical Ctr 1255 Hilyard St	Eugene	OR	97401	**800-288-7444**	541-686-7300
Saint Agnes HealthCare 900 S Caton Ave	Baltimore	MD	21229	**800-875-8750**	410-368-6000
Saint Alexius Hospital *Broadway Campus* 3933 S Broadway	Saint Louis	MO	63118	**800-245-1431**	314-865-7000
Saint Alphonsus Regional Medical Ctr 1055 N Curtis Rd	Boise	ID	83706	**877-401-3627**	208-367-2121

Name / Address	City	State	ZIP	Toll-Free	Phone
Saint Anthony Hospital 1000 N Lee St	Oklahoma City	OK	73101	**800-227-6964**	405-272-7000
Saint Barnabas Medical Ctr 94 Old Short Hills Rd	West Orange	NJ	07052	**888-724-7123**	973-322-5000
Saint Charles Mercy Hospital 2600 Navarre Ave	Oregon	OH	43616	**888-987-6372**	419-696-7200
Saint Cloud Hospital 1406 Sixth Ave	Saint Cloud	MN	56303	**800-835-6652**	320-251-2700
Saint Elizabeth Hospital 1506 S Oneida St	Appleton	WI	54915	**800-223-7332**	920-738-2000
Saint Francis Health Ctr 1700 SW Seventh St	Topeka	KS	66606	**855-578-3726**	785-295-8000
Saint Francis Hospital & Medical Ctr 114 Woodland St	Hartford	CT	06105	**800-993-4312**	860-714-4000
Saint Francis Medical Ctr 601 Hamilton Ave	Trenton	NJ	08629	**888-216-3293**	609-599-5000
Saint John's Hospital 1575 Beam Ave	Maplewood	MN	55109	**888-477-4221**	651-232-7000
Saint Joseph Hospital 700 Broadway	Fort Wayne	IN	46802	**800-258-0974**	260-425-3000
Saint Joseph Mercy Ann Arbor 5301 McAuley Dr	Ypsilanti	MI	48197	**866-522-8268**	734-712-3456
Saint Joseph Mercy Oakland 44405 Woodward Ave	Pontiac	MI	48341	**800-396-1313**	248-858-3000
Saint Joseph's Hospital 2661 County Hwy I	Chippewa Falls	WI	54729	**877-723-1811**	715-723-1811
Saint Joseph's Hospital Health Ctr 301 Prospect Ave	Syracuse	NY	13203	**888-785-6371**	315-448-5111
Saint Luke's Hospital & Regional Trauma Ctr 915 E First St	Duluth	MN	55805	**866-261-5915**	218-249-5555
Saint Luke's Hospital of New Bedford 101 Page St	New Bedford	MA	02740	**800-497-1727**	508-997-1515
Saint Luke's Regional Medical Ctr 2720 Stone Pk Blvd	Sioux City	IA	51104	**800-352-4660**	712-279-3500
Saint Mary Mercy Hospital 36475 Five-Mile Rd	Livonia	MI	48154	**800-464-7492**	734-655-4800
Saint Mary's Health Care System 1230 Baxter St	Athens	GA	30606	**800-233-7864**	706-389-3000
Saint Mary's Health Ctr 6420 Clayton Rd	Richmond Heights	MO	63117	**877-783-4193**	314-768-8000
Saint Mary's Hospital 2251 N Shore Dr *Cust Svc	Rhinelander	WI	54501	**800-578-0840***	715-361-2000
Saint Mary's Hospital & Regional Medical Ctr 2635 N Seventh St	Grand Junction	CO	81502	**800-458-3888**	
Saint Mary's Hospital Medical Ctr 1726 Shawano Ave	Green Bay	WI	54303	**800-666-5606**	920-498-4200
Saint Mary-Corwin Medical Ctr 1008 Minnequa Ave	Pueblo	CO	81004	**800-228-4039**	719-557-4000
Saint Rita's Medical Ctr (SRMC) 730 W Market St	Lima	OH	45801	**800-232-7762**	419-227-3361
Saint Thomas Hospital 4220 HaRding Rd	Nashville	TN	37205	**800-400-5800**	615-222-2111
Saint Vincent Charity Hospital (SVCH) 2351 E 22nd St	Cleveland	OH	44115	**800-750-0750**	216-861-6200
Saint Vincent Hospital 835 S Van Buren St	Green Bay	WI	54301	**800-236-3030**	920-433-0111
Saint Vincent Hospital-Worcester Medical Ctr 123 Summer St	Worcester	MA	01608	**877-633-2368**	508-363-5000
Saint Vincent's Medical Ctr 2800 Main St	Bridgeport	CT	06606	**877-255-7847**	203-576-6000
Salem Hospital 665 Winter St SE	Salem	OR	97301	**800-876-1718**	
Salinas Valley Memorial Hospital (SVMH) 450 E Romie Ln	Salinas	CA	93901	**800-722-4673**	831-757-4333
Samaritan Medical Ctr 830 Washington St	Watertown	NY	13601	**877-888-6138**	315-785-4000
San Francisco General Hospital Medical Ctr 1001 Potrero Ave Ste 1E21	San Francisco	CA	94110	**800-723-7140**	415-206-8426
Sarah Bush Lincoln Health Ctr (SBLHC) 1000 Health Ctr Dr PO Box 372	Mattoon	IL	61938	**800-345-3191**	217-258-2525
Sarasota Memorial Hospital 1700 S Tamiami Trl	Sarasota	FL	34239	**800-764-8255**	941-917-9000
Scheurer Hospital Inc 170 N Caseville Rd	Pigeon	MI	48755	**800-208-9060**	989-453-3223
Schneck Medical Ctr 411 W Tipton St	Seymour	IN	47274	**800-234-9222**	812-522-2349
Scott & White Memorial Hospital 2401 S 31st St	Temple	TX	76508	**800-792-3710**	254-724-2111
Scripps Green Hospital 10666 N Torrey Pines Rd	La Jolla	CA	92037	**800-727-4777**	858-455-9100
Sentara Careplex Hospital 3000 Colliseum Dr	Hampton	VA	23666	**800-736-8272**	757-736-1000
Sentara Obici Hospital 2800 Godwin Blvd	Suffolk	VA	23434	**800-736-8272**	757-934-4000
Sentara Virginia Beach General Hospital 1060 First Colonial Rd	Virginia Beach	VA	23454	**800-736-8272**	757-395-8000
Seton Medical Ctr 1900 Sullivan Ave	Daly City	CA	94015	**800-371-2176**	650-992-4000
Shands Hospital at the University of Florida 1600 SW Archer Rd	Gainesville	FL	32610	**855-483-7546**	352-265-0111
Shannon Medical Ctr (SMC) 120 E Harris Ave	San Angelo	TX	76903	**888-657-5202**	325-653-6741
Sharp Grossmont Hospital (SGH) 5555 Grossmont Ctr Dr	La Mesa	CA	91942	**800-827-4277**	619-740-6000
Shore Memorial Hospital 9507 Hospital Ave PO Box 17	Nassawadox	VA	23413	**800-834-7035**	757-414-8000
Sierra Medical Ctr 1625 Medical Ctr Dr	El Paso	TX	79902	**800-994-6610**	915-747-4000
Sierra Vista Regional Medical Ctr (SVRMC) 1010 Murray Ave	San Luis Obispo	CA	93405	**866-904-6871**	805-546-7600
Sinai Grace Hospital 6071 W Outer Dr	Detroit	MI	48235	**888-362-2500**	313-966-3300
Sinai Hospital of Baltimore 2401 W Belvedere Ave	Baltimore	MD	21215	**800-444-8233**	410-601-9000
Skaggs Community Health Ctr 545 Branson Landing Blvd PO Box 650	Branson	MO	65615	**800-994-6610**	417-335-7000
Skyline Medical Ctr 3441 Dickerson Pike	Nashville	TN	37207	**800-242-5662**	615-769-2000
Soldiers + Sailors Memorial Hospital 32-36 Central Ave	Wellsboro	PA	16901	**800-808-5287**	570-723-7764
Sonora Regional Medical Ctr (SRMC) 1000 Greenly Rd *Compliance	Sonora	CA	95370	**877-336-3566***	209-536-5000
South Nassau Communities Hospital 1 Healthy Way	Oceanside	NY	11572	**877-768-8462**	516-632-3000
South Shore Hospital 55 Fogg Rd	South Weymouth	MA	02190	**800-439-2370**	781-340-8000
Southeast Alabama Medical Ctr 1108 Ross Clark Cir	Dothan	AL	36301	**800-507-7262**	334-793-8111
Southeast Georgia Health System Brunswick Campus 2415 Parkwood Dr	Brunswick	GA	31520	**844-882-7227**	912-466-7000
Southeast Missouri Hospital (SMH) 1701 Lacey St	Cape Girardeau	MO	63701	**800-800-5123**	573-334-4822
Southern Ocean Medical Ctr 1140 Rt 72 W	Manahawkin	NJ	08050	**888-864-4203**	609-978-8900
Southwest General Hospital (SGH) 7400 Barlite Blvd	San Antonio	TX	78224	**877-215-9355**	210-921-2000
Southwestern Medical Ctr (SWMC) 5602 SW Lee Blvd	Lawton	OK	73505	**877-707-1780**	580-531-4700
Southwestern Vermont Medical Ctr 100 Hospital Dr	Bennington	VT	05201	**800-543-1624**	802-442-6361
Spalding Regional Medical Ctr 601 S Eigth St	Griffin	GA	30224	**866-717-5826**	770-228-2721
Sparrow Health System 1215 E Michigan Ave	Lansing	MI	48912	**800-772-7769**	517-364-1000
Spartanburg Regional Medical Ctr (SRMC) 101 E Wood St	Spartanburg	SC	29303	**800-318-2596**	864-560-6000
Spectrum Health Blodgett Campus 100 Michigan St NE	Grand Rapids	MI	49503	**866-989-7999**	616-774-7444
SSM Health 620 E Monroe St	Mexico	MO	65265	**844-776-9355**	573-582-5000
St Agnes Hospital 430 E Div St	Fond du Lac	WI	54935	**800-922-3400**	920-929-2300
St Alexius Medical Ctr 900 E Broadway Ave	Bismarck	ND	58501	**877-530-5550**	701-530-7755
St John Providence Health System 28000 Dequindre	Warren	MI	48092	**866-501-3627**	
St Petersburg General Hospital 6500 38th Ave N	Saint Petersburg	FL	33710	**800-733-0610**	727-384-1414
Stonewall Jackson Memorial Hospital (SJMH) 230 Hospital Plaza	Weston	WV	26452	**866-637-0471**	304-269-8000
Stormont-Vail Regional Health Ctr 1500 SW Tenth Ave	Topeka	KS	66604	**800-432-2951**	785-354-6000
Stoughton Hospital 900 Ridge St	Stoughton	WI	53589	**888-816-3831**	608-873-6611
Straub Clinic & Hospital 888 S King St	Honolulu	HI	96813	**800-232-9491**	808-522-4000
Strong Memorial Hospital *University of Rochester Medical Ctr* 601 Elmwood Ave	Rochester	NY	14642	**800-999-6673**	585-275-2100
Summa Barberton Hospital 155 Fifth St NE	Barberton	OH	44203	**888-905-6071**	330-615-3000
Sumner Regional Medical Ctr 555 Hartsville Pike	Gallatin	TN	37066	**888-863-6198**	615-328-8888
Sutter Auburn Faith Community Hospital (SAFH) 11815 Education St	Auburn	CA	95602	**800-478-8837**	530-888-4500
Sutter Medical Ctr of Santa Rosa 3325 Chanate Rd	Santa Rosa	CA	95404	**800-651-5111**	707-576-4006
SwedishAmerican Hospital 1401 E State St	Rockford	IL	61104	**800-322-4724**	815-968-4400
Tacoma General Hospital 315 MLK Jr Way	Tacoma	WA	98405	**800-552-1419**	253-403-1000
Terre Haute Regional Hospital (THRH) 3901 S Seventh St	Terre Haute	IN	47802	**866-270-2311**	812-232-0021
Terrebonne General Medical Ctr (TGMC) 8166 Main St	Houma	LA	70360	**888-850-6270**	985-873-4141
Texas Healthcare PLLC 2821 Lackland Rd Ste 300	Fort Worth	TX	76116	**800-844-8850**	817-378-3640
Theda Clark Medical Ctr 130 Second St	Neenah	WI	54956	**800-236-3122**	920-729-3100
Thibodaux Regional Medical Ctr (TRMC) 602 N Acadia Rd	Thibodaux	LA	70301	**800-822-8442**	985-447-5500
Thomas Hospital 750 Morphy Ave	Fairhope	AL	36532	**800-422-2027**	251-928-2375
Thomas Jefferson University Hospital 111 S 11th St	Philadelphia	PA	19107	**800-533-3669**	215-955-6000
Thomasville Medical Ctr 207 Old Lexington Rd	Thomasville	NC	27360	**888-844-0080**	336-472-2000
Tift Regional Medical Ctr 1641 Madison Ave	Tifton	GA	31794	**800-648-1935**	229-382-7120
TJ Samson Community Hospital 1301 N Race St	Glasgow	KY	42141	**800-651-5635**	270-651-4444
Torrance Memorial Medical Ctr 3330 Lomita Blvd	Torrance	CA	90505	**866-843-2572**	310-325-9110
Triangle Orthopedic Assoc PA 120 William Penn Plz	Durham	NC	27704	**800-359-3053**	919-220-5255
Trident Medical Ctr 9330 Medical Plz Dr	Charleston	SC	29406	**866-492-9085**	843-797-7000
Trinity Hospital Saint Joseph's One W Burdick Expy	Minot	ND	58701	**800-247-1316**	701-857-5000
Trinity Medical Ctr West 4000 Johnson Rd	Steubenville	OH	43952	**877-271-4176**	740-264-8000
Tristar Southern Hills Medical Ctr 391 Wallace Rd	Nashville	TN	37211	**800-242-5662**	615-781-4000
Tucson Medical Ctr 5301 E Grant Rd	Tucson	AZ	85712	**800-526-5353**	520-327-5461
Tufts Medical Ctr (TMC) 800 Washington St	Boston	MA	02111	**866-220-3699**	617-636-5000
Tulane Medical Ctr (TMC) 1415 Tulane Ave	New Orleans	LA	70112	**800-588-5800**	504-588-5108
Twin County Regional Hospital 200 Hospital Dr	Galax	VA	24333	**800-295-3342**	276-236-8181
UAB Medical West 995 Ninth Ave SW	Bessemer	AL	35022	**800-994-6610**	205-481-7000

				Toll-Free	Phone
UAMS Medical Ctr					
4301 W Markham St	Little Rock	AR	72205	**877-467-6560**	501-686-7000
UC Irvine Healthcare					
101 the City Dr S	Orange	CA	92868	**877-824-3627**	714-456-7890
UH Parma Medical Center (PCGH)					
7007 Powers Blvd	Parma	OH	44129	**855-292-4292**	440-743-3000
United Hospital					
333 N Smith Ave	Saint Paul	MN	55102	**800-869-1320**	651-241-8000
University Health Care System					
1350 Walton Way	Augusta	GA	30901	**866-591-2502**	706-722-9011
University Hospital					
4502 Medical Dr	San Antonio	TX	78229	**866-588-3301**	210-358-4000
University Hospital SUNY Upstate Medical University					
750 E Adams St	Syracuse	NY	13210	**877-464-5540**	315-464-5540
University Hospitals of Cleveland					
11100 Euclid Ave	Cleveland	OH	44106	**866-844-2273**	216-844-1000
University Medical Ctr at Princeton (UMCP)					
253 Witherspoon St	Princeton	NJ	08540	**877-932-8935**	609-497-4304
University of California San Diego Medical Ctr					
200 W Arbor Dr	San Diego	CA	92103	**800-926-8273**	619-543-6222
University of Chicago Medical Ctr					
5841 S Maryland Ave	Chicago	IL	60637	**888-824-0200**	773-702-1000
University of Connecticut Health Ctr					
John Dempsey Hospital					
263 Farmington Ave	Farmington	CT	06030	**800-535-6232**	860-679-2000
University of Illinois Medical Ctr					
1740 W Taylor St	Chicago	IL	60612	**866-600-2273**	312-996-3900
University of Louisville Hospital					
530 S Jackson St	Louisville	KY	40202	**800-891-0947**	502-562-3000
University of Maryland Medical Ctr					
22 S Greene St	Baltimore	MD	21201	**800-492-5538**	410-328-8667
University of Minnesota Medical Ctr Fairview					
Riverside Campus					
2450 Riverside Ave	Minneapolis	MN	55454	**888-702-4073**	612-273-3000
University of Minnesota Medical Ctr Fairview - University Campus					
500 Harvard St	Minneapolis	MN	55455	**800-688-5252**	612-273-3000
University of Nebraska Medical Ctr					
42nd and Emile	Omaha	NE	68198	**800-642-1095**	402-559-4000
University of Pittsburgh Medical Ctr (UPMC)					
Horizon 110 N Main St	Greenville	PA	16125	**888-447-1122**	724-588-2100
South Side 2000 Mary St	Pittsburgh	PA	15203	**800-533-8762**	412-488-5550
University of Texas Medical Branch Hospitals					
301 University Blvd	Galveston	TX	77555	**800-201-0527**	409-772-1011
University of Toledo Medical Center, The					
3000 Arlington Ave	Toledo	OH	43614	**800-321-8383**	419-383-4000
University of Vermont Medical Center, The (FAHC)					
111 Colchester Ave	Burlington	VT	05401	**800-358-1144**	802-847-0000
University of Virginia Health System					
1215 Lee St	Charlottesville	VA	22908	**800-251-3627**	434-924-0211
University of Wisconsin Hospital & Clinics					
600 Highland Ave	Madison	WI	53792	**800-323-8942**	608-263-6400
Upper Valley Medical Ctr (UVMC)					
3130 N County Rd 25-A	Troy	OH	45373	**866-608-3463**	937-440-4000
UVA Culpeper Hospital					
501 Sunset Ln	Culpeper	VA	22701	**866-608-4749**	540-829-4100
Valdese General Hospital (VGH)					
720 Malcolm Blvd Ste 200	Valdese	NC	28690	**800-994-6610**	828-874-2251
Valley Health System					
223 N Van Dien Ave	Ridgewood	NJ	07450	**800-825-5391**	201-447-8000
Valley Medical Ctr					
400 S 43rd St	Renton	WA	98055	**855-923-4633**	425-228-3450
Valley Regional Medical Ctr					
100-A E Alton Gloor Blvd	Brownsville	TX	78526	**877-422-2030**	956-350-7000
Vanderbilt University Medical Ctr					
1215 21st Ave S	Nashville	TN	37232	**877-936-8422**	615-322-5000
Vassar Bros Medical Ctr					
45 Reade Pl	Poughkeepsie	NY	12601	**877-729-2444**	845-454-8500
Vaughan Regional Medical Ctr					
1015 Medical Ctr Pkwy	Selma	AL	36701	**800-994-6610**	334-418-4100
Ventura County Medical Center					
3291 Loma Vista Rd	Ventura	CA	93003	**800-369-7437**	805-652-6000
Walker Baptist Medical Ctr					
3400 Hwy 78 E	Jasper	AL	35501	**877-474-4243**	205-387-4000
Wallace Thomson Hospital					
322 W S St	Union	SC	29379	**800-277-5633***	864-301-2000
*General					
Waukesha Memorial Hospital					
725 American Ave	Waukesha	WI	53188	**800-326-2011**	262-928-1000
Weirton Medical Ctr					
601 Colliers Way	Weirton	WV	26062	**800-994-6610**	304-797-6000
Wentworth-Douglass Hospital					
789 Central Ave	Dover	NH	03820	**877-201-7100**	603-742-5252
Wesley Long Community Hospital					
501 N Elam Ave	Greensboro	NC	27403	**866-391-2734**	336-832-1000
Wesley Medical Ctr					
5001 Hardy St	Hattiesburg	MS	39402	**800-622-8892**	601-268-8000
West Suburban Hospital Medical Ctr					
Three Erie Ct	Oak Park	IL	60302	**866-938-7256**	708-383-6200
West Valley Medical Ctr					
1717 Arlington Ave	Caldwell	ID	83605	**866-270-2311**	208-459-4641
Westerly Hospital					
25 Wells St	Westerly	RI	02891	**800-933-5960**	401-596-6000
Wheaton Franciscan Healthcare					
All Saints 3801 Spring St	Racine	WI	53405	**877-304-6332**	262-687-4011
White County Medical Ctr					
3214 E Race Ave	Searcy	AR	72143	**888-562-7520**	501-268-6121
Whittier Hospital Medical Ctr					
9080 Colima Rd	Whittier	CA	90605	**800-613-4291**	562-945-3561
Wilcox Memorial Hospital (WMH)					
3-3420 Kuhio Hwy	Lihue	HI	96766	**877-709-9355**	808-245-1100
Williamson ARH Hospital					
260 Hospital Dr	South Williamson	KY	41503	**800-283-9375***	606-237-1700
*General					
Wilson Memorial Hospital					
915 W Michigan St	Sidney	OH	45365	**800-589-9641**	937-498-2311
Woodland Heights Medical Ctr					
505 S John Redditt Dr	Lufkin	TX	75904	**800-222-1222**	936-634-8311

				Toll-Free	Phone
Wuesthoff Medical Ctr Rockledge					
110 Longwood Ave	Rockledge	FL	32955	**800-999-6673**	321-636-2211
Wyoming Medical Ctr					
1233 E Second St	Casper	WY	82601	**800-822-7201**	307-577-7201
Yavapai Regional Medical Ctr					
1003 Willow Creek Rd	Prescott	AZ	86301	**877-976-9762**	928-445-2700

373-5 Psychiatric Hospitals

Listings here include state psychiatric facilities as well as private psychiatric hospitals.

				Toll-Free	Phone
Adventist Behavioral Health					
14901 Broschart Rd	Rockville	MD	20850	**800-204-8600**	301-251-4500
Arizona State Hospital					
2500 E Van Buren St	Phoenix	AZ	85008	**877-588-5163**	602-244-1331
Atascadero State Hospital					
10333 S Camino Real	Atascadero	CA	93422	**844-210-6207**	805-468-2000
Aurora Las Encinas Hospital					
2900 E Del Mar Blvd	Pasadena	CA	91107	**800-792-2345**	626-795-9901
Austin State Hospital					
4110 Guadalupe St	Austin	TX	78751	**866-407-3773**	512-452-0381
Banner Behavioral Health Hospital					
7575 E Earll Dr	Scottsdale	AZ	85251	**800-254-4357**	480-941-7500
Brentwood A Behavioral Health Co					
1006 Highland Ave	Shreveport	LA	71101	**877-678-7500**	318-678-7500
Bronx Psychiatric Ctr					
1500 Waters Pl	Bronx	NY	10461	**800-597-8481**	718-931-0600
BryLin Hospitals					
1263 Delaware Ave	Buffalo	NY	14209	**800-727-9546**	716-886-8200
Buffalo Psychiatric Ctr					
400 Forest Ave	Buffalo	NY	14213	**800-597-8481**	716-885-2261
Carrier Clinic					
252 County Rd 601	Belle Mead	NJ	08502	**800-933-3579**	908-281-1000
Catawba Hospital					
5525 Catawba Hospital Dr	Catawba	VA	24070	**800-451-5544**	540-375-4200
Cedar Springs Behavioral Health System					
2135 Southgate Rd	Colorado Springs	CO	80906	**800-888-1088**	719-633-4114
Central Louisiana State Hospital					
242 W Shamrock St	Pineville	LA	71360	**866-666-8335**	318-484-6200
Central Washington Hospital					
1201 S Miller St	Wenatchee	WA	98801	**800-365-6428**	509-662-1511
Chester Mental Health Ctr					
1315 Lehman Dr	Chester	IL	62233	**800-843-6154**	618-826-4571
Chicago Lakeshore Hospital					
4840 N Marine Dr	Chicago	IL	60640	**800-888-0560***	773-878-9700
*Cust Svc					
Clifton T Perkins Hospital Ctr					
8450 Dorsey Run Rd	Jessup	MD	20794	**877-463-3464**	410-724-3000
College Hospital					
10802 College Pl	Cerritos	CA	90703	**800-352-3301**	562-924-9581
College Hospital Costa Mesa					
301 Victoria St	Costa Mesa	CA	92627	**800-773-8001**	949-642-2734
Creedmoor Psychiatric Ctr					
79-25 Winchester Blvd	Queens Village	NY	11427	**800-597-8481**	718-464-7500
Del Amo Hospital					
23700 Camino Del Sol	Torrance	CA	90505	**800-533-5266**	310-530-1151
Delaware Psychiatric Ctr					
1901 N Dupont Hwy Main Bldg	New Castle	DE	19720	**800-652-2929**	302-255-9399
Eastern State Hospital (ESH)					
4601 Ironbound Rd	Williamsburg	VA	23188	**800-994-6610**	757-253-5161
Elmira Psychiatric Ctr					
100 Washington St	Elmira	NY	14901	**800-597-8481**	607-737-4711
Fair Oaks Hospital					
5352 Linton Blvd	Delray Beach	FL	33484	**866-904-6871**	561-498-4440
Fairfax Hospital					
10200 NE 132nd St	Kirkland	WA	98034	**800-435-7221**	425-821-2000
Fairmount Behavioral Health System					
561 Fairthorne Ave	Philadelphia	PA	19128	**800-235-0200**	215-487-4000
Fort Lauderdale Hospital					
1601 E Las Olas Blvd	Fort Lauderdale	FL	33301	**800-585-7527**	954-463-4321
Four Winds Hospital					
800 Cross River Rd	Katonah	NY	10536	**800-528-6624**	914-763-8151
Friends Hospital					
4641 Roosevelt Blvd	Philadelphia	PA	19124	**800-889-0548**	215-831-4600
Georgia Regional Hospital at Savannah					
1915 Eisenhower Dr	Savannah	GA	31406	**800-436-7442**	912-356-2011
Green Oaks Hospital					
7808 Clodus Fields Dr	Dallas	TX	75251	**800-866-6554**	972-991-9504
Griffin Memorial Hospital					
900 E Main St	Norman	OK	73071	**800-955-3468***	405-321-4880
*General					
Hamilton Ctr Inc					
PO Box 4323	Terre Haute	IN	47804	**800-742-0787**	812-231-8323
Hartgrove Hospital					
5730 W Roosevelt Rd	Chicago	IL	60644	**800-478-4783**	773-722-3113
Havenwyck Hospital					
1525 University Dr	Auburn Hills	MI	48326	**800-401-2727**	248-373-9200
Hill Crest Behavioral Health Services					
6869 Fifth Ave S	Birmingham	AL	35212	**800-292-8553**	205-833-9000
Holly Hill Hospital					
3019 Falstaff Rd	Raleigh	NC	27610	**800-447-1800**	919-250-7000
Horsham Clinic					
722 E Butler Pk	Ambler	PA	19002	**800-237-4447**	215-643-7800
Jewish Hospital & St Mary's HealthCare					
2020 Newburg Rd	Louisville	KY	40205	**800-451-3637**	502-451-3330
Kerrville State Hospital					
721 Thompson Dr	Kerrville	TX	78028	**888-963-7111**	830-896-2211
Lakeside Behavioral Health System					
2911 Brunswick Rd	Memphis	TN	38133	**800-232-5253**	901-377-4700
Langley Porter Psychiatric Institute					
401 Parnassus Ave	San Francisco	CA	94143	**800-723-7140**	415-476-7000
Meadows Psychiatric Ctr					
132 The Meadows Dr	Centre Hall	PA	16828	**800-641-7529**	814-364-2161
Memorial Hermann Prevention & Recovery Ctr (MHPARC)					
3043 Gessner	Houston	TX	77080	**800-464-7272**	713-939-7272
Menninger Clinic					
2801 Gessner Dr PO Box 809045	Houston	TX	77080	**800-351-9058**	713-275-5000

				Toll-Free	Phone
Middle Tennessee Mental Health Institute 221 Stewarts Ferry Pike	Nashville	TN	37214	**800-770-8277**	615-902-7400
Mohawk Valley Psychiatric Ctr 1400 Noyes St	Utica	NY	13502	**800-597-8481**	315-738-3800
Napa State Hospital 2100 Napa-Vallejo Hwy	Napa	CA	94558	**866-762-0972**	707-253-5000
New Mexico Behavioral Health Institute 3695 Hot Springs Blvd	Las Vegas	NM	87701	**800-446-5970**	505-454-2100
North Dakota State Hospital 2605 Cir Dr	Jamestown	ND	58401	**888-862-7342**	701-253-3650
Northwest Missouri Psychiatric Rehabilitation Ctr 3505 Frederick Ave	Saint Joseph	MO	64506	**800-273-8255**	816-387-2300
Pembroke Hospital 199 Oak St	Pembroke	MA	02359	**800-222-2237**	781-829-7000
Peninsula Hospital 2347 Jones Bend Rd	Louisville	TN	37777	**800-526-8215**	865-970-9800
Pilgrim Psychiatric Ctr 998 Crooked Hill Rd	West Brentwood	NY	11717	**800-597-8481**	631-761-3500
Pine Rest Christian Mental Health Services 300 68th St SE PO Box 165	Grand Rapids	MI	49501	**800-678-5500**	616-455-5000
Poplar Springs Hospital 350 Poplar Dr PO Box 3060	Petersburg	VA	23805	**866-546-2229**	804-733-6874
Psychiatric Institute of Washington 4228 Wisconsin Ave NW	Washington	DC	20016	**800-369-2273**	202-885-5600
Ridge Behavioral Health System 3050 Rio Dosa Dr	Lexington	KY	40509	**800-753-4673**	859-269-2325
River Park Hospital 1230 Sixth Ave	Huntington	WV	25701	**800-621-2673**	304-526-9111
Riverview Psychiatric Ctr 250 Arsenal St 11 State House Stn	Augusta	ME	04330	**888-261-6684**	207-624-4600
Rogers Memorial Hospital Inc 34700 Valley Rd	Oconomowoc	WI	53066	**800-767-4411**	262-646-4411
Sheppard Pratt Health System (SPHS) 6501 N Charles St	Baltimore	MD	21285	**800-627-0330**	410-938-3000
Spring Grove Hospital Ctr 55 Wade Ave *General	Catonsville	MD	21228	**866-734-3337***	410-402-6000
Spring Harbor Hospital 123 Andover Rd	Westbrook	ME	04092	**888-524-0080**	207-761-2200
Springfield Hospital Ctr 6655 Sykesville Rd	Sykesville	MD	21784	**800-333-7564**	410-970-7000
Thomas B Finan Ctr 10102 Country Club Rd SE PO Box 1722	Cumberland	MD	21502	**888-854-0035**	301-777-2405
Timberlawn Mental Health System 4600 Samuell Blvd	Dallas	TX	75228	**800-426-4944**	214-381-7181
Torrance State Hospital 121 Longview Dr PO Box 111	Torrance	PA	15779	**866-816-9212**	724-459-8000
University Behavioral Ctr 2500 Discovery Dr	Orlando	FL	32826	**800-999-0807**	407-281-7000
Walter P Reuther Psychiatric Hospital 30901 Palmer Rd	Westland	MI	48186	**877-765-8388**	734-367-8400
Western Mental Health Institute 11100 Hwy 64 W	Bolivar	TN	38008	**800-770-8277**	731-228-2000
Western State Hospital 9601 Steilacoom Blvd SW	Tacoma	WA	98498	**877-501-2233**	253-582-8900
Westwood Lodge Hospital 45 Clapboardtree St	Westwood	MA	02090	**800-222-2237**	781-762-7764
William R Sharpe Jr Hospital 936 Sharpe Hospital Rd	Weston	WV	26452	**866-384-5250**	304-269-1210

373-6 Rehabilitation Hospitals

				Toll-Free	Phone
Allied Services Rehabilitation Hospital 475 Morgan Hwy	Scranton	PA	18508	**888-734-2272**	570-348-1300
Bryn Mawr Rehab Hospital 414 Paoli Pike	Malvern	PA	19355	**888-876-8764**	484-596-5400
Burke Rehabilitation Hospital 785 Mamaroneck Ave	White Plains	NY	10605	**888-992-8753**	914-597-2500
Cardinal Hill Healthcare System 2050 Versailles Rd	Lexington	KY	40504	**877-794-7328**	859-254-5701
Charlotte Institute of Rehabilitation 1100 Blythe Blvd	Charlotte	NC	28203	**800-634-2256**	704-355-4300
Craig Hospital 3425 S Clarkson St	Englewood	CO	80113	**800-247-0257**	303-789-8000
Drake Ctr 151 W Galbraith Rd	Cincinnati	OH	45216	**800-948-0003**	513-418-2500
Edwin Shaw Rehab 1621 Flickinger Rd	Akron	OH	44312	**800-221-4601**	330-784-1271
Frazier Rehabilitation Institute 220 Abraham Flexner Way	Louisville	KY	40202	**800-333-2230**	502-582-7400
Gaylord Hospital Gaylord Farms Rd PO Box 400	Wallingford	CT	06492	**866-429-5673**	203-284-2800
HealthSouth Chattanooga Rehabilitation Hospital 3660 Grandview Pkwy Ste 200	Birmingham	AL	35243	**800-765-4772**	205-967-7116
HealthSouth Harmarville Rehabilitation Hospital 320 Guys Run Rd	Pittsburgh	PA	15238	**800-765-4772**	412-828-1300
HealthSouth Hospital of Pittsburgh 320 Guys Run Rd	Pittsburgh	PA	15238	**800-765-4772**	412-828-1300
HealthSouth MountainView Regional Rehabilitation Hospital 1160 Van Voorhis Rd	Morgantown	WV	26505	**800-388-2451**	304-598-1100
HealthSouth Nittany Valley Rehabilitation Hospital 550 W College Ave	Pleasant Gap	PA	16823	**800-842-6026**	814-359-3421
HealthSouth Plano Rehabilitation Hospital 2800 W 15th St	Plano	TX	75075	**800-765-4772**	972-612-9000
HealthSouth Rehabilitation Hospital of Altoona 2005 Vly View Blvd	Altoona	PA	16602	**800-873-4220**	814-944-3535
HealthSouth Rehabilitation Hospital of Austin 1215 Red River	Austin	TX	78701	**800-765-4772**	512-474-5700
HealthSouth Rehabilitation Hospital of Erie 143 E Second St	Erie	PA	16507	**800-765-4772**	814-878-1230
HealthSouth Rehabilitation Hospital of Kingsport 113 Cassel Dr	Kingsport	TN	37660	**800-454-7422**	423-246-7240
Madonna Rehabilitation Hospital 5401 S St	Lincoln	NE	68506	**800-676-5448**	402-489-7102
Magee Rehabilitation Hospital 1513 Race St	Philadelphia	PA	19102	**800-966-2433**	215-587-3000
Marianjoy Rehabilitation Hospital 26 W 171 Roosevelt Rd	Wheaton	IL	60187	**800-462-2366**	630-462-4000
Mary Free Bed Rehabilitation Hospital 235 Wealthy St SE	Grand Rapids	MI	49503	**800-528-8989**	616-242-0300
Methodist Rehabilitation Ctr 1350 E Woodrow Wilson Dr	Jackson	MS	39216	**800-223-6672**	601-981-2611
Northeast Rehabilitation Hospital 70 Butler St	Salem	NH	03079	**800-439-2370**	603-893-2900
Rancho Los Amigos National Rehabilitation Ctr 7601 E Imperial Hwy	Downey	CA	90242	**877-726-2461**	562-401-7111
Rehabilitation Hospital of Indiana 4141 Shore Dr	Indianapolis	IN	46254	**866-510-2273**	317-329-2000
Rehabilitation Hospital of New Mexico 4441 E Lohman Ave	Las Cruces	NM	88011	**888-659-3952**	575-521-6400
Rehabilitation Hospital of the Pacific 226 N Kuakini St	Honolulu	HI	96817	**800-973-4226**	808-531-3511
Rehabilitation Institute of Chicago 345 E Superior St *Admitting	Chicago	IL	60611	**800-354-7342***	312-238-1000
Shadyside Nursing & Rehabilitation Ctr 5609 Fifth Ave	Pittsburgh	PA	15232	**800-366-1232**	412-362-3500
Sierra Providence Physical Rehabilitation Hospital 1740 Curie Dr	El Paso	TX	79902	**800-252-5400**	915-544-3399
Siskin Hospital for Physical Rehabilitation 1 Siskin Plaza	Chattanooga	TN	37403	**800-994-6610**	423-634-1200
Southern Indiana Rehabilitation Hospital 3104 Blackiston Blvd	New Albany	IN	47150	**800-737-7090**	812-941-8300
Spalding Rehabilitation Hospital 900 Potomac St	Aurora	CO	80011	**800-367-3309**	303-367-1166
SSM Rehabilitation Hospital 6420 Clayton Rd	Saint Louis	MO	63117	**800-818-9494**	314-768-5300
TIRR Memorial Hermann Hospital 1333 Moursund St	Houston	TX	77030	**800-447-3422**	713-799-5000

373-7 Specialty Hospitals

				Toll-Free	Phone
Barbara Ann Karmanos Cancer Institute 4100 John R St	Detroit	MI	48201	**800-527-6266**	
Bascom Palmer Eye Institute 900 NW 17th St	Miami	FL	33136	**800-329-7000**	305-326-6000
Brigham & Women's Hospital 75 Francis St	Boston	MA	02115	**800-722-5520**	617-732-5500
Dana-Farber Cancer Institute 44 Binney St	Boston	MA	02115	**866-408-3324**	617-632-3000
Dermatology Assoc of Atlanta 5555 Pchtrdnwyd Ste 190	Atlanta	GA	30324	**800-233-0706**	404-256-4457
Doheny Eye Institute 1450 San Pablo St	Los Angeles	CA	90033	**800-872-2273**	323-442-7100
Eleanor Slater Hospital 14 Harrington Rd	Cranston	RI	02920	**800-438-8477**	401-462-2339
Fox Chase Cancer Ctr 333 Cottman Ave	Philadelphia	PA	19111	**888-369-2427**	215-728-6900
Georgia Cancer Specialists Pc (GCS) 1872 Montreal Rd	Tucker	GA	30084	**800-491-5991**	770-496-9443
H Lee Moffitt Cancer Ctr & Research Institute University of S Florida 12902 Magnolia Dr	Tampa	FL	33612	**800-456-3434**	888-663-3488
Hughston Orthopedic Hospital 100 Frist Ct	Columbus	GA	31908	**866-272-9452**	706-494-2100
Kindred Hospital Atlanta 705 Juniper St	Atlanta	GA	30308	**800-255-0135**	404-873-2871
Kindred Hospital Kansas City 8701 Troost Ave	Kansas City	MO	64131	**800-545-0749**	816-995-2000
Leahi Hospital 3675 Kilauea Ave	Honolulu	HI	96816	**800-845-6733**	808-733-8000
MD Anderson Cancer Ctr 1515 Holcombe Blvd	Houston	TX	77030	**800-889-2094**	713-792-2121
Memorial Sloan-Kettering Cancer Ctr 1275 York Ave	New York	NY	10065	**800-525-2225**	212-639-2000
Midwestern Regional Medical Ctr (MRMC) 2520 Elisha Ave	Zion	IL	60099	**800-615-3055**	847-872-4561
National Jewish Medical & Research Ctr 1400 Jackson St PO Box 17169	Denver	CO	80206	**877-225-5654**	303-388-4461
New York Eye & Ear Infirmary 310 E 14th St	New York	NY	10003	**800-522-4582**	212-979-4000
Odessa Regional Medical Ctr 520 E Sixth St	Odessa	TX	79761	**877-898-6080**	432-582-8000
Roswell Park Cancer Institute Elm and Carlton St	Buffalo	NY	14263	**877-275-7724**	716-845-2300
Saint Vincent Women's Hospital 8111 Township Line Rd	Indianapolis	IN	46260	**800-582-8258**	317-415-8111
Samuel Mahelona Memorial Hospital 4800 Kawaihau Rd	Kapaa	HI	96746	**800-845-6733**	808-822-4961
Siteman Cancer Ctr 4921 Parkview Pl	Saint Louis	MO	63110	**800-600-3606**	314-362-5196
Stanford Cancer Ctr 875 Lake Blake Wilbur Dr	Stanford	CA	94305	**800-422-6237**	650-498-6000
Straith Hospital for Special Surgery 23901 Lahser Rd	Southfield	MI	48034	**800-994-6610**	248-357-3360
Texas Ctr for Infectious Diseases 2303 SE Military Dr	San Antonio	TX	78223	**800-839-5864**	210-534-8857
Texas Orthopedic Hospital 7401 Main St	Houston	TX	77030	**866-783-4549**	713-799-8600
UC Davis Cancer Ctr 4501 X St	Sacramento	CA	95817	**800-362-5566**	916-734-5800

373-8 Veterans Hospitals

Listings for veterans hospitals are organized by states, and then by city names within those groupings.

Toll-Free	Phone

				Toll-Free	Phone
Alexandria Veterans Affairs Medical Ctr					
2495 Shreveport Hwy 71 N	Pineville	LA	71360	800-375-8387	318-473-0010
Altoona VA Medical Ctr					
2907 Pleasant Vly Blvd	Altoona	PA	16602	877-626-2500	
Alvin C York Medical Ctr					
3400 Lebanon Pike	Murfreesboro	TN	37129	800-228-4973	615-867-6000
Batavia VA Medical Ctr					
222 Richmond Ave	Batavia	NY	14020	800-273-8255	585-297-1000
Bath Veterans Affairs Medical Ctr					
76 Veterans Ave	Bath	NY	14810	877-845-3247	607-664-4000
Carl Vinson Veterans Affairs Medical Ctr					
1826 Veterans Blvd	Dublin	GA	31021	800-595-5229	478-272-1210
Central Texas Veterans Health Care System					
1901 Veterans Memorial Dr	Temple	TX	76504	800-423-2111	254-778-4811
Colmery-O'Neil Veterans Affairs Medical Ctr					
2200 SW Gage Blvd	Topeka	KS	66622	800-574-8387	785-350-3111
Dayton Va Medical Ctr					
4100 W Third St	Dayton	OH	45428	800-368-8262	937-268-6511
Denver Veterans Affairs Medical Ctr					
1055 Clermont St	Denver	CO	80220	888-336-8262	303-399-8020
Dwight D Eisenhower V A Medical Ctr					
4101 South 4th St	Leavenworth	KS	66048	800-952-8387	913-682-2000
Erie VA Medical Ctr					
135 E 38th St	Erie	PA	16504	800-274-8387	814-868-8661
Harry S Truman Memorial Veterans Hospital					
800 Hospital Dr	Columbia	MO	65201	877-222-8387	573-814-6000
Huntington Veterans Affairs Medical Ctr					
1540 Spring Valley Dr	Huntington	WV	25704	800-827-8244	304-429-6741
James H Quillen Veterans Affairs Medical Ctr					
Corner of Lamont & Veterans Way					
PO Box 4000	Mountain Home	TN	37684	877-573-3529	423-926-1171
Jerry L Pettis Memorial Veterans Affairs Medical Ctr					
11201 Benton St	Loma Linda	CA	92357	800-827-1000	909-825-7084
John J Pershing Veterans Affairs Medical Ctr					
1500 N Westwood Blvd	Poplar Bluff	MO	63901	888-557-8262	573-686-4151
Louis A Johnson Veterans Affairs Medical Ctr					
1 Medical Ctr Dr	Clarksburg	WV	26301	800-733-0512	304-623-3461
Louis Stokes Cleveland Veterans Affairs Medical Ctr					
10701 E Blvd	Cleveland	OH	44106	888-838-6446	216-791-3800
Malcom Randall VAMC NF/SGVHS					
1601 SW Archer Rd	Gainesville	FL	32608	800-324-8387	352-376-1611
Northern Arizona VA Health Care System					
500 Hwy 89 N	Prescott	AZ	86313	800-949-1005	928-445-4860
Overton Brooks Veterans Affairs Medical Ctr					
510 E Stoner Ave	Shreveport	LA	71101	800-863-7441	318-221-8411
Richard L. Roudebush VA Medical Ctr					
1481 W Tenth St	Indianapolis	IN	46202	888-878-6889	317-988-4498
Sierra NV Healthcare Systems (VA Medical Ctr)					
975 Kirman Ave	Reno	NV	89502	888-838-6256	775-786-7200
Southern Arizona Veterans Healthcare System					
3601 S Sixth Ave	Tucson	AZ	85723	800-470-8262	520-792-1450
Stratton Veterans Affairs Medical Ctr					
113 Holland Ave	Albany	NY	12208	800-223-4810	518-626-5000
Thomas E Creek Veterans Affairs Medical Ctr					
6010 Amarillo Blvd W	Amarillo	TX	79106	800-687-8262	806-355-9703
Tomah Veterans Affairs Medical Ctr					
500 E Veterans St	Tomah	WI	54660	800-872-8662	608-372-3971
Tuscaloosa VA Medical Ctr					
3701 Loop Rd E	Tuscaloosa	AL	35404	888-269-3045	205-554-2000
U.S. Department of Veterans Affairs					
325 E 'H' St	Iron Mountain	MI	49801	800-215-8262	906-774-3300
Castle Point Campus					
41 Castle Pt Rd	Wappingers Falls	NY	12590	877-222-8387	845-831-2000
VA Hudson Valley Health Care System					
Montrose Campus					
2094 Albany Post Rd PO Box 100	Montrose	NY	10548	800-269-8749	914-737-4400
VA Medical Ctr					
4500 S Lancaster Rd	Dallas	TX	75216	800-849-3597	214-742-8387
Veterans Affairs Long Beach Medical Ctr					
5901 E Seventh St	Long Beach	CA	90822	888-769-8387	562-826-8000
Veterans Affairs Medical Ctr					
1700 S Lincoln Ave	Lebanon	PA	17042	800-409-8771	
Veterans Affairs Outpatient Clinic					
1515 W Pleasant St Bldg 1	Knoxville	IA	50138	800-816-8878	641-842-3101
Veterans Affairs Puget Sound Medical Ctr					
1660 S Columbian Way	Seattle	WA	98108	800-329-8387	206-762-1010
WG Bill Hefner Veterans Affairs Medical Ctr					
1601 Brenner Ave	Salisbury	NC	28144	800-469-8262	704-638-9000
White River Junction Veterans Affairs Medical Ctr					
215 N Main St	White River Junction	VT	05009	866-687-8387	802-295-9363

374   HOT TUBS, SPAS, WHIRLPOOL BATHS

				Toll-Free	Phone
Alaglass Swimming Pools					
165 Sweet Bay Rd	Saint Matthews	SC	29135	877-655-7179	
Atlantic Spas & Billiards					
8721 Glenwood Ave	Raleigh	NC	27617	800-849-8827	919-783-7447
Bath-Tec Inc PO Box 1118	Ennis	TX	75120	800-526-3301	972-646-5279
Best Bath Systems					
723 Garber St	Caldwell	ID	83605	866-333-8657	208-342-6823
Cal Spas Inc 1462 E Ninth St	Pomona	CA	91766	800-225-7727	909-623-8781
Hydro Systems Inc					
29132 Ave Paine	Valencia	CA	91355	800-747-9990	661-775-0686
Jason International Inc					
8328 MacArthur Dr	North Little Rock	AR	72118	800-255-5766	501-771-4477
Kallista Inc					
1227 N Eigth St Ste 2	Sheboygan	WI	53081	888-452-5547*	920-457-4441
Cust Svc					
Koral Industries Inc					
1504 S Kaufman St	Ennis	TX	75119	800-627-2441	972-875-6555
Marquis Spas Corp					
596 Hoffman Rd	Independence	OR	97351	800-275-0888	503-838-0888
Master Spas Inc					
6927 Lincoln Pkwy	Fort Wayne	IN	46804	800-860-7727	260-436-9100

				Toll-Free	Phone
Plastic Development Co Inc					
75 Palmer Industrial Rd					
PO Box 4007	Williamsport	PA	17701	800-451-1420	
Royal Baths Manufacturing Co					
14635 Chrisman Rd	Houston	TX	77039	800-826-0074	281-442-3400
Spa Manufacturers					
6060 Ulmerton Rd	Clearwater	FL	33760	877-530-9493	727-530-9493
Spurlin Industries Inc					
625 Main St	Palmetto	GA	30268	800-749-4475	770-463-1644
Thermo Spas Inc					
155 E St	Wallingford	CT	06492	800-876-0158	
Watertech Whirlpool Bath & Spa					
2507 Plymouth Rd	Johnson City	TN	37601	800-289-8827	423-926-1470
Watkins Mfg Corp					
1280 Pk Ctr Dr	Vista	CA	92081	800-999-4688	

375   HOTEL RESERVATIONS SERVICES

				Toll-Free	Phone
AC Central Reservations Inc					
201 Tilton Rd					
London Sq Mall Ste 17B	Northfield	NJ	08225	888-227-6667	609-383-8880
Advance Reservations Inn Arizona					
PO Box 950	Tempe	AZ	85280	800-456-0682	480-990-0682
Alexandria & Arlington Bed & Breakfast Networks (AABBN)					
4938 Hampden Ln Ste 164	Bethesda	MD	20814	888-549-3415	703-549-3415
Alliance Reservations Network					
21640 N 19th Ave Ste C102	Phoenix	AZ	85027	800-419-1545*	602-444-9993
Cust Svc					
Anchorage Alaska Bed & Breakfast Assn (AABBA)					
PO Box 242623	Anchorage	AK	99524	888-584-5147	907-272-5909
B & B Agency of Boston					
47 Commercial Wharf Ste 3	Boston	MA	02110	800-248-9262	
Barclay International Group					
6800 Jericho Tpke	Syosset	NY	11791	800-845-6636	516-364-0064
Bed & Breakfast Atlanta					
790 N Ave Ste 202	Atlanta	GA	30306	800-967-3224	404-875-0525
Bed & Breakfast Cape Cod					
PO Box 2250	Mashpee	MA	02649	800-556-3815	508-255-3824
Bed & Breakfast of Hawaii					
PO Box 449	Kapaa	HI	96746	800-733-1632	808-822-7771
Branson's Best Reservations					
2875 Green Mtn Dr	Branson	MO	65616	800-335-2555	417-339-2204
Branson/Lakes Area Lodging Assn					
PO Box 430	Branson	MO	65615	877-781-1218	417-332-1400
Colonial Williamsburg Reservation Ctr					
PO Box 1776	Williamsburg	VA	23187	800-447-8679	757-229-1000
Greater New Orleans Hotel & Lodging Assn					
2020 St Charles Ave 5th Fl	New Orleans	LA	70130	866-366-1121	504-525-2264
Hawaii's Best Bed & Breakfasts					
571 Pauku St	Kailua	HI	96734	800-262-9912	808-263-3100
Holiday Inn Express & Suites					
5001 Brougham Dr	Drayton Valley	AB	T7A0A1	877-444-3110	780-515-9888
Hot Rooms					
875 N. Michigan Ave Ste 3100	Chicago	IL	60611	800-468-3500	773-468-7666
Jackson Hole Central Reservations (JHCR)					
140 E Broadway Ste 24 PO Box 2618	Jackson	WY	83001	888-838-6606	307-733-4005
Key West Key					
726 Passover Ln	Key West	FL	33040	800-881-7321	
Know Before You Go Reservations					
8000 International Dr	Orlando	FL	32819	800-749-1993	407-352-9813
Leading Hotels of the World					
99 Pk Ave	New York	NY	10017	800-223-6800	212-515-5600
Luxe Worldwide Hotels					
11461 W Sunset Blvd	Los Angeles	CA	90049	866-589-3411	310-440-3090
Nantucket Accommodations					
Two Windy Way	Nantucket	MA	02554	866-743-3330	508-228-9559
National Corporate Housing					
365 Herndon Pkwy Ste 111	Herndon	VA	20170	866-229-4720	
New Otani North America Reservation Ctr					
120 S Los Angeles St	Los Angeles	CA	90012	800-421-8795*	213-629-1200
Cust Svc					
Ocean City Hotel-Motel-Restaurant Assn					
PO Box 340	Ocean City	MD	21843	800-626-2326	410-289-6733
Quikbook					
381 Pk Ave S 3rd Fl	New York	NY	10016	800-789-9887	212-686-7666
Resort 2 Me 975 Cass St	Monterey	CA	93940	800-757-5646	831-642-6622
San Diego Concierge					
4379 30th St Ste 4	San Diego	CA	92104	800-979-9091	619-280-4121
Stay Aspen Snowmass					
425 Rio Grande Pl	Aspen	CO	81611	888-649-5982	970-925-9000
Travel Planners Inc					
381 Pk Ave S	New York	NY	10016	800-221-3531	212-532-1660
Travelocity.com LP					
3150 Sabre Dr	Southlake	TX	76092	888-872-8356	
Vacation Co					
42 New Orleans Rd Ste 102	Hilton Head Island	SC	29928	800-845-7018	843-686-6100
Washington DC Accommodations					
2201 Wisconsin Ave NW Ste C-120	Washington	DC	20007	800-503-3330	202-293-8000
Winter Park Resort					
85 Parsenn Rd	Winter Park	CO	80482	800-903-7275*	970-726-5514
Resv					

376   HOTELS - CONFERENCE CENTER

				Toll-Free	Phone
ACE Conference Ctr					
800 Ridge Pk	Lafayette Hill	PA	19444	800-523-3000	610-825-8000
Airlie Conference Ctr					
6809 Airlie Rd	Warrenton	VA	20187	800-288-9573	540-347-1300
Banff Centre, The					
107 Tunnel Mtn Dr PO Box 1020	Banff	AB	T1L1H5	800-884-7574	403-762-6100
Chaminade					
One Chaminade Ln	Santa Cruz	CA	95065	800-283-6569	831-475-5600

				Toll-Free	Phone
Chateau Elan Resort & Conference Ctr 100 Rue Charlemagne	Braselton	GA	30517	**800-233-9463**	678-425-0900
Chattanoogan, The 1201 Broad St	Chattanooga	TN	37402	**877-756-1684**	423-756-3400
Cheyenne Mountain Conference Resort 3225 Broadmoor Vly Rd	Colorado Springs	CO	80906	**800-428-8886**	719-538-4000
Clarion Hotel & Conference Ctr Antietam Creek 901 Dual Hwy	Hagerstown	MD	21740	**888-528-6738**	301-733-5100
Conference Ctr at NorthPointe 100 Green Meadows Dr S	Lewis Center	OH	43035	**866-233-9393**	614-880-4300
Cook Hotel & Conference Ctr 3848 W Lakeshore Dr	Baton Rouge	LA	70808	**866-610-2665**	225-383-2665
Country Springs Hotel & Conference Ctr 2810 Golf Rd	Pewaukee	WI	53072	**800-247-6640**	262-547-0201
Crystal Mountain Resort 12500 Crystal Mtn Dr	Thompsonville	MI	49683	**800-968-7686**	231-378-2000
Delta Sherbrooke Hotel & Conference Centre 2685 Rue King O	Sherbrooke	QC	J1L1C1	**800-268-1133**	819-822-1989
Dolce Atlanta-Peachtree 201 Aberdeen Pkwy	Peachtree City	GA	30269	**800-983-6523**	770-487-2666
Dolce Hayes Mansion 200 Edenvale Ave	San Jose	CA	95136	**866-981-3300**	408-226-3200
Doral Arrowwood Conference Resort 975 Anderson Hill Rd	Rye Brook	NY	10573	**844-211-0512**	844-214-5500
Emory Conference Ctr Hotel 1615 Clifton Rd	Atlanta	GA	30329	**800-933-6679**	404-712-6000
Evergreen Marriott Conference Resort 4021 Lakeview Dr	Stone Mountain	GA	30083	**800-228-9290**	770-879-9900
Founders Inn 5641 Indian River Rd	Virginia Beach	VA	23464	**800-926-4466**	757-424-5511
Georgetown University Hotel & Conference Ctr 3800 Reservoir Rd NW	Washington	DC	20057	**800-228-9290**	202-687-3200
Glen Cove Mansion Hotel & Conference Ctr 200 Dosoris Ln	Glen Cove	NY	11542	**877-782-9426**	516-671-6400
Grandover Resort & Conference Ctr 1000 Club Rd	Greensboro	NC	27407	**800-472-6301**	336-294-1800
Hamilton Park Hotel & Conference Ctr 175 Pk Ave	Florham Park	NJ	07932	**800-321-6000**	973-377-2424
Heritage Hotel 522 Heritage Rd	Southbury	CT	06488	**800-932-3466**	203-264-8200
Hickory Ridge Marriott Conference Hotel 10400 Fernwood Rd	Bethesda	IL	20817	**800-334-0344**	301-380-3000
Hidden Valley Resort & Conference Ctr 1 Craighead Dr PO Box 4420	Hidden Valley	PA	15502	**800-452-2223**	814-443-8000
Hilton Scranton & Conference Ctr 100 Adams Ave	Scranton	PA	18503	**800-445-8667**	570-343-3000
Hilton University of Florida Conference Ctr 1714 SW 34th St	Gainesville	FL	32607	**800-774-1500**	352-371-3600
Hotel at Auburn University & Dixon Conference Ctr, The 241 S College St	Auburn	AL	36830	**800-228-2876**	334-821-8200
Hotel Roanoke & Conference Ctr 110 Shenandoah Ave	Roanoke	VA	24016	**800-222-8733**	540-985-5900
IBM Palisades Conference Ctr 334 Rt 9 W	Palisades	NY	10964	**800-426-0889**	845-732-6000
Inn at Aspen 38750 Hwy 82	Aspen	CO	81611	**800-222-7736**	
Inn at Virginia Tech & Skelton Conference Ctr 901 Prices Fork Rd MS 0104	Blacksburg	VA	24061	**877-200-3360**	540-231-8000
InterContinental Hotel Cleveland 9801 Carnegie Ave	Cleveland	OH	44106	**877-707-8999**	216-707-4100
Ivey Spencer Leadership Centre 551 Windermere Rd	London	ON	N5X2T1	**888-678-6926**	519-679-4546
James L Allen Ctr 2169 Campus Dr	Evanston	IL	60208	**877-755-2227**	847-467-7000
Kingbridge Centre, The 12750 Jane St	King City	ON	L7B1A3	**800-827-7221**	905-833-3086
Kingsgate Marriott Conference Ctr at the University of Cincinnati 151 Goodman St	Cincinnati	OH	45219	**800-228-9290**	513-487-3800
Kingsmill Resort & Spa 1010 Kingsmill Rd	Williamsburg	VA	23185	**800-832-5665**	757-253-1703
Lakeview Golf Resort & Spa One Lakeview Dr	Morgantown	WV	26508	**800-624-8300**	304-594-1111
Lodge At Breckenridge, The 112 Overlook Dr	Breckenridge	CO	80424	**800-736-1607**	970-453-9300
Marietta Conference Ctr & Resort 500 Powder Springs St	Marietta	GA	30064	**888-685-2500**	770-427-2500
Marriott Montgomery Prattville at Capitol Hill 2500 Legends Cir *Resv	Prattville	AL	36066	**800-593-6429***	334-290-1235
Millennium Broadway Hotel New York 145 W 44th St	New York	NY	10036	**800-622-5569**	212-768-4400
National Ctr for Employee Development (NCED) 2701 E Imhoff Rd	Norman	OK	73071	**866-438-6233**	405-366-4420
NAV Canada Training & Conference Ctr 1950 Montreal Rd	Cornwall	ON	K6H6L2	**877-832-6416**	613-936-5800
Northland Inn & Executive Conference Ctr, The 7025 Northland Dr	Minneapolis	MN	55428	**800-441-6422**	763-536-8300
Oak Brook Hills Marriott Resort 3500 Midwest Rd	Oak Brook	IL	60523	**800-228-9290**	630-850-5555
Oak Ridge Hotel & Conference Ctr 1 Oak Ridge Dr *Sales	Chaska	MN	55318	**800-737-9588***	952-368-3100
Penn Stater Conference Ctr Hotel 215 Innovation Blvd	State College	PA	16803	**800-233-7505**	814-863-5000
Renaissance Portsmouth Hotel & Waterfront Conference Ctr 425 Water St	Portsmouth	VA	23704	**888-839-1775**	757-673-3000
Resort at Squaw Creek 400 Squaw Creek Rd PO Box 3333	Olympic Valley	CA	96146	**800-327-3353**	530-583-6300
Saratoga Hilton 534 Broadway	Saratoga Springs	NY	12866	**800-445-8667**	518-584-4000
Scottsdale Resort & Conference Ctr 7700 E McCormick Pkwy	Scottsdale	AZ	85258	**800-528-0293**	480-991-9000
Skamania Lodge 1131 SW Skamania Lodge Way PO Box 189	Stevenson	WA	98648	**800-221-7117**	509-427-7700
Snowbird Ski & Summer Resort Hwy 210 PO Box 929000	Snowbird	UT	84092	**800-453-3000**	801-742-2222
Stoweflake Mountain Resort & Spa 1746 Mountain Rd PO Box 369	Stowe	VT	05672	**800-253-2232**	802-253-7355

				Toll-Free	Phone
University of Maryland University College Marriott Conference Ctr Hotel 3501 University Blvd E	Adelphi	MD	20783	**800-721-7033**	301-985-7300
White Oaks Conference Resort & Spa 253 Taylor Rd SS4 *Resv	Niagara-on-the-Lake	ON	L0S1J0	**800-263-5766***	905-688-2550
Woodlands Resort & Conference Ctr, The 2301 N Millbend Dr *Resv	The Woodlands	TX	77380	**800-433-2624***	281-367-1100
Wyndham Peachtree Conference Ctr 2443 Hwy 54 W	Peachtree City	GA	30269	**800-996-3426**	770-487-2000

377 HOTELS - FREQUENT STAY PROGRAMS

				Toll-Free	Phone
AmericInn Inn-Pressive Club 250 Lake Dr E	Chanhassen	MN	55317	**800-634-3444**	952-294-5000
Chestnut Mountain Resort 8700 Chestnut Dr	Galena	IL	61036	**800-397-1320**	
Chukchansi Gold Resort & Casino 711 Lucky Ln	Coarsegold	CA	93614	**866-794-6946**	
Danfords Hotel & Marina 25 E Broadway	Port Jefferson	NY	11777	**800-332-6367**	
FairBridge Inns LLC 421 W Riverside Ave Ste 407	Spokane	WA	99201	**877-866-8090**	
Fairmont San Francisco Hotel, The 950 Mason St	San Francisco	CA	94108	**800-257-7544**	415-772-5000
Hospitality International INNcentive Card Program 1726 Montreal Cir	Tucker	GA	30084	**800-247-4677**	
Hyatt Gold Passport Program 9805 Q St PO Box 27089	Omaha	NE	68127	**800-233-1234**	
Inn at Ellis Square 201 W Bay St	Savannah	GA	31401	**877-542-7666**	
Intercontinental San Francisco 888 Howard St	San Francisco	CA	94103	**888-811-4273**	
LeisureLink Inc 90 S 400 W Ste 300	Salt Lake City	UT	84101	**855-840-2249**	
London West Hollywood Hotel 1020 N San Vicente Blvd	West Hollywood	CA	90069	**866-282-4560**	
Oak Plantation Resort & Suites Condominium Association Inc 4090 Enchanted Oaks Cir	Kissimmee	FL	34741	**888-411-4141**	
Omni Hotels Select Guest Loyalty Program 11819 Miami St Third Fl *Cust Svc	Omaha	NE	68164	**800-843-6664***	
Plaza Hotel, The 5th Ave at Central Park S	New York	NY	10019	**888-850-0909**	212-759-3000
Prince Preferred Guest Program 100 Holomoana St	Honolulu	HI	96815	**800-774-6234**	
Purple Sage Motel 1501 E Coliseum Dr	Snyder	TX	79549	**800-388-8255**	325-573-5491
Sandals Life Style 4950 SW 72nd Ave	Miami	FL	33155	**888-726-3257**	876-952-5510
Starwood Hotels Preferred Guest Program 111 Westchester Ave	White Plains	NY	10604	**888-625-4988**	512-834-2426
Wedmore Place LLC 5810 Wessex Hundred	Williamsburg	VA	23185	**866-933-6673**	
Wyndham ByRequest Program PO Box 4090	Aberdeen	SD	57401	**800-996-3426**	

378 HOTELS & HOTEL COMPANIES

SEE ALSO Resorts & Resort Companies ; Hotel Reservations Services ; Hotels - Conference Center ; Hotels - Frequent Stay Programs ; Casino Companies ; Corporate Housing

				Toll-Free	Phone
1886 Crescent Hotel & Spa 75 Prospect Ave	Eureka Springs	AR	72632	**877-342-9766**	479-253-9766
70 Park Avenue Hotel 70 Pk Ave at 38th St	New York	NY	10016	**877-707-2752**	212-973-2400
Academy Hotel Colorado Springs, The 8110 N Academy Blvd	Colorado Springs	CO	80920	**800-766-8524**	719-598-5770
Acadia Inn 98 Eden St	Bar Harbor	ME	04609	**800-638-3636**	207-288-3500
Acapulco Hotel & Resort 2505 S Atlantic Ave	Daytona Beach Shores	FL	32118	**855-922-3224**	386-761-2210
Accent Inns Vancouver Airport 10551 St Edwards Dr	Richmond	BC	V6X3L8	**800-663-0298**	604-273-3311
Accent Inns Vancouver-Burnaby 3777 Henning Dr	Burnaby	BC	V5C6N5	**800-663-0298**	604-473-5000
Acqua Hotel 555 Redwood Hwy	Mill Valley	CA	94941	**888-662-9555**	415-380-0400
Acqualina 17875 Collins Ave	Sunny Isles Beach	FL	33160	**877-312-9742**	305-918-8000
Adams Oceanfront Resort Four Read St	Dewey Beach	DE	19971	**800-448-8080**	302-227-3030
Admiral Fell Inn 888 S Broadway Historic Fell's Pt	Baltimore	MD	21231	**866-583-4162**	410-522-7377
Admiral on Baltimore 2 Baltimore Ave	Rehoboth Beach	DE	19971	**888-882-4188**	302-227-1300
Adolphus, The 1321 Commerce St	Dallas	TX	75202	**800-221-9083**	214-742-8200
Adventureland Inn 305 34th Ave NW	Altoona	IA	50009	**800-910-5382**	515-265-7321
Affina Dumont 150 E 34th St	New York	NY	10016	**866-233-4642**	212-481-7600
Affinia 50 155 E 50th St	New York	NY	10022	**866-246-2203**	212-751-5710
Affinia Chicago 155 E 50th St	New York	NY	10022	**866-246-2203**	212-751-5710
Affinia Gardens 215 E 64th St	New York	NY	10065	**866-233-4642**	212-355-1230
Affinia Manhattan 371 Seventh Ave	New York	NY	10001	**866-246-2203**	212-563-1800
Airport Settle Inn 2620 S Packerland Dr	Green Bay	WI	54313	**800-688-9052**	920-499-1900
Airtel Plaza Hotel 7277 Valjean Ave	Van Nuys	CA	91406	**800-224-7835**	818-997-7676

				Toll-Free	Phone

Ala Moana Hotel
410 Atkinson Dr . . . . Honolulu HI 96814 **800-367-6025** 808-955-4811

Albert at Bay Suite Hotel
435 Albert St . . . . Ottawa ON K1R7X4 **800-267-6644** 613-238-8858

Albion Hotel
1650 James Ave . . . . Miami Beach FL 33139 **877-782-3557*** 305-913-1000
*General

Alexis Hotel 1007 First Ave . . . . Seattle WA 98104 **866-356-8894** 206-624-4844

Alpenhof Lodge
3255 W Village Dr PO Box 288. . . . . .Teton Village WY 83025 **800-732-3244** 307-733-3242

Ambassador Hotel
535 Tchoupitoulas St . . . . .New Orleans LA 70130 **800-455-3417** 504-527-5271

Ambrosia House Tropical Lodging
622 Fleming St . . . . Key West FL 33040 **800-535-9838** 305-296-9838

America's Best Franchising Inc
America's Best Inns & Suites
50 Glen Lake Pkwy NE Ste 350. . . . . Atlanta GA 30328 **800-237-8466** 770-393-2662

AmericInn International LLC
250 Lake Dr E . . . . Chanhassen MN 55317 **800-396-5007*** 952-294-5000
*Resv

Ameristar Casino & Hotel
3200 N Ameristar Dr . . . . Kansas City MO 64161 **888-777-8700** 816-414-7000

Ameristar Casino Hotel Council Bluffs
2200 River Rd .Council Bluffs IA 51501 **866-667-3386** 712-328-8888

Ameritel Inn Boise Towne Square
7965 W Emerald St . . . . Boise ID 83704 **800-600-6001** 208-378-7000

Ameritel Inn Pocatello
1440 Pocatello Bench Rd . . . . Pocatello ID 83201 **800-600-6001** 208-234-7500

Amway Grand Plaza Hotel
187 Monroe Ave NW . . . . Grand Rapids MI 49503 **800-253-3590** 616-774-2000

Anaheim Plaza Hotel & Suites
1700 S Harbor Blvd . . . . Anaheim CA 92802 **800-631-4144** 714-772-5900

Andaluz
125 Second St NW . . . . .Albuquerque NM 87102 **877-987-9090** 505-242-9090

Andaz San Diego 600 F St . . . . .San Diego CA 92101 **877-489-4489** 619-849-1234

Andrews Hotel
624 Post St . . . . .San Francisco CA 94109 **800-926-3739** 415-563-6877

Angler's Inn 265 N Millward . . . . Jackson WY 83001 **800-867-4667** 307-733-3682

Antler Inn
43 W Pearl St PO Box 575 . . . . Jackson WY 83001 **800-483-8667** 307-733-2535

Apple Tree Inn
9508 N Div St . . . . Spokane WA 99218 **800-323-5796** 509-466-3020

Applewood Manor Inn
62 Cumberland Cir . . . . Asheville NC 28801 **800-442-2197** 828-254-2244

Aqua Bamboo 2425 Kuhio Ave . . . . .Honolulu HI 96815 **855-747-0754** 808-922-7777

Aqua Hospitality Corp
445 Seaside Ave . . . . Honolulu HI 96815 **855-747-0755** 808-923-2345

Aqua Waikiki Wave
2299 Kuhio Ave . . . . Honolulu HI 96815 **855-747-0754** 808-922-1262

ARC the Hotel Ottawa
140 Slater St . . . . Ottawa ON K1P5H6 **800-699-2516** 613-238-2888

Arena Hotel
817 The Alameda . . . . .San Jose CA 95126 **800-954-6835** 408-294-6500

Argonaut Hotel
495 Jefferson St . . . . .San Francisco CA 94109 **866-415-0704** 415-563-0800

Arizona Charlie's Boulder Casino & Hotel
4575 Boulder Hwy . . . . .Las Vegas NV 89121 **888-236-9066** 702-951-5800

Arizona Charlie's Decatur Casino & Hotel
740 S Decatur Blvd . . . . .Las Vegas NV 89107 **888-236-8645** 702-258-5200

Arizona Inn 2200 E Elm St . . . . Tucson AZ 85719 **800-933-1093** 520-325-1541

Ashland Springs Hotel
212 E Main St . . . . Ashland OR 97520 **888-795-4545** 541-488-1700

Ashmore Inn & Suites
4019 S Loop 289 . . . . Lubbock TX 79423 **800-785-0061** 806-785-0060

Ashton Hotel 610 Main St . . . . Fort Worth TX 76102 **866-327-4866** 817-332-0100

Asticou Inn
15 Peabody Dr . . . . Northeast Harbor ME 04662 **800-258-3373** 207-276-3344

Aston Hotels & Resorts
2155 Kalakaua Ave Ste 500 . . . . Honolulu HI 96815 **800-775-4228** 808-931-1400

Astor Crowne Plaza
739 Canal St .New Orleans LA 70130 **877-408-9661** 504-962-0500

Astor Hotel, The
924 E Juneau Ave . . . . Milwaukee WI 53202 **800-558-0200** 414-271-4220

Atheneum Suite Hotel & Conference Ctr
1000 Brush Ave . . . . Detroit MI 48226 **800-772-2323** 313-962-2323

Atlantic Eyrie Lodge
Six Norman Rd . . . . Bar Harbor ME 04609 **800-422-2883**

Atlantic Sands Hotel
101 N Boardwalk . . . . Rehoboth Beach DE 19971 **800-422-0600** 302-227-2511

Atrium Hotel
18700 MacArthur Blvd . . . . Irvine CA 92612 **800-854-3012** 949-833-2770

Auberge du Soleil
180 Rutherford Hill Rd . . . . Rutherford CA 94573 **800-348-5406** 707-963-1211

Auberge du Vieux-Port
97 Rue de la Commune E . . . . Montreal QC H2Y1J1 **888-660-7678** 514-876-0081

Auberge Saint-Antoine
Eight rue Saint-Antoine . . . . Quebec QC G1K4C9 **888-692-2211** 418-692-2211

Austin Hotel & Spa
305 Malvern Ave . . . . Hot Springs AR 71901 **877-623-6697** 501-623-6600

Avalon Beverly Hills
9400 W Olympic Blvd . . . . Beverly Hills CA 90212 **800-670-6183** 310-277-5221

Avalon Corporate Furnished Apartments
1553 Empire Blvd . . . . Webster NY 14580 **800-934-9763** 585-671-4421

Avalon Hotel 16 W Tenth St . . . . Erie PA 16501 **888-295-4949** 814-459-2220

Avenue Inn & Spa
33 Wilmington Ave . . . . Rehoboth Beach DE 19971 **800-433-5870**

Avenue Plaza Resort
2111 St Charles Ave . . . . .New Orleans LA 70130 **800-614-8685** 504-566-1212

Ayres Hotel Anaheim
2550 E Katella Ave . . . . Anaheim CA 92806 **800-595-5692** 714-634-2106

Bahama House
2001 S Atlantic Ave . . . . Daytona Beach Shores FL 32118 **888-687-1894**

Balance Rock Inn
21 Albert Meadow . . . . Bar Harbor ME 04609 **800-753-0494** 207-288-2610

Balboa Park Inn
3402 Pk Blvd . . . . .San Diego CA 92103 **800-938-8181** 619-298-0823

Bally's Casino Tunica
1450 Bally's Blvd . . . . .Robinsonville MS 38664 **866-422-5597**

Balmoral Inn
120 Balmoral Ave . . . . Biloxi MS 39531 **800-393-9131** 228-388-6776

Bar Harbor Hotel-Bluenose Inn
90 Eden St . . . . Bar Harbor ME 04609 **800-445-4077** 207-288-3348

Barnstead Inn
349 Bonnet St . . . . Manchester Center VT 05255 **800-331-1619** 802-362-1619

Baronne Plaza Hotel
201 Baronne St . . . . .New Orleans LA 70112 **888-756-0083** 504-522-0083

Barrington Hotel & Suites
263 Shepherd of the Hills Expy . . . . Branson MO 65616 **800-760-8866** 417-334-8866

Bay Club Hotel & Marina
2131 Shelter Island Dr . . . . .San Diego CA 92106 **800-672-0800** 619-224-8888

Bay Park Hotel
1425 Munras Ave . . . . Monterey CA 93940 **800-338-3564*** 831-649-1020
*Resv

Bayfront Inn
138 Avenida Menendez . . . . Saint Augustine FL 32084 **800-558-3455** 904-824-1681

Baymont Inn
4025 McDonald Dr . . . . .Dubuque IA 52003 **800-337-0550** 563-582-3752

Beach Haven Inn
4740 Mission Blvd . . . . .San Diego CA 92109 **800-831-6323** 858-272-3812

Beacher's Lodge
6970 A1A S . . . . Saint Augustine FL 32080 **800-527-8849** 904-471-8849

Beacon Hotel
720 Ocean Dr . . . . Miami Beach FL 33139 **877-674-8200** 305-674-8200

Beacon Hotel & Corporate Quarters
1615 Rhode Island Ave NW . . . . Washington DC 20036 **800-823-1700** 202-296-2100

Beaver Creek Lodge
26 Avon Dale Ln . . . . Beaver Creek CO 81620 **800-525-7280** 970-845-9800

Beechwood Hotel
363 Plantation St . . . . .Worcester MA 01605 **800-344-2589** 508-754-5789

Bell Tower Hotel
300 S Thayer St .Ann Arbor MI 48104 **800-562-3559** 734-769-3010

Bell Tower Inn
1235 Second St SW . . . . Rochester MN 55902 **800-448-7583** 507-289-2233

Bellasera Hotel
221 Ninth St S . . . . Naples FL 34102 **855-990-0301** 239-649-7333

Bellevue Club Hotel
11200 SE Sixth St . . . . Bellevue WA 98004 **800-579-1110** 425-454-4424

Bellmoor, The
Six Christian St . . . . Rehoboth Beach DE 19971 **800-425-2355** 302-227-5800

Belvedere Hotel
319 W 48th St .New York NY 10036 **800-492-8122** 212-245-7000

Ben Lomond Suites LLC
2510 Washington Blvd . . . . .Ogden UT 84401 **877-627-1900** 801-627-1900

Benjamin, The
125 E 50th St .New York NY 10022 **866-233-4642** 212-715-2500

Benson, The
309 SW Broadway . . . . Portland OR 97205 **800-663-1144** 503-228-2000

Berkeley Hotel, The
1200 E Cary St .Richmond VA 23219 **888-780-4422** 804-780-1300

Bernards Inn
27 Mine Brook Rd . . . . Bernardsville NJ 07924 **888-766-0002** 908-766-0002

Bernardus Lodge
415 Carmel Valley Rd . . . . Carmel Valley CA 93924 **800-223-2533** 831-658-3400

Best Western Chincoteague Island
7105 Maddox Blvd . . . . .Chincoteague Island VA 23336 **800-553-6117** 757-336-6557

Best Western International Inc
6201 N 24th Pkwy . . . . Phoenix AZ 85016 **800-528-1234** 602-957-4200

Best Western Laguna Brisas Spa Hotel
1600 S Coast Hwy . . . . Laguna Beach CA 92651 **888-296-6834** 949-497-7272

Best Western Victorian Inn
487 Foam St . . . . Monterey CA 93940 **800-232-4141** 831-373-8000

Betsy Hotel
1440 Ocean Dr . . . . Miami Beach FL 33139 **866-792-3879** 305-531-6100

Beverly Hills Hotel
9641 Sunset Blvd . . . . Beverly Hills CA 90210 **800-283-8885** 310-276-2251

Beverly Hilton
9876 Wilshire Blvd . . . . .Beverly Hills CA 90210 **800-605-8896** 310-274-7777

Beverly Wilshire - A Four Seasons Hotel
9500 Wilshire Blvd . . . . .Beverly Hills CA 90212 **800-545-4000** 310-275-5200

Bienville House Hotel
320 Decatur St . . . . .New Orleans LA 70130 **800-535-7836** 504-529-2345

Billings C'mon Inn Hotel
2020 Overland Ave .Billings MT 59102 **800-655-1170** 406-655-1100

Billings Hotel & Convention Ctr
1223 Mullowney Ln . . . . Billings MT 59101 **800-537-7286** 406-248-7151

Biltmore Greensboro Hotel
111 W Washington St . . . . .Greensboro NC 27401 **800-332-0303*** 336-272-3474
*General

Biltmore Hotel & Suites
2151 Laurelwood Rd . . . . .Santa Clara CA 95054 **800-255-9925** 408-988-8411

Biltmore Hotel Oklahoma
401 S Meridian Ave . . . . Oklahoma City OK 73108 **800-522-6620** 405-947-7681

Biltmore Suites
205 W Madison St . . . . Baltimore MD 21201 **800-868-5064** 410-728-6550

Bismarck Expressway Suites
180 E Bismarck Expy . . . . Bismarck ND 58504 **888-774-5566** 701-222-3311

Blackfoot Inn
5940 Blackfoot Trl SE . . . . .Calgary AB T2H2B5 **800-661-1151** 403-252-2253

Blackwell, The
2110 Tuttle Pk Pl . . . . .Columbus OH 43210 **866-247-4003** 614-247-4000

Blakely New York
136 W 55th St .New York NY 10019 **800-735-0710** 212-245-1800

Blantyre
16 Blantyre Rd PO Box 995 . . . . Lenox MA 01240 **844-881-0104** 413-637-3556

Blue Horizon Hotel
1225 Robson St . . . . Vancouver BC V6E1C3 **800-663-1333** 604-688-1411

Blue Moon Hotel
944 Collins Ave . . . . Miami Beach FL 33139 **800-553-7739** 305-673-2262

Blue Parrot Inn
916 Elizabeth St . . . . Key West FL 33040 **800-231-2473** 305-296-0033

Bluenose Inn & Suites
636 Bedford Hwy . . . . Halifax NS B3M2L8 **800-553-5339** 902-443-3171

Boardwalk Plaza Hotel
Two Olive Ave . . . . Rehoboth Beach DE 19971 **800-332-3224** 302-227-7169

				Toll-Free	Phone
Bodega Bay Lodge					
103 Coast Hwy 1	Bodega Bay	CA	94923	**888-875-2250***	707-875-3525
*Resv					
Bohemian Hotel Celebration					
700 Bloom St	Celebration	FL	34747	**888-249-4007**	407-566-6000
Bond Place Hotel					
65 Dundas St E	Toronto	ON	M5B2G8	**800-268-9390**	416-362-6061
Boone Tavern Hotel of Berea College					
100 S Main St	Berea	KY	40403	**800-366-9358**	859-985-3700
Borgata Hotel Casino & Spa					
1 Borgata Way	Atlantic City	NJ	08401	**877-786-9900**	609-317-1000
Boston Harbor Hotel					
70 Rowes Wharf	Boston	MA	02110	**800-752-7077**	617-439-7000
Boston Park Plaza Hotel & Towers					
50 Pk Plz	Boston	MA	02116	**800-225-2008**	617-426-2000
Boulder Mountain Lodge					
91 Four Mile Canyon Rd	Boulder	CO	80302	**800-458-0882**	303-444-0882
Boulder Station Hotel & Casino					
4111 Boulder Hwy	Las Vegas	NV	89121	**800-683-7777**	702-432-7777
Bourbon Orleans - A Wyndham Historic Hotel					
717 Orleans St	New Orleans	LA	70116	**866-513-9744**	504-523-2222
Bradley Inn					
3063 Bristol Rd	New Harbor	ME	04554	**800-942-5560**	207-677-2105
Brazilian Court, The					
301 Australian Ave	Palm Beach	FL	33480	**800-552-0335**	561-655-7740
Breakers at Waikiki, The					
250 Beach Walk	Honolulu	HI	96815	**800-426-0494**	808-923-3181
Breakers Hotel & Suites					
105 Second St	Rehoboth Beach	DE	19971	**800-441-8009**	302-227-6688
Breakwater Inn					
1711 Glacier Ave	Juneau	AK	99801	**888-586-6303**	907-586-6303
Brent House Hotel					
1512 Jefferson Hwy	New Orleans	LA	70121	**800-535-3986**	504-842-4140
Bridgewater Hotel					
723 First Ave	Fairbanks	AK	99701	**800-528-4916**	
Bristol Hotel					
1055 First Ave	San Diego	CA	92101	**800-662-4477**	619-232-6141
Brookfield Suites Hotel & Convention Ctr					
1200 S Moorland Rd	Brookfield	WI	53005	**800-444-6404**	262-782-2900
Brookshire Suites					
120 E Lombard St	Baltimore	MD	21202	**855-345-5033**	410-625-1300
Brookstown Inn					
200 Brookstown Ave	Winston-Salem	NC	27101	**800-845-4262**	336-725-1120
Brookstreet Hotel					
525 Legget Dr	Ottawa	ON	K2K2W2	**888-826-2220**	613-271-1800
Brown County Inn					
51 State Rd 46	Nashville	IN	47448	**800-772-5249**	812-988-2291
Brown Hotel, The					
335 W Broadway St	Louisville	KY	40202	**888-387-0498**	502-583-1234
Brown Palace Hotel					
321 17th St	Denver	CO	80202	**800-321-2599**	303-297-3111
Brown's Wharf Inn					
121 Atlantic Ave	Boothbay Harbor	ME	04538	**800-334-8110**	207-633-5440
Budget Host International					
2307 Roosevelt Dr	Arlington	TX	76016	**800-283-4678**	817-861-6088
Budget Suites of America					
2770 N Hwy 360	Grand Prairie	TX	75050	**866-877-2000**	972-647-2500
Buena Vista Suites					
8203 World Ctr Dr	Orlando	FL	32821	**800-537-7737***	407-239-8588
*Resv					
Business Inn 180 MacLaren St	Ottawa	ON	K2P0L3	**800-363-1777**	613-232-1121
C'mon Inn Grand Forks					
3051 32nd Ave S	Grand Forks	ND	58201	**800-255-2323**	701-775-3320
California Hotel & Casino					
12 E Ogden Ave	Las Vegas	NV	89101	**800-634-6505**	702-385-1222
Cambridge Suites Hotel Halifax					
1583 Brunswick St	Halifax	NS	B3J3P5	**800-565-1263**	902-420-0555
Cambridge Suites Hotel Toronto					
15 Richmond St E	Toronto	ON	M5C1N2	**800-463-1990**	416-368-1990
Campus Inn & Suites					
390 E Broadway	Eugene	OR	97401	**800-888-6313**	541-343-3376
Canad Inns - Club Regent Casino Hotel					
1415 Regent Ave W	Winnipeg	MB	R2C3B2	**888-332-2623**	204-667-5560
Canad Inns Fort Garry					
1824 Pembina Hwy	Winnipeg	MB	R3T2G2	**888-332-2623**	204-261-7450
Canad Inns Garden City					
2100 McPhillips St	Winnipeg	MB	R2V3T9	**888-332-2623**	204-633-0024
Canad Inns Polo Park					
1405 St Matthews Ave	Winnipeg	MB	R3G0K5	**888-332-2623**	204-775-8791
Canal Park Lodge					
250 Canal Pk Dr	Duluth	MN	55802	**800-777-8560**	218-279-6000
Canandaigua Inn on the Lake					
770 S Main St	Canandaigua	NY	14424	**800-228-2801**	585-394-7800
Canary Hotel					
31 W Carrillo	Santa Barbara	CA	93101	**866-999-5401**	805-884-0300
Cannery Casino & Hotel, The					
Cannery Casino Resorts LLC					
2121 E Craig Rd	North Las Vegas	NV	89030	**866-999-4899**	702-507-5700
Capital Hill Hotel & Suites					
88 Albert St	Ottawa	ON	K1P5E9	**800-463-7705**	613-235-1413
Capital Hotel					
111 W Markham St	Little Rock	AR	72201	**877-637-0037**	501-374-7474
Capitol Plaza Hotel & Conference Ctr					
100 State St	Montpelier	VT	05602	**800-274-5252**	802-223-5252
Capitol Plaza Hotel Jefferson City					
415 W McCarty St	Jefferson City	MO	65101	**800-338-8088**	573-635-1234
Capt Hirams Resort					
1606 Indian River Dr	Sebastian	FL	32958	**888-447-2671**	772-589-4345
Captain Daniel Stone Inn					
10 Water St	Brunswick	ME	04011	**877-573-2374**	207-373-1824
Caribe Royale Orlando All-Suites Hotel & Convention Ctr					
8101 World Ctr Dr	Orlando	FL	32821	**800-823-8300***	407-238-8000
*Resv					
Carlson					
Radisson Hotels & Resorts					
701 Carlson Pkwy	Minnetonka	MN	55305	**800-333-3333**	763-212-5000
Carlson Hotels Worldwide					
Country Inns & Suites by Carlson					
11340 Blondo St Ste 100	Omaha	NE	68164	**800-600-7275**	
Carlton on Madison Ave					
88 Madison Ave	New York	NY	10016	**800-601-8500***	212-532-4100
*Resv					
Carlyle Hotel, The					
1731 New Hampshire Ave NW	Washington	DC	20009	**877-301-0019**	202-234-3200
Carmel River Inn					
26600 Oliver Rd	Carmel	CA	93923	**800-882-8142**	831-624-1575
Carnegie Hotel					
1216 W State of Franklin Rd	Johnson City	TN	37604	**866-757-8277**	423-979-6400
Carolina Inn					
211 Pittsboro St	Chapel Hill	NC	27516	**800-962-8519**	919-933-2001
Carousel Beachfront Hotel & Suites					
11700 Coastal Hwy	Ocean City	MD	21842	**800-641-0011**	410-524-1000
Carousel Inn & Suites					
1530 S Harbor Blvd	Anaheim	CA	92802	**800-854-6767**	714-758-0444
Cartier Place Suite Hotel					
180 Cooper St	Ottawa	ON	K2P2L5	**800-236-8399**	613-236-5000
Casa Madrona Hotel					
801 Bridgeway	Sausalito	CA	94965	**800-288-0502***	415-332-0502
*General					
Casa Monica Hotel					
95 Cordova St	Saint Augustine	FL	32084	**800-648-1888***	904-827-1888
*Help Line					
Casa Munras Hotel					
700 Munras Ave	Monterey	CA	93940	**800-222-2446**	831-375-2411
Casa Via Mar Inn & Tennis Club					
377 W Ch Islands Blvd	Port Hueneme	CA	93041	**800-992-5522**	805-984-6222
Casablanca Hotel					
147 W 43rd St	New York	NY	10036	**888-922-7225**	212-869-1212
Cascades Inn					
3226 Shepherd of the Hills Expy	Branson	MO	65616	**800-588-8424**	417-335-8424
Casino Royale Hotel					
3411 Las Vegas Blvd S	Las Vegas	NV	89109	**800-854-7666**	702-737-3500
Castle in the Sand Hotel					
3701 Atlantic Ave	Ocean City	MD	21842	**800-552-7263**	410-289-6846
Castle Inn & Suites					
1734 S Harbor Blvd	Anaheim	CA	92802	**800-227-8530**	714-774-8111
Castle on the Hudson					
400 Benedict Ave	Tarrytown	NY	10591	**800-616-4487**	914-631-1980
Centennial Hotel					
96 Pleasant St	Concord	NH	03301	**800-360-4839**	603-227-9000
Center Court Historic Inn & Cottages					
1075 Duval St C-19	Key West	FL	33040	**800-797-8787**	305-296-9292
Century Hotel South Beach					
140 Ocean Dr	Miami Beach	FL	33139	**877-659-8855**	305-674-8855
Century Plaza Hotel & Spa					
1015 Burrard St	Vancouver	BC	V6Z1Y5	**800-663-1818**	604-687-0575
Century Suites Hotel					
300 SR-446	Bloomington	IN	47401	**800-766-5446**	812-336-7777
Chamberlain West Hollywood					
1000 Westmount Dr	West Hollywood	CA	90069	**800-201-9652**	310-657-7400
Chancellor Hotel on Union Square					
433 Powell St	San Francisco	CA	94102	**800-428-4748**	415-362-2004
Chandler Inn 26 Chandler St	Boston	MA	02116	**800-842-3450**	617-482-3450
Charles Hotel Harvard Square					
One Bennett St	Cambridge	MA	02138	**800-882-1818**	617-864-1200
Charleston Place					
205 Meeting St	Charleston	SC	29401	**800-611-5545**	843-722-4900
Charter at Beaver Creek					
120 Offerson Rd PO Box 5310	Avon	CO	81620	**800-525-6660**	970-949-6660
Chase Hotel at Palm Springs					
200 W Arenas Rd	Palm Springs	CA	92262	**877-532-4273**	760-320-8866
Chase Park Plaza					
212 N KingsHwy Blvd	Saint Louis	MO	63108	**877-587-2427***	314-633-3000
*Resv					
Chateau Louis Hotel & Conference Centre					
11727 Kingsway	Edmonton	AB	T5G3A1	**800-661-9843**	780-452-7770
Chateau on the Lake					
415 N State Hwy 265	Branson	MO	65616	**888-333-5253**	417-334-1161
Chateau Vaudreuil Suites Hotel					
21700 Rt Transcanada Hwy	Vaudreuil-Dorion	QC	J7V8P3	**800-363-7896**	450-455-0955
Chateau Versailles					
1659 Sherbrooke St W	Montreal	QC	H3H1E3	**888-933-8111**	514-933-3611
Chelsea Savoy Hotel					
204 W 23rd St	New York	NY	10011	**866-929-9353**	212-929-9353
Chesterfield Hotel					
363 Cocoanut Row	Palm Beach	FL	33480	**800-243-7871**	561-659-5800
Chestnut Hill Hotel					
8229 Germantown Ave	Philadelphia	PA	19118	**800-628-9744**	215-242-5905
Chiltern Inn					
11 Cromwell Harbor Rd	Bar Harbor	ME	04609	**800-709-0114**	207-288-3371
Chimo Hotel					
1199 Joseph Cyr St	Ottawa	ON	K1J7T4	**800-387-9779**	613-744-1060
Choice Hotels International Inc					
10750 Columbia Pk	Silver Spring	MD	20901	**800-424-6423**	301-592-5000
NYSE: CHH					
Choice Hotels International, Inc.					
997 New Loudon Rd	Latham	NY	12110	**800-424-6423**	518-785-0931
Chrysalis Inn & Spa					
804 Tenth St	Bellingham	WA	98225	**888-808-0005**	360-756-1005
Churchill Hotel					
1914 Connecticut Ave NW	Washington	DC	20009	**800-424-2464**	202-797-2000
Cincinnatian Hotel					
601 Vine St	Cincinnati	OH	45202	**800-942-9000**	513-381-3000
Circa39 Hotel					
3900 Collins Ave	Miami Beach	FL	33140	**877-824-7223***	305-538-4900
*Resv					
Circus Circus Hotel & Casino Reno					
500 N Sierra St	Reno	NV	89503	**800-648-5010**	775-329-0711
Circus Circus Hotel Casino & Theme Park Las Vegas					
2880 Las Vegas Blvd S	Las Vegas	NV	89109	**800-634-3450***	702-734-0410
*Resv					
Cleftstone Manor					
92 Eden St	Bar Harbor	ME	04609	**888-288-4951**	207-288-8086
Cliff House at Pikes Peak					
306 Canyon Ave	Manitou Springs	CO	80829	**888-212-7000**	

Classified Section

Name	Address	City	State	ZIP	Toll-Free	Phone
Clinton Inn Hotel	145 Dean Dr	Tenafly	NJ	07670	800-275-4411	201-871-3200
Clocktower Inn Hotel	181 E Santa Clara St	Ventura	CA	93001	800-727-1027	805-652-0141
ClubHouse Hotel & Suites Sioux Falls	2320 S Louise Ave	Sioux Falls	SD	57106	866-534-8700	605-361-8700
Coachman Inn	32959 SR-Hwy 20	Oak Harbor	WA	98277	800-635-0043	360-675-0727
Coast Edmonton House Suite Hotel	1090 W Georgia S Ste 900	Vancouver	BC	V6E3V7	800-716-6199	604-682-7982
Coastal Inn Concorde	379 Windmill Rd	Dartmouth	NS	B3A1J6	800-565-1565	902-465-7777
Coastal Inns Inc	111 Warwick St Box 280	Digby	NS	B0V1A0	800-665-7829	800-401-1155
Coastal Palms Hotel	120th St Coastal Hwy	Ocean City	MD	21842	800-641-0011	
Cocca's Inn & Suites	Corner of Wolf Rd & Central Ave	Albany	NY	12205	888-426-2227	518-459-2240
Cohasset Harbor Inn	124 Elm St	Cohasset	MA	02025	800-252-5287	781-383-6650
Colby Hill Inn	33 The Oaks PO Box 779	Henniker	NH	03242	800-531-0330	603-428-3281
Colcord Hotel	15 N Robinson Ave	Oklahoma City	OK	73102	866-781-3800	405-601-4300
Colonnade Hotel	120 Huntington Ave	Boston	MA	02116	800-962-3030	617-424-7000
Colony South Hotel	7401 Surratts Rd	Clinton	MD	20735	800-537-1147	301-856-4500
Colorado Belle Hotel & Casino	2100 S Casino Dr *Resv	Laughlin	NV	89029	877-460-0777*	702-298-4000
Columbia Gorge Hotel	4000 Westcliff Dr	Hood River	OR	97031	800-345-1921	541-386-5566
Columns, The	3811 St Charles Ave	New Orleans	LA	70115	800-445-9308	504-899-9308
Comfort Inn & Suites Milwaukee	916 E State St	Milwaukee	WI	53202	800-424-6423	414-276-8800
Commander Hotel	1401 Atlantic Ave	Ocean City	MD	21842	888-289-6166	410-289-6166
Commonwealth Park Suites Hotel	901 Bank St	Richmond	VA	23219	888-343-7301	804-343-7300
Conch House Heritage Inn	625 Truman Ave	Key West	FL	33040	800-207-5806	305-293-0020
Conch House Marina Resort	57 Comares Ave	Saint Augustine	FL	32080	800-940-6256	904-829-8646
Congress Plaza Hotel & Convention Ctr	520 S Michigan Ave	Chicago	IL	60605	800-635-1666	312-427-3800
Conrad Miami	1395 Brickell Ave	Miami	FL	33131	800-002-6672	305-503-6500
Cooper Hotel & Conference Ctr	12230 Preston Rd	Dallas	TX	75230	800-444-5187	972-386-0306
Copley Square Hotel	47 Huntington Ave	Boston	MA	02116	800-225-7062	617-536-9000
Cornhusker Hotel, The	333 S 13th St	Lincoln	NE	68508	866-706-7706	402-474-7474
Cosmopolitan Hotel Toronto	Eight Colborne St	Toronto	ON	M5E1E1	800-958-3488	416-350-2000
Country Inn at the Mall	936 Stillwater Ave *Resv	Bangor	ME	04401	800-244-3961*	207-941-0200
Country Inn Lake Resort	1332 Airport Rd	Hot Springs	AR	71913	800-822-7402	501-767-3535
Courtyard Fort Lauderdale Beach	440 Seabreeze Blvd	Fort Lauderdale	FL	33316	888-236-2427	954-524-8733
Cove Inn	900 Broad Ave S	Naples	FL	34102	800-255-4365	239-262-7161
Cowboy Village Resort	120 S Flat Creek Dr PO Box 38	Jackson	WY	83001	800-962-4988	307-733-3121
Crest Hotel & Suites	1670 James Ave	Miami Beach	FL	33139	800-531-3880	305-531-0321
Crockett Hotel	320 Bonham St	San Antonio	TX	78205	800-292-1050	210-225-6500
Cross Creek Resort	3815 Pennsylvania 8	Titusville	PA	16354	800-461-3173	814-827-9611
Crown Reef Resort	2913 S Ocean Blvd	Myrtle Beach	SC	29577	877-435-9125	843-626-8077
Crowne Plaza Syracuse	701 E Genesee St	Syracuse	NY	13210	888-227-6963	315-479-7000
Crystal Beach Suites & Health Club	6985 Collins Ave	Miami Beach	FL	33141	888-643-4630	305-865-9555
Crystal Inn	185 S State St Ste 202 *General	Salt Lake City	UT	84111	800-662-2525*	801-320-7200
Crystal Inn Salt Lake City Downtown	230 W 500 S	Salt Lake City	UT	84101	800-662-2525	801-328-4466
Curtis, The	1405 Curtis St	Denver	CO	80202	800-525-6651	303-571-0300
Custom Hotel	8639 Lincoln Blvd	Los Angeles	CA	90045	877-287-8601	310-645-0400
Dahlmann Campus Inn	615 E Huron St	Ann Arbor	MI	48104	800-666-8693	734-769-2200
Daly Seven Inc	4829 Riverside Dr	Danville	VA	24541	800-466-5337	434-822-2161
Dan'l Webster Inn	149 Main St	Sandwich	MA	02563	800-444-3566	508-888-3622
Dauphine Orleans Hotel	415 Dauphine St	New Orleans	LA	70112	800-521-7111	504-586-1800
Davenport Hotel, The	10 S Post St	Spokane	WA	99201	800-899-1482	509-455-8888
Days Inns Worldwide Inc	215 W 94th St Broadway	New York	NY	10025	800-834-2972	212-866-6400
Daytona Beach Resort & Conference Ctr	2700 N Atlantic Ave	Daytona Beach	FL	32118	800-654-6216	386-672-3770
Daytona Inn Beach Resort	219 S Atlantic Ave *General	Daytona Beach	FL	32118	800-874-1822*	386-252-3626
Dearborn Inn the - A Marriott Hotel	20301 Oakwood Blvd	Dearborn	MI	48124	800-228-9290	313-271-2700
Deer Path Inn	255 E Illinois Rd	Lake Forest	IL	60045	800-788-9480	847-234-2280
Deerfoot Inn & Casino	1000 11500 35th St SE	Calgary	AB	T2Z3W4	877-236-5225	403-236-7529
Del Monte Lodge Renaissance Rochester Hotel & Spa, The	41 N Main St	Pittsford	NY	14534	866-237-5979	585-381-9900
DELAMAR Greenwich Harbor	500 Steamboat Rd	Greenwich	CT	06830	866-335-2627	203-661-9800
Delta King Riverboat Hotel	1000 Front St	Sacramento	CA	95814	800-825-5464	916-444-5464
Destination Hotels & Resorts Inc	10333 E Dry Creek Rd Ste 450	Englewood	CO	80112	855-893-1011	303-799-3830
Diamond Head Inn	605 Diamond St	San Diego	CA	92109	888-478-7829	858-273-1900
Dinah's Garden Hotel	4261 El Camino Real	Palo Alto	CA	94306	800-227-8220	650-493-2844
Dolphin Inn	1705 Atlantic Ave	Virginia Beach	VA	23451	800-365-3467	757-491-1420
Don Hall's Guesthouse	1313 W Washington Ctr Rd *General	Fort Wayne	IN	46825	800-348-1999*	260-489-2524
Donatello, The	501 Post St	San Francisco	CA	94102	800-258-2366	415-441-7100
Doubletree Claremont	555 W Foothill Blvd	Claremont	CA	91711	800-222-8733	909-626-2411
Doubletree Hotel Downtown Wilmington Legal District	700 N King St	Wilmington	DE	19801	800-222-8733	302-655-0400
Doubletree North Shore Hotel	9599 Skokie Blvd	Skokie	IL	60077	800-445-8667	847-679-7000
Drake Hotel, The	140 E Walton Pl	Chicago	IL	60611	800-553-7253	312-787-2200
Driftwood Hotel	435 Willoughby Ave	Juneau	AK	99801	800-544-2239	907-586-2280
Driftwood on the Oceanfront	Oceanfront at 16th Ave N	Myrtle Beach	SC	29578	855-741-7986	843-448-1544
Driftwood Shores Resort	88416 First Ave	Florence	OR	97439	800-422-5091	541-997-8263
Driskill Hotel	604 Brazos St	Austin	TX	78701	800-252-9367	512-474-5911
Drury Hotels Company LLC	721 Emerson Rd Ste 400	Saint Louis	MO	63141	800-378-7946	314-429-2255
Dude Rancher Lodge	415 N 29th St	Billings	MT	59101	800-221-3302	406-259-5561
Duke Towers- All Condominium Hotel	807 W Trinity Ave	Durham	NC	27701	866-385-3869	919-687-4444
Duke's 8th Avenue Hotel	630 W Eigth Ave	Anchorage	AK	99501	800-478-4837	907-274-6213
Dunes Manor Hotel	2800 Baltimore Ave	Ocean City	MD	21842	800-523-2888	410-289-1100
Dunhill Hotel	237 N Tryon St	Charlotte	NC	28202	800-354-4141	704-332-4141
Dylan Hotel	52 E 41st St	New York	NY	10017	866-553-9526	212-338-0500
Dynasty Suites	1235 W Colton Ave *General	Redlands	CA	92374	800-874-8958*	909-793-6648
Eagle Mountain House	179 Carter Notch Rd PO Box 804	Jackson	NH	03846	800-966-5779	603-383-9111
East Canyon Hotel & Spa	288 E Camino Monte Vista	Palm Springs	CA	92262	877-324-6835	760-320-1928
Eden House	1015 Fleming St	Key West	FL	33040	800-533-5397	
Edgewater Beach Hotel	1901 Gulf Shore Blvd N	Naples	FL	34102	888-564-1308	
Edgewater Hotel	2411 Alaskan Way Pier 67	Seattle	WA	98121	800-624-0670	206-728-7000
Edgewater Resort	200 Edgewater Cir	Hot Springs	AR	71913	800-234-3687	501-767-3311
Edgewater Resort & Waterpark	2400 London Rd	Duluth	MN	55812	800-777-7925	218-728-3601
Edmonds Harbor Inn & Suites	130 W Dayton	Edmonds	WA	98020	800-441-8033	425-771-5021
El Cortez Hotel & Casino	600 E Fremont St	Las Vegas	NV	89101	800-634-6703	702-385-5200
El Rey Inn	1862 Cerillos Rd	Santa Fe	NM	87505	800-521-1349	505-982-1931
El Tovar Hotel	1 Main Street	Grand Canyon	AZ	86023	888-297-2757	928-638-2631
Elan Hotel	8435 Beverly Blvd	Los Angeles	CA	90048	866-203-2212	323-658-6663
Eldorado Hotel	309 W San Francisco St	Santa Fe	NM	87501	800-955-4455	505-988-4455
Eldorado Hotel Casino	345 N Virginia St *Resv	Reno	NV	89501	800-879-8879*	775-786-5700
Eldridge Hotel	701 Massachusetts St	Lawrence	KS	66044	800-527-0909	785-749-5011
Eliot Hotel, The	370 Commonwealth Ave	Boston	MA	02215	800-443-5468	617-267-1607
Elvis Presley's Heartbreak Hotel	3677 Elvis Presley Blvd	Memphis	TN	38116	877-777-0606	901-332-1000
Embassy Hotel & Suites	25 Cartier St	Ottawa	ON	K2P1J2	800-661-5495	613-237-2111
Embassy West Hotel	1400 Carling Ave	Ottawa	ON	K1Z7L8	800-267-8696	613-729-4331
Emerald Queen Hotel & Casino	5700 Pacific Hwy E	Fife	WA	98424	888-820-3555	253-922-2000
Emerson Resort & Spa	5340 Rt 28	Mount Tremper	NY	12457	877-688-2828	845-688-7900
Emily Morgan Hotel	705 E Houston St	San Antonio	TX	78205	800-824-6674	210-225-5100
Empire Landmark Hotel & Conference Centre	1400 Robson St	Vancouver	BC	V6G1B9	800-830-6144	604-687-0511
Empress Hotel	7766 Fay Ave	La Jolla	CA	92037	888-369-9900	858-454-3001
Enclave Suites of Orlando	6165 Carrier Dr	Orlando	FL	32819	800-457-0077	407-351-1155
Ethan Allen Hotel	21 Lake Ave Ext	Danbury	CT	06811	800-742-1776	203-744-1776
Euro-Suites Hotel	University Centre 501 Chestnut Ridge Rd	Morgantown	WV	26505	800-678-4837	
Evergreen Lodge	250 S Frontage Rd W	Vail	CO	81657	800-284-8245	970-476-7810

				Toll-Free	Phone
Excalibur Hotel & Casino					
3850 Las Vegas Blvd S PO Box 96776	Las Vegas	NV	89109	**877-750-5464**	702-597-7777
Executive Hotel Vintage Court					
650 Bush St	San Francisco	CA	94108	**888-388-3932**	415-392-4666
Executive Inn					
978 Phillips Ln	Louisville	KY	40209	**888-205-8144**	502-367-6161
Executive Inn Group Corp					
Executive Hotels & Resorts					
1080 Howe St Eighth Fl	Vancouver	BC	V6Z2T1	**866-642-6888**	604-642-5250
Executive Pacific Plaza Hotel					
400 Spring St	Seattle	WA	98104	**888-388-3932**	206-623-3900
Executive Suite Hotel					
4360 SpenaRd Rd	Anchorage	AK	99517	**800-770-6366**	907-243-6366
Expressway Hotels					
4303 17th Ave S	Fargo	ND	58103	**877-239-4303**	701-239-4303
Extended Stay America					
11525 N Community House Rd Ste 100	Charlotte	NC	28277	**800-804-3724**	980-345-1600
Crossland Economy Studios					
11525 N Community House Rd Ste 100	Charlotte	NC	28277	**800-804-3724**	980-345-1600
Extended StayAmerica					
11525 N Community House Rd Ste 100	Charlotte	NC	28277	**800-804-3724**	980-345-1600
Extended Stay Hotels					
StudioPLUS Deluxe Studios					
530 Woods Lake Rd	Greenville	SC	29607	**800-804-3724**	864-288-4300
Fairbanks Princess Riverside Lodge					
4477 Pikes Landing Rd	Fairbanks	AK	99709	**800-426-0500**	907-455-4477
Fairmont Hotels & Resorts Inc					
100 Wellington St W TD Ctr Ste 1600	Toronto	ON	M5K1B7	**800-441-3313***	416-874-2600
*General					
Fairmount Hotel, The					
401 S Alamo St	San Antonio	TX	78205	**877-229-8808**	210-224-8800
Falmouth Inn 824 Main St	Falmouth	MA	02540	**800-255-4157**	508-540-2500
Fargo C'mon Inn Hotel					
4338 20th Ave SW	Fargo	ND	58103	**800-334-1570**	701-277-9944
Fenwick Inn					
13801 Coastal Hwy	Ocean City	MD	21842	**800-492-1873**	410-250-1100
Fiesta Henderson					
777 W Lk Mead Pkwy	Henderson	NV	89015	**888-899-7770**	702-558-7000
Fifteen Beacon Hotel					
15 Beacon St	Boston	MA	02108	**877-982-3226**	617-670-1500
Figueroa Hotel					
939 S Figueroa St	Los Angeles	CA	90015	**800-421-9092***	213-627-8971
*General					
Fiksdal Hotel & Suites					
1215 Second St SW	Rochester	MN	55902	**800-366-3451**	507-288-2671
Findlay Inn & Conference Ctr					
200 E Main Cross St	Findlay	OH	45840	**800-825-1455***	419-422-5682
*Cust Svc					
Fireside Inn & Suites					
25 Airport Rd	West Lebanon	NH	03784	**877-258-5900**	603-298-5900
First Gold Hotel					
270 Main St	Deadwood	SD	57732	**800-274-1876**	605-578-9777
Fisherman's Wharf Inn					
22 Commercial St	Boothbay Harbor	ME	04538	**800-628-6872**	207-633-5090
Fitzpatrick Manhattan Hotel					
687 Lexington Ave	New York	NY	10022	**800-367-7701**	212-355-0100
Flagship All Suites Resort					
60 N Maine Ave	Atlantic City	NJ	08401	**800-647-7890**	609-343-7447
Foley House Inn					
14 W Hull St Chippewa Sq	Savannah	GA	31401	**800-647-3708**	912-232-6622
Foot of the Mountain Motel					
200 W Arapahoe Ave	Boulder	CO	80302	**866-773-5489**	303-442-5688
Foothills Inn					
1625 N La Crosse St	Rapid City	SD	57701	**877-428-5666**	605-348-5640
Fort Garry, The					
222 Broadway	Winnipeg	MB	R3C0R3	**800-665-8088**	204-942-8251
Fort Marcy Hotel Suites					
321 Kearney Ave	Santa Fe	NM	87501	**888-667-2775**	505-988-2800
Four Points by Sheraton Charlotte					
315 E Woodlawn Rd	Charlotte	NC	28217	**800-368-7764**	704-522-0852
Four Points by Sheraton French Quarter					
541 Bourbon St	New Orleans	LA	70130	**800-535-7891**	504-524-7611
Four Queens Hotel & Casino					
202 Fremont St	Las Vegas	NV	89101	**800-634-6045**	702-385-4011
Four Sails Resort Hotel					
3301 Atlantic Ave	Virginia Beach	VA	23451	**800-227-4213**	757-491-8100
Four Seasons Hotels Inc					
1165 Leslie St	Toronto	ON	M3C2K8	**800-332-3442**	416-449-1750
Francis Marion Hotel, The					
387 King St	Charleston	SC	29403	**877-756-2121**	843-722-0600
Fremont Hotel & Casino					
200 Fremont St	Las Vegas	NV	89101	**800-634-6460**	702-385-3232
French Quarter Suites Hotel					
1119 N Rampart St	New Orleans	LA	70116	**800-457-2253**	504-524-7725
G6 Hospitality LLC					
Motel 6					
4001 International Pkwy	Carrollton	TX	75007	**800-466-8356**	972-360-9000
Galt House Hotel					
140 N Fourth St	Louisville	KY	40202	**800-843-4258**	502-589-5200
Garden City Hotel					
45 Seventh St	Garden City	NY	11530	**877-549-0400**	516-747-3000
Garden Court Hotel					
520 Cowper St	Palo Alto	CA	94301	**800-824-9028**	650-322-9000
Garden Place Hotel					
6461 Transit Rd	Depew	NY	14043	**877-456-4097**	716-683-7990
Gardens Hotel					
526 Angela St	Key West	FL	33040	**800-526-2664**	305-294-2661
Garfield Suites Hotel					
Two Garfield Pl	Cincinnati	OH	45202	**800-367-2155**	513-421-3355
Garland, The					
4222 Vineland Ave	North Hollywood	CA	91602	**800-238-3759**	818-980-8000
Garrett's Desert Inn					
311 Old Santa Fe Trl	Santa Fe	NM	87501	**800-888-2145**	505-982-1851
Gaslamp Plaza Suites					
520 E St	San Diego	CA	92101	**800-874-8770**	619-232-9500
Gastonian, The					
220 E Gaston St	Savannah	GA	31401	**800-322-6603**	912-232-2869
Gateways Inn 51 Walker St	Lenox	MA	01240	**888-492-9466**	413-637-2532
Gaylord Opryland Hotel & Convention Ctr					
2800 Opryland Dr	Nashville	TN	37214	**888-236-2427**	615-889-1000
General Morgan Inn					
111 N Main St	Greeneville	TN	37743	**800-223-2679**	423-787-1000
Genesee Grande Hotel					
1060 E Genesee St	Syracuse	NY	13210	**800-365-4663**	315-476-4212
Geneva on the Lake					
1001 Lochland Rd	Geneva	NY	14456	**800-343-6382**	315-789-7190
George Washington University Inn					
824 New Hampshire Ave NW	Washington	DC	20037	**800-426-4455**	202-337-6620
Georgetown Inn					
1310 Wisconsin Ave	Washington	DC	20007	**866-971-6618**	202-333-8900
Georgian Court Hotel					
773 Beatty St	Vancouver	BC	V6B2M4	**800-663-1155**	604-682-5555
Georgian Hotel					
1415 Ocean Ave	Santa Monica	CA	90401	**800-538-8147**	310-395-9945
Georgian Resort					
384 Canada St	Lake George	NY	12845	**800-525-3436**	518-668-5401
Georgian Terrace Hotel					
659 Peachtree St NE	Atlanta	GA	30308	**800-651-2316**	404-897-1991
Gershwin Hotel 7 E 27th St	New York	NY	10016	**855-468-3501**	212-545-8000
Gideon Putnam Resort & Spa					
24 Gideon Putnam Rd	Saratoga Springs	NY	12866	**800-452-7275**	518-584-3000
Glacier Bay Country Inn					
35 Tong Rd	Gustavus	AK	99826	**800-628-0912**	
Glass House Inn 3202 W 26th St	Erie	PA	16506	**800-956-7222**	814-833-7751
Glen Grove Suites					
2837 Yonge St	Toronto	ON	M4N2J6	**800-565-3024**	416-489-8441
Glendorn 1000 Glendorn Dr	Bradford	PA	16701	**800-843-8568**	814-362-6511
Glenerin Inn, The					
1695 The Collegeway	Mississauga	ON	L5L3S7	**877-991-9971**	905-828-6103
Glenmore Inn					
2720 Glenmore Trl SE	Calgary	AB	T2C2E6	**800-661-3163**	403-279-8611
Glidden House					
1901 Ford Dr	Cleveland	OH	44106	**866-812-4537**	216-231-8900
Glorietta Bay Inn					
1630 Glorietta Blvd	Coronado	CA	92118	**800-283-9383**	619-435-3101
Gold Coast Hotel & Casino					
4000 W Flamingo Rd	Las Vegas	NV	89103	**800-331-5334**	702-367-7111
Goldbelt Hotel Juneau					
51 Egan Dr	Juneau	AK	99801	**888-478-6909**	907-586-6900
Golden Eagle Resort					
511 Mountain Rd PO Box 1090	Stowe	VT	05672	**800-626-1010**	802-253-4811
Golden Hotel, The					
800 11th St	Golden	CO	80401	**800-233-7214**	303-279-0100
Goldener Hirsch Inn					
7570 Royal St E	Park City	UT	84060	**800-252-3373***	435-649-7770
*Cust Svc					
Good Hotel					
Good Hotel					
112 Seventh St	San Francisco	CA	94103	**800-444-5819**	415-621-7001
Good-Nite Inn Fremont					
4135 Cushing Pkwy	Fremont	CA	94538	**800-648-3466**	510-656-9307
Gouverneur Hotel Montreal (Place-Dupuis)					
1000 Sherbrooke St W Ste 2300	Montreal	QC	H3A3R3	**888-910-1111**	
Governor Calvert House					
58 State Cir	Annapolis	MD	21401	**800-847-8882**	410-263-2641
Governor Hotel					
621 S Capitol Way	Olympia	WA	98501	**800-716-6199**	360-352-7700
Governor's Inn					
210 Richards Blvd	Sacramento	CA	95814	**800-999-6689**	916-448-7224
Grafton on Sunset					
8462 W Sunset Blvd	West Hollywood	CA	90069	**800-821-3660**	323-654-4600
Graham, The					
1075 Thomas Jefferson St NW	Washington	DC	20007	**855-341-1292**	202-337-0900
Gramercy Park Hotel					
2 Lexington Ave	New York	NY	10010	**866-784-1300**	212-920-3300
Grand America Hotel					
555 S Main St	Salt Lake City	UT	84111	**800-621-4505**	801-258-6000
Grand Country Inn					
Grand Country Sq 1945 W Hwy 76	Branson	MO	65616	**888-505-4096**	417-335-3535
Grand Del Mar					
5300 Grand Del Mar Ct	San Diego	CA	92130	**855-314-2030**	858-314-2000
Grand Gateway Hotel					
1721 N LaCrosse St	Rapid City	SD	57701	**866-742-1300**	605-342-8853
Grand Hotel & Suites Toronto					
225 Jarvis St	Toronto	ON	M5B2C1	**877-324-7263**	416-863-9000
Grand Hotel Minneapolis, The					
615 Second Ave S	Minneapolis	MN	55402	**866-843-4726**	612-288-8888
Grand Oaks Hotel					
2315 Green Mountain Dr	Branson	MO	65616	**800-553-6423**	
Grand Summit Hotel					
570 Springfield Ave	Summit	NJ	07901	**800-346-0773**	908-273-3000
Grande Colonial					
910 Prospect St	La Jolla	CA	92037	**888-828-5498**	
Grant Plaza Hotel					
465 Grant Ave	San Francisco	CA	94108	**800-472-6899**	415-434-3883
Granville Island Hotel					
1253 Johnston St	Vancouver	BC	V6H3R9	**800-663-1840***	604-683-7373
*Resv					
Great Divide Lodge					
550 Village Rd PO Box 8059	Breckenridge	CO	80424	**888-400-9590**	970-547-5550
Green Mountain Inn					
18 Main St PO Box 60	Stowe	VT	05672	**800-253-7302**	802-253-7301
Green Valley Ranch Resort Casino & Spa					
2300 Paseo Verde Pkwy	Henderson	NV	89052	**866-782-9487***	702-617-7777
*Resv					
Grey Bonnet Inn					
831 Rt 100 N	Killington	VT	05751	**800-342-2086**	802-775-2537
Greyfield Inn					
Four N Second St Ste 300	Fernandina Beach	FL	32034	**866-401-8581**	904-261-6408
GuestHouse International LLC					
100 Bluegrass Commons Blvd Ste 110	Hendersonville	TN	37075	**800-214-8378**	
Habana Inn					
2200 NW 40th St	Oklahoma City	OK	73112	**800-988-2221**	405-525-0730
Habitat Suites					
500 E Highland Mall Blvd	Austin	TX	78752	**800-535-4663**	512-467-6000

Classified Section

	Toll-Free	Phone
Hacienda The at Hotel Santa Fe		
1501 Paseo del Peralta ....Santa Fe NM 87501	**855-825-9876**	505-955-7805
Halekulani Hotel		
2199 Kalia Rd ....Honolulu HI 96815	**800-367-2343**	808-923-2311
Half Moon Bay Lodge & Conference Ctr		
2400 S Cabrillo Hwy ....Half Moon Bay CA 94019	**800-710-0778**	650-726-9000
Halifax Marriott Harborfront Hotel		
1919 Upper Water St ....Halifax NS B3J3J5	**800-450-4442**	902-421-1700
Halliburton House Inn		
5184 Morris St ....Halifax NS B3J1B3	**888-512-3344**	902-420-0658
Hallmark Inns & Resorts		
15455 Hallmark Dr Ste 200 ....Lake Oswego OR 97035	**888-448-4449**	
Handlery Union Square Hotel		
351 Geary St ....San Francisco CA 94102	**800-995-4874**	415-781-7800
Hanover Inn		
Two E Wheelock St ....Hanover NH 03755	**800-443-7024**	603-643-4300
Harbor Court Hotel		
550 Light St ....Baltimore MD 21202	**800-766-3782**	410-234-0550
Harbor View Hotel		
131 N Water St Martha's Vineyard		
PO Box 7 ....Edgartown MA 02539	**800-225-6005**	508-627-7000
Harborside Hotel & Marina		
55 W St ....Bar Harbor ME 04609	**800-328-5033**	207-288-5033
Harborside Inn		
One Christie's Landing ....Newport RI 02840	**800-427-9444**	401-846-6600
Hard Rock Hotel & Casino Biloxi		
777 Beach Blvd ....Biloxi MS 39530	**877-877-6256**	228-374-7625
Hard Rock Hotel San Diego		
207 Fifth Ave ....San Diego CA 92101	**866-751-7625**	619-702-3000
Harrah's Council Bluffs		
1 Harrahs Blvd ....Council Bluffs IA 51501	**800-342-7724**	712-329-6000
Harrah's Joliet		
151 N Joliet St ....Joliet IL 60432	**800-522-4700**	815-740-7800
Harrah's Las Vegas		
3475 Las Vegas Blvd S ....Las Vegas NV 89109	**800-214-9110**	
Harrah's Reno 219 N Ctr St ....Reno NV 89501	**866-736-6427**	775-788-3044
Harraseeket Inn		
162 Main St ....Freeport ME 04032	**800-342-6423**	207-865-9377
Hartness House Inn		
30 Orchard St ....Springfield VT 05156	**800-732-4789**	802-885-2115
Harvard Square Hotel		
110 Mt Auburn St Harvard Sq. ....Cambridge MA 02138	**800-458-5886**	617-864-5200
Harvest Inn 1 Main St ....Saint Helena CA 94574	**800-950-8466**	707-963-9463
Hassayampa Inn		
122 E Gurley St ....Prescott AZ 86301	**800-322-1927***	
*Cust Svc		
Hastings House Country House Hotel		
160 Upper Ganges Rd ....Salt Spring Island BC V8K2S2	**800-661-9255**	250-537-2362
Hawaiian Inn		
2301 S Atlantic Ave ......Daytona Beach Shores FL 32118	**800-922-3023**	386-255-5411
Hawthorne Hotel		
18 Washington Sq W ....Salem MA 01970	**800-729-7829**	978-744-4080
Hawthorne Inn & Conference Ctr		
420 High St ....Winston-Salem NC 27101	**877-777-3099**	336-777-3000
Heartland Inns 87-2nd St ....Coralville IA 52241	**800-334-3277***	319-351-8132
*Resv		
Helmsley Sandcastle Hotel		
1540 Ben Franklin Dr ....Sarasota FL 34236	**800-225-2181**	941-388-2181
Henley Park Hotel		
926 Massachusetts Ave NW ....Washington DC 20001	**800-222-8474**	202-638-5200
Henlopen Hotel		
511 N Boardwalk ....Rehoboth Beach DE 19971	**800-441-8450**	302-227-2551
Heritage Inn, The		
34521 Postal Ln ....Lewes DE 19958	**800-669-9399**	
Hermitage Hotel		
231 Sixth Ave N ....Nashville TN 37219	**888-888-9414**	615-244-3121
Hermosa Inn		
5532 N Palo Cristi Rd ....Paradise Valley AZ 85253	**800-241-1210**	602-955-8614
Hershey Entertainment & Resorts Co		
27 W Chocolate Ave ....Hershey PA 17033	**800-437-7439**	
Hershey Lodge		
325 University Dr ....Hershey PA 17033	**800-437-7439**	717-533-3311
Hilgard House Hotel & Suites		
927 Hilgard Ave ....Los Angeles CA 90024	**800-826-3934**	310-208-3945
Hilltop Inn of Vermont		
3472 Airport Rd ....Montpelier VT 05602	**877-609-0003**	802-229-5766
Hilton Worldwide		
7930 Jones Branch Dr ....McLean VA 22102	**800-445-8667**	703-883-1000
Historic Bullock Hotel		
633 Main St ....Deadwood SD 57732	**800-336-1876**	
Historic French Market Inn		
509 Decatur St ....New Orleans LA 70130	**800-366-2743**	504-561-5621
Historic Inns of Annapolis		
58 State Cir ....Annapolis MD 21401	**800-847-8882**	410-263-2641
HLC Hotels Inc		
7080 Abercorn St PO Box 13069 ....Savannah GA 31416	**800-344-4378**	912-352-4493
Holiday Inn		
301 Government St ....Mobile AL 36602	**888-465-4329**	251-694-0100
Holiday Inn Express DFW North		
4550 W John Carpenter Fwy ....Irving TX 75063	**800-465-4329**	
Holiday Inn Resort Daytona Beach Oceanfront		
1615 S Atlantic Ave ....Daytona Beach FL 32118	**800-874-0975**	386-255-0921
Hollywood Roosevelt Hotel		
7000 Hollywood Blvd ....Los Angeles CA 90028	**800-950-7667**	323-466-7000
Horton Grand Hotel		
311 Island Ave ....San Diego CA 92101	**800-542-1886**	619-544-1886
Master Hosts Inns & Resorts		
1726 Montreal Cir ....Tucker GA 30084	**800-247-4677**	
Passport Inn		
1726 Montreal Cir ....Tucker GA 30084	**800-251-1962**	
Red Carpet Inn		
1726 Montreal Cir ....Tucker GA 30084	**800-247-4677**	
Hospitality International Inc		
Scottish Inns		
1726 Montreal Cir ....Tucker GA 30084	**800-251-1962**	
Hospitality Suites Resort		
409 N Scottsdale Rd ....Scottsdale AZ 85257	**800-445-5115**	480-949-5115

	Toll-Free	Phone
Hotel & Suites Normandin		
4700 Pierre-Bertrand Blvd ....Quebec QC G2J1A4	**800-463-6721**	418-622-1611
Hotel 1000 1000 First Ave ....Seattle WA 98104	**877-315-1088**	206-957-1000
Hotel 140 140 Clarendon St ....Boston MA 02116	**800-714-0140**	617-585-5600
Hotel 43 981 Grove St ....Boise ID 83702	**800-243-4622**	208-342-4622
Hotel 71		
71 St Pierre St ....Quebec City QC G1K4A4	**888-692-1171**	418-692-1171
Hotel Abri		
127 Ellis St ....San Francisco CA 94102	**866-778-6169**	415-392-8800
Hotel Adagio		
550 Geary St ....San Francisco CA 94102	**800-738-7477**	415-775-5000
Hotel Alex Johnson		
523 Sixth St ....Rapid City SD 57701	**800-888-2539**	605-342-1210
Hotel Allegro Chicago		
171 W Randolph St ....Chicago IL 60601	**800-643-1500**	312-236-0123
Hotel Ambassadeur		
3401 Blvd Ste-Anne ....Qu,bec QC G1E3L4	**800-363-4619**	418-666-2828
Hotel Ambassador		
1324 S Main St ....Tulsa OK 74119	**888-408-8282***	918-587-8200
*General		
Hotel Andra 2000 Fourth Ave ....Seattle WA 98121	**877-448-8600**	206-448-8600
Hotel Andrew Jackson		
919 Royal St ....New Orleans LA 70116	**844-561-5881**	504-561-5881
Hotel Astor		
956 Washington Ave ....Miami Beach FL 33139	**800-270-4981**	305-531-8081
Hotel at Old Town Wichita		
830 E First St ....Wichita KS 67202	**877-265-3869**	316-267-4800
Hotel Avante		
860 E El Camino Real ....Mountain View CA 94040	**800-538-1600**	650-940-1000
Hotel Beacon 2130 Broadway ....New York NY 10023	**800-572-4969**	212-787-1100
Hotel Bedford		
118 E 40th St ....New York NY 10016	**800-221-6881**	212-697-4800
Hotel Bel-Air		
701 Stone Canyon Rd ....Los Angeles CA 90077	**800-648-4097**	310-472-1211
Hotel Bethlehem		
437 Main St ....Bethlehem PA 18018	**800-607-2384**	610-625-5000
Hotel Bijou		
111 Mason St ....San Francisco CA 94102	**877-568-2733**	415-771-1200
Hotel Boulderado		
2115 13th St ....Boulder CO 80302	**800-433-4344**	303-442-4344
Hotel Burnham		
One W Washington St ....Chicago IL 60602	**866-690-1986**	312-782-1111
Hotel Captain Cook		
939 W Fifth Ave ....Anchorage AK 99501	**800-843-1950**	907-276-6000
Hotel Casa del Mar		
1910 Ocean Way ....Santa Monica CA 90405	**800-898-6999**	310-581-5533
Hotel Chateau Bellevue		
16 Rue de la Porte ....Quebec QC G1R4M9	**877-849-1877**	418-692-2573
Hotel Chateau Laurier		
1220 Pl George-V Ouest ....Quebec QC G1R5B8	**877-522-8108**	418-522-8108
Hotel Classique		
2815 Laurier Blvd ....Quebec QC G1V4H3	**800-463-1885**	418-658-2793
Hotel Colorado		
526 Pine St ....Glenwood Springs CO 81601	**800-544-3998**	970-945-6511
Hotel Commonwealth		
500 Commonwealth Ave ....Boston MA 02215	**866-784-4000**	617-933-5000
Hotel Congress		
311 E Congress St ....Tucson AZ 85701	**800-722-8848**	520-622-8848
Hotel Contessa		
306 W Market St ....San Antonio TX 78205	**866-435-0900**	210-229-9222
Hotel de Anza		
233 W Santa Clara St ....San Jose CA 95113	**800-843-3700**	408-286-1000
Hotel Deca		
4507 Brooklyn Ave NE ....Seattle WA 98105	**800-899-0251**	206-634-2000
Hotel Del Sol		
3100 Webster St ....San Francisco CA 94123	**877-433-5765**	415-921-5520
Hotel Deluxe		
729 SW 15th Ave ....Portland OR 97205	**866-895-2094**	503-219-2094
Hotel Derek 2525 W Loop S ....Houston TX 77027	**866-292-4100**	713-961-3000
Hotel Drisco		
2901 Pacific Ave ....San Francisco CA 94115	**800-738-7477**	415-346-2880
Hotel du Pont		
11th & Market Sts ....Wilmington DE 19801	**800-441-9019**	302-594-3100
Hotel Durant		
2600 Durant Ave ....Berkeley CA 94704	**855-687-7262**	510-845-8981
Hotel Edison 228 W 47th St ....New York NY 10036	**800-637-7070**	212-840-5000
Hotel Fort Des Moines		
1000 Walnut St ....Des Moines IA 50309	**800-532-1466**	515-243-1161
Hotel Galvez - A Wyndham Historic Hotel		
2024 Seawall Blvd ....Galveston TX 77550	**800-996-3426**	409-765-7721
Hotel George 15 E St NW ....Washington DC 20001	**800-546-7866***	202-347-4200
*General		
Hotel Grand Pacific		
463 Belleville St ....Victoria BC V8V1X3	**800-663-7550**	250-386-0450
Hotel Grand Victorian		
2325 W Hwy 76 ....Branson MO 65616	**800-324-8751**	417-336-2935
Hotel Granduca		
1080 Uptown Pk Blvd ....Houston TX 77056	**888-472-6382**	713-418-1000
Hotel Griffon		
155 Steuart St ....San Francisco CA 94105	**800-321-2201**	415-495-2100
Hotel Jerome 330 E Main St ....Aspen CO 81611	**855-331-7213**	970-429-5028
Hotel La Jolla		
7955 La Jolla Shores Dr ....La Jolla CA 92037	**800-941-1149**	858-459-0261
Hotel La Rose		
308 Wilson St ....Santa Rosa CA 95401	**800-527-6738**	707-579-3200
Hotel Lawrence		
302 S Houston St ....Dallas TX 75202	**877-396-0334**	214-761-9090
Hotel Le Bleu		
370 Fourth Ave ....Brooklyn NY 11215	**866-427-6073**	718-625-1500
Hotel Le Cantlie Suites		
1110 Sherbrooke St W ....Montreal QC H3A1G9	**800-567-1110**	514-842-2000
Hotel Le Capitole		
972 St Jean St ....Quebec QC G1R1R5	**800-363-4040**	418-694-4040
Hotel Le Clos Saint-Louis		
69 St Louis St ....Quebec QC G1R3Z2	**800-461-1311**	418-694-1311
Hotel Le Germain		
2050 Mansfield St ....Montreal QC H3A1Y9	**877-333-2050**	514-849-2050

				Toll-Free	Phone
Hotel Le Germain Toronto					
30 Mercer St	Toronto	ON	M5V1H3	**866-345-9501**	416-345-9500
Hotel Le Marais					
717 Conti St	New Orleans	LA	70130	**800-935-8740**	504-525-2300
Hotel le Priori					
15 du Sault-au-Matelot St	Quebec	QC	G1K3Y7	**800-351-3992**	418-692-3992
Hotel Le Soleil					
567 Hornby St	Vancouver	BC	V6C2E8	**877-632-3030**	604-632-3000
Hotel Le St-James					
355 St Jacques St	Montreal	QC	H2Y1N9	**866-841-3111**	514-841-3111
Hotel Lombardy					
2019 Pennsylvania Ave NW	Washington	DC	20006	**800-424-5486**	202-828-2600
Hotel Lord-Berri					
1199 Berri St	Montreal	QC	H2L4C6	**888-363-0363**	514-845-9236
Hotel Lucia					
400 SW Broadway	Portland	OR	97205	**877-225-1717**	503-225-1717
Hotel Lumen					
6101 Hillcrest Ave	Dallas	TX	75205	**800-908-1140**	214-219-2400
Hotel Lusso					
808 West Sprague Avenue	Spokane	WA	99201	**800-899-1482***	509-747-9750
*General					
Hotel Madera					
1310 New Hampshire Ave NW	Washington	DC	20036	**800-546-7866**	202-296-7600
Hotel Manoir Victoria					
44 Cote du Palais	Quebec	QC	G1R4H8	**800-463-6283**	418-692-1030
Hotel Maritime Plaza					
1155 Guy St	Montreal	QC	H3H2K5	**877-768-4326**	514-932-1411
Hotel Mark Twain					
345 Taylor St	San Francisco	CA	94102	**877-854-4106**	415-673-2332
Hotel Marlowe Cambridge					
25 Edwind H Land Blvd	Cambridge	MA	02141	**800-825-7140**	617-868-8000
Hotel Max 620 Stewart St	Seattle	WA	98101	**866-833-6299**	206-728-6299
Hotel Mead					
451 E Grand Ave	Wisconsin Rapids	WI	54494	**800-843-6323**	715-423-1500
Hotel Mela 120 W 44th St	New York	NY	10036	**877-452-6352**	212-710-7000
Hotel Metro					
411 E Mason St	Milwaukee	WI	53202	**877-638-7620**	414-272-1937
Hotel Monaco Chicago					
225 N Wabash Ave	Chicago	IL	60601	**800-397-7661**	312-960-8500
Hotel Monaco Denver					
1717 Champa St	Denver	CO	80202	**800-990-1303**	303-296-1717
Hotel Monaco Portland					
506 SW Washington at Fifth Ave	Portland	OR	97204	**866-861-9514**	503-222-0001
Hotel Monaco Salt Lake City					
15 West 200 South	Salt Lake City	UT	84101	**800-805-1801***	801-595-0000
*Resv					
Hotel Monaco San Francisco					
501 Geary St	San Francisco	CA	94102	**866-622-5284**	415-292-0100
Hotel Monaco Seattle					
1101 Fourth Ave	Seattle	WA	98101	**800-715-6513**	206-621-1770
Hotel Monte Vista					
100 N San Francisco St	Flagstaff	AZ	86001	**800-545-3068**	928-779-6971
Hotel Monteleone					
214 Royal St	New Orleans	LA	70130	**800-535-9595**	504-523-3341
Hotel Murano					
1320 Broadway Plz	Tacoma	WA	98402	**888-862-3255**	253-238-8000
Hotel Nikko San Francisco					
222 Mason St	San Francisco	CA	94102	**866-636-4556**	415-394-1111
Hotel Northampton					
36 King St	NorthHampton	MA	01060	**800-547-3529**	413-584-3100
Hotel Oceana					
Santa Barbara					
202 W Cabrillo Blvd	Santa Barbara	CA	93101	**800-965-9776**	805-965-4577
Hotel Omni Mont-Royal					
1050 Sherbrooke St W	Montreal	QC	H3A2R6	**800-843-6664**	514-284-1110
Hotel Orrington					
1710 Orrington Ave	Evanston	IL	60201	**888-677-4648**	847-866-8700
Hotel Pacific					
300 Pacific St	Monterey	CA	93940	**800-554-5542**	831-373-5700
Hotel Palomar San Francisco					
12 Fourth St	San Francisco	CA	94103	**866-373-4941**	415-348-1111
Hotel Park City (HPC)					
2001 Pk Ave	Park City	UT	84060	**866-933-0347**	435-200-2000
Hotel Phillips					
106 W 12th St	Kansas City	MO	64105	**800-433-1426**	816-221-7000
Hotel Plaza Athenee					
37 E 64th St	New York	NY	10065	**800-447-8800**	212-734-9100
Hotel Plaza Quebec					
3031 Laurier Blvd	Sainte-Foy	QC	G1V2M2	**800-567-5276**	418-658-2727
Hotel Plaza Real					
125 Washington Ave	Santa Fe	NM	87501	**855-752-9273**	505-988-4900
Hotel Preston					
733 Briley Pkwy	Nashville	TN	37217	**800-407-4324**	615-361-5900
Hotel Provincial					
1024 Rue Chartres	New Orleans	LA	70116	**800-535-7922**	504-581-4995
Hotel Rex					
562 Sutter St	San Francisco	CA	94102	**800-433-4434***	415-433-4434
*Resv					
Hotel Rodney 142 Second St	Lewes	DE	19958	**800-824-8754**	302-645-6466
Hotel Roger Williams					
131 Madison Ave	New York	NY	10016	**888-448-7788***	212-448-7000
*Resv					
Hotel Rouge					
1315 16th St NW	Washington	DC	20036	**800-738-1202**	202-232-8000
Hotel Royal Plaza					
1905 Hotel Plaza Blvd	Lake Buena Vista	FL	32830	**888-662-4683**	407-828-2828
Hotel Ruby Foo's					
7655 Decarie Blvd	Montreal	QC	H4P2H2	**800-361-5419**	514-731-7701
Hotel Saint Francis					
210 Don Gaspar Ave	Santa Fe	NM	87501	**800-529-5700**	505-983-5700
Hotel Saint Marie					
827 Toulouse St	New Orleans	LA	70112	**800-366-2743**	504-561-8951
Hotel Saint Pierre					
911 Burgundy St	New Orleans	LA	70116	**800-225-4040***	504-524-4401
*Resv					
Hotel San Carlos					
202 N Central Ave	Phoenix	AZ	85004	**866-253-4121**	602-253-4121
Hotel Santa Barbara					
533 State St	Santa Barbara	CA	93101	**888-259-7700**	805-957-9300
Hotel Santa Fe					
1501 Paseo de Peralta	Santa Fe	NM	87501	**855-825-9876**	505-982-1200
Hotel Sax Chicago					
333 N Dearborn St	Chicago	IL	60610	**855-880-1240**	312-245-0333
Hotel Sepia					
3135 Ch St-Louis	Sainte-Foy	QC	G1W1R9	**888-301-6837**	418-653-4941
Hotel Shelley					
844 Collins Ave	Miami Beach	FL	33139	**877-762-3477**	305-531-3341
Hotel Solamar					
435 Sixth Ave	San Diego	CA	92101	**877-230-0300**	619-819-9500
Hotel Strasburg, The					
213 S Holliday St	Strasburg	VA	22657	**800-348-8327**	540-465-9191
Hotel Teatro 1100 14th St	Denver	CO	80202	**888-727-1200**	303-228-1100
Hotel The Queen Mary					
1126 Queens Hwy	Long Beach	CA	90802	**877-342-0738**	562-435-3511
Hotel Triton					
342 Grant Ave	San Francisco	CA	94108	**800-800-1299**	415-394-0500
Hotel Universel					
2300 Ch St-Foy	Qu,bec	QC	G1V1S5	**800-463-4495**	418-653-5250
Hotel Utica 102 Lafayette St	Utica	NY	13502	**877-906-1912**	315-724-7829
Hotel Valencia Santana Row					
355 Santana Row	San Jose	CA	95128	**866-842-0100**	408-551-0010
Hotel Valley Ho					
6850 E Main St	Scottsdale	AZ	85251	**866-882-4484**	844-993-9601
Hotel Victoria 56 Yonge St	Toronto	ON	M5E1G5	**800-363-8228**	416-363-1666
Hotel Viking					
One Bellevue Ave	Newport	RI	02840	**800-556-7126**	401-847-3300
Hotel Vintage Park					
1100 Fifth Ave	Seattle	WA	98101	**800-853-3914**	206-624-8000
Hotel Vitale					
8 Mission St	San Francisco	CA	94105	**888-890-8688**	415-278-3700
Hotel Wales					
1295 Madison Ave	New York	NY	10128	**866-925-3746**	212-876-6000
Hotel XIXe Siecle					
Lhotel					
262 St Jacques St W	Vieux Montreal	QC	H2Y1N1	**877-553-0019**	514-985-0019
Hotel ZaZa Dallas					
2332 Leonard St	Dallas	TX	75201	**800-597-8399**	214-468-8399
Hotel ZaZa Houston					
5701 Main St	Houston	TX	77005	**888-880-3244***	713-526-1991
*Resv					
Humphrey's Half Moon Inn & Suites					
2303 Shelter Island Dr	San Diego	CA	92106	**800-542-7400**	619-224-3411
Hyannis Holiday Motel					
131 Ocean St	Hyannis	MA	02601	**800-423-1551**	508-775-1639
Hyannis Travel Inn 18 N St	Hyannis	MA	02601	**800-352-7190**	508-775-8200
Hyatt Carmel Highlands					
120 Highlands Dr	Carmel	CA	93923	**800-633-7313**	831-620-1234
Grand Hyatt Hotels					
71 S Wacker Dr	Chicago	IL	60606	**800-233-1234***	312-750-1234
*Resv					
Hyatt Place Hotels					
71 S Wacker Dr	Chicago	IL	60606	**888-492-8847**	312-750-1234
Hyatt Regency Hotels					
71 S Wacker Dr	Chicago	IL	60606	**800-233-1234***	312-750-1234
*Resv					
Hyatt Hotels Corp					
Park Hyatt Hotels					
71 S Wacker Dr	Chicago	IL	60606	**800-233-1234***	312-750-1234
*Resv					
Ilikai Hotel & Suites					
1777 Ala Moana Blvd	Honolulu	HI	96815	**866-536-7973**	808-949-3811
Imperial of Waikiki					
205 Lewers St	Honolulu	HI	96815	**800-347-2582**	808-923-1827
Indigo Inn One Maiden Ln	Charleston	SC	29401	**800-845-7639**	843-577-5900
Ingleside Inn					
200 W Ramon Rd	Palm Springs	CA	92264	**800-772-6655**	760-325-0046
Inlet Tower Suites					
1200 L St	Anchorage	AK	99501	**800-544-0786**	907-276-0110
Inn & Spa at Loretto					
211 Old Santa Fe Trl	Santa Fe	NM	87501	**800-727-5531**	505-988-5531
Inn at Camachee Harbor					
201 Yacht Club Dr	Saint Augustine	FL	32084	**800-688-5379**	904-825-0003
Inn at Gig Harbor					
3211 56th St NW	Gig Harbor	WA	98335	**800-795-9980**	253-858-1111
Inn at Harbour Town					
Seven Lighthouse Ln	Hilton Head Island	SC	29928	**800-732-7463***	843-363-8100
*Resv					
Inn at Henderson's Wharf					
1000 Fell St	Baltimore	MD	21231	**888-995-9560**	410-522-7777
Inn at Langley					
400 First St PO Box 835	Langley	WA	98260	**800-843-3779**	360-221-3033
Inn at Mayo Clinic					
4420 Mary Brigh Dr	Jacksonville	FL	32224	**888-255-4458**	904-992-9992
Inn at Montchanin Village					
528 Montchanin Rd	Montchanin	DE	19710	**800-269-2473**	302-888-2133
Inn at Morro Bay					
60 State Pk Rd	Morro Bay	CA	93442	**800-321-9566**	805-772-5651
Inn at Mystic					
3 Williams Ave PO Box 526	Mystic	CT	06355	**800-237-2415**	860-536-9604
Inn at Otter Crest					
301 Otter Crest Loop	Otter Rock	OR	97369	**800-452-2101**	541-765-2111
Inn at Pelican Bay					
800 Vanderbilt Beach Rd	Naples	FL	34108	**800-597-8770**	239-597-8777
Inn at Perry Cabin					
308 Watkins Ln	Saint Michaels	MD	21663	**800-722-2949**	410-745-2200
Inn at Reading, The					
1040 N Pk Rd	Wyomissing	PA	19610	**800-383-9713**	610-372-7811
Inn at Saint John					
939 Congress St	Portland	ME	04102	**800-636-9127**	207-773-6481
Inn at Spanish Head					
4009 SW Hwy 101	Lincoln City	OR	97367	**800-452-8127**	541-996-2161
Inn at the Market					
86 Pine St	Seattle	WA	98101	**800-446-4484**	206-443-3600
Inn At The Quay					
900 Quayside Dr	New Westminster	BC	V3M6G1	**800-663-2001**	604-520-1776

				Toll-Free	Phone
Inn at Union Square					
440 Post St	San Francisco	CA	94102	**800-288-4346**	415-397-3510
Inn at, The Tides, The					
800 Coast Hwy 1 PO Box 640	Bodega Bay	CA	94923	**800-541-7788**	707-875-2751
Inn by the Lake					
3300 Lk Tahoe Blvd	South Lake Tahoe	CA	96150	**800-877-1466**	530-542-0330
Inn of Chicago Magnificent Mile					
162 E Ohio St	Chicago	IL	60611	**800-424-6423***	312-787-3100
*Resv					
Inn of Long Beach					
185 Atlantic Ave	Long Beach	CA	90802	**800-230-7500**	562-435-3791
Inn of the Anasazi					
113 Washington Ave	Santa Fe	NM	87501	**888-767-3966**	505-988-3030
Inn of the Governors					
101 W Alameda St	Santa Fe	NM	87501	**800-234-4534**	505-982-4333
Inn of the Six Mountains					
2617 Killington Rd	Killington	VT	05751	**800-228-4676**	802-422-4302
Inn on Biltmore Estate					
1 Antler Hill Rd	Asheville	NC	28803	**800-411-3812**	828-225-1333
Inn on Fifth 699 Fifth Ave S	Naples	FL	34102	**888-403-8778**	239-403-8777
Inn on Gitche Gumee					
8517 Congdon Blvd	Duluth	MN	55804	**800-317-4979**	218-525-4979
Inn on Lake Superior					
350 Canal Pk Dr	Duluth	MN	55802	**888-668-4352**	218-726-1111
Inn on the Alameda					
303 E Alameda St	Santa Fe	NM	87501	**888-984-2121**	505-984-2121
Inn on the Paseo					
630 Paseo de Peralta	Santa Fe	NM	87501	**855-984-8200**	505-984-8200
Inns at Mill Falls					
312 Daniel Webster Hwy	Meredith	NH	03253	**800-622-6455**	
InnSuites Hospitality Trust InnSuites Hotels & Suites					
475 N Granada Ave Ste 102	Tucson	AZ	85701	**800-842-4242**	520-622-0923
InnSuites Hotel Tempe/Phoenix Airport					
1651 W Baseline Rd	Tempe	AZ	85283	**800-841-4242**	480-897-7900
InnSuites Hotel Tucson City Ctr					
475 N Granada Ave	Tucson	AZ	85701	**888-784-8324**	520-622-3000
Holiday Inn Express					
3 Ravinia Dr Ste 100	Atlanta	GA	30346	**800-725-8232**	770-604-2000
Holiday Inn Hotels & Resorts					
3 Ravinia Dr Ste 100	Atlanta	GA	30346	**800-725-8232**	770-604-2000
InterContinental Hotels Group					
Hotel Indigo					
3 Ravinia Dr Ste 100	Atlanta	GA	30346	**800-334-5194**	770-604-2000
Staybridge Suites					
Three Ravinia Dr Ste 100	Atlanta	GA	30346	**800-465-4329**	770-604-2000
International Hotel					
20 Second Ave SW	Rochester	MN	55902	**800-940-6811**	
International House Hotel					
221 Camp St	New Orleans	LA	70130	**800-633-5770**	504-553-9550
Iroquois New York					
49 W 44th St	New York City	NY	10036	**800-332-7220**	212-840-3080
Island Hotel, The					
690 Newport Ctr Dr	Newport Beach	CA	92660	**866-554-4620**	949-759-0808
Jack London Inn					
444 Embarcadero W	Oakland	CA	94607	**800-549-8780**	510-444-2032
Jackson Hole Lodge					
420 W Broadway PO Box 1805	Jackson	WY	83001	**800-604-9404**	307-733-2992
James Chicago, The					
55 E Ontario	Chicago	IL	60611	**888-526-3778**	312-337-1000
James Gettys Hotel					
27 Chambersburg St	Gettysburg	PA	17325	**888-900-5275**	717-337-1334
Jameson Inns					
Jameson Inns					
115 Ann Denard Dr	Washington	GA	30673	**800-526-3766**	706-678-7925
Janus Hotels & Resorts Inc					
2300 Corporate Blvd NW Ste 232	Boca Raton	FL	33431	**800-327-2110**	561-997-2325
Jared Coffin House					
29 Broad St	Nantucket	MA	02554	**800-248-2405***	508-228-2400
*Cust Svc					
Jefferson Hotel					
101 W Franklin St	Richmond	VA	23220	**800-424-8014**	804-788-8000
Jolly Hotel Madison Towers					
22 E 38th St	New York	NY	10016	**888-726-0528***	212-802-0600
*Resv					
Jolly Roger Inn					
640 W Katella Ave	Anaheim	CA	92802	**888-296-5986**	714-782-7500
Kahala Mandarin Oriental Hotel Hawaii Resort					
5000 Kahala Ave	Honolulu	HI	96816	**800-367-2525**	808-739-8888
Kawada Hotel					
200 S Hill St	Los Angeles	CA	90012	**800-752-9232**	213-621-4455
Kellogg Hotel & Conference Ctr					
219 S Harrison Rd					
Michigan State University Campus	East Lansing	MI	48824	**800-875-5090**	517-432-4000
Kensington Court Ann Arbor					
610 Hilton Blvd	Ann Arbor	MI	48108	**800-344-7829***	734-761-7800
*Orders					
Kensington Park Hotel					
450 Post St	San Francisco	CA	94102	**800-553-1900**	415-202-8700
Kensington Riverside Inn					
1126 Memorial Dr NW	Calgary	AB	T2N3E3	**877-313-3733**	403-228-4442
Kent, The					
1131 Collins Ave	Miami Beach	FL	33139	**866-826-5368**	305-604-5068
Keswick Hall 701 Club Dr	Keswick	VA	22947	**888-778-2565**	434-979-3440
Key Lime Inn					
725 Truman Ave	Key West	FL	33040	**800-549-4430**	305-294-5229
Killington Grand Resort Hotel & Conference Ctr					
4763 Killington Rd	Killington	VT	05751	**800-621-6867**	802-422-5001
Kimball Terrace Inn					
10 Huntington Rd	Northeast Harbor	ME	04662	**800-454-6225**	207-276-3383
Kimberly Hotel					
145 E 50th St	New York	NY	10022	**800-683-0400**	212-755-0400
Kimpton Hotel & Restaurant Group					
422 SW Broadway	Portland	OR	97205	**800-263-2305**	503-228-1212
Kimpton Hotel & Restaurant Group LLC					
222 Kearny St Ste 200	San Francisco	CA	94108	**800-546-7866**	415-397-5572
Kimpton Hotel & Restaurant Group, LLC					
10050 S DeAnza Blvd	Cupertino	CA	95014	**800-499-1408**	408-253-8900
King Kamehameha's Kona Beach Hotel					
75-5660 Palani Rd	Kailua-Kona	HI	96740	**800-367-2111**	808-329-2911
King Pacific Lodge					
255 W First St	North Vancouver	BC	V7M3G8	**855-825-9378**	604-987-5452
Kinzie Hotel 20 W Kinzie St	Chicago	IL	60654	**877-262-5341**	312-395-9000
Kitano New York					
66 Pk Ave E 38th St	New York	NY	10016	**800-548-2666**	212-885-7000
Knob Hill Inn					
960 N Main St PO Box 1327	Ketchum	ID	83340	**800-526-8010**	208-726-8010
Kona Kai Resort					
1551 Shelter Island Dr	San Diego	CA	92106	**800-566-2524**	619-221-8000
L' Appartement Hotel					
455 Sherbrooke W	Montreal	QC	H3A1B7	**800-363-3010**	514-284-3634
L'Ermitage Beverly Hills Hotel					
9291 Burton Way	Beverly Hills	CA	90210	**877-235-7582**	310-278-3344
L'Hotel du Vieux-Quebec					
1190 St Jean St	Quebec	QC	G1R1S6	**800-361-7787**	418-692-1850
L'Hotel Quebec					
3115 des Hotels Ave	Sainte-Foy	QC	G1W3Z6	**800-567-5276**	418-658-5120
La Fonda					
100 E San Francisco St	Santa Fe	NM	87501	**800-523-5002**	505-982-5511
La Pensione Hotel					
606 W Date St	San Diego	CA	92101	**800-232-4683**	619-236-8000
La Posada Hotel & Suites					
1000 Zaragoza St	Laredo	TX	78040	**800-444-2099***	956-722-1701
*Resv					
La Quinta Inn & Suites Secaucus Meadowlands					
350 Lighting Way	Secaucus	NJ	07094	**800-753-3757***	201-863-8700
*General					
Lafayette Hotel					
600 St Charles Ave	New Orleans	LA	70130	**800-366-2743**	504-524-4441
Lafayette Park Hotel					
3287 Mt Diablo Blvd	Lafayette	CA	94549	**877-283-8787**	925-283-3700
Lake Louise Inn					
210 Village Rd PO Box 209	Lake Louise	AB	T0L1E0	**800-661-9237**	403-522-3791
Lake Lure Inn & Spa, The					
2771 Memorial Hwy	Lake Lure	NC	28746	**888-434-4970**	828-625-2526
Lake Placid Lodge					
144 Lodge Way	Lake Placid	NY	12946	**877-523-2700**	518-523-2700
Lakeside Inn					
100 N Alexander St	Mount Dora	FL	32757	**800-556-5016**	352-383-4101
Lakeview on the Lake					
8696 E Lake Rd	Erie	PA	16511	**888-558-8439**	814-899-6948
Lamothe House Hotel					
621 Esplanade Ave	New Orleans	LA	70116	**800-535-7815**	
Lancaster Hotel					
701 Texas St	Houston	TX	77002	**800-231-0336**	713-228-9500
Landmark Inn					
230 N Front St	Marquette	MI	49855	**888-752-6362***	906-228-2580
*General					
Langdon Hall Country House Hotel & Spa					
One Langdon Dr	Cambridge	ON	N3H4R8	**800-268-1898**	519-740-2100
Langham Boston, The					
250 Franklin St	Boston	MA	02110	**800-791-7781**	617-451-1900
Lantern Lodge Motor Inn					
411 N College St	Myerstown	PA	17067	**800-262-5564**	717-866-6536
Las Vegas Club Hotel & Casino (LVC)					
18 E Fremont St	Las Vegas	NV	89101	**800-634-6532**	702-385-1664
Latham Hotel, The					
135 S 17th St	Philadelphia	PA	19103	**877-528-4261**	215-563-7474
Laurel Inn					
444 Presidio Ave	San Francisco	CA	94115	**800-738-7477**	415-567-8467
Le Chamois					
4557 Blackcomb Way	Whistler	BC	V0N1B4	**866-944-7853**	604-932-8700
Le Meridian 20 Sidney St	Cambridge	MA	02139	**800-543-4300**	617-577-0200
Le Meridien Chambers Minneapolis					
901 Hennepin Ave	Minneapolis	MN	55403	**866-961-2861***	612-767-6900
*General					
Le M,ridien Dallas, The Stoneleigh					
2927 Maple Ave	Dallas	TX	75201	**800-650-1458**	214-871-7111
Le Merigot - A JW Marriott Beach Hotel & Spa					
1740 Ocean Ave	Santa Monica	CA	90401	**888-539-7899**	310-395-9700
Le Montrose Suite Hotel					
900 Hammond St	West Hollywood	CA	90069	**800-776-0666**	310-855-1115
Le Nouvel Montreal Hotel & Spa					
1740 Rene-Levesque Blvd W	Montreal	QC	H3H1R3	**800-363-6063**	514-931-8841
Le Parc Suite Hotel					
733 NW Knoll Dr	West Hollywood	CA	90069	**800-578-4837***	310-855-8888
*Resv					
Le Port-Royal Hotel & Suites					
144 St Pierre St	Quebec	QC	G1K8N8	**866-417-2777**	418-692-2777
Le Richelieu Hotel					
1234 Chartres St	New Orleans	LA	70116	**800-535-9653**	504-529-2492
Le Saint Sulpice					
414 Rue St Sulpice	Montreal	QC	H2Y2V5	**877-785-7423***	514-288-1000
*General					
Leisure Sports Inc					
7077 Koll Ctr Pkwy Ste 110	Pleasanton	CA	94566	**888-239-0930**	925-600-1966
Lenox Hotel 61 Exeter St	Boston	MA	02116	**800-225-7676**	617-536-5300
Les Suites Hotel Ottawa					
130 Besserer St	Ottawa	ON	K1N9M9	**866-682-0879**	613-232-2000
Library Hotel					
299 Madison Ave	New York	NY	10017	**877-793-7323**	212-983-4500
Lighthouse Club Hotel					
201 60th St	Ocean City	MD	21842	**888-371-5400**	410-524-5400
Lighthouse Lodge & Suites					
1150 Lighthouse Ave	Pacific Grove	CA	93950	**800-858-1249**	
Linden Row Inn					
100 E Franklin St	Richmond	VA	23219	**800-348-7424**	804-783-7000
Listel Hotel, The					
1300 Robson St	Vancouver	BC	V6E1C5	**800-663-5491**	604-684-8461
Little America Hotel & Resort Cheyenne					
2800 W Lincolnway	Cheyenne	WY	82009	**800-445-6945**	307-775-8400
Little America Hotel & Towers Salt Lake City					
555 S Main St	Salt Lake City	UT	84101	**800-453-9450**	801-258-6568
Little America Hotel Flagstaff					
2515 E Butler Ave	Flagstaff	AZ	86004	**800-352-4386**	928-779-7900

				Toll-Free	Phone

Little America Hotels & Resorts
500 S Main St ....Salt Lake City UT 84101 **800-281-7899** 801-596-5700

Little Nell, The
675 E Durant Ave ....Aspen CO 81611 **888-843-6355** 970-920-4600

Lodge & Spa at Cordillera
2205 Cordillera Way ....Edwards CO 81632 **800-877-3529** 970-926-2200

Lodge At Breckenridge, The
112 Overlook Dr ....Breckenridge CO 80424 **800-736-1607** 970-453-9300

Lodge at the Mountain Village
1415 Lowell Ave ....Park City UT 84060 **800-453-1360** 435-649-0800

Lodge Hotel & Conference Ctr
900 Spruce Hills Dr ....Bettendorf IA 52722 **866-690-4006** 563-359-7141

Lodge on the Desert
306 N Alvernon Way ....Tucson AZ 85711 **877-498-6776** 520-320-2000

Lodgian Inc
2002 Summit Blvd Ste 300.................Atlanta GA 30319 **888-750-5834** 404-364-9400
NYSE: LGN

Lofts Hotel & Suites
55 E Nationwide Blvd ....Columbus OH 43215 **877-902-9022*** 614-461-2663
*General

Lone Oak Lodge
2221 N Fremont St ....Monterey CA 93940 **800-283-5663*** 831-372-4924
*General

Long House Alaskan Hotel
4335 Wisconsin St ....Anchorage AK 99517 **888-243-2133** 907-243-2133

Lonsdale Quay Hotel
123 Carrie Cates Ct ....North Vancouver BC V7M3K7 **800-836-6111** 604-986-6111

Lookout Inn 6901 Lookout Rd ....Boulder CO 80301 **800-530-1513** 303-530-1513

Lord Elgin Hotel
100 Elgin St ....Ottawa ON K1P5K8 **800-267-4298** 613-235-3333

Lord Nelson Hotel & Suites
1515 S Pk St ....Halifax NS B3J2L2 **800-565-2020** 902-423-6331

Lord Stanley Suites on the Park
1889 Alberni St ....Vancouver BC V6G3G7 **888-767-7829** 604-688-9299

Los Angeles Athletic Club
431 W Seventh St ....Los Angeles CA 90014 **800-421-8777** 213-625-2211

LQ Management LLC
La Quinta Inn & Suites
909 Hidden Ridge Ste 600..................Irving TX 75038 **800-753-3757** 214-492-6600

Luxe Hotel Rodeo Drive
360 N Rodeo Dr ....Beverly Hills CA 90210 **800-468-3541** 310-273-0300

Luxe Hotel Sunset Blvd
11461 Sunset Blvd ....Los Angeles CA 90049 **800-468-3541** 310-476-6571

Luxe Worldwide Hotels
11461 W Sunset Blvd ....Los Angeles CA 90049 **866-589-3411** 310-440-3090

Luxor Hotel & Casino
3900 Las Vegas Blvd S ....Las Vegas NV 89119 **800-288-1000*** 702-262-4000
*Resv

MacArthur Place
29 E MacArthur St ....Sonoma CA 95476 **800-722-1866** 707-938-2929

Madison Concourse Hotel & Governors Club
1 W Dayton St ....Madison WI 53703 **800-356-8293** 608-257-6000

Madison Hotel, The
One Convent Rd ....Morristown NJ 07960 **800-526-0729** 973-285-1800

Madison the - A Loews Hotel
667 Madison Ave ....New York NY 10065 **800-235-6397** 212-521-2000

Magnolia Hotel & Spa, The
623 Courtney St ....Victoria BC V8W1B8 **877-624-6654** 250-381-0999

Magnolia Hotel Dallas
1401 Commerce St ....Dallas TX 75201 **888-915-1110** 214-915-6500

Magnolia Hotel Denver
818 17th St ....Denver CO 80202 **888-915-1110** 303-607-9000

Magnolia Hotel Houston
1100 Texas Ave ....Houston TX 77002 **888-915-1110** 713-221-0011

Main Street Station Hotel & Casino
200 N Main St ....Las Vegas NV 89101 **800-713-8933** 702-387-1896

Maison Dupuy Hotel
1001 Toulouse St ....New Orleans LA 70112 **800-535-9177** 504-586-8000

Malaga Inn 359 Church St ....Mobile AL 36602 **800-235-1586** 251-438-4701

Mandarin Oriental Hotel Group (USA)
345 California St Ste 1250............San Francisco CA 94104 **800-526-6566** 415-772-8800

Mandarin Oriental Miami
500 Brickell Key Dr ....Miami FL 33131 **800-526-6566** 305-913-8288

Mandarin Oriental New York
80 Columbus Cir ....New York NY 10023 **866-801-8880** 212-805-8800

Mandarin Oriental San Francisco
222 Sansome St ....San Francisco CA 94104 **800-526-6566** 415-276-9888

Mandarin Oriental Washington DC
1330 Maryland Ave SW ....Washington DC 20024 **888-888-1778** 202-554-8588

Manor House Inn 106 W St ....Bar Harbor ME 04609 **800-437-0088** 207-288-3759

Mansfield, The
12 W 44th St ....New York NY 10036 **800-255-5167** 212-277-8700

Mansion on Forsyth Park
700 Drayton St ....Savannah GA 31401 **888-213-3671** 912-238-5158

Mansion View Inn & Suites
529 S Fourth St ....Springfield IL 62701 **800-252-1083** 217-544-7411

Maple Hill Farm Bed & Breakfast Inn
11 Inn Rd ....Hallowell ME 04347 **800-622-2708** 207-622-2708

Marcus Corp
100 E Wisconsin Ave ....Milwaukee WI 53202 **800-461-9330** 414-905-1000
NYSE: MCS

Marcus Hotels & Resorts
100 E Wisconsin Ave Ste 1950...........Milwaukee WI 53202 **800-294-2812** 414-905-1200

Marina Inn at Grande Dunes
8121 Amalfi Pl ....Myrtle Beach SC 29572 **877-913-1333*** 843-913-1333
*Resv

Mark Spencer Hotel
409 SW 11th Ave ....Portland OR 97205 **800-548-3934** 503-224-3293

Mark Twain Hotel
225 NE Adams St ....Peoria IL 61602 **866-325-6351** 309-676-3600

Market Pavilion Hotel
225 E Bay St ....Charleston SC 29401 **877-440-2250** 843-723-0500

Marquesa Hotel
600 Fleming St ....Key West FL 33040 **800-869-4631** 305-292-1919

Marquette Hotel, The
710 Marquette Ave ....Minneapolis MN 55402 **800-328-4782** 612-333-4545

Marriott Charleston Hotel
170 Lockwood Blvd ....Charleston SC 29403 **888-236-2427** 843-723-3000

Marriott Columbus
800 Front Ave ....Columbus GA 31901 **800-455-9261** 706-324-1800

Marriott International Inc
10400 Fernwood Road ....Bethesda MD 20817 **800-450-4442** 301-380-3000
NASDAQ: MAR
Ritz-Carlton Hotel Co LLC
4445 Willard Ave Ste 800 ....Chevy Chase MD 20815 **800-241-3333** 301-547-4700

Martha Washington Hotel & Spa, The
150 W Main St ....Abingdon VA 24210 **888-999-8078** 276-628-3161

Maryland Inn
16 Church Cir ....Annapolis MD 21401 **800-847-8882** 410-263-2641

Matrix Hotel 10640-100 Ave ....Edmonton AB T5J3N8 **866-465-8150** 780-429-2861

Maumee Bay Lodge & Conference Ctr
1750 Pk Rd Ste 2 ....Oregon OH 43616 **800-282-7275** 419-836-1466

Mayfair Hotel & Spa
3000 Florida Ave ....Coconut Grove FL 33133 **800-433-4555** 305-441-0000

Mayflower Inn
118 Woodbury Rd Rt 47 ....Washington CT 06793 **800-585-7198** 860-868-9466

Mayflower Park Hotel
405 Olive Way ....Seattle WA 98101 **800-426-5100** 206-623-8700

McKinley Grand Hotel
320 Market Ave S ....Canton OH 44702 **877-454-5008** 330-454-5000

MCM Elegante Suites
4250 Ridgemont Dr ....Abilene TX 79606 **888-897-9644** 325-698-1234

Mediterranean Inn
425 Queen Anne Ave N ....Seattle WA 98109 **866-525-4700** 206-428-4700

Meeting Street Inn
173 Meeting St ....Charleston SC 29401 **800-842-8022** 843-723-1882

Menger Hotel
204 Alamo Plz ....San Antonio TX 78205 **800-345-9285** 210-223-4361

Mercer Hotel 147 Mercer St ....New York NY 10012 **888-918-6060** 212-966-6060

Meridian Plaza Resort
2310 N Ocean Blvd ....Myrtle Beach SC 29577 **800-323-3011** 843-626-4734

Metropolitan Hotel Vancouver
645 Howe St ....Vancouver BC V6C2Y9 **800-667-2300** 604-687-1122

Metterra Hotel on Whyte
10454 82nd Ave ....Edmonton AB T6E4Z7 **866-465-8150** 780-465-8150

Meyer Jabara Hotels
1601 Belvedere Rd Ste 407 S ......West Palm Beach FL 33406 **877-696-8671** 561-689-6602

Miami International Airport Hotel
NW 20th St & Le Jeune Rd ....Miami FL 33122 **800-327-1276** 305-871-4100

Michelangelo Hotel
152 W 51st St ....New York NY 10019 **800-237-0990** 212-765-1900

Midtown Hotel
220 Huntington Ave ....Boston MA 02115 **800-343-1177** 617-262-1000

Mill Street Inn 75 Mill St ....Newport RI 02840 **800-392-1316** 401-849-9500

Mills House Hotel
115 Meeting St ....Charleston SC 29401 **800-874-9600** 843-577-2400

Milner Hotel Boston
78 Charles St S ....Boston MA 02116 **877-645-6377** 617-426-6220

Milner Hotels Inc
1538 Centre St ....Detroit MI 48226 **877-645-6377** 313-963-3950

Minto Place Suite Hotel
185 Lyons St N ....Ottawa ON K1R7X5 **800-267-3377** 613-232-2200

Mira Monte Inn & Suites
69 Mt Desert St ....Bar Harbor ME 04609 **800-553-5109**

Mirabeau Park Hotel
1100 N Sullivan Rd ....Spokane Valley WA 99037 **866-584-4674** 509-924-9000

Mirbeau Inn & Spa
851 W Genesee St ....Skaneateles NY 13152 **877-647-2328** 315-685-5006

Mission Inn
3649 Mission Inn Ave ....Riverside CA 92501 **800-843-7755** 951-784-0300

Misty Harbor & Barefoot Beach Resort
118 Weirs Rd ....Gilford NH 03249 **800-336-4789** 603-293-4500

Miyako Hotel Los Angeles
328 E First St ....Los Angeles CA 90012 **800-228-6596** 213-617-2000

MODA Hotel 900 Seymour St ....Vancouver BC V6B3L9 **877-683-5522** 604-683-4251

Mojave A Desert Resort
73721 Shadow Mtn Dr ....Palm Desert CA 92260 **800-391-1104*** 760-346-6121
*Resv

Monarch Hotel & Conference Ctr
12566 SE 93rd Ave ....Clackamas OR 97015 **800-492-8700** 503-652-1515

Mondrian Hotel
8440 Sunset Blvd ....West Hollywood CA 90069 **800-525-8029** 323-650-8999

Monmouth Plantation
36 Melrose Ave ....Natchez MS 39120 **800-828-4531** 601-442-5852

Monte Carlo Inn-Airport Suites
7035 Edwards Blvd ....Mississauga ON L5T2H8 **800-363-6400** 905-564-8500

Monterey Bay Inn
242 Cannery Row ....Monterey CA 93940 **800-424-6242** 831-373-6242

Monterey Hotel
406 Alvarado St ....Monterey CA 93940 **800-727-0960** 831-375-3184

Monterey Inn Resort & Conference Centre
2259 Prince of Wales Dr ....Ottawa ON K2E6Z8 **800-565-1311** 613-288-3500

Monterey Plaza Hotel & Spa
400 Cannery Row ....Monterey CA 93940 **800-334-3999** 831-646-1700

Moody Gardens Hotel
Seven Hope Blvd ....Galveston TX 77554 **888-388-8484** 409-741-8484

Morgans Hotel
237 Madison Ave ....New York NY 10016 **800-606-6090** 212-686-0300

Morgans Hotel Group Co
475 Tenth Ave ....New York NY 10018 **800-606-6090** 212-277-4100
NASDAQ: MHGC

Morrison-Clark Historic Inn & Restaurant
1015 L St NW ....Washington DC 20001 **800-332-7898** 202-898-1200

Mosaic Hotel
125 S Spalding Dr ....Beverly Hills CA 90212 **800-463-4466** 310-278-0303

Mosser Hotel
54 Fourth St ....San Francisco CA 94103 **800-227-3804** 415-986-4400

Motel 6
Red Roof Inn
4001 International Pkwy ....Carrollton TX 75007 **800-466-8356** 972-360-9000

Motel 6 Wichita
465 S Webb Rd ....Wichita KS 67207 **800-466-8356** 316-684-6363

Mount View Hotel & Spa
1457 Lincoln Ave ....Calistoga CA 94515 **800-816-6877** 707-942-6877

Mountain Haus 292 E Meadow Dr ....Vail CO 81657 **800-237-0922** 970-476-2434

Name / Address	City	State	Zip	Toll-Free	Phone
Mountain Lake Hotel 115 Hotel Cir	Pembroke	VA	24136	**800-346-3334**	540-626-7121
Mountain Villas 9525 W Skyline Pkwy	Duluth	MN	55810	**866-688-4552**	218-624-5784
Movie Colony Hotel 726 N Indian Canyon Dr	Palm Springs	CA	92262	**888-953-5700**	760-320-6340
Muse, The 130 W 46th St	New York	NY	10036	**877-692-6873**	212-485-2400
Mutiny Hotel 2951 S Bayshore Dr	Miami	FL	33133	**888-868-8469**	305-441-2100
Napa River Inn 500 Main St	Napa	CA	94559	**877-251-8500**	707-251-8500
Nassau Inn, The 10 Palmer Sq	Princeton	NJ	08542	**800-862-7728**	609-921-7500
National Hotel 1677 Collins Ave	Miami Beach	FL	33139	**800-327-8370**	305-532-2311
Nativo Lodge Hotel 6000 Pan American Fwy NE	Albuquerque	NM	87109	**888-628-4861**	505-798-4300
New Castle Hotels & Resorts 2 Corporate Dr	Shelton	CT	06484	**800-321-2211**	203-925-8370
New Haven Hotel 229 George St	New Haven	CT	06510	**800-644-6835**	203-498-3100
New Haven Premier Suites Hotel Three Long Wharf Dr	New Haven	CT	06511	**866-458-0232**	203-777-5337
New Otani Kaimana Beach Hotel 2863 Kalakaua Ave	Honolulu	HI	96815	**800-356-8264**	808-923-1555
New York Palace Hotel 455 Madison Ave	New York	NY	10022	**800-697-2522**	212-888-7000
New York's Hotel Pennsylvania 401 Seventh Ave	New York	NY	10001	**800-223-8585**	212-736-5000
Newport Beach Hotel & Suites One Wave Ave	Middletown	RI	02842	**800-655-1778**	401-846-0310
Newport Beachside Hotel & Resort 16701 Collins Ave	Miami Beach	FL	33160	**800-327-5476**	305-949-1300
Newport Harbor Hotel & Marina 49 America's Cup Ave	Newport	RI	02840	**800-955-2558**	401-847-9000
Nine Zero Hotel 90 Tremont St	Boston	MA	02108	**866-906-9090**	617-772-5800
Nittany Lion Inn 200 W Pk Ave	State College	PA	16803	**800-233-7505**	814-865-8500
Norwood Hotel 112 Marion St	Winnipeg	MB	R2H0T1	**888-888-1878**	204-233-4475
O Henry Hotel 624 Green Vly Rd	Greensboro	NC	27408	**800-965-8259**	336-854-2000
Oberlin Inn Seven N Main St	Oberlin	OH	44074	**800-376-4173**	440-775-1111
Ocean Five Hotel 436 Ocean Dr *Resv	Miami Beach	FL	33139	**877-666-0505***	305-532-7093
Ocean Forest Plaza 5523 N Ocean Blvd *General	Myrtle Beach	SC	29577	**800-845-6701***	843-497-0044
Ocean Key Resort 424 Atlantic Ave	Virginia Beach	VA	23451	**800-955-9700**	757-425-2200
Ocean Pointe Suites at Key Largo 500 Burton Dr	Tavernier	FL	33070	**800-882-9464**	305-853-3000
Ocean Resort Hotel Waikiki 175 Paoakalani Ave	Honolulu	HI	96815	**877-367-1912**	808-922-3861
Ocean Sky Hotel & Resort 4060 Galt Ocean Dr	Fort Lauderdale	FL	33308	**800-678-9022**	954-565-6611
Ocean Walk Resort 300 N Atlantic	Daytona Beach	FL	32118	**888-743-2561**	386-323-4800
OHANA Waikiki Beachcomber Hotel 2300 Kalakaua Ave	Honolulu	HI	96815	**866-956-4262**	808-922-4646
Old Mill Toronto 21 Old Mill Rd	Toronto	ON	M8X1G5	**866-653-6455**	416-236-2641
Omni Hotels 4001 Maple Ave	Dallas	TX	75219	**800-843-6664**	402-952-6664
Omni La Mansion del Rio 112 College St	San Antonio	TX	78205	**800-292-7300**	210-518-1000
One Washington Cir Hotel One Washington Cir NW	Washington	DC	20037	**800-424-9671**	202-872-1680
Onyx Hotel 155 Portland St	Boston	MA	02114	**866-660-6699**	617-557-9955
Opus Hotel 322 Davie St	Vancouver	BC	V6B5Z6	**866-642-6787**	
Orchard Garden Hotel 466 Bush St	San Francisco	CA	94108	**888-717-2881**	415-399-9807
Orchard Hotel 665 Bush St	San Francisco	CA	94108	**888-717-2881**	415-362-8878
Orchards Hotel, The 222 Adams Rd	Williamstown	MA	01267	**800-225-1517**	413-458-9611
Orchards Inn of Sedona 254 Hwy N 89 A	Sedona	AZ	86336	**855-474-7719**	
Orient Express Hotels Inc 1114 Ave of the Americas *NYSE: OEH*	New York	NY	10036	**800-237-1236**	212-302-5055
Orlando, The 8384 W Third St	Los Angeles	CA	90048	**800-624-6835**	323-658-6600
Orleans Las Vegas Hotel & Casino 4500 W Tropicana Ave	Las Vegas	NV	89103	**800-675-3267**	702-365-7111
Outrigger Enterprises Group 2375 Kuhio Ave	Honolulu	HI	96815	**800-462-6262**	808-921-6941
OHANA Hotels & Resorts 2375 Kuhio Ave	Honolulu	HI	96815	**866-254-1605**	
Outrigger Hotels & Resorts 2375 Kuhio Ave	Honolulu	HI	96815	**800-688-7444**	808-921-6941
Outrigger Waikiki on the Beach 2335 Kalakaua Ave	Honolulu	HI	96815	**800-688-7444**	808-923-0711
Oxford Hotel 1600 17th St	Denver	CO	80202	**800-228-5838**	303-628-5400
Oxford Palace 745 S Oxford Ave	Los Angeles	CA	90005	**800-532-7887**	213-389-8000
Oxford Suites Boise 1426 S Entertainment Ave *General	Boise	ID	83709	**888-322-8001***	208-322-8000
Oxford Suites Spokane Valley 15015 E Indiana Ave	Spokane Valley	WA	99216	**866-668-7848**	509-847-1000
Oxford Suites Spokane-Downtown 115 W N River Dr	Spokane	WA	99201	**800-774-1877**	509-353-9000
Oyster Point Hotel, The 146 Bodman Pl	Red Bank	NJ	07701	**800-345-3484**	732-530-8200
Pacific Beach Hotel 2490 Kalakaua Ave	Honolulu	HI	96815	**800-367-6060**	808-922-1233
Pacific Inn 600 Marina Dr	Seal Beach	CA	90740	**866-466-0300**	562-493-7501
Pacific Inn Resort & Conference Centre 1160 King George Hwy	Surrey	BC	V4A4Z2	**800-667-2248**	604-535-1432
Pacific Shores Inn 4802 Mission Blvd	San Diego	CA	92109	**888-478-7829**	858-483-6300
Pacific Terrace Hotel 610 Diamond St	San Diego	CA	92109	**800-344-3370**	858-581-3500
Painted Buffalo Inn 400 W Broadway PO Box 2547	Jackson	WY	83001	**800-288-3866**	307-733-4340
Palace Casino 158 Howard Ave	Biloxi	MS	39530	**800-725-2239**	228-432-8888
Palace Hotel 2 New Montgomery St	San Francisco	CA	94105	**866-716-8136**	415-512-1111
Palace Station Hotel & Casino 2411 W Sahara Ave *Resv	Las Vegas	NV	89102	**800-634-3101***	702-367-2411
Palmer House Hilton 17 E Monroe St	Chicago	IL	60603	**800-445-8667**	312-726-7500
Palos Verdes Inn 1700 S Pacific Coast Hwy	Redondo Beach	CA	90277	**800-421-9241**	310-316-4211
Pan Pacific Hotel Vancouver 999 Canada Pl Ste 300	Vancouver	BC	V6C3B5	**800-937-1515**	604-662-8111
Pantages Hotel 200 Victoria St	Toronto	ON	M5B1V8	**866-852-1777**	416-362-1777
Par-A-Dice Hotel 21 Blackjack Blvd	East Peoria	IL	61611	**800-727-2342**	309-699-7711
Paramount Hotel 235 W 46th St *Resv	New York	NY	10036	**855-234-2074***	212-764-5500
Paris Las Vegas 3655 Las Vegas Blvd S	Las Vegas	NV	89109	**800-342-7724**	800-522-4700
Park Shore Waikiki Hotel 2586 Kalakaua Ave	Honolulu	HI	96815	**866-536-7975**	808-954-7426
Park South Hotel 124 E 28th St	New York	NY	10016	**800-315-4642**	212-448-0888
Park Vista Resort Hotel 705 Cherokee OrchaRd Rd PO Box 30 *Sales	Gatlinburg	TN	37738	**800-227-5622***	865-436-9211
Parkway Inn 125 N Jackson St PO Box 494	Jackson	WY	83001	**800-247-8390**	
Partridge Inn 2110 Walton Way	Augusta	GA	30904	**800-476-6888**	706-737-8888
Paso Robles Inn 1103 Spring St	Paso Robles	CA	93446	**800-676-1713**	805-238-2660
Peabody Memphis 149 Union Ave	Memphis	TN	38103	**800-732-2639**	901-529-4000
Peacock Suites 1745 S Anaheim Blvd	Anaheim	CA	92805	**800-522-6401**	714-535-8255
Pearl Hotel, The 1410 Rosecrans St	San Diego	CA	92106	**877-732-7573**	619-226-6100
Peery Hotel 110 West 300 South	Salt Lake City	UT	84101	**800-331-0073**	801-521-4300
Pegasus International Hotel 501 Southard St	Key West	FL	33040	**800-397-8148**	305-294-9323
Pelham Hotel 444 Common St	New Orleans	LA	70130	**888-856-4486**	504-522-4444
Penguin Hotel 1418 Ocean Dr	Miami Beach	FL	33139	**800-499-7964**	305-534-9334
Peninsula Beverly Hills 9882 S Santa Monica Blvd	Beverly Hills	CA	90212	**800-462-7899**	310-551-2888
Peninsula Chicago 108 E Superior St	Chicago	IL	60611	**866-288-8889**	312-337-2888
Peninsula New York 700 Fifth Ave	New York	NY	10019	**800-262-9467**	212-956-2888
Penn's View Hotel 14 N Front St	Philadelphia	PA	19106	**800-331-7634**	215-922-7600
Peppermill Hotel & Casino 2707 S Virginia St	Reno	NV	89502	**800-648-6992**	775-826-2121
Pfister Hotel 424 E Wisconsin Ave	Milwaukee	WI	53202	**800-558-8222**	414-273-8222
Phillips Beach Plaza Hotel 1301 Atlantic Ave	Ocean City	MD	21842	**800-492-5834**	410-289-9121
Phoenix Grand Hotel Salem 201 Liberty St SE	Salem	OR	97301	**877-540-7800**	503-540-7800
Phoenix Hotel 601 Eddy St	San Francisco	CA	94109	**800-248-9466**	415-776-1380
Phoenix Park Hotel 520 N Capitol St	Washington	DC	20001	**800-824-5419**	202-638-6900
Piccadilly Inn Hotels 2305 W Shaw Ave	Fresno	CA	93711	**888-286-2645**	559-348-5520
Pier 5 Hotel 711 Eastern Ave	Baltimore	MD	21202	**866-583-4162**	410-539-2000
Pillars Hotel at New River Sound 111 N Birch Rd	Fort Lauderdale	FL	33304	**800-241-3333**	954-467-9639
Pine Crest Inn 85 Pine Crest Ln	Tryon	NC	28782	**800-633-3001**	828-859-9135
Pines Lodge 141 Scott Hill Rd *Resv	Beaver Creek	CO	81620	**800-859-8242***	970-429-5043
Place D'Armes Hotel 625 St Ann St	New Orleans	LA	70116	**800-366-2743**	504-524-4531
Place Louis Riel All-Suite Hotel 190 Smith St	Winnipeg	MB	R3C1J8	**800-665-0569**	204-947-6961
Plains Hotel, The 1600 Central Ave	Cheyenne	WY	82001	**866-275-2467**	307-638-3311
Planters Inn 112 N Market St	Charleston	SC	29401	**800-845-7082**	843-722-2345
Platinum Hotel 211 E Flamingo Rd *General	Las Vegas	NV	89169	**877-211-9211***	702-365-5000
Plaza Hotel & Casino One Main St PO Box 760	Las Vegas	NV	89101	**800-634-6575**	702-386-2110
Plaza on the River Resort Club Hotel 121 W St	Reno	NV	89501	**800-628-5974**	775-786-2200
Plaza Suite Hotel Resort 620 S Peters St	New Orleans	LA	70130	**800-770-6721**	
Plaza Suites Silicon Valley 3100 Lakeside Dr	Santa Clara	CA	95054	**800-345-1554**	408-748-9800

			Toll-Free	Phone

Plump Jack's Squaw Valley Inn
1920 Squaw Vly Rd PO Box 2407 . . . . Olympic Valley CA 96146 — 800-323-7666 — 530-583-1576

Point Plaza Suites & Conference Hotel
950 J Clyde Morris Blvd . . . . Newport News VA 23601 — 800-841-1112 — 757-599-4460

Pontchartrain Hotel
2031 St Charles Ave . . . . New Orleans LA 70130 — 800-777-6193 — 504-524-0581

Port-O-Call Hotel
1510 Boardwalk . . . . Ocean City NJ 08226 — 800-334-4546 — 609-399-8812

Portland Harbor Hotel
468 Fore St . . . . Portland ME 04101 — 888-798-9090 — 207-775-9090

Portland Regency Hotel
20 Milk St . . . . Portland ME 04101 — 800-727-3436 — 207-774-4200

Portofino Hotel & Yacht Club
260 Portofino Way . . . . Redondo Beach CA 90277 — 800-468-4292 — 310-379-8481

Portofino Inn & Suites Anaheim
1831 S Harbor Blvd . . . . Anaheim CA 92802 — 800-398-3963* — 714-782-7600
*Resv

Portola Plaza Hotel
2 Portola Plaza . . . . Monterey CA 93940 — 888-222-5851 — 831-649-4511

Post Hotel, The
200 Pipestone Rd PO Box 69 . . . . Lake Louise AB T0L1E0 — 800-661-1586 — 403-522-3989

Prairie Band Casino & Resort
12305 150th Rd . . . . Mayetta KS 66509 — 888-727-4946 — 785-966-7777

Preferred Hotel Group
Preferred Hotels & Resorts Worldwide Inc
311 S Wacker Dr Ste 1900 . . . . Chicago IL 60606 — 800-650-1281 — 312-913-0400
Summit Hotels & Resorts
311 S Wacker Dr Ste 1900 . . . . Chicago IL 60606 — 800-650-1281 — 312-913-0400

Prescott Hotel
545 Post St . . . . San Francisco CA 94102 — 866-271-3632 — 415-563-0303

President Abraham Lincoln Hotel & Conference Ctr (PALHACC)
701 E Adams St . . . . Springfield IL 62701 — 855-610-8733 — 217-544-8800

Prince Conti Hotel
830 Conti St . . . . New Orleans LA 70112 — 800-366-2743 — 504-529-4172

Prince George Hotel, The
1725 Market St . . . . Halifax NS B3J3N9 — 800-565-1567 — 902-425-1986

Princess Bayside Beach Hotel & Golf Ctr
4801 Coastal Hwy . . . . Ocean City MD 21842 — 888-622-9743* — 410-723-2900
*General

Princess Royale Oceanfront Hotel & Conference Ctr
9100 Coastal Hwy . . . . Ocean City MD 21842 — 800-476-9253 — 410-524-7777

Prospector Hotel
375 Whittier St . . . . Juneau AK 99801 — 800-331-2711 — 907-586-3737

Providence Biltmore Hotel
11 Dorrance St . . . . Providence RI 02903 — 800-294-7709

Publick House Historic Resort
277 Main St Rt 131 . . . . Sturbridge MA 01566 — 800-782-5425* — 508-347-3313
*Cust Svc

Puffin Inn
4400 SpenaRd Rd . . . . Anchorage AK 99517 — 800-478-3346 — 907-243-4044

Quality Inn Halifax Airport Hotel
60 Sky Blvd
Halifax International Airport . . . . Goffs NS B2T1K3 — 800-667-3333 — 902-873-3000

Quality Inn West Harvest
17803 Stony Plain Rd . . . . Edmonton AB T5S1B4 — 800-661-2133 — 780-484-8000

Quarterpath Inn & Suites
614 York St . . . . Williamsburg VA 23185 — 800-581-7245 — 757-220-0960

Quebec Inn
7175 Blvd Hamel Ouest . . . . Quebec City QC G2G1B6 — 800-567-5276 — 418-872-9831

Queen & Crescent Hotel
535 Tchoupitoulas St . . . . New Orleans LA 70130 — 800-455-3417

Queen Anne Hotel
1590 Sutter St . . . . San Francisco CA 94109 — 800-227-3970 — 415-441-2828

Queen Kapiolani Hotel
150 Kapahulu Ave . . . . Honolulu HI 96815 — 866-970-4164 — 808-922-1941

Quimby House Inn
109 Cottage St . . . . Bar Harbor ME 04609 — 800-344-5811 — 207-288-5811

Quincy Hotel
1823 L St NW . . . . Washington DC 20036 — 800-424-2970 — 202-223-4320

Rabbit Hill Inn
48 Lower Waterford Rd
PO Box 55 . . . . Lower Waterford VT 05848 — 800-626-3215 — 802-748-5168

Radisson Butler Blvd
4700 Salisbury Rd . . . . Jacksonville FL 32256 — 888-201-1718 — 904-281-9700

Radisson Chicago-O'Hare Hotel
1450 E Touhy Ave . . . . Des Plaines IL 60018 — 888-201-1718 — 847-296-8866

Radisson Hotel Bloomington Mall of America
1700 American Blvd E . . . . Bloomington MN 55425 — 800-967-9033* — 952-854-8700
*Resv

Radisson Milwaukee North Shore
7065 N Port Washington Rd . . . . Milwaukee WI 53217 — 800-395-7046 — 414-351-6960

Railroad Pass Hotel & Casino
2800 S Boulder Hwy . . . . Henderson NV 89002 — 800-654-0877 — 702-294-5000

Ramada Middletown
425 E Main Rd . . . . Middletown RI 02842 — 800-854-9517 — 401-846-3555

Ramada Plaza & Conference Ctr
4900 Sinclair Rd . . . . Columbus OH 43229 — 800-272-6232 — 614-846-0300

Ranch at Steamboat
1800 Ranch Rd . . . . Steamboat Springs CO 80487 — 888-686-8075 — 970-879-3000

Ranch Inn 45 E Pearl St . . . . Jackson WY 83001 — 800-348-5599 — 307-733-6363

Raphael Kansas City
325 Ward Pkwy . . . . Kansas City MO 64112 — 800-821-5343 — 816-756-3800

Red Jacket Beach Resort
39 Todd Rd . . . . South Yarmouth MA 02664 — 800-227-3263 — 508-398-6941

Red Lion Hotels Corp
201 W N River Dr Ste 100 . . . . Spokane WA 99201 — 800-733-5466*
NYSE: RLH ■ *Resv*

Red Rock Resort Spa & Casino
11011 W Charleston Blvd . . . . Las Vegas NV 89135 — 866-767-7773 — 702-797-7777

Regency Fairbanks Hotel
95 Tenth Ave . . . . Fairbanks AK 99701 — 800-478-1320 — 907-459-2700

Regency Suites Calgary
610 Fourth Ave SW . . . . Calgary AB T2P0K1 — 800-468-4044 — 403-231-1000

Regency Suites Hotel Midtown Atlanta
975 W Peachtree St . . . . Atlanta GA 30309 — 800-642-3629 — 404-876-5003

Remington Suite Hotel
220 Travis St . . . . Shreveport LA 71101 — 800-444-6750 — 318-425-5000

Residence & Conference Centre - Toronto
1760 Finch Ave E . . . . Toronto ON M2J5G3 — 877-225-8664 — 416-491-8811

Rhett House Inn
1009 Craven St . . . . Beaufort SC 29902 — 888-480-9530 — 843-524-9030

Richmond, The
1757 Collins Ave . . . . Miami Beach FL 33139 — 855-627-3767 — 305-538-2331

Rittenhouse Hotel
210 W Rittenhouse Sq . . . . Philadelphia PA 19103 — 800-635-1042 — 215-546-9000

Ritz-Carlton Dallas
2121 McKinney Ave . . . . Dallas TX 75201 — 800-960-7082* — 214-922-0200
*Resv

Riu Hotel Florida Beach
3101 Collins Ave . . . . Miami FL 33140 — 888-666-8816 — 305-673-5333

River's Edge Resort Cottages
4200 Boat St . . . . Fairbanks AK 99709 — 800-770-3343 — 907-474-0286

Riveredge Resort Hotel
17 Holland St . . . . Alexandria Bay NY 13607 — 800-365-6987 — 315-482-9917

Riverside Hotel
620 E Las Olas Blvd . . . . Fort Lauderdale FL 33301 — 800-325-3280 — 954-467-0671

Riverstone Billings Inn
880 N 29th St . . . . Billings MT 59101 — 800-231-7782 — 406-252-6800

Riviera Hotel
1431 Robson St . . . . Vancouver BC V6G1C3 — 888-699-5222 — 604-685-1301

Road King Inn Columbia Mall
3300 30th Ave S . . . . Grand Forks ND 58201 — 800-707-1391

Robert Treat Hotel 50 Pk Pl . . . . Newark NJ 07102 — 800-569-2300 — 973-622-1000

Rock View Resort
1049 Parkview Dr . . . . Hollister MO 65672 — 800-375-9530 — 417-334-4678

Rocklin Park Hotel
5450 China Garden Rd . . . . Rocklin CA 95677 — 888-630-9400 — 916-630-9400

Roger Smith Hotel
501 Lexington Ave . . . . New York NY 10017 — 800-445-0277 — 212-755-1400

Roosevelt Hotel
45 E 45th St . . . . New York NY 10017 — 888-833-3969 — 212-661-9600

Rose Hotel 807 Main St . . . . Pleasanton CA 94566 — 800-843-9540 — 925-846-8802

Rosedale on Robson Suite Hotel
838 Hamilton St . . . . Vancouver BC V6B6A2 — 800-661-8870 — 604-689-8033

Rosellen Suites at Stanley Park
2030 Barclay St . . . . Vancouver BC V6G1L5 — 888-317-6648 — 604-689-4807

Rosen Centre Hotel
9840 International Dr . . . . Orlando FL 32819 — 800-204-7234 — 407-996-9840

Rosen Hotels & Resorts Inc
9840 International Dr . . . . Orlando FL 32819 — 800-204-7234 — 407-996-9840

Rosen Plaza Hotel
9700 International Dr . . . . Orlando FL 32819 — 800-366-9700 — 407-996-9700

Rosen Shingle Creek
9939 Universal Blvd . . . . Orlando FL 32819 — 866-996-9939 — 407-996-9939

Rosewood Hotels & Resorts
500 Crescent Ct Ste 300 . . . . Dallas TX 75201 — 888-767-3966 — 214-880-4200

Roslyn Claremont Hotel
1221 Old Northern Blvd . . . . Roslyn NY 11576 — 800-626-9005 — 516-625-2700

Rough Creek Lodge
5165 County Rd 2013 . . . . Glen Rose TX 76043 — 877-907-0754 — 254-965-3700

Royal Garden at Waikiki Hotel
440 Olohana St . . . . Honolulu HI 96815 — 800-989-0971 — 808-943-0202

Royal Holiday Beach Resort
1988 Beach Blvd . . . . Biloxi MS 39531 — 800-874-0402* — 228-388-7553
*Resv

Royal Regency Hotel
165 Tuckahoe Rd . . . . Yonkers NY 10710 — 800-215-3858

Royal Sonesta Hotel Boston
40 Edwin H Land Blvd . . . . Cambridge MA 02142 — 800-766-3782 — 617-806-4200

Royal Sonesta Hotel New Orleans
300 Bourbon St . . . . New Orleans LA 70130 — 800-766-3782 — 504-586-0300

Royal Sun Inn
1700 S Palm Canyon Dr . . . . Palm Springs CA 92264 — 800-619-4786 — 760-327-1564

Royalton Hotel
44 W 44th St . . . . New York NY 10036 — 800-606-6090 — 212-869-4400

Saint Anthony the - A Wyndham Historic Hotel
300 E Travis St . . . . San Antonio TX 78205 — 800-996-3426 — 210-227-4392

Saint Gregory Luxury Hotel & Suites
2033 M St NW . . . . Washington DC 20036 — 800-821-4367 — 202-530-3600

Saint Michaels Harbour Inn & Marina
101 N Harbor Rd . . . . Saint Michaels MD 21663 — 800-955-9001 — 410-745-9001

Saint Paul Hotel
350 Market St . . . . Saint Paul MN 55102 — 800-292-9292 — 651-292-9292

Saint Regis Hotel
602 Dunsmuir St . . . . Vancouver BC V6B1Y6 — 800-770-7929 — 604-681-1135

Saint Regis Hotel Winnipeg
285 Smith St . . . . Winnipeg MB R3C1K9 — 800-663-7344 — 204-942-0171

Saint Tropez Hotel
Rumor 455 E Harmon Ave . . . . Las Vegas NV 89109 — 877-997-8667 — 702-369-5400

Salisbury Hotel
123 W 57th St . . . . New York NY 10019 — 888-692-5757 — 212-246-1300

Sam's Town Hotel & Casino Shreveport
315 Clyde Fant Pkwy . . . . Shreveport LA 71101 — 877-770-7867

Sam's Town Hotel & Gambling Hall
5111 Boulder Hwy . . . . Las Vegas NV 89122 — 800-897-8696 — 702-456-7777

San Carlos Hotel
150 E 50th St . . . . New York NY 10022 — 800-722-2012 — 212-755-1800

San Joaquin Hotel
1309 W Shaw Ave . . . . Fresno CA 93711 — 800-775-1309* — 559-225-1309
*General

Sands Casino Resort Bethlehem
77 Sands Blvd . . . . Bethlehem PA 18015 — 877-726-3777

Sands Ocean Club Resort
9550 Shore Dr . . . . Myrtle Beach SC 29572 — 888-999-8485*
*General

Sands Regency Casino Hotel
345 N Arlington Ave . . . . Reno NV 89501 — 866-337-1555* — 775-348-2200
*Resv

Sandwich Lodge & Resort
54 Rt 6A - Old King's Hwy
PO Box 1038 . . . . Sandwich MA 02563 — 800-282-5353 — 508-888-2275

Sanibel Inn 937 E Gulf Dr . . . . Sanibel FL 33957 — 866-565-5480 — 239-472-3181

Santa Barbara Inn
901 E Cabrillo Blvd . . . . Santa Barbara CA 93103 — 800-231-0431 — 805-966-2285

Santa Maria Inn
801 S Broadway . . . . Santa Maria CA 93454 — 800-462-4276 — 805-928-7777

				Toll-Free	Phone

Saratoga Hilton
534 Broadway .... Saratoga Springs NY 12866 **800-445-8667** 518-584-4000
Satellite Hotel
411 Lakewood Cir .... Colorado Springs CO 80910 **800-423-8409** 719-596-6800
Savoy Suites Georgetown
2505 Wisconsin Ave NW .... Washington DC 20007 **877-301-0002** 202-337-9700
Scotsman Inn West
5922 W Kellogg St .... Wichita KS 67209 **800-950-7268** 316-943-3800
Sea Ranch Lodge
60 Sea Walk Dr PO Box 44 .... The Sea Ranch CA 95497 **800-732-7262** 707-785-2371
Sea View Hotel
9909 Collins Ave .... Bal Harbour FL 33154 **800-447-1010** 305-866-4441
Seaport Hotel & World Trade Ctr
One Seaport Ln .... Boston MA 02210 **877-732-7678** 617-385-4000
Seaside Inn
541 E Gulf Dr .... Sanibel Island FL 33957 **866-565-5092** 239-472-1400
Seattle Convention Ctr Pike Street
1011 Pike St .... Seattle WA 98101 **800-225-5466** 206-682-8282
Seelbach Hilton Louisville
500 S Fourth St .... Louisville KY 40202 **800-333-3399** 502-585-3200
Senate Luxury Suites
900 SW Tyler St .... Topeka KS 66612 **800-488-3188** 785-233-5050
Sentinel Hotel
614 SW 11th Ave .... Portland OR 97205 **888-246-5631** 503-224-3400
Serrano Hotel
405 Taylor St .... San Francisco CA 94102 **866-575-9941** 415-885-2500
Setai, The
2001 Collins Ave .... Miami Beach FL 33139 **888-625-7500** 305-520-6000
Shades of Green on Walt Disney World Resort
1950 W Magnolia Palm Dr .... Lake Buena Vista FL 32830 **888-593-2242** 407-824-3400
Shelburne Murray Hill
303 Lexington Ave .... New York NY 10016 **866-233-4642** 212-689-5200
Shephard's Beach Resort
619 S Gulfview Blvd .... Clearwater Beach FL 33767 **800-237-8477** 727-441-6875
Sheraton Delfina Santa Monica
530 W Pico Blvd .... Santa Monica CA 90405 **888-627-8532** 310-399-9344
Sheraton Gateway Hotel Los Angeles
6101 W Century Blvd .... Los Angeles CA 90045 **888-627-7104** 310-642-1111
Sherry-Netherland Hotel
781 Fifth Ave .... New York NY 10022 **877-743-7710** 212-355-2800
Shilo Inn Hotel Salt Lake City
206 SW Temple .... Salt Lake City UT 84101 **800-222-2244**
Shilo Inn Suites Hotel Portland Airport
117707 NE Airport Way .... Portland OR 97220 **800-222-2244** 503-252-7500
Shilo Inn Suites Salem
3304 Market St .... Salem OR 97301 **800-222-2244** 503-581-4001
Shilo Inns Suites Hotels
11600 SW Shilo Ln .... Portland OR 97225 **800-222-2244** 503-641-6565
Shutters on the Beach
One Pico Blvd .... Santa Monica CA 90405 **800-334-9000** 310-458-0030
Siena Hotel
1505 E Franklin St .... Chapel Hill NC 27514 **800-223-7379** 919-929-4000
Silver Cloud Hotel Seattle Broadway
1100 Broadway .... Seattle WA 98122 **800-590-1801** 206-325-1400
Silver Cloud Inn Seattle-Lake Union
1150 Fairview Ave N .... Seattle WA 98109 **800-330-5812*** 206-447-9500
*General
Silver Cloud Inn University District
5036 25th Ave NE .... Seattle WA 98105 **800-205-6940** 206-526-5200
Silver King Hotel
1485 Empire Ave .... Park City UT 84060 **888-667-2775** 435-649-5500
Silver Smith Hotel & Suites
10 S Wabash Ave .... Chicago IL 60603 **800-979-0084** 312-372-7696
SilverBirch Hotels & Resorts
1600 - 1030 W Georgia St .... Vancouver BC V6E2Y3 **800-661-1232** 604-646-2447
Silverdale Beach Hotel
3073 NW Bucklin Hill Rd .... Silverdale WA 98383 **800-544-9799** 360-698-1000
Simonton Court Historic Inn & Cottages
320 Simonton St .... Key West FL 33040 **800-944-2687**
Sir Francis Drake Hotel
450 Powell St .... San Francisco CA 94102 **800-795-7129** 415-392-7755
Ski Bromont 150 Champlain .... Bromont QC J2L1A2 **866-276-6668** 450-534-2200
Sky Hotel 709 E Durant Ave .... Aspen CO 81611 **800-882-2582** 970-925-6760
Snell House
21 Atlantic Ave .... Bar Harbor ME 04609 **866-763-5524** 207-288-8004
Snowbird Mountain Lodge
4633 Santeetlah Rd .... Robbinsville NC 28771 **800-941-9290** 828-479-3433
Snowy Owl Inn
41 Village Rd .... Waterville Valley NH 03215 **800-766-9969** 603-236-8383
Sofia Hotel
150 W Broadway .... San Diego CA 92101 **800-826-0009** 619-234-9200
SoHo Grand Hotel
310 W Broadway .... New York NY 10013 **800-965-3000** 212-965-3000
SoHo Metropolitan Hotel
318 Wellington St W .... Toronto ON M5V3T4 **866-764-6638** 416-599-8800
Somerset Inn
2601 W Big Beaver Rd .... Troy MI 48084 **800-228-8769** 248-643-7800
Sonesta Suites Coconut Grove
2889 McFarlane Rd .... Miami FL 33133 **800-766-3782** 305-529-2828
Soniat House
1133 Chartres St .... New Orleans LA 70116 **800-544-8808** 504-522-0570
Sophie Station Suites
1717 University Ave .... Fairbanks AK 99709 **800-528-4916**
South Beach Marina Inn & Vacation Rentals
232 S Sea Pines Dr .... Hilton Head Island SC 29928 **800-367-3909** 843-671-6498
South Pier Inn on the Canal
701 Lake Ave S .... Duluth MN 55802 **800-430-7437** 218-786-9007
South Point Hotel & Casino
9777 Las Vegas Blvd S .... Las Vegas NV 89183 **866-796-7111** 702-796-7111
Southampton Inn
91 Hill St .... SouthHampton NY 11968 **800-832-6500** 631-283-6500
Southernmost On the Beach
508 S St .... Key West FL 33040 **800-354-4455**
Southfork Hotel
1600 N Central Expy .... Plano TX 75074 **877-386-4383** 972-578-8555
Southway Inn 2431 Bank St .... Ottawa ON K1V8R9 **877-688-4929** 613-737-0811
Spindrift Inn
652 Cannery Row .... Monterey CA 93940 **800-841-1879** 831-646-8900

Spring Creek Ranch
1800 Spirit Dance Rd .... Jackson WY 83001 **800-443-6139** 307-733-8833
St James Hotel 406 Main St .... Red Wing MN 55066 **800-252-1875** 651-388-2846
St Julien Hotel & Spa
900 Walnut St .... Boulder CO 80302 **877-303-0900** 720-406-9696
Stamford Suites
720 Bedford St .... Stamford CT 06901 **866-394-4365** 203-359-7300
Stanley Hotel
333 Wonderview Ave .... Estes Park CO 80517 **800-976-1377** 970-586-3371
Star Island Resort
5000 Ave of the Stars .... Kissimmee FL 34746 **800-513-2820** 407-997-8000
Starwood Hotels & Resorts Worldwide Inc
Saint Regis Hotels & Resorts
1111 Westchester Ave .... White Plains NY 10604 **888-625-4988** 914-640-8100
Westin Hotels & Resorts
1111 Westchester Ave .... White Plains NY 10604 **888-625-5144** 914-640-8100
State Plaza Hotel
2117 E St NW .... Washington DC 20037 **800-424-2859** 202-861-8200
Staten Island Hotel
1415 Richmond Ave .... Staten Island NY 10314 **800-230-4134** 718-698-5000
Stockyards Hotel
109 E Exchange Ave .... Fort Worth TX 76164 **800-423-8471** 817-625-6427
Stone Castle Hotel & Conference Ctr, The
3050 Green Mtn Dr .... Branson MO 65616 **800-677-6906** 417-335-4700
Stonebridge Inn
300 Carriage Way PO Box 5008 .... Snowmass Village CO 81615 **800-922-7242** 970-923-2420
Stonewall Jackson Hotel & Conference Ctr
24 S Market St .... Staunton VA 24401 **866-880-0024** 540-885-4848
Stoney Creek Inn
101 Mariner's Way .... East Peoria IL 61611 **800-659-2220** 309-694-1300
Strater Hotel 699 Main Ave .... Durango CO 81301 **800-247-4431** 970-247-4431
Stratford Hotel
242 Powell St .... San Francisco CA 94102 **888-688-0038** 415-397-7080
Strathcona Hotel 60 York St .... Toronto ON M5J1S8 **800-268-8304** 416-363-3321
Strathcona Hotel, The
919 Douglas St .... Victoria BC V8W2C2 **800-663-7476** 250-383-7137
Stratosphere Tower Hotel & Casino
2000 S Las Vegas Blvd .... Las Vegas NV 89104 **800-998-6937** 702-380-7777
Sturbridge Host Hotel & Conference Ctr
366 Main St .... Sturbridge MA 01566 **800-582-3232** 508-347-7393
Suites at Fisherman's Wharf
2655 Hyde St .... San Francisco CA 94109 **800-227-3608** 415-771-0200
Suites Hotel in Canal Park, The
325 Lake Ave S .... Duluth MN 55802 **877-766-2665** 218-727-4663
Summit Lodge & Spa
4359 Main St .... Whistler BC V0N1B4 **888-913-8811** 604-932-2778
Sun Viking Lodge
2411 S Atlantic Ave .... Daytona Beach Shores FL 32118 **800-874-4469** 386-252-6252
Suncoast Hotel & Casino
9090 Alta Dr .... Las Vegas NV 89145 **877-677-7111** 702-636-7111
Sundial Boutique Hotel
4340 Sundial Crescent .... Whistler BC V0N1B4 **800-661-2321** 604-932-2321
Sunset Inn Travel Apartments
1111 Burnaby St .... Vancouver BC V6E1P4 **800-786-1997** 604-688-2474
Sunset Marquis Hotel & Villas
1200 N Alta Loma Rd .... West Hollywood CA 90069 **800-858-9758** 310-657-1333
Sunset Station Hotel & Casino
1301 W Sunset Rd .... Henderson NV 89014 **888-786-7389** 702-547-7777
Surf & Sand Resort
1555 S Coast Hwy .... Laguna Beach CA 92651 **888-869-7569** 949-497-4477
Surfsand Resort
148 W Gower Rd .... Cannon Beach OR 97110 **800-547-6100** 503-436-2274
Surfside Inn
1211 Atlantic Ave .... Virginia Beach VA 23451 **800-437-2497** 757-428-1183
Surrey Hotel 20 E 76th St .... New York NY 10021 **866-233-4642** 212-288-3700
Sutton Place Hotel Edmonton
10235 101st St .... Edmonton AB T5J3E9 **866-378-8866** 780-428-7111
Swag, 2300 Swag Rd .... Waynesville NC 28785 **800-789-7672** 828-926-0430
Taj Boston 15 Arlington St .... Boston MA 02116 **877-482-5267** 617-536-5700
Taj Campton Place
340 Stockton St .... San Francisco CA 94108 **866-969-1825** 415-781-5555
Talbott Hotel
20 E Delaware Pl .... Chicago IL 60611 **800-825-2688** 312-944-4970
Terminal City Club
837 W Hastings St .... Vancouver BC V6C1B6 **888-253-8777** 604-681-4121
Teton Mountain Lodge & Spa
3385 Cody Ln PO Box 564 .... Teton Village WY 83025 **800-631-6271** 307-201-6066
Thayer Hotel
674 Thayer Rd .... West Point NY 10996 **800-247-5047** 845-446-4731
Tickle Pink Inn at Carmel Highlands
155 Highland Dr .... Carmel CA 93923 **800-635-4774** 831-624-1244
Tidewater Inn & Conference Ctr
101 E Dover St .... Easton MD 21601 **800-237-8775** 410-822-1300
Time, The 224 W 49th St .... New York NY 10019 **877-846-3692** 212-246-5252
Tivoli Lodge
386 Hanson Ranch Rd .... Vail CO 81657 **800-451-4756** 970-476-5615
Topaz Hotel 1733 N St NW .... Washington DC 20036 **800-546-7866** 202-393-3000
Town & Country Inn
20 State RT 2 PO Box 220 .... Gorham NH 03581 **800-325-4386*** 603-466-3315
*General
Town & Country Inn & Conference Ctr
2008 Savannah Hwy .... Charleston SC 29407 **800-334-6660** 843-571-1000
Town Inn Suites
620 Church St .... Toronto ON M4Y2G2 **800-387-2755** 416-964-3311
TownHouse Inn
1411 Tenth Ave S .... Great Falls MT 59405 **800-442-4667** 406-761-4600
Townsend Hotel
100 Townsend St .... Birmingham MI 48009 **800-548-4172** 248-642-7900
Trans World Corp (TWC)
545 Fifth Ave Ste 940 .... New York NY 10017 **877-407-9037** 212-983-3355
OTC: TWOC
Travelodge Virginia Beach
1909 Atlantic Ave .... Virginia Beach VA 23451 **800-578-7878** 757-425-0650
Tremont Chicago
100 E Chestnut St .... Chicago IL 60611 **888-627-8281** 312-751-1900
Trianon Old Naples
955 Seventh Ave S .... Naples FL 34102 **877-482-5228** 239-435-9600

			Toll-Free	Phone
Tropical Winds Oceanfront Hotel				
1398 N Atlantic Ave	Daytona Beach FL	32118	800-245-6099	386-258-1016
Tropicana Inn & Suites				
1540 S Harbor Blvd	Anaheim CA	92802	800-828-4898	714-635-4082
Truman Hotel & Conference Ctr				
1510 Jefferson St	Jefferson City MO	65109	800-392-0202	573-635-7171
Trump International Hotel & Tower				
725 Fifth Ave	New York NY	10022	888-448-7867	312-588-8000
Tugboat Inn				
80 Commercial St PO Box 267	Boothbay Harbor ME	04538	800-248-2628	207-633-4434
Tuscany Suites & Casino				
255 E Flamingo Rd	Las Vegas NV	89169	877-887-2261*	702-893-8933
*Resv				
Twin Farms				
452 Royalton Tpke PO Box 115	Barnard VT	05031	800-894-6327	802-234-9999
UMass Hotel at the Campus Ctr				
1 Campus Ctr Way	Amherst MA	01003	877-822-2110	413-549-6000
Umstead Hotel & Spa				
100 Woodland Pond	Cary NC	27513	866-877-4141	919-447-4000
Union Station A Wyndham Historic Hotel				
PO Box 4090	Aberdeen SD	57401	800-996-3426	
University Inn Seattle				
4140 Roosevelt Way NE	Seattle WA	98105	800-733-3855	206-632-5055
University Place				
310 SW Lincoln St	Portland OR	97201	866-845-4647	503-221-0140
US Grant, The				
326 Broadway	San Diego CA	92101	800-237-5029	619-232-3121
US Suites				
4970 Windplay Dr C1	El Dorado Hills CA	95762	800-877-8483*	916-941-7970
*Cust Svc				
Valley River Inn				
1000 Vly River Way	Eugene OR	97401	800-543-8266	541-743-1000
Vanderbilt Grace 41 Mary St	Newport RI	02840	888-826-4255	401-846-6200
Varscona Hotel				
8208 106th St	Edmonton AB	T6E6R9	866-465-8150	780-434-6111
Velvet Cloak Inn, The				
1505 Hillsborough St	Raleigh NC	27605	888-828-0335	919-828-0333
Viceroy Palm Springs				
415 S BelaRdo Rd	Palm Springs CA	92262	866-781-9923	760-320-4117
Viceroy Santa Monica				
1819 Ocean Ave	Santa Monica CA	90401	888-622-4567	310-260-7500
Victoria Inn Winnipeg				
1808 Wellington Ave	Winnipeg MB	R3H0G3	877-842-4667	204-786-4801
Victoria Regent Hotel, The				
1234 Wharf St	Victoria BC	V8W3H9	800-663-7472	250-386-2211
Victorian Condo-Hotel & Conference Ctr				
6300 Seawall Blvd	Galveston TX	77551	800-231-6363	409-740-3555
Villa Florence				
225 Powell St	San Francisco CA	94102	866-980-9684	415-397-7700
Villa Royale Inn				
1620 Indian Trl	Palm Springs CA	92264	800-245-2314	760-327-2314
Village Latch Inn				
101 Hill St PO Box 3000	SouthHampton NY	11968	800-545-2824	631-283-2160
Villagio Inn & Spa				
6481 Washington St	Yountville CA	94599	800-351-1133	707-944-8877
Vintage Inn Napa Valley				
6541 Washington St	Yountville CA	94599	800-351-1133*	
*Cust Svc				
Vintners Inn				
4350 Barnes Rd	Santa Rosa CA	95403	800-421-2584	707-575-7350
Virginian Lodge				
750 W Broadway PO Box 1052	Jackson Hole WY	83001	800-262-4999	307-733-2792
Virginian Suites				
1500 Arlington Blvd	Arlington VA	22209	866-371-1446	703-522-9600
Viscount Gort Hotel				
1670 Portage Ave	Winnipeg MB	R3J0C9	800-665-1122	204-775-0451
Viscount Suite Hotel				
4855 E Broadway Blvd	Tucson AZ	85711	800-527-9666*	520-745-6500
*Resv				
Vista Host Inc				
10370 Richmond Ave Ste 150	Houston TX	77042	800-257-3000	713-267-5800
Voyageur Inn				
200 Viking Dr	Reedsburg WI	53959	800-444-4493	608-524-6431
Voyageur Lakewalk Inn				
333 E Superior St	Duluth MN	55802	800-258-3911	218-722-3911
Waikiki Gateway Hotel				
2070 Kalakaua Ave	Honolulu HI	96815	866-444-4352	808-955-3741
Waikiki Parc Hotel				
2233 Helumoa Rd	Honolulu HI	96815	800-422-0450	808-921-7272
Waikiki Resort Hotel				
2460 Koa Ave	Honolulu HI	96815	800-367-5116	808-922-4911
Waldorf Towers, The				
100 E 50th St	New York NY	10022	800-925-3673	212-355-3100
Warwick Denver Hotel				
1776 Grant St	Denver CO	80203	800-203-3232	303-861-2000
Warwick Melrose Hotel				
3015 Oak Lawn Ave	Dallas TX	75219	800-521-7172	214-521-5151
Warwick New York Hotel				
65 W 54th St	New York NY	10019	800-223-4099	212-247-2700
Warwick Seattle Hotel				
401 Lenora St	Seattle WA	98121	800-426-9280	206-443-4300
Washington Court Hotel				
525 New Jersey Ave NW	Washington DC	20001	800-321-3010	202-628-2100
Washington Duke Inn & Golf Club				
3001 Cameron Blvd	Durham NC	27705	800-443-3853	919-490-0999
Washington Plaza Hotel				
10 Thomas Cir NW				
Massachusetts Ave at 14th St	Washington DC	20005	800-424-1140	202-842-1300
Washington Square Hotel				
103 Waverly Pl	New York NY	10011	800-222-0418	212-777-9515
Waterfront Hotel				
10 Washington St	Oakland CA	94607	888-842-5333	510-836-3800
Waters Edge Hotel				
25 Main St	Tiburon CA	94920	888-662-9555	415-789-5999
Wauwinet, The				
120 Wauwinet Rd PO Box 2580	Nantucket MA	02584	800-426-8718	508-228-0145

			Toll-Free	Phone
Weber's Inn				
3050 Jackson Rd	Ann Arbor MI	48103	800-443-3050*	734-769-2500
*Resv				
Wedgewood Hotel				
845 Hornby St	Vancouver BC	V6Z1V1	800-663-0666	604-689-7777
Wedgewood Resort Hotel				
212 Wedgewood Dr	Fairbanks AK	99701	800-528-4916	
Wellington Hotel				
871 Seventh Ave	New York NY	10019	800-652-1212	212-247-3900
Wellington Resort				
551 Thames St	Newport RI	02840	800-228-2968	401-849-1770
Wentworth Mansion				
149 Wentworth St	Charleston SC	29401	888-466-1886	843-853-1886
Westford Regency Inn & Conference Ctr				
219 Littleton Rd	Westford MA	01886	800-543-7801	978-692-8200
Westgate Branson Woods				
2201 Roark Vly Rd	Branson MO	65616	877-253-8572	417-334-2324
Westgate Painted Mountain Country Club				
6302 E McKellips Rd	Mesa AZ	85215	888-433-3707	480-654-3611
Westin Houston Downtown, The				
1520 Texas Ave	Houston TX	77002	800-427-4697	713-228-1520
Westin San Francisco Market Street				
50 Third St	San Francisco CA	94103	888-627-8561	415-974-6400
Westmark Hotels Inc				
300 Elliott Ave W	Seattle WA	98119	800-544-0970	
White Elephant Inn & Cottages				
50 Easton St	Nantucket MA	02554	800-475-2637	508-228-2500
White Swan Inn				
845 Bush St	San Francisco CA	94108	800-999-9570	415-775-1755
Whitney the - A Wyndham Historic Hotel				
610 Poydras St	New Orleans LA	70130	800-996-3426	504-581-4222
Wickaninnish Inn				
500 Osprey Ln PO Box 250	Tofino BC	V0R2Z0	800-333-4604	250-725-3100
Wild Palms Hotel				
910 E Fremont Ave	Sunnyvale CA	94087	800-738-7477	408-738-0500
Williamsburg Lodge				
310 S England St	Williamsburg VA	23185	800-447-8679*	757-229-1000
*Cust Svc				
Willows Historic Palm Springs Inn				
412 W Tahquitz Canyon Way	Palm Springs CA	92262	800-966-9597	760-320-0771
Willows Hotel 555 W Surf St	Chicago IL	60657	877-207-2111	773-528-8400
Willows Lodge				
14580 NE 145th St	Woodinville WA	98072	877-424-3930	425-424-3900
Wilson Hotel Management Company Inc				
8700 Trl Lk Dr W Ste 300	Memphis TN	38125	800-945-7661	901-346-8800
Windsor Arms Hotel				
18 St Thomas St	Toronto ON	M5S3E7	877-999-2767	416-971-9666
Windsor Court Hotel				
300 Gravier St	New Orleans LA	70130	888-596-0955	504-523-6000
Wonder View Inn & Suites				
50 Eden St PO Box 25	Bar Harbor ME	04609	888-439-8439	207-288-3358
Woodloch Pines Inc				
731 Welcome Lk Rd	Hawley PA	18428	800-966-3562	570-685-8000
Woodmark Hotel on Lake Washington				
1200 Carillon Pt	Kirkland WA	98033	800-822-3700	425-822-3700
Wort Hotel 50 N Glenwood	Jackson WY	83001	800-322-2727*	307-733-2190
*Cust Svc				
AmeriHost Inn				
8001 International Dr	Orlando FL	32819	877-999-3223*	407-351-2420
*Resv				
Baymont Inn & Suites				
PO Box 4090	Aberdeen SD	57401	866-464-2321	
Ramada 949 Route 46	Parsippany NJ	07054	877-212-2733*	
*Resv				
Wyndham Hotel Group				
Travelodge PO Box 4090	Aberdeen SD	57041	800-525-4055*	312-427-8000
*Resv				
Wyndham Vacation Resorts				
6277 Sea Harbor Dr	Orlando FL	32821	800-251-8736	
Wyndham Lake Buena Vista				
1850 Hotel Plaza Blvd	Lake Buena Vista FL	32830	800-624-4109	407-828-4444
Wynfrey Hotel				
1000 Riverchase Galleria	Birmingham AL	35244	800-633-7313	205-987-1600
Wynn Las Vegas				
3131 Las Vegas Blvd S	Las Vegas NV	89109	877-321-9966	702-770-7000
Yarrow Hotel & Conference Ctr				
1800 Pk Ave	Park City UT	84060	800-445-8667	435-649-7000
Yogo Inn 211 E Main St	Lewistown MT	59457	800-860-9646	406-535-8721
Yorktowne Hotel 48 E Market St	York PA	17401	800-233-9324	717-848-1111

379　ICE - MANUFACTURED

			Toll-Free	Phone
Hanover Foods Corp				
1550 York St PO Box 334	Hanover PA	17331	800-888-4646	717-632-6000
OTC: HNFSA				
House of Flavors Inc				
110 N William St	Ludington MI	49431	800-930-7740	231-845-7369
Icemakers Inc				
3711 Fifth Ct N	Birmingham AL	35222	800-467-2181*	205-591-2791
*General				
Reddy Ice Holdings Inc				
8750 N Central Expy Ste 1800	Dallas TX	75231	800-683-4423	214-526-6740
OTC: RDDYQ				

380　ICE CREAM & DAIRY STORES

			Toll-Free	Phone
Baskin-Robbins Inc				
130 Royall St	Canton MA	02021	800-859-5339	781-737-3000
Carvel Express				
200 Glenridge Pt Pkwy Ste 200	Atlanta GA	30342	800-322-4848	
Cloverland Green Spring Dairy Inc				
2701 Loch Raven Rd	Baltimore MD	21218	800-492-0094*	410-235-4477
*Orders				

			Toll-Free	Phone

Cold Stone Creamery Inc
9311 E Via De Ventura ....Scottsdale AZ 85258 **866-452-4252*** 480-362-4800
*Cust Svc

Dairy Queen
7505 Metro Blvd ....Minneapolis MN 55439 **800-883-4279** 952-830-0200

Kilwins Quality Confections Inc (KQC)
1050 Bay View Rd ....Petoskey MI 49770 **888-454-5946**

Royal Crest Dairy Inc
350 S Pearl St ....Denver CO 80209 **888-226-6455** 303-777-2227

381   IMAGING EQUIPMENT & SYSTEMS - MEDICAL

SEE ALSO Medical Instruments & Apparatus - Mfr

			Toll-Free	Phone

Agfa Corp 611 River Dr ....Elmwood Park NJ 07407 **888-274-8626** 201-440-2500

BrainLAB Inc
Three Westbrook Corp Ctr Ste 400 ....Westchester IL 60154 **800-784-7700** 708-409-1343

CIVCO Medical Instruments
102 First St ....Kalona IA 52247 **800-445-6741** 319-656-4447

Dentsply International Inc
221 W Philadelphia St PO Box 872 ....York PA 17405 **800-877-0020** 717-845-7511
NASDAQ: XRAY

Digirad Corp 13950 Stowe Dr ....Poway CA 92064 **800-947-6134** 858-726-1600
NASDAQ: DRAD

Dornier MedTech America Inc
1155 Roberts Blvd ....Kennesaw GA 30144 **800-367-6437** 770-426-1315

Fonar Corp 110 Marcus Dr ....Melville NY 11747 **877-694-2929** 631-694-2929
NASDAQ: FONR

Hitachi Medical Systems America Inc
1959 Summit Commerce Pk ....Twinsburg OH 44087 **800-800-3106** 330-425-1313

Hologic Inc 35 Crosby Dr ....Bedford MA 01730 **800-523-5001** 781-999-7300
NASDAQ: HOLX

iCAD Inc
Four Townsend W Ste 17 ....Nashua NH 03063 **866-280-2239** 603-882-5200
NASDAQ: ICAD

ImageWorks
250 Clearbrook Rd ....Elmsford NY 10523 **800-592-6666** 914-592-6100

Imaging Diagnostic Systems Inc
6531 NW 18th Ct ....Plantation FL 33313 **800-992-9008** 954-581-9800
OTC: IMDS

IRIS International Inc
9172 Eton Ave ....Chatsworth CA 91311 **877-920-4747** 818-709-1244
NASDAQ: IRIS

ITT Night Vision & Imaging
7635 Plantation Rd ....Roanoke VA 24019 **800-448-8678** 540-563-0371

Merge Helathcare
350 N Orleans St First Fl ....Chicago IL 60654 **877-446-3743** 312-565-6868

One Call Medical Inc (OCM)
20 Waterview Blvd PO Box 614 ....Parsippany NJ 07054 **800-872-2875** 973-257-1000

Philips Global PACS
5000 Marina Blvd Ste 100 ....Brisbane CA 94005 **877-328-2808*** 650-228-5555
*Cust Svc

Philips Medical Systems
3000 Minuteman Rd ....Andover MA 01810 **800-934-7372** 978-659-3000

Precision Optics Corp Inc
22 E Broadway ....Gardner MA 01440 **800-447-2812** 978-630-1800
OTC: PEYE

S & S Technology
10625 Telge Rd ....Houston TX 77095 **800-231-1747** 281-815-1300

Shimadzu Medical Systems
20101 S Vermont Ave ....Torrance CA 90502 **800-477-1227*** 310-217-8855
*General

Siemens Medical Solutions Inc
51 Valley Stream Pkwy ....Malvern PA 19355 **800-888-7436** 800-225-5336

SonoSite Inc
21919 30th Dr SE ....Bothell WA 98021 **888-482-9449** 425-951-1200
NASDAQ: SONO

Stereotaxis Inc
4320 Forest Pk Ave ....Saint Louis MO 63108 **866-646-2346** 314-678-6100
NASDAQ: STXS

Topcon Medical Systems Inc
111 Bauer Dr ....Oakland NJ 07436 **800-223-1130** 201-599-5100

Toshiba America Inc
1251 Ave of the Americas Ste 4100 ....New York NY 10020 **800-457-7777** 212-596-0600

Toshiba America Medical Systems Inc
2441 Michelle Dr ....Tustin CA 92780 **800-521-1968*** 714-730-5000
*Cust Svc

Varian Medical Systems Inc
3100 Hansen Way ....Palo Alto CA 94304 **800-544-4636** 650-493-4000
NYSE: VAR

Vision-Sciences Inc
40 Ramland Rd S ....Orangeburg NY 10962 **800-874-9975** 845-365-0600
NASDAQ: VSCI

Wolf X-Ray Corp
100 W Industry Ct ....Deer Park NY 11729 **800-356-9729*** 631-242-9729
*Cust Svc

382   IMAGING SERVICES - DIAGNOSTIC

			Toll-Free	Phone

Alliance Imaging Inc
100 Bayview Cir Ste 400 ....Newport Beach CA 92660 **800-544-3215** 949-242-5300

Center for Diagnostic Imaging
5775 Wayzata Blvd Ste 400 ....Saint Louis Park MN 55416 **877-885-8797** 952-541-1840

Insight Imaging
26250 Enterprise Ct Ste 100 ....Lake Forest CA 92630 **800-344-9555** 949-282-6000

Medical Resources Inc
1455 Broad St ....Bloomfield NJ 07003 **800-537-7272** 973-707-1100

383   INCENTIVE PROGRAM MANAGEMENT SERVICES

SEE ALSO Conference & Events Coordinators
Many of the companies listed here provide travel as a reward for employees or corporate customers in order to boost sales or employee performance. Most of these companies are members of the Society of Incentive & Travel Executives. Some of the companies listed offer merchandise or other types of incentives as well.

			Toll-Free	Phone

Beatty Group International
9800 Beaverton Hillsdale Ste 105 ....Beaverton OR 97005 **800-285-6215** 503-644-3340

Fields Group Inc
12335 Bridgewater Rd ....Indianapolis IN 46256 **800-600-2969** 317-578-4414

ITAGroup
4600 Westown Pkwy ....West Des Moines IA 50266 **800-257-1985**

Marketing Innovators International Inc
9701 W Higgins Rd ....Rosemont IL 60018 **800-543-7373**

MotivAction
16355 36th Ave N Ste 100 ....Minneapolis MN 55446 **866-277-3420** 763-412-3000

Motivation Through Incentives Inc
10400 W 103 St Ste 10 ....Overland Park KS 66214 **800-826-3464**

PROVIDENT TRAVEL
11309 Montgomery Rd ....Cincinnati OH 45249 **800-354-8108** 513-247-1100

Student Advantage LLC
280 Summer St ....Boston MA 02210 **800-333-2920**

USMotivation
7840 Roswell Rd Bldg 100 Third Fl ....Atlanta GA 30350 **866-885-4702**

Viktor Incentives & Meetings
4020 Copper View Ste 130 ....Traverse City MI 49684 **800-748-0478** 231-947-0882

384   INDUSTRIAL EQUIPMENT & SUPPLIES (MISC) - WHOL

			Toll-Free	Phone

AaronEquipment Company Inc
735 E Green St PO Box 80 ....Bensenville IL 60106 **800-492-2766** 630-350-2200

Abatix Corp
2400 Skyline Dr Ste 400 ....Mesquite TX 75149 **800-426-3983** 214-381-0322

Accurate Air Engineering Inc
16207 Carmennita Rd ....Cerritos CA 90703 **800-438-5577** 562-484-6370

AIM Supply Co
7337 Bryan Dairy Rd ....Largo FL 33777 **800-999-0125** 727-544-6211

Aimco 10000 SE Pine St ....Portland OR 97216 **800-852-1368**

Airgas Inc
259 N Radnor-Chester Rd Ste 100 ....Radnor PA 19087 **800-255-2165** 610-687-5253
NYSE: ARG

Alamo Iron Works Inc
943 AT&T Ctr Pkwy ....San Antonio TX 78219 **800-292-7817** 210-223-6161

Atlantic Lift Truck Inc
2945 Whittington Ave ....Baltimore MD 21230 **800-638-4566** 410-644-7777

Austin Pump & Supply Co
PO Box 17037 ....Austin TX 78760 **800-252-9692** 512-442-2348

Barnes Distribution
1301 E Ninth St Ste 700 ....Cleveland OH 44114 **800-726-9626** 216-416-7200

Bearing Distributors Inc
8000 Hub Pkwy ....Cleveland OH 44125 **888-435-7234** 216-642-9100

Berendsen Fluid Power
401 S Boston Ave Ste 1200 ....Tulsa OK 74103 **800-360-2327** 918-592-3781

Bolttech Mannings
501 Mosside Blvd ....North Versailles PA 15137 **888-846-8827** 724-872-4873

Brake Supply Company Inc
5501 Foundation Blvd ....Evansville IN 47725 **800-457-5788** 812-467-1000

Brauer Material Handling Systems Inc
226 Molly Walton Dr ....Hendersonville TN 37075 **800-645-6083** 615-859-2930

Briggs Equipment
10540 N Stemmons Fwy Ste 1525 ....Dallas TX 75220 **800-606-1833** 214-630-0808

Briggs Industrial Equipment
10550 N Stemmons Fwy ....Dallas TX 75220 **800-516-9206** 214-630-0808

C & H Distributors LLC
770 S 70th St ....Milwaukee WI 53214 **800-558-9966*** 414-443-1700
*Sales

Canadian Bearings Ltd
1600 Drew Rd ....Mississauga ON L5S1S5 **800-229-2327** 905-670-6700

Carolina Material Handling Services Inc
PO Box 6 ....Columbia SC 29202 **800-922-6709** 803-695-0149

Cascade Machinery & Electric Inc
4600 E Marginal Way S PO Box 3575 ....Seattle WA 98134 **800-289-0500** 206-762-0500

Cisco-Eagle
2120 Valley View Ln ....Dallas TX 75234 **888-877-3861** 972-406-9330

CMC Construction Services
9103 E Almeda Rd ....Houston TX 77054 **877-297-9111** 713-799-1150

Conveyco Technologies Inc
PO Box 1000 ....Bristol CT 06011 **800-229-8215** 860-589-8215

Cross Co
4400 Piedmont Pkwy ....Greensboro NC 27410 **800-858-1737** 336-856-6000

Cummins Southern Plains Inc
PO Box 90027 ....Arlington TX 76004 **800-516-4354** 817-640-6801

Deacon Industrial Supply Co Inc
165 Boro Line Rd ....King of Prussia PA 19406 **800-726-9800** 610-265-5322

Detroit Pump & Mfg Co
450 Fair St Bldg D ....Ferndale MI 48220 **800-686-1662** 248-544-4242

Dueco
N4 W22610 Bluemound Rd ....Waukesha WI 53186 **800-558-4004** 262-547-8500

Duncan Industrial Solutions
3450 S MacArthur Blvd ....Oklahoma City OK 73179 **800-375-9470** 405-688-2300

DXP Enterprises Inc
7272 Pinemont Dr ....Houston TX 77040 **800-830-3973** 713-996-4700
NASDAQ: DXPE

Eastern Lift Truck Company Inc
549 E Linwood Ave ....Maple Shade NJ 08052 **866-980-7175** 856-779-8880

Edgen Corp
18444 Highland Rd ....Baton Rouge LA 70809 **866-334-3648** 225-756-9868

Endries International Inc
714 W Ryan St PO Box 69 ....Brillion WI 54110 **800-852-5821** 920-756-5381

		Toll-Free	Phone
Engman-Taylor Company Inc (ETCO)			
W142 N9351 Fountain Blvd ....Menomonee Falls WI 53051		800-236-1975	262-255-9300
Enpro Inc 121 S LombaRd Rd ....Addison IL 60101		800-323-2416	630-629-3504
Exterran			
16666 Northchase Dr ....Houston TX 77060		800-975-9090*	281-836-7000
*Sales			
FCx Performance			
3000 E 14th Ave ....Columbus OH 43219		800-253-6223	614-324-6050
Florida Detroit Diesel-Allison Inc			
5040 University Blvd W ....Jacksonville FL 32216		888-812-4440	904-737-7330
Forklifts of Minnesota Inc			
2201 W 94th St ....Bloomington MN 55431		800-752-4300	952-887-5400
FUJIFILM Graphic System USA Inc			
45 Crosby Dr ....Bedford MA 01730		800-755-3854	781-271-4400
FW Webb Co			
160 Middlesex Tpke ....Bedford MA 01730		800-343-7555	781-272-6600
General Tool & Supply Co Inc			
2705 NW Nicolai Blvd ....Portland OR 97210		800-526-9328	503-226-3411
Geneva Scientific Inc			
11 N Batavia Ave ....Batavia IL 60510		800-338-2697	
Gosiger Inc 108 McDonough St ....Dayton OH 45402		877-288-1538	937-228-5174
H G Makelim Co			
219 Shaw Rd ....South San Francisco CA 94080		800-471-0590	650-873-4757
Hagemeyer North America Inc			
1460 Tobias Gadson Blvd ....Charleston SC 29407		877-462-7070	843-745-2400
Haggard & Stocking Assoc			
5318 Victory Dr ....Indianapolis IN 46203		800-622-4824	317-788-4661
Hahn Systems Co Inc			
6312 SE Ave ....Indianapolis IN 46203		800-201-4246	317-243-3796
Harrington Industrial Plastics LLC			
14480 Yorba Ave ....Chino CA 91710		800-213-4528	909-597-8641
HD Supply Waterworks Ltd			
PO Box 1419 ....Thomasville GA 31799		800-492-6909	800-950-7659
Herc-U-Lift Inc			
5655 Hwy 12 W PO Box 69 ....Maple Plain MN 55359		800-362-3500	763-479-2501
Hull Lift Truck Inc			
28747 Old US 33 W ....Elkhart IN 46516		888-284-0364	574-293-8651
IBT Inc 9400 W 55th St ....Merriam KS 66203		800-332-2114	913-677-3151
Illinois Auto Electric Co			
700 Enterprise St ....Aurora IL 60504		800-683-8484	630-862-3300
Indeck Power Equipment Co			
1111 Willis Ave ....Wheeling IL 60090		800-446-3325	847-541-8300
Indoff Inc			
11816 Lackland Rd ....Saint Louis MO 63146		800-486-7867	314-997-1122
Industrial Controls Distributors Inc (ICD)			
1776 Bloomsbury Ave ....Ocean NJ 07712		800-281-4788*	732-918-9000
*Sales			
Industrial Diesel Inc			
8705 Harmon Rd ....Fort Worth TX 76177		800-323-3659	817-232-1071
Industrial Supply Solutions Inc			
520 Elizabeth St ....Charleston WV 25311		800-346-5341	304-346-5341
J. H. Bennett & Company Inc			
PO Box 8028 ....Novi MI 48376		800-837-5426*	248-596-5100
*General			
Jabo Supply Corp			
5164 County Rd 64/66 ....Huntington WV 25705		800-334-5226	304-736-8333
Jefferds Corp			
652 Winfield Rd PO Box 757 ....Saint Albans WV 25177		888-848-6216	304-755-8111
Kennametal Inc			
1600 Technology Way PO Box 231......Latrobe PA 15650		800-446-7738*	724-539-5000
NYSE: KMT ◼ *Cust Svc			
Kimball Midwest			
4800 Robert Rd ....Columbus OH 43228		800-233-1294	614-219-6100
Lewis Goetz & Company Inc			
1571 Grandview Ave ....Paulsboro NJ 08066		800-257-6239	856-579-1421
Lewis-Goetz & Co Inc			
650 Washington Rd Ste 210 ....Pittsburgh PA 15228		888-327-8882	412-341-7100
Lipten Company LLC			
28054 Ctr Oaks Ct ....Wixom MI 48393		800-860-0790	248-374-8910
Logan Corp			
555 Seventh Ave ....Huntington WV 25701		888-853-4751	304-526-4700
M & L Industries Inc			
1210 St Charles St ....Houma LA 70360		800-969-0068*	985-876-2280
*General			
Mac-Gray Corp			
404 Wyman St Ste 400 ....Waltham MA 02451		888-622-4729	781-487-7600
NYSE: TUC			
Machinery Sales Co			
17253 Chestnut St ....City of Industry CA 91748		800-588-8111	626-581-9211
Machinery Systems Inc			
614 E State Pkwy ....Schaumburg IL 60173		888-650-5424	847-882-8085
Mahar Tool Supply Co Inc			
112 Williams St ....Saginaw MI 48605		800-456-2427	989-799-5530
Martin Supply Co			
200 Appleton Ave ....Sheffield AL 35660		800-828-8116	256-383-3131
McCall Handling Co			
8801 Wise Ave Ste 200 ....Dundalk MD 21222		888-870-0685	410-388-2600
McKinley Equipment Corp			
17611 Armstrong Ave ....Irvine CA 92614		800-770-6094	949-261-9222
Medart Inc			
124 Manufacturers Dr ....Arnold MO 63010		800-888-7181*	636-282-2300
*Cust Svc			
Minnesota Supply Company Inc			
6470 Flying Cloud Dr ....Eden Prairie MN 55344		800-869-1028	952-828-7300
Modern Group Ltd			
2501 Durham Rd ....Bristol PA 19007		800-223-3827	215-943-9100
Motion Industries Inc			
1605 Alton Rd ....Birmingham AL 35210		800-526-9328	205-956-1122
MSC Industrial Direct Co			
75 Maxess Rd ....Melville NY 11747		800-645-7270	516-812-2000
NYSE: MSM			
Multiquip Inc			
18910 Wilmington Ave ....Carson CA 90746		800-421-1244	310-537-3700
NC Machinery Co			
17025 W Valley Hwy ....Tukwila WA 98188		800-562-4735	425-251-9800
Nebraska Machinery Co Inc			
3501 S Jeffers St PO Box 809......North Platte NE 69101		800-494-9560	308-532-3100

		Toll-Free	Phone
Nelson-Jameson Inc			
2400 E Fifth St PO Box 647 ....Marshfield WI 54449		800-826-8302	715-387-1151
Newman's Inc			
3003 Texas 225 ....Pasadena TX 77503		800-231-3505	713-675-8631
NSC International			
7090 Central Ave ....Hot Springs AR 71913		800-643-1520	501-525-0133
Nu-Life Environmental Inc			
PO Box 1527 ....Easley SC 29641		800-654-1752	864-855-5155
O Berk Co 3 Milltown Ct ....Union NJ 07083		800-631-7392	908-851-9500
Pacific Power Group			
600 S 56th Pl ....Ridgefield WA 98642		800-882-3860	360-887-7400
Piping & Equipment Inc			
9100 Canniff St ....Houston TX 77017		888-889-9683	713-947-9393
Production Tool Supply			
8655 E Eight Mile Rd ....Warren MI 48089		800-366-3600	586-755-7770
R & M Energy Systems			
301 Premier Rd ....Borger TX 79007		888-262-8645*	806-274-5293
*Sales			
R B M Co			
2700 Texas Ave PO Box 12 ....Knoxville TN 37921		800-521-5656	865-524-8621
Red Ball Oxygen Co Inc			
609 N Market ....Shreveport LA 71107		800-551-8150	318-425-3211
Rem Sales Inc			
910 Gay Hill Rd ....Windsor CT 06095		877-689-1860	860-687-3400
Remstar International Inc			
41 Eisenhower Dr ....Westbrook ME 04092		800-639-5805	
Rex Supply Co			
3715 Harrisburg Blvd ....Houston TX 77003		800-369-0669	713-222-2251
Riekes Equipment Co			
PO Box 3392 ....Omaha NE 68103		800-856-0931	402-593-1181
Robert Dietrick Co Inc			
PO Box 605 ....Fishers IN 46038		866-767-1888	317-842-1991
Robert E Morris Co			
910 Gay Hill Rd ....Windsor CT 06095		877-689-1860	860-687-3300
RS Hughes Company Inc			
10639 Glenoaks Blvd ....Pacoima CA 91331		877-774-8443	818-686-9111
Ryan Herco Products Corp			
3010 N San Fernando Blvd ....Burbank CA 91504		800-848-1141	818-841-1141
S.l.c. Meter Service Inc			
10375 Dixie Hwy ....Davisburg MI 48350		800-433-4332	248-625-0667
Shively Bros Inc			
2919 S Grand Travers St PO Box 1520 ......Flint MI 48501		800-530-9352	810-232-7401
Smith Power Products Inc			
3065 W California Ave ....Salt Lake City UT 84104		800-658-5352	801-415-5000
Sooner Pipe LLC			
1331 Lamar St Ste 970 4 Houston Ctr ....Houston TX 77010		800-888-9161	713-759-1200
Southern Pump & Tank Co			
4800 N Graham St ....Charlotte NC 28269		800-477-2826*	704-596-4373
*Cust Svc			
Strategic Distribution Inc			
1414 Radcliffe St Ste 300 ....Bristol PA 19007		800-322-2644	215-633-1900
Teeco Products Inc			
16881 Armstrong Ave ....Irvine CA 92606		800-854-3463	949-261-6295
Texas Process Equipment Co			
5215 Ted St ....Houston TX 77040		800-828-4114	713-460-5555
Travers Tool Company Inc			
128-15 26th Ave ....Flushing NY 11354		800-221-0270*	718-886-7200
*Cust Svc			
Valtra Inc			
7141 Paramount Blvd ....Pico Rivera CA 90660		800-989-5244	562-949-8625
Vellano Bros Inc			
Seven Hemlock St ....Latham NY 12110		800-342-9855	518-785-5537
Voto Manufacturers Sales Co			
500 N Third St PO Box 1299 ....Steubenville OH 43952		800-848-4010	740-282-3621
Werres Corp 807 E S St ....Frederick MD 21701		800-638-6563	301-620-4000
Wilson Supply Co			
1302 Conti St ....Houston TX 77002		800-874-5930	713-237-3700
Windsor Factory Supply Ltd			
730 N Service Rd ....Windsor ON N8X3J3		800-387-2659	519-966-2202
Yamazen Inc			
735 E Remington Rd ....Schaumburg IL 60173		800-882-8558	847-490-8130

385 INDUSTRIAL MACHINERY, EQUIPMENT, & SUPPLIES

SEE ALSO Rolling Mill Machinery ; Textile Machinery ; Woodworking Machinery ; Furnaces & Ovens - Industrial Process ; Machine Shops ; Material Handling Equipment ; Packaging Machinery & Equipment ; Paper Industries Machinery ; Printing & Publishing Equipment & Systems ; Conveyors & Conveying Equipment ; Food Products Machinery

		Toll-Free	Phone
ABB Inc 501 Merritt 7 ....Norwalk CT 06851		800-626-4999*	203-750-2200
*Prod Info			
Accu Therm Inc			
PO Box 249 ....Monroe City MO 63456		888-925-4332	573-735-1060
Acme Electric			
N85 W12545 Westbrook Crossing			
..............................Menomonee Falls WI 53051		800-334-5214	910-738-1121
Adept Technology Inc			
5960 Inglewood Dr ....Pleasanton CA 94588		800-292-3378	925-245-3400
NASDAQ: ADEP			
Aeroglide Corp			
100 Aeroglide Dr ....Cary NC 27511		800-722-7483	919-851-2000
Alemite LLC			
1057-521 Corporate Ctr Dr Ste 100 ....Fort Mill SC 29715		800-267-8022	803-802-0001
Allentown Equipment			
1733 90th St ....Sturtevant WI 53177		800-553-3414	
American Baler Co			
800 E Centre St ....Bellevue OH 44811		800-843-7512	419-483-5790
AO Smith Water Products Co			
500 Tennessee Waltz Pkwy ....Ashland City TN 37015		800-527-1953	
Apache Stainless Equipment Corp			
200 W Industrial Dr PO Box 538......Beaver Dam WI 53916		800-444-0398	920-356-9900
Ats Systems Oregon Inc			
2121 NE Jack London St ....Corvallis OR 97330		800-564-6253	541-758-3329

Company	Toll-Free	Phone
Azon USA Inc 643 W Crosstown Pkwy .... Kalamazoo MI 49008	800-788-5942	269-385-5942
Bauer-Pileco Inc 100 N FM 3083 E .... Conroe TX 77303	800-474-5326	713-691-3000
Besser Co 801 Johnson St .... Alpena MI 49707	800-530-9980	989-354-4111
Blower Application Company Inc N 114 W 19125 Clinton Dr .... Germantown WI 53022	800-959-0880	262-255-5580
Charles Ross & Son Co 710 Old Willets Path .... Hauppauge NY 11788	800-243-7677	631-234-0500
Chemineer Inc 5870 Poe Ave .... Dayton OH 45414	800-643-0641	937-454-3200
Chief Automotive Systems Inc 1924 E Fourth St .... Grand Island NE 68802	800-445-9262	308-384-9747
Clean Diesel Technologies Inc 4567 Telephone Rd Ste 206 .... Ventura CA 93003 *NASDAQ: CDTI*	800-661-9963	805-639-9458
CMA Dishmachines 12700 Knott St .... Garden Grove CA 92841	800-854-6417	714-898-8781
Corotec Corp 145 Hyde Rd .... Farmington CT 06032	800-423-0348	860-678-0038
CUNO Inc 400 Research Pkwy .... Meriden CT 06450	800-243-6894	203-237-5541
Davis-Ulmer Sprinkler Company Inc One Commerce Dr .... Amherst NY 14228	877-691-3200	716-691-3200
Despatch Industries Inc 8860 207th St W .... Lakeville MN 55044	800-726-0110	952-469-5424
Diamond Power International Inc 2600 E Main St .... Lancaster OH 43130	800-848-5086	740-687-6500
Dings Co 4740 W Electric Ave .... Milwaukee WI 53219	800-494-1918	414-672-7830
Ecodyne Ltd 4475 Corporate Dr .... Burlington ON L7L5T9	888-326-3963	905-332-1404
Enerflex Systems Ltd 1331 Macleod Trail SE Ste 904 .... Calgary AB T2G0K3 *TSE: EFX*	800-242-3178	403-387-6377
Engis Corp 105 W Hintz Rd .... Wheeling IL 60090	800-993-6447	847-808-9400
Equipment Manufacturing Corp (EMC) 14930 Marquardt Ave .... Santa Fe Springs CA 90670	888-833-9000	562-623-9394
FANUC America Corp 3900 W Hamlin Rd .... Rochester Hills MI 48309	800-477-6268	248-377-7000
Farrel Corp 25 Main St .... Ansonia CT 06401	800-800-7290	203-736-5500
Fluid Management Inc 1023 S Wheeling Rd .... Wheeling IL 60090	800-462-2466	847-537-0880
Forward Technology Inc 260 Jenks Ave .... Cokato MN 55321 *Cust Svc	800-307-6040*	320-286-2578
Fusion Inc 4658 E 355th St .... Willoughby OH 44094	800-626-9501	440-946-3300
Gamajet Cleaning Systems Inc 604 Jeffers Cir .... Exton PA 19341 *Sales	877-426-2538*	610-408-9940
General Equipment Co 620 Alexander Dr SW PO Box 334 .... Owatonna MN 55060 *Cust Svc	800-533-0524*	507-451-5510
Genmark Automation Inc 1201 Cadillac Ct .... Milpitas CA 95035	866-467-6268	408-678-8500
George Koch Sons LLC 10 S 11th Ave .... Evansville IN 47712	888-873-5624	812-465-9600
Glastender Inc 5400 N Michigan Rd .... Saginaw MI 48604	800-748-0423	989-752-4275
Gougler Industries Inc 711 Lake St .... Kent OH 44240	800-527-2282	330-673-5826
Graham Corp 20 Florence Ave .... Batavia NY 14020 *NYSE: GHM ▪ *Orders	800-828-8150*	585-343-2216
Gregory Poole Equipment Co 4807 Beryl Rd PO Box 469 .... Raleigh NC 27606	800-451-7278	919-828-0641
Hamon Research-Cottrell Inc 58 E Main St .... Somerville NJ 08876	800-722-7580	908-685-4000
Harrington Hoists Inc 401 W End Ave .... Manheim PA 17545	800-233-3010	717-665-2000
Hfw Industries Inc 196 Philadelphia St PO Box 8 .... Buffalo NY 14207	800-937-9311	716-875-3380
Hosokawa Polymer Systems 63 Fuller Way .... Berlin CT 06037	800-233-6112	860-828-0541
Hydro-Thermal Corp 400 Pilot Ct .... Waukesha WI 53188	800-952-0121	262-548-8900
Jesco-Wipco Industries Inc 950 Anderson Rd PO Box 388 .... Litchfield MI 49252	800-455-0019	517-542-2903
K & B Machine Works Inc 212 Redmond Rd PO Box 10265 .... Houma LA 70363	800-256-1526	985-868-6730
Kobelco Stewart Bolling Inc (KSBI) 1600 Terex Rd .... Hudson OH 44236	800-464-0064	330-655-3111
Koch Membrane Systems Inc 850 Main St .... Wilmington MA 01887	888-677-5624	978-694-7000
Kois Bros Equipment Company Inc 5200 Colorado Blvd .... Commerce City CO 80022	800-672-6010	303-298-7370
Komline-Sanderson Engineering Corp 12 Holland Ave .... Peapack NJ 07977	800-225-5457	908-234-1000
Lawton Industries Inc 4353 Pacific St .... Rocklin CA 95677	800-692-2600	916-624-7895
Lesman Instrument Co 135 Bernice Dr .... Bensenville IL 60106	800-953-7626	630-595-8400
Lightnin 135 Mt Read Blvd .... Rochester NY 14611	877-247-3797	585-436-5550
Littleford Day Inc 7451 Empire Dr .... Florence KY 41042	800-365-8555	859-525-7600
Marathon Equipment Co PO Box 1798 .... Vernon AL 35592	800-633-8974	205-695-9105
Maruka USA Inc 400 Commons Way .... Rockaway NJ 07866	800-631-0426	973-983-1000
Materials Transportation Co (MTC) 1408 S Commerce PO Box 1358 .... Temple TX 76503	800-433-3110	254-298-2900
McNeil & NRM Inc 96 E Crosier St .... Akron OH 44311	800-669-2525	330-253-2525
MEGTEC Systems Inc 830 Prosper Rd .... De Pere WI 54115 *Cust Svc	800-558-5535*	920-336-5715
Michigan Fluid Power Inc 4556 Spartan Industrial Dr SW .... Grandville MI 49418	800-635-0289	616-538-5700
Michigan Wheel Corp 1501 Buchanan Ave SW .... Grand Rapids MI 49507	800-369-4335	616-452-6941
Mico Inc 1911 Lee Blvd .... North Mankato MN 56003	800-477-6426	507-625-6426
Micro-Poise Measurment Systems LLC 1624 Englewood Ave .... Akron OH 44305	800-428-3812	330-784-1251
Minuteman International Inc 111 S Rohlwing Rd .... Addison IL 60101	800-323-9420	630-627-6900
Mississippi Welders Supply Co 5150 W Sixth St PO Box 1036 .... Winona MN 55987	800-657-4422	507-454-5231
Monroe Environmental Corp 810 W Front St .... Monroe MI 48161	800-992-7707	734-242-7654
Moody-Price LLC 18320 Petroleum Dr .... Baton Rouge LA 70809	800-272-9832	
Mueller Steam Specialty 1491 NC Hwy 20 W .... Saint Pauls NC 28384	800-334-6259	910-865-8241
National Super Service Company Inc 3115 Frenchman Rd .... Toledo OH 43607 *Cust Svc	800-677-1663*	419-531-2121
Neumayer Equipment Company Inc 5060 Arsenal St .... Saint Louis MO 63139	800-843-4563	314-772-4501
Nexen Group Inc 560 Oak Grove Pkwy .... Vadnais Heights MN 55127	800-843-7445	651-484-5900
Nilfisk-Advance Inc 14600 21st Ave N .... Plymouth MN 55447 *Cust Svc	800-989-2235*	
Nordson Corp 28601 Clemens Rd .... Westlake OH 44145 *NASDAQ: NDSN*	800-321-2881	440-892-1580
Oil & Gas Equipment Corp Eight Rd 350 .... Flora Vista NM 87415	800-868-9624	505-333-2300
Oscar Wilson Engines & Parts Inc 826 Lone Star Dr .... O Fallon MO 63366	800-233-3723	636-978-1313
Pall Corp 2200 Northern Blvd .... East Hills NY 11548 *NYSE: PLL*	800-645-6532	516-484-5400
Parkson Corp 1401 W Cyperess Creek Rd .... Fort Lauderdale FL 33309	888-727-5766	
Paul Mueller Co 1600 W Phelps St .... Springfield MO 65802 *OTC: MUEL*	800-683-5537	417-831-3000
PDQ Manufacturing Inc 1698 Scheuring Rd .... De Pere WI 54115	800-227-3373	920-983-8333
Peach State Integrated Technologies Inc 3005 Business Pk Dr .... Norcross GA 30071	800-998-6517	678-327-2000
Peerless Manufacturing Co 14651 N Dallas Pkwy Ste 500 .... Dallas TX 75254 *NASDAQ: PMFG*	877-879-7634	214-357-6181
Permadur Industries Inc 186 Rt 206 S .... Hillsborough NJ 08844	800-392-0146	908-359-9767
Peterson Machine Tool Inc 1100 N Union St .... Council Grove KS 66846	800-835-3528	
Phillips Machine Service Inc 367 George St .... Beckley WV 25801	800-733-1521	304-255-0537
Pioneer/Eclipse Corp One Eclipse Rd .... Sparta NC 28675 *Cust Svc	800-367-3550*	336-372-8080
Pipe & Tube Supply Inc 1407 N Cypress .... North Little Rock AR 72114	800-770-8823	501-372-6556
Premier Safety & Service Inc Two Industrial Pk Dr .... Oakdale PA 15071	800-828-1080	724-693-8699
PTI Technologies Inc 501 Del Norte Blvd .... Oxnard CA 93030	800-331-2701	805-604-3700
Pullman/Holt Corp 10702 N 46th St .... Tampa FL 33617	800-237-7582	813-971-2223
R&R Products Inc 3334 E Milber St .... Tucson AZ 85714	800-528-3446	520-889-3593
Rockford Industrial Welding Supply Inc 4646 Linden Rd .... Rockford IL 61109	800-226-1904	815-226-1900
Rotary Lift 2700 Lanier Dr .... Madison IN 47250	800-445-5438	812-273-1622
Salem Tools Inc 1602 Midland Rd .... Salem VA 24153	800-390-4348	540-389-0233
Shop-Vac Corp 2323 Reach Rd .... Williamsport PA 17701	800-356-0783	570-326-0502
SJF Material Handling Equipment 211 Baker Ave .... Winsted MN 55395	800-598-5532	320-485-2824
Sterling Production Control Units 2280 W Dorothy Ln .... Dayton OH 45439	800-968-7728	937-299-5594
STI Electronics Inc 261 Palmer Rd .... Madison AL 35758	888-650-3006	256-461-9191
Super Products LLC 17000 W Cleveland Ave .... New Berlin WI 53151	800-837-9711	262-784-7100
Swiss Precision Instruments Inc 11450 Markon Dr .... Garden Grove CA 92841	888-774-8200	714-799-1555
Synventive Molding Solutions Inc 10 Centennial Dr .... Peabody MA 01960	800-367-5662	978-750-8065
Tennant Co 701 N Lilac Dr .... Minneapolis MN 55422 *NYSE: TNC ▪ *Cust Svc	800-553-8033*	763-540-1200
Thomas Engineering Inc 575 W Central Rd .... Hoffman Estates IL 60192	800-634-9910	847-358-5800
Thompson International Inc PO Box 656 .... Henderson KY 42420	800-626-7054	270-826-3751
Timesavers Inc 11123 89th Ave N .... Maple Grove MN 55369	800-537-3611	763-488-6600
Tool Smith Company Inc 1300 Fourth Ave S PO Box 2384 .... Birmingham AL 35233	800-317-8665	205-323-2576
Unified Brands 1055 Mendell Davis Dr .... Jackson MS 39272	888-994-7636	
USM Corp 32 Stevens St .... Haverhill MA 01830	800-361-2056	978-374-0303
Vacudyne Inc 375 E Joe Orr Rd .... Chicago Heights IL 60411	800-459-9591	708-757-5200
Van Air Systems Inc 2950 Mechanic St .... Lake City PA 16423	800-840-9906	814-774-2631
Vermeer Midsouth Inc 1200 Vermeer Cv .... Cordova TN 38018	800-264-4123	901-758-1928
Videojet Technologies Inc 1500 Mittel Blvd .... Wood Dale IL 60191 *Cust Svc	800-843-3610*	630-860-7300
W M Sprinkman Corp 4234 Courtney Rd PO Box 390 .... Franksville WI 53126	800-816-1610	262-835-2390

			Toll-Free	Phone

Western Hydro Corp
3449 Enterprise Ave . . . . Hayward CA 94545 **800-972-5945** 510-783-9166

WH Bagshaw Company Inc
One Pine St Ext PO Box 766 . . . . Nashua NH 03061 **800-343-7467** 603-883-7758

Windsor K,,rcher Group
1351 W Stanford Ave . . . . Englewood CO 80110 **800-444-7654** 303-762-1800

Yale Carolinas Inc (YCI)
9839 S Tryon St . . . . Charlotte NC 28273 **800-844-1454** 704-588-6930

386 INFORMATION RETRIEVAL SERVICES (GENERAL)

SEE ALSO Investigative Services

			Toll-Free	Phone

AdMobilize LLC
1680 Michigan Ave Ste 736 . . . . Miami FL 33139 **855-236-6245**

Advantix Solutions Group
1202 Richardson Dr Ste 200 . . . . Richardson TX 75080 **866-238-2684**

AirPair Inc
875 Howard St . . . . San Francisco CA 94103 **800-487-0668**

Amigos Library Services
14400 Midway Rd . . . . Dallas TX 75244 **800-843-8482** 972-851-8000

AnswerDash Inc
4000 Mason Rd New Ventures Facility Fluke Hall
. . . . Seattle WA 98195 **800-311-5786**

Apmetrix Inc
5414 Oberlin Dr Ste 200 . . . . San Diego CA 92121 **800-490-3184**

AppsHosting Inc
13772 Goldenwest St Ste 321 . . . . Westminster CA 92683 **877-625-6610**

Arkadin Inc
Five Concourse Pkwy Ste 1600 . . . . Atlanta GA 30328 **866-551-1432**

AroundWire.Com LLC
18107 Sherman Way Ste 206 . . . . Reseda CA 91335 **888-382-3793**

Beepi
5050 El Camino Real Ste 116 . . . . Los Altos CA 94022 **888-542-3374**

Best Telecom Inc
262 E End Ave . . . . Beaver PA 15009 **888-365-2273**

BloomNet Inc
One Old Country Rd Ste 500 . . . . Carle Place NY 11514 **866-256-6663**

Blue Box Group Inc
119 Pine St Ste 200 . . . . Seattle WA 98101 **800-613-4305**

Bocada Inc
5555 Lakeview Dr . . . . Kirkland WA 98033 **866-262-2321** 425-818-4400

BoeFly LLC
50 W 72nd St Ste C6 . . . . New York NY 10023 **800-277-3158**

Broadband Dynamics LLC
8757 E Via De Commercio . . . . Scottsdale AZ 85258 **888-801-1034**

BurrellesLuce
30 B Vreeland Rd PO Box 674 . . . . Florham Park NJ 07932 **800-631-1160** 973-992-6600

C Spire
1018 Highland Colony Pkwy Ste 300 . . . . Ridgeland MS 39157 **855-277-4735**

CallDirek
2200 S Dixie Hwy Ste 401 . . . . Miami FL 33133 **866-673-4735**

Camperoo Inc
2900 Weslayan St Ste 545 . . . . Houston TX 77027 **888-538-8809**

CatholicMatch LLC
211 E Grandview Ave . . . . Zelienople PA 16063 **888-605-3977**

CharityUSA.com LLC
600 University St
Ste 1000 One Union Square . . . . Seattle WA 98101 **888-811-5271** 206-268-5400

Chemical Abstracts Service (CAS)
2540 Olentangy River Rd . . . . Columbus OH 43202 **800-848-6538** 614-447-3600

CloudSway LLC
711 Pacific Ave . . . . Tacoma WA 98402 **855-212-5683**

CompleteCampaigns.com Inc
3635 Ruffin Rd Third Fl . . . . San Diego CA 92123 **888-217-9600**

ComTech21
One Barnes Park S . . . . Wallingford CT 06492 **877-312-5564**

ConvergeOne LLC
175B Rennell Dr . . . . Southport CT 06890 **888-321-6227**

CU Conferences
8711 Watson Rd Ste 200 . . . . St. Louis MO 63119 **888-465-6010**

Curatel LLC
1605 W Olympic Blvd Ste 800 . . . . Los Angeles CA 90015 **866-287-2366**

Custom Toll Free
914 164Th St SE #1670 . . . . Mill Creek WA 98012 **800-222-2222**

CypherWorX Inc
3349 Monroe Ave . . . . Rochester NY 14618 **888-685-4440**

Data Transmission Network Corp
9110 W Dodge Rd Ste 200 . . . . Omaha NE 68114 **800-485-4000** 402-390-2328

Dataium LLC
2525 Perimeter Pl Dr Ste 105 . . . . Nashville TN 37214 **877-896-3282**

Datamir Inc
99 Madison Ave Third Fl . . . . New York NY 10016 **888-764-4959**

Deal Interactive LLC
Three Park Ave 39th Fl . . . . New York NY 10016 **888-415-4888**

DebtFolio Inc
384 Merrow Rd Ste G . . . . Tolland CT 06084 **866-876-3654**

Declara Inc
977 Commercial St . . . . Palo Alto CA 94303 **877-216-0604**

Dialog
2250 Perimeter Pk Dr Ste 300 . . . . Morrisville NC 27560 **800-334-2564** 919-804-6400

DrivingSales LLC
8871 S Sandy Pkwy Ste 250 . . . . Sandy UT 84070 **866-943-8371**

Druva Software Inc
150 Mathilda Place, STE 450 . . . . Sunnyvale CA 94086 **888-248-4976**

DSG Tag Systems Inc
5455 152nd St Ste 214 . . . . Surrey BC V3S5A5 **877-589-8806**

EatStreet Inc
131 W Wilson St Ste 400 . . . . Madison WI 53715 **866-654-8777**

EBSCO Information Services
PO Box 1943 . . . . Birmingham AL 35201 **800-758-5995** 205-991-6600

Edufii Inc
2078 Parker St Ste 200 . . . . San Luis Obispo CA 93401 **800-439-8505**

Ekahau Inc
1851 Alexander Bell Dr Ste 300 . . . . Reston VA 20191 **866-435-2428**

ELM Resources
12950 Race Track Rd Ste 201 . . . . Tampa FL 33626 **866-524-8198**

Environmental Data Resources Inc
440 Wheelers Farms Rd . . . . Milford CT 06460 **800-352-0050** 203-783-0300

eScreen Inc
7500 W 110th St Ste 500 . . . . Overland Park KS 66210 **800-881-0722** 913-327-5915

Everlaw
2020 Milvia St Ste 220 . . . . Berkeley CA 94704 **844-383-7529**

EverTrue LLC
330 Congress St Second Fl . . . . Boston MA 02210 **855-387-8783**

Everwise Corp
1178 Broadway Fourth Fl . . . . New York NY 10001 **888-734-0011**

ezCater Inc
101 Arch St Ste 410 . . . . Boston MA 02110 **800-488-1803**

FamilySearch
35 N W Temple St . . . . Salt Lake City UT 84150 **866-406-1830**

FishHound LLC
15720 Ventura Blvd Ste 220 . . . . Encino CA 91436 **800-469-0224**

Fluidware
12 York St Second Fl . . . . Ottawa ON K1N5S6 **866-218-5127**

FOIA Group Inc (FGI)
1250 Connecticut Ave NW Ste 200 . . . . Washington DC 20036 **888-461-7951**

Forex Newscom
55 Water St 50th Fl . . . . New York NY 10041 **888-503-6739**

Franchise Information Services Inc
4300 Wilson Blvd Ste 480 . . . . Arlington VA 22203 **800-485-9570** 703-740-4700

FTJ FundChoice LLC
2300 Litton Ln Ste 102 . . . . Hebron KY 41048 **800-379-2513**

GigMasters.com Inc
33 S Main St . . . . Norwalk CT 06854 **866-342-9794**

Healthcare Management Systems Inc (HMS)
3102 W End Ave Ste 400 . . . . Nashville TN 37203 **800-383-3317** 615-383-7300

Helpjuice Inc
211 E Seventh St Ste 620 . . . . Austin TX 78701 **888-230-3420**

Homes.com Inc 150 Granby St . . . . Norfolk VA 23510 **866-675-1058**

Host Department LLC
45277 Fremont Blvd Ste 11 . . . . Fremont CA 94538 **866-887-4678**

I Am Athlete LLC
PO Box 667 . . . . Santa Monica CA 90406 **877-462-7979**

IBISWorld Inc
11755 Wilshire blvd 11th fl . . . . Los Angeles CA 90025 **800-330-3772**

InComm Conferencing Inc
208 Harristown Rd Ste 101 . . . . Glen Rock NJ 07452 **877-804-2062**

Infotrieve Inc
20 Westport Rd PO Box 7102 . . . . Wilton CT 06897 **800-422-4633*** 203-423-2130
*Cust Svc

infoUSA Inc 5711 S 86th Cir . . . . Omaha NE 68127 **800-321-0869** 800-835-5856

Infrastructure Networks Inc
1718 Fry Rd Ste 116 . . . . Houston TX 77084 **855-333-4638** 281-740-3226

Innovative Telecom Solutions Inc
Nine Vela Way . . . . Edgewater NJ 07020 **800-510-3000**

Intelletrace Inc
448 Ignacio Blvd . . . . Novato CA 94945 **800-618-5877**

Kaleo Software Inc
841 Apollo St Ste 330 . . . . El Segundo CA 90245 **888-937-8945**

LaughStub LLC
2038 Armacost Ave . . . . Los Angeles CA 90025 **800-927-0939**

LexisNexis Martindale-Hubbell
121 Chanlon Rd . . . . New Providence NJ 07974 **800-526-4902**

Lingo Inc
7901 Jones Branch Dr Ninth Fl. . . . . Mclean VA 22102 **888-546-4699**

LINQ Services
6679 Santa Barbara Rd Ste D . . . . Elkridge MD 21075 **800-421-5467**

LiveMocha Inc
1011 Western Ave, Ste 1000 . . . . Seattle WA 98104 **800-399-6212** 206-257-2500

Merrill DataSite
225 Varick St . . . . New York NY 10014 **866-399-3770**

MessageBank LLC
250 W 57Th St Ste 1001 . . . . New York NY 10107 **800-989-8001** 212-333-9300

MobileIQ Inc
4800 Baseline Rd Ste E104-247 . . . . Boulder CO 80303 **866-261-8600**

MOGL Loyalty Services Inc
9645 Scranton Rd Ste 110 . . . . San Diego CA 92121 **888-664-5669**

Motista Inc
1777 Borel Pl Ste 500 . . . . San Mateo CA 94402 **877-966-8478**

National Technical Information Service (NTIS)
5285 Port Royal Rd . . . . Springfield VA 22161 **800-553-6847*** 703-605-6000
*Orders

NewCloud Networks
160 Inverness Dr W . . . . Englewood CO 80112 **855-255-5001**

Newsbank Inc
5801 Pelican Bay Blvd Ste 600 . . . . Naples FL 34108 **800-243-7694** 239-263-6004

Next Net Media LLC
316 California Ave Ste 804 . . . . Reno NV 89509 **800-737-5820**

Nexxtworks Inc
30798 Us Hwy 19 N . . . . Palm Harbor FL 34684 **888-533-8353**

Niche Directories LLC
909 N Sepulveda Blvd 11th Fl . . . . El Segundo CA 90026 **877-242-9330**

Oklahoma Telephone & Telegraph Inc
26 N Otis Ave . . . . Dustin OK 74839 **800-869-1989**

OneClass
415 Yonge St Unit 1205 . . . . Toronto ON M5B2E7 **855-392-6946**

OneMorePallet.com
9891 Montgomery Rd Ste 122 . . . . Cincinnati OH 45242 **855-438-1667**

OurParents Inc
8521 Leesburg Pk Ste 310 . . . . Vienna VA 22182 **866-629-1634**

Ovid Technologies Inc
333 Seventh Ave 20th Fl. . . . . New York NY 10001 **800-950-2035** 646-674-6300

PackLate.com Inc
100 Four Falls Corporate Ctr
Ste 104 . . . . West Conshohocken PA 19428 **877-472-2552**

PK4 Media Inc
1600 E Franklin Ave Ste C . . . . El Segundo CA 90245 **888-320-6281**

PriceWaiter LLC
426 Market St . . . . Chattanooga TN 37421 **855-671-9889**

Pure Auto LLC
164 Market St Ste 250 . . . . Charleston SC 29401 **877-860-7873**

Purple Communications Inc
595 Menlo Dr . . . . Rocklin CA 95765 **800-900-9478**

				Toll-Free	Phone
Questia Media America Inc					
1 N State St Ste 900	Chicago	IL	60602	800-759-4726	800-889-0097
Rallyorg					
580 Howard St Ste 402	San Francisco	CA	94105	888-648-2220	
Reaslo Inc					
5214F Diamond Heights Blvd Ste 217	San Francisco	CA	94131	888-870-7889	
Rentals Inc					
3585 Engineering Dr	Norcross	GA	30092	888-501-7368	
Reputation Rhino LLC					
711 Third Ave 12th Fl	New York	NY	10017	888-975-3331	
SchoolDocs LLC					
5944 Luther Ln Ste 600	Dallas	TX	75225	866-311-2293	
Scoot & Doodle Inc					
2625 Middlefield Rd Ste 223	Palo Alto	CA	94306	888-563-9224	
Scott Enterprises Inc					
2225 Downs Dr Sixth Fl Exce Stes	Erie	PA	16509	877-866-3445	814-868-9500
Seize The Deal LLC					
1851 N Greenville Ave Ste 100	Richardson	TX	75081	866-210-0881	
Senior-Living.com LLC					
8521 Leesburg Pk Ste 310	Vienna	VA	22182	866-342-4297	
ShopVisible LLC					
945 East Paces Ferry Rd Ste 1475	Atlanta	GA	30326	866-493-7037	
Smarty Ants Inc					
1400 Rollins Rd	Burlingame	CA	94010	877-905-2687	
Social Annex Inc					
5301 Beethoven St Ste 260	Los Angeles	CA	90066	866-802-8806	
Sopheon Corp					
3001 Metro Dr Ste 460	Bloomington	MN	55425	800-367-8358	952-851-7500
SpinGo Solutions Inc					
14193 S Minuteman Dr Ste 100	Draper	UT	84020	877-377-4646	
SpotOn Inc					
2350 Kerner Blvd Ste 380	San Rafael	CA	94901	877-814-4102	
Stickk.com LLC					
39 E 30th St Ste 4	New York	NY	10016	866-578-4255	
TelSpan Inc					
101 W Washington St E Tower Ste 1200	Indianapolis	IN	46204	800-800-1729	
Thomson Financial					
22 Thomson Pl	Boston	MA	02210	888-216-1929	617-856-2000
TodoCast Inc					
31831 Camino Capistrano Ste 301	San Juan Capistrano	CA	92675	866-510-7889	
TouchLogic Corp					
30 Kinnear Ct Ste 602	Richmond Hill	ON	L4B1K8	877-707-0207	
Touchstorm LLC					
355 Lexington Ave 12th Fl	New York	NY	10017	877-794-6101	
Trada Inc 1023 Walnut St	Boulder	CO	80302	877-871-1835	
TruSignal LLC					
25 6th Ave N	St. Cloud	MN	56303	855-569-0426	
US News University Connection LLC					
9417 Princess Palm Ave	Tampa	FL	33619	866-442-6587	
USA Communications Inc					
920 E 56th St Ste B	Kearney	NE	68847	877-234-0102	
uShip Inc 205 Brazos St	Austin	TX	78701	800-698-7447	
Vanilla Forums Inc					
414 McGill St, Ste 800	Montreal	QC	H2Y1S1	866-845-0815	
Vectus Inc					
18685 Main St 101 PMB 360	Huntington Beach	CA	92648	866-483-2887	
Vessel Metrics LLC					
Three Church Cir Ste 325	Annapolis	MD	21401	888-214-1710	
VideoGenie Inc					
314 Lytton Ave Ste 100	Palo Alto	CA	94301	877-392-2235	
Vinely					
One Kendall Sq Bldg 400 B4202	Cambridge	MA	02139	888-294-1128	
Viva Group Inc					
11766 Wilshire Blvd Ste 300	Los Angeles	CA	90025	866-432-7368	
VoIP Innovations Inc					
Eight Penn Ctr W Ste 101	Pittsburgh	PA	15276	877-478-6471	
West Group 610 Opperman Dr	Eagan	MN	55123	800-328-4880*	651-687-7000
*Cust Svc					
WhoKnows Inc					
800 W El Camino Real Ste 180	Mountain View	CA	94040	877-338-2763	
Wholeshare Inc					
2431 Mission St	San Francisco	CA	94110	800-625-4605	
XTRAC LLC 245 Summer St	Boston	MA	02210	855-975-3569	
Yesware Inc					
75 Kneeland St Fl 15	Boston	MA	02111	855-937-9273	
YouVisit LLC					
20533 Biscayne Blvd Ste 1322	Aventura	FL	33180	866-585-7158	
Zenovia Digital Exchange Corp					
3141 Fairview Park Dr Ste 160	Falls Church	VA	22042	855-936-6842	703-813-6400
Zootoo LLC					
400 Plz Dr First Fl	Secaucus	NJ	07094	877-580-7387	

387 INK

				Toll-Free	Phone
Braden Sutphin Ink Co					
3650 E 93rd St	Cleveland	OH	44105	800-289-6872	216-271-2300
Central Ink Corp					
1100 Harvester Rd	West Chicago	IL	60185	800-345-2541	630-231-6500
Color Resolutions International					
575 Quality Blvd	Fairfield	OH	45014	800-346-8570	513-552-7200
Gans Ink & Supply Company Inc					
1441 Boyd St	Los Angeles	CA	90033	800-421-6167	323-264-2200
Independent Ink Inc					
13700 Gramercy Pl	Gardena	CA	90249	800-446-5538	310-523-4657
International Coatings Co					
13929 166th St	Cerritos	CA	90703	800-423-4103	562-926-1010
Matsui International Company Inc					
1501 W 178th St	Gardena	CA	90248	800-359-5679	310-767-7812
Nazdar 8501 Hedge Ln Terr	Shawnee	KS	66227	800-767-9942	913-422-1888
Nor-Cote International Inc					
506 Lafayette Ave	Crawfordsville	IN	47933	800-488-9180	765-362-9180

				Toll-Free	Phone
Reaxis Inc					
941 Robinson Hwy	Mcdonald	PA	15057	800-426-7273	
Sensient Technologies Corp					
777 E Wisconsin Ave 11th Fl	Milwaukee	WI	53202	800-558-9892	414-271-6755
NYSE: SXT					
Sericol Inc					
1101 W Cambridge Dr	Kansas City	KS	66103	800-737-4265	913-342-4060
Siegwerk USA Co					
3535 SW 56th St	Des Moines	IA	50321	800-728-8200	515-471-2100
Sun Chemical Corp					
35 Waterview Blvd	Parsippany	NJ	07054	800-543-2323	973-404-6000
Toyo Ink America LLC					
1225 N Michael Dr	Wood Dale	IL	60191	866-969-8696*	
*General					
US Ink Corp 651 Garden St	Carlstadt	NJ	07072	800-423-8838	201-935-8666

388 INSULATION & ACOUSTICAL PRODUCTS

				Toll-Free	Phone
Anco Products Inc (API)					
2500 S 17th St	Elkhart	IN	46517	800-837-2626	574-293-5574
Applegate Insulation Manufacturing Inc					
1000 Highview Dr	Webberville	MI	48892	800-627-7536	517-521-3545
CertainTeed Corp					
750 E Swedesford Rd	Valley Forge	PA	19482	800-782-8777*	610-341-7000
*Prod Info					
Claremont Sales Corp					
35 Winsome Dr PO Box 430	Durham	CT	06422	800-222-4448	860-349-4499
Dryvit Systems Inc					
1 Energy Way	West Warwick	RI	02893	800-556-7752	401-822-4100
Industrial Insulation Group LLC (IIG)					
2100 Line St	Brunswick	GA	31520	800-334-7997	
Isolatek International Inc					
41 Furnace St	Stanhope	NJ	07874	800-631-9600	973-347-1200
ITW Insulation Systems					
1370 E 40th St Ste 1 Bldg 7	Houston	TX	77022	800-231-1024	
Johns Manville Corp					
717 17th St PO Box 5108	Denver	CO	80217	800-654-3103*	303-978-2000
*Prod Info					
Knauf Insulation					
One Knauf Dr	Shelbyville	IN	46176	800-825-4434	317-398-4434
MIT International					
77 Massachusetts Ave	Cambridge	TX	02139	800-228-9290*	617-253-1000
*General					
Nu-Wool Company Inc					
2472 Port Sheldon Rd	Jenison	MI	49428	800-748-0128	616-669-0100
Rock Wool Manufacturing Co					
1400 Seventh Ct PO Box 506	Leeds	AL	35094	800-874-7625*	205-699-6121
*Sales					
S & S Industries Inc					
115 Clemmons Rd	Mount Juliet	TN	37122	800-762-4104	615-754-8000
Scott Industries Inc					
1573 Hwy 136 W PO Box 7	Henderson	KY	42419	800-951-9276	270-831-2037
Soundcoat Co One Burt Dr	Deer Park	NY	11729	800-394-8913	631-242-2200
Thermafiber Inc					
3711 W Mill St	Wabash	IN	46992	888-834-2371	260-563-2111
Thermwell Products Co					
420 Rt 17 S	Mahwah	NJ	07430	800-526-5265	201-684-4400

389 INSURANCE AGENTS, BROKERS, SERVICES

				Toll-Free	Phone
A Plus Benefits Inc					
395 West 600 North	Lindon	UT	84042	800-748-5102	801-443-1090
Actuarial Systems Corp					
15840 Monte St Ste 108	Sylmar	CA	91342	800-950-2082	
Affinion Group Inc					
6 High Ridge Pk	Stamford	CT	06905	800-251-2148	203-956-1000
Agency Software Inc					
215 W Commerce Dr	Hayden Lake	ID	83835	800-342-7327	208-762-7188
Alliance Worldwide Investigative Group Inc					
Four Executive Park Dr	Clifton Park	NY	12065	800-579-2911	518-514-2944
Amfed LLC					
576 Highland Colony Pkwy	Ridgeland	MS	39157	800-264-8085	601-853-4949
ANCO Insurance					
1111 Briarcrest Dr PO Box 3889	Bryan	TX	77802	800-749-1733	979-776-2626
Andreini & Co					
220 W 20th Ave	San Mateo	CA	94403	800-969-2522	650-573-1111
Aon Risk Services Inc					
200 E Randolph St	Chicago	IL	60601	877-384-4276	312-381-1000
Arthur J Gallagher & Co					
2 Pierce Pl	Itasca	IL	60143	888-285-5106	630-773-3800
NYSE: AJG					
Arthur J. Glatfelter Agency Inc					
PO Box 2726	York	PA	17405	800-233-1957	717-741-0911
Assurity Life Insurance Co					
1526 K St	Lincoln	NE	68508	800-869-0355	402-476-6500
Automobile Protection Corp					
6010 Atlantic Blvd	Norcross	GA	30071	800-230-2434*	
*Cust Svc					
Badger Mutual Insurance Co					
1635 W National Ave	Milwaukee	WI	53204	800-837-7833	414-383-1234
Benefit & Risk Management Services Inc					
10860 Gold Ctr Dr Ste 300	Rancho Cordova	CA	95670	888-326-2555	916-858-2950
Berkley Risk Administrators Company LLC					
222 S Ninth St Ste 1300	Minneapolis	MN	55402	800-449-7707	612-766-3000
Body-Borneman Insurance					
PO Box 584	Boyertown	PA	19512	800-326-5290	610-367-1100
Bollinger Insurance					
101 JFK Pkwy	Short Hills	NJ	07078	800-526-1379	973-467-0444
Callbright Corp					
6700 Hollister	Houston	TX	77040	877-462-2552	
CalSurance					
681 S Parker St Ste 300	Orange	CA	92868	800-762-7800	714-939-0800

Company / Address	City	State	Zip	Toll-Free	Phone
Capital Analysts Inc 218 Glenside Ave	Wyncote	PA	19095	**800-242-1421**	
Casswood Insurance Agency Ltd Five Executive Pk Dr	Clifton Park	NY	12065	**800-972-2242**	518-373-8700
CBIZ Benefits & Insurance Services of Maryland Inc 44 Baltimore St *Cust Svc	Cumberland	MD	21502	**800-615-8418***	301-777-1500
Cross Financial Corp 74 Gilman Rd PO Box 1388	Bangor	ME	04401	**800-999-7345**	207-947-7345
Cumbre Inc 3333 Concours Ste 5100	Ontario	CA	91764	**800-998-7986**	909-484-2456
DailyAccess Corp 307 University Blvd N Bldg 3 Ste 1500	Mobile	AL	36688	**877-859-5735**	251-665-1800
Daniel & Henry Co 1001 Highlands Plaza Dr W Ste 500	Saint Louis	MO	63110	**800-256-3462**	314-421-1525
Distinguished Programs Group LLC, The 1180 Ave Of The Americas 16th Fl	New York	NY	10036	**888-355-4626**	212-297-3100
Dyatech LLC 805 S Wheatley St Ste 600	Ridgeland	MS	39157	**866-651-4222**	601-914-1004
Eagan Insurance Agency Inc 2629 N Cswy Blvd	Metairie	LA	70002	**888-882-9600**	504-836-9600
Elant Inc 46 Harriman Dr	Goshen	NY	10924	**800-501-3936**	
Employers Insurance Company of Nevada 9790 Gateway Dr Ste 100	Reno	NV	89521	**888-682-6671**	
Endurance Specialty Holdings Ltd 767 Third Ave 5th Fl *NYSE: ENH*	New York	NY	10017	**855-838-7792**	212-209-6500
FairMarket Life Settlements Corp 435 Ford Rd Ste 120	St Louis Park	MN	55426	**866-326-3757**	
Farmers Fire Insurance Co 2875 Eastern Blvd	York	PA	17402	**800-537-0928**	717-751-4435
Farris Evans Insurance Agency Inc 1568 Union Ave	Memphis	TN	38104	**800-395-8207**	901-274-5424
Fortun Insurance Agency Inc 365 Palermo Ave	Coral Gables	FL	33134	**877-643-2055**	305-445-3535
Fred Loya Insurance 1800 Lee Trevino Ste 201	El Paso	TX	79936	**800-554-0595**	915-590-5692
Fringe Benefits Management Co 3101 Sessions Rd	Tallahassee	FL	32303	**800-872-0345**	850-425-6200
Frontier Adjusters of America Inc 4745 N Seventh St Ste 320	Phoenix	AZ	85014	**800-426-7228**	
GCube Insurance Services Inc 3101 Wcoast Hwy Ste 100	Newport Beach	CA	92663	**877-903-4777**	949-515-9981
Gebco Insurance Assoc 8600 LaSalle Rd Ste 338	Towson	MD	21286	**800-464-3226**	410-668-3100
Graham Co, The One Penn Sq W 25th Fl	Philadelphia	PA	19102	**888-472-4262**	215-567-6300
Haas & Wilkerson Inc 4300 Shawnee Mission Pkwy	Fairway	KS	66205	**800-821-7703**	913-432-4400
HealthSCOPE Benefits Inc 27 Corporate Hill Dr	Little Rock	AR	72205	**877-240-0135**	501-225-1551
Healy Group Inc, The 53800 Generations Dr	South Bend	IN	46635	**800-667-4613**	574-271-6000
Herbert H. Landy Insurance Agency Inc 75 Second Ave Ste 410	Needham	MA	02494	**800-336-5422**	
Hibbs Hallmark & Co 501 Shelley Dr	Tyler	TX	75701	**800-765-6767**	
Holmes Murphy & Assoc Inc 3001 Westown Pkwy	West Des Moines	IA	50266	**800-247-7756**	515-223-6800
Horton Group, The 10320 Orland Pkwy	Orland Park	IL	60467	**800-383-8283**	708-845-3000
Housing Authority Risk Retention Group Inc PO Box 189	Cheshire	CT	06410	**800-873-0242**	203-272-8220
Hub International Ltd 1065 Ave of the Americas	New York	NY	10018	**800-456-5293**	212-338-2000
Human Arc Corp 1457 East 40th St	Cleveland	OH	44103	**800-828-6453**	216-431-5200
Hunt Insurance Agency Inc 12000 S Harlem Ave	Palos Heights	IL	60463	**800-772-6484**	708-361-5300
Hylant Group 811 Madison Ave	Toledo	OH	43624	**800-249-5268**	419-255-1020
Insurance Services Office Inc (ISO) 545 Washington Blvd	Jersey City	NJ	07310	**800-888-4476**	201-469-2000
InterWest Insurance Services Inc 3636 American River Dr 2nd Fl	Sacramento	CA	95864	**800-444-4134**	916-679-2960
J Smith Lanier & Co 300 W Tenth St	West Point	GA	31833	**800-226-4522**	706-645-2211
Jas. D. Collier & Co 606 S Mendenhall Rd Ste 200 *General	Memphis	TN	38117	**800-511-1548***	
Johns Eastern Co Inc PO Box 110259 Lakewood Branch *General	Sarasota	FL	34211	**800-452-4682***	941-907-3100
Keenan & Assoc 2355 Crenshaw Blvd Ste 200 PO Box 4328	Torrance	CA	90501	**800-654-8102**	310-212-3344
Kraus-Anderson Insurance 420 Gateway Blvd	Burnsville	MN	55337	**800-207-9261**	952-707-8200
Lawley Service Insurance 361 Delaware Ave *Cust Svc	Buffalo	NY	14202	**800-860-5741***	716-849-8618
Le Mars Insurance Co PO Box 1608	Le Mars	IA	51031	**800-545-6480**	
leavitt group Enterprises 216 S 200 W PO Box 130	Cedar City	UT	84720	**800-264-8085**	435-586-6553
Lewer Agency Inc 4534 Wornall Rd	Kansas City	MO	64111	**800-821-7715**	
Lincoln General Insurance Co 3501 Concord Rd	York	PA	17402	**800-876-3350**	717-757-0000
Loomis Co 850 N Pk Rd	Wyomissing	PA	19610	**800-782-0392**	610-374-4040
Lovitt & Touche Inc 7202 E Rosewood St Ste 200 PO Box 32702	Tucson	AZ	85710	**800-426-2756**	520-722-3000
Managed Care of America Inc 1910 Cochran Rd Ste 605	Pittsburgh	PA	15220	**800-922-4966**	412-922-2803
Managed HealthCare Northwest Inc 422 East Burnside St Suite 215 P.O. Box 4629	Portland	OR	97208	**800-648-6356**	503-413-5800
Marshall & Sterling Inc 110 Main St	Poughkeepsie	NY	12601	**800-333-3766**	845-454-0800
McGriff Seibels & Williams Inc 2211 Seventh Ave S PO Box 10265	Birmingham	AL	35233	**800-476-2211**	205-252-9871
Michigan Insurance Co 1700 E Beltline Ne P.O. Box 152120, Suite 100	Grand Rapids	MI	49515	**888-606-6426**	616-447-3600
Miller-Lewis Benefit Consultants 121 E Sixth Ave	Lancaster	OH	43130	**800-734-3198**	740-654-4055
Minnesota Lawyers Mutual Insurance Co 333 S Seventh St Ste 2200	Minneapolis	MN	55402	**800-422-1370**	
MSI Benefits Group Inc 245 Townpark Dr Ste 100	Kennesaw	GA	30144	**800-580-1629**	770-425-1231
Multiplan inc 115 Fifth Ave	New York	NY	10003	**800-922-4362**	212-780-2000
National Farm Life Insurance Co 6001 Bridge St	Fort Worth	TX	76112	**800-772-7557**	817-451-9550
NCCI Holdings Inc 901 Peninsula Corporate Cir *Cust Svc	Boca Raton	FL	33487	**800-622-4123***	561-893-1000
NIA Group Inc / Ste 400	Saddle Brook	NJ	07663	**800-669-6330**	201-845-6600
Northwest Administrators Inc 2323 Eastlake Ave E	Seattle	WA	98102	**877-304-6702**	206-329-4900
Oswald Cos 1100 Superior Ave Ste 1500	Cleveland	OH	44114	**800-975-9468**	216-367-8787
Otis-Magie Insurance Agency Inc 332 W Superior St Ste 700	Duluth	MN	55802	**800-241-2425**	218-722-7753
Pacesetter Claims Service Inc 2871 N Hwy 167	Catoosa	Ok	74015	**888-218-4880**	918-665-8887
Parker Smith & Feek Inc 2233 112th Ave NE *Cust Svc	Bellevue	WA	98004	**800-457-0220***	425-709-3600
Parkville Insurances Services Inc 15242 E Whittier Blvd PO Box 1275	Whittier	CA	90603	**800-350-2702**	562-945-2702
Platinum Select LP 5001 Statesman Dr	Irving	TX	75201	**866-953-0011**	
POMCO 2425 James St	Syracuse	NY	13206	**800-934-2459**	315-432-9171
Protegrity Services Inc 260 Wekiva Springs Rd Ste 1040	Longwood	FL	32779	**800-883-4000**	407-551-3962
Rampart Brokerage Corp 1983 Marcus Ave Ste C130	New Hyde Park	NY	11042	**800-772-6727**	516-538-7000
RC Knox & Co One Goodwin Sq 24th Fl	Hartford	CT	06103	**800-742-2765**	860-524-7600
Reid Jones McRorie & Williams Inc PO Box 18527	Charlotte	NC	28218	**800-785-2604**	704-537-0012
Renaissance Group 981 Worcester St	Wellesley	MA	02482	**800-514-2667**	
Scott Danahy Naylon Company Inc (SDN) 300 Spindrift Dr	Williamsville	NY	14221	**800-728-6362**	716-633-3400
Selectquote Insurance Services 595 Market St 10th Fl	San Francisco	CA	94105	**800-670-3213**	415-543-7338
Senior Market Sales Inc (SMS) 8420 W Dodge Rd Fifth Fl	Omaha	NE	68114	**800-786-5566**	402-397-3311
SilverStone Group 11516 Miracle Hills Dr Ste 100	Omaha	NE	68154	**800-288-5501**	402-964-5400
Stallings Crop Insurance Corp PO Box 6100	Lakeland	FL	33807	**800-721-7099**	863-647-2747
Star Casualty Insurance Company Inc PO Box 451037	Miami	FL	33134	**877-782-7210**	
Starkweather & Shepley Inc 60 Catamore Blvd	East Providence	RI	02914	**800-854-4625**	401-435-3600
Sullivan Curtis Monroe 1920 Main St	Irvine	CA	92614	**800-427-3253**	949-250-7172
Tabb Brockenbrough & Ragland LLC 4905 Dickens Rd	Richmond	VA	23230	**800-296-0531**	804-355-7984
Teachers Protective Mutual Life Insurance Co 116-118 N Prince St	Lancaster	PA	17603	**800-555-3122**	717-394-7156
U S Risk Insurance Group Inc 10210 N Central Expy	Dallas	TX	75231	**800-926-9155**	214-265-7090
Van Dyk Group Inc, The 12800 Long Beach Blvd	Beach Haven	NJ	08008	**800-222-0131**	609-492-1511
Van Gilder Insurance Corp 1515 Wine Coop *General	Denver	CO	80202	**800-872-8500***	303-837-8500
Van Zandt Emrich & Cary Inc 12401 Plantside Dr	Louisville	KY	40299	**800-928-7355**	502-456-2001
VIVA Health Inc 1222 14th Ave S	Birmingham	AL	35205	**800-633-1542**	205-939-1718
Wallace Welch Willingham 300 First Ave S Fifth Fl	Saint Petersburg	FL	33701	**800-783-5085**	727-522-7777
Wharton Group 101 S Livingston Ave	Livingston	NJ	07039	**800-521-2725**	973-992-5775
William Penn Assn 709 Brighton Rd	Pittsburgh	PA	15233	**800-848-7366**	412-231-2979
Willis Group Holdings Ltd 200 Liberty St 1 World Financial Ctr *NYSE: WSH*	New York	NY	10281	**800-234-8596**	212-915-8888
Wolverine Mutual Insurance Co One Wolverine Way	Dowagiac	MI	49047	**800-733-3320**	269-782-3451

390 INSURANCE COMPANIES

SEE ALSO Viatical Settlement Companies ; Home Warranty Services

390-1 Animal Insurance

Company / Address	City	State	Zip	Toll-Free	Phone
Ark Agency 310 Washburne Ave	Paynesville	MN	56362	**800-328-8894**	320-243-7250
Canadian Livestock Insurance 480 University Ave Ste 412	Toronto	ON	M5G1V2	**800-727-1502**	416-510-8191
Equisport Agency Inc 2306 Eastways Rd PO Box 269	Bloomfield Hills	MI	48304	**800-432-1215**	248-644-1215
Henry Equestrian Insurance Brokers 28 Victoria St	Aurora	ON	L4G1P9	**800-565-4321**	905-727-1144

		Toll-Free	Phone

Pet's Health Plan
3840 Greentree Ave SW . . . . .Canton OH 44706 **800-807-6724** 330-484-8080
Veterinary Pet Insurance Inc
PO Box 2344 . . . . .Brea CA 92822 **800-872-7387**

390-2 Life & Accident Insurance

		Toll-Free	Phone

Acacia Life Insurance Co
7315 Wisconsin Ave . . . . .Bethesda MD 20814 **800-444-1889** 301-280-1000
Acacia National Life
7315 Wisconsin Ave . . . . .Bethesda MD 20814 **800-444-1889** 800-368-2745
Advance Insurance Company of Kansas
1133 SW Topeka Blvd . . . . .Topeka KS 66629 **800-530-5989** 785-273-9804
Aetna Inc
151 Farmington Ave . . . . .Hartford CT 06156 **800-872-3862** 860-273-0123
NYSE: AET
Allianz Life Insurance Company of North America
PO Box 1344 .Minneapolis MN 55416 **800-950-5872**
Allstate Life Insurance Co
3100 Sanders Rd Allstate W Plz . . . . .Northbrook IL 60062 **800-366-1411*** 847-402-5000
*Cust Svc
American Amicable Life Insurance Co
PO Box 2549 . . . . .Waco TX 76702 **800-736-7311** 254-297-2777
American Equity Investment Life Insurance Co
6000 Westown Pkwy . . . . .West Des Moines IA 50266 **888-221-1234** 515-221-0002
American Family Life Assurance Company of Columbus (AFLAC)
1932 Wynnton Rd . . . . .Columbus GA 31999 **800-992-3522*** 706-323-3431
*Cust Svc
American Family Life Insurance Co
6000 American Pkwy . . . . .Madison WI 53783 **800-692-6326** 608-249-2111
American Family Mutual Insurance Co
6000 American Pkwy . . . . .Madison WI 53783 **800-374-0008*** 608-249-2111
*Cust Svc
American Income Life Insurance Co (AIL)
1200 Wooded Acres . . . . .Waco TX 76710 **800-433-3405** 254-761-6400
American Republic Insurance Co
601 Sixth Ave . . . . .Des Moines IA 50309 **800-247-2190***
*Cust Svc
American Standard Insurance Company of Wisconsin
6000 American Pkwy . . . . .Madison WI 53783 **800-692-6326** 608-249-2111
American United Life Insurance Co
One American Sq 510A PO Box 6010 . . . . .Indianapolis IN 46282 **800-537-6442** 317-285-1877
Americo Financial Life & Annuity Insurance Co
PO Box 410288 . . . . .Kansas City MO 64141 **800-231-0801**
Ameritas Direct 5900 'O' St . . . . .Lincoln NE 68510 **800-555-4655**
Ameritas Life Insurance Corp
5900 'O' St . . . . .Lincoln NE 68510 **800-745-1112** 402-467-1122
Ameritas Variable Life Insurance Co
5900 'O' St . . . . .Lincoln NE 68510 **800-634-8353** 402-467-1122
Anthem Life Insurance Co
6740 N High St Ste 200 . . . . .Worthington OH 43085 **800-551-7265** 614-436-0688
Arch Insurance Group Inc
One Liberty Plz 53rd Fl . . . . .New York NY 10006 **866-993-9978** 212-651-6500
Assurant Employee Benefits
2323 Grand Blvd . . . . .Kansas City MO 64108 **800-733-7879** 816-474-2345
Aurora National Life Assurance Co
PO Box 4490 . . . . .Hartford CT 06147 **800-265-2652**
Auto-Owners Life Insurance Co
6101 Anacapri Blvd . . . . .Lansing MI 48917 **800-288-8740** 517-323-1200
Baltimore Life Cos
10075 Red Run Blvd . . . . .Owings Mills MD 21117 **800-628-5433** 410-581-6600
Bankers Fidelity Life Insurance Co
4370 Peachtree Rd . . . . .Atlanta GA 30319 **800-241-1439** 404-266-5500
NASDAQ: AAME
Bankers Life & Casualty Co
111 E Wacker Dr Ste 2100 . . . . .Chicago IL 60601 **800-231-9150** 312-396-6000
Banner Life Insurance Co
1701 Research Blvd . . . . .Rockville MD 20850 **800-638-8428** 301-279-4800
Beneficial Financial Group
55 N 300 W . . . . .Salt Lake City UT 84145 **800-233-7979** 801-933-1100
Boston Mutual Life Insurance Co
120 Royall St . . . . .Canton MA 02021 **800-669-2668** 781-463-6068
Central States Health & Life Company of Omaha
1212 N 96th St . . . . .Omaha NE 68114 **800-826-6587** 402-397-1111
CIGNA 900 Cottage Grove Rd . . . . .Hartford CT 06002 **800-997-1654** 860-226-6000
Citizens Insurance Company of America
400 E Anderson Ln . . . . .Austin TX 78752 **800-880-5044** 512-837-7100
Citizens Security Life Insurance Co
12910 Shelbyville Rd Ste 300 . . . . .Louisville KY 40243 **800-843-7752** 502-244-2420
Colonial Life & Accident Insurance Co
1200 Colonial Life Blvd . . . . .Columbia SC 29210 **800-325-4368** 803-213-7250
Colonial Penn Life Insurance Co
399 Market St . . . . .Philadelphia PA 19181 **800-523-9100** 215-928-8000
Columbus Life Insurance Co
400 E Fourth St PO Box 5737 . . . . .Cincinnati OH 45201 **800-677-9595** 800-677-9696
Companion Life Insurance Co
7909 Parklane Rd Ste 200 . . . . .Columbia SC 29223 **800-753-0404** 803-735-1251
Concord Group Insurance Cos
Four Bouton St .Concord NH 03301 **800-852-3380**
Conseco Annuity Assurance Co
11825 N Pennsylvania St . . . . .Carmel IN 46032 **866-595-2255**
Conseco Health Insurance Co
11825 N Pennsylvania St . . . . .Carmel IN 46032 **866-595-2255**
Conseco Senior Health Insurance Co
11825 N Pennsylvania St PO Box 1980 . . . . .Carmel IN 46032 **866-595-2255**
Continental Assurance Co
333 S Wabash Ave . . . . .Chicago IL 60604 **800-251-2148** 312-822-5000
COUNTRY Insurance & Financial Services
1705 Towanda Ave . . . . .Bloomington IL 61701 **888-211-2555** 866-268-6879
ELCO Mutual Life & Annuity
916 Sherwood Dr . . . . .Lake Bluff IL 60044 **888-872-7954** 847-295-6000
Epic Life Insurance Co
1765 W Broadway . . . . .Madison WI 53713 **800-236-8809*** 608-223-2100
*Sales

Equitable Life & Casualty Insurance Co
Three Triad Ctr . . . . .Salt Lake City UT 84180 **877-358-4060***
*Cust Svc
Erie Family Life Insurance Co
100 Erie Insurance Pl .Erie PA 16530 **800-458-0811** 814-870-2000
Farm Bureau Life Insurance Co
5400 University Ave . . . . .West Des Moines IA 50266 **800-247-4170** 515-225-5400
Farm Family Life Insurance Co
PO Box 656 . . . . .Albany NY 12201 **800-948-3276** 518-431-5000
Federal Life Insurance Co Mutual
3750 W Deerfield Rd Ste A . . . . .Riverwoods IL 60015 **800-233-3750** 847-520-1900
Federated Life Insurance Co
121 E Pk Sq PO Box 328 . . . . .Owatonna MN 55060 **800-533-0472** 507-455-5200
Federated Mutual Insurance Co
121 E Pk Sq PO Box 328 . . . . .Owatonna MN 55060 **800-533-0472** 507-455-5200
First Investors Life Insurance Co
Raritan Plz 1 PO Box 7836 . . . . .Edison NJ 08818 **800-423-4026**
First UNUM Life Insurance Co
2211 Congress St . . . . .Portland ME 04122 **800-633-7491** 207-575-2211
FirstCare
1901 W Loop 289 Ste #9 . . . . .Lubbock TX 79407 **800-884-4901** 806-784-4300
Forethought Financial Services Inc
Forethought Ctr . . . . .Batesville IN 47006 **877-454-4777** 713-212-4600
Gerber Life Insurance Co
1311 Mamaroneck Ave . . . . .White Plains NY 10605 **800-704-2180** 914-272-4000
Grange Insurance
671 S High St .Columbus OH 43206 **800-422-0550**
Great-West Life & Annuity Insurance Co
8515 E OrchaRd Rd . . . . .Greenwood Village CO 80111 **800-537-2033** 303-737-3000
Great-West Life Assurance Co
100 Osborne St . . . . .Winnipeg MB R3C3A5 **800-990-6654** 204-946-1190
Greek Catholic Union of the USA
5400 Tuscarawas Rd . . . . .Beaver PA 15009 **800-722-4428** 724-495-3400
Guarantee Trust Life Insurance Co
1275 Milwaukee Ave . . . . .Glenview IL 60025 **800-338-7452** 847-699-0600
Guardian Life Insurance Company of America
Seven Hanover Sq . . . . .New York NY 10004 **888-600-4667** 212-598-8000
GuideOne Mutual Insurance Co
1111 Ashworth Rd . . . . .West Des Moines IA 50265 **877-448-4331** 515-267-5000
Harleysville Life Insurance Co
355 Maple Ave . . . . .Harleysville PA 19438 **800-222-1981***
*General
Harleysville Mutual Insurance Co
355 Maple Ave . . . . .Harleysville PA 19438 **800-523-6344** 215-256-5000
Hartford Life & Accident Insurance Co
One Hartford Plz .Hartford CT 06155 **800-833-5575** 860-547-5000
Harvey Watt & Co
475 N Central Ave . . . . .Atlanta GA 30354 **800-241-6103** 404-767-7501
HCC Life Insurance Co
225 Townpark Dr Ste 145 . . . . .Kennesaw GA 30144 **800-447-0460** 770-973-9851
Horace Mann Life Insurance Co
1 Horace Mann Plaza . . . . .Springfield IL 62715 **800-999-1030** 217-789-2500
Hudson Health Plan Inc
303 S Broadway Ste 321 . . . . .Tarrytown NY 10591 **800-339-4557** 914-631-1611
Humana Inc 500 W Main St . . . . .Louisville KY 40202 **800-486-2620** 502-580-1000
NYSE: HUM
Illinois Mutual Life Insurance Co
300 SW Adams St .Peoria IL 61634 **800-380-6688** 309-674-8255
Indiana Farm Bureau Insurance Co
225 SE St PO Box 1250 . . . . .Indianapolis IN 46206 **800-723-3276** 317-692-7200
Industrial Alliance Insurance & Financial Services
1080 Grande Allee W
PO Box 1907 Stn Therminus . . . . .Quebec City QC G1K7M3 **800-463-6236** 418-684-5000
Insurance Marketing Agencies Inc
306 Main St . . . . .Worcester MA 01608 **800-891-1226** 508-753-7233
Investors Heritage Life Insurance Co (IHLIC)
200 Capital Ave PO Box 717 . . . . .Frankfort KY 40602 **800-422-2011** 502-223-2361
Jackson National Life Insurance Co
One Corporate Way . . . . .Lansing MI 48951 **800-644-4565** 517-381-5500
John Hancock New York
100 Summit Lake Dr 2nd Fl . . . . .Valhalla NY 10595 **800-732-5543** 877-391-3748
Lafayette Life Insurance Co
400 Broadway .Cincinnati OH 45202 **800-443-8793**
Liberty Life Insurance Co
2000 Wade Hampton Blvd . . . . .Greenville SC 29615 **855-428-4363** 864-609-1000
Life Insurance Co of Alabama
302 Broad St . . . . .Gadsden AL 35901 **800-226-2371** 256-543-2022
Life Insurance Company of the Southwest
15455 Dallas Pkwy Ste 800 . . . . .Addison TX 75001 **800-579-2878**
Lincoln Heritage Life Insurance Co
PO Box 29045 . . . . .Phoenix AZ 85038 **800-433-8181**
Lincoln National Life Insurance Co
1300 S Clinton St . . . . .Fort Wayne IN 46802 **800-454-6265** 260-455-2000
London Life Insurance Co
255 Dufferin Ave .London ON N6A4K1 **800-990-6654** 519-432-5281
Loyal American Life Insurance Co
Great American Financial Resources Inc
PO Box 26580 . . . . .Austin TX 78755 **800-315-5522** 800-545-4269
Madison National Life Insurance Company Inc
PO Box 5008 . . . . .Madison WI 53705 **800-356-9601** 608-830-2000
Manulife Mutual Funds
200 Bloor St E N Twr 3 . . . . .Toronto ON M4W1E5 **888-588-7999**
May-mcconville Insurance Brokers Ltd
123 St George St Ste 100 . . . . .London ON N6A3A1 **877-629-6226** 519-673-0880
Medico Group 1515 S 75th St . . . . .Omaha NE 68124 **800-228-6080** 402-391-6900
MetLife Inc 200 Pk Ave . . . . .New York NY 10166 **800-638-5433** 212-578-2211
NYSE: MET
MetLife Investors Insurance Co
Five Pk Plz Ste 1900 . . . . .Irvine CA 92614 **800-848-3854**
Midland National Life Insurance Co
One Sammons Plz . . . . .Sioux Falls SD 57193 **800-923-3223** 605-335-5700
Modern Woodmen of America
1701 First Ave . . . . .Rock Island IL 61201 **800-447-9811** 309-786-6481
Mutual Insurance Company of Arizona
PO Box 33180 . . . . .Phoenix AZ 85067 **800-352-0402** 602-956-5276
Mutual of America Life Insurance Co
320 Pk Ave . . . . .New York NY 10022 **800-468-3785** 212-224-1600

	Toll-Free	Phone
Mutual of Omaha Insurance Co Mutual of Omaha Plaza ... Omaha NE 68175	**800-775-6000**	402-342-7600
Mutual Trust Life Insurance Co 1200 Jorie Blvd ... Oak Brook IL 60522	**800-323-7320**	630-990-1000
National Guardian Life Insurance Co (NGL) 2 E Gilman St ... Madison WI 53703	**800-548-2962**	608-257-5611
National Mutual Benefit 6522 Grand Teton Plaza ... Madison WI 53719	**800-779-1936**	608-833-1936
National Western Life Insurance Co 850 E Anderson Ln ... Austin TX 78752 NASDAQ: NWLI	**800-531-5442**	512-836-1010
Nationwide Life & Annuity Insurance Co One Nationwide Pl ... Columbus OH 43215	**800-882-2822**	614-249-7111
Nationwide Mutual Insurance Company 5100 Rings Rd ... Dublin OH 43017	**800-543-3747**	877-669-6877
New York Life Insurance & Annuity Corp 51 Madison Ave ... New York NY 10010	**800-598-2019**	212-576-7000
North Carolina Mutual Life Insurance Co 411 W Chapel Hill St ... Durham NC 27701	**800-626-1899**	919-682-9201
Ohio State Life Insurance Co PO Box 410288 ... Kansas City MO 64141	**800-752-1387**	
Old American Insurance Co 3520 Broadway ... Kansas City MO 64111	**800-733-6242**	816-753-7000
OneAmerica Financial Partners Inc (PML) PO Box 368 ... Indianapolis IN 46206	**800-249-6269**	317-285-1877
Oxford Life Insurance Co 2721 N Central Ave ... Phoenix AZ 85004 *Cust Svc	**800-308-2318***	602-263-6666
Pacific Guardian Life Insurance Company Ltd 1440 Kapiolani Blvd Ste 1700 ... Honolulu HI 96814	**800-367-5354**	808-955-2236
Pacific Life Insurance Co 700 Newport Ctr Dr ... Newport Beach CA 92660	**800-800-7646**	949-219-3011
Pan-American Life Insurance Co 601 Poydras St ... New Orleans LA 70130 *Life Ins	**877-939-4550***	
Partner Reinsurance Co of the US 1 Greenwich Plaza ... Greenwich CT 06830	**800-831-9146**	203-485-4200
Pekin Life Insurance Co 2505 Ct St ... Pekin IL 61558 OTC: PKIN	**800-322-0160**	309-346-1161
Penn Insurance & Annuity Co 600 Dresher Rd ... Horsham PA 19044 *Cust Svc	**800-523-0650***	215-956-8000
Penn Mutual Life Insurance Co 600 Dresher Rd ... Horsham PA 19044 *Cust Svc	**800-523-0650***	215-956-8000
Penn Treaty Network America Insurance Co 3440 Lehigh St ... Allentown PA 18103	**800-362-0700**	
Physicians Life Insurance Co 2600 Dodge St ... Omaha NE 68131	**800-228-9100**	402-633-1000
Physicians Mutual Insurance Co 2600 Dodge St ... Omaha NE 68131	**800-228-9100**	402-633-1000
Presidential Life Insurance Co 69 Lydecker St ... Nyack NY 10960	**800-926-7599**	845-358-2300
Pro Assurance Corp 1250 23rd St NW Ste 250 ... Washington DC 20037	**800-613-3615**	202-969-1866
Property-Owners Insurance Co PO Box 30660 ... Lansing MI 48909	**800-288-8740**	517-323-1200
Protective Life & Annuity Insurance Co 2801 Hwy 280 S ... Birmingham AL 35223	**844-733-5433**	205-268-1000
Prudential Financial Inc 751 Broad St ... Newark NJ 07102 NYSE: PRU	**800-843-7625**	973-802-6000
RBC Liberty Insurance PO Box 789 ... Greenville SC 29602	**800-551-8354**	864-609-8111
Reliable Life Insurance Co 100 King St W PO Box 557 ... Hamilton ON L8N3K9	**800-465-0661**	905-523-5587
Reliance Standard Life Insurance 2001 Market St Ste 1500 ... Philadelphia PA 19103	**800-351-7500**	267-256-3500
Security Benefit Life Insurance Co One Security Benefit Pl ... Topeka KS 66636	**800-888-2461**	785-438-3000
Security Life Insurance Co of America 10901 Red Cir Dr ... Minnetonka MN 55343	**800-328-4667**	952-544-2121
Security Mutual Life Insurance Co of New York 100 Court St PO Box 1625 ... Binghamton NY 13901	**800-927-8846**	607-723-3551
Security National Financial Corp (SNFC) 5300 South 360 West Ste 250 PO Box 57250 ... Salt Lake City UT 84123 NASDAQ: SNFCA	**800-574-7117**	801-264-1060
Sentry Life Insurance Co 1800 N Pt Dr ... Stevens Point WI 54481	**800-373-6879**	715-346-6000
Settlers Life Insurance Co 1969 Lee Hwy Ste U1 ... Bristol VA 24203	**800-523-2650**	276-645-4300
Shenandoah Life Insurance Co 2301 Brambleton Ave ... Roanoke VA 24015	**800-848-5433**	540-985-4400
Standard Life Insurance Company of Indiana 10689 N Pennsylvania St ... Indianapolis IN 46280	**800-222-3216**	317-574-6201
State Farm Insurance One State Farm Plz ... Bloomington IL 61710	**800-447-4930**	309-766-2311
State Life Insurance Co One American Sq PO Box 368 ... Indianapolis IN 46206 *Cust Svc	**800-537-6442***	317-285-2300
Sun Life Assurance Company of Canada One Sun Life Executive Pk PO Box 9133 ... Wellesley Hills MA 02481	**800-786-5433**	781-237-6030
Thrivent Financial for Lutherans 4321 N Ballard Rd ... Appleton WI 54919	**800-847-4836**	920-684-3225
TIAA-CREF 730 Third Ave ... New York NY 10017	**866-842-2442**	212-490-9000
Transamerica Corporation 4333 Edgewood Rd NE ... Cedar Rapids IA 52499	**800-797-2643***	319-355-3985
Transamerica Occidental Life Insurance Co 1150 S Olive St ... Los Angeles CA 90015 *Cust Svc	**800-852-4678***	213-742-2111
Trustmark Insurance Co 400 Field Dr ... Lake Forest IL 60045	**888-246-9949**	847-615-1500
United Heritage Life Insurance Co PO Box 7777 ... Meridian ID 83680	**800-657-6351**	208-493-6100

	Toll-Free	Phone
United Insurance Holdings Corp 360 Central Ave Ste 900 ... Saint Petersburg FL 33701 NASDAQ: UIHC	**800-861-4370**	800-295-8016
United Investors Life Insurance Co 2801 Hwy 280 S ... Birmingham AL 35223	**800-866-9933**	205-268-1000
United Life Insurance Co PO Box 73909 ... Cedar Rapids IA 52407	**800-332-7977**	319-399-5700
United of Omaha Life Insurance Co Mutual of Omaha Plaza ... Omaha NE 68175	**800-775-6000**	402-342-7600
United Security Life Insurance Company of Illinois (Inc) 6640 S Cicero Ave ... Bedford Park IL 60638	**800-875-4422**	
United World Life Insurance Co Mutual of Omaha Plz ... Omaha NE 68175	**800-775-6000**	402-342-7600
USAA Life Insurance Co (USAA) 9800 Fredericksburg Rd ... San Antonio TX 78288	**800-531-8000**	210-531-8722
Utica National Insurance Group 180 Genesee St ... New Hartford NY 13413	**800-274-1914**	315-734-2000
Variable Annuity Life Insurance Co (VALIC) 2929 Allen Pkwy ... Houston TX 77019	**800-448-2542**	
Washington National Insurance Co 11825 N Pennsylvania St ... Carmel IN 46032	**866-595-2255**	
Western & Southern Life Insurance Co 400 Broadway ... Cincinnati OH 45202	**800-926-1993**	
Western Fraternal Life Assn (WFLA) 1900 First Ave NE ... Cedar Rapids IA 52402	**877-935-2467**	319-363-2653
Western United Life Assurance Co 929 W Sprague Ave PO Box 2290 ... Spokane WA 99210 *General	**800-247-2045***	509-835-2500
Western-Southern Life Assurance Co 400 Broadway ... Cincinnati OH 45202	**866-832-7719**	
William Penn Life Insurance Co of New York 100 Quentin Roosevelt Blvd ... Garden City NY 11530	**800-346-4773**	516-794-3700
Woman's Life Insurance Society 1338 Military St PO Box 5020 ... Port Huron MI 48061	**800-521-9292**	810-985-5191
Woodmen of the World Life Insurance Society 1700 Farnam St ... Omaha NE 68102	**877-664-3332**	

390-3 Medical & Hospitalization Insurance

Companies listed here provide managed care and/or traditional hospital and medical service plans to individuals and/or groups. Managed care companies typically offer plans as Health Maintenance Organizations (HMOs), Preferred Provider Organizations (PPOs), Exclusive Provider Organizations (EPOs), and/or Point of Service (POS) plans. Other types of hospital and medical service plans offered by companies listed here include indemnity plans and medical savings accounts.

	Toll-Free	Phone
AARP Health Care Options PO Box 1017 ... Montgomeryville PA 18936	**800-523-5800**	
Aetna Inc 151 Farmington Ave ... Hartford CT 06156 NYSE: AET	**800-872-3862**	860-273-0123
Aetna US Healthcare Inc 980 Jolly Rd ... Blue Bell PA 19422	**800-872-3862**	215-775-4800
Alberta Blue Cross 10009 108th St NW ... Edmonton AB T5J3C5	**800-661-6995**	780-498-8100
Altius Health Plans 10421 S Jordan Gateway Ste 400 ... South Jordan UT 84095	**800-365-1334**	801-355-1234
American Specialty Health Plans 10221 Wateridge Cir ... San Diego CA 92121	**800-848-3555**	
AMERIGROUP Corp 4425 Corporation Ln ... Virginia Beach VA 23462 NYSE: AGP	**800-600-4441**	757-490-6900
Ameritas Managed Dental Plan Inc 5900 'O' St ... Lincoln NE 68510	**800-404-8019**	402-467-1122
Anthem Blue Cross & Blue Shield 2015 Staples Mill Rd ... Richmond VA 23230	**800-451-1527**	804-354-7000
Anthem Blue Cross & Blue Shield Maine Two Gannett Dr ... South Portland ME 04106 *Cust Svc	**800-482-0966***	207-822-7000
Anthem Blue Cross & Blue Shield of Connecticut 370 Bassett Rd ... North Haven CT 06473	**800-922-1742**	800-922-4670
Anthem Blue Cross & Blue Shield of Nevada 9133 W Russell Rd ... Las Vegas NV 89148	**800-332-3842**	702-228-2583
Anthem Blue Cross Blue Shield Colorado 700 Broadway ... Denver CO 80273	**800-654-9338**	303-831-2131
Arkansas Blue Cross Blue Shield PO Box 2181 ... Little Rock AR 72203	**800-238-8379**	501-378-2000
AvMed 4300 NW 89th Blvd ... Gainesville FL 32606	**800-346-0231**	352-372-8400
Blue Care Network of Michigan 20500 Civic Ctr Dr ... Southfield MI 48076	**800-662-6667**	248-799-6400
Blue Cross & Blue Shield of Alabama 450 Riverchase Pkwy E ... Birmingham AL 35244	**800-292-8868**	205-988-2200
Blue Cross & Blue Shield of Kansas City 2301 Main St ... Kansas City MO 64108	**800-892-6048**	816-395-2222
Blue Cross & Blue Shield of Mississippi PO Box 1043 ... Jackson MS 39215	**800-222-8046**	601-932-3704
Blue Cross & Blue Shield of Montana 560 N Pk Ave PO Box 4309 ... Helena MT 59604	**800-447-7828**	406-437-5000
Blue Cross & Blue Shield of Nebraska 1919 Aksarben Dr PO Box 3248 ... Omaha NE 68180	**800-422-2763**	402-982-7000
Blue Cross & Blue Shield of New Mexico PO Box 27630 ... Albuquerque NM 87125	**800-835-8699**	505-291-3500
Blue Cross & Blue Shield of North Carolina 1965 Ivory Creek Blvd ... Durham NC 27702 *Cust Svc	**800-446-8053***	919-489-7431
Blue Cross & Blue Shield of Oklahoma 1215 S Boulder Ave ... Tulsa OK 74119 *Cust Svc	**800-942-5837***	918-560-3500
Blue Cross & Blue Shield of Rhode Island 500 Exchange St ... Providence RI 02903	**800-637-3718**	401-459-1000
Blue Cross & Blue Shield of Texas Inc 1001 E Lookout Dr ... Richardson TX 75082	**800-521-2227**	972-766-6900
Blue Cross & Blue Shield of Vermont 445 Industrial Ln ... Montpelier VT 05602 *Cust Svc	**800-247-2583***	802-223-6131

				Toll-Free	Phone
Blue Cross Blue Shield of Arizona 2444 W Las Palmaritas Dr	Phoenix	AZ	85021	800-232-2345	602-864-4400
Blue Cross Blue Shield of Delaware PO Box 1991	Wilmington	DE	19899	800-572-4400	800-876-7639
Blue Cross Blue Shield of Georgia 3350 Peachtree Rd NE *Cust Svc	Atlanta	GA	30326	800-441-2273*	404-842-8000
Blue Cross Blue Shield of Kansas 1133 SW Topeka Blvd	Topeka	KS	66629	800-432-0216	785-291-7000
Blue Cross Blue Shield of Louisiana 5525 Reitz Ave	Baton Rouge	LA	70898	800-599-2583	225-295-3307
Blue Cross Blue Shield of Massachusetts 401 Pk Dr	Boston	MA	02215	888-247-2583	617-246-5000
Blue Cross Blue Shield of North Dakota 4510 13th Ave S	Fargo	ND	58121	800-342-4718	701-282-1100
Blue Cross Blue Shield of Wyoming 4000 House Ave	Cheyenne	WY	82001	800-851-9145	307-634-1393
Blue Cross of California Two Gannett Dr	South Portland	ME	04106	800-999-3643	800-482-0966
Blue Cross of Idaho 3000 E Pine Ave	Meridian	ID	83642	800-274-4018	208-345-4550
Blue Cross of Northeastern Pennsylvania 19 N Main St	Wilkes-Barre	PA	18711	800-577-3742*	
BlueCross BlueShield of Western New York 257 W Genesee St	Buffalo	NY	14240	800-888-0757	716-887-6900
Capital District Physicians' Health Plan 500 Patroon Creek Blvd	Albany	NY	12206	888-258-0477	518-641-3000
Capital Health Plan PO Box 15349	Tallahassee	FL	32317	800-390-1434	850-383-3333
Carelink Health Plans 500 Virginia St E Ste 400	Charleston	WV	25301	800-348-2922	304-348-2900
Cdspi 155 Lesmill Rd	Toronto	ON	M3B2T8	800-561-9401	416-296-9401
Centene Corp 7700 Forsyth Blvd NYSE: CNC ■ *General	Saint Louis	MO	63105	800-293-0056*	314-725-4477
Chiropractic Health Plan of California PO Box 190	Clayton	CA	94517	800-995-2442	310-210-5400
CIGNA Healthcare 900 Cottage Grove Rd	Hartford	CT	06152	800-997-1654	860-226-6000
CIGNA Healthcare of North Carolina Inc 701 Corporate Ctr Dr	Raleigh	NC	27607	800-997-1654	919-854-7000
Community Care 218 W Sixth St	Tulsa	OK	74119	800-278-7563	918-594-5200
CompBenefits Corp 100 Mansell Ct E Ste 400	Roswell	GA	30076	800-633-1262	770-552-7101
Comprehensive Health Services Inc (CHSI) 10701 Parkridge Blvd Ste 200	Reston	VA	20191	800-638-8083	703-760-0700
ConnectiCare Inc 175 Scott Swamp Rd *Cust Svc	Farmington	CT	06032	800-251-7722*	860-674-5700
Coventry Health Care Inc 6705 Rockledge Dr Ste 900 NYSE: CVH	Bethesda	MD	20817	866-667-3062	301-581-0600
Coventry Health Care of Delaware Inc 750 Prides Crossing Ste 200	Newark	DE	19713	800-833-7423	
Coventry Health Care of Georgia Inc 1100 Cir 75 Pkwy Ste 1400	Atlanta	GA	30339	800-470-2004	678-202-2100
Coventry Health Care of Iowa Inc 4320 114th St	Urbandale	IA	50322	800-470-6352	515-225-1234
Coventry Health Care of Kansas Inc 8320 Ward Pkwy	Kansas City	MO	64114	800-969-3343	
Coventry Health Care of Louisiana Inc 1720 S Sykes Dr *Sales	Bismarck	ND	58504	800-341-6613*	
Coventry Health Care of Nebraska Inc 15950 W Dodge Rd Ste 100	Omaha	NE	68164	855-449-2889	402-498-9030
Dakotacare 2600 W 49th St PO Box 7406	Sioux Falls	SD	57117	800-325-5598	605-334-4000
Davis Vision Inc 711 Troy-Schenectady Rd	Latham	NY	12110	800-999-5431	
Dean Health Insurance Inc 1277 Deming Way	Madison	WI	53717	800-279-1301	608-836-1400
Delta Dental Insurance Company of Alaska PO Box 1809	Alpharetta	GA	30023	800-521-2651	
Delta Dental of Arizona PO Box 43026	Phoenix	AZ	85080	800-352-6132	
Delta Dental of Arkansas 1513 Country Club Rd PO Box 15965	Sherwood	AR	72120	800-462-5410	501-835-3400
Delta Dental of Colorado 4582 S Ulster St Ste 800	Denver	CO	80237	800-233-0860	303-741-9300
Delta Dental of Georgia PO Box 1803	Alpharetta	GA	30023	800-422-4234	
Delta Dental of Idaho 555 E Parkcenter Blvd PO Box 2870	Boise	ID	83706	800-356-7586	208-489-3580
Delta Dental of Indiana PO Box 30416	Lansing	MI	48909	800-524-0149	
Delta Dental of Iowa 9000 Northpark Dr Ste 13 *Cust Svc	Johnston	IA	50131	800-544-0718*	515-261-5500
Delta Dental of Kansas 1619 N Waterfront Pkwy PO Box 789769	Wichita	KS	67201	800-234-3375	316-264-4511
Delta Dental of Kentucky 10100 Linn Stn Rd PO Box 242810 *Cust Svc	Louisville	KY	40223	800-955-2030*	
Delta Dental of Louisiana PO Box 1803	Alpharetta	GA	30023	800-422-4234	
Delta Dental of Maryland One Delta Dr	Mechanicsburg	PA	17055	800-932-0783	717-766-8500
Delta Dental of Massachusetts 465 Medford St *Cust Svc	Boston	MA	02129	800-872-0500*	617-886-1000
Delta Dental of Michigan PO Box 30416	Lansing	MI	48909	800-524-0149	
Delta Dental of Minnesota PO Box 330	Minneapolis	MN	55440	800-553-9536	651-406-5900
Delta Dental of Mississippi PO Box 1803	Alpharetta	GA	30023	800-422-4234	
Delta Dental of Missouri 12399 Gravois Rd Ste 2	Saint Louis	MO	63127	800-392-1167	314-656-3000
Delta Dental of Montana PO Box 1803	Alpharetta	GA	30023	800-422-4234	
Delta Dental of New Jersey 1639 State Rt 10	Parsippany	NJ	07054	800-624-2633	973-285-4000
Delta Dental of New Jersey Inc PO Box 222	Parsippany	NJ	07054	800-452-9310	
Delta Dental of New Mexico 2500 Louisiana Blvd NE Ste 600	Albuquerque	NM	87110	800-999-0963	505-883-4777
Delta Dental of New York One Delta Dr	Mechanicsburg	PA	17055	800-932-0783	717-766-8500
Delta Dental of Ohio PO Box 30416	Lansing	MI	48909	800-524-0149	
Delta Dental of Oklahoma 16 NW 63rd St Ste 201	Oklahoma City	OK	73116	800-522-0188	405-607-2100
Delta Dental of Pennsylvania One Delta Dr	Mechanicsburg	PA	17055	800-932-0783	
Delta Dental of Rhode Island 10 Charles St	Providence	RI	02904	800-598-6684	401-752-6000
Delta Dental of South Dakota 720 N Euclid Ave PO Box 1157	Pierre	SD	57501	800-627-3961	605-224-7345
Delta Dental of Tennessee 240 Venture Cir *Cust Svc	Nashville	TN	37228	800-223-3104*	615-255-3175
Delta Dental of Texas PO Box 1803	Alpharetta	GA	30023	800-422-4234	
Delta Dental of Utah PO Box 1803	Alpharetta	GA	30023	800-422-4234	
Delta Dental of Virginia 4818 Starkey Rd	Roanoke	VA	24014	800-367-3531	540-989-8000
Delta Dental of West Virginia One Delta Dr	Mechanicsburg	PA	17055	800-932-0783	717-766-8500
Delta Dental of Wisconsin 2801 Hoover Rd PO Box 828	Stevens Point	WI	54481	800-236-3713	715-344-6087
Delta Dental of Wyoming 6234 Yellowstone Rd Ste 100	Cheyenne	WY	82009	800-735-3379	307-632-3313
Delta Dental Plan of North Carolina 343 E Six Forks Rd Ste 180	Raleigh	NC	27609	800-662-8856	919-832-6015
EmblemHealth Co 55 Water St	New York	NY	10041	800-447-8255	646-447-5000
Excellus BlueCross BlueShield PO Box 22999	Rochester	NY	14692	800-278-1247	585-454-1700
Excellus BlueCross BlueShield of Central New York 333 Butternut Dr	Syracuse	NY	13214	800-633-6066	315-671-6400
EyeMed Vision Care 4000 Luxottica Pl	Mason	OH	45040	800-521-3605	513-765-4321
Fallon Community Health Plan Inc 10 Chestnut St Ste 7	Worcester	MA	01608	800-333-2535	508-799-2100
First Choice Health Plan 600 University St Ste 1400	Seattle	WA	98101	800-467-5281	
First Priority Health 19 N Main St	Wilkes-Barre	PA	18711	800-822-8753	
Geisinger Health Plan 100 N Academy Ave	Danville	PA	17822	800-447-4000	570-271-8760
Golden Rule Insurance Co 7440 Woodlands *Cust Svc	Indianapolis	IN	46278	800-444-8990*	
Great American Supplemental Benefits PO Box 26580	Austin	TX	78755	866-459-4272	
Group Health Co-op 320 Westlake Ave N Ste 100	Seattle	WA	98109	888-901-4636	206-448-5600
Hanover Insurance Co 440 Lincoln St	Worcester	MA	01653	800-853-0456	508-855-1000
Harvard Pilgrim Health Care Inc 93 Worcester St	Wellesley	MA	02481	888-888-4742	617-509-1000
Hawaii Dental Service 700 Bishop St Ste 700	Honolulu	HI	96813	800-232-2533	808-521-1431
Hawaii Medical Service Assn 818 Keeaumoku St	Honolulu	HI	96822	800-776-4672	808-948-6111
Health Alliance Plan 2850 W Grand Blvd	Detroit	MI	48202	800-422-4641	313-872-8100
Health Net Inc 21650 Oxnard St NYSE: HNT	Woodland Hills	CA	91367	800-848-4747	818-676-6000
Health Tradition Health Plan 1808 E Main St	Onalaska	WI	54650	800-545-8499	608-781-9692
HealthAmerica Pennsylvania Inc 3721 Tecport Dr PO Box 67103	Harrisburg	PA	17111	800-788-6445	
HealthCare USA 10 S Broadway Ste 1200	Saint Louis	MO	63102	800-213-7792	314-241-5300
HealthPartners Inc PO Box 1309	Minneapolis	MN	55440	800-883-2177	952-883-5000
Healthplex Inc 333 Earl Ovington Blvd *Cust Svc	Uniondale	NY	11553	800-468-0608*	516-542-2200
HealthPlus of Michigan 2050 S Linden Rd	Flint	MI	48532	800-332-9161	810-230-2000
Heritage Summit HealthCare of Florida Inc PO Box 2928	Lakeland	FL	33806	800-282-7644	863-665-6629
Highmark Inc 120 Fifth Ave Pl	Pittsburgh	PA	15222	800-992-0246	412-544-7000
Humana Inc 500 W Main St NYSE: HUM	Louisville	KY	40202	800-486-2620	502-580-1000
Humana Military Healthcare Services 500 W Main St *General	Louisville	KY	40201	800-444-5445*	502-580-3200
Independence Blue Cross 1901 Market St	Philadelphia	PA	19103	800-275-2583	
Independent Health 511 Farber Lakes Dr	Buffalo	NY	14221	800-247-1466	716-631-3001
IOA Re Inc 190 W Germantown Pk Ste 200	East Norriton	PA	19401	800-462-2300	610-940-9000
Kaiser Foundation Health Plan Inc One Kaiser Plz 27th Fl	Oakland	CA	94612	800-464-4000	510-271-5800
Kaiser Permanente 280 W MacArthur Blvd	Oakland	CA	94611	800-464-4000	510-752-1000
Kaiser Permanente Hawaii 711 Kapiolani Blvd	Honolulu	HI	96813	800-966-5955	808-432-0000

				Toll-Free	Phone
Kaiser Permanente Northwest 500 NE Multnomah St Ste 100	Portland	OR	97232	**800-813-2000**	503-813-2000
LA Care Health Plan 555 W Fifth St 29th Fl.	Los Angeles	CA	90013	**888-839-9909**	213-694-1250
Lexington Veteran Affairs Medical Center 1101 Veterans Dr	Lexington	KY	40502	**877-222-8387**	859-233-4511
MEDICA 401 Carlson Pkwy *Cust Svc	Minnetonka	MN	55305	**800-952-3455***	952-992-2900
Medical Benefits Mutual Life Insurance Co 1975 Tamarack Rd	Newark	OH	43058	**800-423-3151**	740-522-8425
Medical Mutual of Ohio 2060 E Ninth St	Cleveland	OH	44115	**800-700-2583**	216-687-7000
Memorial Health Partners 4700 Waters Ave Ste 13	Savannah	GA	31404	**800-537-0690**	912-350-8000
MetLife Inc 200 Pk Ave *NYSE: MET*	New York	NY	10166	**800-638-5433**	212-578-2211
Molina Healthcare Inc 200 Oceangate Ste 100. *NYSE: MOH*	Long Beach	CA	90802	**888-562-5442**	562-435-3666
MVP Health Care 625 State St	Schenectady	NY	12305	**800-777-4793**	518-370-4793
Neighborhood Health Partnership Inc 7600 NW 19th St Ste 200	Miami	FL	33126	**877-972-8845**	
ODS Cos 601 SW Second Ave	Portland	OR	97204	**888-221-0802**	503-228-6554
Oxford Health Plans LLC 48 Monroe Tpke	Trumbull	CT	06611	**800-444-6222**	203-459-9100
Oxford Health Plans (NJ) Inc 111 Wood Ave S Ste 2	Iselin	NJ	08830	**800-201-6920**	732-623-1000
Pacificare of Texas 6200 NW Pkwy	San Antonio	TX	78249	**800-624-7272**	210-474-5000
Paramount Health Care 1901 Indian Wood Cir	Maumee	OH	43537	**800-462-3589**	419-887-2525
Physicians Plus Insurance Corp 2650 Novation Pkwy Ste 200	Madison	WI	53713	**800-545-5015**	608-282-8900
Preferred CommunityChoice PPO 218 W Sixth St	Tulsa	OK	74119	**800-884-4776**	918-594-5200
Preferred Health Systems Inc 8535 E 21st St N	Wichita	KS	67206	**800-990-0345**	316-609-2345
Premera Blue Cross 7001 220th St SW *Cust Svc	Mountlake Terrace	WA	98043	**800-722-1471***	425-918-4000
Premera Blue Cross Blue Shield of Alaska 2550 Denali St Ste 1404 *Cust Svc	Anchorage	AK	99503	**800-508-4722***	907-258-5065
Priority Health 1231 E Beltline NE	Grand Rapids	MI	49525	**800-942-0954**	616-942-0954
Regence Blue Cross Blue Shield of Oregon PO Box 1071	Portland	OR	97207	**888-734-3623**	503-225-5351
Regence BlueCross BlueShield of Utah 2890 E Cottonwood Pkwy *Cust Svc	Salt Lake City	UT	84121	**800-624-6519***	801-333-2100
Rocky Mountain Health Plans 2775 Crossroads Blvd PO Box 10600.	Grand Junction	CO	81502	**800-843-0719**	970-244-7760
SafeGuard Health Enterprises Inc 95 Enterprise Ste 100	Aliso Viejo	CA	92656	**800-880-1800**	949-425-4300
Sagamore Health Network 11555 N Meridian St Ste 400	Carmel	IN	46032	**800-364-3469**	317-573-2886
Scott & White Health Plan 2401 S 31st St	Temple	TX	76508	**800-321-7947**	254-298-3000
Spectera Inc 6220 Old Dobbin Ln Liberty 6, Ste 200	Columbia	MD	21045	**800-638-3120**	
Tufts Associated Health Plans 705 Mt Auburn Street	Watertown	MA	02472	**800-462-0224**	617-972-9400
Union Pacific Railroad Employees' Health Systems 1040 North 2200 West	Salt Lake City	UT	84116	**800-547-0421**	801-595-4300
UnitedHealth Group Inc 9900 Bren Rd E *NYSE: UNH*	Minnetonka	MN	55343	**800-328-5979**	952-936-1300
UnitedHealthcare 9900 Bren Rd E	Minnetonka	MN	55343	**800-362-0655**	952-936-1300
Unity Health Insurance 840 Carolina St	Sauk City	WI	53583	**800-362-3308**	608-643-2491
Univera Healthcare 205 Pk Club Ln	Buffalo	NY	14221	**877-883-9577**	716-847-1480
Voya Services Company 1 Orange Way	Windsor	CT	06095	**855-663-8692**	860-580-4646
Washington Dental Service 9706 Fourth Ave NE	Seattle	WA	98115	**800-367-4104**	206-522-1300
WellCare Group Inc 8735 Henderson Rd Rm 3.	Tampa	FL	33634	**866-765-4385**	813-290-6200
WellCare Health Plans Inc PO Box 31372	Tampa	FL	33631	**866-530-9491**	

390-4 Property & Casualty Insurance

				Toll-Free	Phone
Accident Fund Co 232 S Capitol Ave PO Box 40790 *Mktg	Lansing	MI	48901	**888-276-0327***	517-342-4200
Addison Insurance Co 118 Second Ave SE PO Box 73909	Cedar Rapids	IA	52401	**800-332-7977**	319-399-5700
Aegis Security Inc PO Box 3153	Harrisburg	PA	17105	**800-233-2160**	717-657-9671
Agricultural Workers Mutual Auto Insurance Co PO Box 88	Fort Worth	TX	76101	**800-772-7424**	817-831-9900
ALLIED Group Inc 1100 Locust St	Des Moines	IA	50391	**800-532-1436**	515-508-4211
Allied Insurance 1601 Exposition Blvd	Sacramento	CA	95815	**800-552-2437**	916-924-4000
American Commerce Insurance Co 3590 Twin Creeks Dr	Columbus	OH	43204	**800-848-2945**	614-308-3366
American Family Mutual Insurance Co 6000 American Pkwy *Cust Svc	Madison	WI	53783	**800-374-0008***	608-249-2111

				Toll-Free	Phone
American Modern Home Insurance Co PO Box 5323	Cincinnati	OH	45201	**800-543-2644**	513-943-7200
American National Property & Casualty Co 1949 E Sunshine St	Springfield	MO	65899	**800-333-2860**	417-887-0220
American Southern Insurance Co 3715 Northside Pkwy NW Bldg 400 Ste 800	Atlanta	GA	30327	**800-241-1172**	404-266-9599
AMERISAFE Inc 2301 Hwy 190 W *NASDAQ: AMSF*	DeRidder	LA	70634	**800-256-9052**	337-463-9052
Amerisure Insurance Co 26777 Halsted Rd Ste 200	Farmington Hills	MI	48331	**800-257-1900**	248-615-9000
Amica Mutual Insurance Co 100 Amica Way	Lincoln	RI	02865	**800-652-6422**	
Arbella Mutual Insurance Co 1100 Crown Colony Dr	Quincy	MA	02169	**800-972-5348**	617-328-2800
Armed Forces Insurance Exchange (AFI) PO Box G	Fort Leavenworth	KS	66027	**800-255-0187**	800-255-6792
Arrowpoint Capital Whitehall Corporate Ctr Ste 3 3600 Arco Corporate Dr	Charlotte	NC	28273	**866-236-7750**	704-522-2000
Associated Industries Of Massachusetts Mutual Insurance Com PO Box 4070	Burlington	MA	01803	**866-270-3354**	781-221-1600
AssuranceAmerica Corp 5500 I- N Pkwy Ste 600	Atlanta	GA	30328	**800-450-7857**	770-952-0200
Auto-Owners Insurance Co 6101 Anacapri Blvd	Lansing	MI	48917	**800-346-0346**	517-323-1200
Avemco Insurance Co 411 Aviation Way	Frederick	MD	21701	**800-874-9125**	301-694-5700
Baldwin & Lyons Inc 111 Congressional Blvd Ste 500 *NASDAQ: BWINB*	Carmel	IN	46032	**800-644-5501**	317-636-9800
Berkshire Hathaway Group (BHG) 3024 Harney St	Omaha	NE	68131	**800-223-2064**	402-536-3100
Berkshire Hathaway Homestates Cos (BHHC) PO Box 2048	Omaha	NE	68103	**888-495-8949**	
Bituminous Insurance Cos 320 18th St	Rock Island	IL	61201	**800-475-4477**	
Brotherhood Mutual Insurance Co (BMI) 6400 Brotherhood Way PO Box 2589 *Cust Svc	Fort Wayne	IN	46825	**800-333-3735***	
Brown & Brown Insurance PO Box 1718	Tacoma	WA	98401	**800-562-8171**	253-396-5500
California Casualty Insurance Group 1900 Alameda De Las Pulgas	San Mateo	CA	94403	**866-680-5143**	650-574-4000
Canada Life Assurance Co, The 330 University Ave	Toronto	ON	M5G1R8	**888-252-1847**	416-597-1456
Canal Insurance Co 400 E Stone Ave PO Box 7	Greenville	SC	29601	**800-452-6911**	
Capitol Indemnity Corp 1600 Aspen Commons	Middleton	WI	53562	**800-475-4450**	608-829-4200
Capitol Insurance Cos 1600 Aspen Commons PO Box 5900	Middleton	WI	53562	**800-475-4450**	608-829-4200
Carolina Casualty Insurance Co 4600 Touchton Rd E Bldg 100 Ste 400	Jacksonville	FL	32246	**800-874-8053**	904-363-0900
Central Insurance Cos 800 S Washington St	Van Wert	OH	45891	**800-736-7000**	419-238-1010
Century-National Insurance Co 12200 Sylvan St PO Box 3999 *Cust Svc	North Hollywood	CA	91606	**800-894-8384***	818-760-0880
Chubb & Son 15 Mountain View Rd	Warren	NJ	07059	**800-252-4670**	908-903-2000
Church Mutual Insurance Co 3000 Schuster Ln	Merrill	WI	54452	**800-554-2642**	715-536-5577
Civil Service Employees Insurance Co 2121 N California Blvd Ste 555	Walnut Creek	CA	94596	**800-282-6848**	
Colorado Farm Bureau Mutual Insurance Co PO Box 5647	Denver	CO	80217	**800-315-5998**	303-749-7500
Commerce Insurance Co 211 Main St	Webster	MA	01570	**800-221-1605**	508-943-9000
Concord Group Insurance Cos Four Bouton St	Concord	NH	03301	**800-852-3380**	
Continental Casualty Co 333 S Wabash Ave	Chicago	IL	60685	**800-303-9744**	312-822-5000
Continental Western Group 11201 Douglas Ave	Urbandale	IA	50322	**800-235-2942**	515-473-3000
Cornhusker Casualty Co PO Box 2048	Omaha	NE	68103	**888-495-8949**	
Country Mutual Insurance Co 1701 Towanda Ave *Cust Svc	Bloomington	IL	61701	**888-211-2555***	309-821-3000
Crum & Forster Insurance Inc 305 Madison Ave PO Box 1973	Morristown	NJ	07962	**800-690-5520**	973-490-6600
Cumberland Insurance Group 633 Shiloh Pike	Bridgeton	NJ	08302	**800-232-6992**	
Cumberland Mutual Fire Insurance Co 633 Shiloh Pk	Bridgeton	NJ	08302	**800-232-6992**	
Dairyland Insurance Co 1800 N Pt Dr *Sales	Stevens Point	WI	54481	**866-445-5364***	715-346-6000
Donegal Mutual Insurance Co 1195 River Rd PO Box 302	Marietta	PA	17547	**800-877-0600**	717-426-1931
Economical Insurance Group, The 111 Westmount Rd S PO Box 2000	Waterloo	ON	N2J4S4	**800-265-2180**	519-570-8200
Endurance Reinsurance Corp of America 750 Third Ave Fl 2 & 10	New York	NY	10017	**888-221-3894**	212-471-2800
Erie Indemnity Co *Erie Insurance Group* 100 Erie Insurance Pl *NASDAQ: ERIE*	Erie	PA	16530	**800-458-0811**	814-870-2000
Erie Insurance Exchange 100 Erie Insurance Pl	Erie	PA	16530	**800-458-0811**	814-870-2000
Erie Insurance Property & Casualty Co 100 Erie Insurance Pl	Erie	PA	16530	**800-458-0811**	814-870-2000
Everest Reinsurance Co 477 Martinsville Rd	Liberty Corner	NJ	07938	**800-269-6660**	908-604-3000
Farm Family Casualty Insurance Co PO Box 656	Albany	NY	12201	**800-843-3276**	518-431-5000

	Toll-Free	Phone
Farmers Alliance Mutual Insurance Co		
1122 N Main PO Box 1401 . . . . McPherson KS 67460	800-362-1075	620-241-2200
Farmers Insurance Exchange		
4680 Wilshire Blvd . . . . Los Angeles CA 90010	855-808-6599	323-932-3200
Farmers Mutual Hail Insurance Company of Iowa		
6785 Westown Pkwy . . . . West Des Moines IA 50266	800-247-5248	515-282-9104
Farmers Mutual Insurance Company of Nebraska		
1220 Lincoln Mall . . . . Lincoln NE 68508	800-742-7433	402-434-8300
FCCI Insurance Group		
6300 University Pkwy PO Box 58004 . . . . Sarasota FL 34232	800-226-3224	941-907-3224
Federated Mutual Insurance Co		
121 E Pk Sq PO Box 328 . . . . Owatonna MN 55060	800-533-0472	507-455-5200
Fhm Insurance Co		
4601 Touchton Rd E		
Bldg 300 Ste 3150 . . . . Jacksonville FL 32246	800-393-0001	904-724-9890
Fireman's Fund Insurance Co		
777 San Marin Dr . . . . Novato CA 94998	866-386-3932	800-558-1606
First Insurance Company of Hawaii Ltd		
1100 Ward Ave PO Box 2866 . . . . Honolulu HI 96803	800-272-5202	808-527-7777
Florida Family Insurance Services LLC		
27599 Riverview Ctr Blvd Ste 100		
PO Box 136001 . . . . Bonita Springs FL 34136	888-850-4663	239-495-4700
Florida Farm Bureau Insurance Cos		
5700 SW 34th St . . . . Gainesville FL 32608	866-275-7322	352-378-1321
FM Global		
270 Central Ave PO Box 7500 . . . . Johnston RI 02919	800-343-7722	401-275-3000
Foremost Insurance Co		
5600 Beech Tree Ln . . . . Caledonia MI 49316	800-532-4221	
Frankenmuth Insurance		
1 Mutual Ave . . . . Frankenmuth MI 48787	800-234-4433	989-652-6121
Franklin Mutual Insurance Co		
Five Broad St . . . . Branchville NJ 07826	800-842-0551	973-948-3120
General Star National Insurance Co		
695 E Main St Financial Ctr . . . . Stamford CT 06901	800-431-9994	203-328-5000
Germania Farm Mutual Insurance Assn		
507 Hwy 290 E . . . . Brenham TX 77833	800-392-2202	979-836-5224
Golden Eagle Insurance Corp		
525 B St . . . . San Diego CA 92101	888-398-8924	619-744-6000
Grain Dealers Mutual Insurance Co		
6201 Corporate Dr . . . . Indianapolis IN 46278	800-428-7081	317-388-4500
Great Northern Insurance Co		
15 Mtn View Rd . . . . Warren NJ 07059	800-252-4670*	908-903-2000
*Cust Svc		
Great West Casualty Co		
1100 W 29th St PO Box 277 . . . . South Sioux City NE 68776	800-228-8602	402-494-2084
Grinnell Mutual Reinsurance Co		
4215 Hwy 146 PO Box 790 . . . . Grinnell IA 50112	800-362-2041	641-269-8000
GuideOne Insurance Co		
1111 Ashworth Rd . . . . West Des Moines IA 50265	877-448-4331	515-267-5000
GuideOne Mutual Insurance Co		
1111 Ashworth Rd . . . . West Des Moines IA 50265	877-448-4331	515-267-5000
GuideOne Specialty Mutual Insurance Co		
1111 Ashworth Rd . . . . West Des Moines IA 50265	877-448-4331	515-267-5000
Hagerty Insurance Agency LLC		
141 River's Edge Dr Ste 200		
PO Box 1303 . . . . Traverse City MI 49684	877-922-9701	231-947-6868
Hanover Insurance Co		
440 Lincoln St . . . . Worcester MA 01653	800-853-0456	508-855-1000
Harco National Insurance Co		
PO Box 68309 . . . . Schaumburg IL 60168	800-448-4642	
Harleysville Insurance Co of New Jersey		
112 W Park Dr . . . . Mount Laurel NJ 08054	800-322-5521	856-642-9779
Harleysville Pennland Insurance Co		
355 Maple Ave . . . . Harleysville PA 19438	800-523-6344	215-256-5000
Harleysville Preferred Insurance Co		
355 Maple Ave . . . . Harleysville PA 19438	800-523-6344	215-256-5000
Harleysville Worcester Insurance Co		
120 Front St Ste 400 . . . . Worcester MA 01608	800-225-7387	508-754-6666
Hartford Steam Boiler Inspection & Insurance Co, The (HSB)		
One State St PO Box 5024 . . . . Hartford CT 06102	800-472-1866	
Hartford's Omni Auto Plan		
PO Box 105440 . . . . Atlanta GA 30348	800-243-5860	770-952-4500
Hingham Mutual Fire Insurance Co		
230 Beal St . . . . Hingham MA 02043	800-341-8200	781-749-0841
Hortica Insurance		
One Horticultural Ln PO Box 428 . . . . Edwardsville IL 62025	800-851-7740	618-656-4240
HSB Group Inc 1 State St . . . . Hartford CT 06103	800-472-1866	860-722-1866
ICW Group		
11455 El Camino Real . . . . San Diego CA 92130	800-877-1111	858-350-2400
IMT Group, The		
PO Box 1336 . . . . Des Moines IA 50266	800-274-3531	
Indiana Farmers Mutual Insurance Co		
10 W 106th St . . . . Indianapolis IN 46290	800-666-6460	317-846-4211
Injured Workers Insurance Fund		
8722 Loch Raven Blvd . . . . Towson MD 21286	800-264-4943	410-494-2000
Insurance Company of the West		
11455 El Camino Real . . . . San Diego CA 92130	800-877-1111	858-350-2400
Intact Insurance		
700 University Ave Mn 3 Ste 1500 . . . . Toronto ON M5G0A1	877-341-1464	416-341-1464
James A Scott & Son Inc		
PO Box 10489 . . . . Lynchburg VA 24506	800-365-0101	434-832-2100
Koch Supply & Trading LP		
4111 E 37th St N . . . . Wichita KS 67220	800-245-2243	713-544-4123
Lititz Mutual Insurance Co		
Two N Broad St PO Box 900 . . . . Lititz PA 17543	800-626-4751	717-626-4751
Lumbermen's Underwriting Alliance (LUA)		
1905 NW Corporate Blvd PO Box 3061 . . . . Boca Raton FL 33431	800-327-0630	561-994-1900
Lykes Insurance Inc		
400 N Tampa St . . . . Tampa FL 33602	800-243-0491	813-223-3911
Main Street America Group		
55 W St . . . . Keene NH 03431	800-258-5310	603-352-4000
Manuel Lujan Insurance Inc		
4801 Indian School Rd NE . . . . Albuquerque NM 87110	888-652-7771	505-266-7771
MAPFRE USA Corp 211 Main St . . . . Webster MA 01570	800-922-8276	
Markel Specialty Commercial		
4600 Cox Rd . . . . Glen Allen VA 23060	800-416-4364	
Mercer Insurance Group Inc		
10 N Hwy 31 PO Box 278 . . . . Pennington NJ 08534	800-223-0534	609-737-0426

	Toll-Free	Phone
Merchants Insurance Group		
250 Main St . . . . Buffalo NY 14202	800-462-1077	716-849-3333
Mercury Insurance Group		
4484 Wilshire Blvd . . . . Los Angeles CA 90010	800-956-3728	323-937-1060
NYSE: MCY		
Michigan Millers Mutual Insurance Co		
2425 E Grand River Ave PO Box 30060 . . . . . . Lansing MI 48912	800-888-1914	
Mid-Continent Group		
1437 S Boulder Ave W PO Box 1409 . . . . Tulsa OK 74119	800-722-4994	918-587-7221
Middlesex Mutual Assurance Co		
213 Ct St PO Box 891 . . . . Middletown CT 06457	800-622-3780	
Midwest Employers Casualty Co		
14755 N Outer 40 Dr Ste 300 . . . . Chesterfield MO 63017	877-975-2667	636-449-7000
Millers First Insurance Co		
111 E Fourth St . . . . Alton IL 62002	800-558-0500	618-463-3636
Montgomery Mutual Insurance Co		
13830 Ballantyne Corporate Pl		
Ste 300 . . . . Charlotte NC 28277	800-561-0178	704-759-7661
Mutual of Enumclaw Insurance Co		
1460 Wells St . . . . Enumclaw WA 98022	800-366-5551	360-825-2591
National Farmers Union Property & Casualty Co		
5619 DTC Pkwy Ste 300 . . . . Greenwood Village CO 80111	800-347-1961	303-337-5500
National Fire & Marine Insurance Co		
3024 Harney St . . . . Omaha NE 68131	866-720-7861	402-536-3000
National Grange Mutual Insurance Co		
55 W St . . . . Keene NH 03431	800-258-5310	603-352-4000
National Interstate Corp		
3250 I- Dr . . . . Richfield OH 44286	800-929-1500	330-659-8900
NASDAQ: NATL		
Nationwide Mutual Fire Insurance Co		
1 Nationwide Plaza . . . . Columbus OH 43215	877-669-6877	614-249-7111
Nationwide Mutual Insurance Co		
1 Nationwide Plaza . . . . Columbus OH 43215	877-669-6877	614-249-7111
Nautilus Insurance Group LLC		
7233 E Butherus Dr . . . . Scottsdale AZ 85260	800-842-8972	480-951-0905
New Era Life Insurance Co		
PO Box 4884 . . . . Houston TX 77210	800-552-7879	
New Jersey Manufacturers Insurance Co		
301 Sullivan Way . . . . West Trenton NJ 08628	800-232-6600	609-883-1300
New Mexico Mutual Casualty Co		
PO Box 27825 . . . . Albuquerque NM 87125	800-788-8851	505-345-7260
New York Central Mutual Fire Insurance Co (NYCM)		
1899 Central Plz E . . . . Edmeston NY 13335	800-234-6926	
North American Specialty Insurance Co		
650 Elm St Ste 600 . . . . Manchester NH 03101	800-542-9200	603-644-6600
Northern Security Insurance Co		
PO Box 188 . . . . Montpelier VT 05601	800-451-5000	802-223-2341
Northland Insurance Co		
385 Washington St . . . . Saint Paul MN 55102	800-237-9334	
Northwestern Pacific Indemnity Co		
15 Mtn View Rd . . . . Warren NJ 07059	800-252-4670*	908-903-2000
*Claims		
Odyssey Re Holdings Corp		
300 First Stamford Pl . . . . Stamford CT 06902	866-745-4440	203-977-8000
Ohio Casualty Insurance Co		
9450 SewaRd Rd . . . . Fairfield OH 45014	800-843-6446	513-603-2400
Ohio Indemnity Co		
250 E Broad St 7th Fl . . . . Columbus OH 43215	800-628-8581	614-228-2800
Old Dominion Insurance Co		
4601 Touchton Rd E Ste 330		
Ste 3400 . . . . Jacksonville FL 32246	800-226-0875	904-642-3000
OneBeacon Insurance Group		
601 Carlson Pkwy Ste 600 . . . . Minnetonka MN 55305	877-434-3900	781-332-7000
Oregon Mutual Insurance Co		
PO Box 808 . . . . McMinnville OR 97128	800-888-2141	503-472-2141
Pacific Specialty Insurance Co		
3601 Haven Ave . . . . Menlo Park CA 94025	800-962-1172	
Peerless Insurance Co		
62 Maple Ave . . . . Keene NH 03431	800-542-5385	603-352-3221
Pekin Insurance (FAIA)		
2505 Ct St . . . . Pekin IL 61558	800-322-0160	309-346-1161
Penn Millers Insurance Co		
72 N Franklin St PO Box P . . . . Wilkes-Barre PA 18773	800-233-8347	
Penn National Insurance Co		
2 N Second St PO Box 2361 . . . . Harrisburg PA 17101	800-388-4764	717-234-4941
Pennsylvania Manufacturers Assn Co		
380 Sentry Pkwy . . . . Blue Bell PA 19422	800-222-2749	
Pharmacists Mutual Insurance Co		
808 Hwy 18 W PO Box 370 . . . . Algona IA 50511	800-247-5930*	
*General		
Philadelphia Consolidated Holding Corp		
231 Saint Asaph's Rd Ste 100 . . . . Bala Cynwyd PA 19004	888-647-8639	610-617-7900
Philadelphia Contributionship Insurance Co		
212 S Fourth St . . . . Philadelphia PA 19106	888-627-1752*	215-627-1752
*Cust Svc		
Pinnacol Assurance		
7501 E Lowry Blvd . . . . Denver CO 80230	800-873-7242	303-361-4000
Preferred Employers Insurance Co		
PO Box 85478 . . . . San Diego CA 92186	888-472-9001*	866-472-9602
*Cust Svc		
Preferred Mutual Insurance Co		
One Preferred Way . . . . New Berlin NY 13411	800-333-7642	607-847-6161
Princeton Excess & Surplus Lines Insurance Co		
555 College Rd E . . . . Princeton NJ 08543	800-544-2378	609-243-4200
Princeton Insurance Co		
746 Alexander Rd PO Box 5322 . . . . Princeton NJ 08540	800-334-0588	609-452-9404
Progressive Casualty Insurance Co		
6300 Wilson Mills Rd		
Campus E . . . . Mayfield Village OH 44143	800-776-4737	440-461-5000
Providence Mutual Fire Insurance Co		
340 E Ave . . . . Warwick RI 02886	877-763-1800	401-827-1800
Prudential Financial Inc		
751 Broad St . . . . Newark NJ 07102	800-843-7625	973-802-6000
NYSE: PRU		
QBE Holdings Inc		
Wall St Plz 88 Pine St . . . . New York NY 10005	800-456-1626	212-422-1212
Quincy Mutual Fire Insurance Co		
57 Washington St . . . . Quincy MA 02169	800-899-1116	

	Toll-Free	Phone
Republic Western Insurance Co		
2721 N Central Ave .... Phoenix AZ 85004	**800-528-7134***	
Claims		
RLI Insurance Co		
9025 N Lindbergh Dr .... Peoria IL 61615	**800-331-4929**	309-692-1000
Royal & SunAlliance Insurance Co of Canada (RSA)		
18 York Street Suite 800 .... Toronto ON M5J2T8	**800-268-8406**	416-366-7511
RTW Inc		
8500 Normandale Lk Blvd Ste 1400		
PO Box 390327 .... Bloomington MN 55437	**800-789-2242***	952-893-0403
Sales		
Rural Mutual Insurance Company Inc		
1241 John Q Hammons Dr PO Box 5555 .... Madison WI 53705	**800-362-7881**	608-836-5525
Safe Auto Insurance Co		
Four Easton Oval PO Box 182109 .... Columbus OH 43219	**800-723-3288**	614-231-0200
Safeway Insurance Group		
790 Pasquinelli Dr .... Westmont IL 60559	**800-273-0300**	630-887-8300
Sagamore Insurance Co		
111 Congressional Blvd Ste 500 .... Carmel IN 46032	**800-317-9402**	
Savers Property & Casualty Insurance Co		
26255 American Dr .... Southfield MI 48034	**800-482-2726**	248-204-8299
Scottsdale Insurance Co		
8877 N Gainey Ctr Dr .... Scottsdale AZ 85258	**800-423-7675**	480-365-4000
Secura Insurance Cos		
PO Box 819 .... Appleton WI 54912	**800-558-3405**	920-739-3161
Selective Insurance Company of America		
40 Wantage Ave .... Branchville NJ 07890	**800-777-9656**	973-948-3000
Sentry Insurance Co		
2 Technology Park Dr .... Westford MA 01886	**800-373-6879**	978-392-7119
Sompo Japan Insurance Co of America		
777 Third Ave 28th Fl .... New York NY 10017	**800-208-3614**	212-416-1200
Southern Farm Bureau Casualty Insurance Co		
1800 E County Line Rd Ste 400 .... Ridgeland MS 39157	**800-272-7977**	601-957-7777
SS Nesbitt & Co Inc		
3500 Blue Lake Dr .... Birmingham AL 35243	**800-422-3223**	205-262-2700
Star Insurance Co		
26255 American Dr .... Southfield MI 48034	**800-482-2726**	248-204-8299
State Auto National Insurance Co		
518 E Broad St .... Columbus OH 43215	**800-444-9950**	614-464-5000
State Auto Property & Casualty Insurance Co		
518 E Broad St .... Columbus OH 43215	**800-444-9950**	614-464-5000
State Automobile Mutual Insurance Co		
518 E Broad St .... Columbus OH 43215	**800-444-9950**	614-464-5000
State Compensation Insurance Fund		
1275 Market St .... San Francisco CA 94103	**866-721-3498**	415-565-1234
STOPS Inc		
8855 Grissom Pkwy .... Titusville FL 32780	**866-632-2161**	321-383-4111
Texas Mutual Insurance Co		
6210 E Hwy 290 .... Austin TX 78723	**888-532-5246**	512-224-3800
Tokio Marine Life		
230 Pk Ave .... New York NY 10169	**800-628-2796**	212-297-6600
Topa Insurance Corp		
1800 Ave of the Stars .... Los Angeles CA 90067	**800-949-6505**	310-201-0451
Tower Group Inc		
120 Broadway 14th Fl .... New York NY 10271	**877-883-6599**	212-655-2000
NASDAQ: TWGP		
Transcontinental Insurance Co		
333 S Wabash Ave CNA Ctr .... Chicago IL 60604	**800-437-8854**	312-822-5000
Transportation Insurance Co		
333 S Wabash Ave .... Chicago IL 60604	**800-437-8854**	312-822-5000
ULLICO Casualty Co		
1625 I St NW .... Washington DC 20006	**800-431-5425**	
Unico American Corp		
23251 Mulholland Dr .... Woodland Hills CA 91364	**800-669-9800**	818-591-9800
Union Standard Insurance Co		
122 W Carpenter Fwy 350 .... Irving TX 75039	**800-444-0049**	972-719-2400
United Fire & Casualty Co		
118 Second Ave SE .... Cedar Rapids IA 52407	**800-332-7977**	319-399-5700
NASDAQ: UFCS		
United Heartland Inc		
PO Box 3026 .... Milwaukee WI 53201	**866-206-5851**	
United National Group		
Three Bala Plz E Ste 300 .... Bala Cynwyd PA 19004	**800-333-0352**	610-664-1500
United National Insurance Co		
Three Bala Plz E Ste 300 .... Bala Cynwyd PA 19004	**800-333-0352**	610-664-1500
USA Workers' Injury Network		
1250 S Capital of Texas Hwy		
Bldg 3 Ste 500 .... Austin TX 78746	**800-872-0020***	
Cust Svc		
USAA Property & Casualty Insurance Group		
9800 Fredericksburg Rd .... San Antonio TX 78288	**800-531-8722**	210-531-8722
Utica First Insurance Co		
5981 Airport Rd .... Oriskany NY 13424	**800-456-4556**	315-736-8211
Utica National Insurance Group		
180 Genesee St .... New Hartford NY 13413	**800-274-1914**	315-734-2000
Vermont Mutual Insurance Co		
89 State St PO Box 188 .... Montpelier VT 05601	**800-451-5000**	802-223-2341
Victoria Insurance		
22901 Millcreek Blvd .... Cleveland OH 44122	**800-888-8424**	216-896-6990
Vigilant Insurance Co		
15 Mtn View Rd .... Warren NJ 07059	**800-252-4670***	908-903-2000
Claims		
West Bend Mutual Insurance Co		
1900 S 18th Ave .... West Bend WI 53095	**800-236-5010**	262-334-5571
Western National Mutual Insurance Co		
5350 W 78th St .... Edina MN 55439	**800-862-6070**	952-835-5350
Western Reserve Group, The		
1685 Cleveland Rd .... Wooster OH 44691	**800-362-0426**	330-262-9060
Wisconsin Reinsurance Corp		
2810 City View Dr .... Madison WI 53707	**800-939-9473**	608-242-4500
Zenith Insurance Co		
PO Box 9055 .... Van Nuys CA 91409	**800-440-5020**	818-713-1000
Zenithstar Insurance Co		
Zenith Insurance Co		
1101 Capital of Texas Hwy S Bldg J		
PO Box 163510 .... Austin TX 78746	**800-841-3987**	512-306-1700

390-5 Surety Insurance

	Toll-Free	Phone
AMBAC Assurance Corp		
1 State St Plaza 15th Fl .... New York NY 10004	**800-221-1854**	212-658-7470
American Public Life Insurance Co		
2305 Lakeland Dr PO Box 925 .... Jackson MS 39205	**800-256-8606**	601-936-6600
Bond Pro LLC		
1501 E Second Ave .... Tampa FL 33605	**888-789-4985**	
Catholic Mutual Group		
10843 Old Mill Rd .... Omaha NE 68154	**800-228-6108**	402-551-8765
Central Insurance Cos		
800 S Washington St .... Van Wert OH 45891	**800-736-7000**	419-238-1010
Century Insurance Group		
465 Cleveland Ave .... Westerville OH 43082	**877-855-8462**	614-895-2000
Chubb Specialty Insurance		
82 Hopmeadow St .... Simsbury CT 06070	**800-252-4670**	860-408-2000
CNA Surety Corp		
333 S Wabash Ave .... Chicago IL 60604	**877-672-6115**	312-822-5000
NYSE: L		
Copic Insurance Co		
7351 Lowry Blvd .... Denver CO 80230	**800-421-1834**	720-858-6000
Dentists Insurance Co		
1201 K St 17th Fl .... Sacramento CA 95814	**800-733-0634**	
Doctors' Co, The		
185 Greenwood Rd .... Napa CA 94558	**800-421-2368**	
Euler Hermes ACI		
800 Red Brook Blvd Fourth Fl .... Owings Mills MD 21117	**877-883-3224**	410-753-0753
Everest Reinsurance Co		
477 Martinsville Rd .... Liberty Corner NJ 07938	**800-269-6660**	908-604-3000
Federated Mutual Insurance Co		
121 E Pk Sq PO Box 328 .... Owatonna MN 55060	**800-533-0472**	507-455-5200
Financial Guaranty Insurance Co		
125 Pk Ave Sixth Fl .... New York NY 10017	**800-352-0001**	212-312-3000
Fireman's Fund Insurance Co		
777 San Marin Dr .... Novato CA 94998	**866-386-3932**	800-558-1606
First Insurance Company of Hawaii Ltd		
1100 Ward Ave PO Box 2866 .... Honolulu HI 96803	**800-272-5202**	808-527-7777
Illinois State Medical Inter-Insurance Exchange (ISMIE)		
20 N Michigan Ave Ste 700 .... Chicago IL 60602	**800-782-4767**	312-782-2749
Indemnity Company of California		
17780 Fitch Ste 200 .... Irvine CA 92614	**800-782-1546**	949-263-3300
Insco Dico Group		
17780 Fitch Ste 200 .... Irvine CA 92614	**800-782-1546**	949-263-3300
Insurance Company of the West		
11455 El Camino Real .... San Diego CA 92130	**800-877-1111**	858-350-2400
International Fidelity Insurance Co (IFIC)		
One Newark Ctr 20th Fl .... Newark NJ 07102	**800-333-4167**	973-624-7200
JP Everhart & Co		
1840 N Greenville Ave Ste 178 .... Richardson TX 75081	**888-622-8575**	
Kansas Medical Mutual Insurance Co (KaMMCO)		
623 SW Tenth Ave Ste 200 .... Topeka KS 66612	**800-232-2259**	785-232-2224
Life of the South Insurance Co		
10151 Deerwood Pk Blvd Bldg 100 .... Jacksonville FL 32256	**800-888-2738**	904-350-9660
Louisiana Medical Mutual Insurance Co		
1 Galleria Blvd Ste 700 .... Metairie LA 70001	**800-452-2120**	
MBIA Insurance Corp		
113 King St .... Armonk NY 10504	**800-765-6242**	914-273-4545
Media/Professional Insurance Inc		
1201 Walnut Ste 1800 .... Kansas City MO 64106	**866-282-0565**	816-471-6118
Medical Assurance Inc		
100 Brookwood Pl Ste 300 .... Birmingham AL 35209	**800-282-6242***	205-877-4400
Cust Svc		
Medical Mutual Group		
700 Spring Forest Rd .... Raleigh NC 27609	**800-662-7917**	919-872-7117
Medical Mutual Insurance Company of Maine		
One City Ctr Ste 9 .... Portland ME 04101	**800-942-2791**	207-775-2791
Medical Mutual Liability Insurance Society of Maryland		
225 International Cir PO Box 8016 .... Hunt Valley MD 21030	**800-492-0193**	410-785-0050
Medical Protective Co		
5814 Reed Rd .... Fort Wayne IN 46835	**800-463-3776**	260-485-9622
Mortgage Guaranty Insurance Corp		
270 E Kilbourn Ave .... Milwaukee WI 53202	**800-558-9900**	414-347-6480
NCMIC Insurance Co		
14001 University Ave .... Clive IA 50325	**800-769-2000**	515-313-4500
Norcal Mutual Insurance Company Inc		
560 Davis St .... San Francisco CA 94111	**800-652-1051**	415-397-9700
Old Republic Insured Automotive Services Inc		
8282 S Memorial Dr .... Tulsa OK 74133	**800-331-3780**	918-307-1000
Old Republic Surety		
445 S Moorlands Rd Ste 200 .... Brookfield WI 53005	**800-217-1792**	262-797-2640
Pekin Life Insurance Co		
2505 Ct St .... Pekin IL 61558	**800-322-0160**	309-346-1161
OTC: PKIN		
Penn National Insurance Co		
2 N Second St PO Box 2361 .... Harrisburg PA 17101	**800-388-4764**	717-234-4941
Pennsylvania Medical Society Liability Insurance Co (PMSLIC)		
1700 Bent Creek Blvd		
PO Box 2080 .... Mechanicsburg PA 17050	**800-445-1212**	717-791-1212
PMI Mortgage Insurance Co		
3003 Oak Rd .... Walnut Creek CA 94597	**800-288-1970**	925-658-7878
Podiatry Insurance Company of America		
3000 Meridian Blvd Ste 400 .... Franklin TN 37067	**800-251-5727**	615-984-2005
Pre-Paid Legal Services Inc		
one Pre-Paid Way .... Ada OK 74820	**800-654-7757**	580-436-1234
Princeton Insurance Co		
746 Alexander Rd PO Box 5322 .... Princeton NJ 08540	**800-334-0588**	609-452-9404
ProMutual Group		
101 Arch St 4th Fl .... Boston MA 02110	**800-225-6168**	
Protective Insurance Co		
111 Congressional Blvd Ste 500 .... Carmel IN 46032	**800-644-5501**	317-636-9800
Radian Asset Assurance Inc		
Radian Group Inc, The		
335 Madison Ave 25th Fl .... New York NY 10017	**877-723-4261**	212-983-3100

			Toll-Free	Phone
Radian Group Inc				
1601 Market St	Philadelphia PA	19103	800-523-1988	215-564-6600
NYSE: RDN				
Reciprocal of America				
4200 Innslake Dr Ste 102	Glen Allen VA	23060	800-284-8847	804-747-8600
Republic Mortgage Insurance Co				
101 N Cherry St Ste 101	Winston-Salem NC	27101	800-999-7642	
RLI Insurance Co				
9025 N Lindbergh Dr	Peoria IL	61615	800-331-4929	309-692-1000
Rose & Kiernan Inc				
99 Troy Rd	East Greenbush NY	12061	866-488-6582	518-244-4245
State Volunteer Mutual Insurance Co				
101 W Pk Dr Ste 300	Brentwood TN	37027	800-342-2239	615-377-1999
Surety Group Inc				
3715 Northside Pkwy NW Ste 1-315	Atlanta GA	30327	800-486-8211	404-352-8211
Texas Hospital Insurance Exchange				
8310 N Capital of Texas Hwy Ste 250	Austin TX	78731	800-792-0060	512-451-5775
Texas Lawyers Insurance Exchange (TLIE)				
900 Congress Ave Ste 500	Austin TX	78701	800-252-9332	512-480-9074
Transamerica				
4333 Edgewood Rd NE	Cedar Rapids IA	52499	800-852-4678	319-355-8511
Triad Guaranty Insurance Corp				
101 S Stratford Rd	Winston-Salem NC	27104	888-691-8074*	336-723-1282
*Cust Svc				
ULLICO Casualty Co				
1625 I St NW	Washington DC	20006	800-431-5425	
United Guaranty Corp (UGC)				
230 N Elm St	Greensboro NC	27401	800-334-8966	
United National Group				
Three Bala Plz E Ste 300	Bala Cynwyd PA	19004	800-333-0352	610-664-1500
Utica National Insurance Group				
180 Genesee St	New Hartford NY	13413	800-274-1914	315-734-2000
Victor O Schinnerer & Co Inc				
2 Wisconsin Cir Ste 200	Chevy Chase MD	20815	888-867-9327	301-961-9800
Vision Financial Corp				
PO Box 506	Keene NH	03431	800-793-0223	
Warranty Group Inc, The				
175 W Jackson 11th Fl	Chicago IL	60604	800-621-2130	312-356-3000
Western World Insurance Co				
400 Parson's Pond Dr	Franklin Lakes NJ	07417	888-847-8600	201-847-8600
XL Specialty Insurance Co				
70 Seaview Ave	Stamford CT	06902	877-263-7995	203-964-5200
Zurich North America				
1400 American Ln	Schaumburg IL	60196	800-382-2150	847-605-6000

390-6 Title Insurance

Most title insurance companies also provide other real estate services such as escrow, flood certification, appraisals, etc.

			Toll-Free	Phone
Attorney's Title Insurance Fund Inc				
6545 Corporate Ctr Blvd	Orlando FL	32822	800-336-3863	407-240-3863
Chicago Title & Trust Co				
171 N Clark St	Chicago IL	60601	800-621-1919	312-223-2000
Commonwealth Land Title Insurance Co				
601 Riverside Ave	Jacksonville FL	32204	888-866-3684	
Community Title & Escrow Ltd				
2600 State St Bldg D	Alton IL	62002	800-854-4049	618-466-7755
Dakota Homestead Title Insurance Co				
315 S Phillips Ave	Sioux Falls SD	57104	800-425-0388	605-336-0388
Entitle Direct Group Inc				
281 Tresser Blvd Sixth Fl	Stamford CT	06901	877-936-8485	203-724-1150
Fidelity National Title Group Inc				
601 Riverside Ave	Jacksonville FL	32204	888-866-3684	904-854-8100
Fidelity National Title Insurance Co				
7025 N Scottsdale Rd	Scottsdale AZ	85258	888-934-3354	480-344-6400
Fidelity National Title Insurance Company of Oregon				
900 SW Fifth Ave Mezzanine Level	Portland OR	97204	888-934-3354	503-223-8338
First American Corp				
One First American Way	Santa Ana CA	92707	800-854-3643	714-250-3000
NYSE: FAF				
Hanover Insurance Co				
440 Lincoln St	Worcester MA	01653	800-853-0456	508-855-1000
Meridian Title Corp				
202 S Michigan St	South Bend IN	46601	800-777-1574	574-232-5845
Mississippi Valley Title Insurance Co				
315 Tom Bigbee St	Jackson MS	39201	800-647-2124	601-969-0222
Monroe Title Insurance Corp				
47 W Main St	Rochester NY	14614	800-966-6763	585-232-4950
North American Title Co				
1855 Gateway Blvd Ste 600	Concord CA	94520	800-566-0370	925-935-5599
Northpoint Escrow & Title LLC				
10800 NE Eighth St Ste 200	Bellevue WA	98004	877-678-1678	425-453-8880
Old Republic National Title Insurance Co (ORTIG)				
400 Second Ave S	Minneapolis MN	55401	800-328-4441	612-371-1111
Stewart Information Services Corp				
1980 Post Oak Blvd Ste 800	Houston TX	77056	800-729-1900	713-625-8100
NYSE: STC				
Stewart REI Data Inc				
1980 Post Oak Blvd Ste 800	Houston TX	77056	800-729-1900	212-922-0050
Stewart Title Guaranty Co				
1980 Post Oak Blvd Ste 800	Houston TX	77056	800-729-1900	713-625-8100
Title Guaranty of Hawaii Inc				
235 Queen St	Honolulu HI	96813	800-222-3229	808-533-6261
Title Resources Guaranty Co (TRGC)				
8111 LBJ Fwy Ste 1200	Dallas TX	75251	800-526-8018	972-644-6500
US Recordings Inc				
2925 Country Dr	Little Canada MN	55117	877-272-5250	651-765-6400
USHEALTH Group Inc				
300 Burnett St Ste 200	Fort Worth TX	76102	800-387-9027	

390-7 Travel Insurance

Most of the companies listed here are insurance agencies and brokerages that specialize in selling travel insurance policies, rather than the insurers who underwrite the policies.

			Toll-Free	Phone
All Aboard Benefits				
6162 E Mockingird Ln Ste 104	Dallas TX	75214	800-462-2322	214-821-6677
Continental Assurance Co				
333 S Wabash Ave	Chicago IL	60604	800-251-2148	312-822-5000
Highway To Health Inc				
One Radnor Corporate Ctr Ste 100	Radnor PA	19087	888-243-2358	
Ingle International				
460 Richmond St W Ste 100	Toronto ON	M5V1Y1	800-360-3234	416-730-8488
Insurance Consultants International				
19760 Knights Crossing Ste 1C	Monument CO	80132	800-576-2674	719-573-9080
International SOS Assistance Inc				
3600 Horizon Blvd Ste 300	Trevose PA	19053	888-413-9071	215-244-1500
Pan-American Life Insurance Co				
601 Poydras St	New Orleans LA	70130	877-939-4550*	
*Life Ins				
Travel Insured International				
52-S Oakland Ave PO Box 280568	East Hartford CT	06128	800-243-3174	
Wallach & Company Inc				
107 W Federal St	Middleburg VA	20117	800-237-6615	540-687-3166

391   INTERCOM EQUIPMENT & SYSTEMS

			Toll-Free	Phone
Anacom General Corp				
1240 S Claudina St	Anaheim CA	92805	800-955-9540	714-774-8484
Clever Devices Ltd				
300 Crossways Pk Dr	Woodbury NY	11797	800-872-6129	516-433-6100
Crest Healthcare Supply				
195 Third St	Dassel MN	55325	800-328-8908	320-275-3382
David Clark Company Inc				
360 Franklin St	Worcester MA	01615	800-298-6235*	508-751-5800
*Cust Svc				
Lee Dan Communications Inc				
155 Adams Ave	Hauppauge NY	11788	800-231-1414	631-231-1414

392   INTERIOR DESIGN

			Toll-Free	Phone
24 Asset Management Corp				
2020 Camino del Rio N Ste 900	San Diego CA	92108	855-414-2424	
Accord Creditor Services LLC				
PO Box 10005	Newnan GA	30271	800-373-0760	
Ark TeleServices				
Two E Merrick Rd	Valley Stream NY	11580	800-898-5367	
Arvato Digital Services LLC				
29011 Commerce Ctr Dr	Valencia CA	91355	800-223-1478	
Building Service Inc (BSI)				
W222 N630 Cheaney Rd	Waukesha WI	53186	866-353-3600	262-955-6400
Carenet Healthcare Services				
11845 Interstate 10 W Ste 400	San Antonio TX	78230	800-809-7000	
Cascade Receivables Management LLC				
101 Second St Ste 100	Petaluma CA	94952	888-417-1531	
Cleanwise Inc				
1100 E Woodfield Rd Ste 200	Schaumburg IL	60173	877-255-5230	
CMS Mid-Atlantic Inc				
295 Totowa Rd	Totowa NJ	07512	800-267-1981	
CO-OP Financial Services Inc				
9692 Haven Ave	Rancho Cucamonga CA	91730	800-782-9042	
Decorating Den Systems Inc				
8659 Commerce Dr	Easton MD	21601	800-332-3367	410-822-9001
eCollect LLC				
5000 Euclid Ave Ste 303	Cleveland OH	44103	888-569-6001	
Etheridge Printing Co				
4434 Meriwen Rd	Dallas TX	75244	800-834-2709	214-827-8151
Focus Services Inc				
4102 South 1900 West Ste 7	Roy UT	84067	888-362-8711	
Fortitude Business Solutions LLC				
PO Box 2095	Daphne AL	36526	877-577-2644	
GCS Service Inc				
370 Wabasha St N	St. Paul MN	55102	800-822-2303	
Global R&D Consulting Group				
555 N Point Ctr E	Alpharetta GA	30022	866-770-5577	
Intland GmbH				
968 Inverness Way	Sunnyvale CA	94087	866-468-5210	
iTOK Inc				
3400 North Ashton Blvd Ste 260	Lehi UT	84043	866-515-4865	
Jomax LLC				
14100 N 83rd Ave Ste 235	Peoria AZ	85381	888-866-0721	
Kay Green Design Inc				
859 Outer Rd	Orlando FL	32814	800-226-5186	407-246-7155
Lehman Hardware & Appliances Inc				
4779 Kidron Rd	Dalton OH	44618	888-438-5346	
MGM Mirage Design Group Inc				
3260 Industrial Rd	Las Vegas NV	89109	800-929-1111	702-650-7400
MTI America				
POBox 667140	Pompano Beach FL	33066	800-553-2155	
myFreightWorld LLC				
7133 W 95th St	Overland Park KS	66211	877-549-9438	
Networld Media Group LLC				
13100 Eastpoint Park Blvd Ste 100	Louisville KY	40223	877-441-7545	
Polygon Network PO Box 4806	Dillon CO	80435	800-221-4435	
Primeritus Financial Services Inc				
440 Metroplex Dr	Nashville TN	37211	888-833-4238	
QualiTest Ltd				
1139 Post Rd	Fairfield CT	06824	877-882-9540	
RealtyBid International Inc				
3225 Rainbow Dr Ste 248	Rainbow City AL	35906	877-518-5600	

	Toll-Free	Phone

Regatta Travel Solutions Inc
325 Winding River Ln Ste 201B . . . . Charlottesville VA 22911   **800-605-5093**

Rev.com Inc
251 Kearny St Eighth Fl . . . . .San Francisco CA 94108   **888-369-0701**

Sacor Financial Inc
1911 Douglas Blvd 85-126 . . . . .Roseville CA 95661   **866-556-0231**

Setina Manufacturing Company Inc
2926 Yelm Hwy Se . . . . Olympia WA 98501   **800-426-2627**

Smart LLC
Smart TuitionOne Woodbridge Ctr
Ste 800 . . . . Woodbridge NJ 07095   **866-395-2986**

Training Industry Inc
401 Harrison Oaks Blvd Ste 300 . . . . Cary NC 27513   **866-298-4203**

Venuelabs
505 Fifth Ave S Ste 300 . . . . Seattle WA 98104   **866-333-7328**

Villa Lighting Supply Inc
2929 Chouteau Ave . . . . .Saint Louis MO 63103   **800-325-0963**

Walls 360 Inc
5054 Bond St . . . . .Las Vegas NV 89118   **888-244-9969**

Warranty Life Services Inc
4152 Meridian St Ste 105-29 . . . . .Bellingham WA 98226   **888-927-7269**

Wyse Meter Solutions Inc
RPO Newmarket Court PO Box 95530 . . . . Newmarket ON L3Y8J8   **866-681-9465**

393   INTERNET BACKBONE PROVIDERS

Companies that are, in effect, Internet service providers for Internet Service Providers (ISPs).

	Toll-Free	Phone

BT Americas Inc
2160 E Grand Ave .El Segundo CA 90245   **888-767-2988**   408-330-2700

Cogent Communications Group Inc
1015 31st St NW . . . . Washington DC 20007   **877-875-4432**   202-295-4200
NASDAQ: CCOI

iPass Inc
3800 Bridge Pkwy . . . . Redwood Shores CA 94065   **877-236-3807**   650-232-4100
NASDAQ: IPAS

Level 3 Communications Inc
1025 Eldorado Blvd . . . . Broomfield CO 80021   **877-453-8353**   720-888-1000
NYSE: LVLT

nFrame Inc
701 Congressional Blvd Ste 100 . . . . Carmel IN 46032   **877-570-7827**   317-805-3759

SAVVIS Inc
One Savvis Pkwy . . . . Town & Country MO 63017   **800-728-8471**   314-628-7000

SunGard Availability Services
680 E Swedesford Rd . . . . Wayne PA 19087   **800-468-7483**   484-582-2000

Verio Inc
8005 S Chester St Ste 200 . . . . Centennial CO 80112   **800-438-8374***   561-912-2555
*Sales

Verizon Business
1 Verizon Way . . . . Basking Ridge NJ 07920   **877-297-7816***   908-559-2000
*Cust Svc

XO Communications Inc
13865 Sunrise Vly Dr . . . . Herndon VA 20171   **866-349-0134**   703-547-2000

394   INTERNET BROADCASTING

	Toll-Free	Phone

Audible Inc
One Washington Pk . . . . Newark NJ 07102   **888-283-5051**   973-820-0400

Media Temple Inc
8520 National Blvd Bldg A . . . . Culver City CA 90232   **877-578-4000**

OMT Inc 1-1717 Dublin Ave . . . . Winnipeg MB R3H0H2   **888-665-0501**   204-786-3994

395   INTERNET DOMAIN NAME REGISTRARS

	Toll-Free	Phone

AITDomains.com
421 Maiden Ln . . . . Fayetteville NC 28301   **877-549-2881**

Best Registration Services Inc
1418 S Third St . . . . Louisville KY 40208   **800-977-3475**   502-637-4528

Domain Registration Services
PO Box 447 . . . . Palmyra NJ 08065   **888-339-9001**

Domain-It!
9891 Montgomery Rd . . . . .Cincinnati OH 45242   **866-269-2355***   513-351-4222
*General

DomainPeople Inc
550 Burrard St
Ste 200 Bentall Twr 5 . . . . Vancouver BC V6C2B5   **877-734-3667**   604-639-1680

Dotster
8100 NE Pkwy Dr Ste 300
PO Box 821066 . . . . Vancouver WA 98682   **800-401-5250**   360-449-5800

Dotster Inc PO Box 821066 . . . . Vancouver WA 98682   **800-401-5250**   360-253-2210

Dynadot LLC PO Box 345 . . . . San Mateo CA 94401   **866-652-2039***   650-585-1961
*Cust Svc

easyDNS
219 Dufferin St Ste 304A . . . . Toronto ON M6K3J1   **888-677-4741**   416-535-8672

Name.com LLC
2500 E Second Ave 2nd Fl . . . . Denver CO 80206   **800-365-0006**   720-249-2374

Network Solutions LLC
13861 Sunrise Valley Dr Ste 300 . . . . Herndon VA 20171   **800-361-5712**   703-668-4600

Register.com Inc
575 Eigth Ave Eighth Fl . . . . New York NY 10018   **888-734-4783**

396   INTERNET SEARCH ENGINES, PORTALS, DIRECTORIES

	Toll-Free	Phone

Ancestry 360 W 4800 N . . . . Provo UT 84604   **800-262-3787**   801-705-7000

Ancestry.com 360 W 4800 N . . . . Provo UT 84604   **800-262-3787***   801-705-7000
*Cust Svc

BioSpace Inc
90 New Montgomery St Ste 414 . . . . .San Francisco CA 94105   **888-246-7722**   877-277-7585

CEOExpress Co
1 Broadway 14th Fl . . . . Cambridge MA 02142   **888-686-1181**   617-482-1200

Genealogy.com
360 West 4800 North . . . . Provo UT 84604   **800-262-3787**   801-705-7000

HomeAdvisor
14023 Denver W Pkwy Ste 200 . . . . Golden CO 80401   **800-474-1596**   303-963-7200

Hotelrooms.com Inc
108-18 Queens Blvd . . . . Forest Hills NY 11375   **800-486-7000**   718-730-6000

Internet Public Library
University of Michigan School of Information
304 W Hall . . . . .Ann Arbor MI 48109   **800-545-2433**   734-763-2285

Law Engine
7660-H Fay Avenue Ste 342 . . . . .La Jolla CA 92037   **800-894-2889**   858-456-1234

MindEdge Inc
465 Waverley Oaks Rd Ste 202 . . . . Waltham MA 02452   **877-592-8000**   781-250-1805

NewsHub
100 Lombard St Suite 203 . . . . Toronto ON M5C1M3   **800-889-9487**   416-536-4827

Nursing Ctr
323 Norristown Rd Ste 200 . . . . Ambler PA 19002   **800-346-7844**   800-787-8985

RootsWeb.com 360 W 4800 N . . . . Provo UT 84604   **800-262-3787**   801-705-7000

Tucows Inc 96 Mowat Ave . . . . Toronto ON M6K3M1   **800-371-6992**   416-535-0123
TSE: TC

Wired News
Wired 520 Third St Ste 305 . . . . .San Francisco CA 94107   **800-769-4733**

YELLOWPAGES.com LLC
208 S Akard Ste 1825 . . . . Dallas TX 75202   **866-329-7118**

397   INTERNET SERVICE PROVIDERS (ISPS)

	Toll-Free	Phone

ABT Internet Inc
175 E Shore Rd . . . . Great Neck NY 11023   **800-367-3414**   516-829-5484

Access US
712 N Second St Ste 300 . . . . .Saint Louis MO 63102   **800-638-6373**   314-655-7700

Aplus.net Internet Services
10350 Barnes Canyon Rd . . . . .San Diego CA 92121   **877-275-8763**   858-410-6929

AT & T Inc
175 E Houston St PO Box 2933 . . . . San Antonio TX 78299   **800-351-7221**   210-821-4105
NYSE: AT&T

Cable One Inc
210 E Earll Drive . . . . Phoenix AZ 85012   **877-692-2253**   602-364-6000

Cincinnati Bell Inc
221 E Fourth St . . . . .Cincinnati OH 45202   **800-387-3638**   513-397-9900
NYSE: CBB

ClearSail Communications LLC
3950 Braxton . . . . Houston TX 77063   **888-905-0888**   713-230-2800

Direct Internet Access
141 Desiard St PO Box 7263 . . . . .Monroe LA 71201   **800-296-2249**

DSLextreme.com
21540 Plummer St Ste A . . . . Chatsworth CA 91311   **866-243-8638**

EarthLink Inc
1375 Peachtree St NE . . . . Atlanta GA 30309   **866-383-3080**   404-815-0770
NASDAQ: ELNK

Expedient Communications
810 Parish St . . . . .Pittsburgh PA 15220   **877-570-7827**   412-316-7800

Frontline Communications
PO Box 98 . . . . Orangeburg NY 10962   **888-376-6854**

HughesNet
11717 Exploration Ln . . . . Germantown MD 20876   **866-347-3292**   301-428-5500

Internet America Inc
12853 Capricorn St . . . . .Stafford TX 77477   **800-232-4335**

Net Access Corp
Nine Wing Dr . . . . .Cedar Knolls NJ 07927   **800-638-6336**   973-590-5000

NetZero Inc
21301 Burbank Blvd . . . . .Woodland Hills CA 91367   **800-638-9376**   818-287-3000

New Edge Networks
3000 Columbia House Blvd Ste 106 . . . . Vancouver WA 98661   **877-725-3343**   360-693-9009

Nova Internet Services Inc
PO Box 703696 Ste 230 . . . . .Dallas TX 75370   **877-668-2663**   214-904-9600

ProtoSource Network
2511 W Shaw Ave Ste 102 . . . . Fresno CA 93711   **866-490-8600**

Road Runner Group
60 Columbus Cir 60 Columbus Cir . . . . New York NY 10023   **866-689-3678**   703-345-3422

TOAST.net
4841 Monroe St Ste 307 . . . . Toledo OH 43623   **888-862-7863**   419-292-2200

Verio Inc
8005 S Chester St Ste 200 . . . . Centennial CO 80112   **800-438-8374***   561-912-2555
*Sales

Verizon Business
1 Verizon Way . . . . Basking Ridge NJ 07920   **877-297-7816***   908-559-2000
*Cust Svc

398   INVENTORY SERVICES

	Toll-Free	Phone

Douglas-Guardian Services Corp
14800 St Mary's Ln . . . . Houston TX 77079   **800-255-0552**   281-531-0500

MSI Inventory Service Corp
PO Box 320129 . . . . .Flowood MS 39232   **800-820-1460**   601-939-0130

WIS International
9265 Sky Park Ct Ste 100 . . . . .San Diego CA 92123   **800-268-6848**   858-565-8111

399   INVESTIGATIVE SERVICES

SEE ALSO Security & Protective Services ; Information Retrieval Services (General) ; Public Records Search Services

	Toll-Free	Phone

ASK Services Inc
42180 Ford Rd Ste 101 . . . . Canton MI 48187   **888-416-1313**   734-983-9040

Aurico Reports Inc
116 W Eastman St . . . . Arlington Heights IL 60004   **866-255-1852**

				Toll-Free	Phone

Bombet Cashio & Assoc
11220 N Harrells Ferry Rd . . . . Baton Rouge LA 70816 — **800-256-5333** — 225-275-0796

Capitol Detective Agency
2922 N 18th Pl . . . . Phoenix AZ 85016 — **800-346-0347** — 602-265-3462

Claims Verification Inc
6700 N Andrews Ave Ste 200 . . . . Ft. Lauderdale FL 33309 — **888-284-2000**

Donan Engineering Co Inc
11321 Plantside Dr . . . . Louisville KY 40299 — **800-482-5611**

Douglas Baldwin & Assoc
PO Box 1249 . . . . La Canada CA 91012 — **800-392-3950** — 818-952-4433

Gregg Investigations Inc
222 S Hamilton St Ste 17 . . . . Madison WI 53703 — **800-866-1976**

International Investigators Inc
3216 N Pennsylvania St . . . . Indianapolis IN 46205 — **800-403-8111** — 317-925-1496

Kessler International
45 Rockefeller Plz Ste 2000 . . . . New York NY 10111 — **800-932-2221** — 212-286-9100

Michael Ramey & Assoc Inc
PO Box 744 . . . . Danville CA 94526 — **800-321-0505**

North Winds Investigations Inc
119 S Second St PO Box 1654 . . . . Rogers AR 72756 — **800-530-4514** — 479-925-1612

Owens & Assoc Investigations
8765 Aero Dr Ste 306 . . . . San Diego CA 92123 — **800-297-1343**

Palmer Investigative Services
624 W Gurley St Ste A . . . . Prescott AZ 86304 — **800-280-2951** — 928-778-2951

Research Assoc Inc
27999 Clemens Rd . . . . Cleveland OH 44145 — **800-255-9693** — 440-892-9439

Rick Johnson & Assoc of Colorado
1649 Downing St . . . . Denver CO 80218 — **800-530-2300** — 303-296-2200

Southern Research Company Inc
2850 Centenary Blvd . . . . Shreveport LA 71104 — **888-772-6952** — 318-227-9700

Stewart & Assoc Inc
50 W Douglas St Ste 1200 . . . . Freeport IL 61032 — **888-310-2840** — 815-235-3807

Vericon Resources Inc
3550 Engineering Dr Ste 225 . . . . Norcross GA 30092 — **800-795-3784** — 770-457-9922

VTS Investigations LLC
PO Box 971 . . . . Elgin IL 60121 — **800-538-4464**

Wood & Tait Inc
64-5249 Kaukea Rd . . . . Kamuela HI 96743 — **800-774-8585** — 808-885-5090

400 — INVESTMENT ADVICE & MANAGEMENT

SEE ALSO Securities Brokers & Dealers ; Investment Guides - Online ; Mutual Funds ; Commodity Contracts Brokers & Dealers

				Toll-Free	Phone

Acadian Asset Management Inc
260 Franklin St . . . . Boston MA 02110 — **800-946-0166** — 617-850-3500

Advent Capital Management LLC
1065 Ave of the Americas 31st Fl . . . . . . New York NY 10018 — **888-523-8368** — 212-482-1600

AGF Management Ltd
66 Wellington St W 31st Fl . . . . Toronto ON M5K1E9 — **800-268-8583** — 905-214-8203

AllianceBernstein Holding LP (AB)
1345 Ave of the Americas . . . . New York NY 10105 — **800-221-5672*** — 212-486-5800
NYSE: AB ■ *Cust Svc

American Century Investments Inc
4500 Main St PO Box 419200 . . . . Kansas City MO 64111 — **800-345-2021** — 816-531-5575

Ameriprise Financial Inc
834 Ameriprise Financial Ctr . . . . Minneapolis MN 55474 — **866-673-3673** — 612-671-3131
NYSE: AMP

Ameriprise Financial Services Inc
70100 Ameriprise Financial Ctr . . . . . . Minneapolis MN 55474 — **866-483-8434**

Amivest Capital Management
703 Market St 18th Fl . . . . San Francisco CA 94103 — **800-541-7774**

AmSouth Investment Services Inc (AIS)
250 Riverchase Pkwy E 4th Fl . . . . Birmingham AL 35244 — **866-512-3479**

Analytic Investors LLC
555 W Fifth St 50th Fl . . . . Los Angeles CA 90013 — **800-618-1872** — 213-688-3015

Appleton Partners Inc
One Post Office Sq 6th Fl . . . . Boston MA 02109 — **800-338-0745** — 617-338-0700

Aristotle Capital Management LLC
11100 Santa Monica Blvd Ste 1700 . . . . . Los Angeles CA 90025 — **877-478-4722** — 310-478-4005

AssetMark Inc
1655 Grant St 10th Fl . . . . Concord CA 94520 — **800-664-5345**

Atlantic Trust
100 E Pratt St 23rd Fl . . . . Baltimore MD 21202 — **866-644-4144** — 410-539-4660

Bahl & Gaynor Inc
212 E Third St Ste 200 . . . . Cincinnati OH 45202 — **800-341-1810** — 513-287-6100

Bartlett & Co
600 Vine St Ste 2100 . . . . Cincinnati OH 45202 — **800-800-4612** — 513-621-4612

Becker Capital Management Inc
1211 S W Fifth Ave Ste 2185 . . . . Portland OR 97204 — **800-551-3998** — 503-223-1720

Bessemer Trust Co
630 Fifth Ave 6th Fl . . . . New York NY 10111 — **800-255-7688** — 212-708-9100

Bogdahn Group, The
4901 Vineland Rd Ste 600 . . . . Orlando FL 32811 — **866-240-7932**

Boston Advisors Inc
One Liberty Sq 10th Fl . . . . Boston MA 02109 — **800-523-5903** — 617-348-3100

Boston Financial Data Services
2000 Crown Colony Dr . . . . Quincy MA 02169 — **888-772-2337** — 617-483-5000

Brandes Investment Partners LP
11988 El Camino Real Ste 500 . . . . San Diego CA 92130 — **800-237-7119** — 858-755-0239

Brandywine Capital Associates
113 East Evans St . . . . West Chester PA 19380 — **888-344-2920** — 610-344-2910

Brandywine Global Investment Management LLC
2929 Arch St Eighth Fl . . . . Philadelphia PA 19104 — **800-348-2499** — 215-609-3500

Brown Capital Management Inc
1201 N Calvert St . . . . Baltimore MD 21202 — **800-809-3863** — 410-837-3234

BTS Asset Management Inc
420 Bedford St Ste 340 . . . . Lexington MA 02420 — **800-343-3040**

Cadence Capital Management
265 Franklin St 4th Fl . . . . Boston MA 02110 — **800-298-2194** — 617-624-3500

Calamos Asset Management Inc
2020 Calamos Ct . . . . Naperville IL 60563 — **800-582-6959** — 630-245-7200
NASDAQ: CLMS

Callan Assoc Inc
101 California St Ste 3500 . . . . San Francisco CA 94111 — **800-227-3288** — 415-974-5060

Cambiar Investors Inc
2401 E Second Ave Ste 500 . . . . Denver CO 80206 — **888-673-9950**

Cambria Capital LLC
488 E Winchester St Ste 200 . . . . Salt Lake City UT 84107 — **877-226-0477**

Cameron Thomson Group Ltd
390 Bay St Ste 1706 . . . . Toronto ON M5H2Y2 — **800-395-9943** — 416-350-5009

CapFinancial Partners LLC
4208 Six Forks Rd Ste 1700 . . . . Raleigh NC 27609 — **800-216-0645** — 919-870-6822

Capital Group Cos Inc
333 S Hope St . . . . Los Angeles CA 90071 — **800-421-8511** — 213-615-0514

Capital Growth Management LP
1 International Pl . . . . Boston MA 02110 — **800-345-4048** — 617-737-3225

Capital Research & Management Co (CRMC)
333 S Hope St . . . . Los Angeles CA 90071 — **800-421-4225** — 213-486-9200

Casey Research LLC
PO Box 1427 . . . . Stowe VT 05672 — **888-512-2739** — 602-445-2736

Casgrain & Company Ltd
1200 Mcgill College Ave 21st Fl. . . . . Montreal QC H3B4G7 — **800-361-8738** — 514-871-8080

Churchill Corporate Services
56 Utter Ave . . . . Hawthorne NJ 07506 — **800-941-7458** — 973-636-9400

Clark Capital Management Group Inc (CCMG)
1650 Market St
1 Liberty Pl 53rd Fl. . . . . Philadelphia PA 19103 — **800-766-2264** — 215-569-2224

Cohen & Steers Inc
280 Pk Ave 10th Fl . . . . New York NY 10017 — **800-330-7348** — 212-832-3232
NYSE: CNS

Colony Capital Management
3050 Peachtree Rd NW Suite 200. . . . . Atlanta GA 30305 — **877-365-5050** — 404-365-5050

Columbia Management Investment Advisers LLC
1 Financial Ctr . . . . Boston MA 02111 — **800-426-3750**

Commonwealth Financial Network
29 Sawyer Rd . . . . Waltham MA 02453 — **800-237-0081** — 781-736-0700

Compak Asset Management
1801 Dove St . . . . Newport Beach CA 92660 — **800-388-9700**

Creative Financial Group (CFG)
16 Campus Blvd . . . . Newtown Square PA 19073 — **800-893-4824** — 610-325-6100

Crown Financial Ministries
601 Broad St SE . . . . Gainesville GA 30501 — **800-722-1976** — 770-534-1000

Design ProfessionalXL Group
2959 Salinas Hwy . . . . Monterey CA 93940 — **800-227-4284** — 831-649-5522

Dodge & Cox
555 California St 40th Fl. . . . . San Francisco CA 94104 — **800-254-8494** — 415-981-1710

Driehaus Capital Management Inc
25 E Erie St . . . . Chicago IL 60611 — **800-688-8819** — 312-587-3800

Eagle Asset Management
880 Carillon Pkwy . . . . Saint Petersburg FL 33716 — **800-237-3101**

Earnest Partners LLC
1180 Peachtree St Ste 2300 . . . . Atlanta GA 30309 — **800-322-0068** — 404-815-8772

Edgar Lomax Co
6564 Loisdale Ct Ste 310 . . . . Springfield VA 22150 — **866-205-0524** — 703-719-0026

Elan Financial Services
225 W Sta Sq Dr Ste 620 . . . . Pittsburgh PA 15219 — **877-935-2637**

Estrada Hinojosa & Company Inc
1717 Main St LB47 . . . . Dallas TX 75201 — **800-676-5352** — 214-658-1670

Federated Investors
1001 Liberty Ave
Federated Investors Twr . . . . Pittsburgh PA 15222 — **800-245-0242** — 412-288-1900
NYSE: FII

Fidelity Investments Institutional Services Company Inc
82 Devonshire St . . . . Boston MA 02109 — **800-343-3548** — 617-563-9840

Fiduciary Management Inc of Milwaukee
100 E Wisconsin Ave Ste 2200. . . . . Milwaukee WI 53202 — **800-264-7684** — 414-226-4545

First Pacific Advisors Inc
11400 W Olympic Blvd Ste 1200 . . . . . . Los Angeles CA 90064 — **800-982-4372** — 310-473-0225

Fischer Francis Trees & Watts Inc
200 Pk Ave 11th Fl . . . . New York NY 10166 — **888-367-3389** — 212-681-3000

Fisher Investments
13100 Skyline Blvd . . . . Woodside CA 94062 — **800-550-1071**

FMR Corp 82 Devonshire St . . . . Boston MA 02109 — **800-343-3548**

Ford Equity Research Inc
11722 Sorrento Vly Rd Ste I . . . . San Diego CA 92121 — **800-842-0207** — 858-755-1327

Franklin Resources Inc
One Franklin Pkwy Bdge 970 First Fl . . . . San Mateo CA 94403 — **800-632-2301** — 650-312-2000
NYSE: BEN

Gannett Welsh & Kotler LLC
222 Berkeley St 15th Fl. . . . . Boston MA 02116 — **800-225-4236** — 617-236-8900

Glenmede Trust Co
1650 Market St Ste 1200 . . . . Philadelphia PA 19103 — **800-966-3200** — 215-419-6000

Goldman Sachs Asset Management (GSAM)
200 W St . . . . New York NY 10282 — **800-526-7384** — 212-902-1000

Harris Assoc LP
111 South Wacker Dr Ste 4600 . . . . Chicago IL 60606 — **800-731-0700** — 312-646-3600

Hawthorn PNC Family Wealth
1600 Market St . . . . Philadelphia PA 19103 — **888-947-3762**

HD Vest Financial Services
6333 N State Hwy 161 Fourth Fl. . . . . Irving TX 75038 — **866-218-8206** — 972-870-6000

Henderson Global Investors
One Financial Plz Fl 19. . . . . Hartford CT 06103 — **888-832-6774** — 860-723-8600

Holland Capital Management LP
303 W Madison St Ste 700. . . . . Chicago IL 60606 — **800-295-9779** — 312-553-4830

Hyperion Capital Management Inc
200 Vessey St 3 World Financial Ctr. . . . . New York NY 10281 — **800-497-3746** — 212-549-8400

ICM Asset Management Inc
601 W Main Ave . . . . Spokane WA 99201 — **800-488-4075** — 509-455-3588

IGM Financial Inc
447 Portage Ave 1 Canada Ctr . . . . Winnipeg MB R3C3B6 — **888-746-6344**
NYSE: IGM

Jatheon Technologies Inc
British Colonial Bldg 8 Wellington St E Mezzanine Level
. . . . Toronto ON M5E1C5 — **888-528-4366** — 416-840-0418

Jeffrey Matthews Financial Group LLC, The
30B Vreeland Rd Ste 210 . . . . Florham Park NJ 07932 — **888-467-3636** — 973-805-6222

JPMorgan Fleming Asset Management
PO Box 8528 . . . . Boston MA 02266 — **800-480-4111**

Kayne Anderson Capital Advisors LP
1800 Ave of the Stars Third Fl . . . . Los Angeles CA 90067 — **800-638-1496**

Killen Group Inc
1189 Lancaster Ave . . . . Berwyn PA 19312 — **877-454-5536** — 610-296-7222

			Toll-Free	Phone

Laird Norton Tyee
801 Second Ave Ste 1600 . . . . Seattle WA 98104   **800-426-5105**   206-464-5100

Leerink Swann & Co
1 Federal St 37th Fl . . . . Boston MA 02110   **800-808-7525**

Logan Capital Management Inc
Six Coulter Ave Ste 2000 . . . . Ardmore PA 19003   **800-215-1100**

Loomis Sayles & Company Inc LP
PO Box 219594 . . . . Kansas City MO 64121   **800-343-2029**   800-633-3330

Lord Abbett & Co
90 Hudson St . . . . Jersey City NJ 07302   **888-522-2388**   201-827-2000

Mackenzie Financial Corp
180 Queen St W . . . . Toronto ON M5V3K1   **888-653-7070**   416-922-5322

Madison Investment Advisors Inc
550 Science Dr . . . . Madison WI 53711   **800-767-0300**   608-274-0300

Manchester Financial Inc
2815 Townsgate Rd Ste 100 . . . . Westlake Village CA 91361   **800-492-1107**

Marketocracy Inc
1208 W Magnolia Ste 236 . . . . Fort Worth TX 76104   **877-462-4180**

Marquette Asset Management
60 S Sixth Ste 3900 . . . . Minneapolis MN 55402   **866-661-3770**   612-661-3770

McAdams Wright Ragen Inc
925 Fourth Ave Ste 3900 . . . . Seattle WA 98104   **888-212-8843**   206-664-8850

MFS Investment Management
500 Boylston St . . . . Boston MA 02116   **877-960-6077**   617-954-5000

Morningstar Inc
22 W Washington St . . . . Chicago IL 60606   **800-735-0700***   312-696-6000
NASDAQ: MORN ▩ *Orders

Morrow & Co LLC 470 W Ave . . . . Stamford CT 06902   **800-662-5200**   203-658-9400

Navellier Securities Corp
1 E Liberty St Ste 504 . . . . Reno NV 89501   **800-887-8671**   775-785-2300

Neuberger Berman LLC
605 Third Ave . . . . New York NY 10158   **800-223-6448**

Northern Trust Company of Connecticut
300 Atlantic St Ste 400 . . . . Stamford CT 06901   **866-876-9944**   312-630-0779

Northwestern Mutual Investment Services LLC
611 E Wisconsin Ave Ste 300 . . . . Milwaukee WI 53202   **866-664-7737**

Odlum Brown Ltd
250 Howe St Ste 1100 . . . . Vancouver BC V6C3S9   **866-636-8222**   604-669-1600

Pacific Investment Management Company LLC
840 Newport Ctr Dr . . . . Newport Beach CA 92660   **800-387-4626**   949-720-6000

Payden & Rygel
333 S Grand Ave . . . . Los Angeles CA 90071   **800-572-9336**   213-625-1900

Peninsula Asset Management Inc
1111 Third Ave W Ste 340 . . . . Bradenton FL 34205   **800-269-6417**

Personal Capital Corp
726 Main St . . . . Redwood City CA 94063   **855-855-8005**

Primary Global Research LLC
1975 W El Camino Real Ste 300 . . . . Mountain View CA 94040   **888-893-1688**

Primerica Financial Services
3120 Breckinridge Blvd . . . . Duluth GA 30099   **800-257-4725**   770-381-1000

Prudential Financial Inc
751 Broad St . . . . Newark NJ 07102   **800-843-7625**   973-802-6000
NYSE: PRU

Putnam Investments
30 Dan Rd PO Box 8383 . . . . Canton MA 02021   **888-478-8626**   617-292-1000

PVG Asset Management Corp
24918 Genesee Trl Rd . . . . Golden CO 80401   **800-777-0818**   303-526-0548

QCI Asset Management
40A Grove St . . . . Pittsford NY 14534   **800-836-3960**   585-218-2060

RNC Genter Capital Management
11601 Wilshire Blvd 25th Fl . . . . Los Angeles CA 90025   **800-877-7624**   310-477-6543

Roffman Miller Assoc Inc
1835 Market St Ste 500 . . . . Philadelphia PA 19103   **800-995-1030**   215-981-1030

Ronald Blue & Company LLC
300 Colonial Ctr Pkwy Ste 300 . . . . Roswell GA 30076   **800-841-0362**   770-280-6000

Rothschild North America Inc
1251 Ave of the Americas 51st Fl . . . . New York NY 10020   **844-726-3863**   212-403-3500

Royce & Assoc LLC
745 Fifth Ave 24th Fl . . . . New York NY 10151   **800-221-4268**

RREEF
101 California St 26th Fl . . . . San Francisco CA 94111   **800-222-5885***   415-781-3300
*All

Ruane Cunniff & Goldfarb Inc
9 W 57th St Ste 5000 . . . . New York NY 10019   **800-686-6884**   212-832-5280

Russell Investment Group
909 A St . . . . Tacoma WA 98402   **800-787-7354**

Russell Investments
1301 Second Ave 18th Fl . . . . Seattle WA 98101   **800-426-7969**   206-505-7877

Schultz Collins Lawson Chambers Inc
455 Market St Ste 1250 . . . . San Francisco CA 94105   **877-291-2205**   415-291-3000

Signalert Corp
150 Great Neck Rd Ste 301 . . . . Great Neck NY 11021   **800-829-6229**   516-829-6444

Signator Investors Inc
197 Clarendon St C-8 . . . . Boston MA 02116   **800-543-6611**

Smith Graham & Co
600 Travis St Ste 6900 . . . . Houston TX 77002   **800-739-4470**   713-227-1100

Sovereign Society, The
98 S E Sixth Ave Ste 2 . . . . Delray Beach FL 33483   **888-358-8125**

Stoever Glass & Company Inc
30 Wall St . . . . New York NY 10005   **800-223-3881**

Systematic Financial Management LP
300 Frank W Burr Blvd Seventh Fl
Glenpoint Ctr E 7th Fl . . . . Teaneck NJ 07666   **800-258-0497**   201-928-1982

T Rowe Price Assoc Inc
100 E Pratt St . . . . Baltimore MD 21202   **800-638-7890**   410-345-2000

Tamarac Inc
701 Fifth Ave 14th Fl . . . . Seattle WA 98104   **866-525-8811**

Thompson Siegel & Walmsley Inc
6806 Paragon Pl Ste 300 . . . . Richmond VA 23230   **800-697-1056**   804-353-4500

US Global Investors Inc
7900 Callaghan Rd . . . . San Antonio TX 78229   **800-873-8637**   210-308-1234
NASDAQ: GROW

USAA Investment Management
9800 Fredericksburg Rd
PO Box 659453. . . . . San Antonio TX 78288   **800-531-8722**

Value Line Asset Management
220 E 42nd St . . . . New York NY 10017   **800-634-3583**   212-907-1500

Value Line Inc
220 E 42nd St . . . . New York NY 10017   **800-634-3583***   212-907-1500
NASDAQ: VALU ▩ *Cust Svc

Vanguard Group
455 Devon Pk Dr . . . . Wayne PA 19087   **800-662-7447**   610-669-1000

Vontobel Asset Management Inc
1540 Broad Way Ave 38th Fl . . . . New York NY 10036   **800-445-8872***   212-415-7000
*General

Waddell & Reed Financial Inc
6300 Lamar Ave . . . . Overland Park KS 66201   **888-923-3355**   913-236-2000
NYSE: WDR

WE Donoghue & Company Inc
629 Washington St . . . . Norwood MA 02062   **800-642-4276**

Weiss Research Inc
15430 Endeavour Dr . . . . Jupiter FL 33478   **800-291-8545**

Wentworth Hauser & Violich (WHV)
301 Battery St . . . . San Francisco CA 94111   **800-204-2650**   415-981-6911

Workplace Answers LLC
3701 Executive Ctr Dr Ste 201 . . . . Austin TX 78731   **866-861-4410**

WP Stewart & Company Ltd
527 Madison Ave 20th Fl . . . . New York NY 10022   **888-695-4092**   212-750-8585
OTC: WPSL

Wright Investors' Service
440 Wheelers Farms Rd . . . . Milford CT 06461   **800-232-0013**   203-783-4400

Yacktman Asset Management Co
6300 Bridgepoint Pkwy Bldg 1 Ste 320 . . . . Austin TX 78730   **800-835-3879**   512-767-6700

401   INVESTMENT COMPANIES - SMALL BUSINESS

The companies listed here conform to the Small Business Administration's standards for investing.

			Toll-Free	Phone

Galliard Capital Management Inc
800 La Salle Ave Ste 1100 . . . . Minneapolis MN 55402   **800-717-1617**   612-667-3220

GamePlan Financial Marketing LLC
300 ParkBrooke Pl Ste 200. . . . . Woodstock GA 30189   **800-886-4757***   678-238-0601
*Cust Svc

Hornor Townsend & Kent Inc (HTK)
600 Dresher Rd Ste C1C. . . . . Horsham PA 19044   **800-289-9999**

Impact Seven Inc
147 Lk Almena Dr . . . . Almena WI 54805   **800-685-9353**   715-357-3334

UMB Capital Corp
1010 Grand Blvd . . . . Kansas City MO 64106   **800-821-2171**   816-860-7000

402   INVESTMENT COMPANIES - SPECIALIZED SMALL BUSINESS

Companies listed here conform to the Small Business Administration's requirements for investment in minority companies.

			Toll-Free	Phone

Al Copeland Investments Inc
1001 Harimaw Ct S . . . . Metairie LA 70001   **800-401-0401**   504-830-1000

MMG Ventures LP
826 E Baltimore St . . . . Baltimore MD 21202   **800-248-1960**   410-333-2548

Smith Affiliated Capital (SAC)
800 Third Ave 12th Fl . . . . New York NY 10022   **888-387-3298**   212-644-9440

403   INVESTMENT GUIDES - ONLINE

SEE ALSO Buyer's Guides - Online

			Toll-Free	Phone

Briefing.com Inc
401 N Michigan Ste 2910 . . . . Chicago IL 60611   **800-752-3013***   312-670-4463
*General

EDGAR Online Inc
11200 Rockville Pk Ste 310 . . . . Rockville MD 20852   **800-732-0330**   301-287-0300
NASDAQ: EDGR

eSignal 3955 Pt Eden Way . . . . Hayward CA 94545   **800-815-8256**   510-266-6000

FactSet Research Systems Inc
601 Merritt 7 Third Fl . . . . Norwalk CT 06851   **877-322-8738**   203-810-1000
NYSE: FDS

Harris myCFO Inc
2200 Geng Rd Ste 100 . . . . Palo Alto CA 94303   **866-966-1130**   ·650-210-5000

Hoover's Inc
5800 Airport Blvd . . . . Austin TX 78752   **800-486-8666**   512-374-4500

InvestorPlace.com
2420A Gehman Ln 2420A Gehman Ln . . . . Lancaster PA 17602   **800-219-8592**

Stockwatch
700 W Georgia St PO Box 10371 . . . . Vancouver BC V7Y1J6   **800-268-6397**   604-687-1500

TheStreet.com Inc
14 Wall St 15th Fl . . . . New York NY 10005   **800-562-9571**   212-321-5000
NASDAQ: TST

404   INVESTMENT (MISC)

SEE ALSO Royalty Trusts ; Securities Brokers & Dealers ; Venture Capital Firms ; Franchises ; Investment Guides - Online ; Mortgage Lenders & Loan Brokers ; Mutual Funds ; Investment Newsletters ; Real Estate Investment Trusts (REITs) ; Banks - Commercial & Savings ; Commodity Contracts Brokers & Dealers

			Toll-Free	Phone

ABRY Partners LLC
111 Huntington Ave 29th Fl . . . . Boston MA 02199   **800-777-3674**   617-859-2959

Adams Express Co
Seven St Paul St Ste 1140 . . . . Baltimore MD 21202   **800-638-2479**   410-752-5900
NYSE: ADX

Central Securities Corp
630 Fifth Ave Ste 820 . . . . New York NY 10111   **866-593-2507**   212-698-2020
NYSE: CET

				Toll-Free	Phone
Counsel Corp					
1211 Ave of the Americas Ste 2902	New York	NY	10036	**866-296-3743**	212-696-0100
NYSE: CXS					
DPEC Capital Inc					
135 Fifth Ave	New York	NY	10010	**844-574-3577**	301-590-6500
Enerplus Resources Fund					
333 Seventh Ave SW Ste 3000	Calgary	AB	T2P2Z1	**800-319-6462**	403-298-2200
Fidelity Investments Charitable Gift Fund					
PO Box 770001	Cincinnati	OH	45277	**800-262-6039**	
Haverford Trust Co					
Three Radnor Corp Ctr Ste 450	Radnor	PA	19087	**888-995-1979**	610-995-8700
HomeVestors of America Inc					
6500 Greenville Ave Ste 400	Dallas	TX	75206	**800-442-8937**	972-761-0046
Main Street Capital Corp					
1300 Post Oak Blvd	Houston	TX	77056	**800-966-1559**	713-350-6000
NYSE: MAIN					
Moors & Cabot Inc					
111 Devonshire St	Boston	MA	02109	**800-426-0501**	617-426-0500
Pembina Pipeline Corp					
700 Ninth Ave SW	Calgary	AB	T2P3V4	**888-428-3222**	403-231-7500
TSE: PPL					
Petroleum & Resources Corp					
Seven St Paul St Ste 1140	Baltimore	MD	21202	**800-638-2479**	410-752-5900
NYSE: PEO					
Superior Plus Income Fund					
840-7 Ave SW Ste 1400	Calgary	AB	T2P3G2	**866-490-7587**	403-218-2970
Thomas H Lee Partners					
100 Federal St 35th Fl	Boston	MA	02110	**877-456-3427**	617-227-1050

405 JANITORIAL & CLEANING SUPPLIES - WHOL

				Toll-Free	Phone
AmSan					
3031 N Andrews Ave Exd	Pompano Beach	FL	33064	**866-412-6726**	954-972-1700
Brady Industries Inc					
7055 Lindell Rd	Las Vegas	NV	89118	**800-293-4698**	702-876-3990
Culinary Depot Inc					
Two Melnick Dr	Monsey	NY	10952	**888-845-8200**	
Fitch Co 2201 Russell St	Baltimore	MD	21230	**800-933-4824**	410-539-1953
J. Ennis Fabrics Ltd					
12122 - 68 St	Edmonton	AB	T5B1R1	**800-663-6647**	
Kellermeyer Co					
475 W Woodland Cir	Bowling Green	OH	43402	**800-445-7415**	419-255-3022
Rose Products & Services Inc					
545 Stimmel Rd	Columbus	OH	43223	**800-264-1568**	614-443-7647
Taylor Freezers of California					
221 Harris Ct	South San Francisco	CA	94080	**877-978-4800**	

406 JEWELERS' FINDINGS & MATERIALS

				Toll-Free	Phone
Cyber-Rain Inc					
6345 Balboa Blvd Ste 230	Encino	CA	91316	**877-888-1452**	
David H Fell & Company Inc					
6009 Bandini Blvd	Commerce	CA	90040	**800-822-1996**	323-722-9992
Delta M Corp					
1003 Larsen Dr	Oak Ridge	TN	37830	**800-922-0083**	
Emme E2MS LLC PO Box 2251	Bristol	CT	06011	**800-396-0523**	
Findings Inc 160 Water St	Keene	NH	03431	**800-225-2706**	603-352-3717
Krohn Industries Inc					
PO Box 98	Carlstadt	NJ	07072	**800-526-6299**	201-933-9696
Lee's Morvillo Group					
160 Niantic Ave	Providence	RI	02907	**800-821-1700**	401-353-1740
Paul H Gesswein & Co					
255 Hancock Ave	Bridgeport	CT	06605	**800-544-2043**	203-366-5400
Precision Specialties Co					
1201 East Pecan St	Sherman	TX	75090	**800-527-3295**	
Rainwise Inc					
25 Federal St	Bar Harbor	ME	04609	**800-762-5723**	207-288-5169
Romanoff International Supply Corp					
Nine Deforest St	Amityville	NY	11701	**800-221-7448***	631-842-2400
*Cust Svc					
Stuller Settings Inc					
PO Box 87777	Lafayette	LA	70598	**800-877-7777**	
Victor Settings Inc					
25 Brook Ave	Maywood	NJ	07607	**800-322-9008**	201-845-4433

407 JEWELRY - COSTUME

				Toll-Free	Phone
1928 Jewelry Co					
3000 W Empire Ave	Burbank	CA	91504	**800-227-1928**	818-841-1928
A & Z Hayward Co					
655 Waterman Ave	East Providence	RI	02914	**800-556-7462**	401-438-0550
FGX International Inc					
500 George Washington Hwy	Smithfield	RI	02917	**800-480-4846**	401-231-3800

408 JEWELRY - PRECIOUS METAL

				Toll-Free	Phone
American Achievement Corp					
7211 Cir S Rd	Austin	TX	78745	**800-531-5055**	512-444-0571
Balfour 7211 Cir S Rd	Austin	TX	78745	**800-225-3687**	
Byard F Brogan Inc					
PO Box 0369	Glenside	PA	19038	**800-232-7642**	215-885-3550
Diablo Mfg Company Inc					
900 Golden Gate Terr PO Box 1108	Grass Valley	CA	95945	**800-551-2233***	530-272-2241
*Cust Svc					
Hammerman Bros Inc					
50 W 57th St 12th Fl	New York	NY	10019	**800-223-6436**	212-956-2800

				Toll-Free	Phone
Harry Klitzner Co, The					
530 Wellington Ave Ste 11	Cranston	RI	02910	**800-621-0161**	
Harry Winston Inc					
718 Fifth Ave	New York	NY	10019	**800-988-4110**	212-399-1000
Ira Green Inc					
177 Georgia Ave	Providence	RI	02905	**800-663-7487***	401-467-4770
*General					
Jacmel Jewelry Inc					
3030 47th Ave	Long Island City	NY	11101	**800-945-4300**	
James Avery Craftsman Inc					
145 Avery Rd N	Kerrville	TX	78029	**800-283-1770**	830-895-1122
Jostens Inc					
3601 Minnesota Ave Ste 400	Minneapolis	MN	55435	**800-235-4774**	952-830-3300
Kinsley & Sons Inc					
24 S Church St Ste A	Union	MO	63084	**800-468-4428***	
*General					
Maui Divers of Hawaii					
1520 Liona St	Honolulu	HI	96814	**800-462-4454**	808-946-7979
Mtm Recognition Corp					
3201 SE 29th St	Oklahoma City	OK	73115	**877-686-7464**	405-670-4545
Novell Design Studio					
129 Chestnut St	Roselle	NJ	07203	**888-668-3551**	
OC Tanner Co					
1930 S State St	Salt Lake City	UT	84115	**800-453-7490**	
Oro-Cal Mfg Company Inc					
1720 Bird St	Oroville	CA	95965	**800-367-6225**	530-533-5065
Ostbye & Anderson Inc					
10055 51st Ave N	Minneapolis	MN	55442	**866-553-1515**	763-553-1515
Relios Inc					
6815 Academy Pkwy W NE	Albuquerque	NM	87109	**800-827-6543**	505-345-5304
Robert S Fisher & Company Inc					
280 Sheffield St	Mountainside	NJ	07092	**800-526-8052**	908-928-0002
Stamper Black Hills Gold Jewelry					
7201 S Hwy 16	Rapid City	SD	57702	**800-843-8753***	605-342-0751
*Cust Svc					
Stanley Creations Inc					
1414 Willow Ave	Melrose Park	PA	19027	**800-220-1414**	215-635-6200
Sunshine Minting Inc					
7600 Mineral Dr Ste 700	Coeur d'Alene	ID	83815	**800-274-5837**	208-772-9592
Terryberry Co					
2033 Oak Industrial Dr NE	Grand Rapids	MI	49505	**800-253-0882**	616-458-1391
Tiffany & Co 727 Fifth Ave	New York	NY	10022	**800-526-0649***	212-755-8000
NYSE: TIF ■ *Orders					
Wheeler Mfg Co Inc					
107 Main Ave PO Box 629	Lemmon	SD	57638	**800-843-1937**	605-374-3848
Wright & Lato 2100 Felver Ct	Rahway	NJ	07065	**800-724-1855**	973-674-8700

409 JEWELRY STORES

				Toll-Free	Phone
Ben Bridge Jeweler Inc					
PO Box 1908	Seattle	WA	98111	**888-917-9171***	206-239-6811
*Cust Svc					
Ben Moss Jewellers					
300-201 Portage Ave	Winnipeg	MB	R3B3K6	**888-236-6677**	
Blue Nile Inc					
705 Fifth Ave S Ste 900	Seattle	WA	98104	**800-242-2728**	206-336-6700
NASDAQ: NILE					
Borsheim's Inc					
120 Regency Pkwy	Omaha	NE	68114	**800-642-4438**	402-391-0400
Coleman E Adler & Sons Inc					
722 Canal St Third Fl	New Orleans	LA	70130	**800-925-7912**	504-523-5292
DGSE Cos Inc 11311 Reeder Rd	Dallas	TX	75229	**800-527-5307**	972-484-3662
NYSE: DGSE					
Fantasy Diamond Corp					
1550 W Carrol Ave	Chicago	IL	60607	**800-621-4445**	312-583-3200
Finks Jewelry Inc					
3545 Electric Rd	Roanoke	VA	24018	**800-699-7464**	540-342-2991
Freeman Jewelers Inc					
76 Merchants Row	Rutland	VT	05701	**800-451-4167**	802-773-2792
H Stern Jewelers Inc					
645 Fifth Ave	New York	NY	10022	**800-747-8376**	212-688-0300
Harry Ritchie's Jewelers Inc					
956 Willamette St	Eugene	OR	97401	**800-935-2850***	541-686-1787
*Cust Svc					
Harry Winston Inc					
718 Fifth Ave	New York	NY	10019	**800-988-4110**	212-399-1000
Helzberg Diamonds					
1825 Swift Ave	North Kansas City	MO	64116	**800-669-7780**	816-842-7780
JewelryWeb.com Inc					
98 Cuttermill Rd Ste 464	Great Neck	NY	11021	**800-955-9245**	516-482-3982
Kay Jewelers 375 Ghent Rd	Akron	OH	44333	**800-681-8796**	330-668-5000
Lux Bond & Green Inc					
46 Lasalle Rd	West Hartford	CT	06107	**800-524-7336**	
Reeds Jewelers Inc					
PO Box 2229	Wilmington	NC	28402	**877-406-3266***	910-350-3100
*Orders					
Rogers Jewelry Co					
PO Box 3151	Modesto	CA	95353	**800-877-4221**	
Ross Simons Jewelers Inc					
Nine Ross Simons Dr	Cranston	RI	02920	**800-835-0919**	
Samuels Jewelers					
9607 Research Blvd Ste 100 Bldg F	Austin	TX	78759	**877-202-2870**	512-369-1400
Shane Co					
9790 E Arapahoe Rd	Greenwood Village	CO	80112	**866-467-4263**	
Tiffany & Co 727 Fifth Ave	New York	NY	10022	**800-526-0649***	212-755-8000
NYSE: TIF ■ *Orders					
Trabert & Hoeffer					
111 E Oak St	Chicago	IL	60611	**800-539-3573**	312-787-1654
Van Cleef & Arpels Inc					
744 Fifth Ave	New York	NY	10019	**877-826-2533**	212-896-9284
Zale Corp					
Zales Jewelers Div					
901 W Walnut Hill Ln	Irving	TX	75038	**800-311-5393***	972-580-4000
*Cust Svc					

	Toll-Free	Phone

Zale Corp Bailey Banks & Biddle Div
901 W Walnut Hill Ln ....Irving TX 75038 **800-468-9716*** 866-249-2593
*Cust Svc

410 — JEWELRY, WATCHES, GEMS - WHOL

	Toll-Free	Phone

Alishaev Bros Inc
20 W 47th St Ste 203 ....New York NY 10036 **877-859-6020**
Charles & Colvard Ltd
170 Southport Dr ....Morrisville NC 27560 **877-202-5467**
NASDAQ: CTHR
Circa Inc
415 Madison Ave 19th Fl ....New York NY 10017 **877-876-5493** 212-486-6013
Continental Coin Corp
5627 Sepulveda Blvd ....Van Nuys CA 91411 **800-552-6467** 818-781-4232
Empire Diamond Corp
350 Fifth Ave Ste 4000 ....New York NY 10118 **800-728-3425** 212-564-4777
Gemex Systems Inc
6040 W Executive Dr Ste A...................Mequon WI 53092 **866-694-3639** 262-242-1111
Gerson Co 1450 S Lone Elm Rd ....Olathe KS 66061 **800-444-8172** 913-262-7400
Jewel-Craft Inc
4122 Olympic Blvd ....Erlanger KY 41018 **800-525-5482** 859-282-2400
Joseph Blank Inc
62 W 47th St Ste 808 ....New York NY 10036 **800-223-7666** 212-575-9050
Kendra Scott Design Inc
1400 S Congress Ave Ste A-170 ....Austin TX 78704 **866-677-7023** 512-499-8400
Leo Wolleman Inc
45 W 45th St 10th Fl......................New York NY 10036 **800-223-5667** 212-840-1881
MA Reich & Co Inc
481 Franklin St ....Buffalo NY 14202 **800-746-7062** 716-856-4085
Metal Marketplace International (MMI)
718 Sansom St ....Philadelphia PA 19106 **800-523-9191** 215-592-8777
Mikimoto (America) Company Ltd
680 Fifth Ave Fourth Fl....................New York NY 10019 **800-223-4008** 212-457-4500
World Minerals Inc
130 Castilian Dr ....Goleta CA 93117 **800-893-4445** 805-562-0200

411 — JUVENILE DETENTION FACILITIES

SEE ALSO *Correctional & Detention Management (Privatized) ; Correctional Facilities - State*
Listings are organized alphabetically by states.

	Toll-Free	Phone

Arkansas Juvenile Access & Treatment Ctr
425 W Capitol Ste 1620 ....Little Rock AR 72201 **877-727-3468** 501-324-8900
Cuyahoga Hills Juvenile Correctional Facility
4321 Green Rd ....Highland Hills OH 44128 **800-872-3132** 216-464-8200
Fairbanks Youth Facility
1502 Wilbur St ....Fairbanks AK 99701 **800-478-2686** 907-451-2150
Ferris School
959 Centre Rd ....Wilmington DE 19805 **800-292-9582** 302-993-3800
Johnson Youth Ctr
3252 Hospital Dr ....Juneau AK 99801 **800-780-9972** 907-586-9433
Logansport Juvenile Correctional Facility
1118 S Rd 25 ....Logansport IN 46947 **800-800-5556** 574-753-7571
McLaughlin Youth Ctr
2600 Providence Dr ....Anchorage AK 99508 **800-478-2221** 907-261-4399
New Castle County Detention Ctr
963 Centre Rd ....Wilmington DE 19805 **800-969-4357** 302-633-3100
State Training School
3211 Edgington Ave ....Eldora IA 50627 **800-362-2178** 641-858-5402
Ventura Youth Correctional Facility
3100 Wright Rd ....Camarillo CA 93010 **866-232-5627** 805-485-7951
Woodland Hills Youth Development Ctr
3965 Stewarts Ln ....Nashville TN 37218 **855-418-1622** 615-532-2000

LABELS - FABRIC

SEE *Narrow Fabric Mills*

412 — LABELS - OTHER THAN FABRIC

	Toll-Free	Phone

Accurate Dial & Nameplate Inc
329 Mira Loma Ave ....Glendale CA 91204 **800-400-4455** 323-245-9181
Acro Labels Inc
2530 Wyandotte Rd ....Willow Grove PA 19090 **800-355-2235** 215-657-5366
AME Label Corp
25155 W Ave Stanford ....Valencia CA 91355 **866-278-9268** 661-257-2200
Arch Crown Tags Inc
460 Hillside Ave ....Hillside NJ 07205 **800-526-8353** 973-731-6300
Avery Dennison Corp
207 Goode Ave ....Glendale CA 91203 **888-567-4387*** 626-304-2000
NYSE: AVY ■ *Cust Svc*
Best Label Co
2900 Faber St ....Union City CA 94587 **800-637-5333** 510-489-5400
Blue Ribbon Tag & Label Corp
4035 N 29th Ave ....Hollywood FL 33020 **800-433-4974** 954-922-9292
Brady Corp
6555 W Good Hope Rd ....Milwaukee WI 53223 **800-541-1686*** 414-358-6600
NYSE: BRC ■ *Cust Svc*
Brady Identification Solutions
6555 W Good Hope Rd ....Milwaukee WI 53223 **800-537-8791*** 414-358-6600
Cust Svc
CCL Label Inc
161 Worcester Rd Ste 502 ....Framingham MA 01701 **877-240-9772** 508-872-4511
Cellotape Inc
47623 Fremont Blvd ....Fremont CA 94538 **800-231-0608** 510-651-5551
Clamp Swing Pricing Company Inc
8386 Capwell Dr ....Oakland CA 94621 **800-227-7615** 510-567-1600
Data Label Inc
1000 Spruce St ....Terre Haute IN 47807 **800-457-0676** 812-232-0408

	Toll-Free	Phone

DeskTop Labels
7277 Boone Ave N ....Minneapolis MN 55428 **800-241-9730**
Discount Labels Inc
4115 Profit Ct ....New Albany IN 47150 **800-995-9500**
East West Label Co
1000 E Hector St ....Conshohocken PA 19428 **800-441-7333** 610-825-0410
Ennis Inc PO Box D ....Wolfe City TX 75496 **800-527-1008**
General Data Co Inc
4354 Ferguson Dr ....Cincinnati OH 45245 **800-733-5252** 513-752-7978
Gilbreth Packaging Systems
3001 State Rd ....Croydon PA 19021 **800-630-2413**
Grand Rapids Label Co
2351 Oak Industrial Dr NE ....Grand Rapids MI 49505 **800-552-5215** 616-459-8134
Green Bay Packaging Inc
1700 Webster Ct ....Green Bay WI 54302 **800-236-8400** 920-433-5111
Harris Industries Inc
5181 Argosy Ave ....Huntington Beach CA 92649 **800-222-6866** 714-898-8048
Impact Label Corp
3434 S Burdick St ....Kalamazoo MI 49001 **800-820-0362** 269-381-4280
International Label & Printing Company Inc
2550 United Ln ....Elk Grove Village IL 60007 **800-244-1442**
Labelmaster Co
5724 N Pulaski Rd ....Chicago IL 60646 **800-621-5808** 773-478-0900
Labeltape Inc
5100 Beltway Dr SE ....Caledonia MI 49316 **800-928-4537** 616-698-1830
Lancer Label 301 S 74th St ....Omaha NE 68114 **800-228-7074***
Cust Svc
LGInternational
6700 SW Bradbury Ct ....Portland OR 97224 **800-345-0534** 503-620-0520
McCourt Label Co
20 Egbert Ln ....Lewis Run PA 16738 **800-458-2390** 814-362-3851
MPI Label Systems Inc
450 Courtney Rd ....Sebring OH 44672 **800-423-0442** 330-938-2134
National Printing Converters Inc
18 S Murphy Ave ....Brazil IN 47834 **800-877-6724** 812-448-2555
Northeast Data Services
1316 College Ave ....Elmira NY 14901 **800-699-5636*** 607-733-5541
Cust Svc
Phifer Inc
4400 Kauloosa Ave PO Box 1700 ....Tuscaloosa AL 35401 **800-633-5955** 205-345-2120
Print-O-Tape Inc
755 Tower Rd ....Mundelein IL 60060 **800-346-6311** 847-362-1476
Printed Systems
1265 Gillingham Rd ....Neenah WI 54956 **800-352-2332***
Sales
Quikstik Labels
220 Broadway ....Everett MA 02149 **800-225-3496** 617-389-7570
Reidler Decal Corp
264 Industrial Pk Rd PO Box 8 ....Saint Clair PA 17970 **800-628-7770**
Shamrock Scientific Specialty Systems Inc
34 Davis Dr ....Bellwood IL 60104 **800-323-0249** 708-547-9005
Smyth Cos Inc
1085 Snelling Ave N ....Saint Paul MN 55108 **800-473-3464** 651-646-4544
Spear Inc 5510 Courseview Dr ....Mason OH 45040 **800-627-7327** 513-459-1100
Spinnaker Coating Inc
518 E Water St ....Troy OH 45373 **800-543-9452** 937-332-6500
Tag-It Pacific Inc
21900 Burbank Blvd Ste 270 ....Woodland Hills CA 91367 **877-870-5176** 818-444-4100
Tape & Label Converters Inc
8231 Allport Ave ....Santa Fe Springs CA 90670 **888-285-2462** 562-945-3486
Tapecon Inc 10 Latta Rd ....Rochester NY 14612 **800-333-2407** 585-621-8400
TAPEMARK Co
1685 Marthaler Ln ....West Saint Paul MN 55118 **800-535-1998** 651-455-1611
Valmark Industries Inc
7900 National Dr ....Livermore CA 94550 **800-770-7074** 925-960-9900
Weber Marking Systems Inc
711 W Algonquin Rd ....Arlington Heights IL 60005 **800-843-4242*** 847-364-8500
Sales
Whitlam Label Company Inc
24800 Sherwood Ave ....Center Line MI 48015 **800-755-2235** 586-757-5100
Wright Global Graphics
5115 Prospect St ....Thomasville NC 27360 **800-678-9019** 336-472-4200
WS Packaging Group Inc
2571 S. Hemlock Rd ....Green Bay WI 54229 **800-236-3424** 800-818-5481

413 — LABOR UNIONS

	Toll-Free	Phone

AFT Healthcare
555 New Jersey Ave NW ....Washington DC 20001 **800-238-1133** 202-879-4491
Air Line Pilots Assn
535 Herndon Pkwy ....Herndon VA 20170 **877-331-1223** 703-689-2270
Amalgamated Transit Union (ATU)
5025 Wisconsin Ave NW Third Fl...........Washington DC 20016 **888-240-1196** 202-537-1645
American Federation of Government Employees
80 F St NW ....Washington DC 20001 **888-844-2343** 202-737-8700
American Federation of Labor & Congress of Industrial Organizations (AFL-CIO)
815 16th St NW ....Washington DC 20006 **877-850-4959** 202-637-5000
American Federation of Musicians of the US & Canada (AFM)
1501 Broadway Ste 600 ....New York NY 10036 **800-762-3444** 212-869-1330
American Federation of Teachers (AFT)
555 New Jersey Ave NW ....Washington DC 20001 **800-238-1133** 202-879-4400
Association of Professional Flight Attendants
1004 W Euless Blvd ....Euless TX 76040 **800-395-2732** 817-540-0108
Brotherhood of Locomotive Engineers & Trainmen (BLET)
1370 Ontario St Mezzanine Level ....Cleveland OH 44113 **877-772-5772** 216-241-2630
Directors Guild of America
7920 W Sunset Blvd ....Los Angeles CA 90046 **800-421-4173** 310-289-2000
Glass Molders Pottery Plastics & Allied Workers International Union
608 E Baltimore Pike ....Media PA 19063 **855-670-4787** 610-565-5051
Inlandboatmen's Union of the Pacific (IBU)
1711 W Nickerson St Ste D ....Seattle WA 98119 **800-562-6000** 206-284-6001
International Alliance of Theatrical Stage Employees Moving Picture Technicians (IATSE)
1430 Broadway 20th Fl....................New York NY 10018 **800-456-3863** 212-730-1770
International Assn of Bridge Structural Ornamental & Reinforcing Iron Workers
1750 New York Ave NW Ste 400 ....Washington DC 20006 **800-368-0105** 202-383-4800

			Toll-Free	Phone
International Longshore & Warehouse Union				
1188 Franklin St 4th Fl	San Francisco CA	94109	**866-266-0013**	415-775-0533
International Organization of Masters Mates & Pilots				
700 Maritime Blvd	Linthicum Heights MD	21090	**877-667-5522**	410-850-8700
International Union of Bricklayers & Allied Craftworkers (BAC)				
1776 eye St NW	Washington DC	20006	**888-880-8222**	202-783-3788
International Union of Painters & Allied Trades (IUPAT)				
7234 Pkwy Dr	Hanover MD	21076	**800-554-2479**	410-564-5900
International Union of Police Assn				
1549 Ringling Blvd Ste 600	Sarasota FL	34236	**800-247-4872**	941-487-2560
International Union Security Police & Fire Professionals of America (SPFPA)				
25510 Kelly Rd	Roseville MI	48066	**800-228-7492**	586-772-7250
National Air Traffic Controllers Assn (NATCA)				
1325 Massachusetts Ave NW	Washington DC	20005	**800-266-0895**	202-628-5451
Screen Actors Guild (SAG)				
5757 Wilshire Blvd	Los Angeles CA	90036	**800-724-0767**	323-954-1600
Seafarers International Union				
5201 Auth Way	Camp Springs MD	20746	**800-252-4674**	301-899-0675
Service Employees International Union				
1800 Massachusetts Ave NW	Washington DC	20036	**800-424-8592**	202-730-7000
Sheet Metal Workers International Assn (SMWIA)				
1750 New York Ave NW Sixth Fl	Washington DC	20006	**800-251-7045**	202-783-5880
Shopper Local				
2222 Sedwick Rd # 102	Durham NC	27713	**877-251-4592**	
Transportation Communications International Union				
3 Research Pl	Rockville MD	20850	**877-772-5772**	301-948-4910
Union of American Physicians & Dentists				
180 Grand Ave Ste 1380	Oakland CA	94612	**800-622-0909**	510-839-0193
United Brotherhood of Carpenters & Joiners of America				
101 Constitution Ave NW	Washington DC	20001	**800-530-5090**	202-546-6206
United Food & Commercial Workers International Union (UFCW)				
1775 K St NW	Washington DC	20006	**800-551-4010**	202-223-3111
United Scenic Artists				
29 W 38th St 15th Fl	New York NY	10018	**800-456-3863**	212-581-0300
United Transportation Union				
14600 Detroit Ave	Cleveland OH	44107	**800-558-8842**	216-228-9400
Writers Guild of America West (WGAw)				
7000 W Third St	Los Angeles CA	90048	**800-421-4182**	323-951-4000

414   LABORATORIES - DENTAL

SEE ALSO Laboratories - Medical

			Toll-Free	Phone
1 Biotechnology PO Box 758	Oneco FL	34264	**800-951-4246**	941-355-8451
American Health Associates				
671 Ohio Pk Ste K	Cincinnati IN	45245	**800-522-7556**	
Boos Dental Laboratory				
1000 Boone Ave N Ste 660	Golden Valley MN	55427	**800-333-2667**	763-544-1446
Cleveland HeartLab Inc				
6701 Carnegie Ave Ste 500	Cleveland OH	44103	**866-358-9828**	
Coast2Coast Diagnostics Inc				
600 N Tustin Ave Ste 110	Santa Ana CA	92705	**800-730-9263**	
Cytolab Pathology Services				
6825 216th St Sw	Lynnwood WA	98036	**800-845-6167**	425-712-8020
Dental Technologies Inc (DTI)				
5601 Arnold Rd	Dublin CA	94568	**800-229-0936**	925-829-3611
Elisa Act Biotechnologies				
109 Carpenter Dr	Sterling VA	20165	**800-553-5472**	
ExamWorks Inc				
3280 Peachtree Rd Ste 2625	Atlanta GA	30305	**877-628-4703**	
First Dental Health				
5771 Copley Dr Ste 101	San Diego CA	92111	**800-334-7244**	
Imaging Healthcare Specialists Medical Group Inc				
6256 Greenwich Dr Ste 150	San Diego CA	92122	**866-558-4320**	
Integrated Regional Laboratories Inc				
5361 NW 33rd Ave	Ft. Lauderdale FL	33309	**800-522-0232**	
Kimball Genetics Inc				
8490 Upland Dr Ste 100	Englewood CO	80112	**800-444-9111**	
LifeScan Laboratory Inc				
5255 W Golf	Skokie IL	60077	**800-270-0037**	
Modern Dental Laboratory USA LLC				
13228 SE 30th St Ste C-6	Bellevue WA	98005	**877-711-8778**	
Molecular Imaging Services Inc				
10 Whitaker Ct	Bear DE	19701	**866-937-8855**	
PersonalizeDx				
17500 Red Hill Ave Ste 210	Irvine CA	92614	**877-429-6643**	
Posca Bros Dental Laboratory Inc				
641 W Willow St	Long Beach CA	90806	**800-537-6722**	562-427-1811
Roe Dental Laboratory Inc				
9565 Midwest Ave	Garfield Heights OH	44125	**800-228-6663**	216-663-2233
Roman Research Inc				
800 Franklin St	Hanson MA	02341	**800-225-8652**	

415   LABORATORIES - DRUG-TESTING

SEE ALSO Laboratories - Medical

			Toll-Free	Phone
Bio-Reference Laboratories Inc				
481 Edward H Ross Dr	Elmwood Park NJ	07407	**800-229-5227**	201-421-2001
NASDAQ: BRLI				
LabOne Inc 10101 Renner Blvd	Lenexa KS	66219	**800-646-7788**	913-888-1770
MEDTOX Scientific Inc				
402 W County Rd D	Saint Paul MN	55112	**800-832-3244**	651-636-7466
NASDAQ: MTOX				
US Drug Testing Laboratories Inc				
1700 S Mt Prospect Rd	Des Plaines IL	60018	**800-235-2367**	847-375-0770

416   LABORATORIES - GENETIC TESTING

SEE ALSO Laboratories - Medical

			Toll-Free	Phone
Blood Systems Laboratories				
2424 W Erie Dr	Tempe AZ	85282	**800-288-2199**	602-343-7000

			Toll-Free	Phone
BRT Laboratories Inc				
400 W Franklin St	Baltimore MD	21201	**800-765-5170**	410-225-9595
Cellmark Forensics				
13988 Diplomat Dr Ste 100	Dallas TX	75234	**800-752-2774**	214-271-8400
Center for Genetic Testing at Saint Francis				
6465 S Yale Ave	Tulsa OK	74136	**877-789-6001**	918-502-1720
Clinical Testing & Research Inc				
20 Wilsey Sq	Ridgewood NJ	07450	**888-837-5267**	
Commonwealth Biotechnologies Inc				
601 Biotech Dr	Richmond VA	23235	**800-735-9224**	804-648-3820
DNA Diagnostics Ctr				
1 DDC Way	Fairfield OH	45014	**800-362-2368**	513-881-7800
DNA Paternity Lab of Utah				
2749 E Parleys Way Ste 100	Salt Lake City UT	84109	**800-362-5559**	801-466-3872
Genetic Profiles Corp				
10675 Treena St Ste 103	San Diego CA	92131	**800-551-7763**	
Genetica DNA Laboratories Inc				
8740 Montgomery Rd	Cincinnati OH	45236	**800-433-6848**	513-985-9777
GenQuest DNA Analysis Laboratory				
133 Coney Island Dr	Sparks NV	89431	**877-362-5227**	775-358-0652
Genzyme Genetics				
3400 Computer Dr	Westborough MA	01581	**800-255-7357**	508-898-9001
Identity Genetics Inc				
47047 213th St	Aurora SD	57002	**800-861-1054**	
Laboratory Corp of America Holdings				
358 S Main St	Burlington NC	27215	**800-334-5161**	336-584-5171
NYSE: LH				
LABS Inc				
6933 S Revere Pkwy	Centennial CO	80112	**866-393-2244**	720-528-4750
Maxxam Analytics Inc				
335 LaiRd Rd Unit 2	Guelph ON	N1G4P7	**877-706-7678**	905-288-2150
Medical Genetics Consultants				
819 DeSoto St	Ocean Springs MS	39564	**800-362-4363**	
Memorial Blood Centers (MBC)				
737 Pelham Blvd	Saint Paul MN	55114	**888-448-3253***	651-332-7000
*Cust Svc				
Molecular Pathology Laboratory Network Inc				
250 E Broadway	Maryville TN	37804	**800-932-2943**	865-380-9746
NMS Labs 3701 Welsh Rd	Willow Grove PA	19090	**800-522-6671**	215-657-4900
Paternity Testing Corp (PTC)				
300 Portland St	Columbia MO	65201	**888-837-8323**	573-442-9948
Rhode Island Blood Ctr				
405 Promenade St	Providence RI	02908	**800-283-8385**	401-453-8360
South Texas Blood & Tissue Ctr				
6211 IH-10 W	San Antonio TX	78201	**800-292-5534**	210-731-5555
University of North Texas Health Science Ctr				
3500 Camp Bowie Blvd	Fort Worth TX	76107	**800-687-7580**	817-735-2000

417   LABORATORIES - MEDICAL

SEE ALSO Laboratories - Dental ; Laboratories - Drug-Testing ; Laboratories - Genetic Testing ; Organ & Tissue Banks ; Blood Centers

			Toll-Free	Phone
Accugenix Inc 223 Lake Dr	Newark DE	19702	**800-886-9654**	302-292-8888
Ariosa Diagnostics Inc				
5945 Optical Ct	San Jose CA	95138	**855-927-4672**	
Atherotech Inc				
201 London Pkwy	Birmingham AL	35211	**800-719-9807**	
Aurum Ceramic Dental Laboratories Ltd				
115 17 Ave SW	Calgary AB	T2S0A1	**800-665-8815**	403-228-5120
Bio-Reference Laboratories Inc				
481 Edward H Ross Dr	Elmwood Park NJ	07407	**800-229-5227**	201-421-2001
NASDAQ: BRLI				
Calvert Labs				
1225 Crescent Green Ste 115	Cary NC	27518	**800-300-8114**	919-459-8653
Canadian Medical Laboratories Ltd				
6560 Kennedy Rd	Mississauga ON	L5T2X4	**800-263-0801**	
Cell Signaling Technology Inc				
Three Trask Ln	Danvers MA	01923	**877-678-8324**	978-867-2300
Centrex Clinical Laboratories Inc				
28 Campion Rd	New Hartford NY	13413	**800-753-8653**	315-797-0791
DIANON Systems Inc				
One Forest Pkwy	Shelton CT	06484	**800-328-2666**	203-926-7100
Equipoise Dental Laboratory Inc				
85 Portland Ave	Bergenfield NJ	07621	**800-999-4950**	201-385-4750
Genova Diagnostics				
63 Zillicoa St	Asheville NC	28801	**800-522-4762**	828-253-0621
Global Neuro-Diagnostics LP				
2670 Firewheel Dr Ste B	Flower Mound TX	75028	**866-848-2522**	
Health Network Laboratory				
2024 Lehigh St	Allentown PA	18103	**877-402-4221**	610-402-8170
Keller Laboratories Inc				
160 Larkin Williams Industrial Ct	Fenton MO	63026	**800-325-3056**	636-600-4200
LabOne Inc 10101 Renner Blvd	Lenexa KS	66219	**800-646-7788**	913-888-1770
Laboratory Corp of America Holdings				
358 S Main St	Burlington NC	27215	**800-334-5161**	336-584-5171
NYSE: LH				
Medical Diagnostic Laboratories LLC				
2439 Kuser Rd	Hamilton NJ	08690	**877-269-0090**	609-570-1000
National Genetics Institute				
2440 S Blvd Ste 235	Los Angeles CA	90064	**800-352-7788**	310-996-0036
NMS Labs 3701 Welsh Rd	Willow Grove PA	19090	**800-522-6671**	215-657-4900
North Coast Clinical Laboratory Inc				
2215 Cleveland Rd	Sandusky OH	44870	**800-325-5737**	419-626-6012
Parkway Clinical Laboratories Inc				
3494 Progress Dr	Bensalem PA	19020	**800-327-2764**	215-245-5112
Path Logic Inc				
950 Riverside Pkwy Ste 90	West Sacramento CA	95605	**855-291-4528**	
Physician's Automated Laboratory Inc (PALLAB)				
9830 Brimhall Rd	Bakersfield CA	93312	**800-675-2271**	661-829-2260
Quest Diagnostics at Nichols Institute				
33608 Ortega Hwy	San Juan Capistrano CA	92675	**800-642-4657**	949-728-4000
Quest Diagnostics Inc				
Three Giralda Farms	Madison NJ	07940	**800-222-0446**	201-393-5000
NYSE: DGX				

					Toll-Free	Phone

South Bend Medical Foundation
530 N Lafayette Blvd . . . . South Bend IN 46601 **800-544-0925** 574-234-4176

Specialty Laboratories Inc
27027 Tourney Rd . . . . Valencia CA 91355 **800-421-7110*** 661-799-6543
*Sales

Sunrise Medical Laboratories Inc
250 Miller Pl . . . . Hicksville NY 11801 **800-782-0282*** 631-435-1515
*Cust Svc

US LABS Inc 2601 Campus Dr . . . . Irvine CA 92612 **888-875-2270** 800-710-1800

VCA Antech Inc
12401 W Olympic Blvd . . . . Los Angeles CA 90064 **800-966-1822** 310-571-6500
NASDAQ: WOOF

418 LABORATORY ANALYTICAL INSTRUMENTS

SEE ALSO Glassware - Laboratory & Scientific ; Laboratory Apparatus & Furniture

					Toll-Free	Phone

Abaxis Inc
3240 Whipple Rd . . . . Union City CA 94587 **800-822-2947** 510-675-6500
NASDAQ: ABAX

American Biologics
1180 Walnut Ave . . . . Chula Vista CA 91911 **800-227-4473** 619-429-8200

BD Biosciences
2350 Qume Dr . . . . San Jose CA 95131 **800-223-8226** 408-432-9475

Bio/Data Corp PO Box 347 . . . . Horsham PA 19044 **800-257-3282** 215-441-4000

Bioanalytical Systems Inc
2701 Kent Ave . . . . West Lafayette IN 47906 **800-845-4246** 765-463-4527
NASDAQ: BASI

BioTek Instruments Inc
100 Tigan St PO Box 998 . . . . Winooski VT 05404 **888-451-5171** 802-655-4740

Buehler Ltd
41 Waukegan Rd . . . . Lake Bluff IL 60044 **800-283-4537*** 847-295-6500
*Sales

California Analytical Instruments Inc
1312 W Grove Ave . . . . Orange CA 92865 **800-959-0949** 714-974-5560

Caliper Life Sciences Inc
68 Elm St . . . . Hopkinton MA 01748 **800-762-4000** 508-435-9500

CAO Group Inc
4628 Skyhawk Dr . . . . West Jordan UT 84084 **877-877-9778** 801-256-9282

CDS Analytical Inc
465 Limestone Rd PO Box 277 . . . . . . Oxford PA 19363 **800-541-6593** 610-932-3636

CEM Corp
3100 Smith Farm Rd . . . . Matthews NC 28104 **800-726-3331** 704-821-7015

Cepheid
904 E Caribbean Dr . . . . Sunnyvale CA 94089 **888-838-3222** 408-541-4191
NASDAQ: CPHD

Cetac Technologies Inc
14306 Industrial Rd . . . . Omaha NE 68144 **800-369-2822** 402-733-2829

CMI Inc 316 E Ninth St . . . . Owensboro KY 42303 **866-835-0690** 270-685-6545

CompuMed Inc
5777 W Century Blvd Ste 360 . . . . . Los Angeles CA 90045 **800-421-3395** 310-258-5000

Corning Inc Life Sciences Div
836 N St Bldg 300 Ste 3401 . . . . . . Tewksbury MA 01876 **800-492-1110** 978-442-2200

Datacolor
5 Princess Rd . . . . Lawrenceville NJ 08648 **800-340-1007*** 609-924-2189
*General

FEI Co
5350 NE Dawson Creek Dr . . . . Hillsboro OR 97124 **866-693-3426*** 503-640-7500
NASDAQ: FEIC ■ *Cust Svc

Gambro BCT
10811 W Collins Ave . . . . Lakewood CO 80215 **877-339-4228** 303-231-4357

GrayWolf Sensing Solutions LLC
Six Research Dr . . . . Shelton CT 06484 **800-218-7997** 203-402-0477

Hach Co PO Box 389 . . . . Loveland CO 80539 **800-227-4224** 970-669-3050

Hamilton Co 4970 Energy Way . . . . . . Reno NV 89502 **800-648-5950** 775-858-3000

Harvard Bioscience Inc
84 October Hill Rd . . . . Holliston MA 01746 **800-272-2775** 508-893-8999
NASDAQ: HBIO

Helena Laboratories Inc
1530 Lindbergh Dr . . . . Beaumont TX 77704 **800-231-5663** 409-842-3714

Horiba Instruments Inc
17671 Armstrong Ave . . . . Irvine CA 92614 **800-446-7422** 949-250-4811

hygiena LLC
941 Avenida Acaso . . . . Camarillo CA 93012 **877-494-4364** 805-388-8007

Illumina Inc
9885 Towne Centre Dr . . . . San Diego CA 92121 **800-809-4566** 858-202-4500
NASDAQ: ILMN

Instrumentation Laboratory Inc
180 Hartwell Rd . . . . Bedford MA 01730 **800-955-9525*** 781-861-0710
*Sales

IRIS International Inc
9172 Eton Ave . . . . Chatsworth CA 91311 **877-920-4747** 818-709-1244
NASDAQ: IRIS

ISCO Inc
4700 Superior St PO Box 82531 . . . . . . Lincoln NE 68501 **800-228-4250** 402-464-0231

Labcon North America Inc
3700 Lkeville Hwy . . . . Petaluma CA 94954 **800-227-1466** 707-766-2100

LaMotte Co
802 Washington Ave . . . . Chestertown MD 21620 **800-344-3100** 410-778-3100

Leco Corp
3000 Lakeview Ave . . . . Saint Joseph MI 49085 **800-292-6141** 269-985-5496

Li Cor Inc PO Box 4425 . . . . Lincoln NE 68504 **800-447-3576** 402-467-3576

Luminex Corp
12212 Technology Blvd . . . . Austin TX 78727 **888-219-8020** 512-219-8020
NASDAQ: LMNX

Mandel Scientific Company Inc
Two Admiral Pl . . . . Guelph ON N1G4N4 **888-883-3636** 519-763-9292

Micromeritics Instrument Corp
1 Micromeritics Dr . . . . Norcross GA 30093 **800-229-5052** 770-662-3620

Modal Shop Inc, The
1776 Mentor Ave . . . . Cincinnati OH 45212 **800-860-4867** 513-351-9919

Molecular Devices Inc (MDI)
1311 Orleans Dr Ste 408 . . . . Sunnyvale CA 94089 **800-635-5577** 408-747-1700

Monogram Biosciences Inc
345 Oyster Pt Blvd . . . . . . South San Francisco CA 94080 **800-777-0177** 650-635-1100

MPD Inc 316 E Ninth St . . . . Owensboro KY 42303 **866-225-5673** 270-685-6200

Nova Biomedical Corp
200 Prospect St . . . . Waltham MA 02454 **800-458-5813*** 781-894-0800
*Sales

OI Corp
151 Graham Rd PO Box 9010 . . . . . College Station TX 77842 **800-653-1711** 979-690-1711

Olis Inc
130 Conway Dr Ste A B & C . . . . Bogart GA 30622 **800-852-3504** 706-353-6547

Pall Life Sciences
600 S Wagner Rd . . . . Ann Arbor MI 48103 **800-521-1520** 734-665-0651

Particle Measuring Systems Inc
5475 Airport Blvd . . . . Boulder CO 80301 **800-238-1801*** 303-443-7100
*Cust Svc

Photo Research Inc
9731 Topanga Canyon Pl . . . . Chatsworth CA 91311 **877-424-6423** 818-341-5151

Physical Electronics Inc
18725 Lake Dr E . . . . Chanhassen MN 55317 **800-328-7515** 952-828-6100

Response Biomedical Corp
1781 75th Ave W . . . . Vancouver BC V6P6P2 **888-591-5577** 604-456-6010
TSE: RBM

Sakura Finetek USA Inc
1750 W 214th St . . . . Torrance CA 90501 **800-725-8723** 310-972-7800

Schroer Manufacturing Co
511 Osage Ave . . . . Kansas City KS 66105 **800-444-1579** 913-281-1500

Scientific Industries Inc
70 Orville Dr . . . . Bohemia NY 11716 **888-850-6208** 631-567-4700

SEER Technology Inc
2681 Parleys Way Ste 201 . . . . . . Salt Lake City UT 84109 **877-505-7337** 801-746-7888

Shimadzu Scientific Instruments Inc
7102 Riverwood Dr . . . . Columbia MD 21046 **800-477-1227** 410-381-1227

Soilmoisture Equipment Corp
801 S Kellogg Ave . . . . Goleta CA 93117 **888-964-0040** 805-964-3525

Spectrum Laboratories Inc
18617 Broadwick St . . . . . . Rancho Dominguez CA 90220 **800-634-3300** 310-885-4600

Spectrum Systems Inc
3410 W Nine-Mile Rd . . . . Pensacola FL 32526 **800-432-6119** 850-944-3392

STARR Life Sciences Corp
333 Alegheney Ave Ste 300 . . . . Oakmont PA 15139 **866-978-2779**

Supelco
595 N Harrison Rd . . . . Bellefonte PA 16823 **800-247-6628** 814-359-3441

Tekran Instruments Corp
230 Tech Ctr Dr . . . . Knoxville TN 37912 **888-383-5726** 865-688-0688

Temptronic Corp
41 Hampden Rd . . . . Mansfield MA 02048 **800-558-5080*** 781-688-2300
*Tech Support

Thermo Fisher Scientific Inc
81 Wyman St PO Box 9046 . . . . Waltham MA 02454 **800-678-5599** 781-622-1000
NYSE: TMO

Toptica Photonics Inc
1286 Blossom Dr Ste 1 . . . . Victor NY 14564 **877-277-9897** 585-657-6663

Transgenomic Inc
12325 Emmet St . . . . Omaha NE 68164 **888-233-9283** 402-452-5400
OTC: TBIO

Upchurch Scientific Inc
619 Oak St . . . . Oak Harbor WA 98277 **866-339-4653**

Waters Corp 34 Maple St . . . . Milford MA 01757 **800-252-4752** 508-478-2000
NYSE: WAT

419 LABORATORY APPARATUS & FURNITURE

SEE ALSO Scales & Balances ; Glassware - Laboratory & Scientific ; Laboratory Analytical Instruments

					Toll-Free	Phone

Baker Company Inc
161 Gatehouse Rd PO Box E . . . . Sanford ME 04073 **800-992-2537** 207-324-8773

Bel-Art Products Inc
Six Industrial Rd . . . . Pequannock NJ 07440 **800-423-5278** 973-694-0500

Boekel Scientific
855 Pennsylvania Blvd . . . . Feasterville PA 19053 **800-336-6929** 215-396-8200

Caliper Life Sciences Inc
68 Elm St . . . . Hopkinton MA 01748 **800-762-4000** 508-435-9500

Cole-Parmer Instrument Co
625 E Bunker Ct . . . . Vernon Hills IL 60061 **800-323-4340** 847-549-7600

Corning Inc Life Sciences Div
836 N St Bldg 300 Ste 3401 . . . . . . Tewksbury MA 01876 **800-492-1110** 978-442-2200

Edstrom Industries Inc
819 Bakke Ave . . . . Waterford WI 53185 **800-558-5913** 262-534-5181

Ika-Works Inc
2635 Northchase Pkwy SE . . . . . . Wilmington NC 28405 **800-733-3037** 910-452-7059

Kalamazoo Technical Furniture
6450 Vly Industrial Dr . . . . Kalamazoo MI 49009 **800-832-5227**

Kewaunee Scientific Corp
2700 W Front St PO Box 1842 . . . . . . Statesville NC 28687 **800-824-6626** 704-873-7202
NASDAQ: KEQU

Knf Neuberger Inc
2 Black Forest Rd . . . . Trenton NJ 08691 **800-323-4340** 609-890-8600

Labconco Corp
8811 Prospect Ave . . . . Kansas City MO 64132 **800-821-5525*** 816-333-8811
*Cust Svc

Nalge Nunc International
75 Panorama Creek Dr . . . . Rochester NY 14625 **800-625-4327** 585-586-8800

New Brunswick Scientific Company Inc
44 Talmadge Rd PO Box 4005 . . . . Edison NJ 08818 **800-631-5417*** 732-287-1200
*Cust Svc

Omnicell Inc
1201 Charleston Rd . . . . Mountain View CA 94043 **800-850-6664** 650-251-6100
NASDAQ: OMCL

Pacific Combustion Engineering Co
2107 Border Ave . . . . Torrance CA 90501 **800-342-4442** 310-212-6300

Parr Instrument Co
211 53rd St . . . . Moline IL 61265 **800-872-7720** 309-762-7716

Parter Medical Products Inc
17015 Kingsview Ave . . . . Carson CA 90746 **800-666-8282** 310-327-4417

Percival Scientific Inc
505 Research Dr . . . . Perry IA 50220 **800-695-2743** 515-465-9363

Preston Industries Inc
6600 W Touhy Ave . . . . Niles IL 60714 **800-229-7569** 847-647-0611

				Toll-Free	Phone
Samco Scientific Corp					
81 WYMAN ST PO Box 9046	Waltham	MA	02451	**800-522-3359**	781-622-1000
Thermo Fisher Scientific Inc					
81 Wyman St PO Box 9046	Waltham	MA	02454	**800-678-5599**	781-622-1000
NYSE: TMO					
ThermoGenesis Corp					
2711 Citrus Rd	Rancho Cordova	CA	95742	**800-783-8357**	916-858-5100
NASDAQ: KOOL					
Thomas Scientific					
1654 High Hill Rd PO Box 99	Swedesboro	NJ	08085	**800-345-2100**	856-467-2000
Valley City Mfg Co Ltd, The					
64 Hatt St	Dundas	ON	L9H2G3	**800-306-3319**	905-628-2253

420 LADDERS

				Toll-Free	Phone
ALACO Ladder Co 5167 G St	Chino	CA	91710	**888-310-7040**	909-591-7561
Ballymore Co					
501 Gunnard Carlson Dr	Coatesville	PA	19365	**800-762-8327**	610-593-5062
Cotterman Co					
130 Seltzer Rd	Croswell	MI	48422	**800-552-3337**	810-679-4400
Lynn Ladder & Scaffolding Company Inc					
20 Boston St	Lynn	MA	01904	**800-225-2510**	781-598-6010
Werner Co 93 Werner Rd	Greenville	PA	16125	**888-523-3371**	
Wing Enterprises Inc					
1198 N Spring Creek	Springville	UT	84663	**866-872-5901**	801-489-3684

421 LANDSCAPE DESIGN & RELATED SERVICES

				Toll-Free	Phone
Artistic Maintenance Inc					
23676 Birtcher Dr	Lake Forest	CA	92630	**800-698-9834***	949-581-9817
*General					
Cagwin & Dorward Inc					
1565 S Novato Blvd Ste B	Novato	CA	94947	**800-891-7710**	415-892-7710
Creative Environments					
8920 S Hardy Dr	Tempe	AZ	85284	**855-777-9305**	480-458-4100
Environmental Earthscapes Inc					
5075 S Swan Rd	Tucson	AZ	85706	**800-571-1575**	520-571-1575
Landscape Concepts Management					
31745 Alleghany Rd	Grayslake	IL	60030	**866-655-3800**	847-223-3800
Lipinski Landscape & Irrigation Contractors Inc					
100 Sharp Rd	Marlton	NJ	08053	**800-644-6035**	
Mission Landscape Services Inc					
536 E Dyer Rd	Santa Ana	CA	92707	**800-545-9963**	
Teufel Nursery Inc					
3431 NW John Olsen Pl	Hillsboro	OR	97124	**800-483-8335**	503-646-1111
US Lawns					
4700 Millenia Blvd Ste 240	Orlando	FL	32839	**800-875-2967**	

422 LANGUAGE SCHOOLS

SEE ALSO Translation Services

				Toll-Free	Phone
Agape English Language Institute (AELI)					
610 Pickens St PO Box 12504	Columbia	SC	29201	**877-476-2354**	803-799-3452
American Language Communication Ctr					
229 W 36th St	New York	NY	10018	**800-364-5474**	212-736-2373
AmeriSpan Unlimited					
1334 Walnut St 6 Fl	Philadelphia	PA	19107	**800-879-6640**	215-751-1100
Boston Academy of English					
38 Chauncy St Eighth Fl	Boston	MA	02111	**800-704-9313**	
Boston Academy of English inc					
38 Chauncy St 8th Fl	Boston	MA	02111	**800-704-9313**	
Cultural Ctr for Language Studies					
3191 Coral Way Ste 114	Miami	FL	33145	**800-704-8181**	305-529-2257
Diplomatic Language Services LLC					
1901 N Ft Myer Dr Sixth Fl	Arlington	VA	22209	**800-642-7974**	703-243-4855
ELS Language Centers					
7 Roszel Rd	Princeton	NJ	08540	**800-468-8978**	609-759-5500
ESL Instruction & Consulting Inc					
42 Broad St NW	Atlanta	GA	30303	**877-579-2366**	404-577-2366
Intercultural Communications College					
810 Richards St Ste 200	Honolulu	HI	96813	**800-545-2078**	808-946-2445
International Ctr for Language Studies Inc					
1133 15th St NW Ste 600	Washington	DC	20005	**800-626-2427**	202-639-8800
Language Exchange International					
500 NE Spanish River Blvd Ste 19	Boca Raton	FL	33431	**800-223-5836**	561-368-3913
Lingua School Inc					
225 E Las Olas Blvd Sixth Fl	Fort Lauderdale	FL	33301	**888-654-6482**	954-577-9955
POLY Languages Institute Inc (POLY)					
5757 Wilshire Blvd Ste 510	Los Angeles	CA	90036	**877-738-5787**	323-933-9399

423 LASER EQUIPMENT & SYSTEMS - MEDICAL

SEE ALSO Medical Instruments & Apparatus - Mfr

				Toll-Free	Phone
BioLase Technology Inc					
Four Cromwell	Irvine	CA	92618	**800-699-9462**	888-424-6527
Candela Corp					
530 Boston Post Rd	Wayland	MA	01778	**800-733-8550**	508-358-7400
NASDAQ: CLZR					
Convergent Laser Technologies					
1660 S Loop Rd	Alameda	CA	94502	**800-848-8200**	510-832-2130
Cynosure Inc					
Five Carlisle Rd	Westford	MA	01886	**800-886-2966**	978-256-4200
NASDAQ: CYNO					
Iridex Corp					
1212 Terra Bella Ave	Mountain View	CA	94043	**800-388-4747***	650-940-4700
NASDAQ: IRIX ■ *Cust Svc					
Laserscope 3070 Orchard Dr	San Jose	CA	95134	**800-878-3399**	408-943-0636

				Toll-Free	Phone
Lumenis Ltd					
2033 Gateway Pl Ste 200	San Jose	CA	95110	**877-586-3647**	408-764-3000
PhotoMedex Inc					
147 Keystone Dr	Montgomeryville	PA	18936	**800-366-4758**	215-619-3600
NASDAQ: PHMD					
Spectranetics Corp					
9965 Federal Dr	Colorado Springs	CO	80921	**800-231-0978**	719-447-2000
NASDAQ: SPNC					
Trimedyne Inc					
15091 Bake Pkwy	Irvine	CA	92618	**800-733-5273**	949-559-5300
OTC: TMED					

424 LASERS - INDUSTRIAL

				Toll-Free	Phone
AGL Corp					
2202 N Redmond Rd PO Box 189	Jacksonville	AR	72076	**800-643-9696**	501-982-4433
Coherent Inc					
5100 Patrick Henry Dr	Santa Clara	CA	95054	**800-527-3786***	408-764-4000
NASDAQ: COHR ■ *Sales					
Continuum					
3150 Central Expy	Santa Clara	CA	95051	**888-532-1064**	408-727-3240
Electro Scientific Industries Inc					
13900 NW Science Pk Dr	Portland	OR	97229	**800-331-4708***	503-641-4141
NASDAQ: ESIO ■ *Cust Svc					
GSI Group Inc					
125 Middlesex Tpke	Bedford	MA	01730	**800-342-3757**	781-266-5700
NASDAQ: GSIG					
IPG Photonics Corp					
50 Old Webster Rd	Oxford	MA	01540	**877-980-1550**	508-373-1100
NASDAQ: IPGP					
Laser Excel					
N6323 Berlin Rd PO Box 279	Green Lake	WI	54941	**800-285-6544**	920-294-6544
Leica Geosystems Inc					
3498 Kraft Ave SE	Grand Rapids	MI	49512	**800-367-9453***	616-977-4189
*Sales					
Synrad Inc 4600 Campus Pl	Mukilteo	WA	98275	**800-796-7231**	425-349-3500

425 LAUNDRY & DRYCLEANING SERVICES

SEE ALSO Linen & Uniform Supply

				Toll-Free	Phone
Admiral Inc 10 Taylor Ave	Annapolis	MD	21401	**800-864-4429**	410-267-8381
Coinmach Service Corp					
303 Sunnyside Blvd Ste 70	Plainview	NY	11803	**877-264-6622**	516-349-8555
Crown Management Services Inc					
1501 N Guillemard St	Pensacola	FL	32501	**800-844-5280**	850-438-7578
Martinizing Dry Cleaning					
8944 Columbia Rd Ste J	Loveland	OH	45140	**800-827-0207**	
Nu-Yale Cleaners					
6300 Hwy 62	Jeffersonville	IN	47130	**888-644-7400**	812-285-7400
Pressed4Time Inc					
Eight Clock Tower Pl Ste 110	Maynard	MA	01754	**800-423-8711**	

LAUNDRY EQUIPMENT - HOUSEHOLD

SEE Appliances - Major - Mfr ; Appliances - Whol

426 LAUNDRY EQUIPMENT & SUPPLIES - COMMERCIAL & INDUSTRIAL

				Toll-Free	Phone
Coinmach Service Corp					
303 Sunnyside Blvd Ste 70	Plainview	NY	11803	**877-264-6622**	516-349-8555
Colmac Industries Inc					
PO Box 72	Colville	WA	99114	**800-926-5622**	509-684-4505
Edro Corp					
37 Commerce St	East Berlin	CT	06023	**800-628-6434***	860-828-0311
*Sales					
Ellis Corp					
1400 W Bryn Mawr Ave	Itasca	IL	60143	**800-611-6806**	630-250-9222
GA Braun Inc					
461 E Brighton Ave	Syracuse	NY	13212	**800-432-7286**	315-475-3123
Kemco Systems Inc					
11500 47th St N	Clearwater	FL	33762	**800-633-7055**	727-573-2323
Minnesota Chemical Co					
2285 Hampden Ave	Saint Paul	MN	55114	**800-328-5689**	651-646-7521
Thermal Engineering of Arizona Inc					
2250 W Wetmore Rd	Tucson	AZ	85705	**866-832-7278**	520-888-4000

427 LAW FIRMS

SEE ALSO Litigation Support Services ; Arbitration Services - Legal ; Legal Professionals Associations ; Bar Associations - State

				Toll-Free	Phone
Arnold & Porter LLP					
555 12th St NW	Washington	DC	20004	**877-470-8792**	202-942-5000
Barnes & Thornburg					
11 S Meridian St	Indianapolis	IN	46204	**800-236-1352**	317-236-1313
Boies Schiller & Flexner LLP					
5301 Wisconsin Ave NW	Washington	DC	20015	**877-224-0464**	202-237-2727
Buchanan Ingersoll & Rooney PC					
301 Grant St 1 Oxford Ctr 20th Fl	Pittsburgh	PA	15219	**800-444-6738**	412-562-8800
Cavanagh Law Firm, The					
1850 N Central Ave	Phoenix	AZ	85004	**888-824-3476**	602-322-4000
Clark, Gagliardi & Miller PC					
99 Court St	White Plains	NY	10601	**800-734-5694**	
Cochran Firm LLC					
111 E Main St	Dothan	AL	36301	**800-843-3476**	334-793-1555
Cohen & Grigsby Pc					
625 Liberty Ave	Pittsburgh	PA	15222	**800-235-8619**	412-297-4900

				Toll-Free	Phone
Cooley Godward Kronish LLP 3000 El Camino Real	Palo Alto	CA	94306	**888-654-2411**	650-843-5000
Cozen O'Connor 1900 Market St	Philadelphia	PA	19103	**800-523-2900**	215-665-2000
Day Pitney LLP 242 Trumbull St	Hartford	CT	06103	**800-882-8684**	860-275-0100
Dechert LLP 2929 Arch St Cira Ctr	Philadelphia	PA	19104	**800-328-4880**	215-994-4000
Dickstein Shapiro LLP 1825 Eye St NW	Washington	DC	20006	**800-733-2767**	202-420-2200
Dorsey & Whitney LLP 50 S Sixth St Ste 1500	Minneapolis	MN	55402	**800-759-4929**	612-340-2600
Faegre & Benson LLP 90 S Seventh St 2200 Wells Fargo Bldg	Minneapolis	MN	55402	**800-328-4393**	612-766-7000
Fish & Richardson PC 225 Franklin St 31st Fl	Boston	MA	02110	**800-818-5070**	617-542-5070
Foley & Lardner LLP 777 E Wisconsin Ave	Milwaukee	WI	53202	**855-225-5341**	414-271-2400
Foster Pepper Pllc 1111 Third Ave Ste 3400	Seattle	WA	98101	**800-995-5902**	206-447-4400
Frost Brown Todd LLC 201 E Fifth St 2200 PNC Ctr	Cincinnati	OH	45202	**866-559-6446**	513-651-6800
Fulbright & Jaworski LLP 1301 McKinney St Ste 5100	Houston	TX	77010	**866-385-2744**	713-651-5151
Garden City Group LLC 105 Maxess Rd	Melville	NY	11747	**888-404-8013**	631-470-5000
Gibson Dunn & Crutcher LLP 333 S Grand Ave Ste 4600	Los Angeles	CA	90071	**888-203-1112**	213-229-7000
Goodell Devries Leech & Dann LLP One S St 20th Fl	Baltimore	MD	21202	**888-229-4354**	410-783-4000
Gunster Yoakley & Stewart Pa 777 S Flagler Dr Ste 500 E	West Palm Beach	FL	33401	**800-749-1980**	561-655-1980
Hopkins & Carley A Law Corp PO Box 1469	San Jose	CA	95109	**800-829-3676**	408-286-9800
Hunton & Williams LLP 951 E Byrd St Riverfront Plaza E Tower	Richmond	VA	23219	**800-669-6820**	804-788-8200
John C. Heath, Attorney at Law PLLC 360 N Cutler Dr	Salt Lake City	UT	84054	**800-756-9681**	
Katten Muchin Rosenman LLP 525 W Monroe St Ste 1300	Chicago	IL	60661	**800-449-8114**	312-902-5200
Keller & Heckman LLP 1001 G St NW Ste 500w	Washington	DC	20001	**888-364-1200**	202-434-4100
Kirkland & Ellis LLP 200 E Randolph Dr	Chicago	IL	60601	**800-647-7600**	312-861-2000
Kirkpatrick & Lockhart Preston Gates Ellis LLP 210 Sixth Ave	Pittsburgh	PA	15222	**800-452-8260**	412-355-6500
Larson King LLP 30 E Seventh St Ste 2800	Saint Paul	MN	55101	**877-373-5501**	651-312-6500
Littler Mendelson PC 650 California St 20th Fl	San Francisco	CA	94108	**888-548-8537**	415-433-1940
McGuireWoods LLP 901 E Cary St 1 James Ctr	Richmond	VA	23219	**877-712-8778**	804-775-1000
McKenna Long & Aldridge LLP 303 Peachtree St Ste 5300	Atlanta	GA	30308	**866-643-2933**	404-527-4000
Milbank Tweed Hadley & McCloy LLP 1 Chase Manhattan Plaza	New York	NY	10005	**800-229-0543**	212-530-5000
Miller & Chevalier Chartered 655 15th St NW Ste 900	Washington	DC	20005	**866-628-4282**	202-626-5800
Miller Johnson Snell & Cummiskey PLC 250 Monroe Ave NW Ste 800 PO Box 306	Grand Rapids	MI	49503	**866-667-6572**	616-831-1700
Morgan Lewis & Bockius LLP 1701 Market St	Philadelphia	PA	19103	**866-963-7137**	215-963-5000
Munsch Hardt Kopf Harr Pc 500 N Akard St	Dallas	TX	75201	**800-321-6742**	214-855-7500
Nelson & Kennard 2180 Harvard St Ste 160 PO Box 13807	Sacramento	CA	95853	**866-920-2295**	
Nelson Mullins Riley & Scarborough LLP 1320 Main St 17th Fl	Columbia	SC	29201	**800-237-2000**	803-799-2000
Nysarc Inc 393 Delaware Ave	Delmar	NY	12054	**800-735-8924**	518-439-8311
Orrick Herrington & Sutcliffe LLP 666 Fifth Ave	New York	NY	10103	**866-342-5259**	212-506-5000
Pellettieri Rabstein & Altman 100 Nassau Pk Blvd	Princeton	NJ	08540	**800-432-5297**	609-520-0900
Perkins Coie LLP 1201 Third Ave Ste 4800	Seattle	WA	98101	**888-720-8382**	206-359-8000
Pillsbury Winthrop Shaw Pittman LLP 50 Fremont St	San Francisco	CA	94105	**800-477-0770**	415-983-1000
Polsinelli Shalton Flanigan Suelthaus PC 700 W 47th St Ste 1000	Kansas City	MO	64112	**888-572-7025**	816-753-1000
Proskauer Rose LLP 1585 Broadway	New York	NY	10036	**866-444-3272**	212-969-3000
Quarles & Brady LLP 411 E Wisconsin Ave Ste 2040	Milwaukee	WI	53202	**800-654-2200**	414-277-5000
Rainwater, Holt & Sexton PA 6315 Ranch Dr	Little Rock	AR	72223	**800-434-4800**	
Reminger & Reminger Company LPa 101 W Prospect Ave	Cleveland	OH	44115	**800-486-1311**	216-687-1311
Rodey Dickason Sloan Akin & Robb P A 201 Third St NW Ste 2200	Albuquerque	NM	87102	**800-226-2935**	505-765-5900
Sedgwick Detert Moran & Arnold LLP One Market Plz Steuart Twr Eighth Fl	San Francisco	CA	94105	**800-826-3262**	415-781-7900
Shook Hardy & Bacon LLP 2555 Grand Blvd	Kansas City	MO	64108	**800-821-7962**	816-474-6550
Sidley Austin LLP 1 S Dearborn St	Chicago	IL	60603	**800-306-5230**	312-853-7000
Snell & Wilmer LLP One Arizona Ctr 400 E Van Buren St Ste 1900	Phoenix	AZ	85004	**800-322-0430**	602-382-6000
Spence Law Firm LLC 15 S Jackson St	Jackson	WY	83001	**800-967-2117**	307-733-7290
Squire Patton Boggs 127 Public Sq 4900 Key Tower	Cleveland	OH	44114	**800-743-2773**	216-479-8500
Stark & Stark 993 Lenox Dr Bldg 2	Lawrenceville	NJ	08648	**800-535-3425**	609-896-9060
Stearns Weaver Miller Weissler Alhadeff & Sitterson P.A. 150 W Flagler St Ste 2200	Miami	FL	33130	**866-293-7866**	305-789-3200
Sutherland Asbill & Brennan LLP 999 Peachtree St NE	Atlanta	GA	30309	**855-857-9769**	404-853-8000
Taylor Law Offices Pc 122 E Washington Ave	Effingham	IL	62401	**800-879-2250**	
Thompson Hine LLP 127 Public Sq 3900 Key Ctr	Cleveland	OH	44114	**877-257-3382**	216-566-5500
Thorp Reed & Armstrong LLP 301 Grant St 14th Fl	Pittsburgh	PA	15219	**800-949-3120**	412-394-7711
Vinson & Elkins LLP 1001 Fannin St 1st City Tower Ste 2500	Houston	TX	77002	**877-610-2009**	713-758-2222

428 LAWN & GARDEN EQUIPMENT

SEE ALSO Farm Machinery & Equipment - Mfr

				Toll-Free	Phone
American Biophysics Corp 140 Frenchtown Rd	North Kingstown	RI	02852	**877-699-8727**	800-953-5737
Ames True Temper Inc 465 Railroad Ave	Camp Hill	PA	17011	**800-393-1846**	
Armatron International Inc 15 Highland Ave	Malden	MA	02148	**800-343-3280**	781-321-2300
Artcraft Company Inc, The 200 John L Dietsch Blvd	North Attleboro	MA	02763	**800-659-4042**	508-695-4042
Binkley & Hurst LP 133 Rothsville Stn Rd	Lititz	PA	17543	**800-414-4705**	717-626-4705
Blount Inc Oregon Cutting Systems Div 4909 SE International Way	Portland	OR	97222	**800-223-5168**	503-653-8881
Brinly-Hardy Co 3230 Industrial Pkwy	Jeffersonville	IN	47130	**800-626-5329**	812-218-7200
California Flexrake Corp 9620 Gidley St	Temple City	CA	91780	**800-266-4200**	626-443-4026
Carswell Distributing Co 3750 N Liberty St	Winston Salem	NC	27105	**800-929-1948**	336-767-7700
CMD Products 1410 Flightline Dr Ste D	Lincoln	CA	95648	**800-210-9949**	916-434-0228
Commerce Corp 7603 Energy Pkwy	Baltimore	MD	21226	**800-883-0234**	410-255-3500
Corona Clipper Inc 22440 Tomasco Canyon Rd	Corona	CA	92883	**800-234-2547**	951-737-6515
Dultmeier Sales LLC 13808 Industrial Rd	Omaha	NE	68137	**888-677-5054**	402-333-1444
EarthWay Products Inc 1009 Maple St	Bristol	IN	46507	**800-294-0671**	574-848-7491
Echo Inc 400 Oakwood Rd	Lake Zurich	IL	60047	**800-673-1558**	847-540-8400
Gilmour Mfg Group 492 Drum Ave Somerset *Cust Svc	Somerset	PA	15501	**800-458-0107***	814-443-4802
Grassland Equipment & Irrigation Corp 892-898 Troy Schenectady Rd	Latham	NY	12110	**800-564-5587**	518-785-5841
Harnack Co 6016 Nordic Dr *Cust Svc	Cedar Falls	IA	50613	**800-772-2022***	319-277-0660
Jacobsen 11108 Quality Dr	Charlotte	NC	28273	**866-522-6273**	704-504-6600
Lawn & Golf Supply Co Inc 647 Nutt Rd PO Box 447	Phoenixville	PA	19460	**800-362-5650**	610-933-5801
Lawn Equipment Parts Co 1475 River Rd	Marietta	PA	17547	**800-365-3726**	717-426-5200
Lodi Irrigation 1301 E Armstrong Rd	Lodi	CA	95242	**800-634-7272**	
MacKissic Inc PO Box 111	Parker Ford	PA	19457	**800-348-1117**	610-495-7181
Master Mark Plastics 210 Ampe Dr *Cust Svc	Paynesville	MN	56362	**800-535-4838***	320-845-2111
Melnor Inc 109 Tyson Dr	Winchester	VA	22603	**877-283-0697**	540-722-5600
MTD Products Inc 5965 Grafton Rd	Valley City	OH	44280	**800-800-7310**	330-225-2600
Oliver M Dean Inc 125 Brooks St	Worcester	MA	01606	**800-648-3326**	508-856-9100
Precision Products Inc 316 Limit St *Cust Svc	Lincoln	IL	62656	**800-225-5891***	217-735-1590
Rugg Mfg Company Inc 105 Newton St	Greenfield	MA	01302	**800-633-8772**	413-773-5471
Simplicity Manufacturing Inc PO Box 702	Milwaukee	WI	53201	**800-837-6836**	
Smithco Inc 34 W Ave	Wayne	PA	19087	**877-833-7648**	610-688-4009
Stens Corp 2424 Cathy Ln	Jasper	IN	47546	**800-457-7444**	812-482-2526
Stihl Inc 536 Viking Dr *Cust Svc	Virginia Beach	VA	23452	**800-467-8445***	757-486-9100
Storr Tractor Co 3191 Rt 22	Branchburg	NJ	08876	**800-526-3802**	908-722-9830
Swisher Mower & Machine Company Inc 1602 Corporate Dr	Warrensburg	MO	64093	**800-222-8183**	660-747-8183
Toro Co 8111 Lyndale Ave *NYSE: TTC*	Bloomington	MN	55420	**888-384-9939**	
Toro Company Commercial Products Div 8111 Lyndale Ave *Cust Svc	Bloomington	MN	55420	**800-348-2424***	952-888-8801
Tuff Torq Corp 5943 Commerce Blvd	Morristown	TN	37814	**866-572-3441**	423-585-2000
Weathermatic 3301 W Kingsley Rd	Garland	TX	75041	**888-484-3776**	972-278-6131
Wesspur Tree Equipment 2121 Iron St	Bellingham	WA	98225	**800-268-2141**	360-734-5242

429 LEATHER GOODS - PERSONAL

SEE ALSO Footwear ; Handbags, Totes, Backpacks ; Leather Goods (Misc) ; Luggage, Bags, Cases ; Clothing & Accessories - Mfr

				Toll-Free	Phone
Buxton Co 245 Cadwell Dr PO Box 1650	Springfield	MA	01104	**800-426-3638**	413-734-5900
Carroll Cos Inc 1640 Old Hwy 421 S	Boone	NC	28607	**800-884-2521**	828-264-2521
Coach Inc 516 W 34th St *NYSE: COH*	New York	NY	10001	**800-444-3611**	212-594-1850
Dooney & Bourke Inc 1 Regent St *Cust Svc	East Norwalk	CT	06855	**800-347-5000***	203-853-7515

430 LEATHER GOODS (MISC)

				Toll-Free	Phone
Action Co 1425 N Tennessee St *Sales	McKinney	TX	75069	**800-937-3700***	972-542-8700
Auburn Leather Co 125 N Caldwell St	Auburn	KY	42206	**800-635-0617**	270-542-4116
Carroll Cos Inc 1640 Old Hwy 421 S	Boone	NC	28607	**800-884-2521**	828-264-2521
Gould & Goodrich Leather Inc 709 E McNeil St	Lillington	NC	27546	**800-277-0732**	910-893-2071
Hunter Company Inc 3300 W 71st Ave	Westminster	CO	80030	**800-676-4868**	303-427-4626

431 LEATHER TANNING & FINISHING

				Toll-Free	Phone
Hermann Oak Leather Co 4050 N First St	Saint Louis	MO	63147	**800-325-7950**	314-421-1173

432 LEGISLATION HOTLINES

				Toll-Free	Phone
Alabama *State Legislature* State House 11 S Union St	Montgomery	AL	36130	**800-499-3051**	334-242-7600
Florida *Bill Status* 111 W Madison St Rm 704	Tallahassee	FL	32399	**800-342-1827**	850-488-4371
Maryland *Legislative Services Dept* 90 State Cir	Annapolis	MD	21401	**800-492-7122**	410-946-5400
Massachusetts *Bill Status* 1 Ashburton Pl Rm 1611	Boston	MA	02108	**800-392-6090**	617-727-7030
Nevada *Bill Status* 401 S Carson St	Carson City	NV	89701	**800-978-2878**	775-684-3360
New Jersey *Bill Status* State House Annex PO Box 068	Trenton	NJ	08625	**800-792-8630**	609-292-4840
New York *Bill Status* 202 Legislative Office Bldg	Albany	NY	12248	**800-342-9860**	518-455-4218
North Dakota Legislative Council Services State Capitol Bldg 600 E Blvd Ave	Bismarck	ND	58505	**800-366-6888**	701-328-2916
Washington *Bill Status* PO Box 40600	Olympia	WA	98504	**800-562-6000**	360-786-7573
West Virginia *Bill Status* State Capitol Complex Rm MB27 Bldg 1	Charleston	WV	25305	**877-565-3447**	304-347-4836
Wisconsin *Bill Status* 1 E Main St	Madison	WI	53708	**800-362-9472**	608-266-9960
Wyoming *Legislative Service Office* 3001 E Pershing Blvd	Cheyenne	WY	82002	**800-342-9570**	307-777-7881

433 LIBRARIES

SEE ALSO

				Toll-Free	Phone
Budgetext Corp 1936 N Shiloh Dr	Fayetteville	AR	72704	**800-621-4272**	479-684-3300

433-1 Medical Libraries

				Toll-Free	Phone
Leon S McGoogan Library of Medicine University of Nebraska Medical Ctr 986705 Nebraska Medical Ctr	Omaha	NE	68198	**866-800-5209**	402-559-6221
Moody Medical Library 914 Market st	Galveston	TX	77555	**866-235-5223**	409-772-2371
National Library of Medicine National Institutes of Health 8600 Rockville Pike Bldg 38	Bethesda	MD	20894	**888-346-3656**	301-594-5983
Ruth Lilly Medical Library 975 W Walnut St IB 100	Indianapolis	IN	46202	**877-952-1988**	317-274-7182
State University of New York at Buffalo *Health Sciences Library (HSL)* 3435 Main St Abbott Hall Rm 102	Buffalo	NY	14214	**866-432-5849**	716-829-3900
University of Tennessee Health Science Ctr *Health Sciences Library & Biocommunications Ctr* 877 Madison Ave	Memphis	TN	38103	**877-747-0004**	901-448-5634
University of Texas Southwestern Medical Ctr at Dallas Library, The 5323 Harry Hines Blvd	Dallas	TX	75390	**866-645-6455**	214-648-2001

433-2 Presidential Libraries

				Toll-Free	Phone
Abraham Lincoln Presidential Library & Museum 112 N Sixth St	Springfield	IL	62701	**800-610-2094**	217-557-6250
Dwight D Eisenhower Presidential Library & Museum 200 SE Fourth St	Abilene	KS	67410	**877-746-4453**	785-263-6700
Franklin D Roosevelt Presidential Library & Museum 4079 Albany Post Rd	Hyde Park	NY	12538	**800-337-8474**	845-486-7770
Harry S Truman Presidential Library & Museum 500 W Hwy 24	Independence	MO	64050	**800-833-1225**	816-268-8200
John F Kennedy Presidential Library & Museum Columbia Pt	Boston	MA	02125	**866-535-1960**	617-514-1600
LBJ Library & Museum 2313 Red River St	Austin	TX	78705	**800-874-6451**	512-721-0216
Ronald Reagan Presidential Library & Museum 40 Presidential Dr	Simi Valley	CA	93065	**800-410-8354**	805-577-4000
Rutherford B Hayes Presidential Ctr Spiegel Grove	Fremont	OH	43420	**800-998-7737**	419-332-2081
Woodrow Wilson Presidential Library 20 N Coalter St PO Box 24	Staunton	VA	24401	**888-496-6376**	540-885-0897

433-3 Public Libraries

Listings for public libraries are alphabetized by city name within each state grouping.

				Toll-Free	Phone
Alachua County Library District 401 E University Ave	Gainesville	FL	32601	**866-341-2730**	352-334-3900
Albany Public Library (APL) 161 Washington Ave	Albany	NY	12210	**800-733-2767**	518-427-4300
Allen County Public Library 900 Library Plaza	Fort Wayne	IN	46802	**800-448-6160**	260-421-1200
Alpena County George N Fletcher Public Library 211 N First Ave	Alpena	MI	49707	**877-737-4106**	989-356-6188
Arlington Public Library 101 E Abram St	Arlington	TX	76010	**888-227-7669**	817-459-6900
Arrowhead Library System 210 Dodge St	Janesville	WI	53548	**855-352-9003**	608-758-6690
Atlantic City Free Public Library 1 N Tennessee Ave	Atlantic City	NJ	08401	**800-621-3362**	609-345-2269
Baltimore County Public Library 320 York Rd	Towson	MD	21204	**800-705-3493**	410-887-6100
Bangor Public Library 145 Harlow St	Bangor	ME	04401	**800-442-4293**	207-947-8336
Beauregard Parish Library 205 S Washington Ave	DeRidder	LA	70634	**800-524-6239**	337-463-6217
Bethlehem Area Public Library 11 W Church St	Bethlehem	PA	18018	**800-732-0999**	610-867-3761
Bloomfield Township Public Library 1099 Lone Pine Rd	Bloomfield Hills	MI	48302	**800-318-2596**	248-642-5800
Blue Grass Regional Library 104 E Sixth St	Columbia	TN	38401	**888-345-5575**	931-388-9282
Bolivar County Library 104 S Leflore Ave	Cleveland	MS	38732	**888-268-8076**	662-843-2774
Braille Institute of America Library Services (BILS) 741 N Vermont Ave	Los Angeles	CA	90029	**800-808-2555**	323-660-3880
Bristol Public Library 5 High St	Bristol	CT	06010	**877-603-7323**	860-584-7787
Bronx Library Ctr 310 E Kings Bridge Rd	Bronx	NY	10458	**800-342-3688**	718-579-4244
Brookfield Public Library 1900 N Calhoun Rd	Brookfield	WI	53005	**866-868-3947**	262-782-4140
Brunswick-Glynn County Regional Library 208 Gloucester St	Brunswick	GA	31520	**800-222-6748**	912-267-1212
Cambridge Public Library 244 S Birch St	Cambridge	MN	55008	**877-721-4862**	763-689-7390
Camden County Library 203 Laurel Rd	Voorhees	NJ	08043	**877-222-3737**	856-772-1636
Campbell County Public Library 2101 S 4-J Rd	Gillette	WY	82718	**888-250-1879**	307-682-3223
Canton Public Library 1200 S Canton Ctr Rd	Canton	MI	48188	**888-988-6300**	734-397-0999
Carmel Clay Public Library 55 Fourth Ave SE	Carmel	IN	46032	**800-908-4490**	317-844-3361
Carnegie Regional Library 49 W Seventh St	Grafton	ND	58237	**800-568-5964**	701-352-2754
Carol Stream Public Library 616 Hiawatha Dr	Carol Stream	IL	60188	**800-829-1040**	630-653-0755
Caroline County Public Library 100 Market St	Denton	MD	21629	**800-832-3277**	410-479-1343
Carroll County District Library 70 Second St NE	Carrollton	OH	44615	**800-827-1000**	330-627-2613
Carrollton Public Library 4220 N Josey Ln	Carrollton	TX	75010	**888-727-2978**	972-466-4800
Cerritos Civic Ctr 18025 Bloomfield Ave	Cerritos	CA	90703	**866-402-7433**	562-916-1350
City of Carlsbad Library 1250 Carlsbad Village Dr	Carlsbad	CA	92008	**866-230-2273**	760-434-2870
City of Palm Springs 300 S Sunrise Way	Palm Springs	CA	92262	**800-611-1911**	760-322-7323
Clarksville Montgomery County Public Library 350 Pageant Ln	Clarksville	TN	37040	**877-239-6635**	931-648-8826
Clearwater Public Library 100 N Osceola Ave	Clearwater	FL	33755	**800-342-8060**	727-562-4970
Contra Costa County Library 75 Santa Barbara Rd	Pleasant Hill	CA	94523	**800-984-4636**	925-646-6423
Cullman County Public Library System 200 Clark St NE	Cullman	AL	35055	**800-752-7389**	256-734-1068

Library	Address	City	State	ZIP	Toll-Free	Phone
Cumberland County Public Library	300 Maiden Ln	Fayetteville	NC	28301	866-488-7386	910-483-1580
Cuyahoga County Public Library	2111 Snow Rd	Parma	OH	44134	800-749-5560	216-398-1800
Daly City Public Library	40 Wembley Dr	Daly City	CA	94015	888-227-7669	650-991-8025
Daniel Boone Regional Library	100 W Broadway	Columbia	MO	65203	800-324-4806	573-443-3161
Danville Public Library	319 N Vermilion St	Danville	IL	61832	866-235-6096	217-477-5220
DeKalb County Public Library	215 Sycamore St	Decatur	GA	30030	800-677-1116	404-370-3070
DeKalb Public Library	309 Oak St	DeKalb	IL	60115	888-268-2824	815-756-9568
Delaware County District Library	84 E Winter St	Delaware	OH	43015	866-862-7286	740-362-3861
Des Plaines Public Library	1501 Ellinwood Ave	Des Plaines	IL	60016	800-829-1040	847-827-5551
Deschutes Public Library	507 NW Wall St	Bend	OR	97701	855-268-3767	541-312-1020
DeSoto Public Library	211 E Pleasant Run Rd Ste C	DeSoto	TX	75115	800-886-9008	972-230-9656
Downey City Library (DCL)	11121 Brookshire Ave	Downey	CA	90241	877-846-3452	562-904-7360
Duncanville Public Library	201 James Collins Blvd	Duncanville	TX	75116	866-332-4558	972-780-5050
East Brunswick Public Library	2 Jean Walling Civic Ctr	East Brunswick	NJ	08816	800-829-1040	732-390-6950
East Lansing Public Library	950 Abbott Rd	East Lansing	MI	48823	866-861-2010	517-351-2420
EG Fisher Public Library	1289 Ingleside Ave	Athens	TN	37303	800-552-6843	423-745-7782
El Centro Public Library	539 State St	El Centro	CA	92243	877-482-5656	760-337-4565
Elk Grove Village Public Library	1001 Wellington Ave	Elk Grove Village	IL	60007	800-252-8980	847-439-0447
Englewood Public Library	1000 Englewood Pkwy, Englewood Civic Ctr 1st Fl	Englewood	CO	80110	866-922-9006	303-762-2560
Escanaba Public Library	400 Ludington St	Escanaba	MI	49829	800-992-9012	906-786-4463
Eudora Welty Library, The	300 N State St	Jackson	MS	39201	800-968-5803	601-968-5811
Evanston Public Library	1703 Orrington Ave	Evanston	IL	60201	888-253-7003	847-448-8600
Fall River Public Library	104 N Main St	Fall River	MA	02720	800-331-3764	508-324-2700
Farr Regional Library	1939 61st Ave	Greeley	CO	80634	888-861-7323	970-506-8550
Fayette County Library	216 W Market St	Somerville	TN	38068	866-465-3591	901-465-5248
Fayette County Public Library	531 Summit St	Oak Hill	WV	25901	855-275-5737	304-465-0121
Finger Lakes Library System	119 E Green St	Ithaca	NY	14850	800-909-3557	607-273-4074
First Regional Library	370 W Commerce St	Hernando	MS	38632	800-446-0892	662-429-4439
Flagler County Public Library (FCPL)	2500 Palm Coast Pkwy NW	Palm Coast	FL	32137	877-863-5244	386-446-6763
Forsyth County Public Library	660 W Fifth St	Winston-Salem	NC	27101	866-345-1884	336-703-2665
Fort Smith Public Library	3201 Rogers Ave	Fort Smith	AR	72903	866-660-0885	479-783-0229
Free Library of Philadelphia	1901 Vine St	Philadelphia	PA	19103	800-732-0999	215-686-5322
Fremont Main Library	2400 Stevenson Blvd	Fremont	CA	94538	800-434-0222	510-745-1400
Friendswood Public Library	416 S Friendswood Dr	Friendswood	TX	77546	800-696-3493	281-482-7135
Gaston County Public Library	1555 E Garrison Blvd	Gastonia	NC	28054	888-241-3115	704-868-2164
Genesee District Library	G-4195 W Pasadena Ave	Flint	MI	48504	866-732-1120	810-732-0110
Glendora Public Library & Cultural Ctr	140 S Glendora Ave	Glendora	CA	91741	866-275-3772	626-852-4891
Grace A Dow Memorial Library	1710 W St Andrews Rd	Midland	MI	48640	888-400-5530	989-837-3430
Grande Prairie Public Library	3479 W 183rd St	Hazel Crest	IL	60429	800-321-9511	708-798-5563
Greenville County Library	25 Heritage Green Pl	Greenville	SC	29601	866-275-7273	864-242-5000
Harford County Public Library	1221-A Brass Mill Rd	Belcamp	MD	21017	800-944-7403	410-575-6761
Hastings Public Library	517 W Fourth St	Hastings	NE	68901	800-318-2596	402-461-2346
Helen B Hoffman Plantation Library	501 N Fig Tree Ln	Plantation	FL	33317	800-774-5866	954-797-2140
Henderson County Public Library	301 N Washington St	Hendersonville	NC	28739	866-866-2362	828-697-4725
Henry County Public Library System	1001 Florence McGarity Blvd	McDonough	GA	30252	877-527-3712	770-954-2806
High Point Public Library (HPPL)	901 N Main St	High Point	NC	27262	877-772-8346	336-883-3660
Hillsboro Public Library	2850 NE Brookwood Pkwy	Hillsboro	OR	97124	855-870-0049	503-615-6500
Hilton Head Library	11 Beach City Rd	Hilton Head Island	SC	29926	800-860-1444	843-255-6500
Hockessin Library	1023 Valley Rd	Hockessin	DE	19707	888-352-7722	302-239-5160
Hood County Public Library	222 N Travis St	Granbury	TX	76048	800-452-9292	817-573-3569
Horseshoe Bend Regional Library	207 NW St	Dadeville	AL	36853	855-336-0333	256-825-9232
Houston Public Library	500 McKinney St	Houston	TX	77002	800-318-2596	832-393-1313
Howard County Central Library	10375 Little Patuxent Pkwy	Columbia	MD	21044	800-848-1555	410-313-7800
Huntington Beach Public Library (HBPL)	7111 Talbert Ave	Huntington Beach	CA	92648	800-565-0148	714-842-4481
Hurst Public Library	901 Precinct Line Rd	Hurst	TX	76053	800-344-8377	817-788-7300
Indianhead Federated Library System	1538 Truax Blvd	Eau Claire	WI	54703	800-321-5427	715-839-5082
Iowa City Public Library	123 S Linn St	Iowa City	IA	52240	866-862-6877	319-356-5200
Jackson County Public Library (JCPL)	303 W Second St	Seymour	IN	47274	877-275-7673	812-522-3412
Jefferson-Madison Regional Library	201 E Market St	Charlottesville	VA	22902	866-979-1555	434-979-7151
John F Kennedy Library (JFKL)	190 W 49th St	Hialeah	FL	33012	877-738-5622	305-821-2700
Johnson County Library	PO Box 2933	Shawnee Mission	KS	66201	800-386-8501	913-826-4600
Jones Library Inc	43 Amity St	Amherst	MA	01002	800-439-2370	413-256-4090
Juneau Public Libraries	292 Marine Way	Juneau	AK	99801	800-478-4176	907-586-5324
Kent District Library	814 W River Ctr Dr NE	Comstock Park	MI	49321	877-243-2466	616-784-2007
Kirkwood Library	6000 Kirkwood Hwy	Wilmington	DE	19808	888-352-7722	302-995-7663
Kitsap Regional Library	1301 Sylvan Way	Bremerton	WA	98310	877-883-9900	360-405-9100
Kokomo-Howard County Public Library	220 N Union St	Kokomo	IN	46901	800-257-4762	765-457-3242
LaFayette-Walker County Library	305 S Duke St	La Fayette	GA	30728	877-842-9733	706-638-2992
Lake Agassiz Regional Library (LARL)	118 Fifth St S PO Box 900	Moorhead	MN	56560	800-247-0449	218-233-3757
Lapeer District Library	201 Village W Dr S	Lapeer	MI	48446	866-746-7252	810-664-9521
Lawrence Public Library	707 Vermont St	Lawrence	KS	66044	888-657-7323	785-843-3833
Lawton Public Library	110 SW Fourth St	Lawton	OK	73501	855-895-8064	580-581-3450
Lewis & Clark Library	120 S Last Chance Gulch	Helena	MT	59601	800-733-2767	406-447-1690
Linda Hall Library	5109 Cherry St	Kansas City	MO	64110	800-662-1545	816-363-4600
Lorain Public Library System	351 W Sixth St	Lorain	OH	44052	800-322-7323	440-244-1192
Los Angeles County Public Library	7400 E Imperial Hwy	Downey	CA	90242	888-794-9466	562-940-8462
Lucy Robbins Welles Library	95 Cedar St	Newington	CT	06111	800-842-1423	860-665-8700
Manhattan Public Library	629 Poyntz Ave	Manhattan	KS	66502	800-432-2796	785-776-4741
Mansfield-Richland County Public Library	43 W Third St	Mansfield	OH	44902	877-795-2111	419-521-3100
Marion Public Library	600 S Washington St	Marion	IN	46953	877-275-7673	765-668-2900
Medford Public Library	111 High St	Medford	MA	02155	800-392-6089	781-395-7950
Merced County Library	2100 O St	Merced	CA	95340	866-249-0773	209-385-7643
Meriden Public Library	105 Miller St	Meriden	CT	06450	800-567-0902	203-238-2344
Meridian-Lauderdale County Public Library	2517 Seventh St	Meridian	MS	39301	800-318-2596	601-693-6771
Mesquite Public Library	300 W Grubb Dr	Mesquite	TX	75149	866-797-8268	972-216-6220
Mid-Continent Public Library	15616 E 24 Hwy	Independence	MO	64050	800-318-2596	816-836-5200
Milwaukee Public Library	814 W Wisconsin Ave	Milwaukee	WI	53233	866-947-7363	414-286-3000
Missouri River Regional Library	214 Adams St	Jefferson City	MO	65101	800-949-7323	573-634-2464
Mobile Public Library	701 Government St	Mobile	AL	36602	877-322-8228	251-208-7073
Monroe County Library System	3700 S Custer Rd	Monroe	MI	48161	800-462-2050	734-241-5277
Monroe County Public Library System	700 Fleming St	Key West	FL	33040	877-772-8346	305-292-3595
Monrovia Public Library	321 S Myrtle Ave	Monrovia	CA	91016	888-620-1749	626-256-8274
Monterey Public Library	625 Pacific St	Monterey	CA	93940	800-338-0505	831-646-3932
Mount Laurel Library	100 Walt Whitman Ave	Mount Laurel	NJ	08054	888-576-5529	856-234-7319
Muskegon Area District Library	4845 Airline Rd	Muskegon	MI	49444	877-569-4801	231-737-6248
Nacogdoches Public Library	1112 N St	Nacogdoches	TX	75961	800-252-5400	936-559-2970
Napa City-County Library	580 Coombs St	Napa	CA	94559	877-848-7030	707-253-4241
Nassau Library System	900 Jerusalem Ave	Uniondale	NY	11553	800-662-1220	516-292-8920
New Bedford Free Public Library (NBFPL)	613 Pleasant St	New Bedford	MA	02740	877-336-2627	508-991-6275
New Braunfels Public Library	700 E Common St	New Braunfels	TX	78130	800-434-8013	830-221-4300
New Canaan Library	151 Main St	New Canaan	CT	06840	800-545-2433	203-594-5000
New Castle County Library	750 Library Ave	Newark	DE	19711	877-225-7351	302-731-7550
New Castle Public Library	424 Delaware St	New Castle	DE	19720	877-225-7351	302-328-1995
New Fairfield Free Public Library	2 Brush Hill Rd PO Box F	New Fairfield	CT	06812	877-227-7487	203-312-5679
Northern Waters Library Service	3200 E Lakeshore Dr	Ashland	WI	54806	800-228-5684	715-682-2365
Old Bridge Public Library	One Old Bridge Plz	Old Bridge	NJ	08857	800-829-1040	732-721-5600
Onslow County Public Library	58 Doris Ave E	Jacksonville	NC	28540	800-351-1697	910-455-7350

Classified Section

Library	City	ST	ZIP	Toll-Free	Phone
Orion Township Public Library 825 Joslyn Rd	Lake Orion	MI	48362	877-924-7467	248-693-3000
Owatonna Public Library 105 N Elm St	Owatonna	MN	55060	800-657-3864	507-444-2460
Parkersburg & Wood County Public Library 3100 Emerson Ave	Parkersburg	WV	26104	800-642-8674	304-420-4587
Paul Sawyier Public Library 319 Wapping St	Frankfort	KY	40601	800-829-3676	502-352-2665
Peter White Public Library 217 N Front St	Marquette	MI	49855	800-992-9012	906-228-9510
Pickaway County District Public Library 1160 N Ct St	Circleville	OH	43113	888-268-3756	740-477-1644
Pierce County Library System 3005 112th St E	Tacoma	WA	98446	800-346-0995	253-536-6500
Pima County Public Library 101 N Stone Ave	Tucson	AZ	85701	877-705-5437	520-594-5600
Placer County Library 350 Nevada St	Auburn	CA	95603	800-488-4308	530-886-4500
Ponca City Library 515 E Grand Ave	Ponca City	OK	74601	800-522-8165	580-767-0345
Portage County District Library 10482 S St	Garrettsville	OH	44231	800-500-5179	330-527-4378
Provo City Library 550 N University Ave	Provo	UT	84601	800-914-8931	801-852-6650
Puyallup Public Library 324 S Meridian	Puyallup	WA	98371	866-862-4232	253-841-5454
Racine Public Library 75 Seventh St	Racine	WI	53403	888-529-0061	262-636-9241
Ramapo Catskill Library System 619 Rt 17-M	Middletown	NY	10940	800-327-7343	845-343-1131
Ramsey County Public Library 4570 N Victoria St	Shoreview	MN	55126	888-335-9632	651-486-2200
Rancho Cucamonga Public Library 7368 Archibald Ave	Rancho Cucamonga	CA	91730	800-655-4555	909-477-2720
Rangeview Library District 5877 E 120th Ave	Thornton	CO	80602	800-222-3937	303-288-2001
Richardson Public Library 900 Civic Ctr Dr	Richardson	TX	75080	800-735-2989	972-744-4350
Richmond Public Library 325 Civic Ctr Plaza	Richmond	CA	94804	800-833-2900	510-620-6555
Riverside City Public Library 3581 Mission Inn Ave	Riverside	CA	92501	888-225-7377	951-826-5201
Saint Clair County Library System 210 McMorran Blvd	Port Huron	MI	48060	877-987-7323	810-987-7323
Saint George Library Ctr 5 Central Ave	Staten Island	NY	10301	800-342-3688	718-442-8560
Saint Paul Public Library 90 W Fourth St	Saint Paul	MN	55102	888-335-9632	651-266-7000
San Benito Public Library 101 W Rose St	San Benito	TX	78586	800-444-1187	956-361-3860
San Diego Public Library 820 E St	San Diego	CA	92101	866-470-1308	619-236-5800
Santa Clara County Library 14600 Winchester Blvd	Los Gatos	CA	95032	800-286-1991	408-293-2326
Scott County Library System 13090 Alabama Ave S	Savage	MN	55378	877-772-8346	952-707-1770
Shelbyville-Shelby County Public Library 57 W Broadway	Shelbyville	IN	46176	866-466-1438	317-398-7121
Shenandoah County Library 514 Stoney Creek Blvd	Edinburg	VA	22824	800-829-5137	540-984-8200
Shreve Memorial Library 424 Texas St	Shreveport	LA	71101	866-783-5462	318-226-5897
Somerset County Library 1 Vogt Dr	Bridgewater	NJ	08807	888-313-3532	908-526-4016
Southeastern Library System of Oklahoma (SEPLSO) 401 N Second St	McAlester	OK	74501	800-215-6494	918-426-0456
Southwest Wisconsin Library System 1775 Fourth St	Fennimore	WI	53809	866-866-3393	608-822-3393
St Mary's County Maryland Libraries 23250 Hollywood Rd	Leonardtown	MD	20650	800-783-3625	301-475-2846
Stockton-San Joaquin County Public Library (SSJCPL) 605 N El Dorado St	Stockton	CA	95202	866-805-7323	209-937-8416
Superior Public Library 1530 Tower Ave	Superior	WI	54880	866-894-4899	715-394-8860
Sussex County Library 125 Morris Tpke	Newton	NJ	07860	800-318-2596	973-948-3660
Sutter County Library 750 Forbes Ave	Yuba City	CA	95991	800-533-2873	530-822-7137
Teaneck Public Library 840 Teaneck Rd	Teaneck	NJ	07666	800-245-1377	201-837-4171
Teton County Public Library 125 Virginian Ln	Jackson	WY	83001	800-878-2167	307-733-2164
Timberland Regional Library 415 Tumwater Blvd SW	Tumwater	WA	98501	877-284-6237	360-943-5001
Tippecanoe County Public Library 627 S St	Lafayette	IN	47901	800-542-7818	765-429-0100
Tompkins County Public Library 101 E Green St	Ithaca	NY	14850	800-772-7267	607-272-4557
Troy Public Library 510 W Big Beaver Rd	Troy	MI	48084	855-203-5274	248-524-3538
Tufts Library 46 Broad St	Weymouth	MA	02188	888-283-3757	781-337-1402
Vernon Parish Library 1401 Nolan Trace	Leesville	LA	71446	800-737-2231	337-239-2027
Veterans Memorial Library 301 S University Ave	Mount Pleasant	MI	48858	888-520-8103	989-773-3242
Waco-McLennan County Library 1717 Austin Ave	Waco	TX	76701	800-433-7300	254-750-5941
Walton-De Funiak Library 3 Cir Dr	DeFuniak Springs	FL	32435	800-342-0141	850-892-3624
Warren County-Vicksburg Public Library 700 Veto St	Vicksburg	MS	39180	800-721-7222	601-636-6411
Washington County Library 8595 Central Pk Pl	Woodbury	MN	55125	800-657-3750	651-275-8500
Waterford Township Public Library 5168 Civic Ctr Dr	Waterford	MI	48329	800-318-2596	248-674-4831
Watertown Free Public Library 123 Main St	Watertown	MA	02472	800-829-3676	617-972-6431

Library	City	ST	ZIP	Toll-Free	Phone
Watertown Public Library 100 S Water St	Watertown	WI	53094	800-829-3676	920-262-4090
Weatherford Public Library 1014 Charles St	Weatherford	TX	76086	800-489-0190	817-598-4150
Weber County Library 2464 Jefferson Ave	Ogden	UT	84401	866-678-5342	801-337-2632
Welles-Turner Memorial Library 2407 Main St	Glastonbury	CT	06033	800-411-9671	860-652-7719
Wells County Public Library 200 W Washington St	Bluffton	IN	46714	800-824-6111	260-824-1612
West Allis Public Library 7421 W National Ave	West Allis	WI	53214	800-877-8339	414-302-8500
West Florida Regional Library 200 W Gregory St	Pensacola	FL	32501	800-435-7352	850-436-5060
West Islip Public Library 3 Higbie Ln	West Islip	NY	11795	866-833-1122	631-661-7080
West Orange Public Library 46 Mt Pleasant Ave	West Orange	NJ	07052	800-345-7587	973-736-0198
West Palm Beach Public Library 411 Clematis St	West Palm Beach	FL	33401	866-472-7275	561-868-7700
Westerville Public Library 126 S State St	Westerville	OH	43081	800-816-0662	614-882-7277
Wharton County Library 1920 N Fulton St	Wharton	TX	77488	800-244-5492	979-532-8080
White Plains Public Library 100 Martine Ave	White Plains	NY	10601	877-772-8346	914-422-1400
Willingboro Public Library 220 Willingboro Pkwy	Willingboro	NJ	08046	866-321-9571	609-877-6668
Wilson County Public Library 249 W Nash St	Wilson	NC	27893	877-321-2652	252-237-5355
Woburn Public Library 45 Pleasant St	Woburn	MA	01801	800-392-6089	781-933-0148
Woodland Public Library 250 First St	Woodland	CA	95695	800-321-2752	530-661-5980
Woodridge Public Library 3 Plaza Dr	Woodridge	IL	60517	800-279-0400	630-964-7899
Woonsocket Harris Public Library 303 Clinton St	Woonsocket	RI	02895	800-359-3090	401-769-9044

433-4 Special Collections Libraries

Library	City	ST	ZIP	Toll-Free	Phone
AIDS Library 1233 Locust St 2nd Fl	Philadelphia	PA	19107	877-613-4533	215-985-4851
American Library Assn Library 50 E Huron St	Chicago	IL	60611	800-545-2433	312-944-6780
Association for Research & Enlightenment Library 215 67th St	Virginia Beach	VA	23451	800-333-4499	757-428-3588
Bentley Historical Library 1150 Beal Ave	Ann Arbor	MI	48109	866-233-6661	734-764-3482

433-5 State Libraries

Library	City	ST	ZIP	Toll-Free	Phone
Arkansas State Library 900 W Capitol Ste 100	Little Rock	AR	72201	866-801-3435	501-682-2053
California State Library 900 N St	Sacramento	CA	95814	800-952-5666	916-654-0261
Connecticut State Library 231 Capitol Ave	Hartford	CT	06106	866-886-4478	860-757-6510
Delaware Div of Libraries 497 S Red Haven Ln	Dover	DE	19901	800-829-4059	302-739-4748
Idaho Commission for Libraries (ICFL) 325 W Main St	Boise	ID	83702	800-458-3271	208-334-2150
Kentucky Dept for Libraries & Archives 300 Coffee Tree Rd	Frankfort	KY	40602	800-372-2968	502-564-8300
Massachusetts Board of Library Commissioners 98 N Washington St	Boston	MA	02114	800-952-7403	617-725-1860
Nebraska Library Commission 1200 N St Ste 120	Lincoln	NE	68508	800-307-2665	402-471-2045
Nevada State Library & Archives (NSLA) 100 N Stewart St	Carson City	NV	89701	800-922-2880	775-684-3360
North Dakota State Library (NDSL) 604 E Blvd Ave Dept 250	Bismarck	ND	58505	800-472-2104	701-328-4622
Oklahoma Dept of Libraries 200 NE 18th St	Oklahoma City	OK	73105	800-522-8116	405-521-2502
South Dakota State Library 800 Governors Dr	Pierre	SD	57501	800-423-6665	605-773-3131
State Library of Ohio 274 E First Ave Ste 100	Columbus	OH	43201	800-686-1532	614-644-7061
Tennessee State Library & Archives 403 Seventh Ave N	Nashville	TN	37243	877-850-4959	615-741-2764
Utah State Library 250 N 1950 W Ste A	Salt Lake City	UT	84116	800-662-9150	801-715-6777
Vermont Dept of Libraries 109 State St	Montpelier	VT	05609	888-350-0950	802-828-3261
West Virginia Library Commission 1900 Kanawha Blvd E	Charleston	WV	25305	800-642-9021	304-558-2041
Wisconsin Department of Public Instruction 125 S Webster St PO Box 7841	Madison	WI	53707	800-441-4563	608-266-3390

433-6 University Libraries

Listings for university libraries are arranged by states.

Library	City	ST	ZIP	Toll-Free	Phone
Abilene Christian University Brown Library (ACU) 760 Library Ct	Abilene	TX	79699	800-460-6228	325-674-2000
Andrews University James White Library 4190 Admin Dr	Berrien Springs	MI	49104	800-253-2874	269-471-3264
Angelo State University Henderson Library 2025 S Johnson St	San Angelo	TX	76909	800-946-8627	325-942-2051

		Toll-Free	Phone

Appalachian State University
Belk Library
218 College St PO Box 32026 ....Boone NC 28608   **877-423-0086**   828-262-2300

Ashland University Library
509 College Ave ....Ashland OH 44805   **866-434-5222**   419-289-5400

Barry University
Barry Memorial Library
11300 NE Second Ave ....Miami Shores FL 33161   **800-756-6000**   305-899-3000

Bowling Green State University Jerome Library (BGSU)
1001 E Wooster St ....Bowling Green OH 43403   **866-246-6732**   419-372-2051

Bradley University Cullom-Davis Library
1501 W Bradley Ave ....Peoria IL 61625   **800-858-6843**   309-677-2850

Brown University Rockefeller Library
10 Prospect St ....Providence RI 02912   **877-668-4493**   401-863-2162

Butler University Irwin Library
4600 Sunset Ave ....Indianapolis IN 46208   **888-940-8100**   317-940-9227

California Lutheran University Pearson Library
60 W Olsen Rd ....Thousand Oaks CA 91360   **877-258-3678**   805-493-3250

Calvin College Hekman Library
3201 Burton St SE ....Grand Rapids MI 49546   **800-688-0122**   616-526-6000

Cedarville University Centennial Library
251 N Main St ....Cedarville OH 45314   **800-233-2784**   937-766-7700

Colgate University Case Library
13 Oak Dr ....Hamilton NY 13346   **888-827-4434**   315-228-7300

College of the Holy Cross Dinand Library
1 College St ....Worcester MA 01610   **877-433-1843**   508-793-2642

College of William & Mary Swem Library
PO Box 8794 ....Williamsburg VA 23187   **800-462-3683**   757-221-3072

Cunningham Memorial Library
510 N 6 1/2 St ....Terre Haute IN 47809   **800-851-4279**   812-237-2580

Denison University Doane Library
400 W Loop PO Box L ....Granville OH 43023   **800-336-4766**   740-587-6235

DePauw University West Library
11 E Larabee St ....Greencastle IN 46135   **800-447-2495**   765-658-4420

Drexel University Hagerty Library
33rd St & Market St ....Philadelphia PA 19104   **888-278-8825**   215-895-2767

Duquesne University Gumberg Library
600 Forbes Ave ....Pittsburgh PA 15282   **800-283-3853**   412-396-6130

East Central University Linscheid Library
1100 E 14th St ....Ada OK 74820   **800-772-1213**   580-332-8000

East Stroudsburg University Kemp Library
200 Prospect St ....East Stroudsburg PA 18301   **877-422-1378**   570-422-3465

Eastern Connecticut State University Smith Library
83 Windham St ....Willimantic CT 06226   **800-578-1449**   860-465-4506

Eastern Michigan University Halle Library
955 W Cir Dr ....Ypsilanti MI 48197   **888-888-3465**   734-487-0020

Edinboro University of Pennsylvania Baron-Forness Library (EUB)
200 Tartan Rd ....Edinboro PA 16444   **888-845-2890**   814-732-2273

Ferris State University
FLITE Library
1010 Campus Dr ....Big Rapids MI 49307   **800-433-7747**   231-591-3602

Florida A & M University
Coleman Memorial Library
1500 S Martin Luther King Blvd ....Tallahassee FL 32307   **800-540-6754**   850-599-3370

Francis Marion University Rogers Library
PO Box 100547 ....Florence SC 29502   **800-368-7551**

Franklin & Marshall College Shadek-Fackenthal Library
450 College Ave ....Lancaster PA 17604   **866-366-7655**   717-291-4223

Gallaudet University Library
800 Florida Ave NE ....Washington DC 20002   **800-995-0550**   202-651-5217

Georgia Institute of Technology Library
225 N Ave NW ....Atlanta GA 30332   **888-225-7804**   404-894-4500

Gonzaga University Foley Library
502 E Boone Ave ....Spokane WA 99258   **800-498-5941**   509-323-5931

Grand Valley State University Zumberge Library
One Campus Dr ....Allendale MI 49401   **800-879-0581**   616-331-3252

Grinnell College Burling Library
6th Ave High St ....Grinnell IA 50112   **800-247-0113**   641-269-3371

Hamline University Bush Memorial Library
1536 Hewitt Ave ....Saint Paul MN 55104   **800-753-9753**   651-523-2375
Meader Library
1060 Bishop St ....Honolulu HI 96813   **866-225-5478**   808-544-0210

Hope College Van Wylen Library
53 Graves Pl ....Holland MI 49423   **800-968-7850**   616-395-7790

Indiana University of Pennsylvania Stapleton Library
431 S 11th St ....Indiana PA 15705   **888-342-2383**   724-357-2340

Indiana University-Purdue University Indianapolis
Library
755 W Michigan St ....Indianapolis IN 46202   **888-422-0499**   317-274-0462

Keene State College Mason Library
229 Main St ....Keene NH 03435   **800-572-1909**   603-358-2711

Lawrence University Mudd Library
711 E Boldt Way ....Appleton WI 54911   **888-300-4473**   920-832-6750

Louisiana Tech University Prescott Memorial Library
PO Box 10408 ....Ruston LA 71272   **877-557-2575**   318-257-3555

Marquette University Raynor Memorial Library
1355 W Wisconsin Ave ....Milwaukee WI 53233   **800-876-1715**   414-288-7556

Michigan State University Library
100 Library ....East Lansing MI 48824   **800-500-1554**   517-353-8700

Michigan Technological University J R Van Pelt Library
1400 Townsend Dr ....Houghton MI 49931   **877-688-2586**   906-487-2507

Middlebury College Library
110 Storrs Ave ....Middlebury VT 05753   **800-829-1040**   802-443-5494

Minnesota State University Mankato
Memorial Library
PO Box 8419 ....Mankato MN 56002   **800-722-0544**   507-389-5952

Mount Holyoke College Williston Memorial Library
50 College St ....South Hadley MA 01075   **800-642-4483**   413-538-2000

North Carolina State University Libraries
CB 7111 ....Raleigh NC 27695   **877-601-0590**   919-515-2843

Northeastern Illinois University Williams Library
5500 N St Louis Ave ....Chicago IL 60625   **800-393-0865**   773-442-4470

Northwestern State University Watson Memorial Library
913 University Pkwy ....Natchitoches LA 71497   **888-540-9657**   318-357-4477

Ohio Northern University Heterick Memorial Library
525 S Main St ....Ada OH 45810   **866-943-5787**   419-772-2181
Libraries
1858 Neil Ave Mall ....Columbus OH 43210   **800-555-1212**   614-292-6175

Oral Roberts University Library
7777 S Lewis Ave ....Tulsa OK 74171   **800-678-8876**   918-495-6723

Pacific University Library
2043 College Way ....Forest Grove OR 97116   **800-677-6712**   503-352-1400

Regent University
Library
1000 Regent University Dr ....Virginia Beach VA 23464   **888-249-1822**   757-352-4916

Saginaw Valley State University Zahnow Library
7400 Bay Rd ....University Center MI 48710   **800-968-9500**   989-964-4240

Saint John's University Alcuin Library
2835 Abbey Plaza PO Box 2500 ....Collegeville MN 56321   **800-544-1489**   320-363-2122

Seattle University Lemieux Library
901 12th Ave ....Seattle WA 98122   **800-426-7123**   206-296-6210

Simmons College Beatley Library
300 The Fenway ....Boston MA 02115   **800-831-4284**   617-521-2780

Sixth Floor Museum
411 Elm St Ste 120 Dealey Plz ....Dallas TX 75202   **888-485-4854**   214-747-6660

South Dakota State University Briggs Library
N Campus Dr PO Box 2115 ....Brookings SD 57007   **800-786-2038**   605-688-5106

Southern Illinois University Edwardsville
Lovejoy Library
30 Hairpin Dr PO Box 1063 ....Edwardsville IL 62026   **888-328-5168**   618-650-4636

Stanford University Green Library
557 Escondido Mall ....Stanford CA 94305   **800-521-0600**   650-723-2300

Stetson University DuPont-Ball Library
421 N Woodland Blvd ....DeLand FL 32723   **800-688-0101**   386-822-7183

Syracuse University Bird Library
222 Waverly Ave ....Syracuse NY 13244   **866-722-7858**   315-443-2093

Texas Christian University Mary Couts Burnett Library
2800 S University Dr ....Fort Worth TX 76129   **866-321-7428**   817-257-7000

Texas Tech University Libraries
18th & Boston Ave PO Box 40002 ....Lubbock TX 79409   **888-270-3369**   806-742-2265

Tuskegee University Ford Motor Co Library/Learning Resource Ctr
Hollis Burke Frissell Library Bldg ....Tuskegee AL 36088   **800-622-6531**   334-727-8894

University at Albany University Libraries
1400 Washington Ave ....Albany NY 12222   **800-342-4146**   518-442-3600
Gorgas Library
Information Ctr First Fl ....Tuscaloosa AL 35487   **888-764-5603**   205-348-6047

University of California Davis
Shields Library 100 NW Quad ....Davis CA 95616   **877-772-5772**   530-752-6561

University of California Irvine
Library PO Box 19557 ....Irvine CA 92623   **800-848-4722**   949-824-6836

University of Cincinnati Langsam Library
PO Box 210033 ....Cincinnati OH 45221   **866-397-3382**   513-556-1515

University of Colorado at Colorado Springs
Kraemer Family Library
1420 Austin Bluffs Pkwy
PO Box 7150 ....Colorado Springs CO 80918   **800-990-8227**   719-255-3295

University of Connecticut
Babbidge Library
369 Fairfield Rd Unit 2005 ....Storrs CT 06269   **888-603-9635**   860-486-2219

University of Florida Libraries
PO Box 117001 ....Gainesville FL 32611   **877-351-2377**   352-392-0342

University of Georgia Library
320 S Jackson St ....Athens GA 30602   **877-314-5560**   706-542-0621

University of Illinois Chicago
Daley Library
801 S Morgan St Rm 1-280 ....Chicago IL 60607   **866-904-5843**   312-996-2716

University of Memphis McWherter Library
126 Ned R McWherter Library ....Memphis TN 38152   **866-670-6147**   901-678-2201

University of Miami Richter Library
PO Box 248214 ....Coral Gables FL 33124   **800-708-6754**   305-284-3551

University of Michigan Dearborn
Mardigian Library
4901 Evergreen Rd ....Dearborn MI 48128   **877-619-6650**   313-593-5445

University of Minnesota Crookston
UMC Library
2900 University Ave ....Crookston MN 56716   **800-862-6466**   218-281-8399

University of Minnesota Duluth
UMD Library 416 Library Dr ....Duluth MN 55812   **866-999-6995**   218-726-8102
Williams Library
1 Library Loop ....University MS 38677   **800-891-4596**   662-915-7091

University of Missouri Kansas City
Nichols Library
800 E 51st St ....Kansas City MO 64110   **800-775-8652**   816-235-1534

University of Montana Missoula
Mansfield Library
32 Campus Dr ....Missoula MT 59812   **800-240-4939**   406-243-2053

University of North Texas Libraries
1155 Union Cir PO Box 305190 ....Denton TX 76203   **877-872-0264**   940-565-2413

University of Pennsylvania Van Pelt Library
3420 Walnut St ....Philadelphia PA 19104   **877-784-8379**   215-898-7091
Hillman Library
3960 Forbes Ave ....Pittsburgh PA 15260   **888-465-4329**   412-648-7710

University of Saint Thomas O'Shaughnessy-Frey Library
2115 Summit Ave ....Saint Paul MN 55105   **800-328-6819**   651-962-5494

University of San Francisco Gleeson Library
2130 Fulton St ....San Francisco CA 94117   **800-225-5873**   415-422-5555

University of Southern California
Doheny Memorial Library
3550 Trousdale Pkwy
University Pk Campus ....Los Angeles CA 90089   **800-775-7330**   213-740-4039

University of Tennessee Knoxville
Hodges Library
1015 Volunteer Blvd ....Knoxville TN 37996   **800-426-9119**   865-974-4351

University of Toledo Carlson Library
2801 W Bancroft St MS 509 ....Toledo OH 43606   **800-586-5336**   419-530-2324

University of Utah Marriott Library
Marriott Library 295 S 1500 E ....Salt Lake City UT 84112   **800-458-0145**   801-581-8558

University of Wisconsin Eau Claire
McIntyre Library
105 Garfield Ave ....Eau Claire WI 54702   **877-267-1384**   715-836-3715

University of Wisconsin Stout
Library 315 Tenth Ave E ....Menomonie WI 54751   **866-716-6685**   715-232-1215

University of Wisconsin Superior
Jim Dan Hill Library
PO Box 2000 ....Superior WI 54880   **877-232-1727**   715-394-8343

University of Wyoming Libraries
PO Box 3334 ....Laramie WY 82071   **800-442-6757**   307-766-3190

				Toll-Free	Phone
Virginia Commonwealth University Cabell Library					
901 Pk Ave PO Box 842033	Richmond	VA	23284	**844-352-7399**	804-828-1105
Washington University in Saint Louis Olin Library					
1 Brookings Dr PO Box 1061	Saint Louis	MO	63130	**800-779-3272**	314-935-5400
Weber State University					
Stewart Library					
2901 University Cir	Ogden	UT	84408	**877-306-3140**	801-626-6403
Wells College Long Library					
170 Main St	Aurora	NY	13026	**800-952-9355**	315-364-3266
Wesleyan University Olin Library					
252 Church St	Middletown	CT	06459	**800-421-1561**	860-685-2660
West Chester University Green Library					
700 S High St	West Chester	PA	19383	**800-886-9654**	610-436-1000
Western Michigan University Waldo Library					
1903 W Michigan Ave MS 5353	Kalamazoo	MI	49008	**866-533-3438**	269-387-5202
Wittenberg University Thomas Library					
807 Woodlawn Ave PO Box 7207	Springfield	OH	45504	**800-677-7558**	937-327-7511
Xavier University Library					
3800 Victory Pkwy	Cincinnati	OH	45207	**877-382-2293**	513-745-3881

434   LIBRARY ASSOCIATIONS - STATE & PROVINCE

				Toll-Free	Phone
Minnesota Library Assn (MLA)					
1821 University Ave W Ste S256	Saint Paul	MN	55104	**877-867-0982**	651-999-5343

435   LIGHT BULBS & TUBES

				Toll-Free	Phone
Advanced Lighting Technologies Inc					
32000 Aurora Rd	Solon	OH	44139	**888-440-2358**	440-519-0500
AETEK UV Systems					
1229 Lakeview Ct	Romeoville	IL	60446	**800-333-2304**	630-226-4200
Bayco Products Inc					
640 Sanden Blvd	Wylie	TX	75098	**800-233-2155**	469-326-9400
Empire Wire & Supply					
2119 Austin Ave	Rochester Hills	MI	48309	**800-826-1265**	
Eye Lighting International NA					
9150 Hendricks Rd	Mentor	OH	44060	**888-665-2677***	440-350-7000
*Cust Svc					
Interlectric Corp					
1401 Lexington Ave	Warren	PA	16365	**800-722-2184**	814-723-6061
LCD Lighting Inc					
37 Robinson Blvd	Orange	CT	06477	**800-826-9465**	203-795-1520
Ledtronics Inc					
23105 Kashiwa Ct	Torrance	CA	90505	**800-579-4875**	310-534-1505
Light Sources Inc					
37 Robinson Blvd	Orange	CT	06477	**800-826-9465**	203-799-7877
Litetronics International Inc					
4101 W 123rd St	Alsip	IL	60803	**800-860-3392**	708-389-8000
Magnet Sales & Mfg Company Inc					
11248 Playa Ct	Culver City	CA	90230	**800-421-6692**	310-391-7213
OSRAM Sylvania Glass Technologies					
131 Portsmouth Ave	Exeter	NH	03833	**800-258-8290**	603-772-4331
Philips Lighting Co					
200 Franklin Sq Dr	Somerset	NJ	08873	**800-555-0050**	
Sun Ergoline Inc					
1 Walter Kratz Dr	Jonesboro	AR	72401	**888-771-0996**	
Technical Consumer Products Inc					
325 Campus Dr	Aurora	OH	44202	**800-324-1496**	
Trojan Inc					
198 Trojan St PO Box 850	Mount Sterling	KY	40353	**800-264-0526**	859-498-0526
Ushio America Inc					
5440 Cerritos Ave	Cypress	CA	90630	**800-326-1960**	714-236-8600
UVP Inc 2066 W 11th St	Upland	CA	91786	**800-452-6788***	909-946-3197
*Cust Svc					
Venture Lighting International Inc					
32000 Aurora Rd	Solon	OH	44139	**800-451-2606**	440-248-3510

436   LIGHTING EQUIPMENT - VEHICULAR

				Toll-Free	Phone
Able 2 Products Company Inc					
PO Box 543	Cassville	MO	65625	**800-641-4098**	417-847-4791
Avtec Inc Six Industrial Pk	Cahokia	IL	62206	**800-552-8832**	618-337-7800
JW Speaker Corp					
N 120 W 19434 Freistadt Rd					
PO Box 1011	Germantown	WI	53022	**800-558-7288**	262-251-6660
Luminator 900 Klein Rd	Plano	TX	75074	**800-388-8205**	972-424-6511
Peterson Manufacturing Co					
4200 E 135th St	Grandview	MO	64030	**800-821-3490**	816-765-2000
Truck-Lite Company Inc					
310 E Elmwood Ave	Falconer	NY	14733	**800-562-5012***	716-665-6214
*Cust Svc					
Vehicle Safety Mfg LLC					
408 Central Ave	Newark	NJ	07107	**800-832-7233***	973-643-3000
*General					

437   LIGHTING FIXTURES & EQUIPMENT

				Toll-Free	Phone
Altman Lighting Inc					
57 Alexander St	Yonkers	NY	10701	**800-425-8626**	914-476-7987
American Fluorescent Corp					
2345 Ernie Krueger Cir	Waukegan	IL	60087	**800-873-2326**	847-249-5970
American Louver Co					
7700 N Austin Ave	Skokie	IL	60077	**800-772-0355**	847-470-3300
Brinkmann Corp					
4215 McEwen Rd	Dallas	TX	75244	**800-527-0717**	972-770-8500
Commercial Lighting Industries					
81161 Indio Blvd	Indio	CA	92201	**800-755-0155**	760-343-2704

				Toll-Free	Phone
Con-Tech Lighting					
2783 Shermer Rd	Northbrook	IL	60062	**800-728-0312**	847-559-5500
Cooper Industries					
600 Travis St Ste 5400	Houston	TX	77002	**866-853-4293**	713-209-8400
NYSE: ETN					
Corbett Lighting Inc					
14508 Nelson Ave	City of Industry	CA	91744	**800-533-8769**	626-336-4511
Coronet Lighting					
PO Box 2065	Gardena	CA	90248	**800-421-2748**	310-327-6700
Dazor Manufacturing Corp					
2079 Congressional	Saint Louis	MO	63146	**800-345-9103**	314-652-2400
ELK Lighting					
12 Willow Ln	Nesquehoning	PA	18240	**800-613-3261**	
Elk Lighting Inc					
12 Willow Lane	Nesquehoning	PA	18240	**866-283-1953**	
Energy Focus Inc					
32000 Aurora Rd	Solon	OH	44139	**800-327-7877**	440-715-1300
OTC: EFOI					
Fulton Industries Inc					
135 E Linfoot St PO Box 377	Wauseon	OH	43567	**800-537-5012**	419-335-3015
Gardco Lighting					
1611 Clovis Barker Rd	San Marcos	TX	78666	**800-227-0758**	512-753-1000
GE Lighting Systems Inc					
3010 Spartanburg Hwy	East Flat Rock	NC	28726	**888-694-3533**	828-693-2000
HE Williams Inc					
831 W Fairview Ave	Carthage	MO	64836	**866-358-4065**	417-358-4065
High End Systems Inc					
2105 Gracy Farms Ln	Austin	TX	78758	**800-890-8989**	512-836-2242
Hinkley Lighting					
12600 Berea Rd	Cleveland	OH	44111	**800-446-5539**	216-671-3300
Holophane					
214 Oakwood Ave PO Box 3004	Newark	OH	43058	**866-465-6742**	740-345-9631
Hubbell Lighting Inc					
701 Millennium Blvd	Greenville	SC	29607	**800-465-7051**	864-678-1000
Hydrel 12881 Bradley Ave	Sylmar	CA	91342	**866-533-9901**	
Justice Design Group (JDG)					
500 S Grand Ave Ste 110	Los Angeles	CA	90071	**800-533-4799**	213-437-0102
Kenall Mfg 1020 Lakeside Dr	Gurnee	IL	60031	**800-453-6255**	847-360-8200
Kichler Lighting					
7711 E Pleasant Vly Rd					
PO Box 318010	Cleveland	OH	44131	**866-558-5706**	
Koehler-Bright Star Inc					
380 Stewart Rd	Hanover Township	PA	18706	**800-788-1696***	570-825-1900
*Cust Svc					
Kurtzon Lighting Inc					
1420 S Talman Ave	Chicago	IL	60608	**800-837-8937**	773-277-2121
Lamplight Farms Inc					
W140 N4900 Lilly Rd	Menomonee Falls	WI	53051	**888-473-1088***	262-781-9590
*Cust Svc					
LC Doane Co					
110 Pond Meadow Rd PO Box 700	Ivoryton	CT	06442	**800-447-5006**	860-767-8295
Ledalite Architectural Products					
19750-92A Ave	Langley	BC	V1M3B2	**800-665-5332**	604-888-6811
Legion Lighting Company Inc					
221 Glenmore Ave	Brooklyn	NY	11207	**800-453-4466**	718-498-1770
Lighting Quotient, The					
114 Boston Post Rd	West Haven	CT	06516	**800-222-0193**	203-931-4455
Lights of America					
611 Reyes Dr	Walnut	CA	91789	**800-321-8100***	909-594-7883
*Cust Svc					
Lithonia Lighting					
One Lithonia Way	Conyers	GA	30012	**800-858-7763**	770-922-9000
Luxo Corp					
Five Westchester Plz	Elmsford	NY	10523	**800-222-5896**	914-345-0067
Mag Instrument Inc					
2001 S Hillman Ave	Ontario	CA	91761	**800-289-6241**	909-947-1006
Mercury Lighting Products Company Inc					
20 Audrey Pl	Fairfield	NJ	07004	**800-637-2584**	973-244-9444
Minka Group					
1151 W Bradford Ct	Corona	CA	92882	**800-221-7977**	951-735-9220
Mule Lighting Inc					
46 Baker St	Providence	RI	02905	**800-556-7690**	401-941-4446
Musco Sports Lighting LLC					
100 First Ave W PO Box 808	Oskaloosa	IA	52577	**800-825-6020**	641-673-0411
Nightscaping					
1705 E Colton Ave	Redlands	CA	92374	**800-544-4840**	909-794-2121
North Star Lighting Inc					
2150 Parkes Dr	Broadview	IL	60155	**800-229-4330**	708-681-4330
Norwell Manufacturing Inc					
82 Stevens St	East Taunton	MA	02718	**800-822-2831**	508-823-1751
Pacific Coast Lighting					
20238 Plummer St	Chatsworth	CA	91311	**800-709-9004**	818-886-9751
Paramount Industries Inc					
304 N Howard St	Croswell	MI	48422	**800-521-5405**	810-679-2551
Paul C Buff Inc					
2725 Bransford Ave	Nashville	TN	37204	**800-443-5542**	615-383-3982
Philips Canlyte, Inc					
3015 Louis Amos	Lachine	QC	H8T1C4	**800-668-2770***	514-636-0670
*All					
Philips Day-Brite					
776 S Green St	Tupelo	MS	38804	**800-234-1890**	
Philips Holding USA Inc					
1251 Ave of the Americas	New York	NY	10020	**800-453-6860**	212-536-0500
Prescolite Inc					
701 Millennium Blvd	Greenville	SC	29607	**888-777-4832**	864-678-1000
RAB Lighting					
170 Ludlow Ave	Northvale	NJ	07647	**888-722-1000**	201-784-8600
Rejuvenation Inc					
2550 NW Nicolai St	Portland	OR	97210	**888-401-1900**	503-231-1900
Renova Lighting Systems Inc					
20 Middlesex Rd	Mansfield	MA	02048	**800-635-6682**	401-682-1850
Schonbek Worldwide Lighting Inc					
61 Industrial Blvd	Plattsburgh	NY	12901	**800-836-1892**	518-563-7500
Sea Gull Lighting Products LLC A Generations Brands Co					
301 W Washington St	Riverside	NJ	08075	**800-347-5483**	856-764-0500
SIMKAR Corp					
700 Ramona Ave	Philadelphia	PA	19120	**800-523-3602**	215-831-7700

	Toll-Free	Phone
Spectrolab Inc		
12500 Gladstone Ave ....Sylmar CA 91342	**800-936-4888**	818-365-4611
Stonco Lighting		
2345 Vauxhall Rd ....Union NJ 07083	**800-334-2212**	908-964-7000
Strand Lighting		
10911 Petal St ....Dallas TX 75238	**800-733-0564**	214-647-7880
Streamlight Inc		
30 Eagleville Rd ....Eagleville PA 19403	**800-523-7488**	610-631-0600
Super Sky Products Inc		
10301 N Enterprise Dr ....Mequon WI 53092	**800-558-0467**	262-242-2000
Tech Lighting LLC		
7400 Linda Ave ....Skokie IL 60077	**800-522-5315**	847-410-4400
Tri-Lite Inc		
1642 N Besly Ct ....Chicago IL 60642	**800-322-5250**	773-384-7765
Troy-CSL Lighting Inc		
14508 Nelson Ave ....City of Industry CA 91744	**800-533-8769**	626-336-4511
Western Reflections		
261 Commerce Way ....Gallatin TN 37066	**800-507-8302***	615-451-9700
*Cust Svc		

438 LIME

	Toll-Free	Phone
Carmeuse North America		
11 Stanwix St 11th Fl ....Pittsburgh PA 15222	**866-243-0965**	412-995-5500
Cheney Lime & Cement		
478 Graystone Rd PO Box 160 ....Allgood AL 35013	**800-752-8282**	205-625-3031
Texas Lime Co		
15865 Farm Rd 1434 PO Box 851 ....Cleburne TX 76033	**800-772-8000**	817-641-4433
Western Lime Corp		
206 N Sixth Ave PO Box 57 ....West Bend WI 53095	**800-433-0036**	262-334-2874

439 LIMOUSINE SERVICES

	Toll-Free	Phone
Advantage Limousine Services Inc		
8310 Castleford St Ste 200 ....Houston TX 77040	**888-983-9991**	713-983-9991
Alliance Limousine Inc		
14553 Delano St Unit 210 ....Van Nuys CA 91411	**800-954-5466**	
American Coach Limousine		
1100 Jorie Blvd Ste 314 ....Oak Brook IL 60523	**888-709-5466**	630-629-0001
Arizona Limousines Inc		
8900 N Central Ave Ste 101 ....Phoenix AZ 85020	**800-678-0033**	602-267-7097
Bayview Limousine Service		
15701 Nelson Pl S ....Seattle WA 98188	**800-606-7880**	206-824-6200
Carey Executive Limousine		
245 University Ave ....Atlanta GA 30315	**800-241-3943**	404-223-2000
Carey International Inc		
4530 Wisconsin Ave NW 5th Fl ....Washington DC 20016	**800-336-4646**	202-895-1200
Classic Transportation Group		
1600 Locust Ave ....Bohemia NY 11716	**800-291-8090**	631-567-5100
Elite Limousine Service Inc		
1059 12th Ave Ste E ....Honolulu HI 96816	**800-776-2098**	808-735-2431
Gateway Limousines		
1550 Gilbreth Rd ....Burlingame CA 94010	**800-486-7077**	650-697-5548
International Chauffeured Service Worldwide		
53 E 34th St Fourth Fl ....New York NY 10016	**800-266-5254**	212-213-0302
Mears Transportation Group		
324 W Gore St ....Orlando FL 32806	**800-759-5219**	407-422-4561
Park Cities Limousine		
7129 Harry Hines Blvd ....Dallas TX 75235	**888-559-0708**	214-824-0011
Pontarelli Limousine Service		
2225 W Hubbard St ....Chicago IL 60612	**800-322-5466**	312-226-5466
R & R Limousine		
4403 Kiln Ct ....Louisville KY 40218	**800-582-5576**	502-458-1862
Regency Limousine International		
83-03 24th Ave ....East Elmhurst NY 11370	**866-302-2201**	718-507-4000
Royal Coachman Worldwide		
88 Ford Rd Ste 26 ....Denville NJ 07834	**800-472-7433**	973-400-3200
Starlite Limousines LLC		
PO Box 13542 ....Scottsdale AZ 85267	**800-875-4104**	480-422-3619
US Coachways Inc		
100 St Mary's Ave Ste 2B ....Staten Island NY 10305	**800-359-5991**	718-477-4242

440 LINEN & UNIFORM SUPPLY

	Toll-Free	Phone
Ace ImageWear		
4120 Truman Rd ....Kansas City MO 64127	**800-366-0564**	816-231-5737
Ace-Tex Enterprises		
7601 Central Ave ....Detroit MI 48210	**800-444-3800**	313-834-4000
AmeriPride Services Inc		
10801 Wayzata Blvd ....Minnetonka MN 55305	**800-750-4628***	952-738-4200
*Cust Svc		
ApparelMaster		
123 Harrison Ave ....Harrison OH 45030	**877-543-1678**	513-202-1600
Arrow Uniform Rental Inc		
6400 Monroe Blvd ....Taylor MI 48180	**888-332-7769**	313-299-5000
Cintas Corp		
PO Box 625737 ....Cincinnati OH 45262	**800-786-4367**	513-459-1200
NASDAQ: CTAS		
Continental Linen Services		
4200 Manchester Rd ....Kalamazoo MI 49001	**800-878-4357**	
Coyne Textile Services Inc		
140 Cortland Ave ....Syracuse NY 13202	**800-672-6963**	315-475-1626
Domestic Linen Supply & Laundry Co Inc		
30555 NW Hwy ....Farmington Hills MI 48334	**800-344-3555**	248-737-2000
G & K Services Inc		
5995 Opus Pkwy Ste 500 ....Minnetonka MN 55343	**800-452-2737**	952-912-5500
Healthcare Services Group Inc (HCSG)		
3220 Tillman Dr Ste 300 ....Bensalem PA 19020	**800-486-3289**	215-639-4274
Industrial Towel & Uniform Inc		
2700 S 160th St ....New Berlin WI 53151	**800-767-2487**	262-782-1950

	Toll-Free	Phone
Iron City Uniform Rental		
6640 Frankstown Ave ....Pittsburgh PA 15206	**800-532-2010**	412-661-2001
Model Coverall Service Inc		
100 28th St SE ....Grand Rapids MI 49548	**800-968-6491**	616-241-6491
Morgan Services Inc		
323 N Michigan Ave ....Chicago IL 60601	**888-966-7426**	312-346-3181
Prudential Overall Supply		
PO Box 11210 ....Santa Ana CA 92711	**800-767-5536**	949-250-4855
Roscoe Co		
3535 W Harrison St ....Chicago IL 60624	**888-476-7263***	773-722-5000
*Cust Svc		
Sitex Corp		
1300 Commonwealth Dr ....Henderson KY 42420	**800-278-3537**	270-827-3537
Textile Care Services Inc		
225 Wood Lk Dr SE ....Rochester MN 55904	**800-422-0945**	
Unitech Services Group		
295 Parker St ....Springfield MA 01151	**800-344-3824**	413-543-6911
Valiant Products Corp		
2727 Fifth Ave W ....Denver CO 80204	**800-347-2727***	303-892-1234
*Cust Svc		

441 LIQUOR STORES

	Toll-Free	Phone
ABC Fine Wines & Spirits		
8989 S Orange Ave ....Orlando FL 32824	**800-854-7283**	407-851-0000
Gold Standard Enterprises Inc		
5100 W Dempster St ....Skokie IL 60077	**888-942-9463**	847-674-4200
Pearlstine Distributors Inc (PDI)		
1600 Chrlston Rgonal Pkwy ....Charleston SC 29492	**800-922-1048**	843-388-6800
Spec's Wines Spirits & Finer Foods		
2410 Smith St ....Houston TX 77006	**888-526-8787**	713-526-8787
Touring & Tasting		
125 S Quarantina St ....Santa Barbara CA 93103	**800-850-4370**	805-965-2813
Wine Club, The		
1431 S Village Way ....Santa Ana CA 92705	**800-966-5432**	714-835-6485
Wine.com Inc		
114 Sansome St 3rd Fl ....San Francisco CA 94104	**800-592-5870**	415-291-9500
Zachys Wine & Liquor Inc		
16 E Pkwy ....Scarsdale NY 10583	**800-723-0241**	914-723-0241

442 LITIGATION SUPPORT SERVICES

	Toll-Free	Phone
Al Betz & Assoc Inc		
125 Airport Dr Ste 30 ....Westminster MD 21157	**877-402-3376**	410-875-3376
Alderson Reporting Co		
1155 Connecticut Ave NW Ste 200 ....Washington DC 20036	**800-367-3376**	202-289-2260
Allied Court Reporters Inc		
115 Phenix Ave ....Cranston RI 02920	**888-443-3767**	401-946-5500
Atkinson-Baker Inc (ABI)		
500 N Brand Blvd 3rd Fl ....Glendale CA 91203	**800-288-3376**	818-551-7300
Compex Legal Services Inc		
325 S Maple Ave ....Torrance CA 90503	**800-426-6739***	
*Cust Svc		
Courtroom Sciences Inc		
4950 N O'Connor Rd		
Corporate Plaza 1st Fl ....Irving TX 75062	**800-514-5879**	972-717-1773
DecisionQuest		
21535 Hawthorne Blvd Ste 310 ....Torrance CA 90503	**877-833-2474**	310-618-9600
Depobook Reporting Services		
1600 G St Ste 101 ....Modesto CA 95354	**800-830-8885**	209-544-6466
DepoNet		
2700 Centennial Tower 101 Marietta St		
101 Marietta St ....Atlanta GA 30303	**800-337-6638**	404-495-0777
DOAR Litigation Consulting		
170 Earle Ave ....Lynbrook NY 11563	**800-875-8705**	516-823-4000
FTI Consulting		
909 Commerce Rd Ste 1400 ....Annapolis MD 21401	**800-334-5701**	410-224-8770
NYSE: FCN		
Hahn & Bowersock Corp		
151 Kalmus Dr Ste L1 ....Costa Mesa CA 92626	**800-660-3187**	
Hutchings Court Reporters LLC		
6055 E Washington Blvd Eighth Fl ....Los Angeles CA 90040	**800-697-3210***	323-888-6300
*Cust Svc		
Jane Rose Reporting		
80 Fifth Ave ....New York NY 10011	**800-825-3341**	212-727-7773
Jury Research Institute		
2617 Danville Blvd PO Box 100 ....Alamo CA 94507	**800-233-5879**	925-932-5663
Professional Shorthand Reporters Inc (PSR)		
601 Poydras St Ste 1615 ....New Orleans LA 70130	**800-536-5255**	504-529-5255
Ralph Rosenberg Court Reporters Inc		
1001 Bishop St Ste 2460 ....Honolulu HI 96813	**888-524-5888**	
US Legal Support Inc		
363 N Sam Houston Pkwy E Ste 900 ....Houston TX 77060	**800-567-8757**	713-653-7100
Veritext LLC		
290 W Mt Pleasant Ave Ste 3200 ....Livingston NJ 07039	**800-567-8658**	

443 LIVESTOCK - WHOL

SEE ALSO Cattle Ranches, Farms, Feedlots (Beef Cattle) ; Hog Farms

	Toll-Free	Phone
All West Select Sires		
450 N Hill Blvd ....Burlington WA 98233	**800-426-2697**	
Blue Grass Stockyard		
375 Lisle Industrial Ave		
PO Box 1023 ....Lexington KY 40588	**800-621-3972**	859-255-7701
Empire Livestock Marketing LLC		
5001 Brittonfield Pkwy ....East Syracuse NY 13057	**800-462-8802**	315-433-9129
Equity Co-op Livestock Sales Assn		
401 Commerce Ave ....Baraboo WI 53913	**800-362-3989**	608-356-8311
High Plains Livestock Exchange LLC		
28601 US Hwy 34 ....Brush CO 80723	**866-842-5115**	970-842-5115

Left Column

			Toll-Free	Phone
Kidron Auction Inc				
4885 Kidron Rd	Kidron OH	44636	800-589-9749	330-857-2641
Lewiston Sales Inc				
21241 Dutchmans Crossing Rd	Lewiston MN	55952	800-732-6334	507-523-2112
Prairie Livestock LLC				
2139 Barton Ferry Rd PO Box 636	West Point MS	39773	800-647-6350	662-494-5651
Producers Livestock Marketing Assn				
4809 S 114th St	Omaha NE	68137	800-257-4046	402-597-9189
Stockmen's Livestock Market Inc				
1200 E Hwy 50 PO Box 528	Yankton SD	57078	800-532-0952	605-665-9641
United Producers Inc				
8351 N High St Ste 250	Columbus OH	43235	800-456-3276	
Winner Livestock Auction Co				
31690 Livestock Barn Rd	Winner SD	57580	800-201-0451	605-842-0451

444   LIVESTOCK & POULTRY FEEDS - PREPARED

			Toll-Free	Phone
AC Nutrition 158 N Main St	Winters TX	79567	800-588-3333	325-754-4546
ADM Alliance Nutrition Inc				
1000 N 30th St	Quincy IL	62301	800-292-3333	217-222-7100
AG Partners Inc				
512 S Eigth St PO Box 467	Lake City MN	55041	800-772-2990	651-345-3328
Ag Processing Inc				
12700 W Dodge Rd PO Box 2047	Omaha NE	68103	800-247-1345	402-496-7809
Agri-King Inc				
18246 Waller Rd	Fulton IL	61252	800-435-9560	815-589-2525
Ahrberg Milling Co				
200 S Depot St PO Box 968	Cushing OK	74023	800-324-0267	918-225-0267
Alabama Farmers Co-op Inc				
PO Box 2227	Decatur AL	35601	888-255-2667	256-353-6843
Albion Laboratories Inc				
101 N Main St	Clearfield UT	84015	800-453-2406	801-773-4631
Bagdad Roller Mills Inc				
5740 Elmburg Rd PO Box 7	Bagdad KY	40003	800-928-3333	502-747-8968
Belstra Milling Company Inc				
424 15th St PO Box 460	Demotte IN	46310	800-276-2789	
BioZyme Inc				
6010 Stockyards Expy	Saint Joseph MO	64504	800-821-3070	816-238-3326
Blue Seal Feeds Inc				
2905 US Hwy 61 N	Muscatine IA	52761	866-647-1212*	
*Cust Svc				
Buckeye Nutrition				
330 E Schultz Ave PO Box 505	Dalton OH	44618	800-417-6460	
Cumberland Valley Co-op Assn				
908 Mt Rock Rd	Shippensburg PA	17257	800-488-2197	717-532-2197
D & D Commodities Ltd				
PO Box 359	Stephen MN	56757	800-543-3308	
Darling International Inc				
251 O'Connor Ridge Blvd Ste 300	Irving TX	75038	855-327-7761	972-717-0300
NYSE: DAR				
Diamond V Mills Inc				
PO Box 74570	Cedar Rapids IA	52407	800-373-7234	319-366-0745
Eagle Roller Mill Co				
1101 Airport Rd	Shelby NC	28150	800-223-9108	704-487-5061
Effingham Equity Inc				
201 W Roadway Ave	Effingham IL	62401	800-223-1337	217-342-4101
Elenbaas Co 411 W Front St	Sumas WA	98295	800-808-6954	360-988-5811
First Co-op Assn (FCA)				
960 Riverview Dr PO Box 60	Cherokee IA	51012	877-753-5400	712-225-5400
FL Emmert Co Inc				
2007 Dunlap St	Cincinnati OH	45214	800-441-3343	513-721-5808
Flint River Mills Inc				
1100 Dothan Rd PO Box 280	Bainbridge GA	39817	800-841-8502*	229-246-2232
*Cust Svc				
FM Brown's Sons Inc				
205 Woodrow Ave PO Box 2116	Sinking Spring PA	19608	800-334-8816	610-678-4567
Form-A-Feed Inc (FAF)				
740 Bowman St	Stewart MN	55385	800-422-3649	320-562-2413
Friona Industries LP				
500 S Taylor St Ste 601 PO Box 15568	Amarillo TX	79101	800-658-6014	806-374-1811
Furst-McNess Co				
120 E Clark St	Freeport IL	61032	800-435-5100	815-235-6151
Harvest Land Co-op				
711 Front St PO Box 278	Morgan MN	56266	800-245-5819	507-249-3196
Hog Slat				
200 N Meridian Line Rd	Camden IN	46917	800-949-4647	574-967-3776
Hubbard Feeds Inc				
424 N Riverfront Dr PO Box 8500	Mankato MN	56001	800-869-7219	507-388-9400
JBS United Inc				
4310 State Rd 38 W	Sheridan IN	46069	800-382-9909	317-758-4495
JD Heiskell & Co				
116 W Cedar St	Tulare CA	93274	800-366-1886	559-685-6100
John A Van Den Bosch Co				
4511 Holland Ave	Holland MI	49424	800-968-6477	
Kay Dee Feed Company Inc				
1919 Grand Ave	Sioux City IA	51106	800-831-4815*	712-277-2011
*Cust Svc				
Kemin Industries Inc				
2100 Maury St	Des Moines IA	50317	800-777-8307	515-559-5100
Land O'Lakes Inc Western Feed Div				
4001 Lexington Ave N	Arden Hills MN	55126	800-328-9680	
Lucta USA Inc				
Pine Meadow Corporate Ctr 950 Technology Way Ste 110	Libertyville IL	60048	800-323-5341	847-996-3400
Manna Pro Corp				
707 Spirit 40 Pk Dr Ste 150	Chesterfield MO	63005	800-690-9908	
Mark Hershey Farms Inc				
479 Horseshoe Pk	Lebanon PA	17042	888-801-3301	717-867-4624
Merrick's Inc				
2415 Parview Rd PO Box 620307	Middleton WI	53562	800-637-7425	608-831-3440
Milk Specialties Co				
260 S Washington St	Carpentersville IL	60110	800-323-4274	952-942-7310
Mountaire Corp				
PO Box 1320	Millsboro DE	19966	877-887-1490	302-934-1100
Moyer & Son Inc				
113 E Reliance Rd	Souderton PA	18964	866-669-3747	215-799-2000

Right Column

			Toll-Free	Phone
NRV Inc N8155 American St	Ixonia WI	53036	800-558-0002	920-261-7000
Oberbeck Grain Co				
700 Walnut St	Highland IL	62249	800-632-2012	618-654-2387
OMCO Inc 214 E Mill St	Odon IN	47562	800-525-0272	812-636-7362
Provimi North America Inc				
10 Collective Way	Brookville OH	45309	888-522-2420	937-770-2400
Quali Tech Inc				
318 Lake Hazeltine Dr	Chaska MN	55318	800-328-5870	952-448-5151
Ralco Nutrition Inc				
1600 Hahn Rd	Marshall MN	56258	800-533-5306	
Rangen Inc 115 13th Ave S	Buhl ID	83316	800-657-6446*	208-543-6421
*Cust Svc				
Seminole Feed				
335 NE Watula Ave PO Box 940	Ocala FL	34470	800-683-1881	352-732-4143
Star Milling Co				
24067 Water St	Perris CA	92570	800-733-6455	951-657-3143
Triple Crown Nutrition Inc				
319 Barry Ave S Ste 303	Wayzata MN	55391	800-451-9916	
Trouw Nutrition				
115 Executive Dr	Highland IL	62249	800-365-1357	618-654-2070
Vita Plus Corp				
2514 Fish Hatchery Rd	Madison WI	53713	800-362-8334	608-256-1988
Zeigler Bros Inc				
400 GaRdner Stn Rd PO Box 95	Gardners PA	17324	800-841-6800	717-677-6181

445   LOGGING

			Toll-Free	Phone
Canal Wood LLC 2430 Main St	Conway SC	29526	866-587-1460	843-488-9663
Greif Inc 425 Winter Rd	Delaware OH	43015	877-781-9797	740-549-6000
NYSE: GEF				
Midwest Walnut Co				
1914 Postevin St	Council Bluffs IA	51503	800-592-5688	712-325-9191
Plum Creek Timber Company Inc				
601 Union St Ste 3100	Seattle WA	98101	800-858-5347	206-467-3600
NYSE: PCL				
Roseburg Forest Products Co				
PO Box 1088	Roseburg OR	97470	800-245-1115	541-679-3311

446   LOGISTICS SERVICES (TRANSPORTATION & WAREHOUSING)

SEE ALSO Trucking Companies ; Commercial Warehousing ; Freight Forwarders ; Marine Services ; Rail Transport Services

			Toll-Free	Phone
A Duie Pyle Inc				
650 Westtown Rd	West Chester PA	19382	800-523-5020	610-696-5800
Access Business Group				
7575 Fulton St E	Ada MI	49355	800-253-6500*	616-787-6000
*Cust Svc				
ADS Tactical Inc				
Lynnwood Plz 621 Lynnhaven Pkwy Ste 400	Virginia Beach VA	23452	800-948-9433	757-481-7758
AN Deringer Inc				
64 N Main St	Saint Albans VT	05478	800-448-8108	802-524-8110
APL Logistics Inc				
16220 N Scottsdale Rd Ste 300	Scottsdale AZ	85254	866-896-2005	
Associated Global Systems Inc				
3333 New Hyde Pk Rd	New Hyde Park NY	11042	800-645-8300*	516-627-8910
*Cust Svc				
Atlantic Bulk Carrier Corp				
PO Box 112	Providence Forge VA	23140	800-966-0030	804-966-5459
B-H Transfer Co				
750 Sparta Rd PO Box 151	Sandersville GA	31082	888-786-3664	478-552-5119
Bender Group 345 Parr Cir	Reno NV	89512	800-621-9402	775-788-8800
Bulldog Hiway Express				
3390 Buffalo Ave	Charleston SC	29418	800-331-9515	843-744-1651
Cdo Technologies Inc				
5200 Sprngfeld St Ste 320	Dayton OH	45431	866-307-6616	937-258-0022
Central Transportation Systems Inc				
4105 Rio Bravo Ste 100	El Paso TX	79902	800-283-3106	
CH Robinson Worldwide Inc				
14701 Charlson Rd	Eden Prairie MN	55347	855-229-6128*	952-683-3950
NASDAQ: CHRW ▩ *Cust Svc				
Clean Air Technology Inc				
41105 Capital Dr	Canton MI	48187	800-459-6320	734-459-6320
Clipper Exxpress Inc				
9014 Heritage Pkwy Ste 300	Woodridge IL	60517	800-678-2547	630-739-0700
Coleman American Cos Inc				
PO Box 960	Midland City AL	36350	877-693-7060	334-983-6500
Conley Transport Ii Inc				
2104 Eastline Rd	Searcy AR	72143	800-338-8700	501-268-4672
Coyote Logistics LLC				
191 E Deerpath Rd	Lake Forest IL	60045	877-626-9683	847-295-2424
Crane Worldwide Logistics LLC				
1500 Rankin Rd	Houston TX	77073	888-870-2726	281-443-2777
Daniel F Young Inc				
1235 Westlakes Dr Ste 255	Berwyn PA	19312	866-407-0083	610-725-4000
Danny Herman Trucking Inc				
PO Box 55	Mountain City TN	37683	800-251-7500	423-727-9061
Dennis K Burke Inc				
284 Eastern Ave PO Box 6069	Chelsea MA	02150	800-289-2875	617-884-7800
Dependable Highway Express Inc				
2440 S 48th Ave	Phoenix AZ	85043	800-472-2037	602-278-4401
Dohrn Transfer Co				
625 Third Ave	Rock Island IL	61201	888-364-7621	309-794-0723
DSC Logistics				
1750 S Wolf Rd	Des Plaines IL	60018	800-372-1960	
Exel 570 Polaris Pkwy	Westerville OH	43082	800-272-1052	614-865-8500
Expeditors International of Washington Inc				
1015 Third Ave 12th Fl	Seattle WA	98104	800-284-7474	206-674-3400
NASDAQ: EXPD				
FedEx Supply Chain Services Inc				
5455 Darrow Rd	Hudson OH	44236	800-463-3339	901-369-3600
Fremont Contract Carriers Inc (FCC)				
865 S Bud Blvd	Fremont NE	68025	800-228-9842	

		Toll-Free	Phone
Gypsum Express Ltd			
8280 Sixty Rd PO Box 268	Baldwinsville NY 13027	800-621-7901	315-638-2201
H E Whitlock Inc			
4808 Dillon Dr	Pueblo CO 81008	866-933-0709	
Hanson Logistics			
2900 S State St Ste 4 E	Saint Joseph MI 49085	888-772-1197	269-982-1390
Higher Ed Growth LLC			
5400 S Lakeshore Dr Ste 101	Tempe AZ 85283	866-433-8532	
Horizon Air Freight Inc			
152-15 Rockaway Blvd	Jamaica NY 11434	800-221-6028	718-528-3800
Hub Group Inc			
3050 Highland Pkwy Ste 100	Downers Grove IL 60515	800-377-5833	630-271-3600
NASDAQ: HUBG			
JB Hunt Transport Services Inc			
615 JB Hunt Corporate Dr	Lowell AR 72745	800-643-3622	479-820-0000
NASDAQ: JBHT			
Kenco Group Inc			
2001 Riverside Dr	Chattanooga TN 37406	800-758-3289	
Kintetsu World Express USA Inc			
One Jericho Plz Ste 100	Jericho NY 11753	800-275-4045	516-933-7100
Kuehne & Nagel Inc			
10 Exchange Pl	Jersey City NJ 07302	866-914-0444	201-413-5500
L&B Transport LLC			
708 US190 PO Box 74870	Port Allen LA 70767	800-545-9401	225-387-0894
Landstar Logistics Inc			
13410 Sutton Pk Dr S	Jacksonville FL 32224	800-872-9400	904-398-9400
LeSaint Logistics			
868 W Crossroads Pkwy	Romeoville IL 60446	877-566-9375	630-243-5950
M & J Transportation			
3536 Nicholson Ave	Kansas City MO 64120	866-298-3858	816-231-6733
Matson Logistics Inc			
555 12th St	Oakland CA 94607	800-492-8766	510-628-4000
McElroy Truck Lines Inc			
111 80 Spur PO Box 104	Cuba AL 36907	800-992-7863	205-392-5579
Menlo Worldwide Inc			
Con-Way Inc			
2855 Campus Dr Ste 300	San Mateo CA 94403	800-426-6929	650-378-5200
Meridian IQ			
11501 Outlook St Ste 500	Overland Park KS 66211	877-246-4909	
Metropolitan Trucking Inc (MRTK)			
299 Market St Ste 300	Saddle Brook NJ 07663	800-967-3278	
Midwest Specialized Transportation Inc			
PO Box 6418	Rochester MN 55903	800-927-8007	
Miller Bros Express LC			
560 West 400 North	Hyrum UT 84319	800-366-6239	435-245-6025
Mitsui & Co (USA) Inc			
200 Pk Ave	New York NY 10166	877-248-4237	212-878-4000
National Distributors Inc			
1517 Avco Blvd	Sellersburg IN 47172	800-334-9677	812-246-6306
National Freight Inc (NFI)			
1515 Burnt Mill Rd	Cherry Hill NJ 08003	877-634-3777*	
*General			
Navis Logistics Network			
6551 S Revere Pkwy Ste 250	Centennial CO 80111	800-344-3528	
Oakley Transport Inc			
101 ABC Rd PO Box 4170	Lake Wales FL 33859	800-969-8265	863-638-1435
ODW Logistics Inc			
1580 Williams Rd	Columbus OH 43207	800-743-7062	614-497-1660
Panalpina			
1776 On-the-Green 67 E Pk Pl	Morristown NJ 07960	866-202-0377	973-683-9000
Pegasus Logistics Group Inc			
615 Freeport Pkwy Ste 100	Coppell TX 75019	800-997-7226	469-671-0300
Pierce Distribution Services Co			
PO Box 15600	Loves Park IL 61132	800-466-7397	
Ponvia Technology Inc			
49-T Sherwood Ter	Lake Bluff IL 60045	877-217-0875	
Red Rock Distributing Co			
One NW 50th St	Oklahoma City OK 73118	800-323-7109	405-677-3373
Red Star Oil 802 Purser Dr	Raleigh NC 27603	800-774-6033	919-772-1944
RIM Logistics Ltd			
200 N Gary Ave Ste B	Roselle IL 60172	888-275-0937	630-595-0610
Rinchem Company Inc			
6133 Edith Blvd NE	Albuquerque NM 87107	888-375-2436	505-345-3655
Ryder System Inc			
11690 NW 105th St	Miami FL 33178	800-297-9337	305-500-3726
NYSE: R			
S & H Express Inc			
400 Mulberry St PO Box 20219	York PA 17403	800-637-9782	717-848-5015
Schneider National Inc			
3101 S Packerland Dr PO Box 2545	Green Bay WI 54306	800-558-6767	920-592-2000
Seko Worldwide Inc			
1100 Arlington Heights Rd Ste 600	Itasca IL 60143	800-323-1235	630-919-4800
Shaker Group Inc, The			
862 Albany Shaker Rd	Latham NY 12110	800-267-0314	518-786-9286
Slay Industries Inc			
1441 Hampton Ave	Saint Louis MO 63139	800-852-7529	314-647-7529
Store Opening Solutions (SOS)			
800 Middle Tennessee Blvd	Murfreesboro TN 37129	877-388-9262	
Sunteck Transport Group			
6413 Congress Ave Ste 260	Boca Raton FL 33487	800-759-7910	561-988-9456
PINK: AUTO			
Tbb Global Logistics Inc			
802 Far Hills Dr	New Freedom PA 17349	800-937-8224	717-227-5000
Technical Transportation Inc			
1701 W Northwest Hwy Ste 100	Grapevine TX 76051	800-852-8726	
Thoroughbred Direct Intermodal Services			
5165 Campus Dr Ste 400	Plymouth Meeting PA 19462	877-250-2902	610-567-3360
TRANSFLO Terminal Services Inc			
500 Water St Ste J975	Jacksonville FL 32202	866-872-6735	
Transplace			
3010 Gaylord Pkwy Ste 200	Frisco TX 75034	866-413-9266	
UPS Supply Chain Solutions			
12380 Morris Rd	Alpharetta GA 30005	800-742-5727	913-693-6151
Vimich Traffic Logistics			
12201 Tecumseh Rd E	Tecumseh ON N8N1M3	800-284-1045	
Weber Logistics			
13530 Rosecrans Ave	Santa Fe Springs CA 90670	855-469-3237	

		Toll-Free	Phone
Wiley Sanders Truck Lines Inc			
PO Box 707	Troy AL 36081	800-633-8740	334-566-5184
Wilheit Packaging LLC			
1527 May Dr	Gainesville GA 30507	800-727-4421	770-532-4421
XPO Logistics Inc			
6805 Perimeter Dr	Dublin OH 43016	800-837-7584	614-923-1400

447   LONG-TERM CARE FACILITIES

SEE ALSO Retirement Communities ; Veterans Nursing Homes - State ; Long-Term Care Facilities Operators

Free-standing facilities accredited by the Joint Commission on Accreditation of Healthcare Organizations. Listings in this category are organized alphabetically by states.

		Toll-Free	Phone
Apple Rehab 46 Maple St	Kent CT 06757	800-353-5368*	860-927-5368
*General			
Area Agency On Aging			
9549 Koger Blvd			
Gadsden Bldg Ste 100	St Petersburg FL 33702	800-963-5337	727-570-9696
Area Agency On Aging 10b Inc			
1550 Corporate Woods Pkwy	Uniontown OH 44685	800-421-7277	330-896-9172
Armed Forces Retirement Home - Washington			
3700 N Capitol St NW	Washington DC 20011	800-422-9988*	
*Admissions			
Casa Colina Ctr for Rehabilitation			
255 E Bonita Ave	Pomona CA 91769	800-926-5462	909-596-7733
Central Boston Elder Services Inc			
2315 Washington St	Boston MA 02119	800-922-2275	617-277-7416
Comprehensive Care Management Corp (CCM)			
1250 Waters Pl Tower 1 Ste 602	Bronx NY 10461	877-226-8500	
Diamond Hill Nursing & Rehabilitation			
100 New Tpke Rd	Troy NY 12182	800-697-5374	518-235-1410
Elim Park Baptist Home Inc			
140 Cook Hill Rd	Cheshire CT 06410	800-994-1776	203-272-7550
Extended Care Hospital Westminster			
206 Hospital Cir	Westminster CA 92683	800-236-9747	714-891-2769
Front Porch Communities & Services			
303 N Glenoaks Blvd	Burbank CA 91502	800-233-3709	
Heartland Health Care Ctr Bloomfield Hills			
2975 N Adams Rd	Bloomfield Hills MI 48304	800-622-6757	248-645-2900
Hennis Care Centre			
1720 Cross St	Dover OH 44622	800-241-1044	330-364-8849
Heritage Ctr			
1201 W Buena Vista Rd	Evansville IN 47710	800-704-0700	812-429-0700
Holyoke Rehabilitation Ctr			
260 Easthampton Rd	Holyoke MA 01040	800-811-3535	413-538-9733
Hope Network			
3075 Orchard Vista Dr SE	Grand Rapids MI 49546	800-695-7273	616-301-8000
Jewish Home Lifecare			
120 W 106th St	New York NY 10025	800-544-0304	212-870-5000
Kindred Hospital Greensboro			
2401 Southside Blvd	Greensboro NC 27406	877-836-2671	336-271-2800
Kindred Hospital Philadelphia			
6129 Palmetto St	Philadelphia PA 19111	800-654-5988	215-722-8555
Kindred Hospital Pittsburgh			
7777 Steubenville Pk	Oakdale PA 15071	800-654-5988	412-494-5500
Kula Hospital 100 Keokea Pl	Kula HI 96790	800-845-6733	808-878-1221
La Jolla Nursing & Rehabilitation Ctr			
2552 Torrey Pines Rd	La Jolla CA 92037	800-861-0086	858-453-5810
Lowell Health Care Ctr			
19 Varnum St	Lowell MA 01850	800-811-3535	978-454-5644
ManorCare Health Services - Mountainside			
1180 Rt 22 W	Mountainside NJ 07092	800-366-1232	908-654-0020
North Adams Common Nursing Home			
175 Franklin St	North Adams MA 01247	800-445-4560	413-664-4041
Oklahoma Veterans Ctr Norman			
1776 E Robinson St	Norman OK 73071	800-782-5218	405-360-5600
Presbyterian SeniorCare-Westminster Place			
1215 Hulton Rd	Oakmont PA 15139	877-772-6500	412-828-5600
Pyramid Point Post-Acute Rehabilitation Ctr			
8530 Township Line Rd	Indianapolis IN 46260	800-861-0086	317-876-9955
Redstone Highlands Health Care Ctr			
6 Garden Ctr Dr	Greensburg PA 15601	800-732-0999	724-832-8400
Rest Haven-York			
1050 S George St	York PA 17403	800-368-1019	717-843-9866
River Garden Hebrew Home for the Aged			
11401 Old St Augustine Rd	Jacksonville FL 32258	800-468-3571	904-260-1818
St.Vincent Health			
2001 W 86th St	Indianapolis IN 46260	866-338-2345	317-338-2345
Voorhees Pediatric Facility			
1304 Laurel Oak Rd	Voorhees NJ 08043	888-873-5437	856-346-3300
Watrous Nursing Ctr			
9 Neck Rd	Madison CT 06443	800-353-5368	203-245-9483
Williamstown Commons Nursing & Rehabilitation Ctr			
25 Adams Rd	Williamstown MA 01267	800-445-4560	413-458-2111

448   LONG-TERM CARE FACILITIES OPERATORS

		Toll-Free	Phone
Active Day/Senior Care Inc			
400 Redland Ct Ste 114	Owings Mills MD 21117	866-724-9599	
Aegis Assisted Living			
17602 NE Union Hill Rd	Redmond WA 98052	888-252-3447	425-861-9993
American Religious Town Hall Meeting Inc			
PO Box 180118	Dallas TX 75218	800-783-9828	214-328-9828
CabelTel International Corp			
1603 Lyndon B Johnson Fwy	Dallas TX 75234	888-407-8400	972-407-8400
ElderWood Senior Care			
Seven Limestone Dr	Williamsville NY 14221	888-826-9663	716-633-3900
Emeritus Corp			
3131 Elliott Ave Ste 500	Seattle WA 98121	855-444-7658	206-298-2909
NYSE: ESC			

				Toll-Free	Phone

Five Star Quality Care Inc
400 Centre St . . . . Newton MA 02458 **866-230-1286** 617-796-8387
NYSE: FVE

Genesis HealthCare Corp
101 E State St . . . . Kennett Square PA 19348 **800-944-7776** 610-444-6350

Kindred Healthcare Inc
680 S Fourth Ave . . . . Louisville KY 40202 **800-545-0749** 502-596-7300
NYSE: KND

Odyssey HealthCare Inc
717 N Harwood St . . . . Dallas TX 75201 **888-922-9711** 214-922-9711

Sun Healthcare Group Inc
18831 Von Karman Ste 400 . . . . Irvine CA 92612 **800-729-6600** 949-255-7100
NASDAQ: SUNH

Sunrise Senior Living Inc
7902 Westpark Rd Ste T-900 . . . . McLean VA 22102 **800-929-4124** 703-273-7500
NYSE: SRZ

449   LOTTERIES, GAMES, SWEEPSTAKES

SEE ALSO Games & Gaming

				Toll-Free	Phone

Colorado
Lottery
212 W Third St Ste 210 . . . . Pueblo CO 81003 **800-999-2959** 719-546-2400

Cypress Bayou Casino
832 Martin Luther King Rd . . . . Charenton LA 70523 **800-284-4386**

Idaho
Lottery
1199 Shoreline Ln Ste 100 . . . . Boise ID 83702 **800-432-5688** 208-334-2600

Illinois
Lottery
101 W Jefferson St . . . . Springfield IL 62702 **800-252-1775** 217-524-6435

Indiana
Lottery
201 S Capitol Ave Ste 1100 . . . . Indianapolis IN 46225 **800-955-6886** 317-264-4800

Kansas
Lottery 128 N Kansas Ave . . . . Topeka KS 66603 **800-544-9467** 785-296-5700

Kentucky
Lottery Corp
1011 W Main St . . . . Louisville KY 40202 **800-937-8946** 502-560-1500

Montana Lottery
2525 N Montana Ave . . . . Helena MT 59601 **800-425-1435** 406-444-5825

Nebraska Lottery
1800 "O" St PO Box 98901 . . . . Lincoln NE 68509 **800-587-5200** 402-471-6100

New Hampshire
Lottery Commission
14 Integra St . . . . Concord NH 03301 **800-852-3324** 603-271-3391

Ohio Lottery Commission
615 W Superior Ave . . . . Cleveland OH 44113 **800-686-4208** 216-787-3200

Washington
State Lottery PO Box 43000 . . . . Olympia WA 98504 **800-732-5101** 360-664-4720

450   LUGGAGE, BAGS, CASES

SEE ALSO Handbags, Totes, Backpacks ; Leather Goods - Personal

				Toll-Free	Phone

Anvil Cases
15730 Salt Lake Ave . . . . City of Industry CA 91745 **800-359-2684** 626-968-4100

Brewer-Cantelmo Company Inc
55 W 39th St Ste 205 . . . . New York NY 10018 **800-246-1233** 212-244-4600

Calzone Case Co
225 Black Rock Ave . . . . Bridgeport CT 06605 **800-243-5152*** 203-367-5766
*Cust Svc

CH Ellis Co Inc
2432 SE Ave . . . . Indianapolis IN 46201 **800-466-3351*** 317-636-3351
*Sales

Coach Inc 516 W 34th St . . . . New York NY 10001 **800-444-3611** 212-594-1850
NYSE: COH

Delsey Luggage
6735 Business Pkwy Ste A . . . . Elkridge MD 21075 **800-558-3344** 410-796-5655

Mercury Luggage Manufacturing Co
4843 Victor St . . . . Jacksonville FL 32207 **800-874-1885** 904-334-8801

Platt Luggage Inc
4051 W 51st St . . . . Chicago IL 60632 **800-222-1555** 773-838-2000

SKB Corp 434 W Levers Pl . . . . Orange CA 92867 **800-410-2024*** 714-637-1252
*Sales

Targus Inc 1211 N Miller St . . . . Anaheim CA 92806 **877-482-7487** 714-765-5555

Travelpro USA
700 Banyan Trl . . . . Boca Raton FL 33431 **800-741-7471** 561-998-2824

Zero Manufacturing Inc
500 West 200 North . . . . North Salt Lake UT 84054 **800-959-5050** 801-298-5900

451   MACHINE SHOPS

SEE ALSO Precision Machined Products

				Toll-Free	Phone

Acme Cryogenics Inc
2801 Mitchell Ave . . . . Allentown PA 18103 **800-422-2790** 610-966-4488

American Grinding & Machine Co
2000 N Mango Ave . . . . Chicago IL 60639 **877-988-4343** 773-889-4343

Chalmers & Kubeck Inc
150 Commerce Dr . . . . Aston PA 19014 **800-242-5637** 610-494-4300

Chapel Steel Co
590 N Bethlehem Pk PO Box 1000 . . . . Lower Gwynedd PA 19002 **800-570-7674** 215-793-0899

Femco Machine Co
754 S Main St Ext . . . . Punxsutawney PA 15767 **800-458-3445** 814-938-9763

Furmanite America
101 Old Underwood Rd Unit E . . . . La Porte TX 77571 **800-444-5572** 281-842-5100

Granite State Manufacturing Co
124 Joliette St . . . . Manchester NH 03102 **800-464-7646**

Haas Automation Inc
2800 Sturgis Rd . . . . Oxnard CA 93030 **800-331-6746** 805-278-1800

Hfw Industries Inc
196 Philadelphia St PO Box 8 . . . . Buffalo NY 14207 **800-937-9311** 716-875-3380

Highway Machine Company Inc (HMC)
3010 S Old US Hwy 41 . . . . Princeton IN 47670 **866-990-9462** 812-385-3639

Hughes Supply Company of Thomasville Inc
175 Kanoy Rd PO Box 1003 . . . . Thomasville NC 27360 **800-747-8141** 336-475-8146

Industrial Tool Inc
9210 52nd Ave N . . . . New Hope MN 55428 **800-776-4455*** 763-533-7244
*Sales

J C Steele & Sons Inc
710 S Mulberry St . . . . Statesville NC 28677 **800-278-3353** 704-872-3681

Kurt Manufacturing Co
5280 Main St NE . . . . Minneapolis MN 55421 **800-458-7855** 763-572-1500

Laser Excel
N6323 Berlin Rd PO Box 279 . . . . Green Lake WI 54941 **800-285-6544** 920-294-6544

LaVezzi Precision Inc
999 Regency Dr . . . . Glendale Heights IL 60139 **800-323-1772** 630-582-1230

Lemco Tool Corp
1850 Metzger Ave . . . . Cogan Station PA 17728 **800-233-8713** 570-494-0620

Lith-O-Roll Corp
9521 Telstar Ave . . . . El Monte CA 91731 **800-423-4176** 626-579-0340

Marshall Screw Products Co
3820 Chandler Dr Ne . . . . Minneapolis MN 55421 **800-321-6727**

Micro Instrument Corp (MIC)
1199 Emerson St PO Box 60619 . . . . Rochester NY 14606 **800-200-3150** 585-458-3150

Myrmo & Sons Inc
3600 Franklin Blvd . . . . Eugene OR 97403 **800-683-7040** 541-747-4565

Poly Cycle Inc
5501 Campbells Run Rd . . . . Pittsburgh PA 15205 **800-394-4333** 412-747-1101

Quality Mfg Company Inc (QMI)
PO Box 616 . . . . Winchester KY 40392 **866-460-6459** 859-744-0420

RS Hughes Company Inc Saunders Div
975 N Todd Ave . . . . Azusa CA 91702 **888-932-8836*** 626-691-1111
*Sales

Santinelli International Inc
325 Oser Ave . . . . Hauppauge NY 11788 **800-644-3343** 631-435-3343

Scheirer Machine Company Inc
3200 Industrial Blvd . . . . Bethel Park PA 15102 **800-448-4590** 412-833-6500

Schmiede Corp
1865 Riley Creek Rd PO Box 1630 . . . . . . Tullahoma TN 37388 **800-535-1851** 931-455-4801

Solid Concepts Inc
28309 Ave Crocker . . . . Valencia CA 91355 **888-311-1017** 661-295-4400

Standard Locknut Inc
1045 E 169th St . . . . Westfield IN 46074 **800-783-6887** 317-867-0100

Tier One LLC 31 Pecks Ln . . . . Newtown CT 06470 **877-251-2228** 203-426-3030

Twin City EDM
7940 Rancher Rd NE . . . . Fridley MN 55432 **800-397-0338** 763-783-7808

Unisource Manufacturing Inc
8040 NE 33rd Dr . . . . Portland OR 97211 **800-234-2566** 503-281-4673

Vescio Threading Co
14002 Anson Ave . . . . Santa Fe Springs CA 90670 **800-361-4218** 562-802-1868

Wahlco Inc
2722 S Fairview St . . . . Santa Ana CA 92704 **800-423-5432** 714-979-7300

Warren Fabricating & Machining
3240 Mahoning Ave NW . . . . Warren OH 44483 **800-827-0596** 330-847-0596

Weldmac Manufacturing Co
1451 N Johnson Ave . . . . El Cajon CA 92020 **800-252-1533** 619-440-2300

Windings Inc PO Box 566 . . . . New Ulm MN 56073 **800-795-8533** 507-359-2034

Xtek Inc
11451 Reading Rd . . . . Cincinnati OH 45241 **888-332-9835** 513-733-7800

452   MACHINE TOOLS - METAL CUTTING TYPES

SEE ALSO Machine Tools - Metal Forming Types ; Metalworking Devices & Accessories

				Toll-Free	Phone

Abbco Inc
2401 American Ln . . . . Elkgrove Vlg IL 60007 **866-986-6546** 630-595-7115

Allied Tool Products
9334 N 107th St . . . . Milwaukee WI 53224 **800-558-5147** 414-355-8280

Barnes International Inc
814 Chestnut St PO Box 1203 . . . . Rockford IL 61105 **800-435-4877** 815-964-8661

Crafts Technology
91 Joey Dr . . . . Elk Grove Village IL 60007 **800-323-6802** 847-758-3100

Darex
210 E Hersey St PO Box 730 . . . . Ashland OR 97520 **800-418-1439** 541-488-2224

Davenport Machine Inc
167 Ames St . . . . Rochester NY 14611 **800-344-5748** 585-235-4545

EH Wachs Co
600 Knightsbridge Pkwy . . . . Lincolnshire IL 60069 **800-323-8185** 847-537-8800

Extrude Hone Corp
235 Industry Blvd . . . . Irwin PA 15642 **800-367-1109** 724-863-5900

Flow International Corp
23500 64th Ave S . . . . Kent WA 98032 **800-446-3569** 253-850-3500
NASDAQ: FLOW

GF Machining Solutions
560 Bond St . . . . Lincolnshire IL 60069 **800-282-1336** 847-913-5300

Gleason Corp
1000 University Ave . . . . Rochester NY 14607 **800-727-6333** 585-473-1000

Grob Inc 1731 Tenth Ave . . . . Grafton WI 53024 **800-225-6481** 262-377-1400

Hanchett Manufacturing Inc
906 N State St . . . . Big Rapids MI 49307 **800-454-7463** 231-796-7678

Harding Inc 1 Hardinge Dr . . . . Elmira NY 14902 **800-843-8801** 607-734-2281
NASDAQ: HDNG

Hause Machines
809 S Pleasant St . . . . Montpelier OH 43543 **800-932-8665** 419-485-3158

Huffman Corp
1050 Huffman Way . . . . Clover SC 29710 **888-483-3626** 803-222-4561

Hurco Cos Inc
One Technology Way . . . . Indianapolis IN 46268 **800-634-2416*** 317-293-5309
NASDAQ: HURC ■ *Sales

Hydromat Inc
11600 Adie Rd . . . . Saint Louis MO 63043 **800-552-3288** 314-432-4644

Hypertherm Inc
21 Great Hollow Rd PO Box 5010 . . . . Hanover NH 03755 **800-643-0030** 603-643-3441

Kaufman Mfg Co
547 S 29th St PO Box 1056 . . . . Manitowoc WI 54221 **800-420-6641** 920-684-6641

	Toll-Free	Phone
Kennametal Inc		
1600 Technology Way PO Box 231 . . . . .Latrobe PA 15650	**800-446-7738***	724-539-5000
NYSE: KMT ■ *Cust Svc*		
Klingelhofer Corp		
165 Mill Ln . . . . .Mountainside NJ 07092	**800-879-5546**	908-232-7200
Koike Aronson Inc		
635 W Main St PO Box 307 . . . . .Arcade NY 14009	**800-252-5232**	585-492-2400
Kyocera Tycom Corp		
3565 Cadillac . . . . .Costa Mesa CA 92626	**800-823-7284**	714-428-3600
Makino 7680 Innovation Way . . . . .Mason OH 45040	**888-625-4661**	513-573-7200
McLean Inc		
3409 E Miraloma Ave . . . . .Anaheim CA 92806	**800-451-2424***	714-996-5451
*Cust Svc		
NNT Corp 1320 Norwood Ave .Itasca IL 60143	**800-556-9999**	630-875-9600
North American Products Corp		
1180 Wernsing Rd . . . . .Jasper IN 47546	**800-457-7468***	812-482-2000
*Cust Svc		
Oliver of Adrian Inc		
1111 E Beecher St PO Box 189 . . . . .Adrian MI 49221	**877-668-0885**	517-263-2132
Parker Majestic Inc		
300 N Pike Rd . . . . .Sarver PA 16055	**866-572-7537**	724-352-1551
Peddinghaus Corp		
300 N Washington Ave . . . . .Bradley IL 60915	**800-786-2448**	815-937-3800
Pioneer Broach Co		
6434 Telegraph Rd . . . . .Los Angeles CA 90040	**800-621-1945**	323-728-1263
Rothenberger USA		
4455 Boeing Dr . . . . .Rockford IL 61109	**800-545-7698**	815-397-7617
Rottler Mfg 8029 S 200th St .Kent WA 98032	**800-452-0534**	253-872-7050
S & M Machine Service Inc		
109 E Highland Dr . . . . .Oconto Falls WI 54154	**800-323-1579**	920-846-8130
Sandvik Coromant Co		
1702 Nevins Rd . . . . .Fair Lawn NJ 07410	**800-726-3845***	201-794-5000
*Cust Svc		
Servo Products Co		
34940 Lakeland Blvd . . . . .Eastlake OH 44095	**800-521-7359**	440-942-9999
Setco Sales Co		
5880 Hillside Ave . . . . .Cincinnati OH 45233	**800-543-0470**	513-941-5110
SNK America Inc		
1150 Feehanville Dr . . . . .Mount Prospect IL 60056	**888-765-6224**	847-364-0801
Southwestern Industries Inc		
2615 Homestead Pl . . . . .Rancho Dominguez CA 90220	**800-421-6875**	310-608-4422
Sunnen Products Co		
7910 Manchester Ave .Saint Louis MO 63143	**800-325-3670**	314-781-2100
Technidrill Systems Inc		
429 Portage Blvd . . . . .Kent OH 44240	**800-914-5863**	330-678-9980
Thermal Dynamics Corp		
82 Benning St . . . . .West Lebanon NH 03784	**800-752-7621**	603-298-5711
Tool-Flo Mfg Inc		
7803 Hansen Rd . . . . .Houston TX 77061	**800-345-2815**	713-941-1080
Toyoda Machinery USA Inc		
316 W University Dr . . . . .Arlington Heights IL 60004	**800-257-2985**	847-253-0340
TRU TECH Systems Inc		
24550 N River Rd PO Box 46965 . . . . .Mount Clemens MI 48046	**877-878-8324**	586-469-2700
US Tool Grinding Inc		
701 S Desloge Dr . . . . .Desloge MO 63601	**800-775-8665**	573-431-3856
Vernon Tool Company Ltd		
503 Jones Rd . . . . .Oceanside CA 92054	**800-452-1542**	760-433-5860
WF Meyers Co		
1008 13th St PO Box 426 . . . . .Bedford IN 47421	**800-457-4055**	812-275-4485
Whitney Tool Company Inc		
906 R St PO Box 545 . . . . .Bedford IN 47421	**800-536-1971**	812-275-4491
Wisconsin Machine Tool Corp		
3225 Gateway Rd Ste 100 . . . . .Brookfield WI 53045	**800-243-3078**	262-317-3048

453   MACHINE TOOLS - METAL FORMING TYPES

SEE ALSO Rolling Mill Machinery ; Tool & Die Shops ; Machine Tools - Metal Cutting Types ; Metalworking Devices & Accessories

	Toll-Free	Phone
Advanced Hydraulics Inc		
13568 Vintage Pl . . . . .Chino CA 91710	**888-581-8079**	909-590-7644
Amada America Inc		
7025 Firestone Blvd .Buena Park CA 90621	**800-626-6612**	714-739-2111
Badge A Minit Ltd		
345 N Lewis Ave . . . . .Oglesby IL 61348	**800-223-4103**	815-883-8822
Bliss Clearing Niagara (BCN)		
1004 E State St . . . . .Hastings MI 49058	**800-642-5477**	269-948-3300
Bradbury Company Inc		
1200 E Cole . . . . .Moundridge KS 67107	**800-397-6394**	620-345-6394
Cyril Bath Co		
1610 Airport Rd . . . . .Monroe NC 28110	**800-801-1418**	704-289-8531
DR Sperry & Co		
623 Rathbone Ave . . . . .Aurora IL 60506	**888-997-9297**	630-892-4361
Edwards Manufacturing Co		
1107 Sykes St PO Box 166 . . . . .Albert Lea MN 56007	**800-373-8206**	507-373-8206
Erie Press Systems		
1253 W 12th St PO Box 4061 . . . . .Erie PA 16512	**800-222-3608**	814-455-3941
Grant Assembly Technologies		
90 Silliman Ave . . . . .Bridgeport CT 06605	**800-227-2150**	203-366-4557
Greenerd Press & Machine Company Inc		
41 Crown St . . . . .Nashua NH 03060	**800-877-9110**	603-889-4101
Manor Industries Inc		
24400 Maplehurst . . . . .Clinton Township MI 48036	**800-921-1007**	586-463-4604
Mate Precision Tooling Inc		
1295 Lund Blvd . . . . .Anoka MN 55303	**800-328-4492**	763-421-0230
Murata Machinery USA Inc		
2120 Queen City Dr . . . . .Charlotte NC 28208	**800-428-8469**	
Pacific Press Technologies		
714 Walnut St . . . . .Mount Carmel IL 62863	**800-851-3586**	618-262-8666
Presses Inc 6360 W 73rd St .Chicago IL 60638	**800-927-9393**	708-496-7400
Reed 28 Sword St . . . . .Auburn MA 01501	**800-343-6068**	508-753-6530
Schleuniger Inc		
87 Colin Dr . . . . .Manchester NH 03103	**877-902-1470***	603-668-8117
*Tech Supp		
Strippit Inc/LVD		
12975 Clarence Ctr Rd . . . . .Akron NY 14001	**800-828-1527**	716-542-4511

	Toll-Free	Phone
Tetrahedron Assoc Inc		
PO Box 710157 . . . . .San Diego CA 92171	**800-958-3872**	619-661-0552
Tools for Bending Inc		
194 W Dakota Ave . . . . .Denver CO 80223	**800-873-3305***	303-777-7170
*Cust Svc		
Williams White & Co		
600 River Dr . . . . .Moline IL 61265	**877-797-7650**	
Wysong Inc 4820 US 29 N . . . . .Greensboro NC 27405	**800-299-7664**	336-621-3960

454   MAGAZINES & JOURNALS

SEE ALSO Periodicals Publishers

454-1 Agriculture & Farming Magazines

	Toll-Free	Phone
American Agriculturist		
5227-B Baltimore Pike . . . . .Littlestown PA 17340	**800-441-1410**	717-359-0150
Beef Magazine		
7900 International Dr Ste 300 . . . . .Minneapolis MN 55425	**800-722-5334***	952-851-9329
*Cust Svc		
Dairy Herd Management		
10901 W 84th Terr . . . . .Lenexa KS 66214	**800-255-5113**	913-438-8700
Farm Industry News		
7900 International Dr Ste 300 . . . . .Minneapolis MN 55425	**800-722-5334***	952-851-9329
*Cust Svc		
Farm Journal		
30 S 15th Ste 900 . . . . .Philadelphia PA 19102	**800-331-9310**	215-557-8900
Farm Show Magazine		
20088 Kenwood Trial . . . . .Lakeville MN 55044	**800-834-9665**	
Georgia Farm Bureau News		
1620 Bass Rd . . . . .Macon GA 31210	**800-342-1192**	478-474-8411
Hoard's Dairyman Magazine		
28 Milwaukee Ave W PO Box 801 . . . . .Fort Atkinson WI 53538	**800-245-8222**	920-563-5551
Iowa Farm Bureau Spokesman Magazine		
5400 University Ave . . . . .West Des Moines IA 50266	**866-598-3693**	515-225-5413
Kansas Living Magazine		
2627 KFB Plz . . . . .Manhattan KS 66503	**800-406-3053**	785-587-6000
Pork Report		
1776 NW 114th St PO Box 9114 . . . . .Des Moines IA 50325	**800-456-7675**	515-223-2600
Soybean Digest		
7900 International Dr Ste 300 . . . . .Minneapolis MN 55425	**800-722-5334***	952-851-4667
*Cust Svc		
Tennessee Farm Bureau News		
147 Bear Creek Pike . . . . .Columbia TN 38401	**877-876-2222**	931-388-7812
Texas Agriculture Magazine		
7420 Fish Pond Rd PO Box 2689 . . . . .Waco TX 76710	**800-772-6535**	254-772-3030
Texas Farm Bureau		
7420 Fish Pond Rd PO Box 2689 . . . . .Waco TX 76710	**800-488-7872**	254-772-3030
Top Producer Magazine		
1818 Market St 31st Fl . . . . .Philadelphia PA 19103	**800-320-7992**	

454-2 Art & Architecture Magazines

	Toll-Free	Phone
Architectural Digest		
Four Times Sq 18th Fl .New York NY 10036	**800-365-8032**	
Architectural Record Magazine		
2 Penn Plaza 9th Fl . . . . .New York NY 10121	**800-393-6343**	212-904-2594
Art in America Magazine		
575 Broadway . . . . .New York NY 10012	**800-925-8059***	212-941-2800
*Cust Svc		
Artforum International Magazine		
350 Seventh Ave 19th Fl . . . . .New York NY 10001	**800-966-2783**	212-475-4000
Artist's Magazine, The		
4700 E Galbraith Rd . . . . .Cincinnati OH 45236	**800-422-2550**	513-531-2222
ARTnews Magazine		
48 W 38th St Ninth Fl . . . . .New York NY 10018	**800-284-4625**	212-398-1690
Design/Build Business Magazine		
3030 Salt Creek Ln Ste 200 . . . . .Arlington Heights IL 60005	**800-547-7377**	847-454-2714
HOW Design Magazine		
4700 E Galbraith Rd . . . . .Cincinnati OH 45236	**800-333-1115***	513-531-2690
*Cust Svc		
Metropolis Magazine		
61 W 23rd St Fourth Fl .New York NY 10010	**800-344-3046**	212-627-9977
Pastel Journal		
4700 E Galbraith Rd . . . . .Cincinnati OH 45236	**800-422-2550**	513-531-2222
Southwest Art Magazine		
10901 W 120th Ave Ste 350 . . . . .Broomfield CO 80021	**877-212-1938**	303-442-0427
Sunshine Artist Magazine		
4075 LB McLeod Rd Ste E . . . . .Orlando FL 32811	**800-597-2573**	407-648-7479

454-3 Automotive Magazines

	Toll-Free	Phone
American Iron Magazine		
1010 Summer St . . . . .Stamford CT 06905	**877-693-3572***	203-425-8777
*Cust Svc		
AutoWeek Magazine		
1155 Gratiot Ave . . . . .Detroit MI 48207	**888-288-6954***	313-446-6000
*Circ		
Car Craft Magazine		
6420 Wilshire Blvd . . . . .Los Angeles CA 90048	**800-230-3030**	323-782-2000
Cycle World Magazine		
1499 Monrovia Ave . . . . .Newport Beach CA 92663	**800-456-3084**	949-720-5300
Grassroots Motorsports Magazine		
915 Ridgewood Ave . . . . .Holly Hill FL 32117	**800-520-8292**	386-239-0523
Hemmings Motor News		
222 Main St . . . . .Bennington VT 05201	**800-227-4373**	802-442-3101
Hot Rod Magazine		
6420 Wilshire Blvd . . . . .Los Angeles CA 90048	**800-800-4681***	323-782-2000
*Orders		

Classified Section

				Toll-Free	Phone
Hot Rod Network					
774 S Placentia Ave	Placentia	CA	92870	800-926-8207	
Motor Trend Magazine					
6420 Wilshire Blvd Seventh Fl	Los Angeles	CA	90048	800-800-6848	323-782-2000
Motorcycle Consumer News Magazine					
Three Burroughs	Irvine	CA	92618	888-333-0354	949-855-8822
National Speed Sport News Magazine					
142 F S Cardigan Way	Mooresville	NC	28117	866-455-2531	704-489-5231
Off-Road Magazine					
2400 E Katella Ave Ste 1100	Anaheim	CA	92806	877-462-6752	714-848-8880
Road & Track Magazine					
1499 Monrovia Ave	Newport Beach	CA	92663	800-835-6422	949-720-5300
Sports Car Magazine					
16842 Von Karman Ave Ste 125	Irvine	CA	92606	800-722-7140	949-417-6700
Stock Car Racing Magazine					
PO Box 420235	Palm Coast	FL	32142	800-333-2633	

454-4 Boating Magazines

				Toll-Free	Phone
Blue Water Sailing Magazine					
747 Aquidneck Ave Ste 201 Ste 201	Middletown	RI	02842	888-800-7245	401-847-7612
Power & Motoryacht Magazine					
260 Madison Ave Fourth Fl	New York	NY	10016	800-284-8036	860-767-3200
SAIL Magazine					
98 N Washington St Ste 107	Boston	MA	02114	877-388-7761	617-720-8600
Sailing World Magazine					
55 Hammarlund Way	Middletown	RI	02842	866-436-2460*	401-845-5100
*Cust Svc					
Sea Magazine					
17782 Cowan St Ste C	Irvine	CA	92614	800-873-7327	949-660-6150
Yachting Magazine					
55 Hammarlund Way	Middletown	RI	02842	800-999-0869	

454-5 Business & Finance Magazines

				Toll-Free	Phone
Advisor Today					
2901 Telestar Ct	Falls Church	VA	22042	800-247-4074	
Alaska Business Monthly					
501 W Northern Lights Blvd Ste 100	Anchorage	AK	99503	800-770-4373	907-276-4373
American Banker Magazine					
one State St Plaza 27th Fl	New York	NY	10004	800-221-1809	212-803-8200
American Journalism Review					
University of Maryland					
1117 Journalism Bldg					
1117 Journalism Bldg Rm 2116	College Park	MD	20742	800-827-0771	301-405-8803
Appraisal Journal					
200 W Madison Ste 1500	Chicago	IL	60606	888-756-4624	
Area Development Magazine					
400 Post Ave Ste 304	Westbury	NY	11590	800-735-2732	516-338-0900
Arkansas Business LP					
122 E Second St	Little Rock	AR	72201	888-322-6397	501-372-1443
Banking Strategies Magazine					
115 S LaSalle St Ste 3300	Chicago	IL	60603	888-224-0037	312-553-4600
Black Enterprise Magazine					
130 Fifth Ave	New York	NY	10011	800-727-7777*	212-242-8000
*Cust Svc					
British Standards Institution, The					
12110 Sunset Hills Rd Ste 200	Reston	VA	20190	800-862-4977	703-437-9000
Business Facilities Magazine					
44 Apple St Ste 3	Tinton Falls	NJ	07724	800-524-0337	732-842-7433
Business Insurance Magazine					
711 Third Ave	New York	NY	10017	877-812-1587	212-210-0100
Business Journal, The					
25 E Boardman St	Youngstown	OH	44501	800-837-6397	330-744-5023
California Real Estate Magazine					
525 S Virgil Ave	Los Angeles	CA	90020	888-811-5281	213-739-8200
Central New York Business Journal, The					
269 W Jefferson St	Syracuse	NY	13202	800-836-3539	315-579-3919
CFO Magazine 253 Summer St	Boston	MA	02210	800-772-1119	617-345-9700
Columbus Business First					
303 W Nationwide Blvd	Columbus	OH	43215	800-486-3289	614-461-4040
Communications News					
PO Box 866	Osprey	FL	34229	800-827-9715	941-539-7579
Contract Design Magazine					
770 Broadway	New York	NY	10004	800-697-8859	
Crain's Chicago Business Magazine					
150 N Michigan 16th Fl	Chicago	IL	60601	877-812-1590	312-649-5200
Crain's Cleveland Business Magazine					
700 W St Clair Ave Ste 310	Cleveland	OH	44113	888-909-9111	216-522-1383
Crain's Detroit Business Magazine					
1155 Gratiot Ave	Detroit	MI	48207	888-909-9111	313-446-6000
Crain's New York Business Magazine					
685 Third Ave 3rd Fl	New York	NY	10017	888-909-9111	212-210-0100
Drug Topics Magazine					
24950 Country Club Blvd Ste 200	North Olmsted	OH	44070	877-922-2022*	440-891-2792
*Cust Svc					
E-Commerce Times (ECT)					
16133 Ventura Blvd Ste 700	Encino	CA	91436	877-328-5500	818-461-9700
Editor & Publisher Magazine					
17782 Cowan Ste C	Irvine	CA	92614	855-896-7433	949-660-6150
Employee Benefit News					
1325 G St NW Ste 900	Washington	DC	20005	800-221-1809	202-504-1122
Entrepreneur Magazine					
2445 McCabe Way Ste 400	Irvine	CA	92614	800-274-6229	949-261-2325
Expansion Management Magazine					
1300 E Ninth St	Cleveland	OH	44114	866-505-7173	216-696-7000
Fast Company Magazine					
Seven World Trade Ctr	New York	NY	10007	800-542-6029	212-389-5300
Finance & Commerce					
730 Second Ave S					
US Trust Bldg Ste 100	Minneapolis	MN	55402	800-451-9998	612-333-4244
Fleet Owner Magazine					
11 Riverbend Dr S PO Box 4211	Stamford	CT	06907	800-776-1246	203-358-4205

				Toll-Free	Phone
Forbes Magazine					
60 Fifth Ave	New York	NY	10011	800-295-0893	212-366-8900
Franchising World Magazine					
1501 K St NW Ste 350	Washington	DC	20005	800-543-1038	202-628-8000
Harvard Business Review					
60 Harvard Way	Boston	MA	02163	800-274-3214	617-783-7500
Health Facilities Management Magazine					
155 N Wacker Dr Ste 400	Chicago	IL	60606	800-621-6902	312-893-6800
Hospitals & Health Networks Magazine					
155 N Wacker Ste 400	Chicago	IL	60606	800-621-6902	312-893-6800
HRMagazine 1800 Duke St	Alexandria	VA	22314	800-283-7476	703-548-3440
Human Resource Executive Magazine					
747 Dresher Rd Ste 500	Horsham	PA	19044	888-365-2763	215-784-0910
Inc Magazine					
7 World Trade Ctr	New York	NY	10007	800-234-0999	212-389-5377
Indianapolis Business Journal					
41 E Washington St Ste 200	Indianapolis	IN	46204	800-428-7081	317-634-6200
Journal of Accountancy					
220 Leigh Farm Rd	Durham	NC	27707	888-777-7077	
Journal of Financial Planning Assn					
7535 E Hampden Ave Ste 600	Denver	CO	80231	800-322-4237	303-759-4900
Journal of Housing & Community Development					
630 'I' St NW	Washington	DC	20001	877-866-2476	202-289-3500
Journal of Property Management					
430 N Michigan Ave	Chicago	IL	60611	800-837-0706	
Law Enforcement Technology Magazine					
1233 Janesville Ave	Fort Atkinson	WI	53538	800-547-7377	
Leadership Journal					
465 Gundersen Dr	Carol Stream	IL	60188	800-777-3136	630-260-6200
Lodging Magazine					
385 Oxford Vly Rd Ste 420	Yardley	PA	19067	800-394-5157	215-321-9662
Marketing News					
311 S Wacker Dr Ste 5800	Chicago	IL	60606	800-262-1150	312-542-9000
Meetings & Conventions Magazine					
100 Lighting Way	Secaucus	NJ	07094	877-705-8889	201-902-2000
Mergers & Acquisitions Magazine					
One State St Plz	New York	NY	10004	888-807-8667*	212-803-6051
*Cust Svc					
Mississippi Business Journal					
200 N Congress St	Jackson	MS	39201	800-283-4625	601-364-1000
National Assn of Credit Management					
8840 Columbia 100 Pkwy	Columbia	MD	21045	800-955-8815	410-740-5560
National Notary Magazine					
9350 DeSoto Ave	Chatsworth	CA	91311	800-876-6827*	818-739-4000
*Cust Svc					
National Real Estate Investor Magazine					
6151 Powers Ferry Rd NW Ste 200	Atlanta	GA	30339	877-829-2782	770-955-2500
Palm Beach Daily Business Review					
324 Datura St Ste 140	West Palm Beach	FL	33401	800-777-7300	561-820-2060
PCBE Inc PO Box 1575	Tacoma	WA	98401	800-540-8322	253-404-0891
Pensions & Investments Magazine					
711 Third Ave	New York	NY	10017	888-446-1422*	212-210-0100
*Cust Svc					
Print Magazine					
10151 Carver Rd Ste 200	Blue Ash	OH	45242	877-860-9145	513-531-2690
Purchasing Magazine					
225 Wyman St	Waltham	MA	02451	888-393-5000	
Realtor Magazine					
430 N Michigan Ave Ninth Fl	Chicago	IL	60611	800-874-6500	312-329-8458
Rough Notes Company Inc, The					
11690 Technology Dr	Carmel	IN	46032	800-428-4384	317-582-1600
San Diego Business Journal					
4909 Murphy Canyon Rd Ste 200	San Diego	CA	92123	888-425-7325	858-277-6359
Self-Employed America Magazine					
PO Box 241	Annapolis Junction	MD	20701	800-649-6273	
Selling Power Magazine					
1140 International Pkwy	Fredericksburg	VA	22406	800-752-7355	540-752-7000
Signal Magazine					
4400 Fair Lakes Ct	Fairfax	VA	22033	800-336-4583	703-631-6100
Sloan Management Review					
77 Massachusetts Ave E60-100	Cambridge	MA	02139	800-876-5764	617-253-7170
Staffdigest Magazine					
PO Box 384 Ste H3	Alief	TX	77411	800-444-0674*	281-498-2913
*General					
Strategic Finance Magazine					
10 Paragon Dr Ste 1	Montvale	NJ	07645	800-638-4427	201-573-9000
Training & Development Magazine					
1640 King St	Alexandria	VA	22313	800-628-2783	703-683-8100
Utah Business Magazine					
90 S 400 W Ste 650	Salt Lake City	UT	84101	866-294-1660	801-568-0114
Your Church Magazine					
465 Gundersen Dr	Carol Stream	IL	60188	877-247-4787	630-260-6200

454-6 Children's & Youth Magazines

				Toll-Free	Phone
AppleSeeds Magazine					
30 Grove St Ste C	Peterborough	NH	03458	800-821-0115	
Babybug Magazine					
30 Grove St Ste C	Peterborough	NH	03458	800-821-0115	
Click Magazine					
30 Grove St Ste C	Peterborough	NH	03458	800-821-0115	
Cobblestone Magazine					
30 Grove St Ste C	Peterborough	NH	03458	800-821-0115	603-924-7209
Creative Kids Magazine					
PO Box 8813	Waco	TX	76714	800-998-2208	254-756-3337
Cricket Media Inc					
30 Grove St Ste C	Peterborough	NH	03458	800-821-0115	
Girls' Life Acqusition Co					
4529 Hartford Rd	Baltimore	MD	21214	888-999-3222	410-426-9600
National Geographic Kids Magazine					
1145 17th St NW	Washington	DC	20036	800-647-5463	202-857-7000
New Moon Magazine					
PO Box 161287	Duluth	MN	55816	800-381-4743	218-878-9673
Odyssey Magazine					
30 Grove St Ste C	Peterborough	NH	03458	800-821-0115	603-924-7209

		Toll-Free	Phone

Owl Magazine
10 Lower Spadina Ave Ste 400 .... Toronto ON   M5V2Z2   **800-551-6957**   416-340-2700
Turtle Magazine
1100 Waterway Blvd .... Indianapolis IN   46202   **800-558-2376**   317-634-1100
Wild Animal Baby Magazine
11100 Wildlife Ctr Dr .... Reston VA   20190   **800-822-9919**
Your Big Backyard Magazine
11100 Wildlife Ctr Dr .... Reston VA   20190   **800-822-9919**

454-7 Computer & Internet Magazines

		Toll-Free	Phone

Computer Magazine
10662 Los Vaqueros Cir .... Los Alamitos CA   90720   **800-272-6657***   714-821-8380
*Orders
Computers in Libraries Magazine
143 Old Marlton Pk .... Medford NJ   08055   **800-300-9868**   609-654-6266
Computerworld Magazine
One Speen St .... Framingham MA   01701   **800-343-6474**   508-879-0700
eContent Magazine
143 Old Marlton Pike Ste 3. .... Medford NJ   08055   **800-300-9868**   609-654-6266
Federal Computer Week Magazine
3141 Fairview Pk Dr Ste 777 .... Falls Church VA   22042   **877-534-2208**   703-876-5100
IEEE Computer Graphics & Applications Magazine
10662 Los Vaqueros Cir
PO Box 3014. .... Los Alamitos CA   90720   **800-272-6657**   714-821-8380
IEEE Micro Magazine
10662 Los Vaqueros Cir
PO Box 3014. .... Los Alamitos CA   90720   **800-272-6657**   714-821-8380
Information Today Magazine
143 Old Marlton Pk .... Medford NJ   08055   **800-300-9868**   609-654-6266
InformationWeek Magazine
600 Community Dr .... Manhasset NY   11030   **800-441-8826**   516-562-5000
InfoWorld Magazine
501 Second St Ste 120 .... San Francisco CA   94107   **800-227-8365**   415-243-4344
Law Technology News
120 Broadway 5th Fl. .... New York NY   10271   **800-888-8300***   212-457-7905
*Cust Svc
Macworld Magazine
501 Second St Ste 600 .... San Francisco CA   94107   **800-288-6848***   415-243-0505
*Cust Svc
MultiMedia Schools Magazine
143 Old Marlton Pk .... Medford NJ   08055   **800-300-9868**   609-654-6266
Network World Magazine
492 Old Connecticut Path Ste 200
PO Box 9208. .... Framingham MA   01701   **800-622-1108**
Oracle Magazine
500 Oracle Pkwy MS OPL3. .... Redwood Shores CA   94065   **800-392-2999**   650-506-7000
PC Magazine 28 E 28th St .... New York NY   10016   **800-289-0429**   212-503-3500
Searcher: The Magazine for Database Professionals
143 Old Marlton Pk .... Medford NJ   08055   **800-300-9868**   609-654-6266

454-8 Education Magazines & Journals

		Toll-Free	Phone

Academe Magazine
1133 19th St NW Ste 200 .... Washington DC   20036   **800-424-2973**   202-737-5900
AEA Advocate Magazine
345 E Palm Ln .... Phoenix AZ   85004   **800-352-5411**   602-264-1774
Alabama School Journal
422 Dexter Ave .... Montgomery AL   36104   **800-392-5839**   334-834-9790
American Educator Magazine
555 New Jersey Ave NW .... Washington DC   20001   **800-238-1133**   202-879-4400
American Libraries Magazine
50 E Huron St .... Chicago IL   60611   **800-545-2433**
American Teacher Magazine
555 New Jersey Ave NW .... Washington DC   20001   **800-238-1133**   202-879-4400
Arkansas Educator Magazine
1500 W Fourth St .... Little Rock AR   72201   **800-632-0624**   501-375-4611
Chronicle of Higher Education, The
1255 23rd St NW Ste 700. .... Washington DC   20037   **800-728-2803**   202-466-1000
Colorado School Journal
1500 Grant St .... Denver CO   80203   **800-336-7678**   800-332-5939
Education Ctr Inc
3515 W Market St Ste 200 .... Greensboro NC   27403   **800-714-7991**   336-854-0309
Education Week Magazine
6935 Arlington Rd .... Bethesda MD   20814   **800-346-1834**   301-280-3100
Educational Leadership Magazine
1703 N Beauregard St .... Alexandria VA   22311   **800-933-2723**   703-578-9600
Harvard Educational Review
Eight Story St First Fl .... Cambridge MA   02138   **877-930-4473**   617-495-3432
ISTA Advocate Magazine
150 W Market St Ste 900 .... Indianapolis IN   46204   **800-382-4037**   317-263-3400
KEA News 401 Capital Ave .... Frankfort KY   40601   **800-231-4532**   502-875-2889
Library Journal
160 Varick St 11th Fl .... New York NY   10013   **800-588-1030**   646-380-0700
Louisiana Association of Educators
8322 One Kalais Ave .... Baton Rouge LA   70809   **800-256-4523**   225-343-9243
MAA FOCUS
1529 18th St NW .... Washington DC   20036   **800-741-9415**   202-387-5200
Mailbox Bookbag Magazine
3515 W Market St Ste 200 .... Greensboro NC   27403   **800-714-7991**   336-854-0309
Maine Educator Magazine
35 Community Dr .... Augusta ME   04330   **800-332-8529**   207-622-5866
MEA Voice Magazine
1216 Kendale Blvd PO Box 2573 .... East Lansing MI   48826   **800-292-1934**   517-332-6551
Minnesota Educator Magazine
41 Sherburne Ave .... Saint Paul MN   55103   **800-652-9073**   651-227-9541
Missouri State Teachers Assn
407 S Sixth St .... Columbia MO   65201   **800-392-0532***   573-442-3127
*General
MTA Today Magazine
20 Ashburton Pl .... Boston MA   02108   **800-392-6175**   617-878-8000
NCAE News Bulletin
PO Box 27347 .... Raleigh NC   27611   **800-662-7924**   919-832-3000

		Toll-Free	Phone

NCTM News Bulletin
1906 Assn Dr .... Reston VA   20191   **800-235-7566**   703-620-9840
New Hampshire Educator Magazine
9 S Spring St .... Concord NH   03301   **866-556-3264**   603-224-7751
New York Teacher Magazine
800 Troy-Schenectady Rd .... Latham NY   12110   **800-342-9810**   518-213-6000
NSEA Voice Magazine
605 S 14th St Ste 200. .... Lincoln NE   68508   **800-742-0047**   402-475-7611
Ohio Education Assn (OEA)
225 E Broad St PO Box 2550 .... Columbus OH   43216   **800-282-1500**   614-228-4526
Oklahoma Education Association
323 E Madison PO Box 18485 .... Oklahoma City OK   73154   **800-522-8091**   405-528-7785
Oregon Education Magazine (OEA)
6900 SW Atlanta St Bldg 1 .... Portland OR   97223   **800-858-5505**   503-684-3300
Scholastic Coach & Athletic Director Magazine
557 Broadway .... New York NY   10012   **800-724-6527***   212-343-6100
*General
Teacher Magazine
6935 Arlington Rd Ste 100 .... Bethesda MD   20814   **800-346-1834**   301-280-3100
TSTA Advocate Magazine
316 W 12th St .... Austin TX   78701   **877-275-8782**   512-476-5355
Vermont NEA Today Magazine
10 Wheelock St .... Montpelier VT   05602   **800-649-6375**   802-223-6375
Virginia Journal of Education
116 S Third St .... Richmond VA   23219   **800-552-9554**   804-648-5801
West Virginia School Journal
1558 Quarrier St .... Charleston WV   25311   **800-642-8261**   304-346-5315
Young Children Magazine
1313 L St NW Ste 500 PO Box 97156 .... Washington DC   20005   **800-424-2460**   202-232-8777

454-9 Entertainment & Music Magazines

		Toll-Free	Phone

American Cinematographer Magazine
1782 N Orange Dr .... Los Angeles CA   90028   **800-448-0145**   323-969-4333
Bass Player Magazine
28 E 28th St 12th Fl .... New York NY   10016   **866-246-3595***   212-378-0400
*Cust Svc
Canadian Musician Magazine
4056 Dorchester Rd .... Niagara Falls ON   L2E6M9   **877-746-4692**   905-374-8878
Dance Magazine
333 Seventh Ave 11th Fl. .... New York NY   10001   **800-331-1750**   212-979-4800
Down Beat Magazine
102 N Haven Rd PO Box 906 .... Elmhurst IL   60126   **800-554-7470**   651-251-9682
Entertainment Weekly Magazine
1675 Broadway 29th Fl. .... New York NY   10019   **800-828-6882**   212-522-5600
Film Comment Magazine
165 W 65th St .... New York NY   10023   **888-313-6085**   212-875-5610
Grammy Magazine
3030 Olympic Blvd .... Santa Monica CA   90404   **800-423-2017**   310-392-3777
Guitar Player Magazine
28 E 28th St 12th Fl .... New York NY   10016   **800-289-9839***   212-378-0400
*Cust Svc
Hollywood Reporter
5055 Wilshire Blvd Ste 600 .... Los Angeles CA   90036   **866-525-2150**   323-525-2000
Jazziz Magazine
2650 N Military Trail Ste 140 .... Boca Raton FL   33431   **888-852-9987**   561-893-6868
JazzTimes Magazine
85 Quincy Ave Ste 2 .... Quincy MA   02169   **800-437-5828**   617-706-9110
Keyboard Magazine
28 E 28th St 12th Fl .... New York NY   10016   **800-483-2433***   212-378-0400
*Cust Svc
Live Design 249 W 17th St .... New York NY   10011   **866-505-7173***   212-204-4272
*Sales
Multichannel News
28 E 28th St 12th Fl .... New York NY   10016   **888-343-5563***   917-281-4700
*Cust Svc
Playbill Magazine
525 Seventh Ave Ste 1801 .... New York NY   10018   **800-533-4330**   212-557-5757
Pollstar
4697 W Jacquelyn Ave .... Fresno CA   93722   **800-344-7383**   559-271-7900
Rolling Stone Magazine
1290 Ave of the Americas 2nd Fl .... New York NY   10104   **800-283-1549**
TV Guide Magazine LLC
11 West 42nd St 16th Fl .... New York NY   10036   **800-866-1400**   212-852-7500
Videomaker Magazine
1350 E Ninth St PO Box 4591 .... Chico CA   95927   **800-284-3226**   530-891-8410

454-10 Fraternal & Special Interest Magazines

		Toll-Free	Phone

AARP the Magazine
601 E St NW .... Washington DC   20049   **888-687-2277**   202-434-3525
AAUW Outlook Magazine
1111 16th St NW .... Washington DC   20036   **800-326-2289**   202-785-7700
Adoptive Families Magazine
108 West 39th St Ste 805 .... New York NY   10018   **800-372-3300**   646-366-0830
Columbia Magazine
1 Columbus Plaza .... New Haven CT   06510   **800-380-9995**   203-752-4000
Commentary Magazine
561 7th Ave 16th Fl .... New York NY   10018   **800-829-6270**   212-891-1400
Disabled American Veterans Magazine
3725 Alexandria Pike PO Box 14301 ...... Cold Spring KY   41076   **877-426-2838**   859-441-7300
Eagle Magazine
1623 Gateway Cir S .... Grove City OH   43123   **800-236-5450**   614-883-2200
Elks Magazine
425 W Diversey Pkwy .... Chicago IL   60614   **800-273-8255**   773-755-4700
Kiwanis Magazine
3636 Woodview Trace .... Indianapolis IN   46268   **800-549-2647**   317-875-8755
Ladies Auxiliary VFW Magazine
406 W 34th St .... Kansas City MO   64111   **800-843-1950**   816-561-8655
Lion Magazine
300 W 22nd St .... Oak Brook IL   60523   **800-710-7822***   630-571-5466
*Circ

			Toll-Free	Phone
Phi Delta Kappan Magazine				
408 N Union St	Bloomington IN	47407	800-766-1156	812-339-1156
Royal Neighbor Magazine				
230 16th St	Rock Island IL	61201	800-627-4762	309-788-4561
United Commercial Travellers				
1801 Watermark Dr Ste 100	Columbus OH	43215	800-848-0123	614-228-3276
WOODMEN Magazine				
1700 Farnam St	Omaha NE	68102	800-225-3108	402-342-1890

454-11 General Interest Magazines

			Toll-Free	Phone
Alfred Hitchcock Mystery Magazine				
44 Wall St Ste 904	New York NY	10005	800-220-7443	212-686-7188
Atlantic Monthly Magazine				
600 New Hampshire Ave NW	Washington DC	20037	800-234-2411*	202-266-6000
*Cust Svc				
Better Investing Magazine				
PO Box 220	Royal Oak MI	48068	877-275-6242	248-583-6242
Black Enterprise Magazine				
130 Fifth Ave	New York NY	10011	800-727-7777*	212-242-8000
*Cust Svc				
Booklist Magazine				
50 E Huron St	Chicago IL	60611	800-545-2433	
Bridal Guide Magazine				
330 Seventh Ave 10th Fl	New York NY	10001	800-472-7744	212-838-7733
Canadian Living Magazine				
25 Sheppard Ave W Ste 100	Toronto ON	M2N6S7	800-387-6332	416-733-7600
Christianity Today				
465 Gundersen Dr	Carol Stream IL	60188	800-222-1840*	630-260-6200
*Cust Svc				
College Outlook & Career Opportunities Magazine				
20 E Gregory Blvd	Kansas City MO	64114	800-274-8867	816-361-0616
Consumer Reports Magazine				
101 Truman Ave	Yonkers NY	10703	800-333-0663*	914-378-2000
*Orders				
Cook's Illustrated Magazine				
PO Box 470739	Brookline MA	02447	800-526-8442*	617-232-1000
*Circ				
Cosmopolitan Magazine				
300 W 57th St	New York NY	10019	800-888-2676	212-649-2000
Country Living Magazine				
300 W 57th St	New York NY	10019	800-888-0128	212-649-3204
Country Magazine				
1610 North 2nd St Ste 102	Milwaukee WI	53212	888-861-1265	414-423-0100
Coup de Pouce Magazine				
1100 boul Rene-Levesque O 24e Etage	Montreal QC	H3B4X9	800-528-3836	514-392-9000
Cuisine Magazine				
2200 Grand Ave	Des Moines IA	50312	800-311-3995	
Delicious Living Magazine				
1401 Pearl St Ste 200	Boulder CO	80302	866-458-4935	303-939-8440
Elle Magazine				
1633 Broadway 44th Fl	New York NY	10019	800-876-8775	212-903-5000
Entrepreneur Magazine				
2445 McCabe Way Ste 400	Irvine CA	92614	800-274-6229	949-261-2325
Esquire Magazine				
300 W 57th St 21st Fl	New York NY	10019	800-888-5400	212-649-4020
Essence Magazine				
135 W 50th St Fourth Fl	New York NY	10020	800-274-9398	
Family Cir Magazine				
375 Lexington Ave 9th Fl	New York NY	10017	800-627-4444	
Food & Wine Magazine				
1120 Ave of the Americas	New York NY	10036	800-333-6569	813-979-6625
Franchise Handbook				
5555 N Port Washington Rd Ste 305	Milwaukee WI	53217	800-272-0246	414-882-2878
Futurist Magazine				
7910 Woodmont Ave Ste 450	Bethesda MD	20814	800-989-8274	301-656-8274
Harper's Bazaar Magazine				
300 W 57th St	New York NY	10019	800-285-4274*	212-903-5000
*General				
Harper's Magazine				
666 Broadway 11th Fl	New York NY	10012	800-444-4653	212-420-5720
Interview Magazine				
575 Broadway Fifth Fl	New York NY	10012	800-925-9574	212-941-2900
Latina Media Ventures LLC				
625 Madison Ave 3rd Fl	New York NY	10022	888-489-7753	212-642-0200
Lucky Inc 4 Times Sq	New York NY	10036	888-959-5203	800-405-8085
Marie Claire Magazine				
300 W 57th St 34th Fl	New York NY	10019	800-925-0485	
Martha Stewart Living Magazine				
11 W 42nd St 25th Fl	New York NY	10036	800-999-6518	
Men's Journal LLC				
1290 Ave of the Americas 2nd Fl	New York NY	10104	800-677-6367	
Ms Magazine				
1600 Wilson Blvd Ste 801	Arlington VA	22209	866-672-6363	703-522-4201
National Geographic Adventure Magazine				
1145 17th St NW	Washington DC	20036	800-647-5463	202-857-7000
National Geographic Magazine				
1145 17th St NW	Washington DC	20036	800-647-5463	202-857-7000
New York Review of Books				
435 Hudson St Third Fl	New York NY	10014	800-354-0050	212-757-8070
People Magazine				
Rockefeller Ctr Time & Life Bldg	New York NY	10020	800-541-9000	212-522-3347
Psychology Today Magazine				
115 E 23rd St 9th Fl	New York NY	10010	800-931-2237	212-260-7210
Reminisce Magazine				
750 Third Ave Third Fl	New York WI	10017	888-859-7838	414-423-0100
Saturday Evening Post, The				
1100 Waterway Blvd	Indianapolis IN	46202	800-829-5576	317-634-1100
Self Magazine 4 Times Sq	New York NY	10036	800-274-6111	212-286-2860
Simple & Delicious				
5400 S 60th St	Greendale WI	53129	800-344-6913	414-423-0100
Smithsonian Magazine				
600 Maryland Ave Ste 6001	Washington DC	20024	800-766-2149	202-633-6090
Sun Magazine				
8815 Conroy Windermere Rd Ste 130	Orlando FL	32835	888-218-9968	407-477-2815

			Toll-Free	Phone
Taste of Home Magazine				
5400 S 60th St	Greendale WI	53129	800-344-6913	414-423-0100
Traditional Home Magazine				
1716 Locust St	Des Moines IA	50309	800-374-8791*	515-284-3762
*Circ				
Utne Reader Magazine				
12 N 12th St Ste 400	Minneapolis MN	55403	800-736-8863*	612-338-5040
*Cust Svc				
Vanity Fair Magazine				
Four Times Sq	New York NY	10036	800-365-0635	
Western Living Magazine				
2608 Granville St Ste 560	Vancouver BC	V6H3V3	800-363-3272	604-877-7732
Wilson Quarterly Magazine				
1300 Pennsylvania Ave NW				
1 Woodrow Wilson Plaza	Washington DC	20004	888-947-9018*	202-691-4000
*Orders				
Women's Wear Daily Magazine				
750 Third Ave Fifth Fl	New York NY	10017	800-289-0273	212-630-4600

454-12 Government & Military Magazines

			Toll-Free	Phone
Air Force Magazine				
1501 Lee Hwy	Arlington VA	22209	800-727-3337	703-247-5800
Air Force Times Magazine				
6883 Commercial Dr	Springfield VA	22159	800-368-5718	703-750-7400
ARMY Magazine				
2425 Wilson Blvd	Arlington VA	22201	800-336-4570	703-841-4300
FRA Today 125 NW St	Alexandria VA	22314	800-372-1924	703-683-1400
Governing Magazine				
1100 Connecticut Ave NW Ste 1300	Washington DC	20036	800-940-6039	202-862-8802
Military & Aerospace Electronics Magazine				
98 Spit Brook Rd	Nashua NH	03062	866-423-4837	847-763-9540
Military Engineer Magazine				
607 Prince St	Alexandria VA	22314	800-336-3097*	703-549-3800
*Cust Svc				
Military Officer Magazine				
201 N Washington St	Alexandria VA	22314	800-234-6622	703-549-2311
Navy Times Magazine				
6883 Commercial Dr	Springfield VA	22159	800-368-5718*	703-750-7400
*Cust Svc				
Public Employee Magazine				
1625 L St NW	Washington DC	20036	800-792-0045	202-429-1130
Soldier of Fortune Magazine				
2135 11th St	Boulder CO	80302	800-377-2789	303-449-3750

454-13 Health & Fitness Magazines

			Toll-Free	Phone
American Fitness Magazine				
15250 Ventura Blvd Ste 200	Sherman Oaks CA	91403	800-446-2322	818-905-0040
Cooking Light Magazine				
2100 Lakeshore Dr	Birmingham AL	35209	800-366-4712	205-445-6000
Diabetes Forecast Magazine				
1701 N Beauregard St	Alexandria VA	22311	800-676-4065	703-549-1500
Fitness Rx for Men Magazine				
21 Bennetts Rd	Setauket NY	11733	800-653-1151	631-751-9696
Flex Magazine				
21100 Erwin St	Woodland Hills CA	91367	877-527-8342	412-235-0203
Heart & Soul Magazine				
15480 Annapolis Rd Ste 202-225	Bowie MD	20715	800-834-8813	
Ironman Magazine				
1701 Ives Ave	Oxnard CA	93033	800-447-0008	805-385-3500
Men's Health Magazine				
400 S Tenth St	Emmaus PA	18098	800-666-2303	610-967-5171
Muscle & Fitness Magazine				
21100 Erwin St	Woodland Hills CA	91367	866-688-7679*	818-884-6800
*Orders				
Prevention Magazine				
400 S Tenth St	Emmaus PA	18098	800-813-8070	212-697-2040
Runner's World Magazine				
400 S Tenth St	Emmaus PA	18098	800-666-2828*	610-967-5171
*Cust Svc				
Vegetarian Times				
300 N Continental Blvd Ste 650	El Segundo CA	90245	800-573-1900	310-356-4100

454-14 Hobby & Personal Interests Magazines

			Toll-Free	Phone
American History Illustrated Magazine				
19300 Promenade Dr	Leesburg VA	20176	800-435-0715	310-922-2159
American Photo Magazine				
1633 Broadway 43rd Fl	New York NY	10019	800-274-4514	212-767-6000
Antique Trader 700 E State St	Iola WI	54990	800-258-0929	715-445-2214
AOPA Pilot Magazine				
421 Aviation Way	Frederick MD	21701	800-872-2672	301-695-2000
Arabian Horse World Magazine				
1316 Tamson Dr Ste 101	Cambria CA	93428	800-955-9423	805-771-2300
Bead & Button Magazine				
21027 Crossroads Cir	Waukesha WI	53186	800-533-6644*	262-796-8776
*Cust Svc				
BeadStyle Magazine				
21027 Crossroads Cir	Waukesha WI	53186	800-533-6644*	262-796-8776
*Cust Svc				
Better Homes & Gardens WOOD Magazine				
1716 Locust St	Des Moines IA	50309	800-374-9663	
Bicycling Magazine				
400 S Tenth St	Emmaus PA	18098	800-666-2806	
Bird Talk Magazine				
Three Burroughs	Irvine CA	92618	800-695-6088*	949-855-8822
*Resv				
Birds & Blooms Magazine				
5400 S 60th St	Greendale WI	53129	888-860-8040	414-423-0100

	Toll-Free	Phone
BirdWatching Magazine 25 Braintree Hill Office Pk Ste 404 ... Braintree MA 02184	877-252-8141	
Blood-Horse Magazine PO Box 911088 ... Lexington KY 40591	800-866-2361	859-278-2361
British Heritage Magazine 19300 Promenade Dr ... Leesburg VA 20176	800-358-6327	
Cat Fancy Magazine Three Burroughs ... Irvine CA 92618 *Cust Svc	800-546-7730*	949-855-8822
Ceramics Monthly 600 N Cleveland Ave Ste 210 ... Westerville OH 43082	800-342-3594	614-794-5867
Chess Life Magazine PO Box 3967 ... Crossville TN 38557 *Sales	800-903-8723*	931-787-1234
Classic Trains Magazine 21027 Crossroads Cir PO Box 1612 ... Waukesha WI 53186	800-533-6644	262-796-8776
Coin World Magazine 911 S Vandemark Rd ... Sidney OH 45365	866-519-7298	937-498-0800
Country Woman Magazine 5400 S 60th St ... Greendale WI 53129	800-828-4548	414-423-0100
Crafts 'n Things Magazine PO Box 926 ... Sidney OH 45365	866-222-3621	
Creating Keepsakes Magazine 14850 Pony Express Rd ... Bluffdale UT 84065	888-247-5282	801-816-8300
Daily Racing Form 100 Broadway Seventh Fl ... New York NY 10005 *Cust Svc	800-306-3676*	212-366-7600
Digital Photographer Magazine 12121 Wilshire Blvd 12th Fl ... Los Angeles CA 90025	800-537-4619	310-820-1500
Dog Fancy Magazine Three Burroughs ... Irvine CA 92618 *Cust Svc	800-546-7730*	949-855-8822
Equus Magazine 656 Quince OrchaRd Rd Ste 600 ... Gaithersburg MD 20878 *Cust Svc	800-829-5910*	301-977-3900
Family Handyman Magazine 2915 Commers Dr Ste 700 ... Eagan MN 55121	800-285-4961	
Fine Woodworking Magazine 63 S Main St PO Box 5506 ... Newtown CT 06470	800-283-7252	203-426-8171
Flying Magazine 460 N. Orlando Ave. Suite 200 ... Winter Park FL 32789 *Cust Svc	800-678-0797*	407-628-4802
Horse Illustrated Magazine 3 Burroughs ... Irvine CA 92618	888-588-4677	949-855-8822
McCall's Quilting Magazine 741 Corporate Cir Ste A ... Golden CO 80401	800-944-0736	303-215-5600
Model Airplane News 20 Westport Rd ... Wilton CT 06897	800-827-0323	203-431-9000
Mountain Bike Magazine 400 S Tenth St ... Emmaus PA 18098	800-666-2806	
Nuts & Volts Magazine 430 Princeland Ct ... Corona CA 92879 *Orders	800-783-4624*	951-371-8497
Outdoor Photographer Magazine 12121 Wilshire Blvd 12th Fl ... Los Angeles CA 90025 *Cust Svc	800-283-4410*	310-820-1500
Outside Magazine 400 Market St ... Santa Fe NM 87501 *General	888-909-2382*	505-989-7100
Paper Crafts Magazine 14850 Pony Express Rd ... Bluffdale UT 84065	800-727-2387	801-816-8300
PC Gamer Magazine 4000 Shoreline Ct Ste 400 ... South San Francisco CA 94080	877-404-1337	650-238-2505
Plane & Pilot Magazine 12121 Wilshire Blvd 12th Fl ... Los Angeles CA 90025	800-283-4330	310-820-1500
Popular Woodworking Magazine 4700 E Galbraith Rd ... Cincinnati OH 45236 *Cust Svc	877-860-9140*	513-531-2690
Quilter's Newsletter Magazine 741 Corporate Cir Ste A ... Golden CO 80401	800-477-6089	303-215-5600
Quiltmaker Magazine 741 Corporate Cir Ste A ... Golden CO 80401	800-388-7023	800-881-6634
Radio Control Boat Modeler 88 Danbury Rd ... Wilton CT 06897	888-235-2021	203-431-9000
Rock & Gem Magazine 290 Maple Ct Ste 232 ... Ventura CA 93003	866-377-4666	805-644-3824
Rug Hooking Magazine 5067 Ritter Rd ... Mechanicsburg PA 17055	866-375-8626	717-796-0411
Scale Auto Magazine 21027 Crossroads Cir ... Waukesha WI 53186 *Cust Svc	800-533-6644*	262-796-8776
Shutterbug Magazine 1419 Chaffee Dr Ste 1 ... Titusville FL 32780	800-829-3340	386-447-6318
Smoke Magazine 26 Broadway ... New York NY 10004	800-766-2633	212-391-2060
Threads Magazine 63 S Main St PO Box 5506 ... Newtown CT 06470 *General	800-283-7252*	203-426-8171
Wine Spectator Magazine 387 Pk Ave S Eighth Fl ... New York NY 10016 *Orders	800-752-7799*	212-684-4224
Woodshop News 10 Bokum Rd ... Essex CT 06426	800-444-7686	860-767-8227
Woodsmith Magazine 2200 Grand Ave ... Des Moines IA 50312 *Cust Svc	800-333-5075*	

454-15 Law Magazines & Journals

	Toll-Free	Phone
Alabama Lawyer Magazine 415 Dexter Ave ... Montgomery AL 36104	800-354-6154	334-269-1515
Arizona Attorney Magazine 4201 N 24th St Ste 200 ... Phoenix AZ 85016	866-482-9227	602-252-4804
Arkansas Lawyer Magazine 2224 Cottendale Ln ... Little Rock AR 72202	800-609-5668	501-375-4606
Bench & Bar of Minnesota Magazine 600 Nicollet Mall Ste 380 ... Minneapolis MN 55402	800-366-4812	612-333-1183

	Toll-Free	Phone
Colorado Lawyer Magazine 1900 Grant St Ninth Fl ... Denver CO 80203	800-332-6736	303-860-1115
Florida Bar Journal 651 E Jefferson St ... Tallahassee FL 32399	800-342-8060	850-561-5600
Georgia Bar Journal 104 Marietta St NW Ste 100 ... Atlanta GA 30303	866-773-2782	404-527-8700
Hawaii Bar Journal 1100 Alakea St Ste 1000 ... Honolulu HI 96813	888-586-1056	808-537-1868
Journal of the Kansas Bar Assn 1200 SW Harrison St ... Topeka KS 66612	800-928-3111	785-234-5696
Legal Management: Journal of the Assn of Legal Administrators (ALA) 75 Tri State International Ste 222 ... Lincolnshire IL 60069	800-801-3830	847-267-1252
Maine Bar Journal 124 State St PO Box 788 ... Augusta ME 04332	800-475-7523	207-622-7523
Maryland Bar Journal 520 W Fayette St ... Baltimore MD 21201	800-492-1964	410-685-7878
Michigan Bar Journal 306 Townsend St ... Lansing MI 48933	888-726-3678	517-346-6300
Montana Lawyer Magazine 7 W Sixth Ave Ste 2B ... Helena MT 59601	888-385-9119	406-442-7660
National Jurist Magazine 7670 Opportunity Rd Ste 105 ... San Diego CA 92111	800-296-9656	858-300-3201
New Hampshire Bar News 2 Pillsbury St Ste 300 ... Concord NH 03301	800-868-1212	603-224-6942
New York Law Journal 120 Broadway Fifth Fl ... New York NY 10271	877-256-2472	
Oregon State Bar Bulletin, The 16037 SW Upper Boones Ferry Rd PO Box 231935 ... Tigard OR 97281	800-452-8260	503-620-0222
Pennsylvania Bar News 100 S St ... Harrisburg PA 17101	800-932-0311	717-238-6715
Rhode Island Bar Journal 115 Cedar St ... Providence RI 02903	800-335-5701	401-421-5740
Texas Bar Journal 1414 Colorado St Ste 902 ... Austin TX 78701	800-204-2222	512-463-1463
Washington Lawyer Magazine 1101 K St NW Ste 200 ... Washington DC 20005	877-333-2227	202-737-4700
Washington State Bar News 1325 Fourth Ave Ste 600 ... Seattle WA 98101	800-945-9722	

454-16 Medical Magazines & Journals

	Toll-Free	Phone
Access Magazine 444 N Michigan Ave Ste 3400 ... Chicago IL 60611	800-243-2342	312-440-8900
American Journal of Psychiatry 1000 Wilson Blvd Ste 1825 ... Arlington VA 22209	800-368-5777	703-907-7300
American Nurse Magazine 8515 Georgia Ave Ste 400 ... Silver Spring MD 20910	800-274-4262	301-628-5000
American Psychologist Magazine 750 First St NE ... Washington DC 20002	800-374-2721	202-336-5500
Annals of Internal Medicine Magazine 190 N Independence Mall W ... Philadelphia PA 19106	800-523-1546	215-351-2400
Connecticut Medicine Magazine 160 St Ronan St ... New Haven CT 06511	800-842-8440	203-865-0587
Dental Economics Magazine 1421 S Sheridan Rd ... Tulsa OK 74112	800-331-4463	
Diabetes Advisor Magazine 1701 N Beauregard St ... Alexandria VA 22311	800-342-2383	800-806-7801
Family Practice Management 11400 Tomahawk Creek Pkwy ... Leawood KS 66211	800-274-2237	913-906-6000
Internal Medicine Magazine 5635 Fishers Ln Ste 6000 ... Rockville MD 20852	877-524-9336	240-221-2400
Iowa Medicine Magazine 1001 Grand Ave ... West Des Moines IA 50265	800-747-3070	515-223-1401
Journal of Practical Nursing (JPN) 1940 Duke St Ste 200 ... Alexandria VA 22314	800-655-4845	703-933-1003
Journal of the American Medical Assn (JAMA) PO Box 10946 ... Chicago IL 60654	800-262-2350	312-670-7827
Journal of the American Pharmacists Assn 2215 Constitution Ave NW ... Washington DC 20037	800-237-2742	202-628-4410
Journal of the Louisiana State Medical Society 6767 Perkins Rd Ste 100 ... Baton Rouge LA 70808	800-375-9508	225-763-8500
Journal of the Medical Assn of Georgia 1849 The Exchange Ste 200 ... Atlanta GA 30339	800-282-0224	678-303-9290
Mayo Clinic Proceedings Magazine 200 First St SW Siebens Bldg 7-70 ... Rochester MN 55905 *Cust Svc	800-654-2452*	507-284-2094
Minnesota Medicine Magazine 1300 Godward St NE Ste 2500 ... Minneapolis MN 55413	800-342-5662	612-378-1875
Missouri Medicine Magazine PO Box 1028 ... Jefferson City MO 65102	800-869-6762	573-636-5151
NASW News 750 First St NE Ste 700 ... Washington DC 20002	800-227-3590	202-408-8600
New England Journal of Medicine 10 Shattuck St ... Boston MA 02115	800-843-6356	617-734-9800
Nursing Spectrum Greater New York/New Jersey Metro Magazine 1721 Moon Lk Blvd Ste 540 ... Hoffman Estates IL 60169	800-770-0866	
Ohio Medicine Magazine 3401 Mill Run Dr ... Hilliard OH 43026	800-766-6762	614-527-6762
Pharmacy Today Magazine 2215 Constitution Ave NW ... Washington DC 20037	800-237-2742	202-628-4410
Psychotherapy Networker 5135 MacArthur Blvd NW ... Washington DC 20016	888-883-3782	202-537-8950
Social Work News 750 First St NE Ste 700 ... Washington DC 20002	800-227-3590	202-408-8600
Southern Medical Journal 35 Lakeshore Dr ... Birmingham AL 35209	800-423-4992	205-945-1840
Texas Medicine Magazine 401 W 15th St ... Austin TX 78701	800-880-1300	512-370-1300
US Pharmacist Magazine 100 Ave of the Americas Ninth Fl ... New York NY 10013	800-825-4696	
Virginia Medical News 2924 Emerywood Pkwy Ste 300 ... Richmond VA 23294	800-746-6768	
West Virginia Medical Journal PO Box 4106 ... Charleston WV 25364	800-257-4747	304-925-0342

454-17 Political & Current Events Magazines

				Toll-Free	Phone
American Spectator Magazine					
1611 N Kent St Ste 901	Arlington	VA	22209	**800-524-3469**	703-807-2011
Foreign Affairs					
58 E 68th St	New York	NY	10065	**800-829-5539***	212-434-9527
*Cust Svc					
Freeman, The					
30 S Broadway	Irvington-on-Hudson	NY	10533	**800-960-4333***	914-591-7230
*Sales					
Maclean's Magazine					
One Mt Pleasant Rd 11th Fl	Toronto	ON	M4Y2Y5	**800-268-9119**	416-764-1300
Mother Jones Magazine					
222 Sutter St Ste 600	San Francisco	CA	94108	**800-438-6656**	415-321-1700
Nation Magazine					
33 Irving Pl Eighth Fl	New York	NY	10003	**800-333-8536***	212-209-5400
*Cust Svc					
National Journal					
600 New Hampshire Ave NW	Washington	DC	20037	**800-613-6701**	202-739-8400
New Republic, The					
1331 H St NW Ste 700	Washington	DC	20005	**800-827-1289**	202-508-4444
Newsweek Magazine					
Seven Hanover Sq	New York	NY	10004	**800-631-1040***	
*Cust Svc					
Reason Magazine					
3415 S Sepulveda Blvd Ste 400	Los Angeles	CA	90034	**888-732-7668***	310-391-2245
*Cust Svc					
US News & World Report					
1050 Thomas Jefferson St NW	Washington	DC	20007	**800-836-6397**	212-716-6800

454-18 Religious & Spiritual Magazines

				Toll-Free	Phone
B'Nai B'Rith Magazine					
2020 K St NW Seventh Fl	Washington	DC	20006	**888-388-4224**	202-857-6600
Biblical Archaeology Review					
4710 41st St NW	Washington	DC	20016	**800-221-4644**	202-364-3300
Body & Soul					
42 Pleasant St	Watertown	MA	02472	**800-755-1178**	617-449-5506
Catholic Digest					
PO Box 6015	New London	CT	06320	**800-678-2836**	860-437-3012
Charisma Magazine					
600 Rinehart Rd	Lake Mary	FL	32746	**800-749-6500**	407-333-0600
Christianity Today Magazine					
465 Gundersen Dr	Carol Stream	IL	60188	**800-999-1704**	630-260-6200
Episcopal Life Magazine					
815 Second Ave Episcopal Church Ctr	New York	NY	10017	**800-334-7626**	212-716-6000
Lutheran Magazine					
8765 W Higgins Rd	Chicago	IL	60631	**800-638-3522**	
Moment Magazine					
4115 Wisconsin Ave NW Ste 10	Washington	DC	20016	**800-777-1005**	202-363-6422
Presbyterians Today Magazine					
100 Witherspoon St	Louisville	KY	40202	**800-728-7228**	800-872-3283
Spiritled Woman - Charisma Magazine					
600 Rinehart Rd	Lake Mary	FL	32746	**866-776-6473**	407-333-0600
Today's Christian Woman Magazine					
465 Gundersen Dr	Carol Stream	IL	60188	**877-247-4787***	630-260-6200
*Orders					
US Catholic Magazine					
205 W Monroe	Chicago	IL	60606	**800-328-6515***	312-236-7782
*Cust Svc					

454-19 Science & Nature Magazines

				Toll-Free	Phone
American Scientist Magazine					
3106 E NC Hwy 54					
PO Box 13975	Research Triangle Park	NC	27709	**800-243-6534**	919-549-4691
Archaeology Magazine					
36-36 33rd St	Long Island City	NY	11106	**877-275-9782**	718-472-3050
Audubon Magazine					
225 Varick St Seventh Fl	New York	NY	10014	**800-274-4201***	212-979-3000
*Cust Svc					
Aviation Week & Space Technology Magazine					
1200 G St NW Ste 922	Washington	DC	20005	**800-525-5003**	
BioScience					
1444 'I' St NW Ste 200	Washington	DC	20005	**800-992-2427**	202-628-1500
BioTechniques					
52 Vanderbilt Ave 7th Fl	New York	NY	10017	**800-606-6246**	212-520-2777
Defenders Magazine					
1130 17th St NW	Washington	DC	20036	**800-385-9712**	202-682-9400
E/The Environmental Magazine					
28 Knight St PO Box 5098	Norwalk	CT	06851	**800-321-6742**	203-854-5559
Friends of the Earth Magazine					
1100 15th St NW	Washington	DC	20005	**877-843-8687**	202-783-7400
National Parks Magazine					
777 Sixth St NW Ste 700	Washington	DC	20001	**800-628-7275***	202-223-6722
*General					
National Wildlife Magazine					
11100 Wildlife Ctr Dr	Reston	VA	20190	**800-822-9919***	703-438-6000
*Cust Svc					
Nature					
National Press Bldg 529 14th St NW					
Ste 968	Washington	DC	20045	**800-524-0384**	202-737-2355
Orion Magazine					
187 Main St	Great Barrington	MA	01230	**888-909-6568**	413-528-4422
Physics Today Magazine					
One Physics Ellipse	College Park	MD	20740	**800-344-6902**	301-209-3040
R & D Magazine					
100 Enterprise Dr Ste 600	Rockaway	NJ	07866	**866-885-9794**	973-920-7000
Science Magazine					
1200 New York Ave NW	Washington	DC	20005	**800-731-4939**	202-326-6500

				Toll-Free	Phone
Science News					
1719 N St NW	Washington	DC	20036	**800-552-4412***	202-785-2255
*Cust Svc					
Sierra Magazine					
85 Second St 2nd Fl	San Francisco	CA	94105	**866-338-1015**	415-977-5500
Sky & Telescope Magazine					
90 Sherman St	Cambridge	MA	02140	**800-253-0245**	617-864-7360
Smithsonian Air & Space Magazine					
PO Box 37012	Washington	DC	20013	**800-766-2149***	202-633-6070
*Cust Svc					
Tech Briefs Media Group					
261 Fifth Ave Ste 1901	New York	NY	10016	**888-456-3398**	212-490-3999

454-20 Sports Magazines

				Toll-Free	Phone
Bassmaster Magazine					
3500 Blue Lake Dr Suite 330	Birmingham	FL	35243	**877-227-7872**	
Bowhunting World Magazine					
6121 Baker Rd Ste 101	Minnetonka	MN	55345	**800-766-0039**	952-405-2280
Climbing Magazine					
2291 Arapahoe Ave	Boulder	CO	80302	**800-829-5895**	
Competitor Magazine					
9477 Waples St Ste 150	San Diego	CA	92121	**800-311-1255**	
Ducks Unlimited Magazine					
One Waterfowl Way	Memphis	TN	38120	**800-453-8257**	901-758-3825
Golf Tips Magazine					
12121 Wilshire Blvd Ste 1200	Los Angeles	CA	90025	**877-505-9447**	310-820-1500
Hockey News Magazine					
25 Sheppard Ave Ste 100	Toronto	ON	M2N6S7	**888-361-9768**	
Journal of the Philosophy of Sport					
1607 N Market St	Champaign	IL	61820	**800-747-4457**	217-351-5076
Salt Water Sportsman Magazine					
460 N Orlando Ave Ste 200	Winter Park	FL	32789	**800-759-2127**	407-628-4802
Ski Magazine					
5720 Flatiron Pkwy	Boulder	CO	80301	**888-444-8151**	303-253-6300
Snow Goer Magazine					
3300 Fernbrook Ln N Ste 200	Plymouth	MN	55447	**800-710-5249**	
Sports Afield Magazine					
15621 Chemical Ln	Huntington Beach	CA	92649	**800-451-4788**	714-373-4910
Sports Business Journal					
120 W Morehead St Ste 310	Charlotte	NC	28202	**800-829-9839**	704-973-1410
Sports Spectrum Magazine					
105 Corporate Blvd Ste 2	Indian Trail	NC	28079	**866-821-2971**	704-821-2971
Travel + Leisure Magazine					
1120 Ave of the Americas 10th Fl	New York	NY	10036	**800-452-9292**	212-382-5600

454-21 Trade & Industry Magazines

				Toll-Free	Phone
AAPG Explorer Magazine					
1444 S Boulder Ave	Tulsa	OK	74119	**800-364-2274**	918-584-2555
Aerospace America Magazine					
1801 Alexander Bell Dr Ste 500	Reston	VA	20191	**800-639-2422**	703-264-7500
Air Conditioning Heating & Refrigeration News					
2401 W Big Beaver Rd Ste 700	Troy	MI	48084	**800-837-8337**	248-362-3700
American Salon Magazine					
757 Third Ave 5th Fl	New York	NY	10017	**866-871-0656**	212-895-8200
American Society of Civil Engineers (ASCE)					
1801 Alexander Bell Dr	Reston	VA	20191	**800-548-2723**	703-295-6300
Automotive Executive Magazine					
8400 Westpark Dr	McLean	VA	22102	**800-672-3888**	703-821-7150
Automotive News Magazine					
1155 Gratiot Ave	Detroit	MI	48207	**877-812-1584**	313-446-0450
Bartender Magazine					
PO Box 158	Liberty Corner	NJ	07938	**800-463-7465***	908-766-6006
*Sales					
Builder Magazine					
1 Thomas Cir NW Ste 600	Washington	DC	20005	**800-325-6180**	202-452-0800
Building Design & Construction Magazine					
3030 W Salt Creek Ln					
Ste 201	Arlington Heights	IL	60005	**888-811-3288**	847-391-1000
Chemical Processing Magazine					
555 W Pierce Rd Ste 301	Itasca	IL	60143	**800-343-4048**	630-467-1300
Chemical Week Magazine					
140 East 45th Street					
2 Grand Central Tower,40th Fl	New York	NY	10017	**866-501-7540***	212-884-9528
*Cust Svc					
Civil Engineering Magazine					
1801 Alexander Bell Dr	Reston	VA	20191	**800-548-2723**	703-295-6300
Controller Magazine					
120 W Harvest Dr	Lincoln	NE	68521	**800-247-4890**	402-479-2143
DaySpa Magazine					
7628 Densmore Ave	Van Nuys	CA	91406	**800-442-5667**	818-782-7328
Design News 225 Wyman St	Waltham	MA	02451	**800-869-6882**	763-746-2792
Designfax Magazine					
2506 Tamiami Trail North	Nokomis	FL	34275	**877-245-6247**	941-966-9521
EDN Magazine					
303 Second St	San Francisco	CA	94107	**800-446-6551***	415-947-6000
*Orders					
EE Times Magazine					
600 Community Dr	Manhasset	NY	11030	**800-645-6278**	408-930-7372
Electronic Component News					
100 Enterprise Dr Ste 600	Rockaway	NJ	07866	**877-650-5160**	973-920-7000
Engineering News-Record (ENR)					
Two Penn Plz Ninth Fl	New York	NY	10121	**877-876-8208**	212-904-3507
EPRI Journal					
3420 Hillview Ave	Palo Alto	CA	94304	**800-313-3774**	650-855-2121
Fine Homebuilding Magazine					
63 S Main St PO Box 5506	Newtown	CT	06470	**800-283-7252**	203-426-8171
Food Processing Magazine					
555 W Pierce Rd Ste 301	Itasca	IL	60143	**800-755-5505**	630-467-1300
Giftware News					
20 W Kinzie St 12th Fl	Chicago	IL	60654	**800-229-1967**	312-849-2220

				Toll-Free	Phone
Home Media Retailing					
201 E Sandpointe Ave Ste 500	Santa Ana	CA	92707	800-371-6897	714-759-4661
Institute of Scrap Recycling Industries Magazine					
1615 L St NW Ste 6000	Washington	DC	20036	800-767-7236	202-662-8500
Journal of Petroleum Technology					
222 Palisades Creek Dr	Richardson	TX	75080	800-456-6863	972-952-9393
Journal of Protective Coatings & Linings					
2100 Wharton St Ste 310	Pittsburgh	PA	15203	800-837-8303	412-431-8300
Land Line Magazine					
One NW Oodia Dr	Grain Valley	MO	64029	800-444-5791	816-229-5791
Modern Machine Shop Magazine					
6915 Valley Ave	Cincinnati	OH	45244	800-950-8020	513-527-8800
Nailpro Magazine					
7628 Densmore Ave	Van Nuys	CA	91406	800-442-5667	818-782-7328
Nails Magazine					
3520 Challenger St	Torrance	CA	90503	888-624-5744	310-533-2400
National Fisherman Magazine					
121 Free St	Portland	ME	04101	800-959-5073	207-842-5600
National Fitness Trade Journal					
PO Box 2490	White City	OR	97503	877-867-7835	541-830-0400
Oil & Gas Journal PO Box 2002	Tulsa	OK	74101	800-633-1656	918-831-9423
Plant Services Magazine					
555 W Pierce Rd Ste 301	Itasca	IL	60143	800-872-9141	630-467-1300
Pro Lights & Staging News Magazine					
6000 S Eastern Ste 14-J	Las Vegas	NV	89119	888-667-7438*	702-932-5585
*General					
Proceedings of the IEEE Magazine					
445 Hoes Ln	Piscataway	NJ	08855	800-678-4333	732-562-5478
Qualified Remodeler Magazine					
1233 Janesville Ave	Fort Atkinson	WI	53538	800-547-7377	920-563-6388
Quality Progress Magazine					
600 N Plankinton Ave PO Box 3005	Milwaukee	WI	53201	800-248-1946*	414-272-8575
*Cust Svc					
Women's Wear Daily Magazine					
750 Third Ave Fifth Fl	New York	NY	10017	800-289-0273	212-630-4600
Writer's Digest					
4700 E Galbraith Rd	Cincinnati	OH	45236	800-283-0963*	513-531-2690
*Cust Svc					

454-22 Travel & Regional Interest Magazines

				Toll-Free	Phone
Alaska Magazine					
301 Arctic Slope Ave Ste 300	Anchorage	AK	99518	800-288-5892	386-246-0444
Arizona Highways Magazine					
2039 W Lewis Ave	Phoenix	AZ	85009	800-543-5432	
Baltimore Magazine					
1000 Lancaster St Ste 400	Baltimore	MD	21202	800-935-0838*	410-752-4200
*Cust Svc					
Buffalo Spree Magazine					
100 Corporate Pkwy Ste 220	Buffalo	NY	14226	855-697-7733	716-783-9119
Cape Cod Life Magazine					
13 Steeple St Ste 204 PO Box 1439	Mashpee	MA	02649	800-698-1717	508-419-7381
Caribbean Travel & Life Magazine					
460 N Orlando Ave Ste 200	Winter Park	FL	32789	800-289-9399*	407-628-4802
*Sales					
Chesapeake Bay Magazine					
1819 Bay Ridge Ave Ste 180	Annapolis	MD	21403	800-283-2883	410-263-2662
Chicago Magazine					
435 N Michigan Ave Ste 1100	Chicago	IL	60611	800-999-0879	312-222-8999
Cleveland Magazine					
1422 Euclid Ave Ste 730	Cleveland	OH	44115	800-210-7293	216-771-2833
Connecticut Magazine					
35 Nutmeg Dr	Trumbull	CT	06611	800-645-4328	203-380-6600
Departures Magazine					
1120 Ave of the Americas	New York	NY	10036	800-333-7483	212-642-1999
Down East					
680 Commercial St	Rockport	ME	04856	800-766-1670	207-594-9544
Family Motor Coaching Magazine					
8291 Clough Pk	Cincinnati	OH	45244	800-543-3622	513-474-3622
Guest Informant Magazine					
725 Broad St	Augusta	GA	30901	800-622-6358	706-724-0851
Hamptons Magazine					
67 Hampton Rd Ste 201	SoutHampton	NY	11968	866-891-3144	631-283-7125
Hana Hou Magazine (Hawaiian Airlines)					
1144 Tenth Ave Ste 401	Honolulu	HI	96816	888-733-3336	808-733-3333
Home & Away Magazine					
10703 J St Ste 100	Omaha	NE	68127	800-710-2267	402-592-5000
Honolulu Magazine					
1000 Bishop St Ste 405	Honolulu	HI	96813	800-788-4230	808-534-7546
Houston LifeStyle Magazine					
10707 Corporate Dr Ste 170	Stafford	TX	77477	866-505-4456	281-240-2445
Hudson Valley Magazine					
2678 S Rd 2nd Fl	Poughkeepsie	NY	12601	855-658-1850*	845-463-0542
*General					
Indianapolis Monthly Magazine					
40 Monument Cir Ste 100	Indianapolis	IN	46204	888-403-9005*	317-237-9288
*Circ					
Inland Empire Magazine					
3769 Tibbetts St Ste A	Riverside	CA	92506	800-424-4232*	951-682-3026
*General					
InsideFlyer Magazine					
1930 Frequent Flyer Pt	Colorado Springs	CO	80915	800-767-8896	719-597-8889
Islands Magazine					
460 N Orlando Ave Ste 200	Winter Park	FL	32789	800-250-1523	515-237-3697
Jacksonville Magazine					
1261 King St	Jacksonville	FL	32204	800-962-0214	904-389-3622
Key Magazine PO Box 111266	Memphis	TN	38111	866-446-3674	901-458-3912
Key: This Week in Chicago Magazine					
226 E Ontario St Ste 1	Chicago	IL	60611	877-866-0966	312-943-0838
Los Angeles Confidential Magazine					
8530 Wilshire Blvd Ste 500	Beverly Hills	CA	90211	866-891-3144	310-289-7300
Los Angeles Magazine					
5900 Wilshire Blvd 10th Fl	Los Angeles	CA	90036	800-876-5222*	323-801-0100
*Cust Svc					
Louisville Magazine					
137 W Muhammad Ali Blvd Ste 102	Louisville	KY	40202	866-832-0011	502-625-0100

				Toll-Free	Phone
Memphis Magazine					
460 Tennessee St Ste 200	Memphis	TN	38103	800-288-9999	901-521-9000
Michigan Out-of-Doors Magazine (MOOD)					
2101 Wood St PO Box 30235	Lansing	MI	48912	800-777-6720	517-371-1041
Midwest Living Magazine					
1716 Locust St	Des Moines	IA	50309	800-678-8093	515-284-3808
Milwaukee Magazine					
126 N Jefferson St	Milwaukee	WI	53202	800-662-4818	414-273-1101
Minneapolis-Saint Paul Magazine					
220 S Sixth St Ste 500	Minneapolis	MN	55402	800-999-5589	612-339-7571
MotorHome Magazine					
2750 Park View Ct Ste 240	Oxnard	CA	93036	800-678-1201*	805-667-4100
*Cust Svc					
National Geographic Traveler Magazine					
1145 17th St NW	Washington	DC	20036	800-647-5463	202-857-7000
Nevada Magazine					
401 N Carson St	Carson City	NV	89701	855-729-7117	775-687-5416
New Jersey Monthly Magazine					
55 Pk Pl PO Box 920	Morristown	NJ	07963	888-419-0419	973-539-8230
New Mexico Magazine					
PO Box 12002	Santa Fe	NM	87504	800-898-6639	
New Orleans Magazine					
110 Veterans Blvd Ste 123	Metairie	LA	70005	877-221-3512*	504-828-1380
*Edit					
New York Magazine					
75 Varick St	New York	NY	10013	800-678-0900	212-508-0700
Nob Hill Gazette					
5 Third St Ste 222	San Francisco	CA	94103	866-617-4578	415-227-0190
Ohio Magazine					
1422 Euclid Ave Ste 730	Cleveland	OH	44115	800-210-7293	216-771-2833
Orange Coast Magazine					
3701 Birch St Ste 100	Newport Beach	CA	92660	800-397-8179	949-862-1133
Oregon Coast Magazine					
4969 Hwy 101 Ste 2	Florence	OR	97439	800-348-8401	541-997-8401
Orlando Magazine					
801 N Magnolia Ave Ste 201	Orlando	FL	32803	866-356-3075	407-423-0618
Palm Beach Illustrated Magazine					
1000 N Dixie Hwy Ste C	West Palm Beach	FL	33401	800-308-7346	561-659-6160
Phoenix Magazine					
15169 N Scottsdale Ste C10	Scottsdale	AZ	85254	866-481-6970	480-664-3960
San Francisco Magazine					
243 Vallejo St	San Francisco	CA	94111	866-736-2499	415-398-2800
Southern Accents Magazine					
2100 Lakeshore Dr	Birmingham	AL	35209	877-262-5866	205-445-6000
Southern Living Magazine					
2100 Lakeshore Dr	Birmingham	AL	35209	800-366-4712	205-445-6000
Travel Agent Magazine					
757 Third Ave 5th Fl	New York	NY	10017	855-424-6247	212-895-8200
Travelhost Magazine					
10701 N Stemmons Fwy	Dallas	TX	75220	800-527-1782	972-556-0541
Vermont Life					
One National Life Dr Sixth Fl	Montpelier	VT	05620	800-284-3243	802-828-3241
Western Outdoors Magazine					
185 Avenida La Pata	San Clemente	CA	92673	800-290-2929	949-366-0030
Yankee Magazine					
1121 Main St PO Box 520	Dublin	NH	03444	800-288-4284	603-563-8111

455   MAGNETS - PERMANENT

				Toll-Free	Phone
Electron Energy Corp					
924 Links Ave	Landisville	PA	17538	800-824-2735	717-898-2294
Flexmag Industries Inc					
107 Industry Rd	Marietta	OH	45750	800-543-4426	740-374-8024
Magnetic Component Engineering Inc					
2830 Lomita Blvd	Torrance	CA	90505	800-989-5656	
Magnum Magnetics Corp					
801 Masonic Pk Rd	Marietta	OH	45750	800-258-0991	740-373-7770
Mohr Corp PO Box 1600	Brighton	MI	48114	800-223-6647	810-225-9494

456   MAIL ORDER HOUSES

SEE ALSO Seed Companies ; Art Supply Stores ; Book, Music, Video Clubs ; Checks - Personal & Business ; Computer Stores

				Toll-Free	Phone
Advanced Image Direct					
1415 S Acacia Ave	Fullerton	CA	92831	800-540-3848	714-502-3900
Backcountry.com					
2607 South 3200 West Ste A	West Valley City	UT	84119	800-409-4502*	
*Orders					
Brokers Worldwide					
701C Ashland Ave	Folcroft	PA	19032	800-624-5287	610-461-3661
Chadwick's of Boston					
500 Bic Dr Bldg 4	Milford	CT	06461	877-330-3393	
Cinmar LLC					
5566 W Chester Rd	West Chester	OH	45069	888-263-9850	
Country Home Products Inc					
75 Meigs Road	Vergennes	VT	05491	800-376-9637	802-877-1200
Crutchfield Corp					
One Crutchfield Pk	Charlottesville	VA	22911	800-955-3000*	434-817-1000
*Sales					
Current USA Inc					
1005 E Woodmen Rd	Colorado Springs	CO	80920	800-848-2848*	
*Cust Svc					
Daniel Smith Artist Materials					
PO Box 84268	Seattle	WA	98124	800-426-6740	206-223-9599
Design Toscano Inc					
1400 Morse Ave	Elk Grove Village	IL	60007	800-525-5141	847-952-0100
Digi-Key Corp					
701 Brooks Ave S	Thief River Falls	MN	56701	800-344-4539	218-681-6674
EVINE Live Inc					
6740 Shady Oak Rd	Eden Prairie	MN	55344	800-676-5523	
Fingerhut					
6509 Flying Cloud Dr	Eden Prairie	MN	55344	800-208-2500	

Name / Address	City	State	Zip	Toll-Free	Phone
Forestry Suppliers Inc 205 W Rankin St *Cust Svc	Jackson	MS	39201	**800-752-8460***	601-354-3565
Gaiam Inc 833 W S Boulder Rd Ste C *NASDAQ: GAIA*	Louisville	CO	80027	**877-989-6321**	303-222-3600
Gardens Alive Inc 5100 Schenley Pl	Lawrenceburg	IN	47025	**800-222-1222**	513-354-1482
Hammacher Schlemmer & Co 9307 N Milwaukee Ave	Niles	IL	60714	**800-321-1484**	
Hanna Andersson Corp 1010 NW Flanders St *Cust Svc	Portland	OR	97209	**800-222-0544***	
Harry & David Holdings Inc 2500 S Pacific Hwy *Cust Svc	Medford	OR	97501	**877-322-1200***	
Hello Direct Inc 77 NE Blvd	Nashua	NH	03062	**800-435-5634**	
Houston Numismatic Exchange Inc 2486 Times Blvd	Houston	TX	77005	**800-231-3650**	713-528-2135
J Crew Group Inc 770 Broadway	New York	NY	10003	**800-562-0258**	212-209-2500
Jackson & Perkins Two Floral Ave *Cust Svc	Hodges	SC	29653	**800-292-4769***	
JC Whitney 761 Progress Pkwy	La Salle	IL	61301	**866-529-5530**	
JDR Microdevices Inc 229 Polaris Ave Ste 17	Mountain View	CA	94043	**800-538-5000**	650-625-1400
Lands' End Inc One Lands' End Ln *Orders	Dodgeville	WI	53595	**800-963-4816***	
Levenger 420 S Congress Ave *Cust Svc	Delray Beach	FL	33445	**800-544-0880***	561-276-2436
LL Bean Inc 15 Casco St	Freeport	ME	04033	**800-341-4341**	207-552-3080
Mary Maxim Inc 2001 Holland Ave PO Box 5019	Port Huron	MI	48061	**800-962-9504**	810-987-2000
Miles Kimball Co 250 City Ctr Bldg *Cust Svc	Oshkosh	WI	54906	**855-202-7394***	920-231-3800
Movies Unlimited Inc 3015 Darnell Rd	Philadelphia	PA	19154	**800-668-4344**	215-637-4444
Mystic Stamp Co 9700 Mill St	Camden	NY	13316	**866-660-7147**	315-245-2690
NASCO International Inc 901 Janesville Ave *Orders	Fort Atkinson	WI	53538	**800-558-9595***	920-563-2446
National Wholesale Company Inc 400 National Blvd	Lexington	NC	27292	**800-480-4673**	
Norm Thompson Outfitters Inc 3188 NW Aloclek Dr	Hillsboro	OR	97124	**800-547-1160**	503-614-4600
Northeast Data Services 1316 College Ave *Cust Svc	Elmira	NY	14901	**800-699-5636***	607-733-5541
Now Courier Inc PO Box 6066	Indianapolis	IN	46206	**800-543-6066**	
NRC Sports Inc 603 Pleasant St	Paxton	MA	01612	**800-243-5033**	
Oriental Trading Company Inc 5455 S 90th St	Omaha	NE	68127	**800-875-8480**	402-596-1200
Patagonia Inc 259 W Santa Clara St PO Box 150 *Cust Svc	Ventura	CA	93001	**800-638-6464***	805-643-8616
Phoenix Vintners LLC Four S Main St Ste 2	Ipswich	MA	01938	**877-340-9869**	
Roaman's 2300 SE Ave	Indianapolis	IN	46283	**800-677-0229**	
S & S Worldwide Inc 75 Mill St *Orders	Colchester	CT	06415	**800-243-9232***	860-537-3451
SkyMall Inc 1520 E Pima St	Phoenix	AZ	85034	**800-759-6255**	
Specialty Catalog Corp 400 Manley St	West Bridgewater	MA	02379	**800-364-9060**	508-638-7000
StubHub Inc 199 Fremont St Fl 4	San Francisco	CA	94105	**866-788-2482**	415-222-8400
Sunnyland Farms Inc PO Box 8200	Albany	GA	31706	**800-999-2488**	
Tech4Learning Inc 10981 San Diego Mission Rd Ste 120	San Diego	CA	92108	**877-834-5453**	619-563-5348
Tog Shop Inc 30 Tozer Rd	Beverly	MA	01915	**800-767-6666**	978-922-2040
TravelSmith Outfitters 773 San Marin Dr Ste 2300	Novato	CA	94945	**800-770-3387**	
Unicover Corp One Unicover Ctr *Cust Svc	Cheyenne	WY	82008	**800-443-4225***	307-771-3000
Unistar-Sparco Computers Inc 7089 Ryburn Dr	Millington	TN	38053	**800-840-8400**	901-872-2272
Van Dyke Supply Co 39771 Sd Hwy 34	Woonsocket	SD	57385	**800-279-7985**	704-279-7985
Victorian Trading Co 15600 W 99th St *Cust Svc	Lenexa	KS	66219	**800-700-2035***	913-438-3995
Wild Wings LLC 2101 S Hwy 61	Lake City	MN	55041	**800-445-4833**	651-345-5355
Williams-Sonoma Inc 3250 Van Ness Ave *NYSE: WSM*	San Francisco	CA	94109	**800-838-2589**	415-421-7900
Wintersilks Inc PO Box 196 4th Fl	Jessup	PA	18434	**800-648-7455**	800-718-3687
Women's International Pharmacy Inc PO Box 6468	Madison	WI	53716	**800-279-5708**	608-221-7800
Woodcraft Supply LLC 1177 Rosemar Rd PO Box 1686	Parkersburg	WV	26105	**800-535-4482**	
Zappos.com 400 E Stewart Ave Ste 104	Las Vegas	KY	89101	**800-927-7671**	

457 MALLS - SHOPPING

Name / Address	City	State	Zip	Toll-Free	Phone
Antique Mall 1251 S Virginia St	Reno	NV	89502	**888-316-6255**	775-324-4141
Antique World 11111 Main St	Clarence	NY	14031	**800-321-2211**	716-759-8483
Arizona Mills 5000 Arizona Mills Cir	Tempe	AZ	85282	**877-746-6642**	480-491-7300
Bayshore Town Center 5800 N Bayshore Dr Ste A256	Glendale	WI	53217	**800-235-4636**	414-963-8780
Boulder Arts & Crafts 1421 Pearl St Mall	Boulder	CO	80302	**866-656-2667**	303-443-3683
Boynton Beach Mall 801 N Congress Ave	Boynton Beach	FL	33426	**877-746-6642**	561-736-7902
Bronx Council on the Arts 1738 Hone Ave	Bronx	NY	10461	**866-564-5226**	718-931-9500
Burlington Mall 75 Middlesex Tpke	Burlington	MA	01803	**877-746-6642**	781-272-8667
Concord Mills 8111 Concord Mills Blvd	Concord	NC	28027	**877-789-2327**	704-979-3000
Copley Place 100 Huntington Ave Ste 100	Boston	MA	02116	**877-746-6642**	617-262-6600
Del Amo Fashion Ctr 3525 Carson St	Torrance	CA	90503	**877-746-6642**	310-542-8525
Design Ctr of the Americas (DCOTA) 1855 Griffin Rd	Dania Beach	FL	33004	**877-992-9204**	954-920-7997
Ellenton Premium Outlets 5461 Factory Shops Blvd	Ellenton	FL	34222	**888-267-2121**	941-723-1150
Fairlane Town Ctr 18900 Michigan Ave	Dearborn	MI	48126	**800-992-9500**	
Fallbrook Ctr 6633 Fallbrook Ave	West Hills	CA	91307	**866-718-1649**	818-885-9700
Festival Flea Market Mall 2900 W Sample Rd	Pompano Beach	FL	33073	**800-353-2627**	954-979-4555
Franklin Mills 1455 Franklin Mills Cir *General	Philadelphia	PA	19154	**877-746-6642***	215-632-1500
Gardner Village 1100 West 7800 South	West Jordan	UT	84088	**800-662-4335**	801-566-8903
Genesee Valley Ctr 3341 S Linden Rd	Flint	MI	48507	**866-236-1128**	810-732-4000
Golf Mill Shopping Ctr 239 Golf Mill Ctr	Niles	IL	60714	**866-853-9491**	847-699-1070
Great Lakes Mall 7850 Mentor Ave	Mentor	OH	44060	**877-746-6642**	440-255-6900
Green Hills Antique Mall 4108 Hillsboro Pk	Nashville	TN	37215	**888-316-6255**	615-383-9851
Greenwood Park Mall 1251 US Hwy 31 N	Greenwood	IN	46142	**877-746-6642**	317-881-6758
Grove, The 189 The Grove Dr	Los Angeles	CA	90036	**888-315-8883**	323-900-8080
Historic Old Town Fort Collins 19 Old Town Sq Ste 230	Fort Collins	CO	80524	**866-203-5939**	970-484-6500
Independence Ctr 2035 Independence Ctr Dr	Independence	MO	64057	**877-746-6642**	816-795-8600
Ingram Park Mall 6301 NW Loop 410	San Antonio	TX	78238	**877-746-6642**	210-684-9570
Irving Mall 3880 Irving Mall	Irving	TX	75062	**877-746-6642**	972-255-0571
King of Prussia Mall 160 N Gulph Rd	King of Prussia	PA	19406	**877-746-6642**	610-265-5727
Liberty Tree Mall 100 Independence Way	Danvers	MA	01923	**877-746-6642**	978-777-0794
Lower East Side Business Improvement District 54 Orchard St	New York	NY	10002	**866-224-0206**	212-226-9010
Meyerland Plaza 420 Meyerland Plaza	Houston	TX	77096	**888-675-2275**	713-349-0245
Mill Creek Mall 654 Millcreek Mall	Erie	PA	16565	**800-615-3535**	814-868-9000
Mills at Jersey Gardens, The 651 Kapkowski Rd	Elizabeth	NJ	07201	**877-789-2327**	908-354-5900
North East Mall 1101 Melbourne St Ste 1000	Hurst	TX	76053	**877-746-6642**	817-284-3427
Northgate Mall 401 NE Northgate Way Ste 210	Seattle	WA	98125	**877-789-2327**	206-362-4777
Orland Square 288 Orland Sq	Orland Park	IL	60462	**877-746-6642**	708-349-1646
Outlets at Anthem 4250 W Anthem Way	Phoenix	AZ	85086	**888-482-5834**	623-465-9500
Potomac Mills 2700 Potomac Mills Cir Ste 307	Woodbridge	VA	22192	**877-746-6642**	703-496-9301
Prime Outlets San Marcos 3939 S IH-35	San Marcos	TX	78666	**866-888-5530**	512-396-2200
River Oaks Ctr 96 River Oaks Ctr Dr	Calumet City	IL	60409	**877-746-6642**	708-868-0600
Rolling Oaks Mall 6909 N Loop 1604 E	San Antonio	TX	78247	**877-746-6642**	210-651-5513
Roosevelt Field Mall 630 Old Country Rd	Garden City	NY	11530	**877-746-6642**	516-742-8001
Seminole Towne Ctr 200 Towne Ctr Cir	Sanford	FL	32771	**877-746-6642**	407-323-2262
Shops at Woodlake 725 Woodlake Rd	Kohler	WI	53044	**855-444-2838**	920-459-1713
Solomon Pond Mall 601 Donald Lynch Blvd	Marlborough	MA	01752	**877-746-6642**	508-303-6255
South Coast Plaza 3333 Bristol St	Costa Mesa	CA	92626	**800-782-8888**	
South Shore Plaza 250 Granite St	Braintree	MA	02184	**877-746-6642**	781-843-8200
Southdale Ctr 10 Southdale Ctr	Edina	MN	55435	**877-746-6642**	952-925-7874
Southern Park Mall 7401 Market St	Youngstown	OH	44512	**877-746-6642**	330-758-4511
SouthPark Mall 4400 Sharon Rd	Charlotte	NC	28211	**888-726-5930**	704-364-4411

				Toll-Free	Phone

SouthPointe Pavilions
2910 Pine Lake Rd Ste Q . . . . Lincoln NE 68516 **800-733-2767** 402-421-2114

Spokane Valley Mall
14700 E Indiana Ave . . . . Spokane WA 99216 **800-326-3264** 509-926-3700

Square One Mall
1201 Broadway . . . . Saugus MA 01906 **877-746-6642** 781-233-8787

Stoneridge Shopping Ctr
1 Stoneridge Mall . . . . Pleasanton CA 94588 **877-746-6642** 925-463-2778

Stonestown Galleria
3251 20th Ave . . . . San Francisco CA 94132 **800-326-3264** 415-564-8848

Tacoma Mall
4502 S Steele St Ste 1177 . . . . Tacoma WA 98409 **877-746-6642** 253-475-4565

Tanger Outlet Ctr San Marcos
4015 S IH-35 Ste 319 . . . . San Marcos TX 78666 **800-408-8424** 512-396-7446

Tri-County Mall
11700 Princeton Pike . . . . Cincinnati OH 45246 **866-905-4675** 513-671-0120

Tysons Corner Ctr
1961 Chain Bridge Rd . . . . McLean VA 22102 **877-247-5223** 703-847-7300

University Park Mall
6501 N Grape Rd . . . . Mishawaka IN 46545 **877-746-6642** 574-277-2223

West Point Market
1711 W Market St . . . . Akron OH 44313 **800-838-2156** 330-864-2151

Westchester, The
125 Westchester Ave Ste 925 . . . . White Plains NY 10601 **877-746-6642** 914-421-1333

Westmoreland Mall
5256 Rt 30 E . . . . Greensburg PA 15601 **800-333-7310** 724-836-5025

Woodburn Co Stores
1001 N Arney Rd . . . . Woodburn OR 97071 **866-888-5530** 503-981-1900

458 MALTING PRODUCTS

SEE ALSO Breweries

				Toll-Free	Phone

Premier Malt Products Inc
25760 Groesbeck Hwy Ste 103 . . . . Warren MI 48089 **800-521-1057*** 586-443-3355
*Cust Svc

459 MANAGED CARE - BEHAVIORAL HEALTH

				Toll-Free	Phone

American Behavioral Benefits Managers
2204 Lakeshore Dr Ste 135 . . . . Birmingham AL 35209 **800-925-5327** 205-871-7814

Anthem Inc
120 Monument Cir . . . . Indianapolis IN 46204 **800-999-7222** 317-488-6000

APS Healthcare Inc
44 S Broadway Ste 1200 . . . . White Plains NY 10601 **800-305-3720**

Associated Behavioral Health Care Inc
4700 42nd Ave SW Ste 480 . . . . Seattle WA 98116 **800-858-6702** 206-935-1282

Baxter Assistance Services Inc
2800 E Broadway Ste C-416 . . . . Pearland TX 77581 **866-443-0005**

Bensinger DuPont & Assoc (BDA)
134 N LaSalle St Ste 2200 . . . . Chicago IL 60602 **800-227-8620** 312-726-8620

CIGNA Behavioral Health Inc
11095 Viking Dr Ste 350 . . . . Eden Prairie MN 55344 **800-753-0540** 703-907-7730

Comprehensive EAP
5 Militia Dr . . . . Lexington MA 02421 **800-344-1011**

ComPsych Corp
455 N City Front Plaza Dr
NBC Tower 13th Fl . . . . Chicago IL 60611 **800-851-1714** 312-595-4000

COPE Inc
1120 G St NW Ste 550 . . . . Washington DC 20005 **800-247-3054** 202-628-5100

CorpCare Assoc LLC
7000 Peachtree Dunwoody Rd
Bldg 4 Ste 300 . . . . Atlanta GA 30328 **800-728-9444**

Corporate Care Works
8649 Baypine Rd Ste 101 . . . . Jacksonville FL 32256 **800-327-9757** 904-296-9436

EAP Consultants Inc
3901 Roswell Rd Ste 340 . . . . Marietta GA 30062 **800-869-0276** 770-951-9970

EAP Systems
500 W Cummings Pk . . . . Woburn MA 01801 **800-535-4841** 781-935-8850

FEI Behavioral Health
11700 W Lk Pk Dr . . . . Milwaukee WI 53224 **800-782-1948** 414-359-1055

Gilsbar Inc PO Box 998 . . . . Covington LA 70434 **800-445-7227** 985-892-3520

Holman Group
9451 Corbin Ave . . . . Northridge CA 91324 **800-321-2843** 818-704-1444

Human Management Services Inc
835 Springdale Dr . . . . Exton PA 19341 **800-343-2186** 610-363-6175

Hurst Place
209 Limeridge Rd E . . . . Hamilton ON L9A2S6 **888-521-8300** 289-426-5302

Interface EAP Inc (IEAP)
10370 Richmond Ave Ste 1100
PO Box 421879 . . . . Houston TX 77042 **800-324-4327** 713-781-3364

Magellan Health Services Inc
55 Nod Rd . . . . Avon CT 06001 **800-424-4399** 860-507-1900
NASDAQ: MGLN

Managed Health Network Inc
1600 Los Gamos Dr Ste 300 . . . . San Rafael CA 94903 **800-327-2133**

MENTOR Network, The
313 Congress St 5th Fl . . . . Boston MA 02210 **800-388-5150** 617-790-4800

MHNet Behavioral Health
9606 N MoPac Exwy Ste 600 . . . . Austin TX 78759 **888-646-6889**

Midwest EAP Solutions Inc
1015 W St Germain St Ste 440 . . . . Saint Cloud MN 56301 **800-383-1908** 320-253-1909

National Employee Assistance Services Inc
N 17 W 24100 Riverwood Dr Ste 300 . . . . Waukesha WI 53188 **800-634-6433** 262-574-2500

New Directions Behavioral Health LLC
PO Box 6729 . . . . Leawood KS 66206 **800-528-5763** 913-982-8200

Perspectives Ltd
20 N Clark St Ste 2650 . . . . Chicago IL 60602 **800-866-7556** 312-558-5318

Providence Service Corp
64 E Broadway . . . . Tucson AZ 85701 **800-747-6950** 520-748-7108
NASDAQ: PRSC

Stuecker & Assoc Inc
1930 Bishop Ln Watterson Towers
Ste 1001 . . . . Louisville KY 40218 **800-799-9327** 502-452-9227

				Toll-Free	Phone

United Behavioral Health Inc
425 Market St 27th Fl . . . . San Francisco CA 94105 **800-888-2998** 415-547-5000

ValueOptions Inc
12369 Sunrise Vly Dr Ste C . . . . Reston VA 20191 **877-334-0077** 703-390-6800

460 MANAGEMENT SERVICES

SEE ALSO Hotels & Hotel Companies ; Incentive Program Management Services ; Investment Advice & Management ; Pharmacy Benefits Management Services ; Association Management Companies ; Educational Institution Operators & Managers ; Facilities Management Services

				Toll-Free	Phone

2 Places At 1 Time Inc
270 Peachtree St 20th Fl . . . . Atlanta GA 30303 **877-275-2237**

American Dental Partners Inc
401 Edgewater Pl Ste 430 . . . . Wakefield MA 01880 **800-838-6563** 781-213-6500
NASDAQ: ADPI

AMFM Inc
240 Capitol St Ste 500 . . . . Charleston WV 25301 **800-348-1623** 304-344-1623

Archway Marketing Services Inc
19850 S Diamond Lake Rd . . . . Rogers MN 55374 **866-779-9855** 763-428-3300

Arcweb Technologies LLC
234 Market St Fifth Fl . . . . Philadelphia PA 19106 **800-846-7980**

Bankruptcy Management Solutions Inc
Eight Corporate Park Ste 230 . . . . Irvine CA 92606 **800-634-7734**

Banyan Water Inc
11002-B Metric Blvd . . . . Austin TX 78758 **800-276-1507**

Benefact Consulting Group
6285 Northam Dr Ste 112 . . . . Mississauga ON L4V1X5 **855-829-2225**

Beyond the Arc Inc
2600 Tenth St Ste 616 . . . . Berkeley CA 94710 **877-676-3743**

Birner Dental Management Services Inc
1777 S Harrison St Ste 1400 . . . . Denver CO 80210 **877-898-1083** 303-691-0680

Brillio
100 Town Sq Pl Ste 308 . . . . Jersey City NJ 07310 **800-317-0575**

BSC America Inc
803 Bel Air Rd . . . . Bel Air MD 21014 **800-764-7400**

Carpedia International Ltd
75 Navy St . . . . Oakville ON L6J2Z1 **877-445-8288**

CE Resource Inc
1482 Stone Point Dr Ste 100 . . . . Roseville CA 95661 **800-707-5644**

Chartis Group LLC
220 W Kinzie St Fifth Fl . . . . Chicago IL 60654 **877-667-4700**

Coast Dental Services Inc
4010 W Boy Scout Blvd Ste 1100 . . . . Tampa FL 33607 **800-327-6453** 813-288-1999

Coker Consulting
2400 Lakeview Pkwy Ste 400 . . . . Alpharetta GA 30009 **800-345-5829**

Compmanagement Inc
PO Box 884 . . . . Dublin OH 43017 **800-825-6755** 614-376-5300

Concentra Inc
5080 Spectrum Dr Ste 1200 W . . . . Addison TX 75001 **866-944-6046**

Corizon
105 Westpark Dr Ste 200 . . . . Brentwood TN 37027 **800-729-0069**

CorVel Corp
2010 Main St Ste 600 . . . . Irvine CA 92614 **888-726-7835** 949-851-1473
NASDAQ: CRVL

Corvirtus LLC
1011 N Weber St . . . . Colorado Springs CO 80903 **800-322-5329**

CRAssoc Inc
8580 Cinderbed Rd Ste 2400 . . . . Newington VA 22122 **877-272-8960** 703-550-8145

DealNet Capital Corp
325 Milner Ave Ste 300 . . . . Toronto ON M1B5N1 **855-912-3444**

Designs on Talent LLC
1579 Monroe Dr F155 . . . . Atlanta GA 30324 **888-360-3360**

Enterey Inc
9900 Irvine Ctr Dr Ste 100 . . . . Irvine CA 92618 **800-691-2349**

Ephor Group LLC
24 E Greenway Plz Ste 440 . . . . Houston TX 77046 **800-379-9330**

EPS Corp
150 Paularino Ave Ste A120 . . . . Costa Mesa CA 92626 **866-377-7834**

FCC Services
7951 E Maplewood Ave
Ste 225 . . . . Greenwood Village CO 80111 **888-275-3227**

File Keepers LLC
6277 E Slauson Ave . . . . Los Angeles CA 90040 **800-332-3463** 323-728-3133

Firm Consulting Group
2107 W Cass St Ste B . . . . Tampa FL 33606 **877-636-9525**

First Health Group Corp
Coventry
3200 Highland Ave . . . . Downers Grove IL 60515 **800-247-2898** 630-737-7900

Franchise Brands LLC
325 Bic Dr . . . . Milford CT 06461 **800-797-2308**

Franchise Co, The (TFC)
5399 Eglinton Ave W Ste 110 . . . . Etobicoke ON M9C5K9 **800-294-5591** 416-620-3960

Geo-instruments Inc
24 Celestial Dr Ste B . . . . Narragansett RI 02882 **800-477-2506**

Group Management Services Inc
3296 Columbia Rd Ste 101 . . . . Richfield OH 44286 **888-823-2084** 330-659-0100

Harkcon
1390 Chain Bridge Rd 570 . . . . Mclean VA 22101 **800-499-6456**

HealthAxis Inc
7301 N State Hwy 161 Ste 300 . . . . Irving TX 75039 **888-974-2947** 972-443-5000

Hill Physicians Medical Group Inc
2409 Camino Ramon PO Box 5080 . . . . . . San Ramon CA 94583 **800-445-5747** 925-820-8300

INFOCUS Marketing Inc
4245 Sigler Rd . . . . Warrenton VA 20187 **800-708-5478**

Ingenix Inc
12125 Technology Dr . . . . Eden Prairie MN 55344 **888-445-8745** 952-833-7100

Jolt Consulting Group
112 Spring St Ste 301 . . . . Saratoga Springs NY 12866 **877-249-6262**

Keiro Services
325 S Boyle Ave . . . . Los Angeles CA 90033 **855-872-6060** 323-980-7555

Latitude Consulting Group Inc
100 E Michigan Ave Ste 200 . . . . Saline MI 48176 **888-577-2797**

Lifewings Partners LLC
9198 Crestwyn Hills Dr . . . . Memphis TN 38125 **800-290-9314**

	Toll-Free	Phone
Magellan Medicaid Administration Inc		
4300 Cox Rd ....Glen Allen VA 23060	800-884-2822	804-965-7400
Mattersight Corp		
200 S Wacker Ste 820 ....Chicago IL 60606	877-235-6925	
MavenWire LLC		
630 Freedom Business Ctr		
Third Fl ....King Of Prussia PA 19406	866-343-4870	
Medcor Inc		
4805 W Prime Pkwy ....McHenry IL 60050	877-696-6775	815-363-9500
Metropolitan Health Networks Inc		
777 Yamato Rd Ste 510 ....Boca Raton FL 33431	800-221-5487	561-805-8500
NYSE: MDF		
MHM Services Inc		
1593 Spring Hill Rd Ste 600 ....Vienna VA 22182	800-416-3649	703-749-4600
Modis Inc		
10201 Centurion Pkwy N Ste 400 ....Jacksonville FL 32256	800-372-2788	904-360-2300
MyLLC.com Inc		
5716 Corsa Ave Ste 110 ....Westlake Village CA 91362	888-886-9552	
Netcracker Technology Corp		
95 Sawyer Rd University Ofc Pk III ....Waltham MA 02453	800-477-5785	781-419-3300
New Ventures West		
3502 Geary Blvd Fl 2 ....San Francisco CA 94118	800-332-4618	
Northeast Utilities Service Company Inc		
56 Prospect St ....Hartford CT 06103	800-286-5000	
Partners Benefit Group Inc		
Five Crystal Pond Rd ....Southborough MA 01772	877-993-5600	
Patricia Seybold Group		
210 Commercial St ....Boston MA 02109	855-310-0101	617-742-5200
Pediatrix Medical Group Inc		
1301 Concord Terr ....Sunrise FL 33323	800-243-3839	954-384-0175
PFSweb Inc		
505 Millennium Dr Ste 500 ....Allen TX 75013	888-330-5504	972-881-2900
NASDAQ: PFSW		
Pitney Bowes Management Services		
90 Pk Ave ....New York NY 10016	800-322-8000	212-808-3800
Porter Medical Ctr Inc		
115 Porter Dr ....Middlebury VT 05753	800-994-6610	802-388-4701
Prospect Medical Holdings Inc		
10780 Santa Monica Blvd Ste 400 ....Los Angeles CA 90025	800-708-3230	310-943-4500
Provell Inc		
855 Village Center Drive Suite 116 ....North Oaks MN 55127	800-624-2946	952-258-2000
RBN Energy LLC		
2323 S Shepherd Dr Ste 1010 ....Houston TX 77019	888-400-9838	
Red Spot Interactive		
1001 jupiter park dr ....Jupiter FL 33458	800-401-7931	
Retirement Advantage Inc, The		
47 Park Pl Ste 850 ....Appleton WI 54914	888-872-2364	
RGFCC Corp		
8507 Oxon Hill Rd Ste 301 ....Fort Washington MD 20744	888-389-1230	
RHA Health Services Inc		
17 Church St ....Asheville NC 28801	866-742-2428	828-232-6844
Rideau Inc 473 Deslauriers ....Montreal QC H4N1W2	800-363-6464	
SEA Ltd		
7349 Worthington-Galena Rd ....Columbus OH 43085	800-782-6851	
Select Medical Corp		
4714 Gettysburg Rd ....Mechanicsburg PA 17055	888-735-6332	717-972-1100
Service Intelligence Inc		
1061 Red Venture Dr Ste 175 ....Fort Mill SC 29707	800-263-2980	
Sheridan Healthcare Inc		
1613 NW 136th Ave Ste 200 ....Sunrise FL 33323	800-437-2672	
Solutions AE Inc		
236 Auburn Ave ....Atlanta GA 30303	888-562-4441	
SpawGlass Construction Corp		
13800 W Rd ....Houston TX 77041	800-771-0422	281-970-5300
Spectrum Healthcare Resources Inc		
12647 Olive Blvd Ste 600 ....Saint Louis MO 63141	800-325-3982	
Staples Construction Company Inc		
1501 Eastman Ave ....Ventura CA 93003	800-881-4650	805-658-8786
Summit Energy Services Inc		
10350 Ormsby Pk Pl Ste 400 ....Louisville KY 40223	866-907-8664	502-429-3800
Talent Curve		
14 Bridle Path ....Pittsboro NC 27312	866-494-0248	
Turpin Sales & Marketing Inc		
330 Cold Spring Ave ....West Springfield MA 01089	877-377-7573	
Unisource NTC		
1560 Holly Court Ste 200 ....Thousand Oaks CA 91360	800-736-8470	
Vanir Construction Management Inc		
4540 Duckhorn Dr Ste 300 ....Sacramento CA 95834	888-912-1201	916-575-8887
VetStrategy 780 Hwy 6 N ....Waterdown ON L0R2H1	866-901-6471	
Vetter Health Services Inc		
20220 Harney St ....Elkhorn NE 68022	800-388-4264	402-895-3932
VHA Inc		
220 Las Colinas Blvd E PO Box 140909.............Irving TX 75039	800-842-5146	972-830-7845
Volt VIEWtech Inc		
4761 E Hunter Ave ....Anaheim CA 92807	888-396-9927	714-695-3377
Xand Corp 11 Skyline Dr ....Hawthorne NY 10532	800-522-2823	914-592-8282

461   MANNEQUINS & DISPLAY FORMS

	Toll-Free	Phone
Ronis Bros 39 Harriet Pl ....Lynbrook NY 11563	888-555-1234	516-887-5266
Siegel & Stockman USA		
126 W 25th St ....New York NY 10001	888-515-8949	212-633-0138
Silvestri Studio Inc		
8125 Beach St ....Los Angeles CA 90001	800-647-8874	323-277-4420

462   MARINE SERVICES

SEE ALSO Freight Transport - Deep Sea (Domestic Ports) ; Freight Transport
- Deep Sea (Foreign Ports) ; Freight Transport - Inland Waterways ; Logistics
Services (Transportation & Warehousing)

	Toll-Free	Phone
AEP River Operations		
16150 Main Cir Dr Ste 400....................Chesterfield MO 63017	800-621-3362	636-530-2100

	Toll-Free	Phone
Andrie Inc		
561 E Western Ave ....Muskegon MI 49442	800-722-2421	231-728-2226
Bay Houston Towing Co		
2243 Milford St ....Houston TX 77253	800-324-3755	713-529-3755
Crowley Maritime Corp		
9487 Regency Square Blvd		
Ste 2130 ....Jacksonville FL 32225	800-276-9539	904-727-2200
Edison Chouest Offshore		
16201 E Main St ....Galliano LA 70354	866-925-5161	985-601-4444
Foss Maritime Co		
660 W Ewing St·················.................Seattle WA 98119	800-426-2885	800-562-2711
General Steamship Agencies Inc		
575 Redwood Hwy Ste 200...................Mill Valley CA 94941	855-859-3123	415-389-5200
Great Lakes Towing Co		
4500 Div Ave ....Cleveland OH 44102	800-321-3663	216-621-4854
Hawaiian Tug & Barge		
1331 N Nimitz Hwy PO Box 3288...............Honolulu HI 96817	800-572-2743	808-543-9311
Hopkins-Carter Company Inc		
3300 NW 21st St ....Miami FL 33142	800-595-9656	305-635-7377
Hornbeck Offshore Services Inc		
103 Northpark Blvd Ste 300 ....Covington LA 70433	800-642-9816	985-727-2000
NYSE: HOS		
Kinder Morgan Bulk Terminals Inc		
7116 Hwy 22 ....Sorrento LA 70778	800-232-1627	225-675-5387
Marquette Transportation Company LLC		
5525 Mounes St PO Box 23521 ....New Orleans LA 70123	800-735-5845	504-733-5845
McAllister Towing & Transportation Co Inc		
17 Battery Pl Ste 1200 ....New York NY 10004	888-774-0400	212-269-3200
New York State Canal Corp		
200 Southern Blvd PO Box 189 ....Albany NY 12201	800-422-6254	518-436-2700
Odyssey Marine Exploration Inc		
5215 W Laurel St ....Tampa FL 33607	800-458-4646	813-876-1776
NASDAQ: OMEX		
Sause Bros		
3710 NW Front Ave ....Portland OR 97210	800-488-4167	503-222-1811
Sea Tow Services International Inc		
1560 Youngs Ave PO Box 1178 ....Southold NY 11971	800-473-2869	631-765-3660
SSA Marine		
1131 SW Klickitat Way ....Seattle WA 98134	800-422-3505	206-623-0304
Tidewater Inc		
601 Poydras St Ste 1900 ....New Orleans LA 70130	800-678-8433	504-568-1010
NYSE: TDW		
Virginia International Terminals Inc		
7737 Hampton Blvd Ste D224 ....Norfolk VA 23505	800-541-2431*	757-440-7000
*General		

463   MARKET RESEARCH FIRMS

SEE ALSO

	Toll-Free	Phone
1stWEST Financial Corp		
32186 Castle Court Ste 220 ....Evergreen CO 80439	866-670-3443	
Ameresco Canada Inc		
90 Sheppard Ave E 7th Fl ....North York ON M2N6X3	877-358-3853	416-512-7700
AML Partners LLC		
Four Grand Cove Way ....Edgewater NJ 07020	866-790-5095	201-484-8835
Amphenol Optimize Manufacturing Co		
180 N Freeport Dr Bldg W-10 ....Nogales AZ 85621	800-288-4746	520-397-7015
Arbitron Inc		
9705 Patuxent Woods Dr ....Columbia MD 21046	800-543-7300	410-312-8000
NYSE: ARB		
Bensussen Deutsch & Assoc Inc (BDA)		
15525 Woodinville-Redmond Rd NE ....Woodinville WA 98072	800-451-4764	425-492-6111
Bridge Metrics LLC		
830 S Greenville Ave ....Allen TX 75002	877-801-7158	
C & R Research Services Inc		
500 N Michigan Ave Ste 1200 ....Chicago IL 60611	800-543-9393	312-828-9200
CattleLog		
10305 102nd Terrace ....Sebastian FL 32958	866-239-2665	
comScore Inc		
11950 Democracy Dr # 600 ....Reston VA 20190	866-276-6972	703-438-2000
eXelate		
Seven W 22nd St Ninth Fl. ....New York NY 10010	877-896-3282	646-380-4400
Gallup Organization		
901 F St NW ....Washington DC 20004	877-242-5587	202-715-3030
Gartner Inc		
56 Top Gallant Rd ....Stamford CT 06902	800-863-8863	203-964-0096
NYSE: IT		
GRFI Ltd		
400 E Randolph St Ste 700......................Chicago IL 60601	888-856-5161	
Gulf of Maine Research Institute, The		
350 Commercial St ....Portland ME 04101	866-447-2111	207-772-2321
Harris Interactive Inc		
60 Corporate Woods ....Rochester NY 14623	800-866-7655	585-272-8400
NASDAQ: HPOL		
Information Resources Inc		
150 N Clinton St ....Chicago IL 60661	866-262-5973	312-726-1221
Institute for Corporate Productivity Inc		
411 First Ave S Ste 403 ....Seattle WA 98104	866-375-4427	206-624-6565
International Data Corp (IDC)		
Five Speen St ....Framingham MA 01701	800-343-4952	508-872-8200
Invoke Solutions Inc		
375 Totten Pond Rd ....Waltham MA 02451	866-687-4367	781-810-2700
JD Power & Assoc		
2625 Townsgate Rd Ste 100 ....Westlake Village CA 91361	800-274-5372	805-418-8000
Kazan, McClain, Abrams, Fernandez, Lyons & Farrise PLC		
Jack London Market 55 Harrison St		
Ste 400 ....Oakland CA 94607	877-995-6372	
Knowledge Works Inc		
5750 Old Orchard Rd Ste 250 ....Skokie IL 60077	866-825-3400	847-853-6117
M/A/R/C Research		
1660 Westridge Cir ....Irving TX 75038	800-884-6272	972-983-0400
Maritz Research Inc		
1355 N Hwy Dr ....Fenton MO 63099	877-462-7489	636-827-4000
Market Decisions LLC		
75 Washington Ave Ste 206 ....Portland ME 04101	800-293-1538	207-767-6440

			Toll-Free	Phone
MarketVision Research Inc				
10300 Alliance Rd Ste 200	Cincinnati OH	45242	800-232-4250	513-791-3100
MORPACE International Inc				
31700 Middlebelt Rd Ste 200	Farmington Hills MI	48334	800-881-1723*	248-737-5300
*General				
National Research Corp				
1245 Q St	Lincoln NE	68508	800-388-4264	402-475-2525
NASDAQ: NRCI				
NPD Group Inc				
900 W Shore Rd	Port Washington NY	11050	866-444-1411	516-625-0700
OnCard Marketing Inc				
276 Fifth Ave Ste 608	New York NY	10001	866-996-8729	
Opinion Research Corp (ORC)				
902 Carnegie Ctr Ste 220	Princeton NJ	08540	800-444-4672	
RateHub.ca 103 Balliol St	Toronto ON	M4S1C8	800-679-9622	
RDA Group				
450 Enterprise Ct	Bloomfield Hills MI	48302	800-669-7324	248-332-5000
Reis Inc				
530 Fifth Ave Fifth Fl	New York NY	10036	800-366-7347	212-921-1122
NASDAQ: REIS				
Standards Council of Canada				
270 Albert St Ste 200	Ottawa ON	K1P6N7	800-844-6790	613-238-3222
Strategy Institute				
401 Richmond St W Ste 401	Toronto ON	M5V3A8	866-298-9343	416-944-9200
Walker Information Inc				
301 Pennsylvania Pkwy	Indianapolis IN	46280	800-334-3939	317-843-3939
Westat Inc				
1600 Research Blvd	Rockville MD	20850	800-669-6820	301-251-1500
XtremeEDA Corp				
201-1339 Wellington St W	Ottawa ON	K1Y3B8	800-586-0280	613-728-5912
Zolato Inc				
2801 First Ave Ste 306	Seattle WA	98121	866-557-6716	

464   MARKING DEVICES

			Toll-Free	Phone
American Marking Systems Inc				
1015 Paulison Ave PO Box 1677	Clifton NJ	07011	800-782-6766	973-478-5600
Automark Marking Systems				
13475 Lakefront Dr	Earth City MO	63045	888-777-2303	314-739-0430
Cable Markers Company Inc				
13805-C Alton Pkwy	Irvine CA	92618	800-746-7655	
CH Hanson Co				
2000 N Aurora Rd	Naperville IL	60563	800-827-3398	630-848-2000
Cosco Industries Inc				
7220 W Wilson Ave	Harwood Heights IL	60706	800-296-8970	708-867-5800
Excelsior Marking Products				
888 W Waterloo Rd	Akron OH	44314	800-433-3615	330-745-2300
Hitt Marking Devices Inc				
3231 W MacArthur Blvd	Santa Ana CA	92704	800-969-6699	714-979-1405
Huntington Park Rubber Stamp				
2761 E Slauson Ave PO Box 519	Huntington Park CA	90255	800-882-0029	323-582-6461
Infosight Corp				
PO Box 5000	Chillicothe OH	45601	800-401-0716	740-642-3600
Jackson Marking Products Co				
9105 N Rainbow Ln	Mount Vernon IL	62864	800-782-6722	618-242-1334
La-Co/Markal Co				
1201 Pratt Blvd	Elk Grove Village IL	60007	800-621-4025	847-956-7600
Matthews International Corp Marking Products Div				
6515 Penn Ave	Pittsburgh PA	15206	800-775-7775	412-665-2500
Menke Marking Devices				
13253 Alondra Blvd				
PO Box 2986	Santa Fe Springs CA	90670	800-231-6023	562-921-1380
New Method Steel Stamps Inc				
31313 Kendall Ave	Fraser MI	48026	800-582-0199	586-293-0200
Norwood Marking Systems				
2538 Wisconsin Ave	Downers Grove IL	60515	800-626-3464	630-968-0646
Schwaab Inc				
11415 W Burleigh St	Milwaukee WI	53222	800-935-9877	414-771-4150
Schwerdtle Stamp Co				
166 Elm St	Bridgeport CT	06604	800-535-0004	203-330-2750
Signet Marking Devices				
3121 Red Hill Ave	Costa Mesa CA	92626	800-421-5150	714-549-0341
Stamp-Rite Inc				
154 S Larch St	Lansing MI	48912	800-328-1988	517-487-5071
Tacoma Rubber Stamp & Sign				
919 Market St	Tacoma WA	98402	800-544-7281	253-383-5433
Volk Corp				
23936 Industrial Pk Dr	Farmington Hills MI	48335	800-521-6799*	248-477-6700
*Cust Svc				
Wendell's Inc				
6601 Bunker Lk Blvd NW PO Box 458	Ramsey MN	55303	800-936-3355	763-576-8200

465   MASS TRANSPORTATION (LOCAL & SUBURBAN)

SEE ALSO Bus Services - Intercity & Rural

			Toll-Free	Phone
Alameda-Contra Costa Transit District				
1600 Franklin St 10th Fl	Oakland CA	94612	877-878-8883	510-891-4777
Alaska Marine Highway System				
6858 Glacier Hwy PO Box 112505	Juneau AK	99801	800-642-0066	907-465-3941
Altamont Commuter Express (ACE)				
949 E Ch St	Stockton CA	95202	800-411-7245	
Caledonia Haulers LLC				
420 W Lincoln St PO Box 31	Caledonia MN	55921	800-325-4728	507-725-9000
Cape Cod Regional Transit Authority (CCRTA)				
215 Iyannough Rd PO Box 1988	Hyannis MA	02601	800-352-7155	508-775-8504
Catalina Express Berth 95	San Pedro CA	90731	800-481-3470	310-519-7971
Central Puget Sound Regional Transit Authority				
401 S Jackson St	Seattle WA	98104	800-201-4900	206-398-5000
Cliff Viessman Inc				
215 First Ave PO Box 175	Gary SD	57237	800-328-2408	605-272-5241
Delaware Transit Corp				
119 Lower Beach St Ste 100	Wilmington DE	19805	800-652-3278	302-576-6000

			Toll-Free	Phone
Horizon Freight System Inc				
6600 Bessemer Ave	Cleveland OH	44127	800-480-6829	216-341-7410
Karl's Transport Inc				
PO Box 333	Antigo WI	54409	800-922-8707	715-623-2033
Los Angeles County Metropolitan Transportation Authority				
One Gateway Plz	Los Angeles CA	90012	800-621-7828	213-922-6000
Mission Petroleum Carriers Inc				
8450 Mosley	Houston TX	77075	800-737-9911	713-943-8250
New Jersey Transit Corp				
One Penn Plz E	Newark NJ	07105	800-772-3606*	973-491-7000
*Cust Svc				
Niagara Frontier Transit Metro System Inc				
181 Ellicott St Ste 1	Buffalo NY	14203	877-294-9434	716-855-7300
Norfolk Southern Corp				
3 Commercial Pl	Norfolk VA	23510	800-635-5768*	855-667-3655
NYSE: NSC ■ *Cust Svc				
Northern Indiana Commuter Transportation District				
33 E US Hwy 12	Chesterton IN	46304	800-323-5281	219-926-5744
Office Movers Inc				
6500 Kane Way	Elkridge MD	21075	800-331-4025	410-799-7704
Packard Transport Inc				
24021 S Municipal Dr PO Box 380	Channahon IL	60410	800-467-9260	815-467-9260
Pierce Transit				
3701 96th St SW PO Box 99070	Lakewood WA	98499	800-562-8109	253-581-8000
Regional Transportation Commission of Southern Nevada (RTC)				
600 S Grand Central Pkwy Ste 350	Las Vegas NV	89106	800-228-3911	702-676-1500
Regional Transportation District (RTD)				
1600 Blake St	Denver CO	80202	800-366-7433	303-628-9000
Reliable Carriers Inc				
41555 Koppernick Rd	Canton MI	48187	800-521-6393	734-453-6677
Riverside Transit Agency (RTA)				
1825 Third St PO Box 59968	Riverside CA	92517	800-800-7821	951-565-5000
San Mateo County Transit District				
1250 San Carlos Ave PO Box 3006	San Carlos CA	94070	800-660-4287	650-508-6200
Santa Clara Valley Transportation Authority (VTA)				
3331 N First St	San Jose CA	95134	800-894-9908	408-321-5555
Sonoma County Transit				
355 W Robles Ave	Santa Rosa CA	95407	800-345-7433	707-585-7516
Southern California Regional Rail Authority				
700 S Flower St Ste 2600	Los Angeles CA	90017	800-371-5465	213-452-0200
Suburban Mobility Authority for Regional Transportation (SMART)				
535 Griswold St Ste 600 Buhl Bldg	Detroit MI	48226	866-962-5515	313-223-2100
Utah Transit Authority				
3600 S 700 W PO Box 30810	Salt Lake City UT	84130	888-743-3882	801-262-5626
VIA Metropolitan Transit				
800 W Myrtle St	San Antonio TX	78212	866-362-4200	210-362-2000
Virginia Railway Express (VRE)				
1500 King St Ste 202	Alexandria VA	22314	800-743-3873	703-684-1001
VPSI Inc 1220 Rankin Dr	Troy MI	48083	800-826-7433	248-597-3500
York County Transportation Authority				
1230 Roosevelt Ave	York PA	17404	800-632-9063	717-846-5562

466   MATCHES & MATCHBOOKS

			Toll-Free	Phone
DD Bean & Sons Co				
207 Peterborough St	Jaffrey NH	03452	800-366-2824	603-532-8311
Maryland Match Corp				
605 Alluvion St	Baltimore MD	21230	800-423-0013	410-752-8164
Universal Creative Concepts Corp				
10143 Royalton Rd Unit E	North Royalton OH	44133	800-876-8626	440-230-1366

467   MATERIAL HANDLING EQUIPMENT

SEE ALSO Conveyors & Conveying Equipment

			Toll-Free	Phone
4Front Engineered Solutions Inc				
1612 Hutton Dr Ste 140	Carrollton TX	75006	877-778-3625	972-466-0707
Abell-Howe Crane Inc				
10321 Werch Dr Ste 100	Woodridge IL	60517	800-366-0068	
Advance Lifts Inc				
701 Kirk Rd	Saint Charles IL	60174	800-843-3625	630-584-9881
Air Technical Industries				
7501 Clover Ave	Mentor OH	44060	800-321-9680	440-951-5191
American Crane & Equipment Corp				
531 Old Swede Rd	Douglassville PA	19518	877-877-6778	610-385-6061
American Power Pull Corp				
550 W Linfoot St PO Box 109	Wauseon OH	43567	800-808-5922	419-335-7050
ATAP PO Box 98	Eastaboga AL	36260	800-362-2827	256-362-2221
Autoquip Corp				
1058 W Industrial Rd	Guthrie OK	73044	888-811-9876	405-282-5200
Bayhead Products Corp				
173 Crosby Rd	Dover NH	03820	800-229-4323	603-742-3000
Berns Co 1250 W 17th St	Long Beach CA	90813	800-421-3773	562-437-0471
BGK Finishing Systems				
4131 Pheasant Ridge Dr NE	Minneapolis MN	55449	800-663-5498	763-784-0466
Busse/SJI Corp				
124 N Columbus St	Randolph WI	53956	800-882-4995	
Cascade Corp				
2201 NE 201st Ave	Fairview OR	97024	800-227-2233	503-669-6300
NYSE: CASC				
Clark Material Handling Co				
700 Enterprise Dr	Lexington KY	40510	866-252-5275	859-422-6400
Columbus McKinnon Corp				
140 John James Audubon Pkwy	Amherst NY	14228	800-888-0985	716-689-5400
NASDAQ: CMCO				
Craneveyor Corp				
1524 Potrero Ave	South El Monte CA	91733	888-501-0050	
Crosby Group, The				
2801 Dawson Rd	Tulsa OK	74110	800-772-1500	918-834-4611
Crysteel Mfg Inc				
52182 Ember Rd	Lake Crystal MN	56055	800-533-0494*	507-726-2728
*Orders				

	Toll-Free	Phone
Dematic		
507 Plymouth Ave NE . . . . Grand Rapids MI 49505	877-725-7500*	
*Cust Svc		
Detroit Hoist Co		
6650 Sterling Dr N . . . . Sterling Heights MI 48312	800-521-9126	586-268-2600
Downs Crane & Hoist Company Inc		
8827 Juniper St . . . . Los Angeles CA 90002	800-748-5994	323-589-6061
Drake-Scruggs Equipment Inc		
2000 S Dirksen Pkwy . . . . Springfield IL 62703	877-799-0398	217-753-3871
Escalera Inc		
708 S Industrial Dr PO Box 1359 . . . . Yuba City CA 95993	800-622-1359	530-673-6318
Excellon Automation Inc		
20001 S Rancho Way . . . . Rancho Dominguez CA 90220	800-392-3556	310-668-7700
FL Smidth Inc 2040 Ave C . . . . Bethlehem PA 18017	800-523-9482	610-264-6011
Genie Industries Inc		
18340 NE 76th St . . . . Redmond WA 98052	800-536-1800	425-881-1800
Gunnebo-Johnson Corp		
1240 N Harvard Ave . . . . Tulsa OK 74115	800-331-5460*	918-832-8933
*Sales		
Harlan Materials Handling Corp		
27 Stanley Rd . . . . Kansas City KS 66115	800-255-4262	913-342-5650
Harlo Corp PO Box 129 . . . . Grandville MI 49468	800-391-4151	616-538-0550
Harper Trucks Inc		
PO Box 12330 . . . . Wichita KS 67277	800-835-4099	316-942-1381
Hilman Inc 12 Timber Ln . . . . Marlboro NJ 07746	888-276-5548*	732-462-6277
*Cust Svc		
Indusco Group		
1200 W Hamburg St . . . . Baltimore MD 21230	800-727-0665	410-727-0665
Iowa Mold Tooling Co Inc (IMT)		
500 W US Hwy 18 . . . . Garner IA 50438	800-247-5958	641-923-3711
Kelly Systems Inc		
422 N Western Ave . . . . Chicago IL 60612	800-258-8237	312-733-3224
Konecranes America		
7300 Chippewa Blvd . . . . Houston TX 77086	800-231-0241	281-445-2225
Kornylak Corp		
400 Heaton St . . . . Hamilton OH 45011	800-837-5676	513-863-1277
Landoll Corp 1900 N St . . . . Marysville KS 66508	800-446-5175*	785-562-5381
*Cust Svc		
Leebaw Mfg Company Inc		
PO Box 553 . . . . Canfield OH 44406	800-841-8083	
Lift-All Company Inc		
1909 McFarland Dr . . . . Landisville PA 17538	800-909-1964	717-898-6615
Lovegreen Industrial Services Inc		
2280 Sibley Ct . . . . Eagan MN 55122	800-262-8284	651-890-1166
Magline Inc		
1205 W Cedar St . . . . Standish MI 48658	800-624-5463	
Manitex Inc		
3000 S Austin Ave . . . . Georgetown TX 78626	877-314-3390	512-942-3000
Matot Inc		
2501 Van Buren St . . . . Bellwood IL 60104	800-369-1070	708-547-1888
Maxon Industries Inc		
11921 Slauson Ave . . . . Santa Fe Springs CA 90670	800-227-4116	562-464-0099
Mazzella Lifting Technologies		
21000 Aerospace Pkwy . . . . Cleveland OH 44142	800-362-4601	440-239-7000
McGuire		
W194 N11481 McCormick Dr		
PO Box 309 . . . . Germantown WI 53022	800-624-8473	518-828-7652
Mertz Mfg LLC		
1701 N Waverly St . . . . Ponca City OK 74601	800-654-6433	580-762-5646
Morris Material Handling Inc		
315 W Forest Hill Ave . . . . Oak Creek WI 53154	800-933-3001	414-764-6200
NMC-Wollard Inc		
2021 Truax Blvd . . . . Eau Claire WI 54703	800-656-6867	715-835-3151
North American Industries Inc		
80 Holton St . . . . Woburn MA 01801	800-847-8470	781-897-4100
Nutting		
450 Pheasant Ridge Dr . . . . Watertown SD 57201	800-533-0337	605-882-3000
Ohio Magnetics Inc		
5400 Dunham Rd . . . . Maple Heights OH 44137	800-486-6446	216-662-8484
Pettibone Michigan		
1100 Superior Ave . . . . Baraga MI 49908	800-467-3884	906-353-4800
Positech Corp		
191 N Rush Lk Rd . . . . Laurens IA 50554	800-831-6026	712-841-4548
Process Equipment Inc		
2770 Welborn St PO Box 1607 . . . . Pelham AL 35124	888-663-2028	205-663-5330
Production Equipment Co		
401 Liberty St . . . . Meriden CT 06450	800-758-5697	203-235-5795
Proserv Anchor Crane Group		
455 Aldine Bender PO Box 670965 . . . . Houston TX 77060	800-835-2223	281-405-9048
PTR Baler & Compactor Co		
2207 E Ontario St . . . . Philadelphia PA 19134	800-523-3654	215-533-5100
Pucel Enterprises Inc		
1440 E 36th St . . . . Cleveland OH 44114	800-336-4986	216-881-4604
Raymond Corp 22 S Canal St . . . . Greene NY 13778	800-235-7200*	607-656-2311
*General		
RKI Inc 2301 Central Pkwy . . . . Houston TX 77092	800-346-8988	713-688-4414
Royal Tractor Co Inc		
109 Overland Pk Pl . . . . New Century KS 66031	888-782-7278	913-782-2598
Scott Industrial Systems Inc		
4433 Interpoint Blvd PO Box 1387 . . . . Dayton OH 45401	800-416-6023	937-233-8146
Shepard Niles		
220 N Genesee St . . . . Montour Falls NY 14865	800-481-2260	607-535-7111
Sherman & Reilly Inc		
400 W 33rd St . . . . Chattanooga TN 37401	800-251-7780*	423-756-5300
*Sales		
Solazyme Inc		
225 Gateway Blvd . . . . South San Francisco CA 94080	877-917-9075	650-780-4777
NASDAQ: SZYM		
Southeast Industrial Equipment Inc		
12200 Steele Creek Rd PO Box 39110 . . . . Charlotte NC 28273	800-752-6368	704-399-9700
Southworth Products Corp		
PO Box 1380 . . . . Portland ME 04104	800-743-1000	207-878-0700
Steel King Industries Inc		
2700 Chamber St . . . . Stevens Point WI 54481	800-826-0203	715-341-3120
Streator Dependable Manufacturing Co		
1705 N Shabbona St . . . . Streator IL 61364	800-795-0551	815-672-0551
Taylor-Dunn Manufacturing Co		
2114 W Ball Rd . . . . Anaheim CA 92804	800-688-8680	714-956-4040

	Toll-Free	Phone
Terex Corp Crane Div		
202 Raleigh St . . . . Wilmington NC 28412	877-794-5284	910-395-8500
Terex-Telelect Inc		
500 Oakwood Rd PO Box 1150 . . . . Watertown SD 57201	800-982-8975	605-882-4000
Thern Inc		
5712 Industrial Pk Rd PO Box 347 . . . . Winona MN 55987	800-843-7648	507-454-2996
Triple/S Dynamics Inc		
1031 S Haskell Ave PO Box 151027 . . . . Dallas TX 75315	800-527-2116	214-828-8600
Valley Craft		
2001 S Hwy 61 . . . . Lake City MN 55041	800-328-1480	651-345-3386
WA Charnstrom Co		
5391 12th Ave E . . . . Shakopee MN 55379	800-328-2962*	
*Cust Svc		
Waldon Mfg LLC		
201 W Oklahoma Ave . . . . Fiarview OK 73737	866-283-2759	580-227-3711
Western Hoist Inc		
1839 Cleveland Ave . . . . National City CA 91950	888-994-6478	619-474-3361
Whiting Corp		
26000 Whiting Way . . . . Monee IL 60449	800-861-5744	
Wiggins Lift Company Inc		
2571 Cortez St . . . . Oxnard CA 93031	800-350-7821	805-485-7821
WinHolt Equipment Group		
141 Eileen Way . . . . Syosset NY 11791	800-444-3595	516-222-0335

468   MATTRESSES & ADJUSTABLE BEDS

SEE ALSO Household Furniture

	Toll-Free	Phone
Bechik Products Inc		
1020 Discovery Rd Ste 150 . . . . Eagan MN 55121	800-328-6569	651-698-0364
Bergad Inc 747 Eljer Way . . . . Ford City PA 16226	888-476-8664	724-763-2883
Bowles Mattress Co Inc		
1220 Watt St . . . . Jeffersonville IN 47130	800-223-7509	812-288-8614
Classic Sleep Products Inc		
8214 Wellmoor Ct . . . . Jessup MD 20794	877-707-7533	410-904-0006
Comfortex Inc		
1680 Wilkie Dr PO Box 850 . . . . Winona MN 55987	800-445-4007	507-454-6579
Corsicana Bedding Inc		
PO Box 1050 . . . . Corsicana TX 75151	800-323-4349	903-872-2591
Cotton Belt Inc		
401 E Sater St . . . . Pinetops NC 27864	800-849-4192	252-827-4192
Dreamline Mfg Inc		
1514 S Second St PO Box 1250 . . . . Cabot AR 72023	800-888-3585	501-843-3585
Englander Northeast		
12 Esquire Rd . . . . North Billerica MA 01862	800-370-8700	
Imperial Bedding Co		
720 11th St PO Box 5347 . . . . Huntington WV 25703	800-529-3321	304-529-3321
Jackson Mattress Company Inc		
3154 Camden Rd . . . . Fayetteville NC 28306	800-763-7378	910-425-0131
Jamison Bedding Inc		
PO Box 681948 . . . . Franklin TN 37068	800-255-1883*	615-794-1883
*Cust Svc		
King Koil Licensing Company Inc		
7501 S Quincy St Ste 130 . . . . Willowbrook IL 60527	800-525-8331	
Kingsdown Inc 126 W Holt St . . . . Mebane NC 27302	800-354-5464*	919-563-3531
*Cust Svc		
Kolcraft Enterprises Inc		
10832 NC Hwy 211 E . . . . Aberdeen NC 28315	800-453-7673*	910-944-9345
*Cust Svc		
Leggett & Platt Inc		
Number 1 Leggett Rd PO Box 757 . . . . Carthage MO 64836	800-888-4569	417-358-8131
NYSE: LEG		
Meridian Mattress Factory Inc		
200 Rubush Rd PO Box 5127 . . . . Meridian MS 39301	800-844-3875	601-693-3875
Northwest Bedding		
6102 S Hayford Rd . . . . Spokane WA 99224	800-456-7686	509-244-3000
Omaha Bedding Co		
4011 S 60th St . . . . Omaha NE 68117	800-279-9018	402-733-8600
Restonic Mattress		
201 James E Casey Dr . . . . Buffalo NY 14206	800-898-6075	716-895-1414
Restonic Mattress Corp		
737 Main St . . . . Buffalo NY 14203	800-898-6075	
Riverside Mattress Co		
225 Dunn Rd . . . . Fayetteville NC 28312	888-288-5195	910-483-0461
Serta Mattress/AW Inc		
8415 ARdmore St . . . . Landover MD 20785	888-557-3782	301-322-1000
Sleep Train Inc 2205 Plz Dr . . . . Rocklin CA 95765	800-919-2337	
Southerland Inc		
1973 Southerland Dr . . . . Nashville TN 37207	800-443-1183*	615-226-9650
*Cust Svc		
Tempur-Pedic International Inc		
1713 Jaggie Fox Way . . . . Lexington KY 40511	800-821-6621	
NYSE: TPX		
Therapedic International		
1375 Jersey Ave . . . . North Brunswick NJ 08902	800-233-7467	

469   MEASURING, TESTING, CONTROLLING INSTRUMENTS

SEE ALSO Electrical Signals Measuring & Testing Instruments

	Toll-Free	Phone
ABB Inc 501 Merritt 7 . . . . Norwalk CT 06851	800-626-4999*	203-750-2200
*Prod Info		
All Weather Inc		
1165 National Dr . . . . Sacramento CA 95834	800-824-5873	916-928-1000
AMETEK Inc Test & Calibration Instruments Div		
8600 Somerset Dr . . . . Largo FL 33773	800-733-5427	727-538-6132
AMETEK US Gauge		
820 Pennsylvania Blvd . . . . Feasterville PA 19053	888-631-5454	215-355-6900
Beta LaserMike Inc		
8001 Technology Blvd . . . . Dayton OH 45424	800-886-9935	937-233-9935
Bruel & Kjaer Instruments Inc		
2815 Colonnades Ct Ste A . . . . Norcross GA 30071	800-332-2040	770-209-6907
Cambridge Technology Inc		
25 Hartwell Ave . . . . Lexington MA 02421	800-342-3757	781-541-1600

				Toll-Free	Phone
Canberra Industries Inc					
800 Research Pkwy	Meriden	CT	06450	800-243-3955*	203-238-2351
*Sales					
Clayton Industries					
17477 Hurley St	City of Industry	CA	91744	800-423-4585	626-435-1200
Crane Nuclear Inc					
2825 Cobb International Blvd	Kennesaw	GA	30152	800-795-8013	770-424-6343
Cubic Transportation Systems Inc					
5650 Kearny Mesa Rd	San Diego	CA	92111	800-937-5449	858-268-3100
Danaher Corp					
2200 Pennsylvania Ave NW Ste 800	Washington	DC	20037	800-833-9200	202-828-0850
NYSE: DHR					
Davis Instrument Corp					
3465 Diablo Ave	Hayward	CA	94545	800-678-3669	510-732-9229
Delta Cooling Towers Inc					
PO Box 315	Rockaway	NJ	07866	800-289-3358	973-586-2201
Dynisco LLC 38 Forge Pkwy	Franklin	MA	02038	800-396-4726*	508-541-9400
*General					
Emerson Process Management CSI					
835 Innovation Dr	Knoxville	TN	37932	800-675-4726	865-675-2110
Endevco Corp					
30700 Rancho Viejo Rd	San Juan Capistrano	CA	92675	800-982-6732	949-493-8181
Enidine Inc					
7 Centre Dr	Orchard Park	NY	14127	800-852-8508	716-662-1900
Fairfield Industries Inc					
1111 Gillingham Ln	Sugar Land	TX	77478	800-231-9809	281-275-7500
Fiber Instruments Sales Inc					
161 Clear Rd	Oriskany	NY	13424	800-500-0347*	315-736-2206
*Sales					
Garrett Metal Detectors					
1881 W State St	Garland	TX	75042	800-234-6151	972-494-6151
General Monitors Inc					
26776 Simpatica Cir	Lake Forest	CA	92630	866-686-0741	949-581-4464
George Risk Industries Inc					
802 S Elm St	Kimball	NE	69145	800-523-1227*	308-235-4645
OTC: RSKIA ■ *Sales					
GFI Genfare					
751 Pratt Blvd	Elk Grove Village	IL	60007	877-247-3797	847-593-8855
Gleason M & M Precision Systems Corp					
300 Progress Rd	Dayton	OH	45449	800-727-6333	937-859-8273
Goodrich Corp					
2730 W Tyvola Rd 4 Coliseum Ctr	Charlotte	NC	28217	800-735-7899	704-423-7000
NYSE: GR					
Herman H Sticht Company Inc					
45 Main St Ste 701	Brooklyn	NY	11201	800-221-3203	718-852-7602
Hexagon Metrology Inc					
250 Circuit Dr	North Kingstown	RI	02852	855-443-9638	401-886-2000
Industrial Dynamics Company Ltd					
3100 Fujita St	Torrance	CA	90505	888-434-5832	310-325-5633
Instron Corp Wilson Instruments Div					
825 University Ave	Norwood	MA	02062	800-695-4273	781-828-2500
Interface Inc					
7401 E Butherus Dr	Scottsdale	AZ	85260	800-947-5598	480-948-5555
Kistler Instrument Corp					
75 John Glenn Dr	Amherst	NY	14228	888-547-8537	716-691-5100
Konica Minolta Sensing Americas Inc					
101 Williams Dr	Ramsey	NJ	07446	888-473-2656	201-825-4000
L-3 Avionics Systems					
5353 52nd St SE	Grand Rapids	MI	49512	800-253-9525	616-949-6600
Leica Geosystems Inc					
3498 Kraft Ave SE	Grand Rapids	MI	49512	800-367-9453*	616-977-4189
*Sales					
Ludlum Measurements Inc					
501 Oak St	Sweetwater	TX	79556	800-622-0828	325-235-5494
Magnetic Analysis Corp					
103 Fairview Park Dr	Elmsford	NY	10523	800-463-8622	914-699-9450
Marposs Corp					
3300 Cross Creek Pkwy	Auburn Hills	MI	48326	888-627-7677	248-370-0404
Metrix Instrument Co					
8824 Fallbrook Dr	Houston	TX	77064	800-638-7494	713-461-2131
Metrosonics					
1060 Corporate Ctr Dr	Oconomowoc	WI	53066	800-245-0779	262-567-9157
Metrotech Corp					
3251 Olcott St	Santa Clara	CA	95054	800-446-3392	408-734-1400
MTS Systems Corp					
14000 Technology Dr	Eden Prairie	MN	55344	800-328-2255*	952-937-4000
NASDAQ: MTSC ■ *Cust Svc					
Mustang Dynamometer					
2300 Pinnacle Pkwy	Twinsburg	OH	44087	888-468-7826	330-963-5400
Ohmart/VEGA Corp					
4241 Allendorf Dr	Cincinnati	OH	45209	800-367-5383	513-272-0131
Oxford Instruments Measurement Systems					
300 Bake Ave Ste 150	Concord	MA	01742	800-447-4717	
Preco Electronics Inc					
10335 W Emerald St	Boise	ID	83704	866-977-7326	208-323-1000
Rochester Gauges Inc of Texas					
11616 Harry Hines Blvd	Dallas	TX	75229	800-821-1829	972-241-2161
Rudolph Technologies Inc					
One Rudolph Rd PO Box 1000	Flanders	NJ	07836	877-467-8365	973-691-1300
NASDAQ: RTEC					
Setra Systems Inc					
159 Swanson Rd	Boxborough	MA	01719	800-257-3872	978-263-1400
Sierra Monitor Corp					
1991 Tarob Ct	Milpitas	CA	95035	888-509-1970	408-262-6611
OTC: SRMC					
Sorrento Electronics Inc					
4949 Greencraig Ln	San Diego	CA	92123	800-252-1180	858-522-8300
SuperFlow Technologies Group					
4747 Centennial Blvd	Colorado Springs	CO	80919	800-471-7701	719-471-1746
Testing Machines Inc					
40 McCullough Dr	New Castle	DE	19720	800-678-3221*	302-613-5600
*General					
Thermo Fisher Scientific Inc					
81 Wyman St PO Box 9046	Waltham	MA	02454	800-678-5599	781-622-1000
NYSE: TMO					
Unilux Inc					
59 N Fifth St	Saddle Brook	NJ	07663	800-522-0801	201-712-1266
Vaisala Inc 10-D Gill St	Woburn	MA	01801	888-824-7252	781-933-4500

				Toll-Free	Phone
White's Electronics Inc					
1011 Pleasant Valley Rd	Sweet Home	OR	97386	800-999-9147*	800-547-6911
*Sales					

470　MEAT PACKING PLANTS

SEE ALSO Poultry Processing

				Toll-Free	Phone
Abbyland Foods Inc					
502 E Linden St PO Box 69	Abbotsford	WI	54405	800-732-5483	715-223-6386
Allen Bros Inc					
3737 S Halsted St	Chicago	IL	60609	800-548-7777	773-890-5100
Alpine Meats					
9850 Lowr Sacramento Rd	Stockton	CA	95210	800-399-6328	209-477-2691
American Foods Group Inc					
544 Acme St	Green Bay	WI	54302	800-345-0293	920-437-6330
Carolina Packers Inc					
2999 S Bright Leaf Blvd PO Box 1109	Smithfield	NC	27577	800-682-7675	919-934-2181
Central Nebraska Packing Inc					
2800 E Eigth St	North Platte	NE	69103	800-445-2881*	308-532-1250
*Cust Svc					
Chisesi Bros Meat Packing Co					
5221 Jefferson Hwy	New Orleans	LA	70123	800-966-3550	504-822-3550
Clougherty Packing Co					
3049 E Vernon Ave	Los Angeles	CA	90058	800-846-7635*	
*Sales					
Comer Packing					
1000 Poplar St PO Box 33	Aberdeen	MS	39730	800-748-8916	662-369-9325
ConAgra Foods Retail Products Co Deli Foods Group					
215 W Field Rd	Naperville	IL	60563	877-266-2472	630-857-1000
Cudahy Patrick Inc					
One Sweet Apple-Wood Ln	Cudahy	WI	53110	800-486-6900	414-744-2000
Curtis Packing Co					
2416 Randolph Ave PO Box 1470	Greensboro	NC	27406	800-852-7890	336-275-7684
Eddy Packing Company Inc					
404 Airport Dr	Yoakum	TX	77995	800-292-2361	361-293-2361
Farm Boy Meats					
2761 N Kentucky Ave	Evansville	IN	47711	800-852-3976	812-425-5231
Greater Omaha Packing Company Inc					
3001 L St	Omaha	NE	68107	800-747-5400	402-731-1700
Harris Ranch Beef Co					
16277 S McCall Ave PO Box 220	Selma	CA	93662	800-742-1955	
Hatfield Quality Meats Inc					
2700 Clemens Rd	Hatfield	PA	19440	800-743-1191	215-368-2500
J Freirich Foods Inc					
815 W Kerr St PO Box 1529	Salisbury	NC	28144	800-554-4788	704-636-2621
JH Routh Packing Company Inc					
4413 W Bogart Rd	Sandusky	OH	44870	800-446-6759	419-626-2251
John Morrell & Co					
805 E Kemper Rd	Cincinnati	OH	45246	800-722-1127	513-346-3540
L & H Packing Co					
PO Box 831368	San Antonio	TX	78283	800-999-3241	210-532-3241
Land O'Frost Inc					
16850 Chicago Ave	Lansing	IL	60438	800-323-3308	708-474-7100
Long Prairie Packing Co					
10 Riverside Dr	Long Prairie	MN	56347	800-996-6440	320-732-2171
Morrilton Packing Company Inc					
51 Blue Diamond Dr	Morrilton	AR	72110	800-264-2204	501-354-2474
National Beef Packing Co LLC					
12200 Ambassador Dr Ste 500 PO Box 20046	Kansas City	MO	64163	800-449-2333	
Olymel LP					
2200 Pratte Ave Pratte	Saint-Hyacinthe	QC	J2S4B6	800-361-7990	450-771-0400
Pearl Meat Packing Company Inc					
27 York Ave	Randolph	MA	02368	800-462-3022	781-228-5100
Plumrose USA Inc					
1901 Butterfield Rd Ste 305	Downers Grove	IL	60515	800-526-4909	732-624-4040
Quality Meats & Seafoods					
700 Ctr St	West Fargo	ND	58078	800-342-4250	701-282-0202
Quincy Street Inc					
13350 Quincy St	Holland	MI	49424	800-784-6290	616-399-3330
Rose Packing Company Inc					
65 S Barrington Rd	South Barrington	IL	60010	800-323-7363	847-381-5700
Sam Hausman Meat Packer Inc					
4261 Beacon	Corpus Christi	TX	78403	800-364-5521	361-883-5521
Sam Kane Beef Processors Inc					
9001 Leopard St	Corpus Christi	TX	78409	800-242-4142	361-241-5000
Sioux-Preme Packing Co					
4241 US 75th Ave	Sioux Center	IA	51250	800-735-7675*	
*General					
Smithfield Foods Inc					
200 Commerce St	Smithfield	VA	23430	800-276-6158	757-365-3000
NYSE: SFD					
Superior Farms					
1480 Drew Ave Ste 100	Davis	CA	95618	800-228-5262	530-297-7299
Thompson Packers Inc					
550 Carnation St	Slidell	LA	70460	800-989-6328	985-641-6640
Travis Meats Inc					
7210 Clinton Hwy PO Box 670	Powell	TN	37849	800-247-7606	865-938-9051
Tyson Fresh Meats Inc					
800 Stevens Port Dr	Dakota Dunes	SD	57049	800-416-2269	605-235-2061

471　MEDICAL ASSOCIATIONS - STATE

SEE ALSO Health & Medical Professionals Associations

				Toll-Free	Phone
Alabama Medical Assn					
19 S Jackson St	Montgomery	AL	36104	800-239-6272	
Alaska State Medical Assn					
4107 Laurel St	Anchorage	AK	99508	800-951-8712	907-562-0304
Arizona Medical Assn, The (ArMA)					
810 W Bethany Home Rd	Phoenix	AZ	85013	800-482-3480	602-246-8901
Colorado Medical Society					
7351 Lowry Blvd	Denver	CO	80230	800-654-5653	720-859-1001

				Toll-Free	Phone
Connecticut State Medical Society					
160 St Ronan St	New Haven	CT	06511	**800-406-1527**	203-865-0587
Delmarva Foundation For Medical Care Inc (DFMC)					
28464 Marlboro Ave	Easton	MD	21601	**800-999-3362**	410-822-0697
Hawaii Medical Assn					
1360 S Beretania St Ste 200	Honolulu	HI	96814	**888-536-2792**	808-536-7702
Illinois State Medical Society					
20 N Michigan Ave Ste 700	Chicago	IL	60602	**800-782-4767**	312-782-1654
Indiana State Medical Assn					
322 Canal Walk	Indianapolis	IN	46202	**800-257-4762**	317-261-2060
Iowa Medical Society					
1001 Grand Ave	West Des Moines	IA	50265	**800-747-3070**	515-223-1401
Kansas Medical Society					
623 SW Tenth Ave	Topeka	KS	66612	**800-332-0156**	785-235-2383
Louisiana State Medical Society					
6767 Perkins Rd Ste 100	Baton Rouge	LA	70808	**800-375-9508**	225-763-8500
Maine Medical Assn					
30 Assn Dr	Manchester	ME	04351	**800-772-0815**	207-622-3374
Maryland State Medical Society					
1211 Cathedral St	Baltimore	MD	21201	**800-492-1056**	410-539-0872
Massachusetts Medical Society (MMS)					
860 Winter St	Waltham	MA	02451	**800-322-2303**	781-893-4610
Medical Assn of Georgia (MAG)					
1849 The Exchange Ste 200	Atlanta	GA	30339	**800-282-0224**	678-303-9290
Minnesota Medical Assn					
1300 Godward St NE Ste 2500	Minneapolis	MN	55413	**800-342-5662**	612-378-1875
Missouri State Medical Assn					
113 Madison St	Jefferson City	MO	65101	**800-869-6762**	573-636-5151
Montana Medical Assn					
2021 11th Ave Ste 1	Helena	MT	59601	**877-443-4000**	406-443-4000
New Hampshire Medical Society					
Seven N State St	Concord	NH	03301	**800-564-1909**	603-224-1909
New Jersey Medical Society					
2 Princess Rd	Lawrenceville	NJ	08648	**800-706-7893**	609-896-1766
New Mexico Medical Society (NMMS)					
316 Osuna Rd NE Ste 501	Albuquerque	NM	87107	**800-748-1596**	505-828-0237
New York State Medical Society					
865 Merrick Ave PO Box 5404	Westbury	NY	11590	**800-523-4405**	516-488-6100
North Carolina Medical Society					
222 N Person St	Raleigh	NC	27601	**800-722-1350**	919-833-3836
Ohio State Medical Assn					
3401 Mill Run Dr	Hilliard	OH	43026	**800-766-6762**	614-527-6762
Oregon Medical Assn (OMA)					
11740 SW 68th Pkwy Ste 100	Portland	OR	97223	**877-605-3229**	503-619-8000
Rhode Island Medical Society					
235 Promenade St Ste 500	Providence	RI	02908	**800-343-7776**	401-331-3207
South Carolina Medical Assn					
132 W Pk Blvd	Columbia	SC	29210	**800-327-1021**	803-798-6207
Texas Medical Assn					
401 W 15th St	Austin	TX	78701	**800-880-1300**	512-370-1300
Vermont Medical Society					
134 Main St	Montpelier	VT	05601	**800-640-8767**	802-223-7898
Virginia Medical Society					
4205 Dover Rd	Richmond	VA	23221	**800-746-6768**	804-353-2721
Washington State Medical Assn					
2033 Sixth Ave Ste 1100	Seattle	WA	98121	**800-552-0612**	206-441-9762
West Virginia State Medical Assn					
4307 MacCorkle Ave SE PO Box 4106	Charleston	WV	25364	**800-257-4747**	304-925-0342
Wisconsin State Medical Society					
330 E Lakeside St	Madison	WI	53701	**866-442-3800**	
Wyoming Medical Society					
122 E 17th St	Cheyenne	WY	82001	**888-879-3599**	307-635-2424

472   MEDICAL & DENTAL EQUIPMENT & SUPPLIES - WHOL

				Toll-Free	Phone
A Plus International Inc					
5138 Eucalyptus Ave	Chino	CA	91710	**800-762-1123**	909-591-5168
ABC Home Medical Supply Inc					
15 E Uwchlan Ave Ste 430	Exton	PA	19341	**866-897-8588**	
Ace Medical Inc					
94-910 Moloalo St	Waipahu	HI	96797	**866-678-3601**	808-678-3600
Aeroflow Inc					
3165 Sweeten Creek Rd	Asheville	NC	28803	**888-345-1780**	
Alpha Imaging Inc					
4455 Glenbrook Rd	Willoughby	OH	44094	**800-331-7327**	440-953-3800
American Medical ID					
949 Wakefield Ste 100	Houston	TX	77018	**800-363-5985**	
Ampronix Inc 15 Whatney	Irvine	CA	92618	**800-400-7972**	949-273-8000
Andrew Technologies LLC					
1421 Edinger Ave Ste D	Tustin	CA	92780	**888-959-7674**	
Ansar Group Inc, The					
240 S Eigth St	Philadelphia	PA	19107	**888-883-7804**	215-922-6088
Aqueduct Medical Inc					
665 Third St Ste 20.	San Francisco	CA	94107	**877-365-4325**	
Blue Ridge X-Ray Company Inc					
120 Vista Blvd	Arden	NC	28704	**800-727-7290**	
Burkhart Dental Supply Co					
2502 S 78th St	Tacoma	WA	98409	**800-562-8176***	253-474-7761
*Cust Svc					
Butler Animal Health Supply LLC					
400 Metro Pl N	Dublin	OH	43017	**888-691-2724***	614-761-9095
*PR					
Byram Healthcare Centers Inc					
120 Bloomingdale Rd	White Plains	NY	10605	**800-354-4054**	914-286-2000
CCS Medical Inc					
1505 LBJ Fwy Ste 600	Farmers Branch	TX	75234	**800-726-9811**	800-260-8193
Connect America LLC					
2193 W Chester Pk	Broomall	PA	19008	**800-654-6100**	
Dedicated Distribution Inc					
640 Miami Ave	Kansas City	KS	66105	**800-325-8367**	913-371-2200
Derma Sciences Inc					
214 Carnegie Ctr Ste 100	Princeton	NJ	08540	**800-825-4325**	609-514-4744
Evans-Sherratt Co					
13050 Northend Ave	Oak Park	MI	48237	**800-248-3826**	248-584-5500
Global Medical Imaging LLC					
222 Rampart St	Charlotte	NC	28203	**800-958-9986**	

				Toll-Free	Phone
Global Medical LLC					
8332 Bristol Ct Ste 108	Jessup	MD	20794	**800-528-1001**	
Griswold Machine & Engineering Inc					
8530 M 60	Union City	MI	49094	**800-248-2054**	517-741-4300
Grogans Health Care Supply Inc					
1016 S Broadway St	Lexington	KY	40504	**800-365-1020**	859-254-6661
Henry Schein Inc					
135 Duryea Rd	Melville	NY	11747	**800-582-2702**	631-843-5500
NASDAQ: HSIC					
International Manufacturing Group Inc					
879 F St Ste 120.	West Sacramento	CA	95605	**800-775-6412**	
Iowa Veterinary Supply Co (IVESCO)					
124 Country Club Rd	Iowa Falls	IA	50126	**800-457-0118**	641-648-2529
Jorgensen Laboratories Inc					
1450 Van Buren Ave	Loveland	CO	80538	**800-525-5614**	970-669-2500
Karl Storz Endoscopy-america Inc					
600 Corporate Pt Fl 5	Culver City	CA	90230	**800-321-1304**	310-338-8100
Kentec Medical Inc					
17871 Fitch	Irvine	CA	92614	**800-825-5996**	949-863-0810
Keystone Industries					
480 S Democrat Rd	Gibbstown	NJ	08027	**800-333-3131**	856-663-4700
Leeches USA Ltd					
300 Shames Dr	Westbury	NY	11590	**800-645-3569**	516-333-2570
LENSAR Inc					
2800 Discovery Dr	Orlando	FL	32826	**888-536-7271**	
Life-Assist Inc					
11277 Sunrise Park Dr	Rancho Cordova	CA	95742	**800-824-6016**	
Mabis Healthcare Inc					
1931 Norman Dr	Waukegan	IL	60085	**800-526-4753**	
Mada Medical Products Inc					
625 Washington Ave	Carlstadt	NJ	07072	**800-526-6370**	201-460-0454
Marketlab Inc					
6850 Southbelt Dr	Caledonia	MI	49316	**866-237-3722**	
MC Healthcare Products Inc					
4658 Ontario St	Beamsville	ON	L0R1B4	**800-268-8671**	
McKesson Medical Group Extended Care					
8121 Tenth Ave N	Golden Valley	MN	55427	**800-328-8111**	
McKesson Medical-Surgical					
8741 Landmark Rd	Richmond	VA	23228	**800-446-3008**	415-983-8300
Mesa Laboratories Inc					
12100 W Sixth Ave	Lakewood	CO	80228	**800-992-6372***	303-987-8000
NASDAQ: MLAB *Sales					
Moore Medical Corp					
389 John Downey Dr	New Britain	CT	06050	**800-234-1464***	860-826-3600
*Sales					
Neuro-Tec Inc					
975 Cobb Pl Blvd Ste 301	Kennesaw	GA	30144	**800-554-3407**	
Nihon Kohden America Inc					
90 Icon	Foothill Ranch	CA	92610	**800-325-0283**	949-580-1555
Oakworks Inc					
923 E Wellspring Rd	New Freedom	PA	17349	**800-558-8850**	717-235-6807
Omega Medical Health Systems Inc					
1200 E High St Ste 106	Pottstown	PA	19464	**866-716-6342**	
Omron Healthcare Inc					
1925 W Field Ct	Lake Forest	IL	60045	**877-216-1333**	847-680-6200
Oral-B Laboratories					
600 Clipper Dr Ste 200.	Belmont	CA	94002	**800-566-7252**	
Otto Bock Healthcare North America Inc					
Two Carlson Pkwy N Ste 100	Minneapolis	MN	55447	**800-328-4058**	763-553-9464
Patterson Cos Inc					
1031 Mendota Heights Rd	Saint Paul	MN	55120	**800-328-5536**	651-686-1600
NASDAQ: PDCO					
Pearson Dental Supplies Inc					
13161 Telfair Ave	Sylmar	CA	91342	**800-535-4535**	818-362-2600
Prima Tech USA					
279 Faison McGowan Rd Ste 2.	Kenansville	NC	28349	**888-833-7099**	910-296-6116
Rgh Enterprises Inc					
1810 Summit Commerce Pk	Twinsburg	OH	44087	**800-307-5930**	330-963-6998
Saebo Inc					
2725 Water Ridge Pkwy Ste 320 Six LakePointe Plaza	Charlotte	NC	28217	**888-284-5433**	
SmartScrubs LLC					
3400 E Mcdowell Rd	Phoenix	AZ	85008	**800-800-5788**	
Somagen Diagnostics Inc					
9220 25th Ave	Edmonton	AB	T6N1E1	**800-661-9993**	780-702-9500
Surgical Principals Inc					
1625 S Tacoma Way	Tacoma	WA	98409	**888-801-9251**	
Sysmex America Inc					
One Nelson C White Pkwy	Mundelein	IL	60060	**800-379-7639**	847-996-4500
Tetra Medical Supply Corp					
6364 W Gross Pt Rd	Niles	IL	60714	**800-621-4041***	847-647-0590
*Cust Svc					
Trans Med USA Inc					
31 Progress Ave	Tyngsboro	MA	01879	**800-442-1142**	978-649-1970
Tri State Distribution Inc					
600 Vista Dr	Sparta	TN	38583	**800-392-9824**	
Valeritas Inc					
750 Rt 202 S Ste 600	Bridgewater	NJ	08807	**855-384-8848**	908-927-9920
VWR International					
100 Matsonford Rd Bldg 1 Ste 200.	Radnorpa	PA	19087	**800-932-5000**	610-431-1700
William V MacGill & Co					
1000 N LombaRd Rd	Lombard	IL	60148	**800-323-2841**	630-889-0500
Zee Medical Inc					
22 Corporate Pk	Irvine	CA	92606	**800-435-7763**	

MEDICAL FACILITIES

SEE Substance Abuse Treatment Centers ; Health Care Providers - Ancillary ; Hospices ; Hospitals ; Imaging Services - Diagnostic ; Developmental Centers

			Toll-Free	Phone

SEE ALSO Imaging Equipment & Systems - Medical ; Medical Supplies - Mfr

			Toll-Free	Phone
Accurate Surgical & Scientific Instruments Corp				
300 Shames Dr	Westbury NY	11590	**800-645-3569**	516-333-2570
Accuray Inc				
1310 Chesapeake Terr	Sunnyvale CA	94089	**888-522-3740**	408-716-4600
NASDAQ: ARAY				
Acme United Corp				
60 Round Hill Rd	Fairfield CT	06824	**800-835-2263**	203-254-6060
NYSE: ACU				
Ad-tech Medical Instrument Inc				
1901 William St	Racine WI	53404	**800-776-1555**	262-634-1555
AESCULAP Inc				
3773 Corporate Pkwy	Center Valley PA	18034	**800-282-9000**	
Allied Healthcare Products Inc				
1720 Sublette Ave	Saint Louis MO	63110	**800-444-3954**	314-771-2400
NASDAQ: AHPI				
Altimate Medical Inc				
262 W First St	Morton MN	56270	**800-342-8968**	507-697-6393
Andover Healthcare Inc				
9 Fanaras Dr	Salisbury MA	01952	**800-432-6686**	978-465-0044
Aperio Technologies Inc				
1360 Park Ctr Dr Ste 106	Vista CA	92081	**866-478-4111**	
Aspen Medical Products				
6481 Oak Cyn	Irvine CA	92618	**800-295-2776**	949-681-0200
Atrium Medical Corp				
5 Wentworth Dr	Hudson NH	03051	**800-528-7486**	603-880-1433
B Braun Medical Inc				
824 12th Ave	Bethlehem PA	18018	**800-523-9676**	610-691-5400
Bard Access Systems Inc				
605 North 5600 West	Salt Lake City UT	84116	**800-443-5505**	801-522-5000
Bard Inc Peripheral Vascular				
1625 W Third St	Tempe AZ	85281	**800-321-4254**	480-894-9515
BD Medical 9450 S State St	Sandy UT	84070	**888-237-2762**	801-565-2300
Becton Dickinson & Co				
One Becton Dr	Franklin Lakes NJ	07417	**888-237-2762***	201-847-6800
NYSE: BDX ■ *Cust Svc*				
Becton Dickinson Pharmaceutical Systems				
1 Becton Dr MC407	Franklin Lakes NJ	07417	**800-638-8663**	201-847-6800
Best Vascular				
4350 International Blvd Ste E	Norcross GA	30093	**800-668-6783**	770-717-0904
BioCardia Inc				
125 Shoreway Rd Ste B	San Carlos CA	94070	**800-624-1179**	650-226-0120
Biodex Medical Systems Inc				
20 Ramsay Rd	Shirley NY	11967	**800-224-6339**	631-924-9000
Bioject Medical Technologies Inc				
20245 SW 95 Ave	Tualatin OR	97062	**800-683-7221**	503-692-8001
OTC: BJCT				
BioMerieux Inc				
595 Anglum Rd	Hazelwood MO	63042	**800-634-7656**	314-731-8500
Biomet Microfixation Inc				
1520 Tradeport Dr	Jacksonville FL	32218	**800-874-7711**	904-741-4400
Biosense Webster Inc				
3333 S Diamond Canyon Rd	Diamond Bar CA	91765	**800-729-9010**	909-839-8500
Blackburn's Physicians Pharmacy Inc				
301 Corbet St	Tarentum PA	15084	**800-472-2440**	724-224-9100
Boston Scientific Corp				
One Boston Scientific Pl	Natick MA	01760	**888-272-1001**	508-650-8000
NYSE: BSX				
Braemar Inc				
1285 Corporate Ctr Dr	Eagan MN	55121	**800-328-2719**	651-286-8620
Brava LLC				
14221 SW 142nd St Ste 725	Miami FL	33186	**800-422-5350**	305-856-4242
Cadwell Laboratories Inc				
909 N Kellogg St	Kennewick WA	99336	**800-245-3001**	509-735-6481
Cambridge Heart Inc				
46 Jonspin Rd	Wilmington MA	01887	**888-226-9283**	978-654-7600
CardiacAssist Inc				
240 Alpha Dr	Pittsburgh PA	15238	**800-373-1607**	412-963-7770
Cardica Inc				
900 Saginaw Dr	Redwood City CA	94063	**888-544-7194**	650-364-9975
NASDAQ: CRDC				
Cardiovascular Systems Inc				
651 Campus Dr	St Paul MN	55112	**877-274-0360**	651-259-1600
CareFusion Corp				
3750 Torrey View Ct	San Diego CA	92130	**888-876-4287**	858-617-2000
NYSE: CFN				
CAS Medical Systems Inc				
44 E Industrial Rd	Branford CT	06405	**800-227-4414**	203-488-6056
NASDAQ: CASM				
Celsion Corp				
10220-L Old Columbia Rd	Columbia MD	21046	**888-504-7965**	410-290-5390
NASDAQ: CLSN				
Chad Therapeutics Inc				
2975 Horseshoe Dr S Ste 600	Naples FL	34104	**800-423-8870**	239-687-1285
OTC: CHADQ				
Conmed Corp 525 French Rd	Utica NY	13502	**800-448-6506**	315-797-8375
NASDAQ: CNMD				
ConMed Endoscopic Technologie				
525 French Rd	Utica NY	13502	**800-225-1332**	315-797-8375
CONMED Linvatec				
11311 Concept Blvd	Largo FL	33773	**800-448-6506***	727-392-6464
Cust Svc				
Cook Inc PO Box 4195	Bloomington IN	47402	**800-457-4500**	812-339-2235
Cook Medical Inc				
1186 Montgomery Ln	Vandergrift PA	15690	**800-245-4715***	724-845-8621
General				
Cook Urological Inc				
1100 W Morgan St PO Box 227	Spencer IN	47460	**800-457-4500**	812-829-4891
Cooper Cos Inc				
6140 Stoneridge Mall Rd Ste 590	Pleasanton CA	94588	**888-822-2660**	925-460-3600
NYSE: COO				
CooperSurgical Inc				
95 Corporate Dr	Trumbull CT	06611	**800-645-3760**	203-929-6321

			Toll-Free	Phone
Cordis Corp				
14201 NW 60th Ave	Miami Lakes FL	33014	**800-327-7714**	800-447-7585
Corpak Medsystems Inc				
1001 Asbury Dr	Buffalo Grove IL	60089	**800-323-6305**	847-403-3400
CR Bard Inc Medical Div				
8195 Industrial Blvd	Covington GA	30014	**800-526-4455**	770-784-6100
CR Bard Inc Urological Div				
8195 Industrial Blvd	Covington GA	30014	**800-526-4455**	770-784-6100
Criticare Systems Inc				
N7W22025 Johnson Dr	Waukesha WI	53186	**800-458-4615**	262-798-8282
Cutera Inc				
3240 Bayshore Blvd	Brisbane CA	94005	**888-428-8372**	415-657-5500
NASDAQ: CUTR				
Dale Medical Products Inc				
PO Box 1556	Plainville MA	02762	**800-343-3980**	
Davol Inc				
100 Crossings Blvd	Warwick RI	02886	**800-556-6756***	
Cust Svc				
Encision Inc				
6797 Winchester Cir	Boulder CO	80301	**800-998-0986**	303-444-2600
OTC: ECIA				
Endologix Inc 11 Studebaker	Irvine CA	92618	**800-983-2284**	949-457-9546
NASDAQ: ELGX				
Eternity Healthcare Inc				
Ste 1 8755 Ash St	Vancouver BC	V6P6T3	**855-324-1110**	
ev3 Inc 3033 Campus Dr	Plymouth MN	55441	**800-716-6700**	763-398-7000
G & G Instrument Corp				
466 Saw Mill River Rd	Ardsley NY	10502	**800-882-2288**	914-693-6000
Gaymar Industries Inc				
10 Centre Dr	Orchard Park NY	14127	**800-828-7341**	716-662-2551
GEM Edwards Inc				
5640 Hudson Industrial Pkwy PO Box 429	Hudson OH	44236	**800-733-7976**	
GF Health Products Inc				
2935 NE Pkwy	Atlanta GA	30360	**800-347-5678**	770-447-1609
Haemonetics Corp				
400 Wood Rd	Braintree MA	02184	**800-225-5242**	781-848-7100
NYSE: HAE				
Henry Troemner LLC				
201 Wolf Dr	Thorofare NJ	08086	**800-352-7705**	856-686-1600
Hill-Rom Services Inc				
1069 SR 46 E	Batesville IN	47006	**800-267-2337**	812-934-7777
Hoggan Health Industries Inc				
8020 South 1300 West	West Jordan UT	84088	**800-678-7888**	801-572-6500
Hospira Inc				
275 N Field Dr	Lake Forest IL	60045	**877-946-7747**	224-212-2000
NYSE: HSP				
Hypertension Diagnostics Inc				
2915 Waters Rd Ste 108	Eagan MN	55121	**888-785-7392**	651-687-9999
Implant Sciences Corp				
500 Research Dr	Wilmington MA	01887	**877-732-7333**	978-752-1700
OTC: IMSC				
Inovise Medical Inc				
8770 SW Nimbus Ave Ste D	Beaverton OR	97008	**877-466-8473**	503-431-3800
Insulet Corp				
Nine Oak Park Dr	Bedford MA	01730	**800-591-3455**	781-457-5000
Integra LifeSciences Holdings Corp				
311 Enterprise Dr	Plainsboro NJ	08536	**800-654-2873**	609-275-0500
NASDAQ: IART				
Intuitive Surgical Inc				
1266 Kifer Rd Bldg 101	Sunnyvale CA	94086	**888-868-4647**	408-523-2100
NASDAQ: ISRG				
Joerns Healthcare				
5001 Joerns Dr	Stevens Point WI	54481	**800-826-0270**	715-341-3600
Johnson Matthey Medical Products				
1401 King Rd	West Chester PA	19380	**800-442-1405**	610-648-8000
Kensey Nash Corp				
735 Pennsylvania Dr	Exton PA	19341	**800-322-2885***	484-713-2100
NASDAQ: KNSY ■ *General*				
Kimberly-Clark/Ballard Medical Products				
1400 Holcomb Bridge Rd	Roswell GA	30076	**800-524-3577**	
Knit Rite Inc				
120 Osage Ave	Kansas City KS	66105	**800-821-3094**	913-281-4600
Landice Inc				
111 Canfield Ave	Randolph NJ	07869	**800-526-3423**	973-927-9010
Life-tech Inc PO Box 1849	Stafford TX	77497	**800-231-9841**	281-491-6600
MAQUET Cardiac Assist				
15 Law Dr	Fairfield NJ	07004	**800-777-4222**	973-244-6100
Medovations Inc				
102 E Keefe Ave	Milwaukee WI	53212	**800-558-6408**	414-265-7620
Medtronic Inc				
710 Medtronic Pkwy NE	Minneapolis MN	55432	**800-328-2518***	763-514-4000
NYSE: MDT ■ *Cust Svc*				
Medtronic Neurosurgery				
125 Cremona Dr	Goleta CA	93117	**800-468-9710***	800-633-8766
Cust Svc				
Medtronic Perfusion Systems				
7611 Northland Dr	Brooklyn Park MN	55428	**800-328-3320**	763-391-9000
Megadyne Medical Products Inc				
11506 S State St	Draper UT	84020	**800-747-6110**	801-576-9669
Mercury Medical				
11300 49th St N	Clearwater FL	33762	**800-237-6418**	727-573-0088
Meridian Medical Technologies Inc				
6350 Stevens Forest Rd Ste 301	Columbia MD	21046	**800-638-8093**	443-259-7800
Merit Medical Systems Inc				
1600 W Merit Pkwy	South Jordan UT	84095	**800-356-3748**	801-253-1600
NASDAQ: MMSI				
MicroAire Surgical Instruments Inc				
3590 Grand Forks Blvd	Charlottesville VA	22911	**800-722-0822**	
MiMedx Group Inc				
1775 W Oak Commons Ct Ne	Marietta GA	30062	**888-543-1917**	
Minntech Corp				
14605 28th Ave N	Minneapolis MN	55447	**800-328-3345**	763-553-3300
Mott Corp 84 Spring Ln	Farmington CT	06032	**800-289-6688**	860-747-6333
MPM Medical Inc				
2301 Crown St	Irving TX	75038	**800-232-5512**	972-893-4090
Nephros Inc 41 Grand Ave	River Edge NJ	07661	**800-732-0330**	201-343-5202
OTC: NEPH				
Novosci 2021 Airport Rd	Conroe TX	77301	**800-854-0567**	281-363-4950

				Toll-Free	Phone
Nspire Health Inc					
1830 Lefthand Cir	Longmont	CO	80501	**800-574-7374**	303-666-5555
NuVasive Inc					
7475 Lusk Blvd	San Diego	CA	92121	**800-475-9131**	858-909-1800
NASDAQ: NUVA					
NxStage Medical Inc					
439 S Union St Fifth Fl	Lawrence	MA	01843	**866-697-8243**	978-687-4700
NASDAQ: NXTM					
Ortho Technology Inc					
17401 Commerce Park Blvd	Tampa	FL	33647	**800-999-3161**	813-991-5896
Ortho-Clinical Diagnostics Inc					
1001 US Rt 202 N PO Box 350	Raritan	NJ	08869	**800-828-6316**	
Osteomed Corp					
3885 Arapaho Rd	Addison	TX	75001	**800-456-7779***	972-677-4600
*Cust Svc					
Pacific Bioscience Laboratories Inc					
16275 NE 67th Ct Suite 112	Redmond	WA	98052	**888-525-2747**	425-283-5700
Pilling Surgical					
2917 Weck Dr	Research Triangle Park	NC	27709	**866-246-6990***	919-544-8000
*Cust Svc					
Prodigy Diabetes Care LLC					
2701-A Hutchison McDonald Rd					
PO Box 481928	Charlotte	NC	28269	**800-366-5901**	
Propper Mfg Company Inc					
36-04 Skillman Ave	Long Island City	NY	11101	**800-832-4300***	718-392-6650
*Cust Svc					
ResMed Inc					
9001 Spectrum Ctr Blvd	San Diego	CA	92123	**800-424-0737**	858-836-5000
NYSE: RMD					
Rochester Medical Corp					
1 Rochester Medical Dr	Stewartville	MN	55976	**800-243-3315**	507-533-9600
NASDAQ: ROCM					
Saint Jude Medical					
St Jude Medical Inc	St Paul	MN	55117	**800-328-9634**	651-756-2000
NYSE: STJ					
Salter Labs 100 Sycamore Rd	Arvin	CA	93203	**800-421-0024**	661-854-3166
Sechrist Industries Inc					
4225 E La Palma Ave	Anaheim	CA	92807	**800-732-4747**	714-579-8400
Siemens Medical Solutions Inc					
51 Valley Stream Pkwy	Malvern	PA	19355	**800-888-7436**	800-225-5336
Smith & Nephew Inc Endoscopy Div					
150 Minuteman Rd	Andover	MA	01810	**800-343-5717**	978-749-1000
Smiths Medical MD Inc					
1265 Grey Fox Rd	Saint Paul	MN	55112	**800-258-5361**	651-633-2556
Sorin Group USA Inc					
14401 W 65th Way	Arvada	CO	80004	**800-289-5759**	303-424-0129
Specialty Silicone Fabricators					
3077 Rollie Gates Dr	Paso Robles	CA	93446	**800-394-4284**	805-239-4284
STERIS Corp 5960 Heisley Rd	Mentor	OH	44060	**800-548-4873**	440-354-2600
NYSE: STE					
Stryker Corp					
2825 Airview Blvd	Kalamazoo	MI	49002	**800-616-1406**	269-385-2600
NYSE: SYK					
Synergetics USA Inc					
3845 Corporate Ctr Dr	O'Fallon	MO	63368	**800-600-0565**	636-939-5100
NASDAQ: SURG					
Techno-Aide Inc					
7117 Centennial Blvd	Nashville	TN	37209	**800-251-2629**	615-350-7030
TERATECH Corp					
77-79 Terr Hall Ave	Burlington	MA	01803	**866-837-2766**	781-270-4143
Terumo Cardiovascular Systems Corp					
6200 Jackson Rd	Ann Arbor	MI	48103	**800-262-3304**	734-663-4145
Terumo Medical Corp					
2101 Cottontail Ln	Somerset	NJ	08873	**800-283-7866**	732-302-4900
TFX Medical Inc					
50 Plantation Dr	Jaffrey	NH	03452	**800-548-6600**	603-532-7706
Topcon Medical Systems Inc					
111 Bauer Dr	Oakland	NJ	07436	**800-223-1130**	201-599-5100
Trans1 Inc					
301 Government Ctr Dr	Wilmington	NC	28403	**866-256-1206**	910-332-1700
United States Endoscopy Group Inc					
5976 Heisley Rd	Mentor	OH	44060	**800-769-8226**	440-639-4494
Urologix Inc					
14405 21st Ave N	Minneapolis	MN	55447	**800-475-1403**	763-475-1400
Utah Medical Products Inc					
7043 S 300 W	Midvale	UT	84047	**866-754-9789**	801-566-1200
NASDAQ: UTMD					
Vasamed Inc					
7615 Golden Triangle Dr Ste A	Eden Prairie	MN	55344	**800-695-2737**	
Vascular Solutions Inc					
6464 Sycamore Ct	Minneapolis	MN	55369	**877-979-4300**	763-656-4300
NASDAQ: VASC					
Ventana Medical Systems Inc					
1910 Innovation Pk Dr	Tucson	AZ	85755	**800-227-2155**	520-887-2155
Vital Signs Inc 20 Campus Rd	Totowa	NJ	07512	**800-932-0760**	973-790-1330
W A Baum Company Inc					
620 Oak St	Copiague	NY	11726	**888-281-6061**	631-226-3940
WalkMed Infusion LLC					
96 Inverness Dr E Ste J	Englewood	CO	80112	**800-578-0555**	303-420-9569

474 MEDICAL SUPPLIES - MFR

SEE ALSO Personal Protective Equipment & Clothing

				Toll-Free	Phone
Adhesives Research Inc					
400 Seaks Run Rd PO Box 100	Glen Rock	PA	17327	**800-445-6240**	717-235-7979
Adroit Medical Systems Inc					
1146 CaRding Machine Rd	Loudon	TN	37774	**800-267-6077**	
Advanced Sterilization Products (ASP)					
33 Technology Dr	Irvine	CA	92618	**888-783-7723**	
AESCULAP Inc					
3773 Corporate Pkwy	Center Valley	PA	18034	**800-282-9000**	
Allergan					
2525 Dupont Dr PO Box 19534	Irvine	CA	92612	**800-347-4500**	714-246-4500
Allied Healthcare Products Inc					
1720 Sublette Ave	Saint Louis	MO	63110	**800-444-3954**	314-771-2400
NASDAQ: AHPI					

				Toll-Free	Phone
American Medical Systems Holdings Inc					
10700 Bren Rd W	Minnetonka	MN	55343	**800-328-3881**	952-930-6000
Animas Corp					
200 Lawrence Dr	West Chester	PA	19380	**877-937-7867**	610-644-8990
Armstrong Medical Industries Inc					
575 Knightsbridge Pkwy	Lincolnshire	IL	60069	**800-323-4220***	847-913-0101
*Cust Svc					
Arthrex Inc					
1370 Creekside Blvd	Naples	FL	34108	**800-934-4404**	239-643-5553
Aspen Surgical					
6945 Southbelt Dr SE	Caledonia	MI	49316	**888-364-7004**	616-698-7100
Avery Dennison Corp					
207 Goode Ave	Glendale	CA	91203	**888-567-4387***	626-304-2000
NYSE: AVY ■ *Cust Svc					
Baylis Medical Company Inc					
5959 Trans-Canada Hwy	Montreal	QC	H4T1A1	**800-850-9801**	514-488-9801
Becton Dickinson & Co					
One Becton Dr	Franklin Lakes	NJ	07417	**888-237-2762***	201-847-6800
NYSE: BDX ■ *Cust Svc					
Becton Dickinson Consumer Healthcare					
One Becton Dr	Franklin Lakes	NJ	07417	**888-237-2762**	201-847-6800
Beltone Electronics Corp					
2601 Patriot Blvd	Glenview	IL	60026	**800-235-8663**	847-832-3300
BioHorizons Inc					
2300 Riverchase Ctr	Birmingham	AL	35244	**888-246-8338**	205-967-7880
Biomet Inc					
56 E Bell Dr PO Box 587	Warsaw	IN	46582	**800-348-9500**	574-267-6639
BSN Medical Inc					
5825 Carnegie Blvd	Charlotte	NC	28209	**800-552-1157**	704-554-9933
Burke Inc					
1800 Merriam Ln	Kansas City	KS	66106	**800-255-4147***	
*Sales					
Capstone Therapeutics Corp					
1275 W Washington St Ste 101	Tempe	AZ	85281	**800-937-5520**	602-286-5520
OTC: CAPS					
Centurion Medical Products					
100 Centurion Way	Williamston	MI	48895	**800-248-4058**	517-546-5400
Chattanooga Group					
4717 Adams Rd	Hixson	TN	37343	**800-592-7329**	423-870-2281
Codman & Shurtleff Inc					
325 Paramount Dr	Raynham	MA	02767	**800-225-0460**	800-382-4682
Community Surgical Supply Inc					
1390 Rt 37 W	Toms River	NJ	08755	**800-349-2990**	732-349-2990
Cramer Products Inc					
153 W Warren St	Gardner	KS	66030	**800-345-2231**	913-856-7511
Cyberonics Inc					
100 Cyberonics Blvd					
The Cyberonics Bldg	Houston	TX	77058	**800-332-1375**	281-228-7262
NASDAQ: CYBX					
DeRoyal Industries Inc					
200 DeBusk Ln	Powell	TN	37849	**800-251-9864**	865-938-7828
DJ Orthopedics Inc					
1430 Decision St	Vista	CA	92081	**800-321-9549**	760-727-1280
Dynarex Corporation					
10 Glenshaw St	Orangeburg	NY	10962	**888-335-7500**	845-365-8200
Ehob Inc					
250 N Belmont Ave	Indianapolis	IN	46222	**800-899-5553**	317-972-4600
Ergodyne Corp					
1021 Bandana Blvd E Ste 220	Saint Paul	MN	55108	**800-225-8238**	651-642-9889
Exactech Inc					
2320 NW 66th Ct	Gainesville	FL	32653	**800-392-2832**	352-377-1140
NASDAQ: EXAC					
Female Health Co					
515 N State St Ste 2225	Chicago	IL	60654	**800-860-2442**	312-595-9123
Ferno-Washington Inc					
70 Weil Way	Wilmington	OH	45177	**800-733-3766**	937-382-1451
Fillauer Inc					
PO Box 5189	Chattanooga	TN	37406	**800-251-6398**	423-624-0946
Freeman Manufacturing Co					
900 W Chicago Rd	Sturgis	MI	49091	**800-253-2091**	269-651-2371
GF Health Products Inc					
2935 NE Pkwy	Atlanta	GA	30360	**800-347-5678**	770-447-1609
Halyard Health					
20202 Windrow Dr	Lake Forest	CA	92630	**800-448-3569**	949-206-2700
Hanger Orthopedic Group Inc					
10910 Domain Dr Ste 300	Austin	TX	78758	**877-442-6437**	512-777-3800
Hanger Prosthetics & Orthopedics Inc					
10910 Domain Dr Ste 300	Austin	TX	78758	**877-442-6437**	
Helix Medical LLC					
1110 Mark Ave	Carpinteria	CA	93013	**800-266-4421**	805-684-3304
Helvoet Pharma Inc					
9012 Pennsauken Hwy	Pennsauken	NJ	08110	**800-874-3586**	856-663-2202
Hollister Inc					
2000 Hollister Dr	Libertyville	IL	60048	**800-323-4060**	847-680-1000
Hospira Inc					
275 N Field Dr	Lake Forest	IL	60045	**877-946-7747**	224-212-2000
NYSE: HSP					
Hoveround Corp					
2151 Whitfield Industrial Way	Sarasota	FL	34243	**800-542-7236**	941-739-6200
Howard Leight Industries					
7828 Waterville Rd	San Diego	CA	92154	**800-430-5490**	
Hy-Tape International Inc					
PO Box 540	Patterson	NY	12563	**800-248-0101**	
ICU Medical Inc					
951 Calle Amanecer	San Clemente	CA	92673	**800-824-7890**	949-366-2183
NASDAQ: ICUI					
Ideal Tape Co					
1400 Middlesex St	Lowell	MA	01851	**800-284-3325**	
International Technidyne Corp					
Eight Olsen Ave	Edison	NJ	08820	**800-631-5945**	732-548-5700
Invacare Corp					
One Invacare Way	Elyria	OH	44036	**800-333-6900**	440-329-6000
NYSE: IVC					
Iowa Veterinary Supply Co (IVESCO)					
124 Country Club Rd	Iowa Falls	IA	50126	**800-457-0118**	641-648-2529
Johnson & Johnson Consumer Products Co					
199 Grandview Rd	Skillman	NJ	08558	**866-565-2229**	908-874-1000
Johnson & Johnson Inc					
7101 Notre-Dame E	Montreal	QC	H1N2G4	**800-361-8990**	514-251-5100

			Toll-Free	Phone

K-Tube Technologies
13400 Kirkham Way . . . . Poway CA 92064 — **800-394-0058** — 858-513-9229

Kimberly-Clark/Ballard Medical Products
1400 Holcomb Bridge Rd . . . . Roswell GA 30076 — **800-524-3577**

Kinetic Concepts Inc (KCI)
PO Box 659508 . . . . San Antonio TX 78265 — **800-275-4524***
*Cust Svc

Kloehn Inc
10000 Banburry Cross Dr . . . . Las Vegas NV 89144 — **800-358-4342** — 702-243-7727

Langer Inc
2905 Veterans' Memorial Hwy . . . . Ronkonkoma NY 11779 — **800-645-5520**

LPS Industries Inc
10 Caesar Pl . . . . Moonachie NJ 07074 — **800-275-6577*** — 201-438-3515
*Sales

M & C Specialties Co
90 James Way . . . . SouthHampton PA 18966 — **800-441-6996*** — 215-322-1600
*Cust Svc

Medical Action Industries Inc (MAI)
500 Expy Dr S . . . . Brentwood NY 11717 — **800-645-7042** — 631-231-4600
NASDAQ: MDCI

Medtronic Inc
710 Medtronic Pkwy NE . . . . Minneapolis MN 55432 — **800-328-2518*** — 763-514-4000
NYSE: MDT ■ *Cust Svc

Medtronic Inc Heart Valve Div
710 Medtronic Pwy . . . . Minneapolis MN 55432 — **800-633-8766** — 763-514-4000

Medtronic MiniMed Inc
18000 Devonshire St . . . . Northridge CA 91325 — **800-646-4633**

Medtronic Powered Surgical Solutions
4620 N Beach St . . . . Fort Worth TX 76137 — **800-643-2773** — 817-788-6400

Medtronic Surgical Technologies
6743 Southpoint Dr N . . . . Jacksonville FL 32216 — **800-874-5797** — 904-296-9600

Mentor Corp
201 Mentor Dr . . . . Santa Barbara CA 93111 — **800-525-0245** — 805-879-6000
NASDAQ: MENT

Mettler Electronics Corp
1333 S Claudina St . . . . Anaheim CA 92805 — **800-854-9305** — 714-533-2221

Microtek Medical Holdings Inc
13000 Deerfield Pkwy Ste 300 . . . . Alpharetta GA 30004 — **800-777-7977** — 678-896-4400

Microtek Medical Inc
512 N Lehmberg Rd . . . . Columbus MS 39702 — **800-824-3027** — 662-327-1863

MicroVention Inc
1311 Valencia Ave . . . . Tustin CA 92780 — **800-990-8368** — 714-247-8000

Milestone Scientific Inc
220 S Orange Ave . . . . Livingston NJ 07039 — **800-862-1125** — 973-535-2717
OTC: MLSS

Miracle-Ear Inc
5000 Cheshire Pkwy N Ste 1 . . . . Minneapolis MN 55446 — **800-464-8002**

MP Biomedicals LLC
Three Hutton Ctr Dr Ste 100 . . . . Santa Ana CA 92707 — **800-633-1352** — 949-833-2500

NELCO Inc
Three Gill St Unit D . . . . Woburn MA 01801 — **800-635-2613** — 781-933-1940

Nice-Pak Products Inc
Two Nice-Pak Pk . . . . Orangeburg NY 10962 — **800-999-6423** — 845-365-1700

NorMed 4310 S 131 Pl . . . . Seattle WA 98168 — **800-288-8200**

Ortho Development Corp
12187 S Business Pk Dr . . . . Draper UT 84020 — **800-429-8339** — 801-553-9991

Orthofix Inc
1720 Bray Central Dr . . . . McKinney TX 75069 — **800-527-0404** — 469-742-2500

Osteomed Corp
3885 Arapaho Rd . . . . Addison TX 75001 — **800-456-7779*** — 972-677-4600
*Cust Svc

Pacific Medical Inc
1700 N Chrisman Rd . . . . Tracy CA 95304 — **800-726-9180**

Phonic Ear Inc
2080 Lakeville Hwy . . . . Petaluma CA 94954 — **800-227-0735** — 707-769-1110

Phygen LLC
2301 Dupont Ave Ste 510 . . . . Irvine CA 92612 — **800-939-7008**

Posey Co 5635 Peck Rd . . . . Arcadia CA 91006 — **800-447-6739** — 626-443-3143

Precision Dynamics Corp
13880 Del Sur St . . . . San Fernando CA 91340 — **800-847-0670** — 818-897-1111

Pride Mobility Products Corp
182 Susquehanna Ave . . . . Exeter PA 18643 — **800-800-8586**

Retractable Technologies Inc
511 Lobo Ln . . . . Little Elm TX 75068 — **888-806-2626** — 972-294-1010
NYSE: RVP

Rusch Inc
2917 Weck Dr
PO Box 12600 . . . . Research Triangle Park NC 27709 — **866-246-6990** — 919-544-8000

Sas Safety Corp
3031 Gardenia Ave . . . . Long Beach CA 90807 — **800-262-0200** — 562-427-2775

Siemens Hearing Instruments Inc
10 Constitution Ave PO Box 1397 . . . . Piscataway NJ 08855 — **800-766-4500**

Smith & Nephew Inc
970 Lk Carillon Dr 310 . . . . Saint Petersburg FL 33716 — **800-876-1261*** — 727-392-1261
*Cust Svc

Smith & Nephew Inc Orthopaedic Div
1450 Brooks Rd . . . . Memphis TN 38116 — **800-821-5700** — 901-396-2121

Smiths Medical ASD Inc
160 Weymouth St . . . . Rockland MA 02370 — **800-258-5361** — 781-878-8011

Smiths Medical MD Inc
1265 Grey Fox Rd . . . . Saint Paul MN 55112 — **800-258-5361** — 651-633-2556

Smiths Medical Respiratory Support Products
5200 Upper Metro Pl Ste 200 . . . . Dublin OH 43017 — **800-258-5361** — 214-618-0218

Sonic Innovations Inc
2501 Cottontail Ln Ste 300 . . . . Somerset NJ 08873 — **888-678-4327** — 888-423-7834

Span-America Medical Systems Inc
70 Commerce Ctr . . . . Greenville SC 29615 — **800-888-6752** — 864-288-8877
NASDAQ: SPAN

Spenco Medical Corp
PO Box 2501 . . . . Waco TX 76702 — **800-877-3626** — 254-772-6000

Standard Textile Company Inc
One Knollcrest Dr . . . . Cincinnati OH 45237 — **800-999-0400** — 513-761-9255

Starkey Laboratories Inc
6700 Washington Ave S . . . . Eden Prairie MN 55344 — **800-328-8602** — 952-941-6401

STERIS Corp 5960 Heisley Rd . . . . Mentor OH 44060 — **800-548-4873** — 440-354-2600
NYSE: STE

Sunrise Medical Inc
2842 Business Pk Ave . . . . Fresno CA 93727 — **800-333-4000**

			Toll-Free	Phone

Surgical Appliance Industries Inc
3960 Rosslyn Dr . . . . Cincinnati OH 45209 — **800-888-0867**

Synovis Life Technologies Inc
2575 University Ave . . . . Saint Paul MN 55114 — **800-255-4018** — 651-796-7300
NASDAQ: SYNO

TIDI Products LLC
570 Enterprise Dr . . . . Neenah WI 54956 — **800-521-1314**

TS03 Inc 2505 Dalton Ave . . . . Quebec QC G1P3S5 — **866-715-0003** — 418-651-0003

Utah Medical Products Inc
7043 S 300 W . . . . Midvale UT 84047 — **866-754-9789** — 801-566-1200
NASDAQ: UTMD

Venture Tape Corp
30 Commerce Rd . . . . Rockland MA 02370 — **800-343-1076** — 781-331-5900

Vital Signs Inc 20 Campus Rd . . . . Totowa NJ 07512 — **800-932-0760** — 973-790-1330

Volcano Corp
3661 Vly Centre Dr Ste 200 . . . . San Diego CA 92130 — **800-228-4728**

West Pharmaceutical Services Inc
101 Gordon Dr . . . . Lionville PA 19341 — **800-345-9800** — 610-594-2900
NYSE: WST

Wright Medical Group Inc
5677 Airline Rd . . . . Arlington TN 38002 — **800-238-7188** — 901-867-9971
NASDAQ: WMGI

Wright Medical Technology Inc
5677 Airline Rd . . . . Arlington TN 38002 — **800-238-7188** — 901-867-9971

Zimmer Inc
1800 W Ctr St PO Box 708 . . . . Warsaw IN 46580 — **800-613-6131** — 574-267-6131

475　MEDICAL TRANSCRIPTION SERVICES

Companies listed here have a national or regional clientele base.

			Toll-Free	Phone

FreightPros
3307 Northland Dr Ste 360 . . . . Austin TX 78731 — **888-297-6968**

Thomas Transcription Services Inc
PO Box 26613 . . . . Jacksonville FL 32226 — **888-878-2889** — 904-751-5058

476　MEDICINAL CHEMICALS & BOTANICAL PRODUCTS

SEE ALSO Vitamins & Nutritional Supplements ; Pharmaceutical Companies ; Pharmaceutical Companies - Generic Drugs ; Biotechnology Companies ; Diagnostic Products
Companies listed here manufacture medicinal chemicals and botanical products in bulk for sale to pharmaceutical, vitamin, and nutritional product companies.

			Toll-Free	Phone

Acic Fine Chemicals Inc
81 St Claire Blvd . . . . Brantford ON N3S7X6 — **800-265-6727** — 519-751-3668

Array BioPharma Inc
3200 Walnut St . . . . Boulder CO 80301 — **877-633-2436** — 303-381-6600
NASDAQ: ARRY

Avanti Polar Lipids Inc
700 Industrial Pk Dr . . . . Alabaster AL 35007 — **800-227-0651** — 205-663-2494

Bachem Bioscience Inc
3132 Kashiwa St . . . . Torrance CA 90505 — **800-634-3183** — 310-539-4171

Balchem Corp
52 Sunrise Pk Rd PO Box 600 . . . . New Hampton NY 10958 — **877-407-8289** — 845-326-5613
NASDAQ: BCPC

Bedford Laboratories Inc
300 Northfield Rd . . . . Bedford OH 44146 — **800-562-4797** — 440-232-3320

Ben Venue Laboratories Inc
300 Northfield Rd . . . . Bedford OH 44146 — **800-989-3320*** — 440-232-3320
*General

Bio-Botanica Inc
75 Commerce Dr . . . . Hauppauge NY 11788 — **800-645-5720** — 631-231-5522

Cambrex Corp
1 Meadowlands Plaza 15th Fl . . . . East Rutherford NJ 07073 — **866-286-9133** — 201-804-3000
NYSE: CBM

Charm Sciences Inc
659 Andover St . . . . Lawrence MA 01843 — **800-343-2170** — 978-687-9200

Cyanotech Corp
73-4460 Queen Kaahumanu Hwy
Ste 102 . . . . Kailua-Kona HI 96740 — **800-453-1187*** — 808-326-1353
NASDAQ: CYAN ■ *Sales

Flora Mfg & Distributing Ltd
7400 Fraser Park Dr . . . . Burnaby BC V5J5B9 — **888-436-6697** — 604-436-6000

George Uhe Company Inc
219 River Dr . . . . Garfield NJ 07026 — **800-850-4075** — 201-843-4000

Greer Laboratories Inc
639 Nuway Cir NE PO Box 800 . . . . Lenoir NC 28645 — **800-378-3906*** — 828-754-5327
*Cust Svc

ICC Industries Inc
460 Pk Ave . . . . New York NY 10022 — **800-422-1720** — 212-521-1700

Interchem Corp 120 Rt 17 N . . . . Paramus NJ 07652 — **800-261-7332** — 201-261-7333

Johnson Matthey Inc Pharmaceutical Materials Div
2003 Nolte Dr . . . . Paulsboro NJ 08066 — **800-444-8544** — 856-384-7001

Johnson Matthey Pharma Services
25 Patton Rd . . . . Devens MA 01434 — **800-444-8544** — 978-784-5000

Lannett Company Inc (LCI)
13200 Townsend Rd . . . . Philadelphia PA 19154 — **800-325-9994** — 215-333-9000
NYSE: LCI

LycoRed Corp 377 Crane St . . . . Orange NJ 07051 — **877-592-6733** — 973-882-0322

NHK Laboratories Inc
12230 E Florience Ave . . . . Santa Fe Springs CA 90670 — **866-645-5227** — 562-944-5400

Nutra Pharma Corp
12502 W Atlantic Blvd . . . . Coral Springs FL 33071 — **877-895-5647** — 954-509-0911

Nutraceutix Inc
9609 153rd Ave NE . . . . Redmond WA 98052 — **800-548-3222** — 425-883-9518

One Lambda Inc
21001 Kittridge St . . . . Canoga Park CA 91303 — **800-822-8824** — 818-702-0042

Patheon Inc
2100 Syntex Ct . . . . Mississauga ON L5N7K9 — **866-529-2922** — 905-821-4001

PendoPharm Inc
6111 Royalmount . . . . Montreal QC H4P2T4 — **866-926-7653*** — 514-340-5045
*Cust Svc

				Toll-Free	Phone
Rainbow Light Nutritional Sys Inc					
100 Ave Tea	Santa Cruz	CA	95060	800-635-1233	
Scientific Protein Laboratories Inc					
700 E Main St PO Box 158	Waunakee	WI	53597	800-334-4775	608-849-5944
Siegfried USA LLC					
33 Industrial Pk Rd	Pennsville	NJ	08070	877-763-8630*	856-678-3601
*Cust Svc					
Sigma-Aldrich Corp					
3050 Spruce St	Saint Louis	MO	63103	800-325-3010	314-771-5765
NASDAQ: SIAL					
Spectrum Laboratory Products Inc					
14422 S San Pedro St PO Box 290	Gardena	CA	90248	800-772-8786*	310-516-8000
*General					
SPI Pharma					
Rockwood Office Park Fl 2	Wilmington	DE	19809	800-789-9755	302-576-8567
SST Corp 635 Brighton Rd	Clifton	NJ	07012	800-222-0921	973-473-4300
Starwest Botanicals Inc					
11253 Trade Ctr Dr	Rancho Cordova	CA	95742	800-800-4372*	916-638-8100
*General					
Terry Laboratories Inc					
7005 Technology Dr	Melbourne	FL	32904	800-367-2563	321-259-1630
Tri-K Industries Inc					
Two Stewart Ct PO Box 10	Denville	NJ	07834	800-526-0372	973-298-8850
TSI Health Sciences Inc					
305 E Fourth St E Ste 101	Missoula	MT	59801	877-549-9123	406-549-9123
United-Guardian Inc (UGI)					
230 Marcus Blvd PO Box 18050	Hauppauge	NY	11788	800-645-5566	631-273-0900
NASDAQ: UG					

477 METAL - STRUCTURAL (FABRICATED)

				Toll-Free	Phone
Aerospace America Inc					
900 Harry Truman Pkwy PO Box 189	Bay City	MI	48706	800-237-6414	989-684-2121
Amerimax Bldg Products Inc					
5208 Tennyson Pkwy	Plano	TX	75024	800-448-4033	469-366-3200
Amerimax Home Products Inc					
450 Richardson Dr	Lancaster	PA	17603	800-347-2586	717-299-3711
Anchor Fabrication Ltd					
1200 Lawson Rd	Fort Worth	TX	76131	800-635-0386	817-498-2521
Apex Industries Inc					
100 Millennium Blvd	Moncton	NB	E1E2G8	800-268-3331	506-857-1620
APi Group Inc Fabrication & Mfg Group					
1100 Old Hwy 8 NW	New Brighton	MN	55112	800-223-4922	
Barker Steel Co Inc					
55 Sumner St	Milford	MA	01757	866-977-3227	508-473-8484
Braden Mfg LLC					
5199 N Mingo Rd	Tulsa	OK	74117	800-272-3360	
Central Minnesota Fabricating Inc					
2725 W Gorton Ave	Willmar	MN	56201	800-839-8857	320-235-4181
CENTRIA					
1005 Beaver Grade Rd	Moon Township	PA	15108	800-759-7474	412-299-8000
Chase Industries Inc					
10021 Commerce Park Dr	Cincinnati	OH	45246	800-543-4455	513-860-5565
CMC Alamo Steel Co					
2784 Old Dallas Rd	Waco	TX	76705	800-500-0333	254-799-2471
CMC Capitol City Steel					
14501 S IH 35	Buda	TX	78610	888-682-7337	512-282-8820
CMC Rebar Georgia					
251 Hosea Rd	Lawrenceville	GA	30045	888-682-7337	770-963-6251
Discount RampsCom LLC					
760 S Indiana Ave	West Bend	WI	53095	888-651-3431	262-338-3431
Don Young Co					
8181 Ambassador Row	Dallas	TX	75247	800-367-0390	214-630-0934
Dropbox Inc					
1805 N Second St	Ironton	OH	45638	888-388-7768	
Fabral Inc					
3449 Hempland Rd	Lancaster	PA	17601	800-477-2741	717-397-2741
Garaga Inc 8500 25th Ave	St Georges	QC	G6A1K5	800-464-2724	418-227-2828
GEA PHE Systems North America Inc					
100 Gea Dr	York	PA	17402	800-774-0474	717-268-6200
GLM Industries LP					
1508 - Eighth St	Nisku	AB	T9E7S6	800-661-9828	780-955-2233
Grain Belt Supply Company Inc					
PO Box 615	Salina	KS	67402	800-447-0522	785-827-4491
J. C. Macelroy Company Inc					
PO Box 850	Piscataway	NJ	08855	800-622-3576	732-572-7100
JH Industries Inc					
1981 E Aurora Rd	Twinsburg	OH	44087	800-321-4968	330-963-4105
Linetec 725 S 75th Ave	Wausau	WI	54401	888-717-1472	715-843-4100
Manko Window Systems Inc					
800 Hayes Dr	Manhattan	KS	66502	800-642-1488	785-776-9643
McElroy Metal Inc					
1500 Hamilton Rd	Bossier City	LA	71111	800-562-3576	318-747-8097
Midwest Metal Products Co					
2100 W Mt Pleasant Rd	Muncie	IN	47302	888-741-1044	
Nabco Entrances Inc					
S82W18717 Gemini Dr	Muskego	WI	53150	888-679-3319	262-679-0045
Nucor Corp					
1915 Rexford Rd	Charlotte	NC	28211	800-294-1322	704-366-7000
NYSE: NUE					
Owen Industries Inc					
501 Ave H	Carter Lake	IA	51510	800-831-9252	712-347-5500
Paxton & Vierling Steel Co					
501 Ave H	Carter Lake	IA	51510	800-831-9252	
Pipe Welders Inc					
2965 W State Rd 84	Fort Lauderdale	FL	33312	800-787-8401	954-587-8400
Qualico Steel Co Inc					
PO Box 149	Webb	AL	36376	866-234-5382	334-793-1290
Ralston Metal Products Ltd					
50 Watson Rd S	Guelph	ON	N1L1E2	800-265-7611	
Ranor Inc One Bella Dr	Westminster	MA	01473	800-225-9552	978-874-0591
Rodney Hunt Co 46 Mill St	Orange	MA	01364	800-448-8860	978-544-2511
Schuff Steel Inc					
1920 Ledo Rd	Albany	GA	31707	800-248-5367	229-883-4506
Stupp Bros Inc					
3800 Weber Rd	Saint Louis	MO	63125	800-899-1856	314-638-5000

				Toll-Free	Phone
T. Bruce Sales Inc					
Nine Carbaugh St	West Middlesex	PA	16159	800-944-0738	724-528-9961
Tie Down Engineering Inc					
255 Villanova Dr SW	Atlanta	GA	30336	800-241-1806	404-344-0000
United Window & Door Manufacturing Inc					
24-36 Fadem Rd	Springfield	NJ	07081	800-848-4550	973-912-0600
Val-Fab Inc 218 Jackson St	Neenah	WI	54956	888-482-5322	920-722-1009
Wahlcometroflex Inc					
29 Lexington St	Lewiston	ME	04240	800-272-6652	207-784-2338
WaUSAu Window & Wall Systems					
7800 International Dr	Wausau	WI	54401	877-678-2983	715-845-2161
Wojan Window & Door Corp					
217 Stover Rd	Charlevoix	MI	49720	800-632-9827	231-547-2931
WSF Industries Inc					
Seven Hackett Dr	Tonawanda	NY	14150	800-874-8265	716-692-4930

478 METAL COATING, PLATING, ENGRAVING

				Toll-Free	Phone
Alumicor Ltd					
290 Humberline Dr	Toronto	ON	M9W5S2	877-258-6426	416-745-4222
American Nickeloid Co					
2900 Main St	Peru	IL	61354	800-645-5643	815-223-0373
AST Products Inc					
Nine Linnell Cir	Billerica	MA	01821	877-667-4500	978-667-4500
BL Downey Company LLC					
2125 Gardner Rd	Broadview	IL	60155	800-323-1206	708-345-8000
Charlotte Anodizing Products Inc					
591 E Packard Hwy	Charlotte	MI	48813	800-818-6945	517-543-1911
Chem Processing Inc					
3910 Linden Oaks Dr	Rockford	IL	61109	800-262-2119	815-874-8118
Chemart Co					
15 New England Way	Lincoln	RI	02865	800-521-5001	401-333-9200
Chicago Metallic Corp					
4849 S Austin Ave	Chicago	IL	60638	800-323-7164	708-563-4600
Continental Studwelding Ltd					
35 Devon Rd	Brampton	ON	L6T5B6	800-848-9442	905-792-3650
Deposition Sciences Inc					
3300 Coffey Ln	Santa Rosa	CA	95403	866-433-7724	707-573-6700
East Side Plating Inc					
8400 SE 26th Pl	Portland	OR	97202	800-394-8554	503-654-3774
FW Gartner Thermal Spraying Ltd					
25 Southbelt Industrial Dr	Houston	TX	77047	888-439-4872	713-225-0010
Galvan Industries Inc					
7320 Millbrook Rd	Harrisburg	NC	28075	888-256-6929*	704-455-5102
*General					
GM Nameplate Inc					
2040 15th Ave W	Seattle	WA	98119	800-366-7668	206-284-2200
Hadronics Inc					
4570 Steel Pl	Cincinnati	OH	45209	800-829-0826	513-321-9350
Ingot Metal Company Ltd					
111 Fenmar Dr	Weston	ON	M9L1M3	800-567-7774	416-749-1372
LB Foster Co					
415 Holiday Dr	Pittsburgh	PA	15220	800-255-4500	
NASDAQ: FSTR					
Lorin Industries					
1960 S Roberts St	Muskegon	MI	49443	800-654-1159	231-722-1631
Magnetic Metals Corp					
1900 Hayes Ave	Camden	NJ	08105	800-257-8174	856-964-7842
Master Finish Co					
2020 Nelson SE PO Box 7505	Grand Rapids	MI	49510	877-590-5819	
Metal Cladding Inc					
230 S Niagara St	Lockport	NY	14094	800-432-5513	
Metal Koting - Continuous Colour Coat Ltd					
1430 Martin Grove Rd	Rexdale	ON	M9W4Y1	855-656-8464	416-743-7980
Meziere Enterprises Inc					
220 S Hale Ave	Escondido	CA	92029	800-208-1755	760-746-3273
National Coatings Inc					
3520 Rennie School Rd	Traverse City	MI	49685	888-947-2557	231-943-2557
Nd Industries Inc					
1000 N Crooks Rd	Clawson	MI	48017	800-471-5000	248-288-0000
O E C Graphics Inc					
555 W Waukau Ave PO Box 2443	Oshkosh	WI	54902	800-388-7770	920-235-7770
Pioneer Metal Finishing LLC					
486 Globe Ave	Green Bay	WI	54304	877-721-1100	
Plasma Ruggedized Solutions Inc					
2284 Ringwood Ave Ste A	San Jose	CA	95131	800-994-7527	408-954-8405
Premier Die Casting Co					
1177 Rahway Ave	Avenel	NJ	07001	800-394-3006	732-634-3000
Roesch Inc 100 N 24th St	Belleville	IL	62222	800-423-6243	
Sapa Inc 7933 NE 21st Ave	Portland	OR	97211	800-547-0790	503-802-3000
Towne Technologies Inc					
6-10 Bell Ave PO Box 460	Somerville	NJ	08876	800-837-2515	908-722-9500
Ultra-tech Enterprises Inc					
4701 Taylor Rd	Punta Gorda	FL	33950	800-293-2001	941-575-2000
US Chrome Corp					
175 Garfield Ave	Stratford	CT	06615	800-637-9019	
Willington Cos					
11 Middle River Dr	Stafford Springs	CT	06076	877-892-2966	860-684-4281

479 METAL FABRICATING - CUSTOM

				Toll-Free	Phone
Afco Industries Inc					
3400 Roy St	Alexandria	LA	71302	800-551-6576	
Brakewell Steel Fabricator Inc					
55 Leone Ln	Chester	NY	10918	888-914-9131	845-469-9131
Cross Bros Inc					
5255 Sheila St	Los Angeles	CA	90040	866-939-1057	323-266-2000
CSM Metal Fabricating & Engineering Inc					
1800 S San Pedro St	Los Angeles	CA	90015	800-272-4806	213-748-7321
Demsey Manufacturing Co					
78 New Wood Rd	Watertown	CT	06795	800-533-6739	860-274-6209
Fabricated Components Inc					
PO Box 431	Stroudsburg	PA	18360	800-233-8163	570-421-4110

	Toll-Free	Phone
International Extrusions Inc		
5800 Venoy Rd .... Garden City MI 48135	800-242-8876	734-427-8700
Liquidmetal Technologies Inc (LQMT)		
30452 Esperanza .... Rancho Santa Margarita CA 92688	888-203-1112	949-635-2100
OTC: LQMT		
Lucasey Manufacturing Corp		
2744 E 11th St PO Box 14023 .... Oakland CA 94601	800-582-2739	510-534-1435
MP Metal Products Inc		
W1250 Elmwood Ave .... Ixonia WI 53036	800-824-6744	920-261-9650
NobelClad 5405 Spine Rd .... Boulder CO 80301	800-821-2666*	303-665-5700
*NASDAQ: BOOM ■ *General*		
Sommer Metalcraft Corp		
315 Poston Dr PO Box 688 .... Crawfordsville IN 47933	888-876-6637	765-362-6201
Southwire Company Machinery Div		
One Southwire Dr .... Carrollton GA 30119	800-444-1700	770-832-4242
General		
Unifab Corp 5260 Lovers Ln .... Portage MI 49002	800-648-9569*	269-382-2803
General		
White River Distributors Inc		
720 Ramsey .... Batesville AR 72501	800-548-7219	870-793-2374

480 METAL FORGINGS

	Toll-Free	Phone
Ajax Rolled Ring & Machine Inc		
500 Wallace Way .... York SC 29745	800-727-6333	803-684-3133
Alcoa Wheel Products International		
1600 Harvard Ave .... Cleveland OH 44105	800-242-9898	216-641-3600
Aluminum Precision Products Inc		
3333 W Warner St .... Santa Ana CA 92704	800-411-8983	714-546-8125
Anchor-Harvey Components LLC		
600 W Lamm Rd .... Freeport IL 61032	888-367-4464	815-235-4400
Brainerd Industries Inc		
680 Precision Ct .... Miamisburg OH 45342	800-790-0430	937-228-0488
Ellwood City Forge		
800 Commercial Ave .... Ellwood City PA 16117	800-843-0166	724-752-0055
Federal Flange		
4014 Pinemont St .... Houston TX 77018	800-231-0150	713-681-0606
Ferguson Perforating & Wire Co		
130 Ernest St .... Providence RI 02905	800-341-9800	401-941-8876
Fine Line Production		
2221 Regal Pkwy .... Euless TX 76040	800-887-5625	817-267-6750
Forged Products Inc (FPI)		
6505 N Houston Rosslyn Rd .... Houston TX 77091	800-876-3416	713-462-3416
Forged Vessel Connections Inc		
2525 DeSoto St .... Houston TX 77091	800-231-2701*	713-688-9705
Cust Svc		
Frontier Metal Stamping Inc		
3764 Puritan Way .... Erie CO 80516	888-316-1266	303-458-5129
Green Bay Drop Forge		
1341 State St .... Green Bay WI 54304	800-824-4896	920-432-6401
H & L Tooth Company Inc		
10055 E 56 St N .... Tulsa OK 74117	800-458-6684	918-272-0951
Jorgensen Forge Corp		
8531 E Marginal Way S .... Tukwila WA 98108	800-231-5382	206-762-1100
Kerkau Manufacturing Co		
1321 S Valley Ctr Dr .... Bay City MI 48706	800-248-5060	989-686-0350
KomTeK Technologies		
40 Rockdale St .... Worcester MA 01606	800-669-4500	508-853-4500
Liberty Forge Inc		
PO Box 1210 .... Liberty TX 77575	800-231-2377	936-336-5785
Machine Specialty & Manufacturing Inc		
215 Rousseau Rd .... Youngsville LA 70592	800-256-1292	337-837-0020
Mercer Forge Corp		
200 Brown St .... Mercer PA 16137	800-558-5075	724-662-2750
MMD Equipment		
121 High Hill Rd .... Swedesboro NJ 08085	800-433-1382	856-467-3200
Norforge & Machining Inc		
195 N Dean St .... Bushnell IL 61422	800-839-3706	309-772-3124
Phoenix Forging Company Inc		
800 Front St .... Catasauqua PA 18032	800-444-3674	610-264-2861
Randall Bearings Inc		
1046 Greenlawn Ave PO Box 1258 .... Lima OH 45802	800-626-7071	419-223-1075
Saint Croix Forge Inc		
5195 Scandia Trl .... Forest Lake MN 55025	866-668-7642	651-464-8967
Scot Forge Co		
8001 Winn Rd PO Box 8 .... Spring Grove IL 60081	800-435-6621	847-587-1000
Talan Products Inc		
18800 Cochran Ave .... Cleveland OH 44110	877-419-2805	216-458-0170
Thoro'Bred Inc		
5020 E La Palma Ave .... Anaheim CA 92807	877-585-5152	714-779-2581
Western Forge & Flange Co		
687 County Rd 2201 .... Cleveland TX 77327	800-352-6433	281-727-7060
Wozniak Industries Inc Commercial Forged Products Div		
5757 W 65th St .... Bedford Park IL 60638	800-637-2695	708-458-1220
Wrought Washer Manufacturing Inc		
2100 S Bay St .... Milwaukee WI 53207	800-558-5217	414-744-0771
Young Manufacturing Inc		
2331 N 42nd St .... Grand Forks ND 58203	800-451-9884	701-772-5541

481 METAL HEAT TREATING

	Toll-Free	Phone
Bluewater Thermal Solutions		
201 Brookfield Pwy Ste 102 .... Greenville SC 29607	877-990-0050	864-990-0050
Curtiss-Wright Corp		
10 Waterview Blvd 2nd Fl .... Parsippany NJ 07054	855-449-0995	973-541-3700
NYSE: CW		
FPM LLC		
1501 S Lively Blvd .... Elk Grove Village IL 60007	877-437-6432	847-228-2525
Gibraltar Industries Inc		
3556 Lakeshore Rd .... Buffalo NY 14219	800-247-8368	716-826-6500
NASDAQ: ROCK		
HI TecMetal Group Inc		
1101 E 55th St .... Cleveland OH 44103	877-484-2867	216-881-8100

	Toll-Free	Phone
Industrial Steel Treating Inc		
613 Carroll St .... Jackson MI 49202	800-253-9534	
Rex Heat Treat		
951 W Eigth St PO Box 270 .... Lansdale PA 19446	800-220-4739	215-855-1131
Stahl Specialty Co		
11 E Pacific St PO Box 6 .... Kingsville MO 64061	800-821-7852	816-597-3322

482 METAL INDUSTRIES (MISC)

SEE ALSO Steel - Mfr ; Wire & Cable ; Foundries - Investment ; Foundries - Iron & Steel ; Foundries - Nonferrous (Castings) ; Metal Heat Treating ; Metal Tube & Pipe

	Toll-Free	Phone
Alcoa Inc		
390 Park Ave PO Box 8001 .... New York NY 10022	800-523-9596	412-553-4545
Alcoa Primary Metals		
900 S Gay St Riverview Twr Ste 1100 ..... Knoxville TN 37902	800-852-0238	865-594-4700
Allegheny Technologies Inc		
1000 Six PPG Pl .... Pittsburgh PA 15222	800-258-3586*	412-394-2800
*NYSE: ATI ■ *Sales*		
Allvac Inc		
2020 Ashcraft Ave PO Box 5030 .... Monroe NC 28110	800-841-5491	704-289-4511
Altech LLC		
242 America Pl .... Jeffersonville IN 47130	800-264-8256	812-282-8256
Ampco Metal Inc		
1117 E Algonquin Rd .... Arlington Heights IL 60005	800-844-6008	847-437-6000
Anaheim Extrusion Company Inc		
1330 N Kraemer Blvd PO Box 6380 .... Anaheim CA 92806	800-660-3318	714-630-3111
Arvinyl Metal Laminates Corp		
233 N Sherman Ave .... Corona CA 92882	800-278-4695	
Big River Zinc Corp		
2401 Mississippi Ave .... Sauget IL 62201	800-274-4002	618-274-5000
Broco Inc		
10868 Bell Ct .... Rancho Cucamonga CA 91730	800-845-7259	909-483-3222
Bunting Magnetics Co		
500 S Spencer Ave .... Newton KS 67114	800-835-2526	316-284-2020
Cannon Muskegon Corp		
2875 Lincoln St PO Box 506 .... Muskegon MI 49441	800-253-0371	231-755-1681
Cardinal Aluminum Co		
6910 Preston Hwy .... Louisville KY 40219	800-398-7833*	502-969-9302
Cust Svc		
Chase Brass & Copper Co		
14212 County Rd M 50 PO Box 152 ..... Montpelier OH 43543	800-537-4291	419-485-3193
Chicago Extruded Metals Co (CXM)		
1601 S 54th Ave .... Cicero IL 60804	800-323-8102*	
Cust Svc		
Croft LLC		
107 Oliver Emmerich Dr .... McComb MS 39648	800-437-8421	601-684-6121
Curtis Steel Company LLC (CSC)		
6504 Hurst St PO Box 7469 .... Houston TX 77008	800-749-4621	713-861-4621
Custom Aluminum Products Inc		
414 Div St .... South Elgin IL 60177	800-745-6333	847-717-5000
Doe Run Co		
1801 Pk 270 Dr Ste 300 .... Saint Louis MO 63146	800-356-3786	314-453-7100
Dynamet Inc		
195 Museum Rd .... Washington PA 15301	800-237-9655	724-228-1000
Elmet Industries Inc		
1560 Lisbon St .... Lewiston ME 04240	800-343-8008	207-333-6100
Glines & Rhodes Inc		
189 E St PO Box 2285 .... Attleboro MA 02703	800-343-1196	508-226-2000
H Kramer & Co		
1345 W 21st St .... Chicago IL 60608	800-621-2305	312-226-6600
Haynes International Inc		
1020 W Pk Ave PO Box 9013 .... Kokomo IN 46904	800-354-0806	765-456-6000
NASDAQ: HAYN		
Hoover & Strong Inc		
10700 Trade Rd .... North Chesterfield VA 23236	800-759-9997*	
Cust Svc		
Hussey Copper Ltd		
100 Washington St .... Leetsdale PA 15056	800-733-8866	724-251-4200
Industrial Tectonics Inc		
7222 Huron River Dr .... Dexter MI 48130	800-482-2255	734-426-4681
JW Aluminum		
435 Old Mt Holly Rd .... Mount Holly SC 29445	877-586-5314*	
Sales		
Kaiser Aluminum Corp		
27422 Portola Pkwy Ste 200 .... Foothill Ranch CA 92610	800-873-2011*	949-614-1740
Sales		
Light Metals Corp		
2740 Prairie St SW .... Wyoming MI 49509	888-363-8257	616-538-3030
Linemaster Switch Corp		
29 Plaine Hill Rd .... Woodstock CT 06281	800-974-3668	860-974-1000
Loxcreen Co Inc, The		
1630 Old Dunbar Rd PO Box 4004 .... West Columbia SC 29172	800-330-5699	803-822-8200
Lucas-Milhaupt Inc		
5656 S Pennsylvania Ave .... Cudahy WI 53110	800-558-3856	414-769-6000
Luvata Appleton LLC		
553 Carter Ct .... Kimberly WI 54136	866-488-0217	920-749-3820
Magnat-Fairview Inc		
1102 Sheridan St .... Chicopee MA 01022	800-636-3433	413-593-5742
Magnetech Industrial Services Inc		
800 Nave Rd SE .... Massillon OH 44646	800-837-1614*	330-830-3500
General		
Memry Corp		
Three Berkshire Blvd .... Bethel CT 06801	866-466-3679	203-739-1100
Metglas Inc 440 Allied Dr .... Conway SC 29526	800-581-7654	843-349-7319
Micro Surface Engr Inc		
1550 E Slauson Ave .... Los Angeles CA 90011	800-322-5832	323-582-7348
Midland Industries Inc		
1424 N Halsted St .... Chicago IL 60642	800-662-8228	312-664-7300
Mueller Brass Co		
2199 Lapeer Ave .... Port Huron MI 48060	800-553-3336	810-987-7770
Mueller Industries Inc		
8285 Tournament Dr Ste 150 .... Memphis TN 38125	800-348-8464	901-753-3200
NYSE: MLI		

				Toll-Free	Phone
NetShape Technologies Inc					
31005 Solon Rd	Solon	OH	44139	**866-429-5724**	440-248-5456
NN Inc					
2000 Waters Edge Dr					
Bldg 3 Ste 12	Johnson City	TN	37604	**877-888-0002**	423-743-9151
NASDAQ: NNBR					
Noranda Aluminum Inc					
801 Crescent Ctr Dr Ste 600	Franklin	TN	37067	**800-325-8112**	615-771-5700
Patrick Industries Inc Patrick Metals Div					
5020 Lincolnway E	Mishawaka	IN	46544	**800-922-9692**	574-255-9692
Penn Aluminum International Inc					
1117 N Second St PO Box 490	Murphysboro	IL	62966	**800-445-7366***	618-684-2146
*All					
Revere Copper Products Inc					
One Revere Pk	Rome	NY	13440	**800-448-1776**	315-338-2022
Ross Metals Corp					
27 W 47th St	New York	NY	10036	**800-334-7191**	
Southwire Co					
1 Southwire Dr	Carrollton	GA	30119	**800-444-1700**	770-832-4242
Special Metals Corp					
4317 Middle Settlement Rd	New Hartford	NY	13413	**800-334-8351**	315-798-2900
Taber Extrusions LP					
915 S Elmira Ave	Russellville	AR	72802	**800-563-6853**	479-968-1021
Titanium Metals Corp (TIMET)					
224 Vly Creek Blvd Ste 200	Exton	PA	19341	**800-753-1550**	610-968-1300
NYSE: TIE					
Tree Island Industries					
3933 Boundary Rd PO Box 50	Richmond	BC	V6V1T8	**800-663-0955**	604-524-3744
				*	
US Bronze Powders Inc					
408 Rt 202 N	Flemington	NJ	08822	**800-544-0186***	908-782-5454
*General					
Valmont Industries Inc					
One Valmont Plz	Omaha	NE	68154	**800-825-6668**	402-963-1000
NYSE: VMI					
Victory White Metal Co					
6100 Roland Ave	Cleveland	OH	44127	**800-635-5050**	216-271-1400
Wah Chang					
1600 Old Salem Rd NE	Albany	OR	97321	**888-926-4211**	541-926-4211
Xyron Inc					
8465 N 90th St Ste 6	Scottsdale	AZ	85258	**800-793-3523**	480-443-9419

483 METAL PRODUCTS - HOUSEHOLD

				Toll-Free	Phone
All-Clad Metalcrafters LLC					
424 Morganza Rd	Canonsburg	PA	15317	**800-255-2523***	724-745-8300
*Cust Svc					
Calphalon Corp PO Box 583	Toledo	OH	43697	**800-809-7267**	
Le Creuset of America Inc					
114 Bob Gifford Blvd	Early Branch	SC	29916	**877-418-5547**	803-943-4308
Lifetime Brands Inc					
1000 Steward Ave	Garden City	NY	11530	**800-252-3390**	516-683-6000
NASDAQ: LCUT					
Lifetime Brands Inc Farberware Div					
1000 Stewart Ave	Garden City	NY	11530	**800-999-2811**	516-683-6000
Lifetime Brands Inc Hoffritz Div					
1000 Stewart Ave	Garden City	NY	11530	**800-252-3390**	516-683-6000
ME Heuck Co					
1600 Beech St	Terre Haute	IN	47804	**866-634-3825***	812-238-5000
*Cust Svc					
Meyer Corp 1 Meyer Pl	Vallejo	CA	94590	**800-888-3883***	707-551-2800
*Cust Svc					
Nordic Ware 5005 Hwy 7	Minneapolis	MN	55416	**877-466-7342**	952-920-2888
Saladmaster Inc					
230 Westway Pl Ste 101	Arlington	TX	76018	**800-765-5795**	817-633-3555
Whitesell Corp					
2703 Avalon Ave	Muscle Shoals	AL	35661	**800-826-3317***	256-248-8500
*General					
Wilton Armetale Co					
PO Box 600	Mount Joy	PA	17552	**800-779-4586**	
Wilton Industries Inc					
2240 W 75th St	Woodridge	IL	60517	**800-794-5866**	630-963-7100

484 METAL PRODUCTS (MISC)

				Toll-Free	Phone
Aerodyne Alloys LLC					
350 Pleasant Vly Rd	South Windsor	CT	06074	**800-243-4344**	860-289-6011
Alexandria Extrusion Co					
401 County Rd 22 NW	Alexandria	MN	56308	**800-568-6601**	320-763-6537
Aluchem Inc One Landy Ln	Cincinnati	OH	45215	**800-336-8519**	513-733-8519
Aluminum Ladder Co					
1430 W Darlington St	Florence	SC	29501	**800-752-2526**	843-662-2595
Amatom Electronic Hardware LLC					
Five Pasco Hill Rd	Cromwell	CT	06416	**800-243-6032**	860-828-0847
Bead Industries Inc					
11 Cascade Blvd	Milford	CT	06460	**800-297-4851**	203-301-0270
Carolina Carports Inc					
187 Cardinal Ridge Trl	Dobson	NC	27017	**800-670-4262**	
Flinchbaugh Engineering Inc					
4387 Run Way	York	PA	17406	**866-967-5334**	717-755-1900
General Magnaplate Corp					
1331 Us Rt 1	Linden	NJ	07036	**800-441-6173**	908-862-6200
Lechler Inc					
445 Kautz Rd	Saint Charles	IL	60174	**800-777-2926***	630-377-6611
*Cust Svc					
Liberty Safe & Security Products Inc					
1199 W Utah Ave	Payson	UT	84651	**800-247-5625**	801-925-1000
Metalworking Group Inc					
9070 Pippin Rd	Cincinnati	OH	45251	**800-476-9409**	513-521-4114
Polar Ware Co 502 Hwy 67	Kiel	WI	53042	**800-237-3655***	
*Cust Svc					
Precision Valve Corp					
800 Westchester Ave	Rye Brook	NY	10573	**866-686-8464**	914-969-6500

				Toll-Free	Phone
Viking Materials Inc					
3225 Como Ave SE	Minneapolis	MN	55414	**800-682-3942***	612-617-5800
*General					
Visual Planning Corp					
71 Meadowbank Dr	Ottawa	NY	12919	**888-884-5444**	613-563-8727

485 METAL STAMPINGS

SEE ALSO Metal Stampings - Automotive ; Closures - Metal or Plastics ; Electronic Enclosures

				Toll-Free	Phone
Accurate Perforating Co					
3636 S Kedzie Ave	Chicago	IL	60632	**800-621-0273**	773-254-3232
Acme Metal Cap Inc Co					
33-53 62nd St	Woodside	NY	11377	**800-338-3581**	718-335-3000
Admiral Craft Equipment Corp					
940 S Oyster Bay Rd	Hicksville	NY	11801	**800-223-7750**	516-433-3535
All New Stamping Co					
10801 Lower Azusa Rd	El Monte	CA	91731	**800-877-7775**	
American Metalcraft Inc					
2074 George St	Melrose Park	IL	60160	**800-333-9133**	708-345-1177
American Products LLC					
597 Evergreen Rd	Strafford	MO	65757	**855-736-2135**	417-736-2135
Arrow Tru-Line Inc					
2211 S Defiance St	Archbold	OH	43502	**877-285-7253**	419-446-2785
Ataco Steel Products Corp					
PO Box 270	Cedarburg	WI	53012	**800-536-4822**	262-377-3000
Bazz Houston Co					
12700 Western Ave	Garden Grove	CA	92841	**800-385-9608**	714-898-2666
Btd Mfg Inc					
1111 13th Ave SE	Detroit Lakes	MN	56501	**866-562-3986**	
Dayton Rogers Manufacturing Co					
8401 W 35 W Service Dr	Minneapolis	MN	55449	**800-677-8881**	763-784-7714
Delta Consolidated Industries Inc					
4800 Krueger Dr	Jonesboro	AR	72401	**800-643-0084**	870-935-3711
Diamond Manufacturing Co					
243 W Eigth St	Wyoming	PA	18644	**800-233-9601**	570-693-0300
Diamond Perforated Metals Inc					
7300 W Sunnyview Ave	Visalia	CA	93291	**800-642-4334**	559-651-1889
DORMA Architectural Hardware					
DORMA Dr Drawer AC	Reamstown	PA	17567	**800-523-8483**	717-336-3881
East Moline Metal Products Co					
1201 Seventh St	East Moline	IL	61244	**800-325-4151***	309-752-1350
*Sales					
Fraen Corp					
80 Newcrossing Rd	Reading	MA	01867	**800-370-0078**	781-205-5300
Fulton Industries Inc					
135 E Linfoot St PO Box 377	Wauseon	OH	43567	**800-537-5012**	419-335-3015
GMP Metal Products Inc					
3883 Delor St	Saint Louis	MO	63116	**800-325-9808**	314-481-0300
Hannibal Industries Inc					
3851 S Santa Fe Ave	Los Angeles	CA	90058	**888-246-7074**	323-588-4261
Hendrick Manufacturing Co					
One Seventh Ave	Carbondale	PA	18407	**800-225-7373***	
*Cust Svc					
Heyco Products					
1800 Industrial Way N	Toms River	NJ	08755	**800-526-4182**	732-286-1800
Hobson & Motzer Inc					
30 Air Line Dr PO Box 427	Durham	CT	06422	**800-476-5111**	860-349-1756
HPL Stampings Inc					
425 Enterprise Pkwy	Lake Zurich	IL	60047	**800-927-0397**	847-540-1400
HTT Inc. 1828 Oakland Ave	Sheboygan	WI	53081	**866-270-4710**	920-457-2311
Innovative Stamping Corp					
2068 E Gladwick St	Compton	CA	90220	**800-400-0047**	310-537-6996
Jagemann Stamping Co					
5757 W Custer St PO Box 217	Manitowoc	WI	54221	**888-337-7853**	920-682-4633
Ken-Tron Manufacturing Inc					
PO Box 21250	Owensboro	KY	42304	**800-872-9336**	270-684-0431
Kennedy Manufacturing Co					
1260 Industrial Dr	Van Wert	OH	45891	**800-413-8665**	419-238-2442
Kickhaefer Mfg Co (KMC)					
1221 S Pk St PO Box 348	Port Washington	WI	53074	**800-822-6080**	262-377-5030
Knaack Manufacturing Co					
420 E Terra Cotta Ave	Crystal Lake	IL	60014	**800-456-7865**	815-459-6020
Metal Box International					
11600 W King St	Franklin Park	IL	60131	**800-622-2697***	847-455-8500
*General					
Midwest Wire Products LLC					
649 S Lansing Ave PO Box 770	Sturgeon Bay	WI	54235	**800-445-0225**	920-743-6591
Penn United Technology Inc					
799 N Pike Rd	Cabot	PA	16023	**866-572-7537**	724-352-1507
Quality Perforating Inc					
166 Dundaff St	Carbondale	PA	18407	**800-872-7373**	570-282-4344
RES Mfg Company Inc					
7801 N 73rd St	Milwaukee	WI	53223	**800-334-8044**	414-354-4530
Saunders Manufacturing Co					
65 Nickerson Hill Rd	Readfield	ME	04355	**800-341-4674**	207-685-9860
Stack-On Products Co					
1360 N Old Rand Rd	Wauconda	IL	60084	**800-323-9601**	847-526-1611
Steel City Corp					
190 N Meridian Rd	Youngstown	OH	44501	**800-321-0350**	330-792-7663
Stewart EFI LLC					
45 Old Waterbury Rd	Thomaston	CT	06787	**800-393-5387**	860-283-8213
T & D Metal Products Co					
602 E Walnut St	Watseka	IL	60970	**800-634-7267**	815-432-4938
Waterloo Industries Inc					
139 W Forest Hill Ave	Oak Creek	WI	53154	**800-558-5528***	
*Cust Svc					

486 METAL STAMPINGS - AUTOMOTIVE

SEE ALSO Automotive Parts & Supplies - Mfr

				Toll-Free	Phone
Advance Engineering Co					
7505 Baron Dr	Canton	MI	48187	**800-497-6388**	313-537-3500

			Toll-Free	Phone
American Metal & Plastics Inc				
450 32nd St SW	Grand Rapids MI	49548	**800-382-0067**	616-452-6061
C Cowles & Co Inc				
83 Water St	New Haven CT	06511	**800-624-4483**	203-865-3117
Decoma International Inc				
Magna Exteriors & Interiors				
50 Casmir Ct	Concord ON	L4K4J5	**888-348-2398**	905-669-2888
Lake Air				
7709 Winpark Dr	Minneapolis MN	55427	**888-785-2422**	763-546-0994
Philippi-Hagenbuch Inc				
7424 W Plank Rd	Peoria IL	61604	**800-447-6464**	309-697-9200
Radar Industries				
27101 Grosbeck Hwy	Warren MI	48089	**800-779-0301**	
Spartanburg Steel Products Inc				
1290 New Cut Rd PO Box 6428	Spartanburg SC	29304	**888-974-7500**	864-585-5211
Stewart EFI LLC				
45 Old Waterbury Rd	Thomaston CT	06787	**800-393-5387**	860-283-8213
Syracuse Stamping Co				
1054 S Clinton St	Syracuse NY	13202	**800-581-5555**	315-476-5306

487   METAL TUBE & PIPE

			Toll-Free	Phone
AK Tube LLC				
30400 E Broadway	Walbridge OH	43465	**800-955-8031**	419-661-4150
American Cast Iron Pipe Co (ACIPCO)				
1501 31st Ave N	Birmingham AL	35207	**800-442-2347**	205-325-7701
Atlas Tube 1855 E 122nd St	Chicago IL	60633	**800-733-5683**	773-646-4500
Bull Moose Tube Co				
1819 Clarkson Rd Ste 100	Chesterfield MO	63017	**800-325-4467**	636-537-2600
California Steel & Tube				
16049 Stephens St	City of Industry CA	91745	**800-338-8823**	626-968-5511
Cerro Flow Products Inc				
PO Box 66800	Saint Louis MO	63166	**888-237-7611**	618-337-6000
Charlotte Pipe & Foundry Co				
2109 Randolph Rd	Charlotte NC	28207	**800-438-6091**	704-372-5030
Dixie Pipe Sales Inc				
2407 Broiller PO Box 300650	Houston TX	77054	**800-733-3494**	713-796-2021
Earle M Jorgensen Co				
10650 S Alameda St	Lynwood CA	90262	**800-336-5365***	323-567-1122
*Sales				
Energy Alloys LLC				
350 Glenborough Ste 300	Houston TX	77067	**866-448-9831**	832-601-5800
Felker Bros Corp				
22 N Chestnut Ave	Marshfield WI	54449	**800-826-2304**	715-384-3121
Hanna Steel Corp				
3812 Commerce Ave PO Box 558	Fairfield AL	35064	**800-633-8252**	205-780-1111
Hannibal Industries Inc				
3851 S Santa Fe Ave	Los Angeles CA	90058	**888-246-7074**	323-588-4261
Hydro Aluminum North America				
999 Corporate Blvd Ste 100	Linthicum MD	21090	**888-935-5752**	
International Metal Hose Co				
520 Goodrich Rd	Bellevue OH	44811	**800-458-6855**	419-483-7690
J D Rush C Inc				
5900 E Lerdo Hwy	Shafter CA	93263	**800-537-6284**	661-392-1900
Jackson Tube Service Inc				
8210 Industry Pk Dr	Piqua OH	45356	**800-543-8910**	937-773-8550
Leavitt Tube				
1717 W 115th St	Chicago IL	60643	**800-532-8488**	773-239-7700
LeFiell Manufacturing Co				
13700 Firestone Blvd	Santa Fe Springs CA	90670	**800-451-5971**	562-921-3411
Lock Joint Tube Inc				
515 W Ireland Rd	South Bend IN	46614	**800-257-6859**	574-299-5326
Morris Coupling Co				
2240 W 15th St	Erie PA	16505	**800-426-1579**	814-459-1741
Northwest Pipe Co				
12005 N Burgard	Portland OR	97203	**800-824-9824**	503-285-1400
NASDAQ: NWPX				
Outokumpu Stainless Pipe Inc				
1101 N Main St	Wildwood FL	34785	**800-731-7473**	352-748-1313
Plymouth Tube Co				
29 W 150 Warrenville Rd	Warrenville IL	60555	**800-323-9506***	630-393-3550
*Mktg				
Small Tube Products Company Inc				
PO Box 1017	Duncansville PA	16635	**800-458-3493**	814-695-4491
Southland Tube Inc				
3525 Richard Arrington Blvd N	Birmingham AL	35234	**800-543-9024**	205-251-1884
Stupp Corp				
12555 Ronaldson Rd	Baton Rouge LA	70807	**800-535-9999**	225-775-8800
Synalloy Corp				
775 Spartan Blvd Ste 102				
PO Box 5627	Spartanburg SC	29304	**800-937-5449***	864-585-3605
NASDAQ: SYNL ■ **Orders*				
Tex-Tube Co				
1503 N Post Oak Rd	Houston TX	77055	**800-839-7473**	713-686-4351
Tube Processing Corp				
604 E Le Grande Ave	Indianapolis IN	46203	**800-295-4119**	317-787-1321
Valmont Industries Inc				
One Valmont Plz	Omaha NE	68154	**800-825-6668**	402-963-1000
NYSE: VMI				
Wheatland Tube Co				
700 S Dock St	Sharon PA	16146	**800-257-8182**	
Yarde Metals Inc				
45 Newell St	Southington CT	06489	**800-444-9494**	860-406-6061

488   METAL WORK - ARCHITECTURAL & ORNAMENTAL

			Toll-Free	Phone
Alabama Metal Industries Corp (AMICO)				
3245 Fayette Ave	Birmingham AL	35208	**800-366-2642**	205-787-2611
Alvarado Mfg Company Inc				
12660 Colony St	Chino CA	91710	**800-423-4143**	909-591-8431
American Stair Corp Inc				
642 Forestwood Dr	Romeoville IL	60446	**800-872-7824**	

			Toll-Free	Phone
Ameristar Fence Products Inc				
1555 N Mingo Rd	Tulsa OK	74116	**888-333-3422**	918-835-0898
ATAS International Inc				
6612 Snowdrift Rd	Allentown PA	18106	**800-468-1441**	610-395-8445
Bedford Machine & Tool Inc				
2103 John Williams Blvd	Bedford IN	47421	**800-264-1948**	812-275-1948
Bil-Jax Inc				
125 Taylor Pkwy	Archbold OH	43502	**800-537-0540**	419-445-8915
Brand Energy & Infrastructure Services Inc				
1325 Cobb International Dr Ste A-1	Kennesaw GA	30152	**855-746-4477**	678-285-1400
Chicago Metallic Corp				
4849 S Austin Ave	Chicago IL	60638	**800-323-7164**	708-563-4600
Construction Specialties Inc				
Three Werner Way	Lebanon NJ	08833	**800-972-7214**	908-236-0800
Duvinage Corp				
60 W Oak Ridge Dr	Hagerstown MD	21740	**800-541-2645**	301-733-8255
Fisher & Ludlow Tru-Weld Grating				
2000 Corporate Dr Ste 400	Wexford PA	15090	**800-334-2047**	724-934-5320
Goldline International Inc				
1601 Cloverfield Blvd 100 S Tower				
	Santa Monica CA	90404	**877-376-2646**	310-587-1423
Hafele America Company Inc				
3901 Cheyenne Dr	Archdale NC	27263	**800-423-3531***	336-889-2322
*Cust Svc				
Hapco Inc				
26252 Hillman Hwy	Abingdon VA	24210	**800-368-7171**	276-628-7171
Irvine Access Floors Inc				
9425 Washington Blvd	Laurel MD	20723	**888-458-6339**	301-617-9333
Jerith Mfg Company Inc				
14400 McNulty Rd	Philadelphia PA	19154	**800-344-2242**	215-676-4068
King Architectural Metals Inc				
PO Box 271169	Dallas TX	75227	**800-542-2379**	
Lapmaster International LLC				
501 W Algonquin Rd	Mount Prospect IL	60056	**877-352-8637**	224-659-7101
Lawrence Metal Products Inc				
260 Spur Dr S PO Box 400	Bay Shore NY	11706	**800-441-0019**	
Overly Manufacturing Co				
574 W Otterman St	Greensburg PA	15601	**800-979-7300**	724-834-7300
Spider Staging Corp				
365 Upland Dr	Tukwila WA	98188	**877-774-3370**	206-575-6445
Steel Ceilings Inc				
451 E Coshocton St	Johnstown OH	43031	**800-848-0496**	740-967-1063
Superior Aluminum Products Inc				
555 E Main St PO Box 430	Russia OH	45363	**800-548-8656**	937-526-4065
Tate Access Floors Inc				
7510 Montevideo Rd	Jessup MD	20794	**800-231-7788**	410-799-4200
VELUX America Inc				
450 Old BrickyaRd Rd	Greenwood SC	29648	**866-358-3589**	864-941-4700
Vicwest Corp				
1296 S Service Rd W	Oakville ON	L6L5T7	**800-265-6583**	905-825-2252
Wolf Robotics LLC				
4600 Innovation Dr	Fort Collins CO	80525	**866-965-3911**	970-225-7600
Wooster Products Inc				
1000 Spruce St PO Box 6005	Wooster OH	44691	**800-321-4936**	330-264-2844

489   METALS SERVICE CENTERS

			Toll-Free	Phone
ABC Metals Inc				
500 W Clinton St	Logansport IN	46947	**800-238-8470**	
Accurate Alloys Inc				
5455 Irwindale Ave	Irwindale CA	91706	**800-842-2222**	626-338-4012
Acier Picard Inc				
3000 Rue De L' Etchemin	Levis QC	G6W7X6	**888-834-0646**	418-834-8300
Action Stainless & Alloys Inc				
1505 Halsey Way	Carrollton TX	75007	**800-749-2523**	972-466-1500
Aladdin Steel Inc				
PO Box 89	Gillespie IL	62033	**800-637-4455**	217-839-2121
Alaskan Copper & Brass Co				
3223 Sixth Ave S	Seattle WA	98134	**800-552-7661**	206-623-5800
All Foils Inc				
16100 Imperial Pkwy	Strongsville OH	44149	**800-521-0054**	440-572-3645
All Metals Industries Inc				
PO Box 807	Belmont NH	03220	**800-654-6043**	603-267-7023
Allied Sinterings Inc				
29 Briar Ridge Rd	Danbury CT	06810	**877-875-0464**	
Alro Steel Corp				
3100 E High St	Jackson MI	49204	**800-877-2576**	517-787-5500
Aluminum & Stainless Inc				
PO Box 3484	Lafayette LA	70502	**800-252-9074**	337-837-4381
American Douglas Metals Inc				
783 Thorpe Rd	Orlando FL	32824	**800-428-0023**	407-855-6590
American Strip Steel Inc				
901 Coopertown Rd	Delanco NJ	08075	**800-526-1216**	
AMI Metals Inc				
1738 General George Patton Dr	Brentwood TN	37027	**800-727-1903**	615-377-0400
Amsco Steel Co				
PO Box 11037	Fort Worth TX	76110	**800-772-2743**	817-926-3355
Art Iron Inc 860 Curtis St	Toledo OH	43609	**800-472-1113**	419-241-1261
Atlas Steel Products Co				
7990 Bavaria Rd	Twinsburg OH	44087	**800-444-1682**	330-425-1600
Basic Metals Inc				
W180 Nn11819 River Ln	Germantown WI	53022	**800-989-1996**	262-255-9034
Berlin Metals LLC				
3200 Sheffield Ave	Hammond IN	46327	**800-754-8867**	219-933-0111
BMG Metals Inc				
950 Masonic Ln	Richmond VA	23231	**800-552-1510**	804-226-1024
Bobco Metals Co				
2000 S Alameda St	Los Angeles CA	90058	**877-952-6226**	
Bohler-Uddeholm North America				
2505 Millenium Dr	Elgin IL	60124	**800-638-2520**	630-883-3100
Brown-Strauss Steel				
2495 Uravan St	Aurora CO	80011	**800-677-2778***	303-371-2200
*Sales				
Cambridge Street Metal Corp (CSM)				
82 Stevens St	East Taunton MA	02718	**800-254-7580**	508-822-2278

		Toll-Free	Phone

Chatham Steel Corp
501 W Boundary St . . . . Savannah GA 31401 **800-800-1337** 912-233-5751

Chicago Tube & Iron Co
One Chicago Tube Dr . . . . Romeoville IL 60446 **800-972-0217*** 815-834-2500
*Cust Svc

City Pipe & Supply Corp
PO Box 2112 . . . . Odessa TX 79760 **844-307-4044** 432-332-1541

Clayton Metals Inc
546 Clayton Ct . . . . Wood Dale IL 60191 **800-323-7628**

Columbia Pipe & Supply Co
1120 W Pershing Rd . . . . Chicago IL 60609 **888-429-4635** 773-927-6600

Consolidated Pipe & Supply Inc
1205 Hilltop Pkwy . . . . Birmingham AL 35204 **800-467-7261*** 205-323-7261
*Sales

Consolidated Steel Services Inc
632 Glendale Vly Blvd . . . . Fallentimber PA 16639 **800-237-8783** 814-944-5890

Consumers Pipe & Supply Co
5832 E 61st St . . . . Los Angeles CA 90040 **800-338-7473** 323-685-6870

Contractors Steel Co
36555 Amrhein Rd . . . . Livonia MI 48150 **800-521-3946** 734-464-4000

Damascus Steel Casting Co
Blockhouse Rd Run Extn . . . . New Brighton PA 15066 **800-920-2210** 724-846-2770

Decker Steel & Supply Inc
4500 Train Ave . . . . Cleveland OH 44102 **800-321-6100** 216-281-7900

Dubose National Energy Services Inc
PO Box 499 . . . . Clinton NC 28329 **800-590-2150** 910-590-2151

Eaton Steel Corp
10221 Capital Ave . . . . Oak Park MI 48237 **800-527-3851** 248-398-3434

Ed Fagan Inc
769 Susquehanna Ave . . . . Franklin Lakes NJ 07417 **800-335-6827** 201-891-4003

General Steel Inc PO Box 1503 . . . . Macon GA 31202 **800-476-2794** 478-746-2794

Gibbs Wire & Steel Company Inc
Metals Dr PO Box 520 . . . . Southington CT 06489 **800-800-4422** 860-621-0121

Hanna Steel Corp
3812 Commerce Ave PO Box 558. . . . . Fairfield AL 35064 **800-633-8252** 205-780-1111

Howard Precision Metals Inc
PO Box 240127 . . . . Milwaukee WI 53224 **800-444-0311** 414-355-9611

Hynes Industries
3760 Oakwood . . . . Youngstown OH 44515 **800-321-9257**

JDH Pacific Inc
15301 S Blackburn Ave . . . . Norwalk CA 90650 **800-818-9335** 562-926-8088

Ken-Mac Metals Inc
17901 Englewood Dr . . . . Cleveland OH 44130 **800-831-9503** 440-234-7500

KGS Steel Inc 3725 Pine Ln . . . . Bessemer AL 35022 **800-533-3846** 205-425-0800

Kivort Steel
380 Hudson River Rd . . . . Waterford NY 12188 **800-462-2616** 518-590-7233

Klein Steel Service
105 Vanguarden Pkwy . . . . Rochester NY 14606 **800-477-6789*** 585-328-4000
*Cust Svc

Kreher Steel Company LLC
1550 N 25th Ave . . . . Melrose Park IL 60160 **800-323-0745**

Lapham-Hickey Steel Corp
5500 W 73rd St . . . . Chicago IL 60638 **800-323-8443** 708-496-6111

Lindquist Steels Inc
1050 Woodend Rd . . . . Stratford CT 06615 **800-243-9637**

Livingston Pipe & Tube Inc
1612 Rt 4 N PO Box 300. . . . . Staunton IL 62088 **800-548-7473** 618-635-8700

Loveman Steel Corp
5455 Perkins Rd . . . . Bedford Heights OH 44146 **800-568-3626**

Maas-Hansen Steel Corp
2435 E 37th St PO Box 58364 . . . . Vernon CA 90058 **800-647-8335** 323-586-0171

Majestic Steel USA
5300 Majestic Pkwy . . . . Cleveland OH 44146 **800-321-5590** 440-786-2666

Marmon/Keystone Corp
PO Box 992 . . . . Butler PA 16003 **800-544-1748** 724-283-3000

Matenaer Corp
810 Schoenhaar Dr . . . . West Bend WI 53090 **800-254-0873** 262-338-0700

Mazel & Company Inc
4300 W Ferdinand St . . . . Chicago IL 60624 **800-525-4023** 773-533-1600

McNichols Co
9401 Corporate Lake Dr . . . . Tampa FL 33634 **877-884-4653**

Merfish Pipe & Supply Co
PO Box 15879 . . . . Houston TX 77220 **800-869-5731** 713-869-5731

Merit USA 620 Clark Ave . . . . Pittsburg CA 94565 **800-445-6374**

Metal Supermarkets IP Inc
520 Abilene Dr Second Fl. . . . . Mississauga ON L5T2H7 **866-867-9344** 905-362-8226

Metrolina Steel Inc
2601 Westinghouse Blvd . . . . Charlotte NC 28273 **800-849-7935** 704-598-7007

MultAlloy Inc
8511 Monroe St . . . . Houston TX 77061 **800-568-9551**

Murphy & Nolan Inc
340 Peat St PO Box 6689 . . . . Syracuse NY 13217 **800-836-6385** 315-474-8203

Napco Steel Inc
1800 Arthur Dr . . . . West Chicago IL 60185 **800-292-8010** 630-293-1900

National Specialty Alloys LLC
18250 Keith Harrow Blvd . . . . Houston TX 77084 **800-847-5653*** 281-345-2115
*General

National Tube Supply Co
925 Central Ave . . . . University Park IL 60466 **800-229-6872** 708-534-2700

New Process Steel Corp
5800 Westview Dr . . . . Houston TX 77055 **800-392-4989** 713-686-9631

North American Steel Co
18300 Miles Ave . . . . Cleveland OH 44128 **800-321-9310** 216-475-7300

North Shore Steel
1566 Miles St . . . . Houston TX 77015 **877-453-3533** 713-453-3533

Nucor Steel Memphis Inc
3601 Paul R Lowry Rd . . . . Memphis TN 38109 **888-682-6786**

O'neal Flat Rolled Metals
1229 S Fulton Ave . . . . Brighton CO 80601 **800-336-3365** 303-654-0300

O'Neal Steel Inc
744 41st St N . . . . Birmingham AL 35222 **800-861-8272** 205-599-8000

Olympic Steel Inc
5096 Richmond Rd . . . . Bedford Heights OH 44146 **800-321-6290** 216-292-3800
NASDAQ: ZEUS

OnlineMetals.com
1138 W Ewing . . . . Seattle WA 98119 **800-533-6350**

Owen Industries Inc
501 Ave H . . . . Carter Lake IA 51510 **800-831-9252** 712-347-5500

Pacesetter Steel Service Inc
1045 Big Shanty Rd . . . . Kennesaw GA 30144 **800-749-6505** 770-919-8000

Pacific Steel & Recycling
1401 Third St NW . . . . Great Falls MT 59404 **800-889-6264** 406-771-7222

Paragon Steel Enterprises LLC
4211 County Rd 61 . . . . Butler IN 46721 **800-411-5677** 260-868-1100

Parker Steel Co PO Box 2883 . . . . Toledo OH 43606 **800-333-4140** 419-473-2481

Peerless Steel Corp
2450 Austin . . . . Troy MI 48083 **800-482-3947** 248-528-3200

Peterson Steel Corp
61 W Mountain St . . . . Worcester MA 01606 **800-325-3245** 508-853-3630

Phillips & Johnston Inc
21w179 Hill Ave . . . . Glen Ellyn IL 60137 **877-411-8823** 630-469-8150

Phoenix Metals Co
4685 Buford Hwy . . . . Norcross GA 30071 **800-241-2290** 770-447-4211

Pioneer Steel Corp
7447 Intervale St . . . . Detroit MI 48238 **800-999-9440** 313-933-9400

Posner Industries Inc
8641 Edgeworth Dr . . . . Capitol Heights MD 20743 **888-767-6377** 301-350-1000

Precision Steel Warehouse Inc
3500 Wolf Rd . . . . Franklin Park IL 60131 **800-323-0740** 847-455-7000

Rancocas Metals Corp
35 Indel Ave . . . . Rancocas NJ 08073 **800-762-6382** 609-267-4120

Rolled Alloys Inc
125 W Sterns Rd . . . . Temperance MI 48182 **800-521-0332** 734-847-0561

Rolled Steel Products Corp
2187 Garfield Ave . . . . Los Angeles CA 90040 **800-400-7833** 323-723-8836

Russel Metals Inc
6600 Financial Dr . . . . Mississauga ON L5N7J6 **800-268-0750** 905-819-7777
TSE: RUS

Saginaw Pipe Company Inc
1980 Hwy 31 S PO Box 8 . . . . Saginaw AL 35137 **800-433-1374** 205-664-3670

Service Steel Aerospace Corp
4609 70th St E . . . . Fife WA 98424 **800-426-9794**

Shamrock Steel Sales Inc
238 W County Rd S . . . . Odessa TX 79763 **800-299-2317** 432-337-2317

Siskin Steel & Supply Co Inc
1901 Riverfront Pkwy . . . . Chattanooga TN 37408 **800-756-3671** 423-756-3671

Skyline Steel LLC
Eight Woodhollow Rd Ste 102 . . . . Parsippany NJ 07054 **866-875-9546**

Specialty Pipe & Tube Inc
PO Box 516 . . . . Mineral Ridge OH 44440 **800-842-5839** 330-505-8262

State Pipe & Supply Inc
9615 S Norwalk Blvd . . . . Santa Fe Springs CA 90670 **800-733-6410** 562-695-5555

Staub Metals Corp
7747 E Rosecrans Ave . . . . Paramount CA 90723 **800-447-8282** 562-602-2200

Steel & Pipe Supply Co
555 Poyntz Ave . . . . Manhattan KS 66502 **800-521-2345** 785-587-5100

Steel Supply Co, The
5101 Newport Dr . . . . Rolling Meadows IL 60008 **800-323-7571**

Steel Warehouse Company Inc
2722 W Tucker Dr . . . . South Bend IN 46619 **800-348-2529** 574-236-5100

Supra Alloys Inc
351 Cortez Cir . . . . Camarillo CA 93012 **800-647-8772** 805-388-2138

Sylvania Steel Corp
4169 Holland Sylvania Rd . . . . Toledo OH 43623 **800-435-0986*** 419-885-3838
*General

TCI Aluminum/North Inc
2353 Davis Ave . . . . Hayward CA 94545 **800-824-6197** 510-786-3750

Texas Pipe & Supply Co Inc
2330 Holmes Rd . . . . Houston TX 77051 **800-233-8736** 713-799-9235

ThyssenKrupp Materials NA
22355 W 11 Mile Rd . . . . Southfield MI 48033 **800-926-2600** 248-233-5600

Tioga Pipe Supply Company Inc
2450 Wheatsheaf Ln . . . . Philadelphia PA 19137 **800-523-3678** 215-831-0700

Tomson Steel Co (Inc)
PO Box 940 . . . . Middletown OH 45042 **800-837-3001**

Toyota Tsusho America Inc
805 Third Ave 16th Fl . . . . New York NY 10022 **800-883-0100** 212-355-3600

Triple-S Steel Supply LLC
PO Box 21119 . . . . Houston TX 77226 **800-231-1034** 713-697-7105

Tubular Steel Inc
1031 Executive Pkwy Dr . . . . Saint Louis MO 63141 **800-388-7491** 314-851-9200

Turret Steel Industries Inc
105 Pine St . . . . Imperial PA 15126 **800-245-4800** 724-218-1014

United States Brass & Copper Co Inc
1401 Brook Dr . . . . Downers Grove IL 60515 **800-821-2854** 630-629-9340

Universal Steel Co
6600 Grant Ave . . . . Cleveland OH 44105 **800-669-2645** 216-883-4972

Valiant Steel & Equipment Inc
6455 Old Peachtree Rd . . . . Norcross GA 30071 **800-939-9905** 770-417-1235

Viking Materials Inc
3225 Como Ave SE . . . . Minneapolis MN 55414 **800-682-3942*** 612-617-5800
*General

Vista Metals Inc
65 Ballou Blvd . . . . Bristol RI 02809 **800-431-4113** 401-253-1772

West Central Steel Inc
110 19th St NW PO Box 1178 . . . . Willmar MN 56201 **800-992-8853** 320-235-4070

Willbanks Metals Inc
1155 NE 28th St . . . . Fort Worth TX 76106 **800-772-2352** 817-625-6161

Wisconsin Steel & Tube Corp
1555 N Mayfair Rd . . . . Milwaukee WI 53226 **800-279-8335** 414-453-4441

Wrisco Industries Inc
355 Hiatt Dr Ste B. . . . . Palm Beach Gardens FL 33418 **800-627-2646** 561-626-5700

490　METALWORKING DEVICES & ACCESSORIES

SEE ALSO Tool & Die Shops ; Machine Tools - Metal Cutting Types ; Machine Tools - Metal Forming Types

		Toll-Free	Phone

Acme Industrial Co
441 Maple Ave . . . . Carpentersville IL 60110 **800-323-5582** 847-428-3911

Advanced Machine & Engineering Co
2500 Latham St . . . . Rockford IL 61103 **800-225-4263** 815-962-6076

Allied Machine & Engineering Corp
120 Deeds Dr . . . . Dover OH 44622 **800-321-5537** 330-343-4283

				Toll-Free	Phone
American Cutting Edge Inc 480 Congress Pk Dr	Centerville	OH	45459	**800-543-6860***	888-252-3372
*General					
American Drill Bushings Co (ADB) 5740 Hunt Rd	Valdosta	GA	31606	**800-423-4425**	229-253-8928
ASKO Inc 501 W Seventh Ave	Homestead	PA	15120	**800-321-1310**	412-461-4110
ATI Metal Working Products 1 Teledyne Pl	La Vergne	TN	37086	**888-926-4211**	615-641-4200
Besly Cutting Tools Inc 16200 Woodmint Ln	South Beloit	IL	61080	**800-435-2965**	815-389-2231
Big Kaiser Precision Tooling Inc 641 Fargo Ave	Elk Grove Village	IL	60007	**888-866-5776**	847-228-7660
Buck Chuck Co 2155 Traversefield Dr	Traverse City	MI	49686	**800-228-2825**	
Carbro Corp 15724 Condon Ave PO Box 278	Lawndale	CA	90260	**888-738-4400**	310-643-8400
Carl Zeiss Industrial Metrology 6250 Sycamore Ln N	Maple Grove	MN	55369	**800-752-6181**	763-744-2400
CJT Koolcarb Inc 494 Mission St	Carol Stream	IL	60188	**800-323-2299**	630-690-5933
Cline Tool & Service Co PO Box 866	Newton	IA	50208	**866-561-3022**	641-792-7081
Deltronic Corp 3900 W Segerstrom Ave	Santa Ana	CA	92704	**800-451-6922**	714-545-5800
Detroit Edge Tool Co 6570 E Nevada St	Detroit	MI	48234	**800-404-2038**	313-366-4120
Edmunds Gages 45 Spring Ln	Farmington	CT	06032	**800-878-1622**	860-677-2813
Forkardt 2155 Traverse Field Dr	Traverse City	MI	49686	**800-544-3823**	231-995-8300
Fullerton Tool Company Inc 121 Perry St	Saginaw	MI	48602	**855-722-7243**	989-799-4550
Garr Tool Co 7800 N Alger Rd	Alma	MI	48801	**800-248-9003**	989-463-6171
Gilman USA 1230 Cheyenne Ave PO Box 5	Grafton	WI	53024	**800-445-6267**	262-377-2434
Glastonbury Southern Gage 46 Industrial Pk Rd	Erin	TN	37061	**800-251-4243**	931-289-4243
Guhring Inc 1445 Commerce Ave	Brookfield	WI	53045	**800-776-6170**	262-784-6730
Hannibal Carbide Tool Inc 5000 Paris Gravel Rd	Hannibal	MO	63401	**800-451-9436**	573-221-2775
Hardinge Inc 1 Hardinge Dr	Elmira	NY	14902	**800-843-8801**	607-734-2281
NASDAQ: HDNG					
Hayden Twist Drill & Tool Company Inc 22822 Globe St	Warren	MI	48089	**800-521-1780**	586-754-7700
Hougen Manufacturing Inc 3001 Hougen Dr	Swartz Creek	MI	48473	**800-426-7818***	810-635-7111
*Orders					
Huron Machine Products Inc 228 SW 21st Terr	Fort Lauderdale	FL	33312	**800-327-8186**	
Husqvarna Construction Products 17400 W 119th St	Olathe	KS	66061	**800-288-5040**	
Industrial Tools Inc (ITI) 1111 S Rose Ave	Oxnard	CA	93033	**800-266-5561**	805-483-1111
Jasco Tools Inc 1390 Mt Read Blvd PO Box 60497	Rochester	NY	14606	**800-724-5497**	585-254-7000
Jergens Inc 15700 S Waterloo Rd	Cleveland	OH	44110	**800-537-4367**	877-486-1454
Kennametal Inc 1600 Technology Way PO Box 231	Latrobe	PA	15650	**800-446-7738***	724-539-5000
NYSE: KMT ■ *Cust Svc					
KEO Cutters Inc 25040 Easy St	Warren	MI	48089	**888-390-2050**	586-771-2050
Lancaster Knives Inc 165 Ct St	Lancaster	NY	14086	**800-869-9666**	716-683-5050
Lovejoy Tool Company Inc 133 Main St	Springfield	VT	05156	**800-843-8376**	802-885-2194
Melin Tool Co 5565 Venture Dr Unit C	Cleveland	OH	44130	**800-521-1078**	216-362-4230
Micro 100 Tool Corp 1410 E Pine Ave	Meridian	ID	83642	**800-421-8065**	208-888-7310
NED Corp 31 Town Forest Rd	Oxford	MA	01540	**800-343-6086**	
Niagara Cutter Inc 200 John James Audubon Pkwy	Amherst	NY	14228	**888-689-8400**	716-689-8400
North American Tool Corp 215 Elmwood Ave	South Beloit	IL	61080	**800-872-8277**	815-389-2300
Onsrud Cutter LP 800 Liberty Dr	Libertyville	IL	60048	**800-234-1560**	847-362-1560
OSG Tap & Die Inc 676 E Fullerton Ave	Glendale Heights	IL	60139	**800-837-2223**	630-790-1400
Phillips Corp 7390 Coca Cola Dr	Hanover	MD	21076	**800-878-4242**	410-564-2929
Powers Fasteners Inc Two Powers Ln	Brewster	NY	10509	**800-524-3244**	914-235-6300
Regal-Beloit Corp 200 State St	Beloit	WI	53511	**800-672-6495**	608-364-8800
NYSE: RBC					
Reiff & Nestor Co 50 Reiff St PO Box 147	Lykens	PA	17048	**800-521-3422**	717-453-7113
S-T Industries Inc 301 Armstrong Blvd N	Saint James	MN	56081	**800-326-2039**	507-375-3211
Scotchman Industries Inc 180 E Hwy 14	Philip	SD	57567	**800-843-8844**	605-859-2542
Spiralock Corp 25235 Dequindre Rd	Madison Heights	MI	48071	**800-521-2688**	248-543-7800
Star Cutter Co 23461 Industrial Pk Dr	Farmington	MI	48335	**877-635-3488**	248-474-8200
Starrett Webber Gage Div 24500 Detroit Rd	Cleveland	OH	44145	**800-255-3924**	440-835-0001
Stilson Products 15935 Sturgeon St	Roseville	MI	48066	**888-400-5978**	586-778-1100
Tapmatic Corp 802 S Clearwater Loop	Post Falls	ID	83854	**800-854-6019***	208-773-8048
*General					
Thread Check Inc 390 Oser Ave	Hauppauge	NY	11788	**800-767-7633**	631-231-1515
TM Smith Tool International Corp 360 Hubbard Ave	Mount Clemens	MI	48043	**800-521-4894**	586-468-1465
United Drill Bushing Corp 12200 Woodruff Ave	Downey	CA	90241	**800-486-3466**	562-803-1521
Viking Drill & Tool Inc 355 State St	Saint Paul	MN	55107	**800-328-4655**	651-227-8911
Walker Magnetics Group Inc 20 Rockdale St	Worcester	MA	01606	**800-962-4638**	508-853-3232
Walter USA Inc N22 W23855 Ridgeview Pkwy W	Waukesha	WI	53188	**800-945-5554**	
Zenith Cutter Co 5200 Zenith Pkwy	Loves Park	IL	61111	**800-223-5202**	815-282-5200

491 METALWORKING MACHINERY

SEE ALSO Rolling Mill Machinery

				Toll-Free	Phone
Armstrong Mfg Co 2700 SE Tacoma St	Portland	OR	97202	**800-426-6226**	503-228-8381
Bartell Machinery Systems LLC 6321 Elmer Hill Rd	Rome	NY	13440	**800-537-8473**	315-336-7600
Belvac Production Machinery Inc 237 Graves Mill Rd	Lynchburg	VA	24502	**800-423-5822**	434-239-0358
Eubanks Engineering Co 3022 Inland Empire Blvd	Ontario	CA	91764	**800-729-4208**	909-483-2456
Pannier Corp 207 Sandusky St	Pittsburgh	PA	15212	**877-726-6437**	412-323-4900
Pines Technology 30505 Clemens Rd	Westlake	OH	44145	**800-207-2840**	440-835-5553
Red Bud Industries 200 B & E Industrial Dr	Red Bud	IL	62278	**800-851-4612***	618-282-3801
*Cust Svc					
Rowe Machinery & Automation Inc 76 Hinckley Rd	Clinton	ME	04927	**800-247-2645**	207-426-2351
Sweed Machinery Inc 653 Second Ave PO Box 228	Gold Hill	OR	97525	**800-888-1352***	541-855-1512
*Sales					

492 METERS & OTHER COUNTING DEVICES

				Toll-Free	Phone
AMETEK Inc Dixson Div 287 27 Rd	Grand Junction	CO	81503	**888-302-0639**	970-242-8863
AMETEK Sensor Technology Drexelbrook Div 205 Keith Valley Rd	Horsham	PA	19044	**800-553-9092***	215-674-1234
*Cust Svc					
Auto Meter Products Inc 413 W Elm St	Sycamore	IL	60178	**866-248-6356**	815-895-8141
Badger Meter Inc 4545 W Brown Deer Rd	Milwaukee	WI	53223	**800-876-3837**	414-355-0400
NYSE: BMI					
Clark-Reliance Corp 16633 Foltz Pkwy	Strongsville	OH	44149	**800-238-4027**	440-572-1500
Danaher Controls 1675 Delany Rd	Gurnee	IL	60031	**800-873-8731**	847-662-2666
Duncan Solutions Inc 633 W Wisconsin Ave Ste 1600	Milwaukee	WI	53203	**888-993-8622**	
Electro-Sensors Inc 6111 Blue Cir Dr	Minnetonka	MN	55343	**800-328-6170**	952-930-0100
NASDAQ: ELSE					
Elster American Meter Co 2221 Industrial Rd	Nebraska City	NE	68410	**800-461-4076**	402-873-8200
Engineering Measurements Co (EMCO) 1150 Northpoint Blvd Ste C	Blythewood	SC	29016	**800-575-0394**	
Eugene Ernst Products Company Inc PO Box 925	Farmingdale	NJ	07727	**800-992-2843**	732-938-5641
Greenwald Industries 212 Middlesex Ave	Chester	CT	06412	**800-221-0982**	860-526-0800
Isspro Inc 2515 NE Riverside Way	Portland	OR	97211	**888-447-7776**	503-528-3400
Laser Technology Inc 7070 S Tucson Way	Englewood	CO	80112	**800-280-6113**	303-649-1000
Maxima Technologies Stewart Warner 1811 Rohrerstown Rd	Lancaster	PA	17601	**800-676-1837**	717-581-1000
PMP Corp 25 Security Dr	Avon	CT	06001	**800-243-6628***	860-677-9656
*Cust Svc					
POM Inc 200 S Elmira Ave PO Box 430	Russellville	AR	72802	**800-331-7275**	479-968-2880
Sparling Instruments Company Inc 4097 N Temple City Blvd	El Monte	CA	91731	**800-800-3569***	626-444-0571
*Sales					
Thomas G Faria Corp 385 Norwich-New London Tpke	Uncasville	CT	06382	**800-473-2742**	860-848-9271

493 MICROGRAPHICS PRODUCTS & SERVICES

				Toll-Free	Phone
BMI Imaging Systems 1115 E Arques Ave	Sunnyvale	CA	94085	**800-359-3456**	408-736-7444
Comstor Productivity Ctr Inc 2219 N Dickey Rd	Spokane	WA	99212	**800-776-2451**	509-534-5080
DPF Data Services Group Inc 1990 Swarthmore Ave	Lakewood	NJ	08701	**800-431-4416**	732-370-8840
DST Output 5220 Robert J Mathews Pkwy	El Dorado Hills	CA	95762	**800-441-7587**	916-939-4960
Eye Communication Systems Inc 455 E Industrial Dr	Hartland	WI	53029	**800-558-2153**	262-367-1360
HF Group Inc 203 W Artesia Blvd	Compton	CA	90220	**800-421-5000**	310-605-0755
Indus International Inc 340 S Oak St PO Box 890	West Salem	WI	54669	**800-843-9377**	608-786-0300

494   MILITARY BASES

SEE ALSO Coast Guard Installations

494-1   Air Force Bases

				Toll-Free	Phone
Cannon Air Force Base					
110 E Sextant Ave Ste 1150	Cannon AFB	NM	88103	877-283-3858	575-784-4131
Eielson Air Force Base					
354 Broadway St Unit 2B	Eielson AFB	AK	99702	800-538-6647	907-377-1110
Kirtland Air Force Base					
2000 Wyoming Blvd SE Ste A-1	Kirtland AFB	NM	87117	877-246-1453	505-846-5991
Laughlin Air Force Base					
561 Liberty Dr Ste 3	Laughlin AFB	TX	78843	866-966-1020	830-298-5988
Little Rock Air Force Base					
1250 Thomas Ave	Little Rock AFB	AR	72099	800-557-6815	501-987-1110
Luke Air Force Base					
14185 W Falcon St	Luke AFB	AZ	85309	800-321-1080	623-856-5853
Malmstrom Air Force Base					
7410 Flightline Dr Bldg 300	Malmstrom AFB	MT	59402	866-731-4633	406-731-1110
Maxwell Air Force Base					
55 Le May Plaza S	Maxwell AFB	AL	36112	877-353-6807	334-953-2014
McConnell Air Force Base					
57837 Coffeyville St Ste 271	McConnell AFB	KS	67221	877-272-7337	316-759-6100
Mountain Home Air Force Base					
366 Gunfighter Ave Ste 314	Mountain Home AFB	ID	83648	855-366-0140	208-828-6800
Seymour Johnson Air Force Base					
1510 Wright Bros Ave	Seymour Johnson AFB	NC	27531	800-525-0102	919-722-0027
Shaw Air Force Base					
517 Lance Ave Ste 106	Shaw AFB	SC	29152	800-235-7776	803-895-2019
Sheppard Air Force Base					
419 G Ave Ste 3	Sheppard AFB	TX	76311	877-676-1847	940-676-2511
Tyndall Air Force Base					
445 Suwannee Rd 101	Tyndall AFB	FL	32403	800-356-5273	850-283-1110
Vance Air Force Base					
246 Brown Pkwy	Vance AFB	OK	73705	866-966-1020	580-213-7476
Whiteman Air Force Base					
1081 Arnold Ave Bldg 59 Ste 104	Whiteman AFB	MO	65305	866-363-8667	660-687-6123

494-2   Army Bases

				Toll-Free	Phone
Fort Leonard Wood					
Bldg 744	Fort Leonard Wood	MO	65473	800-350-7746	573-596-0131
Fort Meade					
4550 Parade Field Ln Rm 102	Fort Meade	MD	20755	877-372-3337	301-677-1361
Fort Polk 2030 14th St	Fort Polk	LA	71459	800-752-4658	337-531-2911
Fort Richardson					
Richardson Dr Bldg 600	Fort Richardson	AK	99505	800-984-1517	907-384-0763
Fort Riley					
405 Pershing Ct	Fort Riley	KS	66442	800-273-8255	785-239-2022

494-3   Naval Installations

				Toll-Free	Phone
Naval Air Station Jacksonville					
6801 Roosevelt Blvd	Jacksonville	FL	32212	800-849-6024	904-542-2338
Naval Air Station Joint Reserve Base New Orleans					
301 Russell Ave	New Orleans	LA	70143	800-729-7327	504-678-3254
Naval Air Station Patuxent River					
22268 Cedar Point Road Bldg 409	Patuxent River	MD	20670	877-995-5247	301-342-3000
Naval Base San Diego					
3455 Senn Rd	San Diego	CA	92136	877-995-5247	619-556-1011
Naval Station Mayport					
PO Box 280032	Mayport	FL	32228	800-872-7245	904-270-5401
U.S. Fleet Forces Command					
1562 Mitscher Ave Ste 250	Norfolk	VA	23551	800-473-3549	757-836-3630

495   MILITARY SERVICE ACADEMIES

				Toll-Free	Phone
US Air Force Academy (USAFA)					
2304 Cadet Dr Ste 2300	Air Force Academy	CO	80840	800-443-9266	719-333-1110
US Naval Academy					
121 Blake Rd	Annapolis	MD	21402	888-249-7707*	410-293-1000
*Admissions					

496   MILLWORK

SEE ALSO Shutters - Window (All Types) ; Home Improvement Centers ; Lumber & Building Supplies ; Doors & Windows - Wood

				Toll-Free	Phone
Accent' Windows Inc					
14175 E 42nd Ave	Denver	CO	80239	888-284-3948	303-420-2002
Allen Millwork Inc					
6969 Fern Loop PO Box 6480	Shreveport	LA	71105	800-551-8737	318-629-5300
Anderson Wood Products Co					
1381 Beech St	Louisville	KY	40211	800-825-5591	502-778-5591
Anlin Industries					
1665 Tollhouse Rd	Clovis	CA	93611	800-287-7996	559-322-1531
Brockway-Smith Co (BWAY)					
146 Dascomb Rd	Andover	MA	01810	800-225-7912	978-475-7100
Cascade Wood Products Inc					
PO Box 2429	White City	OR	97503	800-423-3311	541-826-2911
Causeway Lumber Co					
3318 SW Second Ave	Fort Lauderdale	FL	33315	800-375-5050	954-763-1224
Central Woodwork Inc					
870 Keough Rd	Collierville	TN	38017	800-788-3775	901-363-4141
Commercial & Architectural Products Inc					
PO Box 250	Dover	OH	44622	800-377-1221	330-343-6621
Contact Industries Inc					
9200 SE Sunnybrook Blvd Ste 200	Clackamas	OR	97015	800-547-1038	503-228-7361
Cox Interior Inc					
1751 Old Columbia Rd	Campbellsville	KY	42718	800-733-1751	
Graves Lumber Co					
1315 S Cleveland-Massillon Rd	Copley	OH	44321	877-500-5515	330-666-1115
HB&G Inc PO Box 589	Troy	AL	36081	800-264-4424	334-566-5000
Horner Millwork Corp					
1255 Grand Army Hwy	Somerset	MA	02726	800-543-5403	508-679-6479
Huttig Bldg Products Inc (HBP)					
555 Maryville University Dr Ste 400	Saint Louis	MO	63141	800-325-4466	314-216-2600
OTC: HBPI					
Jeld-Wen Inc					
PO Box 1329	Klamath Falls	OR	97601	800-535-3936	
Lafayette Wood-Works Inc					
3004 Cameron St	Lafayette	LA	70506	800-960-3311	337-233-5250
Laflamme Doors & Windows Corp					
39 Industrielle	St. Apollinaire	QC	G0S2E0	800-463-1922	
Louisiana-Pacific Corp					
414 Union St Ste 2000	Nashville	TN	37219	888-820-0325	615-986-5600
NYSE: LPX					
Mann & Parker Lumber Company Inc, The					
335 N Constitution Ave	New Freedom	PA	17349	800-632-9098	717-235-4834
Menzner Lumber & Supply Co					
PO Box 217	Marathon	WI	54448	800-257-1284	
Milliken Millwork Inc					
6361 Sterling Dr N	Sterling Heights	MI	48312	800-686-9218	586-264-0950
New England Garage Door					
15 Campanelli Cir	Canton	MA	02021	800-676-7734	781-821-2737
Polaris Technologies Inc					
500 Victoria Rd	Austintown	OH	44515	800-783-2179	
Quanex Building Products					
2270 Woodale Dr	Mounds View	MN	55112	800-233-4383	763-231-4000
Randall Bros Inc					
665 Marietta St NW	Atlanta	GA	30313	800-476-4539*	404-892-6666
*Cust Svc					
Raynor Garage Doors					
1101 E River Rd	Dixon	IL	61021	800-472-9667	815-288-1431
Shuster's Bldg Components					
2920 Clay Pk	Irwin	PA	15642	800-676-0640	724-446-7000
Somerset Door & Column Co					
174 Sagamore St	Somerset	PA	15501	800-242-7916	814-444-9427
Southern Staircase Inc					
6025 Shiloh Rd Ste E	Alpharetta	GA	30005	800-874-8408	770-888-7333
Sundt Construction					
2620 S 55th St	Tempe	AZ	85282	800-280-3000	480-293-3000
Werzalit of America Inc					
40 Holly Ave	Bradford	PA	16701	800-999-3730	814-362-3881
Woodgrain Millworks Inc					
300 NW 16th St PO Box 566	Fruitland	ID	83619	800-452-3801	208-452-3801
Woodharbor Doors & Cabinetry Inc					
3277 Ninth St SW	Mason City	IA	50401	866-219-9786	641-423-0444
Young Mfg Company Inc					
521 S Main St PO Box 167	Beaver Dam	KY	42320	800-545-6595	270-274-3306

497   MINERAL PRODUCTS - NONMETALLIC

SEE ALSO Insulation & Acoustical Products

				Toll-Free	Phone
Big River Industries Inc					
900 Ashwood Pkwy Ste 500	Atlanta	GA	30338	800-342-5483	770-640-3008
Buffalo Crushed Stone Co Inc					
2544 Clinton St	Buffalo	NY	14224	800-543-3860	716-826-7310
Burgess Pigment Company Inc					
525 Beck Blvd PO Box 349	Sandersville	GA	31082	800-841-8999	478-552-2544
Ceradyne Inc					
3169 Redhill Ave	Costa Mesa	CA	92626	877-992-7749	714-549-0421
NYSE: MMM					
Crystex Composites LLC					
125 Clifton Blvd	Clifton	NJ	07011	800-638-8235	973-779-8866
Eagle-Picher Minerals Inc					
9785 Gateway Dr Ste 1000 PO Box 12130	Reno	NV	89521	800-228-3865*	775-824-7600
*Cust Svc					
Graphel Corp					
6115 Centre Pk Dr PO Box 369	West Chester	OH	45071	800-255-1104	513-779-6166
Graphite Sales Inc					
16710 W Pk Cir Dr	Chagrin Falls	OH	44023	800-321-4147	440-543-8221
Hill & Griffith Co					
1085 Summer St	Cincinnati	OH	45204	800-543-0425	513-921-1075
La Habra Products Inc					
4125 E La Palma Ave Ste 250	Anaheim	CA	92807	866-516-0061	714-778-2266
Miller & Co LLC					
9700 W Higgins Rd Ste 1000	Rosemont	IL	60018	800-727-9847	847-696-2400
Multicoat Corp					
23331 Antonio Pkwy	Rancho Santa Margarita	CA	92688	877-685-8426	949-888-7100
Oil-Dri Corp of America					
410 N Michigan Ave Ste 400	Chicago	IL	60611	800-645-3747	312-321-1515
NYSE: ODC					
Silbrico Corp					
6300 River Rd	Hodgkins	IL	60525	800-323-4287	708-354-3350
US Diamond Wheel Co					
101 Kendall Pt Dr	Oswego	IL	60543	800-223-0457	800-851-1095
USG Corp 550 W Adams St	Chicago	IL	60661	800-874-4968	312-436-4000
NYSE: USG					
Von Roll Isola USA					
200 Von Roll Dr	Schenectady	NY	12306	800-654-7652	518-344-7100

498 MINING - COAL

				Toll-Free	Phone
Alpha Natural Resources Inc					
1 Alpha Pl PO Box 16429	Bristol	VA	24209	**866-322-5742**	276-619-4410
OTC: ANR					
Cloud Peak Energy Inc (RTEA)					
505 S Gillette Ave PO Box 3009	Gillette	WY	82717	**866-470-4300**	307-687-6000
DH Blattner & Sons Inc					
392 County Rd 50	Avon	MN	56310	**800-877-2866**	320-356-7351
JM Huber Corp					
499 Thornall St 8th Fl	Edison	NJ	08837	**877-418-0038**	732-549-8600
Knight Hawk Coal LLC					
500 Cutler-Trico Rd	Percy	IL	62272	**855-611-2625**	618-426-3662
Natural Resource Partners LP					
601 Jefferson St Ste 3600	Houston	TX	77002	**888-334-7102**	713-751-7507
NYSE: NRP					
Peabody Energy Corp					
Peabody Plz 701 Market St	St. Louis	MO	63101	**866-470-4500**	314-342-3400
Westmoreland Coal Co					
9540 S Maroon Cir Ste 200	Englewood	CO	80112	**855-922-6463**	719-442-2600
NASDAQ: WLB					

499 MINING - METALS

				Toll-Free	Phone
Agnico-Eagle Mines Ltd					
145 King St E Ste 500	Toronto	ON	M5C2Y7	**888-822-6714**	416-947-1212
NYSE: AEM					
B2 Gold Corp					
595 Burrard St Ste 3100					
PO Box 49143	Vancouver	BC	V7X1J1	**800-316-8855**	604-681-8371
Badger Mining Corp					
409 S Church St PO Box 328	Berlin	WI	54923	**800-932-7263**	920-361-2388
Barrick Gold Corp					
TD Canada Trust Tower 161 Bay St					
PO Box 212	Toronto	ON	M5J2S1	**800-720-7415**	416-861-9911
NYSE: ABX					
Crystallex International Corp					
Eight King St E Ste 1201	Toronto	ON	M5C1B5	**800-738-1577**	416-203-2448
Eldorado Gold Corp					
550 Burrard St Ste 1188	Vanouver	BC	V6C2B5	**888-353-8166**	604-687-4018
NYSE: ELD					
First Quantum Minerals Ltd					
543 Granville St 8th Fl	Vancouver	BC	V6C1X8	**888-688-6577**	604-688-6577
TSE: FM					
Gold Reserve Inc					
926 W Sprague Ave Ste 200	Spokane	WA	99201	**800-625-9550**	509-623-1500
TSE: GRZ					
Goldcorp Inc					
666 Burrard St Ste 3400	Vancouver	BC	V6C2X8	**800-567-6223**	604-696-3000
NYSE: G					
Golden Star Resources Ltd					
10901 W Toller Dr Ste 300	Littleton	CO	80127	**800-553-8436**	303-830-9000
NYSE: GSS					
IAMGOLD Corp					
401 Bay St Ste 3200 PO Box 153	Toronto	ON	M5H2Y4	**888-464-9999**	416-360-4710
TSE: IMG					
IBC Advanced Alloys Corp					
570 Granville St Ste 1200	Vancouver	BC	V6C3P1	**800-373-3251**	604-685-6263
Kinross Gold Corp					
25 York St 17th Fl	Toronto	ON	M5J2V5	**866-561-3636**	416-365-5123
NYSE: KGC					
Materion Corp					
6070 Parkland Blvd	Mayfield Heights	OH	44124	**800-321-2076**	216-486-4200
NYSE: MTRN					
Meridian Gold Co					
9670 Gateway Dr Ste 200	Reno	NV	89521	**888-231-8191**	775-850-3777
NovaGold Resources Inc					
200 Grandville St Ste 2300					
PO Box 24	Vancouver	BC	V6C1S4	**866-699-6227**	604-669-6227
NYSE: NG					
Pacific Rim Mining Corp					
625 Howe St Ste 1050	Vancouver	BC	V6C2T6	**888-775-7097**	604-689-1976
OTC: PFRMF					
Rubicon Minerals Corp					
800 W Pender St Ste 1540	Vancouver	BC	V6C2V6	**866-365-4706**	604-623-3333
NYSE: RBY					
Sherritt International Corp					
1133 Yonge St	Toronto	ON	M4T2Y7	**800-704-6698**	416-924-4551
TSE: S					
Silver Standard Resources Inc					
999 W Hastings St Ste 1180	Vancouver	BC	V6C2W2	**888-338-0046**	604-689-3846
TSE: SSO					
Stratcor Inc					
1180 Omega Dr Ste 1180	Pittsburgh	PA	15205	**800-573-6052**	412-787-4500
Teck Cominco American Inc					
501 N Riverpoint Blvd Ste 300	Spokane	WA	99202	**888-767-7718**	509-747-6111
US Energy Corp					
877 N Eigth W	Riverton	WY	82501	**800-776-9271**	307-856-9271
NASDAQ: USEG					
Western Copper Corp					
1111 W Georgia St Ste 2050	Vancouver	BC	V6E4M3	**888-966-9995**	604-684-9497
Wharf Resources USA Inc					
10928 Wharf Rd	Lead	SD	57754	**800-567-6223**	605-584-1441

500 MINING - MINERALS

500-1 Chemical & Fertilizer Minerals Mining

				Toll-Free	Phone
American Borate Corp					
5700 Cleveland St Ste 420	Virginia Beach	VA	23462	**800-486-1072**	757-490-2242
New Riverside Ochre Co					
75 Old River Rd SE	Cartersville	GA	30121	**800-248-0176***	770-382-4568
*Orders					
Potash Corp					
1101 Skokie Blvd	Northbrook	IL	60062	**800-667-0403**	847-849-4200
Searles Valley Minerals					
9401 Indian Creek Pkwy Ste 1000	Overland Park	KS	66210	**800-637-2775**	913-344-9500
Solvay Chemicals Inc					
3333 Richmond Ave	Houston	TX	77098	**800-765-8292**	713-525-6800
United Salt Corp					
4800 San Felipe St	Houston	TX	77056	**800-554-8658**	713-877-2600

500-2 Clay, Ceramic, Refractory Minerals Mining

				Toll-Free	Phone
AMCOL International Corp					
2870 Forbs Ave	Hoffman Estates	IL	60192	**800-962-8586***	847-851-1500
NYSE: ACO ■ **General*					
Black Hills Bentonite LLC					
PO Box 9	Mills	WY	82644	**800-788-9443***	307-265-3740
*Orders					
Imerys USA Inc					
100 Mansell Ct E Ste 300	Roswell	GA	30076	**800-374-3224**	770-645-3300
Milwhite Inc					
5487 S Padre Island Hwy	Brownsville	TX	78521	**800-442-0082**	956-547-1970
Riverside Clay Co Inc					
201 Truss Ferry Rd	Pell City	AL	35128	**800-924-0637**	205-338-3346
Riverside Refractories Inc					
201 Truss Ferry Rd	Pell City	AL	35128	**800-924-0637**	205-338-3346
RT Vanderbilt Company Inc					
30 Winfield St	Norwalk	CT	06855	**800-243-6064***	203-853-1400
*Cust Svc					
US Silica Co					
106 Sand Mine Rd PO Box 187	Berkeley Springs	WV	25411	**800-243-7500**	304-258-2500
Wyo-Ben Inc					
1345 Discovery Dr	Billings	MT	59102	**800-548-7055***	406-652-6351
*Cust Svc					

500-3 Minerals Mining (Misc)

				Toll-Free	Phone
Harborlite					
130 Castilian Dr	Santa Barbara	CA	93117	**800-893-4445**	805-562-0200
ILC Resources					
3301 106th Cir	Urbandale	IA	50322	**800-247-2133**	515-243-8106
RT Vanderbilt Company Inc					
30 Winfield St	Norwalk	CT	06855	**800-243-6064***	203-853-1400
*Cust Svc					
Stornoway Diamond Corp					
980 W First St Ste 118	N.Vancouver	BC	V7P3N4	**877-331-2232**	604-983-7750
TSE: SWY					
Vanderbilt Minerals Corp					
30 Winfield St	Norwalk	CT	06855	**800-243-6064**	203-853-1400
WGI Heavy Minerals Inc					
810 E Sherman Ave	Coeur d'Alene	ID	83814	**888-542-7638**	208-666-6000
TSE: WG					

500-4 Sand & Gravel Pits

				Toll-Free	Phone
Best Sand Corp					
11830 Ravenna Rd PO Box 87	Chardon	OH	44024	**800-237-4986**	440-285-3132
Edward C Levy Co					
9300 Dix Ave	Dearborn	MI	48120	**877-938-0007**	313-843-7200
Fisher Sand & Gravel Co					
3948 First ST SW	Underwood	ND	58576	**800-932-8740**	701-442-5600
Hills Materials Co					
3975 Sturgis Rd PO Box 2320	Rapid City	SD	57709	**800-325-7056**	605-394-3300
Janesville Sand & Gravel Co (JSG)					
1110 Harding St	Janesville	WI	53547	**800-955-7702**	608-754-7701
LG Everist Inc					
300 S Phillips Ave Ste 200	Sioux Falls	SD	57117	**800-843-7992**	605-334-5000
Mark Sand & Gravel Co					
525 Kennedy Pk Rd PO Box 458	Fergus Falls	MN	56537	**800-427-8316**	218-736-7523
Pike Industries Inc					
3 Eastgate Pk Rd	Belmont	NH	03220	**800-283-0803**	603-527-5100
Pounding Mill Quarry Corp					
171 St Clair S Crossing	Bluefield	VA	24605	**888-661-7625**	276-326-1145
Unimin 258 Elm St	New Canaan	CT	06840	**800-223-2236**	203-966-8880
US Silica Co					
106 Sand Mine Rd PO Box 187	Berkeley Springs	WV	25411	**800-243-7500**	304-258-2500

500-5 Stone Quarries - Crushed & Broken Stone

				Toll-Free	Phone
Edward C Levy Co					
9300 Dix Ave	Dearborn	MI	48120	**877-938-0007**	313-843-7200
Harney Rock & Paving Co					
457 S Date Ave	Burns	OR	97720	**888-298-2681**	541-573-7855

				Toll-Free	Phone
Hills Materials Co					
3975 Sturgis Rd PO Box 2320	Rapid City	SD	57709	**800-325-7056**	605-394-3300
Hunt Midwest Enterprises Inc					
8300 NE Underground Dr	Kansas City	MO	64161	**800-551-6877**	816-455-2500
Hunt Midwest Mining Inc					
8300 NE Underground Dr	Kansas City	MO	64161	**800-551-6877**	816-455-2500
LG Everist Inc					
300 S Phillips Ave Ste 200	Sioux Falls	SD	57117	**800-843-7992**	605-334-5000
Pike Industries Inc					
3 Eastgate Pk Rd	Belmont	NH	03220	**800-283-0803**	603-527-5100
Pounding Mill Quarry Corp					
171 St Clair S Crossing	Bluefield	VA	24605	**888-661-7625**	276-326-1145
Texas Crushed Stone Co					
5300 S IH-35 PO Box 1000	Georgetown	TX	78627	**800-772-8272**	512-930-0106
Tilcon NY Inc					
162 Old Mill Rd	West Nyack	NY	10994	**800-872-7762**	845-358-4500
Vulcan Materials Co					
1200 Urban Ctr Dr PO Box 385014	Birmingham	AL	35238	**800-615-4331**	205-298-3000
NYSE: VMC					
Vulcan Materials Company Western Div					
3200 San Fernando Rd	Los Angeles	CA	90065	**800-615-4331**	323-258-2777
NYSE: VMC					

500-6 Stone Quarries - Dimension Stone

				Toll-Free	Phone
American Clay Enterprises LLC					
2418 Second St SW	Albuquerque	NM	87102	**866-404-1634**	505-243-5300
Fletcher Granite Company Inc					
534 Groton Rd	Westford	MA	01886	**800-253-8168**	978-251-4031
Pounding Mill Quarry Corp					
171 St Clair S Crossing	Bluefield	VA	24605	**888-661-7625**	276-326-1145

501   MISSILES, SPACE VEHICLES, PARTS

SEE ALSO

				Toll-Free	Phone
Esterline Mason					
13955 Balboa Blvd	Sylmar	CA	91342	**800-232-7700**	818-361-3366
Hi-Shear Technology Corp (HSTC)					
24225 Garnier St	Torrance	CA	90505	**800-733-0321***	310-784-2100
*Mktg					
HITCO Carbon Composites Inc					
1600 W 135th St	Gardena	CA	90249	**800-421-5444**	310-527-0700
International Launch Services (ILS)					
1875 Explorer St Ste 700	Reston	VA	20190	**800-852-4980**	571-633-7400
Lockheed Martin Corp					
6801 Rockledge Dr	Bethesda	MD	20817	**866-562-2363**	301-897-6000
NYSE: LMT					
Lockheed Martin Space Systems Co Michoud Operations					
13800 Old Gentilly Rd	New Orleans	LA	70129	**866-562-2363**	504-257-3311

502   MOBILE HOMES & BUILDINGS

				Toll-Free	Phone
American Homestar Corp					
2450 S Shore Blvd Ste 300	League City	TX	77573	**800-313-5570**	281-334-9700
Cavalier Homes Inc					
32 Wilson Blvd Ste 100	Addison	AL	35540	**800-743-2284**	
Cavco Industries Inc					
1001 N Central Ave Eighth Fl	Phoenix	AZ	85004	**800-790-9111**	602-256-6263
NASDAQ: CVCO					
Destiny Industries LLC					
250 R W Bryant Rd	Moultrie	GA	31788	**866-782-6600**	
Fleetwood Homes of Idaho Inc					
2611 E Comstock Ave	Nampa	ID	83687	**800-334-8958**	208-466-2438
Franklin Homes Inc					
10655 Hwy 43	Russellville	AL	35653	**800-332-4511**	
Giles Industries Inc					
405 S Broad St	New Tazewell	TN	37825	**800-844-4537**	423-626-7243
Hometown America LLC					
150 N Wacker Dr Ste 2800	Chicago	IL	60606	**888-735-4310**	312-604-7500
Horton Homes Inc					
101 Industrial Blvd	Eatonton	GA	31024	**800-657-4000**	706-485-8506
Jacobsen Homes					
600 Packard Ct	Safety Harbor	FL	34695	**800-843-1559**	727-726-1138
Luxury Retreats International Inc					
5530 St Patrick St Ste 2210	Montreal	QC	H4E1A8	**877-993-0100**	514-393-8844
Manufactured Housing Enterprises Inc					
09302 St Rt 6 Rt 6	Bryan	OH	43506	**800-821-0220**	419-636-4511
McGrath RentCorp					
5700 Las Positas Rd	Livermore	CA	94551	**800-962-4284**	925-606-9200
NASDAQ: MGRC					
Nashua Homes of Idaho Inc					
PO Box 170008	Boise	ID	83717	**855-766-0222**	208-345-0222
Nobility Homes Inc					
3741 SW Seventh St	Ocala	FL	34474	**800-476-6624**	352-732-5157
OTC: NOBH					
R-Anell Custom Homes Inc					
235 Anthony Grave Rd	Crouse	NC	28033	**800-951-5511***	704-483-5511
*Cust Svc					
Ritz-Craft Corp of Pennsylvania Inc					
15 Industrial Pk Rd	Mifflinburg	PA	17844	**800-326-9836**	570-966-1053
River Birch Homes Inc					
400 River Birch Dr	Hackleburg	AL	35564	**888-760-3314**	205-935-1997
Satellite Industries Inc					
2530 Xenium Ln N	Minneapolis	MN	55441	**800-328-3332**	
Skyline Corp					
2520 By-Pass Rd	Elkhart	IN	46514	**800-348-7469**	574-294-6521
NYSE: SKY					
Wick Buildings					
405 Walter Rd	Mazomanie	WI	53560	**855-438-9425**	

503   MODELLING AGENCIES

				Toll-Free	Phone
Women Management					
199 Lafayette St 7th Fl	New York	NY	10012	**800-838-3006**	212-334-7480

504   MODELING SCHOOLS

				Toll-Free	Phone
Frederick Taylor University					
346 Rheem Blvd Ste 203	Moraga	CA	94556	**800-988-4622**	

505   MOPS, SPONGES, WIPING CLOTHS

SEE ALSO Brushes & Brooms ; Cleaning Products

				Toll-Free	Phone
A&B Wiper Supply Inc					
5601 Paschall Ave	Philadelphia	PA	19143	**800-333-7247**	215-482-6100
Abco Cleaning Products					
6800 NW 36th Ave	Miami	FL	33147	**888-694-2226**	305-694-2226
Bro-Tex Inc					
800 Hampden Ave	Saint Paul	MN	55114	**800-328-2282**	651-645-5721
Butler Home Products LLC					
237 Cedar Hill St	Marlborough	MA	01752	**888-318-8521**	508-597-8000
Continental Manufacturing Co					
305 Rock Industrial Pk Dr	Bridgeton	MO	63044	**800-325-1051**	314-656-4301
Disco Inc 1895 Brannan Rd	McDonough	GA	30253	**800-325-1051**	770-474-7575
Ettore Products Co					
2100 N Loop Rd	Alameda	CA	94502	**800-438-8673**	510-748-4130
Golden Star Inc					
4770 N Belleview Ave Ste 209	Kansas City	MO	64116	**800-821-2792**	816-842-0233
L C Industries					
1 Signature Dr	Hazlehurst	MS	39083	**877-524-4722**	601-894-1771
Tranzonic Cos					
26301 Curtiss Wright Pkwy Ste 200	Cleveland	OH	44143	**800-553-7979**	216-535-4300
United Textile Company Inc					
751-143rd Ave	San Leandro	CA	94578	**800-233-0077***	510-276-2288
*General					
Wipe-Tex International Corp					
110 E 153rd St	Bronx	NY	10451	**800-643-9607**	718-665-0787

506   MORTGAGE LENDERS & LOAN BROKERS

SEE ALSO Banks - Commercial & Savings

				Toll-Free	Phone
AAA Financial Corp					
4613 N University Dr	Coral Springs	FL	33065	**800-881-2530**	954-344-2530
AMS Servicing LLC					
3374 Walden Ave Ste 120	Depew	NY	14043	**866-919-5608**	
Ascentium Capital LLC					
23970 Hwy 59 N	Kingwood	TX	77339	**866-722-8500**	
BRT Realty Trust					
60 Cutter Mill Rd Ste 303	Great Neck	NY	11021	**800-450-5816**	516-466-3100
NYSE: BRT					
CitiMortgage Inc					
1000 Technology Dr	O'Fallon	MO	63368	**800-283-7918***	
*Cust Svc					
Dominion Lending Centres Inc					
2215 Coquitlam Ave	Port Coquitlam	BC	V3B1J6	**866-928-6810**	
EverHome Mortgage Co					
301 W Bay St	Jacksonville	FL	32202	**800-669-9721***	
*Cust Svc					
Fannie Mae					
3900 Wisconsin Ave NW	Washington	DC	20016	**800-732-6643**	202-752-7000
OTC: FNMA					
First Eastern Mortgage Corp					
100 Brickstone Sq	Andover	MA	01810	**800-777-2240**	978-749-3100
First Equity Mortgage Bankers					
9300 S Dadeland Blvd Ste 500	Miami	FL	33156	**800-973-3654**	305-666-3333
Forest City Residential Management Inc					
50 Public Sq Ste 1515	Cleveland	OH	44113	**800-750-0750**	216-416-3906
Freddie Mac					
8200 Jones Branch Dr	McLean	VA	22102	**800-424-5401**	703-903-2000
North Central Region					
333 W Wacker Dr Ste 2500	Chicago	IL	60606	**800-373-3343**	312-407-7400
Northeast Region					
8200 Jones Branch Dr	McLean	VA	22102	**800-373-3343**	703-903-2000
Southeast/Southwest Region					
2300 Windy Ridge Pkwy Ste 200N	Atlanta	GA	30339	**800-373-3343**	770-857-8800
George Mason Mortgage Corp					
4100 Monu Crnr Dr Ste 100	Fairfax	VA	22030	**800-867-6859**	703-273-2600
Green Tree Servicing LLC					
345 St Peter St	Saint Paul	MN	55102	**800-643-0202**	800-423-9527
Guild Mortgage Co					
5898 Copley Dr Fourth & Fifth Fl	San Diego	CA	92111	**800-365-4441**	
HomeSteps 500 Plano Pkwy	Carrollton	TX	75010	**800-972-7555**	
HSBC Bank USA 2929 Walden Ave	Depew	NY	14043	**800-338-4626**	
Huntington Mortgage Co					
7575 Huntington Pk Dr	Columbus	OH	43235	**800-323-4695**	614-480-6505
Inland Mortgage Corp					
2901 Butterfield Rd	Oak Brook	IL	60523	**800-826-8228**	630-218-8000
LendingTree Inc					
11115 Rushmore Dr	Charlotte	NC	28277	**800-555-8733**	704-541-5351
Lion Inc					
4700 42nd Ave SW Ste 430	Seattle	WA	98116	**800-546-6463**	206-577-1440
loanDepot					
26642 Towne Centre Dr	Foothill Ranch	CA	92610	**888-337-6888**	
Midland Mortgage Co					
PO Box 26648	Oklahoma City	OK	73126	**800-654-4566**	
MMA Capital Management LLC (MuniMae)					
621 E Pratt St Ste 600	Baltimore	MD	21202	**855-650-6932**	443-263-2900
OTC: MMAB					

				Toll-Free	Phone
Mortgage Investors Group					
8320 E Walker Springs Ln	Knoxville	TN	37923	**800-489-8910**	865-691-8910
Mortgage Resources Inc (MRI)					
425 S Woods Mill Rd Ste 100	Chesterfield	MO	63017	**800-965-9910**	314-576-5577
National Rural Utilities Co-op Finance Corp					
2201 Co-op Way	Herndon	VA	20171	**800-424-2954**	703-709-6700
PHH Mortgage Corp					
3000 Leadenhall Rd	Mount Laurel	NJ	08054	**800-210-8849**	
Plaza Home Mortgage Inc					
5090 Shoreham Pl Ste 206	San Diego	CA	92122	**866-260-2529**	858-346-1208
R-B Financial-mortgages Inc					
44028 Mound Rd Ste 3.	Sterling Heights	MI	48314	**800-566-4663***	586-254-8435
*General					
Redwood Trust Inc					
One Belvedere Pl Ste 300	Mill Valley	CA	94941	**866-269-4976**	415-389-7373
NYSE: RWT					
Regions Mortgage Inc					
215 Forrest St	Hattiesburg	MS	39401	**800-986-2462**	
Residential Mortgage LLC					
100 Calais Dr	Anchorage	AK	99503	**888-357-2707**	907-222-8800
Safeguard Properties Inc					
7887 Safeguard Cir	Valley View	OH	44125	**800-852-8306**	216-739-2900
SunTrust Mortgage Inc					
1001 Semmes Ave	Richmond	VA	23224	**800-634-7928**	
Truwest Credit Union					
PO Box 3489	Scottsdale	AZ	85271	**855-878-9378**	480-441-5900
Universal American Mortgage Co					
700 NW 107th Ave 3rd Fl	Miami	FL	33172	**800-741-8262**	
Universal Lending Corp (ULC)					
6775 E Evans Ave	Denver	CO	80224	**800-758-4063**	
Vanderbilt Mortgage & Finance Inc					
500 Alcoa Trl	Maryville	TN	37804	**800-970-7250**	
Wells Fargo Home Mortgage					
2840 Ingersoll Ave	Des Moines	IA	50312	**800-869-3557**	515-237-5196

507 MORTUARY, CREMATORY, CEMETERY PRODUCTS & SERVICES

				Toll-Free	Phone
AJ Desmond & Sons Funeral Directors					
2600 Crooks Rd	Troy	MI	48084	**800-210-7135**	248-362-2500
Baue Funeral Homes					
620 Jefferson St	Saint Charles	MO	63301	**888-724-0073**	
Carriage Services Inc					
3040 Post Oak Blvd Ste 300	Houston	TX	77056	**866-332-8400**	713-332-8400
NYSE: CSV					
Church & Chapel Metal Arts Inc					
2616 W Grand Ave	Chicago	IL	60612	**800-992-1234**	
Dignity Memorial					
1929 Allen Pkwy	Houston	TX	77019	**800-894-2024**	713-522-5141
Forest Lawn Memorial-Parks & Mortuaries					
1712 S Glendale Ave	Glendale	CA	91205	**800-204-3131**	323-254-3131
Neptune Society					
4312 Woodman Ave Third Fl	Sherman Oaks	CA	91423	**888-637-8863**	
Spring Grove Cemetery					
4521 Spring Grove Ave	Cincinnati	OH	45232	**888-853-2230**	513-681-7526
Stewart Enterprises Inc					
1333 S Clearview Pkwy	New Orleans	LA	70121	**877-239-3264**	713-522-5141
NASDAQ: STEI					

508 MOTION PICTURE DISTRIBUTION & RELATED SERVICES

				Toll-Free	Phone
Baker & Taylor Inc					
2550 W Tyvola Rd Ste 300	Charlotte	NC	28217	**800-775-1800**	
Crown Media Holdings Inc					
12700 Ventura Blvd Ste 200	Studio City	CA	91604	**800-479-7328**	818-755-2400
NASDAQ: CRWN					
Extreme Reach Inc					
75 2nd Ave Ste 720	Needham	MA	02494	**888-326-8733**	781-577-2016
NASDAQ: DGIT					
Facets Multimedia Inc					
1517 W Fullerton Ave	Chicago	IL	60614	**800-331-6197***	773-281-9075
*Cust Svc					
First Run Features					
630 Ninth Ave Ste 1213	New York	NY	10036	**800-229-8575**	212-243-0600
Ingram Entertainment Inc					
2 Ingram Blvd	La Vergne	TN	37089	**800-621-1333**	615-287-4000
Insight Media					
2162 Broadway	New York	NY	10024	**800-233-9910**	212-721-6316
Kino International Corp					
333 W 39th St Rm 503	New York	NY	10018	**800-562-3330**	212-629-6880
Kultur International Films Ltd					
PO Box 755	Forked River	NJ	08731	**888-329-2580**	
MPI Media Group					
16101 108th Ave	Orland Park	IL	60467	**800-323-0442**	708-460-0555
Sony Pictures Entertainment Inc					
10202 W Washington Blvd	Culver City	CA	90232	**855-327-7669**	310-244-4000
Twentieth Century Fox Home Entertainment Inc					
2121 Ave of the Stars Suite 100	Los Angeles	CA	90067	**877-369-7867**	310-369-3900
Warner Bros Entertainment Inc					
4000 Warner Blvd	Burbank	CA	91522	**800-778-7879**	818-954-1853

509 MOTION PICTURE PRE- & POST-PRODUCTION SERVICES

				Toll-Free	Phone
Crossman Post Production LLC					
35 Lone Hollow	Sandy	UT	84092	**888-553-1958**	801-553-1958
Go Edit Inc					
5614 Cahuenga Blvd	North Hollywood	CA	91601	**800-833-9200**	818-284-6260
Raleigh Studios Worldwide					
5300 Melrose Ave	Hollywood	CA	90038	**888-960-3456**	323-466-3111

510 MOTION PICTURE PRODUCTION - SPECIAL INTEREST

SEE ALSO Motion Picture & Television Production ; Animation Companies

				Toll-Free	Phone
Active Parenting Publishers					
1955 Vaughn Rd Ste 108	Kennesaw	GA	30144	**800-825-0060**	770-429-0565
American Educational Products Inc					
401 Hickory St PO Box 2121	Fort Collins	CO	80522	**800-289-9299**	970-484-7445
Coastal Training Technologies Corp					
500 Studio Dr	Virginia Beach	VA	23452	**866-333-6888**	757-498-9014
CRM Learning					
2218 Faraday Ave Ste 110	Carlsbad	CA	92008	**800-421-0833**	760-431-9800
Hammond Communications Group Inc					
173 Trade St	Lexington	KY	40511	**888-424-1878**	859-254-1878
Intaglio LLC					
5809 Cross Roads Commerce Pkwy Ste 200	Grand Rapids	MI	49519	**800-632-9153**	616-243-3300
Keystone Learning Systems LLC					
6030 Daybreak Cir Ste A150 116	Clarksville	MD	21029	**800-949-5590**	410-800-4000
Kultur International Films Ltd					
PO Box 755	Forked River	NJ	08731	**888-329-2580**	
Learning Communications LLC					
5520 Trabuco Rd	Irvine	CA	92620	**800-622-3610**	
Medcom Trainex					
6060 Phyllis Dr	Cypress	CA	90630	**800-877-1443***	
*Cust Svc					
Nightingale-Conant Corp					
6245 W Howard St	Niles	IL	60714	**800-557-1660***	
*Cust Svc					
PADI Americas					
30151 Tomas St	Rancho Santa Margarita	CA	92688	**888-725-4801**	949-858-7234

511 MOTION PICTURE & TELEVISION PRODUCTION

SEE ALSO Motion Picture Production - Special Interest ; Animation Companies

				Toll-Free	Phone
Adconion Media Group Ltd					
950 Tower Ln	Santa Monica	CA	94404	**800-542-2811**	650-802-8871
Adm Productions Inc					
40 Seaview Blvd	Port Washington	NY	11050	**800-236-3425**	516-484-6900
Bioquant Image Analysis Corp					
5611 Ohio Ave	Nashville	TN	37209	**800-221-0549**	615-350-7866
Bullfrog Films Inc					
372 Dautrich Rd	Reading	PA	19606	**800-543-3764**	610-779-8226
Cev Multimedia Ltd					
1020 SE Loop 289	Lubbock	TX	79404	**877-610-5017**	806-745-8820
CGI Communications Inc					
130 E Main St Ste 800	Rochester	NY	14604	**800-398-3029**	585-427-0020
Cintrex Audio Visual					
656 Axminister Dr	Fenton	MO	63026	**800-325-9541**	636-343-0178
Columbia TriStar Motion Picture Group					
10202 W Washington Blvd	Culver City	CA	90232	**855-327-7669**	310-244-4000
Eastco Multi Media Solutions Inc					
3646 California Rd	Orchard Park	NY	14127	**800-365-8273**	716-662-0536
High Speed Productions Inc					
1303 Underwood Ave	San Francisco	CA	94124	**888-520-9099**	415-822-3083
Lions Gate Entertainment Corp Lions Gate Television Div					
2700 Colorado Ave Ste 200	Santa Monica	CA	90404	**800-322-2885**	310-449-9200
NBA Entertainment					
450 Harmon Meadow Blvd	Secaucus	NJ	07094	**866-648-4668**	201-865-1500
Pacific Title Archives					
10717 Vanowen St	North Hollywood	CA	91605	**800-968-9111**	818-760-4223
PayReel Inc					
24928 Genesee Trl Rd	Golden	CO	80401	**800-352-7397**	303-526-4900
Sony Pictures Entertainment Inc					
10202 W Washington Blvd	Culver City	CA	90232	**855-327-7669**	310-244-4000
Sony Pictures Television					
10202 W Washington Blvd	Culver City	CA	90232	**888-476-6972**	310-244-4000
Swank Motion Pictures Inc					
10795 Watson Rd	St Louis	MO	63127	**888-248-8757**	314-984-6000
Video Symphony Entertraining Inc					
266 E Magnolia Blvd	Burbank	CA	91502	**888-370-7589**	818-557-6500
Vision Global AR Ltee					
80, Queen St Ste 301	Montreal	QC	H3C2N5	**800-667-7690**	514-879-0020
Warner Bros Entertainment Inc					
4000 Warner Blvd	Burbank	CA	91522	**800-778-7879**	818-954-1853

MOTION PICTURE THEATERS

SEE Theaters - Motion Picture

512 MOTOR SPEEDWAYS

				Toll-Free	Phone
Atlanta Motor Speedway					
PO Box 500	Hampton	GA	30228	**877-926-7849**	770-946-4211
Auto Club Speedway					
9300 Cherry Ave	Fontana	CA	92335	**800-944-7223**	909-429-5000
Bandimere Speedway					
3051 S Rooney Rd	Morrison	CO	80465	**800-664-8946**	303-697-6001
Brainerd International Raceway					
5523 Birchdale Rd	Brainerd	MN	56401	**866-444-4455**	218-824-7223
Bristol Motor Speedway					
151 Speedway Blvd	Bristol	TN	37620	**866-415-4158**	423-989-6933
Darlington Raceway					
1301 Harry Bird Hwy	Darlington	SC	29532	**866-459-7223**	
Heartland Park Topeka					
7530 SW Topeka Blvd	Topeka	KS	66619	**800-437-2237**	785-862-4781
Hickory Motor Speedway					
3130 Hwy 70 SE	Newton	NC	28658	**800-843-8725**	828-464-3655

				Toll-Free	Phone
Holland NASCAR Motorsports Complex					
11586 Holland Glenwood Rd	Holland	NY	14080	**866-655-0257**	716-537-2272
Kentucky Speedway					
1 Speedway Blvd	Sparta	KY	41086	**888-652-7223***	859-567-3400
*Resv					
Las Vegas Motor Speedway					
7000 Las Vegas Blvd N	Las Vegas	NV	89115	**800-644-4444**	702-644-4444
Lime Rock Park					
60 White Hollow Rd	Lakeville	CT	06039	**800-722-3577**	860-435-5000
Los Angeles County Fairplex					
1101 W McKinley Ave	Pomona	CA	91768	**877-859-9909**	909-623-3111
Maple Grove Raceway					
30 Stauffer Pk Ln	Mohnton	PA	19540	**877-814-2538**	610-856-7812
Michigan International Speedway					
12626 US 12	Brooklyn	MI	49230	**800-354-1010**	517-592-6666
Mid-Ohio Sports Car Course					
7721 Steam Corners Rd PO Box 3108	Lexington	OH	44904	**800-643-6446**	419-884-4000
Ocean Speedway Inc					
8070 Soquel Dr Ste 120	Aptos	CA	95003	**800-925-9925**	831-662-9466
Pocono Raceway					
Long Pond Rd PO Box 500	Long Pond	PA	18334	**800-722-3929**	570-646-2300
Road America					
N 7390 Hwy 67	Elkhart Lake	WI	53020	**800-365-7223**	920-892-4576
Road Atlanta Raceway					
5300 Winder Hwy	Braselton	GA	30517	**800-849-7223**	770-967-6143
Sebring International Raceway					
113 Midway Dr	Sebring	FL	33870	**800-626-7223**	863-655-1442
Sonoma Raceway					
Hwy S 37 & 121	Sonoma	CA	95476	**800-870-7223**	707-938-8448
South Boston Speedway					
1188 James D Hagood Hwy					
PO Box 1066	South Boston	VA	24592	**877-440-1540**	434-572-4947
Summit Motorsports Park					
1300 Ohio 18	Norwalk	OH	44857	**800-729-6455**	419-668-5555
Texas Motorplex					
7500 W Hwy 287	Ennis	TX	75119	**800-668-6775**	972-878-2641
Volusia Speedway Park					
1500 W State Rd	De Leon Springs	FL	32130	**800-275-4279**	386-985-4402

513 MOTOR VEHICLES - COMMERCIAL & SPECIAL PURPOSE

SEE ALSO Snowmobiles ; Motorcycles & Motorcycle Parts & Accessories ; All-Terrain Vehicles ; Automobiles - Mfr ; Campers, Travel Trailers, Motor Homes

				Toll-Free	Phone
Allied Body Works Inc					
625 S 96th St	Seattle	WA	98108	**800-733-7450***	206-763-7811
*General					
Auto Crane Co PO Box 580697	Tulsa	OK	74158	**888-848-5445**	918-836-0463
Auto Truck Inc					
1420 Brewster Creek Blvd	Bartlett	IL	60103	**877-284-4440**	630-860-5600
Bianchi Motors Inc					
8430 Peach St PO Box 3086	Erie	PA	16509	**866-979-8132**	
Carnegie Body Co					
9500 Brookpark Rd	Cleveland	OH	44129	**800-362-1989**	216-749-5000
Champion Bus Inc					
331 Graham Rd	Imlay City	MI	48444	**800-776-4943**	810-724-6474
Coach & Equipment Manufacturing Corp					
130 Horizon Pk Dr PO Box 36	Penn Yan	NY	14527	**800-724-8464**	
Columbia ParCar Corp					
1115 Commercial Ave	Reedsburg	WI	53959	**800-222-4653**	608-524-8888
Curtis Industries LLC					
111 Higgins St	Worcester	MA	01606	**800-343-7676**	
Dealers Truck Equipment Co					
2460 Midway St	Shreveport	LA	71108	**800-259-7569**	318-635-7567
Diamond Coach Corp					
2300 W Fourth St PO Box 489	Oswego	KS	67356	**800-442-4645**	620-795-2191
Dick Gores Rv World					
14590 Duval Pl W	Jacksonville	FL	32218	**800-635-7008**	904-741-5100
Douglass Truck Bodies Inc					
231 21st St	Bakersfield	CA	93301	**800-635-7641**	661-327-0258
E-Z-GO					
1451 Marvin Griffin Rd	Augusta	GA	30906	**800-241-5855**	
Fleet Engineers Inc					
1800 E Keating Ave	Muskegon	MI	49442	**800-333-7890***	231-777-2537
*Cust Svc					
Fleet Equipment Corp					
567 Commerce St	Franklin Lakes	NJ	07417	**800-631-0873**	201-337-3294
Fontaine Modification Co					
9827 Mt Holly Rd	Charlotte	NC	28214	**800-366-8246**	704-391-1355
Fontaine Truck Equipment Co					
7574 Commerce Cir	Trussville	AL	35173	**800-874-9780**	205-661-4900
Ford of Ocala Inc					
2816 NW Pine Ave	Ocala	FL	34475	**888-255-1788**	352-732-4800
General Body Manufacturing Co					
7110 Jensen Dr	Houston	TX	77093	**800-395-8585**	713-692-5177
Gillig Corp					
25800 Clawiter Rd	Hayward	CA	94545	**800-735-1500**	510-785-1500
Gowans-Knight Co Inc					
49 Knight St	Watertown	CT	06795	**800-352-4871**	860-274-8801
Graham Cadillac					
1515 W Fourth St	Mansfield	OH	44906	**866-472-4261**	
Hackney & Sons Inc					
911 W 5th St PO Box 880	Washington	NC	27889	**800-763-0700**	252-946-6521
Heil Environmental Ltd					
2030 Hamilton Pl Blvd Ste 200	Chattanooga	TN	37421	**866-367-4345**	423-899-9100
Hercules Manufacturing Co					
800 Bob Posey St	Henderson	KY	42420	**800-633-3031**	270-826-9501
IC Bus LLC					
4201 Winfield Rd	Warrenville	IL	60555	**800-892-7761**	630-753-5000
Johnson Refrigerated Truck Bodies					
215 E Allen St	Rice Lake	WI	54868	**800-922-8360***	715-234-7071
*Sales					
Joyce Koons Buick Gmc					
10660 Automotive Dr	Manassas	VA	20109	**866-224-9293**	703-368-9100
Kidron Inc 13442 Emerson Rd	Kidron	OH	44636	**800-321-5421**	330-857-3011

				Toll-Free	Phone
Knapheide Mfg Co					
1848 Westphalia Strasse PO Box 7140	Quincy	IL	62305	**855-264-4300**	217-222-7131
Labrie Environmental Group					
175 du Pont	Saint-Nicolas	QC	G7A2T3	**800-463-6638**	418-831-8250
Leson Chevrolet Co Inc					
1501 Westbank Express	Harvey	LA	70058	**877-496-2420**	504-366-4381
Liberty Toyota Scion					
4397 Rt 130 S	Burlington	NJ	08016	**888-809-7798**	609-386-6300
Lodal Inc					
620 N Hooper St PO Box 2315	Kingsford	MI	49802	**800-435-3500**	906-779-1700
Luther Brookdale Chevrolet					
6701 Brooklyn Blvd	Brooklyn Center	MN	55429	**800-716-1271**	
LZ Truck Equipment Inc					
1881 Rice St	Saint Paul	MN	55113	**800-247-1082**	651-488-2571
M. H. Eby Inc PO Box 127	Blue Ball	PA	17506	**800-292-4752**	717-354-4971
Matt Castrucci Auto Mall of Dayton					
3013 Mall Pk Dr	Dayton	OH	45459	**855-204-5293**	513-248-3431
Mc-Coy-Mills					
700 W Commonwealth	Fullerton	CA	92832	**888-640-9266***	888-434-3145
*Sales					
McDaniel Motor Co					
1111 Mt Vernon Ave	Marion	OH	43302	**888-350-3802**	740-389-2355
McGuire Cadillac Inc					
910 Rt 1 N	Woodbridge	NJ	07095	**866-552-4208**	
McNeilus Cos Inc					
524 County Rd 34 E PO Box 70	Dodge Center	MN	55927	**800-265-1098**	507-374-6321
Medical Coaches Inc					
399 County Hwy 58	Oneonta	NY	13820	**800-432-1339**	607-432-1333
Mickey Truck Bodies Inc					
1305 Trinity Ave PO Box 2044	High Point	NC	27261	**800-334-9061**	336-882-6806
Mike Castrucci Ford Sales Inc					
1020 SR- 28	Milford	OH	45150	**855-971-6897**	513-831-7010
Miller Industries Inc					
8503 Hilltop Dr	Ooltewah	TN	37363	**800-292-0330**	423-238-4171
NYSE: MLR					
Momentum Bmw Ltd					
10002 SW Fwy	Houston	TX	77074	**800-731-8114**	
Monroe Truck Equipment Inc					
1051 W Seventh St	Monroe	WI	53566	**800-356-8134**	608-328-8127
Morgan Corp					
111 Morgan Way PO Box 588	Morgantown	PA	19543	**800-666-7426**	610-286-5025
Morgan Olson Corp					
1801 S Nottawa Rd	Sturgis	MI	49091	**800-233-4823**	
Morse Operations Inc					
3790 W Blue Herron Blvd	Riviera Beach	FL	33404	**800-755-2593**	
Motor Coach Industries International Co					
1700 E Golf Rd Ste 300	Schaumburg	IL	60173	**800-743-3624**	847-285-2000
Murrays Ford Inc					
3007 Blinker Pkwy	Du Bois	PA	15801	**800-371-6601**	814-371-6600
North Florida Lincoln Mercury					
4620 Southside Blvd	Jacksonville	FL	32216	**888-579-9646**	
Obs Inc					
1324 WTuscarawas St PO Box 6210	Canton	OH	44706	**800-362-9592**	330-453-3725
Omaha Standard Inc					
3501 S 11th St Ste 1	Council Bluffs	IA	51501	**800-279-2201**	712-328-7444
Oshkosh Truck Corp					
2307 Oregon St	Oshkosh	WI	54903	**800-392-9921**	920-235-9150
Parkhurst Manufacturing Co					
18999 Hwy Y	Sedalia	MO	65301	**800-821-7380**	660-826-8685
Pierce Mfg Inc					
2600 American Dr	Appleton	WI	54914	**888-974-3723***	920-832-3000
*Cust Svc					
Porter Truck Sales LP					
135 McCarty St	Houston	TX	77029	**800-956-2408**	713-672-2400
Quad-City Peterbilt Inc					
8100 N Fairmount St	Davenport	IA	52806	**866-601-8607**	
R & S/Godwin Truck Body Co LLC					
5168 S US Hwy 23 PO Box 420	Ivel	KY	41642	**800-826-7413**	606-874-2151
Rapid Chevrolet Company Inc					
2090 Deadwood Ave PO Box 1765	Rapid City	SD	57702	**800-456-2105**	605-343-1282
Rdk Truck Sales Inc					
3214 E Adamo Dr	Tampa	FL	33605	**877-735-4636**	813-241-0711
Reading Truck Body Inc					
201 Hancock Blvd	Reading	PA	19611	**800-458-2226***	
*All					
RKI Inc 2301 Central Pkwy	Houston	TX	77092	**800-346-8988**	713-688-4414
Rocket Supply Corp					
404 N Rt 115 PO Box 98	Roberts	IL	60962	**800-252-6871**	
Rydell Chevrolet Inc					
1325 E San Marnan Dr	Waterloo	IA	50702	**866-697-5167**	319-234-4601
Saf-T-Cab Inc PO Box 2587	Fresno	CA	93745	**800-344-7491**	559-268-5541
Sanders Ford Inc					
1135 Lejeune Blvd	Jacksonville	NC	28540	**888-897-8527***	910-455-1911
*General					
Scania USA Inc					
121 Interpark Blvd Ste 601	San Antonio	TX	78216	**800-272-2642**	210-403-0007
Scelzi Equipment Inc					
1030 W Gladstone St	Azusa	CA	91702	**866-972-3594**	626-334-0573
Schetky Northwest Sales Inc					
8430 NE Killingsworth St	Portland	OR	97220	**800-255-8341**	503-287-4141
Segway Inc 14 Technology Dr	Bedford	NH	03110	**866-473-4929**	603-222-6000
Shealy's Truck Ctr Inc					
1340 Bluff Rd	Columbia	SC	29201	**800-951-8580**	803-771-0176
Snethkamp Chrysler Dodge Jeep Ram					
11600 Telegraph Rd	Redford	MI	48239	**888-455-6146**	313-255-2700
Somerset Welding & Steel Inc					
10558 Somerset Pk	Somerset	PA	15501	**800-777-2671**	814-444-3400
Spartan Motors Inc					
1541 Reynolds Rd	Charlotte	MI	48813	**800-937-5449**	517-543-6400
NASDAQ: SPAR					
STAHL/A Scott Fetzer Co					
3201 W Old Lincoln Way	Wooster	OH	44691	**800-277-8245**	330-264-7441
Sterling Truck Corp					
12120 Telegraph Rd	Redford Township	MI	48239	**800-385-4357***	800-785-4357
*Cust Svc					
Steve Hopkins Inc					
2499 Auto Mall Pkwy	Fairfield	CA	94533	**877-873-3913**	707-427-1000

				Toll-Free	Phone

Steve Landers Toyota
10825 Colonel Glenn Rd .... Little Rock AR 72204 **888-314-4350** 501-568-5800

Superior Trailer Sales Co
501 Hwy 80 .... Sunnyvale TX 75182 **800-637-0324** 972-226-3893

Sutphen Corp PO Box 158 .... Amlin OH 43002 **800-726-7030** 614-889-1005

Sweeney Buick
7997 Market St .... Youngstown OH 44512 **877-360-4928**

Ten-8 Fire Equipment Inc
2904 59th Ave Dr E .... Bradenton FL 34203 **877-989-7660** 941-756-7779

Thomson-Macconnell Cadillac Inc
2820 Gilbert Ave .... Cincinnati OH 45206 **877-472-0738**

Tom Roush Inc
525 W David Brown Dr .... Westfield IN 46074 **877-349-0851** 317-896-5561

Trailercraft Inc
1301 E 64th Ave .... Anchorage AK 99518 **800-478-3238** 907-563-3238

Truck Utilities Inc
2370 English St .... Saint Paul MN 55109 **800-869-1075** 651-484-3305

Tymco Inc
225 E Industrial Blvd PO Box 2368. .... Waco TX 76703 **800-258-9626** 254-799-5546

Unicell Body Co
571 Howard St .... Buffalo NY 14206 **800-628-8914***
*Cust Svc

Vista-pro Automotive LLC
15 Century Blvd Ste 600. .... Nashville TN 37214 **888-250-2676** 615-622-2200

Volvo Honolulu
704 Ala Moana Blvd .... Honolulu HI 96813 **888-892-2456**

Wendle Motors Inc
9000 N Div .... Spokane WA 99218 **888-685-7177**

Wheeled Coach Industries Inc
2737 Forsyth Rd .... Winter Park FL 32792 **800-342-0720** 407-677-7777

Wichita Kenworth Inc
5115 N Broadway .... Wichita KS 67219 **800-825-5558** 316-838-0867

Yark Automotive Group Inc
6019 W Central Ave .... Toledo OH 43615 **866-390-8894**

514　MOTORCYCLES & MOTORCYCLE PARTS & ACCESSORIES

				Toll-Free	Phone

American Honda Motor Company Inc
1919 Torrance Blvd .... Torrance CA 90501 **800-999-1009** 310-783-3170

Corbin
2360 Technology Pkwy .... Hollister CA 95023 **800-538-7035** 831-634-1100

Edelbrock Corp
2700 California St .... Torrance CA 90503 **800-739-3737** 310-781-2222

Fulmer Co 122 Gayoso Ave .... Memphis TN 38103 **800-467-2400** 901-525-5711

Lehman Trikes Inc
125 Industrial Dr .... Spearfish SD 57783 **888-394-3357** 605-642-2111
CVE: LHT

National Cycle Inc
2200 Maywood Dr .... Maywood IL 60153 **877-972-7336** 708-343-0400

Persons Majestic Mfg Co
PO Box 370 .... Huron OH 44839 **800-772-2453** 419-433-9057

Rivco Products Inc
440 S Pine St .... Burlington WI 53105 **888-801-8222** 262-763-8222

Yamaha Motor Corp USA
6555 Katella Ave .... Cypress CA 90630 **800-656-7695***
*Cust Svc

MOTORS - FLUID POWER

SEE Pumps & Motors - Fluid Power

515　MOTORS (ELECTRIC) & GENERATORS

SEE ALSO Automotive Parts & Supplies - Mfr

				Toll-Free	Phone

ADS/Transicoil
Nine Iron Bridge Dr .... Collegeville PA 19426 **800-323-7115** 484-902-1100

Aerotech Inc 101 Zeta Dr .... Pittsburgh PA 15238 **888-492-8950** 412-967-6440

AO Smith Corp
11270 W Pk Pl Ste 170 PO Box 245008. .... Milwaukee WI 53224 **800-359-4065** 414-359-4000
NYSE: AOS

AO Smith Electrical Products Co
531 N Fourth St .... Tipp City OH 45371 **800-543-9450** 937-667-2431

Arco Electric Products Corp
2325 E Michigan Rd .... Shelbyville IN 46176 **800-428-4370** 317-398-9713

Aura Systems Inc
1310 E Grand Ave .... El Segundo CA 90245 **800-909-2872** 310-643-5300
OTC: AUSI

Autotrol Corp
365 E Prairie St PO Box 557 .... Crystal Lake IL 60039 **800-228-6207** 815-459-3080

Bluffton Motor Works LLC
410 E Spring St .... Bluffton IN 46714 **800-579-8527** 260-827-2200

Bodine Electric Co
201 Northfield Rd .... Northfield IL 60093 **800-726-3463** 773-478-3515

Bosch Rexroth Corp
5150 Prairie Stone Pkwy .... Hoffman Estates IL 60192 **800-860-1055** 847-645-3600

CALEX Manufacturing Co
2401 Stanwell Dr .... Concord CA 94520 **800-542-3355** 925-687-4411

Continental Electric Motors Inc
23 Sebago St .... Clifton NJ 07013 **800-335-6718**

Dumore Corp
1030 Veterans St .... Mauston WI 53948 **888-467-8288** 608-847-6420

Elwood Corp High Performance Motors Group
2701 N Green Bay Rd .... Racine WI 53404 **800-558-9489** 262-637-6591

Emoteq Corp 10002 E 43rd St S .... Tulsa OK 74146 **800-221-7572***　918-627-1845
*Sales

Engine Power Source Inc
348 Bryant Blvd .... Rock Hill SC 29732 **800-374-7522** 704-944-1999

Five Star Electric of Houston Inc
19424 Pk Row Ste 100 .... Houston TX 77084 **888-492-7090** 281-492-7090

FLANDERS Inc
8101 Baumgart Rd PO Box 23130 .... Evansville IN 47724 **855-875-5888** 812-867-7421

Franklin Electric Co Inc
9255 Coverdale Rd .... Fort Wayne IN 46809 **800-962-3787** 260-824-2900
NASDAQ: FELE

Generac Power Systems Inc
PO Box 8 .... Waukesha WI 53187 **888-436-3722** 262-544-4811

Glentek Inc
208 Standard St .... El Segundo CA 90245 **877-470-6742** 310-322-3026

Joliet Equipment Corp
One Doris Ave .... Joliet IL 60433 **800-435-9350** 815-727-6606

Kirkwood Industries Inc
1239 Rockside Rd .... Cleveland OH 44134 **800-262-2266** 216-267-6200

Kraft Power Corp
199 Wildwood Ave .... Woburn MA 01801 **800-969-6121** 781-938-9100

Kurz Electric Solutions Inc
1325 McMahon Dr .... Neenah WI 54956 **800-776-3629** 920-886-8200

Martindale Electric Co
1375 Hird Ave .... Lakewood OH 44107 **800-344-9191** 216-521-8567

Molon Motor & Coil Corp
300 N Ridge Ave .... Arlington Heights IL 60005 **800-526-6867** 847-253-6000

Morrill Motors Inc
229 S Main Ave .... Erwin TN 37650 **888-743-7001**

Motor Appliance Corp
555 Spirit of St Louis Blvd .... Saint Louis MO 63005 **800-622-3406** 636-532-3406

Motor Products Owosso Corp
201 S Delaney Rd .... Owosso MI 48867 **800-248-3841**

MTU Onsite Energy Corp
100 Power Dr .... Mankato MN 56001 **800-325-5450** 507-625-7973

Nidec Motor Corp
8050 W Florissant Ave .... Saint Louis MO 63136 **888-637-7333**

PennEngineering & Manufacturing Corp
5190 Old Easton Rd .... Danboro PA 18916 **800-237-4736** 215-766-8853

Petrotech Inc
151 Brookhollow Esplanade .... New Orleans LA 70123 **800-486-8850** 504-620-6600

Piller Inc 45 Turner Rd .... Middletown NY 10941 **800-597-6937**

Polyspede Electronics Company Inc
6770 Twin Hills Ave .... Dallas TX 75231 **888-476-5944** 214-363-7245

RAE Corp 4615 Prime Pkwy .... McHenry IL 60050 **800-323-7049** 815-385-3500

Sag Harbor Industries Inc
1668 Sag Harbor Tpke .... Sag Harbor NY 11963 **800-724-5952** 631-725-0440

Shinano Kenshi Corp
5737 Mesmer Ave .... Culver City CA 90230 **800-755-0752** 818-889-5028

Specialty Motors Inc
25060 Ave Tibbitts .... Valencia CA 91355 **800-232-2612** 661-257-7388

Sterling Electric Inc
7997 Allison Ave .... Indianapolis IN 46268 **800-654-6220***　317-872-0471
*Cust Svc

Stimple & Ward Co
3400 Babcock Blvd .... Pittsburgh PA 15237 **800-792-6457** 412-364-5200

Swiger Coils Systems Inc
4677 Mfg Rd .... Cleveland OH 44135 **800-321-3310** 216-362-7500

Tampa Armature Works Inc
6312 78th St .... Riverview FL 33578 **866-465-8905** 813-621-5661

Toshiba International Corp
13131 W Little York Rd .... Houston TX 77041 **800-231-1412** 713-466-0277

Unitron LP
10925 Miller Rd PO Box 38902 .... Dallas TX 75238 **800-527-1279** 214-340-8600

Vicor Corp 25 Frontage Rd .... Andover MA 01810 **800-869-5300** 978-470-2900
NASDAQ: VICR

Wolverine Power Systems Inc
3229 80th Ave .... Zeeland MI 49464 **800-485-8068** 616-879-0040

Yamaha Motor Corp USA
6555 Katella Ave .... Cypress CA 90630 **800-656-7695***
*Cust Svc

Yaskawa America Inc
2121 Norman Dr S .... Waukegan IL 60085 **800-927-5292** 847-887-7000

516　MOVING COMPANIES

SEE ALSO Trucking Companies
Companies that have the moving of household belongings as their primary business.

				Toll-Free	Phone

Ace World Wide Moving
1900 E College Ave .... Cudahy WI 53110 **800-558-3980** 414-764-1000

Air Van Moving Group
2340 130th Ave NE Ste 201 .... Bellevue WA 98005 **800-989-8905** 425-629-4101

Allied International NA Inc
700 Oakmont Ln .... Westmont IL 60559 **800-444-6787** 630-570-3500

American Red Ball International
9750 Third Ave NE Ste 200. .... Seattle WA 98115 **800-669-6424** 206-526-1730

American Red Ball Transit Company Inc
PO Box 1127 .... Indianapolis IN 46206 **800-733-8139**

Andrews Van Lines Inc
310 S Seventh St .... Norfolk NE 68701 **800-228-8146***　402-371-5440
*Cust Svc

Arnoff Moving & Storage Inc
1282 Dutchess Tpke .... Poughkeepsie NY 12603 **800-633-6683** 845-471-1504

Atlantic Relocation Systems Inc
1314 Chattahoochee Ave NW .... Atlanta GA 30318 **800-241-1140***　404-351-5311
*Cust Svc

Atlas Van Lines Inc
1212 St George Rd .... Evansville IN 47711 **800-638-9797** 812-424-2222

Bekins Van Lines LLC
8010 Castleton Rd .... Indianapolis IN 46250 **800-456-8092**

Berger Transfer & Storage Inc
2950 Long Lk Rd .... Saint Paul MN 55113 **877-268-2101**

Beverly Hills Transfer & Storage Co
15500 S Main St .... Gardena CA 90248 **800-999-7114**

Bohrens Moving & Storage Inc
Three Applegate Dr .... Robbinsville NJ 08691 **800-326-4736** 609-208-1470

Buehler Moving & Storage
3899 Jackson St .... Denver CO 80205 **800-234-6683** 303-388-4000

Callan & Woodworth Moving & Storage
900 Hwy 212 .... Michigan City IN 46360 **800-584-0551** 269-447-1578

Cartwright Cos, The
11901 Cartwright Ave .... Grandview MO 64030 **800-821-2334**

Castine Moving & Storage
1235 Chestnut St .... Athol MA 01331 **800-225-8068** 978-249-9105

			Toll-Free	Phone

Coast to Coast Moving & Storage Co
136 41st St ....Brooklyn NY 11232 | **800-872-6683** | 718-443-5800

Cook Moving Systems Inc
1845 Dale Rd ....Buffalo NY 14225 | **800-828-7144**

Corrigan Moving Systems
23923 Research Dr ....Farmington Hills MI 48335 | **800-267-7442**

Davidson Transfer & Storage Co
1701 Florida Ave NW ....Washington DC 20009 | **800-736-6825** | 202-234-5600

East Side Moving & Storage
4836 SE Powell Blvd ....Portland OR 97206 | **800-547-4600** | 503-777-4181

Graebel Van Lines Inc
16346 Airport Cir ....Aurora CO 80011 | **800-568-0031** | 303-214-6683

Hilford Moving & Storage
1595 Arundell Ave ....Ventura CA 93003 | **800-739-6683** | 805-642-0221

I-Go Van & Storage
9820 S 142nd St ....Omaha NE 68138 | **800-228-9276** | 402-891-1222

Johnson Storage & Moving Co
221 Broadway ....Denver CO 80202 | **800-289-6683** | 303-778-6683

King Relocation Services
13535 Larwin Cir ....Santa Fe Springs CA 90670 | **800-854-3679**

Lido Van & Storage Co Inc
2152 Alton Pkwy Ste N ....Irvine CA 92606 | **800-339-5436** | 949-863-9000

Mayflower Transit LLC
1 Mayflower Dr ....Fenton MO 63026 | **800-325-3924** | 636-305-4000

McCollister's Transportation Group Inc
1800 Rt 130 N PO Box 9 ....Burlington NJ 08016 | **800-257-9595** | 609-386-0600

National Van Lines Inc
2800 W Roosevelt Rd ....Broadview IL 60155 | **877-590-2810** | 708-450-2900

Nationwide Van Lines Inc
1421 NW 65th Ave ....Plantation FL 33313 | **800-310-0056** | 954-585-3945

Nelson Westerberg Inc
1500 Arthur Ave Ste 200 ....Elk Grove Village IL 60007 | **800-245-2080** | 847-437-2080

NorthStar Moving Corp
9120 Mason Ave ....Chatsworth CA 91311 | **800-275-7767** | 818-727-0128

Palmer Moving & Storage
24660 Dequindre Rd ....Warren MI 48091 | **800-521-3954** | 586-436-3804

Paxton Van Lines Inc
5300 Port Royal Rd ....Springfield VA 22151 | **800-336-4536** | 703-321-7600

Pickens-Kane Moving Co
410 N Milwaukee Ave ....Chicago IL 60610 | **888-871-9998** | 312-942-0330

S & M Moving Systems Inc
12128 Burke St ....Santa Fe Springs CA 90670 | **800-528-4561** | 562-567-2100

Security Storage Co
1701 Florida Ave NW ....Washington DC 20009 | **800-736-6825** | 202-234-5600

Smith Dray Line
320 Frontage Rd ....Greenville SC 29611 | **866-642-6389**

Starving Students Moving & Storage Co
1850 Sawtelle Blvd Ste 300 ....Los Angeles CA 90025 | **888-931-6683**

Stevens Worldwide Van Lines
527 W Morley Dr ....Saginaw MI 48601 | **888-860-4566** | 800-678-3836

Suddath Cos
815 S Main St ....Jacksonville FL 32207 | **800-395-7100** | 904-352-2577

Truckin Movers Corp
1031 Harvest St ....Durham NC 27704 | **800-334-1651** | 919-682-2300

Two Men & A Truck International Inc
3400 Belle Chase Way ....Lansing MI 48911 | **800-345-1070** | 517-394-7210

United Van Lines Inc
1 United Dr ....St. Louis MO 63026 | **877-740-3040** | 636-343-3900

Von Paris Enterprises Inc
8691 Larkin Rd ....Savage MD 20763 | **800-866-6355** | 410-888-8500

Wald Relocation Services Ltd
8708 W Little York Rd Ste 190 ....Houston TX 77040 | **800-527-1408** | 713-512-4800

Wheaton Van Lines Inc
8010 Castleton Rd ....Indianapolis IN 46250 | **800-932-7799** | 317-849-7900

517   MUSEUMS

SEE ALSO Museums - Children's ; Museums & Halls of Fame - Sports
Listings for museums are organized alphabetically within state and province groupings.
(Canadian provinces are interfiled among the US states, in alphabetical order.)

			Toll-Free	Phone

390th Memorial Museum
6000 E Valencia Rd ....Tucson AZ 85706 | **800-639-4992** | 520-574-0287

Abraham Lincoln Presidential Library & Museum
112 N Sixth St ....Springfield IL 62701 | **800-610-2094** | 217-557-6250

African American Historical Museum & Cultural Ctr of Iowa
55 12th Ave SE ....Cedar Rapids IA 52406 | **877-526-1863** | 319-862-2101

Alabama Constitution Village
109 Gates Ave ....Huntsville AL 35801 | **800-678-1819** | 256-564-8100

Alaska Native Heritage Ctr
8800 Heritage Ctr Dr ....Anchorage AK 99504 | **800-315-6608** | 907-330-8000

Alaska State Museum
395 Whittier St ....Juneau AK 99801 | **800-440-2919** | 907-465-2901

Alexandria Archaeology Museum
105 N Union St Ste 327 ....Alexandria VA 22314 | **800-367-7623** | 703-746-4399

Alexandria Black History Museum
902 Wythe St ....Alexandria VA 22314 | **800-367-7623** | 703-838-4356

American Airlines CR Smith Museum
4601 Hwy 360 at FAA Rd ....Fort Worth TX 76155 | **877-277-6484** | 817-967-1560

American Jazz Museum
1616 E 18th St ....Kansas City MO 64108 | **800-745-3000** | 816-474-8463

American Royal Museum & Visitors Ctr
1701 American Royal Ct ....Kansas City MO 64102 | **866-844-2295*** | 816-221-9800
*General

American Saddlebred Museum
4083 Iron Works Pkwy ....Lexington KY 40511 | **800-829-4438** | 859-259-2746

Amon Carter Museum
3501 Camp Bowie Blvd ....Fort Worth TX 76107 | **800-573-1933** | 817-738-1933

Antique Car Museum/Grovewood Gallery
111 Grovewood Rd ....Asheville NC 28804 | **877-622-7238** | 828-253-7651

Ardenwood Historic Farm
34600 Ardenwood Blvd ....Fremont CA 94555 | **888-327-2757** | 510-544-2797

Arizona Historical Society Museum
1300 N College Ave ....Tempe AZ 85281 | **800-249-7737** | 480-929-0292

Arizona State Capitol Museum
1700 W Washington St ....Phoenix AZ 85007 | **800-228-4710** | 602-542-4675

			Toll-Free	Phone

Arizona State University Art Museum
10th St & Mill Ave
Nelson Fine Arts Ctr Arizona State University ....Tempe AZ 85287 | **855-278-5080** | 480-965-2787

Arkansas Arts Ctr
501 E Ninth St ....Little Rock AR 72202 | **800-264-2787** | 501-372-4000

Arkansas Museum of Science & History
Museum of Discovery
500 President Clinton Ave Ste 150 ....Little Rock AR 72201 | **800-880-6475** | 501-396-7050

Arkansas State University Museum
PO Box 490 ....State University AR 72467 | **800-342-2923** | 870-972-2074

B & O Railroad Museum
901 W Pratt St ....Baltimore MD 21223 | **800-228-3748** | 410-752-2490

B Carroll Reece Museum
PO Box 70660 ....Johnson City TN 37614 | **855-590-3878** | 423-439-4392

Bailey Matthews Shell Museum
3075 Sanibel-Captiva Rd PO Box 1580 ....Sanibel FL 33957 | **888-679-6450** | 239-395-2233

Baltimore Museum of Art
10 Art Museum Dr ....Baltimore MD 21218 | **800-735-2964** | 443-573-1700

Banneker-Douglas Museum
84 Franklin St ....Annapolis MD 21401 | **877-634-6361** | 410-216-6180

Belle Meade Plantation
5025 Harding Pk ....Nashville TN 37205 | **800-270-3991** | 615-356-0501

Bellevue Arts Museum
510 Bellevue Way NE ....Bellevue WA 98004 | **800-367-2648** | 425-519-0770

Birmingham Civil Rights Institute
520 16th St N ....Birmingham AL 35203 | **866-328-9696** | 205-328-9696

Black Cultural Centre for Nova Scotia
10 Cherry Brook Rd ....Cherry Brook NS B2Z1A8 | **800-465-0767** | 902-434-6223

Bob Bullock Texas State History Museum
1800 N Congress Ave ....Austin TX 78701 | **866-369-7108** | 512-936-8746

Boca Raton Museum of Art
501 Plaza Real Mizner Pk ....Boca Raton FL 33432 | **888-472-4732** | 561-392-2500

Broward County Historical Commission
151 SW Second St ....Fort Lauderdale FL 33301 | **866-682-2258** | 954-765-4670

Buffalo Museum of Science
1020 Humboldt Pkwy ....Buffalo NY 14211 | **866-291-6660** | 716-896-5200

California State Archives
1020 'O' St ....Sacramento CA 95814 | **800-633-5155** | 916-653-7715

California State Railroad Museum
125 'I' St 111 'I' St ....Sacramento CA 95814 | **866-240-4655** | 916-323-9280

Calvert Marine Museum
14200 Solomons Island Rd PO Box 97 ....Solomons MD 20688 | **800-735-2258** | 410-326-2042

Canada Agriculture Museum
Prince of Wales Dr PO Box 9724 Stn T ....Ottawa ON K1G5A3 | **866-442-4416** | 613-991-3044

Canada Science & Technology Museum
1867 St Laurent Blvd PO Box 9724 ....Ottawa ON K1G5A3 | **866-442-4416** | 613-991-3044

Canadian Museum of Civilization
100 Laurier St ....Gatineau QC K1A0M8 | **800-555-5621** | 819-776-7000

Canadian Museum of Contemporary Photography
380 Sussex Dr PO Box 427 Stn A ....Ottawa ON K1N9N4 | **800-319-2787** | 613-990-1985

Canadian Museum of Nature
240 McLeod St ....Ottawa ON K2P2R1 | **800-263-4433** | 613-566-4700

Cathedral Church of Saint Peter & Saint Paul
3101 Wisconsin Ave NW ....Washington DC 20016 | **800-622-6304** | 202-537-6200

Center for Creative Photography
1030 N Olive Rd ....Tucson AZ 85721 | **888-472-4732** | 520-621-7968

Center for Western Studies
2101 S Summit Ave
Augustana College ....Sioux Falls SD 57197 | **800-727-2844** | 605-274-4007

Challenger Learning Ctr (CLC)
316 Washington Ave
Wheeling Jesuit University ....Wheeling WV 26003 | **800-624-6992** | 304-243-2279

Charlotte Nature Museum
1658 Sterling Rd ....Charlotte NC 28209 | **800-935-0553** | 704-372-6261

Cherokee Heritage Ctr & National Museum
21192 S Keeler Dr ....Park Hill OK 74451 | **888-999-6007** | 918-456-6007

Cheyenne Depot Museum
121 W 15th St Ste 300 ....Cheyenne WY 82001 | **800-544-2151** | 307-632-3905

Cincinnati Art Museum
953 Eden Pk Dr ....Cincinnati OH 45202 | **877-472-4226** | 513-721-2787

Cincinnati History Museum
1301 Western Ave
Cincinnati Museum Ctr ....Cincinnati OH 45203 | **800-733-2077** | 513-287-7000

Circus World Museum
550 Water St ....Baraboo WI 53913 | **866-693-1500** | 608-356-8341

Cleveland Museum of Art
11150 E Blvd ....Cleveland OH 44106 | **800-469-4449*** | 216-421-7340
*Sales

Cleveland Museum of Natural History
One Wade Oval Dr University Cir ....Cleveland OH 44106 | **800-317-9155** | 216-231-4600

Cloisters Museum
Fort Tryon Pk ....New York NY 10040 | **800-662-3397** | 212-923-3700

Coe College Permanent Collection of Art
1220 First Ave NE ....Cedar Rapids IA 52402 | **800-273-8255** | 319-399-8500

Colorado Railroad Museum
17155 W 44th Ave ....Golden CO 80403 | **800-365-6263** | 303-279-4591

Conner Prairie Living History Museum
13400 Allisonville Rd ....Fishers IN 46038 | **800-966-1836** | 317-776-6000

Corning Museum of Glass
One Museum Way ....Corning NY 14830 | **800-732-6845*** | 607-937-5371
*Cust Svc

COSI Columbus
333 W Broad St ....Columbus OH 43215 | **888-819-2674** | 614-228-2674

Country Music Hall of Fame & Museum
222 Fifth Ave S ....Nashville TN 37203 | **800-852-6437** | 615-416-2001

Currency Museum of the Bank of Canada
245 Sparks St ....Ottawa ON K1A0G9 | **800-303-1282*** | 613-782-8914
*Hotline

Dayton Art Institute
456 Belmonte Pk N ....Dayton OH 45405 | **800-272-8258** | 937-223-5277

de Saisset Museum at Santa Clara University
500 El Camino Real ....Santa Clara CA 95053 | **866-554-6800** | 408-554-4528

DeGrazia Gallery in the Sun
6300 N Swan Rd ....Tucson AZ 85718 | **800-545-2185** | 520-299-9191

Delaware Art Museum
2301 Kentmere Pkwy ....Wilmington DE 19806 | **800-272-8258** | 302-571-9590

DeWitt Wallace Decorative Arts Museum
325 Francis St ....Williamsburg VA 23185 | **800-447-8679**

		Toll-Free	Phone

Dittrick Museum of Medical History
11000 Euclid Ave . . . . Cleveland OH 44106 · **800-368-4723** · 216-368-3648

Duffy's Collectible Cars
1195 Boyson Rd . . . . Hiawatha IA 52233 · **877-670-3937** · 319-364-7000

Dutton Family Theatre
3454 W 76 Country Blvd . . . . Branson MO 65616 · **888-388-8661** · 417-332-2772

Dwight D Eisenhower Presidential Library & Museum
200 SE Fourth St . . . . Abilene KS 67410 · **877-746-4453** · 785-263-6700

EAA AirVenture Museum
3000 Poberezny Rd . . . . Oshkosh WI 54902 · **888-322-3229** · 920-426-4800

Edgar Allan Poe Museum
1914 E Main St . . . . Richmond VA 23223 · **866-229-8580** · 804-648-5523

Electric City Trolley Station & Museum
300 Cliff St . . . . Scranton PA 18503 · **800-732-0999** · 570-963-6590

Elisabet Ney Museum
304 E 44th St . . . . Austin TX 78751 · **800-680-7289** · 512-458-2255

Empire State Plaza Art Collection
Empire State Plz Curatorial & Services
41st Fl Corning Twr . . . . Albany NY 12242 · **877-659-4377** · 518-474-3899

EnergyExplorium
13339 Hagers Ferry Rd . . . . Huntersville NC 28078 · **800-777-0003** · 980-875-5600

Estes-Winn Memorial Automobile Museum
111 Grovewood Rd . . . . Asheville NC 28804 · **877-622-7238** · 828-253-7651

Exploratorium, The
3601 Lyon St . . . . San Francisco CA 94123 · **800-232-9698** · 415-561-0360

Fireworks Fine Crafts Gallery
3307 Utah Ave S . . . . Seattle WA 98134 · **800-505-8882** · 206-682-8707

Fisheries Museum of the Atlantic
68 Bluenose Dr PO Box 1363 . . . . Lunenburg NS B0J2C0 · **866-579-4909** · 902-634-4794

Fitger's Brewery Museum
600 E Superior St . . . . Duluth MN 55802 · **888-348-4377** · 218-722-8826

Florida Heritage Museum
167 San Marco Ave . . . . Saint Augustine FL 32084 · **800-268-7252** · 904-829-9729

Florida Holocaust Museum
55 Fifth St S . . . . Saint Petersburg FL 33701 · **800-388-4069** · 727-820-0100

Flying Leatherneck Aviation Museum
Anderson Ave MCAS Miramar . . . . San Diego CA 92145 · **877-359-8762** · 858-693-1723

Folk Art Ctr PO Box 9545 . . . . Asheville NC 28815 · **888-672-7717** · 828-298-7928

Forest Lawn Museum
1712 S Glendale Ave . . . . Glendale CA 91205 · **800-204-3131**

Fort Caspar Museum
4001 Fort Caspar Rd . . . . Casper WY 82604 · **800-877-7353** · 307-235-8462

Fort Henry National Historic Site
PO Box 213 . . . . Kingston ON K7L4V8 · **800-437-2233*** · 613-542-7388
*Cust Svc

Fort MacArthur Museum
3601 S Gaffey St . . . . San Pedro CA 90731 · **800-232-5505** · 310-548-2631

Fort McHenry National Monument & Historic Shrine
2400 E Fort Ave . . . . Baltimore MD 21230 · **866-945-7920** · 410-962-4290

Fort Ward Museum & Historic Site
4301 W Braddock Rd . . . . Alexandria VA 22304 · **800-468-8894** · 703-838-4848

Fort Worth Museum of Science & History
1600 Gendy St . . . . Fort Worth TX 76107 · **888-255-9300** · 817-255-9300

Franklin D Roosevelt Presidential Library & Museum
4079 Albany Post Rd . . . . Hyde Park NY 12538 · **800-337-8474** · 845-486-7770

Franklin Institute Science Museum
222 N 20th St . . . . Philadelphia PA 19103 · **800-732-0999** · 215-448-1200

Fraternal Order of Alaska State Troopers Museum
245 W Fifth Ave . . . . Anchorage AK 99501 · **800-770-5050** · 907-279-5050

Geological Museum
1000 E University Ave . . . . Laramie WY 82071 · **800-842-2776** · 307-766-2646

Gerald R Ford Museum
303 Pearl St NW . . . . Grand Rapids MI 49504 · **800-888-9487** · 616-254-0400

Gettysburg Heritage Center
297 Steinwehr Ave . . . . Gettysburg PA 17325 · **800-887-7775*** · 717-334-6245
*General

Gilcrease Museum
1400 N Gilcrease Museum Rd . . . . Tulsa OK 74127 · **888-655-2278** · 918-596-2700

Gillespie Museum of Minerals
421 N Woodland Blvd Unit 8403 . . . . DeLand FL 32723 · **800-688-0101** · 386-822-7330

Glessner House Museum
1800 S Prairie Ave . . . . Chicago IL 60616 · **800-657-0687** · 312-326-1480

Goethe Institut Atlanta/German Cultural Ctr
1197 Peachtree St NE . . . . Atlanta GA 30361 · **888-446-3843** · 404-892-2388

Graceland (Elvis Presley Mansion)
3734 Elvis Presley Blvd . . . . Memphis TN 38116 · **800-238-2000** · 901-332-3322

Grand Rapids Art Museum
101 Monroe Ctr . . . . Grand Rapids MI 49503 · **800-272-8258** · 616-831-1000

Grandmother's Buttons Museum
9814 Royal St . . . . Saint Francisville LA 70775 · **800-580-6941** · 225-635-4107

Greenfield Village
20900 Oakwood Blvd . . . . Dearborn MI 48124 · **800-835-5237** · 313-271-1620

Guggenheim Hermitage Museum
3355 Las Vegas Blvd S
Venetian Resort Hotel & Casino . . . . Las Vegas NV 89109 · **800-329-6109** · 212-423-3575

Guinness World Records Museum
4943 Clifton Hill . . . . Niagara Falls ON L2G3N5 · **866-656-0310** · 905-357-4330

Hale Farm & Village
2686 Oakhill Rd PO Box 296 . . . . Bath OH 44210 · **800-589-9703** · 330-666-3711

Hallie Ford Museum of Art
700 State St . . . . Salem OR 97301 · **844-232-7228** · 503-370-6855

Harry S Truman Presidential Library & Museum
500 W Hwy 24 . . . . Independence MO 64050 · **800-833-1225** · 816-268-8200

Harry S Truman's Little White House Museum
111 Front St Truman Annex . . . . Key West FL 33040 · **800-435-7352** · 305-294-9911

Headley-Whitney Museum
4435 Old Frankfort Pike . . . . Lexington KY 40510 · **800-310-5085** · 859-255-6653

Henricus Historical Park
Henricus Pk Rd . . . . Chester VA 23836 · **800-514-3849** · 804-748-1613

Henry Ford Museum
20900 Oakwood Blvd . . . . Dearborn MI 48124 · **800-733-0345** · 313-271-1620

Heritage of the Americas Museum
12110 Cuyamaca College Dr W . . . . El Cajon CA 92019 · **800-234-1597** · 619-670-5194

Heritage Square Museum
3800 Homer St . . . . Los Angeles CA 90031 · **800-375-1771** · 323-225-2700

High Desert Museum
59800 S Hwy 97 . . . . Bend OR 97702 · **866-632-9992** · 541-382-4754

Historic Annapolis Foundation Museum
77 Main St . . . . Annapolis MD 21401 · **800-603-4020** · 410-268-5576

Historic Jonesborough Visitors Ctr & Museum
117 Boone St . . . . Jonesborough TN 37659 · **866-401-4223** · 423-753-1010

Hollywood Wax Museum
6767 Hollywood Blvd . . . . Hollywood CA 90028 · **800-214-3661** · 323-462-5991

Holocaust Memorial Ctr
28123 OrchaRd Lake Rd . . . . Farmington Hills MI 48334 · **800-875-5275** · 248-553-2400

Honolulu Academy of Arts
900 S Beretania St . . . . Honolulu HI 96814 · **866-385-3849** · 808-532-8700

House of Broel's Historic Mansion & Dollhouse Museum
2220 St Charles Ave . . . . New Orleans LA 70130 · **800-827-4325** · 504-522-2220

Huntsville Museum of Art
300 Church St SW . . . . Huntsville AL 35801 · **800-786-9095** · 256-535-4350

Illinois State Military Museum
1301 N MacArthur Blvd Ste 30 . . . . Springfield IL 62702 · **800-732-8868** · 217-761-3910

Indian Pueblo Cultural Ctr
2401 12th St NW . . . . Albuquerque NM 87104 · **866-855-7902** · 505-843-7270

Indian River Lifesaving Station Museum
25039 Costal Hwy . . . . Rehoboth Beach DE 19971 · **877-987-2757** · 302-227-6991

Indian Temple Mound Museum
107 Miracle Strip Pkwy SW . . . . Fort Walton Beach FL 32548 · **866-847-1301** · 850-833-9500

Institute of Texan Cultures
801 E Durango Blvd . . . . San Antonio TX 78205 · **800-447-3372** · 210-458-2300

Intel Museum
2200 Mission College Blvd . . . . Santa Clara CA 95052 · **800-628-8686** · 408-765-0503

International Civil Rights Ctr & Museum
134 S Elm St . . . . Greensboro NC 27401 · **800-748-7116** · 336-274-9199

International Museum of the Horse
4089 Iron Works Pkwy . . . . Lexington KY 40511 · **800-678-8813** · 859-259-4232

International Women's Air & Space Museum
1501 N Marginal Rd
Burke Lakefront Airport . . . . Cleveland OH 44114 · **877-287-4752** · 216-623-1111

Intrepid Sea-Air-Space Museum
W 46th St & 12th Ave Pier 86 . . . . New York NY 10036 · **877-957-7447** · 212-245-0072

Invent Now, Inc
3701 Highland Park NW . . . . North Canton OH 44720 · **800-968-4332**

Japanese American National Museum
369 E First St . . . . Los Angeles CA 90012 · **800-461-5266** · 213-625-0414

Jewish Museum of Maryland
15 Lloyd St . . . . Baltimore MD 21202 · **800-235-4045*** · 410-732-6400
*All

John E Conner Museum
905 W Santa Gertrudis Ave
700 University Blvd. . . . . Kingsville TX 78363 · **800-726-8192** · 361-593-2810

John F Kennedy Presidential Library & Museum
Columbia Pt . . . . Boston MA 02125 · **866-535-1960** · 617-514-1600

Journey Museum
222 New York St . . . . Rapid City SD 57701 · **877-343-8220** · 605-394-6923

Kansas Museum of History
6425 SW Sixth St . . . . Topeka KS 66615 · **888-537-1222** · 785-272-8681

Kelsey Museum of Archaeology
434 S State St
University of Michigan . . . . Ann Arbor MI 48109 · **800-562-3559** · 734-763-3559

Kenosha Public Museum
5500 First Ave . . . . Kenosha WI 53140 · **888-258-9966** · 262-653-4140

Kent State University Museum
PO Box 5190 . . . . Kent OH 44242 · **800-988-5368** · 330-672-3450

Kentucky Derby Museum
704 Central Ave . . . . Louisville KY 40208 · **800-273-3729** · 502-637-1111

Kings Landing Historical Settlement
5804 Rt 102 . . . . Prince William NB E6K0A5 · **888-666-5547*** · 506-363-4999
*General

Kingsley Plantation
11676 Palmetto Ave . . . . Jacksonville FL 32226 · **877-874-2478** · 904-251-3537

Kruger Street Toy & Train Museum
144 Kruger St . . . . Wheeling WV 26003 · **877-242-8133** · 304-242-8133

Lacrosse Hall of Fame & Museum
113 W University Pkwy . . . . Baltimore MD 21210 · **866-877-7550** · 410-235-6882

Lafayette Museum
1122 Lafayette St . . . . Lafayette LA 70501 · **800-346-1958** · 337-234-2208

Lake Shore Railway Museum
31 Wall St
Lake Shore Historical Society . . . . North East PA 16428 · **800-945-0340** · 814-725-1911

Laura Ingalls Wilder Museum & Home
3068 Hwy A . . . . Mansfield MO 65704 · **877-924-7126**

LBJ Library & Museum
2313 Red River St . . . . Austin TX 78705 · **800-874-6451** · 512-721-0216

Leanin' Tree Museum of Western Art
6055 Longbow Dr . . . . Boulder CO 80301 · **800-525-0656** · 303-530-1442

Louisiana State Museum
751 Chartres St . . . . New Orleans LA 70116 · **800-568-6968** · 504-568-6968

Louisville Science Ctr
727 W Main St . . . . Louisville KY 40202 · **800-591-2203** · 502-561-6100

Loxahatchee River Historical Museum
500 Captian Armours Way
Burt Reynolds Pk . . . . Jupiter FL 33469 · **800-435-7352** · 561-747-8380

Manitou Cliff Dwellings Museum
10 Cliff Rd . . . . Manitou Springs CO 80829 · **800-354-9971** · 719-685-5242

Marbles Kids Museum
201 E Hargett St . . . . Raleigh NC 27601 · **800-745-3000** · 919-834-4040

Marian Koshland Science Museum
Sixth & E Sts NW . . . . Washington DC 20001 · **888-567-4526** · 202-334-1201

Mariners' Museum
100 Museum Dr . . . . Newport News VA 23606 · **800-581-7245** · 757-596-2222

Marjorie Barrick Museum
4505 S Maryland Pkwy . . . . Las Vegas NV 89154 · **877-895-0334** · 702-895-3381

Maryland Historical Society Museum & Library
201 W Monument St . . . . Baltimore MD 21201 · **800-537-5487** · 410-685-3750

Maxwell Museum of Anthropology
University of New Mexico . . . . Albuquerque NM 87131 · **855-227-6231** · 505-277-4405

McWane Science Center
200 19th St N . . . . Birmingham AL 35203 · **877-462-9263** · 205-714-8300

Meadows Museum of Art at Centenary College
2911 Centenary Blvd . . . . Shreveport LA 71104 · **800-234-4448** · 318-869-5169

Memphis Brooks Museum of Art
1934 Poplar Ave Overton Pk . . . . Memphis TN 38104 · **877-829-5500** · 901-544-6200

Meteor Crater & Museum of Astrogeology
Exit 233 Off I-40 Meteor Crater Rd . . . . Winslow AZ 86047 · **800-289-5898**

Name	Address	City	State	ZIP	Toll-Free	Phone
Metropolitan Museum of Art	1000 Fifth Ave	New York	NY	10028	**800-468-7386**	212-879-5500
Mike's Famous Harley-Davidson of Groton	951 Bank St	New London	CT	06320	**800-326-6874**	860-574-9200
Milwaukee Art Museum	700 N Art Museum Dr	Milwaukee	WI	53202	**888-322-3326**	414-224-3200
Minneapolis Institute of Arts	2400 Third Ave S	Minneapolis	MN	55404	**888-642-2787**	612-870-3000
Minnesota Discovery Ctr	1005 Discovery Dr	Chisholm	MN	55719	**800-372-6437**	218-254-7959
Minnesota Historical Society History Ctr Museum	345 Kellogg Blvd W	Saint Paul	MN	55102	**800-657-3773**	651-259-3001
Minnesota State University Moorhead Regional Science Ctr	1104 Seventh Ave S	Moorhead	MN	56563	**800-593-7246**	218-477-2920
Miramont Castle Museum	9 Capitol Hill Ave	Manitou Springs	CO	80829	**888-685-1011**	719-685-1011
Mississippi Agriculture & Forestry Museum/National Agricultural Aviation Museum	1150 Lakeland Dr	Jackson	MS	39216	**800-844-8687**	601-359-1100
Mississippi Museum of Natural Science	2148 Riverside Dr	Jackson	MS	39202	**800-467-2757**	601-576-6000
Mississippi River Museum	125 N Front St	Memphis	TN	38103	**800-507-6507**	901-576-7241
Missouri Veterinary Medical Foundation Museum	2500 Country Club Dr	Jefferson City	MO	65109	**800-632-6900**	573-636-8612
MIT Museum	265 Massachusetts Ave	Cambridge	MA	02139	**800-228-9000**	617-253-4444
Modern Art Museum of Fort Worth	3200 Darnell St	Fort Worth	TX	76107	**866-824-5566**	817-738-9215
Montana Historical Society Museum	225 N Roberts St	Helena	MT	59620	**800-243-9900**	406-444-2694
Musee Conti Historical Wax Museum of New Orleans	917 Rue Conti French Quarter	New Orleans	LA	70112	**800-233-5405**	504-525-2605
Museum of Anthropology	Wake Forest University Wingate Rd PO Box 7267	Winston-Salem	NC	27109	**888-925-3622**	336-758-5282
Museum of Art & Archaeology	1 Pickard Hall	Columbia	MO	65211	**866-447-9821**	573-882-3591
Museum of Contemporary Religious Art	221 N Grand Blvd	Saint Louis	MO	63103	**800-442-1142**	314-977-7170
Museum of Discovery	500 President Clinton Ave Ste 150	Little Rock	AR	72201	**800-880-6475**	501-396-7050
Museum of Early Southern Decorative Arts (MESDA)	924 S Main St	Winston-Salem	NC	27101	**800-441-5303**	336-721-7360
Museum of Flight	9404 E Marginal Way S	Seattle	WA	98108	**877-217-6379**	206-764-5700
Museum of Geology	501 E St Joseph St S Dakota School of Mines & Technology	Rapid City	SD	57701	**800-544-8162**	605-394-2467
Museum of Glass	1801 Dock St	Tacoma	WA	98402	**866-468-7386***	253-284-4750
	*General					
Museum of History & Art	1100 Orange Ave	Coronado	CA	92118	**866-599-7242**	619-435-7242
Museum of International Folk Art	706 Camino Lejo	Santa Fe	NM	87505	**888-670-3655**	505-476-1200
Museum of Making Music	5790 Armada Dr	Carlsbad	CA	92008	**877-551-9976**	760-438-5996
Museum of Natural History & Science	1301 Western Ave Cincinnati Museum Ctr	Cincinnati	OH	45203	**800-733-2077**	513-287-7000
Museum of Nebraska History	15th & P St PO Box 82554	Lincoln	NE	68508	**800-833-6747**	402-471-4754
Museum of Northern Arizona	3101 N Ft Valley Rd	Flagstaff	AZ	86001	**800-423-1069**	928-774-5211
Museum of Science & Industry	5700 S Lk Shore Dr	Chicago	IL	60637	**800-468-6674**	773-684-1414
Museum of the Mountain Man	700 E Hennick St	Pinedale	WY	82941	**877-686-6266**	307-367-4101
Museum of Tolerance	9786 W Pico Blvd	Los Angeles	CA	90035	**800-900-9036**	310-553-8403
Museums at 18th & Vine	1616 E 18th St	Kansas City	MO	64108	**800-734-3447**	816-474-8463
Museums of Oglebay Institute	1330 National Rd	Wheeling	WV	26003	**800-624-6988**	304-242-7272
Mystic Seaport -- The Museum of America & the Sea	75 Greenmanville Ave PO Box 6000	Mystic	CT	06355	**888-973-2767**	860-572-0711
Naples Museum of Art	5833 Pelican Bay Blvd	Naples	FL	34108	**800-597-1900**	239-597-1111
National Afro-American Museum & Cultural Ctr	1350 Brush Row Rd PO Box 578	Wilberforce	OH	45384	**800-752-2603**	937-376-4944
National Border Patrol Museum	4315 Woodrow Bean TransMtn Rd	El Paso	TX	79924	**877-276-8738**	915-759-6060
National Constitution Ctr	525 Arch St Independence Mall	Philadelphia	PA	19106	**866-917-1787**	215-409-6600
National Corvette Museum	350 Corvette Dr	Bowling Green	KY	42101	**800-538-3883**	270-781-7973
National Cowgirl Museum & Hall of Fame	1720 Gendy St	Fort Worth	TX	76107	**800-476-3263**	817-336-4475
National Farm Toy Museum	1110 16th Ave SE	Dyersville	IA	52040	**877-475-2727**	563-875-2727
National Geographic Society Explorers Hall	1145 17th St NW	Washington	DC	20036	**800-647-5463**	
National Inventors Hall of Fame	3701 Highland Park NW Inventure Pl	North Canton	OH	44720	**800-968-4332**	
National Liberty Museum	321 Chestnut St	Philadelphia	PA	19106	**800-732-0999**	215-925-2800
National Mississippi River Museum & Aquarium	350 E Third St	Dubuque	IA	52001	**800-226-3369**	563-557-9545
National Museum of Dentistry	31 S Greene St	Baltimore	MD	21201	**866-787-8637**	410-706-0600
National Museum of Natural History (Smithsonian Institution)	10th St & Constitution Ave NW	Washington	DC	20560	**866-868-7774**	202-633-1000
National Museum of Naval Aviation	1750 Radford Blvd Ste C	Pensacola	FL	32508	**800-247-6289***	850-452-3604
	*General					
National Museum of the American Indian (Smithsonian Institution)	One Bowling Green	New York	NY	10004	**800-242-6624**	212-514-3700

Name	Address	City	State	ZIP	Toll-Free	Phone
National Museum of the Marine Corps	18900 Jefferson Davis Hwy	Triangle	VA	22172	**877-635-1775**	703-221-1581
National Museum of Wildlife Art	2820 Rungius Rd PO Box 6825	Jackson	WY	83002	**800-313-9553**	307-733-5771
National Museum of Women in the Arts	1250 New York Ave NW	Washington	DC	20005	**866-875-4627**	202-783-5000
National Music Museum	414 E Clark St	Vermillion	SD	57069	**877-225-0027**	605-677-5306
National Ornamental Metal Museum	374 Metal Museum Dr	Memphis	TN	38106	**877-881-2326**	901-774-6380
National Railroad Museum	2285 S Broadway St	Green Bay	WI	54304	**866-468-7630**	920-437-7623
National Scouting Museum	1329 W Walnut Hill Ln	Irving	TX	75038	**800-303-3047**	972-580-2100
National Watch & Clock Museum	514 Poplar St	Columbia	PA	17512	**800-368-6511**	717-684-8261
NAUTICUS the National Maritime Ctr	One Waterside Dr	Norfolk	VA	23510	**800-664-1080**	757-664-1000
New Brunswick Museum	One Market Sq	Saint John	NB	E2L4Z6	**888-268-9595**	506-643-2300
New Hampshire Institute of Art	148 Concord St	Manchester	NH	03104	**866-241-4918**	603-623-0313
New Mexico Museum of Art	107 W Palace Ave	Santa Fe	NM	87501	**877-567-7380**	505-476-5072
New Mexico Museum of Space History	Top of Hwy 2001	Alamogordo	NM	88311	**877-333-6589**	575-437-2840
Newark Museum	49 Washington St	Newark	NJ	07102	**888-370-6765**	973-596-6550
Newsome House Museum & Cultural Ctr	2803 Oak Ave	Newport News	VA	23607	**888-493-7386**	757-247-2360
North Carolina Central University Art Museum	1801 Fayetteville St	Durham	NC	27707	**877-667-7533**	919-530-6211
North Dakota Game & Fish Dept	100 N Bismarck Expy	Bismarck	ND	58501	**800-406-6409**	701-328-6300
North Museum of Natural History & Science	400 College Ave	Lancaster	PA	17603	**800-732-0999**	717-291-3941
Nottoway Plantation	31025 Louisiana Hwy 1	White Castle	LA	70788	**866-527-6884**	225-545-2730
Noyes Museum of Art	733 Lily Lake Rd	Oceanville	NJ	08231	**800-852-7899**	609-652-8848
Oakland Museum of California	1000 Oak St	Oakland	CA	94607	**888-625-6873***	510-238-2200
	*General					
Ohio Historical Society	1982 Velma Ave	Columbus	OH	43211	**800-686-6124**	614-297-2300
Oklahoma City Museum of Art	415 Couch Dr	Oklahoma City	OK	73102	**800-579-9278**	405-236-3100
Oklahoma City National Memorial & Memorial Ctr Museum	620 N Harvey Ave	Oklahoma City	OK	73102	**888-542-4673**	405-235-3313
Old Florida Museum	259 San Marco Ave	Saint Augustine	FL	32084	**800-813-3208**	904-824-8874
Old Salem	600 S Main St	Winston-Salem	NC	27101	**800-441-5305**	336-721-7300
Orange County Regional History Ctr	65 E Central Blvd	Orlando	FL	32801	**800-965-2030**	407-836-8500
Oregon Museum of Science & Industry	1945 SE Water Ave	Portland	OR	97214	**800-955-6674**	503-797-4000
Oriental Institute Museum	1155 E 58th St University of Chicago	Chicago	IL	60637	**800-791-9354**	773-702-9514
Orlando Museum of Art	2416 N Mills Ave	Orlando	FL	32803	**800-435-7352**	407-896-4231
Orlando Science Ctr	777 E Princeton St	Orlando	FL	32803	**888-672-4386**	407-514-2000
Pacific Science Ctr	200 Second Ave N	Seattle	WA	98109	**800-664-8775**	206-443-2001
Patriots Point Naval & Maritime Museum	40 Patriots Pt Rd	Mount Pleasant	SC	29464	**800-248-3508**	843-884-2727
Pennsylvania Academy of the Fine Arts Museum (PAFA)	118 N Broad St	Philadelphia	PA	19102	**800-799-7233**	215-972-7600
Pennsylvania Anthracite Heritage Museum	RR1 Bald Mountain Rd	Scranton	PA	18504	**800-732-0999**	570-963-4804
Penobscot Marine Museum	Five Church St PO Box 498	Searsport	ME	04974	**800-268-8030**	207-548-2529
Petersen Automotive Museum	6060 Wilshire Blvd	Los Angeles	CA	90036	**800-546-7866**	323-930-2277
Philadelphia Museum of Art	2600 Benjamin Franklin Pkwy	Philadelphia	PA	19130	**800-732-0999**	215-763-8100
Plaquemine Lock State Historic Site	57730 Main St	Plaquemine	LA	70764	**877-987-7158**	225-687-7158
Polish Museum of America (PMA)	984 N Milwaukee Ave	Chicago	IL	60642	**800-535-2071**	773-384-3352
Polynesian Cultural Ctr	55-370 Kamehameha Hwy	Laie	HI	96762	**800-367-7060**	808-293-3005
Pony Express National Museum	914 Penn St	Saint Joseph	MO	64503	**800-530-5930**	816-279-5059
Port Townsend Marine Science Ctr	532 Battery Way	Port Townsend	WA	98368	**800-566-3932**	360-385-5582
Pueblo Grande Museum & Archaeological Park	4619 E Washington St	Phoenix	AZ	85034	**877-706-4408**	602-495-0901
Queens Museum of Art	New York City Bldg	Queens	NY	11368	**866-867-9665**	718-592-9700
Randall Museum	199 Museum Way	San Francisco	CA	94114	**866-807-7148**	415-554-9600
RCMP Heritage Ctr	5907 Dewdney Ave	Regina	SK	S4T0P4	**866-567-7267**	306-522-7333
Reynolda House Museum of American Art	2250 Reynolda Rd	Winston-Salem	NC	27106	**888-663-1149**	336-758-5150
Reynolds-Alberta Museum	6426 40 Ave PO Box 6360	Wetaskiwin	AB	T9A2G1	**800-661-4726**	780-361-1351
Richmond National Battlefield Park	3215 E Broad St	Richmond	VA	23223	**866-733-7768**	804-226-1981
Roberson Museum & Science Ctr	30 Front St	Binghamton	NY	13905	**888-269-5325**	607-772-0660
Robert C Williams American Museum of Papermaking	500 Tenth St NW	Atlanta	GA	30318	**800-558-6611**	404-894-7840
Robert Hull Fleming Museum	61 Colchester Ave University of Vermont	Burlington	VT	05405	**888-382-1222**	802-656-0750

				Toll-Free	Phone
Rockford Art Museum 711 N Main St	Rockford	IL	61103	**800-521-0849**	815-968-2787
Rocky Mount Museum 200 Hyder Hill Rd PO Box 160	Piney Flats	TN	37686	**888-538-1791**	423-538-7396
Ronald Reagan Presidential Library & Museum 40 Presidential Dr	Simi Valley	CA	93065	**800-410-8354**	805-577-4000
Roscoe Village 600 N Whitewoman St	Coshocton	OH	43812	**800-877-1830**	740-622-7644
Royal British Columbia Museum (RBCM) 675 Belleville St	Victoria	BC	V8W9W2	**888-447-7977**	250-356-7226
Royal Canadian Military Institute 426 University Ave	Toronto	ON	M5G1S9	**800-585-1072**	416-597-0286
Royal Tyrrell Museum of Palaeontology Hwy 838 Midland Provincial Pk	Drumheller	AB	T0J0Y0	**888-440-4240**	403-823-7707
Saint Louis Science Ctr 5050 Oakland Ave	Saint Louis	MO	63110	**800-456-4491**	314-289-4400
Salem Museum 801 E Main St	Salem	VA	24153	**888-827-2536**	540-389-6760
Salem Witch Museum 19 1/2 Washington Sq N	Salem	MA	01970	**800-392-6100**	978-744-1692
San Francisco Museum of Modern Art 151 Third St	San Francisco	CA	94103	**800-792-0754**	415-357-4000
Sauder Village 22611 SR 2 PO Box 235	Archbold	OH	43502	**800-590-9755**	419-446-2541
Sci-Port Discovery Ctr 820 Clyde Fant Pkwy	Shreveport	LA	71101	**877-724-7678**	318-424-3466
Science Central 1950 N Clinton St	Fort Wayne	IN	46805	**866-776-2673**	260-424-2400
Science Museum of Minnesota 120 W Kellogg Blvd	Saint Paul	MN	55102	**800-221-9444**	651-221-9444
Science Museum Oklahoma 2100 NE 52nd St	Oklahoma City	OK	73111	**800-532-7652**	405-602-6664
Shaker Village of Pleasant Hill 3501 Lexington Rd	Harrodsburg	KY	40330	**800-734-5611**	859-734-5411
Sheldon Jackson Museum 104 College Dr	Sitka	AK	99835	**800-587-0430**	907-747-8981
Sixth Floor Museum 411 Elm St Ste 120 Dealey Plz	Dallas	TX	75202	**888-485-4854**	214-747-6660
Smith Robertson Museum & Cultural Ctr 528 Bloom St	Jackson	MS	39202	**800-354-7695**	601-960-1457
Solomon R Guggenheim Museum 1071 Fifth Ave	New York	NY	10128	**800-329-6109**	212-423-3500
Southern University Museum of Art (SUSLA) 3050 Martin Luther King Jr Dr	Shreveport	LA	71107	**800-458-1472**	318-670-6000
Springfield Museums 21 Edwards St	Springfield	MA	01103	**800-625-7738**	413-263-6800
Stan Hywet Hall & Gardens 714 N Portage Path	Akron	OH	44303	**888-836-5533**	330-836-5533
State Historical Society of Missouri, The 1020 Lowry St	Columbia	MO	65201	**800-747-6366**	573-882-1187
Steves Homestead Museum 509 King William St	San Antonio	TX	78204	**800-523-5077**	210-225-5924
Stranahan House Museum Inc 335 SE Sixth Ave	Fort Lauderdale	FL	33301	**800-435-7352**	954-524-4736
Strategic Air & Space Museum 28210 W Pk Hwy	Ashland	NE	68003	**800-358-5029**	402-944-3100
Studebaker National Museum 201 Chapin St	South Bend	IN	46601	**888-391-5600**	574-235-9714
Tampa Bay History Ctr 801 Old Water St	Tampa	FL	33602	**800-352-3671**	813-228-0097
Tampa Museum of Art 120 W Gasparilla Plaza	Tampa	FL	33602	**866-790-4111**	813-274-8130
Taylor & Messick Inc 325 Walt Messick Rd	Harrington	DE	19952	**800-237-1272**	302-398-3729
Tech Museum of Innovation 201 S Market St	San Jose	CA	95113	**800-660-4287**	408-294-8324
Tennessee State Museum 505 Deaderick St	Nashville	TN	37243	**800-407-4324**	615-741-2692
Texas Memorial Museum 2400 Trinity St	Austin	TX	78705	**800-687-4132**	512-471-1604
Toledo Museum of Art 2445 Monroe St	Toledo	OH	43620	**800-644-6862**	419-255-8000
Toronto Aerospace Museum 65 Carl Hall Rd PO Box 1	Toronto	ON	M3K2E1	**866-585-2227**	416-638-6078
Turtle Bay Exploration Park 840 Auditorium Dr	Redding	CA	96001	**800-887-8532**	530-243-8850
Tweed Museum of Art 1201 ordean Ct	Duluth	MN	55812	**866-999-6995**	218-726-8222
University Galleries 400 SW 13th St Fine Arts Bldg B PO Box 115803	Gainesville	FL	32611	**800-745-3000**	352-273-3000
University Museum 3219 Hudson Rd University of Northern Iowa	Cedar Falls	IA	50614	**800-772-2736**	319-273-2188
University of Alaska Museum of the North 907 Yukon Dr	Fairbanks	AK	99775	**866-478-2721**	907-474-7505
University of South Carolina McKissick Museum University of S Carolina 816 Bull St	Columbia	SC	29208	**888-825-9711**	803-777-7251
Upper Room Chapel & Museum 1908 Grand Ave	Nashville	TN	37212	**800-972-0433**	615-340-7200
USS Lexington Museum on the Bay 2914 N Shoreline Blvd	Corpus Christi	TX	78402	**800-523-9539**	361-888-4873
Virginia War Museum 9285 Warwick Blvd	Newport News	VA	23607	**888-493-7386**	757-247-8523
Walker Art Ctr 1750 Hennepin Ave	Minneapolis	MN	55403	**888-339-4496**	612-375-7600
Washington Pavilion of Arts & Science 301 S Main PO Box 984	Sioux Falls	SD	57104	**877-927-4728**	605-367-6000
Weatherspoon Art Museum 500 Tate St	Greensboro	NC	27402	**877-862-4123**	336-334-5770
West Baton Rouge Museum 845 N Jefferson Ave	Port Allen	LA	70767	**888-881-6811**	225-336-2422
West Virginia State Museum 1900 Kanawha Blvd E The Cultural Ctr	Charleston	WV	25305	**800-120-4000**	304-558-0220
Western Museum of Mining & Industry 225 N Gate Blvd	Colorado Springs	CO	80921	**800-752-6558**	719-488-0880
Westville 1850's Village 9294 Singer Pond Rd PO Box 1850	Lumpkin	GA	31815	**888-733-1850**	229-838-6310

				Toll-Free	Phone
Wheelwright Museum of the American Indian 704 Camino Lejo	Santa Fe	NM	87505	**800-607-4636**	505-982-4636
Whitney Museum of American Art 945 Madison Ave	New York	NY	10021	**800-944-8639**	212-570-3600
Will Rogers Memorial Museum 1720 W Will Rogers Blvd	Claremore	OK	74017	**800-324-9455**	918-341-0719
Winterthur Museum & Country Estate 5105 Kennett Pk	Winterthur	DE	19735	**800-448-3883**	302-888-4600
Wisconsin Historical Museum 30 N Carroll St	Madison	WI	53703	**888-748-7479**	608-264-6555
Wisconsin Maritime Museum 75 Maritime Dr	Manitowoc	WI	54220	**866-724-2356**	920-684-0218
Wisconsin State Fair Park 640 S 84th St	West Allis	WI	53214	**800-884-3247**	414-266-7033
Woolaroc Ranch Museum & Wildlife Preserve 1925 Woolaroc Ranch Rd	Bartlesville	OK	74003	**888-966-5276**	918-336-0307
World of Coca-Cola Atlanta 121 Baker St NW	Atlanta	GA	30313	**888-855-5701**	404-676-5151
Yale Ctr for British Art 1080 Chapel St PO Box 208280	New Haven	CT	06510	**877-274-8278**	203-432-2800

518 MUSEUMS - CHILDREN'S

Children's museums are organized alphabetically by states.

				Toll-Free	Phone
Children's Museum of Oak Ridge 461 W Outer Dr	Oak Ridge	TN	37830	**877-524-1223**	865-482-1074
Children's Museum of Richmond 2626 W Broad St	Richmond	VA	23220	**866-737-5965**	804-474-7000
Cinergy Children's Museum 1301 Western Ave Cincinnati Museum Ctr	Cincinnati	OH	45203	**800-733-2077**	513-287-7000
Discovery Ctr of Springfield 438 E St Louis St	Springfield	MO	65806	**888-636-4395**	417-862-9910
Discovery Place 301 N Tryon St	Charlotte	NC	28202	**800-935-0553**	704-372-6261
EdVenture Children's Museum 211 Gervais St	Columbia	SC	29201	**800-915-4522**	803-779-3100
Exploration Place 300 N McLean Blvd	Wichita	KS	67203	**877-904-1444**	316-660-0600
Kansas Cosmosphere & Space Ctr 1100 N Plum St	Hutchinson	KS	67501	**800-397-0330**	620-662-2305
Please Touch Museum Memorial Hall Fairmount Pk 4231 Ave of the Republic	Philadelphia	PA	19131	**800-732-0999**	215-963-0667
Young at Art Children's Museum 751 SW 121st Ave	Davie	FL	33325	**800-435-7352**	954-424-0085

519 MUSEUMS & HALLS OF FAME - SPORTS

				Toll-Free	Phone
1932 & 1980 Lake Placid Winter Olympic Museum Olympic Ctr 2634 Main St	Lake Placid	NY	12946	**800-462-6236**	518-523-1655
American Museum of Fly Fishing 4104 Main Rd	Manchester	VT	05254	**800-333-1550**	802-362-3300
American Water Ski Hall of Fame & Museum 1251 Holy Cow Rd	Polk City	FL	33868	**800-533-2972**	863-324-2472
Baseball Hall of Fame 910 S 3rd St	Minneapolis	MN	55415	**888-375-9707**	612-375-9707
Canadian Golf Hall of Fame & Museum Glen Abbey Golf Course 1333 Dorval Dr Ste 1	Oakville	ON	L6M4X7	**800-263-0009**	905-849-9700
Don Garlits Museums 13700 SW 16th Ave	Ocala	FL	34473	**877-271-3278**	352-245-8661
Green Bay Packers Hall of Fame 1265 Lombardi Ave	Green Bay	WI	54304	**888-442-7225**	920-569-7512
Greyhound Hall of Fame 407 S Buckeye Ave	Abilene	KS	67410	**800-932-7881**	785-263-3000
Harness Racing Museum & Hall of Fame 240 Main St	Goshen	NY	10924	**877-800-8782**	845-294-6330
Hendrick Motorsports Museum 4400 Papa Joe Hendrick Blvd	Charlotte	NC	28262	**877-467-4890**	
International Tennis Hall of Fame & Museum 194 Bellevue Ave	Newport	RI	02840	**800-745-3000**	401-849-3990
Louisville Slugger Museum 800 W Main St	Louisville	KY	40202	**877-775-8443**	502-585-5226
Mississippi Sports Hall of Fame & Museum 1152 Lakeland Dr	Jackson	MS	39216	**800-280-3263**	601-982-8264
Missouri Sports Hall of Fame 3861 E Stan Musial Dr	Springfield	MO	65809	**800-498-5678**	417-889-3100
Motorcycle Hall of Fame Museum 13515 Yarmouth Dr	Pickerington	OH	43147	**800-262-5646**	614-856-2222
Naismith Memorial Basketball Hall of Fame 1000 W Columbus Ave	Springfield	MA	01105	**877-446-6752**	413-781-6500
National Baseball Hall of Fame & Museum 25 Main St	Cooperstown	NY	13326	**888-425-5633**	607-547-7200
National Fresh Water Fishing Hall of Fame 10360 Hall of Fame Dr PO Box 690	Hayward	WI	54843	**866-268-4333**	715-634-4440
National Museum of Racing & Hall of Fame 191 Union Ave	Saratoga Springs	NY	12866	**800-562-5394**	518-584-0400
National Softball Hall of Fame & Museum 2801 NE 50th St	Oklahoma City	OK	73111	**800-654-8337**	405-424-5266
National Sprint Car Hall of Fame & Museum One Sprint Capital Pl	Knoxville	IA	50138	**800-874-4488**	641-842-6176
Negro Leagues Baseball Museum 1616 E 18th St	Kansas City	MO	64108	**888-221-6526**	816-221-1920
North Carolina Sports Hall of Fame 5 E Edenton St NC Museum of History	Raleigh	NC	27601	**877-627-6724**	919-807-7900
Paul W Bryant Museum 300 Paul W Bryant Dr *General	Tuscaloosa	AL	35487	**866-772-2327***	205-348-4668
Texas Sports Hall of Fame 1108 S University Parks Dr	Waco	TX	76706	**800-567-9561**	254-756-1633
U.S. National Ski Hall of Fame 610 Palms Ave	Ishpeming	MI	49849	**800-648-0720**	906-485-6323

Classified Section

				Toll-Free	Phone
University of Iowa Athletics Hall of Fame					
KHF Bldg 446	Iowa City	IA	52242	**877-462-6342**	319-384-1031

520   MUSIC DISTRIBUTORS

				Toll-Free	Phone
A-r Editions Inc					
8551 Research Way Ste 180	Middleton	WI	53562	**800-736-0070**	608-836-9000
Allegro Corp					
20048 NE San Rafael St	Portland	OR	97230	**800-288-2007**	503-491-8480
Baker & Taylor Inc					
2550 W Tyvola Rd Ste 300	Charlotte	NC	28217	**800-775-1800**	
Gotham Distributing Corp					
60 Portland Rd	Conshohocken	PA	19428	**800-446-8426**	610-649-7650
Malaco Music Group Inc					
3023 W Northside Dr	Jackson	MS	39213	**800-272-7936***	601-982-4522
*Cust Svc					
Select-O-Hits Inc					
1981 Fletcher Creek Dr	Memphis	TN	38133	**800-346-0723**	901-388-1190

521   MUSIC PROGRAMMING SERVICES

				Toll-Free	Phone
DMX Music Inc					
1703 W Fifth St Ste 600	Austin	TX	78703	**800-345-5000**	512-380-8500
Muzak LLC					
3318 Lakemont Blvd	Fort Mill	SC	29708	**888-689-2559**	
PlayNetwork Inc					
8727 148th Ave NE	Redmond	WA	98052	**888-964-8274***	425-497-8100
*Sales					

522   MUSIC STORES

SEE ALSO Book, Music, Video Clubs

				Toll-Free	Phone
Amazon.com Inc					
1200 12th Ave S Ste 1200	Seattle	WA	98144	**800-201-7575***	206-266-1000
NASDAQ: AMZN ▪ *Cust Svc					
Best Buy Company Inc					
7601 Penn Ave S	Minneapolis	MN	55423	**888-237-8289**	612-291-1000
NYSE: BBY					
CD Universe					
101 N Plains Industrial Rd	Wallingford	CT	06492	**800-231-7937**	203-294-1648
CD Warehouse					
900 N Broadway	Oklahoma City	OK	73102	**800-641-9394**	919-577-6000
FirstCom Music					
1325 Capital Pkwy Ste 109	Carrollton	TX	75006	**800-858-8880***	972-446-8742
*Cust Svc					
Global Electronic Music Marketplace					
PO Box 2186	La Jolla	CA	92038	**800-207-4366**	858-456-0894
Hastings Entertainment Inc					
3601 Plains Blvd	Amarillo	TX	79102	**877-427-8464***	
NASDAQ: HAST ▪ *Cust Svc					
Mississippi Music Inc					
222 N Main St	Hattiesburg	MS	39401	**800-844-5821**	601-544-5821

523   MUSICAL INSTRUMENT STORES

				Toll-Free	Phone
Alamo Music Ctr					
425 N Main Ave	San Antonio	TX	78205	**800-822-5010**	210-224-1010
American Musical Supply					
PO Box 152	Spicer	MN	56288	**800-458-4076**	320-796-2088
Amro Music Stores					
2918 Poplar Ave	Memphis	TN	38111	**800-626-2676***	901-323-8888
*General					
Brook Mays Music Co					
8605 John Carpenter Fwy	Dallas	TX	75247	**800-637-8966***	214-631-0928
*Cust Svc					
Buddy Rogers Music Inc					
6891 Simpson Ave	Cincinnati	OH	45239	**800-536-2263**	513-729-1950
Cascio Interstate Music					
13819 W National Ave	New Berlin	WI	53151	**800-462-2263**	262-789-7600
Elderly Instruments					
1100 N Washington Ave	Lansing	MI	48906	**888-473-5810**	517-372-7890
First Act Inc					
745 Boylston St	Boston	MA	02116	**888-551-1115**	617-226-7888
Fletcher Music Centers Inc					
3966 Airway Cir	Clearwater	FL	33762	**800-258-1088**	727-571-1088
Foxes Music Co					
416 S Washington St	Falls Church	VA	22046	**800-446-4414**	703-533-7393
Graves Piano & Organ Company Inc					
5798 Karl Rd	Columbus	OH	43229	**800-686-4322**	614-847-4322
International Violin Co Ltd					
1421 Clarkview Rd	Baltimore	MD	21209	**800-542-3538**	410-832-2525
JW Pepper & Son Inc					
2480 Industrial Blvd	Paoli	PA	19301	**800-345-6296**	610-648-0500
Music & Arts Centers Inc					
4626 Wedgewood Blvd	Frederick	MD	21703	**888-731-5396**	
Musician's Friend Inc					
PO Box 7479	Westlake Village	CA	91359	**800-391-8762**	801-501-8110
Musiciansbuy.com Inc					
7830 Byron Dr Ste 1	West Palm Beach	FL	33404	**877-778-7845**	561-842-7451
Quantum Audio Designs Inc					
6408 State Hwy 77	Benton	MO	63736	**888-545-4404**	573-545-4404
Stanton's Sheet Music					
330 S Fourth St	Columbus	OH	43215	**800-426-8742**	614-224-4257
Strait Music Co					
2428 W Ben White Blvd	Austin	TX	78704	**800-725-8877**	512-476-6927
Sweetwater Sound Inc					
5501 US Hwy 30 W	Fort Wayne	IN	46818	**800-222-4700**	260-432-8176

				Toll-Free	Phone
West Music Inc					
1212 Fifth St PO Box 5521	Coralville	IA	52241	**800-373-2000**	319-351-2000
Woodwind & Brasswind					
4004 Technology Dr	South Bend	IN	46628	**800-348-5003**	574-251-3500

524   MUSICAL INSTRUMENTS

				Toll-Free	Phone
Alembic Inc					
3005 Wiljan Ct	Santa Rosa	CA	95407	**800-322-5893**	707-523-2611
Avedis Zildjian Co					
22 Longwater Dr	Norwell	MA	02061	**800-229-8672**	781-871-2200
Burkart-Phelan Inc					
2 Shaker Rd Ste D-107	Shirley	MA	01464	**800-236-4343**	978-425-4500
Carvin Corp					
12340 World Trade Dr	San Diego	CA	92128	**800-854-2235**	858-487-1600
CF Martin & Company Inc					
510 Sycamore St PO Box 329	Nazareth	PA	18064	**888-433-9177**	610-759-2837
Chime Master Systems					
PO Box 936	Lancaster	OH	43130	**800-344-7464**	
Daisy Rock Guitars					
16320 Roscoe Blvd Ste 100	Van Nuys	CA	91410	**877-693-2479**	
Davitt & Hanser Music Co					
3015 Kustom Dr	Hebron	KY	41048	**800-999-5558**	859-817-7100
Deering Banjo Co					
3733 Kenora Dr	Spring Valley	CA	91977	**800-845-7791**	619-464-8252
E & O Mari Inc					
256 Broadway	Newburgh	NY	12550	**800-750-3034**	845-562-4400
Edwards Instrument Co					
530 S Hwy H	Elkhorn	WI	53121	**800-562-6838**	262-723-4221
Ernie Ball					
151 Suburban Rd	San Luis Obispo	CA	93401	**866-823-2255**	805-544-7726
Fender Musical Instruments Corp					
17600 N Perimeter Dr Ste 100	Scottsdale	AZ	85255	**800-488-1818***	480-596-9690
*Cust Svc					
General Music Corp					
1164 Tower Ln	Bensenville	IL	60106	**800-323-0280**	630-766-8230
Getzen Company Inc					
530 S Cty Hwy H PO Box 440	Elkhorn	WI	53121	**800-366-5584**	262-723-4221
GHS Corp					
2813 Wilber Ave	Battle Creek	MI	49037	**800-388-4447**	
Gibson Guitar Corp					
309 Plus Pk Blvd	Nashville	TN	37217	**800-444-2766**	615-871-4500
Gibson Piano Ventures Inc					
309 Plus Pk Blvd	Nashville	TN	37217	**800-444-2766**	615-871-4500
Hammond Suzuki USA Inc					
743 Annoreno Dr	Addison	IL	60101	**888-765-2900**	630-543-0277
Hohner Inc					
1000 Technology Pk Dr	Glen Allen	VA	23059	**800-446-6010**	804-515-1900
J D'Addario & Company Inc					
595 Smith St	Farmingdale	NY	11735	**800-323-2746**	631-439-3300
JD Calato Mfg Company Inc					
4501 Hyde Pk Blvd	Niagara Falls	NY	14305	**800-358-4590***	716-285-3546
*Cust Svc					
La Bella Strings					
256 Broadway	Newburgh	NY	12550	**800-750-3034**	845-562-4400
Lindeblad Piano Restoration					
101 Us 46	Pine Brook	NJ	07058	**888-587-4266**	
Lowrey Organ Co					
847 N Church Ct	Elmhurst	IL	60126	**800-451-5940**	800-451-5939
Lyon & Healy Harps Inc					
168 N Ogden Ave	Chicago	IL	60607	**800-621-3881**	312-786-1881
Maas-Rowe Carillons Inc					
2255 Meyers Ave	Escondido	CA	92029	**800-854-2023**	
Manhasset Specialty Co					
3505 Fruitvale Blvd	Yakima	WA	98902	**800-795-0965**	509-248-3810
Morley Pedals 325 Cary Pt Dr	Cary	IL	60013	**800-284-5172**	847-639-4646
Musicorp					
2456 Remount Rd	North Charleston	SC	29406	**800-845-1922**	843-745-8501
Organ Supply Industries Inc					
2320 W 50th St	Erie	PA	16506	**800-458-0289**	814-835-2244
PianoDisc					
4111 N Fwy Blvd	Sacramento	CA	95834	**800-566-3472**	916-567-9999
Prestini Musical Instruments Inc					
2020 N Aurora Dr	Nogales	AZ	85628	**800-528-6569***	520-287-4931
*General					
Remo Inc 28101 Industry Dr	Valencia	CA	91355	**800-525-5134**	661-294-5600
Saint Louis Music Inc					
1400 Ferguson Ave	Saint Louis	MO	63133	**800-727-4512**	314-727-4512
Schaff Piano Supply Co					
451 Oakwood Rd	Lake Zurich	IL	60047	**800-747-4266**	847-438-4556
Schulmerich Carillons Inc					
Carillon Hill	Sellersville	PA	18960	**800-772-3557**	215-257-2771
Steinway & Sons					
1 Steinway Pl	Long Island City	NY	11105	**800-783-4692**	718-721-2600
Suzuki Musical Instrument Corp					
PO Box 261030	San Diego	CA	92196	**800-854-1594***	619-258-1896
*Cust Svc					
Ultimate Support Systems Inc					
5836 Wright Dr	Loveland	CO	80538	**800-525-5628**	
Wenger Corp					
555 Pk Dr PO Box 448	Owatonna	MN	55060	**800-493-6437**	507-455-4100
Wicks Pipe Organ Co					
1100 Fifth St	Highland	IL	62249	**877-654-2191***	618-654-2191
*Cust Svc					

525   MUTUAL FUNDS

				Toll-Free	Phone
Alerus Retirement Solutions					
Two Pine Tree Dr Ste 400	Arden Hills	MN	55112	**800-795-2697**	
Alger Family of Funds					
PO Box 8480	Boston	MA	02266	**800-992-3863**	
American Century Proprietary Holdings Inc					
PO Box 419200	Kansas City	MO	64141	**800-345-2021**	816-531-5575

	City	State	Zip	Toll-Free	Phone
Aquila Group of Funds 380 Madison Ave Ste 2300	New York	NY	10017	**800-437-1020**	212-697-6666
Artisan Funds PO Box 8412 *Cust Svc	Boston	MA	02266	**800-344-1770***	
Ascendant Advisors LLC Four Oaks Pl 1330 Post Oak Blvd Ste 1550	Houston	TX	77056	**800-552-6010**	
Baron Funds 767 Fifth Ave 49th Fl	New York	NY	10153	**800-992-2766**	212-583-2000
Calvert Investments Inc 4550 Montgomery Ave Ste 1000N	Bethesda	MD	20814	**800-368-2748**	301-951-4800
CGM Funds 38 Newbury St Ste 8	Boston	MA	02116	**800-345-4048**	617-859-7714
Clipper Fund 2949 E Elvira Rd Ste 101	Tucson	AZ	85756	**800-432-2504**	
Davis Funds 2949 E Elvira Rd Ste 101	Tucson	AR	85756	**800-279-0279**	
Dodge & Cox Funds 30 Dan Rd PO Box 8422	Canton	MA	02021	**800-621-3979**	
Domini Social Investments PO Box 9785	Providence	RI	02940	**800-582-6757**	
Dreyfus Family of Funds PO Box 55299	Boston	MA	02205	**800-843-5466**	
Eaton Vance Mutual Funds Two International Pl	Boston	MA	02110	**800-225-6265**	617-482-8260
Fidelity Advisor Funds PO Box 770002	Cincinnati	OH	45277	**800-522-7297**	
Fidelity Investment Funds PO Box 770001	Cincinnati	OH	45277	**800-343-3548**	
Fidelity Investments Institutional Operations Company Inc PO Box 770002	Cincinnati	OH	45277	**877-208-0098**	
First American Funds PO Box 701	Milwaukee	WI	53201	**800-677-3863**	
GAMCO Investors Inc One Corporate Ctr *NYSE: GBL*	Rye	NY	10580	**800-422-3554**	914-921-5100
Glenmede Funds 1650 Market St Ste 1200	Philadelphia	PA	19103	**800-966-3200**	215-419-6000
Goldman Sachs 200 W St *NYSE: GS*	New York	NY	10282	**800-526-7384**	212-902-1000
Hartford Mutual Funds 30 Dan Rd Ste 55022	Canton	MA	02021	**888-843-7824**	
Heartland Funds 789 N Water St Ste 500	Milwaukee	WI	53202	**800-432-7856**	414-347-7777
ICMARC 777 N Capitol St NE Ste 600 *General	Washington	DC	20002	**800-669-7471***	202-962-4600
ING Funds 7337 E Doubletree Ranch Rd	Scottsdale	AZ	85258	**800-992-0180**	
Invesco 11 Greenway Plaza Ste 100	Houston	TX	77046	**800-959-4246**	713-626-1919
Ivy Funds 6300 Lamar Ave	Overland Park	KS	66202	**888-923-3355**	913-236-2000
John Hancock Funds 101 Huntington Ave 10th Fl	Boston	MA	02199	**800-338-8080**	617-375-1500
Lazard Funds 30 Rockefeller Plz 57th Fl	New York	NY	10112	**800-823-6300**	
Loomis Sayles Funds One Financial Ctr	Boston	MA	02111	**800-633-3330**	617-482-2450
Mairs & Power Funds 332 Minnesota St Ste W-1520	Saint Paul	MN	55101	**800-304-7404**	651-222-8478
Manulife Mutual Funds 200 Bloor St E N Twr 3	Toronto	ON	M4W1E5	**888-588-7999**	
MASTER Teacher Inc, The 2600 Leadership Ln	Manhattan	KS	66505	**800-669-9633**	
Monetta Family of Mutual Funds 1776A S Naperville Rd Ste 100	Wheaton	IL	60189	**800-241-9772**	630-462-9800
Morgan Stanley Family of Funds 1585 Broadway	New York	NY	10036	**800-223-2440**	212-761-4000
Mutual Benefit Group 409 Penn St PO Box 577	Huntingdon	PA	16652	**800-283-3531**	814-643-3000
Neuberger Berman Funds PO Box 8403	Boston	MA	02266	**800-877-9700**	212-476-8800
Nicholas Family of Funds 700 N Water St Ste 1010	Milwaukee	WI	53202	**800-227-5987**	414-272-6133
Northern Funds PO Box 75986	Chicago	IL	60675	**800-595-9111**	
Northern Institutional Funds 801 S Canal St C5S	Chicago	IL	60607	**800-637-1380**	
Oak Assoc Funds PO Box 8233	Denver	CO	80201	**888-462-5386**	
Oakmark Family of Funds 330 W nineth St	Kansas City	MO	64105	**800-625-6275**	617-483-8327
OppenheimerFunds Inc 225 Liberty St	New York	NY	10281	**800-525-7048**	
Pax World Fund Family 30 Penhallow St Ste 400	Portsmouth	NH	03801	**800-767-1729**	603-431-8022
PIMCO Institutional Funds PO Box 219024	Kansas City	MO	64121	**800-927-4648**	
Pioneer Funds 60 State St	Boston	MA	02109	**800-225-6292**	617-742-7825
Putnam Family of Funds PO Box 41203	Providence	RI	02940	**800-225-1581**	
Rainier Investment Management Mutual Funds 601 Union St Ste 2801	Seattle	WA	98101	**800-536-4640**	
RidgeWorth Funds 50 Hurt Plaza Ste 1400	Atlanta	GA	30305	**866-595-2470**	
Ross Smith Asset Management Inc 601 10th Ave S W Ste 155	Calgary	AB	T2R0B2	**888-494-6893**	
Rydex Funds 805 King Farm Blvd Ste 600 *Cust Svc	Rockville	MD	20850	**800-820-0888***	301-296-5100
Security Funds One Security Benefit Pl	Topeka	KS	66636	**800-888-2461**	785-438-3000
SEI One Freedom Vly Dr *NASDAQ: SEIC*	Oaks	PA	19456	**800-342-5734**	610-676-1000
Selected Funds PO Box 8243	Boston	MA	02266	**800-243-1575**	
Sequoia Fund Inc 767 Fifth Ave Ste 4701	New York	NY	10153	**800-686-6884**	212-832-5280
Sound Shore Fund 3435 Stelzer Rd	Columbus	OH	43219	**800-754-8758**	
SSgA Funds One Lincoln St	Boston	MA	02111	**800-997-7327**	617-786-3000
State Farm Mutual Funds PO Box 219548	Kansas City	MO	64121	**800-447-4930**	
State Teachers Retirement System of Ohio 275 E Broad St	Columbus	OH	43215	**888-227-7877**	
Steadyhand Investment Funds Limited Partnership 1747 W Third Ave	Vancouver	BC	V6J1K7	**888-888-3147**	
T Rowe Price Mutual Funds 100 E Pratt St	Baltimore	MD	21202	**800-638-5660**	410-345-2000
TCW Group Inc 865 S Figueroa St Ste 1800	Los Angeles	CA	90017	**800-386-3829**	213-244-0000
TFS Capital LLC 10 N High St Ste 500	West Chester	PA	19380	**888-837-4446**	
Thornburg Investment Management Funds 2300 N Ridgetop Rd	Santa Fe	NM	87506	**800-533-9337**	505-984-0200
Torray Fund 7501 Wisconsin Ave Ste 750 W	Bethesda	MD	20814	**800-443-3036**	301-493-4600
Trinity Fiduciary Partners LLC 106 Decker Court Ste 226	Irving	TX	75062	**877-334-1283**	
Victory Funds 4900 Tiedeman Rd PO Box 182593	Brooklyn	OH	44144	**800-539-3863**	
Wilshire Mutual Funds Inc PO Box 219512	Kansas City	MO	64121	**888-200-6796**	

526 NAVIGATION & GUIDANCE INSTRUMENTS & SYSTEMS

	City	State	Zip	Toll-Free	Phone
Adducent Technology Inc 230 Parque Margarita	Rohnert Park	CA	94928	**800-648-0656**	707-478-8136
Alpine Electronics of America 19145 Gramercy Pl	Torrance	CA	90501	**800-257-4631**	310-326-8000
Butler National Corp 19920 W 161st St *OTC: BUKS*	Olathe	KS	66062	**800-690-6903**	913-780-9595
CMI Inc 316 E Ninth St	Owensboro	KY	42303	**866-835-0690**	270-685-6545
Cubic Corp 9333 Balboa Ave PO Box 85587 *NYSE: CUB*	San Diego	CA	92186	**800-937-5449**	858-277-6780
Cubic Defense Systems 9333 Balboa Ave	San Diego	CA	92123	**800-937-5449**	858-277-6780
Del Mar Avionics 1601 Alton Pkwy Ste C	Irvine	CA	92606	**800-854-0481**	949-250-3200
DRS C3 Systems LLC 400 Professional Dr	Gaithersburg	MD	20879	**800-694-5005**	301-921-8100
DRS Technologies Inc Five Sylvan Way	Parsippany	NJ	07054	**800-694-5005**	973-898-1500
DRS Training & Control Systems 645 Anchors St NW	Fort Walton Beach	FL	32548	**800-694-5005**	850-302-3000
Flash Technology Corp 332 Nichol Mill Ln	Franklin	TN	37067	**888-313-5274**	615-503-2000
FLIR Systems Inc 27700-A SW Pkwy Ave *NASDAQ: FLIR*	Wilsonville	OR	97070	**877-773-3547**	503-498-3547
Frontier Electronic Systems Corp 4500 W Sixth Ave	Stillwater	OK	74074	**800-677-1769**	405-624-1769
Garmin Ltd 1200 E 151st St *NASDAQ: GRMN*	Olathe	KS	66062	**888-442-7646**	913-397-8200
General Dynamics C4 Systems 400 John Quincy Adams Rd Bldg 80	Taunton	MA	02780	**877-449-0600**	
Goodrich Corp 2730 W Tyvola Rd 4 Coliseum Ctr *NYSE: GR*	Charlotte	NC	28217	**800-735-7899**	704-423-7000
Innovative Solutions & Support Inc 720 Pennsylvania Dr *NASDAQ: ISSC*	Exton	PA	19341	**866-359-7876**	610-646-9800
Interstate Electronics Corp 602 E Vermont Ave PO Box 3117	Anaheim	CA	92803	**800-854-6979**	714-758-0500
ITT Industries Inc 1133 Westchester Ave *NYSE: ITT*	White Plains	NY	10604	**800-254-2823**	914-641-2000
Jewell Instruments LLC 850 Perimeter Rd	Manchester	NH	03103	**800-227-5955**	603-669-6400
Kollsman Inc 220 Daniel Webster Hwy	Merrimack	NH	03054	**800-772-9603**	603-889-2500
L-3 Avionics Systems 5353 52nd St SE	Grand Rapids	MI	49512	**800-253-9525**	616-949-6600
L-3 Communications Corp Aviation Recorders Div 6000 Fruitville Rd	Sarasota	FL	34232	**877-726-2228**	941-371-0811
L-3 Communications Corp Communication Systems East Div 1 Federal St	Camden	NJ	08103	**800-339-6197**	856-338-3000
L-3 Communications Corp Randtron Antenna Systems Div 130 Constitution Dr *Sales	Menlo Park	CA	94025	**866-900-7270***	650-326-9500
Laitram LLC 200 Laitram Ln	Harahan	LA	70123	**800-535-7631**	504-733-6000
Lockheed Martin Corp 6801 Rockledge Dr *NYSE: LMT*	Bethesda	MD	20817	**866-562-2363**	301-897-6000
Lowrance Electronics Inc 12000 E Skelly Dr	Tulsa	OK	74128	**800-628-4487**	918-437-6881
Lycoming Engines 652 Oliver St	Williamsport	PA	17701	**800-258-3279**	570-323-6181
Mackay Communications Inc 3691 Trust Dr	Raleigh	NC	27616	**877-462-2529**	919-850-3000
Newcon Optik 105 Sparks Ave	North York	ON	M2H2S5	**877-368-6666**	416-663-6963
Onboard Systems International 13915 NW Third Ct	Vancouver	WA	98685	**800-275-0883**	360-546-3072
Oregon Aero Inc 34020 Skyway Dr	Scappoose	OR	97056	**800-888-6910**	503-543-7399
Raymarine Inc 21 Manchester St	Merrimack	NH	03054	**800-539-5539**	603-881-5200
Raytheon Intelligence & Information Systems 1200 S Jupiter Rd	Garland	TX	75042	**800-423-0210**	972-205-5100
Rockwell Collins Inc 400 Collins Rd NE *NYSE: COL*	Cedar Rapids	IA	52498	**888-721-3094**	319-295-1000

	Toll-Free	Phone
Rostra Precision Controls Inc		
2519 Dana Dr ....Laurinburg NC 28352	800-782-3379*	910-276-4853
*Cust Svc		
SELEX Inc		
11300 W 89th St ....Overland Park KS 66214	800-765-0861	913-495-2600
Shadin LP		
6831 Oxford St ....St Louis Park MN 55426	800-328-0584	952-927-6500
Superior Air Parts Inc		
621 S Royal Ln Ste 100 ....Coppell TX 75019	800-420-4727	972-829-4600
Systron Donner Inertial		
355 Lennon Ln ....Walnut Creek CA 94598	866-234-4976	925-979-4400
Trimble Navigation Ltd		
935 Stewart Dr ....Sunnyvale CA 94085	800-827-8000	408-481-8000
NASDAQ: TRMB		
Trutrak Flight Systems Inc		
1500 S Old Missouri Rd ....Springdale AR 72764	866-878-8725	479-751-0250
Tyonek Mfg Group Inc		
229 Palmer Rd ....Madison AL 35758	877-258-6200	256-258-6200
Whistler Group Inc		
13016 N Walton Blvd ....Bentonville AR 72712	800-531-0004*	479-273-6012
*Cust Svc		
Wipaire Inc		
1700 Henry Ave ....South St Paul MN 55075	888-947-2473	651-451-1205
XATA Corp		
965 Prairie Ctr Dr ....Eden Prairie MN 55344	800-745-9282	952-707-5600
Zonar Systems LLC		
18200 Cascade Ave S ....Seattle WA 98188	877-843-3847	206-878-2459

527   NEWS SYNDICATES, SERVICES, BUREAUS

	Toll-Free	Phone
AccountingWEB Inc		
PO Box 2252 ....Westerville OH 43086	866-688-1678	
AccuWeather Inc		
385 Science Pk Rd ....State College PA 16803	800-566-6606*	814-235-8650
*Sales		
American Baptist News Service		
PO Box 851 ....Valley Forge PA 19482	800-222-3872	610-768-2000
American Chiropractor, The		
8619 NW 68Th St ....Miami FL 33166	888-369-1396	
Andrews McMeel Universal		
1130 Walnut ....Kansas City MO 64106	800-851-8923	816-581-7500
Argus Interactive Agency Inc		
217 N Main St Ste 200 ....Santa Ana CA 92701	866-595-9597	
Creators Syndicate Inc		
5777 W Century Blvd Ste 700..........Los Angeles CA 90045	877-563-4645	310-337-7003
Disaster News Network (DNN)		
PO Box 1746 ....Ellicott City MD 21041	888-384-3028	443-393-3330
FurnitureDealer.net Inc		
PO Box 22251 ....Eagan MN 55122	866-387-6357	
Gateway Newstands		
240 Chrislea Rd ....Woodbridge ON L4L8V1	800-942-5351	905-851-9652
Inman News		
1100 Marina Village Pkwy Ste 102......Alameda CA 94501	800-775-4662	510-658-9252
King Features Syndicate Inc		
300 W 57th St 15th Fl............New York NY 10019	800-708-7311	212-969-7550
Los Angeles Times-Washington Post News Service Inc		
1150 15th St NW ....Washington DC 20071	800-627-1150	202-334-6000
Market Wire Inc		
100 N Sepulveda Blvd Ste 325......El Segundo CA 90245	800-774-9473*	310-765-3200
*General		
New York Times News Service Div		
620 Eigth Ave 9th Fl..............New York NY 10018	800-698-4637	212-556-7652
NewRetirement LLC		
1933 Davis St Ste 205 ....San Leandro CA 94111	866-441-0246	415-738-2435
PR Photos		
4521 Pga Blvd ....Palm Beach Gardens FL 33418	866-551-7827	
Religion News Service (RNS)		
529 14th St NW Ste 425 ....Washington DC 20045	800-767-6781	202-463-8777
Softomate LLC		
104 Sixth St Unit B ....Lynden WA 98264	877-243-8735	
United Methodist News Service		
810 12th Ave S ....Nashville TN 37203	800-251-8140	615-742-5470
Washington Post Writers Group		
1150 15th St NW ....Washington DC 20071	800-879-9794	202-334-6375

528   NEWSLETTERS

528-1 Banking & Finance Newsletters

	Toll-Free	Phone
Banking Daily		
1801 S Bell St ....Arlington VA 22202	800-372-1033	
Bankruptcy Court Decisions		
360 Hiatt Dr ....Palm Beach Gardens FL 33418	800-621-5463	561-622-6520
Commercial Lending Litigation News		
360 Hiatt Dr ....Palm Beach Gardens FL 33418	800-621-5463	561-622-6520
Consumer Bankruptcy News		
360 Hiatt Dr ....Palm Beach Gardens FL 33418	800-621-5463	561-622-6520
Credit Union Directors Newsletter		
5710 Mineral Pt Rd ....Madison WI 53705	800-356-9655	608-231-4000
Credit Union Executive Newsletter		
5710 Mineral Pt Rd ....Madison WI 53705	800-356-9655*	608-231-4000
*Circ		
Electronic Commerce & Law Report		
1801 S Bell St ....Arlington VA 22202	800-372-1033	
International Business & Finance Daily		
1801 S Bell St ....Arlington VA 22202	800-372-1033	
International Tax Monitor		
1801 S Bell St ....Arlington VA 22202	800-372-1033	

528-2 Business & Professional Newsletters

	Toll-Free	Phone
American Speaker		
PO Box 787 ....Williamsport PA 17703	800-791-8699	570-567-1982
Antitrust & Trade Regulation Daily		
1801 S Bell St ....Arlington VA 22202	800-372-1033	
CD Publications		
8204 Fenton St ....Silver Spring MD 20910	800-666-6380	301-588-6380
Corporate Writer & Editor		
111 E Wacker Dr Ste 500 ....Chicago IL 60601	800-878-5331	312-960-4140
Customer Communicator, The (TCC)		
712 Main St Ste 187B..............Boonton NJ 07005	800-232-4317	973-265-2300
Daily Report for Executives		
1801 S Bell St ....Arlington VA 22202	800-372-1033	
Daily Tax Report		
1801 S Bell St ....Arlington VA 22202	800-372-1033	
Distribution Ctr Management (DCM)		
712 Main St Ste 187B..............Boonton NJ 07005	800-232-4317	973-265-2300
Downtown Idea Exchange (DIX)		
712 Main St Ste 187B..............Boonton NJ 07005	800-232-4317	973-265-2300
Federal EEO Advisor		
360 Hiatt Dr ....Palm Beach Gardens FL 33418	800-341-7874	561-622-6520
Government Employee Relations Report		
1801 S Bell St ....Arlington VA 22202	800-372-1033	
Human Resources Report		
1801 S Bell St ....Arlington VA 22202	800-372-1033	
International Trade Reporter		
1801 S Bell St ....Arlington VA 22202	800-372-1033	
Journal of Employee Communication Management		
316 N Michigan Ave Ste 400 ....Chicago IL 60601	800-878-5331	312-960-4100
Law Officer's Bulletin		
610 Opperman Dr ....Eagan MN 55123	800-344-5008	651-687-7000
LRP Publications		
360 Hiatt Dr ....Palm Beach Gardens FL 33418	800-341-7874	
Manager's Intelligence Report (MIR)		
316 N Michigan Ave Ste 400 ....Chicago IL 60601	800-878-5331	
Payroll Practitioner's Monthly		
Three Bethesda Metro Ctr Ste 250......Bethesda MD 20814	800-372-1033	
Ragan Communications Inc		
316 N Michigan Ave Ste 400 ....Chicago IL 60601	800-878-5331	312-960-4100
Teamwork Newsletter		
2222 Sedwick Dr ....Durham NC 27713	800-223-8720	
Working Together		
360 Hiatt Dr ....Palm Beach Gardens FL 33418	800-621-5463	561-622-6520

528-3 Computer & Internet Newsletters

	Toll-Free	Phone
Biotechnology Software		
140 Huguenot St Third Fl ....New Rochelle NY 10801	800-654-3237	914-740-2100
Business Intelligence Advisor		
37 Broadway Ste 1 ....Arlington MA 02474	800-964-5118	781-648-8700
Computer Economics Report, The		
2082 Business Ctr Dr Ste 240 ....Irvine CA 92612	800-326-8100	949-831-8700
Cutter Consortium		
37 Broadway Ste 1 ....Arlington MA 02474	800-964-5118	781-648-8700
Cutter IT Journal		
37 Broadway Ste 1 ....Arlington MA 02474	800-964-5118	781-648-8700
Network World Inc		
492 Old Connecticut Path ....Framingham MA 01701	800-622-1108	
Washington Internet Daily		
2115 Ward Ct NW ....Washington DC 20037	800-771-9202	202-872-9200

528-4 Education Newsletters

	Toll-Free	Phone
Early Childhood Report		
360 Hiatt Dr ....Palm Beach Gardens FL 33418	800-621-5463	561-622-6520
Education Grants Alert		
360 Hiatt Dr ....Palm Beach Gardens FL 33418	800-621-5463	561-622-6520
Educational Research Newsletter		
PO Box 2347 ....South Portland ME 04116	800-321-7471	207-632-1954
Library of Congress Information Bulletin		
101 Independence Ave SE ....Washington DC 20540	888-371-5848	202-707-2905
New York Education Law Report		
360 Hiatt Dr ....Palm Beach FL	800-341-7874	561-622-6520
School Law News		
360 Hiatt Dr ....Palm Beach Gardens FL 33418	800-341-7874	
Special Education Report		
360 Hiatt Dr ....Palm Beach Gardens FL 33418	800-621-5463*	561-622-6520
*Sales		

528-5 Energy & Environmental Newsletters

	Toll-Free	Phone
Chemical Regulation Reporter		
1801 S Bell St ....Arlington VA 22202	800-372-1033	
Clean Air Report		
1919 S Eads St Ste 201 ....Arlington VA 22202	800-424-9068	703-416-8516
Coal Outlook		
1200 G St NW Ste 1100 ....Washington DC 20005	800-752-8878	212-904-3070
Daily Environment Report		
1801 S Bell St ....Arlington VA 22202	800-372-1033	
Electric Utility Week		
Two Penn Plz 25th Fl ....New York NY 10121	800-752-8878	212-904-3070
Environment Reporter		
1801 S Bell St ....Arlington VA 22202	800-372-1033	
Environmental Compliance Bulletin		
1801 S Bell St ....Arlington VA 22202	800-372-1033	

	Toll-Free	Phone
Gas Daily		
1200 G St NW Ste 1000 .... Washington DC 20005	**800-752-8878**	202-383-2000
Global Power Report		
Two Penn Plz 25th Fl .... New York NY 10121	**800-752-8878**	
Inside Energy		
Two Penn Plz 25th Fl .... New York NY 10121	**800-752-8878**	
Inside FERC		
Two Penn Plz 25th Fl .... New York NY 10121	**800-752-8878**	
Inside FERC's Gas Market Report		
Two Penn Plz 25th Fl .... New York NY 10121	**800-752-8878**	212-904-3070
Inside NRC		
Two Penn Plz 25th Fl .... New York NY 10121	**800-752-8878**	
Northeast Power Report		
Two Penn Plz 25th Fl .... New York NY 10121	**800-752-8878**	
NuclearFuel		
1200 G St NW Ste 1000 .... Washington DC 20005	**800-228-9290**	202-383-2000
Nucleonics Week		
2 Penn Plaza 25th Fl .... New York NY 10121	**800-752-8878**	212-904-3070
Oil Price Information Service		
3349 Hwy 138 Bldg D Ste D .... Wall NJ 07719	**888-301-2645***	732-901-8800
*Cust Svc		
OPIS		
9737 Washingtonian Blvd Ste 100 ....Gaithersburg MD 20878	**888-301-2645**	301-287-2645
Solid Waste Assn of North America (SWANA)		
1100 Wayne Ave Ste 700 .... Silver Spring MD 20910	**800-467-9262**	301-585-2898
State Environment Daily		
1801 S Bell St .... Arlington VA 22202	**800-372-1033**	
Toxics Law Reporter		
1801 S Bell St .... Arlington VA 22202	**800-372-1033**	
Utility Environment Report		
Two Penn Plz 25th Fl .... New York NY 10121	**800-752-8878**	

528-6 General Interest Newsletters

	Toll-Free	Phone
Bottom Line/Personal		
281 Tresser Blvd Eighth Fl ....Stamford CT 06901	**800-678-5835***	800-274-5611
*Cust Svc		
Kiplinger California Letter		
1729 H St NW .... Washington DC 20006	**800-544-0155**	202-887-6400
NRTA/AARP Bulletin		
601 E St NW .... Washington DC 20049	**888-867-2277**	202-434-2277

528-7 Government & Law Newsletters

	Toll-Free	Phone
Alcoholic Beverage Control		
PO Box 27491 ....Richmond VA 23261	**800-552-3200**	804-213-4565
American Association for Justice		
777 6th St NW Ste 200 .... Washington DC 20001	**800-424-2727**	202-965-3500
Bankruptcy Law Letter		
610 Opperman Dr ....Eagan MN 55123	**800-937-8529**	651-687-7000
BD Week		
9737 Washingtonian Blvd Ste 100 ....Gaithersburg MD 20878	**866-777-8567**	646-223-6771
Bioethics Legal Review		
1617 JFK Blvd Ste 1750 ....Philadelphia PA 19103	**877-256-2472**	215-557-2300
Class Action Litigation Report		
1801 S Bell St .... Arlington VA 22202	**800-372-1033**	
Community Development Digest		
8204 Fenton St .... Silver Spring MD 20910	**800-666-6380**	301-588-6380
Community Health Funding Week		
8204 Fenton St .... Silver Spring MD 20910	**800-666-6380**	301-588-6380
Computer Technology Law Report		
1801 S Bell St .... Arlington VA 22202	**800-372-1033**	
Congress Daily		
600 New Hampshire Ave		
The Watergate .... Washington DC 20037	**800-424-2921**	202-266-7000
Congressional Quarterly Budget Tracker		
77 K St NE .... Washington DC 20002	**800-432-2250**	202-650-6500
Congressional Quarterly HealthBeat		
77 K St NE .... Washington DC 20002	**800-432-2250**	202-650-6500
Congressional Quarterly House Action Reports		
77 K St NE .... Washington DC 20002	**800-432-2250**	202-650-6500
Consumer Financial Services Law Report		
360 Hiatt Dr .... Palm Beach Gardens FL 33418	**800-621-5463**	561-622-6520
Corporate Compliance & Regulatory		
1617 JFK Blvd Ste 1750 ....Philadelphia PA 19103	**877-256-2472**	215-557-2300
Criminal Law Reporter		
1801 S Bell St .... Arlington VA 22202	**800-372-1033**	
Daily Labor Report		
1801 S Bell St .... Arlington VA 22202	**800-372-1033**	
Development Director's Letter		
8204 Fenton St .... Silver Spring MD 20910	**800-666-6380**	301-588-6380
Disability Law Compliance Report		
610 Opperman Dr ....Eagan MN 55123	**800-328-4880***	651-687-7000
*Cust Svc		
e-Commerce Law & Strategy		
1617 JFK Blvd Ste 1750 ....Philadelphia PA 19103	**877-256-2472**	215-557-2300
e-Discovery Law & Strategy		
1617 JFK Blvd Ste 1750 ....Philadelphia PA 19103	**877-256-2472**	215-557-2300
Employment Discrimination Report		
1801 S Bell St .... Arlington VA 22202	**800-372-1033**	
Expert Evidence Report		
1801 S Bell St .... Arlington VA 22202	**800-372-1033**	
Family Law Reporter		
1801 S Bell St .... Arlington VA 22202	**800-372-1033**	
Federal Assistance Monitor		
8204 Fenton St .... Silver Spring MD 20910	**800-666-6380**	301-588-6380
Federal Contracts Report		
1801 S Bell St .... Arlington VA 22202	**800-372-1033**	
Franchising Business & Law Alert		
1617 JFK Blvd Ste 1750 ....Philadelphia PA 19103	**877-256-2472**	215-557-2300
Health Care Fraud Report		
1801 S Bell St .... Arlington VA 22202	**800-372-1033**	

	Toll-Free	Phone
Health Law Reporter		
1801 S Bell St .... Arlington VA 22202	**800-372-1033**	
Homeland Security Funding Week		
8204 Fenton St .... Silver Spring MD 20910	**800-666-6380**	301-588-6380
Hospital Litigation Reporter		
590 Dutch Vly Rd NE .... Atlanta GA 30324	**800-926-7926**	404-881-1141
Hospitality Law		
360 Hiatt Dr .... Palm Beach Gardens FL 33418	**800-621-5463**	561-622-6520
Insurance Coverage Law Bulletin, The		
1617 JFK Blvd Ste 1750 ....Philadelphia PA 19103	**877-256-2472**	215-557-2300
Internet Law & Strategy		
1617 JFK Blvd Ste 1750 ....Philadelphia PA 19103	**877-256-2472**	215-557-2300
IRS Practice Adviser		
1801 S Bell St .... Arlington VA 22202	**800-372-1033**	
Kiplinger Tax Letter		
1729 H St NW .... Washington DC 20006	**800-544-0155**	202-887-6400
Medical Research Law & Policy Report		
1801 S Bell St .... Arlington VA 22202	**800-372-1033**	
Medicare Compliance Alert		
11300 Rockville Pk Ste 1100 ....Rockville MD 20852	**800-929-4824**	301-287-2700
Mergers & Acquisitions Law Report		
1801 S Bell St .... Arlington VA 22202	**800-372-1033**	
Money & Politics Report		
1801 S Bell St .... Arlington VA 22202	**800-372-1033**	
Municipal Litigation Reporter		
590 Dutch Vly Rd NE .... Atlanta GA 30324	**800-926-7926**	404-881-1141
Patent Trademark & Copyright Law Daily		
1801 S Bell St .... Arlington VA 22202	**800-372-1033**	
Pharmaceutical Law & Industry Report		
1801 S Bell St .... Arlington VA 22202	**800-372-1033**	
Privacy & Security Law Report		
1801 S Bell St .... Arlington VA 22202	**800-372-1033**	
Private Security Case Law Reporter		
590 Dutch Vly Rd NE PO Box 13729 .... Atlanta GA 30324	**800-926-7926**	404-881-1141
Real Estate Law Report		
610 Opperman Dr ....Eagan MN 55123	**800-328-4880***	651-687-7000
*Cust Svc		
Roll Call 77 K St NE .... Washington DC 20002	**800-432-2250**	202-650-6500
Securities Law Daily		
1801 S Bell St .... Arlington VA 22202	**800-372-1033**	
Securities Regulation & Law Report		
1801 S Bell St .... Arlington VA 22202	**800-372-1033**	
UCG Holdings		
11300 Rockville Pike Ste 1100 ....Rockville MD 20852	**800-929-4824**	301-287-2700
Virginia Dept of Taxation		
1957 Westmoreland St PO Box 1115 ....Richmond VA 23230	**800-828-1120**	804-367-8037
Workplace Law Report		
1801 S Bell St .... Arlington VA 22202	**800-372-1033**	
World Securities Law Report		
1801 S Bell St .... Arlington VA 22202	**800-372-1033**	

528-8 Health & Social Issues Newsletters

	Toll-Free	Phone
Affordable Housing Update		
8204 Fenton St .... Silver Spring MD 20910	**800-666-6380**	301-588-6380
Aging News Alert		
8204 Fenton St .... Silver Spring MD 20910	**800-666-6380**	301-588-6385
AICR Newsletter		
1759 R St NW .... Washington DC 20009	**800-843-8114**	202-328-7744
American Parkinson's Disease Assn Newsletter		
135 Parkinson Ave ....Staten Island NY 10305	**800-223-2732**	718-981-8001
APCO Bulletin		
351 N Williamson Blvd ....Daytona Beach FL 32114	**888-272-6911**	386-322-2500
Cancer Letter		
PO Box 9905 .... Washington DC 20016	**800-513-7042**	202-362-1809
Cancer Letter Business & Regulatory Report		
PO Box 9905 .... Washington DC 20016	**800-513-7042**	202-362-1809
Children & Youth Funding Report		
8204 Fenton St .... Silver Spring MD 20910	**800-666-6380**	301-588-6380
Congressional Quarterly HealthBeat		
77 K St NE .... Washington DC 20002	**800-432-2250**	202-650-6500
Consumer Reports On Health		
101 Truman Ave .... Yonkers NY 10703	**800-234-1645**	914-378-2000
Dairy Council Digest		
10255 W Higgins Rd Ste 900 .... Rosemont IL 60018	**800-426-8271***	847-803-2000
*Cust Svc		
Disability Funding Week		
8204 Fenton St .... Silver Spring MD 20910	**800-666-6380**	
Dr. Sinatra 95 Old Shoals Rd .... Arden NC 28704	**800-304-1708**	
Environment of Care Leader		
9737 Washintonian Blvd Ste 100 ....Gaithersburg MD 20878	**800-929-4824***	301-287-2700
*Cust Svc		
Harvard Women's Health Watch		
PO Box 9308 ....Big Sandy TX 75755	**877-649-9457**	
Health After 50		
500 Fifth Ave Ste 1900 .... New York NY 10110	**800-829-0422**	
Health Care Daily Report		
1801 S Bell St .... Arlington VA 22202	**800-372-1033**	
Health Care Policy Report		
1801 S Bell St .... Arlington VA 22202	**800-372-1033**	
Health Law Week		
590 Dutch Vly Rd NE .... Atlanta GA 30324	**800-926-7926**	404-881-1141
Healthcare Disparities Report		
8204 Fenton St .... Silver Spring MD 20910	**800-666-6380**	301-588-6385
Home Health Line		
11300 Rockville Pke Ste 1100 ....Rockville MD 20852	**800-929-4824**	301-287-2700
International Medical Device Regulatory Monitor		
300 N Washington St Ste 200 ....Falls Church VA 22046	**888-838-5578**	703-538-7600
Medicare Compliance Alert		
11300 Rockville Pk Ste 1100 ....Rockville MD 20852	**800-929-4824**	301-287-2700
OSHA Up-to-Date Newsletter		
1121 Spring Lk Dr .... Itasca IL 60143	**800-621-7615***	630-285-1121
*Cust Svc		

528-9 Investment Newsletters

				Toll-Free	Phone
Cabot Market Letter					
176 N St PO Box 2049	Salem	MA	01970	800-387-8588*	978-745-5532
*Orders					
Chartist Newsletter					
PO Box 758	Seal Beach	CA	90740	800-942-4278	562-596-2385
Commodity Research Bureau					
330 S Wells St Ste 612	Chicago	IL	60606	800-621-5271	312-554-8456
Dow Theory Forecasts					
7412 Calumet Ave	Hammond	IN	46324	800-233-5922	
Elliott Wave Theorist					
200 Main St	Gainesville	GA	30501	800-336-1618	770-536-0309
Fabian's Investment Resources					
300 New Jersey Ave NW Ste 500	Washington	DC	20001	800-950-8765	267-295-8713
Global Market Perspective					
PO Box 1618	Gainesville	GA	30503	800-336-1618	770-536-0309
Gold Newsletter					
PO Box 84900	Phoenix	AZ	85071	800-877-8847	
Option Advisor					
5151 Pfeiffer Rd Ste 250	Cincinnati	OH	45242	800-448-2080	513-589-3800
Personal Finance Newsletter					
7600A Leesburg Pk W Bldg Ste 300	Falls Church	VA	22043	800-832-2330	703-394-4931
Profitable Investing					
9201 Corporate Blvd	Rockville	MD	20850	800-219-8592	301-250-2200
Richard Young's Intelligence Report					
700 Indian Springs Dr	Lancaster	PA	17601	800-219-8592*	
*Cust Svc					
Systems & Forecasts					
150 Great Neck Rd Ste 301	Great Neck	NY	11021	800-982-4372	516-829-6444
Utility Forecaster					
7600A Leesburg Pk W Bldg Ste 300	Falls Church	VA	22043	800-832-2330	703-394-4931

528-10 Marketing & Sales Newsletters

				Toll-Free	Phone
Book Marketing Update					
P O Box 2887	Taos	NM	87571	888-468-7386	575-751-3398
Downtown Promotion Reporter (DPR)					
712 Main St Ste 187B	Boonton	NJ	07005	800-232-4317	973-265-2300
Marketing Library Services					
143 Old Marlton Pk	Medford	NJ	08055	800-300-9868	609-654-6266
Sales Leader					
2222 Sedwick Dr Ste 101	Durham	NC	27713	800-223-8720	

528-11 Media & Communications Newsletters

				Toll-Free	Phone
Communications Daily					
2115 Ward Ct NW	Washington	DC	20037	800-771-9202	202-872-9200
First Draft					
316 N Michigan Ave Ste 400	Chicago	IL	60601	800-878-5331	800-493-4867
Media Industry Newsletter (MIN)					
110 William St 11th Fl	New York	NY	10038	888-707-5814	212-621-4880
Media Law Reporter					
1801 S Bell St	Arlington	VA	22202	800-372-1033	
Media Relations Report					
316 N Michigan Ave Ste 400	Chicago	IL	60601	800-878-5331	312-960-4100
Speechwriter's Newsletter					
316 N Michigan Ave Ste 400	Chicago	IL	60601	800-878-5331	312-960-4100
State Telephone Regulation Report					
2115 Ward Ct NW	Washington	DC	20037	800-771-9202	202-872-9200
Telecom AM					
2115 Ward Ct NW	Washington	DC	20037	800-771-9202	202-872-9200

528-12 Science & Technology Newsletters

				Toll-Free	Phone
Flame Retardancy News					
49 Walnut Pk Bldg 2	Wellesley	MA	02481	866-285-7215	781-489-7301
Food Ingredient News					
49 Walnut Pk Bldg 2	Wellesley	MA	02481	866-285-7215	781-489-7301
Frost & Sullivan					
7550 IH 10 W Ste 400	San Antonio	TX	78229	877-463-7678	210-348-1000
Genetic Engineering News					
140 Huguenot St 3rd Fl	New Rochelle	NY	10801	800-799-9436	914-740-2100
Geophysical Research Letter					
2000 Florida Ave NW	Washington	DC	20009	800-966-2481	202-462-6900

528-13 Trade & Industry Newsletters

				Toll-Free	Phone
AviationWeek					
1200 G St NW Ste 900	Washington	DC	20005	800-525-5003	
Construction Claims Monthly					
2222 Sedwick Dr	Durham	NC	27713	800-223-8720	
Construction Labor Report					
1801 S Bell St	Arlington	VA	22202	800-372-1033	
Cotton's Week					
7193 Goodlett Farms Pkwy	Cordova	TN	38016	888-232-1738	901-274-9030
Cruise Industry News					
441 Lexington Ave Ste 809	New York	NY	10017	800-333-7300	212-986-1025
DealersEdge					
PO Box 606	Barnegat Light	NJ	08006	800-321-5312	609-879-4456
Funeral Service Insider					
3349 Hwy 138 Bldg D Ste D	Wall	NJ	07719	800-500-4585	
Kiplinger Agriculture Letter					
1729 H St NW	Washington	DC	20006	800-544-0155	202-887-6400

				Toll-Free	Phone
Metals Week 2 Penn Plaza	New York	NY	10121	800-752-8878	
PhotoSource 5106 Louetta Rd	Spring	TX	77379	800-786-6277	281-370-2220
Pro Farmer					
6612 Chancellor Dr Ste 300	Cedar Falls	IA	50613	800-772-0023*	319-277-1278
*Cust Svc					
Questex LLC					
275 Grove St Ste 2-130	Newton	MA	02466	888-552-4346	617-219-8300
Shopping Centers Today					
1221 Ave of the Americas	New York	NY	10020	888-427-2885	646-728-3800
Uniform Commercial Code Law Letter					
610 Opperman Dr	Eagan	MN	55123	800-328-4880*	651-687-7000
*Cust Svc					
Union Labor Report					
1801 S Bell St	Arlington	VA	22202	800-372-1033	

529 NEWSPAPERS

SEE ALSO Newspaper Publishers

529-1 Daily Newspapers - Canada

				Toll-Free	Phone
Calgary Herald					
215-16th St SE PO Box 2400 Stn M	Calgary	AB	T2E7P5	800-372-9219	403-235-7100
Calgary Sun 2615 12th St NE	Calgary	AB	T2E7W9	877-624-1463	403-410-1010
Edmonton Journal					
10006 - 101 St	Edmonton	AB	T5J2S6	800-232-9486	780-429-5100
Edmonton Sun					
4990 92nd Ave Ste 250	Edmonton	AB	T6B3A1	877-468-2401	780-468-0100
Winnipeg Free Press					
1355 Mountain Ave	Winnipeg	MB	R2X3B6	800-542-8900	204-697-7000
L'Acadie-Nouvelle					
476 Boul St-Pierre Ouest PO Box 5536	Caraquet	NB	E1W1B7	800-561-2255	506-727-4444
Chronicle Herald, The					
PO Box 610	Halifax	NS	B3J2T2	800-563-1187	902-426-2811
Journal Le Droit					
47 Clarence St	Ottawa	ON	K1N9K1	800-267-6961	613-562-0555
London Free Press					
369 York St PO Box 2280	London	ON	N6A4G1	866-541-6757	519-679-1111
National Post					
1450 Don Mills Rd Ste 300	Toronto	ON	M3B3R5	800-267-6568	416-383-2300
Ottawa Citizen					
1101 Baxter Rd PO Box 5020	Ottawa	ON	K2C3M4	800-267-6100	613-829-9100
Ottawa Sun PO Box 9729	Ottawa	ON	K1G5H7	877-624-1463	613-739-7000
Record, The 160 King St E	Kitchener	ON	N2G4E5	800-265-8261	519-894-2231
Spectator, The 44 Frid St	Hamilton	ON	L8N3G3	800-263-6902	905-526-3333
Toronto Star One Yonge St	Toronto	ON	M5E1E6	800-268-9756	416-869-4949
Toronto Sun 333 King St E	Toronto	ON	M5A3X5	888-786-7821	416-947-2222
Windsor Star, The					
167 Ferry St	Windsor	ON	N9A4M5	800-265-5647	519-255-5711
Le Devoir					
2050 Bleury St Ninth Fl	Montreal	QC	H3A3M9	800-463-7559	514-985-3333

529-2 Daily Newspapers - US

Listings here are organized by city names within state groupings. Most of the fax numbers given connect directly to the newsroom.

				Toll-Free	Phone
Anniston Star					
4305 McClellan Blvd PO Box 189	Anniston	AL	36202	866-814-9253	256-236-1551
Birmingham News					
2201 Fourth Ave N	Birmingham	AL	35203	800-283-4001	205-325-4444
Decatur Daily					
201 First Ave SE	Decatur	AL	35601	888-353-4612	256-353-4612
Dothan Eagle PO Box 1968	Dothan	AL	36302	800-811-1771	334-792-3141
Gadsden Times 401 Locust St	Gadsden	AL	35901	800-762-2464	256-549-2000
Huntsville Times					
2317 S Memorial Pkwy	Huntsville	AL	35801	800-239-5271	256-532-4000
Montgomery Advertiser					
425 Molton St	Montgomery	AL	36104	877-424-0007	334-262-1611
Tuscaloosa News					
315 28th Ave	Tuscaloosa	AL	35401	800-888-8639	205-345-0505
Anchorage Daily News					
1001 Northway Dr	Anchorage	AK	99508	800-478-4200	907-257-4200
East Valley Tribune					
120 W First Ave	Mesa	AZ	85210	888-887-4286	480-898-6500
Arizona Republic					
200 E Van Buren St	Phoenix	AZ	85004	800-331-9303	602-444-8000
Arizona Daily Star					
4850 S Pk Ave	Tucson	AZ	85714	800-695-4492	520-573-4343
Jonesboro Sun					
518 Carson St	Jonesboro	AR	72401	800-237-5341	870-935-5525
Arkansas Democrat-Gazette					
121 E Capital St	Little Rock	AR	72203	800-482-1121*	501-378-3400
*Cust Svc					
Ventura County Star					
550 Camarillo Ctr Dr	Camarillo	CA	93010	800-221-7827	805-437-0000
Chico Enterprise Record					
400 E Pk Ave PO Box 9	Chico	CA	95927	800-827-1421	530-891-1234
Times-Standard 930 Sixth St	Eureka	CA	95501	800-514-0301	707-498-1817
Fresno Bee 1626 E St	Fresno	CA	93786	800-877-3400	559-441-6111
Daily Review					
22533 Foothill Blvd	Hayward	CA	94541	800-595-9595	510-783-6111
Lodi News-Sentinel					
125 N Church St	Lodi	CA	95240	800-407-7653	209-369-2761
Investor's Business Daily					
12655 Beatrice St	Los Angeles	CA	90066	800-831-2525	310-448-6000
Los Angeles Times					
202 W First St	Los Angeles	CA	90012	800-528-4637	213-237-5000
Appeal-Democrat					
1530 Ellis Lk Dr PO Box 431	Marysville	CA	95901	800-831-2345	530-741-2345
Modesto Bee 1325 H St	Modesto	CA	95354	800-776-4233	209-578-2000
Monterey County Herald					
Eight Upper Ragsdale Dr	Monterey	CA	93940	800-688-1808	831-372-3311

Newspaper / Address	City	ST	ZIP	Toll-Free	Phone
Marin Independent Journal 150 Alameda Del Prado	Novato	CA	94949	877-229-8655	415-883-8600
Desert Sun 750 N Gene Autry Trl	Palm Springs	CA	92263	800-233-3741	760-322-8889
Antelope Valley Press 37404 Sierra Hwy	Palmdale	CA	93550	888-874-2527	661-273-2700
Pasadena Star-News 911 E Colorado Blvd	Pasadena	CA	91106	800-788-1200	626-578-6300
Record Searchlight PO Box 492397	Redding	CA	96049	800-666-1331	530-243-2424
Press-Enterprise 3450 14th St	Riverside	CA	92501	877-473-6397	951-684-1200
Sacramento Bee PO Box 15779	Sacramento	CA	95852	800-284-3233*	916-321-1000
*Cust Svc					
Sun, The 4030 N Georgia Blvd	San Bernardino	CA	92407	800-922-0922	909-889-9666
San Diego Daily Transcript 2131 Third Ave	San Diego	CA	92101	800-697-6397	619-232-4381
San Diego Union-Tribune 350 Camino De La Reina	San Diego	CA	92108	800-244-6397	619-299-3131
San Francisco Chronicle 901 Mission St	San Francisco	CA	94103	866-732-4766	415-777-1111
Tribune, The 3825 S Higuera St	San Luis Obispo	CA	93401	800-477-8799	805-781-7800
San Mateo County Times 477 Ninth Ave Ste 110	San Mateo	CA	94402	800-870-6397	650-348-4321
Orange County Register 625 N Grand Ave	Santa Ana	CA	92701	877-469-7344	714-796-7000
Press Democrat 427 Mendocino Ave	Santa Rosa	CA	95401	800-675-5056	707-546-2020
Daily Breeze 5215 Torrance Blvd	Torrance	CA	90503	800-356-7057	310-540-5511
Vallejo Times Herald 440 Curtola Pkwy	Vallejo	CA	94590	800-600-1141	707-644-1141
Daily Press 13891 Pk Ave PO Box 1389	Victorville	CA	92393	844-287-3897	760-241-7744
San Gabriel Valley Tribune 1210 N Azusa Canyon Rd	West Covina	CA	91790	800-788-1200	626-962-8811
Daily News of Los Angeles 21221 Oxnard St	Woodland Hills	CA	91367	800-559-1950	818-713-3000
Boulder Daily Camera 1048 Pearl St	Boulder	CO	80302	800-783-1202	303-442-1202
Denver Post 101 W Colfax Ave	Denver	CO	80202	800-336-7678	303-820-1010
Durango Herald 1275 Main Ave	Durango	CO	81301	800-530-8318	970-247-3504
Coloradoan, The 1300 Riverside Ave	Fort Collins	CO	80524	877-424-0063	970-493-6397
Daily Sentinel PO Box 668	Grand Junction	CO	81502	800-332-5832	970-242-5050
Loveland Daily Reporter-Herald 201 E Fifth St	Loveland	CO	80537	800-244-5613	970-669-5050
Pueblo Chieftain 825 W Sixth St PO Box 440	Pueblo	CO	81003	800-279-6397	719-544-3520
Connecticut Post 410 State St	Bridgeport	CT	06604	800-293-0795*	203-333-0161
*Edit					
Hartford Courant 285 Broad St	Hartford	CT	06115	800-524-4242	860-241-6200
Journal Inquirer 306 Progress Dr PO Box 510	Manchester	CT	06045	800-237-3606	860-646-0500
Record-Journal 11 Crown St	Meriden	CT	06450	800-228-6915	203-235-1661
New Haven Register 40 Sargent Dr	New Haven	CT	06511	800-925-2509	203-789-5200
Delaware State News 110 Galaxy Dr PO Box 737	Dover	DE	19903	800-282-8586	302-674-3600
Washington Post 1150 15th St NW	Washington	DC	20071	800-627-1150	202-334-6000
El Nuevo Herald 3511 NW 91st Ave	Doral	FL	33172	800-437-2535	305-376-3535
South Florida Sun-Sentinel 200 E Las Olas Blvd	Fort Lauderdale	FL	33301	800-548-6397*	954-356-4000
*Cust Svc					
Northwest Florida Daily News PO Box 2949	Fort Walton Beach	FL	32549	800-755-1185	850-863-1111
Florida Times-Union One Riverside Ave	Jacksonville	FL	32202	800-472-6397	904-359-4111
Ledger, The 300 W Lime St	Lakeland	FL	33815	888-431-7323	863-802-7000
Daily Commercial 212 E Main St	Leesburg	FL	34748	866-273-2273	352-365-8200
Naples Daily News 1075 Central Ave	Naples	FL	34102	800-404-7343	239-262-3161
Orlando Sentinel 633 N Orange Ave	Orlando	FL	32801	800-347-6868	407-420-5000
Seminole Herald PO Box 1667	Sanford	FL	32772	800-955-8770	407-322-2611
Sarasota Herald-Tribune 1741 Main St	Sarasota	FL	34236	866-284-7102	941-953-7755
Highlands Today 315 US Hwy 27 N	Sebring	FL	33870	800-645-3423*	863-386-5800
*General					
Vero Beach Press-Journal PO Box 1268	Vero Beach	FL	32961	866-894-9851	772-562-2315
Palm Beach Post 2751 S Dixie Hwy	West Palm Beach	FL	33405	800-432-7595	561-820-4100
Athens Banner-Herald One Press Pl	Athens	GA	30601	800-533-4252	706-549-0123
Augusta Chronicle 725 Broad St	Augusta	GA	30901	866-249-8223	706-724-0851
Columbus Ledger-Enquirer 17 W 12th St	Columbus	GA	31901	800-282-7859	706-324-5526
Gainesville Times 345 Green St NW	Gainesville	GA	30501	800-395-5005	770-532-1234
Macon Telegraph 120 Broadway	Macon	GA	31201	800-679-6397	478-744-4200
Valdosta Daily Times PO Box 968	Valdosta	GA	31603	800-600-4838	229-244-1880
Honolulu Advertiser 500 Ala Moana Blvd	Honolulu	HI	96813	877-233-1133	808-529-4747
Maui News 100 Mahalani St	Wailuku	HI	96793	888-683-1115	808-244-3981
Idaho Statesman PO Box 40	Boise	ID	83707	800-635-8934	208-377-6400
Post-Register PO Box 1800	Idaho Falls	ID	83403	800-574-6397	208-522-1800
Idaho State Journal 305 S Arthur Ave	Pocatello	ID	83204	800-669-9777	208-232-4161
Telegraph, The PO Box 278	Alton	IL	62002	866-299-9256	618-463-2500
Belleville News-Democrat 120 S Illinois St	Belleville	IL	62220	800-293-0795	618-234-1000
Pantagraph PO Box 2907	Bloomington	IL	61702	800-747-7323	309-829-9000
Southern Illinoisan 710 N Illinois Ave PO Box 2108	Carbondale	IL	62902	800-228-0429	618-529-5454
Chicago Tribune 435 N Michigan Ave	Chicago	IL	60611	800-874-2863	312-222-3232
Commercial-News 17 W N St	Danville	IL	61832	877-732-8258	217-446-1000
Herald & Review 601 E Williams St	Decatur	IL	62523	800-437-2533	217-429-5151
Journal-Standard 27 S State Ave	Freeport	IL	61032	800-325-6397	815-232-1171
Register-Mail 140 S Prairie St PO Box 310	Galesburg	IL	61401	877-732-8258	309-343-7181
Daily Journal 8 Dearborn Sq	Kankakee	IL	60901	866-299-9256	815-937-3300
NASDAQ: DJCO					
News-Tribune 426 Second St	La Salle	IL	61301	800-892-6452	815-223-3200
Macomb Journal 203 N Randolph St	Macomb	IL	61455	800-747-5401	309-833-2114
Reporter 12247 S Harlem Ave	Palos Heights	IL	60463	800-633-4227	708-448-6161
Peoria Journal Star One News Plz	Peoria	IL	61643	800-225-5757	309-686-3000
Quincy Herald-Whig 130 S Fifth St	Quincy	IL	62301	800-373-9444	217-223-5100
Rock Island Argus 1724 Fourth Ave	Rock Island	IL	61201	800-660-2472	309-786-6441
Rockford Register Star 99 E State St	Rockford	IL	61104	800-383-7827	815-987-1200
Shelbyville Daily Union 100 W Main St	Shelbyville	IL	62565	800-772-1213	217-774-2161
State Journal-Register PO Box 219	Springfield	IL	62705	800-397-6397	217-788-1300
Herald Bulletin 1133 Jackson St	Anderson	IN	46016	800-750-5049	765-622-1212
Republic, The 333 Second St	Columbus	IN	47201	800-876-7811	812-372-7811
Truth, The PO Box 487	Elkhart	IN	46515	800-585-5416	574-294-1661
Evansville Courier & Press 300 E Walnut St	Evansville	IN	47713	800-288-3200	812-424-7711
Journal Gazette 600 W Main St	Fort Wayne	IN	46802	888-966-4532	260-461-8773
News-Sentinel 600 W Main St	Fort Wayne	IN	46802	800-444-3303	260-461-8439
Goshen News 114 S Main St PO Box 569	Goshen	IN	46527	800-487-2151	574-533-2151
Indianapolis Star 307 N Pennsylvania St	Indianapolis	IN	46204	800-669-7827	317-444-4000
Kokomo Tribune (KT) 300 N Union St PO Box 9014	Kokomo	IN	46901	800-382-0696	765-459-3121
Journal & Courier 217 N Sixth St	Lafayette	IN	47901	800-407-5813*	765-423-5511
*News Rm					
Chronicle-Tribune 610 S Adams St	Marion	IN	46953	800-955-7888	765-664-5111
Muncie Star-Press 345 S High St	Muncie	IN	47305	800-783-7827	765-747-5700
Times, The 601 W 45th Ave	Munster	IN	46321	800-837-3232	219-933-3200
South Bend Tribune 225 W Colfax Ave	South Bend	IN	46626	800-220-7378	574-235-6464
Tribune-Star PO Box 149	Terre Haute	IN	47808	800-783-8742	812-231-4200
Hawk Eye, The 800 S Main St PO Box 10	Burlington	IA	52601	800-397-1708	319-754-8461
Gazette, The 501 Second Ave SE	Cedar Rapids	IA	52401	800-397-8333	319-398-8333
Daily Nonpareil 535 W Broadway Ste 300	Council Bluffs	IA	51503	800-283-1882	712-328-1811
Quad-City Times 500 E Third St	Davenport	IA	52801	800-437-4641	563-383-2200
Des Moines Register 715 Locust St	Des Moines	IA	50309	800-247-5346	515-284-8000
Telegraph Herald 801 Bluff St	Dubuque	IA	52001	800-553-4801	563-588-5611
Messenger, The 713 Central Ave	Fort Dodge	IA	50501	800-622-6613	515-573-2141
Globe-Gazette 300 N Washington St PO Box 271	Mason City	IA	50402	800-421-0546	641-421-0500
Ottumwa Courier 213 E Second St	Ottumwa	IA	52501	800-532-1504	641-684-4611
Sioux City Journal 515 Pavonia St	Sioux City	IA	51101	800-397-3530	712-293-4300
Pilot Tribune PO Box 1187	Storm Lake	IA	50588	800-447-1985	712-732-3130
Waterloo Cedar Falls Courier PO Box 540	Waterloo	IA	50701	800-798-1730	319-291-1421
Hutchinson News 300 W Second St	Hutchinson	KS	67504	800-766-3311	620-694-5700
Lawrence Journal-World 609 New Hampshire St	Lawrence	KS	66044	800-578-8748	785-843-1000
Topeka Capital-Journal 616 SE Jefferson St	Topeka	KS	66607	800-777-7171	785-295-1111
Wichita Eagle, The 825 E Douglas Ave	Wichita	KS	67202	800-200-8906	316-268-6000
Times-Tribune, The 201 N Kentucky Ave	Corbin	KY	40701	877-629-9722	606-528-2464
News-Enterprise 408 W Dixie Ave	Elizabethtown	KY	42701	877-246-2322	270-769-1200
State Journal, The 1216 Wilkinson Blvd	Frankfort	KY	40601	800-621-3362	502-227-4556
Lexington Herald-Leader 100 Midland Ave	Lexington	KY	40508	800-999-8881	859-231-3100

Classified Section

Newspaper / Address	City	ST	Zip	Toll-Free	Phone
Courier-Journal 525 W Broadway PO Box 740031	Louisville	KY	40201	800-765-4011	502-582-4011
Alexandria Daily Town Talk PO Box 7558	Alexandria	LA	71306	800-523-8391	318-487-6397
Advocate, The 7290 Blue Bonnet Blvd	Baton Rouge	LA	70810	800-960-6397	225-383-1111
Daily Advertiser, The 1100 Bertrand Dr	Lafayette	LA	70506	888-522-6278	337-289-6300
American Press 4900 Hwy 90 E *News Rm	Lake Charles	LA	70615	800-442-2511*	337-494-4080
News-Star 411 N Fourth Ave	Monroe	LA	71201	800-259-7788	318-322-5161
Times-Picayune 3800 Howard Ave	New Orleans	LA	70125	800-925-0000	504-826-3279
Times 222 Lake St	Shreveport	LA	71101	800-551-8892	318-459-3200
Bangor Daily News 491 Main St PO Box 1329	Bangor	ME	04402	800-432-7964	207-990-8000
Sun-Journal PO Box 4400	Lewiston	ME	04243	800-482-0759	207-784-5411
Morning Sentinel 31 Front St	Waterville	ME	04901	800-287-1945	207-873-3341
Baltimore Sun 501 N Calvert St	Baltimore	MD	21278	800-829-8000	410-332-6000
Cumberland Times-News 19 Baltimore St	Cumberland	MD	21502	800-742-8149	301-722-4600
Star Democrat 29088 Airpark Dr PO Box 600	Easton	MD	21601	800-734-3158	410-822-1500
Frederick News Post 200 E Patrick St	Frederick	MD	21701	800-486-1177	301-662-1177
Haverhill Gazette 181 Merrimack St	Haverhill	MA	01831	888-411-3245	978-374-0321
Cape Cod Times 319 Main St	Hyannis	MA	02601	800-451-7887	508-775-1200
Berkshire Eagle 75 S Church St PO Box 1171	Pittsfield	MA	01202	800-234-7404	413-447-7311
Patriot Ledger 400 Crown Colony Dr PO Box 699159	Quincy	MA	02269	888-782-2267	617-786-7000
Daily Telegram 133 N Winter St	Adrian	MI	49221	800-968-5111	517-265-5111
Battle Creek Enquirer 155 W Van Buren St	Battle Creek	MI	49017	800-333-4139	269-964-7161
Bay City Times 311 Fifth St	Bay City	MI	48708	800-727-7661	989-895-8551
Detroit Free Press 615 W Lafayette Blvd	Detroit	MI	48226	800-395-3300	313-222-6400
Detroit News 615 W Lafayette Blvd *General	Detroit	MI	48226	800-395-3300*	313-222-2300
Flint Journal 200 E First St *Circ	Flint	MI	48502	800-875-6200*	810-766-6100
Holland Sentinel 54 W Eigth St	Holland	MI	49423	800-784-6776	616-392-2311
Jackson Citizen Patriot 100 E Michigan Ave Ste 100	Jackson	MI	49201	877-213-3754	
Kalamazoo Gazette 401 S Burdick St	Kalamazoo	MI	49007	800-466-6397	269-345-3511
Lansing State Journal 120 E Lenawee St	Lansing	MI	48919	800-234-1719	517-377-1111
Midland Daily News 124 McDonald St	Midland	MI	48640	877-411-2762	989-835-7171
Muskegon Chronicle 981 Third St	Muskegon	MI	49440	800-783-3161	231-722-3161
Times Herald 911 Military St	Port Huron	MI	48060	800-462-4057	810-985-7171
Saginaw News 203 S Washington Ave	Saginaw	MI	48607	800-875-6397	989-752-7171
Herald-Palladium 3450 Hollywood Rd PO Box 128	Saint Joseph	MI	49085	800-356-4262	269-429-2400
Duluth News-Tribune 424 W First St *Circ	Duluth	MN	55802	800-456-8080*	218-723-5281
Free Press 418 S Second St	Mankato	MN	56001	800-657-4662	507-625-4451
Star Tribune 425 Portland Ave	Minneapolis	MN	55488	800-827-8742	612-673-4000
Saint Cloud Times 3000 7th Street North PO Box 768	Saint Cloud	MN	56303	877-922-1274	320-255-8700
West Central Tribune PO Box 839	Willmar	MN	56201	800-450-1150	320-235-1150
Delta Democrat Times 988 N Broadway St	Greenville	MS	38701	800-273-8255	662-335-1155
Hattiesburg American 825 N Main St	Hattiesburg	MS	39401	800-844-2637	601-582-4321
Clarion-Ledger, The 201 S Congress St	Jackson	MS	39201	877-850-5343	601-961-7000
Meridian Star, The PO Box 1591	Meridian	MS	39302	800-232-2525	601-693-1551
Northeast Mississippi Daily Journal 1242 S Green St	Tupelo	MS	38804	800-264-6397	662-842-2611
Southeast Missourian 301 Broadway St	Cape Girardeau	MO	63701	800-879-1210	573-335-6611
Columbia Daily Tribune 101 N Fourth St	Columbia	MO	65201	800-333-6799	573-815-1700
Jefferson City News Tribune 210 Monroe St	Jefferson City	MO	65101	888-892-6333	573-636-3131
Joplin Globe 117 E Fourth St	Joplin	MO	64801	800-444-8514	417-623-3480
Kansas City Star 1729 Grand Ave	Kansas City	MO	64108	877-962-7827	
Daily American Republic 208 Poplar St PO Box 7	Poplar Bluff	MO	63901	888-276-2242	573-785-1414
Springfield News Leader 651 N Boonville Ave	Springfield	MO	65806	800-695-2005	417-836-1100
Billings Gazette 401 N 28th St	Billings	MT	59101	800-543-2505	406-657-1200
Montana Standard 25 W Granite St	Butte	MT	59701	800-877-1074	406-496-5500
Great Falls Tribune 205 River Dr S	Great Falls	MT	59405	800-438-6600	406-791-1444
Independent Record 317 Cruse Ave	Helena	MT	59601	800-523-2272	406-447-4000
Missoulian PO Box 8029	Missoula	MT	59807	800-366-7102	406-523-5200
Grand Island Independent 422 W First St	Grand Island	NE	68801	800-658-3160	308-382-1000
Lincoln Journal-Star 926 P St	Lincoln	NE	68508	800-742-7315	402-475-4200
Norfolk Daily News PO Box 977	Norfolk	NE	68702	877-371-1020	402-371-1020
Omaha World-Herald 1314 Douglas St	Omaha	NE	68102	800-284-6397	402-444-1000
Nevada Appeal 580 Mallory Way *General	Carson City	NV	89701	877-689-3249*	775-882-2111
Reno Gazette-Journal PO Box 22000	Reno	NV	89520	800-648-5048	775-788-6200
Foster's Daily Democrat 150 Venture Dr	Dover	NH	03820	800-660-8310	603-742-4455
Union Leader 100 William Loeb Dr	Manchester	NH	03109	800-562-8218	603-668-4321
Valley News 24 Interchange Dr	West Lebanon	NH	03784	800-874-2226	603-298-8711
Courier-Post 301 Cuthbert Blvd	Cherry Hill	NJ	08002	800-677-6289	856-663-6000
Asbury Park Press 3601 Hwy 66 PO Box 1550	Neptune	NJ	07754	800-883-7737	732-922-6000
Star-Ledger, The One Star Ledger Plz	Newark	NJ	07102	800-501-2100	973-877-4141
Home News Tribune 92 E Main St Ste 202	Somerville	NJ	08876	800-627-4663	732-246-5500
Albuquerque Journal 7777 Jefferson St NE	Albuquerque	NM	87109	800-990-5765	505-823-7777
Daily Times 201 N Allen Ave	Farmington	NM	87401	877-599-3331	505-325-4545
Las Cruces Sun-News 256 W Las Cruces Ave	Las Cruces	NM	88005	877-827-7200	575-541-5400
Times Union 645 Albany Shaker Rd PO Box 15000	Albany	NY	12212	877-263-7995	518-454-5420
Buffalo News One News Plz PO Box 100	Buffalo	NY	14240	800-777-8640	716-849-4444
Evening Observer 8-10 E Second St PO Box 391	Dunkirk	NY	14048	800-836-0931	716-366-3000
Star-Gazette 201 Baldwin St	Elmira	NY	14902	800-836-8970	607-734-5151
Post-Star 76 Lawrence St	Glens Falls	NY	12801	800-724-2543	518-792-3131
Register-Star 364 Warren St	Hudson	NY	12534	800-836-1616	518-828-1616
Post-Journal 15 W Second St	Jamestown	NY	14701	866-756-9600	716-487-1111
Newsday Inc 235 Pinelawn Rd	Melville	NY	11747	800-639-7329	631-843-2700
Times Herald-Record 40 Mulberry St PO Box 2046	Middletown	NY	10940	800-295-2181	845-341-1100
Financial Times 1330 Ave of the Americas	New York	NY	10019	800-628-8088	212-641-6500
New York Daily News 450 W 33rd St Third Fl	New York	NY	10001	800-692-6397	212-210-2100
New York Post 1211 Ave of the Americas	New York	NY	10036	800-552-7678	212-930-8000
Olean Times-Herald 639 Norton Dr	Olean	NY	14760	800-722-8812	716-372-3121
Daily Star 102 Chestnut St PO Box 250	Oneonta	NY	13820	800-721-1000	607-432-1000
Press-Republican 170 Margaret St PO Box 459	Plattsburgh	NY	12901	800-288-7323	518-561-2300
Poughkeepsie Journal 85 Civic Ctr Plz	Poughkeepsie	NY	12601	800-765-1120	845-437-4800
Democrat & Chronicle 55 Exchange Blvd	Rochester	NY	14614	800-790-9565	585-232-7100
Daily Gazette 2345 Maxon Rd Ext PO Box 1090	Schenectady	NY	12301	800-262-2211	518-374-4141
Post-Standard PO Box 4915	Syracuse	NY	13221	866-447-3787	315-470-0011
Watertown Daily Times 260 Washington St	Watertown	NY	13601	800-642-6222	315-782-1000
Courier-Tribune 500 Sunset Ave	Asheboro	NC	27203	800-488-0444	336-625-2101
Asheville Citizen Times 14 O'Henry Ave	Asheville	NC	28801	800-800-4204	828-252-5622
Times-News PO Box 481	Burlington	NC	27216	800-488-0085	336-227-0131
Charlotte Observer, The 600 S Tryon St	Charlotte	NC	28202	800-332-0686	704-358-5000
Herald-Sun, The 2828 Pickett Rd	Durham	NC	27705	877-627-6724	919-419-6500
Fayetteville Observer 458 Whitfield St	Fayetteville	NC	28306	800-345-9895	910-323-4848
Gaston Gazette 1893 Remount Rd	Gastonia	NC	28054	800-527-5226	704-869-1700
News & Record 200 E Market St	Greensboro	NC	27401	800-553-6880	336-373-7000
Hickory Daily Record 1100 Pk Pl	Hickory	NC	28602	800-849-8586	828-322-4510
Daily News 724 Bell Fork Rd PO Box 196	Jacksonville	NC	28541	800-659-2873	910-353-1171
News & Observer 215 S McDowell St	Raleigh	NC	27602	800-522-4205	919-829-4500
Star-News PO Box 840	Wilmington	NC	28402	800-272-1277	910-343-2000
Winston-Salem Journal 418 N Marshall St	Winston-Salem	NC	27101	800-642-0925	336-727-7211
Bismarck Tribune 707 E Front Ave	Bismarck	ND	58504	866-476-5348	701-223-2500
Forum, The 101 N Fifth St	Fargo	ND	58102	800-747-7311	701-235-7311
Minot Daily News 301 Fourth St SE	Mohall	ND	58761	800-735-3119	701-857-1900
Star Beacon PO Box 2100	Ashtabula	OH	44005	800-554-6768	440-998-2323
Chillicothe Gazette 50 W Main St	Chillicothe	OH	45601	877-424-0215	740-773-2111
Cincinnati Enquirer 312 Elm St	Cincinnati	OH	45202	800-876-4500	513-721-2700
Kentucky Post 421 Gilbert Ave	Cincinnati	OH	45202	877-667-4265	513-721-9900
Plain Dealer 1801 Superior Ave	Cleveland	OH	44114	800-362-0727	216-999-5000

				Toll-Free	Phone
Columbus Dispatch 34 S Third St	Columbus	OH	43215	**800-942-2745**	614-461-5000
Crescent-News 624 W Second St PO Box 249	Defiance	OH	43512	**800-589-5441**	419-784-5441
Chronicle-Telegram 225 E Ave	Elyria	OH	44035	**800-848-6397**	440-329-7000
Record-Courier 1050 W Main St PO Box 5199	Kent	OH	44240	**800-560-9657**	330-541-9400
Lancaster Eagle-Gazette 138 W Chestnut St	Lancaster	OH	43130	**877-513-7355**	740-654-1321
Lima News 3515 Elida Rd	Lima	OH	45807	**800-686-9924**	419-223-1010
News Journal 70 W Fourth St	Mansfield	OH	44903	**800-472-5547**	419-522-3311
Marion Star, The 163 E Center St	Marion	OH	43302	**877-987-2782**	740-387-0400
Times Leader 200 S Fourth St	Martins Ferry	OH	43935	**800-244-5671**	740-633-1131
Medina Gazette 885 W Liberty St	Medina	OH	44256	**800-633-4623**	330-725-4166
Times Reporter 629 Wabash Ave NW	New Philadelphia	OH	44663	**800-686-5577**	330-364-5577
Portsmouth Daily Times PO Box 581	Portsmouth	OH	45662	**866-430-8358**	740-353-3101
Sandusky Register 314 W Market St	Sandusky	OH	44870	**800-466-1243**	419-625-5500
Springfield News-Sun 202 N Limestone St	Springfield	OH	45503	**800-441-6397**	937-328-0300
Blade 541 N Superior St	Toledo	OH	43660	**800-245-3317**	419-724-6000
Tribune Chronicle 240 Franklin St SE	Warren	OH	44482	**888-550-8742**	330-841-1600
News-Herald 7085 Mentor Ave	Willoughby	OH	44094	**800-947-2737**	440-951-0000
Daily Record 212 E Liberty St PO Box 918	Wooster	OH	44691	**800-686-2958**	330-264-1125
Vindicator, The 107 Vindicator Sq PO Box 780	Youngstown	OH	44501	**877-700-4647**	330-747-1471
Times Recorder 34 S Fourth St	Zanesville	OH	43701	**844-265-6246**	740-452-4561
Enid News & Eagle 227 W Broadway PO Box 3451	Enid	OK	73701	**800-299-6397**	580-548-8186
Oklahoman, The 9000 N Broadway	Oklahoma City	OK	73114	**800-375-6397**	405-475-3311
Tulsa World 315 S Boulder Ave	Tulsa	OK	74103	**800-897-3557**	918-583-2161
Albany Democrat-Herald 600 Lyons St SW PO Box 130	Albany	OR	97321	**877-634-2867**	541-926-2211
Bulletin, The 1777 SW Chandler Ave	Bend	OR	97702	**800-503-3933**	541-382-1811
Daily Courier 409 SE Seventh St	Grants Pass	OR	97526	**800-228-0457**	541-474-3700
Medford Mail Tribune PO Box 1108	Medford	OR	97501	**800-452-4011**	541-776-4411
Oregonian 1320 SW Broadway *News Rm	Portland	OR	97201	**800-723-3638***	503-221-8100
News-Review 345 NE Winchester St	Roseburg	OR	97470	**888-459-3830**	541-672-3321
Morning Call PO Box 1260	Allentown	PA	18105	**800-666-5492**	610-820-6500
Altoona Mirror 301 Cayuga Ave	Altoona	PA	16602	**800-222-1962**	814-946-7411
Dispatch, The 116 E Market St	Blairsville	PA	15717	**844-743-2015**	724-459-6100
Sentinel, The 457 E N St	Carlisle	PA	17013	**800-829-5570**	717-243-2611
Express-Times 30 N Fourth St	Easton	PA	18042	**800-360-3601**	610-258-7171
Erie Times-News 205 W 12th St	Erie	PA	16534	**800-352-0043**	814-870-1600
Evening Sun 135 Baltimore St PO Box 514	Hanover	PA	17331	**800-877-3786**	717-637-3736
Patriot-News 812 Market St	Harrisburg	PA	17101	**800-692-7207**	717-255-8100
Hazleton Standard Speaker 21 N Wyoming St *Cust Svc	Hazleton	PA	18201	**800-843-6680***	570-455-3636
Tribune-Democrat 425 Locust St	Johnstown	PA	15907	**855-255-5975**	814-532-5050
Intelligencer Journal Eight W King St PO Box 1328	Lancaster	PA	17603	**800-809-4666**	717-291-8622
Lancaster New Era Eight W King St PO Box 1328	Lancaster	PA	17603	**800-809-4666**	717-291-8733
Meadville Tribune 947 Federal Ct	Meadville	PA	16335	**800-879-0006**	814-724-6370
Philadelphia Inquirer 801 Market St Ste 300 PO Box 8263	Philadelphia	PA	19107	**800-341-3413**	215-854-2000
Pittsburgh Tribune-Review 503 Martindale St 3rd Fl	Pittsburgh	PA	15212	**800-909-8742**	412-321-6460
Scranton Times-Tribune 149 Penn Ave	Scranton	PA	18503	**800-228-4637**	570-348-9100
Centre Daily Times 3400 E College Ave	State College	PA	16801	**800-327-5500**	814-238-5000
Pocono Record 511 Lenox St	Stroudsburg	PA	18360	**800-530-6310**	570-421-3000
Valley News Dispatch 210 Fourth Ave	Tarentum	PA	15084	**877-698-2553**	800-909-8742
Herald-Standard Eight E Church St Ste 18	Uniontown	PA	15401	**800-342-8254**	724-439-7500
Observer-Reporter 122 S Main St	Washington	PA	15301	**800-222-6397**	724-222-2200
Times Leader, The 15 N Main St	Wilkes-Barre	PA	18711	**800-427-8649**	570-829-7101
Williamsport Sun-Gazette 252 W Fourth St	Williamsport	PA	17701	**800-339-0289**	570-326-1551
York Dispatch 205 N George St	York	PA	17401	**800-227-2345**	717-854-1575
Providence Journal 75 Fountain St	Providence	RI	02902	**888-697-7656**	401-277-7303
Anderson Independent-Mail PO Box 2507	Anderson	SC	29622	**800-859-6397**	864-224-4321
Island Packet 10 Buck Island Rd	Bluffton	SC	29910	**877-706-8100**	843-706-8100
State, The 1401 Shop Rd	Columbia	SC	29201	**800-888-5353**	803-771-6161
Greenville News 305 S Main St	Greenville	SC	29601	**800-800-5116**	864-298-4100
Sun News 914 Frontage Rd E	Myrtle Beach	SC	29578	**800-568-1800**	843-626-8555
Spartanburg Herald-Journal 189 W Main St	Spartanburg	SC	29306	**800-922-4158**	864-582-4511
Aberdeen American News 124 S Second St	Aberdeen	SD	57402	**800-925-4100**	605-225-4100
Capital Journal 333 W Dakota Ave	Pierre	SD	57501	**800-537-0025**	605-224-7301
Rapid City Journal 507 Main St	Rapid City	SD	57701	**800-843-2300**	605-394-8300
Argus Leader 200 S Minnesota Ave	Sioux Falls	SD	57104	**800-530-6397**	605-331-2200
Jackson Sun 245 W LaFayette St	Jackson	TN	38301	**800-372-3922**	731-427-3333
Kingsport Times-News 701 Lynn Garden Dr	Kingsport	TN	37660	**800-251-0328**	423-246-8121
Knoxville News-Sentinel 2332 News Sentinel Dr	Knoxville	TN	37921	**800-237-5821**	865-521-8181
Commercial Appeal 495 Union Ave	Memphis	TN	38103	**800-444-6397**	901-529-2345
Citizen Tribune 1609 W First N St PO Box 625	Morristown	TN	37815	**800-624-0281**	423-581-5630
Tennessean 1100 Broadway	Nashville	TN	37203	**800-342-8237**	615-259-8033
Abilene Reporter-News 101 Cypress St	Abilene	TX	79601	**800-588-6397**	325-673-4271
Austin American-Statesman 305 S Congress Ave	Austin	TX	78704	**800-445-9898**	512-445-3500
Bay City Tribune 2901 16th St	Bay City	TX	77414	**877-322-8228**	979-245-5555
Brownsville Herald, The 1135 E Van Buren St	Brownsville	TX	78520	**800-488-4301**	956-542-4301
Brazosport Facts 720 S Main St	Clute	TX	77531	**800-864-8340**	979-265-7411
Caller-Times 820 N Lower Broadway	Corpus Christi	TX	78401	**800-827-2011**	361-884-2011
Dallas Morning News 508 Young St	Dallas	TX	75202	**800-431-0010**	214-977-8222
Denton Record-Chronicle 314 E Hickory St	Denton	TX	76201	**800-275-1722**	940-387-3811
Galveston County Daily News 8522 Teichman Rd PO Box 628	Galveston	TX	77553	**800-561-3611**	409-683-5200
Valley Morning Star PO Box 511	Harlingen	TX	78551	**877-786-7612**	956-430-6200
Houston Chronicle 801 Texas Ave	Houston	TX	77002	**800-735-3800**	713-362-7171
Laredo Morning Times 111 Esperanza Dr	Laredo	TX	78041	**800-232-7907**	956-728-2500
Longview News-Journal 320 E Methvin St	Longview	TX	75601	**800-825-9799**	903-757-3311
Lubbock Avalanche-Journal 710 Ave J	Lubbock	TX	79401	**800-692-4021**	806-762-8844
Lufkin Daily News 300 Ellis Ave	Lufkin	TX	75904	**888-664-8792**	936-632-6631
Monitor, The 1400 E Nolana Loop	McAllen	TX	78504	**800-366-4343**	956-683-4000
Midland Reporter-Telegram PO Box 1650	Midland	TX	79702	**800-542-3952**	432-682-5311
Odessa American PO Box 2952	Odessa	TX	79760	**800-592-4433**	432-337-4661
San Angelo Standard-Times 34 W Harris Ave	San Angelo	TX	76903	**800-588-1884**	325-659-8200
San Antonio Express-News Ave E & Third St	San Antonio	TX	78205	**800-555-1551**	210-250-3000
Herald Democrat 603 S Sam Rayburn Fwy	Sherman	TX	75090	**800-827-7183**	903-893-8181
Texarkana Gazette 315 Pine St *General	Texarkana	TX	75501	**866-747-7424***	903-794-3311
Tyler Morning Telegraph PO Box 2030	Tyler	TX	75710	**800-772-1213**	903-597-8111
Victoria Advocate PO Box 1518	Victoria	TX	77902	**800-234-8108**	361-575-1451
Waco Tribune-Herald 900 Franklin Ave	Waco	TX	76701	**800-678-8742**	254-757-5757
Times Record News PO Box 120	Wichita Falls	TX	76307	**800-627-1646**	940-767-8341
Herald Journal 75 W 300 N	Logan	UT	84321	**800-275-0423**	435-752-2121
Standard-Examiner 332 Standard Way	Ogden	UT	84404	**800-234-5505**	801-625-4200
Daily Herald 1555 N Freedom Blvd	Provo	UT	84604	**800-880-8075**	801-373-5050
Deseret News 30 E 100 S Suite 400 PO Box 1257	Salt Lake City	UT	84110	**800-999-7511**	801-236-6000
Burlington Free Press 100 Bank St	Burlington	VT	05401	**800-427-3124**	802-863-3441
Rutland Herald PO Box 668	Rutland	VT	05702	**800-498-4296**	
Bristol Herald-Courier 320 Bob Morrison Blvd	Bristol	VA	24201	**888-228-2098**	276-669-2181
Free Lance Star 616 Amelia St	Fredericksburg	VA	22401	**800-877-0500**	540-374-5000
News & Advance PO Box 10129	Lynchburg	VA	24506	**800-275-8830**	434-385-5555
Martinsville Bulletin PO Box 3711	Martinsville	VA	24115	**800-234-6575**	276-638-8801
Virginian-Pilot 150 W Brambleton Ave	Norfolk	VA	23510	**800-446-2004**	757-446-2000
Roanoke Times 201 W Campbell Ave SW	Roanoke	VA	24011	**800-346-1234**	540-981-3340
News Leader 11 N Central Ave	Staunton	VA	24401	**800-793-2459**	540-885-7281
Winchester Star Two N Kent St	Winchester	VA	22601	**800-296-8639**	540-667-3200
Daily World 315 S Michigan St	Aberdeen	WA	98520	**800-829-7880**	360-532-4000
Kitsap Sun PO Box 259	Bremerton	WA	98337	**888-377-3711**	360-377-3711
Tri-City Herald 333 W Canal Dr	Kennewick	WA	99336	**800-874-0445**	509-582-1500

Classified Section

Name / Address	City	ST	ZIP	Toll-Free	Phone
Skagit Valley Herald 1000 E College Way PO Box 578	Mount Vernon	WA	98273	800-683-3300	360-424-3251
Peninsula Daily News 305 W First St PO Box 1330	Port Angeles	WA	98362	800-826-7714	360-452-2345
Seattle Post-Intelligencer 101 Elliott Ave W Second Fl	Seattle	WA	98119	800-542-0820	206-448-8000
News Tribune 1950 S State St	Tacoma	WA	98405	800-388-8742	253-597-8742
Columbian 701 W Eigth St PO Box 180	Vancouver	WA	98660	800-743-3391	360-694-3391
Wenatchee World 14 N Mission St	Wenatchee	WA	98801	800-572-4433	509-663-5161
Yakima Herald-Republic PO Box 9668	Yakima	WA	98909	800-343-2799	509-248-1251
Register-Herald 801 N Kanawha St	Beckley	WV	25801	800-950-0250	304-255-4400
Charleston Gazette 1001 Virginia St E	Charleston	WV	25301	800-982-6397	304-348-5140
Clarksburg Exponent Telegram 324 Hewes Ave	Clarksburg	WV	26301	800-982-6034	304-626-1400
Exponent Telegram 324 Hewes Ave	Clarksburg	WV	26301	800-982-6034	
Herald-Dispatch 946 Fifth Ave	Huntington	WV	25701	800-444-2446	304-526-4000
Journal, The 207 W King St	Martinsburg	WV	25402	800-448-1895	304-263-8931
Beloit Daily News 149 State St	Beloit	WI	53511	800-356-3411	608-365-8811
Leader-Telegram 701 S Farwell St	Eau Claire	WI	54701	800-236-8808	715-833-9200
Action Reporter Media N6637 Rolling Meadows Dr PO Box 1955	Fond du Lac	WI	54936	800-261-5325	920-922-4600
Green Bay Press-Gazette PO Box 23430	Green Bay	WI	54305	800-289-8221	920-431-8400
Janesville Gazette One S Parker Dr PO Box 5001	Janesville	WI	53547	800-362-6712	608-754-3311
Kenosha News 5800 Seventh Ave	Kenosha	WI	53140	800-292-2700	262-657-1000
La Crosse Tribune 401 N Third St	La Crosse	WI	54601	800-262-0420	608-782-9710
Capital Times 1901 Fish Hatchery Rd	Madison	WI	53713	800-362-8333	608-252-6400
Wisconsin State Journal 1901 Fish Hatchery Rd	Madison	WI	53713	800-362-8333	608-252-6200
Herald Times Reporter 902 Franklin St	Manitowoc	WI	54221	800-783-7323	920-684-4433
Milwaukee Journal Sentinel 333 W State St	Milwaukee	WI	53201	800-456-5943	414-224-2000
Sheboygan Press 632 Center Ave PO Box 358	Sheboygan	WI	53081	800-686-3900	920-457-7711
Waukesha County Freeman 801 N Barstow St PO Box 7	Waukesha	WI	53187	800-762-6219	262-542-2501
Wausau Daily Herald 800 Scott St	Wausau	WI	54403	800-477-4838	715-842-2101
Wyoming Tribune-Eagle 702 W Lincolnway	Cheyenne	WY	82001	800-561-6268	307-634-3361

529-3 National Newspapers

Name / Address	City	ST	ZIP	Toll-Free	Phone
Circle Media Inc 5817 Old Leeds Rd	Irondale	AL	35210	800-356-9916	
Christian Science Monitor 210 Massachusetts Ave	Boston	MA	02115	800-453-3432	617-450-2000
Wall Street Journal, The 1211 Ave of the Americas *General	New York	NY	10036	800-568-7625*	212-416-2000
USA Today 7950 Jones Branch Dr *Cust Svc	McLean	VA	22108	800-872-0001*	703-854-3400

529-4 Weekly Newspapers

Listings here are organized by city names within state groupings.

Name / Address	City	ST	ZIP	Toll-Free	Phone
Birmingham Times 115 Third Ave W	Birmingham	AL	35204	866-456-4995	205-251-5158
Gardena Valley News 15005 S Vermont Ave	Gardena	CA	90247	800-329-6351	310-329-6351
Independent, The 2250 First St	Livermore	CA	94550	877-952-3588	925-447-8700
Los Angeles Downtown News 1264 W First St	Los Angeles	CA	90026	877-338-1010	213-481-1448
Mammoth Times, The PO Box 3929	Mammoth Lakes	CA	93546	800-427-7623	760-934-3929
Milpitas Post 59 Marylinn Dr	Milpitas	CA	95035	800-870-6397	408-262-2454
Palos Verdes Peninsula News 609 Deep Valley Dr Ste 200	Rolling Hills Estates	CA	90274	877-512-6397	310-372-0388
Paradise Post 5399 Clark Rd	Paradise	CA	95969	855-857-7247	530-877-4413
Aurora Sentinel 14305 E Alameda Ave Ste 200	Aurora	CO	80012	855-269-4484	303-750-7555
Bridgeport News 1000 Bridgeport Ave *Advestisement	Shelton	CT	06484	855-247-8573*	203-926-2080
Milford Mirror 1000 Bridgeport Ave *Advestisement	Shelton	CT	06484	800-372-2790*	203-402-2315
Reminder, The PO Box 210	Vernon	CT	06066	888-456-2211	860-875-3366
Stratford Star 1000 Bridgeport Ave *Advestisement	Shelton	CT	06484	800-372-2790*	203-402-2319
Dialog, The 1925 Delaware Ave	Wilmington	DE	19806	877-225-7870	302-573-3109
Dover Post 1196 S Little Creek Rd	Dover	DE	19901	800-942-1616	302-678-3616
Clay Today 3513 US Hwy 17	Fleming Island	FL	32003	888-434-9844	904-264-3200
Daily Sun 1100 Main St	The Villages	FL	32159	800-726-6592	352-753-1119
Miami Today 710 Brickell Ave	Miami	FL	33131	800-283-2707	305-358-2663
Osceola News-Gazette 108 Church St	Kissimmee	FL	34741	800-281-5303	407-846-7600
Venice Gondolier Sun 200 E Venice Ave	Venice	FL	34285	877-818-6204	941-207-1000
Revue & News, The 319 N Main St	Alpharetta	GA	30004	800-864-5960	770-442-3278
Galena Gazette 716 S Bench St	Galena	IL	61036	800-373-6397	815-777-0019
Granite City Journal Two Executive Dr	Collinsville	IL	62234	800-766-3278	618-877-7700
Times Record 219 S College Ave	Aledo	IL	61231	800-784-6776	309-582-5112
Banner-Gazette 490 E State Rd 60 PO Box 38	Pekin	IN	47165	800-889-3390	812-967-3176
Hendricks County Flyer 8109 Kingston St Ste 500	Avon	IN	46123	800-359-3747	317-272-5800
Papers, The 206 S Main St PO Box 188	Milford	IN	46542	800-733-4111	574-658-4111
Avoyelles Journal 105 N Main St	Marksville	LA	71351	800-565-4321	318-253-5413
Times of Acadiana 1100 Bertrand Dr	Lafayette	LA	70506	877-289-2216	337-289-6300
Coastal Journal 97 Commercial St Ste 3	Bath	ME	04530	800-649-6241	207-443-6241
Baltimore Times 2513 N Charles St	Baltimore	MD	21218	800-944-7403	410-366-3900
Camden Publications 331 E Bell St	Camden	MI	49232	800-222-6336	517-368-0365
Cedar Springs Post 36 E Maple PO Box 370	Cedar Springs	MI	49319	888-937-4514	616-696-3655
Dearborn Times-Herald 13730 Michigan Ave	Dearborn	MI	48126	866-468-7630	313-584-4000
Voice, The 51180 Bedford St	New Baltimore	MI	48047	800-561-2248	586-716-8100
Morrison County Record 216 SE First St	Little Falls	MN	56345	888-637-2345	320-632-2345
Farmington Press 218 N Washington St PO Box 70	Farmington	MO	63640	800-455-0206	573-756-8927
Jefferson County Journal 1405 N Truman Blvd	Festus	MO	63028	800-365-0820	636-937-9811
Press Journal 14522 S Outer 40 Dr	Chesterfield	MO	63017	800-545-6953	314-821-1110
Washington Missourian 14 W Main St PO Box 336	Washington	MO	63090	888-239-7701	636-239-7701
Bellevue Leader 604 Fort Crook Rd N	Bellevue	NE	68005	800-284-6397	402-733-7300
West Nebraska Register PO Box 608	Grand Island	NE	68802	800-652-2229	308-382-4660
Hunterdon County Democrat 8 Minneakoning Rd	Flemington	NJ	08822	888-782-7533	908-782-4747
Twin-Boro News 210 Knickerbocker Rd	Cresskill	NJ	07626	888-473-2673	201-894-6715
Queens Courier 38-15 Bell Blvd	Bayside	NY	11361	800-275-8777	718-224-5863
Journal-Patriot PO Box 70	North Wilkesboro	NC	28659	877-322-8228	336-838-4117
Plains Reporter PO Box 1447	Williston	ND	58802	800-950-2165	701-572-2165
West Fargo Pioneer PO Box 457	West Fargo	ND	58078	888-382-1222	701-282-2443
Cuyahoga Falls News-Press 1050 W Main St PO Box 5199	Kent	OH	44240	800-560-9657	330-541-9421
Dublin Villager 7801 N Central Dr	Lewis Center	OH	43035	866-790-4502	740-888-6100
Early Bird, The 5312 Sebring Warner Rd	Greenville	OH	45331	866-627-4557	937-548-3330
Forest Hills Journal 394 WaRds Corner Rd Ste 170	Loveland	OH	45140	888-894-2113	513-248-8600
Gateway News 1050 West Main St	Kent	OH	44240	800-560-9657	330-541-9400
Hilliard This Week 7801 N Central Dr	Lewis Center	OH	43035	888-837-4342	740-888-6100
Reynoldsburg This Week 7801 N Central Dr	Lewis Center	OH	43035	888-837-4342	740-888-6100
Suburban Press & Metro Press 1550 Woodville Rd	Millbury	OH	43447	800-300-6158	419-836-2221
Westerville This Week 7801 N Central Dr	Lewis Center	OH	43035	888-837-4342	740-888-6100
Northeast Times 2512 Metropolitan Dr	Trevose	PA	19053	800-556-3655	215-355-9009
York Sunday News 1891 Loucks Rd	York	PA	17408	800-483-5517	717-767-6397
Bluffton Today 52 Persimmon St	Bluffton	SC	29910	855-665-8549	843-815-0800
Chronicle Independent 909 W Dekalb St *General	Camden	SC	29020	800-698-3514*	803-432-6157
Georgetown Times 615 Front St	Georgetown	SC	29440	800-772-1213	843-546-4148
Star, The 106 E Buena Vista Ave	North Augusta	SC	29841	888-397-3742	803-279-2793
Valley Town Crier 1811 N 23rd St	McAllen	TX	78501	800-285-5667	956-682-2423
World, The 403 US Rt 302-Berlin	Barre	VT	05641	800-639-9753	802-479-2582
Fauquier Times-Democrat 39 Culpeper St	Warrenton	VA	20186	888-351-1660	540-347-4222
Loudoun Times-Mirror PO Box 359	Leesburg	VA	20178	888-351-1660	703-777-1111
Mechanicsville Local 6400 Mechanicsville Tpke	Mechanicsville	VA	23111	800-468-3382	804-746-1235

		Toll-Free	Phone
Virginia Gazette			
216 Ironbound Rd .... Williamsburg VA 23188		800-944-6908	757-220-1736
Tribune Newspapers of Snohomish County			
127 Ave C Ste B PO Box 499 .... Snohomish WA 98291		877-894-4663	360-568-4121
Country Today			
701 S Farwell St .... Eau Claire WI 54701		800-236-4004	715-833-9270

529-5 Weekly Newspapers - Alternative

		Toll-Free	Phone
Chico News & Review			
353 E Second St .... Chico CA 95928		866-703-3873	530-894-2300
Palo Alto Weekly			
450 Cambridge Ave .... Palo Alto CA 94306		800-766-4466	650-326-8210
San Luis Obispo New Times			
505 Higuera St .... San Luis Obispo CA 93401		800-546-4219	805-546-8208
Orlando Weekly			
1505 E Colonial Dr St Ste 200 .... Orlando FL 32803		800-474-7576	407-377-0400
Creative Loafing Atlanta			
384 Northyards Blvd Ste 600 .... Atlanta GA 30313		888-242-0208	404-688-5623
Chicago Reader			
11 E Illinois St .... Chicago IL 60611		888-473-5362	312-828-0350
Metro Times			
733 St Antoine St .... Detroit MI 48226		866-501-3627	313-961-4060
Minneapolis/St. Paul City Pages			
401 N Third St Ste 550 .... Minneapolis MN 55401		844-387-6962	612-375-1015
Reno News & Review			
708 N Ctr St .... Reno NV 89501		866-703-3873	916-498-1234
Long Island Press			
575 Underhill Blvd Ste 210. .... Syosset NY 11791		800-545-6683	516-284-3300
Syracuse New Times			
1415 W Genesee St .... Syracuse NY 13204		800-856-1900	315-422-7011
Scene			
1468 W Ninth St Ste 805 .... Cleveland OH 44113		877-598-8703	216-241-7550
Eugene Weekly			
1251 Lincoln St .... Eugene OR 97401		866-233-2250	541-484-0519
Memphis Flyer			
460 Tennessee St .... Memphis TN 38103		800-581-5156	901-521-9000
Metro Pulse			
602 S Gay St Ste Mezzanine .... Knoxville TN 37902		800-686-4208	865-522-5399
Nashville Scene			
210 12th Ave S Ste 100 .... Nashville TN 37203		800-577-3917	615-244-7989
Austin Chronicle			
PO Box 49066 .... Austin TX 78765		866-271-4900	512-454-5766
Houston Press			
1621 Milam St Ste 100. .... Houston TX 77002		877-926-8300	713-280-2400
Pacific Northwest Inlander			
9 S Washington St .... Spokane WA 99201		888-431-9911	509-325-0634

530   NURSES ASSOCIATIONS - STATE

SEE ALSO Health & Medical Professionals Associations

		Toll-Free	Phone
Alabama State Nurses Assn (ASNA)			
360 N Hull St .... Montgomery AL 36104		800-270-2762	334-262-8321
Delaware Nurses Assn (DNA)			
4765 Ogletown-Stanton Rd Ste L10 .... Newark DE 19713		800-626-4081	302-733-5880
Georgia Nurses Assn (GNA)			
3032 Briarcliff Rd NE .... Atlanta GA 30329		800-324-0462	404-325-5536
Hawaii Nurses Assn (HNA)			
949 Kapiolani Blvd Ste 107 .... Honolulu HI 96814		800-617-2677	808-531-1628
Idaho Nurses Assn (INA)			
1850 E Southern Ave Ste 1 .... Tempe AZ 85224		888-721-8904	404-760-2803
Louisiana State Nurses Assn, The (LSNA)			
5713 Superior Dr Ste A-6 .... Baton Rouge LA 70816		800-457-6378	225-201-0993
Massachusetts Nurses Assn (MNA)			
340 Tpke St .... Canton MA 02021		800-882-2056	781-821-4625
Michigan Nurses Assn (MNA)			
2310 Jolly Oak Rd .... Okemos MI 48864		888-646-8773	517-349-5640
Minnesota Nurses Assn (MNA)			
345 Randolph Ave Ste 200 .... Saint Paul MN 55102		800-536-4662	651-646-4807
Nebraska Nurses Assn (NNA)			
PO Box 3107 .... Kearney NE 68848		800-582-3014	402-475-3859
New Jersey State Nurses Assn (NJSNA)			
1479 Pennington Rd .... Trenton NJ 08618		888-876-5762	609-883-5335
New York State Nurses Assn (NYSNA)			
11 Cornell Rd .... Latham NY 12110		800-724-6976	518-782-9400
North Carolina Nurses Assn (NCNA)			
103 Enterprise St PO Box 12025 .... Raleigh NC 27605		800-626-2153	919-821-4250
Oregon Nurses Assn (ONA)			
18765 SW Boones Ferry Rd .... Tualatin OR 97062		800-634-3552	503-293-0011
Pennsylvania Assn of Staff Nurses & Allied Professionals (PASNAP)			
One Fayette St Ste 475 .... Conshohocken PA 19428		800-500-7850	610-567-2907
Utah Nurses Assn (UNA)			
4505 S Wastch Blvd Ste 330B .... Salt Lake City UT 84124		800-338-7657	801-272-4510
Vermont State Nurses Assn (VSNA)			
100 Dorset St Ste 13. .... South Burlington VT 05403		800-540-9390	802-651-8886
Washington State Nurses Assn (WSNA)			
575 Andover Pk W Ste 101. .... Seattle WA 98188		800-231-8482	206-575-7979
West Virginia Nurses Assn (WVNA)			
1007 Bigley Ave Ste 308. .... Charleston WV 25302		800-400-1226	304-342-1169

531   OFFICE & SCHOOL SUPPLIES

SEE ALSO Office Supply Stores ; Writing Paper ; Pens, Pencils, Parts ; Printing & Photocopying Supplies

		Toll-Free	Phone
Acroprint Time Recorder Co			
5640 Departure Dr .... Raleigh NC 27616		800-334-7190	919-872-5800
American Product Distributors Inc (APD)			
8350 Arrowridge Blvd .... Charlotte NC 28273		800-849-5842	704-522-9411
American Solutions for Business			
31 E Minnesota Ave PO Box 218 .... Glenwood MN 56334		800-862-3690	

		Toll-Free	Phone
Arlington Industries Inc			
1616 Lakeside Dr .... Waukegan IL 60085		800-323-4147	847-689-2754
Aurora Corp of America			
3500 Challenger St .... Torrance CA 90503		800-327-8508	310-793-5650
Avery Dennison Corp			
207 Goode Ave .... Glendale CA 91203		888-567-4387*	626-304-2000
*NYSE: AVY ▥ *Cust Svc*			
Avery Dennison Worldwide Office Products Div			
207 Goode Ave .... Glendale CA 91203		800-462-8379	626-304-2000
Bartizan Corp			
217 Riverdale Ave .... Yonkers NY 10705		800-899-2278	914-965-7977
Baumgarten's 144 Ottley Dr .... Atlanta GA 30324		800-247-5547	404-874-7675
Business Stationery LLC			
4944 Commerce Pkwy .... Cleveland OH 44128		800-234-9954	216-514-1277
C-Line Products Inc			
1100 E Business Ctr Dr .... Mount Prospect IL 60056		800-323-6084	847-827-6661
Cardinal Office Products Inc			
576 E Main St .... Frankfort KY 40601		800-589-5886	502-875-3300
Case Logic Inc			
6303 Dry Creek Pkwy .... Longmont CO 80503		800-925-8111	303-652-1000
Champion Industries Inc			
PO Box 2968 PO Box 2968. .... Huntington WV 25728		800-624-3431	304-528-2791
OTC: CHMP			
Dahle North America Inc			
49 Vose Farm Rd Ste 110 .... Peterborough NH 03458		800-243-8145	603-924-0003
Deflect-O Corp			
7035 E 86th St .... Indianapolis IN 46250		800-428-4328	
Douglas Stewart Co, The			
2402 Advance Rd .... Madison WI 53718		800-279-2795	608-221-1155
Eaton Office Supply Company Inc			
180 John Glenn Dr .... Buffalo NY 14228		800-365-3237	716-691-6100
GBS Corp			
7233 Freedom Ave NW .... North Canton OH 44720		800-552-2427	330-494-5330
International Imaging Materials Inc			
310 Commerce Dr .... Amherst NY 14228		888-464-4625	716-691-6333
Lakeshore Learning Materials			
2695 E Dominguez St .... Carson CA 90895		800-778-4456	
Lee Products Co			
800 E 80th St .... Bloomington MN 55420		800-989-3544	952-854-3544
Magna Visual Inc			
9400 Watson Rd .... Saint Louis MO 63126		800-843-3399	
Nina Enterprises			
1350 S Leavitt St .... Chicago IL 60608		800-886-8688	312-733-6400
PBS Supply Company Inc			
7013 S 216th St .... Kent WA 98032		877-727-7515	253-395-5550
PerfectData Corp			
1323 Conshohocken Rd .... Plymouth Meeting PA 19462		800-973-7332	
Staples Business Advantage			
500 Staples Dr .... Framingham MA 01702		877-826-7755	
TAB Products Co			
605 Fourth St .... Mayville WI 53050		888-466-8228	
United Stationers Inc			
1 PkwyN Blvd Ste 100 .... Deerfield IL 60015		855-275-6947	847-627-7000
Van Ausdall & Farrar Inc			
6430 E 75th St .... Indianapolis IN 46250		800-467-7474	317-634-2913
Weeks-Lerman Group			
58-38 Page Pl .... Maspeth NY 11378		800-544-5959	718-803-5000

532   OFFICE SUPPLY STORES

		Toll-Free	Phone
Audit & Adjustment Company Inc			
20700 44th Ave W Ste 100 .... Lynnwood WA 98036		800-526-1074	425-776-9797
BenefitHelp Solutions Inc			
10505 SE 17th Ave .... Milwaukie OR 97222		888-398-8057	503-219-3679
Church & Stagg Office Supply Company Inc			
3421 Sixth Ave .... Birmingham AL 35222		800-239-5336	205-251-2951
DBI Inc 912 E Michigan Ave .... Lansing MI 48912		800-968-1324	517-485-3200
Discover Group Inc			
2741 W 23rd St .... Brooklyn NY 11224		866-456-6555	718-456-4500
Eakes Office Plus			
617 W Third St .... Grand Island NE 68801		800-652-9396	308-382-8026
Econ-o-copy Inc			
4437 Trenton St Ste A. .... Metairie LA 70006		877-256-0310	504-457-0032
Egyptian Stationers Inc			
129 W Main St .... Belleville IL 62220		800-642-3949*	618-234-2323
*Cust Svc			
Envoy Plan Services Inc			
901 Calle Amanecer Ste 200. ...... San Clemente CA 92673		800-248-8858	949-366-5070
FASCore LLC			
8515 E Orchard Rd .... Greenwood Village CO 80111		800-232-0859	800-537-2033
Friend's Professional Stationery Inc			
1535 Lewis Ave .... Zion IL 60099		800-323-4394	
Gobin's Inc			
615 N Santa Fe Ave .... Pueblo CO 81003		800-425-2324	719-544-2324
Hurst Group			
257 E Short St .... Lexington KY 40507		800-926-4423	859-255-4422
Kennedy Office Supply			
4211-A Atlantic Ave .... Raleigh NC 27604		800-733-9401	919-878-5400
Koch Bros 325 Grand Ave .... Des Moines IA 50309		800-944-5624	515-283-2451
Latta's School Supply			
1502 Fourth Ave .... Huntington WV 25701		800-624-3501	304-523-8400
McCowan Design & Mfg Ltd			
1760 Birchmount Rd .... Toronto ON M1P2H7		888-782-5189	416-291-7111
Northern Business Products Inc			
PO Box 16127 .... Duluth MN 55816		800-647-8775	218-726-0167
Novacopy Inc			
5520 Shelby Oaks Dr .... Memphis TN 38134		800-264-0637	901-388-3399
Office Depot Inc			
2200 Old Germantown Rd .... Delray Beach FL 33445		800-937-3600	561-438-4800
NASDAQ: ODP			
Opus Framing Ltd			
3445 Cornett Rd .... Vancouver BC V5M2H3		800-663-6953	604-435-9991
Phillips Group			
501 Fulling Mill Rd .... Middletown PA 17057		800-538-7500	717-944-0400
Printers & Stationers Inc			
113 N Ct St .... Florence AL 35630		800-624-5334	256-764-8061

	Toll-Free	Phone
Smith & Butterfield Co Inc		
2800 Lynch Rd ....Evansville IN 47711	**800-321-6543**	812-422-3261
Stationers Inc		
1945 Fifth Ave ....Huntington WV 25703	**800-862-7200**	304-528-2780
Supply Room Cos Inc		
14140 N Washington Hwy ....Ashland VA 23005	**800-849-7239**	804-412-1200
Triplett Office Essentials Corp		
3553 109th St ....Urbandale IA 50322	**800-437-5034**	515-270-9150
Wist Office Products Co		
107 W Julie Dr ....Tempe AZ 85283	**800-999-9478**	480-921-2900
Xpedx 3351 W Addison St ....Chicago IL 60618	**800-678-8536**	773-442-6200

533 OIL & GAS EXTRACTION

	Toll-Free	Phone
A H Belo Corp		
508 Young St PO Box 224866 ....Dallas TX 75202	**800-230-1074**	214-977-8200
NYSE: AHC		
Anadarko Petroleum Corp		
1201 Lk Robbins Dr ....Spring TX 77380	**800-800-1101**	832-636-1000
NYSE: APC		
Apache Corp		
2000 Post Oak Blvd Ste 100 ....Houston TX 77056	**800-272-2434**	713-296-6000
NYSE: APA		
Aramco Services Co		
9009 W Loop S ....Houston TX 77096	**866-287-3592**	713-432-4000
BP Canada Energy Co		
240 Fourth Ave SW ....Calgary AB T2P2H8	**877-833-1359**	403-233-1359
BP PLC 28100 Torch Pkwy ....Warrenville IL 60555	**877-638-5672**	630-420-5111
NYSE: BP		
Cabot Oil & Gas Corp		
840 Gessner Rd Ste 1200 ....Houston TX 77024	**800-434-3985**	281-848-2799
NYSE: COG		
Callon Petroleum Co		
200 N Canal St ....Natchez MS 39120	**800-451-1294**	601-442-1601
NYSE: CPE		
Canadian Natural Resources Ltd (CNRL)		
855 Second St SW Ste 2500 ....Calgary AB T2P4J8	**888-878-3700**	403-517-6700
NYSE: CNQ		
Chevron Corp		
6001 Bollinger Canyon Rd ....San Ramon CA 94583	**800-243-8766***	925-842-1000
NYSE: CVX ■ *Cust Svc		
Cimmaron Field Services Inc		
303 W Wall St Bank of America Tower Ste 600 ....Midland TX 79701	**877-944-2705**	
Comstock Resources Inc		
5300 Town & Country Blvd Ste 500 ....Frisco TX 75034	**800-877-1322**	972-668-8800
NYSE: CRK		
Denbury Resources Inc		
5320 Legacy Dr ....Plano TX 75024	**800-348-9030***	972-673-2000
NYSE: DNR ■ *General		
Devon Energy Corp		
20 N Broadway ....Oklahoma City OK 73102	**877-860-5820**	405-235-3611
NYSE: DVN		
DKRW Advanced Fuels LLC		
5444 Westheimer Ste 1560 ....Houston TX 77056	**855-876-4595**	
EnCana Corp		
855 Second St SW Po Box 2850 ....Calgary AB T2P2S5	**888-568-6322**	403-645-2000
NYSE: ECA		
EQT Corp		
625 Liberty Ave Ste 1700 ....Pittsburgh PA 15222	**800-242-1776**	412-553-5700
NYSE: EQT		
Extreme Plastics Plus Inc		
148 Roush Cir ....Fairmont WV 26554	**866-408-2837**	
Exxon Mobil Corp		
5959 Las Colinas Blvd ....Irving TX 75039	**800-252-1800**	972-444-1000
NYSE: XOM		
GeoResources Inc		
110 Cypress Stn Dr Ste 220 ....Williston ND 58802	**855-538-0599**	281-537-9920
NASDAQ: GEOI		
GMX Resources Inc		
9400 Bdwy Extension Hwy ....Oklahoma City OK 73114	**877-600-0711**	405-600-0711
NYSE: GMXRQ		
Husky Energy Inc		
707 Eigth Ave SW PO Box 6525 ....Calgary AB T2P3G7	**877-262-2111**	403-298-6111
TSE: HSE		
JM Huber Corp		
499 Thornall St 8th Fl ....Edison NJ 08837	**877-418-0038**	732-549-8600
Magnum Hunter Resources		
120 Prosperous Pl Ste 201 ....Lexington KY 40509	**877-778-5463**	859-263-3948
MCW Energy Group Ltd		
344 Mira Loma Ave ....Glendale CA 91204	**800-979-1897**	
Newfield Exploration Co		
363 N Sam Houston Pkwy E Ste 100 ....Houston TX 77060	**866-902-0562**	281-847-6000
NYSE: NFX		
Noble Energy Inc		
100 Glenborough Dr Ste 100 ....Houston TX 77067	**800-220-5824**	281-872-3100
NYSE: NBL		
NW Natural		
220 NW Second Ave PO Box 6017 ....Portland OR 97209	**800-422-4012**	503-226-4211
Ohio Gas Co PO Box 528 ....Bryan OH 43506	**800-331-7396**	419-636-1117
Penn Virginia Corp		
100 Matsonford Rd Ste 200 ....Radnor PA 19087	**877-316-5288**	610-687-8900
NYSE: PVA		
Penn West Petroleum Ltd		
Ninth Ave SW Ste 200 ....Calgary AB T2P1K3	**866-693-2707**	403-777-2500
TSE: PWT		
Petroleum Development Corp (PDC)		
120 Genesis Blvd PO Box 26 ....Bridgeport WV 26330	**800-624-3821**	303-860-5800
NASDAQ: PDCE		
Seneca Resources Corp		
1201 Louisiana St Ste 400 ....Houston TX 77002	**800-365-3234**	713-654-2600
Shell Oil Co		
910 Louisiana St ....Houston TX 77002	**888-467-4355**	713-241-6161
Southwestern Energy Co		
2350 N Sam Houston Pkwy E Ste 300 ....Houston TX 77032	**866-322-0801**	832-796-1000
NYSE: SWN		

	Toll-Free	Phone
Suncor Energy Inc		
150 - 6 Ave SW PO Box 2844 ....Calgary AB T2P3E3	**800-558-9071**	403-296-8000
NYSE: SU		
Sunoco Inc		
1735 Market St Ste LL ....Philadelphia PA 19103	**800-786-6261**	215-977-3000
NYSE: SUN		
Swift Energy Co		
16825 Northchase Dr Ste 400 ....Houston TX 77060	**800-777-2412**	281-874-2700
NYSE: SFY		
Tengasco Inc		
11121 Kingston Pk Ste E ....Knoxville TN 37934	**888-669-0684**	865-675-1554
NYSE: TGC		
Unit Corp		
7130 S Lewis Ave Ste 1000 ....Tulsa OK 74136	**800-722-3612**	918-493-7700
NYSE: UNT		
Wagner Oil Co		
500 Commerce St Ste 600 ....Fort Worth TX 76102	**800-457-5332**	817-335-2222
Warren Resources Inc		
1114 Ave of the Americas 34th Fl ....New York NY 10036	**877-587-9494**	212-697-9660
NASDAQ: WRES		
Wilshire Enterprises Inc		
100 Eagle Rock Ave Ste 100 ....East Hanover NJ 07936	**888-697-3962**	973-585-7770
OTC: WLSE		
XTO Energy Inc		
810 Houston St ....Fort Worth TX 76102	**800-299-2800**	817-870-2800
ZaZa Energy Corp		
1301 McKinney St Ste 3000 ....Houston TX 77010	**866-266-2502**	713-595-1900
NASDAQ: ZAZA		

534 OIL & GAS FIELD EQUIPMENT

	Toll-Free	Phone
Baker Hughes Inc (BHI)		
2929 Allen Pkwy Ste 1200 ....Houston TX 77019	**800-229-7447**	713-439-8600
NYSE: BHI		
Carbo Ceramics Inc		
575 N. Dairy Ashford Rd. Ste. 300 ....Houston TX 77079	**800-551-3247**	281-921-6400
NYSE: CRR		
Cuming Corp 225 Bodwell St ....Avon MA 02322	**800-432-6464**	508-580-2660
Dril-Quip Inc		
13550 Hempstead Hwy ....Houston TX 77040	**877-316-2631**	713-939-7711
NYSE: DRQ		
Drillers Service Inc		
1792 Highland Ave NE PO Box 1407 ....Hickory NC 28601	**800-334-2308**	828-322-1100
FMC Technologies Inc		
1803 Gears Rd ....Houston TX 77067	**800-356-4898**	281-591-4000
NYSE: FTI		
Gearench Inc		
4450 S Hwy 6 PO Box 192 ....Clifton TX 76634	**800-221-1848**	254-675-8651
GEFCO Inc (GEFCO)		
2215 S Van Buren ....Enid OK 73703	**800-759-7441**	580-234-4141
Harbison-Fischer		
901 N Crowley Rd ....Crowley TX 76036	**800-364-7867**	817-297-2211
Kimray Inc		
52 NW 42nd St ....Oklahoma City OK 73118	**866-586-7233**	405-525-6601
M & M Supply Co		
909 W Peach Ave PO Box 548 ....Duncan OK 73534	**800-424-9300**	580-252-7879
Morris Industries Inc		
777 Rt 23 PO Box 278 ....Pompton Plains NJ 07444	**800-835-0777**	973-835-6600
Morrison Bros Co		
570 E Seventh St ....Dubuque IA 52001	**800-553-4840**	563-583-5701
Schramm Inc		
800 E Virginia Ave ....West Chester PA 19380	**888-737-9438**	610-696-2500
ShawCor Ltd 25 Bethridge Rd ....Toronto ON M9W1M7	**800-668-4842**	416-743-7111
TSE: SCL/A		
Southern Company Inc		
3101 Carrier St ....Memphis TN 38116	**800-264-7626**	901-345-2531
Tam International Inc		
4620 Southerland Rd ....Houston TX 77092	**800-462-7617**	713-462-7617
Titan Specialties Inc		
11785 Hwy 152 ....Pampa TX 79065	**800-692-4486***	806-665-3781
*Sales		
Weatherford International Inc		
515 Post Oak Blvd Ste 600 ....Houston TX 77027	**866-398-0010**	713-693-4000
NYSE: WFT		
Winston F2S Corp		
1604 Cherokee Trace ....White Oak TX 75693	**800-527-8465**	903-757-7341

535 OIL & GAS FIELD EXPLORATION SERVICES

	Toll-Free	Phone
Arctic Slope Regional Corp		
1230 Agvik St PO Box 129 ....Barrow AK 99723	**800-770-2772**	907-852-8633
Bill Barrett Corp		
1099 18th St Ste 2300 ....Denver CO 80202	**800-826-6762**	303-293-9100
NYSE: BBG		
Breitburn Energy Partners LP		
515 S Flower St Ste 4800 ....Los Angeles CA 90071	**800-732-0330**	213-225-5900
NASDAQ: BBEP		
Chaparral Energy Inc		
701 Cedar Lake Blvd ....Oklahoma City OK 73114	**866-478-8770**	405-478-8770
Dawson Geophysical Co		
508 W Wall St Ste 800 ....Midland TX 79701	**800-332-9766**	432-684-3000
NASDAQ: DWSN		
EOG Resources Inc		
1111 Bagby Sky Lobby 2 ....Houston TX 77002	**877-363-3647**	713-651-7000
NYSE: EOG		
Equal Energy Ltd		
500 Fourth Ave SW ....Calgary AB T2P2V6	**877-263-0262**	403-263-0262
EXCO Resources Inc		
12377 Merit Dr Ste 1700 ....Dallas TX 75251	**888-788-9449**	214-368-2084
NYSE: XCO		
Fidelity Exploration & Production Co		
1801 California St Ste 2500 ....Denver CO 80202	**800-986-3133**	303-893-3133
Mustang Fuel Corp		
9800 N Oklahoma Ave ....Oklahoma City OK 73114	**800-332-9400**	405-748-9400

				Toll-Free	Phone
New Jersey Natural Gas Co					
1415 Wyckoff Rd	Wall	NJ	07719	**800-221-0051**	732-938-1480
Panhandle Royalty Co					
5400 N Grand Blvd					
Grand Ctr Bldg Ste 300	Oklahoma City	OK	73112	**800-884-4225**	405-948-1560
Patterson-UTI Energy Inc					
450 Gears Rd Ste 500	Houston	TX	77067	**866-387-1933**	281-765-7100
NASDAQ: PTEN					
Power Service Products Inc					
PO Box 1089	Weatherford	TX	76086	**800-643-9089**	817-599-9486
Quicksilver Resources Inc					
777 W Rosedale St Ste 300	Fort Worth	TX	76104	**877-665-8600**	817-665-5000
OTC: KWKAQ					
Rosetta Resources Inc					
717 Texas Ste 2800	Houston	TX	77002	**800-526-2112**	713-335-4000
NASDAQ: ROSE					
Superior Energy Services Inc					
601 Poydras St Ste 2400	New Orleans	LA	70130	**800-259-7774**	504-587-7374
NYSE: SPN					
TGC Industries Inc					
101 E Pk Blvd Ste 955	Plano	TX	75074	**800-223-7470**	972-881-1099
NASDAQ: TGE					
Veritas DGC Inc					
10300 Townpark Dr	Houston	TX	77072	**800-344-4266**	832-351-8300
Walter Oil & Gas Corp					
1100 Louisiana St Ste 200	Houston	TX	77002	**888-756-7880**	713-659-1221

536 OIL & GAS FIELD SERVICES

SEE ALSO Oil & Gas Field Exploration Services

				Toll-Free	Phone
Allamon Tool Company Inc					
18935 Freeport Dr	Montgomery	TX	77356	**877-449-5433**	
Baker Hughes Inc (BHI)					
2929 Allen Pkwy Ste 1200	Houston	TX	77019	**800-229-7447**	713-439-8600
NYSE: BHI					
Central Industries Inc					
11438 Cronridge Dr Ste W	Owings Mills	MD	21117	**800-304-8484**	
Colloid Environmental Technologies Co (CETCO)					
2870 Forbs Ave	Hoffman Estates	IL	60192	**800-527-9948**	847-851-1899
Danos & Curole Marine Contractors Inc					
13083 Louisiana 308	Larose	LA	70373	**800-487-5971**	985-693-3313
Diamond Services Corp					
503 S DeGravelle Rd	Amelia	LA	70340	**800-879-1162**	985-631-2187
Fairweather LLC					
9525 King St	Anchorage	AK	99515	**800-319-8802**	907-346-3247
FESCO Ltd 1000 Fesco Ave	Alice	TX	78332	**800-375-3479**	361-661-7000
Global Industries Ltd					
8000 Global Dr	Sulphur	LA	70665	**800-525-3483**	337-583-5000
Gulf Offshore Logistics LLC					
120 White Rose Dr	Raceland	LA	70394	**866-532-1060**	
Helix Energy Solutions Inc					
400 N Sam Houston Pkwy E Ste 400	Houston	TX	77060	**888-345-2347**	281-618-0400
NYSE: HLX					
Indel-Davis Inc					
4401 S Jackson Ave	Tulsa	OK	74107	**800-331-6300**	918-587-2151
Koch Specialty Plant Services					
12221 E Sam Houston Pkwy N	Houston	TX	77044	**800-765-9177**	713-427-7700
Mansfield Oil Co					
1025 Airport Pkwy SW	Gainesville	GA	30501	**800-695-6626**	
Matrix Service Co					
5100 E Skelly Dr 74135	Tulsa	OK	74135	**866-367-6879**	
NASDAQ: MTRX					
Milbar Hydro-Test Inc					
651 Aero Dr	Shreveport	LA	71107	**800-259-8210**	318-227-8210
Newpark Mats & Integrated Services LLC					
2700 Research Forest Dr Ste 100	The Woodlands	TX	77381	**877-628-7623**	281-362-6800
Oceaneering International Inc					
11911 FM 529	Houston	TX	77041	**877-680-5478**	713-329-4500
NYSE: OII					
Pride International Inc					
5847 San Felipe St Ste 3300	Houston	TX	77057	**877-736-3772**	713-789-1400
Production Management Industries LLC					
9761 Hwy 90 E	Morgan City	LA	70380	**888-229-3837**	985-631-3837
RPC Inc					
2801 Buford Hwy Ste 520	Atlanta	GA	30324	**800-776-9437**	404-321-2140
NYSE: RES					
Supreme Oil Co					
2109 W Monte Vista Rd	Phoenix	AZ	85009	**800-752-7888**	
Team Inc 200 Hermann Dr	Alvin	TX	77511	**800-662-8326**	281-331-6154
NYSE: TISI					
Tiorco Inc					
2452 S Trenton Way Ste M	Denver	CO	80231	**800-525-0578**	303-923-6440
TK Stanley Inc					
6739 Hwy 184	Waynesboro	MS	39367	**800-477-2855**	
Trican Well Service Ltd					
645 Seventh Ave SW Ste 2900	Calgary	AB	T2P4G8	**877-587-4226**	403-266-0202
TSE: TCW					

537 OIL & GAS WELL DRILLING

				Toll-Free	Phone
Callon Petroleum Co					
200 N Canal St	Natchez	MS	39120	**800-451-1294**	601-442-1601
NYSE: CPE					
Cyclone Drilling Inc					
PO Box 908	Gillette	WY	82717	**800-318-3724**	307-682-4161
Diamond Offshore Drilling Inc					
15415 Katy Fwy	Houston	TX	77094	**800-848-1980**	281-492-5300
NYSE: DO					
Doyon Drilling Inc					
11500 C St Ste 200	Anchorage	AK	99515	**800-478-9675**	907-563-5530
GEO Drilling Fluids Inc					
1431 Union Ave	Bakersfield	CA	93305	**800-438-7436**	661-325-5919

				Toll-Free	Phone
Helmerich & Payne Inc					
1437 S Boulder Ave	Tulsa	OK	74119	**800-205-4913**	918-742-5531
NYSE: HP					
Hercules Offshore Inc					
9 Greenway Plaza Ste 2200	Houston	TX	77046	**888-647-1715**	713-350-5100
NASDAQ: HERO					
Justiss Oil Company Inc					
1120 E Oak St	Jena	LA	71342	**800-256-2501**	318-992-4111
Nabors Drilling International Ltd					
515 W Greens Rd Ste 1000	Houston	TX	77067	**877-344-7529**	281-874-0035
Noble Corp					
13135 S Dairy Ashford Rd Ste 800	Sugar Land	TX	77478	**877-285-4162**	281-276-6100
NYSE: NE					
Parker Drilling Co					
1401 Enclave Pkwy Ste 600	Houston	TX	77077	**800-468-9716**	281-406-2000
NYSE: PKD					
Patterson-UTI Energy Inc					
450 Gears Rd Ste 500	Houston	TX	77067	**866-387-1933**	281-765-7100
NASDAQ: PTEN					
Rowan International Inc					
2800 Post Oak Blvd Ste 5450	Houston	TX	77056	**888-385-2663**	713-621-7800
Total Energy Services Ltd					
2550 300-5th Ave SW Ste 2550	Calgary	AB	T2P3C4	**877-818-6825**	403-216-3939
NYSE: TOT					
Transocean Inc					
4 Greenway Plaza	Houston	TX	77046	**877-440-0173**	713-232-7500
NYSE: RIG					
Unit Corp					
7130 S Lewis Ave Ste 1000	Tulsa	OK	74136	**800-722-3612**	918-493-7700
NYSE: UNT					
Vermilion Energy Trust					
3500 520 Third Ave SW	Calgary	AB	T2P0R3	**866-895-8101**	403-269-4884
TSE: VET					

538 OILS & GREASES - LUBRICATING

SEE ALSO Petroleum Refineries ; Chemicals - Specialty

				Toll-Free	Phone
Amsoil Inc 925 Tower Ave	Superior	WI	54880	**800-777-7094***	715-392-7101
*Sales					
Anderol Inc					
215 Merry Ln PO Box 518	East Hanover	NJ	07936	**888-263-3765**	973-887-7410
BG Products Inc					
740 S Wichita St	Wichita	KS	67213	**800-961-6228**	316-265-2686
Blachford Corp 401 Ctr Rd	Frankfort	IL	60423	**800-435-5942**	905-823-3200
BP Lubricants USA Inc					
1500 Valley Rd	Wayne	NJ	07470	**800-333-3991**	973-633-2200
Canada Forgings Inc					
130 Hagar St	Welland	ON	L3B5P8	**800-263-0440**	905-735-1220
Castrol Industrial North America Inc					
150 W Warrenville Rd	Naperville	IL	60563	**877-641-1600**	
Chem-Trend LP					
1445 McPherson Pk Dr	Howell	MI	48843	**800-727-7730**	517-546-4520
Colorado Petroleum Products Co					
4080 Globeville Rd	Denver	CO	80216	**800-580-4080**	303-294-0302
CRC Industries Inc					
885 Louis Dr	Warminster	PA	18974	**800-556-5074***	215-674-4300
*Cust Svc					
D-A Lubricant Co					
1340 W 29th St	Indianapolis	IN	46208	**800-645-5823**	317-923-5321
Elco Corp					
1000 Belt Line St	Cleveland	OH	44109	**800-321-0467**	216-749-2605
Fiske Bros Refining Co					
129 Lockwood St	Newark	NJ	07105	**800-733-4755**	973-589-9150
Fuchs Lubricants Co					
17050 Lathrop Ave	Harvey	IL	60426	**800-323-7755**	708-333-8900
Hangsterfer's Laboratories Inc					
175 Ogden Rd	Mantua	NJ	08051	**800-433-5823**	856-468-0216
Hercules Chemical Company Inc					
111 S St	Passaic	NJ	07055	**800-221-9330**	973-778-5000
Houghton International Inc					
945 Madison Ave PO Box 930	Valley Forge	PA	19482	**888-459-9844**	610-666-4000
Hydrotex Inc					
12920 Senlac D Ste 190	Farmers Branch	TX	75234	**800-527-9439**	
ITW Rocol North America					
3650 W Lake Ave	Glenview	IL	60026	**800-452-5823**	847-657-5278
Jackson Oil & Solvents Inc					
1970 Kentucky Ave	Indianapolis	IN	46221	**800-221-4603**	317-636-4421
Jet-Lube Inc					
4849 Homestead Rd Ste 232	Houston	TX	77226	**800-538-5823**	713-670-5700
Kluber Lubrication North America LP					
32 Industrial Dr	Londonderry	NH	03053	**800-447-2238**	603-647-4104
Leadership Performance Sustainability Laboratories					
4647 Hugh Howell Rd	Tucker	GA	30084	**800-241-8334**	
Lubrication Engineers Inc					
300 Bailey Ave	Fort Worth	TX	76107	**800-537-7683**	817-834-6321
Lubrication Technologies Inc					
900 Mendelssohn Ave N	Golden Valley	MN	55427	**800-328-5573**	763-545-0707
Lubrizol Corp					
29400 Lakeland Blvd	Wickliffe	OH	44092	**800-380-5397**	440-943-4200
NYSE: LZ					
Metalworking Lubricants Co					
25 Silverdome Industrial Park	Pontiac	MI	48342	**800-394-5494**	248-332-3500
Oil Ctr Research LLC					
106 Montrose Ave	Lafayette	LA	70503	**800-256-8977**	337-993-3559
Orelube Corp, The					
20 Sawgrass Dr	Bellport	NY	11713	**800-645-9124**	631-205-9700
Primrose Oil Company Inc					
11444 Benton Dr PO Box 29665	Dallas	TX	75229	**800-275-2772**	972-241-1100
Safariland LLC					
13386 International Pkwy	Jacksonville	FL	32218	**800-347-1200**	
Schaeffer Mfg Company Inc					
102 Barton St	Saint Louis	MO	63104	**800-325-9962***	314-865-4100
*Cust Svc					
Shell Lubricants					
PO Box 2463 909 Fannin St	Houston	TX	77252	**888-743-5586***	713-241-6161
*Cust Svc					

	Toll-Free	Phone
Smitty's Supply Inc		
63399 Hwy 51 N PO Box 530 . . . . Roseland LA 70456	**800-256-7575**	985-748-9687
Southwestern Petroleum Corp		
PO Box 961005 . . . . Fort Worth TX 76161	**800-877-9372**	817-332-2336
Sun Drilling Products Corp		
503 Main St PO Box 129 . . . . Belle Chasse LA 70037	**800-962-6490**	504-393-2778
Texas Refinery Corp		
840 N Main St . . . . Fort Worth TX 76164	**800-827-0711**	817-332-1161
Total Lubricants USA		
5 N Stiles St . . . . Linden NJ 07036	**800-323-3198**	908-862-9300
Valvoline Co		
3499 Blazer Pkwy PO Box 14000 . . . . Lexington KY 40509	**800-832-6825**	859-357-7777
WD-40 Co 1061 Cudahy Pl . . . . San Diego CA 92110	**800-448-9340**	619-275-1400
NASDAQ: WDFC		

539   OPHTHALMIC GOODS

SEE ALSO Personal Protective Equipment & Clothing

	Toll-Free	Phone
Aearo Co		
5457 W 79th St . . . . Indianapolis IN 46268	**877-327-4332**	317-692-6666
Art-Craft Optical Company Inc		
57 Goodway Dr S . . . . Rochester NY 14623	**800-828-8288**	585-546-6640
Bausch & Lomb Inc		
1400 N Goodman St . . . . Rochester NY 14609	**800-553-5340**	585-338-6000
Bausch & Lomb Inc Vision Care Div		
1400 Goodman St N . . . . Rochester NY 14609	**800-828-9030**	585-338-6000
Beitler-Mckee Optical Co		
160 S 22nd St . . . . Pittsburgh PA 15203	**800-989-4700**	412-481-4700
Bolle Inc		
9200 Cody St . . . . Overland Park KS 66214	**800-222-6553**	913-752-3400
CIBA Vision Corp		
11460 Johns Creek Pkwy . . . . Duluth GA 30097	**800-875-3001**	
Conforma Laboratories Inc		
4705 Colley Ave . . . . Norfolk VA 23508	**800-426-1700**	757-321-0200
Cooper Cos Inc		
6140 Stoneridge Mall Rd Ste 590 . . . . . . Pleasanton CA 94588	**888-822-2660**	925-460-3600
NYSE: COO		
CooperVision Inc		
370 Woodcliff Dr Ste 200 . . . . Fairport NY 14450	**800-538-7850**	585-385-6810
Costa Del Mar		
2361 Mason Ave Ste 100 . . . . Daytona Beach FL 32117	**800-447-3700**	386-274-4000
DAC Vision		
3630 W Miller Ste 350 . . . . Garland TX 75041	**800-800-1550**	972-677-2700
Dakota Smith Signature Eyewear		
498 N Oak St . . . . Inglewood CA 90302	**800-765-3937**	310-330-2700
Duffens Langley Optical Co		
8140 Marshall Dr . . . . Lenexa KS 66214	**800-397-2020**	913-492-5379
Eye-Kraft Optical Inc		
8 McLeland Rd . . . . Saint Cloud MN 56303	**888-455-2022**	
Gentex Optics Inc		
324 Main St . . . . Simpson PA 18407	**800-736-0554**	570-282-3550
Homer Optical Company Inc		
2401 Linden Ln . . . . Silver Spring MD 20910	**800-627-2710**	301-585-9060
Icare Industries Inc		
4399 35th St N . . . . Saint Petersburg FL 33714	**877-422-7352**	727-526-0501
IcareLabs		
4399 35th St N . . . . Saint Petersburg FL 33714	**877-422-7352**	
Johnson & Johnson Vision Care Inc		
7500 Centurion Pkwy . . . . Jacksonville FL 32256	**800-843-2020**	800-874-5278
LBI Eyewear		
20801 Nordhoff St . . . . Chatsworth CA 91311	**800-423-5175***	818-407-1890
*Cust Svc		
Maui Jim Inc 721 Wainee St . . . . Lahaina HI 96761	**888-352-2001**	808-661-8841
Night Optics USA Inc		
15182 Triton Ln Ste 101 . . . . Huntington Beach CA 92649	**800-306-4448**	714-899-4475
Oakley Inc 1 Icon . . . . Foothill Ranch CA 92610	**800-403-7449***	949-951-0991
*Cust Svc		
Omega Optical		
13515 N Stemmons Fwy . . . . Dallas TX 75234	**800-366-6342**	972-241-4141
Serengeti Eyewear Inc		
9200 Cody St . . . . Overland Park KS 66214	**800-423-3537***	913-752-3400
*Cust Svc		
Sigma Corp of America		
15 Fleetwood Ct . . . . Ronkonkoma NY 11779	**800-896-6858**	631-585-1144
Signature Eyewear Inc		
498 N Oak St . . . . Inglewood CA 90302	**800-765-3937**	310-330-2700
OTC: SEYE		
Southern Optical Company Inc		
1909 N Church St . . . . Greensboro NC 27405	**800-888-8842**	336-272-8146
STAAR Surgical Co		
1911 Walker Ave . . . . Monrovia CA 91016	**800-352-7842**	626-303-7902
NASDAQ: STAA		
Transitions Optical Inc		
9251 Belcher Rd . . . . Pinellas Park FL 33782	**800-533-2081**	727-545-0400
US Vision Inc		
1 Harmon Dr Glen Oaks Industrial Pk . . . . . . Glendora NJ 08029	**800-524-0789**	856-228-1000
Vision-Ease Lens Inc		
7000 Sunwood Dr NW . . . . Ramsey MN 55303	**800-328-3449***	320-251-8140
*Cust Svc		
Walman Optical Company Inc		
801 12th Ave N . . . . Minneapolis MN 55411	**800-873-9256**	612-520-6000
X-Cel Optical Company Inc		
806 S Benton Dr . . . . Sauk Rapids MN 56379	**800-747-9235***	320-251-8404
*General		
Younger Optics		
2925 California St . . . . Torrance CA 90503	**800-366-5367**	310-783-1533

540   OPTICAL GOODS STORES

	Toll-Free	Phone
Barnett & Ramel Optical Co		
7154 N 16th St . . . . Omaha NE 68112	**800-228-9732**	
Cliff Weil Inc		
8043 Industrial Pk Rd . . . . Mechanicsville VA 23116	**800-446-9345**	804-746-1321

	Toll-Free	Phone
Doctors Vision Ctr		
413 Mill St PO Box 7396 . . . . Rocky Mount NC 27804	**888-414-4442**	252-442-0802
Empire Vision Centers		
2921 Erie Blvd E . . . . Syracuse NY 13224	**877-959-4160**	315-446-5120
Eye Glass World Inc		
296 Grayson Hwy . . . . Lawrenceville GA 30046	**800-637-3597**	
Eye-Mart Express Inc		
13800 Senlac Dr Ste 200 . . . . Dallas TX 75234	**888-372-2763**	972-488-2002
For Eyes/Insight Optical		
285 W 74th Pl . . . . Hialeah FL 33014	**877-688-9891**	305-557-9004
General Vision Services LLC		
520 Eigth Ave 9th Fl . . . . New York NY 10018	**855-653-0586**	212-729-5300
Henry Ford OptimEyes		
655 W 13-Mile Rd . . . . Madison Heights MI 48071	**800-393-2273**	248-588-9300
JAK Enterprises Inc		
8309 N Knoxville Ave . . . . Peoria IL 61615	**800-752-3295**	309-692-8222
JC Penney Optical Co		
821 N Central Expressway . . . . Plano TX 75024	**866-435-7111**	972-516-1393
LensCrafters Inc		
4000 Luxottica Pl . . . . Mason OH 45040	**877-753-6727**	513-765-4321
Magnifying Ctr		
10086 W McNab Rd . . . . Tamarac FL 33321	**800-364-1612**	954-722-1580
Malbar Vision Ctr		
409 N 78th St . . . . Omaha NE 68114	**800-701-3937**	402-391-6600
National Vision Inc		
296 Grayson Hwy . . . . Lawrenceville GA 30045	**800-637-3597***	770-822-3600
*Cust Svc		
Opti Care Eye Health Center		
87 Grandview Ave . . . . Waterbury CT 06708	**800-334-3937**	203-574-2020
Rite-Style Optical Co		
12240 Emmet St . . . . Omaha NE 68164	**800-373-3200**	402-492-8822
Rx Optical 1700 S Pk St . . . . Kalamazoo MI 49001	**800-792-2737**	269-342-0003
Sterling Optical		
520 Eigth Ave 23rd Fl . . . . New York NY 10018	**800-393-7789**	516-390-2117
SVS Vision		
140 Macomb Pl . . . . Mount Clemens MI 48043	**800-787-4600**	586-468-7612
Union Eyecare Centers		
4750 Beidler Rd . . . . Willoughby OH 44094	**800-443-9699**	216-986-9700
United Optical		
2111 Van Deman St . . . . Baltimore MD 21224	**888-267-8422**	
US Vision Inc		
1 Harmon Dr Glen Oaks Industrial Pk . . . . . . Glendora NJ 08029	**800-524-0789**	856-228-1000
Visionworks of America Inc		
175 E Houston St . . . . San Antonio TX 78205	**800-669-1183**	210-340-3531

541   OPTICAL INSTRUMENTS & LENSES

SEE ALSO Laboratory Analytical Instruments

	Toll-Free	Phone
Allergan Inc 2525 Dupont Dr . . . . Irvine CA 92612	**800-347-4500**	714-246-4500
NYSE: AGN		
American Polarizers Inc		
141 S Seventh St . . . . Reading PA 19602	**800-736-9031**	610-373-5177
American Technology Network Corp		
1341 San Mateo Ave . . . . . . South San Francisco CA 94080	**800-910-2862**	650-875-0130
Applied Fiber Inc		
PO Box 1339 . . . . Leesburg GA 31763	**800-226-5394**	229-759-8301
B E Meyers & Co Inc		
9461 Willows Rd NE . . . . Redmond WA 98052	**800-327-5648**	425-881-6648
Burris Company Inc		
331 E Eigth St . . . . Greeley CO 80631	**888-228-7747**	970-356-1670
Bushnell Corp		
9200 Cody St . . . . Overland Park KS 66214	**800-423-3537**	913-752-3400
ChromaGen Vision LLC		
326 W Cedar St Ste 1 . . . . Kennett Square PA 19348	**855-473-2323**	
Conoptics International Sales Corp		
19 Eagle Rd . . . . Danbury CT 06810	**800-748-3349**	203-743-3349
CST/Berger Corp		
255 W Fleming St . . . . Watseka IL 60970	**800-435-1859**	815-432-5237
Deltronic Corp		
3900 W Segerstrom Ave . . . . Santa Ana CA 92704	**800-451-6922**	714-545-5800
Edmund Optics Inc		
101 E Gloucester Pk . . . . Barrington NJ 08007	**800-363-1992**	856-547-3488
Fosta-Tek Optics Inc		
320 Hamilton St . . . . Leominster MA 01453	**866-221-9157**	978-534-6511
G-S Supplies		
408 St Paul St . . . . Rochester NY 14605	**800-295-3050**	585-295-0250
ITT Night Vision & Imaging		
7635 Plantation Rd . . . . Roanoke VA 24019	**800-448-8678**	540-563-0371
Kollmorgen Corp Electro-Optical Div		
50 Prince St . . . . NorthHampton MA 01060	**877-282-1168**	413-586-2330
Meade Instruments Corp		
27 Hubble . . . . Irvine CA 92618	**800-626-3233**	949-451-1450
NASDAQ: MEAD		
Microvision Inc		
6222 185th Ave NE . . . . Redmond WA 98052	**888-822-6847**	425-936-6847
NASDAQ: MVIS		
Mirrotek International LLC		
90 Dayton Ave . . . . Passaic NJ 07055	**888-659-3030**	973-472-1400
Newport Corp 1791 Deere Ave . . . . Irvine CA 92606	**800-222-6440***	949-863-3144
NASDAQ: NEWP ■ *Sales		
Optical Gaging Products Inc		
850 Hudson Ave . . . . Rochester NY 14621	**800-647-4243**	585-544-0450
Parker Hannifin Corp Daedal Div		
1140 Sandy Hill Rd . . . . Irwin PA 15642	**800-245-6903**	724-861-8200
ProPhotonix Inc		
32 Hampshire Rd . . . . Salem NH 03079	**877-941-8631**	603-893-8778
OTC: STKR		
Ross Optical Industries Inc		
1410 Gail Borden Pl . . . . El Paso TX 79935	**800-880-5417**	915-595-5417
Schott North America Inc		
555 Taxter Rd . . . . Elmsford NY 10523	**877-261-2100**	914-831-2200
Seiler Instrument & Mfg Company Inc		
3433 Tree Court Industrial Blvd . . . . Saint Louis MO 63122	**800-489-2282**	314-968-2282
Sorenson Media Inc		
13961 Minuteman Dr Ste 100 . . . . Draper UT 84020	**888-767-3676**	801-501-8650

	Toll-Free	Phone
Stevens Water Monitoring Systems		
12067 NE Glenn Widing Dr Ste 106 .... Portland OR 97220	800-452-5272	503-469-8000
Veeco Instruments Inc		
One Terminal Dr .... Plainview NY 11803	888-248-3326	516-677-0200
NASDAQ: VECO		
Western Ophthalmics Corp		
19019 36th Ave W Ste G. .... Lynnwood WA 98036	800-426-9938	425-672-9332
Zygo Corp		
Laurel Brook Rd .... Middlefield CT 06455	800-994-6669	860-347-8506
NASDAQ: ZIGO		

542   ORGAN & TISSUE BANKS

SEE ALSO Eye Banks

	Toll-Free	Phone
Alamo Tissue Service Ltd		
5844 Rocky Point Dr Ste 167 .... San Antonio TX 78249	800-226-9091	210-738-2663
AlloSource		
6278 S Troy Cir .... Centennial CO 80111	888-873-8330	720-873-0213
Bio-Tissue		
7000 SW 97th Ave Ste 211 .... Miami FL 33173	888-296-8858	305-412-4430
Bone Bank Allografts		
4808 Research Dr .... San Antonio TX 78240	800-397-0088*	210-696-7616
*Sales		
California Cryobank Inc		
11915 La Grange Ave .... Los Angeles CA 90025	866-927-9622	310-443-5244
Community Tissue Services		
3573 Bristol Pike Ste 201 .... Bensalem PA 19020	800-684-7783	215-245-4506
Comprehensive Tissue Ctr		
11402 University Ave Rm 7415 .... Edmonton AB T6G2J3	866-407-1970	780-407-7510
Cryobiology Inc		
4830D Knightsbridge Blvd .... Columbus OH 43214	800-359-4375	614-451-4375
Cryogenic Laboratories Inc		
1944 Lexington Ave N .... Roseville MN 55113	800-466-2796	651-489-8000
Donor Alliance Inc		
720 S Colorado Blvd Ste 800-N .... Denver CO 80246	888-868-4747	303-329-4747
Gift of Hope Organ & Tissue Donor Network		
425 Spring Lake Dr .... Itasca IL 60143	877-577-3747	630-758-2600
Gift of Life Donor Program		
401 N Third St .... Philadelphia PA 19123	800-543-6391	215-557-8090
INDIANA DONOR NETWORK		
3760 Guion Rd .... Indianapolis IN 46222	888-275-4676	317-685-0389
Kentucky Organ Donor Affiliates (KODA)		
106 E Broadway .... Louisville KY 40202	800-525-3456	502-581-9511
LifeBanc		
4775 Richmond Rd Ste 350 .... Cleveland OH 44128	888-558-5433	216-752-5433
LifeCell Corp		
One Millennium Way .... Branchburg NJ 08876	800-226-2714	
Lifeline of Ohio		
770 Kinnear Rd Ste 200 .... Columbus OH 43212	800-525-5667	614-291-5667
LifeLink Tissue Bank		
8510 Sunstate St .... Tampa FL 33634	800-683-2400	813-886-8111
LifeNet		
1864 Concert Dr .... Virginia Beach VA 23453	800-847-7831	757-464-4761
LifeNet Health Northwest		
501 SW 39th St .... Renton WA 98057	800-858-2282	
LifeShare Transplant Donor Services of Oklahoma		
4705 NW Expy .... Oklahoma City OK 73132	888-580-5680	405-840-5551
Louisiana Organ Procurement Agency (LOPA)		
3545 N I-10 Service Rd Ste 300 .... Metairie LA 70002	800-521-4483	
Mid-America Transplant Services (MTS)		
1110 Highlands Plz Dr E Ste 100 .... Saint Louis MO 63110	888-376-4854	314-735-8200
Musculoskeletal Transplant Foundation		
125 May St Ste 300 .... Edison NJ 08837	800-946-9008	732-661-0202
Nevada Donor Network Inc		
2061 E Sahara Ave .... Las Vegas NV 89104	855-683-6667	702-796-9600
New England Organ Bank		
60 First Ave .... Waltham MA 02451	800-446-6362	617-244-8000
OneLegacy Transplant Donor Network		
221 S Figueroa St Ste 500 .... Los Angeles CA 90012	800-786-4077	213-229-5600
Regional Tissue Bank QEII Health Sciences Centre		
5788 University Ave		
Rm 431 MacKenzie Bldg. .... Halifax NS B3H1V7	800-314-6515	902-473-4171
Rocky Mountain Tissue Bank		
2993 S Peoria St Ste 390 .... Aurora CO 80014	800-424-5169	303-337-3330
ScienceCare Inc		
21410 N 19th Ave Ste 126 .... Phoenix AZ 85027	800-417-3747	602-331-3641
Sierra Donor Services		
1760 Creekside Oak Dr Ste 200 .... Sacramento CA 95833	877-401-2546	916-567-1600
South Texas Blood & Tissue Ctr		
6211 IH-10 W .... San Antonio TX 78201	800-292-5534	210-731-5555
Southeast Tissue Alliance (SETA)		
6241 NW 23rd St Ste 400. .... Gainesville FL 32653	866-432-1164	352-248-2114
Wright Medical Technology Inc		
5677 Airline Rd .... Arlington TN 38002	800-238-7188	901-867-9971

543   PACKAGE DELIVERY SERVICES

	Toll-Free	Phone
Crosscountry Courier Inc		
PO Box 4030 .... Bismarck ND 58502	800-521-0287	701-222-8498
DHL Global Mail		
2700 S Commerce Pkwy Ste 400 .... Weston FL 33331	800-805-9306	954-903-6300
Dynamex Inc		
5429 LBJ Fwy Ste 1000 .... Dallas TX 75240	888-478-1660*	214-560-9000
*Cust Svc		
Federal Express Europe Inc		
3610 Hacks Cross Rd .... Memphis TN 38125	800-463-3339	901-369-3600
FedEx Custom Critical Inc		
1475 Boettler Rd .... Uniontown OH 44685	800-463-3339*	234-310-4090
*Cust Svc		
Hot Shot Delivery Inc		
747 N Shepherd Dr Ste 100		
PO Box 701189. .... Houston TX 77007	866-261-3184	713-869-5525

	Toll-Free	Phone
Network Global Logistics (NGL)		
320 Interlocken Pkwy Ste 100. .... Broomfield CO 80021	866-938-1870	
One Source Industries LLC		
185 Technology Dr .... Irvine CA 92618	800-899-4990	
Priority Express Courier		
Five Chelsea Pkwy .... Boothwyn PA 19061	800-526-4646	610-364-3300
Purolator Inc		
5995 Avebury Rd .... Mississauga ON L5R3T8	888-744-7123	905-712-8101
Tricor America Inc		
717 Airport Blvd .... South San Francisco CA 94080	800-669-7874	650-877-3650
Unishippers Assn Inc		
746 E Winchester Ste 200. .... Salt Lake City UT 84107	800-999-8721	
United Parcel Service Inc (UPS)		
55 Glenlake Pkwy NE .... Atlanta GA 30328	800-742-5877*	404-828-6000
NYSE: UPS ■ *Cust Svc		
Washington Express Service LLC		
12240 Indian Creek Ct Ste 100. .... Beltsville MD 20705	800-939-5463	301-210-0899
World Courier Inc		
1313 Fourth Ave .... New Hyde Park NY 11040	800-221-6600	516-354-2600
Worldwide Express		
2828 Routh St Ste 400 .... Dallas TX 75201	800-758-7447	214-720-2400
WPX Delivery Solutions		
3320 W Valley Hwy N Ste 111 .... Auburn WA 98001	800-562-1091	253-876-2760

544   PACKAGING MACHINERY & EQUIPMENT

	Toll-Free	Phone
A-B-C Packaging Machine Corp		
811 Live Oak St .... Tarpon Springs FL 34689	800-237-5975	727-937-5144
ARPAC Group		
9511 W River St .... Schiller Park IL 60176	800-496-7210	847-678-9034
Automated Packaging Systems Inc		
10175 Phillip Pkwy .... Streetsboro OH 44241	800-527-0733*	330-528-2000
*Sales		
B & H Manufacturing Co		
3461 Roeding Rd .... Ceres CA 95307	888-643-0444	209-556-6160
Barry-Wehmiller Cos Inc		
8020 Forsyth Blvd .... Saint Louis MO 63105	800-862-8020	314-862-8000
Barry-Wehmiller Cos Inc Accraply Div		
3580 Holly Ln N .... Plymouth MN 55447	800-328-3997	763-557-1313
Belco Packaging Systems Inc		
910 S Mountain Ave .... Monrovia CA 91016	800-833-1833	626-357-9566
Brenton LLC		
4750 County Rd 13 NE .... Alexandria MN 56308	800-535-2730	320-852-7705
Butler Automatic Inc		
41 Leona Dr .... Middleboro MA 02346	800-544-0070*	508-923-0544
*Cust Svc		
Campbell Wrapper Corp		
1415 Fortune Ave .... De Pere WI 54115	800-727-4210	920-983-7100
Data Technology Inc		
14225 Dayton Cir Ste 4 .... Omaha NE 68137	888-334-9300*	402-891-0711
*General		
Delkor Systems Inc		
8700 Rendova St NE .... Circle Pines MN 55014	800-328-5558	763-783-0855
Dynaric Inc		
5740 Bayside Rd .... Virginia Beach VA 23455	800-526-0827	
E-pak Machinery Inc		
1535 S State Rd 39 .... La Porte IN 46350	800-328-0466	219-393-5541
Elmar Worldwide Inc		
200 Gould Ave PO Box 245 .... Depew NY 14043	800-443-5468*	716-681-5650
Flexicon Corp		
2400 Emrick Blvd .... Bethlehem PA 18020	888-353-9426	610-814-2400
Hartness International Inc		
1200 Garlington Rd PO Box 26509. .... Greenville SC 29616	800-845-8791	864-297-1200
Heat Seal LLC		
4580 E 71st St .... Cleveland OH 44125	800-342-6329	216-341-2022
Kirk Rudy Inc		
125 Lorraine Pkwy .... Woodstock GA 30188	800-897-1910	770-427-4203
Krones Inc		
9600 S 58th St PO Box 321801 .... Franklin WI 53132	800-752-3787	414-409-4000
Lantech Inc		
11000 Bluegrass Pkwy .... Louisville KY 40299	800-866-0322	502-815-9109
Loveshaw Corp		
2206 Easton Tpke .... South Canaan PA 18459	800-747-1586*	570-937-4921
*Cust Svc		
Mooney General Paper Co		
1451 Chestnut Ave PO Box 3800 .... Hillside NJ 07205	800-882-8846	973-926-3800
MTS Medication Technologies Inc		
2003 Gandy Blvd N .... Saint Petersburg FL 33702	800-845-0053*	
*General		
Muller Martini Mailroom Systems Inc		
40 Rabro Dr .... Hauppauge NY 11788	800-331-5674	631-582-4343
National Instrument LLC		
4119 Fordleigh Rd .... Baltimore MD 21215	866-258-1914	410-764-0900
New Jersey Machine Inc		
56 Etna Rd .... Lebanon NH 03766	800-432-2990*	603-448-0300
*Sales		
New Way Packaging Machinery Inc		
210 Blettner Ave .... Hanover PA 17331	844-801-3711	717-637-2133
Ossid Corp		
PO Drawer 1968 4000 College Rd .... Rocky Mount NC 27802	800-334-8369	252-446-6177
Packaging Systems International Inc		
4990 Acoma St .... Denver CO 80216	800-525-6110	303-296-4445
Pearson Packaging Systems		
8120 W Sunset Hwy .... Spokane WA 99224	800-732-7766	509-838-6226
Rollstock Inc		
5720 Brighton Ave .... Kansas City MO 64130	800-295-2949	616-570-0430
Shibuya Hoppmann Corp		
13129 Airpark Dr Ste 120. .... Elkwood VA 22718	800-368-3582*	540-829-2564
*Cust Svc		
Standard Knapp Inc		
63 Pickering St .... Portland CT 06480	800-628-9565*	860-342-1100
*Cust Svc		
Stolle Machinery Co LLC		
6949 S Potomac St .... Centennial CO 80112	800-433-8333	303-708-9044
SWF Cos 1949 E Manning Ave .... Reedley CA 93654	800-344-8951	559-638-8484

			Toll-Free	Phone

Thiele Technologies
315 27th Ave NE .... Minneapolis MN 55418 **800-932-3647** 612-782-1200
Triangle Package Machinery Co
6655 W Diversey Ave .... Chicago IL 60707 **800-621-4170** 773-889-0200
US Digital Media Inc
1929 W Lone Cactus Dr .... Phoenix AZ 85027 **877-992-3766** 623-587-4900

545 PACKAGING MATERIALS & PRODUCTS - PAPER OR PLASTICS

SEE ALSO Coated & Laminated Paper ; Paper Converters ; Plastics Foam Products ; Bags - Paper ; Bags - Plastics ; Blister Packaging

	Toll-Free	Phone

Acme Paper & Supply Company Inc
8229 Sandy Ct PO Box 422 .... Savage MD 20763 **800-462-5812** 410-792-2333
Adhesive Packaging Specialties Inc
PO Box 31 .... Peabody MA 01960 **800-222-1117** 978-531-3300
Admiral Packaging Inc
10 Admiral St .... Providence RI 02908 **800-556-6454** 401-274-7000
Advance Bag & Packaging Technologies
5720 Williams Lk Rd .... Waterford MI 48329 **800-475-2247** 248-674-3126
Alliance Rubber Co
210 Carpenter Dam Rd .... Hot Springs AR 71901 **800-626-5940**
American Packaging Corp
777 Driving Pk Ave .... Rochester NY 14613 **800-551-8801** 585-254-9500
American Packaging Corp Extrusion Div
777 Driving Pk Ave .... Rochester NY 14613 **800-551-8801** 585-254-9500
Apco Extruders Inc
180 National Rd .... Edison NJ 08817 **800-942-8725*** 732-287-3000
*Orders
Automated Packaging Systems Inc
10175 Phillip Pkwy .... Streetsboro OH 44241 **800-527-0733*** 330-528-2000
*Sales
BagcraftPapercon
3900 W 43rd St .... Chicago IL 60632 **800-621-8468** 773-254-8000
Bedford Industries Inc
1659 Rowe Ave .... Worthington MN 56187 **800-533-5314*** 507-376-4136
*Cust Svc
Bemis Co Inc Bemis Clysar Div
2451 Badger Ave .... Oshkosh WI 54903 **888-425-9727** 920-303-7800
Bemis Company Inc Paper Packaging Div
2445 Deer Pk Blvd .... Omaha NE 68105 **800-541-4303**
BPM Inc 200 W Front St .... Peshtigo WI 54157 **800-826-0494** 715-582-4551
Bryce Corp
4505 Old Lamar Ave PO Box 18338 .... Memphis TN 38118 **800-238-7277** 901-369-4400
Burrows Paper Corp Packaging Group
2000 Commerce Ctr Dr .... Franklin OH 45005 **800-732-1933** 937-746-1933
Carton Service Inc
First Quality Dr PO Box 702 .... Shelby OH 44875 **800-533-7744*** 419-342-5010
*General
Cello-Pack Corp
55 Innsbruck Dr .... Cheektowaga NY 14227 **800-778-3111** 716-668-3111
Charter Films Inc
1901 Winter St PO Box 277 .... Superior WI 54880 **877-411-3456** 715-395-8258
Command Plastic Corp
124 W Ave .... Tallmadge OH 44278 **800-321-8001** 330-434-3497
Consolidated Container Co (CCC)
3101 Towercreek Pkwy Ste 300 .... Atlanta GA 30339 **888-831-2184*** 678-742-4600
*Sales
Crawford Industries LLC
1414 Crawford Dr .... Crawfordsville IN 47933 **800-428-0840**
Crown Packaging Corp
17854 Chesterfld Airport Rd .... Chesterfield MO 63005 **800-883-9400** 636-681-8000
Cryovac Food Packaging & Food Solutions
100 Rogers Bridge Rd .... Duncan SC 29334 **800-391-5645**
Curwood Inc
2200 Badger Ave PO Box 2968 .... Oshkosh WI 54903 **800-544-4672** 920-303-7300
DuPont Packaging & Industrial Polymers
Barley Mill Plaza 26-2122
PO Box 80026 .... Wilmington DE 19880 **800-438-7225** 703-305-7666
Exopack LLC
3070 Southport Rd PO Box 5687 .... Spartanburg SC 29302 **877-447-3539** 864-596-7140
Fibercel Packaging LLC
46 Brooklyn St PO Box 610 .... Portville NY 14770 **800-545-8546*** 716-933-8703
*Sales
Fisher Container Corp
1111 Busch Pkwy .... Buffalo Grove IL 60089 **800-837-2247** 847-541-0000
Flextron Industries Inc
720 Mt Rd .... Aston PA 19014 **800-633-2181** 610-459-4600
Flower City Tissue Mills Inc
700 Driving Pk Ave .... Rochester NY 14613 **800-595-2030** 585-458-9200
FPC Flexible Packaging Corp
1891 Eglinton Ave E .... Toronto ON M1L2L7 **888-288-7386** 416-288-3060
General Plastic Extrusions Inc
1238 Kasson Dr .... Prescott WI 54021 **800-532-3888** 715-262-3806
Genpak Corp
68 Warren St .... Glens Falls NY 12801 **800-626-6695** 518-798-9511
Gift Wrap Co
338 Industrial Blvd .... Midway GA 31320 **800-443-4429***
*General
Grayling Industries
1008 Branch Dr .... Alpharetta GA 30004 **800-635-1551** 770-751-9095
Green Bay Packaging Inc
1700 Webster St .... Green Bay WI 54302 **800-236-8400** 920-433-5111
Huhtamaki Inc North America
9201 Packaging Dr .... DeSoto KS 66018 **800-255-4243** 913-583-3025
Indiana Ribbon Inc
106 N Second St .... Wolcott IN 47995 **800-531-3100** 219-279-2112
Innovative Enterprises Inc
25 Town & Country Dr .... Washington MO 63090 **800-280-0300** 636-390-0300
International Paper Co
6400 Poplar Ave .... Memphis TN 38197 **800-223-1268*** 901-419-9000
*NYSE: IP ■ *Prod Info*
LallyPak Inc
1209 Central Ave .... Hillside NJ 07205 **800-523-8484** 908-351-4141
Laminations
3010 E Venture Dr .... Appleton WI 54911 **800-925-2626** 920-831-0596

LPS Industries Inc
10 Caesar Pl .... Moonachie NJ 07074 **800-275-6577*** 201-438-3515
*Sales
Multifilm Packaging Corp
1040 N McLean Blvd .... Elgin IL 60123 **800-837-9727** 847-695-7600
Novacel 21 Third St .... Palmer MA 01069 **877-668-2235** 413-283-3468
Pactiv Corp
1900 W Field Ct .... Lake Forest IL 60045 **888-828-2850** 847-482-2000
Pak West Paper & Packaging
4042 W Garry Ave .... Santa Ana CA 92704 **800-927-7299** 714-557-7420
Perfecseal Inc
3500 N Main St PO Box 2968 .... Oshkosh WI 54903 **888-871-8574** 920-303-7000
Pratt Industries USA
1800C Sarasota Pkwy .... Conyers GA 30013 **800-835-2088** 770-918-5678
Printpack Inc
2800 Overlook PkwyNE .... Atlanta GA 30339 **800-669-6820** 404-460-7000
Rexam Inc
4201 Congress St Ste 340 .... Charlotte NC 28209 **800-944-2217** 704-551-1500
Robinson Industries Inc
3051 W Curtis Rd .... Coleman MI 48618 **877-465-4055** 989-465-6111
Rollprint Packaging Products Inc
320 S Stewart Ave .... Addison IL 60101 **800-276-7629** 630-628-1700
Sabert Corp
2288 Main St Ext .... Sayreville NJ 08872 **800-722-3781**
SI Jacobson Mfg Co
1414 Jacobson Dr .... Waukegan IL 60085 **800-621-5492** 847-623-1414
Tegrant Corp
1401 Pleasant St .... DeKalb IL 60115 **800-633-3962** 815-756-8451
UFP Technologies Inc
172 E Main St .... Georgetown MA 01833 **800-372-3172** 978-352-2200
NASDAQ: UFPT
Unger Co 12401 Berea Rd .... Cleveland OH 44111 **800-321-1418** 216-252-1400
Unicorr
455 Sackett Pt Rd .... North Haven CT 06473 **800-877-6875*** 203-248-2161
*General
Viskase Cos Inc
8205 S Cass Ste 115 .... Darien IL 60561 **800-323-8562** 630-874-0700
Warp Bros Flex-O-Glass Inc
4647 W Augusta Blvd .... Chicago IL 60651 **800-621-3345** 773-261-5200
Wausau Paper Corp
100 Paper Pl .... Mosinee WI 54455 **800-723-0008** 715-693-4470
NYSE: WPP
Weyerhaeuser Co
33663 Weyerhaeuser Way S .... Federal Way WA 98003 **800-525-5440** 253-924-2345
NYSE: WY
Winpak Ltd
100 Salteaux Crescent .... Winnipeg MB R3J3T3 **800-841-2600** 204-889-1015
TSE: WPK
WS Packaging Group Inc
2571 S. Hemlock Rd .... Green Bay WI 54229 **800-236-3424** 800-818-5481
Wynalda Packaging
8221 Graphic Dr NE .... Belmont MI 49306 **800-952-8668*** 616-866-1561
*General

546 PACKING & CRATING

	Toll-Free	Phone

Allied Container Systems Inc
201 N Civic Dr Ste 180 .... Walnut Creek CA 94596 **800-943-6510**
Craters & Freighters
331 Corporate Cir Ste J .... Golden CO 80401 **800-736-3335**
Fapco Inc 216 Post Rd .... Buchanan MI 49107 **800-782-0167** 269-695-6889
Navis Logistics Network
6551 S Revere Pkwy Ste 250 .... Centennial CO 80111 **800-344-3528**
Navis Pack & Ship Centers
6551 S Revere Pkwy Ste 250 .... Centennial CO 80111 **800-344-3528**
Packaging Services of Maryland Inc
16461 Elliott Pkwy .... Williamsport MD 21795 **800-223-6255** 301-223-6200
Southern States Packaging Co
PO Box 650 .... Spartanburg SC 29304 **800-621-2051**
Tech Packaging Inc
13241 Bartram Pk Blvd Ste 601 .... Jacksonville FL 32258 **866-453-8324** 904-288-6403
Unicep Packaging Inc
1702 Industrial Dr .... Sandpoint ID 83864 **800-354-9396** 208-265-9696
Venchurs Packaging
800 Liberty St .... Adrian MI 49221 **855-264-4300** 517-263-8937

547 PAINTS, VARNISHES, RELATED PRODUCTS

	Toll-Free	Phone

Aervoe Industries Inc
PO Box 485 .... Gardnerville NV 89410 **800-227-0196** 775-783-3100
Akron Paint & Varnish Inc
1390 Firestone Pkwy .... Akron OH 44301 **800-772-3452** 330-773-8911
American Safety Technologies Inc
565 Eagle Rock Ave .... Roseland NJ 07068 **800-631-7841** 973-403-2600
Behr Process Corp
3400 W Segerstrom Ave .... Santa Ana CA 92704 **800-854-0133** 714-545-7101
Benjamin Moore & Co
101 Paragon Dr .... Montvale NJ 07645 **800-344-0400** 201-573-9600
BryCoat Inc 207 Vollmer Ave .... Oldsmar FL 34677 **800-989-8788** 727-490-1000
California Products Corp
150 Dascomb Rd .... Andover MA 01810 **800-225-1141** 978-623-9980
Carboline Co
350 Hanley Industrial Ct .... Saint Louis MO 63144 **800-848-4645** 314-644-1000
Coating & Adhesive Corp (CAC)
1901 Popular St PO Box 1080 .... Leland NC 28451 **800-410-2999** 910-371-3184
Color Wheel Paint Mfg Co Inc
2814 Silver Star Rd .... Orlando FL 32808 **855-862-6639** 407-293-6810
DAP Products Inc
2400 Boston St Ste 200 .... Baltimore MD 21224 **800-543-3840*** 410-675-2100
*Cust Svc
Davis Paint Company Inc
1311 Iron St PO Box 7589 .... North Kansas City MO 64116 **800-821-2029** 816-471-4447

	Toll-Free	Phone
Day-Glo Color Corp		
4515 St Clair Ave .... Cleveland OH 44103	**800-424-9300**	216-391-7070
Duckback Products		
2644 Hegan Ln PO Box 980 .... Chico CA 95927	**800-825-5382**	
Dunn-Edwards Corp		
4885 E 52nd Pl .... Los Angeles CA 90058	**800-537-4098**	323-771-3330
DuPont Automotive		
950 Stephenson Hwy PO Box 7013 ...... Troy MI 48007	**800-533-1313**	248-583-8000
DuPont Performance Coatings		
1007 Market St .... Wilmington DE 19898	**800-441-7515**	302-774-1000
Farrell-Calhoun Inc		
221 E Carolina Ave .... Memphis TN 38126	**888-832-7735**	901-526-2211
Ferro Corp		
6060 Parkland Blvd ...... Mayfield Heights IN 44124	**800-321-3314**	216-875-5600
Ferro Corp Plastics Colorants Div		
Three Railroad Ave .... Stryker OH 43557	**800-521-9094**	419-682-3311
FinishMaster Inc		
54 Monument Cir Eighth Fl ...... Indianapolis IN 46204	**888-311-3678**	317-237-3678
Gemini Coatings Inc		
421 SE 27th St .... El Reno OK 73036	**800-262-5710**	405-262-5710
Harrison Paint Co		
1329 Harrison Ave SW .... Canton OH 44706	**800-321-0680**	330-455-5125
HB Fuller Co		
1200 Willow Lk Blvd PO Box 64683 .... Saint Paul MN 55164	**888-423-8553**	651-236-5900
NYSE: FUL		
Hentzen Coatings Inc		
6937 W Mill Rd .... Milwaukee WI 53218	**800-236-6589**	414-353-4200
Insl-X Products Corp		
101 Paragon Dr .... Montvale NJ 07645	**800-225-5554***	
*Cust Svc		
Kelly-Moore Paint Company Inc		
987 Commercial St .... San Carlos CA 94070	**800-874-4436**	650-592-8337
Kenyon Plastering Inc		
4001 W Indian School Rd .... Phoenix AZ 85019	**800-949-4319**	602-233-1191
Kop-Coat Inc		
436 Seventh Ave 1850 Koppers Bldg .... Pittsburgh PA 15219	**800-221-4466**	412-227-2426
Lancaster Distributing Co		
1310 Union St .... Spartanburg SC 29302	**800-845-8287***	864-583-3011
*General		
Lansco Colors		
1 Blue Hill Plaza 11th Fl		
PO Box 1685 .... Pearl River NY 10965	**800-526-2783**	845-507-5942
Mantros-Haeuser & Company Inc		
1175 Post Rd E .... Westport CT 06880	**800-344-4229***	203-454-1800
*General		
Masterchem Industries LLC		
3135 Old Hwy M .... Imperial MO 63052	**866-774-6371**	
Minwax Co		
10 Mountainview Rd ...... Upper Saddle River NJ 07458	**800-523-9299**	
Mobile Paint Manufacturing Co		
4775 Hamilton Blvd .... Theodore AL 36582	**800-621-6952**	251-443-6110
Muralo Company Inc		
148 E Fifth St .... Bayonne NJ 07002	**800-631-3440**	201-437-0770
Neogard Div Jones-blair Co		
2728 Empire Central St .... Dallas TX 75235	**800-492-9400**	214-353-1600
O'Leary Paint		
300 E Oakland Ave .... Lansing MI 48906	**800-477-2066**	517-487-2066
Painters Supply & Equipment Co		
25195 Brest Rd .... Taylor MI 48180	**800-589-8100**	734-946-8119
Parker Paint Mfg Co Inc		
3003 S Tacoma Way .... Tacoma WA 98409	**855-862-6639**	
Penn Color Inc		
400 Old Dublin Pk .... Doylestown PA 18901	**866-617-7366**	215-345-6550
Pioneer Mfg		
4529 Industrial Pkwy .... Cleveland OH 44135	**800-877-1500**	216-671-5500
PPG Industries Inc		
17451 Von Karman Ave .... Irvine CA 92614	**800-544-3338**	949-474-0400
Red Spot Paint & Varnish Co Inc		
1107 E Louisiana St .... Evansville IN 47711	**877-777-4778**	812-428-9100
Republic Powdered Metals Inc		
2628 Pearl Rd .... Medina OH 44256	**800-382-1218**	
RPM International Inc		
2628 Pearl Rd .... Medina OH 44256	**800-776-4488**	330-273-5090
NYSE: RPM		
Rust-Oleum Corp		
11 E Hawthorn Pkwy .... Vernon Hills IL 60061	**800-323-3584**	847-367-7700
Samuel Cabot Inc		
100 Hale St .... Newburyport MA 01950	**800-877-8246**	978-465-1900
Seymour of Sycamore Inc		
917 Crosby Ave .... Sycamore IL 60178	**800-435-4482**	815-895-9101
Sheboygan Paint Company Inc		
1439 N 25th St PO Box 417 .... Sheboygan WI 53082	**800-773-7801**	920-458-2157
Sterling-Clark-Lurton Corp		
PO Box 130 .... Norwood MA 02062	**800-225-9872**	781-762-5400
Textured Coatings Of America		
2422 E 15th St .... Panama City FL 32405	**800-454-0340**	850-769-0347
Tnemec Company Inc		
6800 Corporate Dr .... Kansas City MO 64120	**800-863-6321**	816-483-3400
Troy Corp		
8 Vreeland Rd PO Box 955 .... Florham Park NJ 07932	**800-448-2843**	973-443-4200
Valspar Refinish Inc		
210 Crosby St .... Minneapolis MN 39466	**800-844-3691***	800-845-2500
*Cust Svc		
Whitmore Manufacturing Co		
PO Box 9300 .... Rockwall TX 75087	**800-699-6318**	972-771-1000
Willamette Valley Inc		
1075 Arrowsmith St .... Eugene OR 97402	**800-333-9826**	541-484-9621
WM Barr & Company Inc		
2105 Ch Ave .... Memphis TN 38109	**800-238-2672**	901-775-0100
Wolf Gordon Inc		
33-00 47th Ave .... Long Island City NY 11101	**800-347-0550**	
Yenkin-Majestic Paint Corp		
1920 Leonard Ave .... Columbus OH 43219	**800-848-1898**	614-253-8511

548   PALLETS & SKIDS

	Toll-Free	Phone
Anderson Forest Products Inc		
1267 Old Edmonton Rd PO Box 520 ...... Tompkinsville KY 42167	**800-489-6778**	270-487-6778
Clinch-Tite Corp		
5264 Lake St PO Box 456 .... Sandy Lake PA 16145	**800-241-0900***	724-376-7315
*General		
Hill Wood Products Inc		
9483 Ashawa Rd .... Cook MN 55723	**800-788-9689**	218-666-5933
Hunter Woodworks Inc		
21038 S Wilmington Ave PO Box 4937 .... Carson CA 90749	**800-966-4751**	323-775-2544
Ifco Systems		
6829 Flintlock Rd .... Houston TX 77040	**800-771-1148**	713-332-6200
Pallet Consultants Corp		
PO Box 1692 .... Pompano Beach FL 33061	**888-782-2909**	954-946-2212
Pallet Masters Inc		
655 E Florence Ave .... Los Angeles CA 90001	**800-675-2579**	323-758-6559
PalletOne Inc		
1470 US Hwy 17 S .... Bartow FL 33830	**800-771-1148**	863-533-1147
Potomac Supply Corp		
1398 Kinsale Rd .... Kinsale VA 22488	**800-365-3900***	804-472-2527
*Sales		
Tasler Inc		
1804 Tasler Dr .... Webster City IA 50595	**800-482-7537**	515-832-5200

549   PAPER - MFR

SEE ALSO Packaging Materials & Products - Paper or Plastics

549-1 Coated & Laminated Paper

	Toll-Free	Phone
Appleton Papers Inc		
825 E Wisconsin Ave PO Box 359 .... Appleton WI 54912	**888-593-9546**	920-734-9841
Arkwright Inc		
538 Main St .... Fiskeville RI 02823	**800-556-6866***	401-821-1000
*Cust Svc		
Avery Dennison Worldwide Graphics Div		
250 Chester St Bldg 8 .... Painesville OH 44077	**800-443-9380**	440-358-3700
BPM Inc 200 W Front St .... Peshtigo WI 54157	**800-826-0494**	715-582-4551
Diversified Labeling Solutions		
1285 Hamilton Pkwy .... Itasca IL 60143	**800-397-3013**	630-625-1225
Fortifiber Building Systems Group		
300 Industrial Dr .... Fernley NV 89408	**800-773-4777**	775-333-6400
French Paper Co 100 French St .... Niles MI 49120	**800-253-5952**	269-683-1100
Horizon Paper Co Inc		
1010 Washington Blvd .... Stamford CT 06901	**866-358-0855**	203-358-0855
Lofton Label Inc		
6290 Claude Way ...... Inver Grove Heights MN 55076	**877-447-8118**	651-552-6257
Nashua Corp		
11 Trafalgar Sq 2nd Fl .... Nashua NH 03063	**800-430-7488**	603-880-2323
National/AZON		
1148 Rochester Rd .... Troy MI 48083	**800-325-5939**	
Technicote Westfield Inc		
222 Mound Ave .... Miamisburg OH 45342	**800-358-4448**	937-859-4448
TST/Impreso Inc		
652 Southwestern Blvd .... Coppell TX 75019	**800-527-2878**	972-462-0100
Wausau Paper Corp		
100 Paper Pl .... Mosinee WI 54455	**800-723-0008**	715-693-4470
NYSE: WPP		
Wausau Paper Corp Specialty Paper Div		
100 Paper Pl .... Mosinee WI 54455	**800-723-0008**	715-693-4470

549-2 Writing Paper

	Toll-Free	Phone
Anna Griffin Inc		
99 Armour Dr .... Atlanta GA 30324	**888-817-8170**	404-817-8170
Crane & Co Inc 30 S St .... Dalton MA 01226	**800-268-2281***	
*Cust Svc		
Geographics		
108 Main St Third Fl .... Norwalk CT 06851	**800-436-4919**	
Gordon Paper Company Inc		
PO Box 1806 .... Norfolk VA 23501	**800-457-7366**	757-464-3581
Louisiana Assn For, The Blind, The		
1750 Claiborne Ave .... Shreveport LA 71103	**877-913-6471**	318-635-6471
Mafcote Industries Inc		
108 Main St .... Norwalk CT 06851	**800-221-3056***	203-847-8500
*Cust Svc		
Mohawk Fine Papers Inc		
465 Saratoga St .... Cohoes NY 12047	**800-843-6455**	518-237-1740
Performance Office Papers		
21565 Hamburg Ave .... Lakeville MN 55044	**800-458-7189**	
Rytex Co 100 N Pk Ave .... Peru IN 46970	**800-277-5458**	
Schurman Fine Papers		
500 Chadbourne Rd PO Box 6030 ...... Fairfield CA 94533	**800-789-1649***	
*Sales		
Southworth Co 265 Main St .... Agawam MA 01001	**800-225-1839**	413-789-1200
Specialty Loose Leaf Inc		
One Cabot St .... Holyoke MA 01040	**800-227-3623**	413-532-0106
Top Flight Inc		
1300 Central Ave .... Chattanooga TN 37408	**800-777-3740**	423-266-8171
Wausau Paper Corp		
100 Paper Pl .... Mosinee WI 54455	**800-723-0008**	715-693-4470
NYSE: WPP		
Wausau Paper Corp Printing & Writing Paper Div		
One Clark's Island .... Wausau WI 54403	**800-723-0008**	715-675-3361

Classified Section

Classified Section

550　PAPER - WHOL

		Toll-Free	Phone
Anchor Paper Company Inc			
480 Broadway St . . . . Saint Paul MN 55101		800-652-9755	651-298-1311
AT Clayton & Co Inc			
300 Atlantic St . . . . Stamford CT 06901		800-282-5298	203-658-1200
Atlantic Packaging Co			
806 N 23rd St . . . . Wilmington NC 28405		800-722-5841	910-343-0624
CJ Duffey Paper Co			
528 Washington Ave N . . . . Minneapolis MN 55401		800-752-8190	612-338-8701
Cole Papers Inc			
1300 N 38th St . . . . Fargo ND 58102		800-800-8090	701-282-5311
Dennis Paper Co			
910 Acorn Dr . . . . Nashville TN 37210		800-441-5684	615-883-9010
Field Paper Co 3950 D St . . . . Omaha NE 68107		800-969-3435	402-733-3600
Gould Paper Corp			
11 Madison Ave 14th Fl . . . . New York NY 10010		800-275-4685	212-301-0000
Gpa Specialty Printable Sbstrt			
8740 W 50th St . . . . McCook IL 60525		800-395-9000	773-650-2020
GreenLine Paper Company Inc			
631 S Pine St . . . . York PA 17403		800-641-1117	717-845-8697
Hearn Paper Co			
556 N Meridian Rd . . . . Youngstown OH 44509		800-225-2989	330-792-6533
Kelly Paper Co			
288 Brea Canyon Rd . . . . Walnut CA 91789		800-675-3559	
Lindenmeyr Book Publishing Papers			
521 Fifth Ave 6th Fl . . . . New York NY 10175		800-221-3042	212-551-3900
Lindenmeyr Central			
Three Manhattanville Rd . . . . Purchase NY 10577		800-221-3042	914-696-9300
Lindenmeyr Munroe			
14 Research Pkwy . . . . Wallingford CT 06492		800-842-8480	
Lindenmeyr Munroe Paper Corp			
115 Moonachie Ave . . . . Moonachie NJ 07074		800-221-3042	201-440-6491
Mac Papers			
3300 Phillips Hwy PO Box 5369 . . . . Jacksonville FL 32207		800-622-2968	904-348-3300
Midland Paper			
101 E Palatine Rd . . . . Wheeling IL 60090		800-323-8522	847-777-2700
Millcraft Paper Co			
6800 Grant Ave . . . . Cleveland OH 44105		800-860-2482	216-441-5500
Morrisette Paper Company Inc			
5925 Summit Ave PO Box 20768 . . . . Browns Summit NC 27214		800-822-8882	336-375-1515
Murnane Paper Corp			
345 Fischer Farm Rd . . . . Elmhurst IL 60126		855-632-8191	630-530-8222
Newell Paper Co			
1212 Grand Ave PO Box 631 . . . . Meridian MS 39301		800-844-8894	601-693-1783
PaperDirect Inc			
1005 E Woodmen Rd . . . . Colorado Springs CO 80920		800-272-7377	
Redd Paper Co 3851 Ctr Loop . . . . Orlando FL 32808		800-961-6656	407-299-6656
Roosevelt Paper Co			
One Roosevelt Dr . . . . Mount Laurel NJ 08054		800-523-3470	856-303-4100
Spicers Paper Inc			
12310 Slauson Ave . . . . Santa Fe Springs CA 90670		800-774-2377	562-698-1199
Unisource Worldwide Inc			
6600 Governors Lake Pkwy . . . . Norcross GA 30071		800-864-7687	770-447-9000
White Paper Co 9990 River Way . . . . Delta BC V4G1M9		888-840-7300	604-951-3900

551　PAPER CONVERTERS

		Toll-Free	Phone
Ameri-Fax Corp			
6520 W 20th Ave Ste 2 . . . . Hialeah FL 33016		800-262-8214	
BagcraftPapercon			
3900 W 43rd St . . . . Chicago IL 60632		800-621-8468	773-254-8000
C-P Flexible Packaging			
15 Grumbacher Rd . . . . York PA 17406		800-815-0667	717-764-1193
Caraustar Industries Inc			
5000 Austell-Powder Springs Rd			
Ste 300 . . . . Austell GA 30106		800-223-1373	770-948-3100
Case Paper Company Inc			
500 Mamaroneck Ave Second Fl . . . . Harrison NY 10528		800-222-2922	914-899-3500
Cindus Corp 515 Stn Ave . . . . Cincinnati OH 45215		800-543-4691	
Crusader Paper Company Inc			
350 Holt Rd . . . . North Andover MA 01845		800-421-0007	
Fabricon Products			
1721 W Pleasant Ave . . . . River Rouge MI 48218		800-676-9727	313-841-8200
Graphic Converting LLC			
877 N Larch Ave . . . . Elmhurst IL 60126		800-447-1935	630-758-4100
International Converter Inc			
17153 Industrial Hwy . . . . Caldwell OH 43724		800-848-6623	740-732-5665
Kanzaki Specialty Papers			
1 Monarch Pl Ste 800 . . . . Springfield MA 01144		888-526-9254	
Lauterbach Group Inc			
W222 N5710 Miller Way . . . . Sussex WI 53089		800-841-7301*	262-820-8130
*Sales			
Mafcote Industries Inc			
108 Main St . . . . Norwalk CT 06851		800-221-3056*	203-847-8500
*Cust Svc			
Max International Converters Inc			
2360 Dairy Rd . . . . Lancaster PA 17601		800-233-0222	
Newark Paperboard Products Inc			
20 Jackson Dr . . . . Cranford NJ 07016		800-777-7890	908-276-4000
PAC Paper Inc			
6416 NW Whitney Rd . . . . Vancouver WA 98665		800-223-4981	360-695-7771
Pacon Corp			
2525 N Casaloma Dr . . . . Appleton WI 54912		800-333-2545	
Paper Systems Inc			
185 S Pioneer Blvd . . . . Springboro OH 45066		888-564-6774	937-746-6841
PM Co 9220 Glades Dr . . . . Fairfield OH 45011		800-327-4359	513-825-7626
Protect-All Inc			
109 Badger Pkwy . . . . Darien WI 53114		888-432-8526	
Spinnaker Coating Inc			
518 E Water St . . . . Troy OH 45373		800-543-9452	937-332-6500

		Toll-Free	Phone
TimeMed Labeling Systems Inc			
144 Tower Dr . . . . Burr Ridge IL 60527		800-323-4840*	630-986-1800
*Cust Svc			
Tufco Technologies Inc			
PO Box 23500 . . . . Green Bay WI 54305		800-558-8145	920-336-0054
NASDAQ: TFCO			

552　PAPER FINISHERS (EMBOSSING, COATING, GILDING, STAMPING)

		Toll-Free	Phone
Colad Group 801 Exchange St . . . . Buffalo NY 14210		800-950-1755	716-961-1776
Complemar Partners			
500 Lee Rd Ste 200 . . . . Rochester NY 14606		800-388-7254	585-647-5800
Loroco Industries Inc			
5000 Creek Rd . . . . Cincinnati OH 45242		800-215-9474	513-891-9544
Madison Cutting Die Inc			
2547 Progress Rd . . . . Madison WI 53716		800-395-9405	608-221-3422
McGraphics Inc			
601 Hagan St . . . . Nashville TN 37203		888-280-8200	615-242-8779
Walton Press (WP)			
402 Mayfield Dr . . . . Monroe GA 30655		800-354-0235	770-267-2596

553　PAPER INDUSTRIES MACHINERY

		Toll-Free	Phone
Baumfolder Corp			
1660 Campbell Rd . . . . Sidney OH 45365		800-543-6107	937-492-1281
Cranston Machinery Company Inc			
2251 SE Oak Grove Blvd . . . . Oak Grove OR 97267		800-547-1012	503-654-7751
Entwistle Co Dietzco Div			
6 Bigelow St . . . . Hudson MA 01749		800-445-8909	508-481-4000
Pemco Inc			
3333 Crocker Ave . . . . Sheboygan WI 53082		888-310-1898	920-458-2500

554　PAPER MILLS

SEE ALSO Paperboard Mills ; Pulp Mills

		Toll-Free	Phone
Armor Protective Packaging			
951 Jones St . . . . Howell MI 48843		800-365-1117	517-546-1117
BPM Inc 200 W Front St . . . . Peshtigo WI 54157		800-826-0494	715-582-4551
Burrows Paper Corp			
501 W Main St . . . . Little Falls NY 13365		800-272-7122	315-823-2300
Cauthorn Paper Co			
12124 S Washington Hwy . . . . Ashland VA 23005		800-552-3011	804-798-6999
Climax Manufacturing Co			
7840 SR 26 . . . . Lowville NY 13367		800-225-4629	315-376-8000
FiberMark North America, Inc.			
161 Wellington Rd . . . . Brattleboro VT 05302		800-784-8558*	802-257-0365
*Cust Svc			
Finch Paper LLC			
One Glen St . . . . Glens Falls NY 12801		800-833-9983	518-793-2541
FutureMark Paper Co			
13101 S Pulaski Rd . . . . Alsip IL 60803		866-580-8325	708-272-8700
Green Field Paper Co			
7196 Clairemont Mesa Blvd . . . . San Diego CA 92111		888-402-9979	858-565-2585
Inland Empire Paper Co			
3320 N Argonne . . . . Millwood WA 99212		866-437-7711	509-924-1911
International Paper Co			
6400 Poplar Ave . . . . Memphis TN 38197		800-223-1268*	901-419-9000
NYSE: IP ■ *Prod Info			
Kimberly-Clark Corp			
351 Phelps Dr . . . . Irving TX 75038		888-525-8388	972-281-1200
NYSE: KMB			
Marq Packaging Systems Inc			
3801 W Washington Ave . . . . Yakima WA 98903		800-998-4301	509-966-4300
Monadnock Paper Mills Inc			
117 Antrim Rd . . . . Bennington NH 03442		800-221-2159*	603-588-3311
*Orders			
Pratt Industries USA			
1800C Sarasota Pkwy . . . . Conyers GA 30013		800-835-2088	770-918-5678
Schweitzer-Mauduit International Inc			
100 N Pt Ctr E Ste 600 . . . . Alpharetta GA 30022		800-514-0186	770-569-4271
NYSE: SWM			
Verso Corp			
6775 Lenox Ctr Ct Ste 400 . . . . Memphis TN 38115		877-837-7606	
NYSE: VRS			
West Linn Paper Co			
4800 Mill St . . . . West Linn OR 97068		800-989-3608	503-557-6500
Xamax Industries Inc			
63 Silvermine Rd . . . . Seymour CT 06483		888-926-2988	203-888-7200

555　PAPER PRODUCTS - SANITARY

		Toll-Free	Phone
Associated Hygienic Products LLC			
3400 River Green Ct Ste 600 . . . . Duluth GA 30096		800-757-0927*	770-497-9800
*General			
Atlas Paper Mills LLC			
3301 NW 107th St . . . . Miami FL 33167		800-562-2860	305-636-5740
Hoffmaster 2920 N Main St . . . . Oshkosh WI 54901		800-327-9774	920-235-9330
Kimberly-Clark Corp			
351 Phelps Dr . . . . Irving TX 75038		888-525-8388	972-281-1200
NYSE: KMB			
Nice-Pak Products Inc			
Two Nice-Pak Pk . . . . Orangeburg NY 10962		800-999-6423	845-365-1700
Principle Business Enterprises Inc			
PO Box 129 . . . . Dunbridge OH 43414		800-467-3224	419-352-1551
SCA Americas			
2929 Arch St Ste 2600 . . . . Philadelphia PA 19104		800-328-9043*	610-499-3700
*Cust Svc			

	Toll-Free	Phone

Tranzonic Cos
26301 Curtiss Wright Pkwy Ste 200 .... Cleveland OH　44143　**800-553-7979**　216-535-4300
Wausau Paper Corp
100 Paper Pl .... Mosinee WI　54455　**800-723-0008**　715-693-4470
NYSE: WPP

556　PAPER PRODUCTS - WHOL

	Toll-Free	Phone

American Hotel Register Co
100 S Milwaukee Ave .... Vernon Hills IL　60061　**800-323-5686**　847-743-3000
American Paper & Twine Co
7400 Cockrill Bend Blvd .... Nashville TN　37209　**800-251-2437**　615-350-9000
Atlantic Paper & Twine Co Inc
85 York Ave .... Pawtucket RI　02904　**800-613-0950**　401-725-0950
BGR Inc 6392 Gano Rd .... West Chester OH　45069　**800-628-9195**　513-755-7100
Brame Specialty Company Inc
PO Box 27 .... Durham NC　27702　**800-533-2041**　919-683-1331
Butler-Dearden Paper Service Inc
PO Box 1069 .... Boylston MA　01505　**800-634-7070**　508-869-9000
Central Paper Products Co Inc
350 Gay St Brown Ave Industrial Pk ...... Manchester NH　03103　**800-339-4065**　603-624-4065
Dacotah Paper Co
3940 15th Ave NW .... Fargo ND　58102　**800-270-6352**　701-281-1734
Ernest Paper Products
5777 Smithway St .... Commerce CA　90040　**800-233-7788**
Fleetwood-Signode
2222 Windsor Ct .... Addison IL　60101　**800-862-7997**　630-268-9999
Garland C Norris Co
1101 Terry Rd PO Box 28 .... Apex NC　27502　**800-331-8920**　919-387-1059
Gem State Paper & Supply Co
1801 Highland Ave E .... Twin Falls ID　83303　**800-727-2737**　208-733-6081
H. T. Berry Co Inc PO Box B .... Canton MA　02021　**800-736-2206**　781-828-6000
Heartland Paper Co
808 W Cherokee St .... Sioux Falls SD　57104　**800-843-7922***　605-336-1190
*Cust Svc
Johnston Paper Co 2 Eagle Dr .... Auburn NY　13021　**800-800-7123**　315-253-8435
Landsberg Orora
1640 S Greenwood Ave .... Montebello CA　90640　**888-526-3723***　323-832-2000
*Cust Svc
Leonard Paper Co
725 N Haven St .... Baltimore MD　21205　**800-327-5547***
*Cust Svc
M Conley Co
1312 Fourth St SE .... Canton OH　44707　**800-362-6001**　330-456-8243
Mayfield Paper Co
1115 S Hill St .... San Angelo TX　76903　**800-725-1441**　325-653-1444
National Paper & Sanitary Supply
2511 S 156th Cir .... Omaha NE　68130　**800-647-2737**　402-330-5507
Nichols Paper & Supply Company Inc
PO Box 291 .... Muskegon MI　49443　**800-442-0213**　231-799-2120
Pacific Packaging Products Inc
24 Industrial Way .... Wilmington MA　01887　**800-777-0300**　978-657-9100
Packaging Distribution Services Inc (PDS)
2308 Sunset Rd .... Des Moines IA　50321　**800-747-2699**　515-243-3156
Paterson Pacific Parchment Co
625 Greg St .... Sparks NV　89431　**800-678-8104**　775-353-3000
Phillips Distribution Inc
3000 E Houston St Ste B .... San Antonio TX　78220　**800-580-2397**　210-227-2397
Pollock Paper & Packaging
One Pollock Pl .... Grand Prairie TX　75050　**800-843-7320***　972-263-2126
*Cust Svc
S. Freedman & Sons Inc
3322 Pennsy Dr .... Landover MD　20785　**800-545-7277**　301-322-5000
Saint Louis Paper & Box Co
3843 Garfield Ave .... Saint Louis MO　63113　**800-779-7901**　314-531-7900
Schwarz
8338 Austin Ave .... Morton Grove IL　60053　**800-323-4903**
Shorr Packaging Inc
800 N Commerce St .... Aurora IL　60504　**888-885-0055**　630-978-1000
Snyder Paper Corp
250 26th St Dr SE .... Hickory NC　28602　**800-222-8562**　828-328-2501
TSN Inc
4001 Salazar Way PO Box 679 .... Frederick CO　80530　**888-997-5959***　303-530-0600
*General
Unisource Worldwide Inc
6600 Governors Lake Pkwy .... Norcross GA　30071　**800-864-7687**　770-447-9000

557　PAPERBOARD & CARDBOARD - DIE-CUT

	Toll-Free	Phone

Alvah Bushnell Co
519 E Chelten Ave .... Philadelphia PA　19144　**800-255-7434**　215-842-9520
Blanks/USA Inc
7700 68th Ave N #7 .... Minneapolis MN　55428　**800-328-7311**
Crescent Cardboard Company LLC
100 W Willow Rd .... Wheeling IL　60090　**800-323-1055**
Demco Inc
4810 Forest Run Rd .... Madison WI　53704　**800-356-1200***　608-241-1201
*Orders
GBS Filing Solutions
224 Morges Rd .... Malvern OH　44644　**800-873-4427**　330-494-5330
Tap Packaging Solutions
2160 Superior Ave .... Cleveland OH　44114　**800-827-5679**　216-781-6000
Topps Company Inc
One Whitehall St .... New York NY　10004　**800-489-9149**　212-376-0300
University Products Inc
517 Main St .... Holyoke MA　01040　**800-628-1912**　413-532-3372
Xertrex International Inc
1530 W Glenlake Ave .... Itasca IL　60143　**800-822-2437**　630-773-4020
Xertrex International Inc Tabbies Div
1530 W Glenlake Ave .... Itasca IL　60143　**800-822-2437**　630-773-4160

558　PAPERBOARD MILLS

SEE ALSO Paper Mills ; Pulp Mills

	Toll-Free	Phone

Cascades Inc
404 Marie-Victorin Blvd .... Kingsey Falls QC　J0A1B0　**800-361-4070**　819-363-5100
*TSE: CAS
FiberMark North America, Inc.
161 Wellington Rd .... Brattleboro VT　05302　**800-784-8558***　802-257-0365
*Cust Svc
Green Bay Packaging Inc Mill Div
1700 N Webster Ct Box 19017 ...... Green Bay WI　54307　**800-445-4269**　920-433-5111
International Paper Co
6400 Poplar Ave .... Memphis TN　38197　**800-223-1268***　901-419-9000
*NYSE: IP ■ *Prod Info
Newark Group 20 Jackson Dr ...... Cranford NJ　07016　**800-777-7890**　908-276-4000
Newman & Company Inc
6101 Tacony St .... Philadelphia PA　19135　**800-523-3256**　215-333-8700
Packaging Corp of America
1955 W Field Ct .... Lake Forest IL　60045　**800-456-4725**
*NYSE: PKG
Pactiv Corp
1900 W Field Ct .... Lake Forest IL　60045　**888-828-2850**　847-482-2000
Superior Packaging Solutions
26858 Almond Ave .... Redlands CA　92374　**800-680-2393**

559　PARKING SERVICE

	Toll-Free	Phone

Ace Parking Management Inc
645 Ash St .... San Diego CA　92101　**800-925-7275***　619-233-6624
*General
Baltimore County Revenue Authority
115 Towsontown Blvd E .... Baltimore MD　21286　**888-246-5384**　410-887-3127
Colonial Parking Inc
1050 Thomas Jefferson St NW
Ste 100 .... Washington DC　20007　**877-777-4778**　202-295-8100
Diamond Parking Inc
605 First Ave Ste 6000 .... Seattle WA　98104　**800-340-7275**　206-284-3100
Edison Properties LLC
100 Washington St .... Newark NJ　07102　**888-727-5327**　973-643-0895
Park 'N Fly
2060 Mt Paran Rd Ste 207 .... Atlanta GA　30327　**800-325-4863***
*Cust Svc
Park To Fly Inc
7800 Narcoossee Rd .... Orlando FL　32822　**888-851-8875**　407-851-8875
Parking Panda Corp
3422 Fait Ave .... Baltimore MD　21224　**800-232-6415**
Standard Parking Corp
900 N Michigan Ave Ste 1600 ...... Chicago IL　60611　**888-700-7275**　312-274-2000

PARKS - AMUSEMENT

SEE Amusement Park Companies ; Amusement Parks

560　PARKS - NATIONAL - CANADA

	Toll-Free	Phone

Parks Canada
25-7-N Eddy St .... Gatineau QC　K1A0M5　**888-773-8888**　613-860-1251
Banff National Park
PO Box 900 .... Banff AB　T1L1K2　**877-737-3783**　403-762-1550
Glacier National Park
PO Box 350 .... Revelstoke BC　V0E2S0　**866-787-6221**　250-837-7500
Kluane National Park & Reserve of Canada
PO Box 5495 .... Haines Junction YT　Y0B1L0　**877-852-3100**　867-634-7250
Mingan Archipelago National Park Reserve of Canada
1340 de la Digue St .... Havre-Saint-Pierre QC　G0G1P0　**877-737-3783**　418-538-3331
Mount Revelstoke National Park of Canada
PO Box 350 .... Revelstoke BC　V0E2S0　**866-787-6221**　250-837-7500
Point Pelee National Park of Canada
407 Monarch Ln RR 1 .... Leamington ON　N8H3V4　**888-773-8888**　519-322-2365
Prince Albert National Park of Canada
Northern Prairies Field Unit
PO Box 100 .... Waskesiu Lake SK　S0J2Y0　**877-737-3783***　306-663-4522
*Campground Resv
Prince Edward Island National Park of Canada
2 Palmers Ln .... Charlottetown PE　C1A5V8　**800-663-7192***　902-672-6350
*Campground Resv
Riel House National Historic Site of Canada
330 River Rd .... Winnipeg MB　R2M3Z8　**877-852-3100**　204-257-1783
Wapusk National Park of Canada
PO Box 127 .... Churchill MB　R0B0E0　**888-773-8888**　204-675-8863

561　PARKS - NATIONAL - US

SEE ALSO Parks - State ; Nature Centers, Parks, Other Natural Areas ; Cemeteries - National

	Toll-Free	Phone

Boston Harbor Islands National Recreation Area
408 Atlantic Ave Ste 228. .... Boston MA　02110　**877-874-2478**　617-223-8666
Brice's Crossroads National Battlefield Site
2680 Natchez Trace Pkwy .... Tupelo MS　38804　**800-305-7417**　662-680-4025
Cabrillo National Monument
1800 Cabrillo Memorial Dr .... San Diego CA　92106　**800-236-7916**　619-557-5450
Carl Sandburg Home National Historic Site
81 Carl Sadburg Ln .... Flat Rock NC　28731　**877-642-4743**　828-693-4178
Casa Grande Ruins National Monument
1100 W Ruins Dr .... Coolidge AZ　85128　**877-642-4743**　520-723-3172

				Toll-Free	Phone

Cedar Breaks National Monument
2390 W Hwy 56 Ste 11 . . . . Cedar City UT 84720 **877-642-4743** 435-586-9451

Chaco Culture National Historical Park
PO Box 220 . . . . Nageezi NM 87037 **877-642-4743** 505-786-7014

Chamizal National Memorial
800 S San Marcial St . . . . El Paso TX 79905 **877-642-4743** 915-532-7273

Chattahoochee River National Recreation Area
1978 Island Ford Pkwy . . . . Atlanta GA 30350 **877-874-2478** 678-538-1200

Colonial National Historical Park
PO Box 210 . . . . Yorktown VA 23690 **866-945-7920** 757-898-3400

Colorado National Monument
1750 Rim Rock Dr . . . . Fruita CO 81521 **866-945-7920** 970-858-3617

Cumberland Gap National Historical Park
91 Bartlett Pk Rd PO Box 1848 . . . . Middlesboro KY 40965 **888-831-7526** 606-248-2817

Cumberland Island National Seashore
101 Wheeler St PO Box 806 . . . . Saint Marys GA 31558 **877-860-6787** 912-882-4336

Curecanti National Recreation Area
102 Elk Creek . . . . Gunnison CO 81230 **866-713-9688** 970-641-2337

Cuyahoga Valley National Park
15610 Vaughn Rd . . . . Brecksville OH 44141 **800-445-9667** 216-524-1497

De Soto National Memorial
8300 Desoto Memorial Hwy . . . . Bradenton FL 34209 **888-831-7526** 941-792-0458

Death Valley National Park
PO Box 579 . . . . Death Valley CA 92328 **866-713-9688** 760-786-3200

Eleanor Roosevelt National Historic Site
4097 Albany Post Rd . . . . Hyde Park NY 12538 **800-337-8474** 845-229-9115

Eugene O'Neill National Historic Site
1000 Kuss Rd . . . . Danville CA 94526 **866-945-7920** 925-838-0249

Fort McHenry National Monument & Historic Shrine
2400 E Fort Ave . . . . Baltimore MD 21230 **866-945-7920** 410-962-4290

Fort Vancouver National Historic Site
612 E Reserve St . . . . Vancouver WA 98661 **800-832-3599** 360-816-6230

Gates of the Arctic National Park & Preserve
4175 Geist Rd . . . . Fairbanks AK 99709 **866-869-6887** 907-457-5752

Harry S Truman National Historic Site
223 N Main St . . . . Independence MO 64050 **877-642-4743** 816-254-2720

Jefferson National Expansion Memorial
11 N Fourth St . . . . Saint Louis MO 63102 **855-733-4522** 314-655-1700

Natchez Trace Parkway
2680 Natchez Trace Pkwy . . . . Tupelo MS 38804 **800-305-7417** 662-680-4025

New Orleans Jazz National Historical Park
419 Decatur St . . . . New Orleans LA 70130 **877-520-0677** 504-589-4806

Oregon Caves National Monument
19000 Caves Hwy . . . . Cave Junction OR 97523 **877-245-9022** 541-592-2100

Ozark National Scenic Riverways
404 Watercress Dr PO Box 490 . . . . Van Buren MO 63965 **877-444-6777** 573-323-4236

Pinnacles National Monument
5000 Hwy 146 . . . . Paicines CA 95043 **877-444-6777** 831-389-4485

Point Reyes National Seashore
1 Bear Valley Rd . . . . Point Reyes Station CA 94956 **877-874-2478** 415-464-5100

Poverty Point National Monument
c/o Poverty Pt State Historic Site
PO Box 276 . . . . Epps LA 71237 **888-926-5492** 318-926-5492

Red Hill Patrick Henry National Memorial
1250 Red Hill Rd . . . . Brookneal VA 24528 **800-514-7463** 434-376-2044

Richmond National Battlefield Park
3215 E Broad St . . . . Richmond VA 23223 **866-733-7768** 804-226-1981

San Antonio Missions National Historical Park
2202 Roosevelt Ave . . . . San Antonio TX 78210 **866-945-7920** 210-534-8833

Santa Monica Mountains National Recreation Area
401 W Hillcrest Dr . . . . Thousand Oaks CA 91360 **888-275-8747** 805-370-2300

Shenandoah National Park
3655 US Hwy 211E . . . . Luray VA 22835 **800-732-0911** 540-999-3500

Steamtown National Historic Site
150 S Washington Ave . . . . Scranton PA 18503 **888-693-9391** 570-340-5200

Tupelo National Battlefield
2680 Natchez Trace Pkwy . . . . Tupelo MS 38804 **800-305-7417** 662-680-4025

Voyageurs National Park
360 Hwy 11 E . . . . International Falls MN 56649 **888-381-2873** 218-286-5258

---

562   PARKS - STATE

SEE ALSO Parks - National - Canada ; Parks - National - US ; Nature Centers, Parks, Other Natural Areas

				Toll-Free	Phone

Afton State Park
6959 Peller Ave S . . . . Hastings MN 55033 **800-366-8917** 651-436-5391

Alfred A. Loeb State Park
725 Summer St NE Ste C . . . . Salem OR 97301 **800-551-6949** 503-986-0707

Alsea Bay Historic Interpretive Ctr
725 Summer St NE Ste C . . . . Salem OR 97301 **800-551-6949**

Arkansas Museum of Natural Resources
3853 Smackover Hwy . . . . Smackover AR 71762 **888-287-2757** 870-725-2877

Assateague State Park
7307 Stephen Decatur Hwy . . . . Berlin MD 21811 **888-432-2267** 410-641-2120

Babcock State Park
486 Babcock Rd . . . . Clifftop WV 25831 **800-225-5982** 304-438-3004

Bannack State Park
4200 Bannack Rd . . . . Dillon MT 59725 **855-922-6768** 406-834-3413

Battle Ground Lake State Park
18002 NE 249th St . . . . Battle Ground WA 98604 **888-226-7688** 360-687-4621

Bayou Segnette State Park
7777 Westbank Expy . . . . Westwego LA 70094 **888-677-2296** 504-736-7140

Beacon Rock State Park
34841 State Rd 14 . . . . Skamania WA 98648 **888-226-7688** 509-427-8265

Bear Creek Lake State Park
22 Bear Creek Lk Rd . . . . Cumberland VA 23040 **800-933-7275** 804-492-4410

Beartown State Park
HC 64 PO Box 189 . . . . Hillsboro WV 24946 **800-225-5982*** 304-653-4254
*General

Beaver Creek Nature Area
20641 SD Hwy 1806 25495 485th Ave . . . Fort Pierre SD 57532 **800-710-2267** 605-223-7660

Bennington Battlefield State Historic Site
c/o Grafton Lakes State Pk PO Box 163 . . . . . Grafton NY 12082 **800-456-2267** 518-686-7109

Bentsen-Rio Grande Valley State Park
2800 S Bensen Palm Dr . . . . Mission TX 78572 **800-792-1112** 956-585-1107

Bethpage State Park
Bethpage Pkwy . . . . Farmingdale NY 11735 **800-456-2267** 516-249-0701

Big Foot Beach State Park
1452 Wells St . . . . Lake Geneva WI 53147 **888-936-7463** 262-248-2528

Big Stone Lake State Park
35889 Meadowbrook State Pk Rd . . . . Ortonville MN 56278 **888-646-6367** 320-839-3663

Black River State Forest
101 S Webster St PO Box 7921 . . . . Madison WI 53707 **888-936-7463** 608-266-2621

Bladon Springs State Park
3921 Bladon Rd . . . . Bladon Springs AL 36919 **800-252-7275** 251-754-9207

Blue Licks Battlefield State Resort Park
Hwy 68 . . . . Mount Olivet KY 41064 **800-443-7008**

Blue Mounds State Park
1410 161st St . . . . Luverne MN 56156 **888-646-6367** 507-283-1307

Bob Straub State Park
US 101 . . . . Pacific City OR 97135 **800-551-6949**

Bonnie Lure State Recreation Area
11321 SW Terwilliger Blvd . . . . Portland OR 97219 **800-551-6949**

Boyce Thompson Arboretum State Park
37615 US Hwy 60 . . . . Superior AZ 85273 **800-858-7378** 520-689-2811

Bridal Veil Falls State Scenic Viewpoint
E Bridal Veil Rd PO Box 100 . . . . Bridal Veil OR 97010 **800-551-6949**

Buck's Pocket State Park
393 County Rd 174 . . . . Grove Oak AL 35975 **800-760-4089** 256-659-2000

Buckhorn Lake State Resort Park
4441 Kentucky Hwy 1833 . . . . Buckhorn KY 41721 **800-325-0058**

Caesars Head State Park
8155 Geer Hwy . . . . Cleveland SC 29635 **866-345-7275** 864-836-6115

Caledon State Park
11617 Caledon Rd . . . . King George VA 22485 **800-933-7275** 540-663-3861

Calhoun Falls State Recreation Area
46 Maintenance Shop Rd . . . . Calhoun Falls SC 29628 **866-345-7275** 864-447-8267

California State Railroad Museum
125 "I" St 111 'I' St . . . . Sacramento CA 95814 **866-240-4655** 916-323-9280

Camp Creek State Forest
2390 Camp Creek Rd . . . . Camp Creek WV 25820 **800-225-5982** 304-425-9481

Canaan Valley Resort State Park
230 Main Lodge Rd . . . . Davis WV 26260 **800-622-4121** 304-866-4121

Cane Creek State Park
50 State Pk Rd . . . . Star City AR 71667 **888-287-2757** 870-628-4714

Carley State Park
19041 Hwy 74 . . . . Altura MN 55910 **888-646-6367** 507-932-3007

Carlsbad State Beach
c/o San Diego Coast District Office
4477 Pacific Hwy . . . . San Diego CA 92110 **800-777-0369** 760-438-3143

Casselman River Bridge State Park
580 Taylor Ave Tawes State Ofc Bldg . . . . . . Annapolis MD 21401 **877-620-8367**

Cathedral Caverns State Park
637 Cave Rd . . . . Woodville AL 35776 **800-252-7275** 256-728-8193

Cathedral State Park
Rt 1 12 Cathedral Way . . . . Aurora WV 26705 **800-225-5982** 304-735-3771

Cedars of Lebanon State Park
328 Cedar Forest Rd . . . . Lebanon TN 37087 **800-342-3145** 615-443-2769

Centenary State Historic Site
3522 College St . . . . Jackson LA 70748 **888-677-2364** 225-634-7925

Charles A. Lindbergh State Park
1615 Lindbergh Dr S PO Box 364 . . . . Little Falls MN 56345 **888-646-6367** 320-616-2525

Charles Towne Landing State Historic Site
1500 Old Towne Rd . . . . Charleston SC 29407 **866-345-7275** 843-852-4200

Cheaha Resort State Park
19644 Hwy 281 . . . . Delta AL 36258 **800-610-5801** 256-488-5111

Chemin-A-Haut State Park
14656 State Pk Rd . . . . Bastrop LA 71220 **888-677-2436** 318-283-0812

Cherry Creek State Park
4201 S Parker Rd . . . . Aurora CO 80014 **866-265-6447** 303-699-3860

Chewacla State Park
124 Shell Toomer Pkwy . . . . Auburn AL 36830 **800-252-7275** 334-887-5621

Chickasaw State Park
26955 US Hwy 43 . . . . Gallion AL 36742 **800-760-4089** 334-295-8230

Chicot State Park
3469 Chicot Pk Rd . . . . Ville Platte LA 70586 **888-677-2442** 337-363-2403

Chugach State Park
18620 Seward Highway . . . . Anchorage AK 99516 **800-478-6196** 907-345-5014

Clermont State Historic Site
1 Clermont Ave . . . . Germantown NY 12526 **800-456-2267** 518-537-4240

Cline Falls State Scenic Viewpoint
62976 OB Riley Rd . . . . Bend OR 97701 **800-551-6949**

Connecticut Valley Railroad State Park
1 Railroad Ave PO Box 452 . . . . Essex CT 06426 **866-526-2014** 860-767-0103

Conway Cemetery State Park
c/o Arkansas State Parks
1 Capitol Mall . . . . Little Rock AR 72201 **888-287-2757**

Coopers Rock State Forest
61 County Line Dr . . . . Bruceton Mills WV 26525 **800-225-5982** 304-594-1561

Coquille Myrtle Grove State Natural Site
PO Box 569 . . . . Bandon OR 97411 **800-551-6949**

Cossatot River State Park-Natural Area
1980 Hwy 278 W . . . . Wickes AR 71973 **877-665-6343** 870-385-2201

Cove Lake State Park
110 Cove Lake Ln . . . . Caryville TN 37714 **800-342-3145** 423-566-9701

Crissey Field State Recreation Site
1655 Hwy 101 N . . . . Brookings OR 97415 **800-551-6949** 541-469-2021

Crow Wing State Park
3124 State Pk Rd . . . . Brainerd MN 56401 **888-646-6367** 218-825-3075

Crown Point State Historic Site
21 Grandview Dr . . . . Crown Point NY 12928 **800-456-2267** 518-597-4666

Crystal River Preserve State Park
3266 N Sailboat Ave . . . . Crystal River FL 34428 **800-326-3521** 352-563-0450

Cumberland Falls State Resort Park
7351 Hwy 90 . . . . Corbin KY 40701 **800-325-0063**

Cuyamaca Rancho State Park
13652 Hwy 79 . . . . Julian CA 92036 **800-444-7275** 760-765-0755

Cypremort Point State Park
306 Beach Ln . . . . Cypremort Point LA 70538 **888-867-4510** 337-867-4510

D River State Recreation Site
1110 NW U.S. 101 198 NE 123rd St . . . . Lincoln City OR 97367 **800-551-6949** 541-994-7341

			Toll-Free	Phone

Dabney State Recreation Area
30701 Historic Columbia River Hwy
PO Box 100. . . . . Troutdale OR 97060 **800-551-6949** 503-695-2261

Darlingtonia State Natural Site
84505 Hwy 101 S . . . . Florence OR 97439 **800-551-6949** 541-997-3851

Dash Point State Park
5700 SW Dash Pt Rd . . . . Federal Way WA 98023 **888-226-7688** 253-661-4955

Davy Crockett Birthplace State Park
1245 Davy Crockett Pk Rd . . . . Limestone TN 37681 **800-342-3145** 423-257-2167

Del Rey Beach State Recreation Site
100 Peter Iredale Rd . . . . Hammond OR 97121 **800-551-6949**

Delaware State Park
5202 US Rt 23 N . . . . Delaware OH 43015 **866-644-6727** 740-548-4631

Denali State Park
7278 E Bogard Rd . . . . Wasilla AK 99654 **800-478-6196** 907-745-3975

Depoe Bay Whale Center
Oregon Parks and Recreation Department
58 US-101 198 NE 123rd St. . . . . Depoe Bay OR 97341 **800-551-6949** 541-765-3304

Devil's Den State Park
11333 W Arkansas Hwy 74 . . . . West Fork AR 72774 **888-742-8701** 479-761-3325

Devil's Lake State Recreation Area
198 NE 123rd St . . . . Newport OR 97365 **800-551-6949**

Devil's Punchbowl State Natural Area
198 NE 123rd St . . . . Newport OR 97365 **800-551-6949**

Devils Fork State Park
161 Holcombe Cir . . . . Salem SC 29676 **866-345-7275** 864-944-2639

Disney/Little Blue State Park
Hwy 28 E . . . . Disney OK 74340 **800-622-6317** 918-435-8066

Douthat State Park
14239 Douthat State Pk Rd . . . . Millboro VA 24460 **800-933-7275*** 540-862-8100
*General

Dreher Island State Recreation Area
3677 State Pk Rd . . . . Prosperity SC 29127 **866-345-7275** 803-364-4152

Driftwood Beach State Recreation Site
5580 S Coast Hwy . . . . Newport OR 97366 **800-551-6949**

Dripping Springs State Park
16830 Dripping Springs Rd . . . . Okmulgee OK 74447 **800-622-6317** 918-756-5971

Edisto Beach State Park
8377 State Cabin Rd . . . . Edisto Island SC 29438 **800-315-3087** 843-869-2756

Eldorado Canyon State Park
9 Kneale Rd PO Box B . . . . Eldorado Springs CO 80025 **866-265-6447** 303-494-3943

Ellmaker State Wayside
198 NE 123rd St . . . . Newport OR 97365 **800-551-6949**

Fair Haven Beach State Park
14985 State Park Rd . . . . Sterling NY 13156 **800-456-2267*** 315-947-5205
*General

Fairview-Riverside State Park
119 Fairview Dr . . . . Madisonville LA 70447 **888-677-3247** 985-845-3318

False Cape State Park
4001 Sandpiper Rd . . . . Virginia Beach VA 23456 **800-933-7275*** 757-426-7128
*General

Father Hennepin State Park
41294 Father Hennepin Pk Rd PO Box 397 . . . . Isle MN 56342 **888-646-6367** 320-676-8763

FD Roosevelt State Park
2970 GA Hwy 190 . . . . Pine Mountain GA 31822 **800-864-7275** 706-663-4858

Fillmore Glen State Park
1686 St Rt 38 . . . . Moravia NY 13118 **800-456-2267** 315-497-0130

Fogarty Creek State Recreation Area
5150 Oregon Coast Hwy
198 NE 123rd St . . . . Depoe Bay OR 97341 **800-551-6949**

Fontainebleau State Park
67825 US Hwy 190 . . . . Mandeville LA 70448 **888-677-3668** 985-624-4443

Forestville/Mystery Cave State Park
21071 County 118 . . . . Preston MN 55965 **888-646-6367** 507-352-5111

Former Governors' Mansion State Historic Site
612 E Blvd Ave . . . . Bismarck ND 58505 **866-243-5352** 701-328-2666

Fort Atkinson State Historical Park
PO Box 240 . . . . Fort Calhoun NE 68023 **800-742-7627** 402-468-5611

Fort Cobb Lake State Park
27022 Copperhead Rd . . . . Fort Cobb OK 73038 **800-622-6317** 405-643-2249

Fort Jesup State Historic Site
32 Geoghagan Rd . . . . Many LA 71449 **888-677-5378** 318-256-4117

Fort McAllister State Historic Park
3894 Ft McAllister Rd . . . . Richmond Hill GA 31324 **800-864-7275** 912-727-2339

Fort Pillow State Historic Park
3122 Pk Rd . . . . Henning TN 38041 **800-342-3145** 731-738-5581

Fort Ridgely State Park
72158 County Rd 30 . . . . Fairfax MN 55332 **888-646-6367** 507-426-7840

Fort Rock State Natural Area
c/o LaPine Management Unit
15800 State Recreation Rd . . . . Lake County OR 97739 **800-551-6949**

Fort Saint Jean Baptiste State Historic Site
155 Jefferson St . . . . Natchitoches LA 71457 **888-677-7853** 318-357-3101

Fort Snelling State Park
101 Snelling Lake Rd . . . . Saint Paul MN 55111 **888-646-6367** 612-725-2389

Foss State Park 10252 Hwy 44 . . . . Foss OK 73647 **800-622-6317** 580-592-4433

Frank Jackson State Park
100 Jerry Adams Dr . . . . Opp AL 36467 **800-760-4089** 334-493-6988

Frontenac State Park
29223 County 28 Blvd . . . . Frontenac MN 55026 **888-646-6367** 651-345-3401

Frozen Head State Natural Area
964 Flat Fork Rd . . . . Wartburg TN 37887 **800-342-3145** 423-346-3318

Gambrill State Park
8602 Gambrill Pk Rd . . . . Frederick MD 21702 **800-830-3974** 301-271-7574

George H. Crosby Manitou State Park
c/o Tettegouche State Pk
5702 Hwy 61. . . . . Silver Bay MN 55614 **888-646-6367** 218-226-6365

Giant Springs State Park
4600 Giant Springs Rd . . . . Great Falls MT 59405 **855-922-6768** 406-454-5840

Glacial Lakes State Park
25022 County Rd 41 . . . . Starbuck MN 56381 **888-646-6367** 320-239-2860

Gleneden Beach State Recreation Site
198 NE 123rd St . . . . Newport OR 97365 **800-551-6949**

Golden Gate Canyon State Park
92 Crawford Gulch Rd . . . . Golden CO 80403 **866-265-6447** 303-582-3707

Goose Creek State Park
2190 Camp Leach Rd . . . . Washington NC 27889 **877-722-6762** 252-923-2191

Gooseberry Falls State Park
3206 Hwy 61 . . . . Two Harbors MN 55616 **888-646-6367** 218-834-3855

Government Island State Recreation Area
725 Summer St NE Ste C . . . . Salem OR 97301 **800-551-6949**

Governor Daniel Dunklin's Grave State Historic Site
PO Box 176 2901 Hwy 61. . . . . Jefferson City MO 65102 **800-334-6946**

Governor Patterson Memorial State Recreation Site
5580 S Coast Hwy 5580 S Coast Hwy . . . . Newport OR 97394 **800-551-6949**

Grand Isle State Park
Admiral Craik Dr . . . . Grand Isle LA 70358 **888-787-2559** 985-787-2559

Grand Portage State Park
9393 E Hwy 61 . . . . Grand Portage MN 55605 **888-646-6367** 218-475-2360

Great Plains State Park
22487 E 1566 Rd . . . . Mountain Park OK 73559 **800-622-6317** 580-569-2032

Great River Bluffs State Park
43605 Kipp Dr . . . . Winona MN 55987 **888-646-6367** 507-643-6849

H. B. Van Duzer Forest State Scenic Corridor
198 NE 123rd St . . . . Newport OR 97365 **800-551-6949**

Half Moon Bay State Beach
c/o San Mateo Coast Sector Office
95 Kelly Ave . . . . Half Moon Bay CA 94019 **800-444-7275** 650-726-8819

Hamlin Beach State Park
One Camp Rd . . . . Hamlin NY 14464 **800-456-2267** 585-964-2462

Hampson Archeological Museum State Park
PO Box 156 . . . . Wilson AR 72395 **888-742-8701** 870-655-8622

Hampton Plantation State Historic Site
1950 Rutledge Rd . . . . McClellanville SC 29458 **800-315-3087** 843-546-9361

Harriman State Park
3489 Green Canyon Rd . . . . Island Park ID 83429 **866-634-3246** 208-558-7368

Havenwoods State Forest
6141 N Hopkins St . . . . Milwaukee WI 53209 **888-936-7463** 414-527-0232

Hearst San Simeon State Historical Monument
750 Hearst Castle Rd . . . . San Simeon CA 93452 **800-444-4445** 805-927-2020

Heceta Head Lighthouse State Scenic Viewpoint
93111 Hwy 101 N . . . . Florence OR 97439 **800-551-6949**

Herman Davis State Park
Corner of Ark 18 Baltimore St . . . . Manila AR 72201 **888-287-2757**

Heyburn State Park
57 Chatcolet Rd . . . . Plummer ID 83851 **866-634-3246** 208-686-1308

Hickory Knob State Resort Park
1591 Resort Dr . . . . McCormick SC 29835 **800-491-1764** 864-391-2450

Hoffman Memorial State Wayside
PO Box 569 . . . . Bandon OR 97411 **800-551-6949**

Holliday Lake State Park
2759 State Pk Rd . . . . Appomattox VA 24522 **800-933-7275** 434-248-6308

Honey Creek State Park
901 State Pk Rd . . . . Grove OK 74344 **800-622-6317** 918-786-9447

Hudson River Islands State Park
Schodack State Pk . . . . Schodack Landing NY 12156 **800-456-2267** 518-732-0187

Hueco Tanks State Historic Site
6900 Hueco Tanks Rd Ste 1 . . . . El Paso TX 79938 **800-792-1112** 915-857-1135

Hunting Island State Park
2555 Sea Island Pkwy . . . . Hunting Island SC 29920 **800-315-3087** 843-838-2011

Huntington Beach State Park
16148 Ocean Hwy . . . . Murrells Inlet SC 29576 **800-491-1764** 843-237-4440

Huntington State Park
PO Box 1343 . . . . Huntington UT 84528 **800-322-3770** 435-687-2491

Janes Island State Park
26280 Alfred Lawson Dr . . . . Crisfield MD 21817 **877-620-8367** 410-968-1565

Jenny Wiley State Resort Park
75 Theatre Ct . . . . Prestonsburg KY 41653 **800-325-0142**

Jimmie Davis State Park
1209 State Pk Rd . . . . Chatham LA 71226 **888-677-2263** 318-249-2595

John Boyd Thacher State Park
1 Hailes Cave Rd . . . . Voorheesville NY 12186 **800-456-2267** 518-872-1237

John Burroughs Memorial State Historic Site
c/o Mine Kill State Pk
PO Box 923 Rt 30 . . . . North Blenheim NY 12131 **800-456-2267** 518-827-6111

John Jay Homestead State Historic Site
PO Box 832 . . . . Katonah NY 10536 **800-456-2267** 914-232-5651

John Paul Jones State Historic Site
c/o Bureau of Parks & Lands . . . . Bangor ME 04401 **800-452-1942** 207-941-4014

Jordan Lake State Recreation Area
280 State Pk Rd . . . . Apex NC 27523 **877-722-6762** 919-362-0586

Justin P. Wilson Cumberland Trail State Park
220 Pk Rd . . . . Caryville TN 38555 **800-342-3145** 423-566-2229

Kam Wah Chung State Heritage Site (KWC)
725 Summer St NE Ste C . . . . Salem OR 97301 **800-551-6949** 503-986-0707

Kenlake State Resort Park
542 Kenlake Rd . . . . Hardin KY 42048 **800-325-0143** 270-474-2211

Keystone State Park
1926 S Hwy 151 . . . . Sand Springs OK 74063 **800-654-8240** 918-865-4991

Koberg Beach State Recreation Site
725 Summer St NE Ste C . . . . Salem OR 97301 **800-551-6949** 503-986-0707

Lake Barkley State Resort Park
3500 State Pk Rd . . . . Cadiz KY 42211 **800-325-1708**

Lake Bistineau State Park
103 State Pk Rd . . . . Doyline LA 71023 **888-677-2478** 318-745-3503

Lake Bruin State Park
201 State Pk Rd . . . . Saint Joseph LA 71366 **888-677-2784** 318-766-3530

Lake Carmi State Park
460 Marsh Farm Rd . . . . Enosburg Falls VT 05450 **888-409-7579*** 802-933-8383
*Resv

Lake Cascade State Park
970 Dam Rd . . . . Cascade ID 83611 **866-634-3246** 208-382-6544

Lake Claiborne State Park
225 State Pk Rd . . . . Homer LA 71040 **888-677-2524** 318-927-2976

Lake D'Arbonne State Park
3628 Evergreen Rd . . . . Farmerville LA 71241 **888-677-5200** 318-368-2086

Lake Kegonsa State Park
2405 Door Creek Rd . . . . Stoughton WI 53589 **888-947-2757*** 608-873-9695
*General

Lake Lurleen State Park
13226 Lake Lurleen Rd . . . . Coker AL 35452 **800-760-4089** 205-339-1558

Lake Murray State Park
120 N Robinson Ave Sixth Fl . . . . Oklahoma City OK 73152 **800-652-6552**

Lake Owyhee State Park
725 Summer St NE Ste C . . . . Salem OR 97301 **800-551-6949** 503-986-0707

Lake Wapello State Park
15248 Campground Rd . . . . Drakesville IA 52552 **866-495-4868** 641-722-3371

Park / Address	City	ST	Zip	Toll-Free	Phone
Lake Wissota State Park 18127 County Hwy O	Chippewa Falls	WI	54729	800-847-9367	715-382-4574
Lake Wister State Park 25567 US Hwy 270	Wister	OK	74966	800-622-6317	918-655-7212
Lakepoint Resort State Park 104 Lakepoint Dr	Eufaula	AL	36027	800-544-5253	334-687-8011
LaPine State Park 15800 State Recreation Rd	La Pine	OR	97739	800-551-6949	
LeFleur's Bluff State Park 2140 Riverside Dr	Jackson	MS	39202	800-237-6278	601-987-3923
Lewis & Clark State Recreation Site 725 Summer St NE Ste C	Salem	OR	97301	800-551-6949	503-986-0707
Little Pee Dee State Park 1298 State Pk Rd	Dillon	SC	29536	800-491-1764	843-774-8872
Little Talbot Island State Park 12157 Heckscher Dr	Jacksonville	FL	32226	800-326-3521	904-251-2320
Little White House State Historic Site 401 Little White House Rd	Warm Springs	GA	31830	800-864-7275	706-655-5870
Longfellow-Evangeline State Historic Site 1200 N Main St	Saint Martinville	LA	70582	888-677-2900	337-394-3754
Los Adaes State Historic Site 6354 Hwy 485	Robeline	LA	71469	888-677-5378	318-472-9449
Louisiana State Arboretum 4213 Chicot Pk Rd	Ville Platte	LA	70586	888-677-6100	337-363-6289
Lovers Key State Park 8700 Estero Blvd	Fort Myers Beach	FL	33931	800-326-3521	239-463-4588
Lower Wekiva River Preserve State Park 1800 Wekiwa Cir	Apopka	FL	32712	800-326-3521	407-884-2008
Manhattan Beach State Recreation Site 725 Summer St NE Ste C	Salem	OR	97301	800-551-6949	503-986-0707
Mansfield State Historic Site 15149 Hwy 175	Mansfield	LA	71052	888-677-6267	318-872-1474
Marksville State Historic Site 837 ML King Dr	Marksville	LA	71351	888-253-8954	318-253-8954
Mary Jane Thurston State Park 1466 State Rt 65	McClure	OH	43534	866-644-6727	419-832-7662
Mastodon State Historic Site 1050 Charles J Becker Dr	Imperial	MO	63052	800-334-6946	636-464-2976
Meaher State Park 5200 Battleship Pkwy	Spanish Fort	AL	36577	800-252-7275	251-626-5529
Merkle Wildlife Sanctuary 580 Taylor Ave	Annapolis	MD	21401	877-620-8367	
Middle Bass Island State Park 1719 Fox Rd	Middle Bass Island	OH	43446	866-644-6727	419-285-0311
Millsite State Park Ferron Canyon Rd PO Box 1343	Huntington	UT	84528	800-322-3770	435-384-2552
Minam State Recreation Area 72214 Marina Ln c/o Wallowa Lk Management Unit	Joseph	OR	97846	800-551-6949	
Missouri State Parks PO Box 176	Jefferson City	MO	65102	800-334-6946	
Monte Sano State Park 5105 Nolen Ave	Huntsville	AL	35801	800-252-7275	256-534-3757
Morgan Run Natural Environment Area Benros Ln	Eldersburg	MD	21784	800-830-3974	410-461-5005
Moro Bay State Park 6071 US Hwy 600	Jersey	AR	71651	888-742-8701	870-463-8555
Morro Bay State Park 60 State Pk Rd Morro Bay State Pk Rd	Morro Bay	CA	93442	800-777-0369	
Myakka River State Park 13208 SR 72	Sarasota	FL	34241	800-326-3521	941-361-6511
Myre-Big Island State Park 19499 780th Ave	Albert Lea	MN	56007	888-646-6367	507-379-3403
Natural Bridge Battlefield Historic State Park 7502 Natural Bridge Rd	Tallahassee	FL	32305	800-326-3521	850-922-6007
Natural Bridge State Resort Park 2135 Natural Bridge Rd	Slade	KY	40376	800-325-1710	
Nelson Dewey State Park PO Box 658	Cassville	WI	53806	888-936-7463	608-725-5374
Neskowin Beach State Recreation Site 198 NE 123rd St	Newport	OR	97365	800-551-6949	
New Germany State Park 349 Headquarters Ln	Grantsville	MD	21536	800-830-3974	301-895-5453
Newport State Park 475 County Rd NP	Ellison Bay	WI	54210	800-847-9367	920-854-2500
North Bend Rail Trail Rt 1 PO Box 221	Cairo	WV	26337	800-225-5982	304-643-2931
North Santiam State Recreation Area PO Box 549	Detroit	OR	97342	800-551-6949	
North Toledo Bend State Park 2907 N Toledo Pk Rd	Zwolle	LA	71486	888-677-6400	318-645-4715
Northern Highland - American Legion State Forest 4125 County Hwy M	Boulder Junction	WI	54512	800-847-9367	715-385-2727
Oak Mountain State Park 200 Terr Dr PO Box 278	Pelham	AL	35124	800-252-7275	205-620-2520
OC&E Woods Line State Trail 46000 Hwy 97 N 46000 Hwy 97 N	Chiloquin	OR	97624	800-551-6949	541-883-5558
Occoneechee State Park 1192 Occoneechee Pk Rd	Clarksville	VA	23927	800-933-7275	434-374-2210
Oceanside Beach State Recreation Site 13000 Whiskey Creek Rd W	Tillamook	OR	97141	800-551-6949	
Old Town San Diego State Historic Park 4002 Wallace St	San Diego	CA	92110	800-777-0369	619-220-5422
Oleta River State Park 3400 NE 163rd St	North Miami Beach	FL	33160	800-326-3521	305-919-1846
Oliver Inlet State Marine Park 400 Willoughby Ave PO Box 111071	Juneau	AK	99801	855-277-4491	907-465-4563
Ona Beach State Park 5580 S Coast Hwy	Newport	OR	97366	800-551-6949	
Ontario State Recreation Site 23751 Old Hwy 30	Huntington	OR	97907	800-551-6949	
Osage Hills State Park 2131 Osage Hills State Pk Rd	Pawhuska	OK	74056	800-622-6317	918-336-4141
Oscar Scherer State Park 1843 S Tamiami Trail	Osprey	FL	34229	800-326-3521	941-483-5956
Otter Crest State Scenic Viewpoint 198 NE 123rd St	Newport	OR	97365	800-551-6949	
Otter Point State Recreation Site PO Box 1345	Port Orford	OR	97465	800-551-6949	
Ozark Folk Ctr State Park 1032 Pk Ave	Mountain View	AR	72560	800-264-3655	870-269-3851
Paint Creek State Park 280 Taylor Rd	Bainbridge	OH	45612	866-644-6727	937-981-7061
Palmetto Island State Park 19501 Pleasant Rd	Abbeville	LA	70510	888-677-3668	337-893-3930
Panther State Forest HC 63 PO Box Box 923	Panther	WV	24872	800-225-5982	304-938-2252
Paradise Point State Recreation Site PO Box 1345	Port Orford	OR	97465	800-551-6949	
Paris Mountain State Park 2401 State Pk Rd	Greenville	SC	29609	866-345-7275	864-244-5565
Paul M. Grist State Park 1546 Grist Rd	Selma	AL	36701	800-252-7275	334-872-5846
Paynes Creek Historic State Park 888 Lake Branch Rd	Bowling Green	FL	33834	800-326-3521	863-375-4717
Pennyrile Forest State Resort Park 20781 Pennyrile Lodge Rd	Dawson Springs	KY	42408	800-325-1711	
Picacho State Recreation Area 1416 Ninth St PO Box 942896	Sacramento	CA	95814	800-777-0369	916-653-6995
Pine Grove Furnace State Park 1100 Pine Grove Rd	Gardners	PA	17324	888-727-2757	717-486-7174
Pine Mountain State Resort Park 1050 State Pk Rd	Pineville	KY	40977	800-325-1712	
Pocahontas State Park 10301 State Pk Rd	Chesterfield	VA	23832	800-933-7275	804-796-4255
Pocomoke River State Park 3461 Worcester Hwy	Snow Hill	MD	21863	877-620-8367	410-632-2566
Pocomoke State Forest 580 Taylor Ave	Annapolis	MD	21401	877-620-8367	
Port Hudson State Historic Site 236 Hwy 61	Jackson	LA	70748	888-677-3400	225-654-3775
Potawatomi State Park 3740 County Rd PD	Sturgeon Bay	WI	54235	800-847-9367	920-746-2890
Poverty Point Reservoir State Park 1500 Poverty Pt Pkwy	Delhi	LA	71232	800-474-0392	318-878-7536
Poverty Point State Historic Site 6859 Hwy 577	Pioneer	LA	71266	888-926-5492	318-926-5492
Presque Isle State Park 301 Peninsula Dr Ste 1	Erie	PA	16505	888-727-2757	814-833-7424
Priest Lake State Park 314 Indian Creek Pk Rd *Resv	Coolin	ID	83821	888-922-6743*	208-443-2200
Prompton State Park c/o Lackawanna	North Abington Township	PA	18414	888-727-2757	570-945-3239
Providence Mountains State Recreation Area 1416 Ninth St	Sacramento	CA	95814	800-777-0369	
Ravine Gardens State Park 1600 Twigg St	Palatka	FL	32177	800-326-3521	386-329-3721
Raymond Gary State Park Hwy 70	Fort Towson	OK	74735	800-622-6317	580-873-2307
Raymond R Andy Guest Jr Shenandoah River State Park 350 Daughter of Stars Dr	Bentonville	VA	22610	800-933-7275	540-622-6840
Rebel State Historic Site 1260 Hwy 1221	Marthaville	LA	71450	888-677-3600	318-472-6255
Red Fleet State Park 8750 North Hwy 191	Vernal	UT	84078	800-322-3770	435-789-4432
Rickwood Caverns State Park 370 Rickwood Pk Rd	Warrior	AL	35180	800-252-7275	205-647-9692
Robbers Cave State Park Hwy 2 N	Wilburton	OK	74578	800-654-8240	918-465-2565
Rock Bridge Memorial State Park 5901 S Hwy 163	Columbia	MO	65203	800-334-6946	573-449-7402
Rock Springs Run State Reserve 30601 CR 433	Sorrento	FL	32776	800-326-3521	407-884-2008
Roland Cooper State Park 285 Deer Run Dr	Camden	AL	36726	800-252-7275	334-682-4838
Rough River Dam State Resort Park 450 Lodge Rd	Falls of Rough	KY	40119	800-325-1713	
Saddle Mountain State Natural Area 9500 Sandpiper Ln c/o Nehalem Bay Management Unit PO Box 366	Nehalem	OR	97138	800-551-6949	
Saint Bernard State Park 501 St Bernard Pkwy	Braithwaite	LA	70040	888-677-7823	504-682-2101
Saint Croix State Park 30065 St Croix Pk Rd	Hinckley	MN	55037	888-646-6367	320-384-6591
Saint Mary's River State Park c/o Pt Lookout State Pk 11175 Pt Lookout Rd	Scotland	MD	20687	800-830-3974	301-872-5688
Sakatah Lake State Park 50499 Sakatah Lake State Pk Rd	Waterville	MN	56096	888-646-6367	507-362-4438
Salt Springs State Park c/o Lackawanna	North Abington Twp	PA	18414	888-727-2757	570-945-3239
Sam Houston Jones State Park 107 Sutherland Rd	Lake Charles	LA	70611	888-677-7264	337-855-2665
Sandy Point State Park 1100 E College Pkwy	Annapolis	MD	21409	877-620-8836	410-974-2149
Savanna Portage State Park 55626 Lake Pl	McGregor	MN	55760	888-646-6367	218-426-3271
Schoharie Crossing State Historic Site 129 Schoharie St PO Box 140	Fort Hunter	NY	12069	800-456-2267	518-829-7516
Schuyler Mansion State Historic Site 32 Catherine St	Albany	NY	12202	800-456-2267	518-434-0834
Scioto Trail State Park 144 Lake Rd	Chillicothe	OH	45601	866-644-6727	
Senate House State Historic Site 296 Fair St	Kingston	NY	12401	800-456-2267	845-338-2786
Seneca Fouts Memorial State Natural Area Wygant Trail	Hood River	OR	97014	800-551-6949	
Sequoyah Bay State Park 6237 E 100th St N	Wagoner	OK	74467	800-622-6317	918-683-0878
Sesquicentennial State Park 9564 Two Notch Rd	Columbia	SC	29223	888-245-9300	803-788-2706
Sibley State Park 800 Sibley Pk Rd	New London	MN	56273	888-646-6367	320-354-2055

	Toll-Free	Phone
Snowdale State Park		
501 S 439 .... Salina OK 74361	800-622-6317	918-434-2651
Soldiers Delight Natural Environment Area		
5100 Deer Park Rd .... Owings Mills MD 21117	800-830-3974	410-461-5005
Somers Cove Marina		
715 Broadway PO Box 67 .... Crisfield MD 21817	800-967-3474	410-968-0925
Soudan Underground Mine State Park		
1302 McKinley Park Rd .... Soudan MN 55782	888-646-6367	218-753-2245
South Arkansas Arboretum		
PO Box 7010 .... El Dorado AR 71731	888-287-2757	
South Beach State Park		
5580 S Coast Hwy .... South Beach OR 97366	800-452-5687	541-867-4715
South Toledo Bend State Park		
120 Bald Eaglel Rd .... Anacoco LA 71403	888-398-4770	337-286-9075
Spavinaw State Park		
555 S Main .... Spavinaw OK 74366	800-622-6317	918-589-2651
Split Rock Creek State Park		
50th Ave .... Jasper MN 56144	888-646-6367	507-348-7908
Split Rock Lighthouse State Park		
3755 Split Rock Lighthouse Rd .... Two Harbors MN 55616	800-366-8917	218-595-7625
State Forest State Park		
56750 Hwy 14 .... Walden CO 80480	866-265-6447	970-723-8366
Steinaker State Park		
4335 N Hwy 191 .... Vernal UT 84078	800-322-3770	435-789-4432
Stone Mountain State Park		
3042 Frank Pkwy .... Roaring Gap NC 28668	877-722-6762	336-957-8185
Succor Creek State Natural Area		
1298 Lk Owyhee Dam Rd .... Adrian OR 97901	800-551-6949	
Tettegouche State Park		
5702 Hwy 61 .... Silver Bay MN 55614	800-366-8917	218-226-6365
Three Island Crossing State Park		
1083 S Three Island Pk Dr .... Glenns Ferry ID 83623	866-634-3246	208-366-2394
Tickfaw State Park		
27225 Patterson Rd .... Springfield LA 70462	888-981-2020	225-294-5020
Tokatee Klootchman State Natural Site		
93111 Hwy 101 N .... Florence OR 97439	800-551-6949	
Tombigbee State Park		
264 Cabin Dr .... Tupelo MS 38804	800-467-2757	662-842-7669
Torrey Pines State Reserve		
c/o San Diego Coast District		
4477 Pacific Hwy .... San Diego CA 92110	866-240-4655	858-755-2063
Touvelle State Recreation Site		
8598 Table Rock Rd		
3792 N River Rd .... Central Point OR 97502	800-551-6949	541-983-2277
Tub Springs State Wayside		
12845 Green Springs Hwy		
3792 N River Rd .... Ashland OR 97520	800-551-6949	
Twin Bridges State Park		
14801 Hwy 137 S .... Fairland OK 74343	800-622-6317	918-540-2545
Twin Lakes State Park		
788 Twin Lakes Rd .... Green Bay VA 23942	800-933-7275	434-392-3435
Ukiah-Dale Forest State Scenic Corridor		
Ukiah-Dale Forest State Scenic Corridor		
PO Box 85 .... Ukiah OR 97880	800-551-6949	541-983-2277
Umpqua Lighthouse State Park		
84505 Hwy 101 S .... Florence OR 97439	800-551-6949	
Unicoi State Park & Lodge		
1788 Hwy 356 Rd .... Helen GA 30545	800-573-9659	
Unity Forest State Scenic Corridor		
US-26 23751 Old Hwy 30 .... Ironside OR 97908	800-551-6949	
Unity Lake State Recreation Site		
18998 OR-245 59500 Hwy 26/395 ..... Unity OR 97884	800-551-6949	541-932-4453
Upper Sioux Agency State Park		
5908 Hwy 67 .... Granite Falls MN 56241	800-366-8917	320-564-4777
Van Buren State Park		
12259 Township Rd 218 .... Van Buren OH 45889	866-644-6727	419-832-7662
W.B. Nelson State Recreation Site		
5580 S Coast Hwy .... Newport OR 97366	800-551-6949	
Wah-Sha-She State Park		
HC 75 Hwy 60 .... Copan OK 74022	800-622-6317	918-532-4334
Walt Whitman House State Historic Site		
330 Mickle Blvd .... Camden NJ 08103	800-843-6420	
Watts Towers of Simon Rodia State Historic Park		
1765 East 107th Street		
1925 Las Virgenes .... Calabasas CA 91302	866-240-4655	213-847-4646
White River State Park		
801 W Washington St ...... Indianapolis IN 46204	800-665-9056	317-233-2434
Whitewater State Park		
19041 Hwy 74 .... Altura MN 55910	800-366-8917	507-932-3007
Willamette Stone State Heritage Site		
11321 SW Terwilliger Blvd .... Portland OR 97219	800-551-6949	
Willard Bay State Park		
900 West 650 North Ste A .... Willard UT 84340	800-322-3770	435-734-9494
William M. Tugman State Park		
72549 Hwy 101 .... Lakeside OR 97449	800-551-6949	
Willow River State Park		
1034 County Hwy A .... Hudson WI 54016	800-847-9367	715-386-5931
Winchuck State Recreation Site		
1655 Hwy 101 N .... Brookings OR 97415	800-551-6949	
Winter Quarters State Historic Site		
4929 Hwy 608 .... Newellton LA 71357	888-677-9468	318-467-9750
Yachats Ocean Road State Natural Site		
5580 S Coast Hwy .... Newport OR 97366	800-551-6949	
Youghiogheny River Natural Resources Management Area		
c/o Deep Creek Lake State Pk		
898 State Pk Rd .... Swanton MD 21561	877-620-8367	301-387-5563

563   PARTY GOODS

	Toll-Free	Phone
Amscan Inc		
80 Grasslands Rd .... Elmsford NY 10523	800-444-8887	914-345-2020
Balloons Everywhere Inc		
16474 Greeno Rd .... Fairhope AL 36532	800-239-2000	
Party City Corp		
25 Green Pond Rd Ste 1 .... Rockaway NJ 07866	800-727-8924	973-453-8600

564   PATTERNS - INDUSTRIAL

	Toll-Free	Phone
Freeman Mfg & Supply Co		
1101 Moore Rd .... Avon OH 44011	800-321-8511	440-934-1902
Hub Pattern Corp		
2113 Salem Ave .... Roanoke VA 24016	800-482-3505	540-342-3505

565   PATTERNS - SEWING

	Toll-Free	Phone
Bonfit America Inc		
8460 Higuera St .... Culver City CA 90232	800-526-6348	310-204-7880
McCall Pattern Co		
615 McCall Rd .... Manhattan KS 66502	800-255-2762	

566   PAWN SHOPS

	Toll-Free	Phone
EZCORP Inc 1901 Capital Pkwy .... Austin TX 78746	800-873-7296	512-314-3400
NASDAQ: EZPW		

567   PAYROLL SERVICES

SEE ALSO Professional Employer Organizations (PEOs) ; Data Processing & Related Services

	Toll-Free	Phone
Advantage Payroll Services Inc		
126 Merrow Rd PO Box 1330 .... Auburn ME 04211	800-876-0178*	207-784-0178
*Cust Svc		
Automatic Data Processing Inc (ADP)		
One ADP Blvd .... Roseland NJ 07068	800-225-5237	973-994-5000
NASDAQ: ADP		
CheckPoint HR		
2035 Lincoln Hwy Ste 1080 .... Edison NJ 08817	800-385-0331	732-287-8270
DLH Holdings Corp		
1776 Peachtree St NW Ste 300S ...... Atlanta GA 30309	866-352-5304	770-554-3545
NASDAQ: DLHC		
Employers Resource Management Co		
1301 S Vista Ave Ste 200 .... Boise ID 83705	800-574-4668	208-376-3000
Hiregenics		
47742 Van Dyke Ave .... Shelby Township MI 48317	866-315-5489	
Media Services		
500 S Sepulveda Blvd 4th Fl. ...... Los Angeles CA 90049	800-738-0409	310-440-9600
Paychex Inc		
911 Panorama Trl S .... Rochester NY 14625	800-828-4411	585-385-6666
NASDAQ: PAYX		
SurePayroll		
2350 Ravine Way Ste 100 .... Glenview IL 60025	877-954-7873	847-676-8420

568   PENS, PENCILS, PARTS

SEE ALSO Office & School Supplies ; Art Materials & Supplies - Mfr

	Toll-Free	Phone
Alvin & Company Inc		
1335 Blue Hills Ave .... Bloomfield CT 06002	800-444-2584	860-243-8991
Avery Dennison Corp		
207 Goode Ave .... Glendale CA 91203	888-567-4387*	626-304-2000
*NYSE: AVY ■ *Cust Svc*		
Dixon Ticonderoga Co		
195 International Pkwy .... Heathrow FL 32746	800-824-9430	407-829-9000
Dri Mark Products Inc		
999 S Oyster Bay Rd Ste 312 ...... Bethpage NY 11714	800-645-9118	516-484-6200
Harcourt Pencil Co		
7765 S 175 W .... Milroy IN 46156	800-428-6584	765-629-2244
Listo Pencil Corp		
1925 Union St .... Alameda CA 94501	800-547-8648	510-522-2910
Musgrave Pencil Company Inc		
701 W Ln St .... Shelbyville TN 37160	800-736-2450	931-684-3611
National Pen Corp (NPC)		
12121 Scripps Summit Dr Ste 200 ..... San Diego CA 92131	800-854-1000	858-675-3000

569   PERFORMING ARTS FACILITIES

SEE ALSO Stadiums & Arenas ; Theaters - Broadway ; Theaters - Resident ; Convention Centers
Most of the fax numbers provided for these facilities are for the box office.

	Toll-Free	Phone
A Contemporary Theatre (ACT)		
700 Union St Kreielsheimer Pl .... Seattle WA 98101	888-584-4849	206-292-7660
Adrienne Arsht Ctr for the Performing Arts of Miami-Dade County Inc		
1300 Biscayne Blvd .... Miami FL 33132	877-949-6722	786-468-2000
Alabama Theatre		
4750 Hwy 17 S .... North Myrtle Beach SC 29582	800-342-2262	843-272-1111
Alberta Bair Theater for the Performing Arts		
2722 Third Ave N Ste 200 PO Box 1556 .... Billings MT 59103	877-321-2074	406-256-8915
Andy Williams Moon River Theatre		
2500 Hwy 76 .... Branson MO 65616	800-666-6094	417-334-1800
Artpark 450 S Fourth St .... Lewiston NY 14092	877-325-5787	716-754-9000
Arts Ctr of Coastal Carolina		
14 Shelter Cove Ln .... Hilton Head Island SC 29928	888-860-2787	843-686-3945
Barbara B Mann Performing Arts Hall		
13350 FSW Pkwy .... Fort Myers FL 33919	800-440-7469	239-489-3033
Bass Performance Hall		
4th & Calhoun Sts .... Fort Worth TX 76102	877-212-4280	817-212-4200

	City	State	ZIP	Toll-Free	Phone
Berklee Performance Ctr 136 Massachusetts Ave	Boston	MA	02115	**877-237-5533**	617-747-2261
Blossom Music Ctr Tickets 1145 W Steels Corners Rd	Cuyahoga Falls	OH	44223	**800-745-3000**	330-920-8040
Boisfeuillet Jones Atlanta Civic Ctr 395 Piedmont Ave	Atlanta	GA	30308	**877-430-7596**	404-523-6275
Boston Symphony Hall 301 Massachusetts Ave	Boston	MA	02115	**888-266-1200**	617-266-1492
Broadway Ctr for the Performing Arts 901 Broadway	Tacoma	WA	98402	**800-291-7593**	253-591-5890
Broward Ctr for the Performing Arts 201 SW Fifth Ave	Fort Lauderdale	FL	33312	**877-311-7469**	954-462-0222
Bushnell Ctr for the Performing Arts 166 Capitol Ave	Hartford	CT	06106	**888-824-2874**	860-987-6000
California Ctr for the Arts 340 N Escondido Blvd	Escondido	CA	92025	**800-988-4253**	760-839-4138
California Theatre of Performing Arts 562 W Fourth St	San Bernardino	CA	92401	**800-745-3000**	909-885-5152
Carnegie Hall 881 Seventh Ave	New York	NY	10019	**800-728-3843**	212-247-7800
Carolina Opry 8901 Hwy 17 N Ste A	Myrtle Beach	SC	29572	**800-843-6779**	
Center for the Arts 103 Ctr for the Arts	Buffalo	NY	14260	**800-745-3000**	716-645-2787
Centre in the Square 101 Queen St N	Kitchener	ON	N2H6P7	**800-265-8977**	519-578-1570
Cerritos Ctr for the Performing Arts 12700 Ctr Ct Dr	Cerritos	CA	90703	**800-300-4345**	562-916-8501
Chester Fritz Auditorium 3475 University Ave PO Box 9028	Grand Forks	ND	58202	**800-375-4068**	701-777-3076
Cheyenne Civic Ctr 510 W 20th St	Cheyenne	WY	82001	**877-691-2787**	307-637-6364
Christel DeHaan Fine Arts Ctr 1400 E Hanna Ave University of Indianapolis	Indianapolis	IN	46227	**800-232-8634**	317-788-3566
Cincinnati Playhouse in the Park 962 Mt Adams Cir PO Box 6537	Cincinnati	OH	45202	**800-582-3208**	513-345-2242
Circuit Playhouse, The 51 S Cooper St	Memphis	TN	38104	**888-648-8154**	901-725-0776
Contemporary Arts Ctr 900 Camp St	New Orleans	LA	70130	**800-568-6968**	504-528-3805
Curtis M Phillips Ctr for the Performing Arts 315 Hull Rd PO Box 112750	Gainesville	FL	32611	**800-905-2787**	352-392-1900
Cutler Majestic Theatre at Emerson College 219 Tremont St	Boston	MA	02116	**888-627-7115**	617-824-8000
David A. Straz Jr Ctr for, The Performing Arts, The 1010 N WC MacInnes Pl	Tampa	FL	33602	**800-955-1045**	813-222-1000
Denver Ctr for the Performing Arts 1101 13th St	Denver	CO	80204	**800-641-1222**	303-893-4000
Denver Performing Arts Complex 1245 Champa St 1St Fl	Denver	CO	80204	**800-745-3000**	720-865-4220
Diana Wortham Theatre at Pack Place 2 S Pack Sq	Asheville	NC	28801	**800-999-2160**	828-257-4530
DuPont Theatre 1007 N Market St	Wilmington	DE	19801	**800-338-0881**	302-656-4401
EJ Thomas Performing Arts Hall 198 Hill St University of Akron	Akron	OH	44325	**800-745-3000**	330-972-7570
El Paso Convention & Performing Arts Ctr One Civic Ctr Plz	El Paso	TX	79901	**800-351-6024**	915-534-0600
Evansville Auditorium & Convention Ctr 715 Locust St	Evansville	IN	47708	**844-381-4751**	812-435-5770
Fairfield University Fairfield University 1073 N Benson Rd	Fairfield	CT	06824	**877-278-7396**	203-254-4010
Festival Concert Hall *North Dakota State University* PO Box 5691	Fargo	ND	58105	**800-726-1724**	701-231-7932
Florence Events Ctr 715 Quince St	Florence	OR	97439	**888-968-4086**	541-997-1994
Fox Theater 2001 H St	Bakersfield	CA	93301	**888-825-5484**	661-324-1369
Fox Theatre 660 Peachtree St NE	Atlanta	GA	30308	**855-285-8499**	404-881-2100
Fulton Opera House Foundation 12 N Prince St PO Box 1865	Lancaster	PA	17603	**888-480-1265**	717-397-7425
Gary Soren Smith Ctr for the Fine & Performing Arts *Ohlone College* 43600 Mission Blvd	Fremont	CA	94539	**800-309-2131**	510-659-6031
Grand 1894 Opera House 2020 Postoffice St	Galveston	TX	77550	**800-821-1894**	409-765-1894
Grand Rapids Civic Theatre 30 N Div Ave	Grand Rapids	MI	49503	**866-455-4728**	616-222-6650
Grand, The 818 N Market St	Wilmington	DE	19801	**800-374-7263**	302-658-7897
Greer Garson Theatre Ctr 1600 St Michael's Dr College of Santa Fe	Santa Fe	NM	87505	**800-456-2673**	505-473-6011
Guthrie Theater 818 S Second St *Resv	Minneapolis	MN	55415	**877-447-8243***	612-377-2224
Hale Centre Theater 3333 S Decker Lake Dr	West Valley City	UT	84119	**877-829-5500**	801-984-9000
Heinz Hall for the Performing Arts 600 Penn Ave	Pittsburgh	PA	15222	**800-743-8560**	412-392-4900
Heymann Performing Arts Ctr 1373 S College Rd	Lafayette	LA	70503	**800-745-3000**	337-291-5540
Hollywood Bowl 2301 N Highland Ave	Hollywood	CA	90068	**800-653-8000**	323-850-2000
Hopkins Ctr for the Arts 6041 Wilson Hall	Hanover	NH	03755	**800-451-4067**	603-646-2422
Jefferson Ctr 541 Luck Ave Ste 221	Roanoke	VA	24016	**866-345-2550**	540-343-2624
John Anson Ford Theatres 2580 Cahuenga Blvd E	Hollywood	CA	90068	**800-466-3876**	323-461-3673
John F Kennedy Ctr for the Performing Arts 2700 F St NW	Washington	DC	20566	**800-444-1324**	202-416-8000
Joseph Meyerhoff Symphony Hall 1212 Cathedral St	Baltimore	MD	21201	**877-276-1444**	410-783-8100
Juanita K Hammons Hall for the Performing Arts 901 S National Ave	Springfield	MO	65897	**888-476-7849**	417-836-6776
Kansas City Music Hall 301 W 13th St	Kansas City	MO	64105	**800-821-7060**	816-513-5000
Knoxville Civic Auditorium/Coliseum 500 Howard Baker Jr Ave	Knoxville	TN	37915	**877-995-9961**	865-215-8900
Krannert Ctr for the Performing Arts 500 S Goodwin Ave	Urbana	IL	61801	**800-527-2849**	217-333-6700
Lake Charles Civic Ctr 900 Lakeshore Dr	Lake Charles	LA	70601	**888-620-1749**	337-491-1256
Legends Theater 1600 W Hwy 76	Branson	MO	65616	**800-374-7469**	417-339-3003
Liacouras Ctr 1776 N Broad St	Philadelphia	PA	19121	**800-298-4200**	215-204-2400
Lied Ctr for Performing Arts 301 N 12th St	Lincoln	NE	68588	**800-432-3231**	402-472-4700
Lila Cockrell Theatre 200 E Market St *General	San Antonio	TX	78205	**877-504-8895***	210-207-8500
Long Wharf Theatre 222 Sargent Dr	New Haven	CT	06511	**800-782-8497**	203-787-4282
Lyric Opera House 110 W Mt Royal Ave	Baltimore	MD	21201	**800-872-7245**	410-685-5086
Macon City Auditorium 415 First St	Macon	GA	31201	**877-532-6144**	478-751-9152
Mahaffey Theater for the Performing Arts 400 First St S	Saint Petersburg	FL	33701	**800-435-7352**	727-892-5798
Marcus Ctr for the Performing Arts 929 N Water St	Milwaukee	WI	53202	**888-612-3500**	414-273-7206
Maryland Hall for the Creative Arts 801 Chase St	Annapolis	MD	21401	**866-438-3808**	410-263-5544
McCallum Theatre 73000 Fred Waring Dr	Palm Desert	CA	92260	**866-889-2787**	760-340-2787
Michigan Theater 603 E Liberty St	Ann Arbor	MI	48104	**800-745-3000**	734-668-8397
Morris Performing Arts Ctr 211 N Michigan St	South Bend	IN	46601	**800-537-6415**	574-235-9190
New Jersey Performing Arts Ctr 1 Ctr St	Newark	NJ	07102	**888-466-5722**	973-642-8989
Norwalk Concert Hall 125 E Ave	Norwalk	CT	06851	**800-357-9577**	203-854-7900
Ocean Ctr 101 N Atlantic Ave	Daytona Beach	FL	32118	**800-858-6444**	386-254-4500
Omaha Community Playhouse 6915 Cass St	Omaha	NE	68132	**888-782-4338**	402-553-0800
One World Theatre 7701 Bee Caves Rd	Austin	TX	78746	**888-616-0522**	512-330-9500
Orchestra Hall 1111 Nicollet Mall	Minneapolis	MN	55403	**800-292-4141**	612-371-5600
Orpheum Theatre 409 S 16th St	Omaha	NE	68102	**866-434-8587**	402-345-0202
Pabst Theater 144 E Wells St	Milwaukee	WI	53202	**800-523-7117**	414-286-3205
Palace, Theatre, The 1420 Celebrity Cir Broadway at the Beach	Myrtle Beach	SC	29577	**888-841-2787**	843-448-9224
Pantages Theater 901 Broadway	Tacoma	WA	98402	**800-291-7593**	253-591-5890
Paramount Theatre 123 Third Ave SE	Cedar Rapids	IA	52401	**800-369-8863**	319-398-5226
Parkland College Theatre 2400 W Bradley Ave	Champaign	IL	61821	**800-346-8089**	217-351-2528
Patriots Theater Memorial Dr	Trenton	NJ	08608	**866-847-7682**	609-984-8484
Philharmonic Ctr for the Arts 5833 Pelican Bay Blvd	Naples	FL	34108	**800-597-1900**	239-597-1111
Pikes Peak Ctr 190 S Cascade Ave	Colorado Springs	CO	80903	**866-464-2626**	719-477-2100
Playhouse Square 1501 Euclid Ave Ste 200	Cleveland	OH	44115	**866-546-1353**	216-771-4444
Plaza Live, The 425 N Bumby Ave	Orlando	FL	32803	**877-435-9849**	407-228-1220
Powell Symphony Hall 718 N Grand Blvd	Saint Louis	MO	63103	**800-232-1880**	314-533-2500
Raymond F Kravis Ctr for the Performing Arts 701 Okeechobee Blvd	West Palm Beach	FL	33401	**800-572-8471**	561-832-7469
Rialto Theater 310 S Ninth St	Tacoma	WA	98402	**800-291-7593**	253-591-5890
Robinson Ctr 101 S. Spring St PO Box 3232	Little Rock	AR	72201	**800-844-4781**	501-376-4781
Ruth Eckerd Hall 1111 McMullen Booth Rd	Clearwater	FL	33759	**800-875-8682**	727-791-7060
Ryman Auditorium 116 Fifth Ave N	Nashville	TN	37219	**800-733-6779**	615-458-8700
San Antonio Municipal Auditorium 200 E Market St PO Box 1809	San Antonio	TX	78205	**877-504-8895**	210-207-8500
San Jose Convention Center (SJC) 150 W San Carlos St	San Jose	CA	95110	**800-726-5673**	408-792-4194
San Jose Ctr for the Performing Arts 255 Almaden Blvd	San Jose	CA	95113	**800-726-5673**	408-792-4111
Savannah Civic Ctr 301 W Oglethorp Ave	Savannah	GA	31401	**800-337-1101**	912-651-6550
Scottsdale Ctr for the Performing Arts 7380 E Second St	Scottsdale	AZ	85251	**800-309-8532**	480-994-2787
Severance Hall 11001 Euclid Ave	Cleveland	OH	44106	**800-686-1411**	216-231-7300
Shea's Performing Arts Ctr 646 Main St	Buffalo	NY	14202	**866-341-5945**	716-847-1410
Shepherd of the Hills Homestead & Outdoor Theatre 5586 W Hwy 76	Branson	MO	65616	**800-653-6288**	417-334-4191
Shubert Theater 247 College St	New Haven	CT	06510	**866-889-8061**	203-624-1825
Soldiers & Sailors Memorial Auditorium 399 McCallie Ave	Chattanooga	TN	37402	**800-772-1213**	423-757-5156
Spokane Civic Theatre 1020 N Howard St	Spokane	WA	99201	**800-325-7328**	509-325-1413
Stambaugh Auditorium 1000 Fifth Ave	Youngstown	OH	44504	**866-516-2269**	330-747-5175

	Toll-Free	Phone
Starlight Theatre		
4600 Starlight Rd Swope Pk . . . . Kansas City MO 64132	**800-776-1730**	816-363-7827
State Theatre		
15 Livingston Ave . . . . New Brunswick NJ 08901	**888-636-1133**	732-247-7200
Stranahan Theater		
4645 Heatherdowns Blvd . . . . Toledo OH 43614	**866-381-7469**	419-381-8851
Strand Theatre		
619 Louisiana Ave . . . . Shreveport LA 71101	**800-313-6373**	318-226-1481
Symphony Ctr		
220 S Michigan Ave . . . . Chicago IL 60604	**800-223-7114***	312-294-3000
*Cust Svc		
Tarrytown Music Hall		
13 Main St PO Box 686 . . . . Tarrytown NY 10591	**877-840-0457**	914-631-3390
Tennessee Performing Arts Ctr		
505 Deaderick St . . . . Nashville TN 37219	**866-455-2823**	615-782-4000
University of Texas at Austin Performing Arts Ctr		
E 23rd St & E Robert Dedman Dr . . . . Austin TX 78713	**800-687-6010**	512-471-1444
University of West Florida Ctr for Fine & Performing Arts		
11000 University Pkwy Bldg 82 . . . . Pensacola FL 32514	**800-263-1074**	850-474-2000
Van Wezel Performing Arts Ctr		
777 N Tamiami Trl . . . . Sarasota FL 34236	**800-826-9303**	941-953-3368
Victoria Theatre		
138 N Main St . . . . Dayton OH 45402	**888-228-3630**	937-228-3630
Victoria Vaudeville Theater		
1228 Market St . . . . Wheeling WV 26003	**800-505-7464**	304-233-7464
Virginia Beach Convention Ctr		
2101 Parks Ave Ste 500 . . . . Virginia Beach VA 23451	**800-700-7702**	757-385-4700
Warner Theatre 811 State St . . . . Erie PA 16501	**800-352-0050**	814-452-4857
Warnors Ctr for the Performing Arts		
1400 Fulton St . . . . Fresno CA 93721	**800-320-1733**	559-264-2848
Waterfront Playhouse		
312 Wall St . . . . Key West FL 33040	**800-435-7352**	305-294-5015
Weidner Ctr for the Performing Arts		
2420 Nicolet Dr		
University of Wisconsin at Green Bay . . . . Green Bay WI 54311	**800-895-0071**	920-465-2726
Westport Country Playhouse		
25 Powers Ct . . . . Westport CT 06880	**888-927-7529**	203-227-4177
Wharton Ctr for the Performing Arts		
Michigan State University . . . . East Lansing MI 48824	**800-942-7866**	517-432-2000
Wheeler Opera House		
320 E Hyman St . . . . Aspen CO 81611	**866-449-0464**	970-920-5770
Whiting Auditorium		
1241 E Kearsley St . . . . Flint MI 48503	**888-823-6837**	810-237-7333
Wichita Falls CVB		
1000 Fifth St . . . . Wichita Falls TX 76301	**800-799-6732**	
Williams Performing Arts Ctr		
Abilene Christian University		
1600 Campus Ct . . . . Abilene TX 79601	**800-460-6228**	325-674-2199
Wilma Theater		
265 S Broad St . . . . Philadelphia PA 19107	**800-732-0999**	215-893-9456
Wiltern Theatre		
3790 Wilshire Blvd . . . . Los Angeles CA 90010	**800-348-8499**	213-388-1400
Wolf Trap Foundation for the Performing Arts		
1645 Trap Rd . . . . Vienna VA 22182	**877-965-3872**	703-255-1900

570	PERFORMING ARTS ORGANIZATIONS

SEE ALSO Arts & Artists Organizations

570-1 Dance Companies

	Toll-Free	Phone
Aspen Santa Fe Ballet		
0245 Sage Way . . . . Aspen CO 81611	**866-449-0464**	970-925-7175
Axis Dance Co		
1428 Alice St Ste 200 . . . . Oakland CA 94612	**800-838-3006**	510-625-0110
Ballet Magnificat		
5406 I-55 N . . . . Jackson MS 39211	**866-617-3257**	601-977-1001
Buglisi Dance Theatre		
229 W 42nd St Ste 502 . . . . New York NY 10036	**800-754-0797**	212-719-3301
Carolina Ballet Inc		
3401-131 Atlantic Ave . . . . Raleigh NC 27604	**800-841-2787**	919-719-0800
Cincinnati Ballet		
1555 Central Pkwy . . . . Cincinnati OH 45214	**800-745-3000**	513-621-5219
Collage Dance Theatre		
2934 1/2 Beverly Glen Cir . . . . Los Angeles CA 90077	**866-300-4287**	818-784-8669
Dance Theatre of Harlem Inc		
466 W 152nd St . . . . New York NY 10031	**800-538-2538**	212-690-2800
Dayton Ballet 140 N Main St . . . . Dayton OH 45402	**800-745-3000**	937-449-5060
Dayton Contemporary Dance Co		
840 Germantown St . . . . Dayton OH 45402	**888-228-3630**	937-228-3232
Doug Varone & Dancers		
37 W 32nd St . . . . New York NY 10001	**800-366-2100**	212-279-3344
Houston Ballet		
601 Preston St . . . . Houston TX 77002	**800-828-2787**	713-523-6300
Louisville Ballet		
315 E Main St . . . . Louisville KY 40202	**800-775-7777**	502-583-3150
Mark Morris Dance Group		
3 Lafayette Ave . . . . Brooklyn NY 11217	**800-957-1046**	718-624-8400
Miami City Ballet		
2200 Liberty Ave . . . . Miami Beach FL 33139	**877-929-7010**	305-929-7000
Milwaukee Ballet		
504 W National Ave . . . . Milwaukee WI 53204	**888-612-3500**	414-643-7677
Minnesota Ballet		
301 W First St Ste 800 . . . . Duluth MN 55802	**800-627-3529**	218-529-3742
Oakland Ballet Co		
2201 Broadway Ste 206 . . . . Oakland CA 94612	**866-711-6037**	510-893-3132
Pacific Northwest Ballet		
301 Mercer St . . . . Seattle WA 98109	**800-225-7635**	206-441-2424
Pennsylvania Ballet		
1819 John F Kennedy Blvd . . . . Philadelphia PA 19103	**800-732-0999**	215-551-7000
Pittsburgh Ballet Theatre		
2900 Liberty Ave . . . . Pittsburgh PA 15201	**800-441-1414**	412-281-0360
Sacramento Ballet		
1631 K St . . . . Sacramento CA 95814	**800-925-9989**	916-552-5800
San Francisco Ballet		
455 Franklin St . . . . San Francisco CA 94102	**888-622-2108**	415-865-2000

	Toll-Free	Phone
Tulsa Ballet 1212 E 45th Pl . . . . Tulsa OK 74105	**800-722-9942**	918-749-6030
Virginia Ballet Theatre		
134 W Olney Rd . . . . Norfolk VA 23510	**866-892-6990**	757-622-4822

570-2 Opera Companies

	Toll-Free	Phone
Dallas Opera		
8350 N Central Expy Ste 210 . . . . Dallas TX 75206	**888-353-4537**	214-443-1000
Florentine Opera Co		
700 N Water St Ste 950 . . . . Milwaukee WI 53202	**800-326-7372**	414-291-5700
Florida Grand Opera		
8390 NW 25th St . . . . Miami FL 33122	**800-741-1010**	305-854-1643
Fort Worth Opera		
1300 Gendy St . . . . Fort Worth TX 76107	**877-396-7372**	817-731-0833
Glimmerglass Festival		
7300 State Hwy 80 PO Box 191 . . . . Cooperstown NY 13326	**866-568-2388**	607-547-0700
Houston Grand Opera		
510 Preston St Ste 500 . . . . Houston TX 77002	**800-626-7372**	713-546-0200
Kentucky Opera Assn		
323 W Broadway Ste 601 . . . . Louisville KY 40202	**800-690-9236**	502-584-4500
Minnesota Opera		
620 N First St . . . . Minneapolis MN 55401	**800-676-6737**	612-333-2700
Opera Omaha		
1625 Farnam St Ste 100 . . . . Omaha NE 68102	**877-346-7372**	402-346-4398
Opera San Jose		
2149 Paragon Dr . . . . San Jose CA 95131	**800-745-3000**	408-437-4450
Palm Beach Opera		
415 S Olive Ave . . . . West Palm Beach FL 33401	**800-435-7352**	561-833-7888
Portland Opera		
211 SE Caruthers St . . . . Portland OR 97214	**866-739-6737**	503-241-1407
Santa Fe Opera, The		
301 Opera Dr . . . . Santa Fe NM 87506	**800-280-4654**	505-986-5900
Sarasota Opera		
61 N Pineapple Ave . . . . Sarasota FL 34236	**866-951-0111**	941-366-8450
Seattle Opera PO Box 9248 . . . . Seattle WA 98109	**800-426-1619***	206-389-7600
*Sales		
Toledo Opera		
425 Jefferson Ave Ste 601 . . . . Toledo OH 43604	**866-860-9048**	419-255-7464
Tulsa Opera		
1610 S Boulder Ave . . . . Tulsa OK 74119	**866-298-2530**	918-582-4035
Wichita Grand Opera		
225 W Douglas Ave		
Century II Performing Arts Ctr . . . . Wichita KS 67202	**855-755-7328**	316-683-3444

570-3 Orchestras

	Toll-Free	Phone
Acadiana Symphony Orchestra		
412 Travis St . . . . Lafayette LA 70503	**800-259-8852**	337-232-4277
Austin Symphony Orchestra		
1101 Red River St . . . . Austin TX 78701	**888-462-3787**	512-476-6064
Baltimore Symphony Orchestra		
1212 Cathedral St . . . . Baltimore MD 21201	**877-276-1444**	410-783-8100
Bangor Symphony Orchestra		
PO Box 1441 . . . . Bangor ME 04402	**800-639-3221***	207-942-5555
*General		
Boston Pops		
301 Massachusetts Ave Symphony Hall . . . . Boston MA 02115	**888-266-1200**	617-266-1492
Boston Symphony Orchestra		
301 Massachusetts Ave Symphony Hall . . . . Boston MA 02115	**888-266-1200**	617-266-1492
Chamber Orchestra of Philadelphia		
1520 Locust St Ste 500 . . . . Philadelphia PA 19102	**800-732-0999**	215-545-5451
Chicago Symphony Orchestra		
220 S Michigan Ave . . . . Chicago IL 60604	**800-223-7114**	312-294-3000
Cleveland Orchestra, The		
11001 Euclid Ave Severance Hall . . . . Cleveland OH 44106	**800-686-1141**	216-231-1111
Colorado Symphony Orchestra		
1000 14th St Unit 15 . . . . Denver CO 80202	**877-292-7979**	303-623-7876
Columbus Symphony Orchestra		
55 E State St . . . . Columbus OH 43215	**800-745-3000**	614-228-9600
Corpus Christi Symphony Orchestra		
555 N Carancahua St Tower II Ste 410		
Ste 410 . . . . Corpus Christi TX 78401	**877-286-6683**	361-883-6683
Da Camera of Houston		
1427 Branard St . . . . Houston TX 77006	**800-233-2226**	713-524-7601
Detroit Symphony Orchestra		
3711 Woodward Ave . . . . Detroit MI 48201	**800-434-6340**	313-576-5111
Dubuque Symphony Orchestra		
2728 Asbury Rd Ste 900 . . . . Dubuque IA 52001	**866-803-9280**	563-557-1677
Edmonton Symphony Orchestra		
9720 102nd Ave . . . . Edmonton AB T5J4B2	**800-563-5081**	780-428-1108
Flagstaff Symphony Orchestra		
113 E Aspen Ave # A . . . . Flagstaff AZ 86001	**888-520-7214**	928-774-5107
Illinois Symphony Orchestra		
524 E Capitol Ave . . . . Springfield IL 62701	**800-401-7222**	217-522-2838
Indianapolis Symphony Orchestra		
45 Monument Cir . . . . Indianapolis IN 46204	**800-366-8457**	317-262-1100
Jacksonville Symphony Orchestra (JSO)		
300 W Water St Ste 200 . . . . Jacksonville FL 32202	**877-662-6731**	904-354-5479
Kansas City Symphony		
1020 Central St Ste 300 . . . . Kansas City MO 64105	**877-829-5590**	816-471-1100
Kennedy Ctr Opera House Orchestra		
John F Kennedy Ctr for the Performing Arts		
2700 F St NW . . . . Washington DC 20566	**800-444-1324**	
Lexington Philharmonic		
161 N Mill St . . . . Lexington KY 40507	**888-494-4226**	859-233-4226
Milwaukee Symphony Orchestra		
929 N Water St Ste 700 . . . . Milwaukee WI 53202	**888-367-8101**	414-220-8322
Minnesota Orchestra		
1111 Nicollet Mall Orchestra Hall . . . . Minneapolis MN 55403	**800-292-4141**	612-371-5600
Modesto Symphony Orchestra		
911 13th St . . . . Modesto CA 95354	**877-488-3380**	209-523-4156
National Symphony Orchestra		
2700 F St NW . . . . Washington DC 20566	**800-444-1324**	202-416-8000

				Toll-Free	Phone
New World Symphony					
500 17th St	Miami Beach	FL	33139	800-597-3331	305-673-3330
Orchestra New England					
PO Box 200123	New Haven	CT	06520	800-595-4849	203-777-4690
Orchestre Symphonique de Montreal					
260 de Maisonneuve Blvd W Second Fl	Montreal	QC	H2X1Y9	888-842-9951	514-842-9951
Oregon Symphony Orchestra					
921 SW Washington St Ste 200	Portland	OR	97205	800-228-7343	503-228-4294
Phoenix Symphony					
One N First St Ste 200	Phoenix	AZ	85004	800-776-9080	602-495-1117
Pittsburgh Symphony Orchestra					
600 Penn Ave					
Heinz Hall for the Performing Arts	Pittsburgh	PA	15222	800-743-8560	412-566-7366
Portland Baroque Orchestra					
1020 SW Taylor St Ste 200	Portland	OR	97205	800-494-8497	503-222-6000
River City Brass Band Inc					
500 Grant St Ste 2720	Pittsburgh	PA	15219	800-292-7222	412-434-7222
Saint Louis Symphony Orchestra					
718 N Grand Blvd	Saint Louis	MO	63103	800-232-1880	314-533-2500
Santa Fe Symphony Orchestra & Chorus Inc					
551 W Cordova Rd Ste D Ste D	Santa Fe	NM	87505	800-480-1319	505-983-3530
Sarasota Orchestra					
709 N Tamiami Trl	Sarasota	FL	34236	866-508-0611	941-953-4252
South Bend Symphony Orchestra (SBSO)					
127 N Michigan St	South Bend	IN	46601	800-537-6415	574-232-6343
Spokane Symphony PO Box 365	Spokane	WA	99210	800-899-1482	509-624-1200
Symphony Nova Scotia					
6101 University Ave					
Dalhousie Arts Ctr.	Halifax	NS	B3H4R2	800-874-1669	902-494-3820
Toledo Symphony					
1838 Parkwood Ave	Toledo	OH	43604	800-348-1253	419-246-8000
Vermont Symphony Orchestra					
Two Church St Ste 19.	Burlington	VT	05401	800-876-9293	802-864-5741
Virginia Symphony Orchestra					
861 Glenrock Rd Ste 200	Norfolk	VA	23502	855-876-7677	757-466-3060
Westchester Philharmonic					
123 Main St Lobby Level	White Plains	NY	10601	800-553-0031	914-682-3707
Wheeling Symphony Orchestra					
1025 Main St Ste 811.	Wheeling	WV	26003	800-395-9241	304-232-6191

570-4 Theater Companies

				Toll-Free	Phone
A Contemporary Theatre (ACT)					
700 Union St Kreielsheimer Pl	Seattle	WA	98101	888-584-4849	206-292-7660
Actors Theatre of Louisville					
316 W Main St	Louisville	KY	40202	800-428-5849	502-584-1205
Alabama Shakespeare Festival					
One Festival Dr	Montgomery	AL	36117	800-841-4273	334-271-5300
Corn Stock Theatre					
1700 Pk Rd	Peoria	IL	61604	800-220-1185	309-676-2196
Goodspeed Musicals					
PO Box A	East Haddam	CT	06423	800-262-8721	860-873-8664
Guthrie Theater					
818 S Second St	Minneapolis	MN	55415	877-447-8243*	612-377-2224
*Resv					
Maltz Jupiter Theatre					
1001 E Indiantown Rd	Jupiter	FL	33477	800-445-1666	561-743-2666
Nebraska Repertory Theatre					
12th & R Sts 215 Temple Bldg	Lincoln	NE	68588	800-432-3231	402-472-2072
Northlight Theatre					
9501 Skokie Blvd	Skokie	IL	60077	800-356-9377	847-673-6300
Omaha Community Playhouse					
6915 Cass St	Omaha	NE	68132	888-782-4338	402-553-0800
Pacific Repertory Theater					
PO Box 222035	Carmel	CA	93922	866-622-0709	831-622-0700
Pasadena Playhouse, The					
39 S El Molino Ave	Pasadena	CA	91101	800-733-2767	626-356-7529
People's Light & Theatre Co					
39 Conestoga Rd	Malvern	PA	19355	800-732-0999	610-647-1900
Perseverance Theatre					
914 Third St	Douglas	AK	99824	855-462-8497	907-364-2421
Pittsburgh Public Theater					
621 Penn Ave	Pittsburgh	PA	15222	800-732-0999	412-316-8200
Sacramento Theatre Co					
1419 H St	Sacramento	CA	95814	888-478-2849	916-443-6722
Seattle Repertory Theatre (SRT)					
155 Mercer St PO Box 900923	Seattle	WA	98109	877-900-9285	206-443-2210
Shakespeare Theatre					
516 Eigth St SE	Washington	DC	20003	877-487-8849	202-547-3230
Theatre For A New Audience					
154 Christopher St Ste 3D	New York	NY	10014	866-811-4111	212-229-2819
Theatre IV 114 W Broad St	Richmond	VA	23220	800-235-8687	804-783-1688
Tihati Productions Ltd					
3615 Harding Ave Ste 507	Honolulu	HI	96816	877-846-5554	808-735-0292
Wilma Theater					
265 S Broad St	Philadelphia	PA	19107	800-732-0999	215-893-9456
Yale Repertory Theatre					
1120 Chapel St PO Box 1257	New Haven	CT	06505	800-973-2837	203-432-1234

571	PERFUMES	

SEE ALSO Cosmetics, Skin Care, and Other Personal Care Products

				Toll-Free	Phone
Avon Products Inc					
1345 Ave of the Americas	New York	NY	10017	800-367-2866*	212-282-7000
NYSE: AVP ■ *Cust Svc					
Chanel Inc 15 E 57th St	New York	NY	10022	800-550-0005	212-355-5050
Crabtree & Evelyn Ltd					
102 Peake Brook Rd	Woodstock	CT	06281	800-272-2873	860-928-2761
Eagle Marketing Inc Perfume Originals Products Div					
2412 Sequoia Pk	Yukon	OK	73099	800-233-7424	
Elizabeth Arden Inc					
2400 NE 145th Ave 2nd Fl	Miramar	FL	33027	800-326-7337	954-364-6900
NASDAQ: RDEN					

				Toll-Free	Phone
Key West Aloe					
13095 N Telecom Pkwy	Tampa	FL	33637	800-445-2563	305-293-1885
Parfums de Coeur Ltd					
85 Old Kings Hwy N	Darien	CT	06820	800-887-2738	
ULTA Beauty					
1000 Remington Blvd Ste 120	Bolingbrook	IL	60440	866-983-8582	630-410-4800

572	PERSONAL EMERGENCY RESPONSE SYSTEMS	

				Toll-Free	Phone
AlertOne Services Inc					
1000 Commerce Park Dr Ste 300	Williamsport	PA	17701	866-581-4540*	
*Cust Svc					
Life Alert					
16027 Ventura Blvd	Encino	CA	91436	800-920-3410	818-700-7000
Life Technologies Corp					
3175 Staley Rd	Grand Island	NY	14072	800-955-6288	
LifeFone					
16 Yellowstone Ave	White Plains	NY	10607	888-687-0451	

573	PERSONAL PROTECTIVE EQUIPMENT & CLOTHING	

SEE ALSO Safety Equipment - Mfr ; Safety Equipment - Whol ; Sporting Goods ; Medical Supplies - Mfr

				Toll-Free	Phone
Aearo Co					
5457 W 79th St	Indianapolis	IN	46268	877-327-4332	317-692-6666
Allen-Vanguard Corp					
2400 St Laurent Blvd	Ottawa	ON	K1G5B4	800-644-9078	613-739-9646
Ansell Healthcare Inc					
111 S Wood Ave Ste 200	Iselin	NJ	08830	800-365-2282	732-345-5400
Bell Sports Corp					
6225 N St Hwy 161 Ste 300	Irving	TX	75038	866-525-2357	469-417-6600
Biomarine Inc					
456 Creamery Way	Exton	PA	19341	800-378-2287	610-524-8800
Bullard Co					
1898 Safety Way	Cynthiana	KY	41031	800-227-0423	859-234-6611
David Clark Company Inc					
360 Franklin St	Worcester	MA	01615	800-298-6235*	508-751-5800
*Cust Svc					
Encon Safety Products Co					
6825 W Sam Houston Pkwy N PO Box 3826	Houston	TX	77041	800-283-6266	713-466-1449
Fibre-Metal					
2000 Plainfield Pk PO Box 248.	Cranston	RI	02921	800-430-4110	
Fire-End & Croker Corp					
Seven Westchester Plz	Elmsford	NY	10523	800-759-3473	914-592-3640
Galls Inc 2680 Palumbo Dr	Lexington	KY	40509	800-477-7766	859-266-7227
General Econopak Inc					
1725 N Sixth St	Philadelphia	PA	19122	888-871-8568	215-763-8200
Globe Mfg Co					
37 Loudon Rd PO Box 128.	Pittsfield	NH	03263	800-232-8323	603-435-8323
Graham Medical Products					
2273 Larsen Rd	Green Bay	WI	54303	800-558-6765*	920-494-8701
*Cust Svc					
Handgards Inc					
901 Hawkins Blvd	El Paso	TX	79915	800-351-8161	
HeatMax Inc					
513 Hill Rd PO Box 1191	Dalton	GA	30721	800-432-8629	706-226-1800
Honeywell Safety Products					
2000 Plainfield Pike	Cranston	RI	02921	800-430-4110*	401-943-4400
*Cust Svc					
ILC Dover Inc					
One Moonwalker Rd	Frederica	DE	19946	800-631-9567	302-335-3911
Kappler Inc					
115 Grimes Dr PO Box 490	Guntersville	AL	35976	800-600-4019	256-505-4005
Lakeland Industries Inc					
701-7 Koehler Ave	Ronkonkoma	NY	11779	800-645-9291	631-981-9700
NASDAQ: LAKE					
Landauer Inc					
Two Science Rd	Glenwood	IL	60425	800-323-8830	708-755-7000
NYSE: LDR					
Little Rapids Corp					
2273 Larsen Rd	Green Bay	WI	54303	800-496-3040	920-496-3040
Louis M Gerson Company Inc					
15 Sproat St	Middleboro	MA	02346	800-225-8623	508-947-4000
MCR Safety 5321 E Shelby Dr	Memphis	TN	38118	800-955-6887	901-795-5810
Medline Industries Inc					
1 Medline Pl	Mundelein	IL	60060	800-351-1512*	847-949-5500
*Cust Svc					
Miller Products Company Inc					
2511 S Tricenter Blvd	Durham	NC	27713	800-782-7437	919-313-2100
Moldex Metric Inc					
10111 W Jefferson Blvd	Culver City	CA	90232	800-421-0668	310-837-6500
MTS Safety Products Inc (MTS)					
PO Box 204	Golden	MS	38847	800-647-8168*	
*General					
National Safety Apparel Inc (NSA)					
3865 W 150th St	Cleveland	OH	44111	800-553-0672	
Newtex Industries Inc					
8050 Victor Mendon Rd	Victor	NY	14564	800-836-1001	585-924-9135
Plastic Safety Systems Inc					
2444 Baldwin Rd	Cleveland	OH	44104	800-662-6338	
PolyConversions Inc					
505 Condit Dr	Rantoul	IL	61866	888-893-3330	217-893-3330
Precept Medical Products Inc					
370 Airport Rd PO Box 2400	Arden	NC	28704	800-851-4431	828-681-0209
Saf-T-Gard International Inc					
205 Huehl Rd	Northbrook	IL	60062	800-548-4273	847-291-1600
Safe-T-Gard Corp					
12105 W Cedar Dr	Lakewood	CO	80228	800-356-9026*	303-763-8900
*Cust Svc					
Scott Health & Safety					
4320 Goldmine Rd PO Box 569	Monroe	NC	28110	800-247-7257	704-291-8300
Seattle Manufacturing Corp					
6930 Salashan Pkwy	Ferndale	WA	98248	800-426-6251	360-366-5534

			Toll-Free	Phone
Sellstrom Manufacturing Co				
2050 Hammond Dr	Schaumburg IL	60173	800-323-7402	847-358-2000
Standard Textile Company Inc				
One Knollcrest Dr	Cincinnati OH	45237	800-999-0400	513-761-9255
Steel Grip Inc				
700 Garfield St PO Box 747	Danville IL	61832	800-223-1595	217-442-6240
Steele Inc				
26112 Iowa Ave NE PO Box 7304	Kingston WA	98346	888-783-3538	360-297-4555
Steiner Industries				
5801 N Tripp Ave	Chicago IL	60646	800-621-4515	773-588-3444
Strong Enterprises Inc				
11236 Satellite Blvd	Orlando FL	32837	800-344-6319	407-859-9317
Tingley Rubber Corp				
1551 S Washington Ave Ste 403				
Ste 403	Piscataway NJ	08854	800-631-5498*	
*Cust Svc				
United Pioneer Co				
2777 Summer St Ste 206	Stamford CT	06905	800-466-9823	
Uvex Safety Inc				
900 Douglas Pk	Smithfield RI	02917	800-682-0839*	
*General				
White Knight Engineered Products				
9525 Monroe Rd Ste 100	Charlotte NC	28270	888-743-4700	704-542-6876
Wolf X-Ray Corp				
100 W Industry Ct	Deer Park NY	11729	800-356-9729*	631-242-9729
*Cust Svc				

574
PEST CONTROL SERVICES

			Toll-Free	Phone
Al Hoffer's Pest Protection Inc				
12329 NW 35 St	Coral Springs FL	33065	866-549-7987	
Copesan Services Inc				
W175 N5711 Technology Dr	Menomonee Falls WI	53051	800-267-3726	
Fischer Environmental Service Inc				
1980 Surgi Dr	Mandeville LA	70448	800-391-2565	
Home Paramount Pest Control Cos Inc				
PO Box 850	Forest Hill MD	21050	888-888-4663	410-510-0700
Horizon Termite & Pest Control Corp				
45 Cross Ave	Midland Park NJ	07432	888-612-2847	201-447-2530
Knockout Pest Control Inc				
1009 Front St	Uniondale NY	11553	800-244-7378	516-489-7817
Lawn Doctor Inc 142 SR 34	Holmdel NJ	07733	800-631-5660	
Massey Services Inc				
315 Groveland St E	Orlando FL	32804	888-262-7739	407-645-2500
McCall Service Inc				
2861 College St	Jacksonville FL	32205	800-342-6948	904-389-5561
NaturaLawn of America Inc				
One E Church St	Frederick MD	21701	800-989-5444	301-694-5440
Orkin Exterminating Co Inc				
2170 Piedmont Rd NE	Atlanta GA	30324	844-498-7458	877-250-1652
Presto-X Co				
10421 Portal Rd Ste 101	Gretna NE	68028	800-759-1942	
Schendel Pest Services				
1035 SE Quincy St	Topeka KS	66612	800-591-7378	785-232-9357
Scotts Lawn Service				
14111 Scottslawn Rd	Marysville OH	43040	888-270-3714*	937-644-0011
*Cust Svc				
Smithereen Exterminators Inc				
7400 N Melvina Ave	Niles IL	60714	800-336-3500	847-647-0010
Spring-Green Lawn Care Corp				
11909 Spaulding School Dr	Plainfield IL	60585	800-435-4051	815-436-8777
Terminix International Company LP				
860 Ridge Lk Blvd	Memphis TN	38120	866-399-0453	
TruGreen ChemLawn				
860 Ridge Lk Blvd	Memphis TN	38120	866-369-9539	
Truly Nolen of America Inc				
3636 E Speedway Blvd	Tucson AZ	85716	800-468-7859	800-528-3442
Waltham Services Inc				
817 Moody St	Waltham MA	02453	866-974-7378	781-893-1810
Western Exterminator Co				
305 N Crescent Way	Anaheim CA	92801	800-698-2440	714-517-9000

PESTICIDES

575
PET PRODUCTS

SEE ALSO Leather Goods - Personal ; Livestock & Poultry Feeds - Prepared

			Toll-Free	Phone
Arctic Glacier Holdings Inc				
625 Henry Ave	Winnipeg MB	R3A0V1	888-573-9237	204-772-2473
Bailey Farms LLC				
549 Karem Dr	Marshall WI	53559	800-655-1705	608-655-3439
BioZyme Inc				
6010 Stockyards Expy	Saint Joseph MO	64504	800-821-3070	816-238-3326
Clorox Co 1221 Broadway	Oakland CA	94612	800-424-9300*	510-271-7000
NYSE: CLX ■ *Cust Svc				
Companion Pets Inc (CPI)				
2001 N Black Canyon Hwy	Phoenix AZ	85009	800-646-3611	602-255-0166
Doctors Foster & Smith Inc				
2253 Air Pk Rd PO Box 100	Rhinelander WI	54501	800-826-7206	715-369-3305
Doskocil Mfg Company Inc				
PO Box 1246	Arlington TX	76004	877-738-6283	
Eagle Pack Pet Foods Inc				
200 Ames Pond Dr	Tewksbury MA	01876	800-255-5959	574-259-7834
Efficas Inc				
7007 Winchester Cir Ste 120	Boulder CO	80301	866-446-0388	303-381-2070
FL Emmert Co Inc				
2007 Dunlap St	Cincinnati OH	45214	800-441-3343	513-721-5808
Hartz Mountain Corp, The				
400 Plz Dr	Secaucus NJ	07094	800-275-1414	
Healthy Pet				
6960 Salashan Pkwy	Ferndale WA	98248	800-242-2287	360-734-7415

			Toll-Free	Phone
Hill's Pet Nutrition Inc				
400 SW Eigth St	Topeka KS	66603	800-569-7913*	785-354-8523
*General				
IAMS Co 3700 Ohio 65	Leipsic OH	45856	800-675-3849*	419-943-4267
*Cust Svc				
Jeffers Inc				
310 W Saunders Rd PO Box 100	Dothan AL	36301	800-533-3377	334-793-6257
John A Van Den Bosch Co				
4511 Holland Ave	Holland MI	49424	800-968-6477	
Joy Dog Food				
PO Box 305	Pinckneyville IL	62274	800-245-4125	
Kaytee Products Inc				
521 Clay St	Chilton WI	53014	800-669-9580	920-849-2321
Manna Pro Corp				
707 Spirit 40 Pk Dr Ste 150	Chesterfield MO	63005	800-690-9908	
Mark Hershey Farms Inc				
479 Horseshoe Pk	Lebanon PA	17042	888-801-3301	717-867-4624
Mars Snack Food				
800 High St	Hackettstown NJ	07840	800-551-0895	908-852-1000
MIDWEST Homes for Pets				
3142 S Cowan Rd PO Box 1031	Muncie IN	47302	800-428-8560	765-289-3355
Moyer & Son Inc				
113 E Reliance Rd	Souderton PA	18964	866-669-3747	215-799-2000
Multipet International Inc				
265 W Commercial Ave	Moonachie NJ	07074	800-900-6738	201-438-6600
Natural Life Pet Products Inc				
205 E 29th St	Pittsburg KS	66762	800-367-2391	620-230-0888
Nealanders International Inc				
6980 Creditview Rd	Mississauga ON	L5N8E2	800-263-1939	905-812-7300
Nestle Purina PetCare Co				
801 Chouteau Ave	Saint Louis MO	63102	800-778-7462	314-982-1000
North States Industries Inc				
1507 92nd Ln NE	Blaine MN	55449	800-848-8421	763-486-1756
Orrco Inc				
515 Collins Blvd PO Box 147	Orrville OH	44667	800-321-3085	330-683-5015
Penn-Plax Inc				
35 Marcus Blvd	Hauppauge NY	11788	800-645-6055	631-273-3787
Pet Safe International				
10427 Electric Ave	Knoxville TN	37932	800-732-2677*	865-777-5404
*Cust Svc				
Pet Supermarket Inc				
1100 International Pkwy	Sunrise FL	33323	866-434-1990	954-351-0834
Pet Valu Canada Inc				
225 Royal Crest Crt	Markham ON	L3R9X6	800-845-4759	905-946-1200
PETCO Animal Supplies Inc				
9125 Rehco Rd	San Diego CA	92121	877-738-6742	858-453-7845
PetFoodDirect.com				
189 Main St	Harleysville PA	19438	877-738-3663*	215-513-1999
*Cust Svc				
Petland Inc				
250 Riverside St	Chillicothe OH	45601	800-221-5935	740-775-2464
PetMed Express Inc				
1441 SW 29th Ave	Pompano Beach FL	33069	800-738-6337	954-979-5995
NASDAQ: PETS				
PETsMART Inc				
19601 N 27th Ave	Phoenix AZ	85027	800-738-1385*	623-580-6100
NASDAQ: PETM ■ *Cust Svc				
Prevue Pet Products Inc				
224 N Maplewood Ave	Chicago IL	60612	800-243-3624	312-243-3624
Prince Corp				
8351 County Rd H	Marshfield WI	54449	800-777-2486	715-384-3105
Ralco Nutrition Inc				
1600 Hahn Rd	Marshall MN	56258	800-533-5306	
Rolf C. Hagen Corp				
305 Forbes Blvd	Mansfield MA	02048	800-724-2436*	508-339-9531
*Cust Svc				
Simmons Pet Foods Inc				
316 N Hico	Siloam Springs AR	72761	866-463-6738	
Star Milling Co				
24067 Water St	Perris CA	92570	800-733-6455	951-657-3143
Sunshine Mills Inc				
500 Sixth St SW	Red Bay AL	35582	800-633-3349	256-356-9541
Texas Farm Products Co				
915 S Fredonia St	Nacogdoches TX	75964	800-392-3110	936-564-3711
Triumph Pet Industries Inc				
500 Sixth St SW	Red Bay AL	35582	800-633-3349	256-356-9541
United Pacific Pet				
12060 Cabernet Dr	Fontana CA	92337	800-979-3333	951-360-8550
United Pharmacal Company of Missouri Inc				
3705 Pear St	Saint Joseph MO	64503	800-254-8726	816-233-8800
Wild Birds Unlimited Inc				
11711 N College Ave Ste 146	Carmel IN	46032	800-326-4928	317-571-7100

576
PETROLEUM & PETROLEUM PRODUCTS - WHOL

			Toll-Free	Phone
Allied Oil & Supply Inc				
2209 S 24th St	Omaha NE	68108	800-333-3717	402-344-4343
Atlas Oil Co 24501 Ecorse Rd	Taylor MI	48180	800-878-2000	313-292-5500
Boyett Petroleum				
601 McHenry Ave	Modesto CA	95350	800-545-9212	209-577-6000
BP Lubricants USA Inc				
1500 Valley Rd	Wayne NJ	07470	800-333-3991	973-633-2200
Bretthauer Oil Co				
453 SW Washington St	Hillsboro OR	97123	800-359-3113	503-648-2531
Campbell Oil Company Inc				
611 Erie St S	Massillon OH	44646	800-589-8555	330-833-8555
Cargill Energy				
PO Box 9300	Minneapolis MN	55440	800-227-4455	952-742-7575
Carson Oil Company Inc				
3125 NW 35th Ave PO Box 10948	Portland OR	97296	800-998-7767	503-224-8500
Condon Oil Co				
126 E Jackson St	Ripon WI	54971	800-452-1212	920-748-3186
Consolidated Energy Co				
910 Main St PO Box 317	Jesup IA	50648	800-338-3021	319-827-1211
Dickey Transport				
401 E Fourth St	Packwood IA	52580	800-247-1081	319-695-3601

Petroleum & Petroleum Products - Whol (Cont'd)

				Toll-Free	Phone
Drake Petroleum Co Inc 221 Quinebaug Rd PO Box 866	North Grosvenordale	CT	06255	800-243-6366	
Earhart Petroleum Inc 1494 Lytle Rd	Troy	OH	45373	800-686-2928	937-335-2928
Englefield Oil Co 447 James Pkwy *Cust Svc	Heath	OH	43056	800-837-4458*	740-928-8215
Federated Co-ops Inc 502 S Second St	Princeton	MN	55371	800-638-8228	763-389-2582
Gassco 7515 Lindsay Rd	Bakersfield	CA	93313	800-390-7837	661-832-7406
Gate Petroleum Co 9540 San Jose Blvd PO Box 23627	Jacksonville	FL	32241	866-571-1982	904-737-7220
Global Partners LP 800 S St Ste 200 NYSE: GLP	Waltham	MA	02454	800-685-7222	781-894-8800
Gulf Oil LP 100 Crossing Blvd	Framingham	MA	01702	800-256-4853	508-270-8300
JH Williams Oil Company Inc 1237 E Twiggs St	Tampa	FL	33602	800-683-0536	813-228-7776
Johnson Oil Co (JOC) 1113 E Sara DeWitt Dr	Gonzales	TX	78629	800-284-2432	830-672-9574
Lanman Oil Co Inc PO Box 108	Charleston	IL	61920	800-677-2819	
Leffler Energy Inc 15 Mt Joy St	Mount Joy	PA	17552	800-984-1411	
Licking Valley Oil Inc PO Box 246	Butler	KY	41006	800-899-9449	859-472-7111
Main-Care Energy PO Box 11029	Albany	NY	12211	800-542-5552	
Maritime Energy Inc 234 Pk St PO Box 485	Rockland	ME	04841	800-333-4489	207-594-4487
Martin Eagle Oil Company Inc 2700 James St	Denton	TX	76205	800-316-6148	940-383-2351
Martin Midstream Partners LP 4200 Stone Rd NASDAQ: MMLP	Kilgore	TX	75662	800-256-6644	903-983-6200
Miller Oil Co 1000 E City Hall Ave	Norfolk	VA	23504	800-333-4645	757-623-6600
National Oil & Gas Inc 409 N Main St	Bluffton	IN	46714	800-322-8454	260-824-2220
NOCO Energy Corp 2440 Sheridan Dr	Tonawanda	NY	14150	800-500-6626	716-833-6626
Orange Line Oil Company Inc 404 E Commercial St	Pomona	CA	91767	800-492-6864	909-623-0533
PetroLiance LLC 739 N State St	Elgin	IL	60123	800-628-7231	877-738-7699
Pro Petroleum Inc 4985 N Sloan Ln	Las Vegas	NV	89115	877-791-4900	
R K Allen Oil Inc 36002 AL Hwy 21	Talladega	AL	35161	800-445-5823	256-362-4261
R Kidd Fuels Corp 1172 Twinney Dr	Newmarket	ON	L3Y9E2	866-274-2315	
Ramos Oil Company Inc 1515 S River Rd *Cust Svc	West Sacramento	CA	95691	800-477-7266*	916-371-2570
Reeder Distributors Inc 5450 Wilbarger St	Fort Worth	TX	76119	800-722-3103	817-429-5957
Retif Oil & Fuel Inc 527 Destrehan Ave PO Box 52679	Harvey	LA	70058	800-349-9000	504-349-9000
Rex Oil Co Inc 814 & 1000 Lexington Ave	Thomasville	NC	27360	800-843-0572	336-472-3368
Senergy Petroleum LLC 622 S 56th Ave	Phoenix	AZ	85043	800-964-0076	602-272-6795
Sierra Energy 1020 Winding Creek Rd Ste 100	Roseville	CA	95678	800-576-2264	916-218-1600
Sinclair Marketing 550 E S Temple St	Salt Lake City	UT	84102	800-325-3265	801-524-2700
Southern Maryland Oil Co Inc (SMO) 109 N Maple Ave	La Plata	MD	20646	888-222-3720	
Spencer Cos Inc 120 Woodson St PO Box 18128	Huntsville	AL	35801	800-633-2910	256-533-1150
Sprague Energy 185 International Dr Ste 200	Portsmouth	NH	03801	800-225-1560	603-431-1000
Stern Oil Company Inc PO Box 218	Freeman	SD	57029	800-477-2744	605-925-7999
Sun Coast Resources Inc 6922 Cavalcade St	Houston	TX	77028	800-677-3835	713-429-8492
Taylor Enterprises Inc (TEI) 2586 Southport Rd	Spartanburg	SC	29302	800-922-3149	864-573-9518
Technical Gas Products Inc 66 Leonardo Dr	North Haven	CT	06473	800-847-0745	
Tesoro Corp 1225 17th Street	Denver	CO	80202	800-299-0570	
Texas Enterprises Inc 5005 E Seventh St	Austin	TX	78702	800-545-4412	512-385-2167
Titan Laboratories 1380 Zuni St PO Box 40567	Denver	CO	80204	800-848-4826	
Tower Sales Inc 936 E Grand Ave PO Box 36	Tower City	PA	17980	800-839-1849	717-647-2100
Tulco Oils Inc 5240 E Pine PO Box 582410	Tulsa	OK	74115	800-375-2347	918-838-3354
Turner Gas Company Inc PO Box 26554	Salt Lake City	UT	84126	800-932-4277	801-973-6886
Ullman Oil Inc PO Box 23399	Chagrin Falls	OH	44023	800-543-5195	440-543-5195
Valor Oil 1200 Alsop Ln	Owensboro	KY	42303	800-544-5823	270-683-2461
Vesco Oil Corp 16055 W 12-Mile Rd	Southfield	MI	48076	800-527-5358	
Warren Oil Company Inc PO Box 1507	Dunn	NC	28335	800-779-6456	910-892-6456
Western Petroleum Co 9531 W 78th St	Eden Prairie	MN	55344	800-972-3835	952-941-9090
Western States Petroleum Inc 450 S 15th Ave	Phoenix	AZ	85007	800-220-1353	602-252-4011
World Fuel Services Corp 9800 NW 41st St Ste 400 NYSE: INT	Miami	FL	33178	800-345-3818	305-428-8000

577   PETROLEUM REFINERIES

				Toll-Free	Phone
A H Belo Corp 508 Young St PO Box 224866 NYSE: AHC	Dallas	TX	75202	800-230-1074	214-977-8200
Allegheny Petroleum Products Co 999 Airbrake Ave	Wilmerding	PA	15148	800-600-2900	412-829-1990
BP PLC 28100 Torch Pkwy NYSE: BP	Warrenville	IL	60555	877-638-5672	630-420-5111
Calumet Lubricants Co 2780 Waterfront Pkwy Dr E Ste 200	Indianapolis	IN	46214	800-437-3188	317-328-5660
Calumet Specialty Products Partners LP 2780 Waterfront Pkwy E Dr Ste 200 NASDAQ: CLMT	Indianapolis	IN	46214	800-437-3188	317-328-5660
Chevron Canada Ltd 1200 - 1050 W Pender St	Vancouver	BC	V6E3T4	800-663-1650	604-668-5300
Chevron Corp 6001 Bollinger Canyon Rd NYSE: CVX ■ *Cust Svc	San Ramon	CA	94583	800-243-8766*	925-842-1000
CITGO Petroleum Corp 1293 Eldridge Pkwy	Houston	TX	77077	800-424-9300	832-486-4700
Cross Oil Refining & Marketing Inc 484 E Sixth St	Smackover	AR	71762	800-725-3066	870-881-8700
Ergon Refining 2611 Haining Rd	Vicksburg	MS	39183	877-888-9758	601-933-3000
Exxon Mobil Corp 5959 Las Colinas Blvd NYSE: XOM	Irving	TX	75039	800-252-1800	972-444-1000
Imperial Oil Resources Ltd 237 Fourth Ave SW PO Box 2480 Stn M	Calgary	AB	T2P3M9	800-567-3776	
International Group Inc 85 Old Eagle School Rd	Wayne	PA	19087	800-852-6537	610-687-9030
Motiva Enterprises LLC 700 Milam St	Houston	TX	77002	877-668-4825	713-277-8000
Murphy Oil Corp 200 Peach St	El Dorado	AR	71730	888-289-9314	870-862-6411
SEMCO ENERGY Gas Co 1411 Third St Ste A	Port Huron	MI	48060	800-624-2019	
Sunoco Inc 1735 Market St Ste LL NYSE: SUN	Philadelphia	PA	19103	800-786-6261	215-977-3000

578   PETROLEUM STORAGE TERMINALS

				Toll-Free	Phone
Cary Oil Company Inc 110 Mackenan Dr PO Box 5189	Cary	NC	27511	800-227-9645	919-462-1100
Central Crude Inc 4187 Hwy 3059 PO Box 1863	Lake Charles	LA	70602	800-245-8408	337-436-1000
CHS Inc 3520 E River Rd PO Box 6878	Rochester	MN	55903	888-254-0632	507-289-4086
Jack Becker Distributors Inc 6800 Suemac Pl	Jacksonville	FL	32254	800-488-8411	
Magellan Midstream Partners LP One Williams Ctr NYSE: MMP	Tulsa	OK	74172	800-574-6671	918-574-7000

579   PHARMACEUTICAL & DIAGNOSTIC PRODUCTS - VETERINARY

				Toll-Free	Phone
Abbott Laboratories Animal Health Div 1401 Sheridan Rd	North Chicago	IL	60064	888-299-7416	847-937-6100
Addison Biological Laboratory Inc 507 N Cleveland Ave	Fayette	MO	65248	800-331-2530	660-248-2215
Alltech Inc 3031 Catnip Hill Pike	Nicholasville	KY	40356	800-289-8324	859-885-9613
Bimeda-MTC Animal Health Inc 420 Beaverdale Rd	Cambridge	ON	N3C2W4	888-524-6332	519-654-8000
Bio-Serv 3 Foster Lane Suite 201	Flemington	NJ	08822	800-996-9908	908-284-2155
Bioniche Life Sciences Inc. 231 Dundas St E TSE: BNC	Belleville	ON	K8N1E2	800-265-5464	613-966-8058
Biovet Inc 4375 Ave Beaudry	Saint-Hyacinthe	QC	J2S8W2	888-824-6838	450-771-7291
Biovet USA Inc 9025 Penn Ave S Ste 100	Minneapolis	MN	55431	877-824-6838	952-884-3113
Boehringer Ingelheim Vetmedica Inc 2621 N Belt Hwy	Saint Joseph	MO	64506	800-821-7467	816-233-2571
Cut-Heal Animal Care Products Inc 923 S Cedar Hill Rd	Cedar Hill	TX	75104	800-288-4325	972-293-9700
Darby Group Cos Inc 300 Jericho Quad	Jericho	NY	11753	888-683-5001	516-683-1800
Delmont Laboratories Inc 715 Harvard Ave PO Box 269	Swarthmore	PA	19081	800-562-5541	610-543-3365
DMS Laboratories Inc Two Darts Mill Rd	Flemington	NJ	08822	800-567-4367	908-782-3353
Dominion Veterinary Laboratories Inc 1199 Sanford St	Winnipeg	MB	R3E3A1	800-465-7122	204-589-7361
Elanco Animal Health 2500 Innovation Way	Greenfield	IN	46140	877-352-6261	317-276-2000
Heska Corp 3760 Rocky Mtn Ave NASDAQ: HSKA	Loveland	CO	80538	800-464-3752	970-493-7272
IMMVAC Inc 6080 Bass Ln	Columbia	MO	65201	800-944-7563	573-443-5363
King Bio Pharmaceuticals Inc Three Westside Dr	Asheville	NC	28806	800-543-3245	828-255-0201
Lake Immunogenics Inc 348 Berg Rd	Ontario	NY	14519	800-648-9990	

	Toll-Free	Phone

Lloyd Inc
604 W Thomas Ave PO Box 130 . . . . .Shenandoah IA 51601   **800-831-0004**   712-246-4000

Luitpold Pharmaceuticals Inc
One Luitpold Dr PO Box 9001 . . . . .Shirley NY 11967   **800-645-1706**   631-924-4000

Merial Ltd
3239 Satellite Blvd Bldg 500 . . . . .Duluth GA 30096   **888-637-4251**   678-638-3000

MVP Laboratories Inc
4805 G St . . . . .Omaha NE 68117   **800-856-4648**   402-331-5106

Nutra-Blend Inc
3200 Second St . . . . .Neosho MO 64850   **800-657-5657**

Pfizer Inc Animal Health Group
235 E 42nd St . . . . New York NY 10017   **800-879-3477**   212-573-2323

Renco Corp
116 Third Ave N . . . . .Minneapolis MN 55401   **800-359-8181**   612-338-6124

Texas Vet Lab Inc
1702 N Bell St . . . . .San Angelo TX 76903   **800-284-8403**

Veterinary Pharmacies of America Inc
2854 Antoine Dr . . . . .Houston TX 77092   **877-838-7979**

Vetoquinol Canada Inc
2000 Ch Georges . . . . .Lavaltrie QC J5T3S5   **800-363-1700**   450-586-2252

580   PHARMACEUTICAL COMPANIES

SEE ALSO Vitamins & Nutritional Supplements ; Medicinal Chemicals & Botanical Products ; Pharmaceutical & Diagnostic Products - Veterinary ; Pharmaceutical Companies - Generic Drugs ; Biotechnology Companies ; Diagnostic Products

	Toll-Free	Phone

aaiPharma Inc
1726 N 23rd St . . . . .Wilmington NC 28405   **800-575-4224**

Abbott Laboratories Pharmaceutical Products Div
100 Research Dr Bioresearch Ctr . . . . .Worcester MA 01605   **866-427-8477**   847-937-6100

Accucaps Industries Ltd
2125 Ambassador Dr . . . . .Windsor ON N9C3R5   **800-665-7210**   519-969-5404

Allergan Inc 2525 Dupont Dr . . . . .Irvine CA 92612   **800-347-4500**   714-246-4500
NYSE: AGN

Alva-Amco Pharmacal Cos Inc
7711 Merrimac Ave . . . . .Niles IL 60714   **800-792-2582**   847-663-0700

Amneal Pharmaceuticals LLC
75 Adams Ave . . . . .Hauppauge NY 11788   **866-525-7270**   631-952-0214
NYSE: IPAH

Amphastar Pharmaceuticals Inc
11570 Sixth St . . . . .Rancho Cucamonga CA 91730   **800-423-4136**   909-980-9484

Apotex Inc 150 Signet Dr . . . . .Toronto ON M9L1T9   **800-268-4623**   416-749-9300

Apothecus Pharmaceutical Corp
220 Townsend Sq . . . . .Oyster Bay NY 11771   **800-227-2393**   516-624-8200

AstraZeneca Canada Inc
1004 Middlegate Rd .Mississauga ON L4Y1M4   **800-565-5877**   905-277-7111

AstraZeneca Pharmaceuticals LP
1800 Concord Pk PO Box 15437 . . . . .Wilmington DE 19850   **800-236-9933**

Banner Pharmacaps Inc
4100 Mendenhall Oaks Pkwy . . . . .High Point NC 27265   **866-529-2922***   336-812-3442
*Cust Svc

Bausch & Lomb Inc
1400 N Goodman St .Rochester NY 14609   **800-553-5340**   585-338-6000

Bausch & Lomb Pharmaceuticals Inc
8500 Hidden River Pkwy .Tampa FL 33637   **800-323-0000***   800-553-5340
*Cust Svc

Bayer Corp 100 Bayer Rd . . . . .Pittsburgh PA 15205   **800-422-9374**   412-777-2000

Bayer Inc 77 Belfield Rd .Toronto ON M9W1G6   **800-622-2937**   416-248-0771

Berlex Laboratories Inc
Six W Belt . . . . .Wayne NJ 07470   **888-842-2937**   973-694-4100

Blistex Inc 1800 Swift Dr . . . . .Oak Brook IL 60523   **800-837-1800***
*Cust Svc

Boehringer Ingelheim Ltd
5180 S Service Rd . . . . .Burlington ON L7L5H4   **800-263-9107**   905-639-0333

Boehringer Ingelheim Pharmaceuticals Inc
900 Ridgebury Rd . . . . .Ridgefield CT 06877   **800-243-0127**   203-798-9988

Botanical Laboratories Inc
1441 W Smith Rd . . . . .Ferndale WA 98248   **800-232-4005**   360-384-5656

Bristol-Myers Squibb Canada Inc
2344 Alfred-Nobel Blvd Ste 300 . . . . .Montreal QC H4S0A4   **800-267-0005***   514-333-3200
*Cust Svc

Care-Tech Laboratories Inc
3224 S KingsHwy Blvd . . . . .Saint Louis MO 63139   **800-325-9681**   314-772-4610

CB Fleet Co Inc
4615 Murray Pl . . . . .Lynchburg VA 24502   **866-255-6960**   434-528-4000

Chembio Diagnostics Inc
3661 Horseblock Rd . . . . .Medford NY 11763   **844-243-6246**   631-924-1135
NASDAQ: CEMI

Combe Inc
1101 Westchester Ave . . . . .White Plains NY 10604   **800-431-2610**   914-694-5454

Darby Group Cos Inc
300 Jericho Quad . . . . .Jericho NY 11753   **888-683-5001**   516-683-1800

Dickinson Brands Inc
31 E High St . . . . .East Hampton CT 06424   **888-860-2279**   860-267-2279

DPT Laboratories Ltd
318 McCullough . . . . .San Antonio TX 78215   **866-225-5378**   210-476-8150

Dynavax Technologies Corp
2929 Seventh St Ste 100 . . . . .Berkeley CA 94710   **877-848-5100**   510-848-5100
NASDAQ: DVAX

Edwards Lifesciences Corp
One Edwards Way . . . . .Irvine CA 92614   **800-424-3278**   949-250-2500
NYSE: EW

Eisai Inc
100 Tice Blvd . . . . .Woodcliff Lake NJ 07677   **866-613-4724**   201-692-1100

Eli Lilly & Co
Lilly Corporate Ctr .Indianapolis IN 46285   **800-545-5979***   317-276-2000
NYSE: LLY ■ *Prod Info

Eli Lilly Canada Inc
3650 Danforth Ave . . . . .Toronto ON M1N2E8   **888-545-5972**   416-694-3221

Endo Pharmaceuticals Holdings Inc
100 Endo Blvd . . . . .Chadds Ford PA 19317   **800-462-3636***   610-558-9800
*Cust Svc

First Priority Inc
1590 Todd Farm Dr . . . . .Elgin IL 60123   **800-650-4899**   847-289-1600

	Toll-Free	Phone

Forest Pharmaceutical Inc
13600 Shoreline Dr . . . . .Earth City MO 63045   **800-678-1605**   314-493-7000

G & W Laboratories Inc
111 Coolidge St .South Plainfield NJ 07080   **800-922-1038**   908-753-2000

Galderma Laboratories Inc
14501 N Fwy . . . . .Fort Worth TX 76177   **866-735-4137**   817-961-5000

Germiphene Corp
1379 Colborne St E PO Box 1748 . . . . .Brantford ON N3T5M1   **800-265-9931**   519-759-7100

GlaxoSmithKline Inc
7333 Mississauga Rd N . . . . .Mississauga ON L5N6L4   **800-387-7374**   905-819-3000

Halocarbon Products Corp
PO Box 661 . . . . .River Edge NJ 07661   **800-338-5803**   201-262-8899

Hi-Tech Pharmacal Co Inc
369 Bayview Ave . . . . .Amityville NY 11701   **888-628-0581**   631-789-8228
NASDAQ: HITK

Hoffmann-LaRoche Inc
340 Kingsland St . . . . .Nutley NJ 07110   **800-526-6367**   973-235-5000

Hope Pharmaceuticals Inc
16416 N 92nd St Ste 125 . . . . .Scottsdale AZ 85260   **800-755-9595**

Hospira Inc
275 N Field Dr . . . . .Lake Forest IL 60045   **877-946-7747**   224-212-2000
NYSE: HSP

Humco Holding Group Inc
7400 Alumax Dr . . . . .Texarkana TX 75501   **800-662-3435**   903-334-6200

Immtech Pharmaceuticals
One N End Ave . . . . .New York NY 10282   **877-898-8038**   212-791-2911

InterMune Inc
3280 Bayshore Blvd . . . . .Brisbane CA 94005   **877-862-2292**   415-466-2200
NASDAQ: ITMN

Janssen Healthcare Learning Ctr
PO Box 200 . . . . .Titusville NJ 08560   **800-526-7736**

Janssen Pharmaceutica Inc
1125 Trenton-Harbourton Rd . . . . .Titusville NJ 08560   **800-526-7736**   609-730-2000

Janssen-Ortho Inc
19 Green Belt Dr . . . . .Toronto ON M3C1L9   **800-387-8781**   416-449-9444

Jazz Pharmaceuticals Inc
3180 Porter Dr . . . . .Palo Alto CA 94304   **866-997-3688**   650-496-3777

Juniper Pharmaceuticals Inc
354 Eisenhower Pkwy Plaza 1 2nd Fl . . . . . . .Livingston NJ 07039   **866-566-5636**   973-994-3999
NASDAQ: CBRX

Keryx Biopharmaceuticals Inc
750 Lexington Ave 20th Fl . . . . .New York NY 10022   **800-903-0247**   212-531-5965
NASDAQ: KERX

King Bio Pharmaceuticals Inc
Three Westside Dr . . . . .Asheville NC 28806   **800-543-3245**   828-255-0201

Konsyl Pharmaceuticals Inc
8050 Industrial Pk Rd . . . . .Easton MD 21601   **800-356-6795**   410-822-5192

Kramer Laboratories Inc
8778 SW Eigth St . . . . .Miami FL 33174   **800-824-4894**   305-223-1287

Major Pharmaceutical Co
31778 Enterprise Dr . . . . .Livonia MI 48150   **800-875-0123**   734-743-6161

McNeil Consumer & Specialty Pharmaceuticals
7050 Camp Hill Rd . . . . .Fort Washington PA 19034   **800-962-5357**   215-273-7000

Medical Products Laboratories Inc
9990 Global Rd PO Box 14366 . . . . .Philadelphia PA 19115   **800-523-0191**   215-677-2700

Medicis Pharmaceutical Corp
7720 N Dobson Rd . . . . .Scottsdale AZ 85256   **855-396-2084***   800-321-4576
*Cust Svc

Melaleuca Inc
3910 S Yellowstone Hwy . . . . .Idaho Falls ID 83402   **800-282-3000***   208-522-0700
*Sales

Mentholatum Company Inc
707 Sterling Dr . . . . .Orchard Park NY 14127   **800-688-7660**   716-677-2500

Merck & Company Inc
One Merck Dr PO Box 100 . . . . .Whitehouse Station NJ 08889   **800-672-6372***   908-423-1000
NYSE: MRK ■ *Cust Svc

Mikart Inc
1750 Chattahoochee Ave NW . . . . .Atlanta GA 30318   **888-464-5278**   404-351-4510

Mission Pharmacal
PO Box 786099 . . . . .San Antonio TX 78278   **800-531-3333**   210-696-8400

Mylan
2751 Napa Valley Corporate Dr . . . . .Napa CA 94558   **800-527-4278**   707-224-3200

Mylan Pharmaceuticals Inc
781 Chestnut Ridge Rd . . . . .Morgantown WV 26505   **800-796-9526**

Neos Therapeutics
2940 N Hwy 360 Ste 100 . . . . .Grand Prairie TX 75050   **844-375-8324**   972-408-1300

Novartis Pharmaceuticals Canada Inc
385 boul Bouchard . . . . .Dorval QC H9S1A9   **800-465-2244**   514-631-6775

Novartis Pharmaceuticals Co
10401 Cornhusker Hwy .Waverly NE 68462   **888-669-6682**   402-464-6311

Novartis Pharmaceuticals Corp
1 Health Plaza . . . . .East Hanover NJ 07936   **888-669-6682***   862-778-8300
*Cust Svc

Novo Nordisk of North America Inc
100 College Rd W . . . . .Princeton NJ 08540   **800-727-6500**   609-987-5800

Novo Nordisk Pharmaceuticals Inc
800 Scudders Mill Rd . . . . .Princeton NJ 08536   **800-727-6500***   609-987-5800
*Cust Svc

Numark Laboratories Inc
164 Northfield Ave . . . . .Edison NJ 08837   **800-338-8079**

Odor Management Inc
18-6 E Dundee Rd Ste 101 . . . . .Barrington IL 60010   **800-662-6367**   847-304-9111

Particle Dynamics International LLC
2629 S Hanley Rd . . . . .Saint Louis MO 63144   **800-452-4682**   314-968-2376

Pfizer Canada Inc
17300 TransCanada Hwy . . . . .Kirkland QC H9J2M5   **800-463-6001**   514-695-0500

Pfizer Inc 235 E 42nd St . . . . .New York NY 10017   **800-879-3477**   212-733-2323
NYSE: PFE

Procter & Gamble Pharmaceuticals Canada Inc
PO Box 355 Stn A . . . . .Toronto ON M5W1C5   **800-668-0150**   416-730-4711

Prometheus Laboratories Inc
9410 Carroll Pk Dr . . . . .San Diego CA 92121   **888-892-8391**

ProPhase Labs Inc
621 Shady Retreat Rd . . . . .Doylestown PA 18901   **800-505-2653**   215-345-0919
NASDAQ: PRPH

Protide Pharmaceuticals Inc
505 Oakwood Rd Ste 200 . . . . .Lake Zurich IL 60047   **800-552-3569**   847-726-3100

QLT USA Inc
2579 Midpoint Dr . . . . .Fort Collins CO 80525   **800-901-5241**   970-482-5868

	City	State	ZIP	Toll-Free	Phone
Qualicaps Inc 6505 Franz Warner Pkwy	Whitsett	NC	27377	800-227-7853	336-449-3900
Qualitest Pharmaceuticals 130 Vintage Dr	Huntsville	AL	35811	800-444-4011	
Quintiles Canada Inc 100 Alexis-Nihon Ste 800 *General	Saint Laurent	QC	H4M2P4	866-267-4479*	514-855-0888
Quintiles Transnational Corp 4820 Emperor Blvd	Durham	NC	27703	866-267-4479	919-998-2000
Regis Technologies Inc 8210 Austin Ave	Morton Grove	IL	60053	800-323-8144	847-967-6000
Roxane Laboratories Inc 1809 Wilson Rd *Cust Svc	Columbus	OH	43228	800-520-1631*	614-276-4000
Rules-based Medicine Inc 3300 Duval Rd	Austin	TX	78759	866-726-6277	512-835-8026
Salix Pharmaceuticals Inc 8510 Colonnade Ctr Dr *NASDAQ: SLXP*	Raleigh	NC	27615	800-508-0024	919-862-1000
SciClone Pharmaceuticals Inc 950 Tower Ln Ste 900 *NASDAQ: SCLN*	Foster City	CA	94404	800-724-2566	650-358-3456
Sigma-Tau Pharmaceutical Inc 9841 Washingtonian Blvd Ste 500	Gaithersburg	MD	20878	800-447-0169	301-948-1041
Silipos Inc 7049 Williams Rd	Niagara Falls	NY	14304	800-229-4404	716-283-0700
Solvay America Inc 3333 Richmond Ave *General	Houston	TX	77098	800-365-6565*	713-525-6000
Sovereign Pharmaceuticals Ltd 7590 Sand St	Fort Worth	TX	76118	877-248-0228	817-284-0429
SSS Co 71 University Ave PO Box 4447	Atlanta	GA	30315	800-237-3843	404-521-0857
Sucampo Pharmaceuticals Inc 4520 East-West Hwy 3rd Fl Ste 300 *NASDAQ: SCMP*	Bethesda	MD	20814	800-332-1088	301-961-3400
Taro Pharmaceuticals Inc 130 E Dr	Brampton	ON	L6T1C1	800-268-1975	905-791-8276
UCB Pharma Inc 1950 Lake Pk Dr	Smyrna	GA	30080	800-477-7877	770-970-7500
United Therapeutics Corp 1040 Spring St *NASDAQ: UTHR*	Silver Spring	MD	20910	877-864-8437	301-608-9292
Upsher-Smith Laboratories Inc 6701 Evenstad Dr	Maple Grove	MN	55369	800-654-2299	763-315-2000
Vivus Inc 1172 Castro St *NASDAQ: VVUS*	Mountain View	CA	94040	888-367-6873	650-934-5200
WF Young Inc 302 Benton Dr PO Box 1990	East Longmeadow	MA	01028	800-628-9653	413-526-9999
Wright Group, The 6428 Airport Rd	Crowley	LA	70526	800-201-3096	337-783-3096
ZLB Behring LLC 1020 First Ave PO Box 61501	King of Prussia	PA	19406	800-683-1288	610-878-4000
Zogenix Inc 12400 High Bluff Dr Ste 650	San Diego	CA	92130	866-964-3649	858-259-1165

581 PHARMACEUTICAL COMPANIES - GENERIC DRUGS

SEE ALSO Vitamins & Nutritional Supplements ; Medicinal Chemicals & Botanical Products ; Pharmaceutical & Diagnostic Products - Veterinary ; Pharmaceutical Companies ; Biotechnology Companies ; Diagnostic Products

	City	State	ZIP	Toll-Free	Phone
Apotex Corp 2400 N Commerce Pkwy Ste 400	Weston	FL	33326	877-427-6839	
E Fougera & Co 60 Baylis Rd	Melville	NY	11747	800-645-9833	631-454-6996
Glenwood LLC 111 Cedar Ln	Englewood	NJ	07631	800-542-0772	201-569-0050
Healthpoint 3909 Hulen St *Cust Svc	Fort Worth	TX	76107	800-441-8227*	817-900-4000
Impax Laboratories Inc 3735 Castor Ave *NASDAQ: IPXL*	Philadelphia	PA	19124	877-994-6729	215-613-2400
Mericon Industries Inc 8819 N Pioneer Rd	Peoria	IL	61615	800-242-6464	309-693-2150
Morton Grove Pharmaceuticals Inc 6451 Main St	Morton Grove	IL	60053	800-346-6854	847-967-5600
Mylan Pharmaceuticals ULC 85 Advance Rd	Etobicoke	ON	M8Z2S6	800-575-1379	416-236-2631
Nephron Pharmaceuticals Corp 4121 SW 34th St	Orlando	FL	32811	800-443-4313	407-999-2225
NuCare Pharmaceuticals Inc 622 W Katella Ave	Orange	CA	92867	888-482-9545	
Par Pharmaceutical Cos Inc 300 Tice Blvd *NYSE: PRX*	Woodcliff Lake	NJ	07677	800-828-9393	201-802-4000
Par Pharmaceutical Inc One Ram Ridge Rd	Spring Valley	NY	10977	800-828-9393	201-802-4000
Payless Drug Stores Inc 16100 SW 72nd Ave PO Box 230969	Portland	OR	97224	800-330-3665	503-626-9436
Perrigo Co 515 Eastern Ave *NYSE: PRGO*	Allegan	MI	49010	800-719-9260	269-673-8451
Pharmaceutical Calibrations & Instrumentation LLC 8100 Brownleigh Dr Ste 100-A	Raleigh	NC	27617	877-724-2257	
Skilled Care Pharmacy Inc 6175 Hi Tek Ct	Mason	OH	45040	800-334-1624	513-459-7455
Taro Pharmaceuticals USA Inc 3 Skyline Dr	Hawthorne	NY	10532	800-544-1449	914-345-9001
Teva Pharmaceutical USA 1090 Horsham Rd *NYSE: TEVA*	North Wales	PA	19454	800-545-8800	215-591-3000
TruTouch Technologies Inc 73 Carriage Way	Sudbury	MA	01776	866-721-6221	
UDL Laboratories Inc 1718 Northrock Ct	Rockford	IL	61103	800-435-5272	800-848-0462
USL Pharma 301 S Cherokee St	Denver	CO	80223	800-654-2299	303-607-4500
West-Ward Pharmaceutical Corp 401 Industrial Way W *Cust Svc	Eatontown	NJ	07724	800-631-2174*	732-542-1191
X-Gen Pharmaceuticals Inc 300 Daniels Zenker Dr PO Box 445	Horseheads	NY	14845	866-390-4411	

582 PHARMACY ASSOCIATIONS - STATE

SEE ALSO Health & Medical Professionals Associations

	City	State	ZIP	Toll-Free	Phone
Alabama Pharmacy Assn 1211 Carmichael Way *General	Montgomery	AL	36106	800-529-7533*	334-271-4222
Alaska Pharmacist's Assn 203 W 15th Ave Ste 100	Anchorage	AK	99501	800-228-9290	907-563-8880
California Pharmacists Assn (CPhA) 4030 Lennane Dr	Sacramento	CA	95834	866-365-7472	916-779-1400
Indiana Pharmacists Alliance 729 N Pennsylvania St	Indianapolis	IN	46204	800-516-0313	317-634-4968
Iowa Pharmacy Assn 8515 Douglas Ave Ste 16	Des Moines	IA	50322	866-512-1800	515-270-0713
Kansas Pharmacists Assn 1020 SW Fairlawn Rd	Topeka	KS	66604	888-792-6273	785-228-2327
Kentucky Pharmacists Assn 1228 US 127 S	Frankfort	KY	40601	800-922-1557	502-227-2303
Louisiana Pharmacists Assn 450 Laurel St Ste 1400	Baton Rouge	LA	70801	877-252-5100	225-346-6883
Maryland Pharmacists Assn 1800 Washington Blvd Ste 333	Baltimore	MD	21201	800-833-7587	410-727-0746
Massachusetts Pharmacists Assn 500 W Cummings Pk Ste 3475	Woburn	MA	01801	888-772-7227	781-933-1107
Michigan Pharmacists Assn 815 N Washington Ave	Lansing	MI	48906	866-226-2952	517-484-1466
Minnesota Pharmacists Assn (MPhA) 1935 W County Rd B2	Roseville	MN	55113	800-451-8349	651-697-1771
Mississippi Pharmacists Assn 341 Edgewood Terr Dr	Jackson	MS	39206	800-421-2408	601-981-0416
Nebraska Pharmacists Assn 6221 S 58th St Ste A	Lincoln	NE	68516	866-365-7472	402-420-1500
Texas Pharmacy Assn 12007 Research Blvd Ste 201	Austin	TX	78759	800-505-5463	512-836-8350
Washington State Pharmacy Assn 411 Williams Ave S	Renton	WA	98057	800-562-6000	425-228-7171

583 PHARMACY BENEFITS MANAGEMENT SERVICES

A pharmacy benefits management service (PBM) is a company that manages various pharmacy-related aspects of a health insurance plan, such as the assignment of pharmacy cards, claims filing and processing, formulary management, etc. For the most part, PBM clients are insurance companies, HMOs, or PPOs rather than individuals or pharmacies.

	City	State	ZIP	Toll-Free	Phone
BioScrip 10050 Crosstown Cir Ste 300 *NASDAQ: BIOS*	Eden Prairie	MN	55344	800-444-5951	
Caremark Rx Inc PO Box 832407	Richardson	TX	75083	877-460-7766	
CoreSource Inc 400 Field Dr	Lake Forest	IL	60045	800-832-3332	847-604-9200
CuraScript Inc 6272 Lee Vista Blvd	Orlando	FL	32822	888-773-7376	
Health Smart Rx 1301 E Ninth St	Cleveland	OH	44114	800-681-6912	
Maxor National Pharmacy Services Corp 320 S Polk St Ste 100	Amarillo	TX	79101	800-658-6146	806-324-5400
MedImpact Healthcare Systems Inc 10680 Treena St Ste 500	San Diego	CA	92131	800-788-2949	858-566-2727
Prescription Solutions 3515 Harbor Blvd	Costa Mesa	CA	92626	800-788-4863	
Prime Therapeutics Inc 1305 Corporate Ctr Dr	Eagan	MN	55121	800-858-0723	612-777-4000
ScripNet 10050 Banburry Cross Dr Ste 290	Las Vegas	NV	89144	888-880-8562	702-248-2692
Script Care Inc 6380 Folsom Dr	Beaumont	TX	77706	800-880-9988	
ScriptSave 4911 E Broadway Blvd Ste 200	Tucson	AZ	85711	800-347-5985	
Serve You Custom Prescription Management 10201 Innovation Dr Ste 600	Milwaukee	WI	53226	888-243-6890	414-410-8100

584 PHARMACY MANAGEMENT SERVICES

Companies that provide long-term care pharmacy services to individuals with special needs (e.g., chronic disease or advanced age); and those that provide pharmacy management services to hospitals or other institutions.

	City	State	ZIP	Toll-Free	Phone
Accredo Health Group Inc 1640 Century Ctr Pkwy	Memphis	TN	38134	877-222-7336	901-385-3688
Fisher Bio Svc Inc 14665 Rothgeb Dr	Rockville	MD	20850	888-462-7246	301-315-8460
McKesson Pharmaceutical One Post St	San Francisco	CA	94104	800-571-2889	415-983-8300
Omnicare Inc 201 E 4th St Ste 1900 *NYSE: OCR*	Cincinnati	OH	45202	800-342-5627	800-990-6664

585 PHOTO PROCESSING & STORAGE

	City	State	ZIP	Toll-Free	Phone
Advanced Photographic Solutions 1525 Hardeman Ln	Cleveland	TN	37312	800-241-9234	423-479-5481

			Toll-Free	Phone
Burrell Imaging				
1311 Merrillville Rd	Crown Point IN	46307	800-348-8732	219-663-3210
Candid Color Systems Inc				
1300 Metropolitan Ave	Oklahoma City OK	73108	800-336-4550	405-947-8747
Dale Laboratories				
2960 Simms St	Hollywood FL	33020	800-327-1776	954-925-0103
H & H Color Lab Inc				
8906 E 67th St PO Box 219080	Raytown MO	64133	800-821-1305	816-358-6677
iMemories 9181 E Bell Rd	Scottsdale AZ	85260	800-845-7986	
McKenna Pro Imaging				
2800 Falls Ave	Waterloo IA	50701	800-238-3456*	319-235-6265
*General				
Meisel Visual Imaging				
2019 McKenzie Dr	Carrollton TX	75006	800-527-5186	214-688-4950
Photo USA 2140 Colonial Ave	Roanoke VA	24015	888-234-6320	540-344-0961
Yahoo! Photos				
701 First Ave	Sunnyvale CA	94089	888-267-7574	408-349-3300

586   PHOTOCOPYING EQUIPMENT & SUPPLIES

SEE ALSO Business Machines - Whol

			Toll-Free	Phone
Oce-USA Inc				
5450 N Cumberland Ave Sixth Fl	Chicago IL	60656	800-877-6232	773-714-8500
Sharp Electronics Corp				
One Sharp Plz	Mahwah NJ	07430	800-237-4277	201-529-8200
Toshiba America Inc				
1251 Ave of the Americas Ste 4100	New York NY	10020	800-457-7777	212-596-0600
Xerox Canada Ltd				
5650 Yonge St	North York ON	M2M4G7	800-939-3769	
Xerox Corp				
45 Glover Ave PO Box 4505	Norwalk CT	06856	800-327-9753	203-968-3000
NYSE: XRX				

587   PHOTOGRAPH STUDIOS - PORTRAIT

			Toll-Free	Phone
Cherry Hill Photo Enterprises Inc				
4 East Stow Rd	Marlton NJ	08053	800-969-2440	
CPI Corp				
1706 Washington Ave	Saint Louis MO	63103	800-422-9410	314-231-1575
OTC: CPIC				
Freestyle Photo Biz				
5124 Sunset Blvd	Hollywood CA	90027	800-292-6137	
George STREET Photo & Video LLC				
230 W Huron St Ste 3W	Chicago IL	60654	866-831-4103	
Jostens Inc				
3601 Minnesota Ave Ste 400	Minneapolis MN	55435	800-235-4774	952-830-3300

588   PHOTOGRAPHIC EQUIPMENT & SUPPLIES

SEE ALSO Cameras & Related Supplies - Retail

			Toll-Free	Phone
Agfa Corp 611 River Dr	Elmwood Park NJ	07407	888-274-8626	201-440-2500
Alan Gordon Enterprises Inc				
5625 Melrose Ave	Hollywood CA	90038	800-825-6684	323-466-3561
Anton/Bauer Inc				
14 Progress Dr	Shelton CT	06484	800-422-3473	203-929-1100
Ballantyne Strong Inc				
13710 FNB Pkwy	Omaha NE	68154	800-424-1215*	
*NYSE: BTN ■ *General*				
Beta Screen Corp				
707 Commercial Ave	Carlstadt NJ	07072	800-272-7336	201-939-2400
Carr Corp 1547 11th St	Santa Monica CA	90401	800-952-2398	310-587-1113
Casio Inc 570 Mt Pleasant Ave	Dover NJ	07801	800-634-1895*	973-361-5400
*Cust Svc				
Ceiva Logic Inc				
214 E Magnolia Blvd	Burbank CA	91502	877-693-7263*	818-562-1495
*Tech Supp				
Da-Lite Screen Company Inc				
3100 N Detroit St	Warsaw IN	46581	800-622-3737	574-267-8101
Douthitt Corp 245 Adair St	Detroit MI	48207	800-368-8448	313-259-1565
Draper Shade & Screen Co				
411 S Pearl St	Spiceland IN	47385	800-238-7999	765-987-7999
Identatronics Inc				
165 N Lively Blvd	Elk Grove Village IL	60007	800-323-5403*	847-437-2654
*Cust Svc				
InFocus Corp				
13190 SW 68th Pkwy Ste 200	Portland OR	97223	877-388-8385	503-207-4700
Integrated Design Tools Inc				
1202 E Pk Ave	Tallahassee FL	32301	800-462-4307	850-222-5939
Matthews Studio Equipment Group				
2405 W Empire Ave	Burbank CA	91504	800-237-8263	818-843-6715
Mustek Inc				
15271 Barranca Pkwy	Irvine CA	92618	800-308-7226	949-790-3800
MVM Products LLC				
940 Calle Amanecer Ste K	San Clemente CA	92673	888-246-5832	949-366-1470
Navitar Inc				
200 Commerce Dr	Rochester NY	14623	800-828-6778*	585-359-4000
*Cust Svc				
Nikon Inc				
1300 Walt Whitman Rd	Melville NY	11747	800-645-6687*	631-547-4200
*Cust Svc				
Panavision Inc				
6219 DeSoto Ave	Woodland Hills CA	91367	800-260-1846	818-316-1000
Peter Pepper Products Inc				
17929 S Susana Rd	Compton CA	90221	800-496-0204	310-639-0390
Phase One Inc				
200 Broadhollow Rd Ste 312	Melville NY	11747	888-742-7366	631-757-0400
Reprographics One Inc				
36060 Industrial Rd	Livonia MI	48150	800-333-2600	734-542-8800

			Toll-Free	Phone
Research Technology International Inc				
4700 W Chase Ave	Lincolnwood IL	60712	800-323-7520*	847-677-3000
*Sales				
Schneider Optics Century Div				
7701 Haskell Ave	Van Nuys CA	91406	800-228-1254	818-766-3715
Sharp Electronics Corp				
One Sharp Plz	Mahwah NJ	07430	800-237-4277	201-529-8200
Sony Corp of America				
550 Madison Ave	New York NY	10022	800-282-2848	212-833-6800
Stewart Filmscreen Corp				
1161 W Sepulveda Blvd	Torrance CA	90502	800-762-4999	310-784-5300
Tamron USA Inc				
10 Austin Blvd	Commack NY	11725	800-827-8880*	631-858-8400
*General				
Tiffen Company LLC				
90 Oser Ave	Hauppauge NY	11788	800-645-2522	631-273-2500
Toshiba America Inc				
1251 Ave of the Americas Ste 4100	New York NY	10020	800-457-7777	212-596-0600
Visual Departures Ltd				
2001 W Main St Ste 195	Stamford CT	06902	800-628-2003	
Vivitar Corp 195 Carter Dr	Edison NJ	08817	800-637-1090	732-248-1306
Vutec Corp				
11711 W Sample Rd	Coral Springs FL	33065	800-770-4700	954-545-9000

589   PHOTOGRAPHY - COMMERCIAL

			Toll-Free	Phone
Universal Image				
PO Box 77090	Winter Garden FL	34787	800-553-5499	407-352-5302

590   PHOTOGRAPHY - STOCK

			Toll-Free	Phone
Alaska Stock Images				
2505 Fairbanks St	Anchorage AK	99503	800-487-4285	907-276-1343
Corbis Corp				
710 Second Ave Ste 200	Seattle WA	98104	800-260-0444	206-373-6000
Custom Medical Stock Photo Inc				
3660 W Irving Pk Rd	Chicago IL	60618	800-373-2677	773-267-3100
Image Works PO Box 443	Woodstock NY	12498	800-475-8801	845-679-8500
Photo Researchers Inc				
307 Fifth Ave Third Fl	New York NY	10016	800-833-9033	212-758-3420
Photo Resource Hawaii				
111 Hekili St Ste 241	Kailua HI	96734	888-599-7773	808-599-7773

591   PIECE GOODS & NOTIONS

SEE ALSO Fabric Stores

			Toll-Free	Phone
Advanced Probing Systems Inc				
2300 Central Ave	Boulder CO	80301	800-631-0005	303-939-9384
Associated Fabrics Corp				
15-01 Pollitt Dr Unit 7	Fair Lawn NJ	07410	800-232-4077	
B Berger Co				
1380 Highland Rd	Macedonia OH	44056	800-288-8400*	330-425-3838
*Cust Svc				
Baum Textile Mills Inc				
812 Jersey Ave	Jersey City NJ	07310	866-842-7631	201-659-0444
Blank Quilting Corp				
Blank Quilting				
49 West 37th St 14th fl.	New York NY	10018	800-294-9495	
Blumenthal Lansing Co				
30 Two Bridges Rd Ste 110	Fairfield NJ	07004	800-448-9749	201-935-6220
Bob Barker Company Inc				
PO Box 429	Fuquay Varina NC	27526	800-334-9880	919-552-3431
Brookwood Cos Inc				
25 W 45th St 11th Fl.	New York NY	10036	800-426-5468	212-551-0100
Burch Fabrics Group				
4200 Brockton Dr SE	Grand Rapids MI	49512	800-841-8111	616-698-2800
Criterion Thread Company Inc				
21744 98th Ave	Queens Village NY	11429	800-695-0080*	718-464-4200
*General				
Dunlap Industries Inc				
123 State St	Dunlap TN	37327	800-251-7214	423-949-4021
Duralee Fabrics Ltd Inc				
1775 Fifth Ave	Bay Shore NY	11706	800-275-3872*	631-273-8800
*Cust Svc				
EE Schenck Co				
6000 N Cutter Cir	Portland OR	97217	800-433-0722	503-284-4124
Hanes Cos Inc				
500 N McLin Creek Rd	Conover NC	28613	877-252-3052	828-464-4673
Hoffman California Fabrics Inc				
25792 Obrero Dr	Mission Viejo CA	92691	800-547-0100	
Janlynn Corp				
2070 Westover Rd	Chicopee MA	01022	800-445-5565	413-206-0002
JHB International Inc				
1955 S Quince St	Denver CO	80231	800-525-9007	303-751-8100
Keyston Bros				
2801 Academy Way Ste A	Sacramento CA	95815	800-453-1112	916-646-1834
Marcus Bros Textiles Inc				
980 Ave of the Americas	New York NY	10018	800-548-8295	212-354-8700
McKee Surfaces PO Box 230	Muscatine IA	52761	800-553-9662*	563-263-2421
*Cust Svc				
Miami Corp, The				
720 Anderson Ferry Rd	Cincinnati OH	45238	800-543-0448	513-451-6700
Pine Cone Hill Inc				
125 Pecks Rd	Pittsfield MA	01201	877-586-4771	413-496-9700
Prym-Dritz Corp				
950 Brisack Rd	Spartanburg SC	29303	800-255-7796*	864-576-5050
*Cust Svc				
Robert Allen Fabrics Inc				
225 Foxboro Blvd	Foxboro MA	02035	800-333-3777	

			Toll-Free	Phone
Robert Kaufman Company Inc				
PO Box 59266	Los Angeles CA	90059	**800-877-2066**	310-538-3482
Schott International Inc				
2850 Gilchrist Rd	Akron OH	44305	**877-661-2121**	330-794-2121
Scovill Fasteners Inc				
1802 Scovill Dr	Clarkesville GA	30523	**888-726-8455***	706-754-1000
*Cust Svc				
Spradling International Inc				
200 Cahaba Vly Pkwy PO Box 1668	Pelham AL	35124	**800-333-0955**	205-985-4206
Tiger Button Company Inc				
307 W 38th St Fourth Fl	New York NY	10018	**800-223-2754**	212-594-0570
Transhield Inc				
2932 Thorne Dr	Elkhart IN	46514	**888-731-7700**	574-266-4118
United Notions Inc				
13800 Hutton St	Dallas TX	75234	**800-527-9447**	972-484-8901
US Button Corp				
328 Kennedy Dr	Putnam CT	06260	**800-243-1842**	860-928-2707
Velcro USA Inc				
406 Brown Ave	Manchester NH	03103	**800-225-0180**	603-669-4880
Waterbury Button Co				
1855 Peck Ln	Cheshire CT	06410	**800-928-1812**	
Young Fashions Inc				
10300 Perkins Rd	Baton Rouge LA	70810	**800-824-4154**	225-766-1010

592   PIPE & PIPE FITTINGS - METAL (FABRICATED)

SEE ALSO Metal Tube & Pipe

			Toll-Free	Phone
Alloy Stainless Products Co				
611 Union Blvd	Totowa NJ	07512	**800-631-8372**	973-256-1616
AY McDonald Manufacturing Co				
4800 Chavenelle Rd PO Box 508	Dubuque IA	52002	**800-292-2737***	563-583-7311
*Cust Svc				
Campbell Manufacturing Inc				
127 E Spring St	Bechtelsville PA	19505	**800-523-0224**	610-367-2107
Carpenter Powder Products				
600 Mayer St	Bridgeville PA	15017	**866-790-9092**	412-257-5102
Central Pipe Supply Inc				
101 Ware Rd PO Box 5470	Pearl MS	39288	**800-844-7700**	601-939-3322
Champion Mfg Industries Inc				
6021 N Galena Rd	Peoria IL	61614	**800-452-7473**	309-685-1031
Colonial Engineering Inc				
6400 Corporate Ave	Portage MI	49002	**800-374-0234**	269-323-2495
Douglas Bros				
423 Riverside Industrial Pkwy	Portland ME	04103	**800-341-0926**	207-797-6771
Elkhart Products Corp				
1255 Oak St	Elkhart IN	46514	**800-284-4851**	574-264-3181
Empire Industries Inc				
180 Olcott St	Manchester CT	06040	**800-243-4844**	860-647-1431
General Plug & Mfg Co Inc				
455 Main St	Grafton OH	44044	**800-289-7584**	440-926-2411
H-P Products Inc				
512 W Gorgas St	Louisville OH	44641	**800-822-8356**	330-875-5556
Kelly Pipe Company LLC				
11680 Bloomfield Ave	Santa Fe Springs CA	90670	**800-305-3559**	562-868-0456
McWane Inc				
2900 Hwy 280 Ste 300	Birmingham AL	35223	**877-231-0904**	205-414-3100
MicroGroup Inc				
Seven Industrial Pk Rd	Medway MA	02053	**800-255-8823**	508-533-4925
Mills Iron Works Inc				
14834 Maple Ave	Gardena CA	90248	**800-421-2281**	323-321-6520
Milwaukee Valve Company Inc				
16550 W Stratton Dr	New Berlin WI	53151	**800-348-6544**	262-432-2800
National Excelsior Co				
1999 N Ruby St	Melrose Park IL	60160	**855-373-9235**	708-343-4225
NIBCO Inc				
1516 Middlebury St	Elkhart IN	46515	**800-234-0227**	574-295-3000
Nor-Cal Products Inc				
1967 S Oregon St	Yreka CA	96097	**800-824-4166**	530-842-4457
Parker Hannifin Corp Brass Products Div				
100 Parker Dr	Otsego MI	49078	**800-272-7537**	269-694-9411
Penn Machine Co				
106 Stn St	Johnstown PA	15905	**800-736-6872**	814-288-1547
Piping Technology & Products Inc				
3701 Holmes Rd PO Box 34506	Houston TX	77051	**866-746-9172**	713-422-2271
R & B Wagner Inc PO Box 423	Butler WI	53007	**888-243-6914**	414-214-0444
Richards Industries Inc				
3170 Wasson Rd	Cincinnati OH	45209	**800-543-7311***	513-533-5600
*Cust Svc				
Romac Industries Inc				
21919 20th Ave SE	Bothell WA	98021	**800-426-9341**	425-951-6200
Shaw Group Inc, The				
4171 Essen Ln	Baton Rouge LA	70809	**866-235-5687***	832-513-1000
NYSE: SHAW ▧ *General				
Star Pipe LLC				
4018 Westhollow Pkwy	Houston TX	77082	**800-999-3009**	281-558-3000
Synalloy Corp				
775 Spartan Blvd Ste 102				
PO Box 5627	Spartanburg SC	29304	**800-937-5449***	864-585-3605
NASDAQ: SYNL ▧ *Orders				
Tate Andale Inc				
1941 Lansdowne Rd	Baltimore MD	21227	**800-296-8283**	410-247-8700
Tru-Flex Metal Hose Corp				
2391 S State Rd 263 PO Box 247	West Lebanon IN	47991	**800-255-6291**	765-893-4403
Tube Processing Corp				
604 E Le Grande Ave	Indianapolis IN	46203	**800-295-4119**	317-787-1321
Universal Tube Inc				
2607 Bond St	Rochester Hills MI	48309	**800-394-8823**	248-853-5100
US Pipe & Foundry Co				
Two Chase Corporate Drive				
Suite 200	Birmingham AL	35244	**866-347-7473**	
Victaulic Co				
4901 Kesslersville Rd	Easton PA	18040	**800-742-5842***	610-559-3300
*Sales				
World Wide Fittings Inc				
7501 N Natchez Ave	Niles IL	60714	**800-393-9894**	847-588-2200

593   PIPE & PIPE FITTINGS - PLASTICS

			Toll-Free	Phone
Advanced Drainage Systems Inc				
4640 Trueman Blvd	Hilliard OH	43026	**800-821-6710**	
CertainTeed Corp				
750 E Swedesford Rd	Valley Forge PA	19482	**800-782-8777***	610-341-7000
*Prod Info				
CertainTeed Corp Pipe & Plastics Div				
750 E Swedesford Rd PO Box 860	Valley Forge PA	19482	**800-274-8530**	610-341-7000
Chemtrol Div NIBCO Inc				
1516 Middlebury St	Elkhart IN	46516	**800-234-0227**	574-295-3000
Chevron Phillips Chemical Company Performance Pipe Div				
5085 W Pk Blvd Ste 500	Plano TX	75093	**800-527-0662**	972-599-6600
Diamond Plastics Corp				
1212 Johnstown Rd PO Box 1608	Grand Island NE	68802	**800-782-7473**	308-384-4400
Endot Industries Inc				
60 Green Pond Rd	Rockaway NJ	07866	**800-443-6368**	973-625-8500
Excalibur Extrusions Inc				
110 E Crowther Ave	Placentia CA	92870	**800-648-6804**	714-528-8834
Fernco Inc 300 S Dayton St	Davison MI	48423	**800-521-1283**	810-653-9626
Hancor Inc PO Box 1047	Findlay OH	45839	**888-892-2694**	419-422-6521
Hobas Pipe USA LP				
1413 E Richey Rd	Houston TX	77073	**800-856-7473**	281-821-2200
Isco Industries				
926 Baxter Ave PO Box 4545	Louisville KY	40204	**800-345-4726**	502-583-6591
JM Manufacturing Company Inc				
5200 West Century Blvd	Los Angeles CA	90045	**800-621-4404**	
Lasco Fittings Inc				
414 Morgan St PO Box 116	Brownsville TN	38012	**800-776-2756**	731-772-3180
Maloney Technical Products				
1300 E Berry St	Fort Worth TX	76119	**800-231-7236**	817-923-3344
Mueller Plastics Corp				
3070 E Cedar	Ontario CA	91761	**800-348-8464**	909-930-2060
National Pipe & Plastics Inc				
3421 Old Vestal Rd	Vestal NY	13850	**800-836-4350**	
Nebraska Plastics Inc				
PO Box 45	Cozad NE	69130	**800-445-2887**	308-784-2500
North American Pipe Corp				
2801 Post Oak Blvd Ste 600	Houston TX	77056	**800-370-5247**	713-840-7473
Oil Creek Plastics Inc				
45619 State Hwy 27 PO Box 385	Titusville PA	16354	**800-537-3661**	814-827-3661
Texas United Pipe Inc				
11627 N Houston Rosslyn Rd	Houston TX	77086	**800-966-8741***	281-448-3276
*Sales				
Vinylplex Inc				
1800 Atkinson Ave	Pittsburg KS	66762	**877-779-7473**	620-231-8290
Vinyltech Corp				
201 S 61st Ave	Phoenix AZ	85043	**800-255-3924**	602-233-0071

594   PIPELINES (EXCEPT NATURAL GAS)

			Toll-Free	Phone
BP PLC 28100 Torch Pkwy	Warrenville IL	60555	**877-638-5672**	630-420-5111
NYSE: BP				
Colonial Pipeline Co				
1185 Sanctuary Pkwy Ste 100	Alpharetta GA	30009	**800-275-3004**	678-762-2200
Country Mark Co-op				
1200 Refinery Rd	Mount Vernon IN	47620	**800-832-5490**	
Enbridge Energy Partners LP				
1100 Louisiana Ste 3300	Houston TX	77002	**800-481-2804**	713-821-2000
NYSE: EEP				
Genesis Energy LP				
919 Milam Ste 2100	Houston TX	77002	**800-284-3365**	713-860-2500
NYSE: GEL				
Imperial Oil Resources Ltd				
237 Fourth Ave SW PO Box 2480 Stn M	Calgary AB	T2P3M9	**800-567-3776**	
Kinder Morgan Energy Partners LP				
500 Dallas St Ste 1000	Houston TX	77002	**866-208-3372**	713-369-9000
NYSE: KMI				
Kinder Morgan Management LLC				
500 Dallas St 1 Allen Ctr Ste 1000	Houston TX	77002	**800-781-4152**	713-369-9000
NYSE: KMI				
Magellan Midstream Partners LP				
One Williams Ctr	Tulsa OK	74172	**800-574-6671**	918-574-7000
NYSE: MMP				
MarkWest Energy Partners LP				
1515 Arapahoe St Tower 1 Ste 1600	Denver CO	80202	**800-730-8388**	303-925-9200
NYSE: MWE				
Plains All American Pipeline LP				
333 Clay St Ste 1600	Houston TX	77002	**866-753-3619***	713-646-4100
NYSE: PAA ▧ *Mktg				
Sunoco Inc				
1735 Market St Ste LL	Philadelphia PA	19103	**800-786-6261**	215-977-3000
NYSE: SUN				
Valero LP PO Box 696000	San Antonio TX	78269	**800-333-3377**	866-297-6093

595   PLANETARIUMS

			Toll-Free	Phone
Berea College Weatherford Planetarium				
101 Chestnut St	Berea KY	40404	**800-326-5948**	859-985-3000
Cernan Earth & Space Ctr				
2000 N Fifth Ave Triton College	River Grove IL	60171	**800-972-7000**	708-456-0300
Community College of Southern Nevada Planetarium & Observatory				
3200 E Cheyenne Ave	North Las Vegas NV	89030	**800-630-7563**	702-651-4759
Dreyfuss Planetarium				
49 Washington St	Newark NJ	07102	**888-370-6765**	973-596-6529
Gheens Science Hall & Rauch Planetarium				
Rauch Planetarium				
University of Louisville	Louisville KY	40292	**800-996-7566**	502-852-6664

			Toll-Free	Phone

John Deere Planetarium
820 38th St Augustana College . . . . .Rock Island IL 61201 **800-798-8100** 309-794-7327
Kitt Peak National Observatory
950 N Cherry Ave . . . . .Tucson AZ 85719 **888-809-4012** 520-318-8600
Space Transit Planetarium
3280 S Miami Ave . . . . .Miami FL 33129 **866-268-0250** 305-646-4200

596 PLASTICS - LAMINATED - PLATE, SHEET, PROFILE SHAPES

			Toll-Free	Phone

Connecticut Laminating Company Inc
162 James St . . . . .New Haven CT 06513 **800-753-9119** 203-787-2184
Current Inc
30 Tyler St PO Box 120183. . . . . .East Haven CT 06512 **877-436-6542** 203-469-1337
DuPont Surfaces
4417 Lancaster Pk CRP 728/3105 . . . . .Wilmington DE 19805 **800-448-9835** 302-774-1000
Formica Corp
10155 Reading Rd . . . . .Cincinnati OH 45241 **800-367-6422** 513-786-3400
Franklin Fibre-Lamitex Corp
903 E 13th St . . . . .Wilmington DE 19802 **800-233-9739** 302-652-3621
Hartson-kennedy Cabinet Top Company Inc
522 W 22nd St PO Box 3095 . . . . .Marion IN 46953 **800-388-8144** 765-668-8144
Insulfab Plastics Inc
834 Hayne St . . . . .Spartanburg SC 29301 **800-845-7599** 864-582-7506
Insultab Inc
45 Industrial Pkwy . . . . .Woburn MA 01801 **800-468-4822*** 781-935-0800
*Cust Svc
Iten Industries
4602 Benefit Ave . . . . .Ashtabula OH 44004 **800-227-4836*** 440-997-6134
*Orders
Lakeland Plastics Inc (LP)
1550 McCormick Blvd . . . . .Mundelein IL 60060 **800-454-4006** 847-680-1550
Lamart Corp 16 Richmond St . . . . .Clifton NJ 07015 **800-526-2799** 973-772-6262
Madico Inc
64 Industrial Pkwy . . . . .Woburn MA 01801 **800-456-4331** 781-935-7850
Olon Industries Inc
42 Armstrong Ave . . . . .Georgetown ON L7G4R9 **800-387-2319** 905-877-7300
Petro Plastics Company Inc
450 S Ave . . . . .Garwood NJ 07027 **800-486-4738** 908-789-1200
Reef Industries Inc
9209 Almeda Genoa Rd . . . . .Houston TX 77075 **800-231-6074** 713-507-4200
Rowmark Inc
2040 Industrial Dr . . . . .Findlay OH 45840 **800-243-3339** 419-425-2407
Sabin Corp
3800 Constitution Ave PO Box 788 . . . . .Bloomington IN 47403 **800-457-4500** 812-339-2235
Spaulding Composites Co
55 Nadeau Dr . . . . .Rochester NH 03867 **800-801-0560** 603-332-0555
Techniform Industries Inc
2107 Hayes Ave . . . . .Fremont OH 43420 **800-691-2816** 419-332-8484
V-T Industries Inc
1000 Industrial Pk . . . . .Holstein IA 51025 **800-827-1615** 712-368-4381
Wilmington Fibre Specialty Co
700 Washington St .New Castle DE 19720 **800-220-5132** 302-328-7525
Wilsonart International Inc
2400 Wilson Pl . . . . .Temple TX 76504 **800-433-3222*** 254-207-7000
*Cust Svc

597 PLASTICS - UNSUPPORTED - FILM, SHEET, PROFILE SHAPES

SEE ALSO Blister Packaging

			Toll-Free	Phone

Advance Bag & Packaging Technologies
5720 Williams Lk Rd . . . . .Waterford MI 48329 **800-475-2247** 248-674-3126
AEP Industries Inc
125 Phillips Ave . . . . .South Hackensack NJ 07606 **800-999-2374** 201-641-6600
NASDAQ: AEPI
Allen Extruders Inc
1305 Lincoln Ave . . . . .Holland MI 49423 **800-833-1305** 616-394-3810
Anaheim Custom Extruders
4640 E La Palma Ave . . . . .Anaheim CA 92807 **800-229-2760*** 714-693-8508
*Cust Svc
Arlon Graphics
2811 S Harbor Blvd . . . . .Santa Ana CA 92704 **800-232-7161** 714-540-2811
Atlas Roofing Falcon Foam Div
8240 Byron Ctr Rd SW . . . . .Byron Center MI 49315 **800-917-9138**
Avery Dennison Worldwide Graphics Div
250 Chester St Bldg 8. . . . . .Painesville OH 44077 **800-443-9380** 440-358-3700
Bixby International Corp
1 Preble Rd . . . . .Newburyport MA 01950 **800-466-4102** 978-462-4100
Brandywine Investment Group Homalite Div
11 Brookside Dr . . . . .Wilmington DE 19804 **800-346-7802** 302-652-3686
Catalina Graphic Films Inc
27001 Agoura Rd Ste 100. . . . . .Calabasas Hills CA 91301 **800-333-3136** 818-880-8060
Clopay Plastic Products Co
8585 Duke Blvd . . . . .Mason OH 45040 **800-282-2260** 513-770-4800
CUE Inc
11 Leonberg Rd . . . . .Cranberry Township PA 16066 **800-283-4621** 724-772-5225
Dielectrics Industries Inc
300 Burnett Rd . . . . .Chicopee MA 01020 **800-472-7286** 413-594-8111
Dunmore Corp 145 Wharton Rd . . . . .Bristol PA 19007 **800-444-0242** 215-781-8895
E S Robbins Corp
2802 Avalon Ave . . . . .Muscle Shoals AL 35661 **866-934-6018** 256-248-2400
Enflo Corp 315 Lake Ave . . . . .Bristol CT 06010 **888-887-4093** 860-589-0014
Gary Plastic Packaging Corp
1340 Viele Ave . . . . .Bronx NY 10474 **800-221-8150** 718-893-2200
General Formulations Inc
309 S Union St . . . . .Sparta MI 49345 **800-253-3664** 616-887-7387
Glasforms Inc
1226 Lincoln Ave .San Jose CA 95125 **888-297-3800** 408-297-9300
GSE Lining Technology Inc
19103 Gundle Rd . . . . .Houston TX 77073 **800-435-2008** 281-443-8564
Kama Corp 600 Dietrich Ave . . . . .Hazleton PA 18201 **888-252-6212** 412-553-4545
Kayline Processing Inc
31 Coates St . . . . .Trenton NJ 08611 **800-367-5546*** 609-695-1449
*Sales

			Toll-Free	Phone

Kendall Packaging Corp
10200 N Port Washington Rd . . . . .Mequon WI 53092 **800-237-0951** 262-404-1200
Kimoto Tech Inc
PO Box 1783 . . . . .Cedartown GA 30125 **888-546-6861** 770-748-2643
Lavanture Products Co
22825 Gallatin Way . . . . .Elkhart IN 46514 **800-348-7625** 574-264-0658
Mitsubishi Polyester Film LLC
2001 Hood Rd . . . . .Greer SC 29650 **800-334-1934** 864-879-5000
MPI Technologies 37 E St . . . . .Winchester MA 01890 **888-674-8088** 781-729-8300
Natvar 8720 US Hwy 70 W . . . . .Clayton NC 27520 **800-395-6288** 919-553-4151
New Hampshire Plastics Inc
One Bouchard St .Manchester NH 03103 **800-258-3036** 603-669-8523
Northland Plastics Inc
1420 S 16th St PO Box 290 . . . . .Sheboygan WI 53081 **800-776-7163**
Orcon Corp
1570 Atlantic St . . . . .Union City CA 94587 **800-227-0505*** 510-489-8100
*General
Penn Fibre Plastics
2434 Bristol Rd . . . . .Bensalem PA 19020 **800-662-7366***
*Cust Svc
Petoskey Plastics Inc
One Petoskey St . . . . .Petoskey MI 49770 **800-999-6556** 231-347-2602
Plaskolite Inc
1770 Joyce Ave . . . . .Columbus OH 43219 **800-848-9124** 614-294-3281
Polyvinyl Films Inc
PO Box 753 . . . . .Sutton MA 01590 **800-343-6134** 508-865-3558
Primex Plastics Corp
1235 N 'F' St . . . . .Richmond IN 47374 **800-222-5116** 765-966-7774
Prinsco Inc
108 W Hwy 7 PO Box 265 . . . . .Prinsburg MN 56281 **800-992-1725** 320-978-4116
Raven Industries Inc
205 E Sixth St . . . . .Sioux Falls SD 57104 **800-243-5435** 605-336-2750
NASDAQ: RAVN
Sheffield Plastics Inc
119 Salisbury Rd . . . . .Sheffield MA 01257 **800-254-1707*** 413-229-8711
*Cust Svc
Shepherd CE Company Inc
2221 Canada Dry St .Houston TX 77023 **800-324-6733** 713-924-4300
Shield Pack LLC
411 Downing Pines Rd . . . . .West Monroe LA 71292 **800-551-5185** 318-387-4743
SLM Manufacturing Corp
215 Davidson Ave .Somerset NJ 08873 **800-526-3708** 732-469-7500
Soliant LLC
1872 Hwy 9 Bypass . . . . .Lancaster SC 29720 **800-288-9401** 803-285-9401
Southern Film Extruders Inc
2319 English Rd . . . . .High Point NC 27262 **800-334-6101** 336-885-8091
Summit Plastics Inc
107 S Laurel St . . . . .Summit MS 39666 **800-790-7117** 601-276-7500
Thermoplastic Processes Inc
1268 Valley Rd . . . . .Stirling NJ 07980 **888-554-6400** 908-561-3000
Tredegar Corp Film Products Div
1100 Boulders Pkwy . . . . .Richmond VA 23225 **855-330-1001** 804-330-1000
VCF Films Inc
1100 Sutton Ave . . . . .Howell MI 48843 **888-905-7680**
VPI Corp 3123 S Ninth St . . . . .Sheboygan WI 53081 **800-874-4240*** 920-458-4664
*Orders
Watersaver Company Inc
5870 E 56th Ave . . . . .Commerce City CO 80022 **800-525-2424** 303-289-1818
Zippertubing Inc
7150 W Erie St . . . . .Chandler AZ 85226 **855-289-1874** 480-285-3990

598 PLASTICS FOAM PRODUCTS

			Toll-Free	Phone

Allied Aerofoam Products LLC
216 Kelsey Ln . . . . .Tampa FL 33619 **800-338-9140** 813-626-0090
American Excelsior Co
850 Ave H E PO Box 5067 . . . . .Arlington TX 76005 **800-777-7645**
Barger Packaging Inc
2901 Oakland Ave . . . . .Elkhart IN 46517 **888-525-2845**
Carpenter Co
5016 Monument Ave . . . . .Richmond VA 23230 **800-288-3830** 804-359-0800
Cellofoam North America Inc
1917 Rockdale Industrial Blvd . . . . .Conyers GA 30012 **800-241-3634** 770-929-3688
Chestnut Ridge Foam Inc
PO Box 781 . . . . .Latrobe PA 15650 **800-234-2734*** 724-537-9000
*Cust Svc
Clark Foam Products Corp
655 Remington Blvd . . . . .Bolingbrook IL 60440 **888-284-2290** 630-226-5900
Clayton Corp 866 Horan Dr . . . . .Fenton MO 63026 **800-729-8220*** 636-349-5333
*Cust Svc
Creative Foam Corp
300 N Alloy Dr . . . . .Fenton MI 48430 **800-529-4149** 810-629-4149
Custom Pack Inc
662 Exton Cmns . . . . .Exton PA 19341 **800-722-7005** 610-321-2525
Dart Container Corp
500 Hogsback Rd . . . . .Mason MI 48854 **800-248-5960**
Dow Chemical Company, The
1881 W Oak Pkwy . . . . .Marietta GA 30062 **800-331-6451** 770-428-2684
Elliott Company of Indianapolis Inc
9200 Zionsville Rd . . . . .Indianapolis IN 46268 **800-545-1213*** 317-291-1213
*Orders
Federal Foam Technologies Inc
600 Wisconsin Dr . . . . .New Richmond WI 54017 **800-898-9559** 715-246-9500
Flextron Industries Inc
720 Mt Rd . . . . .Aston PA 19014 **800-633-2181** 610-459-4600
Foam Molders & Specialty Corp
20004 State Rd . . . . .Cerritos CA 90703 **800-378-8987**
Fomo Products Inc
2775 Barber Rd . . . . .Norton OH 44203 **800-321-5585** 330-753-4585
Free Flow Packaging International Inc
1090 Mills Way .Redwood City CA 94063 **800-866-9946** 650-261-5300
Future Foam Inc
1610 Ave N Council Bluffs . . . . .Council Bluffs IA 51501 **800-733-8061** 712-323-9122
FXI 1400 N Providence Rd . . . . .Media PA 19063 **800-355-3626** 610-744-2300
G & T Industries Inc
1001 76th St SW . . . . .Byron Center MI 49315 **800-968-6035**

				Toll-Free	Phone
Gaco Western Inc					
200 W Mercer St Ste 202	Seattle	WA	98119	**800-456-4226**	206-575-0450
General Plastics Mfg Co					
4910 S Burlington Way	Tacoma	WA	98409	**800-806-6051**	253-473-5000
Guardian Packaging Inc					
3615 Security St	Garland	TX	75042	**800-259-1502**	214-349-1500
Hibco Plastics Inc					
1820 Us 601 Hwy	Yadkinville	NC	27055	**800-849-8683**	336-463-2391
Intertrade Industries Ltd					
15632 Commerce Ln	Huntington Beach	CA	92649	**800-944-9277**	714-894-5566
ITW-GaleWrap					
1320 Leslie Dr	Douglasville	GA	30134	**866-425-3727**	
North Carolina Foam Industries Inc					
1515 Carter St	Mount Airy	NC	27030	**800-346-8229**	336-789-9161
Pacific Packaging Products Inc					
24 Industrial Way	Wilmington	MA	01887	**800-777-0300**	978-657-9100
Perfect Turf Inc					
622 Sandpebble Dr	Schaumburg	IL	60193	**888-796-8873**	
Pinova Holdings Inc					
2801 Cook St	Brunswick	GA	31520	**888-807-2958**	
Poly Foam Inc					
116 Pine St S	Lester Prairie	MN	55354	**844-446-4339**	320-395-2551
Poly Molding LLC					
96 Fourth Ave	Haskell	NJ	07420	**800-229-7161**	973-835-7161
RL Adams Plastics Inc					
5955 Crossroads Commerce	Wyoming	MI	49519	**800-968-2241**	616-261-4400
Robbie Manufacturing Inc					
10810 Mid America Ave	Lenexa	KS	66219	**800-255-6328**	913-492-3400
Sekisui Voltek LLC					
100 Shepard St	Lawrence	MA	01843	**800-225-0668**	978-685-2557
Sonoco One N Second St	Hartsville	SC	29550	**800-377-2692**	
NYSE: SON					
Storopack Inc					
12007 S Woodruff Ave	Downey	CA	90241	**800-829-1491**	562-803-5582
ThermoSafe Brands					
3930 N Ventura Dr Ste 450	Arlington Heights	IL	60004	**800-323-7442**	847-398-0110
ThermoServ 3901 Pipestone Rd	Dallas	TX	75212	**800-635-5559**	214-631-0307
Topp Industries Inc					
420 N State Rd 25 PO Box 420	Rochester	IN	46975	**800-354-4534**	574-223-3681
UFP Technologies Inc					
172 E Main St	Georgetown	MA	01833	**800-372-3172**	978-352-2200
NASDAQ: UFPT					
WinCup 4640 Lewis Rd	Stone Mountain	GA	30083	**800-292-2877**	770-938-5281

599   PLASTICS MACHINING & FORMING

SEE ALSO Plastics Molding - Custom

				Toll-Free	Phone
Bardes Plastics Inc					
5225 W Clinton Ave	Milwaukee	WI	53223	**800-558-5161***	
Cust Svc					
Empire West Inc					
9270 Graton Rd PO Box 511	Graton	CA	95444	**800-521-4261**	707-823-1190
Engineered Plastics Inc					
211 Chase St	Gibsonville	NC	27249	**800-711-1740**	336-449-4121
Fabri-Form Co					
200 S Friendship Dr	New Concord	OH	43762	**800-837-2574**	740-826-5000
Fabri-Kal Corp					
600 Plastics Pl	Kalamazoo	MI	49001	**800-888-5054**	269-385-5050
FNW Industrial Plastics Inc					
12500 Jefferson Ave PO Box 2778	Newport News	VA	23602	**800-721-2590**	757-874-7795
Formall Inc					
3908 Fountain Vly Dr	Knoxville	TN	37918	**800-643-3676**	865-922-7514
Inline Plastics Corp					
42 Canal St	Shelton	CT	06484	**800-826-5567**	203-924-2015
Innovize Inc					
500 Oak Grove Pkwy	Saint Paul	MN	55127	**877-605-6580**	
McNeal Enterprises Inc					
2031 Ringwood Ave	San Jose	CA	95131	**800-562-6325**	408-922-7290
Meyer Plastics Inc					
5167 E 65th St	Indianapolis	IN	46220	**800-968-4131**	317-259-4131
Perkasie Industries Corp					
PO Box 179	Perkasie	PA	18944	**800-523-6747***	215-257-6581
Sales					
Placon Corp 6096 McKee Rd	Madison	WI	53719	**800-541-1535**	608-271-5634
Polygon Co					
103 Industrial Pk Dr PO Box 176	Walkerton	IN	46574	**800-918-9261**	574-586-3145
Quadrant Engineering Plastic Products USA					
2120 Fairmont Ave PO Box 14235	Reading	PA	19612	**800-366-0300**	610-320-6600
Ray Products Company Inc					
1700 Chablis Ave	Ontario	CA	91761	**800-423-7859**	909-390-9906
Spaulding Composites Company Fab Div					
55 Nadeau Dr	Rochester	NH	03867	**800-801-0560**	603-332-0555
Total Plastics Inc					
3316 Pagosa Ct	Indianapolis	IN	46226	**800-382-4635**	317-543-3540

600   PLASTICS MATERIALS - WHOL

				Toll-Free	Phone
A Daigger & Company Inc					
620 Lakeview Pkwy	Vernon Hills	IL	60061	**800-621-7193**	847-816-5060
Aetna Plastics Corp					
1702 St Clair Ave	Cleveland	OH	44114	**800-634-3074**	216-781-4421
AIN Plastics Inc					
1750 E Heights Dr	Madison Heights	MI	48071	**877-246-7700***	248-356-4000
Cust Svc					
Aztec Supply					
954 N Batavia St	Orange	CA	92867	**800-836-3210**	714-771-6580
Bamberger Polymers Inc					
Two Jericho Plz Ste 109	Jericho	NY	11753	**800-888-8959**	516-622-3600
Buckley Industries Inc					
1850 E 53rd St N	Wichita	KS	67219	**800-835-2779**	316-744-7587

				Toll-Free	Phone
Calsak Corp					
1411 West 190th St Suite 400	Gardena	CA	90248	**888-663-6005**	310-719-9500
Cope Plastics Inc					
4441 Industrial Dr	Godfrey	IL	62002	**800-851-5510**	618-466-0221
El Mar Plastics Inc					
109 W 134th St	Los Angeles	CA	90061	**800-255-5210**	310-436-6444
H Muehlstein & Company Inc					
10 Westport Rd	Wilton	CT	06897	**800-257-3746**	203-855-6000
Laird Plastics Inc					
6800 Broken Sound Pkwy Ste 150	Boca Raton	FL	33487	**800-243-9696**	561-443-9100
M Holland Co					
400 Skokie Blvd Ste 600	Northbrook	IL	60062	**800-872-7370**	847-272-7370
Momentum Technologies Inc (MTI)					
1507 Boettler Rd	Uniontown	OH	44685	**800-720-0261**	330-896-5900
Nytef Plastics Ltd Inc					
6643 42nd Terr N	West Palm Beach	FL	33407	**800-646-9833**	561-840-9499
Orange County Industrial Plastics Inc					
4811 E La Palma Ave	Anaheim	CA	92807	**800-974-6247**	714-632-9450
Port Plastics Inc					
15325 Fairfield Ranch Rd Ste 150	Chino Hills	CA	91709	**800-800-0039**	480-813-6118
Regal Plastic Supply Co					
111 E Tenth Ave	North Kansas City	MO	64116	**800-627-2102**	816-421-6290
Ryan Herco Products Corp					
3010 N San Fernando Blvd	Burbank	CA	91504	**800-848-1141**	818-841-1141
Seelye Plastics Inc					
9700 Newton Ave S	Bloomington	MN	55431	**800-328-2728**	
Sekisui America Corp					
333 Meadowlands Pkwy 4th Fl	Secaucus	NJ	07094	**866-260-5851***	201-423-7960
General					
Superior Oil Co Inc					
1402 N Capitol Ave Ste 100	Indianapolis	IN	46202	**800-553-5480**	317-781-4400
Tekra Corp					
16700 W Lincoln Ave	New Berlin	WI	53151	**800-448-3572**	262-784-5533

601   PLASTICS MOLDING - CUSTOM

				Toll-Free	Phone
Akron Porcelain & Plastics Co					
2739 Cory Ave PO Box 15157	Akron	OH	44314	**800-737-9664**	330-745-2159
Alladin Plastics Inc					
140 Industrial Dr	Surgoinsville	TN	37873	**877-536-4693**	423-345-2351
American Metal & Plastics Inc					
450 32nd St SW	Grand Rapids	MI	49548	**800-382-0067**	616-452-6061
American Plastic Molding Corp					
965 S Elm St	Scottsburg	IN	47170	**877-527-8427**	812-752-7000
Berry Plastics Corp					
101 Oakley St	Evansville	IN	47710	**877-662-3779**	812-424-2904
Confer Plastics Inc (CPI)					
97 Witmer Rd	North Tonawanda	NY	14120	**800-635-3213**	716-693-2056
Cuyahoga Molded Plastics Corp					
1265 Babbitt Rd	Cleveland	OH	44132	**800-805-9549**	216-261-2744
D-M-E Co					
29111 Stephenson Hwy	Madison Heights	MI	48071	**800-626-6653**	248-398-6000
Double H Plastics Inc					
50 W St Rd	Warminster	PA	18974	**800-523-3932**	215-674-4100
EFP Corp					
223 Middleton Run Rd	Elkhart	IN	46516	**800-205-8537**	574-295-4690
Elgin Molded Plastics					
909 Engle St	Elgin	IL	60120	**800-548-5483**	847-931-2455
Ensinger Putnam Precision Molding					
11 Danco Rd	Putnam	CT	06260	**800-752-7865**	860-928-7911
Evco Plastics					
100 W N St PO Box 497	DeForest	WI	53532	**800-507-6000**	
Filtertek Inc 11411 Price Rd	Hebron	IL	60034	**800-248-2461**	815-648-1001
Flambeau Inc					
15981 Valplast Rd	Middlefield	OH	44062	**800-457-5252**	440-632-1631
Gruber Systems Inc					
25636 Ave Stanford	Valencia	CA	91355	**800-257-4070**	661-257-4060
Kurz-Kasch Inc					
511 Byers Rd	Miamisburg	OH	45342	**888-587-9527**	937-299-0990
Lehigh Valley Plastics Inc					
187 N Commerce Way	Bethlehem	PA	18017	**800-354-5344**	484-893-5500
M & Q Plastic Products Inc					
1120 Welsh Rd Ste 170	North Wales	PA	19454	**800-600-3068**	267-498-4000
Molded Fiber Glass Cos					
2925 MFG PI PO Box 675	Ashtabula	OH	44005	**800-860-0196**	440-997-5851
Molding Corp of America					
10349 Norris Ave	Pacoima	CA	91331	**800-423-2747**	818-890-7877
MXL Industries Inc					
1764 Rohrerstown Rd	Lancaster	PA	17601	**800-233-0159**	717-569-8711
Plaspros Inc					
1143 Ridgeview Dr	McHenry	IL	60050	**800-752-7776**	815-430-2300
Plastic Components Inc					
N 116 W 18271 Morse Dr	Germantown	WI	53022	**877-253-1496**	
Sabin Corp					
3800 Constitution Ave PO Box 788	Bloomington	IN	47403	**800-457-4500**	812-339-2235
Seitz LLC					
212 Industrial Ln	Torrington	CT	06790	**800-261-2011**	860-489-0476
Steere Enterprises Inc					
285 Commerce St	Tallmadge	OH	44278	**800-875-4926**	330-633-4926
Tuthill Corp Plastics Group					
2050 Sunnydale Blvd	Clearwater	FL	33765	**800-634-2695**	727-446-8593
Universal Plastic Mold Inc					
13245 Los Angeles St	Baldwin Park	CA	91706	**888-893-1587**	
Westlake Plastics Co					
PO Box 127	Lenni	PA	19052	**800-999-1700**	610-459-1000
Williams Industries Inc					
2201 E Michigan Rd	Shelbyville	IN	46176	**800-383-4701**	317-392-4701

602   PLASTICS & OTHER SYNTHETIC MATERIALS

	Toll-Free	Phone

Classified Section

602-1 Synthetic Fibers & Filaments

			Toll-Free	Phone
Color-Fi Inc 320 Neeley St	Sumter SC	29150	800-843-6382	803-436-4200
Consolidated Fibers 8100 S Blvd	Charlotte NC	28273	800-243-8621	
Deltech Corp 11911 Scenic Hwy	Baton Rouge LA	70807	800-424-9300	225-775-0150
DuPont Advanced Fibers Systems 5401 Jefferson Davis Hwy	Richmond VA	23234	800-441-7515	804-383-2000
Fairfield Processing Corp 88 Rose Hill Ave	Danbury CT	06810	800-980-8000	203-744-2090
Hexcel Corp 281 Tresser Blvd 16th Fl.	Stamford CT	06901	800-444-3923	800-688-7734
NYSE: HXL				
Honeywell Specialty Materials 101 Columbia Rd	Morristown NJ	07962	800-222-0094	973-455-2145
International Fiber Corp 50 Bridge St	North Tonawanda NY	14120	888-698-1936	716-693-4040
INVISTA 4123 E 37th St N	Wichita KS	67220	877-446-8478	316-828-1000
Nylon Corp of America 333 Sundial Ave	Manchester NH	03103	800-851-2001	603-627-5150
TenCate Grass North America 1131 Broadway St	Dayton TN	37321	800-251-1033	423-775-0792
United Plastic Fabricating Inc 165 Flagship Dr	North Andover MA	01845	800-638-8265	

602-2 Synthetic Resins & Plastics Materials

			Toll-Free	Phone
A Schulman Inc 3550 W Market St	Akron OH	44333	800-547-3746	330-666-3751
NASDAQ: SHLM				
Akcros Chemicals America 500 Jersey Ave	New Brunswick NJ	08901	800-500-7890*	732-220-6882
*Cust Svc				
AlphaGary Corp 170 Pioneer Dr	Leominster MA	01453	800-232-9741	978-537-8071
Asahi Kasei Plastics North America Inc 900 E Van Riper Rd	Fowlerville MI	48836	800-993-5382*	517-223-2000
*Cust Svc				
Bayer Corp 100 Bayer Rd	Pittsburgh PA	15205	800-422-9374	412-777-2000
Bayer Inc 77 Belfield Rd	Toronto ON	M9W1G6	800-622-2937	416-248-0771
Bayer MaterialScience LLC 100 Bayer Rd	Pittsburgh PA	15205	800-662-2927	412-777-2000
Canplas Industries Ltd 500 Veterans Dr	Barrie ON	L4M4V3	800-461-1771	705-726-3361
Cartec International Inc 106 Powder Mill Rd	Canton CT	06019	800-821-4434	860-693-9395
Daikin America Inc 20 Olympic Dr	Orangeburg NY	10962	800-365-9570*	845-365-9500
*Cust Svc				
Dow Chemical Co 2030 Dow Ctr	Midland MI	48674	800-422-8193*	989-636-1463
NYSE: DOW ■ *Cust Svc				
DSM Engineering Plastics Inc 2267 W Mill Rd	Evansville IN	47720	800-333-4237	812-435-7500
DuPont Engineering Polymers Lancaster Pike Rt 141 Barley Mill Plz Bldg 22	Wilmington DE	19805	800-441-7515	302-999-4592
Eastman Chemical Co 200 S Wilcox Dr	Kingsport TN	37660	800-327-8626*	423-229-2000
NYSE: EMN ■ *Cust Svc				
Engineered Polymer Solutions Inc 1400 N State St	Marengo IL	60152	800-654-4242	
Essco Inc 1933 Highland Rd	Twinsburg OH	44087	800-321-2664	216-524-4141
Gallagher Corp 3908 Morrison Dr	Gurnee IL	60031	800-524-8597	847-249-3440
Goldsmith & Eggleton Inc 300 First St	Wadsworth OH	44281	800-321-0954	330-336-6616
Heritage Plastics Inc 1002 Hunt St	Picayune MS	39466	800-245-4623	601-798-8663
Huntsman Corp 500 Huntsman Way	Salt Lake City UT	84108	888-490-8484	801-584-5700
NYSE: HUN				
Indelco Plastics Corp 6530 Cambridge St	Minneapolis MN	55426	800-486-6456	952-925-5075
Interplastic Corp 1225 Wolters Blvd	Saint Paul MN	55110	800-736-5497	651-481-6860
Kraton Performance Polymers Inc 15710 John F Kennedy Blvd Ste 300	Houston TX	77032	800-457-2866	281-504-4950
NYSE: KRA				
Lewcott Corp 86 Providence Rd	Millbury MA	01527	800-225-7725*	508-865-1791
*Sales				
Lord Corp 111 Lord Dr	Cary NC	27511	877-275-5673	919-468-5979
Minova USA Inc 150 Carley Ct	Georgetown KY	40324	800-626-2948	502-863-6800
Mitsui Chemicals America Inc 800 Westchester Ave	Rye Brook NY	10573	800-972-7252	914-701-5245
Neville Chemical Co 2800 Neville Rd	Pittsburgh PA	15225	877-704-4200*	412-331-4200
*Cust Svc				
NOVA Chemicals Corp 1000 Seventh Ave SW PO Box 2518	Calgary AB	T2P5C6	866-289-6682	403-750-3600
Perstorp Polyols Inc 600 Matzinger Rd	Toledo OH	43612	800-537-0280*	419-729-5448
*Cust Svc				
Plastics Color & Compounding Inc 14201 Paxton Ave	Calumet City IL	60409	800-922-9936	
PolyOne Corp 33587 Walker Rd	Avon Lake OH	44012	866-765-9663	440-930-1000
NYSE: POL				

			Toll-Free	Phone
Reichhold Inc 2400 Ellis Rd	Durham NC	27703	800-448-3482	919-990-7500
Resinall Corp PO Box 195	Severn NC	27877	800-421-0561	
RheTech Inc 1500 E N Territorial Rd	Whitmore Lake MI	48189	800-869-1230	734-769-0585
Rogers Corp One Technology Dr	Rogers CT	06263	800-227-6437	860-774-9605
RTP Co 580 E Front St	Winona MN	55987	800-433-4787	507-454-6900
Rutland Plastic Technologies 10021 Rodney St	Pineville NC	28134	800-438-5134	704-553-0046
Sartomer Co 502 Thomas Jones Way	Exton PA	19341	800-345-8247	610-363-4100
Sterling Fibers Inc 5005 Sterling Way	Pace FL	32571	800-342-3779*	850-994-5311
*Cust Svc				
Ticona LLC 8040 Dixie Hwy	Florence KY	41042	800-833-4882	859-372-3244
Tube-Mac Industries Ltd 853 Arvin Ave	Stoney Creek ON	L8E5N8	877-643-8823	905-643-8823
Vi-Chem Corp 55 Cottage Grove St SW	Grand Rapids MI	49507	800-477-8501	616-247-8501
Westlake Chemical Corp 2801 Post Oak Blvd Ste 600	Houston TX	77056	888-953-3623	713-960-9111
NYSE: WLK				

602-3 Synthetic Rubber

			Toll-Free	Phone
Akrochem Corp 255 Fountain St	Akron OH	44304	800-321-2260	330-535-2100
Goodyear Tire & Rubber Co 200 Innovation Way	Akron OH	44316	800-321-2136*	330-796-2121
NASDAQ: GT ■ *Cust Svc				
Lanxess Corp 111 RIDC Pk W Dr	Pittsburgh PA	15275	800-526-9377	412-809-1000
Midwest Elastomers Inc 700 Industrial Dr PO Box 412	Wapakoneta OH	45895	800-786-3539	419-738-8844
Teknor Apex Co 505 Central Ave	Pawtucket RI	02861	800-556-3864	401-725-8000
Textile Rubber & Chemical Company Inc 1300 Tiarco Dr SW	Dalton GA	30721	800-727-8453	706-277-1300

603 PLASTICS PRODUCTS - FIBERGLASS REINFORCED

			Toll-Free	Phone
Crane Composites Inc 23525 W Eames St	Channahon IL	60410	800-435-0080	815-467-8600
Fibergrate Composite Structures Inc 5151 Beltline Rd Ste 700	Dallas TX	75254	800-527-4043	972-250-1633
Glastic Corp 4321 Glenridge Rd	Cleveland OH	44121	800-360-1319	216-486-0100
GMI Composites Inc 1355 W Sherman Blvd	Muskegon MI	49441	800-330-4045	231-755-1611
McClarin Plastics Inc 15 Industrial Dr	Hanover PA	17331	800-233-3189	717-637-2241
Red Ewald Inc 2669 US 181	Karnes City TX	78118	800-242-3524	830-780-3304

604 PLASTICS PRODUCTS - HOUSEHOLD

			Toll-Free	Phone
Eagle Affiliates Inc 1000 S Second St	Plainfield NJ	07063	800-237-9255	908-757-4464
GT Water Products Inc 5239 N Commerce Ave	Moorpark CA	93021	800-862-5647	805-529-2900
Home Products International Inc 4501 W 47th St	Chicago IL	60632	800-327-3534	773-890-1010
Igloo Products Corp 777 Igloo Rd	Katy TX	77494	800-364-5566	713-584-6800
Iris USA Inc 11111 80th Ave	Pleasant Prairie WI	53158	800-320-4747	262-612-1000
Kraftware Corp 270 Cox St	Roselle NJ	07203	800-221-1728*	
*Cust Svc				
Maryland Plastics Inc 251 E Central Ave	Federalsburg MD	21632	800-544-5582*	410-754-5566
*Cust Svc				
Prolon Inc 305 Industrial Ave	Port Gibson MS	39150	800-628-7749	601-437-4211
Sterilite Corp PO Box 524	Townsend MA	01469	800-225-1046	
TAP Plastics Inc 6475 Sierra Ln	Dublin CA	94568	800-894-0827	925-829-4889
Thermos Co 475 N Martingale Rd Ste 1100	Schaumburg IL	60173	800-243-0745	847-439-7821
Tupperware Corp 14901 S Orange Blossom Trail	Orlando FL	32837	800-468-9716*	407-826-5050
NYSE: TUP ■ *Cust Svc				

605 PLASTICS PRODUCTS (MISC)

			Toll-Free	Phone
7-sigma Inc 2843 26th Ave S	Minneapolis MN	55406	888-722-8396	612-722-5358
Acry Fab Inc 584 Progress Way	Sun Prairie WI	53590	800-747-2279	608-837-0045
Aigner Index Inc 23 Mac Arthur Ave	New Windsor NY	12553	800-242-3919	845-562-4510
All States Inc 602 N 12th St	Saint Charles IL	60174	800-621-5837*	773-728-0525
*Cust Svc				
Amerimade Technology Inc 449 Mtn Vista Pkwy	Livermore CA	94551	800-938-3824	925-243-9090
Avery Dennison Fastener Div 224 Industrial Rd	Fitchburg MA	01420	800-225-5913	

				Toll-Free	Phone
AXYS Technologies Inc					
2045 Mills Rd	Sidney	BC	V8L5X2	877-792-7878	250-655-5850
Bemis Manufacturing Co					
300 Mill St	Sheboygan Falls	WI	53085	800-558-7651	920-467-4621
Blackmore Company Inc					
10800 Blackmore Ave	Belleville	MI	48111	800-874-8660	734-483-8661
Burco Molding Inc					
15015 Herriman Blvd	Noblesville	IN	46060	888-883-6656	317-773-5699
C. L. Smith Co					
1311 S 39th St	Saint Louis	MO	63110	800-264-1202	314-771-1202
Coverbind Corp					
3200 Corporate Dr	Wilmington	NC	28405	800-366-6060	910-799-4116
Crystal-Like Plastics					
2547 N Ontario St	Burbank	CA	91504	800-554-6091	323-849-1735
Custom Accents					
1940 Lunt Ave	Elk Grove Village	IL	60007	888-553-6789	847-640-4725
DelStar Technologies Inc					
220 E St Elmo Rd	Austin	TX	78745	800-521-6713	512-447-7000
Den Hartog Industries Inc					
4010 Hospers Dr S PO Box 425	Hospers	IA	51238	800-342-3408	712-752-8432
Engineered Polymers Corp (EPC)					
1020 Maple Ave E	Mora	MN	55051	800-388-2155	320-679-3232
Enor Corp					
245 Livingston St	Northvale	NJ	07647	800-977-6427	201-750-1680
Fiberglass Specialties Inc					
PO Box 1340	Henderson	TX	75653	800-527-1459	903-657-6522
Fusion Optix Inc					
19 Wheeling Ave	Woburn	MA	01801	866-506-8300	781-995-0805
Garner Industries Inc					
7201 N 98th St PO Box 29709	Lincoln	NE	68507	800-228-0275	402-434-9100
Genova Products Inc					
7034 E Court St	Davison	MI	48423	800-521-7488	810-744-4500
GenPore					
1136 Morgantown Rd PO Box 380	Reading	PA	19607	800-654-4391	610-374-5171
Glasteel-stabilit America Inc					
285 Industrial Dr	Moscow	TN	38057	800-238-5546	901-877-3010
GPK Products Inc					
1601 43rd St NW	Fargo	ND	58102	800-437-4670	701-277-3225
Habasit America					
805 Satellite Blvd	Suwanee	GA	30024	800-458-6431	
Hanscom Inc 331 Market St	Warren	RI	02885	877-725-6788	401-247-1999
Harbec Plastics Inc					
369 SR- 104	Ontario	NY	14519	888-521-4416	585-265-0010
Hygolet Inc					
349 SE Second Ave	Deerfield Beach	FL	33441	800-494-6538	954-481-8601
Kalwall Corp					
1111 Candia Rd	Manchester	NH	03109	800-258-9777	603-627-3861
King Plastic Corp					
1100 N Toledo Blade Blvd	North Port	FL	34288	800-780-5502	941-493-5502
Lamvin Inc 4675 N Ave	Oceanside	CA	92056	800-446-6329	760-806-6400
Landmark Plastic Corp					
1331 Kelly Ave	Akron	OH	44306	800-242-1183	330-785-2200
Leaktite Corp					
40 Francis St	Leominster	MA	01453	800-392-0039	978-537-8000
Little Kids Inc					
225 Chapman St Ste 202	Providence	RI	02905	800-545-5437	401-454-7600
LSP Products Group Inc					
3689 Arrowhead Dr	Carson City	NV	89706	800-854-3215	
Magic Plastics Inc					
25215 Ave Stanford	Valencia	CA	91355	800-369-0303	661-257-4485
Mastercraft Mold Inc					
3301 W Vernon Ave	Phoenix	AZ	85009	800-628-1672	602-484-4520
Micro Plastics Inc					
11 Industry Ln Hwy 178 N PO Box 149	Flippin	AR	72634	800-466-1467	870-453-2261
MOCAP Inc 409 Parkway Dr	Park Hills	MO	63601	800-633-6775	314-543-4000
Mold-Rite Plastics LLC					
1 Plant St PO Box 160	Plattsburgh	NY	12901	800-432-5277	518-561-1812
Mylan Technologies Inc					
1000 Mylan Blvd	Canonsburg	PA	15317	800-294-1322	724-514-1800
Neil Enterprises Inc					
450 E Bunker Ct	Vernon Hills	IL	60061	800-621-5584	847-549-7627
Nordson MEDICAL					
3325 S Timberline Rd	Fort Collins	CO	80525	888-404-5837	970-267-5200
Pac Tec 12365 Haynes St	Clinton	LA	70722	877-554-2544	225-683-8602
PI Inc 213 Dennis St	Athens	TN	37303	800-894-4876	423-745-6213
Plastikon Industries Inc					
688 Sandoval Way	Hayward	CA	94544	800-370-0858	510-400-1010
Plastpro Inc					
5200 W Century Blvd 9F	Los Angeles	CA	90045	800-779-0561	310-693-8600
Pleiger Plastics Co					
PO Box 1271	Washington	PA	15301	800-753-4437	724-228-2244
Plitek LLC 69 Rawls Rd	Des Plaines	IL	60018	800-966-1250	
Porex Technologies Corp					
500 Bohannon Rd	Fairburn	GA	30213	800-241-0195*	770-964-1421
*Cust Svc					
Precision Thermoplastic Components Inc					
PO Box 1296	Lima	OH	45802	800-860-4505	419-227-4500
Prism Plastics Inc					
1544 Hwy 65	New Richmond	WI	54017	877-246-7535	715-246-7535
Rayner Covering Systems Inc					
665 Schneider Dr	South Elgin	IL	60177	800-648-0757	847-695-2264
Rogan Corp					
3455 Woodhead Dr	Northbrook	IL	60062	800-584-5662	847-498-2300
Rohrer Corp					
717 Seville Rd PO Box 1009	Wadsworth	OH	44282	800-243-6640	330-335-1541
Rubbermaid Commercial Products (RCP)					
3124 Valley Ave	Winchester	VA	22601	800-347-9800	540-667-8700
Safety Technology International Inc					
2306 Airport Rd	Waterford	MI	48327	800-888-4784	248-673-9898
Shakespeare Monofilaments & Specialty Polymers					
6111 Shakespeare Rd	Columbia	SC	29223	800-845-2110	803-754-7011
Smith McDonald Corp					
1270 Niagara St	Buffalo	NY	14213	800-753-8548	716-684-7200
Spears Manufacturing Co					
PO Box 9203	Sylmar	CA	91392	800-862-1499	818-364-1611
Spilltech Environmental Inc					
1627 Odonoghue St	Mobile	AL	36615	800-228-3877	

				Toll-Free	Phone
Stant Corp					
1620 Columbia Ave	Connersville	IN	47331	800-822-3121	765-825-3121
Steinwall Inc					
1759 116th Ave NW	Coon Rapids	MN	55448	800-229-9199	763-767-7060
Syndicate Sales Inc					
PO Box 756	Kokomo	IN	46903	800-428-0515	765-457-7277
Technetics Group					
3125 Damon Way	Burbank	CA	91505	800-618-4701	818-841-9667
Thombert Inc					
316 E Seventh St N	Newton	IA	50208	800-433-3572	
TMI LLC					
5350 Campbells Run Rd	Pittsburgh	PA	15205	800-888-9750	412-787-9750
Triad Products Co					
1801 W 'B' St	Hastings	NE	68901	888-253-4227*	402-462-2181
*General					
TSE Industries Inc					
4370 112th Terr N	Clearwater	FL	33762	800-237-7634	727-573-7676
Ultra-Poly Corp					
102 Demi Rd PO Box 330	Portland	PA	18351	800-932-0619	570-897-7500
Univenture Inc					
13311 Industrial Pkwy	Marysville	OH	43040	800-992-8262	
Viziflex Seels Inc					
406 N Midland Ave	Saddle Brook	NJ	07663	800-627-7752	
World Class Plastics Inc					
7695 SR- 708	Russells Point	OH	43348	800-954-3140	937-843-4927
Yeti Coolers 3411 Hidalgo St	Austin	TX	78702	888-872-0227	512-394-9384
Zadro Products Inc					
5422 Argosy Ave	Huntington Beach	CA	92649	800-468-4348	714-892-9200
ZAGG Inc					
3855 South 500 West Ste J	Salt Lake City	UT	84115	800-700-9244	801-263-0699

606   PLUMBING FIXTURES & FITTINGS - METAL

				Toll-Free	Phone
Acorn Engineering Co					
15125 Proctor Ave					
PO Box 3527	City of Industry	CA	91744	800-488-8999	626-336-4561
American Brass Manufacturing Co					
5000 Superior Ave	Cleveland	OH	44103	800-431-6440	216-431-6565
Anderson Copper & Brass Co					
4325 Frontage Rd	Oak Forest	IL	60452	800-323-5284	708-535-9030
Bradley Corp					
W 142 N 9101 Fountain Blvd	Menomonee Falls	WI	53051	800-272-3539	262-251-6000
Central Brass Mfg Company Inc					
2950 E 55th St	Cleveland	OH	44127	800-321-8630	216-883-0220
Champion-Arrowhead LLC					
5147 Alhambra Ave	Los Angeles	CA	90032	800-332-4267	323-221-9137
Chicago Faucets A Geberit Co					
2100 S Clearwater Dr	Des Plaines	IL	60018	800-323-5060	847-803-5000
Eljer Inc					
1 Centennial Ave	Piscataway	NJ	08855	800-442-1902	
Fisher Manufacturing Co					
PO Box 60	Tulare	CA	93275	800-421-6162	
Fluidmaster Inc					
30800 Rancho Viejo Rd	San Juan Capistrano	CA	92675	800-631-2011	949-728-2000
Gerber Plumbing Fixtures LLC					
2500 International Pkwy	Woodridge	IL	60517	888-648-6466	
Grohe America Inc					
241 Covington Dr	Bloomingdale	IL	60108	800-444-7643	630-582-7711
Hansgrohe Inc					
1490 Bluegrass Lakes Pkwy	Alpharetta	GA	30004	800-334-0455	770-360-9880
In-Sink-Erator 4700 21st St	Racine	WI	53406	800-558-5712	262-554-5432
Josam Co					
525 W US Hwy 20	Michigan City	IN	46360	800-365-6726	219-872-5531
Keeney Manufacturing Co					
1170 Main St	Newington	CT	06111	800-243-0526*	860-666-3342
*Cust Svc					
Kohler Plumbing North America					
444 Highland Dr	Kohler	WI	53044	800-456-4537	920-457-4441
LDR Industries Inc					
600 N Kilbourn Ave	Chicago	IL	60624	800-545-5230	773-265-3000
Masco Corp 21001 Van Born Rd	Taylor	MI	48180	888-627-6397	313-274-7400
NYSE: MAS					
Microphor Inc 452 E Hill Rd	Willits	CA	95490	800-358-8280*	707-459-5563
*Orders					
Moen Inc					
25300 Al Moen Dr	North Olmsted	OH	44070	800-289-6636*	440-962-2000
*Cust Svc					
Moen Inc CSI Bath Accessories Div					
25300 Al Moen Dr	North Olmsted	OH	44070	800-289-6636	440-962-2000
Oatey Co 4700 W 160th St	Cleveland	OH	44135	800-321-9532*	216-267-7100
*Cust Svc					
Price Pfister Inc					
19701 Da Vinci St	Lake Forest	CA	92610	800-732-8238	949-672-4000
Sloan Valve Co					
10500 Seymour Ave	Franklin Park	IL	60131	800-982-5839	847-671-4300
Speakman Co					
400 Anchor Mill Rd	New Castle	DE	19720	800-537-2107	
Sterling Plumbing					
444 Highland Dr	Kohler	WI	53044	888-783-7546*	920-457-4441
*Cust Svc					
Symmons Industries Inc					
31 Brooks Dr	Braintree	MA	02184	800-796-6667	781-848-2250
T & S Brass & Bronze Works Inc					
PO Box 1088	Travelers Rest	SC	29690	800-476-4103*	864-834-4102
*Cust Svc					
Water Pik Inc					
1730 E Prospect Rd	Fort Collins	CO	80553	800-525-2774	
Water Saver Faucet Co					
701 W Erie St 2nd Fl	Chicago	IL	60654	800-973-7278*	312-666-5500
*Parts					
Waterworks Operating Company LLC					
60 Backus Ave	Danbury	CT	06810	800-899-6757	203-546-6000
Woodford Manufacturing Co					
2121 Waynoka Rd	Colorado Springs	CO	80915	800-621-6032*	
*Sales					

607   PLUMBING FIXTURES & FITTINGS - PLASTICS

	Toll-Free	Phone
Absocold Corp PO Box 1545 .....Richmond IN 47375	800-843-3714	765-935-7501
All-Temp Refrigeration Services Inc 271 Hwy 1085 .....Madisonville LA 70447	888-626-1277	
Apex Piping Systems Inc 302 Falco Dr .....Wilmington DE 19804	888-995-2739	302-995-6136
Applied Mechanical Systems Inc 5598 Wolf Creek Pk .....Dayton OH 45426	888-854-3073	937-854-3073
Aqua Bath Company Inc 921 Cherokee Ave .....Nashville TN 37207	800-232-2284	615-227-0017
Aurora Contractors Inc 100 Raynor Ave .....Ronkonkoma NY 11779	866-423-2197	631-981-3785
Automatic Fire Sprinkler Inc 7272 Mars Dr .....Huntington Beach CA 92647	800-436-2066	714-841-2066
B & B Trade Distribution Centre 675 York St .....London ON N5W2S6	800-265-0382	519-679-1770
Belding Tank Technologies Inc 200 N Gooding St PO Box 160 .....Belding MI 48809	800-253-4252	616-794-1130
Blauch Bros Inc 911 Chicago Ave .....Harrisonburg VA 22802	888-881-3939	540-434-2589
Broadway Mechanical 873 81st Ave .....Oakland CA 94621	800-862-4930	510-746-4000
Brower Mechanical Inc 4060 Alvis Ct .....Rocklin CA 95677	800-360-9276	916-624-0808
C H Garmong & Son Inc 3050 Poplar St .....Terre Haute IN 47803	800-894-2962	812-234-3714
Cambridgeport Air Systems Eight Fanaras Dr .....Salisbury MA 01952	877-648-2872	978-465-8481
Can-am Plumbing Inc 151 Wyoming St .....Pleasanton CA 94566	800-786-9797	925-846-1833
Claybar Constracting Inc 424 Macnab St .....Dundas ON L9H2L3	866-801-9305	905-627-8000
Continental Fire Sprinkler Co 4518 S 133rd St .....Omaha NE 68137	800-543-5170	402-330-5170
D'vontz 7208 E 38th St .....Tulsa OK 74145	877-322-3600	918-622-3600
Dispensing Dynamics International 1020 Bixby Dr .....City of Industry CA 91745	800-888-3698	626-961-3691
Dornbracht Americas Inc 1700 Executive Dr S Ste 600 .....Duluth GA 30096	800-774-1181	
Effective Solar Products LLC 601 Crescent Ave .....Lockport LA 70374	888-824-0090	985-532-0800
Ferrandino & Son Inc 71 Carolyn Blvd .....Farmingdale NY 11735	866-571-4609	516-735-0097
Finken Plumbing Heating & Cooling 628 19th Ave NE .....Saint Joseph MN 56374	877-346-5367	320-258-2005
Fire Fighter Sales & Service Co 791 Commonwealth Dr .....Warrendale PA 15086	888-412-3473	724-720-6000
Florestone Products Company Inc 2851 Falcon Dr .....Madera CA 93637	800-446-8827	559-661-4171
Fujitsu General America Inc 353 Rt 46 W .....Fairfield NJ 07004	888-888-3424	973-575-0380
Ingenuity Ieq 3600 Centennial Dr .....Midland MI 48642	800-669-9726	989-496-2233
Jet Industries Inc 1935 Silverton Rd NE PO Box 7362 .....Salem OR 97303	800-659-0620	503-363-2334
Kinetics Mechanical Service Inc 6691 Brisa St .....Livermore CA 94550	866-567-7378	925-245-6200
KITCO Fiber Optics Inc 5269 Cleveland St .....Virginia Beach VA 23462	866-643-5220	757-518-8100
Kohler Canada Company Hytec Plumbing Products Div 4150 Spallumcheen Dr .....Armstrong BC V0E1B6	800-871-8311	250-546-3067
L B Plastics Inc PO Box 907 .....Mooresville NC 28115	800-752-7739	704-663-1543
Maax Corp 160 St Joseph Blvd .....Lachine QC H8S2L3	888-957-7816	877-438-6229
Maintenx 2202 N Howard Ave .....Tampa FL 33607	855-751-0075	813-254-1656
Matco-Norca Inc Rt 22 .....Brewster NY 10509	800-431-2082	845-278-7570
Meckley Services Inc 5701 General Washington Dr Ste 0 .....Alexandria VA 22312	877-632-5539	703-333-2040
Meier Supply Company Inc 530 Bloomingdale Rd .....Middletown NY 10940	800-418-3216	845-733-5666
Mohr Power Solar Inc 1452 Pomona Rd .....Corona CA 92882	800-637-6527	951-736-2000
National Meter & Automation 7220 S Fraser St .....Centennial CO 80112	877-212-8340	303-339-9100
New Generation Mechanical 1133 Empire Central Dr .....Dallas TX 75247	877-235-5898	972-830-9900
Noveo Technologies Inc 9655 A Ignace St .....Brossard QC J4Y2P3	877-314-2044	450-444-2044
Nupla Corp 11912 Sheldon St .....Sun Valley CA 91352	800-872-7661	818-768-6800
Phybridge Inc 3495 Laird Rd Ste 12 .....Mississauga ON L5L5S5	888-901-3633	905-901-3633
SCI Infrastructure LLC 2825 S 154th St .....Seatac, WA 98188	800-255-0633	206-242-0633
State Supply Co 597 Seventh St E .....Saint Paul MN 55130	877-775-7705	651-774-5985
Sunstore Solar Energy Solutions 3090 S Hwy 14 .....Greer SC 29650	800-571-8310	864-297-6776
Thetford Corp 7101 Jackson Ave PO Box 1285 .....Ann Arbor MI 48106	800-521-3032	734-769-6000
Thetford Corp Recreational Vehicle Group 2901 E Bristol St Ste B .....Elkhart IN 46514	800-831-1076	574-266-7980
Thompson Industrial Services LLC 104 N Main .....Sumter SC 29150	800-849-8040	803-773-8005
Tri-state Fabricators Inc 1146 Ferris Rd .....Amelia OH 45102	888-523-1488	513-752-5005
Tudi Mechanical Systems of Tampa Inc 343 Munson Ave .....Mc Kees Rocks PA 15136	877-367-8834	412-771-4100
Verigent LLC 149 Plantation Ridge Dr Ste 100 .....Mooresville NC 28117	877-637-6422	704-658-3271
Wisco Supply Inc 815 S Saint Vrain St .....El Paso TX 79901	800-947-2689	915-544-8294

	Toll-Free	Phone
Zampell Cos Nine Stanley Tucker Dr .....Newburyport MA 01950	877-926-7355	978-465-0055
Zehnder America Inc 540 Portsmouth Ave .....Greenland NH 03840	888-778-6701	603-422-6700

608   PLUMBING FIXTURES & FITTINGS - VITREOUS CHINA & EARTHENWARE

	Toll-Free	Phone
American Standard Cos Inc Bath & Kitchen Products Div One Centennial Ave PO Box 6820 .....Piscataway NJ 08855	800-442-1902	
Briggs Plumbing Products 300 Eagle Rd .....Goose Creek SC 29445	800-888-4458	
Eljer Inc 1 Centennial Ave .....Piscataway NJ 08855	800-442-1902	
Gerber Plumbing Fixtures LLC 2500 International Pkwy .....Woodridge IL 60517	888-648-6466	
Kohler Plumbing North America 444 Highland Dr .....Kohler WI 53044	800-456-4537	920-457-4441
Mansfield Plumbing Products Inc 150 E First St .....Perrysville OH 44864	877-850-3060	419-938-5211
Microphor Inc 452 E Hill Rd .....Willits CA 95490	800-358-8280*	707-459-5563
*Orders		
Peerless Pottery Inc 319 S Fifth St .....Rockport IN 47635	800-457-5765	800-457-5785
Sterling Plumbing 444 Highland Dr .....Kohler WI 53044	888-783-7546*	920-457-4441
*Cust Svc		
Sunrise Specialty Co 930 98th Ave .....Oakland CA 94603	800-444-4280	510-729-7277
Toto USA Inc 1155 Southern Rd .....Morrow GA 30260	888-295-8134	770-282-8686

609   PLUMBING, HEATING, AIR CONDITIONING EQUIPMENT & SUPPLIES - WHOL

SEE ALSO Refrigeration Equipment - Whol

	Toll-Free	Phone
Aaron & Company Inc PO Box 8310 .....Piscataway NJ 08855	800-734-4822	732-752-8200
AB Young Cos Inc 15305 Stony Creek Way .....Noblesville IN 46060	800-886-7001	317-565-5000
Air Monitor Corp 1050 Hopper Ave .....Santa Rosa CA 95403	800-247-3569	707-544-2706
American Granby Inc 7652 Morgan Rd .....Liverpool NY 13090	800-776-2266	315-451-1100
Applied Membranes Inc 2325 Cousteau Ct .....Vista CA 92081	800-321-9321	760-727-3711
Arizona Partsmaster Inc 7125 W Sherman St PO Box 23169 .....Phoenix AZ 85043	888-924-7278	602-233-3580
Arizona Wholesale Supply Co 2020 E University Dr .....Phoenix AZ 85034	866-977-6849	602-258-7901
Baker Distributing Co PO Box 2954 Ste 100 .....Jacksonville FL 32203	800-217-4698	
Barnett Inc 801 W Bay St .....Jacksonville FL 32204	888-803-4467	904-384-6530
Best Plumbing Specialties 3039 Ventrie Ct .....Myersville MD 21773	800-448-6710	
Broedell Plumbing Supply Inc 1601 Commerce Ln .....Jupiter FL 33458	888-328-2383	561-747-8000
Butcher Distributors Inc 101 Boyce Rd .....Broussard LA 70518	800-960-0008	337-837-2088
Caroplast Inc PO Box 668405 .....Charlotte NC 28266	800-327-5797	704-394-4191
Cleveland Plumbing Supply Company Inc 143 E Washington St .....Chagrin Falls OH 44022	800-331-1078	440-247-2555
Coburn Supply Company Inc 390 Pk St Ste 100 .....Beaumont TX 77701	800-832-8492	409-838-6363
Consolidated Supply Co 7337 SW Kable Ln .....Tigard OR 97224	800-929-5810	503-620-7050
Delta T Inc 8323 Loch Lomond Dr .....Pico Rivera CA 90660	800-928-5828	
Duncan Supply Company Inc 910 N Illinois St .....Indianapolis IN 46204	800-382-5528	317-634-1335
Eastern Pennsylvania Supply Co 700 Scott St .....Wilkes-Barre PA 18705	800-432-8075	570-823-1181
Emerson-Swan Inc 300 Pond St .....Randolph MA 02368	800-346-9219	781-986-2000
Everett J Prescott Inc 32 Prescott St .....Gardiner ME 04345	800-357-2447	207-582-1851
Ferguson Enterprises Inc 12500 Jefferson Ave .....Newport News VA 23602	877-616-2885	757-874-7795
First Supply LLC 6800 Gisholt Dr .....Madison WI 53713	800-236-9795	608-222-7799
Four Seasons Inc 1801 Waters Ridge Dr .....Lewisville TX 75057	800-433-7508	972-316-8100
Fresno Distributing Company Inc 2055 E McKinley Ave .....Fresno CA 93703	800-655-2542	559-442-8800
Frontier Supply Inc 981 Van Horn Rd .....Fairbanks AK 99701	800-478-7867	907-374-3500
Gateway Supply Company Inc 1312 Hamrick St .....Columbia SC 29202	800-922-5312	803-771-7160
Gensco Inc 4402 20th St E .....Tacoma WA 98424	877-620-8203	253-620-8203
Goodin Co 2700 N Second St .....Minneapolis MN 55411	800-328-8433	612-588-7811
Granite Group Wholesalers LLC 6 Storrs St .....Concord NH 03301	800-258-3690	603-224-1901
Hajoca Corp 127 Coulter Ave .....Ardmore PA 19003	888-328-2383	610-649-1430
Hajoca Corp Keenan Supply Div 1341 Philadelphia St .....Pomona CA 91766	800-332-0366	909-613-1363
Harri Plumbing & Heating Inc 809 W 12th St .....Juneau AK 99801	800-478-3190	907-586-3190

					Toll-Free	Phone

Harry Cooper Supply Company Inc
605 N Sherman Pkwy .... Springfield MO 65802 **800-426-6737** 417-865-8392

Hercules Industries Inc
1310 W Evans Ave .... Denver CO 80223 **800-356-5350** 303-937-1000

I D Booth Inc PO Box 579 .... Elmira NY 14902 **888-432-6684** 607-733-9121

JE Sawyer & Company Inc
64 Glen St .... Glens Falls NY 12801 **800-724-3983**

JH Larson Co
10200 51st Ave N .... Plymouth MN 55442 **800-292-7970** 763-545-1717

John M Frey Co Inc
2735 62nd St Ct .... Bettendorf IA 52722 **800-397-3739** 563-332-9200

Johnson Supply Inc
10151 Stella Link Rd .... Houston TX 77025 **800-833-5455** 713-830-2499

Keller Supply Company Inc
3209 17th Ave W .... Seattle WA 98119 **800-285-3302** 206-285-3300

Kelly's Pipe & Supply Co Inc
2124 Industrial Rd .... Las Vegas NV 89102 **888-382-4957**

Koch Air LLC
1900 W Lloyd Expy PO Box 1167 ...... Evansville IN 47712 **877-456-2422** 812-962-5200

Lee Supply Corp
6610 Guion Rd .... Indianapolis IN 46268 **800-873-1103** 317-290-2500

Mdm Supply Inc PO Box 6018 .... Helena MT 59604 **800-949-0005** 406-443-4012

Mid-Lakes Distributing Inc
1029 W Adams St .... Chicago IL 60607 **888-733-2700** 312-733-1033

Mid-States Supply Co
1716 Guinotte Ave .... Kansas City MO 64120 **800-825-1410** 816-842-4290

Morley-Murphy Co
200 S Washington St Ste 305 .... Green Bay WI 54301 **877-499-3171** 920-499-3171

Mountain States Pipe & Supply Co
111 W Las Vegas St .... Colorado Springs CO 80903 **800-777-7173** 719-634-5555

Murray Supply Co (MSC)
102 W Third St .... Winston Salem NC 27101 **800-926-0457** 336-765-9480

New York Replacement Parts Corp
19 School St .... Yonkers NY 10701 **800-228-4718** 914-965-0122

Northwest Pipe Fittings Inc
33 S Eigth St W .... Billings MT 59101 **800-937-4737** 406-252-0142

Peabody Supply Co Inc
PO Box 669 .... Peabody MA 01960 **800-445-5816** 978-532-2200

Plumb Supply Co
1622 NE 51st Ave .... Des Moines IA 50313 **800-483-9511** 515-262-9511

Plumbers Supply Co
1000 E Main St .... Louisville KY 40206 **800-626-5133** 502-582-2261

Plumbing Distributors Inc
1025 Old Norcross Rd .... Lawrenceville GA 30046 **800-262-9231** 770-963-9231

Redlon & Johnson
172 St John St Ste 174 .... Portland ME 04102 **800-905-5250** 207-773-4755

Reeves-Wiedeman Co Inc
14861 W 100th St .... Lenexa KS 66215 **800-365-0024** 913-492-7100

Refrigeration Sales Corp
9450 Allen Dr Ste A .... Valley View OH 44125 **866-894-8200** 216-881-7800

Republic Plumbing Supply Company Inc
890 Providence Hwy .... Norwood MA 02062 **800-696-3900**

Roberts-Hamilton
6601 Pkwy Cir Ste A .... Brooklyn Center MN 55430 **800-888-2222** 763-315-0100

Robertson Heating Supply Co
2155 W Main St .... Alliance OH 44601 **800-433-9532** 330-821-9180

Rundle-Spence Manufacturing Co
PO Box 510008 .... New Berlin WI 53151 **800-783-6060** 262-782-3000

Security Supply Corp
196 Maple Ave .... Selkirk NY 12158 **800-333-2226** 518-767-2226

Standard Air & Lite Corp
2406 Woodmere Dr .... Pittsburgh PA 15205 **800-472-2458** 412-920-6505

TBA LLC
6700 Enterprise Dr .... Louisville KY 40214 **800-626-3525** 502-367-0222

Temperature Systems Inc
5001 Voges Rd .... Madison WI 53718 **800-366-0930** 608-271-7500

Thermal Corp
1264 Slaughter Rd .... Madison AL 35758 **800-633-2962** 256-837-1122

US Airconditioning Distributors
16900 Chestnut St .... City of Industry CA 91748 **800-937-7222** 626-854-4500

Vamac Inc 4201 Jacque St .... Richmond VA 23230 **800-768-2622** 804-353-7811

WA Roosevelt Co
2727 Commerce St .... La Crosse WI 54603 **800-279-2726** 608-781-2000

Waxman Industries Inc
24460 Aurora Rd .... Bedford Heights OH 44146 **800-201-7298** 440-439-1830
OTC: WXMN

Western Nevada Supply Co
950 S Rock Blvd .... Sparks NV 89431 **800-648-1230** 775-359-5800

Woodhill Supply Inc
4665 Beidler Rd .... Willoughby OH 44094 **800-362-6111** 440-269-1100

610   PLYWOOD & VENEERS

SEE ALSO Home Improvement Centers ; Lumber & Building Supplies

					Toll-Free	Phone

Bacon Veneer Co
6951 High Grove Blvd .... Burr Ridge IL 60527 **800-443-7995** 630-323-1414

California Panel & Veneer Co
14055 Artesia Blvd .... Cerritos CA 90703 **800-451-1745** 562-926-5834

Capitol Plywood Inc
160 Commerce Cir .... Sacramento CA 95815 **800-326-1505** 916-922-8861

Columbia Forest Products Inc
7900 Triad Ctr Dr Ste 200 .... Greensboro NC 27409 **800-637-1609** 336-291-5905

Columbia Forest Products Inc Columbia Plywood Div
7900 Triad Ctr Dr Ste 200 .... Greensboro NC 27409 **800-637-1609**

Constantine's Wood Ctr
1040 E Oakland Pk Blvd .... Fort Lauderdale FL 33334 **800-443-9667** 954-561-1716

Darlington Veneer Company Inc
225 Fourth St .... Darlington SC 29532 **800-845-2388** 843-393-3861

Fiber-Tech Industries Inc
2000 Kenskill Ave .... Washington Court House OH 43160 **800-879-4377** 740-335-9400

Flexible Materials Inc
1202 Port Rd .... Jeffersonville IN 47130 **800-244-6492** 812-280-7000

G-L Veneer Co Inc
2224 E Slauson Ave .... Huntington Park CA 90255 **800-588-5003** 323-582-5203

Harbor Sales
1000 Harbor Ct .... Sudlersville MD 21668 **800-345-1712**

Inland Plywood Co
375 N Cass Ave .... Pontiac MI 48342 **800-521-4355** 248-334-4706

Louisiana-Pacific Corp
414 Union St Ste 2000 .... Nashville TN 37219 **888-820-0325** 615-986-5600
NYSE: LPX

Murphy Hardwood Plywood
2350 Prairie Rd .... Eugene OR 97402 **888-461-4545** 541-461-4545

Murphy Plywood Co
2350 Prairie Rd .... Eugene OR 97402 **888-461-4545** 541-461-4545

Norbord Inc
One Toronto St Ste 600 .... Toronto ON M5C2W4 **888-667-2673** 416-365-0705
TSE: NBD

North American Plywood Corp
12343 Hawkins St .... Santa Fe Springs CA 90670 **800-421-1372*** 562-941-7575
*Sales

Phillips Plywood Company Inc
13599 Desmond St .... Pacoima CA 91331 **800-649-6410*** 818-897-7736
*Cust Svc

Plywood Supply Inc
7036 NE 175th St .... Kenmore WA 98028 **888-774-9663** 425-485-8585

Roseburg Forest Products Co
PO Box 1088 .... Roseburg OR 97470 **800-245-1115** 541-679-3311

States Industries Inc
PO Box 7037 .... Eugene OR 97401 **800-626-1981** 541-688-7871

Stimson Lumber Co
520 SW Yamhill St Ste 700 .... Portland OR 97204 **800-445-9758** 503-222-1676

Trimac Panel Products
5201 SW Westgate Dr Ste 200 .... Portland OR 97221 **800-237-8765*** 503-297-1826
*General

United Plywood & Lumber Inc
1640 Mims Ave SW .... Birmingham AL 35211 **800-272-6486** 205-925-7601

611   POINT-OF-SALE (POS) & POINT-OF-INFORMATION (POI) SYSTEMS

					Toll-Free	Phone

3M Digital Signage
600 Ericksen Ave NE Ste 200 .... Bainbridge Island WA 98110 **888-460-8866** 206-855-2000

Checkpoint Systems Inc
101 Wolf Dr .... Thorofare NJ 08086 **800-257-5540** 856-848-1800
NYSE: CKP

Datalogic Scanning
959 Terry St .... Eugene OR 97402 **800-695-5700** 541-683-5700

Kiosk Information Systems Inc (KIS)
346 S Arthur Ave .... Louisville CO 80027 **800-509-5471*** 303-466-5471
*General

Micros Systems Inc
7031 Columbia Gateway Dr .... Columbia MD 21046 **800-937-2211** 443-285-6000
NASDAQ: MCRS

MTI Inc 1050 NW 229th Ave .... Hillsboro OR 97124 **800-426-6844** 503-648-6500

PAR Technology Corp
8383 Seneca Tpke .... New Hartford NY 13413 **800-448-6505** 315-738-0600
NYSE: PAR

SeePoint Technology LLC
2619 Manhattan Beach Blvd .... Redondo Beach CA 90278 **888-587-1777** 310-725-9660

TouchSystems Corp
220 Tradesmen Dr .... Hutto TX 78634 **800-320-5944** 512-846-2424

UTC RETAIL Inc 100 Rawson Rd .... Victor NY 14564 **800-349-0546**

VeriFone Inc
2099 Gateway Pl Ste 600 .... San Jose CA 95110 **800-837-4366** 408-232-7800
NYSE: PAY

VeriFone Systems Inc
2099 Gateway Pl Ste 600 .... San Jose CA 95110 **800-837-4366** 408-232-7800
NYSE: PAY

612   POLITICAL ACTION COMMITTEES

SEE ALSO Civic & Political Organizations

					Toll-Free	Phone

American Academy of Ophthalmology PAC
Governmental Affairs Div
20 F St NW Ste 400 .... Washington DC 20001 **866-561-8558** 202-737-6662

American Apparel & Footwear Assn PAC
1601 N Kent St Ste 1200 .... Arlington VA 22209 **800-520-2262** 703-524-1864

American Assn of Nurse Anesthetists PAC (AANAPAC)
222 S Prospect Ave .... Park Ridge IL 60068 **855-526-2262** 847-692-2051

American Assn of Orthodontists PAC
401 N Lindbergh Blvd .... Saint Louis MO 63141 **800-424-2841** 314-993-1700

American Bankers Assn PAC (ABAPAC)
1120 Connecticut Ave NW .... Washington DC 20036 **800-226-5377**

American Chiropractic Assn PAC (ACA-PAC)
1701 Clarendon Blvd .... Arlington VA 22209 **800-986-4636** 703-276-8800

American Dental Assn
1111 14th St NW Ste 1100 .... Washington DC 20005 **800-353-2237** 202-898-2424

American Family Life Assurance Co PAC (AFLAC PAC)
1932 Wynnton Rd Ste 300 .... Columbus GA 31999 **800-992-3522*** 706-323-3431
NYSE: AFL ■ *Cust Svc

American Hospital Assn PAC (AHAPAC)
325 Seventh St NW .... Washington DC 20004 **800-424-4301** 202-638-1100

American Motorcyclist Assn
101 Constitution Ave NW Ste 800W ... Washington DC 20001 **888-985-6090** 202-742-4301

American Moving & Storage Assn PAC
1611 Duke St .... Alexandria VA 22314 **888-849-2672** 703-683-7410

American Nurses Assn PAC (ANA PAC)
8515 Georgia Ave Ste 400 .... Silver Spring MD 20910 **800-274-4262** 301-628-5000

American Pharmacists Assn PAC
2215 Constitution Ave NW .... Washington DC 20037 **800-237-2742** 202-628-4410

American Society of Travel Agents PAC
1101 King St Ste 490 .... Alexandria VA 22314 **800-275-2782** 703-739-2782

American Veterinary Medical Assn PAC (AVMA)
1910 Sunderland Pl NW .... Washington DC 20036 **800-321-1473** 202-789-0007

Associated General Contractors PAC
2300 Wilson Blvd Ste 400 .... Arlington VA 22201 **800-242-1767** 703-548-3118

				Toll-Free	Phone

Burlington Northern Santa Fe Corp (BNSF)
500 New Jersey Ave NW Ste 550 . . . . Washington DC 20001 **800-964-9386** 202-347-8662

BUSPAC
700 13th St NW Ste 575 . . . . Washington DC 20005 **800-283-2877** 202-842-1645

Coca-Cola Nonpartisan Committee for Good Government
PO Box 1734 . . . . Atlanta GA 30301 **800-438-2653**

College of American Pathologists PAC
1350 I St NW Ste 590 . . . . Washington DC 20005 **800-392-9994** 202-354-7100

Dairy Farmers of America PAC
10220 N Ambassador Dr
Northpointe Twr . . . . Kansas City MO 64153 **888-332-6455** 816-801-6455

DGA-PAC
7920 W Sunset Blvd . . . . Los Angeles CA 90046 **800-421-4173** 310-289-2000

ESOP Assn PAC
1726 M St NW Ste 501. . . . . Washington DC 20036 **866-366-3832** 202-293-2971

FRAN-PAC
1501 K St Ste 350. . . . . Washington DC 20005 **800-543-1038** 202-628-8000

Friends Committee on National Legislation (FCNL)
245 Second St NE . . . . Washington DC 20002 **800-630-1330** 202-547-6000

Human Rights Campaign PAC (HRCPAC)
1640 Rhode Island Ave NW . . . . Washington DC 20036 **800-777-4723** 202-628-4160

IATSE PAC
1430 Broadway 20th Fl. New York NY 10018 **844-422-9273** 212-730-1770

Independent Community Bankers of America PAC
1615 L St Ste 900. . . . . Washington DC 20036 **800-422-8439** 202-659-8111

International Chiropractors Assn PAC (ICA)
6400 Arlington Blvd Ste 800. . . . . Falls Church VA 22042 **800-423-4690** 703-528-5000

Ironworkers Political Action League
1750 New York Ave NW Ste 400. . . . . Washington DC 20006 **800-368-0105** 202-383-4800

Manufactured Housing Institute PAC (MHI PAC)
1655 N Ft Myer Dr Ste 104. . . . . Arlington VA 22209 **800-505-5500** 703-558-0400

MassMutual PAC
1295 State St . . . . Springfield MA 01111 **800-272-2216** 413-788-8411

Mechanical Contractors Assn of America PAC
1385 Piccard Dr . . . . Rockville MD 20850 **877-457-6482** 301-869-5800

NA of Home Builders PAC
1201 15th St NW . . . . Washington DC 20005 **800-368-5242** 202-266-8200

NA of Retired Federal Employees
606 N Washington St . . . . Alexandria VA 22314 **800-627-3394** 703-838-7760

NAADAC PAC
901 N Washington St Ste 600. . . . . Alexandria VA 22314 **800-377-1136** 703-741-7686

NASBIC PAC
1100 H St NW Ste 610 . . . . Washington DC 20005 **800-471-6153** 202-628-5055

National Air Traffic Controllers Assn PAC (NATCA PAC)
1325 Massachusetts Ave NW . . . . Washington DC 20005 **800-266-0895** 202-628-5451

National Confectioners Assn PAC (NCA)
8320 Old Courthouse Rd Ste 300. . . . . Vienna VA 22182 **800-433-1200** 703-790-5750

National Court Reporters Assn PAC
8224 Old Courthouse Rd. . . . . Vienna VA 22182 **800-272-6272** 703-556-6272

National Funeral Directors Assn PAC
13625 Bishop S Dr . . . . Brookfield WI 53005 **800-228-6332** 262-789-1880

National Ground Water Assn PAC
601 Dempsey Rd . . . . Westerville OH 43081 **800-551-7379** 614-898-7791

National Multi Housing Council PAC
1850 M St NW Ste 540. . . . . Washington DC 20036 **866-987-7367** 202-974-2300

National Pork Producers Council PAC
122 C St NW Ste 875 . . . . Washington DC 20001 **800-392-5705** 202-347-3600

National Propane Gas Assn PAC (NPGAPAC)
1899 L St NW Ste 350 . . . . Washington DC 20036 **888-445-1404** 202-466-7200

National Restaurant Assn PAC
2055 L St NW Ste 700 . . . . Washington DC 20036 **888-804-0001** 202-331-5900

National Stone Sand & Gravel Assn PAC
1605 King St . . . . Alexandria VA 22314 **866-722-6959** 703-525-8788

National Sunflower Assn PAC
2401 46th Ave SE Ste 206 . . . . Mandan ND 58554 **888-718-7033** 701-328-5100

NRA Institute for Legislative Action
11250 Waples Mill Rd . . . . Fairfax VA 22030 **800-392-8683**

Outdoor Adv Assn of America Inc (OAAA)
1850 M St NW Ste 1040. . . . . Washington DC 20036 **800-537-0983** 202-833-5566

Petroleum Marketers Assn of America's Small Business Community
1901 N Fort Myer Dr Ste 500 . . . . Arlington VA 22209 **888-372-7341** 703-351-8000

Planned Parenthood Action Fund Inc
1110 Vermont Ave NW . . . . Washington DC 20005 **800-430-4907** 202-973-4800

REITPAC
1875 'I' St NW Ste 600 . . . . Washington DC 20006 **800-362-7348** 202-739-9400

Society of American Florists PAC
1601 Duke St . . . . Alexandria VA 22314 **800-336-4743** 703-836-8700

Title Industry PAC (TIPAC)
1828 L St NW Ste 705 . . . . Washington DC 20036 **800-787-2582** 202-296-3671

613   POLITICAL PARTIES (MAJOR)

SEE ALSO Civic & Political Organizations

				Toll-Free	Phone

Libertarian Party
2600 Virginia Ave NW Ste 200 . . . . Washington DC 20037 **800-353-2887** 202-333-0008

Republican National Committee (RNC)
310 First St SE . . . . Washington DC 20003 **800-445-5768** 202-863-8500

613-1 Democratic State Committees

				Toll-Free	Phone

Florida Democratic Party
214 S Bronough St . . . . Tallahassee FL 32301 **855-352-7233** 850-222-3411

Idaho Democratic Party
943 W Overland Rd . . . . Meridian ID 83642 **800-626-0471** 208-336-1815

Indiana Democratic Party
115 W Washington St Ste 1165 . . . . Indianapolis IN 46204 **800-223-3387** 317-231-7100

Kansas Democratic Party
700 SW Jackson St Ste 706 . . . . Topeka KS 66603 **888-573-3547** 785-234-0425

New Mexico Democratic Party (DPNM)
8214 Second St NW ste A. . . . . Albuquerque NM 87114 **800-624-2457** 505-830-3650

North Carolina Democratic Party
220 Hillsborough St . . . . Raleigh NC 27603 **800-229-3367** 919-821-2777

				Toll-Free	Phone

Pennsylvania Democratic Party
300 N Second St 8th Fl. . . . . Harrisburg PA 17101 **800-437-7439** 717-920-8470

South Carolina Democratic Party
PO Box 5965 . . . . Columbia SC 29250 **800-841-1817** 803-799-7798

Virginia Democratic Party
1710 E Franklin St Second Fl . . . . Richmond VA 23223 **800-322-1144** 804-644-1966

613-2 Republican State Committees

				Toll-Free	Phone

Alabama Republican Party
3505 Lorna Rd Ste 219. . . . . Birmingham AL 35216 **800-274-8683** 205-212-5900

Indiana Republican Party
47 S Meridian St Ste 200 . . . . Indianapolis IN 46204 **800-466-1087** 317-635-7561

Texas Republican Party
1108 Lavaca Ste 500 . . . . Austin TX 78701 **800-525-5555** 512-477-9821

Wyoming Republican Party
1821 Carey Ave PO Box 984. . . . . Casper WY 82003 **800-424-9530** 307-234-9166

614   PORTALS - VOICE

Voice portals permit users to access web-based messaging as well as various types of Internet information (e.g., weather, stock quotes, driving directions, etc.) via the telephone (wired or wireless).

				Toll-Free	Phone

GoSolo Technologies Inc
5410 Mariner St Ste 175. . . . . Tampa FL 33609 **866-246-7656**

615   PORTS & PORT AUTHORITIES

SEE ALSO Airports ; Cruise Lines

				Toll-Free	Phone

Georgia
Ports Authority
PO Box 2406 . . . . Savannah GA 31402 **800-342-8012** 912-964-3811

Hamilton Port Authority
605 James St N 6th Fl . . . . Hamilton ON L8L1K1 **800-263-2131** 905-525-4330

Illinois International Port District
3600 E 95th St . . . . Chicago IL 60617 **800-843-7678** 773-646-4400

Indiana
Port Commission
150 W Market St Ste 100 . . . . Indianapolis IN 46204 **800-232-7678** 317-232-9200

International Port of Dutch Harbor
PO Box 610 . . . . Unalaska AK 99685 **800-526-6731** 907-581-1251

Kodiak Port & Harbor
403 Marine Way . . . . Kodiak AK 99615 **800-563-4254** 907-486-8080

Mississippi State Port Authority at Gulfport
2510 14th St Ste 1450 . . . . Gulfport MS 39501 **877-881-4367** 228-865-4300

North Carolina
State Ports Authority
2202 Burnett Blvd PO Box 9002. . . . . Wilmington NC 28402 **800-334-0682** 910-763-1621

Oregon International Port of Coos Bay
125 Central Ave Ste 300 PO Box 1215 . . . . Coos Bay OR 97420 **800-463-3339** 541-267-7678

Philadelphia Regional Port Authority
3460 N Delaware Ave 2nd Fl. . . . . Philadelphia PA 19134 **800-449-7575** 215-426-2600

Port Canaveral
445 Challanger Rd . . . . Cape Canaveral FL 32920 **888-767-8226** 321-783-7831

Port Freeport PO Box 615 . . . . Freeport TX 77542 **800-362-5743** 979-233-2667

Port Metro Vancouver
999 Canada Pl . . . . Vancouver BC V6C3T4 **888-767-8826** 604-665-9000

Port of Anchorage
2000 Anchorage Port Rd . . . . Anchorage AK 99501 **877-650-8400** 907-343-6200

Port of Astoria
422 Gateway Ave . . . . Astoria OR 97103 **800-860-4093** 503-325-4521

Port of Baltimore
Maryland Port Administration
401 E Pratt St . . . . Baltimore MD 21202 **800-638-7519***
*General

Port of Brownsville
1000 Foust Rd . . . . Brownsville TX 78521 **800-378-5395** 956-831-4592

Port of Corpus Christi
222 Power St . . . . Corpus Christi TX 78401 **800-580-7110** 361-882-5633

Port of Duluth
Duluth Seaway Port Authority
1200 Port Terminal Dr . . . . Duluth MN 55802 **800-232-0703** 218-727-8525

Port of Everett
2911 Bond St Ste 202. . . . . Everett WA 98201 **800-729-7678** 425-259-3164

Port of Lake Charles
150 Marine St . . . . Lake Charles LA 70601 **800-845-7678** 337-439-3661

Port of Milwaukee
2323 S Lincoln Memorial Dr . . . . Milwaukee WI 53207 **800-367-5690** 414-286-3511

Port of New Orleans
1350 Port of New Orleans Pl . . . . New Orleans LA 70130 **800-776-6652** 504-522-2551

Port of Orange
Orange County Navigation Port District
1201 Childers Rd . . . . Orange TX 77630 **800-368-3749** 409-883-4363

Port of Palm Beach
1 E 11th St Ste 400. . . . . Riviera Beach FL 33404 **877-377-1737** 561-842-4201

Port of Pensacola
700 S Barracks St . . . . Pensacola FL 32502 **800-711-1712** 850-436-5070

Port of Port Lavaca-Point Comfort
Calhoun Port Authority
PO Box 397 . . . . Point Comfort TX 77978 **800-933-3643** 361-987-2813

Port of Portland
7200 NE Airport Way PO Box 3529 . . . . Portland OR 97218 **800-547-8411** 503-415-6000

Port of Richmond Commission
900 E Broad St . . . . Richmond VA 23219 **800-467-4943** 804-646-6335

Port of San Diego
3165 Pacific Hwy . . . . San Diego CA 92101 **800-854-2757** 619-686-6200

Port of San Francisco
Pier 1 The Embarcadero . . . . San Francisco CA 94111 **800-479-5314** 415-274-0400

Port of Seattle PO Box 1209 . . . . Seattle WA 98111 **800-426-7817** 206-728-3000

Port of Seward PO Box 167 . . . . Seward AK 99664 **855-445-7131** 907-224-3138

				Toll-Free	Phone
Port of South Louisiana					
171 Belle Terre Blvd PO Box 909	LaPlace	LA	70068	**866-536-8300**	985-652-9278
Port of Stockton					
2201 W Washington St	Stockton	CA	95203	**800-344-3213**	209-946-0246
Port of Vancouver					
3103 NW Lower River Rd	Vancouver	WA	98660	**800-475-8012**	360-693-3611
Sitka Harbor 617 Katlian St	Sitka	AK	99835	**866-948-8683**	907-747-3439
South Carolina					
State Ports Authority					
176 Concord St	Charleston	SC	29401	**800-845-7106**	843-723-8651
Tampa Port Authority					
1101 Channelside Dr	Tampa	FL	33602	**800-741-2297**	813-905-7678
Toledo-Lucas County Port Authority					
1 Maritime Plaza	Toledo	OH	43604	**800-969-4700**	419-243-8251
Wrangell Harbor PO Box 531	Wrangell	AK	99929	**800-347-4462**	907-874-3736

616 POULTRY PROCESSING

SEE ALSO Meat Packing Plants

				Toll-Free	Phone
American Dehydrated Foods Inc					
3801 E Sunshine	Springfield	MO	65809	**800-456-3447**	417-881-7755
Amick Farms Inc					
2079 Batesburg Hwy	Batesburg	SC	29006	**800-926-4257**	803-532-1400
Brakebush Bros Inc					
N4993 Sixth Dr	Westfield	WI	53964	**800-933-2121**	608-296-2121
Claxton Poultry Farms					
8816 Hwy 301 PO Box 428.	Claxton	GA	30417	**888-739-3181**	912-739-3181
Culver Duck Farms Inc					
PO Box 910	Middlebury	IN	46540	**800-825-9225**	574-825-9537
Fieldale Farms Corp					
555 Broiler Blvd	Baldwin	GA	30511	**800-241-5400**	706-778-5100
Foster Farms Inc					
1000 Davis St PO Box 457	Livingston	CA	95334	**800-255-7227**	
House of Raeford Farms Inc					
520 E Central Ave	Raeford	NC	28376	**800-888-7539**	910-875-5161
Jennie-O Turkey Store					
2505 Willmar Ave SW	Willmar	MN	56201	**800-621-3505**	
Koch Foods Inc					
1300 Higgins Rd Ste 100	Park Ridge	IL	60068	**800-837-2778**	847-384-5940
Marshall Durbin Co					
2830 Commerce Blvd	Birmingham	AL	35210	**800-245-8204***	205-380-3251
Sales					
Michael Foods Inc					
301 Carlson Pkwy Ste 400	Minnetonka	MN	55305	**800-328-5474**	952-258-4000
Mountaire Farms					
17269 NC Hwy 71 N	Lumber Bridge	NC	28357	**877-887-1490**	910-843-5942
OK Foods Inc PO Box 1787	Fort Smith	AR	72902	**800-635-9441**	
Olymel LP					
2200 Pratte Ave Pratte	Saint-Hyacinthe	QC	J2S4B6	**800-361-7990**	450-771-0400
Perdue Farms Inc					
31149 Old Ocean City Rd	Salisbury	MD	21804	**800-473-7383**	410-543-3000
Pilgrim's Corp					
1770 Promontory Cir	Greeley	CO	80634	**800-321-1470**	
NASDAQ: PPC					
Sonstegard Foods Co					
1911 W 57th St Ste 102	Sioux Falls	SD	57108	**800-533-3184**	
Tip Top Poultry Inc					
327 Wallace Rd	Marietta	GA	30062	**800-241-5230**	770-973-8070
Tyson Foods Inc					
2210 W Oaklawn Dr PO Box 2020	Springdale	AR	72762	**800-643-3410**	479-290-4000
NYSE: TSN					
Valley Fresh Inc					
3600 E Linwood Ave	Turlock	CA	95380	**800-523-4635**	209-669-5600
Wayne Farms Enterprises LLC					
1020 County Rd 114	Jack	AL	36346	**800-241-3110**	334-897-3435
West Liberty Foods LLC					
228 W Second St	West Liberty	IA	52776	**888-511-4500**	319-627-6000

617 POWER TRANSMISSION EQUIPMENT - MECHANICAL

SEE ALSO Bearings - Ball & Roller

				Toll-Free	Phone
Allied-Locke Industries					
1088 Corregidor Rd	Dixon	IL	61021	**800-435-7752**	815-288-1471
American Metal Bearing Co					
7191 Acacia Ave	Garden Grove	CA	92841	**800-888-3048**	714-892-5527
Ameridrives Couplings					
1802 Pittsburgh Ave PO Box 4000	Erie	PA	16512	**800-352-0141**	814-480-5000
AmeriDrives International					
1802 Pittsburgh Ave	Erie	PA	16502	**800-352-0141**	814-480-5000
Barden Corp 200 Pk Ave	Danbury	CT	06810	**800-243-1060**	203-744-2211
Beemer Precision Inc					
230 New York Dr PO Box 3080.	Fort Washington	PA	19034	**800-836-2340**	215-646-8440
Bird Precision					
One Spruce St PO Box 540569.	Waltham	MA	02454	**800-454-7369***	781-894-0160
Cust Svc					
Bishop-Wisecarver Corp					
2104 Martin Way	Pittsburg	CA	94565	**888-580-8272**	925-439-8272
Buckeye Power Sales Company Inc					
6850 Commerce Ct Dr PO Box 489	Blacklick	OH	43004	**800-523-3587**	614-861-6000
Cangro Industries Long Island Transmission Co					
495 Smith St	Farmingdale	NY	11735	**800-422-9210**	631-454-9000
Carlyle Johnson Machine Co (CJM)					
291 Boston Tpke	Bolton	CT	06043	**888-629-4867**	860-643-1531
Certified Power Inc					
970 Campus Dr	Mundelein	IL	60060	**888-905-7411**	847-573-3800
Diamond Chain Co					
402 Kentucky Ave	Indianapolis	IN	46225	**800-872-4246***	317-638-6431
Cust Svc					
Force Control Industries Inc					
3660 Dixie Hwy	Fairfield	OH	45014	**800-829-3244**	513-868-0900
General Bearing Corp					
44 High St	West Nyack	NY	10994	**800-431-1766***	845-358-6000
Sales					

				Toll-Free	Phone
GGB North America					
700 Mid Atlantic Pkwy PO Box 189	Thorofare	NJ	08086	**888-840-2349**	856-848-3200
Hebeler Corp					
2000 Military Rd	Tonawanda	NY	14150	**800-486-4709**	716-873-9300
Helical Products Co Inc					
901 W McCoy Ln	Santa Maria	CA	93455	**877-353-9873**	805-928-3851
Horton Inc					
2565 Walnut St	Saint Paul	MN	55113	**800-621-1320**	651-361-6400
Kamatics Corp					
1330 Blue Hills Ave	Bloomfield	CT	06002	**866-540-5760**	860-243-9704
Kingsbury Inc					
10385 Drummond Rd	Philadelphia	PA	19154	**866-581-5464***	215-824-4000
Sales					
Linn Gear Co					
100 N Eigth St PO Box 397.	Lebanon	OR	97355	**800-547-2471**	541-259-1211
Magtrol Inc					
70 Gardenville Pkwy W	Buffalo	NY	14224	**800-828-7844**	716-668-5555
Marland Clutch					
485 S Frontage Rd Ste 330.	Burr Ridge	IL	60527	**800-216-3515**	
Maurey Manufacturing Corp					
410 Industrial Pk Rd	Holly Springs	MS	38635	**800-284-2161**	
Nook Industries					
4950 E 49th St	Cleveland	OH	44125	**800-321-7800**	216-271-7900
NSK Corp 4200 Goss Rd	Ann Arbor	MI	48105	**888-446-5675**	800-675-9930
NTN Bearing Corp of America					
1600 E Bishop Ct	Mount Prospect	IL	60056	**800-323-2358**	847-298-7500
OPW Engineered Systems					
2726 Henkle Dr	Lebanon	OH	45036	**800-547-9393***	513-932-9114
Cust Svc					
Peer Bearing Co					
2200 Norman Dr S	Waukegan	IL	60085	**800-433-7337**	847-578-1000
Pic Design Corp					
86 Benson Rd PO Box 1004	Middlebury	CT	06762	**800-243-6125**	203-758-8272
RBC Bearings Inc					
3131 W Segerstrom Ave PO Box 1953	Santa Ana	CA	92704	**866-722-2376**	714-546-3131
Real Goods Solar					
833 W S Boulder Rd	Louisville	CO	80027	**888-567-6527**	
NASDAQ: RSGE					
Regal-Beloit Corp					
200 State St	Beloit	WI	53511	**800-672-6495**	608-364-8800
NYSE: RBC					
Renold Ajax Inc					
100 Bourne St	Westfield	NY	14787	**800-251-9012**	716-326-3121
Schaeffler Group USA Inc					
308 Springhill Farm Rd	Fort Mill	SC	29715	**800-361-5841**	803-548-8500
Solomon Corp					
103 W Main PO Box 245	Solomon	KS	67480	**800-234-2867**	785-655-2191
Stock Drive Products/Sterling Instrument					
2101 Jericho Tpke	New Hyde Park	NY	11040	**800-737-7436**	516-328-3300
TB Wood's Inc					
440 N Fifth Ave	Chambersburg	PA	17201	**888-829-6637**	717-264-7161
US Tsubaki Inc					
301 E Marquardt Dr	Wheeling	IL	60090	**800-323-7790**	847-459-9500
Warner Electric					
449 Gardner St	South Beloit	IL	61080	**800-825-6544**	815-389-3771
Waukesha Bearings Corp					
W 231 N 2811 Roundy Cir E Ste 200	Pewaukee	WI	53072	**888-832-3517**	262-506-3000
Zero-Max Inc					
13200 Sixth Ave N	Plymouth	MN	55441	**800-533-1731**	763-546-4300

618 PRECISION MACHINED PRODUCTS

SEE ALSO Machine Shops ; Aircraft Parts & Auxiliary Equipment

				Toll-Free	Phone
Abbott Interfast Corp					
190 Abbott Dr	Wheeling	IL	60090	**800-877-0789**	847-459-6200
Alger Mfg Company Inc					
724 S Bon View Ave	Ontario	CA	91761	**800-854-9833**	909-986-4591
Bay Swiss Mfg Company Inc					
Five Airpark Vista Blvd	Dayton	NV	89403	**800-247-3207**	775-246-7100
Biddle Precision Components Inc					
701 S Main St	Sheridan	IN	46069	**800-428-4387**	317-758-4451
Boker's Inc					
3104 Snelling Ave	Minneapolis	MN	55406	**800-927-4377**	612-729-9365
Cox Manufacturing Co					
5500 N Loop 1604 E	San Antonio	TX	78247	**800-900-7981**	210-657-7731
Curtis Screw Company Inc					
50 Thielman Dr	Buffalo	NY	14206	**800-914-6276**	716-898-7800
Davies Molding LLC					
350 Kehoe Blvd	Carol Stream	IL	60188	**800-554-9208**	630-510-8188
Elyria Mfg Corp					
145 Northrup PO Box 479	Elyria	OH	44035	**866-365-4171**	440-365-4171
Enoch Manufacturing Co					
14242 SE 82nd Dr PO Box 98	Clackamas	OR	97015	**888-659-2660**	503-659-2660
Fairchild Auto-mated Parts Inc					
10 White St	Winsted	CT	06098	**800-927-2545**	860-379-2725
FCI Inc 4661 Giles Rd	Cleveland	OH	44135	**800-321-1032**	216-251-5200
Gates Albert Inc					
3434 Union St	North Chili	NY	14514	**800-937-9311**	585-594-9401
Greystone of Lincoln Inc					
7 Wellington Rd	Lincoln	RI	02865	**800-446-1761**	401-333-0444
H & H Swiss Screw Machine Products Company Inc					
1478 Chestnut Ave	Hillside	NJ	07205	**800-826-9985**	
Horspool & Romine Manufacturing Inc					
5850 Marshall St	Oakland	CA	94608	**800-446-2263**	
Huron Automatic Screw Co					
PO Box 610068	Port Huron	MI	48061	**800-500-4000**	810-364-6636
Hyland Screw Machine Products					
1900 Kuntz Rd	Dayton	OH	45404	**866-863-7282**	
J T M Technologies Inc					
204 Industrial Ct	Wylie	TX	75098	**877-586-8324**	972-429-6575
Kenlee Precision Corp					
1701 Inverness Ave	Baltimore	MD	21230	**800-969-5278**	410-525-3800
Kerr Lakeside Inc					
26841 Tungsten Rd	Euclid	OH	44132	**800-487-5377**	216-261-2100
Komet Of America Inc					
2050 Mitchell Blvd	Schaumburg	IL	60193	**800-865-6638**	847-923-8400

Name / Address	City	State	Zip	Toll-Free	Phone
Liberty Brass Turning Company Inc 38-01 Queens Blvd	Long Island City	NY	11101	**800-345-5939**	718-784-2911
Metric Machining Co 1425 S Vineyard Ave	Ontario	CA	91761	**800-937-9311**	909-947-9222
Mold-Masters Injectioneering LLC 103 Peyerk Ct Ste E	Romeo	MI	48065	**800-387-2483**	586-752-6551
MSK Precision Products Inc 10101 NW 67th St	Tamarac	FL	33321	**800-992-5018**	954-776-0770
Multimatic Products Inc 390 Oser Ave	Hauppauge	NY	11788	**800-767-7633**	631-231-1515
New Castle Industries Inc 1399 Countyline Rd	New Castle	PA	16101	**800-897-2830**	724-656-5620
Omni-Lite Industries Canada Inc 17210 Edwards Rd	Cerritos	CA	90703	**800-577-6664**	562-404-8510
Precisionform Inc 148 W Airport Rd	Lititz	PA	17543	**800-233-3821**	717-560-7610
Production Products Co 6176 E Molloy Rd	East Syracuse	NY	13057	**800-800-6652**	315-431-7200
RB Royal Industries Inc 1350 S Hickory St PO Box 1168	Fond du Lac	WI	54936	**800-892-1550**	920-921-1550
Roberts Automatic Products Inc 880 Lake Dr	Chanhassen	MN	55317	**800-879-9837**	952-949-1000
RW Screw Products Inc 999 Oberlin Rd SW	Massillon	OH	44647	**866-797-2739**	330-837-9211
SFS intec Inc Spring St & Van Reed Rd	Wyomissing	PA	19610	**800-234-4533**	610-376-5751
Smith & Richardson Manufacturing Co PO Box 589	Geneva	IL	60134	**800-426-0876**	630-232-2581
Sumitomo Metal Industries Ltd 1815 Sandusky St	Fostoria	OH	44830	**866-877-2020**	419-436-4499
Superior Products Inc 3786 Ridge Rd	Cleveland	OH	44144	**800-651-9490**	216-651-9400
Talladega Machinery & Supply Co Inc 301 N Johnson Ave PO Box 736 *Cust Svc	Talladega	AL	35161	**800-289-8672***	256-362-4124
Trace-A-Matic Inc (T-A-M) 1570 Commerce Ave	Brookfield	WI	53045	**877-375-0217**	262-797-7300
Tri Tool Inc 3041 Sunrise Blvd	Rancho Cordova	CA	95742	**800-345-5015**	916-288-6100
Xaloy Inc 1399 Countyline Rd	New Castle	PA	16101	**800-897-2830**	
Yoder 4899 Commerce Pkwy	Cleveland	OH	44128	**800-631-0520**	216-292-4460

619 PREPARATORY SCHOOLS - BOARDING

SEE ALSO

Schools listed here are independent, college-preparatory schools that provide housing facilities for students and teachers. All are members of The Association of Boarding Schools (TABS), and many are considered to be among the top prep schools in the United States.

Name / Address	City	State	Zip	Toll-Free	Phone
American Boychoir School 19 Lambert Dr	Princeton	NJ	08540	**888-269-2464**	609-924-5858
Andrews Osborne Academy 38588 Mentor Ave	Willoughby	OH	44094	**800-753-4683**	440-942-3600
Army & Navy Academy 2605 Carlsbad Blvd PO Box 3000	Carlsbad	CA	92018	**888-762-2338**	760-729-2385
Avon Old Farms School 500 Old Farms Rd	Avon	CT	06001	**800-464-2866**	860-404-4100
Bement School 94 Main St	Deerfield	MA	01342	**877-405-3949**	413-774-7061
Ben Lippen School 7401 Monticello Rd	Columbia	SC	29203	**800-777-2227**	803-786-7200
Berkshire School 245 N Undermountain Rd	Sheffield	MA	01257	**866-738-5500**	413-229-8511
Brewster Academy 80 Academy Dr	Wolfeboro	NH	03894	**800-842-9961**	603-569-7200
CFS the School at Church Farm PO Box 2000	Paoli	PA	19301	**800-439-4745**	610-363-7500
Chaminade College Preparatory School 425 S Lindbergh Blvd	Saint Louis	MO	63131	**877-378-6847**	314-993-4400
Christ School 500 Christ School Rd	Arden	NC	28704	**800-422-3212**	828-684-6232
Christchurch School 49 Seahorse Ln	Christchurch	VA	23031	**800-296-2306**	804-758-2306
Culver Academies 1300 Academy Rd	Culver	IN	46511	**800-528-5837**	574-842-7000
Darlington School 1014 Cave Spring Rd	Rome	GA	30161	**800-368-4437**	706-235-6051
Darrow School 110 Darrow Rd	New Lebanon	NY	12125	**877-432-7769**	518-794-6000
Dunn School 2555 Hwy 154 PO Box 98	Los Olivos	CA	93441	**800-287-9197**	805-688-6471
Episcopal High School 1200 N Quaker Ln	Alexandria	VA	22302	**877-933-4347**	703-933-4062
Fay School 48 Main St	Southborough	MA	01772	**800-933-2925**	508-485-0100
Foxcroft School 22407 Foxhound Ln	Middleburg	VA	20117	**800-858-2364**	540-687-5555
Fryeburg Academy 745 Main St	Fryeburg	ME	04037	**877-935-2013**	207-935-2013
George School 1690 Newtown-Langhorne Rd	Newtown	PA	18940	**888-804-1300**	215-579-6547
Gilmour Academy 34001 Cedar Rd	Gates Mills	OH	44040	**800-533-5140**	440-442-1104
Greenwood School 14 Greenwood Ln	Putney	VT	05346	**800-380-9218**	802-387-4545
Hargrave Military Academy (HMA) 200 Military Dr	Chatham	VA	24531	**800-432-2480**	434-432-2481
Hawaii Preparatory Academy 65-1692 Kohala Mountain Rd	Kamuela	HI	96743	**800-644-4481**	808-881-4007
Hebron Academy Rt 119 PO Box 309	Hebron	ME	04238	**888-432-7664**	207-966-2100
Hill School 717 E High St	Pottstown	PA	19464	**877-651-2800**	610-326-1000
Hillside School 404 Robin Hill Rd	Marlborough	MA	01752	**800-344-8328**	508-485-2824
Holderness School Chapel Ln PO Box 1879	Plymouth	NH	03264	**877-262-1492**	603-536-1747
Howe Military School PO Box 240	Howe	IN	46746	**888-462-4693**	260-562-2131
Indian Springs School 190 Woodward Dr *General	Pelham	AL	35124	**888-843-9477***	205-988-3350
Kent School PO Box 2006	Kent	CT	06757	**800-538-5368**	860-927-6111
Kiski School 1888 Brett Ln	Saltsburg	PA	15681	**877-547-5448**	724-639-3586
Lawrence Academy Powderhouse Rd PO Box 992	Groton	MA	01450	**800-977-4698**	978-448-6535
Lawrenceville School 2500 Main St PO Box 6008	Lawrenceville	NJ	08648	**800-735-2030**	609-896-0400
Linden Hall School for Girls 212 E Main St	Lititz	PA	17543	**800-258-5778**	717-626-8512
MacDuffie School 66 School St	Granby	MA	01033	**877-477-6217**	413-255-0000
Marvelwood School 476 Skiff Mountain Rd	Kent	CT	06757	**800-440-9107**	860-927-0047
Massanutten Military Academy 614 S Main St	Woodstock	VA	22664	**877-466-6222**	540-459-2167
McCallie School 500 Dodds Ave	Chattanooga	TN	37404	**800-234-2163**	423-624-8300
Mercersburg Academy 300 E Seminary St	Mercersburg	PA	17236	**800-588-2550**	717-328-6173
Milton Academy 170 Centre St	Milton	MA	02186	**866-645-8661**	617-898-1798
Milton Hershey School PO Box 830	Hershey	PA	17033	**800-322-3248**	717-520-2100
New York Military Academy 78 Academy Ave	Cornwall On Hudson	NY	12520	**888-275-6962**	845-534-3710
Northfield Mount Hermon School 206 Main St	Northfield	MA	01360	**866-664-4483**	413-498-3227
Northwest School 1415 Summit Ave	Seattle	WA	98122	**800-426-7127**	206-682-7309
Oakwood Friends School 22 Spackenkill Rd	Poughkeepsie	NY	12603	**800-843-3341**	845-462-4200
Oldfields School 1500 Glencoe Rd	Glencoe	MD	21152	**800-767-0700**	410-472-4800
Olney Friends School 61830 Sandy Ridge Rd	Barnesville	OH	43713	**800-303-4291**	740-425-3655
Perkiomen School 200 Seminary St PO Box 130	Pennsburg	PA	18073	**866-966-9998**	215-679-9511
Phelps School 583 Sugartown Rd	Malvern	PA	19355	**800-344-8328**	610-644-1754
Phillips Academy 180 Main St	Andover	MA	01810	**877-445-5477**	978-749-4000
Phillips Exeter Academy 20 Main St	Exeter	NH	03833	**800-245-2525**	603-772-4311
Proctor Academy 204 Main St PO Box 500	Andover	NH	03216	**800-626-4907**	603-735-6000
Purnell School 51 Pottersville Rd PO Box 500	Pottersville	NJ	07979	**800-228-9290**	908-439-2154
Putney School 418 Houghton Brook Rd	Putney	VT	05346	**800-999-9080**	802-387-5566
Rabun Gap-Nacoochee School 339 Nacoochee Dr	Rabun Gap	GA	30568	**800-543-7467**	706-746-7467
Randolph-Macon Academy 200 Academy Dr	Front Royal	VA	22630	**800-272-1172**	540-636-5200
Riverside Military Academy 2001 Riverside Dr	Gainesville	GA	30501	**800-462-2338**	770-532-6251
Saint Andrew's College 15800 Yonge St	Aurora	ON	L4G3H7	**877-378-1899**	905-727-3178
Saint Andrew's School 3900 Jog Rd	Boca Raton	FL	33434	**888-357-7332**	561-210-2000
Saint Bernard Preparatory School 1600 St Bernard Dr SE	Cullman	AL	35055	**800-722-0999**	256-739-6682
Saint Catherine's School 6001 Grove Ave	Richmond	VA	23226	**800-648-4982**	804-288-2804
Saint John's Northwestern Military Academy 1101 N Genesee St	Delafield	WI	53018	**800-752-2338**	262-646-7115
Saint John's Preparatory School 1857 Watertower Rd PO Box 4000	Collegeville	MN	56321	**800-525-7737**	320-363-3321
Saint John's-Ravenscourt School 400 S Dr	Winnipeg	MB	R3T3K5	**800-437-0040**	204-477-2400
Saint Mary's School 900 Hillsborough St	Raleigh	NC	27603	**800-948-2557**	919-424-4000
Saint Michael's University School 3400 Richmond Rd	Victoria	BC	V8P4P5	**800-661-5199**	250-592-2411
San Marcos Academy 2801 Ranch to Market 12 *Admissions	San Marcos	TX	78666	**800-428-5120***	512-353-2400
Scattergood Friends School 1951 Delta Ave	West Branch	IA	52358	**888-737-4636**	319-643-7628
Shattuck-Saint Mary's School 1000 Shumway Ave PO Box 218	Faribault	MN	55021	**800-421-2724**	507-333-1616
Solebury School 6832 Phillips Mill Rd	New Hope	PA	18938	**800-675-6900**	215-862-5261
Storm King School 314 Mountain Rd	Cornwall On Hudson	NY	12520	**800-225-9144**	845-534-9860
Stuart Hall School 235 W Frederick St PO Box 210	Staunton	VA	24402	**888-306-8926**	540-885-0356
Valley Forge Military Academy & College 1001 Eagle Rd	Wayne	PA	19087	**800-234-8362**	610-989-1300
Vermont Academy PO Box 500	Saxtons River	VT	05154	**800-698-8867**	802-869-6229
Virginia Episcopal School 400 VES Rd PO Box 408	Lynchburg	VA	24503	**800-937-3582**	434-385-3607
Wasatch Academy 120 South 100 West	Mount Pleasant	UT	84647	**800-634-4690**	435-462-1400
Wayland Academy 101 N University Ave	Beaver Dam	WI	53916	**800-860-7725**	920-885-3373
Webb School PO Box 488	Bell Buckle	TN	37020	**888-733-9322**	931-389-9322
West Nottingham Academy 1079 Firetower Rd	Colora	MD	21917	**866-381-3684**	410-658-5556
Western Reserve Academy 115 College St	Hudson	OH	44236	**877-486-2048**	330-650-9717

			Toll-Free	Phone
Woodlands Academy of the Sacred Heart				
760 E Westleigh Rd	Lake Forest IL	60045	888-234-3080	847-234-4300
Worcester Academy				
81 Providence St	Worcester MA	01604	800-235-6426	508-754-5302
Wyoming Seminary				
201 N Sprague Ave	Kingston PA	18704	877-996-7361	570-270-2160

620 PREPARATORY SCHOOLS - NON-BOARDING

			Toll-Free	Phone
Iolani School				
563 Kamoku St	Honolulu HI	96826	888-879-8970	808-949-5355

621 PRESS CLIPPING SERVICES

			Toll-Free	Phone
BurrellesLuce				
30 B Vreeland Rd PO Box 674	Florham Park NJ	07932	800-631-1160	973-992-6600
Florida Newsclips LLC				
PO Box 2190	Palm Harbor FL	34682	800-442-0332	
FlyData Inc				
1043 N Shoreline Blvd Ste 200	Mountain View CA	94043	855-427-9787	
InfySource Ltd				
8345 NW 66th St	Miami FL	33166	800-275-7503	
Kentucky Press Assn				
101 Consumer Ln	Frankfort KY	40601	800-264-5721*	502-223-8821
*Cust Svc				
LCS Technologies Inc				
11230 Gold Express Dr Ste 310-140	Gold River CA	95670	855-277-5527	
South Carolina Press Services Inc				
106 Outlet Pointe Blvd PO Box 11429	Columbia SC	29210	888-727-7377	803-750-9561
South Dakota Newspaper Services				
1125 32nd Ave Ste 202	Brookings SD	57006	800-658-3697	605-692-4300
Virginia Press Services Inc				
11529 Nuckols Rd	Glen Allen VA	23059	800-849-8717	804-521-7570
West Virginia Press Association†				
3422 Pennsylvania Ave	Charleston WV	25302	800-235-6881	304-342-6908

622 PRINTED CIRCUIT BOARDS

SEE ALSO Semiconductors & Related Devices ; Electronic Components & Accessories - Mfr

			Toll-Free	Phone
3Dlabs Inc Ltd				
1901 McCarthy Blvd	Milpitas CA	95035	800-464-3348	408-530-4700
Abelconn LLC				
9210 Science Ctr Dr	New Hope MN	55428	800-526-2828	763-533-3533
Acromag Inc 30765 S Wixom Rd	Wixom MI	48393	877-295-7092	248-624-1541
Advanced Circuits Inc				
21101 E 32nd Pkwy	Aurora CO	80011	800-979-4722	303-576-6610
Bourns Inc				
1200 Columbia Ave	Riverside CA	92507	877-426-8767	951-781-5690
Centon Electronics Inc				
15 Argonaut	Aliso Viejo CA	92656	800-836-1986	949-855-9111
Creative Labs Inc				
1901 McCarthy Blvd	Milpitas CA	95035	800-998-1000*	408-428-6600
*Cust Svc				
Crucial Technology				
3475 E Commercial Ct	Meridian ID	83642	800-336-8915	208-363-5790
Data Translation Inc				
100 Locke Dr	Marlborough MA	01752	800-525-8528	508-481-3700
OTC: DATX				
Dataram Corp				
777 Alexander Rd Ste 100	Princeton NJ	08540	800-328-2726	609-799-0071
NASDAQ: DRAM				
Dynatem Inc				
23263 Madero Ste C	Mission Viejo CA	92691	800-543-3830	949-855-3235
GE Fanuc Embedded Systems Inc				
7401 Snaproll NE	Albuquerque NM	87109	888-790-1820	505-875-0600
GoldenRAM Computer Products				
13 Whatney	Irvine CA	92618	800-222-8861	949-460-9000
Hauppauge Computer Works Inc				
91 Cabot Ct	Hauppauge NY	11788	800-443-6284	631-434-1600
Hauppauge Digital Inc				
91 Cabot Ct	Hauppauge NY	11788	800-443-6284	631-434-1600
OTC: HAUP				
Intel Corp				
2200 Mission College Blvd	Santa Clara CA	95052	800-628-8686*	408-765-8080
NASDAQ: INTC ■ *Cust Svc				
Jabil Circuit Inc				
10560 ML King St N	Saint Petersburg FL	33716	877-217-6328	727-577-9749
NYSE: JBL				
Kimball Electronics				
13700 Reptron Blvd	Tampa FL	33626	800-903-8328	813-854-2000
Kimball Electronics Group				
1038 E 15th St	Jasper IN	47549	800-482-1616	812-634-4200
Libra Industries Inc				
7770 Div Dr	Mentor OH	44060	800-825-1674	440-974-7770
Lone Star Circuits				
901 Hensley Ln	Wylie TX	75098	800-303-9266	214-291-1427
Micro Industries Corp				
8399 Green Meadow Dr N	Westerville OH	43081	800-722-1842	740-548-7878
Micron Technology Inc				
8000 S Federal Way	Boise ID	83707	888-363-2589	208-368-4000
NASDAQ: MU				
Natel Engineering Co Inc				
9340 Owensmouth Ave	Chatsworth CA	91311	800-590-5774	818-734-6500
Parallax Inc				
599 Menlo Dr Ste 100	Rocklin CA	95765	888-512-1024	916-624-8333
Promise Technology Inc				
580 Cottonwood Dr	Milpitas CA	95035	800-888-0245*	408-228-1400
*Sales				
Quatech Inc				
5675 Hudson Industrial Pkwy	Hudson OH	44236	800-553-1170	330-655-9000

			Toll-Free	Phone
RadiSys Corp				
5445 NE Dawson Creek Dr	Hillsboro OR	97124	800-950-0044	503-615-1100
NASDAQ: RSYS				
SAE Circuits Colorado Inc				
4820 N 63rd St	Boulder CO	80301	800-234-9001	303-530-1900
SigmaTron International Inc				
2201 Landmeier Rd	Elk Grove Village IL	60007	800-700-9095	847-956-8000
NASDAQ: SGMA				
Sopark Corp 3300 S Pk Ave	Buffalo NY	14218	866-576-7275	716-822-0434
Spectrum Signal Processing by Vecima				
2700 Production Way Ste 300	Burnaby BC	V5A4X1	800-663-8986	604-676-6700
Suntron Corp				
2401 W Grandview Rd	Phoenix AZ	85023	800-690-6903	602-298-4939
TechWorks 4030 W Braker Ln	Austin TX	78759	800-688-7466*	512-794-8533
*Cust Svc				
Unicircuit Inc				
8192 Southpark Ln	Littleton CO	80120	800-648-6449	303-730-0505
Unigen Corp				
45388 Warm Springs Blvd	Fremont CA	94539	800-826-0808	510-668-2088
Westak Inc 1225 Elko Dr	Sunnyvale CA	94089	800-387-3766	408-734-8686
Western Electronics LLC				
1550 S Tech Ln	Meridian ID	83642	888-857-5775	208-955-9700
Wintec Industries Inc				
675 Sycamore Dr	Milpitas CA	95035	866-989-4683	408-856-0500
ZTEST Electronics Inc				
523 Mcnicoll Ave	North York ON	M2H2C9	866-393-4891	416-297-5155

623 PRINTING COMPANIES - BOOK PRINTERS

			Toll-Free	Phone
Adair Printing Technologies				
7850 Second St	Dexter MI	48130	800-637-5025	734-426-2822
Bang Printing Inc				
3323 Oak St	Brainerd MN	56401	800-328-0450	218-829-2877
BOLT Solutions Inc				
90 Park Ave Ste 1700	New York NY	10016	888-608-4646	212-608-4646
CJK 3962 Virginia Ave	Cincinnati OH	45227	800-598-7808	513-271-6035
Claitor's Law Books & Publishing				
PO Box 261333	Baton Rouge LA	70826	800-274-1403	225-344-0476
Cookbook Publishers Inc				
9825 Widmer Rd	Lenexa KS	66215	800-227-7282	913-492-5900
Cushing-Malloy Inc				
1350 N Main St	Ann Arbor MI	48104	888-295-7244	734-663-8554
E & M Bindery Inc				
11 Peekay Dr	Clifton NJ	07014	800-736-2463	973-777-9300
Garlich Printing Co				
525 Rudder Rd	Fenton MO	63026	800-276-2622	636-349-8000
Gospel Publishing House				
1445 N Boonville Ave	Springfield MO	65802	800-641-4310*	417-862-2781
*Orders				
Houchen Bindery LTD				
340 First St	Utica NE	68456	800-869-0420	402-534-2261
Joe Christensen Inc				
1540 Adams St	Lincoln NE	68521	800-228-5030	402-476-7535
John Henry Co				
5800 W Grand River Ave	Lansing MI	48906	800-748-0517	517-323-9000
Jostens Inc				
3601 Minnesota Ave Ste 400	Minneapolis MN	55435	800-235-4774	952-830-3300
Lehigh Phoenix				
18249 Phoenix Dr	Hagerstown MD	21742	800-632-4111*	301-733-0018
*General				
Library Reproduction Service				
14214 S Figueroa St	Los Angeles CA	90061	800-255-5002	310-354-2610
Moran Printing Inc				
5425 Florida Blvd	Baton Rouge LA	70806	800-211-8335	225-923-2550
Mossberg & Company Inc				
301 E Sample St	South Bend IN	46601	800-428-3340	574-289-9253
Publishers Press Inc				
100 Frank E Simon Ave	Shepherdsville KY	40165	800-627-5801	502-955-6526
Rose Printing Company Inc				
2503 Jackson Bluff Rd	Tallahassee FL	32304	800-227-3725	850-576-4151
RR Donnelley				
111 S Wacker Dr	Chicago IL	60606	800-742-4455	
Sheridan Group				
11311 McCormick Rd Ste 260	Hunt Valley MD	21031	800-352-2210	410-785-7277
Smith-Edwards-Dunlap Co				
2867 E Allegheny Ave	Philadelphia PA	19134	800-829-0020	215-425-8800
United Record Pressing LLC				
453 Chestnut St	Nashville TN	37203	866-407-3165	615-259-9396
Versa Press Inc				
1465 Springbay Rd	East Peoria IL	61611	800-447-7829	
Victor Graphics Inc				
1211 Bernard Dr	Baltimore MD	21223	800-899-8303	410-233-8300
Whitehall Printing Co				
4244 Corporate Sq	Naples FL	34104	800-321-9290	
Wright Color Graphics				
9051 Sunland Blvd	Sun Valley CA	91352	877-246-8877	818-246-8877

624 PRINTING COMPANIES - COMMERCIAL PRINTERS

			Toll-Free	Phone
4over Inc				
5900 San Fernando Rd	Glendale CA	91202	877-782-2737	
AlphaGraphics Inc				
215 S State St Ste 320	Salt Lake City UT	84111	800-955-6246	801-595-7270
Amidon Graphics				
1966 Benson Ave	Saint Paul MN	55116	800-328-6502	651-690-2401
Angstrom Graphics Inc				
2025 McKinley St	Hollywood FL	33020	800-634-1262	954-920-7300
Angstrom Graphics Inc				
4437 E 49th St	Cleveland OH	44125	800-634-1262	216-271-5300
Arandell Inc				
N 82 W 13118 Leon Rd	Menomonee Falls WI	53051	800-558-8724	262-255-4400
B H G Inc PO Box 309	Garrison ND	58540	800-658-3485	701-463-2201

				Toll-Free	Phone
Bassett Printing Corp 3321 Fairystone Park Hwy	Bassett	VA	24055	800-336-5102	
Beckmanxmo 376 Morrison Rd	Columbus	OH	43213	800-864-2232	614-864-2232
BFC Forms Service Inc 1051 N Kirk Rd	Batavia	IL	60510	800-774-6840	630-879-9240
Bibbero Systems Inc 1300 N McDowell Blvd	Petaluma	CA	94954	800-242-2376	707-778-3131
Bolger LLC 3301 Como Ave SE	Minneapolis	MN	55414	866-264-3287	651-645-6311
Burton & Mayer Inc W140 N9000 Lilly Rd	Menomonee Falls	WI	53051	800-236-1770	262-781-0770
Canfield & Tack Inc 925 Exchange St *General	Rochester	NY	14608	800-836-0861*	585-235-7710
Century Marketing Solutions LLC 3000 Cameron St	Monroe	LA	71201	800-256-6000	
Challenge Printing Co, The Two Bridewell Pl	Clifton	NJ	07014	800-654-1234	973-471-4700
Champion Industries Inc PO Box 2968 PO Box 2968 *OTC: CHMP*	Huntington	WV	25728	800-624-3431	304-528-2791
ColorDynamics 200 E Bethany Dr	Allen	TX	75002	800-445-0017	972-390-6500
Concord Litho Group 92 Old Tpke Rd	Concord	NH	03301	800-258-3662	603-225-3328
Consolidated Graphics Group Inc 1614 E 40th St *General	Cleveland	OH	44103	888-884-9191*	216-881-9191
Cosmos Communications Inc 11-05 44th Dr	Long Island City	NY	11101	800-223-5751	718-482-1800
Courier Printing One Courier Pl	Smyrna	TN	37167	800-467-0444	615-355-4000
Coyle Reproductions Inc 14949 Firestone Blvd	La Mirada	CA	90638	866-269-5373	714-690-8200
Document Security Systems Inc 28 E Main St Ste 1525 *NYSE: DSS*	Rochester	NY	14614	877-407-8031	585-325-3610
Drug Package Inc 901 Drug Package Ln	O'Fallon	MO	63366	800-325-6137	
Dupli Graphics Corp One Dupli Park Dr	Syracuse	NY	13204	800-724-2477	
DuraColor 1840 Oakdale Ave	Racine	WI	53406	877-899-7900	
Emerald City Graphics 23328 66th Ave S *General	Kent	WA	98032	877-631-5178*	253-520-2600
Flagship Press Inc 150 Flagship Dr	North Andover	MA	01845	800-733-1520	978-975-3100
Fundcraft Publishing Inc PO Box 340	Collierville	TN	38027	800-964-5715	901-853-7070
Gannett Offset 7950 Jones Branch Dr	McLean	VA	22107	800-255-1457	703-750-8673
Gazette Publishing Inc 1114 Broadway	Wheaton	MN	56296	800-567-8303	320-563-8146
Georgia Printco 90 S Oak St	Lakeland	GA	31635	866-572-0146	
Harty Press Inc, The PO Box 324	New Haven	CT	06513	800-654-0562	203-562-5112
Hickory Printing Group Inc 725 Reese Dr SW	Conover	NC	28613	800-442-5679	828-465-3431
IntegraColor 3210 Innovative Way	Mesquite	TX	75149	800-933-9511	972-289-0705
Intelligencer Printing Co 330 Eden Rd	Lancaster	PA	17601	800-233-0107	
Interprint LLC 7111 Hayvenhurst Ave	Van Nuys	CA	91406	800-926-9873	818-989-3600
J & A Printing Inc PO Box 457	Hiawatha	IA	52233	800-793-1781	319-393-1781
John Roberts Co 9687 E River Rd	Coon Rapids	MN	55433	800-551-1534	763-755-5500
Kay Toledo Tag Inc PO Box 5038	Toledo	OH	43612	800-822-8247	419-729-5479
Label Works 2025 Lookout Dr	North Mankato	MN	56002	800-522-3558	
Lane Press Inc 87 Meadowland Dr PO Box 130	Burlington	VT	05402	800-733-3740	802-863-5555
Lew A. Cummings Company Inc Four Peters Brook Dr	Hooksett	NH	03106	800-647-0035	
Litho-Krome Co 5700 Old Brim Dr	Midland	GA	31820	800-572-8028	706-562-7900
Lithographix Inc 12250 Crenshaw Blvd *General	Hawthorne	CA	90250	800-848-2449*	323-770-1000
Lowen Corp PO Box 1528	Hutchinson	KS	67504	800-835-2365	620-663-2161
M & R Sales & Service Inc 1n 372 Main St	Glen Ellyn	IL	60137	800-736-6431	630-858-6101
M. Lee Smith Publishers LLC PO Box 5094	Brentwood	TN	37024	800-274-6774	615-373-7517
Merrill Corp 1 Merrill Cir	Saint Paul	MN	55108	800-688-4400	651-646-4501
Meyers Printing Cos Inc, The 7277 Boone Ave N	Minneapolis	MN	55428	800-927-9709	763-533-9730
Midland Information Resources Co 5440 Corporate Pk Dr	Davenport	IA	52807	800-232-3696	563-359-3696
Minuteman Press International Inc 61 Executive Blvd	Farmingdale	NY	11735	800-645-3006	631-249-1370
Nebraska Printing Company Inc 4411 W Tampa Bay Blvd	Tampa	FL	33614	800-683-2056	813-873-7117
Panel Prints Inc 1001 Moosic Rd	Old Forge	PA	18518	800-557-2635	570-457-8334
PBM Graphics Inc 3700 S Miami Blvd	Durham	NC	27703	800-849-8100	919-544-6222
Platon Digital Graphics 136 Oregon St	El Segundo	CA	90245	800-499-0292	
Print Direction Inc 1600 Indian Brook Way	Norcross	GA	30093	877-435-1672	770-446-6446
PrintingForLess.com Inc 100 PFL Way	Livingston	MT	59047	800-930-6040	

				Toll-Free	Phone
Prisma Graphic Corp 2937 E Broadway Rd	Phoenix	AZ	85040	800-379-5777	602-243-5777
Production Press Inc 307 E Morgan St	Jacksonville	IL	62650	800-231-3880	217-243-3353
ProForma 8800 E Pleasant Vly Rd	Independence	OH	44131	800-825-1525	216-520-8400
Progress Printing Co 2677 Waterlick Rd	Lynchburg	VA	24502	800-572-7804	
Publication Printers Corp 2001 S Platte River Dr	Denver	CO	80223	888-824-0303	303-936-0303
Publishers Printing Co 100 Frank E Simon Ave	Shepherdsville	KY	40165	800-627-5801	502-955-6526
Regal Press Inc, The 129 Guild St	Norwood	MA	02062	800-447-3425	781-769-3900
Rogers Printing Inc PO Box 215	Ravenna	MI	49451	800-622-5591	231-853-2244
Schawk Inc 1695 S River Rd *NYSE: SGK*	Des Plaines	IL	60018	800-621-1909	847-827-9494
Sheridan Group 11311 McCormick Rd Ste 260	Hunt Valley	MD	21031	800-352-2210	410-785-7277
Sir Speedy Inc 26722 Plaza Dr	Mission Viejo	CA	92691	800-854-8297	949-348-5000
Solo Printing Inc 7860 NW 66th St	Miami	FL	33166	800-325-0118	305-594-8699
St Joseph Communications 50 MacIntosh Blvd *General	Concord	ON	L4K4P3	877-660-3111*	905-660-3111
Super Color Digital LLC 16761 Hale Ave	Irvine	CA	92606	800-979-4446	949-622-0010
Times Printing Company Inc 100 Industrial Dr	Random Lake	WI	53075	800-236-4396	920-994-4396
Valassis Communications Inc 19975 Victor Pkwy *NYSE: VCI*	Livonia	MI	48152	800-437-0479	734-591-3000
Vectra Visual 3950 Business Pk Dr	Columbus	OH	43204	800-862-2341	614-351-6868
Victorystore.Com Inc 5200 SW 30th St	Davenport	IA	52802	866-241-2295	
Watson Label Products Corp 10616 Trenton Ave	Saint Louis	MO	63132	800-678-6715	314-493-9300
Weldon Williams & Lick Inc 711 N A St	Fort Smith	AR	72901	800-242-4995	479-783-4113
Xlibris Corp 1663 Liberty Dr Ste 200	Bloomington	IN	47403	888-795-4274	

625   PRINTING & PHOTOCOPYING SUPPLIES

				Toll-Free	Phone
Abco Distribution Inc 6282 Proprietors Rd	Worthington	OH	43085	800-821-9435	
Buckeye Business Products Inc 3830 Kelley Ave	Cleveland	OH	44114	800-837-4323	
Chromaline Corp 4832 Grand Ave	Duluth	MN	55807	800-328-4261	218-628-2217
Color Imaging Inc 4350 Peachtree Industrial Blvd Ste 100	Norcross	GA	30071	800-783-1090	770-840-1090
DuraLine Imaging Inc 110 Commercial Blvd	Flat Rock	NC	28731	866-359-2506	828-692-1301
Graphic Controls LLC 400 Exchange St	Buffalo	NY	14204	800-669-1535	
Hurst Chemical Co 2360 Eastman Ave Ste 108 *Cust Svc	Oxnard	CA	93030	800-723-2004*	
Image One Corp 13201 Capital Ave	Oak Park	MI	48237	800-799-5377	248-414-9955
Ink Technology Corp 18320 Lanken Ave	Cleveland	OH	44119	800-633-2826	216-486-6720
LexJet Corp 1680 Fruitville Rd 3rd Fl	Sarasota	FL	34236	800-453-9538	941-330-1210
Light Impressions 2340 Brighton Henrietta Town Line Rd	Rochester	NY	14623	800-975-6429	
Micro Solutions Enterprises (MSE) 8201 Woodley Ave	Van Nuys	CA	91406	800-673-4968	818-407-7500
NER Data Products Inc 307 S Delsea Dr	Glassboro	NJ	08028	888-637-3282	
Rayven Inc 431 Griggs St N *Cust Svc	Saint Paul	MN	55104	800-878-3776*	651-642-1112
WNC Supply LLC 37841 N 16th St	Phoenix	AZ	85086	800-538-5108	623-594-4602

626   PRINTING & PUBLISHING EQUIPMENT & SYSTEMS

SEE ALSO Printers

				Toll-Free	Phone
Baldwin Technology Co Inc 2 Trap Falls Rd Ste 402 *NYSE: BLD*	Shelton	CT	06484	800-728-5839	203-402-1000
Brackett Inc 451 Forbes Field Bldg 451 J Ste	Topeka	KS	66619	800-255-3506	785-862-2205
Brandtjen & Kluge Inc 539 Blanding Woods Rd	Saint Croix Falls	WI	54024	800-826-7320	715-483-3265
Burgess Industries Inc (BII) 7500 Boone Ave N Ste 111	Brooklyn Park	MN	55428	800-233-2589	763-553-7800
Gravograph-New Hermes Inc 2200 Northmont Pkwy	Duluth	GA	30096	800-843-7637	770-623-0331
Heidelberg USA Inc 1000 Gutenberg Dr *Cust Svc	Kennesaw	GA	30144	888-472-9655*	770-419-6500
LasscoWizer Inc 485 Hague St	Rochester	NY	14606	800-854-6595	585-436-1934

		Toll-Free	Phone

Mark Andy Inc
18081 Chesterfield Airport Rd .... Chesterfield MO 63005 | **800-700-6275** | 636-532-4433
Pamarco Global Graphics
235 E 11th Ave .... Roselle NJ 07203 | **800-526-2180** | 908-241-1200
Presstek Inc 55 Executive Dr .... Hudson NH 03051 | **800-422-3616** | 603-595-7000
NASDAQ: PRST
Rosback Co
125 Hawthorne Ave .... Saint Joseph MI 49085 | **800-542-2420** | 269-983-2582
Stolle Machinery Co LLC
6949 S Potomac St .... Centennial CO 80112 | **800-433-8333** | 303-708-9044
Xerox Corp
45 Glover Ave PO Box 4505 .... Norwalk CT 06856 | **800-327-9753** | 203-968-3000
NYSE: XRX

627   PRISON INDUSTRIES

Prison industries are programs established by federal and state governments that provide work for inmates while they are incarcerated as well as on-the-job training to help them become employable on release. At the same time, prison industries provide quality goods and services at competitive prices.

		Toll-Free	Phone

Alabama Correctional Industries
1400 Lloyd St .... Montgomery AL 36107 | **800-224-7007** | 334-261-3600
Arkansas Correctional Industries (ACI)
2403 E Harding St .... Pine Bluff AR 71601 | **877-635-7213** | 870-850-8431
Badger State Industries (BSI)
3099 E Washington Ave PO Box 8990 ...... Madison WI 53708 | **800-862-1086** | 608-240-5200
Cornhusker State Industries
800 Pioneers Blvd .... Lincoln NE 68502 | **800-348-7537** | 402-471-4597
Correctional Enterprises of Connecticut
24 Wolcott Hill Rd .... Wethersfield CT 06109 | **800-842-1146** | 860-263-6839
Federal Prison Industries Inc
320 First St NW .... Washington DC 20534 | **800-827-3168** |
Georgia Correctional Industries
2984 Clifton Springs Rd .... Decatur GA 30034 | **800-282-7130** | 404-244-5100
Iowa Prison Industries (IPI)
1445 E Grand Ave .... Des Moines IA 50316 | **800-670-4537** | 515-242-5770
Kentucky Correctional Industries
1041 Leestown Rd .... Frankfort KY 40601 | **800-828-9524** | 502-573-1040
Massachusetts Correctional Industries
1 Industries Dr Bldg A PO Box 188 .... Norfolk MA 02056 | **800-222-2211** | 508-850-1070
Missouri Vocational Enterprises
1717 Industrial Dr PO Box 1898 .... Jefferson City MO 65102 | **800-392-8486*** | 573-751-6663
*Sales
New Jersey Bureau of State Use Industries
163 N Olden Ave PO Box 867 .... Trenton NJ 08625 | **800-321-6524** |
New York Correctional Industries
550 Broadway .... Albany NY 12204 | **800-436-6321** | 518-436-6321
Ohio Penal Industries (OPI)
1221 McKinley Ave .... Columbus OH 43222 | **800-237-3454** | 614-752-0287
Oklahoma Correctional Industries
3402 N Martin Luther King Ave .... Oklahoma City OK 73111 | **800-522-3565** | 405-425-7500
PEN Products
2010 E New York St .... Indianapolis IN 46201 | **800-736-2550** | 317-955-6800
Pennsylvania Correctional Industries
PO Box 47 .... Camp Hill PA 17001 | **877-673-3724*** | 717-425-7292
*General
Prison Rehabilitative Industries & Diversified Enterprises Inc (PRIDE)
223 Morrison Rd Ste 200 .... Brandon FL 33511 | **877-283-6819** | 813-324-8700
Rough Rider Industries
3303 E Main Ave .... Bismarck ND 58506 | **800-732-0557** | 701-328-6161
Tennessee Rehabilitative Initiative in Correction (TRICOR)
240 Great Cir Rd Ste 310 .... Nashville TN 37228 | **800-958-7426** | 615-741-5705
West Virginia Correctional Industries
617 Leon Sullivan Way .... Charleston WV 25301 | **800-525-5381** | 304-558-6054

628   PROFESSIONAL EMPLOYER ORGANIZATIONS (PEOS)

Companies listed here contractually assume human resources responsibilities for client companies in exchange for a fee, thus allowing the client company to focus on its true company business. The PEO establishes and maintains an employer relationship with the workers assigned to its client companies, with the PEO and the client company each having specific rights and responsibilities toward the employees.

		Toll-Free	Phone

Adams Keegan Inc
6055 Primacy Pkwy Ste 300 .... Memphis TN 38119 | **800-621-1308** | 901-683-5353
ADP TotalSource Co
10200 Sunset Dr .... Miami FL 33173 | **800-447-3237** | 305-630-1000
Advice Media LLC
PO Box 982064 .... Park City UT 84098 | **800-260-9497** |
Alcott Group
71 Executive Blvd .... Farmingdale NY 11735 | **888-425-2688** | 631-420-0100
Allevity HR & Payroll
870 Manzanita Ct Ste A .... Chico CA 95926 | **800-447-8233** | 530-345-2486
Allied Employer Group
4400 Buffalo Gap Rd Ste 4500 .... Abilene TX 79606 | **800-495-3836** | 325-695-5822
AlphaStaff Inc
800 Corporate Dr Ste 600 .... Fort Lauderdale FL 33334 | **888-335-9545** | 954-267-1760
ALTRES Inc
967 Kapiolani Blvd .... Honolulu HI 96814 | **888-425-8737** | 808-591-4940
Assent Consulting Inc
10054 Pasadena Ave .... Cupertino CA 95014 | **800-747-0940** | 408-366-8820
Axcet HR Solutions
Axet 8325 Lenexa Dr Ste 410 .... Lenexa KS 66214 | **800-801-7557** | 913-383-2999
Barrett Business Services Inc
8100 NE Pkwy Dr Ste 200 .... Vancouver WA 98662 | **800-494-5669** | 360-828-0700
NASDAQ: BBSI
Brandmovers Inc
590 Means St Ste 250 .... Atlanta GA 30318 | **888-463-4933** |
Chipton-ross Inc
343 Main St .... El Segundo CA 90245 | **800-927-9318** | 310-414-7800
Co-Advantage Resources
111 W Jefferson St Ste 100 .... Orlando FL 32801 | **800-868-1016** | 407-422-8448

CrowdSource Solutions Inc
33 Bronze Pointe .... Swansea IL 62226 | **855-276-9376** |
Diversified Hum Res Inc
3020 E Camelback Rd Ste 213 .... Phoenix AZ 85016 | **888-870-5588** | 480-941-5588
Doherty Employment Group
7625 Parklawn Ave .... Edina MN 55435 | **888-297-0495*** | 952-832-8383
*Sales
Employee Management Services
435 Elm St .... Cincinnati OH 45202 | **888-651-1536** | 513-651-3244
Human Capital
2055 Crooks Rd Lowr Level .... Rochester Hills MI 48309 | **888-736-9071** |
Iconma LLC
850 Stephenson Hwy Ste 612 .... Troy MI 48083 | **888-451-2519** |
Innovate E-Commerce Inc
160 N Craig St .... Pittsburgh PA 15213 | **888-771-9606** |
Inspirage Inc
40 Lk Bellevue Dr Ste 100 .... Bellevue WA 98005 | **855-517-4250** |
Marvel Consultants Inc
28601 Chagrin Blvd Ste 210 .... Cleveland OH 44122 | **800-338-1257** | 216-292-2855
Merit Resources Inc
4410 114th St .... Des Moines IA 50322 | **800-336-1931** | 515-278-1931
Mountain Ltd
19 Yarmouth Dr Ste 301 .... New Gloucester ME 04260 | **800-322-8627** | 207-688-6200
Oasis Outsourcing
4511 Woodland Corporate Blvd .... Tampa FL 33614 | **866-709-9401** | 813-864-8321
Oasis Outsourcing Inc
2054 Vista Pkwy Ste 300 .... West Palm Beach FL 33411 | **888-627-4735*** |
*General
Pay Plus Benefits Inc
1110 N Ctr Pkwy Ste B .... Kennewick WA 99336 | **888-531-5781** | 509-735-1143
Pencom Systems Inc
152 Remsen St .... Brooklyn NY 11201 | **800-736-2664** | 718-923-1111
People Lease Inc
689 Town Ctr Blvd Ste B .... Ridgeland MS 39157 | **800-723-3025** | 601-987-3025
Personnel Management Inc
PO Box 6657 .... Shreveport LA 71136 | **800-259-4126** | 318-869-4555
Professional Staff Management Inc
6801 Lake Plaza Dr Suite D-405 .... Indianapolis IN 46220 | **800-967-5515** | 317-816-7007
Progressive Employer Services
6407 Parkland Dr .... Sarasota FL 34243 | **888-925-2990** | 941-925-2990
Qualified Resources International LLC
78 Kenwood St .... Cranston RI 02907 | **866-421-9840** | 401-946-1002
Recon Management Services Inc
3649 S Beglis Pkwy .... Sulphur LA 70665 | **888-301-4662** | 337-583-4662
Red Foundry Inc
1608 S Ashland Ave .... Chicago IL 60608 | **888-406-1099** |
Reserves Network, The
22021 Brookpark Rd .... Cleveland OH 44126 | **866-876-2020** | 440-779-6681
Resource Management Inc
281 Main St Ste 5 .... Fitchburg MA 01420 | **800-508-0048*** |
*Cust Svc
RMPersonnel Inc
4707 Montana Ave .... El Paso TX 79903 | **866-333-7176** | 915-565-7674
Staff Management Inc
5919 Spring Creek Rd .... Rockford IL 61114 | **800-535-3518*** | 815-282-3900
*General
Staff One Inc 8111 LBJ Fwy .... Dallas TX 75251 | **800-771-7823** |
Summit Technical Services Inc
355 Centerville Rd .... Warwick RI 02886 | **800-643-7372** | 401-736-8323
Sycara Inc
6263 N Scottsdale Rd Ste 180 .... Scottsdale AZ 85250 | **855-479-2272** |
TeleSearch Staffing Solutions
251 Re 206 .... Flanders NJ 07836 | **800-499-8367** | 973-927-7870
Tilson HR Inc
1530 American Way Ste 200 .... Greenwood IN 46143 | **800-276-3976** | 317-885-3838
Training Assoc Corp, The
289 Tpke Rd .... Westborough MA 01581 | **800-241-8868** | 508-890-8500
TriNet Group Inc
1100 San Leandro Blvd Ste 300 .... San Leandro CA 94577 | **888-874-6388** | 510-352-5000
VJV IT 96 Linwood Plz .... Fort Lee NJ 07024 | **800-614-7561** |

629   PUBLIC BROADCASTING ORGANIZATIONS

SEE ALSO Radio Networks

		Toll-Free	Phone

Alabama Educational Television Commission
2112 11th Ave S Ste 400 .... Birmingham AL 35205 | **800-239-5233** | 205-328-8756
Alabama Public Television (APT)
2112 11th Ave S Ste 400 .... Birmingham AL 35205 | **800-239-5233** | 205-328-8756
Annenberg Media
1301 Pennsylvania Ave NW ste302 .... Washington DC 20004 | **800-532-7637** |
Arkansas Educational Television Network (AETN)
350 S Donaghey Ave .... Conway AR 72034 | **800-662-2386** | 501-682-2386
Association of Public Television Stations (APTS)
2100 Crystal Dr Ste 700 .... Arlington VA 22202 | **855-948-5853** | 202-654-4200
Blue Ridge Public Television
1215 McNeil Dr .... Roanoke VA 24015 | **888-332-7788** | 540-344-0991
Capitol Steps Productions Inc
210 N Washington St .... Alexandria VA 22314 | **800-733-7837** | 703-683-8330
Commonwealth Club of California
595 Market St Second Fl .... San Francisco CA 94105 | **800-933-7548** | 415-597-6700
Connecticut Public Broadcasting Inc (CPBI)
1049 Asylum Ave .... Hartford CT 06105 | **800-683-2112** | 860-278-5310
Corporation for Public Broadcasting (CPB)
401 Ninth St NW .... Washington DC 20004 | **800-272-2190** | 202-879-9600
East Tennessee Public Communications Corp
1611 E Magnolia Ave .... Knoxville TN 37917 | **844-686-2378** | 865-595-0220
Georgia Public Broadcasting (GPB)
260 14th St NW .... Atlanta GA 30318 | **800-222-6006** |
GPB Education
260 14th St NW .... Atlanta GA 30318 | **888-501-8960** | 404-685-2550
Hawaii Public Television
2350 Dole St .... Honolulu HI 96822 | **800-238-4847** | 808-973-1000
Idaho Public Television (IPTV)
1455 N Orchard St .... Boise ID 83706 | **800-543-6868** | 208-373-7220
Independent Television Service (ITVS)
651 Brannan St Ste 410 .... San Francisco CA 94107 | **800-621-6196** | 415-356-8383

				Toll-Free	Phone
Kentucky Educational Television (KET)					
600 Cooper Dr	Lexington	KY	40502	800-432-0951	859-258-7000
KUAC FM/TV PO Box 755620	Fairbanks	AK	99775	800-727-6543	907-474-7491
Louisiana Public Broadcasting					
7733 Perkins Rd	Baton Rouge	LA	70810	800-973-7246	225-767-5660
Maine Public Broadcasting Network (MPBN)					
65 Texas Ave	Bangor	ME	04401	800-884-1717	207-941-1010
Maryland Public Television (MPT)					
11767 Owings Mills Blvd	Owings Mills	MD	21117	800-223-3678	410-581-4201
Minnesota Public Radio (MPR)					
480 Cedar St	Saint Paul	MN	55101	800-228-7123	651-290-1212
Mississippi Authority for Educational Television					
3825 Ridgewood Rd	Jackson	MS	39211	800-850-4406	601-432-6565
Montana Public Radio					
32 Campus Dr University of Montana	Missoula	MT	59812	800-325-1565	406-243-4931
Montana Public Television					
183 Visual Communications Bldg	Bozeman	MT	59717	800-426-8243	866-832-0829
National Captioning Institute (NCI)					
3725 Concorde Pkwy Ste 100	Chantilly	VA	20151	800-825-6758	703-917-7600
National Educational Telecommunications Assn (NETA)					
939 S Stadium Rd	Columbia	SC	29201	866-270-5141	803-799-5517
Nebraska Educational Telecommunications (NET)					
1800 N 33rd St	Lincoln	NE	68503	800-868-1868	
New Hampshire Public Television (NHPTV)					
268 Mast Rd	Durham	NH	03824	800-639-8408	603-868-1100
Prairie Public Broadcasting Inc					
207 N Fifth St	Fargo	ND	58102	800-359-6900	701-241-6900
Public Broadcasting Council of Central New York					
506 Old Liverpool Rd PO Box 2400	Syracuse	NY	13220	800-451-9269	315-453-2424
Public Broadcasting Northwest Pennsylvania					
8425 Peach St	Erie	PA	16509	800-727-8854	814-864-3001
Rocky Mountain Public Broadcasting Network (RMPB)					
1089 Bannock St	Denver	CO	80204	800-274-6666	303-892-6666
Small Station Assn					
KRWG-TV PO Box 30001 MSCPB 22	Las Cruces	NM	88003	877-308-2408	575-646-2222
Smoky Hills Public Television (SHPTV)					
604 Elm St	Bunker Hill	KS	67626	800-362-9347	785-483-6990
South Dakota Public Broadcasting (SDPB)					
555 N Dakota St PO Box 5000	Vermillion	SD	57069	800-456-0766	605-677-5861
Texas Public Radio (TPR)					
8401 Datapoint Dr Ste 800	San Antonio	TX	78229	800-622-8977	210-614-8977
ThinkTV 110 S Jefferson St	Dayton	OH	45402	800-247-1614	937-220-1600
TRAC Media Services					
3961 E Speedway Blvd Ste 410	Tucson	AZ	85712	888-299-1866	520-299-1866
Twin Cities Public Television Inc					
172 E Fourth St	Saint Paul	MN	55101	866-229-1300	651-222-1717
University of North Carolina Ctr for Public Television (UNC-TV)					
10 TW Alexander Dr					
PO Box 14900	Research Triangle Park	NC	27709	800-906-5050	919-549-7000
Vermont Public Television (VPT)					
204 Ethan Allen Ave	Colchester	VT	05446	800-639-7811	802-655-4800
WAMC/Northeast Public Radio					
318 Central Ave	Albany	NY	12206	800-323-9262	518-465-5233
West Central Illinois Educational Telecommunications Corp					
PO Box 6248	Springfield	IL	62708	800-232-3605	217-483-7887
Wisconsin Educational Communications Board					
3319 W Beltline Hwy	Madison	WI	53713	800-422-9707	608-264-9600
Wisconsin Public Radio (WPR)					
821 University Ave	Madison	WI	53706	800-747-7444	
Wisconsin Public Television (WPT)					
821 University Ave	Madison	WI	53706	800-422-9707	608-263-2121
Wyoming Public Television					
2660 Peck Ave	Riverton	WY	82501	800-495-9788	307-856-6944

630 PUBLIC POLICY RESEARCH CENTERS

				Toll-Free	Phone
AARP Public Policy Institute					
601 E St NW	Washington	DC	20049	888-687-2277	202-434-2277
Acton Institute for the Study of Religion & Liberty					
161 Ottawa Ave NW Ste 301	Grand Rapids	MI	49503	800-345-2286	616-454-3080
Allegheny Institute for Public Policy					
305 Mt Lebanon Blvd Ste 208	Pittsburgh	PA	15234	800-242-2184	412-440-0079
American Enterprise Institute for Public Policy Research (AEI)					
1150 17th St NW Ste 1100	Washington	DC	20036	800-862-5801	202-862-5800
Ashbrook Ctr					
401 College Ave Ashland University	Ashland	OH	44805	877-289-5411	419-289-5411
Atlantic Council of the United States					
1101 15th St NW 11th Fl	Washington	DC	20005	800-311-9410	202-463-7226
Brookings Institution					
1775 Massachusetts Ave NW	Washington	DC	20036	800-275-1447	202-797-6000
Capital Research Ctr					
1513 16th St NW	Washington	DC	20036	800-459-3950	202-483-6900
Carnegie Endowment for International Peace					
1779 Massachusetts Ave NW	Washington	DC	20036	877-866-3070	202-483-7600
Carter Ctr					
One Copenhill Ave 453 Freedom Pkwy	Atlanta	GA	30307	800-550-3560	404-420-5100
Center for Animals & Public Policy					
Tufts Univ School of Veterinary Medicine					
200 Westboro Rd	North Grafton	MA	01536	888-748-8387	508-839-7920
Center for Law & Social Policy (CLASP)					
1015 15th St NW Ste 400	Washington	DC	20005	800-821-4367	202-906-8000
Center for Policy Research					
Syracuse University 426 Eggers Hall	Syracuse	NY	13244	800-325-3535	315-443-3114
Center of the American Experiment (CAE)					
12 S Sixth St 1024 Plymouth Bldg	Minneapolis	MN	55402	800-657-3717	612-338-3605
Committee for Economic Development (CED)					
2000 L St NW Ste 700	Washington	DC	20036	800-676-7353	202-296-5860
Foundation for Economic Education (FEE)					
30 S Broadway	Irvington-on-Hudson	NY	10533	800-960-4333	914-591-7230
Heritage Foundation					
214 Massachusetts Ave NE	Washington	DC	20002	800-546-2843	202-546-4400
Hudson Institute					
1015 15th St NW Ste 600	Washington	DC	20005	888-554-1325	202-974-2400
Independent Institute					
100 Swan Way	Oakland	CA	94621	800-927-8733	510-632-1366

				Toll-Free	Phone
Institute for Humane Studies					
3301 N Fairfax Dr Ste 440	Arlington	VA	22201	800-697-8799	703-993-4880
Institute for Justice					
901 N Glebe Rd Ste 900	Arlington	VA	22203	888-322-6397	703-682-9320
Institute for Policy Studies (IPS)					
1112 16th St NW Ste 600	Washington	DC	20036	877-564-6833	202-234-9382
Institute of Government & Public Affairs					
Univ of Illinois 1007 W Nevada St	Urbana	IL	61801	866-794-3340	217-333-3340
Institute of World Politics					
1521 16th St NW	Washington	DC	20036	888-566-9497	202-462-2101
Malcolm Wiener Ctr for Social Policy					
John F Kennedy School of Government Harvard University					
79 John F Kennedy St	Cambridge	MA	02138	866-845-6596	617-496-4082
Manpower Demonstration Research Corp					
16 E 34th St 19th Fl	New York	NY	10016	800-221-3165	212-532-3200
Margaret Chase Smith Policy Ctr					
University of Maine York Complex Ste 4	Orono	ME	04469	877-486-2364	207-581-1648
Princeton Institute for International & Regional Studies (PIIRS)					
Princeton University Bendheim Hall	Princeton	NJ	08544	888-486-3339	609-258-4852
RAND Corp 1776 Main St	Santa Monica	CA	90401	877-584-8642	310-393-0411
Reason Public Policy Institute					
3415 S Sepulveda Blvd Ste 400	Los Angeles	CA	90034	888-732-7668	310-391-2245
Rockford Institute					
928 N Main St	Rockford	IL	61103	800-383-0680	815-964-5053
World Policy Institute (WPI)					
220 Fifth Ave 9th Fl	New York	NY	10001	800-207-8354	212-481-5005
Worldwatch Institute					
1776 Massachusetts Ave NW	Washington	DC	20036	877-539-9946	202-452-1999

631 PUBLIC RECORDS SEARCH SERVICES

SEE ALSO Investigative Services

				Toll-Free	Phone
Accufax PO Box 35563	Tulsa	OK	74153	800-256-8898	
All-Search & Inspection Inc					
1108 E S Union Ave	Midvale	UT	84047	800-227-3152	801-984-8160
American Driving Records Inc					
2860 Gold Tailings Ct					
PO Box 1970	Rancho Cordova	CA	95670	800-766-6877	916-456-3200
AmRent					
950 Threadneedle Ste 255	Houston	TX	77079	800-324-4595	713-266-1870
Applicant Insight Ltd					
5396 School Rd PO Box 458	New Port Richey	FL	34652	800-771-7703	
Apscreen Inc					
PO Box 80639	Rancho Santa Margarita	CA	92688	800-277-2733	949-646-4003
Background Bureau Inc					
2019 Alexandria Pike	Highland Heights	KY	41076	800-854-3990	859-781-3400
Background Information Services Inc					
1800 30th St Ste 204	Boulder	CO	80301	800-433-6010	303-442-3960
Capitol Services Inc					
800 Brazos St Ste 400	Austin	TX	78701	800-345-4647	
CARCO Group Inc					
5000 Corporate Ct	Holtsville	NY	11742	800-645-4556	631-862-9300
CCH Washington Service Bureau Inc					
1015 15th St NW 10th Fl	Washington	DC	20005	800-955-5219	202-312-6600
CDI Credit Inc					
6160 Peachtree Dunwoody Rd NE					
Ste B-210	Atlanta	GA	30328	800-633-3961	770-350-5070
Charles Jones LLC					
PO Box 8488	Trenton	NJ	08650	800-792-8888	
Colby Attorneys Service Company Inc					
111 Washington Ave Ste 703	Albany	NY	12210	800-832-1220	
CoreLogic SafeRent					
7300 Westmore Rd Ste 3	Rockville	MD	20850	866-873-3651	
CT Lien Solutions					
2727 Allen Pkwy Ste 1000	Houston	TX	77019	800-833-5778	
D+H CollateralGuard RC (CSRS)					
4126 Norland Ave Ste 200	Burnaby	BC	V5G3S8	866-873-9780	604-637-4000
Doc-U-Search Inc					
63 Pleasant St PO Box 777	Concord	NH	03301	800-332-3034	
Driving Records Facilities					
PO Box 1086	Glen Burnie	MD	21061	800-772-5510	
Edge Information Management Inc					
1682 W Hibiscus Blvd	Melbourne	FL	32901	800-725-3343	321-722-3343
Employment Screening Services Inc					
627 E Sprague St Ste 100	Spokane	WA	99202	800-473-7778	509-624-3851
Explore Information Services LLC					
2900 Lone Oak Pkwy Ste 140					
PO Box 21636	St. Paul	MN	55121	800-531-9125	
Fidelifacts					
42 Broadway Ste 1548	New York	NY	10004	800-678-0007	212-425-1520
Government Liaison Services Inc (GLS)					
200 N Glebe Rd Ste 321	Arlington	VA	22203	800-642-6564	703-524-8200
HireRight Inc					
5151 California Ave	Irvine	CA	92617	800-400-2761	949-428-5800
IMI Data Search Inc					
275 E Hillcrest Dr Ste 102	Thousand Oaks	CA	91360	800-860-7779	805-495-1149
Information Management Systems Inc					
114 W Main St Ste 211 PO Box 2924	New Britain	CT	06050	888-403-8347	860-229-1119
KnowX LLC 730 Peachtree St	Atlanta	GA	30308	877-317-5000	404-541-0220
Kress Employment Screening					
320 Westcott St Ste 108	Houston	TX	77007	888-636-3693	713-880-3693
Kroll Background America Inc					
100 Centerview Dr Ste 300	Nashville	TN	37214	800-697-7189	615-320-9800
Laborchex Co, The					
2506 Lakeland Dr Ste 200	Jackson	MS	39232	800-880-0366	601-664-6760
Legal Data Resources Inc					
2816 W Summerdale Ave	Chicago	IL	60625	844-732-2437	773-561-2468
LegalEase Inc					
211 E 43rd St Ste 2203	New York	NY	10017	800-393-1277	212-393-9070
MLQ Attorney Services					
2000 River Edge Pkwy Ste 885	Atlanta	GA	30328	800-446-8794	770-984-7007
OPENonline					
1650 Lk Shore Dr Ste 350	Columbus	OH	43204	888-381-5656	614-481-6999
Orange Tree Employment Screening					
7275 Ohms Ln	Minneapolis	MN	55439	800-886-4777	952-941-9040

			Toll-Free	Phone

Parasec Inc
2804 Gateway Oaks Dr Ste 200
PO Box 160568 . . . . Sacramento CA 95833 **800-533-7272***
*General

Penncorp Servicegroup Inc
600 N Second St Ste 401 . . . . Harrisburg PA 17101 **800-544-9050** 717-234-2300

Property Owners Exchange Inc
6630 Baltimore National Pk
Ste 208 . . . . Catonsville MD 21228 **800-869-3200** 410-719-0100

Questel Orbit
1725 Duke St Ste 625 . . . . Alexandria VA 22314 **800-456-7248** 703-519-1820

Rental Research Services Inc
7525 Mitchell Rd Ste 301 . . . . Eden Prairie MN 55344 **800-328-0333** 952-935-5700

Search Company International
1535 Grant St Ste 140 . . . . Denver CO 80203 **800-727-2120** 303-863-1800

Search Network Ltd
1503 42nd St Ste 210 . . . . West Des Moines IA 50266 **800-383-5050** 515-223-1153

SearchTec Inc
314 N 12th St Ste 100 . . . . Philadelphia PA 19107 **877-273-2724** 215-963-0888

Securitech Inc
8230 E Broadway Blvd Ste E-10 . . . . Tucson AZ 85710 **888-792-4473** 520-721-0305

Superior Information Services Inc
300 Phillips Blvd Ste 500 . . . . Trenton NJ 08618 **800-792-8888** 609-883-7000

TABB Inc PO Box 10 . . . . Chester NJ 07930 **800-887-8222**

Thomson CompuMark
500 Victory Rd . . . . North Quincy MA 02171 **800-692-8833** 617-479-1600

Unisearch Inc
1780 Barnes Blvd SW . . . . Tumwater WA 98512 **800-722-0708** 360-956-9500

USIS
7799 Leesburg Pk Ste 1100-S . . . . . Falls Church VA 22043 **888-270-8978** 703-448-0178

Verified Credentials Inc
20890 Kenbridge Ct . . . . Lakeville MN 55044 **800-473-4934** 952-985-7200

Westlaw Court Express
1100 13th St NW Ste 300 . . . . Washington DC 20005 **877-362-7387** 202-423-2163

632 PUBLIC RELATIONS FIRMS

SEE ALSO Advertising Agencies

			Toll-Free	Phone

Ackermann Public Relations & Marketing
1111 Northshore Dr Ste N-400 . . . . Knoxville TN 37919 **877-325-9453*** 865-584-0550
*General

B & B Media Group
109 S Main St . . . . Corsicana TX 75110 **800-927-0517** 903-872-0517

Boardroom Communications Inc
Bank Of America Plaza 1776 N Pine Island Rd
Ste 320 . . . . Fort Lauderdale FL 33322 **877-773-4761** 954-370-8999

Charles Ryan Assoc Inc
601 Morris St Ste 301 . . . . Charleston WV 25301 **877-342-0161**

Connect PR
One Market St 36th Fl . . . . San Francisco CA 94105 **800-455-8855** 415-222-9691

Hunter Public Relations
41 Madison Ave 5th Fl . . . . New York NY 10010 **866-395-7710** 212-679-6600

McNeely Pigott & Fox
611 Commerce St Ste 2800 . . . . Nashville TN 37203 **800-818-6953** 615-259-4000

MCS Healthcare Public Relations
1420 US Hwy 206 Ste 100 . . . . Bedminster NJ 07921 **888-652-8200** 908-234-9900

Montesquieu Winery
8221 Arjons Dr . . . . San Diego CA 92126 **800-860-2378**

S&S Public Relations Inc
One Northfield Plz Ste 400 . . . . Northfield IL 60093 **800-287-2279**

SHIFT Communications LLC
275 Washington St Ste 410 . . . . Newton MA 02458 **800-494-8477** 617-779-1800

Sitrick & Co
1840 Century Pk E Ste 800 . . . . . . Los Angeles CA 90067 **800-288-8809** 310-788-2850

Thomson Safaris
14 Mt Auburn St . . . . Watertown MA 02472 **800-235-0289** 617-923-0426

PUBLICATIONS

SEE Magazines & Journals ; Newsletters ; Newspapers

633 PUBLISHING COMPANIES

SEE ALSO Magazines & Journals ; Newsletters ; Newspapers ; Book Producers

633-1 Atlas & Map Publishers

			Toll-Free	Phone

DeLorme
Two DeLorme Dr PO Box 298 . . . . Yarmouth ME 04096 **800-452-5931*** 207-846-7000
*Sales

MARCOA Publishing Inc
9955 Black Mtn Rd . . . . San Diego CA 92126 **800-854-2935** 858-695-9600

Rand McNally
9855 Woods Dr PO Box 7600 . . . . Skokie IL 60077 **800-275-7263**

Simon & Schuster Interactive
1230 Ave of the Americas . . . . New York NY 10020 **800-223-2336** 212-698-7000

633-2 Book Publishers

			Toll-Free	Phone

ABC-CLIO Inc 130 Cremona Dr . . . . Goleta CA 93117 **800-368-6868** 805-968-1911

American Printing House for the Blind
1839 Frankfort Ave PO Box 6085 . . . . . . Louisville KY 40206 **800-223-1839** 502-895-2405

Antique Collectors Club
116 Pleasant St . . . . EastHampton MA 01027 **800-254-4100** 413-529-0861

Applewood Books Inc
1 River Rd . . . . Carlisle MA 01741 **800-277-5312*** 781-271-0055
*General

Atlantic Publishing Co
315 E Washington St . . . . Starke FL 32091 **800-814-1132**

Author House
1663 Liberty Dr Ste 200 . . . . Bloomington IN 47403 **888-728-8467** 812-339-6000

Barron's Educational Series Inc
250 Wireless Blvd . . . . Hauppauge NY 11788 **800-645-3476** 631-434-3311

BRB Publications Inc
PO Box 27869 . . . . Tempe AZ 85285 **800-929-3811** 480-829-7475

Brillacademic Publishers Inc
2 liberty Sq 11th Fl . . . . Boston MA 02109 **800-337-9255** 617-263-2323

Browntrout Publishers Inc
201 Continental Blvd . . . . El Segundo CA 90245 **800-777-7812** 310-607-9010

Bureau of National Affairs Inc
1801 S Bell St . . . . Arlington VA 22202 **800-372-1033** 703-341-3000

Bureau of National Affairs Inc BNA Books Div
1801 S Bell St . . . . Arlington VA 22202 **800-372-1033*** 703-341-3500
*Sales

Carroll Publishing Co
4701 Sangamore Rd Ste S-155 . . . . Bethesda MD 20816 **800-336-4240** 301-263-9800

Cengage Learning
PO Box 6904 . . . . Florence KY 41022 **800-354-9706**

Charles C Thomas Publisher
2600 S First St PO Box 19265 . . . . . . Springfield IL 62704 **800-258-8980*** 217-789-8980
*Sales

Chronicle Books
680 Second St . . . . San Francisco CA 94107 **800-722-6657** 415-537-4200

Commemorative Brands Inc
7211 Cir S Rd . . . . Austin TX 78745 **800-225-3687**

Corwin Press Inc
2455 Teller Rd . . . . Thousand Oaks CA 91320 **800-233-9936*** 805-499-9734
*Orders

CRC Press LLC
6000 Broken Sound Pkwy NW Ste 300 . . . . . . Boca Raton FL 33487 **800-272-7737*** 561-994-0555
*Cust Svc

Creative Communications For The Parish Inc
1564 Fencorp Dr . . . . Fenton MO 63026 **800-325-9414** 636-305-9777

Curriculum Assoc Inc
153 Rangeway Rd . . . . North Billerica MA 01862 **800-225-0248**

D & B 103 JFK Pkwy . . . . Short Hills NJ 07078 **800-234-3867** 973-921-5500
NYSE: DNB

Dalmation Press
113 Seaboard Ln Ste C-250 . . . . Franklin TN 37067 **800-815-8696**

Disney Consumer Products
500 S Buena Vista St . . . . Burbank CA 91521 **877-282-8322*** 818-560-1000
*PR

Donning Company Publishers
184 Business Pk Dr Ste 206 . . . . Virginia Beach VA 23462 **800-296-8572**

Dorling Kindersley Publishing
375 Hudson St . . . . New York NY 10014 **800-631-8571*** 646-674-4047
*Cust Svc

Educators Publishing Service Inc (EPS)
625 Mt Auburn St Third Fl
PO Box 9031 . . . . Cambridge MA 02139 **800-225-5750**

EMC-Paradigm Publishing Co
875 Montreal Way . . . . Saint Paul MN 55102 **800-328-1452** 651-290-2800

Encyclopaedia Britannica Inc
331 N La Salle St . . . . Chicago IL 60654 **800-323-1229** 312-347-7159

FA Davis Co
1915 Arch St . . . . Philadelphia PA 19103 **800-323-3555** 215-568-2270

Feminist Press at the City University of New York
365 Fifth Ave Ste 5406 . . . . New York NY 10016 **800-283-3572** 212-817-7922

Financial Publishing Co
PO Box 570 . . . . South Bend IN 46624 **800-433-0090*** 574-243-6040
*Cust Svc

Forbes Inc 60 Fifth Ave . . . . New York NY 10011 **800-295-0893** 212-620-2200

Gale Cengage Learning
27500 Drake Rd . . . . Farmington Hills MI 48331 **800-877-4253*** 248-699-4253
*Cust Svc

Glencoe/McGraw-Hill
8787 Orion Pl . . . . Columbus OH 43240 **800-848-1567**

Goodheart-Willcox Publisher
18604 W Creek Dr . . . . Tinley Park IL 60477 **800-323-0440** 708-687-5000

Government Research Service
1516 SW Boswell Ave . . . . Topeka KS 66604 **800-346-6898** 785-232-7720

Grade Finders Inc PO Box 944 . . . . Exton PA 19341 **800-777-8074** 610-524-7070

Greenwood-Heinemann
361 Hanover St . . . . Portsmouth NH 03801 **800-541-2086** 603-431-7894

Grey House Publishing
4919 Rt 22 PO Box 56 . . . . Amenia NY 12501 **800-562-2139** 518-789-8700

Hachette Book Group
237 Pk Ave . . . . New York NY 10017 **800-759-0190**

Haights Cross Communications
136 Madison Ave 8th Fl . . . . New York NY 10016 **800-338-6519** 212-209-0500

Harlequin Enterprises Ltd
225 Duncan Mill Rd . . . . Don Mills ON M3B3K9 **888-343-9777** 416-445-5860

Harlequin-Silhouette Books
233 Broadway Ste 1001 . . . . New York NY 10279 **800-873-8635** 212-553-4200

HarperCollins Publishers Inc
10 E 53rd St . . . . New York NY 10022 **800-242-7737** 212-207-7000

Harris Connect LLC
1511 Rt 22 Ste C-25 . . . . Brewster NY 10509 **800-516-4915**

Health Communications Inc (HCI)
3201 SW 15th St . . . . Deerfield Beach FL 33442 **800-441-5569*** 954-360-0909
*Cust Svc

Holtzbrinck Publishers
175 Fifth Ave . . . . New York NY 10010 **800-221-7945** 646-307-5151

Houghton Mifflin Harcourt
222 Berkeley St . . . . Boston MA 02116 **877-866-2586** 617-351-5000

Human Kinetics
1607 N Market St . . . . Champaign IL 61820 **800-747-4457** 217-351-5076

HW Wilson Co 10 Estes St . . . . Ipswich MA 01938 **800-653-2726** 978-356-6500

Inner Traditions International
one Pk Row . . . . Rochester VT 05767 **800-246-8648** 802-767-3174

Island Press
2000 M St NW Suite 650 . . . . Washington DC 20036 **800-621-2736** 202-232-7933

iUniverse
1663 Liberty Dr . . . . Bloomington IN 47403 **800-288-4677**

Jane's Information Group
110 N Royal St Ste 200 . . . . Alexandria VA 22314 **800-824-0768** 703-683-3700

Jeppesen Sanderson Inc
55 Inverness Dr E . . . . Englewood CO 80112 **800-621-5377** 303-799-9090

	City	State	ZIP	Toll-Free	Phone
John Wiley & Sons Inc 111 River St *NYSE: JW/A* ■ *Sales	Hoboken	NJ	07030	**800-225-5945***	201-748-6000
Judaica Press Inc 123 Ditmas Ave	Brooklyn	NY	11218	**800-972-6201**	718-972-6200
Kendall/Hunt Publishing Co 4050 Westmark Dr PO Box 1840 *Cust Svc	Dubuque	IA	52002	**800-228-0810***	563-589-1000
Kensington Publishing Corp 119 W 40th St	New York	NY	10018	**800-221-2647**	212-407-1500
Key Curriculum Press 1150 65th St	Emeryville	CA	94608	**800-338-3987**	510-595-7000
Lawyers Diary & Manual 240 Mulberry St PO Box 50	Newark	NJ	07102	**800-444-4041**	973-642-1440
Leadership Directories Inc 104 Fifth Ave 3rd Fl	New York	NY	10011	**800-627-0311**	212-627-4140
Lerner Publishing Group 1251 Washington Ave N	Minneapolis	MN	55401	**800-328-4929**	
LexisNexis Matthew Bender 744 Broad St	Newark	NJ	07102	**800-252-9257**	973-820-2000
Lightning Source 1246 Heil Quaker Blvd	La Vergne	TN	37086	**800-509-4156**	615-213-5815
Linden Publishing 2006 S Mary St *Sales	Fresno	CA	93721	**800-345-4447***	559-233-6633
Little Brown & Co 237 Pk Ave *Cust Svc	New York	NY	10017	**800-759-0190***	212-364-1100
Llewellyn Worldwide Inc 2143 Wooddale Dr	Woodbury	MN	55125	**800-843-6666**	651-291-1970
Lonely Planet Publications 50 Linden St	Oakland	CA	94607	**800-275-8555**	510-893-8555
Marquis Who's Who 300 Connell Dr Ste 2000	Berkeley Heights	NJ	07922	**800-473-7020**	908-673-1000
McFarland & Company Inc 960 NC Hwy 88 W PO Box 611	Jefferson	NC	28640	**800-253-2187**	336-246-4460
McGraw-Hill Higher Education Group 1333 Burr Ridge Pkwy	Burr Ridge	IL	60527	**800-634-3963**	630-789-4000
McGraw-Hill Professional Publishing Group Two Penn Plz 11th Fl	New York	NY	10121	**877-833-5524**	
Mel Bay Publications Inc Four Industrial Dr	Pacific	MO	63069	**800-863-5229**	636-257-3970
Merriam-Webster Inc PO Box 281 *Cust Svc	Springfield	MA	01102	**800-828-1880***	413-734-3134
Microsoft Press one Microsoft Wy *Cust Svc	Redmond	WA	98052	**800-642-7676***	425-882-8080
Midwest Plan Service 122 Davidson Hall ISU	Ames	IA	50011	**800-562-3618**	515-294-4337
Mike Murach & Assoc Inc 4340 N Knoll	Fresno	CA	93722	**800-221-5528**	559-440-9071
National Academy Press 500 Fifth St NW PO Box 285	Washington	DC	20055	**800-624-6242**	202-334-3313
National Braille Press Inc 88 St Stephen St	Boston	MA	02115	**888-965-8965**	617-266-6160
National Register Publishing Co 430 Mountain Ave Suite 400	New Providence	NJ	07974	**800-473-7020**	
National Underwriter Co 5081 Olympic Blvd	Erlanger	KY	41018	**800-543-0874**	
New Generation Research Inc 225 Friend St Ste 801	Boston	MA	02114	**800-468-3810**	617-573-9550
New Readers Press 1320 Jamesville Ave	Syracuse	NY	13210	**800-448-8878**	315-422-9121
Newkirk Products Inc 15 Corporate Cir	Albany	NY	12203	**800-525-4237**	518-862-3200
Nightingale-Conant Corp 6245 W Howard St *Cust Svc	Niles	IL	60714	**800-557-1660***	
No Starch Press Inc 38 Ringold St	San Francisco	CA	94103	**800-420-7240**	415-863-9900
Nolo.com 950 Parker St	Berkeley	CA	94710	**800-728-3555**	
Omnigraphics Inc PO Box 31-1640	Detroit	MI	48231	**800-234-1340**	
Open Court Publishing Co 70 E Lake St Ste 800	Chicago	IL	60601	**800-815-2280**	
Overlook Press 141 Wooster St	New York	NY	10012	**800-527-9703**	212-673-2210
Oxford University Press 198 Madison Ave *Orders	New York	NY	10016	**800-445-9714***	212-726-6000
Pearson Education Inc One Lake St *Cust Svc	Upper Saddle River	NJ	07458	**800-922-0579***	201-236-6716
Pearson Education School Div 1900 E Lk Ave Ofc Ste B-110A	Glenview	IL	60025	**800-348-4474**	
Penguin Group (USA) Inc 375 Hudson St *Sales	New York	NY	10014	**800-847-5515***	212-366-2000
Penguin Random House 1745 Broadway	New York	NY	10019	**800-733-3000**	212-782-9000
Penguin Random House Inc *Bantam Dell Publishing Group* 1745 Broadway 10th Fl.	New York	NY	10019	**888-523-9292**	212-782-9000
Peoples Educational Holdings Inc 299 Market St *OTC: PEDH*	Saddle Brook	NJ	07663	**800-822-1080**	201-712-0090
Perseus Books Group, The 210 American Dr	Jackson	TN	38301	**800-343-4499**	731-426-6061
Price Books & Forms Inc 531 E Sierra Madre Ave	Glendora	CA	91741	**800-423-8961**	
Publications International Ltd 7373 N Cicero Ave *General	Lincolnwood	IL	60712	**800-777-5582***	847-676-3470
Rand McNally 9855 Woods Dr PO Box 7600	Skokie	IL	60077	**800-275-7263**	
Regnery Publishing Inc 300 New Jersey Ave NW	Washington	DC	20001	**888-219-4747**	202-216-0600
Rosen Publishing Group Inc, The 29 E 21st St	New York	NY	10010	**800-237-9932**	
Rowman & Littlefield Publishers Inc 4501 Forbes Blvd Ste 200	Lanham	MD	20706	**800-462-6420**	301-459-3366
RR Bowker LLC 630 Central Ave	New Providence	NJ	07974	**888-269-5372**	908-286-1090
Sage Publications Inc 2455 Teller Rd	Thousand Oaks	CA	91320	**800-818-7243**	805-499-9774
Sams Technical Publishing 9850 E 30th St *Cust Svc	Indianapolis	IN	46229	**800-428-7267***	
Santillana USA Publishing Co 2023 NW 84th Ave	Doral	FL	33122	**800-245-8584**	305-591-9522
School Annual Publishing Co 2568 Park Ctr Blvd Ste B	State College	PA	16801	**800-436-6030**	
Simon & Schuster 1230 Ave of the Americas *Cust Svc	New York	NY	10020	**800-223-2336***	212-698-7000
Slack Inc 6900 Grove Rd	Thorofare	NJ	08086	**800-257-8290**	856-848-1000
Sourcebooks Inc 1935 Brookdale Rd Ste 139	Naperville	IL	60563	**800-432-7444**	630-961-3900
SRDS 1700 Higgins Rd	Des Plaines	IL	60018	**800-851-7737**	847-375-5000
Stackpole Books 5067 Ritter Rd *Sales	Mechanicsburg	PA	17055	**800-732-3669***	717-796-0411
Standard & Poor's Corp 55 Water St	New York	NY	10041	**877-772-5436**	212-438-1000
Sterling Publishing Company Inc 387 Pk Ave S Fifth Fl *Cust Svc	New York	NY	10016	**800-367-9692***	212-532-7160
Storey Publishing LLC 210 Mass Moca Way	North Adams	MA	01247	**800-827-7444**	413-346-2100
Sunset Publishing Corp 80 Willow Rd	Menlo Park	CA	94025	**800-227-7346**	650-321-3600
Taylor & Francis Group 270 Madison Ave	New York	NY	10016	**800-797-3803**	212-216-7855
Technology Marketing Corp One Technology Plz *Cust Svc	Norwalk	CT	06854	**800-243-6002***	203-852-6800
TFH Publications Inc One TFH Plz PO Box 427 *General	Neptune	NJ	07754	**800-631-2188***	732-988-8400
Thomas Publishing Co 5 Penn Plaza	New York	NY	10001	**800-733-1127**	212-695-0500
Thorndike Press 10 Water St Ste 310	Waterville	ME	04901	**800-223-1244**	207-861-7500
Townsend Press 439 Kelley Dr	West Berlin	NJ	08091	**800-772-6410**	856-753-0554
Triumph Learning 136 Madison Ave	New York	NY	10016	**800-221-9372**	
Tuttle Publishing 364 Innovation Dr Airport Industrial Pk *Sales	North Clarendon	VT	05759	**800-526-2778***	802-773-8930
University Press of America 4501 Forbes Blvd Ste 200	Lanham	MD	20706	**800-462-6420**	301-459-3366
Walch Education 40 Walch Dr	Portland	ME	04103	**800-558-2846**	207-772-2846
Walsworth Publishing Co 306 N Kansas Ave	Marceline	MO	64658	**800-972-4968**	660-376-3543
West Group 610 Opperman Dr *Cust Svc	Eagan	MN	55123	**800-328-4880***	651-687-7000
WH Freeman & Co 41 Madison Ave	New York	NY	10010	**800-446-8923**	212-576-9400
Wheatmark Inc 1760 E River Rd Ste 145	Tucson	AZ	85718	**888-934-0888**	520-798-0888
Wilderness Press *c/o Keen Communications* 2204 First Ave S Ste 102	Birmingham	AL	35233	**800-443-7227**	
Wiley Publishing Inc 111 River St	Hoboken	NJ	07030	**800-225-5945**	201-748-6000
William H Sadlier Inc Nine Pine St *OTC: SADL*	New York	NY	10005	**800-221-5175**	
William Morrow & Co 10 E 53rd St	New York	NY	10022	**800-242-7737**	212-207-7000
William S Hein & Company Inc 1285 Main St	Buffalo	NY	14209	**800-828-7571**	716-882-2600
Workman Publishing 225 Varick St	New York	NY	10014	**800-722-7202**	212-254-5900
World Book Inc 233 N Michigan Ave Ste 2000	Chicago	IL	60601	**800-967-5325**	312-729-5800
WW Norton & Company Inc 500 Fifth Ave Sixth Fl	New York	NY	10110	**800-233-4830**	212-354-5500
Zaner-Bloser Inc 1201 Dublin Rd	Columbus	OH	43215	**800-421-3018**	614-486-0221
Zebra Books *Kensington Publishing Corp* 119 W 40th St	New York	NY	10018	**800-221-2647**	212-407-1500

633-3 Book Publishers - Religious & Spiritual Books

	City	State	ZIP	Toll-Free	Phone
American Bible Society 1865 Broadway	New York	NY	10023	**800-322-4253**	212-408-1200
Augsburg Fortress Publishers 100 S Fifth St Ste 600	Minneapolis	MN	55402	**800-426-0115**	612-330-3300
Baker Book House Company Inc 6030 E Fulton St *Orders	Ada	MI	49301	**800-877-2665***	616-676-9185
Baker Book House Company Inc Revell Div 6030 E Fulton St *Orders	Ada	MI	49301	**800-877-2665***	616-676-9185
Bethany House Publishers 11400 Hampshire Ave S	Bloomington	MN	55438	**800-328-6109**	616-676-9185
Brethren Press 1451 Dundee Ave	Elgin	IL	60120	**800-441-3712**	

Classified Section

				Toll-Free	Phone
Broadman & Holman Publishers 127 Ninth Ave N MSN 114	Nashville	TN	37234	800-448-8032	
Concordia Publishing House Inc 3558 S Jefferson Ave *Cust Svc	Saint Louis	MO	63118	800-325-3040*	314-268-1000
Cook Communications Ministries 4050 Lee Vance View	Colorado Springs	CO	80918	800-708-5550	719-536-0100
Deseret Book Co 57 W S Temple	Salt Lake City	UT	84111	800-453-4532	801-534-1515
E-Church Depot 75 Utley Dr Ste 101	Camp Hill	PA	17011	800-233-4443	
Gospel Light Publications 1957 Eastman Ave	Ventura	CA	93003	800-446-7735	805-644-9721
Hay House Inc PO Box 5100	Carlsbad	CA	92018	800-654-5126	760-431-7695
Jewish Publication Society 2100 Arch St Second Fl	Philadelphia	PA	19103	800-234-3151	215-832-0600
NavPress 351 Executive Dr	Carol Stream	CO	60188	800-366-7788	855-277-9400
New Leaf Publishing Group PO Box 726	Green Forest	AR	72638	800-999-3777	870-438-5288
New World Library 14 Pamaron Way	Novato	CA	94949	800-972-6657	415-884-2100
Northwestern Publishing House 1250 N 113th St *Orders	Milwaukee	WI	53226	800-662-6022*	414-475-6600
Oregon Catholic Press (OCP) 5536 NE Hassalo St	Portland	OR	97213	877-596-1653	503-281-1191
Our Sunday Visitor Inc 200 Noll Plaza	Huntington	IN	46750	800-348-2440	260-356-8400
Pauline Books & Media 50 St Paul's Ave *Sales	Boston	MA	02130	800-876-4463*	617-522-8911
Review & Herald Publishing Assn 55 W Oak Ridge Dr	Hagerstown	MD	21740	800-456-3991	301-393-3000
Standard Publishing Co 8805 Governors Hill Dr Ste 400 *Orders	Cincinnati	OH	45249	800-543-1353*	513-931-4050
Standex International Corp Consumer Group 11 Keewaydin Dr *NYSE: SXI*	Salem	NH	03079	800-514-5275	603-893-9701
Thomas Nelson Inc 501 Nelson Pl PO Box 141000	Nashville	TN	37214	800-251-4000	615-889-9000
Tyndale House Publishers Inc 351 Executive Dr	Carol Stream	IL	60188	800-323-9400	
United Methodist Publishing House 201 Eigth Ave S	Nashville	TN	37203	800-672-1789	615-749-6000
Whitaker House/Anchor Distributors 1030 Hunt Vly Cir *General	New Kensington	PA	15068	800-444-4484*	724-334-7000

633-4 Book Publishers - University Presses

				Toll-Free	Phone
Catholic University of America Press 620 Michigan Ave NE 240 Leahy Hall	Washington	DC	20064	800-537-5487	202-319-5052
Columbia University Press 61 W 62nd St 3rd Fl	New York	NY	10023	800-944-8648	212-459-0600
Cornell University Press 750 Cascadilla St PO Box 6525 *Sales	Ithaca	NY	14850	800-666-2211*	607-277-2338
Duke University Press 905 W Main St Ste 18-B *Cust Svc	Durham	NC	27701	888-651-0122*	919-687-3600
Gallaudet University Press 800 Florida Ave NE	Washington	DC	20002	800-621-2736	202-651-5488
Harvard Business School Publishing 60 Harvard Way	Boston	MA	02163	800-795-5200	
Harvard University Press 79 Garden St	Cambridge	MA	02138	800-405-1619	617-495-2600
Indiana University Press 601 N Morton St	Bloomington	IN	47404	800-842-6796	812-855-8817
Johns Hopkins University Press 2715 N Charles St *Orders	Baltimore	MD	21218	800-537-5487*	410-516-6900
Naval Institute Press 291 Wood Rd	Annapolis	MD	21402	800-233-8764	410-268-6110
Ohio University Press 19 Cir Dr The Ridges *Sales	Athens	OH	45701	800-621-2736*	740-593-1154
Oregon State University Press 121 The Vly Library *Orders	Corvallis	OR	97331	800-426-3797*	541-737-3166
Pennsylvania State University Press 820 N University Dr USB1 Ste C	University Park	PA	16802	800-326-9180	814-865-1327
Princeton University Press 41 William St	Princeton	NJ	08540	800-777-4726	609-258-4900
Purdue University Press 504 W State St Stewart Ctr 370 *Orders	West Lafayette	IN	47907	800-247-6553*	765-494-2038
Rutgers University Press 106 Somerset St 3rd Fl	New Brunswick	NJ	08901	800-272-6817	732-745-4935
Stanford University Press 1450 Page Mill Rd	Palo Alto	CA	94304	800-621-2736	650-723-9434
State University of New York Press (SUNY) 22 Corporate Woods Blvd Third Fl	Albany	NY	12211	866-430-7869	518-472-5000
Temple University Press 1852 N 10th St USB 305	Philadelphia	PA	19122	800-621-2736	215-926-2140
Texas A & M University Press John H Lindsey Bldg 4354 TAMU *Orders	College Station	TX	77843	800-826-8911*	979-845-1436
Texas Tech University Press 2903 Fourth St	Lubbock	TX	79409	800-832-4042	806-742-2982
University of Alabama Press, The 200 Hackberry Ln Second Fl PO Box 870380 *Orders	Tuscaloosa	AL	35487	800-621-2736*	205-348-5180
University of Alaska Press 794 University Ave Ste 220	Fairbanks	AK	99709	888-252-6657	907-474-5831
University of Arizona Press, The 1510 E University Blvd PO Box 210055	Tucson	AZ	85721	800-426-3797	520-621-1441
University of Arkansas Press McIlroy House 105 McIlroy	Fayetteville	AR	72701	800-621-2736	479-575-7258
University of California Press 2120 Berkeley Way	Berkeley	CA	94704	800-777-4726	510-642-4247
University of Chicago Press 1427 E 60th St *Sales	Chicago	IL	60637	800-621-2736*	773-702-7700
University of Hawaii Press 2840 Kolowalu St	Honolulu	HI	96822	888-847-7377	808-956-8255
University of Illinois Press 1325 S Oak St	Champaign	IL	61820	866-244-0626	217-333-0950
University of Iowa Press 119 W Pk Rd 100 Kuhl House	Iowa City	IA	52242	800-621-2736	319-335-2000
University of Massachusetts Press PO Box 429	Amherst	MA	01004	800-562-0112	413-545-2217
University of Michigan Press 839 Greene St	Ann Arbor	MI	48104	866-804-0002	734-764-4388
University of Missouri Press 2910 LeMone Blvd	Columbia	MO	65201	800-621-2736	573-882-7641
University of Nebraska Press 1111 Lincoln Mall *Orders	Lincoln	NE	68508	800-755-1105*	402-472-3581
University of North Carolina Press 116 S Boundary St	Chapel Hill	NC	27514	800-848-6224	919-966-3561
University of North Texas Press 1155 Union Cir Ste 311336	Denton	TX	76203	800-826-8911	940-565-2142
University of Pennsylvania Press 3902 Spruce St *Cust Svc	Philadelphia	PA	19104	800-537-5487*	215-898-6261
University of Pittsburgh Press 3400 Forbes Ave 5th Fl *Sales	Pittsburgh	PA	15261	800-621-2736*	412-383-2456
University of South Carolina Press 1600 Hampton St Fifth Fl *Orders	Columbia	SC	29208	800-768-2500*	803-777-5243
University of Texas Press 2100 Comal St *Sales	Austin	TX	78722	800-252-3206*	512-471-7233
University of Utah Press 295 South 1500 East Ste 5400	Salt Lake City	UT	84112	800-621-2736	801-585-0082
University of Virginia Press 210 Sprigg Ln PO Box 400318 *Orders	Charlottesville	VA	22903	800-831-3406*	434-924-3469
University of Washington Press 4333 Brooklyn Ave NE	Seattle	WA	98195	800-537-5487	206-543-4050
University Press of Colorado 5589 Arapahoe Ave Ste 206C	Boulder	CO	80303	800-621-2736	720-406-8849
University Press of Florida 15 NW 15th St *Sales	Gainesville	FL	32611	800-226-3822*	352-392-1351
University Press of Kentucky 663 S Limestone St *Sales	Lexington	KY	40508	800-537-5487*	859-257-8400
University Press of Mississippi 3825 Ridgewood Rd	Jackson	MS	39211	800-737-7788	601-432-6205
University Press of New England (UPNE) One Ct St Ste 250 *Orders	Lebanon	NH	03766	800-421-1561*	603-448-1533
Vanderbilt University Press 2014 Broadway Ste 320	Nashville	TN	37203	800-627-7377	615-322-3585
Wesleyan University Press 215 Long Ln	Middletown	CT	06459	800-421-1561	860-685-7711
Yale University Press 302 Temple St *Sales	New Haven	CT	06511	800-405-1619*	203-432-0960

633-5 Comic Book Publishers

				Toll-Free	Phone
Dark Horse Comics Inc 10956 SE Main St	Milwaukie	OR	97222	800-862-0052	503-652-8815
Diamond Comic Distributors Inc 1966 Greenspring Dr Ste 300	Timonium	MD	21093	800-452-6642	410-560-7100
Fantagraphics Books 7563 Lk City Way NE	Seattle	WA	98115	800-657-1100	206-524-1967

633-6 Directory Publishers

				Toll-Free	Phone
1-800 Attorney Lawyer Holdings LLC 2525 McKinnon Ave Ste 625 *OTC: ATTY*	Dallas	TX	75201	800-288-6763	
ASD Data Services LLC PO Box 1184	Manchester	TN	37349	877-742-7297	
Bresser's Cross Index Directory Co 684 W Baltimore St	Detroit	MI	48202	800-995-0570	313-874-0570
BurrellesLuce 30 B Vreeland Rd PO Box 674	Florham Park	NJ	07932	800-631-1160	973-992-6600
Chain Store Guide 10117 Princess Palm Ave Ste 375	Tampa	FL	33610	800-927-9292	
Cole Information Services 3401 NW 39th St	Lincoln	NE	68524	800-800-3271	402-555-5678
Contractors Register Inc 800 E Main St PO Box 500	Jefferson Valley	NY	10535	800-431-2584	
DAG Media Inc 125-10 Queens Blvd Ste 14	Kew Gardens	NY	11415	800-261-2799	718-263-8454
Dickman Directories Inc 6145 Columbus Pk	Lewis Center	OH	43035	877-836-4154	740-548-6130

				Toll-Free	Phone

Genesis Publisher Services
3310 Eagle Pk Dr NE Ste 200 . . . . Grand Rapids MI 49525 **800-828-1022** 616-831-2800

Haines & Company Inc
8050 Freedom Ave . . . . North Canton OH 44720 **800-843-8452**

HealthLeaders-InterStudy
One Vantage Way Ste B-300 . . . . Nashville TN 37228 **800-643-7600** 615-385-4131

Hoover's Inc
5800 Airport Blvd . . . . Austin TX 78752 **800-486-8666** 512-374-4500

LexisNexis Martindale-Hubbell
121 Chanlon Rd . . . . New Providence NJ 07974 **800-526-4902**

Marc Publishing Co
600 Germantown Pk Ste B . . . . Lafayette Hill PA 19444 **800-432-5478** 610-834-8585

RH Donnelley Corp
1001 Winstead Dr . . . . Cary NC 27513 **844-339-6334** 919-297-1600

Stewart Directories Inc
100 W Pennsylvania Ave PO Box 20250 . . . . Towson MD 21204 **800-311-0786**

University Directories
88 VilCom Cir . . . . Chapel Hill NC 27514 **800-743-5556**

Valley Yellow Pages
1850 N Gateway Blvd . . . . Fresno CA 93727 **800-350-8887** 559-251-8888

World Chamber of Commerce Directory Inc
446 E 29th St . . . . Loveland CO 80538 **888-883-3231** 970-663-3231

Yellow Book USA
398 RXR Plaza . . . . Uniondale NY 11556 **877-237-6120** 917-861-5858

633-7 Music Publishers

				Toll-Free	Phone

Carl Fischer Inc
65 Bleecker St 28th Fl. New York NY 10012 **800-762-2328** 212-777-0900

Hal Leonard Corp
960 E Mark St . . . . Winona MN 55987 **800-321-3408** 507-454-2920

Lorenz Corp 501 E Third St . . . . Dayton OH 45402 **800-444-1144** 937-228-6118

Malaco Music Group Inc
3023 W Northside Dr . . . . Jackson MS 39213 **800-272-7936***
*Cust Svc 601-982-4522

Mel Bay Publications Inc
Four Industrial Dr . . . . Pacific MO 63069 **800-863-5229** 636-257-3970

Theodore Presser Co
588 N Gulph Rd . . . . King of Prussia PA 19406 **800-854-6764** 610-592-1222

633-8 Newspaper Publishers

				Toll-Free	Phone

Afro-American Newspapers Co
2519 N Charles St . . . . Baltimore MD 21218 **800-237-6892** 410-554-8200

Alameda Times-Star
7677 Oakport St Ste 950 . . . . Oakland CA 94604 **866-225-5277** 510-208-6300

Albany Herald Publishing Company Inc
126 N Washington St . . . . Albany GA 31702 **800-234-3725** 229-888-9300

Albert Lea Tribune, The
808 W Front St PO Box 60 . . . . Albert Lea MN 56007 **800-657-4996** 507-373-1411

Arizona Publishing Cos
PO Box 1950 . . . . Phoenix AZ 85001 **800-331-9303** 602-444-8000

Auburn Publishers Inc
25 Dill St . . . . Auburn NY 13021 **800-878-5311** 315-253-5311

Bliss Communications Inc
PO Box 5001 . . . . Janesville WI 53547 **800-362-6712** 608-754-3311

BMH Books
1104 Kings Hwy PO Box 544 . . . . Winona Lake IN 46590 **800-348-2756**

Booth Michigan
169 Monroe Ave Ste 100 . . . . Grand Rapids MI 49503 **800-886-5529** 800-878-1400

Burlington Hawk Eye Co
800 S Main St PO Box 10. . . . . Burlington IA 52601 **800-397-1708** 319-754-8461

Capital Gazette Communications LLC
2000 Capital Dr . . . . Annapolis MD 21401 **888-607-8365** 410-268-5000

Capital Newspapers
1901 Fish Hatchery Rd . . . . Madison WI 53713 **888-798-4468** 920-887-0321

Casa Grande Valley Newspaper Inc
PO Box 15002 . . . . Casa Grande AZ 85130 **800-352-3796** 520-836-7461

Casiano Communications Inc
1700 Fernandez Juncos Ave
PO Box 12130. . . . . San Juan PR 00909 **844-723-2351** 787-728-3000

Cheyenne Newspaper Inc
702 W Lincolnway . . . . Cheyenne WY 82001 **800-561-6268** 307-634-3361

Christian Science Publishing Society
210 Massachusetts Ave P02-15 . . . . Boston MA 02115 **800-456-2220** 617-450-2000

Community Newspaper Co Inc
72 Cherry Hill Dr . . . . Beverly MA 01915 **800-281-6498** 978-739-1300

Consolidated Publishing Co
PO Box 189 . . . . Anniston AL 36202 **866-814-9253** 256-236-1551

Daily Globe, The
118 E McLeod Ave PO Box 548 . . . . Ironwood MI 49938 **800-236-2887** 906-932-2211

Daily Progress
685 W Rio Rd . . . . Charlottesville VA 22902 **866-469-4866** 434-978-7200

Day Publishing Co
47 Eugene O'Neill Dr . . . . New London CT 06320 **800-542-3354** 860-442-2200

Delphos Herald Inc
405 N Main St . . . . Delphos OH 45833 **800-589-6950** 419-695-0015

Denver Newspaper Agency
101 W Colfax Ave . . . . Denver CO 80202 **800-336-7678** 303-954-1010

Derrick Publishing Co
1510 W First St . . . . Oil City PA 16301 **800-352-1002** 814-676-7444

Desert Sun Publishing Co
PO Box 2734 . . . . Palm Springs CA 92263 **800-233-3741***
*Advertising 760-322-8889

Detroit Legal News Co
1409 Allen Rd Ste B . . . . Troy MI 48083 **800-875-5275** 248-577-6100

Dispatch Printing Co
34 S Third St . . . . Columbus OH 43215 **800-282-0263** 614-461-5000

Eagle Publishing Co
75 S Church St . . . . Pittsfield MA 01201 **800-245-0254** 413-447-7311

East Hampton Star Inc, The
153 Main St PO Box 5002 . . . . East Hampton NY 11937 **800-968-7364** 631-324-0002

Eau Claire Press Co
701 S Farwell St . . . . Eau Claire WI 54701 **800-236-8808** 715-833-9200

Edward A Sherman Publishing Co
101 Malbone Rd . . . . Newport RI 02840 **800-320-2378** 401-849-3300

EW Scripps Co
312 Walnut St Ste 2800 . . . . Cincinnati OH 45202 **800-888-3000** 513-977-3000
NYSE: SSP

Express-News Corp
PO Box 2171 . . . . San Antonio TX 78297 **800-555-1551** 210-250-3000

Feather Publishing Co Inc
287 Lawrence St . . . . Quincy CA 95971 **866-849-8390** 530-283-0800

Finger Lakes Times
218 Genesse St PO Box 393 . . . . Geneva NY 14456 **800-388-6652** 315-789-3333

Flashes Publishers Inc
595 Jenner Dr . . . . Allegan MI 49010 **800-968-4415** 269-673-2141

Fort Wayne Newspapers Inc
600 W Main St . . . . Fort Wayne IN 46802 **800-444-3303** 260-461-8444

Forum Communications Co
101 Fifth St N . . . . Fargo ND 58102 **800-747-7311** 701-451-5629

Forward Publishing
125 Maiden Ln . . . . New York NY 10038 **800-266-0773** 212-889-8200

Freedom Communications Inc
17666 Fitch . . . . Irvine CA 92614 **866-262-7678** 949-253-2300

Galesburg Printing & Publishing Co
140 S Prairie St . . . . Galesburg IL 61401 **800-733-2767** 309-343-7181

GateHouse Media Inc
350 Willowbrook Office Pk . . . . Fairport NY 14450 **866-487-9243** 585-598-0030
NYSE: GHSE

Gazette Newspapers Inc
9030 Comprint Ct . . . . Gaithersburg MD 20877 **888-670-7100** 301-948-3120

George J Foster Co Inc
150 Venture Dr . . . . Dover NH 03820 **800-462-2265** 603-742-4455

Hastings & Sons Publishing
38 Exchange St . . . . Lynn MA 01901 **877-226-4267** 781-593-7700

Herald Publishing Co
PO Box 153 . . . . Houston TX 77001 **888-421-1866** 713-630-0391

Herald-Mail Co, The
100 Summit Ave PO Box 439 . . . . Hagerstown MD 21741 **800-626-6397** 301-733-5131

Herald-Star
401 Herald Sq . . . . Steubenville OH 43952 **800-526-7987** 740-283-4711

Hersam Acorn Newspapers
16 Bailey Ave . . . . Ridgefield CT 06877 **800-372-2790** 203-438-6544

High Plains Publishers Inc
1500 W Wyatt Earp Blvd . . . . Dodge City KS 67801 **800-452-7171** 620-227-7171

Home News Enterprises
333 Second St . . . . Columbus IN 47201 **800-876-7811**

Hubbard Publishing Co
127 E Chillicothe Ave PO Box 40 . . . . Bellefontaine OH 43311 **866-632-9992** 937-592-3060

Huse Publishing Co
525 Norfolk Ave PO Box 977 . . . . Norfolk NE 68701 **877-371-1020** 402-371-1020

Independent Publishing Co
1000 Williamston Rd . . . . Anderson SC 29621 **800-859-6397** 864-224-4321

Journal Graphics Inc
2840 NW 35th Ave Ste B . . . . Portland OR 97210 **888-609-6051** 503-790-9100

Journal Publishing Co
1242 S Green St . . . . Tupelo MS 38804 **800-264-6397** 662-842-2611

Keene Publishing Corp
PO Box 546 . . . . Keene NH 03431 **800-765-9994** 603-352-1234

Knight Publishing Co
600 S Tryon St . . . . Charlotte NC 28202 **800-332-0686** 704-358-5000

Lake Charles American Press Inc
PO Box 2893 . . . . Lake Charles LA 70602 **800-737-2283** 337-433-3000

Lakeville Journal Co LLC
33 Bissell St PO Box 1688 . . . . Lakeville CT 06039 **800-553-2234** 860-435-9873

Lancaster Newspapers Inc
Eight W King St PO Box 1328. . . . . Lancaster PA 17603 **800-809-4666** 717-291-8811

Landmark Community Newspapers Inc
601 Taylorsville Rd . . . . Shelbyville KY 40065 **800-939-9322** 502-633-4334

Lawrence Daily Journal-World
609 New Hampshire St PO Box 888 . . . . Lawrence KS 66044 **800-578-8748** 785-843-1000

Livingston County Daily Press & Argus
323 E Grand River Ave . . . . Howell MI 48843 **888-999-1288** 517-548-2000

Lowell Sun Publishing Co
491 Dutton St . . . . Lowell MA 01854 **800-359-1300***
*Cust Svc 978-458-7100

Madison Newspapers Inc
1901 Fish Hatchery Rd . . . . Madison WI 53713 **800-252-7723***
*Sales 608-252-6200

Magic Valley Newspapers
132 Fairfield St W . . . . Twin Falls ID 83301 **800-658-3883** 208-733-0931

Marshall Independent
508 W Main St PO Box 411 . . . . Marshall MN 56258 **877-276-6070** 507-537-1551

McClatchy Co 2100 Q St . . . . Sacramento CA 95816 **866-807-2200** 916-321-1855
NYSE: MNI

McClatchy Newspapers
2100 Q St . . . . Sacramento CA 95816 **866-807-2200** 916-321-1000

Memphis Publishing Co
495 Union Ave . . . . Memphis TN 38103 **800-444-6397***
*Cust Svc 901-529-2666

Meridian Star Inc
814 22nd Ave . . . . Meridian MS 39301 **800-232-2525***
*Cust Svc 601-693-1551

Mid-America Publishing Corp
9 Second St NW . . . . Hampton IA 50441 **800-558-1244** 641-456-2585

Milford Daily News Co
159 S Main St . . . . Milford MA 01757 **800-281-6498** 508-634-7522

Missouri Lawyers Media
319 N Fourth St . . . . Saint Louis MO 63102 **800-635-5297** 314-421-1880

Missourian Publishing Co
14 W Main St . . . . Washington MO 63090 **888-239-7701** 636-239-7701

Moline Dispatch Publishing Co
1720 Fifth Ave . . . . Moline IL 61265 **800-660-2472** 309-764-4344

Morning Call Inc
101 N Sixth St . . . . Allentown PA 18101 **800-666-5492** 610-820-6500

Morris Communications Company LLC
725 Broad St . . . . Augusta GA 30901 **800-622-6358** 706-724-0851

Natchez Newspapers Inc
503 N Canal St . . . . Natchez MS 39120 **877-896-0974** 601-442-9101

Company / Address	City	State	ZIP	Toll-Free	Phone
Native American Times PO Box 411	Tahlequah	OK	74465	800-367-5390	918-708-5838
New Mexico Newspapers Inc PO Box 450	Farmington	NM	87499	866-272-3622	505-325-4545
Northwest Herald Inc PO Box 250	Crystal Lake	IL	60039	800-589-8910	815-459-4040
Oakland Press 48 W Huron St	Pontiac	MI	48342	888-977-3677	248-332-8181
Observer & Eccentric Newspapers 615 W Lafayette Second Level	Detroit	MI	48226	866-887-2737	
Observer Publishing Co 122 S Main St	Washington	PA	15301	800-222-6397	724-222-2200
Oshkosh Northwestern Co 224 State St	Oshkosh	WI	54901	800-924-6168	920-235-7700
Our Sunday Visitor Inc 200 Noll Plaza	Huntington	IN	46750	800-348-2440	260-356-8400
Palm Beach Newspapers Inc PO Box 24700	West Palm Beach	FL	33416	800-432-7595	561-820-4100
Papers Inc 206 S Main St	Milford	IN	46542	800-733-4111	574-658-4111
PG Publishing Co 34 Blvd of the Allies *Cust Svc	Pittsburgh	PA	15222	800-228-6397*	412-263-1100
Phoenix Media Communications Group 126 Brookline Ave	Boston	MA	02215	888-536-7464	617-536-5390
Pipestone Publishing Co PO Box 277	Pipestone	MN	56164	800-325-6440	507-825-3333
Ponca City Publishing Inc PO Box 191	Ponca City	OK	74602	866-765-3311	580-765-3311
Post Publishing Co 131 W Innes St	Salisbury	NC	28144	800-546-5664	704-633-8950
Press-Enterprise Co PO Box 792	Riverside	CA	92502	800-794-6397	951-684-1200
Press-Enterprise Inc 3185 Lackawanna Ave	Bloomsburg	PA	17815	888-484-6345	570-784-2121
Princeton Packet, The 300 Witherspoon St PO Box 350	Princeton	NJ	08542	888-747-1122	609-924-3244
Quincy Newspapers Inc 130 S Fifth St	Quincy	IL	62301	800-373-9444	217-223-5100
Reminder Press Inc 130 Old Town Rd PO Box 27	Vernon	CT	06066	888-456-2211	860-875-3366
Republican Co 1860 Main St	Springfield	MA	01103	800-828-5597	413-788-1000
Republican-American Inc 389 Meadow St	Waterbury	CT	06702	800-992-3232	203-574-3636
Richmond Times-Dispatch PO Box 85333	Richmond	VA	23293	800-468-3382	804-649-6000
Rivertown Newspaper Group 2760 N Service Dr PO Box 15	Red Wing	MN	55066	800-535-1660	651-388-8235
San Angelo Standard Times Inc PO Box 5111	San Angelo	TX	76902	800-588-1884	325-653-1221
Santa Barbara News-Press Publishing Co 715 Anacapa St	Santa Barbara	CA	93101	800-654-3292	805-564-5200
Scripps Howard Inc PO Box 5380	Cincinnati	OH	45202	800-888-3000	513-977-3000
Southern Connecticut Newspapers Inc 9 Riverbend Dr S Bldg 9-A	Stamford	CT	06907	800-542-2517	203-964-2200
Stonebridge Press Inc 25 Elm St	Southbridge	MA	01550	800-536-5836	508-764-4325
Suburban Life Publications 1101 W 31st St Ste 100	Downers Grove	IL	60515	800-397-9397	630-368-1100
Sun Newspapers 5510 Cloverleaf Pkwy	Cleveland	OH	44125	800-362-8008	216-999-3900
TB Butler Publishing Co 410 W Erwin St	Tyler	TX	75702	800-333-9141	903-597-8111
Tennessee Valley Printing Company Inc PO Box 2213	Decatur	AL	35609	888-353-4612	256-353-4612
Times Herald Inc 410 Markley St PO Box 591	Norristown	PA	19404	888-933-4233	610-272-2500
Times News Publishing Co 707 S Main St	Burlington	NC	27215	800-488-0085	336-227-0131
Times-Citizen Communications Inc 406 Stevens St PO Box 640	Iowa Falls	IA	50126	800-798-2691	641-648-2521
Tribune Review Publishing Co 622 Cabin Hill Dr	Greensburg	PA	15601	800-524-5700	724-834-1151
Truth Publishing Company Inc 421 S Second St	Elkhart	IN	46516	800-585-5416	574-294-1661
Western States Weeklies Inc PO Box 600600	San Diego	CA	92160	800-628-9466	619-280-2985
William J Kline & Son Inc One Venner Rd	Amsterdam	NY	12010	800-453-6397	518-843-1100
Wooster Republican Printing Co 212 E Liberty St	Wooster	OH	44691	800-686-2958	330-264-1125
Worcester Telegram & Gazette Inc 20 Franklin St PO Box 15012	Worcester	MA	01615	800-678-6680	508-793-9100
World Publishing Co 315 S Boulder Ave	Tulsa	OK	74102	800-444-6552	918-583-2161
Yankton Press & Dakotan 319 Walnut St PO Box 56	Yankton	SD	57078	800-743-2968	605-665-7811
York Newspaper Co 1891 Loucks Rd	York	PA	17408	800-559-3520	717-767-6397

633-9 Periodicals Publishers

Company / Address	City	State	ZIP	Toll-Free	Phone
Access Intelligence LLC Four Choke Cherry Rd Second Fl	Rockville	MD	20850	800-777-5006	301-354-2000
Advanstar Veterinary Healthcare Communications 8033 Flint St	Lenexa	KS	66214	800-255-6864	913-871-3800
Advertising Specialties Institute 4800 St Rd	Trevose	PA	19053	800-546-1350	215-942-8600
AHC Media LLC 3525 Piedmont Rd NE Bldg 6 Ste 400 *Cust Svc	Atlanta	GA	30305	800-688-2421*	404-262-5476
Alexander Communications Group Inc 712 Main St Ste 187-B	Boonton	NJ	07005	800-232-4317	973-265-2300
American Lawyer Media Inc (ALM) 120 Broadway Fifth Fl	New York	NY	10271	877-256-2472	212-457-9400
American Psychiatric Publishing Inc 1000 Wilson Blvd Ste 1825	Arlington	VA	22209	800-368-5777	703-907-7322
Amos Press Inc 911 S Vandemark Rd	Sidney	OH	45365	866-468-1622	937-498-0850
Annual Reviews 4139 El Camino Way	Palo Alto	CA	94303	800-523-8635	650-493-4400
APN Media LLC PO Box 20113	New York	NY	10023	800-470-7599	212-581-3380
Atlantic Information Services Inc 1100 17th St NW Ste 300	Washington	DC	20036	800-521-4323	202-775-9008
Augsburg Fortress Publishers 100 S Fifth St Ste 600	Minneapolis	MN	55402	800-426-0115	612-330-3300
BCC Research LLC 49 Walnut Pk Bldg 2	Wellesley	MA	02481	866-285-7215	781-489-7301
Boardroom Inc 281 Tresser Blvd 8th Fl	Stamford	CT	06901	800-274-5611	
Bobit Business Media 3520 Challenger St	Torrance	CA	90503	888-239-2455	310-533-2400
Bureau of National Affairs Inc 1801 S Bell St	Arlington	VA	22202	800-372-1033	703-341-3000
Business & Legal Reports Inc (BLR) 141 Mill Rock Rd E	Old Saybrook	CT	06475	800-727-5257	860-510-0100
Business News Publishing Co 2401 W Big Beaver Rd Ste 700	Troy	MI	48084	800-837-7370	248-362-3700
Buyers Laboratory Inc 20 Railroad Ave	Hackensack	NJ	07601	800-578-5902	201-488-0404
Cabot Heritage Corp 176 N St PO Box 2049	Salem	MA	01970	800-654-1514	978-745-5532
Challenge Publications Inc 9509 Vassar Ave Ste A	Chatsworth	CA	91311	800-562-9182	818-700-6868
Cobblestone Publishing Co 30 Grove St Ste C	Peterborough	NH	03458	800-821-0115	603-924-7209
Commodity Information Systems Inc 3030 NW Expy Ste 725	Oklahoma City	OK	73112	800-231-0477	405-604-8726
Conde Nast Publications Inc Four Times Sq	New York	NY	10036	800-897-8666	212-286-2860
Consumers Union of US Inc 101 Truman Ave	Yonkers	NY	10703	800-927-4357	914-378-2000
Cook Communications Ministries 4050 Lee Vance View	Colorado Springs	CO	80918	800-708-5550	719-536-0100
Crain Communications Inc 1155 Gratiot Ave	Detroit	MI	48207	888-288-6954	313-446-6000
CRC Press LLC 6000 Broken Sound Pkwy NW Ste 300 *Cust Svc	Boca Raton	FL	33487	800-272-7737*	561-994-0555
Cutter Information Corp 37 Broadway Ste 1	Arlington	MA	02474	800-964-5118	781-648-8700
Cygnus Business Media Inc 1233 Janesville Ave	Fort Atkinson	WI	53538	800-547-7377	631-845-2700
Deal LLC, The 20 Broad St *Cust Svc	New York	NY	10005	888-667-3325*	212-313-9325
Disney Consumer Products 500 S Buena Vista St *PR	Burbank	CA	91521	877-282-8322*	818-560-1000
Earl G Graves Ltd 130 Fifth Ave 10th Fl *Cust Svc	New York	NY	10011	800-727-7777*	212-242-8000
EGW.com Inc 4075 Papazian Way *Cust Svc	Fremont	CA	94538	800-546-4754*	510-668-0268
Elliott Wave International (EWI) PO Box 1618 *Cust Svc	Gainesville	GA	30503	800-336-1618*	770-536-0309
Elsevier Science Ltd 360 Pk Ave S	New York	NY	10010	888-437-4636	212-989-5800
Entrepreneur Media Inc 2445 McCabe Way Ste 400	Irvine	CA	92614	877-652-5295	949-261-2325
EPM Communications Inc 19 W 21st St Ste 303	New York	NY	10010	888-852-9467	212-941-0099
Ernst Publishing Co LLC one Commerce Plaza 99 Washington Ave Ste 309	Albany	NY	12210	800-345-3822	
Essence Communications Inc 135 W 50th St 4th Fl *Sales	New York	NY	10020	800-274-9398*	
F+W, A Content + eCommerce Company 10151 Carver Rd Ste 200 *Sales	Cincinnati	OH	45236	800-289-0963*	513-531-2690
Forbes Inc 60 Fifth Ave	New York	NY	10011	800-295-0893	212-620-2200
Forecast International 22 Commerce Rd	Newtown	CT	06470	800-451-4975	203-426-0800
Forum Publishing Co 383 E Main St	Centerport	NY	11721	800-635-7654	631-754-5000
Gardner Publications Inc 6915 Valley Ave	Cincinnati	OH	45244	800-950-8020	513-527-8800
Grace Communion International PO Box 5005	Glendora	CA	91740	800-423-4444	626-650-2300
Grand View Media Group Inc (GVMG) 200 Croft St Ste 1	Birmingham	AL	35242	888-431-2877	205-408-3700
Gulf Publishing Company Inc Two Greenway Plz Ste 1020	Houston	TX	77046	800-231-6275	713-529-4301
Hanley-Wood LLC 1 Thomas Cir NW Ste 600	Washington	DC	20005	800-227-8839	202-452-0800
Hart Publications Inc 1616 S Voss Rd Ste 1000	Houston	TX	77057	800-874-2544	713-260-6400
Hatton Brown Publishers Inc PO Box 2268	Montgomery	AL	36102	800-669-5613	334-834-1170
Health Forum 155 North Wacker Drive Suite 400	Chicago	IL	60606	800-621-6902	312-422-2165
Healthy Directions LLC 7811 Montrose Rd	Potomac	MD	20854	866-599-9491	
Highlights for Children Inc 1800 Watermark Dr *Cust Svc	Columbus	OH	43216	800-255-9517*	614-486-0631
Hli Properties Inc PO Box 1052	Fort Dodge	IA	50501	800-247-2000	515-955-1600
Hobsons CollegeView 50 E Business Way Ste 300	Cincinnati	OH	45241	800-927-8439	
Homes & Land Magazine Affiliates LLC 1830 E Pk Ave	Tallahassee	FL	32301	800-277-7800	850-575-0189

Classified Section

					Toll-Free	Phone
Honolulu Publishing Co Ltd	707 Richards St Ste PH3	Honolulu	HI	96813	**800-272-5245**	808-524-7400
Horizon House Publications Inc (HHP)	685 Canton St	Norwood	MA	02062	**800-225-9977**	781-769-9750
IEEE Computer Society Press	10662 Los Vaqueros Cir PO Box 3014	Los Alamitos	CA	90720	**800-272-6657**	714-821-8380
Information Today Inc	143 Old Marlton Pike	Medford	NJ	08055	**800-300-9868**	609-654-6266
InfoWorld Media Group Inc	501 Second St Ste 120	San Francisco	CA	94107	**800-227-8365**	415-243-0500
Inside Washington Publishers	1919 S Eads St Ste 201	Arlington	VA	22202	**800-424-9068**	703-416-8500
Institutional Investor Newsletters	225 Pk Ave S 8th Fl	New York	NY	10003	**800-437-9997**	212-224-3300
International Data Group Inc (IDG)	1 Exeter Plaza 15th Fl	Boston	MA	02116	**800-343-4952*** *Orders	617-534-1200
Internet Business Network	303 Ross Dr	Mill Valley	CA	94941	**866-497-6747**	415-377-2255
JOC Group Inc	2 Penn Plaza E 975 Raymond Blvd	Newark	NJ	07105	**800-223-0243*** *Cust Svc	973-776-7824
JR O'Dwyer Co	271 Madison Ave Sixth Fl	New York	NY	10016	**866-395-7710**	212-679-2471
Kiplinger Washington Editors Inc	1729 H St NW	Washington	DC	20006	**800-544-0155**	202-887-6400
Laurin Publishing Co Inc	100 West St	Pittsfield	MA	01202	**877-422-7300**	413-499-0514
Lawrence Ragan Communications Inc	111 E Wacker Dr Ste 500	Chicago	IL	60601	**800-878-5331**	800-493-4867
Liturgical Publications Inc	2875 S James Dr	New Berlin	WI	53151	**800-876-4574**	262-785-1188
Mary Ann Liebert Publishers Inc	140 Huguenot St Third Fl	New Rochelle	NY	10801	**800-654-3237**	914-740-2100
McKnight's Long-Term Care News	One Northfield Plz Ste 521	Northfield	IL	60093	**800-558-1703**	847-784-8706
Meister Media Worldwide	37733 Euclid Ave	Willoughby	OH	44094	**800-572-7740*** *Orders	440-942-2000
Mergent Inc	477 Madison Ave Ste 410	New York	NY	10022	**800-937-1398**	212-413-7700
Merion Publications Inc	2900 Horizon Dr	King of Prussia	PA	19406	**800-355-1088**	610-278-1400
Miles Media Group Inc	6751 Professional Pkwy W Ste 200	Sarasota	FL	34240	**877-342-2424**	941-342-2300
National Braille Press Inc	88 St Stephen St	Boston	MA	02115	**888-965-8965**	617-266-6160
National Catholic Reporter Publishing Co	115 E Armour Blvd	Kansas City	MO	64111	**800-333-7373**	816-531-0538
Nelson Publishing	2500 Tamiami Trl N	Nokomis	FL	34275	**800-226-6113**	941-966-9521
North American Publishing Co (NAPCO)	1500 Springarden St 12th Fl	Philadelphia	PA	19130	**800-627-2689**	215-238-5300
Northstar Travel Media LLC	100 Lighting Way	Secaucus	NJ	07094	**800-742-7076**	201-902-2000
Our Sunday Visitor Inc	200 Noll Plaza	Huntington	IN	46750	**800-348-2440**	260-356-8400
Pacific Press	1350 N Kings Rd	Nampa	ID	83687	**800-765-6955*** *Cust Svc	208-465-2500
Paisano Publications LLC	28210 Dorothy Dr	Agoura Hills	CA	91301	**800-323-3484**	818-889-8740
PC World Communications Inc	501 Second St	San Francisco	CA	94107	**800-234-3498*** *General	415-243-0505
Photosource International	1910 35th Rd	Osceola	WI	54020	**800-786-6277**	715-248-3800
Platts	Two Penn Plz 25th Fl	New York	NY	10121	**800-752-8878**	212-904-3070
Pohly Co	867 Boylston St 5th Fl	Boston	MA	02116	**800-383-0888**	617-451-1700
PRIMEDIA Inc & Consumer Source Inc	3585 Engineering Dr Ste 100	Norcross	GA	30092	**800-216-1423**	678-421-3000
Progressive Impressions	1 Hardman Dr	Bloomington	IL	61701	**800-644-0444**	309-664-0444
Publications & Communications Inc	13552 Hwy 183 N Ste A	Austin	TX	78750	**800-678-9724**	512-250-9023
Publications International Ltd	7373 N Cicero Ave	Lincolnwood	IL	60712	**800-777-5582*** *General	847-676-3470
Putman Media Inc	555 W Pierce Rd	Itasca	IL	60143	**866-666-6033**	630-467-1301
Randall-Reilly Publishing Co	3200 Rice Mine Rd NE	Tuscaloosa	AL	35406	**800-633-5953*** *Cust Svc	
Reader's Digest Association Inc	44 S Bdwy	White Plains	NY	10601	**800-457-4708**	914-244-2293
RentPath Inc	3585 Engineering Dr Ste 100	Norcross	GA	30092	**800-216-1423**	678-421-3000
Review & Herald Publishing Assn	55 W Oak Ridge Dr	Hagerstown	MD	21740	**800-456-3991**	301-393-3000
Sage Publications Inc	2455 Teller Rd	Thousand Oaks	CA	91320	**800-818-7243**	805-499-9774
Saint Croix Press Inc	1185 S Knowles Ave	New Richmond	WI	54017	**800-826-6622**	715-246-5811
Sandhills Publishing	120 W Harvest Dr	Lincoln	NE	68521	**800-331-1978**	402-479-2181
Schaeffer's Investment Research Inc	5151 Pfeiffer Rd Ste 250	Cincinnati	OH	45242	**800-448-2080**	513-589-3800
Scholastic Corp	557 Broadway	New York	NY	10012	**800-724-6527*** *Cust Svc	212-343-6100
Simba Information	60 Long Ridge Rd Ste 300	Stamford	CT	06902	**888-297-4622**	203-325-8193
Simmons-Boardman Publishing Corp	55 Broad St 26th fl 12th Fl	New York	NY	10004	**800-895-4389**	212-620-7200
Sky Publishing Corp	90 Sherman St	Cambridge	MA	02140	**800-253-0245**	617-864-7360
Slack Inc	6900 Grove Rd	Thorofare	NJ	08086	**800-257-8290**	856-848-1000
Smithsonian Institution Business Ventures Div	600 Maryland Ave SW Ste 6000	Washington	DC	20024	**800-521-5330**	202-633-6080
Source Media Inc	One State St Plz 27th Fl	New York	NY	10004	**800-221-1809**	212-803-8200
Stamats Communications Inc	615 Fifth St SE	Cedar Rapids	IA	52401	**800-553-8878**	319-364-6167
Standard Publishing Co	8805 Governors Hill Dr Ste 400	Cincinnati	OH	45249	**800-543-1353*** *Orders	513-931-4050
Strafford Publications Inc	PO Box 13729	Atlanta	GA	30324	**800-926-7926**	404-881-1141
Sunset Publishing Corp	80 Willow Rd	Menlo Park	CA	94025	**800-227-7346**	650-321-3600
Tax Management Inc	1801 S Bell St	Arlington	VA	22202	**800-372-1033**	703-341-3000
Thompson Publishing Group Inc	805 15th St NW Third Fl	Washington	DC	20005	**800-677-3789*** *Cust Svc	202-872-4000
Transcontinental Inc	1100 Rene-Levesque Blvd W 24th Fl	Montreal	QC	H3B4X9	**800-361-5479**	514-392-9000
TransWorld Business	2052 Corte Del Nogal Ste 100	Carlsbad	CA	92011	**800-788-7072*** *General	760-722-7777
Travelhost Inc	10701 N Stemmons Fwy	Dallas	TX	75220	**800-527-1782**	972-556-0541
United Methodist Publishing House	201 Eigth Ave S	Nashville	TN	37203	**800-672-1789**	615-749-6000
University of Chicago Press Journals Div	PO Box 37005	Chicago	IL	60637	**877-705-1878**	773-702-7700
Value Line Inc	220 E 42nd St *NASDAQ: VALU* ■	New York	NY	10017	**800-634-3583*** *Cust Svc	212-907-1500
Vance Publishing Corp	400 Knightsbridge Pkwy	Lincolnshire	IL	60069	**800-621-2845**	847-634-2600
Vendome Group LLC	216 E 45th St Sixth Fl	New York	NY	10017	**800-519-3692**	
Warren Communications News Inc	2115 Ward Ct NW	Washington	DC	20037	**800-771-9202**	202-872-9200
Yankee Publishing Inc	PO Box 520	Dublin	NH	03444	**800-729-9265**	603-563-8111

633-10 Publishers (Misc)

					Toll-Free	Phone
AM Best Co	Ambest Rd	Oldwick	NJ	08858	**800-424-2378**	908-439-2200
American Printing House for the Blind	1839 Frankfort Ave PO Box 6085	Louisville	KY	40206	**800-223-1839**	502-895-2405
Brodart Company Automation Div	500 Arch St	Williamsport	PA	17701	**800-233-8467**	570-326-2461
Cathedral Press Inc	600 NE Sixth St	Long Prairie	MN	56347	**800-874-8332*** *Cust Svc	320-732-6143
Chalk & Vermilion Fine Arts Inc	55 Old Post Rd Ste 2	Greenwich	CT	06830	**800-877-2250**	203-869-9500
Channing Bete Co	One Community Pl	South Deerfield	MA	01373	**800-477-4776**	413-665-7611
Clement Communications Inc	Three Creek Pkwy PO Box 2208	Boothwyn	PA	19061	**800-253-6368**	610-459-4200
Coastal Training Technologies Corp	500 Studio Dr	Virginia Beach	VA	23452	**866-333-6888**	757-498-9014
Drivers License Guide Co	1492 Oddstad Dr	Redwood City	CA	94063	**800-227-8827**	650-369-4849
EBSCO Publishing Inc	10 Estes St	Ipswich	MA	01938	**800-653-2726**	978-356-6500
Encyclopedia Britannica Inc	331 N Las Salle St	Chicago	IL	60654	**800-323-1229*** *Cust Svc	312-347-7159
Forecast International	22 Commerce Rd	Newtown	CT	06470	**800-451-4975**	203-426-0800
Hadley House Co	4816 Nicollet Ave S	Minneapolis	MN	55419	**800-423-5390**	
Imagination Publishing	600 W Fulton St Ste 600	Chicago	IL	60661	**800-482-0776**	312-887-1000
Interactive Data Corp	32 Crosby Dr	Bedford	MA	01730	**800-228-9715**	781-687-8500
Lifetouch Church Directories	1371 Portland Way N	Galion	OH	44833	**800-521-4611**	419-468-4739
Mergent FIS Inc	580 Kingsley Pk Dr	Fort Mill	SC	29715	**800-342-5647**	
New York Graphic Society Ltd	129 Glover Ave	Norwalk	CT	06850	**800-677-6947**	
OAG Worldwide	3025 Highland Pkwy Ste 200	Downers Grove	IL	60515	**800-342-5624**	630-515-5300
OneSource Information Services Inc	300 Baker Ave	Concord	MA	01742	**800-433-0287**	978-318-4300
San Dieguito Printers	1880 Diamond St	San Marcos	CA	92078	**800-321-5794**	760-744-0910
Somerset Fine Arts	PO Box 869	Fulshear	TX	77441	**800-444-2540*** *Sales	
TechTarget	275 Grove St Ste 800	Newton	MA	02466	**888-274-4111**	617-431-9200
Thomson CenterWatch Inc	100 N Washington St Ste 301	Boston	MA	02114	**800-765-9647*** *Cust Svc	617-948-5100
Wonderlic Inc	400 Lakeview Pkwy Ste 200	Vernon Hills	IL	60061	**877-605-9496**	847-680-4900

633-11 Technical Publishers

					Toll-Free	Phone
Aircraft Technical Publishers	101 S Hill Dr	Brisbane	CA	94005	**800-227-4610**	415-330-9500
Applied Computer Research Inc (ACR)	PO Box 41730	Phoenix	AZ	85080	**800-234-2227**	

Classified Section

				Toll-Free	Phone

Buyers Laboratory Inc
20 Railroad Ave .... Hackensack NJ 07601 — **800-578-5902** — 201-488-0404

Faulkner Information Services
7905 Browning Rd .... Pennsauken NJ 08109 — **800-843-0460** — 856-662-2070

Health Forum
155 North Wacker Drive Suite 400 .... Chicago IL 60606 — **800-621-6902** — 312-422-2165

Information Gatekeepers Inc (IGI)
1340 Soldiers Field Rd Ste 2 .... Brighton MA 02135 — **800-323-1088** — 617-782-5033

JJ Keller & Assoc Inc
3003 Breezewood Ln PO Box 368 .... Neenah WI 54957 — **800-558-5011** — 920-722-2848

Mitchell 1
14145 Danielson St Ste A .... Poway CA 92064 — **888-724-6742** — 858-391-5000

Mitchell International Inc
6220 Greenwich Dr .... San Diego CA 92122 — **800-854-7030** — 858-578-6550

O'Reilly & Assoc Inc
1005 Gravenstein Hwy N .... Sebastopol CA 95472 — **800-998-9938** — 707-829-0515

Thompson Publishing Group Inc
805 15th St NW Third Fl .... Washington DC 20005 — **800-677-3789*** — 202-872-4000
*Cust Svc

634   PULP MILLS

SEE ALSO Paper Mills ; Paperboard Mills

				Toll-Free	Phone

Alberta-Pacific Forest Industries Inc
PO Box 8000 .... Boyle AB T0A0M0 — **800-661-5210** — 780-525-8000

International Paper Co
6400 Poplar Ave .... Memphis TN 38197 — **800-223-1268*** — 901-419-9000
NYSE: IP ▪ *Prod Info

Kimberly-Clark Corp
351 Phelps Dr .... Irving TX 75038 — **888-525-8388** — 972-281-1200
NYSE: KMB

635   PUMPS - MEASURING & DISPENSING

				Toll-Free	Phone

Assay Technology Inc
1382 Stealth St .... Livermore CA 94551 — **800-833-1258** — 925-461-8880

Bennett Pump Co
1218 Pontaluna Rd .... Spring Lake MI 49456 — **800-235-7618** — 231-798-1310

Brooks Utility Products Group
23847 Industrial Park Dr .... Farmington Hills MI 48335 — **888-687-3008** — 248-477-0250

Controlled Access Inc
1515 W 130th St .... Hinckley OH 44233 — **800-942-0829** — 330-273-6185

DICKEY-john Corp
5200 Dickey-John Rd .... Auburn IL 62615 — **800-637-2952** — 217-438-3371

Electro Static Technology
31 Winterbrook Rd .... Mechanic Falls ME 04256 — **866-738-1857** — 207-998-5140

Gagemaker LP
712 Southmore Ave .... Pasadena TX 77502 — **800-767-7633** — 713-472-7360

Gammex Inc
7600 Discovery Dr .... Middleton WI 53562 — **800-426-6391** — 608-828-7000

Gasboy International Inc
7300 W Friendly Ave .... Greensboro NC 27420 — **800-444-5579*** — 336-547-5000
*Sales

Medicomp Inc
7845 Ellis Rd .... Melbourne FL 32904 — **800-234-3278** — 321-676-0010

O'Day Equipment Inc
1301 40th St NW .... Fargo ND 58102 — **800-654-6329** — 701-282-9260

Standard Imaging Inc
3120 Deming Way .... Middleton WI 53562 — **800-261-4446** — 608-831-0025

636   PUMPS & MOTORS - FLUID POWER

				Toll-Free	Phone

Applied Energy Company Inc (AEC)
1205 Venture Ct Ste 100 .... Carrollton TX 75006 — **800-580-1171** — 214-355-4200

Bosch Rexroth Corp
5150 Prairie Stone Pkwy .... Hoffman Estates IL 60192 — **800-860-1055** — 847-645-3600

Bosch Rexroth Corp Piston Pump Div
8 Southchase Ct .... Fountain Inn SC 29644 — **877-266-7811** — 864-967-2777

Fluid Metering Inc
Five Aerial Way Ste 500 .... Syosset NY 11791 — **800-223-3388** — 516-922-6050

Jetstream of Houston LLP
4930 Cranswick .... Houston TX 77041 — **800-231-8192** — 713-462-7000

Permco Inc
1500 Frost Rd .... Streetsboro OH 44241 — **800-628-2801** — 330-626-2801

TII Network Technologies Inc
141 Rodeo Dr .... Edgewood NY 11717 — **888-844-4720** — 631-789-5000
NASDAQ: TIII

Viking Pump Inc
406 State St .... Cedar Falls IA 50613 — **800-123-1234** — 319-266-1741

637   PUMPS & PUMPING EQUIPMENT (GENERAL USE)

SEE ALSO Industrial Machinery, Equipment, & Supplies

				Toll-Free	Phone

Acme Dynamics Inc
3608 Sydney Rd PO Box 1780 .... Plant City FL 33566 — **800-622-9355** — 813-752-3137

Aermotor Pumps Inc
293 Wright St .... Delavan WI 53115 — **800-230-1816**

Air Systems International Inc
829 Juniper Crescent .... Chesapeake VA 23320 — **800-866-8100** — 757-424-3967

American Machine & Tool Company Inc
400 Spring St .... Royersford PA 19468 — **888-268-7867** — 610-948-3800

Ampco Pumps Company Inc
2045 W Mill Rd .... Glendale WI 53209 — **800-737-8671** — 414-643-1852

AR Wilfley & Sons Inc
7350 E Progress Pl Ste 200 .... Englewood CO 80111 — **800-525-9930** — 303-779-1777

Armstrong International Inc
2081 SE Ocean Blvd 4th Fl .... Stuart FL 34996 — **866-738-5125** — 772-286-7175

				Toll-Free	Phone

ASM Industries Inc Pacer Pumps Div
41 Industrial Cir .... Lancaster PA 17601 — **800-233-3861*** — 717-656-2161
*Cust Svc

Beckett Corp
3250 Skyway Cir N .... Irving TX 75038 — **888-232-5388** — 972-871-8000

Blackmer
1809 Century Ave .... Grand Rapids MI 49503 — **888-363-7886** — 616-241-1611

CDS-John Blue Co
290 Pinehurst St .... Huntsville AL 35806 — **800-253-2583** — 256-721-9090

CLYDE UNION Pumps
4600 W Dickman Rd .... Battle Creek MI 49037 — **800-877-7867** — 269-966-4600

Coffin Turbo Pump Inc
326 S Dean St .... Englewood NJ 07631 — **800-568-9798** — 201-568-2826

Corken Inc
3805 NW 36th St .... Oklahoma City OK 73112 — **800-631-4929** — 405-946-5576

Evans-Hydro
18128 S Santa Fe Ave .... Rancho Dominguez CA 90221 — **800-429-7867** — 310-608-5801

Flint & Walling Inc
95 N Oak St .... Kendallville IN 46755 — **800-345-9422*** — 260-347-1600
*Sales

Flowserve Corp
5215 N O'Connor Blvd Ste 2300 .... Irving TX 75039 — **800-350-1082** — 972-443-6500
NYSE: FLS

FMG Enterprises Inc
1125 Memorex Dr .... Santa Clara CA 95050 — **800-327-6177** — 408-982-0110

GIW Industries Inc
5000 Wrightsboro Rd .... Grovetown GA 30813 — **888-832-4449** — 706-863-1011

GPM Industries Inc
110 Gateway Dr .... Macon GA 31210 — **888-476-7867** — 478-471-7867

Graco Inc
88 11th Ave NE PO Box 1441 .... Minneapolis MN 55413 — **800-328-0211*** — 612-623-6000
NYSE: GGG ▪ *Cust Svc

Graymills Corp
3705 N Lincoln Ave .... Chicago IL 60613 — **877-465-7867** — 773-477-4100

Great Plains Industries Inc
5252 E 36th St N .... Wichita KS 67220 — **800-835-0113*** — 316-686-7361
*Sales

Grundfos Pumps Corp
17100 W 118th Terr .... Olathe KS 66061 — **800-345-4555** — 913-227-3400

Hale Products Inc
700 Spring Mill Ave .... Conshohocken PA 19428 — **800-220-4253** — 610-825-6300

Hammelmann Corp
600 Progress Rd .... Dayton OH 45449 — **800-783-4935** — 937-859-8777

Harben Inc
2010 Ronald Regan Blvd .... Cumming GA 30041 — **800-327-5387** — 770-889-9535

Haskel International Inc
100 E Graham Pl .... Burbank CA 91502 — **800-743-2720** — 818-843-4000

Hydromatic Pump Co
740 E Ninth St .... Ashland OH 44805 — **888-957-8677**

Hypro 375 Fifth Ave NW .... New Brighton MN 55112 — **800-424-9776*** — 651-766-6300
*Cust Svc

Imo Pump 1710 Airport Rd .... Monroe NC 28110 — **800-405-0148** — 704-289-6511

Integrated Flow Solutions LLC
6461 Reynolds Rd .... Tyler TX 75708 — **800-859-7867** — 903-595-6511

Kerr Pump & Supply
12880 Cloverdale St .... Oak Park MI 48237 — **800-482-8259** — 248-543-3880

Kimray Inc
52 NW 42nd St .... Oklahoma City OK 73118 — **866-586-7233** — 405-525-6601

Kraft Fluid Systems Inc
14300 Foltz Pkwy .... Strongsville OH 44149 — **800-257-1155** — 440-238-5545

Lehigh Fluid Power Inc
1413 Rt 179 .... Lambertville NJ 08530 — **800-257-9515**

Liberty Pumps Inc
7000 Apple Tree Ave .... Bergen NY 14416 — **800-543-2550** — 585-494-1817

Madden Manufacturing Inc
PO Box 387 .... Elkhart IN 46515 — **800-369-6233** — 574-295-4292

McNally Industries LLC
340 W Benson Ave .... Grantsburg WI 54840 — **800-366-1410** — 715-463-8300

Met-Pro Corp Fybroc Div
700 Emlen Way .... Telford PA 18969 — **800-392-7621** — 215-723-8155

Met-Pro Corp Sethco Div
800 Emlen Way .... Telford PA 18969 — **800-645-0500** — 215-799-2577

Micropump Inc
1402 NE 136th Ave .... Vancouver WA 98684 — **800-222-9565*** — 360-253-2008
*Sales

Moyno Inc
1895 W Jefferson St .... Springfield OH 45506 — **877-486-6966** — 937-327-3111

MP Pumps Inc
34800 Bennett Dr .... Fraser MI 48026 — **800-563-8006** — 586-293-8240

National Pump Company LLC
7706 N 71st Ave .... Glendale AZ 85303 — **800-966-5240** — 623-979-3560

Neptune Chemical Pump Co
PO Box 247 .... Lansdale PA 19446 — **800-255-4017** — 215-699-8700

Neptune-Benson Inc
Six Jefferson St .... Coventry RI 02816 — **800-832-8002** — 401-821-2200

NH Yates & Company Inc
117 Church Ln # C .... Cockeysville MD 21030 — **800-878-8181**

Peerless Pump Co
2005 ML King Jr St PO Box 7026 .... Indianapolis IN 46207 — **800-879-0182** — 317-925-9661

Pentair Water Pool & Spa
1620 Hawkins Ave .... Sanford NC 27330 — **800-831-7133**

Roper Pump Co
3475 Old Maysville Rd .... Commerce GA 30529 — **800-944-6769*** — 706-335-5551
*Sales

Roth Pump Co
PO Box 4330 .... Rock Island IL 61204 — **888-444-7684** — 309-787-1791

RS Corcoran Co
500 N Vine St .... New Lenox IL 60451 — **800-637-1067** — 815-485-2156

Scot Pump
6437 Pioneer Rd PO Box 286 .... Cedarburg WI 53012 — **888-835-0600** — 262-377-7000

Serfilco Ltd
2900 MacArthur Blvd .... Northbrook IL 60062 — **800-323-5431** — 847-559-1777

SHURflo Pump Mfg Company Inc
5900 Katella Ave Ste A .... Cypress CA 90630 — **800-854-3218** — 562-795-5200

Smith Pump Co Inc
301 M B Industrial .... Woodway TX 76712 — **800-299-8909** — 254-776-0377

Standard Alloys & Mfg
PO Box 969 .... Port Arthur TX 77640 — **800-231-8240** — 409-983-3201

					Toll-Free	Phone
Thompson Pump & Mfg Company Inc	4620 City Ctr Dr PO Box 291370	Port Orange	FL	32129	**800-767-7310**	386-767-7310
Tuthill Corp	8500 S Madison St	Burr Ridge	IL	60527	**800-634-2695**	630-382-4900
Vaughan Company Inc	364 Monte-Elma Rd	Montesano	WA	98563	**888-249-2467**	360-249-4042
Veeder-Root Red Jacket Div	125 Powder Forest Dr PO Box 2003	Simsbury	CT	06070	**800-873-3313**	860-651-2700
Viking Pump Inc	406 State St	Cedar Falls	IA	50613	**800-123-1234**	319-266-1741
Wastecorp Inc	PO Box 70	Grand Island	NY	14072	**888-829-2783**	
Waterous Co	125 Hardman Ave	South Saint Paul	MN	55075	**800-488-1228**	651-450-5000
Waukesha Cherry-Burrell Corp (WCB)	611 Sugar Creek Rd	Delavan	WI	53115	**800-252-5200**	262-728-1900
Zoeller Co	3649 Kane Run Rd *OTC: ZOLR*	Louisville	KY	40211	**800-928-7867**	502-778-2731

638 RACING & RACETRACKS

SEE ALSO Motor Speedways

					Toll-Free	Phone
Alameda County Fair Assn (ACFA)	4501 Pleasanton Ave	Pleasanton	CA	94566	**800-874-9253**	925-426-7600
Brainerd International Raceway	5523 Birchdale Rd	Brainerd	MN	56401	**866-444-4455**	218-824-7223
Calder Casino & Race Course	21001 NW 27th Ave	Miami	FL	33056	**800-522-4700**	305-625-1311
Canterbury Park Holding Corp	1100 Canterbury Rd *NASDAQ: CPHC*	Shakopee	MN	55379	**800-340-6361**	952-445-7223
Charlotte Motor Speedway	5555 Concord Pkwy S	Concord	NC	28027	**800-455-3267**	704-455-3200
Churchill Downs Inc	700 Central Ave *NASDAQ: CHDN*	Louisville	KY	40208	**800-994-9909**	502-636-4400
Colonial Downs	10515 Colonial Downs Pkwy	New Kent	VA	23124	**888-482-8722**	804-966-7223
Delaware North Cos Gaming & Entertainment	40 Fountain Plz	Buffalo	NY	14202	**800-828-7240**	716-858-5000
Delaware Park Racetrack & Slots Casino	777 Delaware Pk Blvd	Wilmington	DE	19804	**800-417-5687**	302-994-2521
Delta Downs Racetrack	2717 Delta Downs Dr	Vinton	LA	70668	**800-589-7441**	
Dover Downs Hotel & Casino	1131 N DuPont Hwy *NYSE: DDE*	Dover	DE	19901	**800-711-5882**	302-674-4600
Dover International Speedway	1131 N DuPont Hwy PO Box 843	Dover	DE	19901	**800-441-7223**	302-883-6500
Dover Motorsports Inc	1131 N Dupont Hwy *NYSE: DVD*	Dover	DE	19901	**800-441-7223**	302-883-6500
Fair Grounds Race Course	1751 Gentilly Blvd	New Orleans	LA	70119	**800-262-7983**	504-944-5515
Fair Meadows at Tulsa	4609 E 21st St	Tulsa	OK	74114	**877-781-2660**	918-743-7223
Finger Lakes Gaming & Race Track	5857 Rt 96	Farmington	NY	14425	**877-846-7369**	585-924-3232
Fort Erie Race Track	230 Catherine St PO Box 1130	Fort Erie	ON	L2A5N9	**800-295-3770**	905-871-3200
Fresno District Fair	1121 S Chance Ave	Fresno	CA	93702	**866-275-3772**	559-650-3247
Gillespie County Fairgrounds	530 Fair Dr PO Box 526	Fredericksburg	TX	78624	**800-280-9531**	830-997-2359
Grays Harbor Raceway	32 Elma McCleary Rd PO Box 768	Elma	WA	98541	**800-667-7711**	360-482-4374
Harrington Raceway	15 W Rider Rd	Harrington	DE	19952	**888-887-5687**	302-398-7223
Hazel Park Raceway	1650 E 10 Mile Rd	Hazel Park	MI	48030	**800-794-8001**	248-398-1000
Hollywood Casino at Charles Town Races	750 Hollywood Dr	Charles Town	WV	25414	**800-795-7001**	304-725-7001
Hoosier Park Racing & Casino	4500 Dan Patch Cir	Anderson	IN	46013	**800-526-7223**	765-642-7223
Josephine County Fairgrounds	1451 Fairgrounds Rd PO Box 672	Grants Pass	OR	97527	**800-773-1162**	541-476-3215
Laurel Park	Rt 198 & Racetrack Rd PO Box 130	Laurel	MD	20724	**800-638-1859**	301-725-0400
MetraPark	PO Box 2514	Billings	MT	59103	**800-366-8538**	406-256-2400
Mystique Casino	1855 Greyhound Pk Dr	Dubuque	IA	52001	**800-373-3647**	563-582-3647
Oaklawn Park	2705 Central Ave *General	Hot Springs	AR	71901	**800-625-5296***	501-623-4411
Penn National Gaming Inc	825 Berkshire Blvd Ste 200 *NASDAQ: PENN*	Wyomissing	PA	19610	**877-565-2112**	
Pensacola Greyhound Track	951 Dog Track Rd	Pensacola	FL	32506	**800-345-3997**	850-455-8595
Pinnacle Entertainment Inc	3980 Howard Hughes Pkwy *NYSE: PNK*	Las Vegas	NV	89169	**877-764-8750**	702-541-7777
Ravalli County Fair	100 Old Corvallis Rd	Hamilton	MT	59840	**800-225-6779**	406-363-3411
Remington Park Race Track	One Remington Pl	Oklahoma City	OK	73111	**866-456-9880**	405-424-1000
Retama Park	1 Retama Pkwy	Selma	TX	78154	**800-473-8262**	210-651-7000
Sam Houston Race Park	7575 N Sam Houston Pkwy W	Houston	TX	77064	**800-807-7223**	281-807-8700
Santa Cruz County Fair & Rodeo	3142 Arizona 83 PO Box 85	Sonoita	AZ	85637	**866-394-0121**	520-455-5553
Shoreline Star Greyhound Park & Entertainment Complex LLC	255 Kossuth St	Bridgeport	CT	06608	**888-463-6446**	
Solano County Fair	900 Fairgrounds Dr	Vallejo	CA	94589	**800-700-2482**	707-551-2000
Sonoma County Fairgrounds	1350 Bennett Valley Rd	Santa Rosa	CA	95404	**866-487-9243**	707-545-4200
Sports Creek Raceway	4290 Morrish Rd	Swartz Creek	MI	48473	**844-635-4708**	810-635-3333
Sunland Park Racetrack & Casino	1200 Futurity Dr	Sunland Park	NM	88063	**800-572-1142**	575-874-5200
Tampa Bay Downs Inc	11225 Racetrack Rd	Tampa	FL	33626	**800-200-4434**	813-855-4401
Thistledown Racing Club Inc	21501 Emery Rd	Cleveland	OH	44128	**866-503-3792**	216-662-8600
Turf Paradise Racetrack	1501 W Bell Rd	Phoenix	AZ	85023	**800-639-8783**	602-942-1101
Twin River Casino	100 Twin River Rd	Lincoln	RI	02865	**877-827-4837**	401-475-8505

639 RADIO COMPANIES

					Toll-Free	Phone
Bible Broadcasting Network Inc	11530 Carmel Commons Blvd PO Box 7300	Charlotte	NC	28226	**800-888-7077**	704-523-5555
Bliss Communications Inc	PO Box 5001	Janesville	WI	53547	**800-362-6712**	608-754-3311
Bott Radio Network	10550 Barkley St Ste 100	Overland Park	KS	66212	**800-875-1903**	913-642-7770
Eagle Communications Inc	2703 Hall St Ste 15 Ste 15	Hays	KS	67601	**877-613-2453**	785-625-5910
Eagle Radio Inc	2300 Hall	Hays	KS	67601	**877-613-2453**	785-625-2578
Educational Media Foundation	5700 W Oaks Blvd *General	Rocklin	CA	95765	**800-525-5683***	916-251-1600
Entercom Communications Corp	401 City Ave Ste 809 *NYSE: ETM*	Bala Cynwyd	PA	19004	**800-776-9437**	610-660-5610
Family Radio	290 Hegenberger Rd	Oakland	CA	94621	**800-543-1495**	
Far East Broadcasting Co Inc	15700 Imperial Hwy PO Box 1	La Mirada	CA	90638	**800-523-3480**	
Midwest Communications Inc	904 Grand Ave	Wausau	WI	54403	**877-945-4236**	715-842-1437
Northern Star Broadcasting LLC	3250 Racquet Club Dr	Traverse City	MI	49684	**888-847-2346**	231-922-4981
Saga Communications Inc	73 Kercheval Ave *NYSE: SGA*	Grosse Pointe Farms	MI	48236	**800-777-3674**	313-886-7070
Shamrock Communications Inc	149 Penn Ave	Scranton	PA	18503	**800-228-4637**	570-348-9100
Telesouth Communications Inc	6311 Ridgewood Rd	Jackson	MS	39211	**888-808-8637**	601-957-1700
Withers Broadcasting Co	PO Box 1508	Mount Vernon	IL	62864	**800-333-1577**	618-242-3500
Zimmer Radio Group	3215 Lemone Industrial Blvd Ste 200	Columbia	MO	65201	**800-455-1099**	573-875-1099

640 RADIO NETWORKS

					Toll-Free	Phone
American Family Association	PO Drawer 2440	Tupelo	MS	38803	**800-326-4543**	662-844-5036
Associated Press	1100 13th St NW Ste 700	Washington	DC	20005	**800-824-5498**	202-641-9000
Black Radio Network	166 Madison Ave	New York	NY	10016	**800-226-8276**	212-686-6850
Bott Radio Network	10550 Barkley St Ste 100	Overland Park	KS	66212	**800-875-1903**	913-642-7770
Family Life Communications Inc	PO Box 35300	Tucson	AZ	85740	**800-776-1070**	
Far East Broadcasting Co Inc	15700 Imperial Hwy PO Box 1	La Mirada	CA	90638	**800-523-3480**	
Jones International Ltd	9697 E Mineral Ave	Centennial	CO	80112	**800-525-7002**	
Radio America	1100 N Glebe Rd Ste 900	Arlington	VA	22201	**800-807-4703**	703-302-1000
Relevant Radio	1496 Bellevue St Ste 202 PO Box 10707	Green Bay	WI	54311	**877-291-0123**	920-884-1460
Tiger Financial News Network	601 Cleveland St Ste 618	Clearwater	FL	33755	**877-518-9190**	727-467-9190
United Stations Radio Network	1065 Ave of the Americas 3rd Fl	New York	NY	10018	**866-989-1975**	212-869-1111
Yesterday USA Radio Networks, The	2001 Plymouth Rock Dr	Richardson	TX	75081	**800-624-2272**	972-889-9872

641 RADIO STATIONS

SEE ALSO Internet Broadcasting

					Toll-Free	Phone
AM 570 LA Sports	3400 W Olive Ave Ste 550	Burbank	CA	91505	**866-987-2570**	818-559-2252
CBV-FM 106.3 (CBC)	PO Box 500 Stn A	Toronto	ON	M5W1E6	**866-306-4636**	
CKLW-AM 800 (N/T)	1640 Ouellette Ave	Windsor	ON	N8X1L1	**800-263-2559**	519-258-8888
Family Stations Inc	290 Hegenberger Rd	Oakland	CA	94621	**800-543-1495**	
Fun 101.3 FM	1996 Auction Rd	Manheim	PA	17545	**877-870-5678**	717-653-0800
KABX-FM 97.5 (Oldies)	1020 W Main St	Merced	CA	95340	**800-350-3777**	209-723-2191
KANU-FM 91.5 (NPR)	1120 W 11th St Kansas Public Radio	Lawrence	KS	66044	**888-577-5268**	785-864-4530
KBBY-FM 95.1 (AC)	1376 Walter St	Ventura	CA	93003	**888-288-9242**	805-642-8595

				Toll-Free	Phone
KBHE-FM 89.3 (NPR) 555 N Dakota St PO Box 5000	Vermillion	SD	57069	800-456-0766	605-677-5861
KBIA-FM 91.3 (NPR) 409 Jesse Hall	Columbia	MO	65211	800-292-9136	573-882-3431
KBIG-FM 104.3 (AC) 3400 W Olive Ave Ste 550	Burbank	CA	91505	866-544-6936	818-559-2252
KBRG-FM 100.3 (Span AC) 750 Battery St Ste 200	San Francisco	CA	94111	888-808-1003	415-989-5765
KBYZ-FM 96.5 (CR) 4303 Memorial Hwy	Mandan	ND	58554	888-663-9650	701-663-9600
KCFR-FM 90.1 (NPR) 7409 S Alton Ct	Centennial	CO	80112	800-722-4449	303-871-9191
KCLR-FM 99.3 (Ctry) 3215 Lemone Industrial Blvd Ste 200	Columbia	MO	65201	800-455-5257	573-875-1099
KCMQ-FM 96.7 (CR) 3215 Lemone Industrial Blvd Ste 200	Columbia	MO	65201	800-455-1967	573-875-1099
KCRW-FM 89.9 (NPR) 1900 Pico Blvd	Santa Monica	CA	90405	877-527-9227	310-450-5183
KCSD-FM 90.9 (NPR) 555 N Dakota St PO Box 5000	Vermillion	SD	57069	800-456-0766	605-677-5861
KDON-FM 102.5 (CHR) 903 N Main St	Salinas	CA	93906	888-558-5366	831-755-8181
KFJM-FM 90.7 (AAA) 207 N Fifth St	Fargo	ND	58102	800-366-6888	701-241-6900
KFRG-FM 95.1 (Ctry) 900 E Washington St Ste 315	Colton	CA	92324	888-431-3764	909-825-9525
KGNU-FM 88.5 (Var) 4700 Walnut St	Boulder	CO	80301	800-737-3030	303-449-4885
KGOU-FM 106.3 (NPR) 860 Van Vleet Oval Rm 300	Norman	OK	73019	866-533-2470	405-325-3388
KGY-FM 96.9 (Ctry) 1700 Marine Dr NE	Olympia	WA	98501	855-549-1240	360-943-1240
KHCC-FM 90.1 (NPR) 815 N Walnut St Ste 300	Hutchinson	KS	67501	800-723-4657	620-662-6646
KIXI-AM 880 (Nost) 3650 131st Ave SE Ste 550	Bellevue	WA	98006	866-880-5494	425-562-8964
KNDR-FM 104.7 (Rel) 1400 NE Third St	Mandan	ND	58554	800-767-5095	701-663-2345
KNOW-FM 91.1 (NPR) 480 Cedar St	Saint Paul	MN	55101	800-228-7123	651-290-1500
KNWI-FM 107.1 (Rel) 3737 Woodland Ave Ste 300	West Des Moines	IA	50266	800-701-3123	515-327-1071
KOPN-FM 89.5 (Var) 915 E Broadway	Columbia	MO	65201	800-895-5676	573-874-1139
KPLU-FM 88.5 (NPR) 12180 Pk Ave S	Tacoma	WA	98447	800-677-5758	253-535-7758
KPVU-FM 91.3 (NPR) Prairie View A & M University MS 1415	Prairie View	TX	77446	877-241-1752	936-261-3750
KRCD-FM 103.9 (Span) 655 N Central Ave Ste 2500	Glendale	CA	91203	888-382-1222	818-500-4500
KRKS-FM 94.7 (Rel) 3131 S Vaughn Way Ste 601	Aurora	CO	80014	888-346-4700	303-750-5687
KROX-AM 1260 (Var) 208 S Main St	Crookston	MN	56716	800-222-2537	218-281-1140
KSME-FM 96.1 (CHR) 4270 Byrd Dr	Loveland	CO	80538	877-498-9600	970-461-2560
KTOM-FM 92.7 (Ctry) 903 N Main St *General	Salinas	CA	93906	800-660-5866*	831-755-8181
KTSD-FM 91.1 (NPR) 555 N Dakota St PO Box 5000	Vermillion	SD	57069	800-456-0766	605-677-5861
KTXY-FM 106.9 (AC) 3215 Lemone Industrial Blvd Ste 200	Columbia	MO	65201	800-500-9107	573-875-1099
KUAD-FM 99.1 (Ctry) 600 Main St	Windsor	CO	80550	800-500-2599	
KUAF 91.3 Public Radio 9 S School Ave	Fayetteville	AR	72701	800-522-5823	479-575-2556
KUFM-FM 89.1 (NPR) 32 Campus Dr University of Montana	Missoula	MT	59812	800-325-1565	406-243-4931
KUSP-FM 88.9 (NPR) 203 Eigth Ave	Santa Cruz	CA	95062	800-655-5877	831-476-2800
KUWS-FM 91.3 (NPR) 1805 Catlin Ave	Superior	WI	54880	800-300-8530	715-394-8530
KVLC-FM 101.1 (Oldies) 101 Perkins Dr	Las Cruces	NM	88005	877-527-1011	575-527-1111
KWYR-FM 93.7 (AC) PO Box 491	Winner	SD	57580	800-388-5997	605-842-3333
KXFG-FM 92.9 (Ctry) 900 E Washington Ste 315	Colton	CA	92324	888-431-3764	909-825-9525
Star 92.9 265 Hegeman Ave	Colchester	VT	05446	866-865-7827	802-655-0093
Super Talk 1270 4303 Memorial Hwy	Mandan	ND	58554	844-255-7886	701-663-1270
Triad's 105.7 Man Up, The 2-B PAI Pk	Greensboro	NC	27409	800-950-2482	336-822-2000
WALK-FM 97.5 (AC) 66 Colonial Dr	Patchogue	NY	11772	877-263-7995	631-475-5200
WASH-FM 97.1 (AC) 1801 Rockville Pk Fifth Fl	Rockville	MD	20852	866-927-4361	240-747-2700
WAVA-AM 780 (Rel) 1901 N Moore St Ste 200	Arlington	VA	22209	888-976-6924	703-807-2266
WAVA-FM 105.1 (Rel) 1901 N Moore St Ste 200	Arlington	VA	22209	888-293-9282	703-807-2266
WAYZ-FM 104.7 (Ctry) 10960 John Wayne Dr	Greencastle	PA	17225	888-950-1047	717-597-9200
WBIG-FM 100.3 (Oldies) 1801 Rockville Pk Fifth Fl	Rockville	MD	20852	800-493-1003	240-747-2700
WBRB-FM 101.3 (Ctry) 1065 Radio Pk Dr	Mount Clare	WV	26408	877-232-7121	304-623-6546
WCAT-FM 102.3 (Ctry) 728 N Hanover St	Carlisle	PA	17013	800-932-0505	717-243-1200
WCLT-FM 100.3 (Ctry) PO Box 5150	Newark	OH	43058	800-837-9258	740-345-4004
WCMR-AM 1270 (Rel) PO Box 307	Elkhart	IN	46515	800-522-9376	574-875-5166
WCNY-FM 91.3 (NPR) 506 Old Liverpool Rd	Liverpool	NY	13088	800-451-9269	315-453-2424
WCQR-FM 88.3 (Rel) 2312 Oak St	Gray	TN	37615	888-477-5676	423-477-5676
WCTL-FM 106.3 (Rel) 10912 Peach St	Waterford	PA	16441	800-568-8924	814-796-6000
WDAS-FM 105.3 (Urban AC) 111 Presidential Blvd Ste 100	Bala Cynwyd	PA	19004	800-745-3000	610-784-3333
WDJA-AM 1420 (N/T) 2710 W Atlantic Ave	Delray Beach	FL	33445	877-278-1420	561-278-1420
WDRM-FM 102.1 (Ctry) 26869 Peoples Rd	Madison	AL	35756	866-302-0102	256-309-2400
WEDR-FM 99.1 (Urban) 2741 N 29th Ave	Hollywood	FL	33020	800-843-2677	305-444-4404
WEEI-AM 850 (Sports) 20 Guest St Third Fl	Brighton	MA	02135	888-525-0850	617-779-3500
WEKU-FM 88.9 (Clas) 521 Lancaster Ave 102 Perkins Bldg-EKU	Richmond	KY	40475	800-621-8890	
WEMU-FM 89.1 (NPR) PO Box 980350	Ypsilanti	MI	48198	888-299-8910	734-487-2229
WERU-FM 89.9 (Var) 1186 Acadia Hwy	East Orland	ME	04431	800-643-6273	207-469-6600
WEVO-FM 89.1 (N/T) Two Pillsbury St Ste 600	Concord	NH	03301	800-639-4131	603-228-8910
WFCF-FM 88.5 (Var) Flagler College PO Box 1027	Saint Augustine	FL	32085	800-304-4208	904-819-6449
WFDM-FM 95.9 (N/T) 645 Industrial Dr	Franklin	IN	46131	800-278-9200	317-736-4040
WFHN-FM 107.1 (CHR) 22 Sconticut Neck Rd	Fairhaven	MA	02719	877-854-9467	508-999-6690
WFIU-FM 103.7 Indiana University 1229 E Seventh St	Bloomington	IN	47405	877-285-9348	812-855-1357
WFPG-FM 96.9 (AC) 950 Tilton Rd Ste 200	Northfield	NJ	08225	800-969-9374	609-645-9797
WFRE-FM 99.9 (Ctry) 5966 Grove Hill Rd	Frederick	MD	21703	877-999-9373	301-663-4181
WFUV-FM 90.7 (Var) 441 E Fordham Rd Fordham University	Bronx	NY	10458	888-400-5520	718-817-4550
WGAR-FM 99.5 (Ctry) 6200 Oak Tree Blvd S 4th Fl	Independence	OH	44131	855-222-0995	216-520-2600
WGBG-FM 98.5 (CR) 20200 DuPont Blvd	Georgetown	DE	19947	866-292-5483	302-856-2567
WGCU-FM 90.1 (NPR) 10501 FGCU Blvd S	Fort Myers	FL	33965	888-824-0030	239-590-2300
WGMD-FM 92.7 (N/T) PO Box 530	Rehoboth Beach	DE	19971	800-518-9292	302-945-2050
WGNE-FM 99.9 (Ctry) 6440 Atlantic Blvd	Jacksonville	FL	32211	888-725-2345	904-727-9696
WGTS-FM 91.9 (Rel) 7600 Flower Ave	Takoma Park	MD	20912	877-948-7919	301-891-4200
WGTY-FM 107.7 (Ctry) 1560 Fairfield Rd PO Box 3179	Gettysburg	PA	17325	800-366-9489	717-334-3101
WGY-AM 810 (N/T) 1203 Troy-Schenectady Rd Ste 201 Riverhill Ctr	Latham	NY	12110	800-825-5949	518-452-4800
WHFS-AM 1580 (N/T) 4200 Parliament Pl Ste 300	Lanham	MD	20706	888-432-1580	301-731-1580
WIOQ-FM 102.1 (CHR) 111 Presidential Blvd Ste 100	Bala Cynwyd	PA	19004	800-521-1021	610-784-3333
WJQK-FM 99.3 (Rel) 425 Centerstone Ct	Zeeland	MI	49464	866-931-9936	616-931-9930
WKCQ-FM 98.1 (Ctry) 2000 Whittier St	Saginaw	MI	48601	800-262-0098	989-752-8161
WKDD-FM 98.1 (AC) 7755 Freedom Ave	North Canton	OH	44720	888-533-4582	330-836-4700
WKRR-FM 92.3 (CR) 192 E Lewis St	Greensboro	NC	27406	800-762-5923	336-274-8042
WKSU-FM 89.7 (NPR) 1613 E Summit St	Kent	OH	44242	800-672-2132	330-672-3114
WKVV-FM 101.7 PO Box 2098	Omaha	NE	68103	800-525-5683	
WKZL-FM 107.5 (CHR) 192 E Lewis St	Greensboro	NC	27406	800-682-1075	336-274-8042
WLLL-AM 930 (Rel) PO Box 11375 *Cust Svc	Lynchburg	VA	24506	888-224-9809*	434-385-9555
WMAG-FM 99.5 (AC) 2-B PAI Pk	Greensboro	NC	27409	866-415-4158	336-822-2000
WMGE-FM 94.9 (Span CHR) 7601 Riviera Blvd	Miramar	FL	33023	877-599-2946	954-862-2000
WMIT-FM 106.9 (Rel) Three Porters Cove Rd	Asheville	NC	28805	800-330-9648	828-285-8477
WMPI-FM 105.3 (Ctry) 22 E McClain Ave	Scottsburg	IN	47170	800-441-1053	812-752-3688
WMUM-FM 89.7 (NPR) 243 Carey Salem Rd	Cochran	GA	31014	800-222-4788	478-301-5760
WMZQ-FM 98.7 (Ctry) 1801 Rockville Pk Fifth Fl	Rockville	MD	20852	800-505-0098	240-747-2700
WNCW-FM 88.7 (AAA) PO Box 804	Spindale	NC	28160	800-245-8870	828-287-8000
WNKU-FM 105.9 (Ctry) 301 Landrum Academic Ctr	Highland Heights	KY	41099	855-897-7897	859-572-6500
WODE-FM 99.9 107 Paxinosa Rd W	Easton	PA	18040	800-733-2767	610-258-6155
WOGG-FM 94.9 (Ctry) 123 Blaine Rd	Brownsville	PA	15417	866-983-9898	724-938-2000
WOGL-FM 98.1 (Oldies) Two Bala Plz Ste 800	Bala Cynwyd	PA	19004	800-942-8998	610-668-5998
WOKO-FM 98.9 (Ctry) 70 Joy Dr	South Burlington	VT	05403	800-354-9890	802-862-9890
Woodward Communications Inc 801 Bluff St	Dubuque	IA	52001	800-553-4801	
WPCV-FM 97.5 (Ctry) 404 W Lime St	Lakeland	FL	33815	800-227-9797	863-682-8184
WPGC-FM 95.5 (CHR) 4200 Parliament Pl Ste 300	Lanham	MD	20706	877-955-5267	
WPLM-FM 99.1 (AC) 17 Columbus Rd	Plymouth	MA	02360	877-327-9991	508-746-1390
WPRO-FM 92.3 (CHR) 1502 Wampanoag Trl	East Providence	RI	02915	800-638-0092	401-433-4200

	Toll-Free	Phone
WPST-FM 94.5 (AC) 619 Alexander Rd 3rd Fl .... Princeton NJ 08540	800-248-9778	609-419-0300
WQFL-FM 100.9 (Rel) PO Box 2118 .... Omaha NE 68103	888-937-2471	
WQUN-AM 1220 (Nost) 3085 Whitney Ave .... Hamden CT 06518	800-462-1944	203-582-8984
WRCH-FM 100.5 (AC) 10 Executive Dr .... Farmington CT 06032	800-530-1005	860-677-6700
WRDW-FM 96.5 (Urban) 555 City Line Ave Ste 330 .... Bala Cynwyd PA 19004	866-811-4111	610-667-9000
WRKO-AM 680 (N/T) 20 Guest St Third Fl .... Brighton MA 02135	877-469-4322	617-779-3400
WRVE-FM 99.5 (AC) 1203 Troy-Schenectady Rd Riverhill Ctr Ste 201 .... Latham NY 12110	800-995-9783	518-452-4800
WRVM-FM 102.7 (Rel) PO Box 212 .... Suring WI 54174	888-225-9786	920-842-2900
WSEN-FM 92.1 (CR) 8456 Smokey Hollow Rd PO Box 1050 .... Baldwinsville NY 13027	866-890-6453	315-635-3971
WSHU-FM 91.1 (NPR) 5151 Pk Ave .... Fairfield CT 06825	800-937-6045	203-365-0425
WTFM-FM 98.5 (AC) 222 Commerce St .... Kingsport TN 37660	888-633-5452	423-246-9578
WTSU-FM 89.9 (NPR) Troy University Wallace Hall .... Troy AL 36082	800-800-6616	
WTTS-FM 92.3 (AAA) 400 One City Centre .... Bloomington IN 47404	800-923-9887	812-332-3366
WUMP-AM 730 (Sports) 3280 Peachtree Rd Ste 2300 .... Atlanta GA 30305	866-485-9867	256-830-8300
WUNC-FM 91.5 (NPR) 120 Friday Center Dr PO Box 0915 .... Chapel Hill NC 27517	800-962-9862	919-445-9150
WVPE-FM 88.1 (NPR) 2424 California Rd .... Elkhart IN 46514	888-399-9873	574-262-5660
WVPS-FM 107.9 (NPR) 365 Troy Ave .... Colchester VT 05446	800-639-2192	802-655-9451
WWDC-FM 101.1 (Rock) 1801 Rockville Pk Fifth Fl .... Rockville MD 20852	866-913-2101	240-747-2701
WWFG-FM 99.9 (Ctry) 351 Tilghman Rd .... Salisbury MD 21804	800-664-3764	410-742-1923
WWGR-FM 101.9 (Ctry) 10915 K-Nine Dr .... Bonita Springs FL 34135	877-787-1019	239-495-8383
WWKA-FM 92.3 (Ctry) 4192 N John Young Pkwy .... Orlando FL 32804	866-438-0220	407-298-9292
WXBM-FM 102.7 (Ctry) 6085 Quintette Rd .... Pace FL 32571	844-962-7436	850-994-5357
WYGM-AM 740 (Span) 2500 Maitland Ctr Pkwy Ste 401 .... Maitland FL 32751	800-729-8255	407-916-7800

641-1 Abilene, TX

	Toll-Free	Phone
KEAN-FM 105.1 (Ctry) 3911 S First St .... Abilene TX 79605	800-588-5326	325-676-5326
KGNZ-FM 88.1 (Rel) 542 Butternut St .... Abilene TX 79602	800-588-8801	325-673-3045

641-2 Akron, OH

	Toll-Free	Phone
WAKR-AM 1590 (N/T) 1795 W Market St .... Akron OH 44313	888-723-9688	330-869-9800
WAPS-FM 91.3 (AAA) 65 Steiner Ave .... Akron OH 44301	877-411-3662	330-761-3099
WONE-FM 97.5 (Rock) 1795 W Market St .... Akron OH 44313	888-588-8436	330-869-9800
WQMX-FM 94.9 1795 W Market St .... Akron OH 44313	800-589-6499	330-869-9800

641-3 Albany, NY

	Toll-Free	Phone
WAMC-FM 90.3 (NPR) 318 Central Ave .... Albany NY 12206	800-323-9262	518-465-5233

641-4 Albuquerque, NM

	Toll-Free	Phone
KNML-AM 610 (Sports) 500 Fourth St NW Fifth Fl .... Albuquerque NM 87102	888-922-0610	505-767-6700
KUNM-FM 89.9 (NPR) 1University of New Mexico MSC 06 3520 .... Albuquerque NM 87131	877-277-4806	505-277-4806

641-5 Amarillo, TX

	Toll-Free	Phone
KACV-FM 90 (Alt) PO Box 447 .... Amarillo TX 79178	800-766-0176	
KGNC-AM 710 (N/T) 3505 Olsen Blvd Ste 117 .... Amarillo TX 79109	800-285-0710	806-355-9801
KGNC-FM 97.9 (Ctry) 3505 Olsen Blvd Ste 117 .... Amarillo TX 79109	877-765-9790	806-355-9801
KPRF-FM 98.7 (CHR) 6214 W 34th St .... Amarillo TX 79109	866-930-5225	806-355-9777

641-6 Anchorage, AK

	Toll-Free	Phone
KNBA-FM 90.3 (NPR) 3600 San Geronimo Dr Ste 480 .... Anchorage AK 99508	888-278-5622	907-793-3500
KYMG-FM 98.9 (AC) 800 E Dimond Blvd Ste 3-370 .... Anchorage AK 99515	877-868-8857	907-522-1515

641-7 Ann Arbor, MI

	Toll-Free	Phone
WUOM-FM 91.7 (NPR) 535 W William St Ste 110 .... Ann Arbor MI 48103	888-258-9866	734-764-9210

641-8 Annapolis, MD

	Toll-Free	Phone
WRNR-FM 103.1 112 Main St 3rd Fl .... Annapolis MD 21401	877-762-1031	410-626-0103

641-9 Asheville, NC

	Toll-Free	Phone
WCQS-FM 88.1 (NPR) 73 Broadway .... Asheville NC 28801	866-448-3881	828-210-4800
WKJV-AM 1380 70 Adams Hill Rd .... Asheville NC 28806	800-809-9558	828-252-1380
WKSF-FM 99.9 (Ctry) 13 Summerlin Rd .... Asheville NC 28806	800-303-5477	828-257-2700

641-10 Atlanta, GA

	Toll-Free	Phone
WACG-FM 90.7 (NPR) 2500 Walton Way .... Atlanta GA 30904	800-222-4788	706-737-1661
WCLK-FM 91.9 (Jazz) 111 James P Brawley Dr SW .... Atlanta GA 30314	888-448-3925	404-880-8273

641-11 Augusta, GA

	Toll-Free	Phone
WPRW-FM 107.7 (Urban) 2743 Perimeter Pkwy Bldg 100 Ste 300 .... Augusta GA 30909	800-650-2876	706-396-6000

641-12 Bakersfield, CA

	Toll-Free	Phone
KKBB-FM 99.3 (Oldies) 3651 Pegasus Dr Ste 107 .... Bakersfield CA 93308	866-758-4696	661-393-1900

641-13 Baltimore, MD

	Toll-Free	Phone
WPOC-FM 93.1 (Country) 711 W 40th St Ste 350 .... Baltimore MD 21211	866-962-5487	410-366-7600
WQSR-FM 102.7 (Var) 711 W 40th St .... Baltimore MD 21211	888-410-1027	410-366-7600
WRBS-FM 95.1 (Rel) 3500 Commerce Dr .... Baltimore MD 21227	800-965-9324	410-247-4100
WYPR-FM 88.1 (NPR) 2216 N Charles St .... Baltimore MD 21218	866-789-8627	410-235-1660

641-14 Bangor, ME

	Toll-Free	Phone
WHCF-FM 88.5 (Rel) PO Box 5000 .... Bangor ME 04402	800-947-2577	207-947-2751
WMEH-FM 90.9 (NPR) 63 Texas Ave .... Bangor ME 04401	800-884-1717	207-941-1010
WVOM-FM 103.9 (N/T) 184 Target Industrial Cir .... Bangor ME 04401	800-966-1039	207-947-9100

641-15 Baton Rouge, LA

	Toll-Free	Phone
WBKL-FM 92.7 (Rel) PO Box 2098 .... Omaha NE 68103	800-525-5683	

641-16 Billings, MT

	Toll-Free	Phone
KEMC-FM 91.7 (NPR) 1500 University Dr .... Billings MT 59101	800-441-2941	406-657-2941

641-17 Birmingham, AL

	Toll-Free	Phone
WBHM-FM 90.3 (NPR) 650 11th St S .... Birmingham AL 35233	800-444-9246	205-934-2606
WDXB-FM 102.5 (Ctry) 600 Beacon Pkwy W Ste 400 .... Birmingham AL 35209	877-541-1966	205-439-9600
WJSR-FM 91.1 (CR) Jefferson State Community College 2601 Carson Rd .... Birmingham AL 35215	800-767-4984	205-856-7702

641-18 Bismarck, ND

			Toll-Free	Phone
KXMR-AM 710 (Sports)				
3500 E Rosser Ave PO Box 2156	Bismarck ND	58501	866-522-5710	701-255-1234
KYYY-FM 92.9 (AC)				
3500 E Rosser Ave	Bismarck ND	58501	866-929-9393	701-255-1234

641-19 Boston, MA

			Toll-Free	Phone
WBUR-FM 90.9 (NPR)				
890 Commonwealth Ave	Boston MA	02215	800-909-9287	617-353-0909
WKLB-FM 102.5 (Ctry)				
55 Morrissey Blvd	Boston MA	02125	888-819-1025	617-822-9600
WUMB-FM 91.9 (Folk)				
100 Morrissey Blvd	Boston MA	02125	800-573-2100	617-287-6900

641-20 Branson, MO

			Toll-Free	Phone
KLFC-FM 88.1 (Rel)				
205 W Atlantic St	Branson MO	65616	877-410-8592	417-334-5532

641-21 Buffalo, NY

			Toll-Free	Phone
WDCX-FM 99.5 (Rel)				
625 Delaware Ave Ste 308	Buffalo NY	14202	800-684-2848	716-883-3010

641-22 Burlington, VT

			Toll-Free	Phone
WIZN-FM 106.7 (Rock)				
255 S Champlain St	Burlington VT	05401	888-873-9496	802-860-2440

641-23 Calgary, AB

			Toll-Free	Phone
CHQR-AM 770 (N/T)				
200 Barclay Parade SW Ste 170	Calgary AB	T2P4R5	800-563-7770	403-716-6500

641-24 Casper, WY

			Toll-Free	Phone
KRVK-FM 107.9 (Rock)				
150 N Nichols Ave	Casper WY	82601	800-442-2256	307-266-5252
KTRS-FM 104.7 (CHR)				
150 N Nichols Ave	Casper WY	82601	800-442-2256	307-266-5252
KWYY-FM 95.5 (Ctry)				
150 N Nichols Ave	Casper WY	82601	800-339-4673	307-266-5252

641-25 Cedar Rapids, IA

			Toll-Free	Phone
KCCK-FM 88.3 (Jazz)				
6301 Kirkwood Blvd SW	Cedar Rapids IA	52404	800-373-5225	319-398-5446
WMT-FM 96.5 (AC)				
600 Old Marion Rd NE	Cedar Rapids IA	52402	800-258-0096	319-395-0530

641-26 Champaign, IL

			Toll-Free	Phone
WBGL-FM 91.7 (Rel)				
4101 Fieldstone Road PO Box 111	Champaign IL	61822	800-475-9245*	217-359-8232
*Cust Svc				
WDWS-AM 1400 (N/T)				
2301 S Neil St	Champaign IL	61820	800-223-9397	217-351-5300

641-27 Chattanooga, TN

			Toll-Free	Phone
WUTC-FM 88.1 (NPR)				
615 McCallie Ave				
104 Cadek Hall Dept 1151	Chattanooga TN	37403	800-272-3900	423-425-4756

641-28 Charleston, WV

			Toll-Free	Phone
WQBE-FM 97.5 (Ctry)				
817 Suncrest Pl	Charleston WV	25303	800-222-3697	304-344-9700

641-29 Charlotte, NC

			Toll-Free	Phone
WEND-FM 106.5 (Alt)				
801 Wood Ridge Ctr Dr	Charlotte NC	28217	800-934-1065	704-714-9444
WFAE-FM 90.7 (NPR)				
8801 JM Keynes Dr Ste 91	Charlotte NC	28262	800-876-9323*	704-549-9323
*Cust Svc				
WFNZ-AM 610 (Sports)				
1520 S Blvd Ste 300	Charlotte NC	28203	866-570-9610	704-319-9369
WKKT-FM 96.9 (Ctry)				
801 Wood Ridge Ctr Dr	Charlotte NC	28217	877-903-7867	704-714-9444
WPEG-FM 97.9 (Urban)				
1520 S Blvd Ste 300	Charlotte NC	28203	800-525-0098	704-342-2644
WRFX-FM 99.7 (CR)				
801 Wood Ridge Ctr Dr	Charlotte NC	28217	800-766-9970	704-714-9444

641-30 Chicago, IL

			Toll-Free	Phone
WMBI-FM 90.1 (Rel)				
820 N LaSalle Blvd	Chicago IL	60610	877-376-2194	312-329-4300
WMVP-AM 1000 (Sports)				
190 N State St 7th Fl	Chicago IL	60601	800-438-3776	312-980-1000

641-31 Cincinnati, OH

			Toll-Free	Phone
WAKW-FM 93.3 (Rel)				
6275 Collegevue Pl PO Box 24126	Cincinnati OH	45224	888-542-9393	513-542-9259
WIZF-FM 101.1 (Urban)				
705 Central Ave	Cincinnati OH	45202	866-236-7588	513-679-6000

641-32 Cleveland, OH

			Toll-Free	Phone
WENZ-FM 107.9 (Urban)				
2510 St Clair Ave NE	Cleveland OH	44114	800-440-1079	216-579-1111

641-33 Colorado Springs, CO

			Toll-Free	Phone
KILO-FM 94.3 (Rock)				
1805 E Cheyenne Rd	Colorado Springs CO	80905	800-727-5456*	719-634-4896
*General				
KRCC-FM 91.5 (NPR)				
912 N Weber St	Colorado Springs CO	80903	800-748-2727	719-473-4801
KVOR-AM 740 (N/T)				
6805 Corporate Dr Ste 130	Colorado Springs CO	80919	800-232-6459	719-593-2700

641-34 Columbia, SC

			Toll-Free	Phone
WCOS-FM 97.5 (Ctry)				
316 Greystone Blvd	Columbia SC	29210	800-570-9690	803-343-1100
WHXT-FM 103.9 (Urban)				
1900 Pineview Rd	Columbia SC	29209	877-874-1039	803-695-8600

641-35 Columbus, GA

			Toll-Free	Phone
WKCN-FM 99.3 (Ctry)				
1820 Wynnton Rd	Columbus GA	31906	800-628-2866	706-327-1217

641-36 Columbus, OH

			Toll-Free	Phone
WBNS-FM 97.1 (AC)				
605 S Front St Ste 300	Columbus OH	43215	888-691-9710	614-460-3850
WCOL-FM 92.3 (Ctry)				
2323 W Fifth Ave Ste 200	Columbus OH	43204	800-899-9265	614-486-6101
WLVQ-FM 96.3 (Rock)				
2400 Corporate Exchange Dr Ste 200	Columbus OH	43231	877-736-9696	614-227-9696
WNND-FM 103.5 (NAC)				
4401 Carriage Hill Ln	Columbus OH	43220	877-984-8786	614-451-2191

641-37 Corpus Christi, TX

			Toll-Free	Phone
KEDT-FM 90.3 (NPR)				
4455 S Padre Island Dr Ste 38	Corpus Christi TX	78411	800-307-5338	361-855-2213
KFTX-FM 97.5 (Ctry)				
1520 S Port Ave	Corpus Christi TX	78405	866-975-5389	361-883-5987

641-38 Dallas/Fort Worth, TX

			Toll-Free	Phone
KBFB-FM 97.9 (Urban)				
13331 Preston Rd Ste 1180	Dallas TX	75240	888-362-8683	972-331-5400
KERA-FM 90.1 (NPR)				
3000 Harry Hines Blvd	Dallas TX	75201	800-456-5372	214-871-1390
KLUV-FM 98.7 (Oldies)				
4131 N Central Expy Ste 1000	Dallas TX	75204	855-987-5588	214-525-7000
KRLD-AM 1080 (N/T)				
4131 N Central Expy Ste 100	Dallas TX	75204	800-289-1080	214-525-7000
KVIL-FM 103.7 (AC)				
4131 N Central Expy Ste 1000	Dallas TX	75204	877-787-1037	214-525-7000

641-39 Denver, CO

		Toll-Free	Phone
KUVO-FM 89.3 (Jazz)			
2900 Welton St Ste 200 .... Denver CO 80205		800-574-5886	303-480-9272

641-40 Des Moines, IA

		Toll-Free	Phone
KIOA-FM 93.3 (Oldies)			
1416 Locust St .... Des Moines IA 50309		877-984-8786	515-280-1350

641-41 Duluth, MN

		Toll-Free	Phone
WSCN-FM 100.5 (NPR)			
207 W Superior St Ste 224 .... Duluth MN 55802		800-228-7123	218-722-9411

641-42 El Paso, TX

		Toll-Free	Phone
KINT-FM 93.9 (Span)			
5426 N Mesa St .... El Paso TX 79912		866-560-5673	915-581-1126
KLAQ-FM 95.5 (Rock)			
4180 N Mesa St .... El Paso TX 79902		877-566-8477	915-880-4955

641-43 Erie, PA

		Toll-Free	Phone
WQLN-FM 91.3 (NPR)			
8425 Peach St .... Erie PA 16509		800-727-8854	814-864-3001

641-44 Eugene, OR

		Toll-Free	Phone
KUGN-AM 590 (N/T)			
1200 Executive Pkwy Ste 440 .... Eugene OR 97401		800-590-5846	541-284-8500

641-45 Evansville, IN

		Toll-Free	Phone
WDKS-FM 106.1 (CHR)			
117 SE Fifth St .... Evansville IN 47708		888-454-5477	812-425-4226
WIKY-FM 104.1 (AC)			
1162 Mt Auburn Rd .... Evansville IN 47720		800-454-9459	812-424-8284
WNIN-FM 88.3 (NPR)			
405 Carpenter St .... Evansville IN 47708		855-888-9646	812-423-2973
WSTO-FM 96.1 (CHR)			
1162 Mt Auburn Rd .... Evansville IN 47720		888-685-1961	812-421-9696

641-46 Fairbanks, AK

		Toll-Free	Phone
KUAC-FM 89.9 (NPR)			
312 Tanana Dr Ste 202 PO Box 755620 .... Fairbanks AK 99775		800-727-6543	907-474-7491

641-47 Fargo, ND

		Toll-Free	Phone
KDSU-FM 91.9 (NPR)			
207 Fifth St N .... Fargo ND 58102		800-359-6900	701-241-6900
WDAY-FM 93.7 (CHR)			
1020 25th St S .... Fargo ND 58103		877-478-5437	701-237-5346

641-48 Flagstaff, AZ

		Toll-Free	Phone
KNAU-FM 88.7 (NPR)			
Bldg 83 ,515 E Pine Knoll Dr			
PO Box 5764 .... Flagstaff AZ 86011		800-523-5628	928-523-5628

641-49 Fort Wayne, IN

		Toll-Free	Phone
89.1 WBOI			
3204 Clairmont Ct .... Fort Wayne IN 46808		800-471-9264*	260-452-1189
*General			
WLDE-FM 101.7 (Oldies)			
347 W Berry St Ste 600 .... Fort Wayne IN 46802		888-450-1017	260-423-3676
WOWO-AM 1190 (N/T)			
2915 Maples Rd .... Fort Wayne IN 46816		800-333-1190	260-447-5511

641-50 Fort Smith, AR

		Toll-Free	Phone
KKBD-FM 95.9 (CR)			
311 Lexington Ave .... Fort Smith AR 72901		866-503-1398	479-782-8888
KZBB-FM 97.9 (CHR)			
311 Lexington Ave .... Fort Smith AR 72901		866-503-1398	479-782-8888

641-51 Fresno, CA

		Toll-Free	Phone
KBOS-FM 94.9 (CHR)			
83 E Shaw Ave Ste 150 .... Fresno CA 93710		877-565-9467	559-230-4300
KMJ-AM 580 (N/T)			
1071 W Shaw Ave .... Fresno CA 93711		800-776-5858	559-490-5800
KMJ-FM 105.9 1071 W Shaw Ave ...... Fresno CA 93711		800-491-1899	559-490-5800
KPRX-FM 89.1 (NPR)			
3437 W Shaw Ave Ste 101 .... Fresno CA 93711		800-275-0764	559-275-0764
KSKS-FM 93.7 (Ctry)			
1071 W Shaw Ave .... Fresno CA 93711		800-767-5477	559-490-5800
KSOF-FM 98.9 (AC)			
83 E Shaw Ave Ste 150 .... Fresno CA 93710		800-423-5870	559-230-4300
KVPR-FM 89.3 (NPR)			
3437 W Shaw Ave Ste 101 .... Fresno CA 93711		800-275-0764	559-275-0764
KWYE-FM 101.1 (CHR)			
1071 W Shaw Ave .... Fresno CA 93711		800-345-9101	559-490-5800

641-52 Grand Forks, ND

		Toll-Free	Phone
KFJM-FM 90.7 (AAA)			
207 N Fifth St .... Fargo ND 58102		800-366-6888	701-241-6900

641-53 Grand Rapids, MI

		Toll-Free	Phone
WBCT-FM 93.7 (Ctry)			
77 Monroe Ctr St NW Ste 1000 .... Grand Rapids MI 49503		800-633-9393	616-459-1919
WCSG-FM 91.3 (Rel)			
1159 E Beltline Ave NE .... Grand Rapids MI 49525		800-968-4543	616-942-1500
WGRD-FM 97.9 (Rock)			
50 Monroe Ave NW Ste 500 .... Grand Rapids MI 49503		800-947-3979	616-451-4800
WGVU-FM 88.5 (NPR)			
301 W Fulton St .... Grand Rapids MI 49504		800-442-2771	616-331-6666

641-54 Green Bay, WI

		Toll-Free	Phone
WDUZ-AM 1400 (Sports)			
810 Victoria St .... Green Bay WI 54302		855-724-1075	920-468-4100
WNCY-FM 100.3 (Ctry)			
PO Box 23333 .... Green Bay WI 54305		800-359-1003	920-435-3771
WPNE-FM 89.3 (NPR)			
2420 Nicolet Dr .... Green Bay WI 54311		800-654-6228	920-465-2444
WQLH-FM 98.5 (AC)			
810 Victoria St .... Green Bay WI 54302		855-782-7985	920-468-4100

641-55 Greenville, SC

		Toll-Free	Phone
92.5 WESC-FM			
101 N Main St PO Box 100 .... Greenville SC 29601		800-248-0863	864-242-4660
WJMZ-FM 107.3 (Urban)			
220 N Main St Ste 402 .... Greenville SC 29601		800-767-1073	864-235-1073
WLFJ-FM 89.3 (Rel)			
2420 Wade Hampton Blvd .... Greenville SC 29615		800-447-7234	864-292-6040
WMYI-FM 102.5 (AC)			
101 N Main St Ste 1000 PO Box 100 .... Greenville SC 29601		800-248-0863	864-235-1025
WROQ-FM 101.1 (CR)			
25 Garlington Rd .... Greenville SC 29615		888-257-0058	864-271-9200
WTPT-FM 93.3 (Rock)			
25 Garlington Rd .... Greenville SC 29615		800-774-0093	864-271-9200

641-56 Harrisburg, PA

		Toll-Free	Phone
WHP-AM 580 (N/T)			
600 Corporate Cir .... Harrisburg PA 17110		888-251-7797	717-540-8800
WITF-FM 89.5 (NPR)			
4801 Lindle Rd .... Harrisburg PA 17111		800-366-9483	717-704-3000
WRBT-FM 94.9 (Ctry)			
600 Corporate Cir .... Harrisburg PA 17110		800-682-3047	717-540-8800

641-57 Honolulu, HI

		Toll-Free	Phone
KHJZ-FM 93.9 (CHR)			
650 Iwilei Rd Ste 400 .... Honolulu HI 96817		800-745-3000	808-550-9200
KHVH-AM 830 (N/T)			
650 Iwilei Rd Ste 400 .... Honolulu HI 96817		888-565-8383	808-550-9200

641-58 Hot Springs, AR

		Toll-Free	Phone
KHTO-FM 96.7			
125 Corporate Terr .... Hot Springs AR 71913		866-425-9600	501-525-9700
KLAZ-FM 105.9 (CHR)			
208 Buena Vista Rd .... Hot Springs AR 71913		800-621-3362	501-525-4600

641-59 Houston, TX

		Toll-Free	Phone
KBXX-FM 97.9 (Urban)			
24 Greenway Plaza Ste 900 .... Houston TX 77046		888-407-4747	713-623-2108

				Toll-Free	Phone

KLAT-AM 1010 (Span N/T)
5100 SW Fwy .... Houston TX 77056   **800-646-6779**   713-407-1415
KRBE-FM 104.1 (CHR)
9801 Westheimer Rd Ste 700 .... Houston TX 77042   **888-955-2993**   713-266-1000
KTHT-FM
1990 Post Oak Blvd Ste 2300 .... Houston TX 77056   **877-745-6591**   713-963-1200
KUHF-FM 88.7 (Clas)
4343 Elgin St 3rd Fl .... Houston TX 77204   **877-252-0436**   713-743-0887

641-60 Huntsville, AL

	Toll-Free	Phone

WLRH-FM 89.3 (NPR)
University of Alabama-Huntsville
John Wright Dr .... Huntsville AL 35899   **800-239-9574**   256-895-9574

641-61 Indianapolis, IN

	Toll-Free	Phone

WIBC-FM 93.1 (N/T)
40 Monument Cir Ste 400 .... Indianapolis IN 46204   **800-571-9422**   317-266-9422

641-62 Jackson, MS

	Toll-Free	Phone

WMAE-FM 89.5 (NPR)
3825 Ridgewood Rd .... Jackson MS 39211   **800-850-4406**   601-432-6565

641-63 Jacksonville, FL

	Toll-Free	Phone

WAPE-FM 95.1 (CHR)
8000 Belfort Pkwy Ste 100 .... Jacksonville FL 32256   **800-475-9595**   904-245-8500
WJAX-AM 1220 (Nost)
5353 Arlington Expy .... Jacksonville FL 32211   **800-331-0176**   904-371-1184
WJGL-FM 96.9 (CR)
8000 Belfort Pkwy .... Jacksonville FL 32256   **800-438-1601**   904-245-8500
WXXJ-FM 102.9 (AC)
8000 Belfort Pkwy .... Jacksonville FL 32256   **800-460-6394**   904-245-8500

641-64 Johnson City, TN

	Toll-Free	Phone

WETS-FM 89.5 (NPR)
PO Box 70630 .... Johnson City TN 37614   **888-895-9387**   423-439-6440

641-65 Kansas City, KS & MO

	Toll-Free	Phone

KCUR-FM 89.3 (NPR)
4825 Troost Ave Ste 202 .... Kansas City MO 64110   **855-778-5437**   816-235-1551
KGGN-AM 890 (Rel)
1734 E 63rd St Ste 600 .... Kansas City MO 64110   **800-924-3177**   816-333-0092
KPRS-FM 103.3 (Urban)
11131 Colorado Ave .... Kansas City MO 64137   **800-273-8255**   816-763-2040

641-66 Knoxville, TN

	Toll-Free	Phone

WIVK-FM 107.7 (Ctry)
4711 Old Kingston Pike .... Knoxville TN 37919   **877-995-9961**   865-588-6511
WUOT-FM 91.9 (NPR)
209 Communications Bldg
University of Tennessee .... Knoxville TN 37996   **888-266-9868**   865-974-5375

641-67 Las Vegas, NV

	Toll-Free	Phone

KDWN-AM 720 (N/T)
1455 E Tropicana Ave Ste 800 .... Las Vegas NV 89119   **866-297-5303**   702-730-0300
KMXB-FM 94.1 (AC)
7255 S Tenaya Way Ste 100 .... Las Vegas NV 89113   **866-438-0220**   702-257-9400
KNPR-FM 89.5 (NPR)
1289 S Torrey Pines Dr .... Las Vegas NV 89146   **888-258-9895**   702-258-9895

641-68 Lexington/Frankfort, KY

	Toll-Free	Phone

WKYL-FM 102.1 (NAC)
102 Perkins Bldg 521 Lancaster Ave ... Richmond KY 40475   **800-621-8890**

641-69 Lincoln, NE

	Toll-Free	Phone

KFRX-FM 106.3 (CHR)
3800 Cornhusker Hwy .... Lincoln NE 68504   **800-523-9101**   402-466-1234

641-70 Little Rock, AR

	Toll-Free	Phone

KABZ-FM 103.7 (N/T)
2400 Cottondale Ln .... Little Rock AR 72202   **800-477-1037**   501-661-1037

KKPT-FM 94.1 (CR)
2400 Cottondale Ln .... Little Rock AR 72202   **800-844-0094**   501-664-9410

641-71 Los Angeles, CA

	Toll-Free	Phone

KABC-AM 790 (N/T)
3321 S La Cienega Blvd PO Box 790 .... Los Angeles CA 90016   **800-222-5222**   310-840-4900
KROQ-FM 106.7 (Alt)
5901 Venice Blvd .... Los Angeles CA 90034   **800-520-1067**   323-930-1067
KRTH-FM 101.1 (Oldies)
5670 Wilshire Blvd Ste 200 .... Los Angeles CA 90036   **800-232-5784**   323-936-5784
KUSC-FM 91.5 (Clas)
1149 S Hill St Ste H100
PO Box 7913 .... Los Angeles CA 90015   **877-587-2227**   213-225-7400

641-72 Louisville, KY

	Toll-Free	Phone

WHAS-AM 840 (N/T)
4000 One Radio Dr .... Louisville KY 40218   **800-444-8484**   502-479-2222
WVEZ-FM 106.9 (AC)
612 S 4th St .... Louisville KY 40202   **866-566-2456**   502-589-4800

641-73 Macon, GA

	Toll-Free	Phone

WIBB-FM 97.9 (Urban)
7080 Industrial Hwy .... Macon GA 31216   **800-813-8418**   478-781-1063

641-74 Madison, WI

	Toll-Free	Phone

WERN-FM 88.7 (NPR)
821 University Ave .... Madison WI 53706   **800-747-7444**
WHA-AM 970 (NPR)
821 University Ave .... Madison WI 53706   **800-747-7444**
WHIT-AM 1550 (Nost)
730 Rayovac Dr .... Madison WI 53711   **800-422-7128**   608-273-1000

641-75 Manchester, NH

	Toll-Free	Phone

WMLL-FM 96.5 (CR)
500 Commercial St .... Manchester NH 03101   **800-666-0957**   603-669-5777

641-76 Memphis, TN

	Toll-Free	Phone

600 WREC
2650 Thousand Oaks Blvd Ste 4100 ..... Memphis TN 38118   **800-474-9732**   901-259-1300
Rock 103
2650 Thousand Oaks Blvd Ste 4100 ..... Memphis TN 38118   **800-444-9347**   901-259-1300
WDIA-AM 1070 (Urban)
2650 Thousand Oaks Blvd Ste 4100 ..... Memphis TN 38118   **800-339-4673**   901-259-1300
WHAL-FM 95.7 (Rel)
2650 Thousand Oaks Blvd Ste 4100 ..... Memphis TN 38118   **888-302-6222**   901-259-1300
WKNO-FM 91.1 (NPR)
900 Getwell Rd .... Memphis TN 38111   **800-766-9566**   901-325-6544

641-77 Miami/Fort Lauderdale, FL

	Toll-Free	Phone

WDNA-FM 88.9 (Jazz)
2921 Coral Way .... Miami FL 33145   **877-929-7001**   305-662-8889
WKIS-FM 99.9 (Ctry)
194 NW 187th St .... Miami FL 33169   **866-976-0800**   305-654-1700
WLYF-FM 101.5 (AC)
20450 NW Second Ave .... Miami FL 33169   **877-790-1015**
WMBM-AM 1490 (Rel)
13242 NW Seventh Ave .... North Miami FL 33168   **800-721-9626**   305-769-1100
WMXJ-FM 102.7 (Oldies)
20450 NW Second Ave .... Miami FL 33169   **800-924-1027**   305-521-5100
WSUA-AM 1260 (Span)
2100 Coral Way Ste 201 .... Miami FL 33145   **877-453-5437**   305-285-1260

641-78 Milwaukee, WI

	Toll-Free	Phone

WAUK-AM 540 (Sports)
310 W Wisconsin Ave Ste 100 .... Milwaukee WI 53203   **800-990-3776**   414-273-3776
WHAD-FM 90.7 (NPR)
310 W Wisconsin Ave Ste 750-E .... Milwaukee WI 53203   **800-486-8655**   414-227-2040
WHQG-FM 102.9 (Rock)
5407 W McKinley Ave .... Milwaukee WI 53208   **877-777-1029**   414-978-9000
WUWM-FM 89.7 (NPR)
111 E Wisconsin Ave Ste 700 .... Milwaukee WI 53202   **844-387-6926**   414-227-3355

641-79 Minneapolis/Saint Paul, MN

	Toll-Free	Phone

KFAN-AM 1130 (Sports)
1600 Utica Ave S Ste 400 .... Minneapolis MN 55416   **800-320-5326**   952-417-3000
KQQL-FM 107.9 (Oldies)
1600 Utica Ave S Ste 400 .... Minneapolis MN 55416   **800-745-3000**   952-417-3000

Classified Section

	Toll-Free	Phone
KSTP-AM 1500 (N/T)		
3415 University Ave . . . . .Saint Paul MN 55114	**877-615-1500**	651-646-8255

641-80 Mobile, AL

	Toll-Free	Phone
WBHY-FM 88.5 (Rel)		
PO Box 1328 . . . . Mobile AL 36633	**888-473-8488**	251-473-8488
WHIL-FM 91.3 (NPR)		
166 Reese Phifer Hall		
PO Box 870150. . . . . Tuscaloosa AL 35487	**800-654-4262**	205-348-6644

641-81 Modesto, CA

	Toll-Free	Phone
KMRQ-FM 96.7 (Rock)		
2121 Lancey Dr . . . . Modesto CA 95355	**800-505-3967**	209-866-6677
KQOD-FM 100.1 (Oldies)		
2121 Lancey Dr . . . . Modesto CA 95355	**877-967-6342**	209-551-1306

641-82 Monterey, CA

	Toll-Free	Phone
KHIP-FM 104.3 (CR)		
60 Garden Ct Ste 300 . . . . Monterey CA 93940	**877-762-5104**	831-658-5200

641-83 Naples, FL

	Toll-Free	Phone
WAVV-FM 101.1 (AC)		
11800 Tamiami Trl E . . . . Naples FL 34113	**866-310-9288**	239-775-9288

641-84 Nashville, TN

	Toll-Free	Phone
SuperTalk 99.7 WTN		
10 Music Cir E . . . . Nashville TN 37203	**800-618-7445**	615-321-1067
WLAC-AM 1510 (N/T)		
55 Music Sq W . . . . Nashville TN 37203	**800-688-9522**	615-664-2400
WPLN-FM 90.3 (NPR)		
630 Mainstream Dr . . . . Nashville TN 37228	**877-760-2903**	615-760-2903

641-85 New Orleans, LA

	Toll-Free	Phone
WWNO-FM 89.9 (NPR)		
University of New Orleans		
Lake Frnt Campus. . . . . New Orleans LA 70148	**800-286-7002**	504-280-7000
WYLD-AM 940 (Rel)		
929 Howard Ave . . . . New Orleans LA 70113	**800-899-9265**	504-679-7300

641-86 New York, NY

	Toll-Free	Phone
WABC-AM 770 (N/T)		
2 Penn Plaza 17th Fl. . . . . New York NY 10121	**800-848-9222**	212-613-3800
WAXQ-FM 104.3 (CR)		
32 Ave of the Americas . . . . New York NY 10013	**888-872-1043**	212-377-7900
WCBS-AM 880 (N/T)		
524 W 57th St 8th Fl. . . . . New York NY 10019	**800-242-6397**	212-975-4321
WHTZ-FM 100.3 (CHR)		
32 Ave of the Americas . . . . New York NY 10013	**800-242-0100**	212-377-7900
WLTW-FM 106.7 (AC)		
32 Ave of the Americas 2nd Fl . . . . New York NY 10013	**800-222-1067**	212-377-7900
WQHT-FM 97.1 (Urban)		
395 Hudson St Seventh Fl . . . . New York NY 10014	**800-223-9797**	212-229-9797
WWPR-FM 105.1 (Urban)		
32 Ave of the Americas . . . . New York NY 10013	**800-585-1051**	212-377-7900

641-87 Omaha, NE

	Toll-Free	Phone
Z92 FM 10714 Mockingbird Dr . . . . Omaha NE 68127	**800-955-9230**	402-592-5300

641-88 Orlando, FL

	Toll-Free	Phone
WJHM-FM 102 (Urban)		
1800 Pembrook Dr Ste 400 . . . . Orlando FL 32810	**866-438-0220**	407-919-1000
WOCL-FM 105.9 (Rock)		
1800 Pembrook Dr Ste 400 . . . . Orlando FL 32810	**877-919-1059**	407-919-1000
WOMX-FM 105.1 (AC)		
1800 Pembrook Dr Ste 400 . . . . Orlando FL 32810	**877-919-1051**	407-919-1000
WWKA-FM 92.3 (Ctry)		
4192 N John Young Pkwy . . . . Orlando FL 32804	**866-438-0220**	407-298-9292

641-89 Ottawa, ON

	Toll-Free	Phone
Ottawa-AM 1200 (Sports)		
87 George St . . . . Ottawa ON K1N9H7	**877-670-1200**	613-789-2486

641-90 Pensacola, FL

	Toll-Free	Phone
WPCS-FM 89.5 (Rel)		
PO Box 18000 . . . . Pensacola FL 32523	**800-726-1191**	850-479-6570

641-91 Peoria, IL

	Toll-Free	Phone
WCBU-FM 89.9 (NPR)		
1501 W Bradley Ave . . . . .Peoria IL 61625	**888-488-9228**	309-677-3690
WCIC-FM 91.5 (Rel)		
3902 W Baring Trace . . . . .Peoria IL 61615	**877-692-9242**	
WSWT-FM 106.9 (AC)		
331 Fulton St Ste 1200 . . . . .Peoria IL 61602	**800-597-1069**	309-637-3700

641-92 Philadelphia, PA

	Toll-Free	Phone
WRTI-FM 90.1 (NPR)		
1509 Cecil B Moore Ave 3rd Fl. . . . . Philadelphia PA 19121	**866-809-9784**	215-204-8405

641-93 Phoenix, AZ

	Toll-Free	Phone
KOOL-FM 94.5 (Oldies)		
840 N Central Ave . . . . Phoenix AZ 85004	**800-222-4357**	602-260-9494
KZZP-FM 104.7 (CHR)		
4686 E Van Buren St Ste 300 . . . . Phoenix AZ 85008	**877-541-1966**	602-374-6000

641-94 Pierre, SD

	Toll-Free	Phone
KMLO-FM 100.7 (Ctry)		
214 W Pleasant Dr . . . . Pierre SD 57501	**800-658-5439**	605-224-8686
KPLO-FM 94.5 (Ctry)		
214 W Pleasant Dr . . . . Pierre SD 57501	**800-658-5439***	605-224-8686
*General		

641-95 Pittsburgh, PA

	Toll-Free	Phone
KQV-AM 1410 (N/T)		
650 Smithfield St		
Ste 620 Ctr City Towers . . . . .Pittsburgh PA 15222	**800-289-2642**	412-562-5900
WQED-FM 89.3 (Clas)		
4802 Fifth Ave . . . . .Pittsburgh PA 15213	**800-876-1316**	412-622-1436
WWSW-FM 94.5 (Oldies)		
200 Fleet St 4th Fl . . . . .Pittsburgh PA 15220	**800-653-2258**	412-937-1441

641-96 Portland/Salem, OR

	Toll-Free	Phone
All Classical Portland		
515 NE 15th Ave . . . . Portland OR 97232	**888-306-5277**	503-943-5828
FM NEWS 101 KXL		
1211 SW Fifth Ave . . . . Portland OR 97204	**877-733-1011**	503-517-6000
KEX-AM 1190 (N/T)		
13333 SW 68th Parkway Suite 310. . . . . .Tigard OR 97223	**888-457-4838**	503-323-6400
KGON-FM 92.3 (CR)		
0700 SW Bancroft St . . . . Portland OR 97239	**800-222-9236**	503-223-1441
KINK-FM 101.9 (AAA)		
1211 SW Fifth Ave . . . . Portland OR 97204	**877-567-5465**	503-517-6000
KKRZ-FM 100.3 (CHR)		
13333 SW 68th Pkwy Ste 310 . . . . .Tigard OR 97223	**888-483-0100**	503-460-0100
KNRK-FM 94.7 (Alt)		
0700 SW Bancroft St . . . . Portland OR 97239	**800-777-0947**	503-733-5470
KPDQ-FM 93.9 (Rel)		
6400 SE Lake Rd Ste 350 . . . . Portland OR 97222	**800-845-2162**	503-786-0600
KWJJ-FM 99.5 (Ctry)		
0700 SW Bancroft St . . . . Portland OR 97239	**866-239-9653**	503-733-9653
KXJM-FM 107.5 (AC)		
13333 SW 68th Pkwy Ste 310 . . . . Portland OR 97223	**800-567-1075**	503-248-1075

641-97 Raleigh/Durham, NC

	Toll-Free	Phone
WFXC-FM 107.1 (Urban AC)		
8001-101 Creedmoor Rd . . . . .Raleigh NC 27613	**800-467-3699**	919-848-9736
WFXK-FM 104.3 (Urban AC)		
8001-101 Creedmoor Rd . . . . .Raleigh NC 27613	**800-321-5975**	919-848-9736
WNNL-FM 103.9 (Rel)		
8001-101 Creedmoor Rd . . . . .Raleigh NC 27613	**877-310-9665**	919-848-9736
WPTF-AM 680 (N/T)		
3012 Highwoods Blvd Ste 201 . . . . .Raleigh NC 27604	**800-662-7979**	919-790-9392
WRAL-FM 101.5 (AC)		
3100 Highwoods Blvd Ste 140 . . . . .Raleigh NC 27604	**800-745-3000**	919-890-6101
WSHA-FM 88.9 (Jazz)		
118 E S St . . . . .Raleigh NC 27601	**800-241-0421**	919-546-8430

641-98 Reno/Carson City, NV

	Toll-Free	Phone
KDOT-FM 104.5 (Rock)		
2900 Sutro St . . . . .Reno NV 89512	**800-227-1885**	775-329-9261

Classified Section

				Toll-Free	Phone
KNIS-FM 91.3 (Rel)					
PO Box 21888	Carson City	NV	89721	800-541-5647	775-883-5647
KODS-FM 103.7 (Oldies)					
961 Matley Ln Ste 120	Reno	NV	89502	855-354-9111	775-829-1964
KRNO-FM 106.9 (AC)					
961 Matley Ln Ste 120	Reno	NV	89502	888-505-1261	775-829-1964

641-99 Riverside/San Bernardino, CA

				Toll-Free	Phone
KGGI-FM 99.1 (CHR)					
2030 Iowa Ave Ste A	Riverside	CA	92507	866-991-5444	951-684-1991
KSGN-FM 89.7 (Rel)					
2048 Orange Tree Ln Ste 200	Redlands	CA	92374	888-897-5746	909-583-2150
KVCR-FM 91.9 (NPR)					
701 S Mt Vernon Ave	San Bernardino	CA	92410	800-533-5827	909-384-4444

641-100 Roanoke, VA

				Toll-Free	Phone
WFIR-AM 960 (N/T)					
3934 Electric Rd SW	Roanoke	VA	24018	800-367-7623	540-345-1511
WVTF-FM 89.1 (NPR)					
3520 Kingsbury Ln	Roanoke	VA	24014	800-856-8900	540-989-8900
WXLK-FM 92.3 (CHR)					
3934 Electric Rd SW	Roanoke	VA	24018	800-468-9236	540-774-9200

641-101 Rochester, MN

				Toll-Free	Phone
KLSE-FM 91.7 (Clas)					
206 S Broadway Ste 735	Rochester	MN	55904	800-652-9700	507-282-0910
KWEB-AM 1270 (Sports)					
1530 Greenview Dr SW Ste 200	Rochester	MN	55902	888-519-6683	507-288-3888

641-102 Sacramento, CA

				Toll-Free	Phone
Capital Public Radio Inc					
7055 Folsom Blvd	Sacramento	CA	95826	877-480-5900	916-278-8900
KHTK-AM 1140 (Sports)					
5244 Madison Ave	Sacramento	CA	95841	800-920-1140	916-338-9200
KTKZ-AM 1380 (N/T)					
1425 River Pk Dr Ste 520	Sacramento	CA	95815	888-923-1380	916-924-0710
KXPR-FM 88.9 (Clas)					
7055 Folsom Blvd	Sacramento	CA	95826	877-480-5900	916-278-8900

641-103 Saint Louis, MO

				Toll-Free	Phone
KTRS-AM 550 (N/T)					
638 Westport Plaza	Saint Louis	MO	63146	888-550-5877	314-453-5500

641-104 Salt Lake City, UT

				Toll-Free	Phone
KEGA-FM 101.5 (Ctry)					
50 West Broadway Ste 200	Salt Lake City	UT	84101	866-551-1015	801-524-2600
KLO-AM 1430 (N/T)					
257 East 200 South Ste 400	Salt Lake City	UT	84111	866-627-1430	801-364-9836
KUER-FM 90.1 (NPR)					
101 S Wasatch Dr	Salt Lake City	UT	84112	800-491-1148	801-581-6625
KZHT-FM 97.1 (CHR)					
2801 S Decker Lake Dr	Salt Lake City	UT	84119	800-888-8499	801-908-1300

641-105 San Antonio, TX

				Toll-Free	Phone
930 AM The Answer					
9601 McAllister Fwy Ste 1200	San Antonio	TX	78216	866-308-8867	210-344-8481
KAJA-FM 97.3 (Ctry)					
6222 NW IH-10	San Antonio	TX	78201	800-707-5150	210-736-9700
KISS-FM 99.5 (Rock)					
8122 Datapoint Dr Ste 600	San Antonio	TX	78229	866-333-6747	210-615-5400
KROM-FM 92.9 (Span)					
1777 NE Loop 410 Ste 400	San Antonio	TX	78217	888-382-1222	210-821-6548
KSLR-AM 630 (Rel)					
9601 McAllister Fwy Ste 1200	San Antonio	TX	78216	888-346-4700	210-344-8481
KSTX-FM 89.1 (NPR)					
8401 Datapoint Dr Ste 800	San Antonio	TX	78229	800-622-8977	210-614-8977
KTSA-AM 550 (N/T)					
4050 Eisenhauer Rd	San Antonio	TX	78218	800-299-5872	210-654-5100
WOAI-AM 1200 (N/T)					
6222 NW IH-10	San Antonio	TX	78201	800-707-5150	210-736-9700

641-106 San Diego, CA

				Toll-Free	Phone
KFMB-AM 760 (N/T)					
7677 Engineer Rd	San Diego	CA	92111	800-760-5362	858-292-7600
KLNV-FM 106.5 (Span)					
600 W Broadway Ste 2150	San Diego	CA	92101	800-879-4278	619-235-0600
KPBS-FM 89.5 (NPR)					
San Diego State University					
5200 Campanile Dr	San Diego	CA	92182	888-399-5727	619-265-6438
KSCF-FM 103.7 (N/T)					
8033 Linda Vista Rd	San Diego	CA	92111	888-388-1037	858-571-7600
KSON-FM 97.3 (Ctry)					
1615 Murray Canyon Rd Ste 710	San Diego	CA	92108	800-988-4253	619-291-9797
KYXY-FM 96.5 (AC)					
8033 Linda Vista Rd	San Diego	CA	92111	888-560-9650	858-571-7600

641-107 San Francisco, CA

				Toll-Free	Phone
KGO-AM 810 (N/T)					
55 Hawthorne St	San Francisco	CA	94105	855-847-7247	415-995-5721
KIOI-FM 101.3 (AC)					
340 Townsend St Fourth Fl	San Francisco	CA	94107	800-800-1013	415-975-5555
KITS-FM 105.3 (Alt)					
865 Battery St	San Francisco	CA	94111	800-696-1053	
KKSF-FM 103.7 (NAC)					
340 Townsend St Fourth Fl	San Francisco	CA	94107	866-900-1037	415-975-5555
KMVQ-FM 99.7 (AC)					
865 Battery St	San Francisco	CA	94111	888-456-9970	415-765-4112
KQED-FM 88.5 (NPR)					
2601 Mariposa St	San Francisco	CA	94110	800-723-3566	415-864-2000
KSAN-FM 107.7 (Alt)					
750 Battery St 3rd Fl	San Francisco	CA	94105	888-303-2663	415-995-6800
KYLD-FM 94.9 (Urban)					
340 Townsend St Ste 5101	San Francisco	CA	94107	888-333-9490	415-975-5555

641-108 San Jose, CA

				Toll-Free	Phone
98.5 KFOX					
201 Third St Ste 1200	San Francisco	CA	94103	877-410-5369	
KBAY-FM 94.5 (AC)					
190 Pk Ctr Plz Ste 200	San Jose	CA	95113	800-948-5229	408-287-5775

641-109 Santa Fe, NM

				Toll-Free	Phone
KBAC-FM 98.1 (AAA)					
2502 Camino Entrada Ste C	Santa Fe	NM	87507	888-321-5123	505-988-5222
KSWV-AM 810 (Span)					
102 Taos St	Santa Fe	NM	87505	800-873-3372	505-989-7441
KTRC-AM 1260 (N/T)					
2502 Camino Entrada Ste C	Santa Fe	NM	87507	888-321-5123	505-471-1067

641-110 Savannah, GA

				Toll-Free	Phone
WAEV-FM 97.3 (AC)					
245 Alfred St	Savannah	GA	31408	800-543-3548	912-964-7794
WSVH-FM 91.1 (NPR)					
13040 Abercorn St Ste 8	Savannah	GA	31419	877-472-1227	912-344-3565
WTKS-AM 1290 (N/T)					
245 Alfred St	Savannah	GA	31408	877-263-7995	912-964-7794
WYKZ-FM 98.7 (AC)					
245 Alfred St	Savannah	GA	31408	800-473-8546	912-964-7794

641-111 Seattle/Tacoma, WA

				Toll-Free	Phone
KBKS-FM 106.1 (CHR)					
645 Elliott Ave W Ste 400	Seattle	WA	98119	888-343-1061	206-494-2000
KHHO-AM 850 (Sports)					
645 Elliott Ave W Ste 400	Seattle	WA	98119	800-829-0950	206-494-2000
KJAQ-FM 96.5 (Var)					
1000 Dexter Ave N Ste 100	Seattle	WA	98109	866-416-5225	206-805-1100
KJR-AM 950 (Sports)					
351 Elliott Ave W Ste 300	Seattle	WA	98119	800-829-0950	206-494-2000
KOMO-AM 1000 (N/T)					
140 Fourth Ave N Ste 340	Seattle	WA	98109	888-477-5666	206-404-4000
KPLZ-FM 101.5 (AC)					
140 Fourth Ave N Ste 340	Seattle	WA	98109	888-821-1015	206-404-4000
KUBE-FM 93.3 (AC)					
351 Elliott Ave W Ste 300	Seattle	WA	98119	877-933-9393	206-494-2000
KUOW-FM 94.9 (NPR)					
4518 University Way NE Ste 310	Seattle	WA	98105	800-289-5869	206-543-2710
KZOK-FM 102.5 (CR)					
1000 Dexter Ave N	Seattle	WA	98109	800-252-1025	206-421-1025

641-112 Shreveport, LA

				Toll-Free	Phone
KDAQ-FM 89.9 (NPR)					
One University Pl PO Box 5250	Shreveport	LA	71115	800-552-8502	318-797-5150
KVKI-FM 96.5 (AC)					
6341 W Port Ave	Shreveport	LA	71129	800-487-1840	318-688-1130

641-113 Sioux Falls, SD

				Toll-Free	Phone
KNWC-AM 96.5 (Rel)					
6300 S Tallgrass Ave	Sioux Falls	SD	57108	888-569-5692	605-339-1270
KRRO-FM 103.7 (Rock)					
500 S Phillips Ave	Sioux Falls	SD	57104	877-263-7995	605-331-5350
KRSD-FM 88.1 (Clas)					
480 Cedar St	Saint Paul	MN	55101	800-228-7123	651-290-1500

	Toll-Free	Phone
KTWB-FM 101.9 (Ctry)		
500 S Phillips Ave ....Sioux Falls SD 57104	877-263-7995	605-331-5350

641-114 South Bend, IN

	Toll-Free	Phone
WNDV-FM 92.9 (CHR)		
3371 Cleveland Rd Ste 300 ....South Bend IN 46628	800-242-0100	574-273-9300

641-115 Spokane, WA

	Toll-Free	Phone
KDRK-FM 93.7 (Ctry)		
1601 E 57th Ave ....Spokane WA 99223	877-871-6772	509-448-1000
KZZU-FM 92.9 (CHR)		
500 W Boone Ave ....Spokane WA 99201	866-845-0929	509-324-4200
Spokane Public Radio		
2319 N Monroe St ....Spokane WA 99205	800-328-5729	509-328-5729

641-116 Springfield, IL

	Toll-Free	Phone
WQQL-FM 101.9 (Oldies)		
3501 E Sangamon Ave ....Springfield IL 62707	877-984-8786	217-753-5400

641-117 Springfield, MA

	Toll-Free	Phone
WHYN-AM 560 (N/T)		
1331 Main St Fourth Fl.......................Springfield MA 01103	800-345-9759	413-781-1011
WHYN-FM 93.1 (AC)		
1331 Main St Fourth Fl.......................Springfield MA 01103	888-293-9310	413-781-1011
WSCB-FM 89.9 (Urban)		
263 Alden St ....Springfield MA 01109	800-727-0504	413-748-3000

641-118 Springfield, MO

	Toll-Free	Phone
KGBX-FM 105.9 (AC)		
1856 S Glenstone Ave ....Springfield MO 65804	800-445-1059	417-890-5555
KSMS-FM 90.5 (NPR)		
Missouri State University		
901 S National Ave..........................Springfield MO 65804	800-767-5768	417-836-5878
KSMU-FM 91.1 (NPR)		
Missouri State University		
901 S National Ave..........................Springfield MO 65897	800-767-5768	417-836-5878
KSWF-FM 100.5 (Ctry)		
1856 S Glenstone Ave ....Springfield MO 65804	844-289-7234	417-890-5555
KTOZ-FM 95.5 (AC)		
1856 S Glenstone Ave ....Springfield MO 65804	800-757-9550	417-890-5555
KTTS-FM 94.7 (Ctry)		
2330 W Grand St ....Springfield MO 65802	855-574-2533	417-865-6614
KTXR-FM 101.3 (AC)		
3000 E Chestnut Expy ....Springfield MO 65806	855-586-8852*	417-862-3751
*General		

641-119 Stamford/Bridgeport, CT

	Toll-Free	Phone
WEBE-FM 108 (AC)		
Two Lafayette Sq ....Bridgeport CT 06604	800-932-3108	203-333-9108

641-120 Stockton, CA

	Toll-Free	Phone
KYCC-FM 90.1 (Rel)		
9019 W Ln ....Stockton CA 95210	800-654-5254	209-477-3690

641-121 Syracuse, NY

	Toll-Free	Phone
WHEN-AM 620 (Sports)		
500 Plum St Ste 400..........................Syracuse NY 13204	800-582-7583	315-472-9797

641-122 Tallahassee, FL

	Toll-Free	Phone
WFSQ-FM 91.5 (Clas)		
1600 Red Barber Plaza ....Tallahassee FL 32310	866-321-9378	850-487-3086
WFSU-FM 88.9 (NPR)		
1600 Red Barber Plaza ....Tallahassee FL 32310	800-322-9378	850-487-3086
WTLY-FM 107.1 (AC)		
325 John Knox Rd Bldg G ....Tallahassee FL 32303	855-274-2389	850-422-3107

641-123 Tampa/Saint Petersburg, FL

	Toll-Free	Phone
Cox Media Group Tampa		
11300 Fourth St N Ste 300 ....Saint Petersburg FL 33716	888-723-9388	727-579-2000
WDAE-AM 620 (Sports)		
4002 W Gandy Blvd ....Tampa FL 33611	888-546-4620	813-832-1000
WHPT-FM 102.5 (CR)		
11300 Fourth St N Ste 300 ....Saint Petersburg FL 33716	800-771-1025	727-579-2000

	Toll-Free	Phone
WSUN-FM 97.1 (Alt)		
11300 Fourth St N Ste 300 ....Saint Petersburg FL 33716	877-327-9797	727-579-2000
WUSF-FM 89.7 (NPR)		
4202 E Fowler Ave TVB 100 ....Tampa FL 33620	800-741-9090	813-974-8700
WXGL-FM 107.3 (AC)		
11300 Fourth St N Ste 300 ....Saint Petersburg FL 33716	800-242-1073	727-579-2000

641-124 Toledo, OH

	Toll-Free	Phone
WSPD-AM 1370 (N/T)		
125 S Superior St ....Toledo OH 43604	800-745-3000	419-244-8321
WXKR-FM 94.5 (CR)		
3225 Arlington Ave ....Toledo OH 43614	866-240-9945	419-725-5700

641-125 Topeka, KS

	Toll-Free	Phone
KMAJ-AM 1440 (N/T)		
825 S Kansas Ave Ste 100 ....Topeka KS 66612	877-297-1077	785-272-2122
KMAJ-FM 107.7 (AC)		
825 S Kansas Ave Ste 100 ....Topeka KS 66612	877-297-1077	785-272-2122

641-126 Trenton, NJ

	Toll-Free	Phone
NJTV 825 Eighth Avenue ....New York NY 10019	800-882-6622	609-777-0031
WKXW-FM 101.5 (N/T)		
109 Walters Ave ....Trenton NJ 08638	800-800-7822	609-359-5300

641-127 Tulsa, OK

	Toll-Free	Phone
KRMG-AM 740 (N/T)		
7136 S Yale Ave Ste 500.........................Tulsa OK 74136	855-297-9696	918-493-7400
Public Radio 89.5		
800 Tucker Dr ....Tulsa OK 74104	888-594-5947	918-631-2577

641-128 Tuscaloosa, AL

	Toll-Free	Phone
WTBC-AM 1230 (N/T)		
2110 McFarland Blvd E Ste C...................Tuscaloosa AL 35404	800-518-1977	205-758-5523
WUAL-FM 91.5 (NPR)		
166 Reese Phifer Hall		
PO Box 870150..............................Tuscaloosa AL 35487	800-654-4262	205-348-6644

641-129 Washington, DC

	Toll-Free	Phone
WHUR-FM 96.3 (Urban AC)		
529 Bryant St NW ....Washington DC 20059	877-550-0694	202-806-3500

641-130 West Palm Beach, FL

	Toll-Free	Phone
Sunny 107.9 Radio		
Palm Beach Broadcasting		
701 Northpoint Pkwy Ste 500............West Palm Beach FL 33407	800-919-1079	561-616-4777
WKGR-FM 98.7 (CR)		
3071 Continental Dr ....West Palm Beach FL 33407	877-541-1966	561-616-6600
WMBX-FM 102.3 (Urban)		
701 Northpoint Pkwy Ste 500............West Palm Beach FL 33407	800-969-1023	
WOLL-FM 105.5 (AC)		
3071 Continental Dr ....West Palm Beach FL 33407	888-415-1055	561-616-6600
WXEL-FM 90.7 (NPR)		
3401 S Congress Ave ....West Palm Beach FL 33426	800-915-9935	561-737-8000

641-131 Wichita, KS

	Toll-Free	Phone
KZCH-FM 96.3 (CHR)		
9323 E 37th St N ....Wichita KS 67226	800-800-1013	316-494-6600
KZSN-FM 102.1 (Ctry)		
9323 E 37th St N ....Wichita KS 67226	800-505-0098	316-494-6600

641-132 Wilmington/Dover, DE

	Toll-Free	Phone
WDEL-AM 1150 (N/T)		
2727 Shipley Rd ....Wilmington DE 19810	800-544-1150	302-478-2700
WSTW-FM 93.7 (CHR)		
2727 Shipley Rd ....Wilmington DE 19810	800-544-9370	302-478-2700

641-133 Winnipeg, MB

	Toll-Free	Phone
CKY-FM 102.3 (AC)		
4-166 Osborne St ....Winnipeg MB R3L1Y8	877-413-7970	204-788-3400

641-134 Winston-Salem, NC

	Toll-Free	Phone
WFDD-FM 88.5 (NPR)		
1834 Wake Forest Rd Ste 8850.................Winston-Salem NC 27109	800-262-8850	336-758-8850

642	RADIO SYNDICATORS	

	Toll-Free	Phone
American Urban Radio Networks		
960 Penn Ave Fourth Fl ....Pittsburgh PA 15222	800-456-4211	412-456-4000
Associated Press		
1100 13th St NW Ste 700 ....Washington DC 20005	800-824-5498	202-641-9000
Car Clinic Productions		
5675 N Davis Hwy ....Pensacola FL 32503	888-227-2546	850-478-3139
New Dimensions Radio Broadcasting Network		
PO Box 7847 ....Santa Rosa CA 95407	800-935-8273	707-468-5215
Premiere Radio Networks Inc		
15260 Ventura Blvd Ste 400 .... Sherman Oaks CA 91403	800-276-4431*	818-377-5300
*All		
Radio America		
1100 N Glebe Rd Ste 900 ....Arlington VA 22201	800-807-4703	703-302-1000
Strand Media Group		
3955 Hwy 17 Bypass Ste D		
PO Box 1389....................................Murrells Inlet SC 29576	877-844-1722	843-626-8911
Syndication Networks Corp		
8700 Waukegan Rd Ste 250 ....Morton Grove IL 60053	800-743-1988	847-583-9000
Talk Radio Network (TRN)		
PO Box 3755 ....Central Point OR 97502	888-383-3733	
Transmedia		
719 Battery St ....San Francisco CA 94111	800-229-7234	415-956-3118
WCLV		
1375 Euclid Ave Idea Ctr ....Cleveland OH 44115	877-399-3307	216-916-6301

643	RADIO & TELEVISION BROADCASTING & COMMUNICATIONS EQUIPMENT	

SEE ALSO Telecommunications Equipment & Systems ; Audio & Video Equipment

	Toll-Free	Phone
AheadTek Inc		
6410 Via Del Oro ....San Jose CA 95119	800-971-9191	408-226-9991
Airbiquity Inc		
1011 Western Ave Ste 600 ....Seattle WA 98104	888-334-7741	206-219-2700
Andersen Manufacturing Inc		
3125 N Yellowstone Hwy ....Idaho Falls ID 83401	800-635-6106	208-523-6460
Arris 60 Decibel Rd ....State College PA 16801	800-233-2267	814-238-2461
Arris Group Inc		
3871 Lakefield Dr ....Suwanee GA 30024	866-362-7747	678-473-2000
NASDAQ: ARRS		
Artel Video Systems Corp		
5B Lyberty Way ....Westford MA 01886	800-225-0228	978-263-5775
Atrex Inc		
175 Industrial Loop S ....Orange Park FL 32073	800-874-4505	904-264-9086
Avi Systems Inc		
9675 W 76th St Ste 200 ....Eden Prairie MN 55344	800-488-4954	952-949-3700
Axcera Corp 103 Freedom Dr ....Lawrence PA 15055	800-215-2614	724-873-8100
Blonder Tongue Laboratories Inc		
1 Jake Brown Rd ....Old Bridge NJ 08857	877-407-8033	732-679-4000
NYSE: BDR		
Coaxial Dynamics		
6800 Lake Abrams Dr .... Middleburg Heights OH 44130	800-262-9425	440-243-1100
Cohu Inc		
12367 Crosthwaite Cir ....Poway CA 92064	800-685-5050	858-848-8100
NASDAQ: COHU		
COMARK Communications		
104 Feeding Hills Rd ....Southwick MA 01077	800-288-8364	413-998-1100
Concurrent		
4375 River Green Pkwy Ste 100 ....Duluth GA 30096	877-978-7363	678-258-4000
NASDAQ: CCUR		
Conolog Corp		
Five Columbia Rd ....Somerville NJ 08876	800-526-3984	908-722-8081
OTC: CNLG		
Continental Electronics Corp		
4212 S Buckner Blvd ....Dallas TX 75227	800-733-5011	214-381-7161
Destron Fearing		
490 Villaume Ave ....South Saint Paul MN 55075	800-328-0118	651-552-6300
Eagle Comtronics Inc		
7665 Henry Clay Blvd ....Liverpool NY 13088	800-448-7474	315-622-3402
EFJohnson Technologies		
1440 Corporate Dr ....Irving TX 75038	800-328-3911	972-819-0700
Etm Electromatic Inc		
35451 Dumbarton Ct ....Newark CA 94560	800-883-4386	510-797-1100
GAI-Tronics Corp		
400 E Wyomissing Ave ....Mohnton PA 19540	800-492-1212	610-777-1374
General Dynamics SATCOM Technologies		
1500 Prodelin Dr ....Newton NC 28658	888-874-7646	828-464-4141
Globecomm Systems Inc		
45 Oser Ave ....Hauppauge NY 11788	866-499-0223	631-231-9800
NASDAQ: GCOM		
Harmonic Inc		
4300 N First St ....San Jose CA 95134	800-322-2885	408-542-2500
NASDAQ: HLIT		
Harris Corp		
1025 W NASA Blvd ....Melbourne FL 32919	800-442-7747	321-727-9100
NYSE: HRS		
Harris Corp RF Communications Div		
1680 University Ave ....Rochester NY 14610	866-264-8040	585-244-5830
Hitachi Kokusai Electric America Ltd		
150 Crossways Pk Dr ....Woodbury NY 11797	888-687-6877	516-921-7200
Honeywell International Inc		
101 Columbia Rd PO Box M6/LM ....Morristown NJ 07962	877-841-2840	480-353-3020
NYSE: HON		
ICOM America Inc		
2380 116th Ave NE ....Bellevue WA 98004	800-872-4266	425-454-8155
ID Systems Inc		
123 Tice Blvd Ste 101 ....Woodcliff Lake NJ 07677	866-410-0152	201-996-9000
NASDAQ: IDSY		

	Toll-Free	Phone
Ikegami Electronics USA Inc		
37 Brook Ave ....Maywood NJ 07607	800-368-9171	201-368-9171
Kenwood USA Corp		
2201 E Dominguez St ....Long Beach CA 90810	800-536-9663	310-639-9000
L-3 Communications Corp		
600 Third Ave 34-35 Fl. ....New York NY 10016	800-351-8483	212-697-1111
NYSE: LLL		
L-3 Communications ESSCO		
90 Nemco Way ....Ayer MA 01432	877-282-1168	978-568-5100
L-3 Communications Telemetry West Div		
9020 Balboa Ave ....San Diego CA 92123	800-351-8483	858-694-7500
MCL Inc		
501 S Woodcreek Rd ....Bolingbrook IL 60440	800-743-4625*	630-759-9500
*Support		
MDI Security Systems Inc		
12500 Network Dr Ste 303 ....San Antonio TX 78249	866-435-7634	210-477-5400
MFJ Enterprises Inc		
300 Industrial Pk Rd ....Starkville MS 39759	800-647-1800	662-323-5869
Minerva Networks Inc		
2150 Gold St ....Santa Clara CA 95002	800-806-9594	408-567-9400
Nautel Ltd		
10089 Peggy'S Cove Rd ....Hackett'S Cove NS B3Z3J4	877-662-8835	902-823-3900
ParkerVision Inc		
7915 Baymeadows Way ....Jacksonville FL 32256	800-532-8034	904-737-1367
NASDAQ: PRKR		
Pelco 3500 Pelco Way ....Clovis CA 93612	800-289-9100	559-292-1981
Pico Macom Inc		
8880 Rehco Rd ....San Diego CA 92121	800-421-6511	858-546-5050
RA Miller Industries Inc		
14500 168th Ave PO Box 858. ....Grand Haven MI 49417	888-845-9450	616-842-9450
RELM Wireless Corp		
7100 Technology Dr ....West Melbourne FL 32904	800-648-0947*	321-984-1414
NYSE: RWC ■ *Cust Svc		
RL Drake Co		
9900 Springboro Pike ....Miamisburg OH 45342	800-777-8876	937-746-4556
Rockwell Collins Inc		
400 Collins Rd NE ....Cedar Rapids IA 52498	888-721-3094	319-295-1000
NYSE: COL		
SATCOM Technologies		
1500 Prodelin Dr PO Box 850 ....Newton NC 28658	888-874-7646	828-464-4141
SeaChange International Inc		
50 Nagog Pk ....Acton MA 01720	844-855-8324	978-897-0100
NASDAQ: SEAC		
Secure Communication Systems Inc		
1740 E Wilshire Ave ....Santa Ana CA 92705	866-926-2940	714-547-1174
Shively Labs		
188 Harrison Rd PO Box 389 ....Bridgton ME 04009	888-744-8359	207-647-3327
Sonetics Corp		
7340 Sw Durham Rd ....Portland OR 97224	800-833-4558	
Space Systems/Loral		
3825 Fabian Way ....Palo Alto CA 94303	800-332-6490	650-852-4000
TCI International Inc		
3541 Gateway Blvd ....Fremont CA 94538	800-827-2661	510-687-6100
Tecom Industries Inc		
375 Conejo Ridge Ave ....Thousand Oaks CA 91361	866-840-8550	805-267-0100
Telephonics Corp		
815 Broad Hollow Rd ....Farmingdale NY 11735	877-517-2327	631-755-7000
Thales Communications Inc		
22605 Gateway Ctr Dr ....Clarksburg MD 20871	800-258-4420	240-864-7000
TPL Communications		
3370 San Fernando Rd Unit 206. ....Los Angeles CA 90065	800-447-6937	323-256-3000
Ultra Electronics Flightline Systems Inc		
7625 Omni Tech Pl ....Victor NY 14564	888-959-9001	585-924-4000
Ultra Electronics-DNE Technologies Inc		
50 Barnes Pk N ....Wallingford CT 06492	800-370-4485	203-265-7151
VehSmart Inc		
12180 Ridgecrest Rd Ste 412 ....Victorville CA 92395	855-834-7627	
Vicon Industries Inc		
89 Arkay Dr ....Hauppauge NY 11788	800-645-9116*	631-952-2288
NYSE: VII ■ *Sales		
Wilcom Inc		
73 Daniel Webster Hwy PO Box 508. ....Belmont NH 03220	800-222-1898	603-524-2622
Winegard Co		
3000 Kirkwood St ....Burlington IA 52601	800-288-8094*	319-754-0600
*Cust Svc		

644	RAIL TRANSPORT SERVICES	

SEE ALSO Logistics Services (Transportation & Warehousing)

	Toll-Free	Phone
Aberdeen & Rockfish Railroad Co		
101 E Main St ....Aberdeen NC 28315	800-849-8985	910-944-2341
Buffalo & Pittsburgh Railroad Inc (BPRR)		
1200-C Scottsville Rd Ste 200 ....Rochester NY 14624	800-603-3385	585-463-3307
Burlington Northern & Santa Fe Railway (BNSF)		
2650 Lou Menk Dr ....Fort Worth TX 76131	800-795-2673	
Canadian National Railway Co		
935 Rue de la Gauchetiere O ....Montreal QC H3B2M9	888-668-4626	888-888-5909
TSE: CNR		
Canadian Pacific Railway Co		
401 9 Ave SW Ste 500 ....Calgary AB T2P4Z4	888-333-6370	403-319-7000
CHEP USA 8517 S Pk Cir ....Orlando FL 32819	866-855-2437*	407-370-2437
*Cust Svc		
Chicago Southshore & South Bend Railroad		
505 N Carroll Ave ....Michigan City IN 46360	800-356-2079	219-874-9000
Consolidated Rail Corp		
1717 Arch St Ste 3210 ....Philadelphia PA 19103	800-272-0911	215-209-2000
Dardanelle & Russellville Railroad Co		
4416 S Arkansas Ave ....Russellville AR 72802	888-877-7267	479-968-6455
Georgetown Railroad Co		
5300 SIH-35 PO Box 529 ....Georgetown TX 78626	888-456-6777	512-863-2538
Iowa Interstate Railroad		
5900 Sixth St SW ....Cedar Rapids IA 52404	800-321-3884	319-298-5400
Kansas City Southern Railway Co		
427 W 12th St ....Kansas City MO 64105	800-468-6527	816-983-1303
Montana Rail Link Inc		
101 International Way ....Missoula MT 59808	800-338-4750	406-523-1500

				Toll-Free	Phone

Montreal Maine & Atlantic Railway Ltd
15 Iron Rd .... Hermon ME 04401 **800-635-9449** 800-222-1433

New England Central Railroad (NECR)
7411 Fullerton St Ste 300 .... Jacksonville FL 32256 **877-777-4778** 904-596-1045

New York Susquehanna & Western Railway Corp (NYSW)
One Railroad Ave .... Cooperstown NY 13326 **800-366-6979***
*General

Norfolk Southern Railway Co
Three Commercial Pl .... Norfolk VA 23510 **800-635-5768** 800-453-2530

Providence & Worcester Railroad Co
75 Hammond St .... Worcester MA 01610 **877-373-6374** 508-755-4000
NASDAQ: PWX

Trans-Continental Systems Inc
10801 Evendale Dr .... Cincinnati OH 45241 **800-525-8726** 513-769-4774

Triple Crown Services
2720 Dupont Commerce Ct Ste 200 .... Fort Wayne IN 46825 **800-325-6510** 260-416-3600

Union Pacific Railroad Co
1400 Douglas St .... Omaha NE 68179 **888-870-8777**

Winston-Salem Southbound Railway Co
4550 Overdale Rd .... Winston-Salem NC 27107 **888-780-7245** 336-788-9407

645 RAIL TRAVEL

SEE ALSO Mass Transportation (Local & Suburban)

				Toll-Free	Phone

Dew Distribution Services Inc
2201 Touhy Ave .... Elk Grove Village IL 60007 **800-837-3391**

National Railroad Passenger Corp
60 Massachusetts Ave NE .... Washington DC 20002 **800-872-7245** 202-906-3741

VIA Rail Canada Inc
Three Pl Ville-Marie Ste 500 .... Montreal QC H3B2C9 **800-681-2561** 514-871-6000

646 RAILROAD EQUIPMENT - MFR

SEE ALSO Transportation Equipment & Supplies - Whol

				Toll-Free	Phone

A Stucki Co
2600 Neville Rd .... Pittsburgh PA 15225 **888-266-6630** 412-771-7300

American Railcar Industries Inc
100 Clark St .... Saint Charles MO 63301 **800-489-9888** 636-940-6000
NASDAQ: ARII

CANAC Inc
6505 Trans-Canada Hwy Ste 405 .... St Laurent QC H4T1S3 **800-588-4387** 514-734-4700

Dayton-Phoenix Group Inc
1619 Kuntz Rd .... Dayton OH 45404 **800-657-0707** 937-496-3974

Electro-Motive Diesel Inc
9301 W 55th St .... La Grange IL 60525 **800-255-5355** 708-387-6000

FreightCar America Inc
17 Johns St .... Johnstown PA 15901 **800-458-2235**
NASDAQ: RAIL

GE Transportation Rail
2901 E Lake Rd .... Erie PA 16531 **800-626-2000*** 814-875-2234
*Prod Info

Greenbrier Co
One Centerpointe Dr Ste 200 .... Lake Oswego OR 97035 **800-343-7188** 503-684-7000
NYSE: GBX

Holland Co 1000 Holland Dr .... Crete IL 60417 **800-899-7754** 708-672-2300

Interstate Transport Inc
324 First Ave N .... St Petersburg FL 33701 **866-281-1281** 727-822-9999

LB Foster Co
415 Holiday Dr .... Pittsburgh PA 15220 **800-255-4500**
NASDAQ: FSTR

Loram Maintenance of Way
3900 Arrowhead Dr PO Box 188 .... Hamel MN 55340 **800-328-1466** 763-478-6014

Miner Enterprises Inc
1200 E State St PO Box 471 .... Geneva IL 60134 **888-822-5334** 630-232-3000

MotivePower 4600 Apple St .... Boise ID 83716 **800-445-8667** 208-947-4800

National Railway Equipment Co (NREC)
14400 Robey Ave Ste 2 .... Dixmoor IL 60426 **800-253-2905** 708-388-6002

New York Air Brake Co
748 Starbuck Ave .... Watertown NY 13601 **888-836-6922** 315-786-5200

Nolan Co 1016 Ninth St SW .... Canton OH 44707 **800-297-1383** 330-453-7922

Pacific Coast Container Inc
432 Estudillo Ave .... San Leandro CA 94577 **800-458-4788** 510-346-6100

Salco Products Inc
1385 101st St Ste A .... Lemont IL 60439 **800-535-8990** 630-783-2570

Transco Railway Products Inc
820 Hopley Ave .... Bucyrus OH 44820 **800-472-4592** 419-562-1031

Trinity Mining Service
109 48th St .... Pittsburgh PA 15201 **800-264-2583** 412-682-4700

Trinity Rail Group LLC
2525 N Stemmons Fwy .... Dallas TX 75207 **800-631-4420** 214-631-4420

Union Tank Car Co
175 W Jackson Blvd Ste 2100 .... Chicago IL 60604 **866-535-7685** 312-431-3111

Vapor Bus International
1010 Johnson Dr .... Buffalo Grove IL 60089 **866-375-4126** 847-777-6400

WABCO Locomotive Products
1001 Air Brake Ave .... Wilmerding PA 15148 **877-922-2627*** 412-825-1000
*Cust Svc

Wabtec Corp
1001 Air Brake Ave .... Wilmerding PA 15148 **877-922-2627*** 412-825-1000
NYSE: WAB ■ *Cust Svc

Watco Companies LLC
315 W Third St .... Pittsburg KS 66762 **866-386-9321** 620-231-2230

647 RAILROAD SWITCHING & TERMINAL SERVICES

				Toll-Free	Phone

Belt Railway Co of Chicago
6900 S Central Ave .... Bedford Park IL 60638 **877-772-5772** 708-496-4000

Public Belt Railroad Commission
4822 Tchoupitulas St .... New Orleans LA 70115 **800-524-3421*** 504-896-7410
*Cust Svc

				Toll-Free	Phone

Rail Link Inc
13901 Sutton Pk Dr S Ste 125 .... Jacksonville FL 32224 **877-777-4778** 904-223-1110

Railserve Inc
1691 Phoenix Blvd Ste 110 .... Atlanta GA 30349 **800-345-7245** 770-996-6838

Rescar Inc
1101 31st St Ste 250 .... Downers Grove IL 60515 **800-851-5196** 630-963-1114

Roadrunner Transportation Systems Inc
4900 S Pennsylvania Ave .... Cudahy WI 53110 **800-831-4394** 414-615-1500
NYSE: RRTS

648 REAL ESTATE AGENTS & BROKERS

				Toll-Free	Phone

Assist-2-Sell Inc
1610 Meadow Wood Ln .... Reno NV 89502 **800-528-7816** 775-688-6060

Beach Realty & Construction
4826 N Croatan Hwy .... Kitty Hawk NC 27949 **800-635-1559** 252-261-3815

Bosshardt Realty Services LLC
5542 NW 43rd St .... Gainesville FL 32653 **800-284-6110** 352-371-6100

Bray Real Estate
637 N Ave .... Grand Junction CO 81501 **888-760-4251** 970-242-8450

Brownstone Real Estate Co
1840 Fishburn Rd .... Hershey PA 17033 **877-533-6222** 717-533-6222

Carolina Farms Real Estate
547 S Main St .... King NC 27021 **800-559-2113** 336-983-5263

CENTURY 21 Sweyer & Assoc
1630 Military Cutoff Rd .... Wilmington NC 28403 **800-848-0021** 910-256-0021

Coldwell Banker Gundaker
2458 Old Dorsett Rd Ste 300 .... Maryland Heights MO 63043 **800-325-1978** 314-298-5000

Coldwell Banker Residential Brokerage
600 Grant St Ste 925 .... Denver CO 80203 **800-552-6787*** 303-409-1500
*All

Coldwell Banker Residential Real Estate
5951 Cattleridge Ave .... Sarasota FL 34232 **888-937-6426** 941-378-8211

Conterra Ultra Broadband LLC
2101 Rexford Rd Ste 200E .... Charlotte NC 28211 **800-634-1374** 704-936-1800

Corcoran Group Inc, The
660 Madison Ave .... New York NY 10021 **800-544-4055** 212-355-3550

Dart Appraisalcom
2600 W Big Beaver Rd Ste 100 .... Troy MI 48084 **888-327-8123**

Development Planning & Financing Group Inc
27127 Calle Arroyo
Ste 1910 .... San Juan Capistrano CA 92675 **800-535-5795** 949-388-9269

Equine Canada
2685 Queensview Dr .... Ottawa ON K2B8K2 **866-282-8395** 613-248-3484

ERA Wilder Realty
120A Columbia Ave PO Box 610 .... Chapin SC 29036 **866-593-7653** 803-345-6713

Gove Group Real Estate LLC
70 Portsmouth Ave .... Stratham NH 03885 **866-778-6400** 603-778-6400

H Pearce Real Estate Co
393 State St .... North Haven CT 06473 **800-373-3411** 203-281-3400

Hart Corp 900 Jaymor Rd .... SouthHampton PA 18966 **800-368-4278** 215-322-5100

Hoban & Assoc Dba Coast Real Estate Services
2829 Rucker Ave .... Everett WA 98201 **800-339-3634** 425-339-3638

HomeGain.com Inc
6001 Shellmound St Ste 550 .... Emeryville CA 94608 **888-542-0800** 510-655-0800

HomeServices of America Inc
333 S Seventh St 27th Fl .... Minneapolis MN 55402 **888-485-0018**

Hotpadscom PO Box 53104 .... Washington DC 20009 **888-876-1992** 202-232-1581

Inland Group Inc
2901 Butterfield Rd .... Oak Brook IL 60523 **800-826-8228** 630-218-8000

Inland Real Estate Sales Inc
2901 Butterfield Rd .... Oak Brook IL 60523 **800-828-8999** 630-218-8000

Iowa Realty Company Inc
3501 Westown Pkwy .... West Des Moines IA 50266 **800-247-2430** 515-453-6222

Jack Conway
137 Washington St .... Norwell MA 02061 **800-283-1030** 781-871-0080

Jameson Real Estate LLC
425 W N Ave .... Chicago IL 60610 **888-751-4663** 312-751-0300

Janet Mcafee Inc
9889 Clayton Rd .... Saint Louis MO 63124 **888-991-4800** 314-997-4800

Jersey Cape Realty Inc
739 Washington St .... Cape May NJ 08204 **800-643-0043** 609-884-5800

John Daugherty Realtors
520 Post Oak Blvd Sixth Fl .... Houston TX 77027 **800-231-2821** 713-626-3930

Joyner Fine Properties (JFP)
2727 Enterprise Pkwy PO Box 31355 .... Richmond VA 23294 **800-446-3858** 804-270-9440

Keefe Real Estate
1155 E Geneva St .... Delavan WI 53115 **800-690-2292** 262-728-8757

LG2 Environmental Solutions Inc
88 Riberia St .... St Augustine FL 32084 **800-435-0072** 904-824-8633

Long & Foster Realtors
14501 George Carter Way .... Chantilly VA 20151 **800-237-8800** 703-653-8500

Macdonald Realty
203 5188 Wminster Hwy .... Richmond BC V7C5S7 **877-278-3888** 604-279-9822

MacPherson's Property Management Inc
18551 Aurora Ave N Ste 301 .... Seattle WA 98133 **800-962-6473** 206-542-6363

Mason-McDuffie Real Estate Inc
5724 W Las Positas Blvd .... Pleasanton CA 94588 **888-971-4636** 925-924-4600

MCAP Service Corp
400-200 King St W .... Toronto ON M5H3T4 **800-387-4405** 416-598-2665

Mcenearney Assoc Inc
109 S Pitt St .... Alexandria VA 22314 **877-624-9322** 703-549-9292

National Church Residences Inc
2335 N Bank Dr .... Columbus OH 43220 **800-388-2151**

NP Dodge Real Estate
8701 W Dodge Rd Ste 300 .... Omaha NE 68114 **800-642-5008** 402-397-4900

Ontario Real Estate Assn
99 Duncan Mill Rd .... Don Mills ON M3B1Z2 **866-444-5557** 416-445-9910

Patterson-Schwartz & Assoc Inc
7234 Lancaster Pike Ste 100A .... Hockessin DE 19707 **877-456-4663** 302-234-5270

Preferred Properties of Venice Inc
325 W Venice Ave .... Venice FL 34285 **877-640-7653** 941-485-9602

Premier Realty Group
Two N Sewalls Point Rd .... Stuart FL 34996 **800-915-8517** 772-287-1777

		Toll-Free	Phone

RE/MAX International Inc
5075 S Syracuse St . . . . Denver CO 80237 **800-525-7452*** 303-770-5531
*Cust Svc

RE/MAX of Western Canada Inc
1060 Manhattan Dr Ste 340 . . . . Kelowna BC V1Y9X9 **800-563-3622** 250-860-3628

RE/MAX Ontario-Atlantic
7101 Syntex Dr . . . . Mississauga ON L5N6H5 **888-542-2499** 905-542-2400

RE/MAX Quebec Inc
1500 Cunard St . . . . Laval QC H7S2B7 **800-361-9325** 450-668-7743

Real Estate Institute of Bc
1750 - 355 Burrard St . . . . Vancouver BC V6C2G8 **800-667-2166** 604-685-3702

Real Estate One Inc
25800 NW Hwy Ste 100 . . . . Southfield MI 48075 **800-521-0508** 248-304-6700

Real Living First Service Realty
13155 SW 42nd St Ste 200 . . . . Miami FL 33175 **800-899-8477** 305-551-9400

Real Living Inc
77 E Nationwide Blvd . . . . Columbus OH 43215 **800-848-7400** 614-459-7400

Realestateexpresscom
12977 N 40 Dr Ste 108 . . . . Saint Louis MO 63141 **866-739-7277**

Realty Executives International Inc
7600 N 16th St Ste 100 . . . . Phoenix AZ 85020 **800-252-3366** 602-957-0747

Relocation Center Inc, The
1042 E Juneau Ave . . . . Milwaukee WI 53202 **800-783-5337** 414-226-4200

Rose Assoc Inc
200 Madison Ave . . . . New York NY 10016 **888-475-8860** 212-210-6666

Ross Realty Investments Inc
3325 S University Dr Ste 210 . . . . Davie FL 33328 **800-370-4202** 954-452-5000

Semonin Realtors
4967 US Hwy 42 Ste 200 . . . . Louisville KY 40222 **800-548-1650** 502-425-4760

Silicon Valley Assn of Realtors
19400 Stevens Creek Blvd Ste 100 . . . . Cupertino CA 95014 **877-699-6787** 408-200-0100

Sotheby's International Realty
38 E 61st St . . . . New York NY 10065 **866-899-4747** 212-606-7660

Strother Ventures II Inc
2929 Breezewood Ave Ste 200 . . . . Fayetteville NC 28303 **855-753-6143** 910-864-2327

United Country Real Estate Inc
2820 NW Barry Rd . . . . Kansas City MO 64154 **800-999-1020** 816-420-6200

Watson Realty Co
9101 Camino Media . . . . Bakersfield CA 93311 **800-777-0646** 661-327-5161

Williams & Williams Real Estate Auction
7120 S Lewis Ave Ste 200 . . . . Tulsa OK 74136 **800-801-8003** 918-250-2012

ZipRealty Inc
2000 Powell St Ste 300 . . . . Emeryville CA 94608 **800-225-5947** 510-735-2600
NASDAQ: ZIPR

649   REAL ESTATE DEVELOPERS

SEE ALSO Construction - Building Contractors - Non-Residential ; Construction - Building Contractors - Residential

		Toll-Free	Phone

Al Neyer Inc
302 W Third St Ste 800 . . . . Cincinnati OH 45202 **877-271-6400** 513-271-6400

Alter Group 5500 W Howard St . . . . Skokie IL 60077 **800-637-4842** 847-676-4300

Amerco Real Estate Co
2727 N Central Ave Ste 500 . . . . Phoenix AZ 85004 **800-528-0463*** 602-263-6555
*General

AV Homes Inc
8601 N Scottsdale Rd Ste 225 . . . . Scottsdale AR 85283 **866-392-4286** 480-214-7400
NASDAQ: AVHI

Brooks Resources Corp
409 NW Franklin Ave . . . . Bend OR 97701 **877-475-9779** 541-382-1662

Connell Realty & Development Co
200 Connell Dr . . . . Berkeley Heights NJ 07922 **800-233-3240** 908-673-3700

Cornerstone Group
2100 Hollywood Blvd . . . . Hollywood FL 33020 **800-809-4099** 305-443-8288

CountryTyme Inc
3451 Cincinnati-Zanesville Rd SW . . . . Lancaster OH 43130 **800-213-8365** 740-475-6001

David Weekley Homes Inc
1111 N Post Oak Rd . . . . Houston TX 77055 **800-390-6774** 713-963-0500

Deltona Corp
8014 SW 135th St Rd . . . . Ocala FL 34473 **800-935-6378** 352-347-2322

Double Diamond Co
5495 Belt Line Rd Suite 200 . . . . Dallas TX 75254 **800-324-7438** 214-706-9801

DR Horton Inc
301 Commerce St Ste 500 . . . . Fort Worth TX 76102 **800-846-7866** 817-390-8200
NYSE: DHI

Ergon Properties Inc
PO Box 1639 . . . . Jackson MS 39215 **800-824-2626** 601-933-3174

Fieldstone Homes Two Ada . . . . Irvine CA 92618 **800-665-0661** 949-790-5400

First Hartford Corp
149 Colonial Rd . . . . Manchester CT 06042 **888-646-6555** 860-646-6555
OTC: FHRT

Gilbane Inc
Seven Jackson Walkway . . . . Providence RI 02903 **800-445-2263** 401-456-5890

Hines Interest LP
2800 Post Oak Blvd . . . . Houston TX 77056 **800-891-7017** 713-621-8000

Holiday Builders Inc
2293 W Eau Gallie Blvd . . . . Melbourne FL 32935 **866-431-2533** 321-610-5172

Hunt Midwest Enterprises Inc
8300 NE Underground Dr . . . . Kansas City MO 64161 **800-551-6877** 816-455-2500

Hunt Midwest Residential Development
8300 NE Underground Dr . . . . Kansas City MO 64161 **800-551-6877** 816-455-2500

Inland Real Estate Development Corp
2901 Butterfield Rd . . . . Oak Brook IL 60523 **866-954-5692** 630-218-8000

JA Billipp Co
6925 Portwest Dr Ste 130 . . . . Houston TX 77024 **800-216-9013** 713-426-5000

JMC Communities
2201 Fourth St N Ste 200 . . . . Saint Petersburg FL 33704 **800-741-4106** 727-823-0022

John F Buchan Homes
2821 Northup Way Ste 100 . . . . Bellevue WA 98004 **866-528-2426** 425-827-2266

John Wieland Homes & Neighborhoods
4125 Atlanta Rd SE . . . . Smyrna GA 30080 **800-376-4663** 770-996-2400

KB Home
10990 Wilshire Blvd Seventh Fl . . . . Los Angeles CA 90024 **800-304-0657** 310-231-4000
NYSE: KBH

		Toll-Free	Phone

Legend Homes Corp
12755 SW 69th Ave Ste 100 . . . . Portland OR 97223 **888-782-7937** 503-620-8080

M/I Homes Inc
Three Easton Oval . . . . Columbus OH 43219 **888-644-4111** 614-418-8700
NYSE: MHO

Polygon Northwest Co
11624 SE Fifth St Ste 200 . . . . Bellevue WA 98005 **800-765-9466** 425-586-7700

Richman Group of Cos
340 Pemberwick Rd . . . . Greenwich CT 06831 **800-333-3509** 203-869-0900

Richmond American Homes Inc
4350 S Monaco St . . . . Denver CO 80237 **888-402-4663** 303-773-2727

Robson Communities
9532 E Riggs Rd . . . . Sun Lakes AZ 85248 **800-732-9949**

Schatten Properties Management Company Inc
1514 S St . . . . Nashville TN 37212 **800-892-1315** 615-329-3011

Sea Pines Resort, The
32 Greenwood Dr . . . . Hilton Head Island SC 29928 **866-561-8802** 843-785-3333

Sea Trail Corp
75A Clubhouse Rd . . . . Sunset Beach NC 28468 **888-321-9076** 910-287-1100

Stanley Martin Cos
11111 Sunset Hills Rd Ste 200 . . . . Reston VA 20190 **800-446-4807** 703-964-5000

Stratus Properties Inc
212 Lavaca St Ste 300 . . . . Austin TX 78701 **800-690-0315** 512-478-5788
NYSE: STRS

Toll Bros Inc
250 Gibraltar Rd . . . . Horsham PA 19044 **855-897-8655** 215-938-8000
NYSE: TOL

TransCon Builders Inc
25250 Rockside Rd . . . . Cleveland OH 44146 **800-451-2608** 440-439-2100

Village Green Cos
30833 NW Hwy . . . . Farmington Hills MI 48334 **800-521-2220** 248-851-9600

Villages of Lake Sumter Inc
1000 Lk Sumter Landing . . . . The Villages FL 32162 **800-245-1081** 352-753-2270

WCI Communities Inc
24301 Walden Ctr Dr . . . . Bonita Springs FL 34134 **800-924-4005** 239-498-8200

Weyerhaeuser Co
33663 Weyerhaeuser Way S . . . . Federal Way WA 98003 **800-525-5440** 253-924-2345
NYSE: WY

650   REAL ESTATE INVESTMENT TRUSTS (REITS)

		Toll-Free	Phone

Acadia Realty Trust
1311 Mamaroneck Ave Ste 260 . . . . White Plains NY 10605 **800-937-5449** 914-288-8100
NYSE: AKR

Alexandria Real Estate Equities Inc
385 E Colorado Blvd Ste 299 . . . . Pasadena CA 91101 **800-776-9437** 626-578-0777
NYSE: ARE

Apartment Investment & Management Co
4582 S Ulster St Pkwy Ste 1100 . . . . Denver CO 80237 **888-789-8600*** 303-691-4350
NYSE: AIV ■ *General

Arbor Realty Trust Inc
333 Earle Ovington Blvd Ste 900 . . . . Uniondale NY 11553 **800-272-6710**
NYSE: ABR

AutoStar
114 Ave of the Americas Ste 39 . . . . New York NY 10036 **800-288-6782** 212-930-9400

Benchmark Group
4053 Maple Rd . . . . Amherst NY 14226 **800-876-0160** 716-833-4986

BRT Realty Trust
60 Cutter Mill Rd Ste 303 . . . . Great Neck NY 11021 **800-450-5816** 516-466-3100
NYSE: BRT

Camden Property Trust
11 Greenway Plz Ste 2400 . . . . Houston TX 77046 **800-922-6336** 713-354-2500
NYSE: CPT

Capital Automotive Real Estate Services Inc
8270 Greensboro Dr Ste 950 . . . . McLean VA 22102 **877-422-7288** 703-288-3075

Capstead Mortgage Corp
8401 N Central Expy Ste 800 . . . . Dallas TX 75225 **800-358-2323** 214-874-2323
NYSE: CMO

Chesapeake Lodging Trust (CLT)
1997 Annapolis Exchange Pkwy
Ste 410 . . . . Annapolis MD 21401 **800-698-2820**
NYSE: CHSP

Commercial Properties Realty Trust
402 N Fourth St . . . . Baton Rouge LA 70802 **800-648-9064** 225-924-7206

DiamondRock Hospitality Co (DRHC)
3 Bethesda Metro Ctr Ste 1500 . . . . Bethesda MD 20814 **888-246-5941** 240-744-1150
NYSE: DRH

Dividend Capital Trust
518 17th St Ste 1700 . . . . Denver CO 80202 **866-324-7348** 303-228-2200

Federal Realty Investment Trust
1626 E Jefferson St . . . . Rockville MD 20852 **800-658-8980** 301-998-8100
NYSE: FRT

Franklin Street Properties Corp
401 Edgewater Pl Ste 200 . . . . Wakefield MA 01880 **877-686-9496** 781-557-1300
NYSE: FSP

GE Capital Solutions Franchise Finance
8377 E Hartford Dr Ste 200 . . . . Scottsdale AZ 85255 **866-438-4333**

Health Care Property Investors Inc
1920 Main St Ste 1200 . . . . Irvine CA 92614 **888-604-1990** 949-407-0700

Highwoods Properties Inc
3100 Smoketree Ct Ste 600 . . . . Raleigh NC 27604 **866-449-6637** 919-872-4924
NYSE: HIW

Impac Mortgage Holdings Inc
19500 Jamboree Rd . . . . Irvine CA 92612 **800-597-4101** 949-475-3600
NYSE: IMH

Inland Real Estate Corp
2901 Butterfield Rd . . . . Oak Brook IL 60523 **888-331-4732** 630-218-8000
NYSE: IRC

InnSuites Hospitality Trust
1625 E Northern Ave Ste 105 . . . . Phoenix AZ 85020 **800-842-4242** 602-944-1500
NYSE: IHT

Investors Real Estate Trust
1400 31st Ave Ste 60 . . . . Minot ND 58701 **888-478-4738** 701-837-4738
NYSE: IRET

iStar Financial Inc
1114 Ave of the Americas 39th Fl . . . . New York NY 10036 **888-603-5847** 212-930-9400
NYSE: STAR

		Toll-Free	Phone

Kimco Realty Corp
3333 New Hyde Pk Rd . . . . New Hyde Park NY 11042 — **800-645-6292** — 516-869-9000
NYSE: KIM

Kite Realty Group Trust
30 S Meridian St Ste 1100 . . . . Indianapolis IN 46204 — **888-577-5600** — 317-577-5600
NYSE: KRG

Lexington Corporate Properties Trust
One Penn Plz Ste 4015 . . . . New York NY 10119 — **800-850-3948** — 212-692-7200

Macerich Co, The
401 Wilshire Blvd Ste 700 . . . . Santa Monica CA 90401 — **800-421-7237** — 310-394-6000
NYSE: MAC

Mack-Cali Realty Corp
343 Thornall St . . . . Edison NJ 08837 — **800-317-4445** — 732-590-1000
NYSE: CLI

New York Mortgage Trust Inc (NYMT)
52 Vanderbilt Ave Ste 403 . . . . New York NY 10017 — **800-937-5449** — 212-792-0107
NASDAQ: NYMT

Novastar Financial Inc
2114 Central Ste 600 . . . . Kansas City MO 64108 — **800-591-1137** — 816-237-7000

One Liberty Properties Inc
60 Cutter Mill Rd Ste 303 . . . . Great Neck NY 11021 — **800-937-5449** — 516-466-3100
NYSE: OLP

Parkway Properties Inc
188 E Capitol St Ste 1000 . . . . Jackson MS 39201 — **800-748-1667** — 601-948-4091
NYSE: PKY

Pennsylvania Real Estate Investment Trust
200 S Broad St Third Fl . . . . Philadelphia PA 19102 — **866-875-0700** — 215-875-0700
NYSE: PEI

Plum Creek Timber Company Inc
601 Union St Ste 3100 . . . . Seattle WA 98101 — **800-858-5347** — 206-467-3600
NYSE: PCL

PMC Commercial Trust
17950 Preston Rd Ste 600 . . . . Dallas TX 75252 — **800-486-3223** — 972-349-3200
NASDAQ: CMCT

ProLogis 4545 Airport Way . . . . Denver CO 80239 — **800-566-2706** — 303-375-9292
NYSE: PLD

PS Business Parks Inc
701 Western Ave . . . . Glendale CA 91201 — **888-299-3246*** — 818-244-8080
*NYSE: PSB ▪ *Cust Svc*

Public Storage Inc
701 Western Ave . . . . Glendale CA 91201 — **800-567-0759*** — 818-244-8080
*NYSE: PSA ▪ *Cust Svc*

Regency Centers
One Independent Dr Ste 114 . . . . Jacksonville FL 32202 — **800-950-6333** — 904-598-7000
NYSE: REG

RioCan Real Estate Investment Trust
2300 Yonge St Ste 500 PO Box 2386 . . . . Toronto ON M4P1E4 — **800-465-2733** — 416-866-3033
TSE: REI.UN.CA

Tanger Factory Outlet Centers Inc
3200 Northline Ave Ste 360 . . . . Greensboro NC 27408 — **800-720-6728** — 336-292-3010
NYSE: SKT

Taubman Centers Inc
200 E Long Lk Rd Ste 300 . . . . Bloomfield Hills MI 48303 — **800-297-6003** — 248-258-6800
NYSE: TCO

Transcontinental Realty Investors Inc
1603 Lyndon B Johnson Fwy Ste 800 . . . . Dallas TX 75234 — **800-400-6407** — 469-522-4200
NYSE: TCI

Ventas Inc
353 N Clark St Ste 3300 . . . . Chicago IL 60654 — **877-483-6827**
NYSE: VTR

Vornado Realty Trust
888 Seventh Ave . . . . New York NY 10019 — **800-294-1322** — 212-894-7000
NYSE: VNO

Washington Real Estate Investment Trust (WRIT)
6110 Executive Blvd Ste 800 . . . . Rockville MD 20852 — **800-565-9748** — 301-984-9400
NYSE: WRE

Weingarten Realty Investors
2600 Citadel Plz Dr Ste 300 . . . . Houston TX 77008 — **800-688-8865** — 713-866-6000
NYSE: WRI

Winthrop Realty Trust
7 Bulfinch Pl Ste 500 . . . . Boston MA 02114 — **800-622-6757** — 617-570-4614
NYSE: FUR

WP Carey & Company LLC
50 Rockefeller Plz Second Fl . . . . New York NY 10020 — **800-972-2739** — 212-492-1100
NYSE: WPC

---

651   REAL ESTATE MANAGERS & OPERATORS

SEE ALSO Retirement Communities ; Hotels & Hotel Companies

		Toll-Free	Phone

Acadia Realty Trust
1311 Mamaroneck Ave Ste 260 . . . . White Plains NY 10605 — **800-937-5449** — 914-288-8100
NYSE: AKR

Alexandria Real Estate Equities Inc
385 E Colorado Blvd Ste 299 . . . . Pasadena CA 91101 — **800-776-9437** — 626-578-0777
NYSE: ARE

American Golf Corp
2951 28th St . . . . Santa Monica CA 90405 — **800-238-7267** — 310-664-4000

American Motel Management
2200 Northlake Pkwy Ste 277 . . . . Tucker GA 30084 — **800-580-8258** — 770-939-1801

American Realty Investors Inc
1800 Vly View Ln Ste 300 . . . . Dallas TX 75234 — **800-400-6407** — 469-522-4200
NYSE: ARL

American Spectrum Realty Inc
2401 Fountain View Ste 510 . . . . Houston TX 77057 — **888-315-2776** — 713-706-6200
NYSE: AQQ

Apartment Investment & Management Co
4582 S Ulster St Pkwy Ste 1100 . . . . Denver CO 80237 — **888-789-8600*** — 303-691-4350
*NYSE: AIV ▪ *General*

Associated Estates Realty Corp
One AEC Pkwy . . . . Richmond Heights OH 44143 — **800-440-2372** — 216-261-5000
NYSE: AEC

Bozzuto Group
7850 Walker Dr Ste 400 . . . . Greenbelt MD 20770 — **866-698-7513*** — 301-220-0100
**General*

Brandywine Realty Trust
555 E Lancaster Ave Ste 100 . . . . Radnor PA 19087 — **866-426-5400** — 610-325-5600
NYSE: BDN

Brookfield Properties Corp (BOP)
181 Bay St Ste 330 . . . . Toronto ON M5J2T3 — **800-387-0825** — 416-369-2300
NYSE: BPO

Calista Corp
301 Calista Ct Ste A . . . . Anchorage AK 99518 — **800-277-5516** — 907-279-5516

Camden Property Trust
11 Greenway Plz Ste 2400 . . . . Houston TX 77046 — **800-922-6336** — 713-354-2500
NYSE: CPT

ClubCorp Inc
3030 Lyndon B Johnson Fwy Ste 600 . . . . Dallas TX 75234 — **800-433-5079** — 972-243-6191

ClubLink Corp
15675 Dufferin St . . . . King City ON L7B1K5 — **800-661-1818** — 905-841-3730

Developers Diversified Realty Corp
3300 Enterprise Pkwy . . . . Beachwood OH 44122 — **877-225-5337** — 216-755-5500
NYSE: DDR

Entertainment Properties Trust
909 Walnut Ste 200 . . . . Kansas City MO 64106 — **888-377-7348** — 816-472-1700
NYSE: EPR

Equity Lifestyle Properties Inc
Two N Riverside Plz Ste 800 . . . . Chicago IL 60606 — **800-274-7314** — 312-279-1400
NYSE: ELS

Eugene Burger Management Corp
6600 Hunter Dr . . . . Rohnert Park CA 94928 — **800-788-0233** — 707-584-5123

Federal Realty Investment Trust
1626 E Jefferson St . . . . Rockville MD 20852 — **800-658-8980** — 301-998-8100
NYSE: FRT

General Growth Properties Inc
110 N Wacker Dr . . . . Chicago IL 60606 — **888-395-8037** — 312-960-5000
NYSE: GGP

Grady Management Inc
8630 Fenton St Ste 625 . . . . Silver Spring MD 20910 — **800-544-7239** — 301-587-3330

Gundaker Property Management
2458 Old Dorsett Rd Ste 100 . . . . Maryland Heights MO 63043 — **800-325-1978** — 314-298-5200

Health Care Property Investors Inc
1920 Main St Ste 1200 . . . . Irvine CA 92614 — **888-604-1990** — 949-407-0700

Heitman LLC
191 N Wacker Dr Ste 2500 . . . . Chicago IL 60606 — **800-225-5435** — 312-855-5700

Highwoods Properties Inc
3100 Smoketree Ct Ste 600 . . . . Raleigh NC 27604 — **866-449-6637** — 919-872-4924
NYSE: HIW

Holiday Retirement Corp
5885 Meadows Rd Ste 500 . . . . Lake Oswego OR 97035 — **800-322-0999** — 503-370-7070

Hunt Midwest Enterprises Inc
8300 NE Underground Dr . . . . Kansas City MO 64161 — **800-551-6877** — 816-455-2500

Inland Group Inc
2901 Butterfield Rd . . . . Oak Brook IL 60523 — **800-826-8228** — 630-218-8000

Inland Real Estate Corp
2901 Butterfield Rd . . . . Oak Brook IL 60523 — **888-331-4732** — 630-218-8000
NYSE: IRC

Kimco Realty Corp
3333 New Hyde Pk Rd . . . . New Hyde Park NY 11042 — **800-645-6292** — 516-869-9000
NYSE: KIM

Lexington Corporate Properties Trust
One Penn Plz Ste 4015 . . . . New York NY 10119 — **800-850-3948** — 212-692-7200

Macerich Co, The
401 Wilshire Blvd Ste 700 . . . . Santa Monica CA 90401 — **800-421-7237** — 310-394-6000
NYSE: MAC

Mack-Cali Realty Corp
343 Thornall St . . . . Edison NJ 08837 — **800-317-4445** — 732-590-1000
NYSE: CLI

Mid-Atlantic PenFed Realty Berkshire Hathaway HomeServices (PCR)
3050 Chain Bridge Rd . . . . Fairfax VA 22030 — **800-550-2364** — 703-691-7653

Miller Valentine Group
4000 Miller Valentine Ct . . . . Dayton OH 45439 — **877-684-7687** — 937-293-0900

National Realty & Development Corp
3 Manhattanville Rd . . . . Purchase NY 10577 — **800-932-7368** — 914-694-4444

Omega Healthcare Investors Inc
200 International Cir Ste 3500 . . . . Hunt Valley MD 21030 — **877-511-2891** — 410-427-1700
NYSE: OHI

One Liberty Properties Inc
60 Cutter Mill Rd Ste 303 . . . . Great Neck NY 11021 — **800-937-5449** — 516-466-3100
NYSE: OLP

Parkway Properties Inc
188 E Capitol St Ste 1000 . . . . Jackson MS 39201 — **800-748-1667** — 601-948-4091
NYSE: PKY

Pennsylvania Real Estate Investment Trust
200 S Broad St Third Fl . . . . Philadelphia PA 19102 — **866-875-0700** — 215-875-0700
NYSE: PEI

Professional Community Management Inc
23726 Birtcher Dr . . . . Lake Forest CA 92630 — **800-369-7260**

ProLogis 4545 Airport Way . . . . Denver CO 80239 — **800-566-2706** — 303-375-9292
NYSE: PLD

PS Business Parks Inc
701 Western Ave . . . . Glendale CA 91201 — **888-299-3246*** — 818-244-8080
*NYSE: PSB ▪ *Cust Svc*

Realty Income Corp
600 La Terraza Blvd . . . . Escondido CA 92025 — **877-924-6266** — 760-741-2111
NYSE: O

Regency Centers
One Independent Dr Ste 114 . . . . Jacksonville FL 32202 — **800-950-6333** — 904-598-7000
NYSE: REG

Schatten Properties Management Company Inc
1514 S St . . . . Nashville TN 37212 — **800-892-1315** — 615-329-3011

Sea Island Co
PO Box 30351 . . . . Sea Island GA 31561 — **800-732-4752** — 912-638-3611

Senior Housing Properties Trust
255 Washington St . . . . Newton MA 02458 — **866-511-5038** — 617-796-8350
NYSE: SNH

Stirling Properties
109 Northpark Blvd Ste 300 . . . . Covington LA 70433 — **888-261-2022** — 985-898-2022

Tanger Factory Outlet Centers Inc
3200 Northline Ave Ste 360 . . . . Greensboro NC 27408 — **800-720-6728** — 336-292-3010
NYSE: SKT

Taubman Centers Inc
200 E Long Lk Rd Ste 300 . . . . Bloomfield Hills MI 48303 — **800-297-6003** — 248-258-6800
NYSE: TCO

Transcontinental Realty Investors Inc
1603 Lyndon B Johnson Fwy Ste 800 . . . . Dallas TX 75234 — **800-400-6407** — 469-522-4200
NYSE: TCI

	Toll-Free	Phone
USAA Real Estate Co		
9830 Colonnade Blvd Ste 600 . . . . San Antonio TX 78230	**800-531-8182**	
Ventas Inc		
353 N Clark St Ste 3300 . . . . Chicago IL 60654	**877-483-6827**	
NYSE: VTR		
Village Green Cos		
30833 NW Hwy . . . . Farmington Hills MI 48334	**800-521-2220**	248-851-9600
Vornado Realty Trust		
888 Seventh Ave . . . . New York NY 10019	**800-294-1322**	212-894-7000
NYSE: VNO		
Washington Real Estate Investment Trust (WRIT)		
6110 Executive Blvd Ste 800 . . . . Rockville MD 20852	**800-565-9748**	301-984-9400
NYSE: WRE		
Weingarten Realty Investors		
2600 Citadel Plz Dr Ste 300 . . . . Houston TX 77008	**800-688-8865**	713-866-6000
NYSE: WRI		
Winthrop Realty Trust		
7 Bulfinch Pl Ste 500 . . . . Boston MA 02114	**800-622-6757**	617-570-4614
NYSE: FUR		
WP Carey & Company LLC		
50 Rockefeller Plz Second Fl . . . . New York NY 10020	**800-972-2739**	212-492-1100
NYSE: WPC		

652 REALTOR ASSOCIATIONS - STATE

SEE ALSO Real Estate Professionals Associations
Listed here are the state branches of the National Association of Realtors.

	Toll-Free	Phone
Alabama Assn of Realtors		
522 Washington Ave PO Box 4070 . . . . Montgomery AL 36104	**800-446-3808**	334-262-3808
Arizona Assn of Realtors		
255 E Osborne Rd Ste 200 . . . . Phoenix AZ 85012	**800-426-7274**	602-248-7787
Arkansas Realtors Assn		
11224 Executive Ctr Dr . . . . Little Rock AR 72211	**888-333-2206**	501-225-2020
Colorado Assn of Realtors		
309 Inverness Way S . . . . Englewood CO 80112	**800-944-6550**	303-790-7099
Connecticut Assn of Realtors		
111 Founders Plz Ste 1101 . . . . East Hartford CT 06108	**800-335-4862**	860-290-6601
Delaware Assn of Realtors		
134 E Water St . . . . Dover DE 19901	**800-305-4445**	302-734-4444
Georgia Assn of Realtors		
3200 Presidential Dr . . . . Atlanta GA 30340	**866-280-0576**	770-451-1831
Hawaii Assn of Realtors		
1136 12th Ave Ste 220 . . . . Honolulu HI 96816	**866-693-6767**	808-733-7060
Idaho Assn of Realtors		
10116 W Overland Rd . . . . Boise ID 83702	**800-621-7553**	208-342-3585
Indiana Assn of Realtors		
7301 N Shadeland Ave Ste A . . . . Indianapolis IN 46250	**800-284-0084**	317-842-0890
Iowa Assn of Realtors		
1370 NW 114th St Ste 100 . . . . Clive IA 50325	**800-532-1515**	515-453-1064
Kansas Assn of Realtors		
3644 SW Burlingame Rd . . . . Topeka KS 66611	**800-366-0069**	785-267-3610
Kentucky Assn of Realtors		
161 Prosperous Pl . . . . Lexington KY 40509	**800-264-2185**	859-263-7377
Maryland Assn of Realtors		
2594 Riva Rd . . . . Annapolis MD 21401	**800-638-6425**	410-841-6080
Massachusetts Assn of Realtors		
256 Second Ave . . . . Waltham MA 02451	**800-725-6272**	781-890-3700
Michigan Assn of Realtors		
720 N Washington Ave . . . . Lansing MI 48906	**800-454-7842**	517-372-8890
Minnesota Assn of Realtors		
5750 Lincoln Dr . . . . Minneapolis MN 55436	**800-862-6097**	952-935-8313
Mississippi Assn of Realtors		
4274 Lakeland Dr PO Box 321000 . . . . Jackson MS 39232	**800-747-1103**	601-932-9325
Missouri Assn of Realtors		
2601 Bernadette Pl . . . . Columbia MO 65203	**800-403-0101**	573-445-8400
Montana Assn of Realtors		
One S Montana Ave Ste M1 . . . . Helena MT 59601	**800-477-1864**	406-443-4032
Nebraska Realtors Assn		
800 S 13th St Ste 200 . . . . Lincoln NE 68508	**800-777-5231**	402-323-6500
Nevada Assn of Realtors		
760 Margrave Dr Ste 200 . . . . Reno NV 89502	**800-748-5526**	775-829-5911
New Hampshire Assn of Realtors		
115A Airport Rd . . . . Concord NH 03301	**800-335-4862**	603-225-5549
New York State Assn of Realtors		
130 Washington Ave . . . . Albany NY 12210	**800-462-7585**	518-463-0300
North Carolina Assn of Realtors Inc		
4511 Weybridge Ln . . . . Greensboro NC 27407	**800-443-9956**	336-294-1415
North Dakota Assn of Realtors		
318 W Apollo Ave . . . . Bismarck ND 58503	**800-279-2361**	701-355-1010
Oklahoma Assn of Realtors		
9807 N Broadway . . . . Oklahoma City OK 73114	**800-375-9944**	405-848-9944
Oregon Assn of Realtors		
2110 Mission St SE . . . . Salem OR 97308	**800-252-9115**	503-362-3645
Pennsylvania Assn of Realtors		
4501 Chambers Hill Rd . . . . Harrisburg PA 17111	**800-555-3390**	717-561-1303
Realtors Assn of New Mexico		
2201 Bros Rd . . . . Santa Fe NM 87505	**800-224-2282**	505-982-2442
Rhode Island Assn of Realtors		
100 Bignall St . . . . Warwick RI 02888	**866-438-8345**	401-785-9898
South Carolina Assn of Realtors		
3780 Fernandina Rd . . . . Columbia SC 29210	**800-233-6381**	803-772-5206
South Dakota Assn of Realtors		
204 N Euclid Ave . . . . Pierre SD 57501	**800-227-5877**	605-224-0554
Tennessee Assn of Realtors (TAR)		
901 19th Ave S . . . . Nashville TN 37212	**877-321-1477**	615-321-1477
Texas Assn of Realtors		
1115 San Jacinto Blvd Ste 200 . . . . Austin TX 78701	**800-873-9155**	512-480-8200
Utah Assn of Realtors		
230 W Towne Ridge Pkwy Ste 500 . . . . Sandy UT 84070	**800-594-8933**	801-676-5200
Virginia Assn of Realtors		
10231 Telegraph Rd . . . . Glen Allen VA 23059	**800-755-8271**	804-264-5033
West Virginia Assn of Realtors		
2110 Kanawha Blvd E . . . . Charleston WV 25311	**800-445-7600**	304-342-7600
Wisconsin Realtors Assn		
4801 Forest Run Rd Ste 201 . . . . Madison WI 53704	**800-279-1972**	608-241-2047

	Toll-Free	Phone
Wyoming Assn of Realtors		
951 Werner Ct Ste 300 . . . . Casper WY 82601	**800-676-4085**	307-237-4085

653 RECORDING COMPANIES

	Toll-Free	Phone
American Gramaphone LLC		
9130 Mormon Bridge Rd . . . . Omaha NE 68152	**800-348-3434**	402-457-4341
Integrity Music		
4050 Lee Vance View . . . . Colorado Springs CO 80918	**888-888-4726**	719-536-0100
Malaco Music Group Inc		
3023 W Northside Dr . . . . Jackson MS 39213	**800-272-7936***	601-982-4522
*Cust Svc		
Naxos of America Inc		
1810 Columbia Ave . . . . Franklin TN 37064	**877-629-6723**	615-771-9393
Nightingale-Conant Corp		
6245 W Howard St . . . . Niles IL 60714	**800-557-1660***	
*Cust Svc		
Rhino Records		
3400 W Olive Ave . . . . Burbank CA 91505	**800-827-4466**	800-546-3670
Righteous Babe Records		
341 Delaware Ave PO Box 95 . . . . Buffalo NY 14202	**800-664-3769**	716-852-8020
Smithsonian Folkways Recordings		
600 Maryland Ave SW Ste 200 . . . . Washington DC 20024	**800-410-9815**	202-633-6450
Soar Corp (SOAR)		
5200 Constitution Ave NE . . . . Albuquerque NM 87110	**866-616-4450**	505-268-6110

654 RECORDING MEDIA - MAGNETIC & OPTICAL

SEE ALSO Photographic Equipment & Supplies

	Toll-Free	Phone
Allied Vaughn		
7600 Parklawn Ste 300 . . . . Minneapolis MN 55435	**800-323-0281**	952-832-3100
Ampex Corp		
500 Broadway . . . . Redwood City CA 94063	**800-835-5095**	650-367-2011
Athana Inc		
1624 W 240 St . . . . Harbor City CA 90710	**800-421-1591**	310-539-7280
Cine Magnetics Inc		
100 Business Pk Dr Ste 1 . . . . Armonk NY 10504	**800-431-1102**	914-273-7500
Digital Excellence		
300 York Ave . . . . Saint Paul MN 55101	**800-608-8008**	651-772-5100
Duplication Factory Inc		
4275 Norex Dr . . . . Chaska MN 55318	**800-279-2009**	952-227-8106
Imation Corp One Imation Pl . . . . Oakdale MN 55128	**888-466-3456**	651-704-4000
NYSE: IMN		
Maxell Corp of America		
3 Garret Mountain Plaza		
3rd Fl Ste 300 . . . . Woodland Park NJ 07424	**800-533-2836**	973-653-2400
Optical Disc Solutions Inc		
1767 Sheridan St . . . . Richmond IN 47374	**888-987-6334**	765-935-7574
Peripheral Manufacturing Inc		
4775 Paris St . . . . Denver CO 80239	**800-468-6888**	303-371-8651
TDK USA Corp		
525 RXR Plaza PO Box 9302 . . . . Uniondale NY 11556	**800-285-2783***	516-535-2600
*General		
Verbatim Americas LLC		
1200 W WT Harris Blvd . . . . Charlotte NC 28262	**800-538-8589**	704-547-6500

655 RECREATION FACILITY OPERATORS

SEE ALSO Bowling Centers

	Toll-Free	Phone
Dave & Buster's Inc		
2481 Manana Dr . . . . Dallas TX 75220	**800-842-5369**	214-357-9588

656 RECYCLABLE MATERIALS RECOVERY

Included here are companies that recycle post-consumer trash, tires, appliances, batteries, etc. as well as industrial recyclers of plastics, paper, wood, glass, solvents, and so on.

	Toll-Free	Phone
American Paper Recycling Corp		
301 W Lake St . . . . Northlake IL 60164	**800-762-6790***	708-344-6789
*Cust Svc		
Appliance Recycling Centers of America Inc		
7400 Excelsior Blvd . . . . Minneapolis MN 55426	**800-452-8680**	952-930-9000
NASDAQ: ARCI		
Arrow Value Recovery		
9101 Burnet Rd Ste 203 . . . . Austin TX 78758	**800-393-7627**	
Better Management Corp (BMC)		
41738 Esterly Dr . . . . Columbiana OH 44408	**877-293-4300**	330-482-7070
Clean Earth of North Jersey Inc		
115 Jacobus Ave . . . . South Kearny NJ 07032	**877-445-3478**	973-344-4004
Federal International Inc		
7935 Clayton Rd . . . . Saint Louis MO 63117	**800-972-7277**	314-721-3377
Jupiter Aluminum Corp		
4825 Scott St . . . . Schiller Park IL 60176	**800-392-7265**	847-928-5930
Marborg Industries		
728 E Yanonali St . . . . Santa Barbara CA 93103	**800-798-1852**	805-963-1852
Mervis Industries Inc		
3295 E Main St . . . . Danville IL 61834	**800-637-3016**	217-442-5300
North Shore Recycled Fibers Inc		
53 Jefferson Ave . . . . Salem MA 01970	**800-225-2369**	978-744-4330
Pall Corp		
2200 Northern Blvd . . . . East Hills NY 11548	**800-645-6532**	516-484-5400
NYSE: PLL		
Paper Tigers, The		
2201 Waukegan Rd Ste 180 . . . . Bannockburn IL 60015	**800-621-1774**	847-919-6500
Pioneer Paper Stock		
155 Irving Ave N . . . . Minneapolis MN 55405	**800-821-8512**	612-374-2280

			Toll-Free	Phone
Utah Metal Works Inc (UMW)				
805 Everett Ave PO Box 1073	Salt Lake City UT	84116	**877-221-0099**	877-364-5679

657　RECYCLED PLASTICS PRODUCTS

SEE ALSO Flooring - Resilient

			Toll-Free	Phone
Allen Ventures Inc				
517 State Farm Rd	Deerfield WI	53531	**877-423-9800**	608-423-9800
Amazing Recycled Products Inc				
PO Box 312	Denver CO	80201	**800-241-2174**	303-699-7693
American Recycled Plastic Inc				
773 N. Union Grove Rd	Friendsville TN	37737	**866-674-1525**	865-738-3439
Bedford Technology LLC				
2424 Armour Rd PO Box 609	Worthington MN	56187	**800-721-9037**	507-372-5558
Parkland Plastics Inc				
104 Yoder Dr PO Box 339	Middlebury IN	46540	**800-835-4110**	574-825-4336
Plastic Recycling of Iowa Falls Inc				
10252 Hwy 65	Iowa Falls IA	50126	**800-338-1438**	641-648-5073
Plastiques Cascades Re-Plast				
1350 Ch Quatre-Saisons	Notre-Dame-du-Bon-Conseil QC	J0C1A0	**800-567-5813**	819-336-2440
Renew Plastics				
112 Fourth St PO Box 480	Luxemburg WI	54217	**800-666-5207**	920-845-2326
Resco Plastics Inc				
93783 Newport Ln	Coos Bay OR	97420	**800-266-5097**	541-269-5485
Witt Industries Inc				
4600 Mason-Montgomery Rd	Mason OH	45040	**800-543-7417**	

658　REFRACTORIES - CLAY

			Toll-Free	Phone
BNZ Materials Inc				
6901 S Pierce St Ste 260	Littleton CO	80128	**800-999-0890**	303-978-1199
RENO Refractories Inc				
601 Reno Dr	Morris AL	35116	**800-741-7366**	205-647-0240
RENO Refractories Inc Reftech Div				
601 Reno Dr	Morris AL	35116	**800-741-7366***	
*General				
Resco Products Inc				
Two Penn Ctr W Ste 430	Pittsburgh PA	15276	**888-283-5505**	412-494-4491
Riverside Refractories Inc				
201 Truss Ferry Rd	Pell City AL	35128	**800-924-0637**	205-338-3366
Whitacre Greer Fireproofing Inc				
1400 S Mahoning Ave	Alliance OH	44601	**800-947-2837***	330-823-1610
*Cust Svc				

659　REFRACTORIES - NONCLAY

			Toll-Free	Phone
Fedmet Resources Corp				
PO Box 278	Montreal QC	H3Z2T2	**800-609-5711**	514-931-5711
Inland Refractories Co				
38600 Chester Rd PO Box 239	Avon OH	44011	**800-321-0767**	440-934-6600
Minco Inc 510 Midway Cir	Midway TN	37809	**800-525-9753**	423-422-6051
New Castle Refractories Co Inc				
915 Industrial St	New Castle PA	16102	**888-396-3566**	724-654-7711
Ransom & Randolph Co				
3535 Briarfield Blvd	Maumee OH	43537	**800-800-7496**	419-865-9497
RENO Refractories Inc				
601 Reno Dr	Morris AL	35116	**800-741-7366**	205-647-0240
RENO Refractories Inc Reftech Div				
601 Reno Dr	Morris AL	35116	**800-741-7366***	
*General				
TYK America Inc				
301 BrickyaRd Rd	Clairton PA	15025	**800-569-9359**	412-384-4259
Wahl Refractory Solutions LLC				
767 OH-19	Fremont OH	43420	**800-837-9245**	419-334-2658

660　REFRIGERATION EQUIPMENT - MFR

SEE ALSO Air Conditioning & Heating Equipment - Commercial/Industrial

			Toll-Free	Phone
Advance Energy Technologies Inc				
One Solar Dr	Clifton Park NY	12065	**800-724-0198**	518-371-2140
American Panel Corp				
5800 SE 78th St	Ocala FL	34472	**800-327-3015**	352-245-7055
Applied Process Cooling Corp				
555 Price Ave	Redwood City CA	94063	**877-231-6406**	650-595-0665
Arctic Star Refrigeration Mfg Company Inc				
3540 W Pioneer Pkwy	Arlington TX	76013	**800-229-6562**	817-274-1396
Beverage-Air Corp				
3779 Champion Blvd	Winston-Salem NC	27105	**800-845-9800**	336-245-6400
CrownTonka Inc				
15600 37th Ave N Ste 100	Plymouth MN	55446	**800-523-7337**	763-541-1410
Custom Coolers LLC				
5609 Azle Ave	Fort Worth TX	76114	**800-627-0488**	817-626-3737
Delfield Co				
980 S Isabella Rd	Mount Pleasant MI	48858	**800-733-8821**	989-773-7981
Dole Refrigerating Co				
1420 Higgs Rd	Lewisburg TN	37091	**800-251-8990**	931-359-6211
Eliason Corp 9229 Shaver Rd	Portage MI	49024	**800-828-3655***	269-327-7003
*Cust Svc				
Federal Industries Div Standex Corp				
215 Federal Ave	Belleville WI	53508	**800-356-4206**	
FRL Furniture				
460 Grand Blvd	Westbury NY	11590	**800-529-4375**	516-333-4400
Haws Corp 1455 Kleppe Ln	Sparks NV	89431	**888-640-4297**	775-359-4712
Heatcraft Refrigeration Products				
2175 W Pk Pl Blvd	Stone Mountain GA	30087	**800-321-1881**	770-465-5600

			Toll-Free	Phone
Hill PHOENIX Inc				
1003 Sigman Rd	Conyers GA	30013	**800-518-6630**	770-285-3264
Hussmann Corp				
12999 St Charles Rock Rd	Bridgeton MO	63044	**800-592-2060**	314-291-2000
Ice-O-Matic 11100 E 45th Ave	Denver CO	80239	**800-423-3367**	303-371-3737
IMI Cornelius Inc				
101 Broadway St W	Osseo MN	55369	**800-238-3600**	763-488-8200
International Cold Storage Company Inc				
215 E 13th St	Andover KS	67002	**800-835-0001**	316-733-1385
KDIndustries 1525 E Lake Rd	Erie PA	16511	**800-840-9577**	814-453-6761
Kloppenberg & Co				
2627 W Oxford Ave	Englewood CO	80110	**800-346-3246**	303-761-1615
Kolpak 2915 Tennessee Ave N	Parsons TN	38363	**800-826-7036**	731-847-5328
Kysor Panel Systems				
4201 N Beach St	Fort Worth TX	76137	**800-633-3426**	817-281-5121
Lancer Corp				
6655 Lancer Blvd	San Antonio TX	78219	**800-729-1500**	210-310-7000
Leer LP 206 Leer St	New Lisbon WI	53950	**800-766-5337***	608-562-7100
*Cust Svc				
Manitowoc Ice				
2110 S 26th St	Manitowoc WI	54220	**800-545-5720**	920-682-0161
McCann's Engineering & Manufacturing Co				
4570 W Colorado Blvd	Los Angeles CA	90039	**800-423-2429**	818-637-7200
Micro Matic USA Inc				
10726 N Second St	Machesney Park IL	61115	**866-291-5756**	815-968-7557
MicroMetl Corp				
3035 N Shadeland Ave Ste 300	Indianapolis IN	46226	**800-662-4822**	
Nor-Lake Inc				
727 Second St PO Box 248	Hudson WI	54016	**800-388-5253**	715-386-2323
Norcold Inc 600 S Kuther Rd	Sidney OH	45365	**800-543-1219**	937-493-0033
Perlick Corp				
8300 W Good Hope Rd	Milwaukee WI	53223	**800-558-5592**	414-353-7060
Scotsman Ice Systems				
775 Corporate Woods Pkwy	Vernon Hills IL	60061	**800-726-8762***	847-215-4500
*Cust Svc				
Silver King Refrigeration Inc				
1600 Xenium Ln N	Minneapolis MN	55441	**800-328-3329**	763-923-2441
True Manufacturing Co				
2001 E Terra Ln	O'Fallon MO	63366	**800-325-6152**	636-240-2400
Turbo Refrigerating				
1000 W Ormsby Ave	Louisville KY	40210	**800-853-8648**	502-635-3000
Victory Refrigeration Inc				
110 Woodcrest Rd	Cherry Hill NJ	08003	**800-523-5008**	856-428-4200
Vogt Ice 1000 W Ormsby Ave Ste 19	Louisville KY	40210	**800-853-8648**	502-635-3000
WA Brown & Son Inc				
209 Long Meadow Dr	Salisbury NC	28147	**800-438-2316**	704-636-5131

661　REFRIGERATION EQUIPMENT - WHOL

SEE ALSO Plumbing, Heating, Air Conditioning Equipment & Supplies - Whol

			Toll-Free	Phone
Allied Supply Company Inc				
1100 E Monument Ave	Dayton OH	45402	**800-589-5690**	937-224-9833
Baker Distributing Co				
PO Box 2954 Ste 100	Jacksonville FL	32203	**800-217-4698**	
Broich Enterprises Inc				
6440 City W Pkwy	Eden Prairie MN	55344	**800-853-3508**	952-941-2270
Dennis Supply Co				
PO Box 3376	Sioux City IA	51102	**800-352-4618**	712-255-7637
Don Stevens Inc				
980 Discovery Rd	Eagan MN	55121	**800-444-2299**	651-452-0872
Ernest F Mariani Company Inc				
573 West 2890 South	Salt Lake City UT	84115	**800-453-2927**	
Gustave A Larson Co				
PO Box 910	Pewaukee WI	53072	**800-829-9609**	262-542-0200
Hart & Price Corp				
PO Box 36368	Dallas TX	75235	**800-777-9129**	214-521-9129
Insco Distributing Inc				
12501 Network Blvd	San Antonio TX	78249	**855-282-4295**	210-690-8400
ISI Commercial Refrigeration LP				
9136 Viscount Row	Dallas TX	75247	**800-777-5070**	214-631-7980
Modern Ice Equipment & Supply Co				
5709 Harrison Ave	Cincinnati OH	45248	**800-543-1581**	513-367-2101
RE Lewis Refrigeration Inc				
803 S Lincoln St PO Box 92	Creston IA	50801	**800-264-0767***	641-782-8183
*Cust Svc				
Redico Inc 1850 S Lee Ct	Buford GA	30518	**800-242-3920**	
Rogers Supply Company Inc				
PO Box 740	Champaign IL	61824	**800-252-0406**	217-356-0166
Southern Refrigeration Corp				
3140 Shenandoah Ave	Roanoke VA	24017	**800-763-4433**	540-342-3493
Stafford-Smith Inc				
3414 S Burdick St	Kalamazoo MI	49001	**800-968-2442**	269-343-1240
Supermarket Systems Inc				
6419 Bannington Rd	Charlotte NC	28226	**800-553-1905**	704-542-6000
SWH Supply Co				
242 E Main St	Louisville KY	40202	**800-321-3598**	502-589-9287
Taylor Freezer Sales Company Inc				
2032 Atlantic Ave	Chesapeake VA	23324	**800-768-6945**	
Transport Refrigeration Inc				
301 Lawrence Dr	De Pere WI	54115	**888-502-3569**	920-339-5700
United Refrigeration Inc				
11401 Roosevelt Blvd	Philadelphia PA	19154	**888-578-9100***	215-698-9100
*General				

662　RELOCATION CONSULTING SERVICES

			Toll-Free	Phone
Coldwell Banker Gundaker				
2458 Old Dorsett Rd Ste 300	Maryland Heights MO	63043	**800-325-1978**	314-298-5000
RE/MAX LLC				
5075 S Syracuse St	Denver CO	80237	**800-525-7452**	
RELO Direct Inc				
161 N Clark St Ste 1250	Chicago IL	60601	**800-621-7356**	312-384-5900

				Toll-Free	Phone
Relocation America					
25800 NW Hwy Ste 210	Southfield	MI	48075	877-500-4466	
Runzheimer International					
Runzheimer Pk	Rochester	WI	53167	800-558-1702	262-971-2200
SIRVA Inc 700 Oakmont Ln	Terrace	IL	60181	888-444-4765	630-570-8900
Windermere Relocation Inc					
5424 Sand Point Way NE	Seattle	WA	98105	866-740-9589	206-527-3801

663 REMEDIATION SERVICES

SEE ALSO Waste Management ; Environmental Organizations ; Consulting Services - Environmental

Remediation services include clean-up, restorative, and corrective work to repair or minimize environmental damage caused by lead, asbestos, mining, petroleum, chemicals, and other pollutants.

				Toll-Free	Phone
911 Restoration Enterprises Inc					
7721 Densmore Ave	Van Nuys	CA	91406	888-243-6653	
Antea Group					
5910 Rice Creek Pkwy Ste 100	Saint Paul	MN	55126	800-477-7411	651-639-9449
Carylon Corp					
2500 W Arthington St	Chicago	IL	60612	800-621-4342	312-666-7700
Chemical Waste Management Inc					
1001 Fannin St Ste 4000	Houston	TX	77002	800-633-7871	713-512-6200
Clean Harbors Inc					
42 Longwater Dr PO Box 9149	Norwell	MA	02061	800-282-0058	781-792-5000
NYSE: CLH					
Clean Venture/Cycle Chem Inc					
201 S First St	Elizabeth	NJ	07206	800-347-7672	908-355-5800
Crosby & Overton Inc					
1610 W 17th St	Long Beach	CA	90813	800-827-6729	562-432-5445
Environmental Enterprises Inc (EEI)					
10163 Cincinnati Dayton Rd	Cincinnati	OH	45241	800-722-2818	513-772-2818
MCM Management Corp					
35980 Woodward Ave Ste 210	Bloomfield Hills	MI	48304	800-843-7512	248-932-9600
Perma-Fix Environmental Services Inc					
8302 Dunwoody Pl Ste 250	Atlanta	GA	30350	800-365-6066	770-587-9898
NASDAQ: PESI					
PW Stephens Inc					
15201 Pipeline Ln Unit B	Huntington Beach	CA	92649	800-750-7733	714-892-2028
Safety-Kleen Corp					
2600 N Central Expwy Ste 400	Richardson	TX	75080	800-669-5740	800-323-5040
SEACOR Holdings Inc					
2200 Eller Dr PO Box 13038	Fort Lauderdale	FL	33316	800-516-6203	954-523-2200
NYSE: CKH					
Sevenson Environmental Services Inc					
2749 Lockport Rd	Niagara Falls	NY	14305	800-777-3836	716-284-0431
US Ecology					
300 E Mallard Dr Ste 300	Boise	ID	83706	800-590-5220	208-331-8400
NASDAQ: ECOL					
UXB International Inc					
2020 Kraft Dr Ste 2100	Blacksburg	VA	24060	800-422-4892	540-443-3700
WRR Environmental Services					
5200 Ryder Rd	Eau Claire	WI	54701	800-727-8760	715-834-9624

664 RESEARCH CENTERS & INSTITUTIONS

SEE ALSO Testing Facilities ; Market Research Firms ; Public Policy Research Centers

				Toll-Free	Phone
ADA Technologies Inc					
8100 Shaffer Pkwy Ste 130	Littleton	CO	80127	800-232-0296	303-792-5615
Advanced Cell Diagnostics Inc					
3960 Point Eden Way	Hayward	CA	94545	877-576-3636	510-576-8800
Advion BioSciences Inc					
19 Brown Rd	Ithaca	NY	14850	877-523-8466	607-266-0665
Air Force Research Laboratory (AFRL)					
AFRL/PA					
1864 Fourth St Bldg 15 Rm 225	Wright-Patterson AFB	OH	45433	800-222-0336	
Albany International Research Co					
216 Airport Dr	Rochester	NH	03867	888-797-6735	603-330-5850
American Institute for Cancer Research					
1759 R St NW	Washington	DC	20009	800-843-8114	202-328-7744
American Institutes for Research					
1000 Thomas Jefferson St NW	Washington	DC	20007	877-334-3499	202-403-5000
American Type Culture Collection (ATCC)					
10801 University Blvd PO Box 1549	Manassas	VA	20108	800-638-6597*	703-365-2700
*Cust Svc					
Aptima Inc					
12 Gill St Ste 1400	Woburn	MA	01801	866-461-7298	781-935-3966
Barbara Ann Karmanos Cancer Institute					
4100 John R St	Detroit	MI	48201	800-527-6266	
Battelle Memorial Institute Inc					
505 King Ave	Columbus	OH	43201	800-201-2011	614-424-6424
Berkeley Sensor & Actuator Ctr (BSAC)					
University of California					
497 Cory Hall MC Ste 1774	Berkeley	CA	94720	800-549-1002	510-643-6690
BioLegend Inc					
11080 Roselle St	San Diego	CA	92121	877-246-5343	858-455-9588
bioLytical Laboratories Inc					
1108 - 13351 Commerce Pkwy	Richmond	BC	V6V2X7	866-674-6784	604-204-6784
Biomerix Corp					
47757 Fremont Blvd	Fremont	CA	94538	888-308-3620	510-933-3450
California Pacific Medical Ctr Research Institute					
475 Brannan St Ste 220	San Francisco	CA	94107	855-354-2778	415-600-1600
Center for Automation Research					
University of Maryland					
AV Williams Bldg 115 Rm 4413	College Park	MD	20742	800-868-0094	301-405-4526
Center for Grain & Animal Health Research					
1515 College Ave	Manhattan	KS	66502	800-627-0388	
Center for Research in Mathematics & Science Education					
San Diego State University					
6475 Alvarado Rd Ste 206	San Diego	CA	92120	800-573-8804	619-594-5090
Center for Space Plasma & Aeronomic Research					
University of Alabama Huntsville	Huntsville	AL	35899	800-824-2255	256-961-7403
Center on Education & Training for Employment					
Ohio State University 1900 Kenny Rd	Columbus	OH	43210	800-848-4815	614-292-6869
Center on Human Development & Disability					
University of Washington 1701 NE Columbia Rd					
PO Box 357920	Seattle	WA	98195	800-636-1089	206-543-2832
National Center for Environmental Health					
4770 Buford Hwy Bldg 101	Atlanta	GA	30341	800-232-4636	404-639-3311
National Institute for Occupational Safety & Health					
200 Independence Ave SW	Washington	DC	20201	800-356-4674	404-639-3286
Charles River Laboratories Inc					
251 Ballardvale St	Wilmington	MA	01887	800-522-7287	781-222-6000
NYSE: CRL					
Children's Research Institute					
Children's National Medical Ctr					
111 Michigan Ave NW Research Fl 5	Washington	DC	20010	888-884-2327	
Cincinnati Children's Hospital Research Foundation					
3333 Burnet Ave	Cincinnati	OH	45229	800-344-2462	513-636-4200
CNA Corp					
4825 Mark Ctr Dr	Alexandria	VA	22311	800-344-0007	703-824-2000
Columbia Environmental Research Ctr (CERC)					
4200 New Haven Rd	Columbia	MO	65201	888-283-7626	573-875-5399
Coriell Institute for Medical Research					
403 Haddon Ave	Camden	NJ	08103	800-752-3805	856-966-7377
CureSearch for Children's Cancer					
4600 East-West Hwy Ste 600	Bethesda	MD	20814	800-458-6223	301-718-0047
Dana-Farber Cancer Institute					
44 Binney St	Boston	MA	02115	866-408-3324	617-632-3000
Data Storage Systems Ctr (DSSC)					
Carnegie Mellon University ECE Dept					
5000 Forbes Ave	Pittsburgh	PA	15213	800-864-8287	412-268-6600
Digital Monitoring Products Inc					
2500 N Partnership Blvd	Springfield	MO	65803	800-641-4282	417-831-9362
Digitec Inc					
2731 Van Dorn Rd	Milford	NE	68405	888-761-3382	402-761-3382
Dycor Technologies Ltd					
1851 94 St	Edmonton	AB	T6N1E6	800-663-9267	780-486-0091
Edison Biotechnology Institute					
Ohio University					
Konneker Research Laboratories The Ridges	Athens	OH	45701	800-444-2420	740-593-4713
Eikos Inc 2 Master Dr	Franklin	MA	02038	888-345-6712	508-528-0300
Environmental Management Inc					
5200 NE Hwy 33	Guthrie	OK	73044	800-510-8510	405-282-8510
EPIEN Medical Inc					
4225 White Bear Pkwy Ste 600	St Paul	MN	55110	888-884-4675	651-653-3380
Epitomics Inc					
863 Mitten Rd Ste 103	Burlingame	CA	94010	888-772-2226	650-583-6688
Exponent Inc					
149 Commonwealth Dr	Menlo Park	CA	94025	888-656-3976	650-326-9400
NASDAQ: EXPO					
Aviation Research Div					
800 Independence Ave SW Rm 528A	Washington	DC	20591	866-835-5322	202-267-9251
Florida Solar Energy Ctr					
1679 Clearlake Rd	Cocoa	FL	32922	877-777-4778	321-638-1000
Food & Drug Administration					
National Center for Toxicological Research					
3900 N Ctr Rd	Jefferson	AR	72079	800-638-3321	870-543-7000
Fox Chase Cancer Ctr					
333 Cottman Ave	Philadelphia	PA	19111	888-369-2427	215-728-6900
Friends Research Institute Inc					
1040 Pk Ave Ste 103	Baltimore	MD	21201	800-822-3677	410-823-5116
Gatorade Sports Science Institute					
617 W Main St	Barrington	IL	60010	800-616-4774	
Genemed Biotechnologies Inc					
458 Carlton Ct S San Francisco	San Fransisco	CA	94080	877-436-3633	650-952-0110
General Atomics					
3550 General Atomics Ct					
PO Box 85608	San Diego	CA	92121	800-669-6820	858-455-3000
Glen Research Corp					
22825 Davis Dr	Sterling	VA	20164	800-327-4536	703-437-6191
Goddard Institute for Space Studies					
2880 Broadway	New York	NY	10025	888-661-1620	212-678-5510
H Lee Moffitt Cancer Ctr & Research Institute					
University of S Florida					
12902 Magnolia Dr	Tampa	FL	33612	800-456-3434	888-663-3488
High Performance Computing Collaboratory					
PO Box 9627	Mississippi State	MS	39762	800-521-4041	662-325-8278
Idaho National Laboratory (INL)					
2525 Fremont Ave PO Box 1625	Idaho Falls	ID	83415	866-495-7440	
Institute for Astronomy					
University of Hawaii					
2680 Woodlawn Dr	Honolulu	HI	96822	800-351-1330	808-956-8312
Institute for Research on Poverty					
University of Wisconsin Madison 1180 Observatory Dr					
3412 William H Sewell Social Sciences Bldg	Madison	WI	53706	866-301-1753	608-262-6358
Institute for Systems Research					
University of Maryland					
2173 AV Williams Bldg	College Park	MD	20742	866-675-8967	301-405-6615
Institute of Gerontology					
University of Michigan					
300 N Ingalls St	Ann Arbor	MI	48109	877-865-2167	734-936-2107
Institute of Materials Science					
University of Connecticut					
97 N Eagleville Rd	Storrs	CT	06269	800-528-7411	860-486-4623
Intelligent Mechatronic Systems Inc					
435 King St N	Waterloo	ON	N2J2Z5	866-818-6637	519-745-8887
John F. Kennedy					
Space Ctr	Kennedy Space Center	FL	32899	866-737-5235	321-867-5000
KemPharm Inc					
2656Crosspark Rd Ste 100	Coralville	IA	52241	877-695-3638	319-665-2575
Kendle International Inc					
441 Vine St 1200 Carew Twr	Cincinnati	OH	45202	800-733-1572	513-381-5550
Learning Research & Development Ctr (LRDC)					
University of Pittsburgh					
3939 O'Hara St	Pittsburgh	PA	15260	800-397-0071	412-624-7020
Lerner Research Institute					
9500 Euclid Ave	Cleveland	OH	44195	800-223-2273	216-444-3900

				Toll-Free	Phone

LIMRA International Inc
300 Day Hill Rd .... Windsor CT 06095 **866-540-4505** 860-688-3358

Lincoln Laboratory
Massachusetts Institute of Technology
244 Wood St. .... Lexington MA 02420 **800-445-8667** 781-981-5500

Lineagen Inc
423 Wakara Way Ste 200 .... Salt Lake City UT 84108 **888-888-6736** 801-931-6200

Los Alamos National Laboratory (LANL)
PO Box 1663 .... Los Alamos NM 87545 **877-723-4101** 505-667-7000

Los Angeles Biomedical Research Institute
1124 W Carson St .... Torrance CA 90502 **877-452-2674**

Mailman Research Ctr
McLean Hospital 115 Mill St .... Belmont MA 02478 **800-333-0338** 617-855-2000

Marine Biological Laboratory (MBL)
7 MBL St .... Woods Hole MA 02543 **800-222-1222** 508-548-3705

Market Probe Inc
2655 N Mayfair Rd .... Milwaukee WI 53226 **800-282-1376** 414-778-6000

Martec Group Inc, The
105 W Adams St Ste 2125 .... Chicago IL 60603 **888-811-5755** 312-606-9690

Massa Products Corp
280 Lincoln St .... Hingham MA 02043 **800-962-7543** 781-749-4800

Massey Cancer Ctr
Virginia Commonwealth University
401 College St PO Box 980037 .... Richmond VA 23298 **877-462-7739** 804-828-0450

Mechanical Technology Inc
431 New Karner Rd .... Albany NY 12205 **800-937-5449** 518-533-2200
NASDAQ: MKTY

Memorial Sloan-Kettering Cancer Ctr
1275 York Ave .... New York NY 10065 **800-525-2225** 212-639-2000

Miami Project to Cure Paralysis
1095 NW 14th Terr Lois Pope LIFE Ctr .... Miami FL 33136 **800-782-6387*** 305-243-6001
*General

Michigan Mfg Technology Ctr
47911 Halyard Dr .... Plymouth MI 48170 **888-414-6682**

Monell Chemical Senses Ctr
3500 Market St .... Philadelphia PA 19104 **800-732-0999** 267-519-4700

MSU-DOE Plant Research Laboratory
Michigan State University
106 Plant Biology .... East Lansing MI 48824 **800-875-5090** 517-353-2270

NAHB Research Ctr
400 Prince Georges Blvd .... Upper Marlboro MD 20774 **800-638-8556** 301-249-4000

Nanotechnology Research Ctr
Georgia Institute of Technology
791 Atlantic Dr .... Atlanta GA 30332 **800-424-9300** 404-894-5100

National Biodynamics Laboratory (NBDL)
University of New Orleans College of Engineering
2000 Lakeshore Dr .... New Orleans LA 70148 **888-514-4275**

National Bureau of Economic Research
1050 Massachusetts Ave .... Cambridge MA 02138 **800-621-8476** 617-868-3900

National Ctr for Genome Resources
2935 Rodeo Pk Dr E .... Santa Fe NM 87505 **800-450-4854** 505-995-4451

National Ctr for Mfg Sciences (NCMS)
3025 Boardwalk .... Ann Arbor MI 48108 **800-222-6267** 734-995-0300

National Energy Research Scientific Computing Ctr (NERSC)
Lawrence Berkeley National Laboratory
.... Berkeley CA 94720 **800-666-3772** 510-486-5849

National Energy Technology Laboratory (NETL)
3610 Collins Ferry Rd .... Morgantown WV 26505 **800-432-8330** 304-285-4764

National Hansen's Disease Program (NHDP)
1770 Physicians Pk Dr .... Baton Rouge LA 70816 **800-642-2477** 225-756-3700

National Homeland Security Research Ctr
US Environmental Protection Agency
26 W Martin Luther King Dr .... Cincinnati OH 45268 **888-372-7341** 513-569-7907

National Institute of Standards & Technology (NIST)
100 Bureau Dr Sp 1070 .... Gaithersburg MD 20899 **800-877-8339** 301-975-6478

National Institutes of Health
National Cancer Institute
Public Inquiries Office 6116 Executive Blvd
Rm 3036A .... Bethesda MD 20892 **800-422-6237** 301-435-3848
National Institute of Mental Health
6001 Executive Blvd Rm 8184 MSC 9663 .... Bethesda MD 20892 **866-615-6464** 301-443-4513
National Institute of Neurological Disorders & Stroke
PO Box 5801 .... Bethesda MD 20824 **800-352-9424** 301-496-5751
National Institute on Deafness & Other Communication Disorders
31 Ctr Dr Bldg 31 Rm 3C35 .... Bethesda MD 20892 **800-241-1044** 301-496-7243

National Optical Astronomy Observatories
950 N Cherry Ave .... Tucson AZ 85719 **888-809-4012** 520-318-8163

National Research Ctr for Coal & Energy (NRCCE)
West Virginia University
385 Evansdale Dr PO Box 6064 .... Morgantown WV 26506 **800-624-8301** 304-293-2867

National Technical Information Service (NTIS)
5285 Port Royal Rd .... Springfield VA 22161 **800-553-6847*** 703-605-6000
*Orders

National Undersea Research Ctr for Hawaii & the Western Pacific
University of Hawaii at Manoa .... Honolulu HI 96822 **888-800-0460** 808-956-6335

National Undersea Research Ctr for the Mid-Atlantic Bight
Institute of Marine & Coastal Sciences
Rutgers University 71 Dudley Rd .... New Brunswick NJ 08901 **888-776-6537** 732-932-6555

National Wildlife Health Ctr
6006 Schroeder Rd .... Madison WI 53711 **800-232-4636** 608-270-2400

Natural Resources Research Institute (NRRI)
University of Minnesota Duluth
5013 Miller Trunk Hwy .... Duluth MN 55811 **800-234-0054** 218-720-4294

Naval Surface Warfare Ctr
Dahlgren Div
6149 Welsh Rd Ste 203 .... Dahlgren VA 22448 **877-845-5656**

North American Science Assoc Inc
6750 Wales Rd .... Northwood OH 43619 **866-666-9455** 419-666-9455

Northern Power Systems Inc
29 Pitman Rd .... Barre VT 05641 **877-906-6784** 802-461-2955

Ohio State University Police, The
1680 Madison Ave .... Wooster OH 44691 **800-358-4678** 330-287-0111

Oklahoma Medical Research Foundation (OMRF)
825 NE 13th St .... Oklahoma City OK 73104 **800-522-0211** 405-271-6673

Pacific Disaster Ctr
1305 N Holopono St Ste 2 .... Kihei HI 96753 **888-808-6688** 808-891-0525

Pacific Northwest National Laboratory (PNNL)
902 Battelle Blvd PO Box 999 .... Richland WA 99352 **888-375-7665** 509-375-2121

PAREXEL International Corp
195 W St .... Waltham MA 02451 **800-301-5033** 781-487-9900
NASDAQ: PRXL

Parks Assoc Inc
5310 Harvest Hill Rd Ste 235
PO Box 162 .... Dallas TX 75230 **800-727-5711** 972-490-1113

Peryam & Kroll Research Corp
6323 N Avondale Ave .... Chicago IL 60631 **800-747-5522** 800-281-3155

Phantom Laboratory Inc, The
2727 SR- 29 .... Greenwich NY 12834 **800-525-1190** 518-692-1190

Pittsburgh Supercomputing Ctr
300 S Craig St .... Pittsburgh PA 15213 **800-221-1641** 412-268-4960

Pleora Technologies Inc
340 Terry Fox Dr Suite 300 .... Kanata ON K2K3A2 **888-687-6877** 613-270-0625

Princeton Plasma Physics Laboratory (PPPL)
James Forrestal Campus Princeton University
PO Box 451 .... Princeton NJ 08543 **800-772-2222** 609-243-2750

Providence Health & Services (JWCI)
2200 Santa Monica Blvd .... Santa Monica CA 90404 **800-262-6259** 310-582-7450

Quintiles Transnational Corp
4820 Emperor Blvd .... Durham NC 27703 **866-267-4479** 919-998-2000

Radiant Research Inc
11500 Northlake Dr Ste 320 .... Cincinnati OH 45249 **866-232-8484** 513-247-5500

Research Triangle Institute
3040 Cornwallis Rd
PO Box 12194 .... Research Triangle Park NC 27709 **800-334-8571** 919-541-6000

Ricerca Biosciences LLC
7528 Auburn Rd PO Box 1000 .... Concord OH 44077 **888-742-3722** 440-357-3300

Robotics Institute
Carnegie Mellon University
5000 Forbes Ave .... Pittsburgh PA 15213 **800-767-8483** 412-268-3818

Roswell Park Cancer Institute
Elm and Carlton St .... Buffalo NY 14263 **877-275-7724** 716-845-2300

Roy J Carver Biotechnology Ctr
1206 W Gregory .... Urbana IL 61801 **800-550-3033** 217-333-1695

Salk Institute for Biological Studies
PO Box 85800 .... San Diego CA 92186 **800-245-9757** 858-453-4100

Sandelman & Assoc Inc
257 La Paloma Ste 1 .... San Clemente CA 92672 **888-897-7881** 949-388-5600

SERVE
5900 Summit Ave Ste 201 .... Browns Summit NC 27214 **800-755-3277** 336-315-7400

Siteman Cancer Ctr
4921 Parkview Pl .... Saint Louis MO 63110 **800-600-3606** 314-362-5196

Social & Economic Sciences Research Ctr (SESRC)
Washington State University
Wilson Hall Rm 133 PO Box 644014 .... Pullman WA 99164 **800-932-5393** 509-335-1511

Software Engineering Institute (SEI)
4500 Fifth Ave .... Pittsburgh PA 15213 **888-201-4479** 412-268-5800

Software Engineering Services Corp
1311 Ft Crook Rd S .... Bellevue NE 68005 **800-244-1278** 402-292-8660

Southern Research Institute
2000 Ninth Ave S .... Birmingham AL 35205 **800-967-6774** 205-581-2000

Space Dynamics Laboratory
1695 N Research Pkwy .... North Logan UT 84341 **866-487-2365** 435-797-4600

Space Science & Engineering Ctr
University of Wisconsin
1225 W Dayton St. .... Madison WI 53706 **866-391-1753** 608-262-0544

Stanford Cancer Ctr
875 Lake Blake Wilbur Dr .... Stanford CA 94305 **800-422-6237** 650-498-6000

Synergy Co of Utah LLC, The
2279 S Resource Blvd .... Moab UT 84532 **800-723-0277**

Syracuse Research Corp (SRC)
7502 Round Pond Rd .... North Syracuse NY 13212 **800-724-0451** 315-452-8000

Technology Service Corp
962 Wayne Ave Ste 800 .... Silver Spring MD 20910 **800-324-7700** 301-565-2970

Transportation Research Ctr Inc (TRC Inc)
10820 State Rt 347 PO Box B-67 .... East Liberty OH 43319 **800-837-7872** 937-666-2011

Trex Enterprises Corp
10455 Pacific Ctr Ct .... San Diego CA 92121 **800-626-5885** 858-646-5300

UAB Comprehensive Cancer Ctr
University of Alabama at Birmingham
1824 Sixth Ave S .... Birmingham AL 35294 **800-294-7780** 205-934-4011

UNC Neuroscience Ctr
University of N Carolina
115 Mason Farm Rd CB 7250 .... Chapel Hill NC 27599 **800-862-4938** 919-843-8536

University of Maryland Ctr for Environmental Science (UMCES)
2020 Horn Pt Rd .... Cambridge MD 21613 **866-842-2520** 410-228-9250

US Army Aeromedical Research Laboratory
MCMR-UAC Bldg 6901 .... Fort Rucker AL 36362 **888-386-7635** 334-255-6920

US Army Engineer Research & Development Ctr (ERDC)
3909 Halls Ferry Rd .... Vicksburg MS 39180 **800-522-6937** 601-634-3188

Vanderbilt Kennedy Ctr for Research on Human Development
21st Ave S .... Nashville TN 37203 **800-772-1213** 615-322-8240

Waisman Ctr
University of Wisconsin
1500 Highland Ave .... Madison WI 53705 **888-428-8476** 608-263-5940

WestEd
730 Harrison St Fifth Fl .... San Francisco CA 94107 **877-493-7833** 415-565-3000

Wisconsin National Primate Research Ctr
1220 Capitol Ct .... Madison WI 53715 **800-833-7050** 608-263-3500

Wistar Institute
3601 Spruce St .... Philadelphia PA 19104 **800-724-6633** 215-898-3700

665   RESORTS & RESORT COMPANIES

SEE ALSO Spas - Hotel & Resort ; Hotels - Conference Center ; Hotels & Hotel Companies ; Casinos ; Dude Ranches

Alabama

				Toll-Free	Phone

Joe Wheeler Resort Lodge & Convention Ctr
4401 McLean Dr .... Rogersville AL 35652 **800-544-5639** 256-247-5461

Perdido Beach Resort
27200 Perdido Beach Blvd .... Orange Beach AL 36561 **800-634-8001** 251-981-9811

Alaska

	City	State	ZIP	Toll-Free	Phone
Alyeska Prince Hotel & Resort 1000 Arlberg Ave PO Box 249	Girdwood	AK	99587	**800-880-3880**	907-754-1111

Alberta

	City	State	ZIP	Toll-Free	Phone
Fairmont Banff Springs PO Box 960	Banff	AB	T1L1J4	**800-441-1414**	403-762-2211
Fairmont Chateau Lake Louise 111 Lk Louise Dr	Lake Louise	AB	T0L1E0	**800-441-1414**	403-522-3511
Rimrock Resort Hotel, The 300 Mountain Ave PO Box 1110	Banff	AB	T1L1J2	**888-746-7625**	403-762-3356
Waterton Lakes Lodge Resort 101 Clematis Ave PO Box 4	Waterton Park	AB	T0K2M0	**888-985-6343**	403-859-2150

Arizona

	City	State	ZIP	Toll-Free	Phone
Arizona Biltmore Resort & Spa 2400 E Missouri	Phoenix	AZ	85016	**800-950-0086**	602-955-6600
Arizona Golf Resort & Conference Ctr 425 S Power Rd	Mesa	AZ	85206	**800-528-8282**	480-832-3202
Arizona Grand Resort 8000 S Arizona Grand Pkwy	Phoenix	AZ	85044	**866-267-1321**	602-438-9000
Boulders Resort & Golden Door Spa 34631 N Tom Darlington Dr PO Box 2090	Carefree	AZ	85377	**888-579-2631**	480-488-9009
Camelback Inn JW Marriott Resort Golf Club & Spa 5402 E Lincoln Dr	Scottsdale	AZ	85253	**800-242-2635**	480-948-1700
Canyon Ranch Tucson 8600 E Rockcliff Rd	Tucson	AZ	85750	**800-742-9000**	520-749-9000
Chaparral Suites Resort & Conference Ctr 5001 N Scottsdale Rd	Scottsdale	AZ	85250	**866-534-1797**	480-949-1414
CopperWynd Resort & Club 13225 N Eagle Ridge Dr	Fountain Hills	AZ	85268	**877-707-7760**	480-333-1900
Doubletree Paradise Valley Resort 5401 N Scottsdale Rd	Scottsdale	AZ	85250	**800-222-8733**	480-947-5400
Enchantment Resort 525 Boynton Canyon Rd	Sedona	AZ	86336	**800-826-4180**	
Esplendor Resort at Rio Rico 1069 Camino Caralampi	Rio Rico	AZ	85648	**800-288-4746**	520-281-1901
Fairmont Scottsdale Princess 7575 E Princess Dr	Scottsdale	AZ	85255	**800-257-7544**	480-585-4848
FireSky Resort & Spa 4925 N Scottsdale Rd	Scottsdale	AZ	85251	**800-528-7867**	480-945-7666
Four Seasons Resort Scottsdale at Troon North 10600 E Crescent Moon Dr	Scottsdale	AZ	85262	**800-332-3442**	480-515-5700
Francisco Grande Hotel & Golf Resort 26000 Gila Bend Hwy *General	Casa Grande	AZ	85222	**800-237-4238***	520-836-6444
Gold Canyon Golf Resort 6100 S Kings Ranch Rd	Gold Canyon	AZ	85118	**800-624-6445**	480-982-9090
Hacienda del Sol Guest Ranch Resort 5501 N Hacienda Del Sol Rd	Tucson	AZ	85718	**800-728-6514**	520-299-1501
Harrah's Ak-Chin Casino Resort 15406 Maricopa Rd *General	Maricopa	AZ	85139	**800-427-7247***	480-802-5000
Hilton Sedona Resort & Spa 90 Ridge Trl Dr *General	Sedona	AZ	86351	**877-273-3762***	928-284-4040
JW Marriott Desert Ridge Resort & Spa 5350 E Marriott Dr	Phoenix	AZ	85054	**800-845-5279**	480-293-5000
Lake Powell Resorts & Marinas 100 Lakeshore Dr	Page	AZ	86040	**800-622-6317**	888-896-3829
Legacy Golf Resort 6808 S 32nd St	Phoenix	AZ	85042	**888-828-3673**	602-305-5500
Lodge at Ventana Canyon - A Wyndham Luxury Resort 6200 N Clubhouse Ln	Tucson	AZ	85750	**800-828-5701**	520-577-1400
Loews Ventana Canyon Resort 7000 N Resort Dr	Tucson	AZ	85750	**800-234-5117**	520-299-2020
Los Abrigados Resort 160 Portal Ln	Sedona	AZ	86336	**877-374-2582**	928-282-1777
Millennium Resort Scottsdale McCormick Ranch 7401 N Scottsdale Rd	Scottsdale	AZ	85253	**800-243-1332**	716-681-2400
Orange Tree Golf & Conference Resort 10601 N 56th St	Scottsdale	AZ	85254	**866-729-7159**	480-948-6100
Phoenician, The 6000 E Camelback Rd	Scottsdale	AZ	85251	**800-888-8234**	480-941-8200
Pointe Hilton at Squaw Peak Resort 7677 N 16th St	Phoenix	AZ	85020	**800-685-0550**	602-997-2626
Pointe Hilton Resort at Tapatio Cliffs 11111 N Seventh St	Phoenix	AZ	85020	**800-947-9784**	602-866-7500
Rancho de los Caballeros 1551 S Vulture Mine Rd	Wickenburg	AZ	85390	**800-684-5030**	928-684-5484
Ritz-Carlton Phoenix 2401 E Camelback Rd	Phoenix	AZ	85016	**800-241-3333**	602-468-0700
Royal Palms Resort & Spa 5200 E Camelback Rd	Phoenix	AZ	85018	**800-672-6011**	602-840-3610
Sanctuary on Camelback Mountain 5700 E McDonald Dr	Paradise Valley	AZ	85253	**800-245-2051**	480-948-2100
Scottsdale Camelback Resort 6302 E Camelback Rd	Scottsdale	AZ	85251	**800-891-8585**	480-947-3300
Scottsdale Plaza Resort 7200 N Scottsdale Rd	Scottsdale	AZ	85253	**800-832-2025**	480-948-5000
Sheraton Wild Horse Pass Resort & Spa 5594 W Wild Horse Pass Blvd	Chandler	AZ	85226	**800-325-3535**	602-225-0100
Tanque Verde Guest Ranch 14301 E Speedway Blvd	Tucson	AZ	85748	**800-234-3833**	520-296-6275
Westward Look Resort 245 E Ina Rd	Tucson	AZ	85704	**800-722-2500**	520-297-1151
Wigwam Golf Resort & Spa 300 E Wigwam Blvd	Litchfield Park	AZ	85340	**800-327-0396**	623-935-3811

Arkansas

	City	State	ZIP	Toll-Free	Phone
Arlington Resort Hotel & Spa 239 Central Ave	Hot Springs	AR	71901	**800-643-1502**	501-623-7771
Best Western Inn of the Ozarks 207 W Van Buren	Eureka Springs	AR	72632	**800-552-3785**	479-253-9768

British Columbia

	City	State	ZIP	Toll-Free	Phone
Delta Victoria Ocean Pointe Resort & Spa 45 Songhees Rd	Victoria	BC	V9A6T3	**800-667-4677**	250-360-2999
Delta Whistler Village Suites 4308 Main St	Whistler	BC	V0N1B4	**888-299-3987**	604-905-3987
Fairmont Chateau Whistler 4599 Chateau Blvd	Whistler	BC	V0N1B4	**800-441-1414**	604-938-8000
Harrison Hot Springs Resort & Spa 100 Esplanade Ave	Harrison Hot Springs	BC	V0M1K0	**800-663-2266**	604-796-2244
Hilton Whistler Resort & Spa 4050 Whistler Way	Whistler	BC	V0N1B4	**800-515-4050**	604-932-1982
Holiday Trails Resorts (Western) Inc 53730 Bridal Falls Rd	Rosedale	BC	V0X1X1	**800-663-2265**	604-794-7876
Pan Pacific Whistler Mountainside 4320 Sundial Crescent	Whistler	BC	V0N1B4	**888-905-9995**	604-905-2999
River Rock Casino Resort 8811 River Rd	Richmond	BC	V6X3P8	**866-748-3718**	604-247-8900
Tantalus Resort Lodge 4200 Whistler Way	Whistler	BC	V0N1B4	**888-633-4046**	604-932-4146
Whistler Blackcomb Mountain Ski Resort 4545 Blackcomb Way	Whistler	BC	V0N1B4	**800-766-0449**	604-932-3434

California

	City	State	ZIP	Toll-Free	Phone
Alisal Guest Ranch & Resort 1054 Alisal Rd	Solvang	CA	93463	**800-425-4725**	805-688-6411
Alpine Meadows Ski Resort 2600 Alpine Meadows Rd	Tahoe City	CA	96145	**800-403-0206**	
Bacara Resort & Spa 8301 Hollister Ave	Santa Barbara	CA	93117	**855-968-0100**	805-968-0100
Bahia Resort Hotel 998 W Mission Bay Dr	San Diego	CA	92109	**800-576-4229**	858-488-0551
Barona Resort & Casino 1932 Wildcat Canyon Rd	Lakeside	CA	92040	**888-722-7662**	619-443-2300
Calistoga Ranch 580 Lommel Rd	Calistoga	CA	94515	**800-942-4220**	707-254-2800
Carmel Valley Ranch Resort One Old Ranch Rd	Carmel	CA	93923	**866-405-5037**	831-625-9500
Casa Palmero 1518 Cypress Dr	Pebble Beach	CA	93953	**800-654-9300**	831-622-6650
Chaminade One Chaminade Ln	Santa Cruz	CA	95065	**800-283-6569**	831-475-5600
Claremont Resort & Spa 41 Tunnel Rd	Berkeley	CA	94705	**800-551-7266**	510-843-3000
Costanoa Coastal Lodge & Camp 2001 Rossi Rd	Pescadero	CA	94060	**877-262-7848**	650-879-1100
Desert Hot Springs Spa Hotel 10805 Palm Dr	Desert Hot Springs	CA	92240	**800-808-7727**	760-329-6000
Desert Springs Marriott Resort & Spa 74855 Country Club Dr	Palm Desert	CA	92260	**888-538-9459**	760-341-2211
Doral Desert Princess Palm Springs Resort 67967 Vista Chino	Cathedral City	CA	92234	**800-433-0431**	760-322-7000
Estancia La Jolla Hotel & Spa 9700 N Torrey Pines Rd	La Jolla	CA	92037	**866-437-8262**	858-550-1000
Fairmont Sonoma Mission Inn & Spa, The PO Box 1447	Sonoma	CA	95476	**866-540-4499**	707-938-9000
Fess Parker's Doubletree Resort (FPDTR) 633 E Cabrillo Blvd	Santa Barbara	CA	93103	**800-879-2929**	805-564-4333
Flamingo Resort Hotel & Conference Ctr 2777 Fourth St	Santa Rosa	CA	95405	**800-848-8300**	707-545-8530
Four Seasons Resort Santa Barbara 1260 Ch Dr	Santa Barbara	CA	93108	**800-819-5053**	805-969-2261
Furnace Creek Inn & Ranch Resort Hwy 190 PO Box 187	Death Valley	CA	92328	**800-236-7916**	760-786-2345
Grand Pacific Palisades Resort & Hotel 5805 Armada Dr	Carlsbad	CA	92008	**800-725-4723**	760-827-3200
Greenhorn Creek Resort 711 McCauley Ranch Rd	Angels Camp	CA	95222	**888-736-5900**	209-729-8111
Handlery Hotel & Resort 950 Hotel Cir N	San Diego	CA	92108	**800-676-6567**	619-298-0511
Harrah's Rincon Casino & Resort 777 Harrah's Rincon Way	Valley Center	CA	92082	**800-522-4700**	760-751-3100
Hilton San Diego Resort 1775 E Mission Bay Dr	San Diego	CA	92109	**800-445-8667**	619-276-4010
Hotel Del Coronado 1500 Orange Ave	Coronado	CA	92118	**800-468-3533**	619-435-6611
Indian Springs Resort & Spa 1712 Lincoln Ave	Calistoga	CA	94515	**800-877-3623**	707-942-4913
Indian Wells Resort Hotel 76-661 Hwy 111	Indian Wells	CA	92210	**800-248-3220**	760-345-6466
Inn at Rancho Santa Fe 5951 Linea Del Cielo PO Box 869	Rancho Santa Fe	CA	92067	**800-843-4661**	858-756-1131
Inn at Spanish Bay, The 2700 17-Mile Dr	Pebble Beach	CA	93953	**800-654-9300**	831-647-7500
Knott's Berry Farm Resort 7675 Crescent Ave	Buena Park	CA	90620	**866-752-2444**	714-995-1111
L'Auberge Del Mar 1540 Camino del Mar PO Box 2880	Del Mar	CA	92014	**800-245-9757**	858-259-1515
La Costa Resort & Spa 2100 Costa del Mar Rd	Carlsbad	CA	92009	**800-854-5000**	760-438-9111
La Jolla Beach & Tennis Club 2000 Spindrift Dr	La Jolla	CA	92037	**888-828-0948**	858-454-7126
La Quinta Resort & Club 49-499 Eisenhower Dr	La Quinta	CA	92253	**800-598-3828**	760-564-4111

	City	State	Zip	Toll-Free	Phone
Laguna Cliffs Marriott Resort 25135 Pk Lantern	Dana Point	CA	92629	800-545-7483	949-661-5000
Lake Arrowhead Resort & Spa 27984 Hwy 189	Lake Arrowhead	CA	92352	800-800-6792	909-336-1511
Lakeland Village Beach & Mountain Resort 3535 Lake Tahoe Blvd	South Lake Tahoe	CA	96150	888-484-7094	530-544-1685
Leisure Sports Inc 7077 Koll Ctr Pkwy Ste 110	Pleasanton	CA	94566	888-239-0930	925-600-1966
Lodge at Pebble Beach 1700 17-Mile Dr	Pebble Beach	CA	93953	800-654-9300	831-624-3811
Lodge at Sonoma - A Renaissance Resort & Spa 1325 Broadway	Sonoma	CA	95476	866-263-0758	707-935-6600
Loews Coronado Bay Resort 4000 Coronado Bay Rd	Coronado	CA	92118	800-815-6397	619-424-4000
Mammoth Mountain Resort One Minaret Rd PO Box 24	Mammoth Lakes	CA	93546	800-626-6684	760-934-2571
Meadowood Napa Valley 900 Meadowood Ln	Saint Helena	CA	94574	800-458-8080	707-963-3646
Miramonte Resort & Spa 45000 Indian Wells Ln	Indian Wells	CA	92210	800-237-2926	760-341-2200
Montage Resort & Spa 30801 S Coast Hwy	Laguna Beach	CA	92651	866-271-6953	949-715-6000
Morgan Run Resort & Club 5690 Cancha de Golf *Resv	Rancho Santa Fe	CA	92091	800-378-4653*	858-756-2471
Morongo Casino Resort & Spa 49500 Seminole Dr	Cabazon	CA	92230	800-252-4499	951-849-3080
Mount Shasta Resort 1000 Siskiyou Lk Blvd	Mount Shasta	CA	96067	800-958-3363	530-926-3030
Northstar-at-Tahoe PO Box 129	Truckee	CA	96160	800-466-6784	
Ojai Valley Inn & Spa 905 Country Club Rd	Ojai	CA	93023	800-422-6524	805-640-2068
Pacific Palms Conference Resort 1 Industry Hills Pkwy *Cust Svc	City of Industry	CA	91744	800-524-4557*	626-810-4455
Pala Casino Resort & Spa 35008 Pala-Temecula Rd	Pala	CA	92059	877-946-7252	760-510-5100
Pala Mesa Resort 2001 Old Hwy 395	Fallbrook	CA	92028	800-722-4700	760-728-5881
Palm Mountain Resort & Spa 155 S BelaRdo Rd	Palm Springs	CA	92262	800-622-9451	760-325-1301
Paradise Point Resort & Spa 1404 W Vacation Rd	San Diego	CA	92109	800-344-2626	858-274-4630
Pechanga Resort & Casino 45000 Pechanga Pkwy	Temecula	CA	92592	877-711-2946	951-693-1819
Quail Lodge Resort & Golf Club 8205 Valley Greens Dr	Carmel	CA	93923	866-675-1101	831-624-2888
Rancho Valencia Resort 5921 Valencia Cir PO Box 9126	Rancho Santa Fe	CA	92067	800-548-3664	858-756-1123
Renaissance Esmeralda Resort 44-400 Indian Wells Ln	Indian Wells	CA	92210	888-236-2427	760-773-4444
Resort at Squaw Creek 400 Squaw Creek Rd PO Box 3333	Olympic Valley	CA	96146	800-327-3353	530-583-6300
Ritz-Carlton Half Moon Bay One Miramontes Pt Rd *General	Half Moon Bay	CA	94019	800-241-3333*	650-712-7000
Ritz-Carlton Laguna Niguel, The One Ritz Carlton Dr	Dana Point	CA	92629	800-542-8680	949-240-2000
Saint Regis Monarch Beach Resort & Spa One Monarch Beach Resort	Dana Point	CA	92629	800-722-1543	949-234-3200
San Vicente Inn & Golf Course 24157 San Vicente Rd	Ramona	CA	92065	800-776-1289	760-789-3788
Sea Venture Resort 100 Ocean View Ave	Pismo Beach	CA	93449	800-443-7778	805-773-4994
Shadow Mountain Resort & Club 45-750 San Luis Rey	Palm Desert	CA	92260	800-472-3713	760-346-6123
Silverado Resort & Spa 1600 Atlas Peak Rd	Napa	CA	94558	800-532-0500	707-257-0200
Snow Valley Mountain Resort 35100 State Hwy 18 PO Box 2337	Running Springs	CA	92382	800-680-7669	909-867-2751
Spa Resort, The 100 N Indian Canyon Dr	Palm Springs	CA	92262	800-854-1279	
Squaw Valley USA PO Box 2007	Olympic Valley	CA	96146	800-403-0206	530-583-6955
Tahoe Seasons Resort 3901 Saddle Rd PO Box 16300	South Lake Tahoe	CA	96151	800-540-4874	530-541-6700
Temecula Creek Inn 44501 Rainbow Canyon Rd	Temecula	CA	92592	877-517-1823	855-685-9299
Town & Country Resort Hotel 500 Hotel Cir N	San Diego	CA	92108	800-772-8527	619-291-7131
Two Bunch Palms Resort & Spa 67425 Two Bunch Palms Trl	Desert Hot Springs	CA	92240	800-472-4334	760-329-8791
Ventana Inn 48123 Hwy 1	Big Sur	CA	93920	800-628-6500	831-667-2331
Welk Resort San Diego 8860 Lawrence Welk Dr *Resv	Escondido	CA	92026	800-932-9355*	760-749-3000
Winner's Cir Resort 550 Via de la Valle	Solana Beach	CA	92075	800-874-8770	858-755-6666

Colorado

	City	State	Zip	Toll-Free	Phone
Aspen Meadows Resort 845 Meadows Rd	Aspen	CO	81611	800-452-4240	970-925-4240
Aspen Skiing Co 117 ABC	Aspen	CO	81611	855-754-2863	970-925-1220
Beaver Run Resort & Conference Ctr 620 Village Rd	Breckenridge	CO	80424	800-525-2253	970-453-6000
Broadmoor, The One Lake Ave	Colorado Springs	CO	80906	866-837-9520	719-577-5775
Copper Mountain Resort 209 Ten Mile Cir PO Box 3001	Copper Mountain	CO	80443	888-219-2441	970-968-2882
Crested Butte Mountain Resort (CBMR) 12 Snowmass Rd PO Box 5700	Crested Butte	CO	81224	800-810-7669	970-349-2222
Destination Hotels & Resorts Inc 10333 E Dry Creek Rd Ste 450	Englewood	CO	80112	855-893-1011	303-799-3830
Durango Mountain Resort One Skier Pl	Durango	CO	81301	800-982-6103	970-247-9000
Grand Lodge Crested Butte 12 Snowmass Rd	Crested Butte	CO	81224	877-547-5143	970-349-2222
Hot Springs Lodge & Pool 415 E Sixth St PO Box 308	Glenwood Springs	CO	81602	800-537-7946	970-945-6571
Inverness Hotel & Golf Club 200 Inverness Dr W	Englewood	CO	80112	800-346-4891	303-799-5800
Keystone Resort 21996 Hwy 6 PO Box 38	Keystone	CO	80435	877-625-1556	970-496-2316
Lion Square Lodge & Conference Ctr 660 W Lionshead Pl	Vail	CO	81657	800-525-1943	970-476-2281
Manor Vail Lodge 595 E Vail Vly Dr	Vail	CO	81657	800-950-8245	970-476-5000
Mountain Lodge at Telluride 457 Mtn Village Blvd	Telluride	CO	81435	866-368-6867	970-369-5000
Omni Interlocken Resort 500 Interlocken Blvd	Broomfield	CO	80021	800-843-6664	303-438-6600
Park Hyatt Beaver Creek Resort & Spa 136 E Thomas Pl *Cust Svc	Avon	CO	81620	800-233-1234*	970-949-1234
Peaks Resort & Golden Door Spa 136 Country Club Dr	Telluride	CO	81435	800-789-2220	
Ritz-Carlton Bachelor Gulch 0130 Daybreak Ridge	Avon	CO	81620	800-241-3333	970-748-6200
Saint Regis Resort Aspen 315 E Dean St	Aspen	CO	81611	888-627-7198	970-920-3300
Sonnenalp Resort of Vail 20 Vail Rd	Vail	CO	81657	800-654-8312	970-476-5656
Steamboat Grand Resort Hotel & Conference Ctr 2300 Mt Werner Cir	Steamboat Springs	CO	80487	877-269-2628	970-871-5500
Steamboat Ski & Resort Corp 2305 Mt Werner Cir	Steamboat Springs	CO	80487	877-237-2628	970-879-6111
Torian Plum Condo Resort 1855 Ski Time Sq Dr	Steamboat Springs	CO	80487	800-228-2458	970-879-8811
Vail Cascade Resort & Spa 1300 Westhaven Dr	Vail	CO	81657	800-420-2424	970-476-7111
Vail Resorts Management Co 390 Interlocken Crescent Ste 1000 *NYSE: MTN*	Broomfield	CO	80021	800-842-8062	303-404-1800
Wyndham Vacation Rentals 14 Sylvan Way	Parsippany	NJ	07054	800-467-3529	973-753-6300

Connecticut

	City	State	Zip	Toll-Free	Phone
Heritage Hotel 522 Heritage Rd	Southbury	CT	06488	800-932-3466	203-264-8200
Interlaken Inn 74 Interlaken Rd Rt 12	Lakeville	CT	06039	800-222-2909	860-435-9878
Mohegan Sun Resort & Casino One Mohegan Sun Blvd	Uncasville	CT	06382	888-226-7711	860-862-8150
Saybrook Point Inn & Spa Two Bridge St	Old Saybrook	CT	06475	800-243-0212	860-395-2000
Water's Edge Resort & Spa 1525 Boston Post Rd PO Box 688	Westbrook	CT	06498	800-222-5901	860-399-5901

Florida

	City	State	Zip	Toll-Free	Phone
Amelia Island Plantation 39 Beach Lagoon Rd	Amelia Island	FL	32034	800-834-4900	904-261-6161
Americano Beach Resort 1260 N Atlantic Ave	Daytona Beach	FL	32118	800-874-1824	386-255-7431
Bahia Mar Beach Resort & Yachting Ctr 801 Seabreeze Blvd	Fort Lauderdale	FL	33316	888-802-2442	954-764-2233
Banana Bay Resort 4590 Overseas Hwy	Marathon	FL	33050	866-689-4217	
Banyan Resort 323 Whitehead St	Key West	FL	33040	866-371-9222	305-296-7786
Bay Hill Golf Club & Lodge 9000 Bay Hill Blvd	Orlando	FL	32819	888-422-9445	407-876-2429
Beachcomber Resort Hotel & Villas 1200 S Ocean Blvd	Pompano Beach	FL	33062	800-231-2423	954-941-7830
Biltmore Hotel & Conference Ctr of the Americas 1200 Anastasia Ave *Cust Svc	Coral Gables	FL	33134	800-727-1926*	305-445-1926
Bluewater Bay Resort 2000 Bluewater Blvd	Niceville	FL	32578	800-874-2128	850-897-3613
Boca Raton Resort & Club 501 E Camino Real	Boca Raton	FL	33432	888-543-1224	561-447-3000
Breakers, The One S County Rd	Palm Beach	FL	33480	888-273-2537	561-655-6611
Buena Vista Palace Hotel & Spa 1900 N Buena Vista Dr	Lake Buena Vista	FL	32830	866-397-6516	
Casa Marina Resort & Beach Club 1500 Reynolds St	Key West	FL	33040	888-303-5717	
Casa Ybel Resort 2255 W Gulf Dr	Sanibel Island	FL	33957	800-276-4753	239-472-3145
Club Med Sandpiper 4500 SE Pine Vly St	Port Saint Lucie	FL	34952	888-932-2582	772-398-5100
Deauville Beach Resort 6701 Collins Ave	Miami Beach	FL	33141	800-327-6656	305-865-8511
Disney's Animal Kingdom Lodge 2901 Osceola Pkwy	Lake Buena Vista	FL	32830	855-878-9582	407-938-3000
Don CeSar Beach Resort - A Loews Hotel 3400 Gulf Blvd	Saint Pete Beach	FL	33706	866-563-9792	727-360-1881
Doral Golf Resort & Spa 4400 NW 87th Ave	Miami	FL	33178	800-713-6725	305-592-2000
DoubleTree Resort by Hilton Hotel Grand Key (DGKR) 3990 S Roosevelt Blvd	Key West	FL	33040	888-844-0454	305-293-1818
Eden Roc - A Renaissance Beach Resort & Spa 4525 Collins Ave	Miami Beach	FL	33140	855-433-3676	305-531-0000
Fisher Island Club & Resort One Fisher Island Dr *Resv	Miami	FL	33109	800-537-3708*	305-535-6000
Fontainebleau Miami Beach 4441 Collins Ave	Miami Beach	FL	33140	800-548-8886	305-538-2000

				Toll-Free	Phone
Fort Lauderdale Grande Hotel & Yacht Club					
1881 SE 17th St	Fort Lauderdale	FL	33316	**888-554-2131**	954-463-4000
Four Seasons Resort Palm Beach					
2800 S Ocean Blvd	Palm Beach	FL	33480	**800-432-2335**	561-582-2800
Galleon Resort & Marina					
617 Front St	Key West	FL	33040	**800-544-3030**	305-296-7711
Grand Palms Hotel & Golf Resort					
110 Grand Palms Dr	Pembroke Pines	FL	33027	**800-327-9246**	954-431-8800
Hammock Beach Resort					
200 Ocean Crest Dr	Palm Coast	FL	32137	**866-841-0287**	386-246-5500
HARBORSIDE SUITES AT LITTLE HARBOR					
611 Destiny Dr	Ruskin	FL	33570	**800-327-2773**	
Hard Rock Hotel at Universal Orlando Resort					
5800 Universal Blvd	Orlando	FL	32819	**888-430-4999**	407-503-2000
Hawk's Cay Resort & Marina					
61 Hawk's Cay Blvd	Duck Key	FL	33050	**888-395-5539**	305-743-7000
Hilton Sandestin Beach Golf Resort & Spa					
4000 Sandestin Blvd S	Destin	FL	32550	**800-559-1805**	850-267-9500
Holiday Inn Express & Suites Oceanfront					
3301 S Atlantic Ave	Daytona Beach Shores	FL	32118	**800-633-8464**	386-767-1711
Holiday Inn Resort Lake Buena Vista					
13351 SR 535	Orlando	FL	32821	**866-808-8833***	407-239-4500
*Sales					
Holiday Isle Beach Resort & Marina					
84001 Overseas Hwy	Islamorada	FL	33036	**800-327-7070**	305-664-2321
Innisbrook Resort & Golf Club					
36750 US Hwy 19 N	Palm Harbor	FL	34684	**800-492-6899**	727-942-2000
Inverrary Resort					
3501 Inverrary Blvd	Fort Lauderdale	FL	33319	**800-241-0363**	954-485-0500
Janus Hotels & Resorts Inc					
2300 Corporate Blvd NW Ste 232	Boca Raton	FL	33431	**800-327-2110**	561-997-2325
Jupiter Beach Resort					
Five N A1A	Jupiter	FL	33477	**877-389-0571**	561-746-2511
JW Marriott Orlando Grande Lakes Resort					
4040 Central Florida Pkwy	Orlando	FL	32837	**800-576-5750**	407-206-2300
Key Largo Marriott Bay Resort					
103800 Overseas Hwy	Key Largo	FL	33037	**888-731-9056***	305-453-0000
*Resv					
La Playa Beach & Golf Resort					
9891 Gulf Shore Dr	Naples	FL	34108	**800-237-6883**	239-597-3123
Lago Mar Resort & Club					
1700 S Ocean Ln	Fort Lauderdale	FL	33316	**855-209-5677**	954-678-3915
Little Palm Island Resort & Spa					
28500 Overseas Hwy MM 28.5	Little Torch Key	FL	33042	**800-343-8567**	305-872-2524
Lodge & Club at Ponte Vedra Beach					
607 Ponte Vedra Blvd	Ponte Vedra Beach	FL	32082	**800-243-4304**	888-839-9145
Longboat Key Club					
220 Sands Point Rd	Longboat Key	FL	34228	**800-237-8821**	941-383-8821
Marco Beach Ocean Resort					
480 S Collier Blvd	Marco Island	FL	34145	**800-715-8517**	239-393-1400
Miami Beach Resort & Spa					
4833 Collins Ave	Miami Beach	FL	33140	**866-765-9090**	305-532-3600
Mission Inn Resort & Club					
10400 County Rd 48	Howey in the Hills	FL	34737	**800-874-9053**	352-324-3101
Naples Bay Resort					
1500 Fifth Ave S	Naples	FL	34102	**866-605-1199**	239-530-1199
Naples Beach Hotel & Golf Club					
851 Gulf Shore Blvd N	Naples	FL	34102	**800-237-7600**	239-261-2222
Nickelodeon Family Suites by Holiday Inn					
14500 Continental Gateway	Orlando	FL	32821	**877-642-5111**	407-387-5437
Ocean Key Resort & Spa					
0 Duval St	Key West	FL	33040	**800-328-9815**	305-296-7701
Ocean Manor Resort					
4040 Galt Ocean Dr	Fort Lauderdale	FL	33308	**800-955-0444**	954-566-7500
Ocean Sands Resort & Spa					
1350 N Ocean Blvd	Pompano Beach	FL	33062	**800-721-7033**	954-590-1000
Omni Orlando Resort at Championsgate					
1500 Masters Blvd	Champions Gate	FL	33896	**800-843-6664**	407-390-6664
Orange Lake Country Club Inc (OLCC)					
8505 W Irlo Bronson Memorial Hwy	Kissimmee	FL	34747	**800-877-6522**	407-239-0000
Palms, The					
3025 Collins Ave	Miami Beach	FL	33140	**800-550-0505**	305-534-0505
Park Shore Resort					
600 Neapolitan Way	Naples	FL	34103	**800-548-2077**	239-263-2222
PGA National Resort & Spa					
400 Ave of the Champions	Palm Beach Gardens	FL	33418	**800-633-9150**	561-627-2000
Pier House Resort Caribbean Spa					
One Duval St	Key West	FL	33040	**800-723-2791**	305-296-4600
Plantation Inn & Golf Resort					
9301 W Ft Island Trl	Crystal River	FL	34429	**800-632-6262**	352-795-4211
Plaza Resort & Spa					
600 N Atlantic Ave	Daytona Beach	FL	32118	**800-429-8662**	386-255-4471
Ponte Vedra Inn & Club					
200 Ponte Vedra Blvd	Ponte Vedra Beach	FL	32082	**800-234-7842**	904-285-1111
Portofino Bay Hotel at Universal Orlando - A Loews Hotel					
5601 Universal Blvd	Orlando	FL	32819	**800-235-6397**	407-503-1000
Quality Inn & Suites Naples Golf Resort					
4100 Golden Gate Pkwy	Naples	FL	34116	**800-277-0017**	239-455-1010
Radisson Resort Parkway					
2900 PkwyBlvd	Kissimmee	FL	34747	**800-333-3333**	407-396-7000
Reach Resort					
1435 Simonton St	Key West	FL	33040	**888-318-4316**	305-296-5000
Renaissance Orlando Resort at SeaWorld					
6677 Sea Harbor Dr	Orlando	FL	32821	**800-327-6677**	407-351-5555
Renaissance Resort at World Golf Village					
500 S Legacy Trl	Saint Augustine	FL	32092	**888-740-7020**	904-940-8000
Renaissance Vinoy Resort & Golf Club					
501 Fifth Ave NE	Saint Petersburg	FL	33701	**800-468-3571**	727-894-1000
Resort at Singer Island					
3800 N Ocean Dr	Riviera Beach	FL	33404	**800-721-7033**	561-340-1700
Ritz-Carlton Amelia Island					
4750 Amelia Island Pkwy	Amelia Island	FL	32034	**800-241-3333**	904-277-1100
Ritz-Carlton Key Biscayne					
455 Grand Bay Dr	Key Biscayne	FL	33149	**800-241-3333**	305-365-4500
Ritz-Carlton Naples Golf Resort					
2600 Tiburon Dr	Naples	FL	34109	**888-856-2164***	239-593-2000
*Resv					

				Toll-Free	Phone
Ritz-Carlton Orlando Grande Lakes					
4012 Central Florida Pkwy	Orlando	FL	32837	**800-576-5760**	407-206-2400
Ritz-Carlton Sarasota					
1111 Ritz-Carlton Dr	Sarasota	FL	34236	**800-241-3333**	941-309-2000
Rosen Hotels & Resorts Inc					
9840 International Dr	Orlando	FL	32819	**800-204-7234**	407-996-9840
Royal Pacific Resort at Universal Orlando - A Loews Hotel					
6300 Hollywood Way	Orlando	FL	32819	**800-232-7827**	407-503-3000
Safety Harbor Resort & Spa					
105 N Bayshore Dr	Safety Harbor	FL	34695	**888-237-8772**	727-726-1161
Sandals Resorts International					
4950 SW 72nd Ave	Miami	FL	33155	**888-726-3257**	305-284-1300
Sandestin Golf & Beach Resort					
9300 Emerald Coast Pkwy W	Sandestin	FL	32550	**800-277-0800**	850-267-8000
Sanibel Harbour Marriott Resort & Spa					
17260 Harbour Pt Dr	Fort Myers	FL	33908	**800-767-7777**	239-466-4000
Sawgrass Marriott Resort & Beach Club					
1000 PGA Tour Blvd	Ponte Vedra Beach	FL	32082	**800-228-9290**	904-285-7777
Seminole Hard Rock Hotel & Casino Hollywood					
1 Seminole Way	Hollywood	FL	33314	**888-236-4848**	954-327-7625
Sheraton Sand Key Resort					
1160 Gulf Blvd	Clearwater Beach	FL	33767	**800-456-7263**	727-595-1611
South Seas Island Resort					
5400 Plantation Rd	Captiva	FL	33924	**866-565-5089**	239-472-5111
Standard, The					
40 Island Ave	Miami Beach	FL	33139	**800-327-8363**	305-673-1717
Sundial Beach & Golf Resort					
1451 Middle Gulf Dr	Sanibel	FL	33957	**866-717-2323**	239-472-4151
Sunset Beach Resort					
3287 W Gulf Dr	Sanibel Island	FL	33957	**866-565-5091**	239-472-1700
Trump International Sonesta Beach Resort					
18001 Collins Ave	Sunny Isles Beach	FL	33160	**800-766-3782**	305-692-5600
Vanderbilt Beach Resort					
9225 Gulf Shore Dr N	Naples	FL	34108	**800-243-9076**	239-597-3144
Villas of Grand Cypress Golf Resort					
One N Jacaranda	Orlando	FL	32836	**800-835-7377**	407-239-4700
Walt Disney World Dolphin					
1500 Epcot Resorts Blvd	Lake Buena Vista	FL	32830	**888-828-8850**	407-934-4000
Walt Disney World Swan					
1200 Epcot Resorts Blvd	Lake Buena Vista	FL	32830	**888-828-8850**	407-934-4000
West Wind Inn					
3345 W Gulf Dr	Sanibel	FL	33957	**800-824-0476**	239-472-1541
Westin Key West Resort & Marina					
245 Front St	Key West	FL	33040	**866-837-4250**	305-294-4000

Georgia

				Toll-Free	Phone
Barnsley Gardens					
597 Barnsley Gardens Rd	Adairsville	GA	30103	**877-773-2447**	770-773-7480
Brasstown Valley Resort					
6321 US Hwy 76	Young Harris	GA	30582	**800-201-3205**	706-379-9900
Callaway Gardens					
17800 Hwy 27	Pine Mountain	GA	31822	**800-225-5292**	706-663-2281
Chateau Elan Resort & Conference Ctr					
100 Rue Charlemagne	Braselton	GA	30517	**800-233-9463**	678-425-0900
Forrest Hills Mountain Resort & Conference Ctr					
135 Forrest Hills Rd	Dahlonega	GA	30533	**800-654-6313**	706-864-6456
Jekyll Island Club Hotel					
371 Riverview Dr	Jekyll Island	GA	31527	**800-535-9547**	912-635-2600
King & Prince Beach & Golf Resort					
201 Arnold Rd	Saint Simons Island	GA	31522	**800-342-0212**	912-638-3631
Lake Lanier Islands Resort					
7000 Holiday Rd	Buford	GA	30518	**800-840-5253**	770-945-8787
Reynolds Plantation					
100 Linger Longer Rd	Greensboro	GA	30642	**800-800-5250**	706-467-0600
Ritz-Carlton Lodge Reynolds Plantation					
One Lk Oconee Trl	Greensboro	GA	30642	**800-826-1945**	706-467-0600
Sea Palms Golf & Tennis Resort					
5445 Frederica Rd	Saint Simons Island	GA	31522	**800-841-6268**	912-638-3351
Villas by the Sea Resort					
1175 N Beachview Dr	Jekyll Island	GA	31527	**800-841-6262**	912-635-2521

Hawaii

				Toll-Free	Phone
Fairmont Kea Lani Maui					
4100 Wailea Alanui Dr	Wailea-makena	HI	96753	**800-659-4100**	808-875-4100
Fairmont Orchid Hawaii					
One N Kaniku Dr	Kamuela	HI	96743	**800-845-9905**	808-885-2000
Four Seasons Resort Hualalai					
100 Ka'upulehu Dr	Kailua Kona	HI	96740	**888-340-5662**	808-325-8000
Four Seasons Resort Maui at Wailea					
3900 Wailea Alanui Dr	Wailea	HI	96753	**800-334-6284**	808-874-8000
Grand Hyatt Kauai Resort & Spa					
1571 Poipu Rd	Koloa	HI	96756	**800-233-1234**	808-742-1234
Grand Wailea Resort & Spa					
3850 Wailea Alanui Dr	Wailea	HI	96753	**800-888-6100**	808-875-1234
Hanalei Bay Resort & Suites					
5380 Honoiki Rd	Princeville	HI	96722	**877-344-0688**	808-826-6522
Hapuna Beach Prince Hotel					
62-100 Kauna'oa Dr	Kamuela	HI	96743	**800-882-6060**	808-880-1111
Hawaii Prince Hotel Waikiki, The					
100 Holomoana St	Honolulu	HI	96815	**888-977-4623**	
Hilton Hawaiian Village					
2005 Kalia Rd	Honolulu	HI	96815	**800-445-8667**	808-949-4321
Hilton Waikoloa Village					
425 Waikoloa Beach Dr	Waikoloa	HI	96738	**866-931-1679**	808-886-1234
Hyatt Regency Maui Resort & Spa					
200 Nohea Kai Dr	Lahaina	HI	96761	**800-633-7313**	808-661-1234
Kapalua Villas, The					
2000 Village Rd	Lahaina	HI	96761	**800-545-0018**	808-665-5400
Marriott Kaua'i Resort & Beach Club					
3610 Rice St Kalapaki Beach	Lihue	HI	96766	**800-220-2925**	808-245-5050
Mauna Kea Beach Hotel					
62-100 Maunakea Beach Dr	Island of Hawaii	HI	96743	**866-977-4589**	808-882-7222
Mauna Lani Bay Hotel & Bungalows					
68-1400 Mauna Lani Dr	Kohala Coast	HI	96743	**800-367-2323**	808-885-6622

			Toll-Free	Phone

Napili Kai Beach Club
5900 Honoapiilani Rd .... Lahaina HI 96761 **800-367-5030** 808-669-6271
Outrigger Hotels & Resorts
2375 Kuhio Ave .... Honolulu HI 96815 **800-688-7444** 808-921-6941
Outrigger Kanaloa at Kona
78-261 Manukai St .... Kailua-Kona HI 96740 **800-688-7444** 808-322-9625
Outrigger Reef on the Beach
2169 Kalia Rd .... Honolulu HI 96815 **800-688-7444** 808-923-3111
Prince Resorts Hawaii
100 Holomoana St .... Honolulu HI 96815 **888-977-4623** 808-956-1111
Ritz-Carlton Kapalua
1 Ritz-Carlton Dr Kapalua .... Maui HI 96761 **800-262-8440*** 808-669-6200
*Resv
Royal Lahaina Resort
2780 Kekaa Dr .... Lahaina HI 96761 **800-222-5642** 808-661-3611
Sheraton Kauai Resort
2440 Hoonani Rd .... Koloa HI 96756 **800-325-3535*** 808-742-1661
*Resv
Sheraton Maui Resort
2605 Kaanapali Pkwy .... Lahaina HI 96761 **866-716-8109** 808-661-0031
Sheraton Waikiki
2255 Kalakaua Ave .... Honolulu HI 96815 **800-325-3535** 808-922-4422
Travaasa Hana 5031 Hana Hwy .... Hana HI 96713 **855-868-7282** 808-248-8211
Turtle Bay Resort
57-091 Kamehameha Hwy .... Kahuku HI 96731 **866-475-2567** 808-293-6000
Wailea Beach Marriott Resort & Spa
3700 Wailea Alanui Dr .... Wailea HI 96753 **800-845-5279** 808-879-1922

Idaho

			Toll-Free	Phone

Aston Hotel & Resorts Sunvalley
333 S Main St .... Ketchum ID 83340 **877-997-6667** 208-622-6400
Coeur d'Alene Resort
115 S Second St .... Coeur d'Alene ID 83814 **800-688-5253** 208-765-4000
Red Lion Templin's Hotel on the River
414 E First Ave .... Post Falls ID 83854 **800-733-5466** 208-773-1611
Sun Valley Resort
1 Sun Valley Rd .... Sun Valley ID 83353 **800-786-8259** 208-622-4111

Illinois

			Toll-Free	Phone

Eagle Ridge Inn & Resort
444 Eagle Ridge Dr .... Galena IL 61036 **800-892-2269** 815-777-2444
Eaglewood Resort & Spa
1401 Nordic Rd .... Itasca IL 60143 **877-285-6150** 630-773-1400
Indian Lakes Resort
250 W Schick Rd .... Bloomingdale IL 60108 **800-334-3417** 630-529-0200
Preferred Hotel Group
Preferred Hotels & Resorts Worldwide Inc
311 S Wacker Dr Ste 1900 .... Chicago IL 60606 **800-650-1281** 312-913-0400
Summit Hotels & Resorts
311 S Wacker Dr Ste 1900 .... Chicago IL 60606 **800-650-1281** 312-913-0400

Indiana

			Toll-Free	Phone

Belterra Casino Resort
777 Belterra Dr .... Florence IN 47020 **888-235-8377** 812-427-7777
Fourwinds Resort & Marina
9301 Fairfax Rd .... Bloomington IN 47401 **800-824-2628** 812-824-2628
French Lick Resort
8670 W State Rd 56 .... French Lick IN 47432 **888-936-9360** 812-936-9300
Potawatomi Inn
Pokagan State Pk 6 Ln 100A Lk James ..... Angola IN 46703 **877-768-2928** 260-833-1077

Iowa

			Toll-Free	Phone

Grand Harbor Resort & Waterpark
350 Bell St .... Dubuque IA 52001 **866-690-4006** 563-690-4000

Kentucky

			Toll-Free	Phone

General Butler State Resort Park
1608 US Hwy 227 .... Carrollton KY 41008 **866-462-8853** 502-732-4384
Griffin Gate Marriott Resort
1800 Newtown Pk .... Lexington KY 40511 **800-228-9290** 859-231-5100

Maine

			Toll-Free	Phone

Atlantic Oakes
119 Eden St .... Bar Harbor ME 04609 **800-356-3585** 207-288-5801
Bar Harbor Inn Oceanfront Resort
Newport Dr PO Box 7 .... Bar Harbor ME 04609 **800-248-3351** 207-288-3351
Bethel Inn & Country Club
21 Broad St PO Box 49 .... Bethel ME 04217 **800-654-0125** 207-824-2175
Colony Hotel
140 Ocean Ave .... Kennebunkport ME 04046 **800-552-2363** 207-967-3331
Inn by the Sea
40 Bowery Beach Rd .... Cape Elizabeth ME 04107 **800-888-4287** 207-799-3134
Samoset Resort
220 Warrenton St .... Rockport ME 04856 **800-341-1650** 207-594-2511
Sebasco Harbor Resort
29 Keynon Rd .... Phippsburg ME 04562 **800-225-3819** 207-389-1161
Stage Neck Inn
Eight Stage Neck Rd Rt 1A
PO Box 70 .... York Harbor ME 03911 **800-222-3238** 207-363-3850
Sugarloaf/USA
5092 Access Rd .... Carrabassett Valley ME 04947 **800-843-5623** 207-237-2000
Sunday River Ski Resort
15 S Ridge Rd PO Box 4500 .... Newry ME 04261 **800-543-2754** 207-824-3500

Maryland

			Toll-Free	Phone

Coconut Malorie Resort
200 59th St .... Ocean City MD 21842 **855-826-6361** 443-513-0175
Francis Scott Key Family Resort
12806 Ocean Gateway PO Box 468 ...... Ocean City MD 21842 **800-213-0088** 410-213-0088
Harbourtowne Golf Resort & Conference Ctr
9784 Martingham Dr .... Saint Michaels MD 21663 **800-446-9066** 410-745-9066
Ritz-Carlton Hotel Co LLC, The
4445 Willard Ave Ste 800 .... Chevy Chase MD 20815 **800-241-3333** 301-547-4700
Ritz-Carlton Huntington Hotel & Spa
4445 Willard Ave Ste 800 .... Chevy Chase MD 20815 **800-241-3333** 301-547-4700

Massachusetts

			Toll-Free	Phone

Bayside Resort Hotel
225 Massachusetts 28 .... West Yarmouth MA 02673 **800-243-1114** 508-775-5669
Blue Water Resort
291 S Shore Dr .... South Yarmouth MA 02664 **800-367-9393** 508-398-2288
Canyon Ranch Lenox
165 Kemble St .... Lenox MA 01240 **800-742-9000*** 413-637-4100
*Resv
Cape Codder Resort & Spa
1225 Iyanough Rd Rt 132 Bearse's Way ..... Hyannis MA 02601 **888-297-2200** 508-771-3000
Chatham Bars Inn
297 Shore Rd .... Chatham MA 02633 **800-527-4884** 508-945-0096
Cranwell Resort Spa & Golf Club
55 Lee Rd .... Lenox MA 01240 **800-272-6935** 413-637-1364
New Seabury Resort
20 Red Brook Rd .... Mashpee MA 02649 **877-687-3228** 508-539-8200
Ocean Edge Resort & Golf Club
2907 Main St .... Brewster MA 02631 **800-343-6074** 508-896-9000
Ocean Mist Resort
97 S Shore Dr .... South Yarmouth MA 02664 **800-655-1972** 508-398-2633
Sea Crest Resort & Conference Ctr
350 Quaker Rd .... North Falmouth MA 02556 **800-225-3110** 508-540-9400

Michigan

			Toll-Free	Phone

Bay Valley Hotel & Resort
2470 Old Bridge Rd .... Bay City MI 48706 **888-241-4653** 989-686-3500
Boyne Highlands Resort
600 Highlands Dr .... Harbor Springs MI 49740 **800-462-6963** 231-526-3000
Boyne Mountain Resort
11521 Huffman Lake Rd
PO Box 91252 .... Boyne Falls MI 49713 **800-462-6963** 231-549-6060
Crystal Mountain Resort
12500 Crystal Mtn Dr .... Thompsonville MI 49683 **800-968-7686** 231-378-2000
Evergreen Resort
7880 Mackinaw Trail .... Cadillac MI 49601 **800-634-7302**
Garland Resort
4700 N Red Oak Rd .... Lewiston MI 49756 **877-442-7526** 989-786-2211
Grand Traverse Resort & Spa
100 Grand Traverse Blvd PO Box 404 ...... Acme MI 49610 **800-236-1577** 231-534-6000
Indianhead Mountain Resort
500 Indianhead Rd .... Wakefield MI 49968 **800-346-3426**
Inn at Bay Harbor, The
3600 Village Harbor Dr .... Bay Harbor MI 49770 **800-462-6963** 231-439-4000
Lakewood Shores Resort
7751 Cedar Lake Rd .... Oscoda MI 48750 **800-882-2493** 989-739-2073
Mission Point Resort
6633 Main St .... Mackinac Island MI 49757 **800-833-7711**
Otsego Club
696 M-32 E Main St PO Box 556 .... Gaylord MI 49734 **800-752-5510** 989-732-5181
Shanty Creek Resort
5780 Shanty Creek Rd .... Bellaire MI 49615 **800-678-4111** 231-533-8621
Treetops Resort
3962 Wilkinson Rd .... Gaylord MI 49735 **866-348-5249** 989-732-6711

Minnesota

			Toll-Free	Phone

Arrowwood Resort & Conference Ctr
2100 Arrowwood Ln NW .... Alexandria MN 56308 **866-386-5263*** 320-762-1124
*Resv
Breezy Point Resort
9252 Breezy Pt Dr .... Breezy Point MN 56472 **800-432-3777** 218-562-7811
Caribou Highlands Lodge
371 Ski Hill Rd PO Box 99 .... Lutsen MN 55612 **800-642-6036** 218-663-7241
Carlson
Radisson Hotels & Resorts
701 Carlson Pkwy .... Minnetonka MN 55305 **800-333-3333** 763-212-5000
Cascade Lodge 3719 W Hwy 61 .... Lutsen MN 55612 **800-322-9543** 218-387-1112
Cragun's Conference & Golf Resort
11000 Cragun's Dr .... Brainerd MN 56401 **800-272-4867**
Fair Hills Resort
24270 County Hwy 20 .... Detroit Lakes MN 56501 **800-323-2849*** 218-847-7638
*Resv
Grand Casino Hinckley
777 Lady Luck Dr .... Hinckley MN 55037 **800-472-6321**
Grand Casino Mille Lacs
777 Grand Ave PO Box 343 .... Onamia MN 56359 **800-626-5825**
Grand Portage Lodge & Casino
PO Box 233 .... Grand Portage MN 55605 **800-543-1384** 218-475-2401
Grand View Lodge
23521 Nokomis Ave .... Nisswa MN 56468 **866-801-2951** 218-963-2234
Lake Breeze Motel Resort
9000 Congdon Blvd .... Duluth MN 55804 **800-738-5884** 218-525-6808
Lutsen Resort
5700 W Hwy 61 PO Box 9 .... Lutsen MN 55612 **800-258-8736** 218-663-7212
Madden's on Gull Lake
11266 Pine Beach Peninsula .... Brainerd MN 56401 **800-642-5363** 218-829-2811
Ruttger's Bay Lake Lodge
25039 Tame Fish Lk Rd PO Box 400 ..... Deerwood MN 56444 **800-450-4545** 218-678-2885

				Toll-Free	Phone
Superior Shores Resort 1521 Superior Shores Dr	Two Harbors	MN	55616	800-242-1988	218-834-5671

Mississippi

				Toll-Free	Phone
Beau Rivage Resort & Casino 875 Beach Blvd	Biloxi	MS	39530	888-750-7111	228-386-7111
Gulf Hills Hotel 13701 Paso Rd	Ocean Springs	MS	39564	866-875-4211	228-875-4211
IP Casino Resort & Spa 850 Bayview Ave *Resv	Biloxi	MS	39530	888-946-2847*	228-436-3000
Treasure Bay Casino & Hotel 1980 Beach Blvd *General	Biloxi	MS	39531	800-747-2839*	228-385-6000

Missouri

				Toll-Free	Phone
Dogwood Hills Golf Resort 1252 State Hwy KK	Osage Beach	MO	65065	800-220-6571	573-348-1735
Indian Point Resort 71 Dogwood Pk Trl	Branson	MO	65616	800-888-1891	417-338-2250
Lilleys' Landing Resort 367 River Ln	Branson	MO	65616	866-545-5397	417-334-6380
Lodge of Four Seasons 315 Four Seasons Dr PO Box 215 *Resv	Lake Ozark	MO	65049	888-265-5500*	573-365-3000
Resort at Port Arrowhead, The 3080 Bagnell Dam Blvd PO Box 1930	Lake Ozark	MO	65049	800-532-3575	573-365-2334
Tan-Tar-A Resort Golf Club & Spa 494 Tantara Dr PO Box 188TT *Resv	Osage Beach	MO	65065	800-826-8272*	573-348-3131
Thousand Hills Golf Resort 245 S Wildwood Dr	Branson	MO	65616	877-262-0430	417-336-5873
Welk Resort Branson 1984 State Hwy 165	Branson	MO	65616	800-505-9355	417-336-3575

Montana

				Toll-Free	Phone
Big Sky Resort One Lone Mtn Trl PO Box 160001	Big Sky	MT	59716	800-548-4486	406-995-5000
Fairmont Hot Springs Resort 1500 Fairmont Rd	Fairmont	MT	59711	800-332-3272	406-797-3241
Meadow Lake Resort 100 St Andrews Dr	Columbia Falls	MT	59912	800-321-4653	406-892-8700
Rock Creek Resort 6380 US Hwy 212	Red Lodge	MT	59068	800-667-1119	406-446-1111
Triple Creek Ranch 5551 W Fork Rd	Darby	MT	59829	800-654-2943	406-821-4600

Nebraska

				Toll-Free	Phone
Radisson Palm Beach Shores Resort & Vacation Villas 11340 Blondo S Ste 100	Omaha	NE	68164	800-615-7253	

Nevada

				Toll-Free	Phone
Alexis Park Resort 375 E Harmon Ave	Las Vegas	NV	89169	800-582-2228	702-796-3300
Aquarius Casino Resort 1900 S Casino Dr	Laughlin	NV	89029	888-662-5825	702-298-5111
Atlantis Casino Resort 3800 S Virginia St	Reno	NV	89502	800-723-6500	775-825-4700
Bellagio Hotel & Casino 3600 Las Vegas Blvd S	Las Vegas	NV	89109	888-987-7111	702-693-7111
Casablanca Resort 950 W Mesquite Blvd	Mesquite	NV	89027	800-459-7529	702-346-7529
Club Cal Neva Hotel Casino, The 38 E Second St PO Box 2071	Reno	NV	89501	877-777-7303	775-323-1046
Don Laughlin's Riverside Resort & Casino 1650 Casino Dr	Laughlin	NV	89029	800-227-3849	702-298-2535
Golden Nugget Hotel 129 E Fremont St	Las Vegas	NV	89101	800-634-3454	702-385-7111
Golden Nugget Laughlin 2300 S Casino Dr	Laughlin	NV	89029	800-950-7700	702-298-7111
Grand Sierra Resort & Casino 2500 E Second St	Reno	NV	89595	800-501-2651	775-789-2000
Hard Rock Hotel & Casino 4455 Paradise Rd	Las Vegas	NV	89169	800-693-7625	702-693-5000
John Ascuaga's Nugget Hotel Casino 1100 Nugget Ave	Sparks	NV	89431	800-648-1177	775-356-3300
JW Marriott Resort Las Vegas 221 N Rampart Blvd	Las Vegas	NV	89144	877-869-8777	702-869-7777
Mandalay Bay Resort & Casino 3950 Las Vegas Blvd S	Las Vegas	NV	89119	877-632-7800	702-632-7777
MGM Grand Hotel & Casino 3799 Las Vegas Blvd S	Las Vegas	NV	89109	877-880-0880	702-891-1111
Mirage, The 3400 Las Vegas Blvd S	Las Vegas	NV	89109	800-627-6667	702-791-7111
Monte Carlo Resort & Casino 3770 Las Vegas Blvd S	Las Vegas	NV	89109	800-311-8999	702-730-7777
Planet Hollywood Resort & Casino 3667 Las Vegas Blvd S	Las Vegas	NV	89109	866-919-7472	702-785-5555
Primm Valley Resort & Casino 31900 S Las Vegas Blvd	Primm	NV	89019	800-926-4455	
Ridge Tahoe 400 Ridge Club Dr PO Box 5790	Stateline	NV	89449	800-334-1600	775-588-3553
Riviera Hotel & Casino 2901 Las Vegas Blvd S *Resv	Las Vegas	NV	89109	866-275-6030*	702-734-5110
Treasure Island Hotel & Casino 3300 Las Vegas Blvd S	Las Vegas	NV	89109	800-288-7206	702-894-7111
Tropicana Resort & Casino 3801 Las Vegas Blvd S *Resv	Las Vegas	NV	89109	800-462-8767*	702-739-2222
Venetian Resort Hotel & Casino 3355 Las Vegas Blvd S	Las Vegas	NV	89109	866-659-9643	702-414-1000

New Hampshire

				Toll-Free	Phone
Cranmore Mountain Resort One Skimobile Rd PO Box 1640	North Conway	NH	03860	800-786-6754	603-356-5543
Mount Washington Hotel & Resort Rt 302	Bretton Woods	NH	03575	800-314-1752	603-278-1000
Waterville Valley Resort One Ski Area Rd PO Box 540	Waterville Valley	NH	03215	800-468-2553	603-236-8311
White Mountain Hotel & Resort 2560 W Side Rd PO Box 1828	North Conway	NH	03860	800-533-6301	603-356-7100

New Jersey

				Toll-Free	Phone
Bally's Atlantic City 1900 Pacific Ave	Atlantic City	NJ	08401	800-772-7777	609-340-2000
Caesars Atlantic City Hotel Casino 2100 Pacific Ave	Atlantic City	NJ	08401	800-522-4700	609-348-4411
Montreal Inn Beach Dr & Madison Ave	Cape May	NJ	08204	800-525-7011	609-884-7011
Ocean Place Resort & Spa One Ocean Blvd	Long Branch	NJ	07740	800-411-6493	732-571-4000
Resorts Casino Hotel 1133 Boardwalk	Atlantic City	NJ	08401	800-334-6378	
Tropicana Entertainment 2831 Boardwalk *OTC: TPCA*	Atlantic City	NJ	08401	800-843-8767	
Trump Taj Mahal Casino Resort 1000 Boardwalk & Virginia Ave	Atlantic City	NJ	08401	800-426-2537	609-449-1000

New Mexico

				Toll-Free	Phone
Angel Fire Resort PO Box 130	Angel Fire	NM	87710	800-633-7463	575-377-6401
Inn of the Mountain Gods 287 Carrizo Canyon Rd	Mescalero	NM	88340	800-545-9011	
La Posada de Santa Fe Resort & Spa 330 E Palace Ave	Santa Fe	NM	87501	866-280-3810	505-986-0000
Lifts West Condominium Resort Hotel PO Box 330	Red River	NM	87558	800-221-1859	505-754-2778

New York

				Toll-Free	Phone
Bonnie Castle Resort 31 Holland St	Alexandria Bay	NY	13607	800-955-4511	315-482-4511
Doral Arrowwood Conference Resort 975 Anderson Hill Rd	Rye Brook	NY	10573	844-211-0512	844-214-5500
High Peaks Resort 2384 Saranac Ave	Lake Placid	NY	12946	800-755-5598	518-523-4411
Holiday Valley Resort Rt 219 PO Box 370	Ellicottville	NY	14731	800-323-0020	716-699-2345
Mohonk Mountain House 1000 Mtn Rest Rd	New Paltz	NY	12561	800-772-6646	845-255-1000
Montauk Yacht Club Resort & Marina 32 Star Island Rd	Montauk	NY	11954	888-692-8668	631-668-3100
Otesaga, The 60 Lake St	Cooperstown	NY	13326	800-348-6222	607-547-9931
Point, The PO Box 1327	Saranac Lake	NY	12983	800-255-3530	518-891-5674
Roaring Brook Ranch & Tennis Resort Rte 9N S	Lake George	NY	12845	800-882-7665	518-668-5767
Rocking Horse Ranch Resort 600 Rt 44-55	Highland	NY	12528	800-647-2624	845-691-2927
Sagamore, The 110 Sagamore Rd	Bolton Landing	NY	12814	866-384-1944	518-644-9400
Starwood Hotels & Resorts Worldwide Inc *Saint Regis Hotels & Resorts* 1111 Westchester Ave	White Plains	NY	10604	888-625-4988	914-640-8100
Villa Roma Resort & Conference Ctr 356 Villa Roma Rd	Callicoon	NY	12723	800-533-6767	845-887-4880
Whiteface Club & Resort 373 Whiteface Inn Ln	Lake Placid	NY	12946	800-422-6757	518-523-2551
Woodcliff Hotel & Spa 199 Woodcliff Dr	Fairport	NY	14450	800-365-3065	585-381-4000

North Carolina

				Toll-Free	Phone
Ballantyne Resort Hotel 10000 Ballantyne Commons Pkwy	Charlotte	NC	28277	866-248-4824	704-248-4000
Eseeola Lodge, The 175 Linville Ave PO Box 99	Linville	NC	28646	800-742-6717	828-733-4311
Fontana Village Resort 300 Woods Rd PO Box 68	Fontana Dam	NC	28733	800-849-2258	828-498-2211
Grove Park Inn Resort & Spa 290 Macon Ave	Asheville	NC	28804	800-438-5800	828-252-2711
High Hampton Inn & Country Club 1525 Hwy 107 S	Cashiers	NC	28717	800-334-2551	828-743-2450
Holiday Inn SunSpree Resort Wrightsville Beach 1706 N Lumina Ave	Wrightsville Beach	NC	28480	888-211-9874	910-256-2231
Maggie Valley Resort & Country Club 1819 Country Club Dr	Maggie Valley	NC	28751	800-438-3861	828-926-1616
Mid Pines Inn & Golf Club 1010 Midland Rd	Southern Pines	NC	28387	800-747-7272	910-692-2114
Pine Needles Lodge & Golf Club PO Box 88	Southern Pines	NC	28388	800-747-7272	910-692-7111
Pinehurst Resort & Country Club 80 Carolina Vista Dr	Pinehurst	NC	28374	800-487-4653	910-295-6811
Pinnacle Inn Resort 301 Pinnacle Inn Rd	Beech Mountain	NC	28604	800-405-7888	828-387-2231

	Toll-Free	Phone
Sanderling Resort & Spa 1461 Duck Rd ....Duck NC 27949	800-701-4111	252-261-4111
Waynesville Inn Golf & Country Club, The 176 Country Club Dr ....Waynesville NC 28786	800-627-6250	828-456-3551
Wolf Ridge Ski Resort 578 Vly View Cir ....Mars Hill NC 28754	800-817-4111	828-689-4111

North Dakota

	Toll-Free	Phone
Prairie Knights Casino & Resort 7932 Hwy 24 ....Fort Yates ND 58538	800-425-8277	701-854-7777

Nova Scotia

	Toll-Free	Phone
Atlantica Hotel & Marina Oak Island 36 Treasure Dr PO Box 6 ......Western Shore NS B0J3M0	800-565-5075	902-627-2600
Pines Resort, The 103 Shore Rd PO Box 70 ....Digby NS B0V1A0	800-667-4637	902-245-2511

Ohio

	Toll-Free	Phone
Sawmill Creek Resort 400 Sawmill Creek Dr ....Huron OH 44839	800-729-6455	419-433-3800

Oklahoma

	Toll-Free	Phone
Cherokee Casino & Resort 777 W Cherokee St ....Catoosa OK 74015	800-760-6700	
Lake Murray Resort Park 3323 Lodge Rd ....Ardmore OK 73401	800-622-6317	580-223-6600
Quartz Mountain Resort & Conference Ctr 22469 Lodge Rd ....Lone Wolf OK 73655	877-999-5567	580-563-2424

Ontario

	Toll-Free	Phone
Deerhurst Resort 1235 Deerhurst Dr ....Huntsville ON P1H2E8 *Sales	800-461-6522*	705-789-6411
Delta Meadowvale 6750 Mississauga Rd ....Mississauga ON L5N2L3	800-422-8238	905-821-1981
Fallsview Casino Resort 6380 Fallsview Blvd ....Niagara Falls ON L2G7X5	888-325-5788	
Pinestone Resort 4252 County Rd Ste 21................Haliburton ON K0M1S0	800-461-0357	705-457-1800

Oregon

	Toll-Free	Phone
Black Butte Ranch 12930 Hawks BeaRd Rd PO Box 8000 ....Black Butte Ranch OR 97759	866-901-2961	541-595-1252
Gearhart By the Sea 1157 N Marion Ave ....Gearhart OR 97138	800-547-0115	503-738-8331
Mount Bachelor Village Resort & Conference Ctr 19717 Mt Bachelor Dr ....Bend OR 97702	800-547-5204	541-389-5900
Resort at the Mountain 68010 E Fairway Ave ....Welches OR 97067	877-439-6774	503-622-3101
Salishan Lodge & Golf Resort PO Box 118 ....Gleneden Beach OR 97388	800-452-2300	
Seventh Mountain Resort 18575 SW Century Dr ....Bend OR 97702	800-452-6810	541-382-8711
Sunriver Resort 17600 Ctr Dr PO Box 3609................Sunriver OR 97707	800-547-3922	541-593-1000
Timberline Lodge 27500 E Timberline Rd ....Government Camp OR 97028	800-547-1406	503-272-3311
Village Green Resort & Gardens 725 Row River Rd ....Cottage Grove OR 97424	800-343-7666	541-942-2491

Pennsylvania

	Toll-Free	Phone
Allenberry Resort 1559 Boiling Springs Rd ....Boiling Springs PA 17007	800-430-5468	717-258-3211
Carroll Valley Golf Resort 78 Country Club Trail ....Carroll Valley PA 17320	855-784-0330	717-642-8282
Cove Haven Pocono Palace 5222 Milford Rd ....East Stroudsburg PA 18302	877-822-3333	800-432-9932
Fernwood Resort 5785 Milford Rd ....East Stroudsburg PA 18302	888-337-6966	
Heritage Hills Golf Resort & Conference Ctr 2700 Mt Rose Ave ....York PA 17402	877-782-9752	717-755-0123
Hershey Entertainment & Resorts Co 27 W Chocolate Ave ....Hershey PA 17033	800-437-7439	
Hidden Valley Resort & Conference Ctr 1 Craighead Dr PO Box 4420 ....Hidden Valley PA 15502	800-452-2223	814-443-8000
Hotel Hershey, The 100 Hotel Rd ....Hershey PA 17033	800-437-7439	717-533-2171
Lancaster Host Resort 2300 Lincoln Hwy E ....Lancaster PA 17602 *Resv	800-233-0121*	717-299-5500
Mountain Laurel Resort & Spa Rt 940 PO Box 9................White Haven PA 18661	888-243-9300	570-443-8411
Nemacolin Woodlands Resort & Spa 1001 Lafayette Dr ....Farmington PA 15437	800-422-2736	724-329-8555
Pocono Manor Golf Resort & Spa one Manor Dr Rt 314 ....Pocono Manor PA 18349	800-233-8150	570-839-7111
Seven Springs Mountain Resort 777 Waterwheel Dr ....Champion PA 15622	800-452-2223	814-352-7777
Skytop Lodge One Skytop ....Skytop PA 18357	800-345-7759	570-595-7401
Split Rock Resort 100 Moseywood Rd ....Lake Harmony PA 18624	800-255-7625	570-722-9111

	Toll-Free	Phone
Willow Valley Resort & Conference Ctr 2400 Willow St Pike ....Lancaster PA 17602	800-444-1714	717-464-2711
Woodlands Inn, The 1073 Hwy 315 ....Wilkes-Barre PA 18702	844-779-8472	570-824-9831

Puerto Rico

	Toll-Free	Phone
El Conquistador Resort & Golden Door Spa 1000 El Conquistador Ave ....Fajardo PR 00738 *Resv	888-543-1282*	787-863-1000
Ritz-Carlton San Juan, The 6961 Ave of the Governors Isla Verde ....Carolina PR 00979	800-241-3333	787-253-1700

Quebec

	Toll-Free	Phone
Fairmont Le Chateau Montebello 392 Notre Dame St ....Montebello QC J0V1L0	800-441-1414	819-423-6341
Hotel Cheribourg 2603 Ch du Parc ....Orford QC J1X8C8	877-845-5344	819-843-3308
Hotel du Lac 121 Rue Cuttle ....Mont-Tremblant QC J8E1B9	800-567-8341	819-425-2731
Manoir du Lac Delage 40 Ave du Lac ....Lac Delage QC G3C5C4	888-202-3242	418-848-2551
Westin Resort Tremblant 100 Ch Kandahar ....Mont-Tremblant QC J8E1E2	800-937-8461	819-681-8000

Rhode Island

	Toll-Free	Phone
Castle Hill Inn & Resort 590 Ocean Dr ....Newport RI 02840	888-466-1355	401-849-3800

South Carolina

	Toll-Free	Phone
Barefoot Resort & Golf 4980 Barefoot Resort Bridge Rd ....North Myrtle Beach SC 29582	866-638-4818	843-390-3200
Bay Watch Resort & Conference Ctr 2701 S Ocean Blvd ....North Myrtle Beach SC 29582	866-270-2172	843-272-4600
Beach Colony Resort 5308 N Ocean Blvd ....Myrtle Beach SC 29577 *General	800-222-2141*	843-449-4010
Bluewater Resort 2001 S Ocean Blvd ....Myrtle Beach SC 29577	800-845-6994	843-626-8345
Breakers Resort 3002 N Ocean Blvd ....Myrtle Beach SC 29577	800-952-4507	843-448-8082
Caravelle Resort Hotel & Villas 6900 N Ocean Blvd ....Myrtle Beach SC 29572	800-507-9145	843-918-8000
Caribbean Resort & Villas 3000 N Ocean Blvd ....Myrtle Beach SC 29577	800-552-8509	
Compass Cove Ocean Resort 2311 S Ocean Blvd ....Myrtle Beach SC 29577	800-331-0934	843-448-8373
Coral Beach Resort & Suites 1105 S Ocean Blvd ....Myrtle Beach SC 29577	800-843-2684	800-556-1754
Hilton Myrtle Beach Resort 10000 Beach Club Dr ....Myrtle Beach SC 29572	800-445-8667	843-449-5000
Holiday Inn Oceanfront at Surfside Beach 1601 N Ocean Blvd ....Surfside Beach SC 29575 *Resv	866-661-5139*	843-238-5601
Kiawah Island Golf Resort One Sancturay Beach Dr ....Kiawah Island SC 29455 *Resv	800-654-2924*	843-768-2121
Litchfield Beach & Golf Resort 14276 Ocean Hwy ....Pawleys Island SC 29585	888-766-4633	843-237-3000
Myrtle Beach Resort Vacations 5905 S Kings Hwy PO Box 3936 ....Myrtle Beach SC 29578	888-627-3767	843-238-1559
Mystic Sea Resort 2105 S Ocean Blvd ....Myrtle Beach SC 29577	800-443-7050	843-448-8446
Ocean Reef Resort 7100 N Ocean Blvd ....Myrtle Beach SC 29572	888-322-6411	843-449-4441
Palmetto Dunes Resort 4 Queen Folly Rd ....Hilton Head Island SC 29928	866-380-1778	
Palms Resort 2500 N Ocean Blvd ....Myrtle Beach SC 29577	800-300-1198	843-626-8334
Patricia Grand Resort 2710 N Ocean Blvd ....Myrtle Beach SC 29577	800-255-4763	843-448-8453
Pawleys Plantation 70 Tanglewood Dr ....Pawleys Island SC 29585	800-367-9959	843-237-6000
Player's Club Resort 35 Deallyon Ave ....Hilton Head Island SC 29928	800-497-7529	843-785-3355
Reef Resort 2101 S Ocean Blvd ....Myrtle Beach SC 29577 *Cust Svc	800-845-1212*	843-448-1765
Sand Dunes Resort Hotel 201 74th Ave N ....Myrtle Beach SC 29572	800-726-3783	843-449-3313
Sea Mist Resort 1200 S Ocean Blvd ....Myrtle Beach SC 29577	800-793-6507	843-448-1551
Seacrest Oceanfront Resort on the South Beach 803 S Ocean Blvd ....Myrtle Beach SC 29577	888-889-8113	
Wild Dunes Resort 5757 Palm Blvd ....Isle of Palms SC 29451	800-845-8880	843-886-6000
Wyndham Vacation Resorts King Cotton Villas One King Cotton Rd ....Edisto Beach SC 29438	800-251-8736	843-869-2561

South Dakota

	Toll-Free	Phone
Spearfish Canyon Resort 10619 Roughlock Falls Rd ....Lead SD 57754	877-975-6343	605-584-3435

Tennessee

	Toll-Free	Phone
Brookside Resort 463 E Pkwy ....Gatlinburg TN 37738	800-251-9597	865-436-5611

Texas

	Toll-Free	Phone
Four Seasons Resort & Club Dallas at Las Colinas		
4150 N MacArthur Blvd ....Irving TX 75038	**800-332-3442**	972-717-0700
Hilton Galveston Island Resort		
5400 Seawall Blvd ....Galveston TX 77551	**800-475-3386**	409-744-5000
Houstonian Hotel Club & Spa		
111 N Post Oak Ln ....Houston TX 77024	**800-231-2759***	713-680-2626
*Resv		
Inn of the Hills River Resort		
1001 Junction Hwy ....Kerrville TX 78028	**800-292-5690**	830-895-5000
Omni Barton Creek Resort & Spa		
8212 Barton Club Dr ....Austin TX 78735	**800-336-6158**	512-329-4000
Rancho Viejo Resort & Country Club		
One Rancho Viejo Dr ....Rancho Viejo TX 78575	**800-531-7400**	956-350-4000
Rosewood Hotels & Resorts		
500 Crescent Ct Ste 300..................Dallas TX 75201	**888-767-3966**	214-880-4200
San Luis Resort Spa & Conference Ctr		
5222 Seawall Blvd ....Galveston Island TX 77551	**800-445-0090***	409-744-1500
*Cust Svc		
Silverleaf Resorts Inc		
1221 Riverbend Dr Ste 120..................Dallas TX 75247	**800-613-0310**	214-631-1166
South Shore Harbour Resort & Conference Ctr		
2500 S Shore Blvd ....League City TX 77573	**800-442-5005***	281-334-1000
*Resv		
Tanglewood Resort Hotel & Conference Ctr		
290 Tanglewood Cir ....Pottsboro TX 75076	**800-833-6569**	903-786-2968
Tapatio Springs Golf Resort & Conference Ctr		
One Resort Way ....Boerne TX 78006	**800-999-3299**	

Utah

	Toll-Free	Phone
Alta Lodge PO Box 8040 ....Alta UT 84092	**800-707-2582***	801-742-3500
*Cust Svc		
Canyons Resort, The		
4000 The Canyons Resort Dr ....Park City UT 84098	**888-226-9667**	435-649-5400
Deer Valley Resort Lodging		
PO Box 889 ....Park City UT 84060	**800-558-3337**	435-645-6626
Homestead Resort		
700 N Homestead Dr ....Midway UT 84049	**888-327-7220**	
Little America Hotels & Resorts		
500 S Main St ....Salt Lake City UT 84101	**800-281-7899**	801-596-5700
Park City Mountain Resort (PCMR)		
1345 Lowell Ave PO Box 39 ....Park City UT 84060	**800-222-7275**	435-649-8111
Rustler Lodge		
10380 East Hwy 210 PO Box 8030 ....Alta UT 84092	**888-532-2582**	801-742-2200
Snowbasin Ski Resort		
3925 E Snowbasin Rd ....Huntsville UT 84317	**888-437-5488**	801-620-1100
Snowbird Ski & Summer Resort		
Hwy 210 PO Box 929000 ....Snowbird UT 84092	**800-453-3000**	801-742-2222
Solitude Ski Resort		
12000 Big Cottonwood Canyon ....Brighton UT 84121	**800-748-4754**	801-534-1400
Stein Eriksen Lodge		
7700 Stein Way ....Park City UT 84060	**800-453-1302**	435-649-3700

Vermont

	Toll-Free	Phone
Basin Harbor Club		
4800 Basin Harbor Rd ....Vergennes VT 05491	**800-622-4000**	802-475-2311
Equinox, The		
3567 Main St Rt 7A ....Manchester Village VT 05254	**800-362-4747**	802-362-4700
Hawk Inn & Mountain Resort		
75 Billings Rd ....Plymouth VT 05056	**800-685-4295**	802-672-3811
Inn at Stratton Mountain		
5 Village Lodge Rd ....Stratton Mountain VT 05155	**800-787-2886**	802-297-2500
Jay Peak Resort 830 Jay Peak Rd ....Jay VT 05859	**800-451-4449**	802-988-2611
Killington Resort & Pico Mountain		
228 E Mountain Rd ....Killington VT 05751	**800-621-6867**	802-422-6200
Lake Morey Resort		
One Clubhouse Rd ....Fairlee VT 05045	**800-423-1211**	802-333-4311
Smugglers' Notch Resort		
4323 Vermont Rt 108 S ....Jeffersonville VT 05464	**800-451-8752**	802-644-8851
Stowe Mountain Resort		
5781 Mountain Rd ....Stowe VT 05672	**800-253-4754**	802-253-3000
Stoweflake Mountain Resort & Spa		
1746 Mountain Rd PO Box 369 ....Stowe VT 05672	**800-253-2232**	802-253-7355
Sugarbush Resort & Inn		
1840 Sugarbush Access Rd ....Warren VT 05674	**800-537-8427**	802-583-6300
Topnotch at Stowe Resort & Spa		
4000 Mountain Rd ....Stowe VT 05672	**800-451-8686**	
Trapp Family Lodge		
700 Trapp Hill Rd PO Box 1428 ....Stowe VT 05672	**800-826-7000**	802-253-8511
Woodstock Inn & Resort		
14 The Green ....Woodstock VT 05091	**800-448-7900**	802-457-1100

Virginia

	Toll-Free	Phone
Alamar Resort Inn		
311 16th St ....Virginia Beach VA 23451	**800-346-5681**	757-428-7582
Boar's Head Inn		
200 Ednam Dr ....Charlottesville VA 22903	**800-476-1988**	434-296-2181
Breakers Resort Inn		
16th & Oceanfront ....Virginia Beach VA 23451	**800-237-7532**	757-428-1821
Cavalier Hotel		
4201 Atlantic Ave ....Virginia Beach VA 23451	**800-446-8199**	757-425-8555
Great Wolf Lodge Williamsburg		
549 E Rochambeau Dr ....Williamsburg VA 23188	**800-551-9653**	757-229-9700
Kingsmill Resort & Spa		
1010 Kingsmill Rd ....Williamsburg VA 23185	**800-832-5665**	757-253-1703
OMNI HOMESTEAD RESORT, THE		
7696 Sam Snead Hwy ....Hot Springs VA 24445	**800-838-1766**	540-839-1766
Shenvalee Golf Resort		
9660 Fairway Dr PO Box 930 ....New Market VA 22844	**888-339-3181**	540-740-3181
Turtle Cay Resort		
600 Atlantic Ave ....Virginia Beach VA 23451	**888-989-7788**	757-437-5565
Virginia Beach Resort Hotel & Conference Ctr		
2800 Shore Dr ....Virginia Beach VA 23451	**800-468-2722**	757-481-9000
Virginia Crossings Resort		
1000 Virginia Ctr Pkwy ....Glen Allen VA 23059	**888-444-6553**	804-727-1400
Williamsburg Inn		
136 E Francis St ....Williamsburg VA 23185	**800-447-8679**	757-229-1000

Washington

	Toll-Free	Phone
Alderbrook Resort & Spa		
7101 E SR-106 ....Union WA 98592	**800-622-9370**	360-898-2200
Campbell's Resort		
104 W Woodin Ave PO Box 278 ....Chelan WA 98816	**800-553-8225**	509-682-2561
Desert Canyon Golf Resort		
1201 Desert Canyon Blvd ....Orondo WA 98843	**800-258-4173**	509-784-1111
Freestone Inn at Wilson Ranch		
31 Early Winters Dr ....Mazama WA 98833	**800-639-3809**	509-996-3906
Lake Quinault Lodge		
345 S Shore Rd ....Quinault WA 98575	**800-562-6672**	360-288-2900
Little Creek Casino Resort		
91 W State Rt 108 ....Shelton WA 98584	**800-667-7711**	360-427-7711
Polynesian Resort, The		
615 Ocean Shores Blvd NW ....Ocean Shores WA 98569	**800-562-4836**	360-289-3361
Resort Semiahmoo		
9565 Semiahmoo Pkwy ....Blaine WA 98230	**855-917-3767**	360-318-2000
Rosario Resort & Spa		
1400 Rosario Rd ....Eastsound WA 98245	**800-562-8820**	360-376-2222
Salish Lodge & Spa		
6501 Railroad Ave DE PO Box 1109 ....Snoqualmie WA 98065	**800-272-5474**	425-888-2556
Sun Mountain Lodge		
604 Patterson Lk Rd PO Box 1000 ....Winthrop WA 98862	**800-572-0493**	509-996-2211

West Virginia

	Toll-Free	Phone
Canaan Valley Resort & Conference Ctr		
230 Main Lodge Rd ....Davis WV 26260	**800-622-4121**	304-866-4121
Glade Springs Resort		
255 Resort Dr ....Daniels WV 25832	**866-562-8054**	
Greenbrier, The		
300 W Main St ....White Sulphur Springs WV 24986	**800-453-4858**	304-536-1110
Lakeview Golf Resort & Spa		
One Lakeview Dr ....Morgantown WV 26508	**800-624-8300**	304-594-1111
Oglebay Resort & Conference Ctr		
Rt 88 N Oglebay Pk ....Wheeling WV 26003	**800-624-6988**	304-243-4000
Snowshoe Mountain Resort		
10 Snowshoe Dr ....Snowshoe WV 26209	**877-441-4386**	304-572-1000
Stonewall Resort		
940 Resort Dr ....Roanoke WV 26447	**888-278-8150**	304-269-7400
Woods Resort & Conference Ctr		
Mountain Lk Rd PO Box 5 ....Hedgesville WV 25427	**800-248-2222**	

Wisconsin

	Toll-Free	Phone
Abbey Resort & Fontana Spa		
269 Fontana Blvd ....Fontana WI 53125	**800-709-1323**	262-275-9000
American Club, The		
419 Highland Dr ....Kohler WI 53044	**800-344-2838**	920-457-8000
Chanticleer Inn		
1458 E Dollar Lk Rd ....Eagle River WI 54521	**800-752-9193**	715-479-4486
Chula Vista Resort		
2501 River Rd ....Wisconsin Dells WI 53965	**800-388-4782**	608-254-8366
Devil's Head Resort & Convention Ctr		
S 6330 Bluff Rd ....Merrimac WI 53561	**800-472-6670**	608-493-2251
Fox Hills Resort & Convention Ctr		
250 W Church St ....Mishicot WI 54228	**800-950-7615**	920-755-2376
Grand Geneva Resort & Spa		
7036 Grand Geneva Way ....Lake Geneva WI 53147	**800-558-3417**	262-248-8811
Heidel House Resort		
643 Illinois Ave ....Green Lake WI 54941	**800-444-2812**	920-294-3344
Holiday Acres Resort		
4060 S Shore Dr PO Box 460 ....Rhinelander WI 54501	**800-261-1500**	715-369-1500
Lake Lawn Resort		
2400 E Geneva St ....Delavan WI 53115	**800-338-5253**	262-728-7950
Landmark Resort		
7643 Hillside Rd ....Egg Harbor WI 54209	**800-273-7877**	920-868-3205
Olympia Resort & Spa		
1350 Royale Mile Rd ....Oconomowoc WI 53066	**800-558-9573**	262-369-4999
Osthoff Resort, The		
101 Osthoff Ave PO Box 151 ....Elkhart Lake WI 53020	**800-876-3399**	920-876-3366
Tundra Lodge Resort & Waterpark		
865 Lombardi Ave ....Green Bay WI 54304	**877-886-3725**	920-405-8700

Wyoming

	Toll-Free	Phone
Amangani Resort		
1535 NE Butte Rd ....Jackson WY 83001	**877-734-7333**	307-734-7333
Aramark Parks & Destinations		
27655 Hwy 26 & 287 ....Moran WY 83013	**866-278-4245**	307-543-2847
Four Seasons Resort Jackson Hole		
7680 Granite Loop Rd PO Box 544..................Teton Village WY 83025	**800-914-5110**	307-732-5000
Grand Targhee Resort		
3300 E Ski Hill Rd ....Alta WY 83414	**800-827-4433**	307-353-2300
Grand Teton Lodge Co		
5 Miles N Hwy 89 PO Box 250 ....Moran WY 83013	**800-628-9988***	307-543-2811
*Resv		
Jackson Hole Mountain Resort		
3395 Cody Ln PO Box 290 ....Teton Village WY 83025	**800-450-0477**	307-733-2292
Jackson HoleResort Lodging		
3200 W McCollister Dr		
PO Box 510..................Teton Village WY 83025	**800-443-8613**	307-733-3990

			Toll-Free	Phone
Jackson Lake Lodge PO Box 250	Moran WY	83013	800-628-9988	307-543-2811
Rusty Parrot Lodge & Spa				
PO Box 1657	Jackson WY	83001	800-458-2004	307-733-2000
Snow King Resort				
400 E Snow King Ave Jackson Hole	Jackson WY	83001	800-522-5464	307-733-5200

666   RESTAURANT COMPANIES

SEE ALSO Franchises ; Ice Cream & Dairy Stores ; Bakeries ; Food Service

			Toll-Free	Phone
Al Copeland Investments Inc				
1001 Harimaw Ct S	Metairie LA	70001	800-401-0401	504-830-1000
BAB Inc				
500 Lk Cook Rd Ste 475	Deerfield IL	60015	800-251-6101	
OTC: BABB				
Beef O'Bradys Inc				
5660 W Cypress St Ste A	Tampa FL	33607	800-728-8878	813-226-2333
Bellacino's Corp				
10096 Shaver Rd	Portage MI	49024	877-379-0700	269-329-0782
Bickford's Family Restauarants Inc				
37 Oak St Ext	Brockton MA	02301	800-969-5653	
Bill Miller Bar-B-Q Inc				
430 S Santa Rosa St PO Box 839925	San Antonio TX	78207	800-339-3111	210-225-4461
Bob Evans Farms Inc				
3776 S High St	Columbus OH	43207	800-939-2338	
NASDAQ: BOBE				
Bojangles' Restaurants Inc				
9432 Southern Pine Blvd	Charlotte NC	28273	800-366-9921	704-335-1804
Boston Market Corp				
14103 Denver W Pkwy	Golden CO	80401	800-877-2870*	303-278-9500
*General				
Boston Pizza Restaurants LP				
1501 LBJ Fwy Ste 450	Dallas TX	75234	866-277-8721	972-484-9022
BRAVO | BRIO Restaurant Group				
777 Goodale Blvd Ste 100	Columbus OH	43212	888-452-7286	614-326-7944
Brinker International Inc				
6820 LBJ Fwy	Dallas TX	75240	800-983-4637	972-980-9917
NYSE: EAT				
Brock & Company Inc				
257 Great Vly Pkwy	Malvern PA	19355	866-468-2783	610-647-5656
Bubba Gump Shrimp Co LLC				
2501 Seawall Blvd	Galveston TX	77550	800-552-6379	409-766-4952
Buca di Beppo				
1204 Harmon Pl	Minneapolis MN	55403	866-328-2822	612-288-0138
Buca Inc 1204 Harmon Pl	Minneapolis MN	55403	866-328-2822	612-288-0138
Buck's Pizza Franchising Corp Inc				
PO Box 405	Du Bois PA	15801	800-310-8848	
Buffalo's Franchise Concepts Inc				
9606 Santa Monica Blvd Ste 105	Beverly Hills CA	90210	800-459-4647	310-402-0606
Burger King Corp				
5505 Blue Lagoon Dr	Miami FL	33126	855-673-3725	305-378-3000
Burgerville USA				
109 W 17th St	Vancouver WA	98660	888-827-8369	360-694-1521
California Pizza Kitchen Inc				
18601 Airport Way Ste 135	Santa Ana CA	92707	800-919-3227	949-252-6125
NASDAQ: CPKI				
Captain D's LLC				
624 Grassmere Park Dr Ste 30	Nashville TN	37211	800-314-4819	615-391-5461
Carlson Restaurants				
4201 Marsh Ln	Carrollton TX	75007	800-374-3297	972-662-5400
Cask 'n' Cleaver				
8689 Ninth St	Rancho Cucamonga CA	91730	800-995-4452	909-981-5771
CEC Entertainment Inc				
4441 W Airport Fwy PO Box 152077	Irving TX	75062	888-778-7193	972-258-8507
NYSE: CEC				
Champps Entertainment Inc				
19111 Dallas Pkwy Ste 370	Dallas TX	75287	800-229-2118*	972-581-1171
*General				
Charley's Grilled Subs				
2500 Farmers Dr Ste 140	Columbus OH	43235	800-437-8325	614-923-4700
Chart House Restaurants				
1510 W Loop S	Houston TX	77027	800-552-6379	713-850-1010
Checkers Drive-In Restaurants Inc				
4300 W Cypress St Ste 600	Tampa FL	33607	800-800-8072	813-283-7000
Chick-fil-A Inc				
5200 Buffington Rd	Atlanta GA	30349	800-232-2677	404-765-8000
Cosi Inc				
1751 Lk Cook Rd Ste 600	Deerfield IL	60015	800-822-2076	847-597-8800
NASDAQ: COSI				
Cousins Submarines Inc				
N83 W13400 Leon Rd	Menomonee Falls WI	53051	800-238-9736	262-253-7700
Cracker Barrel Old Country Store Inc				
PO Box 787	Lebanon TN	37088	800-333-9566	615-444-5533
NASDAQ: CBRL				
D'Angelo Sandwich Shops				
600 Providence Hwy	Dedham MA	02026	800-727-2446	781-461-1200
DavCo Restaurants Inc				
1657 Crofton Blvd	Crofton MD	21114	800-523-1411*	410-721-3770
*General				
Del Taco Inc				
25521 Commercentre Dr Ste 200	Lake Forest CA	92630	800-852-7204*	949-462-9300
*Cust Svc				
Denny's Corp				
203 E Main St	Spartanburg SC	29319	800-733-6697*	864-597-8000
NASDAQ: DENN ▨ *Cust Svc*				
Doctor's Assoc Inc				
325 Bic Dr	Milford CT	06461	800-888-4848	203-877-4281
Dolly's Pizza Franchising Inc				
1097 Union Lake Rd	White Lake MI	48386	866-336-5597	248-360-6440
Donatos Pizza				
935 Taylor Stn Rd	Columbus OH	43230	800-366-2667	
Eat'n Park Hospitality Group Inc				
285 E Waterfront Dr PO Box 3000	Homestead PA	15120	800-947-4033	412-461-2000
Edo Japan International Inc				
32 St SE Ste 4838	Calgary AB	T2B2S6	888-336-9888	403-215-8800
El Fenix Corp				
11075 Harry Hines Blvd	Dallas TX	75229	877-591-1918	972-241-2171
El Pollo Loco				
3535 Harbor Blvd Ste 100	Costa Mesa CA	92626	877-375-4968	714-599-5000
Famous Dave's of America Inc				
12701 Whitewater Dr Ste 200	Minnetonka MN	55343	800-929-4040	952-294-1300
NASDAQ: DAVE				
Fatburger North America Inc				
301 Arizona Ave Ste 200	Santa Monica CA	90401	800-315-3901	310-319-1850
Figaro's Italian Pizza Inc				
1500 Liberty St SE Ste 160	Salem OR	97302	888-344-2767	503-371-9318
Firehouse Restaurant Group Inc				
3400 Kori Rd Ste 8	Jacksonville FL	32257	877-309-7332	904-886-8300
Flamers Charbroiled Hamburgers				
1515 International Pkwy Ste 2013	Heathrow FL	32746	866-749-4889	407-574-8363
Fox's Pizza Den Inc				
4425 Willaim Penn Hwy	Murrysville PA	15668	800-899-3697	724-733-7888
Fresh Enterprises Inc				
5900-A Katella Ave Ste 101	Cypress CA	90630	877-225-2373	562-391-2400
Friendly Ice Cream Corp				
1855 Boston Rd	Wilbraham MA	01095	800-966-9970	413-731-4000
Frisch's Restaurants Inc				
2800 Gilbert Ave	Cincinnati OH	45206	800-873-3633	513-961-2660
NYSE: FRS				
Frullati Cafe & Bakery				
9311 E Via de Ventura	Scottsdale AZ	85258	866-452-4252	480-362-4800
Garden Fresh Restaurant Corp				
15822 Bernardo Ctr Dr Ste A	San Diego CA	92127	800-874-1600	858-675-1600
Gates Bar-B-Q				
4621 Paseo Blvd	Kansas City MO	64110	800-662-7427	816-923-0900
Gold Star Chili				
650 Lunken Pk Dr	Cincinnati OH	45226	800-643-0465	513-231-4541
Good Eats Inc				
12200 Stemmons Fwy Ste 100	Dallas TX	75234	800-275-1337	972-241-5500
Great Steak & Potato Co				
9311 E Via de Ventura	Scottsdale AZ	85258	866-452-4252	480-362-4800
Hacienda Mexican Restaurants				
1501 N Ironwood Dr	South Bend IN	46635	800-541-3227	
Hard Rock Cafe International Inc				
6100 Old Pk Ln	Orlando FL	32835	888-686-7625	407-445-7625
Hillstone Restaurant Group				
147 S Beverly Dr	Beverly Hills CA	90212	800-230-9787	310-385-7343
Ho-Lee-Chow				
2204 Danforth Ave	Toronto ON	M4C1K3	800-465-3324	416-996-3333
Home Run Inn Inc				
1300 Internationale Pkwy	Woodridge IL	60517	800-636-9696	630-783-9696
Hoss's Steak & Sea House				
170 Patchway Rd	Duncansville PA	16635	800-992-4677	814-695-7600
Hot Dog on a Stick				
5942 Priestly Dr	Carlsbad CA	92008	877-639-2361	760-930-0456
House of Blues Entertainment Inc				
7060 Hollywood Blvd	Hollywood CA	90028	877-632-7600	323-769-4600
IHOP Corp 450 N Brand Blvd	Glendale CA	91203	800-901-5248	818-240-6055
Il Fornaio America Corp				
770 Tamalpais Dr Ste 400	Corte Madera CA	94925	888-454-6246	415-945-0500
In-N-Out Burger Inc				
4199 Campus Dr Ninth Fl	Irvine CA	92612	800-786-1000*	949-509-6200
*Cust Svc				
International Dairy Queen Corp				
7505 Metro Blvd	Minneapolis MN	55439	866-793-7582	952-830-0200
J Alexander's Inc				
3401 W End Ave Ste 260	Nashville TN	37203	888-528-1991	615-269-1900
NASDAQ: JAX				
Jack in the Box Inc				
9330 Balboa Ave	San Diego CA	92123	800-955-5225	858-571-2121
NASDAQ: JACK				
Jack's Family Restaurants Inc				
2831 19th St S	Homewood AL	35209	800-422-3893	205-879-9321
Jan Cos				
35 Sockanosset Cross Rd	Cranston RI	02920	888-693-6844	401-946-4000
Jerry's Systems Inc				
15942 Shady Grove Rd	Gaithersburg MD	20877	800-990-9176	
Jimmy John's Franchise Inc				
2212 Fox Dr	Champaign IL	61820	800-546-6904	217-356-9900
Joey's Only Seafood Franchising Corp				
514-42nd Ave SE	Calgary AB	T2G1Y6	800-661-2123	403-243-4584
K-Mac Enterprises Inc				
PO Box 6538	Fort Smith AR	72906	800-947-9277	479-646-2053
Kahala Corp				
9311 E Via de Ventura	Scottsdale AZ	85258	866-452-4252	480-362-4800
KFC Corp				
1441 Gardiner Ln	Louisville KY	40213	800-225-5532	818-780-6990
Kimpton Hotel & Restaurant Group LLC				
222 Kearny St Ste 200	San Francisco CA	94108	800-546-7866	415-397-5572
Kona Grill Inc				
7150 E Camelback Rd Ste 220	Scottsdale AZ	85251	866-328-5662	480-922-8100
NASDAQ: KONA				
La Salsa Fresh Mexican Grill				
320 Commerce Ste 100	Irvine CA	92602	866-452-7257	949-270-8900
Landry's Restaurants Inc				
1510 W Loop S	Houston TX	77027	800-552-6379	713-850-1010
Lawry's Restaurants Inc				
234 E Colorado Blvd Ste 500	Pasadena CA	91101	888-552-9797	626-440-5234
Legal Sea Foods Inc				
1 Seafood Way	Boston MA	02210	800-477-5342	617-530-9000
Little Caesars Inc				
2211 Woodward Ave	Detroit MI	48201	800-722-3727	313-983-6409
Luby's Inc				
13111 NW Fwy Ste 600	Houston TX	77040	800-886-4600	713-329-6800
NYSE: LUB				
Malnati Organization Inc				
3685 Woodhead Dr	Northbrook IL	60062	800-568-8646	847-562-1814
Marie Callender Restaurant & Bakery				
27101 Puerta Real Ste 260	Mission Viejo CA	92691	800-776-7437	
Maui Tacos International Inc				
2001 Palmer Ave. Ste 105	Larchmont NY	10538	866-388-3758	
McDonald's Corp				
One McDonald's Plz	Oak Brook IL	60523	800-244-6227	630-623-3000
NYSE: MCD				
Melting Pot Restaurants Inc				
8810 Twin Lakes Blvd	Tampa FL	33614	800-783-0867	813-881-0055

	Toll-Free	Phone
Mexican Restaurants Inc		
1135 Edgebrook St .... Houston TX 77034	800-444-2090	713-943-7574
OTC: CASA		
Monical Pizza Corp		
530 N Kinzie Ave .... Bradley IL 60915	800-929-3227	815-937-1890
Mr Goodcents Franchise Systems Inc		
8997 Commerce Dr .... DeSoto KS 66018	800-648-2368	
Mr Hero Restaurants		
7010 Engle Rd Ste 100 .... Middleburg Heights OH 44130	888-860-5082	440-625-3080
Mr Jim's Pizza Inc		
2521 Pepperwood St .... Dallas TX 75234	800-583-5960	972-267-5467
Nathan's Famous Inc		
One Jericho Plz Second Fl .... Jericho NY 11753	800-628-4267	516-338-8500
NASDAQ: NATH		
NPC International Inc		
7300 W 129th St .... Overland Park KS 66213	866-299-1148	913-327-5555
Orange Julius of America		
7505 Metro Blvd .... Minneapolis MN 55439	866-793-7582	952-830-0200
Palm Management Corp		
1730 Rhode Island Ave NW Ste 900 .... Washington DC 20036	800-388-7256	202-775-7256
Panchero's Mexican Grill		
2475 Coral Ct Ste B .... Coralville IA 52241	888-639-2378	319-545-6565
Panda Express		
1717 Walnut Grove Ave .... Rosemead CA 91770	800-877-8988	626-312-5401
Panda Restaurant Group Inc		
1683 Walnut Grove Ave .... Rosemead CA 91770	800-877-8988	626-799-9898
Papa Gino's Inc		
600 Providence Hwy .... Dedham MA 02026	800-727-2446	781-461-1200
Papa Murphy's International Inc		
8000 NE Pkwy Dr Ste 350 .... Vancouver WA 98662	800-778-7879	360-260-7272
Pappas Restaurants Inc		
13939 NW Fwy .... Houston TX 77040	877-277-2748	713-869-0151
Pappas Seafood House		
13939 NW Fwy .... Houston TX 77040	877-277-2748	713-869-0151
Pat O'Brien's International Inc		
718 St Peter St .... New Orleans LA 70116	800-597-4823	504-525-4823
Penguin Point Franchise Systems Inc		
2691 E US 30 PO Box 975 .... Warsaw IN 46580	800-577-5755	574-267-3107
Perkins Restaurant & Bakery		
6075 Poplar Ave Ste 800 .... Memphis TN 38119	800-877-7375	901-766-6400
Peter Piper Inc		
950 W Behrend Dr Ste 102 .... Phoenix AZ 85027	800-899-3425	480-609-6400
PF Chang's China Bistro Inc		
7676 E Pinnacle Peak Rd .... Scottsdale AZ 85255	866-732-4264	480-888-3000
NASDAQ: PFCB		
Piccadilly Cafeterias Inc		
3332 S Sherwood Forest Blvd .... Baton Rouge LA 70816	800-552-7422	225-293-4853
Piccadilly Circus Pizza		
1007 Okoboji Ave PO Box 188 .... Milford IA 51351	800-338-4340	
Pizza Boli's		
5721 Falls Rd 5725 Falls Rd .... Baltimore MD 21209	800-234-2654	410-323-3278
Pizza Factory Inc		
49430 Rd 426 .... Oakhurst CA 93644	800-654-4840	559-683-3377
Pizza Inn Inc		
3551 Plano Pkwy .... The Colony TX 75056	800-880-9955	469-384-5000
NASDAQ: RAVE		
Pizza Plus Pizza Inc		
299 Franklin Dr .... Blountville TN 37617	800-675-1220	423-279-9335
Pizza Pro Inc		
2107 N Second St PO Box 1285 .... Cabot AR 72023	800-777-7554	501-605-1175
Pizza Ranch Inc		
204 19th St SE .... Orange City IA 51041	800-321-3401	
Pretzelmaker		
1346 Oakbrook Dr Ste 170 .... Norcross GA 30093	877-639-2361	
Quality Dining Inc		
4220 Edison Lakes Pkwy .... Mishawaka IN 46545	800-589-3820	574-271-4600
Quiznos Corp		
1275 Grant St Ste 200 .... Denver CO 80203	866-486-2783	720-359-3300
Red Hot & Blue Restaurants Inc		
1600 Wilson Blvd .... Arlington VA 22209	888-509-7100	703-276-7427
Red Robin Gourmet Burgers Inc		
6312 S Fiddlers Green Cir		
Ste 200-N .... Greenwood Village CO 80111	877-733-6543	303-846-6000
NASDAQ: RRGB		
Restaurant Developers Corp		
7010 Engle Rd Ste 100 .... Cleveland OH 44130	888-860-5082	440-625-3080
Restaurants Unlimited Inc		
411 First Ave S Ste 200 .... Seattle WA 98104	877-855-6106	206-634-0550
Rib Crib Corp		
4535 S Harvard Ave .... Tulsa OK 74135	800-275-9677	918-712-7427
Rocky Rococo		
105 E Wisconsin Ave .... Oconomowoc WI 53066	800-888-7625	262-569-5580
Rubio's Restaurants Inc		
1902 Wright Pl Ste 300 .... Carlsbad CA 92008	800-354-4199	760-929-8226
Ruby Tuesday Inc		
150 W Church Ave .... Maryville TN 37801	800-325-0755	865-379-5700
NYSE: RT		
Russ' Restaurants Inc		
390 E Eigth St .... Holland MI 49423	800-521-1778	616-396-6571
Ruth's Hospitality Group Inc		
1030 W Canton Ave Ste 100` .... Winter Park FL 32789	800-544-0808*	407-333-7440
*NASDAQ: RUTH ▪ *Sales*		
Sagebrush Steakhouse		
129 Fast Ln .... Mooresville NC 28117	877-704-5939	704-660-5939
Shakey's USA		
2200 W Valley Blvd .... Alhambra CA 91803	888-444-6686	626-576-0616
Shari's Restaurant & Pies		
9400 SW Gemini Dr .... Beaverton OR 97008	800-433-5334	503-605-4299
Silver Diner Inc		
12276 Rockville Pk .... Rockville MD 20852	866-561-0518	301-770-0333
Skyline Chili Inc		
4180 Thunderbird Ln .... Fairfield OH 45014	800-443-4371*	513-874-1188
*General		
Snappy Tomato Pizza Co		
6111 A Burgundy Hill Dr .... Burlington KY 41005	888-463-7627	859-525-4680
Sonic Corp		
300 Johnny Bench Dr .... Oklahoma City OK 73104	877-828-7868	405-225-5000
NASDAQ: SONC		

	Toll-Free	Phone
Sonic Drive-in Restaurants		
300 Johnny Bench Dr .... Oklahoma City OK 73104	877-828-7868	405-225-5000
Steak N Shake Co		
3810 W Washington Holt Rd .... Indianapolis IN 46241	877-785-6745	317-241-0483
Stuart Anderson's Black Angus		
4410 El Camino Real .... Los Altos CA 94022	800-382-3852	
Stuckey's Corp		
8555 16th St Ste 850 .... Silver Spring MD 20910	800-423-6171	301-585-8222
Summerwood Corp		
14 Balligomingo Rd .... Conshohocken PA 19428	800-760-0950	610-520-1000
Tacala LLC		
3750 Corporate Woods Dr .... Vestavia Hills AL 35242	800-822-6235	205-443-9600
Taco Cabana Inc		
8918 Tesoro Dr Ste 200 .... San Antonio TX 78217	800-357-9924	210-804-0990
Taco Time International Inc		
9311 E Via de Venutra .... Scottsdale AZ 85258	866-452-4252	480-362-4800
Tacoma Inc		
328 E Church St .... Martinsville VA 24112	800-352-9417	276-666-9417
Tavistock Restaurants LLC		
35 Braintree Hill Office Pk .... Braintree MA 02184	800-424-2753	781-817-4400
Texas Roadhouse Inc		
6040 Dutchmans Ln Ste 400 .... Louisville KY 40205	800-839-7623	502-426-9984
NASDAQ: TXRH		
Thompson Hospitality		
505 Huntmar Pk Dr Ste 350 .... Herndon VA 20170	800-842-2737	703-964-5500
Tim Hortons Inc		
874 Sinclair Rd .... Oakville ON L6K2Y1	888-601-1616	905-845-6511
NYSE: THI		
Tubbys Grilled Submarines		
31920 Groesbeck Hwy .... Fraser MI 48026	800-752-0644	
Uno Chicago Grill		
100 Charles Pk Rd .... Boston MA 02132	866-600-8667	617-323-9200
Uno Restaurant Corp		
100 Charles Pk Rd .... Boston MA 02132	866-600-8667	617-323-9200
Valentino's 2601 S 70th St .... Lincoln NE 68506	888-240-8257	402-434-9350
Village Inn 400 W 48th Ave .... Denver CO 80216	800-800-3644	303-296-2121
Waffle House Inc		
5986 Financial Dr .... Norcross GA 30071	877-992-3353	770-729-5700
Weathervane Seafood Restaurant		
306 US Rt 1 .... Kittery ME 03904	800-914-1774	207-439-0330
World Wrapps		
3023 80th Ave SE Ste 200 .... Mercer Island WA 98040	888-233-9727	206-233-9727
Yoshinoya Beef Bowl		
991 Knox St .... Torrance CA 90502	800-576-8017	310-527-6060
Yum! Brands Inc		
1441 Gardiner Ln .... Louisville KY 40213	800-225-5532	502-874-8300
NYSE: YUM		

667   RESTAURANTS (INDIVIDUAL)

SEE ALSO Restaurant Companies ; Shopping/Dining/Entertainment Districts
Individual restaurants are organized by city names within state and province groupings.
(Canadian provinces are interfiled among the US states, in alphabetical order.)

	Toll-Free	Phone

Alabama

	Toll-Free	Phone
Dreamland BBQ		
1427 14th Ave S .... Birmingham AL 35205	800-752-0544	205-933-2133

Alaska

	Toll-Free	Phone
Alaska Salmon Bake In Alaskaland		
2300 Airport Way .... Fairbanks AK 99701	800-354-7274	907-452-7274
Best Western Grandma's Feather Bed		
9300 Glacier Hwy .... Juneau AK 99801	888-781-5005	907-789-5005
Gold Room 127 N Franklin St .... Juneau AK 99801	800-544-0970	907-586-2660

Alberta

	Toll-Free	Phone
Normand's		
11639 A Jasper Ave .... Edmonton AB T5K2S7	866-308-4438	780-482-2600

Arizona

	Toll-Free	Phone
Grill at Hacienda del Sol		
5501 N Hacienda del Sol Rd .... Tucson AZ 85718	800-728-6514	520-529-3500
L'Auberge de Sedona		
301 L'Auberge Ln .... Sedona AZ 86336	855-905-5745	928-282-1661
T Cook's		
5200 E Camelback Rd .... Phoenix AZ 85018	800-672-6011	602-808-0766

Arkansas

	Toll-Free	Phone
McClard's Bar-B-Q		
505 Albert Pike Rd .... Hot Springs AR 71901	866-622-5273	501-623-9665

California

	Toll-Free	Phone
Abalonetti Seafood Trattoria		
57 Fisherman's Wharf Ste 1 .... Monterey CA 93940	877-643-4972	831-373-1851
Anaheim Marriott		
700 W Convention Way .... Anaheim CA 92802	800-845-5279	714-750-8000
Baja Fresh		
320 Commerce Ste 100 .... Irvine CA 92602	877-225-2373	949-270-8900
Cafe Fina		
47 Fisherman's Wharf Ste 1 .... Monterey CA 93940	800-843-3462	831-372-5200

	Toll-Free	Phone
California Grill		
11999 Harbor Blvd		
Hyatt Regency Orange County...............Garden Grove CA 92840	800-233-1234	714-740-6047
Chinois on Main		
2709 Main St ....Santa Monica CA 90405	888-646-3387	310-392-9025
Duane's		
3649 Mission Inn Ave ....Riverside CA 92501	800-843-7755	951-784-0300
Europa Restaurant		
1620 S Indian Trl ....Palm Springs CA 92264	800-245-2314	760-327-2314
Humphreys Restaurant		
2241 Shelter Island Dr ....San Diego CA 92106	800-377-1177	619-224-3411
Hyatt Regency Huntington Beach Resort & Spa		
21500 Pacific Coast Hwy.............Huntington Beach CA 92648	800-633-7313	714-698-1234
Marine Room, The		
2000 Spindrift Dr ....La Jolla CA 92037	866-644-2351	858-459-7222
Silks 222 Sansome St ....San Francisco CA 94104	800-526-6566	415-986-2020
Sir Winston's Restaurant & Lounge		
1126 Queens Hwy ....Long Beach CA 90802	877-342-0738	562-435-3511
West Coast Club		
21100 Pacific Coast Hwy		
Hilton Waterfront Beach Resort.........Huntington Beach CA 92648	800-548-8690	714-845-8000
Westgate Hotel, The		
1055 Second Ave ....San Diego CA 92101	800-522-1564	619-238-1818

Colorado

	Toll-Free	Phone
Briarhurst Manor		
404 Manitou Ave ....Manitou Springs CO 80829	877-685-1448	719-685-1864
Flying W Ranch Inc		
3330 Chuckwagon Rd ....Colorado Springs CO 80919	800-232-3599	719-598-4000
Greenbriar Inn, The		
8735 N Foothills Hwy ....Boulder CO 80302	800-253-1474	303-440-7979
Thyme on the Creek		
1345 28th St ....Boulder CO 80302	866-866-8086	303-998-3835

Delaware

	Toll-Free	Phone
Green Room at the Hotel duPont		
11th & Market St ....Wilmington DE 19801	800-441-9019	302-594-3100
Melting Pot, The		
1601 Concord Pike		
Ste 43-47 Independence Mall................Wilmington DE 19803	800-783-0867	302-652-6358

District Of Columbia

	Toll-Free	Phone
Charlie Palmer Steak		
101 Constitution Ave NW ....Washington DC 20001	877-632-7800	202-547-8100

Florida

	Toll-Free	Phone
Bahama Breeze		
8849 International Dr ....Orlando FL 32819	877-500-9715	407-248-2499
Blue Heaven 729 Thomas St ....Key West FL 33040	800-986-0958	305-296-8666
Boheme, The		
325 S Orange Ave ....Orlando FL 32801	866-663-0024	407-313-9000
Conch House Restaurant		
57 Comares Ave		
Conch House Marina Resort...............Saint Augustine FL 32080	800-940-6256	904-829-8646
Dave & Buster's		
3000 Oakwood Blvd ....Hollywood FL 33020	844-515-5157	954-923-5505
Islamorada Fish Co		
81532 Overseas Hwy PO Box 283 ......Islamorada FL 33036	800-258-2559	
Lombardi's 401 Biscayne Blvd ....Miami FL 33132	888-286-3792	
Melting Pot of Pensacola, The		
418 Gregory St Ste 500 ....Pensacola FL 32501	800-783-0867	850-438-4030
Melting Pot of Tampa, The		
13164 N Dale Mabry Hwy ....Tampa FL 33618	800-783-0867	813-962-6936
Palm		
5800 Universal Blvd Hard Rock Hotel.............Orlando FL 32819	866-333-7256	407-503-7256

Georgia

	Toll-Free	Phone
Cafe, The		
3434 Peachtree Rd NE		
Ritz-Carlton Buckhead ....Atlanta GA 30326	800-241-3333	404-237-2700
Country's Barbecue		
2016 12th Ave ....Columbus GA 31901	800-285-4267*	706-327-7702
*General		

Hawaii

	Toll-Free	Phone

Illinois

	Toll-Free	Phone
Aria 200 N Columbus Dr ....Chicago IL 60601	888-495-1829	312-444-9494
Captain Merry Guesthouse & Fine Dining		
399 Sinsinawa Ave ....East Dubuque IL 61025	866-351-9586	815-747-3644
Giovanni's Restaurant & Convention Ctr		
610 N Bell School Rd ....Rockford IL 61107	800-383-7829	815-398-6411

Indiana

	Toll-Free	Phone
LaSalle Grill		
115 W Colfax Ave ....South Bend IN 46601	800-382-9323	574-288-1155
Melting Pot of Indianapolis, The		
5650 E 86th St Ste A....................Indianapolis IN 46250	800-783-0867	317-841-3601
Scholars Inn Gourmet Cafe		
717 N College Ave ....Bloomington IN 47404	800-765-3466	812-332-1892

Kentucky

	Toll-Free	Phone
Gratz Park Inn		
120 W Second St ....Lexington KY 40507	800-752-4166	859-231-1777

Louisiana

	Toll-Free	Phone
Arnaud's		
813 Bienville St ....New Orleans LA 70112	866-230-8895	504-523-5433

Maryland

	Toll-Free	Phone
JR's Place for Ribs		
131st St & Coastal ....Ocean City MD 21842	800-879-7742	410-250-3100
Melting Pot of Annapolis, The		
2348 Solomons Island Rd ....Annapolis MD 21401	800-783-0867	410-266-8004

Massachusetts

	Toll-Free	Phone
Bristol, The 200 Boylston St ....Boston MA 02116	800-819-5053	617-338-4400
Capital Grille		
900 Boylston St ....Boston MA 02115	866-518-9113	
Colonial House Inn		
277 Main St Rt 6A ....Yarmouth Port MA 02675	800-999-3416	508-362-4348
KO Prime 90 Tremont St ....Boston MA 02108	866-906-9090	617-772-0202
Palm, The 200 Dartmouth St ....Boston MA 02116	866-333-7256	617-867-9292
Red Inn		
15 Commercial St ....Provincetown MA 02657	866-473-3466	508-487-7334
Water Street		
131 N Water St ....Edgartown MA 02539	800-225-6005	508-627-7000

Michigan

	Toll-Free	Phone
English Inn, The		
677 S Michigan Rd ....Eaton Rapids MI 48827	800-858-0598	517-663-2500
Gandy Dancer 401 Depot St ....Ann Arbor MI 48104	800-552-6379	734-769-0592

Minnesota

	Toll-Free	Phone
Angie's Cantina		
11 E Buchanan St ....Duluth MN 55802	800-706-7672	218-727-6117
Fitger's Brewery Complex		
600 E Superior St ....Duluth MN 55802	888-348-4377	218-722-8826
Grandma's Saloon & Grill		
522 Lake Ave S ....Duluth MN 55802	800-706-7672	218-727-4192
Lindey's Prime Steak House		
3600 N Snelling Ave ....Arden Hills MN 55112	866-491-0538	651-633-9813

Mississippi

	Toll-Free	Phone
Harvey's 424 S Gloster St ....Tupelo MS 38801	888-222-9550	662-842-6763

Missouri

	Toll-Free	Phone
Capitol Plaza Hotel		
415 W McCarty St ....Jefferson City MO 65101	800-338-8088	573-635-1234
Chateau Grille		
415 N State Hwy 265 ....Branson MO 65616	888-333-5253	417-334-1161

Nevada

	Toll-Free	Phone
Atlantis Seafood Steakhouse		
3800 S Virginia St		
Atlantis Casino Resort....................Reno NV 89502	800-723-6500	
Caesar's Palace		
3570 Las Vegas Blvd S		
Caesar's Palace....................Las Vegas NV 89109	800-634-6001	702-731-7110
Canaletto		
3355 Las Vegas Blvd S ....Las Vegas NV 89109	866-659-9643	702-414-1000
Le Cirque		
3600 Las Vegas Blvd S ....Las Vegas NV 89109	888-987-6667	702-693-7111
Lillie's Asian Cuisine		
129 E Fremont St ....Las Vegas NV 89101	800-634-3454	702-385-7111
Nob Hill		
3799 Las Vegas Blvd S		
MGM Grand Hotel....................Las Vegas NV 89109	800-929-1111*	702-891-1111
*Resv		
Osteria Del Circo		
3600 Las Vegas Blvd S ....Las Vegas NV 89109	866-259-7111	888-987-6667
Spago		
3500 Las Vegas Blvd S Ste G1 ....Las Vegas NV 89109	800-241-3333	702-369-6300
SW Steakhouse		
3131 Las Vegas Blvd S ....Las Vegas NV 89109	888-320-7198	702-770-9966
Trattoria Del Lupo		
3950 Las Vegas Blvd S ....Las Vegas NV 89119	800-275-8273	702-740-5522

New Jersey

	Toll-Free	Phone
Sea Blue		
1 Borgata Way ....Atlantic City NJ 08401	877-786-9900*	609-317-1000
*Cust Svc		

New Mexico

	Toll-Free	Phone
Fuego 330 E Palace Ave ....Santa Fe NM 87501	855-811-0050*	505-986-0000
*Sales		

		Toll-Free	Phone
Old House 309 W San Francisco St	Santa Fe NM 87501	**800-955-4455**	505-988-4455

New York

		Toll-Free	Phone
Aureole 135 W 42nd St	New York NY 10036	**800-889-7188**	212-319-1660
Desmond Albany Hotel, The 660 Albany-Shaker Rd	Albany NY 12211	**800-448-3500**	518-869-8100
Kai 20 Jay St Ste 530	Brooklyn NY 11201	**888-832-7832**	718-250-4000
Palm Restaurant 837 Second Ave	New York NY 10017	**866-333-7256**	212-687-2953
Salvatore's Italian Gardens 6461 Transit Rd	Depew NY 14043	**877-456-4097**	716-683-7990

North Carolina

		Toll-Free	Phone
Angus Barn 9401 Glenwood Ave	Raleigh NC 27617	**800-277-2270**	919-781-2444
McCormick & Schmick's 200 S Tryon St	Charlotte NC 28202	**800-552-6379**	704-377-0201
Melting Pot of Charlotte, The 901 S Kings Dr Ste 140B	Charlotte NC 28204	**800-783-0867**	704-334-4400

Ohio

		Toll-Free	Phone
M at Miranova 2 Miranova PL Ste 100	Columbus OH 43215	**877-491-1267**	614-629-0000
Palace, The 601 Vine St	Cincinnati OH 45202	**800-942-9000**	513-381-6006
Tony Packo's 1902 Front St	Toledo OH 43605	**866-472-2567**	419-691-1953

Ontario

		Toll-Free	Phone
Courtyard Cafe 18 St Thomas St *Cust Svc	Toronto ON M5S3E7	**877-999-2767***	416-921-2921
Le Saint Tropez 315 King St W	Toronto ON M5V1J5	**888-627-2357**	416-591-8600

Oregon

		Toll-Free	Phone
Jake's Famous Crawfish 401 SW 12th Ave SW Stark	Portland OR 97205	**800-552-6379**	503-226-1419
Jake's Grill 611 SW Tenth Ave	Portland OR 97205	**800-552-6379**	503-220-1850
McCormick & Schmick's Harborside 0309 SW Montgomery *Resv	Portland OR 97201	**888-262-4386***	503-220-1865

Pennsylvania

		Toll-Free	Phone
Cashtown Inn Restaurant 1325 Old Rt 30	Cashtown PA 17310	**800-367-1797**	717-334-9722
Herr Tavern & Public House 900 Chambersburg Rd	Gettysburg PA 17325	**800-362-9849**	717-334-4332
Petra 3602 W Lake Rd	Erie PA 16505	**866-906-2931**	814-838-7197

Quebec

		Toll-Free	Phone
Laurie Raphael 117 Dalhousie St	Quebec QC G1K9C8	**877-876-4555**	418-692-4555

South Carolina

		Toll-Free	Phone
82 Queen 82 Queen St	Charleston SC 29401	**800-849-0082**	843-723-7591
Grill 225 225 E Bay St	Charleston SC 29401	**877-440-2250**	843-266-4222
Melting Pot of Columbia, The 1410 Colonial Life Blvd	Columbia SC 29210	**800-783-0867**	803-731-8500
Middleton Place 4300 Ashley River Rd	Charleston SC 29414	**800-782-3608**	843-556-6020
Salty Dog Cafe, The 232 S Sea Pines Dr	Hilton Head Island SC 29928	**877-725-8936**	843-671-5199
Signe's Bakery & Cafe 93 Arrow Rd	Hilton Head Island SC 29928	**866-807-4463**	843-785-9118
Sticky Fingers 235 Meeting St	Charleston SC 29401	**800-784-2597**	843-853-7427

Tennessee

		Toll-Free	Phone

Texas

		Toll-Free	Phone
Anaqua Grill 555 S Alamo St	San Antonio TX 78205	**800-845-5279**	210-229-1000
Big Texan Steak Ranch 7701 I-40 E *Cust Svc	Amarillo TX 79118	**800-657-7177***	806-372-6000
Hard Rock Cafe 111 W Crocket St	San Antonio TX 78205	**888-519-6683**	210-224-7625
Hudson's on the Bend 3509 Ranch Rd 620 N	Austin TX 78734	**800-996-7655**	512-266-1369
Kam's 4500 Montrose Blvd	Houston TX 77006	**800-510-3663**	713-529-5057
Landry's Seafood House 6801 Gateway Blvd W	El Paso TX 79925	**800-394-3839**	915-779-2900
Melting Pot of San Antonio, The 14855 Blanco Rd Ste 110	San Antonio TX 78216	**800-783-0867**	210-479-6358

		Toll-Free	Phone
Morton's The Steakhouse 5000 Westheimer Rd	Houston TX 77056	**800-552-6379**	713-629-1946
Noe Restaurant & Bar 4 Riverway	Houston TX 77056	**800-809-6664**	713-871-8177
Spring Creek Barbeque 2340 W I-20 Ste 100	Arlington TX 76017	**888-467-0505**	817-467-0505
Texas Land & Cattle Steak House 9911 W IH-10	San Antonio TX 78230	**855-685-1622**	210-699-8744

Vermont

		Toll-Free	Phone
Trader Duke's 1117 Williston Rd	South Burlington VT 05403	**800-445-8667**	802-660-7523

Virginia

		Toll-Free	Phone
Johnny Rockets 1100 S Hayes St	Arlington VA 22202	**888-856-4669**	703-415-3510
Morrison House 116 S Alfred St	Alexandria VA 22314	**866-834-6628**	703-838-8000

West Virginia

		Toll-Free	Phone
Tidewater Grill 1060 Charleston Town Ctr	Charleston WV 25389	**888-456-3463**	304-345-2620
Whitewater Grille 200 Lee St E	Charleston WV 25301	**800-845-5279**	304-353-3636

Wisconsin

		Toll-Free	Phone
Admiralty Room 666 Wisconsin Ave	Madison WI 53703	**800-922-5512**	608-256-9071
Crawdaddy's 6414 W Greenfield Ave	Milwaukee WI 53214	**800-727-9477**	414-778-2228
Essen Haus 514 E Wilson St	Madison WI 53703	**800-448-0158**	608-255-4674
Packing House 900 E Layton Ave	Milwaukee WI 53207	**800-727-9477**	414-483-5054

Wyoming

		Toll-Free	Phone
Bar-T-5 Covered Wagon Cook Out & Wild West Show 812 Cache Creek Dr	Jackson WY 83001	**800-772-5386**	307-733-5386

668   RETIREMENT COMMUNITIES

SEE ALSO Long-Term Care Facilities
Listed here are senior communities where the majority of residents live independently but where nursing care and/or other personal care is available on-site. The listings in this category are organized alphabetically by state names.

		Toll-Free	Phone
Abbey Delray 2000 Lowson Blvd	Delray Beach FL 33445	**888-791-9363**	561-454-2000
Arbor Acres 1240 Arbor Rd	Winston-Salem NC 27104	**866-658-2724**	336-724-7921
Arbors of Hop Brook 403 W Ctr St	Manchester CT 06040	**866-689-0846**	860-647-9343
Armed Forces Retirement Home - Gulfport 1800 Beach Dr	Gulfport MS 39507	**800-422-9988**	
Army Residence Community 7400 Crestway	San Antonio TX 78239	**800-725-0083**	210-646-5316
Asbury Methodist Village 201 Russell Ave	Gaithersburg MD 20877	**800-327-2879**	301-216-4100
Bermuda Village 142 Bermuda Village Dr *Mktg	Advance NC 27006	**800-843-5433***	
Brittany Pointe Estates 1001 S Valley Forge Rd	Lansdale PA 19446	**800-504-2287**	215-855-4109
Brookdale Senior Living Inc 111 Westwood Pl Ste 400	Brentwood TN 37027	**866-785-9025**	615-221-2250
Cadbury Retirement Community 2150 Rt 38	Cherry Hill NJ 08002	**800-422-3287**	856-667-4550
Capital Manor 1955 Dallas Hwy NW	Salem OR 97304	**800-637-0327**	503-362-4101
Carmel Valley Manor 8545 Carmel Vly Rd	Carmel CA 93923	**800-544-5546**	831-624-1281
Carol Woods Retirement Community 750 Weaver Dairy Rd	Chapel Hill NC 27514	**800-518-9333**	919-968-4511
Carolina Meadows 100 Carolina Meadows	Chapel Hill NC 27517	**800-458-6756**	919-942-4014
Carroll Lutheran Village 300 St Luke Cir	Westminster MD 21158	**877-848-0095**	410-848-0090
Charlestown Retirement Community (CCI) 715 Maiden Choice Ln	Catonsville MD 21228	**800-917-8649**	410-242-2880
Clark-Lindsey Village 101 W Windsor Rd	Urbana IL 61802	**800-998-2581**	217-344-2144
Covenant Village of Golden Valley 5800 St Croix Ave	Minneapolis MN 55422	**877-224-5051**	763-546-6125
Covenant Village of Turlock 2125 N Olive Ave	Turlock CA 95382	**800-485-7844**	209-216-5610
Crestwood Manor 50 Lacey Rd *General	Whiting NJ 08759	**877-467-1652***	732-849-4900
Cross Keys Village 2990 Carlisle Pk PO Box 128 *Mktg	New Oxford PA 17350	**888-624-8242***	717-624-5350
Culpeper Baptist Retirement Community 12425 Military Loop	Culpeper VA 22701	**800-894-2411**	540-825-2411
Deerfield Episcopal Retirement Community 1617 Hendersonville Rd	Asheville NC 28803	**800-284-1531**	828-274-1531
East Ridge Retirement Village 19301 SW 87th Ave	Miami FL 33157	**800-856-8097**	

			Toll-Free	Phone

Edgewater Pointe Estates
23315 Blue Water Cir ....Boca Raton FL 33433 **888-339-2287*** 561-391-6305
*General

Elim Park Place
140 Cook Hill Rd ....Cheshire CT 06410 **800-994-1776** 203-272-3547

Englewood Meridian
3455 S Corona St ....Englewood CO 80113 **855-444-7658** 888-221-7317

Epoch Senior Living
51 Sawyer Rd Ste 500. ....Waltham MA 02453 **877-376-2475** 781-891-0777

Epworth Villa
14901 N Pennsylvania Ave ....Oklahoma City OK 73134 **800-579-8776** 405-752-1200

Eskaton Village
3939 Walnut Ave ....Carmichael CA 95608 **800-300-3929** 916-974-2000

Essex Meadows 30 Bokum Rd ....Essex CT 06426 **800-767-7201** 860-767-7201

Evergreen Woods
88 Notch Hill Rd ....North Branford CT 06471 **866-413-6378*** 203-488-8000
*General

Evergreens, The
309 Bridgeboro Rd ....Moorestown NJ 08057 **877-673-8234** 856-439-2000

Fairhaven 7200 Third Ave ....Sykesville MD 21784 **877-696-6775** 410-795-8801

First Community Village
1800 Riverside Dr ....Columbus OH 43212 **877-364-2570** 614-324-4455

Fleet Landing Retirement Community
1 Fleet Landing Blvd ....Atlantic Beach FL 32233 **877-591-6547*** 904-246-9900
*General

Florida Presbyterian Homes
16 Lk Hunter Dr ....Lakeland FL 33803 **866-294-3352** 863-688-5521

Forest at Duke
2701 Pickett Rd ....Durham NC 27705 **800-474-0258** 919-490-8000

Foxdale Village
500 E Marylyn Ave ....State College PA 16801 **800-253-4951** 814-272-2117

Franciscan Oaks
19 Pocono Rd ....Denville NJ 07834 **800-237-3330** 973-586-6000

Freedom Village
23442 El Toro Rd ....Lake Forest CA 92630 **800-584-8084** 949-472-4700

Friendship Manor
1209 21st Ave ....Rock Island IL 61201 **888-382-1222** 309-786-9667

Friendship Village Kalamazoo
1400 N Drake Rd ....Kalamazoo MI 49006 **800-613-3984** 269-381-0560

Friendship Village of Tempe
2645 E Southern Ave ....Tempe AZ 85282 **800-824-1112** 480-831-5000

Friendsview Retirement Community
1301 E Fulton St ....Newberg OR 97132 **866-307-4371** 503-538-3144

Ginger Cove
4000 River Crescent Dr ....Annapolis MD 21401 **800-299-2683** 410-266-7300

Glen Meadows
11630 Glen Arm Rd ....Glen Arm MD 21057 **800-630-4689**

Golden Oaks Village
5801 N Oakwood Rd ....Enid OK 73703 **800-259-0914** 580-249-2600

Grand Lake Gardens
401 Santa Clara Ave ....Oakland CA 94610 **800-416-6091**

Granite Farms Estates
1343 W Baltimore Pike ....Media PA 19063 **888-499-2287** 610-358-3440

Harbour's Edge
401 E Linton Blvd ....Delray Beach FL 33483 **888-417-9281** 561-272-7979

Harrogate 400 Locust St ....Lakewood NJ 08701 **888-551-5531** 732-905-7070

Havenwood-Heritage Heights Havenwood Campus
33 Christian Ave ....Concord NH 03301 **800-457-6833** 603-224-5363

Heritage Club
2020 S Monroe St ....Denver CO 80210 **888-221-7317** 303-756-0025

Heron Point of Chestertown
501 E Campus Ave ....Chestertown MD 21620 **800-327-9138** 410-778-7300

Indian River Estates
2250 Indian Creek Blvd W ....Vero Beach FL 32966 **800-544-0277*** 772-562-7400
*Mktg

John Knox Village
400 NW Murray Rd ....Lee's Summit MO 64081 **800-892-5669** 816-251-8000

Judson Park
23600 Marine View Dr S ....Des Moines WA 98198 **800-401-4113** 206-824-4000

Kendal at Ithaca
2230 N Triphammer Rd ....Ithaca NY 14850 **800-253-6325** 607-266-5300

Kendal at Longwood & Crosslands
PO Box 100 ....Kennett Square PA 19348 **800-216-1920** 610-388-1441

Kendal at Oberlin
600 Kendal Dr ....Oberlin OH 44074 **800-548-9469***
*Mktg

Kingswood Senior Living Community
10000 Wornall Rd ....Kansas City MO 64114 **888-942-2715*** 816-942-0994
*Sales

Knollwood
6200 Oregon Ave NW ....Washington DC 20015 **800-541-4255** 202-541-0400

La Vida Llena
10501 Lagrima de Oro NE ....Albuquerque NM 87111 **800-922-1344** 505-293-4001

Lake Seminole Square
8333 Seminole Blvd ....Seminole FL 33772 **866-785-9025** 727-391-0500

Lakewood Manor
1900 Lauderdale Dr ....Richmond VA 23238 **866-521-9100** 804-740-2900

Larksfield Place
7373 E 29th St N ....Wichita KS 67226 **866-232-8484** 316-858-3910

Laurel Lake Retirement Community
200 Laurel Lk Dr ....Hudson OH 44236 **866-650-2100**

Lima Estates
411 N Middletown Rd ....Media PA 19063 **888-398-2287** 610-565-7020

Loomis Communities
246 N Main St ....South Hadley MA 01075 **800-865-7655** 413-532-5325

Lutheran Community at Telford
12 Lutheran Home Dr ....Telford PA 18969 **877-343-7518** 215-723-9819

Manor Park Inc
2208 N Loop 250 W ....Midland TX 79707 **800-523-9898** 432-689-9898

Maple Knoll Communities Inc
11100 Springfield Pk ....Cincinnati OH 45246 **800-272-3900** 513-782-2400

Martins Run 100 Halcyon Dr ....Media PA 19063 **877-824-3935** 610-353-7660

Mayflower Retirement Community
1620 Mayflower Ct ....Winter Park FL 32792 **800-228-6518** 407-672-1620

Medford Leas
One Medford Leas Way ....Medford NJ 08055 **800-331-4302** 609-654-3000

Methodist ElderCare Services
5155 N High St ....Columbus OH 43214 **855-636-2225** 614-396-4990

Methodist Manor House
1001 Middleford Rd ....Seaford DE 19973 **800-775-4593** 302-629-4593

Moorings Park
120 Moorings Pk Dr ....Naples FL 34105 **866-802-4302** 239-643-9111

Morningside of Fullerton
800 Morningside Dr ....Fullerton CA 92835 **800-803-7597** 714-256-8000

Mount Miguel Covenant Village
325 Kempton St ....Spring Valley CA 91977 **877-407-4790** 619-479-4790

O'Connor Woods
3400 Wagner Heights Rd ....Stockton CA 95209 **800-957-3308** 209-956-3400

Otterbein Retirement Living Communities
580 N SR 741 ....Lebanon OH 45036 **888-513-9131** 513-933-5400

Panorama City 1751 Cir Ln SE ....Lacey WA 98503 **800-999-9807** 360-456-0111

Passavant Retirement Community
401 S Main St ....Zelienople PA 16063 **888-498-7753** 724-452-5400

Pine Run Community
777 Ferry Rd ....Doylestown PA 18901 **888-992-8992** 215-345-9000

Plymouth Village
900 Salem Dr ....Redlands CA 92373 **800-391-4552** 909-793-9195

Pomperaug Woods
80 Heritage Rd ....Southbury CT 06488 **866-817-8935** 203-262-6555

Presbyterian Homes of SC
2817 Ashland Rd ....Columbia SC 29210 **888-842-4855** 803-772-5885

Providence Life Services
18601 N Creek Dr ....Tinley Park IL 60477 **800-509-2800** 708-342-8100

Regents Point
19191 Harvard Ave ....Irvine CA 92612 **800-347-3735*** 949-988-0849
*General

RiverMead Retirement Community
150 RiverMead Rd ....Peterborough NH 03458 **800-200-5433** 603-924-0062

Rockwood Retirement Community
2903 E 25th Ave ....Spokane WA 99223 **800-727-6650** 509-536-6650

Rogue Valley Manor
1200 Mira Mar Ave ....Medford OR 97504 **800-848-7868** 541-857-7214

Rosewood Retirement Community
1301 New Stine Rd ....Bakersfield CA 93309 **800-984-4216** 661-834-0620

Saint Andrews Estates
6152 Verde Trail N ....Boca Raton FL 33433 **866-897-3490*** 561-487-4728
*Mktg

Seniorsplus
Eight Falcon Rd PO Box 659. ....Lewiston ME 04243 **800-427-1241** 207-795-4010

Shell Point Village
15101 Shell Pt Blvd ....Fort Myers FL 33908 **800-780-1131*** 239-466-1131
*Mktg

Shenandoah Valley Westminster-Canterbury
300 Westminster-Canterbury Dr ....Winchester VA 22603 **800-492-9463** 540-665-5914

Sherwood Oaks
100 Norman Dr ....Cranberry Township PA 16066 **800-642-2217** 724-776-8100

Smith Ranch Homes
400 Deer Vly Rd Ste L......................San Rafael CA 94903 **800-772-6264** 415-491-4918

Solheim Lutheran Home (SLH)
2236 Merton Ave ....Los Angeles CA 90041 **888-257-7518** 323-257-7518

Spanish Cove 11 Palm Ave ....Yukon OK 73099 **800-965-2683**

Spring House Estates
728 Norristown Rd ....Lower Gwynedd PA 19002 **888-365-2287** 215-628-8110

Stratford Court
45 Katherine Blvd ....Palm Harbor FL 34684 **888-434-4648** 727-787-1500

Temple Meridian
4312 S 31st St ....Temple TX 76502 **855-444-7658** 254-771-2350

Terraces at Phoenix, The
7550 N 16th St ....Phoenix AZ 85020 **800-836-4281** 602-906-4024

Valle Verde
900 Calle de los Amigos ....Santa Barbara CA 93105 **800-750-5089** 805-883-4000

Vi 71 S Wacker Dr ....Chicago IL 60606 **800-421-1442** 312-803-8800

Villa Gardens
842 E Villa St ....Pasadena CA 91101 **800-958-4552** 626-463-5329

Villa Pueblo Towers
2501 E 104th Ave ....Thornton CO 80233 **888-808-8828** 303-255-4100

Village on the Green
500 Village Pl ....Longwood FL 32779 **888-541-3443*** 407-682-0230
*Mktg

Village, The
2200 W Acacia Ave ....Hemet CA 92545 **800-257-7888** 951-658-3369

Vista del Monte
3775 Modoc Rd ....Santa Barbara CA 93105 **800-736-1333** 805-687-0793

Vista Grande Villa
2251 Springport Rd ....Jackson MI 49202 **800-889-8499** 517-787-0222

Waterford, The
601 Universe Blvd ....Juno Beach FL 33408 **888-335-1678** 561-627-3800

Wesley Homes
815 S 216th St ....Des Moines WA 98198 **866-937-5390** 206-824-5000

Wesley Towers
700 Monterey Pl ....Hutchinson KS 67502 **888-663-9175** 620-663-9175

Westminster Bradenton Manor
1700 21st Ave W ....Bradenton FL 34205 **866-846-8046** 941-748-4161

Westminster Oaks
4449 Meandering Way ....Tallahassee FL 32308 **866-937-6257** 850-878-1136

Westminster Place
3200 Grant St ....Evanston IL 60201 **800-896-9095** 847-570-3422

Westminster Towers
80 W Lucerne Cir ....Orlando FL 32801 **800-416-2612** 407-841-1310

Westminster Village
803 N Wahneta St ....Allentown PA 18109 **888-563-8147** 610-782-8300

Westminster-Canterbury of Lynchburg
501 VES Rd ....Lynchburg VA 24503 **800-962-3520** 434-386-3500

Westminster-Canterbury on Chesapeake Bay
3100 Shore Dr ....Virginia Beach VA 23451 **800-349-1722** 757-496-1100

Westminster-Canterbury Richmond
1600 Westbrook Ave ....Richmond VA 23227 **800-445-9904** 804-264-6000

White Oak Manor Inc
130 E Main St PO Box 3347................Spartanburg SC 29304 **800-826-6762** 864-582-7503

White Sands of La Jolla
516 Burchett St ....Glendale CA 92037 **800-347-3735** 818-247-0420

Whitney Ctr
200 Leeder Hill Dr ....Hamden CT 06517 **800-237-3847** 203-848-2641

Willamette View
12705 SE River Rd ....Portland OR 97222 **800-446-0670** 503-654-6581

	Toll-Free	Phone
Williamsburg Landing		
5700 Williamsburg Landing Dr .... Williamsburg VA 23185	800-554-5517	757-565-6505
Willow Valley Lakes Manor		
300 Willow Vly Lakes Dr .... Willow Street PA 17584	800-770-5445	717-464-0800
Willows, The 1 Lyman St .... Westborough MA 01581	800-464-8060	508-366-4730

669 RETREATS - SPIRITUAL

The facilities listed here offer basic amenities and services such as bed linens, food preparation, maid service, etc. Although physical activity may play a role in the programs offered, the focus is on the spiritual.

	Toll-Free	Phone
Chopra Ctr at La Costa Resort & Spa		
2013 Costa del Mar Rd ....Carlsbad CA 92009	888-424-6772	760-494-1600
Elat Chayyim		
116 Johnson Rd .... Falls Village CT 06031	800-398-2630	
Expanding Light		
14618 Tyler Foote Rd .... Nevada City CA 95959	800-346-5350	530-478-7518
Harbin Hot Springs		
18424 Harbin Springs Rd PO Box 782 .... Middletown CA 95461	800-622-2477	707-987-2477
Hollyhock		
PO Box 127 ....Mansons Landing BC V0P1K0	800-933-6339	250-935-6576
Kalani Oceanside Retreat		
12-6860 Kapoho Kalapana Rd .... Pahoa HI 96778	800-800-6886	808-965-7828
Kirkridge Retreat & Study Ctr		
2495 Fox Gap Rd .... Bangor PA 18013	800-231-2222	610-588-1793
Laurelville Mennonite Church Ctr		
941 Laurelville Ln .... Mount Pleasant PA 15666	800-839-1021	724-423-2056
Louhelen Baha'i School		
3208 S State Rd .... Davison MI 48423	800-894-9716	810-653-5033
Omega Institute for Holistic Studies		
150 Lake Dr ....Rhinebeck NY 12572	800-944-1001	845-266-4444
Our Lady of Fatima Retreat House		
5353 E 56th St .... Indianapolis IN 46226	800-480-2520	317-545-7681
Pendle Hill		
338 Plush Mill Rd ....Wallingford PA 19086	800-742-3150	610-566-4507
Pumpkin Hollow Farm		
1184 Rt 11 .... Craryville NY 12521	877-325-3583	518-325-3583
Saint Meinrad Archabbey		
200 Hill Dr ....Saint Meinrad IN 47577	800-682-0988	812-357-6585
Satchidananda Ashram Yogaville (SAYVA)		
108 Yogaville Way .... Buckingham VA 23921	800-858-9642*	434-969-3121
*Resv		
Shambhala Mountain Ctr		
151 Shambhala Wy .... Red Feather Lakes CO 80545	888-788-7221	970-881-2184
Spiritual Life Ctr		
7100 E 45th St N .... Wichita KS 67226	800-348-2440	316-744-0167

670 ROLLING MILL MACHINERY

SEE ALSO Metalworking Machinery

	Toll-Free	Phone
Bradbury Company Inc		
1200 E Cole .... Moundridge KS 67107	800-397-6394	620-345-6394
Formtek Metal Forming Inc		
4899 Commerce Pkwy .... Cleveland OH 44128	800-631-0520	216-292-4460
Magnum Integrated Technologies Inc		
200 First Gulf Blvd .... Brampton ON L6W4T5	800-830-0642	905-595-1998
WHEMCO Inc		
5 Hot Metal St ....Pittsburgh PA 15203	800-800-7686	412-390-2700

671 ROYALTY TRUSTS

	Toll-Free	Phone
ARC Resources Ltd		
308 Fourth Ave SW Ste 1200 ....Calgary AB T2P0H7	888-272-4900	403-503-8600
TSE: ARX		
Great Northern Iron Ore Properties		
332 Minnesota St Rm W1290...............Saint Paul MN 55101	800-468-9716	651-224-2385
NYSE: GNI		
Harvest Energy Trust		
330 Fifth Ave SW Ste 2100 ....Calgary AB T2P0L4	866-666-1178	403-265-1178
North European Oil Royalty Trust		
43 W Front St Ste 19A .... Red Bank NJ 07701	800-368-5948	732-741-4008
NYSE: NRT		
Pengrowth Energy Trust		
222 Third Ave SW Ste 2100 ....Calgary AB T2P0B4	800-223-4122	403-233-0224
NYSE: PGH		
Penn West Energy Trust		
425 First St SW Ste 2200 ....Calgary AB T2P3L8	866-693-2707	403-777-2500
Texas Pacific Land Trust		
1700 Pacific Ave Ste 2770 ....Dallas TX 75201	877-231-7500	214-969-5530
NYSE: TPL		

672 RUBBER GOODS

	Toll-Free	Phone
Aero Tec Labs Inc		
45 Spear Rd Industrial Pk ....Ramsey NJ 07446	800-526-5330	201-825-1400
Alliance Rubber Co		
210 Carpenter Dam Rd .... Hot Springs AR 71901	800-626-5940	
Biltrite Corp 51 Sawyer Rd ....Waltham MA 02454	800-877-8775	781-647-1700
BRP Manufacturing Co		
637 N Jackson St ....Lima OH 45801	800-858-0482	419-228-4441
Durable Products Inc		
PO Box 826 .... Crossville TN 38557	800-373-3502	931-484-3502
Flexsys America LP		
260 Springside Dr ....Akron OH 44333	800-455-5622	330-666-4111
Griswold Corp		
One River St PO Box 638 .... Moosup CT 06354	800-472-8788	860-564-3321

	Toll-Free	Phone
Hutchinson Aerospace & Industry Inc		
82 S St ....Hopkinton MA 01748	800-227-7962	508-417-7000
Kent Elastomer Products Inc		
1500 St Claire Ave .... Kent OH 44240	800-331-4762*	330-673-1011
*Cust Svc		
Koneta Inc 1400 Lunar Dr .... Wapakoneta OH 45895	800-331-0775	419-739-4200
Ludlow Composites Corp		
2100 Commerce Dr .... Fremont OH 43420	800-628-5463	
Mitchell Rubber Products Inc		
10220 San Sevaine Way .... Mira Loma CA 91752	800-453-7526	
MSM Industries Inc		
802 Swan Dr ....Smyrna TN 37167	800-648-6648	615-355-4355
Musson Rubber Company Inc		
1320 E Archwood Ave .... Akron OH 44306	800-321-2381*	330-773-7651
*Cust Svc		
National Rubber Technologies Corp		
35 Cawthra Ave .... Toronto ON M6N5B3	800-387-8501	416-657-1111
Pawling Corp		
32 Nelson Hill Rd PO Box 200 .... Wassaic NY 12592	800-431-3456	
Proco Products Inc		
PO Box 590 ....Stockton CA 95201	800-344-3246	209-943-6088
R & K Industrial Products Co		
1945 Seventh St ....Richmond CA 94801	800-842-7655	510-234-7212
Regupol America		
33 Keystone Dr .... Lebanon PA 17042	800-537-8737	
Shercon Inc		
6262 Katella Ave .... Cypress CA 90630	888-227-5847	714-548-3999
SMR Technologies Inc		
93 Nettie Fenwick Rd .... Fenwick WV 26202	800-767-6899	304-846-6636
Teknor Apex Co		
505 Central Ave ....Pawtucket RI 02861	800-556-3864	401-725-8000
Vulcan Corp		
30 Garfield Pl Ste 1040...................Cincinnati OH 45202	800-447-1146*	513-621-2850
*Sales		

673 RUBBER GOODS - MECHANICAL

Mechanical rubber goods are rubber components used in machinery, such as o-rings, sprockets, sleeves, roller covers, etc.

	Toll-Free	Phone
American National Rubber Co		
Main & High St .... Ceredo WV 25507	800-624-3410*	304-453-1311
*Cust Svc		
Armada Rubber Mfg Co		
24586 Armada Ridge Rd PO Box 579 .... Armada MI 48005	800-842-8311	586-784-9135
Atlantic India Rubber Co		
1437 Kentucky Rt 1428 ....Hagerhill KY 41222	800-476-6638	
Fabreeka International Inc		
1023 Tpke St ....Stoughton MA 02072	800-322-7352*	781-341-3655
*Cust Svc		
Finzer Roller Co		
129 Rawls Rd .... Des Plaines IL 60018	888-486-1900	847-390-6200
Griffith Rubber Mills		
2625 NW Industrial St .... Portland OR 97210	800-321-9677	503-226-6971
Holz Rubber Company Inc		
1129 S Sacramento St .... Lodi CA 95240	800-285-1600	209-368-7171
Jamak Fabrication Inc		
1401 N Bowie Dr .... Weatherford TX 76086	800-543-4747	817-594-8771
Jasper Rubber Products Inc		
1010 First Ave ....Jasper IN 47546	800-457-7457	812-482-3242
Lauren Mfg		
2228 Reiser Ave SE .... New Philadelphia OH 44663	855-989-9090	330-339-3373
Lavelle Industries Inc		
665 McHenry St .... Burlington WI 53105	800-528-3553	262-763-2434
Lord Corp 111 Lord Dr .... Cary NC 27511	877-275-5673	919-468-5979
Minor Rubber Company Inc		
49 Ackerman St .... Bloomfield NJ 07003	800-433-6886	973-338-6800
MOCAP Inc 409 Parkway Dr ....Park Hills MO 63601	800-633-6775	314-543-4000
Pamarco 171 E Marquardt Dr .... Wheeling IL 60090	800-323-7735*	847-459-6000
*Sales		
Precision Assoc Inc		
3800 N Washington Ave .... Minneapolis MN 55412	800-394-6590	612-333-7464
Sperry & Rice Mfg Company LLC		
9146 US Hwy 52 .... Brookville IN 47012	800-541-9277	765-647-4141
Thermodyn Corp		
3550 Silica Rd .... Sylvania OH 43560	800-654-6518	419-841-7782
Universal Polymer & Rubber Ltd		
15730 Madison Rd .... Middlefield OH 44062	800-782-2375	440-632-1691

674 SAFETY EQUIPMENT - MFR

SEE ALSO Medical Supplies - Mfr ; Personal Protective Equipment & Clothing

	Toll-Free	Phone
ACR Electronics Inc		
5757 Anglers Ave .... Fort Lauderdale FL 33312	800-432-0227	954-981-3333
Adams Elevator Equipment Co		
6310 W Howard St ....Niles IL 60714	800-929-9247	847-581-2900
ALP Industries Inc		
1229 W Lincoln Hwy .... Coatesville PA 19320	800-220-2571	610-384-1300
Ancra International LLC		
4880 W Rosecrans Ave .... Hawthorne CA 90250	800-973-5092	310-973-5000
Bradley Corp		
W 142 N 9101 Fountain Blvd ....Menomonee Falls WI 53051	800-272-3539	262-251-6000
Carsonite Composites LLC		
19845 US Hwy 76 .... Newberry SC 29108	800-648-7916	803-321-1185
CSE Corp 600 Seco Rd .... Monroeville PA 15146	800-245-2224	412-856-9200
Encon Safety Products Co		
6825 W Sam Houston Pkwy N PO Box 3826 .... Houston TX 77041	800-283-6266	713-466-1449
Gemtor Inc One Johnson Ave ....Matawan NJ 07747	800-405-9048	732-583-6200
Hawkins Traffic Safety Supply		
1255 E Shore Hwy .... Berkeley CA 94710	800-772-3995	800-236-0112
Herbert S Hiller Corp		
401 Commerce Pt ....New Orleans LA 70123	800-833-5211	504-736-0008

				Toll-Free	Phone
Ocenco Inc 10225 82nd Ave	Pleasant Prairie	WI	53158	800-932-2293	262-947-9000
Peerless Chain Co 1416 E Sanborn St	Winona	MN	55987	800-533-8056	507-457-9100
Peerless Industrial Group PO Box 949	Clackamas	OR	97015	800-547-6806	800-873-1916
Plastic Safety Systems Inc 2444 Baldwin Rd	Cleveland	OH	44104	800-662-6338	
Potter-Roemer 17451 Hurley St	City of Industry	CA	91744	800-366-3473	626-855-4890
Reflexite North America 315 S St	New Britain	CT	06051	800-654-7570	860-223-9297
Rite-Hite Corp 8900 N Arbon Dr	Milwaukee	WI	53224	800-456-0600	414-355-2600
Rostra Precision Controls Inc 2519 Dana Dr *Cust Svc	Laurinburg	NC	28352	800-782-3379*	910-276-4853

675 SAFETY EQUIPMENT - WHOL

				Toll-Free	Phone
Allstar Fire Equipment Inc 12328 Lower Azusa Rd	Arcadia	CA	91006	800-425-5787	626-652-0900
Arbill PO Box 820542	Philadelphia	PA	19154	800-523-5367	
Brooks Equipment Company Inc 10926 David Taylor Dr Ste 300	Charlotte	NC	28269	800-826-3473	
Broward Fire Equipment & Service Inc 101 SW Sixth St	Fort Lauderdale	FL	33301	800-866-3473	954-467-6625
Calolympic Glove & Safety Company Inc 1720 Delilah St	Corona	CA	92879	800-421-6630	951-340-2229
Continental Safety Equipment 2935 Waters Rd Ste 140	Eagan	MN	55121	800-844-7003	651-454-7233
Empire Safety & Supply Inc 10624 Industrial Ave	Roseville	CA	95678	800-995-1341	916-781-3003
LaFrance Equipment Corp 516 Erie St	Elmira	NY	14904	800-873-8808	607-733-5511
LN Curtis & Sons 1800 Peralta St	Oakland	CA	94607	800-443-3556	510-839-5111
Mid-Continent Safety 8225 E 35th St N *General	Wichita	KS	67226	800-776-0956*	316-522-0900
Minnesota Conway 575 Minnehaha Ave W St	Saint Paul	MN	55103	800-223-2587	651-251-1880
Nardini Fire Equipment Company Inc 405 County Rd E W	Saint Paul	MN	55126	888-627-3464	651-483-6631
Orr Safety Corp 11601 Interchange Dr	Louisville	KY	40229	800-726-6789	502-774-5791
PK Safety Supply 2005 Clement Ave Bldg 9	Alameda	CA	94501	800-829-9580	510-337-8880
Saf-T-Gard International Inc 205 Huehl Rd	Northbrook	IL	60062	800-548-4273	847-291-1600
Safety Products Inc 3517 Craftsman Blvd	Lakeland	FL	33803	800-248-6860	863-665-3601
Safety Supply South Inc 100 Centrum Dr *Cust Svc	Irmo	SC	29063	800-522-8344*	
Safeware Inc 3200 HubbaRd Rd *Cust Svc	Landover	MD	20785	800-331-6707*	301-683-1234
Sun Devil Fire Equipment Inc 2929 W Clarendon Ave	Phoenix	AZ	85017	800-536-3845	623-245-0636
United Fire Equipment Co 335 N Fourth Ave	Tucson	AZ	85705	800-362-0150	520-622-3639
Wayest Safety Inc 3750 N I-44 Service Rd	Oklahoma City	OK	73112	800-256-1003	405-942-7101
Wenaas AGS Inc 12211 Parc Crest Dr Bldg Ste 100	Stafford	TX	77477	888-576-2668	281-931-4300

676 SALT

SEE ALSO Spices, Seasonings, Herbs

Companies listed here produce salt that may be used for a variety of purposes, including as a food ingredient or for deicing, water conditioning, or other chemical or industrial applications.

				Toll-Free	Phone
Cargill Salt Inc PO Box 5621	Minneapolis	MN	55440	888-385-7258	
Compass Minerals International 9900 W 109th St Ste 100 *NYSE: CMP* ■ *Cust Svc	Overland Park	KS	66210	866-755-1743*	913-344-9200
Morton Salt Inc 123 N Wacker Dr	Chicago	IL	60606	800-725-8847	312-807-2000
United Salt Corp 4800 San Felipe St	Houston	TX	77056	800-554-8658	713-877-2600

677 SATELLITE COMMUNICATIONS SERVICES

SEE ALSO Telecommunications Services ; Internet Service Providers (ISPs) ; Cable & Other Pay Television Services

				Toll-Free	Phone
ARINC Inc 2551 Riva Rd	Annapolis	MD	21401	866-321-6060	410-266-4000
Force10 Networks Inc 1415 N McDowell Blvd	Petaluma	CA	94954	866-600-5100	707-665-4400
Globalstar LP 3200 Zanker Rd Bldg 260	San Jose	CA	95134	877-728-7466	408-933-4000
Lightriver Technologies Inc 2150 John Glenn Dre Ste 200	Concord	CA	94520	888-544-4825	941-552-9410
MDU Communications International Inc 60 D Commerce Way *OTC: MDTV*	Totowa	NJ	07512	866-286-9638	973-237-9499
MTN/ATC Teleports 3044 N Commerce Pkwy	Miramar	FL	33025	877-464-4686	954-538-4000
ORBCOMM 22265 Pacific Blvd Ste 200 *Cust Svc	Dulles	VA	20166	877-538-7764*	703-433-6300
Outerlink Corp 187 Ballardvale St Ste A260	Wilmington	MA	01887	877-688-3770	978-284-6070
Stratos Global Corp 6550 Rock Spring Dr Ste 650	Bethesda	MD	20817	800-563-2255	301-214-8800
ViaSat Inc 6155 El Camino Real *NASDAQ: VSAT*	Carlsbad	CA	92009	877-363-7396	760-476-2200

678 SAW BLADES & HANDSAWS

SEE ALSO Tools - Hand & Edge

				Toll-Free	Phone
California Saw & Knife Works 721 Brannan St	San Francisco	CA	94103	888-729-6533	415-861-0644
Contour Saws Inc 1217 E Thacker St	Des Plaines	IL	60016	800-458-9034	847-824-1146
Diamond Saw Works Inc 12290 Olean Rd	Chaffee	NY	14030	800-828-1180	716-496-7417
Disston Precision Inc 6795 State Rd *Cust Svc	Philadelphia	PA	19135	800-238-1007*	215-338-1200
Great Neck Saw Manufacturing Inc 165 E Second St *Cust Svc	Mineola	NY	11501	800-457-0600*	516-746-5352
ICS Blount Inc 4909 SE International Way	Portland	OR	97222	800-321-1240	
LS Starrett Co 121 Crescent St *NYSE: SCX*	Athol	MA	01331	800-482-8710	978-249-3551
Marvel Mfg Company Inc 3501 Marvel Dr	Oshkosh	WI	54902	800-472-9464	920-236-7200
MK Diamond Products Inc 1315 Storm Pkwy	Torrance	CA	90501	800-421-5830	310-539-5221
MK Morse Co 1101 11th St SE	Canton	OH	44707	800-733-3377	330-453-8187
Simonds International 135 Intervale Rd	Fitchburg	MA	01420	800-343-1616	

679 SAWMILLS & PLANING MILLS

				Toll-Free	Phone
Anthony Forest Products Co 309 N Washington Ave	El Dorado	AR	71730	800-221-2326	870-862-3414
Beadles Lumber Company Inc 900 Sixth St NE PO Box 3457	Moultrie	GA	31776	800-763-2400	229-985-6996
Buse Timber & Sales Inc 3812 28th Pl NE	Everett	WA	98201	800-305-2577	425-258-2577
Buskirk Lumber Co 319 Oak St	Freeport	MI	49325	800-860-9663	616-765-5103
Cersosimo Lumber Co Inc 1103 Vernon St	Brattleboro	VT	05301	800-326-5647	802-254-4508
Collins Cos 1618 SW First Ave Ste 500	Portland	OR	97201	800-329-1219	
Domtar Corp 395 de Maisonneuve W *NYSE: UFS*	Montreal	QC	H3A1L6	877-848-4466	514-848-5555
Fulghum Industries 317 S Main St	Wadley	GA	30477	800-841-5980	478-252-5223
Hampton Affiliates 9600 SW Barnes Rd Ste 200	Portland	OR	97225	888-310-1464	503-297-7691
Hardwoods of Michigan Inc 430 Div St	Clinton	MI	49236	800-327-2812	517-456-7431
Hunt Forest Products 401 E Reynolds Dr PO Box 1263	Ruston	LA	71273	800-390-8589	318-255-2245
Impact Guns 2710 South 1900 West	Ogden	UT	84401	888-505-3086	801-393-2474
Industrial Timber & Lumber Corp (ITL) 23925 Commerce Pk Rd	Beachwood	OH	44122	800-829-9663	216-831-3140
Louisiana-Pacific Corp 414 Union St Ste 2000 *NYSE: LPX*	Nashville	TN	37219	888-820-0325	615-986-5600
Manke Lumber Company Inc 1717 Marine View Dr	Tacoma	WA	98422	800-426-8488	253-572-6252
Parton Lumber Company Inc 251 Parton Rd	Rutherfordton	NC	28139	800-624-1501	828-287-4257
Pike Lumber Company Inc PO Box 247	Akron	IN	46910	800-356-4554	574-893-4511
Plum Creek Timber Company Inc 601 Union St Ste 3100 *NYSE: PCL*	Seattle	WA	98101	800-858-5347	206-467-3600
Robbins Inc 4777 Eastern Ave	Cincinnati	OH	45226	800-543-1913	513-871-8988
Roseburg Forest Products Co PO Box 1088	Roseburg	OR	97470	800-245-1115	541-679-3311
Rushmore Forest Products 23848 Hwy 385 PO Box 619	Hill City	SD	57745	866-466-5254	605-574-2512
Scotch Gulf Lumber 1850 Conception St Rd	Mobile	AL	36610	800-496-3307	251-457-6872
Scotch Lumber Co 119 W Main St PO Box 38	Fulton	AL	36446	800-936-4424	334-636-4424
Scott Industries Inc 1573 Hwy 136 W PO Box 7	Henderson	KY	42419	800-951-9276	270-831-2037
Stimson Lumber Co 520 SW Yamhill St Ste 700	Portland	OR	97204	800-445-9758	503-222-1676
Swaner Hardwood Co Inc 5 W Magnolia Blvd PO Box 4200	Burbank	CA	91503	800-368-1108	818-953-5350
TR Miller Mill Company Inc 215 Deer St PO Box 708	Brewton	AL	36427	800-633-6740	251-867-4331
Universal Forest Products Inc (UFPI) 2801 E Beltline Ave NE *NASDAQ: UFPI*	Grand Rapids	MI	49525	800-598-9663	616-364-6161
USNR 1981 Schurman Way PO Box 310	Woodland	WA	98674	800-289-8767	360-225-8267

	City	State	ZIP	Toll-Free	Phone
Weyerhaeuser Co 33663 Weyerhaeuser Way S *NYSE: WY*	Federal Way	WA	98003	**800-525-5440**	253-924-2345

680 SCALES & BALANCES

SEE ALSO Laboratory Apparatus & Furniture

	City	State	ZIP	Toll-Free	Phone
Avery Weigh-Tronix Inc 1000 Armstrong Dr	Fairmont	MN	56031	**800-458-7062**	507-238-4461
BRK Brands Inc 3901 Liberty St Rd	Aurora	IL	60504	**800-323-9005**	630-851-7330
Cardinal Detecto Scale Manufacturing Co 203 E Daugherty St	Webb City	MO	64870	**800-441-4237**	417-673-4631
Detecto Scale Co 203 E Daugherty St PO Box 151	Webb City	MO	64870	**800-641-2008**	417-673-4631
Emery Winslow Scale Co 73 Cogwheel Ln	Seymour	CT	06483	**800-891-3952**	203-881-9333
Fairbanks Scales Inc 821 Locust St	Kansas City	MO	64106	**800-451-4107**	816-471-0231
Industrial Data Systems Inc 3822 E La Palma Ave	Anaheim	CA	92807	**800-854-3311**	714-921-9212
Intercomp Co 3839 County Rd 116	Medina	MN	55340	**800-328-3336**	763-476-2531
Jarden Consumer Solutions 2381 Executive Ctr Dr	Boca Raton	FL	33431	**800-777-5452**	561-912-4100
Johnson Scale Company Inc 36 Stiles Ln	Pine Brook	NJ	07058	**800-572-2531**	
Measurement Specialties Inc 1000 Lucas Way *NASDAQ: MEAS*	Hampton	VA	23666	**800-745-8008**	757-766-1500
Mettler-Toledo International Inc 5 Barr Rd	Ithaca	NY	14850	**800-836-0836**	
Ohaus Corp 19-A Chapin Rd PO Box 2033	Pine Brook	NJ	07058	**800-672-7722**	973-377-9000
Schenck Trebel Corp 535 Acorn St	Deer Park	NY	11729	**800-873-2357**	631-242-4010
Scientech Inc 5649 Arapahoe Ave	Boulder	CO	80303	**800-525-0522**	303-444-1361
Setra Systems Inc 159 Swanson Rd	Boxborough	MA	01719	**800-257-3872**	978-263-1400
TCI Scales Inc PO Box 1648	Snohomish	WA	98291	**800-522-2206**	425-353-4384
Thayer Scale Corp 91 Schoosett St	Pembroke	MA	02359	**800-225-0450**	781-826-8101
Yamato Corp 1775 S Murray Blvd	Colorado Springs	CO	80916	**800-538-1762**	719-591-1500

681 SCHOOL BOARDS (PUBLIC)

	City	State	ZIP	Toll-Free	Phone
Alamance-Burlington School District 1712 Vaughn Rd	Burlington	NC	27217	**888-764-7001**	336-570-6060
Albuquerque Public Schools (APS) 6400 Uptown Blvd NE	Albuquerque	NM	87110	**866-563-9297**	505-880-3700
Alisal Union Elementary School District 1205 E Market St	Salinas	CA	93905	**800-782-7463**	831-753-5700
Allentown School District (ASD) 31 S Penn St	Allentown	PA	18105	**877-262-1492**	484-765-4000
Ames Community School District 415 Stanton Ave	Ames	IA	50014	**800-262-3867**	515-268-6600
Anchor Bay School District 5201 County Line Rd Ste 100	Casco Township	MI	48064	**800-285-4460**	586-725-2861
Anoka-Hennepin Independent School District 11 2727 N Ferry St	Anoka	MN	55303	**800-729-6164**	763-506-1000
Appling County Board of Education 249 Blackshear Hwy	Baxley	GA	31513	**866-632-9992**	912-367-8600
Arlington Central School District 144 Todd Hill Rd	LaGrangeville	NY	12540	**800-225-2527**	845-486-4460
Arlington School District 315 N French Ave	Arlington	WA	98223	**888-535-0747**	360-618-6200
Armstrong School District 410 Main St	Ford City	PA	16226	**888-573-5733**	724-763-5200
Ashland Independent School District PO Box 3000	Ashland	KY	41105	**800-752-6200**	606-327-2706
Atkinson County School System 98 Roberts Ave E	Pearson	GA	31642	**800-639-0850**	912-422-7373
Auburn City School District PO Box 3270	Auburn	AL	36831	**866-277-9644**	334-887-2100
Ave Intervision LLC 1840 W State St	Alliance	OH	44601	**800-448-9126**	
Bank of Highland Park Financial Corp 1835 First St PO Box 546	Highland Park	IL	60035	**877-651-7800**	847-432-7800
Barney Trucking Inc 235 State Rt 24	Salina	UT	84654	**800-524-7930**	
Bedford Public Schools 1623 W Sterns Rd	Temperance	MI	48182	**866-261-9184**	734-850-6000
Beemac Trucking 2747 Litionville Rd	Ambridge	PA	15003	**800-282-8781**	724-266-8781
Bellefonte Area School District 318 N Allegheny St	Bellefonte	PA	16823	**866-632-9992**	814-355-4814
Beverly Hills Unified School District 255 S Lasky Dr	Beverly Hills	CA	90212	**800-334-5847**	310-551-5100
Bexley City School District 348 S Cassingham Rd	Columbus	OH	43209	**800-282-1780**	614-231-7611
Big Spring Independent School District 708 E 11th Pl	Big Spring	TX	79720	**866-632-9992**	432-264-3600
Boarder to Boarder Trucking Inc PO Box 328	Edinburg	TX	78541	**800-678-8789**	956-316-4444
Breckinridge County School District 86 Airport Rd	Hardinsburg	KY	40143	**800-325-1713**	270-756-2186
Brunswick County Board of Education 35 Referendum Dr	Bolivia	NC	28422	**800-662-7030**	910-253-2900
Bullock Creek Public Schools 1420 S Badour Rd	Midland	MI	48640	**877-706-2508**	989-631-9022
Butler Area School District 110 Campus Ln	Butler	PA	16001	**888-800-5583**	724-287-8720
Cache County School District 2063 N 1200 E	North Logan	UT	84341	**888-837-6437**	435-752-3925
Campbell County Board of Education 101 Orchard Ln	Alexandria	KY	41001	**800-942-3767**	859-635-2173
Canby School District 1130 S Ivy St	Canby	OR	97013	**800-475-7785**	503-266-7861
Charleston County School District (CCSD) 75 Calhoun St	Charleston	SC	29401	**800-255-7688**	843-937-6300
Charlotte-Mecklenburg Schools 701 E ML King Jr Blvd	Charlotte	NC	28202	**800-244-6224**	980-343-3000
Christian County Public Schools 200 Glass Ave PO Box 609	Hopkinsville	KY	42240	**800-274-7374**	270-887-7000
Churchill County School District 545 E Richards St	Fallon	NV	89406	**800-232-6382**	775-423-5184
Circleville City School District 388 Clark Dr	Circleville	OH	43113	**800-418-6423**	740-474-4340
Clark County School District (CCSD) 5100 W Sahara Ave	Las Vegas	NV	89146	**866-799-8997**	702-799-5000
Clio Area School District 430 N Mill St	Clio	MI	48420	**866-984-3962**	810-591-0500
Clovis Unified School District 1450 Herndon Ave	Clovis	CA	93611	**800-498-9055**	559-327-9000
Clyde's Transfer Inc 8015 Industrial Pk Rd	Mechanicsville	VA	23116	**800-342-8758**	804-746-1135
Colorado Springs School District #11 1115 N El Paso St	Colorado Springs	CO	80903	**800-273-8255**	719-520-2000
Conestoga Valley School District 2110 Horseshoe Rd	Lancaster	PA	17601	**800-732-0025**	717-397-2421
Copperas Cove Independent School District 703 W Ave D	Copperas Cove	TX	76522	**866-632-9992**	254-547-1227
Corunna Public School District 124 N Shiawassee St	Corunna	MI	48817	**866-632-9992**	989-743-6338
Culver City Unified School District (CCUSD) 4034 Irving Pl	Culver City	CA	90232	**855-446-2673**	310-842-4220
D & T Trucking Inc 3686 140th St E PO Box 510	Rosemount	MN	55068	**800-624-8130**	651-480-7961
Dallas Independent School District 3700 Ross Ave	Dallas	TX	75204	**866-796-3682**	972-925-3700
Dawson County Board of Education, The 517 Allen St	Dawsonville	GA	30534	**866-632-9992**	706-265-3246
Delaware County Intermediate Unit 200 Yale Ave	Morton	PA	19070	**800-441-3215**	610-938-9000
Denver Public Schools 900 Grant St	Denver	CO	80203	**866-726-0033**	720-423-3200
Des Moines Independent School District 901 Walnut St	Des Moines	IA	50309	**800-452-1111**	515-242-7911
Desoto Parish School District 201 Crosby St	Mansfield	LA	71052	**888-741-0205**	318-872-2836
Detroit Public Schools 3031 W Grand Blvd	Detroit	MI	48202	**800-656-4673**	313-873-7927
Dickenson County School District PO Box 1127	Clintwood	VA	24228	**866-632-9992**	276-926-4643
Duarte Unified School District 1620 Huntington Dr	Duarte	CA	91010	**888-225-7377**	626-599-5000
Durham Academy Inc 3130 Pickett Rd	Durham	NC	27705	**888-904-9149**	919-489-9118
East Maine School District 63 (EMSD) 10150 Dee Rd	Des Plaines	IL	60016	**866-752-6850**	847-299-1900
Eastern Lancaster County School District 669 E Main St PO Box 609	New Holland	PA	17557	**877-935-5655**	717-354-1500
Eastside Union School District 45006 30th St E	Lancaster	CA	93535	**877-263-7995**	661-952-1200
Elzinga & Volkers 86 E Sixth St *General	Holland	MI	49423	**800-632-7734***	616-392-2383
Erie 2-Chautauqua Cattaraugus Boces (ECCB) 8685 Erie Rd	Angola	NY	14006	**800-228-1184**	716-549-4454
Etiwanda School District (ESD) 6061 E Ave	Etiwanda	CA	91739	**800-300-1506**	909-899-2451
Fannin County Board of Education 2290 E First St	Blue Ridge	GA	30513	**800-308-2145**	706-632-3771
Fayette County Board of Education 210 Stonewall Ave	Fayetteville	GA	30214	**800-550-5131**	770-460-3535
First Farmers & Merchants National Bank 816 S Garden St PO Box 1148 *OTC: FIME*	Columbia	TN	38401	**800-882-8378**	931-388-3145
Floyd Blinsky Trucking Inc 210 Keys Rd	Yakima	WA	98901	**800-537-9599**	509-457-3484
Forest Lake Area School District 6100 210th St N	Forest Lake	MN	55025	**866-632-9992**	651-982-8100
Fort Bragg Unified School District 312 S Lincoln St	Fort Bragg	CA	95437	**800-734-7793**	707-961-2850
Franklin Local School District PO Box 428	Duncan Falls	OH	43734	**800-846-4976**	740-674-5203
Fredericksburg City Public Schools 817 Princess Anne St	Fredericksburg	VA	22401	**800-846-4464**	540-372-1130
Fremont Public Schools 220 W Pine St	Fremont	MI	49412	**800-822-9433**	231-924-2350
Fremont Unified School District PO Box 5008	Fremont	CA	94537	**800-544-5248**	510-657-2350
Gainesville City Schools 508 Oak St	Gainesville	GA	30501	**800-533-0682**	770-536-5275
Galveston Independent School District (GISD) 3904 Ave PO Box 660	Galveston	TX	77550	**877-262-1492**	409-766-5100
Garland Independent School District (GISD) 501 S Jupiter PO Box 469026	Garland	TX	75046	**800-252-5555**	972-494-8201
Gladstone School District 115 17789 Webster Rd	Gladstone	OR	97027	**800-328-0272**	503-655-2777
Goliad Independent School District PO Box 830	Goliad	TX	77963	**800-750-9911**	361-645-3259
Granite Falls School District 307 N Alder Ave	Granite Falls	WA	98252	**888-651-8931**	360-691-7717
Gray Transportation Inc 2459 GT Dr	Waterloo	IA	50703	**800-234-3930**	319-234-3930
Greenwood School District 50 1855 Calhoun Rd PO Box 248	Greenwood	SC	29648	**888-260-9430**	864-941-5400

Name / Address	City	State	ZIP	Toll-Free	Phone
Guilford County Schools 617 W Market St	Greensboro	NC	27401	**866-286-7337**	336-370-8100
Gulf Coast Bank & Trust Co 200 St Charles Ave	New Orleans	LA	70130	**800-223-2060**	504-561-6100
Guy Shavender Trucking Inc PO Box 206	Pantego	NC	27860	**800-682-2447**	252-943-3379
Halifax County Public Schools 1030 Mary Bethune St PO Box 1849	Halifax	VA	24558	**800-253-2687**	434-476-2171
Hall County Schools 711 Green St NW Ste 100	Gainesville	GA	30501	**800-505-4732**	770-534-1080
Hamilton County Educational Service Ctr (HCESC) 11083 Hamilton Ave	Cincinnati	OH	45231	**800-964-8211**	513-674-4200
Harnett County Board of Education 1008 11th Street PO Box 1029	Lillington	NC	27546	**800-942-3767**	910-893-8151
Hatboro-Horsham School District 229 Meetinghouse Rd	Horsham	PA	19044	**866-771-3170**	215-672-5660
Hawaii Dept of Education Honolulu District Office 4967 Kilauea Ave	Honolulu	HI	96816	**800-437-8641**	808-733-4950
Hillsborough County Public Schools 901 E Kennedy Blvd	Tampa	FL	33602	**800-962-2873**	813-272-4000
Hillsborough Township Board of Education 379 S Branch Rd	Hillsborough	NJ	08844	**800-272-1325**	908-431-6600
Holiday Express Corp 721 S 28th St	Estherville	IA	51334	**800-831-5078**	712-362-5812
Houston Independent School District 228 McCarty St	Houston	TX	77029	**800-446-2821**	713-556-6000
Hueneme Elementary School Dist 205 N Ventura Rd	Port Hueneme	CA	93041	**866-431-2478**	805-488-3588
Huntsville Board of Education 200 White St	Huntsville	AL	35801	**877-517-0020**	256-428-6800
Idaho Falls School District 91 Education Foundation Inc 690 John Adams Pkwy	Idaho Falls	ID	83401	**888-993-7120**	208-525-7500
Ilex Construction & Woodworking 131 N Washington St Ste 400	Easton	MD	21601	**866-551-4539**	410-820-4393
J.M. Bozeman Enterprises Inc 166 Seltzer Ln *General	Malvern	AR	72104	**800-472-1836***	501-844-4060
Jackson County School District 6 300 Ash St	Central Point	OR	97502	**800-978-3040**	541-494-6200
Jackson County School System 1660 Winder Hwy	Jefferson	GA	30549	**800-760-3727**	706-367-5151
Jacksonville Independent School District PO Box 631	Jacksonville	TX	75766	**866-914-5202**	903-586-6511
Jennings County Schools 34 W Main St	North Vernon	IN	47265	**866-346-3724**	812-346-4483
Julian Charter School Inc 1704 Cape Horn	Julian	CA	92036	**866-853-0003**	760-765-3847
K12 Inc 2300 Corporate Pk Dr *NYSE: LRN*	Herndon	VA	20171	**866-512-2273**	703-483-7000
Lake Superior Ind Sch Dist 381 1640 2 Hwy	Two Harbors	MN	55616	**888-878-0136**	218-834-8201
Lamesa Independent School District PO Box 261	Lamesa	TX	79331	**888-286-6700**	806-872-5461
Lancaster City School District 345 E Mulberry St	Lancaster	OH	43130	**888-647-4729**	740-687-7300
Las Cruces Public Schools 505 S Main St Ste 249	Las Cruces	NM	88001	**888-222-1498**	575-527-5800
Lawrence Public Schools 110 McDonald Dr	Lawrence	KS	66044	**800-772-1213**	785-832-5000
Lenoir County Public School (LCPS) 2017 W Vernon Ave PO Box 729	Kinston	NC	28504	**888-684-8404**	252-527-1109
Lewis S. Mills High School 24 Lyon Rd	Burlington	CT	06013	**800-673-2411**	860-673-0423
Longview School District 2715 Lilac St	Longview	WA	98632	**800-533-7881**	360-575-7000
Los Angeles Unified School District (LAUSD) 333 S Beaudry Ave	Los Angeles	CA	90017	**877-772-6273**	213-241-1000
Madera Unified School District 1902 HowaRd Rd	Madera	CA	93637	**800-322-6384**	559-675-4500
McLeod Express LLC 5002 Cundiff Ct *General	Decatur	IL	62526	**800-709-3936***	
Mecosta-Osceola Intermediate School District 15760 190th Ave	Big Rapids	MI	49307	**877-211-5253**	231-796-3543
Meramec Valley R-3 School District 126 N Payne St	Pacific	MO	63069	**866-632-9992**	636-271-1400
Metropolitan Nashville Public Schools (MNPS) 2601 Bransford Ave	Nashville	TN	37204	**800-848-0298**	615-259-8531
Middlebury Community Schools 57853 Northridge Dr	Middlebury	IN	46540	**866-632-9992**	574-825-9425
Midwestern Intermediate Unit Iv 453 Maple St	Grove City	PA	16127	**800-942-8035**	724-458-6700
Miken Builders Inc 32782 Cedar Dr Unit 1	Millville	DE	19967	**800-888-7501**	302-537-4444
Minneapolis Public Schools 3345 Chicago Ave	Minneapolis	MN	55407	**800-543-7709**	612-668-0000
Mobile County Public Schools 1 Magnum Pass PO Box 180069	Mobile	AL	36618	**800-605-1033**	251-221-4000
Modesto City Schools 426 Locust St	Modesto	CA	95351	**800-942-3767**	209-576-4011
Monticello Central School District 237 Forestburgh Rd	Monticello	NY	12701	**866-805-0990**	845-794-7700
Mooresville Graded School District 305 N Main St	Mooresville	NC	28115	**800-222-1222**	704-658-2530
Mt. Lebanon School District 7 Horsman Dr	Pittsburgh	PA	15228	**800-587-3257**	412-344-2000
Murray Co 1807 Pk 270 Dr Ste 460	Saint Louis	MO	63146	**888-323-5560**	314-576-2818
National Children's Ctr Inc 6200 Second St NW	Washington	DC	20011	**866-632-9992**	202-722-2300
National Outdoor Leadership School 284 Lincoln St	Lander	WY	82520	**800-710-6657**	307-332-5300
Nationwide Magazine & Book Distributors Inc 3000 E Grauwyler Rd PO Box 170427 *General	Irving	TX	75017	**800-777-9068***	972-438-7852
New Brighton Area School District 3225 43rd St	New Brighton	PA	15066	**866-950-1040**	724-843-1795
Niles Community School 111 Spruce St	Niles	MI	49120	**877-622-2321**	269-683-0732
Niskayuna Central School District (NCSD) 1239 Van Antwerp Rd	Schenectady	NY	12309	**866-893-6337**	518-377-4666
Norfolk Public Schools 800 E City Hall Ave	Norfolk	VA	23510	**800-846-4464**	757-628-3843
North Ridgeville City School District 5490 Mills Creek Ln	North Ridgeville	OH	44039	**877-644-6457**	440-327-4444
North Rose-Wolcott Central School District 11631 Salter Colvin Rd	Wolcott	NY	14590	**855-707-2267**	315-594-3141
Northview Public School 4451 Hunsberger NE	Grand Rapids	MI	49525	**866-632-9992**	616-363-4857
Northwest Local School District (NWLSD) 3240 Banning Rd	Cincinnati	OH	45239	**800-374-2806**	513-923-1000
Nye County School District Inc (NCSD) PO Box 113	Tonopah	NV	89049	**800-796-6273**	775-482-6258
Oakland Unified School District 1025 Second Ave	Oakland	CA	94606	**888-604-4636**	510-879-8582
Olympia School District 1113 Legion Way SE	Olympia	WA	98501	**855-846-8376**	360-596-6100
Orange County Public Schools 445 W Amelia St	Orlando	FL	32801	**800-378-9264**	407-317-3200
Ossining Union Free School District 190 Croton Ave	Ossining	NY	10562	**877-769-7447**	914-941-7700
Palm Beach County School District, The 3300 Forest Hill Blvd	West Palm Beach	FL	33406	**866-930-8402**	561-434-8000
Palmerton Area School District 680 Fourth St	Palmerton	PA	18071	**800-732-0999**	610-826-7101
Parkland School District 1210 Springhouse Rd	Allentown	PA	18104	**866-632-9992**	610-351-5503
Peach County School District Inc 523 Vineville St	Fort Valley	GA	31030	**866-632-9992**	478-825-5933
Penns Grove-Carneys Point Regional Board of Education 100 Iona Ave	Penns Grove	NJ	08069	**877-652-7624**	856-299-4250
Person County Public Schools 304 S Morgan St	Roxboro	NC	27573	**866-724-6650**	336-599-2191
Pinelands Regional School District PO Box 248	Tuckerton	NJ	08087	**866-850-0511**	609-296-3106
Pittsylvania County School Board 39 Bank St SE PO Box 232	Chatham	VA	24531	**888-440-6520**	434-432-2761
Plaquemines Parish School Board 557 F Edward Hebert Blvd	Belle Chasse	LA	70037	**877-453-2721**	504-595-6400
Portland Public Schools 501 N Dixon St	Portland	OR	97227	**800-766-8206**	503-916-2000
Princeton Regional School District 25 Valley Rd Administration Bldg	Princeton	NJ	08540	**877-652-2873**	609-806-4200
Prior Lake-Savage Area Public School District 719 4540 Tower St SE	Prior Lake	MN	55372	**855-346-1650**	952-226-0000
Provision Ministry Group PO Box 19700	Irvine	CA	92623	**800-233-3880**	
Puget Sound Educational Service District 800 Oakesdale Ave SW	Renton	WA	98057	**800-664-4549**	425-917-7600
Putnam Valley School District Inc 146 Peekskill Hollow Rd	Putnam Valley	NY	10579	**800-666-5327**	845-528-8143
Rabun County School District 963 Tiger Connector	Tiger	GA	30576	**866-632-9992**	706-212-4350
Romeo Community School District 316 N Main St	Romeo	MI	48065	**888-427-6818**	586-752-0200
Rosetta Stone Ltd 1919 N Lynn St 7th Fl *NYSE: RST*	Arlington	VA	22209	**800-788-0822**	
Ross Valley School District 110 Shaw Dr	San Anselmo	CA	94960	**800-322-6384**	415-454-2162
Salem-Keizer Public Schools 2450 Lancaster Dr NE	Salem	OR	97305	**877-293-1090**	503-399-3000
Salin Bank 8455 Keystone Xing	Indianapolis	IN	46240	**800-320-7536**	317-452-8000
San Antonio Independent School District (SAISD) 141 Lavaca St	San Antonio	TX	78210	**800-943-6422**	210-554-2200
San Jose Unified School District 855 Lenzen Ave	San Jose	CA	95126	**800-433-3243**	408-535-6000
Saucon Valley School District 2097 Polk Vly Rd	Hellertown	PA	18055	**866-632-9992**	610-838-7026
Scarsdale Union Free School District 2 Brewster Rd	Scarsdale	NY	10583	**888-837-6437**	914-721-2410
School Board of Highlands County Florida PO Box 9300	Sebring	FL	33871	**877-357-7456**	863-471-5555
School District of The Chathams 58 Meyersville Rd	Chatham	NJ	07928	**800-225-5425**	973-457-2500
Schuylkill Valley School District 929 Lakeshore Dr	Leesport	PA	19533	**888-883-8237**	610-926-1706
Seguin Independent School District 1221 E Kingsbury St	Seguin	TX	78155	**866-632-9992**	830-372-5771
Sidney Transportation Services 777 W Russell Rd PO Box 748	Sidney	OH	45365	**800-743-6391**	937-498-2323
Southern Regional High School District Board of Education 105 Cedar Bridge Rd	Manahawkin	NJ	08050	**866-850-0511**	609-597-9481
Southgate Community School District 13305 Reeck Rd	Southgate	MI	48195	**888-263-5897**	734-246-4600
Splendora Independent School District 23419 FM 2090 Rd	Splendora	TX	77372	**866-861-2010**	281-689-3128
Springfield Public School District #186 1900 W Monroe St	Springfield	IL	62704	**877-632-7753**	217-525-3000
Sumner School District 1202 Wood Ave	Sumner	WA	98390	**866-548-3847**	253-891-6000
Sunset Ridge School District 29 525 Sunset Ridge Rd	Northfield	IL	60093	**888-331-2195**	847-881-9400
Templeton Unified School District 960 Old County Rd	Templeton	CA	93465	**800-316-6142**	805-434-5800
Tforce Energy Services 6143 S Willow Ste 320	Greenwood Village	CO	80111	**877-234-1444**	
Thunderbird School of Global Management One Global Pl	Glendale	AZ	85306	**800-848-9084**	602-978-7000
Tomball Independent School District 221 W Main St	Tomball	TX	77375	**877-382-4357**	281-357-3100
Toppenish School District 202 306 Bolin Dr	Toppenish	WA	98948	**888-730-1101**	509-865-4455

				Toll-Free	Phone
Tulare Joint Union High School District					
426 N Blackstone Ave	Tulare	CA	93274	**800-942-3767**	559-688-2021
Tulsa Public Schools					
3027 S New Haven Ave	Tulsa	OK	74114	**866-632-9992**	918-746-6800
Twin Falls School District 411					
201 Main Ave W	Twin Falls	ID	83301	**800-726-0003**	208-733-6900
Twin Rivers Unified School District					
3222 Winona Way	North Highlands	CA	95660	**888-674-6854**	916-566-1628
Unified School District of Antigo					
120 S Dorr St	Antigo	WI	54409	**800-795-3272**	715-627-4355
Upper Dauphin Area School District (UDASD)					
5668 State Rt 209	Lykens	PA	17048	**866-632-9992**	717-362-8134
US Special Delivery Inc					
821 E Blvd	Kingsford	MI	49802	**800-821-6389**	906-774-1931
Utica Community Schools (UCS)					
11303 Greendale Dr	Sterling Heights	MI	48312	**800-877-8339**	586-797-1000
Vernon Parish School Board					
201 Belview Rd	Leesville	LA	71446	**800-621-1742**	337-239-3401
W. N. Morehouse Truck Line Inc					
4010 Dahlman Ave	Omaha	NE	68107	**800-228-9378**	402-733-2200
Walker County Board of Education					
1710 Alabama Ave PO Box 311	Jasper	AL	35501	**866-276-7735**	205-387-0555
Washington School District Inc					
201 Allison Ave	Washington	PA	15301	**855-846-8376**	724-223-5085
Westfield Board of Education Inc					
302 Elm St	Westfield	NJ	07090	**800-355-2583**	908-789-4401
Westminster School District					
14121 Cedarwood St	Westminster	CA	92683	**800-678-9133**	714-894-7311
Wharton Independent School District					
2100 N Fulton St	Wharton	TX	77488	**800-818-3453**	979-532-3612
William B Meyer Inc					
255 Long Beach Blvd	Stratford	CT	06615	**800-727-5985**	203-375-5801
Williamsport Area School District					
201 W Third St	Williamsport	PA	17701	**888-448-4642**	570-327-5500
Zanesville City School Board					
160 N Fourth St	Zanesville	OH	43701	**866-280-7377**	740-454-9751

682 SCRAP METAL

SEE ALSO Recyclable Materials Recovery

				Toll-Free	Phone
Advantage Metals Recycling LLC					
3005 Manchester Trfy	Kansas City	MO	64129	**866-527-4733**	816-861-2700
Alter Trading Corp					
700 Office Pkwy	Saint Louis	MO	63141	**888-337-2727**	314-872-2400
AMG Resources Corp					
2 Robinson Plaza # 350	Pittsburgh	PA	15205	**800-633-3606**	412-777-7300
Calbag Metals Co					
2495 NW Nicolai St	Portland	OR	97210	**800-398-3441**	503-226-3441
City Carton Company Inc					
Three E Benton St	Iowa City	IA	52240	**800-369-6112**	319-351-2848
Cleveland Corp					
42810 N Green Bay Rd	Zion	IL	60099	**800-281-3464**	847-872-7200
Cohen Bros Inc					
1723 Woodlawn Ave	Middletown	OH	45044	**800-878-3697**	513-422-3696
Dimco Steel Inc					
3901 S Lamar St	Dallas	TX	75215	**877-428-8336**	214-428-8336
Gachman Metals & Recycling Company Inc					
2600 Shamrock Ave	Fort Worth	TX	76107	**800-749-0423**	817-334-0211
Grossman Iron & Steel					
Five N Market St	Saint Louis	MO	63102	**800-969-9423**	314-231-9423
Iron & Metals Inc					
5555 Franklin St	Denver	CO	80216	**800-776-7910**	303-292-5555
Lionetti Assoc					
450 S Front St	Elizabeth	NJ	07202	**800-734-0910**	908-820-8800
Louis Padnos Iron & Metal Co					
PO Box 1979	Holland	MI	49422	**800-442-3509**	616-396-6521
Mayer Pollock Steel Corp					
Industrial Hwy	Pottstown	PA	19464	**855-773-2848***	610-323-5500
*General					
Mervis Industries Inc					
3295 E Main St	Danville	IL	61834	**800-637-3016**	217-442-5300
Metalico Annaco Inc					
943 Hazel St	Akron	OH	44305	**800-966-1499**	330-376-1400
Metro Metals Northwest					
5611 NE Columbia Blvd	Portland	OR	97218	**800-610-5680**	503-287-8861
OmniSource Corp					
7575 W Jefferson Blvd	Fort Wayne	IN	46804	**800-666-4789**	260-422-5541
Progress Rail Services					
1600 Progress Dr PO Box 1037	Albertville	AL	35950	**800-476-8769**	256-505-6600
PSC 5151 San Felipe Ste 1100	Houston	TX	77056	**800-726-1300**	
SA Recycling LLC					
2411 N Glassell St	Orange	CA	92865	**800-468-7272**	714-632-2000
Sadoff & Rudoy Industries LLP					
240 W Arndt St	Fond du Lac	WI	54936	**877-972-3633***	920-921-2070
*General					
SD Richman Sons Inc					
2435 Wheatsheaf Ln	Philadelphia	PA	19137	**800-648-3576**	215-535-5100
Simon Metals LLC					
2202 E River St	Tacoma	WA	98421	**800-562-8464**	253-272-9364
Sims Bros Inc					
1011 S Prospect St PO Box 1170	Marion	OH	43301	**800-536-7465**	740-387-9041
Sugar Creek Scrap Inc					
1201 W National Ave	West Terre Haute	IN	47885	**800-466-7462**	812-533-2147
Thermo Fluids Inc					
4301 W Jefferson St	Phoenix	AZ	85043	**800-350-7565**	602-272-2400
Tri-State Iron & Metal Co					
1725 E Ninth St	Texarkana	AR	71854	**800-773-8409**	870-773-8409
Tube City IMS Corp (TMS)					
12 Monongahela Ave	Glassport	PA	15045	**800-860-2442**	412-678-6141
NYSE: TMS					
Upstate Shredding LLC					
1 Recycle Dr Tioga Industrial Pk	Owego	NY	13827	**800-245-3133**	607-687-7777
Yaffe Cos Inc, The					
1200 S G St	Muskogee	OK	74403	**800-759-2333**	918-687-7543

683 SCREEN PRINTING

				Toll-Free	Phone
Designer Decal Inc					
1120 E First Ave	Spokane	WA	99202	**800-622-6333**	509-535-0267
Flow-Eze Co 3209 Auburn St	Rockford	IL	61101	**800-435-4873**	815-965-1062
Kay Automotive Graphics					
57 Kay Industrial Dr	Lake Orion	MI	48359	**800-443-0190**	248-377-4999
M & M Designs Inc					
1981 Quality Blvd PO Box 1049	Huntsville	TX	77320	**800-627-0656**	
Motson Graphics Inc					
1717 Bethlehem Pk	Flourtown	PA	19031	**800-972-1986**	215-233-0500
Ram Graphics Inc					
2408 S Pk Ave	Alexandria	IN	46001	**800-531-4656**	
Screen Graphics of Florida Inc					
1801 N Andrews Ave	Pompano Beach	FL	33069	**800-346-4420**	
Vincent Printing Company Inc					
1512 Sholar Ave	Chattanooga	TN	37406	**800-251-7262**	

684 SCREENING - WOVEN WIRE

				Toll-Free	Phone
ACS Industries Inc					
191 Social St	Woonsocket	RI	02895	**866-783-4838**	401-769-4700
Belleville Wire Cloth Inc					
18 Rutgers Ave	Cedar Grove	NJ	07009	**800-631-0490**	973-239-0074
Buffalo Wire Works Co					
1165 Clinton St	Buffalo	NY	14206	**800-828-7028**	716-826-4666
Cleveland Wire Cloth & Manufacturing Co					
3573 E 78th St	Cleveland	OH	44105	**800-321-3234**	216-341-1832
Edward J Darby & Son Inc					
2200 N Eigth St PO Box 50049	Philadelphia	PA	19133	**800-875-6374**	215-236-2203
Gerard Daniel Worldwide					
34 Barnhart Dr	Hanover	PA	17331	**800-232-3332**	717-637-5901
Jelliff Corp					
354 Pequot Ave	Southport	CT	06890	**800-243-0052**	203-259-1615
TWP Inc 2831 Tenth St	Berkeley	CA	94710	**800-227-1570**	510-548-4434
Universal Wire Cloth Co					
16 N Steel Rd	Morrisville	PA	19067	**800-523-0575**	215-736-8981

685 SEATING - VEHICULAR

				Toll-Free	Phone
Freedman Seating Co					
4545 W Augusta Blvd	Chicago	IL	60651	**800-443-4540**	773-524-2440
HO Bostrom Company Inc					
818 Progress Ave	Waukesha	WI	53186	**800-332-5415**	262-542-0222
Milsco Mfg Co					
9009 N 51st St	Milwaukee	WI	53223	**800-255-0337**	414-354-0500
Sears Manufacturing Co					
1718 S Concord St PO Box 3667	Davenport	IA	52808	**800-553-3013***	563-383-2800
*Cust Svc					
Seats Inc					
1515 Industrial St	Reedsburg	WI	53959	**800-443-0615**	608-524-8261

686 SECURITIES BROKERS & DEALERS

SEE ALSO Investment Advice & Management ; Mutual Funds ; Commodity Contracts Brokers & Dealers ; Electronic Communications Networks (ECNs)

				Toll-Free	Phone
1&1 Internet Inc					
701 Lee Rd Ste 300	Chesterbrook	PA	19087	**877-461-2631**	
1st Discount Brokerage Inc					
8927 Hypoluxo Rd Ste A-5	Lake Worth	FL	33467	**888-642-2811**	561-515-3200
AB Watley Direct Inc					
50 Broad St Ste 1614	New York	NY	10004	**877-993-4886**	646-753-9301
Access Securities Inc					
30 Buxton Farm Rd	Stamford	CT	06905	**800-331-6171**	203-322-3377
Allen & Co Inc					
1401 South Florida Avenue	Lakeland	FL	33803	**800-950-2526**	863-688-9000
Ameriprise Brokerage					
70400 Ameriprise Financial Ctr	Minneapolis	MN	55474	**800-535-2001**	
Avisen Securities Inc					
3620 American River Dr Ste 145.	Sacramento	CA	95864	**800-230-7704**	916-480-2747
Baird Patrick & Company Inc					
305 Plz Ten	Jersey City	NJ	07311	**800-221-7747**	201-680-7300
Barclays Capital Inc					
200 Pk Ave	New York	NY	10166	**888-227-2275**	212-412-4000
BaxterBoo					
7025 S Fulton St Ste 150	Centennial	CO	80112	**888-887-0063**	
Bell Supply Inc					
7221 Rt 130	Pennsauken	NJ	08110	**888-834-2371**	856-663-3900
Bernard L Madoff Investment Securities Co					
885 Third Ave 18th Fl	New York	NY	10022	**800-334-1343**	212-230-2424
Berthel Fisher & Co					
701 Tama St Bldg B PO Box 609	Marion	IA	52302	**800-356-5234**	319-447-5700
BHK Securities LLC					
2200 Lakeshore Dr Ste 250	Birmingham	AL	35209	**888-529-2610**	205-322-2025
Blowfish Direct LLC					
11130 Holder St	Cypress	CA	90630	**877-725-6934**	
Bourbon & Boots Inc					
419 Main St	North Little Rock	AR	72114	**855-623-3562**	
Brill Securities Inc					
152 W 57th St 16th Fl.	New York	NY	10019	**800-933-0800**	212-957-5700
Bull Wealth Management Group Inc					
4100 Yonge St Ste 612	Toronto	ON	M2P2B5	**866-623-2053**	416-223-2053
BUYandHOLD.com Securities Corp					
c/o Freedom Investments, Inc					
375 Raritan Ctr Pkwy Ste D	Edison	NJ	08837	**800-646-8212**	

	Toll-Free	Phone
Caldwell Securities Ltd		
150 King St W Ste 1710 ....Toronto ON M5H1J9	800-387-0859	416-862-7755
Calton & Assoc Inc		
14497 N Dale Mabry Hwy ....Tampa FL 33618	800-942-0262	813-264-0440
Ceros Financial Services Inc		
1445 Research Blvd Ste 530..........Rockville MD 20850	866-842-3356	
Cetera Financial Group Inc		
200 N Sepulveda Blvd Ste 1200..........El Segundo CA 90245	866-489-3100	
Charles Schwab & Co Inc		
211 Main St ....San Francisco CA 94105	800-648-5300*	415-667-1009
*Cust Svc		
Chase Plastic Services Inc		
6467 Waldon Ctr Dr ....Clarkston MI 48346	800-232-4273	248-620-2120
City Securities Corp		
30 S Meridian St Ste 600 ....Indianapolis IN 46204	800-800-2489	317-634-4400
CNBS Inc		
7200 W 132nd St Ste 240..........Overland Park KS 66213	800-222-0978	
Corinthian Partners LLC		
10 E 53rd St 28th Fl ....New York NY 10022	800-899-8950	212-287-1500
Credit Suisse		
11 Madison Ave ....New York NY 10010	800-222-8977	212-325-2000
Crowell Weedon & Co		
One Wilshire Blvd 26th Fl...........Los Angeles CA 90017	800-227-0319	213-620-1850
DA Davidson & Company Inc		
Eight Third St N ....Great Falls MT 59401	800-332-5915	406-727-4200
Davenport & Co LLC		
901 E Cary St		
One James Center Ste 1100 ....Richmond VA 23219	800-846-6666	804-780-2000
DiscountMugs.com		
12610 NW 115th Ave ....Medley FL 33178	800-569-1980	
Domestic Securities Inc		
160 Summit Ave ....Montvale NJ 07645	877-690-2274	201-505-9855
Dougherty & Company LLC		
90 S Seventh St Ste 4300..........Minneapolis MN 55402	800-328-4000	612-376-4000
E*Trade Financial Corp		
1271 Ave of the Americas 14th Fl ....New York NY 10020	800-387-2331	
NASDAQ: ETFC		
eBX LLC		
65 Franklin St Ste 201 ....Boston MA 02110	800-958-4813	617-350-1600
ECMD Inc		
Two Grandview St ....North Wilkesboro NC 28659	888-222-3961	336-667-5976
Ellie Fashion Group Inc		
1447 Second St Third Fl..........Santa Monica CA 90401	888-926-9615	
Essex National Securities Inc		
550 Gateway Dr Ste 210 ....Napa CA 94558	855-444-3674	707-258-5000
Fastener Supply Co		
13410 S Ridge Dr PO Box 7369..........Charlotte NC 28241	800-888-9519	704-596-7634
Fieldpoint Private Bank & Trust		
100 Field Pt Rd ....Greenwich CT 06830	877-438-4338	203-413-9300
Financial Service Corp		
2300 Windy Ridge Pkwy Ste 1100 ....Atlanta GA 30339	800-547-2382	770-916-6500
Fincantieri Marine Systems North America Inc		
800-C Principal Ct ....Chesapeake VA 23320	877-436-7643	757-548-6000
First Southwest Co		
325 N St Paul St Ste 800 ....Dallas TX 75201	800-678-3792	214-953-4000
Fisc Investment Services Corp		
1849 Clairmont Rd ....Decatur GA 30033	800-241-3203	404-321-1212
Franklin Templeton Investments		
3344 Quality Dr ....Rancho Cordova CA 95670	800-632-2350	650-312-2000
Freedom Investments Inc		
375 Raritan Ctr Pkwy ....Edison NJ 08837	800-944-4033	
Friedman Billings Ramsey Group Inc		
1001 19th St N ....Arlington VA 22209	800-846-5050	703-312-9500
GE Richards Graphic Supplies Company Inc		
928 Links Ave ....Landisville PA 17538	800-233-0410	717-898-3151
Geary Pacific Corp		
1908 N Enterprise St ....Orange CA 92865	800-444-3279	714-279-2950
George K Baum & Co		
4801 Main St Ste 500 Ste 500 ....Kansas City MO 64112	800-821-7195	816-474-1100
Georgeson Securities Corp		
480 Washington Blvd 27th Fl ....Jersey City NJ 07310	800-428-0717	
Gilford Securities Inc		
777 Third Ave ....New York NY 10017	800-445-3673	212-888-6400
Grace Financial Group LLC		
83 Jobs Ln ....Southampton NY 11968	866-817-6047	631-287-4633
Great Pacific Fixed Income Securities Inc		
151 Kalmus Dr Ste H-8..........Costa Mesa CA 92626	800-284-4804	714-619-3000
Huntleigh Securities Corp		
7800 Forsyth Blvd Fifth Fl ....Saint Louis MO 63105	800-727-5405	314-236-2400
IDI Distributors Inc		
8303 Audubon Rd ....Chanhassen MN 55317	888-843-1318	952-279-6400
Illinois Fair Plan Association		
130 East Randolph Ste 1050..........Chicago IL 60601	800-972-4480	312-861-0385
Industrial Tube & Steel Corp		
4658 Crystal Pkwy ....Kent OH 44240	800-662-9567	330-474-5530
Investrade Discount Securities		
950 N Milwaukee Ave Ste 102 ....Glenview IL 60025	800-498-7120*	847-375-6080
*Cust Svc		
Isaak Bond Investments Inc		
3900 S Wadsworth Blvd Ste 590 ....Lakewood CO 80202	800-279-4426	303-623-7500
ITG Inc		
One Liberty Plz 165 Broadway ....New York NY 10006	800-215-4484	212-588-4000
Janney Montgomery Scott LLC		
1801 Market St ....Philadelphia PA 19103	800-526-6397	215-665-6000
Javelin Capital Markets LLC		
443 Park Ave S 10th Fl ....New York NY 10016	877-528-9244	212-779-2300
JD Ford & Company LLC		
650 S Cherry St Ste 1200 ....Denver CO 80246	888-999-9495	303-333-3673
JJB Hilliard WL Lyons Inc		
500 W Jefferson St ....Louisville KY 40202	800-444-1854	502-588-8400
Kane Reid Securities Group Inc		
13024 Ballantyne Corporate Pl		
Ste 500..........Charlotte NC 28277	877-495-5464	
Katalyst Surgical LLC		
754 Goddard Ave ....Chesterfield MO 63005	888-452-8259	
Knight Capital Group Inc		
545 Washington Blvd ....Jersey City NJ 07310	800-544-7508	201-222-9400
NYSE: KCG		

	Toll-Free	Phone
Kovack Securities Inc		
6451 N Federal Hwy # 1201 ....Fort Lauderdale FL 33308	800-711-4078	954-782-4771
L B L Group		
4281 Katella Ave Ste 221 ....Los Alamitos CA 90720	800-451-8037	714-236-8270
Ladenburg Thalmann Financial Services Inc		
4400 Biscayne Blvd 12th Fl ....Miami FL 33137	800-523-8425	212-409-2000
NYSE: LTS		
Lazard 30 Rockefeller Plz ....New York NY 10112	877-266-8601	212-632-2685
NYSE: LAZ		
Leaders LLC		
Two Portland Fish Pier Ste 301..........Portland ME 04101	888-583-7770	
Lebenthal Wealth Advisors		
230 Park Ave Fl 32 ....New York NY 10169	877-425-6006	212-425-6006
Legg Mason Inc (LMI)		
100 International Dr ....Baltimore MD 21202	800-822-5544	410-539-0000
NYSE: LM		
Leigh Baldwin & Company LLC		
One Hopper St ....Utica NY 13501	800-659-8044	315-734-1410
Loop Capital Markets LLC		
111 W Jackson Blvd Ste 1901 ....Chicago IL 60604	888-294-8898	312-913-4900
LPL Financial Services		
75 State St 24th Fl ....Boston MA 02109	800-877-7210	
Mackie Research Capital Corp		
308-4th Ave SW Ste 2700 ....Calgary AB T2P0H7	888-292-0980	403-292-0970
Mailender Inc		
9500 Glades Dr ....Hamilton OH 45011	800-998-5453	513-942-5453
Mesirow Financial Inc		
350 N Clark St ....Chicago IL 60610	888-681-0082	312-595-6000
Mizuho Securities USA		
1251 Sixth Ave ....New York NY 10020	866-216-1851*	212-282-3000
*Sales		
Morgan Stanley		
1585 Broadway ....New York NY 10036	800-223-2440*	212-761-4000
NYSE: MS ■ *General		
Morgan Stanley Investment Management		
1221 Ave of the Americas 5th Fl ....New York NY 10020	800-223-2440*	212-296-6600
*General		
National Commerce Bank Services Inc		
80 Monroe Ave Ste 250 ....Memphis TN 38103	800-264-2609	
National Securities Corp		
410 Park Ave 14th Fl ....New York NY 10022	800-742-7730	212-417-8000
Needham & Co Inc		
445 Pk Ave 3rd Fl ....New York NY 10022	800-903-3268	212-371-8300
Northern Industrial Sales Ltd		
3526 Opie Cres ....Prince George BC V2N2P9	800-668-3317	250-562-4435
Nuveen Investments Inc		
333 W Wacker Dr ....Chicago IL 60606	800-257-8787	312-917-7700
NYLIFE Securities Inc		
51 Madison Ave Rm 251 ....New York NY 10010	800-695-4785	
Oberweis Securities Inc		
3333 Warrenville Rd Ste 500 ....Lisle IL 60532	800-323-6166	630-577-2300
Octagon Capital Corp		
181 University Ave Ste 400..........Toronto ON M5H3M7	888-478-8888	416-368-3322
Pacific Crest Securities Inc		
111 SW Fifth Ave 42nd Fl ....Portland OR 97204	800-314-9837	503-248-0721
Patriot Flooring Supply Inc		
110 Commerce Way ....Woburn MA 01801	866-444-4433	
PDI Financial Group		
601 N Lynndale Dr ....Appleton WI 54914	800-234-7341	920-739-2303
Pennsylvania Trust Co		
Five Radnor Corp Ctr Ste 450..........Radnor PA 19087	800-975-4316	610-975-4300
People's Securities Inc		
850 Main St ....Bridgeport CT 06601	800-772-4400	203-338-0800
Piper Jaffray Cos		
800 Nicollet Mall Ste 800 ....Minneapolis MN 55402	800-333-6000	612-303-6000
NYSE: PJC		
Planesmart! Aviation LLC		
Addison Airport 15841 Addison Rd ....Addison TX 75001	888-228-4283	972-380-8004
Precision IBC Inc		
8054 Mcgowin Dr ....Fairhope AL 36532	800-544-7069	251-990-6789
Questar Capital Corp		
5701 Golden Hills Dr ....Minneapolis MN 55416	888-446-5872	
R Seelaus & Company Inc		
25 Deforest Ave Ste 304 ....Summit NJ 07901	800-922-0584	
Raymond James Financial Inc		
880 Carillon Pkwy ....Saint Petersburg FL 33716	800-248-8863	727-567-1000
NYSE: RJF		
RBC Capital Markets		
1 Liberty Plaza ....New York NY 10006	800-387-1122	212-428-6200
Robert W Baird & Company Inc		
PO Box 672 ....Milwaukee WI 53201	800-792-2473	414-765-3500
Roosevelt & Cross Inc		
One Exchange Plz 55 Broadway 22nd Fl...........New York NY 10006	800-348-3426	212-344-2500
Royal Alliance Assoc Inc		
One World Financial Ctr 14th Fl ....New York NY 10281	800-821-5100	
Royal Securities Co		
4095 Chicago Dr SW Ste 120..........Grandville MI 49418	800-421-3518	616-538-2550
SagePoint Financial Inc		
2800 N Central Ave Ste 2100 ....Phoenix AZ 85004	800-552-3319	
Samuel A Ramirez & Co Inc		
61 Broadway Ste 2924 ....New York NY 10006	800-888-4086	
Sandler O'Neill + Partners LP		
1251 Avenue of the Americas 6th Fl ....New York NY 10020	800-635-6851	212-466-7800
Schroder Investment Management North America Inc (SIMNA)		
875 Third Ave 22nd Fl ....New York NY 10022	800-730-2932	
Scotia Capital Markets		
One Liberty Plz ....New York NY 10006	877-294-3435	212-225-5000
Securities Service Network Inc		
9729 Cogdill Rd Ste 301 ....Knoxville TN 37932	866-843-4635	
Siebert Brandford Shank & Co LLC		
100 Wall St 18th Fl ....New York NY 10005	800-334-6800	646-775-4850
Silver Legacy Capital Corp		
407 N Virginia St ....Reno NV 89501	800-687-8733	
Stephens Inc 111 Ctr St ....Little Rock AR 72201	800-643-9691	501-377-2000
Sterne Agee & Leach Inc		
800 Shades Creek Pkwy Ste 700 ....Birmingham AL 35209	800-240-1438	205-949-3500
Stifel Financial Corp		
501 N Broadway ....Saint Louis MO 63102	800-679-5446	
NYSE: SF		

	Toll-Free	Phone
Stifel Nicolaus & Co Inc 501 N Broadway .... Saint Louis MO 63102	800-679-5446	314-342-2000
SunTrust Robinson Humphrey Capital Markets 3333 Peachtree Rd NE .... Atlanta GA 30326	800-634-7928	404-926-5000
Tejas Inc 8226 Bee Caves Rd .... Austin TX 78746	800-846-6803	512-306-8222
TradeStation Group Inc 8050 SW Tenth St Ste 2000 .... Plantation FL 33324	800-871-3577	954-652-7000
TradeStation Securities Inc 8050 SW Tenth St Ste 2000 .... Plantation FL 33324	800-808-9336	954-652-7000
Trading Direct 160 Broadway E Bldg Seventh Fl .... New York NY 10038	800-925-8566	212-766-0230
Trumaker Inc 701 Sutter St Fl 5 .... San Francisco CA 94109	855-623-3878	
UBS Financial Services Inc 1285 Ave of the Americas .... New York NY 10019	800-221-3260	212-713-2000
UBS Warburg LLC 677 Washington Blvd .... Stamford CT 06901	800-221-3260	203-719-3000
Vanguard Brokerage Services PO Box 2600 .... Valley Forge PA 19482	800-992-8327	610-669-1000
Wayne Hummer Investments LLC 222 S Riverside Pz 28th Fl .... Chicago IL 60606	800-621-4477	866-943-4732
Western International Securities Inc 70 S Lake Ave Ste 700 .... Pasadena CA 91101	888-793-7717	
William Blair & Company LLC 222 W Adams St .... Chicago IL 60606	800-621-0687	312-236-1600
Winetasting Network, The 578 Gateway Dr .... Napa CA 94558	800-435-2225	
WR Hambrecht & Co 909 Montgomery St 3rd Fl .... San Francisco CA 94133 *Cust Svc	855-753-6484*	415-551-8600

687   SECURITIES & COMMODITIES EXCHANGES

	Toll-Free	Phone
Axial Inc 45 E 20th St 12th Fl .... New York NY 10003	800-860-4519	
Chicago Board Options Exchange (CBOE) 400 S La Salle St .... Chicago IL 60605	800-678-4667	312-786-5600
CME Group Inc 20 S Wacker Dr .... Chicago IL 60606 NASDAQ: CME	866-716-7274	312-930-1000
MAS Capital Inc 2715 Coney Island Ave .... Brooklyn NY 11235	866-553-7493	
Minneapolis Grain Exchange 400 S Fourth St 130 Grain Exchange Bldg .... Minneapolis MN 55415	800-827-4746	612-321-7101
Montreal Exchange 800 Victoria Sq Third Fl PO Box 61 .... Montreal QC H4Z1A9	800-361-5353	514-871-2424
National Stock Exchange (NSX) 440 S LaSalle St Ste 2600 .... Chicago IL 60605	800-843-3924	201-499-3700
NMS Capital Group LLC 433 N Camden Dr Fourth Fl .... Beverly Hills CA 90210	800-716-2080	
NYSE Arce 115 Samsone St .... San Francisco CA 94104	877-729-7291	
NYSE Euronext 11 Wall St .... New York NY 10005 NYSE: NYX	866-873-7422	212-656-3000
Raymond James (USA) Ltd 2200 - 925 W Georgia St .... Vancouver BC V6C3L2	877-570-7558	
Toronto Stock Exchange 130 King St W .... Toronto ON M5X1J2	888-873-8392	416-947-4670
World Currency USA Inc 16 W Main St .... Marlton NJ 08053	888-593-7927	

688   SECURITY PRODUCTS & SERVICES

SEE ALSO Signals & Sirens - Electric ; Audio & Video Equipment ; Fire Protection Systems

	Toll-Free	Phone
ADT Security Services Inc 14200 E Exposition Ave .... Aurora CO 80012	800-238-2455	
Advantor Systems Corp 12612 Challenger Pkwy Ste 300 .... Orlando FL 32809	800-238-2686	407-859-3350
Akal Security Inc Seven Infinity Loop .... Espanola NM 87532	888-325-2527	505-692-6600
Alken Inc 40 Hercules Dr .... Colchester VT 05446	800-357-4777	802-655-3159
Allied Fire & Security Inc 425 W Second Ave .... Spokane WA 99201 *Acctg	888-333-2632*	509-321-8778
AMAG Technology Inc 20701 Manhattan Pl .... Torrance CA 90501	800-889-9138	310-518-2380
American Locker Group Inc 815 S Main St .... Grapevine TX 76051 OTC: ALGI	800-828-9118	817-329-1600
American Locker Security Systems Inc 608 Allen St .... Jamestown NY 14701 *Sales	800-828-9118*	716-664-9600
American Science & Engineering Inc 829 Middlesex Tpke .... Billerica MA 01821 NASDAQ: ASEI	800-225-1608	978-262-8700
American Security Products Inc 11925 Pacific Ave .... Fontana CA 92337	800-421-6142	951-685-9680
APi Systems Group Inc 10575 Vista Park Rd .... Dallas TX 75238 *General	877-828-1200*	214-291-1200
Authentix Inc 4355 Excel Pkwy Ste 100 .... Addison TX 75001	866-434-1402	469-737-4400
BI Inc 6400 Lookout Rd .... Boulder CO 80301	800-241-2911	303-218-1000
Black Hat Inc 1932 First Ave Ste 204 .... Seattle WA 98101	866-203-8081	206-443-5489
Bosch Security Systems 130 Perinton Pkwy .... Fairport NY 14450	800-289-0096	585-223-4060
Brivo Systems LLC 4350 E W Hwy Ste 201 .... Bethesda MD 20814 *Tech Supp	866-692-7486*	301-664-5242

	Toll-Free	Phone
BSM Wireless Inc 75 International Blvd Ste 100 .... Toronto ON M9W6L9	866-768-4771	416-675-1201
Carter Bros LLC 100 Hartsfield Ctr Pkwy Ste 140 .... Atlanta GA 30354	888-818-0152	
Central Signaling 2033 Hamilton Rd .... Columbus GA 31904	800-554-1104	706-322-3756
Checkpoint Systems Inc 101 Wolf Dr .... Thorofare NJ 08086 NYSE: CKP	800-257-5540	856-848-1800
Corby Industries Inc 1501 E Pennsylvania St .... Allentown PA 18109 *Sales	800-652-6729*	610-433-1412
DEI Holdings Inc One Viper Way .... Vista CA 92081 OTC: DEIX	800-876-0800	760-598-6200
Detex Corp 302 Detex Dr .... New Braunfels TX 78130	800-729-3839	830-629-2900
deView Electronics USA Inc 708 Vly Ridge Cir Ste 1 .... Lewisville TX 75057	877-433-8439	214-222-3332
Diebold Inc 5995 Mayfair Rd .... North Canton OH 44720 NYSE: DBD	800-999-3600	330-490-4000
Doyle Security Systems Inc 792 Calkins Rd .... Rochester NY 14623	800-836-9538	585-244-3400
eDist 97 McKee Dr .... Mahwah NJ 07430	800-800-6624	201-512-1400
ELK Products Inc 3266 Us 70 W .... Connelly Springs NC 28612	800-797-9355	828-397-4200
Federal APD Inc (FAPD) 28100 Cabot Dr Ste 200 .... Novi MI 48377	877-992-7749	248-374-9600
Fiber SenSys LLC 2925 NW Aloclek Dr Ste 130 .... Hillsboro OR 97124	800-641-8150	503-692-4430
FireKing Security Group 101 Security Pkwy .... New Albany IN 47150	800-457-2424	812-948-8400
First Action Security Security Team Inc 18702 Crestwood Dr .... Hagerstown MD 21742 *Cust Svc	800-372-7447*	301-797-2124
Fortress Technology Inc 51 Grand Marshall Dr .... Toronto ON M1B5N6	888-220-8737	416-754-2898
GE Analytical Instruments Inc 6060 Spine Rd .... Boulder CO 80301	800-255-6964	303-444-2009
George Risk Industries Inc 802 S Elm St .... Kimball NE 69145 OTC: RSKIA ■ *Sales	800-523-1227*	308-235-4645
Guardian Alarm 20800 Southfield Rd .... Southfield MI 48075	800-782-9688	248-423-1000
Hanchett Entry Systems Inc (HES) 22630 N 17th Ave .... Phoenix AZ 85027	800-626-7590	623-582-4626
HandyTrac Systems LLC 510 Staghorn Ct .... Alpharetta GA 30004	800-665-9994	678-990-2305
Honeywell Security Group Two Corporate Ctr Dr Ste 100 .... Melville NY 11747	800-467-5875	516-577-2000
IDenticard Systems Inc 40 Citation Ln .... Lititz PA 17543	800-233-0298	717-569-5797
Integrated Biometrics Inc 121 Broadcast Dr .... Spartanburg SC 29303	888-840-8034	864-990-3711
Interface Security Systems LLC 6340 International Pkwy Ste 100 .... Plano TX 75093	866-593-3480	972-996-2800
International Electronics Inc 427 Tpke St .... Canton MA 02021	800-343-9502	781-821-5566
Johnson Controls Fire & Security Solutions 4100 Gardian St Ste 200 .... Simi Valley CA 93063	800-229-4076	805-522-5555
KWJ Engineering Inc 8430 Central Ave Ste C .... Newark CA 94560	800-472-6626	510-794-4296
Loomis Fargo & Co 2500 Citywest Blvd Ste 900 .... Houston TX 77042	866-383-5069	713-435-6700
Matrix Systems Inc 1041 Byers Rd .... Miamisburg OH 45342	800-562-8749	937-438-9033
MDI Security Systems Inc 12500 Network Dr Ste 303 .... San Antonio TX 78249	866-435-7634	210-477-5400
MMF Industries 1111 S Wheeling Rd .... Wheeling IL 60090	800-323-8181	
Monitronics International Inc 2350 Valley View Ln Ste 100 .... Dallas TX 75234 *Cust Svc	800-290-0709*	972-243-7443
MorphoTrust USA Inc 296 Concord Rd .... Billerica MA 01821	888-245-1114	978-215-2400
NAPCO Security Systems Inc 333 Bayview Ave .... Amityville NY 11701 NASDAQ: NSSC	800-645-9445	631-842-9400
National Fingerprint Inc 6999 Dolan Rd .... Glouster OH 45732	888-823-7873	740-767-3853
New England Security Inc 10 Industrial Dr .... Westerly RI 02891	800-556-7395	401-596-0660
Norment Security Group Inc 3224 Mobile Hwy .... Montgomery AL 36108	800-466-3007	
Nortek Security & Control LLC 1950 Camino Vida Roble Ste 150 .... Carlsbad CA 92008 *Cust Svc	800-421-1587*	760-438-7000
Optex Inc 13661 Benson Ave Bldg C .... Chino CA 91710	800-966-7839	909-993-5770
Per Mar Security 1910 E Kimberly Rd .... Davenport IA 52807	800-473-7627	563-359-3200
protection One Alarm Monitoring 1035 N Third St Ste 101 .... Lawrence KS 66044	800-438-4357	877-776-1911
PV Labs Inc 1074 Cooke Blvd Ste 400A .... Burlington ON L7T4A8	888-667-7202	905-667-7202
Qualys Inc 1600 Bridge Pkwy .... Redwood Shores CA 94065	866-801-6161	650-801-6100
SAFLOK 31750 Sherman Ave .... Madison Heights MI 48071	800-999-6213	248-837-3700
Seco-Larm USA Inc 16842 Millikan Ave .... Irvine CA 92606	800-662-0800	949-261-2999
Securitas Security Services USA Inc 2 Campus Dr .... Parsippany NJ 07054	800-555-0906	973-267-5300
Security Corp 22325 Roethel Dr .... Novi MI 48375	877-374-5700	
Security Defense Systems Corp 160 Pk Ave .... Nutley NJ 07110	800-325-6339	
Security Signal Devices Inc 1740 N Lemon St .... Anaheim CA 92801	800-888-0444	

			Toll-Free	Phone
Sensormatic Electronics Corp				
6600 Congress Ave	Boca Raton FL	33487	800-327-1765	561-912-6000
Sentry Group				
900 Linden Ave	Rochester NY	14625	800-828-1438*	585-381-4900
*Cust Svc				
Sentry Technology Corp				
1881 Lakeland Ave	Ronkonkoma NY	11779	800-645-4224	
OTC: SKVY				
SIRCHIE Finger Print Laboratories Inc				
100 Hunter Pl	Youngsville NC	27596	800-356-7311	919-554-2244
Sizemore Inc				
2116 Walton Way	Augusta GA	30904	800-445-1748	706-736-1456
Slomin's Inc				
125 Lauman Ln	Hicksville NY	11801	800-252-7663	516-932-7000
Sofradir EC Inc				
373 Rt 46W	Fairfield NJ	07004	800-759-9577	973-882-0211
Southern Folger Detention Equipment Co				
4634 S Presa St	San Antonio TX	78223	888-745-0530	210-533-1231
Teletrac Inc				
7391 Lincoln Way	Garden Grove CA	92841	800-500-6009	714-897-0877
Tyco International Ltd				
Nine Roszel Rd	Princeton NJ	08540	800-685-4509	609-720-4200
NYSE: TYC				
Unisec Inc				
2555 Nicholson St	San Leandro CA	94577	800-982-4587	
Universal Security Instruments Inc				
11407 Cronhill Dr	Owings Mills MD	21117	800-390-4321	410-363-3000
TSE: UUU				
Vector Security Inc				
2000 Ericsson Dr	Warrendale PA	15086	800-832-8575	
Verint Video Solutions				
330 South Service Rd	Melville NY	11747	800-638-5969	800-483-7468
Winner International LLC				
32 W State St	Sharon PA	16146	800-258-2321	724-981-1152

689 SECURITY & PROTECTIVE SERVICES

SEE ALSO Investigative Services

			Toll-Free	Phone
5 Alarm Fire & Safety Equipment LLC				
350 Austin Cir	Delafield WI	53018	800-615-6789	262-646-5911
A10 Networks Inc				
Three W Plumeria Dr	San Jose CA	95134	888-210-6363	408-325-8668
Accuvant Inc				
1125 17th St Ste 1700	Denver CO	80202	800-574-0896	303-298-0600
Allegiance Security Group LLC				
2900 Arendell St Ste 18	Morehead City NC	28557	866-747-2748	252-247-1138
AlliedBarton Security Services				
150 S Warner Rd	King of Prussia PA	19406	866-703-7666	484-654-3800
American Services Inc				
1300 Rutherford Rd	Greenville SC	29609	877-292-7450	864-292-7450
Andy Frain Services Inc				
761 Shoreline Dr	Aurora IL	60504	877-707-4771	630-820-3820
APL Access & Security Inc				
115 S William Dillard Dr	Gilbert AZ	85233	866-873-2288	480-497-9471
ASP Inc				
460 Brant St Ste 212	Burlington ON	L7R4B6	877-552-5535	905-333-4242
Brink's Inc				
555 Dividend Dr Ste 100	Coppell TX	75019	800-274-6575	469-549-6000
Command Security Corp				
388 Westchester Ave Ste 1J/H	Port Chester NY	10573	877-331-8056	914-937-2969
DSX Access Systems Inc				
10731 Rockwall Rd	Dallas TX	75238	888-419-8353	214-553-6140
East Coast Security Services Inc				
68 Stiles Rd	Salem NH	03079	800-639-2086	603-898-6823
Federal Protection Inc				
2500 N Airport Commerce Ave	Springfield MO	65803	800-299-5400	417-869-9192
First Alarm Security & Patrol Inc				
1111 Estates Dr	Aptos CA	95003	800-684-1111	831-476-1111
FJC Security Services Inc				
275 Jericho Tpke	Floral Park NY	11001	888-832-6352	516-328-6000
Fluent Home Ltd				
7319 104 St NW	Edmonton AB	T6E4B9	855-238-4826	
Garda World Security Corp				
1390 Barre St	Montreal QC	H3C1N4	800-859-1599	514-281-2811
TSE: GW				
GHS Interactive Security Inc				
2081 Arena Blvd Ste 260	Sacramento CA	95834	855-208-2447	
Gillmore Security Systems Inc				
26165 Broadway Ave	Cleveland OH	44146	800-899-8995	440-232-1000
Guard Systems Inc				
1190 Monterey Pass Rd	Monterey Park CA	91754	800-606-6711	323-881-6711
Guardian Alarm				
20800 Southfield Rd	Southfield MI	48075	800-782-9688	248-423-1000
Guardian Protection Services Inc				
174 Thorn Hill Rd	Warrendale PA	15086	877-314-7092*	855-779-2001
*Cust Svc				
guardNOW Inc				
16209 Victory Blvd Ste 302	Van Nuys CA	91406	877-482-7366	
Guardsmark Inc				
10 Rockefeller Plz 12th Fl	New York NY	10020	800-238-5878	212-765-8226
Habitec Security Inc				
2926 S Republic Blvd	Toledo OH	43615	888-422-4832	419-537-6768
Hannon Security Services Inc				
9036 Grand Ave S	Minneapolis MN	55420	800-328-3877	952-881-5865
Hepaco Inc				
2711 Burch Dr PO Box 26308	Charlotte NC	28269	800-888-7689	704-598-9782
Houston Harris Div Patrol Inc				
6420 Richmond Ave	Houston TX	77057	877-975-9922	713-975-9922
Information Network Assoc Inc				
5235 N Front St	Harrisburg PA	17110	800-443-0824	717-599-5505
Innovative Industrial Solutions Inc				
2830 Skyline Dr	Russellville AR	72802	888-684-8249	479-968-4266
Intec Video Systems Inc				
23301 Vista Grande Dr	Laguna Hills CA	92653	800-468-3254	949-859-3800
JMG Security Systems Inc				
17150 Newhope St Ste 109	Fountain Valley CA	92708	800-900-4564	714-545-8882

			Toll-Free	Phone
Kent Security Services Inc				
14600 Biscayne Blvd	North Miami Beach FL	33181	800-273-5368	305-919-9400
Law Enforcement Assoc Corp (LEA)				
120 Penmarc Dr Ste 125	Raleigh NC	27616	800-354-9669	919-872-6210
OTC: LAWEQ				
Loomis Armored US Inc				
2500 Citywest Blvd Ste 900	Houston TX	77042	866-383-5069	713-435-6700
Mijac Alarm				
9339 Charles Smith Ave Ste 100	Rancho Cucamonga CA	91730	800-982-7612	909-982-7612
Mircom Technologies Ltd				
25 Interchange Way	Vaughan ON	L4K5W3	888-660-4655	905-660-4655
Murray Guard Inc				
58 Murray Guard Dr	Jackson TN	38305	800-238-3830	731-668-3400
My Alarm Center LLC				
3803 W Chester Pike Ste 100	Newtown Square PA	19073	866-484-4800	
Network Multi-Family Security Corp				
4221 W John Carpenter Fwy	Irving TX	75063	800-541-3138	972-490-9902
New York Merchants Protective Company Inc				
75 W Merrick Rd	Freeport NY	11520	888-696-7911	516-561-5210
Northwest Protective Service Inc				
801 S Fidalgo 2nd Fl	Seattle WA	98108	866-877-1965	206-448-4040
Northwestern Ohio Security Systems Inc				
121 E High St	Lima OH	45801	800-833-6416	614-527-7037
OSI Security Devices Inc				
1580 Jayken Way	Chula Vista CA	91911	800-711-6814	619-628-1000
Pasek Corp				
Nine W Third St	South Boston MA	02127	800-628-2822	617-269-7110
Pierce County Security Inc				
2002 99th St E	Tacoma WA	98445	800-773-4432	253-535-4433
Rapid Focus Security LLC				
253 Summer St Ste 303	Boston MA	02210	855-793-1337	
Rapid Response Monitoring Services Inc				
400 W Division St	Syracuse NY	13204	800-558-7767	
RECON Dynamics LLC				
2300 Carillon Point	Kirkland WA	98033	877-480-3551	
Safeguard Security & Communications Inc				
8454 N 90th St	Scottsdale AZ	85258	800-426-6060	480-609-6200
SDI Chicago				
33 West Monroe Ste 400	Chicago IL	60603	888-968-7734	312-580-7500
Select Engineered Systems				
7991 W 26th Ave	Hialeah FL	33016	800-342-5737	305-823-5410
Sentry Security LLC				
339 Egidi Dr	Wheeling IL	60090	888-272-7080	847-353-7200
St Moritz Security Services Inc				
4600 Clairton Blvd	Pittsburgh PA	15236	800-218-9156	412-885-3144
Stealth Monitoring Inc				
15182 Marsh Lane	Dallas TX	75001	855-783-2584	214-341-0123
Summit Security Services Inc				
390 Rexcorp Plz W Tower - Lobby Level	Uniondale NY	11556	800-615-5888	516-240-2400
Tyco International Ltd				
Nine Roszel Rd	Princeton NJ	08540	800-685-4509	609-720-4200
NYSE: TYC				
UCIT Online Security				
6441 Northam Dr	Mississauga ON	L4V1J2	866-756-7847	905-405-9898
Universal Services of America Inc				
1551 N Tustin Ave Ste 650	Santa Ana CA	92705	866-877-1965	714-619-9700
US Security Assoc Inc				
200 Mansell Ct Fifth Fl	Roswell GA	30076	800-730-9599	770-625-1500
US Security Inc				
4544 NW 10th St	Oklahoma City OK	73127	877-917-5566	405-947-3377
Verant Identification Systems Inc				
2496 Ridge Rd W Ste 203	Rochester NY	14626	866-257-4351	585-214-2451
Vescom Corp 705 Main Rd N	Hampden ME	04444	800-841-1769	207-945-5051
Vinson Guard Service Inc				
955 Howard Ave	New Orleans LA	70113	800-441-7899	504-529-2260
Whelan Security Co				
1699 S Hanley Rd Ste 350	St Louis MO	63144	888-494-3526	314-644-3227

690 SEED COMPANIES

SEE ALSO Farm Supplies
Seed production and development companies (horticultural and agricultural).

			Toll-Free	Phone
AgriGold Hybrids				
5381 Akin Rd	Saint Francisville IL	62460	800-262-7333	618-943-5776
Albert Lea Seed House				
1414 W Main St	Albert Lea MN	56007	800-352-5247	507-373-3161
Ampac Seed Co				
32727 Hwy 99 E	Tangent OR	97389	800-547-3230	541-928-1651
Foremostco Inc				
8457 NW 66th St	Miami FL	33166	800-421-8986	305-592-8986
Harris Moran Seed Co				
PO Box 4938	Modesto CA	95352	800-808-7333	800-320-4672
Johnny's Selected Seeds				
955 Benton Ave	Winslow ME	04901	877-564-6697	207-861-3900
JW Jung Seed Co				
335 S High St	Randolph WI	53956	800-297-3123	
Keithly-Williams Seeds Inc				
420 Palm Ave PO Box 177	Holtville CA	92250	800-533-3465	760-356-5533
Latham Seed Co				
131 180th St	Alexander IA	50420	877-465-2842	641-692-3258
Lebanon Seaboard Corp				
1600 E Cumberland St	Lebanon PA	17042	800-233-0628	717-273-1685
Nunhems USA Inc				
1200 Anderson Corner Rd	Parma ID	83660	800-733-9505*	208-674-4000
*Cust Svc				
Park Seed Co				
One Parkton Ave	Greenwood SC	29647	800-845-3369*	
*Orders				
Pennington Seed Inc				
1280 Atlanta Hwy	Madison GA	30650	800-285-7333	706-342-1234
Red River Commodities Inc				
501 42nd St N	Fargo ND	58102	800-437-5539	701-282-2600
Renee's Garden Seeds Inc				
7389 W Zayante Rd	Felton CA	95018	888-880-7228	831-335-7228

	Toll-Free	Phone
Sand Seed Service Inc		
4765 Hwy 143 .... Marcus IA 51035	**800-352-2228**	712-376-4135
Schlessman Seed Co		
11513 US Rt 250 .... Milan OH 44846	**888-534-7333**	419-499-2572
Seedway LLC 1734 Railroad Pl .... Hall NY 14463	**800-836-3710**	585-526-6391
Sharp Bros Seed Co		
1005 S Sycamore .... Healy KS 67850	**800-462-8483**	620-398-2231
Stock Seed Farms		
28008 Mill Rd .... Murdock NE 68407	**800-759-1520**	402-867-3771
Stratton Seed Co		
1530 Hwy 79 S .... Stuttgart AR 72160	**800-264-4433**	870-673-4433
W Atlee Burpee Co		
300 Pk Ave .... Warminster PA 18974	**800-333-5808***	215-674-4900
*Cust Svc		
Weeks Seed Company Inc		
1050 Moye Blvd .... Greenville NC 27834	**800-322-1234**	252-757-1234
Wetsel Inc		
961 N Liberty St .... Harrisonburg VA 22802	**800-572-4018***	540-434-6753
*Cust Svc		

691   SEMICONDUCTOR MANUFACTURING SYSTEMS & EQUIPMENT

	Toll-Free	Phone
Advanced Energy Industries Inc		
1625 Sharp Pt Dr .... Fort Collins CO 80525	**800-446-9167**	970-221-4670
NASDAQ: AEIS		
Aehr Test Systems		
400 Kato Terr .... Fremont CA 94539	**800-962-4284**	510-623-9400
NASDAQ: AEHR		
Applied Materials Inc		
3050 Bowers Ave PO Box 58039 .... Santa Clara CA 95054	**877-356-9175**	408-727-5555
NASDAQ: AMAT		
Applied Materials/Semitool		
655 W Reserve Dr .... Kalispell MT 59901	**877-356-9175**	406-752-2107
ASML US Inc 8555 S River Pkwy .... Tempe AZ 85284	**800-227-6462**	480-383-4422
Brooks Automation Inc		
15 Elizabeth Dr .... Chelmsford MA 01824	**800-698-6149**	978-262-2400
NASDAQ: BRKS		
BTU International Inc		
23 Esquire Rd .... North Billerica MA 01862	**800-998-0666**	978-667-4111
NASDAQ: BTUI		
Data I/O Corp		
6464 185th Ave NE Ste 101 .... Redmond WA 98052	**800-426-1045**	425-881-6444
NASDAQ: DAIO		
Ebara Technologies Inc		
51 Main Ave .... Sacramento CA 95838	**800-535-5376**	916-920-5451
Engent Inc		
3140 Northwoods Pkwy Ste 300A .... Norcross GA 30071	**888-768-4357**	678-990-3320
Entegris Inc		
129 Concord Rd Bldg 2 .... Billerica MA 01821	**877-695-7654**	978-436-6500
NASDAQ: ENTG		
Fortrend Corp		
687 N Pastoria Ave .... Sunnyvale CA 94085	**888-937-3637**	408-734-9311
I.B.I.S. Inc		
30 Technology Pkwy S Ste 400 .... Norcross GA 30092	**888-477-7989**	770-368-4000
KDF Electronic & Vacuum Services Inc		
10 Volvo Dr .... Rockleigh NJ 07647	**877-533-3343**	201-784-5005
KLA-Tencor Corp		
One Technology Dr .... Milpitas CA 95035	**800-600-2829**	408-875-3000
NASDAQ: KLAC		
Kokusai Semiconductor Equipment Corp		
2460 N First St Ste 290 .... San Jose CA 95131	**800-800-5321**	408-456-2750
Lam Research Corp		
4650 Cushing Pkwy .... Fremont CA 94538	**800-526-7678**	510-572-0200
NASDAQ: LRCX		
Mattson Technology Inc		
47131 Bayside Pkwy .... Fremont CA 94538	**800-315-6607**	510-657-5900
NASDAQ: MTSN		
MaxLinear Inc		
2051 Palomar Airport Rd Ste 100 .... Carlsbad CA 92011	**888-505-4369**	760-692-0711
NYSE: MXL		
N J R Corp		
125 Nicholson Ln .... San Jose CA 95134	**800-800-5441**	408-321-0200
Rudolph Technologies Inc		
One Rudolph Rd PO Box 1000 .... Flanders NJ 07836	**877-467-8365**	973-691-1300
NASDAQ: RTEC		
Spire Corp 1 Patriots Pk .... Bedford MA 01730	**800-510-4815**	781-275-6000
OTC: SPIR		
Tegal Corp		
2201 S McDowell Blvd .... Petaluma CA 94954	**800-828-3425**	707-763-5600
Tokyo Electron America Inc		
2400 Grove Blvd .... Austin TX 78741	**800-828-6596**	512-424-1000
Ultratech Inc		
3050 Zanker Rd .... San Jose CA 95134	**800-222-1213**	408-321-8835
NASDAQ: UTEK		
Universal Instruments Corp (UIC)		
33 Broome Corporate Pk .... Conklin NY 13748	**800-842-9732**	607-779-7522
Varian Semiconductor Equipment Assoc Inc		
35 Dory Rd .... Gloucester MA 01930	**800-344-1111**	978-282-2000
Veeco Instruments Inc		
One Terminal Dr .... Plainview NY 11803	**888-248-3326**	516-677-0200
NASDAQ: VECO		

692   SEMICONDUCTORS & RELATED DEVICES

SEE ALSO Printed Circuit Boards ; Electronic Components & Accessories - Mfr

	Toll-Free	Phone
8x8 Inc 810 W Maude Ave .... Sunnyvale CA 94085	**888-898-8733**	408-727-1885
NASDAQ: EGHT		
Actel Corp		
2061 Stierlin Ct .... Mountain View CA 94043	**800-262-1060**	650-318-4200
Advanced Micro Devices Inc (AMD)		
One AMD Pl PO Box 3453 .... Sunnyvale CA 94088	**800-538-8450**	408-749-4000
NYSE: AMD		

	Toll-Free	Phone
Aeroflex Inc		
35 S Service Rd PO Box 6022 .... Plainview NY 11803	**800-843-1553**	516-694-6700
TSE: ARX		
Altera Corp		
101 Innovation Dr .... San Jose CA 95134	**800-767-3753***	408-544-7000
NASDAQ: ALTR ■ *Cust Svc		
American Arium		
14811 Myford Rd .... Tustin CA 92780	**877-508-3970**	714-731-1661
Analog Devices Inc		
Three Technology Way .... Norwood MA 02062	**800-262-5643**	781-329-4700
NASDAQ: ADI		
Axsun Technologies Inc		
One Fortune Dr .... Billerica MA 01821	**866-462-9786**	978-262-0049
B & B Electronics Manufacturing Co		
PO Box 1040 .... Ottawa IL 61350	**800-346-3119**	815-433-5100
Broadcom Corp		
5300 California Ave .... Irvine CA 92617	**877-577-2726**	949-926-5000
NASDAQ: BRCM		
CEVA Inc 1943 Landings Dr .... San Jose CA 94043	**800-894-0972**	650-417-7900
Cirrus Logic Inc		
2901 Via Fortuna .... Austin TX 78746	**800-888-5016**	512-851-4000
NASDAQ: CRUS		
Conexant Systems Inc		
1901 Main St Ste 300 .... Irvine CA 92614	**888-855-4562**	949-483-4600
Cree Inc 4600 Silicon Dr .... Durham NC 27703	**800-533-2583**	919-313-5300
NASDAQ: CREE		
Cypress Semiconductor Corp		
198 Champion Ct .... San Jose CA 95134	**800-541-4736**	408-943-2600
NASDAQ: CY		
E/g Electro-graph Inc		
2365 Camino Vida Roble .... Carlsbad CA 92011	**800-782-6659**	760-438-9090
Enphase Energy Inc		
1420 N Mcdowell Blvd .... Petaluma CA 94954	**877-797-4743**	707-763-4784
Epson Electronics America Inc		
150 River Oaks Pkwy .... San Jose CA 95134	**800-228-3964**	408-922-0200
Fairchild Imaging Inc		
1801 McCarthy Blvd .... Milpitas CA 95035	**800-325-6975**	408-433-2500
Fairchild Semiconductor Corp		
82 Running Hill Rd .... South Portland ME 04106	**800-341-0392**	207-775-8100
NASDAQ: FCS		
Freescale Semiconductor Inc		
6501 William Cannon Dr W .... Austin TX 78735	**800-521-6274***	512-895-2000
*Tech Supp		
Gel-Pak LLC		
31398 Huntwood Ave .... Hayward CA 94544	**888-621-4147**	510-576-2220
Global Solar Energy Inc		
8500 S Rita Rd .... Tucson AZ 85747	**866-999-8422**	520-546-6313
HEI Inc 1495 Steiger Lk Ln .... Victoria MN 55386	**866-720-2397**	952-443-2500
Hitachi Canada Ltd		
5450 Explorer Dr Suite 501 .... Mississauga ON L4W5N1	**866-797-4332**	905-629-9300
Impinj Inc		
701 N 34th St Ste 300 .... Seattle WA 98103	**866-467-4650**	206-517-5300
Integrated Device Technology Inc		
6024 Silver Creek Vly Rd .... San Jose CA 95138	**800-345-7015**	408-284-8200
NASDAQ: IDTI		
Integrated Silicon Solution Inc (ISSI)		
1940 Zanker Rd .... San Jose CA 95112	**800-379-4774**	408-969-6600
NASDAQ: ISSI		
Intel Corp		
2200 Mission College Blvd .... Santa Clara CA 95052	**800-628-8686***	408-765-8080
NASDAQ: INTC ■ *Cust Svc		
Intermolecular Inc		
3011 N First St .... San Jose CA 95134	**877-251-1860**	408-582-5700
Intersil Corp		
1001 Murphy Ranch Rd .... Milpitas CA 95035	**888-468-3774**	408-432-8888
NASDAQ: ISIL		
Kyocera America Inc		
8611 Balboa Ave .... San Diego CA 92123	**888-955-0800**	858-576-2600
Kyocera Solar Inc		
7812 E Acoma Dr Ste 2 .... Scottsdale AZ 85260	**800-544-6466**	480-948-8003
Lattice Semiconductor Corp		
5555 NE Moore Ct .... Hillsboro OR 97124	**800-528-8423**	503-268-8000
NASDAQ: LSCC		
Linear Technology Corp		
1630 McCarthy Blvd .... Milpitas CA 95035	**888-500-6973**	408-432-1900
NASDAQ: LLTC		
Logic Devices Inc		
1375 Geneva Dr .... Sunnyvale CA 94089	**800-233-2518**	408-542-5400
OTC: LOGC		
LSI Logic Corp		
1320 Ridder Park Dr .... San Jose CA 95131	**800-372-2447**	408-433-8000
NASDAQ: LSI		
M/A-COM Technology Solutions Inc		
100 Chelmsford St .... Lowell MA 01851	**800-366-2266**	978-656-2500
Maxim Integrated Products Inc		
120 San Gabriel Dr .... Sunnyvale CA 94086	**888-629-4642**	408-737-7600
NASDAQ: MXIM		
Medtronic Microelectronics Ctr (MMC)		
710 Medtronic Pkwy .... Minneapolis MN 55432	**800-633-8766**	763-514-4000
Micrel Inc 2180 Fortune Dr .... San Jose CA 95131	**800-538-8450**	408-944-0800
NASDAQ: MCRL		
Microchip Technology Inc		
2355 West Chandler Blvd .... Chandler AZ 85224	**877-860-3951**	480-792-7200
NASDAQ: MCHP		
Microsemi Corp		
2381 Morse Ave .... Irvine CA 92614	**800-713-4113**	949-221-7100
NASDAQ: MSCC		
Mini-Circuits Laboratories Inc		
13 Neptune Ave .... Brooklyn NY 11235	**800-654-7949**	718-934-4500
MoSys Inc		
3301 Olcott St .... Santa Clara CA 95054	**877-360-6690**	408-418-7500
NEC Electronics America Inc		
2801 Scott Blvd .... Santa Clara CA 95050	**800-366-9782***	408-588-6000
*Tech Supp		
NVE Corp		
11409 Vly View Rd .... Eden Prairie MN 55344	**800-467-7141**	952-829-9217
NASDAQ: NVEC		

Company / Address	City	State	ZIP	Toll-Free	Phone
ON Semiconductor Corp 5005 E McDowell Rd *NASDAQ: ON*	Phoenix	AZ	85008	**800-282-9855**	602-244-6600
Optek Technology Inc 1645 Wallace Dr	Carrollton	TX	75006	**800-341-4747**	972-323-2200
Pericom Semiconductor Corp 3545 N First St *NASDAQ: PSEM*	San Jose	CA	95134	**800-435-2336**	408-435-0800
Plascore Inc 615 N Fairview St	Zeeland	MI	49464	**800-630-9257**	616-772-1220
PLX Technology Inc 870 W Maude Ave *NASDAQ: PLXT*	Sunnyvale	CA	94085	**800-759-3735**	408-774-9060
PMC-Sierra Inc 1380 Bordeaux Dr *NASDAQ: PMCS*	Sunnyvale	CA	94089	**866-268-7116**	408-239-8000
Powerex Inc 173 Pavilion Ln	Youngwood	PA	15697	**800-451-1415**	724-925-7272
Powerfilm Inc 2337 230th St	Ames	IA	50014	**888-354-7773**	515-292-7606
QLogic Corp 26650 Aliso Viejo Pkwy *NASDAQ: QLGC*	Aliso Viejo	CA	92656	**800-662-4471**	949-389-6000
Ramtron International Corp 1850 Ramtron Dr *NASDAQ: RMTR*	Colorado Springs	CO	80921	**800-541-4736**	719-481-7000
Raytek Inc 1201 Shaffer Rd Bldg 2	Santa Cruz	CA	95061	**800-227-8074**	831-458-3900
RF Micro Devices Inc 7628 Thorndike Rd *NASDAQ: RFMD*	Greensboro	NC	27409	**800-937-5449**	336-664-1233
Samsung Semiconductors Inc 3655 N First St *General	San Jose	CA	95134	**800-726-7864***	408-544-4000
Seiko Instruments USA Inc 21221 S Western Ave Ste 250 *Sales	Torrance	CA	90501	**800-688-0817***	310-517-7700
Sheldahl Inc 1150 Sheldahl Rd	Northfield	MN	55057	**800-927-3580**	507-663-8000
Silicon Image Inc 1060 E Arques Ave	Sunnyvale	CA	94085	**800-633-8284**	408-616-4000
Silicon Laboratories Inc 400 W Cesar Chavez *NASDAQ: SLAB*	Austin	TX	78701	**877-444-3032**	512-416-8500
Siltronic Corp 7200 NW Front Ave	Portland	OR	97210	**800-922-5371**	503-243-2020
Solar Solutions & Distribution LLC 2500 W Fifth Ave	Denver	CO	80204	**855-765-3478**	303-948-6300
Solatube International Inc 2210 Oak Ridge Way	Vista	CA	92081	**888-765-2882**	760-477-1120
Spectrolab Inc 12500 Gladstone Ave	Sylmar	CA	91342	**800-936-4888**	818-365-4611
SRS Labs Inc 2909 Daimler St *NASDAQ: SRSL* ■ *General	Santa Ana	CA	92705	**800-243-2733***	949-442-1070
STMicroelectronics NV Pmb #192 134 Vintage Park Blvd Ste A	Houston	TX	77070	**888-356-1766**	281-469-2035
Stretch Inc 1322 Orleans Dr	Sunnyvale	CA	94089	**800-468-6853**	408-543-2700
SunPower Corp 77 Rio Robles *NASDAQ: SPWR*	San Jose	CA	95134	**800-786-7693**	408-240-5500
Taiwan Semiconductor Mfg Company Ltd (TSMC) 2585 Junction Ave *NYSE: TSM*	San Jose	CA	95134	**877-248-4237**	408-382-8000
Tellurex Corp 1462 International Dr	Traverse City	MI	49686	**877-774-7468**	231-947-0110
Texas Instruments Inc 12500 TI Blvd *NASDAQ: TXN* ■ *Cust Svc	Dallas	TX	75243	**800-336-5236***	972-995-3773
Thorlabs Quantum Electronics Inc 10335 Guilford Rd	Jessup	MD	20794	**877-226-8342**	240-456-7100
Toshiba America Electronic Components Inc 19900 MacArthur Blvd Ste 400	Irvine	CA	92612	**800-879-4963**	949-623-2900
TriQuint Semiconductor Inc 2300 NE Brookwood Pkwy *NASDAQ: TQNT*	Hillsboro	OR	97124	**855-367-8768**	503-615-9000
United Microelectronics Corp 488 De Guigne Dr *NYSE: UMC*	Sunnyvale	CA	94085	**800-990-1135**	408-523-7800
Veritec Inc 2445 Winnetka Ave N	Golden Valley	MN	55427	**866-546-1011**	763-253-2670
VIA Technologies Inc 940 Mission Ct	Fremont	CA	94539	**888-524-9382**	510-683-3300
Vishay Intertechnology Inc 63 Lancaster Ave *NYSE: VSH*	Malvern	PA	19355	**800-567-6098**	610-644-1300
Vitesse Semiconductor Corp 741 Calle Plano	Camarillo	CA	93012	**800-642-1687**	805-388-3700
Wabash Technologies 1375 Swan St PO Box 829	Huntington	IN	46750	**800-487-6865**	260-355-4100
Wallco Inc 53 E Jackson St # 55	Wilkes Barre	PA	18701	**800-392-5526**	570-823-6181
Xilinx Inc 2100 Logic Dr *NASDAQ: XLNX*	San Jose	CA	95124	**800-594-5469**	408-559-7778

693 SHEET METAL WORK

SEE ALSO Plumbing, Heating, Air Conditioning Contractors ; Roofing, Siding, Sheet Metal Contractors

Company / Address	City	State	ZIP	Toll-Free	Phone
Abalon Precision Mfg Corp 1040 Home St	Bronx	NY	10459	**800-888-2225**	718-589-5682
Air Comfort Corp 2550 Braga Dr	Broadview	IL	60155	**800-466-3779**	708-345-1900
Air Vent Inc 4117 Pinnacle Pnt Dr Ste 400	Dallas	TX	75211	**800-247-8368**	
Aircom Mfg Inc 6205 E 30th St	Indianapolis	IN	46219	**800-925-2426**	317-545-5383
Aluminum Line Products Co 24460 Sperry Cir	Westlake	OH	44145	**800-321-3154**	440-835-8880
Arizona Precision Sheet Metal 2140 W Pinnacle Peak Rd	Phoenix	AZ	85027	**800-443-7039**	623-516-3700
ASC Profiles Inc 2110 Enterprise Blvd *Cust Svc	West Sacramento	CA	95691	**800-360-2477***	916-372-0933
Associated Materials Inc 3773 State Rd	Cuyahoga Falls	OH	44223	**800-257-4335**	330-929-1811
ATS Systems Inc 30222 Esperanza	Rancho Santa Margarita	CA	92688	**800-321-1833**	949-888-1744
Automated Quality Technologies Inc 563 Shoreview Park Rd	St Paul	MN	55126	**800-250-9297**	651-484-6544
Berger Bldg Products Inc 805 Pennsylvania Blvd *Cust Svc	Feasterville	PA	19053	**800-523-8852***	215-355-1200
Captive-aire Systems Inc 4641 Paragon Pk Rd	Raleigh	NC	27616	**800-334-9256**	919-882-2410
Consolidated Systems Inc 650 Rosewood Dr	Columbia	SC	29202	**800-654-1912**	
Contech Construction Products Inc 9025 Centre Pt Dr Ste 400	West Chester	OH	45069	**800-338-1122**	513-645-7000
Crown Products Company Inc 6390 Phillips Hwy	Jacksonville	FL	32216	**800-683-7144**	904-737-7144
Daviess County Metal Sales Inc 9929 E US Hwy 50	Cannelburg	IN	47519	**800-279-4299**	812-486-4299
Durand Forms Inc 6200 Equitable Rd	Kansas City	MO	64120	**800-545-6342**	
Edco & Arrowhead Products Inc 8700 Excelsior Blvd	Hopkins	MN	55343	**800-333-2580**	952-945-2680
Elixir Industries Inc 24800 Chrisanta Dr Ste 210	Mission Viejo	CA	92691	**800-421-1942**	949-860-5000
Epic Metals Corp 11 Talbot Ave	Rankin	PA	15104	**877-696-3742**	412-351-3913
Flexbar Machine Corp 250 Gibbs Rd	Islandia	NY	11749	**800-879-7575**	631-582-8440
FS Tool Corp 71 Hobbs Gate	Markham	ON	L3R9T9	**800-387-9723**	905-475-1999
Gentek Bldg Products Inc 11 Craigwood Rd	Avenel	NJ	07001	**800-548-4542**	732-381-0900
H & H Industrial Corp 7612 Rt 130	Pennsauken	NJ	08110	**800-982-0341**	856-663-4444
HASCO America Inc 270 Rutledge Rd Unit B	Fletcher	NC	28732	**800-387-9609**	828-650-2600
Industrial Louvers Inc 511 Seventh St S	Delano	MN	55328	**800-328-3421**	763-972-2981
JET Equipment & Tools Ltd 49 Schooner St	Coquitlam	BC	V3K0B3	**800-472-7685**	604-523-8665
Jones Metal Products Inc 3201 Third Ave	Mankato	MN	56001	**800-967-1750**	507-625-4436
LB Foster Co 415 Holiday Dr *NASDAQ: FSTR*	Pittsburgh	PA	15220	**800-255-4500**	
Mapes Panels LLC 2929 Cornhusker Hwy PO Box 80069	Lincoln	NE	68504	**800-228-2391**	
Mayco Industries LLC 18 W Oxmoor Rd	Birmingham	AL	35209	**800-749-6061**	205-942-4242
Mayville Products Corp 403 Degner Ave	Mayville	WI	53050	**800-230-0136**	920-387-3000
McCorvey Sheet Metal Works LP 8610 Wallisville Rd	Houston	TX	77029	**800-580-7545**	713-672-7545
Menches Tool & Die Inc 30995 San Benito St	Hayward	CA	94544	**877-592-2328**	510-476-1160
Metal-Fab Inc 3025 May St	Wichita	KS	67213	**800-835-2830**	316-943-2351
Mitchell Metal Products Inc 19250 Hwy 12 E PO Box 789	Kosciusko	MS	39090	**800-258-6137**	662-289-7110
Morse Industries Inc 25811 74th Ave S	Kent	WA	98032	**800-325-7513**	
Murray Sheet Metal Co Inc 3112 Seventh St	Parkersburg	WV	26104	**800-464-8801**	304-422-5431
Napco Ply Gem Inc 5020 Weston Pkwy Ste 400	Cary	MO	27153	**800-786-2726**	888-975-9436
National Metal Fabricators 2395 Greenleaf Ave	Elk Grove Village	IL	60007	**800-323-8849**	847-439-5321
Nu-Way Industries Inc 555 Howard Ave	Des Plaines	IL	60018	**888-488-5631**	847-298-7710
OMAX Corp 21409 72nd Ave S	Kent	WA	98032	**800-838-0343**	253-872-2300
Panavise Products Inc 7540 Colbert Dr	Reno	NV	89511	**800-759-7535**	775-850-2900
Petersen Aluminum Corp 1005 Tonne Rd	Elk Grove Village	IL	60007	**800-323-1960**	847-228-7150
Platt & Labonia Co 70 Stoddard Ave	North Haven	CT	06473	**800-505-9099**	203-239-5681
Rollex Corp 800 Chasa Ave *Cust Svc	Elk Grove Village	IL	60007	**800-251-3300***	847-437-3000
Saint Regis Culvert Inc 202 Morrell St	Charlotte	MI	48813	**800-527-4604**	517-543-3430
Simpson Dura-Vent Inc 877 Cotting Ct	Vacaville	CA	95688	**800-835-4429**	707-446-1786
Southwark Metal Mfg Company Inc 2800 Red Lion Rd	Philadelphia	PA	19114	**800-523-1052**	215-735-3401
Streimer Sheet Metal Works Inc 740 N Knott St	Portland	OR	97227	**888-288-3828**	503-288-9393
Structures Unlimited Inc 88 Pine St	Manchester	NH	03103	**800-225-3895**	603-645-6539
Thybar Corp 913 S Kay Ave	Addison	IL	60101	**800-666-2872**	630-543-5300
United Tool & Stamping Company of North Carolina Inc 2817 Enterprise Ave	Fayetteville	NC	28306	**800-883-6087**	910-323-8588
Valley Joist 3019 Gault Ave N	Fort Payne	AL	35967	**800-263-0324**	256-845-2330
Wilson Tool International Inc 12912 Farnham Ave	White Bear Lake	MN	55110	**800-328-9646**	651-286-6001
Wisco Products Inc 109 Commercial St	Dayton	OH	45402	**800-367-6570**	937-228-2101

					Toll-Free	Phone
Wise Alloys LLC 4805 Second St	Muscle Shoals	AL	35661		**855-287-1922***	256-386-6000
*Sales						

694 SHIP BUILDING & REPAIRING

				Toll-Free	Phone
Cascade General Inc 5555 N Ch Ave	Portland	OR	97217	**855-844-6799**	503-247-1777
Colonna's Shipyard Inc 400 E Indian River Rd	Norfolk	VA	23523	**800-265-6627**	757-545-2414
Continental Maritime of San Diego Inc 1995 Bay Front St	San Diego	CA	92113	**877-631-0020**	619-234-8851
Earl Industries LLC 2 Harper Ave	Portsmouth	VA	23707	**800-433-7300**	757-215-2500
Elevating Boats LLC 201 Dean Ct	Houma	LA	70363	**800-843-2895**	985-868-9655
Essex Boat Works Inc Ferry St PO Box 37	Essex	CT	06426	**866-378-3748**	860-767-8276
Greenbrier Co One Centerpointe Dr Ste 200 *NYSE: GBX*	Lake Oswego	OR	97035	**800-343-7188**	503-684-7000
Leevac Shipyards Inc 111 Bunge St	Jennings	LA	70546	**800-244-3262**	337-824-2210
MARCO Global 4259 22nd Ave W	Seattle	WA	98199	**866-966-2726**	206-285-3200
Northrop Grumman Newport News 13560 Jefferson Ave	Newport News	VA	23603	**888-493-7386**	757-886-7777
Pacific Fisherman Inc 5351 24th Ave NW	Seattle	WA	98107	**877-644-6148**	206-784-2562
Robishaw Engineering Inc 10106 Mathewson Ln	Houston	TX	77043	**800-877-1706**	713-468-1706
Tecnico Corp 831 Industrial Ave *General	Chesapeake	VA	23324	**800-786-2207***	757-545-4013
Trinity Marine Products Inc 2525 N Stemmons Fwy	Dallas	TX	75207	**877-876-5463**	214-589-8446

695 SHUTTERS - WINDOW (ALL TYPES)

				Toll-Free	Phone
Atlantic Premium Shutters 29797 Beck Rd	Wixom	MI	48393	**866-288-2726**	248-668-6408
Champion Window Mfg Inc 12121 Champion Way	Cincinnati	OH	45241	**877-424-2674**	513-346-4600
Commonwealth Laminating & Coating Inc 345 Beaver Creek Dr *General	Martinsville	VA	24112	**888-321-5111***	276-632-4991
Perfect Shutters Inc 12213 Rte 173	Hebron	IL	60034	**800-548-3336**	815-648-2401
Roll Shutter Systems Inc 21633 N 14th Ave	Phoenix	AZ	85027	**800-551-7655**	623-869-7057
Roll-A-Way Inc 1661 Glenlake Ave	Itasca	IL	60143	**866-749-5424**	
Rolling Shield Inc 2500 NW 74th Ave	Miami	FL	33122	**800-474-9404**	
Shutter Mill Inc 8517 S Perkins Rd	Stillwater	OK	74074	**800-416-6455**	405-377-6455
Sunburst Shutters 6480 W Flamingo Rd Ste D	Las Vegas	NV	89103	**877-786-2877**	702-367-1600
Tapco Group 29797 Beck Rd	Wixom	MI	48393	**800-367-8741**	248-668-6400
Vantage Products Corp 960 Almon Rd	Covington	GA	30014	**800-481-3303**	770-788-0136

696 SIGNALS & SIRENS - ELECTRIC

				Toll-Free	Phone
ADDCO LLC 240 Arlington Ave E	Saint Paul	MN	55117	**800-616-4408**	651-488-8600
ECCO 833 W Diamond St	Boise	ID	83705	**800-635-5900**	208-395-8000
Econolite Control Products Inc 3360 E La Palma Av	Anaheim	CA	92806	**800-225-6480**	714-630-3700

697 SIGNS

SEE ALSO Signals & Sirens - Electric ; Displays - Exhibit & Trade Show ; Displays - Point-of-Purchase

				Toll-Free	Phone
Ad Art Co 3260 E 26th St	Los Angeles	CA	90058	**800-266-7522**	323-981-8941
Advance Corp Braille-Tac Div 8200 97th St S	Cottage Grove	MN	55016	**800-328-9451**	651-771-9297
Allen Industries Inc 6434 Burnt Poplar Rd	Greensboro	NC	27409	**800-967-2553**	336-668-2791
APCO Graphics Inc 388 Grant St SE	Atlanta	GA	30312	**877-988-2726**	404-688-9000
Apex Digital Imaging Inc 16057 Tampa Palms Blvd W	Tampa	FL	33647	**866-973-3034**	813-973-3034
Beyond Digital Imaging 36 Apple Creek Blvd	Markham	ON	L3R4Y4	**888-689-1888**	905-415-1888
Brady Corp 6555 W Good Hope Rd *NYSE: BRC* ■ *Cust Svc	Milwaukee	WI	53223	**800-541-1686***	414-358-6600
California Neon Products Inc 4530 Mission Gorge Pl	San Diego	CA	92120	**800-822-6366**	619-283-2191
Century Graphics & Metals Inc 550 S N Lake Blvd Ste 1000	Altamonte Springs	FL	32701	**800-327-5664**	
Colorado Time Systems 1551 E 11th St	Loveland	CO	80537	**800-279-0111**	970-667-1000
Couch & Philippi Inc 10680 Fern Ave PO Box A *Orders	Stanton	CA	90680	**800-854-3360***	714-527-2261
Cummings Signs Inc 15 Century Blvd Ste 200	Nashville	TN	37214	**800-489-7446**	
DiAZiT Company Inc 941 US 1 Hwy PO Box 276 *Cust Svc	Youngsville	NC	27596	**800-334-6641***	919-556-5188
Dualite Sales & Service Inc 1 Dualite Ln	Williamsburg	OH	45176	**800-543-7271**	513-724-7100
Eastern Metal/USA-SIGN 1430 Sullivan St *Sales	Elmira	NY	14901	**800-872-7446***	607-734-2295
Everbrite Inc 4949 S 110th St PO Box 20020	Greenfield	WI	53220	**800-558-3888**	414-529-3500
FASTSIGNS International Inc 2542 Highlander Way	Carrollton	TX	75006	**800-827-7446**	972-447-0777
Formetco Inc 2963 Pleasant Hill Rd	Duluth	GA	30096	**800-367-6382**	770-476-7000
GableSigns Inc 7440 Ft Smallwood Rd	Baltimore	MD	21226	**800-854-0568**	410-255-6400
Gemini Inc 103 Mensing Way	Cannon Falls	MN	55009	**800-538-8377**	507-263-3957
George Patton Assoc Inc 55 Broadcommon Rd	Bristol	RI	02809	**800-572-2194**	401-247-0333
Gopher Sign Co 1310 Randolph Ave	Saint Paul	MN	55105	**800-383-3156**	651-698-5095
Grandwell Industries Inc 121 Quantum St *Cust Svc	Holly Springs	NC	27540	**800-338-6554***	919-557-1221
Graphic Specialties Inc 3110 Washington Ave N	Minneapolis	MN	55411	**800-486-4605**	612-522-5287
Hall Signs Inc 4495 W Vernal Pk	Bloomington	IN	47404	**800-284-7446**	
Hallmark Nameplate Inc 1717 E Lincoln Ave	Mount Dora	FL	32757	**800-874-9063**	352-383-8142
Hawkins Traffic Safety Supply 1255 E Shore Hwy	Berkeley	CA	94710	**800-772-3995**	800-236-0112
Hy-Ko Products Co 60 Meadow Ln	Northfield	OH	44067	**800-292-0550**	330-467-7446
Icon Identity Solutions 1418 Elmhurst Rd	Elk Grove Village	IL	60007	**888-724-0380**	
Insignia Systems Inc 8799 Brooklyn Blvd *NASDAQ: ISIG*	Minneapolis	MN	55445	**800-874-4648**	763-392-6200
International Patterns Inc 50 Inez Dr	Bay Shore	NY	11706	**800-471-6368**	631-952-2000
Kieffer & Company Inc 3322 Washington Ave	Sheboygan	WI	53081	**800-458-4394**	
Lake Shore Industries Inc (LSI) 1817 Poplar St PO BOX 3427	Erie	PA	16508	**800-458-0463**	
LNI Custom Manufacturing Inc 12536 Chadron Ave	Hawthorne	CA	90250	**800-338-3387**	310-978-2000
M-R Sign Company Inc 1706 First Ave N	Fergus Falls	MN	56537	**800-231-5564**	218-736-5681
Magnetsigns Adv Inc 4225 38th St	Camrose	AB	T4V3Z3	**800-219-8977**	780-672-8720
McLoone 75 Sumner St	La Crosse	WI	54603	**800-624-6641**	608-784-1260
National Stock Sign Co 1040 El Dorado Ave	Santa Cruz	CA	95062	**800-462-7726**	831-476-2020
O'Ryan Group Inc 4010 Pilot Ste 108	Memphis	TN	38118	**800-253-0750**	901-794-4610
Pannier Graphics 345 Oak Rd	Gibsonia	PA	15044	**800-544-8428**	724-265-4900
Pattison Sign Group 555 Ellesmere Rd	Scarborough	ON	M1R4E8	**800-268-6536**	416-759-1111
Poblocki Sign Company LLC 922 S 70th St	West Allis	WI	53214	**800-776-7064**	414-453-4010
Precision Solar Controls Inc 2985 Market St	Garland	TX	75041	**800-686-7414**	972-278-0553
Prismaflex Inc 1645 Queens Way E	Mississauga	ON	L4X3A3	**888-454-2244**	905-279-9793
Protection Services Inc 635 Lucknow Rd	Harrisburg	PA	17110	**866-489-1234**	717-236-9307
Quality Manufacturing Inc 969 Labore Industrial Ct	Saint Paul	MN	55110	**800-243-5473**	651-483-5473
Safeway Sign Co 9875 Yucca Rd	Adelanto	CA	92301	**800-637-7233**	760-246-7070
Scioto Sign Company Inc 6047 US Rt 68 N	Kenton	OH	43326	**800-572-4686**	419-673-1261
Scott Sign Systems Inc 7525 Pennsylvania Ave Ste 101	Sarasota	FL	34243	**800-237-9447**	941-355-5171
SFC Graphics 110 E Woodruff Ave	Toledo	OH	43604	**800-537-1130**	419-255-1283
Sign Builders Inc 4800 Jefferson Ave PO Box 28380	Birmingham	AL	35228	**800-222-7330**	
Sign Designs Inc 204 Campus Way	Modesto	CA	95350	**800-421-7446**	209-524-4484
Sign-A-Rama 2121 Vista Pkwy *All	West Palm Beach	FL	33411	**800-776-8105***	561-640-5570
Signs by Tomorrow USA Inc 8681 Robert Fulton Dr	Columbia	MD	21046	**800-765-7446**	410-312-3600
Signs First Corp 720 Wildwood Trace	Winchester	TN	37398	**800-598-5845**	931-636-4031
Signs Now 5368 Dixie Hwy Ste 1	Waterford	MI	48329	**800-356-3373**	248-596-8600
Signtech Electrical Adv Inc 4444 Federal Blvd	San Diego	CA	92102	**877-885-1135**	619-527-6100
Signtronix 1445 W Sepulveda Blvd	Torrance	CA	90501	**800-729-4853**	
Spectrum Corp 10048 Easthaven Blvd	Houston	TX	77075	**800-392-5050**	713-944-6200
Tube Art Group (TAG) 11715 SE Fifth St	Bellevue	WA	98005	**800-562-2854**	206-223-1122
Vomela Specialty Co 274 E Fillmore Ave	Saint Paul	MN	55107	**800-645-1012**	651-228-2200

Classified Section

			Toll-Free	Phone
Walter Haas & Sons Inc				
123 W 23rd St	Hialeah FL	33010	**800-552-3845**	305-883-2257
Werner Tool & Mfg Co Inc				
12301 E McNichols Rd	Detroit MI	48205	**800-362-8491**	313-526-6020
Worldwide Sign Systems				
446 N Cecil St	Bonduel WI	54107	**800-874-3334**	
Young Electric Sign Co				
2401 Foothill Dr	Salt Lake City UT	84109	**888-959-3726**	801-464-4600
Zumar Industries Inc				
9719 Santa Fe Springs Rd	Santa Fe Springs CA	90670	**800-654-7446**	562-941-4633

698 SILVERWARE

SEE ALSO Metal Stampings ; Cutlery

			Toll-Free	Phone
Great American Products Inc				
1661 S Seguin Ave	New Braunfels TX	78130	**800-341-4436**	830-620-4400
Old Newbury Crafters				
36 Main St Ste 2	Amesbury MA	01913	**800-343-1388**	
Olde Country Reproductions Inc				
722 W Market St	York PA	17405	**800-358-3997***	717-848-1859
*Cust Svc				
Pfaltzgraff Co PO Box 21769	York PA	17402	**800-999-2811**	
Salisbury Inc				
29085 Airpark Dr	Easton MD	21601	**855-255-5309**	410-770-4901
Woodbury Pewterers Inc				
860 Main St S	Woodbury CT	06798	**800-648-2014**	

699 SIMULATION & TRAINING SYSTEMS

			Toll-Free	Phone
CAE Inc				
8585 Cote de Liesse	Saint Laurent QC	H4T1G6	**866-999-6223**	514-341-6780
NYSE: CAE				
Cubic Corp				
9333 Balboa Ave PO Box 85587	San Diego CA	92186	**800-937-5449**	858-277-6780
NYSE: CUB				
Cubic Defense Systems				
9333 Balboa Ave	San Diego CA	92123	**800-937-5449**	858-277-6780
DRS C3 Systems LLC				
400 Professional Dr	Gaithersburg MD	20879	**800-694-5005**	301-921-8100
Energy Concepts Inc				
404 Washington Blvd	Mundelein IL	60060	**800-621-1247**	847-837-8191
Evans & Sutherland Computer Corp				
770 Komas Dr	Salt Lake City UT	84108	**800-327-5707***	801-588-1000
OTC: ESCC ▦ *Sales				
Faac Inc				
1229 Oak Valley Dr	Ann Arbor MI	48108	**877-322-2387**	734-761-5836
Meggitt Training Systems Inc				
296 Brogdon Rd	Suwanee GA	30024	**800-813-9046**	678-288-1090
Nida Corp				
300 S John Rodes Blvd	Melbourne FL	32904	**800-327-6432**	321-727-2265

700 SMART CARDS

			Toll-Free	Phone
CardLogix 16 Hughes Ste 100	Irvine CA	92618	**866-392-8326**	949-380-1312
Clever Devices Ltd				
300 Crossways Pk Dr	Woodbury NY	11797	**800-872-6129**	516-433-6100
Credit Card Systems Inc				
180 Shepard Ave	Wheeling IL	60090	**800-747-1269**	847-459-8320
DataCard Corp				
11111 Bren Rd W	Minnetonka MN	55343	**800-328-8623**	952-933-1223
MDI Security Systems Inc				
12500 Network Dr Ste 303	San Antonio TX	78249	**866-435-7634**	210-477-5400

701 SNOWMOBILES

SEE ALSO Sporting Goods

			Toll-Free	Phone
Arctic Cat Inc				
601 Brooks Ave S	Thief River Falls MN	56701	**877-228-2687**	218-681-8558
NASDAQ: ACAT				
Yamaha Motor Corp USA				
6555 Katella Ave	Cypress CA	90630	**800-656-7695***	
*Cust Svc				

SOFTWARE

SEE Computer Software

702 SPAS - HEALTH & FITNESS

SEE ALSO Spas - Hotel & Resort ; Weight Loss Centers & Services ; Health & Fitness Centers

Facilities listed here provide multi-day programs designed to increase health and well-being. Types of programs offered include (but are not limited to) relaxation, smoking cessation, weight loss, and physical fitness.

			Toll-Free	Phone
Cal-a-Vie Spa				
29402 Spa Havens Way	Vista CA	92084	**866-772-4283**	760-945-2055
Calistoga Spa Hot Springs				
1006 Washington St	Calistoga CA	94515	**866-822-5772**	707-942-6269
Cooper Wellness Program				
12230 Preston Rd	Dallas TX	75230	**800-444-5192**	972-386-4777
Cornelia Day Resort				
663 Fifth Ave Eighth Fl	New York NY	10022	**866-663-1700**	212-871-3050
Deerfield Spa				
650 Resica Falls Rd	East Stroudsburg PA	18302	**800-852-4494**	570-223-0160

			Toll-Free	Phone
Duke Diet & Fitness Ctr (DFC)				
501 Douglas St	Durham NC	27705	**800-235-3853**	919-688-3079
Golden Door PO Box 463077	Escondido CA	92046	**866-420-6414**	760-744-5777
Grand Wailea Resort & Spa				
3850 Wailea Alanui Dr	Wailea HI	96753	**800-888-6100**	808-875-1234
Green Mountain at Fox Run				
262 Fox Ln PO Box 358	Ludlow VT	05149	**800-448-8106**	802-228-8885
Green Valley Spa & Resort				
1871 W Canyon View Dr	Saint George UT	84770	**800-237-1068**	
Heartland Spa				
1237 E 1600 N Rd	Gilman IL	60938	**800-545-4853**	
Hills Health Ranch				
4871 Caribou Hwy 97 PO Box 26	108 Mile Ranch BC	V0K2Z0	**800-668-2233**	250-791-5225
Hilton Head Health Institute				
14 Valencia Rd	Hilton Head Island SC	29928	**800-292-2440**	843-785-7292
Hippocrates Health Institute Life-Change Ctr				
1443 Palmdale Ct	West Palm Beach FL	33411	**800-842-2125**	561-471-8876
Kripalu Ctr for Yoga & Health				
57 Interlaken Rd	Stockbridge MA	01262	**800-741-7353**	413-448-3400
Lodge & Spa at Cordillera				
2205 Cordillera Way	Edwards CO	81632	**800-877-3529**	970-926-2200
Miraval AZ Resort & Spa				
5000 E Via Estancia Miraval	Tucson AZ	85739	**800-232-3969**	
New Age Health Spa				
PO Box 658	Neversink NY	12765	**800-682-4348**	845-985-7600
Oaks at Ojai 122 E Ojai Ave	Ojai CA	93023	**800-753-6257**	805-646-5573
Ocean Waters Spa				
600 N Atlantic Ave	Daytona Beach FL	32118	**844-284-2685**	386-267-1660
Ojo Caliente Mineral Springs Resort				
50 Los Banos Dr PO Box 68	Ojo Caliente NM	87549	**800-222-9162**	505-583-2233
Optimum Health Institute				
6970 Central Ave	Lemon Grove CA	91945	**800-993-4325**	619-464-3346
Pritikin Longevity Ctr & Spa				
8755 NW 36th St	Doral FL	33178	**800-327-4914**	305-935-7131
Raj, The 1734 Jasmine Ave	Fairfield IA	52556	**800-248-9050**	641-472-9580
Sagestone Spa & Salon				
Red Mountain Resort				
1275 East Red Mtn Cir	Ivins UT	84738	**877-246-4453**	435-673-4905
Spa at Coeur d'Alene				
115 S Second St	Coeur d'Alene ID	83814	**800-684-0514**	208-765-4000
Spa at Peninsula Beverly Hills				
9882 S Santa Monica Blvd	Beverly Hills CA	90212	**800-462-7899**	310-551-2888
Structure House				
3017 Pickett Rd	Durham NC	27705	**800-553-0052**	919-493-4205
Tennessee Fitness Spa				
299 Natural Bridge Pk Rd	Waynesboro TN	38485	**800-235-8365**	931-722-5589
Tracie Martyn Salon				
59 Fifth Ave Ste 1	New York NY	10003	**866-862-7896**	212-206-9333
Two Bunch Palms Resort & Spa				
67425 Two Bunch Palms Trl	Desert Hot Springs CA	92240	**800-472-4334**	760-329-8791
Uchee Pines Lifestyle Ctr				
30 Uchee Pines Rd PO Box 75	Seale AL	36875	**877-824-3374**	334-855-4764
Vail Cascade Resort & Spa				
1300 Westhaven Dr	Vail CO	81657	**800-420-2424**	970-476-7111

703 SPAS - HOTEL & RESORT

SEE ALSO Spas - Health & Fitness

			Toll-Free	Phone
100 Fountain Spa at the Pillar & Post Inn				
48 John St PO Box 48	Niagara-on-the-Lake ON	L0S1J0	**888-669-5566**	905-468-2123
Abbey Resort & Fontana Spa				
269 Fontana Blvd	Fontana WI	53125	**800-709-1323**	262-275-9000
Ancient Cedars Spa at the Wickaninnish Inn				
500 Osprey Ln PO Box 250	Tofino BC	V0R2Z0	**800-333-4604**	250-725-3113
Aquae Sulis Spa at the JW Marriott Resort Las Vegas				
221 N Rampart Blvd	Las Vegas NV	89144	**877-869-8777**	702-869-7807
Aria Spa & Club at the Vail Cascade Resort				
1300 Westhaven Dr	Vail CO	81657	**888-824-5772**	970-479-5942
Arizona Biltmore Resort & Spa				
2400 E Missouri	Phoenix AZ	85016	**800-950-0086**	602-955-6600
Au Naturel Wellness & Medical Spa at the Brookstreet Hotel				
525 Legget Dr	Ottawa ON	K2K2W2	**888-826-2220**	613-271-1800
Boutique Spa at the Ritz-Carlton Georgetown				
3100 S St NW	Washington DC	20007	**800-241-3333**	202-912-4175
Canyon Ranch SpaClub at the Venetian				
3355 Las Vegas Blvd S Ste 1159	Las Vegas NV	89109	**877-220-2688**	702-414-3606
Cape Codder Resort & Spa				
1225 Iyanough Rd Rt 132 Bearse's Way	Hyannis MA	02601	**888-297-2200**	508-771-3000
Carefree Resort & Conference Ctr				
37220 Mule Train Rd	Carefree AZ	85377	**888-692-4343**	
Carneros Inn, The				
4048 Sonoma Hwy	Napa CA	94559	**888-400-9000**	707-299-4900
Centre for Well-Being at the Phoenician				
6000 E Camelback Rd	Scottsdale AZ	85251	**800-843-2392**	
Chateau Elan Spa at the Chateau Elan Atlanta				
100 Rue Charlemagne	Braselton GA	30517	**800-233-9463**	678-425-0900
Cheeca Lodge & Spa				
81801 Overseas Hwy Mile Marker 82	Islamorada FL	33036	**800-327-2888**	305-664-4651
Cliff Spa at Snowbird				
Hwy 210 PO Box 929000	Snowbird UT	84092	**800-453-3000**	801-933-2225
CopperWynd Resort and Club				
13225 N Eagle Ridge Dr	Fountain Hills AZ	85268	**877-707-7760**	480-333-1831
Cranwell Resort Spa & Golf Club				
55 Lee Rd	Lenox MA	01240	**800-272-6935**	413-637-1364
Disney's Grand Floridian Spa				
4401 Floridian Wy	Lake Buena Vista FL	32830	**800-169-0730**	407-824-2332
Elizabeth Arden Red Door Spa at Mystic Marriott Hotel & Spa				
625 N Rd	Groton CT	06340	**866-449-7390**	860-446-2500
Emerson Resort & Spa				
5340 Rt 28	Mount Tremper NY	12457	**877-688-2828**	845-688-7900
Estancia La Jolla Hotel & Spa				
9700 N Torrey Pines Rd	La Jolla CA	92037	**866-437-8262**	858-550-1000
Four Seasons Spa at the Four Seasons Hotel Las Vegas				
3960 Las Vegas Blvd S	Las Vegas NV	89119	**800-332-3442**	702-632-5302

				Toll-Free	Phone
Four Seasons Spa at the Four Seasons Hotel Los Angeles at Beverly Hills					
300 S Doheny Dr	Los Angeles	CA	90048	**800-819-5053**	310-786-2229
Four Seasons Spa at the Four Seasons Resort Jackson Hole					
7680 Granite Loop Rd PO Box 544	Teton Village	WY	83025	**800-819-5053**	307-732-5120
Four Seasons Spa at the Four Seasons Resort Maui					
3900 Wailea Alanui Dr	Wailea	HI	96753	**800-334-6284**	808-874-2925
Four Seasons Spa at the Four Seasons Resort Santa Barbara					
1260 Ch Dr	Santa Barbara	CA	93108	**800-819-5053***	805-565-8250
*General					
Fox Harb'r Resort & Spa					
1337 Fox Harbour Rd	Wallace	NS	B0K1Y0	**866-257-1801**	902-257-1801
Garden Spa at MacArthur Place					
29 E MacArthur St	Sonoma	CA	95476	**800-722-1866**	707-933-3193
Glacial Waters Spa at Grand View Lodge					
23521 Nokomis Ave	Nisswa	MN	56468	**866-801-2951**	218-963-2234
Grand Hotel Marriott Resort Golf Club & Spa					
One Grand Blvd PO Box 639	Point Clear	AL	36564	**800-544-9933**	251-928-9201
Green Valley Ranch Resort Casino & Spa					
2300 Paseo Verde Pkwy	Henderson	NV	89052	**866-782-9487***	702-617-7777
*Resv					
Greenbrier, The					
300 W Main St	White Sulphur Springs	WV	24986	**800-453-4858**	304-536-1110
Grove Park Inn Resort & Spa					
290 Macon Ave	Asheville	NC	28804	**800-438-5800**	828-252-2711
Hilton Short Hills					
41 JFK Pkwy	Short Hills	NJ	07078	**800-445-8667**	973-379-0100
Hilton Suites Toronto/Markham Conference Centre & Spa					
8500 Warden Ave	Markham	ON	L6G1A5	**800-445-8667**	905-470-8500
Homestead Resort					
700 N Homestead Dr	Midway	UT	84049	**888-327-7220**	
Hyatt Regency Scottsdale Resort at Gainey Ranch					
7500 E Doubletree Ranch Rd	Scottsdale	AZ	85258	**800-233-1234**	480-483-5558
Indian Springs Resort & Spa					
1712 Lincoln Ave	Calistoga	CA	94515	**800-877-3623**	707-942-4913
Jurlique Spa					
4925 N Scottsdale Rd	Scottsdale	AZ	85251	**800-528-7867**	480-424-6072
JW Starr Pass Resort & Spa					
3800 W Starr Pass Blvd	Tucson	AZ	85745	**800-845-5279**	520-792-3500
Kea Lani Spa at the Fairmont Kea Lani Maui					
4100 Wailea Alanui Dr	Maui	HI	96753	**800-659-4100**	808-875-2229
Kohler Waters Spa					
501 Highlands Dr	Kohler	WI	53044	**866-928-3777**	920-457-7777
Lafayette Park Hotel					
3287 Mt Diablo Blvd	Lafayette	CA	94549	**877-283-8787**	925-283-3700
Lake Austin Spa Resort					
1705 S Quinlan Pk Rd	Austin	TX	78732	**800-847-5637**	512-372-7380
Lansdowne Resort					
44050 Woodridge Pkwy	Leesburg	VA	20176	**877-509-8400**	703-729-4036
Living Spa at El Monte Sagrado					
317 Kit Carson Rd	Taos	NM	87571	**888-213-4419**	575-758-3502
Massage Ctr at Mohonk Mountain House					
1000 Mtn Rest Rd	New Paltz	NY	12561	**800-772-6646**	845-255-1000
Mii Amo at Enchantment Resort					
525 Boynton Canyon Rd	Sedona	AZ	86336	**888-749-2137**	928-203-8500
Mirbeau Inn & Spa					
851 W Genesee St	Skaneateles	NY	13152	**877-647-2328**	315-685-5006
Mokara Hotel & Spa					
212 W Crockett St	San Antonio	TX	78205	**866-605-1212**	210-396-5800
Mountain Laurel Spa at Stonewall Resort					
940 Resort Dr	Roanoke	WV	26447	**888-278-8150**	304-269-8881
Na Ho'ola Spa at Hyatt Regency Waikiki Resort					
2424 Kalakaua Ave	Honolulu	HI	96815	**800-233-1234**	808-923-1234
Omni Interlocken Resort					
500 Interlocken Blvd	Broomfield	CO	80021	**800-843-6664**	303-438-6600
Omni Rancho Las Palmas Resort & Spa					
41000 Bob Hope Dr	Rancho Mirage	CA	92270	**866-423-1195**	760-568-2727
Pala Casino Resort & Spa					
35008 Pala-Temecula Rd	Pala	CA	92059	**877-946-7252**	760-510-5100
Peaks Resort & Golden Door Spa					
136 Country Club Dr	Telluride	CO	81435	**800-789-2220**	
Portofino Spa at Portofino Island Resort					
10 Portofino Dr	Pensacola	FL	32561	**866-849-0223**	850-916-5000
Raindance Spa at the Lodge at Sonoma Renaissance Resort					
1325 Broadway	Sonoma	CA	95476	**866-263-0758**	707-935-6600
Resort at Squaw Creek					
400 Squaw Creek Rd PO Box 3333	Olympic Valley	CA	96146	**800-327-3353**	530-583-6300
Revive Spa at the JW Marriott Desert Ridge Resort Phoenix					
5350 E Marriott Dr	Phoenix	AZ	85054	**800-845-5279**	480-293-3700
Ritz-Carlton Hotel Company, The					
1111 Ritz-Carlton Dr	Sarasota	FL	34236	**800-241-3333**	866-922-6882
Ritz-Carlton Tysons Corner, The					
1700 Tysons Blvd	McLean	VA	22102	**800-241-3333**	703-506-4300
Safety Harbor Resort & Spa					
105 N Bayshore Dr	Safety Harbor	FL	34695	**888-237-8772**	727-726-1161
Saint Regis Aspen					
315 E Dean St	Aspen	CO	81611	**888-627-7198***	970-920-3300
*General					
Sea Spa at Loews Coronado Bay Resort					
4000 Loews Coronado Bay Rd	Coronado	CA	92118	**800-815-6397**	619-424-4000
Secret Garden Spa at the Prince of Wales Hotel					
Six Picton St PO Box 46	Niagara-on-the-Lake	ON	L0S1J0	**888-669-5566**	905-468-3246
Senator Inn & Spa of Augusta					
284 Western Ave	Augusta	ME	04330	**877-772-2224**	207-622-8800
Spa & Fitness Club at the Four Seasons Hotel Washington					
2800 Pennsylvania Ave NW	Washington	DC	20007	**800-819-5053**	202-944-2022
Spa at Big Cedar Lodge					
612 Devil's Pool Rd	Ridgedale	MO	65739	**800-225-6343**	417-339-5201
Spa at Eagle Crest Resort					
1522 Cline Falls Hwy PO Box 1215	Redmond	OR	97756	**800-682-4786**	541-923-9647
Spa at Le Merigot JW Marriott Beach Hotel Santa Monica					
1740 Ocean Ave	Santa Monica	CA	90401	**888-236-2427**	310-395-9700
Spa at Pebble Beach					
1518 Cypress Dr	Pebble Beach	CA	93953	**800-654-9300**	831-649-7615
Spa at Pinehurst Resort					
80 Carolina Vista Dr PO Box 4000	Pinehurst	NC	28374	**800-487-4653**	910-235-8320
Spa at the Beverly Wilshire, The					
9500 Wilshire Blvd	Beverly Hills	CA	90212	**800-545-4000**	310-385-7023
Spa at the Bodega Bay Lodge					
103 Coast Hwy 1	Bodega Bay	CA	94923	**888-875-2250**	707-875-3525
Spa at the Breakers					
One S County Rd	Palm Beach	FL	33480	**888-273-2537**	561-653-6656
Spa at the Broadmoor					
One Lake Ave	Colorado Springs	CO	80906	**800-634-7711**	719-634-7711
Spa at the Buena Vista Palace Resort in the Walt Disney World Resort					
1900 Buena Vista Dr					
PO Box 22206	Lake Buena Vista	FL	32830	**866-397-6516**	407-827-3200
Spa at the Camelback Inn JW Marriott Resort Golf Club & Spa					
5402 E Lincoln Dr	Scottsdale	AZ	85253	**800-922-2635**	480-596-7040
Spa at the Chattanoogan					
1201 S Broad St	Chattanooga	TN	37402	**800-619-0018**	423-424-3779
Spa at the Equinox Resort					
3567 Main St Rt 7-A	Manchester Village	VT	05254	**800-362-4747**	
Spa at the Fairmont Inn Sonoma Mission Inn					
100 Boyes Blvd	Sonoma	CA	95476	**877-289-7354**	707-938-9000
Spa at the Hotel Hershey					
100 Hotel Rd	Hershey	PA	17033	**877-772-9988**	717-520-5888
Spa at the JW Marriott Desert Springs Resort Palm Desert					
74855 Country Club Dr	Palm Desert	CA	92260	**800-845-5279**	760-341-2211
Spa at the Norwich Inn					
607 W Thames St	Norwich	CT	06360	**800-275-4772**	860-886-2401
Spa at the PGA National Resort					
450 Ave of the Champions	Palm Beach Gardens	FL	33418	**800-633-9150**	561-627-3111
Spa at the Ponte Vedra Inn & Club					
200 Ponte Vedra Blvd	Ponte Vedra Beach	FL	32082	**800-234-7842**	904-273-7700
Spa at the Ritz-Carlton Amelia Island					
4750 Amelia Island Pkwy	Amelia Island	FL	32034	**800-241-3333**	904-277-1087
Spa at the Ritz-Carlton Bachelor Gulch					
0130 Daybreak Ridge	Avon	CO	81620	**800-241-3333**	970-748-6200
Spa at the Ritz-Carlton Half Moon Bay					
One Miramontes Pt Rd	Half Moon Bay	CA	94019	**800-241-3333**	650-712-7040
Spa at the Ritz-Carlton New Orleans					
921 Canal St	New Orleans	LA	70112	**800-241-3333**	504-670-2929
Spa at the Saddlebrook Resort					
5700 Saddlebrook Way	Wesley Chapel	FL	33543	**800-729-8383**	813-907-4419
Spa at the Sagamore					
110 Sagamore Rd	Bolton Landing	NY	12814	**866-384-1944**	518-743-6081
Spa at the Sanderling Resort					
1461 Duck Rd	Duck	NC	27949	**855-412-7866**	252-261-7744
Spa at the Vail Marriott Mountain Resort					
715 W Lionshead Cir	Vail	CO	81657	**800-648-0720**	970-479-5004
Spa at the Villagio Inn					
6481 Washington St	Yountville	CA	94599	**800-351-1133**	707-948-5050
Spa at White Oaks Conference Resort					
253 Taylor Rd	Niagara-on-the-Lake	ON	L0S1J0	**800-263-5766**	905-641-2599
Spa Esmeralda at the Renaissance Esmeralda Resort					
44400 Indian Wells Ln	Indian Wells	CA	92210	**800-845-5279**	760-836-1265
Spa Gaucin at the Saint Regis Monarch Beach					
One Monarch Beach Resort	Dana Point	CA	92629	**800-722-1543**	949-234-3367
Spa Grande at the Grand Wailea Resort Maui					
3850 Wailea Alanui Dr	Wailea	HI	96753	**800-772-1933**	808-875-1234
Spa La Quinta at La Quinta Resort					
49499 Eisenhower Dr	La Quinta	CA	92253	**877-527-7721**	760-777-4800
Spa Moana at the Hyatt Regency Maui Resort & Spa					
200 Nohea Kai Dr	Lahaina	HI	96761	**800-233-1234**	808-667-4725
Spa Shiki at the Lodge of Four Seasons					
315 Horseshoe Bend Pkwy	Lake Ozark	MO	65049	**800-843-5253**	573-365-8108
Spa Suites at Kahala Hotel & Resort					
5000 Kahala Ave	Honolulu	HI	96816	**800-367-2525**	808-739-8938
Spa Terre at Paradise Point Resort					
1404 Vacation Rd	San Diego	CA	92109	**800-344-2626**	858-581-5998
Spa Terre at the Hotel Viking					
One Bellevue Ave	Newport	RI	02840	**800-556-7126**	401-847-3300
Spa Terre at the Inn & Spa at Loretto					
211 Old Santa Fe Trl	Santa Fe	NM	87501	**800-727-5531**	505-984-7997
Spa Toccare at Borgata Hotel Casino					
1 Borgata Way	Atlantic City	NJ	08401	**877-448-5833**	609-317-7555
Spa Torrey Pines at the Lodge at Torrey Pines					
11480 N Torrey Pines Rd	La Jolla	CA	92037	**800-656-0087**	858-453-4420
SpaHalekulani at the Halekulani Hotel					
2199 Kalia Rd	Honolulu	HI	96815	**800-367-2343**	808-931-5322
Springmaid Beach Resort					
3200 S Ocean Blvd	Myrtle Beach	SC	29577	**866-764-8501**	
Stillwater Spa at the Hyatt Regency Newport					
One Goat Island	Newport	RI	02840	**800-233-1234**	401-851-3225
Taboo Resort Golf & Spa					
1209 Muskoka Beach Rd	Gravenhurst	ON	P1P1R1	**800-461-0236**	
Tampa Marriott Waterside Hotel & Marina					
700 S Florida Ave	Tampa	FL	33602	**888-268-1616**	813-204-6300
Tulalip Resort Casino					
10200 Quil Ceda Blvd	Tulalip	WA	98271	**888-272-1111**	
Vail Mountain Lodge & Spa, The					
352 E Meadow Dr	Vail	CO	81657	**888-794-0410**	970-476-0700
Well Spa at Miramonte Resort					
45000 Indian Wells Ln	Indian Wells	CA	92210	**866-843-9355**	760-837-1652
Westglow Resort & Spa					
224 Westglow Cir	Blowing Rock	NC	28605	**800-562-0807**	828-295-4463
Westin Kierland Resort & Spa					
6902 E Greenway Pkwy	Scottsdale	AZ	85254	**800-354-5892**	480-624-1000
Westin Maui Resort & Spa, The					
2365 Kaanapali Pkwy	Lahaina	HI	96761	**866-716-8112**	808-667-2525
Westin Resort & Spa					
4090 Whistler Way	Whistler	BC	V0N1B4	**888-627-8979**	604-905-5000
Willow Stream Spa at Fairmont Scottsdale Princess					
7575 E Princess Dr	Scottsdale	AZ	85255	**800-908-9540**	480-585-2732
Willow Stream Spa at the Fairmont Banff Springs					
405 Spray Ave	Banff	AB	T1L1J4	**800-404-1772**	403-762-1772
Willow Stream Spa at the Fairmont Empress					
633 Humboldt St	Victoria	BC	V8W1A6	**866-854-7444**	250-995-4650
Wintergreen Resort					
Rt 664 PO Box 706	Wintergreen	VA	22958	**800-266-2444**	855-699-1858

		Toll-Free	Phone

704 SPEAKERS BUREAUS

		Toll-Free	Phone
AEI Speakers Bureau 214 Lincoln St Ste 113 . . . . Allston MA 02134		800-447-7325	617-782-3111
Capitol City Speakers Bureau 1620 S Fifth St . . . . Springfield IL 62703		800-397-3183	217-544-8552
Executive Speakers Bureau 8567 Cordes Cir . . . . Germantown TN 38139		800-754-9404	901-754-9404
Greater Talent Network Inc 437 Fifth Ave Seventh Fl . . . . New York NY 10016		800-326-4211	212-645-4200
Key Speakers Bureau Inc 3500 E Coast Hwy Ste 6 . . . . Corona del Mar CA 92625		800-675-1175	949-675-7856
Leading Authorities Inc 1990 M St Ste 800 . . . . Washington DC 20036		800-773-2537	202-783-0300
National Speakers Bureau 1177 W Bdwy Ste 300 . . . . Vancouver BC V6H1G3		800-661-4110	604-734-3663
National Speakers Bureau Inc 14047 W Petronella Dr Ste 102 . . . . Libertyville IL 60048		800-323-9442	847-295-1122
Speakers Unlimited PO Box 27225 . . . . Columbus OH 43227		888-333-6676	614-864-3703
Steven Barclay Agency 12 Western Ave . . . . Petaluma CA 94952		888-965-7323	707-773-0654

705 SPEED CHANGERS, INDUSTRIAL HIGH SPEED DRIVES, GEARS

SEE ALSO Machine Shops ; Motors (Electric) & Generators ; Power Transmission Equipment - Mechanical ; Aircraft Parts & Auxiliary Equipment ; Automotive Parts & Supplies - Mfr ; Controls & Relays - Electrical

		Toll-Free	Phone
Bison Gear & Engineering Corp 3850 Ohio Ave . . . . Saint Charles IL 60174		800-282-4766	630-377-4327
Cleveland Gear Co 3249 E 80th St . . . . Cleveland OH 44104		800-423-3169	216-641-9000
Columbia Gear Corp 530 County Rd 50 . . . . Avon MN 56310		800-323-9838	320-356-7301
Cone Drive Operations Inc - A Textron Co 240 E 12th St . . . . Traverse City MI 49685 *Sales		888-994-2663*	231-946-8410
Dalton Gear Co 212 Colfax Ave N . . . . Minneapolis MN 55405		800-328-7485	612-374-2150
Designatronics Inc 2101 Jericho Tpke . . . . New Hyde Park NY 11040 *Orders		800-345-1144*	516-328-3300
Fairchild Industrial Products Co 3920 Westpoint Blvd . . . . Winston-Salem NC 27103		800-334-8422	336-659-3400
Hub City Inc 2914 Industrial Ave . . . . Aberdeen SD 57401		800-482-2489	605-225-0360
Kurz Electric Solutions Inc 1325 McMahon Dr . . . . Neenah WI 54956		800-776-3629	920-886-8200
Lenze 630 Douglas St . . . . Uxbridge MA 01569		800-217-9100	508-278-9100
Nuttall Gear LLC 2221 Niagra Falls Blvd . . . . Niagara Falls NY 14304		800-724-6710	716-298-4100
Piller Inc 45 Turner Rd . . . . Middletown NY 10941		800-597-6937	
Regal-Beloit Corp 200 State St . . . . Beloit WI 53511 *NYSE: RBC*		800-672-6495	608-364-8800
Regal-Beloit Corp Durst Div PO Box 298 . . . . Beloit WI 53512		800-356-0775	608-365-2563
Richmond Gear PO Box 238 . . . . Liberty SC 29657 *Sales		800-934-2727*	864-843-9231
Rush Gears Inc 550 Virginia Dr . . . . Fort Washington PA 19034		800-523-2576	215-542-9000
Sterling Electric Inc 7997 Allison Ave . . . . Indianapolis IN 46268 *Cust Svc		800-654-6220*	317-872-0471
Sumitomo Machinery Corp of America 4200 Holland Blvd . . . . Chesapeake VA 23323		800-762-9256	757-485-3355
Superior Gearbox Co 803 W Hwy 32 . . . . Stockton MO 65785		800-346-5745	417-276-5191
TECO-Westinghouse Motor Co 5100 N IH-35 . . . . Round Rock TX 78681		800-451-8798	512-255-4141

706 SPORTING GOODS

SEE ALSO Snowmobiles ; Swimming Pools ; Tarps, Tents, Covers ; Gym & Playground Equipment ; Handbags, Totes, Backpacks ; Motor Vehicles - Commercial & Special Purpose ; Personal Protective Equipment & Clothing ; All-Terrain Vehicles ; Bicycles & Bicycle Parts & Accessories ; Boats - Recreational ; Cord & Twine ; Exercise & Fitness Equipment ; Firearms & Ammunition (Non-Military)

		Toll-Free	Phone
Abel Automatics Inc 165 Aviador St . . . . Camarillo CA 93010		866-511-7444	805-484-8789
Acushnet Co 333 Bridge St . . . . Fairhaven MA 02719		800-225-8500	508-979-2000
AcuSport Corp 1 Hunter Pl . . . . Bellefontaine OH 43311		800-543-3150	937-593-7010
Adams Golf 2801 E Plano Pkwy . . . . Plano TX 75074		800-709-6142	972-673-9000
Adams USA Inc 610 S Jefferson Ave . . . . Cookeville TN 38501		800-251-6857	
Aldila Inc 14145 Danielson St Ste B . . . . Poway CA 92064 *OTC: ALDA*		800-854-2786	858-513-1801
American Sports 74 Albe Dr Ste 1 . . . . Newark DE 19702		866-207-3179	302-369-9480
AMF Bowling Worldwide Inc 7313 Bell Creek Rd . . . . Mechanicsville VA 23111		800-342-5263	
Aqua-Leisure Industries Inc PO Box 239 . . . . Avon MA 02322		866-807-3998	

		Toll-Free	Phone
Aqualung America Inc 2340 Cousteau Ct . . . . Vista CA 92083		800-446-2671	760-597-5000
Atomic USA 2030 Lincoln Ave . . . . Ogden UT 84401		800-258-5020	
Bankshot Sports Organization 842 B Rockville Pike . . . . Rockville MD 20852		800-933-0140	301-309-0260
Bauer Premium Fly Reels 585 Clover Ln Ste 1 . . . . Ashland OR 97520		888-484-4165	541-488-8246
Bell Sports Corp 6225 N St Hwy 161 Ste 300 . . . . Irving TX 75038		866-525-2357	469-417-6600
Big Rock Sports LLC 173 Hankison Dr . . . . Newport NC 28570		800-334-2661	252-808-3500
Biscayne Rod Manufacturing Inc 425 E Ninth St . . . . Hialeah FL 33010		866-969-0808	305-884-0808
Bison Inc 603 L St . . . . Lincoln NE 68508		800-247-7668	402-474-3353
Bravo Sports Corp 12801 Carmenita Rd . . . . Santa Fe Springs CA 90670 *Cust Svc		800-234-9737*	562-484-5100
Bridgestone Golf Inc 15320 Industrial Pk Blvd NE . . . . Covington GA 30014		800-358-6319	770-787-7400
Brine Inc 32125 Hollingsworth Ave . . . . Warren MI 48092		800-968-7845	
Callaway Golf Co 2180 Rutherford Rd . . . . Carlsbad CA 92008 *NYSE: ELY*		800-588-9836	760-931-1771
Cascade Designs Inc 4000 First Ave S . . . . Seattle WA 98134 *Cust Svc		800-531-9531*	206-505-9500
Century Sports Inc 1995 Rutgers University Blvd . . . . Lakewood NJ 08701 *Sales		800-526-7548*	732-905-4422
Century Tool & Mfg 90 McMillen Rd . . . . Antioch IL 60002		800-635-3831	
Champion Shuffleboard Ltd 7216 Burns St . . . . Richland Hills TX 76118		800-826-7856	817-284-3499
Cleveland Golf Co 5601 Skylab Rd . . . . Huntington Beach CA 92647 *Cust Svc		800-999-6263*	
Cobra Mfg Co Inc 7909 E 148th St S . . . . Bixby OK 74008		800-352-6272	918-366-7484
Coleman Co 1100 Stearns Dr . . . . Sauk Rapids MN 56379		800-328-3208	320-252-1642
Coleman Company Inc 3600 N Hydraulic . . . . Wichita KS 67219 *Cust Svc		800-835-3278*	316-832-2653
Columbia Industries Inc PO Box 746 . . . . Hopkinsville KY 42240		800-531-5920	270-881-1300
Confluence Watersports Co 575 Mauldin Rd Ste 200 . . . . Greenville SC 29607		800-595-2925	
Coverstar LLC 1795 West 200 North . . . . Lindon UT 84042		800-617-7283	801-373-4777
Daisy Outdoor Products 400 W Stribling Dr . . . . Rogers AR 72756		800-643-3458	479-636-1200
Daiwa Corp 12851 Midway Pl . . . . Cerritos CA 90703		800-736-4653	562-802-9589
Douglas Industries Inc 3441 S 11th Ave . . . . Eldridge IA 52748		800-553-8907	563-285-4162
Dover Saddlery Inc 525 Great Rd PO Box 1100 . . . . Littleton MA 01460 *NASDAQ: DOVR*		800-406-8204	978-952-8062
Dynastar 1413 Crt Dr . . . . Park City UT 84098		888-243-6722	435-252-3300
Eagle One Golf Products Inc 1340 N Jefferson St . . . . Anaheim CA 92807		800-448-4409	714-983-0050
Ebonite International Inc PO Box 746 . . . . Hopkinsville KY 42241		800-326-6483	270-881-1200
Eppinger Manufacturing Co 6340 Schaefer Rd . . . . Dearborn MI 48126		888-771-8277	313-582-3205
Escalade Inc 817 Maxwell Ave . . . . Evansville IN 47711 *NASDAQ: ESCA ■ *Cust Svc*		800-426-1421*	812-467-1200
Folbot Inc 4209 Pace St . . . . Charleston SC 29405		800-533-5099	843-744-3483
Franklin Sports Inc 17 Campanelli Pkwy PO Box 508 . . . . Stoughton MA 02072		800-225-8649	781-344-1111
G & H Decoys Inc PO Box 1208 . . . . Henryetta OK 74437 *Orders		800-443-3269*	918-652-3314
Gamma Sports 200 Waterfront Dr . . . . Pittsburgh PA 15222		800-333-0337	412-323-0335
Gared Sports Inc 707 N Second St Ste 220 . . . . Saint Louis MO 63102		800-325-2682	314-421-0044
Gill Athletics Inc 2808 Gemini Ct . . . . Champaign IL 61822 *Cust Svc		800-637-3090*	217-367-8438
Goal Sporting Goods Inc 37 Industrial Pk Rd PO Box 236 . . . . Essex CT 06426		800-334-4625	
Goals & Poles 7575 Jefferson Hwy . . . . Baton Rouge LA 70806		800-275-0317	225-923-0622
Goalsetter Systems Inc 1041 Cordova Ave . . . . Lynnville IA 50153		800-362-4625	
Golfsmith International Inc 11000 N IH-35 . . . . Austin TX 78753 *Sales		800-396-0099*	512-821-4050
GolfWorks, The 4820 Jacksontown Rd PO Box 3008 . . . . Newark OH 43055		800-848-8358	740-328-4193
HEAD USA Inc One Selleck St . . . . Norwalk CT 06855		800-874-3235	203-855-8666
HEAD/Penn Racquet Sports 306 S 45th Ave . . . . Phoenix AZ 85043		800-289-7366	
Hillerich & Bradsby Company Inc 800 W Main St . . . . Louisville KY 40202		800-282-2287	502-585-5226
Hireko Trading Company Inc 16185 Stephens St . . . . City of Industry CA 91745		800-367-8912	
Hobie Cat Co 4925 Oceanside Blvd . . . . Oceanside CA 92056		800-462-4349	760-758-9100
Hunter Company Inc 3300 W 71st Ave . . . . Westminster CO 80030		800-676-4868	303-427-4626
Hunter's Specialties Inc 6000 Huntington Ct NE . . . . Cedar Rapids IA 52402		800-530-7149	319-395-0321
Intex Recreation Corp 1665 Hughes Way PO Box 1440 . . . . Long Beach CA 90801 *Cust Svc		800-234-6839*	310-847-6981

Classified Section

			Toll-Free	Phone
Jayhawk Bowling Supply Inc				
355 N Iowa St PO Box 685	Lawrence KS	66044	800-255-6436	785-842-3237
Jerry's Sport Ctr Inc				
100 Capital Rd	Jenkins Township PA	18640	800-234-2612	
Johnson Outdoors Inc				
555 Main St	Racine WI	53403	800-468-9716	262-631-6600
NASDAQ: JOUT				
Jugs Sports				
11885 SW Herman Rd	Tualatin OR	97062	800-547-6843	
K2 Sports 4201 Sixth Ave S	Seattle WA	98108	800-426-1617	206-805-4800
KL Industries Inc				
1790 Sun Dolphin Dr	Muskegon MI	49444	800-733-2727	231-733-2725
Kolpin Powersports				
205 N Depot St PO Box 107	Fox Lake WI	53933	877-956-5746	920-928-3118
Kwik Goal Ltd				
140 Pacific Dr	Quakertown PA	18951	800-531-4252	215-536-2200
Lamartek				
175 NW Washington St	Lake City FL	32055	800-495-1046*	386-752-1087
*Orders				
Lifetime Products Inc				
Freeport Ctr Bldg D-11				
PO Box 160010	Clearfield UT	84016	800-242-3865	801-776-1532
Lobster Sports Inc				
7340 Fulton Ave	North Hollywood CA	91605	800-210-5992	818-764-6000
Louisville Golf Club Co				
2320 Watterson Trail	Louisville KY	40299	800-456-1631	502-491-5490
MacNeill Engineering Company Inc				
140 Locke Dr PO Box 735	Marlborough MA	01752	800-652-4267	508-481-8830
Manns Bait Co				
1111 State Docks Rd	Eufaula AL	36027	800-841-8435	
Maravia Corp of Idaho				
602 E 45th St	Boise ID	83714	800-223-7238	208-322-4949
Mares America Corp				
One Selleck St	Norwalk CT	06855	800-874-3236	203-855-0631
Martin Archery Inc				
3134 Heritage Rd	Walla Walla WA	99362	800-541-8902	509-529-2554
Mizuno USA				
4925 Avalon Ridge Pkwy	Norcross GA	30071	800-966-1211	770-441-5553
Moultrie Feeders				
150 Industrial Rd	Alabaster AL	35007	800-653-3334	205-664-6700
Murrey International Inc				
14150 S Figueroa St	Los Angeles CA	90061	800-421-1022	310-532-6091
National Billiard Manufacturing Co				
3315 Eugenia Ave	Covington KY	41015	800-543-0880	859-431-4129
North Face, The				
14450 Doolittle Dr	San Leandro CA	94577	855-500-8639	877-992-0111
O'Brien International				
14615 NE 91st St	Redmond WA	98052	800-662-7436	425-202-2100
Ocean Kayak				
125 Gilman Falls Ave Bldg B	Old Town ME	04468	800-852-9257	
Oceanic USA				
2002 Davis St	San Leandro CA	94577	800-435-3483	510-562-0500
Old Town Canoe Co				
125 Gilman Falls Ave Bldg B				
PO Box 548	Old Town ME	04468	800-343-1555	207-827-5513
Orvis International Travel				
178 Conservation Way	Sunderland VT	05250	800-547-4322	802-362-8790
Pentair Ltd				
1351 Rt 55	Lagrangeville NY	12540	888-711-7487	845-463-7200
PIC Skate 22 Village Dr	Riverside RI	02915	800-882-3448	401-490-9334
Ping Inc				
2201 W Desert Cove Ave PO Box 82000	Phoenix AZ	85071	800-474-6434	
Poolmaster Inc				
770 Del Paso Rd	Sacramento CA	95834	800-854-1492	916-567-9800
Powell Skate One Corp				
30 S La Patera Ln	Santa Barbara CA	93117	800-288-7528	805-964-1330
Precision Shooting Equipment Inc				
2727 N Fairview Ave	Tucson AZ	85705	800-477-7789	520-884-9065
Prince Global Sports LLC				
One Advantage Ct	Bordentown NJ	08505	800-283-6647*	609-291-5800
*All				
Resilite Sports Products				
PO Box 764	Sunbury PA	17801	800-843-6287	570-473-3529
Riedell Shoes Inc				
122 Cannon River Ave	Red Wing MN	55066	800-698-6893	651-388-8251
Rome Specialty Company Inc Rosco Div				
501 W Embargo St	Rome NY	13440	800-794-8357	315-337-8200
Ross Reels 113 Ponderosa Ct	Montrose CO	81401	866-587-6747	970-249-0606
RSR Group Inc				
4405 Metric Dr	Winter Park FL	32792	800-541-4867	407-677-1000
Saunders Archery Co				
1874 14th Ave PO Box 1707	Columbus NE	68601	800-228-1408*	402-564-7176
*Cust Svc				
Scott Fly Rod Co				
2355 Air Pk Way	Montrose CO	81401	800-728-7208	
Scott USA Inc				
PO Box 2030	Sun Valley ID	83353	800-292-5874	208-622-1000
Sea Eagle Boats Inc				
19 N Columbia St Ste 1	Port Jefferson NY	11777	800-748-8066	631-473-7308
Shakespeare Fishing Tackle Co				
7 Science Ct	Columbia SC	29203	800-466-5643*	803-754-7000
*Cust Svc				
Simms Fishing Products Corp				
101 Evergreen Dr	Bozeman MT	59715	800-217-4667	406-585-3557
Spalding PO Box 90015	Bowling Green KY	42103	855-253-4533	
Sport Supply Group Inc				
1901 Diplomat Dr	Dallas TX	75234	800-527-7510	972-484-9484
Storm Products Inc				
165 South 800 West	Brigham City UT	84302	800-369-4402	435-723-0403
TaylorMade - Adidas Golf				
5545 Fermi Ct	Carlsbad CA	92008	800-555-1212*	760-918-6000
*Cust Svc				
Tecnica USA				
19 Technology Dr	West Lebanon NH	03784	800-258-3897	603-298-8032
Toobs Inc 347 Quintana Rd	Morro Bay CA	93442	800-795-8662	
True Temper Sports				
8275 Tournament Dr Ste 200	Memphis TN	38125	800-355-8783	901-746-2000

			Toll-Free	Phone
Underwater Kinetics (UK)				
13400 Danielson St	Poway CA	92064	800-852-7483	858-513-9100
Weed USA Inc				
5780 Harrow Glen Ct	Galena OH	43021	800-933-3758	740-548-3881
West Coast Trends				
17811 Jamestown Ln	Huntington Beach CA	92647	800-736-4568	714-843-9288
Wiley Waterski and Wakeboard Pro Shop				
1417 S Trenton	Seattle WA	98108	800-962-0785	206-762-1300
Wilson Sporting Goods Co				
8750 W Bryn Mawr Ave	Chicago IL	60631	800-874-5930	773-714-6400
Wittek Golf Supply Co Inc				
3865 N Commercial Ave	Northbrook IL	60062	800-869-1800	847-943-2399
Worldwide Golf Shops Inc				
1430 S Village Way	Santa Ana CA	92705	888-216-5252	714-543-8284
Worth Co, The				
214 Sherman Ave PO Box 88	Stevens Point WI	54481	800-944-1899	715-344-6081
Yakima Bait Company Inc				
PO Box 310	Granger WA	98932	800-527-2711	509-854-1311
Yamaha Motor Corp USA				
6555 Katella Ave	Cypress CA	90630	800-656-7695*	
*Cust Svc				
Yonex Corp				
20140 S Western Ave	Torrance CA	90501	800-449-6639	310-793-3800

707 SPORTING GOODS STORES

			Toll-Free	Phone
Academy Sports & Outdoors				
1800 N Mason Rd	Katy TX	77449	888-922-2336	281-646-5200
Adventure 16 Inc				
4620 Alvarado Canyon Rd	San Diego CA	92120	800-854-2672	619-283-2362
Alabama Outdoors Inc				
3054 Independence Dr	Birmingham AL	35209	800-870-0011	205-870-1919
Altrec.com Inc				
725 SW Umatilla Ave	Redmond OR	97756	800-369-3949	541-316-2400
Apple Saddlery 1875 Innes Rd	Ottawa ON	K1B4C6	800-867-8225	613-744-4040
Athletic Supply Co				
16101 NE 87th St	Redmond WA	98052	800-732-9259	425-882-1456
Austad's Golf				
2801 E 10th St	Sioux Falls SD	57103	800-444-1234*	316-838-5557
*Cust Svc				
Baseball Express Inc				
5750 NW Pkwy Ste 100	San Antonio TX	78249	800-937-4824	210-348-7000
Big 5 Sporting Goods Corp				
2525 E El Segundo Blvd	El Segundo CA	90245	800-898-2994	310-536-0611
NASDAQ: BGFV				
Blade-Tech Industries Inc				
5530 184th St East	Puyallup WA	98375	877-331-5793	253-655-8059
Bob Ward & Sons Inc				
3015 Paxson St	Missoula MT	59801	800-800-5083	406-728-3220
Boyne Country Sports				
1200 Bay View Rd	Petoskey MI	49770	800-462-6963	231-439-4906
Busy Body Home Fitness				
9990 Empire St	San Diego CA	92126	800-466-3348	
Cabela's Inc One Cabela Dr	Sidney NE	69160	800-237-8888	308-254-5505
NYSE: CAB				
Cabela's Outdoor Adventures Inc				
610 Glover Rd Ste A	Sidney NE	69162	800-346-8747	
Century Martial Art Supply Inc				
1000 Century Blvd	Oklahoma City OK	73110	800-626-2787*	405-732-2226
*Sales				
Champs Sports				
311 Manatee Ave W	Bradenton FL	34205	800-991-6813	
D & R Sports Ctr Inc				
8178 W Main St	Kalamazoo MI	49009	800-992-1520	269-372-2277
Dixie Gun Works Inc				
1412 W Reelfoot Ave PO Box 130	Union City TN	38281	800-238-6785*	731-885-0700
*Orders				
Downtown Athletic Store Inc				
1180 Seminole Trail Ste 210	Charlottesville VA	22901	800-348-2649	434-975-3696
Eastern Mountain Sports				
1 Vose Farm Rd	Peterborough NH	03458	888-463-6367	603-924-7231
Fanzz				
2657 South 1030 West	Salt Lake City UT	84119	888-326-9946	801-325-2700
Fitness Zone				
3439 Colonnade Pkwy Se 800	Birmingham AL	35243	800-875-9145	
Gerry Cosby & Company Inc				
11 Pennsylvania Plz	New York NY	10001	877-563-6464	212-563-6464
Golf Etc of America Inc				
2201 Commercial Ln	Granbury TX	76048	800-806-8633	817-579-5263
Golf Shack Inc				
1631 N Bell School Rd	Rockford IL	61107	888-446-5390	815-397-3709
Golfsmith International Inc				
11000 N IH-35	Austin TX	78753	800-396-0099*	512-821-4050
*Sales				
Gym Source 40 E 52nd St	New York NY	10022	800-496-3499	212-688-4222
Hoigaards Inc				
5425 Excelsior Blvd	Minneapolis MN	55416	800-266-8157	952-929-1351
In The Swim Inc				
320 Industrial Dr	West Chicago IL	60185	800-288-7946	630-876-0040
Jan's Mountain Outfitters				
1600 Pk Ave PO Box 280	Park City UT	84060	800-745-1020	435-649-4949
Kittery Trading Post				
301 US 1	Kittery ME	03904	888-587-6246	603-334-1157
MC Sports				
3070 Shaffer Ave SE	Grand Rapids MI	49512	800-626-1762	616-942-2600
Modell's Sporting Goods				
498 Seventh Ave 20th Fl	New York NY	10018	888-645-8667	800-275-6633
NRC Sports Inc				
603 Pleasant St	Paxton MA	01612	800-243-5033	
Outdoor Ventures				
10579 S Main St	Hayward WI	54843	866-710-2846	715-634-4447
Paragon Sporting Goods Corp				
867 Broadway 18th St	New York NY	10003	800-961-3030	212-255-8889
Performance Inc				
One Performance Way	Chapel Hill NC	27514	800-727-2453*	
*Cust Svc				

				Toll-Free	Phone
Peter Glenn Ski & Sports					
2901 W Oakland Pk Blvd	Fort Lauderdale	FL	33311	800-818-0946	954-484-3606
Pro Performance Sports LLC					
2081 Faraday Ave	Carlsbad	CA	92008	877-225-7275	
Recreational Equipment Inc (REI)					
6750 S 228th St	Kent	WA	98032	800-426-4840*	253-395-3780
*Orders					
Ron Jon Surf Shop					
3850 S Banana River Blvd	Cocoa Beach	FL	32931	888-757-8737	321-799-8888
Sport Chalet Inc					
One Sport Chalet Dr	La Canada	CA	91011	888-801-9162	818-949-5300
NASDAQ: SPCHB					
Sports Promotion Network					
PO Box 200548	Arlington	TX	76006	800-460-9989	
Tahoe Mountain Sports					
11200 Donner Pass Rd Ste 5e	Truckee	CA	96161	866-891-9177	
TriSports.com					
4495 S Coach Dr	Tucson	AZ	85714	888-293-3934	
Val Surf Inc					
4810 Whitsett Ave	Valley Village	CA	91607	888-825-7873	818-769-6977
Warrior Custom Golf Inc					
15 Mason Ste A	Irvine	CA	92618	800-600-5113	949-699-2499
Western Power Sports Inc					
601 E Gowen Rd	Boise	ID	83716	800-999-3388	208-376-8400
Wheel & Sprocket Inc					
5722 S 108th St	Hales Corners	WI	53130	866-892-6059	414-529-6600

708 SPORTS COMMISSIONS & REGULATORY AGENCIES - STATE

				Toll-Free	Phone
New York					
Athletic Commission					
123 William St 20th Fl	New York	NY	10038	866-269-3769	212-417-5700

SPORTS FACILITIES

SEE Stadiums & Arenas ; Motor Speedways ; Racing & Racetracks

709 SPORTS TEAMS

SEE ALSO Sports Organizations

				Toll-Free	Phone
Major League Baseball (Office of the Commissioner)					
245 Pk Ave 31st Fl	New York	NY	10167	866-800-1275*	212-931-7800
*Cust Svc					
Atlanta Braves PO Box 4064	Atlanta	GA	30302	800-326-4000	404-522-7630
Cincinnati Reds					
100 Joe Nuxhall Way	Cincinnati	OH	45202	877-647-7337	513-381-7337
Detroit Tigers					
Comerica Pk 2100 Woodward Ave	Detroit	MI	48201	866-800-1275	313-962-4000
Houston Astros					
Minute Maid Pk 501 Crawford St	Houston	TX	77002	800-771-2303	713-259-8000
Kansas City Royals					
Kauffman Stadium 1 Royal Way	Kansas City	MO	64129	800-676-9257*	816-921-8000
*Sales					
Milwaukee Brewers					
Miller Pk 1 Brewers Way	Milwaukee	WI	53214	877-722-6458	414-902-4452
Minnesota Twins					
Metrodome 34 Kirby Puckett Pl	Minneapolis	MN	55415	800-338-9467	612-375-1366
New York Mets					
Shea Stadium 123-01 Roosevelt Ave	Flushing	NY	11368	888-652-7467	718-507-6387
Pittsburgh Pirates					
115 Federal St PO Box 7000	Pittsburgh	PA	15212	800-289-2827	412-321-2827
Seattle Mariners					
Safeco Field 1250 First Ave S	Seattle	WA	98134	800-255-7932	206-346-4000
Texas Rangers					
Rangers Ballpark in Arlington					
1000 Ballpark Way	Arlington	TX	76011	866-800-1275	817-273-5222
Toronto Blue Jays					
One Blue Jays Way Ste 3200	Toronto	ON	M5V1J1	888-654-6529	416-341-1000

710 SPORTS TEAMS - BASKETBALL

SEE ALSO Sports Organizations

710-1 National Basketball Association (NBA)

				Toll-Free	Phone
Cleveland Cavaliers					
Quicken Loans Arena 1 Ctr Ct	Cleveland	OH	44115	800-332-2287	216-420-2000
Golden State Warriors					
1011 Broadway	Oakland	CA	94607	866-648-4668	510-986-2200
Houston Rockets					
1510 Polk St	Houston	TX	77002	866-648-4668	713-758-7200
Los Angeles Clippers					
Staples Ctr 1111 S Figueroa St					
Ste 1100	Los Angeles	CA	90015	855-895-0872	213-742-7100
Los Angeles Lakers					
555 N Nash St	El Segundo	CA	90245	866-648-4668	310-426-6000
Minnesota Timberwolves					
Target Ctr 600 First Ave N	Minneapolis	MN	55403	855-895-0872	612-673-1600
New Jersey Nets					
Nets Champion Ctr					
390 Murray Hill Pkwy	East Rutherford	NJ	07073	800-346-6387	201-935-8888
Phoenix Suns					
US Airways Ctr 201 E Jefferson St	Phoenix	AZ	85004	866-648-4668	602-379-7900
Sacramento Kings					
ARCO Arena 1 Sports Pkwy	Sacramento	CA	95834	866-746-7622	916-928-0000
Seattle SuperSonics					
1201 Third Ave Ste 1000	Seattle	WA	98101	800-743-7021	206-281-5800

710-2 Women's National Basketball Association (WNBA)

				Toll-Free	Phone
Connecticut Sun					
1 Mohegan Sun Blvd	Uncasville	CT	06382	877-329-9622	860-862-4000
Indiana Fever					
Conseco Fieldhouse					
125 S Pennsylvania St	Indianapolis	IN	46204	877-275-9007	317-917-2500
Los Angeles Sparks					
865 S Figueroa St Ste 104	Los Angeles	CA	90017	888-694-3278	213-929-1300
Sacramento Monarchs					
ARCO Arena 1 Sports Pkwy	Sacramento	CA	95834	877-329-9622	916-928-6900
Seattle Storm					
351 Elliott Ave W Ste 500	Seattle	WA	98119	877-329-9622	206-281-5800
Washington Mystics					
627 N Glebe Rd Ste 850	Arlington	VA	22203	877-329-9622	202-266-2200

711 SPORTS TEAMS - FOOTBALL

SEE ALSO Sports Organizations

711-2 Canadian Football League (CFL)

				Toll-Free	Phone
Saskatchewan Roughriders					
1910 Piffles Taylor Way PO Box 1966	Regina	SK	S4P3E1	888-474-3377	306-569-2323

711-3 National Football League (NFL)

				Toll-Free	Phone
Arizona Cardinals					
8701 S Hardy Dr	Tempe	AZ	85284	800-999-1402	602-379-0101
Buffalo Bills					
Ralph Wilson Stadium 1 Bills Dr	Orchard Park	NY	14127	877-228-4257	716-648-1800
Carolina Panthers					
Bank of America Stadium					
800 S Mint St	Charlotte	NC	28202	888-297-8673	704-358-7000
Cincinnati Bengals					
One Paul Brown Stadium	Cincinnati	OH	45202	866-621-8383	513-621-3550
Detroit Lions					
222 Republic Dr	Allen Park	MI	48101	800-745-3000	313-216-4000
Indianapolis Colts					
7001 W 56th St	Indianapolis	IN	46254	800-805-2658	317-297-2658
Kansas City Chiefs					
Arrowhead Stadium 1 Arrowhead Dr	Kansas City	MO	64129	800-332-6048	816-920-9300
Minnesota Vikings					
9520 Viking Dr	Eden Prairie	MN	55344	877-722-6458	952-828-6500
Oakland Raiders					
1220 Harbor Bay Pkwy	Alameda	CA	94502	800-724-3377	510-864-5000
San Diego Chargers					
4020 Murphy Canyon Rd	San Diego	CA	92123	877-242-7437	858-874-4500
Seattle Seahawks					
12 Seahawks Way	Renton	WA	98056	888-635-4295	
Tennessee Titans					
460 Great Cir Rd	Nashville	TN	37228	800-334-4628	615-565-4000

712 SPORTS TEAMS - HOCKEY

SEE ALSO Sports Organizations

				Toll-Free	Phone
Anaheim Ducks					
2695 E Katella Ave	Anaheim	CA	92806	877-945-3946	
Buffalo Sabres					
HSBC Arena 1 Seymour H Knox III Plz	Buffalo	NY	14203	888-467-2273	716-855-4100
Carolina Hurricanes					
RBC Ctr 1400 EdwaRds Mill Rd	Raleigh	NC	27607	800-521-7521	919-467-7825
Edmonton Oilers					
11230 110th St	Edmonton	AB	T5G3H7	866-414-4625	780-414-4000
Los Angeles Kings					
Staples Ctr 1111 S Figueroa St	Los Angeles	CA	90015	888-546-4752	213-742-7100
Minnesota Wild					
317 Washington St	Saint Paul	MN	55102	866-242-5006	651-602-6000
Montreal Canadiens					
Bell Centre					
1260 de la Gauchetiere St W	Montreal	QC	H3B5E8	800-363-8162	514-989-2841
New York Islanders					
1535 Old Country Rd	Plainview	NY	11803	800-843-5678	516-501-6700
Ottawa Senators					
1000 Palladium Dr Scotia Bank Pl	Kanata	ON	K2V1A5	800-444-7367	613-599-0100
Phoenix Coyotes					
6751 N Sunset Blvd Ste 200	Glendale	AZ	85305	877-448-4483	623-772-3200
Pittsburgh Penguins					
1001 Fifth Avenue	Pittsburgh	PA	15219	800-642-7367	412-642-1300
San Jose Sharks					
HP Pavilion at San Jose					
525 W Santa Clara St	San Jose	CA	95113	800-755-5050	408-287-7070
Tampa Bay Lightning					
St Pete Times Forum 401 Channelside Dr	Tampa	FL	33602	800-745-3000	813-301-6500
Vancouver Canucks					
800 Griffiths Way	Vancouver	BC	V6B6G1	877-788-3937	604-899-7400

713 SPORTS TEAMS - SOCCER

SEE ALSO Sports Organizations

				Toll-Free	Phone
Chicago Fire					
7000 S Harlem Ave	Bridgeview	IL	60455	888-657-3473	708-594-7200

Classified Section

					Toll-Free	Phone

Club Deportivo Chivas USA
Home Depot Ctr
18400 Avalon Blvd Ste 500 . . . . Carson CA 90746 **877-244-8271*** 310-630-4550
Sales

Los Angeles Galaxy
Home Depot Ctr 18400 Avalon Blvd
Ste 200 . . . . Carson CA 90746 **877-342-5299** 310-630-2200

Milwaukee Wave LLC
510 W Kilbourn Ave . . . . Milwaukee WI 53203 **800-745-3000** 414-224-9283

New England Revolution
Gillette Stadium 1 Patriot Pl . . . . Foxboro MA 02035 **877-438-7387**

New York Red Bulls
600 Cape May St Eighth Fl . . . . Harrison NJ 07029 **877-727-6223**

714	SPRINGS - HEAVY-GAUGE

					Toll-Free	Phone

Barnes Group Inc
123 Main St . . . . Bristol CT 06011 **800-877-8803** 860-583-7070
NYSE: B

General Wire Spring Co
1101 Thompson Ave . . . . McKees Rocks PA 15136 **800-245-6200** 412-771-6300

Service Spring Corp
4370 Moline Martin Rd . . . . Millbury OH 43447 **800-752-8522** 419-838-6081

Southern Spring & Stamping Inc
401 Sub Stn Rd . . . . Venice FL 34285 **800-450-5882** 941-488-2276

715	SPRINGS - LIGHT-GAUGE

					Toll-Free	Phone

Atlantic Spring
PO Box 650 . . . . Flemington NJ 08822 **877-231-6474** 908-788-5800

Century Spring Corp
222 E 16th St . . . . Los Angeles CA 90015 **800-237-5225** 213-749-1466

Economy Spring & Stamping Co
29 DePaolo Dr PO Box 651 . . . . Southington CT 06489 **800-237-5225** 860-621-7358

General Wire Spring Co
1101 Thompson Ave . . . . McKees Rocks PA 15136 **800-245-6200** 412-771-6300

Hickory Springs Mfg Co
235 Second Ave NW . . . . Hickory NC 28601 **800-438-5341**

Lee Spring Company Inc
140 58th St Ste 3C . . . . Brooklyn NY 11220 **800-110-2500** 718-236-2222

Leggett & Platt Inc
Number 1 Leggett Rd PO Box 757 . . . . . . Carthage MO 64836 **800-888-4569** 417-358-8131
NYSE: LEG

Mid-West Spring & Stamping Co
1404 Joliet Rd Unit C . . . . Romeoville IL 60446 **800-619-0909** 630-739-3800

Newcomb Spring Corp
235 Turner . . . . Southington CT 06489 **888-579-3051** 860-621-0111

Southern Spring & Stamping Inc
401 Sub Stn Rd . . . . Venice FL 34285 **800-450-5882** 941-488-2276

Spring Dynamics Inc
7378 Research Dr . . . . Almont MI 48003 **888-274-8432** 810-798-2622

Spring Engineers Inc
9740 Tanner Rd . . . . Houston TX 77041 **800-899-9488** 713-690-9488

716	STADIUMS & ARENAS

SEE ALSO Performing Arts Facilities ; Convention Centers

					Toll-Free	Phone

Alamodome
100 Montana St . . . . San Antonio TX 78203 **800-884-3663** 210-207-3663

Allen County War Memorial Coliseum
4000 Parnell Ave . . . . Fort Wayne IN 46805 **800-745-3000** 260-482-9502

American Airlines Ctr
2500 Victory Ave . . . . Dallas TX 75219 **800-745-3000** 214-222-3687

Angel Stadium
2000 Gene Autry Way . . . . Anaheim CA 92806 **866-800-1275** 714-940-2000

AT&T Ctr
One AT&T Ctr Pkwy . . . . San Antonio TX 78219 **800-745-3000*** 210-444-5000
Resv

Canal Park Stadium
300 S Main St . . . . Akron OH 44308 **855-977-8225** 330-253-5151

Cleveland Indians Team Shops
2401 Ontario St . . . . Cleveland OH 44115 **800-388-7423** 216-420-4444

Columbus Civic Ctr
400 Fourth St . . . . Columbus GA 31901 **800-745-3000** 706-653-4482

FARGODOME
1800 N University Dr . . . . Fargo ND 58102 **855-694-6367** 701-241-9100

Fenway Park Four Yawkey Way . . . . . Boston MA 02215 **877-733-7699** 617-226-6000

First Niagara Ctr
One Seymour Knox III Plz . . . . Buffalo NY 14203 **888-223-6000** 716-855-4100

Georgia Dome
1 Georgia Dome Dr NW . . . . Atlanta GA 30313 **888-333-4406** 404-223-9200

Honda Ctr
2695 E Katella Ave . . . . Anaheim CA 92806 **877-945-3946** 714-704-2400

HP Pavilion at San Jose
525 W Santa Clara St . . . . San Jose CA 95113 **800-745-3000** 408-287-7070

i Wireless Ctr 1201 River Dr . . . . Moline IL 61265 **800-745-3000** 309-764-2001

Jacksonville Municipal Stadium
1 EverBank Field Dr . . . . Jacksonville FL 32202 **877-452-4784** 904-633-6000

Kauffman Stadium
One Royal Way . . . . Kansas City MO 64129 **800-676-9257** 816-921-8000

Kemper Arena & American Royal Centers
1701 American Royal Ct . . . . Kansas City MO 64102 **800-634-3942** 816-221-5242

Lubbock Municipal Auditorium/Coliseum
1625 13th St . . . . Lubbock TX 79415 **800-735-2989** 806-775-2242

Macon Centreplex Coliseum
200 Coliseum Dr . . . . Macon GA 31217 **877-532-6144** 478-751-9152

MetraPark Arena
308 Sixth Ave N . . . . Billings MT 59101 **800-366-8538** 406-256-2400

MGM Grand Garden Arena
3799 Las Vegas Blvd S . . . . Las Vegas NV 89109 **800-646-9143** 702-891-1111

					Toll-Free	Phone

Michigan Stadium
1201 S Main St
University of Michigan . . . . Ann Arbor MI 48104 **866-296-6849** 734-647-2583

Minute Maid Park
501 Crawford St . . . . Houston TX 77002 **877-927-8767** 713-259-8000

Municipal Auditorium Arena
301 W 13th St . . . . Kansas City MO 64105 **800-821-7060** 816-513-5000

Nassau Veterans Memorial Coliseum
1255 Hempstead Tpke . . . . Uniondale NY 11553 **800-745-3000** 516-794-9300

Nationwide Arena
200 W Nationwide Blvd . . . . Columbus OH 43215 **800-645-2657** 614-246-2000

Norfolk Scope Arena
201 E Brambleton Ave . . . . Norfolk VA 23510 **800-745-3000** 757-664-6464

Olympic Ctr Arena
2634 Main St . . . . Lake Placid NY 12946 **800-462-6236** 518-523-1655

Oriole Park at Camden Yards
333 Camden St . . . . Baltimore MD 21201 **888-848-2473** 410-547-6100

Paul Brown Stadium
1 Paul Brown Stadium . . . . Cincinnati OH 45202 **866-621-8383** 513-621-3550

Petco Park 100 Pk Blvd . . . . San Diego CA 92101 **866-800-1275** 619-795-5000

PNC Arena
1400 EdwaRds Mill Rd . . . . Raleigh NC 27607 **800-745-3000** 919-861-2300

PNC Park 115 Federal St . . . . Pittsburgh PA 15212 **866-800-1275** 412-321-2827

Qualcomm Stadium
9449 Friars Rd . . . . San Diego CA 92108 **800-400-7115** 619-641-3100

Quicken Loans Arena
One Ctr Ct . . . . Cleveland OH 44115 **888-894-9424** 216-420-2000

Qwest Arena
233 S Capitol Blvd . . . . Boise ID 83702 **888-330-8497** 208-424-2200

Richmond Coliseum
601 E Leigh St . . . . Richmond VA 23219 **800-228-9290** 804-780-4970

Roanoke Civic Ctr
710 Williamson Rd . . . . Roanoke VA 24016 **877-482-8496** 540-853-2241

Rockford MetroCentre
300 Elm St . . . . Rockford IL 61101 **800-745-3000** 815-968-5600

Roger Dean Stadium
4751 Main St . . . . Jupiter FL 33458 **800-926-7678** 561-775-1818

Scottsdale Stadium
7408 E Osborn Rd . . . . Scottsdale AZ 85251 **877-229-5042** 480-312-2856

Sioux Falls Arena
1201 NW Ave . . . . Sioux Falls SD 57104 **800-338-3177** 605-367-7288

Sky Sox Stadium
4385 Tutt Blvd
Security Service Field . . . . Colorado Springs CO 80922 **866-698-4253** 719-597-1449

Soldier Field
1410 S Museum Campus Dr . . . . Chicago IL 60605 **800-322-5868** 312-235-7000

Sun Devil Stadium
500 E Veterans Way
Arizona State University . . . . Tempe AZ 85281 **888-786-3857** 480-965-3482

Times Union Ctr
51 S Pearl St . . . . Albany NY 12207 **866-308-3394** 518-487-2000

Toyota Ctr 1510 Polk St . . . . Houston TX 77002 **866-446-8849** 713-758-7200

Tropicana Field
One Tropicana Dr . . . . Saint Petersburg FL 33705 **888-326-7297** 727-825-3137

US Cellular Ctr
370 First Ave E . . . . Cedar Rapids IA 52401 **800-745-3000** 319-398-5211

US Olympic Training Ctr
1750 E Boulder St . . . . Colorado Springs CO 80909 **800-775-8762** 719-866-4618

Valley View Casino Ctr
3500 Sports Arena Blvd . . . . San Diego CA 92110 **800-745-3000** 619-224-4171

Verizon Arena
One Verizon Arena Way . . . . North Little Rock AR 72114 **800-745-3000** 501-340-5660

Webster Bank Arena
600 Main St Second St . . . . Bridgeport CT 06604 **800-745-3000** 203-345-2300

Wrigley Field
1060 W Addison St . . . . Chicago IL 60613 **866-800-1275** 773-404-2827

717	STAFFING SERVICES

SEE ALSO Professional Employer Organizations (PEOs) ; Employment Offices - Government ; Employment Services - Online ; Executive Recruiting Firms

					Toll-Free	Phone

Accounting Principals
10151 Deerwood Park Blvd Ste 400 . . . . . Jacksonville FL 32256 **800-981-3849**

Adecco Inc
175 Broad Hollow Rd . . . . Melville NY 11747 **800-978-3729*** 631-844-7650
General

Advantage Resourcing
220 Norwood Pk S . . . . Norwood MA 02062 **800-343-4314** 781-251-8000

Aerotek Inc 7301 Pkwy Dr . . . . Hanover MD 21076 **800-237-6835** 410-694-5100

Allegis Group Inc
7301 Pkwy Dr . . . . Hanover MD 21076 **800-927-8090** 410-579-3000

Allied Health Group LLC
145 Technology Pkwy NW . . . . Norcross GA 30092 **800-741-4674**

ALTRES Inc
967 Kapiolani Blvd . . . . Honolulu HI 96814 **888-425-8737** 808-591-4940

American Healthcare Services LLC
1000 John R Ste 250 . . . . Troy MI 48083 **866-227-9998** 248-588-9700

AMN Healthcare Services Inc
12400 High Bluff Dr Ste 100 . . . . San Diego CA 92130 **866-871-8519**
NYSE: AHS

APEX Systems Inc
4400 Cox Rd Ste 100 . . . . Glen Allen VA 23060 **800-452-7391** 804-254-2600

AppleOne Employment Services Inc
327 W Broadway . . . . Glendale CA 91204 **800-872-2677** 310-750-3400

Aquent LLC 711 Boylston St . . . . Boston MA 02116 **855-767-6333** 617-535-5000

ARC Industries Inc
2879 Johnstown Rd . . . . Columbus OH 43219 **800-734-7007**

Area Temps Inc
1228 Euclid Ave . . . . Cleveland OH 44115 **866-995-5627** 440-646-1333

Artech Information Systems LLC
240 Cedar Knolls Rd Ste 100 . . . . . . Cedar Knolls NJ 07927 **800-950-9496** 973-998-2500

Bartech Group
17199 N Laurel Pk Dr Ste 224 . . . . Livonia MI 48152 **800-828-4410** 734-953-5050

C & A Industries Inc
13609 California St . . . . Omaha NE 68154 **800-574-9829** 402-891-0009

	Toll-Free	Phone

Calian Technology Ltd
340 Legget Dr Ste 101 .... Ottawa ON K2K1Y6 — **877-225-4264** — 613-599-8600
TSE: CTY

CareerStaff Unlimited Inc
6363 N State Hwy 161 Ste 525 .... Irving TX 75038 — **888-993-4599**

Cejka Search Inc
Four Citypark Dr Ste 300 .... Saint Louis MO 63141 — **800-678-7858** — 314-726-1603

Command Ctr Inc
3901 N Schreiber Wy .... Coeur D Alene ID 83815 — **866-464-5844** — 208-773-7450
OTC: CCNI

CompHealth Inc
6440 S Millrock Dr Ste 175
Ste 175 .... Salt Lake City UT 84121 — **800-453-3030** — 801-930-3000

Compunnel Software Group Inc
103 Morgan Ln Suite 102 .... Plainsboro NJ 08536 — **800-696-8128**

Compuware Corp Professional Services Div
7760 France Ave S Ste 430 .... Bloomington MN 55435 — **800-288-8974** — 612-851-2200

Consultnet LLC
10813 S River Front Pkwy Ste 150 .... South Jordan UT 84095 — **888-215-9675** — 801-208-3700

CPC Logistics Inc
14528 S Outer 40 Rd Ste 210 .... Chesterfield MO 63017 — **800-274-3746** — 314-542-2266

Cross Country Healthcare Inc
6551 Pk of Commerce Blvd .... Boca Raton FL 33487 — **800-347-2264** — 561-998-2232
NASDAQ: CCRN

Davis Cos
325 Donald J Lynch Blvd .... Marlborough MA 01752 — **800-482-9494** — 508-481-9500

DLH Holdings Corp
1776 Peachtree St NW Ste 300S .... Atlanta GA 30309 — **866-352-5304** — 770-554-3545
NASDAQ: DLHC

Duran Human Capital Partners Inc
300 Orchard City Dr Ste 142 .... Campbell CA 95008 — **800-287-9682** — 408-540-0070

Durham Cos Inc
6300 Transit Rd .... Depew NY 14043 — **800-633-7724** — 716-684-3333

Eagle Professional Resources Inc
67 Yonge St Ste 200 .... Toronto ON M5E1J8 — **800-281-2339** — 416-861-0636

Ensearch Management Consultants
905 E Cotati Ave .... Cotati CA 94931 — **888-667-5627**

Entegee Inc
70 BlanchaRd Rd Ste 102 .... Burlington MA 01803 — **800-230-7232** — 781-221-5800

Express Employment Professionals
8516 NW Expy .... Oklahoma City OK 73162 — **800-222-4057** — 405-840-5000

G&A Partners
4801 Woodway Dr Ste 210W .... Houston TX 77056 — **800-253-8562** — 713-784-1181

Gibson Arnold & Assoc
5433 Westheimer Rd Ste 1016 .... Houston TX 77056 — **800-879-2007** — 713-572-3000

Integrity Staffing Solutions Inc
750 Shipyard Dr Ste 200 .... Wilmington DE 19801 — **888-458-8367** — 302-661-8776

Interim HealthCare Inc
1601 Sawgrass Corporate Pkwy .... Sunrise FL 33323 — **800-338-7786** — 954-858-6000

Joule Inc 1245 US Rt 1 S .... Edison NJ 08837 — **800-341-0341** — 732-548-5444

Judge Group Inc
300 Conshohocken State Rd
Ste 300 .... West Conshohocken PA 19428 — **888-228-7162** — 610-667-7700

Kforce Inc 1001 E Palm Ave .... Tampa FL 33605 — **888-663-3626** — 813-552-5000
NASDAQ: KFRC

Kimco Staffing Services Inc
17872 Cowan Ave .... Irvine CA 92614 — **800-649-5627** — 949-752-6996

Labor Finders International Inc
11426 N Jog Rd .... Palm Beach Gardens FL 33418 — **800-864-7749** — 561-627-6507

Lakeshore Staffing Inc
1 N Franklin St .... Chicago IL 60606 — **877-685-2432** — 312-251-7575

LJ Gonzer Assoc Inc
14 Commerce Dr Ste 305 .... Cranford NJ 07016 — **866-692-4538** — 908-709-9494

Lucas Assoc Inc
3384 Peachtree Rd Ste 900 .... Atlanta GA 30326 — **800-515-0819** — 800-466-4489

Lumen Legal
1025 N Campbell Rd .... Royal Oak MI 48067 — **877-933-1330** — 248-597-0400

Marketstar Corp
2475 Washington Blvd .... Ogden UT 84401 — **800-877-8259** — 801-393-1155

Medical Staffing Assoc Inc
6731 Whittier Ave 3rd Fl .... McLean VA 22101 — **800-235-5105**

Medical Staffing Network Holdings Inc
901 Yamato Rd Ste 110 .... Boca Raton FL 33431 — **800-676-8326**

Medvantx Inc
5626 Oberlin Dr Ste 110 .... San Diego CA 92121 — **866-744-0621** — 858-625-2990

Midcom Corp
1275 N Manassero St Ste 200 .... Anaheim CA 92807 — **800-737-1632** — 714-630-1999

Minute Men Staffing Services
3740 Carnegie Ave .... Cleveland OH 44115 — **877-873-8856** — 216-426-9675

National Engineering Service Corp
72 Mirona Rd .... Portsmouth NH 03801 — **800-562-3463** — 603-431-9740

Nursefinders Inc
524 E Lamar Blvd Ste 300 .... Arlington TX 76011 — **800-445-0459** — 817-460-1181

On Assignment Inc
26745 Malibu Hills Rd .... Calabasas CA 91301 — **800-426-9196** — 818-878-7900
NYSE: ASGN

Orion International Consulting Group Inc
912 Capital of Texas Hwy S Ste 220 ...... Austin TX 78746 — **800-336-7466** — 512-327-7111

Oxford Global Resources Inc
100 Cummings Ctr Ste 206L .... Beverly MA 01915 — **800-426-9196** — 978-236-1182

Peak Technical Services Inc
583 Epsilon Dr .... Pittsburgh PA 15238 — **888-888-7325** — 412-696-1080

Principal Technical Services Inc
9960 Research Dr Ste 200 .... Irvine CA 92618 — **888-787-3711**

Productive Data Solutions Inc (PDSINC)
6160 S Syracuse Way
Ste B160 .... Greenwood Village CO 80111 — **800-404-7165** — 303-220-7165

Profiles International Inc
5205 Lk Shore Dr .... Waco TX 76710 — **866-751-1644** — 254-751-1644

RCM Technologies Inc
2500 McClellan Ave Ste 350 .... Pennsauken NJ 08109 — **800-322-2885** — 856-356-4500
NASDAQ: RCMT

Remedy Temp Inc
3820 State St .... Santa Barbara CA 93105 — **800-688-6162** — 805-882-2200

Research Pharmaceutical Services Inc
520 Virginia Dr .... Fort Washington PA 19034 — **866-777-1151*** — 215-540-0700
*General

	Toll-Free	Phone

Resources Global Professionals
17101 Armstrong Ave .... Irvine CA 92614 — **800-900-1131** — 714-430-6400
NASDAQ: RECN

Right at Home Inc
6464 Crt St Ste 150 .... Omaha NE 68106 — **877-697-7537** — 402-697-7537

SEEK Careers/Staffing Inc
PO Box 148 .... Grafton WI 53024 — **800-870-7181** — 262-377-8888

Select Staffing
3820 State St .... Santa Barbara CA 93105 — **800-688-6162** — 805-882-2200

Sigma Systems Inc
201 Boston Post Rd Ste 201 .... Marlborough MA 01752 — **888-867-4462** — 508-925-3200

Silicon Valley Staffing
2200 Powell St Ste 510 .... Emeryville CA 94608 — **877-660-6000** — 510-923-9898

Softworld Inc
281 Winter St Ste 301 .... Waltham MA 02451 — **877-899-1166** — 781-466-8882

Southwest Medical Assoc Inc
638 E Market St PO Box 2168 .... Rockport TX 78382 — **800-929-4854**

Special Counsel Inc
10201 Centurion Pkwy N Ste 400 .... Jacksonville FL 32256 — **800-737-3436** — 904-737-3436

Sterling Computer Corp
600 Stevens Port Dr Ste 200 .... Dakota Dunes SD 57049 — **877-242-4074** — 605-242-4000

Superior Technical Resources Inc
250 International Dr .... Williamsville NY 14221 — **800-568-8310** — 716-929-1400

Surgical Staff Inc
120 St Matthews Ave .... San Mateo CA 94401 — **800-339-9599** — 650-558-3999

TAJ Technologies Inc
1168 Northland Dr .... Mendota Heights MN 55120 — **877-825-2801** — 651-688-2801

Team Health Inc
265 Brookview Ctr Way Ste 400 .... Knoxville TN 37919 — **800-342-2898** — 865-693-1000

TEKsystems Inc 7437 Race Rd .... Hanover MD 21076 — **888-519-0776** — 410-540-7700

Temporary Solutions Inc
10550 Linden Lk Plz Ste 200 .... Manassas VA 20109 — **888-222-0457** — 703-361-2220

Thompson Technologies Inc
114 Townpark Dr Ste 100 .... Kennesaw GA 30144 — **888-794-7947** — 770-794-8380

Transforce Inc
6551 Loisdale Ct Ste 801 .... Springfield VA 22150 — **800-308-6989** — 703-838-5580

True Blue Inc PO Box 2910 .... Tacoma WA 98401 — **800-610-8920** — 253-383-9101
NYSE: TBI

UltraStaff
1818 Memorial Dr Ste 200 .... Houston TX 77007 — **800-522-7707** — 713-522-7100

US Legal Support Inc
363 N Sam Houston Pkwy E Ste 900 ..... Houston TX 77060 — **800-567-8757** — 713-653-7100

VMC Consulting Corp
11611 Willows Rd NE .... Redmond WA 98052 — **877-393-8622** — 425-558-7700

White Glove Placement Inc
85 Bartlett St .... Brooklyn NY 11206 — **866-387-8100** — 718-387-8181

Winston Resources Inc
122 E 42nd St Ste 320 .... New York NY 10168 — **800-494-6786** — 212-557-5000

York Solutions LLC
One Westbrook Corporate Ctr
Ste 910 .... Westchester IL 60154 — **877-700-9675** — 708-531-8362

---

718 — STAGE EQUIPMENT & SERVICES

	Toll-Free	Phone

Apollo Design Technology Inc
4130 Fourier Dr .... Fort Wayne IN 46818 — **800-288-4626** — 260-497-9191

Chapman/Leonard Studio Equipment Inc
12950 Raymer St .... North Hollywood CA 91605 — **888-883-6559** — 818-764-6726

Dreamworld Backdrops
6450 Lusk Blvd Ste E-106 .... San Diego CA 92121 — **800-737-9869**

Grosh Scenic Rentals
4114 Sunset Blvd .... Los Angeles CA 90029 — **877-363-7998**

High End Systems Inc
2105 Gracy Farms Ln .... Austin TX 78758 — **800-890-8989** — 512-836-2242

Janson Industries
1200 Garfield Ave SW .... Canton OH 44706 — **800-548-8982** — 330-455-7029

Musson Theatrical Inc
890 Walsh Ave .... Santa Clara CA 95050 — **800-843-2837** — 408-986-0210

Rosco Laboratories Inc
52 Harbor View Ave .... Stamford CT 06902 — **800-767-2669** — 203-708-8900

Screen Works
2201 W Fulton St .... Chicago IL 60612 — **800-294-8111*** — 312-243-8265
*Cust Svc

Secoa Inc 8650 109th Ave N .... Champlin MN 55316 — **800-328-5519** — 763-506-8800

Syracuse Scenery & Stage Lighting Company Inc
101 Monarch Dr .... Liverpool NY 13088 — **800-453-7775** — 315-453-8096

---

719 — STEEL - MFR

	Toll-Free	Phone

A Finkl & Sons Co
2011 N Southport Ave .... Chicago IL 60614 — **800-343-2562** — 773-975-2510

AK Steel Corp
9227 Centre Pt Dr .... West Chester OH 45069 — **800-331-5050** — 513-425-5000
NYSE: AKS

Aleris International Inc
25825 Science Pk Dr Ste 400 .... Beachwood OH 44122 — **866-266-2586** — 216-910-3400

Allegheny Technologies Inc
1000 Six PPG Pl .... Pittsburgh PA 15222 — **800-258-3586*** — 412-394-2800
NYSE: ATI ▪ *Sales

American Tank & Fabricating Co (AT&F)
12314 Elmwood Ave .... Cleveland OH 44111 — **800-544-5316** — 216-252-1500

ATI Allegheny Ludlum Corp
100 River Rd .... Brackenridge PA 15014 — **800-258-3586*** — 724-224-1000
*Sales

Canam Group Inc
11505 First Ave Bureau 500 .... Saint-Georges QC G5Y7H5 — **877-499-6049** — 418-228-8031
TSE: CAM

Carpenter Specialty Alloys Operations
101 W Bern St .... Reading PA 19601 — **800-654-6543** — 610-208-2000

Carpenter Technology Corp
PO Box 14662 .... Reading PA 19612 — **800-654-6543** — 610-208-2000
NYSE: CRS

			Toll-Free	Phone
Cascade Steel Rolling Mills Inc (CSRM)				
3200 N Hwy 99 W PO Box 687 . . . . McMinnville	OR	97128	**800-283-2776**	503-472-4181
Chicago Heights Steel Acquisition Corp				
211 E Main St . . . . Chicago Heights	IL	60411	**800-424-4487**	708-756-5648
Corey Steel Co				
2800 S 61st Ct . . . . Cicero	IL	60804	**800-323-2750**	708-735-8000
Creform Corp PO Box 830 . . . . Greer	SC	29652	**800-839-8823**	864-989-1700
Crucible Materials Corp				
575 State Fair Blvd . . . . Syracuse	NY	13209	**800-365-1180**	315-487-4111
Electralloy Corp				
175 Main St . . . . Oil City	PA	16301	**800-458-7273**	814-678-4100
Feroleto Steel Company Inc				
300 Scofield Ave . . . . Bridgeport	CT	06605	**800-243-2839**	203-366-3263
Gerdau AmeriSteel Corp				
4221 W Boy Scout Blvd Ste 600 . . . . Tampa	FL	33607	**800-876-7833***	813-286-8383
*Sales				
Gibraltar Industries Inc				
3556 Lakeshore Rd . . . . Buffalo	NY	14219	**800-247-8368**	716-826-6500
NASDAQ: ROCK				
GO Carlson Inc				
350 Marshallton Thorndale Rd . . . . Downingtown	PA	19335	**800-338-5622**	610-384-2800
Greer Steel Co 624 Blvd . . . . Dover	OH	44622	**800-388-2868***	330-343-8811
*Sales				
Gulf Coast Machine & Supply Company Inc				
6817 Industrial Rd . . . . Beaumont	TX	77705	**800-231-3032**	409-842-1311
Intsel Steel Distributors LP				
11310 W Little York . . . . Houston	TX	77041	**800-762-3316**	713-937-9500
Jersey Shore Steel Co				
70 Maryland Ave PO Box 5055 . . . . Jersey Shore	PA	17740	**800-833-0277**	570-753-3000
Kentucky Electric Steel LLC				
2704 S Big Run Rd W . . . . Ashland	KY	41102	**800-333-3012**	606-929-1200
Keystone Steel & Wire Co				
7000 S Adams St . . . . Peoria	IL	61641	**800-447-6444**	
Metalex Corp				
1530 Artaius Pkwy PO Box 399 . . . . Libertyville	IL	60048	**800-323-0792**	847-362-8300
Mill Steel Co				
5116 36th St SE . . . . Grand Rapids	MI	49512	**800-247-6455**	
Niagara Corp				
667 Madison Ave . . . . New York	NY	10021	**877-289-2277**	212-317-1000
Nucor Corp				
1915 Rexford Rd . . . . Charlotte	NC	28211	**800-294-1322**	704-366-7000
NYSE: NUE				
Nucor Corp Cold Finish Div				
2800 N Governor Williams Hwy . . . . Darlington	SC	29540	**800-333-0590**	704-366-7000
Nucor Corp Steel Div				
1455 Hagan Ave . . . . Huger	SC	29450	**800-424-9300**	843-336-6000
Nucor-Yamato Steel Co				
5929 E State Hwy 18 . . . . Blytheville	AR	72315	**800-289-6977**	870-762-5500
Sandmeyer Steel Co				
One Sandmeyer Ln . . . . Philadelphia	PA	19116	**800-523-3663**	215-464-7100
Schnitzer Steel Industries Inc				
3200 NW Yeon Ave . . . . Portland	OR	97210	**800-562-9876**	503-224-9900
NASDAQ: SCHN				
Scion Steel Inc				
21555 Mullin Ave . . . . Warren	MI	48089	**800-288-2127**	586-755-4000
Steel Dynamics Inc				
7575 W Jefferson Blvd Ste 200 . . . . Fort Wayne	IN	46804	**866-740-8700**	260-969-3500
NASDAQ: STLD				
Steel of West Virginia Inc				
17th St & Second Ave . . . . Huntington	WV	25703	**800-624-3492**	304-696-8200
Ulbrich Stainless Steels & Special Metals Inc (USSM)				
57 Dodge Ave . . . . North Haven	CT	06473	**800-243-1676**	203-239-4481
United Performance Metals				
3475 Symmes Rd . . . . Hamilton	OH	45015	**888-282-3292**	513-860-6500
USS-POSCO Industries				
900 Loveridge Rd . . . . Pittsburg	CA	94565	**800-877-7672**	925-439-6000
Worthington Steel Co				
1127 Dearborn Dr . . . . Columbus	OH	43085	**800-944-3733**	614-438-3210

720   STONE (CUT) & STONE PRODUCTS

			Toll-Free	Phone
Akdo Intertrade Inc				
1435 State St . . . . Bridgeport	CT	06605	**800-811-2536**	203-336-5199
AZ Countertops Inc				
1445 S Hudson Ave . . . . Ontario	CA	91762	**800-266-3524**	909-983-5386
Biesanz Stone Co Inc				
4600 Goodview Rd . . . . Winona	MN	55987	**800-247-8322**	507-454-4336
Bristol Memorial Works Inc				
797 King St . . . . Bristol	CT	06010	**888-987-7821**	860-583-1654
Bybee Stone Company Inc				
6293 N Matthews Dr . . . . Ellettsville	IN	47429	**800-457-4530**	812-876-2215
Cold Spring Granite Inc				
17482 Granite W Rd . . . . Cold Spring	MN	56320	**800-328-5040**	320-685-3621
Coldspring				
17482 Granite W Rd . . . . Cold Spring	MN	56320	**800-328-5040**	
Columbus Marble Works Corp				
2415 Hwy 45 N PO Box 791 . . . . Columbus	MS	39703	**800-647-1055***	662-328-1477
*Cust Svc				
Continental Cast Stone Manufacturing Inc				
22001 W 83rd St . . . . Shawnee	KS	66227	**800-989-7866**	
Dakota Granite Co				
48391 150th St PO Box 1351 . . . . Milbank	SD	57252	**800-843-3333**	605-432-5580
Dakota Marble Inc				
902 W 19th St . . . . Yankton	SD	57078	**800-697-7241**	605-665-7241
Glenrock International Inc				
985 E Linden Ave . . . . Linden	NJ	07036	**800-453-6762**	908-862-3433
Keystone Retaining Wall Systems Inc				
4444 W 78th St . . . . Minneapolis	MN	55435	**800-642-3887**	952-897-1040
Kollmann Monumental Works Inc				
1915 W Div St . . . . Saint Cloud	MN	56301	**800-659-8010**	320-251-8010
Little Falls Granite Works				
10802 Hwy 10 PO Box 240 . . . . Little Falls	MN	56345	**800-862-2417**	320-632-9277
Milwaukee Marble & Granite Co				
4535 W Mitchell St . . . . Milwaukee	WI	53214	**877-645-6272**	414-645-0305
Monumental Sales Inc				
537 22nd Ave N PO Box 667 . . . . Saint Cloud	MN	56302	**800-442-1660**	320-251-6585

			Toll-Free	Phone
North Carolina Granite Corp				
151 Granite Quarry Trl PO Box 151 . . . . . . Mount Airy	NC	27030	**800-227-6242**	336-786-5141
Northfield Block Co				
One Hunt Ct . . . . Mundelein	IL	60060	**800-358-3003**	847-949-3600
RJ Marshall Co				
26776 W 12-Mile Rd . . . . Southfield	MI	48034	**888-514-8600***	248-353-4100
*Cust Svc				
Rock of Ages Corp				
560 Graniteville Rd . . . . Graniteville	VT	05654	**800-421-0166**	802-476-3119
Starrett Tru-Stone Technologies Div				
1101 Prosper Dr PO Box 430 . . . . Waite Park	MN	56387	**800-959-0517**	320-251-7171
Vermont Structural Slate Company Inc				
Three Prospect St PO Box 98 . . . . Fair Haven	VT	05743	**800-343-1900**	802-265-4933
Vetter Stone Co (VSC)				
23894 Third Ave . . . . Mankato	MN	56001	**800-878-2850**	507-345-4568
WS Hampshire Inc				
365 Keyes Ave . . . . Hampshire	IL	60140	**800-541-0251**	847-683-4400

721   STUDENT ASSISTANCE PROGRAMS

			Toll-Free	Phone
Alabama				
Prepaid Affordable College Tuition (PACT) Program				
100 N Union St Ste 660 . . . . Montgomery	AL	36130	**800-252-7228**	334-242-7514
Alaska				
Commission on Postsecondary Education				
PO Box 110510 . . . . Juneau	AK	99811	**800-441-2962**	907-465-2962
Arkansas				
Financial Aid Office				
114 Silas Hunt Hall . . . . Fayetteville	AR	72701	**800-547-8839**	479-575-3806
California				
Student Aid Commission				
PO Box 419027 . . . . Rancho Cordova	CA	95741	**888-224-7268**	916-526-8999
Colorado				
CollegeInvest				
1560 Broadway Ste 1700 . . . . Denver	CO	80202	**800-448-2424**	303-376-8800
Council for Opportunity in Education				
1025 Vermont Ave NW Ste 900 . . . . Washington	DC	20005	**800-633-7313**	202-347-7430
District of Columbia				
Tuition Assistance Grant Program				
810 First St NE . . . . Washington	DC	20001	**877-485-6751**	202-727-2824
Dollars for Scholars				
Scholarship America				
1 Scholarship Way . . . . Saint Peter	MN	56082	**800-248-8080**	507-931-1682
EdVest PO Box 55244 . . . . Boston	MA	02205	**888-338-3789**	
FastWeb Inc				
444 N Michigan Ave Ste 3000 . . . . Chicago	IL	60611	**800-829-1040**	444-536-1212
FinAid Page LLC				
PO Box 2056 . . . . Cranberry Township	PA	16066	**800-433-3243**	724-538-4500
Florida				
Student Financial Assistance Office				
1940 N Monroe St Ste 70 . . . . Tallahassee	FL	32303	**888-827-2004**	850-410-5200
Georgia				
Student Finance Commission				
2082 E Exchange Pl Ste 200 . . . . Tucker	GA	30084	**800-505-4732**	770-724-9000
Hawaii				
Postsecondary Education Commission				
2444 Dole St Bachman Hall Rm 209 . . . . Honolulu	HI	96822	**877-531-2333**	808-956-8213
Illinois				
Student Assistance Commission				
1755 Lake Cook Rd . . . . Deerfield	IL	60015	**800-899-4722**	847-948-8500
Indiana				
Students Assistance Commission				
150 W Market St Ste 500 . . . . Indianapolis	IN	46204	**888-528-4719**	317-232-2350
Iowa College Student Aid Commission				
603 E 12th St Fl 5th . . . . Des Moines	IA	50319	**800-383-4222**	515-725-3400
Kentucky (KHEAA)				
Higher Education Assistance Authority				
100 Airport Rd . . . . Frankfort	KY	40602	**800-928-8926**	
Louisiana (LOSFA)				
Office of Student Financial Assistance				
602 N Fifth St PO Box 91202 . . . . Baton Rouge	LA	70802	**800-259-5626**	225-219-1012
Maine (FAME)				
Finance Authority				
5 Community Dr PO Box 949 . . . . Augusta	ME	04332	**800-228-3734**	207-623-3263
Maryland Student Financial Assistance Office				
839 Bestgate Rd Ste 400 . . . . Annapolis	MD	21401	**800-974-0203**	410-260-4565
Michigan (MET)				
Education Trust				
PO Box 30198 . . . . Lansing	MI	48909	**800-638-4543***	517-335-4767
*General				
Michigan				
Student Financial Services Bureau				
Austin Bldg 430 W Allegan . . . . Lansing	MI	48922	**800-642-5626***	888-447-2687
*General				
Minnesota				
Office of Higher Education				
1450 Energy Pk Dr Ste 350 . . . . Saint Paul	MN	55108	**800-657-3866**	651-642-0567
Mississippi				
Student Financial Aid Office				
3825 Ridgewood Rd . . . . Jackson	MS	39211	**800-327-2980**	601-432-6997
Montana				
Higher Education Board of Regents				
2500 Broadway St PO Box 203201 . . . . Helena	MT	59620	**877-501-1722**	406-444-6570
New Hampshire				
Postsecondary Education Commission				
64 South Street Ste 300 . . . . Concord	NH	03301	**800-735-2964**	603-271-2555
New Jersey				
Higher Education Student Assistance Authority				
4 Quakerbridge Plaza PO Box 540 . . . . Trenton	NJ	08625	**800-792-8670**	609-584-4480
New Mexico				
Financial Aid & Student Services Unit				
2048 Galisteo St . . . . Santa Fe	NM	87505	**800-279-9777**	505-476-8400
New York				
Higher Education Services Corp				
99 Washington Ave . . . . Albany	NY	12255	**888-697-4372**	518-473-1574
North Carolina State Education Assistance Authority (NCSEAA)				
PO Box 14103 . . . . Research Triangle Park	NC	27709	**800-700-1775**	919-549-8614

			Toll-Free	Phone

Ohio
Tuition Trust Authority
580 S High St Ste 208 . . . . Columbus OH 43215 **800-233-6734*** 614-752-9400
*Cust Svc

Pennsylvania
Higher Education Assistance Agency
1200 N Seventh St . . . . Harrisburg PA 17102 **800-233-0557**

Rhode Island
Higher Education Assistance Authority (RIHEAA)
560 Jefferson Blvd . . . . Warwick RI 02886 **800-922-9855** 401-736-1100

Scholarship America
One Scholarship Way PO Box 297 . . . . Saint Peter MN 56082 **800-537-4180** 507-931-1682

South Carolina
Higher Education Tuition Grants Commission
115 Atrium Wy Ste 102 . . . . Columbia SC 29203 **877-382-4357** 803-896-1120

Thurgood Marshall Scholarship Fund
80 Maiden Ln Ste 2204 . . . . New York NY 10038 **866-632-9992** 212-573-8888

Utah
Higher Education Assistance Authority
PO Box 145112 . . . . Salt Lake City UT 84114 **877-336-7378** 801-321-7294

Vermont Student Assistance Corp (VSAC)
PO Box 2000 . . . . Winooski VT 05404 **800-642-3177** 802-655-9602

Virginia College Savings Plan
9001 Arboretum Pkwy PO Box 607 . . . . Richmond VA 23236 **888-567-0540** 804-786-0719

West Virginia
Higher Education Policy Commission
1018 Kanawha Blvd E Ste 700 . . . . Charleston WV 25301 **888-825-5707** 304-558-2101

---

722   SUBSTANCE ABUSE TREATMENT CENTERS

SEE ALSO General Hospitals - Canada ; General Hospitals - US ; Psychiatric Hospitals ; Self-Help Organizations

			Toll-Free	Phone

AdCare Hospital of Worcester
107 Lincoln St . . . . Worcester MA 01605 **800-252-6465** 508-799-9000

AREBA Casriel Inc (ACI)
500 W 57th St . . . . New York NY 10019 **800-724-4444** 212-293-3000

Arms Acres
75 Seminary Hill Rd . . . . Carmel NY 10512 **800-989-2676** 845-225-3400

Baltimore Behavioral Health (BBH)
1101 W Pratt St . . . . Baltimore MD 21223 **800-789-2647** 410-962-7180

Betty Ford Ctr
39000 Bob Hope Dr . . . . Rancho Mirage CA 92270 **800-854-9211** 760-773-4100

Bradford Health Services
2101 Magnolia Ave S Ste 518 . . . . Birmingham AL 35205 **800-217-2849** 205-251-7753

Brighton Hospital
12851 E Grand River Ave . . . . Brighton MI 48116 **800-523-8198*** 810-227-1211
*Cust Svc

Central Street Health Ctr
26 Central St . . . . Somerville MA 02143 **800-909-2677** 617-591-6033

Clear Brook Manor
1100 E Northampton St . . . . Laurel Run PA 18706 **800-582-6241**

Conifer Park
79 Glenridge Rd . . . . Schenectady NY 12302 **800-989-6446** 518-399-6446

Cornerstone Medical Arts Ctr Hospital
159-05 Union Tpke . . . . Fresh Meadows NY 11366 **800-233-9999** 718-906-6700

Eagleville Hospital
100 Eagleville Rd . . . . Eagleville PA 19408 **800-255-2019*** 610-539-6000
*General

Fairbanks Hospital
8102 Clearvista Pkwy . . . . Indianapolis IN 46256 **800-225-4673** 317-849-8222

Fellowship Hall Inc
5140 Dunstan Rd . . . . Greensboro NC 27405 **800-659-3381** 336-621-3381

Friary of Lakeview Ctr, The
4400 Hickory Shores Blvd . . . . Gulf Breeze FL 32563 **800-332-2271** 850-932-9375

Gateway Foundation Inc
1080 E Pk St . . . . Carbondale IL 62901 **877-505-4673**

Glenbeigh Health Source
2863 SR 45 . . . . Rock Creek OH 44084 **800-234-1001** 440-563-3400

Greenleaf Ctr
2209 Pineview Dr . . . . Valdosta GA 31602 **800-247-2747** 229-671-6700

Griffin Memorial Hospital
900 E Main St . . . . Norman OK 73071 **800-955-3468*** 405-321-4880
*General

Hampton Behavioral Health Center
650 Rancocas Rd . . . . Westampton NJ 08060 **800-603-6767**

Hazelden Chicago
867 N Dearborn St . . . . Chicago IL 60610 **800-257-7810** 312-943-3534

Hazelden Ctr for Youth & Families (HCYF)
11505 36th Ave N . . . . Plymouth MN 55441 **800-257-7810** 763-509-3800

Hazelden Foundation
15251 Pleasant Vly Rd . . . . Center City MN 55012 **800-257-7810** 651-213-4200

Hazelden New York
322 Eigth Ave 12th Fl . . . . New York NY 10001 **800-257-7800** 212-420-9520

Hazelden Springbrook
1901 Esther St . . . . Newberg OR 97132 **866-866-4662** 503-554-4300

HealthSource Saginaw
3340 Hospital Rd . . . . Saginaw MI 48603 **800-662-6848** 989-790-7700

Impact Drug & Alcohol Treatment Ctr
1680 N Fair Oaks Ave PO Box 93607 . . . . Pasadena CA 91103 **866-734-4200** 626-798-0884

Keystone Ctr
2001 Providence Ave . . . . Chester PA 19013 **800-558-9600** 610-876-9000

La Hacienda Treatment Ctr
145 La Hacienda Way . . . . Hunt TX 78024 **800-749-6160** 830-238-4222

Livengrin Foundation
4833 Hulmeville Rd . . . . Bensalem PA 19020 **800-245-4746** 215-638-5200

Malvern Institute
940 W King Rd . . . . Malvern PA 19355 **888-643-3869** 610-647-0330

Mount Regis Ctr
405 Kimball Ave . . . . Salem VA 24153 **877-217-3447**

Mountain Manor Treatment Ctr
9701 Keysville Rd . . . . Emmitsburg MD 21727 **800-537-3422** 301-447-2361

New Directions Inc
30800 Chagrin Blvd . . . . Cleveland OH 44124 **800-750-6709** 216-591-0324

Phoenix House Foundation Inc (PHF)
164 W 74th St 4th Fl. . . . . New York NY 10023 **800-378-4435** 888-671-9392

			Toll-Free	Phone

Providence Behavioral Health Hospital
1233 Main St . . . . Holyoke MA 01040 **800-274-7724** 413-536-5111

Rimrock Foundation
1231 N 29th St . . . . Billings MT 59101 **800-227-3953** 406-248-3175

Rivervalley Behavioral Health Hospital
1000 Industrial Dr . . . . Owensboro KY 42301 **800-755-8477** 270-689-6800

Samaritan Village
138-02 Queens Blvd . . . . Briarwood NY 11435 **800-532-4357** 718-206-2000

Schick Shadel Hospital
12101 Ambaum Blvd SW . . . . Seattle WA 98146 **800-500-6395**

Serenity Lane 616 E 16th Ave . . . . Eugene OR 97401 **800-543-9905** 541-687-1110

Sierra Tucson Inc
39580 S Lago Del Oro Pkwy . . . . Tucson AZ 85739 **800-842-4487** 520-624-4000

Spencer Recovery Centers Inc
1316 S Coast Hwy . . . . Laguna Beach CA 92651 **800-334-0394**

Substance Abuse Foundation
3125 E Seventh St . . . . Long Beach CA 90804 **888-476-2743** 562-987-5722

Talbott Recovery Campus
5448 Yorktowne Dr . . . . Atlanta GA 30349 **800-445-4232** 770-994-0185

Turning Point Hospital
3015 Veterans Pkwy PO Box 1177 . . . . Moultrie GA 31776 **800-342-1075** 229-985-4815

Turning Point of Tampa
6227 Sheldon Rd . . . . Tampa FL 33615 **800-397-3006** 813-882-3003

Valley Forge Medical Ctr & Hospital
1033 W Germantown Pk . . . . Norristown PA 19403 **888-539-8500** 610-539-8500

Village South Inc
3050 Biscayne Blvd 9th Fl . . . . Miami FL 33137 **800-443-3784** 305-573-3784

Walter B Jones Alcohol & Drug Abuse Treatment Ctr
2577 W Fifth St . . . . Greenville NC 27834 **800-422-1884** 252-830-3426

Willingway Hospital
311 Jones Mill Rd . . . . Statesboro GA 30458 **800-242-9455** 912-764-6236

Wilmington Treatment Ctr
2520 Troy Dr . . . . Wilmington NC 28401 **877-762-3750** 910-762-2727

---

723   SURVEYING, MAPPING, RELATED SERVICES

SEE ALSO Engineering & Design

			Toll-Free	Phone

Cochrane Technologies Inc
PO Box 81276 . . . . Lafayette LA 70598 **800-346-3745** 337-837-3334

Day & Zimmermann Group Inc
1818 Market St . . . . Philadelphia PA 19130 **877-319-0270** 215-299-8000

Huitt-Zollars Inc
1717 McKinney Ave Ste 1400 . . . . Dallas TX 75202 **866-667-6572** 214-871-3311

KCI Technologies Inc
936 Ridgebrook Rd . . . . Sparks MD 21152 **800-572-7496** 410-316-7800

Landiscor
7310 N 16th St Ste 275 . . . . Phoenix AZ 85020 **866-221-8578** 602-248-8989

Print-O-Stat Inc
1011 W Market St . . . . York PA 17404 **800-711-8014** 717-854-7821

Sidwell Co Inc
675 Sidwell Ct . . . . Saint Charles IL 60174 **877-743-9355** 630-549-1000

Teletrac Inc
7391 Lincoln Way . . . . Garden Grove CA 92841 **800-500-6009** 714-897-0877

Wade-Trim Group Inc
500 Griswold Ave Ste 2500 . . . . Detroit MI 48226 **800-482-2864** 313-961-3650

---

724   SWIMMING POOLS

			Toll-Free	Phone

Anthony & Sylvan Pools Corp
3739 Easton Rd Rt 611 . . . . Doylestown PA 18901 **800-366-7958** 215-489-5600

Delair Group LLC
8600 River Rd . . . . Delair NJ 08110 **800-235-0185**

Fox Pool Corp 3490 BoaRd Rd . . . . York PA 17406 **800-723-1011** 717-764-8581

Hornerxpress Inc
5755 Powerline Rd . . . . Fort Lauderdale FL 33309 **800-432-6966** 954-772-6966

Imperial Pools Inc
33 Wade Rd . . . . Latham NY 12110 **800-444-9977** 518-786-1200

Morgan Bldg Systems Inc
2800 McCree Rd . . . . Garland TX 75041 **800-935-0321** 972-864-7300

Radiant Pools Div Trojan Leisure Products LLC
440 N Pearl St . . . . Albany NY 12207 **866-697-5870** 518-434-4161

Viking Pools Inc
121 Crawford Rd PO Box 96 . . . . Williams CA 95987 **800-854-7665** 530-473-5319

Vogue Pool Products
7050 St Patrick St . . . . LaSalle QC H8N1V2 **800-363-3232** 514-363-3232

---

725   SWITCHGEAR & SWITCHBOARD APPARATUS

SEE ALSO Transformers - Power, Distribution, Specialty ; Wiring Devices - Current-Carrying

			Toll-Free	Phone

Bel Fuse Inc
206 Van Vorst St . . . . Jersey City NJ 07302 **800-235-3873** 201-432-0463
NASDAQ: BELFA

Guardian Electric Mfg Company Inc
1425 Lake Ave . . . . Woodstock IL 60098 **800-762-0369** 815-334-3600

HVB AE Power Systems Inc
7250 Mcginnis Ferry Rd . . . . Suwanee GA 30024 **866-362-0798** 770-495-1755

ITW Switches
2550 Mill Brook Dr . . . . Buffalo Grove IL 60089 **800-544-3354** 847-876-9400

Kasa Industrial Controls Inc
418 E Ave B . . . . Salina KS 67401 **800-755-5272** 785-825-7181

Littelfuse Inc
8755 W Higgins Rd Ste 500 . . . . Chicago IL 60631 **800-227-0029*** 773-628-1000
NASDAQ: LFUS ■ *Sales

Lumitex Inc
8443 Dow Cir . . . . Strongsville OH 44136 **800-969-5483** 440-243-8401

Norberg-ies 4237 S 74th E Ave . . . . Tulsa OK 74145 **800-739-9145** 918-665-6888

Otto Engineering Inc
2 E Main St . . . . Carpentersville IL 60110 **888-234-6886** 847-428-7171

					Toll-Free	Phone
Powell Industries Inc						
8550 Mosely Dr	Houston	TX	77075		800-480-7273	713-944-6900
NASDAQ: POWL						
Power Distribution Inc						
4200 Oakleys Ct	Richmond	VA	23223		800-225-4838	804-737-9880
Powercon Corp PO Box 477	Severn	MD	21144		800-638-5055	410-551-6500
Reliance Controls Corp						
2001 Young Ct	Racine	WI	53404		800-634-6155	262-634-6155
Revere Control Systems Inc						
2240 Rocky Ridge Rd	Birmingham	AL	35216		800-536-2525	205-824-0004
Russelectric Inc						
99 Industrial Pk Rd	Hingham	MA	02043		800-225-5250	781-749-6000
S & C Electric Co						
6601 N Ridge Blvd	Chicago	IL	60626		800-621-5546	773-338-1000
Satin American Corp						
40 Oliver Terr	Shelton	CT	06484		877-356-5050	
Superior Electric						
28 Spring Ln Ste 3	Farmington	CT	06032		800-390-6405	860-507-2025
Tapeswitch Corp						
100 Schmitt Blvd	Farmingdale	NY	11735		800-234-8273	631-630-0442

726   TABLE & KITCHEN SUPPLIES - CHINA & EARTHENWARE

SEE ALSO

				Toll-Free	Phone
Heritage Mint Ltd					
PO Box 13750	Scottsdale AZ	85267		888-860-6245	480-860-1300
Homer Laughlin China Co					
672 Fiesta Dr	Newell WV	26050		800-452-4462	304-387-1300
Lenox Corp PO Box 2006	Bristol PA	19007		800-223-4311	
Lipper International Inc					
235 Washington St	Wallingford CT	06492		800-243-3129	203-269-8588
Original Hartstone Pottery, The					
1719 Dearborn St	Zanesville OH	43701		800-339-4278	740-452-9000
Pfaltzgraff Co PO Box 21769	York PA	17402		800-999-2811	

TAPE - ADHESIVE

SEE Medical Supplies - Mfr

727   TAPE - CELLOPHANE, GUMMED, MASKING, PRESSURE SENSITIVE

SEE ALSO Medical Supplies - Mfr

				Toll-Free	Phone
3M Canada Co 300 Tartan Dr	London ON	N5V4M9		888-364-3577	
Adhesive Applications Inc					
41 O'Neill St	EastHampton MA	01027		800-356-3572*	413-527-7120
*General					
Avery Dennison Corp					
207 Goode Ave	Glendale CA	91203		888-567-4387*	626-304-2000
NYSE: AVY ▪ *Cust Svc					
Avery Dennison Specialty Tapes Div					
250 Chester St Bldg 5.	Painesville OH	44077		866-462-8379	626-304-2000
Brady Coated Products					
6555 W Good Hope Rd	Milwaukee WI	53223		800-662-1191	414-358-6600
Brite-Line LLC					
10660 E 51st Ave	Denver CO	80239		888-201-6448	
Decker Tape Products Inc					
Six Stewart Pl	Fairfield NJ	07004		800-227-5252	973-227-5350
DeWAL Industries Inc					
15 Ray Trainor Dr	Narragansett RI	02882		800-366-8356	401-789-9736
Eternabond 75 E Div St	Mundelein IL	60060		888-336-2663	847-837-9400
Gaska-Tape Inc					
1810 W Lusher Ave	Elkhart IN	46517		800-423-1571	574-294-5431
Harris Industries Inc					
5181 Argosy Ave	Huntington Beach CA	92649		800-222-6866	714-898-8048
Holland Mfg Co Inc					
15 Main St PO Box 404	Succasunna NJ	07876		800-345-0492	973-584-8141
JHL Industries					
10012 Nevada Ave	Chatsworth CA	91311		800-255-6636	818-882-2233
Kruse Adhesive Tape Inc					
1610 E McFadden Ave	Santa Ana CA	92705		800-992-7702	714-640-2130
M & C Specialties Co					
90 James Way	SouthHampton PA	18966		800-441-6996*	215-322-1600
*Cust Svc					
Neptco Inc 30 Hamlet St	Pawtucket RI	02861		800-354-5445	401-722-5500
Presto Tape Inc					
1626 Bridgewater Rd	Bensalem PA	19020		800-331-1373	215-245-8555
Pro Tapes & Specialties					
PO Box 53026	Newark NJ	07101		800-345-0234	732-346-0900
Shurtape Technologies LLC					
1712 Eigth St Dr SE	Hickory NC	28602		888-442-8273	828-322-2700
STA Overlaminations					
100 S Puente St	Brea CA	92821		800-235-8273	714-255-7888
Tesa Tape Inc					
5825 Carnegie Blvd	Charlotte NC	28209		800-426-2181	704-554-0707
Tommy Tape 378 Four Rod Rd	Berlin CT	06037		888-866-8273	860-378-0111
Venture Tape Corp					
30 Commerce Rd	Rockland MA	02370		800-343-1076	781-331-5900
VIBAC Canada Inc					
12250 Industrial Blvd	Montreal QC	H1B5M5		800-557-0192	514-640-0250
WTP Inc PO Box 937	Coloma MI	49038		800-521-0731	269-468-3399

728   TARPS, TENTS, COVERS

SEE ALSO Sporting Goods ; Bags - Textile

				Toll-Free	Phone
Aero Industries Inc					
4243 W Bradbury Ave	Indianapolis IN	46241		800-535-9545*	317-244-2433
*Sales					
Anchor Industries Inc					
1100 Burch Dr	Evansville IN	47725		800-544-4445	812-867-2421

				Toll-Free	Phone
Canvas Products Co					
274 S Waterman St	Detroit MI	48209		877-293-1669	
Carefree of Colorado					
2145 W Sixth Ave	Broomfield CO	80020		800-621-2617	303-469-3324
Clamshell Structures Inc					
1101 Maulhardt Ave	Oxnard CA	93030		800-360-8853	805-988-1340
Commonwealth Canvas Inc					
Five Perkins Way	Newburyport MA	01950		877-922-6827	978-499-3900
CR Daniels Inc					
3451 Ellicott Ctr Dr	Ellicott City MD	21043		800-933-2638	410-461-2100
DC Humphrys Inc					
5744 Woodland Ave	Philadelphia PA	19143		800-645-2059*	215-724-8181
*Sales					
Diamond Brand Canvas Products					
145 Cane Creek Industrial Pk Rd					
Ste 1	Fletcher NC	28732		800-459-6262*	828-684-9848
*Sales					
Eide Industries Inc					
16215 Piuma Ave	Cerritos CA	90703		800-422-6827	562-402-8335
Estex Mfg Co Inc					
402 E Broad St PO Box 368	Fairburn GA	30213		800-749-1224	
Fisher Canvas Products Inc					
415 S Mary St	Burlington NJ	08016		800-892-6688	
John Johnson Co					
274 S Waterman St	Detroit MI	48209		800-991-1394	313-496-0600
Johnson Outdoors Inc					
555 Main St	Racine WI	53403		800-468-9716	262-631-6600
NASDAQ: JOUT					
Loop-Loc Ltd					
390 Motor Pkwy	Hauppauge NY	11788		800-562-5667	631-582-2626
Mauritzon Inc					
3939 W Belden Ave	Chicago IL	60647		800-621-4352	773-235-6000
Midwest Canvas Corp					
4635 W Lake St	Chicago IL	60644		800-433-4701*	773-287-4400
*General					
North Sails Group LLC					
125 Old Gate Ln	Milford CT	06460		866-427-4747	203-877-7621
Rainier Industries Ltd					
18375 Olympic Ave S	Tukwila WA	98188		800-869-7162	425-251-1800
Robertson Manufacturing Inc					
112 Woodland Ave	West Grove PA	19390		800-260-5423	610-869-9600
Shur-Co Inc					
2309 Shur-Lok St PO Box 713	Yankton SD	57078		800-474-8756	605-665-6000
Steele Canvas Basket Corp					
201 William St PO Box 6267 IMCN	Chelsea MA	02150		800-541-8929	617-889-0202
Trimaco LLC					
2300 Gateway Centre Blvd Ste 200	Morrisville NC	27560		800-325-7356	919-674-3460
Troy Sunshade Co					
607 Riffle Ave	Greenville OH	45331		800-833-8769	937-548-2466
Universal Fabric Structures Inc					
2200 Kumry Rd	Quakertown PA	18951		800-634-8368	215-529-9921

729   TAX PREPARATION SERVICES

				Toll-Free	Phone
APA Services					
4150 International Plz Tower I					
Ste 510	Fort Worth TX	76109		877-425-5023	
Avitus Group					
P.O. Box 81590	Billings MT	59108		800-454-2446	
BDB Payroll Inc					
768 Bedford Ave	Brooklyn NY	11205		800-729-7687	718-522-2000
Defense Finance & Accounting Service					
8899 E 56th St	Indianapolis IN	46249		888-332-7411	
Eastridge Workforce Solutions					
2375 Northside Dr Ste 360	San Diego CA	92108		877-862-2632	877-337-5422
Employer Flexible					
7850 N Sam Houston Parkway W Ste 100	Houston TX	77064		866-501-4942	
Fesnak & Associates LLP					
1777 Sentry Pkwy W Ste 300	Blue Bell PA	19422		800-274-3978	267-419-2200
Fiducial					
1370 Ave of the Americas 31st Fl	New York NY	10019		866-343-8242	212-207-4700
Fiducial Franchising					
10100 Old Columbia Rd Third Fl	Columbia MD	21046		800-323-9000	410-290-8296
H & R Block Tax Services Inc					
4400 Main St	Kansas City MO	64111		800-472-5625	
Inova Payroll Inc					
176 Thompson Ln Ste 204	Nashville TN	37211		888-244-6106	615-921-0600
Jackson Hewitt Inc					
Three Sylvan Way Ste 301	Parsippany NJ	07054		800-234-1040	
OTC: JHTXQ					
JG Tax Group					
1430 S Federal Hwy	Deerfield Beach FL	33441		866-477-5291	
Knight James E & Associates Pc					
14825 Saint Marys Ln	Houston TX	77079		800-896-4500	281-493-5080
Liberty Tax Service Inc					
1716 Corporate Landing Pkwy	Virginia Beach VA	23454		800-790-3863*	757-493-8855
*Cust Svc					
Paycom					
7501 W Memorial Rd	Oklahoma City OK	73142		800-580-4505	
Payworks Inc					
1565 Willson Pl	Winnipeg MB	R3T4H1		866-788-3500	
PrO Unlimited Inc					
301 Yamato Rd Ste3199	Boca Raton FL	33431		800-291-1099	
Verified Audit Circulation Inc					
900 Larkspur Landing Cir	Larkspur CA	94939		800-775-3332	415-461-6006

730   TELECOMMUNICATIONS EQUIPMENT & SYSTEMS

SEE ALSO Radio & Television Broadcasting & Communications Equipment ; Modems

				Toll-Free	Phone
ADTRAN Inc					
901 Explorer Blvd	Huntsville AL	35806		800-923-8726	256-963-8000
NASDAQ: ADTN					

				Toll-Free	Phone

AltiGen Communications Inc
410 E Plumeria Dr .... San Jose CA 95134 **888-258-4436** 408-597-9000
OTC: ATGN

Amtelco 4800 Curtin Dr .... McFarland WI 53558 **800-356-9148** 608-838-4194

AT & T Inc
175 E Houston St PO Box 2933 .... San Antonio TX 78299 **800-351-7221** 210-821-4105
NYSE: AT&T

Atris Inc
1151 S Trooper Rd Ste E. .... Norristown PA 19403 **800-724-3384**

Audiovox Corp
180 Marcus Blvd .... Hauppauge NY 11788 **800-645-4994** 631-231-7750
NASDAQ: VOXX

Call One Inc
400 Imperial Blvd PO Box 9002 .... Cape Canaveral FL 32920 **800-749-3160** 321-783-2400

Ceragon Networks Inc
10 Forest Ave .... Paramus NJ 07652 **877-342-3247*** 201-845-6955
NASDAQ: CRNT ■ *Tech Supp*

Charles Industries Ltd
5600 Apollo Dr .... Rolling Meadows IL 60008 **800-458-4747** 847-806-6300

CiDRA Corp
50 Barnes Pk N .... Wallingford CT 06492 **877-243-7277** 203-265-0035

CIENA Corp
1201 Winterson Rd .... Linthicum MD 21090 **800-921-1144** 410-694-5700
NASDAQ: CIEN

ClearOne Communications Inc
5225 Wiley Post Way .... Salt Lake City UT 84116 **800-945-7730** 801-975-7200

Comarco Inc
25541 Commerce Ctr Dr .... Lake Forest CA 92630 **800-792-0250** 949-599-7400
OTC: CMRO

Comarco Wireless Technologies Inc
25541 Commerce Ctr Dr .... Lake Forest CA 92630 **800-792-0250*** 949-599-7400
*Cust Svc

Communication Technologies Inc
14151 Newbrook Dr Ste 400. .... Chantilly VA 20151 **888-266-8358** 703-961-9080

Communications Test Design Inc
1339 Enterprise Dr .... West Chester PA 19380 **800-223-3910** 610-436-5203

Compunetix Inc
2420 Mosside Blvd .... Monroeville PA 15146 **800-879-4266** 412-373-8110

Digital Voice Corp
1201 S Beltline Rd Ste 150. .... Coppell TX 75019 **800-777-8329*** 469-635-6500
*Cust Svc

DynaMetric Inc
717 S Myrtle Ave .... Monrovia CA 91016 **800-525-6925** 626-358-2559

Ecessa Corp
2800 Campus Dr Ste 140 .... Plymouth MN 55441 **800-669-6242** 763-694-9949

Electro Standards Laboratories Inc
36 Western Industrial Dr .... Cranston RI 02921 **877-943-1164** 401-943-1164

Electronic Tele-Communications Inc
1915 MacArthur Rd .... Waukesha WI 53188 **888-746-4382** 262-542-5600
OTC: ETCIA

FleetBoss Global Positioning Solutions Inc
241 O'Brien Rd .... Fern Park FL 32730 **877-265-9559** 407-265-9559

Fujitsu America Inc
1250 E Arques Ave .... Sunnyvale CA 94085 **800-538-8460** 408-746-6200

GAI-Tronics Corp
400 E Wyomissing Ave .... Mohnton PA 19540 **800-492-1212** 610-777-1374

Genesys Telecommunications Laboratories Inc
2001 Junipero Serra Blvd .... Daly City CA 94014 **888-436-3797** 650-466-1100

GN US Inc 77 NE Blvd .... Nashua NH 03062 **800-327-2230** 603-598-1100

Harris Corp
1025 W NASA Blvd .... Melbourne FL 32919 **800-442-7747** 321-727-9100
NYSE: HRS

Honeywell International Inc
101 Columbia Rd PO Box M6/LM .... Morristown NJ 07962 **877-841-2840** 480-353-3020
NYSE: HON

Hughes Network Systems LLC
11717 Exploration Ln .... Germantown MD 20876 **888-748-6288** 301-428-5500

I Wireless
4135 NW Urbandale Dr .... Urbandale IA 50322 **888-550-4497*** 515-258-7000
*Cust Svc

iDirect Technologies Inc
13865 Sunrise Valley Dr Ste 100 .... Herndon VA 20171 **888-362-5475** 703-648-8118

Infinera Corp
140 Caspian Ct .... Sunnyvale CA 94089 **877-742-3427** 408-572-5200
NASDAQ: INFN

InnoMedia Inc
128 Baytech Dr .... San Jose CA 95134 **888-251-6250** 408-432-5400

ISCO International LLC
1450 Arthur Ave Ste A .... Elk Grove Village IL 60007 **888-948-4726** 224-222-1666

JTech Communications Inc
6413 Congress Ave Ste 150 .... Boca Raton FL 33487 **800-321-6221**

L-3 Communications Corp
600 Third Ave 34-35 Fl. .... New York NY 10016 **800-351-8483** 212-697-1111
NYSE: LLL

Lantronix Inc
167 Technology Dr .... Irvine CA 92618 **800-526-8766*** 949-453-3990
NASDAQ: LTRX ■ *Orders*

Metro-Tel Corp
11640 Arbor St Ste 100 .... Omaha NE 68144 **888-998-8300** 402-498-2964

Mitel Networks Corp
350 Legget Dr PO Box 13089 .... Kanata ON K2K2W7 **800-722-1301** 613-592-2122

Molex Premise Networks
2222 Wellington Ct .... Lisle IL 60532 **866-733-6659** 630-969-4550

Movius Interactive
11360 Lakefield Dr .... Duluth GA 30097 **800-688-4001*** 770-283-1000
*Tech Supp

NDS Americas
3500 Highland Ave .... Costa Mesa CA 92626 **866-398-8749** 714-434-2100

NEC America Inc
6555 N State Hwy 161 .... Irving TX 75039 **866-632-3226*** 214-262-2000
*Cust Svc

NICE Systems Inc
301 Rt 17 N 10th Fl .... Rutherford NJ 07070 **800-994-4498** 201-964-2600

Norsat International Inc
110-4020 Viking Way .... Richmond BC V6V2N2 **800-644-4562** 604-821-2800
TSE: NII

Numerex Corp
1600 Parkwood Cir Fifth Fl. .... Atlanta GA 30339 **800-665-5686** 770-693-5950
NASDAQ: NMRX

				Toll-Free	Phone

Pics Telecom International Corp
1920 Lyell Ave .... Rochester NY 14606 **800-521-7427** 585-295-2000

Plantronics Inc
345 Encinal St .... Santa Cruz CA 95060 **800-544-4660** 831-426-5858
NYSE: PLT

Polycom Inc
4750 Willow Rd .... Pleasanton CA 94588 **800-765-9266**

Protel Inc 4150 Kidron Rd .... Lakeland FL 33811 **800-925-8882** 863-644-5558

Proxim Wireless Corp
1561 Buckeye Dr .... Milpitas CA 95035 **800-229-1630** 408-383-7600
OTC: PRXM

Pulse Communications Inc
2900 Towerview Rd .... Herndon VA 20171 **800-381-1997*** 703-471-2900
*Cust Svc

RAD Data Communications Ltd
900 Corporate Dr .... Mahwah NJ 07430 **800-444-7234** 201-529-1100

Samsung Telecommunications America LLP
1301 E Lookout Dr .... Richardson TX 75082 **800-726-7864** 972-761-7000

SPL Integrated Solutions
6301 Benjamin Rd Ste 101 .... Tampa FL 33634 **800-292-4125** 813-884-7168

Superior Essex Communications LP
6120 Powers Ferry Rd Ste 150 .... Atlanta GA 30339 **800-551-8948** 770-657-6000

Suttle 1001 E Hwy 212 .... Hector MN 55342 **800-852-8662** 320-848-6711

Symmetricom Inc
2300 Orchard Pkwy .... San Jose CA 95131 **888-367-7966** 408-433-0910
NASDAQ: SYMM

Syntellect Inc
16610 N Black Canyon Hwy Ste 100 .... Phoenix AZ 85053 **800-788-9733**

System Engineering International Inc (SEI)
5115 Pegasus Ct Ste Q. .... Frederick MD 21704 **800-765-4734** 301-694-9601

TAG Solutions LLC
12 Elmwood Rd .... Albany NY 12204 **800-724-0023** 518-292-6500

Technical Communications Corp
100 Domino Dr .... Concord MA 01742 **800-952-4082** 978-287-5100
NASDAQ: TCCO

Tekelec
5200 Paramount Pkwy .... Morrisville NC 27560 **800-633-0738** 919-460-5500
NASDAQ: TKLC

Tel Electronics Inc
313 S 740 E St Suite 1 .... American Fork UT 84003 **800-564-9424** 801-756-9606

Telco Systems Inc
15 Berkshire Rd .... Mansfield MA 02048 **800-227-0937** 781-255-2120

Telect Inc
23321 E Knox Ave .... Liberty Lake WA 99019 **800-551-4567*** 509-926-6000
*Cust Svc

Teo Technologies Inc
11609 49th Pl W .... Mukilteo WA 98275 **800-524-0024** 425-349-1000

Tollgrade Communications Inc
3120 Unionville Rd Ste 400 .... Cranberry Township PA 16066 **800-878-3399*** 412-820-1400
*Cust Svc

Toshiba America Inc
1251 Ave of the Americas Ste 4100 .... New York NY 10020 **800-457-7777** 212-596-0600

Tricomm Services Corp
1247 N Church St Ste 8 .... Moorestown NJ 08057 **800-872-2401** 856-914-9001

TSI Global Cos
700 Fountain Lakes Blvd .... Saint Charles MO 63301 **800-875-5605** 636-949-8889

Uniden America Corp
4700 Amon Carter Blvd .... Fort Worth TX 76155 **800-297-1023*** 817-858-3300
*Cust Svc

UTStarcom Inc
1732 North First St Ste 220 .... San Jose CA 95112 **877-547-6340** 408-453-4557
NASDAQ: UTSI

Valcom Inc 5614 Hollins Rd .... Roanoke VA 24019 **800-825-2661** 540-563-2000

Vbrick Systems Inc
12 Beaumont Rd .... Wallingford CT 06492 **866-827-4251** 203-265-0044

VTech Communications Inc
9590 SW Gemini Dr Ste 120. .... Beaverton OR 97008 **800-595-9511** 503-596-1200

Westell Technologies Inc
750 N Commons Dr .... Aurora IL 60504 **800-323-6883** 630-898-2500
NASDAQ: WSTL

Zhone Technologies Inc
7001 Oakport St .... Oakland CA 94621 **877-946-6320** 510-777-7000
NASDAQ: ZHNE

731   TELECOMMUNICATIONS SERVICES

				Toll-Free	Phone

Access America
673 Emory Vly Rd .... Oak Ridge TN 37830 **800-860-2140** 865-482-2140

Access Point Inc
1100 Crescent Green .... Cary NC 27518 **877-419-4274** 919-851-4838

ACT Conferencing
1526 Cole Blvd Bldg 3 Ste 300. .... Lakewood CO 80401 **800-433-2900** 303-233-3500

Airvoice Wireless LLC
2425 Franklin Rd .... Bloomfield Hills MI 48302 **888-944-2355**

Alaska Communications Systems Group Inc
600 Telephone Ave .... Anchorage AK 99503 **800-808-8083** 907-563-8000
NASDAQ: ALSK

Allstream Corp
200 Wellington St W .... Toronto ON M5V3G2 **888-288-2273*** 416-345-2000
*Cust Svc

AmeriCom Inc PO Box 2146 .... Sandy UT 84091 **800-820-6296** 801-571-2446

AT & T Inc
175 E Houston St PO Box 2933 .... San Antonio TX 78299 **800-351-7221** 210-821-4105
NYSE: AT&T

Auragan LLC PO Box 1501 .... New Canaan CT 06840 **866-644-2872**

Bell Aliant Regional Communications
7 S Maritime Centre
1505 Barrington St .... Halifax NS B3J3K5 **800-555-1212** 800-267-1110
TSE: BA

Bell Canada
1050 Beaver Hall Hill Bureau 3700. .... Montreal QC H2Z1S4 **800-667-0123**

Birch Communications Inc
2300 Main St 6th Fl .... Kansas City MO 64108 **866-424-5100** 816-300-3000

Bledsoe Telephone Co-op Corp (BTC)
338 Cumberland Ave PO Box 609 .... Pikeville TN 37367 **888-382-1222** 423-447-2121

			Toll-Free	Phone
Bluegrass Cellular Inc				
2902 Ring Rd PO Box 5012	Elizabethtown KY	42702	**800-928-2355**	270-769-0339
Broadview Networks Holdings Inc				
800 Westchester Ave Ste N-501	Rye Brook NY	10573	**800-260-8766**	914-922-7000
Cavalier Telephone LLC				
2134 W Laburnum Ave	Richmond VA	23227	**800-683-3944**	800-442-2410
Century Interactive LLC				
8750 N Central Expy Ste 720	Dallas TX	75231	**877-921-7992**	214-446-7867
Cincinnati Bell Inc				
221 E Fourth St	Cincinnati OH	45202	**800-387-3638**	513-397-9900
NYSE: CBB				
Citizens Telephone Co-op				
PO Box 137	Floyd VA	24091	**800-941-0426**	540-745-2111
Co-op Communications Inc				
210 Clay Ave	Lyndhurst NJ	07071	**800-833-2700**	
Commonwealth Telephone Co				
1 Newbury Street Suite 103	Peabody MA	01960	**800-439-7170**	978-536-9500
Comporium Communications				
332 E Main St	Rock Hill SC	29730	**866-922-5922**	888-403-2667
Corporate Telephone Services				
184 W Second St	Boston MA	02127	**800-274-1211**	617-625-1200
CPA2Biz Inc				
100 Broadway Sixth Fl	New York NY	10005	**888-777-7077**	646-233-5000
Criticom Inc				
4211 Forbes Blvd	Lanham MD	20706	**800-449-3384**	301-306-0600
Cypress Communications Inc				
3565 Piedmont Rd NE	Atlanta GA	30305	**844-276-2386**	404-869-2500
Dakota Central Telecommunications Co-op				
630 Fifth St N	Carrington ND	58421	**800-771-0974**	701-652-3184
Deltacom Inc				
7037 Old Madison Pike	Huntsville AL	35806	**800-239-3000**	
deltathree Inc 75 Broad St	New York NY	10004	**888-335-8230**	212-500-4850
PINK: DDDC				
Digerati Technologies Inc				
3463 Magic Dr Ste 355	San Antonio TX	78229	**855-202-5683**	210-614-7240
OTC: DTGI				
Eastex Telephone Co-op Inc				
PO Box 150	Henderson TX	75653	**800-232-7839**	903-854-1000
EATELCORP Inc				
913 S Burnside Ave	Gonzales LA	70737	**800-621-4211**	225-621-4300
Empire Telephone Corp				
34 Main St PO Box 349	Prattsburgh NY	14873	**800-338-3300**	607-522-3712
Etex Telephone Co-op Inc				
1013 Hwy 155 N	Gilmer TX	75644	**877-482-3839**	903-797-2711
Excel Telecommunications				
433 Las Colinas Blvd Ste 400	Irving TX	75039	**877-668-0808**	972-910-1900
FairPoint Communications Inc				
521 E Morehead St Ste 250	Charlotte NC	28202	**866-740-2764**	704-344-8150
NASDAQ: FRP				
Farmers Telecommunications Co-op (FTC)				
144 McCurdy Ave N PO Box 217	Rainsville AL	35986	**866-638-2144**	256-638-2144
Farmers Telephone Co-op Inc				
1101 E Main St	Kingstree SC	29556	**888-218-5050**	843-382-2333
Faxaway 417 Second Ave W	Seattle WA	98119	**800-906-4329**	206-301-7000
FaxBack Inc				
7007 SW Cardinal Ln Ste 105	Portland OR	97224	**800-329-2225**	503-597-5350
Frontier Communications Corp				
Three High Ridge Pk	Stamford CT	06905	**800-877-4390**	203-614-5600
NASDAQ: FTR				
Fusion Telecommunications International Inc				
420 Lexington Ave Ste 1718	New York NY	10170	**888-301-1721**	212-201-2400
OTC: FSNN				
General Communication Inc				
2550 Denali St Ste 1000	Anchorage AK	99503	**800-770-7886**	907-265-5600
NASDAQ: GNCMA				
Golden State Cellular				
17400 High School Rd	Jamestown CA	95327	**800-453-8255**	209-984-8700
Golden West Telecommunications				
415 Crown St PO Box 411	Wall SD	57790	**866-279-2161**	605-279-2161
Granite Telecommunications LLC				
100 Newport Ave Ext	Quincy MA	02171	**866-847-1500**	617-933-5500
Graphnet Inc				
40 Fultron St 28th Fl	New York NY	10038	**800-327-1800**	212-994-1100
GTT Communications Inc				
7900 Tysons One Pl Ste 1450	McLean VA	22102	**866-250-3887**	703-442-5500
NYSE: GTT				
Guadalupe Valley Telephone Co-op (GVTC)				
36101 FM 3159	New Braunfels TX	78132	**800-367-4882**	830-885-4411
Hargray Communications				
856 William Hilton Pkwy				
PO Box 5986	Hilton Head Island SC	29938	**800-726-1266**	843-341-1501
Harrisonville Telephone Co				
213 S Main St PO Box 149	Waterloo IL	62298	**888-482-8353**	618-939-6112
Horry Telephone Co-op Inc (HTC)				
3480 Hwy 701 N PO Box 1820	Conway SC	29528	**800-824-6779**	843-365-2151
Integra Telecom Inc				
1201 NE Lloyd Blvd Ste 500	Portland OR	97232	**866-468-3472***	503-453-8000
*General				
Inter-Community Telephone Co (ICTC)				
PO Box 8	Nome ND	58062	**800-350-9137**	701-924-8815
InterCall				
8420 W Bryn Mawr Ste 1100	Chicago IL	60631	**800-374-2441**	773-399-1600
Intrado Inc				
1601 Dry Creek Dr	Longmont CO	80503	**877-262-3775**	720-494-5800
Iridium Satellite LLC				
6701 Democracy Blvd	Bethesda MD	20817	**866-947-4348**	301-571-6200
IVCi LLC				
601 Old Willets Path	Hauppauge NY	11788	**800-224-7083**	631-273-5800
J2 Global Communications Inc				
6922 Hollywood Blvd Eighth Fl	Los Angeles CA	90028	**888-718-2000***	323-860-9200
*Sales				
Kaplan Telephone Company Inc (KTC)				
220 N Cushing Ave	Kaplan LA	70548	**866-643-7171**	337-643-7171
Kennebec Telephone Company Inc				
220 S Main St	Kennebec SD	57544	**888-868-3390**	605-869-2220
Lambeau Telecom				
1807 N Cntr St	Beaver Dam WI	53916	**800-444-4014***	920-887-3148
*Cust Svc				
LICT Corp				
401 Theodore Fremd Ave	Rye NY	10580	**800-690-6903**	914-921-8821
Lightower Fiber Networks				
80 Central St	Boxborough MA	01719	**888-583-4237**	978-264-6000
Mercury Wireless LLC				
2825 se california ave	Topeka KS	66605	**800-354-4915**	
Midcontinent Communications				
PO Box 5010	Sioux Falls SD	57117	**800-888-1300**	605-274-9810
Molalla Communications Co				
211 Robbins St PO Box 360	Molalla OR	97038	**800-332-2344**	503-829-1100
Net Access Corp				
Nine Wing Dr	Cedar Knolls NJ	07927	**800-638-6336**	973-590-5000
Net2Phone Inc 520 Broad St	Newark NJ	07102	**800-386-6438**	973-438-3111
Network Communications International Corp (NCIC)				
PO Box 551	Longview TX	75601	**800-382-2887**	903-757-4455
New Ulm Telecom Inc				
27 N Minnesota St	New Ulm MN	56073	**888-873-6853**	507-354-4111
OTC: NULM				
North Central Telephone Co-op Corp				
PO Box 70	Lafayette TN	37083	**888-882-1693**	615-666-2151
NTELOS Holdings Corp				
1154 Shenandoah Village Dr				
PO Box 1990	Waynesboro VA	22980	**877-468-3567**	540-946-3500
NASDAQ: NTLS				
NTT DoCoMo USA Inc				
757 Third Ave 16th Fl	New York NY	10017	**888-362-6661**	
O1 Communications Inc				
1515 K St Ste 100	Sacramento CA	95814	**888-444-1111**	
Omnitracs LLC				
10290 Campus Point Dr	San Diego CA	92121	**800-647-3325**	
Otelco Inc 505 Third Ave E	Oneonta AL	35121	**800-344-7483**	205-625-3574
NASDAQ: OTT				
OTZ Telephone Co-op Inc				
PO Box 324	Kotzebue AK	99752	**800-478-3111**	907-442-3114
Panhandle Telecommunication Systems Inc (PTSI)				
2222 NW Hwy	Guymon OK	73942	**800-562-2556**	580-338-2556
Penasco Valley Telecommunications (PVT)				
4011 W Main St	Artesia NM	88210	**800-505-4844**	
Pioneer Long Distance Inc				
PO Box 539	Kingfisher OK	73750	**888-782-2667**	
Pioneer Telephone Assn Inc				
PO Box 707	Ulysses KS	67880	**800-308-7536**	620-356-3211
Pratt Communications				
2913 Tech Ctr	Santa Ana CA	92705	**800-980-2323***	714-540-6840
*General				
Primus Telecommunications (PTGi)				
7901 Jones Ranch Dr Ste 900	McLean VA	22102	**866-385-3360**	703-902-2800
NYSE: PTGI				
PWR LLC 6402 Deere Rd Ste 3	Syracuse NY	13206	**800-342-0878**	315-701-0210
Questar InfoComm Inc				
180 East 100 South				
PO Box 45433	Salt Lake City UT	84145	**800-729-6790**	801-324-5856
Reserve Telephone Company Inc				
PO Box T	Reserve LA	70084	**888-611-6111**	985-536-1111
Rnk Inc 333 Elm St Ste 310	Dedham MA	02026	**877-323-2486**	781-613-6000
Rogers Wireless Communications Inc				
333 Bloor St. E, 4th Fl	Toronto ON	M4W1G9	**800-575-9090**	888-764-3771
Rural Telephone Service Company Inc				
PO Box 158	Lenora KS	67645	**877-625-7872**	785-567-4281
Sage Telecom Inc				
3300 E Renner Rd Ste 350 Bldg 2	Richardson TX	75082	**877-742-5622**	214-495-4700
Securus Technologies Inc				
14651 Dallas Pkwy	Dallas TX	75254	**800-844-6591**	972-277-0300
Shawnee Telephone Co				
PO Box 69	Equality IL	62934	**800-461-3956**	618-276-4211
Shenandoah Telecommunications Co				
500 Shentel Way	Edinburg VA	22824	**800-743-6835**	540-984-5224
NASDAQ: SHEN				
SignalPoint Communications Corp				
433 Hackensack Ave				
Continental Plz 6th Fl	Hackensack NJ	07601	**877-928-3292**	201-968-9797
Skyline Telephone Membership Corp				
PO Box 759	West Jefferson NC	28694	**877-475-9546**	336-877-3111
SkyTel Corp PO Box 2469	Jackson MS	39225	**800-759-8737***	
*Cust Svc				
Smart City Networks				
5795 W Badura Ave Ste 110	Las Vegas NV	89118	**888-446-6911**	702-943-6000
Solarus				
440 E Grand Ave	Wisconsin Rapids WI	54494	**800-421-9282**	715-421-8111
SoundBite Communications Inc				
22 Crosby Dr	Bedford MA	01730	**888-436-3797**	877-768-6324
NASDAQ: SDBT				
South Central Rural Telephone Co-op Corp Inc				
PO Box 159	Glasgow KY	42142	**877-678-2111**	270-678-2111
Southern Communications Services Inc				
5555 Glenridge Connector Ste 500	Atlanta GA	30342	**800-818-5462**	
Spanlink Communications Inc				
605 Hwy 169 N Ste 900	Minneapolis MN	55441	**800-303-1239***	763-971-2000
*Sales				
Startec Global Communications Corp				
11300 Rockville Pike Ste 900	Rockville MD	20852	**800-827-3374**	301-610-4300
T-Mobile USA Inc				
12920 SE 38th St	Bellevue WA	98006	**800-318-9270**	425-383-4000
TDS Telecommunications Corp				
525 Junction Rd	Madison WI	53717	**866-571-6662**	608-664-4000
TelAlaska Inc				
201 E 56th St	Anchorage AK	99518	**888-570-1792**	907-563-2003
Telephone Service Co				
2 Willipie St	Wapakoneta OH	45895	**800-743-5707**	419-739-2200
Teligent Inc				
210 Brookwood Rd	Atmore AL	36502	**888-411-1175**	251-368-8600
TNS Inc				
11480 Commerce Pk Dr Ste 600	Reston VA	20191	**800-240-2824**	703-453-8300
NYSE: TNS				
Total Telcom Inc				
540 1632 Dickson Ave	Kelowna BC	V1Y7T2	**877-860-3762**	
TracFone Wireless Inc				
9700 NW 112th Ave	Miami FL	33178	**800-876-5753**	305-640-2000

			Toll-Free	Phone
Trans National Communications International Inc (TNCI)				
2 Charlesgate W Ste 500	Boston MA	02215	800-800-8400	617-369-1000
Twin Lakes Telephone Co-op				
200 Telephone Ln	Gainesboro TN	38562	800-644-8582*	931-268-2151
*Cust Svc				
United Utilities Inc				
5450 A St	Anchorage AK	99509	800-478-2020	907-561-1674
Unitel Inc PO Box 165	Unity ME	04988	888-760-1048	207-948-3900
Universal Service Administrative Co (USAC)				
2000 L St NW Ste 200	Washington DC	20036	888-641-8722	202-776-0200
Universal Service Administrative Company Schools & Libraries Div				
2000 L St NW Ste 200	Washington DC	20036	888-203-8100	
Upper Peninsula Telephone Co				
PO Box 86	Carney MI	49812	800-950-8506	906-639-2111
US Cellular Corp (USCC)				
8410 W Bryn Mawr Ave Ste 700	Chicago IL	60631	888-944-9400	773-399-8900
NYSE: USM				
USA Datanet Corp				
109 S Warren St Ste 602	Syracuse NY	13202	800-566-8655	
USA Mobility Inc				
6677 Richmond Hwy	Alexandria VA	22306	800-231-2556	703-660-6677
Valley Telephone Co-op Inc				
752 E Maley St	Willcox AZ	85643	800-421-5711	520-384-2231
VeriSign Inc				
350 Ellis St	Mountain View CA	94043	866-893-6565*	650-426-3100
NASDAQ: VRSN ■ *Sales				
Verizon Business				
1 Verizon Way	Basking Ridge NJ	07920	877-297-7816*	908-559-2000
*Cust Svc				
Verizon Wireless				
180 Washington Valley Rd	Bedminster NJ	07921	800-922-0204	908-306-7000
Virgin Mobile USA Inc				
10 Independence Blvd	Warren NJ	07059	888-322-1122	908-607-4000
Voicecom				
5900 Windward Pkwy Ste 500	Alpharetta GA	30005	888-468-3554	
Vonage Holdings Corp				
23 Main St	Holmdel NJ	07733	877-862-2562	732-528-2600
NYSE: VG				
Wabash Telephone Co-op Inc				
PO Box 299	Louisville IL	62858	800-228-9824	618-665-3311
Warwick Valley Telephone Co				
47 Main St PO Box 592	Warwick NY	10990	800-952-7642*	845-986-8080
NASDAQ: WWVY ■ *Cust Svc				
Wavedivision Holdings LLC				
401 Kirkland Prk Pl Ste 500	Kirkland WA	98033	866-928-3123	425-576-8200
West River Telecommunications Co-op				
PO Box 467	Hazen ND	58545	800-748-7220	701-748-2211
WQN Inc				
14911 Quorum Dr Ste 140	Dallas TX	75254	866-661-6176	
OTC: WQNI				
XO Communications Inc				
13865 Sunrise Vly Dr	Herndon VA	20171	866-349-0134	703-547-2000
Yak Communications Corp				
48 Yonge St Ste 1200	Toronto ON	M5E1G6	877-925-4925	
York Telecom Corp				
81 Corbett Way	Eatontown NJ	07724	866-836-8463	732-413-6000

732   TELEMARKETING & OTHER TELE-SERVICES

Both inbound and outbound telephone marketing as well as other tele-services are included here.

			Toll-Free	Phone
Aegis Communications Group Inc				
8201 Ridgepoint Dr	Irving TX	75063	877-892-3447	972-830-1800
Alta Resources				
120 N Commercial St	Neenah WI	54956	877-464-2582	
American Home Base				
428 Childers St	Pensacola FL	32534	800-549-0595*	850-857-0860
*General				
Ameridial Inc				
4535 Strausser St NW	North Canton OH	44720	800-445-7128	
Aria Communications Corp				
717 W Saint Germain St	St. Cloud MN	56301	800-955-9924	
Calling Solutions By Phone Power Inc				
2200 McCullough Ave	San Antonio TX	78212	800-683-5500*	210-822-7400
*Cust Svc				
Connection, The				
11351 Rupp Dr	Burnsville MN	55337	800-883-5777*	952-948-5488
*Sales				
Convergys Corp				
201 E Fourth St	Cincinnati OH	45202	888-284-9900	513-723-7000
NYSE: CVG				
EBSCO TeleServices				
4150 Belden Village Ave NW Ste 401	Canton OH	44718	800-456-5105	330-492-5105
Harte-Hanks Response Management				
2800 Wells Branch Pkwy	Austin TX	78728	800-456-9748	512-434-1100
InfoCision Management Corp				
325 Springside Dr	Akron OH	44333	800-210-6269	330-668-1400
Integretel Inc				
5883 Rue Ferrari	San Jose CA	95138	888-302-2750	408-362-4000
iSky				
1700 Pennsylvania Ave NW Ste 560	Washington DC	20006	855-475-4759	
Lester Inc				
19 Business Pk Dr	Branford CT	06405	800-999-5265	203-488-5265
Lexicon Marketing Corp				
6380 Wilshire Blvd	Los Angeles CA	90048	800-650-4444	323-782-7400
Meyer Assoc Inc				
14 Seventh Ave N	Saint Cloud MN	56303	800-676-9233	320-259-4000
My Receptionist				
800 Wisconsin St PO Box 109	Eau Claire WI	54703	800-686-0162	
ProCom Inc				
28838 US Hwy 69 PO Box 27	Lamoni IA	50140	800-433-9893	641-784-8441
SITEL Corp				
2 American Ctr				
3102 W End Ave Ste 1000	Nashville TN	37203	866-957-4835	615-301-7100
Tele Business USA				
1945 Techny Rd Ste 3	Northbrook IL	60062	877-315-8353	

			Toll-Free	Phone
Telerx 723 Dresher Rd	Horsham PA	19044	800-283-5379	267-942-3300
TeleServices Direct				
5305 Lakeview Pkwy S Dr	Indianapolis IN	46268	888-646-6626	317-216-2240
TeleTech Holdings Inc				
9197 S Peoria St	Englewood CO	80112	800-835-3832*	303-397-8100
NASDAQ: TTEC ■ *General				
TTC Marketing Solutions				
3945 N Neenah	Chicago IL	60634	800-530-7189	
USA 800 Inc				
9808 E 66th Terr PO Box 16795	Kansas City MO	64133	800-821-7539	816-358-1303
West Corp				
11808 Miracle Hills Dr	Omaha NE	68154	800-232-0900*	
*Sales				
Working Solutions				
1820 Preston Pk Blvd Ste 2000	Plano TX	75093	866-857-4800	972-964-4800
Young America Corp				
10 S 5th St 7th Fl	Minneapolis MN	55402	800-533-4529	

TELEVISION - CABLE

SEE Television Networks ; Cable & Other Pay Television Services

733   TELEVISION COMPANIES

			Toll-Free	Phone
Capitol Broadcasting Co Inc				
2619 Western Blvd	Raleigh NC	27606	800-234-4857	919-890-6000
Christian Television Network Inc (CTN)				
6922 142nd Ave N	Largo FL	33771	800-716-7729	727-535-5622
EW Scripps Co				
312 Walnut St Ste 2800	Cincinnati OH	45202	800-888-3000	513-977-3000
NYSE: SSP				
Forum Communications Co				
101 Fifth St N	Fargo ND	58102	800-747-7311	701-451-5629
Freedom Communications Inc				
17666 Fitch	Irvine CA	92614	866-262-7678	949-253-2300
LeSea Broadcasting Corp				
61300 S Ironwood Rd	South Bend IN	46614	800-365-3732	574-291-8200
Media General Broadcast Group				
111 N Fourth St	Richmond VA	23219	800-937-5449	804-649-6000
Quincy Newspapers Inc				
130 S Fifth St	Quincy IL	62301	800-373-9444	217-223-5100
Saga Communications Inc				
73 Kercheval Ave	Grosse Pointe Farms MI	48236	800-777-3674	313-886-7070
NYSE: SGA				
Univision Television Group Inc				
5999 Ctr Dr	Los Angeles CA	90045	800-594-5387	310-846-2800

734   TELEVISION NETWORKS

			Toll-Free	Phone
Accent Health				
60 E 42nd St Ste 1543	New York NY	10165	800-235-4930	
Business News Network (BNN)				
299 Queen St W	Toronto ON	M5V2Z5	855-326-6266	416-384-6600
Cable Public Affairs Ch (CPAC)				
PO Box 81099	Ottawa ON	K1P1B1	877-287-2722	
Christian Broadcasting Network (CBN)				
977 Centerville Tpke CBN Ctr	Virginia Beach VA	23463	800-759-0700	757-226-7000
CRN Digital Talk Radio				
10487 Sunland Blvd	Sunland CA	91040	800-336-2225	818-352-7152
Crown Media Holdings Inc				
12700 Ventura Blvd Ste 200	Studio City CA	91604	800-479-7328	818-755-2400
NASDAQ: CRWN				
Daystar Television Network				
3901 Hwy 121 PO Box 610546	Bedford TX	76021	800-329-0029	817-571-1229
Discovery Communications Inc				
One Discovery Pl	Silver Spring MD	20910	877-324-5850	240-662-2000
NASDAQ: DISCA				
ESPN Deportes				
Two Alhambra Plz Ninth Fl	Coral Gables FL	33134	800-337-6783	305-567-3797
EVINE Live Inc				
6740 Shady Oak Rd	Eden Prairie MN	55344	800-676-5523	
God's Learning Ch (GLC)				
PO Box 61000	Midland TX	79711	800-707-0420	432-563-0420
Hallmark Ch				
12700 Ventura Blvd Ste 200	Studio City CA	91604	888-390-7474	818-755-2400
History Ch				
A&E Television Networks LLC				
235 E 45th St 8th Fl	New York NY	10017	866-582-5613	212-210-1400
Ion Media Networks				
601 Clearwater Pk Rd	West Palm Beach FL	33401	800-987-9936	561-659-4122
Liberty Ch				
1971 University Blvd	Lynchburg VA	24506	800-332-1883	434-582-2000
NASA TV 300 E St SW	Washington DC	20546	877-546-1574	202-358-0000
NFL Network				
345 Park Avenue	New York NY	10154	800-724-3377	212-450-2000
Outdoor Ch				
43445 Business Pk Dr Ste 103	Temecula CA	92590	800-770-5750	951-699-6991
NASDAQ: OUTD				
QVC Inc 1200 Wilson Dr	West Chester PA	19380	800-367-9444	484-701-1000
Resort Sports Network				
Outside Television				
33 Riverside Ave 4th Fl	Westport CT	06880	888-795-9488	203-221-9240
Shopping Ch, The				
Credit Card Dept				
59 Ambassador Dr	Mississauga ON	L5T2P9	888-202-0888	905-362-2020
TCT Ministries Inc				
11717 N Rt 37 PO Box 1010	Marion IL	62959	800-232-9855	618-997-4700
Telelatino Network Inc (TLN)				
5125 Steeles Ave W	Toronto ON	M9L1R5	800-551-8401	416-744-8200
TFC USA				
150 Shoreline Dr	Redwood City CA	94065	800-345-2465	650-508-6000
Trinity Broadcasting Network (TBN)				
PO Box A	Santa Ana CA	92711	888-731-1000	714-832-2950

	Toll-Free	Phone
Weather Ch Inc, The		
300 I N Pkwy Po Box 724554 .... Atlanta GA 30339	866-843-0392	770-226-0000
Worship Network		
PO Box 428 .... Safety Harbor FL 34695	800-728-8723	

735 TELEVISION STATIONS

SEE ALSO Internet Broadcasting

		Toll-Free	Phone
CKVR-TV Ch 3 (Ind)			
299 Queen St W .... Toronto ON	M5V2Z5	866-690-6179	416-384-5000
Global TV 121 Bloor St E .... Toronto ON	M4W3M5	877-345-9195	416-967-1174
Iowa Public Television			
6450 Corporate Dr .... Johnston IA	50131	800-532-1290	515-242-3100
KAFT-TV Ch 13 (PBS)			
350 S Donaghey Ave .... Conway AR	72034	800-662-2386	501-682-2386
KARE-TV Ch 11 (NBC)			
8811 State Hwy 55 .... Golden Valley MN	55427	888-966-4532	763-546-1111
KBHE-TV Ch 9 (PBS)			
555 N Dakota St PO Box 5000 .... Vermillion SD	57069	800-333-0789	
KBYU-TV Ch 11 (PBS)			
2000 Ironton Blvd			
Brigham Young University .... Provo UT	84606	800-298-5298	801-422-8450
KCWY-TV Ch 13 (NBC)			
141 Progress Cir PO Box 1450 .... Mills WY	82644	800-955-5739	307-577-0013
KESQ-TV Ch 3 (ABC)			
42650 Melanie Pl .... Palm Desert CA	92211	888-776-8538	760-568-6830
KETG-TV Ch 9 (PBS)			
350 S Donaghey Ave .... Conway AR	72034	800-662-2386	501-682-2386
KETS-TV Ch 2 (PBS)			
350 S Donaghey Ave .... Conway AR	72034	800-662-2386	501-682-2386
KFBB-TV			
3200 Old Havre Hwy PO Box 1139 .... Black Eagle MT	59414	800-854-7720	406-453-4377
KIMT-TV Ch 3 (CBS)			
112 N Pennsylvania Ave .... Mason City IA	50401	800-323-4883	641-423-2540
KMAX-TV Ch 31 (CBS)			
2713 Kovr Dr .... West Sacramento CA	95605	800-374-8813	916-374-1313
KMIZ-TV Ch 17 (ABC)			
501 Business Loop 70 E .... Columbia MO	65201	800-345-4109	573-449-0917
KMOS-TV Ch 6 (PBS)			
University of Central Missouri .... Warrensburg MO	64093	800-753-3436	
KOMU-TV Ch 8 (NBC)			
5550 Hwy 63 S .... Columbia MO	65201	800-286-3932	573-884-6397
KPDX-TV Ch 49 (PBS)			
14975 NW Greenbrier Pkwy .... Beaverton OR	97006	866-906-1249	503-906-1249
KPLO-TV Ch 6 (CBS)			
501 S Phillips Ave .... Sioux Falls SD	57104	800-888-5356	605-336-1100
KPTV-TV Ch 12 (Fox)			
14975 NW Greenbrier Pkwy .... Beaverton OR	97006	866-906-1249	503-906-1249
KPXE-TV Ch 50 (I)			
4220 Shawnee Mission Pkwy Ste 110 B .... Fairway KS	66205	800-646-7296	913-722-0798
KSMQ-TV Ch 15 (PBS)			
2000 Eigth Ave NW .... Austin MN	55912	800-658-2539	507-433-0678
KSPX-TV Ch 29 (I)			
3352 Mather Field Rd .... Rancho Cordova CA	95670	800-987-9936	916-368-2929
KSTW-TV Ch 11 (CW)			
1000 Dexter Ave N Ste 205 .... Seattle WA	98109	866-313-5789	206-441-1111
KTBN-TV Ch 40 (TBN)			
2442 Michelle Dr .... Tustin CA	92780	888-731-1000	714-832-2950
KTSD-TV Ch 10 (PBS)			
555 N Dakota St PO Box 5000 .... Vermillion SD	57069	800-333-0789	
KTSF-TV Ch 26 (Ind)			
100 Valley Dr .... Brisbane CA	94005	800-772-1213	415-468-2626
KUSD-TV Ch 2 (PBS)			
555 N Dakota St PO Box 5000 .... Vermillion SD	57069	800-333-0789	
KUSM-TV Ch 9 (PBS)			
Visual Communications Bldg Rm 183 .... Bozeman MT	59717	800-426-8243	406-994-3437
KWPX-TV Ch 33 (I)			
8112-C 304th Ave SE PO Box 426 .... Preston WA	98050	888-467-2988	425-222-6010
KWWL-TV Ch 7 (NBC)			
500 E Fourth St .... Waterloo IA	50703	800-947-7746	319-291-1200
Liberman Broadcasting, INC			
1845 Empire Ave .... Burbank CA	91504	866-576-5353	818-729-5300
UNC-TV Ch 4 (PBS)			
10 TW Alexander Dr			
PO Box 14900 .... Research Triangle Park NC	27709	800-906-5050	919-549-7000
WBNX-TV Ch 55 (CW)			
2690 State Rd .... Cuyahoga Falls OH	44223	800-282-0515	330-922-5500
WBRE-TV Ch 28 (NBC)			
62 S Franklin St .... Wilkes-Barre PA	18701	800-367-9222	570-823-2828
WCAX-TV Ch 3 (CBS)			
30 Joy Dr .... South Burlington VT	05403	855-669-9657	802-658-6300
WCBB-TV Ch 10 (PBS)			
1450 Lisbon St .... Lewiston ME	04240	800-884-1717	207-783-9101
WCIA-TV Ch 3 (CBS)			
PO Box 20 .... Champaign IL	61824	800-676-3382	217-356-8333
WDAM-TV Ch 7 (NBC)			
PO Box 16269 .... Hattiesburg MS	39404	800-844-9326	601-544-4730
WDSC-TV			
1200 W International Speedway Blvd			
.... Daytona Beach FL	32114	866-273-5825	386-506-4415
WEAO-TV Ch 49 (PBS)			
1750 Campus Ctr Dr .... Kent OH	44240	800-544-4549	330-677-4549
WEAR-TV Ch 3 (ABC)			
4990 Mobile Hwy .... Pensacola FL	32506	877-903-7867	850-456-3333
WEHT-TV Ch 25 (ABC)			
800 Marywood Dr .... Henderson KY	42420	800-879-8542	270-826-6281
WFFF-TV Ch 44 (Fox)			
298 Mountain View Dr .... Colchester VT	05446	888-344-7233	802-660-9333
WGBH-TV Ch 2 (PBS)			
1 Guest St .... Brighton MA	02135	800-492-1111	617-300-2000
WGGS-TV Ch 16 (Ind)			
3409 Rutherford Rd Ext .... Taylors SC	29687	800-849-3683*	864-244-1616
*General			
WGHP-TV Ch 8 (Fox)			
2005 Francis St .... High Point NC	27263	800-808-6397	336-841-8888

		Toll-Free	Phone
WHLT-TV Ch 22 (CBS)			
5912 Hwy 49 Cloverleaf Mall Ste A .... Hattiesburg MS	39401	866-328-1987	601-545-2077
WKMJ-TV Ch 68 (PBS)			
600 Cooper Dr .... Lexington KY	40502	800-432-0951	859-258-7000
WKNO-TV Ch 10 (PBS)			
7151 Cherry Farms Rd .... Cordova TN	38016	877-717-7822	901-729-8765
WKPC-TV Ch 15 (PBS)			
600 Cooper Dr .... Lexington KY	40502	800-432-0951	859-258-7000
WKPT-TV Ch 19 (ABC)			
222 Commerce St .... Kingsport TN	37660	877-768-5048	423-246-9578
WMTW-TV Ch 8 (ABC)			
99 Danville Corner Rd .... Auburn ME	04210	800-248-6397	207-782-1800
WMYD-TV Ch 20 (MNT)			
2777 Franklin Rd Ste 1220 .... Southfield MI	48034	800-825-0770	248-355-2020
WNEM-TV Ch 5 (CBS)			
107 N Franklin St .... Saginaw MI	48607	800-522-9636	989-755-8191
WNEP-TV Ch 16 (ABC)			
16 Montage Mtn Rd .... Moosic PA	18507	800-982-4374	570-346-7474
WOI-TV Ch 5 (ABC)			
3903 Westown Pkwy .... West Des Moines IA	50266	800-858-5555	515-457-9645
WOWK-TV Ch 13 (CBS)			
555 Fifth Ave .... Huntington WV	25701	800-333-7636	304-525-1313
WPMT-TV Ch 43 (Fox)			
2005 S Queen St .... York PA	17403	866-976-8747	717-843-0043
WPXD-TV Ch 31 (I)			
3975 Varsity Dr .... Ann Arbor MI	48108	888-467-2988	734-973-7900
WSBT-TV Ch 22 (CBS)			
1301 E Douglas Rd .... Mishawaka IN	46545	877-634-7181	574-232-6397
WSET-TV Ch 13 (ABC)			
2320 Langhorne Rd .... Lynchburg VA	24501	800-639-7847	434-528-1313
WTIU-TV Ch 30 (PBS)			
1229 E Seventh St .... Bloomington IN	47405	800-662-3311	812-855-5900
WVIT-TV Ch 30 (NBC)			
1422 New Britain Ave .... West Hartford CT	06110	800-523-9848	860-521-3030
WWMT-TV Ch 3 (CBS)			
590 W Maple St .... Kalamazoo MI	49008	800-875-3333	
WXYZ-TV Ch 7 (ABC)			
20777 W 10-Mile Rd .... Southfield MI	48037	800-825-0770	248-827-7777
WYOU-TV Ch 22 (CBS)			
62 S Franklin St .... Wilkes-Barre PA	18701	855-241-5144	570-961-2222

735-1 Albany, NY

		Toll-Free	Phone
WNYT-TV Ch 13 (NBC)			
715 N Pearl St .... Albany NY	12204	800-999-9698	518-436-4791
WTEN-TV Ch 10 (ABC)			
341 Northern Blvd .... Albany NY	12204	800-888-9836	518-436-4822

735-2 Albuquerque/Santa Fe, NM

		Toll-Free	Phone
KNME-TV Ch 5 (PBS)			
1130 University Blvd NE			
University of New Mexico .... Albuquerque NM	87102	800-328-5663	505-277-2121
KOAT-TV Ch 7 (ABC)			
3801 Carlisle Blvd NE .... Albuquerque NM	87107	877-871-0165	505-884-7777
KRQE-TV Ch 13 (CBS)			
13 Broadcast Plz SW .... Albuquerque NM	87104	800-283-4227	505-243-2285

735-3 Anchorage, AK

		Toll-Free	Phone
KTBY-TV Ch 4 (Fox)			
2700 E Tudor Rd .... Anchorage AK	99507	877-304-1313	907-561-1313
KYUR-TV Ch 13 (ABC)			
2700 E Tudor Rd .... Anchorage AK	99507	877-304-1313	907-561-1313

735-4 Asheville, NC/Greenville, SC/Spartanburg, SC

		Toll-Free	Phone
WLOS-TV Ch 13 (ABC)			
110 Technology Dr .... Asheville NC	28803	800-209-2293	828-684-1340
WMYA-TV Ch 40 (MNT)			
33 Villa Rd .... Greenville SC	29615	800-288-2413	828-684-1340
WSPA-TV Ch 7 (CBS)			
250 International Dr .... Spartanburg SC	29303	800-207-6397	864-576-7777
WYFF-TV Ch 4 (NBC)			
505 Rutherford St .... Greenville SC	29609	800-453-9933	864-242-4404

735-5 Augusta, GA

		Toll-Free	Phone
WRDW-TV Ch 12 (CBS)			
PO Box 1212 .... Augusta GA	30903	866-591-2502	803-278-1212

735-6 Austin, TX

		Toll-Free	Phone
KEYE-TV Ch 42 (CBS)			
10700 Metric Blvd .... Austin TX	78758	800-621-3362	512-835-0042

735-7 Baltimore, MD

		Toll-Free	Phone
WBAL-TV Ch 11 (NBC)			
3800 Hooper Ave .... Baltimore MD	21211	800-622-4121	410-467-3000

735-8 Bangor, ME

		Toll-Free	Phone
WLBZ-TV Ch 2 (NBC)			
329 Mt Hope Ave	Bangor ME 04401	**800-244-6306**	207-942-4821
WVII-TV Ch 7 (ABC)			
371 Target Industrial Cir	Bangor ME 04401	**888-820-8458***	207-945-6457
*General			

735-9 Baton Rouge, LA

		Toll-Free	Phone
KLPB-TV Ch 24 (PBS)			
7733 Perkins Rd	Baton Rouge LA 70810	**800-272-8161**	225-767-5660
WAFB-TV Ch 9 (CBS)			
844 Government St	Baton Rouge LA 70802	**888-677-2900**	225-215-4700
WLPB-TV Ch 27 (PBS)			
7733 Perkins Rd	Baton Rouge LA 70810	**800-272-8161**	225-767-5660

735-10 Billings, MT

		Toll-Free	Phone
KTVQ-TV Ch 2 (CBS)			
3203 Third Ave N	Billings MT 59101	**800-908-4490**	406-252-5611

735-11 Birmingham, AL

		Toll-Free	Phone
WBIQ-TV Ch 10 (PBS)			
2112 11th Ave S Ste 400	Birmingham AL 35205	**800-239-5233**	205-328-8756
WCFT-TV Ch 33 (ABC)			
800 Concourse Pkwy Ste 200	Birmingham AL 35244	**800-819-0121**	205-403-3340
WEIQ-TV Ch 42 (PBS)			
2112 11th Ave S Ste 400	Birmingham AL 35205	**800-239-5233**	205-328-8756
WHIQ-TV Ch 24 (PBS)			
2112 11th Ave S Ste 400	Birmingham AL 35205	**800-239-5233**	205-328-8756
WVTM-TV Ch 13 (NBC)			
1732 Valley View Dr	Birmingham AL 35209	**844-248-7698**	205-933-1313

735-12 Boise, ID

		Toll-Free	Phone
KTVB-TV Ch 7 (NBC)			
5407 Fairview	Boise ID 83706	**800-537-8939**	208-375-7277

735-13 Buffalo, NY

		Toll-Free	Phone
WIVB-TV Ch 4 (CBS)			
2077 Elmwood Ave	Buffalo NY 14207	**800-794-3687**	716-874-4410
WKBW-TV Ch 7 (ABC)			
7 Broadcast Plaza	Buffalo NY 14202	**888-373-7888**	716-845-6100

735-14 Cedar Rapids, IA

		Toll-Free	Phone
KCRG-TV Ch 9 (ABC)			
501 Second Ave SE	Cedar Rapids IA 52401	**800-332-5443**	319-398-8422
KFXA-TV Ch 28 (Fox)			
600 Old Marion Rd NE	Cedar Rapids IA 52402	**800-222-5426**	
KGAN-TV Ch 2 (CBS)			
600 Old Marion Rd NE	Cedar Rapids IA 52402	**800-642-6140**	319-395-9060

735-15 Charleston, WV

		Toll-Free	Phone
WCHS-TV Ch 8 (ABC)			
1301 Piedmont Rd	Charleston WV 25301	**888-696-9247**	304-346-5358

735-16 Charlotte, NC

		Toll-Free	Phone
WAXN-TV Ch 64 (ABC)			
1901 N Tryon St	Charlotte NC 28206	**888-664-6835**	704-335-4786
WJZY-TV Ch 46 (CW)			
3501 Performance Rd	Charlotte NC 28214	**888-369-4762**	704-398-0046
WSOC-TV Ch 9 (ABC)			
1901 N Tryon St	Charlotte NC 28206	**800-247-6299**	704-338-9999

735-17 Chicago, IL

		Toll-Free	Phone
WCPX-TV Ch 38 (I)			
333 S Desplaines St Ste 101	Chicago IL 60661	**800-531-5000**	312-376-8520

735-18 Cincinnati, OH

		Toll-Free	Phone
WKRC-TV Ch 12 (CBS)			
1906 Highland Ave	Cincinnati OH 45219	**877-889-5610**	513-763-5500

735-19 Cleveland/Akron, OH

		Toll-Free	Phone
WDLI-TV Ch 17 (TBN)			
PO Box A	Santa Ana CA 92711	**888-731-1000**	714-832-2950
WKYC-TV Ch 3 (NBC)			
1333 Lakeside Ave E	Cleveland OH 44114	**877-790-7370**	216-344-3333
WOIO-TV Ch 19 (CBS)			
1717 E 12th St	Cleveland OH 44114	**877-929-1943**	216-771-1943

735-20 Columbia, SC

		Toll-Free	Phone
WRLK-TV Ch 35 (PBS)			
1101 George Rogers Blvd	Columbia SC 29201	**800-922-5437**	803-737-3200

735-21 Corpus Christi, TX

		Toll-Free	Phone
KEDT-TV Ch 16 (PBS)			
4455 S Padre Island Dr Ste 38	Corpus Christi TX 78411	**800-307-5338**	361-855-2213
KIII-TV Ch 3 (ABC)			
5002 S Padre Island Dr	Corpus Christi TX 78411	**800-882-9539**	361-986-8300

735-22 Dallas/Fort Worth, TX

		Toll-Free	Phone
KXTX-TV Ch 39 (Tele)			
4805 Amon Carter Blvd	Fort Worth TX 76155	**877-266-8365**	

735-23 Dayton, OH

		Toll-Free	Phone
WPTD-TV Ch 16 (PBS)			
110 S Jefferson St	Dayton OH 45402	**800-247-1614**	937-220-1600

735-24 Denver, CO

		Toll-Free	Phone
KDVR-TV Ch 31 (Fox)			
100 E Speer Blvd	Denver CO 80203	**888-397-3742**	303-595-3131
KRMA-TV Ch 6 (PBS)			
1089 Bannock St	Denver CO 80204	**800-274-6666**	303-892-6666

735-25 Des Moines, IA

		Toll-Free	Phone
WHO-TV Ch 13 (NBC)			
1801 Grand Ave	Des Moines IA 50309	**800-777-8398**	515-242-3500

735-26 Duluth, MN

		Toll-Free	Phone
WDIO-TV Ch 10 (ABC)			
10 Observation Rd	Duluth MN 55811	**800-477-1013**	218-727-6864
WDSE-TV Ch 8 (PBS)			
632 Niagara Ct	Duluth MN 55811	**888-563-9373**	218-788-2831

735-27 El Paso, TX

		Toll-Free	Phone
KVIA-TV Ch 7 (ABC)			
4140 Rio Bravo St	El Paso TX 79902	**800-433-7300**	915-496-7777

735-28 Erie, PA

		Toll-Free	Phone
WQLN-TV Ch 54 (PBS)			
8425 Peach St	Erie PA 16509	**800-727-8854**	814-864-3001
WSEE-TV Ch 35 (CBS)			
3514 State St	Erie PA 16508	**888-346-8982**	814-454-5201

735-29 Evansville, IN

		Toll-Free	Phone
WFIE-TV Ch 14 (NBC)			
1115 Mt Auburn Rd	Evansville IN 47720	**800-832-0014**	812-426-1414
WNIN-TV Ch 9 (PBS)			
405 Carpenter St	Evansville IN 47708	**855-888-9646**	812-423-2973

735-30 Fairbanks, AK

		Toll-Free	Phone
KTVF-TV Ch 11 (NBC)			
3650 Braddock St	Fairbanks AK 99701	**855-255-5975**	907-458-1800
KUAC-TV Ch 9 (PBS)			
University of Alaska PO Box 755620	Fairbanks AK 99775	**800-727-6543**	907-474-7491

735-31 Fargo/Grand Forks, ND

	Toll-Free	Phone
KBME-TV Ch 3 (PBS) 207 N Fifth St .... Fargo ND 58102	800-359-6900	701-241-6900
KFME-TV Ch 13 (PBS) 207 N Fifth St .... Fargo ND 58102	800-359-6900	701-241-6900
KGFE-TV Ch 2 (PBS) 207 N Fifth St .... Fargo ND 58102	800-359-6900	701-241-6900
KVLY-TV Ch 11 (NBC) 1350 21st Ave S .... Fargo ND 58103	800-450-5844	701-237-5211
KXJB-TV Ch 4 (CBS) 1350 21st Ave S .... Fargo ND 58103	877-571-0774	701-237-5211
WDAZ-TV Ch 8 (ABC) 2220 S Washington St .... Grand Forks ND 58201	877-382-4357	701-775-2511

735-32 Fort Smith, AR

	Toll-Free	Phone
KHBS-TV Ch 40 (ABC) 2415 N Albert Pike .... Fort Smith AR 72904 *General	855-253-7122*	479-783-4040

735-33 Fort Wayne, IN

	Toll-Free	Phone
WFWA-TV Ch 39 (PBS) 2501 E Coliseum Blvd .... Fort Wayne IN 46805	888-484-8839	260-484-8839

735-34 Fresno, CA

	Toll-Free	Phone
KFTV-TV Ch 21 (Uni) 601 W Univision Plaza .... Fresno CA 93650	866-783-2645	212-455-5200
KMPH-TV Ch 26 (Fox) 5111 E McKinley Ave .... Fresno CA 93727	800-101-2045	559-453-8850

735-35 Grand Rapids, MI

	Toll-Free	Phone
WGVU-TV Ch 35 (PBS) 301 W Fulton St .... Grand Rapids MI 49504	800-442-2771	616-331-6666
WZPX-TV Ch 43 (I) 2610 Horizon Dr SE Ste E .... Grand Rapids MI 49546	800-987-9936	616-222-4343

735-36 Green Bay, WI

	Toll-Free	Phone
WBAY-TV Ch 2 (ABC) 115 S Jefferson St .... Green Bay WI 54301	800-261-9229	920-432-3331
WLUK-TV Ch 11 (Fox) 787 Lombardi Ave .... Green Bay WI 54304	800-242-8067	920-494-8711

735-37 Honolulu, HI

	Toll-Free	Phone
KHON-TV Ch 2 (Fox) 88 Piikoi St .... Honolulu HI 96814	877-926-8300	808-591-4278
KPXO-TV Ch 66 (I) 875 Waimanu St Ste 630 .... Honolulu HI 96813	800-987-9936	808-591-1275
KWHE-TV Ch 14 (Ind) 1188 Bishop St Ste 502 .... Honolulu HI 96813	800-218-1414	808-538-1414

735-38 Huntsville, AL

	Toll-Free	Phone
WAAY-TV Ch 31 (ABC) 1000 Monte Sano Blvd SE .... Huntsville AL 35801	888-407-4747	256-533-3131
WHNT-TV Ch 19 (CBS) PO Box 19 .... Huntsville AL 35804	800-533-8819	256-533-1919

735-39 Indianapolis, IN

	Toll-Free	Phone
WRTV-TV Ch 6 (ABC) 1330 N Meridian St .... Indianapolis IN 46202	877-667-4265	317-635-9788

735-40 Johnson City, TN

	Toll-Free	Phone
WJHL-TV Ch 11 (CBS) 338 E Main St .... Johnson City TN 37601	800-861-5255	423-926-2151

735-41 Juneau, AK

	Toll-Free	Phone
KJUD-TV Ch 8 (ABC) 2700 E Tudor Rd .... Anchorage AK 99507	877-304-1313	907-561-1313

735-42 Kansas City, KS & MO

	Toll-Free	Phone
KSHB-TV Ch 41 (NBC) 4720 Oak St .... Kansas City MO 64112	800-222-1222	816-753-4141

735-43 Lansing, MI

	Toll-Free	Phone
WILX-TV Ch 10 (NBC) 500 American Rd .... Lansing MI 48911	866-653-4261	517-393-0110

735-44 Las Vegas, NV

	Toll-Free	Phone
KTNV-TV Ch 13 (ABC) 3355 S Valley View Blvd .... Las Vegas NV 89102	800-877-1620	702-876-1313

735-45 Lincoln, NE

	Toll-Free	Phone
KOLN-TV Ch 10 (CBS) 840 N 40th .... Lincoln NE 68503	800-475-1011	402-467-4321
NET Radio 1800 N 33rd St .... Lincoln NE 68503	800-868-1868	

735-46 Little Rock, AR

	Toll-Free	Phone
KTHV-TV Ch 11 (CBS) 720 S Izard St .... Little Rock AR 72201	800-621-3362	501-376-1111

735-47 Louisville, KY

	Toll-Free	Phone
WAVE-TV Ch 3 (NBC) 725 S Floyd St PO Box 32970 .... Louisville KY 40203	800-223-2579	502-585-2201

735-48 Los Angeles, CA

	Toll-Free	Phone
KJLA-TV Ch 57 (Ind) 2323 Corinth Ave .... Los Angeles CA 90064	800-588-5788	310-943-5288

735-49 Madison, WI

	Toll-Free	Phone
NBC15 615 Forward Dr .... Madison WI 53711	800-894-4222	608-274-1515

735-50 Miami/Fort Lauderdale, FL

	Toll-Free	Phone
WPBT-TV Ch 2 (PBS) 14901 NE 20th Ave .... Miami FL 33181	800-222-9728	305-949-8321

735-51 Milwaukee, WI

	Toll-Free	Phone
WVCY-TV Ch 30 (Ind) 3434 W Kilbourn Ave .... Milwaukee WI 53208	800-729-9829	414-935-3000

735-52 Montgomery, AL

	Toll-Free	Phone
WAIQ-TV Ch 26 (PBS) 1255 Madison Ave .... Montgomery AL 36107	800-239-5239	205-328-8756
WAKA-TV Ch 8 (CBS) 3020 Eastern Blvd .... Montgomery AL 36116	800-467-0401	334-271-8888
WNCF-TV Ch 32 (ABC) 3251 Harrison Rd .... Montgomery AL 36109	800-467-0424	334-270-2834

735-53 Naples/Fort Myers, FL

	Toll-Free	Phone
WGCU-TV Ch 30 (PBS) 10501 FGCU Blvd .... Fort Myers FL 33965 *General	888-824-0030*	239-590-2300
WZVN-TV Ch 26 (ABC) 3719 Central Ave .... Fort Myers FL 33901	888-232-8635	239-939-2020

735-54 Nashville, TN

	Toll-Free	Phone
WKRN-TV Ch 2 (ABC) 441 Murfreesboro Rd .... Nashville TN 37210	800-222-5555	615-369-7222

735-55 New Orleans, LA

	Toll-Free	Phone
WDSU-TV Ch 6 (NBC) 846 Howard Ave .... New Orleans LA 70113	888-925-4127	504-679-0600

735-56 New York, NY

	Toll-Free	Phone
WPXN-TV Ch 31 (I) 810 Seventh Ave 30th Fl .... New York NY 10019	800-987-9936	212-603-8419

735-57 Norfolk/Virginia Beach, VA

	Toll-Free	Phone
WTKR-TV Ch 3 (CBS) 720 Boush St .... Norfolk VA 23510	866-347-2423	757-446-1000

735-58 Oklahoma City, OK

	Toll-Free	Phone
KWTV-TV Ch 9 (CBS) 7401 N Kelley Ave .... Oklahoma City OK 73111	888-550-5988	405-843-6641

735-59 Omaha, NE

	Toll-Free	Phone
KETV-TV Ch 7 (ABC) 2665 Douglas St .... Omaha NE 68131	800-279-5388	402-345-7777
KMTV Action 3 News 10714 Mockingbird Dr .... Omaha NE 68127	800-800-6619	402-592-3333
WOWT-TV Ch 6 (NBC) 3501 Farnam St .... Omaha NE 68131	866-434-8587	402-346-6666

735-60 Orlando, FL

	Toll-Free	Phone
WKMG-TV Ch 6 (CBS) 4466 N John Young Pkwy .... Orlando FL 32804	800-435-7352	407-521-1200

735-61 Peoria, IL

	Toll-Free	Phone
WTVP-TV Ch 47 (PBS) 101 State St .... Peoria IL 61602	800-837-4747	309-677-4747

735-62 Phoenix, AZ

	Toll-Free	Phone
KNXV-TV Ch 15 (ABC) 515 N 44th St .... Phoenix AZ 85008	800-222-4357	602-273-1500
KSAZ-TV Ch 10 (Fox) 511 W Adams St .... Phoenix AZ 85003	888-369-4762	602-257-1234

735-63 Pittsburgh, PA

	Toll-Free	Phone
WPXI-TV Ch 11 (NBC) 4145 Evergreen Rd .... Pittsburgh PA 15214	866-347-4434	412-237-1100
WQED-TV Ch 13 (PBS) 4802 Fifth Ave .... Pittsburgh PA 15213	800-876-1316	412-622-1370

735-64 Pocatello, ID

	Toll-Free	Phone
KISU-TV Ch 10 (PBS) Idaho State University CB 8111 921 S Eighth Ave .... Pocatello ID 83209	800-543-6868	208-282-2857
KPVI-TV Ch 6 (NBC) 902 E Sherman St .... Pocatello ID 83201	800-829-3676	208-232-6666

735-65 Portland, ME

	Toll-Free	Phone
WCSH-TV Ch 6 (NBC) One Congress Sq .... Portland ME 04101	800-464-1213	207-828-6666

735-66 Portland, OR

	Toll-Free	Phone
KGW-TV Ch 8 (NBC) 1501 SW Jefferson St .... Portland OR 97201	800-669-9777	503-226-5000

735-67 Providence, RI

	Toll-Free	Phone
WSBE-TV Ch 36 (PBS) 50 Pk Ln .... Providence RI 02907	866-438-0220	401-222-3636

735-68 Raleigh/Durham, NC

	Toll-Free	Phone
WRAL-TV Ch 5 (CBS) 2619 Western Blvd .... Raleigh NC 27606	800-245-9725	919-821-8555
WRAZ-TV Ch 50 (Fox) 512 S Mangum St .... Durham NC 27701	877-369-5050	919-595-5050
WTVD-TV Ch 11 (ABC) 411 Liberty St .... Durham NC 27701	855-324-8477	919-683-1111

735-69 Rapid City, SD

	Toll-Free	Phone
KOTA-TV Ch 3 (ABC) 518 St Joseph St .... Rapid City SD 57701	866-558-4554	605-342-2000

735-70 Richmond, VA

	Toll-Free	Phone
WCVE-TV Ch 23 (PBS) 23 Sesame St .... Richmond VA 23235	800-476-8440	804-320-1301

735-71 Roanoke, VA

	Toll-Free	Phone
WSLS-TV Ch 10 (NBC) PO Box 10 .... Roanoke VA 24022	800-800-9757	540-981-9110

735-72 Rochester, MN

	Toll-Free	Phone
KTTC-TV Ch 10 (NBC) 6301 Bandel Rd NW .... Rochester MN 55901	800-288-1656	507-288-4444
KXLT-TV Ch 47 (Fox) 6301 Bandel Rd NW .... Rochester MN 55901	800-452-4368	507-252-4747

735-73 Sacramento, CA

	Toll-Free	Phone
KVIE-TV Ch 6 (PBS) 2030 W El Camino Ave .... Sacramento CA 95833	800-347-5843	916-929-5843
News10 400 Broadway .... Sacramento CA 95818	866-397-9884	916-441-2345

735-74 Saint Louis, MO

	Toll-Free	Phone
KETC-TV Ch 9 (PBS) 3655 Olive St .... Saint Louis MO 63108	855-482-5382	314-512-9000

735-75 Salt Lake City, UT

	Toll-Free	Phone
KSL-TV Ch 5 (NBC) PO Box 1160 .... Salt Lake City UT 84110	800-862-9098	801-575-5555
KUED-TV Ch 7 (PBS) 101 Wasatch Dr Rm 215 .... Salt Lake City UT 84112	800-477-5833	801-581-7777
KUPX-TV Ch 16 (I) 466C Lawndale Dr .... Salt Lake City UT 84115	888-467-2988	801-474-0016
KUTV-TV Ch 2 (CBS) 299 S Main St Ste 150 .... Salt Lake City UT 84111	866-438-0220	801-839-1234

735-76 San Antonio, TX

	Toll-Free	Phone
KABB-TV Ch 29 (Fox) 4335 NW Loop 410 .... San Antonio TX 78229	800-987-6038	210-366-1129
KLRN-TV Ch 9 (PBS) 501 Broadway St .... San Antonio TX 78215	800-627-8193	210-270-9000
KMYS-TV Ch 35 (MNT) 4335 NW Loop 410 .... San Antonio TX 78229	800-987-6038	210-366-1129

735-77 San Diego, CA

	Toll-Free	Phone
KPBS-TV Ch 15 (PBS) 5200 Campanile Dr .... San Diego CA 92182	888-399-5727	619-594-1515
XETV-TV Ch 6 (CW) 8253 Ronson Rd .... San Diego CA 92111	866-700-6397	858-279-6666

735-78 San Francisco, CA

	Toll-Free	Phone
KQED-TV Ch 9 (PBS) 2601 Mariposa St .... San Francisco CA 94110	866-573-3123	415-864-2000

735-79 Seattle/Tacoma, WA

	Toll-Free	Phone
KBTC-TV Ch 28 (PBS) 2320 S 19th St .... Tacoma WA 98405	888-596-5282	253-680-7700

	Toll-Free	Phone
KCTS-TV Ch 9 (PBS)		
401 Mercer St .... Seattle WA 98109	800-443-9991	206-728-6463
KING 5 Television		
333 Dexter Ave N .... Seattle WA 98109	800-456-3975	206-448-5555

735-80 Shreveport, LA

	Toll-Free	Phone
KTAL-TV Ch 6 (NBC)		
3150 N Market St .... Shreveport LA 71107	800-259-4929	318-629-6000
KTBS-TV Ch 3 (ABC)		
312 E Kings Hwy .... Shreveport LA 71104	866-543-3296	318-861-5800

735-81 Sioux Falls, SD

	Toll-Free	Phone
KDLT-TV Ch 46 (NBC)		
3600 S Westport Ave .... Sioux Falls SD 57106	800-727-5358	605-361-5555
KELO-TV Ch 11 (CBS)		
501 S Phillips Ave .... Sioux Falls SD 57104	800-888-5356	605-336-1100
KTTW-TV Ch 7 (Fox)		
2817 W 11th St .... Sioux Falls SD 57104	800-369-4762	605-338-0017

735-82 South Bend, IN

	Toll-Free	Phone
WNIT-TV Ch 34.1 (PBS)		
300 W Jefferson Blvd PO Box 7034 ...... South Bend IN 46601	877-411-3662	574-675-9648
WSJV-TV Ch 28 (Fox)		
PO Box 28 .... South Bend IN 46624	800-435-3803	574-679-9758

735-83 Spokane, WA

	Toll-Free	Phone
KREM-TV Ch 2 (CBS)		
4103 S Regal St .... Spokane WA 99223	888-404-3922	509-448-2000
KSKN-TV Ch 22 (CW)		
4103 S Regal St .... Spokane WA 99223	888-404-3922	509-448-2000
KSPS Public TV		
3911 S Regal St .... Spokane WA 99223	800-735-2377	509-443-7800

735-84 Springfield, IL

	Toll-Free	Phone
WICS-TV Ch 20 (ABC)		
2680 E Cook St .... Springfield IL 62703	800-263-9720	217-753-5620

735-85 Springfield, MA

	Toll-Free	Phone
WESTERN MASS NEWS		
1300 Liberty St .... Springfield MA 01104	877-872-2756	413-733-4040

735-86 Springfield, MO

	Toll-Free	Phone
KOZK-TV Ch 21 (PBS)		
901 S National Ave .... Springfield MO 65897	866-684-5695	417-836-3500
KSPR-TV Ch 33 (ABC)		
1359 St Louis St .... Springfield MO 65802	888-435-1464	417-831-1333
KYTV-TV Ch 3 (NBC)		
PO Box 3500 .... Springfield MO 65808	888-435-1464	417-268-3000

735-87 Syracuse, NY

	Toll-Free	Phone
WCNY-TV Ch 24 (PBS)		
506 Old Liverpool Rd PO Box 2400 ...... Syracuse NY 13220	800-638-5163	315-453-2424

735-88 Tallahassee, FL

	Toll-Free	Phone
WCTV-TV Ch 6 (CBS)		
1801 Halstead Blvd .... Tallahassee FL 32309	888-297-9461	850-893-6666
WFSU-TV Ch 11 (PBS)		
1600 Red Barber Plz .... Tallahassee FL 32310	800-322-9378	850-487-3170

735-89 Tampa/Saint Petersburg, FL

	Toll-Free	Phone
WFLA-TV Ch 8 (NBC)		
PO Box 1410 .... Tampa FL 33601	800-338-0808	813-228-8888
WFTS-TV Ch 28 (ABC)		
4045 N Himes Ave .... Tampa FL 33607	877-833-2828	813-354-2828
WTSP-TV Ch 10 (CBS)		
11450 Gandy Blvd N .... Saint Petersburg FL 33702	877-762-7824	727-577-1010
WUSF-TV Ch 16 (PBS)		
4202 E Fowler Ave .... Tampa FL 33620	800-654-3703	813-974-4000

735-90 Topeka, KS

	Toll-Free	Phone
KSNT-TV Ch 27 (NBC)		
6835 NW Hwy 24 .... Topeka KS 66618	800-222-8477	785-582-4000

	Toll-Free	Phone
KTWU-TV Ch 11 (PBS)		
1700 College .... Topeka KS 66621	800-866-5898	785-670-1111

735-91 Toronto, ON

	Toll-Free	Phone
CICA-TV Ch 19 (Ind)		
2180 Yonge St Stn Q PO Box 200 ...... Toronto ON M4T2T1	800-613-0513	416-484-2600

735-92 Tulsa, OK

	Toll-Free	Phone
KOTV-TV Ch 6 (CBS) PO Box 6 .... Tulsa OK 74101	888-434-8248	918-732-6000

735-93 Washington, DC

	Toll-Free	Phone
WTTG-TV Ch 5 (Fox)		
5151 Wisconsin Ave NW .... Washington DC 20016	866-756-3587	202-244-5151

735-94 West Palm Beach, FL

	Toll-Free	Phone
WXEL-TV Ch 42 (PBS)		
PO Box 6607 .... West Palm Beach FL 33405	800-915-9935	561-737-8000

735-95 Wichita, KS

	Toll-Free	Phone
KPTS-TV Ch 8 (PBS)		
320 W 21 St .... Wichita KS 67203	800-794-8498	316-838-3090
KSNW-TV 833 N Main St .... Wichita KS 67203	800-325-0778	316-265-3333
KWCH-TV Ch 12 (CBS)		
2815 E 37th St N .... Wichita KS 67219	877-257-6921	316-838-1212

735-96 Winnipeg, MB

	Toll-Free	Phone
CTV-TV Ch 5 (CTV)		
345 Graham Ave Ste 400 .... Winnipeg MB R3C5S6	800-461-1542	204-788-3300

735-97 Youngstown, OH

	Toll-Free	Phone
WFMJ-TV Ch 21 (NBC)		
101 W Boardman St .... Youngstown OH 44503	800-488-9365	330-744-8611

736   TELEVISION SYNDICATORS

Television syndicators are companies that produce programming in-house and market and distribute the programs to networks on a national or regional basis.

	Toll-Free	Phone
Associated Press		
1100 13th St NW Ste 700 .... Washington DC 20005	800-824-5498	202-641-9000
Babe Winkelman Productions		
PO Box 407 .... Brainerd MN 56401	800-333-0471	
Guthy-Renker Television Network		
3340 Ocean Pk Blvd .... Santa Monica CA 90405	800-778-1011	310-581-6250
Independent Television Service (ITVS)		
651 Brannan St Ste 410 .... San Francisco CA 94107	800-621-6196	415-356-8383
Information Television Network		
6650 Pk of Commerce Blvd .... Boca Raton FL 33487	800-463-6488	561-997-5433
National Educational Telecommunications Assn (NETA)		
939 S Stadium Rd .... Columbia SC 29201	866-270-5141	803-799-5517

737   TESTING FACILITIES

	Toll-Free	Phone
Accutest Laboratories		
2235 Rt 130 Bldg B .... Dayton NJ 08810	800-329-0204	732-329-0200
ALine Inc		
2206 E Gladwick St .... Rancho Dominguez CA 90220	877-707-8575	
Altran Solutions USA		
2525 Rt 130 S .... Cranbury NJ 08512	855-425-8726	609-409-9790
Analysts Inc		
22750 Hawthorne Blvd Ste 220 .... Torrance CA 90505	800-336-3637	
Astro Pak Corp		
270 E Baker St Ste 100 .... Costa Mesa CA 92626	866-492-7876	
Bio-Research Products Inc		
323 W Cherry St .... North Liberty IA 52317	800-326-3511	319-626-6707
BIOPAC Systems Inc		
42 Aero Camino .... Goleta CA 93117	877-524-6722	805-685-0066
Camin Cargo Control Inc		
230 Marion Ave .... Linden NJ 07036	800-756-8798	908-862-1899
Celsis International		
600 W Chicago Ave Ste 625 .... Chicago IL 60654	800-222-8260	312-476-1282
Construction Testing & Engineering Inc		
1441 Montiel Road Ste 115 .... Escondido CA 92026	800-576-2271	760-746-4955
CTLGroup 5400 Old OrchaRd Rd .... Skokie IL 60077	800-522-2285	847-965-7500
Dayton T Brown Inc		
1175 Church St .... Bohemia NY 11716	800-232-6300	631-589-6300
Embryotech Laboratories Inc		
140 Hale St .... Haverhill MA 01830	800-673-7500	978-373-7300

				Toll-Free	Phone
EnviroLogix Inc					
500 Riverside Industrial Pkwy	Portland	ME	04103	**866-408-4597**	207-797-0300
Environmental Enterprises Inc (EEI)					
10163 Cincinnati Dayton Rd	Cincinnati	OH	45241	**800-722-2818**	513-772-2818
Everist Genomics Inc					
709 W Ellsworth Rd	Ann Arbor	MI	48108	**855-383-7478**	
Center for Devices & Radiological Health (CDRH)					
10903 New Hampshire Ave					
WO66-5429	Silver Spring	MD	20993	**800-638-2041**	301-796-7100
Forensic Fluids Laboratories Inc					
225 Parsons St	Kalamazoo	MI	49007	**866-492-2517**	269-492-7700
Glidewell Laboratories Inc					
4141 MacArthur Blvd	Newport Beach	CA	92660	**800-854-7256**	
HyGreen Inc					
3630 SW 47th Ave Ste 100	Gainesville	FL	32608	**877-574-9473**	
iHealth Lab Inc					
719 N Shoreline Blvd	Mountain View	CA	94043	**855-816-7705**	
Immuno Concepts NA Ltd					
9825 Goethe Rd Ste 350	Sacramento	CA	95827	**800-251-5115**	916-363-2649
JM Test Systems Inc					
7323 Tom Dr	Baton Rouge	LA	70806	**800-353-3411**	225-925-2029
Kett Engineering Corp					
15500 Erwin St Ste 1029	Van Nuys	CA	91411	**877-372-6799**	818-908-5388
Magna Chek Inc					
32701 Edward Ave	Madison Heights	MI	48071	**800-582-8947**	248-597-0089
Mayer Laboratories Inc					
1950 Addison St Ste 101	Berkeley	CA	94704	**800-426-3633**	510-229-5300
Metcut Research Inc					
3980 Rosslyn Dr	Cincinnati	OH	45209	**800-966-2888**	513-271-5100
National Highway Traffic Safety Administration					
Vehicle Research & Test Ctr					
10820 SR 347 PO Box B37	East Liberty	OH	43319	**800-262-8309**	937-666-4511
National Technical Systems Inc					
24007 Ventura Blvd Ste 200	Calabasas	CA	91302	**800-879-9225**	818-591-0776
NASDAQ: NTSC					
Neuisys LLC					
1500 Pinecroft Rd Ste 212	Greensboro	NC	27407	**877-299-9052**	
SGS Canada Inc					
6490 Vipond Dr	Mississauga	ON	L5T1W8	**877-887-4163***	905-364-3757
*General					
Simco Electronics					
1178 Bordeaux Dr	Sunnyvale	CA	94089	**866-299-6029**	408-734-9750
Southern Petroleum Lab Inc					
8850 Interchange Dr	Houston	TX	77054	**877-775-5227**	713-660-0901
Spectrum Analytical Inc					
830 Silver St	Agawam	MA	01001	**800-789-9115**	413-789-9018
Speedie & Assoc Inc					
3331 E Wood St	Phoenix	AZ	85040	**800-628-6221**	602-997-6391
Syagen Technology Inc					
1411 Warner Ave	Tustin	CA	92780	**877-258-8250**	714-258-4400
TestAmerica Laboratories Inc					
4625 E Cotton Ctr Blvd Ste 189	Phoenix	AZ	85040	**866-785-5227**	602-437-3340
Toxikon Corp 15 Wiggins Ave	Bedford	MA	01730	**800-458-4141**	781-275-3330
Transportation Research Ctr Inc (TRC Inc)					
10820 State Rt 347 PO Box B-67	East Liberty	OH	43319	**800-837-7872**	937-666-2011
TriLink BioTechnologies Inc					
9955 Mesa Rim Rd	San Diego	CA	92121	**800-863-6801**	858-546-0004
Twin City Testing					
662 Cromwell Ave	Saint Paul	MN	55114	**888-645-8378**	651-645-3601
UL LLC 10 Water St	Enfield	CT	06082	**800-903-5660**	860-749-8371
Verichem Laboratories Inc					
90 Narragansett Ave	Providence	RI	02907	**800-552-5859**	401-461-0180
VJ Technologies Inc					
89 Carlough Rd	Bohemia	NY	11716	**800-858-9729**	631-589-8800

738　TEXTILE MACHINERY

				Toll-Free	Phone
Bowman Hollis Manufacturing Inc					
2925 Old Steele Creek Rd	Charlotte	NC	28208	**888-269-2358**	704-374-1500
Eastman Machine Co					
779 Washington St	Buffalo	NY	14203	**800-872-5571**	716-856-2200
Gerber Technology Inc					
24 Industrial Pk Rd W	Tolland	CT	06084	**800-826-3243**	860-871-8082
HH Arnold Co Inc					
529 Liberty St	Rockland	MA	02370	**866-868-9603**	781-878-0346
Hix Corp 1201 E 27th Terr	Pittsburg	KS	66762	**800-835-0606**	620-231-8568
Ioline Corp					
14140 NE 200th St	Woodinville	WA	98072	**800-598-0029**	425-398-8282
Lummus Corp					
225 Bourne Blvd PO Box 929	Savannah	GA	31408	**800-458-6687**	912-447-9000
McCoy-Ellison Inc					
1101 Curtis St PO Box 967	Monroe	NC	28111	**800-811-5348**	704-289-5413
Thermopatch Corp					
2204 Erie Blvd E	Syracuse	NY	13224	**800-252-6555**	315-446-8110
TrimMaster					
4860 N Fifth St Hwy	Temple	PA	19560	**800-356-4237**	610-921-0203
Tubular Textile Machinery					
113 Woodside Dr PO Box 2097	Lexington	NC	27292	**800-531-3715**	336-956-6444
Tuftco Corp					
2318 S Holtzclaw Ave	Chattanooga	TN	37408	**800-288-3826**	423-698-8601
Tuftco Finishing Systems Inc					
100 W Industrial Blvd	Dalton	GA	30720	**800-288-3826**	706-277-1110

739　TEXTILE MILLS

739-1 Broadwoven Fabric Mills

				Toll-Free	Phone
American Cotton Growers Textile Div (ACG)					
PO Box 2827 PO Box 430	Lubbock	TX	79408	**800-333-8011**	806-763-8011
Cone Denim LLC					
804 Green Valley Rd Ste 300	Greensboro	NC	27408	**800-763-0123**	336-379-6220

				Toll-Free	Phone
DeRoyal Textiles					
141 E York St PO Box 400	Camden	SC	29020	**800-845-1062**	803-432-2403
Garnet Hill Inc					
231 Main St	Franconia	NH	03580	**800-870-3513**	603-823-5545
Glen Raven Inc					
232 Glen Raven Rd	Glen Raven	NC	27217	**800-675-0032**	336-227-6211
Hamrick Mills Inc					
515 W Buford St PO Box 48	Gaffney	SC	29341	**800-600-4305**	864-489-4731
Henry Glass & Co					
49 W 37th St	New York	NY	10018	**800-294-9495**	917-229-1080
JB Martin Co					
645 Fifth Ave Ste 400	New York	NY	10022	**800-223-0525**	212-421-2020
KM Fabrics Inc 2 Waco St	Greenville	SC	29611	**800-873-7326**	864-295-2550
Kuraray America Inc					
2625 Bay Area Blvd Ste 600	Houston	TX	77058	**800-423-9762**	
Lantal Textiles Inc					
1300 Langenthal Dr PO Box 965	Rural Hall	NC	27045	**800-334-3309**	336-969-9551
Mount Vernon Mills Inc					
503 S Main St PO Box 100	Mauldin	SC	29662	**800-845-8857**	864-688-7100
Precision Fabrics Group Inc					
301 N Elm St Ste 600	Greensboro	NC	27401	**800-284-8001**	336-510-8000
Scalamandre Silks Inc					
350 Wireless Blvd	Hauppauge	NY	11788	**800-932-4361**	631-467-8800
Trelleborg Coated Systems US Inc					
790 Reeves St	Spartanburg	SC	29301	**800-344-0714**	
Vectorply Corp					
3500 Lakewood Dr	Phenix City	AL	36867	**800-577-4521**	334-291-7704
Warm Co 5529 186th Pl SW	Lynnwood	WA	98037	**800-234-9276**	425-248-2424

739-2 Coated Fabric

				Toll-Free	Phone
Adell Plastics Inc					
4530 Annapolis Rd	Baltimore	MD	21227	**800-638-5218**	410-789-7780
Alpha Assoc Inc					
145 Lehigh Ave	Lakewood	NJ	08701	**800-631-5399**	732-634-5700
Archer Rubber Co					
213 Central St	Milford	MA	01757	**800-804-2074**	508-473-1870
Bondcote Corp PO Box 729	Pulaski	VA	24301	**800-368-2160**	540-980-2640
Cooley Group 50 Esten Ave	Pawtucket	RI	02860	**800-992-0072***	401-724-9000
*Cust Svc					
Dazian Inc					
18 Central Blvd	South Hackensack	NJ	07606	**877-232-9426**	
Deccofelt Corp					
555 S Vermont Ave	Glendora	CA	91740	**800-543-3226***	626-963-8511
*Cust Svc					
Der-Tex Corp One Lehner Rd	Saco	ME	04072	**800-669-0364**	
Duracote Corp					
350 N Diamond St	Ravenna	OH	44266	**800-321-2252**	330-296-3487
Herculite Products Inc					
105 E Sinking Springs Ln	Emigsville	PA	17318	**800-772-0036***	717-764-1192
*Cust Svc					
ICG/Holliston					
905 Holliston Mills Rd PO Box 478	Church Hill	TN	37642	**800-251-0451**	423-357-6141
Middlesex Research Mfg Company Inc					
27 Apsley St	Hudson	MA	01749	**800-424-5188**	978-562-3697
Reflexite Corp 120 Darling Dr	Avon	CT	06001	**800-654-7570**	860-676-7100
Seaman Corp					
1000 Venture Blvd	Wooster	OH	44691	**800-927-8578**	330-262-1111
Taconic					
136 Coonbrook Rd PO Box 69	Petersburg	NY	12138	**800-833-1805**	518-658-3202
Twitchell Corp					
4031 Ross Clark Cir	Dothan	AL	36303	**800-633-7550***	334-792-0002
*General					

739-3 Industrial Fabrics

				Toll-Free	Phone
Albany International Corp					
1373 Broadway PO Box 1907	Albany	NY	12204	**888-797-6735**	518-445-2200
NYSE: AIN					
Amatex Corp					
1032 Stambridge St	Norristown	PA	19404	**800-441-9680**	610-277-6100
AMETEK Inc Chemical Products Div					
455 Corporate Blvd	Newark	DE	19702	**800-441-7777***	302-456-4400
*Orders					
AstenJohnson					
4399 Corporate Rd	Charleston	SC	29405	**800-529-7990**	843-747-7800
Belton Industries Inc					
1205 Hanby Rd PO Box 127	Belton	SC	29627	**800-845-8753**	864-338-5711
BGF Industries Inc					
3802 Robert Porcher Way	Greensboro	NC	27410	**800-476-4845**	
Carthage Mills					
4243 Hunt Rd	Cincinnati	OH	45242	**800-543-4430***	513-794-1600
*Sales					
Clear Edge Technical Fabrics					
7160 Northland Cir N	Minneapolis	MN	55428	**800-328-3036**	763-535-3220
FH Bonn Co					
4300 Gateway Blvd	Springfield	OH	45502	**800-323-0143**	937-323-7024
Firestone Fibers & Textiles Co					
100 Firestone Ln PO Box 1369	Kings Mountain	NC	28086	**800-441-1336**	704-734-2132
Mutual Industries Inc					
707 W Grange St	Philadelphia	PA	19120	**800-523-0888**	215-927-6000
Newtex Industries Inc					
8050 Victor Mendon Rd	Victor	NY	14564	**800-836-1001**	585-924-9135
Sefar Printing Solutions Inc					
111 Calumet St	Depew	NY	14043	**800-995-0531**	716-683-4050
TenCate Geosynthetics North America					
365 S Holland Dr	Pendergrass	GA	30567	**888-795-0808**	706-693-2226
TenCate Protective Fabrics USA					
6501 Mall Blvd	Union City	GA	30291	**800-241-8630**	
Tex-Tech Industries Inc					
1 City Ctr 11th Fl	Portland	ME	04101	**800-441-7089**	207-933-4404
Ultrafabrics LLC					
303 S Broadway	Tarrytown	NY	10591	**888-361-9216**	914-460-1730

739-4 Knitting Mills

Company				Toll-Free	Phone
Apex Mills Corp 168 Doughty Blvd	Inwood	NY	11096	800-989-2739	516-239-4400
Draper Knitting Co 28 Draper Ln	Canton	MA	02021	800-808-7707	781-828-0029
Lace For Less Inc 1500 Main Ave Ste 3	Clifton	NJ	07011	800-533-5223	973-478-2955
Monterey Mills Inc 1725 E Delavan Dr	Janesville	WI	53546	800-255-9665	608-754-2866

739-5 Narrow Fabric Mills

Company				Toll-Free	Phone
Avery Dennison 950 German St	Lenoir	NC	28645	800-444-4947	828-758-2338
Fulflex Inc 32 Justin Holden Dr	Brattleboro	VT	05301	800-283-2500	802-257-5256
Hickory Brands Inc (HBI) 429 27th St NW	Hickory	NC	28601	800-438-5777	
Hope Global Engineered Textile Solutions 50 Martin St *General	Cumberland	RI	02864	800-854-7139*	401-333-8990
JRM Industries Inc One Mattimore St	Passaic	NJ	07055	800-533-2697	973-779-9340
Julius Koch USA Inc 387 Church St *Sales	New Bedford	MA	02745	800-522-3652*	508-995-9565
Murdock Webbing Co 27 Foundry St	Central Falls	RI	02863	800-375-2052	401-724-3000
Name Maker Inc 4450 Commerce Cir PO Box 43821	Atlanta	GA	30336	800-241-2890	404-691-2237
Narrow Fabric Industries Corp 701 Reading Ave	Reading	PA	19611	877-523-6373	610-376-2891
Rhode Island Textile Co 211 Columbus Ave	Pawtucket	RI	02861	800-556-6488	401-722-3700
Ross Matthews Mills Inc 657 Quarry St	Fall River	MA	02723	800-753-7677	508-677-0601
Shelby Elastics Inc 639 N Post Rd PO Box 2405	Shelby	NC	28150	800-562-4507	704-487-4301
Southern Weaving Co 1005 W Bramlett Rd	Greenville	SC	29611	800-849-8962	864-233-1635
Tape Craft Corp 200 Tape Craft Dr *Cust Svc	Oxford	AL	36203	800-521-1783*	
Wayne Mills Co Inc 130 W Berkley St	Philadelphia	PA	19144	800-220-8053	215-842-2134

739-6 Nonwoven Fabrics

Company				Toll-Free	Phone
Aetna Felt Corp 2401 W Emaus Ave	Allentown	PA	18103	800-526-4451	610-791-0900
Airtex Consumer Products a Div of Federal Foam Technologies 150 Industrial Pk Blvd	Cokato	MN	55321	800-851-8887	
Berwick Offray LLC 2015 W Front St *General	Berwick	PA	18603	800-327-0350*	570-752-5934
Cerex Advanced Fabrics Inc 610 Chemstrand Rd	Cantonment	FL	32533	800-572-3739	850-968-0100
Clark-Cutler-McDermott Co (CCMcD) 5 Fisher St	Franklin	MA	02038	800-922-3019	508-528-1200
Fisher Textiles Inc 139 Business Pk Dr	Indian Trail	NC	28079	800-554-8886	704-821-8870
Foss Mfg Co LLC 11 Merrill Industrial Dr PO Box 5000	Hampton	NH	03842	800-343-3277	603-929-6000
Hobbs Bonded Fibers Inc 200 Commerce Dr	Waco	TX	76710	800-433-3357	254-741-0040
National Nonwovens PO Box 150	EastHampton	MA	01027	800-333-3469	413-527-3445
Sellars 6565 N 60th St	Milwaukee	WI	53223	800-237-8454	414-353-5650
Tietex International 3010 N Blackstock Rd	Spartanburg	SC	29301	800-843-8390	864-574-0500

739-7 Textile Dyeing & Finishing

Company				Toll-Free	Phone
Albert Screen Print Inc 3704 Summit Rd	Norton	OH	44203	800-759-2774	330-753-7559
Aurora Textile Finishing Co 911 N Lake St PO Box 70	Aurora	IL	60507	800-864-0303	630-892-7651
Cranston Print Works Co 1381 Cranston St	Cranston	RI	02920	800-876-2756	401-943-4800
Westex Inc 122 W 22nd St	Oak Brook	IL	60523	866-493-7839	773-523-7000

739-8 Textile Fiber Processing Mills

Company				Toll-Free	Phone
Buffalo Industries Inc 99 S Spokane St	Seattle	WA	98134	800-683-0052	206-682-9900
Fabritech Inc 5740 Salmen St	New Orleans	LA	70123	888-733-5009	504-733-5009
JE Herndon Company Inc 1020 J E Herndon Access Rd	Kings Mountain	NC	28086	800-277-0500	704-739-4711
Norman W Paschall Co Inc 1 Paschall Rd	Peachtree City	GA	30269	800-849-1820	770-487-7945

739-9 Yarn & Thread Mills

Company				Toll-Free	Phone
Charles Craft Inc 21381 Charles Craft Ln	Laurinburg-Maxton Airport	Laurinburg NC	28352	800-277-1009	910-844-3521
Coats North America 3430 Toringdon Way Ste 301	Charlotte	NC	28277	800-631-0965	704-329-5800
Eddington Thread Manufacturing Co PO Box 446	Bensalem	PA	19020	800-220-8901	215-639-8900
Glen Raven Inc 232 Glen Raven Rd	Glen Raven	NC	27217	800-675-0032	336-227-6211
Lion Brand Yarn Co 135 Kero Rd	Carlstadt	NJ	07072	800-795-5466	212-243-8995
Parkdale Mills Inc 531 Cotton Blossom Cir	Gastonia	NC	28054	800-331-1843	704-874-5000
Supreme Corp 325 Spence Rd	Conover	NC	28613	888-604-6975	828-322-6975
Swift Spinning Inc 16 Corporate Ridge Pkwy PO Box 8767	Columbus	GA	31907	800-849-1252	706-323-6303
Tuscarora Yarns Inc 8760 E Franklin St	Mount Pleasant	NC	28124	800-849-6527	704-436-6527

740   TEXTILE PRODUCTS - HOUSEHOLD

Company				Toll-Free	Phone
1888 Mills LLC 1520 Kensington Rd Ste 115	Oak Brook	IL	60523	800-346-3660	
Ado Corp 851 Simuel Rd *Cust Svc	Spartanburg	SC	29301	800-845-0918*	
American Textile Co 10 N Linden St *Cust Svc	Duquesne	PA	15110	800-289-2826*	412-948-1020
Biddeford Blankets 300 Terr Dr	Mundelein	IL	60060	800-789-6441	
Carole Fabrics Inc PO Box 1436	Augusta	GA	30903	800-241-0920	706-863-4742
CHF Industries Inc One Pk Ave Ninth Fl *Cust Svc	New York	NY	10016	800-243-7090*	212-951-7800
Crown Crafts Inc 916 S Burnside NASDAQ: CRWS	Gonzales	LA	70737	800-433-9560	225-647-9100
Custom Drapery Blinds & Shutters 3402 E T C Jester	Houston	TX	77018	800-929-9211	713-225-9211
Hollander Home Fashions Corp 6501 Congress Avenue Suite 300	Boca Raton	FL	33487	800-233-7666	561-997-6900
Kaslen Textiles 6099 Triangle Dr	Commerce	CA	90040	800-777-5789	323-588-7700
Kay Dee Designs Inc 177 Skunk Hill Rd	Hope Valley	RI	02832	800-537-3433	401-539-2405
Lafayette Venetian Blind Inc 3000 Klondike Rd. P.O. Box 2838	West Lafayette	IN	47996	800-342-5523	
Louisville Bedding Co 10400 Bunsen Way	Louisville	KY	40299	800-626-2594	502-491-3370
Manual Woodworkers & Weavers Inc 3737 HowaRd Gap Rd	Hendersonville	NC	28792	800-542-3139	828-692-7333
Marietta Drapery & Window Coverings Company Inc 22 Trammel St PO Box 569 *Mktg	Marietta	GA	30064	800-762-4774*	770-428-3335
Pacific Coast Feather Co 1964 Fourth Ave S	Seattle	WA	98134	888-297-1778	206-624-1057
Pendleton Woolen Mills Inc 220 NW Broadway	Portland	OR	97209	800-760-4844	503-226-4801
Riegel Consumer Products 51 Riegel Rd PO Box E	Johnston	SC	29832	800-845-3251	803-275-2541
S Lichtenberg & Co Inc 295 Fifth Ave Rm 918 *Cust Svc	New York	NY	10016	800-682-1959*	212-689-4510
Standard Textile Company Inc Decorative Products One Knollcrest Dr *General	Cincinnati	OH	45237	800-999-0400*	513-761-9255
United Feather & Down Inc 414 E Golf Rd	Des Plaines	IL	60016	800-932-3696	847-296-6610
Wesco Fabrics Inc 4001 Forest St	Denver	CO	80216	800-950-9372	303-388-4101

741   THEATERS - BROADWAY

SEE ALSO Theaters - Resident ; Performing Arts Facilities ; Theater Companies

Company				Toll-Free	Phone
Al Hirschfeld Theatre 302 W 45th St	New York	NY	10036	800-432-7780	212-239-6262
August Wilson 245 W 52nd St	New York	NY	10019	800-432-7250	212-239-6200
Booth Theatre 222 W 45th St	New York	NY	10036	800-432-7780	212-239-6200
Broadhurst Theatre 235 W 44th St	New York	NY	10036	800-447-7400	212-239-6200
Circle in the Square Theatre 1633 Broadway	New York	NY	10019	800-432-7250	212-239-6200
Helen Hayes Theatre 240 W 44th St	New York	NY	10036	800-447-7400	212-239-6200
Imperial Theatre 249 W 45th St	New York	NY	10036	800-447-7400	212-239-6200
Jacobs Theatre 242 W 45th St	New York	NY	10036	800-447-7400	212-239-6200
Longacre Theatre 220 W 48th St	New York	NY	10036	800-447-7400	212-239-6200
Lyceum Theatre 149 W 45th St	New York	NY	10036	800-432-7780	212-239-6200

					Toll-Free	Phone

Majestic Theatre
245 W 44th St .... New York NY 10036 **800-447-7400** 212-239-6200
Minskoff Theatre
200 W 45th St .... New York NY 10036 **800-714-8452** 212-869-0550
Richard Rodgers Theatre
226 W 46th St .... New York NY 10036 **866-755-3075** 212-221-1211
Shubert Theatre
225 W 44th St .... New York NY 10036 **800-432-7250** 212-239-6200

742	THEATERS - MOTION PICTURE

					Toll-Free	Phone

AMC Entertainment Inc
920 Main St .... Kansas City MO 64105 **877-341-6397** 816-221-4000
AMC Star Theatres
25333 W 12-Mile Rd .... Southfield MI 48034 **888-262-4386** 248-368-1802
AMC Theatres
920 Main St .... Kansas City MO 64105 **877-341-6397** 816-221-4000
Brenden Theatres
531 Davis St .... Vacaville CA 95688 **877-638-3456** 707-469-0190
Cinemark USA Inc
3900 Dallas Pkwy Ste 500 .... Plano TX 75093 **800-246-3627** 972-665-1000
Cineplex Entertainment LP
1303 Yonge St .... Toronto ON M4T2Y9 **800-333-0061** 416-323-6600
Kerasotes ShowPlace Theatres LLC
224 N Des Plaines Ave .... Chicago IL 60661 **877-293-2000** 312-756-3360
Landmark Theaters
2222 S Barrington Ave .... Los Angeles CA 90064 **888-724-6362*** 310-473-6701
*Cust Svc
Marcus Corp
100 E Wisconsin Ave .... Milwaukee WI 53202 **800-461-9330** 414-905-1000
NYSE: MCS
Marcus Theatres Corp
100 E Wisconsin Ave Ste 19.. Milwaukee WI 53202 **800-274-0099*** 414-905-1000
*Cust Svc
Regal Entertainment Group
7132 Regal Ln .... Knoxville TN 37918 **877-835-5734*** 865-922-1123
NYSE: RGC ■ *Cust Svc

743	THEATERS - RESIDENT

SEE ALSO Theaters - Broadway ; Performing Arts Facilities ; Theater Companies
All of the theaters listed here are members of the League of Resident Theatres (LORT). In order to become a member of LORT, each theater must be incorporated as a non-profit, IRS-approved organization; must rehearse each self-produced production for a minimum of three weeks; must have a playing season of 12 weeks or more; and must operate under a LORT-Equity contract.

					Toll-Free	Phone

A Contemporary Theatre (ACT)
700 Union St Kreielsheimer Pl .... Seattle WA 98101 **888-584-4849** 206-292-7660
Actors Theatre of Louisville
316 W Main St .... Louisville KY 40202 **800-428-5849** 502-584-1205
Alabama Shakespeare Festival
One Festival Dr .... Montgomery AL 36117 **800-841-4273** 334-271-5300
Asolo Repertory Theatre
5555 N Tamiami Tr .... Sarasota FL 34243 **800-361-8388** 941-351-9010
Goodspeed Musicals
PO Box A .... East Haddam CT 06423 **800-262-8721** 860-873-8664
Guthrie Theater
818 S Second St .... Minneapolis MN 55415 **877-447-8243*** 612-377-2224
*Resv
Maltz Jupiter Theatre
1001 E Indiantown Rd .... Jupiter FL 33477 **800-445-1666** 561-743-2666
Northlight Theatre
9501 Skokie Blvd .... Skokie IL 60077 **800-356-9377** 847-673-6300
Pasadena Playhouse, The
39 S El Molino Ave .... Pasadena CA 91101 **800-733-2767** 626-356-7529
People's Light & Theatre Co
39 Conestoga Rd .... Malvern PA 19355 **800-732-0999** 610-647-1900
Pittsburgh Public Theater
621 Penn Ave .... Pittsburgh PA 15222 **800-732-0999** 412-316-8200
Seattle Repertory Theatre (SRT)
155 Mercer St PO Box 900923 .... Seattle WA 98109 **877-900-9285** 206-443-2210
Shakespeare Theatre
516 Eigth St SE .... Washington DC 20003 **877-487-8849** 202-547-3230
Theatre For A New Audience
154 Christopher St Ste 3D .... New York NY 10014 **866-811-4111** 212-229-2819
Wilma Theater
265 S Broad St .... Philadelphia PA 19107 **800-732-0999** 215-893-9456
Yale Repertory Theatre
1120 Chapel St PO Box 1257.... New Haven CT 06505 **800-973-2837** 203-432-1234

744	THERMAL MANAGEMENT PRODUCTS - PERSONAL

					Toll-Free	Phone

BRK Brands Inc
3901 Liberty St Rd .... Aurora IL 60504 **800-323-9005** 630-851-7330
Chemetron Fire Systems
16 W 361 S Frontage Rd Ste 125 .. Burr Ridge IL 60527 **800-878-5631*** 708-748-1503
*Cust Svc
Fike Corp
704 SW Tenth St .... Blue Springs MO 64015 **877-342-3453** 816-229-3405
Fire & Life Safety America
3017 Vernon Rd Ste 100 ...... Richmond VA 23228 **800-252-5069** 804-222-1381
Firecom Inc 39-27 59th St ...... Woodside NY 11377 **888-347-3269** 718-899-6100
First Alert Inc
3901 Liberty St Rd .... Aurora IL 60504 **800-323-9005** 630-851-7330
Gamewell FCI
12 Clintonville Rd .... Northford CT 06472 **800-606-1983** 203-484-7161
General Monitors Inc
26776 Simpatica Cir .... Lake Forest CA 92630 **866-686-0741** 949-581-4464

					Toll-Free	Phone

Honeywell Fire Solutions
One Fire-Lite Pl .... Northford CT 06472 **800-627-3473** 203-484-7161
Potter Electric Signal Company Inc
5757 Phantom Dr Ste 125 .... Hazelwood MO 63042 **800-325-3936** 314-878-4321
Siemens Bldg Technologies Inc Fire Safety Div
8 Fernwood Rd .... Florham Park NJ 07932 **888-303-3353** 973-593-2600
Silent Knight
7550 Meridian Cir Ste 100 .... Maple Grove MN 55369 **800-328-0103** 763-493-6400
Task Force Tips Inc
3701 Innovation Way .... Valparaiso IN 46383 **800-348-2686** 219-462-6161
Tyco SimplexGrinnell
50 Technology Dr .... Westminster MA 01441 **800-746-7539** 978-731-2500
Viking Corp
210 N Industrial Pk Dr .... Hastings MI 49058 **800-968-9501** 269-945-9501

745	TICKET BROKERS

					Toll-Free	Phone

All American Ticket Service
2616 Philadelphia Pike Ste E .... Claymont DE 19703 **800-669-0571**
Americana Tickets NY
1535 Broadway .... New York NY 10036 **800-833-3121** 212-581-6660
Broadway.com
729 Seventh Ave .... New York NY 10019 **800-762-3929** 212-541-8457
Front Row USA Entertainment
900 N Federal Hwy Ste 200 .... Hallandale FL 33009 **800-277-8499** 305-940-8499
Great Seats Inc
7338 Baltimore Ave Ste 108A .... College Park MD 20740 **800-664-5056** 301-985-6250
Select-A-Ticket Inc
25 Rt 23 S .... Riverdale NJ 07457 **800-735-3288** 973-839-6100
Theatre Development Fund
1501 Broadway 21st Fl .... New York NY 10036 **888-424-4685** 212-221-0885
Ticket Source Inc
5516 E Mockingbird Ln Ste 100 .. Dallas TX 75206 **800-557-6872** 214-821-9011
Tickets.com Inc
555 Anton Blvd 11th Fl .... Costa Mesa CA 92626 **800-352-0212** 714-327-5400
TicketWeb Inc
PO Box 77250 .... San Francisco CA 94103 **866-777-8932***
*Cust Svc
Western States Ticket Service
143 W McDowell Rd .... Phoenix AZ 85003 **800-326-0331** 602-254-3300

746	TILE - CERAMIC (WALL & FLOOR)

					Toll-Free	Phone

American Marazzi Tile Inc
359 Clay Rd .... Sunnyvale TX 75182 **800-289-8453** 972-232-3801
Ann Sacks Tile & Stone Inc
8120 NE 33rd Dr .... Portland OR 97211 **800-278-8453** 503-281-7751
Armstrong World Industries Inc
2500 Columbia Ave .... Lancaster PA 17603 **800-233-3823*** 717-397-0611
NYSE: AWI ■ *Cust Svc
Crossville Porcelain Stone/USA
PO Box 1168 .... Crossville TN 38557 **800-221-9093** 931-484-2110
Dal-Tile International Inc
7834 Hawn Fwy .... Dallas TX 75217 **800-933-8453** 214-398-1411
Epro Tile Inc
10890 E CR 6 .... Bloomville OH 44818 **866-818-3776**
Florida Tile Industries Inc
998 Governors Ln Ste 300 .... Lexington KY 40513 **800-352-8453*** 859-219-5200
*Cust Svc
Florim USA Inc
300 International Blvd .... Clarksville TN 37040 **877-356-7461** 931-645-5100
Interstyle Ceramics & Glass Ltd
3625 Brighton Ave .... Burnaby BC V5A3H5 **800-667-1566** 604-421-7229
Ironrock Capital Inc
1201 Millerton St SE .... Canton OH 44707 **800-325-3945** 330-484-4887
Jefferson Ceramic Tile Company Inc
405 S Main St .... Jefferson WI 53549 **888-739-8399** 920-674-5725
ME Tile 447 Atlas Dr .... Nashville TN 37211 **888-348-8453**
Meredith Collection
1201 Millerton St SE .... Canton OH 44707 **888-325-3945** 330-484-1656
Metropolitan Ceramics
1201 Millerton St SE .... Canton OH 44707 **800-325-3945**
Nudo Products Inc
1500 Taylor Ave .... Springfield IL 62703 **800-826-4132** 217-528-5636
Wood Pro Inc
421 Washington St PO Box 363 .... Auburn MA 01501 **800-786-5577** 508-832-3291

747	TIMBER TRACTS

					Toll-Free	Phone

Haida Corp PO Box 89 .... Hydaburg AK 99922 **800-478-3721** 907-285-3721
Holiday Tree Farms Inc
800 NW Cornell Ave .... Corvallis OR 97330 **800-289-3684** 541-753-3236
Industrial Timber & Lumber Corp (ITL)
23925 Commerce Pk Rd .... Beachwood OH 44122 **800-829-9663** 216-831-3140
JM Huber Corp
499 Thornall St 8th Fl. .... Edison NJ 08837 **877-418-0038** 732-549-8600
McShan Lumber Company Inc
PO Box 27 .... McShan AL 35471 **800-882-3712** 205-375-6277
Moonworks 1137 Park E Dr .... Woonsocket RI 02895 **800-975-6666**
Pike Lumber Company Inc
PO Box 247 .... Akron IN 46910 **800-356-4554** 574-893-4511
Plum Creek Timber Company Inc
601 Union St Ste 3100 .... Seattle WA 98101 **800-858-5347** 206-467-3600
NYSE: PCL
Weyerhaeuser Co
33663 Weyerhaeuser Way S .... Federal Way WA 98003 **800-525-5440** 253-924-2345
NYSE: WY
Yule Tree Farms LLC
PO Box 429 .... Aurora OR 97002 **888-970-8733** 503-651-2114

748 TIMESHARE COMPANIES

SEE ALSO Hotels & Hotel Companies

				Toll-Free	Phone
Bluegreen Corp					
4960 Conference Way N Ste 100	Boca Raton	FL	33431	800-456-2582	561-912-8000
NYSE: BXG					
Central Florida Investments Inc					
5601 Windhover Dr	Orlando	FL	32819	800-218-4363	407-351-3351
Club Intrawest					
375 Water St Ste 326	Vancouver	BC	V6B5C6	800-649-9243	
Disney Vacation Club					
1390 Celebration Blvd	Celebration	FL	34747	800-500-3990	407-566-3100
Festiva Resorts					
One Vance Gap Rd	Asheville	NC	28805	866-933-7848*	828-254-3378
*Resv					
Four Seasons Hotels & Resorts					
1165 Leslie St	Toronto	ON	M3C2K8	800-332-3442	416-449-1750
Hilton Grand Vacations Company LLC					
6355 Metro W Blvd Ste 180	Orlando	FL	32835	800-230-7068	407-722-3100
Hyatt Vacation Ownership Inc					
140 Fountain Pkwy N Ste 570	Saint Petersburg	FL	33716	800-926-4447	727-803-9400
Interval International Inc					
6262 Sunset Dr PO Box 431920	Miami	FL	33143	800-828-8200	305-666-1861
Marriott Vacation Club International					
6649 Westwood Blvd Ste 500	Orlando	FL	32821	800-307-7312	407-206-6000
One Napili Way					
5355 Lower Honoapiilani Hwy	Lahaina	HI	96761	800-841-6284*	808-669-2007
*Cust Svc					
Resort Condominiums International (RCI)					
9998 N Michigan Rd	Carmel	IN	46032	800-338-7777	317-805-8000
Royal Aloha Vacation Club					
1505 Dillingham Blvd Ste 212	Honolulu	HI	96817	800-367-5212	808-847-8050
Silverleaf Resorts Inc					
1221 Riverbend Dr Ste 120	Dallas	TX	75247	800-613-0310	214-631-1166
Starwood Vacation Ownership Inc					
Sheraton Vistana Resort					
8800 Vistana Ctr Dr	Orlando	FL	32821	800-847-8262*	407-239-3100
*Resv					
Sunchaser Vacation Villas					
5129 Riverview Gate Rd	Fairmont Hot Springs	BC	V0B1L1	877-451-1250*	250-345-4545
*Resv					
Tempus Resorts International					
7380 Sand Lake Rd Ste 600	Orlando	FL	32819	877-747-4747	407-226-1000
Vacation Internationale					
1417 116th Ave NE	Bellevue	WA	98004	800-444-6633	425-454-8429
WorldMark the Club					
9805 Willows Rd NE	Redmond	WA	98052	800-722-3487	425-498-1950

749 TIRES - MFR

				Toll-Free	Phone
All Business Machines Inc					
2555 Third St Ste 100	Sacramento	CA	95818	888-880-7801	
Bridgestone Americas Holding Inc					
535 Marriott Dr	Nashville	TN	37214	877-201-2373*	615-937-1000
*Cust Svc					
Carlisle Tire & Wheel Mfg					
23 Windham Blvd	Aiken	SC	29805	800-827-1001*	803-643-2919
*Sales					
Continental Tire North America Inc					
1800 Continental Blvd	Charlotte	NC	28273	877-235-0102	704-583-3900
Cooper Tire & Rubber Co					
701 Lima Ave	Findlay	OH	45840	800-854-6288	419-423-1321
NYSE: CTB					
Dunlop Tires PO Box 1109	Buffalo	NY	14240	800-845-8378	
Goodyear Tire & Rubber Co					
200 Innovation Way	Akron	OH	44316	800-321-2136*	330-796-2121
NASDAQ: GT ■ *Cust Svc					
Hankook Tire America Corp					
1450 Valley Rd	Wayne	NJ	07470	800-426-8252	973-633-9000
Hercules Tire & Rubber Co					
16380 E US Rt 224 - 200	Findlay	OH	45840	800-677-9535	419-425-6400
K&M Tire Inc					
965 Spencerville Rd PO Box 279	Delphos	OH	45833	877-879-5407	419-695-1061
Martin Wheel Company Inc					
342 W Ave	Tallmadge	OH	44278	800-462-7846	330-633-3278
Michelin North America Inc					
1 PkwyS PO Box 19001	Greenville	SC	29602	800-847-3435*	864-458-5000
*Cust Svc					
Mickey Thompson Tires					
4600 Prosper Dr	Stow	OH	44224	800-222-9092	330-928-9092
Mitchell Industrial Tire Co					
2915 Eigth Ave PO Box 71839	Chattanooga	TN	37407	800-251-7226	423-698-4442
Purcell Tire & Rubber Co					
301 N Hall St	Potosi	MO	63664	888-878-2355	573-438-2131
Robbins LLC					
3415 Thompson St	Muscle Shoals	AL	35661	800-633-3312	256-383-5441
SolidBoss Worldwide Inc					
200 Veterans Blvd	South Haven	MI	49090	888-258-7252	269-637-6356
Specialty Tires of America Inc					
1600 Washington St	Indiana	PA	15701	800-622-7327	724-349-9010
Superior Tire & Rubber Corp					
1818 Pennsylvania Ave W PO Box 308	Warren	PA	16365	800-289-1456*	814-723-2370
*Cust Svc					
Tech International					
200 E Coshocton St	Johnstown	OH	43031	800-336-8324	740-967-9015
Titan Tire Co					
2345 E Market St	Des Moines	IA	50317	800-872-2327	515-265-9200
Toyo Tire USA Corp					
6261 Katella Ave Ste 2B	Cypress	CA	90630	800-678-3250	
Yokohama Tire Corp					
601 S Acacia Ave	Fullerton	CA	92831	800-423-4544	714-870-3800

750 TIRES & TUBES - WHOL

				Toll-Free	Phone
Allied Oil & Supply Inc					
2209 S 24th St	Omaha	NE	68108	800-333-3717	402-344-4343
American Tire Depot					
1123 W Commonwealth Ave	Fullerton	CA	92833	855-333-2823	714-525-2306
Bauer Built Inc PO Box 248	Durand	WI	54736	800-268-5114	715-672-4295
Ben Tire Distributors Ltd					
203 E Madison St PO Box 158	Toledo	IL	62468	800-252-8961	
BFGoodrich Tires Inc					
One Pkwy S	Greenville	SC	29602	877-788-8899	
Clark Tire & Auto Supply Co Inc					
220 S Ctr St	Hickory	NC	28602	800-968-3092	828-322-2303
Dapper Tire Company Inc					
4025 Lockridge St	San Diego	CA	92102	800-266-7172	619-266-1397
De Ronde Tire Supply Inc					
95 Rapin Pl	Buffalo	NY	14211	800-227-4647	716-897-6690
East Bay Tire Co					
2200 Huntington Dr Unit C	Fairfield	CA	94533	800-831-8473	707-437-4700
Free Service Tire Co Inc					
PO Box 6187	Johnson City	TN	37602	855-646-1423	423-979-2250
Friend Tire Co					
11 Industrial Dr	Monett	MO	65708	800-950-8473	
Ken Jones Tire Inc					
73 Chandler St	Worcester	MA	01609	800-225-9513	508-755-5255
Kenda USA					
7095 Americana Pkwy	Reynoldsburg	OH	43068	866-536-3287	614-866-9803
Kumho Tire USA Inc					
10299 Sixth St	Rancho Cucamonga	CA	91730	800-445-8646	909-428-3999
Lakin Tire West Inc					
15305 Spring Ave	Santa Fe Springs	CA	90670	800-488-2752	562-802-2752
Michelin North America Inc					
1 PkwyS PO Box 19001	Greenville	SC	29602	800-847-3435*	864-458-5000
*Cust Svc					
Net Driven 280 Eureka St	Batesville	MS	38606	800-647-6133	662-563-1143
Parrish Tire Company Inc					
5130 Indiana Ave	Winston-Salem	NC	27106	800-849-8473	336-767-0202
Piedmont Truck Tires Inc					
PO Box 18228	Greensboro	NC	27419	800-274-8473	336-668-0091
Pomps Tire Service Inc					
1123 Cedar St	Green Bay	WI	54301	800-236-8911	920-435-8301
Reliable Tire Co					
805 N Blackhorse Pk	Blackwood	NJ	08012	800-342-3426*	
*All					
Snyder Tire					
401 Cadiz Rd	Steubenville	OH	43953	800-967-8473	740-264-5543
Southeastern Wholesale Tire Co					
4721 Trademark Dr	Raleigh	NC	27610	800-849-9215*	919-832-3900
*General					
Tire Centers LLC					
310 Inglesby Pkwy	Duncan	SC	29334	800-603-2430	864-329-2700
Tire Rack					
7101 Vorden Pkwy	South Bend	IN	46628	888-541-1777	574-287-2345
Tire Warehouse Inc					
7500 NW 35 Terr	Miami	FL	33122	877-235-0102	305-696-0096
Tire Wholesalers Co Inc					
1783 E 14-Mile Rd	Troy	MI	48083	800-577-3353	248-589-9910
Tire's Warehouse Inc					
240 Teller St	Corona	CA	92879	800-655-8851	951-808-0111
Tire-Rama Inc					
1401 Industrial Ave PO Box 23509	Billings	MT	59104	800-828-1642	406-245-4006
TO Haas Tire Co Inc					
2400 'O' St PO Box 81067	Lincoln	NE	68510	866-393-5204	402-261-2854
Wheels Etc 17521 Mesa St	Hesperia	CA	92345	800-758-4737	909-350-8200

751 TOBACCO & TOBACCO PRODUCTS

				Toll-Free	Phone
Abel Reel, The					
165 Aviador St	Camarillo	CA	93010	866-511-7444	805-484-8789
Albert H Notini & Sons Inc					
225 Aiken St	Lowell	MA	01854	800-366-8464	978-459-7151
Alliance One International Inc					
8001 Aerial Ctr Pkwy PO Box 2009	Morrisville	NC	27560	800-937-5449	919-379-4300
NYSE: AOI					
AMCON Distributing Co					
7405 Irvington Rd	Omaha	NE	68122	888-201-5997	402-331-3727
NYSE: DIT					
Burklund Distributors Inc					
2500 N Main St Ste 3	East Peoria	IL	61611	800-322-2876	309-694-1900
Cigar.com Inc					
1911 Spillman Dr	Bethlehem	PA	18015	800-357-9800	
Commonwealth Altadis Inc					
5900 N Andrews Ave Ste 1000	Fort Lauderdale	FL	33309	800-446-5797*	954-772-9000
*Orders					
Core-Mark International					
395 Oyster Pt Blvd					
Ste 415	South San Francisco	CA	94080	800-622-1713	650-589-9445
Eby-Brown Co					
280 W Shuman Blvd Ste 280	Naperville	IL	60563	800-553-8249	630-778-2800
Finck Cigar Co					
414 Vera Cruz St	San Antonio	TX	78207	800-221-0638*	210-226-4191
*Orders					
Holts Cigar Co					
1522 Walnut St	Philadelphia	PA	19102	800-523-1641	215-732-8500
J Polep Distribution Services Inc					
705 Meadow St	Chicopee	MA	01013	800-447-6537	413-592-4141
JC Newman Cigar Co					
2701 16th St	Tampa	FL	33605	800-477-1884*	813-248-2124
*Orders					
Keilson-Dayton Co					
107 Commerce Pk Dr	Dayton	OH	45404	800-759-3174	937-236-1070

				Toll-Free	Phone

Klafter's Inc
216 N Beaver St .... New Castle PA 16101 **800-922-1233**

National Cigar Corp
407 N Main St PO Box 97 .... Frankfort IN 46041 **800-321-0247**

National Tobacco Company LP
5201 Interchange Way .... Louisville KY 40229 **800-579-0975*** 502-778-4421
*Cust Svc

Philip Morris USA
2325 Bells Rd .... Richmond VA 23234 **800-343-0975** 804-274-2000

Reynolds American Inc
401 N Main St PO Box 2990 .... Winston-Salem NC 27101 **877-703-0386** 336-741-2000
NYSE: LO

Sledd Co 100 E Cove Ext .... Wheeling WV 26003 **800-333-0374*** 304-243-1820
*General

---

752   TOOL & DIE SHOPS

				Toll-Free	Phone

A & M Tool & Die Company Inc
64 Mill St .... Southbridge MA 01550 **800-848-4628** 508-764-3241

A Finkl & Sons Co
2011 N Southport Ave .... Chicago IL 60614 **800-343-2562** 773-975-2510

ABA-PGT Inc
10 Gear Dr PO Box 8270 .... Manchester CT 06040 **877-840-2172** 860-649-4591

Austro Mold Inc
3 Rutter St .... Rochester NY 14606 **800-637-7774** 585-458-1410

Carlson Tool & Manufacturing Corp
W57 N14386 Doerr Way PO Box 85 ...... Cedarburg WI 53012 **800-532-2252** 262-377-2020

Chicago Cutting Die Co
3555 Woodhead Dr .... Northbrook IL 60062 **800-747-3437** 847-509-5800

Cleveland Punch & Die Co
666 Pratt St PO Box 769 .... Ravenna OH 44266 **888-451-4342**

Custom Mold Engineering Inc
9780 S Franklin Dr .... Franklin WI 53132 **800-448-2005** 414-421-5444

D & D Manufacturing Inc
500 Territorial Dr .... Bolingbrook IL 60440 **888-300-6869**

D-M-E Co
29111 Stephenson Hwy ...... Madison Heights MI 48071 **800-626-6653** 248-398-6000

Danly IEM
6779 Engle Rd Ste A-F .... Cleveland OH 44130 **877-534-8986**

Diamond Tool & Die Inc
508 29th Ave .... Oakland CA 94601 **800-227-1084** 510-534-7050

Ehrhardt Tool & Machine Co
25 Central Industrial Dr .... Granite City IL 62040 **877-386-7856** 314-436-6900

General Carbide Corp
1151 Garden St .... Greensburg PA 15601 **800-245-2465** 724-836-3000

General Tool Co
101 Landy Ln .... Cincinnati OH 45215 **800-314-9817** 513-733-5500

GlobalDie
1130 Minot Ave PO Box 1120 .... Auburn ME 04211 **888-271-4735** 207-514-7252

Hill Engineering Inc
373 Randy Rd .... Carol Stream IL 60188 **800-631-0520** 630-834-4430

Hydro Carbide
4439 State Rte 982 .... Latrobe PA 15650 **800-245-2476** 724-539-9701

Hygrade Precision Technologies Inc
329 Cooke St .... Plainville CT 06062 **800-457-1666** 860-747-5773

Indian Creek Fabricators
1350 Commerce Pk Dr .... Tipp City OH 45371 **877-769-5880** 937-667-5818

Jasco Tools Inc
1390 Mt Read Blvd PO Box 60497 .... Rochester NY 14606 **800-724-5497** 585-254-7000

Jones Metal Products Co
200 N Ctr St .... West Lafayette OH 43845 **888-868-6535** 740-545-6381

Lou-Rich Machine Tool Inc
505 W Front St .... Albert Lea MN 56007 **800-893-3235** 507-377-8910

Mate Precision Tooling Inc
1295 Lund Blvd .... Anoka MN 55303 **800-328-4492** 763-421-0230

Mid-State Machine Products Inc
83 Verti Dr .... Winslow ME 04901 **800-341-4672** 207-873-6136

Moeller Mfg Company Inc Punch & Die Div
43938 Plymouth Oaks Blvd .... Plymouth MI 48170 **800-521-7613** 734-416-0000

Mold Base Industries Inc
7501 Derry St .... Harrisburg PA 17111 **800-241-6656**

Mold-A-Matic Corp
147 River St .... Oneonta NY 13820 **866-886-2626** 607-433-2121

Northwestern Tools Inc
3130 Valleywood Dr .... Dayton OH 45429 **800-236-3956** 937-298-9994

Oberg Industries Inc
2301 Silverville Rd PO Box 368 ...... Freeport PA 16229 **866-487-2365** 724-295-2121

Ontario Die Co of America
2735 20th St .... Port Huron MI 48060 **800-763-8272** 810-987-5060

Panoramic Corp
4321 Goshen Rd .... Fort Wayne IN 46818 **800-654-2027**

Paslin Co 25303 Ryan Rd .... Warren MI 48091 **877-972-7546** 586-758-0200

PCS Co 34488 Doreka Dr .... Fraser MI 48026 **800-521-0546** 586-294-7780

Peddinghaus Corp
300 N Washington Ave .... Bradley IL 60915 **800-786-2448** 815-937-3800

Penn United Technology Inc
799 N Pike Rd .... Cabot PA 16023 **866-572-7537** 724-352-1507

Pennsylvania Tool & Gages Inc
PO Box 534 .... Meadville PA 16335 **877-827-8285** 814-336-3136

Porter Precision Products Inc
2734 Banning Rd .... Cincinnati OH 45239 **800-543-7041** 513-923-3777

Producto Machine Co
800 Union Ave .... Bridgeport CT 06607 **800-722-2606*** 203-367-8675
*Cust Svc

Remmele Engineering Inc
10 Old Hwy 8 SW .... New Brighton MN 55112 **800-733-6198*** 651-635-4100
*General

Rome Tool & Die Company Inc
113 Hemlock St .... Rome GA 30161 **800-241-3369** 706-234-6743

RotoMetrics Group
800 Howerton Ln .... Eureka MO 63025 **800-325-3851** 636-587-3600

SB Whistler & Sons Inc
PO Box 270 .... Medina NY 14103 **800-828-1010** 585-318-4630

Specialty Design & Mfg Co
PO Box 4039 .... Reading PA 19606 **800-720-0867** 610-779-1357

				Toll-Free	Phone

SPX Corp OTC Div
655 Eisenhower Dr .... Owatonna MN 55060 **800-533-6127** 507-455-7000

Superior Die Set Corp
900 W Drexel Ave .... Oak Creek WI 53154 **800-558-6040** 414-764-4900

Superior Die Tool & Machine Co
2301 Fairwood Ave .... Columbus OH 43207 **800-292-2181** 614-444-2181

Unipunch Products Inc
311 Fifth St NW .... Clear Lake WI 54005 **800-828-7061**

Walker Tool & Die Inc
2411 Walker Ave NW .... Grand Rapids MI 49544 **877-925-5378** 616-453-5471

Westland Corp
1735 S Maize Rd .... Wichita KS 67209 **800-247-1144** 316-721-1144

Yarema Die & Engineering Co Inc
300 Minnesota Rd .... Troy MI 48083 **800-937-9311** 248-585-2830

---

753   TOOLS - HAND & EDGE

SEE ALSO Saw Blades & Handsaws ; Lawn & Garden Equipment ; Metalworking Devices & Accessories

				Toll-Free	Phone

Allway Tools Inc
1255 Seabury Ave .... Bronx NY 10462 **800-422-5592** 718-792-3636

Ames Taping Tools Inc
3350 Breckinridge Blvd Ste 100 .... Duluth GA 30096 **800-408-2801** 800-303-1827

Ames True Temper Inc
465 Railroad Ave .... Camp Hill PA 17011 **800-393-1846**

Arrow Fastener Co Inc
271 Mayhill St .... Saddle Brook NJ 07663 **800-776-2228** 201-843-6900

BARCO Industries Inc
1020 MacArthur Rd .... Reading PA 19605 **800-234-8665***
*Cust Svc

Bondhus Corp
1400 E Broadway St PO Box 660 ...... Monticello MN 55362 **800-328-8310*** 763-295-2162
*Cust Svc

Cal-Van Tools
4300 Waterleaf Ct .... Greensboro NC 27410 **800-537-1077**

Channellock Inc
1306 S Main St .... Meadville PA 16335 **800-724-3018***
*Cust Svc

Charles GG Schmidt & Company Inc
301 W Grand Ave .... Montvale NJ 07645 **800-724-6438** 201-391-5300

Consolidated Devices Inc (CDI)
19220 San Jose Ave .... City of Industry CA 91748 **800-525-6319** 626-965-0668

Cooper Industries
600 Travis St Ste 5400 .... Houston TX 77002 **866-853-4293** 713-209-8400
NYSE: ETN

Cornwell Quality Tools
667 Seville Rd .... Wadsworth OH 44281 **800-321-8356** 330-336-3506

Danaher Corp
2200 Pennsylvania Ave NW Ste 800 .... Washington DC 20037 **800-833-9200** 202-828-0850
NYSE: DHR

Dasco Pro Inc
340 Blackhawk Pk Ave .... Rockford IL 61104 **800-327-2690** 815-962-3727

Duo-Fast Corp 2400 Galvin Dr ...... Elgin IL 60123 **888-386-3278*** 847-783-5500
*Cust Svc

Empire Level Manufacturing Corp
929 Empire Dr PO Box 800 .... Mukwonago WI 53149 **800-558-0722**

Enderes Tool Co
1103 Hershey St .... Albert Lea MN 56007 **800-874-7776**

Fiskars Brands Inc
2537 Daniels St .... Madison WI 53718 **866-348-5661**

Fletcher-Terry Company Inc
65 Spring Ln .... Farmington CT 06032 **800-843-3826*** 860-677-7331
*Cust Svc

General Machine Products Company Inc
3111 Old Lincoln Hwy .... Trevose PA 19053 **800-345-6009*** 215-357-5500
*Tech Supp

General Tools Mfg Company LLC
80 White St .... New York NY 10013 **800-697-8665** 212-431-6100

Grobet File Company of America Inc
750 Washington Ave .... Carlstadt NJ 07072 **800-847-4188** 201-939-6700

Hexacon Electric Co
161 W Clay Ave .... Roselle Park NJ 07204 **888-765-3371** 908-245-6100

Hyde Tools Co
54 Eastford Rd .... Southbridge MA 01550 **800-872-4933** 508-764-4344

Klein Tools Co
450 Bond St .... Lincolnshire IL 60069 **800-553-4676***
*Cust Svc

Leatherman Tool Group Inc
12106 NE Ainsworth Cir .... Portland OR 97220 **800-847-8665** 503-253-7826

LS Starrett Co
121 Crescent St .... Athol MA 01331 **800-482-8710** 978-249-3551
NYSE: SCX

Mac Tools Inc
505 N Cleveland Ave .... Westerville OH 43082 **800-622-8665** 614-755-7000

Malco Products Inc
14080 State Hwy 55 NW PO Box 400 .... Annandale MN 55302 **800-328-3530** 320-274-8246

Marshalltown Co
104 S Eigth Ave .... Marshalltown IA 50158 **800-888-0127** 641-753-5999

Matco Tools 4403 Allen Rd .... Stow OH 44224 **800-368-6651** 330-926-5332

Mayhew Steel Products Inc
199 Industrial Blvd .... Turners Falls MA 01376 **800-872-0037** 413-863-4860

MIBRO Group 111 Sinnott Rd ...... Toronto ON M1L4S6 **866-941-9006** 416-285-9000

Newell Rubbermaid Inc Irwin Tools Div
8935 Northpointe Executive Dr ...... Huntersville NC 28078 **800-866-5740** 704-987-4555

QEP Co Inc
1001 Broken Sound Pkwy NW Ste A .... Boca Raton FL 33487 **800-777-8665*** 561-994-5550
OTC: QEPC ■ *Sales

Red Devil Inc 1437 S Boulder .... Tulsa OK 74119 **800-423-3845**

Reed Manufacturing Co
1425 W Eigth St .... Erie PA 16502 **800-456-1697** 814-452-3691

Relton Corp
317 Rolyn Dr PO Box 60019 .... Arcadia CA 91066 **800-423-1505*** 323-681-2551
*Cust Svc

Ripley Co 46 Nooks Hill Rd .... Cromwell CT 06416 **800-528-8665** 860-635-2200

Seymour Mfg Co Inc
PO Box 248 .... Seymour IN 47274 **800-815-7253** 812-522-2900

				Toll-Free	Phone

Snap-on Inc 2801 80th St .... Kenosha WI 53143 **877-762-7664** 262-656-5200
NYSE: SNA

Stabila Inc
332 Industrial Dr P.O. Box 402 ....South Elgin IL 60177 **800-869-7460**

Stanley Supply & Services Inc
335 Willow St .... North Andover MA 01845 **888-887-9473*** 978-682-2000
*Cust Svc

Stanley Tools Inc
480 Myrtle St ....New Britain CT 06053 **800-262-2161*** 860-225-5111
*Cust Svc

Stride Tool Inc Imperial Div
30333 Emerald Vly Pkwy .... Glenwillow OH 44139 **888-467-8665** 440-247-4600

Superior Tool Co
100 Hayes Dr Unit C...................Cleveland OH 44131 **800-533-3244*** 216-398-8600
*Cust Svc

Tamco Inc
1466 Delberts Dr .... Monongahela PA 15063 **800-826-2672** 724-258-6622

Triumph Twist Drill Co Inc
1 SW 7th St ....Chisholm MN 55719 **800-942-1501** 218-263-3891

Ullman Devices Corp
664 Danbury Rd ....Ridgefield CT 06877 **800-784-7796** 203-438-6577

Vaughan & Bushnell Manufacturing Co
11414 Maple Ave PO Box 390 ....Hebron IL 60034 **800-435-6000** 815-648-2446

Wall Lenk Corp
1950 Dr Martin Luther King Jr ....Kinston NC 28501 **888-527-4186*** 252-527-4186
*Cust Svc

Warner Manufacturing Co
13435 Industrial Pk Blvd .... Minneapolis MN 55441 **800-444-0606** 763-559-4740

Wheeler-Rex Inc
3744 Jefferson Rd PO Box 688................Ashtabula OH 44005 **800-321-7950** 440-998-2788

Zephyr Mfg Company Inc
201 Hindry Av ....Inglewood CA 90301 **800-624-3944** 310-410-4907

TOOLS - MACHINE

SEE Machine Tools - Metal Cutting Types ; Machine Tools - Metal Forming Types

754 TOOLS - POWER

SEE ALSO Lawn & Garden Equipment ; Metalworking Devices & Accessories

				Toll-Free	Phone

Alpine Power Systems Inc
24355 Capitol ....Redford MI 48239 **877-769-3762** 313-531-6600

American Pneumatic Tool Inc
9949 Tabor Pl ....Santa Fe Springs CA 90670 **800-532-7402** 562-204-1555

Atlas Copco Tools & Assembly Systems
2998 Dutton Rd ....Auburn Hills MI 48326 **800-859-3746** 248-373-3000

Blount Inc Oregon Cutting Systems Div
4909 SE International Way ....Portland OR 97222 **800-223-5168** 503-653-8881

Chicago Pneumatic Tool Co
1800 Overview Dr ....Rock Hill SC 29730 **800-624-4735** 803-817-7000

Cooper Industries
600 Travis St Ste 5400 ....Houston TX 77002 **866-853-4293** 713-209-8400
NYSE: ETN

Dremel Inc 4915 21st St ....Racine WI 53406 **800-437-3635** 262-554-1390

Dynabrade Inc
8989 Sheridan Dr ....Clarence NY 14031 **800-828-7333*** 716-631-0100
*Cust Svc

Enerpac P.O. Box 3241 .... Milwaukee WI 53201 **800-433-2766*** 262-293-1600
*Cust Svc

Florida Pneumatic Manufacturing Corp
851 Jupiter Pk Ln ....Jupiter FL 33458 **800-327-9403** 561-744-9500

Greenlee Textron Inc
4455 Boeing Dr ....Rockford IL 61109 **800-435-0786**

Hilti Inc 5400 S 122nd E Ave ....Tulsa OK 74146 **800-879-8000*** 918-252-6000
*Cust Svc

Hougen Manufacturing Inc
3001 Hougen Dr ....Swartz Creek MI 48473 **800-426-7818*** 810-635-7111
*Orders

Makita USA Inc
14930 Northam St Ste C...............La Mirada CA 90638 **800-462-5482** 714-522-8088

Master Appliance Corp
2420 18th St ....Racine WI 53403 **800-558-9413** 262-633-7791

Milwaukee Electric Tool Corp
13135 W Lisbon Rd ....Brookfield WI 53005 **800-729-3878** 262-781-3600

P & F Industries Inc
445 Broadhollow Rd ....Melville NY 11747 **800-327-9403** 631-694-9800
NASDAQ: PFIN

Paslode
888 Forest Edge Dr ....Vernon Hills IL 60061 **800-682-3428*** 847-634-1900
*Cust Svc

Pioneer Tool & Forge Inc
101 Sixth St ....New Kensington PA 15068 **800-359-6408** 724-337-4700

Pneutek 17 Friars Dr ....Hudson NH 03051 **800-431-8665** 603-883-1660

Powernail Co
1300 Rose Rd ....Lake Zurich IL 60047 **800-323-1653** 847-634-3000

Robert Bosch Tool Corp
1800 W Central Rd ....Mount Prospect IL 60056 **877-267-2499** 224-232-2000

Ryobi Technologies Inc
1428 Pearman Dairy Rd ....Anderson SC 29625 **800-525-2579**

SENCO Products Inc
4270 Ivy Pt Blvd ....Cincinnati OH 45245 **800-543-4596***
*Tech Supp

Shopsmith Inc 6530 Poe Ave ....Dayton OH 45414 **800-543-7586*** 937-898-6070
OTC: SSMH ■ *Cust Svc

Sioux Tools Inc
250 Snap-on Dr ....Murphy NC 28906 **800-722-7290*** 828-835-9765
*Orders

Stanley Assembly Technologies Div
5335 Avion Pk Dr ....Cleveland OH 44143 **877-787-7830** 440-461-5500

Stihl Inc
536 Viking Dr ....Virginia Beach VA 23452 **800-467-8445*** 757-486-9100
*Cust Svc

Thomas C Wilson Inc
21-11 44th Ave ....Long Island City NY 11101 **800-230-2636** 718-729-3360

755 TOUR OPERATORS

SEE ALSO Travel Agencies ; Bus Services - Charter

				Toll-Free	Phone

Academy Bus LLC
111 Paterson Ave ....Hoboken NJ 07030 **800-442-7272** 201-420-7000

Adventure Alaska Tours Inc
PO Box 64 ....Hope AK 99605 **800-365-7057** 907-782-3730

Adventure Connection
PO Box 475 ....Coloma CA 95613 **800-556-6060** 530-626-7385

Adventure Life South America
1655 S Third St W Ste 1...............Missoula MT 59801 **800-344-6118** 406-541-2677

Adventures Out West
1680 S 21st St ....Colorado Springs CO 80904 **800-755-0935**

Africa Adventure Co, The
5353 N Federal Hwy Ste 300 .... Fort Lauderdale FL 33308 **800-882-9453** 954-491-8877

African Travel Inc
330 N Brand Blvd ....Glendale CA 91205 **800-421-8907** 818-507-7893

AHI International Corp
6400 Shafer Ct ....Rosemont IL 60018 **800-323-7373**

Alpine Adventure Trails Tours Inc
7495 Lower Thomaston Rd ....Macon GA 31220 **888-478-4004**

AmaWaterways
26010 Mureau Rd ....Calabasas CA 91302 **800-626-0126**

Ambassadors Group Inc
110 S Ferrall St ....Spokane WA 99202 **800-652-8683** 509-534-6200
NASDAQ: EPAX

American Trails West (ATW)
92 Middle Neck Rd ....Great Neck NY 11021 **800-645-6260** 516-487-2800

AmericanTours International LLC (ATI)
6053 W Century Blvd ....Los Angeles CA 90045 **800-800-8942** 310-641-9953

Anderson Coach & Travel
One Anderson Plz ....Greenville PA 16125 **800-345-3435** 724-588-8310

ATS Tours
300 Continental Blvd Ste 350 ....El Segundo CA 90245 **888-410-5770**

Backroads 801 Cedar St ....Berkeley CA 94710 **800-462-2848** 510-527-1555

Badger Coaches Inc
5501 Femrite Dr ....Madison WI 53718 **800-442-8259** 608-255-1511

Banff Adventures Unlimited
211 Bear St Bison Courtyard ....Banff AB T1L1A8 **800-644-8888** 403-762-4554

Beamers Hells Canyon Tours & Excursions
PO Box 1243 ....Lewiston ID 83501 **800-522-6966** 509-758-4800

Bestway Tours & Safaris
8678 Greenall Ave ....Burnaby BC V5J3M6 **800-663-0844** 604-264-7378

Big Five Tours & Expeditions
1551 SE Palm Ct ....Stuart FL 34994 **800-244-3483** 772-287-7995

Blue Grass Tours Inc
817 Enterprise Dr ....Lexington KY 40510 **800-755-6956** 859-233-2152

Bonaventure Tours
8 Boudreau Ln ....Haute-Aboujagane NB E4P5N1 **800-561-1213** 506-532-3674

Borderland Tours
2550 W Calle Padilla ....Tucson AZ 85745 **800-525-7753** 520-882-7650

Boston Duck Tours Ltd
Four Copley Pl Ste 310.............. Boston MA 02116 **800-226-7442** 617-450-0065

Breakaway Tours
3300 Bloor St Ste 1800 ....Toronto ON M8X2X2 **800-465-4257** 416-915-9880

Brendan Vacations
21625 Prairie St ....Chatsworth CA 91311 **800-421-8446** 800-687-1002

Brewster Rocky Mountain Adventures
PO Box 370 ....Banff AB T1L1A5 **800-691-5085** 403-762-5454

Brewster Travel Canada
100 Gopher St PO Box 1140...............Banff AB T1L1J3 **866-606-6700** 403-762-6700

Burke International Tours Inc
PO Box 890 ....Newton NC 28658 **800-476-3900** 828-465-3900

California Parlor Car Tours
500 Sutter St Ste 401 ....San Francisco CA 94102 **800-227-4250** 415-474-7500

Centennial Travelers
311 S College Ave ....Fort Collins CO 80524 **800-223-0675** 970-484-4988

Churchill Nature Tours
PO Box 429 ....Erickson MB R0J0P0 **877-636-2968** 204-636-2968

City Tours Mainey̆
P.O. Box 167 ....Nobleboro ME 04555 **800-537-5378** 207-563-2288

Classic Student Tours
75 Rhoads Ctr Dr ....Dayton OH 45458 **800-860-0246** 937-439-0032

Club Europa 802 W Oregon St ....Urbana IL 61801 **800-331-1882** 217-344-5863

Coach Tours Ltd
475 Federal Rd ....Brookfield CT 06804 **800-822-6224** 203-740-1118

Contemporary Tours
1400 Old Country Rd Ste 100...............Westbury NY 11590 **800-627-8873** 516-484-5032

Contiki Holidays
801 E Katella Ave 3rd Fl ....Anaheim CA 92805 **800-944-5708** 714-935-0808

Cultural Experiences Abroad (CEA)
2999 N 44th St Ste 200 ....Phoenix AZ 85018 **800-266-4441** 480-557-7900

CYR Bus Tours
153 Gilman Falls Ave ....Old Town ME 04468 **800-244-2335** 207-827-2335

Dash Tours 1024 Winnipeg St ....Regina SK S4R8P8 **800-265-0000** 306-352-2222

Dipert Travel & Transportation Ltd
PO Box 580 ....Arlington TX 76004 **800-433-5335**

Earthwatch Institute
114 Western Ave ....Boston MA 02134 **800-776-0188** 978-461-0081

Educational Tours
1123 Sterling Rd ....Inverness FL 34450 **800-343-9003**

Educational Travel Consultants (ETC)
PO Box 1580 ....Hendersonville NC 28793 **800-247-7969** 828-693-0412

EF Tours One Education St ....Cambridge MA 02141 **800-872-8439** 877-205-9909

Esplanade Tours
160 Commonwealth Ave Ste U-1A .... Boston MA 02116 **800-628-4893** 617-266-7465

Explorica Inc 145 Tremont St .... Boston MA 02111 **888-310-7120**

Fantastic Tours & Travel
6143 Jericho Tpke ....Commack NY 11725 **800-552-6262** 631-462-6262

Festive Holidays Inc
5501 New Jersey Ave .... Wildwood Crest NJ 08260 **800-257-8920** 609-522-6316

Friendly Excursions Inc
PO Box 69 ....Sunland CA 91041 **800-775-5018** 818-353-7726

				Toll-Free	Phone

Frontiers International Travel
PO Box 959 .... Wexford PA 15090 **800-245-1950** 724-935-1577

Gadabout Vacations
1801 E Tahquitz Canyon Way Ste 100 .... Palm Springs CA 92262 **800-952-5068** 760-325-5556

General Tours 53 Summer St .... Keene NH 03431 **800-221-2216**

Gerber Tours Inc
1400 Old Country Rd Ste 100.......... Westbury NY 11590 **800-645-9145** 516-826-5000

Global Educational Tours
7216 Madison Ave Ste U .... Indianapolis IN 46227 **888-508-6877** 317-787-2787

Globus 5301 S Federal Cir .... Littleton CO 80123 **866-755-8581** 303-703-7000

Go Next
8000 W 78th St Ste 345 .... Minneapolis MN 55439 **800-842-9023** 952-918-8950

Go...With Jo! Tours & Travel Inc
910 Dixieland Rd .... Harlingen TX 78552 **800-999-1446** 956-423-1446

Good Time Tours
455 Corday St .... Pensacola FL 32503 **800-446-0886** 850-476-0046

Good Times Travel Inc
17132 Magnolia St .... Fountain Valley CA 92708 **888-488-2287** 714-848-1255

Grand European Tours
6000 Meadows Rd Ste 520.......... Lake Oswego OR 97035 **877-622-9109** 503-718-2262

Green Tortoise Adventure Travel & Hostels
494 Broadway ....San Francisco CA 94133 **800-867-8647** 415-834-1000

Gutsy Women Travel LLC
801 E Katella Ave .... Anaheim CA 92806 **866-464-8879**

Hesselgrave International
PO Box 30768 .... Bellingham WA 98228 **800-457-5522** 360-734-3570

Historic Tours of America Inc
201 Front St Ste 224. .... Key West FL 33040 **800-844-7601*** 305-296-3609
*General

Holiday River Expeditions
544 East 3900 South ....Salt Lake City UT 84107 **800-624-6323** 801-266-2087

Isram World of Travel Inc
233 Pk Ave S 10th Fl .... New York NY 10003 **800-223-7460** 212-661-1193

Julian Tours
1721 Crestwood Dr Ste 110 .... Alexandria VA 22302 **800-541-7936** 703-379-2300

Katmai Coastal Bear Tours
PO Box 1503 .... Homer AK 99603 **800-532-8338** 907-235-8337

Ker & Downey Inc 6703 Hwy Blvd ....Katy TX 77494 **800-423-4236** 281-371-2500

Kincaid Coach Lines Inc
9207 Woodend Rd .... Kansas City KS 66111 **800-998-1901** 913-441-6200

Landmark Tours
1304 University Ave NE Ste 201........... Minneapolis MN 55413 **888-231-8735** 651-490-5408

Lindblad Expeditions
96 Morton St Ninth Fl. .... New York NY 10014 **800-397-3348** 212-765-7740

Macy's Travel
700 Nicollet Mall .... Minneapolis MN 55402 **800-316-6166**

Maupintour Inc
2690 Weston Rd Ste 200 .... Weston FL 33331 **800-255-4266** 954-653-3820

Mayflower Tours Inc
1225 Warren Ave PO Box 490.......Downers Grove IL 60515 **800-323-7604** 630-435-8500

Micato Safaris
15 W 26th St 11th Fl. .... New York NY 10010 **800-642-2861** 212-545-7111

Mid-American Coaches Inc
4530 Hwy 47 .... Washington MO 63090 **866-944-8687**

Midnight Sun Adventure Travel
1027 Pandora Ave ....Victoria BC V8V3P6 **800-255-5057** 250-480-9409

Monograms
5301 S Federal Cir .... Littleton CO 80123 **866-270-9841**

Montana River Outfitters
923 Tenth Ave N .... Great Falls MT 59401 **800-800-8218** 406-761-1677

Mountain Travel Sobek
1266 66th St Ste 4 ....Emeryville CA 94608 **888-831-7526** 510-594-6000

Natural Habitat Adventures
PO Box 3065 .... Boulder CO 80307 **800-543-8917** 303-449-3711

Off the Beaten Path
Seven E Beall St .... Bozeman MT 59715 **800-445-2995** 406-586-1311

Olivia Cruises & Resorts
434 Brannan St ....San Francisco CA 94107 **800-631-6277** 415-962-5700

Onondaga Coach Corp
PO Box 277 .... Auburn NY 13021 **800-451-1570** 315-255-2216

Orange Belt Stages
PO Box 949 .... Visalia CA 93292 **800-266-7433** 559-733-4408

Overseas Adventure Travel
347 Congress St .... Boston MA 02210 **800-221-0814**

Panorama Balloon Tours
2683 Via De La Valle 625G .... Del Mar CA 92014 **800-455-3592**

Perillo Tours
577 Chestnut Ridge Rd .... Woodcliff Lake NJ 07677 **800-431-1515** 201-307-1234

Pilgrim Tours & Travel Inc
3071 Main St PO Box 268 .... Morgantown PA 19543 **800-322-0788** 610-286-0788

Pitmar Tours
7549 140th St Ste 9 ....Surrey BC V3W5J9 **877-596-9670** 604-596-9670

Polynesian Adventure Tours Inc
2880 Kilihau St .... Honolulu HI 96819 **800-622-3011** 808-833-3000

Premier Tours
21 S 12th St Ninth Fl .... Philadelphia PA 19107 **800-545-1910**

Presley Tours Inc
16 Presley Pk Dr PO Box 58 .... Makanda IL 62958 **800-621-6100** 618-549-0704

REI Adventures PO Box 1938 ....Sumner WA 98390 **800-622-2236** 253-437-1100

Richmond Tours
1828 Hylan Blvd ....Staten Island NY 10305 **800-766-3868** 718-979-3111

Rivers Oceans & Mountains Adventures Inc (ROAM)
2485 Hwy 3A .... Nelson BC V1L6K7 **888-639-1114**

Roberts Hawaii Inc
680 Iwilei Rd Ste 700 .... Honolulu HI 96817 **800-831-5541** 808-523-7750

Royal Coach Tours
630 Stockton Ave ....San Jose CA 95126 **800-927-6925** 408-279-4801

RSVP Vacations
2535 25th Ave S .... Minneapolis MN 55406 **800-328-7787** 310-432-2300

Scenic Airlines Inc
3900 Paradise Rd Ste 223 ....Las Vegas NV 89169 **866-235-9422** 702-638-3300

Short Hills Tours
46 Chatham Rd PO Box 310. .... Short Hills NJ 07078 **800-348-6871** 973-467-2113

Silver Fox Tours & Motorcoaches
Three Silver Fox Dr .... Millbury MA 01527 **800-342-5998** 508-865-6000

Silverado Stages Inc
241 Prado Rd ....San Luis Obispo CA 93401 **888-383-8109** 805-545-8400

				Toll-Free	Phone

Sports Leisure Vacations
9812 Old Winery Pl .... Sacramento CA 95827 **800-951-5556** 916-361-2051

Sports Travel Inc
60 Main St PO Box 50 ....Hatfield MA 01038 **800-662-4424** 413-247-7678

Straight A Tours & Travel
6881 Kingspointe Pkwy Ste 18................. Orlando FL 32819 **800-237-5440** 407-896-1242

Student Tours Inc
60 W Ave .... Vineyard Haven MA 02568 **800-331-7093** 508-693-5078

Student Travel Services Inc
1413 Madison Pk Dr .... Glen Burnie MD 21061 **800-648-4849**

Sunny Land Tours Inc
21 Old Kings Rd N Ste B-212 ....Palm Coast FL 32137 **800-783-7839** 386-449-0059

Super Holiday Tours
116 Gatlin Ave .... Orlando FL 32806 **800-327-2116**

Tag-A-Long Expeditions
452 N Main St .... Moab UT 84532 **800-453-3292** 435-259-8946

Tauck World Discovery
10 Norden Pl .... Norwalk CT 06855 **800-468-2825** 203-899-6500

Timberwolf Tours Ltd
51404 RR 264 Ste 34 .... Spruce Grove AB T7Y1E4 **888-467-9697** 780-470-4966

Toto Tours Ltd
1326 W Albion Ave .... Chicago IL 60626 **800-565-1241** 773-274-8686

Travcoa
100 N Sepulveda Blvd Ste 1700 ....El Segundo CA 90245 **800-992-2003** 310-649-7104

Tri-State Travel
4349 Industrial Pk Dr .... Galena IL 61036 **800-779-4869** 815-777-0820

Upstate Tours & Travel
207 Geyser Rd .... Saratoga Springs NY 12866 **800-237-5252** 518-584-5252

USA Student Travel
5080 Robert J Mathews Pkwy ....El Dorado Hills CA 95762 **800-448-4444** 916-939-6805

VBT Bicycling & Walking Vacations
614 Monkton Rd ....Bristol VT 05443 **800-245-3868** 802-453-4811

VentureOut
575 Pierce St Ste 604 ....San Francisco CA 94117 **888-431-6789** 415-626-5678

VIP Tour & Charter Bus Co
129-137 Fox St .... Portland ME 04101 **800-231-2222*** 207-772-4457
*General

Wade Tours Inc
797 Burdeck St ....Schenectady NY 12306 **800-955-9233** 518-355-4500

Walking Adventures International
14612 NE Fourth Plain Rd Ste A........... Vancouver WA 98682 **800-779-0353**

West Coast Connection
1725 Main St Ste 215........... Weston FL 33326 **800-767-0227** 954-888-9780

White Mountain Adventures
131 Eagle Crescent PO Box 4259 ....Banff AB T1L1A6 **800-408-0005** 403-760-4403

White Star Tours
26 E Lancaster Ave .... Reading PA 19607 **800-437-2323** 610-775-5000

Wilderness Travel
1102 Ninth St .... Berkeley CA 94710 **800-368-2794** 510-558-2488

Wings Tours Inc
11350 McCormick Rd Ste 703 .... Hunt Valley MD 21031 **800-869-4647** 410-771-0925

WorldPass Travel Group LLC
5080 Robert J Matthews Pkwy ....El Dorado Hills CA 95762 **800-949-0650** 916-939-6805

WorldStrides
218 W Water St Ste 400 .... Charlottesville VA 22902 **800-999-7676***
*General

756	TOY STORES				

				Toll-Free	Phone

A2Z Science & Nature Store
57 King St .... NortHampton MA 01060 **877-261-6171** 413-586-1611

Alabama Card Systems Inc
500 Gene Reed Dr Ste 102 .... Birmingham AL 35215 **800-985-7507** 205-833-1116

Build-A-Bear Workshop Inc
1954 Innerbelt Business Ctr Dr ....Saint Louis MO 63114 **888-560-2327** 314-423-8000
NYSE: BBW

Creative Kid Stuff
3939 E 46th St .... Minneapolis MN 55406 **800-353-0710** 612-929-2431

Discount School Supplies
Two Lower Ragsdale Rd Ste 125 ....Monterey CA 93940 **800-919-5238**

FAO Schwarz
767 Fifth Ave 58th St .... New York NY 10153 **800-426-8697** 212-644-9400

Learning Express Inc
29 Buena Vista St ....Devens MA 01434 **800-924-2296** 978-889-1000

Mary Maxim Ltd 75 Scott Ave ....Paris ON N3L3G5 **888-442-2266**

MGA Entertainment Inc
16300 Roscoe Blvd Ste 150 .... Van Nuys CA 91406 **800-222-4685** 818-894-2525

757	TOYS, GAMES, HOBBIES				

SEE ALSO Baby Products ; Bicycles & Bicycle Parts & Accessories ; Games & Entertainment Software

				Toll-Free	Phone

Airmate Co Inc
16280 County Rd D .... Bryan OH 43506 **800-544-3614** 419-636-3184

American Girl Inc
8400 Fairway Pl ....Middleton WI 53562 **800-845-0005*** 608-836-4848
*Orders

American Plastic Toys Inc
799 Ladd Rd .... Walled Lake MI 48390 **800-521-7080** 248-624-4881

Atlas Model Railroad Company Inc
378 Florence Ave ....Hillside NJ 07205 **800-872-2521*** 908-687-0880
*Orders

Bachmann Industries Inc
1400 E Erie Ave .... Philadelphia PA 19124 **800-356-3910*** 215-533-1600
*Cust Svc

Ball Bounce & Sport Inc/Hedstrom Plastics
One Hedstrom Dr .... Ashland OH 44805 **800-765-9665** 419-289-9310

Bravo Sports Corp
12801 Carmenita Rd .... Santa Fe Springs CA 90670 **800-234-9737*** 562-484-5100
*Cust Svc

Buffalo Games Inc
220 James E Casey Dr .... Buffalo NY 14206 **855-895-4290**

				Toll-Free	Phone
Cardinal Industries Inc					
21-01 51st Ave	Long Island City	NY	11101	800-524-8697	718-784-3000
Cepia LLC					
121 Hunter Ave Ste 103	Saint Louis	MO	63124	800-225-9319	314-725-4900
Creativity for Kids					
9450 Allen Dr	Cleveland	OH	44125	800-311-8684	216-643-4660
Douglas Cuddle Toys Company Inc					
69 Krif Rd PO Box D	Keene	NH	03431	800-992-9002	603-352-3414
Effanbee Doll Co					
459 Hurley Ave	Hurley	NY	12443	888-362-3655	845-339-8246
Estes-Cox Corp 1295 H St	Penrose	CO	81240	800-525-7561	719-372-6565
Fisher-Price Inc					
636 Girard Ave	East Aurora	NY	14052	800-432-5437	716-687-3000
Gayla Industries Inc					
PO Box 920800	Houston	TX	77292	800-231-7508	905-857-5207
Great Planes Model Distributors					
PO Box 9021	Champaign	IL	61826	800-637-7660	217-398-3630
Guidecraft USA					
55508 Hwy 19 W PO Box U	Winthrop	MN	55396	800-524-3555	507-647-5030
Gund Inc 1 Runyons Ln	Edison	NJ	08817	800-448-4863*	732-248-1500
*Cust Svc					
Hasbro Inc					
1027 Newport Ave	Pawtucket	RI	02861	800-242-7276	401-431-8697
NASDAQ: HAS					
Hasbro Inc Playskool Div					
1027 Newport Ave	Pawtucket	RI	02861	800-242-7276	401-431-8697
International Playthings Inc					
75D Lackawanna Ave	Parsippany	NJ	07054	800-631-1272	973-316-2500
JAKKS Pacific Inc					
21749 Baker Pkwy	Walnut	CA	91789	877-875-2557	909-594-7771
NASDAQ: JAKK					
LeapFrog Enterprises Inc					
6401 Hollis St Ste 100	Emeryville	CA	94608	800-701-5327	510-420-5000
NYSE: LF					
Learning Resources					
380 N Fairway Dr	Vernon Hills	IL	60061	800-222-3909	847-573-8400
LEGO Systems Inc					
555 Taylor Rd	Enfield	CT	06082	877-518-5346	860-763-6731
Lionel .com LLC					
26750 23 Mile Rd	Chesterfield	MI	48051	800-454-6635	586-949-4100
Little Tikes Co, The					
2180 Barlow Rd	Hudson	OH	44236	800-321-0183*	
*Cust Svc					
Losi 4710 E Guasti Rd	Ontario	CA	91761	888-899-5674	909-390-9595
Mag-Nif Inc 8820 E Ave	Mentor	OH	44060	800-869-5463	
Maple City Rubber Co					
55 Newton St PO Box 587	Norwalk	OH	44857	800-841-9434	419-668-8261
Mattel Inc					
333 Continental Blvd	El Segundo	CA	90245	800-524-8697	310-252-2000
NASDAQ: MAT					
Midwest Products Company Inc					
400 S Indiana St	Hobart	IN	46342	800-348-3497*	219-942-1134
*Orders					
Nintendo of America Inc					
4820 150th Ave NE	Redmond	WA	98052	800-255-3700*	425-882-2040
*Cust Svc					
Ohio Art Co 1 Toy St	Bryan	OH	43506	800-800-3141	419-636-3141
OTC: OART					
Patch Products Inc					
1400 E Inman Pkwy	Beloit	WI	53511	800-524-4263	608-362-6896
Pepperball Technologies Inc					
6540 Lusk Blvd Ste C137	San Diego	CA	92121	877-887-3773	858-638-0236
Pioneer National Latex Co					
5000 E 29th St N	Wichita	KS	67220	800-386-4438	316-685-2266
Plaid Enterprises Inc					
3225 Westech Dr	Norcross	GA	30092	800-842-4197	678-291-8100
Poof-Slinky Inc					
4280 S Haggerty Rd PO Box 701394	Canton	MI	48188	800-829-9502	734-454-9552
Pressman Toy Corp					
121 New England Ave	Piscataway	NJ	08854	800-800-0298*	732-562-1590
*Cust Svc					
Radio Flyer Inc					
6515 W Grand Ave	Chicago	IL	60707	800-621-7613	773-637-7100
SIG Mfg Company Inc					
401 S Front St	Montezuma	IA	50171	800-247-5008*	641-623-5154
*Sales					
Spin Master Ltd					
450 Front St W	Toronto	ON	M5V1B6	800-622-8339	416-364-6002
Steiff North America					
24 Albion Rd Ste 220	Lincoln	RI	02865	888-978-3433	401-312-0080
Swibco Inc 4810 Venture Rd	Lisle	IL	60532	877-794-2261	630-968-8900
Tara Toy Corp					
40 Adams Ave	Hauppauge	NY	11788	800-899-8272	631-273-8697
Testor Corp					
440 Blackhawk Pk Ave	Rockford	IL	61104	800-837-8677	815-962-6654
TOMY International Inc					
1111 W 22nd St Ste 320	Oak Brook	IL	60523	800-704-8697	
Tonner Doll Co					
301 Wall St PO Box 4410	Kingston	NY	12402	800-794-2107	845-339-9537
Uncle Milton Industries Inc					
29209 Canwood St Ste 120	Agoura	CA	91301	800-869-7555*	818-707-0800
*General					
Universal Mfg Co Inc					
5030 Mackey S	Overland Park	KS	66203	800-524-5860	913-815-6230
University Games Corp					
2030 Harrison St	San Francisco	CA	94110	800-347-4818	415-503-1600
Upper Deck Co LLC					
5909 Sea Otter Pl	Carlsbad	CA	92010	800-873-7332*	
*Cust Svc					
Vermont Teddy Bear Company Inc					
6655 Shelburne Rd	Shelburne	VT	05482	800-988-8277	802-985-3001
VTech Electronics North America LLC					
1155 W Dundee St Ste 130	Arlington Heights	IL	60004	800-521-2010	847-400-3600
Wham-O Inc					
6301 Owensmouth Ave Ste 700	Woodland Hills	CA	91367	888-942-6650	
William K Walthers Inc					
5601 W Florist Ave	Milwaukee	WI	53218	800-877-7171	414-527-0770
Wizards of the Coast Inc					
1600 Lind Ave SW Ste 400	Renton	WA	98057	800-324-6496	425-226-6500

TRAILERS - TRUCK

SEE Truck Trailers

758 TRAILERS (TOWING) & TRAILER HITCHES

				Toll-Free	Phone
Bright Co-op Inc					
803 W Seale St	Nacogdoches	TX	75964	800-562-0730	936-564-8378
Cequent Towing Products					
47774 Anchor Ct W	Plymouth	MI	48170	800-521-0510	
Cequent Trailer Products					
1050 Indianhead Dr	Mosinee	WI	54455	800-604-9466	715-693-1700
CM Trailers Inc					
200 County Rd PO Box 680	Madill	OK	73446	888-268-7577	580-795-5536
Com-Fab Inc					
4657 Price HilliaRds Rd	Plain City	OH	43064	866-522-1794	740-857-1107
Dethmers Manufacturing Co (DEMCO)					
4010 320th St PO Box 189	Boyden	IA	51234	800-543-3626	712-725-2311
EZ Loader Boat Trailers Inc					
717 N Hamilton St	Spokane	WA	99202	800-398-5623	509-489-0181
Gooseneck Trailer Mfg Co					
4400 E Hwy 21 PO Box 832	Bryan	TX	77808	800-688-5490*	979-778-0034
*Cust Svc					
Load Rite Trailers Inc					
265 Lincoln Hwy	Fairless Hills	PA	19030	800-562-3783	215-949-0500
Midwest Industries Inc					
122 E State Hwy 175	Ida Grove	IA	51445	800-859-3028	712-364-3365
Rigid Hitch Inc					
3301 W Burnsville Pkwy	Burnsville	MN	55337	800-624-7630*	952-895-5001
*Cust Svc					
Sundowner Trailers Inc					
9805 S State Hwy 48	Coleman	OK	73432	800-654-3879	580-937-4255
Take 3 Trailers Inc					
1808 Hwy 105	Brenham	TX	77833	800-428-2533	979-337-9568
Unique Functional Products Corp					
135 Sunshine Ln	San Marcos	CA	92069	800-854-1905	760-744-1610

759 TRAINING & CERTIFICATION PROGRAMS - COMPUTER & INTERNET

				Toll-Free	Phone
Animation Mentor					
1400 65th St Ste 250	Emeryville	CA	94608	877-326-4628	
ASPE Inc					
114 Edinburgh S Dr Ste 200	Cary	NC	27511	877-800-5221	
Global Knowledge Training LLC					
9000 Regency Pkwy Ste 500	Cary	NC	27518	800-268-7737	919-461-8600
Health & Safety Institute Inc					
1450 Westec Dr	Eugene	OR	97402	800-447-3177	
Learning Tree International Inc					
1831 Michael Faraday Dr	Reston	VA	20190	800-843-8733*	703-709-9119
OTC: LTRE ■ *Cust Svc					
MindLeaders.com Inc					
5500 Glendon Ct Ste 200	Dublin	OH	43016	800-223-3732	614-781-7300
New Horizons Computer Learning Centers Inc					
1900 S State College Blvd Ste 450	Anaheim	CA	92806	888-236-3625	714-940-8000
PowerScore Inc					
57 Hasell St	Charleston	SC	29401	800-545-1750	

760 TRAINING PROGRAMS - CORPORATE

				Toll-Free	Phone
ActionCOACH					
5781 S Ft Apache Rd	Las Vegas	NV	89148	888-483-2828	702-795-3188
ClickSafety.com Inc					
2185 N California Blvd Ste 425	Walnut Creek	CA	94596	800-971-1080	
Creative Training Techniques International Inc					
14530 Martin Dr	Eden Prairie	MN	55344	800-383-9210	952-829-1954
Dale Carnegie & Assoc Inc					
290 Motor Pkwy	Hauppauge	NY	11788	800-231-5800	
Don Hutson Organization					
516 Tennessee St Ste 219	Memphis	TN	38103	800-647-9166	901-767-0000
Elite Business Services					
PO Box 9630	Rancho Santa Fe	CA	92067	800-204-3548	
Executive Enterprises Institute					
12 Skyline Dr	Hawthorne	NY	10532	877-334-4273	914-517-1122
Forum Corp					
265 Franklin St 4th Fl	Boston	MA	02110	800-367-8611	617-523-7300
Franklin Covey Co					
2200 West PkwyBlvd	Salt Lake City	UT	84119	800-827-1776	801-817-1776
NYSE: FC					
Fred Pryor Seminars					
9757 Metcalf Ave	Overland Park	KS	66212	800-780-8476	
Frontline Group of Texas LLC					
15021 Katy Fwy Ste 575	Houston	TX	77094	800-285-5512	281-453-6000
HealthStream Inc					
209 Tenth Ave S Ste 450	Nashville	TN	37203	800-933-9293	615-301-3100
NASDAQ: HSTM					
Hinda Incentives Inc					
2440 W 34th St	Chicago	IL	60608	800-621-4112	773-890-5900
Insight Information					
214 King St W Ste 300	Toronto	ON	M5H3S6	888-777-1707	416-777-2020
ITC Learning Corp					
1616 Anderson Rd Ste 109	McLean	VA	22102	800-638-3757	
Jones Knowledge Group Inc					
9697 E Mineral Ave	Centennial	CO	80112	800-350-6914	303-792-3111
Leadership Management Inc					
4567 Lk Shore Dr	Waco	TX	76710	800-568-1241	254-776-2060
Levinson Institute Inc					
28 Main St Ste 100	Jaffrey	NH	03452	800-290-5735	603-532-4700

				Toll-Free	Phone
National Businesswomen's Leadership Assn PO Box 419107	Kansas City	MO	64141	**800-258-7246**	913-432-7755
National Seminars Training 6901 W 63rd St 3rd Fl	Overland Park	KS	66202	**800-258-7246**	913-432-7755
Pacific Institute 1709 Harbor Ave SW	Seattle	WA	98126	**800-426-3660**	206-628-4800
Productivity Inc Four Armstrong Rd Third Fl	Shelton	CT	06484	**800-966-5423**	203-225-0451
Rockhurst University Continuing Education Ctr Inc PO Box 419107	Kansas City	MO	64141	**800-258-7246**	913-432-7755
Safety Sam Inc 2626 S Roosevelt St Ste 2	Tempe	AZ	85282	**866-478-6980**	
Sandler Sales Institute 10411 Stevenson Rd	Stevenson	MD	21153	**800-669-3537**	410-653-1993
SkillSoft PLC 107 NE Blvd	Nashua	NH	03062	**877-545-5763**	603-324-3000
Toastmasters International 23182 Arroyo Vista	Rancho Santa Margarita	CA	92688	**877-738-8118**	949-858-8255
US Learning Inc 516 Tennessee St Ste 219	Memphis	TN	38103	**800-647-9166**	901-767-5700
Veriforce LLC 19221 I-45 S Ste 200	Shenandoah	TX	77385	**800-426-1604**	
Wilson Learning Corp 8000 W 78th St Ste 200	Edina	MN	55439	**800-328-7937**	952-944-2880

761 TRAINING PROGRAMS (MISC)

SEE ALSO Training & Certification Programs - Computer & Internet ; Training Programs - Corporate ; Children's Learning Centers

				Toll-Free	Phone
Academy for Guided Imagery Inc 10780 Santa Monica Blvd Ste 290	Los Angeles	CA	90025	**800-726-2070**	
Audio-Digest Foundation 1577 E Chevy Chase Dr	Glendale	CA	91206	**800-423-2308**	818-240-7500
Canter & Assoc LLC 12975 Coral Tree Pl *Cust Svc	Los Angeles	CA	90066	**800-669-9011***	310-578-4700
Ed Necco & Assoc 178 Private Dr	South Point	OH	45680	**866-996-3226**	513-771-9600
Global University 1211 S Glenstone Ave	Springfield	MO	65804	**800-443-1083**	417-862-9533
Mission Essential Personnel LLC 4343 Easton Commons Ste 100	Columbus	OH	43219	**888-542-3447**	614-416-2345
Outward Bound 910 Jackson St	Golden	CO	80401	**866-467-7651**	207-510-7533
Sailboats Inc 250 Marina Dr	Superior	WI	54880	**800-826-7010**	715-392-7131

762 TRANSFORMERS - POWER, DISTRIBUTION, SPECIALTY

				Toll-Free	Phone
Active Power Inc 2128 W Breaker Ln *NASDAQ: ACPW*	Austin	TX	78758	**800-625-1731**	512-836-6464
AFP Transformers Inc 206 Talmedge Rd	Edison	NJ	08817	**800-843-1215**	732-248-0305
Bodine Co 236 S Mt Pleasant Rd	Collierville	TN	38027	**800-223-5728**	901-853-7211
Controlled Power Co 1955 Stephenson Hwy Ste G	Troy	MI	48083	**800-521-4792**	248-528-3700
DC Group Inc 1977 W River Rd N	Minneapolis	MN	55411	**800-838-7927**	
Delta Star Inc 270 Industrial Rd	San Carlos	CA	94070	**800-892-8673**	
Electric Research & Mfg Co-op Inc PO Box 1228	Dyersburg	TN	38025	**800-238-5587**	731-285-9121
Johnson Electric Coil Co 821 Watson St	Antigo	WI	54409	**800-826-9741**	715-627-4367
Legend Power Systems Inc 8561 Commerce Ct	Burnaby	BC	V5A4N5	**866-772-8797**	604-420-1500
Maruson Technology Corp 18557 Gale Ave	City Of Industry	CA	91748	**888-627-8766**	626-912-8388
Mesta Electronics Inc 11020 Parker Dr	North Huntingdon	PA	15642	**800-535-6798**	412-754-3000
MGM Transformer Co 5701 Smithway St	Commerce	CA	90040	**800-423-4366**	323-726-0888
MTE Corp PO Box 9013	Menomonee Falls	WI	53051	**800-455-4683**	262-253-8200
Niagara Transformer Corp 1747 Dale Rd	Buffalo	NY	14225	**800-817-5652**	716-896-6500
Olsun Electrics Corp 10901 Commercial St	Richmond	IL	60071	**800-336-5786**	
Philips Advance Light Elctro 10275 W Higgins Rd	Rosemont	IL	60018	**800-322-2086**	847-390-5000
PWR LLC 6402 Deere Rd Ste 3	Syracuse	NY	13206	**800-342-0878**	315-701-0210
Raf Technologies Inc 200 Lexington Ave	Deland	FL	32724	**888-876-6424**	386-736-1698
Shape LLC 2105 Corporate Dr	Addison	IL	60101	**800-367-5811**	630-620-8394
T & R Electric Supply Company Inc 308 SW Third St	Colman	SD	57017	**800-843-7994**	605-534-3555
Unique Lighting Systems Inc 1240 Simpson Way	Escondido	CA	92029	**800-955-4831**	
VanTran Industries Inc 7711 Imperial Dr	Waco	TX	76712	**800-433-3346**	254-772-9740
Virginia Transformer Corp 220 Glade View Dr	Roanoke	VA	24012	**800-882-3944**	540-345-9892

763 TRANSLATION SERVICES

SEE ALSO Language Schools

				Toll-Free	Phone
Boston Language Institute Inc 648 Beacon St Kenmore Sq	Boston	MA	02215	**877-998-3500**	617-262-3500
Cosmopolitan Translation Bureau Inc 53 W Jackson Blvd Ste 1260	Chicago	IL	60604	**866-370-1439**	312-726-2610
Interpreters Unlimited Inc 11199 Sorrento Vly Rd Ste 203	San Diego	CA	92121	**800-726-9891**	
Kane Transport Inc 40925 403rd Ave PO Box 126	Sauk Centre	MN	56378	**800-892-8557**	320-352-2762
Language Line Services One Lower Ragsdale Dr Bldg 2	Monterey	CA	93940	**800-752-6096**	
Language Services Associates Inc 455 Business Ctr Dr - Ste 100	Horsham	PA	19044	**800-305-9673**	
Linguistics Systems Inc 201 Broadway	Cambridge	MA	02139	**877-654-5006**	

764 TRANSPLANT CENTERS - BLOOD STEM CELL

				Toll-Free	Phone
Arthur G James Cancer Hospital & Richard J Solove Research Institute *Bone Marrow Transplant Program* 300 W Tenth Ave Ste 519	Columbus	OH	43210	**800-293-5066**	
Beth Israel Deaconess Medical Ctr Hematologic Malignancies/Bone Marrow Transplantation Program 330 Brookline Ave	Boston	MA	02215	**800-439-0183**	617-667-9920
Blood Donor Ctr at Presbyterian/St Luke's Medical Ctr 1719 E 19th Ave	Denver	CO	80218	**800-231-2222**	303-839-6000
Cedars-Sinai Medical Ctr Blood & Marrow Transplant Program 8700 Beverly Blvd AC1060	Los Angeles	CA	90048	**800-265-4186**	310-423-1160
Children's Hospital & Research Ctr at Oakland Blood & Marrow Transplantation Program 747 52nd St	Oakland	CA	94609	**888-433-9042**	510-428-3000
Children's Hospital of New York-Presbyterian *Pediatric Blood & Marrow Transplantation Program* 3959 Broadway 11 Central	New York	NY	10032	**866-463-2778**	212-305-5593
Children's Hospital of Orange County Blood & Donor Services 505 S Main St	Orange	CA	92868	**800-228-5234**	714-532-8339
Children's Hospital of Wisconsin Bone Marrow Transplant Clinic (CHW) 9000 W Wisconsin Ave PO Box 1997	Milwaukee	WI	53226	**877-266-8989**	414-266-2000
Children's Medical Ctr of Dallas Ctr for Cancer & Blood Disorders (CMC) 1935 Medical District Dr	Dallas	TX	75235	**800-222-1222**	214-456-7000
City of Hope National Medical Ctr Hematology & Hematopoietic Cell Transplantation Div 1500 E Duarte Rd	Duarte	CA	91010	**800-535-7119**	626-256-4673
Cleveland Clinic Bone Marrow Transplantation Program 9500 Euclid Ave	Cleveland	OH	44195	**800-223-2273**	216-444-0261
Dana-Farber Cancer Institute Stem Cell/Bone Marrow Transplant Program 44 Binney St Dana Bldg 1B Rm 30	Boston	MA	02115	**866-408-3324**	617-632-3591
Fairfax PET Imaging Ctr 8503 Arlington Blvd Ste 120 Lowr Level	Fairfax	VA	22031	**800-358-8831**	703-698-4441
Fox Chase Cancer Ctr Bone Marrow Transplant Program 333 Cottman Ave	Philadelphia	PA	19111	**888-369-2427**	
Franciscan Alliance, Inc St Francis Hospital 1600 Albany St	Beech Grove	IN	46107	**800-361-0016**	317-528-5500
Froedtert Hospital Bone Marrow Transplant Program 9200 W Wisconsin Ave	Milwaukee	WI	53226	**800-272-3666**	414-805-3666
H Lee Moffitt Cancer Ctr & Research Institute Blood & Marrow Transplantation Program 12902 Magnolia Dr	Tampa	FL	33612	**888-663-3488**	
Helen DeVos Children's Hospital Pediatric Hematology/Oncology Program 100 Michigan NE	Grand Rapids	MI	49503	**866-989-7999**	616-391-9000
Indiana University Cancer Ctr Bone Marrow & Stem Cell Transplant Team 550 N University Blvd	Indianapolis	IN	46202	**888-600-4822**	317-948-6997
James Graham Brown Cancer Ctr 529 S Jackson St	Louisville	KY	40202	**866-530-5516**	502-562-4369
Karmanos Cancer Institute Bone Marrow/Stem Cell Transplant Program 4100 John R Rm 1308-A	Detroit	MI	48201	**800-527-6266**	
Medical City Hospital Transplant Ctr 7777 Forest Ln Bldg A 12 S	Dallas	TX	75230	**800-348-4318**	972-566-7000
Memorial Sloan-Kettering Cancer Ctr Bone Marrow Transplant Service 1275 York Ave	New York	NY	10065	**800-525-2225**	212-639-6009
Mount Sinai Hospital Bone Marrow Transplant Program 19 E 98th St Ste 4B	New York	NY	10029	**866-682-9380**	212-241-6021
North Shore-Long Island Jewish Health System *Bone Marrow & Blood Cell Transplant Program* 300 Community Dr	Manhasset	NY	11030	**888-321-3627**	516-562-8973
Oregon Health & Science University *Bone Marrow Transplant Program (OHSU)* 3181 SW Sam Jackson Pk Rd	Portland	OR	97239	**800-799-7233**	503-494-1617
Roswell Park Cancer Institute Blood & Marrow Transplantation Program Elm & Carlton Sts	Buffalo	NY	14263	**800-685-6825**	716-845-3516
Saint Jude Children's Research Hospital Stem Cell Transplantation Div 262 Danny Thomas Pl	Memphis	TN	38105	**800-822-6344**	901-595-3300
Saint Louis University Cancer Ctr Hematology & Oncology Div 3655 Vista Ave	Saint Louis	MO	63110	**866-977-4440**	314-977-4440
Seattle Cancer Care Alliance 825 Eastlake Ave E PO Box 19023	Seattle	WA	98109	**800-804-8824**	206-288-1024
Shands Hospital at the University of Florida Blood & Bone Marrow Transplant Program 1600 SW Archer Rd PO Box 100403	Gainesville	FL	32610	**800-749-7424**	352-733-0972
Stanford University School of Medicine Blood & Marrow Transplant Program 300 Pasteur Dr Rm H-3249 MC 5623	Stanford	CA	94305	**888-275-5724**	650-723-0822
Texas Transplant Institute 7700 Floyd Curl Dr	San Antonio	TX	78229	**800-298-7824**	210-575-3817
Trustees of the University of Pennsylvania *Bone Marrow & Stem Cell Transplant Program* 3400 Spruce St	Philadelphia	PA	19104	**800-417-9391**	215-662-4533
University Medical Ctr Blood & Marrow Transplantation Program 1501 N Campbell Ave PO Box 24-5176	Tucson	AZ	85724	**800-524-5928**	520-694-0111
University of Illinois Medical Ctr Stem Cell Transplant Unit 1740 W Taylor St	Chicago	IL	60612	**866-600-2273**	312-996-3900
University of Maryland Greenebaum Cancer Ctr 22 S Greene St Ste N9E17	Baltimore	MD	21201	**800-888-8823**	410-328-7904
University of Miami Hospital & Clinics (UMHC) *Sylvester Comprehensive Cancer Ctr* 1475 NW 12th Ave	Miami	FL	33136	**800-545-2292**	305-243-1000
University of Nebraska Medical Ctr Bone Marrow & Stem Cell Transplantation Program (Adults) 987400 Nebraska Medical Ctr	Omaha	NE	68198	**800-922-0000**	402-559-2000
Hematopoietic Cell Transplant Program 2201 Inwood Rd Second Fl	Dallas	TX	75390	**866-645-6455**	214-645-4673
University of Utah Hospital & Clinics (UUHSC) *Blood & Marrow Transplant Program* 50 N Medical Dr *General	Salt Lake City	UT	84132	**800-824-2073***	801-581-2121

Name / Address	City	State	ZIP	Toll-Free	Phone
VA Puget Sound Health Care System - Seattle Div 1660 S Columbian Way	Seattle	WA	98108	800-329-8387	206-762-1010
Winship Cancer Institute of Emory University 1365 Clifton Rd NE	Atlanta	GA	30322	888-946-7447	404-778-1900

765 TRANSPORTATION EQUIPMENT & SUPPLIES - WHOL

Name / Address	City	State	ZIP	Toll-Free	Phone
A & K Railroad Materials Inc 1505 S Redwood Rd *Sales	Salt Lake City	UT	84104	800-453-8812*	801-974-5484
AAR Aircraft Turbine Ctr 1100 N Wood Dale Rd 1 AAR Pl *General	Wood Dale	IL	60191	800-422-2213*	630-227-2000
AAR Corp 1100 N Wood Dale Rd 1 AAR Pl *NYSE: AIR*	Wood Dale	IL	60191	800-422-2213	630-227-2000
AAR Distribution 1100 N Wood Dale Rd 1 AAR Pl	Wood Dale	IL	60191	800-422-2213	630-227-2000
AIRCO Group 1853 S Eisenhower Ct	Wichita	KS	67209	800-835-2243	316-945-0445
AirLiance Materials LLC 450 Medinah Rd *General	Roselle	IL	60172	877-233-5800*	847-233-5800
Airparts Company Inc 2310 NW 55th Ct	Fort Lauderdale	FL	33309	800-392-4999	954-739-3575
Argo International Corp 160 Chubb Ave	Lyndhurst	NJ	07071	877-274-6468	201-561-7010
Atlantic Track & Turnout Co 270 N Broad St	Bloomfield	NJ	07003	800-631-1274	973-748-5885
Birmingham Rail & Locomotive Company Inc PO Box 530157	Birmingham	AL	35253	800-241-2260	205-424-7245
DAC International Inc 6702 McNeil Dr	Austin	TX	78729	800-527-2531	512-331-5323
Defender Industries Inc 42 Great Neck Rd	Waterford	CT	06385	800-628-8225	860-701-3400
Donovan Marine Inc 6316 Humphreys St	Harahan	LA	70123	800-347-4464	504-488-5731
Dreyfus-Cortney & Lowery Bros Rigging 4400 N Galvez St	New Orleans	LA	70117	800-228-7660	504-944-3366
E-Z-GO Division of Textron Inc 1451 Marvin Griffin Rd	Augusta	GA	30906	800-241-5855	706-798-4311
Edmo Distributors Inc 12830 E Mirabeau Pkwy	Spokane Valley	WA	99216	800-235-3300	509-535-8280
ERS Industries Inc 1005 Indian Church Rd	West Seneca	NY	14224	800-993-6446	716-675-2040
Fisheries Supply Co 1900 N Northlake Way	Seattle	WA	98103	800-426-6930	206-632-4462
Freundlich Supply Co Inc 2200 Arthur Kill Rd	Staten Island	NY	10309	800-221-0260	718-356-1500
General Aviation Services LLC 1155 E Ensell Rd	Lake Zurich	IL	60047	800-586-5336	847-726-5000
Heli-Mart Inc 3184 Airway Ave Ste E	Costa Mesa	CA	92626	800-826-6899	714-755-2999
Helicopter Support Inc (HSI) 124 Quarry Rd	Trumbull	CT	06611	800-795-6051	203-416-4000
Industry-Railway Suppliers Inc 811 Golf Ln	Bensenville	IL	60106	800-728-0029	630-766-5708
Intermountain Air LLC 301 N 2370 W	Salt Lake City	UT	84116	800-433-9617	801-322-1645
Jerry's Marine Service 100 SW 16th St	Fort Lauderdale	FL	33315	800-432-2231	954-525-0311
JMA Railroad Supply Co 381 S Main Pl	Carol Stream	IL	60188	800-874-0643	630-653-9224
Kellogg Marine Supply Inc Five Enterprise Dr	Old Lyme	CT	06371	800-243-9303	860-434-6002
O'halloran International Inc PO Box 1804	Des Moines	IA	50305	800-800-6503	515-967-3300
Parker-Hannifin Corp 1160 Ctr Rd	Avon	OH	44011	800-272-5464	440-937-6211
PartsBase Inc 905 Clint Moore Rd *Cust Svc	Boca Raton	FL	33487	888-322-6896*	561-953-0700
Paxton Co 1111 Ingleside Rd	Norfolk	VA	23502	800-234-7290	757-853-6781
Rails Co 101 Newark Way	Maplewood	NJ	07040	800-217-2457	973-763-4320
S-Line Cargo Control & Safety Products 11414 Mathis	Dallas	TX	75234	800-687-9900	
Spencer Industries Inc 19308 68th Ave S	Kent	WA	98032	800-367-5646	253-796-1100
Valley Power Systems Inc 425 S Hacienda Blvd	City of Industry	CA	91745	800-924-4265	626-333-1243
Van Bortel Aircraft Inc 4912 S Collins	Arlington	TX	76018	800-759-4295	817-468-7788
Washington Chain & Supply Inc 2901 Utah Ave S PO Box 3645	Seattle	WA	98124	800-851-3429	206-623-8500
West Marine Inc 500 Westridge Dr *NASDAQ: WMAR*	Watsonville	CA	95076	800-262-8464	831-728-2700
Yingling Aircraft Inc 2010 Airport Rd	Wichita	KS	67209	800-835-0083	316-943-3246
ZAP 501 Fourth St *OTC: ZAAP* ■ *Orders	Santa Rosa	CA	95401	800-251-4555*	707-525-8658

766 TRAVEL AGENCIES

SEE ALSO Tour Operators ; Travel Agency Networks

Name / Address	City	State	ZIP	Toll-Free	Phone
ABC Global Services 6400 Shafer Ct Ste 310	Rosemont	IL	60018	800-722-5179	
Adelman Travel Group 6980 N Port Washington Rd *Cust Svc	Milwaukee	WI	53217	800-248-5562*	414-352-7600
ADTRAV Travel Management 4555 S Lake Pkwy	Birmingham	AL	35244	800-476-2952	205-444-4800
AESU Travel Inc 3922 Hickory Ave	Baltimore	MD	21211	800-638-7640	410-366-5494
Alamo Travel Group Inc 8930 Wurzbach Rd Ste 100	San Antonio	TX	78240	800-692-5266	210-593-0084
Alaska Tour & Travel 9170 Jewel Lk Rd Ste 202 PO Box 221011	Anchorage	AK	99502	800-208-0200	907-245-0200
Alaska Travel Adventures Inc 9085 Glacier Hwy Ste 301	Juneau	AK	99801	800-323-5757	907-789-0052
All Aboard Cruises Inc 11114 SW 127th Ct	Miami	FL	33186	800-883-8657	305-385-8657
All Cruise Travel 1723 Hamilton Ave	San Jose	CA	95125	800-227-8473	408-295-1200
All-Inclusive Vacations Inc 1595 Iris St	Lakewood	CO	80215	866-980-6483	303-980-6483
Apple Vacations Inc 101 NW Pt Blvd	Elk Grove Village	IL	60007	800-517-2000	
Austin Travel 6801 Jericho Tpke Ste 100	Syosset	NY	11791	800-645-7466	516-465-1000
Avanti Destinations Inc 1629 SW Salmon St	Portland	OR	97205	800-422-5053	503-295-1100
Balboa Travel Management Inc 5414 Oberlin Dr Ste 300	San Diego	CA	92121	800-359-8773	858-678-3300
Best Travel Inc 8600 W Bryn Mawr Ave	Chicago	IL	60631	800-840-4822	773-380-0150
Bon Voyage Travel 1640 E River Rd Ste 115	Tucson	AZ	85718	800-439-7963	520-797-1110
Brownell World Travel 216 Summit Blvd Ste 220	Birmingham	AL	35243	800-999-3960	205-802-6222
Burkhalter Travel Agency 6501 Mineral Pt Rd	Madison	WI	53705	800-556-9286	608-833-5200
Carefree Vacations Inc 9710 Scranton Rd Ste 300	San Diego	CA	92121	800-266-3476	858-459-4074
Cass Tours 2621 Green River Rd Ste 105-222	Corona	CA	92882	800-593-6510	951-371-3511
Casto Travel Inc 2560 N First St Ste 150	San Jose	CA	95131	800-832-3445	408-984-7000
City Escape Holidays 13470 Washington Blvd Ste 101	Marina del Rey	CA	90292	800-222-0022	
Classic Custom Vacations 5893 Rue Ferrari	San Jose	CA	95138	800-635-1333	
Clipper Navigation Inc 2701 Alaskan Way Pier 69	Seattle	WA	98121	800-888-2535	206-443-2560
Conlin Travel Inc 3270 Washtenaw Ave	Ann Arbor	MI	48104	800-426-6546	734-677-0900
Corporate Travel Management Group 450 E 22nd St	Lombard	IL	60148	866-545-6789	630-691-8000
Covington International Travel 4401 Dominion Blvd	Glen Allen	VA	23060	800-922-9238	804-747-7077
Crown Travel & Cruises 240 Newton Rd Ste 106	Raleigh	NC	27615	800-869-7447	919-870-1986
Cruise Brokers 2803 W Busch Blvd Ste 100	Tampa	FL	33618	800-409-1919	813-288-9597
Cruise Concepts 1329 Eniswood Pkwy	Palm Harbor	FL	34683	800-752-7963	727-784-7245
Cruise Connection LLC 7932 N Oak Ste 210	Kansas City	MO	64118	800-572-0004	816-420-8688
Cruise Connections Inc 3411 Healy Dr Ste D	Winston-Salem	NC	27103	800-248-7447	
Cruise People Inc 10191 W Sample Rd Ste 215	Coral Springs	FL	33065	800-642-2469	954-753-0069
Cruise People Ltd 1252 Lawrence Ave E Ste 210	Don Mills	ON	M3A1C3	800-268-6523	416-444-2410
Cruise Shop, The 700 Pasquinelli Dr Ste C	Westmont	IL	60559	800-622-6456	630-325-7447
Cruise Vacation Ctr 2042 Central Pk Ave	Yonkers	NY	10710	800-803-7245	
Cruise Web Inc 8100 Corporate Dr Ste 300	Landover	MD	20785	800-377-9383	240-487-0155
CruiseOne Inc 1201 W Cypress Creek Rd Ste 100	Fort Lauderdale	FL	33309	800-278-4731	
Cruises Cruises 6604 Antoine Dr	Houston	TX	77091	800-245-9806	713-681-9866
Cruises Inc 1201 W Cypress Creek Rd Ste 100 *Cust Svc	Fort Lauderdale	FL	33309	888-282-1249*	
Direct Travel 95 New Jersey 17	Paramus	NJ	07652	800-831-1366	201-847-9000
E Tour & Travel 3626 Quadrangle Blvd Ste 400 *Sales	Orlando	FL	32817	800-339-5120*	407-515-2400
Elegant Voyages 1802 Keesling Ct	San Jose	CA	95125	800-555-3534	408-239-0300
Euro Lloyd Travel Inc 1640 Hempstead Tpke	East Meadow	NY	11554	800-334-2724	516-228-4970
Friendly Cruises 3081 S Sycamore Village Dr	Superstition Mountain	AZ	85118	888-842-1786	480-358-1496
Gant Travel Management 304 W Kirkwood Ave Ste 1 *Cust Svc	Bloomington	IN	47404	800-742-4198*	
Gil Tours Travel Inc 1511 Walnut St Ste 200	Philadelphia	PA	19102	800-223-3855	215-568-6655
Giselle's Travel Inc 1300 Ethan Way Ste 100	Sacramento	CA	95825	800-782-5545	916-922-5500
Global Travel 900 W Jefferson St	Boise	ID	83702	800-584-8888	208-387-1000
GOGO WorldWide Vacations 69 Spring St	Ramsey	NJ	07446	800-254-3477	
Golden Sports Tours 301 W Parker Rd Ste 206	Plano	TX	75023	800-966-8258	
Gwin's Travel Planners Inc 212 N Kirkwood Rd	Saint Louis	MO	63122	800-433-9211	314-822-1957
Islands in the Sun Cruises & Tours Inc 121 Bayview	Grasonville	MD	21638	800-278-7786	410-827-3812
Japan Travel Bureau USA Inc 156 W 56th St Third Fl	New York	NY	10019	800-235-3523	212-698-4900

		Toll-Free	Phone

Lawyers' Travel Service
71 Fifth Ave .... New York NY 10003 **800-431-1112***
*General

Liberty Travel Inc
69 Spring St .... Ramsey NJ 07446 **888-271-1584** 201-934-3500

Lorraine Travel Bureau Inc
377 Alhambra Cir .... Coral Gables FL 33134 **800-666-8911** 305-446-4433

Maupin Travel Inc
2501 Blue Ridge Rd .... Raleigh NC 27607 **800-786-2738** 919-821-2146

MC & A Inc
615 Piikoi St Ste 1000 .... Honolulu HI 96814 **877-589-5589***
*General 808-589-5500

Merit Travel Group Inc
111 Peter St Ste 200 .... Toronto ON M5V2H1 **800-268-5940** 416-364-3775

Miller Travel Services Inc
4380 W 12th St .... Erie PA 16505 **800-989-8747** 814-833-8888

Montrose Travel
2355 Honolulu Ave .... Montrose CA 91020 **800-766-4687**

More Hawaii for Less Inc
1200 Quail St Ste 290 .... Newport Beach CA 92660 **800-967-6687** 949-724-5050

National Discount Cruise Co
1401 N Cedar Crest Blvd Ste 56 .... Allentown PA 18104 **800-788-8108** 610-439-4883

Northstar Cruises
80 Bloomfield Ave Ste 102 .... Caldwell NJ 07006 **800-249-9360**

Ocean One Cruise Outlet
3264 Marilynn St .... Lancaster CA 93536 **888-353-1922** 661-949-2873

Omega World Travel Inc
3102 Omega Office Pk Dr .... Fairfax VA 22031 **800-756-6342** 703-359-0200

Orvis International Travel
178 Conservation Way .... Sunderland VT 05250 **800-547-4322** 802-362-8790

Paradise Island Vacations
1000 S Pine Island Rd Ste 800 .... Plantation FL 33324 **888-877-7525***
*Resv 954-809-2000

Pleasant Holidays LLC
2404 Townsgate Rd .... Westlake Village CA 91361 **800-742-9244** 818-991-3390

Premier Golf
4355 River Green Pkwy .... Duluth GA 30096 **866-260-4409** 770-291-4202

Prestige Travel & Cruises Inc
6175 Spring Mountain Rd .... Las Vegas NV 89146 **800-758-5693** 702-251-5552

Professional Travel Inc
25000 Great Northern Corporate Ctr
Ste 170 .... Cleveland OH 44070 **800-247-0060** 440-734-8800

Protravel International Inc
515 Madison Ave 10th Fl .... New York NY 10022 **800-227-1059** 212-755-4550

Regal Travel
615 Piikoi St Ste 104 .... Honolulu HI 96814 **800-799-0865** 808-566-7620

Rich Worldwide Travel Inc
500 Mamaroneck Ave .... Harrison NY 10528 **800-431-1130** 914-835-7600

Roeder Travel Ltd
9805 York Rd .... Cockeysville MD 21030 **800-379-9887** 410-667-6090

Seaside Golf Vacations
218 Main St .... North Myrtle Beach SC 29582 **877-732-6999**

SGH Golf Inc
9403 Kenwood Rd Ste C110 ...... Cincinnati OH 45242 **800-284-8884** 513-984-0414

Sita World Travel Inc
16250 Ventura Blvd .... Encino CA 91436 **800-421-5643** 818-990-9530

Sports Empire PO Box 6169 .... Lakewood CA 90714 **800-255-5258** 562-920-2350

Star Travel Services Inc
1025 Acuff Rd Fourth Fl .... Bloomington IN 47404 **800-542-1687** 812-336-6811

Sterling Cruises & Travel
8700 W Flagler St Ste 105 .... Miami FL 33174 **800-435-7967** 305-592-2522

Stevens Travel Management Inc
119 W 40th St 14th Fl .... New York NY 10018 **800-275-7400** 212-696-4300

Studentcity.com Inc
8 Essex Ctr Dr .... Peabody MA 01960 **888-777-4642**

SunQuest Vacations
77-6435 Kuakini Hwy .... Kailua-Kona HI 96740 **800-367-5168** 808-329-6438

Sunsational Cruises
2470 E Glen Canyon Rd .... Green Valley AZ 85614 **800-239-6252** 480-491-6248

Tenenbaum's Vacation Stores Inc
300 Market St .... Kingston PA 18704 **800-545-7099** 570-288-8747

Tower Travel Management
53 Ogden Ave Ste 2520 ...... Clarendon Hills IL 60514 **800-542-9700**

Tramex Travel Inc
4505 Spicewood Springs Rd Ste 200 .... Austin TX 78759 **800-527-3039** 512-343-2201

Transat AT Inc
300 Leo-Pariseau St Ste 600 ..... Montreal QC H2X4C2 **800-387-0825** 514-987-1616
TSE: TRZ.B

Travel & Transport Inc
2120 S 72nd St .... Omaha NE 68124 **800-228-2545** 402-399-4500

Travel Authority Inc
702 N Shore Dr Ste 300 ...... Jeffersonville IN 47130 **888-501-7010** 812-206-5100

Travel Destinations Management Group Inc
110 Painters Mill Rd .... Owings Mills MD 21117 **800-635-7307** 410-363-3111

Travel Focus
First Class International
8111 LBJ Fwy Ste 900 .... Dallas tx 75251 **800-222-9968** 214-915-9000

Travel Impressions Ltd
465 Smith St .... Farmingdale NY 11735 **800-284-0044** 631-845-8000

Travel Team Inc
2495 Main St .... Buffalo NY 14214 **800-245-8326** 716-862-7600

Travelennium Inc
556 Colonial Rd .... Memphis TN 38117 **800-844-4924** 901-767-0761

Traveline Travel Agencies Inc
4074 Erie St .... Willoughby OH 44094 **888-700-8747** 440-602-8090

Travelong Inc
225 W 35th St Ste 1501 .... New York NY 10001 **800-537-6043** 212-736-2166

TravelStore Inc
11601 Wilshire Blvd .... Los Angeles CA 90025 **800-850-3224** 310-575-5540

Ultramar Travel Management International
14 E 47th St Fifth Fl .... New York NY 10017 **888-856-2929**

Valerie Wilson Travel Inc
475 Pk Ave S .... New York NY 10016 **800-776-1116** 212-532-3400

Virtuoso
505 Main St Ste 5 .... Fort Worth TX 76102 **800-401-4274** 817-870-0300

World Travel Bureau Inc
618 N Main St .... Santa Ana CA 92701 **800-899-3370** 714-835-8111

		Toll-Free	Phone

World Travel Holdings (WTH)
100 Fordham Rd Bldg C Bldg C ..... Wilmington MA 01887 **877-958-7447** 617-424-7990

World Travel Inc
1724 W Schuylkill Rd .... Douglassville PA 19518 **800-341-2014** 610-327-9000

Worldwide Holidays Inc
7800 Red Rd Ste 112 .... South Miami FL 33143 **800-327-9854** 305-665-0841

Worldwide Travel & Cruise Assoc Inc
150 S University Dr Ste E .... Plantation FL 33324 **800-881-8484** 954-452-8800

Wright Travel Inc
2505 21st Ave S Fifth Fl .... Nashville TN 37212 **800-577-0888** 615-783-1111

767   TRAVEL AGENCY NETWORKS

SEE ALSO Travel Agencies

A travel agency network is a consortium of travel agencies in which a host agency provides technology, marketing, distribution, customer support, and other services to the network member agencies in exchange for a percentage of the member agencies' profits.

		Toll-Free	Phone

American Express Company Inc
World Financial Ctr 200 Vesey St ...... New York NY 10285 **800-528-4800** 212-640-2000
NYSE: AXP

Carlson Wagonlit Travel Inc
701 Carlson Pkwy .... Minnetonka MN 55305 **800-213-7295**

CP Franchising LLC
3300 University Dr .... Coral Springs FL 33065 **800-683-0206** 954-344-8060

CruiseOne Inc
1201 W Cypress Creek Rd
Ste 100 .... Fort Lauderdale FL 33309 **800-278-4731**

Ensemble Travel
256 W 38th St 11th Fl. .... New York NY 10018 **800-576-2378** 212-545-7460

Global Travel International
2600 Lk Lucien Dr Ste 201 .... Maitland FL 32751 **800-715-4440** 407-660-7800

MAST Vacation Partners Inc
635 Butterfield Rd Ste 150 ..... Oakbrook Terrace IL 60181 **888-778-4722** 630-889-9817

Nexion
6225 N State Hwy 161 Ste 450 .... Irving TX 75038 **800-949-6410** 408-280-6410

RADIUS
7700 Wisconsin Ave Ste 400 .... Bethesda MD 20814 **800-989-3059** 301-718-9500

Raptim Humanitarian Travel
6420 Inducon Dr W Ste A .... Sanborn NY 14132 **800-272-7846** 716-754-9232

Results Travel
701 Carlson Pkwy .... Minnetonka MN 55305 **800-456-4000** 763-212-5000

Travelex International Inc
2061 N Barrington Rd ...... Hoffman Estates IL 60169 **800-882-0499** 847-882-0400

UNIGLOBE Travel USA LLC
18662 MacArthur Blvd Ste 100. .... Irvine CA 92612 **877-438-4338** 949-623-9000

Vacation.com Inc
1650 King St Ste 450 .... Alexandria VA 22314 **800-843-0733**

Virtuoso
505 Main St Ste 5. .... Fort Worth TX 76102 **800-401-4274** 817-870-0300

WorldClass Travel Network
7831 Southtown Ctr Ste A .... Bloomington MN 55431 **800-234-3576** 952-835-8636

WorldTEK Event & Travel Management
One Audubon Ste 400. .... New Haven CT 06511 **800-233-5989** 203-772-0470

TRAVEL INFORMATION - CITY

SEE Convention & Visitors Bureaus

768   TRAVEL SERVICES - ONLINE

SEE ALSO Hotel Reservations Services

		Toll-Free	Phone

BedandBreakfast.com
700 Brazos St Ste B-700. .... Austin TX 78701 **800-462-2632*** 512-322-2700
*Sales

Cruises.com
100 Fordham Rd Bldg C .... Wilmington MA 01887 **800-288-6006**

Hotwire.com
655 Montgomery St Ste 600. ..... San Francisco CA 94111 **866-468-9473*** 415-343-8400
*Cust Svc

LastMinuteTravel.com Inc
220 E Central Pkwy Ste 4000 .... Altamonte Springs FL 32701 **800-442-0568** 407-667-8700

Lonely Planet Online
150 Linden St .... Oakland CA 94607 **800-275-8555** 510-250-6400

National Recreation Reservation Service (NRRS)
PO Box 140 .... Ballston Spa NY 12020 **877-444-6777** 518-885-3639

Priceline.com LLC
800 Connecticut Ave .... Norwalk CT 06854 **800-774-2354**
NASDAQ: PCLN

ReserveAmerica Holdings Inc
2480 Meadowvale Blvd Ste 120 .... Mississauga ON L5N8M6 **877-444-6777**

Vacation.com Inc
1650 King St Ste 450 .... Alexandria VA 22314 **800-843-0733**

769   TRAVEL & TOURISM INFORMATION - CANADIAN

		Toll-Free	Phone

Nova Scotia Dept of Tourism & Culture
1800 Argyle St PO Box 456 .... Halifax NS B3J2R5 **800-565-0000** 902-425-5781

NWT Tourism PO Box 610 .... Yellowknife NT X1A2N5 **800-661-0788** 867-873-7200

Ontario Tourism Marketing Partnership Corp
10 Dundas St E Ste 900 .... Toronto ON M7A2A1 **800-668-2746** 905-282-1721

Prince Edward Island Tourism
PO Box 2000 .... Charlottetown PE C1A7N8 **800-463-4734** 902-368-4000

Tourism New Brunswick
PO Box 12345 .... Campbellton NB E3N3T6 **800-561-0123**

Tourism Saskatchewan
1621 Albert St .... Regina SK S4P2S5 **877-237-2273** 306-787-9600

Tourism Yukon
PO Box 2703 .... Whitehorse YT Y1A2C6 **800-661-0494**

Travel Manitoba
155 Carlton St Seventh Fl. .... Winnipeg MB R3C3H8 **800-665-0040** 204-927-7800

770   TRAVEL & TOURISM INFORMATION - FOREIGN TRAVEL

SEE ALSO Embassies & Consulates - Foreign, in the US

			Toll-Free	Phone
Anguilla Tourist Marketing Office				
246 Central Ave	White Plains NY	10606	800-553-4939	914-287-2400
Antigua & Barbuda Dept of Tourism & Trade				
305 E 47th St 6th Fl	New York NY	10017	888-268-4227	212-541-4117
Aruba Tourism Authority				
1750 Powder Springs St Ste 190	Marietta GA	30064	800-862-7822	404-892-7822
Bahamas Tourism Office				
1200 S Pine Island Rd Ste 750	Plantation FL	33324	800-327-7678	954-236-9292
Bermuda Dept of Tourism				
675 Third Ave 20th Fl	New York NY	10017	800-223-6106	212-818-9800
Bonaire Government Tourist Office				
80 Broad St Ste 3202 32nd Fl	New York NY	10004	800-328-2288	212-956-5912
Cayman Islands Dept of Tourism				
350 Fifth Ave	New York NY	10118	800-235-5888	212-889-9009
Croatian National Tourist Office				
350 Fifth Ave Ste 4003	New York NY	10118	800-829-4416	212-279-8672
Guided Tours of Trois-Rivieres				
1457 Rue Notre Dame	Trois-Rivieres QC	G9A4X4	800-313-1123	819-375-1122
Hong Kong Tourism Board				
5670 Wilshire Blvd Ste 1230	Los Angeles CA	90036	800-282-4582	323-938-4582
India Tourist Office				
1270 Ave of the Americas Ste 303	New York NY	10020	800-425-1414*	212-586-4901
*General				
Irish Tourist Board				
345 Pk Ave 17th Fl	New York NY	10154	800-223-6470	212-418-0800
Israel Government Tourist Office				
800 Second Ave 16th Fl	New York NY	10017	877-248-8687	212-499-5660
Jamaica Tourist Board				
5201 Blue Lagoon Dr Ste 670	Miami FL	33126	800-233-4582	305-665-0557
Jordan Tourism Board (JTB)				
1307 Dolley Madison Blvd Ste 2A	McLean VA	22101	877-733-5673	703-243-7404
Kenya Tourism Board				
6442 City W Pkwy 6442 City W Pkwy	Minneapolis MN	55344	800-223-6486	310-649-7718
Korea National Tourism Organization				
Two Executive Dr Ste 750	Fort Lee NJ	07024	800-868-7567	201-585-0909
Martinique Promotion Bureau				
444 Madison Ave 16th Fl	New York NY	10022	800-391-4909	
Mexico Tourism Board (CSTM)				
225 N Michigan Ave Ste 1800	Chicago IL	60601	800-446-3942*	
*General				
Monaco Government Tourist Office				
565 Fifth Ave 23rd Fl	New York NY	10017	800-753-9696	212-286-3330
Puerto Rico Tourism Co				
Paseo La Princesa	Old San Juan PR	00902	800-866-7827	787-721-2400
Russian National Tourist Office				
224 W 30th St Ste 701	New York NY	10001	877-221-7120	646-473-2233
Saint Lucia Tourist Board				
800 Second Ave Ninth Fl	New York NY	10017	800-456-3984	212-867-2950
Saint Vincent & the Grenadines Tourist Information Office				
801 Second Ave 21st Fl	New York NY	10017	800-729-1726	212-687-4981
Switzerland Tourism				
608 Fifth Ave Ste 202	New York NY	10020	800-794-7795	212-757-5944
Tourism Malaysia				
818 W Seventh St Ste 970	Los Angeles CA	90017	800-336-6842	213-689-9702
Turks & Caicos Islands Tourism Office				
60 E 42nd St Ste 2817	New York NY	10165	800-241-0824	646-375-8830

771   TREE SERVICES

SEE ALSO Landscape Design & Related Services

			Toll-Free	Phone
Asplundh Tree Expert Co				
708 Blair Mill Rd	Willow Grove PA	19090	800-248-8733	215-784-4200
Davey Tree Expert Co				
1500 N Mantua St	Kent OH	44240	800-445-8733	330-673-9511
FA Bartlett Tree Expert Co				
1290 E Main St	Stamford CT	06902	877-227-8538	203-323-1131
Lewis Tree Service Inc				
300 Lucius Gordon Dr	West Henrietta NY	14586	800-333-1593	585-436-3208
Nelson Tree Service Inc				
3300 Office Pk Dr Ste 205	Dayton OH	45439	800-522-4311	937-294-1313
Trees Inc				
650 N Sam Houston Pkwy E Ste 209	Houston TX	77060	866-865-9617	281-447-1327
West Tree Service Inc				
6300 Forbing Rd	Little Rock AR	72209	800-779-2967	501-568-5111

772   TROPHIES, PLAQUES, AWARDS

			Toll-Free	Phone
Architectural Bronze Aluminum Corp				
655 Deerfield Rd Ste 100	Deerfield IL	60015	800-339-6581	
Bruce Fox Inc				
1909 McDonald Ln	New Albany IN	47150	877-336-9601	812-945-3511
Classic Medallics Inc				
520 S Fulton Ave	Mount Vernon NY	10550	800-221-1348	914-530-6259
F & H Ribbon Co Inc				
3010 S Pipeline Rd	Euless TX	76040	800-877-5775	
Jostens Inc				
3601 Minnesota Ave Ste 400	Minneapolis MN	55435	800-235-4774	952-830-3300
Metallic Arts Inc				
914 N Lake Rd	Spokane WA	99212	800-541-3200	509-489-7173
Regalia Manufacturing Co				
2018 Fourth Ave	Rock Island IL	61201	800-798-7471	309-788-7471
RS Owens & Co				
5535 N Lynch Ave	Chicago IL	60630	800-282-6200	773-282-6000
Trophyland USA Inc				
7001 W 20th Ave	Hialeah FL	33014	800-327-5820	

			Toll-Free	Phone
US Bronze Sign Co				
811 Second Ave	New Hyde Park NY	11040	800-872-5155	516-352-5155
Wilson Trophy Co				
1724 Frienza Ave	Sacramento CA	95815	800-635-5005	916-927-9733

TRUCK BODIES

SEE Motor Vehicles - Commercial & Special Purpose

773   TRUCK RENTAL & LEASING

			Toll-Free	Phone
Carco National Lease Inc				
2905 N 32nd St	Fort Smith AR	72904	800-643-2596	479-441-3200
DeCarolis Truck Rental Inc				
333 Colfax St	Rochester NY	14606	800-666-1169	585-254-1169
Idealease Inc				
430 N Rand Rd	North Barrington IL	60010	800-435-3273	847-304-6000
MHC Kenworth				
1524 N Corrington Ave	Kansas City MO	64120	888-259-4826	816-483-7035
National Truck Leasing System				
450 S Summit Ave	Oakbrook IL	60181	800-729-6857	630-953-8878
PACCAR Leasing Corp				
777 106th Ave NE	Bellevue WA	98004	800-759-2979	425-468-7877
Rush Enterprises Inc				
555 IH 35 S Ste 500	New Braunfels TX	78130	800-973-7874	830-626-5200
NASDAQ: RUSHA				
Ryder System Inc				
11690 NW 105th St	Miami FL	33178	800-297-9337	305-500-3726
NYSE: R				
Star Leasing Co				
4080 Business Pk Dr	Columbus OH	43204	888-771-1004	614-278-9999
Star Truck Rentals Inc				
3940 Eastern Ave SE	Grand Rapids MI	49508	800-748-0468	616-243-7033
U-Haul International Inc				
2727 N Central Ave	Phoenix AZ	85004	800-528-0361	

774   TRUCK TRAILERS

SEE ALSO Motor Vehicles - Commercial & Special Purpose

			Toll-Free	Phone
4-Star Trailers Inc				
10000 NW Tenth St	Oklahoma City OK	73127	800-848-3095	405-324-7827
American Carrier Equipment Trailer Sales LLC				
2285 E Date Ave	Fresno CA	93706	800-344-2174	559-442-1500
Arkansas Trailer Manufacturing Co				
3200 S Elm St	Little Rock AR	72204	800-666-5417	501-666-5417
Beall Corp				
9200 N Ramsey Blvd	Portland OR	97203	855-219-5686	
Brenner Tank LLC				
450 Arlington Ave	Fond du Lac WI	54935	800-558-9750	920-922-5020
Bri-Mar Mfg LLC				
1080 S Main St	Chambersburg PA	17201	800-732-5845	717-263-6116
Circle J Trailers				
312 W Simplot Blvd	Caldwell ID	83605	800-247-2535	208-459-0842
Clement Industries Inc				
PO Box 914	Minden LA	71058	800-562-5948*	318-377-2776
*Cust Svc				
CM Trailers Inc				
200 County Rd PO Box 680	Madill OK	73446	888-268-7577	580-795-5536
Cottrell Inc				
2125 Candler Rd	Gainesville GA	30507	800-827-0132*	770-532-7251
*Sales				
Dakota Mfg Company Inc				
1909 S Rowley St	Mitchell SD	57301	800-232-5682	605-996-5571
East Mfg Corp				
1871 State Rt 44 PO Box 277	Randolph OH	44265	888-405-3278	330-325-9921
Featherlite Trailers				
Hwy 63 & 9 PO Box 320	Cresco IA	52136	800-800-1230	563-547-6000
Fontaine Trailer Co				
430 Letson Rd PO Box 619	Haleyville AL	35565	800-821-6535	205-486-5251
Hesse Inc				
6700 St John Ave	Kansas City MO	64123	800-821-5562	816-483-7808
K-Dee Supply Inc				
621 E Lake St	Lake Mills WI	53551	800-268-3681	920-648-8202
Kentucky Trailer				
7201 Logistics Dr	Louisville KY	40258	888-598-7245	502-637-2551
Kentucky Trailer Technologies				
1240 N Pontiac Trial	Walled Lake MI	48390	866-638-6080	248-960-9700
LBT Inc 11502 "I" St	Omaha NE	68137	888-528-7278	402-333-4900
Ledwell & Son Enterprises				
3300 Waco St	Texarkana TX	75501	888-533-9355	903-838-6531
Mac Trailer Mfg Inc				
14599 Commerce St NE	Alliance OH	44601	800-795-8454	330-823-9900
Magic Tilt Trailers Inc				
2161 Lions Club Rd	Clearwater FL	33764	800-998-8458	727-535-5561
Maurer Mfg				
1300 38th Ave W PO Box 160	Spencer IA	51301	888-274-6010	712-262-2992
MCT Industries Inc				
7451 Pan American Fwy	Albuquerque NM	87109	800-876-8651	505-345-8651
Merritt Equipment Co				
9339 Hwy 85	Henderson CO	80640	800-634-3036	303-289-2286
Mickey Truck Bodies Inc				
1305 Trinity Ave PO Box 2044	High Point NC	27261	800-334-9061	336-882-6806
Midwest Systems				
5911 Hall St	Saint Louis MO	63147	800-383-6281	314-389-6280
Polar Service Centers				
7600 E Sam Houston Pkwy N	Houston TX	77049	800-955-8558	281-459-6400
Polar Tank Trailer Inc				
12810 County Rd 17	Holdingford MN	56340	800-826-6589	320-746-2255
Redneck Trailer Supplies				
2100 NW By-Pass	Springfield MO	65803	877-973-3632	417-864-5210
Rogers Bros Corp				
100 Orchard St	Albion PA	16401	800-441-9880	814-756-4121

			Toll-Free	Phone

Schwend Inc
28945 Johnston Rd . . . . Dade City FL 33523 | **800-243-7757** | 352-588-2220

Summit Trailer Sales Inc
One Summit Plz . . . . Summit Station PA 17979 | **800-437-3729** | 570-754-3511

Timpte Inc
1827 Industrial Dr . . . . David City NE 68632 | **888-256-4884** | 402-367-3056

Towmaster Inc
61381 US Hwy 12 . . . . Litchfield MN 55355 | **800-462-4517** | 320-693-7900

Trail King Industries Inc
147 Industrial Pk Rd . . . . Brookville PA 15825 | **800-545-1549** | 814-849-2342

Trailiner Corp
PO Box 5270 . . . . Springfield MO 65801 | **800-833-8209** | 417-866-7258

Trailstar Mfg Corp
20700 Harrisburg-Westville Rd
PO Box 2086 . . . . Alliance OH 44601 | **800-235-5635** | 330-821-9900

Travis Body & Trailer Inc
13955 FM529 . . . . Houston TX 77041 | **800-535-4372** | 713-466-5888

Trinity Trailer Manufacturing Inc
8200 S Eisenman Rd . . . . Boise ID 83716 | **800-235-6577** | 208-336-3666

Truck Equipment Service Co
800 Oak St . . . . Lincoln NE 68521 | **800-869-0363** | 402-476-3225

Utility Tool & Trailer Co
151 E 16th St PO Box 360 . . . . Clintonville WI 54929 | **800-874-6807** | 715-823-3167

Utility Trailer Mfg Co
17295 E Railroad St . . . . City of Industry CA 91748 | **800-874-6807** | 626-965-1541

Vantage Trailers Inc
29335 Hwy Blvd . . . . Katy TX 77494 | **800-826-8245** | 281-391-2664

Wabash National Corp
1000 Sagamore PkwyS PO Box 6129 . . . . Lafayette IN 47903 | **800-937-4784*** | 765-771-5300
NYSE: WNC ■ *Sales

Wells Cargo Inc
1503 W McNaughton St . . . . Elkhart IN 46514 | **800-348-7553** | 574-264-9661

Western Trailer Co
251 W Gowen Rd . . . . Boise ID 83716 | **888-344-2539** | 208-344-2539

Wilson Trailer Co
4400 S Lewis Blvd . . . . Sioux City IA 51106 | **800-798-2002** | 712-252-6500

Witzco Trailers Inc
6101 McIntosh Rd . . . . Sarasota FL 34238 | **800-363-7237** | 941-922-5301

775 TRUCKING COMPANIES

SEE ALSO Logistics Services (Transportation & Warehousing) ; Moving Companies

			Toll-Free	Phone

A & A Express Inc
PO Box 707 . . . . Brandon SD 57005 | **800-658-3549** | 605-582-2402

AAA Cooper Transportation
1751 Kinsey Rd . . . . Dothan AL 36303 | **800-633-7571** | 334-793-2284

Aaa Moving & Storage Inc
747 E Ship Creek Ave . . . . Anchorage AK 99501 | **866-641-4446** | 907-276-3506

ABF Freight Systems Inc
3801 Old Greenwood Rd . . . . Fort Smith AR 72903 | **800-610-5544** | 479-785-8913

Ace Doran Hauling & Rigging Co Inc
1601 Blue Rock St . . . . Cincinnati OH 45223 | **800-829-0929** | 513-681-7900

Ace Relocation Systems Inc
5608 Eastgate Dr . . . . San Diego CA 92121 | **800-453-0964** | 858-677-5500

Acme Truck Line Inc
121 Pailet Dr . . . . Harvey LA 70058 | **800-825-6246** | 504-368-2510

Alabama Motor Express Inc
10720 E US Hwy 84 E . . . . Ashford AL 36312 | **800-633-7590**

Alan Ritchey Inc
740 S I-35 E Frontage Rd . . . . Valley View TX 76272 | **800-877-0273** | 940-726-3276

All American Moving Group LLC
PO Box 271277 . . . . Memphis TN 38167 | **800-467-2900** | 901-353-3900

All Freight Systems Inc
PO Box 5279 . . . . Kansas City KS 66119 | **800-377-7575** | 913-281-1203

Allegheny Design Management Inc
1154 Parks Industrial Dr . . . . Vandergrift PA 15690 | **800-927-2611** | 724-845-7336

Allied Automotive Group
2302 ParkLake Dr Bldg 15 Ste 600 . . . . Atlanta GA 30345 | **800-476-2058**

Ameril-Co Carriers Inc
1702 E Overland PO Box 1649 . . . . Scottsbluff NE 69361 | **800-445-5400** | 308-635-3157

Amstan Logistics
101 Knightsbridge Dr . . . . Hamilton OH 45011 | **800-322-5546** | 513-863-4627

Anderson Trucking Service Inc
725 Opportunity St PO Box 1377 . . . . Saint Cloud MN 56301 | **800-328-2316** | 320-255-7400

Ards Trucking Company Inc
1702 N Gov Williams Hwy . . . . Darlington SC 29540 | **800-845-7462** | 843-393-5101

ARG Trucking Corp
369 Bostwick Rd . . . . Phelps NY 14532 | **800-334-1314** | 315-789-8871

Arlo G. Lott Trucking Inc
257 S 100 E . . . . Jerome ID 83338 | **800-443-5688** | 208-324-5053

Armellini Express Lines Inc
3446 SW Armellini Ave . . . . Palm City FL 34990 | **800-327-7887** | 772-287-0575

Arnold Transportation Services Inc
9523 Florida Mining Blvd . . . . Jacksonville FL 32257 | **800-846-4321** | 972-986-3154

Associated Petroleum Carriers Inc
PO Box 2808 . . . . Spartanburg SC 29304 | **800-573-9301*** | 864-573-9301
*Cust Svc

Autolog Corp 401 Commerce Rd . . . . Linden NJ 07036 | **800-526-6078**

Averitt Express Inc
1415 Neal St . . . . Cookeville TN 38501 | **800-283-7488**

B-D-R Transport Inc
7994 US Rt 5 . . . . Westminster VT 05158 | **800-421-0126** | 802-463-0606

Baggett Transportation Co
2 S 32nd St . . . . Birmingham AL 35233 | **800-633-8982** | 888-224-4388

Bailey's Express Inc
61 Industrial Pk Rd . . . . Middletown CT 06457 | **800-523-3758** | 860-632-0388

Barlow 1305 Grand Dd SE . . . . Faucett MO 64448 | **800-688-1202** | 816-238-3373

Bastian Trucking Inc
440 South Main . . . . Aurora UT 84620 | **800-452-5126** | 435-529-7453

Baylor Trucking Inc
9269 E State Rd 48 . . . . Milan IN 47031 | **800-322-9567** | 812-623-2020

Bayshore Transportation System Inc
901 Dawson Dr . . . . Newark DE 19713 | **800-523-3319** | 302-366-0220

			Toll-Free	Phone

Beam Mack Sales & Service Inc
2674 W Henrietta Rd . . . . Rochester NY 14623 | **877-650-8789** | 585-424-4860

Beaver Express Service LLC
4310 Oklahoma Ave PO Box 1147 . . . . Woodward OK 73802 | **800-593-2328** | 580-256-6460

Beelman Truck Co
One Racehorse Dr . . . . East Saint Louis IL 62205 | **800-541-5918*** | 618-646-5300
*Sales

Benton Express Inc
1045 S River Industrial Blvd SE . . . . Atlanta GA 30315 | **888-423-6866** | 404-267-2200

Besl Transfer Co
5700 Este Ave . . . . Cincinnati OH 45232 | **800-456-2375** | 513-242-3456

Big G Express Inc
PO Box 1650 . . . . Shelbyville TN 37162 | **800-955-9140** | 800-684-9140

Bilkays Express Co
2400 Bedle Place . . . . Linden NJ 07036 | **800-526-4006** | 908-289-2400

Boyd Bros Transportation Inc
3275 Alabama 30 . . . . Clayton AL 36016 | **800-700-2693** | 334-775-1400

Bryan Systems
14020 US 20A Hwy . . . . Montpelier OH 43543 | **800-745-2796**

Buchanan Hauling & Rigging
4625 Industrial Rd . . . . Fort Wayne IN 46825 | **888-544-4285** | 260-471-1877

Buddy Moore Trucking Inc
PO Box 10047 . . . . Birmingham AL 35202 | **866-704-1598** | 205-949-2260

Bulk Transit Corp
7177 Industrial Pkwy . . . . Plain City OH 43064 | **800-345-2855** | 614-873-4632

Bulkmatic Transport Co
2001 N Cline Ave . . . . Griffith IN 46319 | **800-535-8505**

Burns Motor Freight Inc
500 Seneca Trl N . . . . Marlinton WV 24954 | **800-598-5674** | 304-799-6106

Butler Transport Inc
347 N James St . . . . Kansas City KS 66118 | **800-345-8158** | 913-321-0047

Calex Express Inc
58 Pittston Ave . . . . Pittston PA 18640 | **800-292-2539** | 570-603-0180

California Cartage Company Inc
2931 Redondo Ave . . . . Long Beach CA 90806 | **888-537-1432**

Cardinal Transport Inc
7180 E Reed Rd . . . . Coal City IL 60416 | **800-435-9302** | 815-634-4443

Cedar Rapids Truck Ctr Inc
9201 Sixth St SW . . . . Cedar Rapids IA 52404 | **866-602-1597** | 319-848-6230

Celadon Trucking Services Inc
9503 E 33rd St . . . . Indianapolis IN 46235 | **800-235-2366** | 317-972-7000

Central Freight Lines Inc
PO Box 2638 . . . . Waco TX 76702 | **800-782-5036**

Central Petroleum Transport Inc (CPT)
6115 Mitchell St . . . . Sioux City IA 51111 | **800-798-6357** | 712-258-6357

Central Refrigerated Service Inc
5175 W 2100 S . . . . West Valley City UT 84120 | **800-777-0069** | 801-924-7000

Chadderton Trucking Inc
40 Stewart Way . . . . Sharon PA 16146 | **800-327-6868** | 724-981-5050

Christenson Transportation Inc
2001 W Old Rt 66 . . . . Strafford MO 65757 | **800-880-6711** | 417-866-5993

Coastal Transport Co Inc
1603 Ackerman Rd . . . . San Antonio TX 78219 | **800-523-8612** | 210-661-4287

Coleman American Moving Services Inc
PO Box 960 . . . . Midland City AL 36350 | **877-693-7060** | 866-929-1482

Colonial Freight Systems Inc
10924 McBride Ln . . . . Knoxville TN 37932 | **800-826-1402** | 865-966-9711

Colonial Truck Co
1833 Commerce Rd . . . . Richmond VA 23224 | **800-234-8782** | 804-232-3492

Combined Transport Inc
5656 Crater Lake Ave . . . . Central Point OR 97502 | **800-547-2870** | 541-734-7418

Comcar Industries Inc
502 E Bridgers Ave . . . . Auburndale FL 33823 | **800-524-1101*** | 863-967-1101
*Cust Svc

Con-way Freight
2211 Old Earhart Rd . . . . Ann Arbor MI 48105 | **800-755-2728** | 734-994-6600

Con-way Inc
2855 Campus Dr Ste 300 . . . . San Mateo CA 94403 | **800-755-2728** | 650-378-5200
NYSE: CNW

Cooke Trucking Co Inc
1759 S Andy Griffith Pkwy . . . . Mount Airy NC 27030 | **800-888-9502** | 336-786-5181

Covenant Transport Inc
400 Birmingham Hwy . . . . Chattanooga TN 37419 | **800-334-9686** | 423-821-1212
NASDAQ: CVTI

Cox Transportation Services Inc
10448 Dow Gil Rd . . . . Ashland VA 23005 | **800-288-8118** | 804-798-1477

CR England & Sons Inc
4701 West 2100 South . . . . Salt Lake City UT 84120 | **800-453-8826** | 801-972-2712

Craig Transportation Co
26699 Eckel Rd . . . . Perrysburg OH 43551 | **800-521-9119** | 419-872-3333

Cresco Lines Inc
15220 S Halsted St . . . . Harvey IL 60426 | **800-323-4476** | 708-339-1186

Crete Carrier Corp
400 NW 56th St PO Box 81228 . . . . Lincoln NE 68528 | **800-998-4095*** | 402-475-9521
*Cust Svc

Crossett Inc PO Box 946 . . . . Warren PA 16365 | **800-876-2778***
*General

CRST International Inc
3930 16th Ave SW PO Box 68 . . . . Cedar Rapids IA 52406 | **800-736-2778**

Crysteel Truck Equipment Inc
55248 Ember Rd . . . . Lake Crystal MN 56055 | **800-722-0588*** | 507-726-6041
*General

CTI Inc
11105 Norrth Casa Grande Hwy . . . . Rillito AZ 85654 | **800-362-4952** | 520-624-2348

CTL Distribution Inc
4201 Bonnie Mine Rd . . . . Mulberry FL 33860 | **800-237-9088** | 863-428-2373

D M Bowman Inc
10226 Governor Ln Blvd Ste 4009 . . . . . . Williamsport MD 21795 | **800-326-3274** | 301-582-2784

D&D Sexton Inc PO Box 156 . . . . Carthage MO 64836 | **800-743-0265** | 417-358-8727

D. P. Curtis Trucking Inc
1450 South Hwy 118 . . . . Richfield UT 84701 | **800-257-9151**

Daggett Truck Line Inc
32717 County Rd 10 . . . . Frazee MN 56544 | **800-262-9393** | 218-334-3711

Dahlsten Truck Line Inc
101 W Edgar PO Box 95 . . . . Clay Center NE 68933 | **800-228-4313** | 402-762-3511

Daily Express Inc
1072 Harrisburg Pk . . . . Carlisle PA 17013 | **800-735-3136** | 717-243-5757

Classified Section

			Toll-Free	Phone

Dakota Line Inc
PO Box 476 . . . . Vermillion SD 57069 — **800-532-5682** — 605-624-5228

Dana Transport Inc
210 Essex Ave E . . . . Avenel NJ 07001 — **800-733-3262** — 732-750-9100

Davis Express Inc
PO Box 1276 . . . . Starke FL 32091 — **800-874-4270**

Daylight Transport
1501 Hughes Way Ste 200 . . . . Long Beach CA 90810 — **800-468-9999**

Decker Truck Line Inc
4000 Fifth Ave S . . . . Fort Dodge IA 50501 — **800-247-2537** — 515-576-4141

Dejana Truck & Utility Equipment Company Inc
490 Pulaski Rd . . . . Kings Park NY 11754 — **877-335-2621** — 631-544-9000

Diamond Transportation System Inc
5021 21st St . . . . Racine WI 53406 — **800-927-5702** — 262-554-5400

Dick Lavy Trucking Inc
8848 State Rt 121 . . . . Bradford OH 45308 — **800-345-5289** — 937-448-2104

Dilmar Oil Company Inc
1951 W Darlington St PO Box 5629 . . . . Florence SC 29501 — **800-922-5823**

Dino's Trucking Inc
9615 Continental Indus Dr . . . . Saint Louis MO 63123 — **800-771-7805** — 314-631-3001

Dircks Moving Services Inc
4340 W Mohave St . . . . Phoenix AZ 85043 — **800-523-5038** — 602-267-9401

DistTech Inc
4366 Mt. Pleasant St NW . . . . North Canton OH 44720 — **800-969-5419**

Don Hummer Trucking Corp
1486 Hwy 6 NW PO Box 310 . . . . Oxford IA 52322 — **888-642-7249** — 319-828-2000

Dts Cos Inc 1640 Monad Rd . . . . Billings MT 59101 — **877-896-3420** — 406-245-4695

Duncan & Son Lines Inc
23860 W US Hwy 85 . . . . Buckeye AZ 85326 — **800-528-4283** — 623-386-4511

Eagle Express Lines Inc
715 W 172nd St PO Box 348 . . . . South Holland IL 60473 — **888-868-2501** — 708-333-8400

Eagle Transport Corp
300 S Wesleyan Blvd Ste 202 . . . . Rocky Mount NC 27804 — **800-776-9937** — 252-937-2464

Earl L Henderson Trucking Inc
206 W Main St . . . . Salem IL 62881 — **800-447-8084** — 618-548-4667

Epes Carriers Inc
3400 Edgefield Ct . . . . Greensboro NC 27409 — **800-869-3737** — 336-668-3358

Erickson Transport Corp
2255 N Packer Rd . . . . Springfield MO 65803 — **800-641-4595** — 417-862-6741

Evans Dedicated Systems Inc
PO Box 9 . . . . Maywood CA 90270 — **800-427-6387** — 323-725-2928

EW Wylie Corp
1520 Second Ave NW . . . . West Fargo ND 58078 — **800-437-4132*** — 701-282-5550
*Cust Svc

Falcon Express Inc
2250 E Church St PO Box 4897 . . . . . . Philadelphia PA 19124 — **800-544-6566** — 215-992-3140

FFE Transportation Inc
1145 Empire Central Pl . . . . Dallas TX 75247 — **800-569-9200** — 214-630-8090

First Class Services Inc
9355 US Hwy 60 E . . . . Lewisport KY 42351 — **800-467-8684*** — 270-295-3746
*General

Firstexpress Inc
1135 Freightliner Dr . . . . Nashville TN 37210 — **800-848-9203**

Five Star Trucking Inc
4380 Glenbrook Rd . . . . Willoughby OH 44094 — **800-321-3658** — 440-953-9300

Fort Edward Express Company Inc
1402 Rt 9 . . . . Fort Edward NY 12828 — **800-342-1233** — 518-792-6571

Forward Air Corp
430 Airport Rd PO Box 1058 . . . . Greeneville TN 37744 — **800-726-6654** — 423-636-7100
NASDAQ: FWRD

Frank C. Alegre Trucking Inc
PO Box 1508 . . . . Lodi CA 95241 — **800-769-2440** — 209-334-2112

Fry-Wagner Moving & Storage Co
3700 Rider Trl S . . . . Earth City MO 63045 — **800-899-4035** — 314-291-4100

Godfrey Trucking Inc
6173 West 2100 South . . . . West Valley City UT 84128 — **800-444-7669** — 801-972-0660

Gordon Trucking Inc
151 Stewart Rd SW . . . . Pacific WA 98047 — **800-426-8486** — 253-863-7777

Grammer Industries Inc
18375 E 345 S . . . . Grammer IN 47236 — **800-333-7410** — 812-579-5655

Groendyke Transport Inc
2510 Rock Island Blvd . . . . Enid OK 73701 — **800-843-2103** — 580-234-4663

Guy M Turner Inc
4514 S Holden Rd PO Box 7776 . . . . Greensboro NC 27406 — **800-432-4859** — 336-294-4660

H & M International Transportation Inc
485B Rt 1 S . . . . Iselin NJ 08830 — **800-446-4685** — 732-510-4640

H & W Trucking Company Inc
1772 N Andy Griffith Pkwy
PO Box 1545 . . . . Mount Airy NC 27030 — **800-334-9181** — 336-789-2188

H O Wolding Inc PO Box 217 . . . . Amherst WI 54406 — **800-950-0054** — 715-824-5513

H. F. Campbell & Son
PO Box 260 . . . . Millerstown PA 17062 — **800-233-7112** — 717-589-3194

Hallamore Motor Transportation Inc
795 Plymouth St . . . . Holbrook MA 02343 — **800-242-1300** — 781-767-2000

Hazen Transport Inc
27050 Wick Rd . . . . Taylor MI 48180 — **800-251-2120** — 313-292-2120

Heartland Express Inc
901 N Kansas Ave . . . . North Liberty IA 52317 — **800-654-1175**
NASDAQ: HTLD

High Country Transportation Inc
PO Box 700 . . . . Cortez CO 81321 — **800-635-7687**

Hirschbach Motor Lines Inc
18355 US Hwy 20 . . . . East Dubuque IL 61025 — **800-554-2969** — 402-494-5000

Hodges Trucking Co LLC
4050 W I-40 . . . . Oklahoma City OK 73108 — **888-829-1370** — 405-947-7764

Holman Transportation Services Inc
1010 Holman Ct . . . . Caldwell ID 83605 — **800-375-2416** — 208-454-0779

Hot-Line Freight System Inc
PO Box 205 . . . . West Salem WI 54669 — **800-468-4686** — 608-486-1600

Houff Transfer Inc
46 Houff Rd . . . . Weyers Cave VA 24486 — **800-476-4683** — 540-234-9233

Howard F Baer Inc
1301 Foster Ave . . . . Nashville TN 37210 — **800-447-7430** — 615-255-7351

Howell's Motor Freight Inc
PO Box 12308 . . . . Roanoke VA 24024 — **800-444-0585** — 540-966-3200

HVH Transportation Inc
181 E 56th Ave Ste 200 . . . . Denver CO 80216 — **800-525-4844** — 303-292-3656

Indian River Transport Co
2580 Executive Rd . . . . Winter Haven FL 33884 — **800-877-2430** — 863-324-2430

Interstate Distributor Co
11707 21st Ave S . . . . Tacoma WA 98444 — **800-426-8560**

J A T of Fort Wayne Inc
5031 Industrial Rd . . . . Fort Wayne IN 46825 — **800-522-3306** — 260-482-8447

J P Noonan Transportation Inc
415 W St . . . . West Bridgewater MA 02379 — **800-922-8026** — 508-583-2880

J R C Transportation Inc
47 Maple Ave PO Box 366 . . . . Thomaston CT 06787 — **800-346-3250*** — 860-283-0207
*General

J-Mar Enterprises Inc
PO Box 4143 . . . . Bismarck ND 58502 — **800-446-8283** — 701-222-4518

Jack B Kelley Inc
801 S Fillmore St Ste 505. . . . . Amarillo TX 79101 — **800-225-5525** — 806-353-3553

Jack Cooper Transport Co Inc
1100 Walnut St Ste 2400 . . . . Kansas City MO 64106 — **866-449-6388** — 816-983-4000

Jaro Transportation Services Inc
975 Post Rd PO Box 1890 . . . . Warren OH 44483 — **800-451-3447** — 330-393-5659

Jerry Lipps Inc
3888 Nash Rd PO Box F . . . . Cape Girardeau MO 63702 — **800-325-3331** — 573-335-8204

Jet Star Inc
10825 Andrade Dr . . . . Zionsville IN 46077 — **800-969-4222** — 317-873-4222

JH Walker Trucking Company Inc
152 N Hollywood Rd . . . . Houma LA 70364 — **800-535-5992** — 985-868-8330

Jim Palmer Trucking Inc
9730 Derby Dr . . . . Missoula MT 59801 — **888-698-3422** — 406-721-5151

JNJ Express Inc
3935 Old Getwell Rd PO Box 30983 . . . . . . Memphis TN 38130 — **888-383-7157** — 901-362-3444

Jones Motor Company Inc
900 W Bridge St PO Box 137 . . . . Spring City PA 19475 — **800-825-6637** — 610-948-7900

KAG West
4076 Seaport Blvd . . . . West Sacramento CA 95691 — **800-547-1587** — 916-371-8241

Keim T S Inc
1249 N Ninth St PO Box 226 . . . . Sabetha KS 66534 — **800-255-2450**

Keith Titus Corp
PO Box 920 . . . . Weedsport NY 13166 — **800-233-2126** — 315-834-6681

Kenan Advantage Group Inc (KAG)
4366 Mt Pleasant St NW . . . . North Canton OH 44720 — **800-969-5419** — 330-491-0474

Kenan Transport Co
100 Europa Ctr Ste 320 . . . . Chapel Hill NC 27517 — **866-821-3444** — 919-967-8221

Kenworth Sales Co
2125 Constitution Blvd . . . . West Valley City UT 84119 — **800-222-7831*** — 801-487-4161
*General

KLLM Inc 135 Riverview Dr . . . . Richland MS 39218 — **800-925-5556** — 800-925-1000

Knight Transportation Inc
5601 W Buckeye Rd . . . . Phoenix AZ 85043 — **800-489-2000** — 602-269-2000
NYSE: KNX

Kruepke Trucking Inc
2881 Hwy P . . . . Jackson WI 53037 — **800-798-5000*** — 262-677-3155
*Cust Svc

Kuntzman Trucking Inc
13515 Oyster Rd . . . . Alliance OH 44601 — **800-362-9779** — 330-821-9160

La Rosa Del Monte Express Inc
1133-35 Tiffany St . . . . Bronx NY 10459 — **800-452-7672** — 718-991-3300

Land Span Inc
1120 Griffin Rd . . . . Lakeland FL 33805 — **800-248-4847** — 863-686-6872

Landair Corp
1110 Myers St . . . . Greeneville TN 37743 — **888-526-3247**

Landmark International Trucks Inc
4550 Rutledge Pk . . . . Knoxville TN 37914 — **800-968-9999** — 865-637-4881

Landstar Express America Inc
13410 Sutton Pk Dr S . . . . Jacksonville FL 32224 — **800-872-9400** — 904-398-9400

Landstar Gemini Inc
13410 Sutton Pk Dr S . . . . Jacksonville FL 32224 — **800-872-9400** — 262-250-7582

Landstar Inway Inc
1000 Simpson Rd . . . . Rockford IL 61102 — **800-435-7352** — 815-972-5000

Landstar Ranger Inc
13410 Sutton Pk Dr S . . . . Jacksonville FL 32224 — **800-872-9400** — 904-398-9400

Landstar System Inc
13410 Sutton Pk Dr S . . . . Jacksonville FL 32224 — **800-872-9400** — 904-398-9400
NASDAQ: LSTR

Lawrence Companies (LTS)
872 Lee Hwy PO Box 7667 . . . . Roanoke VA 24019 — **800-336-9626** — 540-966-4000

Lightning Transportation Inc
16820 Blake Rd . . . . Hagerstown MD 21740 — **800-233-0624** — 301-582-5700

Linden Warehouse & Distribution Co Inc
1300 Lower Rd . . . . Linden NJ 07036 — **800-333-2855** — 908-862-1400

Liquid Transport Corp
8470 Allison Pt Blvd Ste 400 . . . . Indianapolis IN 46250 — **800-942-3175** — 317-841-4200

Lisa Motor Lines
1145 Empire Central Pl PO Box 655888 . . . . Dallas TX 75247 — **800-569-9200** — 214-630-8090

Lynden Transport Inc
3027 Rampart Dr . . . . Anchorage AK 99501 — **800-327-9390**

Market Transport Ltd
110 N Marine Dr . . . . Portland OR 97217 — **800-547-0781** — 503-283-2405

Marten Transport Ltd
129 Marten St . . . . Mondovi WI 54755 — **800-395-3000** — 715-926-4216
NASDAQ: MRTN

Martin Enterprises Inc
4315 Meyer Ave . . . . Fort Wayne IN 46806 — **800-348-4759** — 260-447-5591

Matheson Trucking Inc
9785 Goethe Rd . . . . Sacramento CA 95827 — **800-455-7678** — 916-685-2330

Maverick USA Inc
13301 Valentine Rd . . . . North Little Rock AR 72117 — **800-289-6600** — 501-955-1255

Mawson & Mawson Inc
1800 Old Lincoln Hwy PO Box 248 . . . . . . Langhorne PA 19047 — **800-262-9766** — 215-750-1100

May Trucking Co
4185 Brooklake Rd PO Box 9039 . . . . Salem OR 97305 — **800-547-9169**

Mayfield Transfer Company Inc
3200 W Lake St . . . . Melrose Park IL 60160 — **800-222-2959** — 708-681-4440

McKenzie Tank Lines Inc
975 Appleyard Dr . . . . Tallahassee FL 32304 — **800-828-6495** — 850-576-1221

MCT Transportation LLC
1600 E Benson Rd . . . . Sioux Falls SD 57104 — **800-843-9904*** — 605-339-8400
*Cust Svc

Melton Truck Lines Inc
808 N 161 E Ave . . . . Tulsa OK 74116 — **800-545-6651*** — 918-234-8000
*General

				Toll-Free	Phone
Mercer Transportation Co					
1128 W Main St PO Box 35610	Louisville	KY	40232	**800-626-5375**	502-584-2301
Mergenthaler Transfer & Storage					
1414 N Montana Ave	Helena	MT	59601	**800-826-5463***	406-442-9470
*General					
Mid Seven Transportation Co					
2323 Delaware Ave	Des Moines	IA	50317	**800-247-7448**	515-266-5181
Midwest Motor Express Inc					
5015 E Main Ave	Bismarck	ND	58502	**800-741-4097**	701-223-1880
Milan Express Company Inc					
1091 Kefauver Dr PO Box 699	Milan	TN	38358	**800-231-7303**	731-686-7428
Miller Transporters Inc					
5500 Hwy 80 W	Jackson	MS	39209	**800-645-5378***	601-922-8331
*Cust Svc					
Milton Transportation Inc					
5505 State Rt 405 PO Box 355	Milton	PA	17847	**800-776-1150**	570-742-8774
Minuteman Trucks Inc					
2181 Providence Hwy	Walpole	MA	02081	**800-231-8458**	508-668-3112
Murrows Transfer Inc					
PO Box 4095	High Point	NC	27263	**800-669-2928***	336-475-6101
*Cust Svc					
National Carriers Inc					
1501 E Eigth St	Liberal	KS	67901	**800-835-9180**	620-624-1621
National Highway Express Co					
971 Old Henderson St PO Box 20262	Columbus	OH	43220	**800-837-5700**	614-459-4900
Nationwide Truck Brokers Inc (NTB)					
4203 Roger B Chaffee Memorial Blvd SE					
Ste 2	Grand Rapids	MI	49548	**800-446-0682**	616-878-5554
Navajo Express Inc					
1400 W 64 Ave	Denver	CO	80221	**800-525-1969**	303-287-3800
New Penn Motor Express Inc					
625 S Fifth Ave	Lebanon	PA	17042	**800-285-5000***	717-274-2521
*Cust Svc					
Newark School District					
100 E Miller St 4th Fl	Newark	NY	14513	**877-789-2613**	315-332-3230
Nick Strimbu Inc					
3500 PkwyRd	Brookfield	OH	44403	**800-446-8785**	330-448-4046
Northland Trucking Inc					
1515 S 22nd Ave	Phoenix	AZ	85009	**800-214-5564**	602-254-0007
Nussbaum Trucking Inc					
19336 N 1425 East Rd	Normal	IL	61748	**800-322-7305**	309-452-4426
O & S Trucking Inc					
3769 E Evergreen St	Springfield	MO	65803	**800-509-2021**	417-864-4780
Old Dominion Freight Line Inc					
500 Old Dominion Way	Thomasville	NC	27360	**800-432-6335**	336-889-5000
NASDAQ: ODFL					
Oliver Trucking Corp					
1101 Harding Ct	Indianapolis	IN	46217	**888-561-4449**	317-787-1101
Online Transport System Inc					
6311 W Stoner Dr	Greenfield	IN	46140	**866-543-1235**	317-894-2159
Osborn Transportation Inc					
1245 West Grand Ave	Rainbow City	AL	35902	**866-215-3659**	256-442-2514
Overland Express Co					
5539 Harvey Wilson PO Box 262322	Houston	TX	77207	**800-929-7402**	713-672-6161
Ozark Motor Lines Inc					
3934 Homewood Rd	Memphis	TN	38118	**800-264-4100**	901-251-9711
Palmetto State Transportation Company Inc					
1050 Pk W Blvd	Greenville	SC	29611	**800-269-0175**	864-672-3800
PAM Transportation Services Inc					
297 W Henri De Tonti Blvd	Tontitown	AR	72770	**800-879-7261**	479-361-9111
NASDAQ: PTSI					
Pan Western Corp					
4910 Donovan Way Ste A	North Las Vegas	NV	89081	**800-443-1560**	702-632-2931
Paper Transport Inc					
2701 Executive Dr	Green Bay	WI	54304	**800-317-3650**	
Patriot Transportation Holding Inc					
501 Riverside Ave Ste 500	Jacksonville	FL	32202	**877-704-1776**	904-396-5733
NASDAQ: PATI					
Peet Frate Line Inc					
650 S Eastwood Dr PO Box 1129	Woodstock	IL	60098	**800-435-6909**	815-338-5500
Penn's Best Inc					
PO Box 128	Meshoppen	PA	18630	**800-852-3243**	
Phoenix Transportation Services LLC					
335 E Yusen Dr	Georgetown	KY	40324	**800-860-0889**	502-863-0108
Pitt Ohio Express					
15 27th St	Pittsburgh	PA	15222	**800-366-7488***	412-232-3015
*Cust Svc					
Pleasant Trucking Inc					
2250 Industrial Dr PO Box 778	Connellsville	PA	15425	**800-245-2402**	
Pozas Bros Trucking Company Inc					
8130 Enterprise Dr	Newark	CA	94560	**800-874-8383**	510-742-9939
Predator Trucking Co					
3181 Trumbull Ave	McDonald	OH	44437	**888-773-3875**	
Prestera Trucking					
19129 US Rt 52	South Point	OH	45680	**855-761-7943**	740-894-4770
Pride Transport Inc					
5499 W 2455 S	Salt Lake City	UT	84120	**800-877-1320**	801-972-8890
Prime Inc PO Box 4208	Springfield	MO	65808	**800-848-4560***	417-866-0001
*Cust Svc					
Pritchett Trucking Inc					
1050 SE Sixth St PO Box 311	Lake Butler	FL	32054	**800-486-7504**	386-496-2630
Q Carriers Inc					
1415 Maras St	Shakopee	MN	55379	**800-800-4755**	952-445-8718
Quality Distribution Inc					
4041 Pk Oaks Blvd Ste 200	Tampa	FL	33610	**800-282-2031**	
NASDAQ: QLTY					
Queensboro Co					
113 E Broad St PO Box 467	Louisville	GA	30434	**800-236-2442**	478-625-2000
R & R Trucking Inc					
302 Thunder Rd PO Box 545	Duenweg	MO	64841	**800-625-6885**	417-623-6885
RAM Nationwide Inc					
240 W N Bend Rd	Cincinnati	OH	45216	**800-837-0110**	513-821-0010
Rbx Inc PO Box 2118	Springfield	MO	65802	**877-450-2200**	800-245-5507
Refrigerated Food Express Inc					
57 Littlefield St	Avon	MA	02322	**800-342-8822**	508-587-4600
Relco Systems Inc					
7310 Chestnut Ridge Rd	Lockport	NY	14094	**800-262-1020**	716-434-8100
Riechmann Transport Inc					
3328 W Chain of Rocks Rd	Granite City	IL	62040	**800-844-4225**	618-797-6700

				Toll-Free	Phone
Roadtex Transportation Corp					
13 Jensen Dr	Somerset	NJ	08873	**800-762-3839**	
Robert Bearden Inc					
2601 Industrial Pk Dr PO Box 870	Cairo	GA	39828	**888-298-6928**	229-377-6928
Roehl Transport Inc					
1916 E 29th St PO Box 750	Marshfield	WI	54449	**800-826-8367**	715-591-3795
Roger Ward Inc					
17275 Green Mtn Rd	San Antonio	TX	78247	**888-909-3147***	210-655-8623
*General					
Rountree Transport & Rigging Inc					
2640 N Ln Ave	Jacksonville	FL	32254	**800-342-5036**	904-781-1033
Roy Bros Inc					
764 Boston Rd	Billerica	MA	01821	**800-225-0830***	978-667-1921
*Cust Svc					
Royal Trucking Co					
1323 Eshman Ave N PO Box 387	West Point	MS	39773	**800-321-1293**	662-494-1637
RWH Trucking Inc					
2970 Old Oakwood Rd	Oakwood	GA	30566	**800-256-8119**	
S & S Transport Inc					
PO Box 12579	Grand Forks	ND	58208	**800-726-8022**	
S T Bunn Construction					
1904 University Blvd PO Box 20109	Tuscaloosa	AL	35401	**800-297-6302**	205-752-8195
S-j Transportation Co Inc					
PO Box 169	Woodstown	NJ	08098	**800-524-2552**	856-769-2741
Sammons Trucking					
3665 W Broadway	Missoula	MT	59808	**800-548-9276**	406-728-2600
Schilli Transportation Services Inc					
6358 W US Hwy 24	Remington	IN	47977	**800-759-2101**	219-261-2100
Security Van Lines LLC					
100 W Airline Dr PO Box 830	Kenner	LA	70062	**800-218-6915**	800-794-5961
Seward Motor Freight Inc					
PO Box 126	Seward	NE	68434	**800-786-4468**	402-643-4503
Shaffer Trucking Inc					
49 E Main St PO Box 418	New Kingstown	PA	17072	**800-742-3337***	717-766-4708
*Cust Svc					
Sherman Bros Trucking					
32921 Diamond Hill Dr PO Box 706	Harrisburg	OR	97446	**800-547-8980**	541-995-7751
Shetler Moving & Storage Inc					
1253 E Diamond Ave	Evansville	IN	47711	**800-321-5069**	812-421-7750
Shippers Express Co					
1651 Kerr Dr	Jackson	MS	39204	**800-647-2480**	601-948-4251
Short Freight Lines Inc					
459 S River Rd PO Box 357	Bay City	MI	48707	**800-248-0625**	989-893-3505
Simons Trucking Inc					
920 Simon Dr PO Box 8	Farley	IA	52046	**800-373-2580**	563-744-3304
Skinner Transfer Corp					
PO Box 438	Reedsburg	WI	53959	**800-356-9350**	608-524-2326
South Shore Transportation Inc					
4010 Columbus Ave	Sandusky	OH	44870	**888-428-0879**	419-626-6267
Southeastern Freight Lines Inc					
420 Davega Rd	Lexington	SC	29073	**800-637-7335**	803-794-7300
Southern Pan Services Co (SPS)					
2385 Lithonia Industrial Blvd					
PO Box 679	Lithonia	GA	30058	**800-334-9145**	678-301-2400
Southwest Freightlines					
11991 Transpark Dr Horizon City	El Paso	TX	79927	**800-776-5799***	915-860-8592
*General					
Southwestern Motor Transport Inc					
4600 Goldfield	San Antonio	TX	78218	**800-531-1071**	210-661-6791
Spectraserv Inc					
75 Jacobus Ave	South Kearny	NJ	07032	**800-445-4436**	973-589-0277
Star Fleet Inc PO Box 769	Goshen	IN	46527	**877-805-9547**	888-281-8727
Star Transportation Inc					
PO Box 100925	Nashville	TN	37224	**800-333-3060***	615-256-4336
*Cust Svc					
Steelman Transportation					
2160 N Burton	Springfield	MO	65803	**800-488-6287**	417-831-6300
Stevens Transport					
PO Box 279010	Dallas	TX	75227	**800-233-9369**	866-551-0337
Styer Transportation Co					
7870 215th St W	Lakeville	MN	55044	**800-548-9149**	952-469-4491
Summitt Trucking LLC					
1800 Progress Way	Clarksville	IN	47129	**866-999-7799**	812-285-7777
Sunbelt Furniture Express Inc					
PO Box 487	Hickory	NC	28603	**800-766-1117**	828-464-7240
Sunco Carriers Inc					
1025 N Chestnut Rd	Lakeland	FL	33805	**800-237-8288**	863-688-1948
Superior Carriers Inc					
711 Jory Blvd Ste 101-N	Oak Brook	IL	60523	**800-654-7707**	630-573-2555
Swift Transportation Company Inc					
2200 S 75th Ave	Phoenix	AZ	85043	**800-800-2200**	602-269-9700
NYSE: SWFT					
T & T Trucking Inc					
11396 N Hwy 99	Lodi	CA	95240	**800-692-3457***	209-931-6000
*Cust Svc					
T-w Transport Inc					
7405 S Hayford Rd	Cheney	WA	99004	**800-356-4070**	509-623-4004
TanTara Transportation Corp					
2420 Stewart Rd	Muscatine	IA	52761	**800-650-0292**	563-262-8621
Taylor Truck Line Inc					
31485 Northfield Blvd	Northfield	MN	55057	**800-962-5994**	507-645-4531
Teal's Express Inc					
22411 Teal Dr PO Box 6010	Watertown	NY	13601	**800-836-0369**	315-788-6437
Tennessee Steel Haulers Inc					
PO Box 78189	Nashville	TN	37207	**800-776-4004**	615-271-2400
Texas Transeastern Inc					
PO Box 5339	Pasadena	TX	77508	**800-866-8579**	281-604-3100
Tiger Lines LLC Lodi					
927 Black Diamond Way	Lodi	CA	95241	**800-967-8443**	209-334-4100
Total Package Express Inc					
5871 Cheviot Rd	Cincinnati	OH	45247	**800-420-5505**	513-741-5500
TP Trucking LLC					
5630 Table Rock Rd	Central Point	OR	97502	**800-777-1121**	541-664-4776
Trailer Bridge Inc					
10405 New Berlin Rd E	Jacksonville	FL	32226	**800-554-1589**	904-751-7100
OTC: TRBRQ					
Trailer Transit Inc					
1130 E US 20	Porter	IN	46304	**800-423-3647**	219-926-2111

				Toll-Free	Phone
Trans-Carriers Inc					
5135 US Hwy 78	Memphis	TN	38118	**800-999-7383**	901-368-2900
Trans-Phos Inc PO Box 9004	Bartow	FL	33831	**800-940-1575**	863-534-1575
TransAm Trucking Inc					
15910 S 169th Hwy	Olathe	KS	66062	**800-800-5945**	913-782-5300
Transport Corp of America Inc					
1715 Yankee Doodle Rd	Eagan	MN	55121	**800-328-3927**	651-686-2500
Transport Distribution Co					
PO Box 306	Joplin	MO	64802	**800-866-7709**	417-624-3814
Transport Inc					
2225 Main Ave SE	Moorhead	MN	56560	**800-598-7267**	218-236-6300
Transport Service Co					
2001 Spring Rd Ste 400	Oak Brook	IL	60523	**800-323-5561***	630-472-5900
*Sales					
TransWood Carriers Inc					
PO Box 189	Omaha	NE	68101	**888-346-8092**	
Tri Star Freight System Inc					
5407 Mesa Dr	Houston	TX	77028	**800-229-1095**	713-631-1095
Triad Transport Inc					
PO Box 818	McAlester	OK	74502	**800-324-1139**	918-426-4751
Triple Crown Services					
2720 Dupont Commerce Ct Ste 200	Fort Wayne	IN	46825	**800-325-6510**	260-416-3600
Truline Corp					
9390 Redwood St	Las Vegas	NV	89139	**800-634-6489**	702-362-7495
Tryon Trucking Inc					
PO Box 68	Fairless Hills	PA	19030	**800-523-5254**	215-295-6622
Underwood Transfer Company LLC					
940 W Troy Ave	Indianapolis	IN	46225	**800-428-2372**	317-783-9235
United Road Services Inc					
10701 Middlebelt Rd	Romulus	MI	48174	**866-470-0036**	734-947-7900
Universal Truckload Services Inc					
12755 E Nine Mile Rd	Warren	MI	48089	**800-233-9445**	586-920-0100
NASDAQ: UACL					
US Xpress Enterprises Inc					
4080 Jenkins Rd	Chattanooga	TN	37421	**800-251-6291**	423-510-3000
USA Truck Inc					
3200 Industrial Pk Rd	Van Buren	AR	72956	**800-643-9691**	479-471-2500
NASDAQ: USAK					
V & S Midwest Carriers Corp					
2001 Hyland Ave PO Box 107	Kaukauna	WI	54130	**800-876-4330**	920-766-9696
Van Eerden Foodservice Co					
650 Ionia Ave SW	Grand Rapids	MI	49503	**800-833-7374**	616-475-0900
Van Wyk Freight Lines Inc					
PO Box 70	Grinnell	IA	50112	**800-362-2595**	641-236-7551
Vitran Express Canada Inc					
1201 Creditstone Rd	Concord	ON	L4K0C2	**800-263-9588**	416-798-4965
NASDAQ: VTNC					
Vitran Express Inc					
1600 W Oliver Ave	Indianapolis	IN	46221	**800-366-0150**	317-803-4000
Volume Transportation Inc					
6575 Marshall Blvd	Lithonia	GA	30058	**800-879-5565**	770-482-1400
Waggoners Trucking					
5220 Midland Rd	Billings	MT	59101	**800-999-9097**	406-248-1919
Waller Truck Company Inc					
400 S McCleary Rd	Excelsior Springs	MO	64024	**800-821-2196**	816-629-3400
Walpole Inc PO Box 1177	Okeechobee	FL	34973	**800-741-6500**	863-763-5593
Ward Trucking Corp					
PO Box 1553	Altoona	PA	16603	**800-458-3625**	814-944-0803
Warren Transport Inc					
210 Beck Ave	Waterloo	IA	50701	**800-553-2007***	319-233-6113
*General					
Watsontown Trucking Company Inc					
60 Belford Blvd	Milton	PA	17847	**800-344-0313**	570-522-9820
WC McQuaide Inc					
153 Macridge Rd	Johnstown	PA	15904	**800-456-0292**	814-269-6000
Wel Companies Inc					
1625 S Broadway PO Box 5610	De Pere	WI	54115	**800-333-4415**	920-339-0110
Werner Enterprises Inc					
14507 Frontier Rd	Omaha	NE	68138	**800-228-2240**	402-895-6640
NASDAQ: WERN					
Western Co-op Transport Assn					
4501 72nd St SW	Montevideo	MN	56265	**800-992-8817**	320-269-5531
Western Express Inc					
7135 Centennial Pl	Nashville	TN	37209	**800-316-7160**	615-259-9920
White Bros Trucking Co					
4N793 School Rd	Wasco	IL	60183	**800-323-4762**	630-584-3810
White River Paper Co					
1118 Rt 14	Hartford	VT	05047	**800-461-7695**	802-281-4501
Wilhelm Trucking & Rigging Co					
3250 NW St Helens Rd PO Box 10363	Portland	OR	97210	**800-873-4285***	503-227-0561
*Cust Svc					
Willis Shaw Express Inc					
201 N Elm St	Elm Springs	AR	72728	**800-843-9904**	479-248-7261
Wilson Lines of Minnesota Inc					
2131 Second Ave	Newport	MN	55055	**800-525-3333***	651-459-2384
*General					
Wilson Trucking Corp					
137 Wilson Blvd	Fishersville	VA	22939	**866-645-7405**	540-949-3200
Wiseway Motor Freight Inc					
PO Box 838	Hudson	WI	54016	**800-876-1660**	
Woody Bogler Trucking Co					
PO Box 229	Rosebud	MO	63091	**800-899-4120**	573-764-3700
Wragtime Air Freight Inc					
596 W 135th St	Gardena	CA	90248	**800-586-9701**	
Wright Transportation Inc					
2333 Dauphin Island Pkwy	Mobile	AL	36605	**800-342-4598**	251-432-6940
Wyatt Transfer Inc					
3035 Bells Rd PO Box 24326	Richmond	VA	23224	**800-552-5708**	804-743-3800
Wynne Transport Service Inc					
2222 N 11th St	Omaha	NE	68108	**800-383-9330**	402-342-4001
Young's Commercial Transfer					
2075 W Scranton Ave PO Box 871	Porterville	CA	93257	**800-289-1639**	559-784-6651
Yourga Trucking Inc					
100 Shenango St	Wheatland	PA	16161	**800-245-1722**	724-981-3600

776 — TYPESETTING & RELATED SERVICES

SEE ALSO Graphic Design ; Printing Companies - Commercial Printers

				Toll-Free	Phone
Ano-Coil Corp					
60 E Main St	Rockville	CT	06066	**800-492-7286**	860-871-1200
Auto-Graphics Inc					
430 N Vineyard Ave	Ontario	CA	91764	**800-776-6939**	909-595-7004
Blanks Printing & Imaging Inc					
2343 N Beckley Ave	Dallas	TX	75208	**800-325-7651**	214-741-3905
Carey Digital					
1718 Central Pkwy	Cincinnati	OH	45214	**800-767-6071**	513-241-5210
Color Communication Inc					
4000 W Fillmore St	Chicago	IL	60624	**800-458-5743**	
GGS Technical Publications Services					
3265 Farmtrail Rd	York	PA	17406	**800-927-4474**	717-764-2222
Ligature, The					
4909 Alcoa Ave	Los Angeles	CA	90058	**800-944-5440**	323-585-6000
Presstek Inc 55 Executive Dr	Hudson	NH	03051	**800-422-3616**	603-595-7000
NASDAQ: PRST					
Printing Prep Inc					
12 E Tupper St	Buffalo	NY	14203	**877-878-7114**	716-852-5011
Regency Infographics Inc (SED)					
2867 E Allegheny Ave	Philadelphia	PA	19134	**800-829-0020**	215-425-8800
Richards Graphic Communications Inc					
2700 Van Buren St	Bellwood	IL	60104	**866-827-3686**	708-547-6000
Southern Graphic Systems Inc					
502 N Willow Ave	Tampa	FL	33606	**800-777-6789**	813-253-3427
Southern Graphics Systems					
7435 Empire Dr	Florence	KY	41042	**800-777-6789**	859-525-1190
West Essex Graphics Inc (WEG)					
305 Fairfield Ave	Fairfield	NJ	07004	**800-221-5859**	

777 — ULTRASONIC CLEANING EQUIPMENT

SEE ALSO Dental Equipment & Supplies - Mfr

				Toll-Free	Phone
Crest Ultrasonics Corp					
10 Grumman Ave	Trenton	NJ	08628	**800-992-7378**	609-883-4000
Sonicor Inc 82 Otis St	West Babylon	NY	11704	**800-864-5022**	631-920-6555
Sonics & Materials Inc					
53 Church Hill Rd	Newtown	CT	06470	**800-745-1105**	203-270-4600
OTC: SIMA					
Sterigenics					
2015 Spring Rd Ste 650	Oak Brook	IL	60523	**800-472-4508**	630-928-1700

778 — UNITED NATIONS AGENCIES, ORGANIZATIONS, PROGRAMS

				Toll-Free	Phone
Inter-American Development Bank					
1300 New York Ave NW	Washington	DC	20577	**877-782-7432**	202-623-1000

779 — UNITED NATIONS MISSIONS

				Toll-Free	Phone
Canada					
885 Second Ave 14th Fl	New York	NY	10017	**800-267-8376**	212-848-1100
Cuba 315 Lexington Ave	New York	NY	10016	**800-553-3210***	212-689-7215
*General					
Kenya 866 UN Plaza Rm 304	New York	NY	10017	**866-445-3692**	212-421-4740
Libyan Arab Jamahiriya					
309-315 E 48th St	New York	NY	10017	**800-253-9646**	212-752-5775
Mexico 2 UN Plaza 28th Fl	New York	NY	10017	**800-553-3210**	212-752-0220

780 — UNIVERSITIES - CANADIAN

				Toll-Free	Phone
Acadia University					
15 University Ave	Wolfville	NS	B4P2R6	**877-585-1121**	902-542-2201
Alberta College of Art & Design					
1407 14th Ave NW	Calgary	AB	T2N4R3	**800-251-8290**	403-284-7600
Athabasca University					
One University Dr	Athabasca	AB	T9S3A3	**800-788-9041**	780-675-6111
Bethany Bible College					
26 Western St	Sussex	NB	E4E1E6	**888-432-4444**	506-432-4400
Bishop's University					
2600 College St	Sherbrooke	QC	J1M0C8	**800-567-2792**	819-822-9600
Campion College at the University of Regina					
3737 Wascana Pkwy	Regina	SK	S4S0A2	**800-667-7282**	306-586-4242
Canadian College of Naturopathic Medicine					
1255 Sheppard Ave E	Toronto	ON	M2K1E2	**866-241-2266**	416-498-1255
Cape Breton University					
1250 Grand Lk Rd	Sydney	NS	B1P6L2	**888-959-9995**	902-539-5300
Carleton University					
1125 Colonel By Dr	Ottawa	ON	K1S5B6	**888-354-4414**	613-520-7400
Concordia University College of Alberta					
7128 Ada Blvd NW	Edmonton	AB	T5B4E4	**866-479-5200**	780-479-9220
Crandall University					
333 Gorge Rd	Moncton	NB	E1G3H9	**888-968-6228**	506-858-8970
Northern					
1301 Central Ave	Prince Albert	SK	S6V4W1	**800-267-6303**	306-765-3333
First Nations University of Canada					
Saskatoon 226 20th St E	Saskatoon	SK	S7K0A6	**800-267-6303**	306-931-1800
Heritage College & Seminary					
175 Holiday Inn Dr	Cambridge	ON	N3C3T2	**800-465-1961**	519-651-2869
Toronto					
1835 Yonge St Second Fl	Toronto	ON	M4S1X8	**866-838-6542***	
*General					
King's University College					
9125 50th St	Edmonton	AB	T6B2H3	**800-661-8582**	780-465-3500

			Toll-Free	Phone
Laurentian University				
935 Ramsey Lake Rd	Sudbury ON	P3E2C6	800-461-4030	705-675-1151
Laval University				
2325 Rue University	Quebec QC	G1V0A6	877-785-2825	418-656-2131
Mount Royal College				
4825 Mt Royal Gate SW	Calgary AB	T3E6K6	877-440-5001	403-440-6111
Mount Saint Vincent University				
166 Bedford Hwy	Halifax NS	B3M2J6	877-733-6788	902-457-6117
Prairie Bible Institute				
330 Fifth Ave NE PO Box 4000	Three Hills AB	T0M2N0	800-661-2425	403-443-5511
Redeemer University College				
777 Garner Rd E	Ancaster ON	L9K1J4	877-779-0913	905-648-2131
Royal Roads University				
2005 Sooke Rd	Victoria BC	V9B5Y2	800-788-8028	250-391-2511
Ryerson University				
350 Victoria St	Toronto ON	M5B2K3	866-592-8882	416-979-5000
Saint Francis Xavier University				
PO Box 5000	Antigonish NS	B2G2W5	877-867-7839*	902-863-3300
*Admissions				
Saint Paul University				
223 Main St	Ottawa ON	K1S1C4	800-637-6859	613-236-1393
Taylor University College & Seminary				
11525 23rd Ave	Edmonton AB	T6J4T3	800-567-4988	780-431-5200
Thompson Rivers University				
900 McGill Rd PO Box 3010	Kamloops BC	V2C5N3	800-663-1663	250-828-5000
Thorneloe University				
935 Ramsey Lake Rd	Sudbury ON	P3E2C6	800-461-4030*	705-673-1730
*General				
Trent University				
1600 W Bank Dr	Peterborough ON	K9J7B8	888-739-8885	705-748-1011
Trinity Western University				
7600 Glover Rd	Langley BC	V2Y1Y1	888-468-6898	604-888-7511
Universite de Moncton				
Campus Shippagan				
218 Blvd JD Gauthier	Shippagan NB	E8S1P6	800-363-8336	506-336-3400
Edmundston				
165 Blvd Hebert	Edmundston NB	E3V2S8	888-736-8623	506-737-5051
University of Alberta				
Augustana 4901-46th Ave	Camrose AB	T4V2R3	800-661-8714	780-679-1100
University of British Columbia				
2016-1874 E Mall	Vancouver BC	V6T1Z1	877-272-1422	604-822-9836
University of Manitoba				
65 Chancellors Cir				
424 University Ctr	Winnipeg MB	R3T2N2	800-224-7713*	204-474-8880
*Admissions				
University of Moncton				
18 Ave Antonine-Maillet	Moncton NB	E1A3E9	800-363-8336	506-858-4000
University of Ottawa				
550 Cumberland St	Ottawa ON	K1N6N5	877-868-8292	613-562-5800
University of Regina				
3737 Wascana Pkwy	Regina SK	S4S0A2	800-644-4756	306-585-4111
Saint Thomas More College				
1437 College Dr	Saskatoon SK	S7N0W6	800-667-2019	306-966-8900
University of Western Ontario				
King's University College				
266 Epworth Ave	London ON	N6A2M3	800-265-4406	519-433-3491
York University				
4700 Keele St	Toronto ON	M3J1P3	800-426-2255	416-736-2100

781   UNIVERSITY SYSTEMS

Listings are organized by state names.

			Toll-Free	Phone
California State University				
401 Golden Shore	Long Beach CA	90802	800-325-4000	562-951-4000
City University of New York (CUNY)				
535 E 80th St	New York NY	10075	877-769-7441	212-794-5555
Louisiana State University System				
125 E Boyd Dr	Baton Rouge LA	70803	800-227-3002	225-578-3357
New Mexico				
Higher Education Dept				
2048 Galisteo St	Santa Fe NM	87505	800-279-9777	505-476-8400
Pennsylvania				
State System of Higher Education				
2986 N Second St	Harrisburg PA	17110	800-732-0999	717-720-4000
State University of New York, The (SUNY)				
State University Plz	Albany NY	12246	800-342-3811	518-320-1888
University of Alabama System				
401 Queen City Ave	Tuscaloosa AL	35401	800-638-6420	205-348-5861
University of Missouri System				
321 University Hall	Columbia MO	65211	800-225-6075	573-882-2011
University of Nebraska System				
3835 Holdrege St Varner Hall	Lincoln NE	68583	800-542-1602	402-472-2111
University of South Dakota Foundation				
1110 N Dakota St PO Box 5555	Vermillion SD	57069	800-521-3575	605-677-6703
University of Texas System				
601 Colorado St	Austin TX	78701	866-882-2034	512-499-4200
University of Wisconsin System				
1220 Linden Dr 1720 Van Hise Hall	Madison WI	53706	800-442-6461	608-262-2321
West Virginia				
Higher Education Policy Commission				
1018 Kanawha Blvd E Ste 700	Charleston WV	25301	888-825-5707	304-558-2101

782   UTILITY COMPANIES

SEE ALSO Gas Transmission - Natural Gas ; Electric Companies - Cooperatives (Rural)
Types of utilities included here are electric companies, water supply companies, and natural gas companies.

			Toll-Free	Phone
Alabama Gas Corp (Alagasco)				
605 Richard Arrington Jr Blvd N	Birmingham AL	35203	800-292-4005	205-326-8100
Alameda County Water District				
43885 S Grimmer Blvd	Fremont CA	94537	866-275-3772	510-668-4200

			Toll-Free	Phone
Alaska Power & Telephone Co				
193 Otto St PO Box 3222	Port Townsend WA	98368	800-982-0136*	360-385-1733
OTC: APTL ■ *Cust Svc				
Allegheny Power				
800 Cabin Hill Dr	Greensburg PA	15601	800-255-3443*	724-837-3000
*Cust Svc				
Alliant Energy Corp				
4902 N Biltmore Ln Ste 1000	Madison WI	53718	800-255-4268	
NYSE: LNT				
Aqua America Inc				
762 W Lancaster Ave	Bryn Mawr PA	19010	877-987-2782	
NYSE: WTR				
Aquarion Co 835 Main St	Bridgeport CT	06604	800-732-9678	203-336-7662
Arizona Public Service Co (APS)				
400 N Fifth St PO Box 53999	Phoenix AZ	85004	800-253-9405	602-371-7171
ATCO Ltd				
700 909 11th Ave SW	Calgary AB	T2R1N6	800-242-3447	403-292-7500
TSE: ACO/X				
Avista Corp				
1411 E Mission St	Spokane WA	99202	800-936-6629	509-489-0500
NYSE: AVA				
Avista Utilities				
1411 E Mission St	Spokane WA	99252	800-227-9187	
Baltimore Gas & Electric Co				
110 W Fayette St P.O. Box 1475	Baltimore MD	21201	800-685-0123	410-470-7433
Bangor Hydro Electric Co				
PO Box 932	Bangor ME	04402	800-499-6600	207-945-5621
Berkshire Gas Company Inc				
115 Cheshire Rd	Pittsfield MA	01201	800-292-5012	413-442-1511
Brownstown Electric Supply Company Inc				
690 E State Rd 250 PO Box L	Brownstown IN	47220	800-742-8492	812-358-4555
Cabot Oil & Gas Corp				
840 Gessner Rd Ste 1200	Houston TX	77024	800-434-3985	281-848-2799
NYSE: COG				
California ISO				
151 Blue Ravine Rd PO Box 639014	Folsom CA	95630	800-220-4907	916-351-4400
California Water Service Group				
1720 N First St	San Jose CA	95112	800-750-8200	408-367-8200
NYSE: CWT				
Calpine Corp				
717 Texas Ave Ste 1000	Houston TX	77002	800-367-5690	713-830-2000
NYSE: CPN				
Cascade Natural Gas Corp (CNGC)				
8113 W Grandridge Blvd	Kennewick WA	99336	888-522-1130	206-624-3900
Central Hudson Gas & Electric Corp				
284 S Ave	Poughkeepsie NY	12601	800-527-2714	845-452-2700
Central Maine Power Co				
83 Edison Dr	Augusta ME	04336	800-565-0121	207-623-3521
Central Vermont Public Service Corp				
77 Grove St	Rutland VT	05701	800-649-2877	
Citizens Gas & Coke Utility				
2020 N Meridian St	Indianapolis IN	46202	800-427-4217	317-924-3311
City Public Service Board				
PO Box 1771	San Antonio TX	78296	800-870-1006	210-353-2222
Cleco Corp				
2030 Donahue Ferry Rd	Pineville LA	71361	800-622-6537*	318-484-7400
*Cust Svc				
Colorado Springs Utilities				
111 S Cascade Ave				
PO Box 1103	Colorado Springs CO	80903	800-238-5434	719-448-4800
Columbia Gas of Ohio Inc				
200 Civic Ctr Dr	Columbus OH	43215	800-807-9781	614-460-6000
Columbia Gas of Virginia Inc				
8063 Cedon Rd	Woodford VA	22580	800-543-8911*	
*Cust Svc				
Conergy Inc				
2460 W 26th Ave Ste 280C	Denver CO	80211	888-396-6611	
Connecticut Light & Power Co				
107 Selden St	Berlin CT	06037	800-286-2000*	860-665-5000
*Cust Svc				
Consumers Energy Co				
One Energy Plz	Jackson MI	49201	800-477-5050*	517-788-0550
*Cust Svc				
Dakota Gasification Co				
PO Box 5540	Bismarck ND	58506	800-759-0555	701-221-4400
Dayton Power & Light Co				
PO Box 1247	Dayton OH	45401	800-433-8500	937-331-3900
Delmarva Power				
PO Box 231	Wilmington DE	19899	800-898-8042*	
*Cust Svc				
Delta Natural Gas Co Inc				
3617 Lexington Rd	Winchester KY	40391	800-262-2012	859-744-6171
NASDAQ: DGAS				
Dominion East Ohio				
PO Box 26532	Richmond VA	23261	800-362-7557*	
*Cust Svc				
Dominion Hope				
701 E Cary St	Richmond VA	23219	866-366-4357	888-366-8280
Dominion North Carolina Power				
701 E Cary St	Richmond VA	23219	888-667-3000	757-857-2112
Dominion Virginia Power				
120 Tredegar St	Richmond VA	23219	800-688-4673	
Duke Energy Corp				
5400 Westheimer C Mail Drop WP 890	Houston TX	77056	800-521-2232	713-627-5400
Duquesne Light Co				
411 Seventh Ave	Pittsburgh PA	15219	888-393-7000*	412-393-7000
*Cust Svc				
Eastern Shore Natural Gas Co				
1110 Forest Ave Ste 201	Dover DE	19904	877-650-1257	302-734-6720
El Paso Electric Co				
100 N Stanton Stanton Tower	El Paso TX	79901	800-351-1621	915-543-5711
NYSE: EE				
Elizabethtown Gas Co				
One Elizabethtown Plz	Union NJ	07083	800-242-5830	908-289-5000
Empire District Electric Co, The				
602 Joplin St PO Box 127	Joplin MO	64802	800-206-2300	417-625-5100
NYSE: EDE				
Energy West Inc				
1 First Ave S	Great Falls MT	59401	800-570-5688	406-791-7500

Classified Section

				Toll-Free	Phone

Entergy Arkansas Inc
425 W Capitol Ave . . . . Little Rock AR 72201   **800-368-3749**

Entergy Louisiana Inc
639 Loyola Ave . . . . New Orleans LA 70113   **800-368-3749*** 504-576-6116
*Cust Svc

Entergy New Orleans Inc
639 Loyola Ave . . . . New Orleans LA 70113   **800-368-3749***
*Cust Svc

Entergy Texas Inc
350 Pine St . . . . Beaumont TX 77701   **800-368-3749** 409-981-3245

EQT Corp
625 Liberty Ave Ste 1700 . . . . Pittsburgh PA 15222   **800-242-1776** 412-553-5700
NYSE: EQT

Equitable Gas Co
PO Box 6766 . . . . Pittsburgh PA 15212   **800-654-6335**

Erie County Water Authority (ECWA)
295 Main St Rm 350. Buffalo NY 14203   **855-748-1076** 716-849-8484

Eversource
1 Nstar Way NW200 . . . . Westwood MA 02090   **800-592-2000*** 781-441-8011
*Cust Svc

Florida City Gas (FCG)
955 E 25th St . . . . Hialeah FL 33013   **800-993-7546** 305-691-8710

Florida Public Utilities Co (FPUC)
401 S Dixie Hwy . . . . West Palm Beach FL 33401   **800-427-7712**

Gas Co, The
515 Kamake'e St . . . . Honolulu HI 96814   **866-499-3941** 808-535-5933

Georgia Power Co
241 Ralph McGill Blvd NE . . . . Atlanta GA 30308   **866-506-5333*** 404-506-5000
*Cust Svc

Green Mountain Power Corp
163 Acorn Ln . . . . Colchester VT 05446   **888-835-4672** 802-864-5731

Hydro One Inc
483 Bay St 15th Fl . . . . Toronto ON M5G2P5   **888-664-9376** 416-345-5000

Idaho Power Co
1221 W Idaho St . . . . Boise ID 83702   **800-488-6151** 208-388-2200

Intermountain Gas Co Inc
555 S Cole Rd . . . . Boise ID 83709   **800-548-3679*** 208-377-6840
*Cust Svc

Kansas City Power & Light Co
1200 Main . . . . Kansas City MO 64141   **888-471-5275** 816-556-2200

Kansas Gas Service
7421 W 129th St . . . . Overland Park KS 66213   **888-482-4950**

Kinder Morgan Inc
500 Dallas St Ste 1000 . . . . Houston TX 77002   **800-525-3752** 713-369-9000
NYSE: KMI

Kinder Morgan Inc KN Energy Retail Div
370 Van Gordon St . . . . Lakewood CO 80228   **800-232-1627** 303-989-1740

Kissimmee Utility Authority Inc (KUA)
1701 W Carroll St . . . . Kissimmee FL 34741   **877-582-7700** 407-933-7777

Laclede Gas Co
720 Olive St . . . . Saint Louis MO 63101   **800-887-4173** 314-342-0500

Lineage Power Corp
601 Shiloh Rd . . . . Plano TX 75074   **877-546-3243** 972-244-9288

Long Island Power Authority
333 Earle Ovington Blvd Ste 403 . . . . Uniondale NY 11553   **877-275-5472*** 516-222-7700
*Cust Svc

Madison Gas & Electric Co
133 S Blair St . . . . Madison WI 53703   **800-245-1125** 608-252-7000

Marts & Lundy Inc
1200 Wall St W . . . . Lyndhurst NJ 07071   **800-526-9005** 201-460-1660

MEAG Power
1470 Riveredge Pkwy NW . . . . Atlanta GA 30328   **800-333-6324** 770-563-0300

Medley Communications Inc
560-6 Birch St . . . . Lake Elsinore CA 92530   **888-551-7208** 951-245-5200

Metromedia Energy Inc
6 Industrial Way W . . . . Eatontown NJ 07724   **800-828-9427** 732-542-7575

Middle Tennessee Natural Gas Utility District (MTNG)
1036 W Broad St PO Box 670. . . . . Smithville TN 37166   **800-880-6373** 615-597-4300

Middlesex Water Co
1500 Ronson Rd PO Box 1500 . . . . Iselin NJ 08830   **800-549-3802** 732-634-1500
NASDAQ: MSEX

Miller-Eads Company Inc
4125 N Keystone Ave PO Box 55234 . . . . Indianapolis IN 46205   **800-530-0684** 317-545-7101

Minnesota Power
30 W Superior St . . . . Duluth MN 55802   **800-228-4966** 218-722-2625

Missouri Gas Energy
3420 Broadway . . . . Kansas City MO 64111   **800-582-1234** 816-756-5252

Monroe County Water Authority
475 Norris Dr PO Box 10999 . . . . Rochester NY 14610   **866-426-6292** 585-442-2000

Montana-Dakota Utilities Co (MDU)
400 N Fourth St . . . . Bismarck ND 58501   **800-638-3278** 701-222-7900

Mount Carmel Public Utility Co
316 Market St PO Box 220 . . . . Mount Carmel IL 62863   **877-262-7036** 618-262-5151

MRC Global Inc
Two Houston Ctr . . . . Houston TX 77010   **877-294-7574**

National Fuel Gas Distribution Corp
6363 Main St . . . . Williamsville NY 14221   **800-365-3234** 716-857-7000

National Fuel Gas Supply Corp
6363 Main St . . . . Williamsville NY 14221   **800-365-3234*** 716-857-7000
*Cust Svc

National Fuel Resources Inc
165 Lawrence Bell Dr Ste 120. . . . . Williamsville NY 14221   **800-839-9993** 716-630-6778

Nevada Irrigation District (NID)
1036 W Main St . . . . Grass Valley CA 95945   **800-222-4102** 530-273-6185

Nevada Power Co
6226 W Sahara Ave . . . . Las Vegas NV 89146   **800-331-3103*** 702-367-5000
*NYSE: NVE ▪ *Cust Svc

New York State Electric & Gas Corp
Corporate Dr PO Box 5240 . . . . Binghamton NY 13902   **800-572-1111**

NextEra Energy Resources LLC
NextEra Energy Resources LLC
700 Universe Blvd PO Box 14000 . . . . Juno Beach FL 33408   **888-867-3050** 561-691-7171

Nicor Gas 1844 Ferry Rd . . . . Naperville IL 60563   **888-642-6748** 630-983-8888

North Shore Gas Co
3001 Grand Ave . . . . Waukegan IL 60085   **866-556-6004** 847-263-3200

Northern Electric Inc
1275 W 124th Ave . . . . Denver CO 80234   **877-265-0794** 303-428-6969

Northern Kentucky Water District
2835 Crescent Springs Rd
PO Box 18640. . . . . Erlanger KY 41018   **800-772-4636** 859-578-9898

Northwest Natural Gas Co
220 NW Second Ave . . . . Portland OR 97209   **800-422-4012** 503-226-4211
NYSE: NWN

Nova Scotia Power Inc
PO Box 910 . . . . Halifax NS B3J2W5   **800-428-6230** 902-428-6230

NRG Energy Inc
211 Carnegie Ctr . . . . Princeton NJ 08540   **866-735-1214** 609-524-4500
NYSE: NRG

NSTAR Gas One N Star Way . . . . Westwood MA 02090   **800-592-2000**

OG & E Electric Services
PO Box 24990 . . . . Oklahoma City OK 73124   **800-272-9741** 405-553-3000

Ohio Edison Co
76 S Main St PO Box 3637. . . . . Akron OH 44308   **800-736-3402**

Oklahoma Natural Gas Co
401 N Harvey PO Box 401 . . . . Oklahoma City OK 73101   **800-664-5463**

Oncor
1616 Woodall Rodgers Fwy Ste 2M-012 . . . . Dallas TX 75202   **888-313-6862** 214-486-2000

Orange & Rockland Utilities Inc
One Blue Hill Plz . . . . Pearl River NY 10965   **877-434-4100***
*Cust Svc

Otter Tail Power Co
215 S Cascade St . . . . Fergus Falls MN 56537   **800-257-4044** 218-739-8200

Pacific Gas & Electric Co
77 Beale St . . . . San Francisco CA 94105   **800-743-5000*** 415-973-7000
*Cust Svc

Pacific Power & Light
825 NE Multnomah St . . . . Portland OR 97232   **888-221-7070*** 503-813-7100
*Cust Svc

PacifiCorp
825 NE Multnomah St . . . . Portland OR 97232   **888-221-7070** 503-813-5000

Park Water Co
9750 Washburn Rd . . . . Downey CA 90241   **800-727-5987** 562-923-0711

Parkway Electric Inc
11952 James St . . . . Holland MI 49424   **800-574-9553** 616-392-2788

Passaic Valley Water Commission
1525 Main Ave . . . . Clifton NJ 07011   **877-772-7077** 973-340-4300

Pennichuck Corp
25 Manchester St . . . . Merrimack NH 03054   **800-553-5191** 603-882-5191
NASDAQ: PNNW

Peoples Gas Light & Coke Co
130 E Randolph Dr . . . . Chicago IL 60601   **866-556-6001*** 312-240-4000
*Cust Svc

Pepco Energy Services Inc
1300 N 17th St Ste 1600 . . . . Arlington VA 22209   **800-424-8028** 703-253-1800

Piedmont Natural Gas
4720 Piedmont Row Dr PO Box 33068. . . . . Charlotte NC 28210   **800-752-7504** 704-364-3120
NYSE: PNY

Portland General Electric
121 SW Salmon St . . . . Portland OR 97204   **800-542-8818** 503-464-8000
NYSE: POR

PowerSecure International Inc
1609 Heritage Commerce Ct . . . . Wake Forest NC 27587   **866-347-5455** 919-556-3056
NYSE: POWR

PPL Electric Utilities Corp
Two N Ninth St . . . . Allentown PA 18101   **800-342-5775*** 610-774-5151
*Cust Svc

PPL Global LLC
Two N Ninth St . . . . Allentown PA 18101   **800-342-5775** 610-774-5151
NYSE: PPL

Pratt Communications
2913 Tech Ctr . . . . Santa Ana CA 92705   **800-980-2323*** 714-540-6840
*General

PS Energy Group Inc
2987 Clairmont Rd Ste 500 . . . . Atlanta GA 30329   **800-334-7548** 404-321-5711

PSEG Power LLC 80 Pk Plz . . . . Newark NJ 07101   **800-436-7734** 973-430-7000

Public Service of New Hampshire
780 N Commercial St . . . . Manchester NH 03105   **800-662-7764** 603-669-4000

Public Works Commission of The City of Fayetteville North Carolina
955 Old Wilmington Rd
PO Box 1089. . . . . Fayetteville NC 28301   **877-687-7921** 910-483-1382

Puget Sound Energy Inc
10885 NE Fourth St . . . . Bellevue WA 98004   **888-225-5773** 425-452-1234

Questar Gas Co
PO Box 45841 . . . . Salt Lake City UT 84139   **800-323-5517** 801-324-5111

Reliant Energy Retail Services LLC
1201 Fannin St . . . . Houston TX 77002   **866-660-4900** 866-222-7100

Rochester Gas & Electric Corp
89 E Ave . . . . Rochester NY 14649   **800-743-2110**

Roland's Electric Inc
307 Suburban Ave Ste A. . . . . Deer Park NY 11729   **800-981-8010** 631-242-8080

Salt River Project (SRP)
1521 N Project Dr . . . . Tempe AZ 85281   **800-258-4777** 602-236-5900

San Diego Gas & Electric Co
101 Ash St . . . . San Diego CA 92101   **800-411-7343** 619-696-2000

SCANA Energy Marketing Inc
220 Operation Way MC 092 . . . . Cayce SC 29033   **800-472-1051** 803-217-9000

SETEL UC
5121 Maryland Way Ste 300. . . . . Brentwood TN 37027   **800-743-1340** 615-874-6000

SourceGas
655 E Millsap Dr . . . . Fayetteville AR 72703   **800-563-0012**

South Carolina Electric & Gas Co
PO Box 100255 . . . . Columbia SC 29202   **800-251-7234** 803-635-4444

Southern California Edison Co
2244 Walnut Grove Ave . . . . Rosemead CA 91770   **800-655-4555** 626-302-1212

Southern California Gas Co
555 W Fifth St . . . . Los Angeles CA 90013   **800-427-2200** 562-733-1852

Southern Connecticut Gas (SCG)
60 Marsh Hill Rd . . . . Orange CT 06477   **866-268-2887**

Southwest Gas Corp
5241 Spring Mtn Rd PO Box 98510 . . . . Las Vegas NV 89193   **800-748-5539** 702-876-7237
NYSE: SWX

Southwest Gas Corp Northern Nevada Div
400 Eagle Stn Ln . . . . Carson City NV 89701   **877-860-6020**

Southwest Gas Corp Southern Arizona Div
3401 E Gas Rd . . . . Tucson AZ 85714   **877-860-6020**

	Toll-Free	Phone
Southwest Gas Corp Southern California Div		
13471 Mariposa Rd ....Victorville CA 92395	**877-860-6020**	
Southwest Gas Corp Southern Nevada Div		
5241 Spring Mtn Rd ....Las Vegas NV 89150	**877-860-6020**	702-876-7011
Southwestern Energy Co		
2350 N Sam Houston Pkwy E Ste 300 ....Houston TX 77032	**866-322-0801**	832-796-1000
NYSE: SWN		
Spectra Energy Corp		
5400 Westheimer Ct ....Houston TX 77056	**800-700-8744**	713-627-5400
Stream Gas & Electric Ltd		
1950 Stemmons Fwy Ste 3000.................Dallas TX 75207	**866-447-8732**	
Superior Water Light & Power		
2915 Hill Ave PO Box 519 ....Superior WI 54880	**800-227-7957**	715-394-2200
Sweetwater Authority		
PO Box 2328 ....Chula Vista CA 91912	**866-275-3772**	619-420-1413
SWEPCo One Riverside Plz ....Columbus OH 43215	**888-216-3523**	
System Engineering International Inc (SEI)		
5115 Pegasus Ct Ste Q.................Frederick MD 21704	**800-765-4734**	301-694-9601
Texas-New Mexico Power Co (TNMP)		
577 N Garden Ridge Blvd ....Lewisville TX 75067	**888-866-7456**	972-420-4189
Thompson Electric Co (TEC)		
2300 Seventh St PO Box 207 ....Sioux City IA 51105	**800-832-2936**	712-252-4221
Toledo Edison Co PO Box 3687 ....Akron OH 44309	**800-447-3333**	
Trans-Tel Central Inc (TTC)		
2805 Broce Dr ....Norman OK 73072	**800-729-4636**	405-447-5025
Tricomm Services Corp		
1247 N Church St Ste 8 ....Moorestown NJ 08057	**800-872-2401**	856-914-9001
Tucson Electric Power Co		
1 S Church Ave Ste 100 ....Tucson AZ 85701	**800-430-4046**	520-571-4000
TXU Electric 1601 Bryan St ....Dallas TX 75201	**800-242-9113**	214-486-2534
United Electric Supply Inc		
10 Bellecor Dr ....New Castle DE 19720	**800-322-3374**	302-322-3333
United Illuminating Co		
157 Church St ....New Haven CT 06510	**800-722-5584***	203-499-2000
*Cust Svc		
United States Information Systems Inc (USIS)		
35 W Jefferson Ave ....Pearl River NY 10965	**866-222-3778**	845-358-7755
Virginia Natural Gas Inc AGL Resources Inc		
PO Box 4569 ....Atlanta GA 30302	**800-633-4236**	404-584-4000
Wachter Inc 16001 W 99th St ....Lenexa KS 66219	**800-462-9638**	913-541-2500
Ward's Marine Electric Inc		
617 SW Third Ave ....Fort Lauderdale FL 33315	**800-545-9273**	954-523-2815
Washington Gas & Light Co		
6801 Industrial Rd ....Springfield VA 22151	**800-752-7520**	703-750-4440
Washington Gas Energy Services Inc (WGES)		
13865 Sunrise Vly Dr Ste 200 ....Herndon VA 20171	**888-884-9437**	703-793-7500
We Energies		
231 W Michigan St PO Box 2046 ....Milwaukee WI 53203	**800-242-9137**	414-221-2345
Westar Energy PO Box 758500 ....Topeka KS 66675	**800-544-4857**	785-575-6300
Western Massachusetts Electric Co		
1 Federal St Bldg 111-4 ....Springfield MA 01105	**800-286-2000**	413-785-5871
Wisconsin Power & Light Co		
4902 N Biltmore Ln PO Box 77007.........Madison WI 53718	**800-255-4268**	
Wisconsin Public Service Corp		
PO Box 19001 ....Green Bay WI 54307	**800-450-7260**	
Xcel Energy Inc PO Box 840 ....Denver CO 80201	**877-322-8228**	303-571-7511
NYSE: XEL		
Yankee Gas Services Co		
107 Selden St ....Berlin CT 06037	**800-989-0900**	
York Water Co, The		
130 E Market St PO Box 15089 ....York PA 17405	**800-750-5561**	717-845-3601
NASDAQ: YORW		
Yucaipa Valley Water District		
PO Box 730 ....Yucaipa CA 92399	**800-272-8869**	909-797-5117

783   VACUUM CLEANERS - HOUSEHOLD

SEE ALSO Appliances - Small - Mfr

	Toll-Free	Phone
Beam Industries		
1700 W Second St ....Webster City IA 50595	**800-369-2326**	515-832-4620
CentralVac International		
23455 Hellman Ave PO Box 259.............Dollar Bay MI 49922	**800-666-3133**	
Electrolux Home Care Products Inc		
PO Box 3900 ....Peoria IL 61612	**800-282-2886***	
*Cust Svc		
Kirby Co 1920 W 114th St ....Cleveland OH 44102	**800-437-7170**	216-228-2400
Lindsay Manufacturing Inc		
PO Box 1708 ....Ponca City OK 74602	**800-546-3729**	580-762-2457
Metropolitan Vacuum Cleaner Co Inc		
one Ramapo Ave PO Box 149...........Suffern NY 10901	**800-822-1602**	845-357-1600
Oreck Corp 1400 Salem Rd ....Cookeville TN 38506	**800-289-5888**	

784   VALVES - INDUSTRIAL

	Toll-Free	Phone
American Cast Iron Pipe Co (ACIPCO)		
1501 31st Ave N ....Birmingham AL 35207	**800-442-2347**	205-325-7701
Anderson Brass Co		
1629 W Bobo Newsome Hwy ....Hartsville SC 29550	**800-476-9876**	843-332-4111
Armstrong International Inc		
2081 SE Ocean Blvd 4th Fl ....Stuart FL 34996	**866-738-5125**	772-286-7175
Barksdale Inc		
3211 Fruitland Ave ....Los Angeles CA 90058	**800-835-1060**	323-589-6181
Circle Seal Controls Inc		
2301 Wardlow Cir ....Corona CA 92880	**800-991-2726**	951-270-6200
Clow Valve Co		
902 S Second St ....Oskaloosa IA 52577	**800-829-2569**	641-673-8611
Crane Company Stockham Div		
2129 Third Ave SE ....Cullman AL 35055	**800-786-2542**	256-775-3800
Engineered Controls International Inc (ECII)		
100 Rego Dr PO Box 247 ....Elon NC 27244	**800-650-0061**	336-449-7707
Fike Corp		
704 SW Tenth St ....Blue Springs MO 64015	**877-342-3453**	816-229-3405

	Toll-Free	Phone
Flowserve Corp		
5215 N O'Connor Blvd Ste 2300.................Irving TX 75039	**800-350-1082**	972-443-6500
NYSE: FLS		
FMC Technologies Inc		
1803 Gears Rd ....Houston TX 77067	**800-356-4898**	281-591-4000
NYSE: FTI		
Gemini Valve Two Otter Ct ....Raymond NH 03077	**800-370-0936**	603-895-4761
Goulds Pumps Inc Goulds Water Technologies Group		
240 Fall St ....Seneca Falls NY 13148	**800-327-7700**	315-568-2811
Groth Corp		
13650 N Promenade Blvd ....Stafford TX 77477	**800-354-7684**	281-295-6800
High Vacuum Apparatus LLC (HVA)		
12880 Moya Blvd ....Reno NV 89506	**800-551-4422**	775-359-4442
Hoerbiger Corp of America Inc		
3350 Gateway Dr ....Pompano Beach FL 33069	**800-327-8961**	954-974-5700
Hudson Valve Company Inc		
5301 Office Pk Dr Ste 330 ....Bakersfield CA 93309	**800-748-6218**	661-869-1126
Humphrey Products Co		
5070 E N Ave PO Box 2008 ....Kalamazoo MI 49048	**800-477-8707**	269-381-5500
Hydroseal Valve Co Inc		
1500 SE 89th St ....Oklahoma City OK 73149	**800-398-2493**	405-631-1533
ITT Goulds Pumps Industries/Goulds Industrial Pumps Group		
240 Fall St ....Seneca Falls NY 13148	**800-327-7700**	315-568-2811
ITT Industries Inc Engineered Valves Div		
33 Centerville Rd ....Lancaster PA 17603	**800-366-1111**	717-509-2200
Kennedy Valve		
1021 E Water St ....Elmira NY 14902	**800-782-5831**	607-734-2211
KF Industries Inc		
1500 SE 89th St ....Oklahoma City OK 73149	**800-654-4842**	405-631-1533
Kraft Fluid Systems Inc		
14300 Foltz Pkwy ....Strongsville OH 44149	**800-257-1155**	440-238-5545
Leonard Valve Co		
1360 Elmwood Ave ....Cranston RI 02910	**800-222-1208**	401-461-1200
Leslie Controls Inc		
12501 Telecom Dr ....Tampa FL 33637	**800-323-8366**	813-978-1000
Mac Valves Inc 30569 Beck Rd ....Wixom MI 48393	**800-622-8587**	248-624-7700
Marotta Controls Inc		
78 Boonton Ave PO Box 427 ....Montville NJ 07045	**888-627-6882**	973-334-7800
McWane Inc		
2900 Hwy 280 Ste 300 ....Birmingham AL 35223	**877-231-0904**	205-414-3100
Milwaukee Valve Company Inc		
16550 W Stratton Dr ....New Berlin WI 53151	**800-348-6544**	262-432-2800
Mueller Co		
500 W Eldorado St ....Decatur IL 62522	**800-423-1323**	217-423-4471
Mueller Refrigeration Co Inc		
121 Rogers St ....Hartsville TN 37074	**800-937-5449***	615-374-2124
*Cust Svc		
Newport News Industrial Corp		
182 Enterprise Dr ....Newport News VA 23603	**800-627-0353**	757-380-7053
NIBCO Inc		
1516 Middlebury St ....Elkhart IN 46515	**800-234-0227**	574-295-3000
Ogontz Corp		
2835 Terwood Rd ....Willow Grove PA 19090	**800-523-2478**	215-657-4770
Parker Hannifin Corp Hydraulic Valve Div		
520 Ternes Ave ....Elyria OH 44035	**800-272-7537**	440-366-5200
Parker Instrumentation Group		
6035 Parkland Blvd ....Cleveland OH 44124	**800-272-7537**	216-896-3000
Peter Paul Electronics Co Inc		
480 John Downey Dr ....New Britain CT 06051	**800-825-8377**	860-229-4884
PGI International		
16101 Vallen Dr ....Houston TX 77041	**800-231-0233**	713-466-0056
Plast-O-Matic Valves Inc		
1384 Pompton Ave ....Cedar Grove NJ 07009	**800-323-2710**	973-256-3000
Plattco Corp 7 White St ....Plattsburgh NY 12901	**800-352-1731**	518-563-4640
Richards Industries Inc		
3170 Wasson Rd ....Cincinnati OH 45209	**800-543-7311***	513-533-5600
*Cust Svc		
Robert H Wager Co		
570 Montroyal Rd ....Rural Hall NC 27045	**800-562-7024**	336-969-6909
Sherwood		
2200 North Main St ....Washington PA 15301	**888-508-2583**	724-225-8000
United Brass Works Inc		
714 S Main St ....Randleman NC 27317	**800-334-3035**	336-498-2661

785   VALVES & HOSE FITTINGS - FLUID POWER

SEE ALSO Carburetors, Pistons, Piston Rings, Valves

	Toll-Free	Phone
Air-Way Manufacturing Co		
586 N Main St ....Olivet MI 49076	**800-253-1036***	269-749-2161
*Cust Svc		
Arkwin Industries Inc		
686 Main St ....Westbury NY 11590	**800-284-2551**	516-333-2640
Bosch Rexroth PO Box 394 ....Wooster OH 44691	**800-739-7684**	330-263-3300
Bosch Rexroth Corp		
5150 Prairie Stone Pkwy ....Hoffman Estates IL 60192	**800-860-1055**	847-645-3600
Civacon		
4304 N Mattox Rd ....Kansas City MO 64150	**888-526-5657***	816-741-6600
*Sales		
Clippard Instrument Lab		
7390 Colerain Ave ....Cincinnati OH 45239	**877-245-6247**	513-521-4261
Control Flow Inc		
9201 Fairbanks N Houston Rd ....Houston TX 77064	**800-231-9922**	281-890-8300
Daman Products Co Inc		
1811 N Home St ....Mishawaka IN 46545	**800-959-7841**	574-259-7841
Deltrol Fluid Products		
3001 Grant Ave ....Bellwood IL 60104	**800-477-9772**	708-547-0500
Dynaquip Controls		
10 Harris Industrial Pk ....Saint Clair MO 63077	**800-545-3636**	636-629-3700
Fresno Valves & Castings Inc		
7736 E Springfield Ave PO Box 40 ....Selma CA 93662	**800-333-1658**	559-834-2511
Hays Fluid Controls		
114 Eason Rd ....Dallas NC 28034	**800-354-4297**	704-922-9565
Henry Pratt Co		
401 S Highland Ave ....Aurora IL 60506	**877-436-7977**	630-844-4000
Hydraforce Inc		
500 Barclay Blvd ....Lincolnshire IL 60069	**877-237-9101**	847-793-2300

			Toll-Free	Phone

Hyson Products
10367 Brecksville Rd . . . . Brecksville OH 44141 **800-876-4976** 440-526-5900

ITT Aerospace Controls
28150 Industry Dr . . . . Valencia CA 91355 **866-294-8691** 661-295-4000

ITT Industries Inc
1133 Westchester Ave . . . . White Plains NY 10604 **800-254-2823** 914-641-2000
NYSE: ITT

JD Gould Co Inc
4707 Massachusetts Ave . . . . Indianapolis IN 46218 **800-634-6853**

Jetstream of Houston LLP
4930 Cranswick . . . . Houston TX 77041 **800-231-8192** 713-462-7000

Kimray Inc
52 NW 42nd St . . . . Oklahoma City OK 73118 **866-586-7233** 405-525-6601

Mead Fluid Dynamics Inc
4114 N Knox Ave . . . . Chicago IL 60641 **877-632-3872*** 773-685-6800
Cust Svc

Morrison Bros Co
570 E Seventh St . . . . Dubuque IA 52001 **800-553-4840** 563-583-5701

Norgren
5400 S Delaware St . . . . Littleton CO 80120 **800-514-0129** 303-794-5000

Omega Flex Inc
451 Creamery Way . . . . Exton PA 19341 **800-355-1039** 610-524-7272
NASDAQ: OFLX

Parker Fluid Connectors Group
6035 Parkland Blvd . . . . Cleveland OH 44124 **800-272-7537*** 216-896-3000
General

Parker Hannifin Corp Brass Products Div
100 Parker Dr . . . . Otsego MI 49078 **800-272-7537** 269-694-9411

Parker Hannifin Corp General Valve Div
26 Clinton Dr Unit 103 . . . . Hollis NH 03049 **800-272-7537**

Parker Hannifin Corp Skinner Valve Div
95 Edgewood Ave . . . . New Britain CT 06051 **800-825-8305** 860-827-2300

PBM Inc 1070 Sandy Hill Rd . . . . Irwin PA 15642 **800-967-4726** 724-863-0550

Plattco Corp 7 White St . . . . Plattsburgh NY 12901 **800-352-1731** 518-563-4640

Richards Industries Inc
3170 Wasson Rd . . . . Cincinnati OH 45209 **800-543-7311*** 513-533-5600
Cust Svc

Ross Controls
1250 Stephenson Hwy . . . . Troy MI 48083 **800-438-7677** 248-764-1800

Watts Fluidair Inc
Nine Cutts Rd . . . . Kittery ME 03904 **877-467-4323** 207-439-9511

786 VARIETY STORES

			Toll-Free	Phone

99 Cents Only Stores
4000 Union Pacific Ave . . . . Commerce CA 90023 **888-582-5999** 323-980-8145

AC Doctor LLC
2151 W Hillsboro Blvd Ste 400 . . . . Deerfield Beach FL 33442 **866-264-1479**

American Muscle 7 Lee Blvd . . . . Malvern PA 19355 **888-332-7930** 610-251-2397

Andersons Inc Retail Group
480 W Dussel Dr PO Box 119 . . . . Maumee OH 43537 **800-537-3370** 419-893-5050

Armature Dns 2000 Inc
11001 Jean Meunier . . . . Montreal QC H1G4S7 **800-363-7996** 514-324-1141

Big Lots Inc (BLI)
300 Phillipi Rd . . . . Columbus OH 43228 **877-998-1697** 614-278-6800
NYSE: BIG

Black Forest Decor LLC
PO Box 297 . . . . Jenks OK 74037 **800-605-0915**

Building 19 Inc
319 Lincoln St . . . . Hingham MA 02043 **800-225-5061** 781-749-6900

Clubfurniture.com
11535 Carmel Commons Blvd Ste 202 . . . . Charlotte NC 28226 **888-378-8383**

Dollar General Corp
100 Mission Ridge . . . . Goodlettsville TN 37072 **800-777-1410** 615-855-4000
NYSE: DG

Dollar Tree Stores Inc
500 Volvo Pkwy . . . . Chesapeake VA 23320 **877-530-8733**
NASDAQ: DLTR

Easy Ice LLC
925 W Washington St Ste 100 . . . . Marquette MI 49855 **866-327-9423**

Exchange, The
3911 S Walton Walker Blvd . . . . Dallas TX 75236 **800-527-2345** 214-312-2011

Family Dollar Stores Inc
PO Box 1017 . . . . Charlotte NC 28201 **866-377-6420** 704-847-6961
NYSE: FDO

Howell Tractor & Equipment LLC
480 Blaine St . . . . Gary IN 46406 **800-852-8816**

Kryptonite Kollectibles
1441 Plainfield Ave . . . . Janesville WI 53545 **877-646-1728**

Navy Exchange Service Command (NEXCOM)
3280 Virginia Beach Blvd . . . . Virginia Beach VA 23452 **800-628-3924** 757-463-6200

New Vitality
260 Smith St . . . . Farmingdale NY 11735 **888-997-2941**

Overstock.com Inc
6350 South 3000 East . . . . Salt Lake City UT 84121 **800-843-2446*** 801-947-3100
NASDAQ: OSTK *Cust Svc*

Pet Supplies Inc
Customer Service Return Ctr 1 Maplewood Dr
. . . . Hazleton PA 18202 **800-738-7877**

Playscripts
450 Seventh Ave Ste 809 . . . . New York NY 10123 **866-639-7529**

Pride Products Corp
4333 Veterans Memorial Hwy . . . . Ronkonkoma NY 11779 **800-898-5550** 631-737-4444

R J Schinner Company Inc
16950 W Lincoln Ave PO Box 510470 . . . . . . New Berlin WI 53151 **800-234-1460** 262-797-7180

Rally House & Kansas Sampler
9750 Quivira Rd . . . . Lenexa KS 66215 **800-645-5394**

Rennco LLC 300 Elm St . . . . Homer MI 49245 **800-409-5225**

Scout Stuff PO Box 7143 . . . . Charlotte NC 28241 **800-323-0736**

Shoplet.com
39 Broadway Ste 2030 . . . . New York NY 10006 **800-757-3015** 212-619-3353

U-line Corp PO Box 245040 . . . . Milwaukee WI 53224 **800-779-2547** 414-354-0300

787 VENTURE CAPITAL FIRMS

Companies listed here are investors, not lenders.

			Toll-Free	Phone

Adobe Ventures LP
345 Pk Ave . . . . San Jose CA 95110 **877-722-7088** 408-536-6000

American Bullion Inc
12301 Wilshire Blvd Ste 650 . . . . Los Angeles CA 90025 **800-326-9598** 310-689-7720

American Capital Group Inc
8105 Irvine Ctr Dr Ste 250 . . . . Irvine CA 92618 **877-814-6871** 949-485-3005

Ampersand Capital Partners
55 William St Ste 240 . . . . Wellesley MA 02481 **800-477-6834** 781-239-0700

BlackRock Inc
601 Union St 56th Fl . . . . Seattle WA 98101 **800-441-7450** 206-613-6700
NYSE: BLK

Blue Chip Venture Co
312 Walnut St Ste 1120 . . . . Cincinnati OH 45202 **800-775-1812** 513-723-2300

Capital Resource Partners
31 State St 6th Fl . . . . Boston MA 02109 **800-623-2880** 617-478-9600

Capital Southwest Corp
12900 Preston Rd Ste 700 . . . . Dallas TX 75230 **877-870-5176** 972-233-8242
NASDAQ: CSWC

CIBC Wood Gundy Capital
425 Lexington Ave . . . . New York NY 10017 **800-999-6726** 212-856-4000

Code Hennessy & Simmons Inc
10 S Wacker Dr Ste 3175 . . . . Chicago IL 60606 **888-603-5847** 312-876-1840

Connecticut Innovations Inc
865 Brook St Third Fl . . . . Rocky Hill CT 06067 **800-733-4763** 860-563-5851

Cornerstone Equity Investors LLC
281 Tresser Blvd 12th Fl . . . . Stamford CT 06901 **800-438-7465** 212-753-0901

Domain Assoc
1 Palmer Sq Ste 515 . . . . Princeton NJ 08542 **866-803-9204** 609-683-5656

EQUUS Total Return Inc
700 Louisiana St 48th Fl . . . . Houston TX 77002 **888-323-4533**

Frazier Healthcare
601 Union 2 Union Sq Ste 3200 . . . . Seattle WA 98101 **800-638-4817** 206-621-7200

Frontenac Co
135 S La Salle St Ste 3800 . . . . Chicago IL 60603 **800-368-3681** 312-368-0044

Harvest Partners
280 Pk Ave 25th Fl . . . . New York NY 10017 **866-771-1000** 212-599-6300

InterWest Partners
2710 Sand Hill Rd 2nd Fl . . . . Menlo Park CA 94025 **866-803-9204** 650-854-8585

INVESCO Private Capital Inc
1166 Ave of the Americas 26th Fl . . . . . . New York NY 10036 **800-959-4246** 212-278-9000

JatoTech Ventures
6300 Bridgepoint Pkwy Bldg 1 Ste 500 . . . . . Austin TX 78730 **800-626-4686** 512-795-5860

Kleiner Perkins Caufield & Byers (KPCB)
2750 Sand Hill Rd . . . . Menlo Park CA 94025 **877-312-5521** 650-233-2750

MCG Capital Corp
1100 Wilson Blvd Ste 3000 . . . . Arlington VA 22209 **888-748-3526** 703-247-7500
NASDAQ: MCGC

Mesirow Financial Private Equity
350 N Clark St . . . . Chicago IL 60610 **800-453-0600** 312-595-6000

Morgan Stanley Venture Partners
1585 Broadway 38th Fl . . . . New York NY 10036 **866-722-7310** 212-761-4000

MPM Capital Offices
200 Clarendon St 54th Fl . . . . Boston MA 02116 **888-286-8010** 617-425-9200

MRV Communications Inc
20415 Nordhoff St . . . . Chatsworth CA 91311 **800-338-5316*** 818-773-0900
OTC: MRVC *Sales*

MVC Capital Inc
287 Bowman Ave 2nd Fl . . . . Purchase NY 10577 **800-322-2885** 914-510-9400
NYSE: MVC

Needham Capital Partners
445 Pk Ave . . . . New York NY 10022 **800-625-7071** 212-371-8300

Newtek Business Services Inc
1440 Broadway 17th Fl . . . . New York NY 10018 **866-820-8902*** 212-356-9500
NASDAQ: NEWT *Sales*

Northleaf Capital Partners
79 Wellington St W Sixth Fl
PO Box 120 . . . . Toronto ON M5K1N9 **866-964-4141**

Private Capital Management
8889 Pelican Bay Blvd Ste 500 . . . . Naples FL 34108 **800-763-0337** 239-254-2500

Safeguard Scientifics Inc
435 Devon Pk Dr Ste 800 . . . . Wayne PA 19087 **877-506-7371** 610-293-0600
NYSE: SFE

Summit Partners
222 Berkeley St 18th Fl . . . . Boston MA 02116 **800-503-4611** 617-824-1000

TA Assoc Inc
200 Clarendon St 56th Fl . . . . Boston MA 02116 **800-836-8873** 617-574-6700

Technology Funding Inc
460 St Michael's Dr Ste 1000 . . . . Santa Fe NM 87505 **800-821-5323**

Technology Partners
550 University Ave . . . . Palo Alto CA 94301 **800-747-3924** 650-289-9000

TEOCO Corp
12150 Monument Dr Ste 400 . . . . Fairfax VA 22033 **888-868-3626** 703-322-9200

Thomas Weisel Partners Group LLC
One Montgomery St . . . . San Francisco CA 94104 **888-267-3700** 415-364-2500

Tortoise Energy Capital Corp
11550 Ash St Ste 300 . . . . Leawood KS 66211 **866-362-9331** 913-981-1020
NYSE: TYY

UPS Strategic Enterprise Fund
55 Glenlake Pkwy NE Bldg 1 4th Fl . . . . Atlanta GA 30328 **800-742-5877**

Woodside Fund
303 Twin Dolphin Dr Ste 600 . . . . Redwood Shores CA 94065 **888-368-5545** 650-610-8050

788 VETERANS NURSING HOMES - STATE

SEE ALSO Veterans Hospitals

			Toll-Free	Phone

DJ Jacobetti Home for Veterans
425 Fisher St . . . . Marquette MI 49855 **800-433-6760** 906-226-3576

Floyd E Tut Fann State Veterans Home
2701 Meridian St . . . . Huntsville AL 35811 **855-212-8028** 256-851-2807

				Toll-Free	Phone
Grand Island Veterans' Home 2300 W Capital Ave	Grand Island	NE	68803	800-358-8802	308-385-6252
Hastings Veterans Home 1200 E 18th St	Hastings	MN	55033	877-838-3803	651-438-8500
Idaho State Veterans Home-Lewiston 821 21st Ave	Lewiston	ID	83501	877-222-8387	208-799-3422
Idaho State Veterans Home-Pocatello 1957 Alvin Ricken Dr	Pocatello	ID	83201	877-222-8387	208-236-6340
Illinois Veterans Home-Anna 792 N Main St	Anna	IL	62906	888-261-3336	618-833-6302
Iowa Veterans Home 1301 Summit St Bldg 3465	Marshalltown	IA	50131	800-838-4692	515-252-4698
Maine Veterans Home-Augusta 310 Cony Rd	Augusta	ME	04330	888-684-4664	
Maine Veterans Home-Bangor 44 Hogan Rd	Bangor	ME	04401	888-684-4665	207-942-2333
Maine Veterans Home-Caribou 163 Van Buren Rd Ste 2	Caribou	ME	04736	888-684-4667	207-498-6074
Maine Veterans Home-Scarborough 290 US Rt 1	Scarborough	ME	04074	888-684-4666	207-883-7184
Maine Veterans Home-South Paris 477 High St	South Paris	ME	04281	888-684-4668	207-743-6300
Minnesota Veterans Home-Minneapolis 5101 Minnehaha Ave S	Minneapolis	MN	55407	877-838-6757	612-721-0600
Minnesota Veterans Home-Silver Bay 45 Banks Blvd	Silver Bay	MN	55614	877-729-8387	218-226-6300
Mississippi State Veterans' Home Collins 3261 Hwy 49 S	Collins	MS	39428	877-203-5632	601-765-0403
Mississippi State Veterans' Home Kosciusko 310 Autumn Ridge Dr	Kosciusko	MS	39090	877-203-5632	662-289-7044
Missouri Veterans Home-Cape Girardeau 2400 Veterans Memorial Dr	Cape Girardeau	MO	63701	800-392-0210	573-290-5870
Montana Veterans Home 400 Veterans Dr	Columbia Falls	MT	59912	888-279-7532	406-892-3256
New Hampshire Veterans Home 139 Winter St	Tilton	NH	03276	800-735-2964	603-527-4400
New Mexico State Veterans Ctr 992 S Broadway St	Truth or Consequences	NM	87901	800-964-3976	575-894-4200
Ohio Veterans Home 3416 Columbus Ave *Admissions	Sandusky	OH	44870	800-572-7934*	419-625-2454
Oklahoma Veterans Ctr Ardmore 1015 S Commerce	Ardmore	OK	73401	800-941-2160	580-223-2266
Oklahoma Veterans Ctr Norman 1776 E Robinson St	Norman	OK	73071	800-782-5218	405-360-5600
Oklahoma Veterans Ctr Talihina 10014 SE 1138th Ave PO Box 1168	Talihina	OK	74571	800-941-2160	918-567-2251
Oregon Veterans' Home 700 Veterans Dr	The Dalles	OR	97058	800-846-8460	541-296-7190
Thomson-Hood Veterans Ctr 100 Veterans Dr	Wilmore	KY	40390	800-928-4838	859-858-2814
Veterans Home of California-Barstow 100 E Veterans Pkwy	Barstow	CA	92311	800-746-0606	760-252-6200
Veterans Home of California-Chula Vista 700 E Naples Ct	Chula Vista	CA	91911	800-952-5626	
Veterans Home of California-Yountville 1227 O St	Sacramento	CA	95814	800-952-5626	
Wisconsin Veterans Home N2665 County Rd QQ	King	WI	54946	877-944-6667	715-258-5586

789 VETERINARY HOSPITALS

				Toll-Free	Phone
Banfield the Pet Hospital 8000 NE Tillamook St	Portland	OR	97213	866-894-7927	
Pipestone Veterinary Clinic LLC 1300 Hwy 75 S PO Box 188	Pipestone	MN	56164	800-658-2523	507-825-4211
Radiocat 32-A Mellor Ave	Baltimore	MD	21228	800-323-9729	
Summit Pet Product Distributors Inc 420 N Chimney Rock Rd	Greensboro	NC	27410	800-323-2963	336-294-3200
VCA Antech Inc 12401 W Olympic Blvd *NASDAQ: WOOF*	Los Angeles	CA	90064	800-966-1822	310-571-6500
VetSelect Animal Hospital 2150 Old Novi Rd	Novi	MI	48377	800-462-8749	248-624-1100

790 VETERINARY MEDICAL ASSOCIATIONS - STATE

				Toll-Free	Phone
Colorado Veterinary Medical Assn 191 Yuma St	Denver	CO	80223	800-228-5429	303-318-0447
Georgia Veterinary Medical Assn 233 Peachtree St NE Ste 2205	Atlanta	GA	30303	800-853-1625	678-309-9800
Indiana Veterinary Medical Assn 201 S Capitol Ave Ste 405	Indianapolis	IN	46225	800-270-0747	317-974-0888
Iowa Veterinary Medical Assn 1605 N Ankeny Blvd Ste 110	Ankeny	IA	50023	800-369-9564	515-965-9237
Kansas Veterinary Medical Assn 816 SW Tyler St Ste 200	Topeka	KS	66612	888-545-5862	785-233-4141
Kentucky Veterinary Medical Assn 108 Consumer Ln	Frankfort	KY	40601	800-552-5862	502-226-5862
Louisiana Veterinary Medical Assn 8550 United Plz Blvd Ste 1001	Baton Rouge	LA	70809	800-524-2996	225-928-5862
Maine Veterinary Medical Assn (MVMA) 97A Exchange St Ste 305	Portland	ME	04101	800-448-2772	
Maryland Veterinary Medical Assn 8015 Corporate Dr Ste A	Baltimore	MD	21236	888-884-6862	410-931-3332
Minnesota Veterinary Medical Assn 101 Bridgepoint Way Ste 100	South Saint Paul	MN	55075	888-933-5363	651-645-7533
Missouri Veterinary Medical Assn 2500 Country Club Dr	Jefferson City	MO	65109	800-632-6900	573-636-8612
New York State Veterinary Medical Society 100 Great Oaks Blvd Ste 127	Albany	NY	12203	800-876-9867	518-869-7867
North Carolina Veterinary Medical Assn (NCVMA) 1611 Jones Franklin Rd Ste 108	Raleigh	NC	27606	800-446-2862	919-851-5850
Ohio Veterinary Medical Assn (OVMA) 3168 Riverside Dr	Columbus	OH	43221	800-662-6862	614-486-7253
Oklahoma Veterinary Medical Assn PO Box 14521	Oklahoma City	OK	73113	800-248-2862	405-478-1002
Oregon Veterinary Medical Assn 1880 Lancaster Dr NE Ste 118	Salem	OR	97305	800-235-3502	503-399-0311
Puerto Rico Veterinary Medical Assn 352 San Claudio Ave Ste 248	San Juan	PR	00926	888-791-1856	787-283-0565
South Carolina Assn of Veterinarians PO Box 11766	Columbia	SC	29211	800-441-7228	803-254-1027
Tennessee Veterinary Medical Assn PO Box 803	Fayetteville	TN	37334	800-697-3587	931-438-0070
Texas Veterinary Medical Assn 8104 Exchange Dr	Austin	TX	78754	800-711-0023	512-452-4224
Virginia Veterinary Medical Assn (VVMA) 3801 Westerre Pkwy Ste D	Henrico	VA	23233	800-937-8862	804-346-2611
Washington State Veterinary Medical Assn 8024 Bracken Pl SE	Snoqualmie	WA	98065	800-399-7862	425-396-3191
Wisconsin Veterinary Medical Assn (WVMA) 2801 Crossroads Dr Ste 1200	Madison	WI	53718	888-254-5202	608-257-3665
Wyoming Veterinary Medical Assn (WVMA) 1841 W Secluded Ct	Kuna	ID	83634	800-272-1813	208-922-9431

791 VIATICAL SETTLEMENT COMPANIES

A viatical settlement is the sale of an existing life insurance policy by a terminally ill person to a third party in return for a percentage of the face value of the policy paid immediately.

				Toll-Free	Phone
Coventry First LLC 7111 Vly Green Rd	Fort Washington	PA	19034	877-836-8300	
Francis Investment Counsel LLC 21180 W Capitol Dr	Pewaukee	WI	53072	866-232-6457	
Habersham Funding LLC 415 E Paces Ferry Rd NE Terr Level	Atlanta	GA	30305	888-874-2402	404-233-8275
Legacy Benefits Corp 350 Fifth Ave Ste 4320	New York	NY	10118	800-875-1000	
Life Partners Inc (LPI) 204 Woodhew Dr	Waco	TX	76712	800-368-5569	254-751-7797
Life Settlement Solutions Inc 9201 Spectrum Ctr Blvd Ste 105	San Diego	CA	92123	800-762-3387	858-576-8067
Page & Assoc Inc 1979 Lakeside Pkwy Ste 200	Tucker	GA	30084	800-252-5282	
Senior Settlements LLC 1000 S Lenola Rd Bldg 1 Ste 202	Maple Shade	NJ	08052	800-834-0628	856-235-2133

792 VIDEO STORES

SEE ALSO Book, Music, Video Clubs

				Toll-Free	Phone
Amazon.com Inc 1200 12th Ave S Ste 1200 *NASDAQ: AMZN* ■ *Cust Svc	Seattle	WA	98144	800-201-7575*	206-266-1000
Best Buy Company Inc 7601 Penn Ave S *NYSE: BBY*	Minneapolis	MN	55423	888-237-8289	612-291-1000
DVD Empire 2140 Woodland Rd	Warrendale	PA	15086	888-383-1880	
Facets Multimedia Inc 1517 W Fullerton Ave *Cust Svc	Chicago	IL	60614	800-331-6197*	773-281-9075
Family Video 2500 Lehigh Ave	Glenview	IL	60026	888-332-6843	847-904-9000
NetFlix Inc 100 Winchester Cir *NASDAQ: NFLX*	Los Gatos	CA	95032	800-290-8191	408-540-3700

793 VISION CORRECTION CENTERS

				Toll-Free	Phone
Barnet-Dulaney Eye Ctr 4800 N 22nd St	Phoenix	AZ	85016	866-742-6581	602-955-1000
Center for Lasik Ophthalmology Consultants, The 5800 Colonial Dr Ste 103	Margate	FL	33063	800-448-8770	954-969-0090
Eye Centers of Florida (ECOF) 4101 Evans Ave	Fort Myers	FL	33901	888-393-2455	239-939-3456
John-Kenyon Eye Ctr 1305 Wall St Ste 200	Jeffersonville	IN	47130	800-342-5393	
Jones Eye Clinic 4405 Hamilton Blvd PO Box 3246	Sioux City	IA	51104	800-334-2015	712-239-3937
LaserVue Eye Ctr 3540 Mendocino Ave Ste 200	Santa Rosa	CA	95403	888-527-3745	707-522-6200
LCA-Vision Inc 7840 Montgomery Rd *NASDAQ: LCAV*	Cincinnati	OH	45236	800-688-4550	513-792-9292
Minnesota Eye Consultants PA 710 E 24th St Ste 100	Minneapolis	MN	55404	800-526-7632	612-813-3600
Pacific Cataract & Laser Institute 2517 NE Kresky Ave	Chehalis	WA	98532	800-888-9903	360-748-8632
Southwestern Eye Ctr 2610 E University Dr *General	Mesa	AZ	85213	800-224-3339*	480-892-8400
TLC Vision Corp 50 Burnhamthorpe Rd W Ste 101	Mississauga	ON	L5B3C2	877-852-2020	
Will Vision & Laser Centers 8100 NE Pkwy Dr Ste 125	Vancouver	WA	98662	877-542-3937	360-885-1327

794 VITAMINS & NUTRITIONAL SUPPLEMENTS

SEE ALSO Medicinal Chemicals & Botanical Products ; Pharmaceutical Companies ; Pharmaceutical Companies - Generic Drugs ; Diet & Health Foods

				Toll-Free	Phone
ADM Natural Health & Nutrition					
Archer Daniels Midland Co					
4666 Faries Pkwy	Decatur	IL	62526	**800-637-5843**	217-451-7231
Afexa Life Sciences					
9604 20th Ave	Edmonton	AB	T6N1G1	**888-280-0022**	780-432-0022
AST Sports Science Inc					
120 Capitol Dr	Golden	CO	80401	**800-627-2788**	303-278-1420
Atkins Nutritionals Inc					
1050 17th St Ste 1000	Denver	CO	80265	**800-628-5467**	303-633-2840
Beehive Botanicals Inc					
16297 W Nursery Rd	Hayward	WI	54843	**800-233-4483**	715-634-4274
Cc Pollen Co					
3627 E Indian School Rd Ste 209	Phoenix	AZ	85018	**800-875-0096**	602-957-0096
CytoSport Inc					
4795 Industrial Way	Benicia	CA	94510	**888-313-1922**	707-751-3942
Douglas Laboratories Inc					
600 Boyce Rd	Pittsburgh	PA	15205	**800-245-4440**	412-494-0122
Enzymatic Therapy					
825 Challenger Dr	Green Bay	WI	54311	**800-783-2286**	920-469-1313
Foodscience Corp					
20 New England Dr Ste 10	Essex Junction	VT	05452	**800-451-5190**	802-878-5508
Futurebiotics LLC					
70 Commerce Dr	Hauppauge	NY	11788	**800-645-1721**	631-273-6300
Garden of Life Inc					
5500 Village Blvd Ste 102	West Palm Beach	FL	33407	**866-465-0051**	
GNC Inc					
300 Sixth Ave 14th Fl	Pittsburgh	PA	15222	**877-462-4700**	
NYSE: GNC					
Hammer Nutrition Ltd					
4952 Whitefish Stage Rd	Whitefish	MT	59937	**800-336-1977***	406-862-1877
*Cust Svc					
Herbalist, The					
2106 NE 65th St	Seattle	WA	98115	**800-694-3727**	206-523-2600
Integrated BioPharma Inc					
225 Long Ave	Hillside	NJ	07205	**888-319-6962**	973-926-0816
OTC: INBP					
Irwin Naturals					
5310 Beethoven St	Los Angeles	CA	90066	**800-297-3273**	310-306-3636
Jarrow Formulas Inc					
1824 S Robertson Blvd	Los Angeles	CA	90035	**800-726-0886**	310-204-6936
Labrada Nutrition					
403 Century Plz Dr Ste 440	Houston	TX	77073	**800-832-9948**	
Maximum Human Performance Inc (MHP Inc)					
21 Dwight Pl	Fairfield	NJ	07004	**888-783-8844**	973-785-9055
Mega-Pro International Inc					
251 W Hilton Dr	Saint George	UT	84770	**800-541-9469**	435-673-1001
Naturade Products Inc					
2030 Main St Ste 630	Irvine	CA	92614	**800-421-1830**	
Natural Alternatives International Inc					
1185 Linda Vista Dr	San Marcos	CA	92078	**800-848-2646**	760-744-7340
NASDAQ: NAII					
Natural Factors Nutritional Products Ltd					
1550 United Blvd	Coquitlam	BC	V3K6Y7	**800-663-8900**	604-777-1757
Natural Organics Inc					
548 Broadhollow Rd	Melville	NY	11747	**800-645-9500**	
Naturally Vitamins					
4404 E Elwood St	Phoenix	AZ	85040	**800-899-4499**	480-991-0200
Nature's Way Products Inc					
3051 W Maple Loop Dr Ste 125	Lehi	UT	84043	**800-962-8873**	
Nickers International Ltd					
PO Box 50066	Staten Island	NY	10305	**800-642-5377**	718-448-6283
Nutraceutical International Corp					
1400 Kearns Blvd	Park City	UT	84060	**800-669-8877**	435-655-6000
NASDAQ: NUTR					
Pacific Health Laboratories Inc					
100 Matawan Rd Ste 150	Matawan	NJ	07747	**877-363-8769***	732-739-2900
*General					
Paragon Laboratories					
20433 Earl St	Torrance	CA	90503	**800-231-3670**	310-370-1563
Peak Nutrition Inc					
1097 11th St PO Box 87	Syracuse	NE	68446	**800-600-2069***	402-269-2825
*Sales					
Perrigo Co 515 Eastern Ave	Allegan	MI	49010	**800-719-9260**	269-673-8451
NYSE: PRGO					
Phibro Animal Health Corp					
300 Frank W Burr Blvd Ste 21	Teaneck	NJ	07660	**800-223-0434**	201-329-7300
Power Organics					
301 S Old Stage Rd	Mount Shasta	CA	96067	**866-277-3420**	530-926-6684
Prolab Nutrition					
21411 Prairie St	Chatsworth	CA	91311	**800-776-5221**	818-739-6000
SportPharma Inc					
Three Terminal Rd	New Brunswick	NJ	08901	**800-872-0101**	732-545-3130
Swanson Health Products Inc					
PO Box 2803	Fargo	ND	58108	**800-824-4491**	701-356-2700
Synutra International Inc					
2275 Research Blvd Ste 500	Rockville	MD	20850	**866-405-2350**	301-840-3888
NASDAQ: SYUT					
Thayers Natural Pharmaceuticals Inc					
PO Box 56	Westport	CT	06881	**888-842-9371**	
Tishcon Corp					
50 Sylvester St	Westbury	NY	11590	**800-848-8442**	516-333-3050
Twinlab					
600 E Quality Dr	American Fork	UT	84003	**800-645-5626**	801-763-0700
USANA Health Sciences Inc					
3838 West PkwyBlvd	Salt Lake City	UT	84120	**888-950-9595**	801-954-7100
NYSE: USNA					
Wachters' Organic Sea Products Corp					
550 Sylvan St	Daly City	CA	94014	**800-682-7100**	650-757-9851
Wakunaga of America Company Ltd					
23501 Madero	Mission Viejo	CA	92691	**800-421-2998**	949-855-2776
Windmill Health Products					
Six Henderson Dr	West Caldwell	NJ	07006	**800-822-4320**	973-575-6591
Young Living Essential Oils					
3125 Executive Pkwy	Lehi	UT	84043	**866-203-5666**	801-418-8900

795 VOCATIONAL & TECHNICAL SCHOOLS

SEE ALSO Universities - Canadian ; Language Schools ; Military Service Academies ; Children's Learning Centers ; Colleges - Community & Junior ; Colleges - Culinary Arts ; Colleges - Fine Arts ; Colleges & Universities - Four-Year
Listings in this category are organized alphabetically by states.

				Toll-Free	Phone
Enterprise-Ozark Community College					
1975 Ave C	Mobile	AL	36615	**877-701-0033**	251-438-2816
Herzing College Birmingham					
280 W Valley Ave	Birmingham	AL	35209	**800-425-9432**	205-916-2800
ITT Technical Institute Birmingham					
6270 Pk S Dr	Bessemer	AL	35022	**800-488-7033**	205-497-5700
JF Drake State Technical College					
3421 Meridian St N	Huntsville	AL	35811	**888-413-7253**	256-539-8161
Lawson State Community College					
Bessemer 1100 Ninth Ave SW	Bessemer	AL	35022	**800-373-4879**	205-925-2515
MacAurthur					
1708 N Main St PO Box 910	Opp	AL	36467	**877-382-4357**	334-493-3573
Trenholm State Technical College					
1225 Air Base Blvd	Montgomery	AL	36108	**800-917-2081**	334-420-4200
Wallace Community College Selma					
3000 Earl Goodwin Pkwy	Selma	AL	36703	**855-428-8313**	334-876-9227
DeVry University					
Calgary 2700 Third Ave SE	Calgary	AB	T2A7W4	**800-363-5558***	403-235-3450
*General					
DeVry University Phoenix					
2149 W Dunlap Ave	Phoenix	AZ	85021	**800-528-0250***	602-870-9222
*Cust Svc					
ITT Technical Institute Tempe					
5005 S Wendler Dr	Tempe	AZ	85282	**800-879-4881**	602-437-7500
ITT Technical Institute Tucson					
1455 W River Rd	Tucson	AZ	85704	**800-870-9730**	520-408-7488
Southwest Institute of Healing Arts					
1100 E Apache Blvd	Tempe	AZ	85281	**888-504-9106**	480-994-9244
Concorde Career Colleges Inc					
San Bernardino					
201 E Airport Dr	San Bernardino	CA	92408	**800-852-8434**	909-884-8891
DeVry University Fremont					
6600 Dumbarton Cir	Fremont	CA	94555	**800-363-5558**	510-574-1200
DeVry University Long Beach					
3880 Kilroy Airport Way	Long Beach	CA	90806	**800-597-1333**	562-997-5300
DeVry University Pomona					
901 Corporate Ctr Dr	Pomona	CA	91768	**800-243-3660**	909-622-8866
Everest College Alhambra					
2215 W Mission Rd	Alhambra	CA	91803	**888-223-8556**	626-979-4940
Everest College Anaheim					
511 N Brookhurst Ste 300	Anaheim	CA	92801	**888-224-6684**	714-953-6500
Everest College City of Industry					
12801 Crossroads Pkwy S	City of Industry	CA	91746	**888-224-6684**	562-908-2500
Everest College San Bernardino					
217 E Club Ctr Dr Ste A	San Bernardino	CA	92408	**888-224-6684**	909-777-3300
Everest College San Jose					
1245 S Winchester Blvd Ste 102	San Jose	CA	95128	**888-223-8556**	408-246-4171
Everest Institute Long Beach					
2161 Technology Pl	Long Beach	CA	90810	**888-223-8556**	562-624-9530
Golden Gate University					
San Francisco					
536 Mission St	San Francisco	CA	94105	**800-448-4968**	415-442-7000
ITT Technical Institute					
Lathrop 16916 S Harlan Rd	Lathrop	CA	95330	**800-346-1786**	209-858-0077
Oxnard 2051 Solar Dr Ste 150	Oxnard	CA	93036	**800-530-1582**	805-988-0143
Rancho Cordova					
10863 Gold Ctr Dr	Rancho Cordova	CA	95670	**800-488-8466**	916-851-3900
San Bernardino					
670 Carnegie Dr	San Bernardino	CA	92408	**800-888-3801**	909-806-4600
San Dimas					
650 W Cienega Ave	San Dimas	CA	91773	**800-414-6522**	909-971-2300
Sylmar 12669 Encinitas Ave	Sylmar	CA	91342	**800-363-2086**	818-364-5151
Westwood College Inland Empire					
20 W Seventh St	Upland	CA	91786	**866-221-5632**	909-931-7550
Westwood College Los Angeles					
3250 Wilshire Blvd Ste 400	Los Angeles	CA	90010	**866-930-9256**	213-739-9999
Wyotech Sacramento					
980 Riverside Pkwy	West Sacramento	CA	95605	**888-308-7158**	916-376-8888
Bel-Rea Institute of Animal Technology					
1681 S Dayton St	Denver	CO	80247	**800-950-8001**	303-751-8700
Colorado Technical University Denver					
1865 W 121st Ave Bldg C Ste 100	Westminster	CO	80234	**877-250-9372**	303-362-2900
Denver Academy of Court Reporting					
9051 Harlan St Ste 20	Westminster	CO	80031	**866-712-2425**	303-427-5292
Colorado Springs					
1175 Kelly Johnson Blvd	Colorado Springs	CO	80920	**877-784-1997***	719-632-3000
*Help Line					
Everest College Aurora					
14280 E Jewell Ave Ste 100	Aurora	CO	80012	**888-223-8556**	303-745-6244
Everest College Thornton					
9065 Grant St	Thornton	CO	80229	**888-223-8556**	303-457-2757
Jones International University Ltd					
9697 E Mineral Ave	Centennial	CO	80112	**800-811-5663**	303-784-8904
Redstone College					
Denver 10851 W 120th Ave	Broomfield	CO	80021	**800-888-3995**	303-466-1714
Westwood College					
Denver 7350 N Broadway	Denver	CO	80221	**800-281-2978**	303-650-5050
Brown Mackie College Miami					
3700 Lakeside Dr	Miramar	FL	33132	**866-505-0335**	305-341-6600
Concorde Career Colleges inc Miramar					
10933 Marks Way	Miramar	FL	33025	**800-693-7010**	954-731-8880
DeVry University Orlando					
4000 Millenia Blvd	Orlando	FL	32839	**888-857-5757**	407-345-2800

	Toll-Free	Phone

Brandon 3924 Coconut Palm Dr ....Tampa FL 33619 — **877-439-0003*** — 813-621-0041
*Cust Svc

Jacksonville
8226 Phillips Hwy ....Jacksonville FL 32256 — **800-611-2101** — 904-731-4949

Lakeland
995 E Memorial Blvd Ste 110.................Lakeland FL 33801 — **888-223-8556** — 863-686-1444

Largo 1199 E Bay Dr ....Largo FL 33770 — **888-223-8556** — 727-725-2688

Everest University
North Orlando
5421 Diplomat Cir ....Orlando FL 32810 — **888-223-8556** — 407-628-5870

Orange Park
805 Wells Rd ....Orange Park FL 32073 — **888-223-8556** — 904-264-9122

Pompano Beach
225 N Federal Hwy ....Pompano Beach FL 33062 — **888-223-8556** — 954-783-7339

South Orlando
9200 Southpark Ctr Loop ....Orlando FL 32819 — **800-611-2101** — 407-851-2525

Tampa 3319 W Hillsborough Ave ....Tampa FL 33614 — **888-223-8556** — 813-879-6000

Florida Technical College
12900 Challenger Pkwy Ste 130.................Orlando FL 32826 — **888-678-2929*** — 407-447-7300
*General

Full Sail University
3300 University Blvd Ste 160.................Winter Park FL 32792 — **800-226-7625** — 407-679-6333

ITT Technical Institute Fort Lauderdale
3401 S University Dr ....Fort Lauderdale FL 33328 — **800-488-7797** — 954-476-9300

ITT Technical Institute Jacksonville
7011 AC Skinner Pkwy Ste 140 ....Jacksonville FL 32256 — **800-318-1264** — 904-573-9100

ITT Technical Institute Tampa
4809 Memorial Hwy ....Tampa FL 33634 — **800-825-2831** — 813-885-2244

Kaplan University
6301 Kaplan University Ave ....Fort Lauderdale FL 33309 — **866-522-7747** — 954-515-4015

Keiser University
Fort Lauderdale
1500 W Commercial Blvd ....Fort Lauderdale FL 33309 — **800-749-4456** — 954-776-4456

Sarasota 6151 Lk Osprey Dr ....Sarasota FL 34240 — **866-534-7372** — 941-907-3900

Remington College Largo
6302 E Dr Martin Luther King Jr Blvd
Ste 400.................Tampa FL 33619 — **800-560-6192**

Remington College Tampa
6302 E MLK Blvd Ste 400.................Tampa FL 33619 — **800-323-8122*** — 813-935-5700
*General

Stenotype Institute of Jacksonville
3563 Phillips Hwy Bldg E Ste 501 ....Jacksonville FL 32207 — **800-273-5090** — 904-398-4141

Bauder College
384 N Yards Blvd NW Ste 190 ....Atlanta GA 30313 — **800-935-1857** — 404-237-7573

Brown College of Court Reporting & Medical Transcription (BCCR)
1900 Emery St NW Ste 200 ....Atlanta GA 30318 — **800-849-0703** — 404-876-1227

Brown Mackie College Atlanta
4370 Peachtree Rd NE ....Atlanta GA 30319 — **877-479-8419** — 404-799-4500

Central Georgia Technical College
3300 Macon Tech Dr ....Macon GA 31206 — **866-430-0135** — 478-757-3400

Gupton-Jones College of Funeral Service
5141 Snapfinger Woods Dr ....Decatur GA 30035 — **800-848-5352** — 770-593-2257

Herzing College
Atlanta
3393 Peachtree Rd Ste 1003 ....Atlanta GA 30326 — **800-573-4533** — 404-816-4533

Imedex Inc
4325 Alexander Dr ....Alpharetta GA 30022 — **800-243-6969** — 770-751-7332

ITT Technical Institute Kennesaw
2065 Baker Rd NW ....Kennesaw GA 30144 — **800-564-9771** — 770-426-2300

Savannah Technical College
5717 White Bluff Rd ....Savannah GA 31405 — **800-769-6362** — 912-443-5700

Westwood College Atlanta Northlake
2309 Parklake Dr NE ....Atlanta GA 30345 — **866-821-6145** — 770-743-3000

Argosy University Hawaii
400 ASB Tower 1001 Bishop St ....Honolulu HI 96813 — **888-323-2777** — 808-536-5555

Eastern Idaho Technical College
1600 S 25th E ....Idaho Falls ID 83404 — **800-662-0261** — 208-524-3000

ITT Technical Institute Boise
12302 W Explorer Dr ....Boise ID 83713 — **800-666-4888** — 208-322-8844

DeVry University Addison
1221 N Swift Rd ....Addison IL 60101 — **800-346-5420** — 630-953-1300

Midstate College
411 W Northmoor Rd ....Peoria IL 61614 — **800-251-4299** — 309-692-4092

Northwestern College Chicago Campus
4829 N Lipps Ave ....Chicago IL 60630 — **888-205-2283** — 773-777-4220

Westwood College O'Hare Airport
8501 W Higgins Rd Ste 100 ....Chicago IL 60631 — **866-235-2457** — 773-380-6800

Westwood College River Oaks
80 River Oaks Ctr Ste 111.................Calumet City IL 60409 — **888-549-4960** — 708-832-1988

Fort Wayne
3000 E Coliseum Blvd ....Fort Wayne IN 46805 — **866-433-2289*** — 260-484-4400
*General

Merrillville
1000 E 80th Pl Ste 101N ....Merrillville IN 46410 — **800-258-3321** — 219-769-3321

Brown Mackie College
Michigan City
1001 E US Hwy 20 ....Michigan City IN 46360 — **800-519-2416** — 219-877-3100

South Bend
3454 Douglas Rd ....South Bend IN 46635 — **800-743-2447** — 574-237-0774

College of Court Reporting Inc
111 W Tenth St Ste 111 ....Hobart IN 46342 — **866-294-3974** — 219-942-1459

International Business College
5699 Coventry Ln ....Fort Wayne IN 46804 — **800-589-6363** — 260-459-4500

ITT Technical Institute Fort Wayne
2810 Dupont Commerce Ct ....Fort Wayne IN 46825 — **800-866-4488** — 260-497-6200

ITT Technical Institute Indianapolis
9511 Angola Ct ....Indianapolis IN 46268 — **800-937-4488** — 317-875-8640

ITT Technical Institute Newburgh
10999 Stahl Rd ....Newburgh IN 47630 — **800-832-4488** — 812-858-1600

Ivy Tech Columbus College
Columbus 4475 Central Ave ....Columbus IN 47203 — **800-922-4838** — 812-372-9925

Bloomington
200 Daniels Way ....Bloomington IN 47404 — **866-447-0700** — 812-330-6137

Ivy Tech Community College
Central Indiana
50 W Fall Creek Pkwy N Dr ....Indianapolis IN 46208 — **888-489-5463** — 317-921-4800

Kokomo 1815 E Morgan St ....Kokomo IN 46901 — **800-459-0561** — 765-459-0561

Muncie 4301 S Cowan Rd ....Muncie IN 47302 — **800-589-8324** — 765-289-2291

North Central
220 Dean Johnson Blvd ....South Bend IN 46601 — **888-489-3478** — 574-289-7001

Richmond 2357 Chester Blvd ....Richmond IN 47374 — **800-659-4562** — 765-966-2656

Southeast 590 Ivy Tech Dr ....Madison IN 47250 — **800-403-2190** — 812-265-2580

Southern Indiana
8204 old Indiana 311 ....Sellersburg IN 47172 — **800-321-9021** — 812-246-3301

Lincoln College of Technology
7225 Winton Dr Bldg 128.................Indianapolis IN 46268 — **800-228-6232** — 317-632-5553

Mid-America College of Funeral Science (MACFS)
3111 Hamburg Pk ....Jeffersonville IN 47130 — **800-221-6158** — 812-288-8878

AIB College of Business
2500 Fleur Dr ....Des Moines IA 50321 — **800-444-1921** — 515-244-4221

Brown Mackie College Bettendorf
2119 E Kimberly Rd ....Bettendorf IA 52722 — **888-420-1652** — 563-344-1500

Western Iowa Tech Community College
4647 Stone Ave ....Sioux City IA 51102 — **800-352-4649** — 712-274-6400

Brown Mackie College Lenexa
9705 Lenexa Dr ....Lenexa KS 66215 — **800-635-9101** — 913-768-1900

Brown Mackie College Salina
2106 S Ninth St ....Salina KS 67401 — **800-365-0433** — 785-825-5422

Concorde Career Colleges
5800 Foxridge Dr Ste 500.................Mission KS 66202 — **800-693-7010** — 913-831-9977

Wichita Area Technical College
301 S Grove St Bldg A ....Wichita KS 67211 — **866-296-4031** — 316-677-9400

Bowling Green Technical College
1845 Loop Dr ....Bowling Green KY 42101 — **866-590-9238** — 270-901-1000

Brown Mackie College Hopkinsville
4001 Ft Campbell Blvd ....Hopkinsville KY 42240 — **800-359-4753** — 270-886-1302

Brown Mackie College Louisville
3605 Fern Vly Rd ....Louisville KY 40219 — **800-999-7387** — 502-968-7191

Brown Mackie College Northern Kentucky
309 Buttermilk Pk ....Fort Mitchell KY 41017 — **800-888-1445** — 859-341-5627

Gateway Community & Technical College (GCTC)
1025 Amsterdam Rd ....Covington KY 41011 — **855-346-4282** — 859-441-4500

ITT Technical Institute Louisville
9500 Ormsby Stn Rd Ste 100 ....Louisville KY 40223 — **888-790-7427** — 502-327-7424

Louisville Technical Institute
Sullivan College of Technology & Design
3901 Atkinson Sq Dr ....Louisville KY 40218 — **800-844-6528** — 502-456-6509

National College of Business & Technology Florence
8095 Connector Dr ....Florence KY 41042 — **888-956-2732** — 859-525-6510

National College of Business & Technology Pikeville
50 National College Blvd ....Pikeville KY 41501 — **800-664-1886** — 606-478-7200

Owensboro Community & Technical College
4800 New Hartford Rd ....Owensboro KY 42303 — **866-755-6282** — 270-686-4400

Andover College
265 Western Ave ....South Portland ME 04106 — **800-639-3110** — 207-774-6126

Beal College 99 Farm Rd ....Bangor ME 04401 — **800-660-7351** — 207-947-4591

Central Maine Community College
1250 Turner St ....Auburn ME 04210 — **800-891-2002*** — 207-755-5100
*Admissions

Eastern Maine Community College
354 Hogan Rd ....Bangor ME 04401 — **800-286-9357** — 207-974-4600

Southern Maine Community College (SMCC)
Two Ft Rd ....South Portland ME 04106 — **877-282-2182** — 207-741-5500

ITT Technical Institute Owings Mills
11301 Red Run Blvd ....Owings Mills MD 21117 — **877-411-6782** — 443-394-7115

National Labor College
10000 New Hampshire Ave ....Silver Spring MD 20903 — **888-427-8100** — 301-431-6400

Bay State College
122 Commonwealth Ave ....Boston MA 02116 — **800-815-3276** — 617-217-9000

Benjamin Franklin Institute of Technology
41 Berkeley St ....Boston MA 02116 — **877-400-2348** — 617-423-4630

Boston Architectural College
320 Newbury St ....Boston MA 02115 — **877-585-0100** — 617-262-5000

Cambridge College Inc
1000 Mass Ave Ste 31 ....Cambridge MA 02138 — **800-829-4723** — 617-868-1000

ITT Technical Institute Wilmington
200 Ballardvale St Ste 200 ....Wilmington MA 01887 — **800-430-5097** — 978-658-2636

National Aviation Academy
150 Hanscom Dr ....Bedford MA 01730 — **800-659-2080** — 781-274-8448

New England College of Business & Finance
10 High St Ste 204 ....Boston MA 02110 — **888-357-7332** — 617-951-2350

Sanford-Brown College
Boston 126 Newbury St ....Boston MA 02116 — **877-809-2444** — 617-578-7100

Academy of Court Reporting
Clawson 1055 W Maple Rd ....Clawson MI 48017 — **888-314-7780**

Cleary University
3601 Plymouth Rd ....Ann Arbor MI 48105 — **800-686-1883** — 734-332-4477

Livingston 3750 Cleary Dr ....Howell MI 48843 — **800-686-1883** — 517-548-3670

Everest Institute
21107 Lahser Rd ....Southfield MI 48033 — **800-611-2101*** — 248-799-9933
*General

ITT Technical Institute Canton
1905 S Haggerty Rd ....Canton MI 48188 — **800-247-4477** — 734-397-7800

ITT Technical Institute Grand Rapids
1980 Metro Ct SW ....Wyoming MI 49519 — **800-632-4676** — 616-406-1200

ITT Technical Institute Troy
1522 E Big Beaver Rd ....Troy MI 48083 — **800-832-6817** — 248-524-1800

Anoka Technical College
1355 W Hwy 10 ....Anoka MN 55303 — **800-627-3529** — 763-433-1100

Brown College
1345 Mendota Heights Rd ....Mendota Heights MN 55120 — **888-574-3777** — 651-905-3400

Dakota County Technical College
1300 E 145th St ....Rosemount MN 55068 — **877-937-3282** — 651-423-8301

Duluth Business University (DBU)
4724 Mike Colalilo Dr ....Duluth MN 55807 — **800-777-8406** — 218-722-4000

Dunwoody College of Technology
818 Dunwoody Blvd ....Minneapolis MN 55403 — **800-292-4625** — 612-374-5800

Hennepin Technical College
9000 Brooklyn Blvd ....Brooklyn Park MN 55445 — **800-345-4655** — 952-995-1300

Ridgewater College
Hutchinson
Two Century Ave SE ....Hutchinson MN 55350 — **800-722-1151** — 320-234-8500

Willmar
2101 15th Ave NW PO Box 1097 ....Willmar MN 56201 — **800-722-1151** — 320-222-5200

Saint Cloud Technical & Community College
1540 Northway Dr ....Saint Cloud MN 56303 — **800-222-1009** — 320-308-5089

				Toll-Free	Phone
Saint Paul College					
235 Marshall Ave	Saint Paul	MN	55102	**800-227-6029**	651-846-1600
DeVry University Kansas City					
11224 Holmes Rd	Kansas City	MO	64131	**800-821-3766**	816-941-0430
Everest College					
1010 W Sunshine St	Springfield	MO	65807	**888-223-8556**	417-864-7220
ITT Technical Institute Arnold					
1930 Meyer Drury Dr	Arnold	MO	63010	**888-488-1082**	636-464-6600
ITT Technical Institute Earth City					
3640 Corporate Trl Dr	Earth City	MO	63045	**800-235-5488**	314-298-7800
ITT Technical Institute Kansas City					
9150 E 41st Terr	Kansas City	MO	64133	**877-488-1442**	816-276-1400
Vatterott College Berkeley					
8580 Evans Ave	Berkeley	MO	63134	**888-202-2636**	314-264-1000
Vatterott College South County					
12970 Maurer Industrial Dr	Saint Louis	MO	63127	**866-312-8276**	314-843-4200
Vatterott College Springfield					
3850 S Campbell	Springfield	MO	65807	**844-244-3304**	417-831-8116
University of Montana					
College of Technology					
909 S Ave W	Missoula	MT	59801	**800-542-6882**	406-243-7852
Helena College of Technology					
1115 N Roberts St	Helena	MT	59601	**800-827-1000**	406-444-6800
ITT Technical Institute Omaha					
1120 N 103rd Plz Ste 200	Omaha	NE	68114	**800-677-9260**	402-331-2900
Kaplan University Omaha					
5425 N 103rd St	Omaha	NE	68134	**800-987-7734**	402-572-8500
Nebraska College of Technical Agriculture					
404 E 7th	Curtis	NE	69025	**800-328-7847**	308-367-4124
Milford 600 State St	Milford	NE	68405	**800-933-7223**	402-761-2131
ITT Technical Institute Henderson					
168 Gibson Rd	Henderson	NV	89014	**800-488-8459**	702-558-5404
Garrett Mountain					
44 Rifle Camp Rd	Woodland Park	NJ	07424	**800-446-5400**	973-278-5400
Berkeley College					
Paramus 64 E Midland Ave	Paramus	NJ	07652	**800-446-5400**	201-967-9667
Woodbridge					
430 Rahway Ave	Woodbridge	NJ	07095	**800-446-5400**	732-750-1800
DeVry University North Brunswick					
630 US Hwy 1	North Brunswick	NJ	08902	**800-333-3879**	
Divers Academy International					
1500 Liberty Pl	Erial	NJ	08081	**800-238-3483**	
ITT Technical Institute Albuquerque					
5100 Masthead St NE	Albuquerque	NM	87109	**800-636-1114**	505-828-1114
Southwestern Indian Polytechnic Institute					
9169 Coors Blvd NW PO Box 10146	Albuquerque	NM	87120	**800-586-7474**	505-346-2306
American Academy McAllister Institute of Funeral Service					
619 W 54th St 2nd Fl	New York	NY	10019	**866-932-2264**	212-757-1190
Berkeley College New York City					
Three E 43rd St	New York	NY	10017	**800-446-5400**	212-986-4343
Berkeley College White Plains					
99 Church St	White Plains	NY	10601	**800-446-5400**	914-694-1122
College of Westchester (CW)					
325 Central Ave	White Plains	NY	10606	**800-660-7093**	
Commercial Driver Training					
600 Patton Ave	West Babylon	NY	11704	**800-649-7447**	631-249-1330
DeVry University Long Island City					
3020 Thomson Ave	Long Island City	NY	11101	**888-713-3879**	718-472-2728
ITT Technical Institute Albany					
13 Airline Dr	Albany	NY	12205	**800-489-1191**	518-452-9300
ITT Technical Institute Getzville					
2295 Millersport Hwy	Getzville	NY	14068	**800-469-7593**	716-689-2200
ITT Technical Institute Liverpool					
235 Greenfield Pkwy	Liverpool	NY	13088	**877-488-0011**	315-461-8000
Monroe College					
2501 Jerome Ave	Bronx	NY	10468	**800-556-6676**	718-933-6700
TCI College of Technology					
320 W 31st St	New York	NY	10001	**800-878-8246**	212-594-4000
Utica School of Commerce					
201 Bleecker St	Utica	NY	13501	**800-321-4872**	315-733-2307
Wood Tobe-Coburn School					
Eight E 40th St	New York	NY	10016	**800-394-9663**	212-686-9040
Forsyth Technical Community College					
2100 Silas Creek Pkwy	Winston-Salem	NC	27103	**800-870-3676**	336-723-0371
ITT Technical Institute High Point					
4050 Piedmont Pkwy	High Point	NC	27265	**877-536-5231**	336-819-5900
Stanly Community College					
141 College Dr	Albemarle	NC	28001	**877-275-4219**	704-982-0121
Academy of Court Reporting Cleveland					
2044 Euclid Ave	Cleveland	OH	44115	**888-314-7780**	
Academy of Court Reporting Columbus					
150 E Gay St	Columbus	OH	43215	**866-865-8067**	614-221-7770
Bradford School					
2469 Stelzer Rd	Columbus	OH	43219	**800-678-7981**	614-416-6200
Brown Mackie College Findlay					
1700 Fostoria Ave Ste 100	Findlay	OH	45840	**800-842-3687**	419-423-2211
Bryant & Stratton College					
Cleveland 3121 Euclid Ave	Cleveland	OH	44115	**866-948-0571**	216-771-1700
Cincinnati College of Mortuary Science					
645 W N Bend Rd	Cincinnati	OH	45224	**888-377-8433**	513-761-2020
Cleveland Institute of Electronics					
1776 E 17th St	Cleveland	OH	44114	**800-243-6446**	216-781-9400
Davis College 4747 Monroe St	Toledo	OH	43623	**800-477-7021**	419-473-2700
Eastern Gateway Community College					
4000 Sunset Blvd	Steubenville	OH	43952	**800-682-6553**	740-264-5591
Hocking College					
3301 Hocking Pkwy	Nelsonville	OH	45764	**877-462-5464**	740-753-3591
ITT Technical Institute Dayton					
3325 S- Eight Rd	Dayton	OH	45414	**800-568-3241**	937-264-7700
ITT Technical Institute Norwood					
4750 Wesley Ave	Norwood	OH	45212	**800-314-8324**	513-531-8300
ITT Technical Institute Strongsville					
14955 Sprague Rd	Strongsville	OH	44136	**800-331-1488**	440-234-9091
ITT Technical Institute Warrensville Heights					
4700 Richmond Rd	Warrensville Heights	OH	44128	**800-741-3494**	216-896-6500
ITT Technical Institute Youngstown					
1030 N Meridian Rd	Youngstown	OH	44509	**800-832-5001**	330-270-1600

				Toll-Free	Phone
James A Rhodes State College					
4240 Campus Dr	Lima	OH	45804	**866-498-4968**	419-995-8320
Marion Technical College					
1467 Mt Vernon Ave	Marion	OH	43302	**800-772-1213**	740-389-4636
North Central State College					
2441 Kenwood Cir	Mansfield	OH	44906	**888-755-4899**	419-755-4800
Stark State College of Technology					
6200 Frank Ave NW	North Canton	OH	44720	**800-797-8275**	330-494-6170
Zane State College					
1555 Newark Rd	Zanesville	OH	43701	**800-686-8324**	740-454-2501
Indian Capital Technology Ctr					
2403 N 41st St E	Muskogee	OK	74403	**800-757-0877**	918-687-6383
Okmulgee 1801 E Fourth St	Okmulgee	OK	74447	**800-722-4471**	918-293-4678
Spartan College of Aeronautics & Technology					
8820 E Pine St PO Box 582833	Tulsa	OK	74115	**800-331-1204***	918-836-6886
*Admissions					
ITT Technical Institute Portland					
9500 NE Cascades Pkwy	Portland	OR	97220	**800-234-5488**	503-255-6500
American College					
270 S Bryn Mawr Ave	Bryn Mawr	PA	19010	**888-263-7265**	610-526-1000
Cambria-Rowe Business College (CRBC)					
221 Central Ave	Johnstown	PA	15902	**800-639-2273**	814-536-5168
Central Pennsylvania College					
600 Valley Rd PO Box 309	Summerdale	PA	17093	**800-759-2727**	717-732-0702
DuBois Business College					
1 Beaver Dr	Du Bois	PA	15801	**800-692-6213**	814-371-6920
ITT Technical Institute Harrisburg					
449 Eisenhower Blvd Ste 100	Harrisburg	PA	17111	**800-847-4756**	717-565-1700
Johnson College					
3427 N Main Ave	Scranton	PA	18508	**800-293-9675**	570-342-6404
Kaplan Career Institute					
Franklin Mills					
177 Franklin Mills Blvd	Philadelphia	PA	19154	**800-935-1857**	215-612-6600
Penn Commercial Inc					
242 Oak Spring Rd	Washington	PA	15301	**888-309-7484**	724-222-5330
Pennco Tech 3815 Otter St	Bristol	PA	19007	**844-226-0975***	215-785-0111
*General					
Pennsylvania College of Technology					
One College Ave	Williamsport	PA	17701	**800-367-9222***	570-326-3761
*Admissions					
Pennsylvania Institute of Technology (PIT)					
800 Manchester Ave	Media	PA	19063	**800-422-0025***	610-892-1500
*Admissions					
Philadelphia College of Osteopathic Medicine (PCOM)					
4170 City Ave	Philadelphia	PA	19131	**800-999-6998***	215-871-6100
*Admissions					
Pittsburgh Institute of Aeronautics (PIA)					
Five Allegheny County Airport	West Mifflin	PA	15122	**800-444-1440**	412-346-2100
Pittsburgh Institute of Mortuary Science Inc					
5808 Baum Blvd	Pittsburgh	PA	15206	**800-933-5808**	412-362-8500
Pittsburgh Technical Institute (PTI)					
1111 McKee Rd	Oakdale	PA	15071	**800-784-9675**	412-809-5100
Thaddeus Stevens College of Technology (TSCT)					
750 E King St	Lancaster	PA	17602	**800-842-3832**	717-299-7701
Triangle Tech Inc					
Du Bois PO Box 551	Du Bois	PA	15801	**800-874-8324**	814-371-2090
Erie 2000 Liberty St	Erie	PA	16502	**800-874-8324**	814-453-6016
Greensburg					
222 E Pittsburgh St	Greensburg	PA	15601	**800-874-8324**	724-832-1050
Welder Training & Testing Institute					
1144 N Graham St	Allentown	PA	18109	**800-223-9884**	610-820-9551
Williamson Free School of Mechanical Trades, The					
106 S New Middletown Rd	Media	PA	19063	**888-565-1095**	610-566-1776
New England Institute of Technology					
2500 Post Rd	Warwick	RI	02886	**800-736-7744**	401-467-7744
Florence-Darlington Technical College					
2715 W Lucas St	Florence	SC	29502	**800-228-5745**	843-661-8324
Horry-Georgetown Technical College					
Grand Strand Campus					
743 Hemlock Ave	Myrtle Beach	SC	29577	**855-544-4482**	843-477-0808
ITT Technical Institute Greenville					
Six Independence Pointe					
Independence Corporate Pk	Greenville	SC	29615	**800-932-4488**	864-288-0777
Piedmont Technical College					
620 N Emerald Rd	Greenwood	SC	29646	**800-868-5528**	864-941-8324
Spartanburg Community College					
800 Brisack Rd PO Box 4386	Spartanburg	SC	29305	**866-591-3700**	864-592-4800
Tri-County Technical College					
7900 Hwy 76	Pendleton	SC	29670	**866-269-5677**	864-646-8361
Trident Technical College (TTC)					
7000 Rivers Ave					
PO Box 118067	North Charleston	SC	29406	**877-349-7184**	843-574-6111
Southeast Technical Institute					
2320 N Career Ave	Sioux Falls	SD	57107	**800-247-0789**	605-367-8355
Draughons Junior College					
340 Plus Pk Blvd	Nashville	TN	37217	**877-849-7921**	615-361-7555
Fountainhead College of Technology					
3203 Tazewell Pk	Knoxville	TN	37918	**888-218-7335**	865-688-9422
ITT Technical Institute Cordova					
7260 Goodlett Farms Pkwy	Cordova	TN	38016	**866-444-5141**	901-381-0200
ITT Technical Institute Nashville					
2845 Elm Hill Pk	Nashville	TN	37214	**800-331-8386**	615-889-8700
Nashville State Community College (NSCC)					
120 White Bridge Rd	Nashville	TN	37209	**800-272-7363**	615-353-3333
National College of Business & Technology Bristol					
1328 Hwy 11 W	Bristol	TN	37620	**888-956-2732**	423-878-4440
National College of Business & Technology Nashville					
1638 Bell Rd	Nashville	TN	37211	**855-800-1715**	615-333-3344
Northeast State Technical Community College					
2425 Hwy 75 PO Box 246	Blountville	TN	37617	**800-836-7822**	423-323-3191
South College					
3904 Lonas Dr	Knoxville	TN	37909	**877-557-2575**	865-251-1800
Aviation Institute of Maintenance Houston					
7651 Airport Blvd	Houston	TX	77061	**888-349-5387**	713-644-7777
Court Reporting Institute of Dallas					
1341 W Mockingbird Ln Ste 200-E	Dallas	TX	75247	**866-382-1284**	214-350-9722
Court Reporting Institute of Houston					
13101 NW Fwy Ste 100	Houston	TX	77040	**866-996-8300**	713-996-8300

	Toll-Free	Phone
Dallas Institute of Funeral Service 3909 S Buckner Blvd ....Dallas TX 75227	800-235-5444	214-388-5466
DeVry University Houston 11125 Equity Dr ....Houston TX 77041	866-703-3879	713-973-3100
DeVry University Irving 4800 Regent Blvd ....Irving TX 75063	800-633-3879	972-929-6777
ITT Technical Institute Arlington 551 Ryan Plz Dr ....Arlington TX 76011	888-288-4950	817-794-5100
ITT Technical Institute Austin 6330 Hwy 290 E Ste 150 ....Austin TX 78723	800-431-0677	512-467-6800
ITT Technical Institute Houston 15651 N Fwy ....Houston TX 77090	800-879-6486	281-873-0512
ITT Technical Institute Richardson 2101 Waterview Pkwy ....Richardson TX 75080	888-488-5761	972-690-9100
ITT Technical Institute San Antonio 5700 NW Pkwy ....San Antonio TX 78249	800-880-0570	210-694-4612
Wade College 1950 N Stemmons Fwy Ste 2026 ....Dallas TX 75207	800-624-4850	214-637-3530
Westwood College Dallas 8390 LBJ Fwy Ste 100 Executive Ctr 1 ....Dallas TX 75243	800-331-4879	800-281-2978
ITT Technical Institute Murray 920 Levoy Dr ....Murray UT 84123	800-365-2136	801-263-3313
Latter Day Saints Business College 95 North 300 West ....Salt Lake City UT 84101	800-999-5767	801-524-8100
Sterling College PO Box 72 ....Craftsbury Common VT 05827	800-648-3591	802-586-7711
Vermont Technical College PO Box 500 ....Randolph Center VT 05061	800-442-8821	802-728-1000
Bryant & Stratton College Richmond 8141 Hull St Rd ....Richmond VA 23235	866-948-0571	804-745-2444
ITT Technical Institute Norfolk 5425 Robin Hood Rd Ste 100 ....Norfolk VA 23513	888-253-8324	757-466-1260
ITT Technical Institute Richmond 300 Gateway Centre Pkwy ....Richmond VA 23235	888-330-4888	804-330-4992
ITT Technical Institute Springfield 7300 Boston Blvd ....Springfield VA 22153	866-817-8324	703-440-9535
Jefferson College of Health Sciences 101 Elm Ave SE ....Roanoke VA 24031	888-985-8483	540-985-8483
National College of Business & Technology Roanoke Valley 1813 E Main St ....Salem VA 24153	800-664-1886	540-986-1800
DeVry University Federal Way 3600 S 344th Way ....Federal Way WA 98001	877-923-3879	253-943-2800
ITT Technical Institute Seattle 12720 Gateway Dr Ste 100 ....Seattle WA 98168	800-422-2029	206-244-3300
Huntington Junior College 900 Fifth Ave ....Huntington WV 25701	800-344-4522	304-697-7550
West Virginia Junior College Charleston 1000 Virginia St E ....Charleston WV 25301	800-924-5208	304-345-2820
West Virginia Junior College - Bridgeport 176 Thompson Dr ....Bridgeport WV 26330	800-470-5627	304-842-4007
Blackhawk Technical College 6004 S County Rd G ....Janesville WI 53546	800-498-1282	608-758-6900
Bryant & Stratton College Milwaukee 310 W Wisconsin Ave Ste 500-E ....Milwaukee WI 53203	866-948-0571	414-276-5200
Chippewa Valley Technical College 620 W Clairemont Ave ....Eau Claire WI 54701	800-547-2882	715-833-6200
Fox Valley Technical College 1825 N Bluemound Dr PO Box 2277 ....Appleton WI 54912	800-735-3882	920-735-5600
Gateway Technical College 3520 30th Ave ....Kenosha WI 53144	800-247-7122	262-564-2200
Herzing College Madison 5218 E Terr Dr ....Madison WI 53718	800-582-1227	608-249-6611
Lakeshore Technical College 1290 N Ave ....Cleveland WI 53015	888-468-6582	920-693-1000
Milwaukee Area Technical College 700 W State St ....Milwaukee WI 53233	866-211-3380	414-297-6600
Moraine Park Technical College 235 N National Ave ....Fond du Lac WI 54935	800-472-4554	920-922-8611
Northcentral Technical College 1000 W Campus Dr ....Wausau WI 54401	888-682-7144	715-675-3331
Northeast Wisconsin Technical College PO Box 19042 ....Green Bay WI 54307	800-422-6982	920-498-5400
Southwest Wisconsin Technical College (SWTC) 1800 Bronson Blvd ....Fennimore WI 53809	800-362-3322	608-822-3262
Western Technical College 400 Seventh St N ....La Crosse WI 54601	800-322-9982	608-785-9200
Wisconsin Indianhead Technical College New Richmond Campus 1019 S Knowles Ave ....New Richmond WI 54017	800-243-9482	715-246-6561
Rice Lake Campus 1900 College Dr ....Rice Lake WI 54868	800-243-9482	715-234-7082
Superior Campus 600 N 21 St ....Superior WI 54880	800-243-9482	715-394-6677

796 — VOTING SYSTEMS & SOFTWARE

	Toll-Free	Phone
Avante International Technology Inc (AIT) 70 Washington Rd ....Princeton Junction NJ 08550	800-735-5040	609-799-9388
Diebold Inc 5995 Mayfair Rd ....North Canton OH 44720 *NYSE: DBD*	800-999-3600	330-490-4000
Dynapar 1675 Delany Rd ....Gurnee IL 60031 *General	800-873-8731*	
Election Systems & Software Inc 11208 John Galt Blvd ....Omaha NE 68137	877-377-8683*	402-593-0101
Elections USA Inc 1927 E Saw Mill Rd ....Quakertown PA 18951	800-789-8683	215-538-0779
Hart InterCivic 15500 Wells Port Dr PO Box 80649 ....Austin TX 78708	800-223-4278	512-252-6400
MicroVote General Corp 6366 Guilford Ave ....Indianapolis IN 46220	800-257-4901	317-257-4900
UniLect Corp PO Box 3026 ....Danville CA 94526	888-864-5328	925-833-8660

797 — WALLCOVERINGS

	Toll-Free	Phone
Blue Mountain Wallcoverings Inc 15 Akron Rd ....Etobicoke ON M8W1T3	866-563-9872	416-251-1678
Fashion Wallcoverings 4005 Carnegie Ave ....Cleveland OH 44103 *Orders	800-362-9930*	216-432-1600
Goldcrest Wallcoverings PO Box 245 ....Slingerlands NY 12159	800-535-9513	518-478-7214
Thibaut Inc 480 Frelinghuysen Ave ....Newark NJ 07114	800-223-0704	973-643-1118
York Wallcoverings Inc 750 Linden Ave PO Box 5166 ....York PA 17405	800-375-9675	717-846-4456

798 — WAREHOUSING & STORAGE

SEE ALSO Logistics Services (Transportation & Warehousing)

798-1 Commercial Warehousing

	Toll-Free	Phone
Acme Distribution Centers Inc 18101 E Colfax Ave ....Aurora CO 80011	800-444-3614	303-340-2100
All Source Security Container Mfg Corp 40 Mills Rd ....Barrie ON L4N6H4	866-526-4579	705-726-6460
ASW Global LLC 3375 Gilchrist Rd ....Mogadore OH 44260	888-826-5087	330-733-6291
Brundage Management Co Inc 254 Spencer Ln ....San Antonio TX 78201	800-531-7652	210-735-9393
Datalok Co 5990 Malburg Way ....Los Angeles CA 90058	800-232-8256	323-582-6100
DD Jones Transfer & Warehouse Co Inc 2121 Old Greenbrier Rd ....Chesapeake VA 23320	800-335-4787	757-494-0225
Derby Industries LLC 4451 Robards Ln ....Louisville KY 40218	800-569-4812	502-451-7373
Evans Distribution Systems 18765 Seaway Dr ....Melvindale MI 48122	800-653-8267	313-388-3200
Gulf Winds International Inc 411 Brisbane St ....Houston TX 77061	866-238-4909	713-747-4909
Habco Beverage Systems Inc 501 Gordon Baker Rd ....Toronto ON M2H2S6	800-448-0244	416-491-6008
Iron Mountain 745 Atlantic Ave ....Boston MA 02111 *NYSE: IRM*	800-899-4766	617-535-4766
Kenco Group Inc 2001 Riverside Dr ....Chattanooga TN 37406	800-758-3289	
Longistics Transportation Inc 10900 World Trade Blvd ....Raleigh NC 27617	800-289-0082	919-872-7626
Mackinnon Transport Inc 405 Laird Rd ....Guelph ON N1G4P7	800-265-9394	519-821-2311
Monsoon Commerce Solutions Inc 1250 45th St Ste 100 ....Emeryville CA 94608	800-520-2294	510-594-4500
Pacific Storage Co PO Box 334 ....Stockton CA 95201	888-823-5467	209-320-6600
Recall Inc 180 Technology Pkwy NW 180 Technology Pkwy ....Norcross GA 30092	888-732-2556	
Security Storage Co 1701 Florida Ave NW ....Washington DC 20009	800-736-6825	202-234-5600
Tejas Logistics System PO Box 1339 ....Waco TX 76703	800-535-9786	254-753-0301
Tri Union Express Inc 1939 N Lafayette Ct ....Griffith IN 46319	800-228-9098	219-838-5400
W O W Logistics Co 3040 W Wisconsin Ave ....Appleton WI 54914	800-236-3565	920-734-9924

798-2 Refrigerated Storage

	Toll-Free	Phone
Burris Logistics 501 SE Fifth St PO Box 219 ....Milford DE 19963	800-805-8135	302-839-5157
New Orleans Cold Storage & Warehouse Company Inc (NOCS) 3411 JouRdan Rd ....New Orleans LA 70126	800-782-2653	504-944-4400
Perley-Halladay Assn Inc 1037 Andrew Dr ....West Chester PA 19380	800-248-5800	610-296-5800
United Freezer & Storage Co 650 N Meridian Rd PO Box 2446 ....Youngstown OH 44509	800-716-1416	330-792-1739

798-3 Self-Storage Facilities

	Toll-Free	Phone
A-American Self Storage Management Co Inc 11560 Tennessee Ave ....Los Angeles CA 90064	888-333-6479	310-914-4022
Devon Self Storage Holdings LLC 2000 Powell St Ste 1240 ....Emeryville CA 94608	800-326-3199	510-450-1300
Metro Storage LLC 13528 Boulton Blvd ....Lake Forest IL 60045 *Cust Svc	888-498-1660*	847-235-8900
Public Storage Inc 701 Western Ave ....Glendale CA 91201 *NYSE: PSA ■ *Cust Svc*	800-567-0759*	818-244-8080
Sovran Self Storage Inc 6467 Main St ....Buffalo NY 14221 *NYSE: SSS*	800-242-1715	716-633-1850
Stor-All Storage 1375 W Hillsboro Blvd ....Deerfield Beach FL 33442	877-786-7255	954-421-7888

799 WASTE MANAGEMENT

SEE ALSO Remediation Services ; Recyclable Materials Recovery

				Toll-Free	Phone
Athens Services					
14048 Valley Blvd	La Puente	CA	91746	888-336-6100	626-336-3636
Basin Disposal Inc					
2021 N Commercial Ave	Pasco	WA	99301	800-642-6447	509-547-2476
Burrtec Waste Industries Inc					
9890 Cherry Ave	Fontana	CA	92335	888-287-7832	909-429-4200
CalMet Services Inc					
7202 Peterson Ln	Paramount	CA	90723	800-990-6387	562-259-1239
Casella Waste Systems Inc					
25 Greens Hill Ln	Rutland	VT	05701	800-227-3552	802-775-0325
NASDAQ: CWST					
Consolidated Disposal Services Inc					
12949 Telegraph Rd	Santa Fe Springs	CA	90670	800-299-4898	
Deffenbaugh Industries Inc					
2601 Midwest Dr	Kansas City	KS	66111	800-631-3301	913-631-3300
E J Harrison & Sons					
PO Box 4009	Ventura	CA	93007	800-418-7274	805-647-1414
EL Harvey & Sons Inc					
68 Hopkinton Rd	Westborough	MA	01581	800-321-3002	508-836-3000
Exp Pharmaceutical Services Corp					
48021 Warm Springs Blvd	Fremont	CA	94539	800-350-0397	510-476-0909
Gilton Solid Waste Management					
755 S Yosemite Ave	Oakdale	CA	95361	800-894-8980	209-527-3781
Modern Corp					
4746 Model City Rd	Model City	NY	14107	800-662-0012	716-754-8226
N-Viro International Corp					
2254 Centennial Rd	Toledo	OH	43606	800-336-2225	419-535-6374
OTC: NVIC					
National Serv-All Inc					
6231 McBeth Rd	Fort Wayne	IN	46809	800-876-9001	260-747-4117
Oakleaf Waste Management LLC					
415 Day Hill Rd	Windsor	CT	06095	888-625-5323	713-512-6200
Republic Services of Southern Nevada					
770 E Sahara Ave	Las Vegas	NV	89193	800-752-4092	702-735-5151
Rumpke 10795 Hughes Rd	Cincinnati	OH	45251	800-582-3107	
Sanitary Services Co Inc					
21 Bellwether Way Ste 404	Bellingham	WA	98225	888-333-9882	360-734-3490
Stericycle Inc					
28161 N Keith Dr	Lake Forest	IL	60045	866-783-7422	847-367-5910
NASDAQ: SRCL					
Synagro Technologies Inc					
435 Williams Ct Ste 100	Baltimore	MD	21220	800-370-0035	443-489-9017
Texas Disposal Systems Inc (TDS)					
12200 Carl Rd	Creedmoor	TX	78610	800-375-8375	512-421-1300
Triumvirate Environmental					
61 Innerbelt Rd	Somerville	MA	02143	800-966-9282	617-628-8098
Waste Industries USA Inc					
3301 Benson Dr Ste 601	Raleigh	NC	27609	800-647-9946	919-325-3000
Waste Management Inc					
1001 Fannin St Ste 4000	Houston	TX	77002	800-633-7871	713-512-6200
NYSE: WM					
Wheelabrator Technologies Inc					
4 Liberty Ln W	Hampton	NH	03842	800-682-0026	603-929-3000

800 WATER - BOTTLED

				Toll-Free	Phone
Absopure Water Co					
8835 General Dr	Plymouth	MI	48170	800-422-7678	313-898-1200
Calistoga Beverage Co					
865 Silverado Trl	Calistoga	CA	94515	800-365-4446	
Carolina Mountain Water Co					
150 Central Ave	Hot Springs	AR	71902	800-828-0836	
Chester Water Authority					
PO Box 467	Chester	PA	19016	800-793-2323	610-876-8185
Culligan International Co					
9399 W Higgins Rd Ste 1100	Rosemont	IL	60018	800-285-5442	847-430-2800
Distillata Co					
1608 E 24th St	Cleveland	OH	44114	800-999-2906*	216-771-2900
*Cust Svc					
DS Waters of America Inc					
5660 New Northside Dr Ste 500	Atlanta	GA	30328	800-201-6218*	
*Cust Svc					
Glacier Clear Enterprises Inc					
3291 Thomas St	Innisfil	ON	L9S3W3	800-668-5118*	705-436-6363
*Cust Svc					
Mountain Valley Spring Co					
150 Central Ave	Hot Springs	AR	71901	800-828-0836	501-624-1635
Polar Beverages Inc					
1001 Southbridge St	Worcester	MA	01610	800-734-9800*	508-753-4300
*Cust Svc					
Pure-Flo Water Co					
7737 Mission Gorge Rd	Santee	CA	92071	800-787-3356*	619-448-5120
*Cust Svc					

801 WATER TREATMENT & FILTRATION PRODUCTS & EQUIPMENT

				Toll-Free	Phone
Aqua-Aerobic Systems Inc					
6306 N Alpine Rd	Loves Park	IL	61111	800-940-5008	815-654-2501
Aquion Water Treatment Products LLC Rainsoft Div					
2080 E Lunt Ave	Elk Grove Village	IL	60007	800-860-7638	847-437-9400
Atlas Water Systems Inc					
301 Second Ave	Waltham	MA	02451	888-877-0561	781-373-4700
Brita Products Co					
1221 Broadway PO Box 24305	Oakland	CA	94612	800-242-7482	510-271-7000
Bucks County Water & Sewer Authority (BCWSA)					
1275 Almshouse Rd	Warrington	PA	18976	800-222-2068	215-343-2538

				Toll-Free	Phone
Carolina Filters Inc					
109 E Newberry Ave PO Box 716	Sumter	SC	29151	800-849-5646	803-773-6842
Culligan International Co					
9399 W Higgins Rd Ste 1100	Rosemont	IL	60018	800-285-5442	847-430-2800
Deepwater Chemicals Inc					
1210 Airpark Rd	Woodward	OK	73801	800-854-4064	580-256-0500
Dow Liquid Separations					
PO Box 1206	Midland	MI	48642	800-447-4369	989-636-1000
East Valley Water District					
3654 E Highland Ave Ste 18	Highland	CA	92346	866-275-3772	909-889-9501
Energy Recovery Inc					
1717 Doolittle Dr	San Leandro	CA	94577	888-455-2263	510-483-7370
NASDAQ: ERII					
Everpure LLC					
1040 Muirfield Dr	Hanover Park	IL	60133	800-323-7873	630-307-3000
Filterspun					
624 N Fairfield St	Amarillo	TX	79107	800-323-5431	806-383-3840
GE Water & Process Technologies					
4636 Somerton Rd	Trevose	PA	19053	866-439-2837	215-355-3300
Graver Technologies LLC					
200 Lake Dr	Newark	DE	19702	800-249-1990	302-731-1700
Graver Water Systems					
675 Central Ave Ste 3	New Providence	NJ	07974	877-472-8379	908-516-1400
Kinetico Inc					
10845 Kinsman Rd	Newbury	OH	44065	800-944-9283	
Met-Pro Corp Systems Div					
160 Cassell Rd PO Box 144	Harleysville	PA	19438	800-621-0734	215-723-9300
MSC Filtration Technologies					
198 Freshwater Blvd	Enfield	CT	06082	800-237-7359*	860-745-7475
*Cust Svc					
Pall Corp					
2200 Northern Blvd	East Hills	NY	11548	800-645-6532	516-484-5400
NYSE: PLL					
PEP Filters Inc					
322 Rolling Hill Rd	Mooresville	NC	28117	800-243-4583	704-662-3133
Polaris Pool Systems Inc					
2620 Commerce Way	Vista	CA	92081	800-822-7933	760-599-9600
Pro Products LLC					
7201 Engle Rd	Fort Wayne	IN	46804	866-357-5063	260-490-5970
Pure & Secure LLC					
4120 NW 44th St	Lincoln	NE	68524	800-875-5915*	402-467-9300
*Cust Svc					
Severn Trent Services					
580 Virginia Dr Ste 300	Fort Washington	PA	19034	866-646-9201	215-646-9201
Sharp Water Culligan					
129 Columbia Rd	Salisbury	MD	21801	800-439-3853	410-742-3333
Siemens Water Technologies					
181 Thorn Hill Rd	Warrendale	PA	15086	800-424-9300	724-772-0044
Sydnor Hydro Inc					
2111 Magnolia St PO Box 27186	Richmond	VA	23261	800-552-7714	804-643-2725
Taylor Technologies Inc					
31 Loveton Cir	Sparks	MD	21152	800-837-8548*	410-472-4340
*Cust Svc					
Tomco2 Equipment Co					
3340 Rosebud Rd	Loganville	GA	30052	800-832-4262	770-979-8000
Walker Process Equipment					
840 N Russell Ave	Aurora	IL	60506	800-992-5537	630-892-7921
Waterco USA Inc					
1864 Tobacco Rd	Augusta	GA	30906	800-277-4150*	706-793-7291
*General					
Zodiac Pool Systems Inc					
2620 Commerce Way	Vista	CA	92081	800-822-7933	

802 WEB HOSTING SERVICES

SEE ALSO Internet Service Providers (ISPs)
Companies listed here are engaged primarily in hosting web sites for companies and individuals. Although many Internet Service Providers (ISPs) also provide web hosting services, they are not included among these listings.

				Toll-Free	Phone
Baillio's Inc					
5301 Menaul Blvd NE	Albuquerque	NM	87110	800-540-7511	505-883-7511
Catalog.com Inc					
14000 Quail Springs Pkwy Ste 3600	Oklahoma City	OK	73134	888-932-4376	405-753-9300
DataPipe 10 Exchange Pl	Jersey City	NJ	07302	877-773-3306	201-792-4847
Datarealm Internet Services Inc					
PO Box 1616	Hudson	WI	54016	877-227-3783	
Fortress Integrated Technologies					
100 Delawanna Ave	Clifton	NJ	07014	888-734-9320	973-572-1070
Freeservers.com					
1253 N Research Way Ste Q-2500	Orem	UT	84097	800-396-1999	
Global Knowledge Group Inc (GKG)					
302 N Bryan Ave	Bryan	TX	77803	866-776-7584	
Homestead Technologies Inc					
180 Jefferson Dr	Menlo Park	CA	94025	800-797-2958	650-944-3100
Host Depot Inc					
2455 Paces Ferry Rd NW	Atlanta	GA	30339	888-340-3527	770-433-8211
Hostcentric Inc					
70 BlanchaRd Rd 3rd Fl	Burlington	MA	01803	866-897-5418*	602-716-5396
*Tech Supp					
Hostedware Corp					
16 Technology Dr Ste 116	Irvine	CA	92618	800-211-6967	949-585-1500
Hostway Corp					
100 N Riverside Plaza 8th Fl	Chicago	IL	60606	866-467-8929	312-238-0125
INetU Inc					
744 Roble Rd Ste 70	Allentown	PA	18109	888-664-6388	610-266-7441
LightEdge Solutions Inc					
215 10th St Ste 1000	Des Moines	IA	50309	877-771-3343	515-471-1000
Media3 Technologies LLC					
33 Riverside Dr N River Commerce Pk	Pembroke	MA	02359	800-903-9327	781-826-1213
NetNation Communications Inc					
550 Burrard St Ste 200	Vancouver	BC	V6C2B5	888-277-0000	604-688-8946
OLM LLC Four Trefoil Dr	Trumbull	CT	06611	800-741-6813	203-445-7700
Opsource Inc					
5201 Great America Pkwy Ste 120	Santa Clara	CA	95054	800-664-9973	408-567-2000

				Toll-Free	Phone

Pacific Internet
105 W Clay St .... Ukiah CA 95482 **888-722-8638** 707-468-1005

Power Surge Web Solutions
1171 South Robertson Blvd Ste 194 .... Los Angeles CA 90035 **800-867-5055** 312-492-4053

Radiant Communications Corp
1600-1050 W Pender St .... Vancouver BC V6E4T3 **888-219-2111**
CVE: RCN

Salon Media Group Inc
101 Spear St Ste 203 .... San Francisco CA 94105 **800-257-8650** 415-645-9200

SilverSky
440 Wheelers Farms Rd Ste 202 .... Milford CT 06461 **800-234-2175**

Superb Internet Corp
999 Bishop St Ste 1850 .... Honolulu HI 96813 **888-354-6128** 808-544-0387

Telus 1000 Rue de Serigny .... Longueuil QC J4K5B1 **888-709-8759** 450-928-6000

TierraNet Inc
14284 Dani Elson St .... Poway CA 92064 **877-843-7721** 858-560-9416

Verio Inc
8005 S Chester St Ste 200 .... Centennial CO 80112 **800-438-8374*** 561-912-2555
*Sales

VPOP Technologies Inc
1772J Avenida de los Arboles
PO Box 372 .... Thousand Oaks CA 91362 **888-811-8767*** 805-529-9374
*Sales

803   WEB SITE DESIGN SERVICES

SEE ALSO Advertising Agencies ; Advertising Services - Online ; Computer Systems Design Services

				Toll-Free	Phone

Acro Media Inc
2303 Leckie Rd Ste 103 .... Kelowna BC V1X6Y5 **877-763-8844** 250-763-8884

bx.com Inc
1 W Exchange St .... Providence RI 02903 **877-447-2355** 401-274-8991

Paloma Systems Inc
11250 Waples Mill Rd .... Fairfax VA 22030 **855-300-2686** 703-626-5024

Sapient Corp
131 Dartmouth St 3rd Fl .... Boston MA 02116 **866-796-6860** 617-621-0200
NASDAQ: SAPE

Web.com
12808 Grand Bay Pkwy W .... Jacksonville FL 32258 **800-338-1771** 904-680-6600

804   WEIGHT LOSS CENTERS & SERVICES

SEE ALSO Spas - Health & Fitness ; Health & Fitness Centers

				Toll-Free	Phone

American Laser Skincare
24555 Hallwood Ct .... Farmington Hills MI 48335 **877-252-2010** 248-426-8250

Barix Clinics
135 S Prospect St .... Ypsilanti MI 48198 **800-282-0066** 734-547-4700

Companions & Homemakers Inc
613 New Britain Ave .... Farmington CT 06032 **800-348-4663** 860-677-4948

Fit America MD
4864 Arthur Kill Rd .... Staten Island NY 10309 **800-940-7546** 718-227-4980

Greenpath Inc
38505 Country Club Dr .... Farmington Hills MI 48331 **800-550-1961** 248-553-5400

Jazzercise Inc
2460 Impala Dr .... Carlsbad CA 92010 **800-348-4748*** 760-476-1750
*Cust Svc

Jenny Craig International Inc
5770 Fleet St .... Carlsbad CA 92008 **800-443-2331** 760-696-4000

NutriSystem Inc
300 Welsh Rd Bldg 1 .... Horsham PA 19044 **800-585-5483** 215-706-5300
NASDAQ: NTRI

Physicians Weight Loss Centers of America Inc
395 Springside Dr .... Akron OH 44333 **800-205-7887** 330-666-7952

805   WELDING & SOLDERING EQUIPMENT

				Toll-Free	Phone

AGM Industries Inc
16 Jonathan St .... Brockton MA 02301 **800-225-9990** 508-587-3900

American Ultraviolet Co
40 Morristown Rd .... Bernardsville NJ 07924 **800-288-9288** 908-696-1130

Arcos Industries
One Arcos Dr .... Mount Carmel PA 17851 **800-233-8460** 570-339-5200

Argus International Ltd
108 Whispering Pines Dr Ste 110 .... Scotts Valley CA 95066 **800-862-7487** 831-461-4700

BUG-O Systems Inc
161 Hillpointe Dr .... Canonsburg PA 15317 **800-245-3186** 412-331-1776

CK Worldwide Inc
3501 C St NE .... Auburn WA 98002 **800-426-0877** 253-854-5820

Esab Welding & Cutting Products Inc
411 S Ebenezer Rd PO Box 100545 .... Florence SC 29501 **800-372-2123** 843-669-4411

Eureka Welding Alloys Inc
2000 E Avis Dr .... Madison Heights MI 48071 **800-962-8560** 248-588-0001

Eutectic Corp
N 94 W 14355 Garwin Mace Dr ..... Menomonee Falls WI 53051 **800-558-8524** 262-532-4677

Forney Industries Inc
1830 LaPorte Ave .... Fort Collins CO 80521 **800-521-6038**

Goss Inc
1511 William Flynn Hwy .... Glenshaw PA 15116 **800-367-4677** 412-486-6100

Harris Products Group
4501 Quality Pl .... Mason OH 45040 **800-733-4043** 513-754-2000

Industrial Welders & Machinists Inc
610 Opperman Dr .... Eagan MN 55123 **800-455-4565**

JWF Industries
84 Iron St PO Box 1286 .... Johnstown PA 15907 **800-225-9359** 814-539-6922

Lincoln Electric Co
22801 St Clair Ave .... Cleveland OH 44117 **888-935-3878** 216-481-8100

M K Products Inc
16882 Armstrong Ave .... Irvine CA 92606 **800-787-9707** 949-863-1234

Maine Oxy 22 Albiston Way .... Auburn ME 04210 **800-639-1108** 207-784-5788

Merrill Mfg Corp
236 S Genesee St .... Merrill WI 54452 **800-831-6962** 715-536-5533

Miller Electric Mfg Co
1635 W Spencer St .... Appleton WI 54914 **888-843-7693** 920-734-9821

NLC Inc 319 W Main St .... Jackson MO 63755 **800-594-3958*** 573-243-3141
*Sales

Palomar Technologies
2728 Loker Ave W .... Carlsbad CA 92010 **800-854-3467** 760-931-3600

Smith Equipment Mfg Co
2601 Lockheed Ave .... Watertown SD 57201 **866-931-9730*** 605-882-3200
*Cust Svc

Sonobond Ultrasonics Inc
1191 McDermott Dr .... West Chester PA 19380 **800-323-1269** 610-696-4710

Systematics Inc
1025 Saunders Ln PO Box 2429 .... West Chester PA 19380 **800-222-9353** 610-696-9040

Taylor-Winfield Inc
PO Box 779 .... Youngstown OH 44509 **800-523-4899** 330-259-8500

Tuffaloy Products Inc
1400 S Batesville Rd .... Greer SC 29650 **800-521-3722** 864-879-0763

Unitek Miyachi Corp
1820 S Myrtle Ave .... Monrovia CA 91017 **866-751-7378** 626-303-5676

Uniweld Products Inc
2850 Ravenswood Rd .... Fort Lauderdale FL 33312 **800-323-2111** 954-584-2000

Weld Mold Co
750 Rickett Rd .... Brighton MI 48116 **800-521-9755** 810-229-9521

Western Enterprises Inc
875 Bassett Rd .... Westlake OH 44145 **800-783-7890**

806   WHOLESALE CLUBS

				Toll-Free	Phone

Costco Wholesale Corp
999 Lake Dr .... Issaquah WA 98027 **800-774-2678*** 425-313-8100
*NASDAQ: COST ■ *Cust Svc*

807   WIRE & CABLE

				Toll-Free	Phone

Ace Wire & Cable Co Inc
7201 51st Ave .... Woodside NY 11377 **800-225-2354** 718-458-9200

AFC Cable Systems Inc
272 Duchaine Blvd .... New Bedford MA 02745 **800-757-6996** 508-998-1131

Alcan Cable
3 Ravinia Dr Ste 1600 .... Atlanta GA 30346 **800-347-0571** 770-394-9886

Allwire Inc
16395 Ave 24 1/2 PO Box 1000 .... Chowchilla CA 93610 **800-255-3828** 559-665-4893

AmerCable Inc
350 Bailey Rd .... El Dorado AR 71730 **800-643-1516** 870-862-4919

Astro Industries Inc
4403 Dayton-Xenia Rd .... Dayton OH 45432 **800-543-5810** 937-429-5900

Cerro Wire & Cable Company Inc
1099 Thompson Rd SE .... Hartselle AL 35640 **800-523-3869** 256-773-2522

Charter Wire
3700 W Milwaukee Rd .... Milwaukee WI 53208 **800-436-9074** 414-390-3000

Elektrisola Inc
126 High St .... Boscawen NH 03303 **800-325-2022** 603-796-2114

Encore Wire Corp
1329 Millwood Rd .... McKinney TX 75069 **800-962-9473** 972-562-9473
NASDAQ: WIRE

Eubanks Engineering Co
3022 Inland Empire Blvd .... Ontario CA 91764 **800-729-4208** 909-483-2456

Fiberwave Corp
140 58th St Bldg B Unit 6E .... Brooklyn NY 11220 **800-280-9011** 718-802-9011

Gehr Industries
7400 E Slauson Ave .... Los Angeles CA 90040 **800-688-6606** 323-728-5558

Insteel Industries Inc
1373 Boggs Dr .... Mount Airy NC 27030 **800-334-9504** 336-786-2141
NASDAQ: IIIN

Kerite Co 49 Day St .... Seymour CT 06483 **800-777-7483** 203-888-2591

Keystone Consolidated Industries Inc
7000 SW Adams St .... Peoria IL 61641 **800-447-6444***
*Sales

Leggett Wire Co
One Leggett Rd .... Carthage MO 64836 **800-888-4569** 417-358-8131

Major Custom Cable Inc
281 Lotus Dr .... Jackson MO 63755 **800-455-6224**

Mid-South Wire Company Inc
1070 Visco Dr .... Nashville TN 37210 **800-714-7800** 615-743-2850

Mount Joy Wire Corp
1000 E Main St .... Mount Joy PA 17552 **800-321-2305** 717-653-1461

Nichols Wire
1547 Helton Dr .... Florence AL 35630 **800-633-3156** 256-764-4271

Owl Wire & Cable Inc
3127 Seneca Tpke .... Canastota NY 13032 **800-765-9473** 315-697-2011

Rea Magnet Wire Company Inc
3600 E Pontiac St .... Fort Wayne IN 46803 **800-732-9473** 260-421-7321

Ribbon Technology Corp
825 Taylor Stn Rd PO Box 30758 .... Gahanna OH 43230 **800-848-0477** 614-864-5444

Sivaco Wire Group
800 Rue Ouellette .... Marieville QC J3M1P5 **800-876-9473** 450-658-8741

Southwestern Wire Inc
PO Box CC .... Norman OK 73070 **800-348-9473** 405-447-6900

Southwire Co
1 Southwire Dr .... Carrollton GA 30119 **800-444-1700** 770-832-4242

Spotnails
1100 Hicks Rd .... Rolling Meadows IL 60008 **800-873-2239** 847-259-1620

Superior Essex Inc Magnet Wire/Winding Wire Div
1601 Wall St PO Box 1601 .... Fort Wayne IN 46802 **800-551-8948** 260-461-4550

Techalloy Company Inc Baltimore Wire Div
2310 Chesapeake Ave .... Baltimore MD 21222 **800-638-1458** 410-633-9300

Times Fiber Communications Inc
358 Hall Ave PO Box 384 .... Wallingford CT 06492 **800-677-2288** 203-265-8500

Tree Island Steel
12459 Arrow Rt .... Rancho Cucamonga CA 91739 **800-255-6974** 909-594-7511

				Toll-Free	Phone
Wirerope Works Inc 100 Maynard St *Cust Svc	Williamsport	PA	17701	800-541-7673*	570-326-5146
Wrap-On Company Inc 5550 W 70th Pl	Chicago	IL	60638	800-621-6947	708-496-2150

808 WIRE & CABLE - ELECTRONIC

				Toll-Free	Phone
Alpha Wire Co 711 Lidgerwood Ave	Elizabeth	NJ	07207	800-522-5742	908-925-8000
Belden Inc Americas Div 2200 US Hwy 27 S PO Box 1980	Richmond	IN	47375	800-235-3362	765-983-5200
Cables to Go Inc 3599 Dayton Pk Dr	Dayton	OH	45414	800-826-7904	937-224-8646
Champlain Cable Corp 175 Hercules Dr	Colchester	VT	05446	800-451-5162	
CommScope Inc 1100 Commscope Pl SE PO Box 339	Hickory	NC	28603	800-982-1708	828-324-2200
Compulink Inc 1205 Gandy Blvd N	Saint Petersburg	FL	33702	800-231-6685	727-579-1500
Consolidated Electronic Wire & Cable Co 11044 King St	Franklin Park	IL	60131	800-621-4278	847-455-8830
Corning Cable Systems 800 17th St NW	Hickory	NC	28603	800-743-2671	828-901-5000
CXtec 5404 S Bay Rd PO Box 4799 *Orders	Syracuse	NY	13212	800-767-3282*	315-476-3000
Draka Comteq Americas 2512 Penny Rd	Claremont	NC	28610	800-879-9862	828-459-9821
General Cable Corp Four Tesseneer Dr *NYSE: BGC*	Highland Heights	KY	41076	800-572-8000	859-572-8000
Harbour Industries Inc 4744 Shelburne Rd PO Box 188	Shelburne	VT	05482	800-659-4733	802-985-3311
Judd Wire Inc 124 Tpke Rd *Cust Svc	Turners Falls	MA	01376	800-545-5833*	413-863-4357
Madison Cable Corp 125 Goddard Memorial Dr	Worcester	MA	01603	877-623-4766	508-752-2884
Nehring Electric Works Inc 1005 E Locust St	DeKalb	IL	60115	800-435-4481	815-756-2741
Optical Cable Corp (OCC) 5290 Concourse Dr *NASDAQ: OCC*	Roanoke	VA	24019	800-622-7711	540-265-0690
Prestolite Wire Corp 200 Galleria Officentre Ste 212	Southfield	MI	48034	800-498-3132	248-355-4422
Siemon Co 101 Siemon Co Dr	Watertown	CT	06795	866-548-5814	860-945-4200
Superior Essex Inc 6120 Powers Ferry Rd Ste 150 *NASDAQ: SPSX*	Atlanta	GA	30339	800-551-8948	770-657-6000
Trilogy Communications Inc 2910 Hwy 80 E	Pearl	MS	39208	888-713-1414	601-932-4461

809 WIRING DEVICES - CURRENT-CARRYING

				Toll-Free	Phone
Aerospace Optics Inc 3201 Sandy Ln	Fort Worth	TX	76112	888-848-4786	817-451-1141
Amphenol Corp 358 Hall Ave *NYSE: APH*	Wallingford	CT	06492	877-267-4366	203-265-8900
Bizlink Technology Inc 3400 Gateway Blvd	Fremont	CA	94538	800-326-4193	510-252-0786
Burndy LLC 47 E Industrial Park Dr	Manchester	NH	03109	800-346-4175	
Carling Technologies Inc 60 Johnson Ave	Plainville	CT	06062	800-243-8556	860-793-9281
Cherry Corp 11200 88th Ave	Pleasant Prairie	WI	53158	800-510-1689	262-942-6500
Cinch Connectors Inc 1700 Findley Rd	Lombard	IL	60148	800-323-9612	630-705-6000
Cole Hersee Co 20 Old Colony Ave	Boston	MA	02127	800-365-2653	617-268-2100
Component Enterprises Co Inc 235 E Penn St PO Box 189	Norristown	PA	19401	877-232-7253	
Cooper Bussmann Inc 114 Old State Rd	Ellisville	MO	63021	855-287-7626	636-394-2877
Cooper Crouse-Hinds 1201 Wolf St	Syracuse	NY	13208	866-764-5454	315-477-5531
Cooper Industries 600 Travis St Ste 5400 *NYSE: ETN*	Houston	TX	77002	866-853-4293	713-209-8400
Cooper Wiring Devices Inc 203 Cooper Cir *Cust Svc	Peachtree City	GA	30269	866-853-4293*	770-631-2100
Cord Sets Inc 1015 Fifth St N	Minneapolis	MN	55411	800-752-0580	612-337-9700
Cristek Interconnects Inc 5395 E Hunter Ave	Anaheim	CA	92807	888-265-9162	714-696-5200
Curtis Industries Inc 2400 S 43rd St PO Box 343925	Milwaukee	WI	53219	800-657-0853	414-649-4200
Edwin Gaynor Corp 200 Charles St	Stratford	CT	06615	800-342-9667	203-378-5545
EECO Switch 880 Columbia St	Brea	CA	92821	800-854-3808	714-835-6000
Electri-Cord Mfg Co Inc 312 E Main St	Westfield	PA	16950	888-278-8253	814-367-2265
Electroswitch 2010 Yonkers Rd	Raleigh	NC	27604	888-768-2797	919-833-0707
ERICO Products Inc 34600 Solon Rd	Solon	OH	44139	800-813-3378	440-248-0100
ETCO Inc 25 Bellows St	Warwick	RI	02888	800-689-3826	401-467-2400
Glenair Inc 1211 Air Way	Glendale	CA	91201	888-465-4094	818-247-6000
Group Dekko Services LLC 2505 Dekko Dr	Garrett	IN	46738	800-829-3101	260-357-3621
Hoffman Products 9600 Vly View Rd	Macedonia	OH	44056	800-645-2014	216-525-4320
Hubbell Premise Wiring Inc 23 Clara Dr	Mystic	CT	06355	800-626-0005	
Hubbell Wiring Device-Kellems 40 Waterview Dr *Cust Svc	Shelton	CT	06484	800-288-6000*	203-882-4800
ILSCO 4730 Madison Rd *Sales	Cincinnati	OH	45227	800-776-9775*	513-533-6200
Independent Protection Company Inc 1607 S Main St	Goshen	IN	46526	800-860-8388	574-533-4116
Lumens Light & Living 2028 K St	Sacramento	CA	95811	877-445-4486	916-444-5585
Marinco 2655 Napa Valley Corp Dr	Napa	CA	94558	800-307-6702	707-226-9600
McGill Electrical Product Group 9377 W Higgins Rd	Rosemont	IL	60018	800-621-1506	847-268-6000
Mill-Max Mfg Corp 190 Pine Hollow Rd	Oyster Bay	NY	11771	800-333-4237	516-922-6000
Minnesota Wire & Cable Co 1835 Energy Pk Dr	Saint Paul	MN	55108	800-258-6922	651-642-1800
Ohio Associated Enterprises LLC 1382 W Jackson St	Painesville	OH	44077	888-637-4832	440-354-3148
Omnetics Connector Corp 7260 Commerce Cir E *Cust Svc	Minneapolis	MN	55432	800-343-0025*	763-572-0656
Panduit Corp 17301 Ridgeland Ave	Tinley Park	IL	60477	888-506-5400	708-532-1800
Preformed Line Products 660 Beta Dr *NASDAQ: PLPC*	Cleveland	OH	44143	800-622-6757	440-461-5200
Shape LLC 2105 Corporate Dr	Addison	IL	60101	800-367-5811	630-620-8394
Veetronix Inc 1311 W Pacific Ave *General	Lexington	NE	68850	800-445-0007*	308-324-6661
Weidmuller Inc 821 Southlake Blvd *Cust Svc	Richmond	VA	23236	800-849-9343*	804-794-2877
Zierick Manufacturing Corp 131 Radio Cr	Mount Kisco	NY	10549	800-882-8020	914-666-2911

810 WIRING DEVICES - NONCURRENT-CARRYING

				Toll-Free	Phone
Allied Moulded Products Inc 222 N Union St	Bryan	OH	43506	800-722-2679	419-636-4217
Bedford Materials Co Inc 7676 Allegheny Rd	Manns Choice	PA	15550	800-773-4276	
Chase & Sons Inc 295 University Ave	Westwood	MA	02090	800-323-4182	781-332-0700
Conduit Pipe Products Co 1501 W Main St	West Jefferson	OH	43162	800-848-6125	614-879-9114
Cooper B-Line Inc 509 W Monroe St	Highland	IL	62249	800-851-7415	618-654-2184
Cottrell Paper Company Inc 1135 Rock City Rd PO Box 35	Rock City Falls	NY	12863	800-948-3559	518-885-1702
EGS Electrical Group LLC 9377 W Higgins Rd	Rosemont	IL	60018	800-621-1506	847-268-6000
Electri-Flex Co 222 Central Ave	Roselle	IL	60172	800-323-6174	630-529-2920
Flex-Cable Inc 5822 N Henkel Rd	Howard City	MI	49329	800-245-3539	231-937-8000
Gaylord Manufacturing Co 1088 Montclaire Dr	Ceres	CA	95307	800-375-0091	209-538-3313
Hubbell Premise Wiring Inc 23 Clara Dr	Mystic	CT	06355	800-626-0005	
Hubbell RACO 3902 W Sample St	South Bend	IN	46619	800-722-6437	574-234-7151
Hughes Bros Inc 210 N 13th St PO Box 159	Seward	NE	68434	800-869-0359	402-643-2991
Ideal Industries Inc 1000 Pk Ave	Sycamore	IL	60178	800-435-0705	815-895-5181
Joslyn Sunbank Co LLC 1740 Commerce Way	Paso Robles	CA	93446	800-523-0727	805-238-2840
LoDan Electronics Inc 3311 N Kennicott Ave	Arlington Heights	IL	60004	800-401-4995	847-398-5311
MacLean Power Systems 11411 Addison St	Franklin Park	IL	60131	855-677-7447	847-455-0014
MP Husky Corp 204 Old Piedmont Hwy PO Box 16749	Greenville	SC	29605	800-277-4810	864-234-4800
O-Z/Gedney 9377 W Higgins Rd	Rosemont	IL	60018	800-621-1506	847-268-6000
Opti-Com Mfg Network Co Inc 259 Plauche St	New Orleans	LA	70123	800-345-8774	504-736-0331
Rittal Corp One Rittal Pl	Springfield	OH	45504	800-477-4000	937-399-0500
Saginaw Control & Engineering Inc 95 Midland Rd	Saginaw	MI	48638	800-234-6871	989-799-6871
TJ Cope Inc 11500 Norcom Rd	Philadelphia	PA	19154	800-483-3473	215-961-2570
Varflex Corp 512 W Ct St	Rome	NY	13440	800-648-4014	315-336-4400
Virginia Plastics Co Inc 3453 Aerial Way Dr PO Box 4577	Roanoke	VA	24018	877-351-1699	540-981-9700
Weidmann Electrical Technology 1 Gordon Mills Way PO Box 903	Saint Johnsbury	VT	05819	800-242-6748	802-748-8106

WOMEN'S COLLEGES

SEE Colleges - Women's (Four-Year)

811 WOOD MEMBERS - STRUCTURAL

Toll-Free	Phone

			Toll-Free	Phone
Alpine Engineered Products Inc				
1100 Pk Central Blvd S				
PO Box 2225	Pompano Beach FL	33064	**800-786-6086***	954-781-3333
*General				
Armstrong Lumber Co Inc				
2709 Auburn Way N	Auburn WA	98002	**800-868-9066**	253-833-6666
Automated Bldg Components Inc				
2359 Grant Rd	North Baltimore OH	45872	**800-837-2152**	419-257-2152
Buettner Bros Lumber Co				
700 Seventh Ave SW	Cullman AL	35055	**800-500-0669**	256-734-4221
Columbia Forest Products Inc				
7900 Triad Ctr Dr Ste 200	Greensboro NC	27409	**800-637-1609**	336-291-5905
Enwood Structures Inc				
5724 McCrimmon Pkwy PO Box 2002	Morrisville NC	27560	**800-777-8648**	919-518-0464
Fullerton Bldg Systems Inc (FBS)				
34620 250th St PO Box 308	Worthington MN	56187	**800-450-9782**	507-376-3128
HM Stauffer & Sons Inc				
33 Glenola Dr PO Box 567	Leola PA	17540	**800-662-2226**	717-656-2811
Laminate Technologies Inc				
161 Maule Rd	Tiffin OH	44883	**800-231-2523**	
Laminated Wood Systems Inc (LWS)				
1327 285th Rd PO Box 386	Seward NE	68434	**800-949-3526**	402-643-4708
Laminators Inc				
3255 Penn St	Hatfield PA	19440	**877-663-4277**	215-723-8107
Molpus Co, The				
502 Vly View Dr PO Box 59	Philadelphia MS	39350	**800-535-5434**	601-656-3373
Montgomery Truss & Panel Inc				
803 W Main St	Grove City PA	16127	**800-942-8010**	724-458-7500
Robbins Mfg Co				
13001 N Nebraska Ave	Tampa FL	33612	**888-558-8199**	813-971-3030
Shook Builder Supply Co				
1400 16th St NE	Hickory NC	28601	**800-968-0758**	828-328-2051
Southern Components Inc				
7360 Julie Frances Dr PO Box 29010	Shreveport LA	71129	**800-256-2144**	318-687-3330
Stow Co, The				
3311 Windquest Dr	Holland MI	49424	**800-562-4257**	616-399-3311
Structural Wood Corp				
4000 Labore Rd	Saint Paul MN	55110	**800-652-9058**	651-426-8111
Villaume Industries Inc				
2926 Lone Oak Cir	Saint Paul MN	55121	**800-488-3610***	651-454-3610
*Cust Svc				

812   WOOD PRESERVING

			Toll-Free	Phone
Bell Lumber & Pole Co				
778 First St NW PO Box 120786	New Brighton MN	55112	**877-633-4334**	651-633-4334
Brown Wood Preserving Company Inc				
6201 Camp Ground Rd	Louisville KY	40216	**800-537-1765**	502-448-2337
Building Products Plus				
12317 Almeda Rd	Houston TX	77045	**800-460-8627**	
Conrad Forest Products				
68765 Wildwood Dr	North Bend OR	97459	**800-356-7146**	
Cox Industries Inc				
860 Cannon Bridge Rd PO Box 1124	Orangeburg SC	29116	**800-476-4401**	803-534-7467
Elder Wood Preserving Co Inc				
334 Elder Wood Rd	Mansura LA	71350	**800-467-8018**	318-964-2196
Great Southern Wood Preserving Inc				
1100 US Hwy 431 N	Abbeville AL	36310	**800-633-7539**	334-585-2291
JH Baxter & Co				
PO Box 5902	San Mateo CA	94402	**800-556-1098**	650-349-0201
Koppers Inc				
436 Seventh Ave	Pittsburgh PA	15219	**800-321-9876**	412-227-2001
NYSE: KOP				
McFarland Cascade				
1640 E Marc St PO Box 1496	Tacoma WA	98421	**800-426-8430***	253-572-3033
*Cust Svc				
Osmose Inc 980 Ellicott St	Buffalo NY	14209	**800-877-7653**	716-882-5905
Robbins Mfg Co				
13001 N Nebraska Ave	Tampa FL	33612	**888-558-8199**	813-971-3030
Western Wood Preserving Co				
1310 Zehnder St PO Box 1250	Sumner WA	98390	**800-472-7714**	253-863-8191
Wood Preservers Inc				
15939 Historyland Hwy PO Box 158	Warsaw VA	22572	**800-368-2536**	804-333-4022

813   WOOD PRODUCTS - RECONSTITUTED

			Toll-Free	Phone
Cabinet Tronix LLC				
290 Trousdale Dr Ste A	Chula Vista CA	91910	**866-876-6199**	
Geo Products LLC				
8615 Golden Spike Ln	Houston TX	77086	**800-434-4743**	281-820-5493
Homasote Co				
932 Lower Ferry Rd PO Box 7240	West Trenton NJ	08628	**800-257-9491**	609-883-3300
OTC: HMTC				
Panel Processing Inc				
120 N Industrial Hwy	Alpena MI	49707	**800-433-7142**	989-356-9007
Panolam Industries International Inc				
20 Progress Dr	Shelton CT	06484	**800-672-6652**	203-925-1556
Rex Lumber Co 840 Main St	Acton MA	01720	**800-343-0567**	978-263-0055
Tectum Inc 105 S Sixth St	Newark OH	43055	**888-977-9691**	740-345-9691

814   WOOD PRODUCTS - SHAPED & TURNED

			Toll-Free	Phone
A&M Supply Corp				
6701 90th Ave N	Pinellas Park FL	33782	**800-877-8551**	727-541-6631
Brown Wood Products Co				
7040 N Lawndale Ave	Lincolnwood IL	60712	**800-328-5858**	
Chicago Dowel Company Inc				
4700 W Grand Ave	Chicago IL	60639	**800-333-6935**	773-622-2000
Davidson Plyforms Inc				
5505 33rd St SE	Grand Rapids MI	49512	**800-505-4732**	616-956-0033

			Toll-Free	Phone
Frank Edmunds & Co				
6111 S Sayre	Chicago IL	60638	**800-447-3516**	773-586-2772
Jarden Home Brands				
14611 W Commerce Rd	Daleville IN	47334	**800-240-3340***	765-557-3000
*Cust Svc				

815   WOODWORKING MACHINERY

			Toll-Free	Phone
Baker Products				
55480 Hwy 21 N PO Box 128	Ellington MO	63638	**800-548-6914**	573-663-7711
James L. Taylor Manufacturing Co				
108 Parker Ave	Poughkeepsie NY	12601	**800-952-1320**	845-452-3780
Kimwood Corp				
77684 Oregon 99	Cottage Grove OR	97424	**800-942-4401**	541-942-4401
KVAL Inc				
825 Petaluma Blvd S	Petaluma CA	94952	**800-553-5825**	707-762-7367
Memphis Machinery & Supply Co Inc				
2881 Directors Cove	Memphis TN	38131	**800-388-4485**	901-527-4443
Mereen-Johnson Machine Co				
4401 Lyndale Ave N	Minneapolis MN	55412	**888-465-7297**	612-529-7791
Michael Weining Inc				
124 Crosslake Pk Dr PO Box 3158	Mooresville NC	28117	**877-548-0929**	704-799-0100
Oliver Machinery Co				
6902 S 194th St	Kent WA	98032	**800-559-5065**	253-867-0334
Pendu Manufacturing Inc				
718 N Shirk Rd	New Holland PA	17557	**800-233-0471**	717-354-4348
Safety Speed Cut Mfg Co Inc				
13943 Lincoln St NE	Ham Lake MN	55304	**800-772-2327**	763-755-1600
Thermwood Corp				
904 Buffaloville Rd	Dale IN	47523	**800-533-6901***	812-937-4476
OTC: TOOD ▪ *Mktg				
USNR				
1981 Schurman Way PO Box 310	Woodland WA	98674	**800-289-8767**	360-225-8267
USNR Inc				
558 Robinson Rd PO Box 310	Woodland WA	98674	**800-289-8767**	360-225-8267
Viking Engineering & Development Inc				
5750 Main St NE	Fridley MN	55432	**800-328-2403***	763-571-2400
*Sales				
Voorwood Co				
2350 Barney St PO Box 1127	Anderson CA	96007	**800-826-0089**	530-365-3311
Yates-American Machine Company Inc				
2880 Kennedy Dr	Beloit WI	53511	**800-752-6377**	608-364-6333

816   WORLD TRADE CENTERS

			Toll-Free	Phone
Montana World Trade Ctr				
Gallagher Business Bldg University of Montana				
Ste 257	Missoula MT	59812	**888-442-6668**	406-243-6982
Northern California World Trade Ctr				
One Capitol Mall Ste 300	Sacramento CA	95814	**855-667-2259**	
Ronald Reagan Bldg & International Trade Ctr				
1300 Pennsylvania Ave N	Washington DC	20004	**800-734-7393**	202-312-1300
Seaport World Trade Ctr Boston				
200 Seaport Blvd	Boston MA	02210	**800-440-3318**	617-385-4212

817   ZOOS & WILDLIFE PARKS

SEE ALSO Aquariums - Public ; Botanical Gardens & Arboreta

			Toll-Free	Phone
African Lion Safari & Game Farm				
RR 1	Cambridge ON	N1R5S2	**800-461-9453**	519-623-2620
African Safari Wildlife Park				
267 S Lightner Rd	Port Clinton OH	43452	**800-521-2660**	419-732-3606
Arkansas Alligator Farm & Petting Zoo				
847 Whittington Ave	Hot Springs AR	71901	**800-750-7891**	501-623-6172
Assiniboine Park Zoo				
55 Pavilion Crescent	Winnipeg MB	R3P2N6	**877-927-6006**	204-927-8080
Audubon Zoo				
6500 Magazine St	New Orleans LA	70118	**800-774-7394**	504-581-4629
Brevard Zoo				
8225 N Wickham Rd	Melbourne FL	32940	**800-435-7352**	321-254-9453
Bronx Zoo 2300 Southern Blvd	Bronx NY	10460	**800-433-4149**	718-220-5100
Busch Gardens Williamsburg				
1 Busch Gardens Blvd	Williamsburg VA	23185	**800-343-7946**	
Calgary Zoo Botanical Garden & Prehistoric Park				
1300 Zoo Rd NE	Calgary AB	T2E7V6	**800-588-9993**	403-232-9300
Caribbean Gardens				
1590 Goodlette-Frank Rd	Naples FL	34102	**888-520-3756**	239-262-5409
Central Florida Zoological Park				
3755 NW Hwy 17-92 & I-4				
PO Box 470309	Lake Monroe FL	32747	**800-435-7352**	407-323-4450
Cincinnati Zoo & Botanical Garden				
3400 Vine St	Cincinnati OH	45220	**800-944-4776**	513-281-4700
Clyde Peeling's Reptiland				
18628 US Rt 15	Allenwood PA	17810	**800-737-8452**	
Columbian Park Zoo				
1915 Scott St	Lafayette IN	47904	**800-438-9926**	765-807-1540
Columbus Zoo & Aquarium				
4850 W Powell Rd	Powell OH	43065	**800-945-3543**	614-645-3400
Discovery Cove				
6000 Discovery Cove Way Ste B	Orlando FL	32821	**877-434-7268**	407-370-1280
Erie Zoo 423 W 38th St	Erie PA	16508	**877-371-5422**	814-864-4091
Felix Neck Wildlife Sanctuary				
100 Felix Neck Dr	Edgartown MA	02539	**866-627-2267**	508-627-4850
Gator Park 24050 SW Eigth St	Miami FL	33187	**800-559-2205**	305-559-2255
Gatorland				
14501 S Orange Blossom Trl	Orlando FL	32837	**800-393-5297**	407-855-5496
Gladys Porter Zoo				
500 Ringgold St	Brownsville TX	78520	**800-424-8802**	956-546-7187
Good Zoo & Benedum Planetarium				
Rt 88 N Oglebay Pk	Wheeling WV	26003	**800-624-6988**	304-243-4030

			Toll-Free	Phone

Greenville Zoo
150 Cleveland Pk Dr . . . . Greenville SC 29601 **800-877-8339** 864-467-4300
Grizzly & Wolf Discovery Ctr
201 S Canyon St . . . . West Yellowstone MT 59758 **800-257-2570** 406-646-7001
Hutchinson Zoo
6 Emerson Loop E Carey Pk . . . . Hutchinson KS 67501 **800-362-3247** 620-694-2693
Jungle Adventures
26205 E Colonial Dr . . . . Christmas FL 32709 **877-424-2867** 407-568-2885
Kentucky Horse Park
4089 Iron Works Pkwy . . . . Lexington KY 40511 **800-678-8813** 859-233-4303
Louisville Zoo
1100 Trevilian Way . . . . Louisville KY 40213 **866-229-0502** 502-459-2181
Minnesota Zoo
13000 Zoo Blvd . . . . Apple Valley MN 55124 **800-366-7811** 952-431-9200
North Carolina Zoological Park
4401 Zoo Pkwy . . . . Asheboro NC 27205 **800-488-0444** 336-879-7000
Northeastern Wisconsin Zoo
305 E Walnut St Rm 102 PO Box 23600 . . . . Green Bay WI 54301 **888-844-8070** 920-448-6242
Oklahoma City Zoological Park & Botanical Gardens
2101 NE 50th St . . . . Oklahoma City OK 73111 **800-891-2917** 405-424-3344
Pittsburgh Zoo & PPG Aquarium
1 Wild Pl . . . . Pittsburgh PA 15206 **800-732-0999** 412-665-3640
Rosamond Gifford Zoo at Burnet Park
1 Conservation Pl . . . . Syracuse NY 13204 **800-724-5006** 315-435-8511
Safari West Wildlife Preserve & Tent Camp
3115 Porter Creek Rd . . . . Santa Rosa CA 95404 **800-616-2695** 707-579-2551
San Diego Zoo Safari Park
15500 San Pasqual Valley Rd . . . . Escondido CA 92027 **877-363-6237*** 760-747-8702
*Cust Svc
Sarasota Jungle Gardens
3701 Bay Shore Rd . . . . Sarasota FL 34234 **877-681-6547** 941-355-5305
Toledo Zoo 2700 Broadway . . . . Toledo OH 43609 **866-900-1146** 419-385-5721
Tupelo Buffalo Park & Zoo
2272 N Coley Rd . . . . Tupelo MS 38803 **866-272-4766** 662-844-8709
Wild Animal Safari
1300 Oak Grove Rd . . . . Pine Mountain GA 31822 **800-367-2751** 706-663-8744
Wonders of Wildlife
500 W Sunshine St . . . . Springfield MO 65807 **877-245-9453** 417-890-9453

Index to Classified Headings

Citations provided in this index refer to the subject headings under which listings are organized in the Classified Section. The page number given for each citation refers to the page on which a particular subject category begins rather than to a specific company or organization name. "See" and "See also" references are included to help locate appropriate subject categories.

Index

Index

C

Index

Index

E

F

Index

Index

H

Index

Index

Index

Index

Index

Index

Index